Comment utiliser ce dictionnaire

- gender of French nouns
- abbreviations listed in alphabetical position
- language register labels in italics
- one-word compounds given as headwords
- alternative spellings
- irregular plurals
- clear coverage of figurative usage
- alternative pronunciations
- phonetics in latest notation of International Phonetic Alphabet
- superior numbers distinguish between nouns and verbs
- American usage
- modern slang usage
- clear sense distinctions for translations of examples
- superior numbers distinguish further between senses
- detailed grammatical labelling of phrasal verbs
- phrasal verbs marked ▶
- British usage
- proper nouns
- numbers indicate grammatical categories
- full sense indicators in italics

bandan(n)a [bæn'dænə] *n* (*for neck*) ... (*handkerchief*) mouchoir *m*.
B & B [biːən'biː] *n Br abbr* **bed and** ...
bandbox ['bændbɒks] *n* carton ... *fashioned Fig* **she looks as if she's** ... **b.,** elle est tirée à quatre épingles.
banded ['bændɪd] *adj* **(a)** (*fastened*) ... rayé; *Biol* fascié.
banderol(e) ['bændərɒl] *n* bandero...
bandit ['bændɪt] *n* bandit *m*.
banditry ['bændɪtrɪ] *n* brigandage *m*.
bandmaster ['bændmɑːstər] *n Mil etc* chef *m* de musique; (*of brass band*) chef de fanfare.
bandoleer, bandolier [bændə'lɪər] *n* cartouchière *f* (*portée en bandoulière*).
bandsman, *pl* **-men** ['bændzmən] *n* musicien *m* (*d'un orchestre, d'une harmonie*); (*in brass band*) fanfariste *m*.
bandstand ['bændstænd] *n* kiosque *m* à musique.
bandwagon ['bændwæg(ə)n] *n* char *m* des musiciens (*en tête de la cavalcade*); *Fig* **to climb** *or* **jump on the b.,** se mettre dans le mouvement, prendre le train en marche.
bandwidth ['bændwɪdθ] *n Rad* largeur *f* de bande.
bandy¹ ['bændɪ] *vt* (se) renvoyer (*des paroles*); échanger (*des plaisanteries*); **to b. words,** (*quarrel*) se chamailler.
bandy² *adj* aux jambes arquées; **b. legs,** jambes arquées; **to be b., to have b. legs,** avoir les jambes arquées.
▶**bandy about, bandy around** *vtsep* **her name was being bandied about,** on parlait beaucoup d'elle; **decentralization is a word the government bandies about a lot,** la décentralisation est un mot que le gouvernement a toujours à la bouche.
bandy-legged [bændɪ'legɪd, -'legd] *adj* aux jambes arquées.
bane [beɪn] *n Lit* peste *f*; **she is the b. of pretentious authors,** elle est la bête noire des auteurs prétentieux; *F* **he's the b. of my life,** il m'empoisonne l'existence.
baneful ['beɪnful] *adj Lit* funeste; (*influence*) néfaste.
banefully ['beɪnfulɪ] *adv* funestement.
bang¹ [bæŋ] *n* **(a)** coup *m* (violent); détonation *f* (*de fusil etc*); claquement *m* (*de porte*); **the door shut with a b.,** la porte a claqué violemment; **she got a bad b. on the head,** elle a reçu un mauvais coup sur la tête; **to go off with a b.,** (*of firework*) détoner; *F* **to go (off) with a b.,** faire réussite; **(b)** *Am Sl* (*pleasure*) **to get a b. from sth,** prendre son pied à faire qch; **(c)** *Sl* (*of heroin*) injection *f* d'héroïne; **(d)** *Vulg* (*sexual intercourse*) baise *f*.
bang² **1** *vi* **(a)** (*of door*) claquer, battre; **the door banged shut,** la porte a claqué violemment; **to b. at** *or* **on the door,** donner de grands coups dans la porte; **to b. on the table with one's fist,** frapper la table du poing; **(b)** *Sl* (*of heroin addict*) se shooter. **2** *vt* **(a)** frapper (*qch*) (violemment); **to b. one's head,** se cogner la tête; *Fig* **to b. a few heads together,** taper sur la table; **to b. the door,** (faire) claquer la porte; **(b)** *Vulg* baiser (*une femme*).
bang³ **1** *int* pan!, v'lan!, boum!; *Br F* **b. went a fiver!,** j'ai dépensé cinq livres d'un seul coup!; *Br F* **b. went my hopes of a quiet weekend,** tous mes espoirs d'un week-end tranquille se sont envolés d'un seul coup. **2** *adv* **to go b.,** éclater; **he crashed b. into the tree,** il est rentré en plein dans l'arbre; **to fall b. in the middle,** tomber en plein milieu; *F* **b. on time,** exactement à l'heure; *F* **it's b. on,** c'est au poil; *F* **b. up-to-date,** (*equipment etc*) à la pointe de la technologie; (*reference book etc*) vraiment à jour; *Br F* **to be caught b. to rights,** être pris la main dans le sac.
bang⁴ *n* (*also* **bangs**) (*hair*) frange *f*.
▶**bang down** *vtsep* abattre (*un couvercle*); **he banged it down on the table,** il l'a posé avec violence sur la table.
▶**bang into** *vipo* (*collide with*) se heurter contre (*qch, qn*).
▶**bang on** *vi Sl* **he's always banging on about it,** il n'arrête pas de casser les pieds à tout le monde là-dessus.
▶**bang out** *vtsep* jouer (*un air*) tant bien que mal.
▶**bang up** *vtsep Br Sl* boucler (*un prisonnier*).
banger ['bæŋər] *n Br F* **(a)** (*sausage*) saucisse *f*; **bangers and mash,** saucisse-purée *f*; **(b)** (*firework*) pétard *m*; **(c)** (*car*) **old b.,** vieux tacot, vieille guimbarde.
Bangladesh [bæŋglə'deʃ] *n* Bangladesh *m*.
Bangladeshi [bæŋglə'deʃɪ] **1** *n* habitant, -ante du Bangladesh. **2** *adj* (*government etc*) du Bangladesh.
bangle ['bæŋg(ə)l] *n* (*for wrist*) bracelet *m*; (*for ankle*) anneau attaché autour de la cheville.
banish ['bænɪʃ] *vt* **(a)** (*exile*) bannir, exiler, proscrire (*qn*); **(b)** *Fig* (*drive away*) bannir, chasser (*la crainte, les soucis*).
banishment ['bænɪʃmənt] *n* bannissement *m*, proscription *f*, exil *m*; **to go into b.,** partir pour l'exil; **to be sent into b.,** être banni *ou* exilé.

- genre des noms communs
- abré... ...entées dans ...que
- ...veaux de ...es
- articles séparés pour les composés en un seul mot
- variantes orthographiques
- pluriels irréguliers
- sens figurés largement représentés
- variantes de prononciation
- transcription phonétique selon la notation la plus récente de l'Alphabet Phonétique International
- les petits chiffres distinguent noms et verbes
- anglais américain
- sens et mots argotiques
- les zones d'emploi clairement indiquées différencient les traductions
- les petits chiffres distinguent les homographes
- indications détaillées sur la construction des verbes à particule
- repérage des verbes à particule par ▶
- anglais britannique
- noms propres
- les chiffres repèrent les différentes catégories grammaticales
- des éléments en italiques servent à cerner le sens ou le contexte exact

HARRAP'S
SHORTER FRENCH AND ENGLISH DICTIONARY

HARRAP'S
SHORTER FRENCH AND ENGLISH DICTIONARY

HARRAP
EDINBURGH
PARIS NEW YORK

This edition first published in Great Britain 1991
by Harrap Books Ltd
43-45 Annandale Street, Edinburgh EH7 4AZ

Dépôt Légal : juin 1991

The previous edition of
Harrap's Shorter French and English Dictionary
was first published in Great Britain 1982
Reprinted 1983, 1984 (three times), 1985, 1986 (twice)

Printed in new format 1987
Reprinted 1987 (three times), 1988, 1989, 1990
This edition entirely re-set 1991
Reprinted 1992 (twice)

ISBN 0 245-55046-1 (standard edition)
0 245-60355-7 (thumb indexed edition)

Database creation and phototypesetting by
Morton Word Processing Ltd,
Scarborough, England

Printed and bound at
Partenaires, Malesherbes, France

Editorial staff for 1991 edition

Jane Goldie

Michael Wood
Peter Terrell

Sophie Marin-Curtoud
Nadine Mongeard
Philippe Renault

Sophie Curien
Keith Foley
Stuart Fortey
Simon Fraser

Colin Hope
Hugh O'Donnell
Natalie Pomier
John Williams

Copy Editors

Jacqueline Gregan

Diane Robinson
Sheilagh G. F. Wilson

Keyboarders

Susi Hardie

Elizabeth Robertson
Violet Bremner

Project management

LEXUS

Harrap French consultant: Fabrice Antoine

Editorial staff for 1982 edition

Peter Collin
Margaret Ledésert

Helen Knox
René Ledésert

Editorial team and consultants

Reginald Bowen
Fiona Clarke
H. R. Elphick
Ruth Hillmore
F. G. S. Parker
Muriel Holland Smith

Hazel Curties
Flora Elphick
Ian Forbes
Françoise Laurendeau
Gunhild Prowe
Elizabeth A. Strick

Acknowledgement

Harrap would like to thank Michael Janes for his advice and suggestions during the compilation of this dictionary.

Remerciements

Harrap tient à remercier Michael Janes pour ses conseils et remarques au cours de la rédaction de ce dictionnaire.

Trademarks

Words considered to be trademarks have been designated in this dictionary by the symbol ®. However, no judgment is implied concerning the legal status of any trademark by virtue of the presence or absence of such a symbol.

Marques déposées

Les termes considérés comme des marques déposées sont signalés dans ce dictionnaire par le symbole ®. Cependant, la présence ou l'absence de ce symbole ne constitue nullement une indication quant à la valeur juridique de ces termes.

Contents/Table des matières

Preface

For over half a century, Harrap's *Shorter French and English Dictionary* has been a bridge between the English and French languages. The time had come to renovate a solid but ageing edifice, itself a model for more recent reference works within the celebrated Harrap range and elsewhere. An experienced team of French and English lexicographers carried out a programme of reshaping or replacing old material and of adding new. Thousands of new headwords and phrases have been included, mirroring the constant changes affecting both English and French, and existing translations have been revised and updated. More indicating glosses have been built in to point the user clearly towards the correct foreign-language equivalent. Aspects of American English and Canadian French have been incorporated. Entry structure has been revised and the layout made more user-friendly. Our aim has been to produce a dictionary which, by virtue of its readability and comprehensive treatment of English and French, should continue as a standard work of reference bridging the linguistic gap between the English- and French-speaking communities.

Harrap, 1991

Préface

Depuis plus d'un demi-siècle, le *Shorter* de Harrap est un pont privilégié entre l'anglais et le français. Le moment était venu de moderniser cet édifice, toujours solide certes, mais qui avait pris de l'âge, tout en restant la référence pour d'autres ouvrages plus récents, tant dans la gamme prestigieuse de Harrap qu'ailleurs. Une équipe de lexicographes anglais et français chevronnés a été rassemblée pour mener à bien la refonte de l'ouvrage: réorganiser l'information, la corriger et la compléter. Des milliers de nouveaux mots et locutions ont ainsi été inclus et les traductions fournies systématiquement révisées, afin de refléter l'évolution constante que connaissent les deux langues. Un plus grand nombre d'indicateurs ont été introduits afin de guider plus sûrement l'utilisateur vers la meilleure traduction. De nouveaux aspects de l'anglais américain et du français du Canada ont été incorporés. Enfin, la structure des articles a été réorganisée et la présentation générale rendue plus attrayante. L'objectif a été de produire un ouvrage à la fois clair, facile à consulter et exhaustif dans sa présentation de l'anglais comme du français; il restera ainsi un ouvrage de référence indispensable pour renforcer les liens linguistiques entre anglophones et francophones.

Harrap, 1991

HOW TO USE THE DICTIONARY

Entry structure

1. Where a word can be used either as a noun/adjective or as a verb, each is given as a separate headword, for example:

   book[1] *n* **manger**[1] *nm* **thin**[1] *adj*
   book[2] *vt* **manger**[2] *vi* **thin**[2] *vi*

2. Roman numerals (**1, 2, 3** etc) are used to indicate a change of grammatical category, from noun to adjective, for example, or from transitive to intransitive verb.

3. Letters are used within each grammatical category to point to a change in sense, for example:

   briefly *adv* **(a)** (*in a few words*) ...; **(b)** (*for a short time*) ...

4. Within entries a comma is used to separate translations which have the same meaning or use. A semicolon between translations indicates a shift in meaning and is generally accompanied by an indicator to explain this shift.

5. English compounds written as two words are generally listed under the headword which is the first element. English and French compounds which are hyphenated or written as one word are listed as separate headwords.

6. If a headword occurs within an entry in an example or a compound without any change to its form, it is represented by its initial letter only, for example:

   spade *n* ...; **to call a s. a s.,** ...

   If the form of the headword changes (other than for use with a capital letter) it is written in full:

   spade *n* ...; **ace of spades,** ...

   If an English verb is used in an example in which the past participle has the same form as the infinitive, then the form in the example is not abbreviated, for example:

   split: I've split my skirt, j'ai déchiré ma jupe

Indicating material

7. Indicators in italic print and in brackets are used to identify the sense of a word which is being translated, for example:

   caner *vi Arg* (*avoir peur*) to have the jitters; (*se dégonfler*) to chicken out; (*mourir*) to snuff it, to kick the bucket

8. Collocators in italic print and in brackets are used to show which type of word combinations are possible with a particular translation, for example:

   unhealthy *adj* (*person*) maladif; (*state of mind, influence*) malsain; (*air, place*) malsain, insalubre; (*engine*) détraqué

   walk through *vipo* réussir (*ses examens etc*) sans effort

9. Field labels in italic print are used to identify the area of usage for which a translation is being given, for example:

banquier *nm Fin Cartes* banker

shows that the translation of 'banquier' applies both in the financial and the card-playing sense.

10. Style labels are used to identify whether a word or expression is familiar, slang, old-fashioned, literary or vulgar etc, for example:

chier *vi Vulg* to shit, to crap

spiffing *adj Old-fashioned Br F* épatant

yucky *adj F* dégoûtant

wondrous *Arch & Lit* merveilleux

11. The label *Am* is used to refer to North American usage, i.e. Canada and the United States. The label *US* is used to refer to United States usage.

12. The words *or* and *ou* are used:

(i) to separate interchangeable parts of a source language item or a translation, for example:

to stub one's toe on *or* **against sth,** se heurter *ou* se cogner le pied contre qch

(you can say either 'to stub one's toe on sth' or 'to stub one's toe against sth'; either 'se heurter le pied contre qch' or 'se cogner le pied contre qch')

(ii) to separate obviously different parts of a translation, for example:

the scent had gone cold, on avait perdu sa *ou* leur *etc* trace

13. Genders are given for French headwords (*nm* for masculine, *nf* for feminine). Where only *n* is given this means that the headword can be either masculine or feminine.

Pronunciation

14. The phonetics of headwords are given according to the symbols of the International Phonetic Alphabet. For English, received pronunciation (RP) has been taken as the norm. This is generally described as the English of Southern England, though it is perhaps more accurate to call it the English of the speaker who has no regional inflexions. American pronunciation has been given alongside the British where there is a marked difference (tomato [tə'mɑːtəʊ, *Am* tə'meɪtəʊ].

Translations

15. Genders are given for French translations unless the presence in the translation of a non-optional adjective makes the gender self-evident, for example in:

French bean *n* haricot vert

the form of the adjective 'vert' shows that the gender has to be masculine.

Genders are not given for noun translations where the masculine and feminine forms make the gender obvious, for example:

dancer *n* danseur, -euse

Genders are not repeated for a word that occurs more than once within a category. But genders are repeated across categories. So the user should look to the beginning of the category or entry if in doubt as to gender.

16. Feminine forms are given for adjectives which do not follow regular patterns, for example:

    frais, *f* fraîche

    ambigu, -uë

17. Where possible the dictionary gives translations which match the style level of the source language and so the style level is only given once – for the source language. For example:

    bonce *n Br F* (*head*) boule *f*

    bimbo *n Pej* minette *f*

    chien-chien *nm F* doggie

18. Where a translation is not possible (usually because of cultural differences in educational and legal systems etc) an equals sign (=) is used to alert the user to the fact that what follows is not a translation but a definition intended to help them understand the concept.

    A double swung dash (≈) indicates a cultural equivalent.

Phrasal verbs

19. A new feature of this dictionary is the special treatment given to English phrasal verbs. These are given headword status and highlighted by a solid triangle. Phrasal verbs are analysed as follows:

► *vi* (verb, intransitive)

get off: he got off at Victoria Station

listen in: do you mind if I l. in while you talk?

► *vipo* (verb, intransitive with prepositional object)

These are intransitive verbs combined with a particle. Some of them can take an object and some of them must take an object:

join in: they all joined in the chorus
(object 'the chorus' can be omitted)

come across: where did you c. across that word?
(object 'that word' necessary)

Especially in the second type, the combination behaves like a transitive verb and can often form a passive:

a type of virus which had never been come across before

► *vtsep* (verb, transitive, separable)

The two parts of the verb may be separated:

dig up: they're digging the road up, they're digging up the road

A passive form is possible:

the road is being dug up again

If the object of the verb is a personal pronoun (or 'it') then the two parts of the verb must be separated:

look up: I'll l. him up when I'm in Paris

► *vtas* (verb, transitive, always separate)

get over with: she got her work over with as quickly as possible
tide over: can you lend me £5 to t. me over till Monday?

The object cannot come after the particle.

► *vtaspo* (verb, transitive, always separate, with prepositional object)

The particle must always be separate from the verb, and an object must be used both after the verb and after the particle:

keep from: to k. sth from s.o.

COMMENT UTILISER CE DICTIONNAIRE

Structure des articles

1. Lorsqu'un mot peut être utilisé en tant que nom/adjectif et en tant que verbe, il apparaît sous deux mots d'entrée différents. Par exemple:

book[1] *n*	**manger**[1] *nm*	**thin**[1] *adj*
book[2] *vt*	**manger**[2] *vi*	**thin**[2] *vi*

2. Des chiffres (**1, 2, 3** etc) sont utilisés pour indiquer un changement de catégorie grammaticale, de nom à adjectif par exemple, ou encore de verbe transitif à verbe intransitif.

3. Des lettres sont utilisées à l'intérieur de chaque catégorie grammaticale pour marquer un changement de sens. Par exemple:

   briefly *adv* **(a)** (*in a few words*) ...; **(b)** (*for a short time*) ...

4. Au sein des articles, les virgules séparent les traductions ayant le même sens ou le même emploi. Un point virgule séparant deux traductions indique une nuance de sens et est généralement accompagné d'une indication expliquant cette nuance.

5. Les mots composés anglais s'écrivant en deux mots figurent généralement sous le mot d'entrée constituant leur premier élément. Les mots composés anglais et français reliés par un trait d'union ou s'écrivant en un seul mot figurent en tant qu'entrées à part entière.

6. Si un mot d'entrée est repris au sein de l'article dans un exemple ou un groupe de mots sans que sa forme subisse aucun changement, il est représenté par son initiale. Par exemple:

   spade *n* ...; **to call a s. a s.,** ...

   Si sa forme subit un changement (autre que son emploi avec une majuscule), il est écrit en entier:

   spade *n* ...; **ace of spades,** ...

   Si le participe passé d'un verbe anglais apparaît dans un exemple et que sa forme est identique à celle de l'infinitif, il n'est pas abrégé. Par exemple:

   split: I've split my skirt, j'ai déchiré ma jupe

Indications guidant l'utilisateur

7. Les synonymes et explications en italique et entre parenthèses servent à déterminer le sens du mot traduit. Par exemple:

   caner *vi Arg* (*avoir peur*) to have the jitters; (*se dégonfler*) to chicken out; (*mourir*) to snuff it, to kick the bucket.

8. Les exemples types d'emploi apparaissant en italique et entre parenthèses indiquent quel genre de combinaisons sont possibles avec une traduction particulière. Par exemple:

   unhealthy *adj* (*person*) maladif; (*state of mind, influence*) malsain; (*air, place*) malsain, insalubre; (*engine*) détraqué

   walk through *vipo* réussir (*ses examens etc*) sans effort

9. Les champs sémantiques figurant en italique servent à déterminer le domaine d'utilisation de la traduction donnée. Ainsi:

banquier *nm Fin Cartes* banker

montre que la traduction de 'banquier' vaut à la fois pour le domaine financier et pour celui des jeux de cartes.

10. Les indications de niveaux de langue indiquent si un mot ou une expression est, par exemple, familier, argotique, vieilli, littéraire ou vulgaire etc:

chier *vi Vulg* to shit, to crap

spiffing *adj Old-fashioned Br F* épatant

yucky *adj F* dégoûtant

wondrous *Arch & Lit* merveilleux

11. Le signe *Am* désigne un emploi nord-américain – c'est-à-dire du Canada et des États-Unis. Le signe *US* désigne l'emploi étasunien.

12. On a eu recours aux mots *or* et *ou*:

(i) pour séparer les éléments interchangeables d'une locution de la langue de départ ou d'une traduction. Par exemple:

to stub one's toe on *or* **against sth,** se heurter *ou* se cogner le pied contre qch

(on peut dire ou bien 'to stub one's toe on sth' ou 'to stub one's toe against sth'; ou bien 'se heurter le pied contre qch' ou 'se cogner le pied contre qch')

(ii) pour séparer diverses possibilités de traduction, lorsque la différence entre elles apparaît d'elle-même. Par exemple:

the scent had gone cold, on avait perdu sa *ou* leur *etc* trace

13. Les genres sont donnés pour les mots d'entrée français (*nm* pour masculin, *nf* pour féminin). Un mot suivi de *n* uniquement peut avoir les deux genres masculin et féminin.

Prononciation

14. La transcription phonétique des mots d'entrée utilise les symboles de l'alphabet phonétique international. Pour l'anglais, c'est la prononciation consacrée (received pronunciation) qui a été prise comme norme. Celle-ci est traditionnellement définie comme l'anglais parlé dans le Sud de l'Angleterre, bien qu'il soit peut-être plus exact de la décrire comme étant un anglais dépourvu de toute inflexion régionale. La prononciation américaine a été donnée parallèlement à celle d'usage en Grande-Bretagne lorsqu'il existe une différence marquée entre les deux (tomato [tə'mɑːtəʊ, *Am* tə'meɪtəʊ].

Traductions

15. Les genres sont indiqués pour les traductions françaises à moins d'être mis en évidence par un adjectif accompagnant le nom. Ainsi dans:

French bean *n* haricot vert

la forme de l'adjectif 'vert' indique que le genre est masculin.

Les genres ne sont pas donnés lorsque leur indication est rendue superflue par la présence des deux formes masculine et féminine. Par exemple:

dancer *n* danseur, -euse

Les genres ne sont pas répétés lorsqu'une traduction apparaît plus d'une fois dans une même catégorie. Ils sont cependant répétés de catégorie à catégorie. Ainsi un retour en début de catégorie ou d'article permet à l'utilisateur de s'assurer du genre des traductions.

16. Les formes féminines des adjectifs sont indiquées si elles ne suivent pas les modèles réguliers. Par exemple:

    frais, *f* fraîche
    ambigu, -uë

17. Chaque fois que cela est possible, le dictionnaire fournit des traductions qui correspondent au registre de la langue de départ. L'indication de registre n'apparaît donc qu'une fois – pour la langue de départ. Par exemple:

    bonce *n Br F* (*head*) boule *f*
    bimbo *n Pej* minette *f*
    chien-chien *nm F* doggie

18. Si une traduction n'est pas possible (généralement en raison de différences culturelles au niveau du système éducatif ou du système juridique etc) un signe 'égal' (=) attire l'attention de l'utilisateur sur le fait que ce qui suit n'est pas une traduction mais une définition destinée à lui permettre de saisir un concept particulier.

    Le signe '≈' introduit un équivalent culturel.

Verbes composés

19. Une des nouvelles caractéristiques de ce dictionnaire est la façon dont il traite les verbes composés anglais. Ceux-ci ont en effet acquis le statut d'entrées, et sont mis en relief par des triangles pleins. Les verbes composés sont analysés de la façon suivante:

► *vi* (verbe intransitif)

get off: he got off at Victoria Station
il descendit à la gare Victoria
listen in: do you mind if I l. in while you talk?
ça vous dérange si j'écoute pendant que vous parlez?

► *vipo* (verbe intransitif à complémentation)

Il s'agit de verbes intransitifs associés à une particule qui peut ou bien doit être suivie d'un complément d'objet:

join in: they all joined in the chorus
(*le complément* **'the chorus'** *peut être omis)*
ils se mirent tous à chanter (en chœur)

come across: where did you c. across that word?
(*le complément* **'that word'** *est nécessaire*)
où avez-vous trouvé ce mot?

Dans le second cas en particulier, la combinaison verbe/préposition se comporte comme un verbe transitif, et peut généralement se mettre à la voix passive:

a type of virus which had never been come across before
un genre de virus qui n'avait jamais été rencontré auparavant

► *vtsep* (verbe transitif, séparable)

Les deux parties du verbe peuvent être séparées:

dig up: they're digging the road up, they're digging up the road
ils font des travaux sur la route

Il existe une forme passive:

the road is being dug up again
la route est de nouveau en travaux

Si le complément du verbe est un pronom personnel (ou bien 'it'), les deux parties du verbe doivent être séparées:
look up: I'll l. him up when I'm in Paris
je le contacterai quand je serai à Paris

► *vtas* (verbe transitif, toujours séparé)

get over with: she got her work over with as quickly as possible
elle a fini son travail aussi vite que possible
tide over: can you lend me £5 to t. me over till Monday?
pourrais-tu me prêter cinq livres pour me dépanner jusqu'à lundi?

Le complément d'objet ne peut pas suivre la particule.

► *vtaspo* (verbe transitif, toujours séparé, à complémentation)

La particule doit toujours être séparée du verbe, et le verbe et la particule doivent être suivis d'un complément d'objet:
keep from: to k. sth from s.o.
cacher qch à qn

Labels and abbreviations used in the text

Indicateurs de champs sémantiques et abréviations utilisés dans le texte

abbreviation	*abbr, abrév*	abréviation
adjective	*adj*	adjectif
administration	*Admin*	administration
adverb	*adv*	adverbe
agriculture	*Agr*	agriculture
American	*Am*	américain
anatomy	*Anat*	anatomie
antiquity	*Antiq*	antiquité
approximately	*approx*	approximativement
archaic, obsolete	*Arch*	archaïque
archeology	*Archeol, Archéol*	archéologie
architecture	*Archit*	architecture
slang	*Arg*	argot
article	*art*	article
	Art	beaux-arts
astrology	*Astrol*	astrologie
astronomy	*Astron*	astronomie
space travel	*Astronaut*	astronautique
Australian	*Austr*	australien
motoring, road traffic	*Aut*	automobiles, circulation routière
auxiliary	*aux*	auxiliaire
aviation	*Av*	aviation
	Banking, Banque	
art	*Beaux-Arts*	
Belgian	*Belg*	belge
	Billiards, Billard	
biology	*Biol*	biologie
botany	*Bot*	botanique
	Bowling, Boules	
Stock Exchange	*Bourse*	
	Boxing, Boxe	
British	*Br*	britannique
Canadian	*Can*	canadien
	Cards, Cartes	
carpentry	*Carp*	menuiserie
catholicism	*Cathol*	catholicisme
European Community	*CE*	Communauté européenne
ceramics	*Cer, Cér*	céramique
chemistry	*Ch*	chimie
	Chess	échecs
surgery	*Chir*	chirurgie
Church of England	*Church of Eng*	Église anglicane
cinema, films	*Cin*	cinéma, films
commerce	*Com*	commerce
comparative	*comp*	comparatif
compounds	*(compounds)*	mots composés
computing	*Comptr*	informatique, ordinateurs
conditional	*cond*	conditionnel
conjunction	*conj*	conjonction
conjugated like	*conj like*	se conjugue comme
building industry	*Constr*	construction
horseracing	*Courses de chevaux*	
sewing	*Couture*	
cricket	*Cr*	cricket
cookery	*Culin*	cuisine
	Cycling, Cyclisme	
definite	*def, déf*	défini
demonstrative	*dem, dém*	démonstratif
dialect	*Dial*	dialecte
diminutive	*dimin*	diminutif
European Community	*EC*	Communauté européenne
chess	*Échecs*	
ecology	*Ecol, Écol*	écologie
economics	*Econ, Écon*	économie
for example	*eg*	par exemple
Church of England	*Église anglicane*	
electricity	*El, Él*	électricité
electronics	*Electron, Électron*	électronique
children's language	*Enf*	langage des enfants
English	*Eng*	anglais
entomology	*Ent*	entomologie
horseriding	*Équitation*	
fencing	*Escrime*	
especially	*esp*	surtout

et cetera	*etc*	et cetera
euphemism	*Euph*	euphémisme
feminine	*f*	féminin
familiar, colloquial	*F*	familier
football	*Fb*	football
	Fencing	escrime
figurative use	*Fig*	sens figuré
finance	*Fin*	finance
	Fishing	pêche
formal use	*Fml*	langage formel
feminine plural	*fpl*	féminin pluriel
French	*Fr*	français
future tense	*fu*	futur
geography	*Geog, Géog*	géographie
geology	*Geol, Géol*	géologie
geometry	*Geom, Géom*	géométrie
grammar	*Gram*	grammaire
gymnastics	*Gym*	gymnastique
heraldry	*Her, Hér*	héraldique
history	*Hist*	histoire
	Horseracing	courses de chevaux
	Horseriding	équitation
humorous	*Hum*	humoristique
hydraulic engineering	*HydE*	hydraulique
imperative	*imp*	impératif
impersonal	*impers*	impersonnel
imperfect	*impf*	imparfait
indicative	*ind*	indicatif
industry	*Ind*	industrie
indefinite	*indef, indéf*	indéfini
infinitive	*inf*	infinitif
interjection	*int*	interjection
interrogative	*interr*	interrogatif
invariable	*inv*	invariable
ironic	*Iron*	ironique
journalism, press	*Journ*	journalisme, presse
law, legal	*Jur*	juridique, droit
	Knitting	tricot
linguistics	*Ling*	linguistique
literary use	*Lit, Litt*	usage littéraire
literature	*Liter, Littér*	littérature
masculine	*m*	masculin
mathematics	*Math*	mathématiques
mechanical engineering	*MecE*	mécanique
medicine	*Med, Méd*	médecine
carpentry	*Menuis*	menuiserie
meteorology, weather	*Met, Météo*	météorologie, temps
metallurgy	*Metal, Métal*	métallurgie
noun masculine and feminine	*mf*	nom masculin et féminin
military	*Mil*	militaire
mining	*Min*	mines
mineralogy	*Miner, Minér*	minéralogie
masculine plural	*mpl*	masculin pluriel
music	*Mus*	musique
mythology	*Myth*	mythologie
noun	*n*	nom
we	*n.*	nous
swimming	*Natation*	
nautical, naval	*Nau*	nautique, naval
negative	*neg, nég*	négatif
noun feminine	*nf*	nom féminin
noun feminine plural	*nfpl*	nom féminin pluriel
noun masculine	*nm*	nom masculin
noun masculine plural	*nmpl*	nom masculin pluriel
noun plural	*npl*	nom pluriel
nuclear	*Nucl*	nucléaire
numeral	*num*	numéral
obstetrics	*Obst*	obstétrique
occasionally	*occ*	parfois
	Old-fashioned	vieilli
optics	*Opt*	optique
computing	*Ordinat*	ordinateurs, informatique
ornithology	*Orn*	ornithologie
occasionally	*parfois*	
parliament	*Parl*	parlement
fishing	*Pêche*	
pejorative	*Pej, Péj*	péjoratif
personal	*pers*	personnel
petroleum industry	*Petr, Pétr*	industrie pétrolière
pharmacy	*Pharm*	pharmacie
philosophy	*Phil*	philosophie

philately	*Philat*	philatélie
past historic	*p hist*	passé simple
photography	*Phot*	photographie
physics	*Phys*	physique
physiology	*Physiol*	physiologie
plural	*pl*	pluriel
politics	*Pol*	politique
possessive	*poss*	possessif
past participle	*pp*	participe passé
present tense	*pr*	présent
prefix	*pref, préf*	préfixe
preposition	*prep, prép*	préposition
present indicative	*pr ind*	présent de l'indicatif
pronoun	*pron*	pronom
proverb	*Prov*	proverbe
present participle	*prp*	participe présent
present subjunctive	*pr sub*	présent du subjonctif
psychology, psychiatry	*Psy*	psychologie, psychiatrie
past tense	*pt*	prétérit
something	*qch*	quelque chose
someone	*qn*	quelqu'un
registered trademark	®	marque déposée
radio	*Rad*	radio
railways	*Rail*	chemin de fer
regionalism	*Région*	régionalisme
relative	*rel*	relatif
religion	*Rel*	religion
school	*Sch, Scol*	école
Scottish	*Scot*	écossais
	see	voir
	Sewing	couture
singular	*sing*	singulier
skiing	*Ski*	
slang	*Sl*	argot
someone	*s.o.*	quelqu'un
often	*souvent*	
sport	*Sp*	sport
specialized term	*Spec, Spéc*	terme de spécialiste
Stock Exchange	*St Exch*	Bourse
something	*sth*	quelque chose
subjunctive	*sub*	subjonctif
suffix	*suff*	suffixe
Swiss	*Suisse*	
superlative	*superl*	superlatif
surgery	*Surg*	chirurgie
especially	*surtout*	
	Swimming	natation
	Swiss	suisse
technical	*Tech*	technique
telephones	*Tel, Tél*	téléphones
telecommunications	*Telecom, Télécom*	télécommunications
textiles	*Tex*	textiles
theatre	*Th*	théâtre
knitting	*Tricot*	
television	*TV*	télévision
typography, printing	*Typ*	typographie, imprimerie
university	*Univ*	université
United States	*US*	États-Unis
usually	*usu*	généralement
verb	*v*	verbe
you	*v.*	vous
veterinary medicine	*Vet, Vét*	médecine vétérinaire
intransitive verb	*vi*	verbe intransitif
old-fashioned	*Vieilli*	
verb intransitive with prepositional object	*vipo*	verbe intransitif à complémentation
see	*voir*	
pronominal verb	*vpr*	verbe pronominal
transitive verb	*vt*	verbe transitif
verb transitive, always separate	*vtas*	verbe transitif, toujours séparé
verb transitive, always separate, with prepositional object	*vtaspo*	verbe transitif, toujours séparé, à complémentation
verb transitive, separable	*vtsep*	verbe transitif, séparable
vulgar	*Vulg*	vulgaire
zoology	*Zool*	zoologie

Symboles phonétiques de l'anglais

Consonnes

[b] but [bʌt] ; tab [tæb]
[d] dab [dæb] ; madder ['mædər] ; build [bɪld]
[dʒ] jam [dʒæm] ; jail, gaol [dʒeɪl] ; gem [dʒem] ; gin [dʒɪn] ; rage [reɪdʒ] ; edge [edʒ] ; badger ['bædʒər]
[f] fat [fæt] ; laugh [lɑːf] ; ruff, rough [rʌf] ; elephant ['elɪfənt]
[g] go [gəʊ] ; ghost [gəʊst] ; guard [gɑːd] ; again [ə'gen] ; egg [eg] ; exist [eg'zɪst] ; hungry ['hʌŋgrɪ]
[h] hat [hæt] ; cohere [kəʊ'hɪər]
[j] yam [jæm] ; yet [jet] ; youth [juːθ]
[k] cat [kæt] ; kitten ['kɪt(ə)n] ; choir, quire ['kwaɪər] ; cue, queue [kjuː] ; arctic ['ɑːktɪk] ; pique [piːk] ; exercise ['eksəsaɪz]
[l] lad [læd] ; all [ɔːl] ; table ['teɪb(ə)l] ; chisel ['tʃɪz(ə)l]
[m] mat [mæt] ; ram [ræm] ; prism ['prɪz(ə)m]
[n] no, know [nəʊ] ; ban [bæn] ; banner ['bænər] ; pancake ['pænkeɪk] ; nab [næb] ; gnat [næt]
[ŋ] bang [bæŋ] ; sing [sɪŋ] ; singer ['sɪŋər] ; anchor ['æŋkər] ; anger ['æŋgər] ; link [lɪŋk]
[p] pat [pæt] ; top [tɒp]
[r] rat [ræt] ; arise [ə'raɪz] ; barring ['bɑːrɪŋ]
[*r*] (*seulement prononcé en cas de liaison avec le mot suivant*) far [fɑː*r*] ; sailor ['seɪlə*r*] ; finger ['fɪŋgə*r*]
[s] sat [sæt] ; scene [siːn] ; mouse [maʊs] ; ice [aɪs] ; psychology [saɪ'kɒlədʒɪ]
[ʃ] sham [ʃæm] ; dish [dɪʃ] ; sugar ['ʃʊgər] ; ocean ['əʊʃən] ; nation ['neɪʃən] ; machine [mə'ʃiːn]
[t] tap [tæp] ; pat [pæt] ; patter ['pætər] ; trap [træp]
[tʃ] chat [tʃæt] ; search [sɜːtʃ] ; chisel ['tʃɪz(ə)l] ; thatch [θætʃ] ; rich [rɪtʃ]
[θ] thatch [θætʃ] ; ether ['iːθər] ; faith [feɪθ] ; breath [breθ]
[ð] that [ðæt] ; there [ðeər] ; mother ['mʌðər] ; breath [briːð]
[v] vat [væt] ; avail [ə'veɪl] ; rave [reɪv]
[w] wall [wɔːl] ; await [ə'weɪt] ; quite [kwaɪt] ; what [wɒt] ; why [waɪ]
[z] zinc [zɪŋk] ; buzz [bʌz] ; houses ['haʊzɪz] ; business ['bɪznɪs]
[ʒ] pleasure ['pleʒər] ; vision ['vɪʒən] ; beige [beɪʒ]
[χ] loch [lɒχ] (*prononciation écossaise*)

Voyelles

[æ] bat [bæt] ; add [æd]
[ɑː] art [ɑːt] ; ask [ɑːsk] ; car [kɑːr] ; father ['fɑːðər]
[e] bet [bet] ; leopard ['lepəd] ; menace ['menɪs] ; said [sed]
[ɜː] curl [kɜːl] ; herb [hɜːb] ; learn [lɜːn] ; myrrh [mɜːr]
[ə] decency ['diːsənsɪ] ; obey [ə'bəɪ] ; amend [ə'mend] ; delicate ['delɪkət]
[iː] bee [biː] ; fever ['fiːvər] ; see, sea [siː] ; release [rɪ'liːs]
[ɪ] bit [bɪt] ; added ['ædɪd] ; drastic ['dræstɪk] ; sieve [sɪv]
[ɒ] wad [wɒd] ; wash [wɒʃ] ; lot [lɒt] ; what [wɒt]
[ɔː] all [ɔːl] ; haul [hɔːl] ; saw [sɔː] ; caught, court [kɔːt] ; short [ʃɔːt] ; wart [wɔːt] ; thought [θɔːt]
[ʊ] put [pʊt] ; wool [wʊl] ; wood, would [wʊd] ; full [fʊl]
[uː] shoe [ʃuː] ; prove [pruːv] ; threw, through [θruː] ; frugal ['fruːg(ə)l] ; room [ruːm]
[ʌ] cut [kʌt] ; sun, son [sʌn] ; cover ['kʌvər] ; rough [rʌf]

Diphtongues

[aɪ] aisle, isle [aɪl] ; height [haɪt] ; life [laɪf] ; fly [flaɪ] ; beside [bɪ'saɪd]
[aʊ] fowl, foul [faʊl] ; house [haʊs] ; cow [kaʊ]
[eə] bear, bare [beər] ; there, their [ðeər] ; airy ['eərɪ]
[eɪ] date [deɪt] ; day [deɪ] ; rain, rein, reign [reɪn]
[əʊ] low [ləʊ] ; soap [səʊp] ; rope [rəʊp] ; road, rode, rowed [rəʊd] ; sew, so, sow (*verb*) [səʊ]
[ɪə] beer, bier [bɪər] ; appear [ə'pɪər] ; really ['rɪəlɪ]
[ɔɪ] boil [bɔɪl] ; toy [tɔɪ] ; oyster ['ɔɪstər] ; loyal ['lɔɪəl]
[ʊə] poor [pʊər] ; sure [ʃʊər]

French phonetic symbols

Consonants

[b] beau [bo]; abbé [abe]; robe [rɔb]
[d] donner [dɔne]; sud [syd]
[f] feu [fø]; bref [brɛf]; phrase [fraz]
[g] garde [gard]; guerre [gɛr]; second [səgɔ̃]; exister [ɛgziste]
[ʒ] gilet [ʒilɛ]; manger [mɔ̃ʒe]; âge [ɑʒ]
[k] camp [kɑ̃]; képi [kepi]; quatre [katr]; écho [eko]; taxer [takse]; accident [aksidɑ̃]
[l] lait [lɛ]; aile [ɛl]; facile [fasil]
[m] mon [mɔ̃]; flamme [flam]; prisme [prism]
[n] né [ne]; canne [kan]; automne [otɔn]
[ŋ] (*in words of foreign origin*) parking [parkiŋ]; smoking [smɔkiŋ]
[ɲ] campagne [kɔ̃paɲ]; gnaule [ɲol]
[p] pain [pɛ̃]; tape [tap]
[r] rare [rar]; arbre [arbr]; rhume [rym]
[s] sou [su]; rébus [rebys]; cire [sir]; scène [sɛn]; six [sis]
[ʃ] chose [ʃoz]; chercher [ʃɛrʃe]; schisme [ʃism]
[t] table [tabl]; nette [nɛt]; théâtre [teɑtr]
[v] voir [vwar]; vie [vi]; wagon [vagɔ̃]
[w] ouate [wat]; ouest [west]; noir [nwar]; (*also in words of foreign origin*) tramway [tramwɛ]; whist [wist]
[z] cousin [kuzɛ̃]; zéro [zero]; deuxième [døzjɛm]
[j] yacht [jɔt, jat]; piano [pjano]; ration [rasjɔ̃]; voyage [vwajaʒ]; travailler [travaje]; cahier [kaje]
[ɥ] muet [mɥɛ]; huit [ɥit]; luire [lɥir]; aiguille [egɥij]

Vowels

[a] chat [ʃa]; tache [taʃ]; toit [twa]; phare [far]
[ɑ] âge [ɑʒ]; âgé [ɑʒe]; tâche [tɑʃ]
[e] été [ete]; donner, donné [dɔne]; légal [legal]
[ə]* le [lə]; ce [sə]; entremets [ɑ̃trəmɛ]
[ø] feu [fø]; nœud [nø]; heureuse [ørøz]
[œ] seul [sœl]; œuf [œf]; sœur [sœr]; cueillir [kœjir]
[ɛ] elle [ɛl]; très [trɛ]; terre [tɛr]; rêve [rɛv]; père [pɛr]
[i] vite [vit]; signe [siɲ]; sortie [sɔrti]
[ɔ] donner [dɔne]; album [albɔm]; fort [fɔr]
[o] dos [do]; impôt [ɛ̃po]; chaud [ʃo]
[u] tout [tu]; goût [gu]; août [u]; cour [kur]
[y] cru [kry]; ciguë [sigy]; mur [myr]
[ɑ̃] enfant [ɑ̃fɑ̃]; temps [tɑ̃]; paon [pɑ̃]; centre [sɑ̃tr]; branche [brɑ̃ʃ]
[ɛ̃] vin [vɛ̃]; plein [plɛ̃]; thym [tɛ̃]; prince [prɛ̃s]; plainte [plɛ̃t]
[ɔ̃] mon [mɔ̃]; plomb [plɔ̃]; longe [lɔ̃ʒ]; comte [kɔ̃t]
[œ̃] un [œ̃]; lundi [lœ̃di]; humble [œ̃bl]

*The symbol (ə) (in brackets) indicates that the mute e is pronounced in careful speech but not in rapid speech.

ENGLISH-FRENCH

A

A, a[1] [eɪ] *n* **(a)** (la lettre) A, a *m*; **it's spelt with two a's,** cela s'écrit avec deux a; **the car's old, but it gets me from A to B,** c'est une vieille voiture mais elle a le mérite de rouler; **to be A-OK,** *(in health)* tenir la forme; **everything's A-OK,** tout baigne dans l'huile; **the A to Z** ® **of London,** le guide complet de Londres; **an A to Z of Indian Cooking,** un guide détaillé de la cuisine indienne; **he knows the case from A to Z,** il connaît l'affaire à fond; *Am* **A 1** ['eɪ'wʌn] **, A number 1,** de première qualité; **51 A,** *(house number)* 51 bis; **A-bomb,** bombe *f* A; *Br Aut* **A road,** ≈ route nationale; **A-side,** *(of record)* face *f* A; **(b)** *Sch (grade)* **to get an A in French,** avoir un A en français; *Eng Sch* **A level,** ≈ baccalauréat *m*, *F* bac *m*; **(c)** *Mus* la *m*; **in A flat,** en la bémol.

a[2], *before vowel* **an** [ə, ən; *stressed* eɪ, æn] *indef art* **(a)** un, une; **a man,** un homme; **an old man,** un vieillard; **a hill,** une colline; **a hotel** [əhəʊ'tel] , *Old-fashioned* **an hotel** [ənəʊ'tel] , un hôtel; **an hour** [ən'aʊər] , une heure; **a unit** [ə'juːnɪt] , une unité; **an MP** [ən'em'piː] , un député; **a man and (a) woman,** un homme et une femme; **a wife and mother,** une épouse et mère; **so/too high a price,** un prix si/trop élevé;

(b) *(def art in Fr)* **to have a red nose,** avoir le nez rouge; **I have a sore throat,** j'ai mal à la gorge; **to have a taste for sth,** avoir le goût de qch; *Iron* **a fine excuse!,** la belle excuse!; *(generalizing)* **a woman takes life too seriously,** les femmes prennent la vie trop au sérieux;

(c) *(distributive)* **at thirty pence a kilo,** à trente pence le kilo; **five francs a head,** cinq francs par tête; **three times a week/a year,** trois fois par semaine/par an; **fifty kilometres an hour,** cinquante kilomètres à l'heure;

(d) *(partitive in Fr)* **it has given me an appetite,** cela m'a donné de l'appétit;

(e) (= **a certain**) **I know a doctor who ...,** je connais un médecin qui ...; **in a sense,** dans un sens;

(f) (= **the same**) **to come in two at a time,** entrer deux par deux; **of a size,** de la même grandeur *ou* taille;

(g) (= **a single**) **I haven't understood a word,** je n'ai pas compris un seul mot; **I couldn't see a thing,** je n'y voyais rien du tout; **there wasn't a book to be found in the house,** il n'y avait pas un seul livre dans la maison;

(h) *(omitted in Fr)* **he is an Englishman/a father/a barrister,** il est anglais/père/avocat;

(i) **to put an end to sth,** mettre fin à qch; **to make a fortune,** faire fortune; **what a man!,** quel homme!; **what a pity!,** quel dommage!; **as a rule,** en règle générale; **to live like a prince,** vivre en prince; **within a short time,** à bref délai; *(before nouns in apposition)* **Caen, a large town in Normandy,** Caen, ville importante de Normandie.

AA [eɪ'eɪ] *n* **(a)** *(abbr* **anti-aircraft***)* D.C.A.; **(b)** *abbr* **Automobile Association**; **(c)** *(abbr* **Alcoholics Anonymous***)* A.A..

AAA [eɪeɪ'eɪ] *(normally spoken: 3As)* *n* **(a)** *abbr* **Amateur Athletics Association**; **(b)** *abbr* **American Automobile Association**.

Aachen ['ɑːχən, 'ɑːkən] *n* Aix-la-Chapelle.

AB [eɪ'biː] *n* **(a)** *Nau (abbr* **able(-bodied) seaman***)* matelot de deuxième classe; **(b)** *US (abbr* **Artium Baccalaureus***)* = **B.A.**.

ABA [eɪbiː'eɪ] *n* **(a)** *abbr* **Amateur Boxing Association**; **(b)** *abbr* **American Bar Association**.

A & E [eɪən'diː] *n Med (abbr* **accident and emergency***)* = service *m* des urgences, *F* les urgences *fpl*.

aback [ə'bæk] *adv* **to be taken a.,** en rester déconcerté *ou* interdit; **this remark rather took me a.,** cette remarque m'a quelque peu décontenancé.

abacus, *pl* **-ci, -cuses** ['æbəkəs, -saɪ, -kəsɪz] *n* **(a)** *Math* boulier (compteur); **(b)** *Archit* abaque *m*, tailloir *m*.

abaft [ə'bɑːft] *Nau* **1** *adv* sur l'arrière, vers l'arrière. **2** *prep* **a. the mast,** sur l'arrière du mât.

abalone [æbə'ləʊnɪ] *n (shellfish)* ormeau *m*.

abandon[1] [ə'bændən] *n* désinvolture *f*, entrain *m*; *F* **with gay a.,** *(to dance, to spend money etc)* avec une joyeuse désinvolture.

abandon[2] *vt* **(a)** abandonner *(une voiture, un bâtiment)*; délaisser *(sa famille etc)*; *Nau* **to a. ship,** abandonner *ou* évacuer le navire; **(b)** renoncer à *(un projet, un principe etc)*; *Sp* **to a. play,** *(temporarily)* interrompre une partie; *(permanently)* annuler une partie; **to a. all hope,** abandonner tout espoir; **to a. oneself to sth,** s'abandonner à qch, succomber à qch; **she abandoned herself to grief,** elle s'abandonna au chagrin.

abandoned [ə'bændənd] *adj* **(a)** abandonné; **an a. car,** une voiture abandonnée; **(b)** *Old-fashioned (behaviour)* dévergondé; *(woman)* perdu.

abandonment [ə'bændənmənt] *n* abandon *m*.

abase [ə'beɪs] *vt Lit* abaisser, humilier *(qn)*; **to a. oneself,** s'abaisser, s'humilier.

abasement [ə'beɪsmənt] *n Lit* humiliation *f*.

abash [ə'bæʃ] *vt* confondre, décontenancer *(qn)*; **to be** *or* **feel abashed at sth,** rester tout interdit de qch.

abate [ə'beɪt] *vi (of storm etc)* diminuer, faiblir; *(of storm, fear, anger, pain)* se calmer, s'apaiser; *(of flood)* baisser; *(of noise)* diminuer; **the wind abated,** le vent tomba.

abatement [ə'beɪtmənt] *n* diminution *f*, affaiblissement *m*; apaisement *m (d'une tempête)*; abaissement *m (des eaux)*; **noise a. campaign,** campagne *f* contre le bruit.

abattoir ['æbətwɑːr] *n* abattoir *m*.

abbess ['æbɪs] *n* abbesse *f (d'un couvent)*; supérieure *f*.

abbey ['æbɪ] *n* **(a)** abbaye *f*; **(b) a. (church),** (église *f*) abbatiale *f*.

abbot ['æbət] *n* abbé *m (d'un monastère)*; (père *m*) supérieur *m*.

abbreviate [ə'briːvɪeɪt] *vt* abréger *(un mot etc)*.

abbreviation [əbriːvɪ'eɪʃən] *n* abréviation *f*.

ABC, abc [eɪbiː'siː] *n* **(a)** *(alphabet)* ABC *m*, abc *m*; **to know one's ABC,** connaître son alphabet; **(b)** *Fig* b a ba *m (d'un art, d'une science)*.

abdicate ['æbdɪkeɪt] **1** *vt* abdiquer *(un trône, ses responsabilités)*; renoncer à *(un droit, une charge)*. **2** *vi* abdiquer.

abdication [æbdɪ'keɪʃən] *n* abdication *f (d'un trône)*; renonciation *f (à un droit, de ses responsabilités)*.

abdomen ['æbdəmən] *n* abdomen *m*.

abdominal [əb'dɒmɪn(ə)l] *adj* abdominal, -aux.

abduct [əb'dʌkt] *vt Jur* enlever *(qn)*; détourner *(un mineur)*.

abduction [əb'dʌkʃən] *n Jur* enlèvement *m*; détournement *m (de mineur)*; **a. by force,** rapt *m*.

abductor [əb'dʌktər] **1** *n* **(a)** *Jur* ravisseur *m*; auteur *m* d'enlèvement; détourneur *m (de mineur)*; **(b)** *Anat* (muscle *m*) abducteur *m*. **2** *adj Anat (muscle)* abducteur.

abeam [ə'biːm] *adv Nau Av* par le travers.

abed [ə'bed] *adv Arch* au lit.

aberrant [æ'berənt] *adj* aberrant, anormal.

aberration [æbə'reɪʃən] *n* aberration *f*, déviation *f*; écart *m (de conduite)*; égarement *m (des passions etc)*; *Astron Math Opt etc* aberration; **mental a.,** égarement (de l'esprit), aberration, confusion mentale.

abet [ə'bet] *vt* **(-tt-)** encourager *(le crime)*; **to a. s.o. in a crime,** encourager qn à un crime; *Jur* **to aid and a. s.o.,** être le complice de qn.

abetting [ə'betɪŋ] *n Jur* **(aiding and) a.,** complicité *f*.

abeyance [ə'beɪəns] *n* suspension *f (d'une loi)*; **the matter is still in a.,** la question est toujours en suspens; *Jur* la question est toujours pendante; **law in a.,** loi inappliquée; **to fall into a.,** tomber en désuétude; *Jur* **estate in a.,** succession vacante.

abhor [əb'hɔːr] *vt* **(-rr-)** abhorrer *(qn, qch)*, avoir *(qn, qch)* en horreur.

abhorrence [əb'hɒrəns] *n* horreur *f* **(of,** de).

abhorrent [əb'hɒrənt] *adj* odieux, répugnant **(to,** à).

abide [ə'baɪd] *v* (*pt & pp* **abided**) **1** *vt* (*in neg phrases*) **I can't a. him,** je ne peux pas le sentir; **I can't a. that sound/dishonesty,** je ne supporte pas ce bruit/la malhonnêteté. **2** *vi* **(a)** (*of thing*) durer, demeurer; **(b)** *Arch & Lit* rester, demeurer (**with s.o.,** avec qn).

▶**abide by** *vipo* rester fidèle à, tenir (*une promesse*); se conformer à, se soumettre à, respecter (*une règle, une décision, une loi*); **I a. by my decision/what I said,** je maintiens ma décision/mon dire.

abiding [ə'baɪdɪŋ] *adj* permanent; (*impression*) durable.

ability [ə'bɪlɪtɪ] *n* **(a)** (*capability*) capacité *f*; **an a. to do,** (*sth innate*) une capacité de faire; (*sth learned*) une capacité à faire; **(b)** (*skill*) habileté *f*, capacité *f*, compétence *f*; **man of considerable a.,** homme très doué; **she shows artistic a.,** elle manifeste des dons artistiques; **to do sth to the best of one's a.,** faire qch dans la mesure de ses moyens; faire qch de son mieux; **the needs and abilities of each student,** les besoins et les aptitudes de chaque étudiant; **(c)** *Jur* habilité *f* (*à succéder, à tester*); capacité légale.

abject ['æbdʒekt] *adj* **(a)** abject, misérable; **a. poverty,** misère *f*; **(b)** (*despicable*) bas, vil; (*cowardice*) abject; **(c)** (*servile*) servile; **an a. apology,** des excuses abjectes.

abjectly ['æbdʒektlɪ] *adv* (*see adj*) **(a)** abjectement, misérablement; **(b)** bassement; **(c)** avec servilité.

abjuration [æbdʒʊ'reɪʃən] *n* abjuration *f* (**of,** de); reniement *m* (*de sa foi*).

abjure [əb'dʒʊər] *vt* abjurer (*sa religion, ses erreurs*); renier (*sa foi*).

ablation [æb'leɪʃən] *n Geol Surg* ablation *f*.

ablative ['æblətɪv] *Gram* **1** *n* (cas *m*) ablatif *m*; **in the a.,** à l'ablatif; **a. absolute,** ablatif absolu. **2** *adj* (*case*) ablatif.

ablaze [ə'bleɪz] *adv & adj* en feu, en flammes; **to be a.,** flamber; **to set sth a.,** embraser qch; **a. with light,** resplendissant de lumière; **her eyes were a. with anger,** ses yeux étaient enflammés de colère.

able ['eɪb(ə)l] *adj* **(a)** (*person*) capable, compétent; **a very a. man,** un homme de haute capacité; **she's very a.,** elle a des capacités; *Jur* **a. in body and mind,** sain de corps et d'esprit; **to be a. to do sth,** (*know how to*) savoir *ou* être capable de faire qch; (*be physically capable of*) pouvoir faire qch, être en mesure de *ou* à même de faire qch; **I shan't be a. to come,** je ne pourrai pas venir; **someone else will be better a. to help you,** quelqu'un d'autre sera plus à même de vous venir en aide; **I'll do it if I'm a.,** je le ferai si je le peux; **a. to pay,** en mesure de payer; **a. piece of work,** travail compétent *ou* bien fait; **your a. assistance,** votre aide efficace; **(b)** *Jur* apte, habile (*à léguer, à succéder*).

able-bodied ['eɪb(ə)l'bɒdɪd] *adj* fort, robuste; *Mil* bon pour le service; **every a.-b. person helped in the search,** toute personne en état de le faire a participé aux recherches.

ablution [ə'bluːʃən] *n* ablution *f*; *F* **to perform one's ablutions,** faire ses ablutions.

ably ['eɪblɪ] *adv* avec compétence.

abnegate ['æbnɪgeɪt] *vt* renoncer à (*une croyance, un privilège etc*).

abnegation [æbnɪ'geɪʃən] *n* (*of belief etc*) renoncement *m*; **self-a.,** renoncement à *ou* abnégation *f* de soi-même.

abnormal [æb'nɔːm(ə)l] *adj* anormal, -aux.

abnormality [æbnɔː'mælɪtɪ] *n* **(a)** caractère anormal (*de qch*); **(b)** (*event etc*) anomalie *f*, aberration *f*.

abnormally [æb'nɔːm(ə)lɪ] *adv* anormalement.

aboard [ə'bɔːd] **1** *adv* à bord; **to go a.,** monter à bord; **to take sth a.,** embarquer qch; **all a.!,** *Nau* embarquez!; *Rail etc* en voiture!; **welcome a.!,** bienvenue à bord! **2** *prep* dans (*un train, un autobus, un avion*); **a. ship,** à bord (d'un navire).

abode [ə'bəʊd] *n Lit* (*home*) demeure *f*, habitation *f*; *F* **welcome to my humble a.,** bienvenu dans mon petit chez-moi; *Jur* **place of a.,** domicile *m*; **of no fixed a.,** sans domicile fixe.

abolish [ə'bɒlɪʃ] *vt* abolir, supprimer (*un usage, un abus*); abroger (*une loi*).

abolition [æbə'lɪʃən] *n* (*of custom, abuse*) abolition *f*, suppression *f*; abrogation *f* (*d'une loi*); **a. of slavery,** abolition de l'esclavage.

abolitionism [æbə'lɪʃənɪzəm] *n Hist* abolitionnisme *m*.

abolitionist [æbə'lɪʃənɪst] *n & adj Hist* abolitionniste *mf*.

abominable [ə'bɒmɪnəb(ə)l] *adj* abominable; **the a. snowman,** l'abominable homme des neiges.

abominably [ə'bɒmɪnəblɪ] *adv* (*to behave*) abominablement; **it's a. hot,** il fait abominablement chaud.

abominate [ə'bɒmɪneɪt] *vt* abominer, détester (*qn, qch*), avoir (*qn, qch*) en abomination.

abomination [əbɒmɪ'neɪʃən] *n* abomination *f*; **to hold s.o./sth in a.,** avoir qn/qch en abomination; *F* **this coffee's an a.,** ce café est abominable.

aboriginal [æbə'rɪdʒɪn(ə)l] *adj* aborigène, indigène; *Austr* aborigène.

aborigine [æbə'rɪdʒɪnɪ] *n* aborigène *mf*.

abort[1] [ə'bɔːt] *n* **(a)** *Mil Av etc* mission non accomplie; **launch a.,** termination prématurée d'un lancement; **(b)** *Comptr* suspension *f* d'exécution (*d'un programme*).

abort[2] **1** *vi* **(a)** *Obst* avorter; **(b)** *Fig* (*of project*) avorter. **2** *vt* **(a)** *Obst* faire avorter (*une femme*); **(b)** *Fig* faire avorter (*un projet*); **(c)** *Comptr* suspendre l'exécution de (*un programme*).

abortion [ə'bɔːʃən] *n* **(a)** *Obst* avortement *m*; **to have an a.,** se faire avorter; **to perform an a.,** faire un avortement; **a. clinic,** clinique *f* où l'on pratique des avortements; **the a. debate,** le débat sur l'avortement; **a. law,** loi *f* sur l'avortement; **(b)** *Fig* avortement *m* (*d'un projet*); **(c)** *F* (*person, animal*) avorton *m*, monstre *m*; *F* œuvre manquée; **what an a.!,** quelle horreur!

abortionist [ə'bɔːʃənɪst] *n* médecin avorteur; avorteur, -euse.

abortive [ə'bɔːtɪv] *adj* (*plan etc*) avorté, manqué; **a. attempt,** essai qui n'aboutit à rien; coup manqué; *Mil etc* **a. attack,** attaque avortée; **a. mission,** mission non accomplie.

abound [ə'baʊnd] *vi* abonder, foisonner; **literary allusions a. in the book,** les allusions littéraires foisonnent dans le livre; **to a. in** *or* **with sth,** abonder en *ou* de qch, regorger de qch; **the region abounds in oil,** la région abonde en pétrole; **the forest abounds with deer,** la forêt regorge de daims.

about [ə'baʊt] *adv & prep* **(a)** (*around*) autour (de); **the hills (round) a. the town,** les collines à l'entour de la ville; **the people a. us,** les gens auprès de nous *ou* qui nous entourent; **look a. you,** regarde autour de toi; **keep your wits a. you,** garde ta présence d'esprit; *Fml* **to have sth a. one's person,** avoir qch sur soi;

(b) (*in different directions*) de côté et d'autre; **to stroll a.,** se promener de-ci, de-là *ou* de côté et d'autre; **to follow s.o. a.,** suivre qn partout; **to wave one's arms a.,** agiter ses bras en tous sens; **there were clothes all a.,** il y avait des vêtements un peu partout; **don't leave those papers lying a.,** ne laissez pas traîner ces papiers;

(c) (*nearby*) **there was nobody a.,** il n'y avait personne (de visible); **there weren't many people a.,** il n'y avait pas grand monde alentour; **the book was nowhere a.,** le livre n'était nulle part; **he must be somewhere a.,** il doit être quelque part (par là);

(d) (*active*) **to be up** *or* **out and a. again,** (*after illness*) être de nouveau sur pied; **she's usually up** *or* **out and a. by 7 o'clock,** elle est debout généralement à 7 heures; **to be a. early,** être matinal; **there's a great deal of flu a. at present,** il y a beaucoup de grippe actuellement;

(e) (*characteristic of*) **there is something unusual a. him,** il y a dans sa personne quelque chose de pas ordinaire; **there's something a. a horse that ...,** il y a chez le cheval un je ne sais quoi qui ...;

(f) **to do sth turn and turn a.,** faire qch à tour de rôle *ou* tour à tour; **the other way a.,** en sens inverse; **to turn a.,** faire demi-tour; se retourner; *Mil* **a. turn!,** *US* **a. face!,** demi-tour!;

(g) (*approximately*) environ, presque; **there are a. thirty,** il y en a environ trente, il y en a une trentaine; **she's a. my age,** elle a à peu près mon âge; **it will cost a. a hundred francs,** ça coûtera dans les cent francs; **a. one o'clock,** vers une heure; **he's a. as tall as you,** il est à peu près de ta grandeur; **you've got a. as much intelligence as a two-year-old!,** tu es à peu près aussi futé qu'un gamin de deux ans!; **that's a. right,** c'est à peu près ça *ou* cela; **it's a. time,** il serait temps, il commence à être temps; *Iron* il est grand temps; **I've had (just) a. enough of you!,** je commence à en avoir assez de toi!;

(h) (*on the subject of*) au sujet de; **a book a. France,** un livre sur la France; **to enquire a. sth,** se renseigner sur *ou* au sujet de qch; **to speak a. sth,** parler de qch; **to quarrel a. nothing,** se quereller à propos de rien; **what are they talking a.?,** de quoi parlent-ils?; **what's it all a.?,** de quoi s'agit-il?; **I know what it's all a.,** je sais de quoi il s'agit; **how** *or* **what a. a game of bridge/going to Paris?,** si on faisait un bridge/allait à Paris?; **well, what a. it? shall we go?,** alors, qu'est-ce qu'on fait? on y va?; **what a. my bath?,** et mon bain?; **what a. us?,** et nous, alors?; **what a. the children?,** (*what's to be done with them?*) et les enfants?;

what a. money?, (*have you got enough?*) et pour ce qui est de l'argent?;

(i) (*ready, intending*) to be a. to do sth, être sur le point de faire qch; what were you a. to say?, qu'est-ce que vous alliez dire?; he is a. to leave, il est sur le départ; *esp Am* I'm not a. to pay 5,000 francs for that, je n'ai pas l'intention de payer cela 5 000 francs;

(j) (*active in, engaged in*) to go a. one's work/business, vaquer à son travail/ses affaires; while you are a. it, pendant que vous y êtes; be quick a. it!, dépêchez-vous!; what are they a.?, qu'est-ce qu'ils font?

about-face, about-turn [ə'baʊt'feɪs,-'tɜːn] *n* demi-tour *m*; revirement *m* (*d'opinion*); to do an a.-f. *or* a.-t., (*turn around*) faire demi-tour; (*change one's mind*) changer complètement d'avis *ou* d'opinion.

above [ə'bʌv] 1 *adv & prep* (a) au-dessus (de); the water reached a. their knees, l'eau leur montait jusqu'au-dessus des genoux; a. sea level, au-dessus du niveau de la mer; the tenants of the flat a., les locataires du dessus; the sky a. was clear, au-dessus de moi *ou* de nous *etc*, le ciel était clair; heavens a.!, juste ciel!; a voice from a., une voix d'en haut; view from a., vue plongeante; policy imposed from a., politique imposée d'en haut; a mountain rises a. the lake, une montagne s'élève au-dessus du lac *ou* domine le lac; his voice was heard a. the shouting, on entendait sa voix par-dessus le tumulte; a. ground, sur terre; *Min* au jour, à la surface; a. one's station, au-dessus de sa condition; to live a. one's means, vivre au-dessus de ses moyens; temperature a. normal, température supérieure à la normale; a. criticism, hors de l'atteinte de la critique; that's a. me, cela me dépasse; they value friendship a. all else, ils placent l'amitié par-dessus tout; a. all ..., surtout ..., par-dessus tout ...; over and a. that, en plus de cela;

(b) (*of person*) to be a. suspicion, être au-dessus de tout soupçon; I am a. doing that, je me respecte trop pour faire cela; she's not a. telling the occasional lie, elle irait jusqu'au mensonge à l'occasion; he thinks he's a. all that, il pense qu'il est au-dessus de tout ça; *F* to get a. oneself, s'en faire accroire;

(c) (*in rank*) he is a. me (in rank), il est mon supérieur (hiérarchique);

(d) (*of number*) a. twenty, plus de vingt; a. $100, plus de 100 dollars; women aged 18 and a., les femmes âgées de 18 ans et plus; the temperature didn't rise a. 10°C, la température n'a pas dépassé 10°C;

(e) (*upstream*) the Seine a. Paris, la Seine en amont de Paris;

(f) (*north*) a. this latitude, au nord de cette latitude;

(g) (*in book, document etc*) ci-dessus; the paragraph a., le paragraphe ci-dessus; as a., comme ci-dessus.

2 *adj* (*in book etc*) the a. quotation, la citation ci-dessus.

3 *n* the a. is a quotation from Hamlet, le passage ci-dessus est une citation de Hamlet; the a. was the driver of the vehicle, le susdit était le conducteur du véhicule.

aboveboard [ə'bʌvbɔːd] 1 *adv* to play fair and a., jouer cartes sur table. 2 *adj* franc; everything is a., tout est franc et loyal; his conduct was completely a., il a agi en tout bien (et) tout honneur.

above-mentioned, above-named [əbʌv'menʃənd, -'neɪmd] *adj* susmentionné, susdit.

abracadabra [æbrəkə'dæbrə] *n* abracadabra *m*.

abrade [ə'breɪd] 1 *vt* user (*qch*) par le frottement *ou* par abrasion, abraser; écorcher (*la peau*). 2 *vi* s'user par le frottement.

abrasion [ə'breɪʒən] *n* (a) (usure *f* par le) frottement *m*; abrasion *f*; (b) écorchure *f*, éraflure *f* (*de la peau*).

abrasive [ə'breɪsɪv] 1 *adj* (*surface, substance*) abrasif; *Fig* (*person*) caustique; a. paper, papier abrasif. 2 *n* abrasif *m*.

abreast [ə'brest] *adv* de front; three/four a., trois/quatre de front; to march two a., marcher par deux; to march four a., marcher par rangs de quatre; *Nau* (in) line a., en ligne de front; to come a. of a car, arriver à la hauteur d'une voiture; to keep a. of a science, suivre les progrès d'une science; to keep *or* be a. of the times, suivre son temps, être de son temps.

abridge [ə'brɪdʒ] *vt* abréger (*un ouvrage etc*); raccourcir (*un livre, un chapitre*).

abridged [ə'brɪdʒd] *adj* (*édition*) abrégé; a. version, abrégé *m*, résumé *m*.

abridg(e)ment [ə'brɪdʒmənt] *n* (a) (*action*) abrégement *m* (*d'un ouvrage etc*); (b) (*result*) abrégé *m*, résumé *m*.

abroad [ə'brɔːd] *adv* (a) à l'étranger; to live a., vivre à l'étranger; our colleagues from a., nos collègues étrangers; capital invested a., capitaux placés dehors; (b) de tous côtés; scattered a., éparpillé de tous côtés; the news got a., la nouvelle s'est répandue; (c) (*outside*) to venture a., sortir (de la maison).

abrogate ['æbrəgeɪt] *vt* abroger (*une loi*).

abrogation [æbrə'geɪʃən] *n* (*of law*) abrogation *f*.

abrupt [ə'brʌpt] *adj* (a) (*person*) abrupt; (*manière, ton*) brusque; (*départ*) brusque, précipité; (*style*) heurté, saccadé; (*change*) brutal; the evening came to an a. end, la soirée s'acheva brusquement; there was an a. change in the weather, le temps a changé brutalement; (b) (*pente*) abrupt, raide; (*falaise*) escarpé, à pic; (*montée*) ardu, raide.

abruptly [ə'brʌptlɪ] *adv* (*see adj*) (a) abruptement; brusquement; (b) abruptement; à pic; en pente raide.

abruptness [ə'brʌptnɪs] *n* (a) (*of person*) brusquerie *f*, manière *f* brusque; précipitation *f* (*d'un départ*); caractère heurté *ou* saccadé (*du style*); (b) raideur *f* (*d'une pente*).

abscess ['æbses] *n* abcès *m*.

abscond [əb'skɒnd] *vi* se soustraire à la justice; s'enfuir, s'évader (from, de); *F* décamper, filer.

absconder [əb'skɒndər] *n* fugitif, -ive; (*prisoner*) évadé, -ée.

absconding [əb'skɒndɪŋ] 1 *adj* en fuite. 2 *n* évasion *f*, fuite *f*.

►**abseil down** ['æbseɪl] *vi* descendre en rappel.

abseiling ['æbseɪlɪŋ] *n* (*in mountaineering*) rappel *m*.

absence ['æbsəns] *n* (a) absence *f*, éloignement *m* (from, de); during one of his absences abroad, lors d'un de ses voyages à l'étranger; in the a. of the manager, en l'absence du directeur; to be conspicuous by one's a., briller par son absence; *Prov* a. makes the heart grow fonder, = l'éloignement renforce l'affection; *Jur* sentenced in one's a., condamné par contumace; leave of a., congé *m*; *Mil etc* a. without leave, absence illégale; (b) (*lack*) manque *m*; an a. of punctuation, un manque de ponctuation; the a. of references to the crisis, le manque de références à la crise; the a. of a tail in human beings, l'absence de queue chez l'être humain; in the a. of definite information, faute de *ou* à défaut de renseignements précis; (c) a. of mind, distraction *f*, préoccupation *f*.

absent[1] ['æbsənt] *adj* (a) absent (from, de); a. (from school), absent de l'école; to a. friends!, (*toast*) à tous nos amis absents!; *Mil etc* a. without leave, porté manquant; (b) (*lacking*) manquant; this tone was a. from her next speech, ce ton était absent de son discours suivant; in this animal the teeth are a., chez cet animal les dents sont absentes *ou* manquent; (c) an a. stare, un regard absent.

absent[2] [æb'sent] *vt* to a. oneself, s'absenter (from, de).

absentee [æbsən'tiː] *n* (a) absent, -ente; manquant, -ante (*à l'appel*); *Hist* a. landlord, absentéiste *m*; (b) *Ind etc* absentéiste *mf*.

absenteeism [æbsən'tiːɪz(ə)m] *n* absentéisme *m*.

absently ['æbsəntlɪ] *adv* distraitement; d'un air distrait.

absentminded [æbsənt'maɪndɪd] *adj* distrait, préoccupé.

absentmindedly [æbsənt'maɪndɪdlɪ] *adv* distraitement; d'un air distrait; she a. left it on the train, elle l'a laissé dans le train par distraction.

absentmindedness [æbsənt'maɪndɪdnɪs] *n* distraction *f*, préoccupation *f*.

absinth(e) ['æbsɪnθ] *n* absinthe *f*.

absolute ['æbsəluːt] 1 *adj Gram Math etc* absolu; case of a. necessity, cas de nécessité absolue *ou* de force majeure; *F* it's an a. disgrace, c'est un véritable scandale; *F* he's an a. fool, c'est un parfait imbécile; *Pol* a. majority, majorité absolue; a. monarch, roi absolu; a. power, pouvoir absolu; *Math* a. value, valeur absolue; a. zero, zéro absolu. 2 *n Phil* the a., l'absolu *m*.

absolutely [æbsə'luːtlɪ] *adv* absolument; you're a. right, vous avez entièrement *ou* tout à fait raison; that's ridiculous — a., c'est ridicule — (oui,) tout à fait; that's a. untrue!, c'est tout à fait faux!; that's a. disgraceful, c'est absolument honteux; it is a. forbidden, il est formellement interdit; *Gram* verb used a., verbe employé absolument.

absolution [æbsə'luːʃən] *n Rel* absolution *f*; to give s.o. a., donner l'absolution à qn.

absolutism ['æbsəluːtɪz(ə)m] *n Pol* absolutisme *m*.

absolve [əb'zɒlv] *vt* absoudre (*qn*) (of, de); she was absolved from all blame, il fut reconnu qu'elle n'était aucunement responsable.

absorb [əb'sɔːb, -'zɔːb] *vt* (a) absorber (*un liquide, la chaleur etc*); amortir (*un choc, un son*); se charger de (*coûts*); *Com* racheter (*une société*); *Fig* he absorbs information very quickly, il enregistre les informations avec une grande rapidité; these units were absorbed into the new army, ces unités furent intégrées dans le nouveau

corps d'armée; **(b)** (*interest, occupy*) **his business absorbs him,** ses affaires l'absorbent; **to be** *or* **become absorbed in sth,** s'absorber dans qch; **to listen with absorbed interest,** écouter avec un intérêt profond.
absorbency [əb'sɔːbənsɪ, -'zɔːb-] *n* capacité *f* d'absorption.
absorbent [əb'sɔːbənt, -'zɔːb-] *adj & n* absorbant *m*.
absorber [əb'sɔːbər, -'zɔːb-] *n Aut etc* amortisseur *m* (*de choc etc*).
absorbing [əb'sɔːbɪŋ, -'zɔːb-] *adj* **(a)** (*substance*) absorbant; **(b)** (*subject, article, discussion*) absorbant, passionnant.
absorption [əb'sɔːpʃən, -'zɔːb-] *n* **(a)** absorption *f* (*de liquide*); amortissement *m* (*de sons, de chocs etc*); *Com* rachat *m* (*d'une société*); **(b)** (*interest*) absorption *f*; **her a. in the book was so great that ...,** elle était tellement absorbée dans son livre que ... .
abstain [əb'steɪn] *vi* **(a)** s'abstenir; **to a. from (doing) sth,** s'abstenir de (faire) qch; **to a. from meat,** s'abstenir de manger de la viande; **(b)** (*from alcohol*) s'abstenir de boissons alcooliques; **(c)** *Pol* s'abstenir, ne pas voter.
abstainer [əb'steɪnər] *n* **to be a total a.,** ne pas boire d'alcool.
abstemious [əb'stiːmɪəs] *adj* sobre, tempérant; (*repas*) frugal; **he is very a.,** il est très sobre.
abstemiously [əb'stiːmɪəslɪ] *adv* sobrement; (*manger*) frugalement.
abstemiousness [əb'stiːmɪəsnɪs] *n* sobriété *f*, tempérance *f*.
abstention [əb'stenʃən] *n* **(a)** abstention *f*, abstinence *f* (**from,** de); **(b)** *Pol* **there were two abstentions,** il y eut deux abstentions.
abstentionist [ab'stenʃənɪst] *n Pol* abstentionniste *mf*.
abstinence ['æbstɪnəns] *n* **(a)** abstinence *f* (**from,** de); *Rel* **day of a.,** jour *m* d'abstinence; **total a.,** abstinence complète; **(b)** (*de boissons alcooliques*) abstinence *f*.
abstract¹ ['æbstrækt] **1** *adj* **(a)** (*nombre, nom, art*) abstrait; **a. artist,** abstrait *m*; **(b)** *Fml* (*obscure*) abstrait, abstrus. **2** *n* **(a) the a.,** l'abstrait *m*; **in the a.,** dans l'abstrait; **(b)** (*work of art*) peinture *ou* sculpture abstraite.
abstract² *n* résumé *m*, abrégé *m*.
abstract³ [æb'strækt] *vt* **(a)** (*remove*) soustraire, dérober (**sth from s.o.,** qch à qn); détourner (*de l'argent*); *Ch* extraire (par distillation); **(b)** résumer, abréger (*un texte*); dépouiller (*un livre*); relever (*un compte*); **(c)** *Phil* abstraire, faire abstraction de (*une qualité, une conception*).
abstracted [æb'stræktɪd] *adj* distrait.
abstractedly [æb'stræktɪdlɪ] *adv* distraitement; d'un air distrait.
abstraction [æb'strækʃən] *n* **(a)** soustraction *f* (*de papiers etc*); détournement *m* (*d'argent*); *Ch Ind* extraction *f* (par distillation); **(b)** (*abstract idea*) idée abstraite; **to lose oneself in abstractions,** se perdre dans les abstractions; **(c)** (*distraction*) distraction *f*; préoccupation *f* (d'esprit); **in a moment of a.,** dans un moment d'inattention; **(d)** *Phil* abstraction *f*; **(e)** *Art* peinture *ou* sculpture abstraite.
abstractly ['æbstræktlɪ] *adv* abstraitement.
abstruse [əb'struːs] *adj* abstrus.
abstruseness [əb'struːsnɪs] *n* caractère abstrus.
absurd [əb'sɜːd] **1** *adj* absurde; **it's a.!,** c'est ridicule! **2** *n* **the a.,** l'absurde *m*.
absurdity [əb'sɜːdɪtɪ] *n* absurdité *f*; **speech full of absurdities,** discours plein d'absurdités.
absurdly [əb'sɜːdlɪ] *adv* absurdement; *F* **she's a. rich,** elle est ridiculement riche.
abundance [ə'bʌndəns] *n* **(a)** abondance *f*; **in a.,** en abondance, à profusion; **to live in a.,** vivre dans l'abondance; **(b)** *Biol etc* abondance *f* (*d'une espèce etc*); **(c)** *Cards* (*in solo whist*) abondance *f*.
abundant [ə'bʌndənt] *adj* abondant (**in,** en); fertile (*en blé etc*); **there is a. evidence that ...,** il a été amplement démontré que ... .
abundantly [ə'bʌndəntlɪ] *adv* abondamment; en abondance; à foison; **they made their feelings a. clear,** ils exprimèrent leurs sentiments tout à fait clairement.
abuse¹ [ə'bjuːs] *n* **(a)** (*misuse*) abus *m* (**of,** de); emploi abusif (*d'un terme etc*); *Jur* **a. of authority,** abus d'autorité *ou* de pouvoir; **a. of trust,** prévarication *f*; **to remedy an a.,** redresser un abus; **alcohol a.,** l'abus *ou* l'excès *m* d'alcool; **(b)** (*insults*) insultes *fpl*, injures *fpl*; **term of a.,** injure; **to shower a. on s.o.,** accabler qn d'injures; **(c)** (*of child etc*) mauvais traitement.
abuse² [ə'bjuːz] *vt* **(a)** (*misuse*) abuser de (*son autorité, la confiance de qn etc*); mésuser de (*son pouvoir*); faire abus de (*qch*); **a much abused word,** mot employé abusivement; **(b)** (*insult*) injurier, dire des injures à (*qn*); **(c)** (*ill-treat*) maltraiter, houspiller (*qn*); **an abused child,** un enfant maltraité.
abusive [ə'bjuːsɪv] *adj* **(a)** (*emploi*) abusif; **(b)** (*propos*) injurieux; (*homme*) grossier; **he got** *or* **became a.,** il devint grossier.
abusively [ə'bjuːsɪvlɪ] *adv* (*parler*) injurieusement, grossièrement.
▶abut on, abut against [ə'bʌt] *vipo* **(-tt-)** aboutir à, confiner à (*un champ, une rivière etc*); *Constr* s'appuyer *ou* buter contre (*une paroi*); s'arc-bouter contre (*un mur*).
abutment [ə'bʌtmənt] *n Archit Constr* arc-boutant *m*, *pl* arcs-boutants (*d'une muraille*); contrefort *m* (*d'un mur*); butée *f*, culée *f* (*d'un pont*); piédroit *m* (*d'une voûte*).
abysmal [ə'bɪzm(ə)l] *adj* **(a)** sans fond; **a. ignorance,** ignorance profonde; **(b)** *F* (*bad*) atroce.
abysmally [ə'bɪzm(ə)lɪ] *adv* atrocement; **a. ignorant,** d'une ignorance profonde.
abyss [ə'bɪs] *n Geog & Fig* abîme *m*, gouffre *m*; (*in ocean*) abysse *m*, zone abyssale.
abyssal [ə'bɪs(ə)l] *adj* (*depths*) *& Geol* abyssal.
Abyssinia [æbɪ'sɪnɪə] *n* Abyssinie *f*.
Abyssinian [æbɪ'sɪnɪən] **1** *adj* abyssinien, abyssin; (*cat*) abyssin. **2** *n* **(a)** Abyssinien, -ienne; **(b)** *Ling* abyssinien *m*.
AC [eɪ'siː] *n El* (*abbr* **alternating current**) CA *m*.
A/C, a/c *Com* (*abbr* **account**) c..
acacia [ə'keɪʃə] *n* (*shrub*) acacia *m*; **false a.,** faux acacia; robinier *m*.
academia [ækə'diːmɪə] *n Univ* milieu *m* universitaire.
academic [ækə'demɪk] **1** *adj* **(a)** (*carrière, costume etc*) universitaire; **the a. year,** l'année scolaire; **a. excellence,** excellence scolaire; **(b)** (*theoretical*) **a. discussion,** discussion abstraite; **of purely a. interest,** qui n'est intéressant qu'au point de vue théorique; **(c)** *Art* (*peinture etc*) académique. **2** *n* universitaire *mf*.
academically [ækə'demɪklɪ] *adv* académiquement.
academician [əkædə'mɪʃən] *n* académicien *m*; *esp* **Royal A.,** = membre de l'Académie royale des Beaux-Arts.
academicism [ækə'demɪsɪz(ə)m], **academism** [ə'kædəmɪz(ə)m] *n* académisme *m*.
academy [ə'kædəmɪ] *n* **(a)** académie *f*; **the Royal A. (of Arts),** = l'Académie royale des Beaux-Arts; **a. of music,** conservatoire *m*; **fencing a.,** salle *f* d'escrime; **military a.,** école *f* militaire; **(b)** (*school*) *Scot* ≈ lycée *m*; *Br & US* ≈ collège *m* (privé).
acanthus [ə'kænθəs] *n* **(a)** (*shrub*) acanthe *f*; **(b)** *Archit* (feuille *f* d')acanthe *f*.
accede [æk'siːd] *vi* **(a) to a. to the throne,** monter sur le trône; **(b)** (*assent*) **to a. to,** donner son adhésion à (*un traité*); donner suite à (*une demande, une prière*).
accelerate [ək'seləreɪt] **1** *vt* accélérer (*la marche, le pouls, un travail*); presser (*un mouvement, un travail*); précipiter (*les événements*). **2** *vi Aut* accélérer; (*of motion etc*) s'accélérer.
accelerated [ək'seləreɪtɪd] *adj* (*mouvement etc*) accéléré; *Cin* **a. motion,** accéléré *m*.
acceleration [əkselə'reɪʃən] *n* accélération *f*; **negative a.,** accélération retardatrice *ou* négative; *Aut* **the car has good a.,** cette voiture a une bonne accélération; **uniform a.,** vitesse uniformément accélérée.
accelerator [ək'seləreɪtər] *n* **(a)** *Aut* **a. (pedal),** accélérateur *m*; **to step on the a.,** accélérer; **(b)** *Phys* accélérateur *m*.
accent¹ ['æksənt] *n* **(a)** accent *m*; **to have a German/Liverpool a.,** avoir l'accent allemand/de Liverpool; **to speak with an a.,** parler avec un accent; **she speaks French without an a.,** elle parle français sans accent; **(b)** *Lit* **in broken accents,** d'une voix brisée *ou* entrecoupée; **(c)** (*sign*) accent *m*; **acute/grave a.,** accent aigu/grave; **(d)** (*stress*) accent *m*; **the a. is on the final syllable,** l'accent est sur la dernière syllabe; *Fig* **we're putting the a. on efficiency,** on met l'accent sur l'efficacité; *Fig* **fashion with the a. on youth,** mode qui met l'accent sur la jeunesse.
accent² [æk'sent] *vt* accentuer (*une syllabe etc*).
accented [æk'sentɪd] *adj* accentué; *Ling* accentuel.
accentuate [æk'sentʃʊeɪt] *vt* accentuer, faire ressortir (*un détail etc*); accuser (*un contraste*); **the photo accentuated the length of her face,** la photo accentuait la longueur de son visage; **to a. the need for sth,** accentuer la nécessité de qch.
accentuated [æk'sentʃʊeɪtɪd] *adj* fortement marqué; accentué; **the offbeat is a.,** le temps faible est accentué.
accentuation [æksentʃʊ'eɪʃən] *n* accentuation *f* (*d'une voyelle, d'un détail etc*).

accept [ək'sept] **1** *vt* **(a)** accepter (*un cadeau, une invitation, une offre*); agréer (*les salutations, les prières de qn, un prétendant*); admettre (*les raisons, les excuses de qn*); donner son adhésion à (*un traité*); *Com* **to a. a bill,** accepter un effet; **to a. (delivery of) goods,** prendre des marchandises en recette; **the machine won't a. foreign coins,** cette machine n'accepte pas la monnaie étrangère; **please a. my apologies,** je vous prie d'agréer mes excuses; **to be accepted,** (*socially etc*) être accepté; **contrary to accepted opinion,** à l'encontre des idées reçues; **it is generally accepted that ...,** il est généralement admis que ...; **(while) we a. that this may be more expensive ...,** tout en admettant que ceci puisse être plus cher ...; **the accepted custom,** l'usage admis; **I cannot a. that you knew nothing of this,** je n'arrive pas à croire que vous n'avez rien su de ceci;
(b) (*resign oneself to*) accepter; **she just accepts these hardships,** elle accepte tout bonnement ces épreuves; **to a. the inevitable** *or* **one's fate,** se soumettre au destin.
2 *vi* accepter; **they offered me a contract and I accepted,** ils m'ont proposé un contrat que j'ai accepté.

acceptability [əkseptə'bɪlɪtɪ] *n* acceptabilité *f*.

acceptable [ək'septəb(ə)l] *adj* **(a)** acceptable, agréable (**to,** à); **sacrifice a. to God,** sacrifice agréable à Dieu; **your cheque was most a.,** votre chèque est arrivé fort à propos; **a most a. gift,** un cadeau des plus bienvenus; **I trust these terms will be a. to you,** j'espère que ces conditions vous seront acceptables; **(b)** admissible, acceptable; **behaviour of this sort is not a.,** un comportement de la sorte est inacceptable; *F* **just about a.,** tolérable, supportable.

acceptance [ək'septəns] *n* **(a)** (*of gift, invitation, apology etc*) acceptation *f*; accueil *m* favorable (*de qch*); *Com Ind* réception *f* (*d'un article commandé*); **to find a.,** trouver créance; *Com* **to present a bill for a.,** présenter une traite à l'acceptation; **a. bank** *or* **house,** banque *f* d'escompte d'effets étrangers; **a. test** *or* **trial,** essai *m* de réception *ou* de recette; **(b)** (*of one's fate, circumstances*) acceptation *f*.

acceptation [æksep'teɪʃən] *n Fml* acception *f*; **in the full a. of the word,** dans toute l'acception du mot.

acceptor [ək'septər] *n* **(a)** *Com* accepteur *m*; **(b)** *Ch etc* accepteur *m*.

access¹ ['ækses] *n* **(a)** (*to person, place*) accès *m* (**to,** à); **to have a. to sth/s.o.,** avoir accès à qch/auprès de qn; **to give s.o. a. to sth/s.o.,** donner à qn accès à qch/à qn; **we must not give terrorists a. to the media,** nous ne devons pas rendre les médias accessibles aux terroristes; **means of a.,** moyens *mpl* d'accès; *Fml* **difficult of a.,** d'un accès *ou* d'une approche difficile; **burglars gained a. through a window,** les cambrioleurs sont passés *ou* sont entrés par une fenêtre; *Aut* **a. only,** accès interdit (sauf aux riverains); **the husband has unlimited a. to the children,** le mari a un droit de visite illimitée auprès de ses enfants; *Comptr* **a. code/time,** code *m*/temps *m* d'accès; **a. rights,** (*of divorced parent*) droits *mpl* de visite; **a. road,** route *f* d'accès; **(b)** accès *m* (*de colère etc*).

access² *vt Comptr* accéder à, avoir accès à (*des données*).

accessary [ək'sesərɪ] *n* = **ACCESSORY 2 (c)**.

accessibility [æksesɪ'bɪlɪtɪ] *n* accessibilité *f*.

accessible [ək'sesəb(ə)l] *adj* (*endroit, personne etc*) accessible; (*personne*) abordable; **information a. to everyone,** connaissances à la portée de tout le monde; **her latest novel is more a.,** son dernier roman est plus accessible.

accession [ək'seʃən] *n* **(a)** (*to post, power etc*) accession *f* (**to,** à); (*to throne*) avènement *m*, accession (**to,** à); **a. to manhood,** arrivée *f* à l'âge d'homme; **(b)** (*to treaty, demand*) accession *f*, assentiment *m*, adhésion *f* (**to,** à); **(c)** (*increase*) accroissement *m* (par addition); (*item*) addition *f*; **accession(s) book,** registre *m* des additions (*à une bibliothèque*); **a. number,** numéro *m* matricule.

accessory [ək'sesərɪ] **1** *adj* accessoire (**to,** à); (*matériel*) annexe; *Bot* **a. bud** *or* **shoot,** prompt-bourgeon *m*, *pl* prompts-bourgeons. **2** *n* **(a)** accessoire *m*; **car/camera accessories,** accessoires d'automobile/d'appareil; **(b)** (*clothing*) *usu pl* **accessories,** accessoires *mpl*; **(c)** *Jur* complice *m*; **a. to a crime,** complice d'un crime; **a. before the fact,** complice par instigation *ou* par assistance; **a. after the fact,** complice par aide après coup.

accident ['æksɪdənt] *n* accident *m*; *Jur* cas fortuit; **by a.,** accidentellement; (*by chance*) par hasard; **I'm sorry, it was an a.,** je suis désolé, c'était un accident; **an a. in the home/at work,** un accident domestique/de travail; **to have an a.,** être *ou* se trouver victime d'un accident; *F* (*esp of child*) faire pipi dans sa culotte; **car** *or* **road a.,** accident d'automobile; **the victims of the a.,** les victimes de l'accident, les accidentés *mpl*; **accidents will happen,** on ne peut pas parer à tout; **it's no a. that she made the film here,** ce n'est pas par hasard si elle a tourné le film ici; **their last child was an a.,** la naissance de leur dernier enfant fut un accident; **a. and emergency unit,** (*in hospital*) service *m* des urgences, les urgences *fpl*; **a. insurance,** assurance *f* contre les accidents; **a. victim,** victime *f* d'un accident.

accidental [æksɪ'dent(ə)l] **1** *adj* **(a)** (*chance*) accidentel, fortuit; **a. meeting,** rencontre *f* de hasard; **a. death,** mort accidentelle; **(b)** (*incidental*) accessoire, subsidiaire. **2** *n Mus* accident *m*; signe accidentel.

accidentally [æksɪ'dent(ə)lɪ] *adv* **(a)** (*by chance*) accidentellement, par hasard; **(b)** (*not deliberately*) accidentellement, par mégarde; *Hum* **a. on purpose,** comme par hasard, exprès.

accident-prone ['æksɪdəntprəʊn] *adj* prédisposé aux accidents; **he is a.-p.,** il lui arrive toujours des malheurs.

acclaim¹ [ə'kleɪm] *n* **the ballet was performed to great critical a.,** les critiques ont acclamé la représentation du ballet.

acclaim² *vt* **(a)** acclamer; accueillir (*qn*) par des acclamations; **to be acclaimed by the critics,** être acclamé des critiques; **he was acclaimed as the new Caruso,** il fut acclamé et déclaré être le nouveau Caruso; **her acclaimed portrayal of Cleopatra,** sa représentation acclamée de Cléopâtre; **(b)** (*proclaim*) **Charlemagne was acclaimed emperor,** Charlemagne fut acclamé *ou* proclamé empereur.

acclamation [æklə'meɪʃən] *n* acclamation *f*; **carried by a.,** adopté par acclamation.

acclimate [ə'klaɪmeɪt, 'æklɪmeɪt] *vt Am* = **ACCLIMATIZE**.

acclimation [æklɪ'meɪʃən] *n Am* = **ACCLIMATIZATION**.

acclimatization [əklaɪmətaɪ'zeɪʃən] *n* acclimatement *m* (**to,** à); *Fig* acclimatation *f*.

acclimatize [ə'klaɪmətaɪz] **1** *vt* acclimater; naturaliser (*une plante etc*); **to become acclimatized to a new environment,** s'acclimater à un nouvel environnement. **2** *vi* s'acclimater.

accolade ['ækəleɪd] *n* accolade *f*; **the ultimate a.,** la consécration suprême.

accommodate [ə'kɒmədeɪt] **1** *vt* **(a)** loger, recevoir (*tant de personnes*); **restaurant that can a. 50 people,** restaurant où il y a de la place pour 50 personnes; **(b)** (*satisfy*) satisfaire; **we will try to a. you,** nous essaierons de vous satisfaire; **to do sth to a. s.o.,** faire qch pour arranger qn; **(c)** (*provide*) **to a. s.o. with sth,** donner *ou* fournir qch à qn; fournir qn de qch; **to a. s.o. with a loan,** faire un prêt à qn; **(d)** (*reconcile*) accommoder (*ses goûts à ceux d'un autre*); arranger (*une querelle*); concilier (*des opinions*); **to a. oneself to circumstances,** s'adapter aux circonstances. **2** *vi Physiol* (*of eye*) accommoder.

accommodating [ə'kɒmədeɪtɪŋ] *adj* complaisant, obligeant.

accommodation [əkɒmə'deɪʃən] *n* **(a)** (*Am usu* **accommodations**) logement *m*; chambre(s) *f(pl)* (d'hôtel); **to look for a.,** chercher un logement; **furnished a.,** chambres garnies; **hotel a.,** hébergement *m* en hôtel; **there is a. in this hotel for 50 people,** cet hôtel peut loger 50 personnes; **a. address,** adresse *f* de convention; *Nau* **a. ladder,** échelle *f* de commandement *ou* de coupée; **(b)** (*adaptation*) ajustement *m*, adaptation *f* (**to,** à); *Physiol* accommodation *f* (*de l'œil*); **(c)** (*reconciliation*) arrangement *m* (*d'une dispute*); **to come to an a.,** arriver à un compromis; s'arranger (à l'amiable); **(d)** *Fin* avance *f*, prêt *m* (*d'argent*).

accompaniment [ə'kʌmpənɪmənt] *n* **(a)** *Mus* accompagnement *m* (**on the piano,** au piano); **(b)** accompagnement *m*; *Culin* **roast pork with an a. of apple sauce,** rôti de porc avec accompagnement de compote de pommes.

accompanist [ə'kʌmpənɪst] *n Mus* accompagnateur, -trice.

accompany [ə'kʌmpənɪ] *vt* **(a)** accompagner (*qn*); **to be accompanied by s.o.,** être accompagné de qn; **fever accompanied by** *or* **with delirium,** fièvre accompagnée de délire; **a meal accompanied with wine,** un repas accompagné de vin; **(b)** *Mus* accompagner (*qn*) (**on the piano,** au piano); **he accompanied himself on guitar,** il s'accompagna à la guitare.

accomplice [ə'kɒmplɪs, -'kʌm-] *n* complice *mf*; **his accomplices in crime,** les complices de ses crimes.

accomplish [ə'kɒmplɪʃ -'kʌm-] *vt* accomplir, achever,

venir à bout de (*qch*); mener à bonne fin (*une tâche*); effectuer (*un voyage, une traversée*); **to a. one's object,** atteindre son but; **mission accomplished,** mission accomplie.

accomplished [ə'kɒmplɪʃt, -'kʌm-] *adj* **(a)** achevé; **a. fact,** fait accompli; **(b)** (*dancer, pianist*) accompli; **to be very a.,** être très accompli; **an a. performance,** une performance accomplie.

accomplishment [ə'kɒmplɪʃmənt, -'kʌm-] *n* **(a)** accomplissment *m*, achèvement *m* (*d'une tâche etc*); réalisation *f* (*d'un projet*); **(b)** (*thing accomplished*) chose accomplie *ou* réalisée; **(c)** (*talent*) art *m* d'agrément, talent *m* (d'agrément); **she has many accomplishments,** elle est très accomplie, elle possède de nombreux talents.

accord¹ [ə'kɔːd] *n* **(a)** (*agreement*) accord *m*, consentement *m*; **with one a.,** d'un commun accord; **this was in a. with their policy,** ceci était en accord avec leur politique; **(b)** (*pact*) accord *m*; **(c)** (*initiative*) **to do sth of one's own a.,** faire qch de son plein gré *ou* de sa propre volonté.

accord² **1** *vi* s'accorder, être d'accord, concorder (**with,** avec); **this accords with her earlier statement/her views on divorce,** ceci concorde avec sa première déclaration/ses vues sur le divorce. **2** *vt Fml* accorder, concéder (*qch*) (**to,** à); **a privilege/title accorded him by the crown,** un privilège/un titre qui lui a été concédé par la couronne.

accordance [ə'kɔːdəns] *n* accord *m*, conformité *f*; **in a. with your instructions** *or* **wishes,** conformément à vos ordres.

according [ə'kɔːdɪŋ] *adv* **(a)** (*in conj phrase*) **a. to how it is done,** suivant la façon dont on le fait; **a. to whether one is rich or poor,** selon qu'on est riche ou pauvre; **(b)** (*in prep phrase*) **a. to instructions,** selon *ou* suivant *ou* d'après les ordres; **a. to age,** par rang d'âge; **a. to plan,** conformément au plan; **a. to our means,** selon nos moyens; **a. to him,** d'après lui; à ce qu'il dit; **a. to that,** d'après cela; **the Gospel a. to St Luke,** l'Evangile selon saint Luc.

accordingly [ə'kɔːdɪŋlɪ] *adv* **(a) to act a.,** agir en conséquence; **it's a formal dinner, so dress a.,** il s'agit d'un dîner officiel, alors habillez-vous en conséquence; **(b)** (*therefore*) donc; **a. I wrote to him,** je lui ai donc écrit, en conséquence je lui ai écrit.

accordion [ə'kɔːdɪən] *n Mus* accordéon *m*; **piano a.,** accordéon à touches; **a. player,** accordéoniste *mf*; *Sewing etc* **a. pleats,** plis *mpl* en accordéon.

accordionist [ə'kɔːdɪənɪst] *n Mus* accordéoniste *mf*.

accost [ə'kɒst] *vt* accoster, aborder (*qn, un navire*); (*of prostitute*) racoler (*qn*); **she was accosted by a beggar,** elle fut accostée par un mendiant.

account¹ [ə'kaʊnt] *n* **(a)** *Fin Com* compte *m*; **to open an a.,** (*in bank*) ouvrir un compte; **to have an a.** *or US* **a charge a. with s.o.,** avoir un compte chez qn; **put it on** *or* **charge it to my a.,** inscrivez-le *ou* mettez-le à mon compte; **to pay a sum on a.,** payer une somme en acompte *ou* à compte *ou* à valoir; **to settle an a.,** régler une note *ou* un compte; *Fig* régler ses comptes (**with s.o.,** avec qn); **the accounts,** la comptabilité (*d'une entreprise etc*); **accounts department,** (service *m* de) la comptabilité; **profit and loss a.,** compte des profits et pertes; **to keep the accounts,** tenir les livres *ou* les écritures *ou* les comptes;

(b) (*in advertising*) budget *m*; **we were pleased to get Nicol & Co's a.,** nous étions contents d'avoir Nicol et Cie comme clients;

(c) *St Exch* **the A.,** la liquidation (mensuelle); **a. day,** (jour *m* de) liquidation; (jour de) règlement *m*; **dealings for the a.,** négociations *fpl* à terme;

(d) état *m*, note *f* (*de dépenses*); exposé *m* (*de ses opérations*);

(e) (*advantage*) parti *m*; **to turn sth to a.,** tirer parti *ou* avantage de qch; mettre qch à profit; **to turn sth to good a.,** tirer un bon parti de qch;

(f) to call s.o. to a., demander une explication de qn, demander compte à qn (**for sth,** de qch); **those responsible must be brought to a.,** les responsables sont tenus de donner des explications; **to give a good a. of oneself,** s'acquitter bien;

(g) (*importance*) **of no a.,** (*person*) insignifiant, de peu d'importance; **to take sth into a., to take a. of sth,** tenir compte de qch, faire entrer qch en ligne de compte; **taking everything into a.,** tout calcul fait, tout bien calculé; **to leave out of a., to take no a. of,** ne pas tenir compte de (*qch*); ne pas compter (*qch*); négliger (*une circonstance*);

(h) (*because*) **I did it on a. of you,** je l'ai fait à cause de vous; **on a. of sth,** à *ou* pour cause de qch; en raison de qch; **he can't play football on a. of his health,** il ne peut pas jouer au football en raison de sa santé; **on no a., not on any a.,** dans aucun cas;

(i) to act on one's own a., agir de sa propre initiative *ou* de soi-même; **to set up in business on one's own a.,** s'établir à son compte;

(j) récit *m*, relation *f*, narration *f* (*d'un fait*); exposé *m* (*de la situation*); compte rendu (*dans un journal*); **to give an a. of sth,** faire le récit *ou* la relation de qch; **an interesting a. of his travels,** un récit intéressant de ses voyages; **her a. (of the events) was slightly different,** son exposé des événements était légèrement différent; **by all accounts,** au dire de tout le monde.

account² *vt* **to a. s.o. guilty,** tenir qn pour coupable.

►**account for** *vipo* **(a)** (*explain*) rendre compte de (*sa conduite, une dépense*); expliquer (*une circonstance*); (*justify*) justifier (*sa conduite, une dépense*); **that accounts for his interest in baseball,** voilà qui explique son intérêt pour le baseball; **I can't a. for it,** je ne me l'explique pas; **five people have still not been accounted for,** (*after accident etc*) cinq personnes n'ont pas encore été retrouvées; **there is no accounting for tastes,** chacun (à) son goût; **(b)** (*constitute*) constituer; **oil accounts for 10 per cent of exports,** le pétrole constitue dix pour cent des exportations; **(c)** (*destroy*) abattre (*un avion*); couler (*un sous-marin*); tuer (*des troupes*); *Fig* **he accounted for three batsmen,** il a renversé le guichet de trois batteurs.

accountability [əkaʊntə'bɪlɪtɪ] *n* responsabilité *f* (**to,** envers); **local government a. is an important issue,** la nécessité pour les municipalités de rendre compte de leurs actions est une question d'actualité.

accountable [ə'kaʊntəb(ə)l] *adj* **to be a. to s.o. for sth,** être responsable de qch envers qn; **to be a. for a sum of money,** être redevable d'une somme d'argent; **I am a. to no one,** je ne dois rendre compte à personne; **the police must be made more a. for their actions,** la police doit rendre compte de ses actions.

accountancy [ə'kaʊntənsɪ] *n* comptabilité *f*; expertise *f* comptable.

accountant [ə'kaʊntənt] *n Fin* (agent *m*) comptable *m*; **chief a.,** chef *m* de (la) comptabilité; **chartered a.,** *Am* **certified public a.,** = expert *m* comptable.

accounting [ə'kaʊntɪŋ] *n* comptabilité *f*; **cost a.,** comptabilité de prix de revient; **a. machine,** machine *f* comptable; **a. method,** méthode *f* de comptabilité; **a. policy,** politique *f* comptable.

accoutrements [ə'kuːtrəmənts] **,** *US* **accouterments** [ə'kuːtəmənts] *npl* équipement *m* (*du soldat*).

accredit [ə'kredɪt] *vt* **(a)** (*attribute*) attribuer (*qch*); **to a. s.o. with having done sth,** attribuer une action à qn; **this remark is accredited to Napoleon,** cette remarque est attribuée à Napoléon; **(b)** (*appoint, authorize*) accréditer (*un ambassadeur*) (**to a government,** auprès d'un gouvernement).

accredited [ə'kredɪtɪd] *adj* (*person*) accrédité, autorisé; **a. journalist,** journaliste accrédité; **a. college,** école reconnue (par l'Etat).

accretion [ə'kriːʃən] *n* (*through growth*) accroissement *m* organique; (*through addition*) accrétion *f*; accroissement par alluvion *ou* par addition.

accrual [ə'kruːəl] *n Fin* accumulation *f*.

accrue [ə'kruː] *vi* **(a)** *Fin* (*of interest*) s'accumuler; **accrued interest,** intérêt couru, intérêts (ac)cumulés; **(b)** (*of moneys, land etc*) **to a. to s.o.,** revenir à qn.

accumulate [ə'kjuːmjʊleɪt] *vt* accumuler, amasser (*une fortune etc*); amonceler, entasser (*des objets*); emmagasiner (*de l'électricité etc*).

accumulated [ə'kjuːmjʊleɪtɪd] *adj* accumulé; **a. dividends,** dividendes accumulées.

accumulation [əkjuːmjʊ'leɪʃən] *n* **(a)** (*act*) accumulation *f*; amoncellement *m*, entassement *m*; emmagasinage *m* (*de la chaleur, de l'électricité*); **(b)** (*result*) amas *m*, tas *m* (*d'objets, de sable etc*); accumulation *f* (*de faits*).

accumulative [ə'kjuːmjʊlətɪv] *adj* qui s'accumule; *Fin* cumulatif.

accumulator [ə'kjuːmjʊleɪtər] *n* **(a)** (*person*) accumulateur, -trice (*de richesses etc*); **(b)** *MecE Constr El* accumulateur *m*; **(c)** *Horseracing* **a. (bet),** pari *m* avec report.

accuracy ['ækjʊrəsɪ] *n* (*of calculation*) exactitude *f*; (*of firearm, shot etc*) précision *f*; (*of report, statement etc*) justesse *f*; (*of translation*) fidélité *f*; **we can now forecast the weather with far greater a.,** on peut maintenant établir les prévisions météorologiques avec une bien plus grande exactitude.

accurate ['ækjʊrət] *adj* (*calculation*) exact; (*firearm, shot, meter*) précis; (*meter, report*) juste; (*translation*) fidèle; **a. scales,** balance *f* juste; **my typing is much more a.,** ma frappe est beaucoup plus précise; **to be (strictly) a. ...,** pour être tout à fait exact ... .

accurately ['ækjʊrətlɪ] *adv* (*calculer*) exactement; (*calculer, faire un reportage*) avec précision; (*traduire, dessiner*) fidèlement; (*dessiner*) correctement.

accurateness ['ækjʊrətnɪs] *n* exactitude *f*, précision *f*.

accursed [ə'kɜːsɪd] *adj Lit* maudit.

accusation [ækjʊ'zeɪʃən] *n* **(a)** accusation *f*; *Jur* incrimination *f*; **to bring an a. against s.o.,** porter *ou* déposer plainte contre qn; **an a. of bribery was made against him,** on l'a accusé de corruption; **(b)** *Jur* acte *m* d'accusation.

accusative [ə'kjuːzətɪv] *Gram* **1** *n* (cas *m*) accusatif *m*; **in the a.,** à l'accusatif. **2** *adj* (*case*) accusatif.

accuse [ə'kjuːz] *vt* accuser (**s.o. of sth,** qn de qch; **of doing sth,** de faire qch); *Jur* incriminer (*qn*); **you stand accused,** vous êtes inculpé; **are you accusing me of lying?,** vous m'accusez de mentir?; *Iron* **no one could a. her of being punctual,** personne ne saurait l'accuser d'être ponctuelle.

accused [ə'kjuːzd] *n Jur* **the a.,** l'inculpé, -ée; le prévenu, la prévenue (*d'un délit*); l'accusé, -ée (*d'un crime*).

accuser [ə'kjuːzər] *n* accusateur, -trice.

accusing [ə'kjuːzɪŋ] *adj* accusateur, -trice; **an a. look,** un regard accusateur; **she pointed an a. finger at him,** elle dirigea vers lui un doigt accusateur.

accusingly [ə'kjuːzɪŋlɪ] *adv* d'une manière accusatrice.

accustom [ə'kʌstəm] *vt* accoutumer, habituer (**s.o. to sth,** qn à qch; **to do sth,** à faire qch); **habit had accustomed him to her silences,** l'habitude l'avait accoutumé à ses silences; **to a. oneself to,** s'accoutumer à, s'habituer à (*qch*); se faire à (*la discipline etc*).

accustomed [ə'kʌstəmd] *adj* **(a)** accoutumé, habitué (**to,** à); **to be a. to ...,** (*do usually*) avoir coutume de ...; (*have grown used to*) être accoutumé à ...; **I am a. to getting up early,** j'ai l'habitude de me lever de bonne heure; **they weren't a. to strangers/politeness,** ils n'étaient pas habitués aux étrangers/à la politesse; **to get** *or* **grow a. to sth,** s'accoutumer à qch; **her eyes had got a. to the dark,** ses yeux s'étaient accoutumés à l'obscurité; **(b)** (*habitual*) habituel, coutumier.

AC/DC ['eɪsiːdiːsiː] *n El* (*abbr* **alternating current/direct current**) CA/CC *m*; *F Fig* **to be AC/DC,** (*bisexual*) marcher à voile et à vapeur.

ace [eɪs] *n* **(a)** *Cards* as *m*; *F* **to have an a. up one's sleeve,** avoir un as dans sa manche; **(b)** *Tennis* **(service) a.,** ace *m*; **(c)** *F* (*expert*) as *m*; **flying a.,** as de l'aviation; **a. reporter,** journaliste *mf* d'élite; **(d) within an a. of sth,** à deux doigts de qch.

acerbic [ə'sɜːbɪk] *adj* (*fruit, taste*) aigre; *Fig* (*person, comment*) acerbe, mordant.

acerbity [ə'sɜːbɪtɪ] *n* aigreur *f*; acerbité *f*.

acetate ['æsɪteɪt] *n Ch* acétate *m*.

acetic [æ'siːtɪk, -'set-] *adj Ch* (*acide etc*) acétique.

acetone ['æsɪtəʊn] *n Ch* acétone *f*.

acetylene [æ'setɪliːn] *n Ch* acétylène *m*; **a. lamp,** lanterne *f* à acétylène; **a. welding,** soudure *f* autogène.

ache¹ [eɪk] *n* mal *m*, douleur *f*; **stomach a.,** mal de ventre; **to have (a) stomach a.,** avoir mal au ventre; **she's always telling people about all her aches and pains,** elle n'arrête pas de se plaindre de ses maux à tout le monde; **I've just got a few aches and pains, that's all,** j'ai quelques douleurs, c'est tout.

ache² *vi* **my head aches,** j'ai mal à la tête; **it makes my head a.,** cela me donne mal à la tête; **I'm aching all over,** j'ai mal partout; **it makes my heart a.,** cela me serre le cœur; *Fig* **he was aching to join in the fight,** il brûlait de prendre part au combat.

achieve [ə'tʃiːv] *vt* **(a)** (*accomplish*) atteindre à, arriver à (*un but*); **to a. a great deal/very little,** (*in life*) réussir/ne pas réussir; (*of task*) faire/ne pas faire grand-chose; **to a. one's purpose** *or* **ends,** parvenir *ou* en venir à ses fins; **to a. the impossible,** faire l'impossible; **to a. success,** réussir; **we achieved what we set out to do,** nous avons rempli nos objectifs; **I feel that we have achieved something,** j'ai le sentiment que nous sommes arrivés à quelque chose; **he will never a. anything,** il n'arrivera jamais à rien; **this policy achieved very little,** cette politique n'a pas donné de grands résultats; **what will that a.?,** (*of a suggestion etc*) pour en venir à quoi?; **(b)** (*gain*) acquérir (*une honneur*); se faire (*une réputation*); **they achieved a certain notoriety,** ils ont acquis une certaine renommée.

achievement [ə'tʃiːvmənt] *n* **(a)** (*feat*) exploit *m*, (haut) fait *m*; **their real a. lay in ...,** leur véritable prouesse résida dans ...; **getting him to talk about anything is quite an a.,** arriver à le faire parler de quoi que ce soit relève vraiment d'un exploit; **a lasting a.,** une réalisation durable; **her many achievements,** ses nombreux succès; **(b)** accomplissement *m*, réalisation *f*, exécution *f* (*d'un projet etc*).

achievement-orient(at)ed [ə'tʃiːvmənt'ɔːrɪent(eɪt)ɪd] *adj* **to be a.-o.,** mettre l'accent sur le succès; *Pej* être obsédé par le succès.

achiever [ə'tʃiːvər] *n* **to be an a.,** réussir tout ce qu'on entreprend.

Achilles [ə'kɪliːz] *n* Achille *m*; **A. tendon,** tendon *m* d'Achille; *Fig* **gambling is his A. heel,** le jeu est son point faible.

aching ['eɪkɪŋ] *adj* (*dent, tête etc*) qui (*vous*) fait mal; (*jambe*) endolori; **to have an a. heart,** avoir une peine de cœur; *F* **to have an a. void,** avoir l'estomac creux.

achromatic [ækrə'mætɪk] *adj Opt* achromatique.

achy ['eɪkɪ] *adj* courbaturé; *F* **I feel rather a.,** j'ai mal un peu partout.

acid¹ ['æsɪd] *adj* **(a)** acide; **a. drop,** (*sweet*) bonbon acidulé; *Ch* **a. solution,** solution *f* acide; **(b)** (*ton, réponse*) acide.

acid² *n* **(a)** acide *m*; **a. bath,** bain *m* acide; **a. rain,** pluies *fpl* acides; **a. test,** épreuve *f* à la pierre de touche; *Fig* épreuve décisive *ou* concluante; **(b)** *F* (= **LSD**) acide *m*.

acidic [ə'sɪdɪk] *adj* acide; *Fig* (*comment etc*) acerbe.

acidify [ə'sɪdɪfaɪ] *vt* acidifier.

acidity [ə'sɪdɪtɪ] *n* **(a)** acidité *f*; *Med* aigreurs *fpl*; **excessive a. in the stomach,** une acidité gastrique excessive; **(b)** *Fig* aigreur *f* (*d'une réponse*).

acidosis [æsɪ'dəʊsɪs] *n Med* acidose *f*.

acidulate [ə'sɪdjʊleɪt] *vt* aciduler.

acidulous [ə'sɪdjʊləs] *adj* acidulé.

ack-ack ['æk'æk] *n Old-fashioned Mil* (*weapon*) artillerie anti-aérienne; (*system*) ≈ Défense contre avions (D.C.A.); **a.-a. fire,** tir anti-aérien.

acknowledge [ək'nɒlɪdʒ] *vt* **(a)** (*recognize*) reconnaître, avouer (*une erreur, une dette etc*); reconnaître (*un service*); se montrer reconnaissant de, exprimer sa reconnaissance de (*un service*); **they acknowledged him as their king,** il fut reconnu pour roi; **to a. sth as a fact,** faire la constatation de qch; **generally acknowledged as** *or* **to be the best Chinese restaurant in the city,** généralement déclaré être le meilleur restaurant chinois de la ville; **to a. oneself beaten, to a. defeat,** s'avouer *ou* se reconnaître vaincu; **she acknowledged my presence,** elle m'a fait signe qu'elle m'avait vu; **he didn't even a. my presence,** il m'a complètement ignoré; **she never acknowledges me,** (*greets*) elle ne me fait jamais signe; **(b)** (*reply to*) répondre à (*une courtoisie, un salut etc*); **to a. (receipt of) a letter,** accuser réception d'une lettre; *Nau* **to a. a signal,** faire l'aperçu.

acknowledged [ək'nɒlɪdʒd] *adj* (*fait*) reconnu, avéré; (*expert etc*) qui fait autorité; **an a. thief,** un voleur reconnu.

acknowledg(e)ment [ək'nɒlɪdʒmənt] *n* **(a)** reconnaissance *f* (*d'une erreur, d'un service etc*); aveu *m* (*d'une faute*); constatation *f* (*d'un fait*); **I waved/smiled at him, but received no a.,** je lui ai fait signe/ai souri mais il ne m'a pas répondu; **in a. of,** pour témoigner ma *ou* sa *etc* reconnaissance de; **acknowledgments,** (*in book*) remerciements *mpl*; **(b)** reçu *m*, quittance *f* (*d'un paiement*); **a. (of receipt),** accusé *m* de réception (*d'une lettre*).

acme ['ækmɪ] *n Lit* comble *m* (*de la perfection*); sommet *m* (*de la gloire*); apogée *m* (*de la puissance*).

acne ['æknɪ] *n Med* acné *f*.

acolyte ['ækəlaɪt] *n* acolyte *m*.

aconite ['ækənaɪt] *n* (*plant*) & *Pharm* aconit *m*.

acorn ['eɪkɔːn] *n* gland *m* (de chêne).

acotyledon [əkɒtɪ'liːd(ə)n] *n Bot* plante *f* acotylédone.

acoustic [ə'kuːstɪk] *adj* acoustique; (*signal etc*) sonore; *Comptr* **a. coupler,** coupleur *m* acoustique; *Mus* **a. guitar,** guitare *f* acoustique; **a. tile,** carreau *m ou* panneau *m* insonorisant; *Anat* **a. nerve,** nerf acoustique *ou* auditif.

acoustically [ə'kuːstɪklɪ] *adv* acoustiquement.

acoustics [ə'kuːstɪks] *npl* (*with sing or pl verb*) acoustique *f*; **the a. of the hall are good,** cette salle a une bonne acoustique.

acquaint [ə'kweɪnt] *vt* **(a) to a. s.o. with,** informer *ou* avertir qn de (*qch*), faire savoir (*qch*) à qn; apprendre (*un fait*) à qn; mettre qn au courant de (*ses fonctions, la situa-*

tion); **they briefly acquainted me with the facts,** ils me mirent rapidement au courant des faits; **a stay in the jungle had acquainted him with these dangers,** un séjour dans la jungle l'a instruit de ces dangers; **the doctor acquainted himself with her case history,** (*by asking questions*) le médecin s'est informé de ses antécédents médicaux; (*by reading file*) le médecin s'est mis au courant de ses antécedents médicaux;

(b) to be acquainted with s.o., connaître qn; **to be acquainted with sth,** connaître qch, être au fait *ou* au courant de qch; **to become acquainted,** (*of two people*) faire connaissance; **to become acquainted with s.o.,** faire *ou* lier connaissance avec qn; **we soon became** *or* **got acquainted,** nous fîmes vite connaissance; **I got acquainted with him/them/***etc* **later,** j'ai fait sa/leur/*etc* connaissance plus tard; **to become acquainted with the facts,** prendre connaissance des faits; **to become acquainted with one's duties,** s'initier à ses fonctions.

acquaintance [ə'kweɪntəns] *n* **(a)** (*person*) connaissance *f*; **he is an a. (of mine),** je le connais; **a casual a. (of mine),** quelqu'un que je connais de loin; **to have a wide circle of acquaintances,** avoir des relations très étendues; **(b) a. with,** connaissance *f* de (*qn, un fait, une langue*); **to make s.o.'s a.,** faire la connaissance de qn.

acquiesce [ækwɪ'es] *vi* acquiescer, donner son assentiment (**in, to,** à); **to a. in a request,** acquiescer *ou* donner son assentiment à une demande; **to a. in an arrangement,** accepter un arrangement.

acquiescence [ækwɪ'es(ə)ns] *n* acquiescement *m* (**in, to,** à); assentiment *m*, consentement *m*.

acquiescent [ækwɪ'es(ə)nt] *adj* consentant.

acquire [ə'kwaɪər] *vt* acquérir (*une maison, des connaissances, de l'expérience etc*); prendre, contracter (*une habitude*); **we seem to have acquired a cat,** il semble qu'on ait hérité un chat; **to a. a taste for sth,** prendre goût à qch; **gin is an acquired taste,** le gin c'est quelque chose qu'on apprend à aimer; **Proust is an acquired taste,** Proust c'est un auteur qu'on apprend à aimer; **acquired characteristic,** caractère acquis; *Med* **Acquired Immune Deficiency Syndrome,** Syndrome *m* d'immuno-déficience acquise.

acquirement [ə'kwaɪəmənt] *n* acquisition *f* (**of,** de).

acquisition [ækwɪ'zɪʃən] *n* **(a)** (*act*) acquisition *f* (**of,** de); **(b)** (*object, person*) acquisition *f*; **she could be a useful a.,** elle pourrait se révéler être une acquisition utile.

acquisitive [ə'kwɪzɪtɪv] *adj* thésauriseur, -euse; **an a. nature,** une nature avide.

acquit [ə'kwɪt] *vt* (**-tt-**) **(a)** *Jur* acquitter (*un accusé*); **he was acquitted,** il fut acquitté; **to a. s.o. of,** absoudre qn de (*une faute*); décharger qn de (*une accusation*); **(b)** *Fin* acquitter, s'acquitter de, régler (*une dette*); **(c) to a. oneself well/badly/***etc*, bien/mal/*etc* s'en tirer.

acquittal [ə'kwɪt(ə)l] *n* **(a)** *Jur* acquittement *m* (*d'un accusé, d'un débiteur*); décharge *f* (*d'un accusé*); **(b)** exécution *f*, accomplissement *m* (*d'un devoir*).

acquittance [ə'kwɪtəns] *n* *Com Jur* acquit *m*, acquittement *m* (*d'une dette*).

acre ['eɪkər] *n* acre *f* (= 0,4 hectare); (*approx* =) arpent *m*, demi-hectare *m*; **vast acres,** des terres étendues; **acres of forest,** des hectares de forêts.

acreage ['eɪkərɪdʒ] *n* superficie *f* (*en mesures agraires*).

acrid ['ækrɪd] *adj* **(a)** (*goût, fumée*) âcre; **(b)** *Fig* (*style*) mordant; (*critique*) acerbe; (*humeur*) âcre.

acrimonious [ækrɪ'məunɪəs] *adj* acrimonieux; (*person*) acariâtre; **the discussion became a.,** la discussion s'envenimait.

acrimoniously [ækrɪ'məunɪəslɪ] *adv* avec acrimonie.

acrimony ['ækrɪmənɪ], **acrimoniousness** [ækrɪ'məunɪəsnɪs] *n* acrimonie *f*; aigreur *f* (*de ton, de caractère*).

acrobat ['ækrəbæt] *n* acrobate *mf*.

acrobatic [ækrə'bætɪk] *adj* acrobatique; **a. feat,** acrobatie *f*.

acrobatics [ækrə'bætɪks] *npl* (*with sing or pl verb*) acrobatie *f*.

acronym ['ækrənɪm] *n* sigle *m*.

Acropolis [ə'krɒpəlɪs] *n* Acropole *f*.

across [ə'krɒs] *adv & prep* **(a)** (*from one side to the other*) en travers (de); **line drawn a. the page/***etc*, ligne tirée en travers de la page/*etc*; **with his arms folded a. his chest,** les bras croisés sur la poitrine; **they talked to each other a. the table,** ils se parlaient d'un côté de la table à l'autre;

(b) (*of motion*) **to walk a. (a street),** traverser (une rue); **we helped him a. the road,** nous l'avons aidé à traverser la rue; **a. country,** à travers champs; **to swim a. a river,** traverser une rivière à la nage; **to go a. a bridge,** passer (sur) un pont, franchir un pont; **they got the barrel a. the river/road/***etc*, ils ont fait passer le tonneau en travers de la rivière/rue/*etc*; **is he a. the river/road/***etc* **yet?,** est-ce qu'il a enfin traversé la rivière/la rue/*etc*?; **she threw it a. the room/courtyard/***etc*, elle le balança en travers de la pièce/de la cour/*etc*; **to get** *or* **come a.,** (*of play*) passer la rampe, plaire à l'assistance; **to get sth a. to s.o.,** faire comprendre qch à qn;

(c) (*of distance*) **2 km a.,** 2 km de large; **he is broad a. the shoulders,** il est large d'épaules; **the distance a.,** (*width*) la distance en largeur; (*of crossing*) la longueur de la traversée;

(d) (*on the other side*) **a. the street,** de l'autre côté de la rue; **the woman from a. the street,** la femme d'en face; **there's a supermarket just a. the road from us/our house,** il y a un supermarché juste en face/en face de notre maison; **the countries a. the seas,** les pays d'outremer; **just a. the border,** au-delà de la frontière; **from a. the sea,** par-delà la mer;

(e) (*in crossword*) horizontalement.

across-the-board [əkrɒsðə'bɔːd] *adj* général; **an a.-the-b. wage increase,** une augmentation générale des salaires; **a.-the-b. cuts,** réduction linéaire générale (*des droits de douane etc*).

acrostic [ə'krɒstɪk] *n* acrostiche *m*.

acrylic [ə'krɪlɪk] *Ch* **1** *adj* (*fibre, paint etc*) acrylique; **a. garment,** vêtement *m* en acrylique. **2** *n* **(a)** (*resin*) résine *f* acrylique; **(b)** (*material*) fibre *f* acrylique; **(c)** (*garment*) vêtement *m* en acrylique; **(d)** (*paint*) peinture *f* acrylique.

act¹ [ækt] *n* **(a)** acte *m* (*de justice, de bonté etc*); (*deed*) action *f*; **a. of grace,** mesure *f* de grâce; **a. of war,** acte de guerre; *Rel* **a. of faith,** acte de foi; **the Acts of the Apostles,** les Actes des Apôtres; **an a. of folly,** une folie; **the a. of a criminal,** l'action d'un criminel; **to catch s.o. in the (very) a.,** prendre qn sur le fait *ou* en flagrant délit *ou* *F* la main dans le sac; **she was caught in the a. of taking the money,** elle fut surprise en train de voler l'argent; *Jur* **a. of God,** catastrophe naturelle;

(b) *Th* acte *m*; **A. I, scene 1,** Acte I, scène 1;

(c) (*in cabaret, circus etc*) numéro *m* (*d'un artiste*); **circus a.,** numéro de cirque; **to put on an a.,** (*pretend*) jouer la comédie; **it's all an a.,** (*pretence*) c'est du cinéma; *Fig* **to get in on the a.,** se mettre dans le mouvement; *Fig* **to be/to let s.o. in on the a.,** être/mettre qn dans le coup; *F* **to have one's a. together,** (*professionally*) bien connaître son affaire; (*personally*) être un homme *ou* une femme accompli(e), avoir bien sa vie en main; *F* **get your a. together!,** (*professionally*) faites un effort!, *F* vous ne pourriez pas vous secouer, un peu!; (*personally*) prends ta vie en main!;

(d) *Jur Pol* loi *f*; **A. of Parliament,** loi *f*, décret *m*; **Companies A.,** = loi sur les sociétés; **factory a.,** législation industrielle; **land a.,** loi agraire.

act² **1** *vt* jouer, représenter (*une pièce, un personnage*); remplir (*un rôle*); **to a. Hamlet,** jouer Hamlet; **to a. the fool,** faire l'imbécile; **to a. a part,** jouer un rôle; *Fig* feindre, faire *ou* jouer la comédie; **to a. the part of an honest man,** se conduire *ou* agir en honnête homme.

2 *vi* **(a)** (*take action*) agir; **it is time to a.,** il est temps d'agir; **he did not know how to a.,** (*how to behave*) il ne savait comment se conduire; (*what action to take*) il ne savait quel parti prendre; **I acted for the best,** j'ai fait pour le mieux; **to a. for s.o.,** agir au nom de qn; représenter qn; **the police refused to a.,** la police a refusé d'intervenir; **the brake refuses to a.,** le frein ne fonctionne pas;

(b) (*behave*) se comporter, agir; **they a. as if nothing had happened,** ils se comportent comme si rien ne s'était passé; **he acts as if he were** *or* *F* **like he was the boss,** il se comporte comme s'il était le patron *ou* *F* comme si c'était lui le patron; **stop acting like a child!,** arrête de faire l'enfant!;

(c) *Th Cin* jouer; (*pretend*) jouer la comédie; **he can't a.,** c'est un mauvais acteur; **I always wanted to a.,** j'ai toujours voulu être acteur; **to a. in a film,** tourner dans un film; **to a. stupid/all innocent,** faire l'idiot/l'innocent; **to a. as secretary/***etc*, exercer les fonctions de secrétaire/*etc*; **the stick acted as a tent pole,** le bâton servit de montant pour la tente; **the smell acts as a warning to other animals,** les autres animaux sont avertis par l'odeur; **the engine acts as a brake,** le moteur fait fonction de frein.

►**act on** *vi po* **(a)** (*affect*) influer sur, agir sur; (*of remedy etc*) agir sur; **acid acts on metal,** l'acide agit sur le métal; **to a. on the brain/the bowels,** exercer une action sur *ou* agir sur le cerveau/l'intestin; **(b)** (*respond to*) agir d'après, suivre (*un conseil*); exécuter (*un ordre*); donner suite à (*une lettre*); **acting on my lawyer's advice,** conformément aux conseils de mon avocat; **the police acted on the information,** la police agit suite à *ou* après avoir reçu l'information.

►**act out** *vtsep* **to a. out a fantasy,** vivre un fantasme; **local people a. out scenes from the town's history,** les gens du coin font revivre des scènes de l'histoire de leur ville.

►**act up** *vi* (*of child*) se conduire mal; (*of machine*) marcher mal; **the car's acting up again,** la voiture recommence à faire des siennes.

►**act upon** *vipo* = **ACT ON.**

acting ['æktɪŋ] **1** *adj* suppléant, intérimaire; **a. manager,** (*temporary*) directeur *m* intérimaire, gérant *m* provisoire. **2** *n* **(a)** action *f*; **(b)** *Th* jeu *m*, interprétation *f* (*d'un acteur*); **she's done some a.,** elle a fait du théâtre *ou* du cinéma.

action ['ækʃən] *n* **(a)** action *f* (*d'une personne, d'un remède etc*); (*single act*) action, acte *m*, fait *m*; **the a. of water,** le travail des eaux, l'action de l'eau (*sur la berge d'une rivière etc*); **we want a. not words,** nous voulons des actes non des paroles; **to take a.,** agir; (*intervene*) intervenir; **their quick a. prevented more deaths,** leur action rapide a évité d'autres morts; **to take industrial a.,** se mettre en grève; **line of a.,** ligne de conduite; **man of a.,** homme d'action; **sphere of a.,** sphère d'activité; **to put a plan into a.,** mettre un projet à exécution; **to come into a.,** entrer en action *ou* en jeu; **in a.,** (*of machine*) en marche; *F* **she destroys interviewers, you should see her in a.,** elle anéantit les interviewers, tu l'as vue à l'œuvre?; **to bring the law into a.,** faire intervenir la loi; **out of a.,** hors (de) service, en panne; **to put a machine out of a.,** détraquer une machine; **the flu put** *or* **kept him out of a. for a month,** la grippe l'a gardé hors combat pour un mois; **impulsive a.,** action irréfléchie, coup *m* de tête; *Prov* **actions speak louder than words,** les actes en disent plus long que les paroles; *Art* **a. painting,** peinture gestuelle;
(b) *Th Cin TV Liter* action *f* (*d'une pièce*); **the a. takes place in ...,** la scène se passe à ...; *Cin* **a.!,** on tourne!;
(c) (*movement*) action *f*, gestes *mpl* (*d'un joueur*); train *m*, allure *f*, action (*d'un cheval*);
(d) *Tech* mécanisme *m* (*d'une montre etc*); jeu *m* (*d'une pompe, d'une serrure*); mécanique *f* (*d'un piano, d'un orgue*);
(e) *Jur* action *f*; **a. at law, legal a.,** action en justice; (*trial etc*) procès *m*; **a. for libel,** procès *ou* plainte *f* en diffamation; **a. for damages,** action en dommages et intérêts; **to bring an a. against s.o.,** intenter une action *ou* un procès à *ou* contre qn;
(f) *Mil etc* combat *m*, engagement *m*; **naval a.,** engagement naval, opération navale; **to go into a.,** entrer en action, engager le combat; **ready for a.,** prêt à combattre; **to send troops into a.,** faire intervenir *ou* faire donner des troupes; **to see a.,** (*of soldier*) combattre; **to put a gun/plane/***etc* **out of a.,** (*destroy*) mettre un fusil/un avion/*etc* hors de combat; (*disable*) mettre un fusil/un avion/*etc* hors de service *ou F* de cause; **killed in a.,** tué à l'ennemi; **as a result of enemy a.,** à la suite de l'action ennemie;
(g) (*excitement*) action *f*; **there's plenty of a. in the movie,** il y a plein d'action dans ce film; **they were looking for some a.,** (*nightlife etc*) ils cherchaient un peu d'aventure; **where's the a. around here?,** où est-ce que ça bouge ici?;
(h) *Sl* **they want a piece of the a.,** (*profits*) ils veulent une part du gâteau.

actionable ['ækʃənəb(ə)l] *adj Jur* (*mot, action*) qui expose à des poursuites.

action-packed ['ækʃənpækt] *adj* (*film, roman*) plein d'action.

activate ['æktɪveɪt] *vt* **(a)** (*put into operation*) déclencher; **to a. a device,** déclencher un mécanisme; **(b)** *Ch* activer; **activated carbon,** carbon actif *ou* activé; **(c)** *Phys* rendre (*un corps*) radio-actif.

activation [æktɪ'veɪʃən] *n* activation *f*.

active ['æktɪv] **1** *adj* **(a)** (*homme etc*) actif; (*cerveau*) éveillé; (*imagination*) vif; **a. life,** vie active; **to be still a.,** (*of elderly person*) être encore alerte *ou* allant *ou* actif; **to become a.,** (*of volcano*) entrer en activité; **she's very a. in the party,** elle est très active au sein du parti; **to take an a. part in sth,** prendre une part active *ou* effective à qch; *Mil* **on a. service,** en service actif; **to see a. service,** (*fight*) combattre; *Mil* **to be on the a. list,** être sur l'annuaire de l'armée active; *Comptr* **a. program,** programme *m* en cours d'exécution; **(b)** *Gram* (*voice*) actif. **2** *n* *Gram* actif *m*, voix active; **verb in the a. (voice),** verbe *m* à l'actif *ou* à la voix active.

actively ['æktɪvlɪ] *adv* activement; **they were a. seeking peace,** ils cherchaient activement à faire la paix; **to a. dislike s.o.,** avoir une vive aversion pour qn.

activist ['æktɪvɪst] *n Pol* activiste *mf*.

activity [æk'tɪvɪtɪ] *n* activité *f*; **there was little a. in the streets,** il y avait peu d'activité dans les rues; **economic a.,** activité économique; **his numerous activities leave him little leisure,** ses nombreuses occupations lui laissent peu de loisirs.

actor ['æktər] *n* acteur *m*; *Th Cin* acteur, comédien *m*; **to be an a.,** faire du théâtre *ou* du cinéma.

actress ['æktrɪs] *n* actrice *f*; *Th Cin* actrice, comédienne *f*.

actual ['æktʃʊəl] *adj* **(a)** (*concrete*) réel, véritable; (*fait*) positif; (*cas*) concret; **a. size,** grandeur réelle, vraie grandeur; **to give the a. figures,** donner les chiffres mêmes; *F* **in a. fact,** effectivement, en fait; *Com* **a. cost,** coût définitif; **her a. words were ...,** ses paroles véritables furent ...; **his a. name is Jones,** son véritable nom est Jones; **this is the a. house where she was born,** voici en fait la maison où elle est née; *Br F* **the a. managing director visited us today,** le directeur général nous a rendu visite en personne aujourd'hui; *Br F* **it's your a. 24-carat gold,** c'est de l'or à 24-carats, du vrai de vrai; **(b)** (*current*) actuel, présent; **the a. state of affairs,** l'état de choses actuel.

actuality [æktjʊ'ælɪtɪ] *n Fml* **(a)** réalité *f*; **(b)** actualité *f*; le temps présent; **play that lacks a.,** pièce qui n'a aucun rapport avec la vie d'aujourd'hui.

actually ['æktʃʊəlɪ] *adv* **(a)** (*really*) réellement, effectivement; en fait, en réalité; **what a. happened?,** que s'est-il passé au juste?; **what he a. means is ...,** ce qu'il veut vraiment dire est ...; **I didn't a. see it myself,** en réalité, je ne l'ai pas vu de mes propres yeux; **he's not a very nice person a.,** il n'est pas très gentil à vrai dire; **the piano's just for decoration, no one a. plays it,** le piano fait partie du décor, en fait personne n'en joue; **we haven't a. decided yet,** on a pas encore vraiment décidé; **yes, but what will the government a. do?,** oui, mais que va vraiment faire le gouvernement?;
(b) (*even, surprisingly*) **he a. swore,** il est allé (même) jusqu'à lâcher un juron; **she a. said good morning to me,** à mon grand étonnement elle m'a dit bonjour; **he was a. on time for once,** pour une fois il était à l'heure;
(c) (*in fact*) en fait; **a., yes, I do mind, very much!,** mais non, c'est que je ne vous le permets pas en fait!; **I'm not sure, a.,** je n'en suis pas certain en fait; **what do you do? — I'm a lawyer a.,** que faites-vous? — je suis avocat; **a., I rather like it,** à vrai dire, ça me plaît assez;
(d) *Fml* (*at this moment*) actuellement, à présent.

actuarial [æktjʊ'eərɪəl] *adj* actuariel.

actuary ['æktʃʊərɪ] *n* actuaire *m*; **actuaries' tables,** tables *fpl* de mortalité.

actuate ['æktʃʊeɪt] *vt* **(a)** mettre en action, faire marcher (*une machine etc*); **(b)** faire agir (*qn*); **actuated by jealousy,** poussé par la jalousie.

actuation [æktʃʊ'eɪʃən] *n* mise *f* en action (*d'une machine etc*).

acuity [ə'kjuːɪtɪ] *n* acuité *f* (*d'une pointe, de l'esprit, de la douleur etc*); **visual a.,** acuité visuelle.

acumen ['ækjʊmən] *n* pénétration *f*, finesse *f* (d'esprit); perspicacité *f*; **he's got plenty of business a.,** il a un très bon sens des affaires.

acupressure ['ækjʊpreʃər] *n Med* digitopuncture *f*.

acupuncture ['ækjʊpʌŋktʃər] *n Med* acupuncture *f*.

acupuncturist ['ækjʊpʌŋktʃərɪst] *n Med* acupuncteur *m*.

acute [ə'kjuːt] *adj* **(a)** (*pain*) aigu, intense, vif; (*disease, crisis*) aigu; **a. remorse,** remords cruels; **to become more a.,** (*of anxiety etc*) s'aviver; **operation for a. appendicitis,** opération à chaud pour l'appendicite; **to suffer a. embarrassment,** être vivement embarrassé; **an a. shortage of ...,** un manque aigu de ...; **the problem of communication was made more a. by the severe winter,** le problème des communications a été intensifié par la rigueur de l'hiver; **(b)** (*esprit*) fin, perspicace; (*ouïe, odorat*) fin; (*vue*) perçant; **an a. observer,** un observateur pénétrant; **she has an a. awareness of their problems,** elle a une perception pénétrante de leurs problèmes; **an a. businesswoman,** une femme d'affaires avisée *ou* perspicace; **(c)** *Math* (*angle, pointe*) aigu; **(d)** *Gram* (*accent*) aigu.

acute-angled [ə'kjuːtæŋg(ə)ld] *adj* à angle(s) aigu(s).

acutely [ə'kjuːtlɪ] *adv* (*see adj*) **(a)** vivement; intensément; **he felt the loss a.,** il ressentit cette perte intensément; **we are a. aware of that,** nous en sommes extrêmement conscients; **(b)** finement; avec perspicacité.

acuteness [ə'kjuːtnɪs] *n* **(a)** acuité *f* (*d'une douleur*); intensité *f* (*d'une douleur, d'un remords*); caractère aigu (*d'une maladie, d'un accès*); vivacité *f* (*d'un sentiment*); **(b)** pénétration *f*, perspicacité *f* (*de l'esprit*); finesse *f* (*d'ouïe*); acuité *f* (*de la vision, de l'odorat*).

ad [æd] *n F* annonce *f*; **small ads,** petites annonces.

AD [eɪ'diː] *adv* (*abbr* **anno Domini**) après Jésus-Christ; (*written form*) apr. J.-C.; **in 1066 AD,** en 1066 apr. J.-C..

adage ['ædɪdʒ] *n* adage *m*.

adagio [ə'dɑːʒɪəʊ, ə'dɑːdʒ-] *adv & n Mus* adagio *m*.

Adam ['ædəm] *n* Adam *m; Hum* **I don't know you from A.,** je ne vous connais ni d'Ève ni d'Adam; *Hum* **A.'s ale,** de l'eau *f*; **A.'s apple,** pomme *f* d'Adam.

adamant ['ædəmənt] *adj* inflexible, intransigeant; **he is a. on this point,** sur ce point il ne transige pas; **she is a. that she saw him,** elle est inflexible dans sa conviction de l'avoir vu; **they are a. in their conviction,** ils demeurent intransigeants dans leur conviction.

adamantly ['ædəməntlɪ] *adv* inflexiblement; d'une manière intransigeante; **they a. refused,** ils refusèrent d'une manière intransigeante.

adapt [ə'dæpt] **1** *vt* adapter (*une machine, un véhicule etc*); remanier (*une œuvre*); **to a. a novel for the stage,** adapter un roman à la scène; **text adapted from Cicero,** texte d'après Cicéron; **to a. oneself to circumstances/ new surroundings,** s'adapter *ou* s'accommoder aux circonstances/à un nouvel environnement. **2** *vi* (*of person, species*) s'adapter (**to,** à); **failure to a.,** refus de s'adapter.

adaptability [ədæptə'bɪlɪtɪ] *n* faculté *f* d'adaptation; **a. to environment,** adaptabilité *f* au milieu.

adaptable [ə'dæptəb(ə)l] *adj* **(a)** adaptable, ajustable (**to,** à); **(b)** susceptible d'être utilisé (**for,** pour; **to an end,** dans un but); **(c)** (*person, species*) qui s'arrange de tout, qui s'accommode à toutes les circonstances; **she's very a.,** elle est très souple, elle s'adapte facilement.

adaptation [ædæp'teɪʃən] *n* **(a)** adaptation *f*, appropriation *f* (**of sth to sth,** de qch à qch); **a. for the stage,** adaptation à la scène; **(b)** (*novel, play*) adaptation *f*; **(c)** *Biol* adaptation *f*, finalité *f*.

adapted [ə'dæptɪd] *adj* (*roman etc*) adapté (**for the stage,** à la scène); **a telephone a. for use by people with hearing difficulties,** un téléphone adapté à l'usage des malentendants; **a. to sth,** approprié à qch, fait pour qch.

adapter, adaptor [ə'dæptər] *n* **(a)** *El* (*plug*) adaptateur *m*; raccord *m* (*de lampe*); (*with several sockets*) prise *f* multiple; **(b)** *MecE* (*connecting pipes*) raccord *m*; **(c)** *Phot* parquet *m* d'adaptation (*de l'appareil*); **lens a.,** bague *f* porte-objectif; **(d)** (*for record*) centreur *m*; **(e)** (*person*) adaptateur *m*, auteur *m* d'une adaptation.

adaptive [ə'dæptɪv] *adj Biol* (*mécanisme*) adaptif.

ADC [eɪdiː'siː] *n Mil abbr* **aide-de-camp**.

add [æd] **1** *vt* **(a)** ajouter (**to,** à); **this added $40 to the cost,** le prix s'en trouva augmenté de 40 dollars; **to a. water to sth,** ajouter de l'eau à qch; **now a. the eggs,** (*in recipe*) ensuite ajoutez les œufs; **she added her name to the list,** elle inclut son nom à la liste; **the owner added a conservatory,** le propriétaire a ajouté une serre; **this book adds little to the debate,** ce livre n'apporte pas grand-chose au débat; **have you anything you would like to a.?,** aimeriez-vous ajouter quelque chose?;

(b) *Math* additionner; **to a. six to eight,** additionner six et huit, ajouter six à huit; **a. these numbers (together),** additionnez ces nombres, faites l'addition de ces nombres; *Math* **to a. a zero,** apposer un zéro.

2 *vi* (*perform addition*) faire des additions.

▶**add in** *vtsep* ajouter (*du sel*).

▶**add on** *vtsep* ajouter (*une serre*); **should we a. on something as a tip?,** devrait-on laisser un pourboire?

▶**add to** *vipo* (*increase*) faire une addition à, agrandir (*un bâtiment*); augmenter, ajouter à (*une difficulté etc*); rehausser (*la beauté de qn, qch*); accentuer (*une difficulté, une crise*); **the news added to their despondency,** cette nouvelle ajouta à leur abattement; **this will a. to the cost,** ceci va venir s'ajouter au prix; **to a. to my misfortune,** pour mettre le comble à mon malheur.

▶**add up 1** *vi* **(a)** (*calculate*) additionner; **that boy can't a. up,** ce garçon ne sait pas additionner; **(b)** (*give correct total*) faire le compte; **the accounts don't a. up,** ces calculs ne font pas le compte; **(c)** (*make sense*) rimer; **the facts don't a. up,** les faits ne riment à rien; **it just doesn't a. up!,** ça ne rime à rien!; **it's beginning to a. up,** ça devient plus clair. **2** *vtsep* additionner; **to a. up a column of figures,** additionner une colonne de chiffres; **when you a. it all up it was quite cheap,** si on englobe tout, c'était assez bon marché.

▶**add up to** *vipo* **(a)** (*of figures*) s'élever à; **it adds up to £22,** cela s'élève à 22 livres; **(b)** (*amount to*) **is that all you've done? it doesn't a. up to much,** est-ce que c'est tout ce que tu as fait? ça n'avance pas vite; **it all adds up to an enjoyable day out,** tout cela signifie une agréable journée de sortie.

added ['ædɪd] *adj* supplémentaire; **an a. reason was that ...,** une raison supplémentaire était que ...; **a. enjoyment was provided by a jazz band,** un orchestre de jazz a aussi contribué à notre *ou* leur *etc* plaisir; **a. ingredients,** (*on food package*) autres ingrédients; **no a. sugar,** sans ajout de sucre; **no a. preservatives,** sans conservateurs.

addendum, *pl* **-a** [ə'dendəm, -ə] *n* addition *f* (*à un livre etc*); supplément *m*.

adder¹ ['ædər] *n* (*person*) additionneur, -euse; (*machine*) machine *f* à calculer, calculatrice *f*.

adder² *n* (*snake*) vipère *f*.

addict¹ ['ædɪkt] *n* **(a)** personne adonnée à (*l'opium etc*); *Med* intoxiqué, -ée; **(b)** *F* fanatique *mf* (*de football, de la danse etc*); *Br F* **a telly a.,** un fana de la télévision.

addict² [ə'dɪkt] *vt* (*used in passive*) **to be addicted to,** s'adonner à, être adonné à (*l'alcool, l'opium etc*); **to become** *or* **get addicted to drugs/heroin,** devenir toxicomane/héroïnomane.

addiction [ə'dɪkʃən] *n* (*to drugs*) dépendance *f*; (*to chocolate, the cinema etc*) goût immodéré (**to,** pour); **a. to drugs,** la dépendance envers la drogue, la toxicomanie; **my earlier a. to the Italian cinema,** ma passion dévorante d'autrefois pour le cinéma italien; **coffee and cakes at 4.00 had become something of an a. with her,** prendre le café avec de petits gâteaux à 4 heures était devenu une sorte de drogue pour elle.

addictive [ə'dɪktɪv] *adj Med* (*drogue*) qui cause le phénomène de dépendance; *Fig* **soap operas are very a.,** on a du mal à se passer des feuilletons, on devient vite accro aux feuilletons.

adding ['ædɪŋ] *n* addition *f*; **a. machine,** machine *f* à calculer, calculatrice *f*.

addition [ə'dɪʃən] *n* **(a)** addition *f*; **he has just had an a. to his family,** sa famille vient d'augmenter; **additions to the staff,** adjonction *f* de personnel; **the a. of three more musicians,** l'adjonction de trois musiciens supplémentaires; **in a.,** en outre, de plus; **in a. to sth,** en plus de qch; **in a. to that sum,** outre cette somme; **in a. to these misfortunes,** par surcroît de malheur; **to pay sth in a.,** payer un supplément; **(b)** *Constr* rajout *m*, extension *f* (*à un bâtiment*); **the east wing was an eighteenth-century a.,** l'aile est a été ajoutée au dix-huitième siècle; **(c)** *Math* addition *f*.

additional [ə'dɪʃən(ə)l] *adj* additionnel, supplémentaire; **a. postage,** surtaxe *f*; **for each a. 50 grams,** (*in list of postal rates*) au-dessus, par 50 grammes; **a. information can be found on page 28,** se référer à la page 28 pour des informations complémentaires; *Admin* **a. tax,** impôt additionnel; (*because of underpayment*) supplément *m* d'imposition; **for no a. charge,** sans supplément; *Fin Com etc* **a. payment,** supplément; **a. clause,** avenant *m*; **a. security,** contre-caution *f*.

additionally [ə'dɪʃən(ə)lɪ] *adv* en outre (**to,** de); (*to pay*) en supplément (**to,** de).

additive ['ædɪtɪv] *n* additif *m*.

addled ['æd(ə)ld] *adj* **(a)** *Old-fashioned* (*œuf*) pourri, gâté, couvi; **(b) an a. mind,** un esprit confus.

add-on ['ædɒn] *n Comptr* produit *m* supplémentaire *ou* complémentaire.

address¹ [ə'dres, *Am* 'ædres] *n* **(a)** adresse *f* (*d'une personne, d'une lettre*); **what is your a.?,** quelle est ton adresse?; **of no (known) a.,** sans domicile connu; **home** *or* **private/business a.,** adresse privée *ou* personnelle/de bureau; **a Glasgow a.,** une adresse à Glasgow; **not known at this a.,** (*on returned letter*) inconnu à cette adresse; **she no longer lives at that a.,** elle n'est plus à cette adresse; **a. book,** carnet *m* d'adresses; **(b)** (*speech*) discours *m*, allocution *f*; **(c)** (*title*) **form of a.,** titre *m* (*à donner en s'adressant à qn*); **(d)** *Comptr* adresse *f*; **(e)** *Fml* (*skill*) habileté *m*, doigté *m*; **she showed considerable a. in her handling of the situation,** elle fit preuve d'un habileté considérable dans la façon dont elle traita l'affaire; **(f)** *Arch* **to pay one's addresses to a lady,** faire la cour à une femme.

address² *vt* **(a)** adresser (*une lettre, une carte (postale), un colis*) (**to s.o.,** à qn); **it's addressed to you,** ça t'est adressé; **stamped addressed envelope,** enveloppe timbrée avec son adresse; **(b)** (*direct*) adresser (*des reproches, des critiques etc*) (**to s.o.,** à qn); **(c)** (*speak to*) adresser (*une foule*); **to a. s.o.,** adresser la parole à qn; **he addressed her as 'Your Majesty',** il l'a appelée 'Votre Majesté'; **to a. a meeting,** prendre la parole à une réunion; **(d)** (*tackle*) aborder, s'attaquer à (*une question, un problème etc*); *Fml* **to a. oneself to a task,** se mettre à une tâche; **(e)** *Comptr* adresser, accéder à; **(f)** *Golf* viser (*la balle*).

addressee [ædre'siː] *n* destinataire *mf*; receveur *m* (*d'un télégramme etc*).

adduce [ə'djuːs] *vt Fml* alléguer, apporter (*des raisons, des preuves etc*); invoquer, citer (*une autorité*).

adduct [ə'dʌkt] *vt Physiol* déterminer l'adduction de (*un muscle etc*).

adduction [ə'dʌkʃən] *n Fml* **(a)** allégation *f* (*d'une raison*); citation *f*, invocation *f* (*d'une autorité*); **(b)** *Physiol* adduction *f*.

adenoidal [ædɪ'nɔɪd(ə)l] *adj* adénoïdien.

adenoids ['ædɪnɔɪdz] *npl Med* végétations *fpl* (adénoïdes).

adept 1 *adj* [ə'dept] expert, habile (**in sth,** à qch; **at doing sth,** à faire qch). **2** *n* ['ædept] expert, -erte (**in,** en).

adequacy ['ædɪkwəsɪ] *n* (*of arrangements, skills etc*) compétence *f*, capacité *f*; (*of quantity*) suffisance *f*; **they doubted her a. as a mother,** ils doutaient de ses capacités de mère.

adequate ['ædɪkwət] *adj* adéquat, suffisant (**to,** à); **the money we were given was more than a.,** l'argent que l'on nous avait donné était plus que suffisant; **a. supply,** quantité suffisante (*de viande etc*); **a. reward,** récompense adéquate *ou* suffisante; **room of a. size,** pièce d'une grandeur raisonnable; **a. to the task,** (*of tool*) approprié à la tâche; **they had not received a. training for the job,** ils n'avaient pas bénéficié d'une formation adéquate pour le poste; **a. remuneration for the work carried out,** rémunération proportionnée *ou* correspondant au travail accompli.

adequately ['ædɪkwətlɪ] *adv* suffisamment, convenablement.

adhere [əd'hɪər] *vi* adhérer, se coller.

►**adhere to** *vipo* **(a)** (*stick to*) adhérer à, se coller à; **the scab adheres to the wound,** la croûte tient à la plaie; **(b)** observer (*une promesse, une règle etc*); persister dans, s'en tenir à, maintenir (*sa décision*); **to a. to a party,** adhérer *ou* donner son adhésion à un parti; **I don't a. to that philosophy at all,** je n'adhère pas du tout à cette philosophie.

adherence [əd'hɪərəns] *n* **(a)** (*of label etc*) adhérence *f* (**to,** à); **(b)** adhésion *f* (*à un parti*); adhérence *f* (*à une règle etc*).

adherent [əd'hɪərənt] *n* adhérent, -ente; (*to doctrine*) partisan, -ane.

adhesion [əd'hiːʒən] *n* **(a)** (*of label etc*) adhérence *f*; **(b)** (*of person*) adhésion *f* (**to,** à); accession *f* (*à un parti*).

adhesive [əd'hiːsɪv] **1** *adj* (*ruban etc*) adhésif; (*enveloppe*) gommé; **a. stamp,** timbre adhésif *ou* mobile; *Med* **a. plaster,** *Am* **a. tape,** sparadrap *m*. **2** *n* colle *f*, adhésif *m*.

adhesiveness [əd'hiːsɪvnɪs] *n* caractère adhésif.

ad hoc ['æd'hɒk] *adv & adj* ad hoc; **ad h. committee,** comité spécial *ou* ad hoc.

adieu [ə'djuː] *Arch Lit* **1** *int* adieu! **2** *n* **to bid s.o. a.,** dire adieu à qn, faire ses adieux à qn.

ad infinitum ['ædɪnfɪ'naɪtəm] *adv* à l'infini; *F* **he went on talking ad i.,** il parlait à n'en plus finir; **and so on ad i.,** et ainsi de suite ad infinitum.

adipose ['ædɪpəʊs] *adj Biol* (*tissu*) adipeux.

adiposity [ædɪ'pɒsɪtɪ] *n Biol* adiposité *f*.

adjacent [ə'dʒeɪsənt] *adj* (*angle, terrain*) adjacent, contigu, *f* -uë, attenant (**to,** à); (*pays*) limitrophe (**to,** de); **a. rooms,** chambres contiguës; **the two rooms are a.,** les deux pièces sont contiguës; **in an a. street,** dans une rue adjacente; **to be a. to sth,** être contigu à qch; avoisiner qch; *Jur* **a. owner,** riverain *m*.

adjectival [ædʒɪk'taɪv(ə)l] *adj Gram* adjectif, adjectival; **a. clause,** proposition adjective.

adjectivally [ædʒɪk'taɪv(ə)lɪ] *adv* adjectivement; **present participle used a.,** participe présent adjectivé.

adjective ['ædʒɪktɪv] *adj & n Gram* adjectif *m*.

adjoin [ə'dʒɔɪn] **1** *vt* avoisiner (*un lieu*); être contigu à, toucher à, attenir à (*qch*); **our garden adjoins theirs,** notre jardin est contigu au leur. **2** *vi* **the two houses a.,** les deux maisons sont contiguës.

adjoining [ə'dʒɔɪnɪŋ] *adj* contigu, *f* -uë; **garden a. mine,** jardin attenant au mien; **the a. room,** la pièce voisine *ou* à côté.

adjourn [ə'dʒɜːn] **1** *vt* ajourner, différer, remettre, renvoyer (*qch*) (**for a week,** à huitaine); **the trial was adjourned until the next day,** le procès fut ajourné au lendemain. **2** *vi* **(a)** (*of person*) lever la séance, clore les débats; **to a. to the drawing room,** (*after dinner etc*) passer au salon; **shall we a.?,** on passe au salon?; **(b)** (*of meeting etc*) s'ajourner (**until,** à); (*come to a close*) être levé; **the meeting adjourned at 3 o'clock,** la séance a été levée à trois heures.

adjournment [ə'dʒɜːnmənt] *n* ajournement *m*, suspension *f* (*d'une séance etc*); renvoi *m*, remise *f* (*d'une affaire etc*); **a. for a week,** remise à huitaine.

adjudge [ə'dʒʌdʒ] *vt* **(a) to a. s.o. guilty,** déclarer qn coupable; **(b)** adjuger, décerner (*un prix, une récompense*) (**to s.o.,** à qn); **to a. damages,** adjuger *ou* accorder des dommages-intérêts.

adjudicate [ə'dʒuːdɪkeɪt] *vt & vi* juger, décider (*une affaire*); adjuger, décerner (*un prix*); **who is adjudicating?,** (*in competition*) qui sont les membres du jury?; **to a. s.o. bankrupt,** déclarer *ou* mettre qn en faillite.

adjudication [ədʒuːdɪ'keɪʃən] *n* jugement *m*, décision *f*, arrêt *m*; **a. of bankruptcy,** jugement déclaratif de faillite.

adjudicator [ə'dʒuːdɪkeɪtər] *n* **(a)** arbitre *m*; **(b)** (*in competition etc*) membre *m* du jury.

adjunct ['ædʒʌŋkt] *n* **(a)** (*person*) adjoint, -ointe (**to,** de); auxiliaire *mf*; **(b)** (*thing*) accessoire *m* (**of,** de); **(c)** *Gram* complément *m* (*du verbe etc*).

adjust [ə'dʒʌst] **1** *vt* **(a)** régler, ajuster (*une balance, les freins, une montre etc*); étalonner (*un instrument*); rectifier, centrer (*un outil*); mettre (*un microscope, un moteur*) au point; égaliser (*la pression etc*); tarer (*une soupape*); *Nau* compenser, corriger (*les compas*); **to a. the sights of a rifle,** ajuster le tir d'une arme à feu; **to a. the controls of a device,** mettre au point le réglage d'un appareil; **to a. the picture on a television set,** régler l'image d'une télévision; **to a. the length of a strap,** régler la longueur d'une courroie; **she adjusted the seat belt to the correct length,** elle régla la ceinture de sécurité à la bonne longueur; **the seat can be adjusted for height,** la hauteur du siège est réglable;

(b) (*reformulate*) **the figures have been seasonally adjusted,** les chiffres sont les données corrigées des variations saisonnières; **pensions have been adjusted upwards,** les pensions ont été relevées; **to a. an average,** (*in insurance*) répartir une avarie; *Fin* **to a. prices,** ajuster les prix; **the terms of the contract have been adjusted,** les termes du contrat ont été modifiés; **to a. a claim,** (*of insurance company*) régler une demande d'indemnité;

(c) ajuster, arranger (*son chapeau, ses vêtements etc*); **to a. one's dress,** ajuster sa robe;

(d) ajuster (*qch à qch*), **to a. oneself to sth,** s'adapter à qch.

2 *vi* **(a)** (*of person*) s'adapter (**to sth,** à qch); **he found it difficult to a. after his wife died,** il eut des difficultés à se faire à la mort de sa femme;

(b) (*of device*) **the seat adjusts for height,** la hauteur du siège est réglable.

adjustable [ə'dʒʌstəb(ə)l] *adj* ajustable, réglable; *Aut* **a. front seat,** siège avant réglable; **fully a. seat,** siège multipositions; **the seat is a. for height,** la hauteur du siège est réglable; *Br* **a. spanner,** clef anglaise, clef à molette.

adjusted [ə'dʒʌstɪd] *adj Psy* **(well) a.,** (bien) équilibré.

adjuster [ə'dʒʌstər] *n* **(a)** *Fin* **average a.,** dispacheur *m*; **(b)** (*device*) appareil *m* de réglage.

adjusting [ə'dʒʌstɪŋ] *n* **(a)** = **ADJUSTMENT**; **(b) a. screw,** vis *f* de réglage *ou* de rappel.

adjustment [ə'dʒʌstmənt] *n* **(a)** ajustement *m* (*d'une balance*); rectification *f* (*d'un outil, d'un instrument*); réglage *m* (*d'un mécanisme*); tarage *m* (*d'une soupape*); mise *f* au point (*d'un microscope etc*); *Nau* compensation *f*, correction *f* (*des compas*); **fine a.,** réglage de précision; **out of a.,** déréglé, décalé; **to make an a. to sth,** régler qch; **a slight a. improved the picture,** une légère mise au point a amélioré l'image; **the brakes need a.,** les freins ont besoin d'une mise au point;

(b) (*of figures, salaries*) corrigé *m*; (*of prices*) ajustement *m*; **no a. was made for seasonal variation,** il n'y a pas eu de corrigé des variations saisonnières; **we had to make some adjustments to our plans,** nous avons dû modifier quelque peu nos projets; **some adjustments had been made to the text,** des modifications avaient été apportées au texte; **average a.,** (*in insurance*) répartition *f* d'avaries; dispache *f*;

(c) (*adapting*) adaptation *f*, acclimatation *f* (**to,** à);

period of a., période *f* d'adaptation.

adjutant ['ædʒətənt] *n* **(a)** *Mil* (*rank*) capitaine *m* adjudant major; (*assistant*) officier adjoint; **a. general,** adjudant général; **(b) a. (bird),** marabout *m* des Indes, *F* adjudant *m*.

ad lib ['æd'lɪb] *adv* **to speak ad l.**, improviser.

ad-lib¹ ['æd'lɪb] *vi & vtr* (**-bb-**) *F* improviser.

ad-lib² *n F* improvisation *f*.

ad-lib³ *adj F* improvisé; **most of his speech was ad-l.**, la plus grande partie de son discours était improvisée.

ad-libbing [æd'lɪbɪŋ] *n* improvisation *f*.

adman, *pl* **-men** ['ædmæn, -men] *n F* publicitaire *m*.

admass ['ædmæs] *n Br F* le grand public.

admin ['ædmɪn] *n F* administration *f*.

administer [əd'mɪnɪstər] *vt* **(a)** (*manage*) administrer, régir (*un pays*); administrer, gérer (*des affaires, des biens*); appliquer (*les lois*); **(b)** (*give*) administrer (*les derniers sacrements, un médicament*) (**to,** à); faire, adresser (*une réprimande*) (**to,** à); **to a. justice,** dispenser *ou* rendre la justice; *Jur* **to a. an** *or* **the oath to s.o.**, faire prêter serment à qn, assermenter qn.

administration [ədmɪnɪ'streɪʃən] *n* **(a)** administration *f*, gestion *f* (*des affaires, d'une fortune etc*); régie *f* (*d'une succession etc*); **business a.**, gestion *f*; **a background in a.**, une formation en gestion; **(b)** administration *f* (*de la justice, des sacrements, d'un remède*); prestation *f* (*de serment*); *Jur* **letters of a.**, lettres d'administration; **(c)** *esp US* **the A.**, l'administration *f*, le gouvernement.

administrative [əd'mɪnɪstrətɪv] *adj* administratif; **a. skills,** compétences administratives; *Ind* **a. expenses,** frais *mpl* d'administration; *Br* **the a. grade,** (*in civil service*) les fonctionnaires supérieurs.

administratively [əd'mɪnɪstrətɪvlɪ] *adv* administrativement.

administrator [əd'mɪnɪstreɪtər] *n* **(a)** administrateur *m*; gérant *m* (*d'une entreprise*); **(b)** *Jur* curateur *m* (*des biens d'un mineur etc*); administrateur *m* (*d'une succession*).

admirable ['ædmərəb(ə)l] *adj* admirable.

admirably ['ædmərəblɪ] *adv* admirablement; **she succeeded a.**, elle a réussi à merveille.

admiral ['ædmərəl] *n* **(a)** *Nau* amiral *m*; **a. of the fleet, fleet a.**, vice-amiral *m* d'escadre; **(b) red a.**, (*butterfly*) vulcain *m*.

admiralty ['ædmərəltɪ] *n* **(a)** *Nau Hist* **the A.**, = le Ministère de la Marine; **First Lord of the A.**, ≈ Ministre de la Marine; **A. Board,** = division navale du ministère de la Défense; **court of A.**, = tribunal *m* maritime; **(b)** *Geog* **the A. Islands,** les îles *fpl* de l'Amirauté.

admiration [ædmə'reɪʃən] *n* admiration *f* (**of, for,** pour); **I have great a. for doctors,** j'ai beaucoup d'admiration pour les médecins; **to fill s.o. with a.**, remplir qn d'admiration, émerveiller qn; **he is full of a. for her courage,** il est rempli d'admiration pour son courage; **their roads are the a. of the world,** leurs routes font l'admiration du monde entier.

admire [əd'maɪər] *vt* admirer (*qn, qch*); **I a. her as a leader,** je l'admire en tant que dirigeante; **they a. him for sticking to his principles,** ils l'admirent de s'en tenir à ses principes; **to a. oneself in a mirror,** se mirer dans une glace.

admirer [əd'maɪərər] *n* **(a)** admirateur, -trice; **(b)** *Old-fashioned* soupirant *m* (*d'une femme*); *Hum* **is that a letter from one of your admirers?**, est-ce que c'est une lettre de l'un de tes admirateurs?

admiring [əd'maɪrɪŋ] *adj* (*regard, ton etc*) admiratif.

admiringly [əd'maɪrɪŋlɪ] *adv* avec admiration.

admissibility [ədmɪsɪ'bɪlɪtɪ] *n* admissibilité *f* (*d'une preuve etc*); *Jur* recevabilité *f* (*d'un pourvoi, d'un témoignage*).

admissible [əd'mɪsɪb(ə)l] *adj* **(a)** *Jur* (*pourvoi*) recevable; **(b)** (*idea*) acceptable; (*behaviour*) admissible, acceptable; **for them defeat was not a.**, pour eux, la défaite était inacceptable.

admission [əd'mɪʃən] *n* **(a)** admission *f*, accès *m* (*à une école, à un emploi etc*); **to gain a.**, se faire recevoir (*dans une société*); trouver accès (*auprès de qn*); se faire admettre (*dans un endroit*); **free/temporary a.**, (*of imports*) admission en franchise/temporaire; **a. free,** entrée gratuite; **a. is by ticket only,** entrée sur présentation d'un billet seulement; **(b)** (*price*) prix *m* d'entrée; **a. £2,** entrée 2 livres; **(c)** admission *f*, acceptation *f* (*d'un argument, d'une preuve*); *Jur* reconnaissance *f* (*d'un fait allégué*); confession *f* (*d'un crime etc*); aveu *m*; **an a. of guilt,** un aveu de culpabilité; **by** *or* **on his own a.**, de son propre aveu; **(d)** *Tech Aut* admission *f*, adduction *f*, introduction *f*, entrée *f* (*de la vapeur, des gaz etc*); injection *f* (*de l'eau*).

admit [əd'mɪt] *vt* (**-tt-**) **(a)** admettre (*qn à qch, dans un endroit*); laisser entrer (*qn*); **children not admitted,** les enfants ne sont pas admis; **admits one,** (*on ticket*) entrée pour une personne; **he was admitted to hospital,** il a été admis à l'hôpital; **the windows do not a. enough air,** les fenêtres ne laissent pas entrer assez d'air; **(b)** admettre (*une vérité, des excuses*); consentir (*un fait*); reconnaître (*un principe, sa faute*); convenir de (*ses torts*); concéder (*qu'on a tort*); **it must be admitted that ...**, il faut reconnaître que ...; **to a. one's guilt,** se reconnaître *ou* s'avouer coupable; **to a. one's mistake,** admettre sa faute; **I a. (that) I was wrong,** j'ai eu tort, j'en conviens; **it was hot, I must a.**, je dois admettre qu'il a fait chaud; **I had to a. to myself that ...**, j'ai dû m'avouer à moi-même que ...; **he admitted lying,** il reconnut qu'il avait menti.

▶admit of *vipo Fml* (*allow of*) permettre, admettre; **the remark admits of several interpretations,** cette remarque admet plusieurs interprétations; **his conduct admits of no excuse/explanation,** sa conduite est sans excuse/est inexplicable.

▶admit to *vipo* (*confess*) admettre (*qch*).

admittance [əd'mɪtəns] *n* **(a)** permission *f* d'entrer; accès *m* (*à un endroit, auprès de qn*); **to gain a. to a place,** parvenir à entrer dans un lieu; **to refuse s.o. a.**, refuser de laisser entrer qn; **no a.**, entrée interdite, défense d'entrer; **(b)** *El* admittance *f*.

admitted [əd'mɪtɪd] *adj* **(a)** (*usage etc*) admis; **(b)** (*vérité*) reconnu, avoué; **an a. thief,** un voleur avéré.

admittedly [əd'mɪtɪdlɪ] *adv* de l'aveu général; **a. he's right, but ...**, il faut reconnaître qu'il a raison, mais ...; **they got there, two hours late a., but ...**, ils sont arrivés là-bas, avec deux heures de retard, j'en conviens, mais ...; **the car's old a.**, il faut reconnaître que la voiture est vieille.

admixture [əd'mɪkstʃər] *n* **(a)** (*mixture*) mélange *m*; **(b)** *Pharm* (ad)mixtion *f*; **water with an a. of alcohol,** eau additionnée d'alcool.

admonish [əd'mɒnɪʃ] *vt* **(a)** (*reprimand*) admonester, reprendre, faire des remontrances à (*qn*); **he admonished them for their cowardice,** il leur a fait des remontrances pour leur manque de courage; **(b)** *Fml* (*warn*) **to a. s.o. against sth,** mettre qn en garde contre qch; **(c)** *Fml* (*exhort*) **to a. s.o. to do sth,** exhorter qn à faire qch.

admonition [ædmə'nɪʃən] *n* **(a)** (*reprimand*) remontrance *f*, réprimande *f*; *Rel* admonition *f*; **(b)** (*warning*) mise *f* en garde; **(c)** (*exhortation*) exhortation *f*.

ad nauseam [æd'nɔːsɪæm] *adv* jusqu'à la nausée; *F* à n'en plus finir.

ado [ə'duː] *n* agitation *f*, bruit *m*, embarras *m*; **without (any) more a., without further a.**, sans plus de façons *ou* de cérémonie *ou* d'embarras; **to make much a. about nothing,** faire beaucoup de bruit pour rien.

adobe [ə'dəubɪ] *n* (*brick, house*) adobe *m*.

adolescence [ædə'lesəns] *n* adolescence *f*.

adolescent [ædə'lesənt] *adj & n* adolescent, -ente.

Adonis [ə'dəunɪs] *n Myth & Fig* Adonis *m*.

adopt [ə'dɒpt] *vt* **(a)** adopter (*un enfant, une coutume*); **a stray cat adopted us,** un chat abandonné nous a adoptés; **(b)** adopter (*une ligne de conduite, un plan*); choisir, embrasser (*une carrière*); instaurer (*des mesures, une méthode*); se rallier à (*une opinion*); suivre (*un conseil*); *Pol* choisir (*qn comme candidat à un siège*); **to a. a patronizing tone,** prendre un ton protecteur; **(c)** approuver (*les minutes d'un conseil d'administration*).

adopted [ə'dɒptɪd] *adj* (*enfant, mot*) adopté; **a. son,** fils adoptif; **my a. country,** mon pays d'adoption.

adoption [ə'dɒpʃən] *n* **(a)** adoption *f* (*d'un enfant, d'une coutume, d'un pays*); **I am an American by a.**, je suis américain d'adoption; **(b)** adoption *f* (*d'une loi, d'un plan*); choix *m* (*d'une carrière*); instauration *f* (*des mesures, d'une méthode*); *Pol* choix (*de qn comme candidat*).

adoptive [ə'dɒptɪv] *adj* (*enfant, père*) adoptif.

adorable [ə'dɔːrəb(ə)l] *adj* adorable.

adorably [ə'dɔːrəblɪ] *adv* adorablement; à ravir.

adoration [ædə'reɪʃən] *n* adoration *f*.

adore [ə'dɔːr] *vt* adorer (*qn, un dieu*); *F* **I a. those cakes,** j'adore ces gâteaux-là.

adorer [ə'dɔːrər] *n* adorateur, -trice.

adoring [ə'dɔːrɪŋ] *adj* **(a)** (*eyes etc*) adorant; **(b)** (*person*) adorateur, -trice.

adoringly [ə'dɔːrɪŋlɪ] *adv* avec adoration.

adorn [ə'dɔːn] *vt* orner, parer, embellir (**with,** de).

adornment [ə'dɔːnmənt] *n* **(a)** (*act*) ornementation *f*; **(b)** (*object*) ornement *m*, parure *f*.

adrenal [ə'driːn(ə)l] **1** *adj* surrénal, -aux; **a. gland,**

(glande *f*, capsule *f*) surrénale *f*. **2** *n* (glande *f*, capsule *f*) surrénale *f*.

adrenalin(e) [ə'drenəlɪn] *n* adrénaline *f*; *F* **it gets the a. going,** ça fait monter l'adrénaline.

Adriatic [eɪdrɪ'ætɪk] *adj & n* **the A. Sea, the A.,** la mer Adriatique, l'Adriatique *f*.

adrift [ə'drɪft] *adv & adj Nau* à la dérive; **to run** *or* **go a.,** (*of ship*) aller à la dérive, dériver; **they were a. for days,** ils dérivèrent pendant plusieurs jours; **to break a.,** rompre ses amarres; partir en dérive; **to turn a vessel a.,** abandonner *ou* laisser aller un navire à la dérive; *Fig* **young people a. in the big city,** des jeunes à la dérive dans la grande ville; *Fig* **to turn s.o. a.,** abandonner qn; *Fig* **to cut oneself a. from s.o.,** rompre avec qn; *Fig* **to come a.,** (*of rope etc*) se détacher, se défaire; (*of plan etc*) tomber à l'eau.

adroit [ə'drɔɪt] *adj* (*discours*) adroit; (*politique, personne*) adroit, habile; **to be a. at doing,** être habile à faire.

adroitly [ə'drɔɪtlɪ] *adv* adroitement, habilement.

adroitness [ə'drɔɪtnɪs] *n* adresse *f*, dextérité *f*.

adulation [ædjʊ'leɪʃən] *n* adulation *f*, flatterie *f*.

adult ['ædʌlt, ə'dʌlt] *n* adulte *mf*; **a. education,** enseignement *m* pour adultes; **an a. movie,** un film pour adultes; **an a. lion,** un lion adulte.

adulterate [ə'dʌltəreɪt] *vt* adultérer (*une substance*); frelater (*du vin etc*); corrompre (*une langue*); **adulterated milk,** lait additionné de quelque chose.

adulteration [ədʌltə'reɪʃən] *n* adultération *f* (*des médicaments*); frelatage *m* (*des boissons*).

adulterator [ə'dʌltəreɪtər] *n* adultérateur *m*; frelateur *m* (*d'aliments etc*).

adulterer [ə'dʌltərər], **adulteress** [ə'dʌltərəs] *n* adultère *mf*.

adulterous [ə'dʌltərəs] *adj* adultère.

adulterously [ə'dʌltərəslɪ] *adv* par adultère; (*vivre*) en état d'adultère.

adultery [ə'dʌltərɪ] *n* adultère *m*; **to commit a.,** commettre l'adultère.

adulthood ['ædʌlthʊd] *n* âge *m* adulte; **to reach a.,** devenir adulte.

ad valorem ['ædvæ'lɔːrem] *adj & adv Com Ind* **ad v. duty,** droit *m* sur la valeur, droit ad valorem.

advance¹ [əd'vɑːns] *n* **(a)** avance *f*; **with the a. of old age,** avec l'âge; **a. towards sth,** acheminement *m* à *ou* vers qch; **in their a. on the city,** au cours de leur avancée sur la ville; **in a.,** (*go*) en avant; (*arrive*) en avance; **to know in a.,** savoir à l'avance; **in a. of the others,** avant les autres, en avant des autres; **to be in a. of one's time,** être en avance sur son temps, devancer son époque; **to pay in a.,** payer d'avance; **to pay a sum in a.,** (*part payment*) verser une provision; (*total payment*) avancer un paiement; **thanking you in a.,** (*in letter*) en vous remerciant d'avance, avec mes remerciements anticipés; **a. booking,** réservation *f* par avance; **a. guard,** avant-garde *f*; **a. notice** *or* **warning,** préavis *m*; *Mil* **a. party,** (*vanguard*) détachement *m* d'avant-garde; (*scout*) détachement précurseur; **a. payment,** paiement *m* par anticipation;

(b) avancement *m*, progrès *m*, développement *m* (*des sciences etc*); **great advances in medicine,** de grands pas en avant dans le domaine de la médecine; **some advances were made in these decades,** on a fait des progrès au cours de ces décennies;

(c) (*sexual, business overture*) **to make advances to s.o.,** faire une avance *ou* des avances à *ou* auprès de qn;

(d) *Com Fin* avance *f* (*de fonds*); **a. on a contract,** acompte *m* sur contrat; **an a. of £200 on his salary,** une avance de 200 livres sur son salaire;

(e) augmentation *f* (*de prix*); hausse *f*; **any a.?,** (*at auction*) qui dit mieux?; **any a. on a hundred?,** (*at auction*) cent, qui dit mieux?

advance² **1** *vt* **(a)** avancer (*le pied, Chess un pion, la date d'une conférence etc*); faire avancer (*des troupes*);

(b) faire progresser, faire avancer (*les sciences etc*); accélérer (*la croissance, le développement etc*);

(c) avancer (*une idée, une opinion*); mettre en avant, présenter (*une opinion, une observation*); alléguer (*un prétexte*);

(d) *Fin* avancer (*de l'argent*) (**to,** à); **sums advanced,** avances *fpl*, provisions *fpl*;

(e) *Comptr* faire progresser (*le compteur*); faire défiler (*la bande magnétique*); faire avancer (*le papier sur l'imprimante, la carte dans la piste*);

(f) (*promote*) élever, porter, faire avancer (*qn à un grade supérieur*);

(g) (*increase*) augmenter, hausser (*le prix de qch*).

2 *vi* **(a)** (*move forward*) s'avancer (**towards,** vers); (*of troops*) se porter en avant; **to a. on a town/enemy positions/***etc*, avancer sur une ville/des positions ennemies/*etc*; **the season is advancing,** la saison s'avance; **to a. two steps** *or* **paces,** faire deux pas en avant;

(b) (*progress*) avancer (*en âge, dans ses études*); *Biol etc* évoluer; **the work is advancing,** l'ouvrage avance *ou* fait des progrès;

(c) (*of officer etc*) recevoir de l'avancement, monter (en grade);

(d) *Fin* (*of shares etc*) augmenter de prix, hausser; **prices are advancing,** les prix sont à la hausse.

advanced [əd'vɑːnst] *adj* **(a)** (*études, étudiants, opinions*) avancé; (*civilisation*) évolué; (*économie*) développé; (*pays*) développé, industrialisé; (*cours*) supérieur; **to hold very a. ideas,** avoir des idées très avancées; **a class for more a. students,** un cours pour étudiants plus avancés; **a. mathematics,** mathématiques supérieures; **the night is far a.,** il est tard dans la nuit; **the season is a.,** la saison est avancée; **he died at an a. age,** il est mort très vieux; **(b)** *Tech* perfectionné; (*technique*) d'avant-garde; **(c)** *Mil* (*poste*) avancé.

advancement [əd'vɑːnsmənt] *n* **(a)** avancement *m*, progrès *m* (*des sciences*); **economic a.,** essor *m* économique; **(b)** promotion *f* (*d'une personne*); **there is little scope for a.,** il y a peu de possibilités d'avancement; **(c)** *Comptr* progression *f* (*du compteur*); avancement *m*, défilement *m* (*du papier, de la bande*).

advancing [əd'vɑːnsɪŋ] *adj* qui s'avance; **a. storm,** orage qui s'avance.

advantage¹ [əd'vɑːntɪdʒ] *n* **(a)** avantage *m*; **to have/gain the a. over s.o.,** avoir/remporter l'avantage sur qn; **this article has the a. of cheapness,** cet article se recommande par son bon marché; **in this sport size is an a.,** dans ce sport, c'est un avantage d'être grand; *Old-fashioned* **you have the a. of me,** je n'ai pas l'honneur de vous connaître; **you will find it an a. to ...,** vous aurez avantage à ...; **to take a. of sth,** profiter de qch; tirer avantage *ou* profit de qch; **to take a. of the situation,** profiter de l'occasion (**to do,** pour faire); **to take a. of an offer/opportunity,** profiter d'une proposition/occasion; **he took a. of their generosity,** il tira parti de leur générosité; **they'll only take a.,** (*of your generosity etc*) ils ne feront qu'en profiter; **that would be taking a.!,** ce serait prendre un avantage!; **to take a. of s.o.,** abuser de la crédulité *ou* de la bonne volonté de qn; (*sexually*) profiter de l'état de qn; **it is to their a. to keep quiet,** c'est dans leur intérêt de se taire; **that would be to your competitor's a.,** ce serait dans l'avantage de votre concurrent; **the recession/weather worked to their a.,** ils ont été avantagés par la récession/le temps; **to turn sth to a.,** tirer parti de qch, mettre qch à profit; **to turn out to s.o.'s a.,** (*of event*) tourner à l'avantage de qn; profiter à qn; **to show off sth to a.,** faire valoir qch;

(b) *Tennis* avantage *m*.

advantage² *vt* avantager, favoriser (*qn, qch*).

advantageous [ædvən'teɪdʒəs] *adj* avantageux (**to,** pour), profitable, utile (**to,** à).

advantageously [ædvən'teɪdʒəslɪ] *adv* avantageusement, utilement.

advent ['ædvənt] *n* arrivée *f* (*d'une chose importante*); venue *f*, avènement *m* (*de qch, d'un personnage*); **the a. of the railways revolutionized goods transport,** l'introduction du chemin de fer révolutionna le transport des marchandises; **with the a. of McDonald as editor,** avec l'arrivée de McDonald à la rédaction.

Advent ['ædvənt] *n Rel* l'Avent *m*; **the Second A.,** le second Avènement; **A. calendar,** calendrier *m* de l'Avent; **A. Sunday,** le premier dimanche de l'Avent; **A. wreath,** (*for table*) couronne *f* de l'Avent.

Adventist ['ædvəntɪst] *n Rel Hist* Adventiste *mf*; **Seventh-day A.,** Adventiste du septième jour.

adventitious [ædven'tɪʃəs] *adj* adventice; (*accidental*) accidentel, fortuit; (*fait*) accessoire; *Bot* (*roots*) adventif.

adventure¹ [əd'ventʃər] *n* aventure *f*; **after many adventures,** après bien des péripéties; **life of a.,** vie d'aventure *ou* aventureuse; **where's your sense of a.?,** où est ton sens de l'aventure?; **a. playground,** aire *f* de jeux; **a. story,** roman *m* d'aventure(s).

adventure² *vi* s'aventurer, se hasarder (*dans un endroit, dans une entreprise*).

adventurer [əd'ventʃərər] *n* (*explorer*) *& Pej* aventurier *m*.

adventuresome [əd'ventʃəsəm] *adj* (*person*) aventureux; téméraire.

adventuress [əd'ventʃərɪs] *n Pej* aventurière *f*.
adventurous [əd'ventʃərəs] *adj* (*person, life, journey*) aventureux; (*person*) audacieux; **an a. child,** un enfant audacieux; **we had an a. trip,** nous avons eu un voyage plein d'aventures; **be a., try the curry,** sois un peu plus aventureux et essaie le curry, aventure-toi à essayer le curry.
adventurously [əd'ventʃərəslɪ] *adv* aventureusement.
adventurousness [əd'ventʃərəsnɪs] *n* hardiesse *f*, audace *f*; (*liking adventures*) esprit *m* d'aventures.
adverb ['ædvɜːb] *n Gram* adverbe *m*.
adverbial [əd'vɜːbɪəl] *adj Gram* adverbial; **a. phrase,** locution adverbiale.
adverbially [əd'vɜːbɪəlɪ] *adv* adverbialement; **adjective used a.,** adjectif employé comme adverbe.
adversary ['ædvəs(ə)rɪ] *n* adversaire *mf*.
adverse ['ædvɜːs] *adj* **(a)** (*in opposite direction*) contraire, opposé; **a. wind,** vent *m* contraire; **(b)** (*hostile*) hostile (**to,** à, envers); **a. fortune,** fortune *f* adverse; **(c)** (*comments, criticism*) défavorable; (*balance*) déficitaire.
adversely ['ædvɜːslɪ] *adv* **to influence s.o. a.,** exercer une influence défavorable sur qn; **to report a.,** faire un rapport défavorable (**on,** sur).
adversity [əd'vɜːsɪtɪ] *n* adversité *f*; **in a.,** dans l'adversité.
advert ['ædvɜːt] *n F* **(a)** (*publicity*) réclame *f*; **(b)** (*for job etc*) annonce *f*.
advertise ['ædvətaɪz] *vt & vi* **(a)** (*in newspaper*) (faire) annoncer, faire savoir (*un événement*); (*on poster*) afficher (*une vente etc*); **to a. in a paper,** (faire) insérer une annonce dans un journal; **to a. for s.o./sth,** chercher qn/qch par voie d'annonce; **they advertised for an accountant/a nanny,** ils ont passé une annonce pour un comptable/une bonne d'enfants; **house advertised for sale,** (*in newspaper*) maison dont la mise en vente est annoncée; (*in estate agent*) maison dont la mise en vente est affichée; **the job was advertised in the paper/in a shop window,** il y avait une annonce pour cet emploi dans le journal/dans une vitrine;
(b) (*in business*) faire de la réclame *ou* de la publicité (*pour un produit*); **it pays to a.,** la publicité fait gagner de l'argent; **they a. on television,** ils font de la publicité à la télévision; **as advertised,** conforme à la spécification publicitaire; *Fig* **you needn't a. the fact,** vous n'avez pas besoin de le crier sur les toits; *Fig* **you needn't a. your ignorance,** ce n'est pas la peine d'étaler ton ignorance.
advertised ['ædvətaɪzd] *adj Rail etc* **the a. time of departure,** l'heure prévue pour le départ; **the a. programme,** (*on TV*) le programme annoncé.
advertisement [əd'vɜːtɪsmənt] *n* **(a)** (*publicity*) publicité *f*, réclame *f*; *TV etc* spot *m* publicitaire; **an a. for toothpaste, a toothpaste a.,** une publicité pour dentifrice; **bad a.,** contrepublicité *f*; *Fig* **this sort of behaviour is not a good a. for democracy,** ce style de comportement ne fait pas bonne presse à la démocratie; **(b)** (*in newspaper*) annonce *f*; **an a. for a secretary,** une annonce pour une secrétaire; **to reply to** *or* **answer an a.,** répondre à une annonce; **classified advertisements,** petites annonces; **(c)** (*on wall etc*) affiche *f*.
advertiser ['ædvətaɪzər] *n* **(a)** (*on large scale*) annonceur *m*; **one of the biggest advertisers in the world,** l'un des plus gros annonceurs du monde; **(b)** (*in newspaper*) annonceur *m*.
advertising ['ædvətaɪzɪŋ] *n* **(a)** publicité *f*, réclame *f*; **she works in a.,** elle travaille dans la publicité; **there is more a. than news,** il y a plus de publicités que de nouvelles; **a. agency,** bureau *m ou* agence *f* de publicité; **a. agent,** agent *m* de publicité; **a. medium,** organe *m* de publicité; **a. space,** emplacement réservé à la publicité; **(b)** (*in newspaper*) annonces *fpl*.
advice [əd'vaɪs] *n* **(a)** conseil(s) *m(pl)*, avis *m*; **piece of a.,** conseil; **that's good a.,** c'est un bon conseil; **to ask** *or* **seek s.o.'s a.,** demander conseil à qn; **when I want your a. I'll ask for it!,** quand j'aurai besoin de tes conseils, je saurai te les demander!; **to give s.o. a.,** donner conseil à qn; **to take s.o.'s a.,** suivre le conseil de qn; **take my a. and don't have anything to do with them,** suis mon conseil et ne t'en mêle pas; **my a. (to you) would be to buy a new car,** mon conseil serait que tu achètes une nouvelle voiture; **to take medical/legal a.,** consulter un médecin/un avocat; **on s.o.'s a.,** sur l'avis *ou* le conseil de qn; **the magazine is a useful source of a.,** le magazine est une source utile de conseils; **(b)** (*notice*) avis *m*; **as per a.,** suivant avis; **until further a.,** jusqu'à nouvel avis; *Com* **a. note,** lettre *f ou* note *f* d'avis.
advisability [ədvaɪzə'bɪlɪtɪ] *n* opportunité *f*; **a. of doing sth,** opportunité *ou* utilité *f* qu'il y aurait à faire qch; **the a. of this course of action,** l'utilité qu'il y aurait à suivre cette procédure.
advisable [əd'vaɪzəb(ə)l] *n* (*démarche*) recommandable, recommandé, judicieux; **it is a. to book early,** il est recommandé de réserver à l'avance; **I'm going in my old car — is that a.?,** j'y vais dans ma vieille voiture — c'est conseillé?; **it would be a. to ...,** il serait prudent de ...; **it might be a. to ...,** peut-être conviendrait-il de ...; **if you consider** *or* **think it a.,** si bon vous semble.
advise [əd'vaɪz] **1** *vt* **(a)** conseiller (*qn*); recommander, conseiller (*la prudence*); **to a. s.o. to do sth,** conseiller à qn de faire qch; **I strongly a. you to ...,** je vous recommande instamment de ...; **customers are advised to book early,** il est recommandé *ou* conseillé aux clients de réserver à l'avance; **what do you a. me to do?,** que me conseillez-vous?; **you'd be well advised to take an umbrella,** vous feriez mieux de prendre un parapluie; **they were well advised to go by air,** ils ont bien fait de prendre l'avion; **they are advising taking a different route,** ils conseillent de prendre une route différente; **(b)** *Fml* (*inform*) avertir, prévenir, instruire (*qn*) (**of,** de); **to a. s.o. that ...,** avertir *ou* prévenir qn que ... . **2** *vi* servir de conseil.
▶**advise against** *vipo* déconseiller (*qch*); **to a. s.o. against sth,** déconseiller qch à qn.
advisedly [əd'vaɪzɪdlɪ] *adv* de propos délibéré, en connaissance de cause.
adviser, advisor [əd'vaɪzer] *n* conseiller, -ère; **a close a. of the president,** un proche conseiller du président.
advisory [əd'vaɪzərɪ] *adj* (*conseil, comité*) consultatif; **in an a. capacity,** à titre consultatif.
advocacy ['ædvəkəsɪ] *n* plaidoyer *m* (*en faveur d'une cause*).
advocate¹ ['ædvəkət, -eɪt] *n* **(a)** *Jur Scot* avocat *m*; **the Lord A.,** = le Procureur général; **(b)** avocat *m*; défenseur *m* (*d'une cause, d'une doctrine etc*); **the advocates of free trade,** les partisans du libre-échange; *Rel & Fig* **to be** *or* **play Devil's a.,** se faire l'avocat du diable.
advocate² ['ædvəkeɪt] *vt* plaider en faveur de (*qch*); soutenir (*une cause*); préconiser (*l'emploi de qch*); conseiller (*une ligne de conduite*); **she advocates leniency,** elle préconise l'indulgence.
adze, *US* **adz** [ædz] *n* (h)erminette *f*; sape *f* (*d'un piolet*).
Aegean [ɪ'dʒiːən] *adj & n* **(a) the A. sea, the A.,** la mer Égée; **(b)** *Antiq* égéen, -enne.
aegis, *US* **egis** ['iːdʒɪs] *n* égide *f*; **under the a. of ...,** sous l'égide de ... .
aegrotat ['aɪgrəʊtæt] *n Br Univ* équivalence *f* (d'examen) en année supérieure.
aeolian [iː'əʊlɪən] *adj* éolien; *Mus* **a. harp,** harpe éolienne.
aeon, *US* **eon** ['iːən] *n* éternité *f*; **for aeons upon aeons,** pendant des siècles *ou* des éternités.
aerate ['eəreɪt] *vt* **(a)** (*expose to air*) aérer; **(b)** *Physiol* artérialiser (*le sang*); **(c)** *Old-fashioned* gazéifier (*de l'eau, une eau minérale*).
aerated [eə'reɪtɪd] *adj* **(a)** aéré; **(b)** *Old-fashioned* (*water*) gazeux.
aeration [eə'reɪʃən] *n* **(a)** aération *f*; **(b)** *Physiol* artérialisation *f* (*du sang*).
aerial ['eərɪəl] **1** *adj* **(a)** *Av* aérien; **a. warfare,** combat aérien; **a. photography,** photographie aérienne; **(b)** *Bot* aérien; (*orchidée etc*) aéricole; **a. root,** racine aérienne. **2** *n Rad TV* antenne *f*; **transmitting/receiving a.,** antenne d'émission/réceptrice.
aerie ['eərɪ, 'ɪərɪ] *n esp US* aire *f* (*d'un aigle*).
aerobatics [eərəʊ'bætɪks] *npl* (*usu with sing verb*) *Av* acrobaties aériennes.
aerobics [eə'rəʊbɪks] *n* (*usu with sing verb*) aérobic *m*; **to do a.,** faire de l'aérobic; **are you going to a. tonight?,** est-ce que tu vas au cours d'aérobic ce soir?; **a. class/teacher/***etc*, cours *m*/professeur *m*/*etc* d'aérobic.
aerodrome ['eərədrəʊm] *n* aérodrome *m*.
aerodynamic [eərəʊdaɪ'næmɪk] *adj* aérodynamique; **a. centre,** (*in mechanics*) centre *m* aérodynamique; *Phys* centre de poussée; *Av* foyer *m* (*de profil d'aile*); **the car has an a. shape,** cette voiture a un profil *ou* une forme aérodynamique.
aerodynamics [eərəʊdaɪ'næmɪks] *npl* (*usu with sing verb*) aérodynamique *f*.
aerodyne ['eərəʊdaɪn] *n Av* aérodyne *m*.
aero-engine ['eərəʊendʒɪn] *n* moteur *m* d'avion.
aerofoil ['eərəʊfɔɪl], *Am* **airfoil** ['eəfɔɪl] *n Av* plan *m* à profil d'aile; surface portante *ou* sustentrice.
aerogram ['eərəgræm] *n* aérogramme *m*.
aeromodeller ['eərəʊ'mɒdlər] *n* aéromodéliste *m*.

aeromodelling ['eərəʊ'mɒdlɪŋ] *n* aéromodélisme *m*.
aeronaut ['eərənɔːt] *n* aéronaute *mf*.
aeronautic(al) [eərə'nɔːtɪk, -ɪk(ə)l] *adj* aéronautique.
aeronautics [eərə'nɔːtɪks] *npl* (*usu with sing verb*) aéronautique *f*.
aeroplane ['eərəpleɪn] *n esp Br* avion *m*.
aerosol ['eərəsɒl] *n* **(a) a. (can)**, (bombe *f*) aérosol *m*; **(b)** (*substance*) **a. spray**, atomiseur *m*; **a. paint**, peinture *f* aérosol.
aerospace ['eərəspeɪs] *n Ind* aérospatiale *f*; **a. industries**, industries aérospatiales.
aerostat ['eərəstæt] *n Av* aérostat *m*.
aerostatic [eərə'stætɪk] *adj* aérostatique.
aerostatics [eərə'stætɪks] *npl* (*usu with sing verb*) aérostatique *f*.
aesthete, *US* **esthete** [iːs'θiːt] *n* esthète *m*.
aesthetic, *US* **esthetic** [iːs'θetɪk, ɪs-] *adj* esthétique.
aesthetically, *US* **esthetically** [iːs'θetɪklɪ, ɪs-] *adv* esthétiquement.
aestheticism, *US* **estheticism** [iːs'θetɪsɪz(ə)m, ɪs-] *n* esthétisme *m*.
aesthetics, *US* **esthetics** [iːs'θetɪks, ɪs-] *npl* (*usu with sing verb*) esthétique *f*.
aetiology, *US* **etiology** [iːtɪ'ɒlədʒɪ] *n* étiologie *f*.
afar [ə'fɑːr] *adv usu Lit* **from a.**, de loin.
afear(e)d [ə'fɪəd] *adj Arch* effrayé, apeuré; **to be a. of s.o./sth**, être effrayé par *ou* avoir peur de qn/qch.
affability [æfə'bɪlɪtɪ] *n* affabilité *f*, courtoisie *f* (**towards**, envers, avec).
affable ['æfəb(ə)l] *adv* affable, courtois (**to**, envers; **with**, avec).
affably ['æfəblɪ] *adv* avec affabilité, avec courtoisie.
affair [ə'feər] *n* **(a)** (*matter, concern*) affaire *f*; **that's my a.**, ça, c'est mon affaire, ça ne vous regarde pas; **what he does in private is his own a.**, sa vie privée ne regarde que lui; **to put one's affairs in order**, mettre de l'ordre dans ses affaires; **in the present state of affairs**, du train où vont les choses; *Iron* **that's a nice** *or* **fine state of affairs!**, en voilà du propre!; *TV* **Jane Mackay, who reports on affairs in the French capital**, Jane Mackay, notre correspondant à Paris; **affairs of state**, les affaires de l'État; **foreign affairs**, les affaires étrangères; **our home affairs correspondent**, notre spécialiste des affaires intérieures; *Arch* **a. of honour**, affaire d'honneur, duel *m*;
(b) (*sexual*) liaison *f*; **to have an a. with s.o.**, avoir une liaison avec qn; **they're having an a.**, ils ont une liaison; **an a. of the heart**, une affaire de cœur;
(c) (*event*) **the meal will be a lavish a.**, le repas sera un véritable festin; **the festival/play was a dull a.**, ce festival/cette pièce était dépourvu(e) d'intérêt; **it was one of those cheese and wine affairs**, c'était une de ces soirées vin et fromage;
(d) *F* (*thing*) **the cake's one of those fresh-cream affairs**, c'est un de ces gâteaux à la crème fraîche; **the house is a three-storey a.**, il s'agit d'une maison à trois étages; **this workbench is an ingenious a.**, cet établi est vraiment ingénieux.
affect[1] [ə'fekt] *vt* **(a)** atteindre, toucher (*qn*); affecter (*un organe etc*); influer sur (*qch*); altérer (*la santé*); **the economic crisis which is affecting the country at present**, la crise économique qui frappe le pays en ce moment; **it affects me personally**, cela me touche personnellement; **the strike didn't a. us**, nous n'avons pas été touchés par la grève; **pensioners are not affected by this law**, les retraités ne sont pas concernés par cette loi; **those most directly affected**, les premiers intéressés; **(b)** (*move*) affecter, affliger, toucher (*qn*); **to be much affected by sth**, être très affecté *ou* affligé de qch.
affect[2] *vt* **(a)** (*fake*) faire parade de, simuler (*l'indifférence, la douleur*); **to a. an accent**, prendre un accent; **(b)** (*wear, use*) faire qch ostensiblement; **he affects drab colours/a certain style of dress**, il porte ostensiblement des couleurs ternes/un certain style de vêtement.
affectation [æfek'teɪʃən] *n* **(a)** affectation *f*, simulation *f* (*d'intérêt, d'indifférence etc*); **(b)** *Pej* affectation *f*; manque *m* de naturel; apprêt *m* (*de langage*).
affected[1] [ə'fektɪd] *adj* **(a)** *Med* atteint; **to be a. with a disease**, être atteint d'une maladie; **the lung is a.**, le poumon est atteint *ou* attaqué *ou* touché; **apply to the a. part**, appliquer sur les lésions; **(b)** (*emotionally*) ému, touché.
affected[2] *adj* **(a)** *Pej* (*person, manners*) affecté, maniéré, affété; (*style*) maniéré; (re)cherché, apprêté; **(b)** (*indifférence etc*) simulé; **a. cheerfulness**, gaieté *f* d'emprunt.
affectedly [ə'fektɪdlɪ] *adv* avec affectation; d'une manière affectée.
affectedness [ə'fektɪdnɪs] *n* (*no pl*) affectation *f*; manque *m* de naturel; apprêt *m* (*de langage etc*).
affecting [ə'fektɪŋ] *adj* (*spectacle etc*) touchant, attendrissant.
affection [ə'fekʃən] *n* **(a)** affection *f*, tendresse *f*; attachement *m*; **to show s.o. a.**, montrer de l'affection pour qn; **to feel a. for s.o.**, avoir de la tendresse pour qn; **she shows little a.**, elle fait preuve de peu de tendresse; **a rare display of a.**, une rare manifestation de tendresse; **to have an a. for s.o.**, ressentir de l'affection pour qn; **I have a great deal of a. for you**, j'ai beaucoup d'affection pour toi; **with much a.**, (*in letter*) (bien) affectueusement; **he is held in great a.**, il est très aimé; **to gain** *or* **win s.o.'s a.**, se faire aimer de qn; **this town has a special place in my affections**, j'aime tout particulièrement cette ville; **(b)** *Med* affection *f* (*de poitrine, de la peau etc*).
affectionate [ə'fekʃənət] *adj* affectueux; **he's very a. towards his children**, il est très affectueux avec ses enfants; **an a. hug**, une étreinte affectueuse; *Old-fashioned* **your a. nephew**, (*in letter*) votre dévoué neveu.
affectionately [ə'fekʃənətlɪ] *adv* affectueusement; **yours a.**, (*in letter*) bien affectueusement.
affective [ə'fektɪv] *adj* affectif.
affidavit [æfɪ'deɪvɪt] *n Jur* déclaration *f* par écrit et sous serment; **to swear an a.**, certifier sous serment une déclaration (écrite).
affiliate [ə'fɪlɪeɪt] **1** *vt* (*of society etc*) s'affilier (*des membres etc*); **to a. oneself to** *or* **with a society**, s'affilier à une société; **affiliated company**, filiale *f*. **2** *vi* **to a. to** *or* **with a society**, s'affilier à une société.
affiliation [əfɪlɪ'eɪʃən] *n* **(a)** affiliation *f* (*à une société*); **political affiliations**, attaches *fpl* politiques; **(b)** *Jur* procédure *f* en recherche de paternité; **a. order**, assignation *f* d'enfant à un père putatif.
affinity [ə'fɪnɪtɪ] *n* **(a)** *Math Biol* affinité *f*; (**with, to**, avec; **between**, entre); *Ch* **a. for a body**, affinité pour un corps; **(b)** (*relationship*) parenté *f* par alliance; *Jur* affinité *f*.
affirm [ə'fɜːm] *vt* **(a)** affirmer, soutenir (**that**, que); **to a. sth to s.o.**, affirmer qch à qn; **(b)** *Jur* confirmer, homologuer (*une jugement*).
affirmation [æfə'meɪʃən] *n* **(a)** affirmation *f*, assertion *f*; **(b)** *Jur* déclaration solennelle (*tenant lieu de serment*); **(c)** *Jur* confirmation *f*, homologation *f* (*d'un jugement*).
affirmative [ə'fɜːmətɪv] **1** *adj* (*answer*) affirmatif; **to make an a. sign**, faire un signe affirmatif; faire signe que oui. **2** *n* **to answer in the a.**, répondre affirmativement; **the answer is in the a.**, la réponse est affirmative. **3** *int* **a., captain**, affirmatif, mon capitaine.
affirmatively [ə'fɜːmətɪvlɪ] *adv* affirmativement.
affix[1] ['æfɪks] *n Ling* affixe *m*.
affix[2] [ə'fɪks] *vt* attacher (**sth to sth**, qch à qch); apposer (*un sceau, un timbre*) (**to a document**, à, sur un document); **she affixed her signature to the document**, elle apposa sa signature au document.
afflict [ə'flɪkt] *vt* affliger; **to be afflicted with rheumatism**, être affligé de rhumatismes; **to be afflicted at** *or* **by a piece of news**, être affligé *ou* s'affliger d'une nouvelle; *Fig* **the economic problems that a. the nation**, les problèmes économiques qui accablent le pays.
afflicted [ə'flɪktɪd] **1** *adj* affligé. **2** *n* **the a.**, (*used as pl*) les affligés *mpl*.
affliction [ə'flɪkʃən] *n* **(a)** affliction *f*; **deafness is a great a.**, la surdité est une grande affliction; **the afflictions of old age**, les infirmités de la vieillesse; **(b)** *Fig* calamité *f*, revers *m*.
affluence ['æfluəns] *n* **(a)** (*wealth*) abondance *f*, richesse *f*; **to live in a.**, vivre dans l'abondance; **(b)** *Lit* (*large number, quantity*) affluence *f*; foule *f* (*de gens etc*).
affluent ['æfluənt] *adj* **(a)** (*wealthy*) riche; **a. society**, société *f* d'abondance; **(b)** *Lit* (*abundant*) abondant, riche (**in**, en).
affluently ['æfluəntlɪ] *adv* (*vivre*) dans l'abondance.
afford [ə'fɔːd] *vt* **(a)** (*usu with* **can**) avoir les moyens (pécuniaires) de (*faire qch*); être en mesure de (*faire qch*); **an extravagance I could ill a.**, une extravagance qui n'était guère dans mes moyens; **I can't a. it**, mes moyens ne le permettent pas; **we can't a. a new car**, nous ne pouvons pas nous permettre d'acheter une nouvelle voiture; **I can a. to eat out twice a week**, je peux me permettre d'aller au restaurant deux fois par semaine; **give what you can a.**, donnez selon vos possibilités; **I can a. to wait**, je peux attendre; **can you a. the time?**, disposez-vous du temps (nécessaire)?; **I cannot a. to create a bad impression**, cela me nuirait de faire une mauvaise impression; **I can't a. not to go**, je ne peux pas me permettre de ne pas y aller;

(b) *Lit* (*give*) fournir, offrir; **the trees afforded us very little shelter,** les arbres ne nous fournissaient qu'un piètre abri; **it affords me great pleasure,** cela me fait grand plaisir; **kind heaven a. him everlasting rest,** = que Dieu dans sa miséricorde lui donne le repos éternel.

affordable [ə'fɔːdəb(ə)l] *adj* (*price*) abordable; (*house, trip etc*) (d'un prix) abordable.

afforest [ə'fɒrɪst] *vt* boiser (*une terre*).

afforestation [æfɒrɪ'steɪʃən] *n* boisement *m*, afforestation *f*.

affranchise [ə'fræntʃaɪz] *vt* affranchir (*un esclave*).

affranchisement [ə'fræntʃɪzmənt] *n* affranchissement *m* (*d'un serf, d'un esclave*).

affray [ə'freɪ] *n Jur* bagarre *f*, échauffourée *f*.

affront¹ [ə'frʌnt] *n* affront *m*, offense *f* (**to,** à).

affront² *vt* offenser, faire (un) affront à (*qn*); **he was affronted by the suggestion that he should help,** il a été très vexé quand on lui a fait remarquer qu'il pourrait aider.

Afghan ['æfgæn] **1** *adj* afghan; **A. hound,** (*dog*) lévrier afghan. **2** *n* **(a)** Afghan, -ane; **(b)** *Ling* afghan *m*; **(c)** *Am* couverture *f* de laine tricotée (au crochet).

Afghanistan [æf'gænɪstɑːn] *n* Afghanistan *m*.

aficionado [əfɪʃjə'nɑːdəʊ] *n* aficionado *m*.

afield [ə'fiːld] *adv* **to go far a./farther a.,** aller très loin/plus loin; **she rarely ventures farther a. than the next village,** elle s'aventure rarement au-delà du village voisin.

afire [ə'faɪər] *adv & adj Arch & Lit* en feu; *Fig* enflammé.

aflame [ə'fleɪm] *adv & adj Lit* en flammes, embrasé; **the trees were a. with colour,** les arbres étaient flamboyants.

AFL-CIO [eɪefelsiːaɪ'əʊ] *n abbr* **American Federation of Labor and Congress of Industrial Organizations.**

afloat [ə'fləʊt] *adv & adj* **(a)** à flot, sur l'eau; à la mer; **the biggest ship a.,** le plus gros navire à flot; **to be a.,** (*of ship*) être à flot; (*of rumour etc*) courir, circuler; **to keep a ship a.,** maintenir un navire à flot; *Fig* **to keep a.,** (*of company*) se maintenir à flot; (*of person*) surnager; *Fig* **to keep s.o. a. (financially),** renflouer qn; **to be a. in space,** planer dans l'espace; **(b)** (*flooded*) inondé; **the kitchen was a.,** la cuisine était inondée.

aflutter [ə'flʌtər] *adj* excité; **my heart was all a.,** mon cœur battait la chamade.

afoot [ə'fʊt] *adv* **a plan is a. to ...,** on envisage *ou* on a formé un projet pour ...; **there's something a.,** il se prépare *ou* se trame quelque chose.

afore [ə'fɔːr] *Arch* **1** *adv & prep* avant. **2** *conj* avant que + *sub*.

aforementioned [ə'fɔːmenʃənd] *adj esp Jur* susmentionné.

aforesaid [ə'fɔːsed] *adj esp Jur* susdit.

aforethought [ə'fɔːθɔːt] *adj Jur* **with malice a.,** avec préméditation, avec intention criminelle.

a fortiori [ə'fɔːtɪɔːrɪ] *adv* a fortiori.

afoul [ə'faʊl] *adv* **to run a. of the law,** avoir des ennuis avec la police.

afraid [ə'freɪd] *adj* **(a)** (*scared*) pris de peur; **to be a. of s.o./sth,** avoir peur de qn/qch, craindre qn/qch; **don't be a.,** n'ayez pas peur, ne craignez rien; **he felt a.,** il se sentait pris de panique; **if you're not a. of hard work,** si le travail intensif ne vous fait pas peur; **there's nothing to be a. of,** il n'y a pas de raison d'avoir peur; **that's (exactly) what I was a. of!,** c'est bien ce que je craignais!;

(b) (*worried*) **to be a. that ...,** avoir peur *ou* craindre que + *sub* ...; **I was a. you would ask me that question,** je craignais que vous me posiez cette question; **I was a. that might happen,** c'est bien ce que je craignais qu'il arrive; **we were a. you'd be angry,** nous avions peur que tu sois en colère; **I am a. he'll die,** je crains qu'il ne meure;

(c) (*regretful*) **I'm a. so/not,** je crains (bien) que oui/non; **I'm a. she's out,** j'ai bien peur qu'elle soit sortie, je crains bien qu'elle ne soit sortie; **I can't help you, I'm a.,** je suis désolé, je crois que je ne peux rien faire pour vous.

afresh [ə'freʃ] *adv* de nouveau, à nouveau; **to start sth a.,** recommencer qch.

Africa ['æfrɪkə] *n* Afrique *f*; **in A.,** en Afrique.

African ['æfrɪkən] **1** *adj* africain; **an A. American,** un noir américain; **A. violet,** (*plant*) saintpaulia *m*; **A. elephant,** éléphant *m* d'Afrique. **2** *n* Africain, -aine.

Afrikaaner [æfrɪ'kɑːner] **1** *adj* afrikander. **2** *n* Afrikander *mf*.

Afrikaans [æfrɪ'kɑːns] *n Ling* afrika(a)ns *m*.

Afro ['æfrəʊ] **1** *adj* (*coiffure*) afro *inv*. **2** *n* coiffure *f* afro.

Afro-American ['æfrəʊə'merɪkən] **1** *adj* afro-américain. **2** *n* Afro-américain, -aine.

aft [ɑːft] *adv Nau Av* sur *ou* à *ou* vers l'arrière; **to go a.,** aller à l'arrière; **a. of the mast,** sur l'arrière du mât; **to have the wind dead a.,** avoir le vent en poupe.

after ['ɑːftər] **1** *adv* après; **to come a.,** venir après *ou* à la suite; **he was ill for months a.,** il en est resté malade pendant des mois; **soon/long a.,** bientôt/longtemps après; **the night/the week a.,** la nuit/la semaine d'après; **a year a.,** un an après *ou* plus tard; **the day a.,** le lendemain.

2 *prep* **(a)** (*of place*) après; **to run a. s.o.,** courir après qn; **close the door a. you,** fermez la porte après vous; **I called a. him,** je l'ai rappelé; *F* **to be a. s.o./sth,** être en quête de qn/qch; **the police are a. you,** la police est à vos trousses; *F* **what's he a.?,** (*what does he want?*) qu'est-ce qu'il a en tête *ou* derrière la tête?; (*what is he looking for?*) qu'est-ce qu'il cherche?; **are you a. my job?,** est-ce que tu veux me piquer ma place?; **she's a. a full-time job,** elle cherche un travail à temps plein; **they are a. some fun,** ils veulent s'amuser;

(b) (*of time*) après; **to reign a. s.o.,** régner après qn; **a. three days,** trois jours après *ou* plus tard; **a. dinner,** après dîner; **a. this date,** passé cette date; **a. all's said and done,** au bout du compte, finalement; **a. all,** (*all things considered*) après tout; (*don't forget*) au bout du compte; (*in spite of everything*) alors, finalement; **she's only young, a. all,** elle est jeune, c'est tout; **so you went to the party a. all?,** alors, finalement, vous êtes allés à la soirée?; **a. all we've done for you!,** après tout ce que nous avons fait pour toi!; **the day a. the battle,** le lendemain de la bataille; **the day a. tomorrow,** après-demain; **it is a. five (o'clock),** il est cinq heures passées; *Am* **twenty a. four,** quatre heures vingt; **one a. the other,** l'un après l'autre; les uns après les autres; **he read page a. page,** il lut page sur page; **time a. time,** maintes (et maintes) fois; **day a. day,** jour après jour; **year a. year,** une année après l'autre, tous les ans; **street a. street of grey apartment blocks,** rue après rue, les immeubles gris se succédaient; **mile a. mile,** mil(l)e après mil(l)e; **a. dinner speech,** discours *m* d'après-dîner; *Br* **a. hours drinking,** = verres pris après la fermeture des pubs;

(c) (*of order*) après; **a. you,** (*going through door etc*) après vous; (*at a meal*) servez-vous d'abord; **I put Milton a. Dante,** je mets Milton au-dessous de Dante;

(d) (*of manner*) d'après; **landscape a. Turner,** paysage d'après *ou* à la (manière de) Turner; **a man a. my own heart,** un homme qui m'est sympathique; *F* **a. a fashion,** tant bien que mal;

(e) (*about*) **to ask** *or* **inquire a. s.o.,** demander des nouvelles de qn; **Mrs. Smith asked a. you,** Mme Smith a demandé de tes nouvelles;

(f) (*Irish*) **to be a. doing sth,** (*in the middle of*) être en train de faire qch; (*inclined to*) être disposé à faire qch.

3 *conj* (*when subject changes*) après que + *sub*; (*when subject stays the same*) après + *infin*; **I came a. he had gone,** je suis venu après qu'il fût parti; **a. I had seen him I went out,** après l'avoir vu, je suis sorti; **a. doing sth,** après avoir fait qch.

4 *adj* **(a)** (*future*) à venir; **in a. years,** plus tard (dans la vie);

(b) *Nau* arrière; **a. cabin,** cabine *f* sur l'arrière; **a. hold,** cale *f* arrière.

afterbirth ['ɑːftəbɜːθ] *n Obst* placenta *m*.

afterburner ['ɑːftəbɜːnər] *n* dispositif *m* de postcombustion.

aftercare ['ɑːftəkeər] *n* postcure *f*; (*after giving birth*) soins post-natals; (*after operation*) soins post-opératoires; (*of convalescent, delinquent etc*) surveillance *f*.

afterdeck ['ɑːftədek] *n Nau* plage *f* arrière.

aftereffect ['ɑːftərəfekt] *n* (*of drug*) effet *m* secondaire, séquelles *fpl*; *Fig* (*of remark, coup etc*) répercussions *fpl*; **I'm still feeling the aftereffects of last night's drinking,** je ne me suis toujours pas remis de ce que j'ai bu hier soir; *Fig* **famine was one a. of this policy,** cette politique a entraîné la famine.

afterglow ['ɑːftəgləʊ] *n* dernières lueurs, derniers reflets (*du soleil couchant*).

afterlife ['ɑːftəlaɪf] *n* **(a)** *Rel* la vie après la mort; **(b)** (*later life*) suite *f* de la vie; **in a.,** plus tard dans la vie.

aftermath ['ɑːftəmæθ, -mɑːθ] *n* **(a)** suites *fpl* (*d'un événement*); **the a. of war,** (*aftereffects*) les répercussions *fpl* de la guerre; (*period*) l'après-guerre *m*; **(b)** *Agr* regain *m* (*de foin*); arrière-foin *m*.

aftermost ['ɑːftəməʊst] *adj Nau* (*partie*) la plus en arrière, la plus à l'arrière.

afternoon [ɑːftə'nuːn] **1** *n* après-midi *mf inv*; **this a.,** cet(te) après-midi; **in the a.,** (pendant) l'après-midi; **on a sunny a.,** au cours d'une après-midi ensoleillée; **on Tues-**

day a., mardi après-midi; on the a. of Wednesday 22nd March, le mercredi 22 mars après-midi; good a.!, *(hello)* bonjour!; *(goodbye)* au revoir!; a. tea, thé *m*, goûter *m*. 2 *adv esp Am* afternoons, (pendant) l'après-midi.

afterpains ['ɑːftəpeɪnz] *npl Obst* tranchées *fpl*.

afters ['ɑːftəz] *npl (with sing or pl verb) Br F* dessert *m*; what's for a.?, qu'est-ce qu'il y a comme dessert?; there was ice cream for a., il y avait une glace pour le dessert.

after-sales ['ɑːftəseɪlz] *adj Com* après-vente *inv*; a.-s. service, service *m* après-vente.

aftershave ['ɑːftəʃeɪv] 1 *adj (lotion)* après-rasage. 2 *n* lotion *f* après-rasage.

aftershock ['ɑːftəʃɒk] *n (of earthquake)* réplique *f*.

aftertaste ['ɑːftəteɪst] *n* arrière-goût *m*.

afterthought ['ɑːftəθɔːt] *n* réflexion *f* après coup; to be an a., *(of sth added)* être un rajout de dernière minute; as an a., après réflexion; to add sth as an a., ajouter qch après coup.

after-treatment ['ɑːftətriːtmənt] *n* soins ultérieurs *(à donner à un convalescent)*; traitement ultérieur *(d'un produit)*.

afterward ['ɑːftəwəd] *adv esp Am* = AFTERWARDS.

afterwards ['ɑːftəwədz] *adv esp Br* après, plus tard, ensuite; a. they went home, ils rentrèrent ensuite chez eux; I regretted it a., par la suite, je l'ai regretté; a long time a., longtemps après.

again [ə'gen, *occ* ə'geɪn] *adv* (a) de nouveau, encore; once a., encore une fois, une fois de plus, hello, it's me a.!, bonjour, c'est encore moi!; *F* not you a.!, (c'est) toi encore!; *F* not spaghetti a.!, pas encore des spaghettis!; don't do it a.!, ne recommencez pas *ou* plus!; never a., (ne...) jamais plus, plus jamais (... ne); never a.!, *(after bad experience)* plus jamais!; *Lit Fml* never a. will a king rule this land, plus jamais un roi ne régnera dans ce pays; I'm not going to THAT shop a., je ne remettrai jamais les pieds dans ce magasin; a. and a., time and (time) a., maintes et maintes fois; I have told you so a. and a., je vous l'ai dit vingt fois *ou* cent fois; now and a., de temps en temps, de temps à autre; as much a., deux fois autant; half as much a., moitié plus; half as long a., plus long de moitié; different a., encore différent; she was wearing something different a., elle était encore habillée différemment; to begin a., recommencer; to come a., revenir; I've seen him a., je l'ai revu; I hope I shall find it a., j'espère bien le retrouver; *F* what was your name a.?, rappelez-moi votre nom;

(b) *(rhetorical)* de plus, d'ailleurs, en outre; a., I am not sure that ..., d'ailleurs je ne suis pas sûr que ...;

(c) *(on the other hand)* (then) a., d'un autre côté; then a., he may have forgotten, par ailleurs, il se peut qu'il ait oublié; a., others may disagree, d'un autre côté, certains peuvent ne pas être d'accord.

against [ə'genst, *occ* ə'geɪnst] *prep* (a) *(in opposition to)* contre; to fight a. s.o., se battre contre qn; to march a. the enemy, marcher à l'ennemi; to argue a. sth, plaider à contrepied de qch; she was a. the idea, elle s'opposait à l'idée; what have you got a. him/going to Paris?, qu'est-ce que tu as contre lui/le fait d'aller à Paris?; to have nothing a. sth, ne rien avoir contre qch; to be a. s.o., être opposé à qn, être contre qn; you've always been a. me, tu as toujours été contre moi; the war set brother a. brother, la guerre a opposé des hommes contre leurs frères; a. my will, contre mon gré; to act a. the law, agir illégalement; it's a. the law, c'est illégal *ou* contraire à la loi; a. the rules, contraire aux règlements; conditions are a. us, les conditions nous sont défavorables; there is no law a. it, il n'y a pas de loi qui s'y oppose; *Tex* a. the nap, à contre-poil, à rebours, à rebrousse-poil; a. the tide, au contre-sens de la marée; to go a. nature, aller à l'encontre de la nature; it was a race a. time, on n'avait guère le temps de le faire;

(b) *(as protection from)* to warn s.o. a. s.o./sth, mettre qn en garde contre qn/qch; protected a. the cold, protégé contre le froid; a. this eventuality, pour parer à cette éventualité;

(c) *(in contact with)* leaning a. the wall, appuyé contre le mur; to place sth a. a wall, adosser qch à un mur; he banged his head a. the wall, il s'est cogné la tête contre le mur; to come up a., se heurter contre *(qch)*; rencontrer *(des difficultés)*; a cross is placed a. each name/entry, *(beside)* une croix est placée à côté de chaque nom/inscription;

(d) *(in comparison)* three deaths this year (as) a. thirty in 1970, trois morts cette année contre trente en 1970; a. this must be set their extreme youth, en contrepartie, il faut tenir compte de leur extrême jeunesse; to check sth a. a list, vérifier qch d'après une liste; to rise/fall a. the dollar, augmenter/chuter par rapport au dollar;

(e) *(in contrast to)* to show up a. a background, se détacher sur un fond; she was silhouetted a. the sky, sa silhouette se détachait sur le ciel; the red stood out a. the grey, le rouge contrastait avec le gris; a. the light, à contre-jour;

(f) *Fin* en contrepartie; to issue a ticket a. payment of ..., remettre un ticket en contrepartie du paiement de ... .

agape [ə'geɪp] *adv & adj* bouche bée; to stand a., rester bouche bée; with mouth a., bouche bée.

agar(-agar) ['eɪgə('reɪgər)] *n* agar-agar *m*, gélose *f*.

agaric ['ægərɪk] *n (toadstool)* agaric *m*; fly a., (amanite *f*) tue-mouches *m*; fausse oronge.

agate ['ægət] *n Miner* agate *f*.

Agatha ['ægəθə] *n* Agathe *f*.

agave ['ægeɪv, ə'geɪvɪ] *n (plant)* agave *m*.

age¹ [eɪdʒ] *n* (a) âge *m*; to be past middle a., être sur le retour; twenty years of a., âgé de vingt ans; what a. is she?, what's her a.?, quel âge a-t-elle?; children of their own a., des enfants de leur âge; he's your a., il a ton âge; she's the same a. as me *or* as I am, elle a le même âge que moi; they're the same a., they're of an a., ils sont du même âge; when I was your a., quand j'avais votre âge; when you're my a., quand vous aurez mon âge; he doesn't look his a., il ne fait pas son âge; *F* act *or* be your a.!, voyons, tu n'es plus un enfant!; at your a. you should do, à ton âge, tu devrais faire; at that a. children need a lot of attention, c'est un âge où les enfants demandent beaucoup d'attention; 15 is the worst a., kids are so difficult then, à 15 ans les enfants sont si difficiles, c'est vraiment l'âge le pire; at the a. of 33, à l'âge de 33 ans; I'm at an a. where I question things more, je suis arrivé à un âge où l'on se pose plus de questions; to be of an a. to marry, être en âge de se marier; people of all ages, des gens de tout âge; people over the a. of 50, les gens de plus de 50 ans; a. of discretion, âge de raison *ou* de discrétion; *Admin Mil* a. group, classe *f*; the 15-to-20 a. group, le groupe *ou* la classe des 15-20 ans; people of all a. groups, des gens de toutes les tranches d'âge; a. limit, limitation *f* d'âge; is there any a. limit?, y-a-t-il une limite d'âge?; a. ring, cerne *m (d'un arbre)*;

(b) (old) a., vieillesse *f*; wisdom comes with a., la sagesse vient avec l'âge; a. has not been kind to her, elle est marquée par l'âge; the house is falling to pieces with a., la maison tombe de vieillesse *ou* de vétusté; a tree of great a., un très vieil arbre; *Hum* a. before beauty, c'est le bénéfice de l'âge;

(c) *(adulthood)* to be of a., être majeur; to come of a., atteindre sa majorité; coming of a., entrée *f* en majorité; a. of consent, = âge légal auquel une jeune fille peut se marier ou avoir des rapports sexuels; to be under a., *Jur* être mineur; *(not old enough to buy alcohol etc)* ne pas avoir l'âge; full a., âge légal; (état *m* de) majorité;

(d) *(era)* âge *m*, époque *f*, siècle *m*, ère *f*; the a. we live in, notre siècle, le siècle où nous vivons; in our a., à notre époque; she is the product of an earlier a., elle est d'un autre temps; in this a. of consumerism, en cette ère de consumérisme; through the ages, à travers les âges; *Hist* the A. of Reason, le siècle des lumières;

(e) *F (a long time)* it's ages *or* an a. since I saw him, I haven't seen him for ages, il y a une éternité que je ne l'ai pas vu; I've been waiting (for) ages, j'ai attendu pendant des heures.

age² *v* (aged [eɪdʒd], ageing, aging ['eɪdʒɪŋ]) 1 *vi* vieillir, prendre de l'âge; to a. ten years, vieillir de dix ans; he had aged beyond recognition, il avait vieilli à ne plus le reconnaître. 2 *vt* (a) vieillir; rendre *(qn)* vieux; (b) *Ind etc* mûrir *(un produit)*; vieillir *(un métal, le vin, le whisky)*.

aged¹ ['eɪdʒɪd] 1 *adj Lit* âgé, vieux; an a. man, un vieillard. 2 *n* the a., *(used as pl)* les vieillards, les vieux.

aged² [eɪdʒd] *adj* (a) *(of the age of)* a. twenty, âgé de vingt ans; (b) *(older)* I found him greatly a., je l'ai trouvé bien vieilli.

ageing ['eɪdʒɪŋ] 1 *adj* vieillissant; *(makes s.o. look older)* qui fait vieux; a. population, population vieillissante; an a. Don Juan, un Don Juan vieillissant. 2 *n* vieillissement *m (d'une personne, d'un vin etc)*; a. process, processus *m* de vieillissement.

ageism ['eɪdʒɪz(ə)m] *n* âgeisme *m*.

ageist ['eɪdʒɪst] *adj (policy etc)* qui défavorise les personnes âgées.

ageless ['eɪdʒlɪs] *adj* (a) *(young-looking)* toujours jeune;

(b) (*eternal*) éternel.

agency ['eɪdʒənsɪ] *n* **(a)** *Com* agence *f*, bureau *m*; **to have the sole a. for a firm,** être le représentant exclusif d'une maison; **advertising a.,** agence de publicité; **aid a.,** association *f* d'aide aux pays en voie de développement; **news** *or* **press a.,** agence de presse; **employment a.,** agence de placement; **estate a.,** agence immobilière; **travel a.,** agence de tourisme; **(b)** (*action*) action *f*, opération *f*; **the a. of water,** l'action de l'eau; **through s.o.'s a.,** par l'entremise *ou* l'intermédiaire de qn; **(c)** *esp US* (*government department*) organisme gouvernemental.

agenda [ə'dʒendə] *n* ordre *m* du jour, programme *m* (*d'une réunion*); **question on the a.,** question à l'ordre du jour; *Fig* **drugs are back on the a.,** la drogue revient à la une de l'actualité.

agent ['eɪdʒənt] *n* **(a)** *Com* agent *m*, représentant *m*; *Th Cin* agent; **a. for the firm of ...,** représentant de la maison ...; **sole a.,** agent exclusif; **(b) (secret) a.,** agent secret; **double a.,** agent double; **a. provocateur** ['æʒɒnprɒvɒkæ'tɜːr] (*pl* **agents provocateurs**), (agent) provocateur *m*; **(c)** (*instrument*) agent *m*; **to be the a. of sth,** être le moteur *ou* la cause de qch; **the a. of change was the revolution,** l'évolution était due à la révolution; **she was the a. of her own downfall,** elle a causé sa propre perte; **to be a free a.,** *Phil* avoir (le droit d'agir selon) son libre arbitre; *F* **you're a free a.,** tu es libre de faire ce que tu veux; **(d)** agent *m* (*chimique, thérapeutique etc*).

age-old ['eɪdʒəʊld] *adj* (*coutume etc*) séculaire.

agglomerate¹ [ə'glɒmərət] **1** *adj* aggloméré. **2** *n Geol* agglomérat *m*.

agglomerate² [ə'glɒməreɪt] **1** *vt* agglomérer. **2** *vi* s'agglomérer.

agglomeration [əglɒmə'reɪʃən] *n* agglomération *f*.

agglutinate [ə'gluːtɪneɪt] *Physiol Biol Ling* **1** *vt* agglutiner. **2** *vi* s'agglutiner.

agglutination [əgluːtɪ'neɪʃən] *n* agglutination *f*.

aggrandize [ə'grændaɪz] *vt* agrandir (*un État, l'importance de qn*).

aggrandizement [ə'grændɪzmənt] *n* agrandissement *m* (*d'un État etc*).

aggravate ['ægrəveɪt] *vt* **(a)** aggraver (*une faute, une difficulté, un crime, une situation*); empirer (*un mal*); envenimer (*une plaie, une querelle*); augmenter (*l'indignation, la douleur*); *Jur* **aggravated larceny,** vol qualifié; **(b)** *F* (*annoy, anger*) agacer, exaspérer (*qn*).

aggravating ['ægrəveɪtɪŋ] *adj* **(a)** (*circumstance*) aggravant; **(b)** *F* (*exasperating*) exaspérant; **a. child,** enfant insupportable; **it's very a.,** c'est vraiment agaçant.

aggravation [ægrə'veɪʃən] *n* **(a)** aggravation *f* (*d'un crime, d'une maladie*); enveniment *m* (*d'une plaie, d'une querelle*); **(b)** *F* (*of person*) exaspération *f*, agacement *m*; **(c)** *F* (*cause*) circonstance aggravante.

aggregate¹ ['ægrɪgət] **1** *adj* **(a)** collectif; *Econ* global, -aux; **for an a. period of three years,** pendant trois ans en tout; **a. output,** production globale; **(b)** *Bot Geol* agrégé. **2** *n* **(a)** ensemble *m*, total *m*; **world aggregates,** totaux mondiaux; **in the a.,** en somme, dans l'ensemble; *esp Sp* **on a.,** au total; **Milan won on a.,** c'est Milan qui a totalisé le plus de points; **(b)** *Phys* masse *f*, assemblage *m*, agrégation *f*; *Ch Miner* agrégat *m*; **(c)** *Constr* granulat *m*.

aggregate² ['ægrɪgeɪt] **1** *vt* **(a)** *Phys* agréger; **(b)** s'élever à (*un nombre*); monter à (*un total*). **2** *vi Phys* s'agréger.

aggregation [ægrɪ'geɪʃən] *n* **(a)** *Phys* agrégation *f*, agglomération *f*; **(b)** *Econ* **a. of production functions,** agrégation *f* de fonctions de production; **(c)** agrégat *m*.

aggression [ə'greʃən] *n* agression *f*; **an act of a.,** un acte d'aggression; **war of a.,** guerre *f* d'agression.

aggressive [ə'gresɪv] *adj* **(a)** agressif (**towards,** envers); (*regard, air*) cassant; (*politique*) militant; *Psy* **a. impulse,** impulsion agressive; **(b)** (*salesperson etc*) énergique, dynamique.

aggressively [ə'gresɪvlɪ] *adv* (*to behave*) d'une manière agressive; (*to say*) d'un ton agressif; (*to look at*) d'un air agressif.

aggressiveness [ə'gresɪvnɪs] *n* caractère agressif, agressivité *f*.

aggressor [ə'gresər] *n* agresseur *m*; **a. nation,** pays *m* agresseur.

aggrieved [ə'griːvd] *adj* (*expression, tone*) affligé; **to be** *or* **feel a.,** se sentir lésé; (**at, by,** de); *Jur* **the a. party,** la partie lésée.

aggro ['ægrəʊ] *n Br F* **(a)** (*hassle*) enquiquinement *m*; **it's not worth the a.,** ça ne vaut pas le coup de s'enquiquiner; **there's a. with her all the time,** on s'accroche tout le temps avec elle; **(b)** (*fighting*) bagarre(s) *f(pl)*, grabuge *m*.

aghast [ə'gɑːst] *adj* consterné (**at,** de); **to stand a.,** en être tout pantois.

agile ['ædʒaɪl] *adj* (*person, animal, limbs, movement*) agile; leste; (*mind*) adroit, habile, rusé.

agilely ['ædʒaɪlɪ] *adv* (*move, jump*) agilement, avec agilité; (*argue*) adroitement.

agility [ə'dʒɪlɪtɪ] *n* agilité *f*.

aging ['eɪdʒɪŋ] *adj & n* = **AGEING.**

agio ['ædʒɪəʊ] *n Fin* **(a)** (*price*) agio *m*; prix *m* du change; **(b)** (*business*) commerce *m* du change.

agitate ['ædʒɪteɪt] **1** *vt* **(a)** agiter, remuer (*qch*); tourmenter (*la surface de l'eau*); **(b)** agiter, troubler (*qn, l'esprit de qn*). **2** *vi* **to a. for/against sth,** faire de l'agitation *ou* mener une campagne en faveur de/contre qch.

agitated [ædʒɪteɪtɪd] *adj* **(a)** (*water*) agité; **(b)** (*person*) agité, ému, troublé; **now don't get a.!,** allez, calme-toi!

agitation [ædʒɪ'teɪʃən] *n* **(a)** agitation *f* (*de l'air, de la mer*); mouvement *m*; **(b)** (*of person*) agitation *f*, émotion *f*, trouble *m*; *Pol* agitation *f* (*ouvrière etc*); troubles *mpl*; **in a state of a.,** agité.

agitator ['ædʒɪteɪtər] *n* **(a)** (*person*) agitateur, -trice; (*for sth*) contestataire *m*; **(b)** (*machine*) agitateur *m*.

agitprop ['ædʒɪtprɒp] *n* (*activity*) = la propagande et l'agitation.

aglow [ə'gləʊ] *adj* enflammé, embrasé; **the sky was a.,** le ciel était embrasé; **to be a. with colour,** briller de vives couleurs; *Fig* **face a. with delight,** visage rayonnant de joie *ou* tout épanoui; *Fig* **a. with health,** resplendissant de santé.

AGM [eɪdʒiː'em] *n abbr* **annual general meeting.**

agnostic [æg'nɒstɪk] *adj & n* agnostique *mf*.

agnosticism [æg'nɒstɪsɪz(ə)m] *n* agnosticisme *m*.

ago [ə'gəʊ] *adv* **ten years a.,** il y a dix ans; **he arrived an hour a.,** il est arrivé il y a une heure; (*in this place*) il est là depuis une heure; **a little while a.,** tout à l'heure; **long a.,** il y a longtemps; **not long a.,** il n'y a pas longtemps; **not so long ago,** il n'y a pas si longtemps; **how long a. is it since ...?,** combien de temps y a-t-il que ...?, depuis combien de temps ...?; **as long a. as 1840,** déjà en 1840, dès 1840; **I knew her long a.,** je l'ai connue dans le temps.

agog [ə'gɒg] *adv & adj* **to be all a. (with excitement),** être agité *ou* en émoi (**about sth,** à cause de qch); **everyone was a.,** tout le monde était en émoi.

agonize ['ægənaɪz] *vi Lit* être au supplice *ou* au martyre; *Fig* se ronger les sangs.

agonized ['ægənaɪzd] *adj* (*cri*) d'angoisse; **with an a. expression (on her face),** d'un regard plein d'angoisse.

agonizing ['ægənaɪzɪŋ] **1** *adj* (*douleur, peur*) atroce; (*spectacle*) navrant, angoissant; (*situation, decision, dilemma etc*) angoissant. **2** *n* angoisse *f*; **after weeks of a.,** après des semaines d'angoisse.

agonizingly ['ægənaɪzɪŋlɪ] *adv* avec angoisse; **a. slow,** d'une lenteur insupportable.

agony ['ægənɪ] *n* **(a)** (*anguish*) angoisse *f*; **in an a. of fear,** saisi d'une peur atroce; **to be in an a. of suspense,** attendre avec angoisse; **to suffer agonies, to be in a.,** être au supplice *ou* au martyre; *F* **it's a. walking in these shoes,** c'est un véritable supplice de marcher avec ces chaussures; *F* **to pile** *or* **put on the a.,** forcer la dose; *Journ* **a. column,** courrier *m* du cœur; *Journ* **a. aunt,** = responsable de la rubrique courrier du cœur; **(b) (death) a.,** agonie *f*.

agoraphobia [æg(ə)rə'fəʊbɪə] *n Psy* agoraphobie *f*; **to have a.,** souffrir d'agoraphobie.

agoraphobic [æg(ə)rə'fəʊbɪk] *adj & n* qui souffre d'agoraphobie; **to be (an) a.,** souffrir d'agoraphobie.

agrarian [ə'greərɪən] **1** *adj* (*loi, mesure*) agraire; (*parti*) agrarien. **2** *n Pol* agrarien *m*.

agree [ə'griː] **1** *vt* **(a)** (*reach agreement on*) s'accorder *ou* se mettre d'accord sur (*les prix, les conditions etc*); **to be agreed,** (*of date*) à convenir; (*of price*) à débattre; **unless otherwise agreed,** sauf arrangement contraire; **let's a. to differ,** différons à l'amiable;

(b) (*concur*) **I a. that's expensive, but ...,** c'est cher, j'en conviens, mais ...; **I a. that he was mistaken,** j'admets qu'il s'est trompé; **don't you a. that ...?,** ne croyez-vous pas que ...?; **everyone agrees that he's the best singer,** tout le monde s'accorde à dire que c'est le meilleur chanteur;

(c) (*consent*) **to a. to do sth,** accepter *ou* convenir de faire qch, consentir à faire qch; **everyone agrees that ...,** tout le monde accepte que ...; **he agreed to let us go home,** il nous a permis de rentrer à la maison.

2 *vi* **(a)** (*be of same opinion, concur*) être d'accord; (*after discussion*) se mettre d'accord; **everyone agrees,** tout le monde est d'accord; **I'm afraid I can't a.,** (*with you, him* *etc*) j'ai bien peur de ne pas être du même avis; **I think it's too expensive and Peter agrees,** je pense que c'est trop cher et Peter est d'accord avec moi *ou* est du même avis; **in the end she agreed,** (*that it was too expensive*) elle a fini par l'admettre; **we shall never a.,** jamais nous ne mettrons d'accord; **so, we all a.?,** donc, nous sommes tous d'accord?; **it's expensive, I a., but ...,** c'est cher, j'en conviens, mais ...; *F* **I couldn't a. more!,** tu l'as *ou* elle l'a *etc* bien dit!;

(b) (*match*) (*of things*) s'accorder, être d'accord, concorder; (*of ideas, opinions*) se rencontrer; *Gram* s'accorder;

(c) (*accept*) consentir, donner son adhésion (**to,** à); faire droit (**to,** à) (*une requête*); convenir de qch; accepter (*une condition*); **she'll never a.,** elle ne sera jamais d'accord.

►**agree on** *vipo* **(a)** (*of people*) être d'accord sur (*un point*); (*after discussion*) se mettre d'accord sur (*un point*); se mettre d'accord sur, convenir de (*une date*); *Jur* **conditions agreed on,** conditions acceptées d'un commun accord; **(b)** (*of books, versions etc*) s'accorder sur (*un point*).

►**agree to** *vipo* (*accept*) faire droit à (*une requête*); accepter (*une condition, une proposition*); **to a. to sth being done,** accepter que qch se fasse; **they agreed to your visiting us,** ils ont accepté que *ou* ils veulent bien que tu viennes nous voir; **that's already been agreed to,** on l'a déjà accepté.

►**agree upon** *vipo* = **AGREE ON**.

►**agree with** *vipo* **(a)** (*be of same opinion as*) être du même avis que (*qn*), être d'accord avec (*qn*); **he entirely agrees with you,** il est entièrement de votre avis; *F* **I couldn't a. with you more!,** tu l'as bien dit!; **to a. with a theory,** accepter une théorie; **to a. with a decision,** approuver une décision; *F* **I don't a. with all this violence on television,** je n'approuve pas toute cette violence à la télé; **(b)** (*suit*) convenir à (*qn*); (*of food*) réussir à (*qn*); **the climate doesn't a. with him,** le climat ne lui convient pas *ou* ne lui va pas; **(c)** (*coincide*) concorder avec, être en accord avec (*ce que qn a dit*); *Gram* **the verb agrees with the subject in number,** le verbe s'accorde en nombre avec le sujet.

agreeable [ə'griːəb(ə)l] *adj* **(a)** (*pleasant*) agréable (**to,** à); (*person*) aimable (**to,** envers); **if that is a. to you,** si cela vous convient; **(b)** (*willing*) **to be a. to sth/to doing sth,** consentir à qch/à faire qch, accepter qch/de faire qch; **I am (quite) a.,** je veux bien.

agreeably [ə'griːəblɪ] *adv* agréablement.

agreed [ə'griːd] **1** *adj* (*prix etc*) convenu; **they didn't arrive at the a. time,** ils ne sont pas arrivés à l'heure prévue. **2** *int* entendu!, soit!, d'accord!; **it was expensive, a. but ...,** c'était cher, c'est entendu, mais ... .

agreement [ə'griːmənt] *n* **(a)** (*between people*) accord *m* (**on, about,** sur); *Com Ind* entente *f* (*entre producteurs etc*); **to have an a. with s.o.,** conclure un accord *ou* faire un arrangement avec qn; **we had an a.,** nous avions passé un accord; **our a. was that ...,** nous avions convenu que ...; **to be in a. with s.o.,** être d'accord avec qn; **to be in a. with a decision,** approuver une décision; **to come to an a.,** tomber d'accord; **to come to** *or* **arrive at** *or* **reach an a. with s.o.,** se mettre d'accord avec qn; (*compromise*) s'accommoder *ou* s'arranger avec qn; *Com* **as per a.,** comme (il a été) convenu; **by mutual a.,** d'un commun accord; **marketing a.,** accord de commercialisation;

(b) *Jur etc* convention *f*, acte *m*, contrat *m*; **written a.,** convention par écrit; **collective (wage) a.,** convention collective (des salaires); **to enter into** *or* **conclude an a. with s.o.,** passer un traité *ou* un contrat avec qn;

(c) conformité *f*, concordance *f* (*de différentes choses*); *Gram* accord *m* (**with,** avec); **a. of adjectives,** concordance des adjectifs.

agribusiness ['ægrɪbɪznɪs] *n* agro-alimentaire *f*.

agrichemical [ægrɪ'kemɪk(ə)l] *n esp Am* = **AGROCHEMICAL**.

agricultural [ægrɪ'kʌltʃər(ə)l] *adj* (*produit, machine, terre etc*) agricole; (*peuple*) agriculteur; (*instrument*) aratoire; **East Anglia is very a.,** l'East Anglia est une région très agricole; **a. college,** école *f* d'agriculture; **a. economy,** économie *f* du secteur agricole; **a. engineer,** ingénieur *m* agronome; **a. labourer** *or* **worker,** ouvrier *m* agricole.

agricultur(al)ist [ægrɪ'kʌltʃər(əl)ɪst] *n* agriculteur *m*.

agriculture ['ægrɪkʌltʃər] *n* agriculture *f*.

agrochemical [ægrə'kemɪk(ə)l] *n* produit *m* agrochimique.

agronomic [ægrə'nɒmɪk] *adj* agronomique.

agronomist [ə'grɒnəmɪst] *n* agronome *m*.

agronomy [ə'grɒnəmɪ] *n* agronomie *f*.

aground [ə'graʊnd] *adv Nau* échoué; **to run a.,** (*of ship*) (s')échouer; *Fig* (*of policy, project etc*) échouer.

ague ['eɪgjuː] *n Med Arch* fièvre (paludéenne) intermittente.

ah [ɑː] *int* ah!, ha!

aha [ə'hɑː] *int* haha!

ahead [ə'hed] *adv* **(a) to get a.,** (*of person, car etc*) prendre de l'avance; *Fig* (*of person*) avancer (dans sa carrière); **to draw a.,** (*of runner, cyclist etc*) se décoller; *Sp* **to be a. on points,** avoir des points d'avance; **to be a. of s.o.,** être en avant de qn; **to be a. of the bunch,** mener le peloton; **to go on a.,** prendre les devants; **to get a. of s.o.,** dépasser qn; **to be two hours a. of s.o.,** avoir deux heures d'avance sur qn; *Sch* **he is a. of his form,** il est en avance sur sa classe; **to be a. of one's time,** être en avance sur son temps; **to be a. of time,** (*of person*) être *ou* arriver *ou* avoir fini *etc* avant l'heure; (*of clock*) avancer; **you've got your best years a. of you,** vous avez vos meilleures années devant vous; **to look a.,** penser à l'avenir; **how far a. should one book?,** combien de temps faut-il retenir d'avance?; **they went straight a.,** ils allaient (tout) droit devant eux; **go a.!,** (*move*) allez!; (*do it*) vas-y!, allez-y!;

(b) *Nau* **to be a.,** être sur l'avant *ou* en avant (*du navire*); **the ship was right a.,** le navire était droit devant; **to go a.,** aller de l'avant; **full speed a.!,** en avant toute!; **wind a.,** vent debout; **line a.,** en ligne de file *ou* en colonne; **single line a.,** ligne de file.

ahoy [ə'hɔɪ] *int Nau* **boat/ship a.!,** oh(é) du canot!/du navire!

AI ['eɪaɪ] *n abbr* **(a)** *Comptr* **artificial intelligence**; **(b)** *Biol* **artificial insemination**.

aid¹ [eɪd] *n* **(a)** (*help*) aide *f*, assistance *f*, secours *m*; (*to developing countries, for disaster relief*) aide; **with** *or* **by the a. of s.o.,** avec l'aide de qn; **with** *or* **by the a. of sth,** à l'aide de qch; **to go to s.o.'s a.,** aller *ou* se porter au secours de qn; **collection in a. of ...,** quête au profit de ...; *F* **what's (all) this in a. of?,** c'est en quel honneur?; *F* **what's all this noise in a. of?,** qu'est ce que c'est que tout ce bruit?; **mutual a.,** entraide *f*; **mutual-a. society,** société *f* de secours mutuels *ou* d'assistance mutuelle; **legal a.,** aide judiciaire; **medical a.,** soins médicaux; **first a.,** premiers secours (aux blessés); soins d'urgence; **(b)** (*device*) **beauty aids,** produits *mpl* de beauté; **hearing** *or* **deaf a.,** audiophone *m*; *Sch* **audio-visual aids,** matériel audio-visuel.

aid² *vt* (*of person*) aider, assister (*qn*), venir en aide à (*qn*), venir à l'aide de (*qn*); soutenir, venir en aide à (*une entreprise*); (*of treatment etc*) contribuer à (*la guérison de qn*); **to a. one another,** s'aider les uns les autres, s'entraider; *Jur* **to a. and abet s.o.,** être le complice de qn.

AID [eɪaɪ'diː] *n Biol* (*abbr* **artificial insemination by donor**) IAD *f*.

aide [eɪd] *n* aide *mf*; assistant, -e; (*to president etc*) conseiller, -ère.

aide-de-camp ['eɪd'dəkɒŋ] *n* (*pl* **aides-de-camp**) *Mil* aide *m* de camp.

aide-mémoire ['eɪdmemwɑːr] *n* aide-mémoire *m inv*.

aiding ['eɪdɪŋ] *n Jur* **a. and abetting,** complicité *f*.

AIDS, *also* **Aids** [eɪdz] *n Med* sida *m*; **A. sufferer,** sidéen, -enne, malade atteint(e) du sida; **A. clinic,** clinique spécialisée dans le traitement du sida.

aikido [aɪ'kiːdəʊ] *n Sp* aïkido *m*.

ail [eɪl] **1** *vt Arch* **what ails you?,** qu'est-ce que vous avez? **2** *vi* être souffrant.

aileron ['eɪlərɒn] *n Av* aileron *m*.

ailing ['eɪlɪŋ] *adj* (*person*) souffrant; *Fig* (*company, economy*) en mauvaise passe.

ailment ['eɪlmənt] *n* mal *m*; **childish ailments,** maladies infantiles.

aim¹ [eɪm] *n* **(a)** (*action*) action *f* de viser; **to miss one's a.,** (*with firearm etc*) manquer le but *ou* son coup; *Fig* frapper à faux; **to take a. at s.o./sth,** viser qn/qch; **to take a.,** mettre en joue, viser; **he took careful a.,** il visa avec soin; **her a. was good,** elle visait bien; **(b)** (*goal*) but *m*, dessein *m*, visées *fpl*; **his a. was to ...,** il avait pour but de ..., il visait à ...; **she has one a. in life,** sa vie n'a qu'un (seul) but; **with the a. of doing sth,** dans le dessein de faire qch.

aim² **1** *vt* **(a)** lancer (*une pierre*) (**at,** à); porter, allonger (*un coup*) (**at,** à);

(b) pointer (*un fusil etc*); **to a. a gun/a pistol at s.o./sth,** coucher qn/qch en joue avec un fusil/un pistolet; **she aimed the revolver at his head,** elle pointa le revolver sur sa tête; **to a. a camera,** cadrer;

(c) *Fig* **remark aimed at s.o.,** remarque adressée à qn;

to a. **a criticism at s.o.,** porter une critique sur qn; **these measures are aimed at reducing unemployment,** ces mesures visent une réduction du chômage.

2 *vi* **(a) to a. at s.o./sth (with a gun),** ajuster *ou* viser qn/qch, mettre *ou* coucher qn/qch en joue; **I aimed at the tyres,** j'ai visé (dans) les pneus;

(b) *Fig* **to a. at becoming sth, to a. to become sth,** aspirer *ou* viser à devenir qch; **what are you aiming at?,** (*what do you hope to do?*) quel but poursuivez-vous?; (*what do you mean?*) où voulez-vous en venir?; *F* **I a. to go,** j'ai l'intention d'y aller.

aiming ['eɪmɪŋ] *n* visée *f*; *Mil* pointage *m*.

aimless ['eɪmlɪs] *adj* sans but, sans objet; **an a. sort of life,** une vie désœuvrée.

aimlessly ['eɪmlɪslɪ] *adv* sans but, sans objet; **to wander about a.,** aller *ou* errer à l'aventure.

aimlessness ['eɪmlɪsnɪs] *n* manque *m* de but à atteindre; manque d'ambition.

ain't [eɪnt] *Arch & Sl* **(a) = am not, is not, are not,** *see* **BE**; **(b) = have not,** *see* **HAVE²**.

air¹ [eər] *n* **(a)** air *m*; **breath of a.,** souffle *m* d'air; **to go out for a breath of (fresh) a.,** sortir prendre l'air *ou* le frais; **in the open a.,** en plein air, au grand air, à ciel ouvert; *F* **I can't live on a.,** je ne vis pas de l'air du temps; **to walk on a.,** être aux anges; **to be in the a.,** (*of rumour*) circuler; (*of idea*) être dans l'air; (*of project*) être encore vague; **everything's up in the a.,** (*uncertain*) rien n'a été décidé pour l'instant; **the date is still up in the a.,** la date n'a pas encore été fixée; **there's something in the a.,** il y a quelque chose dans l'air; *F* **it's all hot a.,** ce sont des discours en l'air; **castles in the a.,** châteaux en Espagne; **to melt** *or* **vanish into thin a.,** s'évanouir, disparaître (aux yeux de qn); **a. bed,** matelas *m* pneumatique; **a. compressor,** compresseur *m* d'air; **a. duct,** conduite *f* d'air, amenée *f* d'air; **a. filter,** filtre *m* à air; *El* **a. gap,** entrefer *m*; **a. gauge,** micromètre *m* pneumatique; **a. plant,** plante *f* aéricole, (plante) épiphyte *m*; **a. pocket,** *Av* trou *m* d'air; (*hydroelectricity etc*) cantonnement *m* d'air, poche *f* d'air; **a. rifle** *or* **gun,** fusil *m* à air comprimé; **a. temperature,** température ambiante;

(b) *Lit Nau* (*wind*) brise *f*, vent *m*; **there was no a.,** il n'y avait pas de vent;

(c) (*atmosphere*) **high up in the a.,** très haut au-dessus de nous, très haut dans le ciel; **in the a.,** en l'air, dans les airs; **to throw sth (up) in the a.,** jeter qch en l'air; *F* **to go up in the a.,** exploser (*de colère*);

(d) *Av* **by a.,** par avion, par air; **a. hostess,** hôtesse *f* de l'air; **a. mail,** (*service*) poste aérienne; service postal aérien; (*letters etc*) courrier *m* par avion; **by a. mail,** par avion; **a. route,** route aérienne; **a. show,** salon *m* aérien; **a. terminal,** aérogare *f*; **a. traffic,** circulation aérienne, trafic aérien; **a. traffic control,** contrôle aérien; **a. traffic controller,** contrôleur aérien, aiguilleur *m* du ciel; **a. transport,** transports aériens *ou* par avion; **a. travel,** voyages *mpl* par avion;

(e) *Mil Av* **a. attack,** attaque aérienne; **a. base,** base aérienne; **a. commodore,** = général *m* de brigade aérienne; **a. cover,** couverture aérienne, (force *f* de) protection aérienne; **a. defence/reconnaissance,** défense/reconnaissance aérienne; **the A. Force,** l'Armée *f* de l'air, l'Aviation *f*; *Hist* **the A. Ministry,** = le Ministère de l'Air; **a. officer,** officier *m* d'aviation; **a. raid,** raid aérien; (*offensive*) attaque *ou* incursion aérienne; **a. raid precautions,** défense passive; **a. raid warning,** alerte aérienne;

(f) *Rad TV F* **to be on the a.,** (*of person*) parler à la radio; (*of programme*) être radiodiffusé; (*of station*) émettre, faire des émissions; **we're going on the a. in two minutes,** nous sommes à l'antenne dans deux minutes; **the station goes off the a. at midnight,** les programmes finissent à minuit; **to put a play on the a.,** mettre une pièce en ondes;

(g) *Mus* air *m*;

(h) (*look*) air *m*, mine *f*, apparence *f*; **he has an a. about him,** il s'impose; **to carry sth off with an a.,** faire qch avec aplomb; **to give oneself** *or* **to put on airs,** se donner des airs, faire le suffisant *ou* la suffisante.

air² **1** *vt* **(a)** aérer (*une pièce, du linge etc*); éventer (*des vêtements*); mettre (*des vêtements*) à l'air *ou* à l'évent; bassiner (*un lit*); **(b)** *Fig* faire parade de, faire étalage de (*ses opinions, son savoir*); donner libre cours à (*ses sentiments*); exposer (*des griefs, son point de vue*). **2** *vi* **(a)** s'aérer; s'éventer; **(b)** (*of radio or TV programme*) passer.

airborne ['eəbɔːn] *adj* **(a)** (*particles, seeds etc*) en suspension dans l'air; **(b)** (*aircraft*) en vol, sustenté; (*balloon*) en l'air; **to become a.,** (*of aircraft*) décoller; **(c)** *Mil* (*troops, unit*) aéroporté; **a. attack,** attaque exécutée par des troupes aéroportées, assaut vertical; **(d)** *Av* (*équipement, radar*) de bord.

airbrush ['eəbrʌʃ] *n Art etc* aérographe *m*, pistolet vaporisateur.

►**airbrush in** *vtsep Art Phot* ajouter (*un détail*) à l'aide d'un aérographe.

►**airbrush out** *vtsep Art Phot* effacer (*un détail*) au moyen d'un aérographe.

airbrushing ['eəbrʌʃɪŋ] *n Art etc* peinture *f ou* retouchage *m* à l'aérographe.

airbus ['eəbʌs] *n* aérobus *m*, airbus *m*.

air-conditioned ['eəkən'dɪʃənd] *adj* climatisé, à air conditionné.

air-conditioning ['eəkən'dɪʃənɪŋ] *n* climatisation *f*, conditionnement *m* (de l'air).

air-cooled ['eəkuːld] *adj* refroidi par air; *Aut* **a.-c. engine,** moteur *m* à refroidissement par air.

air-cooling ['eəkuːlɪŋ] *n* refroidissement *m* par l'air.

aircraft ['eəkrɑːft] *n inv* avion *m*; **a. carrier,** porte-avions *m inv*; **a. engineering,** ingénierie *f* aéronautique; **a. factory,** usine *f* d'aviation; **a. manufacturer,** constructeur *m* d'avions, avionneur *m*.

aircraftman, *pl* **-men** ['eəkrɑːftmən] *n* = soldat de la Royal Air Force; **leading a.,** = caporal de la Royal Air Force.

aircraftwoman, *pl* **-women** ['eəkrɑːftwʊmən, -wɪmɪn] *n* = femme soldat de la Women's Royal Air Force; **leading a.,** = femme caporal de la Women's Royal Air Force.

aircrew ['eəkruː] *n Av* équipage *m*.

airdrome ['eədrəʊm] *n Am* aérodrome *m*.

airdrop ['eədrɒp] *n Av* largage *m* (de charges).

Airedale ['eədeɪl] *n* (chien *m*) airedale *m*.

airer ['eərər] *n* chevalet *m* (*pour linge*).

airfield ['eəfiːld] *n* champ *m ou* terrain *m* d'aviation, aérodrome *m*.

airflow ['eəfləʊ] *n* **(a)** *Tech etc* écoulement *m* d'air; **smooth/turbulent a.,** écoulement régulier/turbulent; **(b)** *US Aut* **a. body,** carrosserie *f* aérodynamique.

airfoil ['eəfɔɪl] *n Am* = **AEROFOIL.**

airframe ['eəfreɪm] *n* cellule *f* d'avion, fuselage *m*.

airily ['eərɪlɪ] *adv* avec désinvolture; (*to say*) d'un ton dégagé.

airiness ['eərɪnɪs] *n* **(a)** situation aérée (*d'un bâtiment*); bonne ventilation (*d'une pièce*); **(b)** légèreté *f* (*d'esprit*); insouciance *f*, désinvolture *f*.

airing ['eərɪŋ] *n* **(a)** (*of room etc*) ventilation *f*; aérage *m*, aération *f*; **(b)** (*of clothes*) séchage *m*; **a. cupboard,** armoire chauffante; **(c)** (*of new car etc*) présentation *f*; **to give a project an a.,** lancer un ballon d'essai; **(d)** (*walk*) (petite) promenade *f*; **to take an a.,** prendre l'air.

airless ['eəlɪs] *adj* **(a)** (*room, house etc*) privé d'air, renfermé; **(b)** *Tech* sans air; **(c)** (*evening etc*) sans vent, lourd.

airlessness ['eəlɪsnɪs] *n* **(a)** manque *m* d'air (*d'une pièce*); **(b)** lourdeur *f* (*du temps*).

airlift¹ ['eəlɪft] *n Av* pont aérien.

airlift² *vt* transporter (*des vivres*) par avion.

airline ['eəlaɪn] *n* ligne *ou* compagnie aérienne; **to be an a. pilot,** être commandant de bord.

airliner ['eəlaɪnər] *n* avion *m* de ligne.

airlock ['eəlɒk] *n* **(a)** *Constr* écluse *f ou* sas *m* pneumatique *ou* à air (*d'un caisson*); *Nau* sas; *Astronaut* sas (*d'entrée, de sortie*); **(b)** (*in pipe*) poche *f* d'air.

air-mail¹ ['eəmeɪl] *adj* (*letter etc*) (envoyé) par avion.

air-mail² *vt* envoyer (*une lettre etc*) par avion.

airman, *pl* **-men** ['eəmən] *n* **(a)** aviateur *m*; **(b)** *US Mil Av* **a. (basic),** = soldat de la United States Air Force.

airplane ['eəpleɪn] *n Am* avion *m*.

airplay ['eəpleɪ] *n Rad* diffusion *f*; **to get** *or* **receive a.,** (*of record etc*) passer sur les ondes.

airport ['eəpɔːt] *n Av* aéroport *m*; **London A.,** l'aéroport de Londres.

airscrew ['eəskruː] *n Old-fashioned Av* hélice *f*.

air-sea ['eə'siː] *adj* **a.-s. rescue,** sauvetage *m* aéromaritime, sauvetage aérien en mer.

airship ['eəʃɪp] *n* dirigeable *m*.

airsick ['eəsɪk] *adj* **to be a.,** avoir le mal de l'air.

airsickness ['eəsɪknɪs] *n* mal *m* de l'air.

airspace ['eəspeɪs] *n Av etc* espace aérien.

airspeed ['eəspiːd] *n Av* vitesse *f* (*d'un avion*).

airstream ['eəstriːm] *n* courant *m* d'air.

airstrip ['eəstrɪp] *n Av* bande *f ou* piste *f* d'atterrissage.

airtight ['eətaɪt] *adj* (*seal*) hermétique; (*container etc*) à clôture hermétique, étanche (à l'air).

airtime ['eətaɪm] *n Rad TV* **(a)** (*length of programme*) durée *f*; **(b)** (*starting time*) l'heure où commence le programme; **five minutes to a.**, on est à l'antenne dans cinq minutes.

air-to-air ['eətʊ'eər] *adj Mil* (*missile etc*) air-air *inv*.

air-to-ground ['eətə'graʊnd] *adj Mil* (*missile etc*) air-sol *inv*, air-terre *inv*.

air-to-surface ['eətə'sɜːfəs] *adj* (*missile etc*) *Mil* air-sol *inv*; *Nau* air-surface *inv*.

airwaves ['eəweɪvz] *npl Rad F* ondes *fpl*; **the best DJ on the a.**, le meilleur DJ radio.

airway ['eəweɪ] *n* **(a)** *Min* voie *f* d'air *ou* d'aérage, galerie *f* d'aérage; **(b)** *Av* (*route*) route *ou* ligne *ou* voie aérienne; **a. marker**, balise *f* d'entrée de piste; **(c)** *Med* bronches *fpl*; **(d)** *US Rad TV* chaîne *f*.

airwoman, *pl* **-women** ['eəwʊmən, -wɪmɪn] *n* aviatrice *f*.

airworthiness ['eəwɜːðɪnɪs] *n Av* tenue *f* en l'air, navigabilité *f*; **certificate of a.**, certificat *m* de navigabilité.

airworthy ['eəwɜːðɪ] *adj* (*aircraft*) en état de prendre l'air, en bon état de vol *ou* de navigabilité; (*certified*) muni d'un certificat de navigabilité; **to be a.**, tenir l'air.

airy ['eərɪ] *adj* **(a)** (*room, house*) bien aéré, ouvert à l'air; **(b)** (*dress, material*) léger; **the cake was light and a.**, le gâteau était très léger; **(c)** (*person, attitude*) léger, insouciant, désinvolte; **(d)** (*promises*) vaine, illusoire.

airy-fairy ['eərɪ'feərɪ] *adj F* (*person*) farfelu; (*ideas etc*) impraticable, irréalisable.

aisle [aɪl] *n* **(a)** passage *m* (*entre bancs*); couloir *m* (*d'avion*); couloir central (*d'un autobus etc*); allée *f* (*de cinéma etc*); *Th F* **to have them rolling in the aisles**, avoir un succès fou; **a. seat**, (*in plane*) place *f* côté couloir; **(b)** (*in church*) allée centrale; *Fig* **to walk up the a.**, se marier (à l'église).

aitch [eɪtʃ] *n* (la lettre) h *m*; **to drop one's aitches**, ne pas aspirer les h.

aitchbone ['eɪtʃbəʊn] *n Culin* culotte *f* (de bœuf).

ajar [ə'dʒɑːr] *adv & adj* (*door, window*) entrouvert, entrebâillé; **to leave the door a.**, entrebâiller la porte.

aka [eɪkeɪ'eɪ] *adv* (*abbr* **also known as**) alias.

akimbo [ə'kɪmbəʊ] *adv* **with arms a.**, les (deux) poings sur les hanches; **to stand with arms a.**, faire le pot à deux anses.

akin [ə'kɪn] *adv & adj* **a. to s.o./sth**, apparenté à qn/qch; **feeling a. to fear**, sentiment voisin de l'effroi; **this is a. to treachery**, ça ressemble à de la traîtrise.

alabaster ['æləbæstər, -bɑː-] **1** *n* albâtre *m*. **2** *adj* **(a)** (*figurine, vase etc*) en albâtre; **(b)** *Fig* (*complexion, hands etc*) albâtre.

à la carte [ælə'kɑːt] *adj & adv* à la carte.

alacrity [ə'lækrɪtɪ] *n* empressement *m*, promptitude *f*; **he accepted with a.**, il a accepté avec enthousiasme.

Aladdin [ə'lædɪn] *n* Aladin *m*; **the shop is an A.'s cave**, (*full of wonderful things*) cette boutique est une véritable caverne d'Ali Baba.

Alan ['ælən] *n* Alain *m*.

alarm¹ [ə'lɑːm] *n* **(a)** (*signal*) alarme *f*, alerte *f*; **false a.**, fausse alerte; **to raise** *or* **give the a.**, donner l'éveil *ou* l'alerte *ou* l'alarme; **a. signal**, signal *m* d'alarme; **(b)** (*fright, anxiety*) alarme *f*, frayeur *f*; **there's no cause for a.**, il n'y a aucune raison de s'alarmer; **he ran and hid in a.**, effrayé, il s'est caché; **a. call**, (*of bird etc*) cri *m* d'alarme; **(c)** (*warning device*) avertisseur *m*; sonnette *f* d'alarme; (*of burglary*) signalisateur *m* anti-vol; **(d)** (*on clock*) sonnerie *f*; **a. (clock)**, réveille-matin *m inv*, réveil *m*; **to wind up the a.**, remonter la sonnerie; **to set the a. for six o'clock**, mettre le réveil à six heures; **the a. went off at six o'clock**, le réveil a sonné à six heures.

alarm² *vt* **(a)** (*warn, alert*) alarmer, donner l'alarme à (*qn*); alerter (*des troupes*); **(b)** (*frighten*) effrayer; **to be alarmed at sth**, s'alarmer *ou* s'effrayer de qch, être alarmé de qch; **don't be alarmed**, ne vous effrayez pas; **the parents looked alarmed**, les parents semblaient effrayés.

alarming [ə'lɑːmɪŋ] *adj* (*news etc*) alarmant, effrayant.

alarmingly [ə'lɑːmɪŋlɪ] *adv* d'une manière alarmante *ou* effrayante.

alarmist [ə'lɑːmɪst] *adj & n* alarmiste *mf*.

alas [ə'læs] *int Lit* hélas!

Alas *abbr* **Alaska**.

Alaska [ə'læskə] *n* Alaska *m*; *Culin* **baked A.**, omelette norvégienne.

alb [ælb] *n Rel* aube *f*.

Albania [æl'beɪnɪə] *n* Albanie *f*.

Albanian [æl'beɪnɪən] **1** *adj* albanais. **2** *n* **(a)** Albanais, -aise; **(b)** *Ling* albanais *m*.

albatross ['ælbətrɒs] *n* (*bird*) albatros *m*.

albeit [ɔːl'biːɪt] *conj* quoique, bien que; **a brilliant, a. slipshod, writer**, écrivain brillant, bien que négligent.

albinism ['ælbɪnɪz(ə)m] *n* albinisme *m*.

albino, *pl* **-os** [æl'biːnəʊ, -əʊz] **1** *adj* (*person*) albinos; **a. rabbit**, lapin *m* russe. **2** *n* albinos *mf*.

Albion ['ælbɪən] *n Lit* (*England*) Albion *f*; **perfidious A.**, la perfide Albion.

album ['ælbəm] *n* **(a)** (*for photos, comic book*) album *m*; **(b)** (*record*) album *m*.

albumen ['ælbjʊmɪn, æl'bjuːmɪn] *n* **(a)** (*in egg*) albumen *m*, blanc *m* d'œuf; **(b)** (*in blood*) albumine *f*.

albumin ['ælbjʊmɪn, æl'bjuːmɪn] *n Ch* albumine *f*.

alchemist ['ælkəmɪst] *n* alchimiste *m*.

alchemy ['ælkəmɪ] *n* alchimie *f*.

alcohol ['ælkəhɒl] *n* (*drink*) & *Ch* alcool *m*; **I never touch a.**, je ne bois jamais d'alcool; *US Med* **rubbing a.**, = alcool à 90°; **wood a.**, méthanol *m*; **a. content**, teneur *f* en alcool, pourcentage *m* d'alcool.

alcoholic [ælkə'hɒlɪk] **1** *adj* alcoolique; **a. drink**, boisson alcoolisée. **2** *n* (*person*) alcoolique *mf*; **Alcoholics Anonymous**, Alcooliques *mpl* anonymes.

alcoholism ['ælkəhɒlɪz(ə)m] *n* alcoolisme *m*.

alcove ['ælkəʊv] *n* alcôve *f*; niche *f* (*dans un mur*); **dining a.**, coin *m* des repas, coin salle à manger.

aldehyde ['ældɪhaɪd] *n Ch* aldéhyde *f*.

alder ['ɔːldər] *n* (*tree*) aune *m*, aulne *m*.

alderman, *pl* **-men** ['ɔːldəmən] *n* (*for city*) = conseiller municipal; *Br* (*for county*) = conseiller général.

Alderney ['ɔːldənɪ] *n* Aurigny *m*.

ale [eɪl] *n* bière anglaise (légère); ale *f*; **pale/brown a.**, bière blonde/brune; **ginger a.**, = boisson gazeuse au gingembre.

Alec(k) ['ælɪk] *n* (*dimin of* **Alexander**) = Alexandre *m*; *F* **a smart A.**, un je-sais-tout.

alehouse ['eɪlhaʊs] *n Arch* cabaret *m*.

alert¹ [ə'lɜːt] **1** *adj* **(a)** (*temporarily*) alerté, vigilant, éveillé; **to be a. to a danger**, être conscient d'un danger; **(b)** (*naturally*) actif, vif, preste; **a. mind**, esprit présent *ou* vif *ou* éveillé. **2** *n* alerte *f*; **to be on the a.**, être sur le qui-vive, être en état d'alerte; **police were on the a. for an escaped prisoner**, la police était en état d'alerte à la suite de l'évasion d'un prisonnier; **to be on the a. against an attack**, veiller en prévision d'une attaque; **the navy has been put on full a.**, l'alerte générale a été déclarée dans la marine.

alert² *vt* alerter; **troops have been alerted**, les troupes sont en état d'alerte; **to a. s.o. to a danger**, avertir qn d'un danger; **a noise alerted her to the presence of an intruder**, un bruit l'alerta de la présence d'un intrus.

alertness [ə'lɜːtnɪs] *n* **(a)** (*of sentry etc*) vigilance *f*; promptitude *f* **(in doing sth**, à faire qch); **(b)** (*of mind*) vivacité *f*.

Alexander [ælɪg'zɑːndər] *n* Alexandre *m*.

Alexandria [ælɪg'zɑːndrɪə] *n* Alexandrie *f*.

alexandrine [ælɪg'zɑːndraɪn] *adj & n Liter* alexandrin *m*.

alfalfa [æl'fælfə] *n* (*plant*) luzerne *f*.

alfresco [æl'freskəʊ] *adj & adv* en plein air; **a. meal**, repas *m* en plein air.

alga, *pl* **-ae** ['ælgə, 'ældʒiː] *n Bot* algue *f*.

algal ['ælg(ə)l] *adj* **(a)** (*of alga*) des algues; **(b)** (*of cells in lichen*) gonidial, -aux; gonimique.

algebra ['ældʒɪbrə] *n* algèbre *f*.

algebraic(al) [ældʒɪ'breɪɪk, -ɪk(ə)l] *adj* (*signe, somme etc*) algébrique.

Algeria [æl'dʒɪərɪə] *n* Algérie *f*.

Algerian [æl'dʒɪərɪən] **1** *adj* algérien. **2** *n* Algérien, -ienne.

Algiers [æl'dʒɪəz] *n* Alger *m*.

ALGOL, *also* **algol** ['ælgɒl] *n Comptr* algol *m*.

alias ['eɪlɪəs] **1** *adv* alias, autrement dit, autrement nommé; **John X, a. Y**, John X, connu sous le nom de *ou* dit Y. **2** *n* (*pl* **aliases** ['eɪlɪəsɪz]) nom emprunté, nom d'emprunt, faux nom; **to travel under an a.**, voyager sous un faux nom.

alibi ['ælɪbaɪ] *n Jur* alibi *m*; **to produce an a.**, produire *ou* fournir un alibi; **to establish an a.**, prouver *ou* établir son alibi.

alien ['eɪlɪən] **1** *n* **(a)** *Jur* étranger, -ère (non naturalisé, -ée); **undesirable a.**, étranger indésirable; **(b)** (*from outer space*) extra-terrestre *mf*. **2** *adj* **(a)** *Jur* étranger; **(b)** (*from outer space*) extra-terrestre; **(c)** (*unfamiliar*) étranger **(to**, à); (*contrary*) contraire, opposé **(to, à)**; **an action entirely a. to her nature**, une action entièrement contraire à sa nature.

alienable ['eɪlɪənəb(ə)l] *adj Jur* (*bien*) aliénable.

alienate ['eɪlɪəneɪt] *vt* **(a)** (*in personal relationships*) détacher, éloigner, désaffectionner (*qn, les esprits*); **she has alienated many of her colleagues,** elle s'est détachée de beaucoup de ses collègues; **to a. s.o. from his friends,** détacher qn de ses amis; **to a. oneself from s.o.,** se détacher de qn; **these young people feel alienated from society,** ces jeunes gens se sentent en marge de la société; **(b)** *Jur* aliéner (*des biens etc*); **(c)** *Fin* détourner (*une somme*).

alienation [eɪlɪə'neɪʃən] *n* **(a)** aliénation *f* (*de cœurs*); désaffection *f*; **(b)** *Jur* aliénation *f* (*de biens*); **(c)** *Psy* **mental a.,** aliénation mentale.

alight¹ [ə'laɪt] *adj* allumé, en feu; **to catch a.,** s'allumer, prendre feu; **to set sth a.,** mettre le feu à qch, mettre qch en feu; *Fig* **his face was a. with joy,** son visage resplendissait de joie.

alight² *vi* **(a)** *Fml* (*from train, car etc*) descendre (**from,** de); **(b)** (*of bird*) s'abattre, se poser (**on,** sur); (*of falling object, eyes, glance*) se poser (**on,** sur).

align [ə'laɪn] **1** *vt* **(a)** aligner (*des soldats etc*); mettre (*des objets*) en ligne; *Comptr* aligner, cadrer (*des cartes*); dresser (*des arbres etc*); faire coïncider (*les axes*); *Med* dégauchir, redresser (*des organes faussés ou gauchis*); *Electron* aligner, redresser, régler; *Aut* régler le parallélisme de (*les roues*); *Aut* **the wheels were badly aligned,** les roues n'étaient pas centrées; **(b)** *Fin* (*of country*) aligner (*sa monnaie*) (**on,** sur); **(c) to a. oneself with s.o.,** s'aligner sur qn; **they aligned themselves against the President/this policy,** ils se sont ligués contre le président/cette politique. **2** *vi* **(a)** s'aligner, se mettre en ligne; prendre position; **(b)** (*of shafts etc*) coïncider.

alignment [ə'laɪnmənt] *n* **(a)** alignement *m*; tracé *m* (*d'une voie ferrée etc*); *Comptr* alignement, cadrage *m*; *Med* redressage *m*, dégauchissement *m* (*d'organes faussés etc*); centrage *m*, équerrage *m*; *Electron* alignement, redressage, réglage *m*; *Aut* parallélisme *m* (*des roues*); **out of a.,** désaligné; *Constr* hors d'œuvre; *Typ* sortant; *Aut* **front wheel a.,** parallélisme des roues avant; **(b)** *Fin* **a. of currencies,** alignement des monnaies.

alike [ə'laɪk] **1** *adj* semblable, pareil; **they are very much a.,** ils se ressemblent beaucoup; **no two are a.,** il n'y en a pas deux de pareils; **you are all a.!,** vous êtes tous les mêmes! **2** *adv* pareillement, de même; **to treat everybody a.,** traiter tout le monde de la même manière *ou* de la même façon; **we don't think a.,** nous n'avons pas le même point de vue; **dressed a.,** habillé de même, vêtu uniformément; **every day, summer and winter a.,** tous les jours, été comme hiver; **old and young a.,** les vieux comme les jeunes.

aliment ['ælɪmənt] *n* **(a)** *Fml* (*nourishment*) aliment *m*; **(b)** *Scot Jur* = **ALIMONY**.

alimentary [ælɪ'mentərɪ] *adj* **(a)** *Anat* **a. canal,** tube digestif; **(b) a. substances,** substances *fpl* alimentaires.

alimentation [ælɪmen'teɪʃən] *n* alimentation *f*.

alimony ['ælɪmənɪ] *n Jur* pension *f* alimentaire (faite à l'épouse après séparation de corps); **to pay one's wife a.,** fournir des aliments à son épouse.

alive [ə'laɪv] *adj* **(a)** (*person, animal, plant*) **to be (still) a.,** être (encore) vivant *ou* en vie, vivre (encore); **to keep s.o. a.,** maintenir qn en vie; **to come a. again,** (*after apparent death*) revenir à la vie; (*after real death*) ressusciter; **to be burnt/buried a.,** être brûlé/enterré vif; **to be a. and well,** se porter bien; **no one got out of the building a.,** personne n'est sorti vivant de l'immeuble; **Mr Evans was last seen a. on 21st June,** c'est le 21 juin qu'on a vu M. Evans vivant pour la dernière fois; *F* **to be a. and kicking,** être plein de vie; **dead or a.,** mort ou vif; **more dead than a.,** plus mort que vif; **when your father was a.,** du vivant de votre père; **no one a.,** personne au monde;

(b) (*memory, hope, custom*) **in parts of the country her memory is still very much a.,** dans certaines régions, son souvenir est encore très vivant; **to keep a.,** garder, entretenir (*un souvenir, une coutume*); entretenir, ne pas laisser languir (*la conversation*); **to keep a religion a.,** entretenir la pratique d'une religion;

(c) (*awake*) **to be fully a. to,** avoir pleinement conscience de (*qch*); se rendre compte de, comprendre bien (*l'importance de qch*); **I am a. to the fact that ...,** je n'ignore pas que ...; **she's very a. to the latest developments in the industry,** elle est très au courant des nouvelles découvertes industrielles; **she's very a. to the world around her,** elle est très ouverte au monde qui l'entoure;

(d) (*full of vitality*) vif, éveillé: **he came a. when someone mentioned food,** il s'est réveillé quand quelqu'un a parlé de manger; **look a.!,** remuez-vous (donc)!; **the cheese was a. with maggots,** le fromage grouillait de vers; **the street was a. with people,** la rue fourmillait de monde;

(e) *esp US El* **the wire was a.,** le fil était sous tension.

alkali ['ælkəlaɪ] *n Ch* alcali *m*; **a. metal,** métal alcalin.

alkaline ['ælkəlaɪn] *adj Ch* alcalin.

alkaloid ['ælkəlɔɪd] *adj & n Ch* alcaloïde *m*.

all [ɔːl] **1** *adj* tout, tous; **a. France,** toute la France; **a. men,** tous les hommes; **a. the others,** tous les autres; **to be a. things to a. men,** être tout à tous; **a. day,** toute la journée; **a. her life,** toute sa vie; **the people/books had a. disappeared,** les gens/les livres avaient tous disparus; **they are a. smokers,** ce sont tous des fumeurs; **a. the way,** (*of journey*) tout le long du chemin; (*of course of action*) jusqu'au bout; **a. the bread,** tout le pain; **is that a. the luggage you're taking?,** c'est tout ce que vous emportez de bagages?; **for a. his wealth,** en dépit de *ou* malgré sa fortune; **with a. speed,** au plus vite, à toute vitesse; **beyond a. doubt,** sans le moindre doute; **they were here a. morning/night,** ils sont restés ici toute la matinée/la nuit; **at a. hours,** à toute heure; **in a. sorts of ways,** de toutes les façons; **what's a. that noise?,** qu'est-ce que c'est que tout ce bruit?; **a. that's nonsense,** tout ça, c'est des bêtises; **and a. that,** et tout cela, et tout le reste; **you're not as ill as a. that,** vous n'êtes pas aussi *ou* si malade que ça; **of a. the stupid things to say** *or* **do!,** de toutes les idioties possibles!

2 *pron* **(a)** (*with pl*) tous, toutes; **a. are agreed that ...,** tous sont d'accord que ...; **a. of us,** nous tous; **we a. love him,** nous l'aimons tous; **a. of them are blue, they are a. blue,** tous sont bleus, ils sont tous bleus; **a. together,** tous à la fois *ou* ensemble; **a. but he** *or* **him,** tous sauf *ou* excepté lui; **a. and sundry,** tous sans exception;

(b) (*everything*) tout; **almost a.,** presque tout; **a. that glitters is not gold,** tout ce qui brille n'est pas or; **a. will be revealed,** tout sera révélé *ou* dévoilé; **a. is forgiven,** tout est pardonné; **I know it a.,** (*of news etc*) je sais tout cela; (*of poem etc*) je le sais en entier; **take it a.,** prenez le tout; **in the middle of it a.,** au milieu de tout cela; **a. that happens,** tout ce qui arrive; **for a. he may say,** en dépit de ce qu'il dit, quoi qu'il en dise; **that's a.,** c'est tout, voilà tout; **is that a.?,** est-ce tout?; *Iron* n'est-ce que cela?, ce n'est que ça?; **if that's a.,** si ce n'est que cela; **all's well,** tout va bien; **I think that's about a.,** je crois que c'est tout; **a. I said was 'good morning',** tout ce que j'ai dit a été 'bonjour'; **that's a. they ever do, complain,** c'est tout ce qu'ils savent faire, se plaindre; **it was a. I could do not to laugh,** je me tenais à quatre pour ne pas rire; **when all's said and done,** somme toute, en fin de compte; **after a.,** après tout; *F* **he must be a. of sixty,** il doit avoir au moins soixante ans; *F Iron* **it cost a. of £2,** ça a coûté deux livres et pas moins;

(c) once and for a., une fois pour toutes; **for a. I know,** autant que je sache; **for a. I care,** pour (tout) ce que cela me fait; **thirty men in a.,** trente hommes en tout; **above a.,** surtout; **most of a.,** surtout, le plus; **when I was busiest of a.,** au moment où j'étais le plus occupé;

(d) (*everything else*) **and a.,** et (tout) le reste;

(e) *Br Sl* (*nothing*) **damn** *or* **bugger** *or* **sod a.,** rien du tout, rien de rien; **I've done damn a. today,** je n'ai rien fichu aujourd'hui.

3 *adv* **(a)** (*entirely*) tout; **she is a. alone,** elle est toute seule; **to be (dressed) a. in black,** être habillé(e) tout en noir *ou* tout de noir; **she is a. ears/impatience/smiles,** elle est tout oreilles/impatience/sourires; **a. in one piece,** tout d'une pièce; **she is a. for accepting this offer,** elle est tout en faveur d'accepter cette offre; **my wife was a. for calling in a doctor,** ma femme voulait à toute force *ou* à tout prix appeler un médecin; **I'm a. for it,** je suis entièrement pour; **he's not a. bad,** il n'est pas entièrement mauvais; **a. the better/worse (for me),** tant mieux/pis (pour moi); **you will be a. the better for it,** vous vous en trouverez (d'autant) mieux; **the time came a. too soon,** l'heure n'arriva que trop tôt; **a. at once,** (*suddenly*) tout à coup, subitement; (*everything together*) tout d'un coup, tous à la fois; **that's a. nonsense,** tout cela est absurde; **that's a. very well, but ...,** tout cela est bien beau mais ...; **an a. girl band,** un orchestre de filles *ou* composé uniquement de filles; **an a. new outfit,** un ensemble tout neuf; *F* **she's a. upset,** elle est toute triste; *F* **I've come over a. funny,** je me sens tout bizarre; *F* **he's gone a. red,** il est devenu tout rouge; *F* **the dress was a. torn,** la robe était toute déchirée; *F* **he's not a. there,** il est un peu simple d'esprit; **to go a. out,** ne pas s'épargner; **to go a. out to pass one's exams,** faire son maximum pour réussir ses

examens;
(b) *(almost)* **a. but,** presque; **a. but impossible,** presque impossible; **it's a. but done,** c'est pour ainsi dire fini *ou* fait, c'est comme fait;
(c) *(in the slightest)* **at a.,** du tout; **do you know him at a.?,** le connaissez-vous aucunement?; **I didn't speak at a.,** je n'ai pas parlé du tout; **I'm not at a. astonished,** je n'en suis aucunement étonné; **not at a.,** pas du tout, *F* du tout; *(when thanked)* je vous en prie; **nothing at a.,** rien du tout; **if he comes at a.,** s'il lui arrive de venir; **if it is at a. cold,** s'il fait un peu froid; **why do it at a.?,** pourquoi se donner la peine de le faire?;
(d) *(altogether)* **(taking it) a. in a.,** à tout prendre;
(e) *(in games)* **five a.,** *Fb etc* cinq à cinq; *(at dominoes)* cinq partout; *Tennis* **four (games) a.,** quatre (jeux) partout; **fifteen a.,** quinze à.
4 *n* tout *m,* totalité *f;* **to stake one's a.,** risquer le tout pour le tout; **I would give my a. to see her,** je donnerais tout ce que j'ai pour la voir.

all-absorbing [ˈɔːləbˈsɔːbɪŋ] *adj* absorbant, passionnant.

Allah [ˈælə] *n* Allah *m.*

all-American [ˈɔːləˈmerɪkən] *adj* cent pour cent américain.

Allan [ˈælən] *n* Alain *m.*

all-around [ˈɔːləˈraʊnd] *adj Am (athlète)* complet; *(homme)* universel.

allay [əˈleɪ] *vt* **(a)** apaiser, calmer *(une tempête, une colère)*; **(b)** calmer *(la frayeur)*; endormir, dissiper *(les soupçons)*; **(c)** alléger, calmer, soulager *(la douleur)*; apaiser *(la soif, la faim, la fièvre)*.

all-clear [ˈɔːlˈklɪər] *n* (signal *m* de) fin *f* d'alerte; **to give the a.-c.,** *Mil* sonner la fin de l'alerte; *(for project etc)* donner le feu vert; **he gave us the a.-c.,** *(no-one was watching)* il nous a fait signe que la voie était libre.

all-conquering [ˈɔːlˈkɒŋkərɪŋ] *adj (amour etc)* qui triomphe de tout.

allegation [ælɪˈgeɪʃən] *n* allégation *f;* **to make an a.,** alléguer qch.

allege [əˈledʒ] *vt* alléguer, prétendre **(that,** que); **the words alleged to have been spoken by ...,** les propos qui auraient été tenus par ...; **he was alleged to be dead,** on le prétendait *ou* disait mort; **it is alleged that ...,** on prétend que ... .

alleged [əˈledʒd] *adj (attentat, motif etc)* allégué; **the a. thief,** le voleur présumé.

allegedly [əˈledʒɪdlɪ] *adv* prétendument.

allegiance [əˈliːdʒəns] *n* fidélité *f,* obéissance *f* **(to,** à); **to owe a. to a party,** devoir fidélité à un parti; **to renounce one's a. to a party,** se détacher d'un parti; **to owe a. to a king,** devoir fidélité et obéissance à un roi; **to take an oath of a.,** prêter serment d'allégeance.

allegoric(al) [ælɪˈgɒrɪk, -ɪk(ə)l] *adj* allégorique.

allegorically [ælɪˈgɒrɪklɪ] *adv* allégoriquement, sous forme d'allégorie.

allegory [ˈælɪgərɪ] *n* allégorie *f.*

allegretto [ælɪˈgretəʊ] *adv & n Mus* allegretto *m.*

allegro [əˈlegrəʊ, -ˈleɪ-] *adv & n Mus* allegro *m.*

alleluia [ælɪˈluːjə] *int & n* alléluia *m.*

all-embracing [ɔːlɪmˈbreɪsɪŋ] *adj (amour)* qui embrasse tout; **a.-e. knowledge,** vaste érudition *f.*

allergen [ˈælədʒen] *n Med* allergène *m.*

allergic [əˈlɜːdʒɪk] *adj Med* allergique **(to,** à); *Fig* **I'm a. to him,** je ne peux pas le sentir.

allergy [ˈælədʒɪ] *n Med* allergie *f.*

alleviate [əˈliːvɪeɪt] *vt* alléger, soulager *(la douleur)*; adoucir *(le chagrin)*; apaiser *(la soif)*.

alleviation [əliːvɪˈeɪʃən] *n (of pain)* allègement *m,* soulagement *m; (of grief)* adoucissement *m.*

alley [ˈælɪ] *n* **(a)** *(narrow street)* ruelle *f;* **I wouldn't like to meet him in a dark a.!,** je n'aimerais pas le rencontrer dans une impasse sombre!; *F* **a. cat,** chat *m* de gouttière; **(b)** *Sp* **bowling a.,** bowling *m;* **(c)** *(in park etc)* allée *f.*

alleyway [ˈælɪweɪ] *n (street)* ruelle *f;* passage étroit; *Nau Archit* coursive *f.*

alliance [əˈlaɪəns] *n* **(a)** alliance *f; Hist* **the Triple A.,** la Triple Alliance, la Triplice; **to enter into an a.,** s'allier **(with,** avec); **political a.,** apparentement *m;* **to make a political a. with a party,** s'apparenter avec un parti; **in a. with a German firm,** en association avec une firme allemande; **(b)** *(by marriage)* alliance *f.*

allied [ˈælaɪd] *adj* **(a)** allié **(to,** à; **with,** avec); **the A. Powers,** les Puissances alliées; **closely a. industries,** industries *fpl* connexes; **(b)** *Biol Med etc* du même ordre, de la même nature; *Biol (espèce)* voisin.

alligator [ˈælɪgeɪtər] *n* **(a)** *(animal)* alligator *m;* **(b)** *(skin)* crocodile *m;* **a. handbag,** sac *m* à main en croco; **(c)** *Am* **a. pear,** (poire *f* d')avocat *m.*

all-important [ˈɔːlɪmˈpɔːtənt] *adj* de la plus haute *ou* grande importance.

all-in [ˈɔːlɪn] **1** *adj* **(a)** *Com* **a.-in price,** prix *m* tout compris, prix forfaitaire; **a.-in policy,** police *f* tous risques; **(b)** *Sp* **a.-in wrestling,** lutte *f* libre, catch *m;* **a.-in wrestler,** catcheur *m.* **2** *adv Com* tout compris; **the holiday costs £200 a.-in,** les vacances coûtent 200 livres tous frais compris.

all-inclusive [ˈɔːlɪnˈkluːsɪv] *adj (prix)* tout compris.

alliteration [əlɪtəˈreɪʃən] *n* allitération *f.*

alliterative [əˈlɪtərətɪv, -reɪt-] *adj* allitératif.

all-night [ˈɔːlnaɪt] *adj (veillée etc)* de la nuit entière; **an a.-n. party,** une fête qui va durer *ou* qui a duré toute la nuit; *Admin etc* **a.-n. service,** permanence *f* de nuit; *Mil etc* **a.-n. pass,** permission *f* de la nuit.

allocate [ˈæləkeɪt] *vt* allouer, assigner *(qch à qn, à qch)*; **to a. duties,** attribuer *ou* distribuer des fonctions **(to,** à); **to a. a sum to sth,** affecter *ou* assigner une somme à qch; **more money was allocated to defence,** on a affecté plus d'argent à la défense; **you'll need to a. your time carefully,** il va falloir que tu répartisses ton temps avec précaution.

allocation [æləˈkeɪʃən] *n* **(a)** allocation *f,* affectation *f (d'une somme)*; répartition *f (de dépenses, de moyens etc)*; attribution *f (de fonctions)*; **a. of capital,** affectation des investissements; **a. of contract,** adjudication *f;* **a. to lowest tender,** adjudication au mieux-disant; **(b)** *(share)* part assignée; *(money)* somme assignée.

allopathy [æˈlɒpəθɪ] *n Med* allopathie *f.*

allot [əˈlɒt] *vt* **(-tt-) (a)** *(assign)* attribuer, assigner *(qch)* **(to s.o.,** à qn); **to a. sth to** *or* **for an object,** affecter *ou* destiner qch à un but; **in the allotted time,** dans le temps imparti; **(b)** *(distribute)* répartir, distribuer *(des fonctions, des sièges, Fin des actions)*.

allotment [əˈlɒtmənt] *n* **(a)** *(allocation)* attribution *f (de qch à qn)*; affectation *f (d'une somme à un but)*; partage *m,* répartition *f;* distribution *f (des chambres, de fonctions etc)*; lotissement *m (de parts, d'une propriété)*; *Fin* **a. of shares,** attribution *f* d'actions; **letter of a.,** (lettre *f* d')avis *m* de répartition; **(b)** *(share)* portion *f,* part *f,* lot *m;* **(c)** *Br (land)* jardin ouvrier.

all-out [ˈɔːˈlaʊt] *adj F (effort)* suprême, maximum; *(attack)* à fond; **a.-o. strike/war,** grève/guerre totale.

all-over [ˈɔːləʊvər] *adj* **with an a.-o. pattern,** dont le dessin couvre toute la surface.

allow [əˈlaʊ] *vt* **(a)** *(permit)* permettre *(qch)*; **to a. s.o. sth,** permettre qch à qn; **to a. s.o. to do sth,** permettre à qn de *ou* autoriser qn à faire qch; **gambling is not allowed,** les jeux d'argent sont interdits; **she isn't allowed alcohol,** elle n'a pas droit à l'alcool; **to be allowed to compete,** être admis à concourir; **I am allowed to do it,** on me permet *ou* il m'est permis de le faire; **a. me!,** permettez(-moi)!; **a. me to ...,** permettez-moi de ...; **passengers are not allowed on the bridge,** la passerelle est interdite aux voyageurs; **as soon as circumstances a.,** dès que les circonstances le permettront; **to a. oneself to be led/deceived,** se laisser mener/tromper; **I will not a. you to be ill-treated,** je ne vous laisserai pas maltraiter;
(b) *(accept)* faire droit à *(une demande, une réclamation)*; admettre *(une requête)*;
(c) *(grant, allocate)* accorder; **to a. s.o. £1,000 a year,** faire *ou* accorder *ou* allouer à qn une rente de 1 000 livres; **to a. a debtor time to pay,** accorder un délai à un débiteur; *Com Fin* **to a. s.o. a discount,** consentir *ou* accorder *ou* faire un escompte *ou* une remise à qn; **at the end of the six months allowed,** à l'expiration du délai de six mois; **a. 20 minutes to get to the airport,** comptez 20 minutes pour aller à l'aéroport;
(d) *(admit)* admettre **(that,** que);
(e) *Am F* juger, opiner, affirmer **(that,** que).

►**allow for** *vipo* tenir compte de *(qch)*; prévoir *(des difficultés, des retards etc)*; **after allowing for,** déduction faite de; **a. for some wastage,** prévoir plus large; **to a. so much for carriage,** compter tant pour le transport; **you must a. for his being ill,** il faut tenir compte de ce qu'il est malade; **has that been allowed for in your figures?,** en avez-vous tenu compte dans vos estimations?

►**allow of** *vipo Fml* permettre, admettre; **his condition would not a. of his going out,** son état ne lui permettait pas de sortir.

►**allow out** *vtsep* permettre *(à qn)* de sortir; **no-one is allowed out after dark,** personne n'a le droit de sortir après la tombée de la nuit; **some prisoners are allowed**

out at weekends, certains détenus ont la permission de sortir le weekend.

allowable [ə'laʊəb(ə)l] *adj* **(a)** *(permissible)* admissible; **(b)** *Com etc (dépense)* déductible.

allowance [ə'laʊəns] *n* **(a)** pension *f* alimentaire *(donnée volontairement)*; rente *f*; *Am* argent *m* de poche; **to make one's mother an a. of £1,000 a year,** faire à sa mère une rente de 1 000 livres par an; **his parents stopped** *or* **cut off his a.,** ses parents ont arrêté de lui verser de l'argent régulièrement; *(while he was living away from home)* ses parents ont arrêté sa pension;

(b) *Admin etc* allocation *f*; dégrèvement *m* *(pour charges de famille etc)*; **cost-of-living a.,** indemnité *f* de vie chère; *Old-fashioned* **family allowances,** allocations familiales; **supplementary allowances,** majorations *fpl* de pension; *Fin* **personal a.,** abattement personnel (sur l'impôt); *Admin Com* **entertainment a.,** frais *mpl* de représentation; **travel** *or* **travelling a.,** indemnité de déplacement;

(c) (free) luggage a., *(on plane, coach etc)* bagages *mpl* en franchise; **there is an a. of one item of luggage per passenger,** chaque passager n'a droit qu'à un bagage; *Sp* **time a.,** rendement *m* de temps; *Horseracing* **weight a.,** décharge *f*;

(d) *Com Fin* remise *f*, rabais *m*, déduction *f*; **to make an a. on an article,** faire un rabais sur un article;

(e) to make allowance(s) for sth, tenir compte de qch; **to make allowances for s.o.,** avoir de l'indulgence pour qn; **some a. must be made for shrinkage,** il faut tenir compte du rétrécissement;

(f) *Tech* tolérance *f*; *(in minting coins)* faiblage *m*.

alloy[1] ['ælɔɪ] *n* alliage *m*; **a. steel,** acier allié.

alloy[2] [ə'lɔɪ] **1** *vt* allier *(l'or avec l'argent etc)*. **2** *vi* *(of metals)* s'allier (l'un avec l'autre).

alloyed [ə'lɔɪd] *adj (metal etc)* allié (**with,** à, avec).

all-powerful ['ɔːl'paʊəfʊl] *adj* tout-puissant, toute-puissante, *pl* tout-puissants, toutes-puissantes.

all-purpose ['ɔːl'pɜːpəs] *adj* universel; à tout faire; **a.-p. computer,** calculateur universel.

all right [ɔːl'raɪt] *adj* **everything's a. r.,** tout est *ou* va très bien; **it's a. r.,** *(there's no need to worry)* tout va bien, ne vous inquiétez pas; *(to person apologizing)* je vous en prie!; **a. r.!,** bien!, entendu!; **are you a. r.?,** *(are you well?)* est-ce que vous allez bien?; *(did you hurt yourself?)* vous ne vous êtes pas blessé?; *Iron* tu ne te sens pas bien?; **I'm a. r. again now,** *(after being ill)* je suis tout à fait remis maintenant; **it's a. r. for YOU to laugh!,** vous avez beau rire!; **any more? — no, I'm a. r. thanks,** tu en veux encore? — non, ça va merci; **he's** *or* **she's a. r.,** c'est un bon type; *F* **to be a bit of a. r.,** *(of woman)* être une jolie pépée; *(of man)* être un beau mec.

all-round ['ɔːl'raʊnd] *adj* **(a)** *(athlète etc)* complet; **an a.-r. man,** un homme universel; **a.-r. improvement,** amélioration générale *ou* sur toute la ligne; **(b)** *Aut* **car with a.-r. vision,** voiture à carrosserie panoramique.

all-rounder ['ɔːl'raʊndər] *n* homme universel, femme universelle; *(athlete)* athlète complet; *Sch* **a good a.-r.,** un élève complet.

allspice ['ɔːlspaɪs] *n Bot Culin* poivre *m* de la Jamaïque.

all-star ['ɔːl'stɑːr] *adj Th etc* **a.-s. performance,** spectacle joué exclusivement par des vedettes.

all-time ['ɔːl'taɪm] *adj F (record)* sans précédent, inouï; **a.-t. high/low,** record le plus élevé/bas; **the a.-t. greats of rock music,** les plus grands du rock; **one of the a.-t. hits,** un des plus grands succès.

allude [ə'luːd] *vi* **to a. to sth/s.o.,** *(of person)* faire allusion à qch/qn; *(of phrase)* avoir trait à *ou* se rapporter à qch/qn; **I am not alluding to anybody in particular,** je ne vise personne.

allure[1] [ə'lʊər] *n* attrait *m*.

allure[2] *vt* attirer, séduire *(qn)*.

alluring [ə'lʊərɪŋ] *adj* attrayant, attirant, séduisant.

allusion [ə'luːʒən] *n* allusion *f*; **to make an a. to sth,** faire allusion à qch; **in a. to sth,** par allusion à qch.

alluvial [ə'luːvɪəl] **1** *adj Geol (terrain)* alluvial; *(dépôt)* alluvien; **a. plain,** plaine alluviale; **a. deposits,** alluvions *fpl*. **2** *n Austr* alluvions *fpl* aurifères.

alluvium [ə'luːvɪəm] *n Geol* alluvions *fpl*; *(in restricted sense)* limon *m*.

all-weather ['ɔːlweðər] *adj Av etc (avion, atterrissage)* tous temps; *Sp (pitch)* pour tous les temps.

ally[1] ['ælaɪ] *n* **(a)** *(pays, nation)* allié, -ée; *Hist* **the Allies,** les Alliés; **to become allies,** s'allier (ensemble); se coaliser; **(b)** *(person, group)* partisan, -ane; **he found plenty of allies,** il a trouvé beaucoup de partisans *ou* d'adhérents.

ally[2] [ə'laɪ] *vt* allier *(qn, qch)* (**to,** à; **with,** avec); **the country has allied itself with its neighbour,** le pays s'est allié à *ou* avec l'état voisin; **we must a. ourselves with other unions,** nous devons nous allier à *ou* nous associer avec d'autres syndicats; **this newspaper is allied with another,** ce journal est associé avec un autre.

alma mater ['ælmə'meɪtər, -'mɑːtər] *n* = l'université ou l'école où l'on a fait ses études.

almanac ['ɔːlmənæk, 'æl-] *n* almanach *m*.

almighty [ɔːl'maɪtɪ] **1** *adj* tout-puissant, toute-puissante; **an a. row** *or* **din,** un fracas de tous les diables. **2** *n* **the A.,** le Tout-Puissant, le Très-Haut. **3** *adv Am F* très; **he's a. stubborn,** il est têtu comme une mule.

almond ['ɑːmənd] *n* amande *f*; **sweet/bitter a.,** amande douce/amère; **burnt almonds,** amandes grillées, pralines *fpl*; **ground almonds,** amandes pilées; **a. oil,** huile *f* d'amande; **a. paste,** pâte *f* d'amandes; **a.(-shaped) eyes,** yeux *mpl* en amande; **a. tree,** amandier *m*; **a. grove,** amandaie *f*.

almoner ['ɑːmənər, 'æl-] *n* **(a)** *Br (in hospital)* assistant, -e social, -e; **(b)** *Hist* aumônier *m*.

almost ['ɔːlməʊst] *adv* presque, à peu près; **a. blind,** quasi aveugle; **a. nothing,** presque rien; **it's a. six (o'clock),** il est presque six heures; **he a. fell/missed the bus,** il a failli tomber/rater l'autobus.

alms [ɑːmz] *npl* aumône *f*; **to give a. to s.o.,** donner *ou* faire l'aumône à qn, faire la charité à qn; **a. box,** tronc *m* pour les pauvres.

almshouse ['ɑːmzhaʊs] *n* hospice *m*.

aloe ['æləʊ] *n* **(a)** *(plant)* aloès *m*; **(b)** *Pharm* **aloes,** aloès *mpl*; **bitter aloes,** amer *m* d'aloès.

aloft [ə'lɒft] *adv* **(a)** *Nau* dans la mâture; **a. there!,** oh(é) là-haut!; **(b)** *(in sky)* en haut, en l'air.

alone [ə'ləʊn] **1** *adj (not used before noun)* **(a)** *(in isolation)* seul; **he lives (all) a.,** il vit (tout) seul; **I like being a.,** j'aime la solitude; **a. at last!,** enfin seul(s)!; **are we a.?,** est-ce que nous sommes seuls?; **we are not a. in thinking that ...,** nous ne sommes pas seuls à trouver que ...; **you a. can help me,** vous êtes le seul qui puissiez m'aider; **I did it a.,** je l'ai fait tout seul *ou* à moi seul; *Bible* **man does not live by bread a.,** l'homme ne vit pas que de pain; **with that charm which is his a.,** avec ce charme qui lui est propre;

(b) *(undisturbed)* **to let** *or* **leave s.o. a.,** *(not touch, not disturb)* laisser qn tranquille *ou* en paix; *(not interfere with)* laisser qn faire; **leave me a.!,** laissez-moi donc!; *F* fichez-moi la paix!; **to let** *or* **leave sth a.,** *(not get involved)* ne pas se mêler de qch; **leave these things a.,** *(don't touch)* ne touchez pas à tout ça; **a subject better left a.,** un sujet qu'il ne faut toucher que du bout du doigt; **your work is all right, leave it a.,** votre travail est bien, n'y retouchez pas; **let a. ...,** sans parler de ..., sans compter ...; **the soup wasn't even warm, let a. hot!,** la soupe était à peine tiède, encore moins chaude!

2 *adv* seulement; **I want to speak to you a.,** je voudrais vous parler seul à seul; *F* **to go it a.,** faire cavalier seul.

along [ə'lɒŋ] **1** *prep* le long de; **to walk a. the shore,** longer la plage, se promener (tout) le long de la plage; **to go a. a street,** suivre une rue; **to sail a. the coast,** longer *ou* suivre la côte; **to crawl a. the ground,** ramper à la surface du sol; **victorious all a. the line,** victorieux sur toute la ligne; **all a. the street,** tout le long de la rue; **trees a. the river,** arbres qui bordent la rivière, arbres sur le bord de la rivière; **they live somewhere a. this street,** ils habitent quelque part dans cette rue; **it's somewhere a. here,** c'est quelque part dans cette direction *ou* par là.

2 *adv* **to move a.,** avancer; **move a. so I can sit down,** *(in row of seats etc)* pousse-toi que je puisse m'asseoir; *Br* **move a. please,** *(said by policeman)* circulez; **to walk** *or* **stride a.,** avancer à grandes enjambées; **come a. with me,** venez avec moi; **come a.!,** arrivez donc!, venez donc!; *F* **come a. now!,** sois *ou* soyez raisonnable!; **he'll be a. in ten minutes,** il va arriver dans dix minutes; **bring a tent a. (with you),** apportez une tente; *Sl* **get a. (with you)!,** *(go away)* allez!, filez!; *(expressing astonishment, disbelief)* allons donc!; *Am* **a. about four o'clock,** vers quatre heures; *Am* **the afternoon was well a.,** l'après-midi tirait à sa fin; **all a.,** *(all the time)* depuis toujours; **I knew that all a.,** je le savais dès *ou* depuis le commencement, je l'ai toujours su; **I said so all a.,** c'est ce que j'ai toujours dit; **he was lying all a.,** il ne faisait que mentir.

alongshore [ə'lɒŋ'ʃɔːr] *adv* le long de la côte.

alongside [ə'lɒŋ'saɪd] *adv & prep esp Nau* accosté *(le long d'un navire, d'un quai)*; **to come a. (of) a ship,** accoster *ou* aborder un navire; **the police car pulled up a. (us),** la voiture de police nous a accostés; **to walk a. s.o.,** marcher côte à côte avec qn.

aloof [ə'luːf] **1** *adv* **to keep a.,** se tenir à l'écart *ou* à distance *ou* éloigné (**from sth,** de qch); **to stand a. from a cause,** se tenir en dehors d'une cause. **2** *adj* (*person*) distant.

aloofness [ə'luːfnɪs] *n* attitude distante, réserve *f*.

alopecia [æləʊ'piːʃə] *n Med* alopécie *f*.

aloud [ə'laʊd] *adv* à haute voix, (tout) haut; **to read a.,** lire à haute voix; **I was thinking a.,** je pensais à voix haute.

alp [ælp] *n Geog* **(a)** (*pasture*) alpe *f*, pâturage *m* de montagne; **(b) the Alps,** les Alpes; **the Swiss/French Alps,** les Alpes suisses/françaises.

alpaca [æl'pækə] *n* **(a)** (*animal*) alpaca *m*, alpaga *m*; **(b)** *Tex* alpaga *m*; **a. wool,** laine *f* d'alpaga; **a. coat/jacket/etc,** manteau *m*/veste *f*/*etc* en alpaga.

alpenhorn ['ælpənhɔːn] *n Mus* cor *m* des Alpes.

alpha ['ælfə] *n* alpha *m*; *Lit Fig* **a. and omega,** l'alpha et l'oméga; *Phys* **a. rays,** rayons *mpl* alpha.

alphabet ['ælfəbet] *n* alphabet *m*.

alphabetic(al) [ælfə'betɪk, -ɪk(ə)l] *adj* (*ordre etc*) alphabétique.

alphabetically [ælfə'betɪklɪ] *adv* alphabétiquement, par ordre alphabétique.

alphabetize ['ælfəbetaɪz] *vt* classer par ordre alphabétique.

alpine ['ælpaɪn] **1** *n* (*plant*) plante alpine *ou* alpicote. **2** *adj* (*club, chasseur*) alpin; (*site, paysage, climat*) alpestre; (*plante*) alpin, alpestre; **a. range,** chaîne de montagnes alpine.

alpinism ['ælpɪnɪz(ə)m] *n* alpinisme *m*.

alpinist ['ælpɪnɪst] *n* alpiniste *mf*.

already [ɔːl'redɪ] *adv* déjà; (*this early*) dès à présent; **ten o'clock a.!,** déjà dix heures!; **do you want to start a.?,** vous voulez commencer dès à présent?

alright [ɔːl'raɪt] *adj* = **ALL RIGHT**.

Alsatian [æl'seɪʃən] **1** *adj* alsacien; (*vin*) d'Alsace. **2** *n* **(a)** Alsacien, -ienne; **(b)** *Br* (*dog*) berger allemand.

also ['ɔːlsəʊ] *adv* aussi; **he a. saw it,** il l'a vu également, lui aussi l'a vu; **not only ... but a. ...,** non seulement ... mais encore ... *ou* mais aussi ...; **it's very efficient and a. very cheap,** c'est très efficace et de plus, très bon marché; *esp Am* **I study French a.,** j'étudie également le français; *Horseracing* **a. ran,** non classés, ont couru aussi.

also-ran ['ɔːlsəʊræn] *n Horseracing* concurrent qui n'a pas été classé; *F* (*unsuccessful person, thing*) non-valeur *f*.

Alta *abbr* **Alberta**.

altar ['ɔːltər] *n* autel *m*; **to lead s.o. to the a.,** conduire qn à l'autel; *Fig* **they were sacrificed on the a. of the party's interests,** ils ont été sacrifiés dans l'intérêt du parti; **high a.,** maître-autel *m*, *pl* maîtres-autels; **a. boy,** enfant *m* de chœur; **a. cloth,** nappe *f* d'autel; **a. screen,** retable *m*.

altarpiece ['ɔːltəpiːs] *n* retable *m*.

alter ['ɔːltər] **1** *vt* **(a)** changer (*qch, qn*); modifier (*un dessin, son opinion etc*); remanier (*un texte etc*); faire des retouches à (*un vêtement etc*); **that alters the case/the situation,** voilà qui change les choses/la situation; **that doesn't a. the fact that ...,** cela ne change rien au fait que ...; **this has not altered our determination to ...,** ceci n'a pas altéré notre détermination à ...; **the time of the train has been altered,** on a changé l'heure du train; *Nau* **to a. course,** changer de route; **(b)** *Am Austr F* (*castrate*) châtrer. **2** *vi* (*of person, situation*) changer; **her whole outlook has altered,** elle a complètement changé d'horizon.

alteration [ɔːltə'reɪʃən] *n* remaniement *m* (*de qch*); retouche *f* (*à qch*); modification *f* (*apportée à qch*); changement *m*; *Comptr* modification; **slight a.,** petite modification; **there has been an a. in their policy,** ils ont effectué un remaniement de (leur) politique; **subject to a.,** (*programme, timetable etc*) susceptible de révisions, sauf modifications; *Sewing* **alterations in three days,** retouches (aux vêtements) dans un délai de trois jours; **marginal alterations,** (*written*) corrections *fpl* en marge.

altercation [ɔːltə'keɪʃən] *n* altercation *f*, dispute *f*, querelle *f*; **to have an a.,** se disputer.

alter ego ['æltə'riːgəʊ] *n* alter ego *m*.

alternate¹ [ɔːl'tɜːnət] **1** *adj* **(a)** alternatif, alterné, alternant; **she comes on a. days,** elle vient tous les deux jours; **they come on a. days,** ils viennent en alternance un jour sur deux; **a. layers of stone and timber,** couches alternantes *ou* alternées de pierre et de bois; *Av etc* **a. route,** parcours *m* de rechange; **a. airfield,** aérodrome *m* de dégagement; **a. operation,** travail *m* en bascule; **(b)** *Math Bot* (*angle, feuille*) alterne; **(c)** *Liter* (*rime*) croisé; **(d)** *US* = **ALTERNATIVE 1 (a)**. **2** *n esp Am* remplaçant, -ante.

alternate² ['ɔːltəneɪt] **1** *vt* faire alterner (*deux choses*); employer (*deux choses*) tour à tour *ou* alternativement; *Agr* **to a. crops,** alterner des récoltes. **2** *vi* alterner (**with,** avec); se succéder (*tour à tour*).

alternately [ɔːl'tɜːnətlɪ] *adv* alternativement; tour à tour; en alternance; *Bot* **leaves placed a.,** feuilles alternes.

alternating ['ɔːltəneɪtɪŋ] *adj* **(a)** alternant, alterné; **(b)** *El* (*courant*) alternatif; *Tech* (*mouvement*) alternatif, de va-et-vient.

alternation [ɔːltə'neɪʃən] *n* **(a)** alternation *f* (*d'un mouvement*); **(b)** alternance *f* (*du jour et de la nuit, Biol de générations, Geol des couches*); **(c)** *El* alternance *f*.

alternative [ɔːl'tɜːnətɪv] **1** *adj* **(a)** alternatif; autre; **a. proposal,** contre-proposition *f*; **a. route,** route *f* d'emprunt; **an a. site will have to be found,** (*this one is no good*) il faudra trouver un autre lieu; (*in case it is needed*) il faudra trouver un deuxième lieu; **(b)** (*not conventional*) parallèle, alternatif; **a. medicine,** médecine douce; **a. comedy,** comédie alternative. **2** *n* (*choice*) alternative *f*; **there is no a.,** il n'y a pas d'alternative; **they were given the a. of a fine or a month's imprisonment,** on leur a donné le choix entre une amende et un mois de prison; **the a. would be to do,** une autre solution serait de faire; **to have no a.,** ne pas avoir le choix; **he had no a. but to obey,** il n'a pu faire autrement que d'obéir; **there are alternatives to nuclear power,** le nucléaire n'est pas la seule solution possible; **the a. was starvation,** sinon on *ou* il *etc* serait mort de faim.

alternatively [ɔːl'tɜːnətɪvlɪ] *adv* avec l'alternative de ...; (*on the other hand*) ou bien ...; **a. we could go to the beach,** ou bien nous pourrions aller à la plage.

alternator ['ɔːltəneɪtər] *n El* alternateur *m*.

although [ɔːl'ðəʊ] *conj* quoique, bien que + *sub*; **a. I am a father,** tout père que je suis; **a. not beautiful, she was attractive,** sans être belle elle plaisait.

altimeter ['æltɪmiːtər] *n Av* altimètre *m*; **radio a.,** radiosonde *f*.

altitude ['æltɪtjuːd] *n* **(a)** altitude *f*, élévation *f* (*au-dessus du niveau de la mer*); *Av* **what is their a.?,** quelle est leur altitude?; **at these altitudes,** à cette altitude; **a. recorder,** enregistreur *m* d'altitude; **a. sickness,** mal *m* de l'altitude *ou* des aviateurs *ou* des montagnes; **(b)** *Astron* hauteur *f* (*d'un astre, d'un triangle*).

alt key ['ɔːltkiː] *n Comptr* touche *f* alt.

alto ['æltəʊ] *n Mus* **(a)** alto *m*; **a. clef,** clef *f* de troisième ligne; **to sing a.,** chanter la partie alto; **(b)** (*male voice*) haute-contre *f*, *pl* hautes-contre; (*female voice*) contralto *m*; **I'm an a.,** je suis alto; **(c)** (*viola*) alto *m* (à cordes); **a. trombone/saxophone,** trombone *m*/saxophone *m* alto.

altogether [ɔːltə'geðər] **1** *adv* **(a)** (*entirely*) entièrement, tout à fait; **to change sth a.,** changer qch de fond en comble *ou* radicalement; **it's a. out of the question,** c'est absolument impossible; **(b)** (*in total*) en tout; **there were nine of us a.,** nous étions neuf en tout; **a. the bill came to £63,** au total ça a fait 63 livres: **how much is that a.?,** ça fait combien en tout?; **a., it was a memorable occasion,** somme toute, ce fut un événement mémorable; **taking things a.,** à tout prendre. **2** *n F* **in the a.,** complètement nu, en tenue d'Adam; en tenue d'Ève.

altruism ['æltruɪz(ə)m] *n* altruisme *m*.

altruist ['æltruɪst] *n* altruiste *mf*.

altruistic [æltru'ɪstɪk] *adj* altruiste.

alum ['æləm] *n* alun *m*; *Phot* **a. bath,** bain aluné.

alumina [ə'luːmɪnə] *n Miner* alumine *f*.

aluminium [ælju'mɪnɪəm] **,** *Am* **aluminum** [ə'luːmɪnəm] *n* aluminium *m*; **a. foil,** papier *m* aluminium; **a. oxide,** alumine *f*; **a. saucepan,** casserole *f* en aluminium.

aluminize [ə'luːmɪnaɪz] *vt* **(a)** *Metal* combiner avec de l'aluminium; **aluminized steel,** acier *m* à l'aluminium; **(b)** *Tech* aluminer (*un mirroir*); **(c)** *Ch* aluminer; (*in dyeing*) aluner.

aluminum [ə'luːmɪnəm] *n Am* = **ALUMINIUM**.

alumna, *pl* **-ae** [ə'lʌmnə,-iː] *n esp US* ancienne élève (*d'un collège*); ancienne étudiante (*d'une université*).

alumnus, *pl* **-i** [ə'lʌmnəs, -aɪ] *n esp Am* ancien élève (*d'un collège*); ancien étudiant (*d'une université*); **a. association,** association *f* des anciens.

always ['ɔːlwəz, -wɪz, *stressed* -weɪz] *adv* **(a)** (*all the time*) toujours; **nearly** *or* **almost a.,** presque toujours; **a. smiling,** toujours riant; **the office is a. open,** le bureau est ouvert en permanence; **he is a. complaining,** il se plaint tout le temps; **(b)** (*as an alternative*) **I can a. try,** je puis toujours *ou* quand même essayer; **there's a. the old age pension,** en tout cas on aura la retraite de vieillesse.

alyssum ['ælɪs(ə)m] *n* (*plant*) alysson *m*, alysse *m*.

am *see* **BE**.

a.m. ['eɪ'em] *adv* (*abbr* **ante meridiem**) avant midi; **five a.m.,** cinq heures du matin; **we're leaving at six — a.m. or p.m.?,** nous partons à six heures — du matin ou de l'après-midi?

amalgam [ə'mælgəm] *n Metal & Fig* amalgame *m*.

amalgamate [ə'mælgəmeɪt] **1** *vt Metal* amalgamer (*l'or, l'étain*); *Fig* amalgamer (*des idées*); fusionner (*des sociétés, Fin des actions etc*); unifier (*les industries*). **2** *vi* (*of metals, ideas*) s'amalgamer; (*of companies*) fusionner.

amalgamation [əmælgə'meɪʃən] *n Metal* amalgamation *f* (*des métaux*); fusionnement *m* (*de deux sociétés, Fin d'actions*); mélange *m* (*de races etc*); **a. of industries,** unification industrielle.

amaryllis [æmə'rɪlɪs] *n* (*plant*) amaryllis *f* (belle-dame); lis *m* de Saint-Jacques.

amass [ə'mæs] *vt* amasser (*une fortune*); accumuler (*des richesses*).

amateur ['æmətər, -tjʊər, æmə'tɜːr] *n* **(a)** (*non-professional*) amateur *m*, dilettante *m*; **he paints as an a.,** il peint en amateur; *Pej* **he's an a. at painting,** il peint en dilettante; *F* il barbouille; **a. painter/musician,** peintre *m*/musicien *m* amateur; **(b)** *Sp* amateur *m*; **a. championship,** championnat *m* d'amateur; **a. sport,** sport *m* d'amateur; *Horseracing* **a. rider,** gentleman rider *m*; **(c)** (*connoisseur*) amateur *m* (*de peintures etc*).

amateurish [æmə'tɜːrɪʃ] *adj Pej* (*travail etc*) d'amateur; (*acteur, chanteur etc*) amateur.

amateurishly ['æmətɜːrɪʃlɪ] *adv Pej* en amateur.

amateurism ['æmətərɪz(ə)m] *n* **(a)** (*in the arts*) dilettantisme *m*; **(b)** *Sp* amateurisme *m*.

amatory ['æmət(ə)rɪ] *adj* (*sentiment*) amoureux; (*lettre*) d'amour; (*poème*) érotique; **he became rather a.,** il est devenu quelque peu galant.

amaze [ə'meɪz] *vt* confondre, stupéfier, étonner; **his courage amazed me,** son courage m'a stupéfié; **I was amazed at** *or* **by the price,** le prix m'a étonné, j'étais étonné par le prix; **it amazes me that he could have done such a thing,** je m'étonne qu'il ait pu faire une telle chose; **you a. me sometimes,** (*are exasperating*) tu es incroyable quelquefois; *Iron* **you a. me!,** voilà qui m'étonne!, vraiment?

amazement [ə'meɪzmənt] *n* stupéfaction *f*, stupeur *f*, (grand) étonnement *m*; **to listen in a.,** écouter avec stupeur; **to our a.,** à notre grand étonnement; **I heard with a. that ...,** j'ai été stupéfait d'apprendre que ... .

amazing [ə'meɪzɪŋ] stupéfiant, étonnant; (*dexterity*) prestigieux; **it's a.!,** je n'en reviens pas!; **it's a. that no one was hurt,** c'est étonnant mais personne n'a été blessé.

amazingly [ə'meɪzɪŋlɪ] *adv* étonnamment; **a., no one was hurt,** c'est étonnant mais personne n'a été blessé; **he's doing a. well,** (*in business*) il réussit à merveille; (*recovering quickly*) il se remet merveilleusement.

Amazon ['æməz(ə)n] *n* **(a) the (river) A.,** l'Amazone *f*; **the A. basin,** le bassin amazonien; **(b)** *Myth* Amazone *f*, (femme *f*) guerrière *f*; *Fig* femme forte et athlétique.

Amazonian [æmə'zəʊnɪən] *adj* **(a)** de l'Amazone, amazonien; **the A. rainforest,** la forêt tropicale (humide) amazonienne; **(b)** *Myth* d'Amazone; *Fig* (*woman*) fort et athlétique; *Fig* **I like the A. type,** j'aime les femmes fortes et athlétiques.

ambassador [æm'bæsədər] *n* (*diplomat*) & *Fig* ambassadeur *m*, ambassadrice *f*; **the French A. to Japan,** l'ambassadeur de France au Japon.

ambassadorial [æmbæsə'dɔːrɪəl] *adj* (*duties etc*) d'ambassadeur.

ambassadress [æm'bæsədrɪs] *n* (*diplomat*) & *Fig* ambassadrice *f*.

amber ['æmbər] **1** *n* (*colour, stone*) ambre *m*; **yellow a.,** ambre jaune; **he crossed on a.,** (*traffic light*) il a traversé à l'orange. **2** *adj* **(a)** (*necklace*) d'ambre, en ambre; **a. varnish,** vernis *m* au succin; **(b) a.(-coloured),** ambré; **a. light,** (*traffic light*) feu *m* orange.

ambergris ['æmbəgriːs] *n* ambre gris.

ambidextrous [æmbɪ'dekstrəs] *adj* ambidextre.

ambience ['æmbɪəns] *n* ambiance *f*.

ambient ['æmbɪənt] *adj* (*noise, light etc*) ambiant.

ambiguity [æmbɪ'gjuːɪtɪ] *n* **(a)** (*ambiguousness*) ambiguïté *f*; **(b)** (*instance*) équivoque *f*; **his speech was full of ambiguities,** son discours a été très ambigu.

ambiguous [æm'bɪgjʊəs] *adj* **(a)** (*open to different interpretations*) ambigu, *f* -uë, équivoque; **(b)** (*uncertain*) incertain; **an a. conflict,** un conflit d'issue douteuse; **(c)** (*obscure*) difficile à comprendre; **a. style,** style confus.

ambiguously [æm'bɪgjʊəslɪ] *adv* d'une manière ambiguë *ou* équivoque; **an a. worded reply,** une réponse formulée de façon ambiguë.

ambiguousness [æm'bɪgjʊəsnɪs] *n* ambiguïté *f*.

ambition [æm'bɪʃən] *n* ambition *f*; **the a. to succeed,** l'ambition de réussir; **eaten up with a.,** dévoré d'ambition; **to have great ambitions,** avoir de hautes visées; **my parents had great ambitions for me,** mes parents avaient de grands projets pour moi.

ambitious [æm'bɪʃəs] *adj* (*person, project etc*) ambitieux; **to be a. to do sth,** ambitionner de faire qch; **aren't you being rather a.?,** est-ce que tu n'es pas un peu ambitieux?

ambitiously [æm'bɪʃəslɪ] *adv* ambitieusement.

ambitiousness [æmbɪʃəsnɪs] *n* caractère ambitieux.

ambivalence [æm'bɪvələns] *n* ambivalence *f*.

ambivalent [æm'bɪvələnt] *adj* ambivalent.

amble¹ ['æmb(ə)l] *n* (*of horse*) amble *m*, entre pas *m*; (*of person*) pas *m ou* allure *f* tranquille.

amble² *vi* (*of horse*) aller (à) l'amble; **to make a horse a.,** mettre un cheval à l'amble.

►**amble along** *vi* (*of horse*) chevaucher à l'amble; (*of person*) aller *ou* marcher d'un pas tranquille; (*without destination*) flâner.

ambling ['æmb(ə)lɪŋ] *adj* (*cheval*) ambleur, qui va (à) l'amble.

ambrosia [æm'brəʊzɪə] *n Myth* ambroisie *f*.

ambrosial [æm'brəʊzɪəl] *adj* ambrosiaque.

ambulance ['æmbjʊləns] *n* ambulance *f*; **flying a., a. plane,** avion *m* sanitaire; *US Sl* **a. chaser,** = avocat qui encourage les accidentés à porter plainte; **a. crew,** ambulanciers *mpl*; **a. crews are on strike,** les ambulanciers sont en grève; **a. man** *or* **woman,** ambulancier(-brancardier) *m*; **a. post,** poste *m* d'ambulance; **a. ship,** navire *m* hôpital; **a. train,** train *m* sanitaire.

ambulant ['æmbjʊlənt] *adj Med* ambulatoire.

ambulatory¹ ['æmbjʊlətərɪ] *adj* **(a)** ambulant, mobile; *Jur* (*tribunal*) ambulatoire; **(b)** *Med* (*traitement*) ambulatoire; (*malade*) sur pied.

ambulatory² *n* promenoir *m*, préau *m*; (*in a church*) déambulatoire *m*.

ambush¹ ['æmbʊʃ] *n* embuscade *f*, guet-apens *m*, *pl* guets-apens; **to lie in a.,** se tenir en embuscade; *Fig* être à l'affût; **troops in a.,** troupes embusquées; **they were caught in an a.,** ils sont tombés dans un guet-apens.

ambush² *vt* attirer (*l'ennemi*) dans un piège *ou* dans un traquenard; **to be ambushed,** tomber dans une embuscade.

ameba, amebic *US* = **AMOEBA, AMOEBIC**.

ameliorate [ə'miːlɪəreɪt] *Fml* **1** *vt* améliorer. **2** *vi* s'améliorer, s'amender.

amelioration [əmiːlɪə'reɪʃən] *n Fml* amélioration *f*.

amen ['ɑː'men, 'eɪ'men] *int* amen, ainsi soit-il; **and we all say a. to that,** c'est ce que nous souhaitons tous.

amenable [ə'miːnəb(ə)l] *adj* **(a)** (*subject*) sujet **(to,** à); **the case is not a. to ordinary rules,** ce cas n'est pas sujet aux règles ordinaires; **(b)** (*person*) soumis (*à la loi, la discipline*); docile (*aux conseils*); sensible (*à la bonté*); (*child*) soumis, docile; **a. to reason,** raisonnable, disposé à entendre raison.

amend [ə'mend] **1** *vt* amender, modifier (*un projet de loi*); apporter *ou* faire une modification à (*un projet*); rectifier (*un compte*); corriger (*un texte*).

amendment [ə'mendmənt] *n* modification *f*, *Pol* amendement *m* (*d'un projet de loi*); rectification *f* (*d'un compte*); correction *f* (*d'un texte*); redressement *m* (*d'une erreur*); *Pol* **to move an a.,** proposer un amendement **(to a bill,** à un projet de loi).

amends [ə'mendz] *npl* réparation *f*, dédommagement *m*, compensation *f*; **to make a.,** faire amende honorable; **to make a. to s.o. for sth,** dédommager qn de qch.

amenity [ə'miːnɪtɪ] *n* **(a)** agrément *m* (*d'un lieu*); **(b)** (*civilities*) *usu pl* **amenities,** aménités *fpl*, civilités *fpl*; **(c)** (*facilities*) *usu pl* **amenities,** aménagement *m* (*d'un hôtel*); **close to all amenities,** (*in accommodation advertisement*) = proximité tous commerces; *Jur* **compensation for loss of amenities,** dommages-intérêts pour atteinte portée à l'agrément (*d'une propriété*).

America [ə'merɪkə] *n* **(a)** (*continent*) Amérique *f*; **North/South A.,** Amérique du Nord/Sud; **Latin A.,** Amérique latine; **in A.,** en Amérique; **the Americas,** les Amériques; **(b)** (*the United States*) les États-Unis (d'Amérique).

American [ə'merɪkən] **1** *adj* **(a)** (*continental*) américain; **A. Indian,** amérindien, -ienne; **(b)** (*of United States*) américain; *Ling* **A. English,** américain *m*; **A. cloth,** toile cirée; **A. organ,** harmonium *m*. **2** *n* **(a)** (*from continent*)

Américain, -aine; **North A.**, Nord-Américain, -aine; **South A.**, Sud-Américain, -aine; **Native A.**, Amérindien, -ienne; **(b)** (*from United States*) Américain, -aine; *Ling* américain *m*.

Americanism [ə'merɪkənɪzəm] *n Ling* américanisme *m*.

Americanize [ə'merɪkənaɪz] *vt* américaniser.

Amerind ['æmərɪnd] **, Amerindian** [æmə'rɪndiən] **1** *adj* amérindien. **2** *n* Amérindien, -ienne.

amethyst ['æmɪθɪst] *n* améthyste *f*.

amiability [eɪmɪə'bɪlɪtɪ] *n* amabilité *f* (**to,** envers).

amiable ['eɪmɪəb(ə)l] *adj* aimable (**to,** envers); **to be most a.**, être d'une grande amabilité; **to make oneself a. to s.o.**, faire l'aimable auprès de qn.

amiably ['eɪmɪəblɪ] *adv* aimablement, avec amabilité.

amicability [æmɪkə'bɪlɪtɪ] *n* nature *ou* disposition amicale.

amicable ['æmɪkəb(ə)l, ə'mɪk-] *adj* (*manner, relationship etc*) amical; (*person*) bien disposé; **a. designs,** desseins *mpl* pacifiques; **a. agreement,** accord *m* à l'amiable; *Jur* **a. settlement,** arrangement *m* à l'amiable.

amicably ['æmɪkəblɪ, ə'mɪk-] *adv* amicalement; **to live a. together,** vivre en harmonie; **to settle a matter a.**, s'arranger à l'amiable.

amid [ə'mɪd] *prep* au milieu de; **a. all the confusion/noise,** au milieu de tout le désordre/le bruit; **the news came a. revelations of corruption,** la nouvelle survint en plein milieu *ou* au moment des révélations de corruption.

amide ['æmaɪd] *n Ch* amide *m*.

amidships [ə'mɪdʃɪps] *adv Nau* au milieu du navire; **cabin a.**, cabine *f* par le travers; **to put the helm a.**, mettre la barre droite; **helm a.!**, barre à zéro!, zéro (la barre)!

amidst [ə'mɪdst] *prep* = **AMID**.

amino-acid [æ'miːnəʊ'æsɪd] *n Ch* aminoacide *m*.

amiss [ə'mɪs] *adv & adj* **(a)** (*badly*) **to take sth a.**, prendre qch de travers *ou* en mal *ou* en mauvaise part; **he took it very much a.**, il a très mal pris la chose; **(b)** (*out of place*) mal à propos; **a cup of coffee wouldn't come** *or* **go a.**, une tasse de café serait bienvenue; **a few more women presenters on TV wouldn't go a.**, ce ne serait pas un mal que davantage de femmes effectuent la présentation à la télé; **something is a.**, il y a quelque chose qui cloche.

amity ['æmɪtɪ] *n Fml* amitié *f*, concorde *f*; bons rapports (*entre deux pays*); **to live in a. with s.o.**, vivre en amitié *ou* en bonne intelligence avec qn.

ammeter ['æmiːtər] *n* ampèremètre *m*.

ammo ['æməʊ] *n F* = **AMMUNITION**.

ammonia [ə'məʊnɪə] *n Ch* ammoniaque *f*, gaz ammoniac; **a. water,** eau ammoniacale.

ammoniac [ə'məʊnɪæk] **1** *adj* ammoniac, -aque; **sal a.**, sel ammoniac. **2** *n* **(gum) a.**, gomme ammoniaque.

ammoniated [ə'məʊnɪeɪtɪd] *adj Pharm etc* ammoniacé, ammoniaqué.

ammonite ['æmənaɪt] *n* (*fossil*) ammonite *f*.

ammonium [ə'məʊnɪəm] *n Ch* ammonium *m*; **a. carbonate/sulphate,** carbonate *m*/sulfate *m* d'ammonium.

ammunition [æmjʊ'nɪʃən] *n Mil* munitions *fpl*; *Fig* **the scandal provided the opposition with useful a.**, le scandale a procuré à l'opposition un bon moyen d'offensive; *Fig* **protesters used the report as a.**, les manifestants ont utilisé ce rapport comme argument; **blank a.**, munitions à blanc; **dummy a.**, fausses munitions; **live a.**, munitions réelles *ou* pour tir réel; **a. box,** coffre *m* à munitions; **a. depot** *or* **dump,** dépôt *m* de munitions; **a. train,** train *m* de munitions.

amnesia [æm'niːzɪə] *n Med* amnésie *f*.

amnesiac [æm'niːzɪæk], **amnesic** [æm'niːzɪk] *adj* amnésique.

amnesty[1] ['æmnɪstɪ] *n* amnistie *f*.

amnesty[2] *vt* amnistier.

amniocentesis [æmnɪəʊsen'tiːsɪs] *n Med* amniocentèse *f*.

amoeba, *US* **ameba,** *pl* **-as, -ae** [ə'miːbə, -əz, -iː] *n Biol* amibe *f*.

amoebic, *US* **amebic** [ə'miːbɪk] *adj Med* amibien; **a. dysentery,** dysenterie amibienne.

amok [ə'mʌk] *adv* **to run a.**, (*of gunman*) perdre la maîtrise de soi; (*of rioters*) se déchaîner; *F* (*of children etc*) faire les fous.

among [ə'mʌŋ] **, amongst** [ə'mʌŋst] *prep* parmi, entre; **house standing a. trees,** maison située au milieu des arbres *ou* environnée d'arbres; **to wander a. the ruins,** errer dans les ruines; **a. the crowd,** au milieu de la foule, parmi la foule; **to live a. savages,** vivre au milieu des sauvages; **we are a. friends,** nous sommes entre amis; **this expression is current a. young people,** cette expression est courante chez les jeunes; **a. the guests were ...,** au nombre des invités se trouvaient ...; **the orchestra is a. the finest in Europe,** l'orchestre est l'un des meilleurs d'Europe; **not one a. them,** pas un d'entre eux *ou* parmi eux; **a. other things he said that ...,** il a dit entre autres que ...; **they quarrel a. themselves,** ils se disputent entre eux.

amoral [eɪ'mɒrəl] *adj* amoral, -aux.

amorous ['æmərəs] *adj* (*look, advances*) amoureux; **to be of an a. disposition,** être d'un *ou* avoir un tempérament amoureux; **he became quite a.**, il a commencé à me *ou* lui *etc* faire des avances; **a. verse,** poésie *f* érotique.

amorously ['æmərəslɪ] *adv* amoureusement.

amorphous [ə'mɔːfəs] *adj* **(a)** *Ch* amorphe; **(b)** *Fig* (*opinions*) sans forme; (*projet*) vague, amorphe.

amortization [əmɔːtɪ'zeɪʃən] *n* **(a)** *Com Fin* amortissement *m* (*d'une dette etc*); **(b)** *Jur* aliénation *f* en mainmorte.

amortize [ə'mɔːtaɪz] *vt* **(a)** *Com Fin* amortir (*une dette*); **(b)** *Jur* aliéner (*une terre*) en mainmorte.

amount[1] [ə'maʊnt] *n* **(a)** *Com* somme *f*, montant *m*, total *m* (*d'une facture etc*); **please tender the exact a.**, (*on bus etc*) on est prié de faire l'appoint; **(up) to the a. of ...,** jusqu'à concurrence de ...; *Fin* **a. carried forward,** report à nouveau; **(b)** (*quantity*) quantité *f*; **a. of work that an engine will do,** somme de travail que peut rendre *ou* fournir une machine; **in small amounts,** par petites quantités; **no a. of persuasion would make her stay,** il n'y avait pas moyen de la persuader de rester; *F* **he has any a. of money,** il a de l'argent tant et plus.

amount[2] *vi* **(a)** (*of money etc*) s'élever, (se) monter (**to,** à); **transactions amounting to several million pounds,** opérations qui se chiffrent par plusieurs millions de livres; **I don't know what my debts a. to,** j'ignore le montant de mes dettes; **(b)** (*be equivalent*) équivaloir, se réduire, revenir (**to,** à); **these conditions a. to a refusal,** ces conditions équivalent à un refus; **it amounts to the same thing,** cela revient au même; **all that amounts to very little/to nothing,** tout cela ne signifie pas grand-chose/se réduit à rien; *F* **he'll never a. to much,** il ne sera *ou* ne fera jamais grand-chose.

amour [ə'mʊər] *n* intrigue amoureuse, liaison *f*.

amp [æmp] *n* **(a)** *El F* (*abbr* **ampere**) ampère *m*; **a 13-a. plug,** une fiche de 13 ampères; **(b)** *Mus Sl* (*abbr* **amplifier**) ampli *m*.

ampere ['æmpeər] *n El* ampère *m*.

ampersand ['æmpəsænd] *n Typ* et commercial.

amphetamine [æm'fetəmɪn] *n Pharm* amphétamine *f*; **to be on amphetamines,** (*of drug addict*) prendre des amphétamines.

amphibia [æm'fɪbɪə] *npl Zool* amphibiens *mpl*.

amphibian [æm'fɪbɪən] **1** *adj* (*tank, vehicle*) & *Zool* amphibie. **2** *n* **(a)** *Zool* amphibie *m*; **(b)** (*tank*) char *m* amphibie; (*vehicle*) voiture *f* amphibie.

amphibious [æm'fɪbɪəs] *adj* (*animal, avion etc*) amphibie.

amphitheatre, *US* **amphitheater** ['æmfɪθɪətər] *n Archit Th etc* amphithéâtre *m*.

amphora, *pl* **-ae** ['æmfərə, -iː] *n Antiq* amphore *f*.

ample ['æmp(ə)l] *adj* **(a)** (*vêtement, sac*) ample, large; **man of a. proportions,** homme corpulent; **(b)** (*plentiful*) abondant; **a. resources,** d'abondantes ressources; **this will be a.**, ceci sera amplement suffisant; **to have a. means,** avoir de la fortune; **an a. supply of coal for the winter,** largement assez de charbon pour l'hiver; **there are a. supplies of fish this week,** (*in the shops*) il y a gros arrivages de poisson cette semaine; **a. proof,** preuve évidente; **the money is a. for our needs,** nous avons suffisamment d'argent pour nos besoins; **to have a. time,** avoir largement le temps (**to do,** de faire);

ampleness ['æmplnɪs] *n* ampleur *f*, abondance *f* (*de ressources*).

amplification [æmplɪfɪ'keɪʃən] *n* **(a)** (*expansion*) augmentation *f*, extension *f*; **he added some details in a. of his report,** il ajouta des détails supplémentaires à son compte rendu; **(b)** *Phys Electron* amplification *f* (*de puissance, de tension, de son etc*); **(c)** *Opt* grossissement *m* (*d'une lentille etc*).

amplifier ['æmplɪfaɪər] *n* **(a)** *Electron* amplificateur *m*; **a. circuit,** circuit *m* d'amplification; **(b)** *Phot* (lentille *f*) amplificatrice *f*.

amplify ['æmplɪfaɪ] *vt* **(a)** (*expand*) amplifier (*un exposé etc*); ajouter des détails à (*un rapport etc*); **(b)** *Phys Electron* amplifier (*le courant, la puissance, le son etc*).

amplitude ['æmplɪtjuːd] *n* ampleur *f* (*des dimensions, des ressources etc*); étendue *f* (*de l'espace*); *Astron* amplitude *f* (*d'un astre*); *Phys* amplitude (*des oscillations, des vibrations*); *Phys* **magnetic a.**, déclinaison *f* magnétique.

amply ['æmplɪ] *adv* amplement, grandement; **a. rewarded,** largement recompensé.
ampoule ['æmpu:l] *n Med* ampoule *f* (*pour une injection hypodermique*).
amputate ['æmpjʊteɪt] **1** *vt* amputer, faire l'amputation de (*la jambe etc*); **his right leg was amputated,** il a été amputé de la jambe droite. **2** *vi* amputer.
amputation [æmpjʊ'teɪʃən] *n* amputation *f*.
amputee [æmpjʊ'ti:] *n* amputé, -ée.
amuck [ə'mʌk] *adv* = **AMOK.**
amulet ['æmjʊlet] *n* amulette *f*.
amuse [ə'mju:z] *vt* amuser, divertir, faire rire (*qn*); **it amused her to do,** ça l'a amusée de faire; **is something amusing you?,** quelque chose vous amuse?; **to a. oneself,** s'amuser, se divertir; **to a. oneself by** *or* **with doing sth,** (*have fun*) s'amuser *ou* se récréer à faire qch *ou* en faisant qch; (*pass the time*) s'occuper en faisant qch; **to a. oneself with sth,** s'amuser avec qch; **to keep s.o. amused,** (*occupied*) occuper qn; (*entertained*) amuser qn.
amused [ə'mju:zd] *adj* amusé, diverti; **a. smile,** sourire amusé; **to be a. at** *or* **by sth,** être amusé de qch; (*make fun of*) s'amuser de qch.
amusement [ə'mju:zmənt] *n* **(a)** amusement *m*; **his a. was obvious,** son amusement était évident; **she was a source of a. to them,** elle était une source d'amusement pour eux; **smile of a.,** sourire amusé; **to the great a. of the children,** au grand amusement des enfants; **(b)** (*occupation, pastime*) amusement *m*, divertissement *m*, distraction *f*; **we have few amusements here,** nous avons ici peu de distractions; **place of a.,** lieu *m* de divertissement; **a. arcade,** salle *f* de jeux; **a. park,** parc *m* d'attractions.
amusing [ə'mju:zɪŋ] *adj* (*person*) amusant, drôle; (*book, film*) amusant, divertissant, distrayant; **to find sth/s.o. a.,** trouver qch/qn amusant *ou* distrayant.
amusingly [ə'mju:zɪŋlɪ] *adv* d'une manière amusante.
an *see* **A²**.
anabaptist [ænə'bæptɪst] *adj & n Rel Hist* anabaptiste *mf*.
anabolic [ænə'bɒlɪk] *adj* **a. steroid,** stéroïde anabolisant.
anachronism [ə'nækrənɪz(ə)m] *n* anachronisme *m*; **she's an a.,** elle est vieux jeu.
anachronistic [ənækrə'nɪstɪk] *adj* anachronique.
anaconda [ænə'kɒndə] *n* (*snake*) anaconda *m*.
anaemia, *US* **anemia** [ə'ni:mɪə] *n* anémie *f*.
anaemic, *US* **anemic** [ə'ni:mɪk] *adj Med* anémique; *Fig* faible, sans énergie; **to become a.,** s'anémier.
anaesthesia, *US* **anesthesia** [ænəs'θi:zɪə] *n* anesthésie *f*; **general/local a.,** anesthésie générale/locale; **spinal a.,** anesthésie rachidienne.
anaesthetic, *US* **anesthetic** [ænəs'θetɪk] **1** *n* anesthésique *m*; **to give s.o. an a.,** donner un anesthésique à qn; **under (the) a.,** sous l'effet de l'anasthésique. **2** *adj* anesthésique.
anaesthetist, *US* **anesthetist** [ə'ni:sθətɪst] *n* anesthésiste *mf*.
anaesthetize, *US* **anesthetize** [ə'ni:sθətaɪz] *vt Med & Fig* anesthésier.
anagram ['ænəgræm] *n* anagramme *f*.
anal ['eɪn(ə)l] *adj Anat* anal,-aux.
analgesia [ænəl'dʒi:zɪə] *n Med* analgésie *f*.
analgesic [ænəl'dʒi:sɪk, -zɪk] *adj & n Med* analgésique *m*.
analog ['ænəlɒg] **1** *adj Comptr* analogique; **a. computer,** ordinateur *m* analogique; **a. clock,** horloge *f* (à affichage) analogique. **2** *n US* = **ANALOGUE.**
analogical [ænə'lɒdʒɪk(ə)l] *adj* analogique.
analogically [ænə'lɒdʒɪklɪ] *adv* analogiquement, par analogie.
analogize [ə'nælədʒaɪz] **1** *vt* représenter, expliquer (*qch*) par analogie. **2** *vi* raisonner par analogie.
analogous [ə'næləgəs] *adj* analogue (**to, with,** à).
analogously [ə'næləgəslɪ] *adv* d'une manière analogue (**to, with,** à).
analogue, *US* **analog** ['ænəlɒg] *n* analogue *m*.
analogy [ə'nælədʒɪ] *n* analogie *f* (**to, with,** avec; **between,** entre); **by a. with ...,** par analogie avec ...; **to draw an a.,** faire une analogie.
analyse, *US* **analyze** ['ænəlaɪz] *vt esp Ch Math etc* analyser, faire l'analyse de (*qch*); *Gram* analyser (*une phrase, un texte etc*); faire l'analyse logique de (*une phrase*); *Psy* psychanalyser (*qn*); *Com* dépouiller, décomposer (*un compte*).
analysis, *pl* **-es** [ə'næləsɪs, -i:z] *n* analyse *f* (*d'un texte etc*); *Gram* analyse logique (*d'une phrase*); *Psy* psychanalyse *f*; *Am Psy* **to be in a.,** (*of person*) être en analyse; **in the final a.,** (*ultimately*) en fin de compte; *Math* **differential a.,** analyse différentielle; **operations a.,** recherche opérationnelle; *Ch* **qualitative a.,** analyse qualitative; *Phys* **spectral** *or* **spectrum a.,** analyse spectrale; *Comptr etc* **systems a.,** analyse fonctionnelle; **wet/dry a.,** analyse par voie humide/sèche.
analyst ['ænəlɪst] *n Ch Math etc* analyste *mf*; *Econ* économiste-statisticien *m*, *pl* économistes-statisticiens; *Psy* (psych)analyste *mf*.
analytic(al) [ænə'lɪtɪk, -ɪk(ə)l] *adj* analytique; **a. mind,** esprit *m* d'analyse; **a. psychology,** psychologie introspective.
analyze ['ænəlaɪz] *vt US* = **ANALYSE.**
anaphrodisiac [ænæfrə'di:zɪæk] *adj & n Pharm* anaphrodisiaque *m*.
anarchist ['ænəkɪst] *adj & n* anarchiste *mf*.
anarchy ['ænəkɪ] *n* anarchie *f*.
anastigmat [æ'næstɪgmæt] *adj & n Opt Phot* **a. (lens),** objectif *m* anastigmat(ique); anastigmat *m*.
anastigmatic [ænəstɪg'mætɪk] *adj Opt* anastigmat(ique).
anathema [ə'næθəmə] *n Rel & Fig* anathème *m*; **his name is a.,** son nom est maudit; *Fig* **it's** *or* **he's** *etc* **a. to me,** c'est ma bête noire.
anathematize [ə'næθəmətaɪz] *vt* frapper (*qn*) d'anathème.
anatomical [ænə'tɒmɪk(ə)l] *adj* anatomique; **a. specimen,** pièce *f* d'anatomie, préparation *f* anatomique.
anatomically [ænə'tɒmɪklɪ] *adv* anatomiquement.
anatomist [ə'nætəmɪst] *n* anatomiste *mf*.
anatomy [ə'nætəmɪ] *n* **(a)** structure *f* anatomique (*d'un homme, d'un animal*); **(b)** (*science*) anatomie *f*; (*textbook*) cours *m* d'anatomie; **human a.,** anatomie humaine; **(c)** (*dissection*) anatomie *f*, dissection *f*; *Fig* analyse *f*.
ancestor ['ænsestər] *n* ancêtre *m*; *Lit* aïeul *m*, *pl* aïeux; **a. worship,** culte *m* des ancêtres.
ancestral [æn'sestr(ə)l] *adj* **(a)** ancestral, héréditaire, de famille; **it's an a. right,** c'est un droit ancestral; **his a. home,** la demeure de ses ancêtres; **(b)** *Biol* ancestral, -aux.
ancestress ['ænsestrɪs] *n Lit* aïeule *f*.
ancestry ['ænsestrɪ] *n* **(a)** (*descent*) ascendance *f*, race *f*; (*lineage*) lignée *f*, lignage *m*; **both families were of French a.,** l'une et l'autre famille avaient une ascendance française; **(b)** (*no pl*) ancêtres *mpl*, ascendants *mpl*, aïeux *mpl*.
anchor¹ ['æŋkər] *n Nau etc* ancre *f*; *Fig* ancre *ou* planche *f* de salut; **sheet a.,** ancre de veille; **stand by to a.!,** pare à mouiller!; **to let go** *or* **drop the a.,** jeter *ou* mouiller l'ancre; **to weigh a.,** lever l'ancre, appareiller; **to lie** *or* **ride at a.,** être à l'ancre, mouiller; **at a.,** au mouillage; **to slip the a.,** filer (sa chaîne) par le bout; **to drag her a.,** (*of ship*) chasser sur son ancre *ou* sur ses ancres; *Nau* **a. buoy,** bouée *f* de mouillage *ou* d'ancre; *Constr* **a. iron** *or* **tie,** grappin *m*; *Constr* **a. plate** *or* **stay,** plaque *f ou* câble *m* d'ancrage.
anchor² **1** *vt* **(a)** *Nau* ancrer, mouiller (*un navire*); **(b)** (*fix firmly*) *Constr* affermir (*qch*) par des ancres; *Mil* abattre (*une pièce*); *Nau etc* hauban(n)er (*un mât etc*). **2** *vi Nau* jeter l'ancre, mouiller, prendre son mouillage.
anchorage ['æŋkərɪdʒ] *n* **(a)** *Nau* (*act, place*) mouillage *m*; **to leave the a.,** dérader; **(b)** *Nau* (*fee*) droits *mpl* d'ancrage *ou* de stationnement; **(c)** *Constr* ancrage *m*; point *m* d'attache (*d'un tirant etc*).
anchored ['æŋkəd] *adj Nau* ancré, mouillé, à l'ancre; *Fig* **firmly a. faith,** foi solidement ancrée.
anchoring ['æŋkərɪŋ] *n Nau* ancrage *m*, mouillage *m*.
anchorite ['æŋkəraɪt] *n Rel* anachorète *m*.
anchorman ['æŋkəmən] *n* **(a)** *Sp* dernier coureur (*d'une équipe*); *Rugby Fb* pilier *m*; **(b)** *Rad TV* présentateur *m* d'émissions en multiplex.
anchorwoman ['æŋkəwʊmən] *n Rad TV* présentatrice *f* d'émissions en multiplex.
anchovy ['æntʃəvɪ, æn'tʃəʊvɪ] *n* (*fish*) anchois *m*; **a. butter/paste,** beurre *m*/pâte *f* d'anchois.
ancient ['eɪnʃənt] **1** *adj* ancien; (*monument*) historique; (*chêne*) centenaire; *F* (*person*) très vieux; *F* (*thing*) antique, antédiluvien; **family of a. descent,** famille ancienne *ou* de longue lignée; *Jur* **a. lights,** servitude *f* de vue; **A. Rome,** la Rome antique; **the a. world,** le monde antique; **a. history,** histoire ancienne. **2** *npl* **the ancients,** les anciens *mpl*.
ancillary [æn'sɪlərɪ] *adj* subordonné (**to,** à); (*assisting*) auxiliaire; **a. equipment,** matériel *m* annexe *ou* d'appoint, accessoires *mpl*; **a. staff,** (*in hospital*) personnel hospitalier non médical; **a. worker,** (*in hospital*) auxiliaire *mf* de service.
and [ænd, *unstressed* ənd, ən, n] **1** *conj* **(a)** (*connecting words*) et; **a knife a. fork,** un couteau et une fourchette;

my father a. mother are out, mon père et ma mère sont sortis; **four a. five make(s) nine,** quatre plus cinq font neuf; **ham a. eggs,** des œufs au jambon; **now a. then,** de temps en temps; **he came without pencils a. paper,** il est venu sans crayons ni papier; **he speaks English, a. very well too,** il parle anglais et même très bien; **a. (what about) the invalids?,** et les malades?; **the water was nice a. warm,** l'eau était agréablement chaude;

(b) (*connecting clauses*) et; **he could read a. write,** il savait lire et écrire; **move (an inch) a. you're a dead man,** un pas et vous êtes mort; *esp Br* **go a. look for it,** allez le chercher; **come a. see me,** venez me voir; **wait a. see,** attendez voir; *F* **try a. help me,** tâchez de m'aider; **they said goodbye a. left,** ils ont dit au revoir et sont partis; **she stumbled a. fell,** elle est tombée en trébuchant; **to look for sth a. not see it,** chercher qch sans le voir; **I waited an hour a. he still hadn't turned up,** j'ai attendu une heure sans jamais qu'il arrive;

(c) (*with numerals*) et; **two hundred a. two,** deux cent deux; **four a. a half,** quatre et demi; **four a. three quarters,** quatre trois quarts; **an hour a. twenty minutes,** une heure vingt minutes; *Old-fashioned* **five a. twenty,** vingt-cinq; *Br Arch* **three (shillings) a. six(pence),** trois shillings six pence;

(d) (*repetition*) et; **for miles a. miles,** pendant des mil(l)es et des mil(l)es; **better a. better,** de mieux en mieux; **smaller a. smaller,** de plus en plus petit; **I knocked a. knocked (again),** j'ai frappé tant et plus; **over a. over again,** maintes et maintes fois;

(e) (*contrast*) et; **there are doctors a. (there are) doctors,** il y a médecins et médecins;

(f) a. so on, a. so forth, a. so on a. so forth, et ainsi de suite.

2 *n Comptr* (*usu written* **AND**) **A. circuit/element,** circuit *m*/élément *m* ET.

Andalusia [ændə'luːsɪə, -zɪə] *n* Andalousie *f*.

andante [æn'dæntɪ] *adv & n Mus* andante *m*.

andantino [ændæn'tiːnəʊ] *adv & n Mus* andantino *m*.

Andean ['ændiən] *adj* andin, des Andes.

Andes ['ændiːz] *npl* **the A.,** les Andes *fpl*, la Cordillère des Andes.

andiron ['ændaɪən] *n* chenet *m*.

Andorra [æn'dɔːrə] *n* (la république d')Andorre *f*; **A. (City),** Andorre-la-Vieille.

Andrew ['ændruː] *n* André *m*.

androgen ['ændrədʒən] *n Biol* androgène *m*.

anecdotal [ænɪk'dəʊt(ə)l] *adj* anecdotique.

anecdote ['ænɪkdəʊt] *n* anecdote *f*.

anemia, anemic *US* = **ANAEMIA, ANAEMIC**.

anemometer [æne'mɒmɪtər] *n Met* anémomètre *m*.

anemone [ə'nemənɪ] *n* (*flower*) anémone *f*.

aneroid ['ænərɔɪd] *adj Phys* (*baromètre*) anéroïde.

anesthesia, anesthetic *etc US* = **ANAESTHESIA, ANAESTHETIC** *etc*.

anesthesiologist [ænəsθiːzɪ'ɒlədʒɪst] *n Am Med* anesthésiste *mf*.

aneurism, aneurysm ['ænjʊrɪz(ə)m] *n Med* anévrisme *m*, anévrysme *m*.

anew [ə'njuː] *adv Old-fashioned & Am* **(a)** (*again*) de nouveau; **to begin a.,** commencer de nouveau, recommencer; **(b)** (*from beginning*) à nouveau; **to create sth a.,** créer qch à nouveau.

angel ['eɪndʒ(ə)l] *n* **(a)** ange *m*; **the a. of death,** l'ange de la mort; **guardian a.,** ange gardien; **fallen a.,** ange déchu; *F* **an a. passes,** un ange passe; *F* **you a.!, you're an a.!,** tu es un amour!; **be an a.,** sois gentil; **a. face,** visage *m* d'ange *ou* angélique; *Culin* **a. cake, a. food (cake),** = variété de gâteau de Savoie; **(b)** *Th etc F* bailleur *m* de fonds; **(c)** *Av F* écho radar non identifié.

Angela ['ændʒələ] *n* Angèle *f*.

angelfish ['eɪndʒəlfɪʃ] *n* ange *m* de mer, angelot *m*.

angelic [æn'dʒelɪk] *adj* angélique; (*sourire*) d'ange.

angelica [æn'dʒelɪkə] *n Bot Culin etc* angélique *f*.

Angelica [æn'dʒelɪkə] *n* Angélique *f*.

angelically [æn'dʒelɪklɪ] *adv* angéliquement.

angelus ['ændʒələs] *n Rel* angélus *m*.

anger¹ ['æŋgər] *n* colère *f*; **in a fit** *or* **moment of a.,** dans un accès de colère; **to speak in a.,** parler sous le coup de la colère; **the cannon was never fired in a.,** on ne s'est jamais servi de ce canon en temps de guerre.

anger² *vt* irriter (*qn*); mettre (*qn*) en colère; **he is easily angered,** il se met facilement en colère, il est irascible; **these remarks have angered Christians,** ces commentaires ont exaspéré la communauté chrétienne; **he is angered by suggestions that he took bribes,** les suggestions qu'il ait pu accepter des pots de vin l'irritent énormément.

angina [æn'dʒaɪnə] *n Med* angine *f*; **a. pectoris,** angine de poitrine; **to have a.,** avoir une angine.

angle¹ ['æŋg(ə)l] *n* **(a)** *Math & Fig* angle *m*; (*viewpoint*) point *m* de vue; (*of newspaper article etc*) perspective *f*; **acute/obtuse a.,** angle aigu/obtus; **right a.,** angle droit, angle de 90°; **at right angles to ...,** à angle droit avec ..., perpendiculaire à ...; **at an a. of ...,** sous un angle de...; **at an a.,** de biais; **the house stands at an a. to the street,** la maison fait angle sur la rue; **from a different a.,** d'un angle différent; **seen from this a.,** vu sous cet angle; **to study a problem from every a.** *or* **all angles,** étudier un problème sur toutes ses faces *ou* sous tous les angles; *Fig* **what's your a. on this?,** qu'est-ce que vous pensez de ça?; *Astron* **hour a.,** angle horaire; **meridian a.,** angle méridien; *Opt* **a. of incidence,** angle d'incidence; **a. of vision, visual** *or* **viewing a.,** angle de vision, angle visuel; *Phot* **a. of view,** angle de champ; **wide a.,** grand angle; **wide-a. lens,** objectif grand angulaire; *Cin* **a. shot,** prise *f* de vue oblique;

(b) *Mil* angle *m*; **a. of deflection,** angle de dérive; **a. of elevation** *or* **altitude,** angle de hausse *ou* de tir positif; **a. of sight,** angle de mire *ou* de visée;

(c) *Av etc* angle *m*; **a. of attack/of incidence,** *Av* angle d'attaque/d'incidence (*d'un plan dans l'atmosphère*); *Nau* (angle d') incidence *f* du vent sur une voile; **critical a. (of attack), stalling a.,** angle critique; **a. of ascent** *or* **climb,** angle de montée (*d'un avion, d'un projectile*); **helm** *or* **steering a.,** angle de braquage; *Nau* **a. of heel** *or* **list, listing a.,** angle de gîte;

(d) *Constr* coin *m*, encoignure *f*, angle *m* (*d'une pièce*); *Tech* **a. of gradient** *or* **slope,** angle de déclivité; **a. of torque,** angle de torsion; **cutting a.,** angle de coupe; *Constr* **a. bar** *or* **iron** *or* **plate,** cornière *f*, équerre *f*; **a. bracket,** équerre; **a. brace,** *Carp* (*tool*) foret *m* à angle; *Constr* aisselier *m*, contrefiche *f* (*de ferme de toit*); **a. gauge,** goniomètre *m*;

(e) *El Electron* angle *m*; **a. of loss, loss a.,** angle de pertes; **phase a.,** angle de phase.

angle² **1** *vi* **(a)** obliquer, faire des angles; **(b)** *Tennis* jouer à la diagonale. **2** *vt* **(a)** *Tech* angler (*une moulure etc*); **(b)** *usu Pej* orienter (*un compte rendu*); présenter (*des faits*) d'une façon tendancieuse *ou* d'un point de vue préjugé; **studies there are angled towards exams,** les études sont très axées sur les examens à cet endroit-là.

angle³ *vi* pêcher à la ligne; **to a. for trout,** pêcher la truite.

Angle ['æŋg(ə)l] *n Hist* Angle *mf*; **the Angles and Saxons,** les Angles et les Saxons.

▶**angle for** *vipo* chercher (*des compliments, une invitation*); **to a. for promotion,** chercher à être promu.

angled ['æŋg(ə)ld] *adj* **(a)** à angle, aux angles; **acute-a.,** acutangle, aux angles aigus; *Sp* **a. shot,** coup *m* en diagonale; **(b)** (*report etc*) partial, tendancieux.

Anglepoise ® ['æŋg(ə)lpɔɪz] *n* **A.** ® **lamp,** lampe articulée.

angler ['æŋglər] *n* **(a)** (*person*) pêcheur *m* à la ligne; **(b) a. (fish),** poisson grenouille *m*, *pl* poissons grenouilles.

Anglican ['æŋglɪkən] *Rel* **1** *adj* anglican; **the A. Church,** l'Église anglicane. **2** *n* Anglican, -ane.

Anglicanism ['æŋglɪkənɪz(ə)m] *n Rel* anglicanisme *m*.

Anglicism ['æŋglɪsɪz(ə)m] *n* anglicisme *m*.

Anglicist ['æŋglɪsɪst] *n* angliciste *mf*.

Anglicization [æŋglɪsaɪ'zeɪʃən] *n* anglicisation *f*.

Anglicize ['æŋglɪsaɪz] *vt* angliciser.

angling ['æŋglɪŋ] *n* pêche *f* à la ligne.

Anglo-American ['æŋgləʊə'merɪkən] **1** *adj* anglo-américain. **2** *n* Anglo-Américain, -aine, *pl* Anglo-Américains, -aines.

Anglo-Arab ['æŋgləʊ'ærəb] *adj & n* anglo-arabe *m*, *pl* anglo-arabes.

Anglo-Catholic ['æŋgləʊ'kæθ(ə)lɪk] *adj & n Rel* anglo-catholique *mf*.

Anglo-French ['æŋgləʊ'frentʃ] **1** *adj* franco-britannique, *pl* franco-britanniques; *Hist* **the A.-F. wars,** les guerres avec la France. **2** *n Ling* anglo-normand *m*.

Anglo-Indian ['æŋgləʊ'ɪndɪən] **1** *adj* anglo-indien, *pl* anglo-indiens. **2** *n* **(a)** (*person of mixed ancestry*) Eurasien, -ienne; **(b)** (*Briton who has lived in India*) Anglo-Indien, -ienne.

Anglo-Irish ['æŋgləʊ'aɪrɪʃ] **1** *adj* anglo-irlandais. **2** *n* **the A.-I.,** (*used as pl*) les Anglo-Irlandais *mpl*.

Anglophile ['æŋgləʊfaɪl] *n* anglophile *mf*.

Anglophobe ['æŋgləʊfəʊb] *adj & n* anglophobe *mf*.

Anglophobia ['æŋgləʊ'fəʊbɪə] *n* anglophobie *f*.
Anglo-Saxon ['æŋgləʊ'sæks(ə)n] **1** *adj* anglo-saxon. **2** *n* **(a)** (*person*) Anglo-Saxon, -onne, *pl* Anglo-Saxons, -onnes; **(b)** *Ling* anglo-saxon *m*.
Angola [æŋ'gəʊlə] *n* Angola *m*.
angora [æŋ'gɔːrə] *n* **(a) a. (goat/cat/rabbit),** (chèvre *f*/chat *m*/lapin *m*) angora *m*; **(b)** *Tex* angora *m*; **a. wool,** laine *f* angora; **a. jumper,** pull *m* en angora.
angostura [æŋgəs'tjʊərə] *n Pharm etc* angusture *f*; **a. bitters** ®, bitters *mpl* à base d'angusture.
angrily [æŋgrɪlɪ] *adv* (*répondre etc*) avec colère.
angry ['æŋgrɪ] *adj* (*person*) en colère (**at s.o.,** contre qn; **about sth,** à cause de qch); fâché, irrité (**with,** *Am* **at s.o. about sth,** contre qn de qch); (*voice*) irrité; (*speech*) violent; **he is very a.,** il est très en colère *ou* très fâché; **he was a. at being kept waiting,** il était irrité qu'on le fît attendre; **to be a. with oneself,** (*for not doing better*) être mécontent de soi; (*for giving offence, causing pain etc*) s'en vouloir; **to get a.,** se mettre en colère, se fâcher, s'irriter; **to get a. with s.o.,** se fâcher contre qn; **to make s.o. a.,** exaspérer qn, mettre qn en colère; **it makes me very a. when I hear people say things like that,** ça m'exaspère d'entendre dire des choses comme ça; **he sent me an a. letter,** il m'a envoyé une lettre furieuse; **an a. young man,** un contestataire; *Lit* **the a. sea,** la mer courroucée *ou* en courroux; **a. sky,** (*stormy*) ciel *m* à l'orage; *Med* **a. sore,** plaie irritée *ou* enflammée.
angstrom ['æŋstrəm] *n Phys* angström *m*.
anguish ['æŋgwɪʃ] *n* **(a)** (*great anxiety*) angoisse *f*, douleur *f*; **to be in a.,** être dans l'angoisse, être au supplice; **to cause s.o. a.,** angoisser qn; **(b)** *Med* angoisse *f*.
anguished ['æŋgwɪʃt] *adj* angoissé, tourmenté.
angular ['æŋgjʊlər] *adj* **(a)** (*rocher, visage*) anguleux; (*corps*) décharné, osseux; **(b)** (*movement*) saccadé; **(c)** (*vitesse etc*) angulaire.
anhydride [æn'haɪdraɪd] *n Ch* anhydride *m*.
anhydrous [æn'haɪdrəs] *adj Ch* anhydre.
aniline ['ænɪlaɪn] *n Ch* aniline *f*; **a. dyes,** colorants *mpl* azoïques.
animal ['ænɪm(ə)l] **1** *n* animal *m*, *pl* -aux; **to behave like animals,** se comporter comme des animaux; *Fig* **he's an a.,** c'est une brute; *Fig* **she's not a political a.,** elle n'est pas encline à la politique; **draught a.,** bête *f* de trait; **a. husbandry,** élevage *m*; *Art* **a. painter,** animalier *m*; **a. rights,** droits *mpl* des animaux; **a. rights activist,** activiste *mf* pour la défense des droits des animaux. **2** *adj* (*fat, kingdom etc*) animal; **food of a. origin,** aliments d'origine animale; **a. instinct/need,** (*of person*) instinct/besoin animal.
animalcule, *pl* **-cula, -cules** [ænɪ'mælkjuːl, -kjʊlə, -kjuːlz] *n* animalcule *m*.
animate¹ ['ænɪmɪt] *adj* (*alive*) animé, doué de vie; **to become a.,** s'animer.
animate² ['ænɪmeɪt] *vt* animer (*qn, un parti, une conversation*); encourager, stimuler (*qn*).
animated ['ænɪmeɪtɪd] *adj* (*discussion*) animé; **to become a.,** (*of person*) s'animer; (*of discussion*) s'échauffer; *Cin* **a. cartoon,** dessins animés.
animatedly ['ænɪmeɪtɪdlɪ] *adv* (*to say*) d'un ton animé; (*to discuss*) avec animation; (*to speak*) avec vivacité.
animation [ænɪ'meɪʃən] *n* **(a)** (*of person*) animation *f*, vivacité *f*; chaleur *f* (*du style*); feu *m*, entrain *m*, verve *f* (*d'un orateur*); **(b)** (*act*) stimulation *f*; **(c)** *Cin* animation *f*.
animator ['ænɪmeɪtər] *n* animateur, -trice.
animism ['ænɪmɪz(ə)m] *n* **(a)** *Phil* animisme *m*; **(b)** *Phil Rel* spiritualisme *m*.
animist ['ænɪmɪst] *adj & n Phil* animiste *mf*.
animosity [ænɪ'mɒsɪtɪ] *n* animosité *f*; **to feel a. against s.o.,** ressentir de l'animosité contre qn.
animus ['ænɪməs] *n* **(a)** (*hostility*) animosité *f*; **(b)** (*motive, stimulus*) stimulation *f*.
anion ['ænaɪən] *n Phys El* anion *m*.
anise ['ænɪs] *n* (*plant*) anis *m*; **star a.,** anis étoilé; **to flavour sth with a.,** aniser qch.
aniseed ['ænɪsiːd] *n* (graine *f* d')anis *m*; **a. balls,** (*sweets*) bonbons *mpl* à l'anis; *Culin* **a. cake,** gâteau *m* à l'anis.
anisette [ænɪ'zet] *n* (*liqueur*) anisette *f*.
ankle ['æŋk(ə)l] *n* cheville *f* (*du pied*); **a. bone,** astragale *m*; **a. boot,** chaussure montante, bottine *f*; (*fur-lined*) bottillon *m*; **a. joint,** cheville *f ou* attache *f* du pied; **a.-length dress,** robe qui descend jusqu'à la cheville; **a. socks,** socquettes *fpl*; **a. strap,** barette *f* (*de chaussure*); **a. support,** chevillière *f*.
anklet ['æŋklət] *n* **(a)** (*ornament*) bracelet *m ou* anneau *m* de cheville; **(b)** manille *f* (*de forçat*); **(c)** *Am* socquette *f*.
ankylose ['æŋkɪləʊz] *Med* **1** *vt* ankyloser. **2** *vi* s'ankyloser.
ankylosis [æŋkɪ'ləʊsɪs] *n Med* ankylose *f*.
Ann [æn] *n* Anne *f*.
annalist ['ænəlɪst] *n* annaliste *m*.
annals ['æn(ə)lz] *npl* annales *fpl*.
Anne [æn] *n* Anne *f*; *Hist* **A. of Austria,** Anne d'Autriche.
anneal [ə'niːl] *vt Metal* recuire, adoucir (*un métal, le verre*); détremper (*un métal*).
annealing [ə'niːlɪŋ] *n* recuit *m*, recuite *f* (*d'un métal, du verre*); *Metal* adoucissement *m*; **box** *or* **close a.,** recuit en vase clos; **a. furnace,** four *m* à recuire.
annelid ['ænəlɪd] *n Biol* annélide *f*.
annex¹ ['æneks] *n US* = **ANNEXE**.
annex² [æ'neks] *vt* **(a)** (*take possession of*) annexer (*une province*); **(b)** (*attach*) annexer (**sth to sth,** qch à qch); ajouter, joindre (*une pièce à un mémoire*).
annexation [ænek'seɪʃən] *n* annexion *f* (**of,** de); mainmise *f* (**of,** sur).
annexe, *US* **annex** ['æneks] *n* **(a)** (*of building*) annexe *f*; **(b)** (*to document*) annexe *f*.
annihilate [ə'naɪəleɪt] *vt* anéantir, réduire à néant (*une flotte, une armée*); *F* **his opponent annihilated him,** son adversaire l'a pulvérisé.
annihilation [ənaɪə'leɪʃən] *n* **(a)** anéantissement *m* (*d'une flotte, d'un peuple*); **(b)** *Nucl* annihilation *f*; (*of electron and positron*) dématérialisation *f*.
anniversary [ænɪ'vɜːs(ə)rɪ] *n* anniversaire *m*; **it's our wedding a.,** c'est l'anniversaire de notre mariage; **on the a. of ...,** le jour (de l')anniversaire de ... .
anno Domini ['ænəʊ'dɒmɪnaɪ, -niː] **1** *adv* en l'an du Seigneur *ou* de grâce. **2** *n F* vieillesse *f*; **it's just a.d.,** je me fais *ou* vous vous faites *etc* vieux.
annotate ['ænəteɪt] *vt* annoter (*un livre etc*); commenter (*un texte*); **annotated text,** texte avec commentaire.
annotation [ænə'teɪʃən] *n* annotation *f*.
annotator ['ænəteɪtər] *n* annotateur, -trice; commentateur, -trice.
announce [ə'naʊns] *vt* annoncer; **details will be announced nearer the date,** des détails seront donnés à proximité de cette date; **to a. sth over the PA (system),** faire une communication par haut-parleur; **the Prime Minister has announced his cabinet,** le premier ministre a fait connaître la composition de son ministère; **a knock on the door announced their arrival,** un grand coup contre la porte annonça leur arrivée.
announcement [ə'naʊnsmənt] *n* **(a)** annonce *f*, avis *m*; (*of birth, marriage etc*) faire-part *m inv*; *Journ* **a. of death,** avis mortuaire; **here is a passenger a.,** avis voyageurs; **here is a staff a.,** appel de service; **(b)** *Jur* affiche *f* judiciaire.
announcer [ə'naʊnsər] *n* **(a)** annonceur *m*; **(b)** *Rad TV* speaker *m*, speakerine *f*.
annoy [ə'nɔɪ] *vt* (*displease*) contrarier (*qn*); (*irritate*) gêner, fâcher, *F* embêter (*qn*); **he annoys me,** il me fâche, il m'exaspère; **stop annoying your little sister,** cesse de taquiner ta petite sœur; **is the light/noise annoying you?,** est-ce que la lumière/le bruit te dérange?; **it annoys me to have to ...,** cela me fâche d'être obligé de ... .
annoyance [ə'nɔɪəns] *n* (*displeasure*) contrariété *f*; (*irritation*) désagrément *m*, ennui *m*, *F* embêtement *m*; **look of a.,** air contrarié *ou* fâché; **much to his a.,** à son grand mécontentement; **source of a.,** désagrément, cause *f* d'ennuis; **petty annoyances,** petits ennuis.
annoyed [ə'nɔɪd] *adj* (*displeased*) contrarié, ennuyé; (*irritated*) fâché; **a. look/tone,** air/ton ennuyé; **to get a.,** se fâcher (**at sth,** de qch; **with s.o.,** contre qn).
annoying [ə'nɔɪɪŋ] *adj* contrariant, fâcheux, ennuyeux, *F* embêtant; **his a. little habits,** ses petites manies agaçantes; **the a. thing about it is that ...,** le fâcheux de l'affaire c'est que ...; **how a.!,** que c'est embêtant!
annoyingly [ə'nɔɪɪŋlɪ] *adv* d'une façon agaçante *ou F* embêtante; **a., he was late,** c'était ennuyeux qu'il soit en retard.
annual ['ænjʊəl] **1** *adj* (*congé, paiement etc*) annuel; **he has an a. salary of £50,000,** il gagne 50 000 livres par an; **a. accounts,** (*of organization*) bilan annuel; **a. general meeting,** assemblée générale annuelle; **a. instalment,** annuité *f*; **a. report,** rapport annuel (*d'une compagnie*); *Bot* **a. ring,** couche annuelle (*d'un arbre*). **2** *n* **(a)** *Bot* plante annuelle; **(b)** (*publication*) publication annuelle.
annually ['ænjʊəlɪ] *adv* (*in a year*) par an, annuellement; (*every year*) tous les ans.
annuity [ə'njuːɪtɪ] *n* rente *f* (annuelle); **government a.,** rente sur l'État; **perpetual a.,** rente perpétuelle, rente en perpétuel; **life a.,** rente viagère, pension viagère; **to buy an**

a., placer son argent en viager *ou* à fonds perdu; **to pay s.o. an a.**, servir *ou* faire une rente à qn; **a. in redemption of debt,** annuité *f.*

annul [ə'nʌl] *vt* (**-ll-**) annuler, résilier, résoudre (*un contrat, un acte*); annihiler (*un testament*); dénoncer (*un traité*); déclarer nul (*un mariage*); abroger (*une loi*); casser, infirmer (*une décision*).

annular ['ænjʊlər] *adj* (*éclipse, doigt, espace*) annulaire.

annulment [ə'nʌlmənt] *n* annulation *f*, résiliation *f*, résolution *f* (*d'un contrat, d'un acte etc*); cassation *f* (*d'un testament*); dissolution *f* (*d'un mariage*); abrogation *f* (*d'une loi*); abolition *f* (*d'un décret*); **decree of a.**, décret abolitif.

annunciation [ənʌnsɪ'eɪʃən] *n* **(a)** *Rel* **the A.**, l'Annonciation *f*; **(b)** *Fml* proclamation *f*, annonce *f*.

anode ['ænəʊd] *n El* anode *f*, électrode positive; (*in electronic valve or tube*) plaque *f*; **a. voltage,** tension *f* de plaque; **a. current,** courant *m* anodique.

anodyne ['ænəʊdaɪn] **1** *n Med* (*for stress, pain*) calmant *m*; (*for pain*) antalgique *m*, palliatif *m*. **2** *adj Med* palliatif, anodin; *Fig* (*remark*) anodin, qui ne peut blesser personne.

anoint [ə'nɔɪnt] *vt* oindre; **to a. s.o. with oil,** oindre qn d'huile; **to a. s.o. king/bishop,** sacrer qn roi/évêque; **the Lord's Anointed,** l'Oint *m* du Seigneur.

anointing [ə'nɔɪntɪŋ] *n* onction *f*; (*of king, bishop*) sacre *m*.

anomalous [ə'nɒmələs] *adj* **(a)** (*situation*) anormal, -aux; exceptionnel, irrégulier; **(b)** *Bot Med etc* anomal, -aux; *Gram* **a. verb,** verbe anomal.

anomaly [ə'nɒməlɪ] *n* **(a)** *Phys etc* anomalie *f*; **(b)** *Biol etc* anomalie *f*, irrégularité *f*, aberration *f*; **a law full of anomalies,** une loi pleine d'anomalies; **it's an a.**, c'est une anomalie.

anon¹ [ə'nɒn] *adv Arch & Hum* **(a)** (*later*) plus tard; **more of this a.**, je reviendrai sur cela; **(b)** (*soon*) tout à l'heure, bientôt.

anon² *adj abbr* **anonymous.**

anonymity [ænə'nɪmɪtɪ] *n* anonyme *m*, anonymat *m*; **to preserve one's a.**, préserver son anonymat.

anonymous [ə'nɒnɪməs] *adj* (*don, lettre etc*) anonyme; **to remain a.**, garder l'anonymat; **a grey a. building,** un bâtiment gris et sans caractère; **a. letter writer,** corbeau *m*; **a. writer,** anonyme *m*.

anonymously [ə'nɒnɪməslɪ] *adv* anonymement; **to write a.**, écrire sous (le couvert de) l'anonymat.

anorak ['ænəræk] *n* anorak *m*.

anorexia [ænə'reksɪə] *n Med* anorexie *f*; **a. nervosa,** anorexie mentale.

anorexic [ænə'reksɪk] *adj & n Med* anorexique *mf*; *F* **you look a.**, tu n'as plus que la peau sur les os; **she is a.**, elle est anorexique.

another [ə'nʌðər] *adj & pron* **(a)** (*one more*) encore (un); (*second*) un(e) autre, un(e) second(e); **we're thinking of getting a. car,** (*in addition to the one we have*) nous pensons acheter une deuxième voiture; **a. cup of tea,** encore une tasse de thé; **a. fifty years,** encore cinquante ans; **in a. ten years,** dans dix ans d'ici; **a. hour/20 miles and we'll be there,** encore une heure/une vingtaine de mil(l)es et nous y serons; **I don't want a. fish as long as I live,** je ne veux plus un seul poisson de toute ma vie; **without a. word,** sans (un mot de) plus; *F* **have a. (drink)!**, encore un(e)?; **this is not just a. small car,** ce n'est pas seulement une petite voiture parmi d'autres; **he is being called a. Picasso,** c'est le nouveau Picasso;

(b) (*different one*) un(e) autre; **take this cup away and bring me a. (one),** enlevez cette tasse et apportez-m'en une autre; **we're thinking of getting a. car,** (*to replace the car we have*) nous pensons acheter une nouvelle voiture; **a. of the passengers,** quelqu'un d'autre parmi les passagers; **that's (quite) a. matter,** c'est (tout) autre chose; **science is one thing, art is a.**, la science est une chose, l'art en est une autre; **I feel a. man,** je me sens tout autre *ou* tout rajeuni; *Lit* **he loves a.**, il en aime une autre; **she now has a. husband,** elle a maintenant un nouveau mari; **a. athlete would have played safe,** un autre athlète aurait joué la prudence; **a. time,** une autre fois; **let's do it a. way,** faisons autrement; *F* **tell me a.!**, (*you're exaggerating*) ce n'est pas vrai!; **one way or a.**, d'une façon ou d'une autre; **taking one thing with a., we just manage,** l'un dans l'autre, on arrive à joindre les deux bouts; **what with one thing and a., I forgot,** avec tout ça *ou* l'un dans l'autre j'ai oublié;

(c) (*reciprocal*) **one a.**, l'un l'autre, les uns les autres; **love one a.**, aimez-vous les uns les autres; **he and his wife adore one a.**, lui et sa femme s'adorent (l'un l'autre); **they give one a. presents,** ils se donnent des cadeaux (l'un à l'autre); **to help one a.**, s'entraider.

Ansaphone ® ['ɑːnsəfəʊn] *n Tel* répondeur (-)enregistreur *m*.

ANSI [eɪene'saɪ] *n Am* (*abbr* **American National Standards Institute**) = association américaine de normalisation.

answer¹ ['ɑːnsər] *n* **(a)** réponse *f* (*à une question, à une lettre*); réplique *f* (*à une critique*); **she made no a.**, elle n'a pas répondu; **I telephoned/knocked, but there was no a.**, j'ai téléphoné/frappé, mais sans réponse; **there's no a.**, ça ne répond pas; **he has an a. to everything,** il a réponse à tout; *F* **you think you know all the answers, don't you?**, tu crois que tu as réponse à tout, c'est ça?; **his only a. was to burst into tears,** pour toute réponse il a fondu en larmes; **Scotland's a. to Pelé,** le Pelé écossais; *F* **it's the a. to a maiden's prayer,** c'est exactement ce qu'il nous faut; *Hum* **he's not exactly the a. to a maiden's prayer,** il n'a pas été gâté par la nature; **in a. to your letter,** en réponse à votre lettre; *Jur etc* **a. to a charge,** réfutation *f* à une accusation; *Jur* **I have a complete a. to the charge,** je suis prêt à réfuter entièrement cette accusation; *Comptr* **a. mode,** mode *f* réponse;

(b) *Math etc* solution *f* (*d'un problème*); **the a. is 624,** la réponse est 624;

(c) *Mus* (*in counterpoint*) réplique *f*;

(d) *Fencing* riposte *f*.

answer² **1** *vt* répondre à, faire réponse à (*qn*); répondre à (*une question, une lettre*); **letters to be answered,** courrier *m* en cours; **letters answered,** lettres auxquelles on a répondu; **the question is not easy to a.**, c'est une question à laquelle il n'est pas facile de répondre; **to a. the bell/the telephone,** répondre à un coup de sonnette/au téléphone; **to a. the door,** (*go*) aller ouvrir; (*come*) venir ouvrir; **to a. a prayer,** exaucer une prière; *Jur* **to a. a charge,** répondre à *ou* réfuter une accusation; **to a. a description,** répondre à un signalement; **to a. the helm,** (*of ship*) obéir à la barre; **to a. the purpose,** remplir le but; **that will a. my purpose,** cela fera mon affaire. **2** *vi* répondre; **answers to the name of Rover,** (*of dog*) répond au nom de Rover.

►**answer back** **1** *vi* **(a)** (*be impertinent*) répondre, répliquer; **don't a. back!**, pas de réplique!; **(b)** (*defend oneself*) **she's the boss so I can't a. back,** elle est la patronne et je n'ai rien à redire. **2** *vtsep* (*be impertinent to*) répondre à (*qn*).

►**answer for** *vipo* répondre de (*qn*); se porter garant de (*l'intégrité de qn*); **to a. for one's actions,** prendre la responsabilité de ses propres actes; **he has a lot to a. for,** il est responsable pour beaucoup.

►**answer to** *vipo* **(a)** (*be accountable to*) être responsable envers, rendre compte à (*qn*); **you'll have me to a. to,** (*if you do that*) c'est à moi que vous devrez rendre des comptes; **to a. to s.o. for sth,** être responsable envers qn de qch; **(b)** (*correspond to*) répondre à (*un signalement*).

answerable ['ɑːnsərəb(ə)l] *adj* **(a)** garant, responsable (**to s.o. for sth,** envers qn de qch); **to be a. to an authority,** relever d'une autorité; **he is a. to nobody,** il ne doit de comptes à personne; **(b)** (*accusation*) réfutable.

answering ['ɑːnsərɪŋ] *adj* **an a. cry,** un cri jeté en réponse; *Tel* **a. machine,** (*giving message*) répondeur *m* téléphonique; (*giving and taking message*) répondeur (-)enregistreur; *Tel* **a. service,** service *m* de répondeur téléphonique.

ant [ænt] *n* fourmi *f*; **soldier a.**, soldat *m* des bois; **white a.**, fourmi blanche; termite *m*; *F* **to have ants in one's pants,** avoir la bougeotte; **a. bear,** tamanoir *m*; **a. colony,** colonie *f* de fourmis; **a. lion,** fourmi-lion *m*; **a. hill,** fourmilière *f*.

antacid [ænt'æsɪd] *adj & n Med* antiacide *m*.

antagonism [æn'tægənɪz(ə)m] *n* **(a)** (*hostility*) antagonisme *m* (**to, towards s.o./an idea/a policy,** envers qn/une idée/une politique); **(b)** *Biol Ch* **bacterial a.**, antagonisme microbien.

antagonist [æn'tægənɪst] *n* **(a)** (*adversary*) antagoniste *mf*, adversaire *m*; **(b)** *Biol Ch* antagoniste *m*.

antagonistic [æntægə'nɪstɪk] *adj* **(a)** (*opposed*) opposé, contraire (**to,** à); (*milieu*) antagonique; *Anat* (*muscle*) antagoniste; **(b)** (*hostile*) hostile (**to,** à).

antagonize [æn'tægənaɪz] *vt* (*arouse hostility of*) éveiller l'antagonisme *ou* l'hostilité de (*qn*); **to a. the public,** ranger l'opinion contre soi; **don't a. him,** ne te le mets pas à dos.

antarctic [æn'tɑːktɪk] **1** *adj* (*faune etc*) antarctique. **2** *n* **the A.**, l'Antarctique *m*.

Antarctica [æn'tɑːktɪkə] *n* Antarctique *m*.
ante¹ ['æntɪ] *n Cards* (*at poker*) première mise; **to raise** *or* **up the a.,** lever la mise.
ante² *vi Cards* faire une mise.
►**ante up** *vi US F* (*pay*) casquer.
anteater ['æntiːtər] *n* fourmilier *m*; **great a.,** tamanoir *m*; **scaly a.,** pangolin *m*; **spiny a.,** échidné *m*.
antebellum [æntɪ'beləm] *adj US* (*mansion etc*) qui existait avant la guerre Civile.
antecedence [æntɪ'siːd(ə)ns] *n* **(a)** (*precedence*) antériorité *f*; **(b)** (*priority*) priorité *f*; **(c)** *Astron* antécédence *f*.
antecedent [æntɪ'siːd(ə)nt] **1** *adj* antécédent, antérieur (**to,** à); **a. river** *or* **stream,** antécédent *m*. **2** *n* **(a)** *Gram Math* antécédent *m*; **(b)** *Mus* thème *m* (*d'une fugue*); **(c) his antecedents,** (*past*) ses antécédents, son passé; (*ancestors*) ses ancêtres.
antechamber ['æntɪtʃeɪmbər] *n* **(a)** (*room*) antichambre *f*; **(b)** (*in engine*) préchambre *f*; **diesel engine with a.,** moteur *m* diesel à chambre de précombustion.
antedate [æntɪ'deɪt] *vt* **(a)** (*precede*) précéder; venir avant (*un événement*); **(b)** (*give earlier date to*) antidater (*une nomination, un document*).
antediluvian [æntɪdɪ'luːvɪən] *adj* antédiluvien.
antelope ['æntɪləʊp] *n* (*pl* **antelopes, antelope**) antilope *f*; **sable a.,** antilope noire géante.
ante meridian [æntɪmə'rɪdɪən] *adv Fml* du matin.
antenatal [æntɪ'neɪt(ə)l] *adj* prénatal, -als.
antenna [æn'tenə] *n* **(a)** (*pl* **-ae** [-iː]) (*of insect, crustacean*) antenne *f*; (*de mollusque*) tentacule *m*; corne *f* (*de limaçon*); **(b)** (*pl usu* **-as** [-əz]) *esp Am Rad TV* antenne *f*.
antepenult(imate) [æntɪpə'nʌlt, -ɪmət] *adj & n* antépénultième *f*.
anterior [æn'tɪərɪər] *adj* **(a)** antérieur, -eure (**to,** à); *Gram* **past a.,** passé antérieur; **(b)** *Anat* (*muscle etc*) antérieur.
anteroom ['æntɪruːm] *n* antichambre *f*, vestibule *m*.
anthem ['ænθəm] *n Rel* motet *m*; *Lit* chant *m* d'allégresse; **national a.,** hymne national.
anther ['ænθər] *n Bot* anthère *f*.
anthologist [æn'θɒlədʒɪst] *n* anthologue *m*.
anthology [æn'θɒlədʒɪ] *n* anthologie *f*.
Anthony ['æntənɪ] *n* Antoine *m*.
anthracite ['ænθrəsaɪt] *n Min* anthracite *m*.
anthrax ['ænθræks] *n Vet Med* (*disease*) charbon *m*, anthrax *m*; (*sore*) pustule charbonneuse; **a. bacillus,** bacille charbonneux.
anthropoid ['ænθrəpɔɪd] **1** *n* **(a)** anthropoïde *m*; **(b)** *Zool* (singe *m*) anthropomorphe *m*; anthropoïde *m*. **2** *adj* (*apelike*) anthropoïde; (*resembling man*) anthromorphe.
anthropological ['ænθrəpə'lɒdʒɪk(ə)l] *adj* anthropologique.
anthropologist [ænθrə'pɒlədʒɪst] *n* anthropologiste *mf*, anthropologue *mf*.
anthropology [ænθrə'pɒlədʒɪ] *n* anthropologie *f*.
anthropometry [ænθrə'pɒmɪtrɪ] *n* anthropométrie *f*.
anthropomorphism [ænθrəpə'mɔːfɪz(ə)m] *n Phil* anthropomorphisme *m*.
anthropophagous [ænθrə'pɒfəgəs] *adj* anthropophage.
anthropophagy [ænθrə'pɒfədʒɪ] *n* anthropophagie *f*.
anti ['æntɪ, *US* 'æntaɪ] **1** *prep F* anti; **she was a. the idea,** elle était contre l'idée. **2** *adj F* **he's just a.,** il est contre. **3** *n* opposant, -ante.
anti- ['æntɪ, *US* 'æntaɪ] *pref* anti-.
anti-aircraft ['æntɪ'eəkrɑːft] *adj* (*canon etc*) antiaérien; **a.-a. defence,** défense *f* contre avions.
antibacterial [æntɪbæk'tɪərɪəl] *adj Med* antibactérien.
antiballistic [æntɪbə'lɪstɪk] *adj* antiballistique, antimissile; **a. missile,** engin *m ou* fusée *f* antimissile.
antibiotic [æntɪbaɪ'ɒtɪk] **1** *adj* antibiotique. **2** *n* antibiotique *m*; **to be on antibiotics,** être sous antibiotiques.
antibody ['æntɪbɒdɪ] *n Physiol* anticorps *m*.
Antichrist ['æntɪkraɪst] *n* Antéchrist *m*.
antichristian [æntɪ'krɪstʃən] *adj* antichrétien.
anticipate [æn'tɪsɪpeɪt] *vt* **(a)** (*expect*) prévoir, envisager, s'attendre à (*une difficulté, un plaisir etc*); **we don't a. any objections,** nous n'envisageons pas d'objections; **we do not a. any delays,** aucun retard n'est prévu; **to a. that ...,** prévoir que ...; **to a. the worst,** s'attendre au pire;
(b) (*enjoy, count on etc in advance*) anticiper sur (*les événements etc*); savourer (*un plaisir*) d'avance; escompter (*un résultat, un vote etc*); **to a. one's salary,** anticiper sur son salaire;
(c) (*act in advance of*) prévenir (*qn, les ordres de qn*); devancer (*qn, les désirs de qn*); aller au-devant de (*qch*); **you must a. your opponent's moves,** il faut que vous anticipiez les mouvements de votre adversaire; **her writing anticipates the 19th century,** son style présage le dix-neuvième siècle; **don't a. me,** (*in telling story*) attends la suite, laisse-moi finir.
anticipation [æntɪsɪ'peɪʃən] *n* **(a)** (*foresight*) prévision *f*; **in a. of trouble,** en prévision de troubles; **(b)** (*expectation*) anticipation *f*; **they awaited his arrival with eager a.,** ils l'attendaient avec beaucoup d'impatience; **thanking you in a.,** en vous remerciant d'avance.
anticlerical [æntɪ'klerɪk(ə)l] *adj & n* anticlérical, -aux.
anticlericalism [æntɪ'klerɪk(ə)lɪz(ə)m] *n* anticléricalisme *m*.
anticlimax [æntɪ'klaɪmæks] *n* **(a)** retour *m* à l'ordinaire; (*disappointment*) déception *f*; **the party itself was a bit of an a.,** la soirée a été plutôt décevante; **the fifth act forms an a.,** avec le cinquième acte nous retombons dans l'ordinaire *ou* sur terre; **(b)** (*in rhetoric*) anticlimax *m*.
anticline ['æntɪklaɪn] *n* anticlinal *m*, *pl* -aux.
anticlockwise [æntɪ'klɒkwaɪz] *adv & adj Br* en sens inverse des aiguilles d'une montre; **clockwise or a.?,** dans le sens des aiguilles d'une montre ou l'inverse?
anticoagulant [æntɪkəʊ'ægjʊlənt] *adj & n Med* anticoagulant *m*.
anticolonialism [æntɪkə'ləʊnɪəlɪz(ə)m] *n* anticolonialisme *m*.
anticonstitutional [æntɪkɒnstɪ'tjuːʃən(ə)l] *adj* anticonstitutionnel.
antics [æntɪks] *npl* **(a)** (*tricks*) bouffonneries *fpl*, singeries *fpl*; **he's up to his a. again,** le voilà de nouveau qui fait le bouffon *ou* qui fait des farces; **(b)** (*movements*) gambades *fpl*, cabrioles *fpl*.
anticyclone [æntɪ'saɪkləʊn] *n* anticyclone *m*.
anti-dazzle [æntɪ'dæz(ə)l] *adj* anti-aveuglant, *pl* anti-aveuglants; (*headlights*) anti-éblouissant, *pl* anti-éblouissants.
antidepressant [æntɪdɪ'presənt] *adj & n Pharm* euphorisant *m*.
antidote ['æntɪdəʊt] *n* antidote *m* (**to,** contre); contrepoison *m* (**to,** à).
anti-Establishment ['æntɪɪs'tæblɪʃmənt] *adj* anticonformiste.
antifascism [æntɪ'fæʃɪz(ə)m] *n Pol* antifascisme *m*.
antifascist [æntɪ'fæʃɪst] *adj & n* antifasciste *mf*.
antifreeze ['æntɪfriːz] *adj & n Aut* antigel *m*.
antigen ['æntɪdʒen] *n Med* antigène *m*.
anti-glare [æntɪ'gleər] *adj* = **ANTI-DAZZLE.**
Antigua [æn'tiːgə] *n* Antigua *m*.
anti-hero, anti-heroine ['æntɪ'hɪərəʊ, -'herəʊɪn] *n Liter* anti-héros *m*, *pl* anti-héros; anti-héroïne *f*, *pl* anti-héroïnes.
antihistamine [æntɪ'hɪstəmɪn] *Med* **1** *adj* antihistaminique. **2** *n* antihistaminique *m*; **have you taken your a.?,** as-tu pris tes antihistaminiques?
anti-icing [æntɪ'aɪsɪŋ] **1** *n* antigivrage *m*. **2** *adj* antigivre *inv*.
anti-inflationary [æntɪɪn'fleɪʃənərɪ] *adj* (*measures, policy*) anti-inflationniste.
anti-knock [æntɪ'nɒk] *adj & n Aut* antidétonnant *m*.
antilog ['æntɪlɒg] *n Math F* antilog *m*.
antilogarithm [æntɪ'lɒgərɪθəm] *n Math* antilogarithme *m*.
antimacassar [æntɪmə'kæsər] *n* têtière *f* (*de fauteuil etc*).
antimatter ['æntɪmætər] *n* antimatière *f*.
antimilitarism [æntɪ'mɪlɪtərɪz(ə)m] *n* antimilitarisme *m*.
anti-missile [æntɪ'mɪsaɪl] *adj* (*missile*) antimissile.
antimony [æn'tɪmənɪ] *n* antimoine *m*.
antinazi [æntɪ'nɑːtsɪ] *adj & n Pol* antinazi, -ie.
anti-novel ['æntɪnɒv(ə)l] *n Liter* antiroman *m*.
antiparticle ['æntɪ'pɑːtɪk(ə)l] *n Nucl Phys* antiparticule *f*.
antipathetic(al) [æntɪpə'θetɪk, -ɪk(ə)l] *adj* antipathique (**to,** à).
antipathy [æn'tɪpəθɪ] *n* antipathie *f*; **to feel a. for s.o.,** avoir de l'antipathie pour *ou* contre qn.
antipersonnel [æntɪpɜːsə'nel] *adj* (*bomb*) antipersonnel.
antiperspirant [æntɪ'pɜːspɪrənt] *adj & n* déodorant *m*.
antiphon ['æntɪfɒn] *n Rel* (*response*) antienne *f*.
antipodean [æntɪpə'diːən] *adj* **(a)** *Geog* des antipodes; **(b)** *Br* (*from Australia and/or New Zealand*) d'Australie et/ou de Nouvelle-Zélande; **the kangaroo and other a. animals,** le kangarou et d'autres animaux australiens; **(c)** *Fml Fig* à l'antipode (**to,** à).
antipodes [æn'tɪpədiːz] *npl Geog* **the a.,** les antipodes *mpl*; **at the a.,** aux antipodes.
antiproton [æntɪ'prəʊtɒn] *n Phys* antiproton *m*.

antiquarian [æntɪ'kweərɪən] **1** *adj* ancien; **a. collection,** collection *f* d'antiquités; **a. bookshop,** librairie spécialisée dans les vieilles éditions. **2** *n* antiquaire *mf*.

antiquary ['æntɪkwərɪ] *n* (*collector*) amateur *m* d'antiquités; (*dealer*) antiquaire *m*.

antiquated ['æntɪkweɪtɪd] *adj* (*ancient*) vieilli; (*outmoded*) désuet, suranné; **an a. kitchen range,** une cuisinière (à charbon) d'autrefois.

antique [æn'tiːk] **1** *adj* antique, ancien; **a. statue,** statue ancienne; **a. furniture,** meubles *mpl* d'époque. **2** *n* **(a)** *Art* **the a.,** l'antique *m*; **(b)** (*ancient object*) antiquité *f*; (*piece of furniture*) meuble *m* d'époque; **be careful with that, it's an a.,** fais attention, c'est une antiquité; *F* **that television's an a.,** cette télévision est une antiquité; **a. dealer,** antiquaire *mf*; **a. shop,** magasin *m* d'antiquités.

antiquity [æn'tɪkwɪtɪ] *n* **(a)** ancienneté *f* (*d'un usage etc*); **(b)** antiquité *f* (*grecque, romaine*); **the works of art of classical a.,** les antiquités; **women in a.,** la femme dans le monde ancien; **(c) Roman antiquities,** (*remains*) monuments romains.

antiracial [æntɪ'reɪʃəl] *adj* antiraciste.

antiracialism [æntɪ'reɪʃəlɪz(ə)m], **antiracism** [æntɪ'reɪsɪz(ə)m] *n* antiracisme *m*.

antiracist [æntɪ'reɪsɪst] *adj* antiraciste.

antirrhinum [æntɪ'raɪnəm] *n* (*plant*) muflier *m*; *F* gueule-de-loup *f*, *pl* gueules-de-loup.

anti-rust [æntɪ'rʌst] *adj & n* **a.-r. (composition),** (enduit *m*) antirouille *m inv*.

anti-Semite [æntɪ'semaɪt, -siːm-] *n* antisémite *mf*.

anti-Semitic [æntɪsɪ'mɪtɪk] *adj* antisémitique.

anti-Semitism [æntɪ'semɪtɪz(ə)m] *n* antisémitisme *m*.

antisepsis [æntɪ'sepsɪs] *n Med* antisepsie *f*.

antiseptic [æntɪ'septɪk] *Med* **1** *adj* antiseptique. **2** *n* antiseptique *m*; **put some a. on that cut,** mets du désinfectant sur ta coupure, désinfecte ta coupure.

antiserum [æntɪ'sɪərəm] *n Med* antisérum *m*.

antislavery [æntɪsleɪvərɪ] *adj* antiesclavagiste.

antisocial [æntɪ'səʊʃəl] *adj* **(a)** (*behaviour*) antisocial, -aux; **(b)** (*unsociable*) insociable; **he's being very a.,** en ce moment il n'est pas très sociable; **I don't want to be a.,** (*but I've got to go*) je ne veux pas vous fausser compagnie.

antistatic [æntɪ'stætɪk] *adj* antistatique.

anti-submarine [æntɪ'sʌbməriːn] *adj* anti-sous-marin.

anti-tank [æntɪ'tæŋk] *adj Mil* (*défense, roquette etc*) antichar(s).

anti-theft [æntɪ'θeft] *adj* (*serrure etc*) antivol *inv*; **a.-t. device,** antivol *m inv*.

antithesis, *pl* **-es** [æn'tɪθɪsɪs, -iːz] *n* **(a)** (*opposite*) opposé *m*, contraire *m* (**of,** de); **(b)** *Phil* (*in dialectic*) antithèse *f* (**between,** entre; **to, of,** de).

antitoxin [æntɪ'tɒksɪn] *n Med* antitoxine *f*.

antivivisectionist [æntɪvɪvɪ'sekʃənɪst] *n* antivivisection(n)iste *mf*.

antler ['æntlər] *n* andouiller *m* (*d'un cerf etc*); **the antlers,** les bois *mpl*.

Antony ['æntənɪ] *n* Antoine *m*.

antonym ['æntənɪm] *n* antonyme *m*.

Antwerp ['æntwɜːp] *n* Anvers *m*.

anus ['eɪnəs] *n Anat* anus *m*.

anvil ['ænvɪl] *n* **(a)** (*of blacksmith*) enclume *f*; **(b)** *Anat* enclume *f* (*de l'oreille*).

anxiety [æŋ'zaɪətɪ] *n* **(a)** inquiétude *f*; sollicitude *f* (*pour la sûreté de qn*); **deep a.,** anxiété *f*, angoisse *f*; **to cause s.o. great a.,** donner de grandes inquiétudes *ou* bien de soucis à qn; **to be full of a.,** être anxieux; **(b)** (*desire*) désir *m*, souci *m* (**for sth,** de qch); **a. to help/please s.o.,** désir *ou* souci d'aider qn/de plaire à qn; **(c)** *Psy* anxiété *f*; **a. attack,** crise *f* d'angoisse.

anxious ['æŋkʃəs] *adj* **(a)** (*worried*) inquiet, *f* -ète, soucieux (**about,** sur, de, au sujet de); **very** *or* **extremely a.,** tourmenté, angoissé; **the a. faces of relatives,** le visage angoissé des membres de la famille; **to be a. for s.o.,** (*worried*) être inquiet pour qn; (*concerned*) être plein de sollicitude pour qn; **I am a. about ~~his health~~,** sa santé me préoccupe; **(b)** (*worrying*) inquiétant; **an a. moment,** un moment d'anxiété; **it was an a. time for us,** ça a été une période de grande inquiétude pour nous; **(c)** (*eager*) désireux; **to be a. to do sth,** tenir à faire qch, être désireux de faire qch; **why are you so a. to go?,** (*impatient*) pourquoi êtes-vous si impatient de partir?; (*eager*) pourquoi tenez-vous tant à y aller?; **(d)** *Psy* anxieux.

anxiously ['æŋkʃəslɪ] *adv* **(a)** (*worriedly*) avec inquiétude; anxieusement, avec anxiété; **(b)** (*with concern*) avec sollicitude; **(c)** (*with impatience*) avec impatience.

any ['enɪ] **1** *adj* **(a)** (*some, one*) **have you a. milk/books?,** avez-vous du lait/des livres?; **have you a. more milk?,** avez-vous encore du lait?; **is there a. hope?,** y a-t-il de l'espoir?; (*stressed*) y a-t-il aucun espoir?; **if you had a. sense (at all),** si tu avais ne serait-ce qu'un peu de bon sens;

(b) (*in neg sentences or with implied negation*) **not a.,** ne ... aucun, nul; **he hasn't a. reason to complain,** il n'a aucune raison de se plaindre; **he hasn't a. more money,** il n'a plus d'argent; **without a. help,** sans aide; **she is forbidden to do a. work,** tout travail lui est interdit; **it is difficult to find a. explanation for it,** il est difficile d'y trouver une quelconque explication; **complaining won't do a. good,** se plaindre n'avancera à rien;

(c) (*no particular*) n'importe (le)quel; **come a. day (you like),** venez n'importe quel jour; **a. of us,** n'importe qui d'entre nous; **a. man, woman or child,** qui que ce soit, homme, femme, ou enfant; **under a. pretext,** sous n'importe quel prétexte; **a. doctor will tell you that,** n'importe quel médecin vous le dira; **that may happen at a. time,** cela peut arriver n'importe quand; **I expect him a. moment now,** je l'attends d'un instant à l'autre; **take a. two cards,** prenez deux cartes quelconques; *F* **a. old thing,** n'importe quoi; **a. old book,** un livre quelconque; **I don't want just a. (old) wine,** je ne veux pas n'importe quel (vieux) vin;

(d) (*every*) **a. pupil who forgets his books will be punished,** tout élève qui oubliera ses livres sera puni; **at a. rate, in a. case,** en tout cas.

2 *pron* **I haven't got a.,** je n'en ai pas; **I haven't seen a.,** je n'en ai pas vu; **have you a.?,** en avez-vous?; **is there a. more?,** y en a-t-il encore?; **I** *or* **you** *etc* **needn't say a. more,** pas besoin d'en dire davantage; **they won't take a. less,** ils n'accepteront pas moins; **few, if a., can read,** peu, si ce n'est aucun, savent lire; **he has no money and no prospect of a.,** il est sans argent et sans l'espoir d'en avoir; **I don't think a. of the guests have arrived yet,** je ne pense pas qu'aucun des invités soit encore arrivé; **there was no paper in a. of the boxes,** il n'y avait de papier dans aucune des boîtes.

3 *adv* **(a)** (*with comparative*) **I'm not a. better,** je ne vais pas mieux; **I can't speak a. more plainly,** je ne peux pas parler plus clairement; **I can't go a. further,** je ne peux pas aller plus loin; **the weather couldn't be a. worse,** le temps ne pourrait pas être plus mauvais; **I don't see him a. longer** *or* **more,** je ne le vois plus; *F* **a. old how,** n'importe comment; **I didn't do it a. more than you did,** je ne l'ai pas fait plus que vous; **I don't like her a. more than you do,** je ne l'aime pas plus que tu ne l'aimes;

(b) *Am F* **that didn't help us a.,** cela ne nous a été d'aucun secours; **her attitude didn't help a.,** son attitude n'a rien arrangé.

anybody ['enɪbɒdɪ] *pron & n*, **anyone** ['enɪwʌn] *pron* (*no pl*) (**NOTE** *in examples where one of the forms is preferred the word has been printed in full*) **(a)** (*indeterminate*) quelqu'un; (*expecting answer 'no'*) personne; **can you see a. over there?,** voyez-vous quelqu'un là-bas?; **does a. mind if I close the window?,** est-ce que cela gêne quelqu'un si je ferme la fenêtre?; **would a. like some more cake?,** est-ce que quelqu'un voudrait reprendre un peu plus de gâteau?; **does a. dare to say so?,** y a-t-il personne qui ose le dire?; **he knows French if a. does,** il sait le français comme pas un; **she'll know if a. does,** si quelqu'un le sait, c'est bien elle;

(b) (*in neg sentences*) **not a.,** ne ... personne; **you needn't disturb a.,** il est inutile que vous dérangiez personne; **there isn't a. here,** il n'y a personne ici; **there was hardly a.,** il n'y avait presque personne; **I won't speak to a.,** je ne parlerai (pas) à qui que ce soit;

(c) (*no particular person*) n'importe qui; tout le monde; **a. will tell you so,** le premier venu vous le dira; **a. would think he was mad,** on le croirait fou; **a. would have done the same,** tout le monde aurait fait la même chose; **a. but me,** tout autre que moi; **you're not just a.,** tu n'es pas n'importe qui; **a. with any sense,** quiconque a un peu de bon sens; **bring along a. you like,** amenez qui vous voudrez; **I challenge a. to ...,** je défie qui que ce soit de ...; **I haven't met a. else,** je n'ai rencontré personne d'autre; *Sp* **it's anybody's match,** n'importe qui peut gagner *ou* remporter la victoire; **it's a.'s guess!,** qui sait?; *Hum F* **one drink and he's a.'s,** un verre et il est l'homme de tout le monde;

(d) *F* (*person with status*) **is he anybody?,** est-il quelqu'un?; **he never will be anybody,** ce sera toujours une nullité.

anyhow ['enɪhaʊ] *adv* **(a)** *F* (*carelessly*) **to do sth (all) a.,**

faire qch n'importe comment *ou* tant bien que mal, faire qch d'une manière quelconque; **the clothes had been thrown on the bed a.,** les vêtements avaient été jetés n'importe comment sur le lit; **the room looks all a.,** la pièce est en désordre *ou* en pagaille; **(b)** *(anyway)* en tout cas, de toute façon; **a. it's too late,** en tout cas il est trop tard; **a. you can always try,** vous pouvez toujours essayer.

anyone *see* **ANYBODY**.

anyplace ['enɪpleɪs] *adv Am F* = **ANYWHERE**.

anything ['enɪθɪŋ] **1** *pron* **(a)** quelque chose; *(with implied negation)* rien; **can I do a. for you?,** est-ce que je peux vous aider?; **is there a. I can do (to help)?,** puis-je faire quelque chose?; **have you a. to write with?,** avez-vous de quoi écrire?; **is there a. more pleasant than ...?,** est-il rien de plus agréable que ...?; **will there be a. else, madam?,** *(in shop)* vous désirez autre chose, madame?, et avec cela, madame?; **a. bigger than that won't go through a letterbox,** quelque chose de plus volumineux que ça ne passera pas par une boîte aux lettres; **have you a. smaller?,** *(in different size)* est-ce que vous avez la taille en-dessous?; *(money)* avez-vous de la monnaie?; **if a. should happen to me,** s'il m'arrivait quelque chose; **do you see a. of your friend?,** voyez-vous quelquefois votre ami?; **is (there) a. the matter?,** y a-t-il quelque chose qui ne marche pas?;

(b) *(in neg sentences)* **not a.,** ne ... rien; **he doesn't do a.,** il ne fait rien; **I shan't give you a. at all,** je ne vous donnerai rien du tout; **hardly a.,** presque rien; **it doesn't mean a.,** cela ne veut rien dire;

(c) *(no matter what)* n'importe quoi; tout; **he eats a.,** il mange de tout; **a. you like,** tout ce que vous voudrez; **a. will do,** n'importe quoi fera l'affaire; **I love a. French,** j'aime tout ce qui est français; **he would do a. for me,** il ferait tout pour moi; **I would have given a. not to go,** j'aurais tout donné pour ne pas y aller; **he's a. but mad,** il est loin d'être fou; **he's not mad, a. but,** il n'est pas fou, loin de là;

(d) *(adv phrase, intensive) F* **to work like a.,** travailler comme un fou; **it's raining like a.,** il pleut à torrents; **as easy as a.,** facile comme tout.

2 *adv* **she doesn't look a. like her sister,** elle ne ressemble en rien à sa sœur; **is it a. like Chinese food?,** est-ce que ça ressemble un tant soit peu à de la cuisine chinoise?; **it didn't cost a. like £500,** ça a été loin de coûter 500 livres; **the weather wasn't a. like as bad as I'd expected,** le temps a été loin d'être aussi mauvais que ce à quoi je m'étais attendu; **if the food's a. like as good as it was at the last party,** si la nourriture est ne serait-ce qu'aussi bonne qu'à la soirée précédente.

anyway ['enɪweɪ] *adv* = **ANYHOW (b)**.

anywhere ['enɪweər] *adv* **(a)** *(no matter where)* n'importe où; **put it a.,** mettez-le n'importe où; **I'd know him a.,** je le reconnaîtrais entre mille; **it's miles from a.,** c'est au bout du monde *ou* en plein bled; **a. else,** n'importe où ailleurs; **this could be a. in Europe,** ce pourrait être n'importe où en Europe; **has he a. near finished?,** est-il près d'avoir fini?; **(b) not a.,** nulle part, en aucun endroit, en aucun lieu; **I've never been a.,** je ne suis jamais allé nulle part; **you won't find a better curry a.,** vous ne trouverez de meilleur curry nulle part; **I can't find it a.,** je ne le trouve nulle part; *Fig* **we're not getting a.,** nous n'arrivons à rien; **(c)** *(somewhere)* quelque part; **can you see it a.?,** pouvez-vous le voir quelque part?; **have you found a. to live?,** avez-vous trouvé (quelque part) où vous loger?

AOCB [eɪəʊsiː'biː] *abbr* **any other competent business**.

aorta [eɪ'ɔːtə] *n Anat* aorte *f*.

aortic [eɪ'ɔːtɪk] *adj Anat Med (insuffisance etc)* aortique.

apace [ə'peɪs] *adv Arch & Lit* vite, rapidement.

Apache [ə'pætʃɪ] *n* Apache *mf*.

apart [ə'pɑːt] *adv* **(a)** *(at a distance)* **the garage stands a. from the house,** le garage est séparé de la maison; **to hold oneself** *or* **stand a.,** se tenir à l'écart (**from,** de); **the house was set a little way a. from the others,** la maison était un peu à l'écart des autres;

(b) *(separated)* **they are a mile a.,** ils sont à un mil(l)e l'un de l'autre; **lines 10 centimetres a.,** lignes espacées de 10 centimètres; **to stand with one's feet a.,** se tenir les jambes écartées; **they consider themselves in a class a.,** ils se considèrent au-dessus des autres; **place set a. for worship,** endroit destiné au culte; **towns as far a. as New York and Tokyo,** des villes aussi éloignées que New York et Tokyo; **children born two years a.,** des enfants nés à deux ans d'intervalle; **the boys and girls were kept a.,** on tenait séparés les garçons et les filles; **they're never a.,** ils ne se séparent jamais; **they're living a.,** *(because of enforced separation)* ils n'habitent pas ensemble; *(because of divorce, split-up)* ils sont séparés, ils vivent séparément; **it is difficult to tell them a.,** il est difficile de les distinguer l'un de l'autre; **this problem cannot be treated a.,** c'est un problème qu'on ne peut pas considérer séparément;

(c) *(to pieces)* **to take a machine a.,** démonter *ou* désassembler une machine; **my dress is coming a. at the seams,** ma robe commence à se découdre; *F* **to take a room a.,** fouiller une pièce à fond;

(d) joking a., plaisanterie à part;

(e) a. from, à part, sauf; **a. from the fact that ...,** indépendamment du fait que ..., outre (le fait) que ...; **a. from a few mistakes,** à part *ou* sauf quelques erreurs; **a. from him there is nobody who can do it,** à part lui personne ne peut le faire; **I don't know anyone a. from you,** je ne connais personne à part toi.

apartheid [ə'pɑːtaɪt, -heɪt] *n* apartheid *m*.

apartment [ə'pɑːtmənt] *n* **(a)** *Am* appartement *m*; **a. building,** immeuble *m* d'habitation; **(b)** *(room)* pièce *f*; *(luxurious)* salle *f*; *Arch* logement *m*; **state apartments,** grands appartements, salons *mpl* d'apparat; **(furnished) apartments to let,** chambres *fpl* (meublées) à louer.

apathetic [æpə'θetɪk] *adj* apathique, indifférent.

apathetically [æpə'θetɪklɪ] *adv* avec indifférence.

apathy ['æpəθɪ] *n* apathie *f*, indifférence *f*.

ape[1] [eɪp] *n* (grand) singe *m* (sans queue); **the higher apes,** les primates *mpl*; *F* **he's a big a.,** c'est une grande brute; *Sl* **to go a.,** *(become angry)* s'emballer; **to go a. over sth/s.o.,** *(enthuse about)* s'emballer pour qch/qn.

ape[2] *vt* singer *(qn)*.

apelike ['eɪplaɪk] *adj* comme un singe; *(visage)* simiesque.

Apennines (the) [ðiː'æpɪnaɪnz] *npl* les Apennins *mpl*.

aperient [ə'pɪərɪənt] *adj & n Med* laxatif *m*.

aperitif [əperɪ'tiːf] *n* apéritif *m*.

aperture ['æpətjʊər] *n* **(a)** *(opening)* ouverture *f*, orifice *f*; lumière *f (d'une pinnule etc)*; regard *m*, fenêtrelle *f (de fourneau etc)*; **(b)** *Phot* ouverture *f (d'un objectif, du diaphragme)*.

apex, *pl* **apexes, apices** ['eɪpeks, -ɪz, 'eɪpɪsiːz] *n* **(a)** sommet *m (d'un triangle, d'un édifice, d'une montagne)*; point culminant, apogée *m (d'une carrière)*; *Biol* pointe *f*, extrémité *f*; *Biol* sommet *(d'un organe etc)*; **(b)** *Anat* apex *m (du cœur)*; sommet *m (du poumon)*; *Astron* **a. of the sun's motion,** apex de la sphère céleste.

aphasia [ə'feɪzɪə] *n Med* aphasie *f*.

aphid ['eɪfɪd, 'æfɪd] *n (insect)* aphis *m*, puceron *m*.

aphis, *pl* **-ides** ['eɪfɪs, 'æfɪs, -ɪdiːz] *n (insect)* aphis *m*, puceron *m*; **woolly a.,** puceron lanigère.

aphorism ['æfərɪzəm] *n* aphorisme *m*.

aphrodisiac [æfrəʊ'dɪzɪæk] *adj & n* aphrodisiaque *m*.

apiarist ['eɪpɪərɪst] *n* apiculteur *m*.

apiary ['eɪpɪərɪ] *n* rucher *m*.

apiculture ['eɪpɪkʌltʃər] *n* apiculture *f*.

apiculturist [eɪpɪ'kʌltʃərɪst] *n* apiculteur *m*.

apiece [ə'piːs] *adv* chacun; **to cost ten pounds a.,** *(of things)* coûter dix livres (la) pièce; **he gave them five francs a.,** *(to each of them)* il leur donna cinq francs chacun.

aplenty [ə'plentɪ] *adv Am F* en abondance; **there were books a.,** il y avait énormément de livres.

aplomb [ə'plɒm] *n* aplomb *m*.

apocalypse [ə'pɒkəlɪps] *n Rel & Fig* apocalypse *f*; **the A. (of St John),** les Révélations *fpl* de saint Jean, l'Apocalypse; **the four horsemen of the A.,** les quatre cavaliers de l'Apocalypse.

apocalyptic [əpɒkə'lɪptɪk] *adj* apocalyptique.

Apocrypha (the) [ðɪə'pɒkrɪfə] *npl Bible* **(a)** les livres *mpl* deutérocanoniques; **(b)** *(not in Protestant Bible)* les apocryphes *mpl*.

apocryphal [ə'pɒkrɪfəl] *adj* apocryphe; **the story's a.,** je doute que l'histoire soit vraie.

apogee ['æpədʒiː] *n* apogée *m*.

apolitical [eɪpə'lɪtɪk(ə)l] *adj* apolitique.

Apollo [ə'pɒləʊ] *n Myth & Fig* Apollon *m*.

apologetic [əpɒlə'dʒetɪk] *adj* **(a)** *(tone, voice)* d'excuse; **to be very a.,** se confondre en excuses; **she was quite a. about it,** elle s'en est vivement excusée; **(b)** *(book etc)* apologétique.

apologetically [əpɒlə'dʒetɪklɪ] *adv* **(a)** *(in regret)* pour s'excuser, en s'excusant; **(b)** *(in defence)* sous forme d'apologie *ou* de justification.

apologize [ə'pɒlədʒaɪz] *vi* s'excuser; **to a. to s.o. for sth,** s'excuser de qch auprès de qn; faire *ou* présenter des excuses *ou* ses excuses à qn pour qch; **to a. for doing sth,**

s'excuser de faire qch; **I was wrong, I a.,** j'ai eu tort, excusez-moi; **I a. for having kept you waiting,** excusez-moi de vous avoir fait attendre; **I had to a. for you** *or* **your behaviour,** j'ai dû demander qu'on excuse ta conduite.

apology [ə'pɒlədʒɪ] *n* **(a)** excuses *fpl*; **letter of a.,** lettre *f* d'excuses; **to make/offer an a.,** faire/présenter des excuses; **to make/send one's apologies,** faire/envoyer ses excuses; **I owe you an a.,** je vous dois des excuses; *Fig* **an a. for a dinner,** un semblant de dîner; **(b)** *Lit* (*defence*) apologie *f*, justification *f*.

apoplectic [æpə'plektɪk] *adj* (*personne*) apoplectique; (*attaque*) d'apoplexie; **he had an a. fit** *or* **stroke,** il fut frappé d'apoplexie; *F* **she was a. when I told her,** elle a failli avoir une attaque quand je le lui ai dit.

apoplexy ['æpəpleksɪ] *n Med* apoplexie *f*.

apostasy [ə'pɒstəsɪ] *n* apostasie *f*.

apostate [ə'pɒstət] *adj & n* apostat, -ate.

apostatize [ə'pɒstətaɪz] *vi* apostasier (**from one's faith,** sa foi).

apostle [ə'pɒs(ə)l] *n* (*disciple*) *& Fig* apôtre *m*; **the Apostles' Creed,** le Symbole des Apôtres; **a. spoon,** cuiller *f* avec figurine d'apôtre.

apostolic(al) [æpɒs'tɒlɪk, -ɪk(ə)l] *adj Rel* (*bénédiction etc*) apostolique; **a. succession,** succession *f* apostolique.

apostrophe [ə'pɒstrəfɪ] *n Gram Liter* apostrophe *f*.

apostrophize [ə'pɒstrəfaɪz] *vt* **(a)** *Liter* apostropher (*qn*); **(b)** mettre un apostrophe à (*un mot*).

apothecary [ə'pɒθɪkərɪ] *n Arch* apothicaire *m*, pharmacien *m*.

apotheosis, *pl* **-oses** [əpɒθɪ'əʊsɪs, -'əʊsiːz] *n* apothéose *f*.

appal, *US* **appall** [ə'pɔːl] *vt* (*Br* **appals**, *US* **appalls**, *Br & US* **appalled**, **appalling**) consterner (*qn*); **it appals me that ...,** je suis consterné que ... .

Appalachian [æpə'leɪtʃɪən] *adj & n* **the A. Mountains, the Appalachians,** les (monts *mpl*) Appalaches *mpl*.

appalling [ə'pɔːlɪŋ] *adj* (*behaviour, conditions, smell etc*) épouvantable, effroyable; **a. negligence,** une négligence consternante; *F* **to make an a. row,** faire un bruit de tous les diables.

appallingly [ə'pɔːlɪŋlɪ] *adv* épouvantablement, effroyablement; **to behave a. to s.o.,** se conduire épouvantablement mal avec qn; *F* **he's a. stupid,** il est d'une stupidité extraordinaire.

apparatchik [æpæ'rɑːtʃɪk] *n Pol & Fig F* apparatchik *m*.

apparatus, *pl* **-uses** [æpə'reɪtəs, -əsɪz] *n* (*usu no pl*) appareil *m*, dispositif *m*, mécanisme *m*; **a piece of a.,** (*in laboratory*) un appareil; **laboratory a.,** appareils de laboratoire; *Gym* **a. work,** gymnastique *f* aux agrès; *Physiol* **the digestive a.,** l'appareil digestif; *Fig* **the a. of the state,** l'appareil de l'État; *Liter* **critical a., a. criticus,** appareil *ou* apparat *m* critique (*d'un texte*).

apparel [ə'pærəl] *n Arch & Lit Am* vêtement(s) *m(pl)*.

apparent [ə'pærənt] *adj* **(a)** (*clear, obvious*) apparent, manifeste, évident; **his indifference was a.,** son indifférence était manifeste; **the truth became a. to her,** la vérité lui apparut; **it was a. to me that ...,** il m'était évident que ...; **as will soon become a.,** comme on le verra bientôt; *Jur* **heir a.,** héritier présomptif; **(b)** (*seeming*) apparent; **in spite of his a. indifference,** malgré son air d'indifférence; *Econ* **a. consumption,** consommation apparente; *Astron* **a. diameter,** diamètre apparent.

apparently [ə'pærəntlɪ] *adv* apparemment; **he is a. going to Venice,** il paraît qu'il va aller à Venise; **a. not,** il paraît que non.

apparition [æpə'rɪʃən] *n* **(a)** (*ghost*) fantôme *m*, revenant *m*, apparition *f*; **(b)** (*act*) apparition *f*.

appeal¹ [ə'piːl] *n* **(a)** (*call*) appel *m* (**for,** à); recours *m* (*à l'arbitrage etc*); **the president's a. for calm,** l'appel au calme du président; **to make an a. to s.o.'s generosity,** faire appel à la générosité de qn;

(b) *Jur* appel *m*; **a. against a sentence,** appel d'une condamnation; **Court of A.,** cour *f* d'appel; **Supreme Court of A.,** cour de cassation; **without a.,** sans appel; **notice of a.,** intimation *f* (d'appel); **to lodge an a.,** se pourvoir en appel; **acquitted on a.,** acquitté en seconde instance; **military a. court,** conseil *m* de révision;

(c) (*for help*) prière *f*, supplication *f*; **with a look of a.,** d'un air suppliant;

(d) (*attraction*) attrait *m*, attraction *f*; **to have** *or* **hold little a. for s.o.,** ne guère attirer qn; **to have great a.,** (*of thing*) être très attrayant; (*of person*) avoir beaucoup de charme; **their music has a wide a.,** leur musique plaît à beaucoup de personnes différentes; *Com* **sales a.,** attraction commerciale.

appeal² *vi* **(a)** (*make a plea*) **to a. to s.o. for help,** demander de l'aide à qn; **to a. to s.o.'s generosity,** faire appel à la générosité de qn; **I a. to you to ...,** je vous supplie de ...;

(b) (*attract, interest*) attirer (*qn*); **to a. to s.o.'s imagination,** (*of thing*) attirer *ou* séduire *ou* charmer l'imagination; **the plan appeals to me,** le projet me sourit; **it doesn't a. to me,** cela ne me dit rien; **the idea did not a. to him,** l'idée ne l'enchantait guère; **to a. to the emotions/the senses,** faire appel aux sentiments/aux sens; **styles that a. to the young,** modes qui s'adressent aux jeunes;

(c) *Jur etc* interjeter appel; **to a. against a judgment,** appeler d'un jugement; **to a. to another court,** en appeler à un autre tribunal, introduire un recours devant un autre tribunal; **to a. against a decision,** réclamer contre une décision; *Jur* faire opposition à une décision; faire appel (à un tribunal) d'une décision.

appealing [ə'piːlɪŋ] *adj* **(a)** (*imploring*) (*regard, ton etc*) suppliant; **(b)** (*attractive*) (*sourire*) séduisant; (*personnalité*) sympathique; **there's something very a. about puppies,** il y a quelque chose de très attirant chez les chiots; **the idea wasn't very a.,** l'idée n'était pas très attirante.

appealingly [ə'piːlɪŋlɪ] *adv* (*see adj*) **(a)** (*to say*) d'un ton suppliant; (*to look*) d'un air suppliant; **(b) she smiles so a.,** elle a un sourire si sympathique *ou* si attrayant.

appear [ə'pɪər] *vi* **(a)** (*come into view*) paraître, apparaître; se montrer; **a head appeared at the window,** un visage s'est montré à la fenêtre; **a huge lorry suddenly appeared out of the fog,** un gros camion a surgi tout à coup du brouillard; *Lit* **she appeared to him in a dream,** elle lui est apparue en rêve; *F* **she appears at meal times,** elle apparaît au moment des repas; **where did you a. from?,** d'où est-ce que tu es sorti?; **to a. from nowhere,** apparaître de nulle part;

(b) *Jur* comparaître, paraître; **to a. before a court,** comparaître devant un tribunal; **to fail to a.,** faire défaut; **failure to a.,** défaut *m* de comparution; **to a. for s.o.,** représenter qn; (*of counsel*) plaider pour qn;

(c) *Th Cin* paraître; **to a. on the stage,** (*make entrance*) entrer en scène; (*act*) faire du théâtre; *F* **that was when I appeared on the scene,** c'est à ce moment que je suis arrivé;

(d) (*of book*) paraître; (*of newspaper*) sortir;

(e) (*seem*) paraître; **to a. sad,** paraître *ou* sembler triste, avoir l'air triste; **he appeared to hesitate,** il paraissait hésiter, il avait l'air d'hésiter; **she appears to have a lot of friends,** elle semble avoir beaucoup d'amis; **there appears to be a mistake,** il semble(rait) qu'il y ait erreur; **it appears not,** il paraît que non; **it appears to us that the situation is worse,** la situation nous semble pire; **to make it a. that ...,** prétendre que ...;

(f) (*become apparent*) **it appeared later that ...,** on a vu par la suite *ou* plus tard que ...; **as appears from these records,** comme il ressort de ces pièces.

appearance [ə'pɪərəns] *n* **(a)** (*arrival etc*) apparition *f*; entrée *f*; **they were startled by the a. of a teacher,** ils ont été surpris par l'arrivée d'un professeur; **with the a. of fast-food restaurants,** avec l'apparition des restaurants rapides; **to put in an a.,** se montrer;

(b) (*of actor*) entrée *f* en scène; (*of athlete*) entrée sur le terrain de jeu; *Th* **first a. of Miss Kane,** début *m* de Mlle Kane; **to make one's first a.,** débuter, faire ses débuts; **her Olympic a.,** sa participation aux Jeux Olympiques;

(c) *Jur* comparution *f* (*devant un tribunal*);

(d) parution *f* (*d'un livre*);

(e) (*looks, demeanour*) apparence *f*, aspect *m*, air *m*; **from his a. one would say ...,** à son air *ou* son extérieur on dirait ...; **you should not judge by appearances,** il ne faut pas juger selon les apparences; **his beard gave him the a. of a sailor,** avec sa barbe il avait l'air d'un marin; **they gave every a. of being bored,** ils ont donné tous les signes possibles de l'ennui; **an a. of gaiety,** un air de gaieté; **it is like a mushroom in a.,** ça ressemble à un champignon; **at first a.,** à première vue; **appearances are against him,** les apparences sont contre lui; **appearances can be deceptive,** les apparences peuvent être trompeuses; **to all appearance(s),** selon toute apparence, apparemment; **to keep up appearances,** sauver *ou* garder les apparences.

appease [ə'piːz] *vt* apaiser, calmer, tranquilliser (*qn*); apaiser, assouvir (*la faim, une passion*).

appeasement [ə'piːzmənt] *n* **(a)** (*of person*) apaisement *m*, adoucissement *m*; **policy of a.,** politique *f* d'apaisement *ou* de conciliation; **(b)** (*of hunger etc*) assouvissement *m*.

appellant [ə'pelənt] *adj & n Jur* appelant, -ante.
appellate [ə'pelət, -leɪt] *adj Jur* (*juridiction*) d'appel.
appellation [æpe'leɪʃən] *n Fml* appellation *f*, nom *m*.
append [ə'pend] *vt* **(a)** (*attach*) attacher, joindre (*qch*) (**to,** à); **to a. a document to a file,** annexer un document à un dossier; **(b)** (*in writing*) apposer (*sa signature*); ajouter (*des notes marginales*).
appendage [ə'pendɪdʒ] *n* **(a)** (*attachment*) accessoire *m*, apanage *m* (**to,** de); **(b)** *Anat Biol* appendice *m*; annexe *f* (*d'un organe*).
appendectomy [æpen'dektəmɪ], **appendicectomy** [əpendɪ'sektəmɪ] *n Surg* appendicectomie *f*.
appendicitis [əpendɪ'saɪtɪs] *n Med* appendicite *f*.
appendix, *pl* **-ixes, -ices** [ə'pendɪks, -ɪksɪz, -ɪsiːz] *n* **(a)** *Anat* appendice *m*; **to have one's a. (taken) out,** se faire enlever l'appendice; **have you had your a. out?,** tu as encore ton appendice?; *Med* **grumbling a.,** appendicite *f* chronique; **(b)** annexe *f* (*d'un rapport etc*); appendice *m* (*d'un livre*).
appertain [æpə'teɪn] *vi Admin & Lit* **(a)** (*belong*) appartenir (**to,** à); **lands appertaining to the Crown,** terres dépendant de la Couronne; **(b) duties appertaining to my office,** devoirs qui incombent à mes fonctions.
appetite ['æpɪtaɪt] *n* appétit *m* (**for,** pour); **to have a good a.,** avoir bon appétit; **to have a small** *or* **poor a.,** avoir un petit appétit, avoir peu d'appétit; **to have a big a.,** avoir un grand appétit; **to take away** *or* **spoil s.o.'s a.,** couper l'appétit *ou* la faim à qn; **to give s.o. an a., to whet s.o.'s a.,** mettre qn en appétit, donner de l'appétit à qn; **the walk gave him an a.,** la marche lui a ouvert l'appétit; *Fig* **the trip whetted his a. for travel/***etc*, cette excursion a aiguisé son goût des voyages/*etc*; **loss of a.,** manque *m* d'appétit; *Med* inappétence *f*; *Fig* **a. for revenge,** soif *f* de vengeance; *Fig* **she had an enormous a. for books,** elle avait une immense soif de lecture, elle était avide de lecture; *Fig* **to have little a. for a fight,** être peu enclin à une querelle *ou* à se disputer; **sexual a.,** appétit sexuel.
appetizer ['æpɪtaɪzər] *n* **(a)** (*snack*) amuse-gueule *m*, *pl* amuse-gueule(s); **(b)** *Old-fashioned* apéritif *m*.
appetizing ['æpɪtaɪzɪŋ] *adj* (*food*) appétissant, alléchant; (*smell*) alléchant; *Fig* (*water, suggestion etc*) alléchant.
appetizingly [æpɪ'taɪzɪŋlɪ] *adv* d'une façon appétissante.
applaud [ə'plɔːd] **1** *vt* **(a)** applaudir (*qn*); **to be applauded,** être applaudi; **(b)** *Fig* approuver (*une décision etc*); **to a. s.o.'s efforts,** applaudir aux efforts de qn. **2** *vi* (*of audience etc*) battre *ou* claquer des mains.
applause [ə'plɔːz] *n* **(a)** applaudissements *mpl*; **to meet** *or* **be greeted with a.,** être applaudi, soulever les applaudissements; **to win a.,** se faire applaudir (**from,** par, de); **(b)** *Fig* (*approval*) approbation *f*.
apple ['æp(ə)l] *n* pomme *f*; **eating** *or* **dessert a.,** pomme à couteau *ou* à dessert; **cooking a.,** pomme à cuire; **baked a.,** pomme cuite (au four); **stewed apples,** compote *f* de pommes, pommes en compote; *Prov* **an a. a day keeps the doctor away,** = une pomme par jour et vous êtes en bonne santé; *Fig* **he's** *or* **she's** *or* **it's** *etc* **the a. of his eye,** il en prend soin comme de la prunelle de ses yeux; *F* **the Big A.,** = la ville de New-York; **a. (tree),** pommier *m*; **a. brandy,** ≈ calvados *m*; **a. core,** trognon *m* de pomme; **a. green,** (*colour*) vert pomme *inv*; **a. juice,** jus *m* de pomme; **a. orchard,** pommeraie *f*; **a. pie,** (*without top crust*) tarte *f* aux pommes; (*with top crust*) tourte *f* aux pommes; **as American as a. pie,** typiquement américain; *Am F* **a. polisher,** lèche-bottes *m*; **a. sauce,** compote de pommes; **a. tart,** tarte aux pommes.
applecart ['æplkɑːt] *n* voiture *f* à bras (*de marchand des quatre saisons*); *F* **to upset the a.,** brouiller les cartes.
applejack ['æp(ə)ldʒæk] *n esp Am* ≈ calvados *m*.
apple-pie ['æp(ə)lpaɪ] *adj* **in a.-p. order,** admirablement rangé, en ordre parfait; *F* **a.-p. bed,** lit *m* en portefeuille.
appliance [ə'plaɪəns] *n* **(a)** (*machine*) appareil *m*, dispositif *m*; **mechanical a.,** engin *m* mécanique; **electrical/household appliances,** appareils électriques/ménagers; **(b)** (*fire engine*) autopompe *f*, pompe *f* à incendie; **(c)** (*accessory*) accessoire *m* (*d'une machine etc*).
applicable [ə'plɪkəb(ə)l, 'æplɪkəb(ə)l] *adj* applicable (**to,** à); **not a.,** (*on form*) sans rapport; **strike out where not a.,** rayer les mentions inutiles.
applicant ['æplɪkənt] *n* **(a)** candidat, -ate (*à un emploi*); demandeur *m* (*d'un brevet*); *Fin* **a. for shares,** souscripteur *m* d'actions; **(b)** *Jur* demandeur, -deresse, requérant, -ante.
application [æplɪ'keɪʃən] *n* **(a)** application *f*, applicage *m* (**of sth to sth,** de qch à, sur qch); apposition *f* (*d'une couche de vernis etc*); *MecE* **gradual a. of power,** entraînement progressif; **a. of the brake,** freinage *m*, serrage *m* du frein;

(b) (*thing applied*) application *f*; (*of paint*) enduit *m*;

(c) (*use*) application *f* (*d'une théorie, d'un principe, d'une découverte etc*); **practical applications of a process,** réalisations *fpl* d'un procédé; *Comptr* **a. program,** programme *m* d'application;

(d) (*assiduousness*) assiduité *f*, application *f* (*à l'étude etc*); esprit *m* de suite; **a. to a task,** application à un ouvrage;

(e) demande *f* (*d'emploi, de secours, de brevet*); **to make an a. for sth,** formuler une demande pour obtenir qch; **samples are sent on a.,** on envoie des échantillons sur demande; *Fin* **a. for shares,** demande de titres en souscription; **to make a. for shares,** souscrire (à) des actions; **a. form,** (*for job*) formulaire *m* de candidature; (*for shares*) bulletin *m* de souscription.
applicator ['æplɪkeɪtər] *n* (*for glue, eyeshadow etc*) applicateur *m*.
applied [ə'plaɪd] *adj* (*mathématiques etc*) appliqué; (*sciences*) expérimental, -als; **a. psychology,** psychotechnique *f*.
appliqué [æ'pliːkeɪ] *n Sewing* **(a)** (*decoration*) broderie *f* d'application; **(b)** (*technique*) applique *f*.
apply [ə'plaɪ] **1** *vt* **(a)** (*put on*) appliquer (*paint, lotion, bandage*) (**to,** sur); **to a. the brake,** freiner; (*to stationary vehicle*) serrer le frein; **to a. pressure,** (*to stop bleeding etc*) *& Fig* exercer une pression;

(b) (*use*) appliquer (*un système, une théorie etc*); mettre (*un système, une théorie etc*) en pratique; **to a. one's mind to sth,** appliquer son esprit à qch, s'appliquer à qch; **to a. oneself to one's work,** travailler avec application.

2 *vi* **(a) to a. to s.o. for sth,** s'adresser *ou* recourir *ou* avoir recours à qn pour obtenir qch; **to a. for a job,** poser sa candidature à un emploi, solliciter *ou* postuler un emploi; **to a. for a grant,** solliciter une bourse; **a. within,** s'adresser ici; *Fin* **to a. for shares,** souscrire (à) des actions;

(b) (*of law, rule, order*) s'appliquer (**to,** à); **that applies to all of you!,** (*what I've just said*) cela s'adresse à vous tous!
appoint [ə'pɔɪnt] *vt* **(a)** nommer (*un directeur, un comité etc*); constituer (*un comité*); désigner (*un expert*); instituer (*un héritier*); **to a. s.o. (to be) manager,** nommer qn directeur; **to a. s.o. to sth,** nommer qn à qch; **to a. s.o. to do sth,** désigner qn pour faire qch; **to a. s.o. to a post,** désigner qn pour *ou* à un poste; **newly appointed officials,** fonctionnaires entrants *ou* nouvellement nommés; **(b)** fixer, désigner (*l'heure, l'endroit*); arrêter (*un jour*); **(c)** *Jur* léguer, transmettre (*des biens*) avec faculté de distribution.
appointed [ə'pɔɪntɪd] *adj* **(a)** (*official*) nommé; (*agent*) attitré; **(b)** (*heure etc*) convenu, fixé; (*endroit*) convenu, dit; **on the a. day,** le jour convenu; **(c) well-a. house,** maison bien montée *ou* bien agencée *ou* bien installée.
appointee [əpɔɪn'tiː] *n* personne nommée.
appointment [ə'pɔɪntmənt] *n* **(a)** (*meeting*) rendez-vous *m*; (*for business*) entrevue *f*; *Admin* convocation *f*; **to make** *or* **fix an a. with s.o.,** (*for oneself*) donner rendez-vous à qn; (*for s.o. else*) fixer un rendez-vous avec qn; **I've made an a. with the doctor for you,** je t'ai pris un rendez-vous chez le docteur; **please telephone if you cannot make** *or* **keep your a.,** veuillez téléphoner s'il vous est impossible de venir; **she didn't keep our** *or* **the a.,** elle n'est pas venue; **I've got an a. with the doctor,** j'ai rendez-vous chez le médecin; (*announcing arrival to receptionist*) j'ai rendez-vous avec le médecin; **to meet s.o. by a.,** se rencontrer avec qn sur rendez-vous; **by a. only,** sur rendez-vous seulement; **have you an a.?,** avez-vous un rendez-vous?; *Admin* êtes-vous convoqué?;

(b) *Jur* **power of a.,** faculté *f* de distribution (de biens) (*accordée à un légataire*);

(c) nomination *f* (*de qn à un emploi*); *Admin* désignation *f* (*de qn pour un emploi*); *Mil Nau* affectation *f* (*de qn à un navire, une unité*); **by a. to His** *or* **Her Majesty,** (*of company, shop etc*) fournisseur breveté *ou* attitré de sa Majesté; *Journ* **appointments,** offres *fpl* d'emploi; **appointments board,** bureau *m* de placement; *Univ* département *m* d'information et de prospective;

(d) (*post*) place *f*, charge *f*, emploi *m*;

(e) appointments, (*of house*) aménagement *m*, installation *f*.
apportion [ə'pɔːʃən] *vt* répartir (*les frais*); lotir (*une propriété*); **to a. sth to s.o.,** assigner qch à qn; **to a. (out) a sum among several people,** partager *ou* distribuer une somme entre plusieurs personnes; **to a. blame,** répartir la

responsabilité *ou* les responsabilités.

apportionment [ə'pɔːʃənmənt] *n* partage *m*, répartition *f* (*d'impôts, de dépenses etc*); allocation *f* (*de vivres etc*); distribution *f* (*de parts, d'une propriété*); répartition *f* (*de blâme*).

apposite ['æpəzɪt] *adj* approprié (**to,** à); (*remarque*) fait à propos; (*observation*) juste.

apposition [æpə'zɪʃən] *n* **(a)** *Gram etc* apposition *f*; **words in a.,** mots apposés *ou* en apposition; **(b)** *Bot etc* apposition *f*.

appraisal [ə'preɪzəl] *n* évaluation *f*, estimation *f*, appréciation *f*; (*before auction*) prisée *f*; **official a.,** expertise *f*; **self a.,** autocritique *f*.

appraise [ə'preɪz] *vt* priser, estimer, évaluer (*qch*) (**at so much,** à tant); apprécier la valeur de (*qch*); faire l'expertise de (*les dégâts*); **with an appraising eye,** d'un œil critique.

appreciable [ə'priːʃɪəb(ə)l] *adj* (*différence etc*) appréciable; (*changement etc*) sensible; (*variation*) notable.

appreciably [ə'priːʃɪəblɪ] *adv* (*different*) à un degré appréciable; (*changed*) sensiblement.

appreciate [ə'priːʃɪeɪt, -sɪeɪt] **1** *vt* **(a)** (*know the value of, attach importance to*) apprécier, faire cas de (*qch, qn*); **she was never appreciated at her true worth,** elle n'a jamais été appréciée à sa juste valeur; **no one appreciates me,** personne ne m'apprécie à ma juste valeur;

(b) (*be grateful for*) être reconnaissant de, être sensible à; **I greatly a. your kindness,** je suis très sensible à votre gentillesse; **I a. your having done this,** je vous suis reconnaissant d'avoir fait cela; **I a. it,** j'en suis reconnaissant;

(c) (*grasp, understand*) comprendre, se rendre compte de (*qch*); **I fully a. (the fact) that ...,** je me rends bien compte que ...; **he doesn't a. his good fortune,** il ne se rend pas compte à quel point il a de la chance; **while I a. your predicament ...,** tout en comprenant bien votre situation difficile; **we a. the risks involved,** nous sommes conscients des risques que cela implique; **I hadn't appreciated that she was Spanish,** je n'avais pas réalisé qu'elle était espagnole;

(d) *Fin* hausser la valeur de (*qch*).

2 *vi* (*of goods etc*) prendre de la valeur; **the franc has appreciated in terms of other currencies,** le franc s'est apprécié par rapport aux autres monnaies.

appreciation [əpriːʃɪ'eɪʃən, əpriːsɪ-] *n* **(a)** (*evaluation*) appréciation *f*, estimation *f* (*de la valeur de qch*); **to give** *or* **write an a. of a new play,** faire la critique d'une nouvelle pièce; *Sch* **literary a.,** explication *f* de texte; **musical a.,** appréciation musicale;

(b) (*gratitude*) **I should like to express my a. of your kindness,** j'aimerais bien vous dire combien je suis sensible à votre gentillesse; **in a. of her years of loyal service,** pour témoigner de ma *ou* notre *ou* leur *etc* reconnaissance pour ses années de bons et loyaux services; **the audience showed the performers their a. by clapping,** le public a montré qu'il appréciait le spectacle en applaudissant; **he showed no a. of this honour,** il ne s'est pas du tout montré sensible de cet honneur;

(c) (*understanding*) compréhension *f*;

(d) *Fin* (*increase*) accroissement *m* *ou* hausse *f* de valeur; amélioration *f*, valorisation *f*, plus-value *f*, *pl* plus-values; **a. of assets,** plus-value d'actif.

appreciative [ə'priːʃɪətɪv, -sɪətɪv] *adj* **(a)** (*speech, words, review etc*) élogieux; **a few a. words,** quelques paroles élogieuses; **(b)** appréciateur, -trice; **to be a. of music,** apprécier la musique; **an a. audience,** (*liked the performance*) un bon public; (*knowledgeable*) un public capable d'apprécier; **she's a very a. sort of person,** c'est une personne qui sait faire preuve de gratitude; **I'm very a.,** j'en suis reconnaissant.

appreciatively [ə'priːʃɪətɪvlɪ] *adv* **(a)** favorablement; **(b) the audience listened a.,** les auditeurs ont écouté avec appréciation.

apprehend [æprɪ'hend] *vt* **(a)** *Jur* appréhender, arrêter (*qn*); **(b)** *Fml* (*understand*) comprendre (*des faits*); percevoir (*un son*); **(c)** *Arch & Lit* appréhender, craindre (*un danger etc*).

apprehension [æprɪ'henʃən] *n* **(a)** (*fear*) appréhension *f*, crainte *f*; **to give cause for a.,** motiver des craintes; **(b)** *Jur* arrestation *f*; **(c)** *Fml* (*understanding*) perception *f* (*d'un son etc*); compréhension *f* (*des faits*); *Psy* entendement *m*, appréhension *f*; **to be slow of a.,** avoir l'esprit lent.

apprehensive [æprɪ'hensɪv] *adj* (*look, smile etc*) timide, craintif; **to be a. for s.o./for s.o.'s safety,** craindre pour qn/pour la sûreté de qn; **to be a. about sth,** appréhender qch; **I'm feeling a bit a.,** j'appréhende.

apprehensively [æprɪ'hensɪvlɪ] *adv* avec appréhension.

apprentice¹ [ə'prentɪs] *n* apprenti, -ie; *Fig* débutant, -ante; **carpenter's/sorcerer's/***etc* **a.,** apprenti menuisier/sorcier/*etc*.

apprentice² *vt* **to a. s.o. to s.o.,** placer *ou* mettre qn en apprentissage chez qn.

apprenticed [ə'prentɪsd] *adj* en apprentissage (**to s.o.,** chez qn).

apprenticeship [ə'prentɪʃɪp] *n* apprentissage *m*; **to serve an a.,** faire un apprentissage; *Fig* **to serve one's a.,** faire ses débuts.

apprise [ə'praɪz] *vt Fml Lit* **to a. s.o. of sth,** apprendre qch à qn, prévenir *ou* informer qn de qch; **we were not apprised of his arrival,** nous n'avons pas été informés de son arrivée.

appro ['æprəʊ] *n Com F* **on a.,** à l'essai.

approach¹ [ə'prəʊtʃ] *n* **(a)** (*of person*) approche *f*; venue *f* (*du printemps*); approche(s) (*de la mort*); *Av* **a. end of runway,** entrée *f* de piste, seuil *m* de la piste; *Av* **a. aids,** moyens *mpl* d'approche; *Golf* **a. shot,** coup *m* d'approche;

(b) (*to question etc*) approche *f*; démarche *f*, manière *f* *ou* façon *f* d'aborder qch; (*method*) méthode *f*; **his a. to the problem,** sa méthode d'attaque du problème, la façon dont il aborde le problème; **let's try a different a.,** essayons une autre méthode; **I don't like his a.,** je n'aime pas sa façon de s'y prendre;

(c) (*to person*) avance *f*, ouverture *f*; (*for business purposes*) proposition *f*, ouverture;

(d) (*point of entry*) voie *f* d'accès; **the a. to a town,** les abords *mpl ou* les approches *fpl* d'une ville; **all approaches to the town have been sealed off,** tous les abords de la ville ont été bouclés; **a. to a harbour,** atterrage *m*, accès *m* d'un port;

(e) (*approximation*) rapprochement *m*; **it is the nearest a. to perfection,** c'est ce qui s'approche le plus de la perfection.

approach² **1** *vi* approcher, s'approcher; *Golf* jouer le coup d'approche; **Christmas is approaching,** Noël approche.

2 *vt* **(a)** (*get nearer to*) approcher (*qn*); approcher de (*un endroit*); **we are approaching London,** nous approchons de Londres; **I'm approaching forty-five,** je vais sur mes quarante-cinq ans; **the wind was approaching gale force,** le vent soufflait presque en tempête; **something approaching a feeling of relief,** un sentiment proche du soulagement;

(b) (*go up to*) s'approcher de, aborder, approcher (*qn*); (*of company, group, team etc*) pressentir, faire des propositions *ou* des ouvertures à (*qn*); **I was approached by a man in the street,** j'ai été abordé par un homme dans la rue; **to a. s.o. on the subject of ...,** approcher qn au sujet de ...; **to be easy/difficult to a.,** avoir l'abord facile/difficile;

(c) aborder, s'attaquer à (*une question*).

approachable [ə'prəʊtʃəb(ə)l] *adj* **(a)** (*person*) d'un abord facile: **(b)** (*building, place*) accessible, d'un accès facile, facile d'accès; **the town is not a. from the south,** on ne peut pas accéder à la ville par le sud.

approaching [ə'prəʊtʃɪŋ] *adj* (*death*) prochain; (*storm*) qui arrive; **the a. car,** la voiture qui vient *ou* venait en sens inverse.

approbation [æprə'beɪʃən] *n* approbation *f*, jugement *m* favorable; **smile of a.,** sourire approbateur.

appropriate¹ [ə'prəʊprɪət] *adj* (*suitable, fitting*) approprié (**to,** à); (*word, expression*) propre; (*time, clothes*) convenable (**to,** à); (*name, site*) bien choisi; (*music*) de circonstance; (*moment*) opportun; **to take a. action,** prendre les mesures indiquées; **it seemed a. that she should have died in the theatre,** cela semblait être dans l'ordre des choses qu'elle soit morte dans un théâtre.

appropriate² [ə'prəʊprɪeɪt] *vt* **(a)** (*take*) s'approprier (*qch*), s'emparer de (*qch*); (*keep for oneself*) s'attribuer, se destiner, se réserver (*qch*); **to a. s.o.'s ideas,** prendre *ou* dérober ses idées à qn; **(b)** (*set aside*) approprier, appliquer, affecter, consacrer (**sth to, for a purpose,** qch à une destination).

appropriately [ə'prəʊprɪətlɪ] *adv* (*suitably*) de manière appropriée; (*properly*) convenablement, proprement; **a. dressed,** en tenue convenable.

appropriateness [ə'prəʊprɪətnɪs] *n* convenance *f*, justesse *f*, à-propos *m*.

appropriation [əprəʊprɪ'eɪʃən] *n* **(a)** (*taking*) appropriation *f*, prise *f* de possession (**of,** de); **(b)** appropriation *f*, application *f*, affectation *f* (*de qch à un usage*); **(c)** *Fin* affectation *f* de fonds; attribution *f* (*d'une somme*); **(d)** *Pol* crédit *m* (budgétaire).

approval [ə'pruːv(ə)l] *n* **(a)** approbation *f*, agrément *m*; **to meet with s.o.'s a.**, recevoir *ou* obtenir l'approbation de qn; **gesture** *or* **sign of a.**, geste *m ou* signe *m* d'approbation; **to nod a.**, approuver d'un signe de (la) tête; *Com* **on a.**, à condition, à l'essai; **book sent on a.**, livre envoyé à l'examen; **(b)** *Admin* ratification *f*, homologation *f* (*d'un document*); **for (your) a.**, (*of draft letter*) pour approbation.

approve [ə'pruːv] **1** *vt* approuver, sanctionner (*une action*); ratifier, homologuer (*une décision*); agréer (*un contrat*); **read and approved**, lu et approuvé; **approved by the government**, agréé par l'Etat. **2** *vi* être d'accord.

▶**approve of** *vipo* approuver (*qch*); **I don't a. of your friends**, vos amis ne me plaisent pas; **to a. of s.o.'s choice**, applaudir au choix de qn; **I don't a. of the plan**, je ne suis pas d'accord avec ce projet; **she doesn't a. of them smoking**, elle n'est pas d'accord pour qu'ils fument.

approved [ə'pruːvd] *adj* approuvé, agréé; *Admin* **(officially) a.**, homologué; **a. stallion**, étalon autorisé; **a. dealer**, concessionnaire agréé; *Br Arch* **a. school**, école *f* pour les délinquants juvéniles.

approving [ə'pruːvɪŋ] *adj* (*look, smile*) approbateur, -trice.

approvingly [ə'pruːvɪŋlɪ] *adv* avec approbation; (*to look*) d'un air approbateur; (*to say*) d'un ton approbateur.

approx *abbr* **approximately**.

approximate[1] [ə'prɒksɪmɪt] *adj* **(a)** (*calcul etc*) approximatif, approché; **a. value**, valeur approximative; **(b)** *Biol Phys* rapproché, proche, voisin.

approximate[2] [ə'prɒksɪmeɪt] **1** *vt* **to a. a case to another**, rapprocher un cas d'un autre. **2** *vi* **to a. to the truth**, se rapprocher de la vérité.

approximately [ə'prɒksɪmətlɪ] *adv* approximativement, à peu près; **five miles are a. eight kilometres**, cinq mil(l)es valent à peu près huit kilomètres; **his income is a. £5000**, son revenu est d'environ cinq mille livres.

approximation [əprɒksɪ'meɪʃən] *n* approximation *f*; **this is only an a.**, ceci n'est qu'un chiffre approximatif.

appurtenance [ə'pɜːtɪnəns] *n* (*usu pl*) **appurtenances**, accessoires *mpl*; *Jur* **house with all its appurtenances**, immeuble avec ses appartenances et dépendances.

apricot ['eɪprɪkɒt] *n* **(a)** abricot *m*; (*tree*) abricotier *m*; **(b)** (*colour*) abricot *m inv*; **a. dress**, robe *f* (couleur) abricot.

April ['eɪprɪl] *n* avril *m*; **in A.**, en avril, au mois d'avril; **A. showers**, ≈ giboulées de mars; **A. Fool's Day**, le premier avril; **to make an A. fool of s.o.**, faire un poisson d'avril à qn; **A. fool!**, poisson d'avril!

a priori ['eɪpraɪ'ɔːraɪ, æprɪ'ɔːrɪ] *adv & adj* a priori.

apron ['eɪprən] *n* **(a)** (*clothing*) tablier *m*; *F* **to be tied to one's mother's a. strings**, être pendu aux jupons de sa mère; *Tech* **a. lathe**, tour *m* à tablier; *Th* **a. (stage)**, avant-scène *f*, *pl* avant-scènes; **(b)** *Av* aire *f* de manœuvre *ou* de stationnement; tablier *m*, aire en dur (*pour révision et réparation des avions*).

apropos ['æprəpəʊ] **1** *adj* (*remark*) à propos, opportun. **2** *prep* **it was mentioned a. (of) the holidays**, on en a parlé à propos des vacances.

apse [æps] *n* (*in church*) abside *f*.

apt [æpt] *adj* **(a)** (*mot*) juste, fin; (*expression*) heureux, qui convient; **(b) to be a. to do** (*of person, thing*) avoir tendance à faire; **(c)** (*élève etc*) intelligent, habile.

apt *Am abbr* **apartment**.

aptitude ['æptɪtjuːd] *n* aptitude *f* (**for**, à, pour); **to have an a. for studying**, avoir des dispositions pour les études; **to have no a. for French**, n'avoir aucune facilité pour le français; **to show great a.**, montrer de grandes dispositions; **a. test**, test *m* d'aptitude *ou* d'intelligence pratique.

aptly ['æptlɪ] *adv* avec justesse, à propos; **a. chosen name**, nom bien choisi.

aptness ['æptnɪs] *n* **(a)** justesse *f*, à-propos *m* (*d'une expression, d'une citation etc*); **(b)** (*of person, object*) tendance *f* (**to do sth**, à faire qch).

aqualung ['ækwəlʌŋ] *n* scaphandre *m* autonome.

aquamarine [ækwəmə'riːn] **1** *n Miner* aigue-marine *f*, *pl* aigues-marines. **2** *adj* (*dress etc*) bleu vert *inv*.

aquanaut ['ækwənɔːt] *n* aquanaute *mf*.

aquaplane[1] ['ækwəpleɪn] *n Sp* aquaplane *m*.

aquaplane[2] *vi* **(a)** *Sp* faire de l'aquaplane; **(b)** *Aut* faire de l'aquaplaning.

aquaplaning ['ækwəpleɪnɪŋ] *n* **(a)** *Sp* aquaplane *m*; **(b)** *Aut* aquaplaning *m*, effet *m* d'hydroglisseur.

aquarelle [ækwə'rel] *n Art* aquarelle *f*.

aquarium, *pl* **-iums, -ia** [ə'kweərɪəm, -ɪəmz, -ɪə] *n* aquarium *m*.

Aquarius [ə'kweərɪəs] *n Astron* le Verseau.

aquatic [ə'kwætɪk] *adj* (*plant etc*) aquatique; **a. display**, (*by dolphins etc*) numéro *m* aquatique; **a. sports**, sports *mpl* nautiques.

aquatics [ə'kwætɪks] *npl* sports *mpl* nautiques, nautisme *m*.

aquatint ['ækwətɪnt] *n* aquatinte *f*.

aqueduct ['ækwɪdʌkt] *n* aqueduc *m*.

aqueous ['eɪkwɪəs] *adj* aqueux; **a. humour**, humeur aqueuse (*de l'œil*); *Pharm* **a. solution**, soluté *m*.

aquilegia [ækwɪ'liːdʒɪə] *n* (*plant*) aquilégie *f*.

aquiline ['ækwɪlaɪn] *adj* aquilin; **a. nose**, nez aquilin *ou* busqué *ou* en bec d'aigle.

Aquinas [ə'kwaɪnəs] *adj* **Saint Thomas A.**, saint Thomas d'Aquin.

Arab ['ærəb] **1** *adj* **(a)** arabe; **the A. world**, le monde arabe; *Pol* **the A. League**, la Ligue arabe; **(b)** (*horse*) arabe. **2** *n* **(a)** (*person*) Arabe *mf*; **(b)** (*horse*) arabe *m*; **(c)** *Old-fashioned F* **street A.**, gamin *m* des rues.

arabesque [ærə'besk] **1** *adj Art* (*décoration*) arabesque, dans le style arabe. **2** *n* **(a)** (*usu pl*) *Art* arabesque(s) *f(pl)*; **(b)** (*in ballet*) arabesque *f*.

Arabia [ə'reɪbɪə] *n* Arabie *f*; **Saudi A.**, Arabie Saoudite *ou* Séoudite.

Arabian [ə'reɪbɪən] **1** *adj* arabique, arabe; **the A. Gulf**, le golfe Arabique; **the A. Peninsula**, la péninsule d'Arabie; **A. camel**, dromadaire *m*; *Liter* **the A. Nights**, les Mille et une Nuits. **2** *n* Arabe *mf* (*d'Arabie*).

Arabic ['ærəbɪk] **1** *adj* (*langue, littérature*) arabe; **A. scholar**, arabisant *m*; **A. numerals**, chiffres *mpl* arabes; **gum a.**, gomme *f* arabique. **2** *n Ling* arabe *m*.

Arabist ['ærəbɪst] *n* arabisant *m*.

arable ['ærəb(ə)l] *adj* (*terre*) arable.

arachnid [ə'ræknɪd] *n Zool* arachnide *m*.

Aramaic [ærə'meɪɪk] *adj & n Ling* araméen *m*.

arbiter ['ɑːbɪtər] *n* arbitre *m* (*de la mode etc*); **a. of taste**, arbitre des élégances.

arbitrage ['ɑːbɪtrɑːʒ] *n Fin St Exch* arbitrage *m*.

arbitrager ['ɑːbɪtrɑːʒər] *n Fin St Exch* arbitragiste *m*.

arbitrarily [ɑːbɪ'trɑːrɪlɪ] *adv* arbitrairement.

arbitrariness ['ɑːbɪtrərɪnɪs] *n* arbitraire *m* (*d'une décision etc*).

arbitrary ['ɑːbɪtrərɪ] *adj* (*décision etc*) arbitraire.

arbitrate ['ɑːbɪtreɪt] **1** *vt* arbitrer, juger, trancher (*un différend*). **2** *vi* arbitrer.

arbitration [ɑːbɪ'treɪʃən] *n* arbitrage *m*; **to refer a question to a.**, soumettre une question à un arbitrage; *Ind* **to go to a.**, (*of union*) soumettre un différend à l'arbitrage; (*of dispute*) être soumis à l'arbitrage; **a. court, court of a.**, tribunal arbitral; **a. clause**, clause *f* d'arbitrage.

arbitrator ['ɑːbɪtreɪtər] *n* médiateur, -trice; *Jur* arbitre *m*.

arbor[1] ['ɑːbər] *n MecE* arbre *m* (*de roue, de meule*); mandrin *m* (*de tour*); **a. shaft**, joint *m* de cardan; **cutter** *or* **milling a.**, mandrin de fraisage.

arbor[2] *n US* = **ARBOUR**.

arboreal [ɑː'bɔːrɪəl] *adj* **(a)** d'arbre(s); **(b)** (*animal*) arboricole; (*existence*) sur les arbres.

arboriculture ['ɑːbərɪkʌltʃər] *n* arboriculture *f*.

arbour, *US* **arbor** ['ɑːbər] *n* berceau *m* de verdure, charmille *f*; (*on trellis*) tonnelle *f*; **vine a.**, treille *f*.

arbutus [ɑː'bjuːtəs] *n* (*shrub*) arbousier *m*; *Am* **(trailing) a.**, épigée rampante.

arc[1] [ɑːk] *n Math etc* arc *m* (*de cercle etc*); **to describe an a.**, décrire un arc; *Mil* **a. of fire**, champ *m* de tir (*d'un canon etc*); *El* **electric a.**, arc électrique; **a. lamp** *or* **light**, lampe *f* à arc.

arc[2] *vi* (**arcing** ['ɑːkɪŋ]; **arced** [ɑːkt]) *El* faire jaillir un arc, amorcer l'arc; (*of dynamo, commutator*) cracher, projeter des étincelles.

▶**arc over** *vi* (*of dynamo etc*) = **ARC[2]**.

arcade [ɑː'keɪd] *n* **(a)** arcade(s) *f(pl)* (*en bord de rue*); (*for shopping*) galerie *f* (marchande); (*covered passageway*) passage *m* (couvert); **(b)** *Archit* **(blind) a.**, arcature *f*.

arcaded [ɑː'keɪdɪd] *adj* (*street*) bordé d'arcades.

Arcadia [ɑː'keɪdɪə] *n* Arcadie *f*.

Arcadian [ɑː'keɪdɪən] **1** *adj* arcadien. **2** *n* Arcadien, -ienne.

arch[1] [ɑːtʃ] *n* **(a)** *Archit Constr* voûte *f*, arc *m*; *Constr* arche *f* (*d'un pont, d'un viaduc*); voûte (*d'un fourneau*); **a. of a vault**, arceau *m*; **semicircular a.**, arc en plein cintre; **pointed** *or* **gothic a.**, arc brisé; **Tudor a.**, arc en carène; **a. stone**, voussoir *m*; **(b)** *Anat* arc *m* (*des sourcils etc*); arcade *f* (*orbitaire*); crosse *f* (*de l'aorte*); cambrure *f* (*du pied*); **a. support**, cambrure (*pour chaussures*); **to suffer**

from fallen arches, avoir les pieds plats.
arch² 1 *vt* voûter (*une porte, un passage*); arquer, courber (*le dos*); **the cat arches its back,** le chat fait le dos rond. 2 *vi* se voûter, former voûte, bomber.
arch³ *adj* espiègle, malicieux, coquin.
arch⁴ *adj & pref* archi-; grand; insigne; **a. enemy,** adversaire *m ou* ennemi *m* numéro un; **a. traitor,** traître *m* insigne, architraître *m*.
archaeological, *US* **archeological** [ɑːkɪə'lɒdʒɪk(ə)l] *adj* archéologique; **a. dig,** fouilles *fpl* archéologiques.
archaeologically, *US* **archeologically** [ɑːkɪə'lɒdʒɪklɪ] *adv* archéologiquement.
archaeologist, *US* **archeologist** [ɑːkɪ'ɒlədʒɪst] *n* archéologue *mf*.
archaeology, *US* **archeology** [ɑːkɪ'ɒlədʒɪ] *adj* archéologie *f*.
archaic [ɑː'keɪɪk] *adj* archaïque.
archaism ['ɑːkeɪɪz(ə)m] *n* archaïsme *m*.
archangel ['ɑːkeɪndʒ(ə)l] *n* archange *m*.
archbishop [ɑːtʃ'bɪʃəp] *n* archevêque *m*; **a.'s palace,** palais archiépiscopal.
archbishopric [ɑːtʃ'bɪʃəprɪk] *n* archevêché *m*.
archdeacon [ɑːtʃ'diːk(ə)n] *n* archidiacre *m*.
archdiocese [ɑːtʃ'daɪəsɪs, -siːz] *n Rel* archidiocèse *m*, archevêché *m*.
archduchess [ɑːtʃ'dʌtʃɪs] *n* archiduchesse *f*.
archduchy [ɑːtʃ'dʌtʃɪ] *n* archiduché *m*.
archduke [ɑːtʃ'djuːk] *n* archiduc *m*.
arched [ɑːtʃt] *adj* **(a)** *Archit* à arc, en voûte; **a. window,** (*semicircular*) fenêtre cintrée; (*pointed*) fenêtre en arc brisé; **(b)** (*nez etc*) arqué, busqué; (*pied*) cambré; **a. neck,** encolure rouée (*d'un cheval*).
archeological, archeologically *etc US* = **ARCHAEOLOGICAL, ARCHAEOLOGICALLY** *etc*.
archer ['ɑːtʃər] *n* **(a)** *Mil Sp* archer *m*; **(b)** *Astron* **the A.,** le Sagittaire.
archery ['ɑːtʃərɪ] *n* tir *m* à l'arc.
archetypal [ɑːkɪ'taɪp(ə)l] *adj* **the a. English village,** l'archétype du village anglais.
archetype ['ɑːkɪtaɪp] *n* archétype *m*.
archiepiscopal [ɑːkɪɪ'pɪskəp(ə)l] *adj* archiépiscopal, -aux.
Archimedes [ɑːkɪ'miːdiːz] *n* Archimède *m*; *Phys* **Archimedes' principle,** le principe d'Archimède; **Archimedes' screw,** vis *f* d'Archimède.
archipelago, *pl* **-o(e)s** [ɑːkɪ'peləgəʊ, -əʊz] *n Geog* archipel *m*.
architect ['ɑːkɪtekt] *n* architecte *m*; **naval a.,** ingénieur *m* des constructions navales *ou* du génie maritime; *Fig* **she was the a. of the policy,** c'est elle qui a élaboré la politique; *Lit* **to be the a. of one's fortunes,** être l'artisan de sa fortune.
architectural [ɑːkɪ'tektʃər(ə)l] *adj* architectural, -aux.
architecturally [ɑːkɪ'tektʃərəlɪ] *adv* au point de vue architecture.
architecture ['ɑːkɪtektʃər] *n* architecture *f*; *Comptr* architecture.
architrave ['ɑːkɪtreɪv] *n* **(a)** *Archit* architrave *f*; **(b)** *Constr* encadrement *m* (*d'une porte, d'une fenêtre*).
archive¹ ['ɑːkaɪv] *n* (*usu pl*) **archives,** archives *fpl*; *Br* **the National Film A.,** ≈ la Cinémathèque française; **we'll be showing film from the archives,** nous présenterons des extraits d'archives; **a. footage,** extraits *mpl* d'archives; **a. librarian,** archiviste *mf*.
archive² *vt* mettre (*qch*) aux archives.
archivist ['ɑːkɪvɪst] *n* archiviste *mf*.
archly ['ɑːtʃlɪ] *adv* d'un air espiègle *ou* malicieux.
archness ['ɑːtʃnɪs] *n* espièglerie *f*, malice *f*.
archway ['ɑːtʃweɪ] *n* (*corridor*) passage voûté; (*entry*) porte cintrée, voûte *f* d'entrée; (*opening*) arcade *f*.
arcing ['ɑːkɪŋ] *n El* amorçage *m* (*d'arc*); (*of dynamo*) crachement *m*.
arctic ['ɑːktɪk] 1 *adj* (*territoire, cercle, expédition etc*) arctique. 2 *n* **the A.,** l'Arctique *m*; **an expedition to the A.,** une expédition dans l'Arctique.
arc-weld [ɑːk'weld] *vt Tech* souder à l'arc (électrique).
arc-welding [ɑːk'weldɪŋ] *Tech n* soudure *f* à l'arc.
ardent ['ɑːd(ə)nt] *adj* **(a)** (*désir, amour*) passionné; (*admirer*) fervent; **I am an a. admirer of his acting,** j'admire énormément la façon dont il joue; **(b)** *Fml* (*chaleur*) ardent.
ardently ['ɑːd(ə)ntlɪ] *adv* ardemment, avec ardeur.
ardour, *US* **ardor** ['ɑːdər] *n* ardeur *f*.
arduous ['ɑːdjʊəs] *adj* (*sentier, travail*) ardu, pénible.
arduously ['ɑːdjʊəslɪ] *adv* péniblement.
arduousness ['ɑːdjʊəsnɪs] *n* difficulté *f*, dureté *f*.
are *see* **BE**.
area ['eərɪə] *n* **(a)** aire *f*, superficie *f* (*d'un cercle, d'un champ, d'une pièce etc*); surface *f* (*d'ailes, de voiture*); **the room has an a. of 24 square metres** *or* **is 24 square metres in a.,** la pièce a une superficie de 24 mètres carrés, la superficie de la pièce est de 24 mètres carrés; **surface a.,** surface *f*; *MecE etc* **bearing a.,** surface de contact; *Typ* **type a.,** justification *f*;
(b) (*region*) territoire *m*, région *f*; (*of town*) zone *f*, quartier *m*; périmètre *m* (*d'influence etc*); **houses were searched over a wide a.,** on a fouillé les maisons sur un large périmètre; **cotton (growing)/mining a.,** région du coton/minière; *Geog* **drainage** *or* **catchment a.,** aire *f* de drainage; **residential a.,** (*in town*) quartier résidentiel; **industrial/suburban a.,** zone industrielle/suburbaine; **customs a.,** territoire douanier; **currency a.,** zone monétaire; **the Manchester a.,** la région de Manchester; **the Greater London a.,** l'agglomération londonienne, le grand Londres; *Fig* **a. of knowledge,** domaine *m* de connaissance; **problem a.,** domaine problématique; **a. of agreement,** terrain *m* d'entente; *Econ* **economic a.,** secteur *m* économique; **growth a.,** secteur de croissance; *Mil etc* **forward a.,** zone de l'avant, zone avancée; **prohibited** *or* **restricted a.,** zone prohibée; *Comptr* **storage a.,** zone de mémoire; *Rad* **interference** *or* **mush a.,** zone de brouillage; *Anat* **areas of the brain,** territoires cérébraux; *Constr etc* **hard-surfaced a.,** aire en dur; *Av* **landing/servicing a.,** aire d'atterrissage/d'entretien; *Aut* **parking a.,** parking *m*; **service a.,** (*on motorway*) relais *m* d'autoroute; **play a.,** (*in park*) aire de jeu; **dining a.,** (*in living room*) coin *m* salle à manger; (*in kitchen*) coin-repas; *Opt* **light/dark a.,** plage lumineuse/sombre; **a. bombing,** bombardement *m* sur zone; **a. manager,** (*of company*) gestionnaire *mf* de région *ou* de secteur; *Am* **a. rug,** tapis *m*; *Can* carpette *f*;
(c) *Constr* (*also Am* **areaway** ['eərɪəweɪ]) cour *f* d'entrée en sous sol (*sur la rue*); **a. steps,** escalier *m* de service (*du sous-sol*).
areca ['ærɪkə] *n Bot* **a. nut,** noix *f* d'arec; **a. palm (tree),** aréquier *m*.
arena, *pl* **-as** [ə'riːnə, -əz] *n* (*bullring etc*) *& Fig* arène *f*; *Fig* champ *m* (*d'une activité etc*); *Fig* **the political a.,** la scène politique; **to enter the a.,** entrer dans l'arène.
aren't [ɑːnt] **(a)** = **are not,** *see* **BE; (b) a. I?,** = **am I not?,** *see* **BE**.
Argentina [ɑːdʒən'tiːnə] *n* Argentine *f*.
Argentine ['ɑːdʒəntaɪn] *adj & n* **the A. Republic, the A.,** la République argentine, l'Argentine *f*.
Argentinian [ɑːdʒən'tɪnɪən] 1 *adj* argentin. 2 *n* Argentin, -ine.
argon ['ɑːgɒn] *n Ch* argon *m*.
Argonaut ['ɑːgənɔːt] *n* **(a)** *Myth* Argonaute *m*; **(b)** (*mollusc*) **a.,** voilier *m*, argonaute *m*.
arguable ['ɑːgjʊəb(ə)l] *adj* discutable, soutenable, défendable; **that's a.,** c'est discutable; **it is a. that they didn't need our help,** on peut soutenir qu'ils n'auraient pas eu besoin de notre aide.
arguably ['ɑːgjʊəblɪ] *adv* **it's a. the city's best restaurant,** on peut soutenir que c'est le meilleur restaurant de la ville.
argue ['ɑːgjuː] 1 *vt* **(a)** (*debate*) discuter, débattre (*une question*); **she argued the case well,** elle a bien débattu la question; **(b)** (*put a case*) soutenir, maintenir; **she argued that it was impossible,** elle a soutenu *ou* maintenu que c'était impossible. 2 *vi* **(a)** discuter, raisonner (**with s.o. about sth,** avec qn sur qch); (*quarrel*) se disputer (**with s.o. about sth,** avec qn à propos de qch); **to a. about politics,** discuter (de) politique; **those two are always arguing,** ces deux-là sont toujours à se disputer; **he's always arguing,** c'est un argumentateur; **don't a.!,** pas de discussion!; **(b)** (*put a case*) argumenter, plaider; **all this argues in his favour,** tout ceci témoigne en sa faveur.
►**argue against** *vipo* argumenter *ou* plaider contre (*qch*).
►**argue away** 1 *vtsep* (*make disappear*) nier l'importance de (*qch*); **you can't a. the problem away,** tu ne peux pas liquider le problème. 2 *vi* (*argue continuously*) ne pas cesser de se disputer; **they've been arguing away all morning,** ils n'ont pas cessé de se disputer de toute la matinée.
►**argue for** *vipo* argumenter en faveur de (*qch*), plaider pour (*qch*).
►**argue out** *vtsep* (*settle by argument*) résoudre (*une question*) par le débat; **I'll leave you to a. it out between**

you, je vous laisse résoudre la question *ou* le problème.

arguing ['ɑːgjuːɪŋ] *n* argumentation *f*; *F* **and no a.!,** pas de discussion!

argument ['ɑːgjʊmənt] *n* **(a)** (*debate*) discussion *f*, débat *m*; (*quarrel*) dispute *f*; **to have an a. about sth,** (*debate*) discuter de *ou* sur qch; (*quarrel*) se disputer à propos de qch; **I had an a. with my husband,** je me suis disputée avec mon mari; **to get into an a.,** en arriver à se disputer (**with s.o.,** avec qn); **I got into an a. with a man on the bus,** je me suis disputé avec un type dans le bus; **he's always getting into arguments,** il est toujours à se disputer; **to get the best of an a.,** l'emporter dans une discussion; **to obey without a.,** obéir sans discussion;
(b) (*reasoning, case*) argument *m* (**for,** en faveur de; **against,** contre); **to follow s.o.'s (line of) a.,** suivre le raisonnement de qn; **that is another a. for dismissing him,** c'est une raison de plus pour le congédier; **let us suppose for a.'s sake that ...,** supposons à titre d'exemple que ... + *sub*;
(c) *Lit* argument *m* (*d'un ouvrage*).

argumentative [ɑːgjʊ'mentətɪv] *adj* (*person*) raisonneur, disposé à argumenter *ou* à disputailler; **don't be so a.,** arrête de raisonner.

Argy ['ɑːdʒɪ] *n Br Offensive Sl* Argentin *m*.

argy-bargy[1] ['ɑːdʒɪ'bɑːdʒɪ] *n F* chamaillerie *f*.

argy-bargy[2] *vi F* disputailler.

aria ['ɑːrɪə] *n Mus* aria *f*.

arid ['ærɪd] *adj* (*terre, sujet*) aride.

aridity [æ'rɪdɪtɪ] **, aridness** ['ærɪdnɪs] *n* aridité *f*.

Aries ['eəriːz] *n Astrol* le Bélier.

aright [ə'raɪt] *adv Arch & Lit* bien, juste.

arise [e'raɪz] *vi* (**arose** [ə'rəʊz]; **arisen** [ə'rɪz(ə)n]) **(a)** (*of thing*) s'élever, surgir, survenir, se produire; **a storm arose,** il survint une tempête; **if complications a.,** s'il survient des complications; **if the need arises,** si besoin est; **the question has not yet arisen,** la question ne s'est pas encore posée; **should the occasion a.,** (*if necessary*) le cas échéant; (*if possible*) si l'occasion se présente; **(b)** (*result*) émaner, provenir, résulter (**from,** de); **obligations that a. from a clause,** obligations qui émanent d'une clause; **(c)** *Lit* s'élever; **a prophet arose,** un prophète surgit *ou* se révéla; **a., Sir John!,** (*in knighthood ceremony*) relevez-vous Sir John; *Bible* **to a. from the dead,** ressusciter (des morts).

aristocracy [ærɪs'tɒkrəsɪ] *n* (*nobility*) aristocratie *f*; *Fig* **the a. of the fashion world,** le gratin de la mode.

aristocrat ['ærɪstəkræt, ə'rɪs-] *n* aristocrate *mf*.

aristocratic [ærɪstə'krætɪk] *adj* aristocratique.

aristocratically [ærɪstə'krætɪklɪ] *adv* aristocratiquement.

Aristotelian [ærɪstɒ'tiːlɪən] *adj Phil* aristotélicien.

Aristotle ['ærɪstɒt(ə)l] *n* Aristote *m*.

arithmetic [ə'rɪθmətɪk] *n* calcul *m*; (*science*) arithmétique *f*; **mental a.,** calcul mental, calcul de tête; *Sch* **a. book,** arithmétique *f*.

arithmetic(al) [ærɪθ'metɪk, -ɪk(ə)l] *adj* arithmétique.

arithmetically [ærɪθ'metɪklɪ] *adv* arithmétiquement.

Ariz *abbr* **Arizona.**

ark [ɑːk] *n* **(a)** arche *f*; **Noah's a.,** l'arche de Noé; *F* **it looked like it had come out of the a.,** il avait l'air vieux comme Hérode; **(b)** *Jewish Rel* **the A. of the Covenant,** l'Arche *f* d'alliance.

Ark *abbr* **Arkansas.**

arm[1] [ɑːm] *n* **(a)** (*limb*) bras *m* (*de personne, de vertébré, de brachiopode*); **upper a.,** haut *m* du bras, arrière-bras *m inv*; **to carry a child in one's arms,** porter un enfant dans ses bras; **to hold s.o. in one's arms,** (*briefly*) prendre qn dans ses bras; (*for some time*) tenir qn dans ses bras; **child** *or* **infant in arms,** enfant au berceau; **to carry sth under one's a.,** porter qch sous le bras; **to carry a basket over** *or* **on one's a.,** porter un panier au bras; **with a girl on his a.,** une fille à son bras; **to walk a. in a.,** marcher bras dessus bras dessous; **give me your a.,** donne-moi ton bras; **to hold out one's arms,** (*in front*) tendre les bras; (*to sides*) étendre les bras; **to receive s.o. with open arms,** recevoir qn à bras ouverts; **to keep s.o. at a.'s length,** tenir qn à distance;
(b) manche *f* (*de robe etc*); accoudoir *m* (*de fauteuil*); bras *m* (*de mer, d'un fleuve, de fauteuil, de levier*); fléau *m* (*de balance*); bras, patte *f* (*d'ancre*); branche *f* (*d'arbre, de tenailles*); potence *f* (*d'enseigne de boutique etc*); **(pick-up) a.,** (*on record player*) bras de lecture; *Fig* **the secular a.,** le bras séculier; *Fig* **the long a. of the law,** l'autorité de la loi; *F* le représentant de la loi.

arm[2] *n* (*weapon*) (*usu pl*) **arms,** arme *f*; **side arms,** armes blanches; **small arms,** armes portatives; **the arms race,** la course aux armements; **call to arms,** appel *m* aux armes; **nation in arms,** nation *f* en armes; **100,000 men under arms,** 100 000 hommes sous les drapeaux; **to take up arms,** prendre les armes, s'armer (**against,** contre); **to rise up in arms,** se dresser en armes (**against s.o./sth,** contre qn/qch); *Fig* **to be up in arms about sth,** être résolument contre qch; *Mil* **the profession of arms,** le métier *ou* la carrière des armes, le métier militaire; *Her* **arms,** armoiries *fpl*, armes; **the Fleet Air A.,** l'aéronavale *f*; **arms limitation talks,** négociations *fpl* pour la limitation des armements; **arms dealer,** trafiquant *m* d'armes; **arms manufacturer,** armurier *m*, fabricant *m* d'armes; **arms trade,** commerce *m* des armes *ou* d'armes.

arm[3] **1** *vt* **(a)** armer (*qn, un régiment, une place forte etc*); **to a. oneself with an umbrella,** s'armer *ou* se nantir d'un parapluie; *Lit* **to a. oneself with patience,** s'armer de patience; **(b)** armer (*une bombe, une fusée, une torpille, une mine*); **(c)** *Tech* armer (*un aimant, une poutre etc*); renforcer (*une poutre etc*). **2** *vi* s'armer, prendre les armes (**against s.o.,** contre qn); **the country was arming for war,** le pays s'armait pour la guerre.

armada [ɑːˈmɑːdə] *n Hist* armada *f*; *Fig* grande flotte de guerre; **air a.,** flotte aérienne.

armadillo [ɑːmə'dɪləʊ] *n* (*animal*) tatou *m*.

Armageddon [ɑːmə'ged(ə)n] *n Bible* Armageddon *m*.

armament ['ɑːməmənt] *n* **(a)** (*equipment*) armement *m*; (*of ship*) artillerie *f*, munitions *fpl* de guerre; **naval armaments,** armements navals; **(b)** armement *m* (*d'une troupe etc*); **(c)** (*force*) forces *fpl*, armée *f*; *Nau* flotte navale.

armature ['ɑːmətʃər] *n* **(a)** *Biol etc* armure *f*; **(b)** *El* induit *m* (*d'un condensateur, d'une dynamo*); armature *f* (*d'une magnéto, d'une petite dynamo*); **(c)** *Constr* armature *f* (*d'un édifice en ciment etc*); **(d)** *Art* armature *f*.

armband ['ɑːmbænd] *n* brassard *m*; (*for swimmer*) manchon *m*; **black a.,** brassard de deuil.

armchair ['ɑːmtʃeər] *n* fauteuil *m*; **a. strategist/traveller,** stratège *m*/voyageur *m* en chambre.

armed [ɑːmd] *adj* **(a)** (*person, conflict, neutrality*) armé; **a. to the teeth/with a gun,** armé jusqu'aux dents/d'un fusil; **to offer a. resistance,** résister par les armes, se défendre les armes à la main; *Mil* **a. forces,** forces armées; **a. truce,** suspension *f* d'armes; **a. warfare,** guerre *f* par les armes; **(b)** (*bomb, fuse, torpedo, mine etc*) armé; **(c)** *Tech* (*beam, magnet etc*) armé.

Armenia [ɑː'miːnɪə] *n* Arménie *f*.

Armenian [ɑː'miːnɪən] **1** *adj* arménien. **2** *n* **(a)** Arménien, -ienne; **(b)** *Ling* arménien *m*.

armful ['ɑːmfʊl] *n* brassée *f*; **to bring armfuls of flowers** *or* **flowers by the a.,** apporter des fleurs à pleins bras, apporter des brassées de fleurs.

armhole ['ɑːmhəʊl] *n Sewing* emmanchure *f*.

armistice ['ɑːmɪstɪs] *n* armistice *m*; **A. day,** l'anniversaire *m* de l'Armistice (de 1918).

armless ['ɑːmlɪs] *adj* sans bras.

armlet ['ɑːmlɪt] *n* **(a)** bracelet *m* (*porté au-dessus du coude*); **(b)** (*armband*) brassard *m*.

armor *etc US* = **ARMOUR** *etc*.

armorial [ɑː'mɔːrɪəl] *adj* armorial, -aux; **a. bearings,** armoiries *fpl*.

armour[1], *US* **armor** [ɑːmər] *n* (*no pl*) **(a)** *Nau* cuirasse *f*, cuirassement *m*, blindage *m* (*d'un bâtiment*); *Mil* blindage (*d'un véhicule, d'un char de combat etc*); **a.-plated,** *Nau* cuirassé, blindé; *Mil* blindé; **a.-plating,** blindage; **a.-piercing,** (*obus*) perforant, de rupture; **(b)** *Mil* (*units, vehicles*) l'arme blindée, les blindés *mpl*; **(c)** *Tel* armure *f*, armature *f* (*de câble*); *El* blindage *m* (*d'un transformateur etc*); **(d)** *Hist* armure *f* (*de chevalier etc*); **suit of a.,** armure complète; **in full a.,** armé de pied en cap.

armour[2], *US* **armor** *vt* **(a)** *Nau* cuirasser (*un navire*); *Mil* blinder (*un train etc*); **(b)** *El* armer (*un câble*); blinder (*un transformateur*).

armoured, *US* **armored** ['ɑːməd] *adj* **(a)** *Nau* (*croiseur, pont*) cuirassé; *Mil* (*véhicule, train*) blindé; **a. troops,** *US* **a. corps,** les blindés *mpl*; **a. car,** *Mil* engin blindé de reconnaissance; (*used by police*) voiture blindée; (*for cash, gold etc*) fourgon *m* bancaire; **(b)** *Tech Tel* (*câble, tuyau*) armé; *El* (*transformateur*) blindé.

armourer, *US* **armorer** ['ɑːmərər] *n Ind Mil Nau* armurier *m*.

armoury, *US* **armory** ['ɑːmərɪ] *n* **(a)** (*store room*) magasin *m* d'armes; (*in barracks*) armurerie *f*; (*in museum etc*) salle *f* d'armes; **(b)** *US* (*factory*) fabrique *f* d'armes; (*workshop*) armurerie *f*.

armpit ['ɑːmpɪt] *n Anat* aisselle *f*.

armrest ['ɑːmrest] *n Aut etc* accoudoir *m*, appuie-bras *m inv*.

army ['ɑːmɪ] *n Mil* armée *f* (de terre); *Fig* armée (*de fourmis, de fonctionnaires etc*); foule *f*, multitude *f* (*d'hommes etc*); **to be in the a.**, être dans l'armée *ou* au régiment, être soldat *ou* militaire; **to go into** *or* **join the a.**, (*volunteer*) s'engager, s'enrôler, se faire soldat; (*be conscripted*) partir au régiment, entrer au service; **there was enough food for an a.**, il y avait assez de nourriture pour un régiment; **standing** *or* **regular a.**, armée permanente *ou* active; **professional a.**, armée de métier; **a. corps**, corps *m* d'armée; **A. List**, annuaire *m* militaire, cadres *mpl* de l'armée; **a. lorry**, camion *m* militaire; **the Salvation A.**, l'Armée du Salut.

arnica ['ɑːnɪkə] *n* **(a)** (*plant*) arnica *f*, arnique *f*; **(b)** *Pharm* (teinture *f* d')arnica *f*.

aroma [ə'rəʊmə] *n* arôme *m*.

aromatic [ærəʊ'mætɪk] **1** *adj* **(a)** (*herb*) aromatique; (*parfum*) balsamique; **(b)** *Ch* (*série, composé*) aromatique. **2** *n* **(a)** aromate *m*; **(b)** *Ch* **aromatics**, carbures *mpl* aromatiques *ou* à noyau.

around [ə'raʊnd] **1** *adv* **(a)** autour, à l'entour; **all a.**, tout autour, de tous côtés; **the woods (all) a.**, les bois d'alentour; **for miles a.**, sur (un rayon de) plusieurs kilomètres, sur des kilomètres; **people came from miles a.**, les gens sont venus de partout *ou* de très loin;

(b) (*in different directions, places*) **to walk a.**, marcher par-ci, par-là; **to run a.**, courir dans tous les sens; **to throw things a.**, jeter des choses par-ci, par-là; **swivel it a. a little**, fais-le pivoter un peu; *F* **he's now able to get a. again**, il est de nouveau sur pied; *F* **she's been a.**, (*is mature*) elle n'est pas née d'hier; (*sexually*) elle a de l'expérience;

(c) *F* (*in existence, in the area etc*) **this product has been a. for a long time**, ce produit est en circulation depuis longtemps; **I still see her a.**, il m'arrive encore de la voir; **are you a. this weekend?**, tu es là ce weekend?; **there aren't many good translators a.**, il n'y a pas beaucoup de bons traducteurs ces jours-ci; **is he still a.?**, (*in the area*) est-ce qu'il est encore dans les parages *ou* là?; (*alive*) est-ce qu'il est encore de ce monde?;

(d) (*in circular motion*) **to turn a.**, se retourner.

2 *prep* **(a)** autour de; **his arms were a. her neck**, il avait les bras autour de son cou; **she had her family a. her**, elle a été entourée de sa famille; **the people a. him**, les gens qui l'entourent; **we walked a. the lake**, nous avons fait le tour du lac en marchant; *Aut* **it's just a. the bend**, c'est juste au prochain virage;

(b) (*in different parts*) **to travel a. the country**, parcourir le pays; **there were books all a. the room**, il y avait des livres dans toute la pièce;

(c) (*in the region of*) environ; **at a. four o'clock**, sur les quatre heures; **it cost a. £200**, ça a coûté dans les 200 livres;

(d) (*near*) **somewhere a. here**, quelque part par ici.

arousal [ə'raʊz(ə)l] *n* (*from sleep*) éveil *m*, réveil *m*; (*from laziness*) sortie *f*; (*of interest, suspicion*) éveil; (*of anger*) éveil, soulèvement *m*; (*sexual*) excitation *f*.

arouse [ə'raʊz] *vt* (*wake*) réveiller, éveiller (*qn*); (*stir up*) secouer (*qn*) (*de sa paresse, de sa torpeur*); (*sexually*) exciter (*qn*); exciter, éveiller (*un sentiment*); soulever (*des passions*); piquer, éveiller, provoquer (*la jalousie*); chatouiller (*la curiosité*); éveiller (*des soupçons, l'intérêt de qn*); **they aroused her from her sleep**, ils l'ont réveillée; **the crowd was aroused**, la foule était animée.

arpeggio [ɑː'pedʒɪəʊ] *n Mus* arpège *m*.

arr (*abbr* **arrives**) arrive.

arrack ['ærək] *n* (*drink*) arac(k) *m*.

arraign [ə'reɪn] *vt* **(a)** *Jur* poursuivre (*qn*) en justice; **to a. s.o. before a court**, traduire qn en justice *ou* devant un tribunal; **(b)** (*accuse*) accuser, mettre en cause; *Lit* attaquer (*qn, une opinion*).

arraignment [ə'reɪnmənt] *n Jur* **(a)** (*of person*) mise *f* en accusation *ou* en jugement; **(b)** (*charges*) acte *m* d'accusation.

arrange [ə'reɪndʒ] **1** *vt* **(a)** (*put in an order*) disposer, mettre en ordre, ranger, arranger (*les meubles etc*); ordonner (*un cortège etc*); disposer (*des fleurs*); **the chairs were arranged in a circle**, les chaises étaient disposées en cercle; **to a. books in alphabetical order**, ranger des livres par ordre alphabétique;

(b) (*organize*) arranger (*un mariage etc*); organiser (*un concert etc*); **an arranged marriage**, un mariage de convenance; **everything is arranged**, tout est en ordre; **it was arranged that ...**, il fut convenu que ...; **try to a. it**, tâchez d'arranger la chose; **that can be arranged**, cela peut s'arranger; **a. it among yourselves**, arrangez cela entre vous, entendez-vous là-dessus; **the meeting arranged for tomorrow**, la réunion prévue pour demain; **I've got nothing arranged**, je n'ai rien de prévu;

(c) *Mus* **piece arranged for the piano**, morceau adapté *ou* arrangé pour piano.

2 *vi* (*organize*) **to a. to do sth**, (*make preparations*) s'arranger *ou* prendre ses dispositions pour faire qch; (*with s.o. else*) s'arranger avec qn pour faire qch, convenir de faire qch; **to a. for sth to be done**, prendre des dispositions *ou* des mesures pour que qch se fasse; **we arranged to meet**, nous avons prévu de nous rencontrer; **can you a. to have it finished by Friday?**, est-ce que vous pouvez vous arranger pour qu'il soit terminé vendredi?; **they arranged for a taxi to meet me**, ils ont pris des dispositions pour qu'un taxi m'attende.

arrangement [ə'reɪndʒmənt] *n* **(a)** arrangement *m*, disposition *f*, aménagement *m*, mise *f* en ordre (**of**, de); **to make arrangements**, prendre des dispositions *ou* des mesures, faire des préparatifs (**for sth/to do sth/for sth to be done**, pour qch/pour faire qch/pour que qch se fasse); **to make arrangements for a journey**, faire ses préparatifs pour un voyage; **I've made all the arrangements**, j'ai tout arrangé; **flower a.**, (*art*) l'art *m* de disposer les fleurs; (*example*) composition florale;

(b) (*agreement*) accord *m*, entente *f*; *Jur* transaction *f*; *Com etc* **to make an a.** *or* **to come to an a. with s.o.**, faire un arrangement *ou* prendre un arrangement avec qn; **to come to an a. with one's creditors**, parvenir à un accord avec ses créanciers; **the a. was that ...**, (*I or you etc would do*) on avait prévu que ...; **price by a.**, prix à débattre;

(c) *Mus* **a. for piano**, arrangement *m ou* adaptation *f* pour piano.

arranger [ə'reɪndʒər] *n esp Mus* arrangeur, -euse.

arrant ['ærənt] *adj* insigne; (*menteur etc*) fini.

array¹ [ə'reɪ] *n* **(a)** (*display*) étalage *m*; **a bewildering a. of salads**, une profusion stupéfiante de salades; **an imposing a. of tools**, un imposant déploiement d'outils; **(b)** *Mil* rangs *mpl*; **in close a.**, en rangs serrés; **in battle a.**, en ordre de bataille; **(c)** *Math* rangée *f*, tableau *m* (*de chiffres*); **(d)** *Lit* parure *f*, appareil *m*; **in rich a.**, paré de ses plus beaux atours.

array² *vt* **(a)** disposer, déployer (*des troupes etc*) (*en ordre de bataille*); **(b)** *Lit* revêtir, orner, parer (**s.o. in sth**, qn de qch).

arrears [ə'rɪəz] *npl* arriéré *m*, arrérages *mpl*; **I'm £100 in a.**, j'ai cent livres d'arriérés; **rent a.**, arriéré de loyer; **to let one's rent fall into a.**, être en retard pour payer son loyer; **to be in a. with the rent**, être en retard avec *ou* pour le loyer; **work in a.**, travail *m* en retard; **to be paid in a.**, être payé en retard; **I'm a month in a.**, j'ai (pris) un retard d'un mois, je suis en retard d'un mois.

arrest¹ [ə'rest] *n* **(a)** arrestation *f* (*d'un malfaiteur*); *Jur* prise *f* de corps; *Mil Nau* arrêts *mpl*; **under a.**, en état d'arrestation; *Mil Nau* aux arrêts; **warrant of a.**, **a. warrant**, mandat *m* d'arrêt; **several arrests were made**, plusieurs personnes ont été arrêtées; **to make an a.**, (*of police officer*) effectuer un arrêt; *Mil Nau* **open a.**, arrêts simples; *Mil Nau* **close a.**, arrêts forcés *ou* de rigueur; **house a.**, *Mil Nau* arrêts à la chambre; *Pol etc* résidence surveillée; **to be under house a.**, être assigné à la résidence; **(b)** (*of movement, progress etc*) arrêt *m*, suspension *f*; **cardiac a.**, arrêt du cœur; **(c)** *Jur* **a. of judgment**, sursis *m* à l'exécution d'un jugement.

arrest² *vt* **(a)** (*capture*) arrêter (*qn*), mettre (*qn*) en état d'arrestation; *Scot & Nau* saisir (*des biens mobiliers, un navire*); **the arresting officer**, le policier qui a effectué l'arrestation; **you are the arresting officer?**, c'est vous qui avez effectué l'arrestation?; **(b)** (*stop*) arrêter (*le mouvement, le progrès de qn, de qch*); **arrested growth**, arrêt *m* dans la croissance (*de qn*); arrêt dans le développement (*de qch*); *Jur* **to a. judgment**, suspendre l'exécution d'un jugement; **(c)** arrêter, fixer, retenir (*les regards*).

arrester [ə'restər] **(a)** *Tech* intercepteur *m*, séparateur *m*; **spark a.**, pare-étincelles *m inv*; **(b)** *Av* **a. gear**, (*on runway*) dispositif *m* d'arrêt; (*on carrier deck*) dispositif d'appontage.

arresting [ə'restɪŋ] **1** *adj* (*spectacle etc*) frappant, qui arrête l'attention. **2** *n* **(a)** *Jur* arrestation *f*; prise *f ou* appréhension *f* de corps; **(b)** *MecE etc* arrêt *m*; **a. device**, dispositif *m* d'arrêt.

arrhythmia [ə'rɪðmɪə] *n Med* arythmie *f*.

arris ['ærɪs] *n* arête vive (*d'un prisme, d'une cannelure*).

arrival [ə'raɪv(ə)l] *n* **(a)** arrivée *f*; *Com* arrivage *m* (*de marchandises*); *Nau* entrée *f* (*d'un navire*); débarquement *m* (*de passagers*); **port of a.,** port *m* d'arrivée; **on a.,** à l'arrivée (*de qn, de qch*); au débarquement (*de passagers*); **arrivals and departures,** arrivées et départs; **to await a.,** (*on letter*) ne pas faire suivre; **(b)** (*person*) arrivant, -ante; **a new a.,** un nouveau venu, une nouvelle venue; (*baby*) un nouveau-né; (*book*) une dernière parution; **late arrivals,** retardataires *mpl*.

arrive [ə'raɪv] *vi* **(a)** arriver (**at,** à; **in,** dans); **she has just arrived,** elle arrive à l'instant; **he is expected to a. next week,** on attend son arrivée pour la semaine prochaine; **as soon as he arrived,** dès son arrivée; **to a. unexpectedly,** survenir; **to a. at the age of sixty,** atteindre *ou* parvenir à *ou* arriver à l'âge de soixante ans; **to a. at a decision,** arriver à *ou* en venir à *ou* aboutir à une décision; **to a. at a price,** (*of seller*) calculer *ou* fixer un prix; (*of seller and buyer*) convenir d'un prix; **(b)** *F* (*achieve recognition*) réussir, arriver.

arrogance ['ærəgəns] *n* arrogance *f*.

arrogant ['ærəgənt] *adj* arrogant.

arrogantly ['ærəgəntlɪ] *adv* avec arrogance.

arrogate ['ærəgeɪt] *vt Lit & Jur* **(a)** (*appropriate*) **to a. sth to oneself,** s'arroger qch; **(b)** (*attribute*) attribuer injustement (*qch*) (**to s.o.,** à qn).

arrow¹ ['ærəʊ] *n* **(a)** (*missile*) flèche *f*; **to shoot** *or* **let fly an a.,** lancer *ou* décocher une flèche; **to fly straight as an a.,** voler droit comme une flèche; **as swift as an a.,** vif comme l'éclair; *Archit* **a. slit,** arch(i)ère *f*; **(b)** (*on sign etc*) flèche *f* (*indicatrice, de direction*); fiche *f* (*d'arpenteur*); zéro *m* (*d'un vernier*); *Comptr* **a. key,** touche *f* (avec) flèche.

arrow² *vt* marquer (*qch*) d'une flèche; flécher (*une route, une direction*).

►**arrow in** *vtsep* marquer (*une insertion*) d'une flèche.

arrowhead ['ærəʊhed] *n* **(a)** (*on missile*) tête *f ou* fer *m ou* pointe *f* de flèche; **(b)** (*plant*) fléchière *f*, sagittaire *f*, flèche *f* d'eau.

arrowroot ['ærəʊruːt] *n* **(a)** (*plant*) marante *f*; **(b)** *Culin* arrowroot *m*.

arse [ɑːs] *n Vulg* cul *m*, derrière *m*; **to talk out of one's a.,** raconter des conneries; **a. over tit** *or* **tip,** cul par-dessus tête; **to go a. over tip,** tomber à la renverse; **get your a. in gear!,** remuez-vous le cul!; **my a.!,** (*no way, don't believe you etc*) mon cul!

►**arse about** *vi Vulg* faire l'imbécile *ou* l'idiot.

arsehole ['ɑːshəʊl] *n Vulg* **(a)** *Anat* trou *m* du cul *ou* de balle; **(b)** *Fig* connard *m*; **don't be such an a.!,** arrête de faire *ou* de dire des conneries!

arsenal ['ɑːsən(ə)l] *n* arsenal *m*, -aux.

arsenic ['ɑːs(ə)nɪk] *n* arsenic *m*.

arson ['ɑːs(ə)n] *n* incendie *m* volontaire; *Jur* crime *m* d'incendie; **to commit a.,** provoquer (volontairement) un incendie; **police suspect a.,** la police suspecte un incendie criminel.

arsonist ['ɑːsənɪst] *n* incendiaire *mf*.

art¹ [ɑːt] *n* **(a)** art *m*; **the (fine) arts,** les beaux-arts *mpl*; **work of a.,** œuvre *m* d'art; **a. for a.'s sake,** l'art pour l'art; **arts and crafts,** artisanat *m* d'expression; *Sch* travaux manuels; **a. exhibition,** exposition *f* d'art; **a. gallery,** galerie *f*; **a. nouveau,** modern style *m*; **a. school,** école *f* des beaux-arts; **a. student,** élève *mf ou* étudiant, -ante d'une école des beaux-arts;

(b) *Univ* **arts,** lettres *fpl*; **faculty of arts,** faculté des lettres; **arts student,** étudiant, -ante en lettres; **bachelor of arts,** ≈ licencié, -ée ès lettres;

(c) (*technique*) **the a. of war,** l'art *m* militaire, l'art de la guerre; **the black a.,** la magie noire; *Boxing* **the noble a.,** le noble art, la boxe; **there's an a. to doing,** c'est tout un art que de (savoir) faire; **to get** *or* **have sth down to a fine a.,** maîtriser qch jusque dans les moindres détails; **she's got time-saving down to a fine a.,** elle excelle pour ce qui est de l'organisation; **a dying a.,** un art en voie de disparition;

(d) *Pej* stratagème *m*, ruse *f*.

art² *Arch & Bible see* **BE**; **thou a. good,** tu es bon.

artefact ['ɑːtɪfækt] *n* produit œuvré; *Archeol* objet façonné.

arterial [ɑː'tɪərɪəl] *adj Anat Med etc* (*sang etc*) artériel; **a. road,** grande voie de communication.

arteriosclerosis [ɑː'tɪərɪəʊsklə'rəʊsɪs] *n Med* artériosclérose *f*.

artery ['ɑːtərɪ] *n* **(a)** *Anat* artère *f*; **(b)** (*road, river etc*) artère *f*; **main arteries,** grandes voies de communication, grandes artères.

artesian [ɑː'tiːzɪən, -'tiːʒən] *adj* **a. well,** puits artésien.

artful ['ɑːtfʊl] *adj* **(a)** (*person*) rusé, astucieux, malin, *f* -igne; **a. as a monkey,** malin comme un singe; **(b)** (*thing*) ingénieux; **an a. dodge,** un truc ingénieux.

artfully ['ɑːtfʊlɪ] *adv* astucieusement.

artfulness ['ɑːtfʊlnɪs] *n* **(a)** (*of person*) astuce *f*; **(b)** (*of thing*) ingéniosité *f*.

arthritic [ɑː'θrɪtɪk] *adj & n Med* arthritique *mf*.

arthritis [ɑː'θraɪtɪs] *n Med* arthrite *f*; **rheumatoid a.,** rhumatisme articulaire.

arthropod ['ɑːθrəpɒd] *n Zool* arthropode *m*.

arthrosis [ɑː'θrəʊsɪs] *n Med* arthrose *f*.

Arthurian [ɑː'θjʊərɪən] *adj Liter Myth* (*cycle etc*) d'Arthur; (*roman*) arthurien.

artic ['ɑːtɪk] *n Br Sl* (*lorry*) semi-remorque *f*, *pl* semi-remorques.

artichoke ['ɑːtɪtʃəʊk] *n* artichaut *m*; *Culin* **a. hearts,** fonds *mpl ou* cœurs *mpl* d'artichaut; **Jerusalem a.,** topinambour *m*.

article¹ ['ɑːtɪk(ə)l] *n* **(a)** (*object*) article *m*, objet *m*; **a. of clothing,** vêtement *m*; **toilet articles,** produits *mpl* de toilette; **(b)** *Journ etc* article *m* (*de journal, de revue, d'encyclopédie*); **feature a.,** article d'intérêt général; **leading a.,** éditorial *m*, -aux; **(c)** *Com Jur* article *m*, clause *f* (*d'une convention, d'un traité*); **articles of apprenticeship,** contrat *m* d'apprentissage; **articles of war,** *Mil* code *m* (de justice) militaire; *Nau* code de justice maritime; *Nau* **ship's articles,** contrat *m* d'engagement, conditions *fpl* d'embarquement; **a. of faith,** article de foi; **(d)** *Gram* **definite/indefinite a.,** article défini/indéfini.

article² *vt* **to a. s.o. to an attorney/an architect,** placer qn (comme élève) chez un avoué/un architecte; **articled clerk,** clerc d'avoué lié par un contrat d'apprentissage.

articulate¹ [ɑː'tɪkjʊlət] *adj* **(a)** (*speech*) net, distinct; **to be a.,** (*of person*) s'exprimer facilement *ou* avec facilité; **the child gave a very a. account,** l'enfant a fait un compte rendu très clair; **(b)** *Zool* articulé.

articulate² [ɑː'tɪkjʊleɪt] **1** *vt* **(a)** (*pronounce clearly*) articuler (*un mot etc*); **he doesn't a. his words,** son énonciation est mauvaise; **(b)** (*express clearly*) exprimer (*ses pensées, une idée*) clairement. **2** *vi* **(a)** *Anat* articuler (*un squelette etc*); *Anat* s'articuler; **bone that articulates** *or* **is articulated with another,** os qui s'articule *ou* est articulé avec un autre; **(b)** (*in speaking*) articuler.

articulated [ɑː'tɪkjʊleɪtɪd] *adj* **(a)** *Aut* **a. vehicle,** semi-remorque *f*, *pl* semi-remorques; **(b)** *Biol Ling etc* articulé.

articulately [ɑː'tɪkjʊlətlɪ] *adv* **(a)** (*intelligently*) avec facilité; **(b)** (*clearly*) distinctement, nettement.

articulateness [ɑː'tɪkjʊlətnɪs] *n* **(a)** (*of writing, speech*) facilité *f* d'expression; **(b)** (*clarity of sound*) articulation nette, netteté *f* d'énonciation.

articulation [ɑːtɪkjʊ'leɪʃən] *n Biol Ling etc* articulation *f*; *Ling* **faulty a.,** défaut *m* de prononciation.

artifact ['ɑːtɪfækt] *n* = **ARTEFACT**.

artifice ['ɑːtɪfɪs] *n* **(a)** (*trick*) artifice *m*, ruse *f*; **a. of war,** ruse *ou* artifice de guerre; stratagème *m*; **(b)** (*skill*) art *m*, habileté *f*, adresse *f*.

artificial [ɑːtɪ'fɪʃəl] *adj* **(a)** artificiel; *Astron etc* **a. horizon,** horizon artificiel; **a. insemination,** insémination artificielle; **a. insemination by donor,** insémination artificielle avec sperme de donneur; *Comptr* **a. intelligence,** intelligence artificielle; *Comptr* **a. language,** langage artificiel; **a. limb,** prothèse *f* orthopédique; **a. manure,** engrais *mpl* chimiques; **a. respiration,** respiration artificielle; **to give s.o. a. respiration,** faire la respiration artificielle à qn; **a. wood,** similibois *m*; **(b)** (*behaviour, person*) affecté; (*style*) factice, recherché; **she is very a.,** elle manque de naturel.

artificiality [ɑːtɪfɪʃɪ'ælɪtɪ] **(a)** artificialité *f*, nature artificielle (*d'un produit etc*); **(b)** (*of behaviour, person*) caractère artificiel, manque *m* de naturel.

artificially [ɑːtɪ'fɪʃəlɪ] *adv* artificiellement.

artillery [ɑː'tɪlərɪ] *n* artillerie *f*; **field a.,** *Mil* artillerie de campagne; *Nau* artillerie de débarquement; **heavy/light a.,** artillerie lourde/légère; **naval a.,** artillerie navale; **anti-aircraft/anti-tank a.,** artillerie anti-aérienne/anti-chars; **a. fire,** tir *m* d'artillerie; **a. regiment,** régiment *m* d'artillerie.

artilleryman, *pl* **-men** [ɑː'tɪlərɪmən, -men] *n* artilleur *m*.

artisan [ɑːtɪ'zæn] *n* artisan *m*, ouvrier *m*.

artist ['ɑːtɪst] *n* (*actor, painter, singer*) artiste *mf*; **he is an a.,** (*painter*) il est artiste, il est peintre; **pavement a.,** barbouilleur, -euse de trottoir.

artiste [ɑː'tiːst] *n Th* artiste *mf*.

artistic [ɑː'tɪstɪk] *adj* (*style, goût, tempérament*) artiste; (*arrangement*) artistique; (*toilette*) de bon goût; **I'm not at**

all a., je n'ai aucune inclination artistique, je n'ai pas la fibre artistique.

artistically [ɑː'tɪstɪklɪ] *adv* artistement, avec art, artistiquement; **a. speaking,** du point de vue artistique.

artistry ['ɑːtɪstrɪ] *n* art *m* (*avec lequel qch a été ordonné ou truqué etc*).

artless ['ɑːtlɪs] *adj* **(a)** (*natural*) naturel, simple, sans artifice; **(b)** (*naive*) naïf, ingénu.

artlessly ['ɑːtlɪslɪ] *adv* (*see adj*) **(a)** naturellement, simplement, sans artifice; **(b)** naïvement, ingénument.

artlessness ['ɑːtlɪsnɪs] *n* **(a)** (*naturalness*) naturel *m*, simplicité *f*; **(b)** (*naivety*) naïveté *f*, ingénuité *f*.

artwork ['ɑːtwɜːk] *n Art* (*in book production*) (*illustrations*) illustrations *fpl*; (*layout*) mise *f* en page.

arty ['ɑːtɪ] *adj Pej* (*mobilier etc*) qui affiche des goûts artistiques, prétentieux.

arty-crafty ['ɑːtɪ'krɑːftɪ] *adj F* bohème, artiste.

arum ['eərəm] *n Bot* arum *m*; **a. lily,** calla *f*.

Aryan ['eərɪən] *Ling etc* **1** *adj* aryen. **2** *n* Aryen, -enne.

as [əz, *stressed* æz] **1** *adv* **(a)** aussi; **I am as tall as you,** je suis aussi grand que vous; **he's not as tall as you,** il n'est pas aussi *ou* si grand que vous; **I can do that as well as you,** je peux faire cela (tout) aussi bien que vous; **is it as high as that?,** est-ce si haut que ça?; *F* **he was as deaf as a post,** il était sourd comme un pot; **I worked as hard as I could,** j'ai travaillé autant que j'ai pu; **as much for your sake as for mine,** tant pour vous que pour moi; **as soon/as much as possible,** aussitôt/autant que possible;

(b) as for that, as to that, quant à cela, pour cela; **as for you,** quant à vous; **as for money, I can lend you some,** pour ce qui est de l'argent, je peux t'en prêter; **to question s.o. as to his** *or* **her motives,** interroger qn sur ses motifs;

(c) they rose as one man, ils se levèrent comme un seul homme; (*introducing a complement*) **to consider s.o. as a friend,** considérer qn comme un ami; **to treat s.o. as a stranger,** traiter qn en étranger; **to recognize s.o. as one's son,** reconnaître qn pour son fils; **she was often ill as a child,** enfant elle fut souvent malade; elle fut souvent malade dans son enfance; **to use sth as a flag,** se servir de qch comme *ou* en guise de drapeau; **to send sth as a present,** envoyer qch en *ou* comme cadeau; *Th* **Olivier as Hamlet,** Olivier dans le rôle de Hamlet; **to act as interpreter,** servir d'interprète; **I acted in my capacity as a magistrate,** j'ai agi en ma qualité de magistrat; **to be dressed as a boy,** être habillé en garçon; **as a very old friend of your father's,** en tant que vieil ami de votre père; **the novel as social history,** le roman comme histoire sociale; **my rights as a mother,** mes droits de mère; **as one doctor to another,** soit dit entre médecins; **as revenge for ...,** pour se venger de ...; *F* **the Apollo theatre as was,** (*it now has another name*) le théâtre de l'Apollo comme on l'appelait; (*it now has another function*) l'ancien théâtre de l'Apollo; **as it were,** pour ainsi dire.

2 *conj* **(a)** (*time*) **as I was opening the door,** comme j'ouvrais la porte, au moment où j'ouvrais la porte; **he went out (just) as I came in,** il est sorti comme *ou* au moment (même) où j'entrais; **one day as I was sitting ...,** un jour que j'étais assis ...; **she drew back as I advanced,** à mesure que j'avançais, elle reculait; **as and when required,** à discrétion; **as and when I want,** à mon bon plaisir;

(b) (*reason*) puisque, comme; **as he has now left,** puisqu'il *ou* comme il est maintenant parti;

(c) (*expressing degree*) que; (*in similes*) comme; **you are as tall as he is,** vous êtes aussi grand que lui; **you are not as** *or* **not so tall as he is,** vous n'êtes pas si *ou* aussi grand que lui; **I'm not as rich as I was,** je ne suis pas aussi riche que je l'ai été; **I came down as fast as I could,** je suis descendu aussi vite que possible; **he's not such a fool as he looks,** il n'est pas si bête qu'il en a l'air; **a house twice as large (as this),** une maison deux fois plus grande (que celle-ci); **to be as good as one's word,** tenir ses promesses; **by day as well as by night,** le jour comme la nuit, de jour comme de nuit; **as pale as death,** pâle comme un mort; **as white as a sheet,** blanc comme un linge; **it's as easy as anything,** c'est simple comme bonjour, c'est facile comme tout;

(d) (*concessive*) **ignorant as he is,** tout ignorant qu'il est; **much as I like her,** quelle que soit mon affection pour elle; **be that as it may,** quoi qu'il en soit; **covered with dust as he was, he didn't want to come in,** couvert qu'il était de poussière, il ne voulait pas entrer;

(e) (*manner*) comme; **do as you like,** faites comme vous voulez *ou* voudrez; **it happened as I told you,** cela s'est passé comme je vous l'ai dit; **as Mrs Smith remarked ...,** comme Mme Smith l'a fait remarquer ...; **as often happens,** comme il arrive souvent, ainsi qu'il arrive souvent; **leave it as it is,** laissez-le tel quel *ou* tel qu'il est; **as it is, we must ...,** les choses étant ainsi, il nous faut ...; **there are too many cars as it is,** il y a déjà trop de voitures; *Mil Gym* **as you were!,** revenez!, au temps!; **as a man lives, so he dies,** comme on a vécu, ainsi l'on meurt;

(f) (*result*) **he is not so foolish as to believe it,** il n'est pas assez stupide pour le croire; **put on your gloves so as to be ready,** mettez vos gants pour être prêt *ou* de manière à être prêt;

(g) mother is well, as are the children, maman va bien, de même que les enfants.

3 *pron* **beasts of prey, (such) as the lion or tiger,** les bêtes fauves, telles que *ou* comme le lion ou le tigre; **he was a foreigner, as they noticed from his pronunciation,** il était étranger, ce qui se remarquait à sa prononciation; *Eng Dial* **it was her as told me,** c'est elle qui me l'a dit.

asap [eɪesеɪ'piː, 'eɪzæp] (*abbr* **as soon as possible**) = le plus tôt possible.

asbestos [æs'bestəs] *n Miner* amiante *m*.

asbestosis [æsbes'təʊsɪs] *n Med* asbestose *f*.

ascend [ə'send] **1** *vi* monter; *Rel* **He ascended into Heaven,** Il monta aux Cieux. **2** *vt* **(a)** monter sur (*le trône*); **(b)** remonter (*un fleuve*).

ascendancy, -ency [ə'sendənsɪ] *n Lit* ascendant *m* (**over s.o.,** sur qn); **to gain the a. over s.o.,** prendre de l'ascendant sur qn.

ascendant, -ent [ə'sendənt] **1** *adj* **(a)** *Astron Math etc* ascendant; **a. star,** astre ascendant; **(b)** *Bot* (*tige*) montant. **2** *n* **(a)** *Astron* ascendant *m*; **to be in the a.,** être à l'ascendant; *Fig* avoir le dessus, s'affirmer; **his star is in the a.,** son étoile est à l'ascendant, son étoile grandit; **(b)** *Jur* ascendant *m*; **our ascendants and descendants,** nos ascendants et nos descendants.

ascending [ə'sendɪŋ] *adj* **(a)** *Astron Math etc* ascendant; *Met* (*courant*) ascendant; **in a. order,** en ordre croissant; **steeply a. path,** sentier *m* raide; *Jur* **a. line,** ascendance *f*, ligne ascendante; *Mus* **a. scale,** gamme ascendante *ou* montante; **a. series,** progression croissante; **(b)** *Bot* (*tige*) montant.

ascension [ə'senʃən] *n* ascension *f*; **A. Day,** jour *m ou* fête *f* de l'Ascension; **A. (Island),** (l'île *f* de l')Ascension *f*.

ascent [ə'sent] *n* **(a)** ascension *f* (*d'une montagne*); **first a.,** première *f*; **balloon a.,** ascension en ballon; **to make an a.,** faire une ascension; *Fig* **the a. of Napoleon,** l'ascension *ou* l'essor *m* de Napoléon; **(b)** *Tech* montée *f*, remontée *f* (*d'un piston etc*); **(c)** (*slope*) montée *f*, pente *f*; **steep a.,** montée raide; **(d)** *Jur* **line of a.,** ascendance *f*.

ascertain [æsə'teɪn] *vt* constater (*un fait*); s'assurer de, s'informer de (*la vérité de qch*); se rendre compte de (*sa position*); **to a. sth from s.o.,** s'informer de qch auprès de qn; **to a. that all danger is over,** s'assurer qu'il n'y a plus de danger.

ascertainment [æsə'teɪnmənt] *n* constatation *f* (*d'un fait*).

ascetic [ə'setɪk] **1** *adj* (*vie etc*) ascétique. **2** *n* ascète *mf*.

ascetically [ə'setɪklɪ] *adv* ascétiquement; (*vivre*) en ascète.

asceticism [ə'setɪsɪz(ə)m] *n* ascétisme *m*.

ASCII ['æskiː] *n Comptr* (*abbr* **American Standard Code for Information Interchange**) ASCII *m*; **ASCII code,** code *m* ASCII; **ASCII file,** fichier *m* ASCII.

ascorbic [əs'kɔːbɪk] *adj* (*acide etc*) ascorbique.

ascribable [ə'skraɪbəb(ə)l] *adj* attribuable, imputable (**to,** à).

ascribe [ə'skraɪb] *vt* attribuer, imputer (**to,** à); **to what do you a. your success?,** à quoi imputez-vous votre réussite?; **to a. a characteristic to s.o./a meaning to a word,** attribuer *ou* prêter un trait à qn/un sens à un mot.

ascription [ə'skrɪpʃən] *n Fml* attribution *f*, imputation *f* (**of sth to sth,** de qch à qch).

asdic ['æzdɪk] *n Nau* asdic *m*.

asepsis [eɪ'sepsɪs] *n Med* asepsie *f*.

aseptic [eɪ'septɪk] *adj & n Med* aseptique *m*.

asexual [eɪ'seksjʊəl] *adj Biol* asexué, asexuel; *Bot* (*fleur*) neutre; **a. reproduction,** reproduction asexuée.

ash¹ [æʃ] *n Bot* **a. (tree),** frêne *m*; **mountain a.,** sorbier commun *ou* sauvage *ou* des oiseaux *ou* des oiseleurs; **spade with an a. handle,** pelle *f* à la poignée en frêne.

ash² **1** *n* **(a)** cendre(s) *f(pl)*; *Ind etc* escarbilles *fpl*; **cigar a.,** cendre de cigare; **to reduce** *or* **burn sth to ashes,**

réduire qch en cendres; **volcanic a.,** cendres volcaniques; **a. cloud,** nuée *f* de cendres (*au-dessus d'un volcan*); *Lit* **to rake over the ashes of the past,** tisonner les cendres du passé; **to rise from the ashes,** renaître de ses cendres; *Rel* **A. Wednesday,** le mercredi des Cendres; **ashes,** cendres (*des morts*); **ashes to ashes, dust to dust,** (*from funeral service*) cendres aux cendres, poudre à la poudre; **a. heap,** crassier *m*; *Cr* **the Ashes,** = le trophée que les équipes anglaises et australiennes se disputent; **(b)** (*colour*) cendré *m*, gris cendré *m inv*. **2** *adj* (*colour*) gris cendré *inv*.

ashamed [əˈʃeɪmd] *adj* honteux, confus; **to be a. of s.o./sth,** avoir honte de qn/qch; **I am a. of you,** vous me faites honte; **to feel a.,** être couvert de confusion; **you make me feel a.,** (*of myself, you*) vous me faites honte; **I am a. to say that ...,** j'avoue à ma confusion que ...; **I'm not a. to admit it,** je le l'admets sans honte; **you ought to be a. of yourself,** vous devriez avoir honte *ou* être honteux; **there is nothing to be a. of,** il n'y a pas de quoi avoir honte.

ash-blond(e) [ˈæʃˈblɒnd] **1** *adj* (*colour*) blond cendré *inv*. **2** *n* (*person*) **she's an a.-b.,** elle a les cheveux blond cendré.

ashcan [ˈæʃkæn] *n Am* boîte *f* à ordures, poubelle *f*.

ashen¹ [ˈæʃən] *adj* de frêne, en frêne.

ashen² *adj* **(a)** *Lit* (*colour*) cendré; (*face*) pâle comme la mort; **his face turned a.,** il devint blême, son visage blémit; **(b)** (*pluie etc*) de cendres.

ashlar [ˈæʃlər] *n Constr Archit* **(a)** (*stone*) pierre *f* de taille; **(b)** parements *mpl*, revêtement *m* (*des murs d'un édifice*).

ashore [əˈʃɔːr] *adv Nau* **(a)** (*on land*) à terre; **to be a.,** être à terre; **to go a.,** aller *ou* descendre à terre, débarquer; **to set** *or* **put s.o. a.,** débarquer qn; **(b)** (*ship*) échoué; **to be driven a.,** être jeté à la côte; **to run a.,** s'échouer, faire côte.

ashpan [ˈæʃpæn] *n* cendrier *m* (*de poêle*); garde-cendres *m inv*.

ashtray [ˈæʃtreɪ] *n* cendrier *m*.

ashy [ˈæʃɪ] *adj* **(a)** cendreux, couvert de cendres; **(b)** (*colour*) cendré, couleur de la cendre.

Asia [ˈeɪʒə] *n* Asie *f*; **A. Minor,** Asie Mineure.

Asian [ˈeɪʒən] **1** *adj* asiatique, asiate; *Med* **A. flu,** grippe *f* asiatique. **2** *n* Asiatique *mf*.

Asiatic [eɪsɪˈætɪk] **1** *adj* asiatique. **2** *n* Asiatique *mf*.

aside [əˈsaɪd] **1** *adv* de côté, à l'écart, à part; **to pull a.,** écarter (*un rideau etc*); **to lay** *or* **put sth a.,** mettre qch de côté; **stand a.!,** écartez-vous!; **they just stood a. and watched,** ils sont juste restés sur le côté à regarder; **to turn a.,** se détourner **(from,** de); **I took** *or* **drew him a.,** je le pris à part *ou* à l'écart *ou* en particulier; **(leaving) politics a., I think ...,** la politique à part, je pense ...; *Th* **(words spoken) a.,** (paroles dites) en aparté. **2** *prep phrase esp Am* **a. from,** à part; (*except for*) excepté, sauf; **a. from my own interest,** mon propre intérêt à part; **a. from being frightened I was unhurt,** j'en ai été quitte pour la peur. **3** *n Th Fig* aparté *m*; **in an a. to a colleague,** à l'occasion d'un aparté avec un collaborateur.

asinine [ˈæsɪnaɪn] *adj* **(a)** (*stupid*) stupide, sot; **(b)** (*like an ass*) asinien.

ask [ɑːsk] *v* **(asked** [ɑːskt]**) 1** *vt* **(a)** demander; **to a. s.o. sth,** demander qch à qn; **a. him his name/how old he is,** demandez-lui son nom/son âge; **to a. the time,** demander l'heure; **to ask (s.o.) the way,** demander son chemin (à qn); **to a. s.o. a question,** poser une question à qn; **a. any questions you like,** posez toutes les questions que vous voulez; **it may be asked whether ...,** on peut se demander si ...; **I've often asked myself whether ...,** je me suis souvent demandé si, je me suis souvent posé la question si ...; *F* **if you a. me,** à mon avis;

(b) (*request*) demander; **to a. s.o. for sth,** demander qch à qn; **to a. a favour of s.o., to a. s.o. a favour,** demander une faveur à qn; **if it isn't asking too much,** si ce n'est pas trop vous demander; **to a. s.o.'s permission to do sth,** demander à qn la permission de faire qch; **to a. to do sth,** demander à faire qch, demander la permission *ou* l'autorisation de faire qch; **to a. to be excused,** s'excuser de partir; (*in class*) demander la permission de sortir; **to a. s.o. to do sth,** demander à qn *ou* prier qn *ou* solliciter qn de faire qch; **ask him to wait/to come in,** priez-le d'attendre/d'entrer;

(c) (*charge*) **to a. 600 francs for sth,** demander 600 francs pour *ou* de qch; **how much** *or* **what are you asking for it?,** combien en voulez-vous?;

(d) (*question*) interroger (*qn*) **(about,** sur); **he asked me all about my work,** il m'a interrogé longuement sur mon travail;

(e) (*invite*) inviter; **to a. s.o. to lunch,** inviter qn à déjeuner; **I have asked him to come for the weekend,** je l'ai invité à passer le week-end chez nous.

2 *vi* **(a)** (*inquire*) se renseigner **(about,** sur); **if you don't mind me** *or* **my asking,** si vous permettez de vous le demander; **the police were asking about you,** la police a posé des questions à votre sujet;

(b) to a. for s.o., demander à voir qn; **I asked for the manager,** j'ai demandé à parler au gérant; **to a. for sth,** demander qch; (*as a matter of urgency*) solliciter qch; **to a. for something to eat/to drink,** demander à manger/à boire; **to a. for more,** en redemander; **to a. for sth back,** (*that has been lent*) redemander qch; **when I want your opinion I'll a. for it,** lorsque j'aurai besoin de ton avis, je te le demanderai; **to be asking for trouble,** aller au-devant des ennuis; *F* **he's been asking for it!,** il l'a bien cherché!, il ne l'a pas volé!

►**ask after** *vipo* (*show concern for, ask for news of*) demander des nouvelles de (*qn, de la santé de qn*).

►**ask around** *vi* (*enquire*) demander autour de soi, se renseigner.

►**ask back** *vtsep* (*invite to one's home*) inviter à la maison; **do you want to a. them back for a drink after the theatre?,** tu veux les inviter à boire un verre à la maison après le théâtre?

►**ask for** *vipo* **(a)** *see* **ASK 2 (b)**; **(b)** *esp Scot* = **ASK AFTER**.

►**ask in** *vtsep* (*invite*) inviter à entrer; **I would a. you in for tea but ...,** je vous inviterais bien à (entrer) prendre le thé mais ... .

►**ask out** *vtsep* (*on a date etc*) inviter à sortir.

►**ask round** *vtsep* (*invite to one's home*) inviter; **why don't we a. them round for dinner one night?,** pourquoi ne pas les inviter à dîner un soir?

►**ask up** *vtsep* (*invite*) inviter à monter; **they asked us up to their flat,** ils nous ont invités à monter dans leur appartement *ou* chez eux.

askance [əˈskæns, -ɑːns] *adv* de côté, du coin de l'œil, obliquement; **to look a. at s.o./sth,** regarder qn/qch de travers *ou* avec méfiance.

askew [əˈskjuː] *adv* **(a)** de biais, de travers; (*mettre son chapeau*) de guingois; **(b)** (*to cut*) à fausse équerre.

asking [ˈɑːskɪŋ] *n* **(a) it's yours for the a.,** il n'y a qu'à (le) demander; **(b) a. price,** prix demandé.

aslant [əˈslɑːnt] **1** *adv* obliquement, de travers, de biais. **2** *prep* en travers de (*qch*).

asleep [əˈsliːp] *adv & adj* endormi; **to be a.,** dormir; **to be fast** *or* **sound a.,** être profondément endormi *ou* plongé dans le sommeil; **to fall a.,** s'endormir; **my foot is a.,** j'ai le pied engourdi.

ASLEF [ˈæzlef] *n abbr* **Associated Society of Locomotive Engineers and Firemen.**

ASM [eɪeˈsem] *n Mil abbr* **air-to-surface missile.**

asocial [eɪˈsəʊʃəl] *adj* asocial, -aux.

asp [æsp] *n* (*snake*) (vipère *f*) aspic *m*.

asparagus [əˈspærəgəs] *n* (*no pl*) *Culin* asperges *fpl*; **a stick of a.,** une asperge; **a. soup,** soupe *f* aux asperges; *Bot* **a. fern,** asparagus *m*.

aspect [ˈæspekt] *n* **(a)** (*of problem, subject etc*) aspect *m*; **(b)** (*appearance*) air *m* (*de qn, qch*); **man of serious a.,** homme à l'air sérieux; **(c)** (*outlook*) exposition *f*, orientation *f*; **to have a northern a.,** (*of house*) être exposé au nord; **flats with southern a.,** appartements côté midi; **(d)** *Astrol* aspect *m* (*des planètes*); **(e)** *Ling Gram* aspect *m*.

aspen [ˈæspən] *n* (*tree*) (peuplier *m*) tremble *m*; **a. leaf,** feuille *f* de tremble.

asperges [æˈspɜːdʒiːz] , **aspergillum** [æspəˈdʒɪləm] *n Rel* aspergès *m*, goupillon *m*.

asperity [æˈsperɪtɪ] *n* âpreté *f* (*d'un reproche, de la voix*); rigueur *f*, sévérité *f* (*du climat*); rudesse *f* (*de caractère*); aspérité *f* (*de style*).

aspersion [ˈəspɜːʃən] *n* **(a)** calomnie *f*; **to cast aspersions,** répandre des calomnies **(on s.o.,** sur qn); porter atteinte **(on s.o.'s honour,** à l'honneur de qn); **(b)** (*sprinkling*) aspersion *f*.

asphalt¹ [ˈæsfælt] *n Miner Constr* asphalte *m*; *F* bitume *m*; **a. roadway,** chaussée asphaltée.

asphalt² *vt Constr* asphalter, bitumer (*une route etc*).

asphalting [ˈæsfæltɪŋ] *n* asphaltage *m*, bitumage *m*.

asphyxia [æsˈfɪksɪə] *n* asphyxie *f*.

asphyxiate [æsˈfɪksɪeɪt] **1** *vt* asphyxier. **2** *vi* s'asphyxier.

asphyxiation [æsfɪksɪˈeɪʃən] *n* asphyxie *f*.

aspic [ˈæspɪk] *n Culin* aspic *m*; **eggs in a.,** œufs *mpl* en gelée.

aspidistra [æspɪˈdɪstrə] *n* (*plant*) aspidistra *m*.

aspirant [ˈæspɪrənt] *n* candidat, -ate.

aspirate¹ [ˈæspɪrət] *Ling* **1** *adj* aspiré. **2** *n* **(a)** (lettre *f*) aspirée *f*; **(b)** *(h)* (la lettre) h *f*.

aspirate² ['æspɪreɪt] *vt* **(a)** *Ling* aspirer *(une voyelle, l'h)*; **(b)** *Tech* aspirer *(un gaz, un liquide)*; **aspirating filter,** filtre *m* à vide.

aspiration [æspɪ'reɪʃən] *n* **(a)** *Ling Med etc* aspiration *f*; **(b)** *(ambition)* aspiration *f*.

aspirator ['æspɪreɪtər] *n Phys Med* aspirateur *m*.

aspire [ə'spaɪər] *vi* aspirer; **to a. to** *or* **after sth,** aspirer *ou* prétendre *ou* viser à qch, ambitionner qch; **to a. to do sth,** aspirer à *ou* ambitionner de faire qch; **they aspired to greatness,** ils aspiraient à la gloire.

aspirin ['æsprɪn] *n Pharm* **(a)** *(drug)* aspirine *f*; **(b)** *(pill)* comprimé *m* d'aspirine; **take two a.,** prenez deux aspirines.

aspiring [ə'spaɪərɪŋ] *adj* futur *(docteur, danseur, champion etc)*; *(docteur etc)* en herbe; **to be an a. artist/***etc*, avoir l'ambition de devenir artiste/*etc*.

ass¹ [æs] *n* **(a)** *(animal)* âne *m*; **she a.,** ânesse *f*; **a.'s milk,** lait *m* d'ânesse; **wild a.,** hémione *m*; onagre *m*; **(b)** *Old-fashioned (idiot)* âne *m*, idiot, -ote; **don't be a silly a.,** ne fais pas l'imbécile *ou* l'idiot; **to make an a. of oneself,** faire l'idiot *ou* l'imbécile; *(make an exhibition of oneself)* se donner en spectacle.

ass² *n US Vulg* cul *m*; **a nice piece of a.,** un beau cul.

▶ass about *vi F* faire l'imbécile *ou* l'idiot, faire des bêtises.

assail [ə'seɪl] *vt Arch & Lit* assaillir, attaquer *(l'ennemi)*; *Fig* **to a. s.o. with questions,** accabler *ou* assaillir qn de questions; **assailed with doubts,** saisi de doutes.

assailant [ə'seɪlənt] *n* assaillant, -ante, agresseur *m*.

assassin [ə'sæsɪn] *n* assassin *m (d'un homme d'État etc)*; *Hist* **Assassins,** Assassins, Ismaïliens *mpl*.

assassinate [ə'sæsɪneɪt] *vt* assassiner.

assassination [əsæsɪ'neɪʃən] *n* assassinat *m*; **a. attempt,** tentative *f* d'assassinat; **character a.,** assassinat moral.

assault¹ [ə'sɔːlt] *n* **(a)** *Jur* tentative *f* de voie de fait; **unprovoked a.,** agression *f*; **a. and battery,** (menaces *fpl* et) voies *fpl* de fait; coups *mpl* et blessures *fpl*; **criminal a.,** agression *f*; *(attempted rape)* tentative *f* de viol; *(rape)* viol *m*; **indecent a.,** attentat *m* à la pudeur; **(b)** *Mil* assaut *m*, attaque *f* (brusquée); **to take** *or* **carry a town by a.,** prendre une ville d'assaut; **a. craft,** engin *m* d'assaut; *Mil Fig* **a. course,** parcours *m* du combattant.

assault² *vt* **(a)** *(attack)* attaquer *(qn)*; *(sexually)* violenter *(une femme)*; **charged with assaulting s.o.,** accusé de s'être livré à des voies de fait sur qn; **to be assaulted,** *(attacked)* être victime d'une agression; *(sexually)* être victime d'un attentat à la pudeur; **(b)** *Mil* attaquer, assaillir *(une position)*; donner l'assaut à *(une ville etc)*.

assay¹ [ə'seɪ] *n Metal etc* essai *m (d'un métal précieux, d'un minerai)*; *Ch* dosage *m*; *Admin* **a. office,** bureau *m* de garantie *(des métaux précieux)*.

assay² *vt* **(a)** *Metal* essayer, titrer, analyser *(un métal précieux, un minerai)*; faire l'essai de *(un métal)*; coupeller *(l'or etc)*; **(b)** *Lit (attempt)* tenter.

assaying [ə'seɪɪŋ] *n Metal* essai *m*, titrage *m*, analyse *f (d'un minerai etc)*; coupellation *f (de l'or etc)*.

assemblage [ə'semblɪdʒ] *n* **(a)** *Tech* assemblage *m (de pièces de menuiserie etc)*; **(b)** collection *f (d'objets)*.

assemble [ə'semb(ə)l] **1** *vt* **(a)** rassembler *(des personnes)*; réunir *(des personnes, des papiers)*; ameuter *(des révoltés etc)*; convoquer *(un parlement)*; *Mil* rassembler *(des troupes)*; **he addressed the assembled schoolchildren,** il s'est adressé à l'ensemble des élèves réunis; **(b)** *Tech* assembler *(des pièces de menuiserie etc)*; ajuster, assembler, monter *(une machine)*; habiller *(une montre etc)*. **2** *vi (of people)* s'assembler, se rassembler, se réunir; *(of insurgents etc)* s'ameuter.

assembler [ə'semblər] *n Ind* monteur, -euse; *Comptr* assembleur *m*.

assembly [ə'semblɪ] *n* **(a)** *(gathering)* réunion *f*; *Br Sch etc* rassemblement *m*; **place of a.,** lieu *m* de réunion; *Jur* **unlawful a.,** attroupement *m*; **the right of a.,** droit *m* à la liberté de réunion; *Sch* **a. hall,** = hall où le rassemblement a lieu; **a. rooms,** salle *f* des fêtes, salle de danse; *Mil* **a. area,** zone *f* d'attente; **(b)** *Pol etc* assemblée *f*; **the National A.,** l'Assemblée nationale; **(c)** *Ind etc* montage *m*; **a. instructions,** instructions *fpl* de montage *ou* d'assemblage; **a. line,** chaîne *f* de montage; **to work on the a. line,** travailler à la chaîne; **a. shop** *or* **hall,** salle *f ou* atelier *m* de montage; *Comptr* **a. language,** langage assembleur; **(d)** *(group of components)* assemblage *m*.

assent¹ [ə'sent] *n* assentiment *m*, consentement *m*; *Jur* agrément *m*; **the royal a.,** le consentement du souverain; **by common a.,** du consentement de tous.

assent² *vi* accéder, acquiescer, donner son assentiment **(to,** à); **to a. to a bill,** *(of sovereign)* sanctionner une loi.

assert [ə'sɜːt] *vt* **(a)** revendiquer *(ses droits etc)*; **to a. one's claim to ...,** faire valoir ses droits à ...; **to a. oneself,** s'imposer; **you must a. your authority,** il vous faut imposer votre autorité; **(b)** protester de *(son innocence etc)*; affirmer, prétendre, soutenir **(that,** que).

assertion [ə'sɜːʃən] *n* **(a)** *(of right)* revendication *f*; **(b)** *(claim)* assertion *f*, affirmation *f*; **to make an a.,** affirmer qch; **her a. that she was there was unconvincing,** elle était peu convaincante lorsqu'elle affirmait qu'elle était là.

assertive [ə'sɜːtɪv] *adj (tone, manner etc)* autoritaire.

assertiveness [ə'sɜːtɪvnɪs] *n* assurance *f*; **a. training,** cours *m* pour prendre de l'assurance.

assess [ə'ses] *vt* **(a)** estimer *(la valeur de qch)*; juger de *(la qualité d'un produit)*; **to a. the damage,** évaluer les dégâts; *Nau* évaluer l'avarie; *Jur* **to a. the damages,** fixer les dommages et intérêts; *Admin* **to a. s.o. at so much,** imposer *ou* taxer qn à tant; **to a. a property (for taxation),** évaluer une propriété; **if we a. this speech at its true worth,** si nous estimons ce discours à sa juste valeur; **to a. the situation,** évaluer la situation; **how do you a. the team's chances?,** que pensez-vous des chances de l'équipe?; **(b)** répartir, établir *(un impôt)*.

assessment [ə'sesmənt] *n* **(a)** estimation *f (de la valeur de qch)*; évaluation *f (de dégâts, Nau d'avarie, Admin d'une propriété)*; *Jur* **a. of damages,** fixation *f* de dommages et intérêts; *Sch* **continuous a.,** contrôle continu; **they gave their a. of the situation,** ils ont donné leur avis sur la situation *ou* ont dit ce qu'ils pensaient de la situation; **(b)** *Admin* imposition *f (d'une commune, d'un immeuble)*; cotisation *f (du contribuable)*; *(amount)* cote *f*, taxe officielle; **basis of a.,** assiette *f* des impôts; **notice of a.,** avis *m* de contributions; **year of a.,** année *f* d'imposition; **a. on landed property,** cote foncière; **a. on income,** impôt *m* sur le revenu; **(c)** répartition *f*, assiette *f (d'un impôt)*.

assessor [ə'sesər] *n* **(a)** *(of tax)* répartiteur *m*; **(b)** *Jur* assesseur *m (adjoint à un juge)*, juge assesseur.

asset ['æset] *n* **(a)** *(advantage)* avantage *m*; **(b)** *Fin etc (usu pl)* **assets,** actif *m*, avoir(s) *m(pl)*; *Jur* masse *f (d'une succession, d'une société)*; masse active *(d'une liquidation après faillite)*; **a. stripper,** personne *f* qui achète une société pour profiter de la réalisation de l'actif; **a. stripping,** liquidation *f* des actifs; **capital assets,** actif immobilisé; **frozen assets,** fonds bloqués *ou* non liquides; **assets management,** gestion *f* des biens.

asseverate [ə'sevəreɪt] *vt Fml* affirmer (solennellement) **(that,** que); protester de *(son innocence)*.

asshole ['æshəʊl] *n US Vulg* **(a)** *Anat* trou *m* du cul; **(b)** *Fig* connard *m*.

assiduity [æsɪ'djuːɪtɪ] *n* assiduité *f*, diligence *f* **(in doing sth,** à faire qch).

assiduous [ə'sɪdjʊəs] *adj* assidu, diligent; *(work)* assidu.

assiduously [ə'sɪdjʊəslɪ] *adv* assidûment.

assign¹ [ə'saɪn] *n Jur* légataire *m*.

assign² *vt* **(a)** *(allocate)* assigner **(to,** à); *(share out)* donner *(qch)* en partage *(à qn)*; fixer, assigner *(une heure, un lieu)*; assigner, attribuer *(une fonction)* **(to s.o.,** à qn); **to a. s.o. to a task,** assigner une tâche à qn; **they had been assigned to guard duty,** on leur avait assigné la garde; **(b)** *(ascribe)* **to a. a reason for sth,** donner la raison de qch; **to a. a meaning to a word,** attribuer un sens à un mot; **(c)** *Jur* céder, transférer *(une propriété)* **(to s.o.,** à qn); transmettre *(des actions, un brevet)* **(to s.o.,** à qn).

assignation [æsɪg'neɪʃən] *n* **(a)** *(allocation etc)* distribution *f*, répartition *f*, attribution *f (de biens)*; **(b)** *Jur* cession *f*, transfert *m (de biens, de dettes etc)*; transmission *f (d'actions, de brevet)*; **(c)** *Old-fashioned (meeting)* rendez-vous secret; *(with lover)* rendez-vous galant; **to have an a. with s.o.,** avoir un rendez-vous avec qn.

assignment [ə'saɪnmənt] *n* **(a)** distribution *f*, répartition *f*, attribution *f (de biens)*; affectation *f*, allocation *f (de qch à qn)*; **a. of s.o. to a post,** affectation de qn à un poste; *Mil* **he was on a. to headquarters,** il était affecté au quartier général; **(b)** *(task) Sch etc* tâche assignée; *Journ* reportage assigné *(à un tel)*; **dangerous a.,** tâche dangereuse; *Journ* **to be on a.,** être en reportage; **(c)** *Jur etc* cession *f*, transfert *m (de biens, de dettes etc)*; **deed of a.,** acte attributif, acte de transfert.

assimilate [ə'sɪmɪleɪt] **1** *vt* **(a)** *(absorb)* assimiler *(des aliments, des idées, ce qu'on apprend, des immigrants etc)*; **(b)** *(make alike)* **to a. the laws of two countries,** assimiler les lois de deux pays. **2** *vi* **(a)** *(become absorbed)* s'intégrer, être assimilé; **(b)** (*become similar*) **to a. to** *or* **with sth,** s'assimiler à qch; *Ling* (*of consonants*) s'assimiler.

assimilation [əsɪmɪ'leɪʃən] *n* **(a)** assimilation *f* (*des aliments, d'idées etc*); *Bot* photo-synthèse *f*; **(b)** (*process of becoming similar*) assimilation *f* (**to, with,** à); *Ling* assimilation (*de consonnes*); **(c)** (*comparison*) assimilation *f* (**to,** à), comparaison *f* (**to,** avec).

Assisi [ə'si:zɪ, ə'sɪsɪ] *n* Assise *f*; **St. Francis of A.,** saint François d'Assise.

assist [ə'sɪst] **1** *vt* aider (*qn*), prêter son concours *ou* son assistance à (*qn*); seconder (*qn*) (*dans son travail*); **to a. s.o. in (doing) sth,** aider qn à faire qch; **economic growth was assisted by lower interest rates,** des taux d'intérêts plus faibles ont contribué à la croissance économique. **2** *vi* **(a)** (*help*) assister, aider; **(b)** *Arch* (*be present at*) assister (*à une cérémonie etc*).

assistance [ə'sɪstəns] *n* aide *f*, secours *m*, assistance *f*; **to give s.o. a.,** prêter aide *ou* assistance *ou* (son) concours à qn; **to come to s.o.'s a.,** venir à l'aide de *ou* en aide à qn; **with the a. of sth/s.o.,** à l'aide de qch/avec l'aide de qn; **can I be of any** *or* **some a.?,** puis-je être utile à qch?, est-ce que je peux vous aider?; **this theatre receives financial a. from the state,** ce théâtre reçoit des subventions de l'État; *Br Admin Arch* **National A.,** ≈ aide sociale.

assistant [ə'sɪstənt] *n* **(a)** aide *mf*, adjoint, -ointe; **(shop) a.,** vendeur, -euse; **laboratory a.,** laborantin, -ine; **a. manager,** sous-directeur *m*, *pl* sous-directeurs; **a. lecturer,** *esp Am* **a. professor,** ≈ maître assistant (*dans une université*); **(b)** *Sch* assistant, -ante; **French a.,** assistant, -ante de français.

assize [ə'saɪz] *n Jur* **(a)** (*usu pl*) **(court of) assizes, a. court,** (cour *f* d')assises *fpl*; **to be brought before the assizes,** être traduit en cour d'assises; **(b)** *Scot* jugement *m* par jury; **the a.,** le jury.

associate¹ [ə'səʊʃɪət, -sɪət] **1** *n* **(a)** (*in business*) associé, -ée, partenaire *mf*; membre correspondant, associé, -ée (*d'une académie*); **(b)** (*companion*) compagnon *m*, camarade *mf*; **I don't like his associates,** je n'aime pas ses fréquentations; **(c)** *Fml* (*of thing*) accessoire *m* (*de qch*). **2** *adj* associé; **a. company,** société affiliée, filiale *f*; *esp Am* **a. professor,** ≈ professeur de faculté; **a. membership,** (*members*) membres associés; (*participation*) adhésion *f* en tant que membre associé.

associate² **1** *vt* **(a)** (*mentally*) associer (*qn, qch*) (**with s.o.,** avec qn; **with sth,** à qch); **I don't a. the two things,** pour moi, les deux choses sont indépendantes; **(b)** (*in partnership etc*) s'associer; **to a. oneself,** s'associer (**with s.o.,** avec qch); **to be associated with s.o. in an undertaking,** s'associer avec qn pour une entreprise; **we are not associated in any way with that company,** nous n'avons absolument rien à faire avec cette société. **2** *vi* **(a)** (*frequent*) **to a. with s.o.,** fréquenter qn; **to a. with undesirable companions,** avoir de mauvaises fréquentations; **(b)** (*join*) **to a. with s.o. in sth/doing sth,** s'associer *ou* s'unir avec qn pour qch/pour faire qch.

associated [ə'səʊsɪeɪtɪd] *adj* associé.

association [əsəʊsɪ'eɪʃən] *n* **(a)** (*mental*) association *f*; **a. of ideas,** association d'idées; **land full of historic associations,** pays fertile en souvenirs historiques; *Jur* **deed of a.,** acte *m* d'association; **(b)** (*of people*) fréquentation *f* (**with s.o.,** de qn); **through long a. with ...,** à force de fréquenter ...; **in a. with ...,** associé à ..; **to do sth in a. with s.o.,** faire qch en association avec qn; **(c)** (*organization*) association *f*, société *f*; amicale *f* (*de professeurs etc*); **to form an a.,** constituer une société; **trade a.,** association professionnelle; **Young Men's/Women's Christian A.,** Union chrétienne de jeunes gens/de jeunes femmes; **a. football,** football *m* association.

associative [ə'səʊsɪətɪv] *adj* associatif, -ive.

assonance ['æsənəns] *n Ling* assonance *f*.

assorted [ə'sɔ:tɪd] *adj* **(a)** (*sweets etc*) assorti; (*colours*) varié; **box of a. screws,** boîte de vis assorties; **an audience of a. academics and business people,** un public très varié, composé d'universitaires et d'hommes d'affaires; **(b)** (*matched*) assorti; **well a. couple,** époux bien assortis.

assortment [ə'sɔ:tmənt] *n* assortiment *m* (*de bonbons, d'outils etc*); jeu *m* (*d'outils*).

ass(t) *abbr* **assistant.**

assuage [ə'sweɪdʒ] *vt Lit* apaiser (*la colère, la faim*).

assume [ə'sju:m] *vt* **(a)** (*believe without proof*) présumer, supposer (*qch*); tenir (*qch*) comme établi; **I a. that he will come,** je présume qu'il viendra; **he was assumed to be rich,** on le supposait riche; **in the absence of proof he must be assumed to be innocent,** en l'absence de preuves, il doit être présumé innocent; **don't a. that people will like you because you are rich,** ne crois pas que les gens t'aimeront parce que tu es riche; **let us a. that, ...,** mettons *ou* supposons que ...; **assuming that the story is true,** en supposant *ou* en admettant que l'histoire soit vraie; **to a. the worst,** mettre les choses au pis;

(b) (*take over*) prendre sur soi, assumer (*une charge, une responsabilité*); se charger de (*un devoir*); prendre (*le pouvoir, le commandement*); prendre en main (*la conduite des affaires*);

(c) (*adopt*) s'attribuer, s'arroger, s'approprier (*un droit, un titre etc*); adopter, emprunter (*un nom*); *Jur* **to a. ownership,** faire acte de propriétaire;

(d) (*take on*) prendre, se donner (*un air, une mine, un ton*); affecter, revêtir (*une forme, un caractère*); **his voice assumed a tone of authority,** sa voix prit un ton autoritaire;

(e) (*feign*) feindre, simuler (*l'indifférence*); affecter (*une vertu*).

assumed [ə'sju:md] *adj* supposé, feint, faux; **with a. nonchalance,** avec une affectation d'indifférence; **a. name,** nom supposé, nom d'emprunt, nom de guerre; (*of author*) pseudonyme *m*; **a. load,** (*on a bridge etc*) surcharge *f* hypothétique; **a. rate of increase,** taux d'accroissement présumé.

assumption [ə'sʌmpʃən] *n* **(a)** (*supposition*) supposition *f*, hypothèse *f*; *Phil* postulat *m*; **I am going on the a. that ...,** je me fonde sur l'hypothèse que ...; **(b)** (*power, responsibility etc*) prise *f*; **a. of office,** entrée *f* en fonctions; **(c)** action *f* de prendre (*une forme, un caractère*); **(d)** affectation *f* (*de vertu*); **he turned away with an a. of indifference,** il se détourna en feignant l'indifférence; **(e)** (*presumption*) arrogance *f*, prétention(s) *f(pl)*, présomption *f*; **(f)** *Rel* assomption *f* (*de la Vierge*); **Feast of the A.,** fête *f* de l'Assomption.

assurance [ə'ʃʊərəns] *n* **(a)** (*promise*) promesse *f* (formelle); **I can give you an a. that ...,** je peux vous assurer *ou* vous affirmer que ...; **(b)** (*affirmation*) affirmation *f*; **a. to the contrary,** affirmation contraire; **(c)** (*confidence*) assurance *f*; **I have every a. that he will help us,** j'ai la ferme assurance qu'il nous aidera; **(d)** (*self-confidence*) assurance *f*, confiance *f*, aplomb *m*; (*impudence*) hardiesse *f*, présomption *f*; **to answer with a.,** (*self-confidently*) répondre d'un ton assuré *ou* avec assurance; (*impudently*) répondre d'un ton hardi *ou* hardiment; **(e)** (*insurance*) **life a.,** assurance *f* sur la vie, assurance-vie, *pl* assurances-vie; **a. company,** compagnie *f* d'assurances.

assure [ə'ʃʊər] *vt* **(a)** assurer (*qn*); **to a. s.o. of the truth of sth,** assurer qn de la vérité de qch; **to a. s.o. of a fact,** assurer *ou* affirmer un fait à qn; **he assures me that it is true,** il me certifie que c'est vrai; **he will do it, I (can) a. you!,** il le fera, je vous assure!; **(b)** (*ensure*) assurer (*la paix, le bonheur de qn*); **(c)** (*insure*) assurer (*la vie de qn*); **to a. one's life,** s'assurer (*sur la vie*).

assured [ə'ʃʊəd] **1** *adj* **(a)** (*certain*) (*succès etc*) assuré; **they are a. of victory,** ils sont certains de gagner; **you're a. of a warm welcome,** on vous garantit un accueil chaleureux; **(b)** (*self-confident*) sûr de soi. **2** *n* (*in insurance*) assuré, -ée.

assuredly [ə'ʃʊərɪdlɪ] *adv* assurément, sans aucun doute.

Assyria [ə'sɪrɪə] *n Antiq* Assyrie *f*.

Assyrian [ə'sɪrɪən] *Antiq* **1** *adj* assyrien. **2** *n* **(a)** Assyrien, -ienne; **(b)** *Ling* assyrien *m*.

AST [eɪes'ti:] *n Am abbr* **Atlantic Standard Time.**

aster ['æstər] *n* **(a)** (*flower*) aster *m*; **China a.,** aster de Chine; reine-marguerite *f*, *pl* reines-marguerites; **(b)** *Biol* aster *m*.

asterisk¹ ['æst(ə)rɪsk] *n* astérisque *m*.

asterisk² *vt* signaler (*un mot etc*) par une astérisque.

astern [ə'stɜ:n] *Nau* **1** *adv* à l'arrière, sur l'arrière; **two guns a.,** deux canons à l'arrière *ou* en poupe; **to go** *or* **come a.,** faire machine *ou* marche arrière; **full speed a.!,** en arrière à toute vitesse!, en arrière toute!; **to make a boat fast a.,** amarrer un canot derrière; **to fall** *or* **drop a.,** rester en arrière (*d'un autre navire*); **ship right a.,** navire droit derrière. **2** *prep phrase* **a. of a ship,** derrière un navire, sur l'arrière d'un navire, à la traîne; **to pass a. of a ship,** passer sur l'arrière d'un navire.

asteroid ['æstərɔɪd] *Astron* **1** *n* astéroïde *m*. **2** *adj* en forme d'étoile.

asthma ['æsmə] *n* asthme *m*; **to have a.,** avoir de l'asthme; **a. sufferer,** asthmatique *mf*.

asthmatic [æs'mætɪk] *adj & n* asthmatique *mf*.

astigmatic [æstɪg'mætɪk] *adj & n Opt* astigmate *mf*.

astigmatism [ə'stɪgmətɪzəm] *n Opt* astigmatisme *m*.

astir [ə'stɜːr] *adj Old-fashioned* **(a)** *(out of bed)* debout, levé; **to be a. at six o'clock,** être debout à six heures; **(b)** animé; **the whole town was a.,** toute la ville était en émoi.

ASTMS ['æztems] *n abbr* **Association of Scientific, Technical and Managerial Staffs.**

astonish [ə'stɒnɪʃ] *vt* étonner, surprendre *(qn)*, jeter *(qn)* dans l'étonnement; **you a. me,** vous m'étonnez; **to be astonished at seeing sth,** être étonné *ou* s'étonner de voir qch; **I was astonished at** *or* **by the price,** j'ai été surpris par le prix; **I am astonished that ...,** cela m'étonne que + *sub* ...; **to look astonished,** avoir l'air étonné.

astonishing [ə'stɒnɪʃɪŋ] *adj* étonnant, surprenant; **it is a. to me that ...,** je m'étonne que + *sub* ... .

astonishingly [ə'stɒnɪʃɪŋlɪ] *adv* étonnamment; **a. enough, he arrived,** chose étonnante, il est arrivé.

astonishment [ə'stɒnɪʃmənt] *n* étonnement *m*, (grande) surprise *f*; **look of a.,** regard étonné; **I fell back in a.,** j'ai eu un sursaut d'étonnement.

astound [ə'staʊnd] *vt* confondre, frapper de stupeur, stupéfier; **I was astounded by it,** j'en ai été stupéfait; *(appalled)* j'en ai été atterré.

astounding [ə'staʊndɪŋ] *adj* abasourdissant, renversant.

astrakhan [æstrə'kæn] *n (fur)* astrakan *m*; **a. coat,** manteau *m* en astrakan.

astral ['æstrəl] *adj (body etc)* astral.

astray [ə'streɪ] *adv & adj (lost)* égaré; *(morally)* dévoyé; **to go a.,** *(of person, letter etc)* s'égarer; *(morally)* se dévoyer; *(become debauched)* se débaucher; **to lead s.o. a.,** *(with false information)* égarer qn, induire qn en erreur; *(morally)* dévoyer qn, détourner qn de la bonne voie.

astride [ə'straɪd] *adv & prep* **(a)** à califourchon; **to ride a.,** monter à califourchon *(sur un cheval etc)*; **to sit a. sth,** être à cheval *ou* à califourchon sur qch, chevaucher sur qch; **(b) to stand a.,** se tenir (debout) les jambes écartées.

astringent¹ [ə'strɪndʒənt] *adj Med* astringent; *Fig (voice)* péremptoire.

astringent² *n Med* astringent *m*.

astringently [ə'strɪndʒəntlɪ] *adv (to say)* d'une voix péremptoire.

astrologer [ə'strɒlədʒər] *n* astrologue *m*.

astrological [æstrə'lɒdʒɪk(ə)l] *adj* astrologique.

astrology [ə'strɒlədʒɪ] *n* astrologie *f*.

astronaut ['æstrənɔːt] *n* astronaute *mf*.

astronautics [æstrə'nɔːtɪks] *npl (usu with sing verb)* astronautique *f*.

astronomer [ə'strɒnəmər] *n* astronome *m*.

astronomic(al) [æstrə'nɒmɪk, -ɪk(ə)l] *adj (année, unité etc)* astronomique; *Fig* **an a. price,** un prix astronomique.

astronomically [æstrə'nɒmɪklɪ] *adv* astronomiquement; *Fig (to increase)* de façon astronomique.

astronomy [ə'strɒnəmɪ] *n* astronomie *f*.

astrophysics [æstrəʊ'fɪzɪks] *npl (usu with sing verb)* astrophysique *f*.

astute [ə'stjuːt] *adj (shrewd)* astucieux, fin, avisé.

astutely [ə'stjuːtlɪ] *adv* astucieusement, avec finesse, avec une grande pénétration.

astuteness [ə'stjuːtnɪs] *n* astuce *f*, finesse *f*.

asunder [ə'sʌndər] *adv Arch & Lit* **(a)** *(to pieces)* **to tear sth a.,** déchirer qch en deux; **to break a.,** se casser en deux; **(b)** *(separate)* éloignés, écartés (l'un de l'autre).

asylum [ə'saɪləm] *n* **(a)** *(shelter)* asile *m*, (lieu *m* de) refuge *m*; *Hist* asile (inviolable); **to seek a.,** chercher asile; **political a.,** asile politique; **(b)** *Arch (hospital etc)* hospice *m*; *(for lunatics)* asile *m* d'aliénés.

asymmetric(al) [eɪsɪ'metrɪk, -ɪk(ə)l] *adj* asymétrique.

asymmetry [eɪ'sɪmɪtrɪ] *n* asymétrie *f*.

at [æt, *unstressed* ət] *prep* **(a)** *(place)* à; **at the centre/the top,** au centre/sommet; **at table/church/school/the station,** à table/l'église/l'école/la gare; **at my side,** à mes côtés, à côté de moi; **at hand,** sous la main; **at Oxford,** à Oxford; **at sea,** en mer; **at home,** à la maison, chez soi; **at my uncle's/the dentist's,** chez mon oncle/le dentiste; **to sit at the window,** se tenir (au)près de la fenêtre; *US F* **where are we at?,** où en sommes-nous?; **where's he at politically?,** *(what are his views)* quelle est sa politique?; **Paris is where it's at!,** c'est à Paris que ça se passe!; **that's not where I'm at,** *(not my style)* ce n'est pas mon genre; **that's where I was at musically,** c'est ce que j'écoutais (à l'époque);

(b) *(time)* **at six o'clock,** à six heures; **at present,** à présent; **at that time,** à cette époque, en ce temps-là; **at the weekend,** pendant *ou* durant le week-end; **at a time when ...,** dans un moment où ...; **two at a time,** deux par deux, deux à la fois; **at the beginning of the year,** au commencement de l'année; **at the beginning,** au début; **at night,** la nuit, le soir; **at first,** d'abord; **at last,** enfin, à la fin; **at once,** immédiatement;

(c) *(price, speed, height etc)* **at two francs a pound,** à deux francs la livre; **apples at 30p a pound,** des pommes à 30 pence la livre; **at 30 mph,** à 30 mil(l)es l'heure; **at an altitude of 10,000 feet,** à une altitude de 10 000 pieds; **at (the age of) 20,** à 20 ans; **at 5 feet 2 inches he was too short,** avec ses 5 pieds 2 pouces, il était trop petit; **at minus 13°,** à moins 13°; **at a rate of 2 cm a year,** à un rythme de 2 cm par an;

(d) *(state, condition)* **to be at war,** être en guerre; **she's not at her best in the morning,** le matin, elle n'est pas au mieux de sa forme; **at all events,** en tout cas; **we'll leave it at that for today,** nous en resterons là pour aujourd'hui;

(e) *(resulting from)* **at my request,** sur ma demande; **at a word from her, he left the room,** il a suffi qu'elle prononce un mot pour qu'il quitte la pièce; **at a pinch we could all get in the car,** à la limite, nous pourrions tous monter dans la voiture; **at a guess,** en gros, approximativement;

(f) *(skill)* **quick at repartee,** prompt à la repartie; **to be good/bad at mathematics,** être fort/faible en mathématiques; **to be good at games,** être sportif;

(g) *(direction)* **to look at s.o./sth,** regarder qn/qch; **to aim at s.o.,** viser qn; **to laugh at s.o.,** se moquer de qn; **to swear at s.o.,** jurer contre qn; **learn to talk TO people instead of AT them,** apprend à parler aux gens au lieu de parler vers eux; **what are you driving at?,** où voulez-vous en venir?; *F* **she is always (on) at him,** elle est toujours après lui, elle lui casse tout le temps les pieds; **he's been on at me to do,** il me casse les pieds pour que je fasse; **at him!,** *(to dog)* attaque! attaque!;

(h) *(cause)* **to be surprised/delighted at sth,** être étonné/enchanté de qch;

(i) *(activity)* **to be at work,** être au travail; **school children at play,** élèves en récréation; **to be at sth,** être occupé à faire qch, s'occuper de qch; **to keep s.o. at it,** faire trimer qn; **she's at it again!,** voilà qu'elle recommence!, la voilà qui recommence!; **while we are at it,** pendant que nous y sommes; **he's a writer and a poor one at that!,** il est écrivain et encore assez médiocre!

atavism ['ætəvɪz(ə)m] *n* atavisme *m*.

atavistic [ætə'vɪstɪk] *adj* atavique.

ataxia [ə'tæksɪə] , **ataxy** [ə'tæksɪ] *n Med* ataxie *f*; **locomotor a.,** ataxie locomotrice progressive, tabes *m* dorsalis.

ate *see* **EAT**.

atheism ['eɪθɪɪz(ə)m] *n* athéisme *m*.

atheist ['eɪθɪɪst] *n* athée *mf*.

atheistic(al) [eɪθɪ'ɪstɪk, -ɪk(ə)l] *adj* athée.

Athenian [ə'θiːnɪən] **1** *adj* athénien, d'Athènes. **2** *n* Athénien, -ienne.

Athens ['æθənz] *n* Athènes *f*.

athlete ['æθliːt] *n* athlète *mf*; *Med* **a.'s foot,** pied *m* d'athlète, mycose *f*.

athletic [æθ'letɪk] *adj* athlétique; **she's very a.,** c'est une sportive; **an a.-looking young man,** un jeune homme à l'allure sportive; **I don't do anything very a.,** je ne fais pas beaucoup de sport; **a. club,** société *f* d'athlétisme.

athletically [æθ'letɪklɪ] *adv* de façon athlétique.

athletics [æθ'letɪks] *npl (usu with sing verb)* athlétisme *m*.

at-home [ət'həʊm] *n* réception *f*; *(in evening)* soirée *f*.

athwart [ə'θwɔːt] *Nau* **1** *adv* en travers, par le travers. **2** *prep* en travers de.

atishoo [ə'tɪʃuː] *int (sneeze)* atchoum!

Atlantic [ət'læntɪk] **1** *n* **the A. (Ocean),** l'(océan *m*) Atlantique *m*. **2** *adj (coast etc)* atlantique; *Am* **A. Standard Time,** = Temps Universel - 4; **A. liner,** transatlantique *m*.

Atlantis [ət'læntɪs] *n Myth* Atlantide *f*.

atlas ['ætləs] *n* **(a)** *(book) Geog* atlas *m*; **(b)** *Anat* atlas *m*; **(c)** *(paper)* atlas *m*; **an a. folio,** un in-folio format atlas *ou* format atlantique; **(d)** *Archit (pl* **atlantes** [ət'læntiːz]) atlante *m*, télamon *m*.

Atlas ['ætləs] *n* **(a)** *Myth* Atlas *m*; **(b) the A. Mountains,** l'Atlas *m*.

ATM [eɪtiː'em] *n (abbr* **automated teller machine)** D.A.B. *m*.

atmosphere ['ætməsfɪər] *n* **(a)** atmosphère *f (terrestre, planétaire etc)*; *Fig* atmosphère, ambiance *f*; *F* **I don't like atmospheres,** je n'aime pas les milieux où l'on se dispute; **there was an a. in the office today,** il y avait une de ces ambiances au bureau aujourd'hui!; **(b)** *Phys* atmosphère *f*.

atmospheric [ætməs'ferɪk] *adj (pression, condition etc)* atmosphérique.

atmospherics [ætməs'ferɪks] *npl Rad etc* (parasites *mpl*) atmosphériques *fpl*.
atoll ['ætɒl] *n Geog* atoll *m*.
atom ['ætəm] *n Phys* atome *m*; *Fig* **not an a. of common sense,** pas un grain de bon sens; **smashed to atoms,** réduit en miettes *ou* en poudre; **a. bomb,** bombe *f* atomique.
atomic [ə'tɒmɪk] *adj* (*énergie, guerre, Phys poids, nombre etc*) atomique; **the a. age,** l'ère *f ou* l'âge *m* atomique; **a. physicist,** atomiste *m*; **a. reactor,** réacteur *m* nucléaire.
atomics [ə'tɒmɪks] *npl* (*usu with sing verb*) sciences *fpl* atomiques.
atomize ['ætəmaɪz] *vt* atomiser (*un corps*); pulvériser (*un solide*); vaporiser (*un liquide*).
atomizer ['ætəmaɪzər] *n* atomiseur *m*; (*for solids*) pulvérisateur *m*; (*for liquids*) vaporisateur *m*; *Aut* gicleur *m*.
atonal [eɪ'təʊn(ə)l] *adj Mus* atonal, -aux.
▶atone for [ə'təʊn] *vipo* expier, racheter, réparer (*une faute, un péché*).
atonement [ə'təʊnmənt] *n* expiation *f*, réparation *f* (**for,** de); **in a. for a wrong,** en réparation d'un tort; *Rel* **to make a.,** satisfaire; *Jew Rel* **Day of A.,** Fête *f* du Grand Pardon.
atop [ə'tɒp] *adv & prep Lit* en haut (de), au sommet (de); **sitting a. a suitcase,** assis sur une valise.
atrocious [ə'trəʊʃəs] *adj* **(a)** *F* (*very bad*) (*jeu de mots etc*) exécrable; (*chapeau*) affreux; **his French is a.,** son français est très mauvais; **his singing is a.,** il chante affreusement mal; **(b)** (*crime*) atroce; **a. act,** atrocité *f*.
atrociously [ə'trəʊʃəslɪ] *adv* **(a)** *F* (*very badly*) exécrablement; **a. bad,** exécrable; **(b)** (*cruelly*) atrocement.
atrociousness [ə'trəʊʃəsnɪs] *n F* atrocité *f*.
atrocity [ə'trɒsɪtɪ] *n* **(a)** (*act*) atrocité *f*; **to witness atrocities,** assister à des atrocités; **(b)** atrocité *f* (*d'un crime*).
atrophied ['ætrəfɪd] *adj* atrophié.
atrophy¹ ['ætrəfɪ] *n* atrophie *f*.
atrophy² ['ætrəfɪ, -faɪ] **1** *vt* atrophier. **2** *vi* s'atrophier.
attaboy ['ætəbɔɪ] *int F* bravo!, à la bonne heure!
attach [ə'tætʃ] **1** *vt* **(a)** attacher, lier, fixer, accrocher, connecter (*qch*) (**to,** à); interconnecter (*deux choses*); annexer, joindre (*un document*); **the two pieces of paper weren't attached,** (*to each other*) les deux feuilles de papier étaient indépendantes; (*enclosed*) les deux feuilles n'étaient pas jointes; **house with garage attached,** maison avec garage attenant; **the kitten attached himself to her,** (*followed her*) le chaton l'a adoptée;
(b) (*assign*) **I a. no importance to it,** je n'y prête *ou* n'y attache aucune importance; **one cannot a. any blame to him,** on ne peut lui imputer aucune responsabilité; **official temporarily attached to another department,** fonctionnaire détaché à un autre service; **to be attached to a squadron,** (*of ship*) faire partie d'une escadre;
(c) *Jur* mettre une saisie-arrêt sur (*des biens mobiliers, un salaire*).
2 *vi* **(a)** (*of thing*) être relié à *ou* attenant à;
(b) no blame attaches to the crew, l'équipage n'est nullement à blâmer.
attaché [ə'tæʃeɪ] *n* attaché *m*; **military a.,** attaché militaire; **a. case,** attaché-case *m*, mallette *f* (*pour documents*).
attached [ə'tætʃd] *adj* **to be a. to s.o./sth,** être attaché à qn/qch; **she became very a. to the dog,** elle s'est beaucoup attachée au chien; *F* **the only woman not a.,** la seule femme non accompagnée.
attachment [ə'tætʃmənt] *n* **(a)** accessoire *m* (*d'un tour, d'une machine à coudre etc*); **lathe with drilling a.,** tour avec accessoire pour foret; **(b)** (*act*) action *f* d'attacher (*qch à qch*); attachement *m*; **(c)** (*fastener*) attache *f*, lien *m*; **attachments of a muscle,** attaches d'un muscle; **(d)** *Mil* rattachement *m*, stage *m*; **to serve an a. with the French army,** faire un stage dans l'armée française; **(e)** (*fondness*) attachement *m* (**for s.o.,** pour qn; **to sth,** à qch), affection *f* (**for,** pour); **to form an a. for s.o.,** s'attacher à qn, se prendre d'affection pour qn; **(f)** *Jur* arrêt *m*, saisie *f*, saisie-arrêt *f*; **a. of real property,** saisie immobilière; **(g)** *Br Admin* (*to letter etc*) pièce jointe.
attack¹ [ə'tæk] *n* **(a)** *Mil* attaque *f*, assaut *m*; **combined a.,** attaque combinée; **night a.,** attaque de nuit; **to be** *or* **come under a. from s.o.,** être attaqué par qn; **we came under a. at dawn,** on nous a attaqués à l'aube; **to launch an a.,** lancer une attaque; **a. is the best form of defence,** l'attaque est la meilleure forme de défense; *Fig* **an a. on freedom of speech,** une atteinte à la liberté d'expression; **(b)** (*on person*) attentat *m*, agression *f* (*contre qn*); **she was the victim of a vicious a.,** elle a été victime d'une agression; **(c)** (*strong criticism*) attaque *f* (**on s.o.,** contre qn; **on sth,** de qch); **(d)** *Med* attaque *f*, crise *f* (*de goutte etc*); poussée *f* (*de fièvre*); **heart a.,** crise cardiaque; **liver a.,** crise de foie; **a. of nerves,** crise de nerfs; **(e)** *Mus* attaque *f* (*d'une note*).
attack² *vt* **(a)** *Mil* attaquer, assaillir (*l'ennemi*); **to be attacked,** subir une attaque, être attaqué; *Fig* **the government is attacking our rights,** le gouvernement porte atteinte à nos droits; **(b)** (*in street etc*) agresser (*qn*); **(c)** (*criticize*) attaquer (*qn, un projet etc*); s'attaquer à (*qn, un abus etc*); **(d)** (*set about with energy*) s'attaquer à (*un travail, un problème etc*); **(e)** (*of disease*) s'attaquer à, atteindre (*qn, un organe etc*); (*of rust*) attaquer, ronger (*le fer*).
attacker [ə'tækər] *n* attaquant, -ante, agresseur *m*, assaillant, -ante.
attacking [ə'tækɪŋ] *adj* attaquant, assaillant; **a. party,** corps *m* d'attaque.
attain [ə'teɪn] **1** *vt* atteindre, parvenir à, arriver à (*un grand âge, ses fins etc*); s'élever jusqu'à (*un haut rang*); acquérir (*des connaissances*); **to a. one's majority,** arriver à *ou* atteindre sa majorité; **to a. happiness,** atteindre le bonheur. **2** *vi* **to a. to perfection/power,** atteindre la perfection/arriver au pouvoir.
attainable [ə'teɪnəb(ə)l] *adj* accessible; (*dream, ambition etc*) réalisable.
attainment [ə'teɪnmənt] *n* **(a)** (*no pl*) (*achievement*) obtention *f*, réalisation *f*; **for the a. of his purpose,** pour atteindre *ou* pour arriver à ses fins; **(b)** (*skill, achievements*) (*usu pl*) **attainments,** acquisition(s) *f(pl)* de l'esprit, connaissance(s) *f(pl)*; **man of considerable attainments,** homme qui a beaucoup d'instruction *ou* d'acquis; **her linguistic attainments,** sa connaissance des langues.
attempt¹ [ə'tempt] *n* **(a)** (*effort*) tentative *f*, essai *m*, effort *m*; **an a. at a smile,** l'esquisse d'un sourire; **without (making) any a. at concealment,** sans chercher à se cacher; **they made no a. to help,** ils n'ont pas essayé d'aider; **a. to escape,** tentative d'évasion; **to make an a. at (doing) sth** *or* **to do sth,** essayer *ou* tâcher de faire qch, s'essayer à faire qch; **to make an a. on Everest,** tenter l'ascension de l'Everest; **first a.,** coup *m* d'essai, première tentative; **it wasn't bad for a first a.,** ce n'était pas mal pour une première tentative *ou* un premier essai; **at the first a.,** du premier coup; **to make another a.,** renouveler ses tentatives, revenir à la charge; **to give up the a.,** y renoncer; **he died in the a.,** il est mort en essayant; **(b)** (*attack*) attentat *m*; **a. on s.o.'s life,** attentat à la vie de qn; **to make an a. on s.o.'s life,** attenter à la vie de qn; **to make an a. on a record** *or* **to beat a record,** essayer de battre un record.
attempt² *vt* **to a. to do sth,** essayer *ou* tenter *ou* tâcher de faire qch, chercher à faire qch; **he attempted to get up,** il essaya de se lever; **he attempted a smile,** il s'efforça de sourire; **to a. a piece of work,** entreprendre un travail; **to a. the impossible,** tenter l'impossible; **attempted murder/theft,** tentative *f* d'assassinat/de vol.
attend [ə'tend] **1** *vi* **(a)** (*be present*) être présent; **two delegates did not a.,** deux délégués étaient absents; **(b)** (*pay attention*) faire attention; **(c)** *Fml* (*serve*) **to a. on s.o.,** servir qn, être au service de qn. **2** *vt* **(a)** (*go to*) aller à (*l'église, l'école*); (*be present at*) assister à (*une conférence, une réunion*); suivre (*un cours*); **the lectures are well attended,** les cours sont très suivis; **(b)** (*of doctor*) soigner, donner des soins à (*un malade*); **(c)** *Lit* (*accompany*) **success attended my efforts,** mes efforts furent couronnés de succès; **(d)** (*serve*) **we were attended by three waiters,** nous étions servis par trois garçons; **to a. a prince,** suivre *ou* accompagner un prince.
▶attend to *vipo* **(a)** (*deal with*) s'occuper de, se charger de (*une affaire*); vaquer à (*ses occupations etc*); veiller à (*ses intérêts, sa santé etc*); soigner (*sa santé, son style etc*); *Com* exécuter (*une commande*); **I shall a. to it,** je m'en occuperai, je m'en chargerai; **(b)** (*serve*) s'occuper de (*qn*); servir (*un client*); **are you being attended to?,** est-ce qu'on vous sert?; **(c)** (*pay attention to*) faire *ou* prêter attention à (*qch*); **a. to what I'm saying,** écoutez attentivement ce que je dis.
attendance [ə'tendəns] *n* **(a)** (*presence*) présence *f* (*à une réunion*); **regular a.,** assiduité *f*; **school a.,** fréquentation *f* scolaire; **non-a.,** absence *f*; **his a. has been good/bad,** il a été/il n'a pas été assidu; **a. register,** registre *m* de présence; **(b)** (*people present*) assistance *f*; **there was a good a. at the meeting,** il y avait une assistance nom-

breuse à la réunion; **the evening class had to be cancelled because of poor a.,** le cours du soir a dû être annulé pour manque d'élèves; **(c) to be in a. on,** (*of doctor*) donner des soins à (*un malade*); (*of courtier*) être de service auprès de (*un roi etc*); *F* **to dance a. on s.o.,** faire l'empressé auprès de qn.

attendant [ə'tendənt] **1** *n* **(a)** (*official*) surveillant, -ante; *Admin* préposé, -ée; (*in museum etc*) gardien -ienne; (*in theatre*) ouvreuse *f*; (*in public lavatory*) ≈ dame-pipi *f*; (*in car park*) vigile *m*; **(b)** (*usu pl*) **attendants,** suivants *mpl*, gens *mpl* (*d'un roi etc*); **the prince and his attendants,** le prince et sa suite. **2** *adj Lit* **a. on s.o./sth,** qui accompagne qn/qch; *Jur* **a. circumstances,** circonstances concomitantes (*d'un crime etc*).

attending [ə'tendɪŋ] *adj Med* **the a. physician,** le médecin traitant.

attention [ə'tenʃən] *n* **(a)** attention *f* **(to,** à); **a. to truth/detail,** préoccupation *f* de la vérité/des détails; **to pay a. to sth,** faire attention à qch; **to pay a.** *or* **give one's a. to s.o.,** prêter attention à qn; **she didn't pay a. in class,** elle n'a pas été attentive en cours; **to give s.o./sth one's full a.,** consacrer toute son attention à qn/qch; **you have my undivided a.,** je suis tout à vous; **the report will receive our full a.,** nous prêterons une attention toute particulière à ce rapport; **your a. please, ladies and gentlemen,** mesdames et messieurs, votre attention s'il vous plaît; **particular a. should be given to posture,** surveillez tout particulièrement votre attitude; *Admin Com* **for the a. of Mr Green,** à l'attention de M. Green; **to turn one's a. to sth,** diriger son attention vers qch, porter son attention sur qch; **to call** *or* **attract** *or* **draw (s.o.'s) a. to sth,** appeler *ou* attirer l'attention (de qn) sur qch, faire remarquer qch (à qn); **to draw a. to oneself,** se faire remarquer; **it has been brought to our a. that ...,** il a été porté à notre connaissance que ..., on nous a fait savoir *ou* remarquer que ...; **to catch s.o.'s a.,** attirer *ou* fixer l'attention de qn; **to attract everybody's a.,** fixer tous les regards; **to hold** *or* **engage s.o.'s a.,** retenir l'attention de qn; **to be all a.,** être (tout yeux et) tout oreilles; **to get a.,** être considéré; **the child doesn't get much a. at home,** on ne s'occupe pas beaucoup de cet enfant chez lui; **he just does it to get a.,** il ne fait ça que pour se faire remarquer; **she likes being the centre of a.,** elle aime être le centre du monde; (*at party*) elle aime se faire remarquer;
(b) (*maintenance*) soins *mpl*, entretien *m*; **the engine needs** *or* **requires some a.,** le moteur a besoin d'être entretenu; **the batteries require daily/monthly a.,** les accus exigent un entretien journalier/mensuel;
(c) (*often in pl*) attention(s) *f(pl)*, soins *mpl*, prévenance(s) *f(pl)*; *Old-fashioned* **to pay one's attentions to a lady,** faire la cour à une dame;
(d) *Mil* **a.!,** garde-à-vous!; **to come to a.,** se mettre au garde-à-vous; **to stand at a.,** être *ou* se tenir au garde-à-vous.

attentive [ə'tentɪv] *adj* **(a)** (*pupil, listener, audience etc*) attentif **(to,** à); (*in one's work*) soigneux **(to,** de); **(b)** (*anxious to please*) **to be very a. to s.o.,** être aux petits soins pour qn, être très attentionné pour qn, être très empressé auprès de qn; **to be very a. to a lady,** se montrer galant (auprès d'une femme).

attentively [ə'tentɪvlɪ] *adv* attentivement; (*écouter*) avec attention.

attentiveness [ə'tentɪvnɪs] *n* **(a)** (*concentration*) attention *f*; **(b)** (*anxiety to please*) prévenances *fpl*, soins *mpl* **(to, for s.o.,** pour qn).

attenuate [ə'tenjʊeɪt] **1** *vt* atténuer, diminuer (*la gravité de qch etc*); raréfier (*un gaz etc*); **attenuating circumstances,** circonstances atténuantes. **2** *vi* s'atténuer, diminuer.

attenuation [ətenjʊ'eɪʃən] *n* atténuation *f*, diminution *f* (*de qch*).

attest [ə'test] **1** *vt* **(a)** (*affirm, prove*) attester, certifier (*un fait*); **to a. that ...,** attester *ou* certifier que ...; **the document attests the fact that ...,** le document démontre que ...; *Agr* **attested herd,** troupeau tuberculiné; **(b)** (*of witness*) affirmer (*qch*) sous serment; légaliser (*une signature*); **attested copy,** copie certifiée; **(c)** *Jur* assermenter (*qn*). **2** *vi* **to a. to sth,** (*witness*) témoigner de qch; (*bear witness to*) attester qch, se porter garant *ou* témoin de qch.

attestation [æte'steɪʃən] *n Jur* **(a)** déposition *f* (*d'un témoin*), témoignage *m*; **(b)** (*of fact*) attestation *f*; **(c)** légalisation *f* (*d'une signature*); **(d)** (*oath taking*) prestation *f* de serment.

attic ['ætɪk] *n* grenier *m*; **a. room,** mansarde *f*; **a. window,** fenêtre *f* en mansarde; (*skylight*) lucarne *f*.

Attica ['ætɪkə] *n* Attique *f*.

attire[1] [ə'taɪər] *n* **(a)** *Fml* (*clothing*) vêtements *mpl*; costume *m*; **night a.,** vêtements de nuit; **(b)** (*of deer*) ramure *f*.

attire[2] *vt* **(a)** *Arch & Lit* (*usu passive or reflexive*) vêtir, parer; **(b) stag attired,** (*in hunting*) cerf ramé.

attitude ['ætɪtjuːd] *n* **(a)** (*of mind*) attitude *f*, manière *f* de penser *ou* de voir; **what's your a. to people who say it doesn't matter?,** que pensez-vous des gens qui disent que ça n'a pas d'importance?; **old-fashioned attitudes,** des idées démodées; **their a. is that ...,** leur point de vue est que ...; **she takes the a. that ...,** elle considère que ...; **his whole a. is 'I don't care',** tout lui est égal; **I don't like your a.,** je n'aime pas ton attitude; **she's got an a. problem,** elle a un blocage; **(b)** (*pose*) attitude *f*, pose *f*; **to strike an a.,** prendre une attitude dramatique, poser; **(c)** (*of horse*) station *f*; **(d)** *Av etc* attitude *f* (*d'un avion, d'un missile etc sur sa trajectoire*).

attn *abbr* **attention.**

attorney [ə'tɜːnɪ] *n Jur* **(a)** *Arch & Am* **a. (at law),** = avoué *m*; *US* **District A.,** ≈ procureur *m* de la République; **A. General,** *Eng* = Procureur général; *US* = Procureur général d'un État; *Can* = Ministre *m* de la Justice; **(b)** procureur *m*, fondé *m* de pouvoir(s); **power of a.,** procuration *f*, mandat *m*, pouvoirs *mpl*; **full power of a.,** procuration générale.

attract [ə'trækt] *vt* **(a)** attirer (*une foule, l'attention de qn*); **(to,** à, vers); **a magnet attracts iron,** l'aimant attire le fer; **(b)** (*appeal to*) séduire, attirer; (*of person*) attirer; **he is not attracted to her,** elle ne lui plaît pas, *F* elle ne lui dit rien; *Fig* **the prospect of a week in London doesn't a. me,** ça ne me dit rien d'aller passer une semaine à Londres.

attraction [ə'trækʃən] *n* **(a)** (*act, power*) attraction *f*, *Lit* attirance *f* **(to,** vers); **wealth has no a. for her,** elle n'est pas attirée par la richesse; **his a. to her,** son attirance pour elle; *Phys* **molecular a.,** attraction moléculaire; **(b)** (*thing, person*) attraction *f*; **the chief a.,** le clou (*de la fête, du spectacle etc*); **tourist a.,** attraction pour touristes; **the great a. of the day,** la grande attraction du jour; **(c)** (*of person*) (*usu pl*) **physical attractions,** charmes *mpl* physiques; **that's one of my attractions,** cela fait partie de mes charmes.

attractive [ə'træktɪv] *adj* **(a)** (*person, offer, manner*) attrayant, attirant, séduisant; (*house, village*) coquet; **an a. child,** un enfant attachant; **do you find him a.?,** il te plaît?, tu le trouves séduisant?; **this prospect was a.,** j'étais attiré par cette perspective; **in an a. shade of blue,** dans une nuance de bleu très seyante; *Com* **a. prices,** prix intéressants; **(b)** (*magnet etc*) attractif, attirant.

attractively [ə'træktɪvlɪ] *adv* d'une manière attrayante *ou* séduisante; **a. bound in red leather,** élégamment relié de cuir rouge.

attractiveness [ə'træktɪvnɪs] *n* attrait *m*.

attributable [ə'trɪbjʊtəb(ə)l] *adj* attribuable, imputable **(to,** à).

attribute[1] ['ætrɪbjuːt] *n* **(a)** (*quality*) attribut *m*, qualité *f*; **(b)** (*symbol*) symbole *m*, attribut *m*; **(c)** *Gram* épithète *f*.

attribute[2] [ə'trɪbjuːt] *vt* attribuer, imputer **(to,** à); **comedy attributed to Shakespeare,** comédie attribuée à Shakespeare; **you a. to him qualities that he does not possess,** vous lui prêtez des qualités qu'il n'a pas; **she attributes her longevity to her diet,** elle attribue sa longévité à son régime.

attribution [ætrɪ'bjuːʃən] *n* attribution *f*, imputation *f* **(to,** à).

attributive [ə'trɪbjʊtɪv] *Gram* **1** *adj* **a. adjective,** épithète *f*. **2** *n* épithète *f*.

attributively [ə'trɪbjʊtɪvlɪ] *adv* (*mot employé*) avec valeur d'épithète.

attrition [ə'trɪʃən] *n* **(a)** usure *f* par le frottement; **war of a.,** guerre *f* d'usure; **(b)** *Econ Ind* départs *mpl* volontaires.

attune [ə'tjuːn] *vt Lit* accorder, harmoniser **(to,** avec); **ear attuned to every sound,** oreille exercée à saisir tous les sons.

atypic(al) [eɪ'tɪpɪk, -ɪk(ə)l] *adj* atypique.

aubergine ['əʊbəʒiːn] *n Br Culin* aubergine *f*.

auburn ['ɔːbən] *adj* (*cheveux*) châtain roux.

auction[1] ['ɔːkʃən] *n* **(a)** *Com* **(sale by) a., a. sale,** vente *f* à l'enchère *ou* aux enchères; (*for fish, vegetables etc*) (vente à la) criée *f*; **car a.,** vente aux enchères de voitures; **Dutch a.,** vente à la baisse, enchère *f* au rabais; **to sell by a.** *or* *US* **at a.,** vendre aux enchères; (*of fish etc*) vendre à la criée; **to put sth up for a.,** mettre qch aux enchères; **a.**

room, salle *f* des ventes; (*for fish, vegetables etc*) chambre *f* des criées; **(b)** *Cards* enchère *f*; **a. bridge,** bridge *m* aux enchères.

auction² *vt* vendre (*qch*) aux enchères; vendre (*des denrées, un immeuble par autorité de justice*) à la criée.

▶**auction off** *vtsep* vendre (*qch*) aux enchères.

auctioneer [ɔːkʃə'nɪər] *n* **(a)** *Com* commissaire-priseur *m*, *pl* commissaires-priseurs; **(b)** (*at a sale*) directeur *m* de la vente; (*at fish, vegetable market etc*) crieur *m*.

audacious [ɔː'deɪʃəs] *adj* **(a)** (*brave*) audacieux, hardi, intrépide; **(b)** (*insolent*) effronté, hardi.

audaciously [ɔː'deɪʃəslɪ] *adv* (*see adj*) **(a)** audacieusement, avec audace; **(b)** effrontément.

audacity [ɔː'dæsɪtɪ] *n* **(a)** (*bravery*) audace *f*, intrépidité *f*, hardiesse *f*; **(b)** (*nerve*) effronterie *f*; **to have the a. to do sth,** oser faire qch.

audibility [ɔːdɪ'bɪlɪtɪ] *n* perceptibilité *f*, audibilité *f*.

audible ['ɔːdɪb(ə)l] *adj* (*sound*) perceptible (à l'oreille); (*speech, voice*) audible; **he was scarcely a.,** on l'entendait à peine; *Phys* **a. frequency,** fréquence *f* audible.

audibly ['ɔːdɪblɪ] *adv* (*to speak*) de façon à être entendu.

audience ['ɔːdɪəns] *n* **(a)** (*spectators, listeners*) assistance *f*, assistants *mpl*; *Th* spectateurs *mpl*, auditoire *m*, public *m*; *Rad* auditeurs *mpl*; **the whole a. applauded,** toute la salle applaudit; **do we have any Americans in the a.?,** y-a-t-il des Américains dans la salle?; **to perform before a large a.,** jouer *ou* chanter *etc* devant un nombreux public; **(b)** (*with king, pope etc*) audience *f*; **to grant s.o. an a.,** accorder audience à qn; **to hold an a.,** tenir une audience; **a. chamber,** salle *f* d'audience.

audio ['ɔːdɪəʊ] **1** *adj* sonore; **a. cassette,** cassette *f* (audio); **a. equipment,** équipement *m* sonore; *Rad etc* **a. frequency,** audiofréquence *f*, fréquence *f* acoustique. **2** *n* (reproduction *f* du) son *m*.

audiometer ['ɔːdɪəʊmiːtər] *n Tech* audiomètre *m*.

audiotypist ['ɔːdɪəʊtaɪpɪst] *n* audiotypiste *mf*.

audiovisual [ɔːdɪəʊ'vɪzjʊəl] *adj* audiovisuel.

audit¹ ['ɔːdɪt] *n Fin* audit *m* (comptable), apurement *m* (*de comptes*), vérification(s) *f(pl)* comptable(s); *Admin* **A. office,** ≈ la Cour des Comptes; *Econ* **internal a.,** contrôle *m* interne; *Am* **a. trail,** *Can* vérification à rebours.

audit² *vt* **(a)** *Fin* vérifier, apurer, examiner (*des comptes*); **to a. the accounts of a company,** vérifier et certifier la comptabilité d'une société; **(b)** *Am Univ* assister à (*un cours*) en auditeur libre.

auditing ['ɔːdɪtɪŋ] *n* vérification *f* et certification *f* des écritures, apurement *m*.

audition¹ [ɔː'dɪʃən] *n* **(a)** *Th Mus etc* audition *f*, séance *f* d'essai; **(b)** (*hearing*) audition *f*, ouïe *f*.

audition² *Th Mus etc* **1** *vt* auditionner (*qn*) (**for a part,** pour un rôle). **2** *vi* auditionner; **to a. for a part,** auditionner pour un rôle.

auditor ['ɔːdɪtər] *n* **(a)** *Admin* vérificateur *m* des comptes; **(b)** *Com Fin* audit *m*, auditeur *m*; commissaire *m* aux comptes (*d'une société*); censeur *m* (*d'une compagnie d'assurances*); **(c)** auditeur *m* (*d'une conférence etc*).

auditorium [ɔːdɪ'tɔːrɪəm] *n* salle *f* (*de théâtre, de concerts, de conférences etc*).

auditory ['ɔːdɪtrɪ] *adj* (*nerf etc*) auditif; **the a. organ,** l'organe *m* de l'ouïe.

AUEW [eɪjuːiː'dʌb(ə)ljuː] *n abbr* **Amalgamated Union of Engineering Workers**.

Aug *abbr* **August**.

Augean [ɔː'dʒiːən] *adj Myth* **A. Stables,** les écuries *fpl* d'Augias.

auger ['ɔːgər] *n* tarière *f*.

aught [ɔːt] *n Arch & Lit* quelque chose *m*, quoi que ce soit; **for a. I know,** (pour) autant que je sache.

augment [ɔːg'ment] **1** *vt Fml* augmenter, accroître (*qch*) (**with, by,** de); *Mus* **augmented interval,** intervalle augmenté. **2** *vi Fml* augmenter, s'accroître.

augmentation [ɔːgmen'teɪʃən] *n* augmentation *f*, accroissement *m* (*de fortune etc*).

augur¹ ['ɔːgər] *Lit* **1** *vt* augurer, présager, prédire (*qch*); **it augurs no good,** cela ne présage *ou* n'annonce rien de bon. **2** *vi* **it augurs well/ill,** cela est de bon/de mauvais augure (**for,** pour).

augur² *n Antiq & Lit* (*prophet*) augure *m*.

augury ['ɔːgjʊrɪ] *n* **(a)** (*sign*) augure *m*, présage *m*; **(b)** (*practice*) science *f* des augures, science augurale.

august [ɔː'gʌst] *adj* (*assemblée*) auguste; (*maintien*) imposant, majestueux.

August ['ɔːgəst] *n* août *m*; **in A.,** au mois d'août, en août; **(on) the first of A.,** le premier août; **an A. evening,** un soir d'août.

Augustinian [ɔːgə'stɪnɪən] **1** *adj Rel Hist* augustinien; de saint Augustin; **A. monk** *or* **friar,** Augustin *m*. **2** *n Rel* Augustin, -ine.

Augustus [ɔː'gʌstəs] *n* Auguste *m*.

auk [ɔːk] *n* (*bird*) alque *f*; **great a.,** grand pingouin.

auld [ɔːld] *adj Scot* vieux; **a. lang syne,** le temps jadis, le bon vieux temps.

aunt [ɑːnt] *n* tante *f*; *Old-fashioned F* **A. Sally,** (*game*) ≈ jeu de massacre; (*person or thing*) = objet de dérision.

auntie, aunty ['ɑːntɪ] *n F* tatie *f*, tata *f*, tantine *f*.

au pair¹ [əʊ'peər] **1** *n* jeune fille *f* au pair. **2** *adv* **she's staying with them au p.,** elle est chez eux au pair.

au pair² *vi* travailler au pair.

aura ['ɔːrə] *n* **(a)** *Lit* aura *f* (*de sainteté etc*); **(b)** *Med* aura *f*; **epileptic a.,** aura épileptique.

aural ['ɔːrəl] *adj* auditif, sonore; **a. surgeon** *or* **specialist,** auriste *m*; *Rad etc* **a. reception,** réception *f* du son.

aureola [ɔː'riːələ] **, aureole** ['ɔːrɪəʊl] *n* **(a)** *Art* auréole *f*, gloire *f* (*d'un saint*); **(b)** *Astron* auréole *f* (*du soleil*).

auricle ['ɔːrɪk(ə)l] *n Anat* **(a)** (*of heart*) auricule *m*; **(b)** (*external ear*) pavillon *m*.

auricular [ɔː'rɪkjʊlər] **1** *adj* **(a)** *Anat* (*conduit etc*) auriculaire; **(b)** *Fml* (*témoin etc*) auriculaire; *Rel* **a. confession,** confession *f* auriculaire. **2** *n* (doigt *m*) auriculaire *m*.

aurochs ['ɔːrɒks] *n* (*animal*) aurochs *m*.

aurora [ɔː'rɔːrə] *n Lit* aurore *f*; **a. borealis/australis,** aurore boréale/australe.

Aurora [ɔː'rɔːrə] *n Myth* Aurore *f*.

auscultation [ɔːskəl'teɪʃən] *n Med* auscultation *f*; **to examine by a.,** ausculter (*un malade*).

auspices ['ɔːspɪsɪz] *npl* auspices *mpl*; **favourable a.,** d'heureux auspices; **under the a. of the United Nations,** sous l'égide des Nations Unies.

auspicious [ɔː'spɪʃəs] *adj* (*vent etc*) propice, favorable; (*signe*) de bon augure; (*âge*) heureux, prospère; **an a. start to a career,** des débuts favorables dans une carrière; **on this a. occasion,** en ce jour mémorable.

auspiciously [ɔː'spɪʃəslɪ] *adv* sous d'heureux auspices, favorablement; **to begin a.,** commencer heureusement.

auspiciousness [ɔː'spɪʃəsnɪs] *n* heureux auspices *mpl*; aspect *m* favorable *ou* propice (*d'une entreprise etc*).

Aussie ['ɒzɪ] *F* **1** *adj* australien. **2** *n* **(a)** Australien, -ienne; **the Aussies,** les Australiens; **A. Land,** l'Australie *f*; **(b)** *Ling* l'anglais australien; **(c)** (*country*) l'Australie *f*.

austere [ɒ'stɪər] *adj* (*vie, style etc*) austère; (*appartement*) sans luxe, d'un goût sévère; **to lead an a. life,** vivre en ascète.

austerely [ɒ'stɪəlɪ] *adv* austèrement, avec austérité.

austerity [ɒ'sterɪtɪ] *n* (*of life*) austérité *f*; (*of flat, furnishings*) sévérité *f* de goût; **a. measures,** mesures *fpl* d'austérité.

Australasia [ɒstrə'leɪʒɪə, -'leɪʃə] *n Geog* Australasie *f*.

Australasian [ɒstrə'leɪʒɪən, -'leɪʃən] *Geog* **1** *adj* australasien. **2** *n* Australasien, -ienne.

Australia [ɒ'streɪlɪə] *n* Australie *f*; **South A.,** Australie méridionale; **Western A.,** Australie occidentale.

Australian [ɒ'streɪlɪən] **1** *adj* australien. **2** *n* **(a)** Australien, -ienne; **(b)** *Ling* l'anglais australien.

Austria ['ɒstrɪə] *n* Autriche *f*.

Austria-Hungary ['ɒstrɪə'hʌŋgərɪ] *n* Autriche-Hongrie *f*.

Austrian ['ɒstrɪən] **1** *adj* autrichien. **2** *n* Autrichien, -ienne.

Austro-Hungarian ['ɒstrəʊhʌŋ'geərɪən] *adj Hist* austro-hongrois; **the A.-H. Empire,** l'empire d'Autriche-Hongrie.

autarchy ['ɔːtɑːkɪ] *n* autarchie *f*.

autarky ['ɔːtɑːkɪ] *n* autarcie *f*.

authentic [ɔː'θentɪk] *adj* **(a)** (*document, fait, histoire etc*) authentique; **(b)** *Mus* (*mode, cadence*) authentique.

authentically [ɔː'θentɪklɪ] *adv* authentiquement.

authenticate [ɔː'θentɪkeɪt] *vt* **(a)** *Jur* certifier, homologuer, légaliser, valider (*un acte etc*); **(b)** établir l'authenticité de (*qch*); **(c)** *Mil Rad* identifier (*un correspondant*).

authentication [ɔːθentɪ'keɪʃən] *n* **(a)** (*act*) authentication *f*; certification *f* (*d'une signature etc*); homologation *f*, législation *f*, validation *f* (*d'un acte*); **(b)** preuve *f* de l'authenticité (*d'un document etc*); **(c)** *Mil Rad etc* identification *f* (*d'un correspondant*).

authenticity [ɔːθen'tɪsɪtɪ] *n* authenticité *f*.

author ['ɔːθər] *n* auteur *m* (*d'un livre etc*); **to be the a. of one's own misfortunes,** être artisan de ses malheurs.

authoress [ɔːθə'res] *n* femme *f* auteur, écrivain *m*.

authoritarian [ɔːθɒrɪ'teərɪən] *adj & n* autoritaire *m*.

authoritative [ɔː'θɒrɪtətɪv] *adj* **(a)** (*caractère*) autoritaire; (*ton*) d'autorité; **(b)** (*statement, book etc*) qui fait autorité; (*book, document*) de référence; (*document*) qui fait foi, qui fait autorité; **to have sth from an a. source,** avoir qch de source autorisée *ou* de bonne source.

authoritatively [ɔːˈθɒrɪtətɪvlɪ] *adv* **(a)** autoritairement; **(b) I can state it a.,** je puis l'affirmer de bonne source.

authority [ɔːˈθɒrɪtɪ] *n* **(a)** (*power*) autorité *f*; **those in a.,** les autorités; **in a position of a.,** en position d'autorité; **to have** *or* **exercise a. over s.o.,** (*officially*) avoir *ou* exercer une autorité sur qn; (*have power*) avoir de l'ascendant sur qn; **an air of a.,** un air autoritaire; **(b)** (*authorization*) autorisation *f*, mandat *m*; **to have a. to act,** avoir qualité pour agir; **to give s.o. a. to do sth,** autoriser qn à faire qch; **they had the full a. of the law,** ils ont agi avec la pleine autorité de la loi; **to act on s.o.'s a.,** agir sur l'autorité de qn; **to do sth on one's own a.,** faire qch de sa propre autorité; **on what a./on whose a. did they search the house?,** avec quelle autorisation/avec l'autorisation de qui ont-ils perquisitionné la maison?; **(c)** (*of person, book*) **to be an a.,** être expert dans la matière; **to be an a. on sth,** faire autorité en matière de qch; **to have sth on good a.,** tenir *ou* savoir qch de bonne part *ou* de bonne source *ou* de source autorisée; **to quote s.o. as one's a.,** se réclamer de qn; **to quote one's authorities,** citer ses sources *ou* ses auteurs; **she spoke with a.,** elle a parlé avec autorité; **(d)** *Admin* **administrative a.,** service administratif; **the authorities,** les autorités *fpl*; (*government*) l'administration *f*; **he was arrested by the French authorities,** il a été arrêté par les autorités françaises; **the health authorities,** les services d'hygiène; **the military authorities,** les autorités militaires.

authorization [ɔːθəraɪˈzeɪʃən] *n* autorisation *f* (**to do sth,** de faire qch); (*right*) pouvoir *m*, mandat *m*.

authorize [ˈɔːθəraɪz] *vt* autoriser (*qn, qch*) (**to do sth,** à faire qch); **to be authorized to act,** avoir qualité pour agir.

authorized [ˈɔːθəraɪzd] *adj* autorisé; *Mil etc* réglementaire; *Rel* **the A. Version,** = la traduction anglaise de la Bible de 1611; *Admin* **a. charges,** prix homologués; **a. representative,** (*of company*) agent autorisé; **a. signatory,** signataire autorisé.

authorship [ˈɔːθəʃɪp] *n* **(a)** (*of book, plan etc*) paternité *f*; **to establish the a. of a book,** identifier l'auteur d'un livre; **(b)** (*profession*) profession *f ou* qualité *f* d'auteur.

autism [ˈɔːtɪz(ə)m] *n Med* autisme *m*.

autistic [ɔːˈtɪstɪk] *adj Med* autistique, autiste.

auto [ˈɔːtəʊ] *n Am F* automobile *f*, voiture *f*; **a. accident,** accident *m* de voiture.

auto- [ɔːtəʊ] *pref* auto-.

autobank [ˈɔːtəʊbæŋk] *n* distributeur *m* automatique de billets.

autobiographic(al) [ɔːtəʊbaɪəˈgræfɪk, -ɪk(ə)l] *adj* autobiographique.

autobiography [ɔːtəʊbaɪˈɒgrəfɪ] *n* autobiographie *f*.

autocade [ˈɔːtəʊkeɪd] *n US* cortège *m* de voitures.

autocracy [ɔːˈtɒkrəsɪ] *n* autocratie *f*.

autocrat [ˈɔːtəkræt] *n* autocrate *m*.

autocratic(al) [ɔːtəˈkrætɪk, -ɪk(ə)l] *adj* (*government*) autocratique; (*person*) autocrate; (*caractère*) absolu.

autocratically [ɔːtəˈkrætɪklɪ] *adv* autocratiquement.

Autocue ® [ˈɔːtəʊkjuː] *n TV* téléprompteur *m*.

autodidact [ɔːtəʊˈdaɪdækt] *n* autodidacte *mf*.

autofocus [ˈɔːtəʊfəʊkəs] *n* **camera with a.,** appareil *m* autofocus.

autogenous [ɔːˈtɒdʒɪnəs] *adj* autogène.

autogiro [ɔːtəʊˈdʒaɪrəʊ] *n Av* autogyre *m*.

autograph¹ [ˈɔːtəgrɑːf, -græf] **1** *n* autographe *m*; **a. album,** album *m* de signatures. **2** *adj* **a. letter of Byron,** lettre *f* autographe de Byron.

autograph² *vt* écrire son autographe dans (*un livre*); signer, dédicacer (*un exemplaire*); mettre son autographe à (*un document*).

autogyro [ɔːtəʊˈdʒaɪrəʊ] *n Av* autogyre *m*.

automat [ˈɔːtəmæt] *n Old-fashioned Am* restaurant *m* à distributeurs automatiques.

automate [ˈɔːtəmeɪt] *vt* automatiser, rendre automatique.

automated [ˈɔːtəmeɪtɪd] *adj* automatisé; **a. teller machine,** distributeur *m* automatique de billets.

automatic¹ [ɔːtəˈmætɪk] *adj* **(a)** automatique; **fully a.,** entièrement automatique; *Av* **a. pilot,** pilotage *m* automatique; **to be on a. pilot,** (*of aircraft*) être sur le pilotage automatique; *Fig* (*of person*) marcher au radar; **a. pistol,** (pistolet *m*) automatique *m*; *Aut* **a. transmission,** transmission *f* automatique; **a. vending machine,** distributeur *m* automatique; **(b)** (*mouvement*) automatique, inconscient, machinal.

automatic² *n* **(a)** *Aut* voiture *f* automatique; **a Renault ® a.,** une Renault ® (avec boîte de vitesses) automatique; **(b)** (*pistol*) automatique *m*.

automatically [ɔːtəˈmætɪklɪ] *adv* **(a)** automatiquement; **(b)** (*without thinking*) sans réfléchir.

automation [ɔːtəˈmeɪʃən] *n* automatisation *f*.

automatization [ɔːtɒmətaɪˈzeɪʃən] *n* automatisation *f*.

automaton, *pl* **-ons, -a** [ɔːˈtɒmətən, -ənz, -ə] *n* automate *m*.

automobile [ˈɔːtəməʊbiːl] *n Am* automobile *f*, voiture *f*; **a. club,** club *m* automobile.

automotive [ɔːtəʊˈməʊtɪv] *adj* **(a)** (*self-propelled*) automoteur, -trice; **(b)** *esp Am* automobile; **a. engineering,** technique *f* automobile; **a. parts,** pièces *fpl* d'automobile.

autonomous [ɔːˈtɒnəməs] *adj* autonome.

autonomy [ɔːˈtɒnəmɪ] *n* autonomie *f*.

autopilot [ˈɔːtəʊpaɪlət] *n Av* pilotage *m* automatique; **to be on a.,** (*of aircraft*) être sur le pilotage automatique; *Fig* (*of person*) marcher au radar.

autopsy¹ [ˈɔːtɒpsɪ, ɔːˈtɒpsɪ] *n* autopsie *f*; **to carry out an a.,** faire une autopsie; *Fig* faire une analyse; **to carry out** *or* **perform an a. on s.o.,** autopsier qn.

autopsy² *vt* autopsier (*qn*).

autosuggestion [ɔːtəʊsəˈdʒestʃən] *n Psy* autosuggestion *f*.

autumn [ˈɔːtəm] *n* automne *m*; **in a.,** en automne; **an a. evening,** une soirée d'automne; **a. plants,** plantes automnales; **a. crocus,** (*bulb*) colchique *m* d'automne; **a. leaves,** feuilles *fpl* d'automne.

autumnal [ɔːˈtʌmn(ə)l] *adj* automnal, d'automne; **a. equinox,** équinoxe *m* d'automne.

auxiliary [ɔːgˈzɪlɪərɪ, -zɪlərɪ] **1** *adj* (*staff, troops etc*) auxiliaire; (*machine etc*) auxiliaire, de secours; (*chauffage, éclairage*) d'appoint; *Gram* **a. verb,** verbe *m* auxiliaire. **2** *n* auxiliaire *mf*; *Gram* (verbe *m*) auxiliaire *m*; *Mil* **auxiliaries,** (troupes *fpl*) auxiliaires *mpl*.

AV [eɪˈviː] *n* (*abbr* **Authorized Version**) = la traduction anglaise de la Bible de 1611.

avail¹ [əˈveɪl] *n Lit* avantage *m*, utilité *f*; **of no a., without a.,** sans effet; **to be of little a.,** être peu utile *ou* peu avantageux; **to no a.,** sans résultat; **to work to little** *or* **no a.,** travailler sans (grand) résultat.

avail² **1** *vt* **to a. oneself of,** se servir *ou* s'aider de, profiter de (*qch*); user *ou* faire usage de (*un droit*); **to a. oneself of the opportunity to do sth,** saisir l'occasion de faire qch. **2** *vi Lit* **nothing availed against the storm,** contre la tempête nous ne pouvions rien.

availability [əveɪləˈbɪlɪtɪ] *n* disponibilité *f* (*de matériaux, d'hommes etc*); **offer subject to a.,** *Com* dans la limite des stocks disponibles; (*for tickets*) dans la limite des places disponibles.

available [əˈveɪləb(ə)l] *adj* (*person, room, seat etc*) disponible; (*person*) libre; **to try every a. means,** essayer tous les moyens possibles; **they used the time a. to evacuate the area,** ils ont utilisé le temps dont ils disposaient pour évacuer le secteur; **a. funds,** fonds *mpl* liquides *ou* disponibles, disponibilités *fpl*; **capital that can be made a.,** capitaux *mpl* mobilisables; **when are you a. to start work?,** à partir de quand pouvez-vous commencer à travailler?; *Com* **a. in all bookshops,** en vente *ou* disponible chez tous les libraires; *Com* **also a. in white,** existe également en blanc; **illegal drugs are readily a. in the town,** on se procure facilement de la drogue dans cette ville; **pocket calculators weren't a. then,** les calculatrices de poche n'existaient pas à cette époque là; **legal aid should be a. to everyone,** l'assistance juridique devrait être accessible à tous; **I'm catching the first a. flight,** je prends le premier avion.

avalanche [ˈævəlɑːntʃ] *n* avalanche *f* (*de neige, Fig de félicitations, de courrier etc*); **mud a.,** coulée *f* de boue.

avant-garde [ævɒŋˈgɑːd] **1** *n* l'avant-garde *f*. **2** *adj* d'avant-garde, avant-gardiste; **a.-g. films,** films *mpl* d'avant-garde.

avarice [ˈævərɪs] *n* avarice *f*.

avaricious [ævəˈrɪʃəs] *adj* avare, avaricieux.

avariciously [ævəˈrɪʃəslɪ] *adv* avaricieusement.

avast [əˈvɑːst] *int Nau* tiens bon!, tenez bon!, baste!

Av(e) (*abbr* **avenue**) av..

Ave [ˈɑːvɪ] *n* **A. Maria,** avé (Maria) *m inv*.

avenge [əˈvendʒ] *vt* venger (*qn, une injure*); **to a. oneself for an insult,** se venger d'une injure.

avenger [əˈvendʒər] *n* vengeur *m*, vengeresse *f*.

avenging [əˈvendʒɪŋ] *adj* (*angel etc*) vengeur.

avenue ['ævɪnjuː] *n* **(a)** promenade plantée d'arbres; *Fig* **to explore every a.**, explorer toutes les voies; **(b)** (*in street name*) avenue *f*; **(c)** *esp US* (belle) rue *f*; boulevard *m*; **(d)** (*to house*) chemin *m* d'accès.

aver [ə'vɜːr] *vt* (**-rr-**) *Lit* déclarer, affirmer (que).

average[1] ['ævərɪdʒ] **1** *n* **(a)** moyenne *f*; **rough a.**, moyenne approximative; **on a.**, en moyenne; **that gives an a. of 6**, ça fait une moyenne de 6; **above the a.**, au-dessus de la moyenne; *Fb etc* **goal a.**, goal-average *m*, avérage *m*; **(b)** (*marine insurance*) avarie(s) *f(pl)*; **a. adjustment**, dispache *f*. **2** *adj* (*prix, temps, poids etc*) moyen; **the a. Englishman**, l'Anglais moyen; **of a. height**, de taille moyenne; **a. speed**, vitesse moyenne; **the a. reader**, le lecteur moyen; **the food is better than a.**, la nourriture est au-dessus de la moyenne; **in an a. week**, dans une semaine ordinaire; **how was your day? — a.**, comment s'est passée ta journée? — moyen; *F* **a very a. singer**, un chanteur de qualité très moyenne.

average[2] *vt* **(a)** (*amount to on average*) **to a. so much**, donner *ou* atteindre *ou* rendre une moyenne de tant; **sales a. a thousand copies a year**, la vente moyenne *ou* la moyenne des ventes est de mille exemplaires par an; **to a. eight hours work a day**, travailler en moyenne huit heures par jour; **(b)** (*calculate average of*) prendre *ou* établir *ou* faire la moyenne de (*les résultats, les ventes etc*).

►**average out 1** *vtsep* (*calculate average*) **I've averaged out how much I spend a week**, j'ai calculé combien je dépense en moyenne par semaine. **2** *vi* **how does it a. out per week?**, combien ça fait en moyenne par semaine?; **it'll a. out over a month**, sur un mois ça s'équilibrera.

►**average out at** *vipo* (*amount to as an average*) équivaloir en moyenne à.

averse [ə'vɜːs] *adj* opposé; **to be a. to** *or* **from sth**, répugner à qch; **she was a. to doing**, elle a répugné à faire; **he is not a. to a glass of beer**, il prend volontiers un verre de bière.

aversion [ə'vɜːʃən] *n* **(a)** (*feeling*) aversion *f*, répugnance *f*; **to feel** *or* **have an a. to** *or* **for s.o.**, se sentir de l'aversion pour *ou* envers qn; **to feel** *or* **have a great a. to sth/to doing sth**, se sentir une grande répugnance pour qch/à faire qch; **(b)** (*thing*) objet *m* d'aversion; **my pet a.**, ma bête noire.

avert [ə'vɜːt] *vt* **(a)** détourner (*les yeux, son regard, ses pensées*) (**from**, de); **(b)** écarter, éloigner, prévenir (*des soupçons, un danger, un malheur*); conjurer (*une catastrophe*); détourner (*un coup*); parer à (*un accident*).

aviary ['eɪvɪərɪ] *n* volière *f*.

aviation [eɪvɪ'eɪʃən] *n* aviation *f*; **civil/military a.**, aviation civile/militaire; **a. history**, l'histoire *f* de l'aviation.

aviator ['eɪvɪeɪtər] *n Old-fashioned* aviateur, -trice.

aviculture ['eɪvɪkʌltʃər] *n* aviculture *f*.

avid ['ævɪd] *adj* avide (**of, for**, de); **a. reader**, lecteur avide *ou* passionné.

avidity [ə'vɪdɪtɪ] *n* avidité *f* (**for**, de, pour).

avidly ['ævɪdlɪ] *adv* avidement, avec avidité.

avionics [eɪvɪ'ɒnɪks] *n* avionique *f*.

avocado [ævə'kɑːdəʊ] *n* **a. (pear)**, (*fruit*) avocat *m*; (*tree*) avocatier *m*.

avoid [ə'vɔɪd] *vt* éviter (*qn, qch*); se soustraire à (*un châtiment etc*); esquiver (*les attentions de qn, un coup, une difficulté*); **you've been avoiding me**, tu m'évites; **to a. doing sth**, éviter de faire qch; **I could not a. speaking to him**, je ne pouvais faire autrement que de lui parler; **to a. paying tax**, se soustraire à l'impôt; **to a. a collision**, parer à *ou* éviter une collision; **the comparison is hard to a.**, la comparaison est difficile à éviter; **to a. s.o.'s eye**, fuir le regard de qn; **to a. the issue**, éviter *ou* contourner le problème.

avoidable [ə'vɔɪdəb(ə)l] *adj* évitable.

avoidance [ə'vɔɪdəns] *n* action *f* d'éviter; **tax a.**, évasion fiscale; *Jur* **a. of an agreement**, résolution *f ou* résiliation *f* d'un contrat; **condition of a.**, (*in contract*) condition *f* résolutoire.

avoirdupois [ævədə'pɔɪz] *n* **(a)** poids *m* du commerce; **ounce a.**, once *f* avoirdupois; **(b)** *Hum* excès *m* de poids, embonpoint *m*.

avow [ə'vaʊ] *vt* **(a)** *Fml* (*declare*) **to a. oneself a socialist**, se déclarer socialiste; **(b)** (*admit*) avouer, admettre (*une faute*); **to a. oneself beaten**, s'avouer vaincu.

avowed [ə'vaʊd] *adj* (*ennemi etc*) déclaré; **a. atheist**, athée avoué.

avowedly [ə'vaʊədlɪ] *adv* de son propre aveu.

avuncular [ə'vʌŋkjʊlər] *adj* avunculaire.

await [ə'weɪt] *vt Lit* attendre (*qch, qn*); *Com* **awaiting your instructions**, dans l'attente de vos instructions; **soldiers awaiting discharge**, soldats en instance de libération; *Com* **parcel awaiting delivery**, colis en souffrance.

awake[1] [ə'weɪk] *adj* éveillé; **to lie** *or* **keep a.**, rester éveillé; **I was a.**, je ne dormais pas; **to keep s.o. a.**, tenir qn éveillé; **wide a.**, (*alert*) bien éveillé, tout éveillé; *Fig* averti; **to be a. to**, (*aware of*) avoir conscience de (*un danger*); se rendre compte de (*un danger, un fait etc*); (*careful of*) veiller à *ou* sur (*ses intérêts*).

awake[2] *v* (*pt* **awoke** [ə'wəʊk]; *pp* **awoken** [ə'wəʊkən]) **1** *vi* s'éveiller, se réveiller; **to a. from a deep sleep**, se réveiller d'un profond sommeil; **I awoke to the sound of birds singing**, en me réveillant, j'ai entendu chanter les oiseaux; **I awoke to the realization that it was Monday**, je me suis rendu compte, en me réveillant, que c'était lundi; *Fig* **to a. to**, se rendre compte de (*un danger, un fait etc*); prendre conscience de (*un danger*); **to a. from**, revenir de (*une illusion, un rêve etc*). **2** *vt* éveiller, réveiller (*qn, les remords de qn*); éveiller (*la curiosité, les soupçons*); faire naître (*un espoir, une passion*); *Fig* **to a. s.o. to sth**, faire prendre conscience à qn de qch.

awaken [ə'weɪk(ə)n] *vt & vi* – **AWAKE[2]**.

awakening [ə'weɪk(ə)nɪŋ] *n* réveil *m*; *Fig* **a rude a.**, une amère désillusion.

award[1] [ə'wɔːd] *n* **(a)** (*for writer, actor etc*) prix *m*; *Mil etc* distinction *f* honorifique; *Sch etc* récompense *f*; **to make an a.**, décerner un prix *ou* une récompense; **the annual awards ceremony**, la cérémonie annuelle de remise des prix; **(b)** *Jur* (*money*) dommages-intérêts *mpl*; (*decision*) décision *f* (arbitrale), adjudication *f*; **to make an a.**, rendre un jugement (arbitral).

award[2] *vt* adjuger, décerner (*un prix, une récompense*); adjuger (*un marché, un contrat*); conférer (*un bénéfice, une dignité*); accorder (*une augmentation de salaire*); *Jur* **to a. s.o. a sum as damages**, allouer *ou* attribuer à qn une somme à titre de dommages-intérêts.

awarding [ə'wɔːdɪŋ] *n* attribution *f* (*d'un prix, d'un marché etc*).

award-winning [ə'wɔːdwɪnɪŋ] *adj* (*film, book etc*) primé.

aware [ə'weər] *adj* **to be a. of sth**, avoir connaissance *ou* conscience de qch, être au courant de qch; savoir *ou* ne pas ignorer qch; **I wasn't a. of him**, je ne m'étais pas aperçu qu'il était là; **I am a. of all the circumstances**, je connais tous les détails; **I am well** *or* **fully a. that ...**, je n'ignore pas que ...; **were you a. that your husband owed money?**, saviez-vous que votre époux était endetté?; **not that I am a. of**, pas que je sache; **as far as I'm a.**, autant que je sache; **to become a. of**, prendre connaissance de (*un fait*); **I became a. of a smell of burning**, j'ai perçu une odeur de brûlé.

awareness [ə'weənɪs] *n* conscience *f* (*de qch*); **a sudden a.**, une prise de conscience.

awash [ə'wɒʃ] *adj* **(a)** *Nau* (*of submarine etc*) à fleur d'eau; **rocks a. at high tide**, roches couvertes d'eau à marée haute; **(b)** (*flooded*) inondé; **the street was a.**, la rue était inondée.

away [ə'weɪ] **1** *adv* **(a)** (*in opposite direction*) **to turn (one's face) a. from sth**, détourner la tête de qch; **the signpost pointed a. from the village**, le bras du poteau indiquait une direction opposée à celle du village; **to go a.**, partir, s'en aller; **to walk/drive a.**, partir à pied/en voiture; **to run/fly a.**, s'enfuir/s'envoler; **to take sth a.**, emporter qch;

(b) (*at a distance*) **far a.**, dans le lointain, au loin; **a. in the distance**, tout au loin; **the town is five miles a.**, la ville est à (une distance de) cinq mil(l)es; **please stand a little farther a.**, voudriez-vous vous éloigner un peu?; **to keep a.**, se tenir à l'écart; **the church was set a. from the road**, l'église était située à l'écart de la route; **this is far and a. the best**, c'est de beaucoup *ou* sans comparaison le meilleur; **to hold sth a. from sth**, tenir qch éloigné *ou* loin de qch;

(c) (*absent*) **a. from home**, absent (de chez soi); **he is a.**, (*from home, school etc*) il est absent; **to be a. on business**, s'absenter pour affaires; **she is a. on business**, elle s'est absentée pour affaires; **to stay a.**, rester absent, ne pas venir; *Sp* **to play a.**, jouer à l'extérieur;

(d) (*disappearance*) **to melt a.**, (*of snow*) fondre; **to fade or die a.**, (*of sound*) s'éteindre; **to fritter a.**, gaspiller (*son argent, son temps*); **put that knife a.!**, pose ce couteau!; **to do a. with**, abolir (*qch*); tuer (*qn*);

(e) (*continuity*) **to work a.**, travailler toujours; continuer à travailler; **to slave a. at sth**, s'éreinter à qch;

(f) (*elliptical*) **a. with you!**, allez-vous-en!, filez!; **a.**

with him!, emmenez-le!; *Arch & Lit* **we must a.,** il nous faut partir;

(g) (*in motion*) **and they're a!,** (*at the beginning of race etc*) et ils sont partis!; **a couple of drinks and he's a.,** deux coups à boire et il est parti; *F* **well a.,** (*progressing*) bien en train; (*drunk*) soûl;

(h) (*without delay*) **to do sth right** *or* **straight a.,** faire qch tout de suite *ou* sur-le-champ;

(i) (*time*) **a. back,** dès; **I knew him a. back in 1950,** je l'ai connu dès 1950; **that was a. back,** c'était il y a longtemps.

2 *adj Sp* **a. ground,** terrain *m* adverse; **a. match,** match *m* à l'extérieur *ou* sur terrain adverse; **a. team,** équipe visiteuse.

awe¹ [ɔː] *n* (*fear*) crainte *f*; (*respect*) respect *m*, révérence *f*; **to strike s.o. with a.,** (*of person*) imposer à qn un respect mêlé de crainte; (*of object, phenomenon*) frapper qn d'une terreur mystérieuse; **to be in a. of s.o./sth,** (*fear*) craindre *ou* redouter qn/qch; (*respect*) avoir une crainte respectueuse de qn/qch; **to hold s.o. in awe,** redouter qn; **I was in a. of the nuns,** j'étais intimidé par les bonnes sœurs.

awe² *vt* remplir (*qn*) de crainte; intimider, inspirer un respect mêlé de crainte à (*qn*); **the children were awed by the cathedral/the tone of her voice,** les enfants ont été terriblement impressionnés par la cathédrale/le ton de sa voix.

aweigh [ə'weɪ] *adv Nau* **with anchor a.,** l'ancre dérapée; **anchors a.!,** levez l'ancre!

awe-inspiring ['ɔːɪnspaɪərɪŋ] *adj* imposant, impressionnant.

awesome ['ɔːsəm] *adj* **(a)** (= **awe-inspiring**) (*strength*) d'une force impressionnante; **an a. silence,** un silence qui inspire un effroi religieux; **(b)** *US F* (*wonderful*) super.

awe-struck ['ɔːstrʌk] *adj* frappé d'une terreur mystérieuse; (*frightened*) intimidé; **to be a.-s. by s.o./sth,** être terriblement impressionné par qn/qch.

awful ['ɔːfʊl] **1** *adj* **(a)** terrible, effroyable; **to die an a. death,** mourir d'une mort terrible; **that's the a. part of it,** c'est cela le plus terrible; **an a. silence,** un silence effroyable; **(b)** *F* (*very bad*) terrible, affreux, abominable; **it's simply a.,** c'est affreux; **she's an a. woman,** c'est une femme épouvantable; **what a. weather!,** quel temps abominable!; **he's an a. fool,** il est bien bête; **an a. lot of people,** énormément de gens. **2** *adv Sl* terriblement; **I'm a. glad to see you,** je suis rudement content de vous voir; **an a. long time,** terriblement longtemps.

awfully ['ɔːflɪ] *adv* **(a)** terriblement, effroyablement; **(b)** *F* **I'm a. sorry,** je regrette infiniment *ou* énormément; **I'm a. glad,** je suis joliment content; **a. funny,** amusant *ou* drôle comme tout; **thanks a.!,** merci mille fois!

awfulness ['ɔːfulnɪs] *n* **(a)** caractère *m* terrible (*d'une situation*); **(b)** *F* caractère affreux.

awhile [ə'waɪl] *adv Am & Lit* pendant quelque temps, un peu; **wait a.,** attendez un peu.

awkward ['ɔːkwəd] *adj* **(a)** (*movement, person*) gauche, maladroit, disgracieux, balourd; **to be a. with one's hands,** être inhabile de ses mains; **a. sentence,** phrase gauche *ou* mal venue; **(b)** (*embarrassed*) embarrassé, gêné; **I felt very a.,** je me suis senti très gêné *ou* embarrassé; **(c)** (*embarrassing*) fâcheux, embarrassant, gênant; **it would be a. if we met,** une rencontre serait embarrassante; **an a. silence,** un silence gêné; **to arrive at an a. moment,** arriver mal à propos; **to ask a. questions,** poser des questions embarrassantes; **(d)** (*difficult, not straightforward*) incommode, peu commode; (*outil*) peu maniable; (*virage*) difficile, dangereux; **the switch is in an a. place,** l'interrupteur est situé à un endroit peu accessible; **their house is a. to get to,** leur maison est d'un accès difficile; **I'm sorry to be a.,** (*but that doesn't suit me*) je suis désolé d'être peu accommodant; **the a. age,** l'âge ingrat; *F* **he's an a. customer,** c'est un homme difficile, il n'est pas commode.

awkwardly ['ɔːkwədlɪ] *adv* (*see adj*) **(a)** gauchement, maladroitement, disgracieusement; **(b)** d'une manière embarrassée, d'un ton embarrassé *ou* gêné; **(c)** d'une façon gênante *ou* embarrassante; **(d) the lever is a. placed,** le levier est mal placé.

awkwardness ['ɔːkwədnɪs] *n* **(a)** (*clumsiness*) gaucherie *f*, maladresse *f*; (*lack of grace*) manque *m* de grâce balourdise *f*; **(b)** (*embarrassment*) embarras *m*, gêne *f*; **a moment of a.,** un moment de gêne; **(c)** (*inconvenience*) inconvénient *m*, difficulté *f*, incommodité *f* (*d'une situation etc*).

awl [ɔːl] *n* alêne *f*, poinçon *m*, perçoir *m*.

awn [ɔːn] *n Bot* barbe *f* (*de l'orge etc*).

awning ['ɔːnɪŋ] *n* tente *f*, vélum *m*; banne *f* (*de boutique, etc*); bâche *f* (*de charrette*); marquise *f* (*de théâtre, d'hôtel etc*); *Nau* tente, tendelet *m*; cabane *f* (*de canot*); **a. (blind),** store *m* à l'italienne; **rain a.,** taud *m*, taude *f*; **a. deck,** pont-abri *m*, *pl* ponts-abris.

AWOL ['eɪwɒl] *adj* (*abbr* **absent without leave**) **to go AWOL,** s'absenter sans permission; **to be AWOL,** être absent sans permission.

awry [ə'raɪ] *adv & adj* de travers, de guingois; **to go all a.,** (*of plans etc*) aller tout de travers.

axe¹, *US* **ax,** *pl* **axes** [æks, 'æksɪz] *n* **(a)** hache *f*; **ice a.,** piolet *m*; **a. head,** fer *m* de hache; *Fig* **to have an a. to grind,** agir dans un but intéressé; *F* **the project got the axe,** le projet a été abandonné; **two hundred employees got the a.,** deux cent employés ont été mis à la porte; **the department got the a.,** le service a été supprimé; **(b)** *Mus Sl* (*instrument*) boîte *f*.

axe², *US* **ax** *vt F* renvoyer (*qn*); abandonner (*un projet*) (*pour des raisons d'économie*); **to a. public expenditure,** tailler dans les dépenses publiques; **500 jobs axed,** 500 emplois supprimés.

axial ['æksɪəl] *adj* axial, -aux.

axil ['æksɪl] *n Bot* aisselle *f* (*d'une feuille*).

axiom ['æksɪəm] *n* axiome *m*.

axiomatic [æksɪə'mætɪk] *adj* **(a)** axiomatique; **(b)** (*self-evident*) évident.

axis, *pl* **axes** ['æksɪs, 'æksiːz] *n* **(a)** axe *m* (*d'une sphère, d'une plante, d'un cristal, Geol d'un plissement*); **a. of the earth,** axe de la terre; **a. of revolution,** axe de révolution; **(b)** *Anat* axis *m* (*du cou*); **(c)** *Hist* **the A.,** l'Axe *m*.

axle ['æks(ə)l] *n* **(a)** (*of vehicle*) **a. (tree),** essieu *m*; *Rail* **driving a.,** essieu moteur; *Aut* **front/rear a.,** essieu *ou* pont *m* avant/arrière; **a. box,** boîte *f* de l'essieu; **(b)** (*of wheel*) tourillon *m*, arbre *m*, axe *m* (*d'une roue etc*).

ay(e) [aɪ] **1** *int esp Scot* oui, mais oui; *Nau* **a. a., sir!,** oui, commandant! **2** *n* (*in voting*) **ayes and noes,** voix *fpl* pour et contre; **the ayes have it,** les voix pour l'emportent.

azalea [ə'zeɪlɪə] *n* (*plant*) azalée *f*.

azimuth ['æzɪməθ] *n Astron etc* azimut *m*.

Azores (the) [ðiːə'zɔːz] *npl* les Açores *fpl*.

Aztec ['æztek] *Hist* **1** *adj* aztèque. **2** *n* **(a)** Aztèque *mf*; **(b)** *Ling* aztèque *m*.

azure ['æʒər, 'eɪʒər] **1** *n Lit & Her* azur *m*. **2** *adj* d'azur, azuré.

B

B, b [biː] *n* **(a)** (la lettre) B, b *m*; *Sch* ≈ assez bien; **51B,** (*street number*) 51 ter; *Mil* **B company,** deuxième compagnie; **B-movie,** film *m* de série B; **he was a B-movie actor,** c'était un acteur de série B; *Br* **B road,** route *f* secondaire; *Old-fashioned* **B side,** (*of record*) face *f* B; **(b)** *Mus* si *m*; **B flat,** si bémol; **in B flat,** en si bémol; **(c)** *Med* **B-cells,** lymphocytes *mpl* B.

b (*abbr* **born**) né.

BA [biː'eɪ] *n Univ* (*abbr* **Bachelor of Arts**) **to have a BA in history,** ≈ avoir une licence d'histoire; **John Smith, BA,** ≈ John Smith, licencié.

baa¹ [bɑː] *n* bêlement *m*; **b.!,** bê!; **b.-lamb,** (*in children's language*) petit agneau.

baa² *vi* (**baaed, baa'd** [bɑːd]) bêler.

baba ['bɑːbɑː] *n Culin* **rum b.,** baba *m* au rhum.

babbitt ['bæbɪt] *n* **b. (metal),** métal *m* antifriction.

babble¹ ['bæb(ə)l] *n* **(a)** (*chatter*) bavardage *m*; **(b)** (*incoherence*) babillage *m*; **(c)** (*of stream*) murmure *m*.

babble² *vi* **(a)** (*tell secrets*) bavarder, jaser; **(b)** (*be incoherent*) babiller; **(c)** (*of stream*) murmurer, gazouiller.

▸babble away, babble on *vi* bavarder, babiller sans arrêt; **you were babbling away in your sleep last night,** tu n'as pas arrêté de bredouiller en dormant, la nuit dernière; **what are you babbling on about?,** qu'est-ce que tu bredouilles encore?

babbler ['bæblər] *n* **(a)** bavard, -arde; jaseur, -euse (*qui laisse échapper des secrets*); **(b)** (*incoherent talker*) babillard, -arde.

babbling ['bæb(ə)lɪŋ] **1** *adj* **(a)** (*talkative*) bavard, jaseur; **(b)** (*incoherent*) babillard; **b. idiot,** personne qui parle à tort et à travers; **she made me feel like a b. idiot,** elle m'a donné l'impression que je parlais pour ne rien dire; **(c)** (*stream*) murmurant. **2** *n* = **BABBLE¹**.

babe [beɪb] *n* **(a)** *Lit etc* petit enfant, bambin *m*; **a b. in arms,** un enfant porté au bras; *Fig* un naïf, une naïve; **(b)** *Am F* jolie fille; **hi, b.!,** bonjour, ma jolie!

Babel ['beɪb(ə)l] *n* **the Tower of B.,** la Tour de Babel; *Fig* **b. of voices,** brouhaha *m*.

baboon [bə'buːn] *n* (*animal*) babouin *m*; *Fig* singe *m*.

baby¹ ['beɪbɪ] *n* **(a)** bébé *m*; **when I was a b.,** quand j'étais bébé; **she has had a b. boy/girl,** elle a eu un petit garçon/une petite fille; **the b. of the family,** le benjamin; **to behave like a b.,** faire le bébé; **don't be such a b.,** arrête de faire le bébé; **I'm not a b.!,** je ne suis plus un bébé!; **Mum showed him my b. pictures,** Maman lui a montré des photos de moi bébé; *Fig* **to throw the b. out with the bath water,** jeter le bébé avec l'eau du bain; *Fig* **to leave s.o. holding the b.,** laisser payer les pots cassés à qn; *Fig* **the dictionary is his b.,** (*he wrote it*) le dictionnaire est sa création; (*his responsibility*) le dictionnaire est sa responsabilité; **b. elephant/chimpanzee,** bébé éléphant/chimpanzé; **b. boom,** baby-boom *m*; **b. boomer,** enfant *m* du baby-boom; **b.'s breath,** (*flower*) gypsophile *f*; *Am* **b. buggy** *or* **carriage** (*Br* = **pram**), landau *m*, voiture *f* d'enfant; **b. carrots,** de toutes petites carottes; *Mus* **b. grand,** (piano *m*) demi-queue *m*; **b. scales,** pèse-bébé *m*, *pl* pèse-bébés; **b. snatcher,** kidnappeur, -euse; *Fig* (*man*) vieux barbon; (*woman*) = femme qui épouse un garçon beaucoup plus jeune qu'elle; **b. snatching,** enlèvement *m*, rapt *m* d'enfant, kidnapping *m*; *Fig* **I don't go in for b. snatching,** moi, je ne les prends pas au berceau; **b. talk,** babil enfantin; *Am* **b. tooth** (*Br* = **milk tooth**), dent *f* de lait;

(b) *US F* (*girlfriend*) jeune fille *f*, nana *f*; (*boyfriend*) mec *m*; (*as address*) chéri, -ie; (*thing*) machin *m*; **I've been driving this b. for a year,** je conduis cette bagnole depuis un an.

baby² *vt* (**babied**) *Pej* traiter (*qn*) comme un bébé; (*give love and attention to*) dorloter (*qn*).

baby-face ['beɪbɪfeɪs] *n* visage poupin; **he's a real b.-f.,** il a le visage poupin.

baby-faced ['beɪbɪfeɪst] *adj* à visage poupin.

babyhood ['beɪbɪhʊd] *n* première enfance, bas âge.

babyish ['beɪbɪɪʃ] *adj* de bébé.

Babylon ['bæbɪlən] *n Antiq* Babylone *f*.

Babylonia [bæbɪ'ləʊnɪə] *n Antiq* Babylonie *f*.

Babylonian [bæbɪ'ləʊnɪən] *Bible* **1** *adj* babylonien. **2** *n* Babylonien, -ienne.

baby-minder ['beɪbɪmaɪndər] *n* nourrice *f*.

baby-sit ['beɪbɪsɪt] *vi* (**-sat, -sitting**) garder les bébés, *F* faire du baby-sitting.

baby-sitter ['beɪbɪsɪtər] *n* baby-sitter *mf*; *Can* gardienne *f*.

baby-sitting ['beɪbɪsɪtɪŋ] *n* garde *f* des bébés, *F* baby-sitting *m*.

baby-walker ['beɪbɪwɔːkər] *n* trotteur *m*.

baccalaureate [bækə'lɔːrɪət] *n Am Univ* ≈ licence *f*; *Can* baccalauréat *m*.

baccara(t) ['bækərɑː] *n Cards* baccara *m*; **to play b.,** jouer au baccara; **a game of b.,** une partie de baccara.

bacchanal ['bækən(ə)l] *Lit* **1** *adj* bachique. **2** *n* bacchanale *f*, débauche *f* bachique.

bacchanalia [bækə'neɪlɪə] *npl Lit* bacchanales *fpl*.

bacchanalian [bækə'neɪlɪən] *adj Lit* bachique.

baccy ['bækɪ] *n Old-fashioned F* tabac *m*.

bachelor ['bætʃələr] *n* **(a)** célibataire *m*, garçon *m*; **b. flat,** garçonnière *f*; *Old-fashioned* **b. girl,** jeune femme autonome; **b. uncle,** oncle non marié; **(b)** *Univ* ≈ licencié, -ée; **b.'s degree,** *F* **b.'s** licence *f*; **to have a b.'s in French,** avoir une licence de français; **B. of Arts/Science,** ≈ licencié, -ée ès lettres/sciences; **B. of Laws,** ≈ licencié, -ée en droit; **(c)** *Hist* bachelier *m* (*aspirant à la chevalerie*); **knight b.,** chevalier *m*.

bachelorhood ['bætʃələhʊd] *n* célibat *m*, vie *f ou* état *m* de garçon.

bacillary [bə'sɪlərɪ] *adj Biol* bacillaire.

bacillus, *pl* **-i** [bə'sɪləs, -aɪ] *n Biol Med* bacille *m*.

back¹ [bæk] **1** *n* **(a)** dos *m* (*de qn, d'un animal*); (*lower part*) les reins *mpl*; **to fall on one's b.,** tomber à la renverse; **mind your backs!,** attention, s'il vous plaît!; **to be at the b. of sth,** (*behind*) être derrière qch; *Pej* (*responsible for*) être responsable de qch; **to be at the b. of s.o.,** (*support*) soutenir qn; (*chase, harry*) poursuivre qn; **with an army at his b.,** (*supporting him*) soutenu par une armée; **to do sth behind s.o.'s b.,** faire qch à l'insu de qn; **he laughs at you behind your b.,** il se moque de vous quand vous avez le dos tourné; **to talk about s.o. behind their b.,** dire du mal de qn dans son dos; **to turn one's b. on s.o.,** tourner le dos à qn; *Fig* abandonner qn; **to sit** *or* **stand with one's b. to s.o.,** tourner le dos à qn; **sitting with one's b. to the light,** assis à contre-jour; **to be glad to see the b. of s.o.,** être content d'être débarrassé de qn; **I saw him only from the b.,** je ne l'ai vu que de dos; **to be on one's b.,** (*lying down*) être étendu sur le dos; *F* (*ill*) être alité; *F* **I spent three months (flat) on my b.,** j'ai passé trois mois au lit; *F* **get off my b.!,** fiche-moi la paix!; *F* **the boss was on my b. all day,** j'ai eu le patron sur le dos toute la journée; **to put** *or* **get s.o.'s b. up,** mettre qn en colère; **with one's b. to the wall,** adossé au mur; *Fig* (*in difficulties*) au pied du mur; **to put one's b. into it,** s'y mettre énergiquement; **to have b. problems,** avoir des problèmes de dos; **to break one's b.,** se casser les reins; *F* **he won't break his b. working,** il ne se casse pas au travail; **to break the b. of the work,** faire le plus dur *ou* le plus gros du travail; **to break her b.,** (*of ship*) se briser en deux, se casser; **b. pain,** mal *m* de dos; **b. patting,** félicitations *fpl*; **b. slapping,** cordialité exubérante;

(b) dos *m* (*d'un couteau, d'un outil, d'un livre, d'une enveloppe*); envers *m* (*d'un tissu*); verso *m* (*d'une page*); dos, verso (*d'un chèque*); dossier *m* (*d'une chaise etc*); revers *m* (*d'une médaille*); revers, dessus *m* (*de la main*); derrière *m* (*d'une maison*); arrière *m* (*d'une maison, d'une* *voiture, d'un bus*); *F* **you'll feel the b. of my hand in a minute,** tu vas en prendre une; **b. of the mouth,** arrière-bouche *f*; **b. of the throat,** arrière-gorge *f*; *Br F* **to have a face like the b. of a bus,** être moche comme un pou; **carriage at the b. of the train,** voiture *f* en queue de *ou* du train; **to sit in the b.,** (*of car*) monter à l'arrière; **the house has a patio at the b.** *or Am* **in b.,** il y a un patio de l'autre côté de la maison; **the vocabulary is at the b. of the book,** le vocabulaire est à la fin du livre; **the dress fastens at the b.** *or Am* **in b.,** la robe s'agrafe dans le dos; **idea at the b. of one's mind,** idée derrière la tête; **you have your sweater on b. to front,** tu as mis ton pullover à l'envers; *Fig* **she knows the system b. to front,** elle connaît le système d'un bout à l'autre; **he knows London like the b. of his hand,** il connaît Londres comme le fond de sa poche;

(c) *Archit* extrados *m* (*d'une voûte*); fond *m* (*d'une armoire, d'une salle*); *Mus* table *f* du fond (*d'un violon etc*); **the b. of the stage,** le fond de la scène; *F* **to live at the b. of beyond,** habiter un trou perdu; *F* **we're in the b. of beyond,** nous sommes au bout du monde;

(d) *Sp* position *f* d'arrière; **(full) b.,** (*player*) arrière *m*; **right/left b.,** arrière droit/gauche.

2 *adj* **(a)** (*partie, roue etc*) arrière; (*porte, jardin etc*) de derrière; *Fig* **to put sth on the b. burner,** remettre qch à plus tard; **b. axle,** essieu *m* arrière; **b. boiler,** chauffe-eau *m inv* derrière un foyer; **b. door,** porte *f* de service; *Fig* **to come in (to a job) through** *or* **by the b. door,** (*get it through influential contacts*) être pistonné; **the b. page,** la dernière page; *Anat* **b. passage,** rectum *m*; **b. rest,** dossier *m* (*de siège*); **b. room,** pièce *f* qui donne sur l'arrière; *Fig* **b.-room boy,** personne *f* qui travaille dans la coulisse; **b. seat,** siège *m* arrière; *Fig* **to take a b. seat,** (*of job, project*) passer au second plan; (*of person*) s'effacer; *Sp* **b. straight,** (*on track*) ligne opposée; **b. stretch,** (*on race course*) ligne d'en face; **b. yard,** (*of building*) arrière-cour *f*; *Am* jardin *m* de derrière; *Fig* **South America is the United States' b. yard,** l'Amérique du Sud est à la porte des États-Unis; **the 'not-in-my-b.-yard' syndrome,** = attitude de rejet vis à vis de la construction d'une centrale nucléaire etc dans sa commune;

(b) (*in opposite direction*) (*mouvement*) inverse; *Ling* **b. formation,** dérivation régressive;

(c) (*time*) **b. interest,** arrérages *mpl*; **b. list,** (*of publisher*) = liste des titres disponibles et régulièrement réimprimés; *Journ* **b. number** *or* **copy** *or* **issue,** vieux numéro (*d'un journal*); *Fig* **she's a b. number,** elle est démodée; *Com* **b. orders,** commandes *fpl* en attente; *Admin* **b. pay,** rappel *m* de traitement; **b. rent,** arriéré(s) *m(pl)* de loyer;

(d) (*remote*) *Austr* **b. country,** brousse *f*; *Am* **b. road,** petite route;

(e) *Br* **b. shift,** deuxième partie d'une journée de travail.

3 *adv* **(a)** (*of place*) en arrière; **stand b.!,** rangez-vous!; **to step b. a pace,** faire un pas en arrière; **he left him three miles b.,** il l'a laissé à trois mil(l)es d'ici; **far b.,** loin derrière (*les autres etc*); (*seated*) dans les derniers rangs; **house standing b. from the road,** maison écartée du chemin *ou* en retrait; *Am* **b. of sth,** derrière qch;

(b) (*in return, retaliation*) **to hit** *or* **strike b.,** rendre coup pour coup; **to get one's own b.,** prendre sa revanche; **to call s.o. b.,** (*shout, telephone*) rappeler qn; *Tel* **ring** *or* **call me b. in an hour,** rappelez-moi dans une heure; **to come b.,** revenir; **to go b.,** (*return*) retourner **(to,** à); **to go** *or* **turn b.,** (*retrace footsteps*) rebrousser chemin; **to make one's way b.,** s'en retourner;

(c) (*to original starting point*) de retour, **to arrive** *or* **come b.,** rentrer; **when will she be b.?,** quand sera-t-elle de retour?; **I'll be b.,** je serai de retour, *F* vous aurez de mes nouvelles; **I expect him b. tomorrow,** j'attends son retour pour demain; **as soon as I am** *or* **get b.,** dès mon retour; **he's just b. from a trip,** il arrive de voyage; **she's b. at work,** elle a repris son travail; **a few pages b.,** quelques pages plus haut; **b. home,** chez nous; **b. in Britain,** en Grande-Bretagne;

(d) (*of time*) **a few years b.,** il y a (déjà) quelques années; **way b. in the Middle Ages,** il y a bien longtemps au moyen âge; **as far b. as 1914,** déjà en 1914, dès 1914; **b. in 1982,** en 1982.

back² **1** *vt* **(a)** soutenir, appuyer, seconder (*qn*); *Com etc* financer (*qn, un projet etc*); avaliser, endosser (*un effet*); **to b. s.o. in an argument,** donner raison à qn;

(b) *Sp etc* parier *ou* miser sur (*un cheval, une équipe etc*); jouer (*un cheval*); **well-backed horse,** cheval très coté; *Horseracing & Fig* **to b. a winner,** parier *ou* miser sur le gagnant; *Horseracing & Fig* **to b. the wrong horse,** parier *ou* miser sur le mauvais cheval;

(c) (*move*) reculer (*une charrette*); faire reculer (*un cheval*); mettre (*une machine*) en arrière; refouler (*un train*); **to b. one's car into the garage,** entrer en marche arrière dans le garage; *Nau* **to b. the oars, to b. water,** ramer à rebours, déramer;

(d) rentoiler (*un tableau*);

(e) *Nau* masquer, coiffer (*une voile*);

(f) *Mus* accompagner (*qn*).

2 *vi* (*of person*) marcher à reculons; (*of horse*) reculer; *Aut etc* faire marche arrière, reculer; **to b. into the station,** (*of train*) reculer dans la gare.

►**back away** *vi* (*in fear*) reculer (**from,** devant).

►**back down** *vi* **(a)** descendre (*une échelle etc*) à reculons; **(b)** *Fig* (*in argument*) avouer qu'on est dans son tort.

►**back off** *vi* reculer; **the gunman told the police to b. off,** le gangster a dit à la police de reculer.

►**back on to** *vipo* (*of building*) donner par derrière sur (*un jardin*).

►**back out 1** *vi* **(a)** (*of person etc*) sortir à reculons; *Aut* sortir en marche arrière; **(b)** *Fig* (*withdraw*) retirer sa promesse, se dédire; (*of a responsibility*) se défiler; **to b. out of an undertaking,** se retirer d'une entreprise; **he's trying to b. out of it,** il voudrait se dédire. **2** *vtsep* sortir (*une voiture*) en marche arrière.

►**back up 1** *vtsep* **(a)** (*support*) soutenir, appuyer (*qn, qch*); seconder (*qn*); **to b. s.o. up in an argument,** donner raison à qn; **(b)** faire reculer (*une voiture etc*); *Am* **an accident has backed traffic up all the way to the service station,** l'accident a créé un ralentissement jusqu'à la station-service; **(c)** *Comptr* faire une copie de, copier (*des données*). **2** *vi* **(a)** (*of car*) reculer, faire marche arrière; **(b)** *Comptr* faire une copie de secours *ou* un double; **(c)** *US* (*of drains*) être obstrué.

backache ['bækeɪk] *n* mal *m* de reins; **to have b.,** avoir mal aux reins.

backbench ['bæk'bentʃ] *n Br Parl* (*usu pl*) **backbenches,** banquettes *fpl* des députés sans portefeuille; **discontent on the backbenches,** mécontentement parmi les députés sans portefeuille; **she got b. support,** elle a eu le soutien des députés sans portefeuille; **b. MPs.,** députés *mpl* sans portefeuille.

backbencher ['bæk'bentʃər] *n Br Parl* député *m* sans portefeuille.

backbite ['bækbaɪt] *vt* médire de (*qn*).

backbiting ['bækbaɪtɪŋ] *n* médisance *f*.

backboard ['bækbɔːd] *n* (*in basketball*) panneau *m*.

backbone ['bækbəʊn] *n* (*of person, animal*) épine dorsale, colonne vertébrale; (*of fish*) grande arête; **English to the b.,** anglais jusqu'au bout des ongles; **he's got no b.,** il n'a pas de moelle dans les os; **she is the b. of the movement,** c'est elle qui mène le mouvement; **tourism is the b. of the economy,** le tourisme est le pivot de l'économie.

backbreaking ['bækbreɪkɪŋ] *adj* (*travail etc*) éreintant.

backburn¹ ['bækbɜːn] *n Austr* contre-feu *m* (*d'incendie de forêt etc*).

backburn² *vi Austr* allumer un contre-feu.

backchat ['bæktʃæt] *n Br F* **(a)** (*impudence*) impertinence *f*; **none of your b.!,** pas de réplique!; **(b)** (*repartee*) reparties *fpl*.

backcloth ['bækklɒθ] *n Th* toile *f* de fond.

backcomb ['bækkəʊm] *vt* crêper (*les cheveux*).

backdate ['bækdeɪt] *vt* antidater; **increase backdated to July 1st,** augmentation avec effet rétroactif au 1er juillet; **will it be backdated?,** est-ce qu'il aura effet rétroactif?

backdown ['bækdaʊn] *n* retraite *f*, abandon *m* de ses prétentions.

backdrop ['bækdrɒp] *n* **(a)** *Th* toile *f* de fond; **(b)** *Fig* (*background*) toile *f* de fond, arrière-plan *m*, *pl* arrière-plans; **against a b. of continuing violence,** avec, comme arrière-plan *ou* toile de fond, un climat de violence permanente.

backed ['bækt] *adj* **b. on to sth,** adossé à qch.

-backed ['bækt] *suff* **broad-b.,** à large dos, qui a le dos large; **high-b. chair,** chaise *f* à grand dossier.

backer ['bækər] *n* **(a)** *Horseracing* parieur, -euse; **(b)** *Pol etc* partisan *m*; *Com* commanditaire *m*; *Fin* **b. of a bill,** donneur *m* d'aval; *Th etc* **we need a b.,** il nous faut un mécène; **financial b.,** bailleur, -euse de fonds.

backfill¹ ['bækfɪl] *n* (*of trench*) remplissage *m*.

backfill² **1** *vt* remplir (*une tranchée*). **2** *vi* remplir.

backfire¹ [bæk'faɪər] *n* **(a)** (*of engine*) allumage prématuré; retour *m* de flamme (*au carburateur*); (*noise*) pétarade *f*; **(b)** *Am* contre-feu *m* (*d'incendie de forêt etc*).

backfire[2] *vi* **(a)** (*of engine*) s'allumer prématurément; avoir des retours (*au carburateur*); (*make noise*) pétarader; *Fig* **the plan backfired on them,** le projet leur est retombé sur le dos; **(b)** *Am* allumer un contre-feu.

backgammon ['bækgæmən] *n* ≈ (jeu *m* de) jacquet *m*; **b. board,** ≈ jacquet.

background ['bækgraʊnd] *n* **(a)** (*position*) fond *m*, arrière-plan *m*, *pl* arrière-plans; arrière-corps *m inv* (*d'un bas-relief*); **b. of mountains,** fond de montagnes; **in the b.,** dans le fond, à l'arrière-plan; **music was playing in the b.,** il y avait une musique d'ambiance; **against a dark b.,** sur (un) fond sombre; **the protests took place against a b. of repression,** les manifestations se sont inscrites dans un contexte de répression; **to keep (oneself)** *or* **to stay in the b.,** s'effacer; *Fig* **she stays very much in the b.,** elle reste dans l'ombre; **to push s.o. into the b.,** mettre *ou* reléguer qn au second plan; (*outshine*) prendre le pas sur qn; **b. music,** musique d'ambiance *ou* de fond; *Th Cin* fond sonore; **b. noise,** bruit *m* de fond;
(b) (*social class*) origines *fpl*; (*education*) formation *f*, éducation *f*; (*experience*) antécédents *mpl*; contexte *m* historique (*d'un événement*); données *fpl* de base (*d'un problème*); **b. reading,** lectures générales (*autour d'un sujet*); **to do some b. reading,** se documenter; **I need a bit more b.,** j'ai besoin de plus de données; **young man of good b.,** garçon de bonne famille; **to come from a middle-class b.,** venir d'un milieu bourgeois; **what's his professional b.?,** quels sont ses antécédents professionnels?

backhand ['bækhænd] *n* **(a)** *Tennis* revers *m*; **b. stroke,** coup *m* de revers; **her b. is weak,** elle a un mauvais revers; **(b)** (*writing*) écriture renversée *ou* penchée à gauche.

backhanded [bæk'hændɪd] *adj* **(a)** (*coup*) de revers; *Fig* **in a b. way,** déloyalement; **(b)** (*compliment*) équivoque.

backhander ['bækhændər] *n F* **(a)** (*blow*) coup *m* de revers, coup du revers de la main; *Fig* riposte inattendue; attaque déloyale; **(b)** (*bribe*) pot-de-vin *m*.

backing ['bækɪŋ] *n* **(a)** (*support*) soutien *m*, appui *m* (*de qn*); rentoilage *m* (*d'un tableau*); **financial b.,** financement *m* (*de qn, d'un projet etc*); *Fin* **b. of the currency,** garantie *f* de la circulation; **(b)** *Horseracing* paris *mpl* (*sur un cheval*); **(c)** (*movement*) recul *m*, reculement *m* (*d'un cheval, d'une charrette*); refoulement *m* (*d'un train*); marche *f* (en) arrière (*d'une voiture etc*); **(d)** *Mus* accompagnement *m*.

backlash ['bæklæʃ] *n* **(a)** *Fig* contrecoup *m* (*d'un événement*); contre-courant *m* (*politique etc*); **there has been a b. against the policy,** la politique a eu un effet de boomerang; **(b)** *MecE* retour *m* (*de dents, de la denture*).

backless ['bæklɪs] *adj* (*robe etc*) sans dos; (*banc etc*) sans dossier.

backlit ['bæklɪt] *adj Comptr* (*screen*) rétro-éclairé.

backlog ['bæklɒg] *n* arriéré *m* (*de travail*); *Com* **b. of orders,** commandes non exécutées; **to have a b. of correspondence,** avoir du retard dans son courrier, avoir du courrier en souffrance.

backpack[1] ['bækpæk] *n* sac *m* à dos.

backpack[2] *vi* faire de la randonnée et du camping.

backpacking ['bækpækɪŋ] *n* **to go b.,** faire de la randonnée et du camping.

back-pedal [bæk'pedəl] *vi* (**-ll-**, *US* **-l-**) (*on bicycle*) rétropédaler; *Fig* en rabattre, faire marche arrière.

back-pedalling, *US* **-pedaling** ['bækped(ə)lɪŋ] *n* (*on bicycle*) rétropédalage *m*; *Fig* marche *f* arrière.

backscratcher ['bækskrætʃər] *n* gratte-dos *m*; *Fig* = personne qui ne rend un service qu'en échange d'un autre.

backscratching ['bækskrætʃɪŋ] *n Fig* aide mutuellement avantageuse.

back-seat ['bæksiːt] *adj* **b.-s. driver,** personne qui donne des conseils au conducteur; **I don't want any b.-s. driving,** je n'ai pas besoin de conseils pour conduire.

backsheesh, backshish ['bækʃiːʃ] *n* bakchich *m*.

backside [bæk'saɪd] *n F* derrière *m*, postérieur *m*.

backsight ['bæksaɪt] *n* (*on rifle*) hausse *f*.

backslash ['bækslæʃ] *n* (*on keyboard*) oblique *f* inverse.

backslide ['bækslaɪd] *vi* (**backslid**) retomber dans l'erreur *ou* dans le vice.

backsliding ['bækslaɪdɪŋ] *n* rechute *f* dans le vice; (*of criminal*) récidive *f*.

backspace[1] ['bækspeɪs] *n* **b. (key),** (*on keyboard*) touche *f* de rappel arrière, espacement *m* arrière.

backspace[2] *vi* (*on keyboard*) revenir d'un caractère; **b. twice,** revenir de deux caractères.

backstage [bæk'steɪdʒ] *adv Th* (*behind stage*) derrière la scène, dans la coulisse *ou* les coulisses; (*at rear of stage*) à l'arrière-plan; *Fig* en coulisse; *Th* **to help b.,** aider en coulisse(s).

backstairs [bæk'steəz] *n* (*for servants etc*) escalier *m* de service; (*hidden*) escalier dérobé; **b. influence,** protections *fpl* en haut lieu; *F* piston *m*; **b. gossip,** commérages *mpl*.

backstitch[1] ['bækstɪtʃ] *n Sewing* point *m* de piqûre.

backstitch[2] *vi Sewing* coudre au point de piqûre.

backstreet ['bækstriːt] *n* petite rue; **the backstreets of a town,** les bas quartiers d'une ville; **b. abortion,** avortement clandestin; **b. abortionist,** avorteur, -euse clandestin(e).

backstroke ['bækstrəʊk] *n* **(a)** *Swimming* dos crawlé; **the 100 metres b.,** le 100 mètres dos; **(b)** *MecE* course *f* arrière, course de retour (*d'un piston etc*).

backtalk ['bæktɔːk] *n Am* = **BACKCHAT**.

back-to-back [bæktə'bæk] *adj* (*seats, people*) dos à dos; *Am Sp* **to play two games b.-to-b.,** enchaîner deux parties de suite.

backtrack ['bæktræk] *vi* **(a)** revenir sur ses pas; **(b)** *Fig* en rabattre, faire marche arrière; **to b. on a promise/decision,** revenir sur une promesse/une décision.

backup ['bækʌp] *n* soutien *m*, appui *m*; *Mil etc* renforcement *m*; *Med* soins *mpl* supplémentaires; **to ask for b.,** (*of police etc*) demander des renforts; *Comptr* **b. copy/diskette/file,** copie *f*/disquette *f*/fichier *m* de sauvegarde; **b. car,** voiture *f* de rechange; **b. troops,** troupes *fpl* de renfort.

back-up ['bækʌp] *adj Am* **b.-up** (*Br* = **reversing**) **lights,** feux *mpl* de recul.

backward ['bækwəd] **1** *adj* **(a)** (*mouvement etc*) rétrograde; (*regard, pas etc*) en arrière; **b. and forward motion,** mouvement de va-et-vient; **(b)** (*enfant*) arriéré; (*élève*) en retard; (*race*) moins évolué; (*fruit*) tardif; **the b. state of the country,** le retard dont souffre le pays; **to be b. in doing sth,** être lent à faire qch; *Br F* **he isn't b. in coming forward,** il ne fait pas le modeste. **2** *adv* = **BACKWARDS**.

backwardness ['bækwədnɪs] *n* retard *m* (*d'un élève, de la moisson*); (*mental*) arriération mentale, retard; tardiveté *f* (*des fruits*); **b. in doing sth,** hésitation *f* à faire qch.

backwards ['bækwədz] *adv* (*sauter, se pencher*) en arrière; (*aller, marcher*) à reculons; (*tomber*) à la renverse; **to look b.,** jeter un coup d'œil en arrière; (*in time*) remonter dans le passé; **to flow b.,** (*of water*) couler à contre-courant; **to say the alphabet b.,** réciter l'alphabet à rebours; *Fig* **to know sth b.,** connaître qch parfaitement; *Fig* **a step b.,** un pas en arrière; **b. and forwards,** d'avant en arrière et d'arrière en avant; **to walk b. and forwards,** aller et venir; **movement b. and forwards,** mouvement de va-et-vient; **to go b. and forwards,** faire la navette (*entre deux endroits*).

backwash ['bækwɒʃ] *n* remous *m*; *Fig* remous, répercussions *fpl*.

backwater ['bækwɔːtər] *n* **(a)** (*tributary*) bras *m* de décharge (*d'une rivière*); *Fig* **to live in a b.,** habiter un trou perdu; **(b)** (*water*) eau arrêtée (*par un bief etc*).

backwoods ['bækwʊdz] *npl esp Am* forêts *fpl* de l'intérieur; *Fig* **to live in the b.,** habiter un trou perdu *ou* un bled.

backwoodsman, *pl* **-men** [bæk'wʊdzmən] *n* colon *m* des forêts (*de l'Amérique du Nord*); *esp Am F* rustre *m*, rustaud *m*.

baclava [bə'klɑːvə] *n Culin* baklava *m*.

bacon ['beɪkən] *n* bacon *m*; **streaky b.,** ≈ petit salé; *Fig* **to save s.o.'s b.,** sauver la peau de qn; *Fig* **to bring home the b.,** (*provide material support*) faire bouillir la marmite; (*be successful*) réussir.

bacteria *see* **BACTERIUM**.

bacterial [bæk'tɪərɪəl] *adj* bactérien.

bacteriological [bæktɪərɪə'lɒdʒɪk(ə)l] *adj* bactériologique; **b. warfare,** la guerre bactériologique.

bacteriologist [bæktɪərɪ'ɒlədʒɪst] *n* bactériologiste *mf*, bactériologue *mf*.

bacteriology [bæktɪərɪ'ɒlədʒɪ] *n* bactériologie *f*.

bacterium, *pl* **-ia** [bæk'tɪərɪəm, -ɪə] *n* bactérie *f*.

bad [bæd] **1** *adj* (**worse** [wɜːs]; **worst** [wɜːst]) **(a)** (*of poor quality, unfortunate*) mauvais; de mauvaise qualité; **it's not b.,** ce n'est pas mal; *Br F* **it's not half b.,** ce n'est pas mal du tout; **he's/she's not b. looking,** il/elle n'est pas mal; **b. debt,** mauvaise créance; **b. translation,** mauvaise traduction; **to go b.,** (*of food*) se gâter, s'avarier; **to speak b. French,** parler mal le français; **b. at maths,** nul en maths; **to get into b. habits** *or* **ways,** prendre de mauvaises habitudes; **b. light stopped play,** (*at cricket* *match*) la partie a été remise à cause d'un manque de lumière; **is this a b. time to ask for leave?**, le moment est-il mal choisi pour demander des congés?; **it's a b. business!**, c'est une mauvaise affaire!; **to be in a b. way**, être en mauvais état; **he'll come to a b. end**, il finira mal; **to have a b. name**, avoir (une) mauvaise réputation; **it wouldn't be a b. thing** *or* **plan to ...**, on ne ferait pas mal de ...; **things are going from b. to worse**, les choses vont de mal en pis; **a b. apple**, une pomme pourrie; *Fig* une brebis galeuse; **one b. apple spoils the barrel**, pomme pourrie pourrit les autres; *Fig* il ne faut qu'une brebis galeuse pour gâter un troupeau; *Fig* **there's b. blood between them**, il y a du ressentiment *ou* de la rancune entre eux; *F* **he's always turning up like a b. penny**, il revient à tout bout de champ;

(b) (*unpleasant, serious*) mauvais (*nouvelle, odeur, humeur etc*); gros (*rhume*); violent (*mal de tête*); (*accident, faute etc*) grave; **b. weather**, mauvais temps; *Nau* gros temps; *Fig* **she's b. news**, elle ne te *ou* lui *etc* apportera que des ennuis; **to be on b. terms with s.o.**, être mal *ou* en mauvais termes avec qn; **it's (really) too b.!, that's too b.!**, c'est trop fort!, c'est bien dommage!; **it's too b. of him!**, ce n'est vraiment pas bien de sa part!; **if you don't like it, that's just too b.**, tant pis pour vous si vous n'aimez pas;

(c) (*not healthy*) **to be b. for s.o./sth**, ne rien valoir à qn/pour qch; **all that whisky is b. for him**, tout ce whisky ne lui vaut rien; **smoking is b. for you** *or* **your health**, il est mauvais pour la santé de fumer; **my b. leg**, ma jambe malade; **I have a b. heart**, je suis cardiaque; **I'm not so b.**, (*I'm well*) je ne vais pas trop mal; **how's business? — not so b.**, comment vont les affaires? — pas si mal;

(d) (*wicked*) méchant; *F* **he's a b. lot**, c'est un vaurien; **b. language**, gros mots.

2 *adv F* **that looks b.**, (*serious*) c'est (un) mauvais signe; (*in eyes of other people*) c'est mal vu; **to feel b. about sth**, (*regret*) avoir du remords au sujet de qch; **I feel b. about firing him**, ça m'ennuie d'avoir eu à le renvoyer; *F* **she was taken b. yesterday**, (*became ill*) elle est tombée malade hier; *F* **to have it b.**, (*be very much in love*) être mordu.

3 *n* **(a) to take the b. with the good**, accepter la mauvaise fortune aussi bien que la bonne;

(b) to go to the b., (*of person*) mal tourner; (*of business*) être en mauvaise passe;

(c) to be 500 francs to the b., en être de 500 francs (de sa poche);

(d) *F* **to be in b. with s.o.**, être en mauvais termes avec qn.

baddie, baddy ['bædɪ] *n F* méchant *m*.

bade *see* **BID²**.

badge [bædʒ] *n* **(a)** badge *m*; *Mil & Sch* écusson *m*; insigne *m* (*d'un membre d'une société*); médaille *f* (*de porteur etc*); **b. of office**, (*of mayor*) insigne; **(b)** *Fig* symbole *m*, signe distinctif.

badger¹ ['bædʒər] *n* (*animal*) blaireau *m*; **b. baiting**, déterrage *m* du blaireau.

badger² *vt* harceler, tourmenter, importuner (*qn*); **to b. s.o. into granting a favour, to b. a favour out of s.o.**, obtenir une faveur de qn à force d'importunités.

badinage ['bædɪnɑːʒ] *n* badinage *m*.

badly ['bædlɪ] *adv* (**worse** [wɜːs]; **worst** [wɜːst]) **(a)** (*poorly*) mal; **b. dressed**, mal habillé; **to do** *or* **come off b.**, mal réussir; **to be very b. off**, être dans la gêne; *Fig* **I'm very b. off for clothes**, je ne suis pas riche en vêtements; **things are going b.**, les choses vont mal; **to speak English b.**, parler mal l'anglais; **to behave b.**, se conduire mal; **he took it very b.**, il a très mal pris la chose; **to work b.**, (*of machine etc*) mal fonctionner; **(b)** (*seriously*) **b. wounded**, gravement *ou* grièvement blessé; **the b. disabled**, les grands infirmes, les grands mutilés; *Sp etc* **b. beaten**, battu à plate(s) couture(s); **(c)** (*greatly*) **to want sth b.**, avoir grande envie de qch; **if you want it b. enough you'll get it**, quand on veut, on peut; **I need it b.**, j'en ai grand besoin; **he is b. in need of a haircut**, il faudrait vraiment qu'il aille chez le coiffeur.

badminton ['bædmɪntən] *n* (*game*) badminton *m*; **b. court**, terrain *m* de badminton; **b. player**, joueur, -euse de badminton.

bad-mouth ['bædmaʊθ] *vt esp Am* déblatérer sur (*qn*).

badness ['bædnɪs] *n* **(a)** (*of cooking, writing etc*) mauvaise qualité; **(b)** (*of person*) méchanceté *f*.

bad-tempered [bæd'tempəd] *adj* grincheux, acariâtre; **to be b.-t.**, avoir le caractère mal fait; **he is a b.-t. man**, il a mauvais caractère; **I'm a bit b.-t. today**, je ne suis pas de bonne humeur aujourd'hui.

baffle¹ ['bæf(ə)l] *n* **(a)** *Tech* chicane *f*, déflecteur *m*; **b. plate**, plaque-chicane *f*, *pl* plaques-chicanes; **(b)** *Rad* **b. (board)**, écran *m* (*de haut-parleur*).

baffle² *vt* **(a)** confondre, déconcerter, dérouter (*qn*); confondre (*l'imagination etc*); **to b. definition**, échapper à toute définition; **mystery that has baffled all investigators**, mystère qui a déjoué toutes les recherches; **the police admit they are baffled**, la police admet qu'elle est coincée; **I'm baffled as to why she said that**, je ne comprends vraiment pas pourquoi elle a dit ça; **(b)** *Tech* décaler (*des ouvertures etc*); établir des chicanes dans (*un conduit etc*).

baffling ['bæf(ə)lɪŋ] *adj* (*behaviour*) déconcertant; (*mystère etc*) inexplicable.

bag¹ [bæg] *n* **(a)** (*container*) sac *m*; (*handbag*) sac à main; **travel(ling) b.**, sac de voyage; **to pack one's bags**, faire ses bagages; *F* **we've bags of time**, on a tout le temps; *F* **they've bags of money**, ils sont pleins aux as; *F* **there's bags of room**, la place ne manque pas; **b. and baggage**, avec armes et bagages; *Sl* **that's not my b.**, (*I'm not good at it*) ce n'est pas mon fort; (*I'm not interested in it*) ce n'est pas mon genre; *F* **bags under the eyes**, poches *fpl* sous les yeux; *F* **b. lady**, clocharde *f*; **(b)** *Br Sl* **old b.**, vieille chipie; **(c)** (*in hunting*) **the b.**, le tableau; **to make a good b.**, faire un grand abattis de gibier; (*of fighter pilot etc*) avoir un beau tableau de chasse; *F* **in the b.**, dans le sac; *F* **it's in the b.**, c'est du tout cuit; **(d)** *Old-fashioned F* **bags**, pantalon *m*; **(e)** pis *m*, mamelle *f* (*de vache*).

bag² *v* (**-gg-**) **1** *vt* **(a)** (*pack*) mettre (*du charbon, du terreau*) en sac; ensacher (*des pommes, des bonbons*); *Am* (*in supermarket*) emballer (*des achats*); **(b)** *F* (*take*) empocher (*qch*), mettre la main sur (*qch*); accaparer (*les meilleures places*); *Br* **bags I go first!**, c'est moi le premier!; *Br* **bags I sit in front**, c'est moi qui m'assois à l'avant; **(c)** (*kill*) abattre, tuer (*du gibier*); *Av F* abattre (*des avions*). **2** *vi* (se) gonfler, s'enfler; (*of garment etc*) bouffer, avoir trop d'ampleur; **trousers that b. at the knees**, pantalon qui fait des poches aux genoux.

bagatelle [bægə'tel] *n* **(a)** (*trifle*) *& Mus* bagatelle *f*; **(b)** (*game*) billard anglais.

bagel ['beɪg(ə)l] *n esp Am Culin* baguel *m*.

baggage ['bægɪdʒ] *n* **(a)** *esp Am* bagages *mpl*; *Rail* **b. car**, fourgon *m* à bagages; *Av etc* **b. handler**, bagagiste *m*; **b. reclaim**, retrait *m* des bagages; **(b)** *Mil* bagage *m*; **b. waggon**, fourgon *m* à bagages.

baggy ['bægɪ] *adj* (*vêtement*) trop ample; (*pantalon*) flottant, bouffant.

bagpipe(s) ['bægpaɪp, -s] *n(pl)* cornemuse *f*; **to play the b.**, jouer de la cornemuse; **b. player**, joueur, -euse de cornemuse.

bah [bɑː] *int* bah!

Bahama [bə'hɑːmə] *n* **the Bahamas, the B. Islands**, les Lucayes *fpl*, les îles *fpl* Bahamas, l'archipel *m* des Bahamas.

bail¹ [beɪl] *n Jur* (*system*) cautionnement *m*; (*person*) caution *f*, garant *m*; (*money*) caution; **to go** *or* **stand b. for s.o.**, se porter garant *ou* caution de qn, fournir caution pour qn (*pour sa libération provisoire*); **to grant s.o. b.**, (*of judge*) accorder la liberté provisoire à qn sous caution; **she was released on b.**, elle a été libérée sous caution; **to be (out) on b.**, être en liberté provisoire (sous caution); *F* **to jump (one's) b.**, se dérober à la justice (*alors qu'on jouit de la liberté provisoire*).

bail² *vt Jur* (*of judge*) accorder la liberté provisoire à (*qn*) sous caution; (*of lawyer etc*) se porter caution pour (*qn*).

bail³ *n Cr* **bails**, barrettes *fpl*, bâtonnets *mpl*.

bail⁴ *n Nau* écope *f*.

►bail out *vtsep* **(a)** *Jur* se porter garant *ou* caution pour (*qn*); *Fig* tirer (*qn*) d'affaire; *Fig* **I'm not bailing you out again**, c'est la dernière fois que je te tire d'affaire; **(b)** écoper, vider (*un canot, l'eau d'une embarcation*).

bailer ['beɪlər] *n Nau* écope *f*.

Bailey¹ ['beɪlɪ] *n* **the Old B.**, = le tribunal principal de Londres.

Bailey² *n* **B. bridge**, pont *m* Bailey.

bailiff ['beɪlɪf] *n* **(a)** *Jur US* huissier *m*; *Br* **sheriff's b.**, huissier *m*; **(b)** régisseur *m* (*d'un domaine, d'une ferme*); **water b.**, garde-pêche *m*, *pl* gardes-pêche; **(c)** *Hist* bailli *m*.

bailiwick ['beɪlɪwɪk] *n Jur* baillage *m*.

bairn [beə(r)n] *n Scot* enfant *mf*.

bait¹ [beɪt] *n* (*for fish*) amorce *f*, appât *m*; *Fig* appât, leurre *m*; **live b.**, appât vivant; **ground b.**, amorce de fond; **to rise to** *or* **swallow the b.**, mordre à l'hameçon; *Fig* gober *ou* avaler le morceau.

bait[2] *vt* **(a)** (*tease*) harceler (*un animal*); harceler, tourmenter (*qn*); **(b)** (*put bait on*) amorcer (*un hameçon, un piège etc*) (**with,** avec); mettre l'appât à (*la ligne*).

baiting ['beɪtɪŋ] *n* **(a)** (*teasing*) harcèlement *m* (*des animaux*); (*of badger*) déterrage *m*; **(b)** amorçage *m* (*d'un hameçon, d'un piège etc*).

baize [beɪz] *n* feutrine *f*; **green b.,** tapis vert; **green b. door,** porte feutrée.

bake [beɪk] **1** *vt* (faire) cuire (*qch*) au four; cuire (*des briques, la porcelaine etc*); étuver (*un moule*); **to b. bread,** faire cuire le pain; **earth baked by the sun,** sol durci *ou* desséché par le soleil; *F* **I'm baked,** je crève de chaleur. **2** *vi* (*of bread etc*) cuire (au four); **are you going to b. today?,** est-ce que tu vas faire de la pâtisserie aujourd'hui?; *F* **I'm baking,** je crève de chaleur.

baked [beɪkt] *adj* **b. beans,** haricots blancs à la tomate; *Can* fèves *fpl* au lard.

baker ['beɪkər] *n* boulanger *m*, boulangère *f*; **b.'s (shop),** boulangerie *f*; **b.'s dozen,** treize douze, treize à la douzaine, une treizaine.

bakery ['beɪkərɪ] *n* boulangerie *f*.

baking ['beɪkɪŋ] **1** *adj F* **b. hot,** excessivement chaud; (*journée*) torride; **it's b. in here,** on étouffe ici. **2** *n* **(a)** cuisson *f* (*du pain etc*); cuisson, cuite *f* (*des briques etc*); étuvage *m*, étuvement *m* (*des moules*); **I'll do a b. tomorrow,** demain, je ferai de la pâtisserie; **b. sheet,** plaque *f* (à gâteaux); **b. tin,** (*for roast*) plat *m* à rôtir; (*for cake*) moule *m* à gâteau; **b. powder,** levure chimique *ou* artificielle; **b. soda,** bicarbonate *m* de sodium; **(b)** (*batch*) fournée *f* (*de pain*); cuite *f* (*de briques etc*).

baklava [bə'klɑːvə] *n Culin* baklava *m*.

baksheesh ['bækʃiːʃ] *n* bakchich *m*.

Balaclava [bælə'klɑːvə] *n* Balaklava; **B. (helmet),** passe-montagne *m*, *pl* passe-montagnes.

balalaika [bælə'laɪkə] *n Mus* balalaïka *f*.

balance[1] ['bæləns] *n* **(a)** (*steadiness*) équilibre *m*; **to keep one's b.,** se tenir en équilibre; **to lose one's b.,** perdre l'équilibre; *Fig* **to catch s.o. off b.,** prendre qn au dépourvu; **to throw s.o. off (their) b.,** faire perdre l'équilibre à qn; *Fig* interloquer qn; **off b.,** (*esprit*) désaxé, déséquilibré; *Pol* **the b. of power,** l'équilibre des forces; *Pol* **to hold the b. of power,** avoir la possibilité de faire pencher la balance;
(b) *Com Fin* solde *m*, reliquat *m* (*d'un compte*); (*in accounting*) balance *f*, bilan *m*; **credit/debit b.,** solde créditeur/débiteur; **b. carried forward,** report *m* à nouveau; *Fig* **to strike a b.,** (*between two things*) trouver le juste milieu; **b. of trade,** balance du commerce; **b. of payments,** balance des paiements; *Fig* **on b.,** tout bien considéré; **my bank b. is not very big,** mon solde bancaire n'est pas très élevé; **b. sheet,** bilan *m* (d'inventaire);
(c) (*for weighing*) balance *f*; *Astron* **the B.,** la Balance; **Roman b.,** balance romaine; **spring b.,** peson *m*; **to turn the b.,** faire pencher la balance; **to be/hang in the b.,** être/rester en balance; **b. beam,** (*of scales*) fléau *m* de balance; balancier *m*, flèche *f* (*d'une porte d'écluse*); **b. spring,** ressort *m*; **b. (weight),** contrepoids *m*, masse *f* d'équilibrage; **b. (wheel),** balancier (*de montre*); roue *f* de rencontre (*d'un horloge*).

balance[2] **1** *vt* **(a)** mettre *ou* maintenir (*un objet*) en équilibre; équilibrer (*une embarcation*); faire contrepoids à (*qch*); *Aut* équilibrer (*les roues*); **to b. sth on one's head,** porter qch sur sa tête; **one thing balances another,** une chose compense l'autre; **(b)** *Com Fin* balancer, solder, aligner (*un compte*); compenser (*une dette*); équilibrer (*le budget*); **to b. the books,** régler les livres. **2** *vi* **(a)** faire contrepoids; (*of scales*) équilibrer; **the two things b.,** les deux choses se balancent *ou* s'équilibrent; **(b)** *Com Fin* (*of accounts*) se balancer, s'équilibrer, se solder; **account that balances,** compte en balance; **(c)** (*of acrobat*) s'équilibrer; **to b. on one foot,** se tenir en équilibre sur un pied.

►balance against *vtaspo* **to b. one thing against another,** comparer les avantages d'une chose par rapport à une autre; **you have to b. the advantages against the disadvantages,** il faut peser le pour et le contre.

►balance out 1 *vi* (*of figures*) correspondre. **2** *vtsep* (*match*) compléter (*qch*); **they b. each other out,** (*because of their respective skills*) ils se complètent bien.

balanced ['bælənst] *adj* **(a)** (*in weight*) équilibré, compensé; *Fig* (*jugement, esprit*) pondéré; (*reportage*) objectif; **to be well b.,** avoir l'esprit bien équilibré; **(well-) b. diet,** régime (alimentaire) bien équilibré; **(b)** (*in strength, value*) égal; **the two parties are pretty well b.,** les deux parties sont à peu près égales.

balancing ['bælənsɪŋ] *n* **(a)** mise *f* en équilibre; *Rad* neutralisation *f*; *Aut* équilibrage *m* (*des roues*); *Art* balancement *m* (*des figures dans un tableau*); **b. pole,** contrepoids *m* (*de danseur de corde*); *Th* **b. act,** tours *mpl* d'équilibre; *Fig* **a political b. act,** des acrobaties *fpl* politiques; **to do a b. act,** faire de l'équilibrisme; *Fig* **she's doing a b. act between her job and her family,** elle jongle avec son travail et sa famille; **(b)** *Com Fin* **b. of accounts,** règlement *m ou* solde *m ou* alignement *m* des comptes; **(c)** ajustement *m* (*de deux choses*); compensation *f* (*de qch par qch*).

balcony ['bælkənɪ] *n* **(a)** (*on house*) balcon *m*; **(b)** *Th* fauteuils *mpl* de première *ou* deuxième galerie, balcon *m*; **we always sit in the b.,** nous prenons toujours des places au balcon; **there are two b. seats left,** il reste deux places au balcon.

bald [bɔːld] *adj* **(a)** (*person*) chauve; (*pneu*) lisse; **his b. head,** son crâne chauve; **he is going b.,** il commence à perdre ses cheveux; *F* **b. as a coot** *or* **an egg,** chauve comme un œuf; **b. eagle,** aigle *m* à tête blanche; **b. patch,** commencement *m* de tonsure; **(b)** *Fig* (*style etc*) dépouillé; **b. statement of (the) facts,** simple exposition des faits, exposition des faits sans glose.

balderdash ['bɔːldədæʃ] **1** *n* bêtises *fpl*, balivernes *fpl*; **to talk b.,** dire des bêtises *ou* des balivernes. **2** *int* balivernes!

bald-headed [bɔːld'hedɪd] *adj* (= **bald**) *F Fig* **to go b.-h. into** *or* **at sth,** foncer tête baissée dans qch.

balding ['bɔːldɪŋ] *adj* qui devient chauve.

baldly ['bɔːldlɪ] *adv Fig* (*to write*) d'un style dépouillé; (*to say*) sèchement.

baldness ['bɔːldnɪs] *n* **(a)** (*of person*) calvitie *f*; **(b)** *Fig* maigreur *f* (*du style etc*).

bale[1] [beɪl] *n Com* balle *f*, ballot *m* (*de marchandises*); **b. of paper,** ballot de dix rames de papier.

bale[2] *vt* emballotter, paqueter (*des marchandises*).

bale[3] *n* = **BAIL**[4].

►bale out 1 *vi Av* sauter en parachute d'un avion en perdition; **he baled out over the Atlantic,** il s'est éjecté de l'avion au-dessus de l'Atlantique. **2** *vtsep* = **BAIL OUT (b).**

Balearic [bælɪ'ærɪk] *adj* **the B. Islands,** les îles *fpl* Baléares.

baleen ['beɪliːn] *n* (*of whale*) fanon *m* de baleine.

baleful ['beɪlfʊl] *adj Lit* sinistre, maléfique.

balefully ['beɪlfʊlɪ] *adv* sinistrement.

baler[1] ['beɪlər] *n* **(a)** (*machine*) presse *f* à balles *ou* à emballer; *Agr* **pick-up b.,** ramasseuse-presse *f*, *pl* ramasseuses-presses; **(b)** (*person*) emballeur, -euse.

baler[2] *n Nau* écope *f*.

baling ['beɪlɪŋ] *n* mise *f* en balles, paquetage *m*; **b. machine,** presse *f* à balles *ou* à emballer.

baling out *n* saut *m* en parachute.

balk[1] [bɔːk] *n* **(a)** *Agr* billon *m*; **(b)** (*obstacle*) pierre *f* d'achoppement, obstacle *m*; **(c)** *Constr* (grosse) poutre *f*, solive *f*.

balk[2] **1** *vt* déjouer, frustrer, contrarier (*les desseins de qn*); contrecarrer (*qn*). **2** *vi* (*of horse*) refuser, (se) dérober; **to b. at a fence,** (*of horse*) refuser un obstacle; *Fig* **to b. at,** s'arrêter *ou* reculer *ou* hésiter devant (*une difficulté, une dépense*).

Balkan ['bɔːlkən] **1** *adj* **the B. States,** les États *mpl* balkaniques; **the B. Peninsula,** la péninsule des Balkans. **2** *npl* **the Balkans,** (*region*) les États *mpl* balkaniques; (*mountains*) les (monts *mpl*) Balkans *mpl*.

Balkanize ['bɔːlkənaɪz] *vt* balkaniser, libaniser (*un territoire*).

ball[1] [bɔːl] *n* **(a)** boule *f* (*de croquet, de neige*); balle *f* (*de cricket, de tennis etc*); ballon *m* (*d'enfant, de football*); bille *f* (*de billard*); boulet *m* (*de canon*); pelote *f* (*de laine, de ficelle*); **to wind wool into a b.,** mettre de la laine en pelote; **b. game,** (*played with ball*) jeu *m* de ballon; *Am* base-ball *m*; **b. games not allowed,** (*notice*) ballons interdits; *Am* **to go to the b. game,** aller au match de base-ball; *Fig* **that's a whole new b. game,** c'est une situation tout à fait nouvelle; **black b.,** (*for voting*) boule noire; **b. lightning,** éclair *m* en boule; **b. of earth,** motte *f*; **b. of fire,** boule de feu; *Fig* **to be a b. of fire,** être plein de vie; **to knock the balls about,** *Tennis* peloter; *Billiards* caramboler les billes; *Fb* **to kick the b. about,** s'amuser avec le ballon; *Cr* **no b.,** balle nulle; **to play b.,** jouer à la balle; *Am* jouer au base-ball; *Fig* coopérer, jouer le jeu; *Fig* **to be on the b.,** (*quick-witted*) avoir de la présence d'esprit; (*knowledgeable*) connaître son affaire; *Fig* **to keep the b. rolling,** (*in conversation*) soutenir la conversation; *Fig* **to start the b. rolling,** mettre le bal en train; *Fig* **the b. is in your court,** c'est à vous de jouer; *Fig* **to have the**

b. at one's feet, avoir la balle *ou* la partie belle; *Tennis* **b. boy/girl,** ramasseur/ramasseuse de balles;

(b) *MecE* bille *f* (*de roulement*); **b. bearing,** roulement *m* à billes; **b. cage,** cage *f* à billes; **b. cock,** robinet *m ou* soupape *f* à flotteur; **b.(-and socket) joint,** *Anat* énarthrose *f*; *MecE* joint *m* à rotule, articulation *f* à genouillère; *Constr* **b. mill,** moulin *m* à boulets; **b. race,** (*channel, groove*) chemin *m ou* voie *f* de roulement; (*in ball bearing*) cage à billes; **b. valve,** soupape à boulet;

(c) *Vulg* **balls,** couilles *fpl*; **balls!,** (*rubbish*) quelles conneries!; **b. to him!,** qu'il aille se faire foutre!; *Fig* **to have s.o. by the balls,** mettre à qn le couteau sous la gorge;

(d) lentille *f* (*de pendule*);

(e) éminence métatarsienne (*du pied*); globe *m* (*de l'œil*); **b. of the thumb,** (éminence *f*) thénar *m*;

(f) loupe *f* (*de fer fondu*);

(g) *Vet* (*bolus*) boulette *f*.

ball[2] **1** *vt* **(a)** baller (*le fer*); *Tex* mettre (*la laine*) en pelote; **(b)** *Vet* administrer une boulette à (*un cheval*). **2** *vi* s'agglomérer.

ball[3] *n* (*dance*) bal *m*, *pl* bals; **to open the b.,** ouvrir le bal; *F* **to have (oneself) a b.,** bien s'amuser; **b. dress** *or* **gown,** robe *f* de bal.

▶**ball up** *vtsep Am Vulg* = **BALLS UP**.

ballad ['bæləd] *n* **(a)** *Mus* romance *f*; **(b)** *Lit* ballade *f*.

ballast[1] ['bæləst] *n* **(a)** *Nau Av* lest *m*; **ship in b.(-trim),** navire *m* sur lest; **to take in b.,** faire son lest; **to discharge b.,** se délester, jeter du lest; **b. tank,** ballast *m* (*de sous-marin*); *Fig* **I'm carrying a bit too much b.,** j'ai un peu de poids en excédent; **(b)** *Constr* pierraille *f*, cailloutage *m*; *Rail* ballast *m*, empierrement *m*; *Rail etc* **b. bed,** coffre *m*, empierrement (*de la voie*); encaissement *m* (*d'une route*); *Rail* **b. truck** *or* **car,** wagon *m* de terrassement.

ballast[2] *vt* **(a)** *Nau Av* lester; **(b)** *Constr* empierrer, ensabler, caillouter; *Rail* ballaster.

ballerina [bælə'riːnə] *n* ballerine *f*.

ballet ['bæleɪ, *esp Am* bæ'leɪ] *n* ballet *m*; **I'm going to the b. this evening,** je vais voir un ballet ce soir; **b. dancer,** danseur, -euse de ballet; (*woman*) ballerine *f*; **b. lesson/school,** cours *m*/école *f* de danse; **b. shoe,** chausson *m* de danse.

ballistic [bə'lɪstɪk] *adj* balistique; **b. missile,** missile *m* balistique.

ballistics [bə'lɪstɪks] *npl* (*usu with sing verb*) balistique *f*.

balloon[1] [bə'luːn] *n* **(a)** (*toy*) ballon *m* d'enfant; *Av* ballon; *Sp* montgolfière *f*; *Fig* **when the b. goes up,** quand l'action commence; *Fig* **to go down like a lead b.,** (*of suggestion, joke*) tomber à plat; **b. barrage,** barrage *m* de ballons; **(b)** *Ch* **b. (flask),** ballon *m*; **b. glass,** verre *m* ballon; **(c)** (*in cartoons, comic strips*) bulle *f*, phylactère *m*.

balloon[2] *vi* (*of skirt, sail etc*) ballonner; (*of cheeks*) gonfler.

ballooning [bə'luːnɪŋ] *n* **(a)** (*sport*) aérostation *f*; **(b)** ballonnement *m* (*d'un vêtement, d'une voile etc*).

balloonist [bə'luːnɪst] *n* aéronaute *m*, aérostier *m*.

ballot[1] ['bælət] *n* (*process*) tour *m* de scrutin; (*vote*) scrutin *m*, vote *m*; **to vote by b.,** voter au scrutin; **to put sth to the b.,** soumettre qch à un vote; **second b.,** ballottage *m*, deuxième tour de scrutin; **b. paper,** bulletin *m* de vote; **b. (ball),** boule *f* de scrutin.

ballot[2] **1** *vt Pol* appeler (*des syndiqués*) à voter. **2** *vi* **(a)** *Pol* voter au scrutin; **to b. for/against s.o.,** voter pour/contre qn; **(b)** *Arch* (*draw lots*) tirer au sort; **to b. for a place/***etc*, tirer une place/*etc* au sort.

balloting ['bælətɪŋ] *n* **(a)** *Pol* élection *f* au scrutin; **(b)** *Arch* tirage *m* au sort.

ballpark ['bɔːlpɑːk] *n Am* terrain *m* de base-ball; *Fig* **b. figure,** estimation *f*, approximation *f*; *Fig* **are we in the same b.?,** est-ce qu'on est sur la même longueur d'ondes?

ballplayer ['bɔːlpleɪər] *n Am Sp* joueur *m* de base-ball.

ballpoint ['bɔːlpɔɪnt] *n* **b. (pen),** stylo *m* (à) bille.

ballroom ['bɔːlruːm] *n* salle *f* de bal, salle de danse; **b. dancing,** danses *fpl* de bal *ou* de salon; **b. dancing championship,** championnat *m* de danses de salon; **to go b. dancing,** aller danser.

▶**balls up** *vtsep Br Vulg* foutre (*qch*) en l'air.

balls-up ['bɔːlzʌp] *n Vulg* **to make a (right) b.-up,** faire une connerie *ou* une couillonnade; **to make a (right) b.-up of sth,** foutre qch en l'air.

bally ['bælɪ] *adj Old-fashioned Br F* sacré, satané.

ballyhoo[1] [bælɪ'huː] *n Sl* **(a)** (*publicity*) battage *m* (publicitaire); **(b)** (*deception*) baratin *m*; **to see through the b.,** ne pas être dupe.

ballyhoo[2] *vt esp Am* faire du battage (publicitaire) pour promouvoir (*un livre, un spectacle*).

balm [bɑːm] *n Pharm & Fig* baume *m*; **b. to the soul,** baume au cœur.

balminess ['bɑːmɪnɪs] *n* **(a)** (*mildness*) **the b. of the evening air,** l'air embaumé du soir; **(b)** *Br F* = **BARMINESS**.

Balmoral [bɑːl'mɒrəl] *n* (*shoe*) balmoral *m*.

balmy ['bɑːmɪ] *adj* **(a)** (*like balm*) balsamique; **(b)** (*air, temps*) embaumé, parfumé; *Lit* doux; **(c)** *Br F* = **BARMY**.

baloney [bə'ləʊnɪ] **1** *n Am* (*sausage*) saucisse bolognaise; *F* **it's all b.,** (*nonsense*) c'est des histoires *ou* de la fantaisie; (*lies*) c'est du chiqué *ou* du boniment. **2** *int* quel baratin!

balsa ['bɔːlsə] *n* **b. (wood),** balsa *m*; **b. wood raft,** radeau *m* en bois de balsa.

balsam ['bɔːlsəm] *n* **(a)** (*substance*) baume *m*; **(b)** (*plant*) balsamine *f*; **b. fir,** (*tree*) sapin baumier.

Baltic ['bɔːltɪk] **1** *n* **the B. (Sea),** la (mer) Baltique. **2** *adj* balte, baltique; **B. port,** port *m* balte; **B. States,** les pays *mpl* baltes.

baluster ['bæləstər] *n* balustre *m*; **balusters,** rampe *f* d'escalier.

balustrade [bælə'streɪd] *n* balustrade *f*.

bamboo [bæm'buː] *n* bambou *m*; **b. cane,** bambou, bamboche *f*; **b. chair,** chaise *f* en bambou; *Pol* **b. curtain,** rideau *m* de bambou; *Culin* **b. shoots,** pousses *fpl* de bambou.

bamboozle [bæm'buːz(ə)l] *vt F* mystifier, enjôler, embobiner (*qn*); **you've been bamboozled,** on vous a refait; **to b. s.o. out of sth,** (*cheat*) refaire qn de qch; (*trick*) soutirer qch à qn; **to b. s.o. into sth,** embobiner qn pour qu'il fasse qch.

ban[1] [bæn] *n* interdiction *f*; *Hist* ban *m*, bannissement *m*, proscription *f*; *Rel* interdit *m*; **atomic test b.,** interdiction des essais nucléaires; **to put/lift a b. on sth,** interdire/lever l'interdiction sur qch; **is there a b. on smoking?,** est-il interdit de fumer?

ban[2] *vt* (-nn-) interdire (*qn, qch*); **play banned by the censor,** pièce interdite par la censure; **b. the bomb!,** non à la bombe atomique!; **to b. nuclear testing,** interdire les essais nucléaires; **to be banned from driving,** se voir retirer son permis de conduire; **he should be banned for life,** (*from driving*) on devrait lui interdire de conduire à vie; **dogs have been banned from the beach,** les chiens sont interdits sur la plage.

banal [bə'nɑːl] *adj* banal, ordinaire.

banality [bə'nælɪtɪ] *n* banalité *f*.

banana [bə'nɑːnə] *n* banane *f*; *F* **to go bananas,** (*become excited*) devenir surexcité; (*become angry*) s'énerver; *F* **you're bananas!,** (*crazy*) tu es fou!; **b. boat,** bananier *m*; *Pej* **b. republic,** république bananière; **b. (tree),** bananier *m*; **b. plantation,** bananeraie *f*; **b. skin,** (*of fruit*) *& Fig* peau *f* de banane; *Culin* **b. split,** banana split *m*.

band[1] [bænd] *n* **(a)** (*of metal, material*) lien *m*; (*of metal, for reinforcing*) frette *f*; cercle *m* (*d'un tonneau*); bandage *m* (*d'une roue*); bande *f* (*de papier, de toile*); ruban *m* (*d'un chapeau*); bague *f* (*de cigare*); **crêpe b.,** (*round arm*) brassard *m* de crêpe *ou* de deuil; **steel b.,** ruban d'acier; **(b)** bande *f*, raie *f* (*de couleur etc*); **bands of the spectrum,** bandes du spectre; **(c)** *Rad* bande *f* de fréquence; **(d)** (*range*) tranche *f*; **children in the 10-15 age b.,** les enfants dans la tranche des 10-15 ans; **(e)** *MecE etc* bande *f*, courroie *f* (*de transmission*); **b. saw,** scie *f* à ruban; *Ind* **b. conveyor,** tapis roulant; **(f)** *Rel* **bands,** rabat *m*; **(g)** alliance *f* (*de mariage*); **b. of gold,** alliance en or.

band[2] *vt* bander (*un ballot*).

band[3] *n* **(a)** bande *f*, troupe *f*, compagnie *f*; *Pej* clique *f* (*de personnes*); **(b)** *Mus* orchestre *m*; (*rock music etc*) groupe *m*; **to be** *or* **play in a b.,** faire partie d'un orchestre *ou* d'un groupe.

▶**band together** *vi* (*unite*) se liguer (**to do,** pour faire).

bandage[1] ['bændɪdʒ] *n Med* bandage *m*, bande *f*; (*blindfold*) bandeau *m*; **to have** *or* **wear a b. on one's arm, to have one's arm in a b.,** avoir le bras bandé; **to put a b. on s.o./sth,** bander qn/qch.

bandage[2] *vt* bander (*qn, une plaie*); mettre un pansement sur (*une plaie*).

▶**bandage up** *vtsep* bander (*qn*); **I'll b. this up for you,** je vais te faire un bandage; **I bandaged her up with towels,** je lui ai fait un bandage avec des serviettes de toilette.

bandaging ['bændɪdʒɪŋ] *n* bandage *m*; (*of finger*) pansement *m*.

Band-Aid ® ['bændeɪd] *n esp Am* sparadrap *m*; *Fig* **a b.-a. solution/measure/***etc*, une solution/une mesure/*etc* d'attente *ou* provisoire.

bandan(n)a [bæn'dænə] *n* (*for neck*) foulard *m*; (*handkerchief*) mouchoir *m*.

B & B [biːən'biː] *n Br abbr* **bed and breakfast**.

bandbox ['bændbɒks] *n* carton *m* à chapeau(x); *Old-fashioned Fig* **she looks as if she's just stepped out of a b.**, elle est tirée à quatre épingles.

banded ['bændɪd] *adj* **(a)** (*fastened*) à bandes; **(b)** (*striped*) rayé; *Biol* fascié.

banderol(e) ['bændərɒl] *n* banderole *f*.

bandit ['bændɪt] *n* bandit *m*.

banditry ['bændɪtrɪ] *n* brigandage *m*.

bandmaster ['bændmɑːstər] *n Mil etc* chef *m* de musique; (*of brass band*) chef de fanfare.

bandoleer, bandolier [bændə'lɪər] *n* cartouchière *f* (*portée en bandoulière*).

bandsman, *pl* **-men** ['bændzmən] *n* musicien *m* (*d'un orchestre, d'une harmonie*); (*in brass band*) fanfariste *m*.

bandstand ['bændstænd] *n* kiosque *m* à musique.

bandwagon ['bændwæg(ə)n] *n* char *m* des musiciens (*en tête de la cavalcade*); *Fig* **to climb** *or* **jump on the b.**, se mettre dans le mouvement, prendre le train en marche.

bandwidth ['bændwɪdθ] *n Rad* largeur *f* de bande.

bandy¹ ['bændɪ] *vt* (se) renvoyer (*des paroles*); échanger (*des plaisanteries*); **to b. words,** (*quarrel*) se chamailler.

bandy² *adj* aux jambes arquées; **b. legs,** jambes arquées; **to be b., to have b. legs,** avoir les jambes arquées.

►bandy about, bandy around *vtsep* **her name was being bandied about,** on parlait beaucoup d'elle; **decentralization is a word the government bandies about a lot,** la décentralisation est un mot que le gouvernement a toujours à la bouche.

bandy-legged [bændɪ'legɪd, -'legd] *adj* aux jambes arquées.

bane [beɪn] *n Lit* peste *f*; **she is the b. of pretentious authors,** elle est la bête noire des auteurs prétentieux; *F* **he's the b. of my life,** il m'empoisonne l'existence.

baneful ['beɪnfʊl] *adj Lit* funeste; (*influence*) néfaste.

banefully ['beɪnfʊlɪ] *adv* funestement.

bang¹ [bæŋ] *n* **(a)** coup *m* (violent); détonation *f* (*de fusil etc*); claquement *m* (*de porte*); **the door shut with a b.**, la porte a claqué violemment; **she got a bad b. on the head,** elle a reçu un mauvais coup sur la tête; **to go off with a b.**, (*of firework*) détoner; *F* **to go (off) with a b.**, faire réussite; **(b)** *Am Sl* (*pleasure*) **to get a b. from sth,** prendre son pied à faire qch; **(c)** *Sl* (*of heroin*) injection *f* d'héroïne; **(d)** *Vulg* (*sexual intercourse*) baise *f*.

bang² **1** *vi* **(a)** (*of door*) claquer, battre; **the door banged shut,** la porte a claqué violemment; **to b. at** *or* **on the door,** donner de grands coups dans la porte; **to b. on the table with one's fist,** frapper la table du poing; **(b)** *Sl* (*of heroin addict*) se shooter. **2** *vt* **(a)** frapper (*qch*) (violemment); **to b. one's head,** se cogner la tête; *Fig* **to b. a few heads together,** taper sur la table; **to b. the door,** (faire) claquer la porte; **(b)** *Vulg* baiser (*une femme*).

bang³ **1** *int* pan!, v'lan!, boum!; *Br F* **b. went a fiver!**, j'ai dépensé cinq livres d'un seul coup!; *Br F* **b. went my hopes of a quiet weekend,** tous mes espoirs d'un week-end tranquille se sont envolés d'un seul coup. **2** *adv* **to go b.**, éclater; **he crashed b. into the tree,** il est rentré en plein dans l'arbre; **to fall b. in the middle,** tomber en plein milieu; *F* **b. on time,** exactement à l'heure; *F* **it's b. on,** c'est au poil; *F* **b. up-to-date,** (*equipment etc*) à la pointe de la technologie; (*reference book etc*) vraiment à jour; *Br F* **to be caught b. to rights,** être pris la main dans le sac.

bang⁴ *n* (*also* **bangs**) (*hair*) frange *f*.

►bang down *vtsep* abattre (*un couvercle*); **he banged it down on the table,** il l'a posé avec violence sur la table.

►bang into *vipo* (*collide with*) se heurter contre (*qch, qn*).

►bang on *vi Sl* **he's always banging on about it,** il n'arrête pas de casser les pieds à tout le monde là-dessus.

►bang out *vtsep* jouer (*un air*) tant bien que mal.

►bang up *vtsep Br Sl* boucler (*un prisonnier*).

banger ['bæŋər] *n Br F* **(a)** (*sausage*) saucisse *f*; **bangers and mash,** saucisse-purée *f*; **(b)** (*firework*) pétard *m*; **(c)** (*car*) **old b.**, vieux tacot, vieille guimbarde.

Bangladesh [bæŋglə'deʃ] *n* Bangladesh *m*.

Bangladeshi [bæŋglə'deʃɪ] **1** *n* habitant, -ante du Bangladesh. **2** *adj* (*government etc*) du Bangladesh.

bangle ['bæŋg(ə)l] *n* (*for wrist*) bracelet *m*; (*for ankle*) anneau attaché autour de la cheville.

banish ['bænɪʃ] *vt* **(a)** (*exile*) bannir, exiler, proscrire (*qn*); **(b)** *Fig* (*drive away*) bannir, chasser (*la crainte, les soucis*).

banishment ['bænɪʃmənt] *n* bannissement *m*, proscription *f*, exil *m*; **to go into b.**, partir pour l'exil; **to be sent into b.**, être banni *ou* exilé.

banisters ['bænɪstəz] *npl* rampe *f* (*d'escalier*); **to slide down the b.**, glisser le long de la rampe d'escalier.

banjo, *pl* **-os, -oes** ['bændʒəʊ, -əʊz] *n Mus* banjo *m*.

banjoist ['bændʒəʊɪst] *n* joueur, -euse de banjo.

bank¹ [bæŋk] *n* **(a)** berge *f* (*d'une rivière, d'un canal etc*); bord *m*, rive *f* (*d'une rivière, d'un lac*); **the banks,** le rivage; **(b)** (*on side of road etc*) talus *m*; (*manmade*) terrasse *f*, levée *f* de terre; (*in garden*) glacis *m*; *Constr* banquette *f*, remblai *m*; *Rail* rampe *f*; *Horseracing* banquette (irlandaise); **b. of flowers,** tertre *m* de fleurs; **(c)** *Geog* banc *m* (*de sable, de coquillages, de roches*); **the Banks of Newfoundland,** le Banc de Terre-Neuve; **(d)** (*dike*) digue *f*; **(e)** banc *m* (*de brouillard, de nuages*); **(f)** *Av* inclinaison *f*; (*turn*) virage incliné.

bank² **1** *vt* contenir (*une rivière*) par des berges; *Constr* **to b. a road,** surhausser *ou* relever un virage; **banked corner,** dévers *m*. **2** *vi* **(a)** (*of snow, clouds, mist etc*) s'entasser, s'accumuler; **(b)** *Av* s'incliner sur l'aile; (*turn*) virer (sur l'aile).

bank³ *n* **(a)** *Com Fin* banque *f*; (*branch of specific bank*) agence *f*; (*for coins*) tirelire *f*; **is there a b. nearby?**, y a-t-il une banque par ici?; **the B. of England,** la Banque d'Angleterre; **b. account,** compte *m* en banque; **b. balance,** solde *m* bancaire; *Br* **b. card,** carte *f* bancaire; **b. charges,** frais *mpl* bancaires; **b. clerk,** employé, -ée de banque; *Br* **b. holiday,** (jour *m* de) fête légale (*où les banques n'ouvrent pas*); **b. manager,** directeur *m* de banque; **my b. manager,** mon banquier; **b. robber,** dévaliseur *m* de banque; **b. statement,** relevé *m* bancaire; *Can* état *m* de compte; **(b)** (*in game*) banque *f* (*de celui qui tient le jeu*); **to break the b.**, faire sauter la banque; *Fig* **it won't break the b.**, (*of expenditure*) ça ne va pas me *ou* nous *etc* ruiner; **(c)** *Med* banque *f* (*de sang etc*).

bank⁴ **1** *vt* mettre *ou* déposer (*de l'argent*) en banque. **2** *vi* **(a)** **to b. with s.o.**, avoir un compte en banque chez qn; **who do you b. with?**, à quelle banque êtes-vous?; **do you b. with us?**, avez-vous un compte chez nous?; **(b)** (*in game*) tenir la banque.

bank⁵ *n* **(a)** *Nau* banc *m* (*de rameurs*); rang *m* (*d'avirons*); travée *f* (*de sièges*); **(b)** rang *m* (*de touches, de clavier*); *Cin* rampe *f* (*de projecteurs*); *Mus* clavier *m* (*d'un orgue*); **(c)** *Ind* groupe *m*, batterie *f* (*de chaudières, de transformateurs etc*); *Aut* rangée *f* (*de cylindres*); *Tel* groupe (*de broches, de contacts*).

►bank on *vipo* compter sur (*qch*); miser sur (*un événement*); **to b. on success,** escompter un succès; **I wouldn't b. on her being there,** ça m'étonnerait qu'elle soit là; **don't b. on it,** ne comptez pas là-dessus.

►bank up *vtsep* remblayer, terrasser (*de la terre etc*); **to b. up the fire,** recharger le feu.

bankable ['bæŋkəb(ə)l] *adj Fin* (*effet etc*) bancable; *Fig* **to be b.**, (*of film star etc*) être une valeur sûre; *Fig* **a b. idea,** une idée qui vaut de l'or.

bankbook ['bæŋkbʊk] *n* livret *m ou* carnet *m* de banque.

banker ['bæŋkər] *n* **(a)** *Fin* banquier *m*; **b.'s draft,** chèque *m* bancaire *ou* de banque; **b.'s order,** ordre *m* de transfert permanent; **(b)** (*in game*) banquier *m*, tailleur *m*; **to be b.**, tenir la banque.

banking¹ ['bæŋkɪŋ] *n* **(a)** *Constr* remblayage *m*; surhaussement *m*, relèvement *m* (*d'un virage*); **(b)** *Av* inclinaison *f*; (*turning*) virage incliné.

banking² *n* **(a)** (*business*) affaires *fpl ou* opérations *fpl* de banque; **b. hours,** horaires *mpl* de la banque; **home b.**, opérations bancaires informatisées effectuées à domicile; **(b)** (*profession*) profession *f* de banquier, la banque; **she's in b.**, elle travaille dans la banque.

banking up *n* haussement *m* du niveau (*d'une rivière*).

banknote ['bæŋknəʊt] *n* billet *m* de banque.

bankroll ['bæŋkrəʊl] *vt Am F* financer (*qn, un projet*).

bankrupt¹ ['bæŋkrʌpt] **1** *n* failli, -ie; **fraudulent b.**, banqueroutier, -ière; *Jur* **undischarged b.**, failli non réhabilité. **2** *adj* failli; **to go b.**, (*of person, business*) faire faillite; (*fraudulently*) faire banqueroute; **to be b.**, être en faillite; **to adjudge** *or* **adjudicate s.o. b.**, déclarer *ou* mettre qn en faillite; *Fig* **to be morally b.**, avoir perdu toute crédibilité morale.

bankrupt² *vt* **(a)** mettre (*qn*) en faillite; **(b)** *F* ruiner (*qn*).

bankruptcy ['bæŋkrəptsɪ] *n* **(a)** faillite *f*; **fraudulent b.**, banqueroute *f*; **(b)** *F* ruine *f*.

banner ['bænər] **1** *n* (*flag*) bannière *f*; **the Star-Spangled B.**, la bannière étoilée; *Journ* **b. heading** *or* **headline,** manchette *f*. **2** *adj Am* (*year etc*) excellent.

bannisters ['bænɪstəz] *npl* = **BANISTERS.**

banns [bænz] *npl* bans *mpl* (*de mariage*); **to put up** *or*

publish the b., (faire) publier les bans.

banquet¹ ['bæŋkwɪt] *n* banquet *m*; **b. hall,** salle *f* de banquet; **b. facilities,** (*notice in hotel etc*) possibilité d'organiser des banquets.

banquet² **1** *vt* offrir un banquet à (*qn*). **2** *vi* banqueter.

banquette [bæŋ'ket] *n esp Am* (*seat*) banquette *f*.

banshee [bæn'ʃiː] *n Myth* ≈ dame blanche.

bantam ['bæntəm] *n* **(a)** (*chicken*) coq *m ou* poule *f* (de) bantam; **(b)** *Boxing* = **BANTAMWEIGHT**.

bantamweight ['bæntəmweɪt] *n* poids *m* coq, poids bantam; **b. champion,** champion *m* poids coq *ou* bantam.

banter ['bæntər] *n* (*jokes*) badinage *m*; (*teasing*) raillerie *f*.

bantering ['bæntərɪŋ] *adj* (*ton etc*) railleur.

Bantu ['bæntuː] **1** *adj* bantou. **2** *n* **(a)** Bantou, -oue; **(b)** *Ling* bantou *m*.

banyan ['bænjən] *n* (*tree*) banian *m*.

BAOR [biːeɪəʊ'ɑːr] *n abbr* **British Army of the Rhine**.

bap [bæp] *n Br Culin* petit pain rond au lait.

baptism ['bæptɪz(ə)m] *n* baptême *m*; *Fig* **b. of fire,** baptême du feu.

baptismal [bæp'tɪzm(ə)l] *adj* (*registre*) baptistaire; (*nom*) de baptême; **b. font,** fonts *mpl* baptismaux.

baptist ['bæptɪst] *n* **(a)** **(St.) John the B.,** saint Jean-Baptiste; **(b)** *Rel* baptiste *mf*; **the B. doctrine,** baptisme *m*.

baptist(e)ry ['bæptɪstrɪ] *n* baptistère *m*.

baptize [bæp'taɪz] *vt* baptiser (*qn, un navire etc*); **to be baptized,** recevoir le baptême; **to be baptized (in the name of) John,** être baptisé du nom de Jean.

bar¹ [bɑːr] *n* **(a)** barre *f* (*de fer, de savon, de chocolat etc*); tablette *f* (*de chocolat*); lingot *m* (*d'or*); élément *m* (*d'un feu électrique*); raie *f* (*de couleur*); barrette *f* (*d'une médaille*); barre *f* (*dans un gymnase*); **with b.,** (*of medal*) ≈ avec palme; **bars,** barreaux *mpl* (*d'une fenêtre, d'une cage, d'une prison*); **to be behind (prison) bars,** être derrière les barreaux *ou* sous les verrous;
(b) (*obstacle*) empêchement *m*, obstacle *m*; (*in river, harbour*) barre *f* (*de sable*), traverse *f*; **to be a b. to sth,** être un empêchement *ou* faire obstacle à qch;
(c) (*in court*) barre *f* (*des accusés*); barreau *m* (*des avocats*); **the prisoner at the b.,** l'accusé, -ée; **to read for the b.,** faire son droit; **to be called to the b.,** être reçu au barreau, être reçu avocat; *F* **the B.,** l'Ordre *m* des avocats;
(d) (*establishment*) bar *m*, café *m*, *F* bistro *m*; comptoir *m* (*d'un café*); *F* **he's always propping up the b.,** c'est un vrai pilier de café *ou* de bar; *Am* **b. fly,** pilier de bar;
(e) (*line*) barre *f*, ligne *f*, trait *m*; *Mus* mesure *f*; *Mus* **b. (line),** barre; **double b.,** double barre; *Comptr* **b. code,** code *m* (à) barres; **b. code reader,** lecteur *m* de code barres; **b. chart** *or* **graph** *or* **diagram,** histogramme *m*;
(f) *Met* bar *m*.

bar² *vt* (**-rr-**) **(a)** (*lock*) barrer (*une porte etc*); mettre des barreaux à (*une fenêtre*); **to b. the door against s.o.,** barrer la porte à qn; **(b)** (*obstruct*) barrer (*un chemin*); **to b. s.o.'s way,** barrer la route à qn, couper (le) chemin à qn; **to b. s.o. from sth,** (*keep out*) exclure qn de qch, interdire qch à qn; **he's been barred from the club,** il a été exclu du club; **she's been barred from playing,** elle a été interdite de jeu; **(c)** (*forbid*) défendre, prohiber, interdire (*une action*); exclure (*un sujet de conversation*); *Jur* opposer une fin de non-recevoir à (*une action*); **to b. s.o. from doing sth,** défendre à qn de faire qch.

bar³ *prep* (*except*) excepté, sauf, à part, à l'exception de; **b. one,** sauf un, sauf une; **b. none,** sans exception.

bar⁴ *n* (*fish*) maigre *m*.

barb¹ [bɑːb] *n* **(a)** barbillon *m*, dardillon *m* (*d'un hameçon*); barbelure *f* (*d'une flèche*); ardillon *m* (*d'un crochet*); picot *m* (*de fil de fer barbelé*); barbe *f*, bavure *f* (*de métal*); **(b)** (*on fish, animal*) barbillon *m*; *Bot* arête *f*, barbe *f* (*d'une plume*).

barb² *vt* garnir de barbelures *ou* de barbillons; **to b. a hook,** relever le barbillon d'un hameçon.

Barbados [bɑː'beɪdɒs] *n* Barbade *f*.

barbarian [bɑː'beərɪən] *adj & n* barbare *mf*.

barbaric [bɑː'bærɪk] *adj* barbare; *Fig* (*primitive*) rude, primitif.

barbarism ['bɑːbərɪz(ə)m] *n* **(a)** barbarie *f*; *Fig* rudesse *f*; **(b)** *Gram Ling* barbarisme *m*.

barbarity [bɑː'bærɪtɪ] *n* **(a)** (*cruelty*) barbarie *f*, cruauté *f*; **(b)** (*action*) acte *m* de barbarie, cruauté *f*.

barbarous ['bɑːbərəs] *adj* barbare.

barbarously ['bɑːbərəslɪ] *adv* cruellement.

Barbary ['bɑːbərɪ] *n* **the B. States,** la Barbarie, les États *mpl* barbaresques; **B. ape,** magot *m*; **B. horse,** cheval *m* barbe.

barbecue¹ ['bɑːbɪkjuː] *n* (*fireplace, party*) barbecue *m*; **to cook sth on the b.,** faire cuire qch sur le barbecue; **to have a b.,** faire un barbecue.

barbecue² *vt* griller (*de la viande*) sur un barbecue; **barbecued chicken,** poulet rôti au barbecue.

barbed [bɑːbd] *adj* **(a)** barbelé; **b. arrow,** flèche barbelée; **b. wire,** (fil *m* de fer) barbelé *m*; **b.-wire fence,** clôture *f* de barbelé; **b.-wire entanglements,** barbelés *mpl*; **(b)** *Fig* (*comment etc*) acerbe; **(c)** *Bot* hameçonné.

barbel ['bɑːb(ə)l] *n* **(a)** (*fish*) barbeau *m* (commun); **(b)** (*on fish*) barbillon *m*.

barbell ['bɑːbel] *n Gym* barre *f* à disques.

barber ['bɑːbər] *n* (*for men*) coiffeur *m*; *Old-fashioned* barbier *m*; **I'm going to the b.'s,** je vais chez le coiffeur.

barbershop ['bɑːbəʃɒp] *n Am* salon *m* de coiffure (*pour hommes*); *Mus* **b. harmony,** chants *mpl* à quatre voix d'hommes; **b. quartet,** = groupe de quatre hommes ou femmes chantant en harmonie étroite; **to sing in a b. quartet,** faire partie d'un quatuor qui chante en harmonie étroite.

barbican ['bɑːbɪkən] *n* (*fortification*) barbacane *f*.

barbie ['bɑːbiː] *n Austr F* barbecue *m*.

Barbie ® ['bɑːbiː] *n* **B. doll,** poupée *f* Barbie.

barbitone ['bɑːbɪtəʊn] *n Pharm* véronal *m*.

barbiturate [bɑː'bɪtjʊreɪt] *n Ch* barbiturique *m*.

barbituric [bɑːbɪ'tjuːrɪk] *adj* barbiturique.

barcarol(l)e ['bɑːkərəʊl] *n Mus* barcarolle *f*.

Barcelona [bɑːsɪ'ləʊnə] *n* Barcelone *f*.

bard¹ [bɑːd] *n* **(a)** (*poet*) poète *m*; *Lit* **the B.,** Shakespeare; **(b)** (*Celtic*) barde *m*.

bard² *n Culin* barde *f*.

bard³ *vt Culin* barder (*un poulet*).

bardic ['bɑːdɪk] *adj* (*poésie*) des bardes.

bare¹ ['beər] *adj* **(a)** (*tête, jambe etc*) nu; (*poitrine*) découvert; (*placard, rayon*) vide; (*arbre*) dénudé, dépouillé; (*pays*) nu, dénudé; *El* (*fil*) dénudé; **to fight with b. hands,** se battre à mains nues; **I'll kill him with my b. hands,** je le tuerai de mes propres mains; **stop walking around in your b. feet,** arrête de marcher pieds nus n'importe où; **to lie** *or* **sleep on the b. boards,** coucher sur la dure; **the b. facts,** le fait brutal; **the b. bones of the case are ...,** les grandes lignes de cette affaire sont ...; **to lay b.,** mettre à nu, exposer (*une surface, des fautes, son cœur*); dévoiler (*un secret, une fraude*); déchausser (*des fondations, des racines etc*); **(b)** (*just sufficient*) **to earn a b. living,** gagner tout juste *ou* à peine de quoi vivre; **the b. minimum,** le strict minimum; **the b. necessities (of life),** juste ce qu'il faut pour vivre; *Sch* **he got a b. pass,** il a été reçu sans mention; **b. majority,** faible majorité.

bare² *vt* mettre (*qch*) à nu; découvrir (*la tête*), déchausser (*des racines etc*); **to b. one's teeth,** montrer ses dents; **to b. one's heart** *or* **soul,** ouvrir son cœur, mettre son âme à nu.

bareback ['beəbæk] **1** *adv* **to ride b.,** monter (un cheval) à nu *ou* à cru. **2** *adj* **b. rider,** cavalier, -ière qui monte à cru.

barefaced ['beəfeɪst] *adj F* (*mensonge etc*) éhonté, effronté.

barefoot(ed) ['beəfʊt, -ɪd] **1** *adj* aux pieds nus. **2** *adv* nu-pieds, pieds nus; **she goes b. whenever possible,** elle marche pieds nus dès que cela est possible.

barehanded [beə'hændɪd] **1** *adj* aux mains nues. **2** *adv* les mains nues.

bareheaded [beə'hedɪd] **1** *adj* à la tête nue. **2** *adv* nu-tête, (la) tête nue.

bare-legged [beə'leg(ɪ)d] **1** *adj* aux jambes nues. **2** *adv* (les) jambes nues.

barely ['beəlɪ] *adv* (*just*) à peine, tout juste; **I b. know her,** je la connais à peine; **he can b. read and write,** c'est tout juste s'il sait lire et écrire; **you've b. got here and you're leaving,** vous êtes à peine arrivé que vous partez déjà; **b. furnished room,** (*lacking furniture*) pièce avec très peu de meubles; (*poorly furnished*) pièce pauvrement meublée.

bareness ['beənɪs] *n* **(a)** dénuement *m* (*d'une chambre etc*); **(b)** pauvreté *f* (*de style etc*).

bargain¹ ['bɑːgɪn] *n* **(a)** (*deal*) marché *m*, affaire *f*; **a good/bad b.,** une bonne/mauvaise affaire; **to make** *or* **strike a b. with s.o.,** conclure *ou* faire un marché avec qn; **I'll make a b. with you,** on fait un marché; **I thought we had a b.,** je croyais qu'on s'était mis d'accord; **you haven't kept your side of the b.,** vous n'avez pas respecté notre accord; **to drive a hard b.,** chercher à gagner le dernier centime; **into the b.,** par-dessus le marché, en plus; **it's a b.!,** c'est entendu!; **(b)** (*good buy*) **a real b.,** une véritable occasion; **b. basement** *or* **counter,** rayon *m* des soldes; *Fig* **b. basement price,** prix *m* de bazar; **b. hunter,** chercheur, -euse d'occasions; **to go b. hunting,** fouiner (pour des affaires), faire les soldes; **b. offer,** offre avantageuse, occasion; **b. price,** prix exceptionnel; *Com* **b. sale,** (vente *f* de) soldes *mpl*.

bargain² *vi* entrer en négociations, négocier; **to b. with s.o.,** (*in market place*) marchander avec qn.

►bargain for, bargain on *vipo* compter sur; **I didn't b. for** *or* **on that,** je ne m'attendais pas à cela; **he got more than he bargained for,** il ne s'attendait pas à cela; *Pej* il a eu du fil à retordre.

bargaining ['bɑːgɪnɪŋ] *n* (*in market etc*) marchandage *m*; *Ind* négociations *fpl*; **b. agent,** agent-négociateur *m*; **b. unit,** unité *f* de négociation.

barge [bɑːdʒ] *n* chaland *m*, péniche *f*; (*with sails*) gabare *f*, barge *f*; *Nau* deuxième canot *m* (*d'un navire de guerre*).

►barge in *vi* **(a)** (*enter noisily*) faire irruption; **(b)** (*interrupt*) intervenir mal à propos; **don't keep barging in with questions,** arrête de me *ou* nous *etc* interrompre avec tes questions.

►barge into *vipo* **(a)** (*collide with*) venir se heurter contre (*qn, qch*); se cogner sur (*qn*); se cogner contre (*qch*); **(b)** (*enter noisily*) faire irruption dans (*une pièce*).

bargee [bɑː'dʒiː] **,** *Am* **bargeman** ['bɑːdʒmən] *n* marinier *m*.

bargepole ['bɑːdʒpəʊl] *n* gaffe *f*; *Fig* **I wouldn't touch it with a b.,** (*it's disgusting*) ça me dégoûterait d'y toucher; (*it's risky for me*) je ne veux rien avoir à faire avec ça; (*it's risky for you*) je ne voudrais rien avoir à faire avec ça.

baritone ['bærɪtəʊn] *n Mus* (*voice, singer, instrument*) baryton *m*.

barium ['beərɪəm] *n Ch* baryum *m*; *Med* **b. meal,** sulfate *m* de baryum.

bark¹ [bɑːk] *n* **(a)** écorce *f* (*d'arbre*); **to strip the b. off a tree,** écorcer un arbre; **(b)** (*for tanning*) tan *m*.

bark² *vt* écorcer (*un arbre*); *Fig* **to b. one's shins,** s'écorcher *ou* s'érafler les jambes (**on,** sur).

bark³ *n* **(a)** (*of dog*) aboiement *m*, aboi *m*; glapissement *m* (*du renard*); *Fig* **his b. is worse than his bite,** il aboie plus qu'il ne mord; **(b)** *F* (*cough*) toux sèche; **she has a dreadful b.,** elle tousse terriblement.

bark⁴ 1 *vi* (*of dog*) aboyer (**at,** après, contre, à); (*of fox*) glapir; *Fig* **to b. up the wrong tree,** suivre une fausse piste. **2** *vt* (*of person*) dire (*qch*) d'un ton sec *ou* cassant.

bark⁵ *n* **(a)** *Nau* trois-mâts *m*; **(b)** *Lit* barque *f*.

►bark out *vtsep* dire (*qch*) d'un ton sec *ou* cassant; **to b. out an order,** donner un ordre d'un ton sec.

barkeep(er) ['bɑːkiːp, -ər] *n Am* garçon *m* de comptoir, barman *m*.

barker¹ ['bɑːkər] *n* (*at fair*) aboyeur *m*.

barker² *n* (*machine*) écorceuse *f*.

barking ['bɑːkɪŋ] **1** *adj* **(a)** (*chien*) aboyeur; (*renard*) glapissant; **(b)** *F* (*cough*) sec. **2** *n* aboiement *m* (*d'un chien*); glapissement *m* (*d'un renard*).

barley ['bɑːlɪ] *n* orge *f*; **b. meal/sugar,** farine *f*/sucre *m* d'orge; **b. water,** tisane *f* d'orge.

barleycorn ['bɑːlɪkɔːn] *n* grain *m* d'orge.

barm [bɑːm] *n* levure *f* (*de bière*); (*yeast*) levain *m*.

barmaid ['bɑːmeɪd] *n Br* serveuse *f* (*dans un bar*), barmaid *f*.

barman, *pl* **-men** ['bɑːmən] *n* garçon *m* de comptoir, barman *m*.

barminess ['bɑːmɪnɪs] *n Br F* loufoquerie *f*.

barmy ['bɑːmɪ] *adj* **(a)** *Br F* (*crazy*) toqué, loufoque; **(b)** (*bread, cake*) contenant de la levure; (*beer*) en fermentation.

barn [bɑːn] *n* **(a)** grange *f*; (*for cows*) étable *f*; (*for horses*) écurie *f*; **he couldn't hit a b. door,** (*he's a poor shot*) c'est un mauvais tireur; **they live in an old b. of a house,** ils habitent dans une vieille bicoque; **were you born in a b.?,** (*when someone does not close a door*) où est-ce que tu as été élevé?; **b. dance,** danse *f* folklorique; **b. owl,** chouette-effraie *f*; **(b)** *Am Rail* dépôt *m* de tramways.

barnacle ['bɑːnək(ə)l] *n* (*mollusc*) anatife *m*, *F* bernacle *f*; **(acorn) b.,** balane *m*, gland *m* de mer; **b. goose,** (*bird*) bernacle *f*, bernache *f* (nonnette).

barney ['bɑːnɪ] *n Br F* (*argument*) dispute *f*; **I had a bit of a b. with the bus driver,** je me suis légèrement heurté au conducteur du bus; **we've had a b.,** nous nous sommes disputés; **to get into a b. with s.o.,** se disputer avec qn; **I had a bit of a b. with a bus,** (*of car driver*) j'ai eu des problèmes avec un bus.

barnstorm ['bɑːnstɔːm] *vi* **(a)** *Br* faire une tournée théâtrale; **(b)** *Am Pol* faire une tournée électorale.

barnstormer ['bɑːnstɔːmər] *n* **(a)** *Br* acteur, -trice ambulant, -e; **(b)** *Am Pol* orateur électoral.

barnyard ['bɑːnjɑːd] *n* basse-cour *f*, *pl* basses-cours; **b. humour,** humour *m* au ras de pâquerettes.

barometer [bə'rɒmɪtər] *n* (*instrument*) *& Fig* baromètre *m*; **the b. is at fair,** le baromètre est au beau fixe; **b. reading,** hauteur *f* barométrique.

barometric [bærə'metrɪk] *adj* (*pression etc*) barométrique.

baron ['bærən] *n* (*nobleman*) *& Fig* baron *m*; *Culin* **b. of beef,** double aloyau *m*.

baroness ['bærənes] *n* baronne *f*.

baronet ['bærənet] *n* baronnet *m*.

baronetcy ['bærənɪtsɪ] *n* dignité *f* de baronnet; **to be given a b.,** être élevé au rang de baronnet.

baronial [bə'rəʊnɪəl] *adj* baronnial; **b. hall,** demeure seigneuriale.

barony ['bærənɪ] *n* **(a)** (*domain*) baronnie *f*; **(b)** (*in Ireland*) subdivision *f* d'un comté; **(c)** *Scot* grande propriété terrienne.

baroque [bə'rɒk] *adj & n Art Mus* baroque *m*.

barque [bɑːk] *n Nau* trois-mâts *m* barque.

barrack¹ ['bærək] *n* **(a)** *Mil* (*usu pl*) (*with sing or pl verb*) **barracks,** caserne *f*, quartier *m*; **to be confined to barracks,** être consigné; **b. square,** cour *f* du quartier *ou* de caserne; **(b)** *Can* ≈ gendarmerie *f*; **(c)** *Pej F* (*house etc*) caserne *f*.

barrack² *vt Mil* caserner (*des troupes*).

barrack³ *vt Br F* (*jeer at*) se moquer de (*qn*).

barrackroom ['bærəkruːm] *n* chambre *f*; **b. language,** langage *m* de corps de garde *ou* de caserne; **b. lawyer,** chicanier, -ière.

barracuda [bærə'kjuːdə] *n* (*fish*) barracuda *m*, bécune *f*.

barrage¹ ['bærɑːʒ] *n* (*dam*) *& Mil* barrage *m*; *Fig* torrent *m* (*de questions, d'injures*); *Br* **b. balloon,** ballon *m* de barrage *ou* de protection.

barrage² *vt* **to b. s.o. with questions,** assommer qn de questions.

barred [bɑːd] *adj* **(a)** (*door*) barré; (*window*) muni de barreaux; **(b)** *Jur* **b. by limitation,** (*droit*) périmé.

barrel ['bær(ə)l] *n* **(a)** (*container*) tonneau *m*, barrique *f*, fût *m* (*de vin etc*); baril *m* (*de pétrole*); caque *f*, baril (*de harengs etc*); *Fig* **to scrape the bottom of the b.,** gratter le fonds du panier; *F* **to have s.o. over a b.,** coincer qn; **(b)** *Am F* grande quantité (**of,** de); **she's a b. of fun** *or* **laughs,** c'est un sacré boute-en-train; **(c)** (*cylinder, tube*) cylindre *m*, partie *f* cylindrique; caisse *f* (*d'un tambour*); canon *m* (*de fusil, de serrure, de clef*); corps *m*, barillet *m* (*de pompe*); cylindre, barillet (*de serrure*); fusée *f*, mèche *f*, tambour *m* (*de cabestan, de treuil*); *Mil* tube *m* (*de canon*); **b. organ,** orgue *m* de Barbarie; *Av* **b. roll,** tonneau *m*; *Archit* **b. vault,** voûte *f* en berceau.

►barrel along *vi* (*in car etc*) foncer.

barren ['bær(ə)n] **1** *adj* (*femme, terrain*) stérile; *Fig* (*sujet*) maigre; **mind b. of ideas,** esprit dépourvu d'idées; **he's going through a b. period,** (*of author*) il n'a pas beaucoup d'inspirations ces temps-ci; **b. lands,** lande(s) *f(pl)*. **2** *npl Am* **barrens,** lande(s) *f(pl)*.

barrenness ['bærənnɪs] *n* stérilité *f*.

barrette [bə'ret] *n esp Am* (*Br* = **hair slide**) barrette *f*.

barricade¹ ['bærɪkeɪd, bærɪ'keɪd] *n* barricade *f*.

barricade² *vt* barricader.

►barricade in *vtsep* barricader (*qn*) dans une pièce *etc*; **they barricaded themselves in,** ils se sont barricadés.

►barricade off *vtsep* barrer (*une rue*).

barrier ['bærɪər] *n* barrière *f*; *Mil etc* barrage *m* (*d'obstacles*); *Fig* **this created a b. between them,** cela a créé une barrière entre eux; **the language b.,** la barrière linguistique; **b. methods of contraception,** moyens *mpl* mécaniques de contraception; **b. cream,** (*for skin*) crème protectrice *ou* de protection; *Geog* **b. ice,** banquise *f*; **b. reef,** récif *m* en barrière; *Geog* **the Great B. Reef,** la Grande Barrière.

barring ['bɑːrɪŋ] **1** *n* **(a)** barrage *m* (*d'une porte etc*); **(b)** interdiction *f* (*d'une action etc*). **2** *prep* (*except*) excepté, sauf, à part; **b. accidents,** sauf accident, sauf imprévu.

barrister ['bærɪstər] *n Br Jur* ≈ avocat, -ate.

barrow¹ ['bærəʊ] *n* (*in garden etc*) brouette *f*; *esp Br* (*handcart*) voiture *f ou* charrette *f* à bras; *Rail* diable *m*; *Br* **b. boy,** marchand *m* des quatre saisons.

barrow² *n Archeol* tumulus *m*; tertre *m* (*funéraire*).

Bart *abbr* **baronet.**

bartender ['bɑːtendər] *n* garçon *m* de comptoir, barman *m*.

barter¹ ['bɑːtər] *n* troc *m*; **b. society,** société *f* vivant du troc.

barter² **1** *vt* troquer (*qch*) (**for,** contre). **2** *vi* faire du troc.
Bartholomew [bɑːˈθɒləmjuː] *n* Barthélemy *m*; *Hist* **the Massacre of St. B.,** le Massacre de la Saint-Barthélemy.
barytone [ˈbærɪtəʊn] *n* = **BARITONE.**
basal [ˈbeɪsəl] *adj* fondamental.
basalt [ˈbæsɔːlt] *n* basalte *m*.
basaltic [bəˈsɔːltɪk] *adj* basaltique.
bascule [ˈbæskjuːl] *n* *Constr* bascule *f*; **b. bridge,** pont (-levis) *m* à bascule, *pl* ponts-levis à bascule.
base¹ [beɪs] *n* **(a)** (*foundation*) fondement *m*, base *f*; *Constr* soubassement *m*; (*of column, statue*) socle *m*; sole *f*, embase *f* (*de machine-outil etc*); *Phot* support *m* (*du film, de l'émulsion*); *El* culot *m* (*d'une lampe*); *Rail* patin *m* (*de rail*); *Fin* **b. rate,** taux *m* de base; **(b)** *Math Ch etc* base *f*; *Ling* base, racine *f*; **(c)** *Mil etc* base *f* (*d'opérations, de ravitaillement*); **b. camp,** camp *m* de base; **(d)** (*in baseball*) base *f*, piquet *m*; *Fig* **to get to first b.,** faire les premiers pas (*vers un objectif*); **he didn't even get to first b. with her,** il n'a pas fait le moindre progrès avec elle; **to be off b.,** (*mistaken*) se tromper; *Am F* être fou *ou* cinglé.
base² *vt* **(a)** (*found*) baser, fonder (*un calcul, un espoir*) (**on,** sur); baser (*un roman, un film*) (**on,** sur); asseoir, fonder, appuyer (*une opinion*) (**on,** sur); **to b. oneself on sth,** se baser sur qch; **(b)** (*have as headquarters*) (*usu passive*) **to be based in Manchester,** être basé à Manchester.
base³ *adj* **(a)** (*ignoble*) (*homme*) vil; (*motif*) bas, indigne; (*action*) ignoble, indigne; **(b)** (*inferior*) **b. metals,** métaux vils; **(c)** (*counterfeit*) **b. coin(age),** fausse monnaie.
baseball [ˈbeɪsbɔːl] *n* *Sp* base-ball *m*; **b. player,** baseballeur *m*, joueur *m* de base-ball; **b. game,** partie *f* de base-ball.
baseboard [ˈbeɪsbɔːd] *n* *Am* (*Br* = **skirting board**) plinthe *f*; **b. heater,** plinthe électrique.
Basel [ˈbɑːz(ə)l] *n* Bâle *f*.
baseless [ˈbeɪslɪs] *adj* sans base, sans fondement.
baseline [ˈbeɪslaɪn] *n* *Tennis* ligne *f* de fond; *Art* ligne de fuite.
basement [ˈbeɪsmənt] *n* (*in house, shop*) sous-sol *m*; **in the b.,** au sous-sol; **b. flat,** (appartement *m* de) sous-sol.
baseness [ˈbeɪsnɪs] *n* bassesse *f* (*d'une action etc*).
bash¹ [bæʃ] *n* *F* **(a)** (*dent*) coup *m*, enfoncement *m*; **the saucepan has had a b.,** la casserole est bosselée *ou* cabossée; **(b)** (*blow*) coup *m*; (*with fist*) coup de poing violent; *Br F* **to have a b. at sth,** tenter le coup; **I'll have a b. at mending it,** je vais tenter le coup de le réparer.
bash² *vt F* **to b. one's head,** se cogner la tête.
▶**bash about** *vtsep Br F* (*beat, damage*) battre, maltraiter, rudoyer (*qn*); maltraiter (*une valise*).
▶**bash down** *vtsep Br F* (*smash*) enfoncer (*une porte*).
▶**bash in** *vtsep Br F* (*smash*) enfoncer (*une porte*); **I'll b. your face in,** je te casse la gueule.
▶**bash into** *vipo Br F* se heurter contre (*qn*).
▶**bash on** *vi Br F* continuer.
▶**bash up** *vtsep Br F* tabasser (*qn*); abîmer (*une voiture*).
bashful [ˈbæʃfʊl] *adj* **(a)** (*timid*) modeste, timide; **b. lover,** amoureux transi; **(b)** (*modest*) modeste, pudique.
bashfully [ˈbæʃfʊlɪ] *adv* (*see adj*) **(a)** modestement, timidement; **(b)** pudiquement.
bashfulness [ˈbæʃfʊlnɪs] *n* **(a)** (*timidity*) modestie *f*, timidité *f*; **(b)** (*modesty*) modestie *f*, pudeur *f*.
bashing [ˈbæʃɪŋ] *n F* volée *f* de coups, rossée *f*; *Mil etc* **to take** *or* **get a b.,** prendre quelque chose.
basic [ˈbeɪsɪk] **1** *adj* (*principe etc*) fondamental; (*vérité*) premier; *Ling* (*vocabulaire*) de base; **to learn some b. French,** apprendre les bases du français; *Econ* **b. commodity,** denrée *f* de base; *Ind* **b. pay,** salaire *m* de base; **b. slag,** scorie *f* basique. **2** *npl* **basics,** choses essentielles; (*of a language*) éléments *mpl*.
BASIC [ˈbeɪsɪk] *n* *Comptr* langage *m* BASIC.
basically [ˈbeɪsɪklɪ] *adv* fondamentalement, au fond.
basil [ˈbæz(ə)l] *n* *Bot Culin* basilic *m*.
basilica [bəˈzɪlɪkə] *n* *Archit* basilique *f*.
basilisk [ˈbæzɪlɪsk] *n* *Myth* basilic *m*; *Fig Lit* **a b. stare,** un regard assassin.
basin [ˈbeɪs(ə)n] *n* **(a)** (*bowl*) bassin *m*; (*for soup etc*) écuelle *f*, bol *m*; (*for milk*) jatte *f*; vasque *f*, coupe *f* (*d'une fontaine*); (*for washing up etc*) bassine *f*, cuvette *f*; **hand b.,** lavabo *m*; **(b)** (*of river*) bassin *m*; **the Paris B.,** le Bassin parisien; **coal b.,** bassin houiller; **(c)** *Nau* bassin *m*; (*in canal, river*) garage *m*; **tidal b.,** bassin à flot; **dry b.,** garage à sec.
basinful [ˈbeɪs(ə)nfʊl] *n* (*of soup*) plein bol, bolée *f*; (*of water*) pleine cuvette; *Sl* **to have had a b.,** en avoir ras le bol, en avoir marre.
basis, *pl* **bases** [ˈbeɪsɪs, -iːz] *n* **(a)** base *f* (*de négociations etc*); fondement *m* (*d'une opinion etc*); assiette *f* (*d'un impôt*); **on the b. of ...,** sur la base de ...; **(b)** *Math* matrice *f* de base.
bask [bɑːsk] *vi* **to b. in the sun,** se chauffer (au soleil); *F* lézarder; *Fig* **to b. in s.o.'s favour,** jouir de la faveur de qn; **basking shark,** pèlerin *m*.
basket [ˈbɑːskɪt] *n* (*with or without handles*) corbeille *f*; (*with handles*) panier *m*; (*carried on back*) hotte *f*; (*for coal etc*) banne *f*, manne *f*; (*plaited shopping basket*) cabas *m*, couffin *m*; (*for carrying baby*) couffin; (*in basketball*) panier; *Fig* **b. of currencies,** panier de monnaies; **oyster b.,** cloyère *f*; **laundry b.,** corbeille à linge; **linen b.,** panier à linge; **picnic b.,** (*containing food, plates etc*) panier de pique-nique; (*fitted with plates, cutlery*) mallette *f* de pique-nique; *Br F* **(you) silly b.!,** espèce d'idiot!; **(economic) b. case,** pays invalide sur le plan économique; **b. chair,** chaise *f* en rotin *ou* osier; **b. hilt,** (*of sword*) (garde *f* en) coquille *f*; **b. making,** vannerie *f*; **b. maker,** vannier *m*.
basketball [ˈbɑːskɪtbɔːl] *n* basket-ball *m*, *F* basket *m*; **b. player,** basketteur, -euse.
basketful [ˈbɑːskɪtfʊl] *n* plein panier.
basketry [ˈbɑːskɪtrɪ] *n* vannerie *f*.
basketwork [ˈbɑːskɪtwɜːk] *n* vannerie *f*.
Basle [bɑːl] *n* Bâle *f*.
basque [bɑːsk] *n* (*bodice*) basque *f*.
Basque [bɑːsk] **1** *adj* basque; **the B. Country,** le Pays basque. **2** *n* **(a)** Basque *mf*; **(b)** *Ling* basque *m*.
bass¹ [bæs] *n* (*fish*) (*freshwater*) perche commune; (*saltwater*) bar *m*; **striped b.,** bar rayé.
bass² [beɪs] **1** *n* (*voice, singer, instrument*) basse *f*; (*double bass*) contrebasse *f*; **he sings b.,** il chante dans les basses; **deep b.,** basse profonde. **2** *adj Mus* (*voice, part*) de basse; **b. clef,** clef *f* de fa; **b. drum,** grosse caisse; **b. guitar,** basse *f*; **b. tones,** sons *mpl* graves.
bass³ [bæs] *n* **(a)** *Bot* liber *m*; **(b)** (*material*) tille *f*, filasse *f*; **b. rope,** bastin *m*.
basset [ˈbæsɪt] *n* (*dog*) **b. (hound),** basset *m*.
bassinet(te) [bæsɪˈnet] *n Arch* **(a)** (*cradle*) moïse *m*; **(b)** (*pram*) voiture *f* d'enfant (*en osier*).
bassist [ˈbeɪsɪst] *n Mus* bassiste *mf*.
basso [ˈbæsəʊ] *n* **b. profundo,** (voix *f* de) basse profonde.
bassoon [bəˈsuːn] *n* *Mus* basson *m*; **double b.,** contrebasson *m*.
bassoonist [bəˈsuːnɪst] *n Mus* basson *m*, bassoniste *m*.
bast [bæst] *n* = **BASS³.**
bastard [ˈbæstəd, ˈbɑː-] **1** *n* **(a)** bâtard, -arde; *Jur* enfant naturel(le); **(b)** *Sl* salaud *m*; **you b.!,** espèce de salaud!; **a b. of a job,** une saloperie de travail; **it's a b.,** (*of work, problem*) c'est vachement difficile. **2** *adj* **(a)** (*child*) bâtard; **(b)** (*irregular*) bâtard; **b. file,** lime bâtarde; **b. hand,** (écriture *f*) bâtarde *f*; **b. size,** (*of paper, book etc*) format bâtard; *Typ* **b. title,** faux titre.
bastardize [ˈbæstədaɪz, ˈbɑː-] *vt* **(a)** (*debase*) corrompre; **(b)** déclarer (*un enfant*) illégitime.
bastardy [ˈbæstədɪ] *n* bâtardise *f*; *Jur* **b. case,** action *f* en désaveu de paternité.
baste¹ [beɪst] *vt* *Sewing* bâtir, faufiler (*un corsage etc*).
baste² *vt* *Culin* arroser (*un rôti*) (*de sa graisse, de son jus*).
basting¹ [ˈbeɪstɪŋ] *n* *Sewing* bâti *m*, faufilure *f*; glacis *m* (*de doublure*); **b. thread,** faufil *m*, bâti *m*.
basting² *n* *Culin* arrosement *m*, arrosage *m* (*d'un rôti*).
bastion [ˈbæstɪən] *n* (*fortification*) & *Fig* bastion *m*.
bat¹ [bæt] *n* chauve-souris *f*, *pl* chauves-souris; *Fig* **to go down the road like a b. out of hell,** descendre la rue comme un bolide; *Br F* **to have bats in the belfry,** avoir une araignée au plafond.
bat² *n* **(a)** batte *f* (*de cricket, de base-ball etc*); raquette *f* (*de ping-pong*); **he's a good b.,** il manie bien la batte; *F* **to do sth off one's own b.,** faire qch de sa propre initiative; *esp Am* **to do sth right off the b.,** faire qch tout de suite; *esp Am* **to go to b. for s.o.,** (*intercede for*) intervenir *ou* intercéder pour *ou* en faveur de qn; **(b)** *Am* **to go on a b.,** se soûler.
bat³ *vi* (-tt-) manier la batte (*au cricket, au base-ball*); *Cr* être au guichet.
bat⁴ *vt* battre (*des paupières*); *Fig* **he didn't b. an eyelid,** il n'a pas sourcillé *ou* tiqué.
batch [bætʃ] *n* fournée *f* (*de pain, F de prisonniers*); tas *m*, paquet *m* (*de lettres*); lot *m* (*de marchandises etc, Comptr de données*); gâchée *f* (*de ciment, de béton*); *Comptr* **b. file,** fichier séquentiel; *Comptr* **b. processing,** traitement *m* par lots.
bated [ˈbeɪtɪd] *adj* **with b. breath,** (*attendre, regarder*) en

retenant son haleine.

bath¹, *pl* **baths** [bɑːθ, bɑːðz] *n* **(a)** (*washing*) bain *m*; **to take** *or* **have a b.**, prendre un bain, se baigner; **to give a child a b.**, baigner un enfant; **to run a b.**, faire couler un bain; *Old-fashioned Br* **public baths**, (*for washing*) bains publics; (*for swimming*) piscine *f*; **steam b.**, étuve *f* humide (*de hammam*); *Med* bain de vapeur; *Br* **the Order of the B.**, l'Ordre *m* du Bain; **b. pearls**, perles *fpl* de bain; **b. mat**, descente *f ou* tapis *m* de bain; **b. salts**, sels *mpl* de bain; **b. towel**, serviette *f* de bain; **b. water**, eau *f* du bain; **my b. water's too hot**, mon bain est trop chaud; **b. wrap**, sortie *f* de bain; **(b)** (*tub*) baignoire *f*; *Phot etc* cuvette *f*; **hip b.**, **sitz b.**, bain *m* de siège.

bath² **1** *vt* baigner, donner un bain à (*qn*). **2** *vi* prendre un bain.

bathe¹ [beɪð] *n* bain *m* (*de rivière, de mer*); baignade *f*; **to go for a b.**, (aller) se baigner.

bathe² **1** *vt* (*wash*) baigner; *Am* baigner (*un enfant*); *Med* laver, lotionner (*une plaie*); **to b. one's face**, se baigner la figure; **face bathed in tears**, visage baigné de larmes; **bathed in perspiration**, trempé de sueur, en nage. **2** *vi* **(a)** (*swim*) se baigner; prendre un bain (*de mer, de rivière*); **(b)** *Am* prendre un bain (*dans la baignoire*).

bather ['beɪðər] *n* baigneur, -euse.

bathers [beɪðəs] *npl Austr F* maillot *m*.

bathing ['beɪðɪŋ] *n* **(a)** (*swimming*) bains *mpl* de mer *ou* de rivière, baignades *fpl*; **b. cap**, bonnet *m* de bain; **b. costume** *or* **suit**, maillot *m* de bain; **b. place**, baignade; **b. resort**, station *f* balnéaire; **b. trunks**, caleçon *m ou* slip *m* de bain; **(b)** *Med* lotion *f* (*d'une plaie etc*).

bathos ['beɪθɒs] *n* chute *f* du sublime au ridicule.

bathrobe ['bɑːθrəʊb] *n* peignoir *m*.

bathroom ['bɑːθruːm] *n* salle *f* de bain(s); **to go to the b.**, aller aux toilettes; **b. scales**, pèse-personne *m*, *pl* pèse-personnes.

bathtub ['bɑːθtʌb] *n* baignoire *f*.

batik ['bætɪk, bə'tiːk] *n* batik *m*; **b. skirt/***etc*, jupe *f*/*etc* en batik.

batman, *pl* **-men** ['bætmən] *n Mil* ordonnance *mf*.

baton ['bætən] *n* **(a)** bâton *m* (*de maréchal etc*); *Sp* (*in relay race*) témoin *m*; *Mus* (*of conductor*) baguette *f*, bâton; **orchestra under the b. of John Smith**, orchestre sous la direction de John Smith; **(b)** *Br* bâton *m* (*d'agent de police*); **b. charge**, charge *f* à la matraque; *Mil* **b. round**, balle *f* en plastique.

bats [bæts] *adj Br F* loufoque, toqué.

batsman, *pl* **-men** ['bætsmən] *n Cr* batteur *m*.

battalion [bə'tæljən] *n Mil* **(a)** bataillon *m*; **b. commander**, commandant *m* de bataillon; **tank b.**, **armoured b.**, bataillon de chars; **(b)** *US* groupe *m* (*d'artillerie*).

batten¹ ['bæt(ə)n] *n* **(a)** *Carp etc* (*for joint*) couvre-joint *m*, *pl* couvre-joints; (*lathe*) latte *f*, liteau *m*; planche *f* (*de parquet*); **(b)** *Nau* barre *f*, latte *f*, tringle *f*; **(c)** *Th* **the battens**, les herses *fpl* (*d'éclairage*).

batten² *vt* **(a)** *Carp* latter, voliger; **(b)** *Nau* **to b. down the hatches**, condamner les panneaux; *Fig* se préparer à affronter la crise *ou* la situation *etc*.

▶**batten on** *vipo* s'enrichir aux dépens de (*qn*).

batter¹ ['bætər] *n Cr* batteur *m*.

batter² *n Culin* pâte *f*; **pancake b.**, pâte à crêpes.

batter³ *vt* **(a)** maltraiter (*un enfant etc*); **(b)** bosseler (*une casserole, un chapeau etc*); **(c)** *Mil* battre en brèche, canonner (*une ville*); **(d)** *Typ* endommager (*des caractères*).

▶**batter down** *vtsep* abattre, démolir (*une porte etc*); battre (*un mur*) en brèche.

▶**batter in** *vtsep* enfoncer (*une porte etc*); **the victim's skull was battered in**, la victime a eu le crâne défoncé.

battered ['bætəd] *adj* **(a)** (*visage*) meurtri; **b. wives**, femmes battues; **b. child** *or* **baby**, enfant maltraité, enfant martyr; **(b)** (*mobilier etc*) délabré; (*chapeau*) cabossé; (*casserole etc*) bossué, bosselé; **a b. old car**, une vieille voiture délabrée.

battering ['bætərɪŋ] *n* (*of child, wife*) mauvais traitements *mpl*; **b. ram**, bélier *m*.

battery ['bæt(ə)rɪ] *n* **(a)** *Jur* voie *f* de fait; **assault and b.**, voies de fait; **(b)** *Mil* batterie *f*; **(c)** (*set, group*) batterie *f* (*de fours à coke etc*); *Psy* batterie (*de tests*); **(d)** *El* (*for calculator, watch etc*) pile *f*; (*for car*) batterie *f*; **dry b.**, (batterie de) piles sèches; **(storage) b.**, accumulateur *m*, *F* accu *m*; **to be b. operated** *or* **powered**, (*of radio, toy*) fonctionner sur piles; **batteries not included**, (*notice in catalogue*) livré sans piles; **(e)** (*for poultry*) batterie *f*; **b. farming**, élevage *m* en batterie(s); **b. hen**, poulet *m* de batterie; **(f)** (*in baseball*) **the b.**, le lanceur et le receveur.

batting ['bætɪŋ] *n Cr etc* maniement *m* de la batte.

battle¹ ['bæt(ə)l] *n* bataille *f*, combat *m*; **to fight/win a b.**, livrer/gagner une bataille; **killed in b.**, tué à l'ennemi; **to join b. with s.o.**, entrer en lutte avec qn, livrer bataille à qn; **that's half the b.**, c'est bataille à moitié gagnée; **the first blow is half the b.**, le premier coup en vaut deux; **pitched b.**, bataille rangée; *Hist* **the B. of Britain**, la Bataille d'Angleterre; **b. area**, zone *f* de bataille *ou* d'engagement; *Nau* **b. cruiser**, croiseur *m* de combat; **b. cry**, cri *m* de guerre; **b. fleet**, flotte *f* de ligne *ou* de combat; **b. royal**, (*fight involving several people*) mêlée générale, bagarre *f*; (*argument*) dispute violente.

battle² **1** *vi* se battre, lutter **(with s.o. for sth**, avec qn pour qch); **to b. with** *or* **against a fire**, combattre *ou* lutter contre un incendie. **2** *vt Am* combattre (*une doctrine etc*); **to b. one's way through difficulties**, se frayer un chemin à travers les difficultés.

battle-axe ['bæt(ə)læks] *n* hache *f* d'armes; *Pej Fig* (*woman*) virago *f*, mégère *f*.

battledore ['bæt(ə)ldɔːr] *n Sp* raquette *f*; **to play at b. and shuttlecock**, jouer au volant.

battledress ['bæt(ə)ldres] *n Mil* tenue *f* de campagne.

battlefield ['bæt(ə)lfiːld], **battleground** ['bæt(ə)lgraʊnd] *n Mil & Fig* champ *m* de bataille.

battlements ['bæt(ə)lmənts] *npl* parapet *m*, rempart *m*; *Archit* créneaux *mpl*.

battleship ['bæt(ə)lʃɪp] *n Nau* cuirassé *m*; *Hist* bâtiment *m* de ligne; **pocket b.**, cuirassé de poche.

batty ['bætɪ] *adj F* toqué, timbré.

batwing ['bætwɪŋ] *adj* en forme d'aile de chauve-souris; **b. sleeves**, manches *fpl* kimono.

bauble ['bɔːb(ə)l] *n* babiole *f*, colifichet *m*.

baud [bɔːd] *n Comptr* baud *m*; **at 2,400 b.**, à (une vitesse de) 2 400 bauds.

baulk [bɔːk] *n & v* = **BALK¹·²**.

bauxite ['bɔːksaɪt] *n Miner* bauxite *f*.

Bavaria [bə'veərɪə] *n* Bavière *f*.

Bavarian [bə'veərɪən] **1** *adj* bavarois; *Culin* **B. cream**, bavarois *m*. **2** *n* Bavarois, -oise.

bawdiness ['bɔːdɪnɪs] *n* (*of talk, words*) obscénité *f*; (*of humour, joke, poetry*) paillardise *f*.

bawdy ['bɔːdɪ] *adj* (*talk, words*) obscène; (*humour, joke, poetry*) paillard, grivois; **b. joke**, histoire paillarde *ou* cochonne.

bawdyhouse ['bɔːdɪhaʊs] *n Arch* maison *f* de prostitution.

bawl [bɔːl] **1** *vi* **(a)** (*shout*) hurler, brailler, crier à tue-tête, *F* beugler; *Sl* gueuler **(at s.o.**, contre qn); **(b)** *F* (*weep*) brailler. **2** *vt Sl* gueuler (*un ordre*).

▶**bawl out** *vtsep* **(a)** (*shout*) gueuler (*un ordre*); **(b)** *F* (*scold*) engueuler (*qn*).

bawling ['bɔːlɪŋ] *n* **(a)** (*shouting*) hurlement *m*, braillement *m*; **(b)** (*weeping*) braillement *m*; **stop that b.**, arrête de brailler.

bawling out *n* engueulade *f*; **to give s.o. a b. out**, engueuler qn.

bay¹ [beɪ] *n* (*shrub*) **sweet b.**, **b. laurel**, laurier commun, laurier des poètes; *Culin* **b. leaf**, feuille *f* de laurier; **b. tree**, laurier *m*; **b. wreath**, couronne *f* de laurier(s).

bay² *n Geog* baie *f*; (*small*) anse *f*; **Hudson B.**, la Baie d'Hudson; **the B. of Biscay**, le golfe de Gascogne.

bay³ *n* **(a)** (*alcove*) enfoncement *m*; baie *f* (*d'une porte etc*); *Mil* (*in trench*) niche *f*; *Br Rail* quai *m* subsidiaire, quai en cul-de-sac; *Av* **bomb b.**, soute *f* à bombes; *Aut* **parking b.**, place *f* de stationnement; **loading b.**, quai *m* de chargement; **b. window**, fenêtre *f* en baie *ou* en saillie; **(b)** (*of bridge, roof etc*) travée *f*; (*of joists*) claire-voie *f*, *pl* claires-voies.

bay⁴ *n* **to keep** *or* **hold the enemy at b.**, tenir l'ennemi en échec; *F* **I'm managing to keep my cold at b.**, jusqu'ici, j'ai réussi à passer à côté du rhume; **to bring a stag to b.**, mettre un cerf aux abois, forcer *ou* acculer un cerf; **to be at b.**, (*of stag*) être aux abois *ou* à l'accul.

bay⁵ *vi* (*of hound*) aboyer, donner de la voix; **to b. (at) the moon**, hurler *ou* aboyer à la lune.

bay⁶ *adj & n* (*cheval*) bai *m*.

bayberry ['beɪbərɪ] *n Bot* **(a)** (*fruit*) baie *f* de laurier; **(b)** (*tree*) piment *m* de la Jamaïque; **(c)** *Am* (*shrub*) cirier *m*.

baying ['beɪɪŋ] *n* (*of hound*) aboiement *m*.

bayonet¹ ['beɪənɪt] *n Mil* baïonnette *f*; **with fixed bayonets**, baïonnette au canon; *Mil* **b. charge**, charge *f* à la baïonnette; *El* **b. holder** *or* **socket**, douille *f* à baïonnette (*de lampe électrique*); *MecE etc* **b. joint**, joint *m* en baïonnette.

bayonet² *vt* (**-t-**) percer (*qn*) d'un coup de baïonnette.

bazaar [bə'zɑːr] *n* **(a)** (*in Middle East*) bazar *m*; **(b)** (*in aid* *of charity*) vente *f* de charité.

bazooka [bəˈzuːkə] *n Mil* bazooka *m*.

BBC [biːbiːˈsiː] *n* (*abbr* **British Broadcasting Corporation**) **what's on BBC?**, qu'est-ce qui passe sur la BBC?; **BBC programme**, émission *f* de la BBC.

BC [biːˈsiː] **1** *adv* (*abbr* **before Christ**) avant Jésus-Christ; **in (the year) 25 BC**, en (l'an) 25 avant J.-C.. **2** *n Can Geog* (*abbr* **British Columbia**) C.-B. *f*.

BCG [biːsiːˈdʒiː] *n Med* (*abbr* **bacille Calmette-Guérin**) B.C.G. *m*.

be [biː] *vi* (*pr ind* **am** [æm], **are** [ɑːr], **is** [ɪz], *pl* **are**; *past ind* **was** [wɒz], **were** [wɜːr], **was**, *pl* **were**; *pr sub* **be**; *past sub* **were**; *prp* **being** [ˈbiːɪŋ]; *pp* **been** [biːn]; *imp* **be**; **I am, he is, she is, it is, we are, you are, they are** *can be shortened into* **I'm, he's, she's, it's, we're, you're, they're**; **is not, are not, was not, were not** *into* **isn't, aren't, wasn't, weren't**) **(a)** (*specifying attribute*) être; **Mary is pretty**, Marie est jolie; **the weather was fine**, le temps était beau; **time is money**, le temps, c'est de l'argent; **he's a bit odd, is Bob**, c'est un drôle de garçon que Bob; **his father is a doctor**, son père est médecin; **he is an Englishman**, il est anglais, c'est un Anglais; **are they English?**, sont-ils anglais?; **if I were you**, à votre place, si j'étais vous; **as it is, we must go**, les choses étant ainsi il nous faut partir; **unity is strength**, l'union fait la force; **three and two are five**, trois et deux font cinq; **money isn't everything**, l'argent ne fait pas tout;

(b) (*specifying location, time, health, price*) **the books are on the table**, les livres sont *ou* se trouvent sur la table; **I was at the meeting**, j'ai assisté à la réunion; **where am I?**, où suis-je?; **I don't know where I am**, (*I am lost*) je ne sais pas où je suis; (*I have lost my place*) je ne sais pas où j'en suis; **where was I?**, (*after digression when talking*) où en étais-je?; **you never know where you are with him**, avec lui on ne sait jamais à quoi s'en tenir; **here I am**, me voici; **ah, there you are!**, vous voilà donc!; **how are you?**, comment allez-vous?, comment vous portez-vous?; **I am better**, je vais mieux, je me sens mieux; **how much is that?**, (*one item*) combien cela coûte-t-il?, c'est combien?; (*several items*) c'est combien?, combien ça fait?; **how far is it to London?**, combien y a-t-il d'ici à Londres?; **when is the concert?**, quand le concert aura-t-il lieu?; **today is the tenth**, nous sommes (aujourd'hui) le dix (du mois); **tomorrow is Friday**, demain, c'est vendredi;

(c) to be cold/hot, (*of person*) avoir froid/chaud; (*of water etc*) être froid/chaud; **to be ashamed of s.o./sth**, avoir honte de qn/qch; **to be hungry/thirsty**, avoir faim/soif; **to be right/wrong**, avoir raison/tort; **my hands are cold**, j'ai froid aux mains; **to be twenty (years old)**, avoir vingt ans, être âgé de vingt ans; **the wall is six metres high**, le mur a six mètres de haut; **he was so foolish as to do it**, il a eu la sottise de le faire;

(d) (*exist, remain*) **to be or not to be**, être ou ne pas être; **business is not what it was**, les affaires ne sont plus ce qu'elles étaient; **that may be**, cela se peut; **to see things as they are**, voir les choses comme elles sont; **be that as it may**, quoi qu'il en soit; **let me be!**, laissez-moi tranquille!; **there is, there are**, (*impersonal*) il y a; **there is a man in the garden**, il y a un homme dans le jardin; **what is there to see?**, qu'est-ce qu'il y a à voir?; **there will be dancing**, on dansera; **there were a dozen of us**, nous étions une douzaine;

(e) (*go, come*) **I have been to see David**, j'ai été voir David; **I have been to the museum**, j'ai visité le musée; **I have never been to Venice**, je n'ai jamais été à Venise; **he was into the room like a flash**, il est entré dans la pièce en un éclair; **where have you been?**, où étais-tu?; **has anyone been?**, est-il venu quelqu'un?; **has the postman been?**, est-ce que le facteur est passé?; *Br Sl* **(now) you've been and gone and done it!**, vous en avez fait une belle!; **be off (with you)!**, partez!;

(f) *impers* **it is six o'clock**, il est six heures; **it is late**, il est tard; **it is a fortnight since I saw him**, il y a quinze jours que je ne l'ai vu; **it is the tenth today**, nous sommes (aujourd'hui) le dix (du mois); **it is my birthday tomorrow**, demain, c'est mon anniversaire; **it is fine/cold**, il fait beau (temps)/froid; **it is easy to do it**, il est facile de le faire; **it is right that ...**, il est juste que +*sub* ...; **it is said that ...**, on dit que ...; **it is for you to decide**, c'est à vous de décider; **what is it?**, (*what do you want?*) que voulez-vous?; (*what is wrong?*) qu'est-ce qu'il y a?; **as it were**, pour ainsi dire, en quelque sorte; *F* **what's it to be?**, (*in pub, bar*) qu'est-ce que vous prenez?; (*make up your mind*) décidez donc!;

(g) (*auxiliary*) (*forming continuous tenses*) **I am/was doing sth**, je fais/faisais qch; (*be in the process of*) je suis/j'étais en train de faire qch; **they are always laughing**, ils sont toujours à rire; **the house is being built**, la maison est en construction; **I have (just) been writing**, je viens d'écrire; **I have been waiting for a long time**, il y a longtemps que j'attends, j'attends depuis longtemps; (*with a few intransitive verbs as aux of perfect*) **the sun is set**, le soleil est couché; **the guests were all gone**, les invités étaient tous partis; (*forming passive*) **he was killed**, il a été tué; **she is respected by all**, elle est respectée de tous; **he was always being laughed at**, on se moquait toujours de lui; **she is to be pitied**, elle est à plaindre; **what's to be done?**, que faire?; (*denoting future*) **I am to see them tomorrow**, je dois les voir demain; **he was never to see them again**, il ne devait plus les revoir; **is the house going to be sold?**, est-ce qu'on va vendre la maison?; (*necessity, duty*) **am I to do it or not?**, faut-il que je le fasse ou non?;

(h) the bride to be, la mariée; **the mother to be**, la future maman; *F* **a has-been**, un homme fini, une femme finie; **I am all for reform**, je suis pour *ou* je suis partisan de la réforme; **I'm all for staying here**, je ne demande qu'à rester ici; **what are you at?**, que faites-vous?; **while we're at it**, pendant que nous y sommes; **she is always at him**, elle l'embête tout le temps;

(i) (*in tag questions*) **so you're back, are you?**, alors, vous voilà de retour?; **she is beautiful, isn't she?**, elle est belle, n'est-ce pas?; **they're big, aren't they?**, ils sont grands, n'est-ce pas?

beach[1] [biːtʃ] *n* plage *f*; **sandy b.**, plage de sable; **to go to the b.**, aller à la plage; *Fig* **you're not the only pebble on the b.**, (*to boyfriend, girlfriend*) un(e) de perdu(e), dix de retrouvé(e)s; (*don't be selfish*) tu n'es pas tout seul au monde; **b. ball**, ballon *m* de plage; **b. buggy**, buggy *m*; **b. hut**, cabine *f* (*de bains, de plage*); **b. wear**, vêtements *mpl* de plage.

beach[2] *vt* échouer (*un navire*); tirer (*une embarcation*) à sec.

beachcomber [ˈbiːtʃkəʊmər] *n* **(a)** (*person*) batteur *m* de grève; **(b)** (*wave*) vague déferlante.

beachhead [ˈbiːtʃhed] *n Mil* tête *f* de pont (*de débarquement*).

beacon [ˈbiːk(ə)n] *n* **(a)** *Nau Av* (*lighthouse*) phare *m*; (*marking channel, runway*) balise *f*; (*light, signal*) feu *m*; *Fig* phare; *Nau Av* **radio b.**, radiophare *m*; **marker b.**, radiobalise *f*; **radar b.**, balise radar; radar *m* de radionavigation; **b. light**, feu de balisage; **(b)** *Arch* (*fire*) feu *m* d'alarme; (*location*) tour *f ou* colline *f* du feu d'alarme.

bead[1] [biːd] *n* **(a)** (*ornament*) perle *f* (*de verroterie, d'émail etc*); **(string of) beads**, collier *m*; **beads of dew**, perles de rosée; **there were beads of perspiration on his forehead**, la sueur perlait sur son front; **(b)** (*for prayers*) grain *m*; **(string of) beads**, chapelet *m*; **to tell one's beads**, égrener *ou* dire son chapelet; *Archit* **b. moulding**, patenôtre *f*; **(c)** bulle *f* (*sur le vin*); **(d)** *Archit Carp* perle *f*, baguette *f*; **(e)** guidon *m*, mire *f* (*de fusil*); **(f)** *Metal* cordon *m* de soudure.

bead[2] **1** *vt* **(a)** couvrir *ou* orner (*qch*) de perles; **(b)** *Archit Carp* appliquer une baguette sur (*qch*). **2** *vi* (*of liquid*) perler, faire la perle, faire chapelet.

beaded [ˈbiːdɪd] *adj* **(a)** (*material*) perlé; **(b)** *Archit Carp* **b. strip**, chapelet *m*.

beading [ˈbiːdɪŋ] *n* **(a)** (*decoration*) garniture *f* de perles; **(b)** *Archit Carp* baguette *f*; **(c)** (*of tyre*) talon *m*, bourrelet *m*.

beady [ˈbiːdɪ] *adj* (*yeux*) en vrille; **b. eyed**, aux yeux en vrille; *Br F* **I've got my b. eye on you**, je t'ai à l'œil.

beagle [ˈbiːg(ə)l] *n* (*dog*) beagle *m*, briquet *m*.

beagling [ˈbiːglɪŋ] *n* chasse *f* au briquet.

beak [biːk] *n* **(a)** bec *m* (*d'oiseau, de tortue, de cruche, de vase etc*); *F* nez crochu (*d'une personne*); **(b)** *Br Sl* (*judge*) juge *m*; (*headmaster*) dirlo *m*.

beaked [biːkt] *adj* (*animal*) à bec; (*nez*) crochu; **b. whale**, hyperoodon *m*.

beaker [ˈbiːkər] *n* **(a)** *Lit* (*without stem*) gobelet *m*; timbale *f*; (*with stem*) coupe *f*; **(b)** *Ch* vase *m* à bec.

be-all and end-all [ˈbiːɔːləˈnendɔːl] *n* **(a)** (*aim*) but *m* suprême, fin *f* des fins; **(b)** *Hum Pej* **he thinks he's the be-a. and e.-a.**, il se prend pour quelqu'un.

beam[1] [biːm] *n* **(a)** *Constr* poutre *f* (en bois), solive *f*, madrier *m*; (*small*) poutrelle *f*; **b. and joists**, solivure *f*; **ceiling b.**, doubleau *m*; **cross b.**, sommier *m*, traverse *f*; *Gym* **(balance) b.**, poutre horizontale; **cross b.**, portique *m*; **(b)** (*width*) **(breadth of) b.**, largeur *f* (*d'un navire*); **broad in the b.**, (*ship*) à larges baux; *F* (*person*) aux larges hanches; **(c)** travers *m* (*d'un navire*); **on the port/starboard b.,** par le travers bâbord/tribord; **(d)** rayon *m* (*de lumière, de soleil*); faisceau *m* (*d'un phare*); *Fig* grand *ou* large sourire (*de joie*); **(e)** *El* faisceau *m*; **electronic/radar b.,** faisceau électronique/radar; **radio b.,** faisceau hertzien; *Av* **radio landing b.,** axe balisé d'atterrissage; *F* **you are completely off b.,** (*mistaken*) tu dérailles.

beam² **1** *vt* **(a)** *Telecom* transmettre (*un message*) par ondes dirigées; **to be beamed in on Orly,** (*of aircraft*) être dirigé sur Orly; **(b)** *Fig* (*of person*) **she beamed her thanks,** elle a souri largement en guise de remerciement. **2** *vi* (*of sun*) rayonner; (*of person*) rayonner (de joie); **beaming with health,** resplendissant de santé.

beam-ends [biːˈmendz] *npl* (*of ship*) baux *mpl*; **to be on her b.-e.,** (*of ship*) être accoté *ou* sur le côté; *Fig* **to be on one's b.-e.,** être *ou* se trouver à bout de ressources.

beaming [ˈbiːmɪŋ] *adj* (*soleil, visage*) rayonnant, radieux; (*smile*) radieux, large.

bean [biːn] *n* **(a)** (*vegetable*) **broad b.,** fève *f*; **French b.,** *Am* **string b.,** haricot vert, *Can* fève verte; **runner b.,** haricot d'Espagne; *Br* **butter b.,** *Am* **Lima b.,** haricot de Lima; **kidney b., haricot b.,** haricot Soissons; **soya b.,** graine *f* de soya *ou* de soja, pois chinois; *Culin* **dried beans, haricot beans,** haricots secs; *F* **to be full of beans,** être plein de verve *ou* d'entrain; *F* **it isn't worth a b.,** ça ne vaut pas un radis; *F* **he hasn't a b.,** il n'a pas un radis; *F* **to spill the beans,** vendre la mèche; *Am Fig* **not to know beans about sth,** savoir que dalle sur qch; *Old-fashioned* **old b.,** mon vieux; *Culin* **b. sprout,** germe *m* de soja; **(b)** grain *m* (*de café*); graine *f*, fève *f* (*de cacao*); **(c)** *Am Sl* (*head*) boule *f*.

beanbag [ˈbiːnbæg] *n* **(a)** (*bag*) balle lestée; **(b)** (*cushion, chair*) fauteuil *m* poire.

beanery [ˈbiːnərɪ] *n US* = petit restaurant pas cher.

beanfeast [ˈbiːnfiːst] **, beano** [ˈbiːnəʊ] *n Old-fashioned Br F* (*meal*) régal *m*; (*festive occasion*) bombe *f*.

beanpole [ˈbiːnpəʊl] *n* rame *f* pour haricots; *Fig* (*person*) manche *m* à balai, échalas *m*.

beanstalk [ˈbiːnstɔːk] *n* tige *f* de fève *ou* de haricot.

bear¹ [ˈbeər] *n* **(a)** (*animal*) *& Fig* ours *m*; **to be like a b. with a sore head,** être d'une humeur massacrante; **the Great B. Lake,** le grand lac de l'Ours; *Astron* **the Great/Little B.,** la Grande/Petite Ourse; **she b.,** ourse *f*; **b. cub,** ourson *m*; **b. garden,** fosse *f* aux ours; *Fig* pétaudière *f*; *Fig* **to turn the place into a b. garden,** mettre le désordre partout; *Fig* **the room was like a b. garden,** la pièce était sens dessus dessous; **b. pit,** fosse *f* aux ours; *F* **b. hug,** forte étreinte; **to give s.o. a b. hug,** serrer qn très fort dans ses bras; **(b)** *St Exch* baissier *m*, joueur *m* à la baisse; **b. market,** marché *m* à la baisse; **to go a b.,** spéculer à la baisse; **to sell a b.,** vendre à découvert.

bear² *v* (-r-) *St Exch* **1** *vt* **to b. the market,** chercher à faire baisser les cours. **2** *vi* spéculer à la baisse.

bear³ *vt* (*pt* **bore** [bɔːr]; *pp* **borne** [bɔːn]) **(a)** (*carry*) porter (*un fardeau, des armes, un nom, une date etc*); **the document bears your signature,** le document porte votre signature; **I still b. the scars,** (*of attack etc*) j'en porte encore les cicatrices; *Fig* j'en garde encore les cicatrices; **to b. s.o. a grudge,** garder rancune à qn; **she doesn't b. him any grudge,** (*for what he did*) elle ne lui en tient absolument pas rigueur; **to b. sth in mind,** (*remember*) se souvenir de qch; (*take into account*) tenir compte de qch; **b. us in mind if ever you want to sell it,** pensez à nous si jamais vous décidez de le vendre; **it bears no relation/resemblance to ...,** cela n'a aucun rapport/aucune ressemblance avec ...; **to b. witness to sth,** rendre *ou* porter témoignage de qch, témoigner de qch; **he bore himself with dignity,** il est resté très digne; **to be borne backwards** *or* **along** *or* **away,** être refoulé *ou* emporté;

(b) (*tolerate*) supporter, soutenir (*un poids*); supporter (*la souffrance, les conséquences*); souffrir (*la douleur etc*); **we will b. the costs,** nous prendrons les frais en charge; **to b. the responsibility of sth,** avoir la responsabilité de qch; **she bears a heavy responsibility,** elle porte une lourde responsabilité; **his language does not b. repeating,** son langage n'est pas à répéter; **he could b. it no longer,** il ne pouvait plus y tenir; **I can't b. this,** je ne peux pas supporter ça; **to grin and b. it,** faire contre mauvaise fortune bon cœur; **you'll just have to grin and b. it,** tu n'as qu'à faire contre mauvaise fortune bon cœur; **I can't b. (the sight of) him,** je ne peux pas le souffrir *ou* le sentir; **I can't b. the idea of it,** je ne peux pas en souffrir *ou* en supporter l'idée; **it doesn't b. thinking about,** l'idée en est insupportable;

(c) (*move, lie*) **to b. the right/left,** (*of person, road*) tourner à droite/à gauche; (*of person*) prendre à droite/à gauche; **to b. round,** (*of ship*) arriver en grand; *Nau* **the cape bears north-north-west,** on relève le cap au nord-nord-ouest;

(d) (*give birth to*) (*see also* **born**) donner naissance à (*un enfant*); **she has borne him three sons,** elle lui a donné trois fils;

(e) (*yield*) **capital that bears interest,** capital *m* qui porte intérêt; **to b. fruit,** (*of tree*) porter fruit; *Fig* (*of work etc*) porter fruit, fructifier; **my enquiries bore fruit,** mes recherches ont été couronnées de succès.

▶**bear away** **1** *vtsep* emporter, enlever (*qch*). **2** *vi Nau* **to b. away (for a point),** laisser arriver, laisser porter (*sur une pointe, sur un cap*).

▶**bear down** **1** *vi* (*of woman in labour*) pousser. **2** *vtsep* (*usu passive*) **to be borne down by poverty,** être accablé par la misère.

▶**bear down (up)on** *vipo Nau* foncer, laisser porter, fondre sur (*l'ennemi*); *Nau* courir sur (*qch*); (*of person, car etc*) foncer sur (*qn*).

▶**bear on** *vipo* **(a)** (*place weight on*) buter *ou* appuyer sur (qch); **beam bearing on two uprights,** poutre qui s'appuie sur deux montants; **to bring all one's strength to b. on a lever,** s'appuyer de toutes ses forces sur un levier; **to bring all one's energies to b. on sth,** apporter *ou* consacrer toute son énergie à qch; **to bring one's mind to b. on sth,** porter son attention sur qch; **to bring influence/pressure to b. on s.o.,** exercer une influence/une pression sur qn; **it was gradually borne in upon him that ...,** peu à peu il s'est rendu compte que ...; **(b)** (*be relevant to*) avoir rapport à (*qch*); **I don't see how that bears on what I'm doing,** je ne vois pas le rapport que ça a avec ce que je fais.

▶**bear out** *vtsep* **(a)** (*carry*) emporter (*un cadavre etc*); **(b)** (*confirm*) confirmer, justifier (*une assertion*); **to b. s.o. out, to b. out what s.o. has said,** corroborer ce que qn a dit.

▶**bear up** **1** *vtsep* soutenir (*qn, qch*). **2** *vi* **to b. up under misfortune,** faire face *ou* tenir tête au malheur; **b. up!,** tenez bon!, du courage!; *Br F* **how are you? — bearing up,** comment ça va?, ça va? — je me défends.

▶**bear upon** *vipo* = **BEAR ON.**

▶**bear with** *vipo* **(a)** (*tolerate*) supporter (*la mauvaise humeur de qn etc*); **(b)** (*be patient with*) être patient avec (*qn*).

bearable [ˈbeərəb(ə)l] *adj* supportable; **the situation is no longer b.,** la situation n'est plus tenable.

bearably [ˈbeərəblɪ] *adv* d'une façon supportable.

bear-baiting [ˈbeəbeɪtɪŋ] *n* combats *mpl* d'ours et de chiens.

beard¹ [bɪəd] *n* (*of man, animal*) barbe *f*; *Bot* arête *f* (*d'épi*); **to have a b.,** porter la barbe; **to grow a b.,** se laisser pousser la barbe; **a week's b.,** une barbe de huit jours.

beard² *vt* braver, défier, narguer (*qn*); *Fig* **to b. the lion in his den,** affronter la colère de qn.

bearded [ˈbɪədɪd] *adj* (*homme, blé, poisson*) barbu.

-bearded [ˈbɪədɪd] *suff* **black-/white-/***etc* **b.,** à barbe noire/blanche/*etc*.

beardless [ˈbɪədlɪs] *adj* imberbe, sans barbe.

bearer [ˈbeərər] *n* **(a)** porteur *m* (*de nouvelles, de brancard, d'un chèque*); titulaire *mf* (*d'un passeport*); **the b. of this letter,** le porteur de cette lettre; **the bearers,** (*at funeral*) les porteurs; **to be a good b.,** (*of tree*) bien donner; *Fin* **b. bond/cheque,** titre *m*/chèque *m* au porteur; **(b)** *Constr MecE* support *m*; **b. joist,** lambourde *f* (de parquet).

bearing [ˈbeərɪŋ] **1** *adj* (*essieu etc*) porteur; **b. wall,** mur *m* d'appui; **b. surface,** surface *f* d'appui (*d'une poutre*); tablette *f* (*d'une solive*); *MecE* surface portante *ou* de portage.

2 *n* **(a)** port *m* (*d'armes, de nouvelles*);

(b) (*deportment*) port *m*, maintien *m*;

(c) *Constr etc* (appareil *m* d')appui *m* (*d'un pont métallique*); surface *f* d'appui (*d'une poutre*); portée *f* (*de poutres*); chape *f* (*d'une balance*); *Archit* dé *m*;

(d) *MecE* palier *m*; **self-lubricating b.,** palier graisseur; **ball/roller/needle b.,** roulement *m* à billes/à rouleaux/à aiguilles;

(e) (*direction*) orientation *f*; (*in surveying*) gisement *m*, azimut *m*; *Nau Av* relèvement *m*, position *f*; **true b.,** (*in surveying*) azimut *ou* gisement géographique; *Nau Av* relèvement vrai; **compass b.,** relèvement au compas; **to take the ship's bearings,** faire le point; **to take one's bearings,** s'orienter, se repérer; **to lose one's bearings,** perdre sa direction *ou* sa route; *F* perdre le nord; **to get**

one's bearings, retrouver sa direction *ou* sa route;
(f) (*connection*) rapport *m* (**on a question,** avec une question); **it has no b. on the matter,** (*of fact etc*) cela n'a aucun rapport avec l'affaire.

-bearing ['beərɪŋ] *suff* **fruit-b.,** fructifère, qui porte des fruits; **interest-b. capital,** capital *m* qui rapporte; **silver-b.,** argentifère; **wool-b.,** lanifère.

bearish ['beərɪʃ] *adj* **(a)** (*manières*) d'ours; (*person*) bourru; **(b)** *St Exch* (*marché*) à la baisse; **b. tendency,** tendance *f* à la baisse.

bearskin ['beəskɪn] *n* **(a)** peau *f* d'ours (*garnie de son poil*); **b. rug,** peau d'ours; **(b)** *Mil* bonnet *m* à poil.

beast [biːst] *n* **(a)** bête *f*; **wild b.,** (*not domesticated*) bête sauvage; (*fierce*) bête féroce; **the king of the beasts,** le roi des animaux; **b. of prey,** carnassier *m*; **b. of burden,** (*ass etc*) *& Fig* bête de somme; *Bible* **the B.,** l'Antéchrist *m*; **beasts,** (*on farm*) bétail *m*, bestiaux *mpl*, cheptel *m*; **(b)** *Fig* (*brute*) animal *m*, brute *f*, abruti *m*; *F* (*unkind person*) goujat *m*; **to sink to the level of a b.,** s'avilir; **the little b.,** le petit diable; **he's a perfect b.!,** c'est une rosse!; **it was a b. of a day,** il a fait un temps abominable *ou* un temps de chien; **a b. of a job,** (*employment*) un sale métier; (*task*) un travail de chien.

beastliness ['biːstlɪnɪs] *n* bestialité *f*, brutalité *f*.

beastly ['biːstlɪ] **1** *adj* **(a)** bestial; **(b)** *Fig* (*person*) brutal; (*unpleasant*) sale, dégoûtant; **a b. job,** (*employment*) un sale métier; (*task*) un travail de chien; **what b. weather!,** quel sale temps! **2** *adv F* terriblement; **it's b. cold,** il fait bigrement froid.

beat[1] [biːt] *n* **(a)** (*stroke, blow*) battement *m* (*du cœur, d'un mouvement, d'horloge*); son *m* (*du tambour*); *Mus* mesure *f*, temps *m*; **music with a strong b.,** musique avec un fort rythme; **(b)** *Br* ronde *f* (*d'un agent de police*); **policeman on the b.,** agent qui fait sa ronde; *F* **it's off my b. altogether,** cela ne relève pas de ma compétence, ce n'est pas de mon ressort.

beat[2] *v* (*pt* **beat**; *pp* **beaten** ['biːt(ə)n]) **1** *vt* **(a)** battre (*qn, qch*); **to b. s.o. with a stick,** donner des coups de bâton à qn; **to b. s.o. black and blue,** meurtrir *ou* rouer qn de coups; **to b. s.o. to death,** assommer qn (*à coups de trique etc*); **to b. sth flat,** aplatir qch à coups de marteau *ou* de hache *etc*; **to b. one's breast,** se frapper la poitrine; **to b. a carpet,** battre un tapis; **to b. eggs,** battre des œufs; **to b. a drum,** battre du tambour; *Mil* **to b. the retreat,** battre la retraite; **to b. a retreat,** *Mil* battre en retraite; *Fig* se retirer, se dérober; **to b. time (to music),** battre la mesure; **to b. a wood (for game),** battre *ou* traquer un bois; **the world is beating a path to her door,** tout le monde se rue sur elle; *F* **b. it!,** (*go away*) file!, fiche le camp!; **to b. its wings,** (*of bird*) battre des ailes;
(b) (*conquer*) battre, vaincre (*l'ennemi*); battre (*un record*); (*get ahead of*) devancer (*qn*); **to b. s.o. at chess,** battre qn aux échecs; **they were beaten,** ils ont été vaincus; *F* **that beats me!,** ça me dépasse!; *F* **that beats everything!,** ça c'est le comble *ou* le bouquet!; *F* **you can't b. a good book,** rien de tel qu'un bon livre; *F* **I got up early to b. the traffic,** je me suis levé tôt pour éviter les embouteillages; *F* **he beat me to it,** (*arrived, telephoned before me*) il m'a devancé; (*took the seat I wanted*) il m'a fauché ma place;
(c) *US Sl* (*cheat, get the better of*) rouler, refaire (*qn*); **to b. the customs,** frauder la douane.
2 *vi* **(a)** (*of heart, rain*) battre; **the waves b. against the shore,** les vagues déferlent sur le rivage;
(b) *Nau* **to b. to windward,** louvoyer;
(c) *Fig* **to b. about** *or Am* **around the bush,** tourner autour du pot; **not to b. about the bush,** (*in deeds*) aller droit au but, ne pas y aller par quatre chemins; (*in words*) répondre sans ambages *ou* carrément.

beat[3] *adj F* **(a) you have** *or* **you've got me b.,** (*defeated*) je m'avoue vaincu; (*puzzled*) tu me prends de court; **it's got** *or* **it has me b. why she did it,** je ne comprends pas pourquoi elle a fait ça; **(b)** (*very tired*) crevé; **dead b.,** complètement crevé.

beat[4] *n Old-fashioned F* beatnik *m*.

►**beat back** *vi* repousser (*qn, l'ennemi*); rabattre (*les flammes*).

►**beat down 1** *vtsep* **(a)** (r)abattre (*qch*); enfoncer (*une porte*); damer (*la terre*); *Fig* **to b. down the price of sth,** (*by bargaining*) faire baisser le prix de qch; **to b. s.o. down,** faire baisser le prix à qn. **2** *vi* (*of rain*) s'abattre; **the sun is beating down on our heads,** le soleil nous tape sur la tête.

►**beat in** *vtsep* enfoncer, défoncer (*une porte etc*).

►**beat off** *vtsep* repousser (*qn, un assaut*).

►**beat out** *vtsep* **(a)** (*extinguish*) éteindre (*des flammes*); **(b)** (*flatten*) battre, aplatir (*le fer*); marteler, écolleter (*l'or etc*); débosseler (*un panneau*); **(c)** *Mus* **to b. out a rhythm,** *F* **to b. it out,** marquer un rythme; **(d) to b. s.o.'s brains out,** assommer qn, décerveler qn; **to b. one's brains out,** se creuser la tête *ou* la cervelle; **(e) to b. the dust out of sth,** battre qch pour en faire sortir la poussière.

►**beat up 1** *vtsep* **(a)** (*attack*) tabasser (*qn*); **(b)** fouetter (*des œufs*); **(c)** rabattre, traquer (*le gibier*). **2** *vi Nau* louvoyer *ou* gagner vers la terre.

►**beat up on** *vipo esp Am F* battre, maltraiter (*sa femme*); **stop beating up on yourself,** arrête de culpabiliser.

beaten ['biːt(ə)n] *adj* **(a)** (*or, fer*) battu, martelé; **b. earth,** terre battue; *Fig* **house off the b. track,** maison écartée; **(b)** (*ennemi*) battu, vaincu.

beater ['biːtər] *n* **(a)** (*person*) batteur, -euse; (*in hunting*) rabatteur *m*, traqueur *m*; **(b)** (*stick etc*) batte *f*; *Mus* tringle *f* (*de triangle*); **(egg) b.,** fouet *m*; (*in papermaking*) pilon *m*; *Tex* volant *m*.

beatific [biːə'tɪfɪk] *adj* (*vision etc*) béatifique; (*sourire*) béat.

beatifically [biːə'tɪfɪklɪ] *adv* d'un air béatifique.

beatification [biːætɪfɪ'keɪʃən] *n Rel* béatification *f*.

beatify [biː'ætɪfaɪ] *vt Rel* béatifier (*qn*).

beating ['biːtɪŋ] **1** *adj* (*cœur*) palpitant; (*pluie*) battant. **2** *n* **(a)** battement *m* (*d'ailes, du cœur etc*); *Tech* battage *m*; rabattage *m*, rabat *m* (*du gibier*); traque *f* (*d'un bois*); *Nau* louvoyage *m*; **(b)** (*thrashing*) raclée *f*, rossée *f*; **to give s.o. a b.,** rosser qn; **(c)** défaite *f* (*dans un match etc*); **to get a good b.,** être battu à plate(s) couture(s).

beatitude [biː'ætɪtjuːd] *n* béatitude *f*; *Bible* **the Beatitudes,** les Béatitudes.

beatnik ['biːtnɪk] *n* beatnik *mf*.

beat-up ['biːtʌp] *adj* (*car etc*) déglingué.

beau, *pl* **beaus, beaux** [bəʊ, bəʊz] *n* **(a)** (*dandy*) élégant *m*, dandy *m*; **(b)** *Arch & US* prétendant *m* (*d'une jeune fille*), galant *m*.

beaut [bjuːt] *F* **1** *n* **what a b.!,** quelle merveille!; **what a b. of a car!,** quelle voiture!; **it's a real b.,** c'est une véritable merveille. **2** *adj Aust* (*meal*) délicieux; (*weather*) superbe; (*car*) génial.

beautician [bjuː'tɪʃən] *n* esthéticien, -ienne; (*make-up artist*) visagiste *mf*.

beautiful ['bjuːtɪfʊl] **1** *adj* **(a)** (*person, place*) (très) beau, (très) belle; **a b. face,** un très beau visage; **at twenty she was b.,** à vingt ans c'était une beauté; **the b. people,** le beau monde; **(b)** (*dîner, temps etc*) magnifique. **2** *n* **the b.,** le beau.

beautifully ['bjuːtɪfʊlɪ] *adv* (*intensifier*) admirablement, à merveille; **that will do b.,** cela fera l'affaire parfaitement *ou* à merveille.

beautify ['bjuːtɪfaɪ] *vt* embellir, enjoliver.

beauty ['bjuːtɪ] *n* **(a)** (*appearance*) beauté *f*; **to be in the flower of one's b.,** être dans toute sa beauté; **the beauties of nature,** les beautés de la nature; **that's the b. of it,** c'est justement ce qu'il y a de bien avec ça; **b. aids** *or* **preparations,** produits *mpl* de beauté; **b. competition,** concours *m* de beauté; **b. parlour** *or* **salon,** institut *m* de beauté; **b. queen,** reine *f* d'un concours de beauté; **b. spot,** (*place*) site *m ou* coin *m* pittoresque; (*on skin*) grain *m* de beauté; (*artificial*) mouche *f*;
(b) (*person, object*) **she was a b. in her day,** elle a été une beauté dans son temps; **B. and the Beast,** la Belle et la Bête; **the Sleeping B.,** la Belle au bois dormant; *F* **isn't it a b.?,** (*of flower*) n'est-ce pas qu'elle est jolie?; (*of car*) n'est-ce pas qu'elle est chouette?; **it's a b.,** c'est un rêve; *Sl* **he fetched him a b. on the chin,** il lui a flanqué un coup magnifique *ou* formidable au menton; **that black eye is a b.,** cet œil au beurre noir est une splendeur.

beaver ['biːvər] *n* (*animal, fur*) castor *m*; *F* **to work like a b.,** travailler comme quatre; **an eager b.,** un zélé, une zélée; **b. lamb (coat),** (manteau *m* en) mouton doré.

►**beaver away** *vi* travailler d'arrache-pied (**at,** à).

becalmed [bɪ'kɑːmd] *adj* (*ship*) accalminé, encalminé.

became *see* **BECOME.**

because [bɪ'kɒz, -kəz] **1** *conj* parce que; **I eat b. I'm hungry,** je mange parce que j'ai faim; **I was all the more astonished b. I had been told ...,** j'en fus d'autant plus étonné qu'on m'avait assuré ...; **b. he dashed off a sonnet he thinks himself a poet,** pour avoir bâclé un sonnet il se croit poète; **why? — just b.,** pourquoi? — parce que. **2** *prep phrase* **b. of sth,** à cause de qch; **he has been retired b. of his illness,** on l'a mis à la retraite en raison de *ou* vu sa maladie; **I said nothing b. of the children,** je n'ai rien dit à cause des enfants.

béchamel ['beʃəmel] *n Culin* **b. sauce,** béchamel *f*, sauce *f* (à la) béchamel.

beck [bek] *n* **to have s.o. at one's b. and call,** avoir qn à ses ordres *ou* à sa disposition; **to be at s.o.'s b. and call,** obéir aux moindres volontés de qn, être aux ordres de qn.

beckon ['bek(ə)n] *vt & vi* faire signe (**to s.o.,** à qn); appeler (*qn*) du doigt *ou* de la main; **to b. s.o. in,** faire signe à qn d'entrer.

become [bɪ'kʌm] *v* (*pt* **became** [bɪ'keɪm]; *pp* **become**) **1** *vi* **(a)** devenir, se faire (*prêtre, médecin etc*); devenir (*grand, roi, l'ennemi de qn etc*); **to b. old/thin,** vieillir/maigrir; **to b. suspicious of s.o.,** concevoir des soupçons à propos de *ou* sur qn; **the murmurs became louder,** les murmures se faisaient plus forts; **custom that has become law,** usage qui a passé en loi; **to b. accustomed/attached/interested,** s'accoutumer/s'attacher/s'intéresser; **to b. known,** (*of person*) commencer à être connu; **it will soon b. clear that ...,** il sera bientôt évident que ...; **(b) what has become of Tom?,** qu'est devenu Tom?; **what will b. of him?,** que va-t-il devenir?; **I don't know what has become of her,** je ne sais pas ce qu'elle est devenue. **2** *vt* (*of behaviour etc*) convenir à, être propre à (*qn, qch*); (*of clothes, colour etc*) aller bien à (*qn*).

becoming [bɪ'kʌmɪŋ] *adj* **(a)** (*proper*) convenable, bienséant; **(b)** (*colour, clothes*) seyant, qui sied, qui va bien (**to,** à); **b. dress,** robe avantageuse; **that's a very b. dress,** c'est une robe très seyante; **green looks very b. on you,** le vert te va très bien.

becquerel [bek(ə)'rel] *n Phys* becquerel *m*.

bed¹ [bed] *n* **(a)** lit *m*; **single b.,** lit pour une personne; **double b.,** lit de *ou* pour deux personnes; **twin beds,** lits jumeaux; **camp b.,** lit de camp; **we've got a spare b.,** (*you can stay the night*) nous avons de quoi vous coucher; **b. of state,** lit de parade; **the marriage b.,** le lit conjugal; **to sleep in separate beds,** faire lit à part; **to be in b.,** (*for night*) être couché; (*through illness*) être alité, être au lit, garder le lit; **to go to b.,** se coucher; *Journ* **the paper has gone to b.,** le journal est bouclé; **to take/keep to one's b.,** prendre/garder le lit; **to keep s.o. in b.,** garder qn au lit; **I'm going home to b.,** je vais rentrer me coucher; **to put a child to b.,** coucher un enfant, mettre un enfant au lit; *F* **to go to b. with a man/woman,** coucher avec un homme/une femme; **it's time for b.,** c'est l'heure d'aller au lit; **to make the beds,** faire les lits; *Fig* **you've made your b. and now you must lie in it,** comme on fait son lit, on se couche; **place the roast on a b. of vegetables,** placez le rôti sur un lit de légumes; **b. and breakfast,** (*at hotel*) chambre *f* et petit déjeuner; *esp Br* **we stayed in a b. and breakfast,** nous avons dormi dans un bed and breakfast; *F* **to get out of b. on the wrong side,** se lever du pied gauche; **to turn down the b.,** faire la couverture; **b. head,** chevet *m*; tête *f* (de lit); **b. jacket,** liseuse *f*; **b. linen,** literie *f*; **b. settee,** canapé-lit *m*, *pl* canapés-lits;
(b) lit *m* (*d'une rivière, de la mer*); fond *m* (*de billard*); **filter b.,** lit de filtrage;
(c) (*in garden*) planche *f*, carré *m* (*de légumes*); **flower b.,** parterre *m*; **oyster b.,** banc *m* d'huîtres; (*on oyster farm*) parc *m* à huîtres;
(d) *Geol* assise *f*, couche *f*; *Miner* gisement *m*;
(e) *Constr etc* assise *f*, lit *m* (*de béton*); assise (*de pierres*); *Rail* infrastructure *f*;
(f) *MecE* banc *m* (*de tour*); sommier *m* (*d'une machine*); table *f* (*de raboteuse*); *Av* berceau *m* (*de moteur*); **(engine) b.,** support *m*, bâti *m*.

bed² *vt* (**-dd-**) *Old-fashioned* coucher avec (*une femme*).

►bed down 1 *vi* (*of animal*) se gîter; *F* (*of person*) se coucher. **2** *vtsep* faire la litière à (*les chevaux*).

►bed in *vtsep* repiquer (*des plantes*).

►bed out *vtsep* dépoter (*des plantes*).

B Ed [biː'ed] *n abbr* **Bachelor of Education**.

bedbug ['bedbʌg] *n* punaise *f* des lits.

bedchamber ['bedtʃeɪmbər] *n Arch* chambre *f* à coucher; **Lady of the B.,** (*at court*) dame *f* du lit.

bedclothes ['bedkləʊðz] *npl* couvertures *fpl* et draps *mpl* de lit; **to turn down the b.,** faire la couverture (de lit).

beddable ['bedəb(ə)l] *adj F* baisable.

bedding ['bedɪŋ] *n* **(a) b. plants,** plants *mpl* à repiquer; **b. roses,** roses *fpl* pour massifs *ou* pour corbeilles; **(b)** (*for bed*) literie *f*; **(c)** (*for animals*) litière *f*.

bedding out *n* dépotage *m*, dépotement *m* (*de plantes*).

bedevil [bɪ'dev(ə)l] *vt* (**-ll-,** *US* **-l-**) **(a)** (*torment*) taquiner, tourmenter (*qn*); **(b)** gâcher (*qch*); **industrial relations bedevilled by politics,** rapports entre patrons et ouvriers envenimés par la politique.

bedfellow ['bedfeləʊ] *n* camarade *mf* de lit; **they make strange bedfellows,** c'est une association inattendue, c'est un couple disparate.

bedlam ['bedləm] *n* **(a)** *Fig* charivari *m*, tohu-bohu *m*; **the meeting was absolute b.,** la réunion était un véritable tohu-bohu; **(b)** *Arch* maison *f* de fous *ou* d'aliénés.

Bedouin ['bedʊɪn] **1** *adj* bédouin. **2** *n* (*pl* **Bedouin(s)**) Bédouin, -ine.

bedpan ['bedpæn] *n* bassin *m* de lit.

bedpost ['bedpəʊst] *n* colonne *f* de lit.

bedraggled [bɪ'dræg(ə)ld] *adj* (*muddy*) crotté, taché de boue; (*wet*) trempé (*d'eau*); (*clothing*) dépenaillé; **you look a bit b.,** tu as l'air un peu dépenaillé.

bedridden ['bedrɪd(ə)n] *adj* alité, cloué au lit.

bedrock ['bedrɒk] *n Geol* roche *f* de fond; *Fig* fondement *m* (*de sa croyance etc*); **to get down to b.,** voir au fond des choses.

bedroll ['bedrəʊl] *n US Mil* matériel *m* de couchage.

bedroom ['bedruːm] *n* chambre *f* à coucher; **spare b.,** chambre d'ami; **b. furniture/curtains/***etc*, meubles *mpl*/rideaux *mpl*/*etc* de chambre à coucher; **b. slippers,** pantoufles *fpl*; *Th* **b. farce,** comédie *f* leste.

Beds *abbr* **Bedfordshire**.

bedside ['bedsaɪd] *n* chevet *m*; **to have a good b. manner,** (*of doctor*) avoir un comportement agréable au chevet du malade; **b. lamp,** lampe *f* de chevet; **b. rug,** descente *f* de lit; **b. table,** table *f* de nuit *ou* de chevet.

bed-sittingroom [bed'sɪtɪŋruːm], **bed-sit(ter)** ['bedsɪt, -ər] *n Br* chambre meublée.

bedsock ['bedsɒk] *n* chausson *m* de nuit.

bedsore ['bedsɔːr] *n* escarre *f* (*produite par le séjour au lit*); *Med* décubitus *m*.

bedspread ['bedspred] *n* dessus *m* de lit.

bedstead ['bedsted] *n* châlit *m*, bois *m* de lit.

bedtick¹ ['bedtɪk] *n Am* (*bug*) punaise *f* des lits.

bedtick², bedticking ['bedtɪk, -ɪŋ] *n* toile *f* à matelas.

bedtime ['bedtaɪm] *n* heure *f* du coucher; **b.!,** c'est l'heure d'aller au lit!; **what is your b.?,** à quelle heure vous couchez-vous?; **it's past your b.,** vous devriez être déjà couché; **it's long past my b.,** je devrais être couché depuis longtemps; **b. stories,** histoires *fpl* pour l'heure du coucher *ou* pour endormir.

bed-wetter ['bedwetər] *n* (*child*) enfant incontinent *ou F* qui fait pipi au lit; **to be a b.-w.,** être incontinent, *F* faire pipi au lit.

bed-wetting ['bedwetɪŋ] *n* incontinence *f* nocturne.

bee [biː] *n* **(a)** abeille *f*; **queen b.,** reine *f* des abeilles; *Fig* **she's the queen b. around here,** c'est elle qui commande, c'est elle la patronne; **honey b.,** abeille domestique; **working b.,** abeille ouvrière; **bees' nest,** nid *m* d'abeilles; **to keep bees,** élever des abeilles; *Fig* **to be a busy b.,** être très actif; **to have a b. in one's bonnet,** avoir une idée fixe; **he's got a b. in his bonnet about this,** c'est pour lui une idée fixe; *Br F* **she thinks she's the b.'s knees,** elle se croit sortie de la cuisse de Jupiter; **she thinks he's the b.'s knees,** pour elle, c'est une merveille; (*plant*) **b. balm,** monarde *f* d'Amérique; **b. orchid,** (*plant*) ophrys *f* abeille; **(b)** *Am* réunion *f* (*pour travaux en commun*); **(c)** *Old-fashioned* (*competition*) concours *m*; **spelling b.,** concours (oral) d'orthographe.

beech [biːtʃ] *n* (*tree*) hêtre *m*; **copper b.,** hêtre rouge *ou* pourpre; **b. (wood),** bois *m* de hêtre; **b. furniture,** meubles *mpl* en hêtre; **b. mast,** faînes *fpl* (*comme nourriture de pourceaux*).

beechnut ['biːtʃnʌt] *n* faîne *f*.

bee-eater ['biːiːtər] *n* (*bird*) guêpier *m* (d'Europe).

beef¹ [biːf] *n* **(a)** (*no pl*) *Culin* bœuf *m*; **roast b.,** rôti *m* de bœuf, rosbif *m*; **salt b.,** bœuf salé; **corned b.,** corned beef *m*, conserve *f* de bœuf, *F* singe *m*; **b. stew,** ragoût *m* de bœuf, bœuf mode; *Fig* **to have plenty of b.,** avoir du muscle, être costaud; **b. cattle,** bœufs de boucherie; **b. tea,** bouillon *m* de bœuf; **(b)** *US* (*animal*) (*pl* **beeves** [biːvz], **beefs** [biːfs]) bœuf(s) *m(pl)* à l'engrais; **a b.,** un bœuf, une vache; **b. farm,** élevage *m* de bœufs; **b. farmer,** éleveur *m* de bœufs; **(c)** (*complaint*) (*pl* **beefs**) *F* plainte *f*, grief *m*; **he enjoys a good b.,** il aime ronchonner *ou* rouspéter; **what's your b.?,** qu'est-ce que tu as à ronchonner?; **my main b. is that ...,** ce qui m'énerve le plus c'est que ... .

beef² *F vi* ronchonner, rouspéter.

►beef up *vtsep F* gonfler l'importance de (*qch*); renforcer (*l'armée*).

beefburger ['biːfbɜːgər] *n* hamburger *m*.

beefcake ['biːfkeɪk] *n F* poitrine (d'homme) nue; **look at all that b.,** (*on beach etc*) regarde tous ces athlètes.

beefeater ['biːfiːtər] *n F* = hallebardier de service à la

Tour de Londres.

beefing [bi:fɪŋ] *n F* ronchonnement *m*, rouspétance *f*.

beefsteak ['bi:fsteɪk] *n Culin* bifteck *m*; *Am* **b. tomato,** ≈ marmande *f*.

beefy ['bi:fɪ] *adj F* **(a)** (*muscular*) musclé, costaud; **(b)** (*fleshy*) bien en chair.

beehive ['bi:haɪv] *n* **(a)** (*for bees*) ruche *f*; **(b)** (*hairstyle*) coiffure toute en hauteur.

beekeeper ['bi:ki:pər] *n* apiculteur, -trice.

beekeeping ['bi:ki:pɪŋ] *n* apiculture *f*.

beeline ['bi:laɪn] *n Fig* **to make a b. for sth,** aller droit *ou* directement vers qch.

Beelzebub [bɪ'elzɪbʌb] *n* **(a)** *Bible* Belzébuth *m*; **(b)** (*devil*) le Diable.

been *see* **BE**.

beep[1] [bi:p] *n* bip-bip *m* (*d'un satellite etc*); coup *m* (*de klaxon*).

beep[2] **1** *vi* (*of satellite etc*) faire bip-bip. **2** *vt* **(a)** *Aut* **to b. the horn,** klaxonner; **(b)** appeler (*qn*) au récepteur d'appel; **I'm being beeped,** (*of doctor etc*) mon récepteur d'appel retentit.

beeper ['bi:pər] *n* récepteur *m* de poche.

beeping [bi:pɪŋ] *n* bip-bip *m* (*d'un satellite etc*).

beer [bɪər] *n* bière *f*; **draught b.,** bière au tonneau *ou* à la pompe *ou* sous pression; **bottled b.,** bière en bouteille; **to order a b.,** demander une bière; **does anybody want to go for a b.?,** on va boire une bière?; **will you join me in a b.?,** (*have one too*) est-ce que tu prendras une bière aussi?; **life's not all b. and skittles,** la vie n'est pas qu'une partie de rigolade; **ginger b.,** = boisson gazeuse au gingembre; **b. barrel/bottle,** tonneau *m*/bouteille *f* à bière; **b. cellar,** brasserie *f*; **b. garden,** café *m* en plein air; **b. glass,** verre *m* à bière; (*big*) chope *f*; **b. mat,** sous-bock *m inv*.

beery ['bɪərɪ] *adj* **(a)** (*atmosphère etc*) qui sent la bière; **(b)** **b. voice,** voix avinée.

beeswax ['bi:zwæks] *n* cire *f* d'abeilles; **b. (polish),** cire *f* à parquet.

beet [bi:t] *n* **(a)** betterave *f*; **fodder b.,** betterave fourragère; **sugar b.,** betterave à sucre; **b. sugar,** sucre *m* de betterave; **b. industry,** industrie betteravière; **(b)** *Am* = **BEETROOT**.

beetle[1] ['bi:t(ə)l] *n* (*insect*) coléoptère *m*.

beetle[2] *n* (*for beating, pounding*) (*large*) masse *f* (*en bois*); (*small*) maillet *m*; (*for paving*) hie *f*, demoiselle *f*; (*for quarrying*) batterand *m*; *Constr* **b. head,** mouton *m*.

beetle[3] *vi* (*of cliff*) surplomber.

beetle[4] *adj* **b. brows,** (*overhanging eyebrows*) sourcils proéminents; (*bushy eyebrows*) sourcils touffus.

►**beetle along** *vi* mettre les bouts.

►**beetle away, beetle off** *vi F* décamper.

beetle-browed [bi:t(ə)l'braʊd] *adj* (*with overhanging eyebrows*) aux sourcils proéminents; (*with bushy eyebrows*) aux sourcils touffus.

beetling ['bi:tlɪŋ] *adj* (*cliff, rock etc*) surplombant, en surplomb.

beetroot ['bi:tru:t] *n* betterave *f* (potagère).

befall [bɪ'fɔ:l] *vt* (*conj like* **fall**; *used only in third person*) *Lit* arriver à, survenir à (*qn*).

befit [bɪ'fɪt] *vt* (**-tt-**) *Lit* (*used only in third person*) convenir à (*qn, qch*); **as befits her position,** comme il convient à son rang; **it does not b. a man to ...,** ce n'est pas le fait d'un homme de ... .

befitting [bɪ'fɪtɪŋ] *adj* convenable, seyant (**for s.o./sth,** à qn/qch).

before [bɪ'fɔ:r] **1** *adv* **(a)** (*of time*) auparavant, avant; **two days b.,** deux jours avant *ou* auparavant; **the day b.,** la veille; **the year b.,** l'année d'avant, un an auparavant; **she had come two years b.,** elle était venue deux ans auparavant; **a moment b.,** un moment auparavant *ou* plus tôt; **I have seen him b.,** je l'ai déjà vu; **I have never seen him b.,** je ne l'ai jamais vu (de ma vie); **we've met b.,** nous nous sommes déjà rencontrés; **I've told you b.,** (*don't do that*) je te l'ai déjà dit; **she gave me the same advice as b.,** elle m'a redonné le même conseil; **to go on as b.,** faire comme par le passé; **you should have told me so b.,** vous auriez dû me le dire plus tôt;

(b) (*of place*) en avant, devant; **to go on b.,** marcher en avant; **this page and the one b.,** cette page et la précédente.

2 *prep* **(a)** (*of place*) devant; **b. my (very) eyes,** sous mes (propres) yeux; **b. God and man,** devant Dieu et les hommes; **to appear b. the judge,** comparaître par-devant le juge; **that is the task b. us,** c'est là la tâche qui nous incombe;

(b) (*of time*) avant; **b. that, she was a teacher,** auparavant, elle était professeur; **where did you go b. that?,** où est ce que vous êtes allé avant ça?; **b. long,** avant longtemps, sous peu; **not b. Easter,** pas avant Pâques; **it ought to have been done b. now,** ce devrait déjà être fait; **to arrive an hour b. time,** arriver avec une heure d'avance; *F* **it's not b. time, and not b. time,** ce n'est pas trop tôt; **I got here b. you,** je vous ai devancé; **you were here b. me,** (*in queue*) vous étiez avant moi; **the day b. the battle,** la veille de la bataille; **two days b. Christmas,** l'avant-veille de Noël; **b. answering,** avant de répondre; **take the medicine b. meals,** prenez ce médicament avant les repas;

(c) (*of order*) **b. anything (else) I must have ...,** il me faut avant tout ...; **death b. dishonour,** plutôt la mort que le déshonneur; **ladies b. gentlemen,** les dames d'abord; **this word should come b. that one,** ce mot devrait être placé devant celui-là; **the welfare of the country comes b. everything,** le bien de la patrie prime tout; **she puts family b. friends,** pour elle, la famille est plus importante que les amis.

3 *conj* **(a)** (*of time*) avant que (ne) + *sub*; **come and see me b. you leave,** venez me voir avant de partir *ou* avant votre départ; **I saw him the day b. he died,** je l'ai vu la veille de sa mort; **don't come in b. I call you,** n'entrez pas avant que *ou* sans que je vous appelle; **it was long b. he came,** (*it happened before that*) c'était longtemps avant qu'il arrive; **how long will it be b. you hear?,** est-ce que tu mettras longtemps à entendre?; *F* **b. you know where you are, b. I** *or* **he** *etc* **knew where I** *or* **he** *etc* **was,** en moins de rien; **b. I forget, they expect you this evening,** j'oubliais de vous dire qu'on vous attend ce soir; **b. I forget, will you ...,** j'oubliais de te demander de ...;

(b) (*of order*) **I will die b. I yield,** je préfère mourir plutôt que de céder;

(c) (*or else*) avant que (ne) + *sub*; **get out b. I throw you out,** sortez avant que je vous jette dehors; **tell me b. I die of curiosity,** dis-le moi ou je vais mourir de curiosité; **give it to her b. she cries,** donne-le lui avant qu'elle ne se mette à pleurer.

beforehand [bɪ'fɔ:hænd] *adv* au préalable, à l'avance, d'avance; **to come an hour b.,** venir une heure à l'avance; **I must tell you b. that ...,** il faut vous dire d'avance *ou* au préalable que ...; **if I come I shall let you know b.,** si je viens je vous préviendrai; **we should make sure b.,** nous ferions mieux de nous en assurer d'abord.

befriend [bɪ'frend] *vt* (*make friends with*) se lier avec (*qn*).

befuddle [bɪ'fʌd(ə)l] *vt* **(a)** (*confuse*) brouiller les idées de (*qn*); **(b)** (*make drunk*) griser (*qn*); **befuddled (with drink),** éméché.

beg [beg] *v* (**-gg-**) **1** *vi* (*for money*) mendier; (*plead*) supplier; **these jobs go begging,** ce sont des emplois qui trouvent peu d'amateurs; **I'm not going to b.,** je ne vais pas supplier; **to sit up and b.,** (*of dog*) faire le beau; **to b. for mercy,** demander grâce; **I b. of you!,** je vous en prie! **2** *vt* **to b. s.o. to do sth,** prier *ou* supplier qn de faire qch; **to b. a favour of s.o.,** demander instamment un service à qn; **she begged to be sent back to school,** elle supplia qu'on la renvoie à l'école; *Fml* **I b. to inform you that ...,** j'ai l'honneur de vous faire savoir que ...; **I b. your pardon,** je vous demande pardon; **to b. forgiveness,** implorer le pardon; **I b. to differ,** permettez-moi d'être d'un autre avis; **to b. the question,** faire une pétition de principe; (*evade the issue*) contourner le problème.

►**beg off** *vi* (*from a meeting party etc*) demander à être excusé.

beget [bɪ'get] *vt* (*pt* **begot** [bɪ'gɒt], *Bible* **begat** [bɪ'gæt]; *pp* **begotten** [bɪ'gɒt(ə)n]) **(a)** *Bible Lit* engendrer, procréer; **Abraham begat Isaac,** Abraham engendra Isaac; *Bible* **the only begotten Son of the Father,** le Fils unique du Père; **(b)** *Lit Fig* causer, susciter; **discord begets crime,** la discorde enfante le crime.

beggar[1] ['begər] *n* **(a)** (*in street*) mendiant, -ante, gueux, -euse; *Prov* **beggars can't be choosers,** ne choisit pas qui emprunte, faute de souliers on va nu-pieds; **(b)** *esp Br* (*person*) individu *m*; **poor b.!,** pauvre diable!; **lucky b.!,** chançard!, veinard!; **you little b.!,** petit coquin!, petit espiègle!

beggar[2] *vt* (**beggared** ['begəd]) **(a)** **to b. s.o.,** réduire qn à la mendicité; **they are beggaring themselves doing it,** en faisant cela, ils vont tout droit à la ruine; **(b)** *Fig* **to b. description,** être indescriptible.

beggarly ['begəlɪ] *adj* (*very poor*) minable, misérable; (*salaire*) dérisoire, minable.

beggar-my-neighbour ['begəmɪ'neɪbər] *n Cards*

bataille *f*.

beggary ['begərɪ] *n* mendicité *f*; **to be reduced to b.**, être réduit à la mendicité.

begging ['begɪŋ] **1** *adj* (*frère, ordre*) mendiant; **b. letter**, lettre quémandant de l'argent. **2** *n* mendicité *f*; **to live by b.**, vivre d'aumône; **b. bowl**, sébile *f* (*de mendiant*); **b. the question**, pétition *f* de principe; (*avoiding the issue*) fait *m* de contourner un problème.

begin [bɪ'gɪn] *vt & vi* (*pt* **began** [bɪ'gæn]; *pp* **begun** [bɪ'gʌn]) commencer (*un discours, une tâche etc*); entamer, amorcer (*une conversation etc*); attaquer (*un repas etc*); **b. at the beginning**, commencez par le commencement; **before winter begins**, avant le début de l'hiver; **the day began well/badly**, la journée s'annonça bien/mal; **to b. a fresh chapter**, entamer un nouveau chapitre; **to b. to do sth, to b. doing sth**, commencer à faire qch, se mettre à faire qch; **to b. to laugh/cry, to b. laughing/crying**, se mettre à rire/à pleurer; **to b. to boil/melt**, entrer en ébullition/en fusion; **he soon began to complain**, il ne tarda pas à se plaindre; **we began** *or* **we were beginning to get hungry**, nous commencions à avoir faim; **it doesn't b. to compare with ...**, cela est loin d'être comparable à ...; **I couldn't (even) b. to explain/describe/***etc*, c'est presque impossible de t'expliquer/de te décrire/*etc*; **to b. by doing sth**, débuter *ou* commencer par faire qch; **the play begins with a prologue**, la pièce débute par un prologue; **to b. again**, recommencer.

►**begin with** *vi* commencer par; **to b. with**, (*in the first place*) premièrement, pour commencer; (*at first*) au départ; **what did you have to b. with?**, (*in restaurant etc*) par quoi avez-vous commencé?

beginner [bɪ'gɪnər] *n* **(a)** (*novice*) débutant, -ante; **English for beginners**, anglais pour débutants; **b.'s class**, cours de débutant; **b.'s luck**, aux innocents les mains pleines; **she just had b.'s luck**, elle a profité de la chance du débutant; **(b)** *Th* **beginners please!**, en scène pour le un!

beginning [bɪ'gɪnɪŋ] *n* commencement *m*, début *m* (*d'un discours, d'une carrière etc*); origine *f*, naissance *f* (*du monde etc*); **in the b.**, au commencement, au début; **from the b.**, dès le commencement; **from b. to end**, depuis le commencement jusqu'à la fin; **at the b. of the week**, au début de la semaine; **at the b. of term**, à la rentrée (des classes); **the first beginnings of civilization**, les rudiments de la civilisation; **I have the beginnings of a cold**, je couve un rhume; **to make a b.**, commencer, débuter.

begone [bɪ'gɒn] *pp Arch & Lit* (*used as imp*) va-t'en!, allez-vous-en!

begonia [bɪ'gəʊnɪə] *n* (*plant*) bégonia *m*.

begrudge [bɪ'grʌdʒ] *vt* donner (*qch*) à contrecœur; **to b. doing sth**, faire qch à contrecœur; **I b. spending so much money**, c'est à contrecœur que je dépense une telle somme; **to b. s.o. sth**, envier qch à qn; **they b. him his food**, on lui mesure *ou* reproche sa nourriture.

beguile [bɪ'gaɪl] *vt Lit* **(a)** (*charm*) enjôler, séduire (*qn*); **to b. s.o. with promises**, bercer qn de promesses; **(b)** (*while away*) **to b. the time**, faire passer le temps.

beguiling [bɪ'gaɪlɪŋ] *adj* (*sourire*) enjôleur, séduisant.

begum ['beɪgəm] *n* bégum *f*.

behalf [bɪ'hɑːf] *n* **on b. of s.o.**, au nom de qn, de la part de qn; *Com* au compte *ou* à l'acquit de qn; **he is acting on my b.**, il agit pour moi *ou* pour mon compte; **don't be uneasy on my b.**, ne vous inquiétez pas à mon sujet; **speaking on my own b.** *or* **on b. of myself**, en mon (propre) nom; **on b. of myself and my husband**, de la part de mon mari et moi.

behave [bɪ'heɪv] *vi* **(a)** se comporter, se conduire; **to b. well to(wards) s.o.**, bien agir envers qn; **what a way to b.!**, quelles manières!; **to know how to b.**, savoir vivre; **I'll teach him how to b.!**, je lui apprendrai la politesse!; **b. yourself!**, (*to child, husband etc*) tiens-toi (comme il faut)!; (*to child*) sois sage!; **(b)** (*of machine*) marcher, fonctionner.

-behaved [bɪ'heɪvd] *suff* **well-b.**, sage, qui se conduit bien; **badly-b.**, qui se conduit *ou* qui se tient mal.

behaviour, *US* **behavior** [bɪ'heɪvjər] *n* **(a)** (*of person*) comportement *m* (**towards**, envers); (*of pupil*) conduite *f* (**to(wards) s.o.**, avec, envers qn); **good b.**, bonne conduite; **to be on one's best b.**, se surveiller; **I want you to be on your best b.**, j'espère que tu te surveilleras; **b. pattern**, type *m* de comportement; **(b)** fonctionnement *m* (*d'une machine*); tenue *f* (*d'une voiture*).

behavioural, *US* **behavioral** [bɪ'heɪvjər(ə)l] *adj* (*psychology etc*) du comportement.

behaviourism, *US* **behaviorism** [bɪ'heɪvjərɪz(ə)m] *n* behavio(u)risme *m*.

behead [bɪ'hed] *vt* décapiter.

beheading [bɪ'hedɪŋ] *n* décapitation *f*.

behemoth [bɪ'hiːmɒθ] *n Fig* monstre *m*.

behest [bɪ'hest] *n Lit* commandement *m*, ordre *m*; **at whose b.?**, sur l'ordre de qui?

behind [bɪ'haɪnd] **1** *adv* derrière, par derrière; **to attack s.o. from b.**, attaquer qn par derrière; **to come b.**, venir derrière, suivre; **to fall** *or* **lag b.**, s'attarder; **to stay** *or* **remain b.**, (*be at the back*) rester *ou* demeurer en arrière; (*not leave*) ne pas partir; **I'll stay b. and wait for them**, je resterai derrière pour les attendre; **I left my umbrella b.**, (*at home*) j'ai oublié mon parapluie à la maison; (*at s.o. else's home*) j'ai oublié mon parapluie (chez eux); **to be b. with** *or* **in one's work**, être en retard dans son travail; **to be b. with the rent**, être en retard pour payer son loyer; *Sp* **they are only three points b.**, ils ne sont qu'à trois points; **the other cars followed close b.**, les autres voitures suivaient de très près.

2 *prep* derrière; **he hid b. it**, il s'est caché derrière; **look b. you**, regardez derrière vous; **garden b. the house**, jardin derrière la maison; **I'm right b. you**, (*at your back*) je suis juste derrière toi; *Fig* (*I support you*) je suis avec toi; **to walk** *or* **follow close b. s.o.**, marcher sur les talons de qn; *Fig* **he has the minister b. him**, il a le ministre derrière *ou* avec lui, il est protégé par le ministre; **what's b. all this?**, qu'y a-t-il derrière tout cela?; **the reasons b. sth**, les raisons de qch; **to be b. schedule**, avoir du retard; **to put sth b. one**, rejeter le souvenir de qch; **let's put it all b. us**, oublions tout cela; **it's all b. me now**, c'est passé pour moi; **she's ten minutes b. the leaders**, (*in race*) elle a dix minutes de retard sur le peloton de tête; **b. the times**, (*country*) arriéré, attardé; **you're behind the times**, (*old-fashioned*) tu n'es pas à la page; (*not aware of latest developments*) tu retardes d'un métro.

3 *n F* derrière *m*; **to kick s.o.'s b.**, botter le derrière de *ou* à qn.

behindhand [bɪ'haɪndhænd] *adv* en arrière, en retard; **to be b. with the rent**, être en retard pour le loyer; **I am b. with my work**, je suis en retard dans mon travail.

behold [bɪ'həʊld] *vt* (*pt & pp* **beheld** [bɪ'held]) *Lit* voir; **b.!**, voyez!

beholden [bɪ'həʊld(ə)n] *adj* **to be b. to s.o.**, être redevable à qn, être obligé à *ou* envers qn (**for**, de); **I'm b. to you**, je vous suis redevable.

beholder [bɪ'həʊldər] *n* **beauty is in the eye of the b.**, il n'y a point de laides amours.

behove [bɪ'həʊv] **,** *US* **behoove** [bɪ'huːv] *vt impers Arch* incomber à; **it behoves him to ...**, il lui appartient de ... .

beige [beɪʒ] *adj & n* (*colour*) beige *m*.

being ['biːɪŋ] **1** *n* existence *f*, être *m*; **those to whom I owe my b.**, ceux qui m'ont donné le jour; **to come into b.**, prendre forme, prendre naissance; **the company is still in b.**, la société existe toujours; **all my b. rebels at the idea**, tout mon être se révolte à cette idée; **a human b.**, un être humain; **human beings**, le genre humain, les (êtres) humains *mpl*; **the Supreme B.**, l'Être suprême. **2** *adj* **for the time b.**, pour le moment, temporairement; **this is my home for the time b.**, voici où j'habite provisoirement.

Beirut [beɪ'ruːt] *n* Beyrouth *m*.

bejewelled, *US* **bejeweled** [bɪ'dʒuːəld] *adj* paré de bijoux.

belabour, *US* **belabor** [bɪ'leɪbər] *vt* **(a)** (*beat*) rouer (*qn*) de coups; *Fig* **to b. a point**, insister lourdement sur un point; **(b)** (*criticize*) accabler (*qn*) d'injures.

belated [bɪ'leɪtɪd] *adj* (*voyageur etc*) attardé; (*renseignement, invitation etc*) tardif; (*invité etc*) en retard; **to wish you a b. happy birthday**, pour te souhaiter un bon anniversaire avec un peu de retard.

belay [bɪ'leɪ] *vt* **(a)** *Nau* tourner, amarrer (*une manœuvre*); **(b)** (*of mountaineer*) assurer (*la corde*).

belaying [bɪ'leɪɪŋ] *n* **(a)** *Nau* tournage *m*, amarrage *m*; **b. pin** *or* **cleat**, cabillot *m*, taquet *m*; **(b)** (*in mountaineering*) assurance *f* (*de la corde*).

belch[1] [beltʃ] *n* **(a)** (*of person*) éructation *f*, renvoi *m*, *F* rot *m*; **he gave a b.**, il a fait un rot; **(b)** vomissement *m* (*de flammes etc*).

belch[2] *vi* avoir un renvoi, éructer, *F* roter; **he belched all through the meal**, il a roté pendant tout le repas.

►**belch forth, belch out** *vtsep* vomir (*des flammes, de la fumée etc*).

beleaguer [bɪ'liːgər] *vt* assiéger (*une ville*); *Fig* critiquer, s'attaquer à (*un projet, une idéologie etc*).

beleaguered [bɪ'liːgəd] *adj* (*city etc*) assiégé; *Fig* (*project, ideology etc*) qui fait l'objet de nombreuses

critiques *ou* de réactions hostiles.
belfry ['belfrɪ] *n* beffroi *m*, clocher *m*.
Belgian ['beldʒən] **1** *adj* belge; (*history, ambassador*) de Belgique. **2** *n* Belge *mf*.
Belgium ['beldʒəm] *n* Belgique *f*.
belie [bɪ'laɪ] *vt* (*prp* **belying** [bɪ'laɪɪŋ]) démentir (*une promesse etc*); **his appearance belies it,** il n'en a pas l'air.
belief [bɪ'liːf] *n* **(a)** conviction *f*; *Rel* croyance *f*; **b. in ghosts,** croyance aux revenants; **b. in God,** croyance en Dieu; **she did it in the b. that,** elle l'a fait en étant persuadée que; **it is beyond b.,** c'est incroyable; **to the best of my b.,** pour autant que je sache; **it is my b. that ...,** je suis convaincu que ..., j'ai la conviction que ...; **(b)** (*trust*) foi *f*, confiance *f* (*en qn, en qch*).
believable [bɪ'liːvəb(ə)l] *adj* croyable.
believe [bɪ'liːv] **1** *vt* croire (*une nouvelle etc*); ajouter foi à (*une rumeur*); **I b. that it is true,** je crois que c'est vrai; **I b. (that) I am right,** je crois avoir raison; **I b. him to be alive,** je le crois vivant; **she is believed to be in Paris,** on la croit à Paris; **the house was believed to be haunted,** la maison passait pour être hantée; **he believes himself to have been unfairly treated,** il se croit (la) victime d'une injustice; **I b. not,** (*I don't think so*) je crois que non; **I b. so,** (*I think so*) je crois que oui; **I don't b. a word of it,** je n'en crois rien *ou* pas un mot; **I don't know what to b.,** je ne sais que croire; **I could scarcely** *or* **hardly b. my eyes,** j'en croyais à peine mes yeux; **you can't b. everything you read in the papers,** il ne faut pas croire tout ce qu'on lit dans les journaux; **seeing is believing,** voir c'est croire; **to make s.o. b. that ...,** faire croire à qn que ...; *F* **don't you b. it!,** n'en croyez rien!; **I can well b. it,** je suis prêt à le croire, je veux bien le croire; **b. it or not, he fell for her!,** il s'est épris d'elle, figure-toi! *ou* crois-le ou non!; **would you b. it!,** vous vous rendez compte!; **to b. s.o.,** croire qn, accorder créance au dire de qn; **if he is to be believed,** à l'en croire, s'il faut l'en croire; *F* **she's a smart one, b. me!** *or F* **b. you me!,** c'est une maline, crois-moi!; **I wouldn't have believed it of you,** je n'aurais pas cru ça de toi; *F* **I don't b. it!,** c'est pas vrai!
2 *vi* **to b. in (one) God,** croire en (un seul) Dieu; **to b. in ghosts,** croire aux revenants; **I b. in his innocence,** je crois en son innocence; **to b. in sth,** (*support*) être partisan de qch, être pour qch; **to b. in s.o.,** (*trust*) avoir confiance en qn; **I don't b. in doctors,** je n'ai pas confiance dans les médecins.
believer [bɪ'liːvər] *n Rel* croyant, -ante; **to be a b. in sth,** croire à qch; (*supporter of*) être partisan de qch, être pour qch; **I am not a b. in patent medicines,** je ne crois pas à l'efficacité des spécialités pharmaceutiques; **I'm a great b. in newborn babies being breast-fed,** je suis très en faveur de l'allaitement au sein pour les nouveau-nés.
Belisha [bə'liːʃə] *n Old-fashioned Br* **B. beacon,** = sphère orange lumineuse (indiquant un passage clouté).
belittle [bɪ'lɪt(ə)l] *vt* rabaisser, déprécier, amoindrir (*qn, le mérite de qn*); décrier (*qn*); **to b. oneself,** (*disparage*) se déprécier; (*demean*) se déconsidérer (*aux yeux de qn, auprès de qn*).
bell[1] [bel] *n* **(a)** cloche *f*; (*small*) clochette *f*; (*in house*) sonnette *f*; (*fixed*) timbre *m*; (*for cattle etc*) clochette, clarine *f*; *Br F* **to give s.o. a b.,** (*telephone*) passer un coup de fil à qn; **electric b.,** sonnerie *f* (électrique); **set of bells,** sonnerie *f* (*d'une église*); **great b.,** (*of a church*) bourdon *m*; **there's the b.,** (*of the door*) on sonne; **to ring the b.,** (*of the door*) sonner; (*handbell*) agiter la sonnette; *Fig* **that rings a b.,** cela me rappelle *ou* me dit quelque chose; **for whom the b. tolls,** pour qui sonne le glas; *Nau* **to strike the bells,** piquer l'heure; **six bells,** six coups (de cloche); Nau **b. buoy,** bouée *f* à cloche; **b. heather,** (*plant*) bruyère cendrée; *Ch* **b. jar,** cloche; **b. pull,** (*in room*) cordon *m* de sonnette; (*at door*) poignée *f* de sonnette; **b. push,** bouton *m* de sonnette; **b. tent,** tente *f* conique; **b. tower,** clocher *m*, campanile *m*;
(b) calice *m* (*d'une fleur*); pavillon *m* (*d'une trompette etc*); campane *f* (*d'une colonne*); vase *m* (*de chapiteau*); cône *m*, cloche *f* (*d'un haut fourneau*).
bell[2] **1** *vt* attacher une clochette autour du cou de (*une vache*). **2** *vi* (*of skirt etc*) faire cloche, ballonner.
bell[3] *n* bramement *m* (*du cerf*).
bell[4] *vi* (*of deer*) bramer.
►**bell out** *vi* (*of tube etc*) s'évaser, renfler.
belladonna [belə'dɒnə] *n Bot Pharm* belladone *f*.
bell-bottomed ['belbɒtəmd] *adj* **b.-b. trousers,** = **BELL-BOTTOMS.**
bell-bottoms ['belbɒtəmz] *npl* pantalon *m* à pattes d'éléphant.
bellboy ['belbɔɪ] *n Am* groom *m* (*d'hôtel*).
belle [bel] *n* beauté *f*; **the b. of the ball,** la reine *ou* la beauté du bal.
bellflower ['belflaʊər] *n* campanule *f*.
bellhop ['belhɒp] *n Am F* groom *m* (*d'hôtel*).
bellicose ['belɪkəʊs] *adj* belliqueux.
bellicosity [belɪ'kɒsɪtɪ] *n* (*of speech, behaviour*) caractère belliqueux, agressivité *f*; (*of person*) humeur belliqueuse.
belligerence [be'lɪdʒərəns] *n* belligérence *f*.
belligerent [be'lɪdʒərənt] **1** *adj* (*person, country*) belligérant; (*tone of voice, attitude, person etc*) belliqueux, agressif. **2** *n* belligérant, -ante.
bellow[1] ['beləʊ] *n* (*of bull*) beuglement *m*, mugissement *m*; (*of person*) braillement *m*.
bellow[2] **1** *vi* (*of bull*) beugler, mugir; (*of person*) brailler. **2** *vt* brailler (*un ordre*); *F* beugler (*une chanson*).
►**bellow out** *vtsep* = **BELLOW[2] 2.**
bellowing ['beləʊɪŋ] *n* beuglement *m*, mugissement *m* (*d'un animal*); braillement *m* (*d'une personne*).
bellows ['beləʊz] *npl* **(a) (a pair of) b.,** un soufflet (*pour le feu*); **(b)** soufflerie *f* (*d'un orgue*).
bell-ringer ['belrɪŋər] *n* carillonneur *m*.
bell-ringing ['belrɪŋɪŋ] *n* (*sound*) carillonnement *m*; (*art*) art *m* campanaire.
bell-shaped ['belʃeɪpt] *adj* en forme de cloche.
bellwether ['belweðər] *n* (*sheep*) bélier *m*.
belly[1] ['belɪ] *n* **(a)** ventre *m* (*de l'homme*); panse *f* (*d'un animal*); *Sl* panse, bedaine *f*; *Culin* **b. of pork,** poitrine *f* de porc; **to have an empty b.,** avoir l'estomac creux; **to have a full b.,** avoir le ventre plein; **his eyes are bigger than his b.,** il a les yeux plus grands que le ventre; **to do a b. flop** (*of diver*) faire un plat; **b. dance,** danse *f* du ventre; **b. dancer,** danseuse *f* du ventre; **b. laugh,** rire rabelaisien *ou* énorme; **(b)** ventre *m* (*d'une cruche, d'un avion, d'un navire etc*); panse *f* (*d'une cruche*); *Av* **b. tank,** réservoir ventral; *Av* **b. landing,** atterrissage *m* sur le ventre; **(c)** *Mus* table *f* d'harmonie (*d'un violon etc*); **(d)** *Nau* creux *m*, renflement *m* (*d'une voile*).
belly[2] *Nau* **1** *vt* (*of wind*) enfler, gonfler (*les voiles*). **2** *vi* (*of sail*) faire (le) sac, s'enfler, se gonfler.
►**belly out** *vtsep & vi* = **BELLY[2].**
bellyache[1] ['belɪeɪk] *n* **(a)** *F* mal *m* au ventre; **(b)** *Sl* (*complaints*) rouspétance *f*.
bellyache[2] *vi Sl* ronchonner, rouspéter, *Sl* râler; **he's always bellyaching about something,** il faut toujours qu'il rouspète après qch.
bellyacher ['belɪeɪkər] *n Sl* **to be a b.,** être un râleur.
bellyaching ['belɪeɪkɪŋ] *n Sl* rouspétance *f*, jérémiades *fpl*; **I don't want any b.,** je n'accepterai aucune rouspétance; **your constant b. is driving me up the wall,** tes jérémiades incessantes me fatiguent.
bellybutton ['belɪbʌt(ə)n] *n F* nombril *m*.
belly-flop ['belɪflɒp] *vi F* (*of diver*) faire un plat.
bellyful ['belɪfʊl] *n* plein ventre, *F* ventrée *f*; *F* **to have had a b.,** (*of food*) en avoir tout son soûl; (*more than can be tolerated*) en avoir ras le bol, en avoir marre; **I've had a b. of him,** j'en ai marre de lui.
bellyland ['belɪlænd] *vi Av* atterrir sur le ventre.
belong [bɪ'lɒŋ] *vi* **(a)** (*be property of*) **to b. to,** appartenir à, être à; **that book belongs to me,** ce livre m'appartient *ou* est à moi; **to b. to the Crown,** (*of land etc*) dépendre de la Couronne; **(b)** (*be connected*) être propre (*à qch*); **to what category do they b.?,** à quelle catégorie appartiennent-ils?; **to b. to a society,** faire partie d'une société; **do you b. to this club?,** êtes-vous membre de ce cercle?; **I b. here,** (*come from*) je suis d'ici; (*feel at ease*) je me sens chez moi ici; **to feel that one doesn't b.,** se sentir isolé *ou* intrus; **(c)** (*usually go*) **this is where the spoons b.,** c'est ici qu'on range les cuillers; **things that b. together,** choses qui vont ensemble; **to put things back where they b.,** remettre les choses à leur place.
belonging [bɪ'lɒŋɪŋ] *n* **to feel a sense of b.,** se sentir tout de suite bien.
belongings [bɪ'lɒŋɪŋz] *npl* affaires *fpl*.
beloved **1** *adj* [bɪ'lʌvd] aimé; bien-aimé; **b. by all,** aimé de tous *ou* par tout le monde; **the b. wife of ...,** l'épouse bien-aimée de ... . **2** *n* [bɪ'lʌvɪd] bien-aimé, -ée, chéri, -ie; **my b.,** mon bien-aimé, ma bien-aimée; *Rel* **dearly b.,** mes bien chers frères.
below [bɪ'ləʊ] **1** *adv* en bas, (au-)dessous; **remain b.,** restez en bas; **voices from b.,** des voix qui venaient d'en bas; **the tenants (of the flat) b.,** les locataires du dessous; **on the floor b.,** à l'étage d'en dessous; *F* **ten (degrees) b.,** moins dix; **it's ten (degrees) b.,** il fait moins dix; **the engine will start at temperatures of ten b.,** le moteur

peut démarrer à une température de moins dix degrés; **here b. (on earth),** ici-bas; *Nau* **all hands b.!,** tout le monde en bas!; **the passage quoted b.,** (*immediately afterwards*) le passage cité ci-dessous; (*further on*) le passage cité plus loin *ou* ci-après.

2 *prep* au-dessous de; **b. the knee,** au-dessous du genou; **b. (the) average,** au-dessous de la moyenne; **people b. the age of 65,** les gens âgés de moins de 65; *F* **I'm feeling a bit b. par,** je ne suis pas dans mon assiette; **temperature b. normal,** température inférieure à la normale; **ten degrees b. zero,** dix degrés au-dessous de zéro; **b. sea level,** au-dessous du niveau de la mer; **b. the surface,** sous la surface; **b. the bridge,** (*downstream*) en aval du pont.

belt[1] [belt] *n* **(a)** (*round waist*) ceinture *f*; *Mil* ceinturon *m*; **to tighten one's b.,** serrer sa ceinture; *Fig* se boucler *ou* se serrer la ceinture; *F* **I'm a b. and braces type,** (*very cautious*) je suis du genre à penser que deux précautions valent mieux qu'une; *Aut Av* **seat b., safety b.,** ceinture de sécurité; **to be a brown/black b.,** (*in judo*) être ceinture marron/noire; *Boxing* **to hold the b.,** être le champion; **blow below the b.,** coup bas; *Fig* **to have sth under one's b.,** (*completed*) en avoir fini avec qch; *Fig* **to hit s.o. below the b.,** donner à qn un coup en traître *ou* un coup bas; **that was a bit below the b.,** (*of joke, remark*) c'était un coup bas; **(b)** *Tech* courroie *f* (*de transmission*); *Constr etc* **b. conveyor,** transporteur *m* à courroie *ou* à ruban *ou* à bande; **(c)** (*area*) région *f*, zone *f*; *Archit Astron* bande *f*; *Am* **b. line,** ligne *f* (de chemin de fer) de ceinture; **the belts of Jupiter,** les zones *ou* les bandes de Jupiter; **(d)** *F* (*blow*) gifle *f*.

belt[2] *vt* **(a)** *F* (*hit with belt*) donner des coups de ceinture à (*qn*); (*hit with hand*) gifler; **(b)** ceinturer, ceindre (*qn, qch*).

►belt along *vi F* courir *ou* aller *ou* conduire à toute vitesse.

►belt out *vtsep F* vociférer, gueuler (*un ordre etc*); gueuler, brailler (*une chanson*).

►belt up *vi* **(a)** *Br Sl* se taire; **b. up!,** ta gueule!; **(b)** *Aut F* attacher sa ceinture de sécurité.

belted ['beltɪd] *adj* ceinturé; **b. overcoat,** pardessus *m* avec ceinture.

belting ['beltɪŋ] *n* **(a)** (*belts*) ceinture(s) *f(pl)*, courroie(s) *f(pl)*; (*material*) matière *f* à courroies; **(b)** *F* **to give s.o. a (good) b.,** gifler qn; *Sch* administrer une correction à qn (avec une ceinture).

beltway ['beltweɪ] *n US* périphérique *m*.

belvedere ['belvɪdɪər] *n Archit* belvédère *m*, mirador *m*.

bemoan [bɪ'məʊn] *vt* pleurer (*qch*); **to b. the loss of sth,** se lamenter de *ou* pleurer la perte de qch; **to b. one's fate,** pleurer sur son sort; **she was bemoaning the fact that they had no money,** elle se lamentait de ce qu'ils n'avaient pas d'argent.

bemuse [bɪ'mjuːz] *vt Lit* (*confuse*) confondre (*qn*).

bemused [bɪ'mjuːzd] *adj* perplexe.

ben [ben] *n Geog Scot* sommet *m*, pic *m*; **B. Nevis,** le Ben Nevis.

bench [bentʃ] *n* **(a)** (*seat*) (*in park, garden*) banc *m*; (*upholstered*) banquette *f*; gradin *m* (*d'amphithéâtre*); *Sp* banc (*pour les joueurs qui ne sont pas sur le terrain*); *Jur* siège *m* (*du juge*); *Jur* banc (*des magistrats, des témoins*); *Aut* **b. seat,** banquette *f*; *Parl* **the Front B.,** le banc ministériel; *Br Jur* **the B.,** (*magistrates*) la magistrature; (*court*) la Cour; **to be on the B.,** (*as a magistrate*) être magistrat; (*as a judge*) siéger au tribunal; *Sp* **to be on the b.,** (*waiting to play*) attendre son tour; (*as punishment*) avoir été retiré du jeu *ou* renvoyé du terrain;

(b) (*work table*) établi *m* (*de menuisier*); banc *m*, marbre *m* (*d'ajusteur*); tablette *f* (*de serre*); **b. test,** essai *m* au banc; *Ch etc* **laboratory b.,** paillasse *f*;

(c) (*platform*) banc *m*; estrade *f* (*sur laquelle on exhibe un chien etc à une exposition*); *US* **b. show,** exposition canine;

(d) (*ledge*) banquette *f* (*de terre*); accotement *m*, berme *f* (*d'un chemin*); *Constr* gradin *m*.

bench-mark ['bentʃmɑːk] *n Comptr & Fig* référence *f*; (*in surveying*) repère *m* (de nivellement); *Comptr* **b.-m. programme,** programme *m* d'évaluation des performances; *Can Admin* **b.-m. position,** poste-repère *m*.

bend[1] [bend] *n Nau* (*knot*) nœud *m*.

bend[2] *n* **(a)** courbure *f*; (*of road*) tournant *m*, virage *m*, courbe *f*; (*of pipe*) coude *m*; (*of river*) boucle *f*; *Anat* saignée *f* (*du bras*); **bends for 3 kilometres,** (*road sign*) virages sur 3 kilomètres; *Aut* **to take a b. at speed,** prendre un virage à toute vitesse; *F* **to be round the b.,** être fou *ou* cinglé; *F* **you're driving me** *or* **sending me round the b.,** tu me rends cinglé *ou* fou; **(b)** *Med F* **the bends,** bends *mpl*; **to have the bends,** souffrir des bends; **(c)** inclination *f* (*du corps*).

bend[3] *v* (*pt* **bent** [bent]; *pp* **bent**, *Arch* **bended**) **1** *vt* **(a)** courber (*de l'osier, le corps*); ployer, fléchir (*le genou*); baisser (*la tête*); arquer (*le dos*); cambrer, cintrer (*un tuyau, un rail*); cambrer, arquer (*du bois, du fer*); dévirer (*du bois*); *Phys* réfracter (*la lumière*); infléchir (*un rayon*); tendre, bander (*un arc, un ressort*); **to b. one's head over a book,** pencher la tête sur un livre; **to b. s.o. to one's will,** plier qn à sa volonté; **to b. a rod/a key (out of shape),** forcer *ou* fausser une barre de fer/une clef;

(b) *Fig* forcer, donner *ou* faire une entorse à (*la loi, une règle etc*); *Br F* **to b. the elbow,** lever le coude; *Br F* **to b. s.o.'s ear,** casser les oreilles à qn.

2 *vi* (*of rod, branch etc*) plier, ployer; (*of branch, person*) se courber; (*of person*) se pencher; (*of road, river*) tourner, faire un tournant; **to b. under a strain,** (*of wood, iron*) arquer; (*of steel plate etc*) s'envoiler; (*of rod, wheel*) se voiler; **to b. to s.o.'s will,** se plier à *ou* fléchir devant la volonté de qn; **old man bending under a heavy load,** vieillard courbé sous un pesant fardeau; **to b. over s.o.,** se pencher sur qn.

►bend back 1 *vtsep* replier; recourber (*une lame etc*); réfléchir (*la lumière*). **2** *vi* (*of person*) se pencher en arrière; (*of blade*) se recourber; (*of light*) se réfléchir.

►bend down 1 *vtsep* courber, ployer (*une branche*); **the tree was bent down by the weight of the fruit,** l'arbre penchait sous le poids des fruits. **2** *vi* (*of person*) se courber, se baisser.

►bend forward *vi* se pencher en avant.

►bend over 1 *vi* (*of person*) se pencher; *Fig* **to b. over backwards,** se mettre en quatre (**to do,** pour faire). **2** *vtsep* replier (*une tôle etc*).

bended ['bendɪd] *adj Lit* **on one's b. knees,** (*demander qch*) à genoux; *Fig* **to go down on one's b. knees to s.o.,** (*beg*) supplier qn.

bender ['bendər] *n Sl* soûlerie *f*; **to go on a b.,** se soûler.

bending ['bendɪŋ] *n* **too much b. is bad for the back,** il est mauvais pour le dos de se pencher trop souvent; *Tech* **b. moment,** moment de flexion *ou* fléchissant; *Tech* **b. strength,** résistance *f* à la flexion; *Tech* **b. test,** essai *m ou* épreuve *f* de ployage *ou* de flexion.

beneath [bɪ'niːθ] **1** *adv* dessous, au-dessous; **from b.,** de dessous. **2** *prep* **to marry b. one,** faire une mésalliance; **b. contempt,** complètement méprisable, indigne d'attention; **he would consider it b. him to complain,** il dédaignerait de se plaindre; **to be b. s.o.'s dignity,** (*of behaviour etc*) ne pas être digne de qn; **the plank gave way b. me,** la planche a cédé sous mon poids.

Benedictine [benɪ'dɪktɪn] **1** *n* **(a)** *Rel* Bénédictin, -ine; **(b)** (*also* [-tiːn]) (*liqueur*) Bénédictine *f*. **2** *adj Rel* bénédictin.

benediction [benɪ'dɪkʃən] *n* bénédiction *f*; (*at meals*) bénédicité *m*.

benefaction [benɪ'fækʃən, 'benɪ-] *n Lit* **(a)** (*kindness*) bienfaisance *f*; **(b)** (*act of kindness*) bienfait *m*; (*help*) œuvre *f* de bienfaisance *ou* de charité; (*donation*) don *m* charitable.

benefactor, -tress ['benɪfæktər, -trɪs] *n* bienfaiteur, -trice.

benefice ['benɪfɪs] *n Rel Hist* bénéfice *m*.

beneficence [bɪ'nefɪs(ə)ns] *n Lit* **(a)** (*kindness*) bienfaisance *f*; **(b)** (*act of charity*) œuvre *f* de bienfaisance.

beneficent [bɪ'nefɪsənt] *adj Lit* bienfaisant.

beneficial [benɪ'fɪʃəl] *adj* **(a)** (*doing good*) salutaire, avantageux; **b. to the health,** salutaire pour la santé; **b. to business,** avantageux pour les affaires *ou* aux affaires; **(b)** *Jur* **b. owner** *or* **occupant,** usufruitier, -ière.

beneficiary [benɪ'fɪʃərɪ] *adj & n Jur* bénéficiaire *mf*; ayant droit *m*, *pl* ayants droit; **the main beneficiaries of the new law will be working mothers,** ce sont les mères qui travaillent qui bénéficieront le plus de cette nouvelle loi.

benefit[1] ['benɪfɪt] *n* **(a)** (*advantage*) avantage *m*, profit *m*; **to derive b. from sth,** profiter de qch; **in order to derive full b. from the medicine,** de façon à tirer tout le profit de ce médicament; **I get** *or* **gain no b. from it,** il ne m'en revient aucun avantage; **it's of no b. to anyone,** personne n'en tire profit; **I'm not doing this for my own b.,** je ne fais pas ça pour mon plaisir; **fringe benefits,** avantages accessoires; (*for employees*) compléments *mpl* de salaire en nature; **with the b. of hindsight,** avec du recul; **performance for the b. of the blind,** représentation au profit des aveugles; **for the b. of the others,** à l'intention des autres; **that remark was for my b.,** cette remarque était à mon intention; **for the b. of one's health,** dans l'intérêt de sa santé; *Jur* **b. of the doubt,** bénéfice *m* du doute; **to give s.o. the b. of the doubt,** accorder à qn le bénéfice du doute; *F Hum* **to live with s.o. without b. of clergy,** se marier avec qn de la main gauche;

(b) *Th* **b. (performance),** représentation *f* au bénéfice de qn; *Sp* **a b. match to raise money for the victims' families,** un match organisé au bénéfice des familles des victimes;

(c) *Admin* (*allowance*) indemnité *f*, allocation *f*; **social security benefits,** prestations sociales; **unemployment b.,** indemnité de chômage; **sickness b.,** indemnité de maladie, secours médical; **maternity b.,** allocation de maternité.

benefit² **1** *vt* faire du bien à, être avantageux à, profiter à (*qn, qch*); **a steady exchange rate benefits trade,** un change stable est avantageux pour le commerce *ou* favorise le commerce; **who(m) does it b.?,** qui en bénéficie?; **it will b. mankind,** c'est l'humanité toute entière qui en profitera. **2** *vi* **to b. by** *or* **from sth,** profiter de qch, tirer avantage de qch; **you will b. by a holiday,** un congé vous fera du bien; **who benefits most from his death?,** qui tire le plus de profit de sa mort?; **to b. from a rise in prices,** profiter *ou* tirer profit d'une hausse de prix.

Benelux ['benɪlʌks] *n Pol* Bénélux *m*; **the B. countries,** les pays *mpl* du Bénélux.

benevolence [bɪ'nevələns] *n* bienveillance *f*, bonté *f*; **act of b.,** acte *m* de bienveillance.

benevolent [bɪ'nevələnt] *adj* **(a)** (*kindly disposed*) bienveillant (**to,** envers); **(b)** (*charitable*) bienfaisant, charitable (**to,** envers); **b. society,** association *f* de bienfaisance; *Fig Hum* **I'm not a b. society,** je ne suis pas l'Armée du Salut.

benevolently [bɪ'nevələntlɪ] *adv* (*see adj*) **(a)** avec bienveillance; **(b)** bénévolement.

Bengal [beŋ'gɔːl] *n* Bengale *m*.

Bengali [beŋ'gɔːlɪ] **, Bengalese** [beŋgə'liːz] **1** *adj* bengali, bengalais. **2** *n* **(a)** Bengali *mf inv*, Bengalais, -aise; **(b)** *Ling* bengali *m*.

benighted [bɪ'naɪtɪd] *adj* **(a)** (*country etc*) plongé dans (les ténèbres de) l'ignorance; **(b)** *Arch* (*voyageur etc*) surpris par la nuit.

benign [bɪ'naɪn] *adj* (*smile etc*) bénin, *f* bénigne; (*propitious*) favorable; (*climate*) doux, *f* douce; *Med* **b. tumour,** tumeur bénigne.

Benjamin ['bendʒəmɪn] *n* Benjamin *m*; *Arch* **the B. of the family,** le benjamin de la famille.

benny ['benɪ] *n Am Sl* (*drug*) (comprimé *m* de) benzédrine *f*.

bent¹ [bent] *n* penchant *m*, inclination *f*, disposition *f* (**for,** pour); **to follow one's b.,** suivre son penchant *ou* son inclination; **to have a natural b. for music,** avoir des dispositions naturelles pour la musique.

bent² *see* **BEND³**.

bent³ *adj* **(a)** (*branch*) courbé, plié, arqué; (*essieu, levier*) coudé; (*dos, vieillard*) voûté; (*out of shape*) faussé, fléchi, gauchi; **to become b.,** (*with age*) se voûter, s'affaisser; **b. chassis,** châssis tordu; **(b)** *Sl* (*fonctionnaire, politicien, policier*) malhonnête, corrompu, vénal; **(c)** *Old-fashioned* homosexuel, inverti; **(d)** (*determined*) déterminé, résolu (**(up)on doing sth,** à faire qch); **he is b. on seeing me,** il veut absolument me voir; **b. on self-destruction,** obstiné à se perdre; **the government is b. on eliminating dissent,** le gouvernement est résolu à éliminer toute opposition.

bentwood ['bentwʊd] *adj* (*chaise*) en bois courbé.

benumb [bɪ'nʌm] *vt* engourdir.

benzene ['benziːn] *n Ch* benzène *m*.

benzin(e) ['benziːn, ben'ziːn] *n Ch Ind* benzine *f*.

benzodiazepine [benzəʊdaɪ'eɪzəpiːn] *n Pharm* (*tranquillizer*) benzodiazépine *f*.

benzol ['benzɒl] *n Ch* benzol *m*.

bequeath [bɪ'kwiːð] *vt* léguer (*qch*) (**to,** à).

bequest [bɪ'kwest] *n* legs *m*; **it was a b. from my grandmother,** je l'ai hérité de ma grand-mère; **she made a b. of £2,000 to her favourite charity,** elle a légué 2 000 livres à l'œuvre de bienfaisance qu'elle préférait.

berate [bɪ'reɪt] *vt* réprimander (*qn*).

Berber ['bɜːbər] **1** *adj* berbère. **2** *n* **(a)** Berbère *mf*; **(b)** *Ling* berbère *m*.

bereave [bɪ'riːv] *vt* (*pt & pp usu* **bereft** [bɪ'reft]) priver, déposséder (**s.o. of sth,** qn de qch); **he has been bereaved,** il est en deuil; **bereft of all hope,** privé de tout espoir, ayant perdu tout espoir.

bereaved [bɪ'riːvd] **1** *adj* affligé (*d'un deuil*); (*family, parents etc*) du mort, de la morte. **2** *n* **the b.,** (*used as pl*) la famille du mort *ou* de la morte.

bereavement [bɪ'riːvmənt] *n* deuil *m*; **owing to a recent b.,** en raison d'un deuil récent; **she has suffered a b.,** elle a été affligée par un deuil.

beret ['bereɪ, 'berɪ] *n* béret *m*; *Mil* **the red berets,** les bérets rouges, les parachutistes *mpl*.

berg [bɜːg] *n F* iceberg *m*.

bergamot ['bɜːgəmɒt] *n* (*plant*) bergamote *f*.

beriberi ['berɪ'berɪ] *n Med* béribéri *m*.

berk [bɜːk] *n Br Sl* **you great b.!,** espèce d'idiot!

Berks *abbr* **Berkshire**.

Berlin [bɜː'lɪn] *n* Berlin; **East/West B.,** Berlin Est/Ouest; **the B. Wall,** le mur de Berlin.

Berliner [bɜː'lɪnər] *n* Berlinois, -oise.

berm(e) [bɜːm] *n* **(a)** (*fortification*) berme *f*; **(b)** (*path*) berme *f*, banquette *f*.

Bermuda [bə'mjuːdə] *n* les Bermudes *fpl*; **B. shorts,** *F* **bermudas,** bermuda *m*; *Nau* **B. rig,** gréement *m* Marconi; **B. Triangle,** triangle *m* des Bermudes.

Bern(e) [bɜːn] *n* Berne *f*.

Bernese [bɜː'niːz, 'bɜː-] **1** *adj* bernois; **the B. Alps,** les Alpes bernoises. **2** *n* Bernois, -oise.

berried ['berɪd] *adj* **(a)** *Bot* à baies, couvert de baies; **(b)** (*crustacé*) œuvé.

berry¹ ['berɪ] *n* **(a)** (*fruit*) baie *f*; **to pick berries,** cueillir des baies; **coffee b.,** fruit *m* du caféier, cerise *f* de caféier; **(b)** œufs *mpl* (*de crustacé, de poisson*); **lobster in b.,** homard œuvé.

berry² *vi* **to go berrying,** aller à la cueillette des baies.

berserk [bə'zɜːk] *adj* (*personne, rage*) furieux; *F* **to go b.,** devenir fou furieux.

berth¹ [bɜːθ] *n* **(a)** *Nau Rail* couchette *f* (*de passager, de voyageur*); *Nau* cadre *m* (*d'officier, d'homme d'équipage*); *F* lit *m*; *F* **I can give you a b. for the night,** je peux te coucher pour la nuit; **(b)** (*for ship*) poste *m* à quai; **(anchoring) b.,** poste *m* de mouillage *ou* d'amarrage; **(c)** *Nau* évitée *f*, évitage *m*; **to give a ship a wide b.,** éviter *ou* parer un navire, passer au large d'un navire; *Fig* **to give s.o. a wide b.,** ne pas se mettre sur le chemin de qn; **(d)** *F* (*job*) emploi *m*; **to find a soft b.,** trouver un emploi pépère.

berth² **1** *vt* (*of helmsman*) accoster (*un navire*) le long du quai, amener *ou* amarrer (*un navire*) à quai; (*of port official*) donner *ou* assigner un poste à (*un navire*); **where is she berthed?,** à quel quai se trouve-t-il? **2** *vi* **(a)** (*of ship*) aborder à quai, se ranger à quai; **when do we b.?,** quand accostons-nous?; **(b) to b. forward/aft,** (*of passengers, crew*) coucher à l'avant/à l'arrière.

berthing ['bɜː'θɪŋ] *n* (*of ship*) abordage *m* à quai.

beryl ['berɪl] *n Miner* béryl *m*.

beryllium [be'rɪlɪəm] *n Ch* béryllium *m*.

beseech [bɪ'siːtʃ] *vt* (*pt & pp* **besought** [bɪ'sɔːt]) *Lit* supplier, implorer (**s.o. to do sth,** qn de faire qch); **help me, I b. you,** aidez moi, je vous en supplie.

beseeching [bɪ'siːtʃɪŋ] *adj* (*air, ton*) suppliant.

beset [bɪ'set] *vt* (*pt & pp* **beset**; *prp* **besetting**) (*of misfortunes, temptations etc*) assaillir (*qn*); **beset with dangers/difficulties,** environné *ou* entouré de dangers/de difficultés; **to be beset by doubts,** être assailli de doutes.

besetting [bɪ'setɪŋ] *adj* (*idea, thought etc*) obsédant; **it's his b. sin,** c'est son grand défaut *ou* son péché mignon.

beside [bɪ'saɪd] *prep* **(a)** (*place*) à côté de, auprès de (*qn, qch*); **seated b. me,** assis à côté de moi, assis à mes côtés; **a house b. the lake,** une maison au bord du lac; **(b)** (*comparison*) à côté de, auprès de (*qn, qch*); **b. him everyone else appears slow,** à côté de lui tous les autres paraissent lents; **(c)** (*in addition to*) en dehors de; **other people b. ourselves,** d'autres (personnes) que nous; **(d)** (*wide of*) **b. the question** *or* **the point,** à côté de la question, hors de propos, en dehors du sujet; **that is b. the point,** cela n'a rien à voir à l'affaire; **whether you arrrived or not is b. the point,** que tu sois arrivé ou non n'est pas le problème; **b. oneself with joy/anger/***etc*, fou de joie/colère/*etc*.

besides [bɪ'saɪdz] **1** *adv* **(a)** (*in addition*) en outre, en plus; **many more b.,** encore bien d'autres; **nothing b.,** rien de plus; **(b)** (*moreover*) d'ailleurs, du reste, et en outre. **2** *prep* (*in addition to*) excepté, hormis; (*as well as*) sans compter; **ten of us, b. myself,** dix d'entre nous, sans me compter; **there are others b. him,** il y en a d'autres que lui; **have you got it in anything b. black?,** est-ce que vous l'avez dans d'autres couleurs qu'en noir?; **what else can you do b. type?,** que savez-vous faire en dehors de taper à la machine?; **b. being an excellent singer, she also plays the violin,** c'est une excellente chanteuse, et en plus elle joue du violon; **b. which, he was unwell,** sans compter qu'il était indisposé.

besiege [bɪ'siːdʒ] *vt* assiéger (*une ville*); *Fig* faire le siège de; **we have been besieged with requests to ...,** nous

avons été assaillis de demandes de ... .
besmirch [bɪ'smɜːtʃ] *vt Lit* salir, tacher (*qch*); salir, ternir (*la mémoire de qn etc*).
besom ['biːzəm] *n* balai *m* (de jonc).
besotted [bɪ'sɒtɪd] *adj* **(a)** entiché (**with s.o.,** de qn); **(b)** abruti (*par l'opium, la boisson*).
bespatter [bɪ'spætər] *vt* éclabousser; **bespattered with mud,** tout couvert de boue.
bespectacled [bɪ'spektək(ə)ld] *adj* qui porte des lunettes, portant lunettes, à lunettes.
bespoke [bɪ'spəʊk] *adj esp Br* (*vêtement*) (fait) sur commande *ou* mesure; **b. tailor/shoemaker,** tailleur *m*/cordonnier *m* à façon.
Bess [bes] *n* (*dimin of* **Elizabeth**) Lisette *f*, Babette *f*; *Eng Hist* **Good Queen B.,** = la reine Elisabeth Ière d'Angleterre.
best¹ [best] **1** *adj* (*superl of* **good**) **(a)** meilleur, meilleure; **the b. man on earth,** le meilleur homme du monde; **may the b. man win,** que le meilleur gagne; **my b. dress,** ma plus belle robe; **to be dressed in one's b. clothes,** être sur son trente-et-un; **I am acting in your b. interests,** j'agis au mieux de vos intérêts; **with the b. will in the world,** avec la meilleure volonté du monde; **b. friend,** ami, -ie intime *ou* de cœur; **the b. part of the year,** la plus grande partie de l'année; **I waited for the b. part of an hour,** j'ai attendu une petite heure; **to know what is b. for s.o.,** savoir ce qui va *ou* convient le mieux à qn; **it is b. to ...,** le mieux c'est de ...; **the b. thing you can do , the b. course to take, the b. way is to ...,** ce qu'il y a de mieux à faire c'est de ...; **it would be b. to, the b. plan would be to ...,** le mieux serait de ...; **I thought it (would be) b. to stay,** j'ai pensé qu'il valait mieux rester; **b. before date,** (*for foodstuffs*) date *f* limite de consommation; (*for batteries, car oil etc*) date limite d'utilisation; **b. man,** (*at wedding*) garçon *m* d'honneur; *esp Am Cin* **b. boy,** aide-électricien *m*; *Br Culin* **b. end,** (*of lamb*) = filet *m*; **b. seller,** (*book, record*) best-seller *m*, meilleure vente; **to be a b. seller,** (*of book, record*) être un best-seller *ou* une des meilleures ventes; (*of author, musician*) être un auteur *ou* un musicien *etc* à succès;
(b) at b., au mieux; **at b. he will get 2,000 votes,** au mieux, il aura 2 000 suffrages; **your article is at b. unhelpful, at worst obstructive,** au mieux votre article n'apporte rien d'utile, au pire c'est un obstacle.
2 *n* **(a)** le meilleur, la meilleure; (*neuter*) le mieux; **to be dressed in one's b.,** être sur son trente-et-un; **I keep it for b.,** (*of dress, suit etc*) je le garde pour des occasions spéciales; **he can sing with the b.,** il chante comme pas un; **we are the b. of friends,** nous sommes les meilleurs amis du monde; **I am in the b. of health,** je me porte à merveille, je suis en excellente santé; **the b. of it is that ...,** le plus beau de l'affaire c'est que ...; **this is the b. there is,** voici ce qu'il y a de meilleur *ou* de mieux; *F* **the b. of luck!,** bonne chance!; **all the b.!,** meilleurs souhaits!; *Am* **my brother sends his b.,** bien des choses de la part de mon frère; **to do one's b.** *or* **the b. one can to ...,** faire ce qu'on peut *ou* de son mieux pour ...; **I did my b. to comfort her,** je la consolai de mon mieux; **I did my b.,** j'ai fait de mon mieux; **your b. wasn't good enough,** tu as peut-être fait de ton mieux mais ça n'a pas suffi; **he did his b. to smile,** il s'efforça de sourire; **I am doing my (level) b.** *or* **the b. I can for you,** je fais tout ce que je peux pour vous; **that's the b. I can offer,** c'est ce que je peux vous offrir de mieux; **is that the b. you can do?,** vous ne pouvez pas faire mieux?; **do the b. you can,** (*given the circumstances*) arrangez-vous; (*in exam*) faites de votre mieux; **to look one's b.,** être *ou* paraître à son avantage; **she looks her b. in the morning,** elle est à son avantage le matin; **to be at one's b.,** être en train *ou* en forme; **I am not at my b. in the morning,** je ne suis pas au mieux de ma forme le matin; **you haven't seen the house at its b.,** tu n'as pas vu la maison sous son meilleur jour; **that is Dickens at his b.,** voilà du meilleur Dickens; **to get the b. out of s.o.,** encourager qn à faire de son mieux; **to get** *or* **have the b. of it** *or* **of the bargain,** faire une bonne affaire; **to have the b. of an argument,** l'emporter dans une discussion; **to get the b. of s.o. in an argument,** l'emporter sur qn dans une discussion; **to hope for the b.,** ne pas désespérer, avoir bon espoir; **we must hope for the b.,** il faut être optimiste; **to make the b. of sth,** s'accommoder de qch; **you'll just have to make the b. of it,** il faudra t'y faire; **to make the b. of things** *or* **a bad job,** faire avec ce qu'on a; **to make the b. of the circumstances,** s'adapter aux circonstances; **let's make it the b. of five,** jouons au premier qui remporte trois jeux *ou* parties sur cinq; *Br F* **six of the b.,** une fessée magistrale;
(b) at the b., au mieux; **he was undemonstrative at the b. of times,** même dans ses meilleurs moments il était peu démonstratif; **to act for the b.,** agir pour le mieux; **I did it for the b.,** j'ai fait pour le mieux; **it's all for the b.,** tout est pour le mieux; **I meant it for the b.,** je l'ai fait *ou* dit *etc* dans une bonne intention; **to do sth to the b. of one's ability,** faire qch de son mieux; **to the b. of my belief/knowledge,** à ce que je crois/autant que je sache; **to the b. of my judgment,** autant que je peux en juger.
3 *adv* (*superl of* **well**) **he does it (the) b.,** c'est lui qui le fait le mieux; **I comforted her as b. I could,** je la consolai de mon mieux; **I got down as b. I could,** je suis descendu comme j'ai pu; **you know b.,** c'est vous (qui êtes) le mieux placé pour en juger; **mother knows b.,** maman sait mieux que personne; **do as you think b.,** faites comme bon vous semble(ra); **he had b. agree,** il ferait mieux d'accepter; **the b. dressed man,** l'homme le mieux habillé; **the b. known book,** le livre le mieux *ou* le plus connu; **the b.-looking women,** les femmes les plus jolies; **to come off b.,** (*in argument, discussion*) l'emporter, avoir l'avantage, avoir le dessus.
best² *vt* (*in argument etc*) l'emporter sur (*qn*).
bestial ['bestɪəl] *adj* bestial.
bestiality [bestɪ'ælɪtɪ] *n* bestialité *f*.
bestially ['bestɪəlɪ] *adv* bestialement.
bestir [bɪ'stɜːr] *vt* **(-rr-) to b. oneself,** se remuer, se démener, s'activer.
bestow [bɪ'stəʊ] *vt Lit* accorder, donner (**sth (up)on s.o.,** qch à qn); **to b. a favour on s.o.,** accorder une faveur à qn.
bestride [bɪ'straɪd] *vt* (*pt* **bestrode** [bɪ'strəʊd]; *pp* **bestridden** [bɪ'strɪd(ə)n]) **(a)** (*straddle*) être à cheval *ou* à califourchon sur (*qch*); **(b)** (*cross*) enjamber (*un fossé etc*).
best-selling [best'selɪŋ] *adj* (*livre, auteur*) à grand succès; (*livre, article etc*) de grosse vente; **this is one of our b.-s. items,** c'est l'un des articles que nous vendons le mieux.
bet¹ [bet] *n* pari *m*; **to make** *or* **lay a b.,** parier, faire un pari; *F* **your best b. would be to ...,** ce que vous avez de mieux à faire c'est de ...; *F* **it's my b.** *or* **my b. is that he'll come,** je parie qu'il viendra; **to win/lose a b.,** gagner/perdre un pari.
bet² *v* (*pt* **bet**; *pp* **bet**, *occ* **betted**) **1** *vt* parier (*une somme*); **I'll b. you that ...,** je vous parierais que ..., parions que ...; **to b. ten to one that ...,** parier à dix contre un que ...; *F* **I'll b. you anything (you like) that ...,** j'en donnerais ma tête à couper que ...; *F* **I b. you don't!,** chiche (que tu ne le feras pas)!; *F* **b. you I will!,** chiche (que je le fais)! **2** *vi* **to b. on a horse,** miser sur *ou* jouer un cheval; **to b. with s.o.,** parier avec qn; **to b. on sth,** parier sur qch; *F* **you b.!,** pour sûr!
beta-blocker ['biːtəblɒkər] *n* (*drug*) bêtabloquant *m*.
betel ['biːt(ə)l] *n* (*for chewing*) *& Bot* bétel *m*; **b. nut,** (noix *f* d')arec *m*; **b. (nut) palm,** arec, aréquier *m*.
Bethlehem ['beθlɪhem, -lɪəm] *n Bible* Bethléem *m*.
betide [bɪ'taɪd] *vt Arch & Lit* (*used only in*) **woe b. him/you/***etc*, malheur *ou* gare à lui/à toi/*etc*.
betray [bɪ'treɪ] *vt* **(a)** (*be disloyal to*) trahir (*qn, sa patrie, sa foi etc*); **to b. s.o.'s trust,** trahir la confiance de qn; **(b)** (*disclose*) révéler, laisser voir, trahir (*son ignorance, son émotion*); trahir, livrer, révéler (*un secret*).
betrayal [bɪ'treɪəl] *n* **(a)** (*disloyalty*) trahison *f* (**of,** de); **b. of trust,** abus *m* de confiance; **(b)** (*disclosure*) révélation *f* (*de son ignorance etc*).
betrayer [bɪ'treɪər] *n* **(a)** (*of country etc*) traître, -esse; **(b)** révélateur, -trice (*d'un secret*).
betrothal [bɪ'trəʊðəl] *n Lit* fiançailles *fpl*.
betrothed [bɪ'trəʊðd] *adj & n Lit* fiancé, -ée.
better¹ ['betər] **1** *adj* (*comp of* **good**) meilleur; **they have seen b. days,** ils ont connu des jours meilleurs; **you will find no b. hotel,** vous ne trouverez pas mieux comme hôtel; **he's a b. man than you,** il vous est supérieur; **you are b. than I am,** vous êtes plus fort que moi; **he is no b. than his brother,** il ne vaut pas mieux que son frère; **to appeal to s.o.'s b. feelings,** faire appel aux bons sentiments de qn; **I had hoped for b. things,** j'avais espéré mieux; **to get b.,** (*of person*) se remettre, se rétablir; (*of things*) s'améliorer; (*of wine etc*) se bonifier; **the weather is b.,** il fait meilleur; **to be b.,** (*in health*) aller *ou* se porter mieux; **I hope you will soon be b.,** j'espère que vous serez bientôt rétabli; **it is b. that it should be so,** il vaut mieux qu'il en soit ainsi; **it is b. to do without it,** mieux vaut *ou* il vaut mieux s'en passer; **it would be b. for you to go,** (*to that place*) il vaudrait mieux que vous y

alliez; **that's b.**, voilà qui est mieux; **nothing could be b., it couldn't be b.**, c'est on ne peut mieux; **it would be b. if you called me tomorrow,** ce serait mieux que tu m'appelles demain; **for the b. part of the day,** pendant la plus grande partie du jour; *Br F* **my b. half,** ma (chère) moitié, ma légitime; (*man*) mon homme; *Br* **to go one b. than s.o.**, *Am* **to go s.o. one b.**, (r)enchérir *ou* surenchérir *ou* faire une surenchère sur qn.

2 *n* **(a) I expected b. of you,** je m'attendais à mieux de ta part; **one's betters,** (*socially*) ses supérieurs; (*more experienced*) ses aînés, ceux qui ont de l'expérience; **(b) change for the b.**, changement *m* en bien; (*in state of health*) amélioration *f*; **he has changed for the b.**, (*his character has improved*) il a changé à son avantage; **things are taking a turn for the b.**, les choses prennent meilleure tournure; **to get the b. of s.o.**, l'emporter sur qn, prendre le dessus sur qn; **to get the b. of,** surmonter, vaincre (*un obstacle etc*); maîtriser (*sa colère etc*); **his anger/shyness got the b. of him,** sa colère/timidité a eu raison de lui; **to be (all) the b. for doing sth,** se trouver mieux d'avoir fait qch; **I'm all the b. for seeing you,** ça me fait du bien de te voir; **I'd feel all the b. for a holiday,** je partirais volontiers en vacances; **I think all the b. of you for it,** je vous en estime d'autant plus; **you will be all the b. for it,** vous vous en trouverez (d'autant) mieux; **all the b. (for me)!**, tant mieux (pour moi)!

3 *adv* (*comp of* **well**) mieux; **so much the b.**, tant mieux; **to take s.o. for b. or for worse,** (*in marriage ceremony*) s'unir à qn pour le meilleur comme pour le pire; **b. and b.**, de mieux en mieux; **I know that b. than you,** je sais cela mieux que vous; **I am feeling b.**, je me sens mieux; **you are looking b.**, tu as meilleure mine; **to know s.o. b.**, mieux connaître qn; **the more I know him the b. I like him,** plus je le connais plus je l'aime; **I can understand it all the b. because ...,** je le conçois d'autant mieux que ...; **you had b. stay,** il vaut mieux que vous restiez; **I had b. begin by ...,** je ferai bien de commencer par ...; **we'd b. be going back,** il est temps de rebrousser chemin; **you had b. not,** ne vous en avisez pas; **to think b. of it,** changer d'opinion, se raviser; **you'll think b. of it,** vous en reviendrez; **to think b. of s.o. for doing sth,** estimer qn davantage d'avoir *ou* pour avoir fait qch; **that's b. still,** (*what you have done*) c'est encore mieux; **b. still you could come tomorrow,** mieux encore tu pourrais venir demain, ce qui serait mieux c'est que tu viennes demain; **b. dressed,** mieux habillé; **b. known,** plus connu; **b. looking,** (*more attractive*) plus beau *ou* joli; **b. tempered,** d'une humeur plus égale; **to be b. off,** (*wealthier*) être plus à son aise (matériellement); (*well situated*) se trouver dans de meilleures conditions; **he is b. off where he is,** il est bien mieux où il est; **you're b. off without him,** tu es bien mieux sans lui; **the children of b.-off parents,** les enfants dont les parents sont aisés.

better² *vt* **(a)** (*improve*) améliorer (*qch*), rendre (*qch*) meilleur; **to b. oneself,** améliorer sa condition; **(b)** (*surpass*) surpasser (*un exploit, un ouvrage*); **can you b. that?**, pouvez-vous faire mieux que cela?

better³, bettor ['betər] *n* parieur, -euse.

betterment ['betəmənt] *n* amélioration *f*.

betting ['betɪŋ] *n* (*bets*) les paris *mpl*; (*price*) cote *f*; **the b. ran high,** on a parié gros; **the b. is twenty to one,** la cote est à vingt contre un; **the b. is that ...,** il y a fort à parier que ...; **b. book,** carnet *m* de paris; **b. slip,** bulletin *m* de pari; **b. shop,** = bureau du pari mutuel.

between [bɪ'twiːn] **1** *prep* entre (*deux maisons etc*); **a table stood b. him and the door,** une table le séparait de la porte; **to stand b. two opponents,** s'interposer *ou* intervenir entre deux adversaires; **no one can come b. us,** personne ne peut nous séparer; **to be b. life and death,** être entre la vie et la mort; **to be something b. ... and ...,** tenir le milieu entre ... et ...; **b. eight and nine o'clock,** entre huit et neuf heures; **b. now and Monday,** d'ici (à) lundi; **b. twenty and thirty,** de vingt à trente; **you must choose b. them,** il faut choisir entre eux; **to distinguish b. A, B and C,** distinguer entre A, B et C; **we bought it b. us,** nous l'avons acheté à nous deux *ou* à nous trois *etc*; **b. the two/the three of them,** à eux deux/trois; **they scored 1,500 b. them,** (*of two people*) ils ont marqué 1 500 à eux deux; (*of more than two people*) ils ont marqué 1 500 à eux tous; **they shared the loot b. them,** ils se sont partagé le butin; **b. ourselves ...,** entre nous ...; **this is strictly b. ourselves** *or* **b. you and me,** que cela reste entre nous; *F* **b. you (and) me and the gatepost,** (soit dit) entre nous; **there is no love lost b. them,** ils ne peuvent pas se souffrir *ou* se sentir.

2 *adv* **(in) b.**, entre les deux; (*in the intervening time*) dans l'intervalle.

between-decks [bɪ'twiːn'deks] *Nau* **1** *adv* dans l'entrepont. **2** *n* l'entrepont *m*.

between-season [bɪ'twiːn'siːz(ə)n] *n* demi-saison *f*, *pl* demi-saisons.

betweentime(s) [bɪ'twiːntaɪm, -z] **, betweenwhile(s)** [bɪ'twiːnwaɪl, -z] *adv* dans l'intervalle, entre-temps.

betwixt [bɪ'twɪkst] *adv F* **it's b. and between,** c'est entre les deux.

bevel¹ ['bev(ə)l] *n* biseau *m*; **b. cut,** fausse coupe; **b. drive,** transmission *f* par pignons; **b. edge,** bord biseauté *ou* en chanfrein; **b. gear,** engrenage à biseau; **b. rule** *or* **square,** fausse équerre.

bevel² *v* (**-ll-**, *US* **-l-**) **1** *vt* biseauter, chanfreiner (*qch*); tailler (*qch*) en biseau; **to b. off a corner,** dégraisser un coin. **2** *vi* aller en biseau.

bevelled, *US* **beveled** ['bevəld] *adj* (*bord*) biseauté, en biseau, en chanfrein.

bevelling, *US* **beveling** ['bev(ə)lɪŋ] *n* biseautage *m*, équerrage *m*, chanfreinage *m*.

beverage ['bevərɪdʒ] *n* boisson *f*; *Can* **b. room,** bar *m*.

bevy ['bevɪ] *n* **(a)** (*group*) bande *f*, troupe *f*; **b. of girls,** bande de jeunes filles; **(b)** volée *f* (*d'alouettes, de cailles*); harde *f*, troupe *f* (*de chevreuils*).

bewail [bɪ'weɪl] *vt* pleurer (*qch*); se lamenter sur (*son sort*).

beware [bɪ'weər] *vi* (*used only in inf and imp*) se méfier, *Lit* se défier (**of s.o.**, de qn); se garder (**of sth,** de qch), prendre garde (**of sth,** à qch); **b.!**, prenez garde!; **b. of pickpockets,** attention aux pickpockets; **b. of the dog,** ≈ chien méchant; **to b. of doing sth,** se garder de faire qch.

bewilder [bɪ'wɪldər] *vt* **(a)** (*puzzle*) désorienter, dérouter (*qn*); (*because of one's character*) troubler (*qn*); **(b)** (*confuse*) confondre (*qn*).

bewildered [bɪ'wɪldəd] *adj* **(a)** (*puzzled*) désorienté; (*air*) perplexe; **(b)** (*confused*) confondu.

bewildering [bɪ'wɪldərɪŋ] *adj* déroutant.

bewilderment [bɪ'wɪldəmənt] *n* **(a)** (*puzzlement*) perplexité *f*; trouble *m*; **(b)** (*confusion*) confusion *f*.

bewitch [bɪ'wɪtʃ] *vt* ensorceler, jeter un sort sur (*qn*); *Fig* enchanter (*qn*).

bewitching [bɪ'wɪtʃɪŋ] *adj* (*sourire*) ravissant.

bey [beɪ] *n* bey *m*.

beyond [bɪ'jɒnd] **1** *adv* au-delà, par-delà, plus loin; **the ocean and the lands b.**, l'océan et les terres au-delà.

2 *prep* **(a)** (*of place*) au-delà de, par-delà; **the house is b. the church,** la maison est au-delà de *ou* plus loin que l'église; **b. the seas,** par-delà les *ou* au-delà des mers; **to be b. the pale,** être au ban de la société;

(b) (*of time*) **b. a certain date,** passé une certaine date; **b. the usual hour,** plus tard que d'ordinaire;

(c) (*surpassing*) **b. all praise,** au-dessus de tout éloge; **to live b. one's means,** vivre au-dessus de ses moyens; **it's b. me,** cela me dépasse, je n'y comprends rien; **it's b. me how they can do it,** je ne comprends vraiment pas comment ils peuvent le faire; **circumstances b. our control,** circonstances indépendantes de notre volonté; **it's b. my power,** cela passe ma capacité; **it's b. my power to save him,** je suis impuissant à le sauver; **I will not go b. what I said,** je m'en tiens à ce que j'ai dit; **b. doubt,** hors de doute, sans le moindre doute; **b. question,** indiscutablement, incontestablement; **to be b. question,** être indiscutable *ou* incontestable; **fact b. doubt** *or* **question,** fait avéré; **b. belief,** incroyable, à ne pas y croire; **b. measure,** outre mesure, sans mesure; **that's (going) b. a joke,** cela dépasse les bornes (de la plaisanterie); **b. repair,** irréparable; **she is b. recovery,** (*of sick person*) il n'est plus possible de la sauver;

(d) (*except*) **he has nothing b. his wages,** il n'a rien que son salaire.

3 *n* **the b.**, l'au-delà *m*; **at the back of b.**, tout au bout du monde; **he lives at the back of b.**, il habite un trou perdu.

bezel ['bezəl] *n* **(a)** biseau *m*, bezel *m* (*d'une pierre taillée*); **(b)** chaton *m* (*de bague*).

BF [biː'ef] *n Sl abbr* **bloody fool.**

bi-annual [baɪ'ænjuəl] *adj* semestriel.

bi-annually [baɪ'ænjuəlɪ] *adv* deux fois par an.

bias¹ ['baɪəs] *n* **(a) to have a b. towards,** avoir un parti pris pour (*qn, qch*); **to be without b.**, être sans parti pris; **(b)** *Sewing* biais *m*; **material cut on the b.**, étoffe coupée en *ou* de biais; **b. binding,** ruban *m* en biais; **(c)** *Bowling* décentrement *m*; déviation *f* (*due au décentrement*); **(d)** *Electron* **grid b.**, polarisation *f* de la grille; **b. winding,** enroulement *m* de polarisation.

bias² *vt* (*pt & pp* **bias(s)ed**) **(a)** rendre (*qn*) partial; influencer, prévenir (*qn*) (**towards, in favour of,** en faveur de; **against,** contre); **(b)** *Bowling* altérer le centre de gravité de (*la boule*); **(c)** *Electron* polariser (*la grille*).

bias(s)ed ['baɪəst] *adj* **(a)** partial; **b. opinion,** opinion préconçue; **to be b.,** être partial; **you're b. in her favour,** tu as un parti pris pour elle; **(b)** *Tex* (*tissu*) en fil biais; **(c)** (*bowling ball*) décentré; **(d)** (*in statistics*) **b. sample,** échantillon biaisé *ou* avec erreur systématique; **b. error,** erreur *f* systématique.

bib [bɪb] *n* **(a)** bavette *f*, bavoir *m* (*d'enfant*); **(b)** bavette *f* (*de tablier*); *F* **in one's best b. and tucker,** sur son trente-et-un.

bible ['baɪb(ə)l] *n* Bible *f*; *Fig* **this dictionary is his b.,** il fait de ce dictionnaire sa bible; **B. class,** classe *f* d'instruction religieuse; **B. stories,** histoires tirées de la Bible.

bible-bashing ['baɪb(ə)lbæʃɪŋ] *n Pej* **b.-b. preacher,** évangéliste *m* de bazar.

biblical ['bɪblɪk(ə)l] *adj* biblique.

bibliographer [bɪblɪ'ɒgrəfər] *n* bibliographe *mf*.

bibliographic(al) [bɪblɪə'græfɪk, -ɪk(ə)l] *adj* bibliographique.

bibliography [bɪblɪ'ɒgrəfɪ] *n* bibliographie *f*.

bibliophile ['bɪblɪəfaɪl] *n* bibliophile *mf*.

bibulous ['bɪbjʊləs] *adj Fml* (*person*) adonné à la boisson.

bicameral [baɪ'kæmərəl] *adj* bicaméral; **b. system,** bicaméralisme *m*, bicamérisme *m*.

bicarb [baɪ'kɑːb] *n F* bicarbonate *m* de soude.

bicarbonate [baɪ'kɑːbəneɪt] *n* bicarbonate *m* (*de soude etc*).

bicentenary [baɪsen'tiːnərɪ], *US* **bicentennial** ['baɪsen'tenɪəl] *adj & n* bicentenaire *m*.

biceps ['baɪseps] *n Anat* biceps *m*.

bicker ['bɪkər] *vi* se quereller, se chamailler.

bickering ['bɪkərɪŋ] *n* querelles *fpl*, chamailleries *fpl*.

bickie ['bɪkɪ] *n Br F* biscuit *m*.

bicolour(ed), *US* **bicolor(ed)** [baɪ'kʌlər, -ləd] *adj Bot etc* bicolore.

biconcave [baɪ'kɒnkeɪv] *adj* biconcave.

biconvex [baɪ'kɒnveks] *adj* biconvexe.

bicycle¹ ['baɪsɪk(ə)l] *n* bicyclette *f*, vélo *m*; **to ride a b.,** faire de la bicyclette *ou* du vélo; **b. clip,** pince *f* à vélo; **b. path** *or* **track,** piste *f* cyclable.

bicycle² *vi* (*for exercise*) faire de la bicyclette; (*travel*) aller à bicyclette (**to,** à).

bid¹ [bɪd] *n* **(a)** (*offer*) enchère *f*, offre *f*, mise *f*; (*in bridge*) appel *m*; (*in solo whist, boston*) demande *f*; *Cards* **b. of two diamonds,** appel de deux carreaux; *Cards* **no b.!,** je passe!; **higher** *or* **further b.,** offre supérieure, surenchère *f*; **to put a b. in on a flat,** faire une offre pour un appartement; **closing** *or* **last b.,** dernière mise, dernière enchère; **takeover b.,** offre publique d'achat; **to make a b.,** faire une offre; *Fig* **to make a b. for power,** (*legally*) viser au pouvoir; (*illegally*) tenter un coup d'état; **she failed in her b. to beat the world record,** elle a échoué dans sa tentative de battre le record du monde; **(b)** *US* soumission *f* (*dans une adjudication*); **to make a b.,** soumissionner.

bid² *vt & vi* (*pt* **bade** [bæd, beɪd], **bid**; *pp* **bidden** [bɪd(ə)n], **bid**) **(a)** (*pt & pp* **bid**) **to b. for sth,** (*offer*) faire une offre pour qch; **what am I bid for this table?,** qu'est-ce que vous m'offrez pour cette table?; **to b. ten pounds,** faire une offre de dix livres; *Cards* **to b. three diamonds,** demander *ou* appeler trois carreaux; **(b)** *US* faire une soumission (**on sth,** pour qch); **(c)** (*greet*) **to b. s.o. welcome,** souhaiter la bienvenue à qn; **to b. s.o. goodbye,** dire au revoir *ou* faire ses adieux à qn; **(d)** (*seem probable*) **the weather bids fair to be fine** *or* **to improve,** le temps s'annonce beau; **(e)** *Arch & Lit* (*order*) commander, ordonner (**s.o. do sth,** à qn de faire qch); **to b. s.o. (to) be silent,** ordonner à qn de se taire, commander le silence à qn.

biddable ['bɪdəb(ə)l] *adj* (*child etc*) obéissant, docile.

bidder ['bɪdər] *n* (*at sale*) enchérisseur *m*; (*at cards*) demandeur, -euse, déclarant, -ante; **there were no bidders,** il n'y a pas eu de preneurs; **the highest b.,** le plus offrant.

bidding ['bɪdɪŋ] *n* **(a)** (*at sale*) enchères *fpl*, mises *fpl*; **to start the b. at £5,000,** commencer les enchères à 5 000 livres; **the b. is against you,** est-ce que vous voulez surenchérir?; **(b)** (*order*) commandement *m*, ordre *m*; **to do s.o.'s b.,** exécuter les ordres de qn.

bide [baɪd] *vt* (**bided**) to b. one's time, attendre le bon moment.

bidet ['biːdeɪ] *n* bidet *m*.

biennial [baɪ'enɪəl] **1** *adj* **(a)** biennal; **(b)** (*plant*) bisannuel. **2** *n Bot* plante bisannuelle.

biennially [baɪ'enɪəlɪ] *adv* tous les deux ans.

bier [bɪər] *n* bière *f* (*pour un cercueil, un mort*).

biff¹ [bɪf] **1** *n Sl* baffe *f*. **2** *int* v'lan!, pan!

biff² *vt Sl* flanquer une baffe à (*qn*).

bifocal [baɪ'fəʊk(ə)l] **1** *adj Opt* bifocal. **2** *npl* **bifocals,** verres bifocaux *ou* à double foyer.

bifurcate ['baɪfəkeɪt] *vi* bifurquer.

bifurcation [baɪfə'keɪʃən] *n* bifurcation *f*.

big [bɪg] **1** *adj* (**bigger** ['bɪgər]; **biggest** ['bɪgɪst]) (*tall, large*) grand; (*bulky*) gros; **b. hotel,** grand hôtel; **b. man,** (*tall*) homme de grande taille; (*fat*) gros homme; *F* (*important*) homme important; **b. enough to defend oneself,** de taille à se défendre; *F* **to earn b. money,** gagner gros; **b. drop in prices,** forte baisse de prix; **to be doing a b. trade,** faire de grosses affaires; *F* **he had b. ideas,** il voyait grand; *F* **I've got b. plans for you,** j'ai de grands projets pour toi; *F* **b. money** *or Am* **bucks,** fric *m*; *F* **there's b. money in professional tennis,** il y a du fric dans le tennis professionnel; *F* **the b. screen,** le grand écran; **the b. (white) Chief, b. Daddy,** le grand chef; **that's b. of you,** c'est généreux *ou* magnanime de votre part; *Iron* grand merci!; **the b. names in the theatre world,** les grands noms du théâtre; *F* **b. shot** *or* **noise** *or* **gun,** gros bonnet, grosse légume; *Th* **the b. scene,** la grande scène; *Sp* **the b. match,** le grand match; *Sp* **b. field (of starters),** champ fourni; **to grow big(ger),** (*taller*) grandir; (*fatter*) grossir; *F* **he's getting too b. for his boots** *or Am* **britches,** il se croit important; **you're the biggest fool of the lot!,** c'est toi le plus bête de tous!; **he's not a b. eater,** ce n'est pas un gros mangeur; *F* **you've got a b. mouth,** (*you let the secret out*) tu n'es pas capable de la fermer; **the b. toe,** le gros orteil; **the B. Bang,** *Br Fin F* = la déréglementation de la bourse de Londres en octobre 1986; *Astron* le big bang; **b. drum,** grosse caisse; *F* **a b. A,** un A majuscule; *F* **the B. Apple,** = la ville de New York; **my b. brother,** mon frère aîné; **B. Brother,** chef *m* d'un État autoritaire; (*government*) État qui exerce un paternalisme autoritaire; *F* **B. Brother is watching you,** on t'a à l'œil; **to be in the b. time,** être en haut de l'échelle, être le dessus du panier; **b.-time actor,** acteur de premier rang; **b. top,** (*of circus*) chapiteau *m*; *Aut* **b. end,** tête *f* de bielle; **the b. game,** les grands fauves; **b. game hunter,** chasseur de grands fauves; *Arch Lit* **to be b. with child,** être sur le point d'enfanter; **b. with consequences,** gros *ou* lourd de conséquences; *F* **to be b. on sth,** (*keen*) aimer beaucoup qch; **Walkmans ® were b. last year,** les Walkmans ® ont bien marché l'année dernière.

2 *adv* **to talk b.,** (*boast*) se vanter, faire l'important; **to think b.,** avoir des idées larges, voir grand; *F* **to go over** *or* **down b.,** décrocher le grand succès; *F* **the last song went down b. with the audience,** la dernière chanson a fait un tabac auprès du public.

bigamist ['bɪgəmɪst] *n* bigame *mf*; **he/she is a b.,** c'est un/une bigame.

bigamous ['bɪgəməs] *adj* bigame; **b. marriage,** bigamie *f*.

bigamy ['bɪgəmɪ] *n* bigamie *f*; **to commit b.,** être coupable de bigamie.

big-bellied [bɪg'belɪd] *adj* (*fat*) ventru, pansu; **she's b.-b.,** (*of pregnant woman*) elle a un gros ventre.

big-boned [bɪg'bəʊnd] *adj* fortement charpenté.

biggish ['bɪgɪʃ] *adj* (*tall*) assez grand; (*fat*) assez gros.

bighead ['bɪghed] *n F* **(a)** crâneur, -euse; **(b)** *Am* (*conceitedness*) suffisance *f*, prétention *f*.

bigheaded [bɪg'hedɪd] *adj F* crâneur.

bigheadedness [bɪg'hedɪdnɪs] *n F* suffisance *f*, prétention *f*.

big-hearted [bɪg'hɑːtɪd] *adj* **to be b.-h.,** avoir du cœur.

bight [baɪt] *n* **(a)** *Geog* crique *f*, anse *f* (*peu profonde et assez étendue*); renfoncement *m* (*d'une côte*); **the Great Australian B.,** la Grande Baie Australienne, le Grand Golfe Australien *ou* de l'Australie; **(b)** *Nau* double *m*, bal(l)ant *m*, anse *f* (*d'un cordage*).

bigness ['bɪgnɪs] *n* (*tallness*) grande taille; (*fatness*) grosseur *f*; (*of thing*) grandes dimensions.

bigot ['bɪgət] *n* sectaire *mf*.

bigoted ['bɪgətɪd] *adj* sectaire; **don't be so b.,** ne sois pas si borné.

bigotry ['bɪgətrɪ] *n* sectarisme *m*.

bigwig ['bɪgwɪg] *n F* gros bonnet, grosse légume.

bijou ['biːʒuː] *n* (*trinket*) objet *m* d'art de facture délicate; **b. flat** *or* **residence,** petit appartement coquet.

bike¹ [baɪk] *n F* (*bicycle*) vélo *m*; (*motorbike*) moto *f*; *Br Sl* **on your b.!,** (*go away*) tire-toi!

bike[2] *vi F* faire du vélo; (*on motorbike*) faire de la moto; **we biked there,** nous y sommes allés à *ou* en vélo *ou* moto.

biker ['baɪkər] *n* cycliste *mf*; (*on motor bike*) *& Pej* motard *m*.

bikini [bɪ'kiːnɪ] *n* bikini *m*.

bilabial [baɪ'leɪbɪəl] *adj & n Ling* (consonne *f*) bilabiale *f*.

bilateral [baɪ'lætər(ə)l] *adj* (*accord etc*) bilatéral.

bilaterally [baɪ'lætər(ə)lɪ] *adv* bilatéralement.

bilberry ['bɪlbərɪ] *n* airelle *f*, myrtille *f*.

bile [baɪl] *n Physiol* bile *f*; **b. duct,** canal *m* biliaire.

bilestone ['baɪlstəʊn] *n* calcul *m* biliaire.

bilge [bɪldʒ] *n* **(a)** *Nau* fond *m* de cale; **b. pump,** pompe *f* de drain *ou* de cale; **b. (water),** eau *f* de cale; *F* **to talk a lot of b.,** dire des bêtises; **(b)** bouge *m* (*d'une barrique*).

bilharzia [bɪl'hɑːtsɪə] *n Med* **(a)** (*disease*) bilharziose *f*; **(b)** (*parasite*) bilharzia *f*, bilharzie *f*.

biliary ['bɪlɪərɪ] *adj Physiol* biliaire.

bilingual [baɪ'lɪŋgwəl] *adj* bilingue.

bilingualism [baɪ'lɪŋgwəlɪz(ə)m] *n* bilinguisme *m*.

bilious ['bɪlɪəs] *adj* **(a)** bilieux; (*tempérament*) colérique; **b. attack,** crise *f* de foie; *Fig* **b. yellow/green,** jaunâtre/verdâtre; **(b)** *F* (*bad-tempered*) colérique.

biliousness ['bɪlɪəsnɪs] *n* affection bilieuse.

bilk [bɪlk] *vt Old-fashioned F* tromper (*qn*); **he bilked her (out) of all her money,** il lui a extirpé tout son argent.

bill[1] [bɪl] *n* **(a)** bec *m* (*d'oiseau, d'ancre*); **(b)** *Geog* bec *m*, promontoire *m*.

bill[2] *vi* (*of birds*) se becqueter; *F* **to b. and coo,** (*of couple*) faire les tourtereaux, se faire des mamours.

bill[3] *n* **(a)** *Com* note *f*, facture *f*; (*in restaurant*) addition *f*; **have you paid the b.?,** (*for gas, electricity*) as-tu payé la facture *ou F* la note?; (*in restaurant*) as-tu payé l'addition?; **to make out a b.,** rédiger une facture;

(b) *Am* (*money*) billet *m* de banque; **five-dollar b.,** billet de cinq dollars;

(c) *Com Fin* effet *m* (de commerce); **bills,** valeurs *fpl*; papier *m* (bancable); **long(-dated)/short(-dated) bills,** papier *ou* effets à longue/courte échéance; **day b.,** effet à date fixe; **b. of exchange,** lettre *f* de change; **b. book,** carnet *m* d'échéances; **b. broker,** courtier *m ou* agent *m* de change; **Exchequer b.,** bon *m* du Trésor britannique;

(d) *Th etc* affiche *f*; (*for political party*) placard *m*; **(stick) no bills!,** défense d'afficher; **to head** *or* **top the b.,** (*of actor*) être en tête d'affiche; **to fill the b.,** (*of play*) tenir l'affiche; *F* **that will fill** *or* **fit the b.,** cela fera l'affaire; **double b.,** programme de deux pièces *ou* films *etc*;

(e) (*list*) **b. of fare,** carte *f* du jour, menu *m*; *Nau* **b. of health,** patente *f* de santé; *Fig* **the doctor gave me a clean b. of health,** le docteur m'a trouvé en parfait état de santé; **the investigators gave the engine a clean b. of health,** les enquêteurs ont conclu que le moteur était en parfait état; **b. of lading,** connaissement *m*; *US Rail* feuille *f* d'expédition; **b. of entry,** déclaration *f* d'entrée (en douane); **b. of sale,** acte *m ou* contrat *m* de vente; **wages b.,** masse globale des salaires; *Constr* **b. of quantities,** devis *m*;

(f) *Pol* projet *m* de loi; (*private*) proposition *f* de loi; **to pass/reject a b.,** adopter/repousser un projet de loi; *Hist* **B. of Rights,** *Br* = la loi de 1689 déterminant les droits du citoyen anglais; *US* = les amendements de 1791 à la Constitution de 1787;

(g) *Jur* résumé *m* des chefs d'accusation (*présenté au jury*); *US* **to find a true b. against s.o.,** (*of Grand Jury*) déclarer fondés les chefs d'accusation.

bill[4] *vt* **(a)** envoyer une facture à (*qn*) (**for,** pour); **(b)** *Th etc* annoncer, afficher (*qch*); **billed as the greatest show on earth,** (*of event*) annoncé *ou* affiché comme le plus grand spectacle du monde.

Bill [bɪl] *n* (*dimin of* **William**) = Guillaume *m*; *Br F* **Old B., the B.,** (*police*) les flics *mpl*, les poulets *mpl*.

billboard ['bɪlbɔːd] *n esp Am* panneau *m* d'affichage.

billet[1] ['bɪlɪt] *n* **(a)** *Mil* (*requisition*) billet *m* de logement; **(b)** *Mil* (*accommodation*) logement *m* (*chez l'habitant*); cantonnement *m* (*en ville*); logement (*d'un évacué*); **(c)** *Old-fashioned Br F* situation *f*, emploi *m*.

billet[2] *v* (**-t-**) **1** *vt* **(a)** loger (*des troupes, un évacué*) (**on s.o.,** chez qn); **to b. troops on** *or* **in a town,** cantonner des troupes dans une ville. **2** *vi* loger (**with,** chez).

billet[3] *n* **(a)** rondin *m*, bille *f*, billette *f* (*de bois de chauffage etc*); **(b)** *Metal* billette *f*, larget *m* (*d'acier*).

billeting ['bɪlɪtɪŋ] *n* (*in private house*) logement *m* chez l'habitant; (*on town*) cantonnement *m*; **b. officer,** officier de cantonnement.

billfold ['bɪlfəʊld] *n Am* (*wallet*) portefeuille *m*.

billhook ['bɪlhʊk] *n* (*for pruning, chopping*) serpe *f*, croissant *m* (*à élaguer*); (*small*) serpette *f*.

billiard ['bɪljəd] *n* **(a)** (*usu pl with sing verb*) **billiards,** (jeu *m* de) billard *m*; **to play billiards,** jouer au billard; **bar billiards,** billard russe; **b. ball/cue,** bille *f*/queue *f* de billard; **b. room,** (salle *f* de) billard; **b. table,** billard; **(b)** *Am* (*shot*) carambolage *m*.

billing ['bɪlɪŋ] *n Th* affichage *m*; **to get top b.,** (*of actor*) être en tête d'affiche.

billion ['bɪljən] *n Br* (*one million million*) billion *m*; *Am* (*one thousand million*) milliard *m*.

billionaire [bɪljə'neər] *n* milliardaire *mf*.

billow[1] ['bɪləʊ] *n* lame *f* (*de mer*); *Lit* **the billows,** les flots *mpl*; **billows of smoke,** des nuages de fumée.

billow[2] *vi* (*of sea*) se soulever en vagues; (*of crowds, flames etc*) ondoyer; **the sails billowed in the wind,** les voiles se gonflaient au vent.

billowy ['bɪləʊɪ] *adj* (*flot, mer*) houleux.

billposter ['bɪlpəʊstər] **, billsticker** ['bɪlstɪkər] *n* afficheur *m*, colleur *m* d'affiches; (*for political party*) placardeur *m*; **billposters will be prosecuted,** ≈ défense d'afficher.

billposting ['bɪlpəʊstɪŋ] **, billsticking** ['bɪlstɪkɪŋ] *n* affichage *m*; (*for political party*) placardage *m*.

billy, *pl* **billies** ['bɪlɪ, -z] *n* **(a)** *Austr New Zealand* gamelle *f*; bouilloire *f* (*à thé*); **to boil the b.,** faire du thé; **(b) b. (club),** gourdin *m*; *Am* (*for police*) matraque *f*.

Billy ['bɪlɪ] *n* (*dimin of* **William**) = Guillaume *m*.

billycan ['bɪlɪkæn] *n* = **BILLY (a)**.

billy-goat ['bɪlɪgəʊt] *n* bouc *m*.

billy-o(h) ['bɪlɪəʊ] *n Br Old-fashioned F* **it's raining like b.-o.,** il pleut à verse; **to run like b.-o.,** courir très vite *ou* à toutes jambes.

bimbo ['bɪmbəʊ] *n Pej* minette *f*.

bimetallic [baɪmɪ'tælɪk] *adj* **(a)** *Econ* (*système*) bimétallique; **(b)** *Tech* **b. strip,** bilame *f*.

bimetallism [baɪ'metəlɪz(ə)m] *n Econ* bimétallisme *m*.

bimonthly [baɪ'mʌnθlɪ] **1** *adj* **(a)** (*every two months*) bimestriel; **(b)** (*twice a month*) bimensuel. **2** *n* (*magazine*) (*every two months*) revue *ou* publication bimestrielle; (*twice monthly*) bimensuel *m*. **3** *adv* (*see adj*) **(a)** tous les deux mois; **(b)** bimensuellement, deux fois par mois.

bin [bɪn] *n* coffre *m*, huche *f*, bac *m*; (*dustbin*) poubelle *f*; **litter b.,** boîte *f* à ordures; **wine b.,** casier *m* à bouteilles, porte-bouteilles *m inv*; **cement b.,** silo *m* à ciment; *Min* **ore b.,** réservoir *m ou* caisson *m* à minerai; *Sl* **loony b.,** maison *f* de fous.

binary ['baɪnərɪ] **1** *adj Math etc* binaire; **b. code/number,** code *m*/nombre *m* binaire; *Astron* **b. star,** binaire *f*; *Mil* **b. weapon,** arme *f* binaire. **2** *n Astron* binaire *f*.

bind[1] [baɪnd] *n* **(a)** *F* (*nuisance*) scie *f*; **what an awful b.!,** quelle barbe!; **to be in a b.,** (*difficult situation*) être dans une mauvaise passe; **I'm in a bit of a b.,** j'ai un petit problème; **(b)** (*tie*) sarment *m*, tige *f*, liane *f* (*de houblon etc*); *Mus* ligature *f*, liaison *f*; **(c)** *Min* couche *f* d'argile dure (*entre deux couches de houille*).

bind[2] *v* (*pt & pp* **bound** [baʊnd]) **1** *vt* **(a)** (*attach*) attacher, lier (*qch*) (**to,** à); lier, attacher, ligoter (*un prisonnier*); lier (*une gerbe*); **to b. s.o. hand and foot,** lier pieds et poings à qn; *Fig* **I am bound hand and foot,** (*powerless*) je suis pieds et poings liés; **they are bound together by a close friendship,** ils sont liés d'une étroite amitié; **they are very much bound up with each other,** ils sont très attachés l'un à l'autre; **the present is bound up with the past,** le présent se relie au passé; **to b. one's skis,** fixer ses skis;

(b) (*dress*) bander, panser (*une blessure*);

(c) (*cover*) relier (*un livre*); **bound in boards,** cartonné; **bound in cloth,** relié toile;

(d) (*cause to cohere*) lier, agglutiner (*du sable etc*); cohérer, fixer (*la poussière d'une route*); **stones bound together with cement,** pierres liées avec du ciment;

(e) (*of obligation, promise etc*) lier, engager (*qn*); **to b. s.o. to pay a debt,** astreindre *ou* obliger qn à payer une dette; **to b. oneself to do sth,** s'engager à faire qch; **to be bound to do sth,** être obligé *ou* tenu de faire qch; **to be bound by an oath,** être engagé sous serment, être lié par un serment; **he's bound to come,** (*sure to come*) il ne peut pas manquer de venir; **it's bound to rain tomorrow,** il pleuvra sûrement demain; **it's bound to happen,** c'est fatal; *F* **he'll come, I'll be bound,** il viendra, j'en suis sûr *ou* je vous le promets; *Am* **he's bound (and determined) to come and see you,** il veut absolument venir vous voir;

(f) *Sewing* border (*un manteau, un chapeau*); brider (*une boutonnière*).

2 *vi* (*of gravel etc*) se lier, s'agglomérer, s'agglutiner; (*of cement*) durcir, prendre.

►**bind over** *vtsep Jur* **to b. s.o. over to keep the peace,** exiger de qn sous caution qu'il ne se livrera à aucune voie de fait; **to be bound over,** être sommé (par un magistrat) d'observer une bonne conduite.

►**bind up** *vtsep* **(a)** (*tie*) lier une gerbe; **(b)** (*dress*) bander, panser (*une blessure*).

binder ['baɪndər] *n* **(a)** (*for papers*) relieur *m*; **(b)** (*of books*) relieur, -euse; **(c)** *Agr* (*machine*) lieuse *f* (*de gerbes*); (*for hay*) botteleuse *f*; **b. twine,** ficelle *f* à lier; **(d)** *Sewing* ourleur *m* (*d'une machine à coudre*); **(e)** *Culin* liant *m* (*d'une sauce*); *Constr* matériau *m* d'agrégation; (*for road surface*) liant, agglomérant *m*; **(f)** (*beam, girder*) *Carp* entrait *m*; sommier *m* (*de plancher*); *Constr* parpaing *m*; **(g)** *Com* convention *f* liant le vendeur.

bindery ['baɪnd(ə)rɪ] *n* atelier *m* de reliure.

binding ['baɪndɪŋ] **1** *adj* **(a)** (*agent*) agglomérant, agglutinant; **(b)** (*contract etc*) obligatoire (**upon s.o.,** pour qn); **b. agreement,** obligation *f* irrévocable; **agreement b. (up)on s.o.,** contrat qui lie qn; **decision b. on all parties,** décision obligatoire pour tous; **(c)** *Med* astringent, constipant. **2** *n* **(a)** *Sp* fixation *f* (*de ski*); **safety (release) bindings,** fixations de sécurité; **(b)** reliure *f* (*d'un livre*); **quarter b.,** demi-reliure *f*; **cloth b.,** reliure en toile; **limp b.,** cartonnage *m* souple; **perfect b.,** reliure arraphique *ou* sans couture; **(c)** *Constr* agglutination *f*; agrégation *f*; liant *m*, agglomérant *m* (*d'une route*); **b. material,** matière agglomérante *ou* d'agrégation; **(d)** bordure *f*, liséré *m* (*d'une robe etc*).

bindweed ['baɪndwiːd] *n* (*plant*) liseron *m*.

binge [bɪndʒ] *n F* bombe *f*; **to go on a b.,** (*of drinking*) prendre une cuite; (*of eating*) *F* se gaver; (*of shopping*) *F* faire une razzia.

bingo ['bɪŋgəʊ] **1** *n* bingo *m*; *Br F* **to go to the b.,** aller jouer au bingo; **b. hall,** lieu *m* où l'on joue au bingo. **2** *int* et voilà!

binman ['bɪnmæn] *n Br* éboueur *m*.

binnacle ['bɪnək(ə)l] *n Nau* habitacle *m*.

binocular [bɪ'nɒkjʊlər, baɪ-] *adj* (*vision etc*) binoculaire.

binoculars [bɪ'nɒkjʊləz] *npl* jumelles *fpl*; **to look at sth through b.,** regarder qch avec des jumelles.

binomial [baɪ'nəʊmɪəl] **1** *adj Math* (*facteur etc*) binôme; **the b. theorem,** le binôme de Newton, le théorème de Newton. **2** *n* binôme *m*.

biochemic(al) [baɪəʊ'kemɪk, -ɪk(ə)l] *adj* biochimique; **b. oxygen demand,** demande *f* biochimique en oxygène.

biochemist [baɪəʊ'kemɪst] *n* biochimiste *mf*.

biochemistry [baɪəʊ'kemɪstrɪ] *n* biochimie *f*.

biodegradability [baɪəʊdɪgreɪdə'bɪlɪtɪ] *n* (*of plastic etc*) biodégradabilité *f*.

biodegradable [baɪəʊdɪ'greɪdəb(ə)l] *adj* (*plastic etc*) biodégradable.

bioethics [baɪəʊ'eθɪks] *n* bioéthique *f*; **b. debate,** débat sur la bioéthique.

biogenesis [baɪəʊ'dʒenɪsɪs] *n Biol* biogenèse *f*.

biographer [baɪ'ɒgrəfər] *n* biographe *mf*, auteur *m* d'une biographie.

biographic(al) [baɪə'græfɪk, -ɪk(ə)l] *adj* biographique; **b. novel,** vie *ou* biographie romancée.

biography [baɪ'ɒgrəfɪ] *n* biographie *f*.

biologic(al) [baɪə'lɒdʒɪk, -ɪk(ə)l] *adj* biologique; **b. clock,** horloge *f* physiologique *ou* biologique; **my b. clock is running down,** (*of woman*) je deviens trop vieille pour avoir un enfant; **b. control,** (*of insects*) élimination des insectes par des méthodes biologiques; **b. warfare,** guerre *f* bactériologique.

biologically [baɪə'lɒdʒɪklɪ] *adv* biologiquement.

biologist [baɪ'ɒlədʒɪst] *n* biologiste *mf*.

biology [baɪ'ɒlədʒɪ] *n* biologie *f*.

biomass ['baɪəʊmæs] *n* biomasse *f*.

biomaterial [baɪəʊmə'tɪərɪəl] *n* biomatériau *m*.

biometrics [baɪəʊ'metrɪks] *npl* (*usu with sing verb*) biométrie *f*.

bionics [baɪ'ɒnɪks] *npl* (*usu with sing verb*) bionique *f*.

biophysics [baɪəʊ'fɪzɪks] *npl* (*usu with sing verb*) biophysique *f*.

biopsy ['baɪɒpsɪ, baɪ'ɒpsɪ] *n Surg* biopsie *f*; **to do** *or* **perform a b.,** effectuer une biopsie.

biorhythm ['baɪəʊrɪð(ə)m] *n* rythme *m* biologique, biorythme *m*.

bioscope ['baɪəskəʊp] *n Cin* **(a)** *Old-fashioned* bioscope *m*; **(b)** (*in South Africa*) cinéma *m*.

biosphere ['baɪəsfɪər] *n* biosphère *f*.

biosynthesis [baɪəʊ'sɪnθɪsɪs] *n* biosynthèse *f*.

biotechnology [baɪəʊtek'nɒlədʒɪ], *F* **biotech** ['baɪəʊtek] *n* biotechnologie *f*.

biotope ['baɪətəʊp] *n Biol* biotope *m*, habitat *m*.

bipartisan [baɪpɑːtɪ'zæn] *adj Pol etc* biparti, bipartite.

bipartite [baɪ'pɑːtaɪt] *adj* **(a)** *Biol* biparti, bipartite; **(b)** *Jur* (*document*) rédigé en double.

biped ['baɪped] *adj & n* bipède *m*.

biplane ['baɪpleɪn] *n Av* (avion *m*) biplan *m*.

bipolar [baɪ'pəʊlər] *adj El Physiol etc* bipolaire.

birch¹ [bɜːtʃ] *n* **(a)** (*tree*) bouleau *m*; **b. (wood),** (bois *m* de) bouleau; **(b) b. (rod),** verge *f*; **to give s.o. the b.,** donner le fouet à qn, fouetter qn.

birch² *vt* donner le fouet à (*qn*), fouetter (*qn*).

birching ['bɜːtʃɪŋ] *n* fouettée *f*; **to give s.o. a b.,** fouetter qn.

bird [bɜːd] *n* **(a)** oiseau *m*; **(farmyard) b.,** volaille *f*; **cage b.,** oiseau d'appartement; *F* **a little b. told me,** mon petit doigt me l'a dit; **night b.,** oiseau de nuit *ou* nocturne; *Fig* noctambule *mf*; **b. of passage,** oiseau passager *ou* de passage; **I'm just a b. of passage,** je ne suis que de passage; **b. of prey,** oiseau de proie, rapace *m*; **b. of paradise,** oiseau de paradis, paradisier *m*; *F* **to give s.o. the b.,** (*dismiss them*) envoyer promener qn; *Th etc* huer *ou* siffler qn; **to get the b.,** (*be dismissed*) être renvoyé; *Th* être hué *ou* sifflé; **to eat like a b.,** avoir un appétit d'oiseau; *Prov* **the early b. catches the worm,** l'avenir appartient à ceux qui se lèvent tôt; **to be an early b.,** être matinal; *Prov* **a b. in the hand is worth two in the bush,** un tiens vaut mieux que deux tu l'auras; *Fig* **the b. has flown,** l'oiseau s'est envolé; *Prov* **birds of a feather flock together,** qui se ressemble s'assemble; **you and your father are birds of a feather,** toi et ton père, vous ne valez pas mieux l'un que l'autre; *Euph* **it's time you talked to him about the birds and the bees,** (*facts of life*) il serait temps de lui expliquer que les bébés ne naissent pas dans les choux; *F* **it's (strictly) for the birds,** c'est de la roupie de sansonnet; **b. call,** cri *m* d'oiseau; (*lure*) appeau *m*, pipeau *m*, chanterelle *f*; **b. fancier,** connaisseur *m* en oiseaux; (*breeder*) oiselier *m*; (*of farm birds*) aviculteur *m*; **b.'s nest,** nid *m* d'oiseau; *Culin* **b.'s nest soup,** soupe aux nids d'hirondelles; **b. sanctuary,** réserve *f* ornithologique; **b. shot,** cendrée *f*; *Av* **b. strike,** = collision d'un avion avec un oiseau; **b. table,** mangeoire *f* pour les oiseaux (*dans un jardin*);

(b) *F* type *m*, individu *m*; **he's a queer b.,** c'est un drôle d'oiseau; **a home b.,** un casanier, une casanière;

(c) *Br Sl* (*in prison*) taule *f*, tôle *f*; **to do b.,** faire de la taule;

(d) *Br Sl* (*woman*) nana *f*;

(e) *Sp* pigeon artificiel; volant *m* (*de jeu de badminton*);

(f) *Mil F* engin téléguidé.

birdbath ['bɜːdbɑːθ] *n* bain *m* pour les oiseaux.

bird-brained ['bɜːdbreɪnd] *adj F* écervelé; **to be b.-b.,** avoir une cervelle de moineau.

birdcage ['bɜːdkeɪdʒ] *n* cage *f* (d'oiseau); (*large*) volière *f*.

birdcatcher ['bɜːdkætʃər] *n* oiseleur *m*.

bird-dog ['bɜːddɒg] *vt Am* surveiller (*qn*) de près.

bird-house ['bɜːdhaʊs] *n* volière *f*.

birdie ['bɜːdɪ] *n F* **(a)** *Golf* (trou fait en) un coup de moins que la normale; **(b)** (*in children's language*) gentil petit oiseau.

birdlike ['bɜːdlaɪk] *adj* comme (d')un oiseau; (*appetite*) d'oiseau.

birdlime ['bɜːdlaɪm] *n* glu *f*.

bird-nesting ['bɜːdnestɪŋ] *n* **to go b.-n.,** = rechercher des nids pour collecter les œufs.

birdseed ['bɜːdsiːd] *n* graines *fpl* pour oiseaux.

bird's-eye ['bɜːdzaɪ] *n* **(a) b.-e. view,** vue *f* à vol d'oiseau; *Phot* photographie aérienne oblique; *Cin* prise *f* de vues en plongeon; *Fig* **b.-e. view of the situation,** résumé *m* de la situation; **(b)** *Bot* véronique *f*; **b.-e. mahogany,** acajou moucheté; **b.-e. maple,** érable madré *ou* à broussin; **(c)** *Tex* œil-de perdrix *m*, *pl* œils-de-perdrix.

bird's-foot ['bɜːdzfʊt] *n* (*plant*) pied-d'oiseau *m*, *pl* pieds-d'oiseau; **b.-f. trefoil,** lotier *m*, corne *f* du diable.

bird-watcher ['bɜːdwɒtʃər] *n* observateur, -trice d'oiseaux.

bird-watching ['bɜːdwɒtʃɪŋ] *n* observation *f* des oiseaux (*dans leur milieu naturel*); **to go b.-w.,** aller observer les oiseaux.

biretta [bɪ'retə] *n Rel Cathol* barrette *f*.

biro ® ['baɪrəʊ] *n* stylo *m* (à) bille.

birth [bɜːθ] *n* **(a)** (*of child, nation, industry*) naissance *f*; genèse *f* (*d'une idée etc*); **to give b. to a child,** mettre un enfant au monde, donner naissance à un enfant; **she has given b. to a daughter,** elle a eu une fille; **he weighed**

only 1 kilo at b., il ne pesait qu'un kilo à la naissance; **will the father be present at the b.?**, le père assistera-t-il à l'accouchement?; **it was a difficult b.**, c'était un accouchement difficile; **Irish by b.**, Irlandais de naissance; **from b.**, (*aveugle etc*) de naissance; (*délicat*) dès *ou* depuis sa naissance; **b. certificate**, (*original*) acte *m* de naissance; (*copy*) extrait *m* de naissance; **b. control**, contrôle *m ou* limitation *f* des naissances; **b. rate**, (taux *m* de) natalité *f*; **premature b.**, accouchement prématuré *ou* avant terme; **b. pangs**, douleurs *fpl* d'accouchement; *Fig* accouchement difficile (*d'un nouveau système etc*); **(b)** mise *f* bas (*d'un animal*); **to give b. to a litter**, mettre bas une portée.

birthday ['bɜːθdeɪ] *n* (*anniversary*) anniversaire *m*; (*day of birth*) jour *m* de naissance; *F* **to be in one's b. suit**, être dans le *ou* en costume d'Adam *ou* d'Ève; **happy b.!**, bon *ou* joyeux anniversaire!; **b. card**, carte *f* d'anniversaire; **b. present**, cadeau *m* d'anniversaire; *Br* **B. Honours**, = distinctions honorifiques accordées à l'occasion de l'anniversaire du souverain.

birthing ['bɜːθɪŋ] *n esp Am Med* **b. room**, salle *f* d'accouchement.

birthmark ['bɜːθmɑːk] *n* envie *f*, tache *f* de vin.

birthplace ['bɜːθpleɪs] *n* lieu *m* de naissance; *Fig* berceau *m* (*d'une religion etc*).

birthright ['bɜːθraɪt] *n* **(a)** droit *m* de naissance, droit du sang; (*inheritance*) patrimoine *m*; *Fig* **clean air is everyone's b.**, tout le monde a le droit de respirer; **(b)** (*of firstborn*) droit *m* d'aînesse.

birthstone ['bɜːθstəʊn] *n Astrol etc* pierre *f* porte-bonheur.

biryani [bɪr'jɑːnɪ] *n* (*plat indien*) biriani *m*.

Biscay ['bɪskeɪ] *n Geog* **the Bay of B.**, le golfe de Gascogne.

biscuit ['bɪskɪt] *n* **(a)** *Br* biscuit *m*; *Am* petit gâteau (feuilleté); **(sweet) biscuits**, gâteaux secs; **ship's b.**, biscuits de mer; **dog b.**, biscuit de chien; **b. barrel**, boîte *f ou* seau *m* à biscuits; **b. factory**, biscuiterie *f*; *Old-fashioned F* **that takes the b.!**, ça, c'est le bouquet!; **(b)** *Cer* **b. ware**, biscuit *m*; **(c)** (*colour*) biscuit *m*.

bisect [baɪ'sekt] **1** *vt Math etc* couper *ou* diviser (*une ligne, un angle*) en deux parties égales. **2** *vi* (*of road etc*) bifurquer.

bisection [baɪ'sekʃən] *n* bissection *f*.

bisector [baɪ'sektər] *n* ligne *f* de bissection, bissectrice *f*.

bisexual [baɪ'seksjʊəl] *adj Bot Psy* bis(s)exué, bis(s)exuel; **he's b.**, il est bisexuel.

bishop ['bɪʃəp] *n* **(a)** *Rel* évêque *m*; **b.'s palace**, palais épiscopal, évêché *m*; **(b)** *Chess* fou *m*; **(c)** *Culin* (*mulled wine*) bi(s)chof *m*.

bishopric ['bɪʃəprɪk] *n* (*office or diocese*) évêché *m*.

bismuth ['bɪzməθ] *n Miner Pharm* bismuth *m*.

bison ['baɪsən] *n* bison *m* (*de l'Amérique septentrionale*).

bisque¹ [bɪːsk] *n Cer* biscuit *m*.

bisque² *n Culin* bisque *f* (*de homard etc*).

bistre ['bɪstər] *adj & n* bistre *m*.

bisulphite [baɪ'sʌlfaɪt] *n Ch* bisulfite *m*; **sodium b.**, bisulfite de sodium *ou* de soude.

bit¹ [bɪt] *n* **(a)** mors *m* (*d'une bride*); **to champ at the b.**, (*of horse*) mâcher son mors; (*of person*) ronger son frein; **to take the b. between one's teeth**, (*of horse, person*) prendre le mors aux dents, s'emballer; **(b)** mèche *f* (*de vilebrequin*); foret *m* (*de perceuse*); mors *m* (*d'une tenaille, d'un étau*); ciseau *m* (*d'un rabot*); **copper** *or* **soldering b.**, fer *m* à souder, soudoir *m*.

bit² *n* **(a)** (*piece*) morceau *m* (*de pain etc*); bout *m* (*de papier, de ficelle etc*); brin *m* (*de paille etc*); **he has eaten every b.**, il a tout mangé; *F* **she's a nice b. of stuff** *or* **skirt**, c'est une jolie fille; **made of bits and pieces** *or F* **bits and bobs**, fait de pièces et de morceaux *ou F* de bric et de broc; *F* **my bits and pieces**, mes affaires; *Th Cin* **b. part**, rôle *m* de figurant; **a (little) b. of hope**, un petit brin d'espoir; **to do one's b.**, y aller de sa personne, y mettre du sien; *F* **to make a b.**, (*earn money*) faire sa pelote; **to make a b. on the side**, faire de la gratte;

(b) a b., un peu (**of**, de); **a tiny** *or* **little b.**, un tout petit peu; **I'm a b. late**, je suis un peu en retard; **I'm a b. hungry**, j'ai un peu faim, *F* j'ai un petit creux; **he's a b. jealous**, il est quelque peu jaloux; **she's a b. of an artist**, elle est un peu artiste; *F* **he's a b. of a lad**, (*likes a good time*) il aime faire la bombe; (*runs after women*) il aime courir les jupons; **wait a b.!**, attendez un peu!; **that takes a b. of doing**, ça c'est bien compliqué; **a good b. older**, sensiblement plus âgé; **every b. as good/interesting/***etc* **as**, aussi bon/intéressant/*etc* que; *F* **it's a b. much!**, ça c'est vraiment trop fort!; **b. by b.**, peu à peu, petit à petit; **not a b. (of it)!**, pas du tout!; **I don't care a b.**, cela m'est bien égal; **it's not a b. of use**, cela ne sert absolument à rien; **a b. of news**, une nouvelle; **a b. of luck**, une chance; **to tear sth to bits**, déchirer qch en morceaux; **smashed to bits**, brisé (en mille morceaux); **to take sth to bits**, démonter qch; **in bits**, en morceaux;

(c) *F* (*coin*) pièce *f*; *Br Arch* **threepenny b.**, pièce de trois pence; *Am* **two bits**, vingt-cinq cents.

bit³ *n Comptr* bit *m*.

bitch¹ [bɪtʃ] *n* **(a)** (*dog*) chienne *f*; femelle *f* (*de renard etc*); **terrier b.**, terrier *m* femelle; **(b)** *Sl* (*woman*) garce *f*; **(c)** *Sl* **a b. of a job**, un travail de chien.

bitch² *v Sl* **1** *vt* gâcher (*un travail*); **he bitched up the whole business for us**, il nous a tout bousillé. **2** *vi* (*complain*) rouspéter; **stop bitching about the weather**, arrête de rouspéter après le temps; **bitching session**, séance *f* de défoulement.

bitchy ['bɪtʃɪ] *adj Sl* (*woman*) garce; (*remark etc*) vache; **that was a b. thing to do!**, quel tour de vache!; **to be b.**, (*of woman*) être garce; (*of man*) être mauvaise langue.

bite¹ [baɪt] *n* **(a)** coup *m* de dent; (*in dentistry*) articulé *m* dentaire; *esp Am F* **to put the b. on s.o.**, (*try to extort money from*) toucher qn; **(b)** (*in fishing*) touche *f*; **I haven't had a b. all day**, je n'ai pas eu une seule touche de toute la journée; **(c)** morsure *f* (*d'un chien etc*); piqûre *f*, morsure (*d'un insecte*); **(d)** *F* (*of food*) bouchée *f*, morceau *m*; **would you like a b. (to eat)?**, voulez-vous manger quelque chose?; **I haven't had a b. all day**, je n'ai rien mangé de la journée; **to take a big b. out of sth**, mordre dans qch à pleines dents; *Fig* **the repairs took a big b. out of our savings**, les réparations ont écorné *ou* fait un trou dans nos économies; **you don't get two bites at the cherry**, l'occasion ne se présente qu'une fois; **(e)** piquant *m* (*d'une sauce, d'un vin*); *Tech* mordant *m* (*de lime etc*).

bite² *vt & vi* (*pt* **bit** [bɪt]; *pp* **bitten** [bɪt(ə)n]) **1** *vt* **(a)** mordre (*qn*), donner un coup de dent à (*qn, qch*); (*of insect*) piquer; **the dog bit him in the leg**, le chien l'a mordu à la jambe; **to b. one's lips**, se mordre les lèvres; **to b. one's nails**, se ronger les ongles; **to b. one's tongue**, (*with teeth*) & *Fig* se mordre la langue; **to b. the dust**, mordre la poussière; *Prov* **once bitten twice shy**, chat échaudé craint l'eau froide; **to b. the bullet**, faire contre mauvaise fortune bon cœur; **to get bitten**, (*by dog*) se faire mordre; (*by insect*) se faire piquer; *F* **what's bitten him?**, quel chien l'a mordu?, quelle mouche l'a piqué?; *F* **to be bitten by the collecting bug**, être pris par la folie de la collection; *Fig* **to b. the hand that feeds you**, cracher dans la soupe; *Austr F* **to b. s.o.**, (*for money*) taper qn;

(b) (*of wind, cold*) couper (*le visage etc*); (*of pepper*) piquer (*la langue*); **acid bites metal**, l'acide ronge *ou* attaque le métal.

2 *vi* **(a)** (*of fish*) mordre (à l'hameçon); **does the dog b.?**, est-ce que le chien est méchant?;

(b) (*of screw, file*) mordre (**on**, sur); (*of tool*) mordre, s'engager; (*of anchor*) mordre, prendre fond; **screw that won't b.**, vis qui foire.

▸**bite back** *vtsep* ravaler (*une réplique*).

▸**bite off** *vtsep* enlever *ou* détacher (*qch*) d'un coup de dent(s); *F* **to b. s.o.'s head off**, rembarrer qn; **to b. off more than one can chew**, tenter qch au-dessus de ses forces.

biter ['baɪtər] *n Prov* **the b. bit**, l'arroseur arrosé.

biting ['baɪtɪŋ] *adj* (*cold*) cuisant, âpre, perçant; (*wind*) cinglant, piquant; (*style, wit*) mordant, caustique; **b. irony**, ironie amère.

bit-mapped ['bɪtmæpt] *adj Comptr* (*image*) dessiné point par point.

bitter ['bɪtər] **1** *adj* (*goût, bière, personne*) amer; (*vin*) acerbe; (*vent*) aigre, piquant; (*temps*) rigoureux; (*froid, vent*) glacial, cinglant; (*ennemi*) implacable; (*conflit*) aigu; (*ton*) aigre, âpre; **not being promoted was a b. pill to swallow**, ça a été dur à avaler pour moi *ou* lui *etc* de ne pas être promu; **b. hatred**, haine acharnée; **b. tears**, larmes amères; **b. disappointment**, cruelle déception; **b. experience**, expérience cruelle; **to feel** *or* **be b. about sth**, ressentir de l'amertume de qch; **she's very b. about it**, elle est très amère à ce sujet; *Fig* **to go on/resist to the b. end**, aller/résister jusqu'au bout. **2** *n* **(a)** *Br* bière amère; **(b) bitters**, bitter(s) *m(pl)*, amer(s) *m(pl)*.

bitterly ['bɪtəlɪ] *adv* (*dire*) amèrement, avec amertume; (*pleurer*) amèrement; **it was b. cold**, il faisait un froid de loup; **I've regretted it b. ever since**, je n'ai cessé de le regretter amèrement; **b. disappointed**, cruellement déçu; **to be b. opposed to sth**, être farouchement opposé à qch.

bittern ['bɪtən] *n* (*bird*) butor *m*.

bitterness ['bɪtənɪs] *n* amertume *f* (*d'une boisson, de la douleur, d'une personne*); rigueur *f* (*du temps*); âpreté *f* (*du temps, des reproches*); aigreur *f*, acrimonie *f* (*de paroles, d'une querelle*).

bittersweet ['bɪtəswiːt] **1** *adj* aigre-doux, *f* -douce; *Fig* (*memory, romance*) doux-amer. **2** *n* (*plant*) douce-amère *f*, *pl* douces-amères.

bitty ['bɪtɪ] *adj F* (*livre etc*) d'un style décousu.

bitumen ['bɪtjʊmɪn] *n* **(a)** *Ch Miner* bitume *m*; **(b)** *Austr F* route goudronnée.

bituminous [bɪ'tjuːmɪnəs] *adj* bitumineux; **b. coal,** houille grasse *ou* collante.

bivalent [baɪ'veɪlənt] *adj Ch* bivalent.

bivalve ['baɪvælv] *adj & n* (*mollusc*) bivalve *m*.

bivouac¹ ['bɪvʊæk] *n Mil etc* bivouac *m*.

bivouac² *vi* (**bivouacked**; **bivouacking**) bivouaquer.

biweekly [baɪ'wiːklɪ] **1** *adj* **(a)** (*every two weeks*) de tous les quinze jours, bimensuel; **(b)** (*twice a week*) bihebdomadaire. **2** *adv* (*see adj*) **(a)** tous les quinze jours; **(b)** deux fois par semaine.

bizarre [bɪ'zɑːr] *adj* bizarre.

bizarrely [bɪ'zɑːlɪ] *adv* bizarrement.

bizarreness [bɪ'zɑːnɪs] *n* bizarrerie *f*.

B/L, b/l *Com* (*abbr* **bill of lading**) connt.

blab¹ [blæb] *n* = **BLABBER¹**.

blab² *v* (-bb-) *F* **1** *vi* **(a)** (*betray secret*) vendre la mèche; **(b)** (*prattle*) jaser, bavarder. **2** *vt* divulguer, laisser échapper (*un secret*).

►**blab out** *vtsep* = **BLAB² 2**.

blabber¹ ['blæbər], *esp US* **blabbermouth** ['blæbəmaʊθ] *n F* jaseur, -euse, bavard, -e.

blabber² *vi* jaser, bavarder.

black¹ [blæk] **1** *adj* **(a)** (*coffee, dress, hair etc*) noir; **b. horse,** cheval moreau; *Hist* **the B. Death,** la Peste Noire; *Old-fashioned Br Jur* **the B. cap,** le bonnet noir (*que coiffait le juge en prononçant une condamnation à mort*); **to be in s.o.'s b. books,** être mal vu de qn; *Fig* **to be the b. sheep of the family,** être le mouton noir de la famille; *Ind* **to declare a ship/a firm b.,** mettre un navire/une entreprise à l'index; **b. with age,** noirci par le temps; **it** *or* **the night was pitch b.,** il faisait noir comme dans un four; **to look as b. as thunder,** avoir l'air furieux; **to give s.o. a b. look,** jeter un regard noir à qn; **things are looking b.,** les affaires prennent une mauvaise tournure; **to paint things blacker than they are,** noircir la situation; **she's not as b. as she's painted,** elle n'est pas si mauvaise qu'on le dit; **a b. man/woman,** un Noir/une Noire; **his hands were b.,** il avait les mains sales *ou* toutes noires; **the B. Country,** le Pays Noir (de l'Angleterre); **b. and tan,** (*dog*) noir et feu *inv*; (*drink*) = mélange de bière et de porter; *Br Mil Hist* **the B. and Tans,** = police auxiliaire envoyée en Irlande pour combattre l'IRA; **b. belt,** (*in judo*) ceinture noire; *Av* **b. box,** boîte noire; **b. bread,** pain *m* de seigle; *Scot* **b. bun,** = sorte de pain au raisin; **b. economy,** économie souterraine; **b. eye,** œil poché, *F* œil au beurre noir; **B. Forest,** Forêt-Noire; **B. Forest gateau,** forêt *m* noire; *Met* **b. ice,** verglas *m*; *Old-fashioned Br F* **B. Maria,** panier *m* à salade; **b. mark,** mauvais point; **that earned him a b. mark,** ça a été un mauvais point pour lui; *Culin* **b. pudding,** boudin noir; **B. Sea,** Mer Noire; **b. spot,** *Aut etc* point noir; (*on furniture etc*) noircissure *f*; **b. swan,** cygne noir; **b. tie,** nœud papillon noir; **is it b. tie?,** est-ce que la tenue habillée est de rigueur?; **b. widow (spider),** veuve noire;
(b) (*nuage, ciel etc*) sombre; *Fig* (*humour, plaisanterie, comédie*) macabre; **he's in one of his b. moods,** il est dans un de ses mauvais jours; **it's a b. day for Britain,** c'est un mauvais jour pour la Grande-Bretagne; **b. magic,** la magie noire; **b. mass,** messe noire; **b. market,** marché noir; **b. marketeer,** profiteur *m* du marché noir; **to buy/sell on the b. market,** acheter/vendre au marché noir; **the b. market in jeans,** le marché noir du jean.
2 *n* **(a)** noir *m*; **she always wears b.,** elle porte toujours du noir, elle est toujours en noir; *Fin F* **in the b.,** solvable, sans dettes; **to work in b. and white,** (*of artist*) faire du dessin à l'encre *ou* au crayon noir; **I have his consent in b. and white,** j'ai son consentement par écrit; **I should like to have it in b. and white,** je voudrais avoir cela noir sur blanc; **she sees everything in b. and white,** pour elle, c'est tout l'un ou tout l'autre; **the b.,** (*in roulette*) le noir; (*in snooker*) la bille noire;
(b) (*horse*) cheval noir.

black² *vt* **(a)** noircir (*qch*); **to b. one's face,** se charbonner le visage; **to b. s.o.'s eye,** pocher l'œil à qn, *F* faire à qn un œil au beurre noir; **(b)** *Ind* refuser de travailler avec (*une compagnie, un homme non syndiqué*); mettre (*un navire, une entreprise*) à l'index; **(c)** cirer (*des chaussures*).

Black [blæk] *n* Noir, -e.

►**black out 1** *vi* **(a)** (*faint*) perdre connaissance, s'évanouir; (*lose memory*) avoir un trou de mémoire; **(b)** occulter *ou* voiler *ou* masquer les lumières, faire le black-out; *Th* éteindre la rampe, couper la lumière; *Cin* fermer en fondu. **2** *vtsep* **(a)** (*completely*) éteindre les lumières dans, faire le black-out dans (*une maison*); (*partially*) voiler *ou* masquer les lumières dans (*une maison etc*); **(b)** *Rad TV* **industrial action has blacked out this evening's programmes,** un mouvement de grève a interrompu les programmes de la soirée; **(c)** effacer, rayer (*qch*) (*d'un gros trait noir*).

►**black up** *vi Th* se maquiller en noir.

black-and-blue [blækən'bluː] *adj* **to beat s.o. b.-and-b.,** meurtrir *ou* rosser qn de coups; **to be b.-and-b. all over,** être tout meurtri (de coups); **her face was b.-and-b.,** son visage était couvert de coups.

black-and-tan [blækən'tæn] *adj* **b.-and-tan terrier,** chien noir et feu *inv*.

black-and-white [blækən'waɪt] *n* (*photograph*) photo *f* noir et blanc; **b.-and-w. film,** film *m* (en) noir et blanc; **b.-and-w. postcard,** carte *f* en noir et blanc; **b.-and-w. television,** télévision *f* (en) noir et blanc.

blackball¹ ['blækbɔːl] *n* (*in balloting*) noire *f*.

blackball² *vt* blackbouler (*qn*).

blackballing ['blækbɔːlɪŋ] *n* blackboulage *m*.

blackbeetle ['blækbiːt(ə)l] *n F* (*insect*) blatte *f*, cafard *m*, cancrelat *m*.

blackberry ['blækb(ə)rɪ] *n* mûre *f*; **b. bush,** ronce *f ou* mûrier *m* des haies; **b. jam,** confiture *f* de mûres; **b. tart,** tarte *f* aux mûres.

blackberrying ['blækberɪɪŋ] *n* **to go b.,** aller cueillir des mûres, aller à la cueillette des mûres.

blackbird ['blækbɜːd] *n* **(a)** merle *m* (noir); **(b)** *Am* (variété *f* d')étourneau *m*.

blackboard ['blækbɔːd] *n* tableau noir.

black-bordered [blæk'bɔːdəd] *adj* à bordure noire.

blackcap ['blækkæp] *n* (*bird*) fauvette *f* à tête noire.

blackcock ['blækkɒk] *n* (*bird*) tétras *m* lyre; coq *m* des bouleaux.

blackcurrant ['blækkʌrənt] *n* (*bush, fruit*) cassis *m*.

blacken ['blæk(ə)n] **1** *vt* noircir (*un mur, Fig la réputation de qn*); obscurcir (*le ciel*); (*with smoke*) enfumer (*du papier, du verre*); *Fig* **to b. s.o.'s character,** calomnier qn. **2** *vi* (se) noircir, devenir noir; *Fig* (*of face*) s'assombrir; **to b. with age,** (*of painting*) pousser *ou* tirer au noir.

blackening ['blæk(ə)nɪŋ] *n* noircissement *m*.

black-eyed ['blækaɪd] *adj* **b.-e. pea,** dolique *m*.

blackfly ['blækflaɪ] *n F* (*insect*) mouche noire.

blackguard ['blægɑːd] *n Arch* fripouille *f*, canaille *f*.

blackhead ['blækhed] *n F* point noir (*sur le visage*).

blackheart ['blækhɑːt] *adj & n* **b. (cherry),** guigne noire.

blacking ['blækɪŋ] *n* **(a)** noircissement *m*; **(b)** *Ind* mise *f* à l'index (*d'un navire, d'une entreprise*); **(c)** *Arch* cirage *m* (*à chaussures*).

blackish ['blækɪʃ] *adj* noirâtre, tirant sur le noir.

blackjack¹ ['blækdʒæk] *n* **(a)** (*weapon*) nerf *m* de bœuf; **(b)** *Cards* vingt-et-un *m*.

blackjack² *vt* frapper avec un nerf de bœuf.

blacklead ['blækled] *vt Old-fashioned* passer (*un poêle etc*) à la mine de plomb.

blackleg¹ ['blækleg] *n Ind F* jaune *m*, briseur *m* de grève.

blackleg² *vi* (-gg-) *Ind* briser une grève, être un briseur de grève.

blacklist¹ ['blæklɪst] *n* liste noire; **to be on the b.,** être noté *ou* suspect.

blacklist² *vt* inscrire *ou* mettre (*qn, une entreprise etc*) sur la liste noire.

blackmail¹ ['blækmeɪl] *n* chantage *m*; extorsion *f* (*sous menace de scandale*); **emotional b.,** chantage aux sentiments.

blackmail² **1** *vt* soumettre (*qn*) à un chantage, *F* faire chanter (*qn*); **to be blackmailed,** être victime d'un chantage; **I'm being blackmailed for £5,000,** je suis victime d'un chantage, on me réclame 5 000 livres; **to b. s.o. into resigning/etc,** faire chanter qn pour qu'il démissionne/*etc*. **2** *vi* faire du chantage.

blackmailer ['blækmeɪlər] *n* maître-chanteur *m*, *pl* maîtres-chanteurs.

blackness ['blæknɪs] *n* **(a)** (*of hair etc*) noirceur *f*; **(b)** (*of sky*) obscurité *f*.

blackout ['blækaʊt] *n* **(a)** (*during war*) black-out *m*; *Fig* **to impose a news b.,** interdire la divulgation d'une information; (*in general*) imposer le black-out sur l'information; **(b)** *El* panne *f* d'électricité; **(c)** *Cin* fermeture *f* en fondu; **(d)** (*loss of consciousness*) évanouissement *m*; (*memory lapse*) trou *m* de mémoire.

Blackshirt ['blækʃɜːt] *n Pol* fasciste *m*, chemise noire.

blacksmith ['blæksmɪθ] *n* forgeron *m*; (*who shoes horses*) maréchal-ferrant *m*.

blackthorn ['blækθɔːn] *n* **(a)** (*shrub*) épine noire, prunier épineux, prunellier *m*; **(b)** (*stick*) gourdin *m* (d'épine).

blacktop ['blæktɒp] *n esp Am* **(a)** (*substance*) bitume *m*; **(b)** (*road*) route bitumée.

blackwater ['blækwɔːtər] *adj Med* **b. fever,** hématurie *f*.

bladder ['blædər] *n* **(a)** (*for urine*) vessie *f*; **to have a full b.,** avoir la vessie pleine; **(b)** (*sac*) vésicule *f*; **gall b.,** vésicule biliaire; **air b.,** (*of fish*) vésicule aérienne; (*of algae*) vésicule aérocyste; *Vet* cysticerque *m*; **(c)** vessie *f* (*de ballon*).

bladderwort ['blædəwɜːt] *n* (*plant*) utriculaire *f*.

bladderwrack ['blædəræk] *n* (*seaweed*) goémon jaune vésiculeux.

blade [bleɪd] *n* **(a)** lame *f* (*de couteau, d'épée, de patin, Bot de feuille*); couperet *m* (*de la guillotine*); feuille *f*, lame (*d'une scie*); **(b)** pale *f* (*d'aviron, d'hélice*); pelle *f* (*d'aviron*); ailette *f* (*de ventilateur, de turbine*); aube *f* (*de roue hydraulique*); fer *m* (*de bêche*); *Rail* aiguille *f* (*de croisement*); *Aut* balai *m* (*d'un essuie-glace*); *Phot* **blades of a shutter,** pales *ou* secteurs *mpl* d'un obturateur; **(c)** brin *m* (*d'herbe*); pampe *f* (*de blé*); *Bot* limbe *m*; **(d)** *Arch* (*sword*) sabre *m*, épée *f*.

bladed ['bleɪdɪd] *adj* à lame(s), à aile(s), à pales; **three-b.,** (*canif*) à trois lames; (*hélice*) à trois pales.

blah(-blah) ['blɑː(blɑː)] *n F* bla-bla *m*, baratin *m*; **it's all b.(-b.),** tout ça c'est du baratin; **it was very b.-b.,** (*of meeting etc*) ce n'était que du bavardage.

blame¹ [bleɪm] *n* **(a)** (*reproof*) reproches *mpl*; **to deserve b.,** mériter des reproches; **to be free from b.,** être au-dessus de tout reproche; **(b)** (*responsibility*) faute *f*; **to lay** *or* **put the b. (for sth) on s.o., to lay the b. (for sth) at s.o.'s door,** rejeter *ou* faire retomber le blâme *ou* la faute (de qch) sur qn; **to bear** *or* **take the b.,** endosser la faute *ou* la responsabilité; **to shift the b. onto s.o. else,** se décharger d'une faute sur qn; **where does the b. lie?,** à qui la faute?; **the b. lies with her,** c'est sa faute *ou* à cause d'elle.

blame² *vt* blâmer, condamner (*qn*); **to b. s.o. for sth,** blâmer qn de qch, reprocher qch à qn; **he can't be blamed for it,** on ne peut pas l'en blâmer; **I b. him, not her,** c'est à lui que je fais des reproches, pas à elle; **I b. myself,** je me sens responsable; **don't b. me,** ne me condamne pas; **I don't b. you,** (*I would have done the same*) je ne te le reproche pas; **I have nothing to b. myself for,** je n'ai rien à me reprocher; **to have only oneself to b., to have nobody to b. but oneself,** n'avoir à s'en prendre qu'à soi-même; **he is to b.,** c'est de sa faute; **the bad weather was to b.,** c'était à cause du mauvais temps; **the accident was blamed on the bad weather,** on a mis l'accident sur le compte du mauvais temps; **she was in no way to b.,** elle n'était en aucun cas à blâmer; **to b. sth on s.o.,** rejeter la faute *ou* la responsabilité de qch sur qn.

blamed [bleɪmd] *adj esp US Euph* sacré.

blameless ['bleɪmlɪs] *adj* innocent, irréprochable, irrépréhensible; (*vie*) sans reproche, irréprochable; **none of us is b.,** nous sommes tous responsables.

blamelessly ['bleɪmlɪslɪ] *adv* irréprochablement.

blanch [blɑːntʃ] **1** *vt* (*des légumes, des fruits*) blanchir. **2** *vi* (*of person*) blêmir, pâlir.

blancmange [blə'mɒnʒ] *n Culin* blanc-manger *m*, *pl* blancs-mangers.

bland [blænd] *adj* **(a)** (*person, speech*) affable; *Pej* doucereux, mielleux; (*sourire*) narquois; **(b)** (*air, food, drink*) doux, *f* douce; *Pej* fade.

blandly ['blændlɪ] *adv* avec affabilité; *Pej* mielleusement.

blandish ['blændɪʃ] *vt* cajoler, caresser, flatter.

blandishments ['blændɪʃmənts] *npl* cajoleries *fpl*, câlineries *fpl*, flatterie *f*.

blank¹ [blæŋk] *adj* **(a)** (*papier*) blanc, *f* blanche; (*page*) vierge, blanc; (*porte, fenêtre*) feint, aveugle; (*cartouche*) à blanc; **b. cheque,** chèque *m* en blanc; *Fig* carte blanche; **to give s.o. a b. cheque to do sth,** donner carte blanche à qn pour faire qch; *Com Fin* **b. credit,** crédit *m* en blanc; **b. space,** espace *m* vide, blanc *m*; **b. verse,** vers blancs *ou* non rimés; **b. voting paper,** bulletin blanc; *Cards* **to be b. in clubs,** ne pas avoir de trèfles dans son jeu; **(b)** (*existence*) vide; (*regard*) sans expression; **he gave me a b. look,** il m'a regardé d'un air sans expression; **my mind went b.,** je me sentais la tête vide; **to look b.,** avoir l'air confondu *ou* déconcerté *ou* ahuri; **a look of b. astonishment,** un air ébahi *ou* confondu; **(c)** (*impossibilité, refus*) absolu.

blank² *n* **(a)** (*in document etc*) blanc *m*, vide *m*; (*in memory*) trou *m*, lacune *f*, vide; *Am* formulaire *m*, formule *f* (*de télégramme etc*); *Mil* cartouche *f* à blanc; blanc (*de cible*); **to fire blanks,** tirer à blanc; **to leave blanks,** laisser des blancs; **his mind is a b.,** (*he has lost his memory*) il ne se souvient de rien; (*for the moment*) il a *ou* se sent la tête vide; *Cards* **to have a b. in clubs,** ne pas avoir des trèfles dans son jeu; **(b)** (*domino*) blanc *m*; (*in lottery*) billet blanc *ou* perdant; **to draw a b.,** (*in lottery*) tirer un mauvais numéro; *Fig* (*be unsuccessful*) éprouver une déception; *Am* (*be unable to remember*) avoir un trou de mémoire; **(c)** (*in minting coins*) flan *m* (*de métal*); *Metal MecE* flan; masselotte *f*; galette *f*; **(d)** *Typ* tiret *m* (*remplaçant un mot grossier etc*).

▶**blank off** *vtsep* obturer (*un orifice*).

▶**blank out 1** *vtsep* cacher; (*obscure*) obscurcir; **she's blanked out the memory,** elle a délibérément effacé cet événement de sa mémoire. **2** *vi* (*of person*) avoir un trou de mémoire.

blanket¹ ['blæŋkɪt] *n* couverture *f* (*de lit, de cheval*); *Fig* manteau *m* (*de brouillard etc*); *Fig* couche *f* (*de neige*); *Old-fashioned F* **to be born on the wrong side of the b.,** (*be illegitimate*) être un enfant bâtard; *Med* **b. bath,** = toilette d'un malade alité faite par une infirmière; *Sewing* **b. stitch,** point *m* de languette; **b. term,** terme général.

blanket² *vt* mettre une couverture à (*qch*); **the mountain was blanketed in fog/snow,** la montagne était couverte d'un manteau de brouillard/de neige.

blankly ['blæŋklɪ] *adv* (*regarder qn*) (*without expression*) sans expression, d'un air incompréhensif; (*in confusion*) d'un air déconcerté.

blankness ['blæŋknɪs] *n* **(a)** (*of person*) air confus *ou* décontenancé; **(b)** vide *m*, néant *m* (*de la pensée etc*); vacuité *f* (*d'un regard*).

blare¹ ['bleər] *n* sonnerie *f*, son *m*, accents cuivrés (*de la trompette*); **the b. of the brass band,** le son éclatant de la fanfare; **the b. of car horns,** le son de klaxons de voiture.

blare² *vi* (*of trumpet*) sonner; (*of car horn*) retentir; (*of radio*) *F* gueuler; **the band blared,** la fanfare éclata.

▶**blare away** *vi* (*of radio etc*) *F* gueuler.

▶**blare out 1** *vi* (*of trumpet*) sonner; (*of voice*) résonner; **his voice blared out over the loudspeaker,** sa voix résonnait dans les haut-parleurs. **2** *vtsep* (*of loudspeaker, band*) faire retentir.

blarney¹ ['blɑːnɪ] *n* cajolerie *f*, boniments *mpl*, flatterie séduisante; **don't give me any of your b.,** arrête tes boniments.

blarney² *vt* cajoler (*qn*), séduire (*qn*) par des propos flatteurs.

Blarney ['blɑːnɪ] *n F* **to have kissed the B. Stone,** avoir le don de la flatterie *ou* de la cajolerie.

blasé ['blɑːzeɪ] *adj* blasé; **she's very b. about going to Australia,** pour ce qui est des voyages en Australie elle est très blasée.

blaspheme [blæs'fiːm] **1** *vi* blasphémer. **2** *vt* **to b. the name of God,** blasphémer le saint nom de Dieu.

blasphemer [blæs'fiːmər] *n* blasphémateur, -trice.

blasphemous ['blæsfəməs] *adj* (*person*) blasphémateur, -trice; (*words etc*) blasphématoire, impie.

blasphemously ['blæsfəməslɪ] *adv* avec blasphème, avec impiété; **to speak b.,** blasphémer.

blasphemy ['blæsfəmɪ] *n* blasphème *m*.

blast¹ [blɑːst] *n* **(a)** (*gust*) bouffée *f* de vent, coup *m* de vent; rafale *f* (*de vent*); **b. of steam,** jet *m* de vapeur; **(b)** coup *m* (*de sifflet, de sirène*); *Mil* **whistle b.,** commandement *m* au sifflet; **b. on the trumpet,** sonnerie *f* de trompette; **(c)** *Metal* air *m*, vent *m* (*de la soufflerie*); soufflerie *f*, soufflage *m* (*d'un haut fourneau*); **b. furnace,** haut fourneau; **to be in b.,** (*of furnace*) être allumé *ou* en marche; **to be** *or* **be working at full b.,** être en pleine activité, travailler à plein rendement; *F* **to turn the radio on full b.,** faire gueuler *ou* brailler la radio; **(d)** souffle *f* (*d'une bombe, d'une explosion etc*); *Min* explosion *f*, coup *m* de mine; charge *f* d'explosif; **to fire a b.,** faire jouer une mine, faire partir un pétard; **a lot of people were killed by the b.,** beaucoup de gens ont été tués par l'explosion; **b. hole,** *Min* pétard *m*, trou *m* de mine; *Mil* fourneau *m* de mine.

blast² *int* mince!, zut!

blast³ 1 *vt* **(a)** *Min* faire sauter (*qch*) (*à la dynamite etc*); **(b)** (*of frost*) brûler, flétrir (*une plante*); (*of lightning*) foudroyer (*un arbre etc*); *Fig* **to b. s.o.'s hopes,** anéantir les espoirs de qn; **(c)** *F* envoyer *(qn)* au diable; **b. it!,** zut!; **b. you/him!,** que le diable t'emporte/l'emporte!; **(d)** *F (criticize)* démolir *(qn, qch)*. **2** *vi (of brass instrument)* sonner; *(of radio etc)* hurler, brailler.

►**blast away** *vi* **(a)** *(of radio etc)* hurler, brailler; **(b)** *(with gun, rifle etc)* tirer en rafales.

►**blast off** *vi (of rocket, missile)* décoller, être mis à feu.

blasted ['blɑːstɪd] *adj* **(a)** *(lande)* désolé; *(chêne)* foudroyé; **(b)** *F* sacré; **you b. idiot!,** espèce d'idiot!

blasting ['blɑːstɪŋ] *n* **(a)** travail *m* aux explosifs; exploitation *f* à la mine; **beware of b.!,** attention aux coups de mine!; **(b)** foudroiement *m (d'un arbre)*; *Fig* destruction *f*, anéantissement *m (d'un espoir etc)*; **(c)** *(severe criticism)* critique *f* féroce; **his latest novel got a b. from reviewers,** son dernier roman a été démoli par les critiques.

blastoderm ['blæstəʊdɜːm] *n Biol* blastoderme *m*.

blastoff ['blɑːstɒf] *n* décollage *m (d'une fusée)*; **b. is at 2 o'clock,** la fusée décollera à deux heures.

blatancy ['bleɪtənsɪ] *n* **(a)** caractère flagrant *(d'une injustice, d'un crime etc)*; **(b)** *(of person, manners)* vulgarité criarde.

blatant ['bleɪtənt] *adj* **(a)** *(injustice)* criant; *(mensonge)* flagrant; **don't be so b.,** *(in your approach)* sois un peu plus diplomate; **(b)** *(person, manners)* d'une vulgarité criarde.

blatantly ['bleɪtəntlɪ] *adv (see adj)* **(a)** d'une manière flagrante; **(b)** avec une vulgarité criarde.

blather¹ ['blæðər] *n F* paroles *fpl* en l'air, bêtises *fpl*.

blather² *vi F* parler à tort et à travers, dire des bêtises.

blaze¹ [bleɪz] *n* **(a)** *(fire)* flamme(s) *f(pl)*, feu *m*; *(in fireplace)* flambée *f*; **many people died in the b.,** beaucoup de gens ont péri dans les flammes; **in a b.,** en feu, en flammes; **b. of anger,** éclat *m* de colère; **in a b. of anger,** enflammé de colère; **(b)** flamboiement *m (du soleil)*; éclat *m (des couleurs, des diamants etc)*; **the garden was a b. of colour,** le jardin était resplendissant de couleur; **in the full b. of publicity,** sous les feux de la rampe; **(c)** *F* **go to blazes!,** allez au diable!; **what the blazes does he want?,** qu'est-ce qu'il veut au juste?, que diable veut-il?; **to work like blazes,** travailler furieusement; **to run like blazes,** courir comme un dératé; **what the blazes is she doing?,** qu'est-ce qu'elle est donc en train de faire?, que diable est-elle en train de faire?

blaze² *vi* **(a)** *(of fire etc)* flamber; **a fire was blazing in the grate,** un feu flambait au foyer; **the house was blazing,** *(on fire)* la maison était embrasée; **to b. with anger,** *(of person)* être enflammé de colère; **his eyes were blazing with anger,** ses yeux lançaient des éclairs de colère; **(b)** *(of sun, colours)* flamboyer.

blaze³ *n* **(a)** *(on face of horse, ox)* marque allongée blanche; **(b)** *(on tree)* **b. (mark),** blanchis *m*, griffe *f*.

blaze⁴ *vt* griffer, blanchir, marteler *(un arbre)*; **to b. a trail,** tracer un chemin; *Fig* faire œuvre de pionnier; poser des jalons *(dans une science etc)*.

►**blaze down** *vi (of sun)* taper; **the sun was blazing down on the beach,** le soleil dardait *ou* déversait ses rayons sur la plage.

►**blaze up** *vi (of fire)* s'embraser; s'enflammer; *F (of person)* s'emporter *(de colère)*.

blazer ['bleɪzər] *n (vêtement)* blazer *m*.

blazing ['bleɪzɪŋ] **1** *n* martelage *m*, griffage *m (des arbres)*. **2** *adj* **(a)** *(on fire)* en feu, enflammé; *(navire)* embrasé; **(b)** *(feu, soleil)* flambant, ardent; **b. star,** *Her* comète *f*; *Bot* alétris *m*; **(c)** *F (mensonge)* éclatant; **a b. row,** une dispute violente.

blazon¹ ['bleɪzən] *n Her* blason *m (composant un écu)*; *(coat of arms)* armoiries *fpl*; *(flag)* étendard armorié.

blazon² *vt* **(a)** *Her (describe)* blasonner *(des armoiries)*; *(mark, identify)* marquer *(qch)* aux armoiries de qn; **(b)** embellir, orner *(de dessins héraldiques)*.

►**blazon abroad** *vtsep* publier *(une nouvelle)* à son de trompe.

►**blazon out** *vtsep* publier *ou* proclamer *(qch)* à son de trompe.

bldg *abbr* **building**.

bleach¹ [bliːtʃ] *n (for hair)* décolorant *m*; **(household) b.,** eau *f* de Javel.

bleach² **1** *vt Tex etc* blanchir; *Ch etc* décolorer *(les cheveux)*; **hair/sheets bleached by the sun,** cheveux/draps décolorés par le soleil. **2** *vi Tex etc* blanchir; *Ch etc* se décolorer; **do not b.,** *(washing instruction)* ne pas passer à l'eau de Javel.

bleachers ['bliːtʃəz] *npl Am Sp* gradins *mpl*.

bleaching ['bliːtʃɪŋ] *n Tex etc* blanchiment *m*; *(of hair)* & *Ch* décoloration *f*; **b. agent,** *Tex* produit blanchissant; *Ch* décolorant *m*.

bleak¹ [bliːk] *adj* **(a)** *(temps)* morne, triste; *(terrain)* exposé au vent; *(vent)* froid; **(b)** *Fig (avenir)* lugubre; *(sourire)* pâle; **the prospects are b.,** les perspectives sont peu encourageantes.

bleak² *n (fish)* ablette *f*.

bleakly ['bliːklɪ] *adv* d'un air morne, tristement.

bleakness ['bliːknɪs] *n (of weather)* aspect *m* morne, tristesse *f*; *Fig* **the b. of the future,** l'absence de futur.

blearily ['blɪərɪlɪ] *adv (to look at s.o.)* les yeux troubles.

bleary ['blɪərɪ] *adj* **(a)** *(eyes)* trouble; **(b)** *(outline)* vague, imprécis.

bleary-eyed [blɪərɪ'aɪd] *adj* aux yeux troubles; **to be b.-e. with lack of sleep,** avoir les yeux brouillés (à cause du manque de sommeil).

bleat¹ [bliːt] *n (of sheep)* bêlement *m*; *Fig (complaint)* plainte *f*.

bleat² *vi* **(a)** *(of sheep)* bêler; *(of ram)* blatérer; *(of goat, old man etc)* chevroter; **(b)** *Fig (complain)* se plaindre; *(talk nonsense)* dire des bêtises; **what's he bleating about?,** de quoi se plaint-il?

bleating ['bliːtɪŋ] **1** *adj* bêlant; *(voice)* chevrotant. **2** *n* **(a)** *(of sheep)* bêlement *m*; **(b)** *(complaining)* plaintes *fpl*.

bleed [bliːd] *v (pt & pp* **bled** [bled]) **1** *vi* **(a)** saigner; **his nose is bleeding,** il saigne du nez; **to b. to death,** mourir d'avoir perdu trop de sang; *Iron* **my heart bleeds for you/her/***etc*, j'en ai le cœur brisé pour toi/elle/*etc*; **(b)** *(of tree etc)* pleurer, perdre sa sève; **(c)** *Constr etc (of riveted joints)* fuir; **b. valve,** soupape *f* de purge; **(d)** *(of colour)* s'étendre, couler *(au lavage)*. **2** *vt* **(a)** *Med* saigner *(qn)*; *F* **to b. s.o.,** *(for money)* saigner qn; **to b. s.o. white,** saigner qn à blanc; **(b)** *MecE* purger *(les freins, une canalisation etc)*.

bleeder ['bliːdər] *n* **(a)** *Sl Pej* salaud *m*; **poor b.,** pauvre type; **(b)** *Tech* dispositif *m* de drainage, purgeur *m*.

bleeding ['bliːdɪŋ] **1** *adj* **(a)** saignant; **with a b. heart,** le cœur brisé; *Fig* **b. heart,** *Fig* personne au grand cœur; *(plant)* cœur-de-Marie *m*, *pl* cœurs-de-Marie; cœur-de-Jeannette *m*, *pl* cœurs-de-Jeannette; **(b)** *Br Sl* sacré; **you b. liar!,** sacré menteur! **2** *n* **(a)** hémorragie *f*; *Bot* écoulement *m* de sève; *(of vine etc)* pleurs *mpl*; **b. at the nose,** saignement *m* de nez; **I can't stop the b.,** je n'arrive pas à arrêter le sang; **(b)** *Arch Med* saignée *f*; **(c)** *Constr etc* fuite *f (d'eau, de gaz etc)*.

bleeding-heart [bliːdɪŋ'hɑːt] *adj* **b.-h. liberals,** = des sentimentaux.

bleep¹ [bliːp] **1** *vi (of satellite, radio signal)* faire bip-bip. **2** *vt* appeler *(qn)* par l'intermédiaire d'un interphone *ou* d'une radio *etc*.

bleep²(-bleep) *n* bip-bip *m (d'un satellite etc)*.

bleeper ['bliːpər] *n* récepteur *m* d'appel *ou* de poche.

bleeping ['bliːpɪŋ] *n* bip-bip *m (d'un satellite etc)*.

blemish¹ ['blemɪʃ] *n* **(a)** *Fig (flaw)* défaut *m*; imperfection *f (physique ou morale)*; **there's not a b. on her record,** il n'y a rien à redire à ses états de service; **(b)** *(mark)* tache *f*, tare *f*; **there's not a b. on it,** *(of piece of furniture etc)* il n'y a pas un défaut.

blemish² *vt* **(a)** *Fig* tacher, entacher, ternir *(une réputation etc)*; **(b)** abîmer, gâter *(une œuvre d'art etc)*.

blench¹ [blentʃ] *vi* sourciller, broncher; **without blenching,** sans sourciller.

blench² *vi* blêmir; **to b. with terror,** pâlir de terreur.

blend¹ [blend] *n* mélange *m (de thés, de whiskys, de tabacs)*.

blend² **1** *vt* mélanger *(des thés, des cafés, des whiskys)*; **to b. sth with sth,** mêler qch à *ou* avec qch; **to b. one colour with another,** *(mix)* mélanger une couleur avec une autre, fondre deux couleurs; *(harmonize)* allier *ou* marier deux couleurs. **2** *vi* se mêler, se mélanger, se confondre **(into,** en); *(of voices etc)* se marier harmonieusement; *(of colours)* s'allier, se marier; *(of ideas etc)* fusionner; **oil does not b. with water,** l'huile ne se dissout pas dans l'eau; **the colours b. well,** les couleurs sont bien agencées *ou* vont bien ensemble.

►**blend in** **1** *vi (harmonize)* s'harmoniser, se marier **(with,** avec); **that new building doesn't b. in with its surroundings,** ce nouveau bâtiment ne se marie pas bien avec son environnement. **2** *vtsep (mix)* incorporer *(la farine)*.

blender ['blendər] *n (kitchen appliance)* mixer *m*, mixeur *m*.

blending ['blendɪŋ] *n* mélange *m (de thés, de tabacs etc)*; alliance *f (de deux qualités)*; *(in winemaking)* assemblage *m*, coupage *m*; *Ch Metal* alliage *m (de métaux)*.

bless [bles] *vt (pt & pp* **blessed** [blest]; *pp Arch* **blest**

[blest]) **(a)** (*of God, priest*) bénir (*le peuple*); consacrer, bénir (*une cloche*); **God b. you!,** que (le bon) Dieu vous bénisse!; **b. you!,** (*when s.o. sneezes*) à vos souhaits!; *F* **b. you for doing the washing-up,** merci bien d'avoir fait la vaisselle; **(b) to be blessed with sth,** jouir de qch; avoir le bonheur de posséder qch; **to be blessed with a cheerful disposition,** être doué d'un heureux caractère; **they have been blessed with two fine children,** ils ont eu la chance d'avoir deux enfants adorables; *Hum* **they are blessed with eight children,** ils ont huit enfants sur les bras; *F* **he hasn't a penny to b. himself with,** il n'a pas le sou; **(c) to b. God,** bénir *ou* adorer Dieu; **(d)** *Old-fashioned* **b. me!, (God) b. my soul!,** mon Dieu!; **well, I'm blest!,** par exemple!; **I'm blest if I know,** que le diable m'emporte si je le sais.

blessed ['blesɪd] *adj* **(a)** *Cathol etc* bienheureux; **the late king, of b. memory,** le feu roi, d'heureuse mémoire; *Bible* **b. are the poor in spirit,** heureux les pauvres en esprit; **(b)** *F* **every b. day,** tous les jours que Dieu fait; **the whole b. day,** toute la sainte journée; **the whole b. lot,** tout le bazar, tout le bataclan.

blessedness ['blesɪdnɪs] *n* félicité *f*; *Rel* béatitude *f*.

blessing ['blesɪŋ] *n* bénédiction *f*; **to give** *or* **pronounce the b.,** donner la bénédiction; **to ask** *or* **say a b.,** (*at meal*) dire le bénédicité; **the blessings of God,** les grâces *fpl* de Dieu; **the blessings of civilisation,** les avantages *mpl ou* bienfaits *mpl* de la civilisation; **it turned out to be a b. in disguise,** à la longue j'ai *ou* il a *etc* pu m'en *ou* s'en *etc* féliciter; **losing my job was a b. in disguise,** finalement ça a été une bonne chose de perdre mon travail; **to count one's blessings,** s'estimer heureux avec ce qu'on a; **count your blessings,** ne te plains pas, estime-toi heureux; **to give a plan one's b.,** donner sa bénédiction à un projet; **it's a b. no-one was hurt,** c'est une bénédiction que personne n'ait été blessé.

blest [blest] **1** *adj* bienheureux. **2 the B.,** (*used as pl*) les Bienheureux *mpl*, les saints *mpl* au Paradis.

blether¹ ['bleðər] *n F* **(a)** (*talk*) paroles *fpl* en l'air; bêtises *fpl*; **(b)** (*person*) = personne qui parle à tort et à travers.

blether² *vi F* parler à tort et à travers, dire des bêtises; **blethering idiot,** espèce *f* d'idiot.

blight¹ [blaɪt] *n* **(a)** *Agr* rouille *f* (*des céréales*); brunissure *f* (*des pommes de terre*); cloque *f* (*des pêches etc*); **(b)** *Fig* influence *f* néfaste; **his arrival cast a b. over the company,** son arrivée a jeté un froid sur la compagnie.

blight² *vt Agr* rouiller (*le blé*); (*of wind*) flétrir; **blighted leaf,** feuille cloquée; *Fig* **to b. s.o.'s hopes,** ruiner les espérances de qn; *Fig* **a marriage blighted by money problems,** un mariage assombri par des problèmes d'argent.

blighter ['blaɪtər] *n F* **(a)** individu *m*, type *m*; **poor b.,** pauvre type; **(you) lucky b.!,** veinard!; **(b)** *Pej* salaud *m*; **the little b.,** le petit coquin.

Blighty ['blaɪtɪ] *n Old-fashioned Br Mil F* l'Angleterre *f*, le pays.

blimey ['blaɪmɪ] *int Br Sl* mince alors!

blimp [blɪmp] *n* **(a)** *Av* (petit) dirigeable *m* de reconnaissance; **(b)** *Fig* réactionnaire endurci; **a real Colonel B.,** une vraie culotte de peau, un scro(n)gneugneu.

blind¹ [blaɪnd] **1** *adj* **(a)** aveugle; **b. from birth,** aveugle de naissance; **b. in one eye,** borgne; **a b. man/woman,** un/une aveugle; **b. man's bluff,** (*game*) colin-maillard *m*; **to play b. man's bluff,** jouer à colin-maillard; **to be struck b.,** être frappé de cécité; **he's as b. as a bat,** il est myope comme une taupe; **b. with anger,** aveuglé par la colère; **b. obedience,** soumission aveugle; **to turn a b. eye on** *or* **to sth,** fermer les yeux sur qch, refuser de voir qch; *Av* **b. flying,** vol *m* sans visibilité, vol en P.S.V. (*pilotage sans visibilité*); *F* **he didn't take a b. bit of notice,** il n'a pas fait la moindre attention; **to be b. to s.o.'s faults,** ne pas voir *ou* être aveugle aux défauts de qn; *Prov* **love is b.,** l'amour est aveugle; **in a b. stupor,** (*drunk*) complètement soûl, bourré; **b. spot,** *Anat* papille *f* optique; (*on road*) angle mort; *Fig* côté faible (*de qn*); **I have a b. spot where maths are concerned,** (*don't understand them*) je n'y connais rien en mathématiques;

(b) (*bend*) masqué, sans visibilité; **b. ditch,** saut *m* de loup; *Med* **double b. test,** = épreuve pratiquée à l'insu du malade et du médecin; *F* **b. date,** rendez-vous *m* (*avec qn qu'on ne connaît pas*); inconnu(e) (*avec qui on a rendez-vous*); **I have a b. date tonight,** j'ai un rendez-vous avec un(e) inconnu(e); **I've fixed you up with a b. date,** je t'ai organisé une rencontre avec une personne que tu ne connais pas; *Rugby* **b. side,** côté fermé;

(c) (*trou, fistule*) borgne; (*chemin, tunnel*) sans issue; *Archit* faux (*porte*); (*fenêtre, porte*) feint, aveugle; **b. alley,** impasse *f*, cul-de-sac *m*, *pl* culs-de-sac; *Fig* impasse; **b.-alley job,** occupation *f ou* situation *f* sans avenir; *Rail* **b. siding,** cul-de-sac.

2 *n* **the b.,** (*used as pl*) les aveugles *mpl*; **she goes to the b. school,** elle est dans une école pour aveugles *ou* pour non-voyants.

3 *adv* **to fire b.,** tirer au jugé; *Av* **to fly b.,** voler à l'aveuglette; *Culin* **to bake b.,** cuire un fond de tarte (sans rien dessus); **bake b. for five minutes,** cuire le fond de tarte cinq minutes; *F* **to go at a thing b.,** se lancer à l'aveuglette dans une entreprise; **b. drunk,** complètement ivre *ou* soûl.

blind² *vt* **(a)** aveugler (*qn*); frapper (*qn*) de cécité; (*dazzle*) aveugler, éblouir (*qn*); **blinded ex-service men,** aveugles *mpl* de guerre; **blinded by passion,** aveuglé par la passion; **love blinded her to his faults,** aveuglée par l'amour, elle n'a pas vu ses défauts; **to b. s.o. to the facts,** cacher les faits à qn; *Fig* **don't b. me with science,** pas la peine de m'éblouir avec ta science; **(b)** *Constr* ensabler (*une chaussée, une voie ferrée*); *Mil Min* blinder (*une galerie etc*).

blind³ *n* **(a)** *Br* (*at window*) store *m* (à l'italienne); **shop b.,** (*over pavement*) banne *f*; **(b)** (*pretext*) prétexte *m*, masque *m*; **his attitude was only a b.,** son attitude n'était qu'un prétexte; **(c)** *Am* œillère *f* (*de cheval*).

blinder ['blaɪndər] *n* **(a)** *Br Sl* **to go on a b.,** (*get very drunk*) se bourrer (la gueule); **(b)** *Sp* (*outstanding feat*) **he played a b. of a game,** il a eu un jeu spectaculaire; **the first goal was a b.,** le premier but a été spectaculaire; **(c)** *Am* (*for horse*) œillère *f*.

blindfold¹ ['blaɪndfəʊld] **1** *adj* les yeux bandés; *Chess* **b. player,** joueur *m* qui joue sans voir l'échiquier. **2** *adv* (*recklessly*) aveuglément; **I can do it b.,** (*I am very familiar with the task*) je pourrais le faire les yeux fermés. **3** *n* bandeau *m* sur les yeux; **they put a b. over my eyes,** ils m'ont mis un bandeau sur les yeux.

blindfold² *vt* bander les yeux à *ou* de (*qn*), couvrir les yeux de (*qn*) avec un bandeau.

blinding ['blaɪndɪŋ] **1** *adj* aveuglant; **b. headache,** mal de tête fou; *Aut* **b. headlights,** phares éblouissants *ou* aveuglants. **2** *n* **(a)** éblouissement *m* (*par des phares etc*); **(b)** *Constr* ensablement *m*; *Mil* blindage *m*; **(c)** *Constr* couche *f* de sable (*sur une route*).

blindly ['blaɪndlɪ] *adv* **(a)** (*look at*) sans le *ou* la *etc* voir; (*grope*) à l'aveuglette; (*obey*) aveuglément; **(b)** (*unthinkingly*) à l'aveugle, sans réflexion.

blindness ['blaɪndnɪs] *n* **(a)** cécité *f*; **(b)** *Fig* aveuglement *m*; **b. to the facts,** refus *m* d'envisager les faits.

blindstitch ['blaɪndstɪtʃ] *n Sewing* point perdu.

blindworm ['blaɪndwɜːm] *n* orvet *m*.

blink¹ [blɪŋk] *n* **(a)** (*of eyes*) battement *m*, clignotement *m ou* clignement *m* de paupières; **(b)** (*of light*) lueur momentanée; **(c)** *Br Sl* **on the b.,** (*of television set etc*) en panne, qui fait des siennes.

blink² *vi* **(a)** battre *ou* cligner des paupières, clignoter; **(b)** (*of light*) clignoter, vaciller; **(c) to b. at the fact that ...,** nier le fait que ...; **to b. at the facts** fermer les yeux sur la vérité.

▶blink away *vtsep* refouler (*une larme*) d'un battement de paupières.

blinker¹ ['blɪŋkər] *n* **(a)** (*for horse*) & *Fig* œillère *f*; **(b)** phare *m* à éclats (*sur un aérodrome*); *Aut* clignotant *m*.

blinker² *vt* mettre des œillères à (*un cheval*); *Fig* **that's very blinkered thinking on their part,** ils ont des œillères.

blinking ['blɪŋkɪŋ] **1** *adj* **(a)** (*eyes*) clignotant; **(b)** (*light*) papillotant, clignotant; **(c)** *Old-fashioned Br F* **what a b. nuisance!,** quelle barbe!; **b. idiot!,** espèce d'idiot!; **a b. good meal,** un repas sacrément bon; **I b. well DID see her there,** je l'y ai vue de mes propres yeux. **2** *n* **(a)** (*of eyes*) clignotement *m*; **(b)** (*of light*) papillotage *m*.

blintz(e) [blɪnts] *n Am Culin* crêpe fourrée (*au fromage, aux fruits etc*).

blip [blɪp] *n* (*of radar*) spot *m* (*sur l'écran*); (*noise*) top *m* d'écho.

bliss [blɪs] *n* béatitude *f*, félicité *f*; **breakfast in bed — what b.!,** le petit déjeuner au lit — quelle joie!

blissful ['blɪsfʊl] *adj* (bien)heureux; **b. days,** jours sereins; **to be in b. ignorance,** être dans l'ignorance la plus totale.

blissfully ['blɪsfʊlɪ] *adv* heureusement; **b. happy,** au comble du bonheur; **to be b. unaware that ...,** n'avoir aucun soupçon que ... .

blister¹ ['blɪstər] *n* **(a)** (*on skin*) ampoule *f*, cloque *f*; **(b)**

(*on paint*) cloque *f*, boursouflure *f*; (*on glass*) bulle *f*; *Metal* soufflure *f*; **(c)** *Com* **b. pack,** (*for pills etc*) conditionnement transparent par plusieurs unités; (*for larger items*) emballage *m* coque; **(d)** *Med Arch* vésicatoire *m*.

blister[2] **1** *vt* **(a)** provoquer des ampoules sur (*la main etc*); **to have a blistered heel,** avoir une ampoule au talon; **(b)** *Med Arch* appliquer un vésicatoire sur (*la peau*). **2** *vi* **(a)** se couvrir d'ampoules; **(b)** (*of paint*) cloquer, gondoler.

blistering ['blɪstərɪŋ] **1** *adj* **(a)** (*sun, heat*) brûlant, ardent; **(b)** (*remark etc*) cinglant, mordant, caustique; (*attaque*) foudroyant; **(c)** *Med Arch* (*emplâtre*) vésicant. **2** *n* **(a)** formation *f* d'ampoules (*à la peau*); **(b)** cloquage *m*, gondolage *m* (*de la peinture*); **(c)** *Med Arch* vésication *f*.

blithe ['blaɪð] *adj* joyeux, folâtre.

blithely ['blaɪðlɪ] *adv* joyeusement, allègrement; **she b. ignored him,** elle l'a ignoré avec désinvolture.

blithering ['blɪðərɪŋ] *adj F* sacré; **b. idiot!,** espèce d'idiot!

BLitt [biː'lɪt] *n* (*abbr* **Bachelor of Letters**) B. ès L..

blitz[1] [blɪts] *n* blitz *m*, bombardement aérien; *Fig* **to have a b. on sth,** s'attaquer à qch; *Fig* **the b. of holiday advertisements starts immediately after Christmas,** dès que les fêtes sont finies, on est bombardé de publicité par les agences de voyage.

blitz[2] *vt* bombarder; **the house was blitzed,** la maison a été endommagée *ou* détruite par un bombardement.

blizzard ['blɪzəd] *n* blizzard *m*, tempête *f* de neige.

bloat [bləʊt] **1** *vt* boursoufler, gonfler, bouffir. **2** *vi* se gonfler, se bouffir.

bloated ['bləʊtɪd] *adj* gonflé, bouffi, boursouflé; **to feel b.,** (*because of water retention, overeating*) se sentir gonflé.

bloater ['bləʊtər] *n Com* hareng bouffi.

blob [blɒb] *n* tache *f* (*de couleur*); pâté *m* (*d'encre*).

bloc [blɒk] *n Pol etc* bloc *m*.

block[1] [blɒk] *n* **(a)** bloc *m* (*de marbre etc*); tronçon *m* (*de bois*); quartier *m* (*de roche*); carreau *m* (*de pierre taillée*); brique *f* (*de verre*); tête *f* à perruque (*de coiffeur*); forme *f* (*pour chapeaux*); **like a b. of stone,** (*transfixed*) immobile; (*unfeeling*) dur; (*not speaking*) silencieux, muet; *Am* **to be on the b.,** (*up for auction*) être mis aux enchères; *Aut* **engine b.,** bloc moteur; **blocks,** (*for children*) (jeu *m* de) cubes *mpl*; **b. diagram,** schéma fonctionnel;

(b) (*for chopping*) billot *m*; *Hist* **to perish on the b.,** périr sur le billot;

(c) (*for getting on horse*) montoir *m*; (*for athletes*) bloc *m* de départ;

(d) (*chock*) tin *m*, cale *f*; **angle blocks,** coins *mpl*; **to put a car up on blocks,** mettre une voiture sur cales;

(e) sabot *m* (*de frein*);

(f) *Sl* tête *f*, caboche *f*; **I'll knock your b. off!,** je vais t'amocher la figure!;

(g) *esp Am* bloc *m ou* pâté *m* de maisons (*entre quatre rues*); **he lives two blocks from us,** il habite à deux rues de nous; **it's two blocks north/south of here,** c'est à deux rues d'ici vers le nord/sud; **we live on the same b.,** nous habitons dans le même pâté de maisons; **to walk round the b.,** faire le tour du pâté de maisons; **b. of flats,** immeuble divisé en appartements; **office b.,** immeuble de bureaux; **b. association,** association *f* de riverains;

(h) *Austr* quartier *m* (*d'une ville*); lot *m* (*de terrains*);

(i) bloc *m* (*de papier, à dessin*); *Fin* **b. of shares,** tranche *f* d'actions; **b. booking,** location *f* (*de places de théâtre etc*) en bloc;

(j) **traffic b.,** embouteillage *m*; **mental b.,** blocage *m* psychologique; **I have a mental b. about computers,** je fais un blocage psychologique avec les ordinateurs;

(k) *Rail* canton *m*, tronçon *m* (*de ligne*); **b. system,** bloc-système *m*; **b. section,** cantonnement *m*;

(l) (*in engraving*) (*wood*) planche *f*; bois *m*; *Typ* (*metal*) cliché *m*; **b. process,** phototypographie *f*; *Typ* **b. letter,** lettre moulée; **b. letters,** le moulé; **to write sth in b. capitals,** écrire qch en majuscules d'imprimerie; *Carp* **sandpaper b.,** cale *f*; **mitre b.,** boîte *f* à onglets;

(m) *Nau etc* (*casing*) chape *f*; (*pulley*) poulie *f*; **b. and tackle,** moufle *f*; palan *m*;

(n) *Comptr* bloc *m*.

block[2] *vt* **(a)** bloquer, obstruer (*un passage etc*); bloquer, enrayer (*une roue*); entraver, gêner (*la circulation*); arrêter (*le progrès*); **to b. s.o.'s way,** barrer le passage *ou* le chemin à qn; **to b. the view,** cacher la vue; *Parl* **to b. a bill,** faire obstruction à un projet de loi; **(b)** *Cr* arrêter (*la balle*) sans la relancer, bloquer (*la balle*); (*in dominoes*) fermer (*le jeu*); *Fb etc* gêner (*un adversaire*); *Cards* **to b. a suit,** faire une impasse; **(c)** gaufrer, frapper (*la couverture d'un livre*); enformer (*un chapeau*); cambrer la forme de (*un soulier*); **(d)** *Comptr* (*text*) bloquer.

▶**block in** *vtsep esp Aut* empêcher (*qn*) de sortir, bloquer le passage à (*qn*); **the man next door has blocked me in again,** le voisin m'a encore empêché de sortir (*du garage, du parking etc*).

▶**block off** *vtsep* barrer (*une rue*).

▶**block out** *vtsep* **(a)** (*prevent entry of*) empêcher d'entrer *ou* de passer; **those trees b. out all the sun,** ces arbres empêchent le soleil de passer; **(b)** (*draft*) ébaucher, esquisser (*un livre, un projet*).

▶**block up** *vtsep* **(a)** (*close*) boucher, bloquer, fermer (*un trou*); boucher, murer (*une porte, une fenêtre*); *Nau* bâcler (*un port*); **(b)** (*clog*) obstruer, engorger (*un tuyau etc*); boucher (*un évier*); **my nose is blocked up,** j'ai le nez bouché.

blockade[1] [blɒ'keɪd] *n* **(a)** *Mil Nau* blocus *m*; **to run the b.,** forcer le blocus; **b. runner,** forceur *m* de blocus; **(b)** *Am* encombrement *m*, embouteillage *m* (*d'une rue*).

blockade[2] *vt* **(a)** bloquer (*une ville, un port*); faire le blocus de (*une place forte*); **(b)** *Am* bloquer (*la circulation*); encombrer (*une rue*).

blockage ['blɒkɪdʒ] *n* obstruction *f* (*d'un tuyau, d'une artère etc*); embouteillage *m* (*d'une rue*).

blockbuster ['blɒkbʌstər] *n Mil* bombe *f* de très gros calibre; **his speech was a real b.,** (*influential*) son discours a eu une très grande portée; (*upset people*) son discours a causé beaucoup de consternation; **this show will be a b.,** ce spectacle aura un succès fou; **a b. of a film,** un film à grand spectacle *ou* commercial.

blockhead ['blɒkhed] *n F* lourdaud *m*.

blockhouse ['blɒkhaʊs] *n Mil* blockhaus *m*.

blocking ['blɒkɪŋ] *n* **(a)** encombrement *m*, embouteillage *m* (*d'une rue*); murage *m* (*d'une porte etc*); blocus *m* (*d'un port*); *Rail* **b. device,** dispositif bloqueur; **(b)** *El* blocage *m* (*du courant*); **(c)** (*of book binding*) gaufrage *m*, frappe *f*.

bloke [bləʊk] *n Br F* (*man*) type *m*.

blond, *f* **blonde** [blɒnd] *adj & n* blond, *f* blonde.

blood[1] [blʌd] *n* sang *m*; **to give b.,** (*of donor*) donner du sang; **his b. will be on your hands,** tu auras son sang sur les mains, tu seras responsable de sa mort; *Fig* **to sweat b.,** suer sang et eau; *Fig* **his b. is up,** il est furieux; **it makes my b. boil/run cold,** cela me fait bouillir/me glace le sang; **to commit a crime in cold b.,** commettre un crime de sang-froid; *Fig* **the committee needs new** *or* **fresh b.,** le comité a besoin d'être rajeuni; **to shed** *or* **spill b.,** verser le sang; **to draw b.,** faire saigner qn; *F* **to be out for b.,** chercher à se venger; *F* **to be after** *or* **out for s.o.'s b.,** vouloir se venger de qn, en vouloir à qn; **the boss is after your b.,** le patron en a après toi; *Prov* **it's like trying to get b. out of a stone,** c'est comme si on se heurtait à un mur; **the theatre is in her b.,** (*she comes from a theatrical family*) elle a le théâtre dans le sang; **the call of b.,** la voix du sang; **b. is thicker than water,** nous sommes unis par la voix *ou* la force du sang; **prince of the b.,** prince *m* du sang; *Prov* **b. will tell,** bon sang ne peut mentir; **warm the milk until it is at b. heat,** chauffe le lait jusqu'à ce qu'il atteigne la température du corps; **b. bank,** banque *f* du sang; **b. bath,** carnage *m*, massacre *m*; **b. blister,** pinçon *m*; **b. brother,** frère *m* de sang; **b. cell,** globule sanguin; **b. count,** numération *f* globulaire; **b. donor,** donneur, -euse de sang; *Sp Med* **b. doping,** = transfusion sanguine (*comme méthode de dopage*); **b. group,** groupe sanguin; **what b. group are you?,** quel est votre groupe sanguin?; **b. horse,** (cheval *m*) pur-sang *m inv*; **b. money,** prix *m* du sang; **b. orange,** sanguine *f*; **b. plasma,** plasma sanguin; **b. poisoning,** septicémie *f*, toxémie *f*; **b. pressure,** tension *f* (artérielle); **to have high b. pressure,** avoir beaucoup de tension *ou* une tension élevée; **to take** *or* **measure s.o.'s b. pressure,** prendre la tension de qn; **b. pudding** *or* **sausage,** boudin noir; **b. red,** (*colour*) rouge sang *inv*; **b. relation,** parent(e) par le sang; **b. sample,** prise *f* de sang; **b. serum,** sérum sanguin; **b. sports,** la chasse; **b. test,** examen *m ou* prise de sang; **I'm having a b. test** *or* **my b. tested tomorrow,** on doit me faire une prise de sang demain; **b. transfusion,** transfusion de sang *ou* sanguine; **to give s.o. a b. transfusion,** faire une transfusion de sang *ou* sanguine à qn; **b. vessel,** vaisseau sanguin.

blood[2] *vt* **(a)** donner (*aux chiens*) le goût du sang; initier (*un chasseur débutant*) (*en l'aspergeant du sang de la bête morte*); **(b)** *Fig* initier (*qn*); *Mil* **to b. the troops,** donner aux troupes le baptême du feu.

blood-and-thunder [blʌdən'θʌndər] *adj* (*film, roman etc*) sensationnel, mélodramatique.

bloodcurdling ['blʌdkɜːdlɪŋ] *adj* (*story, scream*) à vous tourner les sangs, à (vous) figer le sang.

blooded ['blʌdɪd] *adj* (*horse etc*) **to be b.**, avoir du sang de race.
bloodhound ['blʌdhaʊnd] *n* (*dog, Fig detective*) limier *m*.
bloodiness ['blʌdɪnɪs] *n* état sanglant; (*of battle*) sauvagerie *f*.
bloodless ['blʌdlɪs] *adj* **(a)** (*victoire etc*) sans effusion de sang; **(b)** (*pale*) exsangue, pâle; (*unfeeling*) insensible, froid; (*lifeless*) sans vitalité; (*personne*) qui n'a pas de sang dans les veines.
bloodlessly ['blʌdlɪslɪ] *adv* sans effusion de sang.
blood-letting ['blʌdletɪŋ] *n* **(a)** = **BLOODSHED**; **(b)** *Med Arch* saignée *f*.
blood-red [blʌd'red] *adj* rouge (comme du) sang.
bloodshed ['blʌdʃed] *n* **(a)** effusion *f* de sang; **without b.**, sans verser de sang; **(b)** (*slaughter*) carnage *m*.
bloodshot ['blʌdʃɒt] *adj* (*œil*) injecté de sang; **to become b.**, (*of eye*) s'injecter.
bloodstain ['blʌdsteɪn] *n* tache *f* de sang.
bloodstained ['blʌdsteɪnd] *adj* taché *ou* souillé de sang, ensanglanté.
bloodstock ['blʌdstɒk] *n* chevaux *mpl* pur sang.
bloodstone ['blʌdstəʊn] *n Miner* jaspe sanguin.
bloodstream ['blʌdstriːm] *n Physiol* le sang.
bloodsucker ['blʌdsʌkər] *n* sangsue *f*; *Fig* sangsue, parasite *m*.
bloodsucking ['blʌdsʌkɪŋ] *adj* hématophage; *Fig* vampirique.
bloodthirsty ['blʌdθɜːstɪ] *adj* (*person*) sanguinaire; (*film, book*) très violent.
bloody¹ ['blʌdɪ] **1** *adj* **(a)** ensanglanté, taché de sang; **B. Mary**, *Hist* la reine Mary I (d'Angleterre); (*drink*) = mélange de vodka et de jus de tomate; **(b)** *Br Sl* (*intensifier*) sacré; **a b. liar**, un sacré menteur; **(you) b. fool!**, sacré imbécile! **2** *adv Br Sl* **it's b. hot!**, quelle sacrée chaleur!; **he can b. well do it himself!**, il n'a qu'à se démerder tout seul; **I b. well AM going out**, j'ai bien l'intention de sortir (et personne ne m'en empêchera); **I'm b. tired**, je suis complètement crevé; **b. hell!**, merde, bon sang!
bloody² *vt* (*pt & pp* **bloodied**) ensanglanter; souiller (*ses mains etc*) de sang.
bloody-minded [blʌdɪ'maɪndɪd] *adj Br Sl* **he's just b.-m.**, c'est un mauvais coucheur; **don't be so b.-m.**, arrête d'emmerder le monde.
bloody-mindedness [blʌdɪ'maɪndɪdnɪs] *n Sl* **it's sheer b.-m.**, ce n'est rien que pour emmerder le monde.
bloom¹ [bluːm] *n* **(a)** (*flower*) fleur *f*; **to burst into b.**, fleurir; **flower in b.**, fleur éclose; **the roses are in b.**, les roses sont ouvertes; **in full b.**, épanoui, en pleine floraison; **in the b. of youth**, à *ou* dans la fleur de l'âge *ou* de la jeunesse; **(b)** velouté *m*, pruine *f*, duvet *m* (*du raisin, d'une pêche*); efflorescence *f*, fleur *f* (*du soufre sur le caoutchouc etc*); *Ch* **cobalt/zinc b.**, fleur de cobalt/zinc.
bloom² *vi* (*of plant*) fleurir, être en fleur; *Fig* (*of child*) profiter.
bloomer ['bluːmər] *n Br F* bévue *f*, gaffe *f*; **to make a b.**, faire une gaffe.
bloomers ['bluːməz] *npl* culotte bouffante (*de femme*).
blooming ['bluːmɪŋ] **1** *adj* **(a)** (*flower*) fleurissant, en fleur; *Fig* florissant; **b. with health**, resplendissant de santé; **(b)** *Br F* (*intensifier*) **you b. idiot!**, sacré idiot!; **it's a b. lie!**, ça, pour un mensonge!; **the woman's a b. genius**, cette femme est un sacré génie *ou* en a dans la tête. **2** *adv* **I b. well will go!**, et moi je te dis que j'irai! **3** *n* floraison *f*, fleuraison *f*.
blooper ['bluːpər] *n Am F* = **BLOOMER**.
blossom¹ ['blɒs(ə)m] *n* fleur *f* (*des arbres*); **tree in b.**, arbre *m* en fleur(s); **apple/cherry/orange/***etc* **b.**, fleur de pommier/de cerisier/d'oranger/*etc*.
blossom² *vi* (*of tree*) fleurir; *Fig* **she had blossomed into a charming young woman**, elle était devenue une charmante jeune femme.
►**blossom out** *vi* = **BLOSSOM²**.
blossoming ['blɒs(ə)mɪŋ] *n* fleuraison *f*, floraison *f*; *Fig* épanouissement *m*.
blot¹ [blɒt] *n* tache *f*; (*of ink*) pâté *m*; *Fig* **a b. on s.o.'s honour**, une tache à l'honneur de qn; *Fig* **to be a b. on the landscape**, (*of building*) gâcher le paysage.
blot² *v* (**-tt-**) **1** *vt* **(a)** (*stain*) tacher, souiller, ternir; (*with ink*) faire des pâtés sur (*qch*); *Fig* **to b. one's copybook**, ternir sa réputation; **(b)** sécher l'encre de (*une lettre etc*); passer le buvard sur (*l'encre*). **2** *vi* (*of blotting paper*) boire l'encre.
►**blot out** *vtsep* (*obliterate*) effacer (*un souvenir etc*); rayer, barrer (*un mot*); (*of fog etc*) cacher, masquer (*l'horizon etc*).
blotch¹ [blɒtʃ] *n* **(a)** tache *f*, éclaboussure *f* (*d'encre, de couleur*); **(b)** tache *f* rouge (*sur la peau*).
blotch² **1** *vt* couvrir (*la peau*) de taches *ou* de rougeurs; **cold blotches the skin**, le froid marbre la peau. **2** *vi* **this pen blotches**, ce stylo fuit.
blotchy ['blɒtʃɪ] *adj* tacheté; (*teint*) brouillé, couperosé; (*peau*) couvert de rougeurs.
blotter ['blɒtər] *n* **(a)** (*for ink*) (bloc *m*) buvard *m*; **(b)** *Com* brouillard *m*, main courante; **(c)** *US Admin* registre *m* (*d'arrestations etc*); (*in prison*) livre *m* d'écrou.
blotting ['blɒtɪŋ] *n* **(a)** séchage *m* (*au papier buvard*); **b. paper**, (papier *m*) buvard *m*; **b. pad**, (bloc *m*) buvard; (*large*) sous-main *m inv*; **(b)** maculage *m* (*du papier*).
blotto ['blɒtəʊ] *adj Br Sl* bourré.
blouse [blaʊz] *n* **(a)** corsage *m*, chemisier *m* (*de femme*); **(b)** *Am* vareuse *f* (*de marin etc*).
blow¹ [bləʊ] *n* **(a)** souffle *m*; **give your nose a good b.**, (*to child*) mouche-toi bien; *Vulg* **to give s.o. a b. job**, sucer qn, faire une pipe à qn; **(b)** (*of wind*) coup *m* de vent.
blow² *v* (*pt* **blew** [bluː]; *pp* **blown** [bləʊn]) **1** *vi* **(a)** (*of wind*) souffler; **the wind is blowing**, il y a *ou* il fait du vent; **it's blowing hard**, le vent souffle fort, il fait grand vent; **it was blowing a gale**, le vent soufflait en tempête; **the wind was blowing down the chimney**, le vent s'engouffrait dans la cheminée; **my papers blew out of the window**, mes papiers se sont envolés par la fenêtre; **the door blew open**, le vent a ouvert la porte; **the wind's blowing from the west**, le vent souffle de l'ouest;
(b) (*of person, animal*) souffler; (*of whale*) rejeter l'eau par les évents; **to b. on one's fingers**, souffler dans ses doigts;
(c) *esp Am F* (*boast*) se vanter;
(d) (*of fuse*) sauter; (*of boiler etc*) exploser.
2 *vt* **(a)** **the wind is blowing the rain against the windows**, le vent chasse la pluie contre les vitres; **to b. a ship ashore**, (*of wind*) pousser un navire à la côte; **to be blown out to sea**, être poussé au large; *Prov* **it's an ill wind that blows nobody any good**, à quelque chose malheur est bon;
(b) (*of person*) donner un coup de (*sifflet*); sonner de (*la trompette*); **to b. the dust off sth**, souffler sur qch pour enlever la poussière; **to b. s.o. a kiss**, envoyer un baiser à qn; **to b. one's nose**, se moucher; **to b. the horn**, sonner du cor; *F* **to b. one's own trumpet**, chanter ses propres louanges;
(c) faire (*des bulles de savon*); souffler (*le verre*); vider (*un œuf*);
(d) essouffler (*un cheval etc*);
(e) *El* faire sauter (*les plombs*); *Aut* **to b. a gasket**, faire sauter un joint; *F Fig* **to b. a fuse** *or* **a gasket** *or* **one's stack** *or* **top**, sortir de ses gonds; **to b. a safe**, faire sauter un coffre-fort; **to b. the gaff**, vendre la mèche; *Sl* **the Grand Canyon blew my mind**, le Grand Canyon m'a enthousiasmé, j'étais ébloui par le Grand Canyon; *Sl* **the prices blew my mind**, j'ai été affolé par les prix;
(f) *F* (*ruin, spoil*) gâcher, bousiller (*qch*); louper (*une occasion*);
(g) *F* gaspiller (*son argent*); **he blew all his savings on a car**, il a mis toutes ses économies dans une voiture;
(h) *F* **b. the expense!**, je me moque de la dépense!; **I'll be blowed if ...**, que le diable m'emporte si ...; **well, I'm blowed!**, ça, par exemple!; **b. it!**, zut!
blow³ *n* coup *m* (*de poing etc, Fig du sort*); **at the first b.**, du premier coup; **at a (single) b.**, d'un (seul) coup; **to strike a b.**, porter *ou* asséner *ou* donner un coup; **to come to blows, to exchange blows**, en venir aux coups *ou* aux mains; **to return b. for b.**, rendre coup pour coup; **to strike a b. for/against sth**, se battre pour/contre qch; **it came as a crushing b. to us**, ce fut un coup d'assommoir pour nous; **his death is a sad b. to his family**, sa mort est un rude coup pour sa famille; **b. to s.o.'s pride**, atteinte à la vanité de qn.
blow⁴ *vi* (*pt* **blew** [bluː]; *pp* **blown** [bləʊn]) *Lit* (*of flower*) s'épanouir; **full-blown roses**, roses fraîches écloses.
►**blow about** **1** *vi* (*of leaves etc*) voler çà et là. **2** *vtsep* agiter, faire voler (*qch*); disperser (*les feuilles etc*).
►**blow away** **1** *vtsep* **(a)** (*of wind etc*) emporter (*qch*); **(b)** *Sl* (*kill*) descendre (*qn*). **2** *vi* (*of papers etc*) s'envoler; **his hat blew away in the wind**, son chapeau s'est envolé à cause du vent; **all my cares have blown away**, tous mes soucis se sont évanouis.
►**blow down** **1** *vtsep* (*of wind*) abattre, renverser (*une barriere etc*); abattre (*un arbre*). **2** *vi* (*of fence etc*) s'abattre, se renverser; (*of tree*) s'abattre.

▶**blow in 1** *vtsep* **(a)** (*of wind etc*) enfoncer (*un carreau, une porte*); **(b)** (*of person*) souffler; **b. some more air in,** souffle un peu plus dedans. **2** *vi* **(a)** (*of window etc*) s'enfoncer; **(b) the dust is blowing in,** le vent fait entrer la poussière; **(c)** *F* (*of person*) arriver à l'improviste; **when did you b. in?,** quand es-tu arrivé?

▶**blow off 1** *vtsep* **(a)** (*of wind etc*) emporter (*un chapeau etc*); (*person*) souffler (*la poussière*); **to b. off steam,** (*from machine*) lâcher de la vapeur; *Fig* se défouler; **(b)** (*with gun, explosives*) faire exploser (*qch*); **the gunman threatened to b. their heads off,** l'homme au pistolet a menacé de leur faire sauter la cervelle. **2** *vi* (*of hat etc*) s'envoler.

▶**blow out 1** *vtsep* **(a)** souffler (*une bougie*); **(b)** chasser, expulser (*de l'air*); gonfler (*ses joues*); **to b. out one's brains,** se faire sauter la cervelle; **to blow s.o.'s brains out,** faire sauter la cervelle à qn; **to b. itself out,** (*of storm*) se dissiper, se calmer. **2** *vi* **(a)** (*of candle*) s'éteindre; **(b)** *Min* (*of shot*) faire canon; *Aut etc* (*of gasket*) sauter; (*of tyre*) éclater; *El* (*of fuse*) sauter.

▶**blow over 1** *vtsep* (*of wind*) renverser (*une table etc*). **2** *vi* (*fall down*) se renverser; (*of storm*) se calmer, se dissiper; (*of argument*) se calmer; **the scandal soon blew over,** le scandale a été vite oublié.

▶**blow up 1** *vi* (*of mine*) éclater, sauter; (*of boiler etc*) crever, exploser; *Fig* éclater (de rage); **the argument blew up out of nowhere,** la dispute a commencé sans raison; **to b. up into a crisis,** (*of situation*) prendre les proportions d'une crise; **there's a gale blowing up,** il se prépare une tempête. **2** *vtsep* **(a)** faire sauter, (faire) exploser (*une mine etc*); faire sauter (*un édifice*); *F* engueuler (*qn*); **(b)** gonfler (*un pneu, un ballon etc*); **(c)** *Phot* agrandir (*une photo*); **I'd like this photograph blown up,** j'aimerais un agrandissement de cette photo; **(d)** *F* exagérer (*un incident etc*); **you're blowing this up out of all proportion,** tu en fais un drame.

blow-by-blow [bləʊbaɪ'bləʊ] *adj* (*account*) minutieux, détaillé.

blowcock ['bləʊkɒk] *n* robinet *m* d'extraction *ou* de vidange.

blow-dry¹ ['bləʊdraɪ] *n* (*at hairdresser's*) séchage *m* (libre); **a cut and b.-d.,** une coupe et un séchage libre.

blow-dry² 1 *vt* sécher (avec un séchoir) (*ses cheveux*). **2** *vi* sécher (avec un séchoir).

blow-drying ['bləʊdraɪɪŋ] *n* **too much b.-d. can damage your hair,** à force d'être séchés au séchoir, les cheveux s'abîment.

blower ['bləʊər] *n* **(a)** (*person*) souffleur, -euse (*de verre etc*); **(b)** (*device*) écran *m* à tirage, tablier *m*, rideau *m* (*de cheminée*); *Ind etc* ventilateur soufflant; *Agr* ensileuse *f*; insufflateur *m* (*à poudre insecticide*); **(c)** *F* téléphone *m*; (*speaking tube*) porte-voix *m inv*; **get him on the b. for me,** joignez-le au téléphone pour moi; **(d)** *Min* échappement *m* de gaz; soufflard *m* (*de grisou*).

blowfly, *pl* **-flies** ['bləʊflaɪ, -flaɪz] *n* mouche *f* de la viande, mouche bleue.

blowgun ['bləʊgʌn] *n Am* (*for darts*) sarbacane *f*.

blowhard ['bləʊhɑːd] *n F* (*boaster*) vantard, -arde.

blowhole ['bləʊhəʊl] *n* **(a)** *Zool* évent *m* (*d'une baleine*); **(b)** (*in ice*) = trou où un phoque etc vient respirer; **(c)** bouche *f* d'aération (*d'un tunnel*).

blowing ['bləʊɪŋ] *n* **(a)** soufflement *m* (*du vent*); **(b)** soufflage *m* (*du verre etc*).

blowlamp ['bləʊlæmp] *n* **(a)** chalumeau *m*, lampe *f* à souder *ou* à braser; **(b)** brûloir *m* (*de peintre en bâtiments*).

blown [bləʊn] *adj* **(a)** (*person*) essoufflé, hors d'haleine; **(b)** *El* **b. fuse,** fusible fondu; plomb sauté.

blowout ['bləʊaʊt] *n* **(a)** *Sl* grande bouffe, gueuleton *m*; **we had a b. last night,** on a fait un gueuleton hier soir; **(b)** *Aut etc* éclatement *m* (*de pneu*); **(c)** *Min etc* éruption *f* (*de gaz, de pétrole etc*) au cours d'un sondage; **(d)** *El* soufflage *m* d'étincelles; **magnetic b.,** souffleur *m* magnétique; **(e)** *Metal* mise *f* hors feu (*d'un haut fourneau*).

blowpipe ['bləʊpaɪp] *n* **(a)** (*for darts*) sarbacane *f*; **(b)** *Ch Metal* chalumeau *m*; (*of glassblower*) canne *f*, fêle *f*; **(c)** *Mus* porte-vent *m inv* (*de cornemuse*).

blowtorch ['bləʊtɔːtʃ] *n Am* = **BLOWLAMP.**

blow-up ['bləʊʌp] *n F* **(a)** (*argument*) dispute *f*, querelle *f*; (*tantrum*) accès *m* de fureur; **we had a b.-up last night,** nous nous sommes disputés hier soir; **(b)** *Phot* agrandissement *m*.

blow-valve ['bləʊvælv] *n* reniflard *m* (*de chaudière à vapeur*).

blowy ['bləʊɪ] *adj* (*day etc*) venteux.

blowzy ['blaʊzɪ] *adj* (*woman*) mal soigné.

blubber¹ ['blʌbər] *n* graisse *f ou* lard *m* de baleine; *F* (*on person*) graisse.

blubber² *vi F* chialer, pleurer comme un veau (**over,** sur); **stop blubbering,** arrête de chialer!

bludgeon¹ ['blʌdʒən] *n* gourdin *m*, matraque *f*.

bludgeon² *vt* matraquer (*qn*); **he was bludgeoned to death,** il a été matraqué à mort; *Fig* **to b. s.o. into doing sth,** forcer qn à faire qch par des méthodes brutales.

blue¹ [bluː] **1** *adj* **(a)** (*dress, sky etc*) bleu; **face b. with cold,** visage violacé par le froid; *F* **to be in a b. funk,** avoir la trouille; *F* **to scream** *or* **yell b. murder,** hurler; **to go b.,** virer au bleu; (*of person*) prendre un teint violacé; *F* **I've told you so until I'm b. in the face,** je me tue à te le dire; *F* **she can complain until she's b. in the face,** elle peut se plaindre autant qu'elle veut; **once in a b. moon,** en de rares occasions; *Med* **b. baby,** enfant bleu; **b. blood,** sang bleu; **b. cheese,** fromage bleu; **b. ribbon,** (*first prize*) premier prix; **b. rinse,** (*for hair*) rinçage colorant qui donne des reflets bleutés; **b. whale,** rorqual bleu;

(b) *F* (*depressed*) triste, déprimé; **to feel b.,** avoir le cafard;

(c) *F* (*indecent*) obscène, vert; **to tell b. stories,** en raconter des vertes; **b. film,** film *m* porno;

(d) *Pol* conservateur, -trice.

2 *n* **(a)** (*colour*) bleu *m*; *Fig* **a bolt from the b.,** un événement imprévu; *Fig* **her resignation was** *or* **came like a bolt from the b.,** sa démission a été une véritable surprise; *Fig* **he arrived out of the b.,** il est arrivé à l'improviste;

(b) the blues, *F* (*depression*) des idées noires, le cafard; *Mus* le blues;

(c) *Pol* conservateur, -trice; **a true b.,** un patriote; *Pol* un conservateur;

(d) *Sp* **(Oxford/Cambridge** *etc***) b.,** sportif chevronné (de l'université d'Oxford/de Cambridge *etc*);

(e) *Mil* **the Blues,** *Br* la Cavalerie de la Maison du Souverain; *US Hist* l'armée *f* du Nord.

blue² *vt* **(a)** *F* **to b. one's money,** gaspiller *ou* claquer son argent; **don't tell me you've blued the lot!,** ne me dis pas que tu as tout claqué!; **she blued £300 on a dress,** elle a claqué 300 livres dans une robe; **(b)** bleuir (*qch*), teindre (*qch*) en bleu.

Bluebeard ['bluːbɪəd] *n* Barbe-bleue *m*.

bluebell ['bluːbel] *n* (*flower*) **(a)** jacinthe *f* sauvage *ou* des bois; **(b)** *Scot* campanule *f*.

blueberry ['bluːb(ə)rɪ] *n* (*shrub, fruit*) airelle *f*, myrtille *f*; *Can* bleuet *m*; *Can* **b. pie,** tarte *f* aux bleuets.

bluebird ['bluːbɜːd] *n* rouge-gorge bleu.

blue-black [bluː'blæk] *adj* noir tirant sur le bleu; (*ink*) bleu-noir.

bluebottle ['bluːbɒt(ə)l] *n* **(a)** (*insect*) mouche *f* de la viande; **(b)** *Old-fashioned Br F* (*policeman*) flic *m*.

blue-chip ['bluːtʃɪp] *adj St Exch* **b.-c. stocks,** actions triées sur le volet; **b.-c. company,** affaire *f* de premier ordre.

blue-collar [bluː'kɒlər] *adj* **b.-c. worker,** ouvrier *m*, travailleur manuel, *Can* col bleu; **b.-c. union,** syndicat ouvrier.

blue-eyed ['bluːaɪd] *adj* aux yeux bleus; *Br F* **b.-e. boy,** (*at home*) le chouchou de sa maman; (*at work*) le favori du patron.

bluegrass ['bluːgrɑːs, -æs] *n US* **(a) the B. state,** Kentucky *m*; **(b)** *Mus* folklore *m* du Kentucky.

blueness ['bluːnɪs] *n* couleur bleue, bleu *m*.

blue-pencil ['bluːpens(ə)l] *vt* censurer (*un article*).

blueprint ['bluːprɪnt] *n* **(a)** plan (détaillé), projet *m*, épure *f*; **(b)** (*photograph*) dessin négatif, photocalque *m*.

blue-ribbon ['bluːrɪb(ə)n] *adj Am* **b.-r. committee,** = comité sélect; **b.-r. jury,** jury spécial.

bluestocking ['bluːstɒkɪŋ] *n Pej* (*woman*) bas-bleu *m*, *pl* bas-bleus.

bluff¹ [blʌf] **1** *adj* **(a)** (*cliff, coast*) escarpé, à pic; *Nau* **b. (bowed),** (*navire*) à proue renflée, renflé de l'avant; **(b)** (*person*) carré et sincère. **2** *n* cap *m ou* falaise *f* à pic, à-pic *m inv*.

bluff² *n* **(a)** (*at poker*) bluff *m*; **to call s.o.'s b.,** (*at poker*) inviter l'adversaire à mettre cartes sur table; *Fig* prendre qn au mot; **(b)** (*deception*) bluff *m*, battage *m*; **piece of b.,** coup *m* de bluff.

bluff³ 1 *vt Cards etc* bluffer (*qn*); **he bluffed her into agreeing,** il le lui a fait accepter par le bluff. **2** *vi* faire du bluff *ou* de l'épate; *Cards* faire cassade.

bluffer ['blʌfər] *n* bluffeur, -euse.

▶**bluff out** *vtsep* (*use cleverness*) **to b. one's way out of a tricky situation,** se tirer d'affaire par un coup de bluff; **we'll just have to b. it out,** nous n'aurons qu'à bluffer.

blunder[1] ['blʌndər] *n* bévue *f*, gaffe *f*.

blunder[2] *vi* faire une bévue *ou* une gaffe; **to b. along,** s'avancer d'un pas maladroit; **to b. against** *or* **into s.o./sth,** se heurter contre qn/qch, heurter qn/qch; **she blundered into a situation she knew nothing about,** elle s'est trouvée prise dans une situation dont elle ignorait tout; **he managed to b. through,** il s'en est tiré tant bien que mal.

blunderbuss ['blʌndəbʌs] *n Hist* (*gun*) tromblon *m*.

blunderer ['blʌndərər] *n* gaffeur, -euse.

blundering ['blʌndərɪŋ] **1** *adj* maladroit. **2** *n* maladresse *f*.

blunt[1] [blʌnt] *adj* **(a)** (*knife, cutting edge etc*) émoussé; (*needle, pencil*) épointé; (*instrument*) contondant; **(b)** *Fig* (*person, question etc*) brusque; (*person, reply etc*) carré; (*fact*) brutal; (*refusal*) tranché.

blunt[2] *vt* **(a)** émousser (*un couteau etc*); épointer (*un crayon etc*); **(b)** *Fig* émousser (*les sentiments, la colère de qn*); **(c)** arrondir (*un angle*).

bluntly ['blʌntlɪ] *adv* (*to ask*) brusquement; (*to reply*) carrément, brutalement; **to put it b. ...,** pour dire les choses comme elles sont; **to speak b.,** parler net *ou* carrément.

bluntness ['blʌntnɪs] *n* **(a)** (*of knife etc*) manque *m* de tranchant; **(b)** *Fig* (*of person*) brusquerie *f*, sans-façon *m*; **b. of speech,** franc-parler *m*.

blur[1] [blɜːr] *n* **(a)** forme confuse; *Phot* flou *m*; **without my glasses, everything is a b.,** sans mes lunettes je suis complètement dans le brouillard; **b. of tears,** voile *m* de larmes; **(b)** tache *f*, macule *f*, barbouillage *m* (*d'encre etc*); *Typ* frison *m*.

blur[2] *vt* (**-rr-**) **(a)** brouiller, troubler; **eyes blurred with tears,** yeux voilés *ou* brouillés de larmes; **the haze has blurred the outline of the mountain,** la brume a estompé les contours de la montagne; **(b)** barbouiller (*d'encre etc*); *Typ* maculer, mâchurer.

blurb [blɜːb] *n F* baratin *m* publicitaire; (*on book*) annonce *f* sur la jaquette d'un livre.

blurred [blɜːd] *adj* (*photographie*) flou; (*contours*) noyé, indécis, flou; (*souvenirs*) confus, estompé; *Med* **b. vision,** vue trouble.

blurring ['blɜːrɪŋ] *n* **(a)** maculage *m*, barbouillage *m*; **(b)** *Opt* halo *m*, flou *m*.

▶blurt out *vtsep* lâcher (à l'étourdie), laisser échapper (*un secret*); **he blurted out the truth,** il a révélé *ou* trahi la vérité; **'he's dead', she blurted out,** 'il est mort', a-t-elle lâché.

blush[1] [blʌʃ] *n* **(a)** rougeur *f* (*de modestie, de honte*); **a b. rose to her cheeks,** le sang lui est monté au visage; **to hide one's blushes,** baisser le nez d'embarras; *Lit* **the first b. of dawn,** les premières rougeurs de l'aube; **b. wine,** vin rosé; **(b)** *Fml* aspect *m*; **at (the) first b.,** à l'abord, au premier abord, au premier aspect.

blush[2] *vi* (*of person*) rougir; **to b. for** *or* **with shame,** rougir de honte; **to b. crimson,** devenir tout rouge; **to b. to the roots of one's hair,** rougir jusqu'à la racine des cheveux; *Fig* **to b. to admit sth,** rougir de devoir admettre qch.

blusher ['blʌʃər] *n* (*for face*) blush *m*, fard *m* à joues.

blushing ['blʌʃɪŋ] **1** *adj* (*person*) rougissant; **the b. bride,** la mariée rougissante. **2** *n* rougissement *m*.

bluster[1] ['blʌstər] *n* fureur *f*, fracas *m* (*de l'orage*); *Fig* (*of person*) fanfaronnade(s) *f(pl)*.

bluster[2] *vi* (*of wind*) souffler en rafales; *Fig* parler haut; (*boast*) faire de l'esbroufe; **he blusters to cover up his ignorance,** il parle haut pour cacher son ignorance.

blustering ['blʌstərɪŋ] **1** *adj* (*vent*) violent; *Fig* (*person, tone*) fanfaron. **2** *n* fanfaronnade(s) *f(pl)*.

blustery ['blʌst(ə)rɪ] *adj* (*vent*) violent; (*jour*) venteux.

blvd (*abbr* **boulevard**) boul., bd..

BMA [biːe'meɪ] *n Br* (*abbr* **British Medical Association**) = Association médicale britannique.

BO [biː'əʊ] *n F* (*abbr* **body odour**) = odeur corporelle; **to have BO,** sentir (la transpiration), sentir mauvais.

boa ['bəʊə] *n* (*snake*) boa *m*; **b. constrictor,** boa constricteur, constrictor *m*; **feather b.,** (*scarf*) boa.

boar ['bɔːr] *n* (*animal*) verrat *m*; **wild b.,** sanglier *m*; (*young*) marcassin *m*; **b. hunting,** la chasse au sanglier; *Culin* **b.'s head,** hure *f* de sanglier.

board[1] [bɔːd] *n* **(a)** planche *f*; (*thick*) madrier *m*; (*for bread*) planche à (couper le) pain; (*for notices*) panneau *m* de publicité *ou* d'affichage; (*inscribed with information*) écriteau *m*; *Sch* **to write sth on the b.,** écrire qch au tableau; *Th* **the boards,** la scène, les planches;

(b) *Admin etc* conseil *m*, comité *m*; **to be on the b.,** (*of company*) faire partie du conseil, être membre du conseil; **advisory b.,** comité consultatif; **disciplinary b.,** conseil de discipline; **medical b.,** conseil de santé; *Br* **National Coal B.,** = administration des charbonnages; **b. of directors,** conseil d'administration (*d'une société*); **b. of enquiry,** commission *f* d'enquête; **b. of examiners,** jury *m* d'examen; *Admin* **B. of Trade,** *Br* = Ministère du Commerce; *US* = chambre de commerce; **b. of trustees,** conseil de gestion (*d'un musée etc*); **b. meeting,** réunion *f* du conseil (d'administration);

(c) (*table*) table *f*; (*food*) table, nourriture *f*; tableau *m* (*de jeu*); (*for draughts*) damier *m*; (*for chess*) échiquier *m*; **b. and lodging, full b.,** pension *f* (complète); **with b. and lodging,** nourri et logé; *Fig* **to sweep the b.,** faire table rase; **b. game,** jeu *m* de société;

(d) *Nau* bord *m*; **on b.,** à bord; **to take goods on b.,** embarquer des marchandises; *Fig* **to take on b.,** (*work, responsibility*) accepter; (*problem*) assumer; (*comments, information*) assimiler; **to go on b.,** monter à bord, s'embarquer; **to go by the b.,** (*of mast etc*) s'en aller par-dessus bord; *Fig* (*of plan, hopes*) être abandonné; (*of reputation*) être perdu; *Fig* **to let sth go by the b.,** abandonner qch, laisser tomber qch;

(e) (*in bookbinding*) carton *m*; **the boards,** les plats *mpl* (*d'un livre*); **in paper boards,** cartonné; **limp boards,** cartonnage *m* souple.

board[2] **1** *vt* **(a)** *Nau* (*come alongside*) aborder, accoster; *Admin* arraisonner (*un navire*); (*of passengers*) aller *ou* monter à bord de (*un navire, un avion*); monter dans (*un train, un autobus*); **(b)** cartonner (*un livre*); rebrousser (*le cuir*). **2** *vi* **(a)** être en pension; **I b. at Mrs Brown's** *or* **with Mrs Brown,** je suis en pension chez Mme Brown; **(b)** *Av* **flight 123 is now boarding,** l'embarquement a commencé pour le vol 123.

▶board in *vtsep* = **BOARD UP**.

▶board out 1 *vtsep* mettre (*des enfants*) en pension; placer (*des enfants*) dans une famille. **2** *vi* (*of student, lodger*) prendre ses repas à l'extérieur.

▶board up *vtsep* condamner (*une porte, une fenêtre*).

boarder ['bɔːdər] *n* **(a)** (*lodger*) pensionnaire *mf*; *Sch* interne *mf*; **she takes in boarders,** elle prend des pensionnaires; **(b)** *Nau* abordeur *m*.

boarding ['bɔːdɪŋ] *n* **(a)** *Nau Av* embarquement *m*; *Admin* arraisonnement *m*; *Nau* (*by pirates, enemy*) abordage *m*; **flight 123 is now ready for b.,** le vol 123 est maintenant prêt pour l'embarquement; *Av* **in preparation for b., please extinguish all cigarettes,** veuillez éteindre vos cigarettes en vue de l'embarquement; **b. party,** (*for inspection*) détachement *m* de visite; (*of pirates etc*) détachement d'abordage; *Av* **b. card,** carte *f* d'embarquement; **(b) b. house,** pension *f* de famille; **b. kennels,** (*for dog*) = chenil où l'on peut faire garder les chiens pendant les vacances; **b. school,** pensionnat *m*; **he's being sent to b. school,** on l'envoie en pension; **(c)** *Constr* planchéiage *m*; cartonnage *m* (*d'un livre*); rebroussement *m* (*du cuir*); **(d)** (*no pl*) planches *fpl*; *Constr* bardage *m*.

boardroom ['bɔːdruːm] *n* salle *f* de réunion du conseil d'administration.

boardwalk ['bɔːdwɔːk] *n Am* = passage ou trottoir constitué de planches en bois (au bord de la mer).

boast[1] [bəʊst] *n* vantardise *f*; **it is their b. that ...,** ils se vantent que ... .

boast[2] **1** *vi* se vanter; **to b. of** *or* **about sth,** se vanter ou se faire gloire de qch; **without wishing to b.,** sans vanité. **2** *vt* revendiquer (*qch*); **the school boasts a fine library,** l'école est fière de posséder une belle bibliothèque.

boaster ['bəʊstər] *n* vantard, -arde.

boastful ['bəʊstfʊl] *adj* vantard.

boastfully ['bəʊstfʊlɪ] *adv* avec vantardise.

boasting ['bəʊstɪŋ] *n* vantardise *f*.

boat[1] [bəʊt] *n* **(a)** *Nau* bateau *m*; (*small*) canot *m*, embarcation *f*; **I came by b.,** je suis venu sur *ou* par le bateau; **we're all in the same b.,** nous sommes tous dans le même cas *ou* logés à la même enseigne; *Fig* **to miss the b.,** manquer le coche; **sailing b.,** bateau à voiles; **b. deck,** pont *m* des embarcations; **b. drill,** manœuvres *fpl* d'évacuation; **b. neck,** (*on dress, jumper*) encolure *f* bateau; **b. people,** boat people *mpl*; **b. race,** course *f* à l'aviron; **b. stations!,** chacun à son poste d'abandon!; **b. train,** train assurant un service en correspondance avec une compagnie maritime; **(b)** (*for sauce, gravy*) saucière *f*.

boat[2] *vi* se promener en bateau; (*in rowboat etc*) canoter, faire du canotage.

boatbuilder ['bəʊtbɪldər] *n* constructeur *m* de canots *ou* de bateaux de plaisance.
boater ['bəʊtər] *n* (*hat*) canotier *m*; **straw b.,** chapeau *m* de paille.
boathook ['bəʊthʊk] *n Nau* gaffe *f*.
boathouse ['bəʊthaʊs] *n* hangar *m* à bateaux.
boating ['bəʊtɪŋ] *n* canotage *m*; **to go b.,** faire du canotage; **b. song,** barcarolle *f*.
boatload ['bəʊtləʊd] *n* cargaison *f* (*de bois etc*); plein bateau (*de personnes*).
boatman, *pl* **-men** ['bəʊtmən] **(a)** (*operator*) batelier *m*; **(b)** (*custodian*) gardien *m* de canots; (*renter*) loueur *m* de canots; **(c)** (*insect*) **(water)b.,** corise *f*.
boatswain ['bəʊs(ə)n] *n Nau* maître *m* d'équipage, maître principal de manœuvre, bosco *m*.
boatyard ['bəʊtjɑːd] *n* chantier *m* de construction pour canots et bateaux de plaisance.
bob¹ [bɒb] *n* **(a)** (coupe *f* au) carré *m*; **to wear one's hair in a b.,** avoir les cheveux coupés au carré; **(b)** *Sp* bob(sleigh) *m*; **(c)** lentille *f* (*d'un pendule*); plomb *m* (*d'un fil à plomb*); poids *m* (*au bout de la queue d'un cerf-volant*); bouchon *m* (*de ligne à pêche*); paquet *m* de vers (*pour la pêche à l'anguille*).
bob² *vt* (**-bb-**) **to have one's hair bobbed,** se faire couper les cheveux au carré.
bob³ 1 *vi* s'agiter; **to b. for apples,** = essayer d'attraper avec les dents des pommes flottant dans une bassine d'eau; **to b. down,** se baisser subitement; **to b. up,** surgir brusquement, revenir à la surface; *Fig* réapparaître d'une façon inattendue; **to b. up and down in the water,** danser sur l'eau; **to b. under,** (*of fisherman's float*) plonger. **2** *vt* **to b. a curtsey,** faire une petite révérence.
bob⁴ *n* **(a)** (*tap*) petit coup; **(b)** (*curtsey*) petite révérence.
bob⁵ *n inv Br F Arch* shilling *m*; **that must cost a few b.,** ça ne doit pas être donné; **he's not short of a b. or two,** il n'est pas dans l'indigence, il a de quoi.
Bob [bɒb] *n* (*dimin of* **Robert**) = Robert *m*; *F* **and Bob's your uncle!,** ça y est!, et voilà!
bobbin ['bɒbɪn] *n* **(a)** *Tex* bobine *f* (*de la navette*); (*for lace*) fuseau *m*; **b. frame,** bobinoir *m*; **b. winder,** bobineuse *f*; **(b)** *El* corps *m* de bobine.
bobble ['bɒb(ə)l] *n F* (*on hat etc*) pompon *m*.
bobby ['bɒbɪ] *n Am* **b. pin,** pince *f* (à cheveux); **b. socks,** socquettes *fpl*.
Bobby ['bɒbɪ] *n* **(a)** (*dimin of* **Robert**) = Robert *m*; **(b)** *Old-fashioned Br F* (*policeman*) flic *m*.
bobbysoxer ['bɒbɪsɒksər] *n Am F* = adolescente (*qui porte des socquettes*).
bobcat ['bɒbkæt] *n Am* (*animal*) lynx *m* rufus.
bobsled¹ ['bɒbsled], **bobsleigh¹** ['bɒbsleɪ] *n* bob(sleigh) *m*; **b. race,** course *f* de bob.
bobsled², bobsleigh² *vi* faire du bob(sleigh).
bobtail ['bɒbteɪl] *n* **(a)** queue écourtée (*d'un cheval, d'un chien*); **(b)** (*dog*) anglais *m* sans queue, bobtail *m*.
bock [bɒk] *n* (*glass*) bock *m*; **b. (beer),** bière brune (allemande).
bod [bɒd] *n F* type *m*; **any old b.,** n'importe qui.
BOD [biːəʊ'diː] *n* (*abbr* **biochemical oxygen demand**) DOB *f*.
bode [bəʊd] *vt & vi Arch & Lit* présager; **to b. well/ill,** être de bon/de mauvais augure (**for,** pour).
bodge [bɒdʒ] *vt* bousiller, saboter (*un travail*); **to b. sth up,** (*make temporary or unskilful repair*) rafistoler qch, faire une réparation de fortune sur qch.
bodice ['bɒdɪs] *n* corsage *m* (*d'une robe*).
bodily ['bɒdɪlɪ] **1** *adj* corporel, physique; (*maladie*) du corps; **one's b. needs,** ses besoins matériels; **b. harm,** lésion corporelle; **to be in b. fear of s.o.,** craindre d'être attaqué par qn. **2** *adv* **(a)** (*forcibly*) corporellement; **he was carried b. to the door,** on l'a saisi (à bras-le-corps) et transporté jusqu'à la porte; **(b)** (*as a whole*) entièrement, en masse.
bodkin ['bɒdkɪn] *n* passe-lacet *m*, *pl* passe-lacets; *Sewing* poinçon *m*.
body ['bɒdɪ] *n* **(a)** corps *m* (*d'une personne, d'un animal*); (*corpse*) cadavre *m*, corps; **the human b.,** le corps humain; **to throw oneself b. and soul into sth,** se jeter à corps perdu *ou* corps et âme dans qch; **to have just enough to keep b. and soul together,** avoir tout juste de quoi vivre; **the resurrection of the b.,** la résurrection des morts; **over my dead b.!,** à mon corps défendant!; **b. bag,** = sac servant au transport de dépouilles mortelles; *Fig* **b. blow,** choc *m*; **b. building,** culture *f* physique, culturisme *m*; **b. builder,** culturiste *m*; *Aut* carrossier *m*; *Art* **b. colour,** gouache *f*; **b. count,** comptage *m* du nombre de morts; **b. language,** langage *m* du corps; **I could tell by his b. language,** je le savais d'après la façon dont il se tenait; **b. lotion,** lait *m* pour le corps; **b. odour,** odeur corporelle; **b. popper,** danseur, -euse de smurf; **b. popping,** smurf *m*; **b. scrub,** produit exfoliant pour le corps; *Aut* **b. shop,** atelier *m* de carrosserie; **b. stocking,** body *m*; **b. warmer,** petit gilet chaud;
(b) sève *f*, générosité *f* (*d'un vin*); corps *m*, consistance *f* (*d'un papier, d'une peinture etc*); vigueur *f* (*des cheveux*); **wine with b.,** vin généreux; **to get b.,** (*of wine*) prendre du corps; *Mus* **to give b. to the tone,** nourrir le son;
(c) (*group*) corps *m*; recueil *m* (*de lois*); étendue *f* (*d'eau*); **large b. of people,** foule nombreuse, assistance nombreuse; **there is a large b. of support for the policy,** un grand nombre de personnes sont en faveur de la politique; **b. of troops,** troupe armée; **the main b.,** le gros (de l'armée); **to come in a b.,** venir en masse; **electoral b.,** collège électoral; **governing b.,** conseil *m* de direction; **learned b.,** corps savant; **public b.,** corporation *f*; **b. corporate,** personne morale; **b. politic,** corps politique;
(d) (*main part*) corps *m* (*de document, de bâtiment etc*); vaisseau *m*, nef *f* (*d'église*); tronc *m* (*d'arbre, d'homme*); coffre *m* (*d'un instrument de musique*); fuselage *m* (*d'avion*); nacelle *f* (*d'une voiture d'enfant*); ventre *m* (*de haut fourneau*); coque *f* (*de chaudière*); fût *m* (*d'un cric, d'un tambour*); *Aut etc* carrosserie *f*; *Typ* pause *f* (*d'un a, d'un d*); *Aut* **standard b.,** carrosserie de série; *Typ* **b. type,** caractères *mpl* de texte;
(e) *Phys etc* corps *m*; *Astron* **heavenly b.,** corps céleste, astre *m*.
bodycheck ['bɒdɪtʃek] *n Sp* (*in ice hockey*) interception *f*; (*in wrestling*) coup *m* de bélier.
bodyguard ['bɒdɪgɑːd] *n* **(a)** (*no pl*) gardes *mpl* du corps; **(b)** (*individual*) garde *m* du corps, *F* gorille *m*.
bodywork ['bɒdɪwɜːk] *n Aut* **(a)** (*structure*) carrosserie *f*; **(b)** (*repairs*) travail *m* de carrosserie.
Boer [bʊər, 'bəʊər] **1** *adj* boer; **the B. War,** la guerre des Boers. **2** *n* Boer *mf*.
boffin ['bɒfɪn] *n F* savant *m*.
bog [bɒg] *n* **(a)** (*marsh*) marécage *m*; **peat b.,** tourbière *f*; *Miner* **b. iron,** fer *m* des lacs *ou* des marais; **(b)** *Br Sl* (*lavatory*) chiottes *fpl*.
►**bog down** *vtsep* (*usu passive*) **to get bogged down,** (*of car etc*) s'embourber, s'enfoncer dans une fondrière; *F* (*of person, discussion etc*) se trouver dans une impasse; **don't let's get bogged down in details,** ne nous perdons pas dans les détails.
bogey ['bəʊgɪ] *n* **(a)** (*source of fear*) spectre *m*, hantise *f*; **unionization is the b. of the company,** la syndicalisation est la hantise de la société; **(b)** *F* (*in nose*) crotte *f* de nez; **(c)** *Golf* un coup au-dessus de la normale; **(d)** (*spirit*) fantôme *m*, spectre *m*, épouvantail *m*; *Arch* diable *m*.
bogeyman, *pl* **-men** ['bəʊgɪmæn, -men] *n* **the b.,** croque-mitaine *m*, le Père Fouettard; **the b. will get you,** le Père Fouettard va venir te chercher.
boggle ['bɒg(ə)l] **1** *vi* **(a) to b. at doing sth,** rechigner à faire qch; **(b)** *F* **the mind boggles,** cela confond l'imagination. **2** *vt* **it boggles the mind,** cela confond l'imagination.
boggy ['bɒgɪ] *adj* marécageux.
bogie ['bəʊgɪ] *n Rail* bog(g)ie *m*.
bogus ['bəʊgəs] *adj* faux, *f* fausse; *Com* **b. company,** société *f* fantôme; *F* **he's completely b.,** il est faux comme un jeton.
Bohemia [bəʊ'hiːmɪə] *n* **(a)** *Geog* Bohême *f*; **(b)** (vie *f* de) bohème *f*.
Bohemian [bəʊ'hiːmɪən] **1** *adj* **(a)** *Geog* bohémien; **(b)** (*vie etc*) de bohème. **2** *n* **(a)** *Geog* Bohémien, -ienne; **(b)** (*arty type*) bohème *mf*; (*gipsy*) bohémien, -ienne.
boil¹ [bɔɪl] *n Med* furoncle *m*.
boil² *n* **to come to the b.,** (*of water etc*) commencer à bouillir, entrer en ébullition; **let the water come to a** *or* **the b.,** attendre que l'eau arrive à ébullition; **the water is on the b.,** l'eau bout; **to bring the water to the b.,** amener l'eau à l'ébullition; *Fig* **their romance has gone off the b.,** leur histoire tourne au ralenti, leur histoire ne marche plus très fort; **to go off the b.,** (*of athlete, actor etc*) perdre son entrain.
boil³ 1 *vi* **(a)** (*of water etc*) bouillir; (*violently*) bouillonner; **to begin to b.,** entrer en ébullition; *Culin* **allow to b. gently,** laissez mijoter; **to let the kettle b. dry,** laisser évaporer complètement l'eau de la bouilloire; **the kettle's boiling,** la bouilloire siffle; **are the potatoes boiling?,** est-ce que les pommes de terre bouillent?; *F* **to keep the pot boiling,** faire bouillir la marmite; **it makes me** *or* **my**

blood b.!, ça me fait bouillir le sang!; **to b. with rage,** bouillir de colère; *F* **I'm boiling!,** (*very hot*) je crève de chaleur!;
(b) (*of sea etc*) bouillonner, tourbillonner.
2 *vt* **(a)** faire bouillir (*de l'eau etc*); *Culin* faire cuire (*qch*) à l'eau; cuire (*du sucre*); **to b. the kettle,** (*by gas*) mettre la bouilloire sur le feu; (*by electricity*) brancher la bouilloire; **to b. an egg,** faire cuire un œuf à la coque; *Hum* **he can't b. an egg,** (*does not know how to cook*) il n'est même pas capable de faire cuire un œuf; *Sl* **go (and) b. your head!,** va te faire cuire un œuf!;
(b) (*in papermaking*) décreuser (*des fibres végétales*).
▶**boil away** *vi* **(a)** continuer à bouillir; **(b)** (*evaporate*) s'évaporer.
▶**boil down 1** *vtsep* réduire (*une solution*); (faire) réduire (*un sirop etc*); *Fig* condenser (*un article etc*). **2** *vi* (*of sauce etc*) se réduire.
▶**boil down to** *vipo F* se ramener *ou* se résumer *ou* revenir à; **what her story boils down to is that ...,** ce à quoi se résume son histoire, c'est que ...; **this is what it all boils down to,** voilà à quoi cela revient *ou* se résume.
▶**boil over** *vi* **(a)** (*of liquid*) s'en aller, se sauver; (*of pot etc*) déborder; **(b)** *F* (*become angry*) exploser (de colère); **I boiled over when she said that,** j'ai explosé quand elle a dit ça; **(c)** (*worsen*) s'empirer; **the dispute is in danger of boiling over into a strike,** le conflit risque de virer à la grève.
boiled [bɔɪld] *adj* bouilli; *Culin* cuit à l'eau; **b. egg,** œuf *m* à la coque; **lightly** *or* **soft b. egg,** œuf mollet; **b. sweet,** sucre *m* d'orge; **b. potatoes,** pommes *fpl* de terre à l'eau.
boiler ['bɔɪlər] *n* **(a)** chaudière *f*; **double b.,** bain-marie *m*, *pl* bains- marie; **b. maker,** chaudronnier *m*; **b. room,** salle *f* des chaudières; *Nau* chambre *f* de chauffe; **b. suit,** bleu *m* de chauffe; **(b)** *Culin* poule *f* (à la casserole).
boilerman, *pl* **-men** ['bɔɪləmən] *n* chauffeur *m*.
boiling ['bɔɪlɪŋ] **1** *adj* **(a)** (*water*) bouillant; **(b)** (*sea*) bouillonnant, tourbillonnant. **2** *adv* **b. hot,** tout bouillant; **it's been a b. hot day,** il a fait horriblement chaud aujourd'hui; *F* **I'm b. hot,** je crève de chaleur. **3** *n* **(a)** bouillonnement *m*, ébullition *f*; **b. point,** point *m* d'ébullition; *Fig* **I reached b. point when he said ...,** j'ai failli sortir de mes gonds *ou* exploser quand il a dit ...; **(b)** (*in papermaking*) décreusage *m* (*des fibres végétales*); **(c)** *Br F* **the whole b.,** tout (le tas).
boiling-water ['bɔɪlɪŋwɔːtər] *adj Nucl Phys* **b.-w. reactor,** réacteur *m* à eau bouillante.
boisterous ['bɔɪst(ə)rəs] *adj* (*person*) turbulent; (*noisy*) bruyant, tapageur; (*wind*) violent; (*sea*) tumultueux; **b. spirits,** gaieté débordante *ou* tapageuse.
boisterously ['bɔɪst(ə)rəslɪ] *adv* bruyamment; tumultueusement.
bold [bəʊld] **1** *adj* **(a)** (*fearless*) hardi; (*courageous*) courageux; (*reckless*) audacieux, téméraire; (*tone, look*) assuré, confiant; **to put on a b. front,** s'armer de courage; **to put a b. face** *or* **front on it,** payer d'audace; **b. stroke,** (*fearless*) coup hardi; (*reckless*) coup d'audace; **b. enterprise,** entreprise audacieuse; **if I may be** *or* **make so b.,** si je puis prendre une telle liberté; **she made so b. as to ask what my salary was,** elle ne s'est pas gênée pour me demander combien je gagnais; **(b)** (*impudent*) impudent, effronté; **as b. as brass,** d'un air effronté; **(c)** *Art etc* (*style, trait, coup de pinceau*) hardi; (*coloris*) vigoureux; **b. features,** traits accusés; *Typ* **b. type** *or* **face,** caractères gras. **2** *n Typ* **in b.,** en gras.
boldly ['bəʊldlɪ] *adv* (*see adj*) **(a)** hardiment; courageusement; audacieusement; **to state sth b.,** affirmer qch avec confiance; **to treat a subject b.,** traiter un sujet hardiment; **(b)** effrontément; **(c)** avec hardiesse.
boldness ['bəʊldnɪs] *n* **(a)** hardiesse *f* (*de conduite etc*); (*courage*) courage *m*; (*recklessness*) audace *f*; **(b)** (*impudence*) effronterie *f*, impudence *f*; **(c)** *Art* hardiesse *f* (*de style, de pinceau*).
bole [bəʊl] *n* fût *m*, tronc *m* (*d'un arbre*).
bolero [bə'leərəʊ] *n* **(a)** (*dance, music*) boléro *m*; **(b)** (*also* ['bɒlərəʊ]) (*jacket*) boléro *m*.
boletus [bɒ'liːtəs] *n* (*fungus*) bolet *m*; **edible b.,** cèpe *m*.
Bolivia [bə'lɪvɪə] *n* Bolivie *f*.
Bolivian [bə'lɪvɪən] **1** *adj* bolivien. **2** *n* Bolivien, -ienne.
boll [bəʊl] *n Bot* capsule *f* (*du cotonnier, du lin*); **b. weevil,** anthonome *m* (*du cotonnier*).
bollard ['bɒləd] *n* **(a)** *Nau* bitte *f* (*d'amarrage, de tournage*); **(b)** *Br* (*on road*) borne *f*.
bollocking ['bɒləkɪŋ] *n Sl* (*severe reprimand*) engueulade *f*; **he got a b. from the boss,** il s'est fait engueuler par le patron.
bollocks ['bɒləks] *npl Vulg* couilles *fpl*; **b.!,** c'est de la merde!
▶**bollocks up** *vtsep Vulg* bousiller (*qch*).
Bologna [bə'lɒnjə] *n* Bologne *f*.
Bolognese [bɒlə'niːz, -eɪz] **1** *adj* bolognais. **2** *n* Bolognais, -aise.
boloney [bə'ləʊnɪ] *n* = **BALONEY**.
Bolshevik ['bɒlʃɪvɪk] **, Bolshevist** ['bɒlʃɪvɪst] *adj & n* bolchevik *mf*, bolcheviste *mf*.
Bolshevism ['bɒlʃəvɪz(ə)m] *n* bolchevisme *m*.
bolshie, bolshy ['bɒlʃɪ] *F* **1** *adj* **he's b.,** c'est un mauvais coucheur; **he turned b.,** il a commencé à râler; **she's in a b. mood,** elle est de très mauvais poil. **2** *n* rouge *mf*.
bolster¹ ['bəʊlstər] *n* **(a)** traversin *m* (*de lit*); **(b)** *MecE* coussinet *m*; *Metal* contre poinçon *m*, *pl* contre poinçons; **(c)** *Constr* racinal *m*, -aux; chapeau *m* (*de poteau*); **(d)** *Nau* coussin *m* (*de capelage, de ferrure*).
bolster² *vt* (*strengthen*) donner (*du courage, de la confiance*); **to b. s.o.'s confidence,** donner de la confiance à qn; **to b. one's courage,** se donner du courage.
▶**bolster up** *vtsep Fig* appuyer, soutenir (*qn*); étayer (*une théorie*); *Fin* **to b. up the pound,** renforcer la livre.
bolt¹ [bəʊlt] *n* **(a)** (*closing device*) verrou *m* (*de porte*); pêne *m* (*de serrure*); **(b)** *MecE* boulon *m*; cheville *f*; goupille *f*; **nuts and bolts,** visserie *f*; *Fig* **the nuts and bolts,** (*practical details*) les détails pratiques *ou* matériels; **(c)** *F* fuite *f*; **to make a b. for it,** décamper, déguerpir; **she made a b. for the door,** elle se précipita vers la porte; **b. hole,** trou *m* de refuge (*d'un animal*); *Mil* abri *m* de bombardement; *Fig* échappatoire *f*, porte *f* de sortie; **to arrange a b. hole for oneself,** se ménager une porte de sortie; **this is my b. hole,** c'est mon échappatoire; **(d)** (*of lightning*) éclair *m*; **it's like a b. from the blue,** c'est comme un coup de foudre; **(e)** (*roll*) **a b. of cloth,** une coupe de drap; **(f)** *Arch* carreau *m* (*d'arbalète*); **he has shot his b.,** (*is exhausted*) il est épuisé; *Fig* (*of politician etc*) il a joué sa dernière carte.
bolt² **1** *vt* **(a)** (*close*) verrouiller; fermer (*une porte*) à *ou* au verrou; **to b. oneself in,** s'enfermer au verrou; **(b)** *MecE* boulonner, cheviller; **(c)** *F* bouffer (*son dîner*). **2** *vi* **(a)** (*of door etc*) se verrouiller; **(b)** (*of horse*) s'emballer, prendre le mors aux dents; *F* (*of person*) décamper, déguerpir; **(c)** (*of plant*) monter en graine.
bolt³ *adv* **b. upright,** droit comme un piquet.
▶**bolt down 1** *vipo* descendre rapidement (*l'escalier*). **2** *vtsep* **to b. down one's food** *or* **a meal,** manger avec un lance-pierres; **don't b. your food down,** (*even though you're hungry*) ne te jette pas sur la nourriture comme ça; (*even though you're late*) n'avale pas à cette vitesse.
▶**bolt in 1** *vi* (*enter quickly*) entrer comme un bolide; **she came bolting in to tell them the news,** elle s'est ruée dans la pièce pour leur donner les nouvelles. **2** *vtsep* (*lock in*) enfermer (*qn*).
▶**bolt out 1** *vi* (*leave quickly*) sortir comme un bolide; **they bolted out of the door,** ils sont sortis en courant. **2** *vtsep* (*lock out*) enfermer (*qn*) dehors.
bolus ['bəʊləs] *n Pharm* bol *m*.
bomb¹ [bɒm] *n Mil etc* bombe *f*; **the b.,** la bombe atomique; **to release** *or* **drop a b.,** jeter *ou* lâcher *ou* larguer une bombe; *F* **this room looks as if a b. had hit it,** cette pièce est un véritable champ de bataille; *Br F* **to go like a b.,** (*of car*) bomber; (*of party*) battre son plein; (*of play, show etc*) casser la baraque, marcher très bien; *F* **it costs a b.,** ça coûte les yeux de la tête; *Am* **it's a b.,** (*of musical, play etc*) c'est un navet; **b. attack,** bombardement *m*; *Av* **b. bay,** soute *f* à bombes; **b. crater,** entonnoir *m*, cratère *m*; **b. disposal,** déminage *m*; **b. disposal expert,** démineur *m*; **b. hoax,** fausse alerte à la bombe; **b. scare,** alerte *f* à la bombe.
bomb² **1** *vt* bombarder, lancer des bombes sur (*une ville etc*). **2** *vi Am* (*of play etc*) faire un flop.
▶**bomb along 1** *vi* (*of car, driver*) bomber, aller à toute vitesse. **2** *vipo* **to b. along the road,** bomber sur la route.
▶**bomb down** *vipo* (*of car, driver*) **to b. down the road at 100 mph,** foncer à 160 (km/h).
▶**bomb off** *vi* (*of car, driver*) partir comme un bolide *ou* en trombe.
▶**bomb out** *vtsep* **they have been bombed out of their homes,** ils sont à la rue parce que leurs maisons ont été bombardées.
bombard [bɒm'bɑːd] *vt Mil etc* bombarder; *Fig* **to b. s.o. with questions,** assaillir qn de questions.
bombardier [bɒmbə'dɪər] *n* **(a)** *Mil* brigadier *m*; **(b)** *US Av* bombardier *m*.

bombardment [bɒm'bɑːdmənt] *n Mil etc* bombardement *m*.

bombasine, bombazine ['bɒmbəziːn] *n Tex* bombasin *m*.

bombast ['bɒmbæst] *n* emphase *f*, boursouflure *f* (*de style*).

bombastic [bɒm'bæstɪk] *adj* (*style*) ampoulé, boursouflé, emphatique.

bombastically [bɒm'bæstɪklɪ] *adv* d'un style ampoulé *ou* emphatique.

bomber ['bɒmər] *n* **(a)** (*aircraft*) bombardier *m*; **(b)** (*person*) *Mil* grenadier *m*; *Av* bombardier *m*; (*terrorist*) terroriste *mf* qui se sert de bombes; **b. jacket,** bomber *m*.

bombing ['bɒmɪŋ] *n Av* bombardement *m*; **b. raid,** bombardement aérien; **b. run,** course *f* de visée.

bombproof ['bɒmpruːf] *adj* à l'épreuve des bombes; **b. shelter,** abri blindé.

bombshell ['bɒmʃel] *n* **(a)** obus *m*; **(b)** *Fig* coup *m* de foudre; **this news came as a b. to us,** cette nouvelle nous a atterrés; **(c)** *F* (*attractive woman*) beauté *f*.

bombsight ['bɒmsaɪt] *n Av* viseur *m ou* collimateur *m* de bombardement.

bombthrower ['bɒmθrəʊər] *n* **(a)** (*device*) lance-bombes *m inv*; **(b)** (*person*) lanceur *m* de bombes.

bona fide ['bəʊnə'faɪdɪ] **1** *adj* **(a)** (*genuine*) authentique; **(b)** (*in good faith*) (*purchaser*) de bonne foi; (*offer*) sérieux. **2** *n* **one's bona fides** [-faɪdɪz], sa bonne foi, sa sincérité.

bonanza [bə'nænzə] **1** *n* **to strike a b.,** rencontrer un riche filon. **2** *adj* **b. year,** année *f* de prospérité *ou* d'abondance.

Bonapartist ['bəʊnəpɑːtɪst] *n & adj* bonapartiste *mf*.

bonbon ['bɒnbɒn] *n* bonbon *m*.

bonce [bɒns] *n Br F* (*head*) boule *f*.

bond¹ [bɒnd] *n* **(a)** (*chain, rope*) lien *m*; *Lit* **bonds,** fers *mpl*, liens; **to burst one's bonds,** rompre *ou* briser ses liens *ou* ses fers;
(b) (*tie*) lien *m* (*d'osier, pour fagots etc*); *Constr etc* attache *f*; *Rail* éclisse *f* (*de rail conducteur*); *Carp* assemblage *m*; *Ch* liaison *f*; (*of glue*) adhérence *f*; *Constr* **(system of) b.,** appareil *m* (en liaison); *Fig* **bonds of friendship,** liens d'amitié; **there is a very close b. between us,** nous sommes très liés;
(c) (*commitment*) engagement *m*, contrat *m*; *Jur* obligation *f*; **my word is my b.,** (*you can trust me*) je vous donne ma parole d'honneur; (*I cannot back out*) j'ai donné ma parole d'honneur; **mortgage b.,** titre *m* hypothécaire;
(d) *Fin* bon *m*; *Am* obligation *f*; **registered b.,** bon nominatif; **Treasury b.,** bon du trésor;
(e) *Jur* caution *f*;
(f) *Com* **to be in b.,** être à l'entrepôt *ou* en dépôt; **to take goods out of b.,** dédouaner des marchandises.

bond² *vt* **(a)** *Constr* (en)lier, liaisonner (*des pierres*); appareiller (*un mur, des moellons*); **(b)** coller (*des métaux etc*); **(c)** *Com* entreposer, mettre en dépôt *ou* à l'entrepôt (*des marchandises*).

bondage ['bɒndɪdʒ] *n* **(a)** *Lit* esclavage *m*, asservissement *m*; **(b)** *Hist* servage *m*; **(c)** (*sexual practice*) = pratique sexuelle qui fait intervenir l'utilisation de liens.

bonded ['bɒndɪd] *adj* **(a)** *Constr* (*masonry*) en liaison; **(b)** *Com* (*goods*) en dépôt, en entrepôt; **b. warehouse,** entrepôt *m* en douane; **(c)** *Fin* (*dette*) garanti par obligations.

bondholder ['bɒndhəʊldər] *n Fin* obligataire *m*; détenteur *m ou* porteur *m* de bons *ou* d'obligations.

bonding ['bɒndɪŋ] *n* **(a)** *Constr* liaison *f* (*de pierres*); appareillage *m* (*d'un mur*); **(b)** collage *m* (*des métaux*); **(c)** *Com* entreposage *m* (*de marchandises*).

bondstone ['bɒndstəʊn] *n Constr* parpaing *m*.

bone¹ [bəʊn] *n* **(a)** (*of human, animal*) os *m*; (*of fish*) arête *f*; *F* **he's nothing but skin and bones,** il est maigre comme un clou, il n'a que la peau et les os; **to be as dry as a b.** *or* **b. dry,** (*of earth*) être desséché; (*of well*) être à sec; (*of washing*) être complètement sec; **he won't make old bones,** il ne fera pas de vieux os; **chilled** *or* **frozen to the b.,** gelé jusqu'aux os; **to cut expenses to the b.,** (*greatly reduce*) réduire les dépenses au minimum; **to work one's fingers to the b.,** se tuer à travailler; **to be b. idle** *or* **lazy,** être paresseux comme une couleuvre; **I feel it in my bones,** j'en ai le pressentiment; **b. of contention,** sujet *m* de dispute; *F* **to have a b. to pick with s.o.,** avoir un compte à régler avec qn; **to make no bones about doing sth,** ne pas hésiter à faire qch; **he made no bones about it,** il y est allé carrément; **she made no bones about her displeasure,** elle n'a pas caché son mécontentement; **near** *or* **close to the b.,** (*joke etc*) risqué, d'un goût douteux; **b. ash,** cendre *f ou* poudre *f* d'os; *Cer* **b. china,** porcelaine tendre anglaise; **b. meal,** (*fertiliser*) engrais *m* d'os (broyés);
(b) armature *f* (*d'un bustier etc*);
(c) **bones,** (*of the dead*) ossements *mpl*.

bone² *vt* **(a)** désosser (*la viande*); ôter les arêtes de (*un poisson*); **(b)** garnir (*un corset*) de baleines.
▶bone up on *vipo Sl* (*study*) potasser (*qch*).

boned [bəʊnd] *adj* **(a)** (*meat*) désossé; (*fish*) sans arêtes; **(b)** (*corset*) baleiné.

bone-dry ['bəʊn'draɪ] *adj* (*earth*) desséché; (*well*) à sec; (*washing*) complètement sec.

bonehead ['bəʊnhed] *n F* (*stupid person*) idiot, -ote; (*stubborn person*) tête *f* de bois.

boneless ['bəʊnlɪs] *adj* **(a)** (*meat*) sans os; (*from which bones have been removed*) désossé; (*fish*) sans arêtes; **(b)** *Fig* (*weak*) mou, sans caractère.

boner ['bəʊnər] *n Am F* (*mistake*) gaffe *f*; **I made a real b.,** j'ai fait une de ces gaffes!

boneshaker ['bəʊnʃeɪkər] *n F* **(a)** (*car*) vieux clou, vieille guimbarde; **(b)** *Arch* vélocipède *m* à bandages de fer.

bonfire ['bɒnfaɪər] *n* (*with fireworks*) feu *m* de joie; (*for burning leaves etc*) feu de jardin; **to make a b.,** faire un feu (*avec des feuilles mortes etc*); *Br* **B. Night,** = célébration de l'échec de la tentative de faire sauter le Parlement.

bonhomie ['bɒnɒmiː] *n* bonhomie *f*, jovialité *f*.

bonito [bə'niːtəʊ] *n* (*fish*) bonite *f*.

bonk [bɒŋk] **1** *vt & vi Br F Hum* (*have sex*) faire des galipettes, faire crac-crac (**s.o.,** avec qn). **2** *vt F* (*hit*) cogner.

bonkers ['bɒŋkəz] *adj Br Sl* cinglé.

bonnet ['bɒnɪt] *n* **(a)** (*hat*) bonnet *m*, béret *m* (écossais); capote *f*, bonnet (*de femme, d'enfant*); **(b)** *Br Aut* capot *m*; *Nau* couvercle *m*, chapeau *m* (*de cheminée*); *MecE* chapeau, capot, couvercle (*de soupape, de vanne*); *Aut* **to have a look under the b.,** regarder sous le capot.

bonny ['bɒnɪ] *adj esp Scot* joli; **a b. baby,** un bébé magnifique.

bonsai ['bɒnsaɪ] *n* bonsaï *m*.

bonus, *pl* **-uses** ['bəʊnəs, -əsɪz] *n* gratification *f*, bonification *f*; (*esp at work*) prime *f*; **to work on a b. system,** travailler à la prime; **cost-of-living b.,** indemnité *f* de vie chère *ou* de cherté de vie; **no-claims b.,** (*in insurance*) bonus *m*; *Com etc* **Christmas b.,** gratification de fin d'année; **productivity** *or US* **merit b.,** prime de rendement.

bony ['bəʊnɪ] *adj* **(a)** (*person*) à *ou* aux gros os; (*corps, contours*) anguleux; (*doigt, visage*) décharné; (*meat*) plein d'os; (*fish*) plein d'arêtes; **(b)** (*like bone*) osseux.

boo¹ [buː] **1** *int* hou!; *F* **he wouldn't say b. to a goose,** c'est un timide. **2** *n* huée *f*; **her arrival was greeted with boos,** elle s'est fait huer à son arrivée.

boo² *vt & vi* **to b. (at) s.o.,** huer *ou* chahuter qn; **to be booed off the stage,** quitter la scène au milieu des huées.

boob¹ [buːb] *n Sl* **(a)** (*fool*) idiot, -ote, crétin *m*; *esp Am* **b. tube,** (*television*) télé *f*; **(b)** (*mistake*) gaffe *f*; **(c)** (*breast*) néné *m*; **b. tube,** bustier *m*.

boob² *vi Sl* faire une gaffe.

boo-boo ['buːbuː] *n F* (*blunder*) gaffe *f*, bourde *f*; **to make a b.-b.,** faire une gaffe *ou* une bourde.

booby ['buːbɪ] *n* **(a)** *Old-fashioned* idiot, -ote, crétin *m*, nouille *f*; *US Sl* **b. hatch,** (*mental hospital*) maison *f* de fous; **b. trap,** attrape-nigaud *m*, *pl* attrape-nigauds; *Mil* piège *m*; mine-piège *f*, *pl* mines-pièges; **to set a b. trap for s.o.,** tendre un piège à qn; **(b)** le dernier (*dans un concours etc*); **b. prize,** = prix décerné par plaisanterie à celui qui vient en dernier; **(c)** (*bird*) fou *m*.

booby-trap ['buːbɪtræp] *vt* piéger (*une voiture etc*).

boogie-woogie ['buːgɪ'wuːgɪ] *n Mus* boogie-woogie *m*.

booing ['buːɪŋ] *n* huées *fpl*, chahutage *m*.

book¹ [bʊk] *n* **(a)** (*for reading, of Bible*) livre *m*; livret *m*, libretto *m* (*d'un opéra*); recueil *m* (*de chansons, de prières etc*); *Tel* annuaire *m*; **a b. on** *or* **about gardening,** livre de jardinage; **old books,** vieux bouquins; (*antiques*) vieilles éditions; **the b. trade,** l'industrie *f* du livre, la librairie; **school b.,** livre scolaire, livre de classe; **not published in b. form,** inédit en librairie; **by** *or* **according to the b.,** selon les règles; **to go by the b.,** suivre les règles; **to be a closed b. to s.o.,** (*of subject*) être du chinois pour qn; **she's a closed b. to me,** (*I don't understand her*) je n'arrive pas à la cerner; *Old-fashioned* **the good B.,** la Bible; **to swear on the B.,** prêter serment sur la Bible; *Tel* **I'm in the b.,** (*listed in directory*) je suis dans l'annuaire; **she's an open b.,** elle ne peut rien cacher (*de ses sentiments etc*); **in my b.,** d'après moi; **that doesn't suit my b.,** ça ne me convient pas; **b. club,** club *m* du livre; **b. end,**

serre-livres *m inv*; **b. fair,** salon *m* du livre; **b. post,** service postal des imprimés; **b. review,** revue *f* littéraire; **b. review page,** (*in newspaper*) chronique *f* littéraire; **b. token,** bon-cadeau *m ou* chèque-cadeau *m* pour des livres; **(b)** *Com Fin etc* registre *m*; *Sch* cahier *m*; **account b.,** livre *m* de comptes; **to keep the books of a firm,** tenir les livres d'une maison; **to be in s.o.'s good books,** être dans les petits papiers de qn, être bien vu de qn; **to be in s.o.'s bad books,** être mal vu *ou* mal noté de *ou* par qn; **to bring s.o. to b. for sth,** forcer qn à rendre compte de qch; *F* **to throw the b. at s.o.,** accabler qn d'accusations; **I'll throw the b. at you!,** vous allez entendre parler de moi!; *Nau* **ship's books,** livres de bord; **signal b.,** tome *m* des signaux; *Horseracing* **to make a b.,** faire un pari; **we've opened a b. on how late he'll be,** nous parions sur l'étendue de son retard; **b. of matches,** pochette *f* d'allumettes; **b. of needles,** sachet *m ou* jeu *m* d'aiguilles; **b. of stamps/tickets,** carnet *m* de timbres/billets; **b. matches,** allumettes plates; *Com* **b. value,** valeur *f* comptable.

book[2] **1** *vt* **(a)** (*write down*) inscrire, enregistrer (*une commande etc*); *F* (*of policeman*) dresser une contravention à (*qn*); *US* arrêter (*qn*); (*of referee*) donner un avertissement à (*un joueur*); **I was booked for speeding yesterday,** hier j'ai eu une contravention pour excès de vitesse; **(b)** (*reserve*) retenir, réserver (*une place, une chambre*); louer (*une place*) d'avance; *Rail Av* réserver (*un billet, une place*); *Th etc* engager (*un artiste*); **I've booked you on the next flight,** je vous ai réservé une place sur le prochain vol; **fully booked,** (*of theatre, flight*) complet; **I'm booked for this evening,** je suis pris ce soir. **2** *vi Rail etc* réserver une place *ou* un billet; **to b. through to Nice,** prendre un billet direct pour Nice.

▶**book in 1** *vi* (*of hotel guest*) se faire inscrire sur le registre. **2** *vtsep* inscrire (*qn*) au registre.

▶**book out 1** *vi* (*of hotel guest*) quitter un hôtel. **2** *vtsep* **I booked them out at noon,** ils ont réglé leur note à midi.

▶**book up 1** *vi* (*make reservations*) réserver; **have you booked up for a holiday?,** est-ce que vous avez réservé pour vos vacances? **2** *vtsep* (*usu passive*) **the hotel is all booked up,** l'hôtel est complet; **I'm booked up for this evening,** je suis pris ce soir.

bookable ['bʊkəb(ə)l] *adj Th etc* (*seat*) qui peut être réservé *ou* loué à l'avance.

bookbinder ['bʊkbaɪndər] *n* relieur, -euse.

bookbinding ['bʊkbaɪndɪŋ] *n* reliure *f*.

bookcase ['bʊkkeɪs] *n* bibliothèque *f*.

bookie ['bʊkɪ] *n Horseracing F* bookmaker *m*, book *m*.

booking ['bʊkɪŋ] *n* **(a)** (*of order*) enregistrement *m*, inscription *f*; **(b)** réservation *f* (*d'une chambre, d'une place etc*); *Th etc* engagement *m* (*d'un artiste*); location *f* (*de places, de billets*); **do you have a b.?,** (*to hotel guest*) avez-vous réservé?; **you have a b. in the name of Smith,** (*to hotel clerk*) j'ai réservé au nom de Smith; **b. clerk,** employé, -ée du guichet; **b. office,** guichet *m* de réservation *ou* de location.

bookish ['bʊkɪʃ] *adj* **(a)** (*studious*) studieux; **(b)** *Pej* (*person, style*) pédant *f*.

book-keeper ['bʊkkiːpər] *n Com* comptable *m*.

book-keeping ['bʊkkiːpɪŋ] *n Com* comptabilité *f*; **single-entry b.-k.,** comptabilité en partie simple; **double-entry b.-k.,** comptabilité en partie double.

book-learning ['bʊklɜːnɪŋ] *n* érudition *f*; *Pej* savoir acquis dans les livres.

booklet ['bʊklɪt] *n* brochure *f*; (*small book*) plaquette *f*.

booklover ['bʊklʌvər] *n* bibliophile *m*.

bookmaker ['bʊkmeɪkər] *n Horseracing* bookmaker *m*.

bookmark(er) ['bʊkmɑːk, -ər] *n* signet *m*.

bookmobile ['bʊkməbiːl] *n esp US* (*mobile library*) bibliobus *m*.

bookplate ['bʊkpleɪt] *n* ex-libris *m inv*.

bookrest ['bʊkrest] *n* appui-livre(s) *m inv*, porte-livres *m inv*.

bookseller ['bʊkselər] *n* libraire *m*; **secondhand b.,** bouquiniste *m*.

bookselling ['bʊkselɪŋ] *n* (commerce *m* de) librairie *f*.

bookshelf, *pl* **-shelves** ['bʊkʃelf, -ʃelvz] *n* rayon *m* (à livres).

bookshop ['bʊkʃɒp] *n* librairie *f*.

bookstall ['bʊkstɔːl] *n* **(a)** (*in street*) étalage *m* de livres; **secondhand b.,** étalage de bouquiniste; **(b)** (*in station*) bibliothèque *f* de gare.

bookstore ['bʊkstɔːr] *n Am* librairie *f*.

bookworm ['bʊkwɜːm] *n* **(a)** *Fig* dévoreur, -euse de livres, bouquineur, -euse; **I've always been a b.,** j'aime bouquiner depuis toujours; **(b)** (*insect*) anobion *m*, ptine *m*.

boom[1] [buːm] *n* **(a)** (*at harbour mouth*) barrage flottant, barre *ou* estacade flottante; **(b)** *Nau* bout-dehors *m* (*de foc*), *pl* bouts-dehors; **cargo b.,** corne *f* de charge; **derrick b.,** mât *m* de charge; **swinging b.,** tangon *m*; **(c)** flèche *f* (*d'une grue*); *Cin TV* perche *f* (*de microphone*), *F* girafe *f*.

boom[2] *n* grondement *m*, retentissement *m* (*du canon, du tonnerre, des vagues*); mugissement *m* (*du vent*); tons *mpl* sonores (*de la voix*); ronflement *m* (*de l'orgue*); bourdonnement *m* (*de cloches*).

boom[3] *vi* (*of wind etc*) retentir, gronder, mugir (sourdement); (*of guns*) gronder, tonner; (*of organ*) ronfler; (*of bells*) bourdonner; **his voice boomed,** sa voix retentissait.

boom[4] *n Com Fin etc* boom *m*, période *f* d'essor, vague *f* de prospérité; **b. town,** (*growing*) ville *f* champignon; (*prosperous*) ville prospère.

boom[5] *vi* (*of trade, business etc*) être en plein essor.

▶**boom out 1** *vi* (*sound loudly*) résonner; **the president's voice was booming out over the loudspeakers,** la voix du président résonnait dans les haut-parleurs. **2** *vtsep* (*utter loudly*) hurler (*un ordre*).

boomerang[1] ['buːməræŋ] *n* (*for throwing*) & *Fig* boomerang *m*; **to throw a b.,** lancer un boomerang.

boomerang[2] *vi* faire boomerang; *Fig* **the joke boomeranged on him,** la plaisanterie lui est retombée dessus.

booming ['buːmɪŋ] *adj* (*vent*) mugissant; (*tonnerre*) retentissant; **b. voice,** voix retentissante.

boon[1] [buːn] *n* **(a)** (*useful item*) bienfait *m*, avantage *m*; **I found it a great b.,** cela m'a rendu grand service; **(b)** *Arch Lit* faveur *f*.

boon[2] *adj* **b. companion,** gai *ou* bon compagnon.

boondocks ['buːndɒks], **boonies** ['buːniːz] *npl Am F* (grande) banlieue *f*; **to live in the boonies,** habiter à Perpète(-les-Oies).

boor ['bʊər] *n* rustre *m*, rustaud *m*.

boorish ['bʊərɪʃ] *adj* rustre, rustaud, grossier.

boorishly ['bʊərɪʃlɪ] *adv* grossièrement, de façon rustre.

boorishness ['bʊərɪʃnɪs] *n* grossièreté *f*.

boost[1] [buːst] *n* **(a) to give a b. to,** faire de la réclame *ou* du battage pour (*un produit*); relancer (*une industrie, la production etc*); augmenter (*le recrutement, la vente de qch etc*); relever (*le moral*); *F* pistonner (*qn*); **(b)** *El* survoltage *m*; *Av* surpression *f*.

boost[2] *vt* **(a)** faire de la réclame *ou* du battage pour (*un produit*); relancer (*une industrie, la production etc*); augmenter (*le recrutement, le nombre, les prix etc*); relever (*le moral*); *F* pistonner (*qn*); **(b)** augmenter (*la vitesse, l'énergie, la pression de qch*); *El* survolter.

booster ['buːstər] *n* **(a)** *El* survolteur *m*; **(b)** (*of missile*) propulseur *m* auxiliaire de départ; **b. rocket,** fusée *f* de démarrage; **(c)** *Av* démarreur *m* auxiliaire, accélérateur *m* (de décollage); **(d)** *Tech* surpresseur *m*; **b. station,** station *f* auxiliaire de pompage, station relais; **(e)** *Electron* préamplificateur *m* d'antenne; **(f)** *Ch* renforçateur *m*; **(g)** *Med* **b. dose/injection,** dose *f*/injection *f ou* piqûre *f* de rappel.

boot[1] [buːt] *n* **(a)** (*footwear*) (*short*) bottine *f*; (*high*) botte *f*; **laced b.,** brodequin *m*; **fur-lined b.,** bottillon *m*; **riding boots,** bottes à l'écuyère; *F* **the boot's on the other foot,** les rôles sont renversés; *F* **you can bet your boots that ...,** je te garantis que ...; *F* **to give s.o. the (order of the) b.,** mettre *ou* flanquer qn à la porte; *F* **to get the b.,** être mis à la porte; *F* **as tough as old boots,** dur comme tout; **to die with one's boots on,** (*in battle*) mourir les bottes aux pieds; *Fig* rester fidèle au poste jusqu'à la mort; *US Mil Sl* **b. camp,** = camp d'entraînement des nouvelles recrues;
(b) *Ind* hotte *f*, trémie *f* (*pour alimenter une machine etc*); **charging b.,** entonnoir *m*;
(c) *Br Aut* coffre *m*; **b. sale,** ≈ brocante *f*;
(d) (*kick*) coup *m* de pied; **to give a ball a b.,** donner un coup de pied dans un ballon; *F* **to put the b. in,** (*kick someone*) donner des coups de pied; *Fig* (*get tough*) serrer la vis.

boot[2] **1** *vt F* flanquer des coups de pied à (*qn*); **to b. s.o. out,** (*dismiss*) flanquer qn à la porte; **her parents booted her out of the house,** ses parents l'ont mise à la porte. **2** *vi* (*of computer*) s'amorcer.

boot[3] *n* (*only in the phrase*) **to b.,** par surcroît, en sus, par-dessus le marché; **and a liar/a thief to b.,** et par-dessus le marché c'est un menteur/un voleur.

▶**boot up** *Comptr* **1** *vi* (*of computer*) s'amorcer. **2** *vtsep* amorcer (*un ordinateur*).

bootblack ['buːtblæk] *n* cireur *m* (*de chaussures*).

bootee [buː'tiː] *n* **(a)** (*short boot*) bottillon *m*; **(b)** bottine *f* d'enfant; chausson tricoté (*de bébé*).

booth [buːð, buːθ] *n* baraque *f*, tente *f* (*de marché, de*

forains); *Tel* cabine *f*; *US* stand *m* (*d'exposition*); **polling b.**, isoloir *m*; *Cin* **projection b.**, cabine de projection.
bootjack ['buːtdʒæk] *n* tire-botte *m*, *pl* tire-bottes.
bootlace ['buːtleɪs] *n* lacet *m* (de botte).
bootleg¹ ['buːtleg] *adj* (*whisky*) de contrebande; (*record, video*) piraté.
bootleg² *v* (**-gg-**) **1** *vt* transporter *ou* produire *ou* vendre (*de l'alcool*) illégalement; **bootlegged videos are on sale,** des cassettes vidéo piratées sont en vente. **2** *vi* trafiquer (*surtout en boissons alcooliques*); faire de la contrebande.
bootlegger ['buːtlegər] *n* contrebandier *m*; *Hist US* bootlegger *m*.
bootlegging ['buːtlegɪŋ] *n* contrebande *f* (*surtout de l'alcool*).
bootlick ['buːtlɪk] *vi* faire du lèche-bottes.
bootlicker ['buːtlɪkər] *n F* lèche-bottes *m inv*.
bootlicking ['buːtlɪkɪŋ] *n* **b. is his speciality,** il est spécialiste du lèche-bottes.
bootloader ['buːtləʊdər] *n Comptr* chargeur-amorce *m*.
bootmaker ['buːtmeɪkər] *n* bottier *m*; cordonnier *m*.
bootstrap ['buːtstræp] *n* **(a)** languette *f* (*sur une botte*); *Fig* **to pull oneself up by one's bootstraps,** se faire tout seul; **(b)** *Comptr* amorce *f*, programme *m* d'amorcement; **b. loader,** chargeur-amorce *m*; **b. routine,** routine *f* d'amorçage.
booty ['buːtɪ] *n* butin *m*.
booze¹ [buːz] *vi F* boire comme un trou, lever le coude, picoler; **he's gone out boozing,** il est allé boire.
booze² *n Sl* boisson *f* (alcoolique); **there's no more b.,** il n'y a plus rien à boire; **to go on the b.,** se mettre à boire.
boozer ['buːzər] *n Sl* **(a)** (*drunkard*) ivrogne *m*, soûlard *m*; **he's a real b.,** c'est un véritable ivrogne!; **(b)** *Br* (*pub*) troquet *m*; **I'll see you in the b. at seven,** je te verrai au troquet à sept heures.
booze-up ['buːzʌp] *n Br Sl* beuverie *f*, soûlerie *f*; **we're having a b.-up on Friday,** on va faire la fête vendredi.
boozy ['buːzɪ] *adj F* soûlard; (*breath*) qui sent l'alcool; **a b. evening,** une soirée passée à boire; **a b. old man,** un vieil ivrogne.
bop¹ [bɒp] *n* **(a)** *Mus* bop *m*; **(b)** *F* (*at disco*) danse *f*; **to go for a b.,** aller danser.
bop² *vi F* (*at disco*) danser.
bop³ *n F* (*blow*) coup *m*; **you've had a b. on the head,** tu as reçu un coup sur la tête.
bop⁴ *vt F* donner un coup à (*qn*); **he bopped me on the head,** il m'a donné un coup sur la tête.
bo-peep [bəʊ'piːp] *n F* cache-cache *m inv*.
bopper ['bɒpər] *n* (*likes dancing*) danseur, -euse acharné(e).
boracic [bə'ræsɪk] *adj Ch* (*acide*) borique; *Pharm* **b. ointment,** pommade boriquée.
borage ['bɒrɪdʒ] *n Culin* bourrache *f*.
borax ['bɔːræks] *n Ch etc* borax *m*.
bordeaux [bɔː'dəʊ] *n* (*wine*) bordeaux *m*.
border¹ ['bɔːdər] *n* **(a)** bord *m* (*d'un chemin, d'une route, d'une précipice etc*); lisière *f* (*d'un tissu etc*); bordure *f* (*d'un mouchoir, d'un massif de fleurs, d'un trottoir etc*); marge *f*; **(b)** frontière *f* (*entre deux pays*); **to cross the b.,** passer la frontière; **the B.,** (*in Britain*) la frontière écossaise (et les comtés limitrophes); (*in US*) la frontière entre les États-Unis et le Mexique; **the Borders, the B. country,** (*in Britain*) = les comtés limitrophes de la frontière entre l'Ecosse et l'Angleterre; **b. guard,** garde-frontière *m*, *pl* gardes-frontière; **b. town,** ville *f* frontière; **b. region,** région frontalière; **(c)** galon *m* (*d'un habit*); bordure *f* (*d'un tableau, d'un tapis etc*); bord *m* (*d'une assiette*); encadrement *m* (*d'un panneau*); carnèle *f* (*d'une pièce de monnaie*); **(d)** (*in garden*) plate-bande *f*, *pl* plates-bandes.
border² *vt* **(a)** border (*un habit, un chemin etc*); lisérer (*un mouchoir*); encadrer (*un panneau*); **(b)** border; confiner à *ou* avec (*un pays etc*); **the countries that b. the Mediterranean,** les pays qui bordent la Méditerranée.
►**border on** *vipo* **(a)** (*of territory*) toucher à, confiner à (*un autre pays*); **the two countries b. on one another,** les deux pays se touchent; **his estate borders on mine,** sa terre tient à la mienne; **(b)** (*be equivalent to*) approcher de, être voisin de (*la folie etc*); friser (*le mensonge etc*); toucher à (*l'absurde*); **he was bordering on sixty,** il frisait la soixantaine.
borderer ['bɔːdərər] *n* habitant, -ante de la frontière (*surtout de la frontière d'Ecosse*); frontalier, -ière.
bordering ['bɔːdərɪŋ] *adj* **(a)** (*pays*) contigu, *f* -uë, limitrophe (**on,** de); **countries b. the Mediterranean,** pays en bordure de la Méditerranée; **(b) emotion b. on terror,** émotion voisine de la terreur.
borderland ['bɔːdəlænd] *n* pays frontalier *ou* limitrophe; *Fig* frontière *f* (**between sleeping and waking,** entre le sommeil et le réveil).
borderline ['bɔːdəlaɪn] *n* ligne *f* de séparation (*entre deux catégories etc*); frontière *f* (*entre deux Etats*); *Fig* **the b. between sanity and insanity,** la limite entre le bon sens et la folie; **a b. case,** un cas-limite.
bore¹ ['bɔːr] *n* **(a)** (*diameter*) calibre *m*, alésage *m* (*d'un tuyau etc*); calibre (*d'une arme à feu*); **(b)** (*cylinder*) âme *f* (*d'une arme à feu*); **smooth/rifled b.,** âme lisse/rayée; **(c)** *Min* trou *m* de sonde, sondage *m*, forage *m*.
bore² *vt & vi* foncer (*un puits*); forer, percer (*un trou*); aléser (*un cylindre*); **to b. into wood,** (*of insect*) creuser un trou *ou* une galerie dans le bois; **to b. through sth,** percer qch; *Min* **to b. for water/minerals,** faire un sondage *ou* sonder pour trouver de l'eau/des minéraux.
bore³ *n* **(a)** personne ennuyeuse, *F* raseur, -euse; **what a b. (he is)!,** ce qu'il est barbant *ou* rasoir!; **she's a crashing b.,** elle est d'un ennui; **he's a real b. on the subject of gardening,** il est vraiment barbant quand il parle de jardinage; **(b)** (*thing*) corvée *f*, *F* scie *f*; **what a b.!,** quelle corvée!
bore⁴ *vt* ennuyer, *F* raser, barber (*qn*); *F* **it bores me rigid** *or* **stiff** *or* **to death** *or* **to tears,** ça me fait mourir *ou* crever d'ennui; **he bores me rigid** *or* **stiff** *etc*, il m'ennuie à mourir.
bore⁵ *n* (*wave*) mascaret *m*.
bore⁶ *see* **BEAR³**.
Boreal ['bɔːrɪəl] *adj* (*forest*) boréal.
bored [bɔːd] *adj* (*look etc*) d'ennui; **you look b.,** on dirait que tu t'ennuies vraiment; **to be** *or* **get b.,** s'ennuyer; **I'm never b.,** je ne m'ennuie jamais; **she is b. with it/him,** cela/il l'ennuie; (*has had enough of*) elle en a assez/elle en a assez de lui.
boredom ['bɔːdəm] *n* ennui *m*.
borehole ['bɔːhəʊl] *n Min* (*exploratory*) trou *m* de sonde, sondage *m*; (*for mine*) trou de mine.
borer ['bɔːrər] *n* **(a)** (*person*) foreur *m*, perceur *m*; sondeur *m* (*de puits*); **(b)** (*device*) foret *m*, tarière *f*; perçoir *m*; (*of cylinder*) alésoir *m*; *Min* fleuret *m*, sonde *f*; **(c)** (*mollusc*) taret *m*; **(d)** (*insect*) insecte térébrant.
boring¹ ['bɔːrɪŋ] **1** *adj* (*insect*) térébrant. **2** *n* percement *m* (*d'un trou etc*); *MecE* forage *m*, perçage *m*; (*of cylinder*) alésage *m*; *Min* sondage *m*, forage; **to make borings,** faire des sondages; **b. mill,** aléseuse fraiseuse; **b. machine,** *MecE* foreuse *f*, perceuse *f*; (*for cylinders*) alésoir *m*; *Min etc* sondeuse *f*, sonde *f*; **b. tool,** *MecE* outil *m* à aléser; alésoir *m*; *Min etc* outil de sondage, sonde *f*.
boring² *adj* ennuyeux, *F* barbant, rasoir; **what a b. evening!,** quelle soirée ennuyeuse!
boric ['bɔːrɪk] *adj Ch* (*acid etc*) borique.
born [bɔːn] **1** *v* (*pp of* **bear³** *used in formation of passive verb*) **to be b.,** naître; **I was b. in London,** je suis né à Londres; **the house where I was b.,** ma maison natale; **he is French b.,** il est français de naissance; **when I was b.,** lors de ma naissance; **he was b. in 1930,** il est né en 1930; **to be b. deaf/blind,** être sourd/aveugle de naissance; **to be b. lucky,** être né coiffé; *F* **do you think I was b. yesterday?,** croyez-vous que je suis né d'hier?; **I wasn't b. yesterday,** je ne suis pas né d'hier *ou* de la dernière pluie; *Fig* **crime b. of poverty,** crime né de la misère. **2** *adj* **he's a b. storyteller,** c'est un conteur né; **a Londoner b. and bred,** un vrai Londonien de Londres; **in all my b. days,** de toute ma vie.
born-again ['bɔːnəgen] *adj Rel & Hum* régénéré; **b.-a. Christian,** chrétien régénéré; *Fig* **b.-a. vegetarian,** personne devenue végétarienne (et qui essaye de convaincre les autres).
borne *see* **BEAR³**.
Borneo ['bɔːnɪəʊ] *n* Bornéo *m*.
borough ['bʌrə] *n* **(a)** *esp Br* (*town*) ville *f* (*avec municipalité*); **b. council,** conseil municipal; **(b)** *Pol* circonscription électorale (urbaine).
borrow ['bɒrəʊ] **1** *vt* emprunter (**from,** à); **may I b. your pen?,** pourriez-vous me prêter votre stylo?; *Fin etc* **to b. money from s.o.,** faire un emprunt à qn, emprunter à qn; **can I b. the car?,** puis-je prendre la voiture?; **to b. an idea from s.o.,** emprunter une idée à qn; **this word was borrowed from Latin,** ce mot est un emprunt au latin. **2** *vi* emprunter; **to b. from s.o.,** (*money*) faire un emprunt à qn, emprunter à qn.
borrowed ['bɒrəʊd] *adj* **b. capital,** capitaux empruntés *ou* d'emprunt; **he's living on b. time,** (*close to death*) il ne lui reste que peu de temps à vivre; (*is very old*) il a déjà

dépassé l'âge où la plupart des gens meurent.

borrower ['bɒrəʊər] *n* emprunteur, -euse.

borrowing ['bɒrəʊɪŋ] *n* (*action, money*) emprunt *m*.

borsch [bɔːʃ] *n Culin* bortsch *m*.

borstal ['bɔːst(ə)l] *n Br Admin* maison *f* de redressement (*pour jeunes délinquants âgés de 15 à 21 ans*); **b. boy,** jeune délinquant.

borzoi ['bɔːzɔɪ] *n* (*dog*) lévrier *m* russe, barzoï *m*.

bosh [bɒʃ] *n & int F* bêtises *fpl*, blague *f*.

bos'n ['bəʊs(ə)n] *n* = **BOATSWAIN.**

bosom ['bʊzəm] **1** *n* poitrine *f* (*d'une personne*); seins *mpl* (*d'une femme*); *Fig* **in the b. of one's family,** au sein de sa famille; *Fig* **in the b. of the Church,** dans le giron de l'Église. **2** *adj* **b. friend,** ami intime; **they are b. friends,** ils sont très intimes.

bosomy ['bʊzəmɪ] *adj* qui a une poitrine opulente.

Bosp(h)orus (the) [ðə'bɒsfərəs], ['bɒspərəs] *n* le Bosphore.

boss[1] [bɒs] *n* **(a)** (*knob*) protubérance *f*; *Archit Metal Zool etc* bosse *f*; (*on furniture*) capiton *m*; **(b)** *MecE* mamelon *m*, portée *f*; *Av* moyeu *m* (*de l'hélice*); **centre b.,** (*of wheel, crank*) tourteau *m*.

boss[2] *F* **1** *n* patron, -onne, chef *m*; *Am Pol* chef d'un parti; **the trade-union bosses,** les grands chefs du syndicat; **show them who's (the) b.,** montre-leur qui est le patron; **she's the b. here,** c'est elle qui porte la culotte. **2** *adj esp Am* épatant, merveilleux.

boss[3] *vt F* mener, diriger (*qn, qch*); **to b. the show,** faire la loi.

▶**boss about, boss around** *vtsep* donner des ordres à (*qn*); **stop bossing me about!,** j'en ai assez de vous et de vos ordres!

boss-eyed ['bɒsaɪd] *adj Br F* qui louche; **to be b.-e.,** avoir un œil qui dit merde à l'autre.

bossiness ['bɒsɪnɪs] *n F* (*of person, manner*) façons *fpl* autoritaires.

bossy ['bɒsɪ] *adj F* autoritaire; **he's so b.,** il veut toujours faire la loi; **don't be so b.,** arrête de jouer au petit chef.

bosun ['bəʊs(ə)n] *n* = **BOATSWAIN.**

botanic(al) [bə'tænɪk, -ɪk(ə)l] *adj* botanique; **b. garden(s),** jardin *m* botanique.

botanist ['bɒtənɪst] *n* botaniste *mf*.

botanize ['bɒtənaɪz] *vi* herboriser.

botany ['bɒtənɪ] *n* botanique *f*; **B. wool,** laine très fine (importée d'Australie).

botch[1] [bɒtʃ] *n F* travail mal fait *ou* bousillé; **you've made an awful b. of it,** tu l'as bien bousillé *ou* loupé.

botch[2] *vt F* bousiller, louper (*un travail etc*).

▶**botch up** *vtsep* rafistoler (*qch*), **botched-up work,** travail mal torché *ou* loupé.

botcher ['bɒtʃər] *n F* bousilleur *m*.

botch-up ['bɒtʃʌp] *n* = **BOTCH[1].**

both [bəʊθ] **1** *adj & pron* tous (les) deux, toutes (les) deux; l'un(e) et l'autre; **b. brothers, b. (of) the brothers,** les deux frères; **b. (of them) are dead,** ils sont morts tous (les) deux; **he has two houses, b. of which are vacant,** il a deux maisons, qui sont vides toutes les deux; **she kissed him on b. cheeks,** elle l'a embrassé sur les deux joues; **to hold sth in b. hands,** tenir qch à deux mains; **on b. sides,** des deux côtés; **b. alike,** l'un comme l'autre; **b. of us saw it,** nous deux l'avons vu, nous l'avons vu tous (les) deux; **look b. ways,** (*when crossing street*) regarde des deux côtés; **you can't have it b. ways,** on ne peut pas avoir le beurre et l'argent du beurre; *Nau* **stop b. engines,** stoppez partout. **2** *adv* **b. you and I,** (et) vous et moi; **she is b. intelligent and beautiful,** elle est à la fois intelligente et belle.

bother[1] ['bɒðər] *n* **(a)** (*trouble*) ennui *m*, *F* embêtement *m*; **I'm in a bit of (a) b., I'm having a bit** *or* **a spot of b.,** j'ai des ennuis (**with,** avec); **to be in b. with the police,** avoir des ennuis avec la police; **if it's not too much b.,** si cela ne vous dérange pas trop; **it's not worth the b.,** cela ne vaut pas la peine; **I hate to be a b., but ...,** je suis désolé de vous déranger, mais ...; **it's no b. at all,** ça ne m'ennuie pas du tout; **(b)** *Br Sl* (*fighting*) bagarre *f*; **there was a bit of b. in the pub,** il y a eu un peu de bagarre dans le pub.

bother[2] **1** *vt* **(a)** (*annoy*) ennuyer, *F* embêter (*qn*); (*disturb*) déranger (*qn*); (*be in the way of*) gêner (*qn*); **does the light b. you?,** est-ce que la lumière vous gêne *ou* dérange?; **don't b. me!,** laissez-moi tranquille!; **I can't be bothered to do it,** je n'ai pas envie de le faire; **b. (it)!,** zut!; **b. the man!,** qu'il aille au diable!; **my back's still bothering me,** (*giving pain*) mon dos me gêne encore; **his old wound bothers him in damp weather,** sa vieille blessure le fait souffrir par temps humide; **I hate to b. you but ...,** je suis désolé de vous déranger, mais ...;

(b) (*worry*) inquiéter (*qn*); **to be bothered about sth,** s'inquiéter de qch, se faire du mauvais sang pour qch; **don't b. yourself** *or* **your head about me,** ne vous inquiétez pas de moi; *F* **I'm not bothered!,** cela m'est bien égal!, je m'en fiche!; **he didn't even b. to apologize,** il ne s'est même pas excusé; **don't b. to ring me up/to turn the lights off,** ce n'est pas la peine de me téléphoner/d'éteindre la lumière; **don't b.!,** (*I can get on without you*) ce n'est pas la peine!, ne te donne pas de mal!

2 *vi* s'inquiéter (**about,** de); s'occuper (**with,** de); prendre *ou* se donner la peine (**to do sth,** de faire qch); **he doesn't b. about anything,** il ne s'inquiète de rien.

botheration [bɒðə'reɪʃən] *F int* zut!

bothersome ['bɒðəsəm] *adj* importun, gênant.

bottle[1] ['bɒt(ə)l] *n* **(a)** bouteille *f*; (*small, for perfume etc*) flacon *m*; (*wide-mouthed*) bocal *m*; (*for baby*) biberon *m*; *Med* urinal *m* de lit, *F* pistolet *m*; **bring your own b.,** (*on invitation*) chacun doit amener une bouteille; (*notice in restaurant*) = les clients peuvent apporter leur vin puisque le restaurant n'a pas de licence; **he drank the whole b.,** il a bu toute la bouteille; **I'm just giving the baby her b.,** je suis juste en train de donner son biberon au bébé; **brought up on the b.,** (*of baby*) élevé *ou* allaité au biberon; **stone b.,** cruchon *m*; **b. of wine,** bouteille de vin; *F* **to be fond of the b.,** aimer la bouteille; **to be on the b.,** s'adonner à la boisson; **to hit the b.,** boire (trop); **he then hit the b.,** il s'est mis alors à boire; **b. bank,** dépôt *m* de bouteilles; *Pej* **b. blonde,** (*with dyed hair*) blonde décolorée; **b. green,** vert bouteille; *Boxing* **b. holder,** soigneur *m*, second *m*; **b. opener,** ouvre-bouteille(s) *m inv*, décapsuleur *m*; **b. party,** = soirée à laquelle chacun apporte à boire;

(b) *Br Sl* (*courage, nerve*) cran *m*, culot *m*; **to have a lot of b.,** avoir beaucoup de cran *ou* de culot.

bottle[2] *vt* mettre (*du vin*) en bouteilles; conserver (*des fruits, etc*) en bocal.

▶**bottle out** *vi Br Sl* (*be too frightened*) se dégonfler.

▶**bottle up** *vtsep* étouffer (*ses sentiments*); refouler, ravaler (*sa colère*).

bottlebrush ['bɒt(ə)lbrʌʃ] *n* **(a)** (*for cleaning*) goupillon *m*; **(b)** (*plant*) callistemon *m*.

bottled ['bɒt(ə)ld] *adj* (*vin, bière, gaz etc*) en bouteille(s); **b. fruit,** fruits *mpl* en bocaux; **people are being recommended to drink b. water,** on recommande à la population de boire de l'eau minérale.

bottle-feed ['bɒt(ə)lfiːd] *vi* nourrir (*un bébé*) au biberon; **b.-fed,** élevé *ou* allaité au biberon.

bottleneck ['bɒt(ə)lnek] *n* **(a)** goulot *m* (*de bouteille*); **(b)** *Fig* (*in road*) rétrécissement *m* de la chaussée; (*traffic jam*) embouteillage *m*, bouchon *m*; (*in production etc*) goulet *m ou* goulot *m* d'étranglement.

bottle-washer ['bɒt(ə)lwɒʃər] *n* **(a)** (*person*) laveur, -euse de bouteilles; *Fig* factotum *m*; *F* **head cook and b.-w.,** = homme ou femme qui mène toute l'affaire; **(b)** (*machine*) rince-bouteilles *m inv*.

bottling ['bɒt(ə)lɪŋ] *n* (*of wine*) mise *f* en bouteille(s); (*of fruit*) mise en bocaux.

bottom[1] ['bɒtəm] *n* **(a)** bas *m* (*d'une colline, d'un escalier, d'une page*); fond *m* (*d'un puits, d'une boîte, de la mer*); ballast *m*, assiette *f* (*d'une chaussée etc*); **at the b. of the garden,** au fond du jardin; **I found the keys at the b. of my bag,** j'ai trouvé mes clés au fond de mon sac; **he's at the b. of the class,** il est le dernier de sa classe; **at the b. of the page,** au *ou* en bas de la page; **to send a ship to the b.,** envoyer un bâtiment par le fond; **to go to the b.,** (*of ship*) couler à fond; **to strike** *or* **touch b.,** (*of ship*) toucher le fond; **to touch b.,** (*of swimmer*) *& Fig* toucher le fond; **prices have reached rock b.,** les prix sont au plus bas; **from the b. of one's heart,** du fond du cœur; **to get to the b. of sth** *or* **of things,** découvrir la cause *ou* l'origine de qch, aller au fond des choses; **to be at the b. of sth,** (*be the instigator*) être derrière qch, être l'instigateur de qch; (*be the cause*) être la cause de qch; **b. line,** (*of balance sheet*) solde final; (*end result, outcome*) résultat *m*; **all she cares about is the b. line,** il n'y a que le résultat qui l'intéresse; **the b. line is that he is unsuited to the job,** la conclusion est qu'il n'est pas fait pour ce travail; **that's the b. line,** c'est la seule chose qui compte; **b. half,** partie inférieure; **b. book (of a pile),** livre qui est en bas *ou* tout en dessous; **b. end of the table,** (bas) bout de la table; **b. stair,** marche *f* du bas, première marche (*en montant*); dernière marche (*en descendant*); **b. price,** prix plancher; **at rock b. prices,** aux plus bas prix; *Aut* **in b. gear,** en première (vitesse); *F* **you can bet your b. dollar that ...,**

vous pouvez être sûr que ...; *Br* **b. drawer,** (*trousseau*) trousseau *m*; **b. fishing,** pêche *f* à la ligne de fond;

(b) siège *m* (*d'une chaise*) **the b. of my glass/plate,** (*inside*) le fond de mon verre/assiette; (*outside*) le dessous de mon verre/assiette; **to put sth b. up(wards),** mettre qch sens dessus dessous; **box with a false b.,** boîte à double fond; **to knock the b. out of,** défoncer (*une boîte etc*); *Fig* démolir (*un argument*); **the b. has fallen out of the market,** le marché s'est effondré; *F* **bottoms up!,** (*empty your glass*) cul sec!; (*cheers*) à votre santé!; *Billiards* **to put b. on a ball,** faire de l'effet à revenir *ou* de l'effet rétrograde;

(c) *F* derrière *m* (*d'une personne*);

(d) bottoms, (*of pyjamas*) pantalon *m ou* bas *m* de pyjama;

(e) *Nau* carène *f*, fond *m* (*d'un navire*).

bottom² **1** *vt* mettre un siège à (*une chaise*). **2** *vi* (*of ship etc*) toucher le fond.

►bottom out *vi* atteindre son niveau le plus bas; **the government hopes that inflation/unemployment has bottomed out,** le gouvernement espère que l'inflation/le chômage n'augmentera pas plus.

bottomless ['bɒtəmlɪs] *adj* **(a)** (*puits etc*) sans fond; **it's like pouring money into a b. pit,** c'est comme jeter de l'argent par les fenêtres; **(b)** (*réserve*) inépuisable.

bottommost ['bɒtəmməʊst] *adj* le plus bas.

botulism ['bɒtjʊlɪz(ə)m] *n Med* botulisme *m*.

bouclé ['buːkleɪ] *adj & n Tex* bouclé *m*; **b. wool,** bouclette *f*; **b. sweater,** pull *m* en bouclette.

boudoir ['buːdwɑːr] *n* boudoir *m*.

bouffant ['buːfɒn] *adj* (*hair*) gonflant; (*sleeve, skirt*) bouffant.

bougainvillea [buːgən'vɪlɪə] *n* (*plant*) bougainvillée *f*.

bough [baʊ] *n* branche *f*, rameau *m* (*d'arbre*).

bought *see* **BUY²**.

bouillon ['buːjɒn] *n Culin* bouillon *m*, consommé *m*; *Am* **b. cube,** cube *m* de bouillon *ou* de consommé; *Am* **b. cup,** tasse *f* à bouillon *ou* à consommé.

boulder ['bəʊldər] *n* (gros) bloc *m* de pierre; *Geol* **b. clay,** argile *f* à blocaux.

boulevard ['buːləvɑːd] *n Am* **(a)** (*street*) boulevard *m*; **(b)** (*on road*) terre-plein *m* (central), *pl* terre-pleins (centraux).

bounce¹ [baʊns] *n* **(a)** (*of ball*) rebond *m*, rebondissement *m*; **to catch the ball on the b.,** prendre la balle au bond; *Am F* **to get the b.,** (*from job*) se faire virer; **she gave him the b.,** (*from relationship*) elle l'a plaqué, elle l'a viré; **(b)** *F* (*of person*) vitalité *f*; **he's as full of b. as ever,** il est toujours aussi plein d'énergie.

bounce² **1** *vi* (*of ball etc*) rebondir; **to b. into/out of a room,** (*of person*) entrer dans/sortir d'une pièce en coup de vent *ou* en trombe; **cheque that bounces,** chèque sans provision, chèque en bois; **the cheque bounced,** le chèque a été refusé (parce qu'il était sans provision *ou* en bois); **I don't want the cheque to b.,** (*the cheque that I have written*) je ne veux pas que le chèque soit refusé parce que mon compte n'est pas approvisionné. **2** *vt* **(a)** faire rebondir (*une balle*); **to b. a baby on one's knee,** faire sauter un bébé sur ses genoux; **(b)** *Am F* (*from job, nightclub etc*) flanquer (*qn*) à la porte; **to b. a cheque,** (*of bank*) refuser un chèque sans provision *ou* en bois.

►bounce back *vi* (*of ball*) rebondir; *Fig* (*of actor etc*) faire son retour (*après un échec*); (*from illness*) se remettre; *Fig* **she will b. back from this disappointment,** elle se remettra de sa déception.

►bounce off **1** *vtaspo* faire rebondir (*qch*) contre (*un mur*); faire rebondir (*qch*) sur (*le sol*); *Fig* **to b. an idea off s.o.,** lancer une idée à qn (pour voir sa réaction); **to b. radio waves off a satellite,** faire se réfléchir des ondes radio sur un satellite. **2** *vipo* (*of ball, rain, bullets etc*) rebondir contre (*la chaussée, les maisons etc*); *Fig* **criticism bounces off him,** (*does not penetrate*) la critique ne lui fait aucun effet.

bouncer ['baʊnsər] *n F* **(a)** videur *m* (*dans une boîte de nuit etc*); (*who refuses entry*) physionomiste *m*; **(b)** chèque *m* sans provision *ou* en bois; **(c)** *Cr* balle *f* qui rebondit en hauteur.

bouncing ['baʊnsɪŋ] *adj* (*ball*) rebondissant; *Fig* (*baby*) plein de vie et de santé.

bouncy ['baʊnsɪ] *adj* **(a)** (*ball*) qui rebondit; (*hair*) plein de vigueur; **(b)** *Fig* (*person*) dynamique.

bound¹ [baʊnd] *n* (*usu pl*) (*limit*) limite(s) *f(pl)*, bornes *fpl*; **out of bounds,** défendu; *Mil etc* consigné; *Golf Fb etc* hors des limites, hors du jeu; **to go beyond the bounds of reason,** dépasser les bornes de la raison; **it is not beyond the bounds of possibility,** c'est dans le domaine du possible; **my fury knew no bounds,** je n'ai pu contenir ma fureur; **to keep within bounds,** rester dans la juste mesure, user de modération; **to keep one's imagination/spending within bounds,** mettre un frein à *ou* modérer son imagination/ses dépenses.

bound² *n* (*jump*) bond *m*, saut *m*; **at one b.,** d'un (seul) bond, d'un saut, d'un seul élan; **to advance by leaps and bounds,** avancer à pas de géant.

bound³ *vi* bondir, sauter; (*of ball etc*) rebondir; **to b. forward,** bondir en avant.

bound⁴ *adj Nau* **ship b. for America,** navire en partance pour *ou* en route pour l'Amérique; **a plane b. for Paris,** un avion à destination de Paris; **the plane which was b. for Paris crashed,** l'avion qui volait à destination de Paris s'est écrasé; **where are you b. for?,** où allez-vous?

bound⁵ *vt* (*usu passive*) limiter, délimiter (*un quartier*); être limitrophe de (*un pays, un départment*); **France is bounded by Spain in the south,** l'Espagne est limitrophe de la France au sud; **an area bounded by Smith Street on the west, James Avenue on the south,** une zone délimitée par la rue Smith à l'ouest et l'avenue James au sud.

bound⁶ *see* **BIND²**.

boundary ['baʊnd(ə)rɪ] *n* limite *f*, bornes *fpl*; (*between countries*) frontière *f*; *Cr* **to hit** *or* **score a b.,** envoyer la balle jusqu'aux limites du terrain; **the boundaries of human knowledge,** les frontières *ou* limites de la connaissance humaine; **the mountains form the b.,** les montagnes constituent la frontière; **b. adjustment,** rectification *f* de frontière; **b. line,** ligne frontière, ligne de démarcation; *Sp* ligne du jeu; **b. stone,** borne *ou* pierre *f* de bornage.

bounden ['baʊndən] *adj Lit* **b. duty,** devoir impérieux; **it's your b. duty to help,** il est de ton devoir impérieux d'aider.

bounder ['baʊndər] *n Old-fashioned F* goujat *m*.

boundless ['baʊndlɪs] *adj* sans bornes, illimité, infini.

bounteous ['baʊntɪəs] *adj Lit* **(a)** (*harvest etc*) abondant; **(b)** (*person*) libéral, généreux.

bounteousness ['baʊntɪəsnɪs] *n Lit* **(a)** (*of harvest etc*) abondance *f*; **(b)** (*of person*) bonté *f*, générosité *f*.

bountiful ['baʊntɪfʊl] *adj Lit* **(a)** (*ample, in large quantities*) bienfaisant; **b. rains,** pluies fécondes; **a b. supply of fish,** une provision abondante de poisson; **fish is in b. supply this week,** il y a du poisson en quantité abondante cette semaine; **(b)** (*generous*) généreux, libéral.

bounty ['baʊntɪ] *n* **(a)** (*reward*) indemnité *f*; prime *f* (*à l'exportation etc*); *esp Am* **b. hunter,** chasseur *m* de primes; **(b)** *Lit* (*of person*) bonté *f*, générosité *f*, libéralité *f*.

bouquet *n* **(a)** [bəʊ'keɪ, buː-] bouquet *m* (*de fleurs*); **(b)** [buː'keɪ] bouquet *m* (*du vin*).

bourbon ['bɜːb(ə)n] *n* whisky *m* de maïs.

Bourbon ['bʊəb(ə)n] *n Hist* Bourbon; **B. biscuit,** = biscuit au chocolat fourré de crème.

bourdon ['bʊəd(ə)n] *n Mus* (*of organ, bagpipes*) bourdon *m*.

bourgeois ['bʊəʒwɑː] *adj & n usu Pej* bourgeois, -oise.

bourgeoisie [bʊəʒwɑː'ziː] *n* bourgeoisie *f*.

bout [baʊt] *n* **(a)** (*at games etc*) tour *m*, reprise *f*; **the b. will be fought at Wembley,** (*boxing match*) le combat sera disputé à Wembley; **boxing b.,** combat de boxe; **fencing b.,** assaut *m* d'armes; **wrestling b.,** assaut de lutte; **(b)** accès *m*, poussée *f* (*de fièvre*); quinte *f* (*de toux*); (*of drinking*) soûlerie *f*.

boutique [buː'tiːk] *n* petit magasin de modes; (*in department store*) boutique *f*.

bovine ['bəʊvaɪn] **1** *adj Zool* bovin; *Fig* (*esprit*) lourd; *Vet* **b. spongiform encephalopathy,** encéphalite bovine spongiforme. **2** *npl Zool* les bovins *m*.

bovver ['bɒvər] *n Br Sl* (*hooliganism, rowdiness*) = comportement violent; **b. boots,** rangers *mpl*; **b. boys,** voyous *mpl*.

bow¹ [bəʊ] *n* **(a)** (*of archer*) arc *m*; **to draw a b.,** bander *ou* tendre un arc; *Fig* **to have two strings** *or* **more than one string to one's b.,** avoir deux cordes *ou* plus d'une corde à son arc; *Fig* **I have still one** *or* **another string to my b.,** il me reste encore une ressource; **b. legs,** jambes arquées *ou* torses; **b. window,** fenêtre *f* en saillie (courbe) *ou* en rotonde; **(b)** *Mus* archet *m* (*de violon etc*); (*movement*) coup *m* d'archet; **(c)** nœud *m* (*de ruban*); **b. tie,** nœud (de) papillon; **(d)** *Tech* arceau *m*, anse *f* (*de cadenas*); anneau *m* (*de clef*); collier *m* (*d'éperon*); **b. compass,** compas *m* à balustre.

bow² *vt* **(a)** courber (*qch*); **(b)** *Mus* gouverner l'archet dans *(un passage)*; **bowed instrument,** instrument à archet.

bow[3] [baʊ] *n* salut *m*; *(from waist)* révérence *f*; *(from neck)* inclination *f* de tête; **to make a deep** *or* **low b. to s.o.,** saluer qn profondément; **to take a b.,** *(of performer)* saluer; **to take one's final b.,** *(retire from stage etc permanently)* faire ses adieux.

bow[4] **1** *vi* **(a)** s'incliner; **to b. to s.o.,** s'incliner devant qn; **to b. and scrape,** faire des salamalecs *ou* des courbettes; **(b)** se soumettre *(à la volonté de qn, une décision etc)*; **to b. to the inevitable,** s'incliner devant les faits; **I bowed to her (greater) wisdom,** je me suis incliné devant tant de sagesse. **2** *vt* incliner, baisser *(la tête)*; fléchir *(le genou)*; courber, voûter *(le dos, les épaules de qn)*; **to become bowed,** se voûter.

bow[5] *n* **(a)** *Nau (often pl)* avant *m*, étrave *f*, bossoir *m*; **on the port/starboard b.,** par le bossoir bâbord/tribord; **to cross the bows of a ship,** couper la route d'un navire; **b. rope,** amarre *f* de bout *ou* de l'avant; **b. wave,** lame *f* d'étrave; **(b)** *(in rowing)* nageur *m* de tête *ou* de l'avant; **b. oar,** aviron *m* de l'avant.

►**bow down 1** *vi (incline one's head)* s'incliner; **to b. down before s.o.,** faire des courbettes devant qn; *(very deeply)* se prosterner devant qn; *Fig* **the teachers b. down before the headmaster,** les professeurs s'écrasent devant le directeur. **2** *vtsep (of poverty etc)* accabler *(qn)*; **he is bowed down by care,** il est accablé par les soucis.

►**bow out** *vi F (leave job, relationship etc voluntarily)* tirer sa révérence; **when the company automated, he bowed out,** lorsque la société s'est automatisée il a décidé de leur tirer sa révérence.

bowdlerize ['baʊdləraɪz] *vt* expurger, aseptiser *(une œuvre littéraire)*.

bowed [baʊd] *adj* **with b. head,** la tête inclinée; la tête baissée *(de honte etc)*; **b. with age,** courbé par le fardeau des ans; **b. with grief,** accablé de douleur.

bowel ['baʊəl] *n Anat* intestin *m*; **the bowels,** les intestins; **b. complaint,** affection intestinale; **b. movement,** transit intestinal; **have you had a b. movement today?,** est-ce que vous êtes allé (à la selle) aujourd'hui?; *Lit* **the bowels of the earth,** les entrailles *fpl ou* le sein de la terre.

bower ['baʊər] *n* **(a)** *(in wood, garden)* berceau *m* de verdure, charmille *f*; *(made of trellis work)* tonnelle *f*; **(b)** *Poet Arch* appartement *m (d'une dame)*, boudoir *m*.

bowerbird ['baʊəbɜːd] *n* oiseau *m* à berceau.

bowfronted [bəʊ'frʌntɪd] *adj (chest etc)* à devant bombé; *(house)* à fenêtres en saillie.

bowhead ['bəʊhed] *n (whale)* baleine boréale.

bowing ['baʊɪŋ] *n* saluts *mpl*; **b. and scraping,** courbettes *fpl*, salamalecs *mpl*.

bowl[1] [bəʊl] *n* **(a)** *(for soup, cereal etc)* bol *m*; coupe *f (de cristal etc)*; *(for washing hands, dishes)* cuvette *f*; bassin *m (d'évier)*; *(plastic)* bassine *f*; cuvette *(de W.C.)*; **goldfish b.,** bocal *m* à poissons rouges; **a b. of milk,** *(contents)* *(for person)* un bol de lait; *(for cat)* une jatte de lait; **(b)** fourneau *m*, godet *m (de pipe à tabac)*; cuilleron *m (de cuiller)*; coupe *f (de verre à pied)*; culot *m (de lampe)*; plateau *m (de balance)*; *Nau* cuvette *f (du compas)*; **(c)** *Geog* cuvette *f*, bassin *m*; *US (for concerts etc)* amphithéâtre *m*.

bowl[2] *n Sp* boule *f*; **(game of) bowls,** *(on grass)* (jeu *m* de) boules; *(in bowling alley)* (partie *f* de) bowling *m*; **to play (at) bowls,** *(on grass)* jouer aux boules; *(in bowling alley)* jouer au bowling.

bowl[3] **1** *vt* **(a)** rouler, faire courir *(un cerceau)*; **(b)** *Sp* lancer, rouler *(la boule)*; **(c)** *Cr* lancer, servir *(la balle)*; renverser le guichet à *(qn)*. **2** *vi* **(a)** jouer aux boules *ou* au bowling; **(b)** *Cr* lancer *ou* servir la balle; **well bowled!,** bien lancé!

►**bowl along** *vi (in car, train)* rouler rapidement.

►**bowl out** *vtsep Cr* renverser le guichet de *(qn)*.

►**bowl over** *vtsep* **(a)** *(knock down)* renverser *(les quilles, qn etc)*; **(b)** *F (astonish)* sidérer, renverser *(qn)*; **I was bowled over by winning first prize,** j'ai été sidéré de gagner le premier prix; **her beauty bowled him over,** sa beauté l'a renversé.

bowlegged [bəʊ'legɪd] *adj* aux jambes arquées.

bowler[1] ['bəʊlər] *n* **(a)** *(in bowls)* *(on grass)* joueur *m* de boules, bouliste *m*; *(in bowling alley)* joueur de bowling; **(b)** *Cr* lanceur *m*, serveur *m*.

bowler[2] *n* **b. (hat),** (chapeau *m*) melon *m*.

bowlful ['bəʊlfʊl] *n* plein bol *(de qch)*; jatte *f (de lait etc)*; cuvette *f*, bassinée *f (d'eau etc)*.

bowline ['bəʊlɪn] *n Nau* **(a)** *(rope)* bouline *f*; **(b)** *(knot)* nœud *m* de chaise, nœud d'agui.

bowling ['bəʊlɪŋ] *n* **(a)** *(game)* *(on grass)* jeu *m* de boules; *(tenpin)* bowling *m*; **b. alley,** bowling; **(b)** *(action)* lancement *m* de la boule *ou Cr* de la balle.

bowsaw ['bəʊsɔː] *n (tool)* scie *f* à archet *ou* à arc *ou* à chantourner.

bowser ['baʊzər] *n Petr* camion-citerne *m*, *pl* camions-citernes.

bowsprit ['bəʊsprɪt] *n Nau* beaupré *m*.

bowstring ['bəʊstrɪŋ] *n* corde *f* d'arc.

bow-wow ['baʊ'waʊ] **1** *int* oua-oua! **2** *n F (in children's language)* toutou *m*.

box[1] [bɒks] *n* **(a) b. (tree),** buis *m*; **(b)** *(wood)* (bois *m* de) buis *m*.

box[2] *n* **(a)** *(container)* boîte *f*; *(small)* coffret *m*; *(large)* coffre *m*, caisse *f*; *(for food etc)* bac *m*; *Rel* **alms b.,** tronc *m*; *Mil* **ammunition b.,** coffre à munitions; **cardboard b.,** (boîte en) carton *m*; **cash b.,** caisse; **deed b.,** coffret à documents; **jewel b.,** coffre à bijoux; **post** *or* **letter b.,** boîte à *ou* aux lettres; **p. office b., PO B.,** boîte postale, B.P.; **strong b., safety deposit b.,** coffre-fort *m*, *pl* coffres-forts; **tool b.,** boîte à outils; *Gym* **(vaulting) b.,** cheval *m* de bois; **window b.,** caisse *ou* bac à fleurs *(pour fenêtres, balcons)*; **b. camera,** appareil *m* rigide *ou* en box; *US* **b. canyon,** cañon *ou* canyon encaissé; **b. kite,** cerf-volant *m* cellulaire, *pl* cerfs-volants cellulaires; **b. number 12,** référence 12; **write to b. number 12,** *(in newspaper advertisement)* écrire en rappelant la référence 12; **b. office,** *(in theatre, cinema)* bureau *m* de location; *Fig (profits)* caisse *f*; **the film did well at the b. office,** le film a enregistré beaucoup d'entrées; *Sewing* **b. pleat,** pli creux *ou* rond; **b. spanner/wrench,** clef *f*/clé *m* à douille *ou* en tube; **b. spring,** *(for mattress)* sommier *m* à ressorts;

(b) *(contents)* boîte *f (de chocolats, d'allumettes etc)*; caisse *f (de marchandises etc)*; **Christmas b.,** ≈ étrennes *fpl*;

(c) *Br F* **the b.,** la télé; **is there anything on the b. tonight?,** il y a quelque chose à la télé ce soir?;

(d) *(enclosed space)* stalle *f (d'écurie)*; *Th* loge *f*; *(on ground floor)* baignoire *f*; *Tel* cabine téléphonique; **horse b.,** *Aut* van *m*; *Rail* wagon *m* à chevaux; **loose b.,** box *m*, *pl* boxes; **shooting b.,** pavillon *m* de chasse; **stage b.,** loge d'avant-scène;

(e) *Tech* boîte *f (d'essieu, de frein)*; moyeu *m (de roue)*; palâtre *m*, palastre *m (d'une serrure)*; *Typ* cassetin *m*; **b. girder,** poutre *f* caisson; **b. key,** clef *f* à douille; **b. screw,** douille taraudée, écrou *m*; **b. section,** section *f* rectangulaire;

(f) case *f (à remplir sur une formule etc)*; pavé *m (d'organigramme)*; encadré *m (dans un journal)*; *Aut* **b. junction,** zone quadrillée.

box[3] *vt* emboîter, encaisser, encartonner *(qch)*; mettre *(qch)* en boîte.

box[4] *n (blow)* **b. (on the ear),** gifle *f*, claque *f*, taloche *f*; **to give s.o. a b. on the ear,** donner une taloche à qn.

box[5] **1** *vt* **to b. s.o.'s ears,** gifler qn, *F* flanquer une gifle *ou* une claque *ou* une taloche à qn. **2** *vi Sp* boxer, faire de la boxe; *(of two opponents)* se boxer.

►**box in** *vtsep* **(a)** *(surround)* coincer *(qn)*; **the defence seem to have him boxed in,** la défense semble l'avoir coincé; **(b)** *(enclose)* encastrer *(une baignoire, un évier)*; **don't you feel boxed in in such a small room?,** tu ne te sens pas un peu à l'étroit *ou* coincé dans une pièce aussi petite?

box-calf ['bɒkskɑːf] *n (leather)* box-calf *m*, *F* box *m*.

boxcar ['bɒkskɑːr] *n Am Rail* wagon *m*, fourgon *m*.

boxed [bɒkst] *adj Com etc* en boîte; *(jewellery)* en étui; **b. in,** *(bath etc)* encastré; *(surrounded)* coincé; *(confined)* coincé, à l'étroit.

boxer ['bɒksər] *n* **(a)** *(fighter)* boxeur *m*, pugiliste *m*; **b. shorts,** *(underwear)* caleçon *m*; **(b)** *(dog)* boxer *m*.

Boxer ['bɒksər] *n Hist* Boxer *m* (chinois); **the B. Rebellion,** la révolte des Boxers.

boxful ['bɒksfʊl] *n* pleine boîte, plein coffre, pleine caisse *(de qch)*.

boxing[1] ['bɒksɪŋ] *n Sp* la boxe; **b. glove,** gant *m* de boxe; **b. match,** match *m* de boxe.

boxing[2] *n* emboîtement *m*, encaissement *m*.

Boxing ['bɒksɪŋ] *n Br* **B. Day,** la Saint-Étienne, le lendemain de Noël.

box-office ['bɒksɒfɪs] *adj (success, failure)* populaire; **she's always a big b.-o. draw,** elle est sûre de faire des entrées.

box-pleated ['bɒkspliːtɪd] *adj (skirt etc)* à plis creux *ou* ronds.

boxroom ['bɒksruːm] *n* débarras *m*.

boxwood ['bɒkswʊd] *n* (bois *m* de) buis *m*.

boy [bɔɪ] *n* **(a)** garçon *m*; **boys will be boys,** il faut bien que jeunesse se passe; **she ought to have been a b.,** c'est un garçon manqué; **b. scout,** boy-scout *m*, scout *m*;
(b) *Sch* élève *m*; **day b.,** externe *m*; **an old b.,** un ancien élève; *F* **the old b. network,** = le réseau des relations entre anciens camarades d'école ou de collège;
(c) (*man*) *F* **a nice old b.,** un vieillard sympathique; **one of the boys,** un joyeux vivant; **he's having a night out with the boys,** il est sorti avec ses copains; **come on boys!,** allons-y les gars!; *esp Am* **oh b.!,** ben alors!, dis donc!; *esp Am* **b., am I glad to be home!,** dis donc, qu'est-ce que je suis content d'être rentré à la maison!; *Old-fashioned Br* **I say, old b.!,** dis, mon vieux!; *Br F* **the boys in blue,** (*police*) = la police; *Sl* **the big boys,** les grosses légumes;
(d) (*employee*) (*in Africa etc*) domestique *m*, boy *m*; **errand b.,** (*to fetch things*) garçon *m* de courses; (*to deliver things*) garçon livreur; **office b.,** garçon de bureau; **ship's b.,** mousse *m*; **stable b.,** garçon d'écurie.

boycott¹ ['bɔɪkɒt] *n* boycottage *m*; **to put under a b., to put a b. on,** boycotter (*qn, une entreprise etc*).

boycott² *vt* boycotter (*qn, une entreprise etc*).

boyfriend ['bɔɪfrend] *n* (petit) ami *m*; *Can F* chum *m*.

boyhood ['bɔɪhʊd] *n* (*when very young*) enfance *f*, première jeunesse; (*in teens*) adolescence *f* (d'un garçon); **b. friends,** amis *fpl* d'enfance (d'un garçon).

boyish ['bɔɪɪʃ] *adj* **(a)** (*hopes, enthusiasm*) d'enfant; **(b)** (*nature, apparence*) jeune; **b. good looks,** (*of man*) air gamin; (*of woman*) air de garçonnet *ou* de jeune garçon; **(c)** (*manières*) de garçon.

boyishness ['bɔɪɪʃnɪs] *n* manières *fpl ou* air *m* de garçon *ou* de jeune homme.

boy-meets-girl ['bɔɪmiːts'gɜːl] *adj* **b.-m.-g. story,** (*book, film*) histoire *f* d'amour (conventionnelle).

bozo ['bəʊzəʊ] *n Am Sl* (*stupid man*) idiot *m*.

BR [biː'ɑːr] *n* (*abbr* **British Railways**) = service national des chemins de fer britannique.

bra [brɑː] *n* soutien-gorge *m*, *pl* soutiens-gorge; **b. top,** brassière *f*.

brace¹ [breɪs] *n* **(a)** *Constr etc* (*in tension*) attache *f*, lien *m*; (*for framework*) entretoise *f*, étrésillon *m*; (*in compression*) contrefiche *f*, moise *f*; **anchor b.,** ancre *f*, ancrure *f*; **cross** *or* **diagonal b.,** écharpe *f*, diagonale *f*; *Aut* croisillon *m* (du châssis); **(b)** (*on teeth*) appareil *m* dentaire; (*on leg*) armature *f* orthopédique; (*on torso*) corset *m*; **(c)** *Br* **braces,** bretelles *fpl* (de pantalon); **(d)** couple *f* (*de perdrix, de faisans*); paire *f* (*de pistolets etc*); **two b. of partridges,** deux couples de perdrix; **(e)** (*drill*) **b. (and bit),** vilebrequin *m* (et sa mèche); **ratchet b.,** *MecE* perçoir *m ou* foret *m* à rochet; *Carp* vilebrequin à cliquet; *Aut* **wheel b.,** vilebrequin (à roues); **(f)** *Nau* bras *m* (*de vergue*); **main b.,** grand bras; **(g)** *Mus Typ* accolade *f*.

brace² *vt* **(a)** *Constr etc* ancrer (*une construction*); armer (*une poutre*); entretoiser, étrésillonner (*une charpente*); moiser (*des étais*); affermir (*un mur*) par des ancres; *Av* croisillonner (*une aile*); **(b)** fortifier (*le corps*); tonifier (*les nerfs*); **to b. s.o. up,** (re)donner de la vigueur *ou* du courage à qn, remonter qn; **to b. oneself to do sth,** rassembler ses forces pour faire qch, s'armer de (tout son) courage pour faire qch; **b. yourself!,** (*hold tight*) tiens bon!; (*be brave*) du courage!; **b. yourself for a shock,** prépare-toi à recevoir un choc; **(c)** tendre, bander (*l'arc*); **to b. (the skin of) a drum,** tendre la peau d'un tambour, bander un tambour; **to b. the knees,** tendre les jarrets; **(d)** *Typ* accoler (*des mots*); **(e)** *Nau* brasser (*les vergues*); **to b. round,** contrebrasser.

bracelet ['breɪslɪt] *n* **(a)** (*jewellery*) bracelet *m*; **chain b.,** gourmette *f*; **b. watch,** montre-bracelet *f*, *pl* montres-bracelets, bracelet-montre *m*, *pl* bracelets-montres; **(b)** *F* **bracelets,** (*handcuffs*) bracelets *mpl*; **put the bracelets on him,** passe-lui les bracelets.

bracer ['breɪsər] *n F* petit verre (*de spiritueux*).

brachial ['brækɪəl, 'breɪk-] *adj Anat* brachial, -aux.

brachiopod ['brækɪəpɒd] *n* (*mollusc*) brachiopode *m*.

brachycephalic [brækɪsɪ'fælɪk] *adj* brachycéphale.

bracing ['breɪsɪŋ] **1** *adj* (*air, climate etc*) fortifiant, vivifiant, tonifiant. **2** *n* **(a)** *Constr etc* ancrage *m*; (*of framework*) entretoisement *m*; armement *m* (*d'une poutre*); renforcement *m* (*d'un mur*); *Av* croisillonnage *m*; **b. strut,** jambe *f* de force; **(b)** retrempe *f* (*du corps*); tonification *f* (*des nerfs*); **(c)** *Nau* brassage *m* (*des vergues*).

bracken ['bræk(ə)n] *n* (*plant*) fougère *f* à l'aigle.

bracket¹ ['brækɪt] *n* **(a)** *Constr etc* console *f*; *Archit* corbeau *m*; *Constr MecE* tasseau *m*, patte *f* (*de fixation, de sustentation*); applique *f* (*pour lampe*); **b. lamp,** (lampe *f* d')applique; **(b)** *Typ etc* (*square*) crochet *m*; (*round*) parenthèse *f*; (*connecting two lines*) accolade *f*; **in brackets,** entre parenthèses *ou* crochets *ou* accolades; **(c)** *Admin* tranche *f* (*de revenus, d'imposition*); fourchette *f* (*de salaires*); **the 15-to-20 age b.,** le groupe *ou* la classe des 15 à 20 ans; **people in the upper income brackets,** les gens dans les tranches de revenu les plus élevées; **what tax b. are you in?,** dans quelle tranche d'imposition es-tu?

bracket² *vt* (-t-) mettre (*des mots etc*) entre crochets *ou* parenthèses; (*in a vertical list*) réunir (*des mots*) par une accolade; *Fig* associer les noms de (*deux personnes*); *Fig* associer (*deux idées*); *Fig* placer (*deux candidats*) ex aequo; **bracketed together,** (*of candidates*) classé ex aequo; **his name has often been bracketed with hers,** son nom a souvent été associé au sien.

bracketing ['brækɪtɪŋ] *n* (*action*) mise *f* entre crochets *ou* parenthèses.

brackish ['brækɪʃ] *adj* (*eau*) saumâtre.

bract [brækt] *n Bot* bractée *f*.

brad [bræd] *n* pointe *f*; clou à tête perdue *ou* étêté.

bradawl ['brædɔːl] *n* (*tool*) alêne plate; poinçon *m*.

bradycardia [brædɪ'kɑːdɪə] *n Med* bradycardie *f*.

brae [breɪ] *n Scot* pente *f*, côte *f*, colline *f*.

brag¹ [bræg] *n* vantardise *f*, hâblerie *f*.

brag² *vi* (-gg-) hâbler, se vanter; **to b. of** *or* **about sth,** se vanter de qch; **stop bragging,** arrête de te vanter; **you've got nothing to b. about,** tu n'as pas de quoi te vanter; **it's not something I b. about,** ce n'est pas quelque chose dont je me vante.

braggart ['brægət] *adj & n* vantard, -arde, hâbleur, -euse.

bragging ['brægɪŋ] **1** *adj* vantard, hâbleur, -euse. **2** *n* vantardise *f*, hâblerie *f*.

Brahman ['brɑːmən] *n* brahmane *mf*.

Brahmanism ['brɑːmənɪz(ə)m] *n* brahmanisme *m*.

Brahmin ['brɑːmɪn] *n* **(a)** (*in India*) brahmane *mf*; **(b)** *US F* intellectuel, -elle.

braid¹ [breɪd] *n* **(a)** *esp Am* tresse *f*, natte *f* (*de cheveux*); **she wears her hair in braids,** elle a les cheveux tressés *ou* nattés; **(b)** (*on cushion etc*) galon *m*, ganse *f*, passepoil *m*; (*on clothing as ornament*) galon, soutache *f*; cordonnet *m*, lacet *m* (*de bordure*); **gold b.,** (*of officers*) galon; **(c)** *El* guipage *m* (*de fils conducteurs*).

braid² *vt* **(a)** tresser (*de la paille*); *esp Am* tresser, natter (*ses cheveux*); **(b)** galonner, soutacher (*un vêtement*); passementer (*le bord d'une chaise etc*).

braiding ['breɪdɪŋ] *n* **(a)** (*of hair*) tressage *m*, nattage *m*; **(b)** (*decoration*) (*on cushion*) (garniture *f* de) galon *m*; (*on clothing*) soutache *f*.

Braille [breɪl] *n* Braille *m*; **to read B.,** lire le Braille; **in B.,** en Braille; **B. alphabet,** alphabet *m* Braille.

brain¹ [breɪn] *n* **(a)** (*organ*) cerveau *m*; **electronic b.,** cerveau électronique; **to be b. dead,** (*of accident victim*) être en coma dépassé, avoir un électroencéphalogramme plat; *F* **to have money on the b.,** être obsédé par l'argent; *F* **to have a tune on the b.,** être hanté *ou* obsédé par un air; **she had a b. scan,** on lui a fait un scanner du cerveau; **b. death,** coma dépassé; **b. disease,** maladie cérébrale; *Old-fashioned* **b. fever,** fièvre cérébrale; **b. surgeon,** neurochirurgien *m*; **b. surgery,** neurochirurgie *f*; **b. stem,** pédoncule cérébral; **b. tumour,** tumeur *m* au cerveau; *F* **b. wave,** idée *f ou* trait *m* de génie, idée lumineuse;
(b) brains, *Culin* cervelle *f* (*de veau etc*); (*of person*) intelligence *f*; **he has brains** *or* **a good b.,** il est intelligent; **he's the brains of the family,** c'est lui le plus intelligent de la famille; **she's the brains of the business,** c'est elle le cerveau de l'entreprise; **to rack one's brains,** se creuser la cervelle *ou* le cerveau, se casser la tête; **use your brains,** sers-toi de ton cerveau; **to pick s.o.'s brains,** = faire appel à qn pour lui demander une idée ou un renseignement;
(c) *F* (*intelligent person*) cerveau *m*; **to call in the best brains,** faire appel à tous les talents; **brains trust,** *Am* **b. trust,** brain-trust *m*, *pl* brain-trusts; *F* **the b. drain,** l'exode *m ou* la fuite des cerveaux.

brain² *vt* défoncer le crâne à (*qn*); *Sl* (*hit over head*) assommer (*qn*).

brainbox ['breɪnbɒks] *n Sl* **(a)** (*skull*) boîte cranienne; **(b)** (*intelligent person*) as *m*, bête *f*; **she's a real b.,** c'est une vraie bête (à concours).

brainchild ['breɪntʃaɪld] *n* idée originale (*de qn*).

brain-fever ['breɪnfiːvər] *adj* **b.-f. bird,** coucou *m* épervier.

brainless ['breɪnlɪs] *adj* sans cervelle; *F* (*stupid*) stupide;

he's a b. idiot, c'est un idiot sans cervelle.

brainpower ['breɪnpaʊər] *n* intelligence *f*.

brainstorm ['breɪnstɔːm] *n* **(a)** (*disorder*) transport *m* au cerveau; **I must have had a b.,** j'ai dû avoir un moment d'égarement; **(b)** *Am F* (*brilliant idea*) idée *f* de génie.

brainstorming ['breɪnstɔːmɪŋ] *n* brainstorming *m*; **we had a b. session,** nous nous sommes réunis pour plancher sur le problème.

brainwash ['breɪnwɒʃ] *vt* soumettre (*qn*) à un lavage de cerveau; **he's been brainwashed,** on lui a fait un lavage de cerveau; **to b. s.o. into doing sth,** convaincre qn de faire qch à force de lavage de cerveau; *Hum* convaincre qn de faire qch.

brainwashing ['breɪnwɒʃɪŋ] *n* lavage *m* de cerveau.

brainwork ['breɪnwɜːk] *n* travail intellectuel, travail cérébral.

brainworker ['breɪnwɜːkər] *n* intellectuel, -elle, travailleur intellectuel.

brainy ['breɪnɪ] *adj F* intelligent, calé.

braise [breɪz] *vt Culin* braiser (*qch*), cuire (*qch*) à l'étouffée; **braised beef,** bœuf braisé; **braised chicken,** poulet *m* en cocotte.

braising ['breɪzɪŋ] *n* cuisson *f* à l'étouffée; **b. beef,** bœuf *m* à braiser.

brake¹ [breɪk] *n* (*undergrowth*) fourré *m*, hallier *m*.

brake² *n Tex* (*for flax, hemp*) brisoir *m*, broie *f*; *Agr* **b. (harrow),** brise-mottes *m inv*.

brake³ *vt Tex* briser, broyer, macquer (*du lin, du chanvre*).

brake⁴ *n* (*on car, train etc*) frein *m*; **to apply** *or* **put on the brake(s),** (*in traffic*) freiner; (*after parking*) mettre *ou* serrer le frein; **to slam on the brakes,** freiner d'un coup sec, *F* piler; **to release the brake(s),** desserrer le frein; *Fig* **to put a b. on a project,** donner un coup de frein à un projet; **air b.,** (*on car, train*) frein pneumatique *ou* à air comprimé; *Av* frein aérodynamique, aérofrein *m*; **b. fluid,** liquide *m* pour freins (hydrauliques); **b. horsepower,** puissance *f* au frein; **b. lining,** garniture *f* de frein; **b. pedal,** pédale *f* de frein; **b. shoe,** patin *m*, sabot *m* de frein; *Rail* **b. van,** wagon-frein *m*, *pl* wagons-freins; (*guard's van*) fourgon *m*.

brake⁵ *vi* (*in traffic*) freiner; (*after parking*) serrer *ou* mettre le frein; **to b. hard,** freiner d'un coup sec, *F* piler.

brake⁶ *n* = **BREAK³**.

brakesman, *Am* **brakeman,** *pl* **-men** ['breɪk(s)mən] *n Rail etc* garde-frein(s) *m*, *pl* gardes-frein(s).

braking ['breɪkɪŋ] *n* (*in traffic*) freinage *m*; (*abrupt*) coup *m* de frein; (*after parking*) serrage *m* des freins; **b. distance,** distance *f* d'arrêt *ou* de freinage.

bramble ['bræmb(ə)l] *n* **(a)** (*shrub*) ronce *f ou* mûrier *m* des haies; **brambles,** (*thorns*) ronces; **(b)** (*fruit*) mûre *f* (de ronce), mûre sauvage; **b. jelly,** gelée *f* de mûres.

brambly ['bræmblɪ] *adj* plein *ou* couvert de ronces.

bran [bræn] *n* (*of oats, wheat*) son *m*; **b. flakes,** son en flocons; **b. mash,** (*animal feed*) son mouillé; **b. tub,** = baquet rempli de son où l'on plonge la main pour en retirer une surprise.

branch¹ [brɑːntʃ] *n* **(a)** branche *f*, rameau *m* (*d'un arbre*); **the branches,** le branchage, les branches; **(b)** branche *f*, embranchement *m* (*d'une route, d'un chemin de fer*); branche, bras *m* (*d'un fleuve*); branche (*de chandelier, d'une famille, d'une science etc*); *Min* rameau *m* (*d'une galerie*); *Anat Math* branche (*d'artère, d'une courbe*); **the different branches of industry,** les différentes branches de l'industrie; *Rail* **b. line,** (ligne *f* d')embranchement; **(c)** *Admin Com* succursale *f* (*d'une société, d'une banque*); **b. office,** agence *f*; **(d)** *Mil* arme *f* (*du service*); service *m*, direction *f* (*de l'administration*); bureau *m* (*d'état-major*); **(e)** *Comptr* branchement *m*.

branch² *vi* **(a)** (*of road etc*) bifurquer; **at the point where the road branches,** à la bifurcation de la route; **(b)** (*of tree*) faire des branches.

►**branch off** *vi* (*of road*) bifurquer; **we b. off here,** nous bifurquons ici; **the road branches off to the left,** la route bifurque vers la gauche.

►**branch out** *vi* (*of organization etc*) étendre ses activités, se diversifier; **to b. out into ...,** étendre ses activités à ...; (*of person*) étendre ses activités *ou* son commerce à ...; **I'm going to b. out on my own one of these days,** un de ces jours je vais aller faire cavalier seul.

branched [brɑːntʃd] *adj* **(a)** *Bot* branchu, rameux; **(b)** (*candlestick*) à (plusieurs) branches.

branchia, *pl* **-iae** ['bræŋkɪə, -iːː] *n* (*of aquatic animals*) branchies *fpl*; (*of fish*) ouïes *fpl*.

branchiate ['bræŋkɪət] *adj* branchié.

branchiopod, *pl* **-s** ['bræŋkɪəpɒd, -z] *n* (*crustacean*) branchiopode *m*.

brand¹ [brænd] *n* **(a)** *Com* marque *f* (de fabrique); *Fig* **I have my own b. of humour,** j'ai un humour qui m'est propre *ou* qui n'appartient qu'à moi; **a good b. of cigars,** une bonne marque de cigares; **b. image,** image *f* de marque; **b. leader,** (*on market*) marque dominante; **b. loyalty,** (*of consumer*) fidélité *f* à la marque; **b. manager,** chef *m* de produit *ou* de marque; **b. name,** marque; **b. new,** tout neuf, flambant neuf; **(b)** (*on cattle*) marque *f* (*faite au fer rouge*); *Hist* flétrissure *f*, stigmate *m*; (*branding iron*) fer rouge; **the cattle have his b. on them,** le bétail porte sa marque; **(c)** (*burning wood*) brandon *m*, tison *m*; **(d)** *Poet* (*torch*) flambeau *m*; **(e)** *Agr* brûlure *f*; rouille *f* (*des plantes*).

brand² *vt* **(a)** (*label, identify*) marquer (*qn, un animal, une marchandise*) au fer rouge; *Hist* flétrir (*un criminel*); marquer (*un esclave*); **to be branded on s.o.'s memory,** (*of sight, scene*) être gravé dans la mémoire de qn; **the experience branded them for life,** l'expérience les a marqués à vie; **(b)** (*stigmatize*) flétrir, stigmatiser (*qn*); **to b. s.o. a liar/coward/***etc*, coller à qn une étiquette de menteur/lâche/*etc*, stigmatiser qn en le traitant de menteur/lâche/*etc*; **to be branded as a swindler,** être noté (d'infamie) comme escroc.

branded ['brændɪd] *adj* **(a)** (*cattle, criminal etc*) marqué au fer rouge; **to be b.,** porter la marque; **(b)** (*produit*) de marque.

branding ['brændɪŋ] *n* (*of cattle*) marquage *m* au fer rouge.

brandish ['brændɪʃ] *vt* brandir (*une arme etc*).

brandy ['brændɪ] *n* cognac *m*; **liqueur b.,** fine *f*; **b. and soda,** ≈ fine à l'eau; *Br Culin* **b. butter,** (*for Christmas pudding*) = beurre parfumé au cognac; **b. snap,** (*biscuit*) galette *f* au gingembre.

brash [bræʃ] *adj* (*impudent*) effronté, présomptueux, impudent; (*showing off*) exubérant; (*rash*) impétueux; (*colour*) cru; **a b. young man,** un jeune homme effronté.

brashly ['bræʃlɪ] *adv* (*with impudence*) effrontément, présomptueusement, impudemment; (*when showing off*) avec exubérance; (*rashly*) impétueusement.

brashness ['bræʃnɪs] *n* (*impudence*) effronterie *f*, impudence *f*; (*showing off*) exubérance *f*; (*rashness*) impétuosité *f*.

brass [brɑːs] *n* **(a)** (*metal*) cuivre *m* jaune, laiton *m*; **as bold as b.,** d'un air effronté; **to get down to b. tacks,** en venir aux faits; **I haven't got a b. farthing,** (*any money*) je n'ai pas un rond *ou* un clou; **it's not worth a b. farthing,** ça ne vaut pas un clou; *Mil F* **the top** *or US* **high b.,** les gros bonnets, *Sl* les grosses légumes; *Br F* **it's a bit b. monkeys today,** (*very cold*) on se les caille; **b. foundry,** fonderie *f* de cuivre; *Mil F* **b. hat,** officier *m* d'état-major; *Mus* **b. instrument,** instrument *m* à vent en cuivre; **b. plate,** plaque *f* de cuivre; (*of doctor, lawyer etc*) plaque; **(b)** (*item(s)*) les cuivres *mpl* (*du ménage etc*); (*in church*) plaque tombale en cuivre; *MecE* coussinet *m* de bielle *ou* de palier; coquille *f* (*de coussinets*); **to do the b.** *or* **brasses,** faire les cuivres; **horse b.,** médaillon *m* de cuivre (fixé sur le harnachement du cheval); **the b.,** (*in band, orchestra*) les cuivres; **b. band,** fanfare *f*; **b. rubbing,** décalquage par frottement d'une plaque tombale en cuivre; **(c)** *Br F* argent *m*, galette *f*; **(d)** *Br F* (*cheek, nerve*) **b. (neck),** culot *m*; **to have the b. to do sth,** avoir le culot de faire qch; **what a b. neck!,** quel culot!; **to have a b. neck,** avoir du culot, être culotté; *Can* avoir du front tout le tour de la tête.

►**brass off** *vtsep Br F* (*usu passive*) **to be brassed off,** en avoir marre, en avoir ras-le-bol; **I'm brassed off with waiting,** j'en ai marre *ou* ras-le-bol d'attendre.

brasserie ['bræsərɪ] *n* (*restaurant, bar*) brasserie *f*.

brassica ['bræsɪkə] *n Bot* brassica *m*.

brassie ['brɑːsɪ] *n Golf* brassie *m*.

brassière ['bræsɪər, 'bræz-] *n* (*underwear*) soutien-gorge *m*, *pl* soutiens-gorge.

brassiness ['brɑːsɪnɪs] *n* **(a)** sons cuivrés (*d'une musique*); **(b)** *F* (*insolence*) culot *m*.

brassware ['brɑːsweər] *n* dinanderie *f*.

brasswork ['brɑːswɜːk] *n* dinanderie *f*, chaudronnerie *f* d'art.

brassy¹ ['brɑːsɪ] *n Golf* brassie *m*.

brassy² *adj* **(a)** (*colour etc*) qui ressemble au cuivre; (*cheap jewellery*) qui fait toc; **(b)** (*son*) cuivré, claironnant; **(c)** (*person*) effronté.

brat [bræt] *n usu Pej* gosse *mf*, môme *mf*; (*spoilt young adult*) morveux, morveuse.

bravado [brə'vɑːdəʊ] *n* bravade *f*.

brave¹ [breɪv] **1** *adj* courageux, brave, vaillant; **be b. for a little bit longer,** courage, il n'y en a plus pour très longtemps *ou* c'est bientôt fini; **as b. as a lion,** courageux comme un lion; **to put a b. face on it,** faire bonne contenance. **2** *n* (*Am Indian warrior*) brave *m*.

brave² *vt* braver, défier (*qn*); braver, affronter (*un danger etc*).

bravely ['breɪvlɪ] *adv* courageusement, vaillamment.

bravery ['breɪvərɪ] *n* courage *m*, bravoure *f*, vaillance *f*; **she was decorated for b.,** elle a été décorée pour son courage.

bravo [brɑː'vəʊ] *int* bravo!

bravura [bræ'vuːrə] *n Mus* morceau *m* de bravoure.

brawl¹ [brɔːl] *n* rixe *f*, bagarre *f*; **drunken b.,** querelle *f* d'ivrognes.

brawl² *vi* (*of person*) se bagarrer.

brawler ['brɔːlər] *n* bagarreur, -euse.

brawling ['brɔːlɪŋ] *n* rixe *f*, bagarre *f*.

brawn [brɔːn] *n* **(a)** *F* muscles *mpl*; **to have plenty of b.,** avoir du biceps; **he's got more b. than brains,** il a du muscle mais pas grand-chose dans la tête; **(b)** *Br Culin* fromage *m* de tête.

brawny ['brɔːnɪ] *adj* (*arm*) fort, musculeux; (*person*) musclé, bien bâti.

bray¹ [breɪ] *n* braiment *m* (*d'un âne*).

bray² *vi* (*of donkey*) braire.

braze [breɪz] *vt Tech* (*using solder*) braser (*qch*); (*using brass*) souder (*qch*) au laiton.

brazen ['breɪz(ə)n] *adj* **(a)** (*bold*) effronté, impudent, cynique; **b. lie,** mensonge audacieux *ou* effronté; **(b)** *Lit* d'airain; **b. vessel,** vase *m* d'airain.

►**brazen out** *vtsep* **to b. it out,** (*cope with difficult situation by being insolent*) s'en tirer par des fanfaronnades, payer d'effronterie, payer de toupet.

brazenly ['breɪz(ə)nlɪ] *adv* effrontément, cyniquement, sans honte.

brazier ['breɪzɪər] *n* brasero *m*.

brazil [brə'zɪl] *n* **b. nut,** noix *f* d'Amérique *ou* du Brésil.

Brazil [brə'zɪl] *n* Brésil *m*.

Brazilian [brə'zɪlɪən] **1** *adj* brésilien. **2** *n* Brésilien, -ienne.

brazing ['breɪzɪŋ] *n* (*with solder*) brasage *m*, brasure *f*; (*with brass*) soudure *f* au laiton; **b. lamp,** lampe *f* à braser.

breach¹ [briːtʃ] *n* **(a)** infraction *f*, contravention *f* (*aux règles, au devoir etc*); violation *f* (*de la loi etc*); manquement *m* (*au devoir, à l'honneur, à la discipline etc*); rupture *f* (*de contrat*); **the company is suing him for b. of contract,** la société lui fait un procès pour rupture de contrat; **the company is in b. of the law,** la société est dans une position de violation de la loi; **b. of faith,** manque *m* de foi; **b. of trust,** (*by friend*) abus *m* de confiance; (*by official*) prévarication *f*; *Jur* violation d'un des devoirs d'un mandataire; **b. of good manners,** manque de savoir-vivre; **to commit a b. of etiquette,** manquer au protocole; **b. of professional secrecy,** violation du secret professionnel; **b. of privilege,** atteinte portée aux privilèges; **b. of the peace,** atteinte à l'ordre public; *Old-fashioned Jur* **b. of promise,** rupture de promesse de mariage;

(b) brouille *f*, rupture *f* (*entre deux amis etc*);

(c) trou *m*, brèche *f* (*dans un mur etc*); *Mil* **to stand in the b.,** monter sur la brèche; **to make a b. in the enemy's lines,** percer les lignes de l'ennemi; *Fig* **to step into the b.,** se porter volontaire pour remplacer qn, remplacer qn au pied levé.

breach² *vt* ouvrir une brèche dans (*une digue, un mur*); battre (*un mur*) en brèche; *Mil* percer (*les lignes ennemies*).

bread [bred] *n* **(a)** pain *m*; **a loaf of b.,** un pain; **b. and butter,** pain beurré; **a slice of b. and butter,** une tartine de beurre, une tartine beurrée; *Fig* **poetry doesn't earn you your b. and butter,** la poésie ne nourrit pas son homme; *Fig* **the customers are our b. and butter,** les clients sont notre gagne-pain; *Fig* **he knows which side his b. is buttered on,** il sait où est son avantage *ou* son intérêt; *Fig* **to earn one's daily b.,** gagner sa vie *ou* son pain; **to be on b. and water,** être au pain (sec) et à l'eau; *Fig* **to take the b. out of s.o.'s mouth,** en lever le pain de la bouche de qn; *Rel* **give us this day our daily b.,** donnenous aujourd'hui notre pain de ce jour; **b. bin,** (*horizontal*) boîte *f* à pain; (*vertical*) huche *f* à pain; **b. knife,** couteau *m* à pain; *Culin* **b. pudding,** gâteau *m* de pain; *Culin* **b. sauce,** sauce *f* à la mie de pain; **b. slicer** *or* **cutter,** tranche-pain *m inv*;

(b) *Old-fashioned Sl* (*money*) galette *f*, blé *m*, avoine *f*.

bread-and-butter [bredən'bʌtər] *adj F* **b.-and-b. letter,** lettre *f* de remerciements (*envers son hôte*); **b.-and-b. issues,** problèmes essentiels, questions essentielles.

breadbasket ['bredbɑːskɪt] *n* **(a)** corbeille *f* à pain; *Am Fig* région productrice de céréales panifiables; **the b. of the world,** la principale région productrice de céréales panifiables dans le monde; **(b)** *Old-fashioned Sl* estomac *m*, bedaine *f*.

breadboard ['bredbɔːd] *n* **(a)** planche *f* à pain; **(b)** *Electron etc* montage expérimental.

breadcrumb¹ ['bredkrʌm] *n* miette *f* (de pain); *Culin* **breadcrumbs,** chapelure *f*; **fried in breadcrumbs,** pané; **to coat fish with breadcrumbs,** enrober du poisson de chapelure.

breadcrumb² *vt* enrober (*du poisson*) de chapelure.

breadfruit ['bredfruːt] *n* (*fruit*) fruit *m* à pain; **b. tree,** artocarpe *m*, arbre *m* à pain.

breadline ['bredlaɪn] *n Am* = queue (du public) pour toucher les bons de pain ou pour recevoir de la nourriture gratuite; **on the b.,** indigent, sans ressources.

breadth [bredθ] *n* **(a)** (*width*) largeur *f*; (*of material*) lé *m*, laize *f*; **finger's b.,** travers *m* de doigt; **(b)** *Fig* largeur *f* (*de pensée, d'esprit, de vues*); facture *f* large (*d'un tableau*); ampleur *f* (*de style, de son*).

breadwinner ['bredwɪnər] *n* soutien *m* de famille; **to be the b.,** faire bouillir la marmite.

break¹ [breɪk] *n* **(a)** brisure *f*, cassure *f* (*dans une assiette etc*); trouée *f*, percée *f*, brèche *f* (*dans une haie*); éclaircie *f* (*à travers les nuages*); *El* rupture *f* (*du circuit*); *Lit* **b. of day,** point *m* du jour; **b. in the weather,** changement *m* du temps; **b. in the voice,** *Physiol* mue *f* (*à la puberté*); altération *f* de la voix (*par l'émotion*); *Mus* passage *m* d'un registre à l'autre; *Typ* **b. line,** dernière ligne (*d'un alinéa*);

(b) (*interruption*) lacune *f* (*dans une succession*); *Rad TV* coupure *f* (*dans un programme pour y introduire une publicité*); interruption *f* (*en cas de panne*); brisure *f* (*d'une ligne*); *Constr* brisis *m* (*d'un comble*); angle *m* (*d'un mur*); **b. of continuity,** solution *f* de continuité; **b. in a journey,** arrêt *m* en cours de route; **without a b.,** sans s'arrêter;

(c) (*breach*) rupture *f* (*entre deux amis, deux pays*); **the b. with his wife is final,** la rupture avec sa femme est définitive; **b. with a tradition,** rupture avec une tradition; **in a b. with tradition,** en rupture avec la tradition;

(d) (*rest*) (moment *m* de) repos *m*, répit *m*; pause *f*, arrêt *m* (*dans un travail, une conversation etc*); (*for coffee, tea*) pause; *Sch* intervalle *m* (*entre les classes*); récréation *f* (*d'interclasse*); (*holiday*) vacances *fpl*; *Mus* pause; (*in jazz*) break *m*; **an hour's b. for lunch,** une heure de pause pour le déjeuner; **a weekend in the country makes a pleasant b.,** un week-end à la campagne offre un repos agréable;

(e) *F* (*escape*) évasion *f*; **to make a b. for it,** s'évader; **to make the b.,** larguer les amarres;

(f) *F* (*chance*) chance *f*; **a good/bad b.,** une bonne/mauvaise chance; **we had a lucky b.,** nous avons eu de la veine; **give him a b.,** donnez-lui une chance; (*he won't do it again*) donnez-lui une seconde chance;

(g) *Billiards etc* (*opening shot*) l'acquit *m*; série *f*, suite *f* (*de coups gagnants*); *Tennis* rupture *f* (*du service de l'adversaire*); **she had a b. of serve in the first set,** (*she lost her serve*) elle a eu une rupture de service au cours du premier set; *Tennis* **to have two b. points,** avoir deux points de plus que son adversaire quand on reçoit le service.

break² *v* (*pt* **broke** [brəʊk]; *pp* **broken** ['brəʊk(ə)n]) **1** *vt* **(a)** casser (*un verre, un œuf, un bâton, un jouet etc*); briser (*un verre, un carreau, les liens d'amitié etc*); rompre (*un bâton, une corde, Nau les amarres etc*); entamer (*la peau*); *Jur* (*illegally*) briser (*les scellés*); (*legally*) lever (*les scellés*); *Tex* battre, teiller (*le lin*); *Min* concasser (*le minerai*); *El* interrompre (*le courant*); couper (*un circuit*); *Av* franchir (*le mur du son*); **to b. sth into pieces,** mettre qch en morceaux; **to b. one's arm/neck,** se casser le bras/le cou; *Fig* **to b. the ice,** rompre la glace; **to b. a branch from a tree,** détacher une branche d'un arbre; **to b. ground,** *Agr* défricher un terrain; *Constr etc* donner les premiers coups de pioche; *Fig* **to b. (new** *or* **fresh) ground,** faire œuvre de pionnier, faire une percée; **to b. a ten pound note,** entamer un billet de dix livres; **to b. a dinner set,** dépareiller un service de table; *El* **b. switch,** disjoncteur *m*, interrupteur *m*;

(b) (*interrupt*) rompre (*le silence, le jeûne etc*); **to b. step,** rompre le pas; **to b. ranks,** rompre les rangs; **to b. the thread of a story,** interrompre *ou* couper le fil d'une narration; **to b. one's journey,** s'arrêter en route, faire une étape; *Nau* faire escale; *Av* **to b. one's journey in Singapore,** faire (une) escale à Singapour;

(c) (*weaken impact of*) amortir (*une chute, la force de* *qch*); arrêter (*le vent*); rompre (*le courant*); **to b. the force of a blow,** amortir *ou* rompre un coup;

(d) (*overcome, destroy*) briser (*la résistance de qn*); abattre, dompter (*l'orgueil de qn*); ruiner (*la santé de qn*); briser (*une grève etc*); écarter (*un alibi*); battre (*un record*); *Mil* casser (*un officier*); dresser, entraîner (*un cheval*); corriger (*une mauvaise habitude*); **to b. s.o. into the work,** rompre qn à un travail; **to b. s.o. of a habit,** corriger *ou* guérir qn d'une habitude; **to b. oneself of a habit,** se corriger *ou* se défaire d'une habitude; **to b. s.o.,** ruiner qn; (*of grief etc*) briser qn; **to b. the bank,** (*when gambling*) faire sauter la banque; *Hum* **one night out won't b. the bank,** une sortie ne va pas me *ou* vous *etc* ruiner; *Tennis* **to b. one's opponent's service,** gagner le service de son adversaire; **to b. s.o.'s heart,** briser le cœur à qn; **to b. s.o.'s spirit,** briser le courage de qn;

(e) (*fail to respect*) violer, enfreindre, ne pas observer (*une loi, une règle, une trêve etc*); manquer à (*sa parole, un rendez-vous etc*); rompre (*un contrat etc*); **to b. the peace,** troubler l'ordre public; **to b. one's word to s.o.,** manquer à sa parole envers qn; **to b. gaol,** s'évader du prison; **to b. cover,** (*of animal*) débucher; *Mil Sch* **to b. bounds,** violer la consigne; **insolence that has broken all bounds,** insolence qui ne connaît plus de bornes *ou* qui dépasse les bornes;

(f) (*reveal, disclose*) *Nau* déferler (*un drapeau*); **to b. the news of sth to s.o.,** apprendre qch à qn; **to b. bad news gently to s.o.,** apprendre une mauvaise nouvelle doucement à qn; *Physiol* **to b. wind,** lâcher un vent.

2 *vi* (a) (*of glass, egg, toy etc*) se casser; (*of glass, window*) se briser; (*of wood, rope*) se rompre; (*of limb*) se fracturer, se casser; (*of bubble, abscess*) crever; (*of wave*) se briser, déferler; (*of troops*) se débander; **to b. in two/into pieces,** se casser en deux/en morceaux; **the sea breaks against the rocks,** la mer se brise sur les rochers; **my waters have broken,** (*of pregnant woman*) je perds mes eaux;

(b) (*of heart*) se briser, se fendre; (*of health*) s'altérer; **to b. under torture,** s'effondrer sous la torture; **to b. with s.o./with a tradition,** rompre avec qn/avec une tradition;

(c) (*of weather*) changer; (*of fine weather*) se gâter; (*of heatwave*) passer, prendre fin; (*of voice*) *Physiol* muer; (*with emotion*) se briser, s'étrangler;

(d) (*of storm*) éclater, se déchaîner; (*of news, scandal*) éclater; **day was beginning to b.,** le jour commençait à se lever; **to b. free from one's bonds,** briser ses liens;

(e) *Billiards* donner l'acquit.

break³ *n* (a) (*carriage*) break *m*; (b) *Aut* **shooting b.,** break *m* (de chasse).

break⁴ *vt* = **BRAKE³**.

▶**break away 1** *vtsep* détacher (*qch*) (**from,** de). **2** *vi* (a) (*escape*) s'évader; **she broke away from the guards,** elle a échappé à la surveillance de ses gardiens; (b) (*cut ties with*) se dégager, détacher (**from,** de); (*of province*) se séparer (*d'un Etat*); **when did you b. away from your family?,** quand est-ce que tu as coupé les ponts avec ta famille?; *Pol* **to b. away from a party,** lâcher *ou* abandonner un parti; **it was the year France broke away from NATO,** c'était l'année où la France a quitté l'OTAN; (c) (*crumble*) se détacher (**from,** de); **the merest touch and the surface breaks away,** la surface se détache au moindre contact.

▶**break back** *vi Tennis* = gagner le service de son adversaire après avoir eu une rupture de son propre service.

▶**break down 1** *vtsep* (a) (*destroy*) enfoncer (*une porte*); abattre, démolir (*un mur etc*);

(b) (*overcome*) briser (*la résistance*); vaincre, surmonter (*des préjugés*); **to b. down all opposition,** vaincre toute opposition;

(c) (*separate into parts*) concasser, broyer; *Ch* décomposer (*une substance*); *Ch* dissocier (*des molécules*); *Fin etc* décomposer (*un compte*); analyser (*un compte, une statistique*); **we need to b. the figures down a bit further,** il faut que nous décomposions *ou* ventilions les chiffres un peu plus.

2 *vi* (a) (*fail*) (*of health*) s'altérer, se détraquer; (*of the mind*) s'ébranler, sombrer; (*of car, machinery*) tomber en panne; (*of ship*) subir une avarie; **that's where your argument breaks down,** c'est là que ton argument ne tient plus debout;

(b) (*collapse*) (*of plan, negotiations*) échouer; (*of resistance, hopes*) s'effondrer; (*of person*) (*have nervous breakdown*) faire une dépression nerveuse; (*burst into tears*) éclater en sanglots, fondre en larmes; (*confess*) faire des aveux complets, passer aux aveux; **their marriage seems to be breaking down,** leur mariage semble être en train d'échouer;

(c) (*be separable*) se décomposer; **the substance breaks down into a number of components,** la substance se décompose en un certain nombre de composants.

▶**break even** *vi* (a) (*of person*) équilibrer son budget; (*of company*) rentrer dans ses frais; **the company is just about breaking even,** la société arrive tout juste à rentrer dans ses frais; (b) *Cards* cesser la partie à jeu égal.

▶**break in 1** *vtsep* (a) (*destroy*) enfoncer (*une porte etc*); (b) (*accustom to being used*) dresser (*un cheval*); culotter (*une pipe*); briser (*des souliers neufs*); *Am* roder (*une voiture*); **to b. s.o./oneself in to sth,** rompre qn/se rompre à qch; **I'm getting these shoes broken in at last,** ces chaussures commencent enfin à se faire. **2** *vi* (a) (*to interrupt*) intervenir, s'interposer; faire irruption (**on s.o.,** chez qn); **to b. in on a conversation,** interrompre une conversation; **I really must b. in at this point,** (*and say something*) il faut vraiment que je vous arrête à ce stade; (b) (*of burglar*) s'introduire *ou* entrer *ou* pénétrer par effraction.

▶**break into** *vipo* (a) (*burgle*) entrer de force dans, s'introduire *ou* entrer *ou* pénétrer par effraction dans (*une maison etc*); (*of burglar*) cambrioler (*une maison*); **to b. into the till,** forcer la caisse; (b) (*begin suddenly*) **to b. into laughter,** éclater de rire; **to b. into a song,** se mettre à entonner un air; **to b. into a trot,** prendre le trot, se mettre *ou* passer au trot; **her face broke into a smile,** son visage s'épanouit en un sourire; (c) (*use part of*) entamer (*des provisions, un billet d'une livre etc*); (d) (*interrupt*) interrompre (*une conversation*).

▶**break loose** *vi* se dégager de ses liens; s'évader (**from,** de); (*of ship*) partir en dérive; **all hell has broken loose,** les diables sont déchaînés.

▶**break off 1** *vtsep* (a) (*remove*) casser, rompre (*qch*); détacher (*qch*) (**from,** de); **I've broken the handle off a cup,** j'ai cassé l'anse d'une tasse;

(b) (*end*) abandonner (*un travail etc*); rompre (*des négociations etc*); **to b. off relations with s.o.,** rompre avec qn; **talks with the union have been broken off,** les discussions avec le syndicat ont été interrompues;

(c) (*end relationship*) rompre; **it wouldn't surprise me if they broke it off,** ça ne me surprendrait pas s'ils rompaient; **I've broken it off with him,** j'ai rompu avec lui.

2 *vi* (a) (*become detached*) se casser net, se détacher net; se détacher (**from,** de); **the handle just broke off in my hand,** l'anse vient de me rester dans la main;

(b) (*stop*) **to b. off for ten minutes,** prendre dix minutes de repos; **to b. off for lunch,** s'arrêter pour déjeuner; **can we b. off for the rest of the day?,** est-ce que nous pouvons nous arrêter pour le restant de la journée?;

(c) (*stop talking*) s'interrompre, se taire; **to b. off in the middle of a speech,** s'arrêter *ou* s'interrompre au milieu d'un discours.

▶**break open 1** *vtsep* (*open by force*) enfoncer (*une porte*); forcer (*une serrure, un coffre-fort*); éventrer (*une caisse*); **to b. a desk open,** forcer un bureau. **2** *vi* (*of box etc*) s'ouvrir.

▶**break out 1** *vi* (a) (*escape*) s'échapper, s'évader (*d'une prison etc*); (b) (*of argument, war, riots*) éclater; (*of fire*) se déclarer; **a quarrel broke out between them,** ils se sont mis à se quereller; (c) (*develop*) **to b. out into a sweat,** se mettre à transpirer; **to b. out in spots,** (*of face etc*) se couvrir de boutons; **the baby is breaking out into a rash,** le bébé est en train de faire une éruption; (d) (*say suddenly*) lancer *ou* déclarer brusquement. **2** *vipo* (a) *F* ouvrir (*une bouteille de vin*); (b) *Am* (*prepare for use*) sortir (*qch*) de sa cachette; déployer (*un drapeau*).

▶**break through 1** *vipo* enfoncer (*une barrière etc*); se frayer un chemin à travers (*une barrière, une foule etc*); faire une brèche dans (*un mur etc*); *Av* franchir (*le mur du son*); (*of sun*) percer (*les nuages*); **once you b. through her shyness,** une fois que vous pénétrez sa réserve. **2** *vi* (*of sun*) percer.

▶**break up 1** *vtsep* (a) (*reduce to pieces*) mettre *ou* briser (*qch*) en morceaux; démolir (*un bâtiment, un navire etc*); morceler (*une propriété*); démembrer (*un empire*); disperser (*une foule, une famille*); rompre (*une coalition*); *Ch* résoudre (*un composé*); *Agr* ameublir (*le sol*); **to b. up a word into syllables,** décomposer un mot en syllabes;

(b) (*bring to an end*) détruire (*un mariage*); dissoudre (*une assemblée*); mettre fin à (*une conférence*); **to b. up a fight,** séparer des combattants; *F* **b. it up!,** la paix!

2 *vi* (a) (*disintegrate*) (*of ship, empire etc*) se démembrer; (*of road surface*) se désagréger; (*of ice*) débâcler; (*of group*) se disjoindre; (*of crowd etc*) se disperser; (*of clouds*) se dissiper, se disperser; *Fig F* **I just broke up,** (*with laughter*) j'ai été pris d'un fou rire; **ship breaking up,** navire en perdition;

(b) (*end*) (*of celebration*) prendre fin; *Sch* entrer en vacances; **when did the party finally b. up?,** quand est-ce que la soirée s'est finalement terminée?; **the meeting broke up in confusion,** la séance fut levée dans le tumulte; *Sch* **we b. up on the 4th,** nos vacances commencent le 4; **the schools will be breaking up for summer soon,** les écoles vont bientôt fermer pour l'été;

(c) (*end relationship*) rompre; **I've heard that they're breaking up,** j'ai appris qu'ils sont en train de rompre; **their marriage has broken up,** leur mariage s'est brisé *ou* a cassé;

(d) (*of weather*) se gâter.

breakable ['breɪkəb(ə)l] **1** *adj* cassable; (*fragile*) cassant, fragile. **2** *npl* **breakables,** objets *mpl* fragiles.

breakage ['breɪkɪdʒ] *n* rupture *f* (*d'une chaîne, d'un arbre d'hélice etc*); bris *m*, fracture *f* (*de verre etc*); **have there been any breakages?,** (*was anything broken?*) est-ce qu'il y a eu de la casse?; **to pay for breakages,** payer la casse.

breakaway ['breɪkəweɪ] *n* **(a)** sécession *f* (**from,** de); **b. union,** syndicat dissident; **(b)** *Sp* séparation *f* (*de deux boxeurs*); *Fb* échappée *f* (*de l'ailier etc*); **(c)** (*in race*) faux départ; **(d)** *Rail* dérive *f* (de wagons); **(e)** *Austr* ruée *f* (*d'un troupeau*).

break-dance ['breɪkdɑːns] *vi* danser le smurf.

break-dancer ['breɪkdɑːnsər] *n* danseur, -euse de smurf.

break-dancing ['breɪkdɑːnsɪŋ] *n* smurf *m*.

breakdown ['breɪkdaʊn] *n* **(a)** insuccès *m*, échec *m* (*d'une tentative*); rupture *f* (*des négociations*); écroulement *m* (*d'un système*); arrêt complet (*dans un service*); **(b)** détérioration *f* (spectaculaire), délabrement *m* (*de la santé*); **she's had a b.,** (*and has not yet recovered*) elle fait une dépression; *Hum* **I'm going to have a b.,** je vais craquer; **nervous b.,** dépression nerveuse; **mental b.,** effondrement de la raison; **(c)** *Aut etc* panne *f*; **I've had a b.,** je suis tombé en panne; **b. service,** service *m* de dépannage; **b. gang,** équipe *f* de dépannage; **b. van** *or* **truck,** dépanneuse *f*, camion *m* de dépannage; **(d)** (*into component parts*) analyse *f* (*statistique etc*); décomposition *f* (*d'un compte etc*); répartition *f*, classement *m* (*de la population par classes, âges etc*); **(e)** *El* claquage *m*; **b. voltage,** tension *f* de claquage; **(f)** *Ch* dissociation *f*.

breaker ['breɪkər] *n* **(a)** casseur, -euse (*de pierres*); **b.'s yard,** chantier *m* de démolition (*de voitures, navires etc*); **(b)** dresseur, -euse (*de chevaux etc*); **(c)** violateur, -trice (*d'une loi etc*); **(d)** (*apparatus*) brisoir *m*; *Constr etc* concasseur *m*; casse-pierre(s) *m inv*; **ice b.,** *Nau* brise-glace(s) *m inv*; *Fig* = technique utilisée dans une réunion, un stage etc pour faciliter le contact entre les participants; *El* **circuit b.,** coupe-circuit *m inv*, disjoncteur *m*; **(e)** (*wave*) vague déferlante *ou* brisante.

breakeven ['breɪkiːv(ə)n] **1** *adj* à budget équilibré; **b. point,** seuil *m* de rentabilité; **b. prices,** prix permettant de rentrer dans ses frais. **2** *n* seuil *m* de rentabilité; **to reach b.,** atteindre le seuil de rentabilité.

breakfast[1] ['brekfəst] *n* petit déjeuner; **to have (one's) b.,** déjeuner, prendre le *ou* son (petit) déjeuner; **while we were at b.,** pendant que nous déjeunions; **what do you want for b.?,** qu'est-ce que tu veux pour le petit déjeuner?; **b. cup (and saucer),** déjeuner; **b. cereals,** céréales *fpl* (en flocons); **b. meeting,** réunion *f* pendant le petit déjeuner; **b. television,** programmes télévisés matinaux.

breakfast[2] *vi* déjeuner (le matin).

break-in ['breɪkɪn] *n* **(a)** (*by burglar etc*) effraction *f*; **(b)** *MecE & Am Aut etc* rodage *m*.

breaking ['breɪkɪŋ] *n* **(a)** bris *m* (*d'un carreau etc*); rupture *f* (*du silence etc*); interruption *f* (*d'un voyage*); *Tex* battage *m*, teillage *m* (*du lin*); *Min* concassage *m* (*du minerai*); *El* interruption (*du courant*); rupture (*du circuit*); *Av* franchissement *m* (*du mur du son*); *Jur* **b. and entering,** entrée *f* par effraction (*dans une maison*); *Jur* **b. of seals,** (*illegal*) bris *m* des scellés; (*legal*) levée *f* des scellés; **b. of new ground,** *Agr* défrichage *m*; (*research, science etc*) œuvre *f* de pionnier;

(b) (*disintegration*) brisement *m* (*des flots*); *Med* percement *m* (*d'un abcès*); *Med* fracture *f* (*d'un os etc*); **b. of the voice,** *Physiol* mue *f*; (*with emotion*) altération *f* de la voix; *MecE* **b. strain,** tension *f* de rupture; **b. point,** *MecE* point *m* de rupture; *MecE* limite *f* critique (*de la résistance*); *Fig* limite (*des forces etc*); **she has reached b. point,** elle est au bout du rouleau, elle est à bout; **their marriage has reached b. point,** leur mariage a atteint le point critique; **to try s.o.'s patience to b. point,** pousser à bout la patience de qn;

(c) dressage *m* (*d'un cheval*);

(d) amortissement *m* (*d'une chute, de la force de qch*);

(e) action *f* de briser (*une grève, le cœur de qn*); destruction *f* (*de la puissance de qn*);

(f) violation *f* (*de la loi, d'un traité etc*); rupture *f* (*d'une promesse*); **b. of one's word,** manquement *m* à sa parole.

breakneck ['breɪknek] *adj* **b. speed,** vitesse *ou* allure folle *ou* vertigineuse.

break-out ['breɪkaʊt] *n* évasion *f* (*de prison etc*).

breakthrough ['breɪkθruː] *n* **(a)** *Mil* percée *f* (*des lignes ennemies*); **(b)** (*achievement*) (*action*) percée *f* (*technologique*); (*result*) invention *f* révolutionnaire; **to make a b.,** faire une percée.

break-up ['breɪkʌp] *n* **(a)** dissolution *f* (*d'un empire, d'une assemblée*); destruction *f* (*d'un mariage etc*); délabrement *m* (*de la santé*); bris *m* (*d'un navire etc*); **(b)** changement *m* (*du temps*); débâcle *f* (*des glaces*).

breakwater ['breɪkwɔːtər] *n* **(a)** (*wall*) brise-lames *m inv*, môle *m*; (*jetty*) jetée *f*; **(b)** éperon *m* (*d'un pont*).

bream [briːm] *n* (*fish*) brème *f*; **sea b.,** dorade *f*, brème de mer.

breast[1] [brest] *n* **(a)** (*of woman*) sein *m*; **child at the b.,** enfant au sein; **b. cancer,** cancer *m* du sein; **b. feeding,** allaitement *m* (au sein); **(b)** (*chest*) poitrine *f* (*de personne, d'animal*); poitrail *m* (*de cheval*); devant *m* (*d'une chemise etc*); *Culin* blanc *m* (*de volaille*); **to make a clean b. of it,** tout avouer; **b. high** *or* **deep,** (*water etc*) jusqu'à la poitrine; **b. pocket,** (*of shirt, jacket*) poche *f* poitrine, *pl* poches poitrine; **inside b. pocket,** poche poitrine intérieure, poche portefeuille; **(c)** *Tech* ventre *m* (*de haut fourneau*); *Constr* **chimney b.,** manteau *m* de cheminée; *HydE* **b. wheel,** roue *f* de côté; **(d)** *Min* front *m* de taille *ou* d'abattage.

breast[2] *vt Lit* affronter, faire front à (*un danger*); affronter, gravir (*une colline*); **to b. the waves,** (*of swimmer*) fendre la lame; *Sp* **to b. the tape,** être le premier à franchir la ligne d'arrivée.

breastbone ['brestbəʊn] *n* (*of person, animal*) sternum *m*; (*of bird*) bréchet *m*.

breast-feed ['brestfiːd] *v* (*pt & pp* **-fed** [-fed]) **1** *vt* nourrir (*un enfant*) au sein, allaiter (*un enfant*). **2** *vi* allaiter; **she's decided to b.-f.,** elle a décidé d'allaiter.

breast-feeding ['brestfiːdɪŋ] *n* allaitement *m*.

breastplate ['brestpleɪt] *n* (*armour*) cuirasse *f*.

breaststroke ['bres(t)strəʊk] *n* (*in swimming*) brasse *f*; **I can only do b.,** je ne sais nager que la brasse.

breastwork ['brestwɜːk] *n* parapet *m*.

breath [breθ] *n* haleine *f*, souffle *m*; **to draw b.,** respirer; **give me time to draw b.,** donnez-moi le temps de souffler; **to draw** *or* **take a deep** *or* **long b.,** respirer profondément *ou* à pleins poumons; **to pause for b.,** (*when speaking*) s'arrêter pour reprendre sa respiration; **to draw one's last b.,** rendre le dernier soupir; **to have bad b.,** avoir mauvaise haleine; **the b. of life,** le souffle vital *ou* de la vie; *Fig* **music is the very b. of life to me,** je ne pourrais pas vivre sans musique; **all in the same b.,** tout d'une haleine; **but in the next b. he said the opposite,** mais quelques secondes plus tard il a dit le contraire; **they are not to be mentioned in the same b.,** on ne saurait les comparer; **to hold one's b.,** retenir son souffle; **to gasp for b.,** haleter; **to waste one's b.,** perdre son temps en discours inutiles; **I'm wasting my b.,** je perds mon temps, je me fatigue pour rien; **save your b.,** ne te fatigue pas; **to be short of b.,** être essoufflé, avoir la respiration coupée; **out of b.,** hors d'haleine, à bout de souffle, essoufflé; **to get out of b.,** perdre haleine, s'essouffler; **to take s.o.'s b. away,** couper la respiration *ou* le souffle à qn; *Fig* ébahir *ou* interloquer qn; **to get one's b. (back), to recover** *or* **catch one's b.,** reprendre haleine; **under one's b.,** (*parler*) d'une voix très basse, à voix basse; (*jurer*) en sourdine; **the first b. of spring,** les premiers effluves du printemps; **a b. of wind/of air,** un souffle de vent/d'air; **to go out for a b. of (fresh) air,** sortir prendre l'air; **there isn't a b. of wind today,** il n'y a pas un souffle de vent aujourd'hui; *Ling* **b. consonant,** consonne soufflante; *Admin* **b. test,** alco(o)test *m*.

breathalyse, *US* **breathalyze** ['breθəlaɪz] *vt* faire subir l'alco(o)test à (*qn*).

breathalyser, *US* **breathalyzer** ['breθəlaɪzər] *n Admin* **b. test,** alco(o)test *m*.

breathe [briːð] **1** *vi* **(a)** respirer, souffler; **to b. hard,** haleter; **to b. heavily,** (*noisily*) respirer bruyamment; (*with difficulty*) respirer péniblement; **you can't b. in**

here, (*it's too hot*) on ne peut pas respirer ici; **I feel as if I can't b.,** je me sens oppressé; **to b. again,** (*with relief*) respirer de nouveau; **to b. on one's fingers,** souffler dans ses doigts; *F* **to b. down s.o.'s neck,** (*supervise*) talonner qn, être sur le dos de qn; (*look over their shoulder*) regarder par-dessus l'épaule de qn; **the police are breathing down our necks,** (*very close to arresting us*) la police nous talonne; **there's a police car breathing down our necks,** on a une voiture de police au cul;

(b) (*of voice, instrument, wind*) soupirer, souffler doucement; **open the bottle to let the wine b.,** ouvre la bouteille pour permettre au vin de respirer.

2 *vt* **(a)** respirer (*l'air*);

(b) exhaler, laisser échapper (*un soupir*); murmurer (*une prière*); **to b. a sigh of relief,** pousser un soupir de soulagement; *Lit* **to b. one's last,** rendre le dernier soupir, rendre l'âme; **don't b. a word (of it)!,** n'en soufflez (pas un) mot!; **to b. fire,** (*be very angry*) cracher des flammes; **to b. new life into sth,** insuffler une force nouvelle à qch; **he was breathing whisky fumes all over me,** il me soufflait des relents de whisky en pleine figure;

(c) *Ling* aspirer (*un son, une consonne*).

►breathe in *vi* aspirer; (*on doctor's instructions*) inspirer.

►breathe out *vi* expirer.

breathed [breθt, briːðd] *adj Ling* (*consonant*) sourd, fort; (*vowel*) aspiré.

breather ['briːðər] *n* **(a)** *F* moment *m* de repos (pour souffler); **to give s.o. a b.,** laisser souffler qn, laisser un moment de répit à qn; **to go for a b.,** aller respirer un peu d'air, sortir prendre l'air; **to take a b.,** faire une pause; **(b) heavy b.,** personne qui respire bruyamment; *Hum F* homme qui donne des coups de téléphone anonymes, *F* corbeau *m*.

breathing ['briːðɪŋ] *n* **(a)** (*of person*) respiration *f*; **heavy b.,** (*noisy*) respiration bruyante; (*difficult*) respiration pénible; **b. apparatus,** *Min etc* appareil *m* respiratoire, masque *m* de protection; (*for diver*) scaphandre *m*; **b. space,** (*rest, respite*) répit *m*, relâche *f*; (*place*) place *f ou* espace *m* pour respirer; **(b)** *Ling* aspiration *f* (*d'un son*).

breathless ['breθlɪs] *adj* **(a)** (*out of breath*) hors d'haleine, à bout de souffle, essoufflé, haletant; **b. with running,** hors d'haleine *ou* essoufflé d'avoir couru; **b. chase,** poursuite *f* à perte d'haleine; **(b)** *Fig* **to hold s.o. b.,** (*of film etc*) tenir qn en haleine *ou* en suspens; **b. silence** *or* **hush,** silence absolu; **b. suspense,** attente fiévreuse.

breathlessly ['breθlɪslɪ] *adv* (*see adj*) **(a)** tout haletant; **(b)** (*attendre, écouter*) en retenant son souffle.

breathlessness ['breθlɪsnɪs] *n* essoufflement *m*; (*of patient*) manque *m* de souffle, oppression *f*.

breathtaking ['breθteɪkɪŋ] *adj* **it's b.,** (*of view, stupidity*) c'est à vous couper le souffle.

breathtakingly ['breθteɪkɪŋlɪ] *adv* (*beautiful, stupid*) étonnamment, extraordinairement.

breath-test ['breθtest] *vt* faire subir l'alco(o)test à.

breathy ['breθɪ] *adj* **(a) b. voice,** voix haletante; **(b)** *Mus* (*voice*) qui manque d'attaque.

breech [briːtʃ] *n* **(a)** *Obst* **b. (delivery** *or* **birth),** accouchement *m* par le siège; **b. presentation,** présentation *f* par le siège; **(b) (pair of) breeches** ['brɪtʃɪz] , culotte *f*; **knee breeches,** culotte; **riding breeches,** culotte de cheval; **(c)** (*of firearm*) culasse *f*, tonnerre *m*; **b. action** *or* **mechanism,** mécanisme *m* de culasse; **(d)** *Nau* **breeches buoy,** bouée *f* culotte.

breed¹ [briːd] *n* race *f* (*d'hommes, d'animaux*); *Fig* **she is one of the new b. of executive,** elle fait partie de la nouvelle race *ou* génération de cadres; **a new b. of modems,** une nouvelle génération de modems; **thatchers are a dying b.,** les couvreurs sont une race en voie de disparition.

breed² *v* (*pt & pp* **bred** [bred]) **1** *vt* **(a)** produire, procréer (*des enfants, des petits*); *Fig* faire naître; **dirt breeds disease,** la malpropreté engendre la maladie; **all these rumours are breeding insecurity,** toutes ces rumeurs engendrent l'insécurité; **(b)** élever (*du bétail, des lapins etc*); **to be town/country bred,** (*of person*) avoir été élevé à la ville/à la campagne; *Prov* **what's bred in the bone will come out in the flesh,** bon chien chasse de race. **2** *vi* **(a)** (*of animals*) se multiplier, se reproduire; (*of people*) se reproduire; *Fig* (*of opinions etc*) se propager; **(b)** (*of person*) faire de l'élevage (*d'animaux domestiques etc*).

breeder ['briːdər] *n* **(a)** reproducteur, -trice; *Nucl Phys* **b. reactor,** surgénérateur *m*, *F* couveuse *f*; **(b)** éleveur, -euse (*d'animaux*); **poultry b.,** aviculteur, -trice; **silkworm b.,** sériciculteur *m*.

breeding ['briːdɪŋ] *n* **(a)** reproduction *f*, multiplication *f* (*des êtres*); **b. ground,** endroit fréquenté par certains animaux à l'époque de la reproduction; *Fig* foyer *m*, lieu *m* de prédilection, terrain *m* propice; **b. ground of anarchists,** pépinière *f* d'anarchistes; **b. ground of crime/violence,** terrain propice au crime/à la violence; **damp areas are a b. ground for germs,** les zones humides constituent un terrain propice *ou* un lieu de prédilection pour les microbes; **(b)** élevage *m* (*d'animaux domestiques etc*); **animal kept for b. purposes,** (animal *m*) reproducteur *m*; **sheep b.,** élevage des moutons; **silkworm b.,** sériciculture *f*; **b. stock,** animaux élevés en vue de la reproduction; **(c)** éducation *f* (*d'un enfant etc*); **(good) b.,** bonne éducation, bonnes manières, savoir-vivre *m*; **to lack b.,** manquer de savoir-vivre *ou* d'éducation.

breeze¹ [briːz] *n* brise *f*; **gentle** *or* **light b.,** petite *ou* légère brise; **land b.,** brise de terre; **sea b.,** brise de mer *ou* du large; *Nau* **strong** *or* **stiff b.,** vent frais, grosse brise; **fresh b.,** bonne brise; *esp Am F* **it was a b.,** (*easy*) c'était simple comme bonjour, c'était un jeu d'enfant.

breeze² *n* (*ashes*) braise *f* de houille; charbonnaille *f*; **coke b.,** grésillon *m* de coke, poussier *m* de coke; **b. concrete,** ciment *m* de laitier; **b. block** *or* **brick,** parpaing *m*.

►breeze in *vi* (*quickly*) entrer en coup de vent; (*casually*) entrer d'une façon désinvolte.

►breeze out *vi* (*quickly*) sortir en coup de vent; (*casually*) sortir d'une façon désinvolte.

►breeze through 1 *vi* (*pass exam with ease*) réussir les doigts dans le nez. **2** *vipo* réussir (*un examen*) les doigts dans le nez.

►breeze up *vi Nau* (*of wind*) fraîchir.

breezeway ['briːzweɪ] *n US* passage couvert (*souvent entre la maison et le garage*).

breezily ['briːzɪlɪ] *adv* (*in lively fashion*) avec verve; (*casually*) avec désinvolture.

breezy ['briːzɪ] *adj* **(a)** (*jour, endroit etc*) venteux; **(b)** *F* (*pleasant*) jovial; (*casual*) désinvolte; (*speech*) plein de verve.

Bremen ['breɪmən] *n* Brême.

Bren [bren] *n Mil* **B. (gun),** fusil-mitrailleur *m*; **B. carrier,** chenillette *f* porte-fusil-mitrailleur, *pl* chenillettes porte-fusil(s)-mitrailleur(s).

brent [brent] *n* **b. (goose),** bernache *f* cravant.

brethren *see* **BROTHER 1 (c)** .

Breton ['bretɒn] **1** *adj* breton. **2** *n* **(a)** Breton, -onne; **(b)** *Ling* breton *m*.

breve [briːv] *n* **(a)** (*accent*) brève *f*; **(b)** *Mus* brève *f*, carrée *f*; **b. rest,** demi-bâton *m*, *pl* demi-bâtons; **(c)** *Hist* bref *m* (*du pape*).

brevet ['brevɪt, *esp Am* brə'vet] *n Mil* brevet *m* d'honorariat.

breviary ['briːvɪərɪ] *n Rel* bréviaire *m*.

brevity ['brevɪtɪ] *n* **(a)** brièveté *f*, concision *f* (*de style*); laconisme *m* (*d'expression*); **(b)** brièveté *f*, courte durée (*de la vie etc*).

brew¹ [bruː] *n* **(a)** (*of beer*) cuvée *f*; **home b.,** bière *ou* cidre de ménage; **(b)** infusion *f* (*de thé*).

brew² 1 *vt* **(a)** brasser (*de la bière*); **home brewed,** (*beer, cider*) de ménage; **(b)** faire infuser (*du thé*); préparer (*un bol de punch*). **2** *vi* (*of tea etc*) infuser; **there's a storm brewing,** un orage couve *ou* se prépare; *Fig* il y a de l'orage dans l'air; *Fig* **there's something brewing,** il y a quelque chose dans l'air *ou* qui se prépare.

►brew up *vi Br F* faire infuser le thé.

brewer ['bruːər] *n* brasseur *m*; **b.'s yeast,** levure *f* de bière.

brewery ['brʊərɪ] *n* brasserie *f*.

brewing ['bruːɪŋ] *n* **(a)** brassage *m* (*de la bière*); **the b. industry,** la brasserie; **(b)** infusion *f* (*du thé*); préparation *f* (*d'un bol de punch*).

briar¹ ['braɪər] *n* **(a)** (*shrub*) bruyère *f*; **(b)** (*pipe*) bruyère *f*.

briar² *n* = **BRIER¹**.

briarroot ['braɪəruːt] , **briarwood** ['braɪəwʊd] *n* racine *f* de bruyère.

bribable ['braɪbəb(ə)l] *adj* corruptible.

bribe¹ [braɪb] *n* paiement *m* illicite, *F* pot-de-vin *m*, *pl* pots-de-vin; **to take a b.** *or* **bribes,** se laisser corrompre; **he was accused of taking bribes,** on l'a accusé de toucher des pots-de-vin.

bribe² *vt* corrompre, soudoyer, *F* graisser la patte à (*qn*); **to b. s.o. to silence,** acheter le silence de qn; *Fig* **I bribed her with some chocolate to go to bed,** je lui ai donné du chocolat pour la faire se mettre au lit.

bribery ['braɪbərɪ] *n* corruption *f*; **open/not open to b.,**

corruptible/incorruptible.

bribing ['braɪbɪŋ] *n* corruption *f*, *F* graissage *m* de patte; subornation *f* (*de témoins*).

bric-a-brac ['brɪkəbræk] *n* (*no pl*) bric-à-brac *m*.

brick[1] [brɪk] *n* **(a)** brique *f*; **air b.**, brique perforée; **fire b.**, brique réfractaire; *Prov* **one cannot make bricks without straw,** on ne peut pas faire de miracles; *F* **to come down on s.o. like a ton of bricks,** tomber sur le dos à qn; **to drop a b.**, faire une bourde *ou* une gaffe; **box of (building) bricks,** (*toys*) jeu *m* de cubes *ou* de construction; **b. kiln,** four *m* à briques; **b. partition,** cloison *f* de briques; **b. (red),** rouge brique *inv*; **b. wall,** mur *m* en briques; *Fig* **to run up** *or* **bang one's head against a b. wall,** se heurter à l'impossible *ou* à un obstacle infranchissable; **it's like talking to a b. wall,** (*he or she etc won't listen*) c'est comme parler à un mur *ou* à un sourd; **(b)** *Old-fashioned Br F* **he's a b.**, c'est un chic type; **(c)** bloc *m* (*de thé etc*); pain *m* (*de savon, de glace etc*).

brick[2] *vt* briqueter (*qch*), garnir (*qch*) de briques.

►brick up *vtsep* murer, maçonner (*une fenêtre*).

brickbat ['brɪkbæt] *n* (*weapon*) fragment *m* de brique; *Fig* insulte *f*; **she got a lot of brickbats for her performance,** son interprétation lui a valu des critiques.

brickfield ['brɪkfiːld] *n* briqueterie *f*.

bricklayer ['brɪkleɪər] , *Br F* **brickie** ['brɪkɪ] *n* maçon *m*.

bricklaying ['brɪkleɪɪŋ] *n* briquetage *m*.

brickmaker ['brɪkmeɪkər] *n* briquetier *m*.

brickwork ['brɪkwɜːk] *n* briquetage *m*, maçonnerie *f* de brique; **brickworks,** briqueterie *f*.

brickyard ['brɪkjɑːd] *n* briqueterie *f*.

bridal ['braɪd(ə)l] *adj* nuptial, de noce(s); **b. veil,** voile *m* de mariée; **b. suite,** (*in hotel*) appartement *m* pour jeunes mariés.

bride [braɪd] *n* (*about to be married*) fiancée; (*married*) jeune mariée; **the b. and (bride)groom,** (*about to be married*) les futurs époux; (*married*) les jeunes mariés; **with his young b.**, avec sa jeune épouse.

bridegroom ['braɪdgruːm] *n* (*about to be married*) fiancé; (*married*) jeune marié.

bridesmaid ['braɪdzmeɪd] *n* demoiselle *f* d'honneur (*de la mariée*).

bride-to-be ['braɪdtə'biː] *n* future mariée.

bridge[1] [brɪdʒ] *n* **(a)** pont *m*; **to cross a b.**, traverser un pont; *Fig* **we'll cross that b. when we get** *or* **come to it,** chaque chose en son temps; **loading b.**, pont de chargement; **b. building,** construction *f* de ponts, pontage *m*; *Mil* **b. train,** (*bridges*) train *m* de pontons; (*builders*) corps *m* des pontonniers;

(b) (*in wrestling*) pont *m*; **to make a b.**, ponter;

(c) (*in billiards etc*) chevalet *m*;

(d) *Nau* passerelle *f*; **fore b.**, passerelle de commandement; **b. house,** rouf-passerelle *m*;

(e) *El etc* pont *m*, shunt *m*; **impedance b.**, pont d'impédance; **inductance b.**, pont d'induction; **induction b.**, balance *f* d'induction; **measuring b.**, pont de mesure; **b. circuit/connection/network/rectifier,** montage *m*/couplage *m*/réseau *m*/redresseur *m* en pont; **b. piece,** pont polaire (*d'accus*);

(f) dos *m*, arête *f* (*du nez*); chevalet *m* (*d'un violon*); arcade *f* (*d'une paire de lunettes*); autel *m* (*d'une chaudière*);

(g) (*in mouth*) bridge *m*.

bridge[2] *vt* construire un pont sur (*un cours d'eau*); **to b. a gap,** relier les bords d'une brèche; *Fig* combler une lacune; (*esp for supplies*) faire la soudure; **that will b. (over) the difficulty,** cela nous aidera à surmonter la difficulté.

bridge[3] *n Cards* bridge *m*; **to play b.**, jouer au bridge, bridger; **game of b.**, (partie *f* de) bridge; **auction b.**, bridge aux enchères; **contract b.**, bridge contrat; **b. player,** bridgeur, -euse; *Br Culin* **b. roll,** petit pain (au lait).

bridgehead ['brɪdʒhed] *n Mil & Fig* tête *f* de pont.

bridgework ['brɪdʒwɜːk] *n* **(a)** construction *f* de ponts; **(b)** (*in mouth*) bridge *m*.

bridging ['brɪdʒɪŋ] *n* **(a)** construction *f* d'un pont, pontage *m* (*sur un fleuve*); **b. party,** équipe *f* de pontonniers; **(b)** comblement *m* (*d'une lacune*); *El Electron* shuntage *m*; *El Electron* **b. connection,** montage *m* en pont; **b. loan,** crédit *m* de relais *ou* provisoire; *Constr Carp* **b. piece,** entretoise *f*; *Cin* **b. title,** titre *m* de liaison.

bridle[1] ['braɪd(ə)l] *n* **(a)** (*for horse*) bride *f*; *Fig* frein *m*; **b. bit,** mors *m* de bride; **b. path,** route cavalière; (*in forest etc*) piste cavalière; **b. rein,** rênes *fpl* de bride; **(b)** *Nau* branche *f*.

bridle[2] **1** *vt* brider (*un cheval*); *Fig* maîtriser, mettre un frein à (*ses passions*). **2** *vi* (*of horse*) redresser la tête; *Fig* (*of person*) se rebiffer; *Fig* **she bridled at the implication,** elle s'est rebiffée contre l'insinuation.

brief[1] [briːf] **1** *adj* (*letter, interval etc*) court; (*discussion, explanation etc*) bref, succinct, concis; (*exposé*) sommaire; (*séjour etc*) passager, de courte durée; **I caught a b. glimpse of her,** je n'ai fait que l'entrevoir; **he was wearing a very b. pair of shorts,** il portait un short très court; **for a b. period,** pendant peu de temps; **in b.**, en raccourci, en résumé; **to be b.**, pour vous dire la chose en deux mots, bref. **2** *npl* **briefs,** (*for man, woman*) slip *m*; **bikini briefs,** (slip) bikini *m*.

brief[2] *n* **(a)** *Jur* dossier *m* (*d'une procédure*); **to take a b.**, accepter un dossier; **to hold a b.**, être chargé d'une cause; **to hold a b. for s.o.**, représenter qn en justice; **to hold a watching b. for s.o.**, veiller (en justice) aux intérêts de qn; *US Jur* **b. (of argument),** conclusions *fpl* (*présentées à la cour avant l'audience*); *Fig* **I don't hold any** *or* **I hold no b. for him,** ce n'est pas mon affaire de plaider sa cause; *Fig* **I hold no b. for this policy,** je n'adhère absolument pas à cette politique; **(b)** (*of committee etc*) *& Pol* mission *f*; *Av Com etc* instructions *fpl*; **(c)** *Rel* bref *m*; **apostolic b.**, bref apostolique; **(d)** *Br Sl* (*lawyer*) avocat *m*.

brief[3] *vt* **(a)** *Eng Jur* confier une cause à (*un avocat*); **(b)** *Av Com etc* donner une mission à (*qn*); munir (*qn*) d'instructions, fournir des directives à (*qn*); **to b. s.o. on sth,** donner des informations sur qch à qn, faire l'exposé de qch à qn; **have you been briefed?,** est-ce que vous êtes au courant?, est-ce que vous savez de quoi il s'agit?; **was the Prime Minister briefed?,** est-ce que le Premier Ministre a été renseigné sur la question?

briefcase ['briːfkeɪs] *n* serviette *f*; (*for carrying under arm*) porte-documents *m inv*.

briefing ['briːfɪŋ] *n* **(a)** *Eng Jur* **b. of a barrister,** ≈ constitution *f* d'avoué; **(b)** (*orders*) instructions *fpl*, directives *fpl* (*de mission*); (*meeting*) réunion *f* d'information; *Av* briefing *m*; **they gave me a final b.**, ils m'ont donné les dernières directives; **b. room,** salle *f* de réunion.

briefly ['briːflɪ] *adv* **(a)** (*in a few words*) brièvement, en peu de mots, en bref; **(b)** (*for a short time*) (pendant) un instant.

briefness ['briːfnɪs] *n* (*of time, visit*) brièveté *f*; (*of speech*) concision *f*.

brier[1] ['braɪər] *n* **(a)** (*shrub*) églantier *m*; **wild b.**, églantier commun, rosier *m* sauvage; **sweet b.**, églantier odorant; **b. rose,** églantine *f*; **(b) briers,** ronces *fpl*.

brier[2] *n* = **BRIAR**[1].

brierroot ['braɪəruːt], **brierwood** ['braɪəwʊd] *n* = **BRIARROOT, BRIARWOOD**.

brig [brɪg] *n* **(a)** *Nau* brick *m*; **(b)** *Am Nau* prison *f*, cellule *f* (*à bord d'un navire*).

Brig [brɪg] *n Mil abbr* **Brigadier**.

brigade [brɪ'geɪd] *n* **(a)** *Mil* brigade *f*; **infantry b.**, régiment *m* d'infanterie; *US* **artillery b.**, brigade d'artillerie; *Fig* **one of the old b.**, un vieux de la vieille; **(b)** corps organisé (*pour un service public etc*).

brigadier [brɪgə'dɪər] *n Mil* **b. (general),** général *m* de brigade.

brigand ['brɪgənd] *n Old-fashioned* brigand *m*, bandit *m*.

brigandage ['brɪgəndɪdʒ] *n Old-fashioned* brigandage *m*.

bright [braɪt] **1** *adj* **(a)** (*star, metal, gem etc*) brillant; (*sun*) éclatant; (*fire, light etc*) vif, *f* vive; (*day, weather etc*) clair; (*colour*) vif, éclatant; (*sound*) clair; **b. eyes,** yeux brillants *ou* lumineux; **b. intervals,** (*in weather forecast*) éclaircies *fpl*; **to become brighter,** s'éclaircir; **b. red,** rouge vif; **b. future,** avenir brillant *ou* qui promet; **the company's future looks b.**, cette société est très prometteuse; **it was the only b. spot in the day,** c'était la seule chose positive de la journée; **the only b. spot in the play was her acting,** son jeu était le seul intérêt de la pièce; **brighter days,** des jours plus heureux; **the unemployment situation is looking a bit brighter,** la situation de l'emploi commence à s'améliorer; **to look on the b. side of things,** prendre les choses par le bon côté; *Fig* **the b. lights,** (*big city*) la ville; *Fig* **as soon as he could, he headed for the b. lights of the city,** dès qu'il a pu, il a cherché à s'installer en ville;

(b) (*cheerful, lively*) vif, animé, sémillant; (*face, smile*) gai;

(c) (*clever*) éveillé, intelligent; **a b. idea,** une idée lumineuse; **he's not very b.**, ce n'est pas un as; *Iron* **that's b.!**, c'est vraiment intelligent.

2 *adv* **to get up/leave/***etc* **b. and early,** se lever/partir/*etc* de bonne heure.

3 *npl US Aut* **brights,** les pleins phares; **put the brights on,** mets en (pleins) phares.

brighten ['braɪt(ə)n] **1** *vt* faire briller, faire reluire (*qch*);

aviver (*une couleur*); égayer (*une salle, qn*); fourbir (*le métal*). **2** *vi* (*of person, face*) s'épanouir; (*become less bad-tempered*) se dérider; (*of weather*) s'éclaircir; (*of the future*) s'éclaircir, devenir moins sombre; **his eyes brightened,** ses yeux s'allumèrent *ou* brillèrent.

▶**brighten up** *vtsep & vi* = **BRIGHTEN**.

brightening ['braɪt(ə)nɪŋ] *n* **(a)** éclaircissement *m* (*du ciel, du temps*); **(b)** avivage *m* (*de couleurs*).

bright-eyed ['braɪtaɪd] *adj* aux yeux brillants; *Fig* (*eager*) enthousiaste; *F* **b.-e. and bushy-tailed,** (*eager*) très enthousiaste; (*alert*) en pleine forme.

brightly ['braɪtlɪ] *adv* **(a)** brillamment; **the sun was shining b.,** le soleil était éclatant; **to burn b.,** (*of fire*) être vif; **b. lit,** (*street etc*) vivement éclairé; **b. polished,** reluisant d'éclat; **(b)** (*to say*) d'un ton vif, gaiement.

brightness ['braɪtnɪs] *n* éclat *m* (*du soleil, d'une lampe, d'un son*); intensité *f* (*d'éclairage*); luminosité *f* (*d'une surface*); clarté *f* (*du jour, d'un son*); vivacité *f* (*de l'intelligence, d'une couleur*); intelligence *f* (*d'un enfant etc*); brillant *m* (*de l'acier*); *Opt* brillance *f*; *TV* **b. (control),** (dispositif *m* de réglage de la) luminosité.

brill[1] [brɪl] *n* (*fish*) barbue *f*.

brill[2] *adj Br F* (*abbr* **brilliant**) super *inv*.

brilliance ['brɪljəns], **brilliancy** ['brɪljənsɪ] *n* **(a)** éclat *m*, brillant *m*, lustre *m*; netteté *f* (*du son*); *Opt etc* luminance *f*; **(b)** intelligence *f* remarquable (*de qn*); brillant *m* (*d'esprit, de style etc*); habileté *f* remarquable (*d'un chirurgien etc*).

brilliant[1] ['brɪljənt] *adj* **(a)** (*lighting*) intense, brillant; (*sun*) brillant, éclatant; **(b)** *Fig* (*person*) très intelligent, très doué; (*idea*) lumineux; (*success*) éclatant; **she was b. in her last film,** elle était formidable dans son dernier film; **he made a b. speech,** il a fait un discours remarquable; **he's not b.,** il n'est pas brillant; *F* **I'm not feeling very b.,** (*I feel ill*) je ne suis pas dans mon assiette.

brilliant[2] *n* **(a)** (*diamond, cut*) brillant *m*; **(b)** *Typ* corps *m* 3.5.

brilliantine ['brɪljəntiːn] *n* (*for hair*) brillantine *f*.

brilliantly ['brɪljəntlɪ] *adv* **(a)** brillamment; **the sun was shining b.,** le soleil était éclatant; **b. lit,** vivement éclairé; **(b) b. intelligent,** d'une intelligence brillante; *Mus* **to play b.,** jouer avec brio.

brim[1] [brɪm] *n* bord *m* (*de verre, de chapeau etc*); **to fill a glass to the b.,** remplir un verre à ras bord.

brim[2] *vi* (**-mm-**) (*of vessel*) être plein jusqu'au bord; **eyes brimming with tears,** yeux noyés de larmes; **to be brimming with ideas,** (*of person*) déborder d'idées.

▶**brim over** *vi* déborder, regorger (**with sth,** de qch); *Fig* **brimming over with health/life/ideas,** débordant de santé/de vie/d'idées.

brimful ['brɪmfʊl] *adj* (*glass etc*) plein jusqu'au bord; **to fill a glass b.,** remplir un verre à ras bord; *Fig* **b. of health/of life/of ideas,** débordant de santé/de vie/d'idées.

-brimmed [brɪmd] *suff* **broad/narrow-b.,** à larges bords/à bords étroits.

brimless ['brɪmlɪs] *adj* (*chapeau*) sans bord(s).

brimstone ['brɪmstəʊn] *n* **(a)** *Arch* soufre *m* (brut); **(b) b. (butterfly),** citron *m*.

brindle(d) ['brɪnd(ə)l, -d] *adj* moucheté, tacheté.

brine [braɪn] *n* saumure *f*; **tuna packed in b.,** thon mariné.

bring [brɪŋ] *vt* (*pt & pp* **brought** [brɔːt]) **(a)** (*lead, carry*) amener (*qn, un animal*); apporter (*qch, une lettre, une nouvelle etc*); **b. your friend,** amenez votre ami; **she brought a lot of luggage (with her),** elle a apporté beaucoup de bagages; **what brings you to London?,** qu'est-ce qui vous amène à Londres?; **to b. a child into the world,** mettre au monde un enfant; *Jur* **to b. before a court,** faire comparaître (*qn*) devant un tribunal; soumettre *ou* déférer (*un litige*) à un tribunal; *Jur* **to b. an action against s.o.,** intenter un procès contre *ou* à qn; *Jur* **to b. an accusation** *or* **a charge against s.o.,** porter une accusation contre qn;

(b) (*lead to, cause*) **to b. s.o. (good) luck/bad luck,** porter bonheur/malheur à qn; **the announcement brought an angry reaction,** la nouvelle a suscité la colère; **production has been brought to a standstill,** la production a été paralysée; **to b. new hope to s.o.,** redonner de l'espoir à qn; **you've brought it on yourself,** vous l'avez voulu; **to b. tears to s.o.'s eyes,** faire venir les larmes aux yeux de qn; **to b. discord into a family,** semer la discorde dans une famille; **it has brought me great happiness,** cela m'a apporté un grand bonheur;

(c) (*cause to come to a particular condition*) **to b. s.o. to his senses,** ramener qn à la raison; **to b. s.o. into the conversation,** mêler qn à la conversation; **to b. water to a boil,** faire bouillir de l'eau; **to b. sth into question,** mettre qch en question; **to b. sth into disrepute,** discréditer qch; **to b. sth to s.o.'s attention,** appeler *ou* attirer l'attention de qn sur qch; **to b. sth to mind,** rappeler qch; **to b. sth to light,** déterrer (*des objets anciens, des manuscrits*); révéler (*un crime, un secret*); **to b. sth to an end,** mettre fin à qch; **to b. sth to a successful conclusion,** faire aboutir qch; **to b. sth home to s.o.,** faire sentir qch à qn; **to b. oneself to do sth,** se résoudre *ou* se décider à faire qch; **he cannot b. himself to speak about it,** il lui est trop pénible d'en parler;

(d) (*be sold for*) **the house won't b. very much,** la maison ne rapportera pas beaucoup.

▶**bring about** *vtsep* **(a)** (*cause*) amener, causer, occasionner (*qch*); amener, ménager (*une réconciliation*); entraîner (*la ruine de qn*); provoquer (*un accident etc*); opérer (*un changement, un miracle*); **(b)** *Nau* retourner, faire virer (*un navire*).

▶**bring along** *vtsep* amener (*qn*).

▶**bring away** *vtsep* (*carry*) rapporter (*qch*); **I brought away a lot of happy memories from my stay in France,** j'ai gardé de mon séjour en France le souvenir de beaucoup de moments heureux.

▶**bring back** *vtsep* **(a)** (*carry*) rapporter (*qch*); (*lead*) ramener (*qn*); *Jur* **to b. a case back before the court,** ressaisir le tribunal d'un différend; **(b)** (*of letter, song etc*) rappeler (*des souvenirs*); **it brings back my childhood to me,** cela me rappelle mon enfance; **(c)** (*restore*) rétablir (*la liberté, la discipline, la monarchie etc*); ramener (*la confiance*); **the electors will decide whether the government should be brought back,** les électeurs décideront si le gouvernement doit être maintenu; **a couple of days in bed will b. him back to normal,** quelques jours au lit le remettront d'aplomb; **to b. s.o. back to health,** rétablir la santé de qn; **to b. s.o. back to life,** ramener qn à la vie.

▶**bring down** *vtsep* **(a)** (*destroy*) abattre (*un arbre, du gibier, un avion*); descendre (*une perdrix, un avion*); mettre à bas, faire crouler, faire effondrer (*un mur, une maison*); *Th F* **to b. the house down,** faire crouler la salle (sous les applaudissements); **(b)** (*cause to fall*) terrasser (*un adversaire*); faire tomber (*un gouvernement*); **(c)** (*lead, carry*) faire descendre (*qn*); descendre (*un objet*) (**from,** de); **(d)** (*reduce*) abaisser, faire baisser (*le prix*); avilir (*la monnaie, les prix*); abaisser, réduire (*la natalité*); réduire (*une enflure*); faire baisser (*la fièvre*); **(e)** (*of pilot*) faire atterrir (*un avion*); **(f)** (*cause to appear, esp of a person in authority*) attirer (*qn*); **stop making so much noise or you'll b. the headmaster down on us,** ne fais pas tant de bruit, tu vas attirer le proviseur.

▶**bring forth** *vtsep Arch & Lit* mettre au monde (*des enfants*); (*of animal*) mettre bas (*des petits*); (*of plant*) produire (*des fruits*).

▶**bring forward** *vtsep* **(a)** (*carry, lead*) avancer (*une chaise etc*); amener, faire avancer, faire approcher (*qn*); produire (*un témoin*); avancer, présenter (*un argument*); alléguer (*une preuve*); **(b)** (*advance*) avancer (*une réunion etc*); **the meeting has been brought forward from the 14th to the 7th,** la séance a été avancée du 14 au 7; **(c)** *Com* reporter (*une somme*); **brought forward,** report *m*.

▶**bring in** *vtsep* **(a)** (*lead, carry*) introduire, faire entrer (*qn*); apporter, rentrer (*qch*); **b. him in,** faites-le entrer; **to b. in the harvest,** rentrer la moisson; **(b)** (*introduce*) introduire, lancer (*une mode etc*); déposer, présenter (*un projet de loi*); **new legislation will be brought in next year,** une nouvelle loi sera présentée l'an prochain; **(c)** (*involve*) faire intervenir (*qn*); **the company is bringing consultants in,** la société fait appel à des experts-conseils; **(d)** (*earn*) **to b. in interest,** rapporter, porter intérêt; **investment that brings in 10%,** placement qui rend 10%; **this land brings her in an income of £5,000,** cette terre lui vaut 5000 livres de rente; **how much money is he bringing in?,** combien est-ce qu'il gagne?; **(e)** *Jur* **to b. in a verdict,** rendre un verdict; **(f) to b. in the New Year,** (*celebrate it*) fêter le nouvel an.

▶**bring off** *vtsep* **(a)** (*from ship*) débarquer (*qn*); **(b)** (*complete successfully*) réussir (*un coup etc*); **they brought it off,** ils ont réussi.

▶**bring on** *vtsep* **(a)** (*cause to appear*) produire, occasionner (*une maladie etc*); provoquer (*une crise d'asthme etc*); **(b)** (*of sun etc*) faire pousser (*les plantes*); (*of teacher, trainer*) faire faire des progrès à (*qn*); **(c)** *Th* amener *ou* apporter sur la scène; **in the second act an elephant is brought on,** au second acte on fait paraître en scène un éléphant; **please b. on our next contestant,** au concurrent suivant; **(d) I brought it on myself,** (*it was my own fault*) c'est entièrement de ma faute.

►**bring out** *vtsep* **(a)** *(lead)* sortir *(qch)*; faire sortir *(qn)*; **(b)** *(cause to appear)* révéler, faire ressortir *(le sens de qch)*; faire valoir *(une couleur, un détail etc)*; publier, sortir *(un livre)*; **to b. out the best/the worst in s.o.,** faire ressortir les bonnes/les mauvaises qualités de qn; **the sun has brought out the roses,** le soleil a fait épanouir les roses; **strawberries b. her out in a rash,** les fraises lui donnent de l'urticaire; **(c)** *Fig* **to b. s.o. out,** *(make less shy)* faire sortir qn de sa réserve.

►**bring over** *vtsep (lead, carry)* amener *(qn)*; amener, apporter *(qch)*; **they're bringing people over from France to testify,** ils font venir des gens de France pour qu'ils témoignent.

►**bring round** *vtsep* **(a)** *(lead, carry)* amener *(qn)*; amener, apporter *(qch)*; **b. her round to meet us some time,** amène-la un jour, qu'on puisse faire sa connaissance; **(b)** *(restore to consciousness)* faire reprendre connaissance à, ranimer *(qn)*; **(c)** *(restore to good mood)* remettre *(qn)* de bonne humeur; **(d)** *(persuade)* convertir *(qn)* **(to an opinion,** à une opinion); **(e)** *(steer)* (r)amener *(la conversation)* **(to a subject,** sur un sujet); **(f)** *Nau etc* faire virer *(un navire etc)*.

►**bring through** *vtas* **(a)** *(treat with success)* guérir *(qn)*; **(b)** *(lead with success)* conduire qn à la réussite; **she brought all of us through the exam,** grâce à elle, nous avons tous réussi l'examen.

►**bring to** *vtsep* **(a)** faire reprendre connaissance à, ranimer *(qn)*; **(b)** *Nau* mettre *(un navire)* en panne.

►**bring together** *vtsep* réunir *(des personnes, des documents)*; mettre *(des personnes)* en contact; rassembler *(des documents)*; **he brought them together again,** *(for a meeting)* il les a réunis; *(after a quarrel)* il les a réconciliés; *Jur* **to b. the parties together,** mettre les parties en présence.

►**bring up 1** *vtsep* **(a)** *(carry, lead upstairs)* monter *(qch)*; faire monter *(qn)*; *(carry, lead forward)* apporter, approcher, avancer *(qch)*; amener, faire approcher *(qn)*; faire avancer *(des troupes)*; amener *(des renforts)*; **to be brought up before the magistrate,** comparaître devant le tribunal;

(b) *(vomit)* vomir *(qch)*; **to b. up one's food,** vomir;

(c) *(rear)* élever *(des enfants)*; **I was brought up by an aunt,** j'ai été élevé par une tante; **I was brought up to be polite,** j'ai été élevé dans la politesse; **well/badly brought up child,** enfant bien/mal élevé;

(d) *(mention)* soulever *(une question)*, mettre *(une question)* sur le tapis; **to b. sth up against s.o.,** objecter qch à qn; *Jur* faire état de qch contre un accusé;

(e) *Nau* mouiller, arrêter *(un navire)*; **to be brought up short by a roadblock/an accident,** *(of car)* s'arrêter brusquement à cause d'un barrage/d'un accident; **to be brought up short by s.o.'s indifference,** *(when talking)* être refroidi par l'indifférence de qn.

2 *vi Nau (of ship)* mouiller.

bring-and-buy ['brɪŋən'baɪ] *adj Br* **b.-and-b. sale,** vente *f* de charité.

bringing-up ['brɪŋɪŋ'ʌp] *n (of child)* éducation *f*.

brink [brɪŋk] *n* bord *m (d'un précipice, d'un fleuve)*; *Fig* **to stand shivering on the b.,** hésiter à faire le plongeon; *Fig* **on the b. of ...,** tout près de ...; *Fig* **to be on the b. of,** être au bord de *(les larmes)*; être à la veille de *(une découverte, la ruine)*; être à deux doigts de *(la ruine, la mort)*; *Fig* **I was on the b. of telling him,** j'étais à deux doigts de le lui dire; *Fig* **to be on the b. of extinction,** *(of animal)* être en voie de disparition.

brinkmanship ['brɪŋkmənʃɪp] *n* bravade *f*; **he's a master in the art of b.,** c'est un maître dans l'art de savoir jusqu'où il peut aller *ou Iron* jusqu'où il peut aller trop loin.

briny ['braɪnɪ] **1** *adj* saumâtre, salé. **2** *n F* **the b.,** la mer, la grande bleue.

briquette [brɪ'ket] *n (of coal)* briquette *f*.

brisk [brɪsk] *adj* **(a)** *(person, attitude, tone)* déterminé; **(b)** *(movement)* vif, actif, animé; *Com (commerce)* actif; *(demande)* animé; **at a b. pace,** à vive allure; **to take a b. walk,** se promener à bon pas; **business is b.,** les affaires marchent bien; **(c)** *(air)* vivifiant; *(temps)* frais; *Nau (vent)* rond.

brisket ['brɪskɪt] *n Culin* poitrine *f*, avant-cœur *m (de bœuf)*.

briskly ['brɪsklɪ] *adv* **(a)** *(to say)* avec détermination; **(b)** *(to move)* vivement, activement; **to step out b.,** marcher avec entrain.

briskness ['brɪsknɪs] *n* **(a)** *(of person, voice)* détermination *f*; **(b)** *(of movement)* vivacité *f*, activité *f*, animation *f*, entrain *m*; activité *(des affaires, du marché)*; **(c)** fraîcheur *f (de l'air etc)*.

bristle¹ ['brɪs(ə)l] *n* **(a)** soie *f (de porc, de chenille)*; soie, poil *m (de brosse)*; poil raide *(de la barbe)*; **(b)** *Bot* soie *f*, poil *m*.

bristle² **1** *vi (of animal, hair etc)* se hérisser; *Fig* se rebiffer, se hérisser. **2** *vt (of animal)* hérisser *(ses poils, ses soies)*.

►**bristle up** *vi & vtsep* = **BRISTLE²**.

►**bristle with** *vipo* grouiller de; **the room was bristling with security men,** la pièce grouillait de membres de la sécurité.

bristly ['brɪslɪ] *adj* **(a)** couvert de soies *ou* de poils raides; *(moustache)* hérissé, raide; **(b)** *Bot* poilu, garni de soies.

bristol ['brɪst(ə)l] *n Br Sl (breast)* nichon *m*.

Bristol ['brɪst(ə)l] *n* **B. board,** carton *m* Bristol, bristol *m*; *Nau & Fig* **(shipshape and) B. fashion,** en bon ordre.

Brit [brɪt] *n F (abbr* **Briton***)* Britannique *mf*, Anglais, -aise, *Pej* rosbif *mf*; **she's a B.,** c'est une rosbif; **I met a lot of other Brits,** j'ai rencontré beaucoup d'autres Anglais.

Britain ['brɪt(ə)n] *n* **(Great) B.,** la Grande-Bretagne.

Britannia [brɪ'tænɪə] *n* (nom *m* symbolique de) la Grande-Bretagne; *Com* **B. metal,** métal anglais.

Britannic [brɪ'tænɪk] *adj* **His** *or* **Her B. Majesty,** Sa Majesté britannique.

Briticism ['brɪtɪsɪz(ə)m] *n Ling* anglicisme *m*.

British ['brɪtɪʃ] **1** *adj* britannique, de la Grande-Bretagne; *(in Fr usu)* anglais, d'Angleterre; **B. Columbia,** la Colombie britannique; **the B. Isles,** les îles Britanniques; **the B. consul,** le consul d'Angleterre; **B. goods,** produits anglais, marchandises anglaises; **B. English,** l'anglais britannique; **B. Standards Institution,** = association britannique de normalisation; **B. summer time,** = heure d'été en Grande-Bretagne; **B. Telecom,** Télécommunications *fpl* britanniques; **B. thermal unit,** = 1055,06 joules. **2** *n* **the B.,** *(used as pl)* les Britanniques *mpl*, les Anglais *mpl*.

Britisher ['brɪtɪʃər] *n Am* natif, -ive de (la) Grande-Bretagne, Britannique *mf*, *F* Anglais, -aise.

Briton ['brɪt(ə)n] *n* **(a)** Britannique *mf*, Anglais, -aise; **(b)** *Hist* Breton, -onne *(de la Grande-Bretagne)*.

Brittany ['brɪtənɪ] *n* Bretagne *f*.

brittle ['brɪt(ə)l] **1** *adj* fragile, cassant; *Fig* **in a b. voice,** d'une voix crispée. **2** *n* = bonbon croquant à base de mélasse et de noix.

brittleness ['brɪt(ə)lnɪs] *n (of bones)* fracture *f*; *Fig* **the b. of her voice,** sa voix crispée.

broach¹ [brəʊtʃ] *n* **(a)** *Culin* broche *f (à rôtir)*; **(b)** *(tool)* équarrissoir *m*; mèche *f* de foret; *(for tapping cask)* perçoir *m*.

broach² *vt* équarrir, brocher; percer *(un fût)*; *Fig* entamer, aborder *(une question etc)*; **to b. the subject,** faire une entrée en matière; **I broached with your mother the subject of your leaving school,** j'ai abordé la question de ton départ de l'école avec ta mère.

broad [brɔːd] **1** *adj* **(a)** *(wide)* large; **the road is 15 metres b.,** la route a 15 mètres de large; **a b. smile,** un large sourire; **to have a b. back,** avoir une forte carrure; *Fig* avoir bon dos; **in b. daylight,** en plein jour; *Fig* au grand jour, devant tout le monde; *Fig* **it's as b. as it's long,** cela revient au même, c'est tout un, c'est blanc bonnet et bonnet blanc; **b. views** *or* **ideas** *or* **outlook,** idées larges *ou* tolérantes; **b. bean,** fève *f*; *Am Sp* **b. jump,** saut *m* en longueur; *Ling* **b. vowel,** voyelle large;

(b) *(règle)* général; *(distinction)* sommaire; **b. outline,** aperçu *m (d'un projet etc)*; **term used in its broadest sense,** terme employé dans un sens (très) large; **the project has b. support,** le projet est largement soutenu;

(c) *(accent)* prononcé; **to speak b. Scots/Yorkshire,** parler avec un accent écossais/du Yorkshire prononcé; **b. humour,** humour de mauvais goût *ou* peu délicat; **b. joke,** grosse plaisanterie.

2 *n* **(a) the b. of the back,** le milieu du dos;

(b) *Br* **the Norfolk Broads,** la région de lacs du Norfolk;

(c) *esp US Sl* nana *f*.

broad-brimmed ['brɔːd'brɪmd] *adj (chapeau)* à large bord.

broadcast¹ ['brɔːdkɑːst] *v (pt & pp* **broadcast)** **1** *vt* **(a)** *Rad TV* transmettre, (radio)diffuser, téléviser *(un programme etc)*; **the match will be broadcast live,** le match sera diffusé en direct; **commentary broadcast from Paris,** radioreportage *m* depuis Paris; **(b)** *Agr* semer *(du grain)* à la volée; *Fig* répandre *(une nouvelle)*. **2** *vi* **(a)** *(on radio)* parler *ou* chanter *etc* à la radio; *(on television)* paraître *ou* se produire à la télévision; **(b)** *(of radio or TV authority)* émettre.

broadcast² **1** *n Rad TV* émission *f*; *Rad* programme radiodiffusé; *TV* programme télévisé; **simultaneous/recorded/live b.,** émission simultanée/en différé/en direct. **2** *adj* **(a)** *Rad* radiodiffusé; *TV* diffusé, télévisé; **b. announcement,** *Rad* annonce *f* par radio; *TV* annonce télévisée; **b. account,** reportage *m* radio(phonique) (*d'un match etc*); **(b)** *Agr* semé à la volée; **b. sowing,** semis *m* à la volée. **3** *adv Agr* **to sow b.,** semer à la volée.

broadcaster ['brɔːdkɑːstər] *n Rad* reporter radio(phonique); *Rad TV* speaker, speakerine.

broadcasting ['brɔːdkɑːstɪŋ] *n* **(a)** *Rad* radiodiffusion *f*; *TV* diffusion *f*; **she works in b.,** *Rad* elle fait de la radio; *TV* elle fait de la télévision; **(television) b.,** télévision *f*; **news b.,** *Rad TV* reportage *m*; *Rad* reportage radio(phonique); *TV* téléreportage *m*; **the British B. Corporation,** la Corporation Britannique de radiodiffusion; **this is the end of today's b.,** voici la fin de nos émissions pour aujourd'hui; **b. station,** *Rad* station *f* de radio; *TV* chaîne *f* de télévision; **B. House,** = siège de la BBC; **(b)** *Agr* semis *m* à la volée.

broadcloth ['brɔːdklɒθ] *n Tex* **(a)** drap noir fin (*pour vêtements d'hommes*); **(b)** *Am* popeline *f*.

broaden ['brɔːd(ə)n] **1** *vt* élargir; **to b. s.o.'s outlook** *or* **horizons,** élargir l'horizon de qn; **travel broadens the mind,** les voyages élargissent l'esprit. **2** *vi* s'élargir.

▶**broaden out** *vi* (*of river, road, valley*) s'élargir.

broad-leaved [brɔːd'liːvd] *adj* (*tree*) à larges feuilles, latifolié.

broadloom ['brɔːdluːm] *adj* (*tapis*) grande largeur.

broadly ['brɔːdlɪ] *adv* **(a)** largement; **smiling b.,** avec un large sourire; **(b)** généralement; **b. speaking,** généralement parlant, d'une façon générale; **(c)** (*parler*) avec un accent prononcé.

broad-minded [brɔːd'maɪndɪd] *adj* **to be b.-m.,** avoir l'esprit large, être tolérant, être large d'esprit; **b.-m. people,** les gens tolérants; **she takes a b.-m. attitude to that kind of thing,** elle est très tolérante pour ce genre de chose.

broad-mindedness [brɔːd'maɪndɪdnɪs] *n* largeur *f* d'esprit, tolérance *f*.

broadness ['brɔːdnɪs] *n* largeur *f*.

broadsheet ['brɔːdʃiːt] *n* **(a)** *Journ* journal *m* grand format; **(b)** (*pamphlet*) feuille imprimée.

broad-shouldered [brɔːd'ʃəʊldəd] *adj* large d'épaules, aux larges épaules.

broadside ['brɔːdsaɪd] *n Nau* **(a)** flanc *m*, travers *m* (*du navire*); **collision b. on,** abordage *m* par le travers; **(b)** (*from guns*) bordée *f*; **to fire a b.,** tirer une bordée.

broad-spectrum [brɔːd'spektrəm] *adj* (*antibiotic*) au spectre d'action très large.

broadways, broadwise ['brɔːdweɪz, -waɪz] *adv* dans le sens de la largeur.

brocade[1] [brə'keɪd] *n Tex* brocart *m*; **b. curtains/skirt/***etc*, des rideaux/une jupe/*etc* en brocart.

brocade[2] *vt Tex* brocher; **brocaded gown,** robe *f* de brocart.

broccoli ['brɒkəlɪ] *n* (*vegetable*) brocoli *m*; **eat your b.,** mange tes brocolis.

brochure ['brəʊʃjʊər, -ʃər] *n* brochure *f*; (*folding*) dépliant *m*.

brogue[1] [brəʊg] *n* chaussure *f* de marche *ou* de golf.

brogue[2] *n Br* accent irlandais; *Am* accent *m*.

broil[1] [brɔɪl] *n* (*quarrel*) querelle *f*; (*disturbance*) échauffourée *f*; (*brawl*) rixe *f*.

broil[2] *vt & vi* **(a)** *Am Culin* (*under grill*) passer (*qch*) au gril; (*over fire*) griller (*qch*), (faire) cuire (*qch*) sur le gril; **(b)** *F* **we were broiling (hot),** on grillait; **a broiling hot day,** un jour où il fait une chaleur à crever.

broiler ['brɔɪlər] *n* **(a)** *Am* gril *m*, rôtissoire *f*; **put it under the b. for a few minutes,** passez-le au gril pendant quelques minutes; **(b) b. (fowl),** poulet *m* de chair (à rôtir); **b. house,** batterie *f* (pour l'élevage des poulets de chair); **(c)** *F* **it's a real b. (of a day),** on crève de chaleur.

broke [brəʊk] *adj F* fauché, à sec; **to go b.,** (*of company*) faire faillite; **to be (stony, dead) b.,** être sans le sou, être fauché, être à sec; *Sl* **to go for b.,** tout miser; *Austr* **to be b. for a feed,** avoir faim.

broken ['brəʊk(ə)n] *adj* **(a)** (*un verre, un œuf, un bâton, un jouet etc*) cassé; (*un verre, un carreau, les liens d'amitié etc*) brisé; (*un bâton, une corde, Nau les amarres etc*) rompu; (*limb*) fracturé, cassé; (*coke, gravier*) concassé; (*stones*) (con)cassé; *Com* **b. lots,** articles dépareillés; **(b)** (*terrain*) accidenté; (*chemin*) raboteux, défoncé; (*rivage*) tourmenté; (*contour*) irrégulier; **forest b. by large clearings,** forêt trouée de grandes clairières; **(c)** (*sommeil*) interrompu; (*words*) entrecoupé; **voice b. with sobs,** voix entrecoupée de sanglots; **in a b. voice,** d'une voix saccadée; **to speak b. English,** estropier l'anglais; **(d)** (*mariage*) en ruine; (*cœur*) brisé; (*promesse*) violé, manqué; **b. home,** foyer détruit; **a b. man,** (*financially*) un homme ruiné; (*by grief etc*) un homme abattu *ou* découragé.

broken-down [brəʊk(ə)n'daʊn] *adj* (*car etc*) en panne; (*mechanism*) détraqué; (*house, furniture*) délabré; (*horse*) fourbu.

brokenhearted [brəʊk(ə)n'hɑːtɪd] *adj* au cœur brisé; **to die b.,** mourir de douleur *ou* de chagrin.

brokenly ['brəʊk(ə)nlɪ] *adv* (*parler*) par saccades.

broken-winded [brəʊk(ə)n'wɪndɪd] *adj Vet* (*cheval*) poussif.

broker ['brəʊkər] *n* **(a)** *Com* courtier *m* (de commerce); **bill b.,** courtier de change; **insurance b.,** courtier d'assurances; **(b)** *St Exch* agent *m* de change; **outside b.,** courtier *m* libre; **(c)** (*secondhand dealer*) brocanteur, -euse.

brokerage ['brəʊkərɪdʒ] *n Fin* **(a)** (*fee*) (frais *mpl* de) courtage *m*; **(b) b. house,** (*business*) maison *f* de courtage.

broking ['brəʊkɪŋ] *n Fin* (*profession*) courtage *m*.

brolly ['brɒlɪ] *n Br F* pépin *m*.

bromeliad [brəʊ'miːlɪæd] *n Bot* broméliacée *f*.

bromide ['brəʊmaɪd] *n* **(a)** *Ch Typ* bromure *m*; **potassium b.,** bromure de potassium; *Phot* **b. (paper),** papier *m* au gélatinobromure (d'argent); **(b)** *Fig* banalité *f*.

bronchial ['brɒŋkɪəl] *adj Anat* (*artère, asthme etc*) bronchique; **the b. tubes,** les bronches *fpl*; *Med* **b. pneumonia,** broncho-pneumonie *f*.

bronchitic [brɒŋ'kɪtɪk] *adj & n Med* bronchitique *mf*.

bronchitis [brɒŋ'kaɪtɪs] *n Med* bronchite *f*; **she has b.,** elle a une bronchite.

bronchopneumonia [brɒŋkəʊnjuː'məʊnɪə] *n Med* broncho-pneumonie *f*.

bronco ['brɒŋkəʊ] *n* cheval sauvage *ou* non dressé de l'Amérique.

broncobuster ['brɒŋkəʊbʌstər] *n Am* dresseur *m* de chevaux.

brontosaur(us) ['brɒntəsɔːr, brɒntə'sɔːrəs] *n* brontosaure *m*.

bronze[1] [brɒnz] **1** *n* **(a)** (*metal*) bronze *m*; **the B. Age,** l'âge *m* de bronze; **(b)** *Art* (objet *m* en) bronze *m*; **(c)** *F Sp etc* médaille *f* de bronze. **2** *adj* **(a)** (*statue*) de *ou* en bronze; *Sp etc* **b. medal,** médaille *f* de bronze; **(b)** (*colour*) (couleur *f*) bronze *inv*.

bronze[2] **1** *vt* bronzer (*le fer etc*); mordorer (*le cuir, des souliers*); **bronzed by the sun,** (*of person*) bronzé. **2** *vi Phot* se métalliser.

bronzed [brɒnzd] *adj* (*teint*) bronzé, basané.

bronzing ['brɒnzɪŋ] *n* bronzage *m*.

brooch [brəʊtʃ] *n* broche *f* (*de diamants etc*).

brood [bruːd] *n* **(a)** couvée *f* (*de poussins*); volée *f* (*de pigeons*); naissain *m* (*d'huîtres, de moules*); **b. hen,** (poule *f*) couveuse *f*; **b. mare,** (jument *f*) poulinière *f*; **b. cell,** (*in beehive*) cellule *f* d'incubation; **(b)** *Fig* (*children*) enfants *mpl*; *Pej* marmaille *f*; **(c)** *Fig Pej* race *f* (*de scélérats etc*).

brood[2] *vi* (*of hen*) couver; *Fig* broyer du noir; **to b. about** *or* **on** *or* **over,** remâcher (*le passé*); ruminer (*une idée*); **she's brooding about the exam,** (*which she has sat*) elle repense à son examen; (*which she will sit*) elle n'arrête pas de penser à son examen; **stop brooding about what he said,** arrête de ruminer ce qu'il a dit; **to b. over things,** remuer *ou* repasser des idées dans sa tête; *Lit* **night broods over the scene,** la nuit plane sur la scène.

brooder ['bruːdər] *n* **(a)** (poule *f*) couveuse *f*; **(b)** (*enclosure*) couveuse *f* (artificielle); **(c)** *Fig* rêveur, -euse; **he's such a b.,** il s'inquiète pour un rien.

broody ['bruːdɪ] *adj* (*poule*) couveuse, qui demande à couver; *Fig* (*person*) pensif, rêveur; **to feel b.,** (*of woman*) être en mal d'enfant.

brook[1] [brʊk] *n* ruisseau *m*; **b. trout,** saumon *m* de fontaine.

brook[2] *vt Lit* (*used only in neg sentences*) (ne pas) souffrir; **the matter brooks no delay,** l'affaire n'admet aucun retard; **he will b. no insolence,** il ne supporte pas d'impertinence; **I will b. no refusal,** je n'accepterai aucun refus.

broom [bruːm] *n* **(a)** (shrub) genêt *m* (à balai); **(b)** (*for sweeping*) balai *m*; *Fig* **a new b.,** = personne nouvellement arrivée qui veut remanier l'organisation de l'entreprise.

broomstick ['bruːmstɪk] *n* manche *m* à balai.

Bros *npl Com* (*abbr* **Brothers**) **Thomas B.,** maison *f* Thomas frères.

broth [brɒθ] *n Culin* (*clear*) bouillon *m*; (*with vegetables etc*) potage *m*; **Scotch b.,** soupe *f* (de mouton) avec orge et légumes.

brothel ['brɒθ(ə)l] *n* maison *f* de prostitution, bordel *m*;

Jur maison de débauche.

brother ['brʌðər] **1** *n* **(a)** (*sibling*) frère *m*; **half b.,** demi-frère; **older b.,** frère aîné; **younger b.,** (frère) cadet *m*; *Com* **Thomas Brothers,** maison *f* Thomas frères; **(b)** *Rel* frère *m* (*d'une communauté*); **lay b.,** frère lai; **(c)** (*fellow member, pl usu* **brethren** ['breðrɪn]) frère *m* (*d'une société religieuse*); confrère *m* (*d'un corps de métier*); **brothers!,** (*at union meeting etc*) camarades!; **brothers in arms,** frères d'armes; **b. officers,** officiers *mpl* du même régiment; **his b. officers,** les autres officiers de son régiment. **2** *int esp Am F* bon sang!

brotherhood ['brʌðəhʊd] *n* **(a)** (*relationship*) fraternité *f*; **(b)** (*organization*) confraternité *f*, société *f*; (*religious*) confrérie *f*; **(c)** *esp US* syndicat ouvrier.

brother-in-law ['brʌðərɪnlɔː] *n* (*pl* **brothers-in-law**) beau-frère *m*, *pl* beaux-frères.

brotherliness ['brʌðəlɪnɪs] *n* **(a)** (*of relation*) amour fraternel; **(b)** (*of organization*) confraternité *f*.

brotherly ['brʌðəlɪ] *adj* (*amour etc*) fraternel.

brouhaha ['bruːhɑːhɑː] *n* brouhaha *m*.

brow [braʊ] *n* **(a)** *Anat* front *m*; **to knit one's brows,** froncer les sourcils; **(b)** front *m* (*de colline*); bord *m* (*de précipice etc*); **the b. of a hill,** (*on road*) le haut d'une côte.

browbeat ['braʊbiːt] *vt* intimider, rudoyer (*qn*); **to b. s.o. into doing sth,** rabrouer qn pour lui faire faire qch.

browbeating ['braʊbiːtɪŋ] *n* intimidation *f*.

brown¹ [braʊn] **1** *adj* (*eyes, hair*) brun; (*coat, shoe, eyes*) marron *inv*; **to be b.,** (*of person*) être hâlé *ou* bronzé; **to be as b. as a berry,** (*tanned*) être tout bronzé *ou* noir; **b. ale,** = bière brune; **b. bear,** ours brun; **b. bread,** pain bis; **b. hair,** cheveux bruns *ou* châtains; **light b. hair,** cheveux châtain clair; **b. owl,** (*bird*) chat-huant *m*; **B. Owl,** (*in Guides*) cheftaine *f*; **b. paper,** papier *m* d'emballage, papier kraft; **b. rice,** riz brun; **b. sugar,** cassonade *f*; **b. trout,** truite saumonée. **2** *n* brun *m*, marron *m*.

brown² **1** *vt* **(a)** (*of sun*) brunir, bronzer; **face browned by the sun,** teint bruni *ou* hâlé au soleil; **(b)** *Culin* faire rissoler (*la viande*); faire dorer (*le poisson*); faire roussir (*du beurre, une sauce*); praliner (*des amandes*). **2** *vi* **(a)** (se) brunir; **his face browns easily,** son visage (se) brunit facilement; **(b)** *Culin* rissoler.

▶**brown off** *vtsep F esp Br* (*usu passive*) **to be browned off,** être découragé; **I'm browned off with always having to do the dishes,** j'en ai marre de devoir toujours faire la vaisselle; **he's very browned off with you,** il en a vraiment marre de toi.

brown-bag [braʊn'bæg] *vi & vtr Am F* **to b.-b. (it),** = apporter son déjeuner (sur son lieu de travail).

brown-bagger [braʊn'bægər] *n Am F* = personne qui apporte son déjeuner sur son lieu de travail.

brown-eyed [braʊ'naɪd] *adj* aux yeux bruns.

brown-haired [braʊn'heəd] *adj* aux cheveux bruns.

brownie ['braʊnɪ] *n* **(a)** (*elf*) lutin *m* (bienfaisant), farfadet *m*; **(b) B.,** (*guide*) jeannette *f*; **B. points,** bons points; *Fig* **to win** *or* **get b. points,** se faire bien voir; **(c)** *Am Culin* = petit gâteau au chocolat et aux noisettes.

browning ['braʊnɪŋ] *n* **(a)** (*by sun*) brunissement *m*, bronzage *m*; **(b)** *Culin* pralinage *m* (*des amandes*); **(c)** *Culin* colorant brun (*pour les sauces*).

Browning ['braʊnɪŋ] *n* (*gun*) browning *m*.

brownish ['braʊnɪʃ] *adj* brunâtre.

brown-nose ['braʊnnəʊz] *Am Sl* **1** *vi* faire du lèche-cul. **2** *vt* faire du lèche-cul à (*qn*).

brown-noser ['braʊnnəʊzər] *n Am Sl* lèche-cul *m*.

brownout ['braʊnaʊt] *n US El* baisse *f* de tension; **parts of New York had another b. last night,** il y a eu encore une baisse de tension (électrique) sur certains quartiers de New York hier soir.

browse [braʊz] *vt & vi* brouter (*l'herbe*); paître; **to b. (on) leaves,** brouter des feuilles; *Fig* **to b. (among books),** feuilleter des livres, bouquiner; *Fig* **I'm just browsing thank you,** (*in shop*) je regarde, merci.

brucellosis [bruːsɪ'ləʊsɪs] *n Med Vet* brucellose *f*.

bruise¹ [bruːz] *n* meurtrissure *f*, contusion *f*, *F* bleu *m*; (*on fruit*) talure *f*, meurtrissure; **she just has cuts and bruises,** (*of accident victim*) elle a juste quelques coupures et quelques bleus.

bruise² **1** *vt* **(a)** meurtrir, contusionner (*une partie du corps*); meurtrir, taler (*un fruit*); **to b. one's arm,** se meurtrir au bras *ou* le bras; **(b)** broyer, écraser, concasser (*une substance*); égruger (*le blé*). **2** *vi* (*of person*) se faire des bleus; (*of fruit etc*) se meurtrir; **he bruises easily,** il se fait des bleus très facilement; *Fig* il est sensible.

bruiser ['bruːzər] *n F* (*boxer*) boxeur *m*; (*bully*) cogneur *m*.

bruising ['bruːzɪŋ] *n* **(a)** (*on skin*) contusion *f*; **there is some b. round the throat,** il y a quelques contusions autour de la gorge; **(b)** (*of substance*) broyage *m*, écrasement *m*, concassage *m*; (*of wheat*) égrugeage *m*.

brumbie, brumby ['brʌmbɪ] *n Austr F* cheval sauvage *ou* non dressé.

brunch [brʌntʃ] *n F* brunch *m*.

brunette [bruː'net] *n* brune *f*, brunette *f*; **she's a b.,** elle est brune.

brunt [brʌnt] *n* choc *m*; **the b. of his argument,** le point principal de sa thèse; **to bear the b. of,** soutenir le plus fort de (*l'attaque, la tempête etc*); soutenir le poids de (*la colère de qn*); **to bear the b. of the expense,** supporter la plus grande partie des frais.

brush¹ [brʌʃ] *n* **(a)** (*undergrowth*) broussailles *fpl*; *US Austr etc* (*backwoods*) brousse *f*; **b. harrow,** herse *f* d'épines; **b. fire,** incendie *m* de forêt;

(b) (*for hair etc*) brosse *f*; (*for sweeping*) balai *m*; **clothes b.,** brosse à habits; **dustpan and b.,** balayette *f* et ramasse-poussière *m inv*; **flat b.,** queue-de morue *f*, *pl* queues-de morue; **hard b.,** (*for shoes etc*) brosse à décrotter; (*for pans etc*) brosse à récurer; **hat b.,** brosse à chapeau; **(paint) b.,** pinceau *m*, brosse; **paste b.,** pinceau à colle; **scrubbing b.,** brosse dure; **shaving b.,** blaireau *m*; **washing-up b.,** lavette *f*;

(c) *Art* touche *f* (*de peintre*); **to paint with a full b.,** peindre dans la pâte;

(d) queue *f* (*de renard*);

(e) *El* balai *m* (*de commutateur, de génératrice*); **(contact) b.,** frotteur *m*; **carbon b.,** balai en charbon; **b. holder,** porte-balai(s) *m inv*;

(f) **to give sth a b.,** donner un coup de brosse à qch; **to give one's hair a b.,** se donner un coup de brosse;

(g) (*encounter*) rencontre *f*, échauffourée *f* (*avec l'ennemi*); **at the first b.,** au premier abord; *F* **to have a b. with the police,** avoir des ennuis avec la police.

brush² *vt* **(a)** brosser (*un habit, les cheveux*); balayer (*un tapis*); **to b. one's hair,** se brosser les cheveux; **to b. one's teeth,** se brosser *ou* se laver les dents; **to b. sth clean,** nettoyer qch avec une brosse *ou* à la brosse; **(b)** effleurer, raser, frôler, érafler (*une surface*); **(c)** gratter (*la laine, le nylon*).

▶**brush against** *vipo* frôler *ou* friser (*qn*) en passant; frôler, érafler (*qch*); **he brushed against me in the street,** il m'a frôlé (en passant à côté de moi) dans la rue.

▶**brush aside** *vtsep* écarter (*qn, une difficulté*).

▶**brush away** *vtsep* **(a)** (*remove*) enlever (*de la boue etc*) d'un coup de brosse *ou* de balai; essuyer furtivement (*une larme*); **b. the leaves away from the path,** balaye les feuilles qui sont sur le chemin; **(b)** (*treat as unimportant*) écarter (*qn, une difficulté etc*); *F* envoyer promener (*qn*); **to b. away criticism,** ignorer les critiques.

▶**brush down** *vtsep* donner un coup de brosse à (*qn*); brosser (*un cheval*).

▶**brush off** **1** *vtsep* **(a)** (*remove*) enlever (*de la boue etc*) d'un coup de brosse *ou* de balai; **to b. the dust off sth,** enlever la poussière de qch (à la brosse, en brossant); **b. those flies off,** chasse ces mouches; **(b)** *F* (*reject*) envoyer promener (*qn*); **he never brushes anyone off,** il n'envoie jamais les gens promener; **to b. off pleas for help,** refuser son aide à qn. **2** *vi* (*of dirt etc*) s'enlever à la brosse.

▶**brush over** *vtsep* enduire (*une surface*) à la brosse; badigeonner (*une surface*) (**with,** de).

▶**brush past** *vipo* = **BRUSH AGAINST**.

▶**brush up** *vtsep* **(a)** (*collect*) ramasser (*les miettes*) (avec la brosse); **(b)** *F* (*improve*) se remettre à (*un sujet*); (*for an exam etc*) réviser (*un sujet*); **to b. up one's French,** dérouiller son français; **(c)** gratter (*la laine*); **(d)** brosser, donner un coup de brosse à (*un chapeau etc*).

brushdown ['brʌʃdaʊn] *n* **to give s.o. a b.,** donner un coup de brosse à qn; **to give a horse a b.,** brosser *ou* panser un cheval.

brushed [brʌʃt] *adj Tex* (*wool, nylon*) gratté.

brushing ['brʌʃɪŋ] *n* (*of hair etc*) brossage *m*; (*of carpet*) balayage *m*.

brushoff ['brʌʃɒf] *n F* **to give s.o. the b.,** envoyer promener qn.

brush-up ['brʌʃʌp] *n* coup *m* de brosse; **to have a wash and b.-up,** faire un brin de toilette.

brushwood ['brʌʃwʊd] *n* **(a)** (*undergrowth*) broussailles *fpl*; **(b)** (*worthless wood*) mort-bois *m*; (*for fire etc*) menu bois; (*twigs*) brindilles *fpl*.

brushwork ['brʌʃwɜːk] *n* **(a)** travail *m* au pinceau; **(b)** *Art* touche *f* (*du peintre*).

brusque [bruːsk] *adj* brusque; (*ton*) rude, bourru.

brusquely ['bru:sklı] *adv* brusquement.
brusqueness ['bru:sknıs] *n* brusquerie *f*; (*of tone*) rudesse *f*.
Brussels ['brʌs(ə)lz] *n* Bruxelles; **B. sprouts,** choux *mpl* de Bruxelles.
brutal ['bru:t(ə)l] *adj* brutal, -aux; **the b. truth,** la vérité brutale.
brutality [bru:'tælıtı] *n* brutalité *f* (**to,** envers); *Jur* sévices *mpl* (**to,** envers).
brutalize ['bru:təlaız] *vt* **(a)** (*make brutal*) rendre (*qn*) brutal; **(b)** (*ill-treat*) brutaliser, maltraiter (*qn*).
brutally ['bru:təlı] *adv* brutalement.
brute [bru:t] **1** *n* (*animal*) (bête *f*) brute *f*; *Fig* brute; **you b.!,** espèce d'animal!; **what a b.!,** quel animal!; *F* **a b. of a job,** un travail de chien. **2** *adj* **b. beast,** bête brute; *Fig* **b. strength** *or* **force,** la force brutale; **by b. force,** de vive force; **you'll have to use b. force,** il faudra user de la manière forte.
brutish ['bru:tıʃ] *adj* bestial, -aux; *Fig* (*stupid*) abruti; (*violent*) brutal, -aux.
brutishly ['bru:tıʃlı] *adv* comme une brute.
bryony ['braıənı] *n* (*plant*) bryone *f*, couleuvrée *f*.
BSc [bi:es'si:] *n abbr* **Bachelor of Science**.
BSE [bi:es'i:] *n* (*abbr* **bovine spongiform encephalopathy**) EBS *f*.
BSI [bi:es'aı] *n abbr* **British Standards Institution**.
BST [bi:es'ti:] *n abbr* **British Summer Time**.
BT [bi:'ti:] *n abbr* **British Telecom**.
bubble¹ ['bʌb(ə)l] *n* **(a)** bulle *f* (*d'air, de savon*); (*in boiling liquid*) bouillon *m*; (*in glass*) soufflure *f*; *Cer* cloche *f*; *Metal* boursouflement *m*; *Ch etc* barbotage *m*; **to blow bubbles,** faire des bulles de savon; *Br Culin F* **b. and squeak,** = réchauffé en friture de pommes de terres et de choux; **b. bath,** bain *m* de mousse; **b. gum,** bubble-gum *m*; **b. pack,** (*for pills etc*) conditionnement par plusieurs unités, plaquette *f*; (*for large item*) emballage *m* coque; **(b)** *Fig* projet *m* chimérique.
bubble² *vi* (*of boiling liquid etc*) bouillonner; *Ch Ind* (*of gas through liquid*) barboter; (*of liquid poured*) faire glouglou, glouglouter.
►**bubble over** *vi* déborder (en bouillonnant, en moussant); **to b. over with vitality/with high spirits,** déborder de vie/de gaieté; **to b. over with joy,** pétiller de joie; **he was bubbling over with laughter,** il ne se retenait pas de rire.
bubbling ['bʌb(ə)lıŋ] **1** *adj* bouillonnant. **2** *n* **(a)** bouillonnement *m*; **(b)** *Ch etc* barbotage *m*.
bubbly ['bʌblı] **1** *adj* plein de bulles; *Fig* pétillant. **2** *n F* champagne *m*; (*sparkling wine*) vin mousseux.
bubonic [bju:'bɒnık] *adj Med* (*peste*) bubonique.
buccaneer¹ [bʌkə'nıər] *n* boucanier *m*, flibustier *m*.
buccaneer² *vi* faire le boucanier.
buck¹ [bʌk] *n* **(a)** daim *m*, chevreuil *m* (mâle); **(b)** mâle *m* (*du renne, du chamois etc*); **b. rabbit,** lapin *m* (mâle); **(c)** *esp US Pej* (jeune) Noir *m*; (jeune) Indien *m* (*d'Amérique*); **b.'s fizz,** = cocktail fait à partir de champagne et de jus d'orange; **(d)** *Am F* dollar *m*; **to make a fast b.,** faire du fric; **(e)** chevalet *m*, chèvre *f* (*de sciage*); *Gym* cheval *m*; **(f)** (*of horse*) saut *m* de mouton.
buck² **1** *vi* **(a)** (*of horse*) faire le saut de mouton; (*of aircraft*) se cabrer; **(b)** *Am* (*of person*) résister, se regimber; **to b. against sth,** s'opposer à qch. **2** *vt* **(a)** (*of horse etc*) **to b. s.o. off,** désarçonner qn; **(b) you can't b. the system,** on ne peut rien faire contre l'ordre établi; **to b. a trend,** aller à l'encontre d'une tendance; **to b. the question,** renvoyer la balle.
buck³ *n US Cards* = objet que l'on place devant un joueur pour marquer que c'est à lui de donner; *F* **to pass the b. to s.o.,** (*at poker*) passer la parole au suivant; *F Fig* **to pass the b.,** (*shift blame*) mettre l'affaire sur le dos de qn; (*make s.o. else decide*) passer la décision à qn; *F Fig* **the b. stops here,** (*with me*) en fin de compte, c'est moi qui en suis responsable *ou* c'est moi le responsable; (*with you*) en fin de compte, c'est toi qui en es responsable *ou* c'est toi le responsable.
►**buck for** *vipo Am F* (*strive to achieve*) chercher à obtenir (*qch*); **to b. for promotion,** chercher à obtenir une promotion à tout prix.
►**buck up** *F* **1** *vtsep* remonter le moral à, ragaillardir (*qn*); **that will b. you up,** ça vous remontera *ou* vous retapera; **to b. one's ideas up,** s'améliorer, se montrer à la hauteur. **2** *vi* (*become more cheerful*) reprendre courage; (*hurry*) se hâter, se remuer; **b. up!,** (*be cheerful*) courage!; (*hurry*) dépêche-toi!, *F* grouille-toi!
bucked [bʌkt] *adj F* (*happier*) ragaillardi; (*delighted*) enchanté; **I was really b. to hear the news,** (*it cheered me up*) ça m'a remonté le moral d'apprendre la nouvelle; (*I was delighted*) j'ai été enchanté d'apprendre la nouvelle.
bucket¹ ['bʌkıt] *n* **(a)** seau *m*; **a b. of water,** un seau d'eau; *Br F* **it's coming down in buckets,** il pleut à verse *ou* à seaux; *Sl* **to kick the b.,** casser sa pipe; **b. chain,** = chaîne de personnes qui se passent des seaux d'eau (*en cas d'incendie*); **(b)** *Min Ind* baluchon *m*, baquet *m*; benne *f* (*d'une grue, de téléphérique*); auget *m*, auge *f* (*d'une roue hydraulique*); godet *m*, louchet *m* (*d'une drague*); **b. dredger,** drague *f* à godets; **b. elevator,** élévateur *m* à godets; *Aut* **b. seat,** baquet; *F* **b. shop,** *Fin* bureau *m* d'un courtier marron; *esp Br* = agence de voyages bon marché; **b. wheel,** roue *f* à augets.
bucket² *vi* (*move jerkily*) cahoter; **the car bucketed down the street,** la voiture a cahoté tout le long de la rue.
►**bucket along** *vi* (*of car etc*) aller à une vitesse folle.
►**bucket down** *vi* pleuvoir à verse *ou* à seaux.
bucketful ['bʌkıtfʊl] *n* (*pl* **bucketsful, bucketfuls**) plein seau.
bucking ['bʌkıŋ] *n* sauts *mpl* de mouton (*d'un cheval*).
buckle¹ ['bʌk(ə)l] *n* **(a)** (*fastener*) boucle *f* (*d'une courroie, d'une ceinture etc*); **(b)** (*deformation*) gauchissement *m*, voile *m* (*d'une roue etc*).
buckle² **1** *vt* **(a)** (*fasten*) boucler (*une valise etc*); agrafer (*une ceinture etc*); attacher (*une ceinture de sécurité*); **(b)** (*deform*) déjeter, gauchir (*du métal*); voiler (*une roue*); tordre (*une plaque d'accumulateur etc*). **2** *vi* (*of metal etc*) se déjeter, gauchir; (*of wheel, sheet iron*) se voiler; *Fig* (*under attack*) céder; (*under criticism*) se décomposer.
►**buckle down, buckle to** *vi* (*set to work*) s'y mettre; **to b. down to a task,** s'appliquer *ou* s'atteler à un travail; **isn't it time you buckled down to your homework?,** il serait peut-être temps de faire tes devoirs, non?; **he buckled down and finished cleaning the car,** il s'est armé de courage et a fini de nettoyer la voiture.
►**buckle up** **1** *vi* **(a)** *Aut* attacher sa ceinture de sécurité; **(b)** = **BUCKLE² 2. 2** *vtsep* = **BUCKLE² 1.**
buckled ['bʌk(ə)ld] *adj* **(a)** (*fastened*) (*belt*) bouclé; **(b)** (*deformed*) (*metal*) déjeté, gauchi; (*wheel*) voilé; (*accumulator plate*) tordu.
buckler ['bʌklər] *n* (*shield*) (*worn on arm*) écu *m*, bouclier *m*; (*carried*) targe *f*; *Arch Fig* bouclier.
buckling¹ ['bʌk(ə)lıŋ] *n* **(a)** (*of bell*) agrafage *m*; **(b)** (*of metal etc*) déformation *f*, gauchissement *m*; (*of wheel, sheet iron*) voilure *f*.
buckling² ['bʌklıŋ] *n* hareng cuit et fumé.
buckram ['bʌkrəm] *n Tex* bougran *m*.
Bucks *abbr* **Buckinghamshire.**
bucksaw ['bʌksɔ:] *n* (*tool*) scie *f* à bûches.
buckshee [bʌk'ʃi:] *Old-fashioned Br F* **1** *adj & adv F* gratis *inv;* **we got in b.,** on est entré gratis *ou* sans payer. **2** *n* **a bit of b.,** (*extra ration*) du rab.
buckshot ['bʌkʃɒt] *n* (*ammunition*) chevrotines *fpl*.
buckskin ['bʌkskın] *n* peau *f* de daim; **b. breeches** (*pl* **buckskins**), culotte *f* de peau (de daim).
buckthorn ['bʌkθɔ:n] *n* (*shrub*) nerprun *m*.
bucktooth ['bʌktu:θ] *n* **to have buckteeth,** avoir des dents de lièvre.
buckwheat ['bʌkwi:t] *n Agr* sarrasin *m*; **b. cake,** galette *f* de blé noir.
bucolic [bju:'kɒlık] **1** *adj* (*vie, poésie, poète*) bucolique. **2** *npl* **bucolics,** bucoliques *fpl*.
bud¹ [bʌd] *n* (*on plant*) bourgeon *m*; bouton *m* (*de fleur*); **to be in b.,** (*of tree*) bourgeonner.
bud² *v* **(-dd-)** **1** *vi* (*of tree, plant*) bourgeonner; (*of flower*) boutonner. **2** *vt* greffer (*un arbre fruitier*) par œil détaché; écussonner (*un arbre*).
Buddha ['bʊdə] *n* (le) Bouddha.
Buddhism ['bʊdız(ə)m] *n* bouddhisme *m*.
Buddhist ['bʊdıst] **1** *n* bouddhiste *mf*. **2** *adj* bouddhique, bouddhiste.
budding ['bʌdıŋ] **1** *adj* (*plante, arbre*) bourgeonnant; *Fig* (*artiste, avocat etc*) en herbe; (*passion*) naissant; **a b. genius,** un génie en herbe; **a b. rose,** une rose en bouton. **2** *n* (*of plant, tree*) bourgeonnement *m*.
buddleia ['bʌdlıə] *n* (*shrub*) buddleia *f*.
buddy ['bʌdı] *n F* ami *m*, amie *f*, copain *m*, copine *f*; *esp Am* **b. movie,** buddy-movie *m*, film *m* qui raconte les histoires de deux copains.
buddy-buddy ['bʌdıbʌdı] *adj esp Am* (*close, friendly*) copain, *f* copine (**with,** avec); **I'm very b.-b. with her,** je suis très copain avec elle; **those two are very b.-b.,** ils sont très copain-copain.
budge [bʌdʒ] **1** *vi* **(a)** (*give way*) bouger, céder, reculer; **to**

refuse to b., refuser de bouger; **I won't b. an inch,** je ne reculerai pas d'un centimètre; **(b)** (*move*) bouger, remuer; **if you (so much as) b.,** si vous faites le moindre mouvement. **2** *vt* **(a) I couldn't b. him,** il est resté inébranlable; **(b) he couldn't b. it,** il ne pouvait pas le bouger.

budgerigar ['bʌdʒərɪgɑːr] *n* (*bird*) perruche *f*.

budget¹ ['bʌdʒɪt] *n Fin etc* budget *m*; **to balance the b.,** équilibrer le budget; **we are within b.,** (*at the moment*) nous n'avons pas dépassé le budget; **the concert hall was finished within b.,** la salle de concert a été finie sans dépasser le budget; **it was finished well below b.,** c'est revenu bien moins cher que prévu; *F* **I'm on a b. this month,** je fais des économies ce mois-ci; **recipes for b. meals,** recettes *fpl* économiques; **family/household b.,** budget familial/du ménage; *Can* **to bring down the b.,** présenter le budget; *Parl* **to pass the b.,** voter le budget; **b. account,** (*in store*) = compte permanent; (*in bank*) compte crédit (pour régler les factures de la vie courante); *Com* **b. prices,** prix raisonnables *ou* avantageux; *Can & Br* **b. speech,** = discours à l'occasion de la présentation du budget au parlement; **b. estimates,** prévisions *fpl* budgétaires; **b. holiday,** des vacances économiques *ou* pas chères.

budget² **1** *vi Fin etc* budgétiser. **2** *vt* **to b. one's time,** organiser son temps.

▶budget for *vipo* **(a)** (*allow for in accounts*) porter *ou* inscrire (*qch*) au budget; budgétiser, prévoir (*une dépense*); **we didn't b. for all these car repair bills,** nous n'avions pas prévu toutes ces dépenses pour la réparation de la voiture; **(b)** (*save up for*) économiser pour (*ses vacances*).

budgetary ['bʌdʒɪtərɪ] *adj Fin etc* budgétaire.

budgeting ['bʌdʒɪtɪŋ] *n* budgétisation *f*.

budgie ['bʌdʒɪ] *n F* (*bird*) perruche *f*.

buff¹ [bʌf] **1** *n* **(a)** (*leather*) (peau *f* de) buffle *m*; *Metal* **b. stick,** polissoir *m*; **(b)** (*colour*) couleur *f* chamois; **(c)** *F* **in the b.,** tout nu; **(d)** (*fan*) enthousiaste *mf*; **he is a film b.,** c'est un cinéphile; **she's a history b.,** elle est passionnée d'histoire; **computer buffs,** les mordus *ou* les passionnés d'informatique. **2** *adj* de couleur chamois.

buff² *vt* **(a)** *Metal* polir, émeuler (*un métal etc*) (au buffle); **to b. one's nails,** se polir les ongles; **(b)** effleurer (*les peaux*).

buffalo, *pl* **-oes** ['bʌfələʊ, -əʊz] *n* **(a)** buffle *m*; **water b.,** karbau *m*; **young b.,** bufflon *m*; **(b)** *US* bison *m*.

buffer¹ ['bʌfər] *n* appareil *m* de choc, amortisseur *m*; *Rail* tampon *m* (de choc); (*at end of line*) butoir *m*, heurtoir *m*; *El Electron* (circuit *m*) tampon; *Comptr* tampon, mémoire *f* intermédiaire; *F* **to act as a b.,** (*between people*) faire tampon; *Mil* **recoil b.,** frein *m*, amortisseur de recul; *Rad* **b. stage,** étage *m* tampon *ou* intermédiaire; *Pol* **b. state,** état *m* tampon; *Econ* **b. stocks,** stocks régulateurs.

buffer² *n F* **old b.,** vieille ganache, vieux bonze.

buffer³ *n* (*for polishing*) polissoir *m*.

buffet¹ ['bʌfɪt] *n* (*with fist*) coup *m*; (*slap*) gifle *f*.

buffet² *vt* bourrer (*qn*) de coups, tomber sur (*qn*) à coups de poing; **buffeted by the waves/the wind,** (*of ship*) battu *ou* ballotté par les vagues/secoué par le vent.

buffet³ *n* **(a)** ['bʌfɪt] (*piece of furniture*) buffet *m*; **(b)** ['bʊfeɪ] buffet *m*; *Rail* **b. car,** voiture-buffet, *pl* voitures-buffets; **cold b.,** (*on menu*) viandes froides, assiette anglaise; (*meal*) buffet froid; **b. lunch,** lunch *m*.

buffeting ['bʌfɪtɪŋ] *n* succession *f* de coups *ou* de chocs.

buffing ['bʌfɪŋ] *n* **(a)** *Metal etc* polissage *m*, émeulage *m*; bufflage *m*; **b. wheel,** meule *f* à polir *ou* à buffler, disque *m* en buffle; **(b)** (*of hide*) effleurage *m*.

buffoon [bə'fuːn] *n* bouffon *m*, paillasse *m*, clown *m*; **to act** *or* **play the b.,** faire le bouffon.

buffoonery [bə'fuːnərɪ] *n* bouffonneries *fpl*.

bug¹ [bʌg] *n* **(a)** (*insect*) **(bed) b.,** punaise *f* (des lits); *esp Am* insecte *m*; *US* **potato b.,** doryphore *m*; **(b)** *F* virus *m*, microbe *m*; **to catch a b.,** attraper un microbe; **there's a b. going round,** il y a un virus qui traîne; *Fig* **to have** *or* **have been bitten by the skiing b.,** avoir la passion *ou* la folie du ski; **(c)** *Comptr* bogue *f*; **(d)** (*concealed listening device*) micro clandestin.

bug² **1** *vt F* **(a)** camoufler des micros clandestins dans (*une pièce*); brancher (*un téléphone*) sur table d'écoute; intercepter (*une conversation*); **(b)** (*annoy*) taper sur les nerfs à (*qn*); (*of person*) emmerder (*qn*); **stop bugging me about it,** arrête de m'emmerder *ou* de m'embêter avec ça; **it really bugs me to think of her having all that money,** ça me tape vraiment sur les nerfs de savoir qu'elle a tout cet argent. **2** *vi Am* (*of eyes*) être globuleux.

bugaboo ['bʌgəbuː] *n esp Am* = **BUGBEAR.**

bugbear ['bʌgbeər] *n F* (*goblin*) croquemitaine *m*; *Fig* épouvantail *m*; **maths is my b.,** les maths, c'est mon cauchemar.

bug-free [bʌg'friː] *adj* **(a)** *Comptr* (*program*) exempt d'erreurs *ou* de bogues; **(b)** (*room*) sans micros clandestins; (*having no insects*) d'où les insectes ont été chassés.

bugger¹ ['bʌgər] *n* **(a)** *Sl* salaud *m*; **silly b.!,** espèce d'idiot!; **poor b.,** pauvre type; **a b. of a job,** un travail de chien; **she knows b. all about it,** elle n'y entrave que dalle; **(b)** *Jur* pédéraste *m*.

bugger² *vt* **(a)** *Sl* **b. (it)!,** merde!; **(b)** *Jur* sodomiser (*qn*); **(c)** *Sl* **to be buggered,** (*tired*) être crevé; (*broken*) être foutu.

▶bugger about, bugger around *Sl* **1** *vi* lambiner. **2** *vtsep* emmerder (*qn*).

▶bugger off *vi Sl* foutre le camp; **b. off!,** (*go away*) fous le camp!; (*leave me alone*) fous-moi la paix!

▶bugger up *vtsep Sl* (*spoil*) gâcher (*la journée de qn*); bousiller (*un projet, la télé, un stylo*); **having to work overtime buggered up my weekend,** ça m'a gâché mon week-end de devoir faire des heures supplémentaires; **you've buggered the whole thing up,** tu as tout gâché.

buggery ['bʌgərɪ] *n Jur* sodomie *f*.

bugging ['bʌgɪŋ] *n* (*of room*) installation *f* des micros clandestins; (*of telephone*) mise *f* sur table d'écoute; **b. device,** micro clandestin.

buggy ['bʌgɪ] *n* **(a)** (*carriage*) boghei *m*, buggy *m*; **(American) b.,** américaine *f*; **beach** *or* **dune b.,** buggy; **moon b.,** jeep *f* lunaire; **(b)** *Am* (*for baby*) landau *m*.

bughouse ['bʌghaʊs] *US Sl* **1** *n* (*for the insane*) maison *f* de fous. **2** *adj* (*insane*) fou, *f* folle, à enfermer.

bugle¹ ['bjuːg(ə)l] *n Mil* clairon *m*; **key(ed) b.,** bugle *m*; **b. call,** coup *m ou* sonnerie *f* de clairon.

bugle² *n* (*plant*) bugle *f*.

bugler ['bjuːglər] *n* (sonneur *m* de) clairon *m*.

build¹ [bɪld] *n* **(a)** carrure *f*, taille *f*, conformation *f* (*d'une personne*); **man of powerful b.,** homme à forte membrure; **of slight b.,** fluet; **(b)** construction *f*; façons *fpl* (*d'un navire etc*); style *m* (*d'un édifice*).

build² *v* (*pt & pp* **built** [bɪlt]) **1** *vt* bâtir (*une maison etc*); construire (*un navire, un pont, une route etc*); édifier (*un temple*); faire (*son nid etc*) (**with,** avec); **the walls were built of granite,** les murs étaient (bâtis) en granit; **the stables are built on to the house,** les écuries tiennent à la maison; **the house is being built,** la maison est en construction; **to b. one's hopes on sth,** fonder *ou* baser ses espoirs sur qch; **I'm building my hopes on you,** je compte sur vous. **2** *vi* **to b. on a piece of land,** bâtir un terrain; **to b. on sand,** bâtir sur le sable.

▶build in *vtsep* (*incorporate*) intégrer, incorporer (*qch*); *Constr* encastrer (*une armoire, une poutre etc*); **to b. in safety features,** intégrer des dispositifs de sécurité.

▶build into *vtaspo* incorporer (*certaines caractéristiques*) dans (*un produit*).

▶build on **1** *vipo* (*use as a foundation*) mettre à profit (*sa réussite*); **to b. on a promise,** miser *ou* faire fond sur une promesse. **2** *vtsep* (*add to existing structure*) ajouter (*une véranda*).

▶build up **1** *vtsep* **(a)** (*increase*) développer (*la demande*); *Mil etc* constituer (*des réserves*); mettre sur pied (*des unités, des renforts etc*); **don't b. your hopes up,** ne te fais pas d'illusions;

(b) (*create*) bâtir, échafauder, construire (*une théorie, un système*); développer (*un commerce*); se faire (*une réputation*); constituer (*une collection, une bibliothèque*); **to b. up custom** *or* **a clientele,** (*of company*) constituer une clientèle; **his father built the company up from nothing,** son père a créé la société à partir de rien; *Med etc* **to b. up an immunity,** développer une immunité;

(c) (*strengthen*) affermir (*la santé*); reconstituer (*ses forces*); **the children need vitamins to b. them up,** les enfants ont besoin de vitamines pour se retaper;

(d) (*usu passive*) **this area has been very much built up,** on a beaucoup construit par ici;

(e) (*publicize*) faire de la publicité pour (*qn, un produit etc*);

(f) (*make higher*) rehausser (*un mur*); (*rebuild*) réparer (*un mur*).

2 *vi* (*of pressure, tension etc*) s'accumuler, augmenter; (*of traffic*) devenir dense; (*of snow*) s'amonceler.

builder ['bɪldər] *n Constr* entrepreneur *m* en bâtiment; constructeur *m* (*de navires etc*); *Fig* créateur *m*, fondateur *m* (*d'un empire etc*).

building ['bɪldɪŋ] *n* **(a)** (*action*) construction *f*; **the b. trade,** le bâtiment; **b. block,** (*toy*) cube *m* de construction; **b. contractor,** entrepreneur *m* de bâtiment; **b. estate,** lotissement *m*; **b. materials,** matériaux *mpl* de construction; **b. plot,** terrain *m* à bâtir; **b. site,** (*vacant land*) terrain à bâtir; (*where work is going on*) chantier *m* (de construction); *Br* **b. society,** = coopérative ou société immobilière; **b. slip,** (*for ship*) cale *f* de construction; **b. workers,** ouvriers *mpl* du bâtiment; **(b)** (*house, factory etc*) bâtiment *m*, immeuble *m*; (*large*) édifice *m*; **public b.,** édifice public; (*monument*) monument *m*; **farm buildings,** bâtiments *ou* dépendances *fpl* d'une ferme.

build-up ['bɪldʌp] *n* **(a)** accumulation *f*, augmentation *f* (*de la pression, de la tension*); *Phys* manifestation croissante (*d'un phénomène*); **traffic b.-up,** bouchon *m*; **(b)** élaboration *f*, développement *m* (*d'un système etc*); **(c)** *Mil* mise *f* sur pied (*d'unités, de renforts etc*); constitution *f* (*de réserves en hommes, de matériel etc*); **(d)** (*for film etc*) campagne *f* publicitaire; **her latest book is getting a lot of b.-up,** on fait beaucoup de battage autour de son dernier livre.

built [bɪlt] *adj* bâti; **British b.,** de construction anglaise; **solidly b.,** solidement bâti; **a powerfully b. man,** un homme à forte membrure.

built-in ['bɪl'tɪn] *adj* (*armoire, baignoire, poutre*) encastré; (*placard*) incorporé; **b.-in obsolescence,** (*in machine*) obsolescence programmée; *Fig* **b.-in resistance to ...,** opposition congénitale à ... .

built-up ['bɪl'tʌp] *adj* (*poutre*) composé, rapporté; (*épaules d'un complet*) surhaussé; (*talons*) compensé; **b.-up area,** agglomération *f* (urbaine).

bulb [bʌlb] *n* **(a)** bulbe *m*, oignon *m* (*de tulipe etc*); **(b)** *El* ampoule *f*, lampe *f*; **(c)** *Phys* boule *f*, cuvette *f*, ampoule *f*, réservoir *m* (*de thermomètre*); *Ch* (*flask*) ballon *m*; *Culin* (*of baster*) poire *f*; **(d)** *Anat* bulbe *m* (*pileux, aortique etc*).

bulbous ['bʌlbəs] *adj* bulbeux; **b. root,** (*of plant*) racine bulbeuse; **b. nose,** gros nez.

Bulgaria [bʌl'geərɪə] *n* Bulgarie *f*.

Bulgarian [bʌl'geərɪən] **1** *adj* bulgare. **2** *n* **(a)** Bulgare *mf*; **(b)** *Ling* bulgare *m*.

bulge[1] [bʌldʒ] *n* (*in wall*) bombement *m*, ventre *m*, renflement *m*; (*on face*) protubérance *f*; (*of bottle, vase*) panse *f*; *Archit* jarret *m*; (*in tyre*) soufflure *f*; *Mil* saillant *m* (*du front*); *Econ F* poussée *f*; **this dress shows all my bulges,** cette robe me moule trop.

bulge[2] *vi* **to b. (out),** bomber, ballonner; (*stick out*) faire saillie; (*of wall etc*) se déjeter; *Archit* jarreter; **his eyes were bulging,** il avait les yeux exorbités; **sack bulging with potatoes,** sac bourré de pommes de terre.

bulging ['bʌldʒɪŋ] **1** *adj* (*front etc*) bombé; (*ventre*) ballonnant; (*yeux*) protubérant; (*joues*) bouffi; (*sac etc*) bourré, plein à craquer; (*mur*) qui fait ventre. **2** *n* bombement *m*, renflement *m* (*d'un mur etc*); (*of stomach*) ballonnement *m*.

bulimia [bjuː'lɪmɪə, bʊ'l-] *n Med* boulimie *f*.

bulk[1] [bʌlk] *n* **(a)** grandeur *f*, grosseur *f*, masse *f*, volume *m*; encombrement *m* (*d'un colis*); **(b) the b.,** la masse, la plupart (*des hommes*); le gros (*de l'armée*); la plus grosse partie (*de ses biens etc*); **(c)** *Comptr* volume *m*, masse *f* (*d'informations*); *Nau* charge *f*; chargement arrimé; *Com etc* **in b.,** en bloc, globalement; **to buy in b.,** acheter par grosses quantités; **b. buying,** achat massif *ou* en gros; **to sell in b.,** vendre en vrac; *Nau* **b. carrier,** navire *m* pour le transport en vrac (*du pétrole etc*), vraquier *m*; **b. concrete,** béton *m* en masse; **b. rate,** (*for sending letters*) affranchissement *m* à forfait.

bulk[2] **1** *vi* (*of material, wood etc*) (se) gonfler (*par l'humidité*); *Fig* **to b. large,** occuper une place importante (**in s.o.'s eyes,** aux yeux de qn). **2** *vt* réunir, grouper (*plusieurs colis*) en un seul; entasser (*des marchandises*) en vrac.

bulkhead ['bʌlkhed] *n* (*on ship etc*) cloison *f*.

bulkiness ['bʌlkɪnɪs] *n* **(a)** volume excessif; (*of parcel*) encombrement *m*; **(b)** (*of sweater*) épaisseur *f*.

bulky ['bʌlkɪ] *adj* **(a)** (*parcel etc*) volumineux, encombrant; (*livre*) épais; *Nau* **b. cargo,** chargement volumineux; **(b)** (*sweater*) gros.

bull[1] [bʊl] **1** *n* **(a)** taureau *m*; *Astron* **the B.,** le Taureau; **to take the b. by the horns,** prendre le taureau par les cornes; **like a b. in a china shop,** comme un éléphant dans un magasin de porcelaine; **to go at sth like a b. at a gate,** foncer tête baissée *ou* la tête la première dans qch; **b. calf,** jeune taureau, taurillon *m*; **(b)** mâle *m* (*de l'éléphant, de la baleine etc*); **b. elephant,** éléphant *m* mâle; **(c)** *Br Mil Sl* fourbissage *m*; **(d)** *Sl* connerie *f*; **he talks a lot of b.,** il raconte des conneries; **(e)** *St Exch* spéculateur *m* à la hausse, haussier *m*; **b. transaction,** opération *f* à la hausse; **(f)** (*of target*) noir *m*, blanc *m*, mouche *f*; **he got six bulls,** il a fait mouche six fois; **(g)** (*dog*) bouledogue *m*; **b. bitch/pup,** chienne *f*/chiot *m* de bouledogue; **b. terrier,** bull-terrier *m*, *pl* bull-terriers; **b. mastiff,** molosse *m*. **2** *int* foutaise!

bull[2] *St Exch* **1** *vt* **to b. the market,** chercher à faire monter les cours. **2** *vi* spéculer à la hausse.

bull[3] *n Rel* bulle *f*; **Papal b.,** bulle du Pape.

bulldog ['bʊldɒg] *n* bouledogue *m*; *F Fig* personne d'un courage obstiné; *Br Univ* appariteur *m* du censeur (*aux universités d'Oxford et de Cambridge*); **b. clip,** pince *f* à dessin.

bulldoze ['bʊldəʊz] *vt* dégager, déblayer (*un terrain*) (au bulldozer); démolir (*une maison etc*) (au bulldozer); *Fig* **to b. s.o. into doing sth,** pousser qn à faire qch; **I was bulldozed into it,** on m'a poussé à le faire.

bulldozer ['bʊldəʊzər] *n Constr* bulldozer *m*, bouteur *m*.

bullet ['bʊlɪt] *n* balle *f* (*de fusil, de revolver*); **riddled with bullets,** criblé de balles; *F* **to stop a b.,** recevoir une balle; **b. hole,** trou *m* de balle; **b. train,** (*in Japan*) = train à grande vitesse; **b. wound,** blessure *f* par balle.

bullet-headed ['bʊlɪthedɪd] *adj* **(a)** à tête ronde; **(b)** *US Fig* entêté.

bulletin ['bʊlɪtɪn] *n* bulletin *m*, communiqué *m*; **news b.,** flash *m* (spécial); **b. board,** tableau *m* d'affichage.

bulletproof ['bʊlɪtpruːf] *adj* à l'épreuve des balles; (*gilet etc*) antiballes, pare-balles *inv*.

bullfight ['bʊlfaɪt] *n* course *f ou* combat *m* de taureaux, corrida *f*.

bullfighter ['bʊlfaɪtər] *n* matador *m*.

bullfighting ['bʊlfaɪtɪŋ] *n* combats *mpl* de taureaux, courses *fpl* de taureaux; (*as an art*) tauromachie *f*.

bullfinch ['bʊlfɪntʃ] *n* (*bird*) bouvreuil *m* (pivoine).

bullfrog ['bʊlfrɒg] *n* grenouille *f* taureau.

bull-headed ['bʊlhedɪd] *adj F* d'une impétuosité de taureau; **to go at sth b.-h.,** foncer la tête la première.

bullhorn ['bʊlhɔːn] *n Am* porte-voix *m inv*.

bullion ['bʊljən] *n* (*gold*) or *m* en barres *ou* en lingot(s); (*silver*) argent *m* en lingot(s); *Fin* métal *m*; **b. van,** fourgon *m* bancaire.

bullish ['bʊlɪʃ] **(a)** *St Exch* (*market, trend*) à la hausse; **(b)** *Fig* (*optimistic*) optimiste; **to be b. about sth,** être optimiste pour qch.

bull-necked ['bʊlnekt] *adj* au cou de taureau.

bullock ['bʊlək] *n* bœuf *m*; **young b.,** bouvillon *m*; **b. cart,** char *m* à bœufs.

bullpen ['bʊlpen] *n US* (*in police station*) = grande cellule commune.

bullring ['bʊlrɪŋ] *n* arène *f* (*pour les courses de taureaux*).

bull's-eye ['bʊlzaɪ] *n* **(a)** noir *m*, mouche *f* (*d'une cible*); **to hit the** *or* **get a b.-e.,** (*in archery*) faire mouche, mettre dans le noir; (*at darts*) mettre dans le mille; *Fig* **to hit the b.-e.,** (*of remark*) faire mouche; **(b)** (*in glass*) boudine *f*; **b.-e. panes,** carreaux *mpl* à boudines *ou* en culs-de-bouteille; **(c)** (*sweet*) gros bonbon à la menthe; **(d)** *Nau* verre mort, lentille *f*.

bullshit[1] ['bʊlʃɪt] *Vulg* **1** *n* foutaise *f*; **he's a real b. artist,** (*talks a lot of nonsense*) il ne dit que des conneries; (*he can impress people*) c'est un vrai baratineur. **2** *int* foutaise!

bullshit[2] *vi Vulg* dire des conneries.

bullshitter ['bʊlʃɪtər] *n Vulg* personne qui dit des conneries.

bully[1] ['bʊlɪ] *n* tyran *m*, brutal *m*; *Sch* brimeur *m*; **don't be such a b.,** ne sois pas si tyrannique.

bully[2] *vt* brutaliser, rudoyer (*qn*); **to b. s.o. into doing sth,** faire faire qch à qn à force de menaces; **he bullies his wife,** il brutalise sa femme; **she bullies her little sister,** elle est très brutale avec sa petite sœur.

bully[3] *int Old-fashioned F* **b. for you!,** (*what luck*) vous avez de la chance!; (*well done*) bravo pour vous!

bully[4] *adj F* **b. beef,** bœuf *m* de conserve, *F* singe *m*.

►**bully off** *vi* (*in hockey*) engager (le jeu), mettre la balle en jeu.

bullyboy ['bʊlɪbɔː] *n* voyou *m*, dur *m*; **b. tactics,** tactiques *mpl* de voyou.

bullying ['bʊlɪɪŋ] **1** *adj* brutal, -aux. **2** *n* intimidation *f*; (*among children*) brimades *fpl*; **b. is not a problem in this school,** il n'y a pas de problèmes de brimades dans cette école.

bully-off ['bʊlɪɒf] *n* (*in hockey*) engagement *m* (du jeu).

bulrush ['bʊlrʌʃ] *n* (*plant*) jonc *m* des marais.

bulwark ['bʊlwɜːk] *n* **(a)** (*fortification*) & *Fig* rempart *m*; **(b)** *Nau* **bulwarks,** pavois *m*, bastingage *m*.

bum[1] [bʌm] *n Br F* derrière *m*; **b. bag** banane *f*.

bum[2] *esp Am Sl* **1** *adj* moche, minable; **b. advice,** des conseils minables; **b. check,** chèque *m* en bois; **b. rap,** (*false charge*) accusation inventée de toutes pièces; (*unfair* *punishment*) punition *f* injuste; **b. steer,** tuyau *m* bidon. **2** *n* **(a)** (*worthless person*) fainéant *m*; (*tramp*) clochard *m*, trimardeur *m*; **to give s.o. the b.'s rush,** (*from relationship, meeting*) virer qn avec perte et fracas; **to give a suggestion/an idea the b.'s rush,** ne tenir aucun compte d'une suggestion/idée; **(b) to be on the b.,** (*live off other people*) vivre aux dépens des autres; (*travel round country*) vagabonder.

bum³ *v* (-mm-) *Am Sl* **1** *vi* (*beg*) taper les autres, vivre aux dépens des autres, vivre en parasite. **2** *vt* **to b. a cigarette from** *or* **off s.o.,** taper qn d'une cigarette; **to b. a ride,** faire de l'auto-stop.

►**bum around** *vi Am Sl* glander, glandouiller.

►**bum around with** *vipo Am Sl* fréquenter (*qn*).

bumble ['bʌmb(ə)l] *vi* (*be inefficient*) = papillonner à droite et à gauche sans rien faire correctement.

bumblebee ['bʌmb(ə)lbiː] *n F* bourdon *m*.

bumbler ['bʌmb(ə)lər] *n F* **an old b.,** un vieux maladroit.

bumbling ['bʌmb(ə)lɪŋ] *adj* **b. fool** *or* **idiot,** idiot bon à rien.

bumboat ['bʌmbəʊt] *n Nau* bateau *m* à provisions.

bumf [bʌmf] *n* **(a)** *F* (*useless paper*) paperasse *f*; **(b)** *Sl* (*lavatory paper*) papier *m* hygiénique, papier cul.

bumfreezer ['bʌmfriːzər] *n Br Sl* = veste qui arrive au ras des fesses.

bummaree [bʌmə'riː] *n Old-fashioned Br* **(a)** (*au marché de Billingsgate*) courtier *m* en poisson; **(b)** (*au marché de Smithfield*) porteur *m*.

bummer ['bʌmər] *n Sl* (*something worthless*) fiasco *m*; **don't go and see this film, it's a b.,** ne va pas voir ce film, il est nul.

bump¹ [bʌmp] *n* **(a)** (*collision*) choc *m*; (*jolt*) secousse *f*; (*of car etc against sth*) heurt *m*, cahot *m* (*d'une voiture*); heurt d'un canot par le poursuivant (*dans une bumping race*); **to give s.o. a b. start,** pousser la voiture de qn pour la faire démarrer; **to sit down with a b.,** faire un casse-cul; **(b)** (*lump*) inégalité *f* (*d'un chemin, d'une surface etc*); (*as result of being hit*) bosse *f*; (*in phrenology*) protubérance *f*, *F* bosse (*du crâne*); **(c)** *Av* trou *m* d'air.

bump² *vt* cogner, frapper; heurter (*le canot qu'on poursuit*) (*dans une bumping race*); **to b. one's head on** *or* **against sth,** se cogner la tête contre qch.

bump³ *adv & int* pan!, boum!; *F* **things that go b. in the night,** des bruits étranges qui se font entendre pendant la nuit.

►**bump along** *vi* (*in cart etc*) cahoter.

►**bump into** *vipo* **(a)** (*collide with*) se cogner *ou* se heurter *ou* buter contre (*qch*); (*of vehicle*) tamponner (*une voiture*); **(b)** (*meet*) rencontrer (*qn*) par hasard.

►**bump off** *vtsep Sl* supprimer (*qn*), faire la peau à (*qn*).

►**bump up** *vtsep F* gonfler (*les prix*) (d'une façon exagérée).

bumper ['bʌmpər] *n* **(a)** *Br Aut* pare-choc(s) *m*; **front/rear b.,** pare-choc(s) avant/arrière; **the cars were b. to b.,** les voitures se suivaient pare-choc(s) contre pare-choc(s); **(b)** rasade *f* (*de champagne etc*); **b. crop** *or* **harvest,** récolte magnifique *ou* exceptionnelle; **it's been a b. year for tourism,** ça a été une année exceptionnelle pour le tourisme.

bumpety-bump ['bʌmpɪtɪ'bʌmp] *adv F* en cahotant; **my heart went b.-b.,** mon cœur faisait boum-boum.

bumph [bʌmf] *n* = **BUMF**.

bumping ['bʌmpɪŋ] *n* (*collision*) heurtement *m*; (*in cart etc*) cahotement *m*; **b. race,** course-poursuite *f* (*dans laquelle chaque bateau doit rattraper le précédent et de son avant en heurter l'arrière*).

bumpkin ['bʌmpkɪn] *n* **country b.,** rustre *m*, rustaud *m*.

bump-start ['bʌmpstɑːt] *vt Aut* **to b.-s. a car,** pousser une voiture pour la faire démarrer.

bumptious ['bʌmpʃəs] *adj* orgueilleux, suffisant, outrecuidant; **to be b.,** faire l'important.

bumpy ['bʌmpɪ] *adj* **(a)** (*chemin etc*) cahoteux, défoncé, inégal; *Av* (*vol*) chahuté; *Fig* **we've got a b. road ahead of us,** nous avons une période difficile devant nous; **(b)** (*forehead etc*) couvert de bosses.

bun [bʌn] *n* **(a)** *Culin* petit pain au lait; **Bath b.,** = petit pain saupoudré de sucre; *Old-fashioned F* **b. fight,** (*tea party*) réunion *f* pour le thé; **(b)** (*in hair*) chignon *m*; **she wears her hair in a b.,** elle porte un chignon; **(c)** *F* **buns,** miches *fpl* (*d'un homme*); **he has a nice pair of buns,** il a un beau cul.

bunch¹ [bʌntʃ] *n* **(a)** botte *f* (*de radis etc*); bouquet *m* (*de fleurs*); grappe *f* (*de raisin*); touffe *f* (*d'herbes*); houppe *f* (*de plumes*); trousseau *m* (*de clefs*); régime *m* (*de bananes*); **to wear one's hair in bunches,** porter des couettes; **(b)** groupe *m* (*de personnes*); *US* troupeau *m* (*de bestiaux*); **he's the best** *or* **the pick of the b.,** c'est lui le meilleur (de la bande); **they're quite an intelligent b.,** c'est un groupe plutôt intelligent; *Sp* **the b.,** le peloton; *Am F* **thanks a b.,** merci beaucoup.

bunch² *vt* botteler (*des radis etc*); lier (*des fleurs etc*) en bouquet.

►**bunch together** *vi* (*of people*) se presser en foule, se serrer, se tasser, se pelotonner.

►**bunch up** *vi* (*of material*) retrousser.

bundle¹ ['bʌnd(ə)l] *n* paquet *m* (*de linge etc*); ballot *m* (*de marchandises, d'effets*); baluchon *m* (*d'effets*); botte *f* (*d'asperges etc*); faisceau *m* (*de cannes, de nerfs, de fils etc*); liasse *f* (*de billets de banque, de papiers*); fagot *m* (*de bois*); tas *m* (*de choses diverses*); *Am F* **to make a b.,** (*lot of money*) faire sa pelote; *Am F* **thanks a b.,** merci beaucoup; *Am F* **to go a b. on sth,** (*like*) aimer qch beaucoup; *F* **she's a b. of nerves,** c'est un paquet de nerfs; *F* **my driving test was not exactly a b. of fun,** mon permis de conduire n'a pas vraiment été de la rigolade.

bundle² *vt* empaqueter (*qch*), mettre *ou* lier (*qch*) en paquet; botteler (*du foin*); mettre (*des documents*) en liasse; *F* **to b. papers into a drawer,** fourrer des papiers dans un tiroir.

►**bundle off** *vtsep* **(a)** (*send hastily*) envoyer (*qn, qch*) à la hâte *ou* sans attendre; **the baby was bundled off to hospital,** le bébé a été envoyé à l'hôpital sans attendre; **they bundled me off the train,** ils m'ont fait descendre du train en toute hâte; **(b)** *Pej* se débarrasser de (*qn*) (sans cérémonie); **his father bundled him off to boarding school,** son père l'a expédié en pension.

►**bundle out** *vtsep* faire sortir (*qn*) à la hâte.

►**bundle up 1** *vtsep* **(a)** (*make parcel of*) = **BUNDLE²**; **(b)** (*collect*) ramasser (*ses affaires*) à la hâte. **2** *vi* (*wear warm clothes*) emmitoufler; **b. up, it's cold outside,** emmitoufle-toi bien, il fait froid dehors.

bung¹ [bʌŋ] *n* bonde *f*, bondon *m* (*de fût*).

bung² *vt* **(a)** boucher (*un orifice*); **(b)** *F* mettre, fourrer (*qch*); **b. it in a drawer,** fourre-le dans un tiroir; **b. it over,** (*throw it*) balance-le.

►**bung up** *vtsep F* (*block*) boucher (*un évier*); **I'm** *or* **my nose is all bunged up,** j'ai le nez complètement bouché.

bungalow ['bʌŋgələʊ] *n* bungalow *m*.

bungee ['bʌndʒiː] *n* **b. (cord),** tendeur *m*.

bunghole ['bʌŋhəʊl] *n* bonde *f* (*de fût*).

bungle¹ ['bʌŋg(ə)l] *n* gâchis *m*, bousillage *m*; **to make a b. of sth,** bousiller *ou* gâcher qch.

bungle² **1** *vt* gâcher, *F* bousiller, louper (*un travail*). **2** *vi* s'y prendre maladroitement.

bungler ['bʌŋglər] *n* bousilleur, -euse; gâcheur, -euse (*de travail*); (*clumsy person*) maladroit, -e.

bungling ['bʌŋglɪŋ] **1** *adj* maladroit. **2** *n* bousillage *m*, gâchis *m*.

bunion ['bʌnjən] *n Med* inflammation *f* de la base du gros orteil, *F* oignon *m*.

bunk¹ [bʌŋk] *n* **(a)** *Nau Rail etc* couchette *f*; **b. beds,** lits superposés; (*collapsible*) lits gigognes; **(b)** *F* logement *m*.

bunk² *vi Nau* être logé (**forward,** à l'avant).

bunk³ *n F* **to do a b.,** déguerpir, décamper.

bunk⁴ *n Old-fashioned F* bêtises *fpl*.

►**bunk down** *F vi* **(a)** (*go to bed*) aller se coucher; **(b)** (*sleep*) passer la nuit (**with friends,** chez des amis).

bunker¹ ['bʌŋkər] *n* **(a)** (*in home*) coffre *m* à charbon; *Nau* soute *f* (*à charbon, mazout etc*); réservoir *m*, caisse *f* (*à huile*); **(b)** *Golf* banquette *f*, bunker *m*; **(c)** *Mil* blockhaus *m*.

bunker² **1** *vt Nau* **(a)** mettre (*du combustible*) en soute; **(b)** *Golf* **to be bunkered,** se trouver dans le sable. **2** *vi Nau* se ravitailler en charbon, charbonner.

bunkhouse ['bʌŋkhaʊs] *n Am* baraquement pourvu de couchettes (*pour bûcherons etc*).

bunkum ['bʌŋkəm] *n F* foutaise *f*.

bunny ['bʌnɪ] *n F* **(a)** (*in children's language*) **b. (rabbit),** Jeannot lapin *m*, petit lapin; **(b) b. (girl),** = employée de boîte de nuit Playboy ® (habillée en lapin).

Bunsen ['bʌns(ə)n] *n Ch etc* **B. burner,** bec *m* Bunsen.

bunting¹ ['bʌntɪŋ] *n* (*bird*) bruant *m*.

bunting² *n* **(a)** (*flags*) drapeaux *mpl*, fanions *mpl*; **decorated with b.,** pavoisé; **(b)** *Tex* étamine *f*.

buoy¹ [bɔɪ] *n Nau* bouée *f*.

buoy² *vt Nau* baliser (*un chenal*); marquer (*une épave*).

►**buoy up** *vtsep Fig* soutenir, appuyer (*qn*); *Nau* faire flotter (*un objet*); *Fig* **buoyed up with new hope,** animé *ou* soutenu par un nouvel espoir.

buoyancy ['bɔɪənsɪ] *n* **(a)** *Nau Av* flottabilité *f* (*d'un objet*); **centre of b.,** centre *m* de poussée; **b. bag/tank,**

ballonnet *m*/réservoir *m* de flottabilité; **b. chamber,** *Nau* flotteur *m* (*d'une torpille*); *Nau Av* chambre *f* de flottabilité; **(b)** *Fig* entrain *m*, allant *m*, optimisme *m*; *Com* fermeté *f* (*du marché*); **man full of b.,** homme qui a du ressort.

buoyant ['bɔɪənt] *adj* **(a)** flottable; **salt water is more b. than fresh,** l'eau salée porte mieux que l'eau douce; *Constr* **b. foundation,** radier *m* en béton; **(b)** (*person*) optimiste, plein d'entrain, allègre; *Com* (*marché*) soutenu; **b. step,** pas *m* élastique; **the market is b.,** le marché reste ferme.

buoyantly ['bɔɪəntlɪ] *adv* avec entrain, avec optimisme.

BUPA ['bu:pə] *n* (*abbr* **British United Provident Association**) service *m* de santé privé.

bur [bɜ:r] *n* = **BURR¹(a).**

Burberry ® ['bɜ:bərɪ] *n* **(a)** imperméable *m* (de la marque Burberry); **(b)** vêtement *m* de la marque Burberry.

burble ['bɜ:b(ə)l] *vi* **(a)** (*of stream*) murmurer; *Fig* (*of person*) murmurer (des sons inarticulés); *Pej F* (*of person*) débiter des inepties; **(b)** glousser (**with laughter,** de rire).

►**burble away, burble on** *vi F* débiter des inepties.

burbot ['bɜ:bət] *n* (*fish*) lotte *f*, barbot *m*, barbot(t)e *f*.

burden¹ ['bɜ:d(ə)n] *n* **(a)** fardeau *m*, charge *f*; **b. of taxation,** poids de la fiscalité *ou* des impôts; *Jur* **b. of proof,** charge *ou* fardeau de la preuve; **the b. of proof rests with him,** c'est à lui que la preuve incombe; **I am a b. to you,** je suis un fardeau pour toi; **to make s.o.'s life a b.,** rendre la vie dure à qn; **(b)** *Nau* charge *f*, contenance *f* (*d'un navire*); substance *f* (*d'un discours, d'une plainte*); **(c)** *Old-fashioned* refrain *m* (*d'une chanson*).

burden² *vt* (*load*) charger, alourdir, accabler (**s.o. with sth,** qn de qch); **to b. one's memory with useless facts,** se charger la mémoire de faits inutiles; **burdened estate,** domaine grevé d'hypothèques *ou* hypothéqué; **I'm sorry to b. you with my worries,** je suis désolé de vous accabler avec mes soucis; **she is burdened with a retarded child,** elle a un enfant handicapé à sa charge.

burdensome ['bɜ:d(ə)nsəm] *adj* onéreux (**to,** à).

burdock ['bɜ:dɒk] *n* (*weed*) bardane *f*, glouteron *m*.

bureau, *pl* **-eaux** ['bjʊərəʊ, -əʊz] *n* **(a)** (*furniture*) bureau *m*; (*with roll top*) secrétaire *m*; *US* commode *f*; **(b)** (*office*) bureau *m*; *US* (*government department*) bureau, service *m*.

bureaucracy [bjʊə'rɒkrəsɪ] *n Pej* bureaucratie *f*.

bureaucrat ['bjʊərəkræt] *n Pej* bureaucrate *m*.

bureaucratic [bjʊərə'krætɪk] *adj Pej* bureaucratique.

burette, *US* **buret** [bjʊ'ret] *n Ch* éprouvette graduée, burette *f*.

burg [bɜ:g] *n Am F* (*village*) bourg *m*; (*town*) municipalité *f*, ville *f*; **there's nothing happening in this b.,** il ne se passe rien dans ce coin *ou* bled.

burgeon ['bɜ:dʒən] *vi Lit* bourgeonner.

burger [bɜ:gər] *n F* hamburger *m*.

burgess ['bɜ:dʒɪs] *n* **(a)** (*in England*) citoyen *m*; **(b)** *Eng Hist* député *m* (*représentant une ville*); **(c)** *US* = conseiller municipal.

burgher ['bɜ:gər] *n US* citoyen *m*.

burglar ['bɜ:glər] *n* cambrioleur *m*; **b. alarm,** alarme *f* anti-vol; **b. proof,** inviolable.

burglarize ['bɜ:gləraɪz] *vt Am* cambrioler.

burglary ['bɜ:glərɪ] *n* cambriolage *m*; (*breaking and entering*) vol *m* avec effraction.

burgle ['bɜ:g(ə)l] *vt* cambrioler, dévaliser (*une maison*).

Burgundian [bɜ:'gʌndɪən] **1** *adj* bourguignon. **2** *n* Bourguignon, -onne.

Burgundy ['bɜ:gəndɪ] *n* **(a)** *Geog* Bourgogne *f*; **(b)** (*wine*) bourgogne *m*, vin *m* de Bourgogne; **(c)** (*colour*) bordeaux *m*.

burial ['berɪəl] *n* enterrement *m*, inhumation *f*; **b. ground,** cimetière *m*; **b. mound,** tumulus *m*; **b. place,** (lieu *m* de) sépulture *f*; (*for radioactive substances*) dépôt souterrain; **b. service,** office *m* des morts.

burin ['bjʊərɪn] *n* (*for engraving*) burin *m*.

burk [bɜ:k] *n Br Sl* **you (great) b.!,** espèce d'idiot!

burlap ['bɜ:læp] *n* toile *f* d'emballage.

burlesque¹ [bɜ:'lesk] **1** *adj* burlesque. **2** *n* **(a)** (*satire*) burlesque *m*; (*caricature*) parodie *f*; **(b)** *US* revue *f* vulgaire, striptease *m*.

burlesque² *vt* parodier (*qn, qch*), tourner (*qn, qch*) en ridicule.

burliness ['bɜ:lɪnɪs] *n* **(a)** (*build*) forte carrure; **(b)** *Am* (*brusqueness*) brusquerie *f*.

burly ['bɜ:lɪ] *adj* **(a)** (*well built*) solidement bâti, robuste, de forte carrure; **(b)** *Am* (*brusque*) brusque, bourru.

Burma ['bɜ:mə] *n* Birmanie *f*.

Burmese [bɜ:'mi:z] **1** *adj* birman; **B. cat,** chat birman ganté. **2** *n* **(a)** Birman, -ane; **(b)** *Ling* birman *m*.

burn¹ [bɜ:n] *n* **(a)** *Med etc* brûlure *f*; **the child suffered severe burns,** l'enfant a subi de graves brûlures; **(b)** *Astronaut* allumage *m*; poussée *f* (*d'une fusée*).

burn² *v* (*pt & pp* **burnt** [bɜ:nt], *occ* **burned**) **1** *vt* **(a)** brûler (*qch, qn*); **to b. coal/oil/gas,** (*of boiler*) chauffer au charbon/au mazout/au gaz; *Fig* **to b. one's boats** *or* **one's bridges,** brûler ses vaisseaux; **to b. the candle at both ends,** brûler la chandelle par les deux bouts; **to b. the midnight oil,** travailler *ou* veiller fort avant dans la nuit; **to b. sth to ashes,** réduire qch en cendres; *Old-fashioned F* **to be burnt,** (*of police informer*) être brûlé; **to be burnt alive, to be burnt to death,** être brûlé vif; **the house was burned to the ground,** la maison a été complètement brûlée; **to b. one's fingers,** se brûler les doigts; *Fig* **he got his fingers burnt, he burnt his fingers over it,** il s'est fait échauder (dans cette affaire); **to b. a hole in sth with a cigarette/the iron,** faire un trou dans qch avec une cigarette/le fer à repasser; *Fig* **money burns a hole in his pocket,** l'argent lui brûle les doigts; **to have money to b.,** avoir de l'argent à n'en savoir que faire; **acids b. into metal,** les acides rongent le métal; **mustard burns the tongue,** la moutarde brûle la langue; **I burned my tongue,** je me suis brûlé la langue;

(b) *Ind* cuire (*des briques, du charbon de bois*); vulcaniser, cuire (*le caoutchouc*);

(c) *Culin* brûler (*le rôti, une casserole*).

2 *vi* **(a)** brûler; (*of house etc*) être en feu; (*of wound, eyes*) cuire; **to make the fire b.,** faire flamber *ou* faire marcher le feu; **to b. low,** (*of fire*) baisser; **a candle burning in the window,** une bougie qui brûle à la fenêtre; **his cheeks were burning with shame,** il avait les joues rouges de honte; **to b. with impatience,** griller d'impatience; *F* **her ears must have been burning,** les oreilles ont dû lui tinter, elle a dû avoir les oreilles qui sifflent; **magnesium burns white,** le magnésium brûle avec une flamme blanche;

(b) (*of mixture in engine*) exploser;

(c) *Culin* (*of meat, toast etc*) brûler; (*of sauce, milk etc*) attacher.

burn³ *n Scot* ruisseau *m*.

►**burn down 1** *vtsep* brûler, incendier (*une ville etc*); détruire (*une maison*) par le feu. **2** *vi* **(a)** (*of building etc*) être détruit par le feu *ou* par un incendie; **(b)** (*of fire*) baisser; **the fire had burned down,** le feu était bas.

►**burn in** *vtsep Comptr* roder.

►**burn off** *vtsep* brûler (*la peinture, les broussailles etc*); décaper (*la peinture*) à la lampe à brûler; enlever (*de la rouille etc*) au feu.

►**burn out 1** *vtsep Aut etc* brûler (*la garniture des freins*); *El* brûler, court-circuiter (*une bobine*); griller (*une lampe*); **the building was burnt out,** le feu a complètement détruit l'intérieur de la maison; **to b. itself out,** (*of fire*) s'éteindre; **to b. oneself out,** se ruiner la santé, s'épuiser (par excès de travail). **2** *vi* (*of fire, oil, lamp, candle etc*) s'éteindre; (*of candle*) brûler jusqu'au bout; (*of electric lamp*) claquer, griller; *Fig* **social workers b. out at an early age,** les travailleurs sociaux s'épuisent très tôt.

►**burn up 1** *vtsep* **(a)** (*consume*) brûler (entièrement), consumer; **to b. up energy,** brûler *ou* consommer de l'énergie; **(b)** (*of sun*) griller, flétrir (*les feuilles etc*); *F* (*make angry*) foutre (*qn*) en pétard. **2** *vi* **(a)** *F* (*get angry*) s'enflammer de colère, s'emporter; **(b)** (*of rocket*) brûler, se consumer; (*of person with high temperature*) être brûlant.

burner ['bɜ:nər] *n* (*on stove*) brûleur *m*, feu *m*; bec *m* (*de gaz, pour acétylène etc*); brûleur (*à gaz*).

burn-in ['bɜ:nɪn] *n Comptr* (*of machine*) rodage *m*.

burning ['bɜ:nɪŋ] **1** *adj* (*fever, thirst, desire etc*) brûlant, ardent; (*charbon*) embrasé, allumé, ardent; (*ville, maison*) incendié, enflammé, en feu; (*chaleur*) brûlant, torride; **b. question,** question brûlante; **b. sun,** soleil ardent *ou* brûlant; *F* **I'm b. (hot),** je brûle de chaleur; **b. bush,** *Bible* buisson ardent; (*shrub*) fraxinelle *f*. **2** *n* **(a)** incendie *m* (*d'une maison etc*); *Ch etc* combustion *f*; *Hist* **b. (at the stake),** supplice *m* du bûcher; **there's a smell of b.,** cela sent le brûlé; **b. sensation,** (*heat*) sensation de chaleur (excessive); (*discomfort*) sensation de brûlure; (*pain*) douleur cuisante; **(b)** *Culin* coup *m* de feu; *Metal* brûlure *f* (*de l'acier*); **(c)** cuisson *f* (*de briques, de tuiles etc*); (*batch*) fournée *f* (*de briques etc*).

burnish¹ ['bɜ:nɪʃ] *n* (*on metal*) bruni *m*; (*on furniture*) poli *m*, brillant *m*.

burnish² **1** *vt* brunir (*un métal*); polir, lisser (*un meuble*); *Phot* satiner (*une épreuve*). **2** *vi* se polir, prendre de l'éclat.

burnisher ['bɜ:nɪʃər] *n* **(a)** (*person*) brunisseur, -euse; **(b)** (*instrument*) brunissoir *m*, polissoir *m*.

burnishing ['bɜ:nɪʃɪŋ] *n* brunissage *m*, polissage *m*, lissage *m*.

burnous(e) [bɜːˈnuːs] *n* burnous *m* (*d'Arabe*).

burnt [bɜːnt] *adj* **(a)** (*person, thing*) brûlé; (*odeur, goût*) de brûlé, de roussi; **to be b. beyond recognition,** être carbonisé; *Prov* **a b. child dreads** *or* **fears the fire,** chat échaudé craint l'eau froide; *Culin* **b. almonds,** amandes grillées; **b. sugar,** caramel *m*; **(b)** (*earth, clay*) cuit; **(c) b. out,** (*volcan*) éteint; (*maison, voiture etc*) réduit à l'état de carcasse par le feu; (*tube*) brûlé; (*roulement*) grippé; *El* (*bobine, ampoule*) grillé; *Fig* **b.-out case,** homme *ou* femme qui a épuisé son talent.

burp¹ [bɜːp] *n* éructation *f*, *F* rot *m*.

burp² **1** *vi* éructer, *F* roter. **2** *vt* faire roter (*un bébé*).

burr¹ [bɜːr] *n* **(a)** *Bot* teigne *f* (*de bardane*); **to stick to s.o. like a b.,** se cramponner *ou* s'accrocher à qn; **(b)** (*on tree*) broussin *m*; **b. walnut,** (plaqué *m* en) ronce *f* de noyer; **(c)** (*on metal*) bavure *f*, barbe *f*; **to take the burrs off metal,** ébarber le métal; **(d)** (*file*) fraise *f*.

burr² *n* **(a)** *Ling* r *m* de la gorge; **to speak with a b.,** grasseyer; **(b)** ronflement *m* (*d'une machine*).

burr³ **1** *vt* **to b. one's r's,** prononcer l'r de la gorge, grasseyer. **2** *vi* (*of machine etc*) ronfler.

burro [ˈbʊrəʊ] *n US* âne *m*.

burrow¹ [ˈbʌrəʊ] *n* terrier *m*; renardière *f* (*de renard*); clapier *m* (*de lapin*).

burrow² **1** *vi* (*of rabbits etc*) (*dig*) fouir la terre; (*go to ground*) (se) terrer; (*of moles*) tracer; *Fig* **to b. into the archives,** fouiller *ou* fouiner dans les archives; **to b. in one's pocket/bag,** fourrager dans sa poche/son sac. **2** *vt* creuser, pratiquer (*un trou, un terrier*); **to b. one's way underground,** creuser (un chemin) sous terre; **to b. one's head into s.o.'s shoulder,** enfouir sa tête dans l'épaule de qn; **to b. the ground,** (*of rabbits*) percer la terre.

burrowing [ˈbʌrəʊɪŋ] *adj* (*animal*) fouisseur; (*insecte*) fossoyeur, mineur.

bursar [ˈbɜːsər] *n Sch* **(a)** (*official in charge of finance*) économe *mf*, intendant, -ante; **(b)** *esp Scot* (*student*) boursier, -ière.

bursary [ˈbɜːsərɪ] *n* **(a)** (*office*) économat *m*, intendance *f*; **(b)** *esp Scot* bourse *f* (d'études); **b. student,** boursier, -ière.

bursitis [bɜːˈsaɪtɪs] *n Med* bursite *f*; **I have b. in my shoulder,** j'ai une bursite à l'épaule.

burst¹ [bɜːst] *n* **(a)** éclatement *m*, explosion *f* (*d'une bombe, d'une chaudière etc*); **(b)** jaillissement *m*, jet *m* (*de flamme*); coup *m* (*de tonnerre*); (*of gunfire*) rafale *f*; (*of machine gun*) giclée *f*; éclat *m* (*de rire etc*); explosion *f* (*de colère*); élan *m* (*d'éloquence*); salve *f* (*d'applaudissements*); poussée *f* (*d'activité*); accès *m* (*d'enthousiasme*); *Sp* **b. of speed,** emballement *m*; **to put on a b. of speed,** s'emballer; **final b.,** finish *m*.

burst² *v* (*pt & pp* **burst**) **1** *vi* (*of boiler, bomb etc*) éclater, exploser, faire explosion; (*of boiler*) sauter; (*of abscess*) crever, percer; (*of bubble, cloud*) crever; (*of bud*) éclore; (*of storm*) éclater; *Hum* **he'll b. if he eats any more,** il va éclater s'il mange davantage; **we've got a burst pipe,** (*in house*) nous avons un tuyau qui a éclaté; **to b. in pieces,** voler en éclats; **her heart was ready to b.,** son cœur se brisait; **to be bursting at the seams,** (*of dress etc*) se découdre; *Fig* (*of building etc*) être plein à éclater; **to be bursting with pride,** crever d'orgueil; **to be bursting with health,** déborder de santé; **to be bursting with impatience,** bouillir d'impatience; **I was bursting to tell him so,** je mourais d'envie de le lui dire; **a cry burst from his lips,** un cri s'échappa de ses lèvres; **to b. upon s.o.'s sight,** se présenter aux yeux de qn; **to b. upon s.o.'s ears,** (*of sound*) venir (subitement) frapper les oreilles de qn; **the truth burst upon me,** soudain la vérité m'apparut.

2 *vt* faire éclater (*qch*); crever, éclater (*un ballon, un pneu*); faire sauter (*une chaudière*); rompre (*ses liens*); **to b. a blood vessel,** se rompre un vaisseau sanguin; *Fig* prendre un coup de sang; **to b. its banks,** (*of river*) crever *ou* rompre ses berges.

▶**burst in** **1** *vtsep* enfoncer (*une porte*). **2** *vi* faire irruption; (*of person*) entrer en trombe *ou* en coup de vent; **to b. in on s.o.,** faire irruption (chez qn); **to b. in on a conversation,** interrompre brusquement une conversation.

▶**burst into** *vipo* **(a)** (*enter noisily*) entrer dans (*une pièce*) en coup de vent *ou* en trombe; **(b)** (*suddenly start*) se mettre à (*faire qch*) tout d'un coup; **to b. into flame(s),** s'enflammer brusquement; **to b. into song,** entonner une chanson; **to b. into blossom,** (*of tree*) commencer à fleurir; **to b. into laughter/tears,** éclater de rire/fondre en larmes.

▶**burst open** **1** *vtsep* ouvrir (*une porte*) subitement; (*of police etc*) enfoncer, briser (*une porte etc*); faire sauter (*le couvercle, la serrure*). **2** *vi* (*of door etc*) s'ouvrir tout d'un coup.

▶**burst out** *vi* **(a)** (*suddenly say*) s'écrier; **to b. out laughing/crying,** éclater de rire/fondre en larmes; **(b)** (*leave noisily*) quitter (*une pièce*) en coup de vent ou en trombe.

▶**burst through** *vipo* enfoncer (*un cordon de police*); **to come bursting through a door,** enfoncer une porte; **to b. through a cloud,** (*of sun*) percer un nuage.

bursting [ˈbɜːstɪŋ] **1** *adj* (*boiler, bomb*) sur le point d'éclater; (*abscess*) sur le point de crever. **2** *n* éclatement *m*, explosion *f* (*d'une bombe etc*); crevaison *f* (*d'un pneu*); rupture *f* (*de barrage*).

burton [ˈbɜːt(ə)n] *n Br Sl* **to have gone for a b.,** (*be dead*) être mort; (*be missing*) être manquant; (*of hopes*) être tombé à l'eau; *Av* avoir fait un trou dans l'eau; (*of plate etc*) être cassé; (*of iron, television etc*) être foutu; (*of ball etc*) être perdu pour de bon.

bury [ˈberɪ] *vt* (*pt & pp* **buried**) **(a)** enterrer, inhumer, ensevelir (*un mort*); (*at sea*) immerger (*un mort*); enterrer, enfouir (*qch, un animal*); **to b. s.o. alive,** enterrer qn vif;

(b) (*of snow, earthquake*) ensevelir (*une ville, une maison*); **buried treasure,** trésor enterré *ou* enfoui; *El* **buried cable,** câble souterrain; **I found the letter buried under my papers,** j'ai trouvé la lettre enfouie sous mes papiers; *F* **to b. the hatchet,** enterrer la hache de guerre; **to b. itself,** (*of animal*) se terrer, s'enfouir; **to b. oneself in the country,** s'enterrer à la campagne; **to b. oneself in one's work,** se plonger *ou* s'enfoncer *ou* s'absorber dans son travail; **to b. one's face in one's hands,** se cacher la figure dans les mains; **to b. one's hands in one's pockets,** fourrer les *ou* ses mains dans ses poches; *Fig* **to b. one's head in the sand,** se cacher la tête dans le sable, pratiquer la politique de l'autruche; **she always has her head buried in a book,** elle est toujours plongée dans un livre.

burying [ˈberɪɪŋ] **1** *adj* (*insecte*) enfouisseur; **b. beetle,** nécrophore *m*. **2** *n* enterrement *m*, ensevelissement *m*; **b. ground,** cimetière *m*.

bus¹, *pl* **buses,** *US* **busses** [bʌs, ˈbʌsɪz] *n* **(a)** bus *m*, autobus *m*; (*on country services*) car *m*; **to go by b.,** aller en bus; **to miss the b.,** manquer *ou* rater le bus; *Fig F* manquer le coche; *F* **old b.,** (*car*) vieille bagnole; (*aircraft*) coucou *m*; **b. lane,** (*in town*) couloir *m ou* voie *f* d'autobus; **b. shelter,** abribus *m*; **b. station,** gare routière; **b. route/stop,** trajet *m*/arrêt *m* de bus; *esp US* **b. boy,** (*in restaurant*) aide-serveur *m*, *pl* aides-serveurs; **(b)** *Electron* bus *m*.

bus² **1** *vi* voyager en autobus. **2** *vt* transporter (*qn, qch*) par autobus *ou* en car; **the children are bus(s)ed to school,** les enfants sont emmenés à l'école par autobus; **are you bus(s)ing it?,** tu y vas en autobus?

busbar [ˈbʌzbɑːr] *n Electron* bus *m*.

busby [ˈbʌzbɪ] *n Mil* bonnet *m* de hussard.

bush¹ [bʊʃ] *n* **(a)** buisson *m*; (*of lilac etc*) arbrisseau *m*; (*small*) arbuste *m*; **rose b.,** rosier *m*; **red-currant b.,** groseillier *m*; **(b)** (*clump of bushes*) fourré *m*, taillis *m*; **(c)** queue *f* (*du renard*); **(d)** (*in Africa, Austr*) **the b.,** la brousse; **to take to the b.,** *Austr* **to go b.,** prendre la brousse; **b. hat,** chapeau *m* de brousse; *Av* **b. pilot,** pilote *m* de ligne opérant sur une région peu habitée *ou* sur la brousse *ou Can* sur le Grand Nord; **b. shirt, b. jacket,** = saharienne *f*; *F* **b. telegraph,** téléphone *m* arabe.

bush² *n esp Am MecE* bague *f*; (*between bearing and shaft*) coussinet *m*.

bush³ *vt MecE* baguer, manchonner; mettre un coussinet à (*un palier etc*).

bushbaby [ˈbʊʃbeɪbɪ] *n* (*animal*) galago *m*.

bushbuck [ˈbʊʃbʌk] *n* (*animal*) guib *m*.

bushed [bʊʃt] *adj* **(a)** *F* (*exhausted*) fatigué, éreinté; **(b)** *Can* désorienté; **(c)** *Austr* perdu *ou* égaré dans la brousse; *Fig* désorienté.

bushel [ˈbʊʃəl] *n* **(a)** (*unit of measurement*) boisseau *m* (= *approx* 36 litres); *Fig* **to hide one's light under a b.,** cacher son talent; **(b)** *US F* grande quantité.

bushfire [ˈbʊʃfaɪər] *n* feu *m* de brousse.

bushing¹ [ˈbʊʃɪŋ] *n esp Am MecE* bague *f*; (*between bearing and shaft*) coussinet *m*.

bushing² *n* **(a)** (*action*) manchonnage *m*; **(b)** (*device*) manchon *m*, coussinet *m* métallique.

bushman, *pl* **-men** [ˈbʊʃmən] *n* **(a)** colon *m* (*de la brousse australienne*); **(b)** personne qui connaît la brousse; (*lives in bush*) broussard *m*.

Bushman [ˈbʊʃmən] **1** *adj* boschiman. **2** *n* **(a)** Boschiman,

-ane; **(b)** *Ling* boschiman *m*.

bushw(h)acker ['bʊʃwækər] *n esp Am* **(a)** colon *m ou* habitant, -ante de la brousse; **(b)** *(bandit)* bandit *m* (de la brousse).

bushy ['bʊʃɪ] *adj* **(a)** *(country)* buissonneux, broussailleux; *(eyebrows)* broussailleux; *(beard)* fourni; *(hair)* épais, touffu, embroussaillé; **(b)** *(shrub)* buissonnant.

busily ['bɪzɪlɪ] *adv* *(to prepare)* activement; *(to search)* d'un air affairé.

business ['bɪznɪs] *n* **(a)** *(affair)* affaire *f*; **to have b. with s.o.,** avoir affaire avec qn; **what's your b. (with him)?,** que (lui) voulez-vous?; **it is/it is not my b. to ...,** c'est/ce n'est pas à moi de ...; **it's not your b., it's none of your b.,** ce n'est pas votre affaire, cela ne vous regarde pas; **you have no b. (being) in here,** vous n'avez rien à faire ici; **you had no b. telling her,** ce n'était pas à toi de le lui dire; **mind your own b.,** occupez-vous de ce qui vous regarde; **to make it one's b. to do sth,** prendre sur soi de faire qch; **to go about one's b.,** vaquer à ses affaires; *esp Fml* **I sent him about his b.,** *(dismissed him)* je l'ai envoyé promener; **let's get down to b.!,** maintenant, allons-y!; **can we get down to b.?,** est-ce qu'on peut commencer?, est-ce qu'on peut se mettre au travail?; **we got through a lot of b.,** nous avons abattu de la besogne; **to mean b.,** être sérieux; **the b. before a meeting,** l'ordre *m* du jour; **it's a bad** *or* **sad** *or* **sorry b.,** c'est une malheureuse *ou* triste affaire; **I'm sick of the whole b.,** j'en ai assez de toute cette affaire; **she can ride a bike like nobody's b.,** *(does it very well)* elle fait du vélo mieux que personne; **they're working like nobody's b.,** *(very hard)* ils travaillent plus que quiconque; *Euph* **has the dog done its b.?,** est-ce que le chien a fait ses besoins?;

(b) *(trade)* métier *m*; *(commerce)* commerce *m*; *(dealings)* les affaires *fpl*; *(company, firm)* entreprise *f*; **to carry on a b.,** exercer un métier *ou* un commerce; **to go into** *or* **to set up in b. as a grocer,** s'établir épicier; **to be in/go into b. on one's own** *or* **for oneself,** être/s'établir *ou* s'installer à son compte; **what's his line of b.?, what b. is he in?,** qu'est-ce qu'il fait (comme métier)?; **she's in b.,** elle est dans les affaires; *Fig* **now we're in b.,** maintenant nous pouvons y aller; **I'm not in the b. of solving your problems,** ce n'est pas à moi de résoudre tes problèmes; **to go out of b.,** *(of firm)* faire faillite; **to go to London on b.,** aller à Londres pour affaires; **I'm here on b.,** je suis ici pour affaires; **a profitable piece of b.,** une affaire profitable; **to lose b.,** perdre de la clientèle; **to do b. with s.o.,** faire des affaires avec qn; **shop with a thriving b.,** commerce qui marche bien; **it's good/bad for b.,** c'est bon/mauvais pour les affaires; **how's b.?,** comment vont les affaires?; **b. is b.,** les affaires sont les affaires; **b. is slow,** les affaires ne vont pas; **she has a good head for b.,** elle a le sens des affaires; **to talk b.,** parler affaires; **the tourist trade is big b. today,** le tourisme est une affaire de grande importance aujourd'hui; **looking for b.?,** *(said by prostitute)* tu viens, chéri?; **he is the owner of a small b.,** *(factory)* il est propriétaire d'une petite entreprise; *(shop)* il est propriétaire d'un petit commerce; **he worked up a small firm into a big b.,** à partir d'une petite maison il a créé une grosse entreprise; **b. administration,** gestion commerciale; **b. card,** carte *f* (de visite); **b. career,** carrière *f* d'affaires; **b. class,** *(in aircraft)* classe *f* affaires; **to travel b. class,** voyager en classe affaires; *esp Am* **b. cycle,** cycle *m* économique; *F* **b. end,** *(of knife, hatchet etc)* côté *ou* extrémité coupante *ou* tranchante; **b. hours,** heures *fpl* de bureau *ou* de travail *ou* d'ouverture; **b. lunch/trip,** déjeuner *m*/voyage *m* d'affaires; **b. manager,** directeur commercial; *Journ Rad TV* **b. news,** chronique *f* économique; **b. park,** parc commercial; **b. reply envelope,** enveloppe *f* T; **b. school,** école *f* de commerce; **b. studies,** études commerciales; *Comptr* **b. systems,** logiciels *mpl* de bureautique; **b. traveller,** personne qui voyage pour affaires;

(c) *Th* jeux *mpl* de scène.

businesslike ['bɪznɪslaɪk] *adj* *(person)* sérieux; *(attitude, appearance)* professionnel; *(manner)* sérieux, avisé; *(transaction)* régulier, sérieux; *(thing)* pratique; *(style)* net, précis.

businessman, *pl* **-men** ['bɪznɪsmæn, -men] *n* homme *m* d'affaires; *(shopkeeper)* commerçant *m*; **big b.,** homme d'affaires important.

businesswoman, *pl* **-women** ['bɪznɪswʊmən, -wɪmɪn] *n* femme *f* d'affaires; *(shopkeeper)* commerçante *f*; **she's a good b.,** elle s'entend aux affaires.

busing ['bʌsɪŋ] *n* = **BUSSING.**

busk [bʌsk] *vi esp Br* chanter *ou* jouer d'un instrument dans les rues.

busker ['bʌskər] *n esp Br* musicien ambulant *ou* des rues.

busman, *pl* **-men** ['bʌsmən] *n F* **to take a b.'s holiday,** faire la même chose pendant ses loisirs que pendant son travail; **that's a bit of a b.'s holiday,** vous appelez ça des vacances!

bussing ['bʌsɪŋ] *n* *(of schoolchildren etc)* transport *m* par autobus.

bust¹ [bʌst] *n* **(a)** poitrine *f* *(de femme)*; **she's got a big b.,** elle a une grosse poitrine; **what b. are you?,** combien est-ce que vous faites de tour de poitrine?; **what b. is this dress?,** combien cette robe fait-elle de tour de poitrine?; **it's too tight round the b.,** c'est trop serré à la poitrine; **(b)** *(by sculptor)* buste *m*.

bust² *adj F* *(cup, plate)* cassé; *(balloon etc)* crevé; *(iron, radio)* foutu; **to go b.,** *(of company)* faire faillite; *(of individual)* perdre tout son argent.

bust³ *F* **1** *vi* (se) casser, *(of ballon)* (se) crever. **2** *vt* **(a)** casser *(qch)*; crever *(un ballon etc)*; *Am* **to b. s.o.'s nose,** donner un coup de poing à qn sur le nez; *Am Vulg* **to b. one's ass doing sth,** se crever le cul à faire qch; **(b)** arrêter *(un voleur etc)*; écraser *(une bande de trafiquants etc)*; **he was busted for armed robbery,** il s'est fait choper pour vol à main armée; **you're busted,** tu es fait; **(c)** *Am esp Mil* *(reduce in rank)* rétrograder *(qn)*; **he's been busted to private again,** il a été rétrogradé au rang de simple soldat encore une fois; **(d)** *Am* dresser *(des chevaux sauvages)*.

bust⁴ *n F* *(by police)* *(of thief etc)* arrestation *f*; *(raid)* rafle *f*; *(search)* perquisition *f*.

►**bust up** *vtsep F* **(a)** rompre, briser *(un mariage, une amitié etc)*; **to b. up a meeting,** interrompre une réunion; **(b)** *(damage, destroy)* saccager *(un bar, un appartement)*.

bustard ['bʌstəd] *n* *(bird)* outarde *f*.

buster ['bʌstər] *n Am F* *(child)* (petit) garçon *m*; *(man)* homme *m*, type *m*; **hi, b.!,** *(as address) Sl* alors, mon pote!

bustle¹ ['bʌs(ə)l] *n* mouvement *m*, remue-ménage *m*; **the b. in the streets,** l'animation *f* des rues.

bustle² **1** *vi* **to b. (about),** s'activer, s'affairer; **the streets are bustling with people,** les rues grouillent de monde. **2** *vt* faire dépêcher *(qn)*; **to b. s.o. out of the house,** pousser qn dehors.

bustle³ *n* tournure *f* *(de derrière de jupe)*.

bustling ['bʌs(ə)lɪŋ] *adj* *(person)* affairé; *(street)* animé.

bust-up ['bʌstʌp] *n F* **(a)** *(in business)* faillite *f*; destruction *f* *(d'un mariage)*; **(b)** *(quarrel)* brouille *f*; **to have a b.-up,** se brouiller; **(c)** *(brawl)* bagarre *f*.

busty ['bʌstɪ] *adj F* *(femme)* à la poitrine plantureuse.

busy¹ ['bɪzɪ] *adj* **(busier, busiest) (a)** *(with work)* occupé, affairé; *(with hobbies etc)* actif; **not now — I'm b.,** pas maintenant — je suis occupé; **my work keeps me b. all the morning,** mon travail m'occupe toute la matinée; **to keep (oneself) b.,** s'occuper; **to be b. with sth,** être occupé à *ou* de qch; **to be b. doing sth,** être occupé à faire qch; **to get b.,** se mettre à la tâche *ou* au travail; *F* **get b.!,** grouille-toi!; *F* **b. Lizzie,** *(plant)* impatiente *f*, impatiens *f* balsamine;

(b) *(jour etc)* chargé; *(route)* à grande circulation; *Rail* *(ligne)* à grand trafic; **I've had a b. day,** j'ai eu une journée occupée; **b. street,** *(full of people)* rue mouvementée *ou* animée *ou* passante; *(full of shoppers)* rue très affairée *ou* très commerçante; **the hotel industry is at its busiest in August,** l'industrie hôtelière est au plus haut de son activité au mois d'août; **we're not b. at the moment,** *(of business etc)* nous travaillons au ralenti en ce moment; **this is a b. time of year for us,** *(of business etc)* nous travaillons beaucoup à cette période de l'année;

(c) *esp Am Tel* occupé; **the line is b.,** la ligne est occupée; **b. signal** *or* **tone,** tonalité *f* indiquant que la ligne est occupée; **I keep getting the b. signal,** ça sonne toujours occupé.

busy² *vt* **to b. oneself with sth,** s'occuper à *ou* de qch; **to b. oneself (with) doing sth,** s'occuper à *ou* de faire qch.

busybody ['bɪzɪbɒdɪ] *n* **he's an awful b.,** il se mêle des affaires de tout le monde.

but [bʌt] **1** *conj* **(a)** *(coordinating)* mais; **he is small b. strong,** il est petit mais fort; **b. I tell you I saw it!,** (mais) puisque je vous dis que je l'ai vu!; **he can't do anything b. shout,** il ne peut rien faire d'autre que de crier;

(b) *(subordinating)* **I can't go out for a minute b. something happens,** je ne peux pas sortir une minute sans qu'il se passe quelque chose; *Arch & Lit* **I cannot b. believe that ...,** il m'est impossible de ne pas croire que ...; **it never rains b. it pours,** un malheur ne vient jamais seul; **what could I do b. invite him?,** que pouvais-je faire d'autre que de l'inviter?;

(c) *(intensive)* **not merely once, b. twice,** pas une fois, mais deux; **nobody, b. nobody,** personne, mais absolument personne.

2 *adv* *(only)* seulement, ne ... que; *esp Lit* **he's b. a boy,** ce n'est qu'un garçon; **had I b. known!,** si j'avais su!; **one can b. try,** on peut toujours essayer; **it seems b. yesterday,** cela ne semble pas plus tard qu'hier; **if I could b. see him!,** si je pouvais seulement le voir!

3 *prep* **(a)** *(except)* **any day b. tomorrow,** n'importe quel jour excepté *ou* sauf demain; **all b. he** *or* **him,** tous excepté *ou* sauf lui; **none b. he,** personne d'autre que lui; **anyone b. me,** tout autre que moi; **nobody b. me knew about it,** personne d'autre que moi n'était au courant; **anything b. that,** n'importe quoi plutôt que cela; **he is anything b. a hero,** il est loin d'être un héros; **it's nothing b. laziness,** ce n'est que de la paresse; **there is nothing for it b. to obey,** il n'y a qu'à obéir; **he is anything b. happy,** il n'est pas du tout heureux;

(b) the last b. one, l'avant-dernier; **the next house b. one,** la deuxième maison (à partir d'ici);

(c) b. for, sans; **b. for the rain I should have gone out,** sans la pluie je serais sorti; **he wouldn't have left b. for me,** *(it was my fault)* il ne serait pas parti si je n'avais pas été là; *(it was for my sake)* il ne serait pas parti si ça n'avait pas été pour moi; **b. for you I would have been killed,** si vous n'aviez pas été là, j'aurais été tué.

4 *n* **there is a b.,** il y a un mais; **I don't want any buts,** je ne veux pas de mais.

butane ['bju:teɪn] *n Ch* butane *m*.

butch [bʊtʃ] *F* **1** *adj* *(man, woman)* très masculin; **to be b.,** *(of woman)* être lesbienne. **2** *n* **(a)** lesbienne *f*, gouine *f* (d'apparence masculine); **(b)** *(man)* costaud *m*, dur *m*.

butcher¹ ['bʊtʃər] *n* **(a)** boucher, -ère; **to go to the b.'s,** aller chez le boucher; **b.'s block,** billot *m* de boucher; **b.'s boy,** garçon boucher; **b.'s shop** *or* **trade,** boucherie *f*; **(b)** *Pej* boucher *m*, massacreur *m*; **(c)** *F* *(surgeon)* boucher *m*, charcutier *m*.

butcher² *vt* **(a)** abattre *(un animal)*; *US* dépecer *(une bête)*; **(b)** *Pej* massacrer, égorger *(qn)*; **he butchered that song,** il a massacré cette chanson; **(c)** *F* *(of surgeon)* charcuter *(un patient)*.

butchery ['bʊtʃərɪ] *n* **(a)** *(trade)* boucherie *f*; **(b)** *Pej* *(bloodshed)* boucherie *f*, massacre *m*.

butler ['bʌtlər] *n* maître *m* d'hôtel *(d'une maison privée)*; **b.'s pantry,** office *f*.

butt¹ [bʌt] *n* **(a)** *(cask)* barrique *f*, futaille *f*; **(b)** tonneau *m* *(pour l'eau de pluie etc)*.

butt² *n* **(a)** souche *f* *(d'arbre etc)*; billot *m* *(d'arbre)*; mégot *m* *(de cigare etc)*; **(b)** *Am F* *(of person)* derrière *m*; **get off your b. and do something!,** remue-toi le cul et fais quelque chose!; **(c) b. (end),** gros bout, talon *m*, pommeau *m*; gros brin *(d'une canne à pêche)*; **(d)** *Billiards* masse *f*, talon *m* *(de la queue)*; **(e) b. (end),** crosse *f* *(de fusil)*; **(f)** *Carp* **b. (end),** about *m*; **b. joint,** joint *m* bout à bout; **b. hinge,** charnière *f*; *Metal* **b. welding,** soudure *f* bout à bout.

butt³ **1** *vt* **(a)** *Carp etc* (r)abouter, rabouter *(deux pièces)*; **(b)** étayer, buter *(une poutre etc)* **(against,** contre**)**. **2** *vi* *(of prop etc)* s'étayer, buter **(against,** contre**)**.

butt⁴ *n* **(a)** *Mil* butte *f* *(de tir)*; **the butts,** le champ de tir; **(b)** *(target)* but *m*; *(of joke)* souffre-douleur *m inv*.

butt⁵ *n* coup *m* de (la) tête; coup de corne *(d'un bélier etc)*; **head b.,** *(in wrestling)* coup de tête.

butt⁶ *vt* donner contre *(qn, qch)* de la tête; *(of ram)* donner un coup de corne à *(qn)*.

►**butt against** *vipo* donner du front *ou* buter contre *(qn, qch)*.

►**butt in** *vi* intervenir sans façon dans la conversation.

►**butt into** *vipo* **to b. into the conversation,** intervenir sans façon dans la conversation.

butter¹ ['bʌtər] *n* **(a)** beurre *m*; **unsalted b.,** beurre doux; **salt(ed) b.,** beurre salé; **dairy b.,** beurre laitier; *Culin* **melted b.,** beurre fondu; *Fig* **b. wouldn't melt in her mouth,** elle fait la sainte nitouche, on lui donnerait le bon Dieu sans confession; **b. bean,** haricot blanc; **b. dish,** beurrier *m*; **b. knife,** couteau *m* à beurre; **(b) cocoa/peanut b.,** beurre *m* de cacao/cacahuètes.

butter² *vt* **(a)** beurrer *(du pain)*; **(b)** *Culin* accommoder *(des légumes etc)* au beurre.

►**butter up** *vtsep F* passer la pommade à *(qn)*.

butterball ['bʌtəbɔ:l] *n US F* personne boulotte.

buttercup ['bʌtəkʌp] *n* *(flower)* renoncule *f* des champs; *F* bouton *m* d'or, bassinet *m* des champs.

butterfat ['bʌtəfæt] *n* matière grasse *(du lait)*.

butterfingered ['bʌtəfɪŋgəd] *adj F* maladroit, empoté; **he's b.,** tout lui glisse des mains *ou* des doigts.

butterfingers ['bʌtəfɪŋgəz] *n F* maladroit, -e, empoté, -ée.

butterfly ['bʌtəflaɪ] *n* *(insect)* papillon *m* (diurne); *Fig* personne frivole, papillon; *F* **to have butterflies (in one's stomach),** avoir l'estomac noué, avoir le trac; **b. bow,** nœud *m* papillon; **b. net,** filet *m* à papillons; *Tech* **b. nut,** écrou *m* à oreilles *ou* à ailettes, écrou ailé, (écrou) papillon; **b. valve,** (soupape *f* à) papillon; vanne *f*; *Swimming* **b. (stroke),** (nage *f*, brasse *f*) papillon.

buttermilk ['bʌtəmɪlk] *n* babeurre *m*.

butterscotch ['bʌtəskɒtʃ] *n* caramel *m* (dur) au beurre.

buttery¹ ['bʌtərɪ] *n* **(a)** dépense *f*, office *f* *(surtout dans les universités anglaises)*; **b. hatch,** passe-plats *m inv*; **(b)** buffet *m* *(où l'on sert des repas légers)*.

buttery² *adj* **(a)** de beurre; **(b)** *(like butter)* butyreux.

butting ['bʌtɪŋ] *n* coups *mpl* de tête *ou* de cornes.

buttock ['bʌtək] *n* fesse *f*; **the buttocks,** le derrière, les fesses; **cross b.,** *(in wrestling)* ceinture *f* arrière *ou* à rebours, tour *m* de hanche.

button¹ ['bʌtən] *n* **(a)** *(on dress etc)* bouton *m*; **as bright as a b.,** brillant comme un sou neuf; *(child)* vif, éveillé; *Am* **she's as cute as a b.,** elle est trognon; **b. nose,** petit nez; **buttons,** groom *m*; **(b)** bouton *m*, pressoir *m* *(de sonnerie électrique etc)*; poussoir *m* *(d'une montre à répétition)*; bouton *(de fleuret, de queue de violon)*; mouche *f* *(de fleuret)*; taquet *m* *(d'aviron)*; **chocolate buttons,** *(sweets)* pastilles *fpl* de chocolat; **b. rose,** bouton de rose; **b. mushroom,** champignon *m* de couche; **(c)** *Am* *(badge)* badge *m*.

button² **1** *vt* **(a)** boutonner *(qch)*; *F* **b. your lip, keep your lip buttoned,** ferme-la, la ferme; **(b)** *Fencing* moucheter *(une épée)*. **2** *vi* *(of garment)* (se) boutonner; **dress that buttons behind,** robe qui (se) boutonne par derrière.

►**button up** *vtsep* **(a)** boutonner *(qch)*; **buttoned up,** *(person)* boutonné jusqu'au menton; **(b)** *Fig* **to have sth all buttoned up,** avoir qch tout cuit.

button-down ['bʌtəndaʊn] *adj* *(collar)* à pointes boutonnées; **b.-d. shirt,** chemise à col boutonné.

buttoned-up [bʌtən'dʌp] *adj F* silencieux, renfermé.

buttonhole¹ ['bʌtənhəʊl] *n* **(a)** *(in jacket, shirt etc)* boutonnière *f*; *Sewing* **b. stitch,** point de boutonnière; **(b)** *Surg* boutonnière *f*, petite incision; **(c)** *(flower)* (fleur portée à la) boutonnière *f*.

buttonhole² **1** *vt* **(a)** *F* **to b. s.o.,** agrafer *ou* cueillir qn (au passage); **(b)** *Sewing* festonner. **2** *vi Sewing* faire une boutonnière.

button-through ['bʌtənθru:] *adj* **b.-t. (dress),** robe *f* chemisier; **b.-t. skirt,** jupe boutonnée jusqu'en bas.

buttress¹ ['bʌtrɪs] *n Archit* contrefort *m*; **flying b.,** arc-boutant *m*, *pl* arcs-boutants.

buttress² *vt Constr* arc-bouter; *Constr & Fig* étayer.

butty ['bʌtɪ] *n Eng Dial* sandwich *m*.

buxom ['bʌksəm] *adj* **(a)** *(full-bosomed)* à la forte poitrine; **(b)** *(plump)* aux formes rebondies *ou* plantureuses.

buy¹ [baɪ] *n* achat *m*; **a good b.,** une occasion, une affaire; **a bad b.,** un mauvais achat.

buy² *vt* *(pt & pp* **bought** [bɔ:t]*)* **(a)** acheter *(qch)* **(from,** à**)**; **to b. sth cheap,** acheter qch (à) bon marché; **money cannot b. it,** cela ne se paie pas; **money can't b. you love/health/happiness,** l'amour/la santé/le bonheur ne s'achète pas; **a dearly bought advantage,** un avantage chèrement payé; **to b. s.o. sth,** acheter qch à qn; *F* **he's bought it,** *(is dead)* il a passé l'arme à gauche; *Fig* **to b. time,** gagner du temps; **(b)** *Pej* corrompre, suborner *(un témoin etc)*; **(c)** *F* *(believe)* gober; **I won't b. that!,** tu ne me feras pas gober ça!; **I'll b. it!,** je te crois.

►**buy back** *vtsep* racheter *(une maison etc)*.

►**buy in** *vtsep* **(a)** s'approvisionner de *(denrées etc)*; **(b)** *(at auction)* racheter *(pour le compte du vendeur)*.

►**buy into** *vipo* *(purchase share in)* acheter une part de *(une entreprise)*.

►**buy off** *vtsep F* acheter *(qn)*.

►**buy out** *vtsep* **(a)** *Com* désintéresser *(un associé etc)*; **he was bought out for £50,000,** on lui a acheté sa part pour 50 000 livres; **the other shareholders have been bought out,** on a racheté la part des autres actionnaires; **(b)** *Mil* racheter *(qn)*; **to b. oneself out,** se racheter.

►**buy up** *vtsep Com* acheter *(qch)* en masse; rafler, accaparer *(des denrées etc)*; *F* **you must have bought up the entire store,** tu as dû dévaliser tout le magasin.

buyer ['baɪər] *n* **(a)** *(consumer)* acheteur, -euse; **prospective b.,** acheteur potentiel *ou* éventuel; *Fin* **buyers' market,** marché demandeur; **(b)** *(for shop)* acheteur, -euse; **head b.,** acheteur principal.

buying ['baɪɪŋ] *n* achat(s) *m(pl)*; **b. and selling,** achat et vente.
buying back *n* rachat *m*.
buying out *n* **(a)** *Com* désintéressement *m* (*d'un associé*); **(b)** *Mil* rachat *m* (*de qn*).
buying up *n* accaparement *m* (*de denrées*).
buy-out ['baɪaʊt] *n Com* (*of company*) rachat *m*.
buzz¹ [bʌz] *n* **(a)** bourdonnement *m* (*d'un insecte etc*); bruissement *m* (*d'abeilles*); bruit confus, brouhaha *m* (*de conversation*); vrombissement *m* (*d'un avion*); *Rad* ronflement *m*; *Fig* **b. word,** mot en vogue; **to give s.o. a b.,** *Tel F* donner un coup de fil à qn; *Sl* (*thrill*) faire planer qn; *Sl* **being recognized gives him a b.,** ça le fait planer d'être reconnu; **(b)** (*rumour, gossip*) rumeur *f*; **what's the latest b.?,** quelle est la dernière rumeur?; **the b. is that he's been fired,** on murmure qu'il a été renvoyé.
buzz² **1** *vi* (*of insect etc*) bourdonner; (*of aircraft etc*) vrombir; **the whole town was buzzing with excitement,** la ville était en pleine agitation. **2** *vt* **(a)** *Av etc F* frôler (*un avion, un navire*); raser (*un bâtiment, une ville*); **(b)** *F* donner un coup de téléphone à (*qn*); (*in office*) appeler (*qn*) à l'interphone; **I'll b. Mr Smith and tell him you're here,** je vais appeler M. Smith (à l'interphone) et lui dire que vous êtes là.
►**buzz about, buzz around** *vi F* s'activer.
►**buzz off** *vi F* s'en aller, décamper; **b. off!,** va-t-en!, file!
buzzard ['bʌzəd] *n* (*bird*) buse *f*, busard *m*.
buzzer ['bʌzər] *n* **(a)** *Nau Ind* sirène *f*; **(b)** *Tel etc* (*noise*) sonnerie *f* (ronflante); (*device*) avertisseur *m* sonore; **(c)** *El* trembleur *m*.
buzzing ['bʌzɪŋ] *n* bourdonnement *m* (*d'un insecte, Med des oreilles*).
by¹ [baɪ] **1** *prep* **(a)** (*near*) (au)près de, à côté de (*qn, qch*); (*in compass reading*) quart; **sitting by the fire,** assis près du feu; **by the sea,** au bord de la mer; **X-by-Y,** (*in place names*) X-lès-Y, X-lez-Y; **X-by-Sea,** X-sur-Mer; **by oneself,** (*alone*) seul; (*isolated*) à l'écart; **north by east,** nord quart nord-est; **north-east by north,** nord-nord-est quart nord; *Nau* **by the head/stern,** sur nez/cul;
(b) (*via*) par; **to go by the same road,** aller par la même route; **by land and sea,** par terre et par mer;
(c) (*agency, means*) par, de; **to be punished by s.o.,** être puni par qn; **to be loved by s.o.,** être aimé *ou* se faire aimer de qn; **to have a child by s.o.,** avoir un enfant de qn; **she has a daughter by her first marriage** *or* **husband,** elle a une fille de son premier mariage *ou* mari; **to die by one's own hand,** mourir de ses propres mains; **he took me by the arm/hand,** il m'a pris par le bras/la main; **made by hand,** fait à la main; **to call s.o. by his name,** appeler qn par son nom; **to live by one's work,** vivre de son travail; **what do you mean by that?,** qu'entendez-vous par là?; **by force,** de force; **by way of a joke,** par plaisanterie; **by chance,** par hasard; **cheerful by nature,** gai de caractère *ou* par nature; **to do sth (all) by oneself,** faire qch (tout) seul; **by heart,** par cœur; **to divide by three,** diviser par trois; **three metres by two,** trois mètres sur deux; **by land/sea,** par (voie de) terre/mer; **to travel by rail,** voyager par le *ou* en chemin de fer; **to come by car/motorcycle,** venir en voiture/à motocyclette; **to earn one's living by teaching,** gagner sa vie en enseignant; **I shall gain/lose by (doing) it,** j'y gagnerai/j'y perdrai; **to begin/end by laughing,** commencer/finir par rire; **we shall lose nothing by waiting,** nous ne perdrons rien pour attendre;
(d) (*according to*) à; **by my watch,** à ma montre; **to set one's watch by the time signal,** régler sa montre sur le signal horaire; **to judge s.o. by appearances,** juger qn sur les apparences; **I can tell it by your face,** on le voit à votre visage; **to sell sth by the pound/dozen,** vendre qch à la livre/douzaine; **to rent a house by the year,** louer une maison à l'année;
(e) (*in measurements, numbers*) **by degrees,** par degrés; **by turn(s),** tour à tour; **one by one,** un à un; **to come in by twos** *or* **two by two,** entrer deux par deux; **by twos and threes,** par deux ou trois; **little by little,** peu à peu, petit à petit; **day by day,** jour par jour, de jour en jour;
(f) (*during*) **by day,** de jour, le jour; **by night,** de nuit, la nuit; **by daylight,** au jour;
(g) (*time*) **he will be here by three o'clock,** il sera ici avant *ou* pour trois heures; **you will hear from us by Monday,** vous aurez de nos nouvelles d'ici lundi; **he ought to be here by now** *or* **by this time,** il doit *ou* il devrait être déjà ici; **by the time (that) you have finished, I shall be gone,** quand vous aurez fini je serai parti; **you shall have it by tomorrow,** vous l'aurez pour demain; **they were tired by the end of the day,** ils étaient fatigués à la fin de la journée; **by 1970,** (*talking about the past*) en 1970; **by 2025,** (*talking about the future*) d'ici à 2025;
(h) (*to the extent of*) de; **longer by two metres,** plus long de deux mètres; **by far,** de beaucoup; **they overcharged me by ten per cent,** ils m'ont compté dix pour cent en trop;
(i) **I know him by name/sight,** je le connais de nom/vue; **to do one's duty by s.o.,** faire son devoir envers qn; *F* **it's all right by me!,** ça (me) va!, d'accord!;
(j) (*in oaths*) **by God,** au nom de Dieu; **to swear by all one holds sacred,** jurer par tout ce qu'on a de plus sacré;
(k) *Mil* **by the right!,** guide à droit!
2 *adv* **(a)** (*near*) près; **close by,** tout près, ici près, tout à côté; **by and large,** dans l'ensemble;
(b) (*aside*) de côté; **to lay** *or* **set** *or* **put sth by,** mettre qch de côté; **to put** *or* **lay money by,** mettre de l'argent de côté;
(c) **to go** *or* **pass by,** (*elapse*) passer; **the time goes by,** le temps passe; **to come** *or* **stop by,** (*to see s.o., fetch sth*) passer;
(d) **by and by,** (*soon*) bientôt, tantôt; (*in the immediate future*) tout à l'heure; **by the by(e), by the way,** à propos.
bye¹ [baɪ] *n* **(a)** *Cr* balle passée; **(b)** *Sp* **to have a b.,** (*of player*) être exempt (*d'une épreuve, d'un match dans un tournoi*); **(c)** **by the b. ...,** à propos ... .
bye² *int F* au revoir!; **b. for now!,** à bientôt!
bye-bye ['baɪ'baɪ] *F* **1** *int* salut!, au revoir! **2** *n* (*in children's language*) **to go to b.-b., to go b.-byes,** aller faire dodo.
bye-law ['baɪlɔː] *n* arrêté municipal.
by-election ['baɪɪlekʃən] *n Pol* élection partielle.
bygone ['baɪgɒn] **1** *adj* passé, ancien, d'autrefois; **in b. days,** autrefois, dans l'ancien temps. **2** *npl* **bygones,** le passé; **let bygones be bygones,** oublions le passé, passons l'éponge (là-dessus).
bylaw ['baɪlɔː] *n* arrêté municipal.
by-line ['baɪlaɪn] *n* **(a)** *Journ* signature *m*; **a report under the by-l. of Mary Jones,** un reportage signé Mary Jones; **(b)** *Sp* limites *fpl* du terrain.
BYO [biːwaɪ'jəʊ] *n Austr* (*abbr* **bring your own**) = restaurant qui ne sert pas d'alcool et où on peut amener sa boisson.
BYOB [biːwaɪjəʊ'biː] *adj F* (*abbr* **bring your own bottle**) **is it BYOB?,** (*of party etc*) est-ce qu'on doit amener de la boisson?
bypass¹ ['baɪpɑːs] *n* **(a)** route *f* d'évitement; **(b)** *Med* pontage *m*; **she's had a b.** *or* **b. surgery,** on lui a fait un pontage; **(c)** *Tech* (conduit *m* de) dérivation *f*; **b. valve,** soupape *f* de dérivation; *Av* **b. ratio,** taux *m* de dilution; **(d)** *El* dérivation *f*.
bypass² *vt* **(a)** (*of road, person*) contourner, éviter (*une ville etc*); *Fig* laisser (*qn*) de côté; court-circuiter (*un intermédiaire etc*); **(b)** *Tech* amener (*la vapeur etc*) en dérivation; **(c)** *El* mettre hors circuit.
by-play ['baɪpleɪ] *n Th etc* (*action*) jeu *m* accessoire, jeu de second plan; (*speech*) aparté mimé, jeu muet.
by-product ['baɪprɒdʌkt] *n Ind* sous-produit *m*, *pl* sous-produits; *Fig* effet *m* secondaire.
byre ['baɪər] *n esp Scot* étable *f* à vaches.
byroad ['baɪrəʊd] *n* chemin détourné.
bystander ['baɪstændər] *n* spectateur, -trice; **innocent bystanders were hurt,** des spectateurs innocents ont été blessés.
byte [baɪt] *n Comptr* **(eight-bit) b.,** octet *m*; **four-bit b.,** quartet *m*.
byway ['baɪweɪ] *n* chemin détourné, voie indirecte; **byways of history,** à-côtés *mpl* de l'histoire.
byword ['baɪwɜːd] *n* **(a)** *Arch* proverbe *m*, dicton *m*; *Fig* **to have become a b.,** être devenu proverbial; **she is a b. for punctuality,** elle est l'exemple même de la ponctualité; **(b)** **to be the b. of the village,** (*of person*) être la fable *ou* la risée du village.
Byzantine [bɪ'zæntaɪn] *Hist & Fig* **1** *adj* byzantin; **the B. Empire,** l'Empire byzantin, l'Empire romain d'Orient. **2** *n* Byzantin, -ine.
Byzantium [bɪ'zæntɪəm, baɪ-] *n Antiq* Byzance *f*.

C

C, c [siː] *n* **(a)** (la lettre) C, c *m*; *US F* **C note,** billet *m* de cent dollars; *Am Med F* **C-section,** (opération *f*) césarienne *f*; **(b)** *Mus* ut *m*, do *m*; **(c)** *Sch* (*grade*) **to get a C,** avoir une note médiocre (*pour un devoir*).
C (*abbr* **centigrade**) C..
ca (*abbr* **circa**) env..
CA [siːˈeɪ] *n Br Fin abbr* **chartered accountant.**
CAA [siːeɪˈeɪ] *n Br Av Admin* (*abbr* **Civil Aviation Authority**) = organisme de réglementation de l'aviation civile.
cab [kæb] *n* **(a)** taxi *m*; *Arch* fiacre *m*; **to call** *or* **hail a c.,** appeler *ou* héler un taxi; **hansom c.,** cab *m*; **c. driver,** chauffeur *m* de taxi; **c. rank,** station *f* de taxis; **(b)** (*of truck, train, crane etc*) cabine *f*; **driver's c.,** cabine *ou* poste *m* de conduite.
cabal [kəˈbæl] *n* **(a)** (*plot*) cabale *f*, brigue *f*; **(b)** (*group*) coterie *f*.
cabaret [ˈkæbəreɪ] *n* **(a) c. (show),** spectacle *m* de music-hall *ou* de cabaret (*donné dans un restaurant etc*); (*in restaurant*) attractions *fpl*; **she's in c.,** c'est une artiste de cabaret; **c. act/artist,** numéro *m*/artiste *mf* de cabaret; **(b)** (*nightclub, restaurant*) cabaret *m*.
cabbage [ˈkæbɪdʒ] *n* **(a)** chou *m*, *pl* choux; **red c.,** chou rouge; **c. white,** (*butterfly*) piéride *f* du chou; **c. lettuce,** laitue pommée; **c. palm,** (*tree*) palmiste *m*; **c. rose,** rose *f* chou, *pl* roses chou; **(b)** *Fig* (*person*) légume *m*; **the accident left him a c.,** l'accident en a fait un légume, depuis l'accident il n'est plus qu'un légume.
cab(b)alistic [kæbəˈlɪstɪk] *adj* cabalistique.
cabbie, cabby [ˈkæbɪ] *n F* chauffeur *m* de taxi.
caber [ˈkeɪbər] *n Scot* tronc *m* (*de mélèze, de pin etc*); *Sp* **tossing the c.,** = concours de lancement d'un tronc de mélèze.
cabin [ˈkæbɪn] *n* **(a)** (*hut*) cabane *f*, case *f*; *Br Rail* poste *m* *ou* cabine *f* d'aiguillage; **log c.,** cabane en rondins; **(b)** *Nau* cabine *f*; (*on barge etc*) cabane *f*; *Av* cabine, habitacle *m*; *Old-fashioned Nau* **c. boy,** mousse *m*; *Av* **c. crew,** équipage *m*; *Nau* **c. cruiser,** yacht *m* de croisière (à moteur); **c. trunk,** malle *f* de cabine.
cabinet [ˈkæbɪnɪt] *n* **(a)** (*piece of furniture*) meuble *m* à tiroirs; (*of television, loudspeaker etc*) coffret *m*; **filing c.,** classeur *m*; (*for index cards*) fichier *m*; **bathroom c.,** armoire *f* à pharmacie; **(b)** *Pol* cabinet *m*, ministère *m*; **to form a c.,** former un ministère; **shadow c.,** conseil *m* de ministres fantôme; **c. minister,** ministre *m* (d'État), membre du cabinet (ministériel); **c. reshuffle,** remaniement ministériel; **(c)** *Arch* (*room*) cabinet *m*.
cabinet-maker [ˈkæbɪnɪtmeɪkər] *n* ébéniste *m*.
cabinet-making [ˈkæbɪnɪtmeɪkɪŋ] *n* ébénisterie *f*.
cable¹ [ˈkeɪb(ə)l] *n* **(a)** *Nau etc* câble *m*; **anchor c.,** câble d'ancre; **c. car,** (*on cable railway*) funiculaire *m*; (*overhead*) (cabine *f* de) téléphérique *m*; **cable('s) length,** (*measure*) encâblure *f*; *Knitting* **c. needle,** aiguille *f* à torsades; **c. railway,** (chemin *m* de fer) funiculaire *m*; *Phot* **c. release,** déclencheur *m*; **c. ship,** câblier *m*; *Knitting* **c. stitch,** torsade *f*; **(b)** *El* câble *m*, (fil *m*) conducteur *m*; **to lay a c.,** poser un câble; **overhead/underground/submarine c.,** câble aérien/souterrain/sous-marin; **twin c.,** câble à deux conducteurs; **c. (television),** (télévision *f* par) câble; **(c)** *Telecom* câble *m*, câblogramme *m*; **c. address,** adresse *f* télégraphique.
cable² *Telecom* **1** *vt* **(a)** câbler (*un message*); **to c. s.o.,** câbler à qn, aviser qn par câble; **to c. sth to s.o.,** câbler qch à qn. **2** *vi* câbler; **to c. to s.o.,** câbler à qn.
cablegram [ˈkeɪb(ə)lgræm] *n Telecom* câblogramme *m*.
cableway [ˈkeɪb(ə)lweɪ] *n* téléphérique *m*.
cabling [ˈkeɪb(ə)lɪŋ] *n* **(a)** *El etc* câbles *mpl*; **a hundred metres of c.,** cent mètres de câble; **(b)** *Telecom* envoi *m* d'un câblogramme.
cabman, *pl* **-men** [ˈkæbmən] *n* chauffeur *m* de taxi.
cabochon [ˈkæbəʃɒn] *n* (*gem*) cabochon *m*.
caboodle [kəˈbuːd(ə)l] *n F* **the whole (kit and) c.,** tout le bazar *ou* bataclan.
caboose [kəˈbuːs] *n* **(a)** *Am Rail* fourgon *m* de queue (*d'un train de marchandises*); **(b)** *Am Sl* (*jail*) tôle *f*, taule *f*; **(c)** *Can* baraquement *m* mobile (*pour bûcherons etc*); **(d)** *Nau* cuisine *f*, coquerie *f*.
cacao [kəˈkɑːəʊ, kəˈkeɪəʊ] *n Bot* **(a) c. (bean),** (graine *f* de, fève *f* de) cacao *m*; **c. pod,** cabosse *f*; **(b) c. (tree),** cacaotier *m*, cacaoyer *m*.
cache¹ [kæʃ] *n* **(a)** (*of arms, drugs etc*) dépôt *ou* réserve caché(e) *ou* clandestin(e); **(b)** (*place*) cachette *f* (*d'explorateur*); **(c)** *Comptr* **c. (memory),** antémémoire *f*, mémoire-cache *f*.
cache² *vt* **(a)** (*store*) cacher (*qch*); **(b)** *Comptr* mettre (*des données*) en antémémoire *ou* en mémoire-cache.
cachet [ˈkæʃeɪ] *n Pharm* cachet *m* (*d'aspirine etc*); *Fig* **to have a certain c.,** avoir un certain cachet.
cack-handed [kækˈhændɪd] *adj F* **(a)** (*clumsy*) empoté; **(b)** (*left-handed*) gaucher.
cackle¹ [ˈkæk(ə)l] *n* **(a)** (*of hen*) caquet *m*; **(b)** *Fig F* (*talking*) caquet *m*; (*laughter*) rire saccadé; **cut the c.!,** la ferme!
cackle² *vi* **(a)** (*of hen*) caqueter; (*of goose*) cacarder; **(b)** *Fig F* (*talk*) caqueter, cailleter; (*laugh*) faire entendre un rire saccadé.
cacophonous [kəˈkɒfənəs] *adj* cacophonique.
cacophony [kæˈkɒfənɪ] *n* cacophonie *f*.
cactus, *pl* **-ti** [ˈkæktəs, -tiː, -taɪ] *n* (*plant*) cactus *m*.
cad [kæd] *n Old-fashioned Br* salaud *m*, canaille *f*.
CAD [kæd] *n Comptr* (*abbr* **computer-assisted design**) CAO *f*.
cadastral [kəˈdæstrəl] *adj* (*registre etc*) cadastral, -aux.
cadaver [kəˈdævər] *n esp Am & Med* cadavre *m*.
cadaverous [kəˈdævərəs] *adj* **(a)** (*pale*) (*teint etc*) cadavéreux; **(b)** (*haggard*) émacié, décharné.
CAD/CAM [ˈkædkæm] *n Comptr* (*abbr* **computer-assisted design/computer-assisted manufacture**) CAOFAO *f*.
caddie¹ [ˈkædɪ] *n Golf* caddie *m*; **c. car(t),** poussette *f* (pour crosses de golf).
caddie² *vi Golf* **to c. for s.o.,** servir de caddie à qn.
caddy¹ [ˈkædɪ] *n* **tea c.,** boîte *f* à thé.
caddy² *n & vi* = **CADDIE¹,².**
cadence [ˈkeɪdəns] *n* cadence *f*, rythme *m*; *Mus* cadence; **perfect/imperfect c.,** cadence parfaite/imparfaite.
cadenza [kəˈdenzə] *n Mus* cadence *f* (*d'un concerto*).
cadet [kəˈdet] *n Mil etc* élève *m* d'une école militaire, élève officier; *Sch* élève de la préparation militaire; **c. corps,** peloton *m* de préparation militaire.
cadge [kædʒ] **1** *vt F* mendier, quémander; taxer, taper (*de l'argent, une cigarette*) **(from,** à); écornifler (*un repas*); **can I c. a lift?,** ça ne t'ennuierait pas de me déposer? **2** *vi* mendier; **he's always cadging,** il mendie toujours.
cadger [ˈkædʒər] *n F* quémandeur, -euse; (*of cigarette, money*) tapeur, -euse; (*of meal*) écornifleur *m*.
Cadiz [kəˈdɪz] *n* Cadix.
cadmium [ˈkædmɪəm] *n Miner* cadmium *m*.
cadre [kɑːdər] *n Mil* cadre *m*.
caecum, *US* **cecum,** *pl* **-a** [ˈsiːkəm, -ə] *n Anat* cæcum *m*.
Caesar [ˈsiːzər] *n* César *m*; **Julius C.,** Jules César.
Caesarean, Caesarian [sɪˈzeərɪən] **1** *n* **(a)** *Obst* (opération *f*) césarienne *f*; **it was a C.,** on lui a fait une césarienne; **to be a C.,** (*of baby*) être né par césarienne; **she has to have a C.,** il va falloir lui faire une césarienne; **the baby was born by C.,** l'enfant est né par césarienne; **(b)** *Hist* Césarien, -ienne. **2** *adj Obst* césarien; **c. section,** césarienne *f*.
caesura [sɪˈzjʊərə] *n Liter* césure *f*.
café [ˈkæfeɪ] *n* ≈ café-restaurant *m*, *pl* cafés-restaurants; (*in France*) café *m*; **transport c.,** ≈ restaurant *m* de routiers.
cafeteria [kæfɪˈtɪərɪə] *n* caféteria *f*, (restaurant *m*) self-

service *m*, *pl* self-services, self *m inv*.

caff [kæf] *n Br F* ≈ café *m*.

caffeine ['kæfiːn] *n* caféine *f*; **I need my dose of c. to get through the morning,** il me faut ma dose de caféine pour tenir toute la matinée; **c. free,** (*without caffeine*) sans caféine; (*decaffeinated*) décaféiné.

caftan ['kæftæn] *n* (*garment*) caf(e)tan *m*.

cage[1] [keɪdʒ] *n* **(a)** (*for birds, animals etc*) cage *f*; *Mil* **prisoners' c.,** parc *m ou* cage à prisonniers (de guerre); *Anat* **rib c.,** cage thoracique; **c. bird,** oiseau *m* de volière *ou* d'appartement; **(b)** (*of lift*) (*open*) cage *f*; (*enclosed*) cabine *f*; **(c)** *Min* cage *f* d'extraction.

cage[2] *vt* mettre (*un oiseau etc*) en cage; emprisonner, encager (*qn*); **caged animal,** animal en cage *ou* en captivité.

cagey ['keɪdʒɪ] *adj F* (*cautious*) prudent, circonspect; (*not frank*) cachottier; **to be c. about one's age,** ne pas vouloir avouer son âge; **she's being very c.,** elle n'en parle pas.

cagoule [kə'guːl] *n* anorak léger.

cahoots [kə'huːts] *npl F* **to be in c. with s.o.,** être de mèche avec qn.

caiman ['keɪmən] *n* (*animal*) caïman *m*.

Cain [keɪn] *n Bible* Caïn *m*; *F* **to raise C.,** (*make noise*) faire un bruit *ou* un fracas de tous les diables; (*make scene*) faire une scène monumentale.

cairn ['keən] *n* **(a)** (*of stones*) cairn *m*, tumulus *m* de pierres; **(b)** (*dog*) **c. (terrier),** terrier *m* cairn.

cairngorm [keən'gɔːm] *n* (*gem*) pierre *f* de cairngorm.

Cairo ['kaɪrəʊ] *n* le Caire.

caisson ['keɪs(ə)n] *n* **(a)** (*for working underwater*) caisson *m*; *Med* **c. disease,** maladie *f* des caissons; **(b)** *Nau* bateau-porte *m* (*de bassin de radoub*), *pl* bateaux-portes; **(c)** *Mil* caisson *m*.

cajole [kə'dʒəʊl] *vt* enjôler; **to c. s.o. into doing sth,** persuader qn de faire qch.

cajolery [kə'dʒəʊlərɪ] *n* cajolerie(s) *f(pl)*.

Cajun ['keidʒən] **1** *adj* (*language, music, recipe*) cajun *inv*. **2** *n* **(a)** (*person*) Cajun *mf*; **(b)** *Ling* cajun *m*.

cake[1] [keɪk] *n* **(a)** *Culin* gâteau *m*; (*small*) pâtisserie *f*; **(small) cakes,** (petits) gâteaux, pâtisseries; **fruit c.,** cake *m*; **sponge c.,** = gâteau de Savoie, gâteau mousseline; *Iron* **that takes the c.!,** ça c'est le comble *ou* le bouquet!; *Fig* **it's a piece of c.,** c'est simple comme bonjour, c'est du gâteau!; *Fig* **they're going** *or* **selling like hot cakes,** ça se vend comme des petits pains; *Prov* **you can't have your c. and eat it,** on ne peut pas avoir le beurre et l'argent du beurre; **c. mix,** préparation *f* pour gâteau; **c. shop,** pâtisserie *f*; **c. tin,** moule *m* à gâteau; **c. stand,** présentoir *m* à gâteaux; **(b)** *Old-fashioned* pain *m* (*de savon etc*); tablette *f* (*de chocolat, de couleur*); **a great c. of mud,** un gros paquet de boue; *Agr* **oil** *or* **linseed c.,** (*animal feed*) tourteau *m* de lin; tourte *f* (*pour engrais*).

cake[2] *vi* (*solidify*) s'agglutiner, s'agglomérer; (*of mud*) sécher; (*of blood etc*) coaguler.

caked [keɪkt] *adj* (*solidified*) agglutiné; **c. with mud/blood,** plaqué de boue/sang.

Cal *abbr* **California.**

CAL [siːeɪ'el] *Comptr* (*abbr* **computer-aided learning**) EAO *m*.

calabash ['kæləbæʃ] *n* **(a) c. (gourd),** calebasse *f*, gourde *f*; **c. tree,** calebassier *m*; **(b)** (*bottle*) calebasse *f*, gourde *f*; **(c)** (*pipe*) pipe *f* en (forme de) calebasse.

calaboose ['kæləbuːs] *n US Sl* taule *f*, tôle *f*; **ten days in the c.,** dix jours de taule *ou* tôle.

calamitous [kə'læmɪtəs] *adj* calamiteux, désastreux.

calamity [kə'læmɪtɪ] *n* désastre *m*, calamité *f*.

calcareous [kæl'keərɪəs] *adj Geol etc* calcaire.

calceolaria [kælsɪə'leərɪə] *n* (*plant*) calcéolaire *f*.

calcification [kælsɪfɪ'keɪʃən] *n* calcification *f*.

calcify ['kælsɪfaɪ] *Ch etc* **1** *vt* calcifier; pétrifier (*le bois etc*). **2** *vi* se calcifier.

calcination [kælsɪ'neɪʃən] *n Ch Ind* calcination *f*; (*of carbonate*) frittage *m*; (*of gypsum*) cuisson *f*; (*of ore*) grillage *m*.

calcine ['kælsaɪn] **1** *vt Ch Ind* calciner; fritter (*des carbonates etc*); cuire (*le gypse etc*); *Metal* griller (*le minerai*). **2** *vi* se calciner.

calcium ['kælsɪəm] *n Ch* calcium *m*; **cheese is high in c.,** il y a beaucoup de calcium dans le fromage; **c. carbide/chloride,** carbure *m*/chlorure *m* de calcium.

calculable ['kælkjʊləb(ə)l] *adj* calculable; (*sum of money*) chiffrable.

calculate ['kælkjʊleɪt] **1** *vt* **(a)** *Math etc* calculer, évaluer; estimer (*une distance*); faire le compte de (*sa fortune*); **(b)** (*plan, design*) calculer, faire (*qch*) délibérément *ou* avec préméditation; **the remark was calculated to shock,** la remarque était délibérément choquante; **(c)** *Am F* (*think*) croire, supposer (**that,** que). **2** *vi esp Am* (*rely*) **to c. on sth/on doing sth,** compter sur qch/compter faire qch.

calculated ['kælkjʊleɪtɪd] *adj* (*insolence etc*) délibéré, calculé; (*crime*) prémédité; **c. risk,** risque calculé; **c. to do sth,** fait pour faire qch; **words c. to reassure us,** paroles propres à nous rassurer.

calculating ['kælkjʊleɪtɪŋ] **1** *adj* (*person*) calculateur, -trice; **this was not the action of a c. murderer,** ce n'était pas un meurtre prémédité. **2** *n* calcul *m*; (*estimate*) estimation *f*; **c. machine,** machine *f* à calculer.

calculation [kælkjʊ'leɪʃən] *n* calcul *m*; **to make a c.,** effectuer un calcul; **to upset s.o.'s calculations,** déjouer les calculs de qn; **according to my calculations,** selon mes estimations *ou* mes calculs.

calculator ['kælkjʊleɪtər] *n* **(a)** (*machine*) machine *f* à calculer; (*pocket*) calculatrice *f*; **(b)** (*tables*) barème *m*; **(c)** (*person*) calculateur, -trice.

calculus ['kælkjʊləs] *n* **(a)** *Math* calcul *m*; **differential/integral c.,** calcul différentiel/intégral; **(b)** *Med* (*pl* **calculi** ['kælkjʊlaɪ]) calcul *m* (*vésical etc*); **urinary c.,** urolithe *m*.

Calcutta [kæl'kʌtə] *n* Calcutta.

Caledonia [kælɪ'dəʊnɪə] *n Lit & Antiq* (*Scotland*) Calédonie *f*.

Caledonian [kælɪ'dəʊnɪən] *Lit & Antiq* **1** *adj* calédonien. **2** *n* Calédonien, -ienne.

calendar ['kælɪndər] *n* (*of dates*) *& Rel* calendrier *m*; annuaire *m* (*d'une université, d'une institution etc*); *Jur* rôle *m* des causes; (*criminal law*) rôle des assises; *US* ordre *m* du jour (*du Congrès*); **I'll check my c.,** je vais vérifier mon agenda; **the club has a full c. this month,** le club a un calendrier chargé ce mois-ci; **an important date in the publishing c.,** une date importante dans le calendrier de l'édition; **Julian/Gregorian c.,** calendrier julien/grégorien; **tear-off c.,** éphéméride *m*; **c. month,** mois civil *ou* de calendrier; **c. year,** année civile.

calends ['kælɪndz] *npl Antiq* calendes *fpl*.

calf[1], *pl* **calves** [kɑːf, kɑːvz] *n* **(a)** (*animal*) veau *m*; **cow in** *or* **with c.,** vache pleine; **buffalo c.,** buffletin *m*; **elephant c.,** éléphanteau *m*; **sea c.,** phoque commun; **whale c.,** baleineau *m*; *F* **c. love,** les premières amours; **it was just c. love,** c'était un amour de jeunesse; **(b)** (*leather*) veau *m*; **c. binding,** (*of book*) reliure *f* en veau; **(c)** (*détaché d'un iceberg*) glaçon *m*.

calf[2], *pl* **calves** *n* mollet *m* (*de la jambe*); **c.-length boots,** demi-bottes *fpl*.

calfskin ['kɑːfskɪn] *n* (cuir *m* de) veau *m*; **c. wallet,** portefeuille *m* en veau.

caliber ['kælɪbər] *n US* = **CALIBRE.**

calibrate ['kælɪbreɪt] *vt Tech* étalonner (*un compteur etc*); calibrer (*un tube*); graduer (*un thermomètre*); tarer (*un ressort*); *Mil* vérifier le calibre de (*un canon*).

calibration [kælɪ'breɪʃən] *n* étalonnage *m* (*d'un compteur etc*); calibrage *m* (*d'un tube*); tarage *m* (*d'un ressort*).

calibre, *US* **caliber** ['kælɪbər] *n* calibre *m*, alésage *m* (*d'un canon, d'un tube*); *Fig* calibre (*d'une personne*); **a man of your c.,** un homme de votre calibre *ou* envergure; **a very high c. translator,** un traducteur de très grande envergure.

calico ['kælɪkəʊ] **1** *n Tex* calicot *m*; *Com* blanc *m* de coton; *US* calicot imprimé, indienne *f*; *Sewing* percaline *f* (*pour doublures*); **printed c.,** calicot imprimé, indienne *f*. **2** *adj* **(a)** *Tex* de calicot; **(b)** *US* (*cow*) varié, bigarré; (*material*) à pois.

California [kælɪ'fɔːnɪə] *n* Californie *f*.

Californian [kælɪ'fɔːnɪən] **1** *adj* californien. **2** *n* Californien, -ienne.

caliper ['kælɪpər] *n* = **CALLIPER.**

caliph ['keɪlɪf] *n* calife *m*.

caliphate ['keɪlɪfɪt] *n* califat *m*.

calisthenics [kælɪs'θenɪks] *npl* (*usu with sing verb*) callisthénie *f*.

calk[1] [kɔːk] *n* (*on shoe, horseshoe*) crampon *m*.

calk[2] *vt Art etc* décalquer.

calk[3] *vt* calfater, étouper (*un navire*).

call[1] [kɔːl] *n* **(a)** (*shout*) appel *m*, cri *m*; (*of bird*) cri; **bird c.,** (*instrument*) pipeau *m*;

(b) (*summons*) (*of person*) appel *m*; sonnerie *f* (*de clairon*); batterie *f* (*de tambour*); *Nau* coup *m* de sifflet; **c. for help,** appel au secours; **to come at/answer s.o.'s c.,** venir/répondre à l'appel de qn; **on c.,** de garde; **to be within c.,** être à portée de voix; **to give s.o. a c.,** appeler qn; (*waken*) réveiller qn; *Euph* **to obey** *or* **answer a c. of nature,** faire ses besoins; *F* **to have a close c.,** l'échapper belle; **that was a close c.!**, on l'a échappé belle!, ça n'est pas passé loin!; *Th* **curtain c.**, rappel *m* (d'un acteur); **to take a curtain c.**, paraître devant le rideau; **roll c.**, appel nominal; **c. button**, bouton *m* d'appel; **bugle/trumpet c.**, coup *ou* appel de clairon/de trompette;

(c) *Rel* vocation *f*; **he felt a c. (to the ministry)**, il se sentait la vocation (pour l'Église);

(d) *Tel* **(telephone) c.**, coup *m* de téléphone *or F* de fil, *Fml* appel *m* téléphonique; **to make a c.**, passer un coup de téléphone; **to give s.o. a c.**, téléphoner à qn, appeler qn (au téléphone); **you have a c. from Canada**, on vous appelle du Canada; **you had a c. from Pam**, Pam t'a appelé; **there was a c. for you**, il y a eu un coup de téléphone *ou* un appel pour toi; **will you accept the c.?**, (*when charges are reversed*) est-ce que vous prenez *ou* acceptez l'appel?; **to put a c. through**, donner la communication; **to return s.o.'s c.**, rappeler qn; **local c.**, communication urbaine *ou* locale; **personal** *or esp Am* **person to person c.**, appel avec préavis *ou* de personne à personne; **reversed charge c.**, *Am* **collect c.**, communication en P.C.V.; **c. girl**, prostituée *f* sur rendez-vous téléphonique, call-girl *f*; *Telecom* **c. key**, touche *f* d'appel; *Rad Nau* **c. letters/sign**, lettres *fpl*/indicatif *m* d'appel;

(e) (*visit*) visite *f*; *Com* passage *m* (*d'un représentant*); **to pay** *or* **make a c. on s.o.**, rendre (une) visite à qn; **to return s.o.'s c.**, rendre sa visite à qn; *Euph* **to pay a c.**, aller se laver les mains; *Nau* **port of c.**, port *m* d'escale; *Fig* étape *f*; **official c.**, visite officielle;

(f) (*demand*) demande *f*; **there's not much c. for ...**, il n'y a pas une forte demande de ...; **there's not much c. for them**, ce n'est pas un article très demandé;

(g) (*need*) besoin *m*; **there's no c. for rudeness!**, pas besoin *ou* ce n'est pas la peine d'être impoli!;

(h) *Cards* (*at bridge*) appel *m*; (*at solo whist, boston*) demande *f*; **c. for trumps**, invite *f* d'atout; **a c. of three diamonds**, une annonce de trois carreaux;

(i) *Tennis Cr* décision *f* de l'arbitre;

(j) *Fin* demande *f* (*d'argent*); appel *m* de fonds *ou* de versement; **payable at c.**, remboursable sur demande *ou* à vue; **money at** *or* **on c., c. money**, prêts *mpl* au jour le jour, argent *m* à court terme; *St Exch* **c. option**, option *f* d'achat.

call² **1** *vt* **(a)** (*in order to attract attention*) appeler (*qn*); crier (*le nom de qn*); **'come quickly', he called**, 'venez vite', a-t-il crié; **to c. the banns**, publier les bans; **to c. a halt**, faire halte; **to c. a halt to sth**, crier *ou* dire halte à qch; **to c. the roll**, faire l'appel;

(b) (*summon*) appeler (*qn, les pompiers, un ascenseur*); héler (*un taxi*); convoquer (*une assemblée*); décréter, ordonner (*une grève*); *Jur* appeler (*une cause*); *Th* rappeler (*un acteur*); **to c. s.o.'s attention to sth**, attirer l'attention de qn sur qch; **to c. the doctor**, faire venir *ou* appeler le médecin; **to be called away**, être appelé dehors; **I was called to the manager's office**, j'ai été appelé dans le bureau du directeur; **c. me at six o'clock**, réveillez-moi à six heures;

(c) *Tel* téléphoner à, appeler (*qn*); **I called her house**, j'ai téléphoné chez elle; **I got the impression it was a case of 'don't c. us, we'll c. you'**, j'ai eu l'impression que ça voulait dire 'on vous écrira';

(d) (*name*) appeler; **he is called Martin**, (*that is his name*) il s'appelle Martin; (*by other people*) on l'appelle Martin; **to c. s.o. after s.o.**, donner le nom de qn à qn; **to c. oneself a colonel**, s'attribuer le titre de colonel; **c. yourself a carpenter!**, et tu te prétends menuisier!; **and they c. themselves socialists!**, et ils se disent socialistes!; **do you c. that clean?**, c'est ce que tu appelles propre?; **c. me by my Christian** *or* **first name**, appelez-moi par mon prénom; **to c. s.o. names**, injurier qn, invectiver qn; **to c. s.o. a liar/a child**, traiter *ou* qualifier qn de menteur/d'enfant; **we'll c. it three**, mettons trois, va pour trois; **I c. that a dirty trick**, voilà ce que j'appelle un sale tour;

(e) *Cards* appeler, déclarer (*deux carreaux etc*); **to c. spades**, déclarer pique.

2 *vi* **(a)** (*to attract s.o.'s attention*) appeler (**to s.o.**, qn); (*of bird etc*) crier; **the bird was calling to its mother**, l'oiseau appelait sa mère;

(b) (*summon*) **duty calls**, le devoir m'appelle; *Mil* **to c. to arms**, battre la générale;

(c) (*knock on door etc*) passer, se rendre, se présenter (chez qn); **to c. (on s.o.)**, (*visit*) faire une visite (chez qn); **has anyone called?**, est-il venu quelqu'un?; **I called at your house**, je suis passé chez vous; **I must c. at the grocer's**, il faut que je passe chez l'épicier; **to c. again**, repasser (chez qn); **the train calls at every station**, le train s'arrête *ou* fait halte à toutes les gares; *Nau* **to c. at a port**, (*of ship*) faire escale à un port;

(d) *Tel* appeler; **who's calling, please?, may I ask who's calling?**, c'est de la part de qui, s'il vous plaît?;

(e) *Cards* appeler (l'atout); (*at poker*) forcer l'adversaire à déclarer son jeu.

►**call back** **1** *vtsep* (*summon again*) & *Tel* rappeler (*qn*); **they called her back for a second interview**, ils l'ont rappelée pour un deuxième entretien; **to c. s.o. back from vacation**, demander à qn de rentrer de vacances. **2** *vi* **(a)** (*return*) repasser; **I shall c. back for it**, je repasserai le prendre; **(b)** *Tel* rappeler; **if you'd like to c. back in an hour**, si vous voulez rappeler dans une heure.

►**call down** **1** *vtsep* **they called her down from upstairs**, ils l'ont appelée en criant du bas de l'escalier. **2** *vi* **I called down after him**, je l'ai appelé du haut de l'escalier.

►**call for** *vipo* **(a)** (*summon*) appeler, faire venir (*qn*); faire apporter (*qch*); commander (*une consommation etc*); **to c. for help**, crier au secours, appeler à l'aide;

(b) (*collect*) venir prendre, venir chercher (*qn, qch*); **I'll c. for you at nine**, je viendrai vous chercher à neuf heures; **to be (left till) called for**, (*by messenger*) à remettre au messager; (*of letter etc sent by post*) pour attendre l'arrivée; (*on envelope*) poste restante; *Rail* en gare;

(c) (*request, demand*) demander, exiger (*une explication, des excuses*); **the opposition were calling for his resignation**, l'opposition exigeait sa démission; **some union members are calling for industrial action**, certains syndicalistes appellent à une action revendicative; **the police are calling for tougher penalties**, la police réclame des sanctions plus fermes; **to c. for volunteers**, demander des volontaires; *Cards* **to c. for trumps**, inviter l'atout;

(d) (*require*) demander, comporter, réclamer, exiger (*l'attention, des réformes*); **situation that calls for tactful handling**, situation qui demande à être gérée avec tact; *F* **this calls for a celebration/a drink!**, il faut fêter/arroser ça!; **that sort of behaviour isn't called for**, on se passe bien de ce genre de comportement.

►**call in** **1** *vtsep* **(a)** (*into building, office etc*) faire entrer (*qn*), demander à (*qn*) d'entrer; **c. Miss Smith in, please**, faites entrer Mlle Smith, s'il vous plaît; **she called the children in**, elle a fait rentrer les enfants;

(b) (*withdraw from circulation*) retirer (*une monnaie, un livre*) de la circulation; **to c. in one's money**, faire rentrer ses fonds; **to c. in a loan**, (*of bank*) demander le remboursement d'un prêt;

(c) (*for advice, help*) faire appel à, avoir recours à (*un spécialiste*); **the army was called in**, on a fait appel à l'armée.

2 *vi* **(a)** (*visit*) rendre visite; **to c. in at s.o.'s house/at the grocer's**, passer chez qn/ chez l'épicier; **to c. in to see s.o.**, aller *ou* venir voir qn; **I'll c. in on my way home**, je passerai te voir en rentrant chez moi;

(b) (*by telephone*) passer un coup de fil *ou* de téléphone; **nurses called in and offered to help**, des infirmières ont téléphoné pour offrir leur aide; **to c. in sick**, téléphoner pour prévenir qu'on est malade.

►**call off** *vtsep* **(a)** (*cancel*) décommander, annuler (*un rendez-vous*); annuler (*une grève, un match*); rompre, annuler (*un marché*); **the holiday will have to be called off**, il faudra annuler les vacances; **they were going to get married, but they called it off**, ils étaient sur le point de se marier mais ils ont tout annulé; **(b)** (*tell to come away*) rappeler (*un chien*).

►**call on** *vipo* **(a)** (*request*) **to c. on s.o. for sth**, demander instamment qch à qn, réclamer qch à qn; **to c. on s.o. to do sth**, sommer qn de faire qch, appeler qn à faire qch, en appeler à qn pour qu'il fasse qch; **I c. on the government to act**, je demande instamment au gouvernement d'agir; **I now c. on Mr Stewart**, (*to speak*) la parole est à M. Stewart; **the limited resources the police can c. on**, les ressources limitées que la police peut mettre en œuvre; **(b)** (*visit*) rendre visite à (*qn*); (*drop in*) aller *ou* passer *ou* se rendre chez (*qn*), aller voir (*qn*); **(c)** invoquer (*le nom de Dieu*).

►**call out** **1** *vtsep* **(a)** (*summon*) faire sortir (*qn*), prier (*qn*) de sortir; appeler (*les pompiers*); **to c. out workers (on strike)**, donner l'ordre de grève à des ouvriers; **(b)** (*shout*) crier, déclarer; **she called out the winning number**, elle a annoncé le numéro gagnant. **2** *vi* appeler; **to c. out for sth**, appeler pour demander qch.

►**call up** *vtsep* **(a)** (*summon*) faire monter (*qn*); *Mil etc* appeler (*des renforts*); **we waited at the foot of the**

stairs until we were called up, nous avons attendu au pied de l'escalier jusqu'à ce qu'on nous dise de monter; **(b)** (*evoke*) invoquer (*un esprit*); évoquer (*une idée, un souvenir*); **(c)** *Tel* appeler (*qn*) au téléphone; **he keeps calling me up,** il n'arrête pas de me téléphoner; **(d)** *Mil Nau* mobiliser (*un réserviste*), appeler (*un réserviste*) sous les drapeaux *ou* sous les armes; **to be called up,** être mobilisé; **(e)** *Fin* **called-up capital,** capital appelé.

callable ['kɔːlɪb(ə)l] *adj Fin* (*loan*) remboursable avant échéance.

callbox ['kɔːlbɒks] *n* cabine *f* téléphonique.

callboy ['kɔːlbɔɪ] *n Th etc* avertisseur *m*.

caller [kɔːlər] *n* **(a)** visiteur, -euse; **to be a frequent c. at s.o.'s house,** être un habitué *ou* venir fréquemment chez qn; **(b)** *Tel* personne qui passe l'appel; **one minute please, c.,** un instant s'il vous plaît.

calligrapher [kə'lɪgrəfər] *n* calligraphe *m*.

calligraphy [kə'lɪgrəfɪ] *n* calligraphie *f*.

calling ['kɔːlɪŋ] *n* **(a)** (*shouting*) appel *m*, cri(s) *m(pl)*; **(b)** (*summoning*) convocation *f* (*d'une assemblée etc*); **(c)** (*visit, visiting*) visite *f* (**on,** à); *Am* **c. card,** carte *f* de visite; **(d)** (*vocation*) vocation *f* (**for,** pour); **I felt no/a c. for a religious life,** je n'avais aucune/j'avais une vocation pour une vie religieuse; **(e)** (*profession*) vocation *f*, profession *f*, métier *m*.

calling in *n* retrait *m* (*de monnaies*).

calling off *n* **(a)** (*cancellation*) (*of appointment, match, holidays*) annulation *f*; rupture *f* (*d'un marché*); **the c. off of the strike,** l'annulation de l'ordre de grève; **(b)** (*of dog, guards etc*) rappel *m*.

calling up *n* **(a)** (*of idea, memory*) évocation *f*; **(b)** (*by telephone*) appel *m* au téléphone; **(c)** *Mil Nau* appel *m* sous les drapeaux *ou* sous les armes.

calliper ['kælɪpər] *n* **(a)** *Tech* **c. compasses, (pair of) callipers,** compas *m* de calibre *ou* à calibrer; **(b)** *Med* **c. (splint),** attelle-étrier *f*, *pl* attelles-étriers.

callisthenics [kælɪs'θenɪks] *npl* (*usu with sing verb*) callisthénie *f*.

callosity [kæ'lɒsɪtɪ] *n* callosité *f*.

callous ['kæləs] *adj* **(a)** (*person, heart*) insensible, endurci; (*person*) dur, sans cœur; (*treatment, behaviour*) dur, brutal; (*remark*) dur; **to be c. to s.o.,** être dur avec qn; **the c. way in which the government has reacted,** la dureté de la réaction du gouvernement; **(b)** (*skin, feet, hands*) calleux.

calloused ['kæləst] *adj* (*skin, feet, hands*) calleux.

callously ['kæləslɪ] *adv* (*behave*) sans pitié, sans cœur; (*treat*) sans pitié; (*say, answer*) durement.

callousness ['kæləsnɪs] *n* (*of person, heart*) insensibilité *f* (**to,** à); (*of person, treatment, behaviour*) dureté *f*; (*of person*) manque *m* de cœur *ou* de pitié.

callow ['kæləʊ] *adj* **(a) c. youth,** jeune homme imberbe *ou* sans expérience; **(b)** (*fledgling*) sans plumes.

callowness ['kæləʊnɪs] *n* jeunesse *f*; (*immaturity*) manque *m* de maturité.

call-up ['kɔːlʌp] *n Br Mil* appel *m* sous les drapeaux; **c.-up papers,** fascicule *m* de mobilisation; **to receive one's c.-up papers,** être appelé sous les drapeaux.

callus ['kæləs] *n* cal *m*, *pl* cals, durillon *m*.

calm¹ [kɑːm] **1** *n* (*peace*) *& Nau* calme *m*; tranquillité *f*, sérénité *f* (*d'esprit*); **the government appealed for c.,** le gouvernement appela au calme; *Nau* **dead** *or* **flat c.,** calme plat; **period of c.,** accalmie *f*; *Nau & Fig* **c. before a storm,** calme avant la tempête. **2** *adj* (*peaceful*) calme, tranquille; (*esprit*) rassis, posé; (*sea*) calme, mou, *f* molle; (*day*) sans vent; **to remain** *or* **keep c.,** rester calme; **to grow calmer,** se calmer; **a sea as c. as a millpond,** une mer d'huile.

calm² *vt* calmer, apaiser (*la tempête, la colère etc*); remettre, détendre, tranquilliser (*l'esprit*); atténuer, adoucir (*la douleur*); **this will c. your nerves,** cela vous calmera; **c. yourself,** remettez-vous!, calmez-vous!

▶**calm down 1** *vi* (*of person*) se calmer; (*of storm, grief etc*) se calmer, s'apaiser, se modérer; (*of grief*) s'adoucir; *Nau* (*of sea, wind*) calmir; **things have calmed down,** (*after the crisis, busy spell etc*) les choses se sont calmées. **2** *vtsep* calmer (*qn*).

calming ['kɑːmɪŋ] **1** *adj* (*effet etc*) tranquillisant, calmant. **2** *n* apaisement *m* (*des flots, de la colère etc*); adoucissement *m* (*de la douleur*).

calmly ['kɑːmlɪ] *adv* avec calme, tranquillement; **she c. shot him,** elle lui tira dessus en restant très calme; **he just c. wrote out a huge cheque,** il a sans plus de cérémonies signé un gros chèque.

calmness ['kɑːmnɪs] *n* tranquillité *f*, calme *m*.

caloric [kə'lɒrɪk] *n Phys* calorique *m*.

calorie ['kælərɪ] *n Phys* calorie *f*; **to be low in calories,** (*of food*) être faible en calories; **low-c. diet, c. controlled diet,** régime hypocalorique *ou* de basses calories *ou* faible en calories; **calories per serving,** nombre de calories par portion; *F* **to watch the calories,** surveiller sa ligne.

calorific [kælə'rɪfɪk] *adj Phys* (*valeur etc*) calorifique.

calumniate [kə'lʌmnɪeɪt] *vt* calomnier.

calumny ['kæləmnɪ] *n* calomnie *f*.

Calvary ['kælvərɪ] *n* **(Mount) C.,** le Calvaire; *Fig* calvaire *m*.

calve [kɑːv] *vi* (*of cow, iceberg*) vêler.

calving ['kɑːvɪŋ] *n* (*of cow, iceberg*) vêlage *m*, vêlement *m*; **at c. time,** pendant le vêlement.

Calvinism ['kælvɪnɪz(ə)m] *n Rel Hist* calvinisme *m*.

Calvinist ['kælvɪnɪst] *n & adj Rel Hist* calviniste *mf*.

calypso [kə'lɪpsəʊ] *n Mus* calypso *m*.

calyx, *pl* **-yxes, -yces** ['keɪlɪks, -ɪksiːz, -ɪsiːz] *n Bot* calice *m*.

cam [kæm] *n Tech etc* came *f*.

CAM [kæm] *n Comptr* (*abbr* **computer-assisted manufacture**) FAO *f*.

camber¹ ['kæmbər] *n* (*of road*) bombement *m*; (*of beam*) cambrure *f*; *Nau* tonture *f* (*du pont*); *Av* flèche *f* (*d'aile*).

camber² **1** *vt* bomber (*une chaussée*); cambrer (*une poutre*). **2** *vi* (*of road*) bomber; (*of beam*) cambrer.

Cambodia [kæm'bəʊdɪə] *n* Cambodge *m*.

Cambodian [kæm'bəʊdɪən] **1** *adj* cambodgien. **2** *n* **(a)** Cambodgien, -ienne; **(b)** *Ling* cambodgien *m*.

cambric ['kæmbrɪk, 'keɪm-] *n Tex* batiste *f* (*de lin*).

Cambs *abbr* **Cambridgeshire.**

camcorder ['kæmkɔːdər] *n Phot* caméscope *m*.

camel ['kæməl] *n* **(a)** (*animal*) chameau *m*; **she c.,** chamelle *f*; **Bactrian c.,** chameau (bactrien); **Arabian c.,** dromadaire *m*; **c. driver,** chamelier *m*; *Mil* **c. corps,** compagnies *fpl* de méharistes; **(b)** (*colour*) chameau *m inv*.

camelhair ['kæməlheər] *n* poil *m* de chameau; **c. brush,** pinceau *m* en petit-gris (*pour l'aquarelle*); **c. coat,** manteau *m* en poil de chameau.

camellia [kə'miːlɪə] *n* (*flower*) camélia *m*.

cameo ['kæmɪəʊ] *n* **(a)** (*gem*) camée *m*; **c. (brooch),** camée en broche; **(b)** *Th Cin* **c. (role),** petit rôle (*joué par un acteur connu*).

camera ['kæmərə] *n* **(a)** *Phot* appareil *m* (photographique); *TV Cin* caméra *f*; **I'm no good with a c.,** je ne suis pas doué pour prendre des photos; **I know nothing about cameras,** je n'y connais rien en appareils photos; **in front of the c.,** devant les caméras; **on c.,** à l'écran; **reflex c.,** appareil reflex; **film** *or* *Am* **movie c.,** caméra *f*; **television c.,** caméra de télévision; **(b)** *Opt* **c. obscura,** chambre noire; **(c)** *Jur* **in c.,** à huis clos; **the trial was held in c.,** le procès a eu lieu à huis clos.

cameraman, *pl* **-men** ['kæmərəmən] *n Cin TV* cameraman *m*, *pl* cameramen; **assistant c.,** opérateur *m*.

camera-shy ['kæmərəʃaɪ] *adj* **he is c.-s.,** il n'aime pas être pris en photo *ou* être filmé.

camerawork ['kæmərəwɜːk] *n* photographie *f*.

Cameroun [kæmə'ruːn] *n* **the Republic of C.,** la République fédérale du Cameroun.

camomile ['kæməmaɪl] *n Bot Culin* camomille *f*; **c. tea,** (tisane *f* de) camomille.

camouflage¹ **1** ['kæməflɑːʒ] *n Mil etc & Fig* camouflage *m*; *Mil* **c. painting/net(ting),** peinture *f*/filet *m* de camouflage.

camouflage² *vt* camoufler; *Fig* **the President's rhetoric camouflaged his true intentions,** la rhétorique du Président a dissimulé ses véritables intentions.

camp¹ [kæmp] **1** *n* camp *m*, campement *m*; **to pitch c.,** établir un camp; **to strike** *or* **break c.,** lever le camp; *Fig* **to go over to the other c.,** passer dans l'autre camp; *Fig* **to have a foot in both camps,** manger à deux râteliers; **concentration c.,** camp de concentration; **gipsy c.,** camp *ou* campement de gitans; **holiday c.,** camp de vacances; (*for children*) ≈ colonie *f* de vacances; **labour c.,** camp de travail; **c. bed,** lit *m* de camp; *Mil* **c. follower,** (*prostitute*) prostituée *f*; (*civilian*) civil *m* qui accompagne une armée; *Fig* compagnon *m* de route; **c. site,** emplacement *m* du camp; (*specially designed*) (terrain *m* de) camping *m*; **c. stool** *or* **chair,** pliant *m*, chaise pliante. **2** *adj Th F* **(a)** affecté, poseur; **(b)** *Sl* homosexuel, tapette.

camp² **1** *vi* camper. **2** *vt Th F* **to c. it up,** outrer (le mauvais goût).

▶**camp out** *vi* camper.

campaign¹ [kæm'peɪn] *n* campagne *f*; **on c.,** en campagne; **to lead** *or* **conduct a c. against s.o.,** mener (une) campagne contre qn; **advertising c.,** campagne publicitaire; *Mil* **c. medal,** médaille commémorative.

campaign² *vi Mil* faire (une) campagne, faire des campagnes; *Pol* faire campagne; **she campaigned on an anti-drug platform,** elle a axé sa campagne sur la lutte contre la drogue; **they campaigned for his release,** ils ont lutté pour sa libération.

campaigner [kæm'peɪnər] *n* (*activist*) militant, -ante (*pour, contre qch*); *Mil* **old c.,** vieux soldat, vieux troupier; *Fig* vétéran *m*.

campanologist [kæmpə'nɒlədʒɪst] *n* spécialiste *mf* de l'art campanaire, carillonneur *m*.

campanology [kæmpə'nɒlədʒɪ] *n* art *m* campanaire, art du carillon.

campanula [kæm'pænjʊlə] *n* (*flower*) campanule *f*.

camper ['kæmpər] *n* (*person*) campeur, -euse; (*vehicle*) camping-car *m*, *pl* camping-cars.

campfire ['kæmpfaɪər] *n* feu *m* de camp.

camphor ['kæmfər] *n* camphre *m*; **c. oil,** essence *f* de camphre; **c. tree,** camphrier *m*.

camphorated ['kæmfəreɪtɪd] *adj* camphré; **c. oil,** huile camphrée.

camping ['kæmpɪŋ] *n* camping *m*; **to go c.,** faire du camping; **c. site,** (terrain *m* de) camping; **c. equipment** *or* **gear,** matériel *m ou* équipement *m* de camping; **c. gas,** camping-gaz *m inv*.

campion ['kæmpɪən] *n* (*plant*) lychnide *f*, lychnis *m*; **white c.,** compagnon blanc.

campus ['kæmpəs] *n* campus *m* (universitaire); **they live on c.,** (*of students*) ils vivent sur le campus.

camshaft ['kæmʃɑːft] *n* arbre *m* à came(s).

can¹ [kæn] *n* **(a)** (*for drink, esp Am food*) boîte *f*; **c. opener,** ouvre-boîte(s) *m*, *pl* ouvre-boîtes; **(b)** bidon *m*, broc *m*, pot *m* (*pour liquides*); boîte *f* (*à lait, d'un film*); *F* **to carry the c.,** payer les pots cassés; *F* **I'm not carrying the c. for you,** je ne vais pas payer les pots cassés pour toi; *F* **in the c.,** (*of film*) prêt à monter; *Fig* (*of deal etc*) dans la poche; *F* **c. of worms,** problème insoluble; *F* **don't let's open up that c. of worms,** ne nous occupons pas de ce problème pour le moment; *Am* **trash** *or* **garbage c.,** poubelle *f*; **watering c.,** arrosoir *m*; **(c)** *Sl* (*prison*) *F* taule *f*, tôle *f*; **(d)** *Am Sl* (*lavatory*) **the c.,** les cabinets *mpl*, les toilettes *fpl*.

can² *vt* (-nn-) **(a)** (*put in cans*) mettre *ou* conserver (*de la viande etc*) en boîte; **canned fruit,** fruits en conserve *ou* en boîte; *Sl* **c. it!,** (*shut up!*) la ferme!; **(b)** *US Sl* (*dismiss*) congédier, renvoyer (*qn*); **(c)** *Rad TV* enregistrer, transcrire; **canned laughter,** rires enregistrés; *F* **canned music,** musique *f* en boîte; **(d)** *F* **to get canned,** se soûler.

can³ [*stressed* kæn; *unstressed* k(ə)n] *modal aux v* (*pr* **can**; *neg* **cannot** ['kænɒt] (*US* **can not** ['kæn'nɒt]); *pt & cond* **could** [kʊd]; *no inf, prp & pp*; *defective parts are supplied from* **to be able to**; **cannot** *and* **could not** *are often contracted into* **can't** [kɑːnt], **couldn't** ['kʊdnt]) **(a)** (*be able to*) pouvoir; **I c. do it,** je peux le faire; **we cannot** *or US* **c. not possibly do it,** nous ne pouvons absolument pas le faire; **I will come as soon/as often as I c.,** je viendrai aussitôt/aussi souvent que possible; **he will do what he c.,** il fera ce qu'il pourra; **I will help you all I c., I will do all I c. to help you,** je vous aiderai de mon mieux, je ferai tout mon possible pour vous aider; **I can't very well accept,** il m'est difficile d'accepter; *F* **c. do!,** ça va!, bien sûr!; *F* **no c. do,** c'est impossible; **(it) can't be helped!,** tant pis!; **it can't be done,** il est impossible de le faire; **how could he say that?,** comment a-t-il pu dire cela?; **how c. you say that?,** comment peux-tu dire une chose pareille?; **what c. it be?,** qu'est ce-que cela peut bien être?; **c. it be true?,** serait-ce vrai?; **(it) could be,** c'est possible; **I never COULD understand maths,** je n'ai jamais été capable de comprendre les maths; **what CAN he want?,** qu'est-ce qu'il peut bien me *ou* nous *etc* vouloir?; **how COULD you!,** à quoi pensiez-vous?; **he could not have been kinder,** il n'aurait pu être plus aimable;

(b) (*know how to*) savoir; **I c. swim,** je sais nager; **a man who c. cook,** un homme qui sait faire la cuisine; **she c. play the violin,** elle joue du violon;

(c) (*indicating possibility*) **you don't know how hot it c. get,** vous ne savez pas à quel point il peut faire chaud; **the crossing c. be rough,** il arrive que la traversée soit mauvaise; **adults c. grow to 20 feet,** un adulte peut mesurer jusqu'à 20 pieds;

(d) (*indicating permissibility*) **when c. I move in?,** quand pourrai-je emménager?; **could you be quiet please?,** pourriez-vous vous taire, s'il vous plaît?; **you c. go,** vous pouvez vous retirer; **c. I ask you something?,** est-ce que je peux vous demander quelque chose?; **you can't smoke in here,** il est défendu de fumer ici;

(e) (*asking help*) **c. you help me?,** peux-tu m'aider?; (*asking more politely*) pourrais-tu m'aider?; **could you get me some water?,** pourriez-vous m'apporter de l'eau?;

(f) (*making suggestion*) **we could always telephone,** nous pourrions toujours téléphoner; **you could go to the beach,** tu pourrais aller à la plage; **I c. help if you like,** je peux t'aider si tu veux;

(g) (*not translated*) **I c. see nothing,** je n'y vois rien, je ne vois rien; **c. you see that hill?,** est-ce que tu vois cette colline?; **I could hear them talking,** je les entendais parler; **I c. see you don't believe me,** je vois bien que vous ne me croyez pas; **how c. you tell?,** comment le savez-vous?;

(h) (*in conditional*) **he could have done it,** il aurait pu le faire; **I could not have asked for anything better,** je n'aurais pas désiré mieux; **I could weep/could have wept,** j'ai/j'avais envie de pleurer; **I could have smacked his face!,** je l'aurais giflé!; **you could have warned me!,** tu aurais pu me prévenir!;

(i) (*elliptically*) **I cannot but believe him,** je suis bien forcé de le croire; **you c. but try,** vous pouvez toujours essayer.

Canada ['kænədə] *n* Canada *m*; **in C.,** au Canada; **C. Day,** la fête du Canada; **C. goose,** (*bird*) bernache *f* du Canada.

Canadian [kə'neɪdɪən] **1** *adj* canadien; *Ling* **C. French/English,** le français/l'anglais du Canada. **2** *n* Canadien, -ienne.

Canadianism [kə'neɪdɪənɪz(ə)m] *n* canadianisme *m*.

canal [kə'næl] *n* **(a)** (*waterway*) canal *m*, -aux; **slip c.,** canal maritime; **c. boat** *or* **barge,** péniche *f*; *Geog* **the C. zone,** la zone du Canal de Panama; **(b)** *Anat etc* canal *m*; **alimentary c.,** canal alimentaire; **auditory c.,** conduit auditif.

canalization [kænəlaɪ'zeɪʃən] *n* canalisation *f*.

canalize ['kænəlaɪz] *vt* **(a)** canaliser (*une rivière etc*); *Fig* canaliser; *Fig* **to c. efforts/energy into sth,** canaliser ses efforts/son énergie dans *ou* pour qch; **(b)** canaliser, poser les conduites dans (*une ville*).

canapé ['kænəpeɪ] *n Culin* canapé *m*.

canard ['kænɑːd, kə'nɑːd] *n* canard *m*, fausse nouvelle.

canary [kə'neərɪ] *n* (*bird*) serin *m*, canari *m*; *Bot* **c. grass,** alpiste *m*; **c. seed,** (grains *mpl* de) millet *m*; **c. yellow,** jaune canari.

Canary [kə'neərɪ] *n* **the C. Islands, the Canaries,** les îles *fpl* Canaries.

canasta [kə'næstə] *n Cards* canasta *f*; **to play c.,** jouer à la canasta.

cancan ['kænkæn] *n* cancan *m*; **c. dancer,** danseuse *f* de cancan.

cancel ['kæns(ə)l] *vt* (-ll-, *US* -l-) **(a)** annuler (*un chèque, une dette, une commande*); annuler, résilier, résoudre (*un marché, un contrat*); révoquer (*un acte, un testament*); rappeler (*un message*); révoquer, contremander (*un ordre*); supprimer (*un train*); décommander (*une réunion, une invitation, une réservation etc*); oblitérer (*un timbre*); *Mil* lever (*une consigne*); **to c. each other,** (*of two bookkeeping entries*) s'annuler, se contrepasser; **500, no c. that, 350 ...,** 500, ou plutôt, 350 ...; **(b)** *Math* éliminer (*des facteurs équivalents d'une fraction*).

►**cancel out** *vtsep Math* (*of terms*) annuler, éliminer; **to c. each other out,** s'annuler, s'éliminer; *Fig* **inflation cancelled out the increase in salary,** l'inflation a annulé la hausse des salaires.

cancellation [kænsə'leɪʃən] *n* annulation *f*; résiliation *f* (*d'une commande, d'une vente, d'un contrat*); (*of stamp*) oblitération *f*; **c. of an order,** révocation *f* d'un ordre; **there have been several cancellations,** (*in restaurant, hotel*) il y a plusieurs réservations qui ont été annulées.

cancer ['kænsər] *n* **(a)** *Med* cancer *m*; **to have c.,** avoir le cancer; *Fig* **we must remove the c. of militarism,** il faut enrayer le cancer du militarisme; **c. of the lung, lung c.,** cancer du poumon; **c. patient,** cancéreux, -euse; **c. specialist,** cancérologue *mf*; **c. research,** cancérologie *f*; **(b)** *Astron* **C.,** le Cancer; **(c)** *Geog* **the Tropic of C.,** le tropique du Cancer.

cancer-causing ['kænsəkɔːzɪŋ] *adj* (*substance etc*) cancérigène.

cancerous ['kæns(ə)rəs] *adj Med* cancéreux.

candelabra, *pl* **-as** [kændɪ'lɑːbrə, -əz] **, candelabrum,** *pl* **-a** [kændɪ'lɑːbrəm, -ə] *n* candélabre *m*.

candid ['kændɪd] *adj* franc, *f* franche, sincère; **c. camera,** caméra invisible *ou* cachée.

candidacy ['kændɪdəsɪ] *n* candidature *f*.

candidate ['kændɪdeɪt] *n* (*for job, office*) candidat *m* (**for,** à); **to stand as c. for sth,** se présenter comme candidat à qch, poser sa candidature à qch; **presidential c.,** candidat aux élections présidentielles; **successful candidates will have at least two years experience,** les candidats retenus auront au moins deux ans d'expérience.
candidature ['kændɪdətʃər] *n* candidature *f*.
candidly ['kændɪdlɪ] *adv* franchement, sincèrement.
candidness ['kændɪdnɪs] *n* franchise *f*, sincérité *f*.
candied ['kændɪd] *adj Culin* glacé, confit (au sucre); **c. peel,** zeste confit.
candle¹ ['kænd(ə)l] *n* **(wax) c.,** bougie *f*; **(tallow) c.,** chandelle *f*; **church c.,** cierge *m*; **Roman c.,** (*firework*) chandelle romaine; *Fig* **to burn the c. at both ends,** brûler la chandelle par les deux bouts; *Fig* **he can't hold a c. to you,** il n'est rien à côté de vous; **c. grease,** suif *m*.
candle² *vt* mirer (*des œufs*).
candlelight ['kænd(ə)laɪt] *n* lumière *f* de chandelle *ou* de bougie; **by c.,** à la chandelle, à la bougie.
candle-lit ['kænd(ə)lɪt] *adj* (*room*) éclairé à la bougie; (*meal*) aux chandelles.
Candlemas ['kænd(ə)lmæs] *n Rel* la Chandeleur.
candlestick ['kænd(ə)lstɪk] *n* chandelier *m*, bougeoir *m*.
candlewick ['kænd(ə)lwɪk] *n* **(a)** *Tex* candlewick *m*, chenille *f* de coton; **c. bedspread/dressing gown,** dessus *m* de lit/robe *f* de chambre en chenille de coton; **(b)** mèche *f* de bougie *ou* de chandelle.
candour, *US* **candor** ['kændər] *n* franchise *f*, sincérité *f*.
candy¹ ['kændɪ] *n Culin* **(a) (sugar) c.,** sucre candi; **stick of (sugar) c.,** sucre d'orge; **c. apple,** pomme *f* d'amour; **(b)** *Am* (*sweet, confectionery*) bonbon *m*; *F* **it's like taking c. from a baby,** c'est simple comme bonjour; **c. store,** confiserie *f*.
candy² **1** *vt* faire candir (*le sucre*); glacer (*des fruits*). **2** *vi* (*of sugar*) se cristalliser.
candyfloss ['kændɪflɒs] *n Culin* barbe *f* à papa.
candy-striped ['kændɪstraɪpt] *adj Tex* pékiné.
candy-striper ['kændɪstraɪpər] *n US Med F* = bénévole *mf*.
cane¹ [keɪn] *n* **(a)** *Bot etc* canne *f*, jonc *m*; (*of bamboo*) (canne de) bambou *m*; (*of rattan*) rotin *m*; **c. chair/furniture,** siège *m*/meubles *mpl* en rotin; **c.-seated chair,** chaise cannée; **raspberry c.,** tige *f* de framboisier; **sugar c.,** canne à sucre; **c. sugar,** sucre *m* de canne; **(b)** (*walking stick*) canne *f*; **(c)** (*switch*) badine *f*; (*for punishment*) canne *f*; **to get the c.,** recevoir des coups de bâton.
cane² *vt* **(a)** (*beat*) battre *ou* frapper (*qn*) à coups de canne, donner des coups de canne à (*qn*); **(b)** canner (*une chaise*).
canine ['keɪnaɪn, 'kæ-] **1** *adj* de chien; (*race, species*) canin; **c. devotion,** dévotion *f* de chien; **c. tooth,** (dent *f*) canine *f*, (dent) œillère *f*. **2** *n* **(a)** (*tooth*) (dent *f*) canine *f*, (dent) œillère *f*; **(b)** (*animals*) **canines,** canidés *mpl*.
caning ['keɪnɪŋ] *n* **(a)** (*punishment*) (volée *f* de) coups *mpl* de canne; **(b)** (*in furniture*) cannage *m*.
canister ['kænɪstər] *n* boîte *f* (en fer blanc).
canker ['kæŋkər] *n* **(a)** *Med* ulcère rongeur; *Fig* chancre *m*; **(b)** *Vet* (*in horse's hoof*) crapaud *m*; (*of dog etc*) gale *f* de l'oreille; **(c)** *Bot* chancre *m*; (*in wood*) nécrose *f*.
cankerworm ['kæŋkəwɜːm] *n* ver rongeur (des plantes).
cannabis ['kænəbɪs] *n* cannabis *m*; **c. resin,** cannabine *f*.
cannery ['kænərɪ] *n* conserverie *f*.
cannibal ['kænɪb(ə)l] *n & adj* cannibale *mf*.
cannibalism ['kænɪbəlɪz(ə)m] *n* cannibalisme *m*.
cannibalize ['kænɪbəlaɪz] *vt Tech Aut etc* démonter (*une machine etc*) pour en réutiliser les pièces.
cannily ['kænɪlɪ] *adv esp Scot* prudemment.
canning ['kænɪŋ] *n* (*of food*) mise *f* en conserve *ou* en boîte; **c. industry,** industrie *f* de conserves alimentaires.
cannon¹ ['kænən] *n* **(a)** (*usu inv*) *Mil* (*on aircraft*) canon *m*; *Am Fig* **he's a loose c.,** on ne sait pas trop ce qu'il va faire; **c. shot,** (*ball*) boulet *m* de canon; (*act, noise*) coup *m* de canon; **c. fodder,** chair *f* à canon; **(b)** *Billiards* carambolage *m*; **c. off the cushion,** bricole *f*.
cannon² *vi* (**-n-**) *Billiards* faire un carambolage, caramboler; **to c. off the cushion,** (*of player*) jouer la bricole.
►**cannon into** *vipo* se heurter contre (*qn, qch*).
cannonade¹ [kænə'neɪd] *n Old-fashioned Mil* canonnade *f*.
cannonade² *vt Old-fashioned Mil* attaquer (*une ville*) à coups de canon.
cannonball ['kænənbɔːl] *n Mil* boulet *m* de canon.
canny ['kænɪ] *adj esp Scot* (*cautious*) prudent, circonspect; (*aware*) avisé; (*clever*) rusé; (*thrifty*) économe; **c. answer,** réponse *f* de Normand.
canoe¹ [kə'nuː] *n* canoë *m*; (*with double-ended paddle*) périssoire *f*; **dugout c.,** pirogue *f*; *Fig* **to paddle one's own c.,** conduire seul sa barque.
canoe² *vi* (*pp & pt* **canoed**; *prp* **canoeing**) faire du canoë *ou* de la périssoire.
canoeing [kə'nuːɪŋ] *n* canoë *m*.
canoeist [kə'nuːɪst] *n* canoéiste *mf*.
canon¹ ['kænən] *n* **(a)** *Rel* canon *m* (*de la messe etc*); **c. law,** droit *m* canon; **(b)** *Lit* canon *m*; **(c)** *Mus* canon *m*.
canon² *n Rel* chanoine *m*.
cañon ['kænjən] *n Geog* cañon *m*, canyon *m*.
canonical [kə'nɒnɪk(ə)l] **1** *adj Rel* **(a)** (*devoir etc*) canonical; (*droit, épître, résidence etc*) canonique; *Fig* autorisé, accepté; **c. hours,** *Cathol* heures canoniales; *Church of Eng* heures pendant lesquelles il est permis de célébrer les mariages; **c. dress,** vêtements sacerdotaux; **(b)** *Mus* (*passage*) en forme de canon. **2** *npl* **canonicals,** vêtements sacerdotaux.
canonization [kænənaɪ'zeɪʃən] *n Rel* canonisation *f*.
canonize ['kænənaɪz] *vt Rel* canoniser (*qn*); *Fig* sanctionner (*un usage*).
canoodle [kə'nuːd(ə)l] *vi Old-fashioned* se faire des mamours.
canopy ['kænəpɪ] *n* dais *m* (*d'un trône*); baldaquin *m* (*de lit*); hotte *f* (*de foyer*); (*over doorway*) auvent *m*, marquise *f*; calotte *f* (*de parachute*); *Av* verrière *f* (*d'habitacle*); *Archit* gable *m*, gâble *m* (*de comble, de fenêtre*); *Rel* ciel *m* (*d'autel etc*); *Fig* **c. of leaves,** voûte *f* de feuillage *ou* de verdure.
cant¹ [kænt] *n* **(a)** *Carp Constr etc* (*slope*) inclinaison *f*, dévers *m*; *Rail* surélévation *f*, dévers (*du rail extérieur*); **to give sth a c.,** incliner qch; **to have a c.,** pencher; **(b)** (*edge*) *Archit Carp* chanfrein *m*, biseau *m*; *Tech* arête *f* (*de boulon*).
cant² **1** *vt* **(a)** (*turn over*) renverser, retourner (*qch*); *Nau* chavirer (*un canot pour le réparer*); **(b)** (*tilt*) dévoyer, incliner (*une poutre, un montant*); incliner, pencher (*un fût*); *Rail* surhausser (*le rail extérieur*); **(c)** *Carp etc* biseauter, écorner. **2** *vi* **(a)** *Carp Constr etc* s'incliner; **(b)** (*tilt*) se trouver incliné, pencher; **(c)** *Nau* (*of ship*) éviter.
cant³ *n* **(a)** (*of thieves, beggars*) argot *m*; **(b)** (*hypocritical talk*) langage *m* hypocrite; **c. phrase,** cliché *m*.
cant⁴ *vi* **(a)** faire l'hypocrite; **(b)** (*of thieves, beggars etc*) parler en argot.
Cantab (*abbr* **Cantabrigiensis**) de l'Université de Cambridge.
cantaloup(e) ['kæntəluːp] *n* (*melon*) cantaloup *m*.
cantankerous [kæn'tæŋk(ə)rəs] *adj* (*bad-tempered*) revêche, acariâtre; (*irritable*) querelleur, -euse.
cantata [kæn'tɑːtə] *n Mus* cantate *f*.
canteen [kæn'tiːn] *n* **(a)** (*in school, factory etc*) cantine *f*; **(b)** *Mil* (*shop*) magasin *m* à l'usage des soldats; (*water bottle*) bidon *m*; (*mess tin*) gamelle *f*; **(c) c. of cutlery,** ménagère *f*.
canter¹ ['kæntər] *n Horseriding* petit galop.
canter² **1** *vi* aller au petit galop. **2** *vt* faire aller (*un cheval*) au petit galop.
Canterbury ['kæntəb(ə)rɪ] *n* Cantorbéry *m*; **C. bell(s),** (*flower*) campanule *f*.
canticle ['kæntɪk(ə)l] *n* cantique *m*.
cantilever ['kæntɪliːvər] *n Archit* encorbellement *m*; *Av* cantilever *m*; *Constr etc* **c. beam,** poutre *f* en porte-à-faux; **c. bridge,** pont *m* cantilever.
canto ['kæntəʊ] *n Lit* chant *m* (*d'un poème*).
Cantonese [kæntə'niːz] **1** *adj* cantonais. **2** *n* **(a)** Cantonais, -aise; **(b)** *Ling* cantonais *m*.
cantor ['kæntɔːr] *n Rel* chantre *m*.
Canuck [kə'nʌk, kə'nʊk] *n US Pej* Canadien, -ienne français, -e.
canvas ['kænvəs] *n* **(a)** *Tex* (grosse) toile *f*; toile de tente; (*for tapestry*) canevas *m*; *Mil etc* **under c.,** sous la tente; **c. bucket,** seau *m* en toile; **c. shoes,** chaussures *fpl* de toile; espadrilles *fpl*; *Sewing* **c. work,** tapisserie *f ou* broderie *f* sur canevas *ou* sur toile; **(b)** *Art* tableau *m*, toile *f*; **(c)** *Boxing* tapis *m*; **(d)** *Nau* (*sails*) voile(s) *f(pl)*; **under c.,** sous voile.
canvass¹ ['kænvəs] *n* = **CANVASSING**.
canvass² **1** *vt* **(a)** *Pol Com* solliciter (*des suffrages, des commandes*); **to c. s.o.,** (*for vote*) solliciter la voix de qn; (*for custom*) solliciter la clientèle de qn; *Pol* **to c. a district,** faire une tournée électorale dans une région; *Com* **to c. for customers,** prospecter un quartier *ou* une région en y recherchant la clientèle; **(b)** (*debate, discuss*) discuter (*une affaire*); examiner minutieusement (*une question*); **(c)** *Am Pol* pointer, vérifier (*des suffrages*). **2** *vi* **(a)** *Pol* faire

campagne, faire une tournée électorale; **candidates were out canvassing today,** les candidats ont fait une tournée électorale aujourd'hui; **(b)** *Com* faire du démarchage; **she made extra money canvassing,** elle complétait ses revenus en faisant du démarchage; **(c)** (*debate, discuss*) débattre; **(d)** *Am Pol* vérifier (*les suffrages*).

canvasser ['kænvəsər] *n Pol etc* solliciteur, -euse; *Com* prospecteur, -trice; **no canvassers,** (*notice on door*) pas de représentants.

canvassing ['kænvəsɪŋ] *n* **(a)** *Pol Com* sollicitation *f* (*de suffrages, de commandes*); *Pol* propagande électorale; **(b)** (*debate*) discussion *f*; **(c)** *Am Pol* pointage *m*, vérification *f* (*des suffrages*).

canyon ['kænjən] *n Geog* canyon *m*, cañon *m*.

cap¹ [kæp] *n* **(a)** (*headgear*) bonnet *m*; (*with peak*) casquette *f*; toque *f* (*universitaire, de jockey*); képi *m* (*de militaire*); bonnet, béret *m* (*de marin*); **bathing** *or* **swimming c.,** bonnet de bain, baigneuse *f*; *Sp* **to win one's c.,** être sélectionné pour représenter l'équipe nationale; *Sch* **in c. and gown,** en costume académique; *Fig* **to come** *or* **go c. in hand,** se présenter chapeau bas *ou* humblement (**to s.o.,** devant qn); *Fig* **if the c. fits, (wear it)!,** qui se sent morveux se mouche!; *Fig* **to put on one's thinking c.,** méditer une question; *Min* **c. lamp,** photophore *m*;

(b) (*cover*) *Tech* chapeau *m* (*de protection*); capuchon *m* (*d'un stylo, de valve à pneu*); calotte *m* (*d'une pompe*); capsule *f* (*de bouteille*); chapeau, couvercle *m* (*de palier, de soupape*); (*for tooth*) couche *f* d'émail (*naturelle, artificielle*); *Phot* **lens c.,** bouchon *m* d'objectif; *F* **(Dutch) c.,** diaphragme *m* (contraceptif);

(c) (*upper part*) chapiteau *m* (*de colonne*); chapeau *m* (*de champignon*); comble *m* en dôme, lanterne *f* (*de bâtiment*);

(d) (*for toy gun*) amorce *f*, capsule *f*; **percussion c.,** amorce;

(e) *Orn* capuchon *m*, chapeau *m* (*d'un oiseau*).

cap² *vt* (**-pp-**) **(a)** (*put cap on*) coiffer (*qn*) d'un bonnet *ou* d'une casquette; **(b)** *Tech etc* coiffer, couronner, recouvrir (**sth with sth,** qch de qch); coiffer (*une fusée, un pieu*); capsuler (*une bouteille*); (*over cork*) surboucher (*une bouteille*); **(c)** (*surpass*) surpasser (*qch*); **to c. a quotation,** renchérir sur une citation; **that caps everything** *or* **the lot** *or* **it all!,** ça c'est le comble! *ou* le bouquet!; **(d)** *Scot New Zealand Sch* conférer un diplôme à (*un candidat*); **(e)** *Sp* **to be capped for England,** jouer dans l'équipe d'Angleterre.

cap³ *n Typ F* majuscule *f*; **put in small caps,** à imprimer en petites capitales.

CAP [siːeɪ'piː] *n abbr* **Common Agricultural Policy**.

capability [keɪpə'bɪlɪtɪ] *n* **(a)** capacité *f* (**to do sth,** pour faire qch); **we have the military c. to ...,** nous avons les capacités militaires de ...; **to have capabilities,** (*of person*) être doué, avoir des moyens; **(b)** (*of improvement etc*) susceptibilité *f*.

capable ['keɪpəb(ə)l] *adj* **(a)** capable (**of sth,** de qch; **of doing sth,** de faire qch); **to show what one is c. of,** montrer ce dont on est capable; **c. of love,** capable de sentiments; **I'm perfectly c. of walking upstairs by myself, thank you!,** je suis tout à fait capable de monter l'escalier tout seul, merci!; **the machine is c. of producing 300 items a minute,** cette machine a une capacité de production de 300 pièces à la minute; **she's not c. of lying,** elle est incapable de mentir; **that man's c. of anything,** cet homme est capable de tout; **(b)** (*person*) capable, compétent; **the business is in c. hands,** l'affaire est en bonnes mains; **(c) c. of improvement,** susceptible.

capably ['keɪpəblɪ] *adv* avec compétence, d'une manière compétente.

capacious [kə'peɪʃəs] *adj* vaste, spacieux; (*clothing*) ample.

capacitance [kə'pæsɪtəns] *n El* capacité *f*.

capacitate [kə'pæsɪteɪt] *vt Jur* donner pouvoir *ou* qualité à (*qn*) (**to act,** pour agir).

capacitor [kə'pæsɪtər] *n El* condensateur *m*.

capacity [kə'pæsɪtɪ] *n* **(a)** capacité *f* (*d'un cylindre etc*); contenance *f* (*d'un tonneau etc*); **the stadium has a c. of 50,000,** le stade peut accueillir 50 000 personnes; **to play to c.,** *Th etc* jouer à bureaux fermés; *Sp* jouer à guichets fermés; *F* **he has a remarkable c. for whisky,** il peut absorber des quantités extraordinaires de whisky; **cubic c.,** volume *m*; **seating c.,** nombre *m* de places (*dans un autobus, un théâtre etc*); **storage c.,** *Ind etc* capacité de stockage; *Comptr* capacité de mémoire;

(b) *Ind etc* rendement *m*; **to work at full c.,** travailler à plein rendement; **carrying c.,** (*of vehicle*) charge *f* utile; **lifting c.,** (*of crane*) puissance *f* de levage; **production c.,** capacité *f* de production;

(c) *El* capacité *f*;

(d) (*aptitude*) capacité *f* (**for,** pour, de); aptitude *f* (**for doing sth,** à faire qch); **c. for work/love,** capacité de travailler/d'aimer; **to the utmost of my c.,** dans toute la mesure de mes moyens;

(e) *Jur* **to have c./no c. to act,** avoir/ne pas avoir qualité pour agir;

(f) (*position*) **in the c. of ...,** en qualité de ...; **to act in one's official c.,** agir dans l'exercice de ses fonctions; **in my c. as chairwoman,** en ma qualité de présidente.

cape¹ [keɪp] *n* **(a)** pèlerine *f*, cape *f*; (*small*) collet *m*; **(b)** *Rel* camail *m*, *pl* camails.

cape² *n* cap *m*, promontoire *m*; **the C. (of Good Hope),** le Cap (de Bonne-Espérance); **C. Town,** le Cap; **C. Coloured,** métis, -isse (de l'Afrique du Sud).

caper¹ ['keɪpər] *n* **(a)** *Bot Culin* câpre *f*; **(b)** (*plant*) câprier *m*.

caper² *n* **(a)** (*movement*) cabriole *f*, gambade *f*; **to cut a c.,** faire des cabrioles; **(b)** (*trick*) astuce *f*, ruse *f*, farce *f*; **I've had enough of that kid's capers,** j'en ai assez de ces gamineries; **what a c.!,** quel cirque!; **(c)** *US Sl* (*robbery*) hold-up *m inv*.

caper³ *vi* **to c. (about),** faire des cabrioles, cabrioler, gambader.

capercaillie, capercailzie [kæpə'keɪljɪ] *n* (*bird*) grand tétras, (grand) coq *m* de bruyère.

capful ['kæpfʊl] *n* un plein bouchon, une pleine mesure (*d'un liquide, de lessive etc*).

capillary [kə'pɪlərɪ] **1** *adj* (*tube, pression etc*) capillaire; *Anat* **the c. vessels,** les vaisseaux capillaires. **2** *npl Anat* **the capillaries,** les capillaires *mpl*.

capital¹ ['kæpɪt(ə)l] *adj* **(a)** capital, -aux; **c. letter,** (lettre *f*) capitale *f*, (lettre) majuscule *f*; **a c. A,** un grand A, un A majuscule; **he's lazy with a c. L,** c'est un paresseux avec un grand P; **c. city,** (ville *f*) capitale *f*; **(b)** *Jur* **c. crime** *or* **offence,** crime capital *ou* puni de mort; **c. punishment,** peine capitale, peine de mort; **(c)** (*important*) capital, -aux; **c. sin,** péché capital; **c. error,** erreur fatale; *Nau* **c. ship,** bâtiment *m* de ligne; **of c. importance,** d'une importance capitale; **(d)** *Old-fashioned F* excellent.

capital² *n* **(a)** *Typ* capitale *f*, majuscule *f*; **(write in) block capitals,** (*on form*) (écrire en) capitales d'imprimerie; **(b)** (*city*) (ville *f*) capitale *f*; **(c)** *Fin* capital *m*, capitaux *mpl*, fonds *m*(*pl*); **to live on one's c.,** vivre sur son capital; *Fig* **to make c. out of sth,** profiter *ou* tirer parti de qch; *Fig* **they're trying to make political c. out of the scandal,** ils essaient de récupérer ce scandale; **working c.,** fonds *ou* capital d'exploitation; **c. assets,** actif immobilisé; **c. equipment,** immobilisations *fpl*; **c. expenditure,** dépenses *fpl* en immobilisations, frais *mpl* d'équipement; **c. gain,** plus-value *f* (en capital); **to make a c. gain on sth,** faire une plus-value sur qch; **c. gains tax,** impôt *m* sur les plus-values (en capital); **c. goods,** moyens *mpl* de production; **c.-intensive,** (*industry etc*) qui nécessite un investissement important; **c. investment,** investissement *m* de capitaux.

capital³ *n Archit* chapiteau *m*.

capitalism ['kæpɪtəlɪz(ə)m] *n* capitalisme *m*.

capitalist ['kæpɪtəlɪst] *n* capitaliste *mf*.

capitalist(ic) ['kæpɪtəlɪst, -'lɪstɪk] *adj* (*system, society etc*) capitaliste.

capitalization [kæpɪtəlaɪ'zeɪʃən] *n* **(a)** *Fin* capitalisation *f* (*des intérêts etc*); *Fig* profit *m* (**on,** de); **(b)** *Typ* emploi *m* des majuscules.

capitalize ['kæpɪtəlaɪz] *vt* **(a)** *Fin* capitaliser (*une rente etc*); **(b)** *Typ* écrire (*un mot*) avec une majuscule.

▶**capitalize on** *vipo Fig* tourner (*qch*) à son avantage.

capitally ['kæpɪt(ə)lɪ] *adv Old-fashioned F* admirablement (bien), à merveille.

capitation [kæpɪ'teɪʃən] *n Econ* capitation *f*; *Admin* **c. grant,** allocation *f* (de tant) par tête.

Capitol (the) [ðə'kæpɪtɒl] *n* le Capitole (*de Rome, de Washington etc*).

capitulate [kə'pɪtjʊleɪt] *vi* capituler (**to,** devant).

capitulation [kəpɪtjʊ'leɪʃən] *n* **(a)** (*surrender*) capitulation *f*; **(b)** (*list*) énumération *f* des chapitres *ou* des articles (*d'un traité etc*).

capon ['keɪpən] *n Culin* chapon *m*.

cappucino [kæpʊ'tʃiːnəʊ] *n* cappucino *m*; **two cappucinos,** deux cappucinos.

caprice [kə'priːs] *n* **(a)** caprice *m*, lubie *f*; **(b)** *Mus* caprice *m*.

capricious [kə'prɪʃəs] *adj* capricieux.

capriciously [kə'prɪʃəslɪ] *adv* capricieusement.

Capricorn ['kæprɪkɔːn] *n Astron* le Capricorne; *Geog* **the Tropic of C.,** le tropique du Capricorne.

capsicum ['kæpsɪkəm] *n* **(a)** *Culin* (*hot*) piment *m*; (*mild*) poivron *m*; **(b)** (*plant*) piment *m*.

capsize [kæp'saɪz] **1** *vi* (*of boat*) chavirer; **we capsized,** nous avons chaviré. **2** *vt* faire chavirer (*une embarcation*).

capstan ['kæpst(ə)n] *n* **(a)** *Nau etc* cabestan *m*; **(b)** *Tech* (*of lathe*) revolver *m*; **c. lathe,** tour *f* à revolver.

capsular ['kæpsjʊlər] *adj Biol etc* capsulaire.

capsule ['kæpsjuːl] *n* capsule *f*; **space c.,** cabine *ou* capsule spatiale.

Capt *n abbr* **Captain.**

captain[1] ['kæptɪn] *n* **(a)** chef *m*, capitaine *m*; *Nau* capitaine, commandant *m* (*d'un navire*); *Av* commandant de bord; capitaine (*des pompiers*); *Sp* capitaine *ou* chef d'équipe; (*in Girl Guides*) chef(e)taine *f*; *US* (*in restaurant*) maître *m* d'hôtel; *Fig* **the great captains of industry,** les grands capitaines *ou* les chefs de l'industrie; **(b)** (*rank*) *Mil & US Air Force* capitaine *m*; (*WRAC*) première classe; *Nau* capitaine de vaisseau; (*US police*) = officier de police responsable d'un quartier; **c. of the fleet,** capitaine de pavillon; *Br* **group c.,** colonel *m* (d'aviation); **C. James Brown,** (*in title*) le capitaine James Brown.

captain[2] *vt Sp* être capitaine *ou* chef de (*une équipe*); conduire, mener (*une expédition etc*); commander (*une compagnie etc*); *Sp* **he captained the side in the World Cup,** c'était lui le capitaine de l'équipe pour la Coupe du Monde.

captaincy ['kæptɪnsɪ] *n* **(a)** *Mil Nau* grade *m* de capitaine; **(b)** *Sp* commandement *m* de l'équipe.

caption[1] ['kæpʃən] *n* (*of cartoon, photograph, illustration*) légende *f*; *Cin* sous-titre *m*, *pl* sous-titres (*d'un film muet*); (*heading*) chapeau *m*.

caption[2] *vt* légender, écrire la légende de (*une illustration*).

captious ['kæpʃəs] *adj* (*reasoning*) captieux, sophistique; (*person*) pointilleux, chicaneur.

captivate ['kæptɪveɪt] *vt* charmer, captiver, séduire (*tous les cœurs etc*).

captivating ['kæptɪveɪtɪŋ] *adj* (*person, smile*) séduisant; (*personality*) captivant; (*smile*) enchanteur.

captivation [kæptɪ'veɪʃən] *n* séduction *f*; ensorcellement *m*.

captive ['kæptɪv] **1** *adj* captif; **he was taken c.,** on l'a fait prisonnier; **c. balloon,** ballon captif; **c. market,** clientèle captive; **he had a c. audience,** le public était forcé de l'écouter; **c. state,** état *m* de captivité. **2** *n* captif, -ive, prisonnier, -ière.

captivity [kæp'tɪvɪtɪ] *n* captivité *f*; **their c. lasted six months,** ils sont restés six mois en captivité; **animals in c.,** animaux en captivité.

captor ['kæptər] *n* ravisseur, -euse.

capture[1] ['kæptjər] *n* **(a)** capture *f*, prise *f* (*d'un navire, d'un prisonnier, d'un animal etc*); **(b)** *Comptr* (*of data*) saisie *f*; **(c)** (*thing or person taken*) prise *f*.

capture[2] *vt* capturer (*un navire, un malfaiteur, un animal etc*); prendre (*une ville*) (**from,** sur); s'emparer de (*un malfaiteur*); captiver (*l'attention, l'imagination de qn*); (*of artist, painting*) saisir (*une ressemblance*); *Comptr* (*data*) saisir; **to c. the moment,** (*of photographer, photograph*) saisir l'instant; **to c. s.o./sth on film,** immortaliser qn/qch sur la pellicule; **the movie captures the mood of those years,** ce film immortalise l'ambiance de ces années-là; *Com* **to c. a market,** accaparer un marché.

capuchin ['kæpʊʃɪn] *n* **(a)** (*monkey*) capucin *m*; **(b)** (*cloak*) mante *f* à capuchon.

Capuchin ['kæpʊʃɪn] *n Rel* capucin, -ine.

car [kɑːr] *n* **(a)** *Aut* **(motor) c.,** voiture *f*, automobile *f*; **sports c.,** voiture (de) sport; **racing c.,** voiture de course; **to go by c.,** aller en voiture; **c. bomb,** voiture piégée; **c. industry/manufacturer,** industrie *f*/constructeur *m* automobile; *Br* **c. park,** parc *m* de stationnement, parking *m*; **c. phone,** téléphone *m* de voiture; **(b)** *Am Rail* voiture *f*, wagon *m*; **freight c.,** wagon à *ou* de marchandises; **dump c.,** wagon à bascule; *Br & Am Rail* **dining** *or* **restaurant c.,** wagon-restaurant *m*, *pl* wagons-restaurants; **buffet** *or* **refreshment c.,** voiture-bar *f*, *pl* voitures-bars; **sleeping c.,** wagon-lit *m*, *pl* wagons-lits; **(c)** (*cabin*) nacelle *f* (*d'un pont transbordeur, Av d'un ballon*); *Am* cabine *f* (*d'un ascenseur*); **(d)** *Lit* (*chariot*) char *m*.

carafe [kə'ræf, -'rɑːf] *n* carafe *f*; (*small*) carafon *m*.

caramel ['kærəməl] *n* **(a)** *Culin* caramel *m*; **c. cream, cream c.,** crème *f* caramel; **c. custard,** crème (renversée) au caramel; **(b)** (*sweet*) caramel *m*; **(c)** (*colour*) (couleur *f*) caramel *m inv*.

caramelize ['kærəməlaɪz] *Culin* **1** *vt* caraméliser. **2** *vi* se caraméliser.

carapace ['kærəpeɪs] *n Zool* carapace *f*.

carat ['kærət] *n* **(a)** (*for gold*) carat *m* (de fin); **eighteen-c. gold,** or à dix-huit carats; **(b)** (*for diamonds*) **metric c.,** carat *m* (de 200 milligrammes).

caravan ['kærəvæn] *n* **(a)** *Br* (*pulled by car*) caravane *f*; **c. site,** camping *m* (pour caravanes); **(b)** (*horse-drawn*) roulotte *f* (*de romanichel, de forains*); **(c)** (*in desert*) caravane *f*; **to travel in c.,** voyager en convoi; **c. route,** piste *f* caravanière.

caravan(n)ing ['kærəvænɪŋ] *n* caravaning *m*; **to go on a c. holiday,** faire du caravaning.

caraway ['kærəweɪ] *n* (*plant*) carvi *m*, cumin *m* des prés; **c. seeds,** graines *fpl* de carvi.

carbide ['kɑːbaɪd] *n Ch Ind* carbure *m*.

carbine ['kɑːbaɪn] *n Mil* **(a)** carabine *f*; **(b)** *US* mitraillette *f*.

carbohydrate [kɑːbəʊ'haɪdreɪt] *n* **(a)** *Ch* hydrate *m* de carbone; **(b) carbohydrates,** (*in food*) les glucides *mpl*.

carbolic [kɑː'bɒlɪk] *adj Ch* phénique; **c. acid,** acide *m* phénique, phénol *m*.

carbon ['kɑːbən] *n Ch* carbone *m*; **powdered c.,** charbon *m* en poudre; **c. (copy),** (*of letter etc*) double *m ou* copie *f ou* exemplaire *m* (au carbone); *Fig* **she is a c. copy of her mother,** c'est une copie conforme de sa mère; **c. dating,** (*in archaeology*) datation *f* au carbone 14; **c. dioxide,** gaz *m* carbonique; **c. electrode,** électrode *f* de charbon; **c. (paper),** (papier *m*) carbone; **c. monoxide,** oxyde *m* de carbone; **c. steel,** acier enrichi en carbone.

carbonaceous [kɑːbə'neɪʃəs] *adj Ch* carboné; *Geol* carbonifère.

carbonate ['kɑːbəneɪt] *n Ch* carbonate *m*.

carbonated ['kɑːbəneɪtɪd] *adj* gazéifié, gazeux; **c. water,** eau gazeuse.

carbonic [kɑː'bɒnɪk] *adj Ch* carbonique.

carboniferous [kɑːbə'nɪfərəs] *adj & n* carbonifère *m*.

carbonization [kɑːbənaɪ'zeɪʃən] *n* carbonisation *f* (*du bois etc*); *Aut etc* encrassement *m*, calaminage *m*.

carbonize ['kɑːbənaɪz] **1** *vt Ch* carboniser; *Aut* carburer; *Ind* carboniser, charbonner (*du bois etc*). **2** *vi Aut etc* s'encrasser, se calaminer.

car-boot ['kɑːbuːt] *n Br* **c.-b. sale,** = vente à la brocante à l'arrière d'une voiture; **there's a c.-b. sale this Sunday,** il y a une foire à la brocante dimanche.

carborundum [kɑːbə'rʌndəm] *n* carborundum *m*.

carboy ['kɑːbɔɪ] *n* bonbonne *f*, ballon *m*.

carbuncle ['kɑːbʌŋk(ə)l] *n* **(a)** *Med* furoncle *m*; **(b)** (*gem*) escarboucle *f*.

carburettor, *US* **carburetor** ['kɑːbjʊretər] *n Aut* carburateur *m*.

carcass ['kɑːkəs] *n* **(a)** cadavre *m*, carcasse *f* (*d'un animal*); **(b)** carcasse *f* (*d'une maison, d'un navire*); charpente *f* (*d'une maison*).

carcinogen [kɑː'sɪnədʒen] *n Med* substance *f* cancérigène *ou* cancérogène.

carcinogenic [kɑːsɪnəʊ'dʒenɪk] *adj Med* cancérigène.

carcinoma [kɑːsɪ'nəʊmə] *n Med* carcinome *m*.

card[1] [kɑːd] *n* **(a)** *Cards* **(playing) c.,** carte *f* à jouer; **court c.,** *Am* **face c.,** figure *f*; **pack** *or Am* **deck of cards,** jeu *m* de cartes; **to play cards,** jouer aux cartes; **to win at cards,** gagner aux cartes; **to play one's cards well,** bien jouer ses cartes; *Fig* jouer la bonne carte, bien se débrouiller; **play your cards right and you could get promoted,** si tu joues la bonne carte, tu peux avoir une promotion; **to play one's last c.,** jouer sa dernière carte *ou* son va-tout; **to hold all the winning cards,** avoir tous les atouts dans son jeu *ou* en main; **to hold one's cards close to one's chest,** cacher son jeu; **to put one's cards on the table,** mettre cartes sur table; *Fig* **to have a c. up one's sleeve,** avoir encore une ressource; **it is on** *or Am* **in the cards that ...,** il est bien possible que, il se pourrait fort bien que ...; *Old-fashioned F* **he's a (great) c.,** c'est un original; **c. player,** joueur -euse de cartes; **c. game,** (*type*) jeu *m* de cartes; (*occasion*) partie *f* de cartes; **c. table,** table de jeux;

(b) (*with printed information*) carte *f*; (*postcard*) carte (postale); *Golf* carte du parcours; *Sp* programme *m* des courses; **visiting c.,** carte de visite; **business c.,** carte de visite; **this is my c.,** voici ma carte; *Br F* **to get one's cards,** être renvoyé; **invitation c.,** carte d'invitation; **birthday/Christmas c.,** carte d'anniversaire/de Noël; **greetings c.,** carte de vœux; **cigarette c.,** image offerte avec un paquet de cigarettes; **identity c.,** carte d'identité; **banker's c., cheque c.,** carte bancaire; **score c.,** carton

m; **punched c.**, carte perforée; **smart c.**, carte à puce;
(c) (*for card index*) fiche *f*; **c. index** *or* **file,** fichier *m*; **c. catalogue,** fichier;
(d) (*for wool, buttons*) carte *f*;
(e) (*cardboard*) carton *m*.
(f) *Comptr* carte *f*.

card² *n Tex* carde *f*, peigne *m*.

card³ *vt Tex* carder, peigner (*la laine etc*).

cardamom ['kɑːdəmən] *n* **(a)** (*plant*) cardamome *m*; **(b)** *Culin* (*spice*) graine *f* de cardamome.

cardboard ['kɑːdbɔːd] *n* carton *m*, cartonnage *m*; **corrugated c.**, carton ondulé; **c. box,** carton *m*, boîte *f* en carton.

card-carrying ['kɑːdkærɪŋ] *adj* **a c.-c. member of the party,** un membre qui a la carte du parti.

cardiac ['kɑːdɪæk] *adj Anat Med* cardiaque; **c. arrest,** arrêt cardiaque *ou* du cœur; **he suffered c. arrest,** il a eu un arrêt cardiaque.

cardigan ['kɑːdɪgən] *n* cardigan *m*, gilet *m* (de laine).

cardinal ['kɑːdɪn(ə)l] **1** *adj* **(a)** cardinal, -aux; **c. numbers,** nombres cardinaux; **c. error,** erreur fondamentale; **the four c. points,** les quatre points cardinaux; **c. virtues,** vertus cardinales; **c. flower,** cardinale *f*; **(b)** (*colour*) pourpre, cardinal *inv*. **2** *n Rel* cardinal *m*, -aux.

carding ['kɑːdɪŋ] *n* cardage *m*, peignage *m*; **c. machine,** cardeuse *f*.

cardiogram ['kɑːdɪəʊgræm] *n Med* cardiogramme *m*.

cardiograph ['kɑːdɪəʊgræf] *n Med* cardiographe *m*.

cardiologist [kɑːdɪ'ɒlədʒɪst] *n Med* cardiologue *mf*.

cardiology [kɑːdɪ'ɒlədʒɪ] *n Med* cardiologie *f*.

cardiovascular [kɑːdɪəʊ'væskjʊlər] *adj Med* (*disease etc*) cardio-vasculaire, *pl* cardio-vasculaires; **c. accident,** accident *m* cardio-vasculaire.

cardphone ['kɑːdfəʊn] *n Tel* publiphone *m* à carte.

cardsharp(er) ['kɑːdʃɑːp, -ər] *n* fileur *m* de cartes.

care¹ [keər] *n* **(a)** (*worry*) souci *m*, inquiétude *f*; **to be full of cares,** être plein de soucis; **to be free of c.,** être insouciant; **life of c.,** vie pleine de soucis; **cares of State,** responsabilités *fpl* d'Etat;
(b) (*attention*) soin(s) *m(pl)*, attention *f*; **constant c.,** soins continuels *ou* assidus; **to do sth with great c.,** faire qch avec beaucoup de soin; **to put a lot of c. into sth,** mettre beaucoup de soin à faire qch; **c. for details,** attention aux détails; **to drive without due c.,** conduire avec négligence; **to take c. of,** (*look after*) prendre soin de (*qn*); avoir soin de (*qch*); (*deal with*) s'occuper de (*qn, qch*); **they took c. of me when I was ill,** ils ont pris soin de moi quand j'étais malade; **he doesn't take c. of his bicycle,** il ne prend *ou* n'a aucun soin de son vélo; **my bank manager takes c. of all that,** le directeur de ma banque prend tout cela en charge; **they didn't receive the proper c. in hospital,** ils n'ont pas reçu les soins appropriés à l'hôpital; **this should take c. of that grease,** cela devrait enlever cette saleté; **to take c. to do sth,** avoir (bien) soin *ou* prendre (bien) garde de faire qch; **they took c. not to mention this fact,** ils ont pris garde de ne pas mentionner ce fait; **take c. when you cross the road,** fais attention en traversant la rue; **take c.!,** (*look out!*) faites attention!, prenez garde!; **cheerio, take c.,** au revoir; **take c. of yourself,** (*look after yourself*) soignez-vous bien; **to take c. of one's health,** ménager sa santé; **with c.,** (*on parcel etc*) fragile;
(c) (*looking after*) soin(s) *m(pl)*, charge *f*; entretien *m* (*d'une machine etc*); **hair/shoe c.,** (*in advertising etc*) soins des cheveux/entretien des chaussures; *Admin* **children in c.,** enfants à l'Assistance (publique); **to go into c.,** (*of child*) aller à l'Assistance (publique); **to put a child in c.,** mettre un enfant à l'Assistance (publique); **she's been in c. since she was three,** elle est à l'Assistance (publique) depuis l'âge de trois ans; **to put s.o./sth in s.o.'s c.,** confier qn/qch aux soins de qn; **write to me c. of Mrs Smith** *or* **c/o Mrs Smith,** *or US* **in c. of Mrs Smith,** écrivez-moi aux bons soins de Mme Smith *ou* chez Mme Smith; **to be in** *or* **under s.o.'s c.,** être confié aux soins de qn.

care² **1** *vi* (*be concerned*) se soucier, s'occuper, se préoccuper (**about,** de); **people who c.,** des gens compatissants; **no one seems to c. about the environment/the elderly,** personne ne semble se préoccuper de l'environnement/des personnes âgées; **no-one seems to c.,** personne ne s'y intéresse; **of course we c. about you!,** mais bien sûr qu'on t'aime; **that's all he cares about,** il n'y a que cela qui l'intéresse; **I don't c. what he says,** peu m'importe ce qu'il dit; **what do I c.?,** que m'importe?, qu'est-ce que cela me fait?; **who cares?,** qu'est-ce que ça fait?; **I don't c. whether he likes it or not,** que cela lui plaise ou non, ça m'est parfaitement égal; **do you really c.?,** (*how I am, what my feelings are etc*) est-ce que ça t'intéresse vraiment?; **she just doesn't c.,** elle s'en moque complètement, *F* elle n'en a rien à faire; **for all I c.,** pour (tout) ce que ça me fait; **I don't c.!,** ça m'est égal!, je m'en fiche!; **as if I cared!, I couldn't c. less,** je m'en fiche éperdument, je m'en fous, **couldn't-c.-less attitude,** je-m'en-foutisme *m*.
2 *vt* (*like*) **would you c. to come with me?,** voulez-vous m'accompagner?, aimeriez-vous m'accompagner?; **if you c. to join us,** (*where we're going*) si cela vous dit de venir avec nous *ou* d'être des nôtres; (*at our table*) si cela vous dit de partager notre table.

►**care for** *vipo* **(a)** (*tend*) soigner (*des malades, des enfants*); **to look well cared for,** (*of animal, child etc*) avoir un air soigné *ou* une apparence soignée; **(b)** (*like*) **I don't c. for this music,** cette musique ne me dit rien; **he doesn't c. for her,** elle ne lui plaît pas; **would you c. for some tea?,** voudriez-vous du thé?; **(c)** (*love*) aimer, tenir à (*qn*); **if you really c. for her ...,** si tu tiens vraiment à elle.

careen [kə'riːn] **1** *vt Nau* **(a)** abattre *ou* mettre (un navire) en carène; **(b)** (*clean*) caréner (*un navire*). **2** *vi* **(a)** *Nau* (*of ship*) se coucher; **(b)** *Am* (*of car etc*) pencher sur le côté.

careening [kə'riːnɪŋ] *n Nau* carénage *m*.

career¹ [kə'rɪər] *n* carrière *f*; **the accident ended his dancing c.,** cet accident a mis fin à sa carrière de danseur; *Sch Univ etc* **careers service,** service *m* d'orientation professionnelle; **c. diplomat,** diplomate *m* de carrière; **c. woman,** = femme qui poursuit une carrière; **careers officer,** conseiller, -ère d'orientation; **job with c. prospects,** perspectives de carrière.

career² *vi* courir rapidement *ou* follement; **to c. along,** aller à toute vitesse; **to c. into a lorry,** (*of vehicle*) foncer dans un camion; **the car careered off the road,** la voiture a quitté la route à vive allure.

careerist [kə'rɪərɪst] *n Pej* arriviste *mf*, carriériste *mf*.

carefree ['keəfriː] *adj* (*person*) insouciant; (*person, existence*) sans souci; **c. childhood,** enfance insouciante.

careful ['keəfʊl] *adj* **(a)** soigneux (**of,** de), attentif (**of,** à); *Fml* **to be c. of one's reputation,** être soucieux *ou* jaloux de sa réputation; **to be c. with one's money,** regarder à la dépense; **to be c. to do sth,** avoir soin de faire qch, veiller à faire qch; **she was c. not to mention this,** elle a fait bien attention de ne pas mentionner cela; **be c. you don't fall** *or* **not to fall,** faites attention à *ou* de ne pas tomber; **be c. what you say,** faites attention à ce que vous dites; **we are very c. (about) who we employ,** nous faisons très attention quand nous engageons quelqu'un; **(be) c.!,** faites attention!; **c. English speech,** l'anglais parlé surveillé; **c. consideration of a question,** examen attentif *ou* approfondi d'une question;
(b) (*prudent*) prudent, circonspect; **you can't be too c. these days,** de nos jours, on n'est jamais trop prudent; **c. answer,** une réponse bien pesée *ou* réfléchie; **a c. driver,** un conducteur prudent.

carefully ['keəfʊlɪ] *adv* **(a)** soigneusement, avec soin; (*to listen*) attentivement; **(b)** (*to drive*) prudemment.

carefulness ['keəfʊlnɪs] *n* **(a)** soin *m*, attention *f*; **(b)** prudence *f*.

careless ['keəlɪs] *adj* **(a)** (*negligent*) négligent, sans soin; (*work*) négligé; (*error*) d'inattention; **accused of c. driving,** accusé de négligence au volant; **to be c. about one's appearance,** être négligé de sa personne; **she's very c. about her things,** elle n'attache aucune importance à ses biens; **(b)** (*unconcerned*) insouciant, peu soucieux (**of, about,** de); **a c. person,** un *ou* une sans-souci *inv*; *Fml* **he's c. of his friendships,** il fait peu de cas de ses amis; **a c. remark,** une observation inconsidérée *ou* irréfléchie *ou* faite à la légère; **with a c. wave of her hand,** en faisant un léger geste de la main.

carelessly ['keəlɪslɪ] *adv* (*see adj*) **(a)** négligemment, sans soin; **(b)** avec insouciance; **he threw the towel c. over his shoulder,** il lança nonchalamment la serviette par dessus son épaule.

carelessness ['keəlɪsnɪs] *n* **(a)** (*negligence*) manque *m* de soin, négligence *f*; **(b)** insouciance *f*; inattention *f*, étourderie *f*.

carer ['keərər] *n* = personne qui a à sa charge un parent handicapé ou âgé.

caress¹ [kə'res] *n* caresse *f*.

caress² *vt* caresser.

caret ['kærət] *n Typ* signe *m* d'omission.

caretaker ['keəteɪkər] *n* concierge *mf* (*d'un immeuble*

etc); gardien *m* (*d'un musée etc*); *Pol* **c. government,** gouvernement *m* intérimaire.
careworn ['keəwɔːn] *adj* (*visage etc*) rongé *ou* usé par les soucis.
cargo, *pl* **-oes** ['kɑːgəʊ, -əʊz] *n Nau Av* cargaison *f*, chargement *m*; **a c. of wheat,** une cargaison de blé; **full c.,** plein chargement; **general** *or* **mixed c.,** cargaison mixte; **c. boat** *or* **ship,** cargo *m*; **c. plane,** avion-cargo *m*, *pl* avions-cargos, cargo aérien.
Caribbean [kærɪ'biːən, *US* kə'rɪbɪən] *adj & n* **the C. (Sea),** la Mer des Caraïbes *ou* des Antilles; **the C. islands,** les Antilles *fpl*.
caribou ['kærɪbuː] *n* (*animal*) caribou *m*, *pl* -ous.
caricature¹ ['kærɪkətjər] *n* caricature *f*.
caricature² *vt* caricaturer.
caricaturist [kærɪkə'tjuːrɪst] *n* caricaturiste *m*.
caries ['keəriːz] *n Med* carie *f*.
carillon [kə'rɪljən] *n Mus* carillon *m*.
caring ['keərɪŋ] *adj* (*person, society etc*) compatissant, humain, humanitaire; **she's a c. person,** c'est une personne très humaine *ou* généreuse; **the c. professions,** = la profession médicale et para-médicale; les travailleurs sociaux.
carless ['kɑːlɪs] *adj* sans voiture.
carload ['kɑːləʊd] *n* **(a)** (*of motor car*) pleine voiture; **a c. of people/furniture,** une voiture pleine de passagers/de meubles; **(b)** *Am Rail* (*contents*) plein wagon (de marchandises); (*quantity needed to fill car*) quantité *f* (de marchandises) nécessaire pour remplir un wagon.
Carmelite ['kɑːməlaɪt] *n* **C. (nun),** carmélite *f*.
carmine ['kɑːmaɪn] **1** *n* carmin *m*. **2** *adj* carminé, carmin *inv*; (*lèvres*) de carmin.
carnage ['kɑːnɪdʒ] *n* carnage *m*.
carnal ['kɑːn(ə)l] *adj* charnel; (*sensual*) sensuel; (*sexual*) sexuel; **c. sins,** péchés *mpl* de la chair; **c. knowledge,** connaissance charnelle; **to have c. knowledge of s.o.,** avoir des relations sexuelles avec qn.
carnally ['kɑːn(ə)lɪ] *adv* charnellement.
carnation¹ [kɑː'neɪʃən] **1** *n* (*colour*) incarnat *m*; (*of flesh tones*) carnation *f*. **2** *adj* (*teint*) incarnat, incarnadin.
carnation² *n* (*flower*) œillet *m*.
carnival ['kɑːnɪv(ə)l] *n* **(a)** carnaval *m*, fête *f*; **we went to Rio during C.,** nous sommes allés à Rio pendant le Carnaval; **a c. atmosphere,** une ambiance de fête; **(b)** carnaval *m*, -als (*avant le carême*).
carnivora [kɑː'nɪvərə] *npl Zool* carnivores *mpl*.
carnivore ['kɑːnɪvɔːr] *n* (*animal*) carnivore *m*; (*plant*) plante *f* carnivore.
carnivorous [kɑː'nɪv(ə)rəs] *adj* **(a)** (*animal*) carnivore, carnassier; **(b)** (*person, plant*) carnivore.
carob ['kærəb] *n* **(a)** (*tree*) caroubier *m*; **(b)** *Culin* caroube *m*.
carol¹ ['kær(ə)l] *n* chant *m*, chanson *f*; **Christmas c.,** chant de Noël; **c. singer,** chanteur, -euse (de chants de Noël); **to go c. singing,** aller chanter des chants de Noël.
carol² *vi & vt* (**-ll-**, *US* **-l-**) **(a)** (*sing carols*) chanter des chants de Noël; **(b)** *Lit* chanter (joyeusement); (*of lark*) tire-lirer.
Carolina [kærə'laɪnə] *n* Caroline *f*; **South/North C.,** Caroline du Sud/du Nord; **the Carolinas,** la Caroline du Sud et la Caroline du Nord.
Carolingian [kærə'lɪndʒɪən] *Hist* **1** *adj* carolingien. **2** *n* Carolingien, -ienne.
carom ['kærəm] *n Am Billiards* carambolage *m*.
carotid [kə'rɒtɪd] *Anat Med* **1** *adj* **c. artery,** artère *f* carotide. **2** *n* (artère *f*) carotide *f*.
carouse [kə'raʊz] *vi Arch* faire la fête *ou F* la bombe.
carousel [kærə'sel] = **CARROUSEL**.
carp¹ [kɑːp] *n inv* (*fish*) carpe *f*.
carp² *vi* épiloguer, gloser; **to c. at s.o.,** censurer qn; **to c. at sth,** trouver à redire à qch.
Carpathian [kɑː'peɪθɪən] *adj & n* **the C. Mountains, the Carpathians,** les (Monts *mpl*) Carpates *mpl*.
carpel ['kɑːp(ə)l] *n Bot* carpelle *m*, carpophylle *m*.
carpenter¹ ['kɑːpɪntər] *n* charpentier *m*, menuisier *m* en bâtiments; (*makes smaller objects*) menuisier; *Nau* **ship's c.,** matelot *m* charpentier.
carpenter² **1** *vi* faire de la charpenterie. **2** *vt* charpenter (*qch*).
carpentry ['kɑːpɪntrɪ] *n* charpenterie *f*; (*smaller items*) menuiserie *f*; **she likes (doing) c.,** elle aime la menuiserie; **that's a nice piece of c.,** c'est un beau travail de menuiserie.
carpet¹ ['kɑːpɪt] *n* **(a)** tapis *m*; (*fitted*) moquette *f*; **to lay a c.,** poser un tapis; *Fig* **to put out the red c. for s.o., to give s.o. the red c. treatment,** dérouler le tapis rouge devant qn; *Fig* **to sweep under the c.,** enterrer (*une question*); *Fig* **to be on the c.,** (*of question*) être sur le tapis; (*of person*) être sur la sellette; *Fig* **to have** *or* **put s.o. on the c.,** réprimander qn; **c. slippers,** pantoufles *fpl*; **c. tack,** fixe-tapis *m inv*; **c. tile,** dalle *f* (de moquette); **(b)** *Fig* tapis *m* (*de verdure, de fleurs etc*).
carpet² *vt* **(a)** recouvrir (*le plancher*) d'un tapis *ou* d'une moquette; moquetter (*une pièce*); **all the rooms are carpeted,** il y a de la moquette dans toutes les chambres; *Fig* **the pond was carpeted with weed,** le bassin était tapissé d'algues; **(b)** *Old-fashioned F* réprimander (*qn*).
carpetbagger ['kɑːpɪtbægər] *n esp US* **(a)** *Pol F* candidat (au parlement) étranger à la circonscription; **(b)** *Hist* profiteur *m*.
carpeting ['kɑːpɪtɪŋ] *n* **(a)** (*action*) pose *f* de tapis *ou* de moquette; **(b)** (*carpets*) moquette *f*.
carpet-sweeper ['kɑːpɪtswiːpər] *n* balai *m* mécanique.
carping ['kɑːpɪŋ] **1** *adj* (*person, criticism*) pointilleux, malveillant. **2** *n* censure *f*.
carport ['kɑːpɔːt] *n Aut* abri-garage *m*, *pl* abris-garages.
carriage ['kærɪdʒ] *n* **(a)** (*vehicle*) voiture *f*; (*together with horses and driver*) équipage *m*; **open/closed c.,** voiture découverte/fermée; **c. and pair,** voiture à deux chevaux; **baby c.,** voiture d'enfant; **invalid c.,** voiture d'infirme; **c. clock,** = horloge à boîtier rectangulaire muni d'une poignée; **c. drive,** avenue *f* pour voitures; **c. entrance,** porte cochère; *esp Am* **the c. trade,** la clientèle haut de gamme; **(b)** *Br Rail* voiture *f*, wagon *m*; **(c)** *Tech* chariot *m* (*d'un tour, d'une machine à écrire etc*); *Mil* **gun c.,** affût *m*; *Nau* **launching c.,** chariot (de torpille); **c. return (key),** (*on keyboard*) retour *m* de chariot; **(d)** (*transport*) port *m*, transport *m*; *Com* (*cost*) (frais *mpl* de) port; *Com* **c. free,** franc de port, franco; **c. paid,** (en) port payé; **c. forward,** (en) port dû; **(e)** port *m*, maintien *m*, tenue *f* (*d'une personne*); **free** *or* **easy c.,** allure dégagée.
carriageway ['kærɪdʒweɪ] *n Br Aut* chaussée *f*; **dual c.,** route à quatre voies.
carrier ['kærɪər] *n* **(a)** *Med etc* porteur, -euse (*d'une maladie, de germes, de bacilles*); **(b)** *Com* (*company*) commissionnaire expéditeur, transporteur *m*; (*by road*) camionneur *m*; (*airline*) transporteur *m*; *Jur* voiturier *m*; *Jur* **common c.,** voiturier public; **(c)** (*container*) porte-bagages *m inv* (*de bicyclette etc*); cartouche *f* (*pour pigeon voyageur etc*); **c. (bag),** (grand) sac *m* (*en papier, en plastique*); **(d)** *Ind* (*conveyor*) transporteur *m*; *Nau* **aircraft c.,** porte-avions *m inv*; *Av* **troop c.,** (avion *m* de) transport *m* de troupes; *Mil* **armoured personnel c.,** véhicule blindé de transport de troupes; *Nau* **bulk c.,** navire *m* pour le transport en vrac (*du grain etc*); **c. pigeon,** pigeon voyageur.
carrier-based ['kærɪə'beɪst] *adj Av Nau* embarqué; **c.-b. aircraft,** l'aviation embarquée.
carrion ['kærɪən] *n* (*no pl*) charogne *f*; **c. crow,** corneille noire, corbine *f*.
carrot ['kærət] *n* carotte *f*; **a pay rise is the c. management is holding out to the unions,** le patronat tente d'amadouer les syndicats en promettant une hausse des salaires; **which will the government use with the strikers — the c. or the stick?,** quelle méthode le gouvernement va-t-il adopter face aux grévistes, la carotte ou le bâton?; *F* **carrots, c. top,** (*hair*) cheveux *mpl* roux *ou* carotte; (*person*) rouquin *m*, poil *m* de carotte.
carroty ['kærətɪ] *adj F* (*person, hair*) roux, *f* rousse.
carrousel [kærə'sel] *n* **(a)** (*for slides*) magasin *m*; **(b)** (*at airport*) carrousel *m* (pour bagages); **(c)** *Am* chevaux *mpl* de bois; **(d)** (*at fairground*) manège *m*.
carry ['kærɪ] *v* (**carried**) **1** *vt* **(a)** porter (*un enfant, un fardeau etc*); transporter (*des marchandises, des passagers etc*); camionner (*des marchandises*); (*on one's person*) porter (*un revolver, une montre*) sur soi; **we had to c. him,** nous avons dû le porter; **I don't c. much money about** *or* **on me,** je n'ai jamais beaucoup d'argent sur moi; **the bus carried us to our destination,** l'autobus nous a conduits *ou* transportés à notre destination; **a memory that he will c. with him to the grave,** un souvenir qu'il emportera dans la tombe; **the truck is carrying explosives,** le camion transporte des explosifs; **we were carrying livestock,** (*of ship*) nous avions du bétail à bord; **to c. sth in one's head,** retenir qch dans sa tête; **to c. weight/authority,** (*of person, opinion*) avoir du poids/de l'autorité; **to c. interest,** (*of money*) porter intérêt; **to c. a child,** (*be pregnant*) porter un enfant, être enceinte;
(b) (*of wires etc*) conduire, transmettre (*le son etc*); (*of pipes*) amener (*l'eau etc*);

(c) (*capture, win*) enlever (*une forteresse*); emporter (*une position*) d'assaut; **to c. all before one,** (*be successful*) remporter tous les prix; (*win support, approval*) vaincre toutes les résistances, triompher sur toute la ligne; *Hum* **she carries all before her,** il y a du monde au balcon; **to c. one's point,** établir la validité d'un argument;

(d) (*pass*) adopter (*une proposition*); (*secure passage of*) faire adopter *ou* passer (*une proposition*); **the bill was carried,** le projet a été adopté;

(e) *Com* tenir (*un article*); avoir (*des marchandises*) en magasin *ou* en dépôt; **to c. an advertisement/article,** comporter une publicité/un article; **do you c. bathroom accessories?,** (*to sales assistant*) est-ce que vous vendez des accessoires pour salles de bain?;

(f) (*hold*) **to c. oneself well/badly,** se tenir bien/mal; **to c. one's head high,** porter la tête haute;

(g) *Archit Constr* porter, supporter (*une poutre, une voûte*);

(h) *Math* **to c. a figure,** retenir un chiffre; **c. two and seven are nine,** deux de retenue et sept font neuf.

2 *vi* **(a)** (*of sound, gun etc*) porter; **her voice carries well,** elle a une voix qui porte bien;

(b) *US Pol* (*of resolution etc*) passer;

(c) *Sl* avoir de la drogue sur soi; **he was arrested for carrying,** il a été arrêté parce qu'il avait de la drogue sur lui.

►**carry along** *vtsep* emporter, entraîner (*qn, qch*); **mud carried along by the stream,** boue charriée par le ruisseau.

►**carry away** *vtsep* **(a)** (*take*) emporter, enlever (*qch*); entraîner, emmener (*qn*); **(b)** (*make excited, over-enthusiastic*) **he let his enthusiasm c. him away,** il s'est laissé emporter par son enthousiasme; **don't get carried away!,** ne te laisse pas emporter!; *Iron F* ne t'emballe pas!; **she gets carried away by the sound of her own voice,** elle se berce au son de sa voix.

►**carry back** *vtsep* **(a)** (*bring*) rapporter (*qch*); ramener (*qn*); **(b)** (*take*) reporter (*qch*); remmener (*qn*); **that carries me back to my youth,** cela me rappelle ma jeunesse.

►**carry forward** *vtsep* **(a)** (*bring, take*) avancer (*qch*); **(b)** (*in book-keeping*) **to c. an item forward,** reporter un article; **carried forward,** report *m*, à reporter.

►**carry off** *vtsep* **(a)** (*bring, take*) emporter (*qch*); emmener (*qn*); (*capture*) enlever, emporter (*qn*); **(b)** (*win*) remporter (*le prix*); **(c)** (*be successful in*) faire passer, faire accepter (*qch d'insolite*); **to c. it off,** réussir le coup; **they managed to c. the robbery off,** ils ont mené à bien le cambriolage; **it's a difficult role and he didn't quite c. it off,** c'est un rôle difficile, et il n'a pas su se montrer à la hauteur; **(d)** (*of disease*) emporter (*qn*).

►**carry on 1** *vtsep* poursuivre, continuer (*un travail*); continuer (*une tradition*); exercer (*un commerce, un métier*); entretenir (*une correspondance*); soutenir (*une conversation*).

2 *vi* **(a)** (*continue*) continuer; **just c. on with what you were doing,** continuez ce que vous étiez en train de faire; **to c. on during s.o.'s absence,** continuer le travail *ou* diriger les affaires pendant l'absence de qn; *Admin* assurer l'intérim; **c. on!,** continuez!; **I shall c. on to the end,** j'irai jusqu'au bout;

(b) *F* (*behave*) se comporter; **I don't like the way she carries on,** je n'aime pas ses façons; **from the way he carries on anyone'd think ...,** vu la façon dont il se comporte, on croirait vraiment ...;

(c) *F* (*behave badly*) faire des scènes, s'emporter; **don't c. on like that!,** ne vous emballez pas comme ça!;

(d) *F* (*have an affair*) avoir une liaison (**with,** avec); **are you carrying on behind my back?,** est-ce que tu as une liaison sans que je le sache?

►**carry out** *vtsep* **(a)** (*bring, take*) porter (*qch*) dehors *ou* hors de la salle *etc*; transporter (*qn*) au grand air; **(b)** (*do, execute*) mettre à exécution (*un projet, une menace, une décision*); effectuer (*une expérience*); remplir (*les instructions de qn*); exécuter (*un programme*); exercer (*un mandat*); donner suite à (*une idée, Com une commande*); satisfaire à (*une obligation, un désir*); se décharger de (*une commission*); mener à bonne fin (*un travail*); s'acquitter de (*une tâche, une fonction*); appliquer (*la loi, un principe*); **to c. out a procedure,** suivre un mode de procédure.

►**carry through** *vtsep* **(a)** (*complete*) mener (*une entreprise*) à bien *ou* à bonne fin *ou* à bon terme; exécuter (*un travail, un calcul*); **(b) his strong constitution carried him through his illness,** sa forte santé l'aida à surmonter cette maladie.

carryall ['kærɪɔːl] *n* (sac *m*) fourre-tout *m inv*.

carrycot ['kærɪkɒt] *n* porte-bébé *m inv*.

carrying ['kærɪɪŋ] **1** *adj* **(a) c. party,** équipe *f* de porteurs; **(b) c. axle,** (*of locomotive*) essieu porteur. **2** *n* **(a)** port *m*, transport *m*; **c. capacity,** (*of vehicle*) charge *f* utile; **(b)** adoption *f*, vote *m* (*d'un projet de loi etc*).

carrying-on ['kærɪɪŋ'ɒn] *n F* (*foolish behaviour*) **carrying(s)-on,** cirque *m*.

carry-on[1] ['kærɪ'ɒn] *n F* scène *f*; **what a c.-on just to buy a ticket!,** quelle histoire rien que pour acheter un billet!

carry-on[2] *adj* (*luggage*) à main.

carsick ['kɑːsɪk] *adj* **to be c.,** avoir mal au cœur en voiture.

carsickness ['kɑːsɪknɪs] *n* mal *m* au cœur (en voiture).

cart[1] [kɑːt] *n* charrette *f* (*à deux roues*); (*with four wheels*) chariot *m*; (*small*) carriole *f*; *Fig* **to put the c. before the horse,** mettre la charrue devant les bœufs; **bullock** *or* **ox c.,** char *m* à bœufs; **tip c.,** tombereau *m*; **c. track,** chemin charretier.

cart[2] *vt* charrier, voiturer (*qch*).

►**cart about, cart around** *vtsep F* (trans)porter (*des colis*); trimbal(l)er (*une valise*).

►**cart away, cart off** *vtsep F* enlever, emporter (*des ordures etc*); **they carted him away** *or* **off,** ils l'ont emmené.

cartage ['kɑːtɪdʒ] *n* **(a)** (*in cart*) charroi *m*, charriage *m*; (*in lorry*) camionnage *m*; **(b)** (*cost*) (prix *m* de) camionnage *m*.

cartel [kɑː'tel] *n Ind etc* cartel *m*; **oil/steel/***etc* **c.,** cartel du pétrole/de l'acier/*etc*; **to form a c.,** former un cartel.

carter ['kɑːtər] *n* charretier *m*.

Cartesian [kɑː'tiːzɪən] *adj Phil* cartésien.

carthorse ['kɑːthɔːs] *n* cheval *m* de charrette.

Carthusian [kɑː'θjuːzɪən] *adj & n* **(a)** *Rel* chartreux, -euse; **(b)** *Br Sch* (élève ou ancien élève) de l'école de Charterhouse.

cartilage ['kɑːtɪlɪdʒ] *n* cartilage *m*.

cartload ['kɑːtləʊd] *n* charretée *f*, voiturée *f* (**of,** de); (*of tip cart*) tombereau *m* (*de charbon, de fumier*).

cartographer [kɑː'tɒgrəfər] *n* cartographe *m*.

cartography [kɑː'tɒgrəfɪ] *n* cartographie *f*.

cartomancy ['kɑːtəmænsɪ] *n* cartomancie *f*.

carton ['kɑːtən] *n Com* **(a)** (*box*) (boîte *f* en) carton *m*; **(b)** (*container*) (*for yoghurt, cream etc*) pot *m* (*en carton, en plastique*); (*for milk, orange juice etc*) brick *m*; **a c. of cigarettes,** une cartouche de cigarettes.

cartoon [kɑː'tuːn] *n* **(a)** (*in newspaper etc*) dessin *m* (*humoristique, satirique*); *Cin* dessin animé; **c. character,** personnage *m* de bande dessinée; **strip c., c. strip,** bande dessinée; **(b)** (*caricature*) portrait caricaturé, caricature *f*; **(c)** *Art* carton *m*.

cartoonist [kɑː'tuːnɪst] *n* **(a)** dessinateur, -trice (*de dessins humoristiques, satiriques*); **(b)** (*caricaturist*) caricaturiste *m*.

cartridge ['kɑːtrɪdʒ] *n* **(a)** *Mil* cartouche *f* (*d'arme à feu*); gargousse *f* (*de grosse pièce*); **blank c.,** cartouche à blanc; **c. clip,** chargeur *m*; **c. belt,** (*for soldier*) ceinture-cartouchière *f*, *pl* ceintures-cartouchières; (*for machine gun*) bande-chargeur souple *ou* articulée (*pl* bandes-chargeurs); **(b)** (*container, unit*) cartouche *f* (*de film, d'encre, El de fusible etc*); (*on record-player*) cellule *f* de lecture; (*for tape recorder*) cassette *f*; **c. pen,** stylo *m* à plume *ou* à cartouche; **(c)** *Ind Art* **c. paper,** papier *m* à cartouches, papier-cartouche *m*.

cartwheel ['kɑːtwiːl] *n* roue *f* de charrette; *Gym* **to turn cartwheels,** faire la roue; **to do a c.,** faire une roue.

cartwright ['kɑːtraɪt] *n* charron *m*.

carve [kɑːv] **1** *vt* **(a)** sculpter (*du marbre etc*); graver, ciseler (*un dessin, un nom etc sur le marbre etc*); **to c. a statue in** *or* **out of marble,** sculpter une statue dans le marbre; **carved lion,** lion sculpté; **(b)** (*meat*) découper; (*poultry*) dépecer. **2** *vi* **(a)** sculpter (**in,** dans); **(b)** (*of material*) **wood that carves well/badly,** bois qui se prête bien/mal à la sculpture.

►**carve out** *vtsep* sculpter, tailler, découper; **to c. out a statue,** sculpter une statue; *Fig* **the company carved out a niche in this market,** la société s'est taillé une place sur le marché; *Fig* **to c. out a career for oneself,** se faire une place (dans une profession).

►**carve up** *vtsep* **(a)** (*cut*) (*meat*) découper; (*poultry*) dépecer; *F Fig* **to c. s.o. up,** défigurer qn; *Fig* **Europeans carved up the continent (among themselves),** les Européens se sont partagé le continent; **(b)** *Aut F* (*overtake dangerously*) faire une queue de poisson à (*qn*); **did you**

see how that idiot carved me up?, tu as vu la queue de poisson que m'a fait cet imbécile?

carver ['kɑːvər] *n* **(a)** (*sculptor*) sculpteur *m* (*sur bois*); (*on marble*) ciseleur *m*; **(b)** (*of meat*) découpeur, -euse; (*knife*) couteau *m* à découper; (*chair*) fauteuil *m* de table (*qu'occupe le chef de famille*).

carving ['kɑːvɪŋ] *n* **(a)** *Art* sculpture *f*; (*on wood, metal*) gravure *f*; (*on metal, stone*) ciselure *f*; **wood c.,** sculpture sur bois; **(b)** découpage *m* (*de la viande*); **c. knife/fork,** couteau *m*/fourchette *f* à découper.

carwash ['kɑːwɒʃ] *n Aut* lave-auto *m*.

caryatid [kærɪ'ætɪd] *n Archit* cariatide *f*.

cascade¹ [kæs'keɪd] *n* (*waterfall*) & *Fig* cascade *f*.

cascade² *vi* (*of water etc*) tomber en cascade; *Fig* **balloons cascaded down from the ceiling,** des ballons sont tombés en cascade depuis le plafond.

case¹ [keɪs] *n* **(a)** (*instance, situation*) cas *m*; **a c. in point,** un cas d'espèce; **to put the c. clearly,** exposer clairement le cas *ou* la situation; **if that is the c.,** s'il en est ainsi; **should that be the c.,** le cas échéant; **that would meet the c.,** cela ferait (bien) l'affaire; **it's a c. of now or never,** il s'agit de saisir l'occasion *ou* de faire vite; **in c. of emergency/accident/need,** en cas d'urgence/d'accident/de besoin; **in c. he isn't there,** au cas *ou* dans le cas où il n'y serait pas; **just in c.,** à titre de précaution; **just in c. it rains I'll take an umbrella,** je prends un parapluie, juste au cas où il pleuvrait; **I'll take an umbrella, just in c.,** je prends un parapluie au cas où; **in any c.,** (*at any rate*) en tout cas; (*besides*) de toute façon; **in that c.,** en ce cas; **in such a c., in such cases,** en pareil cas, en pareille circonstance; **in these cases it's best to wait,** dans de telles circonstances, il vaut mieux attendre; **in his c.,** dans son cas; **their c. is typical,** leur cas est typique; **let's take the c. of the Smith family,** prenons le cas de la famille Smith; **as the c. may be,** selon le cas, selon les circonstances; **in most cases,** dans la plupart des cas;
(b) *Med* cas *m* (*de jaunisse, de scarlatine etc*); (*patient*) malade *mf*; **heart c.,** cardiaque *mf*; *F* **he's a c.,** c'est un drôle de type; **c. history,** antécédents *mpl*; histoire *f* de la maladie; **c. load,** (nombre *m* de) dossiers *mpl* (*d'un médecin, d'une assistante sociale etc*); **c. study,** étude *f* de cas;
(c) *Jur etc* affaire *f*; **famous cases,** causes *fpl ou* affaires célèbres; **the police are working on the c.,** la police enquête sur cette affaire; **to state the c.,** faire l'exposé des faits; **to put the c. for the prisoner,** présenter la défense du prévenu; **the c. for the Crown,** (*in criminal trial*) l'accusation *f*; **there is no c. against you,** vous êtes hors de cause; **the c. for s.o./sth,** les arguments *mpl* en faveur de qn/qch; **to put up a strong c. for s.o.,** (*defend*) prendre le parti de qn, défendre qn; (*recommend*) recommander qn très chaudement; **civil/criminal c.,** affaire civile/criminelle; **divorce c.,** procès *m* en divorce; **test c.,** cas *m* dont la solution fait jurisprudence; **c. law,** jurisprudence *f*;
(d) *Gram* cas *m*; **c. endings,** flexions casuelles.

case² *n* **(a)** (*large*) **(packing) c.,** caisse *f*, boîte *f* (d'emballage); **c. of wine,** caisse de vin;
(b) (*for specific object*) étui *m* (*à lunettes, à cigarettes etc*); coffret *m*, écrin *m* (*pour bijoux*); trousse *f* (*d'instruments*); boîte *f* (*de violon*); gaine *f* (*de poignard, de pistolet, de momie*); **record c.,** mallette *f* porte-disques; **dressing c.,** nécessaire *m ou* trousse de toilette; **card c.,** porte-cartes *m inv*; **(display) c.,** vitrine *f*; **the crown was displayed in a glass c.,** la couronne était exposée dans une vitrine;
(c) (*suitcase*) valise *f*; (*briefcase*) porte-documents *m inv*;
(d) (*outer part*) coffre *m*, caisse *f* (*de piano*); buffet *m* (*d'orgue*); caisse (*d'horloge*); boîtier *m* (*de montre etc*); palastre *m*, coffre (*de serrure*); douille *f*, étui *m* (*de cartouche*); chemise *f*, enveloppe *f* (*de cylindre de moteur*); bâche *f* (*de turbine*); *Aut* carter *m* (*du différentiel etc*); *Aut* **crank c.,** carter (du moteur);
(e) (*in bookbinding*) couverture *f*;
(f) *Typ* casse *f*; **lower c.,** bas *m* de casse; **lower-c. letter,** minuscule *f*; **upper c.,** haut *m* de casse; **upper-c. letter,** (lettre *f*) majuscule *f*, (lettre) capitale *f*.

case³ *vt* **(a)** (*put in box*) encaisser, emballer (*des marchandises*), mettre (*des marchandises*) en caisse(s); **(b)** (*put outer layer on*) envelopper (**with,** de); chemiser (*une chaudière, un cylindre*); bâcher (*une turbine*); **(c)** (*in bookbinding*) cartonner (*un livre*); **(d)** *Sl* **to c. a joint,** examiner les lieux, prospecter (*avant un cambriolage*).

casebook ['keɪsbʊk] *n* **(a)** *Jur* recueil *m* de jurisprudence; **(b)** *Med* dossier médical.

case-harden ['keɪshɑːd(ə)n] *vt Metal* cémenter, aciérer (*le fer*); tremper *ou* durcir (*l'acier*) à la surface.

case-hardened ['keɪshɑːd(ə)nd] *adj Metal* cémenté, aciéré, trempé à la surface; (*moulé*) en coquille; *F* (*person*) endurci.

case-hardening ['keɪshɑːd(ə)nɪŋ] *n Metal* cémentation *f* (*de l'acier*).

casein ['keɪsiːn] *n Ch Ind* caséine *f*.

casement ['keɪsmənt] *n* **(a)** châssis *m* de fenêtre à deux battants; **c. window,** fenêtre *f* à deux battants, croisée *f*; **(b)** *Lit* fenêtre *f*.

casework ['keɪswɜːk] *n Med* traitement individuel; (*social work*) assistance individuelle.

caseworker ['keɪswɜːkər] *n* assistant(e) social(e).

cash¹ [kæʃ] *n* (*no pl*) argent comptant, espèces *fpl*, numéraire *m*; **I haven't got any c.,** (*no money*) je n'ai pas d'argent; (*no change*) je n'ai pas de monnaie; **to pay in c.,** payer comptant; *esp Am* **will that be c. or charge?,** vous payez comptant ou vous le portez à votre compte?; **c. (purchases) only,** (*notice at checkout*) paiements en liquide seulement; **c. on delivery,** paiement à la livraison, (livraison) contre remboursement; **c. reduction,** = réduction accordée si on paie en liquide; **c. and carry,** emporter-comptant *m*; **c. in hand,** fonds *mpl ou* espèces en caisse; **it's all c. in hand in this sort of work,** dans cette branche, tout se paye de la main à la main; **petty c.,** petite caisse; *Fin* **c. flow,** cash-flow *m*, trésorerie *f*; **c. flow forecast,** prévision *f* de trésorerie; *F* **I've got a c. flow problem,** j'ai un problème de trésorerie; *F* **I'm short of c.,** je suis à sec; **to keep the c.,** tenir la caisse; **c. box,** caisse, cassette *f*; *Agr* **c. crop,** culture qui rapporte de l'argent; **c. desk** *or* **point,** caisse; **c. dispenser,** distributeur *m* automatique, *Can* guichet *m* automatique; **c. card,** carte *f* de retrait; **c. register,** caisse enregistreuse; **c. payment,** paiement *m* (au) comptant; *Com* **c. balance,** solde actif, solde de caisse; **c. price,** prix *m* au comptant; **c. transaction/sale,** transaction *f*/vente *f* au comptant; **c. discount, discount for c.,** escompte *m* de caisse.

cash² *vt* toucher (*un chèque, un mandat-poste etc*); encaisser (*un effet, un coupon*); escompter (*un effet*); changer (*un billet de banque*); **to c. a cheque for s.o.,** verser à qn le montant d'un chèque.

►cash in *vtsep Fin* (*exchange for money*) **to c. in premium bonds/savings stamps,** se faire rembourser des bons à lots/des bons d'épargne; *Sl* **to c. in one's chips** *or* **checks,** (*die*) casser sa pipe.

►cash in on *vipo F* (*derive benefit from*) tirer profit de (qch); **she cashed in on the popularity of country music,** elle a profité de la popularité de la country music.

►cash up *vi Br Fin* faire les comptes.

cash-book ['kæʃbʊk] *n* livre *m* de caisse.

cashew [kæ'ʃuː] *n* **c. (nut tree),** acajou *m* à pommes, anacardier *m*; **c. (nut),** (noix *f* de) cajou *m*.

cashier¹ [kæ'ʃɪər] *n* caissier, -ière.

cashier² *vt Mil Nau* casser (*un sous-officier*); réformer (*un officier, par mesure disciplinaire*).

cashless ['kæʃlɪs] *adj* **the c. society,** la société démonétisée; **c. transaction,** transaction *f* sans argent.

cashmere ['kæʃmɪər] *n Tex* cachemire *m*; **c. shawl,** (châle *m* de) cachemire; **c. sweater,** pull *m* en cachemire.

casing ['keɪsɪŋ] *n* **(a)** (*process*) encaissage *m* (*de marchandises*); clissage *m* (*d'une bouteille*); cartonnage *m* (*d'un livre*); tubage *m*, cuvelage *m* (*d'un puits de mine etc*); **(b)** (*outer layer*) enveloppe *f*, garniture *f* (*d'une pompe etc*); blindage *m*, chemise *f* (*d'un cylindre*); huche *f*, bâche fermée (*d'une turbine*); cage *f*, coquille *f* (*d'une machine*); boîte *f*, caisse *f* (*de l'embrayage*); revêtement *m* (*d'une maçonnerie*); *Min* boisage *m* (*d'un puits, d'une galerie etc*); *Nau Arch* entourage plein; cadre *m* (*d'une hélice*); manchon *m* (*de gouvernail*); *Constr* coffrage *m* (*pour béton armé*); *MecE* gainage *m*; *Metal* manteau *m* (*d'un moule*); *Aut* carter *m* (*du différentiel, d'embrayage*); **tyre c.,** enveloppe (extérieure) de pneu.

casino [kə'siːnəʊ] *n* casino *m*.

cask [kɑːsk] *n* **(a)** barrique *f*, fût *m*, futaille *f*, tonneau *m*; *Com* **wine in the c.,** vin *m* en fût *ou* en cercles, vin en pièce; **(b)** (*for dry goods*) boucaut *m*.

casket ['kɑːskɪt] *n* **(a)** coffret *m* (*à bijoux*); cassette *f* (*pour bijoux, argent*); **(b)** *esp Am* (*coffin*) cercueil *m*; **(c)** (*for ashes*) urne *f*.

Caspian ['kæspɪən] *adj* caspien; **the C. Sea,** la mer Caspienne.

Cassandra [kə'sændrə] *n Myth* Cassandre *f*; *Fig* oiseau *m* de malheur.

cassata [kə'sɑːtə] *n Culin* cassate *f*.

cassava [kə'sɑːvə] *n Bot* cassave *f*, manioc *m*; **c. (flour),** farine *f* de cassave, manioc.
casserole¹ ['kæsərəʊl] *n Culin* **(a)** *Br* (*receptacle*) cocotte *f*; **(b)** (*food*) ragoût *m* en cocotte; **beef c..** ragoût de bœuf.
casserole² *vt* cuire (*de la viande etc*) en cocotte.
cassette [kæ'set] *n* **(a)** (*audio, video etc*) *& Comptr* cassette *f*; **c. player,** lecteur *m* de cassette; **c. recorder,** enregistreur *m* à cassette; **(b)** *Phot* chargeur *m*.
cassock ['kæsək] *n Rel* soutane *f*.
cassowary ['kæsəweərɪ] *n* (*bird*) casoar *m*.
cast¹ [kɑːst] *n* **(a)** *Th Cin TV* distribution *f*; **members of the c.,** membres de la troupe *ou* de la distribution; **with the following c.,** avec la distribution suivante, avec le concours de; **a c. of three/thousands,** avec trois acteurs/des milliers d'acteurs; **all-star c.,** distribution ne comportant que des vedettes; **the film has an all-star c.,** il y a une pléiade de vedettes dans ce film;
(b) (*act of throwing*) jet *m* (*d'une pierre etc*); coup *m* (*de dés, de filet*); (*in fishing*) lancer *m* (*de la ligne, de la mouche, du filet*); **at a single c. of the dice,** d'un seul coup de dés;
(c) *Med* appareil plâtré; *Art Metal etc* (*mould*) moule *m* en creux; (*item*) pièce moulée; (*of plaster*) plâtre *m*; **plaster c.,** moulage *m* au plâtre; **to take a c. of sth,** mouler qch; (*in plaster*) tirer un plâtre de qch; **to have one's arm in a c.,** avoir le bras dans le plâtre;
(d) (*squint*) **to have a c. in one's eye,** avoir une coquetterie dans l'œil;
(e) *Lit* **a man of his c.,** un homme de sa trempe; **c. of features,** physionomie *f*;
(f) (*of earthworm*) déjections *fpl*;
(g) (*skin of insect, snake*) dépouille *f*;
(h) (*regurgitated food*) pelote régurgitée (*par les hiboux, les faucons*);
(i) (*twist, warp etc*) voilure *f* (*d'une poutre etc*);
(j) *Typ* cliché *m*.
cast² *v* (*pt & pp* **cast**) **1** *vt* **(a)** jeter, lancer (*une pierre etc*); porter, projeter (*une ombre*); lancer (*un filet, la ligne*); **the die is cast,** le dé *ou* le sort en est jeté; **she cast her eyes over the letter,** elle a parcouru la lettre; **this cast doubt on his ability,** cela jeta un doute sur ses capacités; **to c. sth aside,** se défaire de qch; *Nau* **to c. the lead,** donner un coup de sonde; **to c. its slough,** (*of reptile*) jeter sa dépouille; **to c. a shoe,** (*of horse*) perdre un fer; **to c. a stream,** pêcher au lancer;
(b) *Pol etc* donner (*une voix*); **to c. a vote for the greens,** voter pour les écologistes;
(c) *Th Cin TV* distribuer les rôles de (*une pièce*); **to c. s.o. for a part,** assigner *ou* attribuer un rôle à qn; **she was cast as** *or* **in the role of Desdemona,** on lui a donné le rôle de Desdémone, elle a joué (le rôle de) Desdémone.
(d) tirer, faire dresser (*un horoscope*); **to c. a spell over s.o.,** ensorceler qn, envoûter qn.
(e) *Art Metal etc* fondre (*du métal*); mouler, couler (*un cylindre etc*); sabler (*une médaille*); couler (*une statue*); **the statue had been cast in bronze,** cette statue avait été coulée dans le bronze; **cast in one piece,** coulé en bloc;
(f) *Nau* virer (*un navire*).
2 *vi* **to c. for fish,** pêcher au lancer.
cast³ *adj Art Metal* coulé, fondu; **c. steel,** fonte *f* d'acier, acier fondu; **c. iron,** (fer *m* de) fonte, fonte de fer; *Cer* **c. ware,** pièces coulées; *Fig* **c. iron alibi,** alibi *m* irréfutable; *Fig* **c. iron guarantee,** garantie *f* en béton.
▶**cast about, cast around** *vi* chercher; **to c. around for something to say,** chercher quelque chose à dire.
▶**cast away** *vtsep Nau* **to be cast away,** faire naufrage.
▶**cast back** *vtsep* **to c. one's mind back (to sth),** se rappeler qch; **c. your mind back a week,** souvenez-vous de *ou* rappelez-vous la semaine dernière.
▶**cast down** *vtsep* **(a)** baisser (*les yeux*); **(b)** *Lit* **to be cast down,** être abattu *ou* découragé *ou* déprimé.
▶**cast off** **1** *vtsep* **(a)** (*reject*) rejeter, repousser (*qn*); **he was cast off by his family,** il était rejeté par sa famille; **(b)** (*shed*) se dépouiller de (*sa réserve*); **(c)** *Knitting* arrêter (*des mailles*); **(d)** *Nau* larguer (*les amarres*). **2** *vi* **(a)** *Nau* (*of ship*) démarrer, larguer les amarres; **(b)** *Knitting* arrêter les mailles.
▶**cast on** *Knitting* **1** *vtsep* monter (*des mailles*). **2** *vi* monter les mailles.
▶**cast out** *vtsep* **(a)** (*reject*) rejeter (*qn*); **(b)** (*exorcise*) chasser, exorciser (*des démons*).
▶**cast up** *vtsep* **(a) to c. sth up to s.o.,** reprocher qch à qn; **(b)** (*of sea*) rejeter; **flotsam cast up on the shore,** épaves rejetées sur la plage.
castanets [kæstə'nets] *npl* **(pair of) c.,** (paire *f* de) castagnettes *fpl*.
castaway ['kɑːstəweɪ] *n* naufragé, -ée.
caste [kɑːst] *n* caste *f*; **high/low-c.,** de haute/basse caste; *Fig* **to lose c.,** déroger (à son rang), déchoir (de son rang).
casteless ['kɑːstlɪs] *adj* sans caste.
castellated ['kæstɪleɪtɪd] *adj Archit Mil etc* crénelé.
caster ['kɑːstər] *n* **(a)** *Art Metal etc* fondeur *m*; mouleur, -euse (*de plâtre etc*); (*machine*) fondeuse *f*; **(b)** = **CASTOR (a), (b).**
castigate ['kæstɪgeɪt] *vt Fml* **(a)** (*punish*) châtier, corriger (*qn*); **(b)** (*criticize*) critiquer sévèrement (*qn, un ouvrage*).
castigation [kæstɪ'geɪʃən] *n* **(a)** (*punishment*) châtiment *m*, correction *f*; **(b)** (*criticism*) critique *f* sévère.
Castile [kæ'stiːl] *n* Castille *f*; **New C.,** Nouvelle-Castille.
Castilian [kæs'tɪlɪən] **1** *adj* castillan. **2** *n* **(a)** (*person*) Castillan, -ane; **(b)** *Ling* castillan *m*.
casting ['kæstɪŋ] **1** *adj* **c. vote,** voix prépondérante (*accordée au président d'une assemblée ou d'un conseil quand les avis sont également partagés*); **the chairman has the c. vote,** la voix du président est prépondérante. **2** *n* **(a)** (*throwing*) jet *m* (*d'une pierre etc*); (*in fishing*) (pêche *f* au) lancer *m*; **c. net,** épervier *m*; **(b)** *Art Metal etc* (*process*) coulée *f*, coulage *m*, moulage *m*, fonte *f*; (*individual item*) pièce coulée, pièce de fonte; **sand c.,** coulée en sable; **heavy castings,** grosses pièces; **die c.,** pièce moulée sous pression; **(c)** *Th Cin* distribution *f* des rôles, casting *m*; *F* **she got the part through the c. couch,** elle a eu son rôle en couchant avec le metteur en scène; **c. director,** directeur *m* de casting.
casting off *n Knitting* fermeture *f* (de mailles).
casting on *n Knitting* montage *m* (de mailles).
castle¹ ['kɑːs(ə)l] *n* **(a)** château *m* (*royal, seigneurial*); (*fortress*) château fort; **to build castles in the air** *or* **in Spain,** bâtir des châteaux en Espagne; *Prov* **an Englishman's home is his c.,** charbonnier est maître chez lui; **(b)** *Chess* tour *f*.
castle² *vt & vi Chess* roquer.
castling ['kɑːs(ə)lɪŋ] *n Chess* roque *f*.
cast-off ['kɑːstɒf] **1** *n* **(a)** (*item of clothing*) **I used to wear my brother's c.-offs,** je portais les vêtements que mon frère ne mettait plus; **(b)** *Fig* laissé-pour-compte, laissée-pour-compte; **one of society's c.-offs,** un laissé-pour-compte de la société. **2** *adj* **c.-o. clothing,** vêtements *mpl* de rebut.
castor ['kɑːstər] *n* **(a)** poivrière *f*; saupoudroir *m* (*à sucre etc*); *Culin* **c. sugar,** sucre *m* semoule; **(b)** (*on chair etc*) roulette *f*; **the desk's on castors,** le bureau est sur roulettes; **(c)** *Pharm* **c. oil,** huile *f* de ricin.
castrate [kæs'treɪt] *vt* châtrer (*une bête, un homme*); castrer, émasculer (*un homme*); *Fig* (*un texte etc*) mutiler, expurger.
castration [kæs'treɪʃən] *n* (*of animal, man*) castration *f*; (*of man*) émasculation *f*; *Fig* (*of text etc*) mutilation *f*, expurgation *f*.
castrato, *pl* **-ti** [kæ'strɑːtəʊ, -tɪ] *n Mus* castrat *m*.
casual ['kæʒjʊ(ə)l] **1** *adj* (*meeting*) fortuit, accidentel; (*remark*) désinvolte; (*glance*) au hasard; (*person*) insouciant; **to engage in c. conversation,** parler de choses et d'autres *ou* de la pluie et du beau temps; **to throw out a c. suggestion,** suggérer qch en passant; **they were very c. about the danger,** ils se moquaient du danger; **c. clothes, (clothes for) c. wear,** tenue *f* de loisirs; **c. labour,** main-d'œuvre occasionnelle *ou* temporaire; **c. sex,** rapports accidentels. **2** *npl* **casuals,** (*shoes*) mocassins *mpl*.
casually ['kæʒjʊ(ə)lɪ] *adv* fortuitement, par hasard, en passant; **to reply c.,** répondre d'un air indifférent *ou* négligemment.
casualty ['kæʒjʊəltɪ] *n* (*victim*) victime *f* (*d'un accident, d'un incendie, d'un tremblement de terre*); (*in war, road accident*) blessé, -ée; (*in road accident*) accidenté, -ée; **there were no casualties,** il n'y a pas eu de victimes; *Mil* **casualties,** pertes *fpl*; *Fig Pol* **the party had many casualties in the last election,** le parti a perdu beaucoup de députés aux dernières élections; *Fig* **freedom of speech was one of the first casualties of the military takeover,** la suppression de la liberté d'expression a été une des premières conséquences fâcheuses de la prise du pouvoir par les militaires; *Fig* **these children are the casualties of the divorce rate,** ces enfants sont les victimes du divorce; *Mil* **c. list** *or* **return,** état *m* des pertes; *Med* **c. ward,** salle *f* des accidentés; *Med* **c. (department),** service *m* des urgences (*d'un hôpital*); *Med* **she was taken to c.,** elle a été emmenée aux urgences.
casuist ['kæzjʊɪst] *n* casuiste *m*.
casuistry ['kæzjʊɪstrɪ] *n* casuistique *f*.

cat [kæt] *n* **(a)** chat *m*, *f* chatte; **Siamese c.**, chat siamois; **tabby c.**, chat tigré; **tom c.**, matou *m*; *F* **ginger** *or* **marmalade c.**, chat roux tigré; **alley c.**, chat de gouttière; **wild c.**, chat sauvage; **civet c.**, **musk c.**, civette *f*; **the big cats**, les grands félins; **it smelled of cats**, ça sentait la pisse de chat; *Sl* **that looks like something the cat's brought in**, ça, c'est dégoûtant; **to quarrel like c. and dog**, s'entendre comme chien et chat; *F* **c. got your tongue?**, tu as perdu ta langue?; *F* **he thinks he's the c.'s whiskers**, il se croit quelqu'un; *Fig* **to see which way the c. jumps**, voir d'où vient le vent; **to play a c.-and-mouse game with s.o.**, jouer au chat et à la souris avec qn; *Prov* **while the cat's away the mice (will) play**, quand le chat n'est pas là, les souris dansent; *F* **to be like a c. on hot bricks**, ne pas tenir en place; *F* **to let the c. out of the bag**, vendre la mèche; *F* **to put the c. among the pigeons**, mettre le loup dans la bergerie; *F* **there's no** *or* **there isn't enough room to swing a c.**, il n'y a pas de place pour se retourner; **c. show**, exposition féline; **c. flap**, chatière *f*; **c. litter**, litière *f* de chat; *F* **c. burglar**, cambrioleur *m* par escalade; **c.'s cradle**, jeu *m* du berceau (*joué avec une ficelle*); **c.'s eye**, *Aut* catadioptre *m*, cataphote ® *m*; (*gem*) œil-de-chat *m*, *pl* œils-de-chat;
(b) (*person*) *US Sl* (*man*) type *m*, individu *m*; *Pej* (*woman, girl*) salope *f*;
(c) **c.(-o'-nine-tails)**, martinet *m* à neuf cordes;
(d) *Nau* **c. (purchase, tackle)**, capon *m*.

CAT [kæt] *n Med* (*abbr* **computerized axial tomography**) **CAT scan**, tomographie *f*.

cataclysm ['kætəklɪz(ə)m] *n* cataclysme *m*.

cataclysmic [kætə'klɪzmɪk] *adj* cataclysmique.

catacomb ['kætəkəʊm] *n* (*usu pl*) **catacombs**, catacombes *fpl*.

catafalque ['kætəfælk] *n* catafalque *m*.

Catalan ['kætəlæn] **1** *adj* catalan. **2** *n* **(a)** (*person*) Catalan, -ane; **(b)** *Ling* catalan *m*.

catalepsy ['kætəlepsɪ] *n Med* catalepsie *f*.

cataleptic [kætə'leptɪk] *adj & n Med* cataleptique *mf*.

catalogue¹, *US* **catalog** ['kætəlɒg] *n* **(a)** *Com* catalogue *m*; **mail-order c.**, catalogue de vente par correspondance; **trade c.**, album(-tarif) *m*, tarif-album *m*; **c. number**, référence *f*; **(b)** (*list*) catalogue *m*, liste *f*, répertoire *m*; **the holiday was a c. of disasters**, les vacances ont été une suite de catastrophes; **subject c.**, catalogue méthodique.

catalogue², *US* **catalog** *vt* cataloguer.

cataloguing, *US* **cataloging** ['kætəlɒgɪŋ] *n* catalogage *m*.

Catalonia [kætə'ləʊnɪə] *n* Catalogne *f*.

catalysis [kə'tælɪsɪs] *n Ch* catalyse *f*.

catalyst ['kætəlɪst] *n Ch & Fig* catalyseur *m*.

catalytic [kætə'lɪtɪk] *adj Ch* catalytique; *Fig* catalyseur; *Aut* **c. converter**, pot *m* catalytique.

catamaran [kætəmə'ræn] *n Nau* catamaran *m*.

cataplasm ['kætəplæz(ə)m] *n Med* cataplasme *m*.

catapult¹ ['kætəpʌlt] *n Br* (*for stones etc*) fronde *f*; (*on aircraft carrier*) catapulte *f*.

catapult² **1** *vt* catapulter, projeter (*qn, qch*); catapulter (*un avion*); **he catapulted the stone over the wall**, il a lancé la pierre par dessus le mur; *Fig* **these reforms catapulted the country into the 20th century**, ces réformes ont propulsé le pays dans le XXᵉ siècle; **to c. s.o. to stardom**, (*of film etc*) propulser qn vers la célébrité. **2** *vi* entrer en trombe (**into a room**, dans une pièce).

cataract ['kætərækt] *n* (*in river etc*) *& Med* cataracte *f*.

catarrh [kə'tɑːr] *n Med* catarrhe *m*; **bronchial c.**, bronchite *f*.

catarrhal [kə'tɑːr(ə)l] *adj* (*cough*) catarrhal, -aux; (*person*) catarrheux.

catastrophe [kə'tæstrəfɪ] *n* catastrophe *f*; **the victims of the c.**, les sinistrés *mpl*.

catastrophic [kætə'strɒfɪk] *adj* (*effect etc*) catastrophique.

catastrophically [kætə'strɒfɪklɪ] *adv* d'une façon catastrophique.

catatonia [kætə'təʊnɪə] *n Med* catatonie *f*.

catatonic [kætə'tɒnɪk] *adj* catatonique; **to be c.**, (*of psychiatric patient*) être catatonique.

catcall¹ ['kætkɔːl] *n Th etc* (coup *m* de) sifflet *m* (*dirigé contre un acteur etc*).

catcall² **1** *vt* siffler (*un acteur*). **2** *vi* (*of audience*) siffler.

catch¹ [kætʃ] *n* **(a)** prise *f* au vol (*d'une balle, d'un ballon*); **that was a good c.**, bien joué!; **to play c.**, (*of children*) jouer au ballon; **c. phrase**, scie *f*; *Th* phrase comique (répétée); *Agr* **c. crop**, culture dérobée;
(b) (*fishing*) prise *f*, pêche *f*; **to have a good c.**, faire (une) bonne pêche; **the day's c.**, la pêche de la journée;
(c) (*person as marriage partner*) parti *m*; **he's** *or* **she's no great c.**, ce n'est pas un bon parti;
(d) (*fastening*) (*on door etc*) loquet *m*, loqueteau *m*; (*of window*) loqueteau; (*of buckle*) ardillon *m*; (*of clasp knife*) mouche *f*; (*on garment*) agrafe *f*; *MecE* crochet *m* d'arrêt; (*of wheel, winch, shaft etc*) cliquet *m*; **safety c.**, (*on gun*) cran *m* de sûreté;
(e) (*disadvantage*) attrape *f*; **there's a c. in it**, c'est une attrape; **that's** *or* **there's the c.**, voilà le hic; *Sch etc* **c. question**, colle *f*; **c. 22 situation**, cercle vicieux;
(f) **with a c. in one's voice**, d'une voix entrecoupée;
(g) *Mus* chanson *f* à reprises, canon *m*;
(h) (*in rowing*) attaque *f*.

catch² *v* (*pt & pp* **caught** [kɔːt]) **1** *vt* **(a)** attraper, saisir (*une balle etc*); attraper, prendre (*un poisson, un voleur etc*); pêcher (*un poisson*); saisir (*un voleur*); **c.!**, (*when throwing sth to s.o.*) attrape!; **well caught!**, bien joué!; *Nau* **to c. the wind**, (*of sail etc*) prendre le vent; **I caught him as he fell**, je l'ai retenu *ou* attrapé au moment où il tombait; **I caught him by the hand**, je l'ai attrapé par la main; **to c. s.o. doing sth** *or* **in the act** *or* **red-handed**, prendre qn en flagrant délit; **don't get caught!**, ne te fais pas prendre!; **you'll be in trouble if your mother catches you**, tu vas avoir des problèmes si ta mère te surprend; **caught you!**, je t'y prends!; **you won't c. me doing that again**, on ne m'y reprendra plus; **to be caught in a storm**, être surpris par un orage; **you might c. her if you run**, vous pouvez la rattraper si vous courez; **you're unlikely to c. her at home**, je ne pense pas que tu la trouveras chez elle; **you've caught me in the middle of a meeting**, tu m'as interrompu au milieu d'une réunion; **we caught him in a good mood**, nous l'avons pris dans un moment de bonne humeur; *F* **c. you later!**, on se voit plus tard!;
(b) (*not miss*) attraper (*un train etc*); *F* arriver à temps pour voir (*un film*); *F* **c. this outstanding singer next month**, ne manquez pas ce chanteur étonnant le mois prochain; *F* **I caught the last half hour of the documentary**, j'ai réussi à voir la dernière demi-heure du documentaire;
(c) (*perceive*) saisir, percevoir (*des sons*); **to c. a glimpse of** *or* **sight of sth**, apercevoir qch; **I caught a few words**, j'ai entendu *ou* j'ai saisi quelques mots; **I didn't c. what you were saying**, je n'ai pas entendu ce que vous disiez; **I caught a hint of bitterness**, (*in what she said*) j'ai senti un peu d'amertume dans ses paroles; **the author has caught the mood of the time**, l'auteur a su rendre l'ambiance de l'époque,
(d) (*make impression on*) frapper (*la vue, l'oreille*); attirer (*l'attention de qn*); **to c. the chairman's eye**, (*at meeting etc*) attirer l'attention du président; **nothing in the shop caught my fancy**, je n'ai rien trouvé qui me plaisait dans la boutique; **their story caught the imagination of the public**, l'imagination du public a été stimulée par leur histoire;
(e) (*entangle*) **I caught my dress on a nail**, j'ai accroché ma robe à un clou; **he caught his foot on a root and fell**, il s'est pris le pied dans une racine et il est tombé; **don't c. your fingers in the door!**, ne te coince pas les doigts dans la porte!; **there's something caught in the door**, il y a quelque chose de coincé dans la porte;
(f) (*contract*) attraper (*une maladie*); *Fig* contracter (*une habitude*); prendre (*l'accent du pays*); **to c. (a) cold**, s'enrhumer, attraper un rhume; **I caught this cold from you**, c'est toi qui m'a passé ce rhume; **to c. fire** *or US* **on fire**, prendre feu;
(g) (*of blow, object*) **the punch caught me in the chest**, j'ai reçu le coup de poing en plein dans la poitrine; **the stone caught her on the arm**, elle a reçu la pierre sur le bras; *Boxing* **he caught him with a left to the chin**, il lui a porté un gauche au menton; *F* **you'll c. it!**, tu vas écoper quelque chose!;
(h) *F* (*fool*) attraper, avoir (*qn*); **you won't c. me!**, ça ne prend pas (avec moi)!
2 *vi* **(a)** attraper; **(here) c.!**, tiens, attrape!; **I'm hopeless at catching**, je n'arrive jamais à attraper (*la balle etc*);
(b) (*engage*) (*of cog wheel*) mordre; (*of gearing*) quotter;
(c) (*of fire*) prendre, s'allumer;
(d) *Culin* (*of stew etc*) attacher.

▶**catch at** *vipo* (*grab at*) essayer de saisir (*qch*); (*hold on to*) s'accrocher à (*qch*); **he caught at her sleeve**, il s'est accroché à sa manche.

▶**catch on** *vi* **(a)** (*become popular*) (*of fashion etc*) réussir, avoir du succès; (*of tune*) accrocher; **the game**

never caught on in Europe, ce jeu n'a jamais eu de succès en Europe; **(b)** *F* (*understand*) saisir, piger; **he still hasn't caught on,** il n'y est pas.

▶**catch out** *vtsep* (*trap*) (*by difficult question*) prendre, piéger (*qn*); (*of circumstances*) surprendre; **the police caught her out when they asked her ...,** la police l'a piégée en lui demandant ...; **to c. s.o. out in a lie,** prendre qn à mentir; **a lot of investors got caught out when the stock market collapsed,** beaucoup d'investisseurs se sont fait piéger quand la bourse s'est effondrée; **we got caught out by the rain,** nous avons été surpris par la pluie.

▶**catch up 1** *vi* (*close gap, get closer*) se rapprocher, rattraper; **the runners behind are catching up,** les coureurs qui sont derrière se rapprochent; **we caught up with them at the lights,** nous les avons rattrapés au feu rouge; **our competitors are catching up with us,** nos concurrents nous rattrapent; **to c. up on** *or* **with one's work/sleep,** rattraper du travail/du sommeil; *F* **it will c. up with you (one of these days),** ça va vous retomber sur le nez. **2** *vtsep* **(a)** (*overtake*) rattraper (*qn*); **(b)** (*become entangled*) **I got caught up in a discussion,** j'ai été entraîné dans une discussion; **I got really caught up in what I was doing,** j'étais complètement absorbé dans ce que je faisais; **they were caught up in a traffic jam for hours,** ils ont été bloqués dans un embouteillage pendant des heures; **to be caught up in a wave of enthusiasm,** être entraîné dans un mouvement d'enthousiasme.

catch-all ['kætʃɔːl] *n Am F* fourre-tout *m inv*; **c.-a. category/clause,** catégorie *f*/clause *f* fourre-tout.

catch-as-catch-can ['kætʃəz'kætʃ'kæn] *n* (*wrestling*) catch *m*, lutte *f* libre.

catcher ['kætʃər] *n* **(a)** attrapeur, -euse, preneur, -euse; **rat c.,** preneur de rats; **mole c.,** taupier *m*; **(b)** *Baseball* attrapeur *m*, receveur *m*.

catching ['kætʃɪŋ] **1** *adj* (*disease, habit etc*) contagieux, -ieuse; (*laughter, melancholy*) communicatif. **2** *n* **(a)** (*capture*) prise *f*, capture *f*; **(b)** (*of toothed wheel*) engrenure *f*; (*of gearing*) quottement *m*.

catchment ['kætʃmənt] *n* captation *f*, captage *m* (*d'eaux*); **c. area** *or* **basin,** bassin *m* hydrographique; **c. area,** (*of airport, school*) zone desservie.

catchpenny ['kætʃpenɪ] *n* attrape-nigaud *m*, *pl* attrape-nigaud(s); **c. scheme** *or* **show,** attrape-nigaud.

catchphrase ['kætʃfreɪz] *n* (*of comedian etc*) slogan *m*.

catchword ['kætʃwɜːd] *n* **(a)** *Pol etc* mot *m* de ralliement; **(b)** *Th* (*cue*) réplique *f*; **(c)** (*of comedian etc*) slogan *m*.

catchy ['kætʃɪ] *adj* (*tune*) entraînant, facile à retenir; (*slogan*) facile à retenir.

catechism ['kætəkɪz(ə)m] *n* catéchisme *m*.

catechist ['kætəkɪst] *n* catéchiste *mf*.

catechize ['kætəkaɪz] *vt* **(a)** *Rel* catéchiser; **(b)** *Fig* (*question*) interroger, questionner (*qn*).

catechumen [kætɪ'kjuːmən] *n* catéchumène *mf*.

categoric(al) [kætɪ'gɒrɪk, -ɪk(ə)l] *adj* (*réponse, refus etc*) catégorique.

categorically [kætɪ'gɒrɪklɪ] *adv* (*to answer, refuse etc*) catégoriquement.

categorize ['kætɪgəraɪz] *vt* classer par catégories; **I don't like being categorized,** je n'aime pas qu'on me colle une étiquette.

category ['kætɪgərɪ] *n* (*class*) catégorie *f*; **these facts fall into another c.,** ces faits entrent dans une autre catégorie.

catenary [kə'tiːnərɪ] *adj* (*railway*) caténaire.

cater ['keɪtər] *vt* **we're having the meal catered,** nous faisons fournir le repas.

▶**cater for** *vipo* **(a)** (*provide with food*) approvisionner (*qn*), pourvoir à la nourriture de (*qn*); **(b)** (*provide with special requirement*) **parties catered for,** (*notice in hotel etc*) = banquets, noces; **hotel that caters for English visitors,** hôtel qui s'adresse surtout à la clientèle anglaise; **to c. for all tastes,** pourvoir à tous les goûts; **the hotel doesn't c. for children,** l'hôtel ne prévoit pas d'aménagements pour les enfants; **I hadn't catered for that,** (*allowed for*) je n'avais pas prévu ça.

▶**cater to** *vipo* satisfaire à (*les besoins*).

cater-corner(ed) ['keɪtəkɔːnər, -əd] *adj & adv Am* diagonalement opposé(s).

caterer ['keɪtərər] *n Com* traiteur *m*.

catering ['keɪtərɪŋ] *n* restauration *f*; *Av* service traiteur; **to work in c.,** travailler dans la restauration; **who did the c. at your wedding?,** qui a préparé le repas *ou* le buffet à votre mariage?; **the c. industry,** la restauration; **c. manager,** chef *m ou* responsable *mf* de la restauration; **c. firm,** entreprise *f* de restauration.

caterpillar ['kætəpɪlər] *n* **(a)** (*insect*) chenille *f*; **(b)** *Tech* **c. (tread** *or* **track),** chenille *f*; **c. tractor,** tracteur *m* à chenilles.

caterwaul ['kætəwɔːl] *vi* **(a)** (*of cat*) miauler; **(b)** *Fig* hurler (comme les chats la nuit).

caterwauling ['kætəwɔːlɪŋ] *n* **(a)** miaulements *mpl* (*de chats*); **(b)** *Fig* hurlements *mpl*.

catfish ['kætfɪʃ] *n* **(a)** silure *m*, poisson-chat *m*, *pl* poissons-chats; **(b)** (*wolffish*) blennie *f*.

catgut ['kætgʌt] *n* **(a)** *Mus* corde *f* de boyau; **c. strings,** cordes en boyau de chat (*pour violon*); **(b)** *Med* catgut *m*.

catharsis [kə'θɑːsɪs] *n Psy* catharsis *f*.

cathartic [kə'θɑːtɪk] *adj Psy* cathartique.

cathedral [kə'θiːdrəl] *n* cathédrale *f*; **c. town,** ville épiscopale, évêché *m*.

Catherine ['kæθrɪn] *n* Catherine *f*; *Hist* **C. the Great,** la Grande Catherine; **C. wheel,** (*firework*) soleil *m*, roue *f* à feu.

catheter ['kæθɪtər] *n Med* sonde *f* (creuse), cathéter *m*; **indwelling c.,** sonde intérieure *ou* à demeure; **he has to have a c.,** il faut qu'on lui pose un cathéter.

cathode ['kæθəʊd] *n El* cathode *f*; **photo(electric) c.,** cathode photoélectrique; **c. beam/ray/screen,** faisceau *m*/rayon *m*/écran *m* cathodique; **c. ray tube,** tube *f* à rayons cathodiques, tube cathodique.

catholic ['kæθlɪk] *adj* (*wide-ranging*) éclectique; (*broad-minded*) à l'ésprit large; (*universal*) universel; **to be c. in one's tastes,** avoir des goûts éclectiques.

Catholic ['kæθlɪk] **1** *adj Rel* catholique; **I believe in one holy, c. and apostolic Church,** je crois en l'Église, une, sainte, catholique et apostolique. **2** *n* catholique *mf*; **she's become a C.,** elle est devenue catholique.

Catholicism [kə'θɒlɪsɪz(ə)m] *n Rel* catholicisme *m*.

catkin ['kætkɪn] *n Bot* chaton *m*.

catlick ['kætlɪk] *n F* **to have** *or* **give oneself a c.,** se laver le bout du nez, faire une toilette de chat.

catmint ['kætmɪnt] *n* (*plant*) cataire *f*, herbe *f* aux chats.

catnap[1] ['kætnæp] *n F* sieste *f* (de courte durée), somme *m*.

catnap[2] *vi F* faire la sieste *ou* un somme.

catnip ['kætnɪp] *n* (*plant*) cataire *f*, herbe *f* aux chats.

catspaw, cat's-paw ['kætspɔː] *n* **to be s.o.'s c.,** être la dupe de qn; **to be made a c. of,** être dupé.

catsuit ['kætsuːt] *n* combinaison-pantalon *f*.

catsup ['kætsəp] *n US Culin* ketchup *m*.

cattery ['kætərɪ] *n* pension *f* pour chats.

cattiness ['kætɪnɪs] *n F* vacherie *f*, rosserie *f*, méchanceté *f*.

cattle ['kæt(ə)l] *n* (*no pl*) bétail *m*, bestiaux *mpl*; **horned c.,** bêtes *fpl* à cornes, bovins *mpl*; **we were herded onto trucks like c.,** on nous a entassés dans des camions comme du bétail; **c. breeding,** élevage *m* du bétail; *Rail* **c. truck** *or Am* **car,** wagon *m* pour le bétail *ou* les bestiaux; **c. crossing,** passage *m* de troupeaux; **c. market,** (*for animals*) *& Fig* marché *m* aux bestiaux; **c. show,** comice *m* agricole.

cattle-cake ['kæt(ə)lkeɪk] *n* tourteau *m*.

cattle-grid ['kæt(ə)lgrɪd] *n* = grille placée sur un fossé pour empêcher le passage du bétail.

cattleman, *pl* **-men** ['kæt(ə)lmən, -men] *n Am* bouvier *m*.

catty ['kætɪ] *adj F* **(a)** (*esp woman*) vache, rosse, méchant; **c. remark,** vacherie *f*, rosserie *f*; **(b) there's a c. smell,** ça sent la pisse de chat.

catty-corner(ed) ['kætɪ'kɔːnər, -əd] *adj & adv Am* diagonalement opposé(s).

catwalk ['kætwɔːk] *n* passerelle *f*; *Nau* coursive *f*; (*for models*) podium *m* de défilé de mode.

Caucasian [kɔː'keɪʒən, -'keɪzɪən] **1** *adj* **(a)** *Geog Ling* caucasien; **(b)** (*in ethnology*) caucasien. **2** *n* Caucasien, -ienne; (*white person*) membre *m* de la race blanche.

Caucasus (the) [ðə'kɔːkəsəs] *n* le Caucase.

caucus ['kɔːkəs] *n esp US Pol* **(a)** (*group*) bloc *m*; **(b)** (*meeting*) réunion *f* du bloc.

caudal ['kɔːd(ə)l] *adj Zool* caudal, -aux; **c. fin,** (nageoire *f*) caudale *f*; **c. feathers,** plumes caudales.

caught *see* **CATCH**[2].

caul [kɔːl] *n* coiffe *f* (de nouveau-né); **born with a c.,** né coiffé.

cauldron ['kɔːldrən] *n* chaudron *m*.

cauliflower ['kɒlɪflaʊər] **,** *Br F* **cauli** ['kɒlɪ] *n* chou-fleur *m*, *pl* choux-fleurs; *Culin* **c. cheese,** chou-fleur au gratin; *Boxing etc* **c. ear,** oreille *f* en chou-fleur *ou* en feuille de chou.

caulk [kɔːk] *vt* calfater, étouper (*un navire*).

caulking ['kɔːkɪŋ] *n* calfatage *m*; **c. iron,** calfait *m*, burin *m*.

causal [ˈkɔːz(ə)l] *adj* causal.
causality [kɔːˈzælɪtɪ] *n* causalité *f*.
causally [ˈkɔːzəlɪ] *adv* **to be c. connected,** avoir un rapport de cause à effet.
causative [ˈkɔːzətɪv] *adj Gram* (*verbe*) causatif.
cause¹ [kɔːz] *n* **(a)** (*origin*) cause *f*; **c. and effect,** la cause et l'effet; **no effect without a c.,** point d'effet sans cause; **to be the c. of an accident,** être (la) cause d'un accident; **this is a common c. of bankruptcy,** c'est une cause courante de faillite;
(b) (*reason*) raison *f*, motif *m*, sujet *m*; **c. for litigation,** matière *f* à procès; **I have c. to be thankful,** j'ai lieu d'être reconnaissant; **you've no c. to be indignant,** vous n'avez pas lieu d'être indigné, vous n'avez pas de quoi être indigné; **to have good c. for doing sth,** avoir de bonnes raisons pour faire qch; **to give serious c. for complaint,** donner de grands sujets de plainte; **his condition is giving c. for concern,** son état donne des raisons de s'inquiéter; **and with good c.,** et pour cause; **without c.,** sans raison;
(c) (*movement etc*) cause *f*; **to win s.o. over to one's c.,** gagner qn à sa cause; **to make common c.,** faire cause commune (**with,** avec); **in the c. of justice,** pour (la cause de) la justice; **to work for a good c.,** travailler pour une bonne cause; **it's for a good c.,** c'est pour une bonne cause; *F* **it's all in a good c.,** ce n'est pas du temps perdu;
(d) *Jur* cause *f*; **to plead s.o.'s c.,** plaider la cause de qn.
cause² *vt* causer, occasionner (*un malheur, du retard etc*); faire arriver (*un accident*); provoquer (*la gaîté, un accident*); faire naître (*une querelle*); susciter (*de l'étonnement*); **to c. a fire,** provoquer un incendie; **to c. trouble,** (*disturbance*) semer la perturbation; (*problems*) causer des ennuis; **to c. a sensation,** faire sensation; **all the worry you've caused us,** toute l'inquiétude que tu nous as causée; **to c. s.o./sth to do sth,** faire faire qch à qn/qch; **a dog caused him to swerve,** un chien lui a fait faire une embardée; **to c. s.o. to be punished,** faire punir qn.
causeway [ˈkɔːzweɪ] *n* chaussée *f*, levée *f*, digue *f* (*coupant à travers des marécages*).
caustic [ˈkɔːstɪk] **1** *adj* caustique; **c. soda,** soude *f* caustique, hydrate *m* de soude; *Fig* **c. wit,** esprit mordant. **2** *n Ch Med* caustique *m*.
cauterization [kɔːtəraɪˈzeɪʃən] *n Med* cautérisation *f*.
cauterize [ˈkɔːtəraɪz] *vt Med* cautériser.
cautery [ˈkɔːtərɪ] *n* cautère *m*.
caution¹ [ˈkɔːʃən] *n* **(a)** (*prudence*) précaution *f*, prévoyance *f*, prudence *f*; **with great c.,** avec beaucoup de circonspection; **c. is advised,** on conseille la prudence; **(b)** (*warning*) avis *m*, avertissement *m*; **c.! steep gradient/pressurized container,** Attention! Descente rapide/Récipient sous pression; **(c)** *Jur Sp etc* (*reprimand*) réprimande *f*; **he has been let off with a c.,** il s'en est tiré avec une réprimande; **(d)** *Mil* commandement *m* préparatoire.
caution² *vt* **(a)** (*warn*) avertir (*qn*), mettre (*qn*) en garde; **to c. s.o. against sth,** prévenir qn contre qch; **(b)** *Jur* prévenir (*un suspect*) que ce qu'il dira peut être utilisé contre lui au cours des poursuites du procès; **(c)** (*reprimand*) menacer (*qn*) de poursuites à la prochaine occasion, réprimander (*qn*).
cautious [ˈkɔːʃəs] *adj* circonspect; (*driver, remark*) prudent; **to be c. in doing sth,** faire qch avec circonspection; **to play a c. game,** jouer serré.
cautiously [ˈkɔːʃəslɪ] *adv* (*to proceed*) avec précaution, avec circonspection; (*to drive*) prudemment.
cautiousness [ˈkɔːʃəsnɪs] *n* circonspection *f*; (*of driver, remark*) prudence *f*.
cavalcade [kævəlˈkeɪd] *n* cortège *m*; (*on horseback*) cavalcade *f*.
cavalier [kævəˈlɪər] **1** *n Hist* cavalier *m*. **2** *adj* cavalier, désinvolte; **this is a very c. attitude,** c'est une attitude bien cavalière; **with a c. air,** avec désinvolture.
Cavalier [kævəˈlɪər] *n Eng Hist* royaliste *m*; **the Cavaliers and Roundheads,** les Cavaliers et les Têtes rondes.
cavalry [ˈkævəlrɪ] *n* cavalerie *f*; **c. officer,** officier *m* de cavalerie.
cavalryman, *pl* **-men** [ˈkævəlrɪmən, -men] *n Mil* cavalier *m*, soldat *m* de cavalerie.
cave¹ [keɪv] *n* caverne *f*, grotte *f*; **c. art,** art *m* rupestre; **c. dweller,** (*troglodyte*) troglodyte *mf*; (*in prehistoric times*) homme *m ou* femme *f* des cavernes; **c. dwelling,** maison *f* troglodyte; **c. paintings,** peintures *fpl* rupestres.
cave² *vi* faire de la spéléologie.
cave³ [ˈkeɪvɪ, ˈkɑːveɪ] *int Br Sch F Arch* attention!, pet!
►**cave in** *vi* **(a)** (*of ground, structure etc*) céder, s'affaisser, s'effondrer; (*of structure, beam*) s'infléchir; **(b)** *F* (*of person*) céder, se soumettre.
caveat [ˈkævɪæt] *n* **(a)** (*warning*) avertissement *m* (**against,** contre); **(b)** *Jur* opposition *f* (**to,** à).
cave-in [ˈkeɪvɪn] *n* (*of ground, structure etc*) affaissement *m*, effondrement *m*; (*of structure, beam*) infléchissement *m*.
caveman, *pl* **-men** [ˈkeɪvmæn, -mən] *n* (*troglodyte*) troglodyte *mf*; (*prehistoric man*) homme *m* des cavernes; *Fig* primitif *m*.
caver [ˈkeɪvər] *n* spéléologue *mf*.
cavern [ˈkævən, -ɜːn] *n* caverne *f*.
cavernous [ˈkævənəs] *adj* (*room etc*) caverneux; (*eye-sockets*) cave, creux; (*yawn*) profond.
caviar(e) [ˈkævɪɑːr] *n* caviar *m*; *Prov* **(it's) c. to the general,** c'est comme donner de la confiture aux cochons.
cavil [ˈkævɪl] *vi* (**-ll-**, *US* **-l-**) chicaner, ergoter (**at, about sth,** sur qch).
caving [ˈkeɪvɪŋ] *n* spéléologie *f*.
caving in *n* effondrement *m*, affaissement *m*.
cavitation [kævɪˈteɪʃən] *n Tech* cavitation *f*.
cavity [ˈkævɪtɪ] *n* cavité *f*, creux *m*; *Constr* **c. wall,** mur *m* double; **(dental) c.,** cavité dentaire.
cavort [kəˈvɔːt] *vi* faire des cabrioles, cabrioler.
cavy [ˈkeɪvɪ] *n* (*animal*) cobaye *m*, cochon *m* d'Inde.
caw¹ [kɔː] *vi* (*of crow etc*) croasser.
caw² *n* (*of crow etc*) croassement *m*.
cawing [ˈkɔːɪŋ] *n* croassement *m*.
cayenne [keɪˈen] *n* **c. (pepper),** (poivre *m* de) cayenne *m*.
cayman [ˈkeɪmən] *n* (*animal*) caïman *m*; **C. Islands,** îles *fpl* Cayman.
CB [siːˈbiː] *n* (*abbr* **Citizen's Band**) CB *f*.
CBC [siːbiːˈsiː] *n TV Rad* (*abbr* **Canadian Broadcasting Corporation**) (societé *f*) Radio-Canada *f*; **she works for the CBC,** elle travaille pour Radio-Canada.
CBE [siːbiːˈiː] *n abbr* **Commander of the Order of the British Empire**.
CBI [siːbiːˈaɪ] *n Br Ind* (*abbr* **Confederation of British Industry**) = patronat *m* britannique.
CBS [siːbiːˈes] *n abbr* **Columbia Broadcasting System**.
cc [siːˈsi] **1** *n abbr* **(a)** (*on memorandum*) **carbon copy** *or* **copies**; **(b) cubic centimetres**. **2** *vt* envoyer une copie à.
CC [siːˈsiː] *n abbr* **county council**.
CD [siːˈdiː] *n* **(a)** *Admin* (*abbr* **Corps Diplomatique**) = Corps *m* Diplomatique; **a car with CD plates,** une voiture du Corps Diplomatique; **(b)** (*abbr* **compact disc**) = (disque *m*) compact *m*; **CD player,** lecteur *m* de (disques) compacts.
Cdr *n abbr Mil* **Commander**.
Cdre *n abbr Nau* **Commodore**.
CD-ROM [siːdiːˈrɒm] *n Comptr* (*abbr* **compact disc-read only memory**) CD-ROM *m*; **available on CD-ROM,** existe en CD-ROM.
cease¹ [siːs] *n* **without c.,** sans cesse.
cease² **1** *vi* cesser (**doing sth,** de faire qch); **hostilities have ceased,** les hostilités ont cessé; **they have ceased to exist,** ils n'existent plus; **it never ceases to amaze me that ...,** cela m'étonne toujours que ...; **without ceasing,** sans arrêt. **2** *vt* cesser; *Mil* **to c. fire,** cesser le feu.
cease-fire [ˈsiːsfaɪər] *n* cessez-le-feu *m inv*.
ceaseless [ˈsiːslɪs] *adj* incessant, continuel; **their c. efforts to have the law changed,** leurs efforts continuels pour faire changer la loi.
ceaselessly [ˈsiːslɪslɪ] *adv* sans cesse, continuellement.
cecum [ˈsiːkəm] *n US* = **CAECUM**.
cedar [ˈsiːdər] *n Bot* **c. (tree),** cèdre *m*; **c. of Lebanon,** cèdre du Liban; **c. panelling,** lambris *mpl* en cèdre; *Am* **c. closet,** placard *m* en cèdre (*pour éloigner les mites*).
cede [siːd] *vt esp Jur* céder (*un bien immobilier, une province, une dette*) (**to,** à); **to c. a point,** (*in an argument*) concéder un point.
cedilla [sɪˈdɪlə] *n* cédille *f*.
CEGB [siːiːdʒiːˈbiː] *n Eng El* (*abbr* **Central Electricity Generating Board**) ≈ EDF *f*.
ceiling [ˈsiːlɪŋ] *n* **(a)** plafond *m* (*d'une pièce, d'une voiture etc*); **c. light,** plafonnier *m*; **c. tile,** dalle *f* pour plafond; *F* **to hit the c.,** (*become angry*) entrer dans une colère noire; **(b)** *Econ etc* plafond *m*; **c. price,** prix *m* plafond; **to reach a c.,** (*of prices etc*) plafonner; **(c)** *Av* plafond *m*; **to fly at the c.,** plafonner; **(d)** *Met* plafond *m* (nuageux).
celadon [ˈselədɒn] *n* (*porcelain*) céladon *m*; **c. green,** (vert *m*) céladon.
celandine [ˈseləndaɪn] *n* (*flower*) **greater c.,** chélidoine *f*; grande éclaire; **lesser c.,** ficaire *f*; petite éclaire.

celebrant ['selıbrənt] *n Rel* célébrant *m*, officiant *m*.

celebrate ['selıbreıt] **1** *vt* **(a)** (*commemorate, mark*) célébrer, commémorer (*un événement*); *F* fêter (*qch*); **the city is celebrating the anniversary of its founding,** la ville célèbre l'anniversaire de sa fondation; **the players celebrated their win,** les joueurs ont célébré *ou* fêté leur victoire; **to c. s.o.'s birthday,** fêter l'anniversaire de qn; **let's open a bottle of wine to c. the occasion,** ouvrons une bouteille de vin pour marquer l'occasion; **(b)** *Rel* célébrer (*la messe, un mariage, une fête*). **2** *vi* faire la fête; **will you be celebrating tonight?,** tu vas arroser ça *ou* tu vas faire la fête ce soir?; **let's c.,** faisons la fête.

celebrated ['selıbreıtıd] *adj* célèbre (**for sth,** par qch).

celebration [selı'breıʃən] *n* **(a)** (*party, drink etc*) festivités *fpl*, réunion *f*, dîner *m* (*pour fêter qch*); **the Independance Day celebrations,** les festivités à l'occasion de l'anniversaire de l'Indépendance; *F* **this calls for a c.!,** il faut fêter ça!, ça s'arrose!; **(b)** *Rel* célébration *f* (*de la communion, d'une fête*).

celebrity [sı'lebrıtı] *n* **(a)** (*person*) célébrité *f*; **c. football match,** = match de football dans lequel une des équipes est composée de célébrités; **(b)** (*fame*) célébrité *f*, renommée *f*.

celeriac [sı'lerıæk] *n* céleri-rave *m*, *pl* céleris-raves.

celerity [sı'lerıtı] *n Fml* célérité *f*.

celery ['selərı] *n* céleri *m*; **head of c.,** pied *m* de céleri; **stick of c.,** branche *f* de céleri; **c. soup,** soupe *f* au céleri.

celestial [sı'lestıəl] *adj* (*sphère etc*) céleste.

celiac ['si:lı'æk] *adj & n US* = **COELIAC**.

celibacy ['selıbəsı] *n* chasteté *f* (*pendant une longue période ou à un moment déterminé*); (*not being married*) célibat *m*.

celibate ['selıbət] **1** *adj* (*chaste*) chaste; (*unmarried*) célibataire; (*vie*) de chasteté, de célibataire. **2** *n* célibataire *mf*.

cell [sel] *n* **(a)** (*in prison*) cellule *f*, cachot *m*; **they spent a night in the cells,** ils ont passé la nuit en cellule; **(b)** (*of monk, hermit*) cellule *f*; **(c)** (*in beehive*) cellule *f*, alvéole *m*; **(d)** *El Electron etc* élément *m* (*de pile*); **dry c.,** pile sèche; **wet c.,** pile à liquide; **storage c.,** (*of accumulator*) élément d'accumulateur; **photoelectric/photovoltaic c.,** cellule *f* photoélectrique/photovoltaïque; **solar c.,** pile solaire; **(e)** *Biol* cellule *f*; **c. wall,** paroi *f* cellulaire; *Anat* **blood c.,** globule *m*; **(f)** *Pol* **communist c.,** cellule *f ou* noyau *m* communiste.

cellar ['selər] *n* cave *f*; chai *m* (*de négociant en vins*); **wine c.,** cave à vin; **to keep a good c.,** avoir une bonne cave.

cellist ['tʃelıst] *n Mus* violoncelliste *mf*.

cello ['tʃeləʊ] *n Mus* violoncelle *m*; **c. concerto,** concerto *m* pour violoncelle.

cellular ['seljʊlər] *adj Biol* (*structure etc*) cellulaire; *Tex* **c. blanket,** couverture *f* alvéolaire; **c. board,** (*cardboard*) carton ondulé; *Electron* **c. logic,** logique *f* cellulaire; *Telecom* **c. phone,** téléphone *m* cellulaire.

cellulite ['seljʊlaıt] *n* cellulite *f*.

celluloid ['seljʊlɔıd] *n* (*no pl*) celluloïd(e) *m*; *Cin* **on c.,** sur la pellicule; **c. epic,** film *m* à grand spectacle, épopée *f* cinématographique.

cellulose ['seljuləʊs] **1** *adj* celluleux. **2** *n* cellulose *f*.

Celsius ['selsıəs] *n* (*no pl*) *Phys* **C. thermometer,** thermomètre *m* de Celsius; **ten degrees C.,** dix degrés Celsius.

Celt [kelt] *n* Celte *mf*.

Celtic ['keltık] *Ling* **1** *adj* celtique, celte. **2** *n* le celtique, les langues *fpl* celtiques *ou* celtes.

cement¹ [sı'ment] *n* **(a)** *Constr* ciment *m*; **Portland c.,** ciment de Portland; **quick-setting c.,** ciment à prise rapide; **c. mixer,** bétonnière *f*; **c. path,** allée *f* en ciment; **c. powder,** poudre *f* à ciment; **(b)** (*binding element*) ciment *m*; mastic *m*.

cement² *vt* **(a)** (*join*) cimenter (*des pierres, des briques*); cimenter, consolider (*la paix, une amitié*); **(b)** (*coat*) cimenter, enduire d'une couche de ciment (*une paroi etc*); **(c)** (*in dentistry*) mastiquer, obturer (*une dent*); **(d)** *Metal* cémenter (*le fer*).

cementation [si:men'teıʃən] *n* **(a)** cimentation *f*; **(b)** *Metal* cémentation *f*.

cemetery ['semətrı] *n* cimetière *m*.

cenotaph ['senətæf] *n* cénotaphe *m*.

censer ['sensər] *n Rel* encensoir *m*.

censor¹ ['sensər] *n* **(a)** *Admin Mil* censeur *m*; **the film c.,** la censure cinématographique; *Mil Cin etc* **to get past the c.,** échapper à la censure; **(b)** *Antiq* censeur *m*.

censor² *vt* interdire, censurer (*une pièce de théâtre*); soumettre (*une pièce etc*) à des coupures; caviarder (*un article*); censurer (*un film*); supprimer, couper (*une scène*); **to be censored,** (*banned*) être interdit *ou* supprimé par la censure; (*cut*) (*of book, screenplay*) être expurgé; (*of play*) être soumis à des coupures.

censoring ['sensərıŋ] *n* censure *f* (*des journaux etc*).

censorious [sen'sɔ:rıəs] *adj* porté à censurer, sévère (**of,** pour).

censorship ['sensəʃıp] *n* censure *f*; **there is no longer any c. of his films,** ses films ne sont plus censurés; **postal c.,** contrôle postal; **c. of the press,** régime préventif.

censurable ['senʃərəb(ə)l] *adj* censurable, blâmable.

censure¹ ['senʃər] *n Fml* censure *f*, blâme *m*, condamnation *f*; *Jur* réprimande *f*; **he deserves c.,** il mérite des reproches; *Pol* **vote of c.,** motion *f* de censure.

censure² *vt Fml* censurer; (*condemn*) blâmer, condamner; (*criticize*) critiquer.

census ['sensəs] *n* recensement *m*; **to take a c.,** faire un recensement; *US* **C. Bureau,** Bureau *m* des statistiques.

cent [sent] *n* **(a)** (*coin, sum*) cent *m*; *F* sou *m*; **to pay to the last c.,** payer jusqu'au dernier sou; **(b) per c.,** pour cent; **ten per c.,** dix pour cent; *Ch etc* **thirty per c. solution,** solution à trente pour cent; **a hundred per c. efficient,** cent pour cent efficace; **I'm ninety per c. sure,** je suis sûr à quatre-vingt dix pour cent.

centaur ['sentɔ:r] *n Myth* centaure *m*.

centenarian [sentı'neərıən] **1** *n* (*person*) centenaire *mf*. **2** *adj* centenaire.

centenary [sen'ti:nərı] **1** *n* (anniversaire *m*) centenaire *m*; **c. celebrations,** célébrations *fpl* du centenaire. **2** *adj* centenaire.

centennial [sen'tenıəl] **1** *adj* centenaire. **2** *n Am* = **CENTENARY**.

center, centerboard *etc US* = **CENTRE, CENTREBOARD** *etc*.

centigrade ['sentıgreıd] *adj* centigrade; **c. thermometer,** thermomètre *m* centigrade.

centigramme, *US* **centigram** ['sentıgræm] *n* centigramme *m*.

centilitre, *US* **centiliter** ['sentıli:tər] *n* centilitre *m*.

centimetre, *US* **centimeter** ['sentımi:tər] *n* centimètre *m*; **square/cubic c.,** centimètre carré/cube.

centipede ['sentıpi:d] *n* scolopendre *f*, *F* mille-pattes *m inv*.

central ['sentr(ə)l] **1** *adj* **(a)** (*in location*) central, -aux; *Comptr* **c. processing unit,** unité centrale de traitement; **c. nervous system,** système nerveux central; *Br* **c. reserve,** (*on road*) terre-plein *m*, *pl* terre-pleins; **c. point,** centre *m*; **in a c. position,** situé au centre; **the office is very c.,** (*in town*) le bureau est situé en plein centre; **c. heating,** chauffage central; **does the flat have c. heating?,** est-ce qu'il y a le chauffage central dans l'appartement?; **c. locking,** (*on car*) verrouillage central; **c. bank,** banque centrale; **C. America,** Amérique Centrale; **(b)** (*in importance*) central, -aux; **the c. character,** le personnage central; **c. to the debate is the question of safety,** la question de la sécurité se situe au cœur du débat. **2** *n Am Tel* central *m* (téléphonique).

centralize ['sentrəlaız] **1** *vt* centraliser. **2** *vi* se centraliser.

centralized ['sentrəlaızd] *adj* (*power, planning etc*) centralisé; **c. data capture,** saisie centralisée; **c. management,** gestion intégrée; **c. storage,** mémoire centrale.

centrally ['sentrəlı] *adv* centralement; **c. situated,** situé dans le centre; **c. heated,** avec chauffage central; **the flat is c. heated,** l'appartement a le chauffage central.

centre¹, *US* **center** ['sentər] *n* **(a)** centre *m* (*d'un cercle, de la terre, d'une ville etc*); milieu *m* (*d'une table etc*); corps *m*, centre (*d'une roue*); *Med* foyer *m* (*d'infection*); **in the c.,** au centre, au milieu; **the great urban centres,** les grandes agglomérations urbaines; **commercial/industrial c.,** centre commercial/industriel; **civic/community c.,** centre civique/social; **shopping c.,** centre commercial; *Old-fashioned* **music c.,** combiné *m* stéréo; *Phys* **c. of gravity,** centre de gravité; *Journ* **c. spread,** pages centrales; **c. of attraction,** *Phys* centre d'attraction *ou* de gravitation; *Fig* clou *m* (*d'une fête etc*); **the animals/children were the c. of attraction,** les animaux/enfants étaient le centre d'attraction;

(b) *Pol* Centre *m*; *Pol* **the c. party,** les membres *mpl* du Centre; **to be left/right of c.,** être du centre gauche/droit;

(c) *Sp Rugby* centre *m*; *Fb etc* **c. forward,** avant-centre *m*; **c. half,** demi-centre *m*;

(d) *MecE etc* (*of lathe*) pointe *f*; **out of c.,** décentré; **c. punch,** pointeau *m*; *Tech* **ten centimetres c. to c.,** dix centimètres centre à centre.

centre^2, *US* **center** *vt* **(a)** *Tech* centrer (*une roue, une pièce sur le tour etc*); **to c. a line,** (*when typing*) centrer une ligne; **(b)** *Cin Phot* centrer, cadrer (*une photo*); **(c)** *Fb etc* centrer (*le ballon etc*).

►**centre on, centre round 1** *vipo* être centré *ou* axé sur (*qch*); **the debate centres on the President's ability to govern,** le débat est centré *ou* axé sur la capacité du Président à gouverner. **2** *vtsep* (*usu passive*) **to be centred on s.o./sth,** se concentrer sur qn/qch; **all his thoughts were centred on the coming match,** toutes ses pensées étaient concentrées sur le match à venir.

centreboard, *US* **centerboard** ['sentəbɔːd] *n Nau* dérive centrale.

centrefold, *US* **centerfold** ['sentəfəuld] *n* (*in magazine, newspaper*) double page centrale détachable; **to do a c.,** (*for magazine*) poser comme pin-up; **c. girl,** = pin-up *f*.

centrepiece, *US* **centerpiece** ['sentəpiːs] *n* (pièce *f* de) milieu *m* de table.

centrifugal [sentrɪ'fjʊg(ə)l] *adj* (*force, pompe etc*) centrifuge.

centrifuge^1 ['sentrɪfjuːdʒ] *vt* centrifuger (*un liquide*).

centrifuge^2 *n* centrifugeur *m*, centrifugeuse *f*.

centring, *US* **centering** ['sent(ə)rɪŋ] *n* **(a)** *MecE* centrage *m*, guidage *m* (*d'une pièce sur le tour etc*); (*of line, text*) centrage; **c. tool,** centreur *m*; **(b)** *Constr* cintrage *m* (*d'une voûte*).

centripetal [sen'trɪpɪtəl] *adj* (*force etc*) centripète.

centrist ['sentrɪst] *Pol* **1** *n* centriste *mf*. **2** *adj* centriste.

century ['sentʃərɪ] *n* **(a)** siècle *m*; **in the nineteenth c.,** au dix-neuvième siècle; **the wedding of the c.,** le mariage du siècle; **trees centuries old,** arbres *mpl* séculaires; **(b)** *Cr* centaine *f*, série *f* de cent.

CEO [siːiː'əʊ] *n esp Am Com* (*abbr* **chief executive officer**) président-directeur général; **President and CEO,** P.-D.G. *m*.

cephalic [se'fælɪk] *adj* (*veine, index etc*) céphalique.

ceramic [sə'ræmɪk] **1** *adj* céramique; **c. hob,** (*on cooker*) plaque *f* vitro-céramique. **2** *npl* **ceramics,** la céramique.

cereal ['sɪərɪəl] *n* céréale *f*; **(breakfast) cereals,** céréales (en flocons); **c. crops,** céréales.

cerebellum [serɪ'beləm] *n Anat* cervelet *m*.

cerebral ['serɪbrəl, *US* sə'riːbrəl] *adj* **(a)** *Anat* cérébral, -aux; **c. palsy,** infirmité motrice cérébrale; **(b)** (*intellectual*) cérébral; **his style is far too c. for me,** son style est bien trop cérébral pour moi.

cerebrum ['serɪbrəm] *n Anat* cerveau *m*.

ceremonial [serɪ'məʊnɪəl] **1** *adj* de cérémonie; **c. visit,** visite *f* de cérémonie. **2** *n* cérémonial *m*.

ceremonially [serɪ'məʊnɪəlɪ] *adv* en grande cérémonie.

ceremonious [serɪ'məʊnɪəs] *adj* cérémonieux.

ceremoniously [serɪ'məʊnɪəslɪ] *adv* cérémonieusement, avec cérémonie.

ceremony ['serɪmənɪ] *n* **(a)** cérémonie *f*; **with c.,** avec cérémonie, solennellement; **without c.,** sans formalités; **to stand on c.,** faire des cérémonies; **we don't stand on c.,** nous ne faisons pas de cérémonies; **master of ceremonies,** maître *m* des cérémonies; **(b)** (*event*) cérémonie *f*; **the marriage c.,** la cérémonie du mariage.

cert [sɜːt] *n F* (= **certainty**) **a dead c.,** une certitude (absolue), un coup sûr, une affaire sûre; *Horseracing* un gagnant sûr; **it's a c.,** c'est couru.

certain ['sɜːt(ə)n] *adj* **(a)** (*sure*) (*succès etc*) infaillible, assuré; **they face c. death/dismissal,** leur mort/renvoi est assuré(e); **it's absolutely c.,** c'est sûr et certain; **there is c. to be some opposition to the bill,** il n'y a pas de doute que la loi rencontrera une opposition; **he is c. to come,** il viendra à coup sûr; **to my c. knowledge, they are ...,** je sais pertinemment qu'ils sont ...; **to be c. of sth,** (*person*) être certain *ou* sûr de qch; **I am almost c.,** j'en suis presque sûr; **I am c. that he will come,** je suis certain *ou* sûr qu'il viendra; **to know sth for c.,** tenir qch pour certain, être bien sûr de qch; **I cannot say for c.,** je ne saurais dire avec certitude; **you shall have it tomorrow for c.,** vous l'aurez demain sans faute; **to make c. that ...,** (*find out, ensure*) s'assurer que ...; **I made c. (that) the information was correct,** je me suis assuré que les informations étaient exactes; **I'd better make c.,** je ferais mieux de m'en assurer; **she made c. that everyone found out,** elle s'est assurée que tout le monde le saurait; **to make c. of sth,** (*find out*) s'assurer de qch; (*make sure to get sth*) s'assurer qch; **I made c. of the date,** je me suis assuré de la date; **to make c. of a seat,** s'assurer une place; **he made c. of her co-operation,** il s'est assuré sa collaboration;
(b) (*particular*) **there are c. things that ...,** il y a certaines choses que ...; **only c. animals are sacred,** seuls certains animaux sont sacrés; **women of a c. age,** les femmes d'un certain âge; **a c. person,** une certaine personne; **c. people,** (de) certaines gens, certains *mpl*; **a c. Mr Thomas,** un certain M. Thomas; **he used to write to me on a c. day,** il m'écrivait à jour fixe.

certainly ['sɜːtənlɪ] *adv* (*definitely*) à coup sûr; (*admittedly*) certes; **she c. knows her facts,** elle sait assurément *ou* parfaitement de quoi elle parle; **it c. won't be ready tomorrow,** ça ne sera jamais prêt pour demain; **you shall c. have it tomorrow,** vous l'aurez demain sans faute; **may I? — c.!** *or* **you c. may!,** vous permettez? — je vous en prie! *ou* bien sûr! *ou* certainement; **c. not!,** bien sûr que non!

certainty ['sɜːtəntɪ] *n* **(a)** (*sureness*) certitude *f* (*d'un fait à venir*); **there is no c. that we will win,** nous n'avons aucune certitude de gagner; **(b)** (*thing*) chose certaine; **I know it for a c.,** je le sais à coup sûr; **it's a dead c.,** c'est une certitude absolue; **(c)** (*conviction*) certitude *f* (morale), conviction *f*; **she said it with some c.,** elle a dit cela avec une certaine conviction.

certifiable ['sɜːtɪfaɪəb(ə)l] *adj* que l'on peut certifier; **c. lunatic,** aliéné interdit; *F* **he's c.,** il est fou à lier.

certificate [sə'tɪfɪkət] *n* **(a)** certificat *m*; **medical c.,** certificat médical; **health c.,** billet *m* de santé; *Fin etc* **bearer c.,** titre *m* au porteur; **share** *or* **stock c.,** certificat d'action(s); **(government) savings c.,** bon *m* d'épargne; *Com* **c. of origin,** certificat d'origine; *Av* **c. of airworthiness,** certificat de navigabilité; *Aut* **test c.,** = certificat d'aptitude à rouler; **(b)** (*professional, educational*) certificat *m* (d'aptitude), diplôme *m*, brevet *m*; *Nau* **master's c.,** brevet de capitaine; *Br Sch* **C. of Secondary Education,** = certificat de fin d'études secondaires; **(c)** *Admin* acte *m*; **birth/marriage c.,** acte *ou* extrait *m* de naissance/acte de mariage; **death c.,** acte de (constat de) décès.

certificated [sə'tɪfɪkeɪtɪd] *adj* diplômé, titré.

certification [sɜtɪfɪ'keɪʃən] *n* certification *f*, authentification *f*.

certified ['sɜːtɪfaɪd] *adj* **(a)** (*having certificate*) diplômé; *US Sch* **c. teacher,** instituteur diplômé; *Am Com* **c. public accountant,** expert *m* comptable; **(b)** (*guaranteed*) *Com* **c. cheque,** chèque certifié; *US* **c. letter,** lettre recommandée; **(c)** (*declared insane*) déclaré atteint d'aliénation mentale.

certify ['sɜːtɪfaɪ] **1** *vt* **(a)** certifier, déclarer, attester (*qch*); constater (*un décès*); **to c. that sth is true,** attester *ou* porter témoignage que qch est vrai; **this is to c. that A. Gooch has ...,** (*on certificate*) ce document certifie que A. Gooch a ...; *Arch* **to c. s.o. a lunatic,** (*of doctor*) déclarer qn atteint d'aliénation mentale; *F* **you ought to be certified,** tu es complètement fou; **(b)** (*guarantee*) authentifier, homologuer, légaliser (*un document*); **(c)** diplômer, breveter (*qn*). **2** *vi* **to c. to sth,** attester qch.

certitude ['sɜːtɪtjuːd] *n* certitude *f*.

cervical ['sɜːvɪk(ə)l, sɜː'vaɪk(ə)l] *adj Anat* **(a)** (*pertaining to the cervix*) du col de l'utérus; **c. cancer,** cancer *m* du col de l'utérus; **c. smear,** frottis *m* du col de l'utérus; **(b)** (*of the neck*) cervical; **c. vertebra,** vertèbre cervicale.

cervix, *pl* **-vices** ['sɜːvɪks, -vɪsiːz] *n Anat* **(a) c. (uteri),** col *m* de l'utérus; **(b)** (*neck*) cou *m*.

cessation [se'seɪʃən] *n* cessation *f*, arrêt *m*; **c. of work,** suspension *f ou* interruption *f* du travail.

cession ['seʃən] *n* cession *f* (*d'un territoire*); *Jur* cession de biens (*aux créanciers*).

cesspit ['sespɪt] *n* **(a)** *Agr* fosse *f* à fumier et à purin; **(b)** = **CESSPOOL**.

cesspool ['sespuːl] *n* fosse *f* d'aisances; fosse de curage (*d'un égout*); *Fig* **the district is a c. of drug-dealing and prostitution,** le quartier est un cloaque où règnent le trafic de drogue et la prostitution.

Ceylon [sɪ'lɒn] *n Hist* Ceylan *m*.

cf [siː'ef] (*abbr* **confer**) cf.

CFC [siːef'siː] *npl* **CFCs** (*abbr* **chlorofluorocarbons**) CFC *mpl*.

cg (*abbr* **centigram**) cg.

ch (*abbr* **chapter**) Ch.

CH [siː'eɪtʃ] *n abbr* **central heating**.

Chad [tʃæd] *n* Tchad *m*.

chafe [tʃeɪf] **1** *vt* **(a)** user *ou* échauffer (*qch*) par le frottement; irriter (*la peau*); érailler (*un cordage*); **the boots chafed her ankles,** les bottes lui ont irrité les chevilles; **apply to chafed skin,** (*of lotion etc*) appliquer sur la peau irritée; **(b)** (*annoy*) irriter, énerver (*qn*); **(c)** (*warm*) frictionner (*les membres de qn*). **2** *vi* **(a)** s'user par le frottement; (*of skin*) s'irriter, s'écorcher; (*of rope*) s'érailler; **(b)** (*of person*) **to c. at** *or* **under sth,** s'irriter de *ou* contre qch, s'énerver de qch; **to c. under restraint,** ronger son frein.

chaff[1] [tʃɑːf] *n* **(a)** *Agr* (*husks*) balle(s) *f(pl)* (*du grain*); (*straw*) (*small pieces*) menue paille; (*cut up*) paille hachée; **(b)** *Electron* ruban *m* métallique antiradar; **(c)** (*teasing*) raillerie *f*, taquinerie *f*.

chaff[2] *vt* **(a)** (*tease*) railler, taquiner (*qn*); *F* chiner (*qn*); **(b)** *Agr* hacher (*la paille*).

chaffinch ['tʃæfɪntʃ] *n* (*bird*) pinson *m*.

chafing ['tʃeɪfɪŋ] *n* **(a)** irritation *f*, écorchement *m* (*de la peau*); usure *f*, friction *f*, frottement *m* (*d'une courroie, d'un pneu etc*); **(b)** friction *f* (*des membres*); **(c)** *Old-fashioned Culin* **c. dish,** réchaud *m* de table.

chagrin[1] ['ʃægrɪn] *n* chagrin *m*, dépit *m*; **to my c.,** à mon dépit.

chagrin[2] *vt esp Lit* chagriner (*qn*); **to be chagrined at sth,** être vexé de *ou* par qch.

chain[1] [tʃeɪn] *n* **(a)** chaîne *f*; (*small, for medallion etc*) chaînette *f*; **he wore a silver c. round his neck,** il portait une chaîne en argent autour du cou; **to put a dog on the c.,** mettre un chien à la chaîne; **prisoner in chains,** prisonnier enchaîné; *Fig* **to break or burst one's chains,** rompre ses chaînes; **to have nothing to lose but one's chains,** n'avoir rien d'autre à perdre que ses chaînes; **to form a chain,** former *ou* faire la chaîne (*pour passer des seaux etc*); **to pull the c.,** (*in WC*) tirer la chasse d'eau; **c. of events,** suite *f ou* série *f* d'événements; *Aut* **snow chains,** chaînes (à neige); *Nau* **anchor c.,** chaîne d'ancrage; **bicycle c.,** chaîne de bicyclette; *Aut* **drive** *or* **driving** *or* **transmission c.,** chaîne de transmission; **bucket c.,** chaîne à augets *ou* à godets; **watch c.,** chaîne de montre; **safety c.,** (*for door*) chaîne de sûreté; (*for bracelet etc*) chaînette de sûreté; **c. gang,** chaîne de forçats; **c. link,** chaînon *m ou* maillons de chaîne; **c. armour, c. mail,** mailles *fpl*; (*suit*) cotte *f* de mailles; **c. guard,** (*on bicycle etc*) carter *m*; **c. saw,** tronçonneuse *f*; *Agr* **c. harrow,** herse *f* à chaînons; **c. well,** puits *m* à chaînes *ou* aux chaînes; **c. conveyor,** transporteur *m* à chaîne; *Sewing* **c. stitch,** point *m* de chaînette; **c. letter,** chaîne; **c. smoker,** personne qui fume des cigarettes à la file; *Ind* **c. work,** travail *m* à la chaîne;

(b) *Geog* chaîne *f* (*de montagnes*); (*small*) chaînon *m*;

(c) *Com* **a c. of stores/restaurants,** une chaîne de magasins/restaurants; **fast food c.,** chaîne de restauration rapide; **c. store,** magasin *m* à succursales (multiples); (*branch*) succursale *f* (*de grand magasin*);

(d) *Phys Ch etc* chaîne *f* (*de désintégration etc*); *Phys Ch & Fig* **c. reaction,** réaction *f* en chaîne;

(e) (*measurement*) longueur *f* de 20 m 116; **surveyor's c., measuring c.,** chaîne *f* d'arpenteur *ou* d'arpentage.

chain[2] *vt* fermer (*une porte etc*) avec une chaîne; **to c. s.o./sth to sth,** attacher qn/qch à qch avec une chaîne *ou* des chaînes; **she chained herself/the bicycle to the railings,** elle s'est attachée/a attaché sa bicyclette à la palissade avec une chaîne *ou* des chaînes; **to c. s.o.,** enchaîner qn; *Fig* **chained to one's desk,** cloué à son bureau.

►**chain down** *vtsep* retenir (*qch*) par une chaîne; enchaîner (*qn*).

►**chain up** *vtsep* mettre (*un chien*) à la chaîne; **people could be chained up in prison for years,** les gens pouvaient être enchaînés en prison pendant des années.

chain-smoke ['tʃeɪnsməʊk] **1** *vi* fumer des cigarettes à la file. **2** *vt* fumer à la file.

chair[1] [tʃeər] *n* **(a)** chaise *f*; **folding c.,** chaise pliante, pliant *m*; **easy c.,** fauteuil *m*; **grandfather c.,** fauteuil à oreillettes; **rocking c.,** fauteuil à bascule, *Can* berceuse *f*; **deck c.,** chaise longue, transatlantique *m*, *F* transat *m*; **high c.,** chaise haute (*pour enfants*); *Old-fashioned* **Bath c., invalid c.,** voiture *f* de malade, fauteuil roulant; **musical chairs,** (*game*) jeu *m ou* polka *f* des chaises; **c. attendant,** loueur, -euse de chaises, chaisière *f* (*dans un parc etc*); *Ski* **c. lift,** télésiège *m*; **(b)** *Univ* chaire *f* (*de professeur de faculté*); **to endow a c. in mathematics,** (*of company*) financer une chaire en mathématiques; **(c)** (*in meeting*) fauteuil *m* (*de président*); (*chairperson*) président, -ente; **to be in the c.,** occuper le fauteuil présidentiel, présider (*la séance*); **(d)** *US F* **the c.,** la chaise électrique; *F* **to go to the c.,** passer sur la chaise électrique; **(e)** *Rail* coussinet *m*, chaise *f* (de rail).

chair[2] *vt* **(a)** (*preside over*) présider (*une réunion*); **(b)** (*after victory etc*) porter (*qn*) en triomphe.

chairback ['tʃeəbæk] *n* dossier *m* de chaise.

chairman, *pl* **-men** ['tʃeəmən] *n* président, -ente; *Com* président-directeur général (*d'une maison*); **to act as c.,** présider (la séance); **Mr C./Madam C.,** Monsieur le Président/Madame la Présidente.

chairmanship ['tʃeəmənʃɪp] *n* présidence *f*; **under the c. of Mr Stevens,** sous la présidence de M. Stevens.

chairperson ['tʃeəpɜːsən] *n* président, -ente.

chairwoman, *pl* **-women** ['tʃeəwʊmən, -wɪmɪn] *n* présidente *f*.

chalet ['ʃæleɪ] *n* chalet *m*.

chalice ['tʃælɪs] *n* **(a)** *Rel* calice *m*; **(b)** *Arch & Lit* coupe *f* (à boire).

chalk[1] [tʃɔːk] *n* (*for writing etc*) *& Geol* craie *f*; *Art* (crayon *m*) pastel *m*; *Billiards* blanc *m*; **they are as different as c. and cheese,** c'est le jour et la nuit; *F* **not by a long c.,** pas du tout; **by a long c.,** de beaucoup; **c. hills/cliffs,** collines/falaises crayeuses; **a set of coloured chalks,** un assortiment de craies de couleur; **French c.,** craie de tailleur; *Art* **c. drawing,** pastel; **c. line** *or* **mark,** (*drawn*) trait *m* à la craie; *Carp etc* (*string*) cordeau *m* (blanchi à la craie); (*made by string*) ligne faite au cordeau.

chalk[2] *vt* marquer (*qch*) à la craie; (*write*) écrire (à la craie); *Carp etc* **to c. a line,** tringler une ligne (*au cordeau*); *Billiards* **to c. one's cue,** frotter sa queue de blanc.

►**chalk up** *vtsep* **(a)** (*write*) écrire (*qch*) à la craie; **instructions had been chalked up on the blackboard,** les ordres avaient été écrits à la craie sur le tableau; **(b)** (*give credit in shop*) mettre (*qch*) sur l'ardoise de qn; **(c)** (*achieve*) remporter (*une victoire, un succès*); **the team chalked up another win today,** l'équipe a remporté une nouvelle victoire aujourd'hui; **(d)** (*register as*) **to c. sth up to experience,** mettre qch au compte de l'expérience.

chalkpit ['tʃɔːkpɪt] *n* carrière *f* de craie, crayère *f*.

chalky ['tʃɔːkɪ] *adj* **(a)** (*terrain*) crayeux; (*sol, eau*) calcaire; (*dépôt*) calcique; **(b)** (*colour*) pâle, terreux; **c. white,** blanc comme de la craie; (*because of illness*) blanc comme un cachet d'aspirine.

challenge[1] ['tʃælɪndʒ] *n* **(a)** défi *m*; *Sp* défi, challenge *m*; *Mil* interpellation *f* (*par une sentinelle*); **to accept** *or* **take up a c.,** relever un défi; **a c. to s.o.'s leadership,** une tentative de remplacer qn au pouvoir; **this work is a real c. to me,** ce travail est une vraie gageure pour moi; **environmental problems are the major c. for our generation,** les problèmes d'environnement constituent la principale gageure *ou* le principal défi pour notre génération; *Sp* **c. match,** challenge; *Sp* **c. cup,** coupe-challenge *f*, *pl* coupes-challenge; **(b)** *Jur* récusation *f* (*du jury*).

challenge[2] *vt* **(a)** *Sp* **to c. s.o.,** (*to fight*) provoquer qn (au combat); **to c. s.o. to do sth,** défier qn de faire qch; **to c. s.o. to single combat,** provoquer qn en combat singulier; **to c. s.o. to a game of chess,** défier qn aux échecs; **to c. s.o. to a game of tennis,** défier qn à une partie de tennis; **(b)** (*question etc*) protester contre, disputer (*une affirmation*); mettre en question *ou* en doute *ou* en cause (*la parole de qn*); contester (*les titres de qn*); **their position was challenged by younger artists,** leur position a été remise en question par des artistes plus jeunes; **to c. s.o.'s right to do sth,** contester à qn le droit de faire qch; **(c)** (*stimulate*) représenter une gageure; **you need a job that will c. you,** il te faut un travail qui représente une gageure pour toi; **(d)** *Mil* (*of sentry*) interpeller (*qn*); **(e)** *Jur* récuser (*un juré*).

challenger ['tʃælɪndʒər] *n* **(a)** (*to fight*) provocateur, -trice; *Sp* challenger *m*; *Sp* **the holder and the c.,** le détenteur et le challenger; **(b)** *Jur* récusant, -ante.

challenging ['tʃælɪndʒɪŋ] *adj* **(a)** (*look, remark etc*) provocateur, -trice; (*air*) de défi; **(b)** (*job*) stimulant, qui représente une gageure.

chamber ['tʃeɪmbər] *n* **(a)** chambre *f* (*de commerce, de métiers*); *Pol* Chambre (haute, basse); *Pol* **double c. system,** système bicaméral; **(b)** *Jur* **chambers,** cabinet *m* de consultation (*d'un avocat*); étude *f* (*d'un avoué*); **in chambers,** en chambre du conseil; **to hear a case in chambers,** juger une cause en référé; **(c)** *Metal* laboratoire *m* (*de fourneau*); *Phys* chambre *f* (*d'ionisation, à détente*); (*of firearm*) chambre; *Ind* **lead c.,** chambre de plomb; **compression c.,** (*in engine*) chambre de compression; **air c.,** chambre à air (*d'une pompe*); **deposition c.,** chambre de déposition; **(d)** *Biol etc* alvéole *m*; **(e)** *Arch & Lit* salle *f*; **audience c.,** salle d'audience; **council c.,** salle du conseil; **c. music,** musique *f* de chambre; *Lit* **(bed-)c.,** chambre *f* (à coucher); **c. pot,** pot *m* de chambre; **(f) the chambers of a revolver,** les alvéoles *mpl* d'un revolver.

chamberlain ['tʃeɪmbəlɪn] *n* chambellan *m*.

chambermaid ['tʃeɪmbəmeɪd] *n* femme *f* de chambre

(d'hôtel).

chameleon [kə'miːlɪən] *n* (*animal*) *& Fig* caméléon *m*.

chamfer[1] ['tʃæmfər] *n* **(a)** *Carp etc* biseau *m*, chanfrein *m*; arête *f* (*de moulure*); **(b) hollow c.,** cannelure *f*.

chamfer[2] *vt* **(a)** *Carp etc* biseauter, chanfreiner (*une planche etc*); abattre (*une arête*); **(b)** (*cut grooves in*) canneler (*une colonne etc*).

chamois *n* **(a)** ['ʃæmwɑː] (*deer*) chamois *m*; **(b)** ['ʃæmɪ] **c. (leather),** (*for washing car*) (cuir *m* de) chamois *m*, peau *f* de chamois.

champ[1] [tʃæmp] *n Sp F* champion *m*.

champ[2] *vt* (*of horse etc*) mâcher bruyamment (*le fourrage*); ronger, mâcher, mâchonner (*le mors*); *F* **to c. at the bit,** (*of person*) ronger son frein.

champagne [ʃæm'peɪn] *n* **(a)** (*wine*) vin *m* de Champagne, champagne *m*; **(b)** (*colour*) champagne *m*.

Champagne [ʃæm'peɪn] *n* (*region*) Champagne *f*.

champers ['ʃæmpəz] *n F* (*champagne*) champ *m*.

champion[1] ['tʃæmpɪən] **1** *n* **(a)** *Sp* champion, -ionne; **world c.,** champion du monde; **a c. footballer,** un champion du football; **(b)** (*of cause*) champion, -ionne, partisan, -ane. **2** *adj Br Dial* **that's c.!,** à la bonne heure!, bravo!

champion[2] *vt* soutenir, défendre, se faire le champion de (*une cause*).

championship ['tʃæmpɪənʃɪp] *n* **(a)** *Sp etc* championnat *m*; **c. match,** match *m* de championnat; **(b)** (*of cause*) défense *f*.

chance[1] [tʃɑːns] *n* **(a)** hasard *m*, chance *f*; **game of c.,** jeu *m* de hasard; **by c.,** par hasard; **somebody I met by c.,** quelqu'un que j'ai rencontré par hasard; **do you by any c. know his address?,** sauriez-vous son adresse par hasard?; **to leave nothing to c.,** ne rien laisser au hasard; **to leave everything to c.,** s'en remettre au hasard; **to do sth on the off c.,** faire qch à tout hasard; **I went on the off c. that they would be there,** j'y suis allé à tout hasard au cas où ils y seraient; **to look to** *or* **have an eye to the main c.,** veiller à ses propres intérêts; **c. would be a fine thing!,** ah, si seulement je pouvais!; **c. discovery,** découverte accidentelle *ou* fortuite; **c. meeting,** rencontre de hasard, rencontre fortuite;

(b) (*opportunity*) occasion *f*; **now's your c.,** vous avez la partie belle; **it's your last c.,** c'est votre dernière chance; **it's a c. in a million,** c'est une occasion qui ne se présentera pas deux fois; **I had a c. to work in the States,** j'ai eu l'occasion de travailler aux États-Unis; **I go to the theatre when I get the c.,** je vais au théâtre quand j'en ai l'occasion; **can you translate this for me when you get a c.?,** est-ce que tu peux me traduire ceci dès que tu en auras le temps?; **there are no second chances, there is no second c.,** on n'a qu'une seule chance; **to give s.o. a c.,** (*in a job*) mettre qn à l'essai; (*to do better*) donner une chance à qn; **give me another c.,** donne-moi une autre chance; **you didn't give me a c.!,** (*to tell you*) tu ne m'en as pas laissé le temps!; *F* **given half a c. she'd play tennis every day,** si elle le pouvait elle jouerait au tennis tous les jours;

(c) (*possibility*) **to have** *or* **stand a c.,** (*of succeeding*) avoir des chances de succès; **he never had a c., the truck was coming straight at him,** il n'a rien pu faire, le camion se dirigeait droit vers lui; **she stands a good c. of being chosen,** elle a de bonnes chances d'être choisie; **he hasn't the slightest c.** *or* **an earthly c. of succeeding,** il n'a pas la moindre chance de réussir; **to have an even** *or* **a fifty-fifty c.,** avoir des chances égales; **there's little/no/a good c. of that happening,** il y a peu de chance/aucune chance/de bonnes chances que cela se produise; **do you think they'll win? — no c.!,** est-ce que tu crois qu'ils vont gagner? - certainement pas!; **can I stay the night? — no c.!,** est-ce que je peux passer la nuit ici? - pas question!; **(the) chances are (that) he'll forget,** il y a fort à parier qu'il oubliera;

(d) (*risk*) risque *m*; **she takes too many chances,** elle prend trop de risques; **to take a c.,** courir un risque; **he took a c. on them not finding out,** il a couru le risque qu'ils le découvrent; **I'll have to take a c. on that,** j'en prends le risque; **I'm taking no chances,** je ne veux rien risquer, je ne veux pas prendre de risques; **to take a sporting c.,** tenter le coup; **to take one's c.,** risquer sa chance.

chance[2] **1** *vi Lit* **to c. to do sth,** faire qch par hasard. **2** *vt* risquer; **to c. it** *or* **one's luck** *or* **one's arm,** risquer le coup, tenter sa chance, tenter le coup.

►**chance on, chance upon** *vipo* (*find by accident*) tomber (par hasard) sur (*qn,qch*).

chancel ['tʃɑːns(ə)l] *n Archit* chœur *m*; **c. screen,** jubé *m*.

chancellery ['tʃɑːnsələrɪ] *n* chancellerie *f*.

chancellor ['tʃɑːnsələr] *n* **(a)** *Univ Rel* chancelier *m*; **(b)** *Pol* **C.,** chancelier *m*; *Br Jur* **the Lord (High) C.,** le Grand Chancelier, ≈ Ministre *m* de la Justice; *Br Pol* **C. (of the Exchequer),** Chancelier de l'Échiquier, ≈ Ministre des Finances.

chancer ['tʃɑːnsər] *n Br Sl* risque-tout *mf inv*.

chancery ['tʃɑːnsərɪ] *n* **(a)** *Jur Br* **(Court of) C.,** cour *f* de la chancellerie; *US* **(court of) c.,** cour d'équité; **(b)** (*of embassy*) chancellerie *f*; **(c)** (*in wrestling*) **hold in c.,** cravate *f*.

chancre ['ʃæŋkər] *n Med* chancre *m*.

chancy ['tʃɑːnsɪ] *adj F* (*uncertain*) incertain; (*risky*) risqué.

chandelier [ʃændə'lɪər] *n* lustre *m*.

chandler ['tʃɑːndlər] *n Com* **ship('s) c.,** fournisseur *m* de navires; **corn c.,** marchand de blé *ou* de grains.

change[1] [tʃeɪndʒ] *n* **(a)** changement *m* (*d'air, d'occupation etc*); changement, variation *f* (*du temps*); altération *f* (*du visage, de la voix*); revirement *m* (*d'opinion*); **c. of address,** changement de domicile; **to have a c. of opinion** *or* **of heart,** changer d'avis; **c. for the better/worse,** amélioration *f*/altération (*de la santé etc*); **there's been a c. in the weather,** il y a eu un changement de temps; **a c. in the law,** un changement de la loi; **sudden c. of fortune,** revirement *m* de fortune; **there is no/little c. in the situation,** il n'y a pas/il y a peu de changement dans la situation; **there are going to be some changes in this office!,** il va y avoir du nouveau dans ce bureau!; **some changes were made to the timetable,** des changements *ou* des modifications ont été apporté(e)s à l'horaire; **you need a c.,** il vous faut un changement d'air *ou* d'occupation; **the c. will do you good,** le changement te fera du bien; **this trip will be a bit of a c. for you,** ce voyage vous changera un peu; **he was early for a c.,** pour une fois il était en avance; **for a c., why don't you wash the dishes?,** pour changer pourquoi tu ne fais pas la vaisselle?; **it** *or* **that makes a c.,** ça change un peu; **yes, it makes a c., doesn't it?,** oui, ça change (un peu) (de l'ordinaire) n'est-ce pas?; **to gain by the c.,** gagner au change; **it was a c. from the old system,** ça changeait du système précédent; **c. of life,** *F* **the c.,** (*of woman*) retour *m* d'âge; **to go through the c.,** (*of woman*) traverser la ménopause; *Aut etc* **oil c.,** vidange *f*; *Th* **scene c.,** changement de décor; *Mus* **chord c.,** changement d'accord; **c. of clothes,** vêtements *mpl* de rechange;

(b) (*money*) monnaie *f*; **small** *or* **loose c.,** petite monnaie; **to get c.,** faire de la monnaie; **to get c. for £5,** faire la monnaie de 5 livres; **have you got c. for a £10 note?,** est-ce que tu as de la monnaie sur un billet de 10 livres?; **you may keep the c.,** vous pouvez garder le reste; **that machine doesn't give c.,** la machine ne rend pas la monnaie; **you won't get much change out of £100,** (*if you buy that*) il ne va pas te rester beaucoup sur tes 100 livres; *F* **he won't get much c. out of me,** il en sera pour ses frais avec moi; **c. machine,** changeur *m* de monnaie;

(c) (*in bell-ringing*) **to ring the changes,** carillonner avec variations *ou* avec permutations; *Fig* **to ring the changes on,** ressasser, rabâcher, broder des variations sur (*un sujet*); varier, donner de la variété à (*un menu, un programme etc*).

change[2] **1** *vt* **(a)** (*alter*) changer, modifier (*ses projets, son genre de vie etc*); **to c. one thing into another,** changer une chose en une autre; **the witch changed him into a frog,** la sorcière l'a transformé en crapaud; **to c. one's ways** *or* **one's habits,** se refaire; **to c. one's mind** *or* **one's opinion,** changer d'avis; **to c. the subject,** changer de sujet, parler d'autre chose; **to c. colour,** changer de couleur *ou* de visage;

(b) (*replace*) changer (*les draps*); **to c. one's clothes,** se changer; **to c. one's dress/one's shoes,** changer de robe/de chaussures; *F* **to c. the baby,** changer le bébé; *Aut* **to c. a tyre,** remplacer un pneu; *Aut* **to c. the oil,** faire la vidange; *Aut* **to c. gear,** changer de vitesse; **to c. channels,** (*on TV*) changer de chaîne; **to c. one's seat/trains,** changer de place/de train;

(c) (*exchange*) **to c. one thing for another,** changer *ou* troquer une chose pour *ou* contre une autre; **to c. places** *or* **seats with s.o.,** changer de place avec qn; *Fig* **I wouldn't (like to) c. places with him,** je ne changerais pas avec lui; **I've changed doctors,** j'ai changé de docteur; **to c. sides,** changer de parti; **to c. the guard,** relever la garde; *Fin* **to c. a note,** (*into foreign currency*) changer un billet (de banque); (*into coins*) faire de la monnaie sur un billet (de banque); **to c. dollars into francs,** changer des dollars contre des francs *ou* en francs; **they won't c. pounds,** ils ne changeront pas des livres.

2 *vi* **(a)** (*alter*) (se) changer, se modifier, varier; (*of moon*) changer de quartier; (*of luck*) tourner; **she's changed (since I last saw her),** elle a changé depuis la dernière fois que je l'ai vue; **some things never c.,** certaines choses ne changent jamais; **the situation hasn't changed,** la situation n'a pas changé; **to c. for the better,** changer en mieux, s'améliorer; (*of weather*) tourner au beau; **to c. for the worse,** changer en mal; **to c. into sth,** (se) changer *ou* se transformer en qch; **the lights changed from green to amber,** les feux sont passés du vert à l'orange; **to c. from one system to another,** passer d'un système à un autre; **the wind has changed,** le vent a tourné;

(b) (*put on other clothes*) se changer; **to c. into another dress,** changer de robe; **to c. into trousers,** se mettre en pantalon;

(c) (*of passenger*) changer (de train, d'avion *etc*); **we had to c. twice/at Milan,** il a fallu que nous changions deux fois/à Milan; **do we c. here?,** est-ce qu'on change (de train, de car, d'avion) ici?; **all c.!,** tout le monde descend!;

(d) (*of sentries, Nau of watches, Ind of shifts*) se relever.

▶**change down** *vi Aut* (*use lower gear*) rétrograder; **to c. down into second,** passer en seconde.

▶**change over** *vi* **(a)** (*convert*) passer (d'un système à un autre); **the UK changed over to decimal currency in 1971,** le Royaume-Uni est passé à la monnaie décimale en 1971; **(b)** (*switch*) **let's c. over,** (*exchange jobs etc*) on échange; *TV* **to c. over (to another channel),** passer sur une autre chaîne; *TV* **c. over for the news,** change de chaîne pour regarder les informations.

▶**change up** *vi Aut* (*use higher gear*) passer à une vitesse supérieure.

changeability [tʃeɪndʒə'bɪlɪtɪ], **changeableness** ['tʃeɪndʒəb(ə)lnɪs] *n* variabilité *f* (*du temps etc*); inconstance *f*, versatilité *f* (*de caractère*).

changeable ['tʃeɪndʒəb(ə)l] *adj* changeant; (*weather*) variable, instable; (*vent*) inégal; **c. character,** caractère changeant *ou* instable.

changeless ['tʃeɪndʒlɪs] *adj* immuable, inaltérable.

changeling ['tʃeɪndʒlɪŋ] *n* = enfant de fées, substitué à un enfant qu'elles ont volé.

changeover ['tʃeɪndʒəʊvər] *n* **(a)** (*to new system*) changement *m*, passage *m*; **(b)** (*great change*) changement radical, renversement *m* (*politique etc*); **(c)** (*of guards etc*) relève *f*.

changer ['tʃeɪndʒər] *n Tech* changeur *m*; **record c.,** changeur de disques.

changing ['tʃeɪndʒɪŋ] **1** *adj* changeant; (*expression etc*) mobile. **2** *n* changement *m*; **the c. of the guard,** la relève de la garde; *Sp etc* **c. room,** vestiaire *m*.

channel[1] ['tʃæn(ə)l] *n* **(a)** (*of river*) lit *m*; (*waterway*) détroit *m*, canal *m*; passe *f*, chenal *m* (*d'un port*); **the (English) C.,** la Manche; **on the other side of the C.,** outre-Manche; **the C. Islands,** les îles Anglo-Normandes; **the C. Tunnel,** le tunnel sous la Manche;

(b) (*for complaint, inquiry etc*) voie *f*; **to go through official channels,** suivre la filière *ou* la voie hiérarchique; **through diplomatic channels,** par voie diplomatique; **during the cold war there were still channels of communication open,** pendant la guerre froide, la communication n'était pas totalement interrompue entre les deux blocs; **channels of communication are still open,** (*between us*) on est toujours en relation, le dialogue continue;

(c) *TV* chaîne *f*; *Rad* station *f*;

(d) *El Electron etc* voie *f*; (*on stereo*) sortie *f*; (*on magnetic tape*) piste *f*; (*de bande perforée*) canal *m*;

(e) (*tube, pipe*) canal *m*, conduit *m*;

(f) (*for irrigation*) rigole *f*;

(g) (*groove*) (*in wood*) rainure *f*; (*on column*) cannelure *f*.

channel[2] *vt* **(-ll-,** *US* **-l-) (a)** (*direct*) canaliser, diriger, orienter (*des efforts, des ressources etc*) (**towards,** vers; **into,** dans); acheminer, canaliser (*des informations*); **(b)** (*cut channels in*) creuser des rigoles dans (*un terrain*).

chant[1] [tʃɑːnt] *n* **(a)** chant scandé, slogans scandés (*de manifestants*); **the shouting had become a c.,** les cris étaient devenus des slogans (scandés); **(b)** *Mus* chant *m* (monotone); *Rel* psalmodie *f*; **plain c.,** plain-chant *m*, *pl* plains-chants; **Gregorian c.,** chant grégorien.

chant[2] *vt* **(a)** scander (*des slogans*); **the crowd chanted her name,** la foule a scandé son nom; **(b)** *Rel* psalmodier.

chantey ['ʃæntɪ] *n US* chanson *f* de marin.

chanting ['tʃɑːntɪŋ] **1** *adj* (*voice etc*) monotone, traînant. **2** *n* **(a)** chant scandé, slogans scandés (*de manifestants*); **(b)** *Rel* psalmodie *f*.

chantry ['tʃɑːntrɪ] *n Arch Rel* = fondation de messes pour le repos de l'âme du fondateur; **c. priest,** prêtre *m* de la fondation.

chaos ['keɪɒs] *n* chaos *m*; **in a state of c.,** dans le chaos, dans la confusion; *Journ* **c. as bus drivers strike,** confusion due à la grève des chauffeurs de bus; *F* **it was c. in the post office,** c'était la pagaille dans le bureau de poste.

chaotic [keɪ'ɒtɪk] *adj* chaotique.

chaotically [keɪ'ɒtɪklɪ] *adv* chaotiquement.

chap[1] [tʃæp] *n F* type; *m*; **the c. in the shop said ...,** le type dans la boutique a dit ...; **a good c.,** un bon type; **a young c.,** un jeune type; **an odd c.,** un drôle de type; **be a good c.,** sois sympa; *Old-fashioned* **I say, old c.!,** dis, mon vieux!

chap[2] *n* gerçure *f*, crevasse *f* (*sur la peau*).

chap[3] *v* **(-pp-) 1** *vt* gercer, crevasser (*la peau*); **to get chapped,** (*of hands*) se gercer, se crevasser. **2** *vi* se gercer, se crevasser.

chap[4] *n* (*usu pl*) bajoue(s) *f*(*pl*) (*d'un cochon*); *Culin* **Bath c.,** joue *f* de porc fumée.

chap[5] *n* (*abbr* **chapter**) chap.

chapel ['tʃæp(ə)l] *n* **(a)** chapelle *f* (*d'un collège etc*); oratoire *m* (*particulier*); chapelle latérale (*d'une cathédrale etc*); **C. royal,** chapelle d'un palais royal; **c. of ease,** (église *f*) succursale *f*; **mortuary c., c. of rest,** = chapelle ardente; **Lady c.,** chapelle de la Vierge; **(b)** temple *m* (*protestant*); **are you church or c.?,** êtes-vous anglican ou dissident?; **(c)** (*of print union, NUJ*) branche *f* du syndicat; **Father** *or* **Mother of C.,** chef *m* de l'atelier.

chaperon(e)[1] ['ʃæpərəʊn] *n* chaperon *m* (*d'une jeune fille*); **to act as c.,** servir de chaperon; *Fig* **the foreign journalists had a c.,** les journalistes étrangers avaient un guide.

chaperon[2] *vt* **(-n-)** chaperonner (*une jeune fille*).

chaplain ['tʃæplɪn] *n Rel* aumônier *m*; **army c.,** aumônier militaire.

chaplaincy ['tʃæplɪnsɪ] *n* aumônerie *f*.

chappie ['tʃæpɪ] *n F Old-fashioned* = **CHAP[1]**.

chapter ['tʃæptər] *n* **(a)** (*of book*) chapitre *m*; **to give c. and verse for sth,** citer ses autorités à l'appui d'une affirmation; **a new c. in one's life,** un nouveau chapitre de sa vie; **a c. of accidents,** une suite de malheurs, *F* la série noire; **(b)** *Rel* chapitre *m* (*de chanoines, de moines*); **c. house,** salle *f* capitulaire; **(c)** (*of society etc*) groupe *m*; **a Hell's Angel c.,** une bande de Hell's Angels.

char[1] [tʃɑːr] *v* **(-rr-) 1** *vt* carboniser, réduire (*du bois, des os*) en charbon *ou* en cendres; **the charred remains of a building,** les restes carbonisés d'un bâtiment. **2** *vi* se carboniser.

char[2] *n Br Sl* (*tea*) thé *m*.

char[3] *n Br F* (*charlady*) femme *f* de ménage.

char[4] *vi Br F* faire des ménages.

char[5] *n* (*fish*) omble *m* (chevalier).

charabanc ['ʃærəbæŋ] *n Br Arch* autocar *m*.

character ['kærɪktər] *n* **(a)** *Liter Th etc* personnage *m*; **a c. straight out of a novel,** un vrai personnage de roman; **in c.,** *Th etc* dans son rôle, dans la peau du personnage; (*of person's action*) qui s'accorde bien avec son caractère; **out of c.,** *Th etc* pas dans le rôle; (*of person's action*) qui ne s'accorde guère avec son caractère; **his behaviour was totally out of c.,** ça ne lui ressemble pas du tout de se conduire comme ça; **c. actor,** acteur *m* de genre; **c. part,** rôle chargé; **c. dance,** danse *f* de caractère;

(b) caractère *m*, marque distinctive (*de qn, d'une race, d'un livre etc*); **face full of c.,** physionomie qui a du caractère; **region with a c. of its own,** région qui a un caractère particulier; **these old buildings have c.,** ces vieux bâtiments ont du caractère; **books of this c.,** les livres de ce genre; *Biol* **hereditary/acquired c.,** caractère héréditaire/acquis;

(c) (*moral qualities*) caractère *m*; **man of (strong) c.,** homme de caractère *ou* de volonté; *Fml* **a person of good c.,** une personne honorable; **c. building,** formation *f* du caractère; **a c. reference,** une référence (attestant l'honorabilité de qn);

(d) (*reputation*) réputation *f*; *Arch* (*written reference*) certificat *m* (*de moralité, de bonne conduite*); **place of a very dubious c.,** endroit mal famé;

(e) (*person*) **a suspicious c.,** un individu suspect *ou* louche; **he's a c.!,** c'est un numéro!;

(f) *Typ etc* caractère *m*; **in Greek characters,** en caractères grecs; *Comptr* **special** *or* **binary c.,** caractère spécial *ou* binaire; *Comptr* **c. set,** jeu *m* de caractères.

character-forming ['kærɪktəfɔːmɪŋ] *adj* qui forme le caractère; *Hum* **it's c.-f.,** ça forme le caractère.

characteristic [kærɪktə'rɪstɪk] **1** *adj* (*signe, goût etc*) caractéristique; **this attitude is c. of her,** cette attitude la caractérise *ou* lui est particulière; *Admin* **c. signs,** signalement *m*, signes particuliers. **2** *n* **(a)** trait *m ou* signe *m* de caractère, trait caractéristique, particularité *f*; **(b)** *Math* caractéristique *f* (*d'un logarithme*).

characteristically [kærɪktə'rɪstɪklɪ] *adv* d'une manière caractéristique.

characterization [kærɪktəraɪ'zeɪʃən] *n* caractérisation *f*.

characterize ['kærɪktəraɪz] *vt* **(a)** (*of writer*) caractériser (*un personnage, un siècle*); **(b)** (*be characteristic of*) être caractéristique de (*qn*); **the long pauses that c. his speech,** les longs silences qui caractérisent son discours.

characterless ['kærɪktəlɪs] *adj* sans caractère.

charade [ʃə'rɑːd] *n* (*in game*) charade *f*; *Fig* **we had to go through the c. of filling out the forms again,** il a fallu recommencer ce cirque consistant à remplir les formulaires.

charades [ʃə'rɑːdz] *npl* (*game*) charades *fpl*; **to play c.,** jouer aux charades.

charcoal ['tʃɑːkəʊl] *n* **(a)** charbon *m* de bois; *Med* **c. biscuit,** biscuit *m* au charbon de bois; **animal c.,** noir animal, charbon animal; **(b)** *Art* fusain *m*; **c. drawing,** (dessin *m* au) fusain.

charcoal-broiled ['tʃɑːkəʊl'brɔɪld] *adj* (*steak etc*) grillé au charbon de bois.

charcoal-burner ['tʃɑːkəʊlbɜːnər] *n* **(a)** (*person*) charbonnier *m*; **(b)** (*stove*) réchaud *m* à charbon de bois.

chard [tʃɑːd] *n Culin* **Swiss c.,** bette *f*, blette *f*.

charge¹ [tʃɑːdʒ] *n* **(a)** (*cost*) frais *mpl*, prix *m*; *Admin* droits *mpl*; *Jur* privilège *m*, droit *m*; **list of charges,** tarif *m*; **scale of charges,** barème *m* des prix; **no c. for admission,** (*in museum etc*) entrée gratuite; **to make a c. for sth,** compter qch; **free of c.,** gratis, (à titre) gratuit, à titre gracieux; *Com Banking* exempt de frais, sans frais; *esp Am* **will that be cash or c.?,** vous payez comptant ou vous le portez à votre compte?; *Jur* **charges on an estate,** charges *fpl* d'une succession; **service c.,** prestation *f* de service; **extra c.,** supplément *m*; **bank charges,** frais bancaires; **minimum c.,** (*in taxi*) prise *f* en charge; (*in café, restaurant*) = prix minimum à payer; **c. account,** compte crédit d'achats; *Br* **c. card,** (*for use in shop*) = carte de crédit d'un magasin particulier;

(b) *Jur* (*accusation*) chef *m* d'accusation, acte *m* d'accusation; (*by public prosecutor*) réquisitoire *m*; **to bring** *or* **lay a c. against s.o.,** porter une accusation *ou* porter plainte contre qn; **on a c. of having ...,** sous l'inculpation d'avoir ...; **what's the c.?,** de quoi est-il *ou* suis-je accusé?; **he denies the c.,** il nie les accusations; **c. sheet,** (*in police station*) cahier *m* des délits et écrous; **c. room,** bureau *m* (*de poste de police*);

(c) (*responsibility*) garde *f*, soin *m*; **to place sth in s.o.'s c.,** confier qch à qn *ou* à la garde de qn *ou* aux mains de qn; **to have c. of sth,** avoir qch en garde; **to take c. of sth/s.o.,** se charger de qch/qn; **when the fire broke out a policeman took c.,** lorsque l'incendie s'est déclaré un policier s'est chargé de tout; **Jane's in c. of sales,** Jane est chargée *ou* responsable des ventes; **the director is in overall c.,** le directeur est responsable de l'entreprise dans son ensemble; **he was put in c. of 100 men,** on a mis 100 hommes sous sa responsabilité; **who is in c.?,** qui est (le) responsable?; **I want to speak to the person in c.,** je veux parler au responsable *ou* à la personne responsable; **who was in c. of the vehicle?,** qui était au volant?; *Mil* **the captain in c.,** le capitaine de service; *Jur* **to take s.o. in c.,** arrêter qn; **c. hand,** chef *m* d'équipe; *Br* **c. nurse,** infirmier *m* en chef;

(d) (*person, thing entrusted*) personne *ou* chose confiée à la garde de qn;

(e) *Mil* charge *f*, attaque *f*; **bayonet c.,** charge *ou* assaut *m* à la baïonnette; **to sound the c.,** sonner la charge;

(f) charge *f* (*d'une cartouche, d'une mine etc*); (*of kiln, blast furnace etc*) fournée *f*; *El* charge *f*; *Fig* **the word has an emotional c.,** le mot a une charge affective; *Mil* **blank c.,** charge de salut;

(g) (*of clergy*) cure *f*;

(h) *Her* meuble *m* (*de l'écu*).

charge² **1** *vt* **(a)** (*of seller*) compter, demander (*un prix*) (**for sth,** pour qch); *Com Fin* charger (*un compte*) (**with,** de); **he charged me £15,** il m'a compté 15 livres; **how much do you c. for an hour?,** combien prenez-vous de l'heure?; **to c. a fee,** percevoir un droit; *Tel* **calls charged for,** conversations taxées; **to c. the postage to the customer,** débiter les frais postaux au client; **commission charged by the bank,** commission prélevée par la banque; **c. it to my account/the bill,** portez-le sur mon compte/la note;

(b) *Jur* **to c. s.o. (with a crime)** inculper qn (d'un crime); **he wasn't charged,** il n'a pas été inculpé; **to c. s.o. with assault and battery,** inculper qn de coups et blessures; **charged with ...,** inculpé de ...; *US* **to c. that ...,** alléguer que ...;

(c) (*entrust, order*) **to c. s.o. with a commission,** charger qn d'une commission; **to c. s.o. to do sth,** ordonner à qn de faire qch;

(d) *Mil* (*attack*) charger, faire une charge contre (*l'ennemi*);

(e) *El* charger (*un conducteur d'électricité, un accumulateur etc*) (**with,** de); *El* **charged conductor,** conducteur chargé *ou* sous tension; *Fig* **a highly charged atmosphere,** une atmosphère très tendue;

(f) *Her* charger (*une pièce de blason d'une autre*).

2 *vi* **(a)** *Mil* charger, faire une charge; *F* (*run heavily*) se précipiter, foncer; **he charged in,** il est entré en coup de vent; **the crowd charged across the square,** la foule s'est élancée à travers la place;

(b) (*require payment*) faire payer (**for sth,** pour qch); **do you c. for delivery?,** est-ce qu'il y a des frais de livraison?;

(c) (*of battery*) se charger.

▶**charge up** **1** *vtsep* **(a)** (*in shop etc*) **to c. sth up,** mettre qch sur le compte de qn; **(b)** (*battery*) charger. **2** *vi* (*of battery*) se charger.

chargeable ['tʃɑːdʒəb(ə)l] *adj* **(a)** (*person*) inculpable (**with,** de); **(b)** *Com etc* (*item, repair etc*) à la charge (**to,** de).

chargé d'affaires ['ʃɑːʒeɪdæ'feər] *n* chargé *m* d'affaires.

charger ['tʃɑːdʒər] *n* **(a)** *El* chargeur *m* (*d'accumulateur*); chargeuse *f* mécanique (*de haut fourneau etc*); **(b)** (*horse*) cheval *m* de bataille.

charging ['tʃɑːdʒɪŋ] *n* chargement *m*; *El* **battery c.,** (re)charge *f* des accus.

charily ['tʃeərɪlɪ] *adv* **(a)** (*cautiously*) avec précaution, avec prudence; **(b)** (*meanly*) avec parcimonie.

chariot ['tʃærɪət] *n* char *m*.

charioteer [tʃærɪə'tɪər] *n* conducteur *m* de char.

charisma [kæ'rɪzmə] *n* charisme *m*; **to have c.,** avoir du charisme.

charismatic [kærɪz'mætɪk] *adj* charismatique.

charitable ['tʃærɪtəb(ə)l] *adj* **(a)** (*person, action*) charitable; **c. donation,** don *m* à une œuvre de bienfaisance; *Fig* **the critics were not c.,** les critiques n'ont pas été très bienveillants; **(b)** (*organization, work*) de bienfaisance, de charité; *Jur* **c. trust,** œuvre *f* de charité.

charitably ['tʃærɪtəblɪ] *adv* charitablement.

charity ['tʃærɪtɪ] *n* **(a)** (*money, food*) charité *f*, aumônes *fpl*, bienfaisance *f*; **to live on c.,** vivre d'aumônes; **I don't want your c.,** je ne veux pas qu'on me fasse l'aumône; **c. ball,** bal *m* de bienfaisance; **c. organization,** société *f* de bienfaisance; **c. run,** course *f* à pied au profit d'une œuvre de bienfaisance; **(b)** (*organization*) œuvre *f* de bienfaisance; **registered c.,** œuvre d'utilité publique; **(c)** (*kindness*) charité *f*; **out of c.,** par charité; *Prov* **c. begins at home,** charité bien ordonnée commence par soi(-même).

charlady ['tʃɑːleɪdɪ] *n Br* femme *f* de ménage.

charlatan ['ʃɑːlət(ə)n] *n* charlatan *m*.

charleston ['tʃɑːlstən] *n* (*dance*) charleston *m*.

Charley, Charlie ['tʃɑːlɪ] *n* (*dimin of* **Charles**) Charlot *m*; *Cin* **Charlie Chaplin,** Charlot; *Br F* **I felt a right** *or* **a proper C.,** je me sentais vraiment idiot; *Am F* **to have a charley horse,** avoir mal à la jambe.

charlotte ['ʃɑːlət] *n Culin* **apple c.,** charlotte *f* aux pommes.

charm¹ [tʃɑːm] *n* **(a)** (*attractiveness*) charme *m*, agrément *m*; attrait *m* (*de la jeunesse etc*); **a film of great c.,** un film plein de charme; **the village has a quiet c.,** le village a un charme tranquille; **to be devoid of c.,** manquer de charme; *F* **to turn on the c.,** faire du charme; **(physical) charms,** (*of woman*) charmes, attraits, appas *mpl*; **the c. of it is that it's easy to use,** ce qu'il y a de bien avec ça, c'est que c'est facile à utiliser; **(b)** (*spell*) charme *m* (**against,** contre); sortilège *m*, sort *m*, enchantement *m*; **to be under a c.,** être sous (le coup d') un charme; *F* **it works like a c.,** ça marche à merveille; **(c)** (*talisman*) amulette *f*, fétiche *m*; **(lucky) c.,** breloque *f*, porte-bonheur *m inv*; **c. bracelet,** bracelet *m* porte-bonheur.

charm² *vt* charmer, enchanter (*qn*); charmer (*un*

serpent); **he leads a charmed life,** sa vie est sous un charme.

charmer ['tʃɑːmər] *n* **(a)** (*charming person*) charmeur, -euse, séducteur, -trice; **he's quite a c.,** c'est un charmeur; **(b)** (*magician*) charmeur, -euse; **snake c.,** charmeur de serpents.

charming ['tʃɑːmɪŋ] *adj* (*person, village, story*) charmant; (*person, house, smile, story*) exquis; **Prince C.,** le Prince Charmant; **c. child,** enfant adorable.

charmingly ['tʃɑːmɪŋlɪ] *adv* d'une façon charmante.

charnel ['tʃɑːn(ə)l] *n* **c. house,** charnier *m*, ossuaire *m*.

charring ['tʃɑːrɪŋ] *n* carbonisation *f*.

chart¹ [tʃɑːt] *n* **(a)** *Math etc* (*graph*) graphique *m*; (*diagram*) diagramme *m*; (*table*) tableau *m*; *Med* **temperature c.,** feuille *f* de température; *Com* **colour c.,** nuancier *m*; *Mus* **(pop) charts,** palmarès *m*, hit-parade *m*; **c. topper,** numéro un; **it's number one in** *or* **top of the charts,** c'est le numéro un au palmarès; **(b)** *Nau* carte *f* (*marine, aéronautique*); **c. room,** cabine *f* des cartes.

chart² **1** *vt* **(a)** *Nau* hydrographier, faire l'hydrographie de (*une mer etc*); porter (*un rocher etc*) sur une carte; **(b)** porter (*la température d'un malade etc*) sur la feuille; (*plot a graph of*) établir le graphique de (*une série de relèvements etc*); *Fig* **the book charts the rise of the labour movement,** ce livre retrace la montée du mouvement travailliste. **2** *vi Mus F* (*of record*) être classé; **it charted at 16,** il a été classé 16ème.

charter¹ ['tʃɑːtər] *n* **(a)** *Hist Jur* charte *f* (*d'une ville, d'une université etc*); statuts *mpl* (*d'une société*); *Pol* **the Atlantic C.,** la Charte de l'Atlantique; **(b)** (*of plane, ship, bus*) affrètement *m*; **c. plane,** (*for passengers, cargo*) avion affrété *ou* nolisé; (*very small, for passengers*) avion-taxi *m*, *pl* avions-taxis; (*for passengers, at reduced fare*) (avion *m*) charter *m*; **c. flight,** vol *m* d'affrètement; **on c.,** (*to a company*) affrété; (*to an individual*) loué.

charter² *vt* **(a)** (*hire*) affréter, noliser (*un navire, un avion*); prendre (*un navire*) à fret; **to c. a coach,** affréter un car; **(b)** accorder une charte à (*une compagnie etc*).

chartered ['tʃɑːtəd] *adj* **(a)** (*navire, avion*) affrété, nolisé; **(b)** (*compagnie, banque*) privilégié; *Br* **c. accountant,** expert *m* comptable.

charterer ['tʃɑːtərər] *n Nau* affréteur *m*.

chartering ['tʃɑːtərɪŋ] *n* (*of plane, ship, bus*) affrètement *m*.

charwoman, *pl* **-women** ['tʃɑːwʊmən, -wɪmɪn] *n Br* femme *f* de ménage.

chary ['tʃeərɪ] *adj* (*cautious*) prudent, circonspect; **to be c. of doing sth,** hésiter à faire qch; **to be c. of praise,** (*sparing with it*) être avare de compliments.

chase¹ [tʃeɪs] *n* **(a)** (*pursuit*) chasse *f*, poursuite *f*; **to give c. to s.o.,** donner la chasse à qn; **in c. of s.o.,** à la poursuite de qn; **a car c.,** une poursuite en voitures; **paper c.,** rallye-paper *m*, *pl* rallye-papers; **(b)** *Horseracing* steeple *m*; **(c)** (*animal(s) hunted*) gibier chassé; **the c.,** la chasse à courre.

chase² **1** *vt* (*pursue*) poursuivre; donner la chasse à (*un voleur, l'ennemi etc*); courir après (*une femme, un homme*); chasser (*le cerf*); **to c. a dog away,** chasser un chien; **to c. s.o. out of the house,** chasser qn de la maison. **2** *vi* **I've been chasing around all day,** j'ai couru dans tous les sens toute la journée.

chase³ *vt* **(a)** (*engrave*) ciseler, bretteler (*l'or, l'argent*); relever (*le métal*) en bosse; **chased work,** ouvrage ciselé; **(b)** (*emboss*) repousser (*le métal*); **chased silver,** argent repoussé.

chase⁴ *n Typ* châssis *m* (*de mise en pages*).

►**chase after** *vipo F* courir après (*un homme, une femme*); partir à la poursuite de (*qch*); **we've been all over town chasing after that spare part,** nous avons dû parcourir la ville à la recherche de cette pièce détachée.

►**chase up** *vtsep* **(a)** (*insistently contact or try to contact*) **it was only by chasing them up that ...,** ce n'est qu'à force de les rappeler que ...; **we had to keep chasing up the woman in the consulate,** il a fallu que nous rappelions sans cesse l'employée du consulat; **we finally chased him up in the library,** finalement on l'a trouvé dans la bibliothèque; **(b)** (*to make insistent inquiries about*) activer (*une affaire*); **I'll c. the matter up for you,** je vais me renseigner pour vous.

chaser ['tʃeɪsər] *n F* **(a)** (*drink*) (*after beer*) = verre d'alcool qu'on prend après un verre de bière; (*after whisky*) = verre de bière etc qu'on prend après un whisky; **(b)** **woman c.,** coureur *m* de jupons.

chasing ['tʃeɪsɪŋ] *n* **(a)** (*of gold, silver*) ciselage *m*, ciselure *f*, brettelure *f*; **c. hammer,** marteau *m* à chasser; **(b)** (*of metal*) repoussage *m*.

chasm ['kæz(ə)m] *n* **(a)** (*abyss*) abysse *m*, abîme *m*, gouffre béant; **(b)** *Fig* abîme *m* (*entre deux personnes*); **the c. between their political viewpoints,** l'abîme qui sépare leurs points de vue politiques.

chassis ['ʃæsɪ] *n Aut Av etc* châssis *m*.

chaste [tʃeɪst] *adj* **(a)** (*sexually*) chaste; (*in behaviour*) pudique; **(b)** *Lit* (*speech, taste, style*) pur, sobre, simple.

chastely ['tʃeɪstlɪ] *adv* (*see adj*) **(a)** chastement; **(b)** sobrement.

chasten ['tʃeɪs(ə)n] *vt esp Lit* **(a)** (*of providence, suffering etc*) châtier, éprouver (*qn*); (*humble*) rabattre la présomption *ou* l'orgueil de (*qn*); (*subdue*) assagir (*qn*); **he was in a chastened mood,** il était abattu; **(b)** (*moderate*) châtier (*ses passions*).

chasteness ['tʃeɪstnɪs] *n* chasteté *f*.

chastise [tʃæs'taɪz] *vt Fml* châtier; corriger (*un enfant*).

chastisement [tʃæs'taɪzmənt] *n Fml* châtiment *m*; correction *f* (*d'un enfant*).

chastity ['tʃæstɪtɪ] *n* **(a)** (*sexual*) célibat *m*; virginité *f*; **(b)** (*of behaviour, speech, thought*) chasteté *f*, pudeur *f*, pureté *f*.

chasuble ['tʃæzjʊb(ə)l, 'tʃæzəb(ə)l] *n Rel* chasuble *f*.

chat¹ [tʃæt] *n* causerie *f*, causette *f*, bavardage *m*; **to have a c. with s.o.,** bavarder avec qn; **the c. at work is all about cars,** au travail, on ne discute que de voitures; *TV* **c. show,** talk-show *m*, *pl* talk-shows.

chat² *vi* (**-tt-**) causer, bavarder; **to c. with s.o.,** bavarder avec qn, faire la causette avec qn; **they spend all day chatting,** ils passent toute la journée à bavarder; **to c. about one thing and another,** parler de choses et d'autres.

►**chat up** *vtsep F* (*s.o. of the opposite sex*) baratiner (*une fille, un type*); *Fig* **to c. up a client,** baratiner un client.

chattel ['tʃæt(ə)l] *n Jur* bien *m* meuble, bien mobilier; **chattels,** biens *mpl*; **goods and chattels,** biens et effets *mpl*.

chatter¹ ['tʃætər] *n* (*of people*) bavardage *m*; (*of birds*) caquet(age) *m*, jacasserie *f*; (*of monkeys*) babil *m*; (*of teeth*) claquement *m*.

chatter² *vi* (*of person*) bavarder, jaser; (*of birds*) caqueter, jacasser; (*of monkeys*) babiller; (*of teeth*) claquer; **my teeth were chattering,** je claquais des dents.

chatterbox ['tʃætəbɒks] *n F* grand(e) bavard(e), moulin *m* à paroles.

chatterer ['tʃætərər] *n* bavard, -arde, jaseur, -euse.

chattering ['tʃætərɪŋ] *n* (*of bird*) caquetage *m*; (*of people*) bavardage *m*; (*of teeth*) claquement *m*.

chatty ['tʃætɪ] *adj* (*person*) bavard; (*letter*) plein de bavardages; (*article etc*) écrit sur le ton de la conversation; **Mr Smith was very c.** *or* **in a very c. mood today,** M. Smith était très bavard aujourd'hui; **the interview with the President was rather too c.,** il y avait un peu trop de bavardages dans l'entretien avec le Président.

chauffeur¹ ['ʃəʊfər] *n Aut* chauffeur *m* (*employé par un particulier*); **c.-driven,** (*car*) conduit par un chauffeur.

chauffeur² *vt* accompagner, conduire (*qn*); conduire (*une voiture*); **we were chauffeured to the airport,** on nous a conduits à l'aéroport.

chauvinism ['ʃəʊvɪnɪz(ə)m] *n* chauvinisme *m*.

chauvinist ['ʃəʊvɪnɪst] **1** *n* **(a)** chauvin, -ine; **(b)** *F* **(male) c.,** macho *m*. **2** *adj* **(a)** chauvin; **(b)** *F* **(male) c.,** macho, machiste; *F* **male c. pig,** phallocrate *m*.

chauvinistic [ʃəʊvɪ'nɪstɪk] *adj* chauvin, chauviniste.

cheap [tʃiːp] **1** *adj* **(a)** (*inexpensive*) (à) bon marché, (à) bon compte, pas cher; **it works out cheaper to take a whole bottle,** cela revient moins cher de prendre la bouteille entière; **the cheapest,** le meilleur marché, le moins cher; *F* **he's very c.,** (*of shopkeeper*) il n'est pas cher; **a c. day out,** une journée économique; **to do sth on the c.,** (*at little cost*) faire qch à peu de frais; (*meanly*) faire qch chichement; **to buy sth on the c.,** acheter qch au rabais *ou* à bas prix; **dirt c.,** pour rien; **c. fare/rate,** tarif/taux réduit; **(b)** *Pej* (*of little worth*) de peu de valeur; (*émotion*) superficiel; **it's c. and nasty,** c'est de la camelote; **a c. remark,** une remarque facile; **that was a c. thing to do,** ça n'était pas bien de faire ça; *F* **to feel c.,** avoir honte; **to make oneself c.,** se déprécier; **(c)** *Am Pej* (*mean*) pingre. **2** *adv F* = **CHEAPLY**.

cheapen ['tʃiːp(ə)n] *vt* **(a)** (*degrade*) diminuer la valeur de (*qch*); **to c. oneself,** se déprécier; **(b)** (*lower price of*) (ra)baisser *ou* faire baisser le prix de (*qch*).

cheap-jack ['tʃiːpdʒæk] *n* camelot *m*.

cheaply ['tʃiːplɪ] *adv* **(a)** (à) bon marché, à bas prix; (*to do, to travel*) à peu de frais; **it's possible to eat out c. in**

Brussels, à Bruxelles, on peut manger dehors pour pas cher; **he got off c.,** il s'en est tiré à bon compte; **(b)** (*to say*) mesquinement.

cheapness ['tʃi:pnɪs] *n* **(a)** bas prix (*de qch*); **(b)** *Pej* peu *m* de valeur, basse qualité (*de qch*).

cheapo ['tʃi:pəʊ] *F* **1** *adj* (*inexpensive*) bon marché, pas cher. **2** *n* **it's a real c.,** c'est un truc pas cher.

cheapskate ['tʃi:pskeɪt] *n F* radin *m*.

cheat¹ [tʃi:t] *n* **(a)** (*at games*) tricheur, euse; **(b)** (*dishonest person*) trompeur, -euse (*par habitude*); (*crook*) escroc *m*; (*imposter*) imposteur *m*.

cheat² **1** *vt* **(a)** (*at games*) tricher (*qn*); **(b)** (*be dishonest to*) tromper; (*defraud*) frauder (*qn*); **to c. s.o. out of sth,** escroquer qch à qn. **2** *vi* **(a)** (*at games*) tricher, truquer; **(b)** (*be dishonest*) frauder.

►cheat on *vipo* **(a)** (*be unfaithful to*) tromper (*sa femme, son mari*); **(b)** (*be dishonest about*) frauder sur (*les dépenses*).

cheating ['tʃi:tɪŋ] *n* **(a)** (*dishonesty*) tromperie *f*; **(b)** *Cards* tricherie *f*.

check¹ [tʃek] *n* **(a)** (*inspection, examination*) contrôle *m*; vérification *f* (*d'un compte etc*); **to keep a c. on sth,** contrôler qch; **let's run a c. on Porsche owners in the area,** contrôlons les propriétaires de Porsche de la région; **cross c.,** recoupement *m*; *Aut etc* **spot c.,** (*on the spot*) vérification sur place; (*surprise*) contrôle-surprise *m*, *pl* contrôles-surprises; **radar speed c.,** contrôle de vitesse par radar; **c. list,** liste *f* de contrôle; *Am* **c. (mark),** (*tick*) coche *f*;
(b) *Am* (*bill in restaurant etc*) note *f*;
(c) *Am* (*for deposited item*) billet *m*, ticket *m*; *Rail etc* **luggage c.,** bulletin *m* de bagages *ou* d'enregistrement; **cloakroom c.,** bulletin *m* de consigne;
(d) *US* (*gambling chip*) jeton *m* de présence (*à une séance*); *Sl* **to hand in** *or* **cash in one's checks,** casser sa pipe;
(e) *US Fin* = **CHEQUE**;
(f) (*restraint*) frein *m*; **to keep** *or* **hold the enemy in c.,** tenir l'ennemi en échec; **to keep one's feelings in c.,** se contraindre, se contenir; *Pol* **a system of checks and balances,** une politique de restriction et d'équilibre; **there is no effective c. on presidential power,** il n'y a pas de limitation réelle du pouvoir du président; *Tech* **c. valve,** soupape *f ou* clapet *m* de retenue;
(g) (*reversal*) revers *m*;
(h) (*halt*) arrêt *m*, pause *f*; **(sudden) c.,** à-coup *m*;
(i) *Chess* échec *m*; **c.!,** échec au roi!

check² **1** *vt* **(a)** (*verify, examine etc*) vérifier (*un compte, la pression etc*); compulser (*un document*) sur l'original; *Typ* (*go over*) réviser (*des épreuves*); *Typ* (*compare*) conférer (*des épreuves*); **I'll c. the arrival time/when they're supposed to arrive,** je vérifierai l'heure d'arrivée/ quand ils sont censés arriver; **to c. names on a list/***etc*, pointer *ou F* cocher des noms sur une liste/*etc*; **to c. sth against sth,** comparer qch à qch; **c. these names against the ones on the list,** vérifie que ces noms sont les mêmes que ceux de la liste; *Sch* **c. your work before handing it in,** relisez votre travail avant de le rendre; **to c. goods,** vérifier *ou* recenser des marchandises; *Com* **to c. the books,** pointer les écritures; **checked and double checked,** vérifié et revérifié; **to c. that ...,** s'assurer que ...;
(b) (*officially inspect*) contrôler (*les billets*);
(c) *Am* (*of customer*) (faire) enregistrer (*ses bagages*); (*at restaurant etc*) mettre (*son chapeau, son pardessus*) au vestiaire; (*of employee*) enregistrer (*des bagages*); prendre (*un chapeau, un pardessus*);
(d) *Am* (*mark with tick*) cocher;
(e) (*halt*) faire échec à, arrêter net (*qn, qch*); enrayer (*une crise, la hausse des prix*); arrêter (*une attaque*);
(f) (*restrain*) refouler, retenir (*ses larmes, sa colère*); modérer (*sa violence*); réprimer, refréner (*une passion*);
(g) *Chess* mettre (*le roi*) en échec, faire échec à (*le roi*);
(h) *Fml* (*reprimand*) réprimander (*un enfant etc*).
2 *vi* **(a)** (*verify etc*) vérifier; **they usually have vacancies, but it's a good idea to c.,** d'ordinaire, ils ont de la place, mais il vaut mieux s'en assurer; **we checked with the university,** nous avons vérifié à l'université;
(b) (*halt*) hésiter, s'arrêter (**at,** devant).

check³ *n Tex* carreau *m*; **c. material/shirt,** tissu *m*/ chemise *f* à carreaux.

►check in **1** *vi* **(a)** (*at hotel*) remplir la fiche d'entrée *ou* le registre; **(b)** (*at airport*) se faire enregistrer. **2** *vtsep* **(a)** (*of receptionist*) enregistrer l'arrivée de (*qn*); **I checked them in myself,** j'ai enregistré leur arrivée moi-même; **(b)** (*make reservation for*) faire une réservation pour (*qn*); **they checked the actress into a four-star hotel,** ils ont fait une réservation pour l'actrice dans un hôtel quatre étoiles; **(c)** (*at airport etc*) enregistrer (*les bagages*).

►check off *vtsep Am* cocher (*un nom*).

►check on *vipo* vérifier, recouper (*des informations etc*); **to c. on s.o.,** enquêter sur qn (*du point de vue de la sécurité etc*).

►check out **1** *vi* **(a)** (*leave hotel*) quitter un hôtel; **they checked out last night,** ils ont quitté l'hôtel la nuit dernière; **(b)** *Sl* (*of story, statement*) tenir debout; **it doesn't c. out,** ça ne tient pas debout, ça ne marche pas. **2** *vtsep* **(a)** (*investigate*) vérifier, recouper (*des informations etc*); enquêter sur (*qn*) (*du point de vue de la sécurité etc*); *Sl* **there's a new night-club we could c. out,** il y a une nouvelle boîte que nous pourrions tester; **(b)** (*of receptionist*) enregistrer le départ de (*qn*).

►check over *vipo* (*look over*) vérifier (*qch*).

►check through *vtsep* **(a)** (*examine*) contrôler, examiner; **they checked through everyone's hand luggage,** ils ont contrôlé tous les bagages à main; **(b)** (*send by plane*) faire envoyer (par avion); **I'd like my luggage checked through to Los Angeles,** je voudrais faire envoyer directement mes bagages à Los Angeles.

►check up *vi* (*make sure*) vérifier, s'assurer de (*qch*).

►check up on *vipo* = **CHECK ON**.

checkbook ['tʃekbʊk] *n Am* = **CHEQUEBOOK**.

checked [tʃekt] *adj* (*tissu etc*) à carreaux, quadrillé.

checker¹ ['tʃekər] *n* **(a)** (*person*) contrôleur, -euse; **(b)** *Comptr* **grammar/spelling c.,** correcteur grammatical/ orthographique.

checker² *vt Am* = **CHEQUER**.

checkerboard ['tʃekəbɔ:d] *n Am* damier *m*.

checkered ['tʃekəd] *adj Am* = **CHEQUERED**.

checkers ['tʃekəz] *npl Am* jeu *m* de dames.

check-in ['tʃekɪn] *n Av* **(a)** enregistrement *m* (*des passagers*); **c.-in time,** heure *f* d'enregistrement; **(b) c.-in. (desk),** guichet *m* d'enregistrement.

checking ['tʃekɪŋ] *n* **(a)** (*verification, examination*) contrôle *m*, vérification *f*; (*more detailed*) pointage *m*; **(b)** (*of luggage etc*) enregistrement *m*; **(c)** *Am Fin* **c. account,** compte courant; **(d)** (*of horse*) parade *f*.

checkmate¹ ['tʃekmeɪt] *n Chess* échec *m* et mat; *Fig* échec complet.

checkmate² *vt Chess* faire (*le roi*) échec et mat; *Fig* faire échec et mat à (*qn*); contrecarrer, déjouer (*les projets de qn*).

checkout ['tʃekaʊt] *n* **(a)** (*in supermarket*) **c. (point, desk),** caisse *f*; **(b)** (*in hotel*) **c. time is 12 noon,** les clients doivent quitter la chambre avant midi (le jour du départ).

checkpoint ['tʃekpɔɪnt] *n* contrôle *m*.

checkrein ['tʃekreɪn] *n US Horseriding* fausses rênes.

checkroom ['tʃekru:m] *n Am* vestiaire *m*.

checkup ['tʃekʌp] *n* **(a)** *Med* examen médical complet, check-up *m*; **to give s.o. a c.,** faire le bilan de santé de qn; **to have a c.,** se faire faire un check-up; **it's just a c.,** c'est juste une visite de routine; **(b)** (*inspection*) vérification *f*, inspection *f*; (*of machinery*) révision *f*.

cheddar ['tʃedər] *n* (fromage *m* de) cheddar *m*.

cheek¹ [tʃi:k] *n* **(a)** *Anat* joue *f*; **flabby cheeks,** bajoues *fpl*; **to dance c. to c.,** danser joue contre joue; **c. by jowl with s.o.,** côte à côte avec qn; **to turn the other c.,** tendre l'autre joue; **(b)** (*buttock*) fesse *f*; **(c)** *Br F* impertinence *f*, toupet *m*, culot *m*; **he's got a c.,** il est culotté *ou* gonflé; **that's enough of your c.!,** (ne) te fiche pas de moi!; **the c.!,** quel culot *ou* toupet!; **(d)** *Tech* (*of vice*) mâchoire *f*; *Nau* (*of mast*) jottereau *m*; (*of rudder*) safran *m*; (*of harness*) branche *f*.

cheek² *vt Br F* dire des impertinences à (*qn*), faire l'insolent avec (*qn*).

cheekbone ['tʃi:kbəʊn] *n* pommette *f*; **high** *or* **prominent cheekbones,** pommettes saillantes.

cheekily ['tʃi:kɪlɪ] *adv Br F* (*to do*) d'une manière impertinente *ou* effrontée; (*to say*) d'un air impertinent *ou* effronté.

cheekiness ['tʃi:kɪnɪs] *n Br F* effronterie *f*.

cheeky ['tʃi:kɪ] *adj Br F* effronté, insolent; **don't be c.!,** pas d'insolence!

cheep¹ [tʃi:p] *n* (*of young birds*) piaulement *m*, piaulis *m*; *F* **you can't get a c. out of her,** elle ne dit jamais mot.

cheep² *vi* (*of young birds*) piauler.

cheer¹ [tʃɪər] *n* **(a)** (*shout*) hourra *m*; **cheers,** acclamations *fpl*, bravos *mpl*; **to give three cheers,** pousser trois hourras; **three cheers for Mary!,** un ban pour Mary!, vive Mary!; **(b)** *F* **cheers!,** (*toast*) (à votre) santé!; *Br* (*at parting*) à bientôt; *Br* (*thanks*) merci!; **(c)** *Lit* (*spirits*) bonne disposition (*d'esprit*); **be of good c.!,** prenez courage!; **we were of good c.,** nous étions de bonne humeur.

cheer[2] **1** *vt* **(a)** (*shout for*) acclamer (*qn*); **(b)** (*encourage, make happier*) remonter le moral de (*qn*). **2** *vi* (*shout*) pousser des hourras *ou* des acclamations.

►cheer on *vtsep* (*support*) encourager.

►cheer up 1 *vi* (*become more cheerful*) s'égayer; **she cheered up a bit in the afternoon,** elle est devenue un peu plus gaie dans l'après-midi; **the weather's cheered up,** le temps s'est amélioré; **c. up!,** courage! **2** *vtsep* **(a)** (*make more cheerful*) remonter le moral de (*qn*); **(b)** (*make brighter*) éclaircir; **the new curtains really do c. the room up,** les nouveaux rideaux éclaircissent vraiment la pièce.

cheerful ['tʃɪəfʊl] *adj* (*person*) gai, de bonne humeur, allègre; (*face, view etc*) riant; (*room*) gai, d'aspect agréable; (*conversation, music etc*) égayant; (*news etc*) encourageant; **that's a c. thought!,** ça c'est encourageant!; *Iron* comme vous êtes optimiste!; **it's nice to see a c. face,** c'est agréable de voir un visage souriant; **you're c. this morning,** tu es de bonne humeur ce matin.

cheerfully ['tʃɪəfʊlɪ] *adv* **(a)** (*happily*) gaiement, avec entrain, allègrement; **(b)** (*willingly*) de bon cœur, volontiers, **they c. gave up their free time,** ils ont renoncé de bon cœur à leur temps libre; **(c)** (*without compunction*) sans remords; **she would c. leave the work for the others,** elle laisserait sans remords le travail aux autres; **I could quite c. strangle him,** je l'étranglerais volontiers.

cheerfulness ['tʃɪəfʊlnɪs] *n* (*of person*) gaieté *f*, bonne humeur; (*of room*) aspect *m* agréable.

cheerily ['tʃɪərɪlɪ] *adv* gaiement, avec gaieté, de bonne humeur.

cheerio [tʃɪərɪ'əʊ] *int Br F* (*at parting*) à bientôt!; (*in drinking a toast*) à la vôtre!, à la tienne!

cheerleader ['tʃɪəliːdər] *n Am* meneur, -euse de ban.

cheerless ['tʃɪəlɪs] *adj* morne, triste, sombre.

cheery ['tʃɪərɪ] *adj* **(a)** (*person, smile, wave*) joyeux, gai, réjoui, guilleret; **(b)** (*news etc*) encourageant, réconfortant.

cheese [tʃiːz] *n Culin* **(a)** fromage *m*; **blue c.,** (fromage) bleu *m*; **cream c.,** fromage frais; **cottage c.,** caillé *m*; *Culin* **cauliflower/macaroni c.,** chou-fleur *m*/macaronis *mpl* au gratin; **toasted c.,** toast *m* au fromage; **quince c.,** pâte *f* de coings; *Phot F* **say c.!,** souriez!; **c. sandwich,** sandwich *m* au fromage; **the c. industry,** l'industrie fromagère; **c. maker** *or* **manufacturer,** fromager, -ère; **c. biscuit,** (*for cheese*) biscuit salé; (*with cheese on*) biscuit au fromage; **c. straws,** allumettes *f* au fromage; **(b)** (*individual item*) (*pl* **cheeses**) **a c.,** un fromage (entier); meule *f* (de fromage).

►cheese off *vtsep* (*usu pass*) *Br Sl* **to be cheesed (off),** en avoir marre (**with,** de).

cheeseboard ['tʃiːzbɔːd] *n* **(a)** (*for cutting cheese*) plateau *m* à fromage; **(b)** (*as part of meal*) plateau *m* de fromages; **a selection from our** *or* **the c.,** (*in restaurant etc*) une sélection de fromages.

cheeseburger ['tʃiːzbɜːgər] *n Culin* cheeseburger *m*.

cheesecake ['tʃiːzkeɪk] *n* **(a)** *Culin* cheesecake *m*; **(b)** *Am F* (*no pl*) pin-up *f inv*.

cheesecloth ['tʃiːzklɒθ] *n* gaze *f*, étamine *f*.

cheeseparing ['tʃiːzpeərɪŋ] **1** *adj* parcimonieux; **c. economy,** économies *fpl* de bouts de chandelle. **2** *n* parcimonie *f*, lésine *f*.

cheesy ['tʃiːzɪ] *adj* **(a)** (*in taste*) qui a un goût de fromage; (*in smell*) qui sent le fromage, parfumé au fromage; **(b)** *Am F* (*poor quality*) moche.

cheetah ['tʃiːtə] *n* (*animal*) guépard *m*.

chef [ʃef] *n Culin* chef *m* (de cuisine).

chemical ['kemɪk(ə)l] **1** *adj* chimique; **c. company,** industrie *f* de produits chimiques; **c. engineering,** génie *m* chimique; **c. engineer,** ingénieur *m* chimiste; **c. warfare,** guerre *f* chimique; **c. dependency,** toxicodépendance *f*. **2** *n* produit *m* chimique.

chemically ['kemɪk(ə)lɪ] *adv* chimiquement.

chemist ['kemɪst] *n* **(a)** *esp Br Com* pharmacien, -ienne; **c.'s (shop),** pharmacie *f*; **(b)** (*scientist*) chimiste *m*.

chemistry ['kemɪstrɪ] *n* chimie *f*; **organic/inorganic c.,** chimie organique/minérale; **industrial** *or* **technical c.,** chimie industrielle; *Fig* **there was a certain c. between the members of the band,** il y avait une certaine entente entre les musiciens; **the c. between us is good,** nous avons de bons rapports, ça passe bien entre nous.

chemotherapy [kiːmə'θerəpɪ], *F* **chemo** ['kiːməʊ] *n Med* chimiothérapie *f*; **to have c.,** avoir de la chimiothérapie.

cheque, *Am* **check** [tʃek] *n Fin* chèque *m*; **who should I make the c. out to?,** à quel ordre dois-je faire *ou* écrire le chèque?; **to cash a c.,** toucher un chèque; **to stop a c.,** suspendre le paiement d'un chèque; **c. for ten pounds,** chèque de dix livres; **crossed c.,** chèque barré; **blank c.,** chèque en blanc; **traveller's c.,** chèque de voyage; **c. without cover,** *F* **dud c.,** chèque en bois; **c. card,** = carte bancaire délivrée avec un chéquier.

chequebook, *Am* **checkbook** ['tʃekbʊk] *n Fin* carnet *m* de chèques, chéquier *m*; *Pej* **c. journalism,** = le fait pour un journaliste d'offrir des sommes importantes pour obtenir l'exclusivité d'un récit, d'un témoignage etc.

chequer, *Am* **checker** ['tʃekər] *vt* **(a)** (*mark with check pattern*) quadriller (*un tissu etc*); marquer *ou* diviser (*qch*) en carreaux; **(b)** (*variegate with colour*) diaprer, bigarrer.

chequered, *Am* **checkered** ['tʃekəd] *adj* **(a)** (*pattern*) quadrillé, à carreaux, en damier; **(b)** (*variegated*) diapré, bigarré; *Fig* (*life*) mouvementé, plein de vicissitudes; **she's had a somewhat c. career,** elle a eu une carrière un peu mouvementée.

cherish ['tʃerɪʃ] *vt* **(a)** (*hold dear*) bercer, caresser (*un espoir*); nourrir, entretenir (*une idée, une opinion*); **to c. illusions,** se nourrir d'illusions; **his most cherished hopes,** ses espérances les plus chères; **to c. a memory,** chérir un souvenir; **(b)** (*love, look after*) chérir; soigner tendrement (*un enfant*).

cheroot [ʃə'ruːt] *n* cigare *m* à bouts coupés.

cherry ['tʃerɪ] **1** *n* **(a)** (*fruit*) cerise *f*; **wild c.,** merise *f*; **c. brandy,** cherry-brandy *m*, *F* cherry *m*; *F* **to take two bites at the c.,** s'y prendre à deux fois; **c. tart,** tarte *f* aux cerises; **c. stone,** noyau *m* de cerise; **(b) c. (tree),** cerisier *m*; **wild c. (tree),** merisier *m*; **c. orchard,** cerisaie *f*; **(c) c.-red,** rouge *m* cerise. **2** *adj* **c.(-red),** cerise *inv*.

cherub, *pl* **cherubs,** *Bible* **cherubim** ['tʃerəb, -z, -əbɪm] *n Bible* chérubin *m*; *Art* angelot *m*, ange joufflu; *Fig* **a little c.,** (*child*) un petit ange.

cherubic [tʃɪ'ruːbɪk] *adj Bible Art* chérubique, de chérubin; *Fig* (*smile, face etc*) d'ange.

chervil ['tʃɜːvɪl] *n Bot Culin* cerfeuil *m*.

Ches *abbr* **Cheshire**.

Cheshire ['tʃeʃər] *n* **C. cheese,** fromage *m* de Chester, chester *m*; **to grin like a C. cat,** sourire jusqu'aux oreilles.

chess [tʃes] *n* jeu *m* d'échecs; **a c. game, a game of c.,** une partie d'échecs; **to play c.,** jouer aux échecs; **c. player,** joueur, -euse d'échecs.

chessboard ['tʃesbɔːd] *n* échiquier *m*.

chessman, *pl* **-men** ['tʃesmən], **chesspiece** ['tʃespiːs] *n* pièce *f* (du jeu d'échecs).

chest [tʃest] *n* **(a)** *Anat* poitrine *f*; poitrail *m* (*de cheval*); **cold on the c., c. cold,** rhume *m* de poitrine; **to get sth off one's c.,** dire ce qu'on a sur le cœur; **c. size,** tour *m* de poitrine; **what c. (size) are you?,** quel est votre tour de poitrine?; **(b)** (*box*) coffre *m*, caisse *f*; **c. of drawers,** commode *f*; **tea c.,** caisse à thé; **medicine c.,** (coffret *m* de) pharmacie *f*.

chesterfield ['tʃestəfiːld] *n* (*sofa*) canapé rembourré et capitonné (à deux accoudoirs).

chestnut ['tʃesnʌt] **1** *n* **(a) (sweet, Spanish) c.,** châtaigne *f*; (*when cooked*) marron *m*; **horse c.,** marron (d'Inde); *F* **an old c.,** plaisanterie usée; **(b) (sweet) c. (tree),** châtaignier *m*, marronnier *m*; **horse c. (tree),** marronnier d'Inde; **(c)** (*wood*) châtaignier *m*; **(d)** (*colour*) châtain *m*; **(e)** (*horse*) alezan *m*. **2** *adj* **(a)** (*hair*) châtain; **(b)** (*horse*) alezan.

chesty ['tʃestɪ] *adj F* **to be c.,** être bronchitique.

chevron ['ʃevrən] *n Her & Mil* chevron *m*.

chew[1] [tʃuː] *n* **(a)** (*action*) **to have a c. at sth,** mâchonner qch; **(b)** (*of tobacco*) chique *f*.

chew[2] *vt* mâcher, mastiquer (*des aliments etc*); chiquer (*du tabac*); mâchonner (*un cigare*); **to c. the cud,** (*of cow*) ruminer; *F* **to c. the rag** *or* **the fat,** (*chat*) parler *ou* discuter à n'en plus finir; (*complain*) ronchonner.

►chew on *vipo* **(a)** (*gnaw*) mâchouiller, ronger (*qch*); **he chewed on his pipe stem,** il mâchouillait le tuyau de sa pipe; **(b)** (*consider*) réfléchir sur (*qch*); **how much longer do you need to c. on it?,** combien te faut-il encore de temps pour réfléchir à la question?

►chew out *vtsep Am F* (*reprimand*) engueuler (*qn*).

►chew over *vtsep F* (*think over*) méditer sur (*qch*).

►chew up *vtsep* (*damage by chewing*) abîmer à force de mâchonner; **the dog has chewed up the newspaper,** le chien a mangé le journal; *Fig* **the machine chewed up the bank card,** la machine a détérioré la carte bancaire.

chewing ['tʃuːɪŋ] *n* mastication *f*, mâchement *m*, mâchonnement *m*; **c. gum,** chewing-gum *m*; **c. tobacco,** tabac *m* à chiquer.

chewy ['tʃuːɪ] *adj* **(a)** *Pej* (*meat etc*) difficile à mâcher; **(b)** (*sweet*) mou, tendre.
chic [ʃiːk, ʃɪk] **1** *adj* élégant, chic. **2** *n* chic *m*.
chicanery [ʃɪ'keɪnərɪ] *n* chicanerie *f*, chicane *f*.
chicano [tʃɪ'kænəʊ] *n US* citoyen, -enne d'origine mexicaine.
chichi ['ʃiːʃiː] *F* **1** *adj* prétentieux. **2** *n* prétention *f*.
chick [tʃɪk] *n* **(a)** (*young bird*) poussin *m*; **(b)** *esp US F* (*young woman*) fille *f*, nana *f*.
chickadee [tʃɪkə'diː] *n Am* (*bird*) mésange *f* (à tête noire).
chicken ['tʃɪkɪn] **1** *n* **(a)** (*bird*) poulet *m*; *Prov* **don't count your chickens before they are hatched,** il ne faut pas vendre la peau de l'ours avant de l'avoir tué; **free-range c.,** poulet fermier; *Am* **prairie c.,** tétras *m* cupidon, cupidon *m* des prairies, *Can* poule *f* des prairies; **c. liver,** foie *m* de volaille; **c. sandwich,** sandwich *m* au poulet; **c. farm,** élevage *m* avicole; **c. farmer,** aviculteur *m*; **c. feed,** nourriture *f* pour les volailles; *F Fig* **this is c. feed by comparison,** par comparaison c'est de la gnognote; **c. run,** enclos *m* (*d'un poulailler*); **c. wire,** grillage *m*; **(b)** *F* (*coward*) lâche *m*, froussard, -arde; **(c)** *Am Sl* (*young person*) mineur, -e, gamin, -e; **she's no (spring) c.,** elle n'est plus dans sa première jeunesse; **(d)** *Am Sl* **c. hawk,** = pédophile *m*. **2** *adj F* lâche, froussard.
►chicken out *vi F* flancher, se dégonfler; **he chickened out at the last minute,** à la dernière minute il s'est dégonflé; **she chickened out of her dental appointment,** elle avait rendez-vous chez le dentiste mais elle s'est dégonflée.
chickenhearted [tʃɪkɪn'hɑːtɪd], **chickenlivered** [tʃɪkɪn'lɪvəd] *adj F* poltron, froussard.
chickenpox ['tʃɪkɪnpɒks] *n Med* varicelle *f*; **to have c.,** avoir la varicelle.
chickpea ['tʃɪkpiː] *n* (*seed*) pois *m* chiche.
chickweed ['tʃɪkwiːd] *n* (*plant*) mouron *m* des oiseaux, morgeline *f*.
chicory ['tʃɪkərɪ] *n* **(a)** (*plant*) chicorée *f*; *Am* chicorée (frisée); *Br Culin* endive *f*; **(b) (ground) c.,** (poudre *f* de) chicorée *f*.
chide [tʃaɪd] *vt Arch & Lit* (*pt* **chided** *or* **chid**; *pp* **chided** *or* **chidden**) réprimander, gronder (*qn*).
chief [tʃiːf] **1** *n* (*pl* **chiefs**) chef *m* (*de tribu, de bande, de service*); *Mil* **c. of staff,** chef d'état-major; *Am* **fire/police c.,** chef des pompiers/de la police; *F* **the c.,** le patron; *F* **he's the big white c.,** c'est lui le grand patron; **in c.,** en chef; *Mil Nau* **Commander-in-c.,** commandant *m* en chef; **editor in c.,** rédacteur *m* en chef. **2** *adj* principal, (en) chef; **my c. assistant,** mon principal collaborateur; *Am* **c. executive officer,** (*of company*) directeur général; **c. reason,** raison majeure; *US Pol* **C. Executive,** chef *m* de l'Exécutif, Président des États-Unis; *Br* **C. Inspector,** (*of police*) inspecteur principal.
chiefly ['tʃiːflɪ] *adv* **(a)** (*above all*) surtout, avant tout; **(b)** (*principally*) principalement.
chieftain ['tʃiːftən] *n* chef *m* (*de clan*).
chiffon ['ʃɪfɒn] *n Tex* mousseline *f* de soie.
chignon ['ʃiːnjɒn] *n* chignon *m*.
chihuahua [tʃɪ'wɑːwɑː] *n* (*dog*) chihuahua *m*.
chilblain ['tʃɪlbleɪn] *n Med* engelure *f*; **to have chilblains,** avoir des engelures.
child, *pl* **children** [tʃaɪld, 'tʃɪldrən] *n* enfant *mf*; *Lit* descendant, -ante; **be a good c.!,** sois sage!; **to treat s.o. like a c.,** traiter qn en petit garçon *ou* en petite fille; **I'm not a c.!,** je ne suis pas un môme!; *Old-fashioned* **come here, c.!,** viens ici, petit(e)!; **the c. in all of us,** l'enfant qui est en chacun; **our children's children,** les enfants de nos enfants; **children's literature,** littérature enfantine *ou* pour enfants; **ever since I was a c.,** depuis mon enfance; *Old-fashioned* **I have known him from a c.,** (*when he was a child*) je l'ai connu enfant; (*when I was a child*) je le connais depuis mon enfance; **it's c.'s play,** c'est un jeu d'enfant; **c. abuse,** mauvais traitement d'enfant; **c. welfare,** protection *f* de l'enfance; **c. labour,** travail *m* des enfants; **c. murder,** infanticide *m*; **c. wife,** mariée *f* qui est toujours enfant; *Br Admin* **c. benefit,** ≈ allocation familiale; **c. minder,** gardienne d'enfants; **the children of Israel,** les enfants d'Israël.
child-bearing ['tʃaɪldbeərɪŋ] *n* maternité *f*; **after 20 years of c.-b.,** après 20 ans de maternités successives; **of c.-b. age,** en âge d'avoir des enfants; **past c.-b.,** (*femme*) trop âgée pour avoir des enfants; **to have c.-b. hips,** avoir les hanches larges.
childbirth ['tʃaɪldbɜːθ] *n* accouchement *m*; **to die in c.,** mourir en couches.
child-friendly [tʃaɪld'frendlɪ] *adj* (*area, city*) aménagé pour les enfants; (*furniture, house*) conçu pour les enfants.
childhood ['tʃaɪldhʊd] *n* enfance *f*; **to be in one's second c.,** être retombé en enfance; **c. memory,** souvenir *m* d'enfance; **c. sweetheart,** amour *m* d'enfance.
childish ['tʃaɪldɪʃ] *adj* **(a)** *Pej* enfant, puéril; **don't be so c.,** ne faites pas l'enfant, ne soyez pas aussi puéril; **c. remarks,** observations puériles *ou* enfantines; **(b)** enfantin, d'enfant, d'enfance; (*question*) naïf; **c. games,** jeux enfantins.
childishness ['tʃaɪldɪʃnɪs] *n Pej* enfantillage *m*, puérilité *f*.
childless ['tʃaɪldlɪs] *adj* sans enfant(s); (*mariage*) stérile; **she died c.,** elle est morte sans enfants.
childlike ['tʃaɪldlaɪk] *adj* enfantin; (*question*) naïf; (*sourire*) d'enfant; **he was c. in his curiosity,** il avait une curiosité enfantine.
childproof ['tʃaɪldpruf] *adj* (*lock*) ne pouvant pas être ouvert par les enfants.
Chile ['tʃɪlɪ] *n* Chili *m*.
Chilean ['tʃɪlɪən] **1** *adj* chilien. **2** *n* Chilien, -ienne.
chili ['tʃɪlɪ] *n esp Am* = **CHILLI**.
chill¹ [tʃɪl] *n* **(a)** *Med* coup *m* de froid; **to catch a c.,** prendre froid, attraper un refroidissement; **c. of fear,** frisson *m* de crainte; **his laugh sent a c. down my spine,** son rire m'a fait froid dans le dos; **(b)** froideur *f* (*de l'eau, du marbre etc*); froid *m*, fraîcheur *f*; **there's a c. in the air,** le fond de l'air est frais; **to take the c. off,** (*water*) (faire) tiédir; (*wine*) chambrer; **to cast a c. over the company,** jeter un froid sur l'assemblée.
chill² *adj* froid, glacé; (*vent*) frais.
chill³ **1** *vt* **(a)** refroidir, glacer (*qn, qch*); faire frissonner (*qn*); **chilled with fear,** transi de peur; **chilled to the bone,** gelé jusqu'aux os; **(b)** réfrigérer (*la viande etc*); mettre (*le vin*) au frais; **chilled meat,** viande réfrigérée *ou* frigorifiée; **chilled products,** produits frigorifiés; **best served chilled,** (*on label*) servir glacé. **2** *vi* se refroidir, se glacer.
chilli ['tʃɪlɪ] *n Culin* **c. (pepper),** piment *m* (rouge); **c. con carne,** chili *m* con carne; **c. sauce,** sauce *f* aux piments; **c. powder,** poudre *m* de piment.
chilliness ['tʃɪlɪnɪs] *n* (*of air*) froid *m*, froideur *f;* (*of person, welcome*) froideur.
chilling ['tʃɪlɪŋ] **1** *adj* (*wind, welcome*) glacial, -als; (*story, events*) qui donne la chair de poule. **2** *n* réfrigération *f* (*des aliments*); glacement *m* (*du corps etc*).
chilly ['tʃɪlɪ] *adj* **(a)** (*weather etc*) frais, *f* fraîche; **it's c. this morning,** il fait frais ce matin; **(b)** (*person*) frileux; **to feel c.,** avoid froid; **(c)** (*person, manner, welcome*) froid; (*politesse*) glacial.
chime¹ [tʃaɪm] *n* **c. (of bells),** carillon *m*; **can you hear the chimes of St. Mary's?,** est-ce que vous entendez le carillon de St. Mary?; **to ring the chimes,** carillonner; **door chimes,** carillon de porte.
chime² **1** *vi* (*of clock, bells*) carillonner. **2** *vt* sonner (*les cloches*) en carillon; (*of clock*) carillonner (*l'heure*).
►chime in *vi F* placer son mot, intervenir; **they all chimed in at once,** ils sont tous intervenus en même temps.
chimera [kaɪ'mɪərə, kɪ-] *n Myth & Fig* chimère *f*.
chiming ['tʃaɪmɪŋ] **1** *adj* carillonnant; (*pendule etc*) à carillon. **2** *n* carillonnement *m*, carillon *m*.
chimney ['tʃɪmnɪ] *n* **(a)** (*on house etc*) cheminée *f*; **to have the chimneys swept,** faire ramoner les cheminées; *F* **to smoke like a c.,** (*of person*) fumer comme un sapeur; **c. breast,** manteau *m* de (la) cheminée; **c. stack,** (*of house*) tuyau *m* de cheminée; (*of factory*) cheminée d'usine; **c. sweep,** ramoneur *m*; **c. corner,** coin *m* du feu; **(b)** (*on oil lamp*) verre *m* (*de lampe*); **(c)** (*in mountaineering*) cheminée *f*.
chimneypiece ['tʃɪmnɪpiːs] *n esp Br* (manteau *m* de) cheminée *f*.
chimneypot ['tʃɪmnɪpɒt] pot *m* de cheminée.
chimpanzee [tʃɪmpæn'ziː], *F* **chimp** [tʃɪmp] *n* chimpanzé *m*.
chin [tʃɪn] *n* menton *m*; **to keep one's c. up,** tenir bon, tenir le coup; **to take sth on the c.,** faire face à qch; **double c.,** double menton; **receding c.,** menton fuyant; **c. strap,** jugulaire *f* (*de casque etc*).
china ['tʃaɪnə] *n* (*no pl*) (*material*) porcelaine *f*; (*plates etc*) vaisselle *f* (de porcelaine); **made of c.,** en porcelaine; **I bought some c.,** j'ai acheté de la vaisselle en porcelaine; *Br F* **my old c.!,** mon vieux!; **c. clay,** kaolin *m*; **c. plate,** assiette *f* en porcelaine; **c. doll,** poupée *f* en porcelaine.
China ['tʃaɪnə] *n* Chine *f*; **the C. Sea,** la mer de Chine; **C.**

tea, thé *m* de Chine; **the Great Wall of C.,** la muraille de Chine.

Chinaman, *pl* **-men** ['tʃaɪnəmən] *n Old-fashioned* Chinois *m*.

Chinatown ['tʃaɪnətaʊn] *n* quartier chinois; **in C.,** dans le quartier chinois.

chinchilla [tʃɪn'tʃɪlə] *n* (*rodent, fur*) chinchilla *m*; **c. coat/jacket/*etc*,** manteau *m*/veste *f*/*etc* en chinchilla.

chin-chin ['tʃɪn'tʃɪn] *int F* (*as a toast*) santé!, à la vôtre!, à la tienne!

chine[1] [tʃaɪn] *n* **(a)** *Anat* échine *f*; **(b)** *Culin* échinée *f*.

chine[2] *vt* (*of butcher*) fendre (*une carcasse*).

Chinese [tʃaɪ'niːz] **1** *adj* chinois; **the C. Ambassador,** l'ambassadeur *m* de Chine; *Culin* **C. cabbage** *or* **leaves,** bettes *fpl*; **C. white,** blanc *m* de Chine; **C. lantern,** lanterne vénitienne. **2** *n* **(a)** Chinois, -oise; **(b)** *Ling* chinois *m*; **(c)** *F* (*food*) **do you like c.?,** vous aimez bien manger chinois?; **I feel like a c. tonight,** j'ai envie de manger chinois ce soir.

chink[1] [tʃɪŋk] *n* (*gap*) fente *f*, crevasse *f*, lézarde *f* (*dans un mur etc*); entrebaillement *m* (*de la porte*); *Fig* **a c. in s.o.'s armour,** une faille dans la cuirasse de qn.

chink[2] *n* (*sound*) tintement *m*.

chink[3] **1** *vt* faire sonner (*son argent*); faire tinter (*des verres etc*). **2** *vi* sonner (sec).

Chink [tʃɪŋk] *n Offensive Sl* Chinetoque *mf*.

Chinky ['tʃɪŋkɪ] *n Pej* **(a)** *Br Sl* (*restaurant*) (restaurant *m*) chinois *m*; **(b)** *Br Sl* (*meal*) repas chinois; **(c)** *Offensive Sl* (*person*) Chinetoque *mf*.

chinless ['tʃɪnlɪs] *adj* au menton fuyant; *Br F* **c. wonder,** = jeune homme (de bonne famille) aimable mais mou.

Chino ['tʃiːnəʊ] *n Tex* chino *m*; **chinos,** (*trousers*) chinos *mpl*; **a pair of chinos,** une paire de chinos.

chintz [tʃɪnts] *n Tex* chintz *m*, perse *f*, indienne *f*; **c. curtains,** rideaux *mpl* de perse.

chinwag ['tʃɪnwæg] *n Br F* causette *f*; **to have a c.,** tailler une bavette (**with,** avec).

chip[1] [tʃɪp] *n* **(a)** (*small piece*) éclat *m*, copeau *m* (*de bois*); écaille *f*, éclat (*de marbre*); paille *f* (*de laminage*); **diamond chips,** semence *f* de diamants; *Fig* **he's a c. off the old block,** c'est son père tout craché;

(b) (*piece missing*) brisure *f*, écornure *f* (*d'assiette*); brèche *f* (*de lame de couteau*); *Fig* **to have a c. on one's shoulder,** être aigri, porter rancune (à tout le monde);

(c) *Br Culin* (*usu pl*) **chips,** frites *fpl*; **c. cutter,** coupe-frites *m inv*; **c. pan,** friteuse *f*; **c. basket,** panier *m* de friteuse; **c. shop,** friterie *f*;

(d) *Am Culin* **chips,** (pommes *fpl*) chips *mpl*;

(e) *Cards etc* jeton *m*; *Fin* **blue chips,** valeurs sûres; **when the chips are down,** aux moments critiques; *Sl* **he's had his chips,** il est cuit *ou* fichu;

(f) *Comptr* **(silicon) c.,** pastille *f*, *F* puce *f*; **there are 20 megabytes of memory on this c.,** il y a vingt méga-octets de mémoire sur cette puce; **c. manufacturer,** fabricant *m* de pastilles de silicium; **c. technology,** technologie *f* des pastilles.

chip[2] *v* **(-pp-)** **1** *vt* **(a)** (*cut at*) tailler par éclats; hacher (*le bois*); cliver (*la pierre*); enlever (*du marbre*) au burin *ou* au ciseau; **(b)** (*damage*) ébrécher (*un couteau, une assiette*); écorner (*un meuble*); écailler (*de l'émail*); **(c)** *Golf* prendre (*la balle*) en dessous. **2** *vi* **(a)** (*of stone, china*) s'écailler, s'ébrécher; **(b)** *Golf* prendre la balle en dessous.

►chip in **1** *vi* **(a)** *F* (*contribute*) donner (*dans une collecte*); apporter sa contribution (*dans une discussion*); **they chipped in to buy her a present,** ils ont tous donné pour lui acheter un cadeau; **if everyone chips in with an idea,** si tout le monde y va de son idée; **(b)** *F* (*interrupt*) mettre son grain de sel; **(c)** *Cards* miser. **2** *vtsep* (*contribute*) donner (*qch*); **everyone chipped in £5,** tout le monde a donné 5 livres.

►chip off **1** *vi* (*fall, break off*) s'écailler; **the paint is chipping off,** la peinture s'écaille. **2** *vtsep* (*break off*) **to chip a piece off a plate,** ébrécher une assiette; **I don't want any pieces chipped off,** (*those plates etc*) je ne veux pas d'ébréchures.

chipboard ['tʃɪpbɔːd] *n Carp* (panneau *m* de) bois aggloméré.

chipmunk ['tʃɪpmʌŋk] *n* (*animal*) tamia rayé, chipmunk *m*, écureuil rayé, *Can* suisse rayé *ou* barré.

chipolata [tʃɪpə'lɑːtə] *n esp Br Culin* **c. (sausage),** chipolata *f*.

chipped [tʃɪpd] *adj* **(a)** (*knife, plate*) ébréché; (*enamel*) écaillé; **(b)** *Culin Br* **c. potatoes,** pommes (de terre) frites; *Am* **c. beef,** = bœuf séché ou fumé coupé en tranches fines.

chipper ['tʃɪpər] *adj Am F* (*person*) gai, vif, en train.

chipping ['tʃɪpɪŋ] *n* (*breaking*) écaillement *m* (*de pierre, de métal etc*); clivage *m* (*de pierre*); **chippings,** éclats *mpl* (*de pierre*); graillons *mpl* (*de marbre*); **(wood) chippings,** copeaux *mpl* (de bois); **loose chippings,** (*road sign*) gravillons *mpl*, *Can* gravelle *f*.

chippy ['tʃɪpɪ] *n Br* **(a)** *F* (*fish and chip shop*) friterie *f*; **(b)** *Sl* (*carpenter*) charpentier *m*.

chiromancer ['kaɪərəʊmænsər] *n* chiromancien, -ienne.

chiromancy ['kaɪərəʊmænsɪ] *n* chiromancie *f*.

chiropodist [kɪ'rɒpədɪst] *n Med* pédicure *mf*.

chiropody [kɪ'rɒpədɪ] *n Med* pédicurie *f*.

chiropractic [kaɪrə'præktɪk] *n Med* chiropraxie *f*.

chiropractor ['kaɪrəpræktər] *n* chiropracteur *m*.

chirp[1] [tʃɜːp] *n* pépiement *m*, gazouillement *m*, gazouillis *m* (*d'oiseaux*); piaulement *m* (*d'un poussin*); cri *m*, chant *m*, grésillement *m* (*du grillon*).

chirp[2] *vi* **(a)** (*of bird*) pépier, gazouiller; (*of chicken*) piauler; (*of grasshopper*) chanter; **(b)** (*of person*) babiller, *Sl* couiner.

chirpily ['tʃɜːpɪlɪ] *adv* gaiement, gaillardement.

chirpiness ['tʃɜːpɪnɪs] *n F* humeur gaie.

chirpy ['tʃɜːpɪ] *adj F* d'humeur gaie, gaillard.

chirrup[1] ['tʃɪrəp] *n* **(a)** = **CHIRP[1]**; **(b)** (*to encourage a horse*) claquement *m* de langue.

chirrup[2] *vi* **(a)** = **CHIRP[2]**; **(b)** (*to encourage a horse*) faire claquer sa langue.

chisel[1] ['tʃɪz(ə)l] *n* ciseau *m* (*de menuisier etc*); **wood c.,** ciseau à bois; **hollow c.,** gouge *f*; **cold c.,** ciseau à froid, burin *m*.

chisel[2] *vt* **(-ll-,** *US* **-l-)** **(a)** *Carp* ciseler (*le bois, la pierre*); buriner, ciseler (*le métal*); **to c. sth off,** enlever qch au ciseau; **(b)** *Sl* (*cheat*) rouler (*qn*).

chiselled ['tʃɪz(ə)ld] *adj* **delicately chiselled features,** visage délicatement ciselé.

chit[1] [tʃɪt] *n F* (*child*) mioche *mf*, gosse *mf*, gamin, -ine; (*girl*) jeune fille *ou* femme.

chit[2] *n F* (*note*) petit mot, billet *m*; (*for money owed*) facture *f*, note *f*.

chitchat ['tʃɪttʃæt] *n F* bavardage *m*, papotage *m*.

chitterlings, chitlings, chitlins ['tʃɪtəlɪŋz, 'tʃɪtlɪŋz, 'tʃɪtlɪns] *npl Culin* andouillettes *fpl*.

chivalrous ['ʃɪvəlrəs] *adj* courtois; *Hist* chevaleresque.

chivalrously ['ʃɪvəlrəslɪ] *adv* courtoisement; *Hist* chevaleresquement.

chivalry ['ʃɪvəlrɪ] *n* **(a)** (*behaviour*) courtoisie *f*; **it's nice to see c. is not dead,** ça fait plaisir de voir qu'il y a encore des gens qui font preuve de courtoisie; **(b)** (*of medieval knights*) chevalerie *f*; **in the days of c.,** aux temps de la chevalerie.

chives [tʃaɪvz] *npl Bot Culin* ciboulette *f*, civette *f*.

chiv(v)y ['tʃɪvɪ] *vt Br F* **(a)** (*pester*) harceler; **we had to c. him into doing it,** nous avons dû le harceler pour qu'il le fasse; **(b)** (*hunt*) poursuivre, chasser; **go and c. them along,** presse-les, va leur dire de se dépêcher.

chlamydia [klə'mɪdɪə] *n Med* chlamydia *m*.

chloral ['klɔːr(ə)l] *n Ch* chloral *m*.

chlorate ['klɔːreɪt] *n Ch* chlorate *m*.

chloric ['klɔːrɪk] *adj Ch* chlorique; **c. acid,** acide *m* chlorique.

chloride ['klɔːraɪd] *n Ch* chlorure *m*; **c. of silver,** chlorure d'argent.

chlorinate ['klɒrɪneɪt] *vt* (*water*) chlo(ru)rer.

chlorination [klɒrɪ'neɪʃən] *n* chloruration *f*; **c. barrel,** baril *m* de chloruration; **c. plant,** (*equipment*) appareil *m* de chloruration; **c. plant** *or* **works,** usine *f* de chloruration.

chlorine ['klɔːriːn] *n Ch* chlore *m*.

chlorinize ['klɔːrɪnaɪz] *vt* = **CHLORINATE.**

chlorite ['klɔːraɪt] *n* **(a)** *Ch* chlorite *m*; **(b)** *Miner* chlorite *f*.

chloroform[1] ['klɒrəfɔːm] *n Ch* chloroforme *m*.

chloroform[2] *vt* chloroformer (*qn*).

chlorophyl(l) ['klɒrəfɪl] *n Ch Bot* chlorophylle *f*.

chocaholic [tʃɒkə'hɒlɪk] *n F* accro *m* du chocolat.

choc-ice ['tʃɒkaɪs] *n Culin F* esquimau *m*.

chock[1] [tʃɒk] *n* accotoir *m*; *Av* cale *f*; *Nau* support *m* (*d'ancre etc*); *Av* **to remove the chocks,** enlever les cales.

chock[2] *vt* **(a)** **to c. (up),** caler, accorer, accoter (*un tonneau etc*); accoter, caler (*une roue*); **(b)** (*in engineering etc*) coincer (*une pièce*).

chock-a-block ['tʃɒkə'blɒk], **chock-full** ['tʃɒk'fʊl] *adj F* plein à craquer, bourré (**of, with,** de).

chocolate ['tʃɒklət] **1** *n* chocolat *m*; **c. bar, bar of c.,** tablette *f* de chocolat; **milk c.,** chocolat au lait; **plain c.,** chocolat à croquer; **white c.,** chocolat blanc; **cooking c.,** chocolat à cuire; **drinking c.,** (*drink*) chocolat; (*powder*) chocolat en poudre; **hot c.,** chocolat chaud; **a c.,** un chocolat; **box of chocolates,** boîte *f* de chocolats; **c.**

biscuit/ice cream/cake/etc, biscuit *m*/glace *f*/gâteau *m*/*etc* au chocolat; *esp Am* **c. chip cookies,** biscuits aux pépites *ou Can* brisures de chocolat; **c. factory,** chocolaterie *f*. **2** *adj* (de couleur) chocolat *inv*; **c. brown,** brun chocolat *inv*.

choice¹ [tʃɔɪs] *n* **(a)** (*preference*) préférence *f*; **Spain would be my c.,** c'est à l'Espagne que je donnerais ma préférence; **to make** *or* **take one's c.,** faire son choix, choisir; **by** *or* **out of c.,** par goût; **to do sth of one's own c.,** faire qch volontairement; **(b)** (*thing chosen*) choix *m*; **the red wine was her c.,** le vin rouge était son choix; **(c)** (*alternative*) alternative *f*; **to have the c. of two evils,** avoir le choix entre deux maux; **what c. did she have?,** (*rhetorical*) qu'est-ce qu'elle pouvait faire d'autre?; **you have no c. in the matter,** vous n'avez pas le choix; **(d)** (*selection*) assortiment *m*, choix *m*; **available in a c. of colours,** disponible dans un choix de couleurs; **there isn't much c.,** il n'y a pas grand choix; **to have a wide c.,** avoir amplement de quoi choisir.

choice² *adj* **(a)** (*well chosen*) bien choisi; **in a few c. sentences,** en quelques phrases bien choisies; *Hum* **she used some c. language,** elle a utilisé un langage choisi; **(b)** *Com* choisi, recherché; (*article*) de choix; (*vin*) fin; (*liqueur*) de marque.

choir ['kwaɪər] *n* **(a)** *Mus* chœur *m* (de chanteurs), chorale *f*; **she's in the c.,** elle est dans le chœur *ou* dans la chorale; **male-voice c.,** orphéon *m*; *Rel* **c. school,** maîtrise *f*, manécanterie *f*; **(b)** *Archit* chœur *m* (*d'église*); **c. stall,** stalle *f*; **c. screen,** jubé *m*.

choirboy ['kwaɪəbɔɪ] *n Rel* jeune choriste, petit chanteur.

choirmaster ['kwaɪəmɑːstər] *n Rel* maître *m* de chapelle *ou* de chœur.

choke¹ [tʃəʊk] *n* **(a)** *Aut* starter *m*; buse *f* (*du carburateur*); **to pull out the c.,** mettre le starter; **you've given it too much c.,** tu as mis trop de starter; **(b)** (*in voice*) étranglement *m*; **(c)** *Av* étouffoir *m*; **(d)** (*of artichoke*) foin *m*; **(e)** *El* **c. (coil),** bobine *f* d'impédance; self *f*; **(f)** (*on gun barrel*) étranglement *m*.

choke² **1** *vt* **(a)** (*strangle*) étouffer, suffoquer (*qn*); (*of weeds*) étouffer (*les fleurs*); **voice choked with sobs,** voix suffoquée *ou* entrecoupée par les sanglots; **c. chain,** (*for dog*) collier étrangleur; **(b)** (*block*) obstruer, boucher (*un tuyau etc*) (**with,** de). **2** *vi* **(a)** (*become stifled*) étouffer, étrangler (**with,** de); **he was choking with anger,** il suffoquait de colère; **to c. with laughter,** s'étrangler de rire; **I choked on a bone,** je me suis étranglé avec un os; **(b)** (*become blocked*) s'engorger, s'obstruer, se boucher (**with,** de); (*of filter etc*) se colmater; **(c)** *Sl* (*die*) clamser.

▶**choke back** *vtsep* (*suppress*) refouler (*ses larmes, ses paroles*), ravaler (*ses larmes, sa colère*).

▶**choke up** *vtsep* (*block*) boucher, obstruer; **the drain is all choked up with leaves,** la bouche d'égout est complètement obstruée par les feuilles.

choked [tʃəʊkt] *adj Br F* (*disappointed*) déçu; (*annoyed*) ennuyé.

choker ['tʃəʊkər] *n* **(a)** (*necklace*) collier *m* de chien; **(b)** (*of clergyman*) col droit blanc.

choking ['tʃəʊkɪŋ] **1** *adj* étouffant, suffocant; **he made a c. sound,** il a fait un bruit comme quelqu'un qui s'étouffe. **2** *n* étouffement *m*, suffocation *f*.

cholera ['kɒlərə] *n Med Vet* choléra *m*.

choleric ['kɒlərɪk, kə'lerɪk] *adj Fml* colérique, coléreux.

cholesterol [kɒ'lestərɒl] *n Ch* cholestérol *m*; **watch your c. level,** surveillez votre taux de cholestérol.

chomp¹ [tʃɒmp] *vt & vi* mâchouiller *ou* mâchonner bruyamment.

chomp² *n* mâchonnement bruyant.

choo-choo ['tʃuːtʃuː] *n Br F* (*in children's language*) petit train; **the train goes c.-c.,** le train fait tchou-tchou.

chook [tʃuːk] *n Austral F* (*chicken*) poulet *m*.

choose [tʃuːz] *v* (*pt* **chose** [tʃəʊz]; *pp* **chosen** ['tʃəʊz(ə)n]) **1** *vt* **(a)** choisir, porter son choix sur (*qch*); **there is nothing to c. between them,** l'un vaut l'autre, ils se valent; **I didn't c. to go there,** je n'ai pas choisi d'y aller; **(b)** (*decide*) décider, choisir; **since you chose not to accept,** puisque vous avez décidé de ne pas accepter. **2** *vi* faire un choix, choisir; **c. for yourself,** je vous laisse le choix; **to pick and c.,** se montrer difficile, faire le difficile; **I'll do as I c.,** je ferai comme il me plaît *ou* comme bon me semble; **to c. from** *or* **between several people,** choisir entre *ou* parmi plusieurs personnes.

choosing ['tʃuːzɪŋ] *n* choix *m*; **it was none of my c.,** ce n'est pas moi qui l'ai choisi.

choosy ['tʃuːzɪ] *adj F* difficile; **I'm not c.,** (*at this moment*) ça m'est égal; (*in general*) je ne suis pas difficile; **don't be so c.,** ne fais pas le difficile; **he isn't too c. who he does business with,** il n'est pas très difficile quant aux gens avec lesquels il traite.

chop¹ [tʃɒp] *n* **(a)** (*blow*) coup *m* (*de hache, de couperet*); *F* **to get the c.,** (*of person*) se faire saquer, être mis à la porte; (*of project*) être annulé; (*of chapter*) être supprimé; **(b)** *Culin* côtelette *f* (*de mouton, de porc*); **loin c.,** côte première; **c. suey,** chopsouy *m*; **(c)** (*in karate etc*) coup porté avec le tranchant de la main; *Tennis* **c. (stroke),** volée coupée-arrêtée; *Billiards* **c. (shot),** coup piqué.

chop² *v* (**-pp-**) **1** *vt* **(a)** couper, fendre (*du bois*); hacher (*de la viande*); casser; **to c. sth in pieces,** couper qch en morceaux, hacher qch; **to c. sth finely,** hacher qch menu; **(b)** *Tennis* couper (*la balle*). **2** *vi* **to c. at sth,** (*cut sth*) donner des coups de hache à qch; (*aim blows at sth*) tenter de porter un coup à qch; *F* **c., c.!** vite, vite!

chop³ *vi* **(a) to c. and change,** tergiverser; **he's always chopping and changing,** il change d'opinion à tout bout de champ; **(b)** *Nau* **to c. (round),** (*of wind*) changer, sauter; **(c)** *Arch* faire le troc.

▶**chop down** *vtsep* abattre (*un arbre etc*).

▶**chop off** *vtsep* trancher, couper (*qch*); **to c. s.o.'s head off,** trancher la tête à qn.

▶**chop up** *vtsep* couper (*qch*) en morceaux.

chophouse ['tʃɒphaʊs] *n* = restaurant où on sert surtout des côtelettes et des steaks.

chopper ['tʃɒpər] *n* **(a)** (*tool*) couperet *m*, hachoir *m*; **meat c.,** feuille *f* de boucher; **(b)** (*person*) fendeur, -euse (*de bois*); **(c)** *F* (*helicopter*) hélicoptère *m*; **(d)** (*motorcycle*) moto *f*; (*bicycle*) vélo *m* cross; **(e)** *Electron* hacheur *m*, vitreur *m*.

choppers ['tʃɒpəz] *npl F* (*false teeth*) ratelier *m*; (*teeth*) ratiches *fpl*.

chopping ['tʃɒpɪŋ] *n* coupe *f* (*du bois*); **c. block,** billot *m*; **c. board,** hachoir *m*; **c. knife,** couperet *m*, hachoir *m*.

choppy ['tʃɒpɪ] *adj* (*lac*) clapoteux; (*mer*) agité.

chops [tʃɒps] *npl* bajoues *fpl*; **to licks one's c.,** se lécher les babines.

chopsticks ['tʃɒpstɪks] *npl* baguettes *fpl*.

choral ['kɔːr(ə)l] *adj Mus* choral, -als; **c. society,** (société *f*) chorale *f*; **c. music,** musique chorale; **c. symphony,** symphonie *f* avec chœur.

choral(e) [kə'rɑːl] *n Mus* **(a)** (*hymn*) choral *m*, *pl* -als; **(b)** *US* chorale *f*.

chord¹ [kɔːd] *n Mus* accord *m*; **broken c.,** arpège *m*.

chord² *n* **(a)** corde *f* (*d'une harpe*); *Fig* **to touch the right c.,** faire vibrer la corde sensible; **(b)** *Math* corde *f* (*d'un arc*).

chore [tʃɔːr] *n* **(a)** (*usu pl*) **chores,** travail quotidien (*d'un ménage*); occupations *fpl* du ménage; **the daily chores,** les travaux quotidiens; **to do the chores,** faire le ménage; **(b)** (*unwelcome task*) corvée *f*; **singing had become a c.,** chanter était devenu une corvée.

choreograph ['kɒrɪəgræf] *vt* faire la chorégraphie de (*un ballet, un spectacle*).

choreographer [kɒrɪ'ɒgrəfər] *n* chorégraphe *mf*.

choreographic [kɒrɪə'græfɪk] *adj* chorégraphique.

choreography [kɒrɪ'ɒgrəfɪ] *n* chorégraphie *f*.

chorister ['kɒrɪstər] *n* choriste *mf*.

chortle¹ ['tʃɔːt(ə)l] *n F* gloussement *m* (de joie); **she gave a c.,** elle a gloussé.

chortle² *vi F* glousser (de joie).

chorus¹, *pl* **-uses** ['kɔːrəs, -əsɪz] *n* **(a)** (*of song*) refrain *m*; **to join in the c.,** chanter le refrain en chœur; **(b)** (*group of singers, actors*) chœur *m*; **in the c.,** (*of musical*) dans les chœurs; **to sing in c.,** chanter en chœur; **no!, they shouted in c.,** non!, se sont-ils exclamés en chœur; **(c) c. of praise,** concert *m* de louanges; **c. girl,** girl *f* (de music-hall).

chorus² *v* (**-s-**) **1** *vi* faire chœur, reprendre en chœur. **2** *vt* répéter (*qch*) en chœur, répondre (*qch*) en chœur; **'yes please!', they chorused,** 'oui s'il vous plaît', ont-ils répondu en chœur.

chorusmaster ['kɔːrəsmɑːstər] *n* maître *m* de chant.

chosen ['tʃəʊz(ə)n] **1** *adj* choisi; **the c. people,** les élus *mpl*. **2** *n* **the c.,** (*used as pl*) les élus *mpl*.

chou(x) [ʃuː] *n Culin* **c. pastry,** pâte *f* à choux.

chough [tʃʌf] *n* (*bird*) crave *m* à bec rouge.

chow [tʃaʊ] *n* **(a)** (*dog*) chow-chow *m*; **(b)** *F* (*food*) boustifaille *f*; **c. time,** l'heure *f* du repas.

chow-chow ['tʃaʊtʃaʊ] *n* (*dog*) chow-chow *m*.

chowder ['tʃaʊdər] *n Am Culin* = soupe aux poissons ou fruits de mer.

Christ [kraɪst] **1** *n* le Christ, Jésus-Christ; **the C. Child,** l'Enfant Jésus. **2** *int* bon Dieu!

christen ['krɪs(ə)n] *vt* **(a)** baptiser (*qn, un navire*); **to c. a child George,** baptiser un enfant (sous le nom de) Georges;

(b) (*use for first time*) étrenner (*qch*).

Christendom ['krɪs(ə)ndəm] *n* la chrétienté.

christening ['krɪs(ə)nɪŋ] *n* baptême *m*; **c. ceremony,** cérémonie *f* du baptême; **c. robe,** (*for baby*) robe *f* de baptême.

Christian ['krɪstʃən] *Rel* **1** *n* chrétien, -ienne; **are you a C.?,** êtes-vous chrétien? **2** *adj* **(a)** chrétien; **C. Scientist,** scientiste chrétien; **C. burial,** sépulture *f* en terre sainte; **C. name,** nom *m* de baptême, prénom *m*; **(b)** *F* (*good, kind*) chrétien, de chrétien; **that's not a very c. attitude,** ce n'est pas une attitude très chrétienne.

Christianity [krɪstɪ'ænɪtɪ] *n* christianisme *m*; **in a spirit of C.,** en chrétien.

Christianize ['krɪstʃənaɪz] *vt* christianiser, convertir au christianisme.

Christmas ['krɪsməs] *n* Noël *m*; **C. Day,** le jour de Noël; **C. Eve,** la veille de Noël; **at C.,** à (la) Noël; **to spend C. at home,** passer Noël chez soi; **Merry** *or* **Happy C.!,** joyeux Noël!; **Father C.,** le père Noël; **C. dinner/present/tree,** repas *m*/cadeau *m*/arbre *m* de Noël; **C. stocking,** ≈ soulier *m ou* sabot *m* de Noël; **C. carol,** noël *m*; **C. pudding,** pudding *m* de Noël, plum-pudding *m*; *Bot* **C. rose,** rose *f* de Noël.

Christmastide ['krɪsməstaɪd] *n Old-fashioned* époque *f ou* saison *f* de Noël; **at C.,** à la Noël.

Christopher ['krɪstəfər] *n* Christophe *m*.

chromatic [krəʊ'mætɪk] *adj Mus Phys* chromatique; *Phys* **c. aberration,** aberration *f* chromatique.

chrome [krəʊm] *n* **(a)** **c. (steel),** acier chromé *ou* au chrome; **c. nickel,** nickel-chrome *m*; **(b)** *Art* **c. yellow,** jaune *m* de chrome; **(c)** (*in dyeing*) bichromate *m* de potasse; **c. leather,** cuir chromé.

chromium ['krəʊmɪəm] *n Ch* chrome *m*; **c. plating,** chromage *m*; **c.-plated,** chromé.

chromosome ['krəʊməsəʊm] *n Biol* chromosome *m*.

chronic ['krɒnɪk] *adj* **(a)** *Med & Fig* chronique; **c. ill health,** maladie *f* chronique; **a c. invalid,** un *ou* une chronique; *Fig* **a c. exaggerator,** une personne qui a pour habitude d'exagérer; **c. unemployment,** chômage chronique; **(b)** *Br F* (*very bad*) atroce; **their singing was c.,** la manière dont ils chantaient était atroce.

chronically ['krɒnɪklɪ] *adv* chroniquement.

chronicle¹ ['krɒnɪk(ə)l] *n* chronique *f*; *Bible* **Chronicles,** les Chroniques.

chronicle² *vt* **to c. events,** faire la chronique des événements.

chronicler ['krɒnɪklər] *n* chroniqueur *m*.

chronological [krɒnə'lɒdʒɪk(ə)l] *adj* (*ordre etc*) chronologique.

chronologically [krɒnə'lɒdʒɪklɪ] *adv* chronologiquement, par ordre chronologique.

chronology [krə'nɒlədʒɪ] *n* chronologie *f*.

chronometer [krə'nɒmɪtər] *n* chronomètre *m*.

chronometry [krə'nɒmɪtrɪ] *n* chronométrie *f*.

chrysalid ['krɪsəlɪd], **chrysalis,** *pl* **chrysalises** ['krɪsəlɪs, 'krɪsəlɪsɪz] *n Ent* chrysalide *f*.

chrysanthemum [krɪ'sænθəməm] *n* (*flower*) chrysanthème *m*.

chub [tʃʌb] *n* (*fish*) chevesne *m*, meunier *m*.

chubbiness ['tʃʌbɪnɪs] *n* (*of person*) apparence potelée.

chubby ['tʃʌbɪ] *adj* (*person, hands*) potelé; (*person*) boulot, dodu, grassouillet; (*face*) joufflu; (*cheeks*) rebondi.

chuck¹ [tʃʌk] *vt* **(a)** *F* (*throw*) jeter, lancer (*une pierre etc*); **to c. one's money about** *or* **around,** gaspiller son argent; **(b) to c. s.o. under the chin,** donner une tape à qn sous le menton; **(c)** *F* (*finish with*) lâcher (*un emploi*); plaquer, virer (*qn*); **(d)** *F* (*throw away*) balancer, foutre en l'air; **(e)** *Br* **c. it!,** (*stop it!*) arrête!

chuck² *n* **(a)** *F* **to give s.o. the c.,** balancer qn, vider qn; **(b)** (*under the chin*) petite tape.

chuck³ *n* **(a)** *Tech* (*for lathe, drill*) mandrin *m*; foret *m* (*pour tour*); **c. drill, c. key,** foret pour tour; **(b)** *Culin* paleron *m* (*de bœuf*); *Am F* **c. wagon,** = charrette *f* qui transporte la nourriture (*à des moissonneurs, des cowboys etc*).

►**chuck away** *vtsep F* balancer (*qch*), foutre (*qch*) en l'air; **that's just chucking money away,** ça c'est du gaspillage.

►**chuck in** *vtsep F* (*finish with*) lâcher (*un emploi*); plaquer, virer (*qn*); **he chucked it all in and bought a farm,** il a tout plaqué pour acheter une ferme; **to c. one's hand in,** *Cards* jeter ses cartes sur la table; *Fig* (*admit defeat*) s'avouer battu, quitter la partie.

►**chuck out** *vtsep F* **(a)** (*throw away*) jeter (*qch dont on n'a plus besoin*); **(b)** (*from pub, house etc*) flanquer (*qn*) à la porte, balancer, vider (*qn*); *Br* **chucking-out time,** l'heure *f* de la fermeture (des pubs).

►**chuck up** *vtsep F* (*finish with*) abandonner (*un travail*); lâcher (*son emploi*); **she chucked everything up and became a nurse,** elle a tout plaqué pour devenir infirmière.

chucker-out ['tʃʌkə'raʊt] *n Br F* videur *m* (*dans une boîte de nuit etc*).

chuckle¹ ['tʃʌk(ə)l] *n* rire étouffé, petit rire; **to give a c.,** lâcher un petit rire.

chuckle² *vi* rire tout bas *ou* en soi-même (**at, over,** de).

chuff [tʃʌf] *vi* (*of engine etc*) souffler, haleter.

chuffed [tʃʌft] *adj Br F* ravi, tout content (**about,** de); **I'm really c. with myself,** je suis tout content de moi.

chug¹ [tʃʌg] *n* souffle *m* (*d'une machine à vapeur*).

chug² *vi* (**-gg-**) (*of engine etc*) souffler, haleter.

►**chug along** *vi F* (*move slowly*) avancer à grand peine; **we were chugging along at 30 km/h,** nous avancions péniblement à 30 km/h.

chum [tʃʌm] *n F* camarade *mf*, copain *m*, copine *f*.

►**chum up with** *vipo F* (**-mm-**) se lier d'amitié avec (*qn*).

chummy ['tʃʌmɪ] *adj F* amical, bon copain; **she's quite c. with the boss,** elle est assez copine avec le patron.

chump [tʃʌmp] *n* **(a)** *F* (*foolish person*) idiot, -ote; **(b)** (*large piece*) gros bout, gros morceau (*de qch*); tronçon *m* (*de bois*); *Culin* **c. chop,** côtelette *f* d'agneau (*coupée dans le gigot*); **(c)** *Sl* (*head*) trognon *m*, caboche *f*; **off one's c.,** timbré, maboul.

chunder ['tʃʌndər] *vi esp Austr Sl* dégueuler.

chunk [tʃʌŋk] *n* gros morceau (*de pain, de fromage etc*); quignon *m* (*de pain*); tronçon *m* (*de bois*).

chunky ['tʃʌŋkɪ] *adj F* **(a)** (*person*) trapu; **(b)** gros (*morceau, pullover etc*); (*verre*) solide.

Chunnel ['tʃʌn(ə)l] *n F* **the C.,** le tunnel sous la Manche.

church [tʃɜːtʃ] *n* église *f*; (*Protestant*) temple *m*; **to go to c.,** (*Catholic*) aller à l'église, (*Protestant*) aller au temple; **I saw her in c. on Sunday,** je l'ai vue à l'église dimanche; **the C. of England, the Anglican C.,** l'Église anglicane; **to go into the C.,** entrer dans les ordres; **High C.,** = section de l'Église anglicane qui se rapproche du catholicisme en matière de rituel; **the (Roman) Catholic C.,** l'Église catholique; **c. hall,** salle paroissiale; **c. service,** office *m*; **c. wedding,** mariage religieux.

churchgoer ['tʃɜːtʃgəʊər] *n Rel* pratiquant, -ante; **an occasional c.,** une personne qui va à l'église de temps en temps.

churchgoing ['tʃɜːtʃgəʊɪŋ] *Rel* **1** *adj* pratiquant. **2** *n* pratique *f* (de sa religion).

churchman, *pl* **-men** ['tʃɜːtʃmən] *n Rel* **(a)** (*clergyman*) homme *m* d'église, ecclésiastique *m*; **(b)** (*member of a church*) membre *m* d'une église; (*in England*) membre de l'Église anglicane.

churchwarden [tʃɜːtʃ'wɔːd(ə)n] *n* **(a)** *Rel* marguillier *m*, fabricien *m*; **(b) c. (pipe),** longue pipe (*en terre blanche*), pipe hollandaise.

churchwoman, *pl* **-women** ['tʃɜːtʃwʊmən, -wɪmɪn] *n Rel* **(a)** (*clergywoman*) femme *f* d'église; **(b)** (*member of a church*) femme *f* membre d'une église.

churchy ['tʃɜːtʃɪ] *adj F Pej* bigot, bondieusard.

churchyard ['tʃɜːtʃjɑːd] *n* (*graveyard*) cimetière *m*; (*grounds*) enclos *m* d'église.

churlish ['tʃɜːlɪʃ] *adj* **(a)** (*rude*) mal élevé, qui n'a pas de savoir-vivre; (*behaviour, person*) grossier; **it would be c. to refuse,** ce serait grossier de refuser; **(b)** (*grumpy*) hargneux, grincheux.

churlishness ['ʃɜːlɪʃnɪs] *n* **(a)** (*rudeness*) grossièreté *f*; manque *m* de savoir-vivre; **(b)** (*grumpiness*) tempérament hargneux.

churn¹ [tʃɜːn] *n Agr* **(a)** (*for butter*) baratte *f*; **(b)** (*for milk*) bidon *m* à lait.

churn² **1** *vt* baratter (*la crème*); battre (*le beurre*); **to c. up the foam,** (*of ship's screw*) brasser l'écume; *Fig* **to c. a thought (over) in one's mind,** agiter une pensée dans son esprit. **2** *vi* (*of sea*) bouillonner; *Fig* **my stomach's churning,** (*with nerves, excitement*) j'ai l'estomac noué.

►**churn out** *vtsep F* (*mass produce*) pondre (*des livres etc*) en série; débiter (*des objets*).

churning ['tʃɜːnɪŋ] *n* barattage *m*.

chute [ʃuːt] *n* **(a)** glissière *f*; **rubbish** *or Am* **garbage c.,** vide-ordures *m inv*; **(b)** *Sp* piste *f* (*pour luges, toboggans*); (*in swimming pool*) toboggan *m*; **(c)** (*waterfall*) chute *f* d'eau; **(d)** *F* parachute *m*.

chutney ['tʃʌtnɪ] *n Culin* condiment *m* (*à la pomme etc*).

CIA ['siːaɪeɪ] *n US Admin* (*abbr* **Central Intelligence Agency**) = centrale américaine de renseignements.

ciborium, *pl* **-ia** [sɪ'bɔːrɪəm, -ɪə] *n Rel* **(a)** (*vessel*) ciboire

m; **(b)** (*canopy*) tabernacle *m*.
cicada [sɪ'kɑːdə, -'keɪdə] *n* (*insect*) cigale *f*.
cicely ['sɪsəlɪ] *n* (*plant*) **(sweet) c.,** myrrhe *f*.
Cicero ['sɪsərəʊ] *n* Cicéron *m*.
CID ['siːaɪdiː] *n Br Admin* (*abbr* **Criminal Investigation Department**) ≈ P.J. *f*; **Joanna Smith, CID,** ≈ Joanna Smith, de la P.J..
cider ['saɪdər] *n* **(a)** *Br* cidre *m*; **c. apples,** pommes *fpl* à cidre; **c. vinegar,** vinaigre *m* de cidre; **(b)** *Am* (*apple juice*) jus *m* de pommes; **hard c.,** cidre *m*.
cif ['siːaɪef] *n Com* (*abbr* **cost, insurance and freight**) CAF *m*.
cigar [sɪ'gɑːr] *n* cigare *m*; **c. case,** étui *m* à cigares; **c. cutter,** coupe-cigares *m inv*; **c. holder,** fume-cigare *m*, *pl* fume-cigare(s); **c. lighter,** (*in car*) allume-cigare(s) *m*.
cigarette, *occ US* **cigaret** [sɪgə'ret] *n* cigarette *f*; **c. advertising,** publicité *f* pour les cigarettes; **c. ash,** cendre *f* de cigarette; **c. card,** image offerte avec un paquet de cigarettes; **c. case,** étui *m* à cigarettes, porte-cigarettes *m inv*; **c. end,** bout *m* de cigarette, *Sl* mégot *m*; **c. holder,** fume-cigarette *m*, *pl* fume-cigarette(s); **c. lighter,** briquet *m*; (*in car*) allume-cigare(s) *m*; **c. machine,** (*vending machine*) distributeur *m* automatique de cigarettes; (*for rolling cigarettes*) machine *f ou* moule *m* à cigarettes, rouleuse *f*; **c. packet,** paquet *m* de cigarettes; **c. paper,** papier *m* à cigarettes; **c. smoke,** fumée *f* de cigarette; **c. smoker,** fumeur, -euse de cigarettes.
C(-)in(-)C [siːɪn'siː] *n Mil Nau abbr* **Commander in Chief.**
cinch [sɪntʃ] *n* **(a)** (*something very easy*) **it's a c.,** c'est facile à faire; **it'll be a c.,** ça va être simple comme bonjour *ou* un jeu d'enfant; **(b)** *F* (*certainty*) certitude *f*; **it's a c.,** c'est certain *ou* couru; **(c)** *Am* (*for horse*) sangle *f*, sous-ventrière *f*, *pl* sous-ventrières.
cinder ['sɪndər] *n* cendre *f*; **burnt to a c.,** (*of meat, toast etc*) complètement carbonisé; **cinders,** cendres; *Ind etc* escarbilles *fpl*; *Metal* laitier *m*, scorie *f*, scories *fpl*, crasse *f*; *Ind* **c. chute,** tuyau *m* de vidange des escarbilles; *Geol* **c. cone,** cône *m* de scories; *Sp* **c. track,** (piste *f*) cendrée *f*.
Cinderella [sɪndə'relə] *n Liter* Cendrillon *f*; *Fig* **poetry has been the C. of the arts,** la poésie a été le parent pauvre des arts.
cine ['sɪnɪ] *pref Cin* **c. camera,** caméra *f*; **c. film,** film *m*; **c. projector,** projecteur *m* de cinéma.
cinema ['sɪnəmə] *n Cin* **(a)** (*art*) cinéma *m*; **French c.,** le cinéma français; **(b)** *Br* (*place*) cinéma *m*.
cinematic [sɪnə'mætɪk] *adj Cin* cinématique.
cinematograph [sɪnə'mætəgræf] *n Old-fashioned* cinématographe *m*.
cineraria [sɪnə'reərɪə] *n* (*plant*) cinéraire *f*.
cinnabar ['sɪnəbɑːr] *n* **(a)** *Miner* cinabre *m*; **(b)** *Ind* (*colour*) vermillon *m*.
cinnamon ['sɪnəmən] *n* **(a)** *Culin* cannelle *f*; **c. stick,** bâton *m* de cannelle; **(b)** *Bot* **c. (tree),** cannelier *m*; **(c)** (*colour*) cannelle *inv*.
cinq(ue)foil ['sɪŋkfɔɪl] *n* **(a)** (*plant*) potentille rampante, quintefeuille *f*; **(b)** *Archit* quintefeuille *m*.
cipher¹ ['saɪfər] *n* **(a)** (*secret writing*) chiffre *m*, code *m*; (*message*) message chiffré *ou* codé; (*signal*) signal chiffré *ou* codé; (*key*) clef *f*; **to write a message in c.,** transmettre une dépêche en chiffre *ou* en code *ou* en écriture chiffrée *ou* codée; **c. key,** clef de chiffre *ou* de code; **c. clerk,** chiffreur, -euse; **c. machine,** (*encoder*) machine *f* à chiffrer *ou* à coder; (*decoder*) machine à déchiffrer *ou* à décoder; **(b)** (*monogram*) chiffre *m*, monogramme *m*; **(c)** *Math* zéro *m*; *Fig* **he's a mere c.,** c'est un homme nul *ou* un zéro *ou* une nullité.
cipher² *vt* chiffrer (*une dépêche*); (*send*) transmettre en chiffre *ou* en code.
ciphering ['saɪfərɪŋ] *n* chiffrage *m*, chiffrement *m*, codage *m*.
circa ['sɜːkə] *prep* (*of time*) aux alentours de; (*of amount*) environ.
circadian [sɜː'keɪdɪən] *adj* circadien; **c. rhythm,** rythme circadien.
circle¹ ['sɜːk(ə)l] *n* **(a)** *Math etc* cercle *m*; **to draw a c.,** tracer un cercle; **to stand in a c.,** (*of people*) se tenir en cercle, faire cercle; **the chairs were arranged in a c.,** les chaises étaient disposées en cercle; **to go round in circles,** tourner en rond; **to have circles round one's eyes,** avoir les yeux cernés; *Aut* **turning c.,** cercle de braquage; **polar c.,** cercle polaire; **Arctic/Antarctic C.,** cercle (polaire) arctique/antarctique; *Gym* **to do a c. (on the horizontal bar),** faire le grand soleil; *Archeol* **stone c.,** cercle de pierres; **(b)** (*movement*) révolution *f*, orbite *f* (*d'une planète*); **to come full c.,** (*physically*) compléter son orbite; (*of argument, person*) revenir à son point de départ; (*of fashion, history*) être un éternel recommencement; **(c)** *Th* **dress c.,** (premier) balcon *m*, corbeille *f*; **upper c.,** seconde galerie; **(d)** (*group*) cercle *m*, groupe *m*; **a c. of friends,** un cercle d'amis; **the family c.,** le sein de la famille; **in certain circles,** dans certains milieux; **in theatrical circles,** dans le monde du théâtre; **the inner c.,** le cercle intime (d'amis).
circle² **1** *vt* **(a)** faire le tour de (*qch*); *Gym* **to c. the bar,** faire le grand soleil; **(b)** *Lit* (*place round*) ceindre, entourer (**with,** de). **2** *vi* **(a) to c. round sth,** tourner *ou* tournoyer autour de qch; **the planes are circling overhead,** les avions décrivent des cercles au-dessus de nos têtes; **(b)** *Mil* se rabattre (**round,** sur).
circuit ['sɜːkɪt] *n* **(a)** *El* circuit *m*; **in/out of c.,** en/hors de circuit; **short c.,** court-circuit *m*, *pl* courts-circuits; *Electron* **anode c.,** circuit anodique; **grid c.,** circuit de grille; *Tel* **trunk c.,** circuit interurbain; *Comptr* **c. board,** plaquette *f*, carte *f* de circuits; **c. breaker,** coupe-circuit *m inv*, disjoncteur *m*, interrupteur *m*; **(b)** (*journey, movement around*) révolution *f* (*du soleil*); tournée *f* (*de juge d'assises etc*); *Th* (*tour*) tournée dramatique; **to make one c. of the track,** faire un tour de circuit; **to make the c. of the town,** faire le tour de la ville; **to go on c.,** (*of judge*) aller en tournée; **to make a wide c.,** faire un grand détour; **(c)** (*route, places visited*) circonscription *f* de tournée, ressort *m* (*d'un juge d'assises*); (*series of venues etc*) circuit *m*; **the hottest cabaret act on the club c.,** le meilleur numéro de cabaret de la tournée des clubs; **(d)** *Sp* (*motor racing*) circuit *m*, parcours *m*.
circuitous [sə'kjuːɪtəs] *adj* (*chemin*) détourné, indirect; **by c. means,** par des moyens détournés.
circuitously [sə'kjuːɪtəslɪ] *adv* (*agir*) par des moyens indirects *ou* détournés.
circuitry ['sɜːkɪtrɪ] *n* (*no pl*) *Electron* circuits *mpl*; **the c. on this board is really simple,** le montage de cette plaquette est vraiment simple.
circular ['sɜːkjʊlər] **1** *adj* (*mouvement*) circulaire; **c. arc,** arc *m* de cercle; **c. letter,** (lettre *f*) circulaire *f*; *Tech* **c. saw,** scie *f* circulaire. **2** *n* (lettre *f*) circulaire *f*; (*publicity material*) prospectus *m*; *Journ* **the Court c.,** la Cour au jour le jour.
circularization [sɜːkjʊləraɪ'zeɪʃən] *n* expédition *f ou* envoi *m* de circulaires *ou* de prospectus (**of,** à).
circularize ['sɜːkjʊlərаɪz] *vt* envoyer des circulaires *ou* des prospectus à (*ses clients etc*).
circulate ['sɜːkjʊleɪt] **1** *vi* (*of thing, person*) circuler; **to c. freely,** (*of money*) circuler librement; **I ought to c.,** (*at party*) je devrais aller voir les autres invités. **2** *vt* **(a)** faire circuler (*l'air, le vin etc*); **(b)** mettre en circulation (*de l'argent, des nouvelles etc*); répandre, faire circuler (*une nouvelle etc*).
circulating ['sɜːkjʊleɪtɪŋ] **1** *adj* circulant; **c. library,** bibliothèque ambulante; *Math* **c. fraction,** fraction *f* périodique. **2** *n* circulation *f*.
circulation [sɜːkjʊ'leɪʃən] *n* **(a)** circulation *f* (*de l'air, d'un liquide, de nouvelles etc*); *Fin* roulement *m* (*de fonds*); **to put a book into c.,** mettre un livre en circulation; **for private c.,** (*in publishing*) hors commerce; **newspaper with a large c.,** journal à grand tirage; **a c. of 500,000,** un tirage de 500 000 exemplaires; **(b)** *Physiol* circulation *f* (*du sang etc*); **to have poor c.,** souffrir d'une mauvaise circulation (du sang); **to restore the c. in one's legs,** se dégourdir les jambes; **(c)** (*of money*) cours *m* (de la monnaie); **to put forged notes into c.,** mettre de faux billets en circulation; **notes in c.,** billets circulants; **these old coins are still in c.,** ces vieilles pièces sont encore en circulation; *Fig F* **to be in/out of c.,** (*of person*) être/ne plus être dans le circuit.
circulatory [sɜːkjʊ'leɪt(ə)rɪ, 'sɜːkjʊlət(ə)rɪ] *adj Anat etc* circulatoire; de la circulation.
circumcise ['sɜːkəmsaɪz] *vt* circoncire (*un petit garçon*).
circumcision [sɜːkəm'sɪʒən] *n* circoncision *f*; *Rel* **the C.,** la (fête de la) Circoncision.
circumference [sə'kʌmfərəns] *n* circonférence *f*; **thirty metres in c.,** trente mètres de circonférence.
circumflex ['sɜːkəmfleks] **1** *n Gram* accent *m* circonflexe. **2** *adj* circonflexe.
circumlocution [sɜːkəmlə'kjuːʃən] *n* circonlocution *f*; **without c.,** sans ambages.
circumnavigate [sɜːkəm'nævɪgeɪt] *vt* faire (par mer) le tour de (*qch*).
circumnavigation [sɜːkəmnævɪ'geɪʃən] *n* circumnavi-

gation *f*.

circumscribe ['sɜːkəmskraɪb] *vt* **(a)** (*limit*) limiter, restreindre (*un champ d'opérations, des pouvoirs*); **(b)** *Math* circonscrire (*un cercle etc*).

circumscribed ['sɜːkəmskraɪbd] *adj* **(a)** (*limited*) restreint, limité; **(b)** *Math* (*cercle etc*) circonscrit.

circumscription [sɜːkəm'skrɪpʃən] *n* **(a)** (*limitation*) restriction *f*, limitation *f* (*de l'action de qn etc*); **(b)** *Math* circonscription *f*.

circumspect ['sɜːkəmspekt] *adj* circonspect; (*person*) avisé; (*conduct*) prudent; (*speech*) mesuré.

circumspection [sɜːkəm'spekʃən] *n* circonspection *f*.

circumspectly ['sɜːkəmspektlɪ] *adv* avec circonspection; (*to behave*) prudemment.

circumstance ['sɜːkəmstəns] *n* **(a)** (*situation*) (*usu pl*) **circumstances,** circonstances *fpl*; **extenuating circumstances,** circonstances atténuantes; **in** *or* **under the circumstances,** dans ces circonstances, en de telles circonstances; **in** *or* **under no circumstances,** en aucun cas, sous aucun prétexte; **that depends on circumstances,** c'est selon; **he was the victim of c.,** il a été la victime des circonstances; **by force of circumstances,** par la force des choses; **(b)** *Fml* (*financial situation*) **in easy circumstances,** à l'aise; **if his circumstances allowed,** si ses moyens le permettaient; **(c)** *Lit* (*detail*) circonstance *f*, détail *m*; **(d) with pomp and c.,** en grande cérémonie, en grand apparat.

circumstantial [sɜːkəm'stænʃəl] *adj* **(a)** circonstanciel; **c. evidence,** preuves indirectes; **(b)** (*secondary*) accessoire, secondaire; **(c)** (*detailed*) circonstancié, détaillé.

circumstantiate [sɜːkəm'stænʃɪəɪt] *vt* donner des détails circonstanciés sur (*un rapport*).

circumvent [sɜːkəm'vent] *vt* circonvenir (*qn, une manœuvre*); **to c. the law,** contourner la loi.

circumvention [sɜːkəm'venʃən] *n* circonvention *f* (*de la loi etc*).

circus, *pl* **-uses** ['sɜːkəs, -əsɪz] *n* **(a)** (*show, troupe*) & *Antiq* cirque *m*; **to join a c.,** entrer dans un cirque; **let's go to the c.,** allons au cirque; *Av* **flying c.,** parade aérienne itinéraire; **travelling c.,** cirque forain; **c. act,** numéro *m* de cirque; **(b)** *Br* (*in names of crossroads*) rond-point *m*, *pl* ronds-points, cirque *m*.

cirrhosis [sɪ'rəʊsɪs] *n Med* cirrhose *f*; **c. of the liver,** cirrhose du foie; **to have c.,** avoir une cirrhose.

cirrus, *pl* **-ri** ['sɪrəs, -raɪ] *n Met* cirrus *m*; *Bot* vrille *f*; *Biol* cirr(he) *m*.

cisalpine [sɪs'ælpaɪn] *adj* cisalpin; *Hist* **C. Gaul,** la Gaule cisalpine.

cissy ['sɪsɪ] *F Pej* **1** *n* mauviette *f*, poule mouillée. **2** *adj* (*cowardly*) mollasse, mollasson; (*effeminate*) qui fait pédale, qui fait tapette.

Cistercian [sɪ'stɜːʃən] *adj & n Rel* cistercien, -ienne; **the C. Order,** l'ordre *m* de Cîteaux.

cistern ['sɪstən] *n Tech* réservoir *m* à eau (*sous les combles*); (*in lavatory*) réservoir de chasse d'eau; (*underground*) citerne *f*; réservoir (*d'une pompe*).

citadel ['sɪtədəl, -del] *n* **(a)** (*fortress*) citadelle *f*; **(b)** (*in Salvation Army*) temple *m*.

citation [saɪ'teɪʃən] *n* **(a)** citation *f* (*d'un auteur, d'une autorité*); (*passage quoted*) citation empruntée à un auteur; **(b)** *Mil* citation *f* (*à l'ordre du jour*); **(c)** *Jur* citation *f* à comparaître.

cite [saɪt] *vt* **(a)** (*quote*) citer (*un passage, un auteur, un exemple*); alléguer (*un auteur, une autorité*); **(b)** *Mil* citer (*un militaire pour son héroïsme*); **(c)** *Jur* **to c. s.o. before a court,** citer qn devant un tribunal.

citizen ['sɪtɪzən] *n* **(a)** (*of nation, city, town*) citoyen, -enne; **a good c.,** un bon citoyen; **private c.,** simple particulier; **fellow citizens,** concitoyens; **c.'s band (radio),** (radio *f* de la) citizen band *f*; **c. of the world,** citoyen du monde *ou* de l'univers; **a c. army,** armée *f* de citoyens; **(b)** *Am* civil *m* (*par opposition à l'armée, la marine*); **c. rights,** droits *mpl* civiques.

citizenry ['sɪtɪzənrɪ] *n* ensemble *m* des citoyens.

citizenship ['sɪtɪzənʃɪp] *n* (*of nation*) citoyenneté *f*, nationalité *f*; (*of city, town*) droit *m* de cité *ou* de bourgeoisie; **French c.,** citoyenneté française; **to be granted full c. of a country,** se voir accorder la citoyenneté d'un pays; **good c.,** civisme *m*.

citrate ['sɪtreɪt] *n Ch* citrate *m*.

citric ['sɪtrɪk] *adj Ch* (*acide etc*) citrique.

citron ['sɪtrən] *n* **(a)** (*fruit*) cédrat *m*; **(b) c. (tree),** cédratier *m*.

citronelle [sɪtrə'nel] *n* (*plant*) citronnelle *f*.

citrus ['sɪtrəs] *adj* **c. fruit,** agrume *m*.

city ['sɪtɪ] *n* (grande) ville; *Lit* cité *f*; *Br* **(cathedral) c.,** ville épiscopale, évêché *m*; **the Holy C.,** la Cité sainte; **the Celestial C.,** la Cité céleste; **the Eternal C.,** la Ville éternelle; **the C. of Manchester,** la ville de Manchester; **c. children,** les enfants des grandes villes; **c. life,** la vie citadine; **c. street,** rue *f* d'une grande ville; **c. hall,** hôtel *m* de ville; *Am Fig* **you can't win against c. hall,** on ne peut pas gagner contre la municipalité; *Journ* **c. editor,** *Am* rédacteur de la chronique du jour; *Br* rédacteur de la rubrique financière.

City ['sɪtɪ] *n* **the C.,** (*district*) la Cité de Londres; (*financial world*) le monde de la finance.

city-state [sɪtɪ'steɪt] *n* état-cité *m*, *pl* états-cités.

civet ['sɪvɪt] *n* (*animal, scent*) civette *f*.

civic ['sɪvɪk] *adj* (*duty, pride etc*) civique; **the c. authorities,** les autorités municipales; **c. buildings,** bâtiments *mpl* de la municipalité; **c. rights,** droits civils; *Br* **c. centre,** centre civique *ou* social.

civics ['sɪvɪks] *npl* (*usu with sing verb*) *Sch* instruction *f* civique.

civies ['sɪvɪz] *npl* vêtements civils.

civil ['sɪv(ə)l] *adj* **(a)** (*society, law, year etc*) civil; **c. action** *or* **proceedings,** action civile; **c. aircraft,** les appareils de l'aviation civile; **c. aviation,** aviation civile; *Jur* **c. death,** mort civile; **c. defence,** protection civile; **c. engineer,** ingénieur constructeur; ingénieur des travaux publics; **c. engineering,** génie civil; **c. law,** (*Roman law*) droit romain, droit civil, = le code civil; **in c. life,** dans le civil; *Br Admin* **the C. List,** la liste civile (du souverain); **C. List pension,** pension sur les fonds de la Couronne; **c. marriage,** mariage civil; *Jur* **c. rights,** droits civils; **c. rights activist/lawyer,** activiste/avocat cherchant à protéger les droits civils; **c. rights movement,** mouvement *m* des droits civils; **c. servant,** fonctionnaire *m* (de l'État); **the C. Service,** l'Administration (civile), *Can* la Fonction publique; **to be in the c. service,** être fonctionnaire; **c. war,** guerre civile;

(b) (*polite*) poli, civil; **he was very c. to me,** il s'est montré très aimable; **keep a c. tongue in your head!,** soyez plus poli!

civilian [sɪ'vɪljən] **1** *n* civil *m*. **2** *adj* civil; **c. clothes,** tenue civile; **in c. life,** dans le civil.

civility [sɪ'vɪlɪtɪ] *n* courtoisie *f*, politesse *f*; **exchange of civilities,** échange *m* d'amabilités.

civilization [sɪvɪlaɪ'zeɪʃən] *n* civilisation *f*; *F* **it's miles from c.,** c'est à des kilomètres de toute civilisation.

civilize ['sɪvɪlaɪz] *vt* civiliser.

civilized ['sɪvɪlaɪzd] *adj* (*life, people*) civilisé; **the little girl is really quite c.,** la petite fille est très bien élevée; **their divorce was a very c. affair,** ils ont divorcé comme des gens civilisés; **can't you eat in a c. manner?,** tu ne peux pas manger convenablement?

civilizing ['sɪvɪlaɪzɪŋ] *adj* (*influence*) qui adoucit les mœurs; **the new teacher had a c. influence on them,** le nouveau professeur semble les avoir calmés.

civvies ['sɪvɪz] *npl* vêtements civils.

civvy ['sɪvɪ] *adj Sl* civil; **to get back to c. street,** rentrer dans le civil.

cl (*abbr* **centilitre**) cl..

clack[1] [klæk] *n* **(a)** (*sound*) bruit sec, claquement *m*; **click-c.,** clic-clac *m*; **(b)** *Tech* **c. (valve),** (soupape *f* à) clapet *m*; **(mill) c.,** traquet *m*; **(c)** *F* (*talk*) caquet *m*, jacasserie *f*.

clack[2] *vi* **(a)** (*make sound*) claquer, faire clic-clac; **(b)** (*talk*) jacasser.

clad[1] [klæd] *see* **CLOTHE**.

clad[2] *vt* (**-dd-**) *Tech* revêtir (*un pan de mur, une tôle etc*) (**with,** de).

cladding ['klædɪŋ] *n Tech* revêtement *m*.

claim[1] [kleɪm] *n* **(a)** (*demand*) demande *f*; revendication *f*, réclamation *f*; **pay claims,** revendications salariales;

(b) (*right*) droit *m*, titre *m*, prétention *f* (**to sth,** à qch); **to have a c. to sth,** avoir droit à qch; **what is her c. to the throne?,** quel est son titre à la couronne?; **his only c. to fame,** la seule chose notable qu'il ait faite; **they have no c. to the land,** ils n'ont aucun droit sur le terrain; **to lay c. to,** (*property etc*) prétendre à, revendiquer son droit à; (*ability etc*) s'attribuer qch; **legal c. to sth,** titre juridique à qch; **to put in a c.,** faire valoir ses droits; **exaggerated claims have been made for this medicine,** on a exagéré l'efficacité de ce médicament;

(c) *Jur* réclamation *f*; **to make** *or* **put in a c. for damages,** demander une indemnité, réclamer des dommages-intérêts; **to put in a c.,** (*in insurance*) réclamer une indemnité (d'assurance); **to have no c. whatever on**

s.o., n'avoir aucun recours contre qn; *Fig* **to have a c. on s.o.**, avoir prise sur qn; *Fig* **I have many claims on my time**, je suis très pris; **c. form**, formulaire *m* de demande d'indemnité;

(d) *esp Am Austr Min* concession *f* (minière).

claim² **1** *vt* **(a)** (*demand as a right*) réclamer (*un droit, les soins de qn, un territoire*); revendiquer (*un droit*); exiger, demander (*du respect, de l'attention*); *Jur* requérir; **to c. sth from s.o.**, réclamer qch à qn; **to c. a privilege**, prétendre à un privilège; **to c. the right to do sth**, prétendre avoir *ou* revendiquer le droit de faire qch; **to c. responsibility for an attack**, (*of terrorist*) revendiquer un attentat;

(b) (*affirm*) prétendre, avancer, affirmer, soutenir (**that**, que); **to c. to be an expert**, se faire passer pour expert; **I don't c. to be an expert, but ...**, je ne prétends pas être un expert, mais ...; **to c. acquaintance with s.o.**, prétendre connaître qn;

(c) (*collect, take*) récupérer (*les bagages*); (*lost property*) réclamer; **have you claimed your allowance?**, est-ce que tu as réclamé ton allocation?; **has anyone arrived to c. her?**, (*of unidentified child*) est-ce que quelqu'un est venu la chercher?; **the sea claims many victims**, la mer fait de nombreuses victimes.

2 *vi* (*put in a claim for sth*) faire une demande.

claimant ['kleɪmənt] *n* (*to throne*) prétendant, -ante; (*for social security etc*) revendicateur, -trice; *Jur* réclamant, -ante; demandeur, -eresse; *Br Admin* personne qui effectue une demande; (**to sth**, de qch); **rightful c.**, ayant droit *m*, *pl* ayants droit.

claiming ['kleɪmɪŋ] *n* réclamation *f*, revendication *f* (*d'un droit etc*).

clairvoyance [kleə'vɔɪəns] *n* **(a)** (*second sight*) voyance *f*, don *m* de seconde vue; **(b)** (*shrewdness*) clairvoyance *f*.

clairvoyant [kleə'vɔɪənt] **1** *adj* **(a)** doué de seconde vue; **(b)** (*shrewd*) clairvoyant. **2** *n* voyant, -ante, extra-lucide *mf*, *pl* extra-lucides.

clam [klæm] *n* (*mollusc*) palourde *f*, clam *m*; *F Fig* (*quiet person*) personne taciturne; **to shut up like a c.**, refuser de dire quoi que ce soit; *Am* **c. chowder**, soupe *f* aux palourdes.

▶**clam up** *vi Sl* (**-mm-**) se taire; **don't c. up on me**, parle-moi.

clambake ['klæmbeɪk] *n Am* **(a)** (*picnic*) pique-nique où l'on mange des fruits de mer; **(b)** *F* (*noisy gathering*) grande réunion tapageuse.

clamber¹ ['klæmbər] *n* **it was quite a c.**, c'était une sacrée grimpette.

clamber² *vi* grimper (des pieds et des mains) en se hissant; **to c. up a wall**, escalader un mur; **he clambered over the pile of bricks**, il a escaladé le tas de briques; **they clambered out**, (*from car etc*) ils sont sortis en se hissant.

clamminess ['klæmɪnɪs] *n* moiteur froide (*de la peau*); humidité froide (*de l'air*).

clammy ['klæmɪ] *adj* (*hands, skin*) (froid et) moite; (*atmosphere*) (froid et) humide.

clamor ['klæmər] *n & vi US* = **CLAMOUR**.

clamorous ['klæmərəs] *adj Lit* bruyant, braillard; (*foule*) vociférant.

clamorously ['klæmərəslɪ] *adv Lit* bruyamment, à grands cris.

clamour¹, *US* **clamor** ['klæmər] *n* **(a)** (*noise*) clameur *f*, cris *mpl*, vociférations *fpl*; **(b)** (*protest*) tollé *m*; **there was a great c.**, ça a été un tollé général.

clamour², *US* **clamor** *vi* vociférer, crier, pousser des clameurs; **to c. for sth**, réclamer *ou* demander qch à grands cris.

clamp¹ [klæmp] *n Tech* crampon *m*, presse *f*; *Constr* agrafe *f*; collier *m* (*de tuyau*); *Carp* **(G-) c.**, serre-joints *m*, presse *f* à ris, mordache *f* (*d'étau*); pince *f* (*pour fils*); *Surg* clamp *m*; **(bar) c.**, barre *f* de pression; **vice c.**, mâchoire *f*.

clamp² *vt* **(a)** cramponner, serrer; mettre (*qch*) sous presse; *Constr etc* agrafer (*deux pierres*); brider (*un tuyau*); bloquer (*un instrument de précision*); caler (*un télescope*); *Surg* clamper; **to c. two pieces of wood together**, bloquer deux morceaux de bois l'un contre l'autre; **(b)** *Aut* mettre un sabot à (*une voiture*).

clamp³ *n Agr* **(a)** silo *m* (temporaire) (*de pommes de terre*); **(b)** meule *f* (*de briques en cuisson*).

clamp⁴ *vt* **(a)** *Agr* mettre (*des pommes de terre*) en silo; **(b)** mettre (*des briques*) en meule.

▶**clamp down** **1** *vtsep* fixer (*qch*) par un crampon. **2** *vi F* (*become stricter*) sévir (**on**, contre).

clampdown ['klæmpdaʊn] *n* raffermissement *m* des mesures (**on**, contre); **as a result of the c.**, suite au raffermissement.

clamping ['klæmpɪŋ] *n* agrafage *m*, serrage *m*; fixation *f* (*d'un outil*); *Surg* clampage *m*.

clan [klæn] *n* **(a)** (*d'une tribu*) *& Scot* clan *m*; *Fig* bande *f*, clique *f*; **the head of the c.**, le chef de clan; **gathering of the clans**, réunion *f* d'adhérents *ou* de partisans; **c. name**, nom clanique; **c. tartan**, les couleurs du clan.

clandestine [klæn'destɪn] *adj* clandestin.

clandestinely [klæn'destɪnlɪ] *adv* clandestinement.

clang¹ [klæŋ] *n* son *m ou* bruit *m* métallique, bruit retentissant.

clang² **1** *vi* retentir, résonner, rendre un son métallique; **the gate clanged shut**, le portail s'est refermé avec un bruit métallique. **2** *vt* faire résonner (*une cloche etc*).

clanger ['klæŋər] *n Br F* **to drop a c.**, faire une gaffe *ou* une boulette, gaffer.

clank¹ ['klæŋk] *n* bruit sec (*de chaînes, de fers*).

clank² **1** *vi* (*of chain, bucket*) rendre un bruit métallique, cliqueter. **2** *vt* faire cliqueter (*des chaînes etc*).

clannish ['klænɪʃ] *adj Pej* qui a l'esprit de clan; (*groupe etc*) fermé.

clansman, *pl* **-men**, **clanswoman**, *pl* **-women** ['klænzmən, -mən, -wʊmən, -wɪmɪn] *n* = membre d'un clan.

clap¹ [klæp] *n* **(a)** battement *m* (*de mains*); tape *f* (*de la main*); **to give s.o. a c.**, applaudir qn; **(b) c. of thunder**, coup *m* de tonnerre.

clap² *v* (**-pp-**) **1** *vt* **(a) to c. one's hands**, battre des mains; **to c. s.o. on the back**, donner à qn une tape sur le dos; **to c. a performer**, applaudir un artiste; **(b)** (*put*) mettre, *F* coller; **to c. s.o. in irons**, mettre qn aux fers; **to c. s.o. in prison**, fourrer qn en prison; *F* **to c. eyes on s.o.**, voir qn (tout à coup), apercevoir qn; **I've never clapped eyes on her before**, je ne l'ai jamais vue de ma vie. **2** *vi* **(a)** (*of person, audience etc*) frapper des *ou* dans ses mains, applaudir; **(b)** (*of wings*) battre.

clap³ *n Sl* (*gonorrhoea*) chaude-pisse *f*; (*for women*) blennorragie *f*; **he's got a dose of the c.**, il a la chaude-pisse; **to give s.o. the c.**, passer la chaude-pisse à qn.

▶**clap on** *vtsep Nau* **to c. on more sail**, augmenter de toile; **he clapped his hat on**, il a enfoncé son chapeau sur la tête.

clapboard ['klæpbɔːd] *n Am Constr* planche *f* à clin.

clapometer [klæ'pɒmɪtər] *n TV etc* applaudimètre *m*.

clapped [klæpd] *adj Sl* **c. out**, éreinté, fourbu.

clapper ['klæpər] *n* **(a)** battant *m* (*de cloche, de moulin à blé*); claquet *m* (*de moulin*); clapet *m* (*de pompe*); **c. ring**, bélière *f* (*de cloche*); **c. valve**, (soupape *f* à) clapet; **(b)** (*noise-maker*) claquette *f*, claquoir *m*; crécelle *f* (*de crieur public*); *Agr* moulin *m* à claquet (*pour effrayer les oiseaux*); *Sl* **like the clappers**, (*travailler*) comme un enragé; (*courir*) comme un dératé; **(c)** (*person*) applaudisseur, -euse.

clapperboard ['klæpəbɔːd] *n Cin* claquette *f* (*de synchronisation*).

clapping ['klæpɪŋ] *n* applaudissements *mpl*.

claptrap ['klæptræp] **1** *n* baratin *m*; **to talk c.**, raconter des histoires. **2** *adj* (*discours*) creux, sans sincérité.

claque [klæk] *n Th* claque *f*.

claret ['klærət] **1** *n* **(a)** (*wine*) bordeaux *m* rouge; **(b)** (*colour*) bordeaux *m inv*. **2** *adj* **c.(-coloured)**, bordeaux *inv*.

clarification [klærɪfɪ'keɪʃən] *n* **(a)** (*further explanation*) clarification *f*; éclaircissement *m*, élucidation *f* (*d'une question etc*); **(b)** *Tech* clarification *f* (*d'un liquide*); soutirage *m*, collage *m* (*du vin*).

clarify ['klærɪfaɪ] **1** *vt* **(a)** clarifier (*sa pensée etc*); éclaircir (*l'esprit, la vision etc*); élucider (*une question*); **(b)** *Culin* clarifier (*le beurre, un sirop*); coller (*le vin*). **2** *vi* (*of liquid, one's thoughts*) se clarifier, s'éclaircir.

clarinet [klærɪ'net] *n Mus* clarinette *f*.

clarinettist [klærɪ'netɪst] *n Mus* clarinettiste *mf*.

clarion ['klærɪən] *n Lit* clairon *m*; **the speech was a c. call to ...**, le discours était un appel à ... .

clarity ['klærɪtɪ] *n* clarté *f*.

clash¹ [klæʃ] *n* **(a)** (*noise*) fracas *m*; résonnement *m* (*de cloches etc*); cliquetis *m* (*d'épées etc*); son strident (*de cymbales*); tumulte *m* (*d'armes*); **(b)** (*conflict*) conflit *m*, choc *m* (*d'opinions*); (*between people*) affrontement *m*; (*between mobs*) échauffourée *f*; désaccord *m*, opposition *f* (*d'intérêts, de doctrines*); **an armed c.**, un conflit armé; **clashes on the border**, des affrontements à la frontière; **there was a c. (between them) over the method to be used**, il y a eu un conflit entre eux quant aux méthodes à utiliser; **a c. of personalities, personality c.**, incompatibilité *f* de caractères; **(c)** discordance *f* (*des couleurs, des styles*).

clash² **1** *vi* **(a)** (*of cymbals, bells etc*) résonner (bruyamment); (*of arms*) s'entrechoquer; **(b)** (*come into conflict*) entrer en conflit, s'affronter; **police clashed with protestors,** il y a eu des heurts entre la police et les manifestants; *Fig* **they clashed over how to solve the problem,** ils sont entrés en conflit quant à la manière de résoudre le problème; **their personalities c.,** leurs personalités se heurtent, il y a incompatibilité entre leurs caractères; **(c)** (*of colours*) jurer, détonner; (*of literary styles*) être discordant; **the two dates c.,** les deux réunions *etc* tombent le même jour. **2** *vt* faire résonner (*des cymbales etc*); sonner ensemble (*les cloches*).

clashing ['klæʃɪŋ] **1** *adj* **(a)** (*sound*) bruyant, retentissant; **(b)** (*opinions*) opposé; (*colours, styles*) discordant. **2** *n* = **CLASH¹**.

clasp¹ [klɑːsp] *n* **(a)** (*fastener*) agrafe *f* (*de broche, de médaille, d'album etc*); fermeture *f* (*de collier etc*); fermoir *m*, fermail *m* (*de livre, de porte-monnaie*); **c. knife,** couteau pliant à plusieurs lames; **(b)** (*grip*) étreinte *f*, enlacement *m*; serrement *m* (*de mains*).

clasp² *vt* **(a)** (*fasten*) agrafer (*un bracelet etc*); **(b)** (*grip*) serrer, étreindre, enlacer (*qn*); embrasser (*qch, les genoux de qn*); prendre (*qch*) dans ses bras; **to be clasped in each other's arms,** se tenir étroitement embrassés; **to c. s.o.'s hand,** serrer la main à qn; **to c. one's hands,** joindre les mains.

class¹ [klɑːs] *n* **(a)** (*in social hierarchy*) classe *f*; **the upper classes,** la haute société; **the middle class(es),** la classe moyenne; **the working classes,** la classe ouvrière; **working-c. family,** famille ouvrière; **c. distinction,** distinction *f* entre les classes; **c. traitor,** personne qui renie ses origines sociales; **c. war, the c. struggle,** la lutte des classes;

(b) *F* (*quality*) classe *f*; **to have c.,** avoir de la classe; **that's what I call c. furniture,** ça, c'est que j'appelle des meubles classes;

(c) *Sch* (*lesson*) leçon *f*, classe *f*; **the French c.,** la classe de français; **evening c.,** cours *m* du soir; **day release classes,** la scolarité à temps partiel; **dancing c.,** cours de danse; **in c.,** en classe;

(d) *Am Sch* promotion *f*; **the c. of '89,** la promotion 1989;

(e) (*category*) catégorie *f*, sorte *f*, genre *m*; *Biol* classe *f*; (*in marine insurance*) cote *f* (*d'un navire*) (*à la Lloyd*); **in a c. by itself,** (*article*) unique; **he's in a c. by himself,** il surpasse tout le monde; **first-c.,** (*passenger, ticket, compartment*) de première classe; *Nau etc* **tourist/cabin/economy c.,** classe touriste/cabine/économique; *Br Univ* **first-/second-c. degree,** ≈ licence *f* avec mention bien/avec mention; **first-c. player/hotel/***etc*, joueur, -euse/hôtel *m*/*etc* de premier ordre; **of Olympic c.,** digne de participer aux Jeux Olympiques; *Mil US* **private first c.,** soldat *m* de première classe.

class² *vt* **(a)** classer, assimiler (*qn, qch*) **(with,** à); **classed first,** classé premier; **(b)** (*in marine insurance*) coter (*un navire*); **ship classed A1,** navire classé suivant cote A1.

classic ['klæsɪk] **1** *adj* classique; **c. records of the sixties,** des classiques de la musique des années soixante; *F* **a c. example,** un exemple classique *ou* typique; *Horseracing* **c. race,** course *f* classique. **2** *n* (*author, book etc*) & *Horseracing* classique *m*; **a c. of romantic poetry,** un classique de la poésie romantique; **classics,** (*usu with sing verb*) les humanités *fpl*; le latin et le grec; **a classics degree,** une licence en sciences humaines.

classical ['klæsɪk(ə)l] *adj* **(a)** (*civilization etc*) de l'antiquité; **c. Greece,** la Grèce antique; **the c. world,** le monde de l'antiquité; **in c. times,** dans l'antiquité; **c. scholar,** humaniste *m*; **(b)** *Mus Art Liter etc* classique.

classically ['klæsɪk(ə)lɪ] *adv* classiquement; **c. trained,** (*pianist etc*) ayant reçu une formation classique.

classicism ['klæsɪsɪz(ə)m] **(a)** *Art Liter Archit etc* classicisme *m*; **(b)** *Ling* tour emprunté *ou* locution empruntée aux langues classiques.

classicist ['klæsɪsɪst] *n* **(a)** *Sch* (*student*) humaniste *m*; (*advocate of classical studies*) partisan, -ane des études classiques; **(b)** *Art Liter Archit etc* classique *m*.

classification [klæsɪfɪ'keɪʃən] *n* **(a)** (*action*) classification *f* (*des plantes, des animaux*); classement *m* (*de papiers, de concurrents, de livres etc*); **(b)** (*category*) classification *f*, classe *f*; (*in marine insurance*) cote *f* (*d'un navire*).

classified ['klæsɪfaɪd] *adj* classifié, classé; (*document, information*) secret; *Journ* **c. advertisements,** petites annonces; *Sp* **c. results,** résultats *mpl* et classements *mpl*.

classifier ['klæsɪfaɪər] *n* (*person*) classificateur, -trice.

classify ['klæsɪfaɪ] *vt* **(a)** classifier, classer; **their music is classified as jazz,** leur musique est classée comme étant du jazz; **(b)** (*make secret*) classer secret (*un document etc*).

classless ['klɑːslɪs] *adj* (*société*) sans classes.

classmate ['klɑːsmeɪt] *n Sch* **(a)** (*in same class*) camarade *mf* de classe; **(b)** *Am* (*in same year*) camarade *mf* de promotion.

classroom ['klɑːsruːm] *n Sch* (salle *f* de) classe *f*.

classy ['klɑːsɪ] *adj F* bon genre; (*restaurant etc*) chic.

clatter¹ ['klætər] *n* bruit *m*, vacarme *m*, fracas *m*; bruit (*de vaisselle*); clic-clac *m* (*de sabots*); ferraillement *m* (*d'une machine*).

clatter² **1** *vi* faire du bruit; **we could hear him clattering about in the attic,** on l'entendait qui faisait un bruit de tous les diables dans le grenier; **the old cart clattered by,** le vieux chariot est passé en faisant du bruit; **to come clattering down,** dégringoler avec fracas, faire un bruit de dégringolade. **2** *vt* faire résonner; **don't c. your spoons!,** ne faites pas de bruit avec vos cuillers!

Claudius ['klɔːdɪəs] *n Antiq* Claude *m*.

clause [klɔːz] *n* **(a)** *Jur* clause *f*, article *m* (*d'un traité, d'une loi*); disposition *f* (*testamentaire, d'une loi*); **penalty c.,** clause pénale; **arbitration c.,** clause compromissoire; **(restrictive) clauses,** modalités *fpl*; **(b)** *Gram* proposition *f*.

claustrophobia [klɔːstrə'fəʊbɪə, klɒs-] *n Med* claustrophobie *f*.

claustrophobic [klɔːstrə'fəʊbɪk, klɒs-] *adj & n Med* claustrophobe *mf*; **this room feels quite c.,** cette pièce donne une impression de claustrophobie; **I feel c.,** j'ai un sentiment de claustrophobie.

clavichord ['klævɪkɔːd] *n Mus* clavicorde *m*.

clavicle ['klævɪk(ə)l] *n Anat* clavicule *f*.

claw¹ [klɔː] *n* **(a)** griffe *f* (*de chat etc*); serre *f* (*d'oiseau de proie*); pince *f* (*d'une écrevisse*); **to sharpen its claws,** (*of cat*) se faire les griffes; **to draw in its claws,** faire patte de velours; **c.-footed,** (*table etc*) à pied de griffon; *Fig* **to have** *or* **get one's claws in s.o.,** (*dislike*) s'en prendre à qn; (*trap*) mettre le grappin sur qn; **(b)** *Tech* (*of bench*) valet *m*; (*of vice*) mordache *f*; (*of winch, shaft etc*) cliquet *m*; (*of crane*) patte *f*; (*of hammer*) panne fendue; **c. hammer,** marteau *m* à panne fendue; *Aut* **c. clutch,** embrayage *m* à griffes.

claw² **1** *vt* (*scratch*) griffer, égratigner; donner un coup de griffe à (*qn*). **2** *vi* **to c. at sth,** s'accrocher à qch, agripper qch; (*of cat*) saisir qch avec ses griffes.

►**claw back** *vtsep* **(a)** (*regain*) regagner péniblement; **(b)** *Fin* récupérer (*une dépense*).

clay [kleɪ] *n* argile *f*, (terre-)glaise *f*; **boulder c.,** argile à blocaux; *Cer etc* **china c.,** terre *f* à porcelaine, kaolin *m*; **modelling c.,** pâte *f* à modeler; **potter's c.,** terre à *ou* de potier, (terre-) glaise; *Lit* **idol with feet of c.,** idole aux pieds d'argile; *Lit* **mortal c.,** le corps humain; *Sp* **c. pigeon,** pigeon artificiel; **c. soil,** sol argileux *ou* glaiseux; **c. pipe,** pipe *f* de *ou* en terre; *Tennis* **to play on c.,** jouer sur la terre battue; **c. court,** court *m* en terre battue; **to be a good c. court player** *or* **good on c.,** jouer bien sur la terre battue.

clayey ['kleɪɪ] *adj* (*soil*) argileux, glaiseux.

claymore ['kleɪmɔːr] *n Scot Hist* = sabre à deux tranchants utilisé par les Écossais.

clean¹ [kliːn] **1** *adj* **(a)** propre, net; (*eau*) pur, clair; (*papier*) blanc; (*cassure*) franc, net; (*saut*) franc; (*blessure*) pas infecté; (*blague*) décent; **to put on c. clothes,** mettre des vêtements propres; **cats are very c. animals,** les chats sont des animaux très propres; **to make a c. break,** (*in relationship*) en finir une bonne fois pour toutes; **c. timber,** bois uni *ou* sans malandres; *Typ* **c. proof,** (*with few corrections*) épreuve non chargée *ou* peu chargée; (*final*) épreuve pour bon à tirer; **c. driving licence,** permis *m* de conduire vierge; *Fin* **c. bill,** effet *m* libre; **c. hands,** mains *fpl* propres; (*from crime*) mains nettes; **c. living,** vie réglée; **good c. fun,** amusement innocent; **to keep sth c.,** tenir qch propre; *F* **keep it c.!,** (*the joke, story etc*) pas de grossièretés!; *Med* **c. room,** pièce aseptisée;

(b) **c. (out)lines,** contours nets; **car with c. lines,** voiture qui a de la ligne;

(c) *Sp* (*joueur, boxeur*) impeccable.

2 *adv F* absolument, tout à fait; **I c. forgot,** j'ai complètement oublié; **they got c. away,** ils se sont échappés sans laisser de traces; **we're c. out of soap powder,** nous n'avons plus de lessive en poudre du tout; **to cut c. through sth,** couper *ou* traverser qch de part en part; **to jump c.,** (*of horse*) sauter franchement; *F* **to come c.,** avouer, dire toute la vérité.

clean² *n* nettoyage *m*; **to give sth a c.,** nettoyer qch.

clean³ **1** *vt* nettoyer (*qch*); récurer (*des casseroles*); balayer (*les rues*); curer (*un puits*); *Culin* vider (*le *poisson*); lessiver, décrasser (*une chaudière*); ramoner (*les tubes*); *Med* nettoyer (*une plaie, un ulcère*); *Tech* nettoyer, dessabler (*une pièce coulée*); **to c. one's teeth,** se laver les dents; **to c. one's nails,** se curer les ongles; **to c. one's plate,** faire assiette nette; *Am* **to c. house,** faire le ménage. **2** *vi* faire le nettoyage; **to go out cleaning,** faire des ménages.

►**clean out** *vtsep* **(a)** nettoyer (*une armoire etc*); curer, décrasser (*un fourneau*); vidanger, décombler (*une fosse etc*); ébouer (*une chaudière*); déboucher (*un tuyau*); **(b)** *F* (*leave without money*) nettoyer (*qn*), laisser (*qn*) sans un rond; **they cleaned out the safe,** ils ont vidé le coffre; **cleaned out,** nettoyé (à sec), fauché; **(c)** (*buy, take all of*) **to c. a shop out of sugar,** dévaliser un magasin de son stock de sucre.

►**clean up 1** *vtsep* **(a)** enlever, ramasser (*des saletés etc*); nettoyer (*une salle etc*); *Fig* assainir (*la télévision*); **to c. oneself up,** se débarbouiller; *Fig* **to c. up a town,** nettoyer une ville (*d'ennemis, de gangsters etc*); **(b)** *Am Sl* **to c. up a thousand dollars,** gagner *ou* ramasser mille dollars. **2** *vi* **(a)** (*in room, building etc*) faire le nettoyage; (*wash oneself*) se débarbouiller; **(b)** (*put back in order*) mettre tout en ordre; **I hate cleaning up after parties,** j'ai horreur de ranger après les soirées; **(c)** (*repair damage*) réparer le désordre; **people have begun cleaning up after the earthquake,** les gens ont commencé à réparer les dégâts après le tremblement de terre; **(d)** *Am Sl* (*make a lot of money*) taper dans le mille.

clean-cut ['kliːn'kʌt] *adj* (*lines*) d'une grande netteté; (*opinion*) net, bien défini; (*order*) précis; (*division*) net.

cleaner ['kliːnər] *n* **(a)** (*person*) nettoyeur, -euse; (*in home, office*) personne qui fait le ménage; **window c.,** laveur *m* de carreaux *ou* de vitres; **(dry) c.,** nettoyeur à sec; **to take sth to the cleaners,** faire nettoyer qch; *Sl* **to take s.o. to the cleaners,** (*cheat*) nettoyer qn, plumer qn; (*defeat*) battre qn à plates coutures; **(b)** (*device*) nettoyeuse *f*; **air c.,** épurateur *m* d'air; **window c.,** lave-vitres *m inv*; **pipe c.,** cure-pipe *m*, *pl* cure-pipes; **(c)** (*product*) produit *m* pour nettoyer; (*for clothes*) détachant *m*.

cleaning *n* ['kliːnɪŋ] nettoyage *m*, nettoiement *m*; curage *m* (*d'un puits*); décrassage *m* (*des chaudières*); ramonage *m* (*des tubes*); décapage *m* (*d'une surface à repeindre*); *Culin* vidage *m* (*du poisson*); **c. woman,** (*in home, office*) femme *f* de ménage; **(household) c. materials,** produits *mpl* d'entretien.

cleaning up *n* nettoyage *m* (*d'une salle, d'un quartier criminel etc*).

cleanliness ['klenlɪnɪs] *n* propreté *f*; **c. of habit,** habitudes de propreté; *Prov* **c. is next to godliness,** la propreté du corps s'apparente à la pureté de l'âme.

clean-living ['kliːn'lɪvɪŋ] *adj* (*person*) réglé, qui mène une vie réglée.

cleanly[1] ['kliːnlɪ] *adv* proprement, nettement; **to break c.,** se casser net.

cleanly[2] ['klenlɪ] *adj* (*person*) propre (par habitude); **c. habits,** habitudes *fpl* de propreté.

cleanness ['kliːnnɪs] *n* propreté *f* (*des habits, de langage, d'un appartement etc*); pureté *f* (*de l'eau*); netteté *f*, pureté (*de lignes*).

clean-out ['kliːnaʊt] *n* nettoyage *m*; **to give a room a c.-o.,** nettoyer une pièce.

cleanse [klenz] *vt* démaquiller (*le visage*); *Med* nettoyer (*une plaie*); purifier, dépurer (*le sang*); épurer (*l'air etc*); assainir, curer, débourber (*un égout etc*); *Arch & Lit* purifier (*le cœur, l'âme etc*).

cleanser ['klenzər] *n* (*for skin*) démaquillant *m*.

clean-shaven ['kliːn'ʃeɪv(ə)n] *adj* sans barbe ni moustache; (*visage*) entièrement rasé; **he was c.-s.,** il était glabre.

cleansing ['klenzɪŋ] *n Med* nettoyage *m* (*d'une plaie*); purification *f* (*du sang, de l'âme*); épuration *f* (*d'un gaz*); assainissement *m*, curage *m* (*d'un chenal, d'un égout*); **c. cream/milk** *or* **lotion,** (*for skin*) crème *f*/lait *m* de démaquillage; **c. pads,** disques-lotion *mpl*.

cleanup ['kliːnʌp] *n* (*d'une pièce, d'une ville capturée*) nettoyage *m*; **to give sth a c.,** nettoyer qch.

clear[1] [klɪər] **1** *adj* **(a)** (*ciel, teint, œil, son etc*) clair; (*temps*) clair, dégagé; **c. water,** eau claire *ou* limpide; **on a c. day,** par temps clair; **as c. as daylight** *or* **crystal,** clair comme le jour *ou* comme de l'eau de roche; *TV* **the picture was very c.,** l'image était très nette; *F* **as c. as mud,** clair comme du jus de boudin; **c. conscience,** conscience tranquille; **my conscience is c.,** j'ai la conscience tranquille; **c. voice,** voix claire *ou* nette;

(b) (*manifest*) clair, net; (*signe*) évident; **c. case of bribery,** cas *m* manifeste de corruption; **the meaning of the sentence was c.,** le sens de la phrase était clair; **to make one's meaning** *or* **oneself c.,** se faire comprendre; **have I made myself c.?,** est-ce que je me suis bien fait comprendre?; **to make it c. to s.o. that ...,** bien faire comprendre à qn que ...; **she made it quite c. that ...,** elle lui *ou* nous *etc* a bien fait comprendre que ...; **the letter doesn't make it c. when they will arrive,** la lettre n'indique pas clairement quand ils vont arriver; **I want to be quite c. on this point,** je tiens à ce qu'il n'y ait aucun malentendu sur ce point; **is that c.?,** (*do you understand?*) c'est clair?; **it is c. that ...,** il est clair *ou* évident que ...; **it was not c. who had won,** on ne savait pas exactement qui avait gagné; **it is not yet c. whether ...,** on ne sait pas encore si ...;

(c) (*not confused*) net; **c. thinker** *or* **mind,** esprit *m* lucide; **I want to keep a c. head,** je veux garder les idées claires;

(d) (*certain*) **to be c. about sth,** être convaincu *ou* certain de qch; **are you c. about what you have to do,** es-tu sûr de ce que tu as à faire?; **there's something I'm not c. about,** il reste quelque chose dont je ne suis pas sûr; **I wasn't c. what she meant,** je n'étais pas sûr de ce qu'elle a voulu dire;

(e) (*unqualified*) **c. profit,** bénéfice clair et net; **a c. ten thousand a year,** un revenu (clair et) net de dix mille livres; **c. majority,** majorité absolue; *Sp* **c. winner,** vainqueur détaché; *Jur* **three c. days,** trois jours francs;

(f) (*unobstructed, free*) libre; (*vue etc*) dégagé; **to be c. of sth,** (*of person*) être débarrassé de qch; **we were c. of the last checkpoint,** nous avions dépassé le dernier poste de contrôle; **the sea is c. of ice,** la mer est libre; **the exhaust pipe is 30 cm c. of the ground,** le tuyau d'échappement est à 30 cm du sol; *Av* **you are c. to take off,** vous êtes autorisé à *ou* vous pouvez décoller; *Rail* **c. road, road c., line c.,** voie libre, signal effacé; **all c.!,** (*there's no traffic, no-one is watching*) vous pouvez y aller, c'est libre; *Mil* fin *f* d'alerte; *Nau* paré!;

2 *adv* **to jump five centimetres c. of the bar,** franchir la barre avec cinq centimètres de reste; **to hang c. of the ground,** être suspendu de manière à ne pas toucher le sol; *Nau* **to steer c. of a rock,** passer au large d'un écueil; **to stand c.,** s'écarter, se garer (*pour éviter un danger*); **to keep** *or* **steer** *or* **stand c. of sth,** rester *ou* se tenir à distance de qch; éviter qch; **stand c. of the doors!,** attention aux portes!; *Rail* = attention au départ!; **they pulled him c. of the wreckage,** ils l'ont dégagé de l'épave; **to get c. of s.o.,** échapper à qn; **to get c.,** se tirer d'embarras, se tirer d'affaire.

3 *n* **(a)** (*of person*) **to be in the c.,** (*free from suspicion*) être libre de tout soupçon; (*free from debt*) ne pas avoir de dettes;

(b) *Mil etc* **despatch sent in c.,** dépêche *f* en clair.

clear[2] 1 *vt* **(a)** (*free of obstacles*) dégager (*une route, un terrain, une entrée*); désencombrer (*une salle etc*); défricher (*un terrain*); faire évacuer (*les rues, une salle*); *Rad etc* éliminer (*l'interférence*); déboucher, dégorger (*un tuyau*); *Jur* **to c. the court,** faire évacuer la salle; **to c. one's conscience,** décharger sa conscience; **he cleared a space on the floor,** il a dégagé un espace sur le sol; **they cleared 20 acres of forest,** ils ont défriché 8 hectares de forêt; **to c. a way** *or* **a passage for s.o.,** ouvrir un passage à qn; **to c. a way for oneself,** se frayer un passage; **to c. the table,** (*after meal*) enlever le couvert, débarasser la table; *Nau* **to c. the decks for action,** faire le branle-bas de combat; *Fig* **to c. the decks,** déblayer le terrain; *Comptr* **to c. the screen,** vider l'écran; **the rain had cleared the streets,** la pluie avait vidé les rues; **to c. slums,** supprimer des taudis; *Mil* **to c. an area of mines,** déminer un terrain; **fresh air clears the head,** un peu d'air frais vous éclaircit les idées; *Com* **to c. goods,** (*in sale etc*) solder *ou* liquider des marchandises; *Rail* **to c. the line,** dégager la voie; (*after an accident*) déblayer la voie;

(b) (*exonerate*) justifier, innocenter (*qn*) (**of a charge,** d'une accusation); disculper (*qn*) (*d'un soupçon*); **he was cleared of all blame,** il a été lavé de tout blâme; **to c. oneself,** se justifier;

(c) éclaircir (*le brouillard etc*); **to c. the air,** (*of thunderstorm*) rafraîchir l'air; (*of discussion etc*) mettre les choses au point; **to c. one's throat,** se racler la gorge;

(d) (*remove*) **to c. sth from sth,** enlever qch de sur qch; **he cleared the plates from the table,** il a enlevé les assiettes de sur la table; **c. all this out of here,** débarrassez-moi de tout cela;

(e) (*empty*) **to c. the letterbox,** lever le courrier; *Med*

to c. the bowels, purger *ou* dégager les intestins;

(f) (*go past, over etc without touching*) **to c. a barrier (by 10 centimetres),** franchir une barrière (avec 10 centimètres de reste); **to c. a ditch,** sauter *ou* franchir un fossé; *Nau* **to c. the harbour,** sortir du port, quitter le port; **the ship just cleared the bottom,** le bateau a évité le fond de justesse;

(g) (*make a profit of*) **to c. 10%,** gagner *ou* réaliser 10%, faire une bénéfice net de 10%; **I cleared a hundred pounds,** j'ai touché *ou* cela m'a rapporté cent livres net;

(h) *Banking* compenser, virer (*un chèque*);

(i) *Admin* (*authorize*) expédier (*un navire*); dédouaner (*des marchandises*); **to c. s.o.,** (*for security purposes*) attribuer à qn un certificat de sécurité; **he's been cleared,** l'enquête de sécurité a été favorable; **to c. sth with s.o.,** (*obtain permission for*) donner l'autorisation de qch à qn; *F* **I'll need to c. it with the boss,** il faut que j'obtienne la permission du patron; **to c. an article for publication,** (*ask for authorization*) demander l'autorisation de publier un article; (*authorize*) autoriser la publication d'un article; **the plane was cleared for take-off,** l'avion a été autorisé à décoller, l'avion a reçu l'autorisation de décollage;

(j) *Fin* acquitter (*une dette*); purger (*une hypothèque*); solder, liquider, arrêter (*un compte*); **to c. one's property of debt,** purger son bien de dettes;

(k) (*free from impurities*) clarifier (*un liquide*); purifier (*le sang*).

2 *vi* **(a)** (*of the weather*) s'éclaircir; (*of the sky*) se découvrir; (*of mist*) se dissiper; (*of sky*) se dégager;

(b) (*of cheque*) être viré;

(c) (*of liquid*) se clarifier.

►**clear away 1** *vtsep* (*remove*) enlever, ôter (*qch*); enlever (*les débris, des livres*); écarter (*un obstacle*); ranger (*ses affaires*). **2** *vi* **(a)** (*of mist*) se dissiper; **(b)** (*after meal*) desservir.

►**clear off 1** *vtsep* (*remove*) retirer, enlever; **c. all those papers off the table,** retire *ou* enlève tous ces papiers de sur la table. **2** *vi Br F* (*leave*) filer, décamper; **my wife cleared off,** ma femme s'est tirée; **c. off!,** tire-toi!, casse-toi!, dégage!, fous le camp!

►**clear out 1** *vtsep* (*empty*) vider (*une armoire*); débarrasser (*un grenier*); décombler (*un puits*); *F* mettre (*qn*) à sec. **2** *vi Br F* (*leave building, room etc*) filer, déguerpir, se sauver; (*leave home, spouse*) se tirer; **c. out!,** filez!, hors d'ici!

►**clear up 1** *vtsep* **(a)** (*tidy*) (re)mettre (*une pièce*) en ordre; ranger (*ses affaires*); **we had to c. up the mess,** (*after party*) il a fallu tout ranger *ou* nettoyer; *Fig* il a fallu tout arranger; **(b)** (*settle, clarify*) éclaircir, dissiper (*un malentendu*); éclaircir (*un mystère, un doute*); dénouer, démêler (*une situation, une intrigue*); résoudre (*une difficulté*); tirer (*une affaire*) au clair; **(c)** (*cure*) guérir. **2** *vi* **(a)** (*of weather*) s'éclaircir, se (re)mettre au beau; **(b)** (*of mystery etc*) s'éclaircir, s'élucider; **(c)** (*of rash, headache etc*) disparaître.

clearance ['klɪərəns] *n* **(a)** (*removal*) **slum c.,** élimination *f* des taudis; **c. area,** quartier *m* (insalubre) à démolir; *Com* **c. sale,** vente *f* de soldes, liquidation *f*;

(b) (*of land*) défrichement *m*;

(c) *Banking* (*of a cheque*) compensation *f*;

(d) (*authorization*) autorisation *f*; *Nau* départ *m* (*du port*); (*by customs*) acquit(tement) *m* (*de marchandises*); dédouanage *m*, dédouanement *m*; **we got c. to inspect the documents,** nous avons eu l'autorisation d'examiner les documents; *Av* **flight c.,** autorisation de vol; *Admin Mil* **security c.,** (*check*) contrôle *m* de sécurité (*sur qn*); (*document*) certificat *m* de sécurité;

(e) *Tech* (*space*) espace *m* libre; jeu *m* (*d'un piston etc*); jour *m*, écartement *m* (*entre barreaux*); entrefer *m* (*entre tôles etc*); débattement *m* (*de parties qui pourraient se heurter*); *Constr* (*of bridge, doorway etc*) hauteur *f* libre; **c. angle,** angle *m* d'incidence;

(f) *Fb* dégagement *m*.

clear-cut ['klɪə'kʌt] *adj* (*outline, feature*) nettement dessiné; (*opinion*) bien défini, tranché; (*order*) précis; (*division*) net, brutal.

clear-headed ['klɪə'hedɪd] *adj* **(a)** (*of sound judgment*) qui voit juste; (*drawing correct conclusions*) perspicace; **(b)** (*mentally alert*) à l'esprit net.

clearing ['klɪərɪŋ] *n* **(a)** (*unblocking, freeing of obstacles*) dégagement *m*, déblaiement *m* (*d'une voie*); enlèvement *m* (*de débris*); défrichement *m* (*d'un terrain*); curage *m* (*des fossés*); éclaircissement *m* (*d'une forêt*);

(b) (*emptying*) évacuation *f* (*d'une salle*); levée *f* (*du courrier*); *Mil* **c. station,** centre *m* de triage *ou* d'évacuation (*de blessés*);

(c) franchissement *m* (*d'une barrière*);

(d) *Fin* liquidation *f*, solde *m* (*de marchandises*); acquittement *m* (*de dettes*); liquidation (*d'un compte*); affranchissement *m* (*d'un bien*);

(e) *Banking* compensation *f* (*de chèque*); clearing *m*; **c. bank,** banque *f* de virement *ou* de clearing; **c. house,** *Banking* comptoir général de virement, clearing (house) *m*; *Br Univ* = organisme de tri des demandes d'entrée à l'université;

(f) *Nau Av* (*authorization to land, leave*) expédition *f* (*d'un navire*); dédouanement *m* (*des marchandises*);

(g) (*in forest*) éclaircie *f*, clairière *f*;

(h) clarification *f* (*d'un liquide*).

clearing away *n* enlèvement *m* (*de débris, des couverts*).

clearing up *n* **(a)** (*of house etc*) remise *f* en ordre; (*after earthquake, flood, bombing etc*) déblaiement *m*; **(b)** (*of mystery, doubt*) éclaircissement *m*.

clearly ['klɪəlɪ] *adv* **(a)** (*to see*) clair; (*to explain, write, speak*) clairement, d'une manière claire; (*to hear*) distinctement; (*to distinguish*) clairement, nettement; **c. legible,** bien lisible; **is that c. understood?,** c'est bien compris?; **(b)** (*obviously, plainly*) évidemment; **he is c. wrong,** il est évident qu'il a tort; **they are c. different,** il est évident qu'ils sont différents; **c., this can't be right,** c'est faux, il n'y a aucun doute là-dessus; **c., we'll have to pay,** nous devrons payer, c'est certain; **this is c. unacceptable,** c'est tout à fait inacceptable; **c. not,** manifestement pas.

clearness ['klɪənɪs] *n* **(a)** clarté *f*, limpidité *f* (*de l'eau, de l'atmosphère etc*); **(b)** netteté *f* (*d'une image, des idées*).

clearout ['klɪəraʊt] *n* action *f* de débarrasser (*une chambre, un grenier etc*); **to have a c.,** faire du rangement.

clear-sighted [klɪə'saɪtɪd] *adj* **(a)** (*having good judgement*) clairvoyant, qui voit juste; **(b)** (*having good sight*) à la vue nette.

clear-sightedness [klɪə'saɪtɪdnɪs] *n* **(a)** (*good judgement*) clairvoyance *f*; **(b)** (*good sight*) netteté *f* de vision.

clear-up ['klɪərʌp] *n* (*of room etc*) remise *f* en ordre; **this place needs a good c.-up,** cet endroit a bien besoin d'être remis en ordre.

clearway ['klɪəweɪ] *n Br* grande route à stationnement interdit.

cleat [kliːt] *n* **(a)** (*bracket*) tasseau *m* (*de bois*); attache *f* (*de poutre*); **(b)** *esp Nau* **(belaying) c.,** taquet *m* (*de tournage*); **(c)** *El* serre-câble(s) *m inv*, serre-fils *m inv*.

cleavage ['kliːvɪdʒ] *n* **(a)** (*of breasts*) naissance *f* des seins; **what a c.!,** quel décolleté!; **it fell down her c.,** c'est tombé dans son décolleté; **to show a lot of c.,** (*of woman*) être décolletée jusqu'au nombril; (*of dress*) être très décolleté; **(b)** (*split*) fissure *f*, scission *f* (*dans un parti*); **(c)** (*splitting*) fendage *m*; *Geol Ch* clivage *m*; *Biol* division *f*.

cleave [kliːv] *v* (*pt* **cleaved, cleft** [kleft], *Lit* **clove** [kləʊv]; *pp* **cleaved, cleft,** *Lit* **cloven** ['kləʊv(ə)n]) **1** *vt Lit* fendre (*le bois*); cliver (*un cristal*); (*of bird, ship*) fendre (*l'air, les eaux*). **2** *vi* **(a)** *Lit* **to c. (asunder),** se fendre, se feuilleter; **(b)** (*of crystals*) se cliver.

►**cleave to** *vipo* (*pt & pp* **cleaved**) *Lit* être fidèle à (*qn, un parti, un principe*).

cleaver ['kliːvər] *n* fendoir *m*; (*for meat*) couperet *m*; (*for wood*) merlin *m*.

clef [klef] *n Mus* clef *f*; **bass c.,** clef de fa; **C c.,** clef d'ut.

cleft [kleft] **1** *n* fente *f*, fissure *f*, crevasse *f*. **2** *adj* fendu; **c. stick,** piquet fourchu; *Fig* **to be in a c. stick,** se trouver dans une impasse; *Med* **c. palate,** palais fendu.

clematis ['klemətɪs, klə'meɪtɪs] *n* (*plant*) clématite *f*.

clemency, *pl* **-cies** ['klemənsɪ, -sɪz] *n* **(a)** (*mercy*) clémence *f*, indulgence *f* (**to,** envers); **to show c.,** faire preuve de clémence; **(b)** (*of weather*) douceur *f*.

clement ['klemənt] *adj Fml* **(a)** (*person*) clément, indulgent (**to,** envers, pour); **(b)** (*weather*) doux, clément.

clementine ['kleməntiːn, -aɪn] *n* (*fruit*) clémentine *f*.

clench [klen(t)ʃ] **1** *vt* **(a)** serrer (*les dents, le poing*); **between clenched teeth,** (*to say*) les dents serrées; **to c. sth in one's hand,** serrer qch dans la main; **(b)** *Tech* river (*un clou*). **2** *vi* (*of teeth, hands*) se serrer; (*of hands*) se crisper.

Cleopatra [klɪə'pætrə] *n Antiq* Cléopâtre *f*; **C.'s needle,** l'Obélisque *m* de Cléopâtre.

clerestory ['klɪəstɔːrɪ] *n Arch* fenêtres hautes.

clergy ['klɜːdʒɪ] *n Rel* (*no pl*) **(a)** (*with sing verb*) clergé *m*; **(b)** (*with pl verb*) ecclésiastiques *mpl*.

clergyman, *pl* **-men** ['klɜːdʒɪmən] *n Rel* ecclésiastique *m*; pasteur *m* (*protestant*); prêtre *m* (*catholic*).

clergywoman, *pl* **-women** [klɜːdʒɪwʊmən, -wɪmɪn] *n Rel* femme *f* pasteur.

cleric ['klerɪk] *n Rel* ecclésiastique *m*.

clerical ['klerɪk(ə)l] *adj* **(a)** *Com* (*work*) d'écritures, de bureau; (*staff*) de bureau; **c. error,** faute *f* de copiste; (*in book-keeping*) erreur *f* d'écritures; **(b)** *Rel* clérical, -aux; **c. dress,** habit *m* ecclésiastique; **c. collar,** col droit blanc.

clericalism ['klerɪk(ə)lɪz(ə)m] *n Rel* cléricalisme *m.*

clerk¹ [klɑːk, *Am* klɜːrk] *n* **(a)** (*in office*) employé, -ée de bureau; clerc *m* (*d'avoué*); **bank c.,** employé, -ée de banque; **filing c.,** *US* **file c.,** employé, -ée au classement; **records c.,** archiviste *m*; **shipping c.,** expéditionnaire *m*, employé, -ée de l'expédition; *Rail* **booking c.,** employé, -ée du guichet; *Jur* **c. of the court,** greffier *m* (*du tribunal*); *Constr* **c. of (the) works,** conducteur *m* des travaux; *Sp* **c. of the course,** commissaire *m* de la piste; **(b)** *Am* vendeur, -euse (*de magasin*); **(c)** *Am* (*receptionist*) préposé, -ée à la réception; **(d)** *Rel* **c. (in holy orders),** ecclésiastique *m.*

clerk² *vi* **(a)** (*work in office etc*) travailler comme employé -ée de bureau; **(b)** *Am* (*in shop*) travailler comme vendeur, -euse.

clever ['klevər] *adj* **(a)** (*intelligent*) intelligent; (*chien etc*) savant; (*ouvrage*) bien fait; (*plan, dispositif*) ingénieux; *Sch* **c. at mathematics,** fort en mathématiques; **he was too c. for us,** il nous a roulés; **(b)** *Pej* malin; *Br F* **a c. Dick,** un monsieur je-sais-tout; *Br* **she's too c. by half,** elle est bien trop maligne; **don't get c. with me,** ne fais pas le malin avec moi; **(c)** (*skilful*) habile, adroit; **to be c. with one's hands,** être adroit *ou* agile de ses mains; **c. at doing sth,** habile à faire qch; *F* **to play it c.,** jouer serré.

cleverly ['klevəlɪ] *adv* **(a)** (*intelligently*) avec intelligence; (*planned*) ingénieusement; **the dog had c. worked out how to ...,** le chien avait astucieusement découvert comment ...; **(b)** habilement, adroitement.

cleverness ['klevənɪs] *n* **(a)** intelligence *f*; ingéniosité *f* (*d'une invention etc*); **(b)** *Pej* le fait de jouer au malin; **(c)** (*with hands*) habileté *f*, adresse *f*, dextérité *f.*

cliché ['kliːʃeɪ] *n Typ & Fig* cliché *m.*

clichéd ['kliːʃeɪd] *adj* (*has become a cliché*) qui est devenu cliché; (*sounds like a cliché*) qui fait cliché.

cliché-ridden ['kliːʃeɪrɪd(ə)n] *adj* bourré de clichés.

click¹ ['klɪk] *n* **(a)** bruit sec, clic *m* (*d'un pistolet qu'on arme etc*); (*of tongue*) coup *m* de langue; (*of camera*) déclic *m*; *Horseriding* appel *m* de langue; *Ling* clic; *Fig* **something went c.,** (*became clear*) quelque chose a fait clic; *Ent* **c. beetle,** élatère *m*, *F* taupin *m*; **(b)** *Tech* cliquet *m*, détente *f*; **c. and ratchet,** encliquetage *m.*

click² **1** *vi* **(a)** (*make sound*) cliqueter, faire tic-tac; **cameras were clicking,** on entendait les déclics des appareils; **to c. together,** (*of two parts*) s'assembler avec un bruit sec; *F* **to c. shut,** (*of door etc*) se refermer avec un bruit sec; **(b)** *F* (*become clear*) faire clic; **now it's clicked,** ça a fait clic, j'ai *ou* il a *etc* pigé, j'y suis, il y est *etc*; **(c)** *F* (*of two people*) s'entendre à merveille dès l'abord; **to c. with the public,** (*of play, film*) faire un tabac. **2** *vt* **to c. one's heels,** (faire) claquer les talons (*en saluant*); **to c. one's tongue,** claquer la langue.

►**click on** *vi* **(a)** *Br F* (*understand*) piger; **(b)** *Comptr* cliquer.

clicking ['klɪkɪŋ] *n* (*noise*) cliquetis *m.*

client ['klaɪənt] *n Com* client, -ente (*d'un magasin, dans les professions libérales*); (*of stockbroker*) donneur *m* d'ordres.

clientele [kliːɒn'tel] *n* clientèle *f* (*d'un magasin, dans les professions libérales etc*).

cliff [klɪf] *n* falaise *f*; (*in mountains*) à-pic *m*, *pl* à-pics.

cliffhanger ['klɪfhæŋər] *n Journ* = roman-feuilleton dont chaque épisode se termine par un suspense; **the election/race was a c.,** le résultat de l'élection/de la course a été douteux jusqu'au dernier moment.

climacteric [klaɪ'mæktərɪk] *n* climatère *m.*

climactic [klaɪ'mæktɪk] *adj* arrivé à son apogée; (*point*) culminant.

climate ['klaɪmət] *n Met & Fig* climat *m.*

climatic [klaɪ'mætɪk] *adj Met* (*zone, influence etc*) climatique.

climatologist [klaɪmə'tɒlədʒɪst] *n Met* climatologue *mf.*

climatology [klaɪmə'tɒlədʒɪ] *n Met* climatologie *f.*

climax¹ ['klaɪmæks] *n* **(a)** apogée *m*, faîte *m*, point culminant (*de la renommée etc*); **the c. of the festivities,** l'apogée des réjouissances; **to reach a c.,** (*of music*) atteindre son point culminant; **to work up to a c.,** (*in rhetoric*) procéder par gradation (ascendante); *Th etc F* corser l'action; **as a c. to the entertainment ...,** comme bouquet de la fête ...; **(b)** (*sexual*) orgasme *m.*

climax² *vi* (*have an orgasm*) jouir, avoir un orgasme; (*reach orgasm*) atteindre l'orgasme.

climb¹ [klaɪm] *n* montée *f*, ascension *f* (*d'une paroi abrupte*); course *f* (*dans les montagnes*); côte *f*, montée (*d'une route etc*); *Aut* **hill c.,** course de côte; *Av* **rate of c.,** vitesse ascensionnelle *ou* de montée; **a short c. takes you to the village,** une petite montée vous mène au village; **there are some good climbs in these mountains,** il y a de bonnes courses dans ces montagnes.

climb² **1** *vi* (*up a tree*) grimper; (*up a ladder*) monter; (*up a rock face*) escalader; (*up stairs*) monter, gravir; **to c. up a mountain,** faire l'ascension d'une montagne; **to c. over the wall,** escalader le mur; **to c. on (to) the roof,** monter *ou* grimper sur le toit; **to c. down a ladder,** descendre d'une échelle; **to c. out of a hole,** grimper *ou* se hisser en dehors d'un trou; **to c. into bed,** grimper dans son lit; *Fig* **to c. to power,** s'élever au pouvoir; *Fig* **to c. (socially, in the world),** faire son chemin, parvenir; **(b)** (*go mountain climbing*) faire des ascensions; (*go rock climbing*) faire de la varappe; **(c)** (*of road*) monter; (*of prices*) monter, augmenter; **(d)** *Av* prendre de l'altitude, monter; **the plane climbed 200 feet,** l'avion a pris 60 mètres d'altitude. **2** *vt* grimper à (*un arbre*); monter à (*une échelle*); escalader (*une falaise*); monter, gravir (*un escalier*).

►**climb down** *vi* **(a)** (*descend*) descendre, redescendre; **it took them a day to c. down,** il leur a fallu une journée pour redescendre; **(b)** *Fig* en rabattre, reculer; **management later climbed down,** la direction en a ensuite rabattu.

climb-down ['klaɪmdaʊn] *n F* reculade *f.*

climber ['klaɪmər] *n* **(a)** (*of mountain*) alpiniste *mf*; (*of rock face*) varappeur, -euse; grimpeur, -euse (*à un arbre*); *Fig* **(social) c.,** arriviste *mf*; **(b)** *Bot* plante grimpante.

climbing ['klaɪmɪŋ] **1** *adj* (*plante*) grimpant; (*oiseau*) grimpeur; *Av* (*vol*) ascendant. **2** *n* (*of mountain*) escalade *f*; (*of hill*) montée *f*; ascension *f* (*d'un arbre*); *Av* remontée *f* (*après descente*); **rock c.,** varappe *f*; **mountain c.,** alpinisme *m*; **social c.,** arrivisme *m*; **c. frame,** (*for children*) cage *f* à écureuil; **c. irons,** (*for mountaineer*) crampons *mpl*, grappins *mpl*; étriers *mpl* (*pour l'ascension des arbres*); **c. wall,** (*indoors*) mur *m* d'escalade.

clime [klaɪm] *n Lit* (*climate*) climat *m*; (*country*) contrée *f.*

clinch¹ [klɪntʃ] *n* **(a)** *F* étreinte *f* (*d'amoureux*); **to go into a c.,** s'étreindre; **(b)** *Boxing* clinch *m*; **to break a c.,** briser un corps à corps; **to go into a c.,** se prendre corps à corps; **(c)** *Tech* rivet *m*, crampon *m*; **c. nail,** clou rivé *ou* à river; **(d)** *Nau* étalingure *f.*

clinch² **1** *vt* **(a)** (*settle*) conclure, clore (*un marché*); confirmer (*un argument*); **that clinches it!,** (*settles the matter*) voilà qui tranche la question!; (*forces a decision*) cela me décide!; **(b)** *Tech* river (*un clou*); abattre, aplatir (*un rivet, la pointe du clou*); **(c)** *Nau* étalinguer (*une chaîne*). **2** *vi* **(a)** *Boxing* en venir aux prises, se prendre corps à corps; **(b)** *F* (*of lovers*) s'étreindre.

clincher ['klɪntʃər] *n F* **(a)** (*argument*) argument *m* irréfutable; **(b)** *Sp* but *ou* point décisif.

cling¹ [klɪŋ] *vi* (*pt & pp* **clung** [klʌŋ]) (*of person*) s'attacher, s'accrocher (**to sth/s.o.,** à qch/qn); *Pej* se coller (**to s.o.,** à qn); (*of burr*) s'attraper (**to,** à); (*of plant*) s'accrocher (*au mur*); **he clung to the rope for dear life,** il s'agrippa à la corde; **the two children clung to each other,** les deux enfants se sont serrés l'un contre l'autre; *Fig* **to c. to one's children/wife/***etc*, s'accrocher à ses enfants/sa femme/*etc*; *Fig* **to c. to an opinion,** rester attaché à une opinion, s'obstiner dans une opinion; *Fig* **to c. to a hope,** se raccrocher à un espoir; **to c. to the figure,** (*of garment*) mouler le corps.

cling² *n* **c. (peach),** pavie *f.*

clingfilm ['klɪŋfɪlm] *n Br* Scellofrais ® *m.*

clinging ['klɪŋɪŋ] *adj* (*person*) qui s'attache; *Pej* qui colle; (*plant, person*) qui s'accroche; (*vêtement*) collant; (*tissu*) qui moule le corps; (*parfum*) tenace; **c. parents,** parents qui ne laissent pas partir leurs enfants; *Am F* **c. vine,** pot-de-colle *m.*

clingstone ['klɪŋstəʊn] *n* **c. (peach),** pavie *f.*

clingy ['klɪŋɪ] *adj Pej* **she's so c.,** (*of child*) elle est toujours dans mes jupes; **he's the c. type,** c'est le genre collant.

clinic ['klɪnɪk] *n* **(a)** *Med* dispensaire *m*; **(b)** *Br Med* (*nursing home*) clinique *f*; **(c)** *Fig* (*at a DIY shop etc*) atelier *m* de démonstration.

clinical ['klɪnɪk(ə)l] *adj Med & Fig* clinique; (*thermomètre*) médical.

clink¹ [klɪŋk] *n* tintement *m*, choc *m* (*de verres*).

clink² **1** *vi* (*of glasses etc*) tinter. **2** *vt* faire tinter; **to c. glasses,** choquer les verres, trinquer.

clink³ *n Sl* (*prison*) taule *f*, tôle *f*; **to be in c.,** être au bloc.

clinker ['klɪŋkər] *n* **(a)** *Constr* brique hollandaise (*pour* *carrelage*); (*vitrified*) brique vitrifiée, brique à four; **(b)** (*ash*) mâchefer *m* (*de forge etc*), escarbilles *fpl.*

clinker-built ['klɪŋkəbɪlt] *adj Nau* bordé à clin(s).

clip¹ [klɪp] *n* **(a)** pince *f*, serre *f*; (*brooch*) clip *m*; pince (*pour mise en plis*); (*hair ornament*) barrette *f*; **paper c.,** trombone *m*; **tie c.,** pince à cravate; **bicycle** *or* **trouser c.,** pince à pantalon, pince-pantalon *m inv*, *Surg* **artery c.,** pince hémostatique; **(b)** *El* cosse *f* (*de fil, de câble*); **(c)** *Rail* serre-rail(s) *m inv*, crapaud *m.*

clip² *vt* (-pp-) pincer, serrer; **to c. papers together,** agrafer des papiers.

clip³ *n* **(a)** tondage *m* (*de chien etc*); **to give one's nails a c.,** se couper les ongles; **(b)** *Sl* (*blow*) **c. (on the ear),** taloche *f*; **(c)** *Sl* **c. joint,** = boîte de nuit ou restaurant où l'on reçoit le coup de fusil; **(d)** *Cin* extrait *m* de film; *TV* clip *m*; **a c. from the video of the concert,** un clip de la vidéo du concert; **(e)** *US* (*from newspaper*) coupure *f.*

clip⁴ *vt* **(a)** tondre (*un chien, le gazon*); couper, tailler (*une haie*); rogner, cisailler (*la monnaie*); couper, cisailler (*une tôle*); **to c. the wings of a bird,** rogner les ailes à une volaille; *Fig* **to c. s.o.'s wings,** couper les ailes à qn; **to c. ten seconds off a record,** améliorer un record de dix secondes; *Tennis* **to c. the line,** (*of ball*) mordre la ligne; **(b)** poinçonner (*un billet de chemin de fer*); **(c)** *Sl* **to c. s.o.'s ear,** flanquer une taloche à qn.

►clip on 1 *vtsep* attacher (*qch*). **2** *vi* s'attacher.

clipboard ['klɪpbɔːd] *n* planchette *f* porte-papiers.

clip-clop ['klɪpklɒp] *n* = le bruit que font les chevaux en se déplaçant.

clip-on ['klɪpɒn] *adj* qui s'attache avec une agrafe; **c.-on tie,** cravate *f* à système.

clipped [klɪpt] *adj* (*pronunciation*) écourté; **c. speech,** manière de parler saccadée.

clipper ['klɪpər] *n* **(a)** (*person*) tondeur, -euse; **(b)** *Nau Arch* clipper *m.*

clippers ['klɪpəz] *npl* (*for the hair etc*) tondeuse *f*; **hedge c.,** taille-buissons *m inv*; **nail c,** coupe-ongles *m inv.*

clippie ['klɪpɪ] *n Old-fashioned Br F* receveuse *f* (d'autobus).

clipping ['klɪpɪŋ] *n* **(a)** (*from newspaper*) coupure *f*; **(b) clippings,** (*from nail*) rognures *fpl*; (*from hair*) mèches *fpl* de cheveux coupés; (*from hedge*) bouts *mpl* de branches; **(c)** tondage *m* (*de chien etc*); **(d)** poinçonnage *m* (*de billets*).

clique [kliːk] *n* coterie *f*; *Pej* clique *f.*

cliqu(e)y ['kliːkɪ], **cliquish** ['kliːkɪʃ] *adj F* qui a l'esprit de clique.

clitoris ['klɪtərɪs] *n Anat* clitoris *m.*

cloak¹ [kləʊk] *n* manteau *m*; *Fig* **under the c. of night,** sous le couvert de la nuit; *Fig* **c.-and-dagger story,** roman *m* de cape et d'épée.

cloak² *vt Fig* couvrir, revêtir (*qn*) d'un manteau; masquer, voiler (*ses projets, ses pensées*).

cloakroom ['kləʊkruːm] *n* (*for coats etc*) vestiaire *m*; *Br* (*lavatory*) toilettes *fpl*; **ladies' c.,** dames; **c. attendant,** préposé, -ée au vestiaire; *Br* préposé, -ée aux cabinets de toilette.

clobber¹ ['klɒbər] *n Br F* **(a)** (*clothes*) frusques *fpl*, hardes *fpl*; **(b)** (*belongings*) effets *mpl*; **all my c.,** toutes mes affaires.

clobber² *vt Sl* (*hit*) frapper; (*beat up*) rosser (*qn*); (*rebuke*) tancer, étriller (*qn*); (*defeat heavily*) battre (*un adversaire*) à plate(s) couture(s).

clobbering ['klɒbərɪŋ] *n Sl* **to get a c.,** (*be beaten up*) prendre une dérouillée; (*be rebuked*) prendre un savon; (*be heavily defeated*) ramasser une pâtée.

cloche [klɒʃ, kləʊʃ] *n* (*in gardening and hat*) cloche *f.*

clock¹ [klɒk] *n* **(a)** horloge *f*; (*small*) pendule *f*; *F* **to watch the c.,** (*of employee*) avoir les yeux rivés sur l'horloge, ne penser qu'à l'heure de la sortie; **a full hour by the c.,** une bonne heure d'horloge; **to sleep the c. round,** faire le tour du cadran; **to work round the c.,** travailler vingt-quatre heures sur vingt-quatre; **a race against the c.,** une course contre la montre; **to beat the c.,** arriver *ou* finir avant l'heure; **to put** *or* **turn the c. back,** (*in spring time*) retarder la pendule; *Pej Fig* régresser; *Fig* **the measures will turn the c. back to Victorian times,** les mesures nous feront retourner à l'époque victorienne; *Fig* **you can't turn the c. back,** on ne peut pas revenir en arrière; **ship's c.,** horloge marine *ou* de bord; *Aut* **dashboard c.,** pendule de tableau de bord; **grandfather c.,** horloge de parquet; **travelling c.,** pendulette *f*; **eight-day c.,** huitaine *f*; **digital c.,** horloge digitale, horloge à affichage digital; *Tel* **speaking c.,** horloge parlante; **time c.,** (*in factory etc*) pendule de pointage;

(b) *Aut* (*speedometer*) compteur *m* de vitesse; (*milometer*) compteur *m*; (*in taxi*) compteur horokilométrique; **there were 15,000 miles on the clock,** il y avait 15 000 mil(l)es au compteur;

(c) *Comptr* horloge *f.*

clock² *vt F* **(a)** (*time*) chronométrer (*un coureur etc*); **(b)** (*reach*) faire (*une certaine vitesse*); *Aut* **to c. ninety,** taper le 145; **(c)** *Br Sl* (*see*) repérer (*qn*).

►clock in 1 *vi* (*have a time of*) faire un temps; **for the hundred metres she clocked in at nine seconds,** elle a fait neuf secondes sur le 100 mètres; **the last of the marathon runners clocked in at six hours,** le dernier marathonien a effectué le parcours en six heures; **(b)** *Ind* (*record arrival at work*) pointer à l'arrivée; **you clocked in 10 minutes late,** vous avez pointé avec 10 minutes de retard. **2** *vtsep Ind* pointer pour (*qn*).

►clock off 1 *vi Ind* (*record departure from work*) pointer à la sortie. **2** *vtsep* pointer pour (*qn*).

►clock on = **CLOCK IN 1(b), 2.**

►clock out = **CLOCK OFF 1, 2.**

►clock up *vtsep* (*achieve*) atteindre, parvenir à (*un total*); **she has clocked up 700 kilometres in two days,** elle a fait 700 kilomètres en deux jours.

clocking ['klɒkɪŋ] *n Sp* chronométrage *m.*

clocking in *n Ind* pointage *m* à l'arrivée.

clocking off *n Ind* pointage *m* à la sortie.

clocking on *n Ind* = **CLOCKING IN.**

clocking out *n Ind* = **CLOCKING OFF.**

clocklike ['klɒklaɪk] *adj* (*d'une régularité*) d'horloge.

clockmaker ['klɒkmeɪkər] *n* horloger *m.*

clock-watcher ['klɒkwɒtʃər] *n F* employé, -ée qui ne pense qu'à l'heure de sortie.

clockwise ['klɒkwaɪz] *adv & adj* dans le sens des aiguilles d'une montre.

clockwork ['klɒkwɜːk] *n* rouage *m* d'horloge; (*in toy etc*) mécanisme *m* à ressort; **c. train,** (*toy*) chemin *m* de fer mécanique; **as regular as c.,** réglé comme du papier à musique; **everything is done with c. precision,** tout est réglé comme du papier à musique; **everything's going like c.,** tout va *ou* marche comme sur des roulettes.

clod [klɒd] *n* **(a)** (*of earth*) motte *f*; **c. breaker** *or* **crusher,** (*rouleau m*) brise-mottes *m inv*; *Old-fashioned F* **c. crushers,** godasses *fpl*; **(b)** *F* (*stupid, clumsy person*) rustre *m*, lourdaud *m*; **you great c.!,** espèce de lourdaud!

clodhopper ['klɒdhɒpər] *n F* **(a)** (*person*) rustre *m*, lourdaud *m*; **(b) clodhoppers,** (*shoes*) godasses *fpl.*

clog¹ [klɒg] *n* **(a)** (*shoe*) gros brodequin à semelle de bois; **(wooden) c.,** sabot *m*; *F* **to pop one's clogs,** (*die*) casser sa pipe; **c. dance,** sabotière *f*; **(b)** (*for preventing movement*) entrave *f* (*pour cheval*); billot *m* (*pour vache*); *Fig* embarras *m*, entrave.

clog² *v* (-gg-) **1** *vt* **(a)** (*block*) boucher, obstruer (*une artère, un tuyau etc*); encrasser (*une arme à feu, une machine*); colmater (*un filtre*); **our boots got clogged with mud,** nos bottes se sont crottées dans la boue; **(b)** (*prevent from moving*) entraver (*un animal*); *Fig* entraver, gêner (*une entreprise etc*). **2** *vi* se boucher, s'obstruer, s'encrasser; (*of filter*) se colmater.

►clog up *vtsep* = **CLOG² 1(a), 2.**

clogging ['klɒgɪŋ] *n* (*of pipe etc*) obstruction *f*; (*of firearm*) encrassement *m*; colmatage *m* (*d'un filtre*); empâtement *m* (*d'une lime etc*).

cloister¹ ['klɔɪstər] *n* **(a)** *Archit* (*usu pl*) **cloisters,** cloître *m* (*d'un couvent, d'une église etc*); **(b)** *Rel* monastère *m.*

cloister² *vt* cloîtrer.

cloistered ['klɔɪstəd] *adj* **(a)** (*life*) de cloître, cloîtré; **(b)** *Archit* entouré d'un cloître.

clone¹ [kləʊn] *n Bot Biol Comptr etc* clone *m.*

clone² *vt Bot Biol* cloner.

close¹ [kləʊs] **1** *adj* **(a)** (*in distance*) rapproché; **the two islands are very c.,** les deux îles sont très rapprochées; **we must be c. now,** nous devons être près maintenant; **our office is c. to the town hall,** notre bureau est près de la mairie; **was I c.?,** (*of person guessing*) je brûlais?; **to be c. to tears,** être au bord des larmes; **c. intervals,** intervalles rapprochés; **c. proximity,** proximité immédiate; **I saw him at c. quarters,** je l'ai vu de près; **in c. quarters,** à l'étroit; **c. combat,** *Mil* (combat *m*) corps à corps *m*; *Nau* combat bord à bord; **c. range,** courte portée; **to fire at c. range,** tirer à bout portant; *Mus* **c. harmony,** tessiture limitée;

(b) (*in relationship*) proche; **to be c. to s.o.,** être proche de qn; **he and his brother/the two brothers are very c.,** lui et son frère/les deux frères sont très proches; **Italian is c. to French,** l'italien est proche du français; **c. relative,** un parent proche; **c. friend,** ami intime; **to be in c. contact,** être en contact étroit;

(c) (*tight*) ajusté, serré; (*clothes*) ajusté, près du corps; *Tech* **c. fit,** montage *ou* ajustage serré;

(d) (*careful*) minutieux, attentif; (*attention*) soutenu; (*observateur*) attentif; (*étude*) minutieux; **on closer examination,** en y regardant de plus près; **after c. consideration,** après mûre considération; **to keep (a) c. watch on s.o./sth,** surveiller qn/qch de près;

(e) (*blockade, imprisonment*) rigoureux;

(f) (*copy, resemblance*) exacte; **c. translation,** traduction exacte *ou* fidèle *ou* serrée;

(g) *Ling* **c. vowel,** voyelle fermée *ou* entravée;

(h) (*air*) enfermé; (*smell*) de renfermé; (*weather*) lourd; (*secret, silence*) impénétrable;

(i) (*dense*) serré, dense; (*thicket, woods*) épais, touffu; **c. grain,** (*of metal, stone, wood etc*) grain serré; **c. texture,** (*of metal, stone etc*) (con)texture serrée, tissu serré; **in c. order,** *Mil* en rangs serrés; *Nau* à distance serrée; **in c. ranks,** en rangs serrés;

(j) (*contest*) à forces égales; **c. election,** élection vivement contestée; **c. match,** match serré; *Sp* **c. finish,** arrivée serrée; **a c. shave,** un rasage de près; *Fig* **that was a close shave** *or* **thing** *or* **call,** nous l'avons échappé belle, il était moins cinq;

(k) (*reserved, secretive*) peu communicatif, réservé; **to keep sth c.,** ne rien dire de qch; **to play a c. game,** jouer serré;

(l) (*mean*) ladre, *F* pingre;

(m) (*in hunting*) **c. season,** période *f* d'interdiction, chasse fermée.

2 *adv* **(a)** (*near*) près, de près, auprès; **to be** *or* **follow c. behind s.o.,** suivre qn de près; **to stand c. against a wall,** se coller contre un mur; **houses c. together,** maisons serrées les unes contre les autres; **to sit/stand c. together,** être/se tenir serrés *ou* coude à coude; **sit closer (together)!,** serrez-vous!; **to keep c.,** rester tout-près; **c. to** *or* **by s.o./sth,** (tout) près de *ou* à proximité de qn/qch; **he lives c. to here,** il demeure tout près *ou* à deux pas (d'ici); **to come** *or* **draw c./closer to s.o.,** s'approcher/se rapprocher de qn; **put it closer to the door,** mets le plus près de la porte; **to keep c. to s.o.,** se tenir tout près de qn; **ship c. to the shore,** navire près de terre; **c. to the ground,** au ras du sol; **to cut c.,** couper (*les cheveux etc*) ras; **to keep c. to the text,** serrer le texte de près; **she came c. to losing her job,** elle a failli perdre son emploi; **to come c. to death,** frôler la mort (de près); **to come c. to the world record,** frôler le record du monde; **c. at hand, c. by,** tout près, tout contre; *Nau* **to stand c. in (to the land),** serrer la terre; **c. on nine (o'clock),** tout près de neuf heures; **to be c. on fifty,** friser la cinquantaine;

(b) **c. shut,** bien fermé; (*blocked*) bouché.

close² *n* **(a)** *Br* (*street*) impasse *f*, cul-de-sac *m*, *pl* culs-de-sac; **(b)** (*of cathedral*) enceinte *f*; **(c)** *Br* (*field*) clos *m*, enclos *m*.

close³ [kləʊz] *n* fin *f*, conclusion *f*, terminaison *f* (*d'une action, d'un discours etc*); fin, bout *m* (*de l'année*); clôture *f*, levée *f* (*d'une séance*); fin (*du jour*); **at c. of business,** à la fin de la journée (de travail); *Cr* **at c. of play,** à la fin de la journée; *Lit* **at c. of day,** à la chute du jour; **the year is drawing to a c.,** l'année tire à sa fin.

close⁴ **1** *vt* **(a)** (*shut, block*) fermer (*une porte, les yeux, un livre etc*); fermer, replier (*un parapluie*); barrer (*une rue*); *Nau* bâcler (*un port*); *Rail* bloquer (*une section*); **road closed to motor traffic,** route interdite à la circulation automobile; **cold closes the pores,** le froid resserre les pores; **to c. the books,** (*in book-keeping*) régler les livres;

(b) (*bring to an end*) conclure, terminer (*une série, une affaire etc*); conclure (*une vente*); lever, clore (*une séance*); arrêter (*un marché*); fermer (*un débat*); fermer, clôturer (*un compte*); *St Exch* liquider (*une opération*); *Jur* clôturer (*une faillite*); **to declare the discussion closed,** prononcer la clôture des débats;

(c) **to c. (the) ranks,** serrer les rangs.

2 *vi* **(a)** (*of door etc*) (se) fermer; (*of wound, hole etc*) se refermer; **the theatre will c. for a month,** le théâtre fermera ses portes pendant un mois; **theatres c. on Good Friday,** les théâtres font relâche le vendredi saint;

(b) (*end*) finir, se terminer; *St Exch* **the shares closed at 1,** les actions ont terminé à 1; **I will c. with a story,** pour terminer je vais vous raconter une histoire.

►**close down 1** *vtsep* fermer (*une usine etc*). **2** *vi* **(a)** (*of factory etc*) fermer, cesser la production, chômer; (*of shop*) fermer boutique; **(b)** *Rad TV* terminer l'émission.

►**close in 1** *vi* **(a)** (*approach*) **night is closing in,** la nuit tombe; **(b)** (*get shorter*) **the days are closing in,** les jours (se) raccourcissent. **2** *vtsep* (*enclose*) clôturer (*un terrain etc*); entourer (*un édifice etc*) d'une clôture.

►**close in on** *vipo* cerner (*qn*) de près; **darkness closed in on us,** la nuit nous enveloppa.

►**close round** *vipo* cerner, se presser autour de (*qn*).

►**close up 1** *vi* **(a)** (*of aperture*) s'obturer; (*of wound, hole etc*) se refermer; **(b)** (*of people*) se serrer, se tasser; *Mil etc* **c. up!,** serrez (les rangs)!; **(c)** (*of shopkeeper*) fermer. **2** *vtsep* **(a)** (*seal*) boucher, obturer (*une ouverture etc*); **(b)** faire la fermeture de (*un magasin*); **the house is all closed up,** tout est fermé; **(b)** *Typ* rapprocher (*les caractères*); *Mil etc* serrer (*les rangs*).

►**close with** *vipo* **to c. with s.o.,** (*conclude a deal*) conclure le marché avec qn; (*in fighting*) en venir aux mains avec qn.

close-cropped ['kləʊs'krɒpt] *adj* (*hair*) coupé ras; (*grass*) rasé *ou* tondu de près.

closed [kləʊzd] *adj* **(a)** (*door etc*) fermé; *El* (*circuit*) fermé; (*pipe etc*) obturé, bouché; **behind c. doors,** dans le privé; **with eyes c.,** les yeux fermés; **road c.,** rue barrée; **c.,** (*notice*) *Th* relâche; (*on shop*) fermé; **c. season,** (*in hunting*) période *f* d'interdiction, chasse fermée; **c. professions,** professions fermées; *Ind* **c. shop,** atelier *m ou* chantier *m etc* qui n'admet pas de travailleurs non syndiqués; **c.-shop policy,** exclusivité syndicale; **c.-circuit television,** télévision *f* à circuit fermé.

close-down ['kləʊzdaʊn] *n* **(a)** (*of factory etc*) fermeture *f*, clôture *f*; **(b)** *TV Rad* fin *f* d'émission.

close-fisted [kləʊs'fɪstɪd] *adj* avare, pingre.

close-fitting [kləʊs'fɪtɪŋ] *adj* (*vêtement*) ajusté, collant.

close-knit [kləʊs'nɪt] *adj* (*community etc*) lié *ou* joint étroitement.

close-lipped [kləʊs'lɪpt] *adj* **to be c.-l. about sth,** être énigmatique quant à qch.

closely ['kləʊslɪ] *adv* **(a)** (*ressembler*) exactement; (*examiner*) de près, attentivement; (*suivi, observé, traduit*) de près; (*connected, guarded, related*) étroitement; **you are the most c. concerned,** c'est vous le premier intéressé; **c. cut,** tondu ras; **c. contested,** vivement contesté; **to watch s.o. c.,** surveiller qn de près; **to listen c.,** écouter attentivement; **(b)** (*densely*) l'un près de l'autre; **c. packed in a box,** serré dans une boîte; **two c. written pages,** deux pages d'une écriture serrée; **(c)** **c. shut,** bien fermé; (*blocked*) bien bouché.

close-mouthed [kləʊs'maʊθd] *adj* = **CLOSE-LIPPED**.

closeness ['kləʊsnɪs] *n* **(a)** (*nearness*) rapprochement *m*, proximité *f* (**to,** de); **(b)** (*of relationship, contact etc*) intimité *f* (**to s.o.,** avec qn); **(c)** (*of description*) exactitude *f*; (*of translation*) fidélité *f*, exactitude; **(d)** (*stuffiness*) manque *m* d'air; **(e)** (*of weather*) lourdeur *f*; **(f)** (*reserve, secretiveness*) réserve *f*, caractère réservé (*de qn*); **(g)** avarice *f*, pingrerie *f*.

close-range ['kləʊsreɪndʒ] *adj Mil* **c.-r. weapon,** arme *f* à courte portée.

close-run ['kləʊsrʌn] *adj* (*election, race*) serré; **it was a c.-r. thing,** on a joué très serré.

close-set ['kləʊs'set] *adj* (*eyes etc*) rapproché.

close-shaven ['kləʊs'ʃeɪv(ə)n] *adj* rasé de près.

closet¹ ['klɒzɪt] **1** *n* **(a)** *esp Am* placard *m*, armoire *f*; *F* **to come out of the c.,** (*of homosexual*) se déclarer *ou* se révéler homosexuel; **(b)** (*room*) cabinet *m*, bureau *m*; **(c)** *Arch* **(water) c.,** les cabinets *mpl*. **2** *adj Am* **(a)** (*secret*) confidentiel; **c. discussions,** discussions confidentielles; **(b)** (*private*) privé, personnel; **c. thoughts,** des pensées personnelles.

closet² *vt* **(-t-)** **to be closeted with s.o.,** être en tête-à-tête avec qn.

close-up ['kləʊsʌp] *n Cin TV* plan rapproché, gros plan; *TV* plan serré; **in c.-up,** en plan serré, en gros plan; **c.-up detail,** détail vu de près; *Fig* **the programme gives us a c.-up of life in prison,** l'émission nous fait entrer de plain-pied dans la vie carcérale.

closing ['kləʊzɪŋ] **1** *adj* **(a)** (*final*) dernier, final, -als; **c. date,** date *f* limite; **the c. date for applications is ...,** le registre d'inscriptions sera clos le ...; **the c. bid,** la dernière enchère; **c. speech,** discours de fin de séance; **c. prices,** derniers cours; **(b)** qui (se) ferme. **2** *n* **(a)** (*shutting, blocking*) fermeture *f* (*des magasins, d'une usine etc*); clôture *f* (*d'un théâtre etc*); barrage *m* (*d'une rue*); cicatrisation *f* (*d'une blessure*); **c. time,** heure *f* de fermeture; *Br Com* **early c. day,** = jour où les magasins sont fermés l'après-midi; **(b)** (*ending*) clôture *f* (*d'un compte etc*); levée *f* (*d'une séance*); arrêté *m*, règlement *m* (*d'un compte*).

closing down *n* (*of factory*) fermeture *f*.

closure ['kləʊʒər] *n* **(a)** (*of factory etc*) fermeture *f*; **(b)** clôture *f*, fermeture *f* (*d'une séance etc*); *Parl* clôture; **to**

move the c., voter la clôture.

clot¹ [klɒt] *n* **(a)** (*of blood*) caillot *m*; **(b)** *Br F* (*stupid person*) idiot, -ote, imbécile *mf*.

clot² *v* **(-tt-) 1** *vi* (*of blood*) se figer, se coaguler. **2** *vt* caillebotter (*la crème*); figer (*le sang*).

cloth, *pl* **cloths** [klɒθ, klɒθs] *n* **(a)** (*material*) étoffe *f*; (*linen, cotton*) toile *f*; **c. maker** *or* **manufacturer,** fabricant *m* de draps; **c. binding,** reliure *f* en toile; **American c.,** molesquine *f*, moleskine *f*; **c. of gold,** drap *m* d'or; *Br* **c. cap,** casquette *f*; **(b)** (*individual piece*) linge *m*; (*for cleaning*) chiffon *m*; (*tablecloth*) nappe *f*; (*on billiard table*) tapis *m*; *Th* toile *f* (de décor); **(floor) c.,** serpillière *f*; **to clean, simply wipe with a wet c.,** pour nettoyer, passer un chiffon humide; **(c)** *F* **the c.,** (*costume*) l'habit *m* ecclésiastique, la soutane; (*the clergy*) le clergé; **a man of the c.,** un membre du clergé.

cloth-bound ['klɒθbaʊnd] *adj* relié toile.

clothe [kləʊð] *vt* (*pt & pp* **clad** [klæd] *or* **clothed** [kləʊðd]) vêtir, habiller (*qn*) (**in, with,** de); **three children to feed and c.,** trois enfants à nourrir et à habiller; **warmly/lightly clad,** chaudement/légèrement vêtu.

cloth-eared ['klɒθɪəd] *adj F* (*deaf*) sourd.

clothes [kləʊðz] *npl* vêtements *mpl*, habits *mpl*; **old c.,** vieux habits; **in one's best c.,** endimanché; **to put on/take off one's c.,** s'habiller/se déshabiller; **to go to bed with one's c. on** *or* **in one's c.,** se coucher tout habillé; **with no c. on,** nu; **dirty c.,** linge sale; **(dirty) c. basket,** panier *m* à linge; **c. brush,** brosse *f* à habits; **c. hook,** patère *f* à habits; **c. peg,** pince *f* à linge; **c. prop** *or* **pole,** perche *f* de corde à linge.

clotheshorse ['kləʊðzhɔːs] *n* séchoir *m* (à linge); *esp Am Fig* **she's a c.,** à part les nippes, rien ne l'intéresse.

clothesline ['kləʊðzlaɪn] *n* corde *f* à linge.

clothespin ['kləʊðzpɪn] *n Am* pince *f* à linge.

clothier ['kləʊðɪər] *n Com* **(a)** (*clothes seller*) marchand, -ande de confections; (*cloth seller*) marchand de draps; **(b)** (*clothmaker*) fabricant, -ante de draps.

clothing ['kləʊðɪŋ] *n* (*no pl*) **(a)** (*clothes*) habillement *m*, vêtements *mpl*; **dirty c.,** linge *m* sale; **take plenty of warm c.,** prends beaucoup de vêtements chauds; **articles of c.,** vêtements; **the c. trade,** l'industrie du vêtement; **(b)** **c. a family of six ...,** habiller une famille de six personnes ... .

clotted ['klɒtɪd] *adj* (*sang*) coagulé; **c. cream,** crème caillée *ou* caillebottée (*par l'échaudage*).

clotting ['klɒtɪŋ] *n* (*of cream*) caillement *m*; coagulation *f* (*du sang etc*).

cloud¹ [klaʊd] *n* **(a)** *Met* nuage *m*; *Lit* nuée *f*, nue *f*; **there wasn't a c. in sight,** il n'y avait pas un nuage en vue; *Fig* **to have one's head in the clouds,** être dans les nuages *ou* dans la lune; *F* **to be on c. nine,** être aux anges; *Prov* **every c. has a silver lining,** dans toute chose il y a un bon côté; *Fig* **to be under a c.,** (*suspected*) être l'objet de soupçons; (*out of favour*) être en défaveur; **he left the firm under a c.,** il a quitté la société dans une atmosphère de scandale étouffé; **c. bank,** banc *m* de nuages; **rain c.,** nuage de pluie; **(b)** (*of smoke, dust*) nuage *m*, voile *m*; (*of dust*) tourbillon *m*; *Nucl* **c. chamber,** chambre *f* de détente *ou* d'ionisation; **(c)** (*in liquid*) nuage *m*, turbidité *f*; (*in precious stone*) nuée *f*; **(d)** (*swarm*) nuée *f* (*de sauterelles etc*).

cloud² 1 *vt* couvrir, voiler (*le ciel*); troubler, rendre trouble (*un liquide*); ternir (*un miroir*); troubler (*le bonheur de qn*); ternir (*la réputation de qn*); **eyes clouded with tears,** yeux voilés de larmes; **to c. the issue,** embrouiller la question. **2** *vi* (*of sky*) se couvrir *ou* se voiler de nuages.

►cloud over *vi* (*of sky*) se couvrir *ou* se voiler de nuages; **it clouded over in the afternoon,** ça s'est couvert dans l'après-midi.

►cloud up 1 *vi* (*of sky*) se couvrir; **it's clouding up,** ça se couvre; **the mirror had clouded up,** le miroir s'était couvert de buée. **2** *vtsep* embuer (*les fenêtres*).

cloudburst ['klaʊdbɜːst] *n* trombe *f* d'eau, rafale *f* de pluie.

cloud-cuckoo-land ['klaʊd'kʊkuːlænd] *n* **you're living in c.-c.-l. if you think ...,** tu rêves en couleurs si tu penses que ...; **that's c.-c.-l.,** c'est de la fantaisie.

clouded ['klaʊdɪd] *adj* (*ciel*) couvert (de nuages); (*liquide*) trouble; **to become c.,** (*of sky*) se couvrir; (*of mind*) s'obscurcir.

cloudiness ['klaʊdɪnɪs] *n* **(a)** (*of sky*) aspect nuageux; **(b)** (*of liquid*) turbidité *f*.

cloudless ['klaʊdlɪs] *adj* (*ciel*) sans nuages.

cloudy ['klaʊdɪ] *adj* **(a)** (*weather*) couvert; (*sky*) nuageux; **it's c.,** le temps est couvert; **a c. day,** un jour nuageux; **(b)** (*liquid*) trouble; (*wine*) louche; *Med* (*urine*) chargé.

clout¹ [klaʊt] *n* **(a)** *F* **to have (plenty of) c.,** (*be powerful*) être puissant; (*be influential*) avoir de l'influence *ou* du piston; **(b)** *F* (*blow*) taloche *f*, calotte *f*; **(c)** *Br Arch* (*cloth*) chiffon *m*.

clout² *vt F* **to c. s.o. on** *or* **over the head,** flanquer une taloche à qn, talocher qn.

clove¹ [kləʊv] *n Bot Culin* **c. of garlic,** gousse *f* d'ail.

clove² *n* **(a)** *Bot Culin* clou *m* de girofle; **oil of cloves,** essence *f* de girofle; **c. tree,** giroflier *m*; **(b)** (*flower*) **c. pink,** œillet-giroflée *m*, *pl* œillets-giroflées, œillet *m* des fleuristes.

clove³ *see* **CLEAVE.**

clove⁴ *n Nau* **c. hitch,** demi-clef *f*, *pl* demi-clefs.

cloven ['kləʊv(ə)n] *adj* **c. foot** *or* **hoof,** pied fourchu (*d'un ruminant, du diable*).

cloven-footed, -hoofed ['kləʊv(ə)n'fʊtɪd,'-huːft] *adj Zool* au pied fourchu.

clover ['kləʊvər] *n* (*plant*) trèfle *m*; **c. leaf,** feuille *f* de trèfle; **four-leaved c.,** trèfle à quatre feuilles; *F* **to be** *or* **live in c.,** vivre comme un coq en pâte.

cloverleaf, -leafs, -leaves ['kləʊvəliːf, -liːfs, -liːvz] *n Constr* **c. (intersection),** croisement *m* *ou* carrefour *m* en trèfle (à quatre feuilles).

clown¹ [klaʊn] *n* clown *m* (*de cirque*); *Th & Fig* bouffon *m*, pitre *m*.

clown² *vi* faire le clown *ou* le pitre.

clowning ['klaʊnɪŋ] *n Th & Fig* bouffonnerie *f*, pitrerie *f*; clownerie *f* (*de cirque*).

cloy [klɔɪ] *vt* (*of food etc*) rassasier, écœurer; *Lit* **delights that never c.,** plaisirs dont on ne se lasse pas.

cloying ['klɔɪɪŋ] *adj* rassasiant; (*sentiment*) écœurant.

club¹ [klʌb] *n* **(a)** (*association*) association *f*, société *f*; (*political, literary etc*) club *m*; **I've got a cold — join the c.!,** j'ai un rhume - on est deux!; *F* **to be in the c.,** (*of woman*) avoir un polichinelle dans le tiroir; **c. chair,** (fauteuil *m*) club; **literary c.,** cercle *m* littéraire; **gambling c.,** cercle de jeu; **fan c.,** fan club *m*; **youth c.,** foyer *m* des jeunes; (*associated with church*) patronage *m*; **football/tennis/yacht c.,** club de football/tennis/yachting; **book c.,** club du livre; *Culin esp Am* **c. sandwich,** sandwich *m* club; **c. tie,** cravate *f* aux couleurs d'une association sportive; **(b)** (*nightclub*) boîte *f* (de nuit); **the London c. scene,** les milieux nocturnes londoniens; **(c)** (*weapon etc*) massue *f*, gourdin *m*; *Golf* club *m*, crosse *f*; *Gym* **Indian c.,** bouteille *f* en bois; *Med* **c. foot,** pied bot; **(d)** *Cards* trèfle *m*; **ace of clubs,** as *m* de trèfle.

club² *vt* **(-bb-)** (*hit*) frapper (*qn*) avec une massue *ou* avec un gourdin; **to c. s.o. to death,** tuer qn à coups de gourdin.

►club together *vi* se cotiser, mettre son argent en commun; **to c. together to do sth,** se cotiser pour faire qch.

clubber [klʌbər] *n F* fêtard *m*, adepte *mf* de boîte de nuit.

clubbing ['klʌbɪŋ] *n F* **to go clubbing,** aller en boîte.

clubfooted ['klʌbfʊtɪd] *adj Med* qui a le pied bot.

clubhouse ['klʌbhaʊs] *n* club *m*; *Golf Tennis etc* pavillon *m*.

clubroom ['klʌbruːm] *n* salle *f* de réunion (*d'un cercle etc*).

cluck¹ [klʌk] *n* (*of hens*) gloussement *m*.

cluck² *vi* (*of hen*) glousser; *F* (*of person*) faire claquer sa langue.

clucking ['klʌkɪŋ] *n* gloussement *m*.

clue [kluː] *n* **(a)** indication *f*; (*to crime*) indice *m*; **to get** *or* **find the c. to sth,** trouver *ou* découvrir la clef de qch; **her hat provides a c. to her profession,** on devine sa profession à son chapeau; **to give s.o. a c.,** mettre qn sur la voie *ou* sur la piste; *F* **I haven't got a c.,** je n'en sais rien, je n'en ai pas la moindre idée; *F* **he hasn't got a c. what he's doing,** il fait n'importe quoi; **(b)** (*in crossword*) définition *f*; **what's the c. to 13 down?,** quelle est la définition du 13 vertical?

►clue in *vtsep F* (*inform*) renseigner (*qn*), mettre (*qn*) à la page.

►clue up *vtsep F usu passive* **I'm not very clued up on astrophysics,** je ne suis pas très calé en astrophysique.

clueless ['kluːlɪs] *adj F* **he's quite c.,** il ne sait rien de rien.

clump¹ [klʌmp] *n* **(a)** (*cluster*) groupe *m*, bouquet *m* (*d'arbres*); massif *m* (*d'arbustes, de fleurs*); touffe *f* (*de fleurs*); **(b)** (*lump*) bloc *m*, masse *f* (*de bois, d'argile etc*); **(c)** (*sound*) (bruit *m* de) pas lourd.

clump² 1 *vi* **(a)** (*group*) se grouper en masse compacte; **(b)** (*of person*) **to c. (about),** marcher lourdement. **2** *vt* grouper en masse compacte; planter (*des arbustes etc*) en massif.

clumsily ['klʌmzɪlɪ] *adv* **(a)** (*to move*) maladroitement, gauchement; **(b)** (*drawn*) grossièrement; **c. built,** mal bâti; **(c)** (*to break bad news etc*) gauchement, sans tact.

clumsiness ['klʌmzɪnɪs] *n* **(a)** maladresse *f*, gaucherie *f*; **(b)** (*of shape*) grossièreté *f*, lourdeur *f*; (*of sentence*) lourdeur, maladresse *f*; **(c)** (*in relationship*) manque *m* de tact.

clumsy ['klʌmzɪ] *adj* **(a)** (*person, movement etc*) maladroit, gauche; **c. boots,** godillots *mpl*; **(b)** (*shape*) lourd, disgracieux; (*phrase, excuse*) maladroit, gauche; **c. verse,** vers mal faits; **c. forgery,** contre-façon grossière.

clung *see* **CLING**[1].

cluster[1] ['klʌstər] *n* bouquet *m* (*de fleurs, de cerises*); grappe *f* (*de raisins, de cerises*); épi *m*, nœud *m* (*de diamants*); amas *m* (*d'étoiles*); peloton *m* (*d'abeilles etc*); groupe *m*, rassemblement *m* (*de personnes*); agglomération *f* (*d'îles*); pâté *m* (*de maisons*); faisceau *m* (*d'ampoules électriques*); *Mil* **c. bomb,** bombe *f* à fragmentation.

cluster[2] **1** *vt* grouper (en grappes); rassembler (*des objets*) en groupes. **2** *vi* (*of fruit*) se former *ou* croître en grappes; **to c. round s.o./sth,** (*of people*) se grouper *ou* se rassembler autour de qn/qch; **to c. together,** (*of particles etc*) se conglomérer.

clutch[1] [klʌtʃ] *n* **(a)** *Aut etc* embrayage *m*; **to let in the c.,** embrayer; **to release** *or* **let out the c.,** débrayer; **automatic c.,** embrayage automatique, autodébrayage *m*; **disc/plate c.,** embrayage à disque/à plateau; **c. disc/plate,** disque *m*/plateau *m* d'embrayage; **c. pedal,** pédale *f* d'embrayage *ou* de débrayage; **(b)** (*action*) action *f* de saisir; **to make a c. at sth,** essayer de saisir qch; **c. bag,** *Am* **c. purse,** pochette *f*; **(c)** griffe *f* (*d'un animal*); serre *f* (*d'un oiseau de proie*); **to fall into s.o.'s clutches,** tomber sous la patte de qn; **to escape from s.o.'s clutches,** se tirer des pattes de qn.

clutch[2] **1** *vt* saisir, étreindre; **to c. sth with both hands,** saisir qch à deux mains; **to c. hold of sth,** s'agripper *ou* se cramponner à qch. **2** *vi* **to c. at sth,** s'agripper *ou* se cramponner à qch.

clutch[3] *n* couvée *f* (*d'œufs, de poussins*).

clutter[1] ['klʌtər] *n* encombrement *m*, confusion *f*; entassement *m* (*de mobilier etc*); **everything's in a c.,** tout est en désordre *ou* en pagaille.

clutter[2] *vt* encombrer (*une pièce, un bureau*) (**with,** de); **to c. one's mind with useless facts,** charger sa mémoire de faits inutiles.

►**clutter up** *vtsep* = **CLUTTER**[2].

cluttered ['clʌtəd] *adj* encombré (**with,** de).

cm (*abbr* **centimetre**) cm..

CND [siːen'diː] *n Br* (*abbr* **Campaign for Nuclear Disarmament**) = campagne pour le désarmement nucléaire.

c/o (*abbr* **care of**) a.b.s..

Co, co [kəʊ] *n Com* (*abbr* **company**) Cie; *Fig* **Jane and co,** Jane et compagnie.

CO [siː'əʊ] *n Mil abbr* **Commanding Officer**.

coach[1] [kəʊtʃ] *n* **(a)** *Br* (*motor vehicle*) car *m*; **c. station,** gare routière; *Am Av* **c. class,** seconde classe, classe économie; **c. fare,** tarif *m* économie *ou* de seconde classe; **(b)** *Rail* voiture *f*, wagon *m*; **(c)** (*trainer*) *Sch* répétiteur *m*; *Sp* entraîneur *m*; **(d)** (*horse-drawn*) carrosse *m*; *Arch* **stage c.,** diligence *m*; **c. and four,** carrosse à quatre chevaux; **c. house,** remise *f*.

coach[2] **1** *vt Sch* donner des leçons particulières à (*qn*); *Sp* entraîner (*une équipe*); **the police coached the witness,** la police a préparé le témoin à la déclaration; **to c. s.o. in French,** donner des leçons particulières en français à qn; *Th* **to c. s.o. for a part,** faire répéter son rôle à qn. **2** *vi Sch* donner des leçons particulières.

coachbuilder ['kəʊtʃbɪldər] *n Aut etc* carrossier *m*.

coaching ['kəʊtʃɪŋ] *n* **(a)** *Sch* leçons particulières, répétitions *fpl*; *Sp* entraînement *m*; **(b)** *Arch* **c. inn,** relais *m*.

coachman, *pl* **-men** [kəʊtʃmən] *n* cocher *m*.

coachwork ['kəʊtʃwɜːk] *n Aut* carrosserie *f*.

coagulant [kəʊ'ægjʊlənt] *n* coagulant *m*.

coagulate [kəʊ'ægjʊleɪt] **1** *vt* coaguler. **2** *vi* se coaguler.

coagulation [kəʊægjʊ'leɪʃən] *n* coagulation *f*.

coal[1] [kəʊl] *n* charbon *m*; **the c. (mining) industry,** l'industrie houillère; *Fig* **to carry coals to Newcastle,** porter de l'eau à la rivière; *Fig* **to haul s.o. over the coals,** réprimander qn vertement, laver la tête à qn; **smokeless c.,** charbon sans fumée; **coking c.,** charbon à coke; **live coals,** braise *f*, charbon ardent; **c. basin,** bassin houiller; **c. bunker,** coffre *m* à charbon; **c. cellar,** cave *f* au charbon; *Min* **c. cutter,** (*person*) haveur *m*; (*machine*) haveuse *f*; **c. gas,** gaz *m* de houille; **c. merchant,** négociant *m* en charbon, marchand *m* de charbon; **c. mine,** mine *f* de charbon, houillère *f*; **c. miner,** mineur *m*, houilleur *m*; **c. mining,** exploitation *f* du charbon *ou* de la houille; **c. scuttle,** seau *m* à charbon, charbonnière *f*; **c. shovel,** pelle *f* à charbon; **c. strike,** grève *f* des mineurs; **c. tar,** goudron *m* de houille.

coal[2] **1** *vt* **(a)** (*supply with coal*) approvisionner (*un navire*) de charbon; **to c. ship,** charbonner; **(b)** (*convert to coal*) charbonner (*du bois*). **2** *vi Nau* charbonner.

coal-black ['kəʊl'blæk] *adj* noir comme du charbon.

coalesce [kəʊə'les] *vi* s'unir, se fondre (ensemble); *Ch* se combiner; (*of parties etc*) fusionner.

coalescence [kəʊə'lesəns] *n* coalescence *f*, union *f*, fusion *f*; *Ch* combinaison *f*.

coalface ['kəʊlfeɪs] *n Min* front *m* de taille.

coalfield ['kəʊlfiːld] *n Min* bassin houiller.

coal-fired [kəʊl'faɪəd] *adj Ind* alimenté au charbon.

coalition [kəʊə'lɪʃən] *n* coalition *f*; *Pol* **to form a c.,** se coaliser; **a c. government,** une coalition gouvernementale.

coalman, *pl* **-men** ['kəʊlmæn, -men] *n* (petit) marchand *m* de charbon, charbonnier *m*.

coalshed ['kəʊlʃed] *n* hangar *m* à charbon.

coal-tar ['kəʊl'tɑːr] *n* **c.-t. soap,** savon *m* au coaltar.

coaltit ['kəʊltɪt] *n* (*bird*) mésange noire.

coarse [kɔːs] *adj* **(a)** (*vulgar*) grossier, vulgaire; (*language*) grossier; **c. joke,** plaisanterie grossière; **(b)** (*material*) gros, grossier, rude; **c. features,** traits grossiers *ou* lourds; **c. hair,** cheveux raides et épais; **c. salt,** gros sel; **c. sandpaper,** papier de verre épais; **c. cut,** haché; (*tabac*) de grosse coupe; **the c. weave of the material,** le tissage lâche du tissu; **(c) c. fish,** poissons d'eau douce (*sauf truites et saumons*).

coarsely ['kɔːslɪ] *adv* **(a)** (*vulgarly*) grossièrement, vulgairement; **(b)** (*ground*) grossièrement; (*chopped etc*) gros.

coarsen ['kɔːs(ə)n] **1** *vt* rendre plus grossier *ou* plus rude. **2** *vi* devenir plus grossier.

coarseness ['kɔːsnɪs] *n* **(a)** (*vulgarity*) grossièreté *f*, brutalité *f*; grossièreté (*d'une plaisanterie etc*); **(b)** (*roughness*) rudesse *f* (*de la peau, des cheveux*); grosseur *f* de fil (*d'une étoffe*); gros grain (*du bois*).

coast[1] [kəʊst] *n* **(a)** (*of sea*) côte *f*, rivage *m*; (*extensive*) littoral *m*; **from c. to c.,** d'une mer à l'autre, d'un océan à l'autre; **the country's Caribbean c.,** la côte caraïbe du pays; **two miles off the c. of France,** à deux mil(l)es de la côte française; **the country has no sea c.,** ce pays n'est bordé par aucune mer; *Br* **the c.,** (*seaside*) la côte; *F* **the c. is clear,** le champ est libre; **(b)** (*act of going downhill*) (*on bicycle, in car etc*) descente *f* en roue libre; (*on sledge*) descente (en toboggan); **(c)** *US* (*slope for sledges*) piste *f* (de toboggan).

coast[2] *vi* **(a)** (*on bicycle, in car*) avancer en roue libre; (*downhill*) descendre en roue libre; (*on sledge*) descendre une côte en toboggan *ou* en luge; *Fig* **he coasted home,** (*in race*) il a gagné sans effort; *Fig* **she coasted through her exams,** elle a passé ses examens sans difficulté; *Fig* **you're coasting,** (*not working hard*) tu ne te foules pas; **(b)** *Nau* **to c. (along),** suivre la côte; *Com* caboter.

coastal ['kəʊst(ə)l] *adj* côtier; **c. navigation,** navigation côtière, cabotage *m*; **c. defence,** défense côtière; **c. waters,** eaux territoriales.

coaster ['kəʊstər] *n* **(a)** *Nau* (*ship*) cabotier *m*, caboteur *m*; **(b)** (*for wine bottle*) dessous *m* de bouteille *ou* de carafe; (*for glass*) dessous de verre.

coastguard ['kəʊstgɑːd] *n* **(a)** (*no pl*) la garde des côtes; **c. vessel** *or* **cutter,** garde-côte *m*, *pl* gardes-côte; **(b)** (*also* **coastguard(s)man** [kəʊst'gɑːd(z)mən]) garde-côte *m*, *pl* gardes-côte.

coasting ['kəʊstɪŋ] *n* **(a)** (*on bicycle, in car*) course *f* en roue libre; (*downhill*) descente *f* en roue libre; (*on sledge*) descente en luge; **(b)** navigation côtière; **c. vessel,** caboteur *m*.

coastline ['kəʊstlaɪn] *n* littoral *m*.

coat[1] [kəʊt] *n* **(a)** (*short*) veste *f*, veston *m*; (*long*) manteau *m*; (*for men*) manteau, pardessus *m*; **tail c.,** queue *f* de pie; **morning c.,** jaquette *f*; **car c.,** manteau trois quarts; **lab c.,** blouse blanche; *Hist* **c. of mail,** cotte *f* de mailles; **c. dress,** robe-manteau *f*, *pl* robes-manteaux; **c. hanger,** cintre *m*; porte-vêtements *m inv*; **c. hook,** patère *f*; **(b)** *Her* **c. of arms,** armes *fpl*, armoiries *fpl*, écusson *m*; **(c)** (*of dog, horse*) robe *f*; (*of big cat*) pelage *m*; **(d)** (*of snow etc*) manteau *m*, couche *f*; **(e)** (*of paint*) couche *f*, application *f*; (*of varnish*) pelure *f*; (*of tar*) enduit *m*.

coat[2] *vt* enduire (*qch de peinture, de goudron etc*); enrober (*qch de chocolat etc*); dragéifier (*une pilule*); revêtir, armer (*un câble*) (**with,** de); coucher (*du papier*); **to c. sth with**

dust, couvrir qch de poussière.
coated ['kəʊtɪd] *adj* enduit, (re)couvert, enrobé **(with,** de); *(électrode)* enrobé; *(langue)* chargé, pâteux; *(papier)* couché; *Phot (objectif)* bleuté, traité; **c. with dust,** couvert de poussière.
coating ['kəʊtɪŋ] *n* **(a)** enduit *m*, couche *f (de peinture etc)*; pelure *f (de vernis)*; pellicule *f (de gélatine)*; **covered in a chocolate c.** *or* **a c. of chocolate,** recouvert d'une couche de chocolat; *Tech* **protective c.,** couche protective; **(b)** *(act)* enduisage *m*.
coatrack ['kəʊtræk] *n* portemanteau *m*.
coat-tails ['kəʊt'teɪlz] *npl* basques *fpl ou* pan *m* d'un habit; *Am* **to ride on s.o.'s c.-t.,** se faire élire dans le sillage de qn.
coauthor¹ [kəʊ'ɔːθər] *n* coauteur *m*.
coauthor² *vt* coécrire *(un livre)*.
coax [kəʊks] *vt* cajoler, enjôler, câliner; **to c. s.o. to do** *or* **into doing sth,** encourager qn à faire qch (en le cajolant).
coaxial ['kəʊæksɪəl] *adj Electron* coaxial; **c. cable,** câble coaxial.
coaxing ['kəʊksɪŋ] **1** *adj (ton etc)* cajoleur. **2** *n* cajolerie *f*; **he took a lot of c.,** il s'est bien fait tirer l'oreille.
cob [kɒb] *n* **(a)** *(horse)* cob *m*, bidet *m*; **(b) c. (swan),** cygne *m* mâle; **(c)** *(hazelnut)* aveline *f*, grosse noisette; **(d) (corn) c.,** *(with grain)* épi *m* de maïs; *(without grain)* rafle *f*; *Culin* **corn on the c.,** maïs en épi; **(e)** *(loaf)* pain rond.
cobalt ['kəʊbɔːlt] *n Ch* cobalt *m*; **c. bloom,** fleur *f* de cobalt; **c. blue,** bleu *m* de cobalt; **c. bomb,** bombe *f* au cobalt.
cobber ['kɒbər] *n Austr F* copain *m*, pote *m*.
cobble¹ ['kɒb(ə)l] *n* galet *m*, caillou *m (de chaussée)*.
cobble² *vt* paver *(une cour)* de galets.
cobble³ *vt Old-fashioned Br* réparer *(des chaussures)*.
▶**cobble together** *vtsep (do hastily)* bricoler, faire à la hâte; **he cobbled together an article,** il a bricolé un article.
cobbled ['kɒb(ə)ld] *adj (path, street)* pavé.
cobbler ['kɒblər] *n* **(a)** *Br (shoe repairer, maker of shoes)* cordonnier *m*; **(b)** *Am Culin* = dessert chaud à base de fruits recouvert d'une génoise.
cobblers ['kɒbləz] **1** *npl Br Sl* **(a)** *(rubbish)* conneries *fpl*; **that's c.,** c'est des conneries tout ça; **(b)** *(testicles) Vulg* couilles *fpl*. **2** *int Br Sl* foutaise!
cobblestone ['kɒb(ə)lstəʊn] *n* caillou *m (de chaussée)*.
cobloaf ['kɒbləʊf] *n* pain rond.
cobnut ['kɒbnʌt] *n* aveline *f*, grosse noisette.
COBOL ['kəʊbɒl] *n Comptr* Cobol *m*.
cobra ['kəʊbrə] *n (snake)* cobra *m*.
cobweb ['kɒbweb] *n (web)* toile *f* d'araignée; *(thread)* fil *m* d'araignée; **to brush** *or* **sweep away the cobwebs from sth,** ôter les toiles d'araignées de qch; *Fig* **to go for a walk to blow away the cobwebs,** prendre l'air pour se rafraîchir les idées.
coca ['kəʊkə] *n Bot Pharm* coca *m or f*.
cocaine [kə'keɪn] *n Pharm* cocaïne *f*; **c. addict,** cocaïnomane *mf*.
coccyx ['kɒksɪks] *n Anat* coccyx *m*.
cochineal ['kɒtʃɪniːl] *n* cochenille *f*.
cock¹ [kɒk] *n* **(a)** coq *m*; **fighting c.,** coq de combat; *Fig* **c. of the walk** *or* **of the roost,** coq du village; **c. bird,** oiseau *m* mâle; **c. pheasant,** coq faisan; **c. canary,** serin *m*; **c. sparrow,** moineau *m* mâle; **c. lobster,** homard *m* mâle; **(b)** *Vulg (penis)* bit(t)e *f*; **(c)** *Tech etc (in plumbing)* robinet *m*; *Nau* **sea c.,** robinet de prise d'eau à la mer; **(d)** *(on firearm)* chien *m*; **at full c.,** au cran d'armé; *Fig* **to go off at half c.,** partir au quart de tour; **(e)** *Br Sl (form of address)* **wotcher c.!,** salut mon vieux!; **(f)** *(of balance)* aiguille *f*; *(of sundial)* style *m*; **(g)** *Agr* meule *f (de foin)*.
cock² *vt* **(a) to c. one's eye at s.o./sth,** donner un coup d'œil à qn/qch; **(b)** *(of horse etc)* **to c. (up) its ears,** dresser les oreilles; **(c) to c. one's hat,** *(put on one side)* mettre son chapeau de côté; *(raise)* relever son chapeau; **(d)** armer *(un fusil etc)*.
▶**cock up** *Br Sl* **1** *vtsep* bousiller *(qch)*. **2** *vi* merder.
cockade [kɒ'keɪd] *n* cocarde *f*.
cock-a-doodle-doo ['kɒkəduːd(ə)l'duː] *int F* cocorico!
cock-a-hoop ['kɒkə'huːp] *adj & adv* (en) jubilant; *(having done sth)* triomphant; **all c.-a-h.,** fier comme Artaban.
cock-a-leekie [kɒkə'liːkɪ] *n Scot Culin* **c. (soup),** = bouillon de volaille aux poireaux et aux pruneaux.
cock-and-bull ['kɒk(ə)n'bʊl] *adj F* **c.-a.-b. story,** histoire abracadabrante.
cockatoo [kɒkə'tuː] *n (bird)* cacatoès *m*.
cockchafer ['kɒktʃeɪfər] *n (beetle)* hanneton *m*.
cockcrow ['kɒkkrəʊ] *n* chant *m* du coq; **to rise at c.,** se lever au (premier) chant du coq *ou* à l'aube.
cocked [kɒkd] *adj* **c. hat,** chapeau *m* à cornes; *F* **to knock s.o. into a c. hat,** battre qn à plate(s) couture(s), démolir qn.
cocker ['kɒkər] *n* **c. (spaniel),** (épagneul *m*) cocker *m*.
cockerel ['kɒk(ə)r(ə)l] *n* jeune coq *m*, coquelet *m*.
cockeyed ['kɒkaɪd] *adj F* **(a)** *(absurd)* absurde; *(story)* qui ne tient pas debout; **(b)** *(person)* qui louche.
cockfight ['kɒkfaɪt] *n* combat *m ou* joute *f* de coqs.
cockfighting ['kɒkfaɪtɪŋ] *n* combats *mpl ou* concours *mpl* de coqs.
cockiness ['kɒkɪnɪs] *n F* **because of his c.,** parce qu'il était trop sûr de soi *ou Pej* puant.
cocking ['kɒkɪŋ] *n (of firearm)* armement *m*.
cockle¹ ['kɒk(ə)l] *n (flower)* **(corn) c.,** nielle *f* des champs.
cockle² *n (mollusc)* coque *f*, fausse praire; *Fig* **that will warm the cockles of your heart,** voilà qui vous réchauffera le cœur.
cockleshell ['kɒk(ə)lʃel] *n* **(a)** *(boat)* coquille *f* de noix; **(b)** coquille *f* de coque.
Cockney ['kɒknɪ] **1** *adj* cockney. **2** *n* **(a)** *(person)* Cockney *mf (des quartiers de l'est de Londres)*; **(b)** *(dialect)* cockney *m*.
cockpit ['kɒkpɪt] *n* **(a)** *(of plane)* poste *m* de pilotage, cockpit *m*; *(of racing car)* poste du pilote; **(b)** *(in cockfighting)* arène *f* de combats de coqs.
cockroach ['kɒkrəʊtʃ] *n (insect)* blatte *f*, cafard *m*.
cockscomb ['kɒkskəʊm] *n* **(a)** *(on bird)* crête *f* de coq; **(b)** *(flower)* (amarante *f*) crête-de-coq *f*, *pl* crêtes-de-coq.
cocksure ['kɒk'ʃʊər] *adj* sûr de soi, suffisant, outrecuidant.
cocktail ['kɒkteɪl] *n Culin* cocktail *m*; **fruit c.,** salade *f* de fruits *(servie dans un verre)*; **prawn c.,** crevettes à la mayonnaise; **Molotov c.,** cocktail Molotov; **c. cabinet,** bar *m* (à cocktails); **c. mixer** *or* **shaker,** shaker *m*; **c. party,** cocktail; **c. stick,** pique *f*; **c. dress,** robe de cocktail.
cockup ['kɒkʌp] *n Br Sl* couillonnade *f*; **it was a complete c.,** c'était un vrai bordel; **you made a complete c. of that,** tu as fait un beau bordel, tu as bien merdé.
cocky ['kɒkɪ] *adj F* trop sûr de soi, *Pej* puant; **don't get c.!,** ne fais pas ton malin!
cocoa ['kəʊkəʊ] *n* **(a)** *(powder or drink)* cacao *m*; **c. bean,** graine *f ou* fève *f* de cacao; **c. butter,** beurre *m* de cacao; **(b)** *(colour)* chocolat *inv*.
coconut ['kəʊkənʌt] *n* (noix *f* de) coco *m*; **c. palm** *or* **tree,** cocotier *m*; **c. milk/butter,** lait *m*/beurre *m* de coco; **c. oil,** huile *f* de coprah; **c. fibre,** fibre *f* de coco, coir *m*; **c. matting,** natte *f* en fibres de coco; **c. shy,** jeu *m* de massacre *(où on essaie d'abattre des noix de coco)*.
cocoon¹ [kə'kuːn] *n* cocon *m (de ver à soie etc)*.
cocoon² *vt* envelopper **(in,** dans); *Fig* **workers in the public sector have been cocooned from unemployment,** les travailleurs du secteur public ont été protégés du chômage.
cod [kɒd] *n (fish)* morue *f*; **fresh c.,** morue fraîche, cabillaud *m*; **dried c.,** morue sèche, merluche *f*; **c.'s roe,** œufs *mpl* de morue.
COD [siːəʊ'diː] *Com (abbr* **cash** *or Am* **collect on delivery)** contre remboursement.
coda ['kəʊdə] *n Mus* coda *f*.
coddle ['kɒd(ə)l] *vt* **(a)** *(spoil)* choyer, dorloter *(qn)*; **to c. oneself,** se dorloter; **(b)** *Culin* faire cuire *(des œufs)* en cocotte.
code¹ [kəʊd] *n* **(a)** *Telecom etc* code *m (télégraphique etc)*; **c. letter/number,** indicatif littéral/numérique; *Tel* **(dialling) c.,** indicatif (départemental); **c. word,** mot convenu; **(b)** *(secret)* code *m*, chiffre *m*; **c. letter,** lettre *f* code; **c. name,** nom *m* de code; **to write a message in c.,** chiffrer un message; **the letter was in c.,** la lettre était codée; **c. message,** message chiffré; **c. book,** *(for encoding)* code *ou* carnet *m* de chiffrement; *(for decoding)* code *ou* carnet de déchiffrement; **(c)** *Comptr* code *m*; **computer c.,** code machine; **c. translation,** transcodage *m*; **(d)** *(rules etc)* code *m*; **c. of honour,** code *ou* règles *fpl* de l'honneur; **Highway C.,** = Code de la route; **c. of criminal procedure,** code d'instruction criminelle.
code² *vt* **(a)** coder, mettre en code *ou* en chiffre *(un message etc)*; **(b)** *Comptr* coder, écrire *(une séquence etc)*.
coded ['kəʊdɪd] *adj* **(a)** *(message etc)* chiffré; **(b)** *Comptr* codé.
co-defendant ['kəʊdɪ'fendənt] *n* coaccusé, -ée; *(civil law)* codéfendeur *m*.
codeine ['kəʊdiːn] *n Pharm* codéine *f*.
coder ['kəʊdər] *n* **(a)** chiffreur *m*; **(b)** *Comptr* codeur *m*,

codifieur *m*.

codex, *pl* **-ices** ['kəʊdeks, -ɪsiːz] *n* manuscrit *m* (ancien).

codger ['kɒdʒər] *n Old-fashioned Br F* type *m*; **an old c.,** un vieux bonhomme.

codicil ['kɒdɪsɪl] *n Jur* codicille *m* (*d'un testament*).

codification [kəʊdɪfɪ'keɪʃən] *n* codification *f*.

codify ['kəʊdɪfaɪ] *vt* codifier (*les lois etc*).

coding ['kəʊdɪŋ] *n* **(a)** codification *f*, codage *m*; **(b)** *Comptr* (*providing codes*) codage *m*; (*system of codes*) codes *mpl*; **c. error,** erreur *f* de codage.

co-director ['kəʊdɪ'rektər] *n* codirecteur, -trice.

cod-liver ['kɒdlɪvər] *adj Pharm* **c.-l. oil,** huile *f* de foie de morue.

co-driver ['kəʊ'draɪvər] *n Sp* copilote *m*.

codswallop ['kɒdzwɒləp] *n Br Sl* bêtises *fpl*, tissu *m* d'âneries; **it's a load of (old) c.,** c'est du bidon.

co-ed ['kəʊ'ed] *F* **1** *adj* (*school*) mixte; **to go co-ed,** (*of school*) devenir mixte. **2** *n* **(a)** *Br* (*school*) école mixte; **(b)** *US* (*pupil*) élève *f* d'une école mixte.

coeducation ['kəʊedjʊ'keɪʃən] *n* coéducation *f*, enseignement *m* mixte.

coeducational ['kəʊedjʊ'keɪʃənəl] *adj* coéducationnel; **c. school,** école *f* mixte.

coefficient [kəʊɪ'fɪʃənt] *n Math & Phys* coefficient *m*.

coeliac, *US* **celiac** ['siːlɪæk] **1** *adj* cœliaque; **c. disease,** maladie *f* cœliaque. **2** *n Am Med F* = personne atteinte de maladie cœliaque.

coerce [kəʊ'ɜːs] *vt* **(a)** (*compel*) forcer, contraindre (**s.o. into doing sth,** qn à faire qch); **(b)** (*restrain*) réprimer par la force.

coercion [kəʊ'ɜːʃən] *n* coercition *f*, contrainte *f*; *Jur* coaction *f*; **to act under c.,** agir par contrainte.

coexist ['kəʊɪg'zɪst] *vi* coexister (**with,** avec); **the two species c. peacefully,** les deux espèces coexistent pacifiquement.

coexistence ['kəʊɪg'zɪstəns] *n* coexistence *f* (**with,** avec); *Pol* **peaceful c.,** coexistence pacifique.

coexistent ['kəʊɪg'zɪstənt] *adj* coexistant (**with,** avec).

C of E [siːə'viː] *adj Rel* (*abbr* **Church of England**) anglican.

coffee ['kɒfɪ] *n* **(a)** café *m*; **two coffees, please,** deux cafés, s'il vous plaît; **will you have a c.?,** tu prends un café?; **instant c.,** café instantané; **ground c.,** café moulu; **black c.,** café noir; *Br* **white c.,** café crème, café au lait; **c. and rolls,** (*ordering breakfast*) café complet; **c. bar,** café; **c. bean,** grain *m* de café; **c. break,** pause-café *f*, *pl* pauses-café; **c. cream,** (*sweet*) chocolat fourré au café; **c. cup,** tasse *f* à café; **c. grounds,** marc *m* de café; **c. machine,** (*in public place*) distributeur *m* de boissons; (*in home*) cafetière *f* (électrique); **c. mill,** moulin *m* à café; **c. pot,** cafetière; **c. shop,** café; **c. spoon,** cuillère *f* à café; (*small*) cuillère à moka; **c. table,** table *f* de salon; **c. tree,** caféier *m*; **(b)** (*colour*) **c.(-colour),** (*dark*) café *inv*; (*light*) café au lait *inv*.

coffee-(coloured) ['kɒfɪ(kʌləd)] *adj* (*dark*) café *inv*; (*light*) café au lait *inv*.

coffee-table ['kɒfɪteɪb(ə)l] *adj* **c.-t. book,** livre de grand format profusément illustré.

coffer[1] ['kɒfər] *n* **(a)** coffre *m*; **the coffers of State,** les fonds publics; **(b)** *Archit* caisson *m* (*de plafond*); **(c)** (*in dam, lock etc*) chambre *f*, bassin *m*, sas *m* (*d'écluse*); **(d)** = **COFFERDAM**.

coffer[2] *vt* **(a)** *Min Constr* coffrer (*un puits*); **(b)** diviser (*un plafond*) en caissons; **coffered ceiling,** plafond *m* à caissons.

cofferdam ['kɒfədæm] *n HydE* coffre *m*, batardeau *m*; caisson *m* hydraulique.

coffering ['kɒfərɪŋ] *n Min etc* coffrage *m*.

coffin ['kɒfɪn] *n* **(a)** cercueil *m*, bière *f*; *F* **that's another nail in his c.,** (*he's closer to death*) c'est (pour lui) un pas de plus vers la tombe; (*he's closer to defeat, disaster etc*) c'est (pour lui) un pas de plus vers l'échec; *Sl* **c. nail,** (*cigarette*) clope *f*; **(b)** (*of horse*) cavité *f* du sabot.

cofounder [kəʊ'faʊndər] *n* cofondateur, -trice.

cog [kɒg] *n Tech* **(a)** dent *f* (*d'une roue dentée*); **the cogs,** la denture; *Fig* **I'm only a c. in the machinery,** je ne suis qu'un rouage de la machine; **c. rail,** crémaillère *f*; **c. railway** *or US* **railroad,** chemin *m* de fer à crémaillère; **(b)** (*wheel*) pignon *m*, roue dentée.

cogency ['kəʊdʒənsɪ] *n* force *f*, puissance *f*.

cogent ['kəʊdʒənt] *adj* **(a)** (*convincing*) (*argument*) irrésistible; (*motif*) puissant; (*raison*) valable, convaincant; **(b)** (*relevant*) (*cas*) urgent.

cogently ['kəʊdʒəntlɪ] *adv* avec force; incontestablement.

cogitate ['kɒdʒɪteɪt] **1** *vi* méditer, réfléchir (**on, over,** sur). **2** *vt* projeter, imaginer (*un plan etc*).

cogitation [kɒdʒɪ'teɪʃən] *n* réflexion *f*, cogitation (**on, over,** sur).

cognac ['kɒnjæk] *n* cognac *m*.

cognate ['kɒgneɪt] **1** *n* **(a)** *Gram* mot *m* de même origine; **(b)** *Jur* cognat *m*. **2** *adj* **(a)** qui a du rapport (**with sth,** avec qch), qui est parent (**with sth,** de qch); **(b)** *Gram* de même origine.

cognition [kɒg'nɪʃən] *n Phil Psy* connaissance *f*, cognition *f*.

cognizance ['kɒgnɪzəns, 'kɒnɪzəns] *n* **(a)** (*knowledge*) connaissance *f*, perception *f*; *Jur* connaissance; **to take c. of sth,** prendre connaissance de qch; **(b)** *Jur* (*of a court*) compétence *f*; **within** *or* **under the c. of a court,** du ressort d'une cour.

cognizant ['kɒgnɪzənt, *Jur* 'kɒnɪzənt] *adj* **(a)** ayant connaissance (**of,** de); **to be c. of a fact,** être instruit d'un fait; **(b)** *Jur* **court c. of an offence,** tribunal compétent pour juger un délit.

cognoscente, *pl* **-ti** [kɒnjəʊ'ʃentɪ, kɒgnə-] *n* connaisseur, -euse, spécialiste *mf*.

cogwheel ['kɒgwiːl] *n Tech* roue à dents *ou* dentée, roue d'engrenage.

cohabit [kəʊ'hæbɪt] *vi* cohabiter, vivre maritalement (**with,** avec).

cohabitation [kəʊhæbɪ'teɪʃən] *n* cohabitation *f* (**with,** avec).

cohabitee [kəʊhæbɪ'tiː] *n* concubin, -ine.

cohere [kəʊ'hɪər] **1** *vi* **(a)** (*of whole, of parts*) se tenir ensemble, rester uni(s); **(b)** (*of argument, style*) se suivre (*logiquement*); **(c)** *Phys* être cohérent. **2** *vt* faire tenir ensemble (*des matériaux etc*).

coherence [kəʊ'hɪərəns] *n* (*of argument, style*) suite *f* (logique), cohérence *f*.

coherent [kəʊ'hɪərənt] *adj* **(a)** (*whole*) cohérent; **(b)** (*plan, speech etc*) conséquent, cohérent; (*thinker*) qui a de la suite dans ses idées; (*argument*) bien développé; *F* **the man wasn't c.,** il racontait n'importe quoi; **(c)** *Phys* cohérent.

coherently [kəʊ'hɪərəntlɪ] *adv* (*speak*) d'une manière cohérente, avec cohérence.

cohesion [kəʊ'hiːʒən] *n* cohésion *f*.

cohesive [kəʊ'hiːsɪv] *adj* **(a)** cohésif; *Phys* (*force*) de cohésion; **(b)** (*capable of cohesion*) cohésif, susceptible de cohésion.

cohort ['kəʊhɔːt] *n Antiq Mil* cohorte *f*; *Fig* **he was there with his cohorts,** il était là avec ses suiveurs.

coiffure [kwɑː'fjʊər] *n* coiffure *f*.

coil[1] [kɔɪl] *n* **(a)** rouleau *m* (*de corde*); *Nau* glène *f*; cueille *f* (*de filin, de câble*); roue *f* (*de câble*); rouleau, torque *f* (*de fil métallique*); **(b)** (*single loop*) pli *m*, repli *m* (*d'un cordage*); repli, nœud *m*, anneau *m* (*d'un serpent*); **(c)** (*in hairdressing*) rouleau *m* (de cheveux), chignon *m*; **(d)** (*coiled tube*) serpentin *m*; **(e)** *Med* (*contraceptive*) stérilet *m*; **(f)** *El* bobine *f*.

coil[2] **1** *vt* (en)rouler, gléner (*un cordage etc*); *El* bobiner (*des fils*); **to c. itself up,** (*of snake*) s'enrouler, se lover; *Nau etc* **to c. (down) a rope,** lover un cordage. **2** *vi* serpenter.

coiled [kɔɪld] *adj* (en)roulé, gléné; (*ressort*) en spirale; (*serpent*) lové.

coin[1] [kɔɪn] *n* **(a)** pièce *f* de monnaie; **a 10p c.,** une pièce de 10 pence; **gold coins,** pièces d'or; **(b)** (*no pl*) monnaie(s) *f(pl)*, pièces *fpl*, espèces *fpl*; **small c., subsidiary c.,** monnaie divisionnaire; **c. and bullion,** métal monnayé et métal en barres; *Fig* **to pay s.o. back in their own c.,** rendre la pareille à qn.

coin[2] *vt* **(a) to c. money,** frapper de la monnaie; *F* **he's simply coining money** *or* **coining it,** il fait des affaires en or; **(b)** monnayer (*des lingots*); **(c)** (*invent*) inventer, créer (*un mot nouveau*); **to c. a phrase,** pour inventer un idiotisme; *Iron* pour se servir du cliché habituel.

coinage ['kɔɪnɪdʒ] *n* **(a)** monnayage *m*; frappe *f* (*de la monnaie*); **(b)** (*invention*) invention *f*, création *f*; **the word is a recent c.,** c'est un mot nouveau; **(c)** (*currency*) système *m* monétaire (*d'un pays*); **(d)** (*coins*) monnaie(s) *f(pl)*, numéraire *m*.

coincide [kəʊɪn'saɪd] *vi* **(a)** (*in space, time*) coïncider (**with,** avec); **events that c.,** événements qui concourent; **her arrival coincided with that of the President,** son arrivée a coïncidé avec celle du président; **(b)** (*agree*) coïncider, s'accorder, être d'accord (**with,** avec).

coincidence [kəʊ'ɪnsɪdəns] *n* **(a)** coïncidence *f*, rencontre *f* (*d'événements*); **what a c.!,** quelle coïncidence!; **(b)** (*in space, time*) coïncidence *f*; *El* **phase c.,** concordance *f* de phase.

coincidental [kəʊɪnsɪ'dent(ə)l] *adj* (*effet*) de coïncidence; (*fait*) de pure coïncidence.
coiner ['kɔɪnər] *n* **(a)** monnayeur *m*; (*counterfeiter*) faux monnayeur; **(b)** (*of word, expression*) inventeur, -trice.
coin-op ['kɔɪnɒp] *n F* laverie *f* automatique.
coin-operated ['kɔɪnɒpəreɪtɪd] *adj* automatique; **c.-o. laundry,** laverie *f* automatique.
coitus ['kəʊɪtəs, kɔɪ-] *n* coït *m*; **c. interruptus,** rapport interrompu.
coke[1] [kəʊk] *n* coke *m*; **c. oven,** four *m* à coke.
coke[2] **1** *vt* coké(i)fier, convertir (*de la houille*) en coke. **2** *vi* (*of coal*) se coké(i)fier, se convertir en coke.
coke[3] *n Sl* (*cocaine*) neige *f*, blanche *f*, coke *f*.
Coke ® [kəʊk] *n F* Coca ® *m*.
coking ['kəʊkɪŋ] **1** *adj* (*charbon etc*) cokéfiable. **2** *n* cokéfaction *f*, coké(i)fication *f*.
col [kɒl] *n Geog* col *m*.
col. *abbr* **column.**
Col *abbr* **(a) Colombia; (b) Colorado.**
COLA ['kəʊlə] *n Am Admin* (*abbr Can* **cost of living allowance** *or US* **adjustment**) *Can* IVC *f*.
colander ['kʌləndər, kɒl-] *n Culin* passoire *f*.
cold[1] [kəʊld] **1** *adj* **(a)** (*temps, bain, repas etc*) froid; **it's c.,** il fait froid; **it's getting colder,** la température baisse; **a c. snap,** chute *f* de température; **to get** *or* **grow c.,** se refroidir; **that coffee will be c. by now,** ce café va être froid maintenant; **the c. tap,** le robinet d'eau froide; *F* **out c.,** sans connaissance, inanimé; **to knock s.o. (out) c.,** étendre qn raide (*d'un coup*); **to give s.o. the c. shoulder,** tourner le dos à qn, snober qn; **to be** *or* **feel c.,** (*of person*) avoir froid; **you're cold,** (*in game*) tu gèles; **my hands are c.,** j'ai les mains froides, j'ai froid aux mains; **my feet are as c. as ice,** j'ai les pieds glacés; *Fig* **to have c. feet,** avoir la frousse; **c. cream,** cold-cream *m*; **c. engine,** moteur froid; *Met* **c. front,** front froid; **c. meat,** viande froide; **c. meats,** *Am* **c. cuts,** assiette anglaise; **c. scent,** piste froide; **the scent had gone c.,** (*in hunting*) & *Fig* on avait perdu sa *ou* leur *etc* trace; **c. start,** (*of car*) & *Comptr* démarrage *m* à froid; **c. store,** chambre froide *ou* frigorifique; *Com* **c. storage,** conservation *f* par le froid; *Fig* **to put in c. storage,** mettre (*un projet*) en veilleuse; *Sl* **c. turkey,** manque *m* de drogues; **to quit smoking c. turkey,** arrêter de fumer du jour au lendemain; *Pol* **c. war,** guerre froide; **c. warrior,** partisan, -ane de la guerre froide;
(b) (*person, manner, welcome etc*) froid; **to be c. with s.o.,** se montrer froid avec qn; **a c. intellectual play,** une pièce intellectuelle sans émotions; *F* **that leaves me c.,** cela me laisse froid; **he's a c. fish,** c'est un pisse-froid;
(c) *Tech* **c. riveting,** rivure *f* à froid;
(d) *Nucl F* non radioactif.
2 *adv* **(a)** *Am* (tout) net, carrément; **to turn s.o. down c.,** envoyer promener qn;
(b) *Surg* **to operate c.,** (*unprepared*) opérer à froid.
cold[2] *n* **(a)** froid *m*; **I feel the c.,** je suis très frileux; **to protect oneself against the c.,** se protéger contre le froid; *Fig* **to leave s.o. out in the c.,** laisser qn à l'écart; *Fig* **to be left out in the c.,** rester sur le carreau; *Fig* **to come in from the c.,** rentrer en faveur; **c. wave,** vague *f* de froid; coup *m* de froid; **(b)** *Med* **(common) c.,** rhume *m*; **to have a c.,** être enrhumé, avoir un rhume; **bad** *or* **heavy c.,** gros rhume; **c. in the head, head c.,** rhume de cerveau; **chest c.,** rhume de poitrine; **to catch (a) c.,** s'enrhumer; *Fin F* boire un bouillon; *F* **you'll catch your death of c.,** vous allez attraper la mort; **c. remedy,** remède *m* contre le froid; **c. sore,** herpès *m*.
cold-blooded ['kəʊld'blʌdɪd] *adj* (*unemotional*) froid, insensible; (*murderer etc*) sans pitié; (*murder etc*) accompli de sang-froid; (*animal*) à sang froid; **reptiles are c.-b.,** les reptiles sont des animaux à sang froid.
cold-bloodedly ['kəʊld'blʌdɪdlɪ] *adv* de *ou* avec sang-froid, froidement; (*unemotionally*) avec insensibilité.
cold-bloodedness ['kəʊld'blʌdɪdnɪs] *n* sang-froid *m*; insensibilité *f*.
cold-hearted [kəʊld'hɑːtɪd] *adj* froid, insensible.
coldly ['kəʊldlɪ] *adv* froidement; (*regarder qn, qch*) avec froideur.
coldness ['kəʊldnɪs] *n* **(a)** froideur *f*; froidure *f* (*du climat etc*); **(b)** (*of welcome, person etc*) froid *m*; **there is a c. between them,** il y a un froid entre eux.
cold-pressed ['kəʊldpresd] *adj Tech* embouti à froid.
cold-shoulder ['kəʊld'ʃəʊldər] *vt* tourner le dos à (*qn*), snober (*qn*).
coleseed ['kəʊlsiːd] *n Bot* (graine *f* de) colza *m*.
coleslaw ['kəʊlslɔː] *n Culin* salade *f* de chou cru.
colic ['kɒlɪk] *n Med Vet* colique *f*.
colitis [kə'laɪtɪs] *n Med* colite *f*.
collaborate [kə'læbəreɪt] *vi* (*in work*) & *Pej* collaborer (**with,** avec; **on,** à).
collaboration [kəlæbə'reɪʃən] *n* collaboration *f*; **in c. with,** en collaboration avec.
collaborator [kə'læbəreɪtər] *n* (*in work*) & *Pej* collaborateur, -trice; (*on book etc*) coauteur *m*.
collage ['kɒlɑːʒ] *n Art* collage *m*.
collapse[1] [kə'læps] *n* **(a)** écroulement *m*, effondrement *m* (*d'un édifice, d'espoirs*); éboulement *m* (*de terre, de sable*); dégonflement *m* (*d'un ballon*); affaissement *m* (*d'un pneu*); débâcle *f* (*d'un établissement, d'un pays*); *MecE etc* déformation *f* (*d'une plaque etc*); *Com* chute subite (*de prix*); *Fin* effondrement (*du marché*); dégringolade *f* (*du franc etc*); **the c. of the economy,** l'effondrement de l'économie; **(b)** *Med* perte *f* de connaissance; collapsus *m* (*pulmonaire*); **(c)** (*moral*) effondrement moral.
collapse[2] **1** *vi* **(a)** (*of building, institution etc*) s'écrouler, s'effondrer; (*of balloon etc*) se dégonfler; *MecE etc* (*of support, wheel etc*) gauchir, se déformer; (*of prices*) s'effondrer; **(b)** (*of person*) s'effondrer; s'affaisser subitement; **I collapsed from the heat,** je me suis évanoui tellement il faisait chaud; **he collapsed into an armchair,** il s'effondra dans un fauteuil; *F* **I feel like I'm about to c.,** je sens que je vais m'effondrer; *Med* **her lung has collapsed,** elle a eu *ou* fait un collapsus pulmonaire. **2** *vt* plier (*une table etc*).
collapsed [kə'læpsd] *adj Med* **c. lung,** collapsus *m* pulmonaire.
collapsible [kə'læpsəb(ə)l] *adj* (*chair, boat etc*) pliant, repliable; (*handle etc*) rabattable; *Aut* **c. hood,** capote pliante *ou* rabattable.
collar[1] ['kɒlər] *n* **(a)** col *m* (*de chemise etc*); tour *m* de cou (*en fourrure etc*); **to seize** *or F* **grab s.o. by the c.,** prendre *ou* saisir qn au collet; **to get hot under the c.,** se ficher en rogne; **lace c.,** collerette *f* en dentelle; **detachable c.,** faux col; **Peter Pan c.,** col Claudine; **clerical c.,** col romain; **(b) (dog) c.,** collier *m* de chien; *F* (*clergyman's*) col romain; **horse c.,** collier de cheval; **(c)** *MecE* collier *m*, bague *f*; (*of axle, pipe*) collet *m*; *Nau* collier (*d'étai*); *Constr* **c. beam** *or* **tie,** entrait retroussé; (*between rafters*) traversière *f*; **(d)** *Zool* (*marking*) collier *m* (*d'oiseau, de quadrupède*); **(e)** *Bot* collet *m* (*de racine*); **(f)** *Culin* roulade *f* (*de bœuf, de veau, de poisson*).
collar[2] *vt* **(a)** colleter (*qn*), saisir *ou* prendre (*qn*) au collet; *Fig* empoigner, pincer (*qn, qch*); **(b)** *Tech* baguer, fretter.
collarbone ['kɒləbəʊn] *n Anat* clavicule *f*.
collared ['kɒləd] *adj MecE* (*manchon*) à frettes.
collate [kɒ'leɪt] *vt* rassembler (*des documents, des données*); (*in bookbinding*) assembler, collationner (*les feuilles*); collationner (*un texte*) (**with,** avec).
collateral [kə'lætər(ə)l] **1** *n* **(a)** *Fin* nantissement *m*; **what can you provide as c.?,** qu'est-ce que vous pouvez fournir en nantissement?; **(b)** (*descendant*) collatéral *m*; (*blood vessel*) collatéral. **2** *adj* **(a)** (*knowledge, fact*) concomitant; (*phenomenon*) correspondant, parallèle; **(b)** (*cause etc*) accessoire, subsidiaire; *Com Jur* **c. security,** garantie additionnelle, nantissement *m* subsidiaire; **(c)** (*street etc*) collatéral, -aux, parallèle; (*branch, family*) collatéral, -ale.
collating [kɒ'leɪtɪŋ] *n* collationnement *m*; (*in bookbinding*) assemblage *m*.
collation [kə'leɪʃən] *n* **(a)** rassemblement *m* (*de documents, de données*); (*in bookbinding*) assemblage *m*, collationnement *m* (*des feuilles*); collation *f* (*de textes*); **(b)** *Old-fashioned Culin* collation *f*; **cold c.,** repas froid.
colleague ['kɒliːg] *n* collègue *mf*; (*doctor, lawyer*) confrère *m*.
collect[1] ['kɒlekt] *n Rel* (*prayer*) collecte *f*.
collect[2] [kə'lekt] **1** *vt* **(a)** collectionner (*des timbres, des livres etc*); **I c. paintings,** je fais collection de peintures; **she has collected more than 2,000 records,** elle a une collection de plus de 2 000 disques;
(b) (*gather*) rassembler (*une foule, ses effets*); assembler (*des matériaux*); réunir (*des amis*); recueillir (*des données, des nouvelles*); récolter (*des documents etc*); lever (*les lettres*), faire la levée (*des lettres*); *Mil* ramasser (*les blessés*); **he had collected several parking fines,** il avait totalisé plusieurs P.V.; **that metal tray is there to c. the drips,** le plateau métallique sert à recueillir les gouttes; **I'll c. you at midday,** je passerai vous prendre à midi;
(c) *Fin* percevoir (*les impôts*); toucher (*une traite*); recouvrer (*une créance*);
(d) (*recover*) aller chercher (*sa valise etc*);
(e) recueillir, rassembler (*ses idées*); recueillir (*ses forces*); **to c. oneself,** se reprendre, se calmer; **to c. one's thoughts,** se recueillir.

2 *vi* (*of people*) s'assembler, se rassembler, se réunir; (*of things*) s'amasser; **a pile of rubbish collected outside the door,** un tas d'ordures s'amassa devant la porte.

collect³ *adj & adv Am* en port dû; **to send a telegram c.,** envoyer un télégramme en port dû; *Tel* **c. call,** communication *f* en P.C.V.; **to call (s.o.) c.,** appeler (qn) en P.C.V.

collectable [kə'lektəb(ə)l] *n* objet *m* de collection.

collected [kə'lektɪd] *adj* **(a)** (*assembled*) réuni, recueilli; **the c. works of Jane Austen,** les œuvres complètes de Jane Austen; **(b)** (*calm*) (plein) de sang-froid.

collectible [kə'lektəb(ə)l] *n* objet *m* de collection.

collecting [kə'lektɪŋ] *n* = **COLLECTION (b)** *&* **(c)**; **c. point,** poste *m* de ramassage *ou* de rassemblement (*du personnel, du matériel etc*).

collection [kə'lekʃən] *n* **(a)** (*of stamps, butterflies etc*) collection *f*; recueil *m* (*de chansons*); *Sewing etc* **spring c.,** collection de printemps;

(b) (*gathering*) rassemblement *m*, assemblage *m* (*de personnes, de choses*); ramassage *m* (*des blessés*); recouvrement *m* (*d'une somme*); perception *f* (*des impôts*); encaissement *m* (*d'un billet*); levée *f* (*des lettres*); captage *m* (*d'eau, de courant électrique etc*); recueil *m* (*de données*); **there is no c. on Sunday,** (*from letterbox*) il n'y a pas de levée le dimanche; **c. times are 8.45 and 17.30,** les levées sont à 8h45 et à 17h30;

(c) (*accumulation*) amas *m*, assemblage; (*of people*) assemblée *f*; **a c. of rubbish had built up outside the door,** des ordures s'étaient amassées devant la porte;

(d) (*in church etc*) quête *f*, collecte *f*; **to take up a c.,** faire la quête; **c. box,** tronc *m* (*d'église, de quêteur*); **c. plate,** plat *m* de quête.

collective [kə'lektɪv] **1** *adj* **(a)** collectif; *Jur* **c. ownership,** propriété collective; (*of building*) copropriété *f*; **c. farm,** ferme collective; **c. agreement,** convention collective; *Econ* **c. bargaining,** (négociation *f* de) convention collective; *Gram* **c. noun,** nom collectif; **(b)** *Bot* (*fruit*) multiple. **2** *n* **(a)** *Gram* collectif *m*; **(b)** (*farm etc*) coopérative *f*.

collectively [kə'lektɪvlɪ] *adv* collectivement; (*possédé etc*) en commun; **c. owned building,** immeuble en copropriété.

collectivism [kə'lektɪvɪz(ə)m] *n Econ* collectivisme *m*.

collectivist [kə'lektɪvɪst] *adj & n Econ* collectiviste *mf*.

collectivity [kɒlek'tɪvɪtɪ] *n* **(a)** collectivité *f*; **(b)** (*property*) propriété *f* en commun.

collectivization [kəlektɪvaɪ'zeɪʃən] *n* collectivisation *f*.

collectivize [kə'lektɪvaɪz] *vt* collectiviser.

collector [kə'lektər] *n* **(a)** collectionneur, -euse (*de peintures, de timbres-poste*); **these records have become c.'s items,** ces disques sont devenus des pièces de collection; **(b)** *Com etc* quêteur, -euse (*d'aumônes*); collecteur, -trice (*de cotisations*); *Rail* **ticket c.,** contrôleur *m* (*de billets*); encaisseur *m* (*de la compagnie du gaz etc*); *Admin* percepteur *m* (*des contributions directes*); receveur *m* (*des contributions indirectes*); **(c)** *MecE etc* collecteur *m* (*d'huile, de vapeur etc*); récepteur *m* (*de trop-plein etc*).

colleen ['kɒliːn] *n* (*in Ireland*) jeune fille *f*.

college ['kɒlɪdʒ] *n* **(a) c. of education,** *Old-fashioned* **(teachers') training c.,** = école normale; **agricultural c.,** = institut *m* agronomique; **military/navy c.,** école militaire/navale; **(b)** (*British university*) collège *m*; **c. team,** l'équipe du collège; **he played rugby for his c.,** il a joué au rugby pour son collège *ou* dans l'équipe de son collège; **(c)** *Sch* = lycée *m*; **technical c.,** = lycée technique; **Eton C.,** le collège d'Eton; **(d)** *Rel* collège *m*; *Rel* **the Sacred C., the C. of Cardinals,** le Sacré Collège, le Collège des cardinaux; *Pol* **electoral c.,** collège électoral; **(e)** *Culin* **c. pudding,** = (variété de) pouding *m* aux raisins.

collegiate [kə'liːdʒɪət] *adj* collégial, -aux; **c. church,** collégiale *f*.

collide [kə'laɪd] *vi* (*of vehicles etc*) se heurter, se tamponner, entrer en collision; **to c. with,** rencontrer, heurter, tamponner (*qch*); entrer en collision avec (*qch*); *Nau* aborder (*un navire*); **to c. with s.o.,** (*of person*) se heurter à *ou* contre qn.

collie ['kɒlɪ] *n* (*dog*) chien de berger écossais, colley *m*.

collier ['kɒlɪər] *n* **(a)** *Nau* (navire *m*) charbonnier *m*; **(b)** *Min* (*person*) houilleur *m*, mineur *m* (*de charbon*).

colliery ['kɒlɪərɪ] *n Min* houillère *f*, mine *f* de charbon.

collision [kə'lɪʒən] *n* **(a)** collision *f*; tamponnement *m* (*de trains*); abordage *m*, collision (*de navires*); *Fig* conflit *m* (*d'intérêts*); **head-on c.,** collision frontale; **to come into c. with,** tamponner (*un train, une voiture*), entrer en collision avec (*un train, un navire etc*); aborder (*un navire*); **c. course,** cap *m* de collision; *Nau* **to be on a c. course,** être sur un cap de collision; *Fig* **they are on a c. course,** ils vont se rentrer dedans; **(b)** *Nucl Phys* choc *m*, collision *f* (*des particules*).

colloquial [kə'ləʊkwɪəl] *adj* familier, de (la) conversation; (*langue*) parlé; **c. English,** l'anglais parlé.

colloquialism [kə'ləʊkwɪəlɪz(ə)m] *n* expression familière.

colloquially [kə'ləʊkwɪəlɪ] *adv* familièrement, en style familier; **known c. as ...,** communément appelé ... .

collude [kə'luːd] *vi* comploter, être de connivence (**with s.o.,** avec qn).

collusion [kə'luːʒən] *n* collusion *f*; **to act in c. with s.o.,** agir de complicité *ou* de connivence avec qn; **to be in c. with s.o.,** être d'intelligence *ou* de connivence avec qn.

collywobbles ['kɒlɪwɒb(ə)lz] *npl F* **to have the c.,** (*an upset stomach*) avoir mal au ventre; (*be nervous*) avoir la frousse.

Colo *abbr* **Colorado.**

Colombia [kə'lʌmbɪə] *n* Colombie *f*.

Colombian [kə'lʌmbɪən] **1** *adj* colombien. **2** *n* Colombien, -ienne.

colon¹ ['kəʊlən] *n Anat* côlon *m*.

colon² *n* deux-points *m*; *Typ* comma *m*.

colonel ['kɜːn(ə)l] *n Mil US Av* colonel *m*; **he was made a c.,** il a été fait colonel.

colonial [kə'ləʊnɪəl] *adj & n* colonial, -aux; *US Archit etc* (*style*) du dix-huitième siècle, colonial; **in c. times,** au temps des colonies.

colonialism [kə'ləʊnɪəlɪz(ə)m] *n* colonialisme *m*.

colonialist [kə'ləʊnɪəlɪst] *adj & n* colonialiste *mf*.

colonist ['kɒlənɪst] *n* colon *m*.

colonization [kɒlənaɪ'zeɪʃən] *n* colonisation *f*.

colonize ['kɒlənaɪz] **1** *vt* coloniser. **2** *vi* former une colonie; s'établir (dans un pays nouveau).

colonizer ['kɒlənaɪzər] *n* colonisateur *m*.

colonnade [kɒlə'neɪd] *n Archit* colonnade *f*

colony ['kɒlənɪ] *n* **(a)** colonie *f*; **to live in the colonies,** vivre aux colonies; *Hist* **the Colonies,** = Les Colonies; **the English c. in Paris,** la colonie anglaise à Paris; **a c. of writers,** une colonie d'écrivains; **(b)** (*of animals*) colonie *f*.

colophon ['kɒləfən] *n Typ* chiffre *m* (*de l'éditeur, de l'imprimeur*); marque *f* typographique.

color, color-blind *etc US* = **COLOUR, COLOUR-BLIND** *etc*.

Colorado [kɒlə'rɑːdəʊ] *n* **C. beetle,** doryphore *m*.

coloration [kʌlə'reɪʃən] *n* coloration *f*, coloris *m*; (*of textiles etc*) colorisation *f*.

coloratura [kɒlərə'tʊərə] *n Mus* **(a)** chant agrémenté de fioritures; **c. aria,** air *m* coloratur; **(b) c. (soprano),** coloratur *f*.

colossal [kə'lɒs(ə)l] *adj* **(a)** (*statue etc*) colossal, -aux; **(b)** *Fig* (*succès, mensonge etc*) colossal.

colossus, *pl* **-i, -uses** [kə'lɒsəs, -aɪ, -əsɪz] *n* colosse *m*; **the C. of Rhodes,** le Colosse de Rhodes.

colostomy [kə'lɒstəmɪ] *n Surg* colostomie *f*; **to have a c.,** subir une colostomie.

colour¹, *US* **color** ['kʌlər] *n* **(a)** couleur *f*; **what c. is it?,** de quelle couleur est-ce?; **it's the c. of a ripe cherry,** ça a la couleur d'une cerise mûre; **a dark grey c.,** une couleur gris foncé; **it's a sort of greenish/blueish c.,** c'est d'un certain vert/bleu; **it's a sort of cream/rust c.,** c'est un peu couleur crème/rouille; **the c. problem,** le problème des races de couleur; **c. bar,** *US* **c. line,** discrimination *ou* ségrégation raciale; **local c.,** couleur locale; **the political c. of a journal,** la couleur d'un journal; **to give** *or* **lend c. to a story,** rendre une histoire vraisemblable; **to put a false c. on things,** mal voir les choses; **to see sth in its true colours,** voir qch sous son vrai jour; *Fig* **I've still to see the c. of his money,** je n'ai pas encore vu la couleur de son argent; **c. blindness,** daltonisme *m*; *Comptr* **c. graphics/printer,** graphisme *m*/imprimante *f* en couleur; **c. photography/television,** photographie *f*/télévision *f* en couleur(s); **c. photocopying,** photocopie *f* en couleurs; **c. print,** reproduction *f* en couleurs; **c. scheme,** (*in room etc*) couleurs, coloris *mpl*; *Journ* **c. supplement,** supplément *m* couleurs;

(b) *Art etc* coloris *m*; **light colours,** coloris clairs; **c. value,** valeur *f* chromatique;

(c) matière colorante; **oil c.,** couleur *f* à l'huile; **to paint in water c.,** peindre à l'aquarelle; **box of colours,** boîte *f* de couleurs;

(d) (*complexion*) teint *m*, couleurs *fpl*; **to lose c.,** perdre ses couleurs; **a week in the country will bring the c. to her cheeks,** une semaine à la campagne, et elle reprendra des couleurs; **indignation brought the c. to his cheeks,** l'indignation colorait ses joues; **to have a fresh c.,** avoir le teint frais; *Br* **to be off c.,** ne pas être dans son assiette; **the joke was off c.,** la plaisanterie était d'un goût douteux; **(e)** (*in insignia etc*) couleurs *fpl* (*d'un parti*); *Nau* pavillon *m*, couleurs; **to show** *or* **display one's colours,** montrer son pavillon; *Mil* **(regimental) colours,** le fanion du régiment; **to serve with the colours,** servir sous les drapeaux; **with colours flying,** (à) enseignes déployées; **to pass (an examination) with flying colours,** être reçu brillamment; **to sail under false colours,** naviguer sous un faux pavillon; **to show oneself in one's true colours,** se révéler tel qu'on est; *Fig* **to nail one's colours to the mast,** prendre un parti irrévocable; **c. party,** garde *f* du drapeau; **c. bearer,** porte-drapeau *m inv*; **c. sergeant,** sergent chef (*de la garde du drapeau*); **(f)** *Sp Horseracing* couleurs *fpl* (*d'un jockey, d'une équipe*); *Sp Sch* **to get one's colours,** recevoir une haute distinction sportive.

colour[2], *US* **color 1** *vt* **(a)** colorer; colorier (*une carte, un dessin*); enluminer (*une gravure*); **to c. sth blue,** colorer qch en bleu; **(b)** (*present advantageously*) donner de l'éclat à (*une description*); imager (*son style*); **(c)** (*bias*) présenter (*un fait*) sous un faux jour; **resentment will c. one's opinions,** le ressentiment agit sur *ou* fausse les opinions. **2** *vi* **(a)** (*of person*) rougir; **(b)** (*of thing*) se colorer; (*of fruit etc*) tourner.

►colour in *vtsep* (*add colour to black and white illustration*) colorier; coloriser (*film, photo*).

colour-blind, *US* **color-** ['kʌləblaɪnd] *adj* daltonien, atteint de daltonisme.

colour-coded, *US* **color-** [kʌlə'kəʊdɪd] *adj* (*tools etc*) repéré par des couleurs.

coloured, *US* **colored** ['kʌləd] *adj* coloré; (*drawing*) colorié; (*shirt*) de couleur; **c. person,** personne *f* de couleur; **gaily c. butterfly,** papillon *m* multicolore; **brightly c. clothing,** des vêtements aux couleurs vives; **highly c. narrative,** récit coloré.

Coloured, *US* **Colored** ['kʌləd] *n* **(Cape) C.,** (*in South Africa*) métis, -isse.

coloureds, *US* **coloreds** ['kʌlədz] *npl* **(a)** (*clothes*) couleurs *fpl*; **separate whites and c.,** (*washing instructions*) lavez les couleurs et le blanc séparément; **(b)** gens *mpl* de couleur.

colourful, *US* **colorful** ['kʌləfʊl] *adj* (*ciel etc*) coloré; (*style*) coloré, pittoresque; **a c. character,** un original; **c. language,** langage coloré.

colouring, *US* **coloring** ['kʌlərɪŋ] *n* **(a)** coloration *f*; coloriage *m* (*des cartes etc*); **c. book,** livre de coloriage; **(b)** (*shade*) coloris *m* (*de la peinture, du style*); **(c)** (*complexion*) teint *m* (*d'une personne*); **(d)** (*exaggeration*) apparence *f*.

colouring-in, *US* **coloring-** ['kʌlərɪŋ'ɪn] *adj* **c.-in book,** livre *m* de coloriage.

colourless, *US* **colorless** ['kʌləlɪs] *adj* **(a)** (*clear*) sans couleur, incolore; **water is c.,** l'eau est incolore; **(b)** (*pale*) terne, incolore; (*visage*) blême; (*teint*) délavé; (*lumière*) pâle, falot; **(c)** (*dull*) (*style*) insipide, fade; (*voice*) terne; (*person*) sans caractère.

colourlessness, *US* **colorlessness** ['kʌləlɪsnɪs] *n* (*see adj*) **(a)** absence *f* de couleur; **(b)** décoloration *f* (*du teint*); **(c)** fadeur *f* (*du style*); manque *m* de personnalité.

colourway ['kʌləweɪ] *n* coloris *m*.

colt [kəʊlt] *n* poulain *m*, jeune cheval mâle; *Fig* débutant, -ante, novice *mf*.

Colt ® [kəʊlt] *n* colt *m*, revolver *m*.

coltish ['kəʊltɪʃ] *adj* **(a)** (*immature*) sans expérience; **(b)** (*playful*) folâtre.

coltsfoot ['kəʊltsfʊt] *n* (*plant*) pas-d'âne *m*.

Columbia [kə'lʌmbɪə] *n* **(a) British C.,** Colombie-Britannique *f*; **(b) (District of) C.,** (District fédéral de) Columbia *f*.

columbine ['kɒləmbaɪn] *n* (*plant*) ancolie *f*.

Columbine *n Th* Colombine *f*.

Columbus [kə'lʌmbəs] *n* **Christopher C.,** Christophe Colomb.

column ['kɒləm] *n* **(a)** (*of smoke, mercury*) & *Archit etc* colonne *f*; *Anat* **spinal c.,** colonne vertébrale; *Aut* **steering c.,** colonne de direction; *Av* **control c.,** levier *m* de commande; **(b)** *Mil Nau* colonne *f*; **to march in c./in two columns,** marcher en colonne/en deux colonnes; **supply/relief c.,** colonne de ravitaillement/de secours; *Pol* **fifth c.,** cinquième colonne; **(c)** *Journ* colonne *f*; (*feature*) rubrique *f*; **two c. page,** page de deux colonnes; **sports c.,** rubrique *ou* chronique sportive; **advertising costs £17 per single c. centimetre,** la publicité coûte 17 livres pour chaque centimètre d'une colonne.

columnist ['kɒləmɪst, -əmnɪst] *n* **(a)** *Journ* chroniqueur *m*, courriériste *m*; **sports c.,** rubriqueur *m* aux sports; **(b)** *Pol* **fifth c.,** membre *m* de la cinquième colonne.

colza ['kɒlzə] *n* (*plant*) colza *m*; **c. oil,** huile *f* de colza.

COM [kɒm] *n Comptr* (*abbr* **Computer Output Microfilm**) **COM unit,** unité d'impression sur microfilm; **COM plotter,** traceur C.O.M.; **COM printer,** imprimante sur microfilm.

coma ['kəʊmə] *n Med* coma *m*; **to go into/be in a c.,** entrer/être dans le coma.

comatose ['kəʊmətəʊs] *adj Med* **(a)** (*state*) comateux; **(b)** (*person*) dans le coma.

comb[1] [kəʊm] *n* **(a)** peigne *m*; **to run a c. through one's hair,** se donner un coup de peigne; **c. maker** *or* **manufacturer,** peignier *m*; **(b)** *Tex* peigne *m*; **(c)** (*for painting*) peigne *f* (*à décor, à fileter*); **(d)** (*of cock*) crête *f*; **(e)** (*honeycomb*) rayon *m*; **honey in the c.,** miel *m* en rayon.

comb[2] *n* **to give one's hair a c.,** se donner un coup de peigne.

comb[3] *vt* **(a)** peigner (*les cheveux de qn*); **to c. one's hair,** se peigner; **to c. down a horse,** étriller un cheval; **(b)** *Tex etc* peigner, carder (*la laine etc*); **combed cotton,** coton peigné; **(c)** (*search thoroughly*) ratisser, passer au peigne fin; **she combed the book for references to the crisis,** elle a passé le livre au peigne fin *ou* au crible pour trouver les références à la crise.

►comb out *vtsep* **(a)** (*untangle*) démêler (*les cheveux*); **(b)** carder (*un matelas etc*); **(c)** (*remove*) **to c. the knots out of one's hair,** démêler ses cheveux.

combat[1] ['kɒmbæt] *n* combat *m*; **in c.,** au combat; *Hist* **single c.,** combat singulier; **close c.,** combat rapproché; **mock c.,** combat simulé; **aerial c.,** combat aérien; **c. mission,** mission *f* tactique; **women are now used in a c. role,** les femmes sont maintenant sur le terrain; **c. zone,** zone *f* de combat; **camouflaged c. clothing,** tenue *f* léopard; *US* **c. fatigue,** psychose *f* traumatique.

combat[2] *v* (-t-) **1** *vt* lutter contre, combattre (*une maladie, un préjugé, le crime*). **2** *vi* combattre (**with, against,** contre).

combatant ['kɒmbətənt] *adj & n* combattant, ante.

combination [kɒmbɪ'neɪʃən] *n* **(a)** combinaison *f*; concours *m* (*de sons, de circonstances*); *Ch* combiné *m*, combinaison; **nitrogen in c. with oxygen,** l'azote combiné avec l'oxygène; **an interesting c. of flavours,** un mélange intéressant de parfums; **(b)** (*of people, workers etc*) association *f*; **to enter into a c. with ...,** s'associer avec ...; **(c)** (*for lock*) combinaison *f*; **what is the c.?,** quelle est la combinaison?; **c. lock,** serrure *f* à combinaisons *ou* à code; **(d)** *Br* **(motorcycle) c.,** (motocyclette *f* avec) sidecar *m*; **(e)** *Old-fashioned Br* (*clothing*) **(pair of) combinations,** combinaison-culotte *f*, *pl* combinaisons-culottes.

combine[1] ['kɒmbaɪn] *n* **(a)** *Com Fin* combinaison financière, cartel *m*, trust *m*; **(b)** *Agr* **c. (harvester),** moissonneuse-batteuse *f*, *pl* moissonneuses-batteuses.

combine[2] [kəm'baɪn] **1** *vt* combiner; allier (*des qualités etc*) (**with,** à); (*of person*) (ré)unir, allier; **to c. forces,** joindre ses forces; **to c. strength of body with strength of mind,** allier la force du corps à celle de l'âme; **to c. business with pleasure,** joindre l'utile à l'agréable; **the play combines drama and music,** la pièce allie la fiction et la musique. **2** *vi* (*of people*) s'unir, se réunir, s'associer, s'allier; se liguer (**against,** contre); (*of workers*) se syndiquer; *Pol* (*of parties*) fusionner; *Ch* (*of elements*) se combiner; **everything combined to give me this impression,** tout concourait à me donner cette impression.

combined [kəm'baɪnd] *adj* (*travail*) fait en collaboration; (*mouvement*) d'ensemble; (*efforts*) réuni; *Rail* **c. rail and road ticket,** billet *m* mixte; **the c. sound of a pneumatic drill and the traffic,** le bruit d'un marteau piqueur additionné à celui de la circulation; *Mil etc* **c. operation,** opération combinée *ou* interarmées; **c. force,** force *f* mixte; **c. fleets,** flottes combinées.

combing ['kəʊmɪŋ] *n* **(a)** coup *m* de peigne; **(b)** *Tex* peignage *m*, cardage *m*; **(c)** (*search*) ratissage *m* (*par la police*); **(d) combings,** (*of hair*) cheveux *mpl* (*sur la brosse etc*).

combining [kəm'baɪnɪŋ] *n* combinaison *f*; *Gram* **c. form,** affixe *m*.

combo ['kɒmbəʊ] *n Mus* petite formation musicale.

combust [kəm'bʌst] *vi Tech* brûler.

combustible [kəm'bʌstɪb(ə)l] **1** *adj* combustible. **2** *n* matière *f* inflammable; (*fuel*) combustible *m*.

combustion [kəm'bʌstʃən] *n* combustion *f*; **spontan-**

eous c., inflammation spontanée; **internal c. engine,** moteur *m* à combustion interne; **c. chamber,** chambre *f* de combustion.

come [kʌm] *vi* (*pt* **came** [keɪm]; *pp* **come**) **(a)** venir, arriver (**to,** à); arriver (**from,** de); **he came up to me,** il est venu à moi; **they still haven't c.,** ils ne sont pas encore venus; **here c. the children,** voici les enfants qui arrivent; **here he comes!,** le voilà qui arrive!; **I'm coming with you,** je viens avec vous, je vous accompagne; **she comes this way every week,** elle passe par ici tous les huit jours; **they don't c. here often,** ils ne viennent pas souvent ici; **we're coming to a crossroads,** nous arrivons à un croisement; **c. here!,** venez ici!; (*to dog*) (viens) ici!; **coming!,** je viens!, j'arrive!; **(are you) coming?,** (*with me, us etc*) tu viens?; **c. and see/do/***etc*, viens voir/faire/*etc*; **I have come to see you,** je viens vous voir; **to c. for s.o./sth,** venir chercher qn/qch; **to c. to s.o. for advice,** venir demander conseil à qn; **you've come to the wrong person,** vous vous adressez à la mauvaise personne; **I was coming to the end of my stay,** la fin de mon séjour approchait; **when you come to the last coat of paint ...,** quand tu en seras à la dernière couche de peinture ...; **to c. to the throne,** monter sur le trône; **a crisis is coming,** une crise se prépare; **the fireworks c. next,** le feu d'artifice est après; **what are things coming to?,** où allons-nous?; **letters came pouring in,** ce fut une avalanche de lettres; **he has come a long way,** il arrive de loin; *Fig* il a fait son chemin; **to c. and go,** aller et venir; **the idea came to me that ...,** il m'est venu à l'esprit que ...; **suddenly it came to me,** (*remembered*) tout d'un coup je m'en suis souvenu; (*had idea*) tout d'un coup j'ai eu une idée; **a smile came to her lips,** un sourire parut sur ses lèvres; **c. now!, c., c.!,** allons! voyons!; *Prov* **easy c. easy go,** ce qui vient par la flûte s'en va par le tambour; **to c. to oneself,** (*regain consciousness*) reprendre connaissance; (*recover one's reason*) recouvrer sa raison; **she's as obstinate/intelligent/***etc* **as they c.,** il n'y a pas plus têtue/intelligente/*etc* qu'elle; **he had it coming to him,** il n'a eu que ce qu'il mérite; **I don't know whether I'm coming or going,** je perds la tête *ou* les pédales; *F* **c. summer (and) we shall meet again,** vienne l'été, on se retrouvera tous; **she will be ten c. January,** elle aura dix ans en janvier; **I've got £500 coming to me,** je vais (bientôt) toucher 500 livres; **he never lets anything c. between him and his football,** avec lui le football passe avant tout;

(b) (*happen*) **we must take things as they c.,** il faut prendre les choses comme elles viennent; **c. what may,** advienne que pourra, quoi qu'il arrive *ou* advienne; **how does the door c. to be open?,** d'où vient que la porte est ouverte?; *F* **how c.?,** pourquoi?; **now that I c. to think of it,** maintenant que j'y pense;

(c) (*originate*) **word that comes from Latin,** mot qui (pro)vient du latin; **this is surprising coming from him,** cela étonne de sa part;

(d) (*be included*) **that doesn't c. within my duties,** cela ne rentre pas dans mes fonctions;

(e) (*be*) **that comes easy/natural(ly) to him,** cela lui est facile/naturel; **it came as a shock to me,** cela a été un choc pour moi; **gold watches don't c. cheap,** les montres en or ne sont pas données;

(f) **to c. apart,** se décoller; **to c. apart** *or* **undone** *or* **unstitched,** (*of seam etc*) se découdre; **to c. undone/untied/loose,** (*of tie, knot, bootlaces etc*) se dénouer/se délacer/se défaire;

(g) in the years/days/*etc* **to c.,** dans les années/les jours/*etc* à venir; **that will not be for some time to c.,** cela n'arrivera pas d'ici à quelque temps;

(h) (*of butter*) prendre forme; (*of fruit etc*) venir; (*of teeth*) sortir;

(i) *F* **that's coming it a bit strong,** ça, c'est un peu fort; **to c. the heavy husband,** prendre un ton de mari autoritaire; **don't c. it with me,** (*don't pretend*) ne me la fais pas; (*don't exaggerate*) n'exagère pas;

(j) *F* (*reach orgasm*) jouir.

▶come about *vi* **(a)** (*of event, occurrence etc*) arriver, se passer, se produire; **it came about that,** il arriva *ou* il advint que ...; **(b)** *Nau* virer de bord; (*of the wind*) tourner.

▶come across 1 *vipo* (*find*) trouver, rencontrer (*qn, qch*) par hasard *ou* sur son chemin, tomber sur (*qn*). **2** *vi* **(a)** (*make an impression*) **they c. across as nice people,** ils m'ont paru gentils; **the story doesn't c. across so well on the screen,** l'histoire ne rend pas très bien à l'écran; **how did her story c. across?,** quelle impression est-ce que son histoire t'a faite *ou* donnée?; **(b)** *F* (*pay up*) payer ce que l'on doit; **(c)** (*tell the truth*) se décider à dire la vérité.

▶come across with *vipo F* (*supply*) filer (*l'argent*).

▶come after 1 *vipo* **(a)** (*chase*) poursuivre, courir après; **she came after me with a knife,** elle m'a poursuivi avec un couteau; **(b)** (*follow*) suivre; **n comes after k in the alphabet,** le n vient après le k dans l'alphabet; **what comes after the dancing?,** qu'est-ce qu'il y a après la danse? **2** *vi* (*follow*) suivre; **the recession came after,** la récession a suivi.

▶come along *vi* **(a)** (*hurry*) **c. along!,** allons-y!; (*come here*) amène-toi!, arrive!; **(b)** (*make progress*) **how's the work coming along?,** comment se passe le travail?; **the preparations are coming along fine,** les préparatifs avancent bien; **(c)** (*arrive*) arriver; **everything was peaceful until he came along,** tout était calme avant qu'il n'arrive; **then the baby came along,** ensuite, le bébé est arrivé; **these things c. along when you least expect them,** ces choses-là arrivent quand on s'y attend le moins; **(d)** (*accompany*) venir avec qn; **the children came along,** les enfants sont venus avec nous.

▶come at *vipo* **(a)** (*attack*) attaquer (*qn*); **he came at me with a baseball bat,** il m'a attaqué avec une batte de base-ball; **(b)** parvenir à (*la vérité etc*).

▶come away *vi* **(a)** (*leave*) partir, s'éloigner; **why not c. away with us to Paris for the weekend?,** pourquoi ne pas venir avec nous à Paris ce week-end?; **c. away from that cat — it's got fleas,** éloigne-toi de ce chat, il est plein de puces; **(b)** (*become detached*) se détacher; (*when glued*) se décoller; **the handle came away (in his hand),** l'anse lui est restée dans la main.

▶come back *vi* **(a)** (*return*) revenir; **to c. back (home),** rentrer; **it's all coming back to me,** cela me revient à la mémoire; **her name will c. back to me later,** son nom me reviendra plus tard; **to c. back to what I was saying ...,** pour en revenir à ce que je disais ...; **I'll c. back to you on that when I've got more information,** je vous en reparlerai quand j'aurai plus de détails; **(b)** (*of fashion etc*) revenir en vogue; **(c)** (*from losing position etc*) remonter; **after losing popularity the group are coming back,** après avoir perdu de sa popularité, le groupe redevient à la mode; **(d)** *F* (*retort*) répliquer, riposter.

▶come by 1 *vipo* (*acquire*) **how did you c. by this camera/those bruises?,** comment as-tu fait pour avoir cet appareil-photo/ces bleus? **2** *vi* **(a)** (*go past*) passer; **I heard him c. by,** je l'ai entendu passer; **(b)** (*visit*) passer; **I'll c. by next week if that suits you,** je passerai la semaine prochaine si cela vous convient.

▶come down *vi* **(a)** (*descend*) descendre (*l'échelle, l'escalier*); faire la descente de (*la montagne etc*); *Av* (*crash*) s'écraser; (*land*) atterrir; **the rain was starting to c. down,** la pluie commençait à tomber; **to c. down to breakfast,** descendre déjeuner; **the plane came down in the sea,** (*crashed*) l'avion est tombé en mer; (*landed*) l'avion a amerri; **to c. down (in the world),** déchoir; **to c. down to earth,** descendre des nues;

(b) (*decrease*) (*of temperature, prices*) baisser; **he'll come down a few pounds if you bargain,** il baissera son prix de quelques livres si tu marchandes;

(c) (*be lowered*) **hemlines are coming down this year,** les jupes rallongent cette année;

(d) (*decide*) décider; **to c. down in s.o.'s favour,** se décider en faveur de qn; **the committee came down in favour of a ten per cent increase,** le comité se décida en faveur d'une augmentation de dix pour cent;

(e) (*reach*) **her hair came down to her waist,** ses cheveux lui venaient jusqu'à la taille; **the curtains should c. right down to the floor,** les rideaux devraient tomber jusqu'au sol;

(f) (*be an inheritance*) être un héritage; (*of tale, tradition*) venir (*de nos aïeux*); **the necklace came down to her from her great-aunt,** elle tient ce collier de sa grand-tante; **the tales that have c. down to us,** les contes qui nous sont parvenus;

(g) (*collapse*) (*of tree etc*) s'abattre; (*of structure*) s'écrouler; **a lot of trees came down in the storm,** de nombreux arbres se sont abattus pendant l'orage; **these houses are coming down soon,** on démolira bientôt ces maisons;

(h) (*be removed*) être enlevé *ou* défait *ou* décroché; **the Christmas decorations are coming down today,** aujourd'hui, on défait les décorations de Noël; **that disgusting poster is coming down now!,** enlève-moi tout de suite cet affreux poster!;

(i) (*be a question of*) se résumer, revenir (**to,** à); **the whole difficulty comes down to this question,** toute la difficulté se réduit à cette question; **it all comes down to**

money, ce n'est qu'une question d'argent;

(j) *Am F* (*to happen*) se faire.

▶**come down on** *vipo* **(a)** *F* (*criticize, punish*) tomber sur le dos de qn; **one mistake and he'll c. down on you like a ton of bricks,** si tu fais la moindre erreur, il te tombe dessus à bras raccourcis; **(b)** (*decide in favour of*) **he'll see what happens and c. down on the winning side,** il verra ce qui se passe et se mettra du côté des vainqueurs; **to c. down on s.o.'s side,** décider en faveur de qn.

▶**come down with** *vipo* (*succumb to*) tomber malade de (*une grippe*); **I always c. down with a cold at this time of year,** j'attrape toujours un rhume à cette saison.

▶**come forward** *vi* (*present oneself*) se proposer (*pour faire qch*); **no one has come forward with any alternative ideas,** personne n'a proposé d'autres idées; **the police have appealed for witnesses to c. forward,** la police a demandé aux témoins de se faire connaître; *Iron* **he's not backward in coming forward,** il ne se gêne pas.

▶**come in** *vi* **(a)** (*enter*) entrer; **to c. in again,** rentrer; **c. in!,** entrez!; *Br F* **Mrs Brown comes in twice a week,** Madame Brown vient faire le ménage deux fois par semaine; **Mr Jones isn't coming in today,** (*to office etc*) M. Jones n'est pas là aujourd'hui; *Fig & Cin* **this is where we came in,** on a déjà vu ça;

(b) (*of tide*) monter; (*of ship*) arriver; (*of year*) commencer; (*of funds*) rentrer; (*of custom etc*) s'introduire; *Pol* (*of party*) arriver *ou* parvenir au pouvoir; *Cr* (*of batsman*) venir prendre son tour au guichet; **we don't have much (money) coming in,** il n'y a pas beaucoup d'argent qui rentre; *Sp* **to c. in first/second,** arriver premier/second; **this fashion is coming in again,** cette mode reprend; *Rad TV* **reports are coming in of a coup,** on nous annonce qu'il y a eu un coup d'état;

(c) (*have a role*) avoir un rôle à jouer (*dans une affaire*); **and where do I c. in?,** et moi, quel sera mon rôle?; *F* **that's where I c. in,** voilà où je peux vous aider, voilà où j'interviens; **to c. in useful to s.o./for sth/for doing sth,** servir à qn/à qch/à *ou* pour faire qch; **extra money always comes in useful** *or* **handy,** l'argent en plus est toujours utile *ou* bienvenu;

(d) (*join an enterprise etc*) **they were the founder members of the alliance — the others didn't come in till later,** ce sont les membres fondateurs de l'union, les autres ne s'y sont associés que plus tard; **to c. in with s.o.,** s'associer à qn;

(e) (*contact by radio*) répondre.

▶**come in for** *vipo* (*receive*) **to c. in for praise/criticism,** être félicité/critiqué; **the government came in for a lot of criticism over its handling of the crisis,** le gouvernement a été très critiqué pour la façon dont il gère la crise; **to c. in for a share of sth,** avoir part à qch.

▶**come in on** *vipo* (*be given a part in*) prendre part à; **they let him c. in on the deal,** ils l'ont laissé prendre part à l'affaire.

▶**come into** *vipo* **(a)** (*enter*) entrer dans (*une chambre*); **to c. into the world,** venir au monde; **to c. into power,** arriver *ou* parvenir au pouvoir; **when does the law c. into effect,** quand la loi prend-elle effet?; **to c. into possession of sth,** entrer en possession de qch; **how did this painting c. into your possession?,** comment êtes-vous entré en possession de ce tableau?; **to c. into s.o.'s mind,** (*of idea*) se présenter à l'esprit de qn; **(b)** (*inherit*) hériter (de) (*qch*); recueillir (*une succession*); *F* **to c. into the money,** (*inherit it*) hériter d'une somme d'argent; (*win it*) gagner une somme d'argent; **(c)** (*be involved in*) **ability doesn't c. into it,** le talent n'entre pas en compte.

▶**come of** *vipo* **(a)** (*result from*) **what will c. of it?,** qu'en adviendra-t-il?, qu'en résultera-t-il?; **no good will c. of it,** cela tournera mal; **that's what comes of being too ambitious,** voilà ce qui arrive quand on est trop ambitieux; **(b)** (*derive from*) **to c. of a good family,** être issu d'une bonne famille; **(c) to c. of age,** (*reach legal status*) atteindre la majorité.

▶**come off 1** *vi* **(a)** (*become detached*) (*of button etc*) se détacher, sauter; (*of paint, stain etc*) s'enlever, partir; (*of fabric etc*) se décoller; **does this bit c. off?,** est-ce que ça s'enlève?; **the colour came off on my dress,** la couleur a déteint sur ma robe; **the chain has come off,** (*of bicycle*) la chaîne a sauté; **the top of the pen had come off,** le bouchon du stylo avait sauté.

(b) (*fall from horse, motorbike etc*) tomber;

(c) (*take place*) avoir lieu; **the wedding didn't come off,** le mariage n'a pas eu lieu;

(d) (*succeed*) réussir, aboutir; **did it come off all right?,** ça s'est bien passé?; **my little trip abroad didn't come off,** mon petit voyage à l'étranger est tombé à l'eau; **the experiment came off,** l'expérience a réussi;

(e) (*acquit oneself*) **to c. off badly/with flying colours,** mal s'en tirer/s'acquitter brillamment;

(f) (*escape*) **they came off without a scratch,** ils s'en sont tirés sans une égratignure;

(g) *Sl* (*reach orgasm*) jouir.

2 *vipo* **(a)** (*climb down from, leave*) descendre de (*un mur, une échelle etc*); **to c. off a ship/plane,** (*of passengers, goods*) débarquer d'un navire/d'un avion; **the workers had just come off the late shift,** les ouvriers venaient de quitter la dernière équipe de relais;

(b) (*fall from*) tomber de (*un cheval, une moto etc*);

(c) (*become detached from*) **the handle has come off the knife,** le manche s'est détaché du couteau;

(d) (*be removed from*) **that stain will never c. off the carpet,** cette tache ne partira jamais du tapis;

(e) c. off it!, arrête ton baratin; **c. off it — he's not 21!,** arrête de dire n'importe quoi, il n'a pas 21 ans!

▶**come on** *vi* **(a) c. on!,** en avant!; (*with motion*) arrivez!; *F* (*as challenge*) viens-y donc!; *F* (*expressing incredulity*) allons donc!; **c. on, let's have a game!,** allons! faisons une partie!;

(b) (*make progress*) (*of plants etc*) se développer; (*of people*) faire des progrès; **Jackie's French is really coming on,** le français de Jackie s'améliore vraiment; **Jackie is really coming on with her French,** Jackie fait de gros progrès en français; **how's the work coming on?,** comment le travail avance-t-il?; **the building work is coming on fine,** la construction avance bien;

(c) (*start*) (*of winter etc*) venir, arriver; (*of night*) tomber; (*of symptoms*) apparaître; **I feel a cold coming on,** je sens que je suis en train de m'enrhumer; **I have a sore throat coming on,** je commence à avoir mal à la gorge;

(d) *Th* (*appear*) entrer en scène;

(e) (*be shown*) passer; **the play/film is coming on next week,** on va donner la pièce/le film va passer la semaine prochaine; **when does that programme c. on?,** quand passe cette émission?

▶**come out** *vi* **(a)** (*from room, prison, hospital etc*) sortir; *F* (*of homosexual*) se déclarer *ou* se révéler être homosexuel; **to c. out of a place/a room,** sortir d'un lieu/d'une pièce;

(b) (*become detached*) (*of filling*) partir;

(c) *esp Br Ind* **to c. out (on strike),** se mettre en grève;

(d) (*emerge*) **they came out of that business looking rather foolish,** à l'issue de cette affaire ils avaient l'air plutôt ridicule; **to c. badly/well out of an affair,** se tirer mal/bien se tirer d'une affaire; *Sch* **to c. out first/second,** sortir premier/second, être reçu premier/second;

(e) (*appear*) (*of sun, stars*) paraître; (*of buds*) éclore; *Phot* (*of image*) se développer; (*of rash, pimples*) sortir, se montrer; **to c. out in a rash,** (*of person*) avoir une éruption (*de boutons, de plaques etc*);

(f) (*become known*) (*of the truth*) être découvert; (*of election, sports results etc*) être révélé *ou* communiqué; **as soon as the news came out ...,** dès qu'on a su la nouvelle ...; **it came out that ...,** il s'avéra que ..., il se trouva que ...;

(g) (*be published, issued*) (*of book, journal*) paraître, sortir; (*of record*) sortir; **the magazine comes out on a Wednesday,** ce magazine paraît le mercredi; **when does that film c. out?,** quand est-ce que ce film sort?;

(h) *Phot* **he always comes out well,** il est toujours bien sur les photos; **these photos have come out well,** ces photos sont bien sorties;

(i) (*of stain*) s'enlever, s'effacer; **the colour comes out of this material,** c'est une étoffe qui déteint;

(j) *Math* (*be solved*) se résoudre; **to c. out at ...,** (*of average, total etc*) être de ..., se monter à ...; **everything will c. out (all) right in the end,** tout va s'arranger à la fin;

(k) *Br* (*of debutante*) débuter, faire son entrée dans le monde;

(l) (*decide*) **to c. out strongly,** se prononcer avec vigueur (**for,** pour; **against,** contre); **we've come out against the idea of moving,** on a renoncé à déménager; **the committee came out in her favour,** le comité s'est décidé en sa faveur.

▶**come out with** *vipo F* (*say*) sortir, dire; **to c. out with a remark,** lâcher *ou* laisser échapper une observation; **I'm always wondering what he'll c. out with next,** je me demande toujours ce qu'il va sortir; **she finally came out with what was bothering her,** elle a fini par dire ce qui la tracassait.

▶**come over 1** *vi* **(a)** (*travel, walk etc across*) traverser (*la mer, les champs*); **to c. over from a place,** arriver *ou* venir d'un lieu (*situé de l'autre côté de la mer, du pont, de la montagne etc*); **a lot of Americans came over during the war,** de nombreux Américains sont venus (en Europe) pendant la guerre; **friends are coming over from Canada,** des amis arrivent du Canada; **some friends are coming over,** (*who live not far away*) des amis viennent me *ou* nous voir; **c. over tomorrow,** passe demain; **he came over and spoke to me,** il est venu me parler;

(b) (*change allegiance*) **to c. over to s.o.'s side,** passer dans le parti de qn *ou* du côté de qn; **to c. over to s.o.'s way of thinking,** se rallier à l'opinion de qn;

(c) (*make impression*) **how did she come over?,** quelle impression vous a-t-elle fait?; **he doesn't c. over well on television,** il manque de relief à la télévision; **her voice comes over well,** sa voix passe bien; **he comes over as (being) rather pompous,** il a l'air d'être assez solennel;

(d) *F* (*suddenly become*) **to c. over funny,** être pris d'un malaise.

2 *vipo* (*affect*) envahir, gagner (*qn*); **a change has come over him,** il a bien changé; **what has come over you?,** qu'est-ce qui vous prend?

▶**come round** *vi* **(a)** (*travel*) faire le tour; **the road is blocked, I've had to c. round by the village,** la route est bloquée, j'ai dû faire un détour par le village; **(b)** *F* (*visit*) **c. round and see me one day,** venez me voir un de ces jours; **(c)** (*arrive*) **the weekend will soon c. round,** le weekend viendra bientôt; **birthdays seem to c. round more often after you're 40,** les anniversaires semblent être plus fréquents après 40 ans; **(d)** (*regain consciousness*) reprendre connaissance, revenir à soi; **(e) to c. round to s.o.'s way of thinking,** se convertir à l'opinion de qn; **he has c. round,** il a cédé; **(f)** *Nau* (*of ship*) venir dans le vent; (*of wind*) remonter.

▶**come through 1** *vi* **(a)** (*penetrate*) (*of tooth*) percer; (*of water*) pénétrer; **(b)** (*survive*) **he came through without a scratch,** il s'en est tiré indemne; **(c)** (*arrive*) (*of message etc*) arriver; **my visa is taking a long time to c. through,** mon visa met du temps à arriver *ou* à me parvenir; **the news has just come through,** la nouvelle vient d'arriver. **2** *vipo* **(a)** (*penetrate*) **water is coming through the roof,** l'eau s'infiltre par le toit; **the nail has come through the wood,** le clou a traversé le bois; **(b)** (*survive*) survivre; **he came through the war without a scratch,** il a survécu à la guerre sans une égratignure; **I'm sure you will c. through this crisis,** je suis sûr que tu te sortiras de cette crise; **(c)** (*succeed*) **she came through her exams with flying colours,** elle a réussi ses examens.

▶**come to 1** *vi* **(a)** = **COME ROUND (d)**; **(b)** *Nau* (*of ship*) lofer, venir dans le vent.

2 *vipo* **(a)** (*amount to*) s'élever à; **the bill came to $80,** la note s'éleva à 80 dollars; **how much does it c. to?,** combien cela fait-il?; **the plan never came to anything,** le projet n'a abouti à rien; **that nephew of yours will never c. to anything,** ton neveu n'arrivera jamais à rien;

(b) (*be a question of*) **when it comes to music I haven't got a clue,** je ne m'y connais absolument pas en musique; **c. to that, what are you doing here?,** au fait, qu'est-ce que vous faites ici?; **if it comes to that ...,** à ce compte-là; **it comes to this** *or* **that ...,** cela revient à ceci que ...; **when it comes to buying a car, find yourself a reputable dealer,** si vous voulez acheter une voiture adressez-vous à un concessionnaire d'expérience;

(c) (*get as far as*) en venir à (*qch*); **I wish she'd c. to the point,** si seulement elle en venait au fait; **if it comes to a fight, we outnumber them,** si on en vient à se battre, nous sommes plus nombreux qu'eux;

(d) it's really come to something when ..., si ce n'est pas malheureux que ...; **what is the world coming to?,** où est-ce qu'on va!

▶**come together** *vi* **(a)** (*gather*) s'assembler, se réunir; (*of troops*) opérer une jonction; **(b)** (*meet*) se rencontrer; **the two leaders came together in June,** les deux dirigeants se sont rencontrés en juin; **the two roads c. together at this point,** les deux routes se croisent à cet endroit.

▶**come up** *vi* **(a)** (*go up, go upstairs, climb etc*) (*by stairs, on ladder etc*) monter; (*up a hill*) gravir; **would you like to c. up (to my room** *etc*) **for tea?,** vous voulez monter prendre un thé?; **a man came up from the office downstairs,** un homme est monté du bureau d'en-dessous; **to c. up after a dive,** revenir à la surface après un plongeon;

(b) *Br* **to c. up to town,** venir en ville, venir à Londres;

(c) (*approach*) **a man came up (to me) and started talking,** un homme est venu vers moi et a commencé à (me) parler; **a police car came up alongside ours,** une voiture de police s'est mise à la hauteur de la nôtre; **it's coming up to 10 o'clock,** il est presque 10 heures; *Tennis* **to c. up to the net,** monter au filet;

(d) (*appear*) apparaître; (*of plant*) sortir de terre, pousser; (*of sun*) se lever; **some words came up on the screen,** quelques mots sont apparus sur l'écran; *Nau* **to c. up on the horizon,** (*of land etc*) commencer à paraître à l'horizon; **there's a cabaret act coming up (next),** il y a un numéro de cabaret tout de suite après; **there are some interesting films coming up on television,** il y a quelques films intéressants qui vont passer à la télévision;

(e) (*be on the way*) **your coffee, coming up, sir,** (voilà) votre café, monsieur!;

(f) (*arise*) (*of opportunity, question etc*) se présenter; (*of problem etc*) survenir, surgir; **I'll let you know if anything comes up,** (*if I find further information*) s'il y a du nouveau, je vous tiendrai au courant; (*that is suitable*) je vous tiendrai au courant si je vois quelque chose qui vous convienne; **call me if something comes up that you can't handle,** appelle-moi s'il y a quelque chose qui te pose problème; *Jur* **to c. up before the Court,** comparaître (devant le tribunal); **the case comes up (for trial) tomorrow,** la cause sera entendue demain; **two houses in our street are coming up for sale soon,** dans notre rue, deux maisons seront bientôt à vendre; **to c. up (for discussion),** venir sur le tapis; **this question has never yet come up,** cette question n'a encore jamais été soulevée; **the subject came up twice in the conversation,** le sujet est revenu deux fois dans la conversation;

(g) (*shine, look clean*) **the sideboard came up beautifully,** le buffet est devenu splendide.

▶**come up against** *vipo* **(a)** (*encounter*) se heurter à; **the reformers came up against some pretty strong opposition,** les réformateurs se sont heurtés à une opposition plutôt violente; **who does she c. up against in the next round?,** qui doit-elle affronter dans la prochaine manche?; **(b)** (*hit, come into contact with*) rencontrer; **his hand came up against something cold,** sa main rencontra quelque chose de froid; **the tunnellers came up against solid rock,** les ouvriers qui creusaient le tunnel se sont trouvés face à de la roche dure.

▶**come upon** *vipo* (*find*) trouver (*qch*) par hasard; rencontrer (*qn*) par hasard; surprendre (*un secret*).

▶**come up to** *vipo* **(a)** (*reach*) atteindre (*qch*); **the water came up to my knees,** l'eau me montait jusqu'aux genoux; **I only c. up to her shoulder,** je ne lui arrive qu'aux épaules; **we're coming up to the half-way mark,** nous en sommes maintenant à la moitié (du parcours); **(b)** (*equal*) égaler; **to c. up to s.o.'s expectations,** répondre à l'attente de qn; **to c. up to standard,** être au niveau.

▶**come up with** *vipo* (*produce*) **she's come up with a solution,** elle a trouvé une solution; **he comes up with some terrible jokes,** il sort parfois d'horribles plaisanteries.

comeback ['kʌmbæk] *n* **(a)** (*return*) retour *m* (en vogue); retour au pouvoir (*d'un homme politique etc*); retour à la scène *ou* à l'écran (*d'un acteur*); (*of sportsperson*) retour; **to make a c.,** faire son retour; **(b)** *F* (*reply*) réplique *f*; **(c)** (*justification for complaint*) **to have no c.,** n'avoir aucune raison de se plaindre.

COMECON ['kɒmɪkɒn] *n* (*abbr* **Council for Mutual Economic Aid**) COMECON.

comedian [kə'mi:dɪən] *n* **(a)** comique *m* (*de music-hall etc*); **(b)** *Th* (*actor*) comédien, -ienne.

comedienne [kəmi:dɪ'en] *n* **(a)**(comic) actrice comique (*de music-hall etc*); **(b)** *Th* (*actress*) comédienne *f*.

comedown ['kʌmdaʊn] *n F* **(a)** (*loss of status*) déchéance *f*; **(b)** (*disappointment*) désillusion *f*.

comedy ['kɒmɪdɪ] *n* **(a)** (*genre*) comédie *f*, le genre comique; **c. of manners,** comédie de mœurs; **musical c.,** comédie musicale; **c. actor/actress,** acteur/actrice de comédie; **(b)** (*play, film*) comédie *f*; *TV* **(situation) c.,** comédie de situation; **we weren't taken in by her little c.,** sa petite comédie n'a pas pris.

come-hither [kʌm'hɪðər] *adj F* (*regard*) aguichant.

comely ['kʌmlɪ] *adj Lit* (*person*) avenant, beau, *f* belle.

come-on ['kʌmɒn] *n Sl* incitation *f*; **it was a c.-on to get buyers interested,** c'était pour attirer les clients; **to give s.o. the c.-on,** encourager les avances sexuelles de qn.

comer ['kʌmər] *n* **open to all comers,** ouvert à tout venant; **I'm ready to take on all comers,** je suis prêt à me

battre avec n'importe qui.
comestible [kə'mestɪb(ə)l] **1** *adj esp Am* comestible. **2** *npl* **comestibles,** comestibles *mpl.*
comet ['kɒmɪt] *n Astron* comète *f.*
come-to-bed [kʌmtə'bed] *adj* **she has c.-to-b. eyes,** elle a un regard à la suivez-moi-jeune-homme.
comeuppance [kʌm'ʌpəns] *n F* **she got her c.,** elle n'a que ce qu'elle mérite.
comfort¹ ['kʌmfət] *n* **(a)** (*ease etc*) confort *m*; **to live in c.,** vivre à l'aise; **the boots are fur-lined for extra c.,** les bottes sont fourrées pour plus de confort; **to do sth in the c. of one's own home,** faire qch confortablement chez soi; *US* **c. station,** toilettes *fpl*; **(b) comforts,** commodités *fpl*; **tobacco was one of the soldiers' few comforts,** le tabac était l'un des seuls plaisirs des soldats; **(c)** (*consolation*) consolation *f*; **to take c.,** se consoler; **that's cold c.,** c'est là une piètre consolation; **too close for c.,** plutôt dangereux; **she is a great c. to me,** elle me rend la vie douce; **she was a great c. to us,** elle nous a beaucoup réconfortés; **some c. you are!,** tu parles d'une consolation!; **it's a c. to know that ...,** c'est une satisfaction que ...; **there was little c. in the news that ...,** la nouvelle que ... était peu réconfortante; **(d)** (*well-being*) bien-être *m.*
comfort² *vt* **(a)** (*console*) consoler, soulager (*qn*); **to be comforted,** être consolé, se consoler (**by,** de); **they comforted the wounded,** ils ont réconforté les blessés; **it comforted him to know she had had a decent burial,** ça l'a réconforté de savoir qu'elle avait eu un enterrement décent; **(b)** (*of beverage etc*) réconforter.
comfortable ['kʌmfətəb(ə)l] *adj* **(a)** (*bed, armchair, hotel etc*) confortable; (*dress*) commode; (*warmth, sensation*) agréable, doux, *f* douce; **you will be more c. in this armchair,** vous serez mieux dans ce fauteuil; **to make oneself c.,** se mettre à son aise; **to be c.,** être à l'aise *ou* à son aise; **to feel c.,** se trouver bien *ou* à son aise; **he couldn't get c. in bed,** il ne savait pas comment se mettre dans le lit pour être à l'aise; **she makes people feel c.,** elle met les gens à l'aise; **(b)** (*of patient*) **to be c.,** ne pas souffrir; **he had a c. night,** la nuit a été bonne; **(c)** (*free from worry*) (*majority, lead*) confortable; **I wouldn't feel c. accepting that money,** je ne me sentirais pas tranquille d'accepter cet argent; **c. income,** revenu suffisant; **to be in c. circumstances,** mener une vie aisée; **two hours will give you a c. margin,** en deux heures, tu auras largement le temps.
comfortably ['kʌmftəblɪ] *adv* confortablement, commodément, agréablement; **to be c. off,** être à l'aise; **to live c.,** vivre à l'aise *ou* à son aise; **we can get there c. in an hour,** une heure suffira amplement pour y aller.
comforter ['kʌmfətər] *n* **(a)** (*person*) consolateur, -trice; **(b)** *US* édredon *m*; **(c)** *Br* (*scarf*) cache-nez *m inv* (*de laine*); **(d)** (*for baby*) tétine *f*, sucette *f.*
comforting ['kʌmfətɪŋ] *adj* réconfortant; **c. words,** paroles *fpl* de consolation *ou* de réconfort.
comfortless ['kʌmfətlɪs] *adj* (*room etc*) sans confort, peu confortable; (*person*) désolant; (*prospect*) décourageant.
comfy ['kʌmfɪ] *adj F* = **COMFORTABLE (a).**
comic ['kɒmɪk] **1** *adj* (*chanson etc*) comique; **c. opera,** opéra *m* bouffe; *Journ* **c. strip,** bande dessinée, B.D. *f.* **2** *n* **(a)** (*performer*) comédien, -ienne (*de music-hall*); comique *m*; **(b)** (*magazine*) **c. (book),** bande dessinée, B.D. *f*; **(c)** *Am F* (*in newspaper*) **comics,** (la page des) bandes dessinées.
comical ['kɒmɪk(ə)l] *adj* comique, drôle; **what a c. idea!,** quelle drôle d'idée!
comically ['kɒmɪklɪ] *adv* comiquement, drôlement.
coming ['kʌmɪŋ] **1** *adj* (*année, semaine*) qui vient; (*orage*) qui approche; **c. generations,** les générations futures. **2** *n* venue *f*, arrivée *f* (*de qn*); approche *f* (*de la nuit*); avènement *m* (*du Messie*); **the second C.,** le second avènement; **comings and goings,** allées *fpl* et venues.
comma ['kɒmə] *n* virgule *f*; **inverted commas,** guillemets *mpl*; **to put a word in inverted commas,** mettre un mot entre guillemets.
command¹ [kə'mɑːnd] *n* **(a)** (*order*) ordre *m*, commandement *m*; **to give a c.,** donner un ordre; **to do sth at s.o.'s c.,** agir sur les ordres de qn; **to be at s.o.'s c.,** être aux ordres de qn; **word of c.,** commandement; *Th* **c. performance,** représentation commandée par le souverain;
(b) *Mil* (*authority*) ordre *m*; commandement *m* (*d'une armée, d'une expédition*) (**of,** de; **over,** sur); gouvernement *m* (*d'une place forte*); **he was given the c. of a division/fleet,** on lui a confié le commandement d'une division/de la flotte; **to be in c. of a battalion,** avoir le commandement d'un bataillon, commander un bataillon; **to be in c. of a pass/***etc*, (*hold it*) commander un défilé/*etc*; **c. of the seas,** maîtrise *f* des mers; **c. over oneself,** maîtrise de soi; **who is in c.?,** qui commande?; **to be first/second in c.,** commander en premier/en second; **under (the) c. of ...,** sous le commandement de ...; **to be responsible for one's c.,** être responsable de ses troupes; *Av* **bomber/fighter c.,** aviation *f* de bombardement/de chasse; **Scottish/Northern c.,** (*area*) la région militaire d'Écosse/du Nord; **air/naval c.,** région aérienne/maritime;
(c) (*knowledge*) connaissance *f*, maîtrise *f* (*d'une langue*); **to have a c. of several languages,** posséder plusieurs langues; **she has a good c. of (the) English (language),** elle a une bonne maîtrise de l'anglais;
(d) *Comptr* commande *f*; **c. language,** langage *m* de commande.
command² **1** *vt* **(a)** (*order*) ordonner, commander (**sth,** qch; **s.o. to do sth,** à qn de faire qch); **he did what** *or* **as I commanded him,** il a fait ce que je lui ai commandé *ou* ordonné;
(b) (*be in command of*) commander (*un navire, un régiment*);
(c) (*have at one's disposal*) avoir (*qch*) à sa disposition; **all the skill he could c.,** toute l'habileté qu'il possédait;
(d) (*inspire*) inspirer (*le respect, l'admiration*); forcer (*l'attention*); **to c. a high price,** se vendre à un haut prix;
(e) (*of fort etc*) dominer (*une ville, l'entrée d'un détroit etc*); **window that commands a view over the valley,** fenêtre qui donne sur la vallée.
2 *vi* commander.
commandant [kɒmən'dænt] *n* commandant *m* (*d'un camp etc*).
commandeer [kɒmən'dɪər] *vt Mil* réquisitionner; *Fig* **the boss commandeered our photocopier,** le patron a accaparé notre photocopieuse.
commander [kə'mɑːndər] *n Mil* commandant *m* (*d'armée, de compagnie etc*); chef *m* (*de section*); *Mil Av* chef *m* de bord (*d'un avion etc*); *Nau* capitaine *m* de frégate; **c.-in-chief,** commandant en chef; **one of the great commanders of history,** un des grands chefs de l'histoire; *Mil Av* **wing c.,** lieutenant-colonel *m* (*d'aviation*), *pl* lieutenants-colonels; *Nau* **lieutenant c.,** capitaine de corvette.
commanding [kə'mɑːndɪŋ] *adj* **(a)** *Mil* **c. officer,** officier commandant, chef *m* de corps; **who is your c. officer?,** qui est votre chef de corps?; **(b)** (*tone*) d'autorité, de commandement; (*air*) imposant; (*beauty*) majestueux; **(c)** (*place*) éminent; (*position*) dominant.
commandment [kə'mɑːndmənt] *n* commandement (divin); **the Ten Commandments,** les Dix Commandements; **to keep the commandments,** observer les commandements.
commando [kə'mɑːndəʊ] *n Mil* commando *m.*
commemorate [kə'meməreɪt] *vt* commémorer (*qn, le souvenir de qn*).
commemoration [kəmemə'reɪʃən] *n* **(a)** commémoration *f*; **in c. of s.o./sth,** en commémoration de qn/qch; **(b)** *Rel* commémoraison *f.*
commemorative [kə'memərətɪv] *adj* commémoratif (**of,** de); *Rel* **c. prayer,** commémoraison *f.*
commence [kə'mens] *vt & vi* commencer (*qch, à faire qch, par faire qch*); *Mil* entamer (*les opérations*); *Fml* **he commenced speaking,** il commença à parler.
commencement [kə'mensmənt] *n* commencement *m*, début *m.*
commencing [kə'mensɪŋ] *adj* qui commence; **a c. salary of ...,** un salaire de début de ... .
commend [kə'mend] *vt* **(a)** (*praise*) faire l'éloge de (*qn*); louer (*qn, qch*); **to c. s.o. for bravery,** louer qn de sa bravoure; **(b)** (*recommend*) **a course of action that did not c. itself to me,** une ligne de conduite à laquelle je ne pouvais pas donner mon approbation; **the train journey has little to commend it,** je ne vous recommande pas le voyage en train; **(c)** *Lit* (*entrust*) **to c. sth to s.o.'s care,** recommander *ou* confier qch aux soins de qn; **to c. one's soul to God,** recommander son âme à Dieu; **(d)** *Fml* (*remember*) **c. me to Dr Smith,** rappelez-moi au bon souvenir du Docteur Smith.
commendable [kə'mendəb(ə)l] *adj* louable; (*action*) digne d'éloges; **with c. promptness,** avec une louable promptitude.
commendably [kə'mendəblɪ] *adv* d'une manière louable.
commendation [kɒmen'deɪʃən] *n* **(a)** (*praise*) éloge *m* (**of,** de); **(b)** *Arch* **letters of c.,** lettres *fpl* de recommandation.
commensurable [kə'mensərəb(ə)l, -ʃər-] *adj* **(a)** *Math* commensurable (**with, to,** avec); **(b)** =

COMMENSURATE (b)

commensurate [kə'mensərət, -ʃər-] *adj* **(a)** (*of same proportions*) coétendu (**with,** à); **(b)** (*proportionate*) proportionné (**to, with,** à); **the salary offered will be c. with experience,** le salaire sera en fonction de l'expérience.

comment¹ ['kɒment] *n* observation *f*, commentaire *m*; **to make a c. on sth,** faire des observations sur qch; **no c.,** sans commentaire; **to refrain from c.,** s'abstenir de faire des commentaires.

comment² **1** *vt* observer (*que*). **2** *vi* **(a) to c. on,** faire des observations sur (*qch*); **nobody commented on it,** cela n'a suscité aucun commentaire; **(b) to c. on a text,** commenter un texte.

commentary ['kɒmənt(ə)rɪ] *n* **(a)** *TV Rad* commentaire *m*; **with c. by Terry Davis,** commenté par Terry Davis; **running c.,** (*on a match*) commentaire point par point; **(b)** (*on text etc*) commentaire *m*, glose *f*.

commentate ['kɒmənteɪt] *vi TV Rad* faire le commentaire (**on an event,** d'un événement).

commentator ['kɒmənteɪtər] *n* **(a)** *TV Rad* commentateur, -trice; **sports c.,** commentateur sportif; **(b)** (*on text*) commentateur, -trice.

commerce ['kɒmɜːs] *n* commerce *m*; **Chamber of C.,** Chambre *f* de commerce.

commercial [kə'mɜːʃəl] **1** *adj* **(a)** commercial, -aux; (*port, tribunal etc*) de commerce; (*véhicule*) utilitaire; (*valeur*) marchand; **the c. world,** le commerce; **c. bank,** banque *f* de commerce; **c. law,** droit commercial; *Old-fashioned* **c. traveller,** représentant *m*; **c. artist,** artiste *mf* en publicité; **c. radio/television,** radio/télévision commerciale; **(b)** *usu Pej* (*esprit*) mercantile, commercial; (*record, music*) commercial. **2** *n Rad TV* publicité *f*.

commercialism [kə'mɜːʃəlɪz(ə)m] *n* esprit commercial; *Pej* mercantilisme *m*.

commercialization [kəmɜːʃəlaɪ'zeɪʃən] *n* commercialisation *f*.

commercialize [kə'mɜːʃəlaɪz] *vt* commercialiser.

commercially [kə'mɜːʃəlɪ] *adv* commercialement.

commie ['kɒmɪ] *n & adj F* communiste *mf*.

commiserate [kə'mɪzəreɪt] *vi* **to c. with s.o.,** témoigner de la commisération à qn.

commiseration [kɒmɪzə'reɪʃən] *n* commisération *f*, compassion *f* (**with,** pour).

commissariat [kɒmɪ'sɛərɪət] *n Mil* **(a)** (*department*) intendance *f* (*militaire*); **(b)** (*food*) les vivres *mpl*.

commissary ['kɒmɪsərɪ] *n* **(a)** *US Mil* (*store*) dépôt *m* de vivres; **(b)** *US Mil* (*officer*) officier *m* d'intendance; **(c)** (*delegate*) commissaire *m*, délégué *m*.

commission¹ [kə'mɪʃən] *n* **(a)** *Com* (*payment*) commission *f*; **sale on c.,** vente *f* à la commission; **three per cent c.,** trois pour cent de commission; **c. agent,** représentant *m* à la commission; *Horseracing* bookmaker *m*; **(b)** *Com etc* (*order*) ordre *m*, mandat *m*, commande *f*, mission *f*; **work done on c.,** travail fait sur commande; **to carry out a c.,** s'acquitter d'une commission; **(c)** (*investigating body*) commission *f* (*parlementaire etc*); **fact-finding c.,** commission d'enquête; **(d)** *Nau etc* armement *m* (*d'un navire*); *Mil* = brevet (d'officier); **to put a ship into c.,** armer un navire; **in c.,** (*navire*) en commission; (*avion, usine*) en service; *Fig* **she'll be out of c. for a month,** (*as a result of injury, illness*) elle sera hors circuit pendant un mois; **to resign one's c.,** démissionner, donner sa démission; **to get a** *or* **one's c.,** être nommé officier; **(e)** (*of a crime*) perpétration *f*.

commission² *vt* **(a)** (*order*) commissionner (*qn*) (**to do sth,** pour faire qch); commander (*un livre, un tableau*); **to c. an artist to paint a portrait,** faire à un artiste la commande d'un portrait; **to be commissioned to do sth,** être chargé de faire qch; **(b)** (*appoint*) préposer *ou* déléguer (*qn*) à une fonction; investir (*qn*) d'un pouvoir; *Mil* nommer (*un officier*) à un commandement; **(c)** *Nau etc* armer (*un navire*); mettre (*un avion, une usine*) en service.

Commission [kə'mɪʃən] *n EC* Commission *f*.

commissionaire [kəmɪʃə'neər] *n* commissionnaire *m*; chasseur *m* (*d'hôtel*).

commissioned [kə'mɪʃənd] *adj* **(a)** *Nau* (*navire*) armé; **(b)** *Mil* **c. officer,** officier *m*; **to be c.,** être nommé officier.

commissioner [kə'mɪʃənər] *n* commissaire *m*; (*member of a commission*) membre *m* d'une commission; (*delegate*) délégué *m* d'une commission; **c. of police,** = préfet *m* de police; **c. for oaths,** =officier ministériel (*le plus souvent un solicitor*) ayant qualité pour recevoir les déclarations sous serment.

commissioning [kə'mɪʃənɪŋ] *n* **(a)** nomination *f* (*d'un officier*) à un commandement; **(b)** *Nau* armement *m* (*d'un navire*).

commit [kə'mɪt] *vt* **(-tt-)** **(a)** (*carry out*) commettre, *Jur* perpétrer (*un crime, un délit*); commettre (*une erreur, une indiscrétion*); **to c. suicide,** se suicider;

(b) (*dedicate*) engager (*sa parole d'honneur etc*); **to c. oneself,** se compromettre; **without committing myself,** sans m'engager; **he had committed 2,000 troops to the defence of the village,** il avait assigné 2 000 soldats à la défense du village;

(c) (*entrust*) confier, remettre (**s.o./sth to s.o.'s care,** qn/qch aux soins *ou* à la garde de qn); livrer (*un corps*) (**to the earth,** à la terre); rendre (*son âme*) (**to God,** à Dieu); **to c. sth to writing,** coucher qch par écrit; **to c. sth to memory,** apprendre qch par cœur;

(d) *Jur* **to c. s.o. to prison, to c. s.o.,** envoyer qn en prison; **to c. s.o. for trial,** mettre qn en accusation; (*send to assizes*) renvoyer (*un prévenu*) aux assises;

(e) *Pol* renvoyer (*un projet de loi*) à une commission.

commitment [kə'mɪtmənt] *n* **(a)** (*obligation*) engagement *m* (*financier ou autre*); **I cannot do it because of other commitments,** d'autres obligations m'empêchent de le faire; **to make a c.,** s'engager; **(b)** (*to a cause etc*) engagement *m* (**to,** à); **no one doubts their c.,** personne ne doute de leur engagement; **(c)** *Jur* emprisonnement *m*; **(d)** (*act of entrusting*) dépôt *m* (*d'un document chez un notaire etc*).

committal [kə'mɪt(ə)l] *n* **(a)** *Jur* emprisonnement *m*, mise *f* en prison; internement *m* (*d'un aliéné*) dans un hôpital psychiatrique; **c. for trial,** détention préventive; **c. order,** ordre *m* d'internement; **(b)** (*of corpse*) mise *f* en terre; **(c)** (*of crime*) perpétration *f*.

committed [kə'mɪtɪd] *adj* engagé (**to,** dans); **a c. socialist,** un socialiste engagé; **c. to the struggle,** engagé dans la lutte; **he didn't seem very c.,** son engagement ne semblait pas être très ferme.

committee [kə'mɪtɪ] *n* comité *m*; commission *f*; **to be on** *or* **sit on a c.,** être membre *ou* faire partie d'un comité; *Parl* **standing c.,** commission permanente; **select c.,** conseil *m ou* commission d'enquête; **C. of Ways and Means,** = Commission du budget; **c. meeting,** réunion *f* d'un comité; **c. member,** membre *m* d'un comité.

committeeman [kə'mɪtɪmən, -mæn] *n esp US* homme *m* membre d'un *ou* plusieurs comités.

committeeperson [kə'mɪtɪpɜːsən] *n esp US* membre *m* d'un *ou* plusieurs comités.

committeewoman [kə'mɪtɪwʊmən] *n esp US* femme *f* membre d'un *ou* plusieurs comités.

commode [kə'məʊd] *n* **(a)** (*with drawers*) commode *f*; **(b)** (*toilet*) **(night) c.,** chaise percée.

commodious [kə'məʊdɪəs] *adj* spacieux.

commodity [kə'mɒdɪtɪ] *n Econ etc* marchandise *f*, produit *m*; **coffee is the staple c. of Brazil,** le café est la ressource principale du Brésil; **primary** *or* **basic c.,** produit de base; **c. market,** marché *m* de matières premières.

commodore ['kɒmədɔːr] *n Nau* chef *m* de division; (*of convoy*) chef de convoi; (*Merchant Navy*) capitaine le plus ancien; (*of yacht club*) président *m*; *Mil Av* **air c.,** général *m* de brigade.

common¹ ['kɒmən] *adj* **(a)** (*frequent*) ordinaire; fréquent, qui arrive souvent; **mixed marriages are c. here,** les mariages mixtes sont courants ici; **c. name,** nom vulgaire (*d'une plante*); **in c. use,** d'usage courant; **in c. parlance,** en langage ordinaire; **it is c. (practice) to ...,** il est d'usage de ...; **c. decency,** politesse *f*; **this is c. knowledge,** tout le monde le sait; **the agreement is c. knowledge,** l'accord est connu de tous; **c. or garden cabbage,** chou commun; *Hum* **I'm just a c. or garden lexicographer,** je suis un lexicographe lambda; *Mus* **c. time,** mesure à quatre temps; **the c. cold,** le rhume; **c. sense,** le bon sens, le sens commun; **c. sense dictates that ...,** le bon sens conseille de faire ...; **she has a great deal of c. sense,** elle a beaucoup de bon sens; **it's only c. sense to ...,** c'est raisonnable de ...;

(b) (*shared*) commun; **c. wall,** mur commun *ou* mitoyen; **c. property,** choses communes; *F* **the C. Market,** le Marché commun; **we have c. interests,** nous avons des intérêts communs; **to make c. cause with s.o.,** s'allier à qn; *Jur* **c. land,** champs communs; *Sch* **c. room,** (*for pupils*) salle commune; (*for teachers*) salle des professeurs; *Gram* **c. noun,** nom commun; *Math* **c. divisor** *or* **factor,** commun diviseur; **there is no c. ground between them,** il n'y a pas de terrain d'entente entre eux; *Am St Exch* **c. stock,** actions *fpl* ordinaires;

(c) (*average*) **the c. people,** les gens du peuple; **the c. man,** l'homme moyen; **he lacks the c. touch,** il ne sait pas parler aux gens;

(d) *Pej* (*vulgar*) vulgaire, trivial; (*accent*) plébéien; **he's rather a c. little man,** il est assez vulgaire; **c. expression,** expression triviale; **he's nothing but a c. thief,** ce n'est qu'un vulgaire voleur.

common² *n* **(a) to have sth in c. with s.o.,** avoir qch en commun avec qn; **they have nothing in c.,** ils n'ont rien en commun; **(b)** (*land*) terrain communal; *Jur* vaine pâture; **the village c.,** les communaux du village; **(c)** *Jur* **(right of) c.,** (droits *mpl* de) servitude *f*, droit de (vaine) pâture.

commoner ['kɒmənər] *n* **(a)** roturier, -ière; **(b)** *Jur* usager *m* d'une servitude *ou* du droit de vaine pâture; **(c)** *Univ* (*at Oxford*) étudiant ordinaire (*qui n'est pas boursier*).

common-law ['kɒmənlɔː] *adj Jur* **c.-l. husband/wife,** concubin *m*/concubine *f*; **c.-l. marriage,** concubinage légal.

commonly ['kɒmənlɪ] *adv* **(a)** (*frequently*) communément, ordinairement, généralement; **what is c. known as ...,** ce qu'en langage courant on appelle ...; **(b)** *Pej* (*vulgarly*) vulgairement, de façon vulgaire.

commonness ['kɒmənnɪs] *n* **(a)** (*frequency*) fréquence *f* (*d'un événement*); **(b)** *Pej* (*vulgarity*) vulgarité *f*.

commonplace ['kɒmənpleɪs] **1** *n* lieu commun; (*platitude*) banalité *f*, platitude *f*; **c. book,** recueil *m* de faits notables. **2** *adj* banal, -als; **such operations are becoming c.,** de telles opérations deviennent de plus en plus banales.

commons ['kɒmənz] *npl* **(a)** (*people*) le peuple, le tiers état; **the (House of) C.,** la Chambre des Communes; **(b) to be on short c.,** faire maigre chère.

commonwealth ['kɒmənwelθ] *n* **(a) the British C. (of Nations),** le Commonwealth, la Communauté britannique; **C. country,** pays *m* du Commonwealth; **(b)** (*state*) état *m*; **the C.,** la chose publique.

commotion [kə'məʊʃən] *n* **(a)** (*noise*) agitation *f*, commotion *f*; **in a state of c.,** en émoi; **to create a c.,** faire de l'éclat; **what's all the c. about?,** pourquoi toute cette agitation?; **(b)** (*unrest*) troubles *mpl*.

comms package ['kɒmz'pækɪdʒ] *n Comptr* logiciel *m* de communication.

communal ['kɒmjʊn(ə)l] *adj* communal, communautaire; **c. life,** la vie commune *ou* communautaire; **c. violence,** violence *f* au sein d'une communauté; *Jur* **c. estate,** communauté (conjugale); **c. property,** biens en commun *ou* copropriété.

communally [kə'mjuːnəlɪ] *adv* communalement.

commune¹ ['kɒmjuːn] *n* **(a)** communauté *f* (*de hippies etc*); **(b)** *Admin* (*in some countries*) commune *f*.

commune² [kə'mjuːn] *vi* **(a)** *Lit* s'entretenir (**with s.o.,** avec qn); **to c. with nature,** être en communion avec la nature; **(b)** *US Rel* communier.

communicable [kə'mjuːnɪkəb(ə)l] *adj* (*disease*) transmissible.

communicant [kə'mjuːnɪkənt] *n Rel* communiant, -ante.

communicate [kə'mjuːnɪkeɪt] **1** *vi* **(a) to c. with s.o.,** communiquer avec qn; entrer en communication *ou* en relations avec qn; **to c. by letter,** communiquer par lettre; **he finds it difficult to c.,** il lui est difficile d'entrer en rapport avec les autres; **we can't seem to c.,** on a du mal à communiquer; **we've stopped communicating,** on a cessé de communiquer, on ne se parle plus; **(b)** (*connect*) **rooms that c. with one another,** chambres qui communiquent entre elles; **(c)** *Rel* communier, recevoir la communion. **2** *vt* communiquer, faire parvenir (*une nouvelle etc*); passer (*une maladie*); communiquer (*une émotion*); communiquer (*la chaleur etc*).

communicating [kə'mjuːnɪkeɪtɪŋ] *adj* communicant; **c. rooms,** chambres communicantes; **c. door,** porte *f* de communication.

communication [kəmjuːnɪ'keɪʃən] *n* **(a)** (*contact*) **to be in c. with ...,** être en relation avec ...; **to be in close c. with one another,** être en relations suivies; **to break off all c. with s.o.,** rompre toutes relations avec qn; **communications between the two have broken down,** les relations entre les deux sont rompues; **(b)** (*message etc*) communication *f*, renseignement *m*; **(c)** (*of information, feeling etc*) communication *f* (**of sth to s.o.,** de qch à qn); **communications satellite,** satellite *m* de communications; **c. problem,** problèmes *mpl* de communication; **c. skills,** (*of person*) dons *mpl* de communication; *Comptr* **communications software,** logiciel *m* de communication *ou* de transmission; **(d)** (*means*) voie *f* d'accès; **line of c.,** voie d'intercommunication; *Mil* ligne *f* de communication; **means of c.,** moyens *mpl* de communication; (*transport*) moyens de transport; *Br Rail* **c. cord,** corde *f* de signal d'alarme; **(e)** *Mil* transmissions *fpl*, liaison(s) *f(pl)*; **radio c.,** liaison par radio.

communicative [kə'mjuːnɪkətɪv] *adj* communicatif, expansif; **she's not very c.,** elle n'est pas très expansive.

communion [kə'mjuːnjən] *n* **(a)** *Rel* **the (Holy) C.,** la sainte communion; **c. wine,** (*in Protestant church*) vin *m* de communion; *Cathol* vin de messe; **c. cup,** calice *m*; **to administer Holy C. to s.o.,** administrer la sainte communion à qn; **to take (Holy) C.,** communier; **the c. of saints,** la communion des saints; **(b)** *Lit* communication *f* (**with s.o.,** avec qn).

communiqué [kə'mjuːnɪkeɪ] *n* communiqué *m*; **joint c.,** communiqué commun.

communism ['kɒmjʊnɪz(ə)m] *n* communisme *m*.

communist ['kɒmjʊnɪst] *adj & n* communiste *mf*.

community [kə'mjuːnɪtɪ] *n* **(a)** (*group*) communauté *f*; **the European Economic C.,** la Communauté Économique Européenne; **c. centre,** centre social; *Br* **C. charge,** = impôt local; *US* **c. chest,** fonds *m* de secours; **c. singing,** = chansons populaires reprises en chœur par l'assistance; **c. spirit,** esprit *m* de communauté;

(b) (*village etc*) commune *f*; **Redford is a small mining c.,** Redford est une petite commune minière; **a c. of 2,000,** une commune de 2 000 habitants;

(c) *Rel* communauté *f* (religieuse); ordre *m* (monastique);

(d) the c., le public; **harmful to the c.,** nuisible à la communauté; **relations between the police and the c.,** les relations entre la police et le public;

(e) (*something shared*) communauté *f* (*de biens, d'intérêts etc*); solidarité *f* (*d'intérêts*); communauté, identité *f* (*de goûts etc*).

commutable [kə'mjuːtəb(ə)l] *adj* **(a)** *Jur* (*sentence*) commuable; **(b)** (*interchangeable*) permutable, interchangeable.

commutation [kɒmjʊ'teɪʃən] *n* commutation *f*; *Jur* **c. of sentence,** commutation de peine; *US Rail* **c. ticket,** carte *f* d'abonnement.

commutator ['kɒmjʊteɪtər] *n El* commutateur *m*.

commute¹ [kə'mjuːt] *n US F* trajet *m* (*de qn qui fait la navette entre son travail et son domicile*).

commute² **1** *vi* faire la navette entre sa résidence et son travail; **I c. every day,** je fais le trajet tous les jours. **2** *vt* **(a)** échanger (**for, into,** pour, contre); **to c. an annuity into** *or* **for a lump sum,** racheter une rente par un versement global; **(b)** *Jur* **to c. a penalty into** *or* **for another,** commuer une peine en une autre; **(c)** (*exchange*) interchanger; **(d)** *Metal* transformer.

commuter [kə'mjuːtər] *n* navetteur, -euse; **I've been a c. for fifteen years,** ça fait quinze ans que je fais la navette (entre chez moi et le travail); **c. belt,** (grande) banlieue *f*.

compact¹ [kəm'pækt] *adj* (*neige, sol etc*) compact; (*terrain*) liant; (*style*) concis; (*appartement, cuisine etc*) petit mais bien agencé; (*téléphone, ordinateur etc*) petit mais pratique; (*personne*) petit mais solide; **c. disc,** disque compact; **c. disc player,** lecteur *m* de disques compacts.

compact² ['kɒmpækt] *n* **(a)** (*for powder*) poudrier *m* (*de sac à main*); **(b)** *Am Aut* voiture petite et économique.

compact³ [kɒm'pækt] *vt* rendre (*qch*) compact; tasser (*de la neige*); *Constr* compacter.

compact⁴ ['kɒmpækt] *n* convention *f*, accord *m*.

compactly [kəm'pæktlɪ] *adv* d'une manière compacte.

compactness [kəm'pæktnɪs] *n* caractère compact (*d'une masse etc*); concision *f* (*de style*).

companion¹ [kəm'pænjən] *n* **(a)** compagnon *m*, *f* compagne; (*of an order*) compagnon; **c. in arms,** compagnon d'armes; **(lady) c.,** dame *f* de compagnie; **(b)** (*title of book*) manuel *m*, vade-mecum *m inv*; **(c)** (*other of a pair*) **c. volume,** pendant *m* (*à un livre etc*).

companion² *n Nau* **c. (hatch),** capot *m* (*de descente*); **c. ladder,** échelle *f* de commandement.

companionable [kəm'pænjənəb(ə)l] *adj* sociable.

companionably [kəm'pænjənəblɪ] *adv* de manière sociable.

companionship [kəm'pænjənʃɪp] *n* compagnie *f*; (*comradeship*) camaraderie *f*; **the dog provides c. for her,** le chien lui fait de la compagnie *ou* lui tient compagnie.

companionway [kəm'pænjənweɪ] *n Nau* escalier *m* des cabines.

company ['kʌmpənɪ] *n* **(a)** (*companionship*) compagnie *f*; **to be in s.o.'s c.,** être en compagnie de qn; **I feel relaxed in her c.,** je me sens bien en sa compagnie; **I like his c.,** j'aime sa compagnie *ou* être avec lui; **to keep s.o. c.,** tenir compagnie à qn; **he's very good c.,** c'est un compagnon agréable; **it's nice to have c.,** c'est agréable d'avoir de la compagnie; **she needs the c. of children of her own**

age, elle a besoin d'être avec des enfants de son âge; **to be fond of one's own c.,** aimer être seul; *Prov* **two's c., three's a crowd,** deux s'amusent, trois s'embêtent; **to part c. with s.o.,** (*split up*) se séparer de qn; (*disagree*) ne plus être d'accord avec qn;

(b) (*acquaintances*) compagnie *f*, société *f*; **a man is known by the c. he keeps,** on connaît un homme par ses fréquentations; **to get into bad c.,** faire de mauvaises fréquentations;

(c) (*people present*) assemblée *f*; **present c. excepted,** les présents exceptés; **a very gloomy c.,** une assemblée très lugubre; **the most daring of the c.,** les plus audacieuses des personnes présentes;

(d) (*guest(s)*) invités *mpl*; **we have c. to dinner today,** nous avons du monde à dîner aujourd'hui; *F* **we've got c.!,** (*unexpected visitors*) tiens, voilà du monde!; (*unwelcome presence*) nous avons de la compagnie;

(e) *Com Ind* société *f*; **joint stock c.,** société par actions; **limited liability c.,** société à responsabilité limitée; *Br* **public limited c.,** = société anonyme; **insurance c.,** compagnie d'assurances; **companies' act,** loi *f* sur les sociétés; **(the firm of) Thomas and C.** (*usu* **& Co.**), (la maison) Thomas et Compagnie (et Cie); **it isn't c. policy,** ce n'est pas la politique de la maison *ou* de la société; **c. car,** voiture *f* de fonction; **c. director,** administrateur *m*; **c. secretary,** secrétaire général; **on c. time,** (*to make telephone call etc*) pendant les heures de travail;

(f) *Th* troupe *f*; **touring c.,** troupe en tournée;

(g) *Nau* **the ship's c.,** l'équipage *m* (*au complet, y compris les officiers*);

(h) *Mil* compagnie *f*; **c. officer,** officier *m* de compagnie;

(i) (*of girl guides*) compagnie *f*;

(j) (*guild*) corporation *f* de marchands.

comparable ['kɒmpərəb(ə)l] *adj* comparable (**with,** avec; **to,** à); **the two situations are not c.,** les deux situations ne sont pas comparables.

comparative [kəm'pærətɪv] **1** *adj* **(a)** comparatif; *Gram* **c. adverb,** adverbe comparatif; **c. degree,** le comparatif; **c. grammar/philology,** la grammaire/la philologie comparée; **(b)** (*relative*) (*coût*) comparatif; **he's a c. stranger to me,** je ne le connais guère. **2** *n Gram* comparatif *m*; **in the c.,** au comparatif.

comparatively [kəm'pærɪtɪvlɪ] *adv* **(a)** (*in comparison*) comparativement (**to,** à), par comparaison (**to,** avec); **(b)** (*easy, expensive etc*) relativement.

compare¹ [kəm'peər] *n Lit* **beyond c.,** sans comparaison; **beauty without c.,** beauté sans pareille.

compare² **1** *vt* **(a)** comparer, rapprocher (*des faits, des idées*); confronter (*des résultats etc*); **to c. sth to sth,** (*liken*) comparer qch à qch; (*contrast*) comparer qch avec qch; **to c. sth with sth,** (*contrast*) comparer qch avec qch; **compared with** *or* **to ...,** en comparaison de ..., à côté de ..., par rapport à ...; **to c. notes,** échanger ses impressions; **(b)** *Gram* former les degrés de comparaison de (*un adjectif, un adverbe*). **2** *vi* être comparable (**with,** à); **he can't c. with you,** il ne vous est pas comparable; **it can't c.,** il ne supporte pas la comparaison; **to c. favourably with sth,** ne le céder en rien à qch; **the French car compares well with the Italian one,** la voiture française tient la comparaison avec l'italienne.

comparing [kəm'peərɪŋ] *n* comparaison *f* (*de deux personnes, de deux choses*); rapprochement *m* (*de faits*).

comparison [kəm'pærɪs(ə)n] *n* comparaison *f*; **to make** *or* **draw a c. between sth and sth,** faire la comparaison de qch avec qch; **in** *or* **by c.,** en comparaison; **in c. with ...,** en comparaison de ..., par rapport à ..., à côté de ...; **without c., beyond all c.,** sans comparaison; **there is no c.,** il n'y a pas de comparaison; *Gram* **degrees of c.,** degrés *mpl* de comparaison.

compartment [kəm'pɑːtmənt] *n* **(a)** *Rail* compartiment *m*; **smoking c.,** compartiment fumeurs; **sleeping c.,** compartiment lit (*dans un wagon-lit*); *Aut* **glove c.,** boîte *f* à gants, vide-poches *m inv*; **luggage c.,** soute *f* à bagages; **(b)** (*of a drawer etc*) case *f*; **secret c.,** compartiment secret.

compartmentalize [kɒmpɑːt'ment(ə)laɪz] *vt* compartimenter.

compass ['kʌmpəs] *n* **(a)** (*in surveying*) & *Nau etc* (*with moving needle*) boussole *f*; (*with moving card*) compas *m*; **pocket c.,** boussole de poche; **mariner's c.,** compas (de mer); **steering c.,** compas de route; **c. error,** erreur *f* du compas; **the points of the c.,** les aires *fpl* de vent; **c. card,** rose *f* des vents; *Nau* **to take a c. bearing,** prendre un relèvement au compas; **(b) (a pair of) compasses,** un compas; **(c)** (*scope*) étendue *f* (*du savoir*); espace *m* (*de temps*); portée *f* (*de l'esprit*); *Mus* étendue, diapason *m*, registre *m* (*de la voix*); **beyond the c. of the human mind,** que l'esprit humain ne saurait embrasser; **(d)** limite(s) *f(pl)*, borne(s) *f(pl)* (*d'un endroit*); **(e)** *Constr* **c. brick,** brique *f* circulaire; **c. window,** fenêtre *f* en saillie ronde; *Carp* **c. saw,** scie *f* à guichet.

compassion [kəm'pæʃən] *n* compassion *f*; **to arouse c.,** faire pitié, exciter la compassion; **to show c.,** montrer de la compassion; **you have no c.,** tu n'as pas de pitié.

compassionate [kəm'pæʃənət] *adj* compatissant (**to,** à; **towards,** pour); **on c. grounds,** pour des raisons d'humanité; **c. leave,** permission exceptionnelle (*pour raisons familiales*).

compassionately [kəm'pæʃənətlɪ] *adv* avec compassion.

compatibility [kəmpætə'bɪlɪtɪ] *n* (*of people*) & *Comptr* compatibilité *f*.

compatible [kəm'pætəb(ə)l] *adj* (*person*) & *Comptr* compatible (**with,** avec).

compatibly [kəm'pætəblɪ] *adv* d'une manière compatible (**with,** avec).

compatriot [kəm'pætrɪət, -'peɪ-] *n* compatriote *mf*.

compel [kəm'pel] *vt* (**-ll-**) contraindre, forcer, obliger (*qn*) (**to do sth,** à faire qch); **to be compelled to do sth,** être contraint *ou* obligé de faire qch; **to c. s.o.'s admiration/respect,** forcer l'admiration/le respect de qn.

compelling [kəm'pelɪŋ] *adj* (*force, curiosité etc*) irrésistible; **her book makes c. reading,** son livre est prenant; **a c. speaker,** un orateur qui attire son auditoire; **c. need,** nécessité contraignante.

compellingly [kəm'pelɪŋlɪ] *adv* irrésistiblement.

compendium, *pl* **-ums** [kəm'pendɪəm, -z] *n* (*summary*) abrégé *m*, précis *m*, compendium *m*; **c. of laws,** recueil *m* des lois; *Br* **c. of games,** malle *f* de jeux.

compensate ['kɒmpenseɪt] **1** *vt* **(a)** dédommager, indemniser (*qn*) (**for,** de); (*pay*) rémunérer (*qn*); **(b)** *Tech* compenser (*une pendule etc*); **to c. one another,** (*of factors etc*) se compenser. **2** *vi* **(a) to c. for sth,** racheter qch, compenser qch; **skill may c. for lack of strength,** l'adresse peut compenser *ou* racheter le manque de force; **(b)** *Psy* compenser.

compensated ['kɒmpenseɪtɪd] *adj El etc* compensé.

compensating ['kɒmpenseɪtɪŋ] *adj* compensateur, -trice; *MecE El etc* (*circuit etc*) compensateur; *Tech El* (*soupape, bobine etc*) de compensation; **c. errors,** erreurs *fpl* qui se compensent.

compensation [kɒmpen'seɪʃən] *n* **(a)** compensation *f*; (*for loss, injury*) dédommagement *m*; (*for damage*) indemnité *f*, indemnisation *f*; **all of the victims will receive c.,** toutes les victimes recevront une indemnité; **in c.,** à titre de compensation; **(b)** *Psy* compensation *f*.

compensator ['kɒmpenseɪtər] *n El Phys etc* compensateur *m*; *Aut* palonnier *m* (*du frein*).

compensatory [kɒmpen'seɪt(ə)rɪ] *adj* compensateur, -trice.

compère¹ ['kɒmpeər] *n Th TV etc* animateur *m*, présentateur, -trice (*d'un programme*).

compère² *vt Th TV etc* présenter, animer (*un programme*).

compete [kəm'piːt] *vi* **to c. with s.o.,** faire concurrence à qn, concurrencer qn; **to c. with one another,** se faire concurrence; **we can't c.,** nous ne sommes pas concurrentiels; **to c. for a prize,** concourir pour un prix; **to c. with s.o. for a prize,** disputer un prix à qn; **children here aren't encouraged to c.,** ici, les enfants ne sont pas encouragés à la compétition.

competence ['kɒmpɪtəns] *n* **(a)** (*ability*) compétence *f*, aptitude *f* à (faire) qch, capacité *f* pour (faire) qch; **I don't have the c.,** je n'ai pas les compétences *ou* la compétence; **(b)** (*scope of functions*) attributions *fpl* (*d'un fonctionnaire*); *Jur* compétence *f*; **to be within/beyond the c. of a court,** être/ne pas être de la compétence *ou* du ressort d'un tribunal.

competency ['kɒmpɪtənsɪ] *n* = **COMPETENCE.**

competent ['kɒmpɪtənt] *adj* **(a)** (*able*) capable; (*médecin, travail etc*) compétent; **c. knowledge of English,** bonne connaissance de l'anglais; **c. to do sth,** capable de faire qch; (*qualified*) qualifié pour faire qch; **(b)** *Jur* (*tribunal*) compétent; **c. to inherit,** habile à succéder.

competently ['kɒmpɪtəntlɪ] *adv* avec compétence.

competition [kɒmpɪ'tɪʃən] *n* **(a)** (*rivalry*) rivalité *f*, concurrence *f*; **to enter into c. with s.o.,** concurrencer *ou* faire concurrence à qn; **there was a lot of c. for the job,** il y avait beaucoup de concurrence pour cette place; **to be in c.,** être en compétition; **(b)** *Sp etc* concours *m*; compétition *f* (sportive); **a poetry c.,** un concours de poésie; **c. for**

a prize, concours pour un prix; **to win a prize in open c.,** remporter un prix au concours; **to be good enough to take part in competitions,** être assez bon pour faire de la compétition; **that's him out of the c.,** le voilà hors compétition; **you're up against some tough c.,** vous êtes en face d'adversaires de taille; **(c)** *Com Econ* concurrence *f*; **free c.,** libre concurrence; **unfair c.,** concurrence déloyale; **the company has to stay ahead of the c.,** l'entreprise doit rester plus compétitive que les autres.

competitive [kəm'petɪtɪv] *adj* **(a) she's very c.,** c'est une battante; **c. spirit,** esprit *m* de concurrence; **c. examination,** concours *m*; **c. sports,** (sports *mpl* de) compétition *f*; **(b)** *Com Econ* (*prix etc*) concurrentiel, compétitif; (*produit*) concurrent; **in c. conditions,** en conditions de concurrence; **British industry must be more c.,** l'industrie britannique doit devenir plus compétitive.

competitively [kəm'petɪtɪvlɪ] *adv* **(a)** en esprit de concurrence; **gained** *or* **obtained c.,** obtenu au concours; **(b)** *Com Econ* **c. priced,** à prix compétitifs.

competitiveness [kəm'petɪtɪvnɪs] *n* **(a)** compétitivité *f*; **(b)** *Com Econ* concurrence *f* (*d'un produit sur le marché*).

competitor [kəm'petɪtər] *n* **(a)** *Sp* concurrent, -ente; adversaire *mf*; (*in a contest*) compétiteur, -trice (**for a prize,** pour un prix); **(b)** *Com* (*company, person*) concurrent.

compilation [kɒmpɪ'leɪʃən] *n* **(a)** (*activity*) compilation *f* (*d'un dictionnaire etc*); **(b)** (*list etc*) compilation *f*; **c. album,** (*record*) album *m* de compilation.

compile [kəm'paɪl] *vt Comptr etc* compiler.

compiler [kəm'paɪlər] *n* (*of dictionary etc*) compilateur, -trice, rédacteur, -trice; *Comptr* compilateur *m*.

compiling [kəm'paɪlɪŋ] *n* = **COMPILATION (a).**

complacency [kəm'pleɪsənsɪ] *n* **(a)** (*self-satisfaction*) contentement *m* de soi; **this is no time for c.,** l'heure n'est pas à la complaisance; **(b)** (*satisfaction*) satisfaction *f*, contentement *m*.

complacent [kəm'pleɪsənt] *adj* (*person*) content de soi, suffisant; (*look*) suffisant; (*optimism*) béat; **a c. remark,** une remarque lénifiante.

complacently [kəm'pleɪsəntlɪ] *adv* **(a)** (*smugly*) d'un air suffisant; **(b)** (*with satisfaction*) avec contentement, avec satisfaction.

complain [kəm'pleɪn] *vi* **(a)** se plaindre (**of,** de); **he's always complaining,** il se plaint toujours; **to c. that ...,** se plaindre + *sub or ind*; **I have nothing to c. of, I can't c.,** je n'ai pas à me plaindre; **she complained of giddiness,** elle se plaignit d'un étourdissement; **(b)** (*officially*) se plaindre (**to,** à), réclamer (**against sth,** contre qch).

complainant [kəm'pleɪnənt] *n Jur* plaignant, -ante.

complaint [kəm'pleɪnt] *n* **(a)** (*grievance*) grief *m*, sujet *m* de plainte; **I have no cause** *or* **grounds for c.,** je n'ai aucun motif de plainte; **I've got no c. against you,** je n'ai rien à te reprocher; **(b)** (*official*) plainte *f*, réclamation *f*; **to lodge** *or* **make a c. against s.o.,** porter plainte contre qn; *Admin Com* **complaints office,** service *m* des réclamations; **(c)** *Jur US* plainte *f* en justice; **(d)** (*illness*) maladie *f*; **liver c.,** maladie de *ou* affection *f* du foie.

complaisance [kəm'pleɪzəns] *n* complaisance *f*.

complaisant [kəm'pleɪz(ə)nt] *adj* complaisant.

complement[1] ['kɒmplɪmənt] *n* **(a)** (*of bus etc*) charge complète (*de voyageurs*); *Nau etc* effectif *m*; **full c.,** effectif complet; **engine-room c.,** personnel *m* des machines; **(b)** *Gram Math* complément *m* (*d'un verbe, d'un angle etc*); *Gram* attribut *m*.

complement[2] *vt* compléter, être *ou* faire le complément de (*qch*).

complementary [kɒmplɪ'ment(ə)rɪ] *adj* (*angle, couleur, Comptr opération etc*) complémentaire.

complete[1] [kəm'pliːt] *adj* **(a)** complet, entier; (*repos*) complet; *El* (*circuit*) total; **c. surprise,** surprise totale; **is the pack c.?,** le jeu est-il complet?; *Com* **c. with battery,** livré avec pile; **my happiness is c.,** rien ne manque à mon bonheur; **to give a c. account,** donner tous les détails; **a visit to Brussels would not be c. without a meal here,** la visite de Bruxelles ne serait pas complète sans un repas ici; **c. (and utter) failure,** échec total; **the operation has been a c. success,** l'opération a pleinement réussi; **(b)** (*finished*) terminé; **my report is not yet c.,** mon rapport n'est pas encore achevé.

complete[2] *vt* **(a)** (*finish*) compléter (*qch*); achever, terminer (*un travail etc*); mener à bien (*une tâche*); accomplir (*son apprentissage*); **(b)** (*find missing parts of*) compléter (*une collection, un nombre*); appareiller (*un service à thé*); **c. these sentences,** (*in exercise etc*) complétez les phrases suivantes; *Com* **to c. an order,** compléter une commande; **(c)** (*fill in*) remplir (*une formule, un questionnaire*).

completely [kəm'pliːtlɪ] *adv* complètement, totalement.

completeness [kəm'pliːtnɪs] *n* état complet.

completion [kəm'pliːʃən] *n* achèvement *m* (*d'un ouvrage*); complètement *m* (*d'une collection*); **in process of c.,** en (cours d') achèvement; **near c.,** près d'être achevé; **to reach c.,** s'achever; **occupation on c. (of contract),** (*of property*) prise *f* de possession dès la signature du contrat.

complex ['kɒmpleks] **1** *adj* (*question, phrase*) complexe; *Math* **c. number,** nombre *m* complexe. **2** *n* **(a)** (*building(s)*) complexe *m*; **industrial c.,** complexe industriel; **shopping c.,** centre commercial; **(b)** *Psy* complexe *m*; **Oedipus c.,** complexe d'Œdipe; **inferiority c.,** complexe d'infériorité; *F* **he has a c. about his teeth,** il fait un complexe à cause de *ou* pour ses dents; *F* **you'll give her a c.,** tu vas lui donner un complexe.

complexion [kəm'plekʃən] *n* **(a)** teint *m*; **to have a dark/fair c.,** avoir le teint foncé/clair; **to have a good c.,** avoir une belle peau; **(b)** *Fig* nature *f*, caractère *m* (*de qch*); **that puts a new** *or* **a different c. on it,** voilà qui change la situation.

complexity [kəm'pleksɪtɪ] *n* complexité *f*.

compliance [kəm'plaɪəns] *n* **(a)** action *f* de conformer (**with,** à); **in c. with your wishes,** conformément à vos désirs; **(b)** *Pej* soumission *f* (abjecte).

compliant [kəm'plaɪənt] *adj* **(a)** complaisant, accommodant; **(b)** *Pej* servile.

complicate ['kɒmplɪkeɪt] *vt* compliquer (**with,** de); **that complicates matters,** cela complique la situation.

complicated ['kɒmplɪkeɪtɪd] *adj* compliqué; **to become c.,** (*of situation etc*) se compliquer.

complication [kɒmplɪ'keɪʃən] *n* complication *f*; **c. of circumstances,** engrenage *m* de circonstances; *Med* **if no complications set in,** s'il ne survient pas de complications; **you're always making complications!,** tu compliques toujours les choses!

complicity [kəm'plɪsɪtɪ] *n* complicité *f* (**in,** à).

compliment[1] ['kɒmplɪmənt] *n* **(a)** compliment *m*; **to pay a c. to s.o., to pay s.o. a c.,** faire *ou* adresser un compliment à qn; **my compliments to the chef,** mes compliments au chef; **(b)** (*courtesy*) **to pay one's compliments to s.o.,** faire une visite (de politesse) à qn; **to present** *or* **send one's compliments to s.o.,** se rappeler au bon souvenir de qn; *Old-fashioned* **to present** *or* **send one's compliments to a lady,** présenter ses hommages à une dame; **my compliments to your mother,** mes hommages à votre mère; **with the compliments of the chef,** avec les compliments du chef; **compliments of the season,** meilleurs vœux (*de Nouvel An, Noël etc*).

compliment[2] *vt* complimenter, féliciter (*qn*), faire des compliments à (*qn*); **to c. s.o. on** *or* **on doing sth,** féliciter qn de *ou* d'avoir fait qch; **she complimented him on his English/haircut,** elle l'a félicité pour son anglais/sa coupe de cheveux.

complimentary [kɒmplɪ'ment(ə)rɪ] *adj* **(a)** flatteur, -euse (**about,** pour); **they weren't very c. about my paintings,** ils n'ont pas été très élogieux pour mes tableaux; **c. remarks,** compliments *mpl*, félicitations *fpl*; **(b)** (*free*) gratuit, gracieux; **c. ticket,** billet *m* de faveur; **c. copy,** (*of book*) exemplaire envoyé à titre gracieux.

complin(e) ['kɒmplɪn] *n Rel* complies *fpl*.

comply [kəm'plaɪ] *vi* **to c. with,** se conformer à, accomplir (*une clause d'un traité, une formalité etc*); se soumettre à (*la loi*); observer, satisfaire à (*une règle*); accéder, répondre à (*une demande, un désir*); déférer à (*un avis, une opinion*); obéir à (*un ordre*); **we asked them to move but they did not c.,** nous leur avons demandé de circuler mais ils n'ont pas obéi.

component [kəm'pəʊnənt] **1** *adj* **c. parts,** parties constituantes; *Ind* pièces détachées. **2** *n* composant *m*, partie composante; *Ind* pièce détachée; *Phys Ch* composant.

comport [kəm'pɔːt] *Fml* **1** *vt* **to c. oneself,** se comporter. **2** *vi* s'accorder (**with,** à).

comportment [kəm'pɔːtmənt] *n Fml* conduite *f*, maintien *m*, comportement *m*.

compos ['kɒmpɒs] *adj Jur* **c. mentis,** sain d'esprit.

compose [kəm'pəʊz] **1** *vt* **(a)** composer (*un poème, une symphonie etc*); *Typ* composer (*une ligne*); **(b)** (*make up*) constituer; **to be composed of sth,** se composer *ou* être composé de qch; **(c)** *Art* arranger (*les personnages d'un tableau*); **(d)** (*calm*) calmer, tranquilliser (*l'esprit*); **to c. one's thoughts,** se recueillir (*avant d'agir*); **c. yourself!,** calmez-vous!; **(e)** régler (*un différend etc*). **2** *vi Mus* composer.

composed [kəm'pəʊzd] *adj* calme.
composer [kəm'pəʊzər] *n Mus* compositeur, -trice.
composing [kəm'pəʊzɪŋ] *n Mus Typ etc* composition *f*.
composite ['kɒmpəzɪt] **1** *adj Bot (fleur)* composé; *Archit (chapiteau)* composite; *Cin* **c. shot,** impression combinée. **2** *n* composé *m*; *Bot* composée *f*.
composition [kɒmpə'zɪʃən] *n* **(a)** composition *f (de qch)*, action *f* de composer; **a sonata of his own c.,** une sonate de sa composition; **(b)** *(piece of music)* composition *f*; **a musical c.,** une composition musicale; **(c)** composition *f (de l'air, de l'eau, d'un comité etc)*; **(d)** *Art (distribution of elements)* composition *f*; **(e)** *(mixture)* mélange *m*, composé *m*; *Constr* stuc *m*; simili marbre *m*; **(f)** *Sch* dissertation *f*, rédaction *f*, composition *f*; *Old-fashioned* **prose c.,** thème *m*; **(g)** *Com* arrangement *m*, accommodement *m (avec des créanciers)*; concordat préventif *(à la faillite)*; **to make a c.,** composer.
compositor [kəm'pɒzɪtər] *n Typ* compositeur *m*.
compost¹ ['kɒmpɒst] *n (for garden)* compost *m*.
compost² *vt* composter.
composure [kəm'pəʊʒər] *n* calme *m*, sang-froid *m*; **to regain one's c.,** (re)trouver son sang-froid, se calmer.
compote ['kɒmpɒt] *n Culin* compote *f (de fruits)*.
compound¹ ['kɒmpaʊnd] **1** *adj* composé, combiné; *Archit (ordre)* composite; *Gram (mot, nom)* composé; *Mus (mesure, nom)* composé; *Surg (fracture)* compliqué; *Math (nombre)* complexe; *Metal El (acier, enroulement, moteur)* compound *inv*; **c. fertilizer,** engrais complet; **c. entry,** *(in bookkeeping)* article composé; *Fin* **c. interest,** intérêts composés. **2** *n (combination)* (corps *m*) composé *m*; *Tech* composition *f*, mastic *m*; *Gram* mot composé; **chemical c.,** composé chimique.
compound² [kəm'paʊnd] **1** *vt* **(a)** *(worsen)* aggraver *(un problème etc)*; *Jur* **to c. a felony,** pactiser avec un crime; **(b)** combiner *(des éléments)*; préparer *(une drogue)*; **(c)** *(settle)* accommoder, arranger *(un différend)*; **to c. a debt,** faire une transaction pour le règlement d'une dette. **2** *vi* **(a)** s'arranger, composer (**with s.o.,** avec qn); transiger *(avec sa conscience)*; **(b)** *Com* arriver à un concordat *(avec ses créanciers)*.
compound³ ['kɒmpaʊnd] *n (place)* enceinte *f (d'une résidence etc)*; cour *f (d'une prison)*; *(in South Africa) (for miners)* quartier *m* des noirs *(dans une mine d'or etc)*; *(for livestock)* parc *m* à bétail.
comprehend [kɒmprɪ'hend] *vt* comprendre.
comprehensible [kɒmprɪ'hensəb(ə)l] *adj* compréhensible, intelligible.
comprehensibly [kɒmprɪ'hensəblɪ] *adv* d'une manière compréhensible *ou* intelligible.
comprehension [kɒmprɪ'henʃən] *n* entendement *m*; **it is above** *or* **beyond my c.,** cela dépasse mon entendement; **she looked at him in dawning c.,** elle l'a regardé en commençant à comprendre; **then c. dawned,** puis j'ai *ou* il a *etc* pigé; *Sch* **c. (test),** test *m* de compréhension.
comprehensive [kɒmprɪ'hensɪv] **1** *adj* **(a)** *(wide-ranging) (terme etc)* compréhensif; *(étude, vue)* d'ensemble; **c. knowledge,** vastes connaissances; *Br Sch* **c. school,** = collège d'enseignement secondaire; = lycée polyvalent; **c. programme,** programme détaillé et complet; **c. insurance,** assurance tous-risques; **(b)** *Phil* **the c. faculty,** la faculté de comprendre *ou* de concevoir. **2** *n Br Sch* = collège d'enseignement secondaire; = lycée polyvalent.
compress¹ ['kɒmpres] *n Med* compresse *f*; **to apply a cold c. to sth,** appliquer une compresse froide à qch.
compress² [kəm'pres] **1** *vt* **(a)** comprimer *(un gaz, l'air etc)*; bander *(un ressort)*; *(of compressor)* refouler *(l'air etc)*; **(b)** condenser *(un discours etc)*; concentrer *(son style)*. **2** *vi (of gas etc)* se comprimer; *(of spring)* fléchir.
compressed [kəm'presd] *adj* comprimé; **c. air,** air comprimé; **c. lips,** des lèvres serrées *ou* pincées.
compression [kəm'preʃən] *n* **(a)** compression *f (d'un gaz, d'un ressort etc)*; bande *f (d'un ressort)*; **force of c.,** effort *m* de compression; **c. chamber/period/pump,** chambre *f*/période *f*/pompe *f* de compression; **c. stroke,** *(in engine)* (temps *m* de) compression; **c. ratio,** compression volumétrique; **(b)** *(of thought, style etc)* concentration *f*.
compressive [kəm'presɪv] *adj* compressif, de compression; **c. strain,** déformation occasionnée par la compression; **c. strength,** résistance *f* à la compression; **c. stress,** effort *m* de compression.
compressor [kəm'presər] *n* compresseur *m (de gaz, d'air etc)*; **air c.,** motocompresseur *m*; *Comptr* **c. program,** programme *m* de compression.
comprise [kəm'praɪz] *vt* contenir; **the flat comprises** *or* **is comprised of three rooms,** l'appartement comprend trois pièces.
compromise¹ ['kɒmprəmaɪz] *n* compromis *m*, transaction *f*; **to agree to a c.,** consentir à transiger; **to make** *or* **reach** *or* **arrive at a c.,** composer (**with s.o.,** avec qn); transiger; **policy of no c.,** politique intransigeante; **there must be no c.,** il ne faut pas faire de compromis.
compromise² **1** *vt* compromettre *(qn, son honneur etc)*; transiger sur *(un différend)*; **to c. one's principles,** transiger sur ses principes; **to c. oneself with s.o.,** se compromettre avec qn; **he has been compromised,** il a été compromis. **2** *vi* transiger, composer; **to c. with s.o.,** s'accommoder avec qn; **if he agrees to c.,** s'il accepte un compromis; **let's c.,** faisons un compromis.
compromising ['kɒmprəmaɪzɪŋ] *adj (situation etc)* compromettant.
comptroller [kən'trəʊlər] *n Admin* administrateur *m*; contrôleur *m*; vérificateur *m (de comptes)*.
compulsion [kəm'pʌlʃən] *n* **(a)** compulsion *f*; **under c.,** par contrainte; **to be under c. to do sth,** être astreint à faire qch; **(b)** *Psy* compulsion *f*; **he felt a c. to kiss her,** il se sentit irrésistiblement poussé à l'embrasser.
compulsive [kəm'pʌlsɪv] *adj Psy etc* compulsif; *(fumeur, joueur, menteur)* invétéré; **I am a c. eater,** je ne peux pas m'empêcher de manger; **c. eating is a sign of stress,** le fait de ne pas pouvoir s'empêcher de manger est un signe de stress; **we are all c. in our own way,** nous sommes tous gouvernés par nos compulsions.
compulsively [kəm'pʌlsɪvlɪ] *adv* par besoin; **to smoke c.,** ne pas pouvoir s'empêcher de fumer.
compulsorily [kəm'pʌlsərɪlɪ] *adv* obligatoirement; *Admin* **to be retired c.,** être mis à la retraite d'office.
compulsory [kəm'pʌlsərɪ] *adj* **(a)** obligatoire, forcé; **c. liquidation,** liquidation forcée; **c. school attendance,** scolarité *f* obligatoire; **military service/Latin is c.,** le service militaire/le latin est obligatoire; **(b)** *(coercive)* coercitif; **c. powers,** pouvoirs coercitifs.
compunction [kəm'pʌŋkʃən] *n* remords *m*; **without c.,** sans remords *ou* scrupule.
computation [kɒmpjʊ'teɪʃən] *n Fml* compte *m*, calcul *m*, supputation *f*, estimation *f*; **to make a c. of,** faire le calcul de, calculer *(qch)*; estimer *(les dépenses etc)*; **electronic c.,** calcul électronique.
compute [kəm'pjuːt] **1** *vt* calculer; **computed distance,** distance estimée. **2** *vi* faire des calculs.
computer [kəm'pjuːtər] *n Comptr (machine)* ordinateur *m*; **she's in computers,** elle est dans l'informatique; **to have sth on c.,** avoir qch sur ordinateur; **analog/digital c.,** calculateur analogique/numérique; **the c. age,** l'ère *f* des ordinateurs; **c. aided design,** conception assistée par ordinateur; **c. aided instruction,** enseignement assisté par ordinateur; **c. aided manufacturing,** fabrication assistée par ordinateur; **c. analyst,** analyste *mf* en informatique; *Am* **c. camp,** colonie de vacances centrée sur l'informatique; **to go on a c. course,** aller à un cours d'informatique; **c. dating,** = rencontres organisées par ordinateur; **c. expert,** informaticien, -ienne; **c. game,** jeu *m* informatique; **c. graphics,** infographie *f*; **c. hacker,** pirate *mf* informatique; **to be c. literate,** s'y connaître en informatique; **c. output,** sortie *f* d'ordinateur; **c. program/language/instruction,** programme *m*/langage *m*/instruction *f* machine; **c. printout,** listing *m*; **c. programmer,** programmeur, -euse; **c. programming,** programmation *f*; **c. room,** salle *f* des ordinateurs; **c. science,** informatique *f*; **c. scientist,** informaticien, -ienne; **c. translation,** traduction *f* par ordinateur.
computerization [kəmpjuːtəraɪ'zeɪʃən] *n* informatisation *f*.
computerize [kəm'pjuːtəraɪz] *vt* informatiser; équiper *(une organisation)* d'ordinateurs.
computerized [kəm'pjuːtəraɪzd] *adj* **c. data,** données *fpl* informatiques; **c. type setting,** composition *f* par ordinateur.
computing [kəm'pjuːtɪŋ] *n* calcul *m*, estimation *f*; **c. machine,** machine *f* à calcul; **c. power,** puissance *f* de calcul.
comrade ['kɒmreɪd, -rəd] *n* camarade *m*, compagnon *m*; *(as term of address)* camarade *mf*; **comrades in arms,** compagnons d'armes; *Pol* **C. Jones,** camarade Jones.
comradeship ['kɒmreɪdʃɪp, -rəd-] *n* camaraderie *f*.
comsat ['kɒmsæt] *n Astronaut* satellite *m* de communication.
con¹ [kɒn] *n F* **c. (trick),** arnaque *f*, escroquerie *f*; **what a c.!,** quelle arnaque!; **c. man,** arnaqueur *m*, filou *m*, escroc *m*; **c. woman,** arnaqueuse *f*, escroc.
con² *vt* (-nn-) *F* arnaquer, escroquer *(qn)*; **I've been**

conned, on m'a eu, je me suis fait arnaquer; **they were conned out of £500,** ils se sont fait arnaquer de cinq cents livres; **to c. s.o. into doing sth,** persuader qn à faire qch par la ruse.

con³ *n* **the pros and (the) cons,** le pour et le contre.

con⁴ *n Sl* (*convict*) taulard *m*, tôlard *m*.

con⁵ *vt* (**-nn-**) *Nau* gouverner, piloter; **conning tower,** kiosque *m* (*d'un sous-marin*).

Con *Pol abbr* **Conservative.**

concave ['kɒnkeɪv] *adj* concave, incurvé.

concavity [kɒn'kævɪtɪ] *n* concavité *f*.

conceal [kən'siːl] *vt* cacher (*qn, qch*); dissimuler (*la vérité etc*); masquer (*ses projets, une fenêtre*); voiler (*ses pensées, ses desseins*); **to c. oneself,** se cacher; **to c. one's intentions,** cacher *ou* déguiser son jeu; **to c. sth from s.o.,** (*hide*) cacher qch à qn; (*not tell*) taire qch à qn.

concealed [kən'siːld] *adj* caché; dissimulé; (*virage*) masqué; (*éclairage*) indirect; **danger! c. entrance,** danger! entrée cachée.

concealment [kən'siːlmənt] *n* (**a**) action *f* de (se) cacher; (*of feelings etc*) dissimulation *f*, déguisement *m*; dissimulation (*de certains faits*); **to keep s.o. in c.,** tenir qn caché; **a place of c.,** une cachette; *Fin* **c. of assets,** dissimulation d'actif.

concede [kən'siːd] *vt* concéder (*un privilège etc, Sp un corner etc*); *Pol Sp etc* **to c. defeat,** s'avouer vaincu; **to c. that one is wrong,** admettre qu'on a tort.

conceit [kən'siːt] *n* vanité *f*, suffisance *f*; **eaten up with c.,** pétri *ou* pourri d'amour-propre.

conceited [kən'siːtɪd] *adj* suffisant, vaniteux, prétentieux; **I don't want to sound c. but ...,** je ne veux pas avoir l'air prétentieux mais ...; **he is unbearably c.,** il est d'une suffisance insupportable.

conceitedly [kən'siːtɪdlɪ] *adv* avec suffisance, avec vanité, avec prétention; **he c. imagined that ...,** il a eu la prétention d'imaginer que ... .

conceivable [kən'siːvəb(ə)l] *adj* concevable, imaginable; **it is c.,** cela se conçoit; **it is c. that ...,** il est concevable que ... + *sub*; **by every c. means,** par tous les moyens imaginables; **what c. reason could I have?,** quelle raison concevable pourrais-je avoir?

conceivably [kən'siːvəblɪ] *adv* d'une façon concevable; **she could c. have done it,** il est concevable qu'elle l'ait fait.

conceive [kən'siːv] **1** *vt* (**a**) (*form*) concevoir (*un projet*); **to c. a dislike for s.o.,** prendre qn en aversion; (**b**) (*imagine*) **I cannot c. why ...,** je n'imagine pas pourquoi ...; **it is difficult to c. how ...,** il est difficile de concevoir *ou* d'imaginer comment ...; (**c**) concevoir (*un enfant*); **to be conceived,** (*of child*) être conçu. **2** *vi* (*become pregnant*) concevoir; devenir enceinte.

►**conceive of** *vipo* imaginer (*qch*).

concentrate¹ ['kɒnsəntreɪt] *n* concentré *m* (*de tomates etc*); (*mineral*) minerai concentré; **made from c.,** (*of orange juice*) fabriqué à partir de concentré.

concentrate² **1** *vt* concentrer (*des troupes, son attention etc*); grouper (*des efforts*); **the presence of danger helped to c. our minds,** la présence du danger nous a aidés à nous concentrer; **with concentrated fury,** avec une fureur intense; **industry is concentrated in the south,** l'industrie est concentrée dans le sud; **concentrated milk,** lait concentré. **2** *vi* (**a**) (*mentally*) se concentrer; **try to c.,** (*said by teacher etc*) essayez de vous concentrer; **the noise made it hard to c.,** le bruit faisait qu'il était difficile de se concentrer; **to c. on sth** *or* **on doing sth,** porter toute son attention sur qch, s'appliquer à faire qch; (**b**) se concentrer; **population tends to c. in cities,** la population tend à se concentrer dans les villes.

concentration [kɒnsən'treɪʃən] *n* (**a**) (*mental*) concentration *f*, application *f* (*de l'esprit*); **to lose one's c.,** être déconcentré, perdre sa concentration; **the work requires c.,** le travail demande de la concentration; (**b**) concentration *f* (*des troupes etc*); **c. of effort,** convergence *f* des efforts; **c. camp,** camp *m* de concentration; *Ch* **(degree of) c.,** titre *m* (*d'un acide etc*); **the large urban concentrations,** les grandes agglomérations urbaines.

concentric [kɒn'sentrɪk] *adj Math* concentrique.

concept ['kɒnsept] *n* concept *m*; **this is a difficult c. for children,** c'est un concept difficile à comprendre pour les enfants.

conception [kən'sepʃən] *n* (**a**) conception *f* (*d'un enfant, d'une idée etc*); (**b**) (*idea*) **to have a clear c. of sth,** se représenter clairement qch par la pensée; **he has no c. of how long the work takes,** il n'a aucune idée du temps que le travail prend.

conceptual [kən'septjʊəl] *adj* conceptuel.

conceptualize [kən'septjʊəlaɪz] *vt & vi* conceptualiser.

concern¹ [kən'sɜːn] *n* (**a**) (*interest*) intérêt *m* (**in,** dans); **it's no c. of mine,** cela ne me regarde pas, cela ne me concerne pas; **it's no c. of yours,** cela ne vous intéresse *ou* regarde pas; (**b**) (*worry, compassion*) souci *m*, anxiété *f*, inquiétude *f*; sollicitude *f*; **to show c.,** se montrer inquiet; **my only c. has been to ensure ...,** ma seule préoccupation a été d'assurer ...; **there is no cause for c.,** il n'y a pas de raison de s'inquiéter; **to express c. about sth,** exprimer de l'inquiétude au sujet de qch; (**c**) *Com Ind* entreprise *f*; **a large publishing c.,** une grande maison d'édition; **going c.,** affaire *f* qui marche; **to be sold as a going c.,** (*of shop etc*) à vendre avec fonds.

concern² *vt* (**a**) (*be of interest to, affect*) concerner, regarder, toucher, intéresser (*qn, qch*); se rapporter à (*qn, qch*); avoir rapport à (*qch*); **this does not c. you,** (*does not apply to you*) ceci ne vous concerne *ou* touche pas; (*is not your business*) ceci ne vous regarde pas; **matters that c. the public,** choses qui intéressent le public; **to whom it may c.,** à qui de droit; **to c. oneself with** *or* **about** *or* **in sth,** s'intéresser à qch, s'occuper de qch; **I do not c. myself with what people say,** je ne m'occupe pas de ce que les gens disent; **where work is/children are concerned,** en ce qui concerne le travail/les enfants; **to be concerned in** *or* **with sth,** s'intéresser à *ou* s'occuper de qch; **the parties concerned,** les intéressés; *Com etc* **the department concerned,** le service compétent; **as far as I am concerned,** en ce qui me concerne, quant à moi; **as far as this question is concerned,** en ce qui concerne cette question;

(**b**) (*be about*) traiter de (*qn, qch*); **this book is concerned with politics,** ce livre traite de la politique; **it concerns your mother,** (*she's ill, has had an accident etc*) c'est au sujet de votre mère;

(**c**) (*usu passive*) (*worry*) **to be concerned about s.o./sth,** s'inquiéter *ou* être inquiet de qn/qch; **I am concerned for his health,** l'état de sa santé me donne des inquiétudes; **I am not concerned about what they say,** je ne m'inquiète guère de ce qu'on dit.

concerned [kən'sɜːnd] *adj* (*smile,look*) inquiet, soucieux; **he didn't seem at all c.,** il n'avait pas du tout l'air inquiet.

concerning [kən'sɜːnɪŋ] *prep* concernant, en ce qui concerne, au sujet de, à l'égard de (*qn, qch*); **information c. the crime,** des informations au sujet du *ou* concernant le délit.

concert¹ ['kɒnsət] *n* (**a**) *Mus* concert *m*; **to go to a c.,** aller à un concert; **to give a c.,** donner un concert; **c. performer,** concertant, -ante, concertiste *mf*; **c. hall,** salle *f* de concert; **c. grand,** piano *m* de concert; **c. pitch,** diapason *m*; *Fig* **to be at c. pitch,** être prêt; (**b**) (*association*) concert *m*; **to act in c. (with s.o.),** agir de concert (avec qn).

concert² [kən'sɜːt] **1** *vt* concerter (*des mesures etc*). **2** *vi* se concerter, tenir conseil (**with,** avec).

concerted [kən'sɜːtɪd] *adj* (*plan, effort etc*) concerté; **c. action,** action concertée *ou* d'ensemble.

concertgoer [kɒnsətgəʊər] *n* amateur *m* de concerts.

concertina¹ [kɒnsə'tiːnə] *n* (**a**) *Mus* concertina *m*; (**b**) *Rail* **c. vestibule,** soufflet *m* (*entre voitures*).

concertina² *vi* (**concertinaed** [-nəd]) (*of car etc in collision*) s'écraser en accordéon.

concertmaster ['kɒnsətmɑːstər] *n Am* (*of orchestra*) premier violon.

concerto [kən'tʃɜːtəʊ] *n Mus* concerto *m*; **piano/violin c.,** concerto pour piano/violon.

concession [kən'seʃən] *n* concession *f* (*de terrain, d'opinion etc*); *Com* réduction *f*; *Min* **mining c.,** concession minière; **to make concessions,** faire des concessions; **the only c. the film makes to reality is ...,** la seule concession que le film fait à la réalité est ...; *esp Br* **c. ticket,** (*for theatre, cinema*) ticket *m* à prix réduit.

concessionary [kən'seʃən(ə)rɪ] *Com* **1** *adj* (*compagnie etc*) concessionnaire; (*subside etc*) concédé; (*tarif etc*) réduit. **2** *n* = **CONCESSION(N)AIRE.**

concession(n)aire [kənseʃə'neər] *n Com* concessionnaire *mf*.

conch [kɒŋk, kɒn(t)ʃ] *n* (**a**) (*mollusc*) conque *f*; (**b**) = **CONCHA.**

concha, *pl* **-ae** ['kɒŋkə, -iː] *n* (**a**) *Anat* conque *f* (*de l'oreille*); oreille *f* externe; (**b**) *Archit* voûte *f* d'abside.

conchie, conchy ['kɒntʃɪ] *n Old-fashioned F abbr* **conscientious objector.**

conciliate [kən'sɪlɪeɪt] *vt* (**a**) (*win over*) gagner la bonne volonté de (*qn*); (**b**) (*reconcile*) concilier, réconcilier (*des* *théories contraires, des intérêts opposés*).

conciliation [kənsılı'eıʃən] *n* conciliation *f*; *Jur* **court of c.,** bureau *m* de conciliation; **c. board,** (*in industrial dispute*) conseil *m* d'arbitrage, = conseil des prud'hommes.

conciliatory [kən'sılıət(ə)rı] *adj* conciliatoire, conciliant; (*esprit*) de conciliation.

concise [kən'saıs] *adj* concis; (*style*) dense; (*dictionnaire*) abrégé.

concisely [kən'saıslı] *adv* brièvement, avec concision.

conciseness [kən'saısnıs] , **concision** [kən'sıʒən] *n* concision *f*; **to aim at c.,** serrer son style.

conclave ['kɒnkleıv] *n* **(a)** (*meeting*) assemblée *f*, réunion *f* (*à huis clos*); **to be in c. with s.o.,** tenir conseil avec qn; **(b)** *Cathol* conclave *m*.

conclude [kən'klu:d] **1** *vt* **(a)** (*finish*) terminer, conclure, finir, achever (*un discours, un ouvrage*); clôturer (*une session*); **(b)** (*infer*) conclure; **from this I c. that ...,** de ceci je conclus que ...; **(c)** (*sign etc*) conclure (*la paix, un traité etc*); arranger, régler (*une affaire, un contrat*). **2** *vi* (*at end of speech etc*) **to c.,** en conclusion, pour conclure.

concluding [kən'klu:dıŋ] *adj* (*mot, chapitre*) final, -als; **c. remarks,** remarques pour conclure.

conclusion [kən'klu:ʒən] *n* **(a)** (*inference*) conclusion *f*; **without coming to a c.,** sans rien conclure; **to draw a c. from sth,** tirer une conclusion de qch; **to come to the c. that ...,** conclure que ...; **it was a foregone c.,** c'était prévu; **to jump to a c.,** tirer une conclusion hâtive; **draw your own conclusions,** à vous d'en juger, tirez vos propres conclusions; **(b)** (*end*) fin *f*, conclusion *f* (*d'une lettre etc*); clôture *f* (*d'une session etc*); **in c.,** pour conclure, en conclusion; **to bring a matter to a successful c.,** mener une affaire à bonne fin; **(c)** (*of treaty etc*) conclusion *f*.

conclusive [kən'klu:sıv] *adj* (*argument*) concluant, décisif; (*test*) probant.

conclusively [kən'klu:sıvlı] *adv* décisivement; **it has been c. shown that ...,** il a été montré de façon décisive que ... .

concoct [kən'kɒkt] *vt* **(a)** (*make*) composer (*un cocktail etc*); confectionner, mitonner (*un plat*); **(b)** (*think out*) imaginer, inventer, concocter (*un plan*); machiner (*un complot*).

concoction [kən'kɒkʃən] *n* **(a)** (*of food etc*) confectionnement *m*, confection *f*; **(b)** (*drink, dish etc*) mélange *m*; **(c)** (*of plan*) élaboration *f*; (*of plot*) machination *f*; **a c. of lies,** un tissu de mensonges.

concomitant [kən'kɒmıtənt] **1** *adj* concomitant (**with,** de). **2** *n* événement concomitant.

concord ['kɒŋkɔ:d] *n* **(a)** concorde *f* (*entre personnes*); *Lit* **to live in c.,** vivre dans la concorde (**with,** avec); **(b)** *Gram* concordance *f*; **(c)** *Mus* accord consonant.

concordance [kən'kɔ:dəns] *n* **(a)** concordance *f*, accord *m* (**with,** avec); harmonie *f*; **(b)** *Liter* index *m*, concordance *f* (*de la Bible*).

concordant [kən'kɔ:dənt] *adj* **(a)** qui s'accorde, concordant (**with,** avec); **(b)** *Mus* harmonieux.

concordat [kɒn'kɔ:dæt] *n* concordat *m*.

concourse ['kɒnkɔ:s] *n* **(a)** (*of railway station*) hall *m*; **(b)** (*gathering place*) lieu *m* de rassemblement; **(c)** (*crowd*) foule *f*, rassemblement *m*, affluence *f* (*de personnes*).

concrete¹ ['kɒnkri:t] **1** *n Constr* béton *m* (de ciment); **reinforced c.,** béton armé; **c. mixer,** bétonnière *f*; *Fig* **c. jungle,** forêt *f* de béton. **2** *adj* (*exemple, terme*) concret; **c. music,** musique concrète; **c. suggestion/proposal,** suggestion *f*/proposition *f* concrète *ou* pratique.

concrete² [kən'kri:t] **1** *vt* **(a)** ['kɒnkri:t] *Constr* bétonner (*une paroi etc*); **(b)** (*make solid*) concréter, solidifier (*une matière*). **2** *vi* se solidifier.

concreting ['kɒnkri:tıŋ] *n Constr* bétonnage *m*.

concretion [kən'kri:ʃən] *n Med Geol etc* concrétion *f*.

concubine ['kɒŋkjubaın] *n* **(a)** concubine *f*; **(b)** (*in polygamy*) seconde femme.

concur [kən'kɜ:r] *vi* (**-rr-**) **(a)** (*agree*) être d'accord (**with s.o.,** avec qn), être du même avis (**with s.o.,** que qn); **(b)** (*of events*) concourir, coïncider; **to c. in a result,** concourir à un résultat.

concurrence [kən'kʌrəns] *n* **(a)** concours *m* (*de circonstances*); coopération *f* (*de personnes*); (*in time*) simultanéité *f*; **(b)** (*agreement*) accord *m*, concours *m*; (*assent*) assentiment *m*, consentement *m* (**in,** à).

concurrent [kən'kʌrənt] *adj* **(a)** concourant; (*in time*) simultané; *Math* **c. lines,** lignes concourantes; *Jur* **two c. sentences,** confusion *f* de deux peines; **c. cause,** cause contribuante; **(b)** (*in agreement*) concordant, d'accord; **c. views,** des opinions concordantes.

concurrently [kən'kʌrəntlı] *adv* concurremment (**with,** avec); *Jur* **the two sentences to run c.,** avec confusion des deux peines.

concuss [kən'kʌs] *vt* **(a)** *Med* commotionner (*le cerveau*); **she was badly concussed in the accident,** elle a subi de graves commotions lors de l'accident; **(b)** (*shake*) ébranler, secouer (*qch*).

concussion [kən'kʌʃən] *n* **(a)** *Med* commotion *f* (*cérébrale*); **suffering from c.,** commotionné; **(b)** secousse *f*, choc *m*.

condemn [kən'dem] *vt* **(a)** condamner (*qn*); **to c. s.o. to death,** condamner qn à (la) mort; **to be condemned to sth/to do sth,** être condamné à qch/à faire qch; **(b)** (*declare unsafe etc*) déclarer (*qch*) non utilisable; *Mil* réformer (*du matériel*); **the bridge has been condemned as unsafe,** le pont a été fermé à la circulation à cause de son état dangereux; **these slums have been condemned (as unfit for habitation),** ces taudis ont été condamnés à être démolis; **this meat has been condemned,** cette viande a été jugée impropre à la consommation; **(c)** (*censure*) censurer, blâmer (*qn, une politique etc*); condamner (*un abus etc*); **she condemned the remarks as pure prejudice,** elle a condamné les remarques comme relevant de simples préjugés.

condemnation [kɒndem'neıʃən] *n* **(a)** (*of prisoner*) condamnation *f*; **(b)** (*censure*) censure *f*, blâme *m*, condamnation *f*; **(c)** *Mil* réforme *f* (*du matériel*).

condemned [kən'demd] *adj* **(a)** **c. man,** condamné *m*; **c. cell,** cellule *f* des condamnés; **(b)** (*building*) condamné; (*meat*) jugé impropre à la consommation.

condensation [kɒnden'seıʃən] *n Phys Ch Met etc* condensation *f* (*d'un gaz, d'un liquide, d'un discours etc*); **the windows were covered in c.,** les fenêtres étaient couvertes de condensation.

condense [kən'dens] *Phys Chem Met etc* **1** *vt* condenser (*un gaz, un liquide etc*); serrer (*son style*); concentrer (*un produit*); concentrer (*un faisceau de rayons*); **to c. a chapter into a single paragraph,** condenser un chapitre en un seul paragraphe. **2** *vi* se condenser.

condensed [kən'densd] *adj* (*lait*) concentré, condensé.

condenser [kən'densər] *n* **(a)** *El* condensateur *m*; **(b)** (*for condensing liquids*) condenseur *m*; **surface c.,** condenseur par surface; *Nau* **freshwater c.,** distillateur *m*.

condensing [kən'densıŋ] *n* condensation *f*.

condescend [kɒndı'send] *vi* **(a)** (*accept reluctantly*) daigner, condescendre (**to sth,** à qch; **to do sth,** à faire qch); **(b)** (*do sth beneath one*) s'abaisser, condescendre (**to do,** à faire, jusqu'à faire); **(c)** (*be condescending*) se montrer condescendant (**to s.o.,** envers qn).

condescending [kɒndı'sendıŋ] *adj* (*air, sourire, remarque etc*) condescendant.

condescendingly [kɒndı'sendıŋlı] *adv* d'une manière condescendante, avec condescendance.

condescension [kɒndı'senʃən] *n* condescendance *f* (**to,** envers, pour).

condiment ['kɒndımənt] *n Culin* condiment *m*, assaisonnement *m*; **c. set,** assortiment *m* de condiments.

condisciple [kɒndı'saıp(ə)l] *n* condisciple *m*.

condition¹ [kən'dıʃən] *n* **(a)** (*state*) état *m*, situation *f*; état d'entretien (*du matériel etc*); **road conditions,** l'état des routes; **in good c.,** en bon état; **in bad c., in a poor c.,** en mauvais état; **you're in no c. to drive,** (*you're ill, tired, drunk*) tu n'es pas en état de conduire; **you shouldn't be carrying this case in your c.,** (*to pregnant woman*) tu ne devrais pas porter cette valise dans ton état; **to keep oneself in c.,** (*of person*) se maintenir en forme; **I'm out of c.,** je ne suis pas en forme; **horse in c.,** cheval en chair *ou* en condition;

(b) (*circumstances*) situation *f*, condition *f*; **the c. of the workers,** la situation des travailleurs; **working conditions,** conditions de travail (*dans une usine*); **normal working conditions,** (*of machine*) régime *m* de marche normal; **weather conditions,** conditions météorologiques; **the human c.,** la condition humaine;

(c) (*requirement*) condition *f*; **to impose conditions on s.o.,** (im)poser des conditions à qn; **conditions of sale,** conditions de vente; **conditions of a contract,** stipulations *fpl* d'un contrat; **on c. that ...,** à (la) condition que ...; **you can borrow the book, on one c.,** tu peux emprunter le livre, à une condition; **it was a c. of the lease that ...,** l'une des stipulations du bail était que ...; **under these conditions,** dans ces conditions;

(d) *Med* maladie *f*, affection *f* (*cardiaque etc*);

(e) (*social position*) condition sociale.

condition² *vt* **(a)** *Psy* conditionner (*un sujet*) (**to do,** à faire); **(b)** *Ind Com* conditionner (*la soie, la laine etc*);

vérifier l'état de (*une marchandise*); **c. your hair after you shampoo,** appliquer du démêlant après votre shampooing; **(c)** (*subject to a condition*) soumettre (*qch*) à une condition, conditionner (*qch*).

conditional [kən'dɪʃən(ə)l] **1** *adj Gram* (*proposition*) conditionnel; **c. acceptance of an offer,** acceptation provisoire d'une offre; **my promise was c.,** ma promesse était conditionnelle; **c. on sth,** dépendant de qch; *Gram* **c. mood,** mode conditionnel. **2** *n Gram* **in the c.,** (*verbe*) au conditionnel.

conditionally [kən'dɪʃən(ə)lɪ] *adv* conditionnellement.

conditioned [kən'dɪʃənd] *adj* **(a)** *Psy* **c. reflex,** réflexe conditionné; **(b) air c.,** climatisé; **(c)** *Gram* conditionné.

conditioner [kən'dɪʃənər] *n Ind* appareil *m* à conditionner (*la soie etc*); **air c.,** climatiseur *m*; **fabric c.,** assouplissant *m*; **hair c.,** démêlant *m*.

conditioning [kən'dɪʃənɪŋ] *n* **(a)** *Psy* conditionnement *m*; **(b) air c.,** climatisation *f*; **(c)** *Com Ind* (*of textiles*) conditionnement *m*; **c. cream,** crème démêlante (*pour les cheveux*).

condo ['kɒndəʊ] *n F* = **CONDOMINIUM (b)**.

condole [kən'dəʊl] *vi* **to c. with s.o.,** faire *ou* exprimer ses condoléances à qn.

condolence [kən'dəʊləns] *n* condoléance *f*; **to offer s.o. one's condolences,** présenter ses condoléances à qn; **letter of c.,** lettre *f* de condoléance.

condom ['kɒndəm] *n* préservatif *m*.

condominium [kɒndə'mɪnɪəm] *n* **(a)** (*shared sovereignty*) condominium *m*; **the territory was made a c.,** le territoire fut placé sous un régime de condominium; **(b)** *Am* (*building*) immeuble *m* en copropriété; (*apartment*) appartement *m* dans un immeuble en copropriété; (*ownership*) copropriété *f*.

condone [kən'dəʊn] *vt* trouver des excuses pour (*qch*); *Jur* pardonner (*un adultère*); **I am not condoning the crime ...,** je ne cherche pas à excuser le crime ... .

condor ['kɒndɔːr] *n* (*bird*) condor *m*.

conduce [kən'djuːs] *vi* (*of action or thing*) contribuer, tendre (**to,** à).

conducive [kən'djuːsɪv] *adj* qui contribue (*à qch*), favorable (*à qch*); **this weather is not c. to work,** ce temps n'incite pas au travail.

conduct¹ ['kɒndʌkt] *n* **(a)** *F* (*behaviour*) conduite *f* (**towards s.o.,** à l'égard de, avec, envers qn); **his c. was disgraceful,** sa conduite était honteuse; **insolent c.,** insolence *f*; **good c. certificate,** certificat *m* de moralité; *Sch* **good c. prize,** prix de bonne conduite; *Mil Nau* **c. book,** registre *m* de punitions; **(b)** (*management*) conduite *f*, gestion *f*; **the lawyer's c. of the case,** la manière dont l'avocat a mené l'affaire; **(c) safe c.,** sauf-conduit *m*, *pl* sauf-conduits.

conduct² [kən'dʌkt] **1** *vt* **(a)** (*manage, direct*) mener, gérer (*des affaires*); diriger (*des opérations*); effectuer (*une expérience*); *Mus* diriger (*un orchestre*); *Rel* diriger (*un office*); **to c. a campaign against s.o.,** mener une campagne contre qn; *Jur* **to c. one's own case,** plaider soi-même sa cause; **(b)** *F* **to c. oneself,** se comporter, se conduire (bien, mal); **(c)** (*lead*) conduire, (a)mener (*qn*); **conducted tours,** visites guidées; **to give s.o. a conducted tour,** faire faire à qn une visite guidée; **(d)** *El Phys* être conducteur de; **substance that conducts heat/electricity,** substance qui conduit la chaleur/l'électricité. **2** *vi Mus* être chef d'orchestre; **who's conducting?,** qui est le chef d'orchestre?, qui dirige?

conducting [kən'dʌktɪŋ] *n* **(a)** conduite *f* (*d'une entreprise etc*); art *m* de diriger (*un orchestre*); **(b)** conduite *f* (*de touristes etc*).

conduction [kən'dʌkʃən] *n Phys* conduction *f*, transmission *f* (*de la chaleur etc*); *El* conduction.

conductive [kən'dʌktɪv] *adj Phys El* conducteur, -trice.

conductivity [kɒndʌk'tɪvɪtɪ] *n Phys* conductivité *f*; **thermal c.,** conductibilité thermique.

conductor [kən'dʌktər] *n* **(a)** (*on bus*) receveur *m*; **(b)** *Mus* chef *m* d'orchestre; *Am Rail* chef *m* de train; **(c)** *Phys El* conducteur *m* (*de l'électricité etc*); **c. wire,** fil *m* conducteur; **lightning c.,** paratonnerre *m*; **non c.,** non-conducteur *m*; *Rail* **c. rail,** rail *m* conducteur.

conductress [kən'dʌktrɪs] *n Br* receveuse *f* (*d'un autobus*).

conduit ['kɒndjʊɪt] *n* **c. (pipe),** conduit *m*, tuyau conducteur; (*in machine*) tuyau de communication; *El* tube *m*.

cone [kəʊn] *n* **(a)** *Math* cône *m*; *Opt* cône (*de lumière*); *Culin* cornet *m* (*de glace*); **truncated c.,** cône tronqué; *Nau etc* **signal c.,** cône de signalisation; **traffic c.,** cône de signalisation pour la circulation routière; **(b)** *Metal* cône *m* de fermeture; *MecE* **driving c.,** cône de commande; *Av* **nose c.,** cône avant; **(c)** *Bot* pomme *f*, cône *m* (*de pin*); **c.-bearing,** conifère; **(d)** *Geol* cône *m* (*d'un volcan*); **(e)** *Anat* cône *m* (*de la rétine*).

cone-shaped ['kəʊnʃeɪpt] *adj* en forme de cône, conique.

coney ['kəʊnɪ] *n Arch* lapin *m*; **c. (skin),** peau *f* de lapin.

confab ['kɒnfæb] *n F* (*conversation*) colloque *m*; (*chat*) causerie *f*; **to have a c.,** (*confer*) conférer; (*chat*) bavarder, causer.

confection [kən'fekʃən] *n* **(a)** *esp Am Culin* (*cake, sweet*) friandise *f*; (*preserve*) conserve *f*; **(b)** *Pharm* confection *f*; **(c)** (*making*) confectionnement *m*, confection *f* (*de qch*).

confectioner [kən'fekʃənər] *n Com* (*selling sweets*) confiseur, -euse; (*making, selling cakes*) pâtissier, -ière; **c.'s (shop),** confiserie *f*; **J. Smith bakers & confectioners,** boulangerie-pâtisserie J. Smith; **c.'s custard,** crème pâtissière; *Am* **c.'s sugar,** sucre *m* glace.

confectionery [kən'fekʃən(ə)rɪ] *n Culin* (*sweets*) confiserie *f*.

confederacy [kən'fed(ə)rəsɪ] *n* **(a)** (*alliance*) confédération *f* (*d'États*); *US Hist* **the C.,** les États Confédérés; **(b)** (*conspiracy*) conspiration *f*.

confederate¹ [kən'fed(ə)rət] **1** *adj* confédéré; *US Hist* **the C. States,** les États confédérés. **2** *n* **(a)** confédéré *m*; **(b)** *Jur & Fig* complice *mf*.

confederate² [kən'fedəreɪt] **1** *vt* confédérer (*des États*); **to c. oneself with ...,** se liguer avec .... **2** *vi* **(a)** (*join*) se confédérer (**with,** avec); **(b)** (*conspire*) conspirer (**with,** avec; **against,** contre).

confederation [kənfedə'reɪʃən] *n* confédération *f*.

confer [kən'fɜːr] *v* (**-rr-**) **1** *vt* conférer (*un titre*) (**on,** à); adjuger (*une récompense*) (**on,** à). **2** *vi* conférer, entrer en consultation (**with,** avec; **on, about,** sur); **contestants are not allowed to c.,** les concurrents n'ont pas le droit de se consulter.

conference ['kɒnfərəns] *n* **(a)** conférence *f*; **press** *or* **news c.,** conférence de presse; **to be in c.,** être en conférence (**with,** avec); **round-table c.,** table ronde; **we hope to get management to the c. table,** nous espérons réunir la direction en table ronde; **c. call,** *Tel* réunion *f* téléphone; **c. room,** salle *f* de conférence; **(b)** (*of professional association etc*) congrès *m*, conférence *f*; **international c.,** congrès international; **at a c.,** à un congrès; *Pol* **Party C.,** congrès annuel du parti.

conferment [kən'fɜːmənt] *n* collation *f* (*d'un titre, d'un grade*).

confess [kən'fes] **1** *vi* **(a)** (*of criminal*) faire des aveux; **to c. to a crime,** avouer un crime;

(b) (*admit*) **to c. to sth,** avouer qch; **she confessed to having left the window open,** elle a avoué avoir laissé la fenêtre ouverte; **to c. to a liking for ...,** avouer avoir un penchant *ou* un faible pour ...;

(c) *Rel* (*of sinner*) se confesser (**to s.o.,** à qn, auprès de qn).

2 *vt* **(a)** (*admit*) confesser, avouer (*une faute*); **to c. that ...,** confesser que ...; **I must c. that ...,** je dois avouer que ..., je dois reconnaître que ...; **I was wrong, I c.,** j'admets que j'ai eu tort; **I don't understand either, I must c.,** je dois avouer que je ne comprends pas non plus; **medical experts c. themselves helpless,** les médecins s'avouent impuissants;

(b) *Rel* (*of sinner*) confesser, se confesser de (*ses péchés*); **to c. oneself,** se confesser (**to s.o.,** à qn, auprès de qn);

(c) *Rel* (*of priest*) confesser (*un pénitent*).

confession [kən'feʃən] *n* **(a)** confession *f*, aveu *m* (*de qch*); **to make a full c.,** faire des aveux complets; **I have a c. to make,** j'ai un aveu à faire; **on their own c.,** de leur propre aveu; **that would be a c. of failure,** ça reviendrait à s'avouer vaincu; **(b)** *Rel* confession *f*; **the seal of c.,** le secret de la confession, le secret du confessionnal; **to go to c.,** aller à confesse; **to hear s.o.'s c.,** (*of priest*) confesser qn; **c. of faith,** confession de foi.

confessional [kən'feʃən(ə)l] **1** *adj* confessionnel. **2** *n Rel* confessionnal *m*; **the secrets of the c.,** les secrets *mpl* du confessionnal.

confessor [kən'fesər] *n Rel* **(a)** (*priest*) confesseur *m*; **(b)** (*sinner*) personne qui se confesse; **(c)** (*of one's faith*) confesseur *m*; *Hist* **Edward the C.,** Édouard le Confesseur.

confetti [kən'fetɪ] *npl* confettis *mpl*.

confidant, *f* **confidante** [kɒnfɪ'dænt] *n* confident, -ente.

confide [kən'faɪd] *vt* confier (*un secret*) (**to s.o.,** à qn); **she confided to me that ...,** elle m'a confié que ...; **to c. sth to s.o.'s care,** confier qch à la garde de qn.

►**confide in** *vipo* se confier à (*qn*).
confidence ['kɒnfɪdəns] *n* **(a)** (*trust*) confiance *f* (**in,** en); **to place** *or* **put one's c. in s.o.,** placer *ou* mettre sa confiance en qn, faire confiance à qn; **to win s.o.'s c.,** gagner la confiance de qn; **to have every c. in s.o.,** faire toute confiance à qn; **she has no c. in her own ability,** elle n'a aucune confiance en soi; **with complete c.,** en toute assurance; *Parl* **vote of c.,** vote *m* de confiance; **motion of no c.,** motion *f* de censure; **c. trick,** escroquerie *f*, abus *m* de confiance; **c. trickster,** escroc *m*;
(b) (*assurance*) assurance *f*, confiance *f*; **full of c.,** (*person*) plein d'assurance *ou* de confiance en soi; (*letter, article*) qui dénote une grande assurance; **with c.,** (*agir etc*) avec confiance, avec assurance; **to lack c.,** manquer de confiance en soi, manquer d'assurance;
(c) (*secret*) confidence *f*; **to be in s.o.'s c.,** (*share secrets*) partager les secrets de qn; (*be in the secret*) être dans le secret; **to exchange confidences,** échanger des confidences; **to take s.o. into one's c.,** se confier à qn; **in c.,** confidentiellement, en confidence; **remarks made in c.,** des remarques formulées confidentiellement; **to make a c. to s.o.,** faire une confidence à qn.
confident ['kɒnfɪdənt] *adj* assuré, sûr (**of,** de); (*remark*) plein d'assurance; (*article*) qui dénote l'assurance *ou* la confiance en soi; **are you feeling c.?,** tu te sens sûr de toi?; **we are c. that ...,** nous sommes persuadés que ...; **I'm c. about this translation,** je suis sûr que cette traduction est bonne; **c. of success,** sûr de réussir; **be c.!,** aie confiance en toi!; **c. hope,** ferme espoir *m*.
confidential [kɒnfɪ'denʃəl] *adj* **(a)** (*information, report, tone etc*) confidentiel; **keep it c.,** n'en parlez à personne; **(b)** (*attached to one person*) (*poste*) de confiance; (*secrétaire*) particulier; **c. agent,** homme *m* de confiance.
confidentiality [kɒnfɪdenʃɪ'ælɪtɪ] *n* (*of information, report*) caractère confidentiel.
confidentially [kɒnfɪ'denʃəlɪ] *adv* confidentiellement, en confidence.
confidently ['kɒnfɪdəntlɪ] *adv* (*with trust*) avec confiance, en toute confiance; (*with assurance*) avec assurance, d'un ton assuré.
confiding [kən'faɪdɪŋ] *adj* **c. nature,** caractère confiant.
configuration [kənfɪgjʊ'reɪʃən] *n* (*shape*) *& Comptr* configuration *f*.
configure [kən'fɪgər] *vt Comptr* configurer.
confine [kən'faɪn] *vt* **(a)** (*in prison etc*) (r)enfermer (*qn*); **to be confined to one's room,** (être obligé de) garder la chambre; **to be confined to bed,** être alité; *Mil* **to be confined to barracks,** être consigné; **confined air,** air confiné; **confined space,** espace restreint; **the kitchen is very confined,** la cuisine est très petite; **(b)** (*limit*) **to c. oneself to sth/to doing sth,** se borner *ou* se limiter *ou* s'en tenir à qch/à faire qch; **let us c. ourselves to the question of ...,** tenons-nous en à la question de ...; **c. your answer to the matter in hand,** limitez votre réponse à l'affaire qui nous occupe; **(c)** *Obst* **to be confined,** accoucher.
confinement [kən'faɪnmənt] *n* **(a)** (*in prison*) emprisonnement *m*; **three months' c.,** trois mois de prison; **solitary c.,** régime *m* cellulaire; **to be in solitary c.,** être en cellule; **(b)** (*limitation*) limitation *f*, restriction *f* (**to,** à); **(c)** *Obst* couches *fpl*, accouchement *m*.
confines ['kɒnfaɪnz] *npl Lit* confins *mpl* (*d'un lieu etc*); **within the confines of this subject,** dans les limites du sujet.
confirm [kən'fɜːm] **1** *vt* **(a)** (*corroborate*) confirmer, corroborer (*une nouvelle, des soupçons*); confirmer (*une réservation*); *Av* **flight confirmed,** vol confirmé; **not confirmed,** (*of concert, film etc*) à confirmer; **to c. that ...,** confirmer que ...; **she confirmed that she would attend the interview,** elle a confirmé qu'elle se rendrait à l'entretien;
(b) (*reinforce*) (r)affermir, assurer (*son pouvoir*); confirmer (*qn dans une opinion*); **to c. s.o.'s fears,** confirmer les craintes de qn;
(c) (*approve, validate*) confirmer (*un traité, un privilège etc*); approuver (*une nomination*); entériner (*une décision*); valider (*une élection*);
(d) *Rel* confirmer, donner la confirmation à (*qn*); **to be confirmed,** recevoir la confirmation.
2 *vi* confirmer; **please c. in writing,** veuillez confirmer par écrit.
confirmation [kɒnfə'meɪʃən] *n* **(a)** (*of news, doubts, reservation etc*) confirmation *f*; **written c.,** confirmation écrite; **there has been no c. of the rumour,** la rumeur n'a pas été confirmée; **(b)** (*reinforcement*) (r)affermissement *m* (*de l'autorité de qn*); **(c)** (*validation*) confirmation *f* (*d'un traité etc*); corroboration *f* (*d'un témoignage etc*); *Jur* homologation *f*; **in c. of ...,** à l'appui de ...; (*a reservation*) pour confirmer ...; **(d)** *Rel* confirmation *f*.
confirmed [kən'fɜːmd] *adj* (*habitude*) invétéré; (*ivrogne*) incorrigible; **c. bachelor,** célibataire endurci.
confiscate ['kɒnfɪskeɪt] *vt* confisquer (**from s.o.,** à qn).
confiscation [kɒnfɪs'keɪʃən] *n* confiscation *f*.
confiscatory [kɒnfɪs'keɪtərɪ] *adj* (*power*) de confiscation.
conflagration [kɒnflə'greɪʃən] *n Fml* (grand) incendie *m*; *Fig* conflagration *f*.
conflict¹ ['kɒnflɪkt] *n* conflit *m* (*de personnes*); conflit, antagonisme *m* (*de lois, de sentiments, d'intérêts*); **there is no c. of interests,** il n'y a pas de conflit d'intérêts; **a c. of interest situation,** une situation entraînant un conflit d'intérêts; **armed c.,** conflit armé; **to come into/to be in c.,** entrer/être en conflit (**with,** avec); **this was in c. with her principles,** c'était en conflit *ou* en contradiction avec ses principes.
conflict² [kən'flɪkt] *vi* être en conflit *ou* en désaccord (**with sth,** avec qch); **this conflicts with his earlier statement,** ceci est en contradiction avec sa déclaration précédente; **duties that c. with each other,** fonctions *fpl* incompatibles; **it conflicts with another appointment,** j'ai *ou* elle a *etc* un autre rendez-vous à cette heure.
conflicting [kən'flɪktɪŋ] *adj* (*opinions*) opposé (**with,** à); (*advice, evidence*) contradictoire; **c. interests,** des intérêts incompatibles.
confluence ['kɒnfluəns] *n Geog* confluent *m*, confluence *f* (*de deux cours d'eau, deux glaciers*).
conform [kən'fɔːm] **1** *vi* **(a)** se conformer (**to sth,** à qch); **to c. to a standard,** (*of equipment*) être conforme à *ou* répondre à une norme; **to c. to the law,** obéir aux lois; **to c. (in shape) to another part,** (*of a part*) être identique à une autre pièce; **(b)** *Rel Pol etc* faire acte de soumission; **when fashion changed, she refused to c.,** lorsque la mode a changé, elle a refusé de suivre le mouvement. **2** *vt* conformer (**sth to sth,** qch à qch).
conformable [kən'fɔːməb(ə)l] *adj* **(a)** (*thing*) conforme (**to,** à); **(b)** (*person*) accommodant, docile (**to,** à).
conformism [kən'fɔːmɪz(ə)m] *n Rel etc* conformisme *m*.
conformist [kən'fɔːmɪst] *n Rel etc* conformiste *mf*.
conformity [kən'fɔːmɪtɪ] *n* **(a)** conformité *f* (**to, with,** à); **in c. with ...,** conformément à ...; **action in c. with the law,** action conforme à la loi; **(b)** *Rel* conformisme *m*.
confound [kən'faʊnd] *vt* **(a)** (*confuse, surprise*) bouleverser, troubler (*qn*); **(b)** (*bring to nothing*) déconcerter, renverser (*les plans de qn*); réduire à rien (*un espoir*); **(c)** *Lit* (*put in confusion*) mettre la confusion dans (*qch*), **to c. sth with sth,** confondre qch avec qch; **(d)** (*curse*) *F* envoyer (*qn*) au diable; *Lit* **c. him!,** que le diable l'emporte!; **c. it!,** zut alors!
confounded [kən'faʊndɪd] *adj F* sacré; **you c. idiot!,** espèce d'idiot!
confront [kən'frʌnt] *vt* **(a)** (*face*) affronter, faire face à (*l'ennemi, un danger*); tenir tête à (*l'ennemi*); **to c. the issue,** faire face au problème; **to c. s.o. with,** confronter qn avec (*des témoins etc*); mettre qn en présence *ou* en face de (*qch*); **she confronted him with his responsibilities,** elle l'a mis face à ses responsabilités; **(b)** (*be faced with*) être en face de, se trouver en présence de (*qn,qch*); **to be confronted by** *or* **with a difficulty,** se trouver en face d'une difficulté.
confrontation [kɒnfrʌn'teɪʃən] *n* **(a)** (*of two people, armies etc*) affrontement *m* (**with,** avec); **he tried to avoid a c.,** il a essayé d'éviter un affrontement; **(b)** (*bringing into contact*) confrontation *f* (*de témoins etc*).
confrontational [kɒnfrʌn'teɪʃən(ə)l] *adj* (*situation*) d'affrontement; (*policy*) de confrontation.
Confucian [kən'fjuːʃən] *adj Phil* confucéen, -enne, confucianiste.
confuse [kən'fjuːz] *vt* **(a)** (*make unsure*) embrouiller (*qn*); **to get confused,** s'embrouiller, s'y perdre; **(b)** (*put into disorder*) compliquer, brouiller; mettre la confusion dans (*les choses*); **to c. the issue,** compliquer les choses; **it'll only c. matters,** ça ne fera que compliquer les choses; **(c)** (*mix up*) confondre (*des dates, des noms etc*); **he always confuses the two,** il confond toujours les deux; **to c. sth with sth/s.o. with s.o.,** confondre qch avec qch/qn avec qn; **I always c. him with** *or* **and his brother,** je le confonds toujours avec son frère; **(d)** (*embarrass*) rendre (*qn*) confus; **to get confused,** se troubler.
confused [kən'fjuːzd] *adj* **(a)** (*unsure, bewildered*) embrouillé; (*esprit, conscience*) trouble; (*souvenir*) confus; **to**

get c., s'embrouiller; **I'm c.**, (*why did he do it?*) je suis perdu, je n'y comprends rien; **she's still a little c.**, (*because of shock, anaesthetic etc*) elle n'a pas encore les idées claires; (*does not understand*) elle est encore un peu embrouillée; **(b)** (*disordered*) confus, enchevêtré; (*discours*) confus; **c. voices,** voix confuses.

confusing [kən'fjuːzɪŋ] *adj* embrouillant; **it's very c.**, on s'y perd.

confusion [kən'fjuːʒən] *n* **(a)** (*bewilderment*) confusion *f*; *Med* état confusionnel, confusion mentale; **in his c. he forgot his hat,** dans sa confusion il a oublié son chapeau; **to add to the c. ...,** pour ajouter à la confusion ...; **this news added to her c.**, cette nouvelle a ajouté à sa confusion; **there's still some c. about the exact number killed,** on n'est pas encore sûr du bilan; **it will only lead to c.**, ce ne va faire qu'embrouiller les choses; **(b)** (*disorder*) confusion *f*, désordre *m*; **everything was in c.**, tout était en désordre, tout était pêle-mêle; **to spread c. everywhere,** jeter partout le désordre; **(c) c. of sth with sth,** confusion *f* de qch avec qch; **there has been a c. of names,** il y a eu confusion de noms.

confutation [kɒnfjuː'teɪʃən] *n* réfutation *f* (*d'un argument*).

confute [kən'fjuːt] *vt* **(a)** (*prove wrong*) convaincre (*qn*) d'erreur; **(b)** (*disprove*) réfuter (*un argument*).

congeal [kən'dʒiːl] **1** *vi* geler; (*of fat, oil, blood*) se figer; (*of blood*) se coaguler. **2** *vt* (*set*) faire coaguler; faire cailler (*le sang*); faire figer (*l'huile*).

congenial [kən'dʒiːnɪəl] *adj* **(a)** (*esprit*) sympathique, aimable; (*travail*) agréable (**to,** à); **to find s.o. c.**, trouver qn sympathique; **an evening spent in c. company,** une soirée passée en compagnie de gens sympathiques; **(b)** *Lit* **c. with sth,** (*compatible*) du même caractère *ou* de la même nature que qch; **we have c. tastes,** nous avons des goûts en commun.

congenital [kən'dʒenɪt(ə)l] *adj* (*defect, idiot etc*) congénital, -aux.

conger ['kɒŋgər] *n* **c. (eel),** congre *m*.

congest [kən'dʒest] **1** *vt* **(a)** encombrer, embouteiller (*la circulation, les rues etc*); **(b)** *Med* (*with blood, mucus*) congestionner. **2** *vi* **(a)** (*of traffic etc*) s'accumuler; **(b)** *Med* (*with blood*) se congestionner; (*of respiratory tract*) se bloquer; (*of nose*) se boucher.

congested [kən'dʒestɪd] *adj* **(a)** (*traffic etc*) encombré, embouteillé; (*rue*) encombré; **the c. state of the roads,** l'encombrement *m* des routes; **(b)** *Med* (*with blood*) congestionné; (*respiratory tract*) bloqué; (*nose*) bouché.

congestion [kən'dʒestʃən] *n* **(a)** encombrement *m* (*de circulation etc*); (*actual instance*) embouteillage *m*; **the new road will relieve the c. in the town,** la nouvelle route va décongestionner la ville; **(b)** *Med* (*with blood*) congestion *f*; (*with mucus*) blocage *m*, obstruction *f* (*des voies respiratoires*).

conglomerate¹ [kən'glɒmərət] *n* *Econ* conglomérat *m*; *Geol* conglomérat, aggloméré *m*.

conglomerate² [kən'glɒməreɪt] **1** *vt* conglomérer. **2** *vi* se conglomérer; *Geol* s'agglomérer.

conglomeration [kənglɒmə'reɪʃən] *n* conglomération *f*; agrégation *f* (*de roches etc*); *Fig* **a c. of ideas,** conglomération d'idées.

Congo ['kɒŋgəʊ] *n* **the (River) C.**, le Congo; *Old-fashioned* **the (Belgian) C.**, le Congo (belge).

congrats [kən'græts] *npl* *Br* *F* = **CONGRATULATIONS**.

congratulate [kən'grætjʊleɪt] *vt* féliciter (*qn*) (**on,** de); **I c. you,** je vous en félicite, (je vous en fais) mes compliments; **to c. oneself on sth/on having done sth,** se féliciter de qch/d'avoir fait qch.

congratulations [kəngrætjʊ'leɪʃənz] *npl* félicitations *fpl*; **to send one's c.**, envoyer ses félicitations; **give her my c.**, transmets-lui mes félicitations; **c.!**, je vous en félicite!, félicitations!; **c. on passing your exams,** félicitations pour avoir réussi tes examens; **c. are in order, I hear,** j'apprends que les félicitations sont de mise.

congratulatory [kən'grætjʊleɪtərɪ] *adj* (*lettre etc*) de félicitation(s).

congregate ['kɒŋgrɪgeɪt] *vi* se rassembler, s'assembler.

congregation [kɒŋgrɪ'geɪʃən] *n* **(a)** (*in church*) assemblée *f* des fidèles, assistance *f*; **I'm not a member of your c.**, je ne fais pas partie de votre paroisse, je ne viens pas à l'église ici; **(b)** rassemblement *m*; **(c)** *Univ* (*at Oxford, Cambridge*) assemblée générale (*des professeurs etc*).

congregational [kɒŋgrɪ'geɪʃən(ə)l] *adj* *Rel* en assemblée; **c. worship,** culte public; **the C. Church,** l'Église *f* congrégationaliste.

congress ['kɒŋgres] *n* **(a)** (*conference*) congrès *m* (*de l'enseignement, d'une Eglise, d'hommes d'Etat etc*); **(b)** *Fml* (*sexual*) rapports sexuels.

Congress ['kɒŋgres] *n* *US Pol* Congrès *m*.

congressional [kɒŋ'greʃən(ə)l] *adj* (*réunion etc*) du congrès, congressionnel.

Congressional [kɒŋ'greʃən(ə)l] *adj* *US Pol* (*committee, election*) du Congrès.

Congressman, -woman, *pl* **-men, -women** ['kɒŋgresmæn, -wʊmən, -men, -wɪmɪn] *n* *Pol esp US* membre *m* du Congrès.

congruence ['kɒŋgrʊəns] *n* **(a)** conformité *f* (**with,** avec); **(b)** *Math* congruence *f* (**with,** à).

congruent ['kɒŋgrʊənt] *adj* **(a)** conforme (**with,** à); **(b)** *Math* (*triangle*) congru.

congruity [kɒŋ'gruːɪtɪ] *n* *Fml* conformité *f* (**with,** à).

congruous ['kɒŋgrʊəs] *adj* *Fml* conforme (**with,** à).

conic ['kɒnɪk] *adj* *Math* conique; **c. sections,** sections coniques.

conical ['kɒnɪk(ə)l] *adj* conique; **c. projection,** (*in mapmaking*) projection *f* conique.

conifer ['kɒnɪfər] *n* (*tree*) conifère *m*.

coniferous [kə'nɪfərəs] *adj* *Bot* conifère; (*forêt*) de conifères.

conjectural [kən'dʒektʃər(ə)l] *adj* conjectural, -aux.

conjecture¹ [kən'dʒektʃər] *n* conjecture *f*; **to hazard a c.**, risquer une hypothèse *ou* une supposition; **a matter of c.**, une question hypothétique; **it's sheer c.**, ce ne sont que des suppositions.

conjecture² *vt* conjecturer, supposer.

conjoin [kən'dʒɔɪn] *Fml* **1** *vt* unir, réunir. **2** *vi* s'unir.

conjoint [kɒn'dʒɔɪnt] *adj* *Fml* conjoint, associé.

conjointly [kɒn'dʒɔɪntlɪ] *adv* *Fml* conjointement, ensemble.

conjugal ['kɒndʒʊg(ə)l] *adj* conjugal, -aux; **c. rights,** droits conjugaux.

conjugate¹ ['kɒndʒʊgeɪt] *adj* *Math Opt Ch* conjugué.

conjugate² **1** *vt* *Gram* conjuguer (*un verbe*). **2** *vi* **(a)** *Gram* se conjuguer; **(b)** *Biol* (*of cells*) se conjuguer.

conjugation [kɒndʒʊ'geɪʃən] *n* **(a)** *Gram* conjugaison *f*; **(b)** *Biol* conjugaison, zygose *f*.

conjunct [kən'dʒʌŋkt] *Fml* **1** *adj* conjoint. **2** *n* **(a)** associé, -ée; **(b)** chose liée (*à une autre*).

conjunction [kən'dʒʌŋkʃən] *n* **(a)** conjonction *f*; **in c. with,** conjointement avec (*qn*); concurremment avec (*qch*); *Astron* **planets in c.**, planètes en conjonction; **(b)** *Gram* conjonction *f*.

conjunctive [kən'dʒʌŋktɪv] *adj* (*tissu etc*) conjonctif.

conjunctivitis [kəndʒʌŋktɪ'vaɪtɪs] *n* *Med* conjonctivite *f*; **to have c.**, avoir de la conjonctivite.

conjuncture [kən'dʒʌŋktʃər] *n* *Fml* conjoncture *f*, circonstance *f*.

conjuration [kɒndʒʊ'reɪʃən] *n* *Fml* conjuration *f*.

conjure ['kʌndʒər] **1** *vi* faire des tours de passe-passe. **2** *vt* **(a)** (*produce*) **to c. sth out of sth,** faire *ou* fabriquer qch comme par enchantement à partir de qch; **they conjured a bottle of wine out of nowhere** *or* **thin air,** ils ont fait apparaître une bouteille de vin comme par enchantement; **(b)** [kən'dʒʊər] (*entreat*) conjurer (**s.o. to do sth,** qn de faire qch).

▶**conjure up** *vtsep* **(a)** (*call to mind*) évoquer (*des images, des souvenirs*); **(b)** (*call up*) faire apparaître (*un esprit etc*); **(c)** (*produce*) **to c. up sth (out of sth),** faire *ou* fabriquer qch comme par enchantement (à partir de qch); **they conjured up some armchairs,** ils ont déniché deux fauteuils d'on ne sait où.

conjurer, conjuror ['kʌndʒərər] *n* prestidigitateur *m*, illusionniste *mf*.

conjuring ['kʌndʒərɪŋ] *n* prestidigitation *f*; **c. trick,** tour *m* de passe-passe.

conk¹ [kɒŋk] *n* *Sl* **(a)** *Br* (*nose*) blair *m*, pif *m*; **(b)** (*head*) caboche *f*; **(c)** (*blow*) gnon *m*; **I gave him a c. on the nose,** je lui ai fait un gnon sur le nez.

conk² *vt* *Sl* faire un gnon à (*qn*).

▶**conk out** *vi* *Sl* **(a)** (*of machinery etc*) tomber en panne; **(b)** (*lose consciousness*) s'évanouir; **(c)** (*go to sleep*) s'endormir; **(d)** *US* (*die*) mourir.

conker ['kɒŋkər] *n* *Br F* marron *m* d'Inde; **conkers,** = jeu consistant à démolir le marron de son adversaire.

Conn *abbr* **Connecticut**.

connect¹ [kə'nekt] **1** *vt* **(a)** (*join*) (re)lier, (ré)unir, rattacher (*qch*) (**to,** à); faire communiquer (**with,** avec); *MecE etc* embrayer (*deux arbres*); joindre (*des tuyaux*); *El* interconnecter (*des circuits*); connecter (*des fils*); **a road connects the two cities, the two cities are connected**

by a road, une route relie les deux villes, les deux villes sont reliées par une route; **a corridor connects the room to the library,** un corridor fait communiquer la pièce et la bibliothèque; **connected by telephone,** relié par téléphone; *Tel* **will you c. me with reservations please?,** est-ce que vous pouvez me passer votre service des réservations?; *Tel* **to c. two subscribers,** mettre deux abonnés en communication; **the telephone/electricity hasn't been connected,** le téléphone/l'électricité n'a pas été branché(e); **c. this wire to the other terminal,** connectez ce fil à l'autre borne;

(b) (*link*) associer (**s.o./sth with s.o./sth,** qn/qch avec qn/à qch); **there is nothing to c. the two crimes,** il n'y a aucun lien entre les deux crimes; **at first I didn't c. the name with the face,** au début je n'ai pas fait le lien entre le nom et le visage; **to be connected with ...,** (*of person*) avoir des relations *ou* des rapports avec ...; (*of thing*) se rattacher *ou* se rapporter à ...; **questions connected with a subject,** questions relatives à un sujet; **to be connected with a family,** (*of person*) être allié avec une famille.

2 *vi* **(a)** (*of wires*) être relié (**with,** à); (*of roads*) se rejoindre; (*of rooms*) communiquer (**with,** avec); **this road connects with the ...,** cette route rejoint la ...; **the tunnels don't c.,** les deux tunnels ne sont pas reliés *ou* ne communiquent pas;

(b) to c. with a train/a flight, (*of train, plane*) assurer la correspondance avec un train/un vol; (*of person*) prendre la correspondance avec un train/un vol;

(c) *F* (*of blow*) atteindre son but.

connect² *n Comptr* connexion *f*; **c. time,** durée *f* (d'établissement) de la connexion.

▶**connect up** *vtsep* raccorder (*des tuyaux*); connecter (*des fils électriques*).

connected [kə'nektɪd] *adj* **(a)** (*linked*) (*sciences, faits etc*) connexe; (*faits, événements*) lié; **to be well c.,** (*of person*) être bien apparenté; **(b)** (*coherent*) (*discours*) suivi, cohérent; **(c)** *Bot Jur* connexe.

connecting [kə'nektɪŋ] *adj* de connexion; **c. cable,** câble *m* de connexion; **c. piece,** pièce *f* de raccordement; **c. rod,** bielle *f*; **c. wire,** fil *m* de connexion; **c. pipe,** tuyau *m* de communication *ou* de jonction; **c. door,** porte *f* de communication; **c. rooms,** (*in hotel*) pièces communicantes; **c. flight** *or* **train** *etc*, correspondance *f*.

connection [kə'nekʃən] *n* **(a)** (*link*) rapport *m*, liaison *f* (*des choses*); connexion *f* (*des idées*); **close c. between two facts,** relation étroite entre deux faits; **I didn't make the c.,** je n'ai pas fait le rapprochement; **in c. with ...,** à propos de ..., relatif à ...; **in this c.,** à ce propos, à cet égard;

(b) (*personal relationship*) relations *fpl*, rapports *mpl*; **to form a c. with s.o.,** établir des rapports avec qn; **I have broken off all c. with him,** j'ai cessé toutes relations avec lui; **to establish a business c. with a firm,** entrer en relations (d'affaires) avec une maison;

(c) (*acquaintance*) relation *f*; **she has important connections,** elle a des relations en haut lieu;

(d) (*family relationship*) parenté *f*; **the Royal Family's Spanish c.,** les cousins espagnols de la famille royale; **to form a c. by marriage with a good family,** s'allier à *ou* avec une bonne famille; **there's no c. with the Bedford Smythes,** il n'y a pas de lien de parenté avec les Smythe de Bedford;

(e) (*relative*) parent, -ente; (*by marriage*) allié, -ée; **he** *or* **she is a c. of mine,** c'est un(e) de mes parent(e)s; **I've got Scottish connections,** j'ai de la famille en Écosse;

(f) *MecE etc* connexion *f*; assemblage *m*, raccordement *m* (*de tuyaux, fils etc*); accouplement *m*, embrayage *m*, engrenage *m* (*des organes d'une machine*); *El* raccordement, connexion, branchement *m*; *Tel* communication *f*; *Comptr* connexion, liaison *f*; *El* **wrong c.,** fausse connexion; *Tel* **we had a very bad c.,** on a eu une très mauvaise ligne;

(g) (*connecting device*) raccord *m*, attache *f* (*entre deux tuyaux, fils etc*); *El* contact *m*; prise *f* (*de courant*); **flexible c.,** raccord souple; **earth** *or US* **ground c.,** *El* prise *f* de terre; *Aut etc* mise *f* à la masse;

(h) (*in journey*) correspondance *f*; (*train, plane etc*) train *ou* avion *ou* bateau correspondant; **I missed my c.,** j'ai manqué *ou* raté ma correspondance.

connective [kə'nektɪv] **1** *adj Biol* **c. tissue,** tissu conjonctif. **2** *n Gram* conjonction *f* de coordination.

connector [kə'nektər] *n El* connecteur *m*; *MecE etc* raccord *m*.

connexion [kə'nekʃən] *n* = **CONNECTION**.

conniption [kə'nɪpʃən] *n Am F* crise *f* de rage.

connivance [kə'naɪvəns] *n* connivence *f*; **c. at** *or* **in a crime,** complicité *f* dans un crime; **to be in c. with s.o.,** être de connivence avec qn.

connive [kə'naɪv] *vi* être de connivence (**with,** avec; **to do,** pour faire); **to c. at,** fermer les yeux sur (*un abus etc*); être de connivence dans (*un crime*).

connoisseur [kɒnɪ'sɜːr] *n* (bon) connaisseur *m* (**of, in,** en); **to be a c.,** s'y connaître (**of,** en).

connotation [kɒnə'teɪʃən] *n* connotation *f* (*d'un terme*); **unfortunate c.,** connotation malheureuse.

connote [kɒ'nəʊt] *vt* (*of word*) suggérer, comporter (*une notion, une idée*); **the word connotes courage,** le mot suggère une idée de courage.

connubial [kə'njuːbɪəl] *adj Fml* conjugal, -aux.

conquer ['kɒŋkər] *vt* **(a)** conquérir (*un pays, le monde, l'amour de qn*); **(b)** (*overcome*) vaincre, surmonter (*une difficulté, sa timidité, ses craintes*); vaincre (*l'inflation, une maladie*); dompter (*ses passions*); **Everest was conquered in 1953,** la première ascension du Mont Everest a eu lieu en 1953.

conquering ['kɒŋkərɪŋ] *adj* (*army, hero*) conquérant, victorieux.

conqueror ['kɒŋkərər] *n* **(a)** conquérant *m* (*d'un pays*); *Hist* **(William) the C.,** Guillaume le Conquérant; **(b)** (*victor*) vainqueur *m*.

conquest ['kɒŋkwest] *n* (*victory, prize*) *& Fig* conquête *f*; *Hist* **the (Norman) C.,** la conquête de l'Angleterre (1066); *Fig* **his many conquests,** ses nombreuses conquêtes; *Fig* **to make a c. of s.o.,** faire la conquête de qn.

Cons *Pol abbr* **Conservative**.

consanguine [kɒn'sæŋgwɪn] *adj* consanguin.

consanguinity [kɒnsæŋ'gwɪnɪtɪ] *n* consanguinité *f*.

conscience ['kɒnʃəns] *n* conscience *f*; **to have a clear** *or* **an easy c.,** avoir la conscience tranquille; **to have a guilty** *or* **bad c.,** avoir mauvaise conscience; **to have sth on one's c.,** avoir qch (qui pèse) sur la conscience; **it's on my c.,** (*what I did*) je l'ai sur la conscience; **it's on my c. that I left him alone,** le fait de l'avoir laissé tout seul me pèse *ou* me reste sur la conscience; **I can't sleep with that on my c.,** je ne peux pas dormir avec ça sur la conscience; **to have no c.,** n'avoir point de conscience; **a matter of c.,** une affaire de conscience; **freedom of c.,** liberté *f* de conscience; **one cannot in all c. believe that ...,** on ne peut pas raisonnablement croire que ...; **c. clause,** clause *f* de conscience; **c. money,** somme restituée par remords de conscience.

conscience-stricken ['kɒnʃəns'strɪk(ə)n] *adj* pris de remords.

conscientious [kɒnʃɪ'enʃəs] *adj* **(a)** (*worker, work*) consciencieux; (*work*) fait en conscience; **(b) c. objector/objection,** objecteur *m*/objection *f* de conscience.

conscientiously [kɒnʃɪ'enʃəslɪ] *adv* (*to work*) consciencieusement.

conscious ['kɒnʃəs] **1** *adj* **(a)** (*awake*) **to be c.,** avoir sa connaissance; **to become c.,** reprendre connaissance; **he's not c. yet,** *Med* il n'a pas encore repris connaissance; *Hum* (*he's still in bed*) il n'a pas encore fait surface;

(b) (*aware*) conscient; **to be c. of sth,** avoir conscience de qch, être conscient de qch; **to become c. of sth,** s'apercevoir de qch; **I wasn't c. of having annoyed you,** je n'étais pas conscient de vous avoir fâché; **to be c. that ...,** être conscient du fait que ...; **fashion c.,** qui suit de près la mode; **health c.,** qui se préoccupe de sa santé;

(c) (*intentional*) conscient; **it was not a c. decision to employ more young people,** le fait d'employer plus de jeunes ne relève pas d'une décision consciente;

(d) *Phil Psy* conscient; **the c. mind,** la conscience; **man as a c. being,** l'homme en tant qu'être conscient; **to have a c. dislike of s.o.,** éprouver une aversion consciente pour qn.

2 *n Phil Psy* **the c.,** le conscient.

consciously ['kɒnʃəslɪ] *adv* consciemment; (*deliberately*) sciemment.

consciousness ['kɒnʃəsnɪs] *n* **(a)** connaissance *f*; **to lose c.,** perdre connaissance; **to regain c.,** reprendre connaissance, revenir à soi; **(b)** (*awareness*) conscience *f*, sentiment *m* (**of,** de); **the organization aims to raise people's c. of these problems,** l'organisation a pour objet de faire prendre davantage conscience de ces problèmes aux gens *ou* de sensibiliser les gens à ces problèmes; **c. raising,** sensibilisation *f*; **(c)** *Phil* conscience *f*.

conscript¹ ['kɒnskrɪpt] *Mil n* conscrit *m*; **c. army,** armée *f* de conscrits.

conscript² [kən'skrɪpt] *vt* enrôler, engager (*des troupes*) par la conscription; **to be conscripted,** être conscrit.

conscription [kən'skrɪpʃən] *n Mil* conscription *f*.

consecrate ['kɒnsɪkreɪt] *vt* **(a)** *Rel* consacrer (*une église etc*); bénir (*le pain etc*); sacrer (*un roi, un évêque*); **(b)** (*dedicate*) consacrer; **to c. one's life to sth,** consacrer sa vie *ou* se vouer à qch.
consecrated ['kɒnsɪkreɪtɪd] *adj Rel* (*church etc*) consacré; (*bread*) bénit, consacré; **in c. ground,** en terre sainte *ou* bénite.
consecration [kɒnsɪ'kreɪʃən] *n* **(a)** consécration *f* (*d'une église etc*); bénédiction *f* (*d'un drapeau*); sacre *m* (*d'un roi, d'un évêque*); **(b)** (*dedication*) dévouement *m*.
consecutive [kən'sekjʊtɪv] *adj* consécutif; **on three c. days,** trois jours de suite; **these numbers are not c.,** ces numéros ne se suivent pas; *Gram* **c. clause,** proposition consécutive.
consecutively [kən'sekjʊtɪvlɪ] *adv* **two days c.,** deux jours de suite, deux jours consécutifs; **to deal with problems c.,** traiter les problèmes l'un après l'autre.
consensus [kən'sensəs] *n* consensus *m*, unanimité *f* (*d'opinions, de témoignages etc*); **the c. was that the new road was unnecessary,** l'opinion générale était que la nouvelle route n'était pas nécessaire; *F* **what is the c. of opinion?,** quelle est l'opinion générale?; **to reach a c.,** arriver à un consensus.
consent[1] [kən'sent] *n* consentement *m*, assentiment *m*; **to give one's c. to sth,** donner son consentement à qch; **I'll never give my c.,** je n'y consentirai jamais, je ne donnerai jamais mon accord; **do I have your c.?,** est-ce que j'ai votre accord?; **by common c.,** de l'aveu de tout le monde; **by mutual c.,** de gré à gré; (*divorce*) par consentement mutuel; *Jur* **age of c.,** âge *m* nubile.
consent[2] *vi* **to c. to sth/to do sth,** consentir à qch/à faire qch; **I c.,** j'y consens.
consenting [kən'sentɪŋ] *adj* consentant; **c. adult,** adulte consentant.
consequence ['kɒnsɪkwəns] *n* **(a)** (*result*) conséquence *f*, suites *fpl*; **the c. is that ...,** il en résulte *ou* il s'ensuit que ...; **in c., as a c.,** par conséquent; **in c. of ...,** par suite de ...; **this decision had dire consequences for the region,** cette décision a comporté des conséquences terribles pour la région; **to take the consequences,** accepter les conséquences; **(game of) consequences,** (jeu *m* des) petits papiers; **(b)** (*importance*) importance *f*, conséquence *f*; **it is of no c.,** cela n'a pas d'importance, cela ne fait rien; **it is of some c. to me,** ça a de l'importance pour moi; **he is of no c.,** il ne compte pas; **a woman of c.,** une femme avec qui il faut compter.
consequent ['kɒnsɪkwənt] *adj* **(a)** (*resulting*) résultant; **c. upon sth,** qui est la conséquence de qch, qui résulte de qch; **a glut and the c. drop in prices,** un surplus et la baisse des prix qui en résulte; **(b)** (*in logic*) conséquent; **to be c.,** être logique.
consequential [kɒnsɪ'kwenʃəl] *adj* (*resulting*) conséquent (**to,** à), consécutif (**to,** à); *Jur* **c. effects,** répercussions *fpl* (*d'une action*); **c. damages,** dommages indirects.
consequently ['kɒnsɪkwentlɪ] *adv & conj* par conséquent, donc.
conservancy [kən'sɜːvənsɪ] *n* **(a)** (*body*) commission *f* de conservation (*d'une forêt, d'un fleuve etc*); **(b)** (*conservation*) conservation *f*, protection *f* (*des forêts etc*).
conservation [kɒnsə'veɪʃən] *n* **(a)** conservation *f*; **c. of energy,** économies *fpl* d'énergie; **(b)** (*of environment*) protection *f* de l'environnement; **c. area,** zone protégée; **c. expert,** expert *m* de la protection de l'environnement.
conservationist [kɒnsə'veɪʃənɪst] *n* partisan, -ane de la protection de l'environnement.
conservatism [kən'sɜːvətɪz(ə)m] *n Pol* conservatisme *m*.
conservative [kən'sɜːvətɪv] **1** *adj* **(a)** conservateur, -trice; (*evaluation*) prudent; **at a c. estimate,** au minimum, au bas mot; **(b)** *Pol* conservateur, -trice; **the C. Party,** le parti conservateur. **2** *n Pol* conservateur, - trice.
conservatively [kən'sɜːvətɪvlɪ] *adv* **it was c. estimated ...,** selon des estimations modérées ... .
conservatoire [kən'sɜːvətwɑːr] *n* conservatoire *m* (*de musique*).
conservatory [kən'sɜːvətrɪ] *n* **(a)** (*attached to house*) véranda *f*; **(b)** = **CONSERVATOIRE**.
conserve[1] ['kɒnsɜːv] *n Culin* conserve *f* (*de fruits*).
conserve[2] [kən'sɜːv] *vt* conserver, préserver (*un monument ancien etc*); **to c. water/energy,** faire des économies d'eau/d'énergie.
consider [kən'sɪdər] *vt* **(a)** (*think over*) considérer (*une question*); songer à, réfléchir à (*qch*); interroger (*les faits*); envisager (*une possibilité*); prendre (*une offre*) en considération; étudier (*une proposition*); **I will c. it,** j'y réfléchirai; **all things considered,** tout bien considéré, tout compte fait; **he was considering whether to go out when ...,** il se demandait s'il sortirait quand ...; **have you considered (buying) a larger model?,** est-ce que vous avez envisagé d'acheter un modèle plus grand?; **the jury retired to c. its verdict,** le jury se retira pour délibérer;
(b) (*take into account*) avoir égard à (*la sensibilité de qn*); regarder à (*la dépense*); **he is a man to be considered,** c'est un homme dont il faut tenir compte; **we hadn't considered this possibility,** nous n'avions pas envisagé cette possibilité; **when one considers that ...,** quand on pense que ...; **c. that 2 million people live there,** songe que 2 millions de personnes vivent là; **c. the cost!,** pensez au coût!; **we c. that he ought to do it,** à notre avis il doit le faire; **you ought to have considered my feelings,** tu aurais dû penser à moi;
(c) (*regard*) considérer; **I c. him a friend,** je le considère comme un ami; **c. it done,** considérez cela comme fait; **c. yourself dismissed,** tenez-vous pour congédié; **to c. oneself happy,** s'estimer heureux; **I c. it my duty to ...,** j'estime qu'il est de mon devoir de ... .
considerable [kən'sɪdərəb(ə)l] *adj* **(a)** grand; bon (*partie*); (*différence*) sensible; **a c. number of ...,** un nombre considérable de ...; **the new car attracted c. attention,** la nouvelle voiture a fait l'objet d'une attention considérable; **(b)** (*worthy of attention*) digne d'attention; (*person*) notable, important.
considerably [kən'sɪdərəblɪ] *adv* considérablement.
considerate [kən'sɪdərət] *adj* prévenant, plein d'égards, (**towards, to,** pour, envers); **it's very c. of you,** c'est très aimable de votre part; **try to be more c.,** essaye d'être un peu plus prévenant; **that wasn't very c. of you,** ce n'était pas très gentil de ta part.
considerately [kən'sɪdərətlɪ] *adv* avec considération, avec prévenance.
consideration [kənsɪdə'reɪʃən] *n* **(a)** (*deliberation*) **under c.,** (*of question, candidate etc*) à l'étude; **to give c. to a question,** mettre une question à l'étude; **I'll give it some c.,** j'y penserai; **after due c.,** après mûre réflexion, toute réflexion faite; **to take sth into c.,** prendre qch en considération, tenir compte de qch, prendre qch en ligne de compte; **taking all things into c.,** tout bien considéré; **taking her age into c.,** si l'on tient compte de son âge; **to leave sth out of c.,** ne pas tenir compte de qch;
(b) (*factor*) facteur *m*; **there is another c.,** il y a autre chose dont il faut tenir compte; **money is always the first c.,** la question d'argent vient toujours en premier; **on no c.,** à aucun prix; **money is no c.,** l'argent n'entre pas en ligne de compte;
(c) (*regard*) considération *f*; **to have no c. for anyone,** n'avoir de considération pour personne; **show some c.!,** fais preuve d'un peu de considération!; **out of c. for s.o.,** par égard pour qn; **to treat s.o. with c.,** ménager qn;
(d) (*payment*) compensation *f*, rémunération *f*; *Com etc* **for a c.,** moyennant paiement; **he will do it for a c.,** il le fera si vous le payez; **in c. of your services,** en récompense de vos services.
considered [kən'sɪdəd] *adj* (*thought out*) **it is my c. opinion that ...,** après mûre réflexion je pense que ...; **(b)** (*thought of*) **to be highly c.,** être très estimé.
considering [kən'sɪdərɪŋ] *prep* eu égard à (*qch*); **c. his age,** étant donné son âge; **c. the circumstances,** vu les circonstances; **c. that ...,** vu *ou* attendu que ...; **c. (that) he is so young,** étant donné qu'il est si jeune; *F* **it's not so bad c.,** ce n'est pas si mauvais après tout *ou* malgré tout.
consign [kən'saɪn] *vt* **(a)** (*entrust*) confier, remettre (**sth to s.o.'s care,** qch à qn); **to c. a body to the grave,** livrer un corps à la tombe; **(b)** *Com* consigner, expédier (*des marchandises*) (**to s.o.,** à qn); envoyer (*des marchandises*) en consignation (*à qn*).
consignee [kɒnsaɪ'niː] *n* consignataire *mf*.
consignment [kən'saɪnmənt] *n* **(a)** (*goods*) livraison *f*, arrivage *m* (*de marchandises*); **(b)** envoi *m*, expédition *f* (*de marchandises*); **c. note,** bordereau *m* de consignation; *Rail* récépissé *m*; *Com* **on c.,** en consignation; **to send s.o. goods on c.,** livrer à qn une marchandise en dépôt permanent; **your c. of books has duly arrived,** votre envoi de livres nous est bien parvenu.
consignor [kən'saɪnər] *n Com* consignateur, -trice, expéditeur, -trice.
►**consist in** [kən'sɪst] *vipo* consister à (*qch*).
►**consist of** *vipo* consister en, se composer de qch; **inheritance consisting of a house,** héritage consistant en une maison.
consistency [kən'sɪstənsɪ] *n* **(a)** (*of liquid etc*) consistance

f; **to be the c. of sth,** avoir la consistance de qch; **(b)** (*of actions etc*) uniformité *f* (*de conduite etc*); cohérence *f* (*d'un raisonnement etc*); logique *f* (*dans les idées*); **to lack c.,** manquer de suite; **c. check,** contrôle *m* d'uniformité.

consistent [kən'sɪstənt] *adj* **(a)** (*person*) conséquent; (*conduct etc*) uniforme; (*reasoning etc*) cohérent; *Comptr* cohérent; **(b)** (*compatible*) compatible, d'accord (**with,** avec); **this action is not c. with his character,** cette action n'est pas en harmonie avec son caractère.

consistently [kən'sɪstəntlɪ] *adv* **(a)** (*behave*) régulièrement; **she has c. denied the accusation,** elle a constamment nié l'accusation; **(b)** (*in logic*) logiquement.

consistory [kən'sɪstərɪ] *n Rel* consistoire (*pontifical*); **C. Court,** tribunal *m* ecclésiastique.

consolation [kɒnsə'leɪʃən] *n* consolation *f*; **words of c.,** paroles consolatrices; **that's one c.,** c'est déjà une consolation; **it wasn't much c. to reflect that tomorrow was her birthday,** c'était une piètre consolation de penser que son anniversaire était le lendemain; **if it's any c.,** si ça peut te consoler; **c. prize,** prix *m* de consolation.

console¹ [kən'səʊl] *vt* consoler (*qn*) (**for,** de); **c. yourself with the thought that it's Friday tomorrow,** console-toi en pensant que c'est vendredi demain.

console² ['kɒnsəʊl] *n* **(a)** console *f* (*d'orgue*); *Rad TV* meuble *m* pour radio *ou* télévision; *Av* tableau *m* de bord; *Electron* console; *Comptr* **c. (desk), control c.,** pupitre *m* de commande; **(b)** *Archit* console *f* (*d'un balcon etc*); **c. table,** (table *f*) console.

consolidate [kən'sɒlɪdeɪt] **1** *vt* consolider, (r)affermir (*des fondements etc*); *Mil etc* consolider (*une position*); consolider, unir (*deux envois, deux entreprises etc*); *Fin* consolider (*une dette*). **2** *vi* se consolider.

consolidated [kən'sɒlɪdeɪtɪd] *adj* consolidé; *Fin* **c. annuities,** fonds consolidés.

consolidation [kənsɒlɪ'deɪʃən] *n* **(a)** consolidation *f*, (r)affermissement *m* (*de fondements, de pouvoir etc*); tassement *m* (*de l'opinion publique*); **(b)** *Jur* consolidation *f* (*de la dette publique etc*); unification *f* (*des lois*); *Fin* regroupement *m* (*d'actions*).

consoling [kən'səʊlɪŋ] *adj* consolateur, -trice.

consols ['kɒnsɒlz, kən'sɒlz] *npl Br Fin* (fonds *mpl*) consolidés *mpl*.

consonance ['kɒnsənəns] *n* **(a)** *Mus Ling* consonance *f*; **(b)** (*of ideas etc*) accord *m*, conformité *f*.

consonant ['kɒnsənənt] **1** *n Ling* consonne *f*; **2** *adj Fml* **c. with,** en accord avec, conforme à.

consort ['kɒnsɔːt] *n* **(a)** (*spouse*) époux, -ouse; **prince c.,** prince consort; **(b)** *Nau* **to sail in c.,** naviguer de conserve.

►**consort with** *vipo* s'associer avec (*qn*), frayer avec (*qn*), fréquenter (*qn*).

consortium [kən'sɔːtɪəm] *n Com Fin* consortium *m*.

conspicuous [kən'spɪkjʊəs] *adj* **(a)** (*easily visible*) visible, apparent, manifeste; (*monument, landmark*) voyant; **in a c. position,** bien en évidence; *Hum Fig* **to be c. by one's absence,** briller par son absence; **(b)** (*striking*) remarquable, frappant; **c. gallantry,** acte de bravoure insigne; **to make oneself c.,** se faire remarquer (**by, through,** par); **c. consumption,** consommation *f* ostentatoire *ou* ostensible.

conspicuously [kən'spɪkjʊəslɪ] *adv* (*see adj*) **(a)** visiblement, manifestement; **(b)** remarquablement.

conspicuousness [kən'spɪkjʊəsnɪs] *n* **(a)** (*visibility*) évidence *f*, visibilité *f* (*de qch*); éclat *m* (*d'un uniforme etc*); **(b)** (*striking nature*) caractère *m* insigne (*d'une action*).

conspiracy [kən'spɪrəsɪ] *n* conjuration *f*, complot *m*; *Jur* association *f* de malfaiteurs; **c. of silence,** conspiration *f* du silence; **c. to obtain documents illegally,** conspiration pour obtenir des documents de façon illégale; **there's a c. against me,** il y a un complot contre moi; **it's a c.,** c'est un complot; **c. theory,** théorie *f* de complot; **c. theorist,** partisan *m* de la théorie de complot.

conspirator [kən'spɪrətər] *n* conspirateur, -trice, conjuré, -ée.

conspiratorial [kənspɪrə'tɔːrɪəl] *adj* (*air*) de conspirateur; **she gave me a c. wink,** elle m'a jeté un coup d'œil de conspiratrice.

conspire [kən'spaɪər] *vi* **(a)** conspirer (**against,** contre; **with,** avec); **to c. to do sth,** comploter de faire qch; **(b)** (*of events etc*) concourir (*à produire un effet*); **everything conspired to make him late,** tout a contribué à le mettre en retard; **circumstances conspired against me,** les circonstances se sont liguées contre moi.

constable ['kʌnstəb(ə)l, kɒn-] *n* **(police) c.,** = agent *m* de police; **good evening, c.,** bonsoir, monsieur l'agent; **special c.,** = supplétif *m*; **chief c.,** = commissaire (central) de police.

constabulary [kən'stæbjʊlərɪ] *n* (*no pl*) *also Hum* la police; **the Kent c.,** = la gendarmerie du Kent.

constancy ['kɒnstənsɪ] *n* **(a)** constance *f*, fermeté *f* (*de caractère*); fidélité *f* (*d'un ami*); **(b)** constance *f* (*de la température*); régularité *f* (*du vent etc*).

constant ['kɒnstənt] **1** *adj* constant; (*équilibre*) stable; (*pression*) invariable; incessant, continuel; (*soin, travail*) assidu, soutenu; (*ami*) fidèle; **through c. repetition,** à force de répéter; **there was c. pressure for reform,** il y avait une pression constante pour qu'une réforme soit mise en œuvre; **c. stream of insults,** un flot d'injures ininterrompu. **2** *n Math Phys* constante *f*; **time c.,** constante de temps.

constantly ['kɒnstəntlɪ] *adv* constamment; continuellement.

constellation [kɒnstə'leɪʃən] *n* constellation *f*.

consternation [kɒnstə'neɪʃən] *n* consternation *f*; atterrement *m*; **look of c.,** air consterné; **they looked at each other in c.,** ils se regardaient atterrés; **to our c.,** à notre consternation.

constipate ['kɒnstɪpeɪt] *vt Med* constiper.

constipated ['kɒnstɪpeɪtɪd] *adj Med* constipé; **to be c.,** être constipé.

constipating ['kɒnstɪpeɪtɪŋ] *adj Med* constipant, qui constipe.

constipation [kɒnstɪ'peɪʃən] *n Med* constipation *f*.

constituency [kən'stɪtjʊənsɪ] *n* **(a)** (*voters*) électeurs *mpl* (*d'une circonscription*); **(b)** (*district*) circonscription électorale; *Br* **the c. party,** la section locale du parti.

constituent [kən'stɪtjʊənt] **1** *adj* constituant, constitutif, composant. **2** *n* **(a)** *Pol* mandant *m* (*d'un député*); **my constituents,** mes électeurs; **(b)** (*element*) élément constitutif; composant *m*; *Ling* constituant *m*; **(c)** *Jur* commettant *m*.

constitute ['kɒnstɪtjuːt] *vt* **(a)** constituer (*un tribunal*); faire (*le bonheur de qn etc*); **to c. a threat to ...,** constituer une menace pour ...; **the countries that c. the EEC,** les pays qui constituent la CEE; **factors that c. an offence,** éléments constitutifs d'un délit; **(b)** (*appoint*) **to c. s.o. arbitrator,** constituer qn arbitre.

constitution [kɒnstɪ'tjuːʃən] *n* **(a)** *Pol* constitution *f* (*d'un État*); **(b)** (*of person*) constitution *f*; **to have a strong** *or* **an iron c.,** avoir une bonne constitution *ou* une santé de fer; **(c)** (*make up*) constitution *f*, composition *f* (*de qch*).

constitutional [kɒnstɪ'tjuːʃən(ə)l] **1** *adj* **(a)** *Pol* (*monarque, régime*) constitutionnel; **the president's actions are not c.,** les actions du président sont anticonstitutionnelles; **(b)** *Med* (*affection*) diathésique. **2** *n* (petite) promenade *f*.

constitutionally [kɒnstɪ'tjuːʃən(ə)lɪ] *adv* **(a)** *Pol* constitutionnellement; **(b)** (*by nature*) **c. lazy,** paresseux de nature *ou* par nature.

constitutive [kən'stɪtjuːtɪv] *adj* constitutif; **c. elements,** éléments constitutifs.

constrain [kən'streɪn] *vt* **(a)** (*compel*) contraindre, forcer (*qn*) (**to do,** à, de faire); **to find oneself constrained to do sth,** se voir contraint de faire qch; **(b)** (*of clothing etc*) gêner (*les mouvements*); (*of person*) retenir (*qn*) de force, contenir (*qn*).

constrained [kən'streɪnd] *adj* (*air*) gêné; (*voix*) forcé; (*sourire*) embarrassé.

constraint [kən'streɪnt] *n* **(a)** (*restriction*) contrainte *f*; *Jur etc* coercition *f*; **to put s.o. under c.,** retenir qn de force; **(b)** (*of manner*) gêne *f*, contrainte *f*; **(c)** (*self-control*) retenue *f*; **without c.,** dégagé.

constrict [kən'strɪkt] *vt* resserrer, étrangler, rétrécir (*une ouverture*); serrer, gêner (*le corps etc*).

constriction [kən'strɪkʃən] *n* resserrement *m*, rétrécissement *m*; *Med* constriction *f*.

constrictor [kən'strɪktər] *n* **(a)** *Anat* (muscle *m*) constricteur *m*; **(b) boa c.,** boa *m* constricteur.

construct¹ [kən'strʌkt] *vt* construire (*un édifice, une machine*); confectionner (*un roman*); **well/badly constructed,** (*phrase, play*) bien/mal agencé *ou* construit.

construct² ['kɒnstrʌkt] *n* construction *f*; (*idea*) construction mentale *ou* de l'esprit.

construction [kən'strʌkʃən] *n* **(a)** *Ind Nau etc* construction *f* (*d'un édifice, d'un bâtiment, d'une machine etc*); **under c.,** en (cours de) construction; **1,000 tons of concrete were used in the c. of the building,** 1 000 tonnes de béton ont été utilisées pour la construction du bâtiment; **c. site,** chantier *m* de construction; **c. workers/industry,** ouvriers *mpl*/industrie *f* de la construction; **(b)** (*manner*) manière dont une machine *etc* a été réalisée; **compact c.,**

réalisation peu encombrante; **(c)** *(thing constructed)* construction *f*; *(building)* édifice *m*; **all-metal c.,** construction entièrement métallique; **(d)** *Gram etc* construction *f (d'une phrase etc)*; **(e)** *(interpretation)* interprétation *f (d'une action etc)*; **to put a good/bad c. on s.o.'s words/ actions,** interpréter en bien/en mal les paroles/actions de qn; **to put another c. on sth,** interpréter qch d'une autre façon.

constructional [kən'strʌkʃən(ə)l] *adj (défaut)* de construction; **c. engineering,** construction *f* mécanique.

constructive [kən'strʌktɪv] *adj* **(a)** *(positive)* constructif; *(esprit)* créateur; **have you got anything c. to say?,** est-ce que vous avez quelque chose de constructif à dire?; **c. criticism,** critique constructive; **(b)** *Jur* par interprétation; par déduction.

constructively [kən'strʌktɪvlɪ] *adv (to criticize)* d'une manière constructive.

constructor [kən'strʌktər] *n* constructeur *m*.

construe [kən'struː] *vt (interpret)* interpréter *(les paroles de qn)*; *Old-fashioned Sch* analyser, décomposer *(une phrase)*; **my remarks were construed correctly,** mes remarques ont été correctement interprétées; **the phrase can be construed to mean two things,** on peut interpréter l'expression de deux manières différentes; *Gram* **preposition construed with the dative,** préposition qui gouverne le datif.

consul ['kɒns(ə)l] *n* **(a)** *(diplomat)* consul *m*; **c. general,** consul général; **(b)** *Antiq & Fr Hist* consul *m*.

consular ['kɒnsjʊlər] *adj* consulaire.

consulate ['kɒnsjʊlət] *n* **(a)** *(office)* consulat *m*; **c. general,** Consulat Général; **(b)** *Antiq* consulat *m*; *Fr Hist* **the C.,** le Consulat.

consult¹ [kən'sʌlt] *n F* = **CONSULTATION.**

consult² **1** *vt* consulter *(un médecin, un dictionnaire)* **(on, about,** sur). **2** *vi* consulter (avec qn); **to c. together,** se consulter.

consultancy [kən'sʌltənsɪ] *n* **(a)** *Br Med* **to be appointed to a c.,** être nommé médecin *ou* chirurgien consultant; **(b)** *Ind* **c. firm,** cabinet *m* d'experts-conseils; **(c)** *(service)* consultation *f*.

consultant [kən'sʌltənt] *n* **(a)** *Br Med* chirurgien consultant; **(b)** *Ind etc* conseiller *m*, expert-conseil *m*, *pl* experts-conseils; **engineering c.,** ingénieur *m* conseil; **management c.,** conseiller *m*, ingénieur conseil *ou* en organisation; **beauty c.,** esthéticien, -ienne; *(for face)* visagiste *mf*.

consultation [kɒnsəl'teɪʃən] *n (with one person)* consultation *f*; *(as a group)* délibération *f*; *(of dictionary etc) & Jur* consultation *f*; **in c. with s.o.,** en consultation avec qn; **to hold a c.,** délibérer, conférer; **can I have a c.?,** *(ask your advice)* est-ce que je peux vous demander (un) conseil?

consultative [kən'sʌltətɪv] *adj (committee)* consultatif.

consulting [kən'sʌltɪŋ] **1** *adj (médecin)* consultant; *(ingénieur)* conseil. **2** *n Med etc* **c. room,** cabinet *m* de consultation.

consumable [kən'sjuːməb(ə)l] *n* **computer consumables,** petit matériel informatique.

consume [kən'sjuːm] **1** *vt (eat, drink)* consommer *(des vivres)*; *(exhaust)* épuiser *(ses vivres, ses provisions etc)*; *(of fire)* consumer, dévorer *(un bâtiment etc)*; **they had consumed six bottles of wine,** ils avaient consommé six bouteilles de vin; **engine that consumes a ton of coal per hour,** machine qui brûle une tonne de charbon par heure; **the discussion consumed many hours,** la discussion a pris de nombreuses heures; **to be consumed with,** brûler de *(désir)*; être rongé de *(jalousie)*; être miné par *(l'envie)*. **2** *vi (be consumer)* consommer.

consumer [kən'sjuːmər] *n* consommateur, -trice *(d'une denrée etc)*; **gas/electricity consumers,** abonnés *mpl* au gaz/à l'électricité; **c. protection society,** association *f* de défense des consommateurs; *Econ* **c. council,** comité *m* (consultatif) des consommateurs; **c. goods,** biens *mpl* de consommation; **c. durables,** biens de consommation durables; **c. nondurables,** biens *ou* produits *mpl* de grande consommation; **the c. society,** la société de consommation; **c. magazine,** magazine pour les consommateurs; **c. resistance,** résistance *f ou* réticence *f* des consommateurs; **c. advocate,** défenseur *m* des intérêts des consommateurs.

consumerism [kən'sjuːmərɪz(ə)m] *n* consumérisme *m*.

consummate¹ ['kɒnsəmɪt] *adj (art)* consommé, achevé; *(menteur)* achevé; **to be a c. master of one's craft,** connaître à fond son métier.

consummate² ['kɒnsəmeɪt] *vt* consommer *(un mariage etc)*.

consummation [kɒnsə'meɪʃən] *n* **(a)** *(of marriage etc)* consommation *f*; **(b)** *(achievement)* achèvement *m*, fin *f*, perfection *f*; **(c)** *(of a skill, art)* perfection *f*; **(d)** *(of desires)* comble *m*.

consumption [kən'sʌmpʃən] *n* **(a)** consommation *f (des denrées etc)*; consommation, dépense *f (de chaleur, de charbon, d'essence)*; *(by fire etc)* destruction *f*; **for current c.,** destiné à la consommation courante; **unfit for human c.,** impropre à la consommation; *Econ* **home c.,** consommation intérieure; *Fig* **the president's remarks were strictly for home c.,** les remarques du président ne s'adressaient qu'à son pays; **(b)** *Old-fashioned Med* phtisie *f*.

consumptive [kən'sʌmptɪv] *adj & n Old-fashioned Med* phtisique *mf*.

cont (a) *abbr* **contents**; **(b)** *(abbr* **continued)** suite.

contact¹ ['kɒntækt] *n* **(a)** *(act of touching)* contact *m*; **the substance must not come into c. with the air,** la substance ne doit pas entrer au contact de l'air; **point of c.,** point *m* de contact *ou* de tangence *(de deux courbes etc)*; *Opt* **c. (lens),** verre *m ou* lentille *f* de contact; **to wear c. lenses** *or* **contacts,** porter des lentilles de contact; *Photo* **c. print,** épreuve *f* par contact; **c. sport,** sport *m* de contact;

(b) *(of humans)* rapport *m*, contact *m*; **preliminary contacts,** prise *f* de contact; **to be in/to come into c. with s.o.,** être/entrer en contact *ou* en rapport avec qn; **are you still in c.?,** *(of two people)* est-ce que vous êtes toujours en contact?; **he didn't get in c. (with me/***etc***),** il n'est pas entré en contact (avec moi/*etc*); **she hadn't come into c. with poverty,** elle ne s'était pas trouvée au contact de la pauvreté; **anyone who has come into c. with the sick man,** quiconque s'est trouvé au contact de l'homme malade; **the two leaders are in close c.,** les deux dirigeants sont en contact étroit; **to make c. with s.o.,** *(by radio etc)* contacter qn, prendre contact avec qn; **after three days they made c. with civilization,** après trois jours ils ont pris contact avec la civilisation; **to make eye c. with s.o.,** rencontrer le regard de qn; **we made eye c.,** nos regards se sont croisés; *Mil* **to establish c. with the enemy,** prendre contact avec l'ennemi;

(c) *Med* personne ayant approché un malade contagieux; **sexual c.,** partenaire sexuel;

(d) *(acquaintance etc)* relation *f*; **I have a c. who may be able to help you,** je connais quelqu'un qui pourrait vous aider; **who's our c. in Paris?,** qui est la personne à contacter à Paris?;

(e) *El etc (state)* contact *m*; *(part)* contact, touche *f*; **c. to earth,** contact avec la terre; **c. breaker,** dispositif *m* de rupture, (inter)rupteur *m*; **sliding c.,** contact glissant.

contact² *vt* se mettre en contact *ou* en rapport *ou* en relation avec *(qn)*, *F* contacter *(qn)*; **I can be contacted at this address,** on peut me contacter à cette adresse.

contagion [kən'teɪdʒən] *n* contagion *f*.

contagious [kən'teɪdʒəs] *adj (disease, laughter etc)* contagieux; *(laughter)* communicatif; *Vet* **c. disease,** épizootie *f*; **c. abortion,** brucellose *f*.

contagiousness [kən'teɪdʒəsnɪs] *n* contagiosité *f*; **the c. of laughter,** la contagion du rire.

contain [kən'teɪn] *vt* **(a)** *(hold)* contenir; **a jug containing only a few drops of milk,** un pot qui ne contenait que quelques gouttes de lait; **(b)** *(include)* contenir, renfermer; *(of book etc)* contenir; **medicine that contains arsenic,** médicament où il entre de l'arsenic; **ore containing a high percentage of iron,** minerai à forte teneur en fer; **the document contains a reference to ...,** le document contient une référence à ...; **(c)** *(control)* contenir, maîtriser *(son indignation)*; retenir *(ses sentiments)*; contenir *(l'inflation etc)*; circonscrire *(une épidémie, une idéologie)*; **he was unable to c. his laughter,** il ne pouvait pas s'empêcher de rire; *Lit* **I could no longer c. myself,** je ne pouvais plus me retenir davantage; **(d)** *Mil* contenir *(l'ennemi)*; **containing force,** corps de troupes destiné à arrêter l'ennemi.

container [kən'teɪnər] *n* **(a)** récipient *m*; réservoir *m*; bac *m (pour aliments)*; *El* bac *(d'accumulateur)*; *Com etc* boîte *f*, récipient; coffret *m (pour bande magnétique etc)*; **(b)** *(for transport)* conteneur *m*; **c. ship,** navire *m* porte-conteneurs; **c. port,** port destiné à recevoir des navires porte-conteneurs.

containerization [kənteɪnəraɪ'zeɪʃən] *n* conteneurisation *f*; *(of port)* conversion *f* à la conteneurisation.

containerize [kən'teɪnəraɪz] *vt* mettre en conteneur, conteneuriser; *(port)* convertir à la conteneurisation.

containment [kən'teɪnmənt] *n* **(a)** *(of disease, ideology)* action *f* de circonscrire; **(b)** *Nucl Phys* confinement *m*.

contaminate [kən'tæmɪneɪt] *vt* contaminer; **contaminated air,** air vicié; *Fig* **he had been contaminated by contact with political activists,** il a été contaminé au contact d'activistes.

contamination [kəntæmɪ'neɪʃən] *n* contamination *f* (*bactérienne, radioactive etc*).

contango, *pl* **-oes** [kən'tæŋgəʊ, -əʊz] *n St Exch* report *m*; taux *m* du report.

contd *adj* (*abbr* **continued**) suite *f*; **c. on p14,** suite à la page 14; **to be c.,** à suivre.

contemplate ['kɒntempleɪt] **1** *vt* **(a)** (*look at*) contempler (*qn, qch*); *Fig* **to c. one's navel,** se regarder le nombril, faire du nombrilisme; **(b)** (*envisage*) prévoir, envisager (*qch*), avoir (*qch*) en vue; **we don't c. moving soon,** nous n'envisageons pas de déménager dans l'immédiat; **(c)** (*consider*) **to c. doing sth,** se proposer de *ou* songer à faire qch; **to c. suicide,** songer au suicide; **that was never contemplated,** il n'a jamais été question de cela. **2** *vi* se recueillir, méditer.

contemplation [kɒntem'pleɪʃən] *n* **(a)** contemplation *f* (*d'un tableau, d'une vitrine etc*); **(b)** (*meditation*) recueillement *m*, méditation *f*, contemplation *f*.

contemplative [kən'templətɪv] *adj Rel* (*life, order*) contemplatif.

contemporaneous [kəntempə'reɪnɪəs] *adj* contemporain (**with,** de).

contemporaneously [kəntempə'reɪnɪəslɪ] *adv* **c. with ...,** en même temps que ... .

contemporary [kən'temp(ə)rərɪ] **1** *adj* **(a)** (*of same time*) contemporain, -aine (**with,** de); **(b)** (*present day*) contemporain; **c. events,** événements actuels. **2** *n* **our contemporaries,** nos contemporains *mpl*; **the two composers were not contemporaries,** les deux compositeurs ne vivaient pas à la même époque; **she and I are contemporaries,** elle et moi, nous sommes de la même génération.

contempt [kən'tempt] *n* mépris *m*, dédain *m*; **to hold s.o./sth in c.,** mépriser qn/qch; **to treat s.o./sth with c.,** traiter qn/qch avec dédain *ou* mépris; **beneath c.,** tout ce qu'il y a de plus méprisable; **her c. for the law/our opinions/***etc*, son mépris de la loi/nos opinions/*etc*; **I have nothing but c. for him,** je n'éprouve que du mépris à son égard; *Jur* **c. of court,** outrage *m* au tribunal, offense *f* à la cour; (*non-appearance*) refus *m* de comparaître.

contemptible [kən'temptəb(ə)l] *adj* méprisable; (*conduite*) indigne.

contemptibly [kən'temptɪblɪ] *adv* avec mépris.

contemptuous [kən'temptjʊəs] *adj* (*air*) méprisant; (*geste, parole*) de mépris; **he was c.,** il était méprisant; **c. of sth,** dédaigneux de qch.

contemptuously [kən'temptʊəslɪ] *adv* avec mépris, avec dédain.

contend [kən'tend] **1** *vi* combattre, lutter (**with, against,** contre); disputer (**with,** avec; **about,** sur); **the difficulties with which I have to c.,** les difficultés avec lesquelles je suis aux prises. **2** *vt* **to c. that ...,** prétendre *ou* soutenir que... .

contender [kən'tendər] *n* concurrent, -ente; (*in election*) candidat, -ate; (*for a title*) challenger *m* (**for sth,** de qch).

contending [kən'tendɪŋ] *adj* **the c. parties,** les concurrents *mpl;* **the c. armies,** les armées opposées.

content[1] ['kɒntent] *n* **(a) contents,** contenu *m* (*d'un livre, d'un film etc*); **average contents,** (*on label*) contenu moyen; **(table of) contents,** (*of book*) table *f* de matières; **(b)** *Ch Miner etc* teneur *f*, titre *m*; **gold/moisture c.,** teneur en or/humidité; **high protein c.,** haute teneur en protéines; **peanut butter has a high protein c.,** le beurre de cacahuètes est riche en protéines; **(c)** (*capacity*) contenu *m*, volume *m* (*d'un solide*); capacité *f* (*d'un vase*); **there is more emphasis on style than on c.,** une plus grande importance est accordée au style qu'au fond.

content[2] [kən'tent] *n* contentement *m*, satisfaction *f*; **to one's heart's c.,** à cœur joie.

content[3] *adj* satisfait (**with,** de); **they were poor but c.,** ils étaient pauvres mais heureux; **to be c. with sth,** se contenter de qch; **you'll have to be c. with beer,** il faudra que tu te contentes de bière; **he's quite c. to stay at home,** il ne demande pas mieux que de rester à la maison; **she's never c. to just watch a film — she has to make comments,** il ne lui suffit pas de regarder un film — il faut qu'elle fasse des commentaires.

content[4] *vt* **(a)** contenter, satisfaire (*qn*); **(b) to c. oneself with (doing) sth,** se contenter de (faire) qch.

contented [kən'tentɪd] *adj* content, satisfait; (*sourire*) de satisfaction.

contentedly [kən'tentɪdlɪ] *adv* avec contentement; **to live c.,** vivre heureux.

contentedness [kən'tentɪdnɪs] *n* contentement *m* (*de son sort*).

contention [kən'tenʃən] *n* **(a)** (*struggle*) lutte *f*, dispute *f*; **bone of c.,** pomme *f* de discorde; **(b)** (*competition*) émulation *f*; **(c)** (*affirmation*) affirmation *f*; **my c. is that ...,** je soutiens que ... .

contentious [kən'tenʃəs] *adj* **(a)** (*issue etc*) contentieux; **(b)** (*person, humour*) querelleur, -euse.

contentment [kən'tentmənt] *n* contentement *m*.

contest[1] ['kɒntest] *n* **(a)** (*competition*) concours *m*; **speed c.,** course *f* de vitesse; **beauty c.,** concours de beauté; **(b)** (*struggle*) combat *m*, lutte *f* (**with,** avec, contre; **between,** entre); **(c)** *US Jur* **no c.,** pas de témoins à charge.

contest[2] [kən'test] **1** *vt* **(a)** contester, disputer (*une question*) (**with, against,** avec); *Pol* se porter candidat pour (*un siège au Parlement*); **to c. an election,** disputer *ou* se présenter à une élection; **to c. the victory with s.o.,** disputer la victoire à qn; *Sp* **to c. a race,** se mettre sur les rangs; *Pol* **a hotly contested seat,** un siège très disputé; **(b)** *Jur etc* (*call into question*) attaquer (*un testament*); contester (*une succession*); **to c. s.o.'s right to do sth,** contester à qn le droit de faire qch. **2** *vi* se disputer (**with, against,** avec); **to c. for a prize,** disputer un prix.

contestant [kən'testənt] *n* concurrent *m*; (*in boxing, wrestling etc*) combattant *m*.

contestation [kɒntes'teɪʃən] *n Fml* **(a)** contestation *f* (*d'un droit etc*); **(b)** (*affirmation*) affirmation *f*, prétention *f*; **his c. was that ...,** il soutenait que ... .

context ['kɒntekst] *n* contexte *m*; **what's the c.?,** quel est le contexte?; **in this c.,** à ce propos; **in/out of c.,** en/hors de son contexte; **she was quoted out of c.,** on a cité ses paroles hors de leur contexte; **in the c. of an international recession,** dans le contexte d'une récession au niveau international.

context-dependent ['kɒntekstdɪ'pendənt] *adj* **to be c.-d.,** dépendre du contexte.

contextual [kən'tekstjʊəl] *adj* contextuel.

contextualize [kən'tekstjʊəlaɪz] *vt* placer (*qch*) dans son contexte.

contiguous [kən'tɪgjʊəs] *adj* **(a)** contigu, -uë (**to,** à, avec), attenant (**to,** à); **(b)** (*neighbouring*) voisin (**to,** de); **(c)** (*preceding in time*) qui précède immédiatement; (*following in time*) qui suit immédiatement.

continence ['kɒntɪnəns] *n* **(a)** (*control of bladder, bowel*) continence *f*; **(b)** (*sexual*) chasteté *f*.

continent[1] ['kɒntɪnənt] *n Geog* continent *m*; **the five continents,** les cinq parties du monde; *esp Br* **the C.,** l'Europe continentale; **on the C.,** en Europe (continentale), outre-Manche.

continent[2] *adj* **(a)** (*in control of bladder, bowel*) continent; **(b)** (*sexually*) chaste.

continental [kɒntɪ'nent(ə)l] **1** *adj* **(a)** *Geog* continental, -aux; **c. drift,** dérive *f* des continents; **c. shelf,** plate-forme continentale; **(b)** (*European*) de l'Europe continentale; **C.** *or* **c. breakfast,** = petit-déjeuner se composant de croissants et de pain; **c. quilt,** couette *f*, *Swiss* duvet *m*. **2** *n* (*European*) continental, -ale, habitant, -ante de l'Europe (continentale).

contingency [kən'tɪndʒənsɪ] *n* **(a)** (*unexpected event*) éventualité *f*; **to provide for every c.,** parer à toute éventualité; **prepared for all contingencies,** préparé à toutes les éventualités; **contingencies,** (*item on balance sheet*) frais divers; **to allow for contingencies,** parer à l'imprévu; **c. plan,** plan *m* d'urgence; **c. fund,** caisse *f* de prévoyance; **(b)** contingence *f* (*d'événements*); éventualité *f* (*d'un événement*).

contingent [kən'tɪndʒənt] **1** *adj* **(a)** (*conditional*) conditionnel; **c. on sth,** sous (la) réserve de qch; **to be c. upon sth,** (*of event*) dépendre de qch; **(b)** *Phil* contingent; **(c)** (*accidental, uncertain*) éventuel, fortuit. **2** *n Mil etc* contingent *m*; **the annual c. (of recruits),** le contingent annuel, *F* la classe; **there was a c. of holiday makers on the train,** il y avait un contingent de vacanciers dans le train.

continual [kən'tɪnjʊəl] *adj* continuel, incessant.

continually [kən'tɪnjʊəlɪ] *adv* continuellement, sans cesse.

continuance [kən'tɪnjʊəns] *n Fml* **(a)** continuation *f* (*d'une action*); **(b)** (*duration*) continuation *f*, durée *f*.

continuation [kəntɪnjʊ'eɪʃən] *n* **(a)** (*action*) continuation *f* (*d'une route, d'une histoire etc*); **(b)** (*result*) prolongement *m* (*d'un mur etc*); suite *f* (*d'un roman*); **to be a c. of ...,** faire suite à ...; **(c)** *St Exch* report *m*.

continue [kən'tɪnjuː] **1** *vt* **(a)** continuer (*un ouvrage, une activité etc*); prolonger (*une droite*); poursuivre (*un travail, un voyage*); continuer, reprendre (*une conversation*); perpétuer (*la race, une tradition*); **to c. one's studies,**

poursuivre ses études; (*later in life*) reprendre ses études; *Journ* **to be continued,** à suivre; **continued on page 30,** suite à la page 30; **to c. to do sth** *or* **doing sth,** continuer à *ou* de faire qch; **after lunch we continued working,** après le déjeuner nous avons repris notre travail; **she continued to support reform,** elle a continué à soutenir la réforme; **inflation continued to rise,** l'inflation a continué à augmenter;

(b) *Jur* ajourner (*un procès*).

2 *vi* **(a)** continuer; (*of line*) se prolonger; **the situation cannot c.,** la situation ne peut pas durer; **the situation continued into the 1960s,** la situation s'est prolongée dans le courant des années 1960; **to c. in office,** garder sa charge; (*of political party*) rester au pouvoir; **she will c. as director until December,** elle gardera les fonctions de directrice jusqu'à décembre; **his bad luck continues,** ses malheurs se poursuivent; **to c. on one's way,** continuer son chemin; **they continued to Rome,** ils ont poursuivi leur chemin jusqu'à Rome;

(b) (*resume talking*) continuer; **'and then', he continued,** 'et puis', continua-t-il.

continued [kən'tɪnjuːd] *adj* (*effort, intérêt*) soutenu.

continuing [kən'tɪnjuːɪŋ] *adj* continu; (*interest*) soutenu; **the c. story of a small American town,** (*TV serial etc*) la suite de l'histoire d'une petite ville américaine; **the c. violence in the province,** la violence continue dans la province; **c. education,** formation permanente *ou* continue; **c. education class,** cours *mpl* de formation permanente *ou* continue.

continuity [kɒntɪ'njuːɪtɪ] *n* **(a)** continuité *f*; **to break the c. of s.o.'s ideas,** couper le fil des idées de qn; **(b)** *Cin* scénario *m*, découpage *m*; **c. man,** découpeur *m*; **c. girl,** scripte *f*, secrétaire *f* de plateau; *El* **c. check,** contrôle *m* de continuité; **c. checker,** appareil *m* de contrôle de la continuité; **to check c.,** contrôler la continuité.

continuous [kən'tɪnjʊəs] *adj* continu, -e; **c. succession,** suite ininterrompue (*de visites etc*); *El* **c. waves,** ondes entretenues; *Cin* **c. performance,** spectacle permanent; *Comptr* **c. paper** *or* **stationery,** papier en continu.

continuously [kən'tɪnjʊəslɪ] *adv* continuellement, continûment, sans interruption.

contort [kən'tɔːt] *vt* tordre (*les traits etc*); **face contorted by pain,** visage tordu par la douleur.

contortion [kən'tɔːʃən] *n* crispation *f* (*des traits etc*); (*of body*) contorsion *f*.

contortionist [kən'tɔːʃənɪst] *n* contorsionniste *mf*.

contour ['kɒntʊər] *n* contour *m* (*d'un objet*); profil *m* (*du terrain*); **the contours of the hill,** les contours de la colline; **c. (line),** (*on map*) courbe *f* de niveau, courbe hypsométrique; **c. map,** carte *f* en courbes de niveau.

contra ['kɒntrə] **1** *prep* (*abbr* **con.**) contre **2** *n* (*in bookkeeping*) **c. entry,** écriture *f* inverse.

contraband ['kɒntrəbænd] *n* contrebande *f*; **c. goods,** marchandises *fpl* de contrebande.

contrabass ['kɒntrəbeɪs] *n Mus* contrebasse *f* (*à cordes*).

contrabassoon [kɒntrəbə'suːn] *n Mus* contrebasson *m*.

contraception [kɒntrə'sepʃən] *n* contraception *f*, **male c.,** contraception masculine; **method of c.,** méthode contraceptive.

contraceptive [kɒntrə'septɪv] *Med* **1** *n* contraceptif *m*; **male c.,** contraceptif masculin; **to use a c.,** utiliser un contraceptif. **2** *adj* **c. advice,** conseils *mpl* sur la contraception; **c. device,** contraceptif *m*; **c. method,** méthode contraceptive; **c. pill,** pilule contraceptive; **c. sponge,** éponge contraceptive.

contract¹ ['kɒntrækt] *n* **(a)** pacte *m*, contrat *m*; **marriage c.,** contrat de mariage; **to bind oneself by c.,** s'engager par contrat; **have you (got) a c.?,** est-ce que tu as un contrat?; **that isn't in my c.,** ce n'est pas dans mon contrat; **to be under c.,** être sous contrat; **she is under c. to the studio,** elle est sous contrat avec le studio; **to enter into a c.,** (*of person*) passer (un) contrat (**with,** avec);

(b) (*of sale*) acte *m* de vente; **simple c.,** convention verbale; **law of c.,** droit *m* des contrats;

(c) *Ind Com* marché *m*; **they were given a c. to build a new road/*etc*,** ils se sont vu attribuer un marché pour construire une nouvelle route; **to put work out to c.,** faire effectuer un travail en sous-traitance; **to tender for a c.,** soumissionner à une adjudication; **conditions of c.,** cahier *m* des charges; **breach of c.,** rupture *f* de contrat; **c. work,** travail *m* à l'entreprise *ou* à forfait;

(d) *Cards* **c. bridge,** bridge *m* contrat.

contract² [kən'trækt] **1** *vt* **(a)** contracter (*une obligation, une maladie*); prendre (*une habitude*); **to c. debts,** s'endetter; **she has contracted to make two films,** elle a signé un contrat pour faire deux films; **(b)** *Com* **to c. to do sth,** entreprendre de faire qch. **2** *vi Com* **to c. for a supply of sth,** entreprendre une fourniture de qch; **to c. for work,** entreprendre des travaux à forfait.

contract³ **1** *vt* contracter (*les métaux, les muscles etc*); crisper (*les traits*); rétrécir (*un tissu, une ouverture*); resserrer (*les tissus*); *Ling* **to c. 'shall not' into 'shan't',** contracter 'shall not' en 'shan't'. **2** *vi* se contracter, se rétrécir; **the pupil contracts in bright light,** la pupille se contracte à la lumière intense; *Ling* **'cannot' contracts into 'can't',** 'cannot' se contracte en 'can't'.

▶**contract in** *vi Br* (*insurance*) signifier son intention de souscrire.

▶**contract out** **1** *vi Br* signifier son intention de ne pas souscrire à (*un régime d'assurance ou de retraite*). **2** *vtsep Com* sous-traiter (*du travail*) (**to,** à).

contracting [kən'træktɪŋ] **1** *adj* **c. parties,** contractants *mpl*. **2** *n* **(a)** affermage *m* (*pour annonces etc*); **(b)** *Ind* recours *m* à l'entreprise.

contraction [kən'trækʃən] *n* **(a)** contraction *f*, rétrécissement *m* (*de la pupille etc*); retrait *m* (*des métaux lors du refroidissement*); contraction (*d'un muscle*); *Obst* **contractions have begun,** les contractions ont commencé; **(b)** *Ling* (*of two words*) contraction *f*; (*word*) mot contracté; **(c) c. of debts,** endettement *m*.

contractor [kən'træktər] *n Com* entrepreneur *m*; **army c.,** fournisseur *m* de l'armée; **haulage/building c.,** entrepreneur de transports/de bâtiments.

contractual [kən'træktjʊəl] *adj* contractuel; **c. obligations,** obligations contractuelles.

contradict [kɒntrə'dɪkt] *vt* contredire (*qn*); démentir (*qn, un bruit*); **don't c. me, young man!,** ne me contredisez pas, jeune homme!; **to c. oneself,** se contredire; **the statements of the witnesses c. each other,** les dépositions des témoins se contredisent.

contradiction [kɒntrə'dɪkʃən] *n* **(a)** (*act*) contradiction *f*, démenti *m* (*d'une nouvelle*); **(b)** (*statement*) contradiction *f*; **this was a c. of what they had previously said,** c'était un démenti de ce qu'ils avaient dit auparavant; **in c. with,** en contradiction avec, incompatible avec; **c. in terms,** contradiction dans les termes; **the contradictions in his character,** les contradictions de son caractère; **(c)** *Phil* contradiction *f*, incompatibilité *f* (*entre deux principes*).

contradictory [kɒntrə'dɪktərɪ] *adj* **(a)** (*statement etc*) contradictoire, opposé (**to,** à); **(b)** (*person*) raisonneur, -euse; **don't be so c.,** ne sois pas aussi raisonneur.

contradistinction ['kɒntrədɪs'tɪŋkʃən] *n* opposition *f*, contraste *m*; **in c. to ...,** par opposition à ... .

contraflow ['kɒntrəfləʊ] *n* **c. system,** système *m* de circulation à contre-sens; **6 miles of c. (traffic),** circulation à contre-sens sur 6 mil(l)es.

contraindication ['kɒntrəɪndɪ'keɪʃən] *n Med* contre-indication *f*, *pl* contre-indications.

contralto [kən'træltəʊ] *adj & n Mus* contralto *m*.

contraption [kən'træpʃən] *n F* machin *m*, engin *m*, truc *m*.

contrapuntal [kɒntrə'pʌnt(ə)l] *adj Mus* (*morceau, accompagnement etc*) en contrepoint.

contrarily [kən'treərɪlɪ] *adv* contrairement.

contrariness [kən'treərɪnɪs] *n* disposition *f* à tout contrarier, esprit *m* de contradiction, esprit contrariant.

contrariwise ['kɒntrərɪwaɪz] *adv* **(a)** (*on the other hand*) au contraire; **(b)** (*in the opposite direction*) en sens opposé; **(c)** [kən'treərɪwaɪz] *F* (*perversely*) par esprit de contradiction.

contrary ['kɒntrərɪ] **1** *n* contraire *m*; **on the c.,** au contraire; **unless you hear to the c.,** sauf avis contraire. **2** *adj* **(a)** (*opposite*) contraire (**to,** à); (*interests etc*) opposé (**to,** à), en opposition (**to,** avec); **c. to nature,** contre (la) nature; **c. to reason,** contraire à la raison; **(b)** (*unfavourable*) **c. winds,** vents *mpl* contraires; **(c)** *F* [kən'treərɪ] (*person*) opiniâtre, qui a l'esprit de contradiction; (*remark*) formulé par esprit de contradiction. **3** *adv* contrairement (**to,** à); **to act c. to instructions,** contrevenir aux ordres reçus; **c. to my expectations,** contre mon attente; **c. to what I was told,** contrairement à ce qu'on m'a dit.

contrast¹ ['kɒntrɑːst] *n* (*difference*) & *TV Phot Art* contraste *m* (**between,** entre); **the c. between brother and sister could not have been greater,** le contraste entre le frère et la sœur n'aurait pas pu être plus grand; **in c. with sth/s.o.,** par contraste avec qch/qn; **to form a c. to ...,** faire contraste avec ...; **by c. the president's adviser was almost optimistic,** par contraste, le conseiller du président était presque optimiste; **as a c. to ...,** comme contraste à ... .

contrast² [kən'trɑːst] **1** *vt* faire contraster, mettre en contraste (**with,** avec); **she contrasted the attitudes of the 1950s with those of today,** elle a mis en contraste *ou* en opposition les attitudes des années 1950 avec celles d'aujourd'hui. **2** *vi* contraster (**with,** avec); **this statement contrasts with his earlier remarks,** cette déclaration contraste avec ses remarques précédentes; **to c. strongly,** trancher (**with,** sur).

contrasting [kən'trɑːstɪŋ] *adj* qui fait contraste; (*colours*) contrastant.

contravene [kɒntrə'viːn] *vt* **(a)** transgresser, enfreindre (*la loi etc*); être en contravention avec (*une règle*); **(b)** (*dispute, contradict*) aller à l'encontre de (*qch*).

contravention [kɒntrə'venʃən] *n* (*of law*) contravention *f*, infraction *f*; **to act in c. of a rule/a right,** agir en opposition avec une règle/un droit.

contribute [kən'trɪbjuːt] **1** *vt* contribuer pour (*une somme*); **to c. one's share,** payer sa part; **to c. sth to sth,** apporter qch à qch; **she contributed $50,000 to the cause,** elle a versé 50 000 dollars au profit de la cause; **he didn't c. anything to the discussion,** il n'a rien apporté à la discussion. **2** *vi* contribuer; **if everyone contributes we'll be able to get a bigger present,** si tout le monde contribue *ou* participe, nous pourrons acheter un cadeau plus important; **he rarely contributes to discussions,** il contribue rarement aux discussions; **to c. to a charity,** contribuer à une bonne œuvre; **to c. to a newspaper,** collaborer à un journal; **to c. to the success,** aider au succès; **everything contributed to make him happy,** tout contribuait à le rendre heureux.

contribution [kɒntrɪ'bjuːʃən] *n* **(a)** contribution *f*; participation *f* (*à un repas, un cadeau etc*); **I've already made a c.,** (*to s.o. collecting for charity*) j'ai déjà donné; **contributions welcome,** (*to charity*) les contributions sont les bienvenues; *Fin* **c. of capital,** apport *m* de capitaux; **their c. to the carnival was a brass band,** leur participation au carnaval s'est concrétisée par une fanfare; **(b)** *Journ* article écrit pour un journal.

contributor [kən'trɪbjʊtər] *n* **(a)** contributaire *mf*; **(b)** *Journ* collaborateur, -trice (**to a paper,** d'un journal).

contributory [kən'trɪbjʊtərɪ] *adj* contribuant; **c. causes,** causes contribuantes; *Jur* **c. negligence,** manque *m* de précautions (*de la part d'un accidenté*).

contrite [kən'traɪt, 'kɒntraɪt] *adj* contrit, pénitent, repentant.

contritely [kən'traɪtlɪ] *adv* d'un air contrit *ou* pénitent; avec contrition.

contrition [kən'trɪʃən] *n* contrition *f*, pénitence *f*.

contrivance [kən'traɪvəns] *n* **(a)** (*device*) appareil *m*, dispositif *m*, engin *m*; **(b)** (*action*) invention *f* (*d'un appareil etc*); **(c)** (*skill*) ingéniosité *f*; **(d)** (*invention*) invention *f*; combinaison *f*; **(e)** *Pej* machination *f*.

contrive [kən'traɪv] *vt* inventer, concevoir (*un appareil etc*); **to c. (a means) to do sth,** trouver moyen de faire qch; **she contrived to get herself mentioned in the article,** elle a trouvé le moyen pour qu'on parle d'elle dans l'article.

contrived [kən'traɪvd] *adj* forcé, qui manque de naturel.

control¹ [kən'trəʊl] *n* **(a)** (*authority*) autorité *f*; **state c.,** étatisme *m*; **to have c. of a business,** être à la tête d'une entreprise; **the government exercises strict c. over how funds are invested,** le gouvernement exerce un contrôle strict sur la manière dont les fonds sont investis;

(b) (*power*) contrôle *m*; (*over oneself*) maîtrise *f*; **circumstances beyond our c.,** circonstances indépendantes de notre volonté; **these things are beyond our c.,** ces choses-là ne se commandent pas; **to keep s.o. under strict c.,** surveiller qn de près; **the state has no c. over the media,** l'état n'a aucun contrôle sur les médias; **she has no c. over the children,** elle n'a aucune autorité sur les enfants; **things/the situation had got out of c.,** les choses/la situation étaient/était devenue(s) incontrôlable(s); **the children/horses were out of c.,** les enfants/les chevaux étaient incontrôlables; **she soon had the horse under c.,** elle est vite parvenue à contrôler le cheval; **self c.,** contrôle de soi-même; **to lose c. of oneself,** ne plus être maître de soi; **to regain c. of oneself,** se ressaisir; **to keep one's feelings under c.,** contrôler *ou* maîtriser ses sentiments; **everything is under c.,** (*almost ready*) tout est fin prêt; (*there's no need to panic*) tout va bien; **to have c. over sth/s.o.,** avoir le contrôle de qch/qn; **to be in c. of sth/s.o.,** avoir le contrôle de qch/qn; **the government is now firmly back in c.,** le gouvernement a maintenant fermement repris le contrôle; **to bring under c.,** maîtriser (*un incendie etc*); enrayer (*une maladie*); **to take c.,** prendre le contrôle (**of,** de);

(c) *Econ etc* (*measure*) contrôle *m* (*des changes*); contrôle, réglementation *f* (*des loyers*); **new government controls on financial practices,** nouvelles réglementations gouvernementales sur les pratiques financières; **birth c.,** contrôle *ou* limitation *f* des naissances;

(d) (*verification*) témoin *m*; **c. experiment,** expérience *f* de contrôle; **c. group,** (*in experiment*) groupe *m* témoin;

(e) *Tech* (*action*) commande *f* (*d'un mécanisme*); manœuvre *f* (*d'un train, d'un avion, d'un navire etc*); *El Electron etc* contrôle *m* (*de fréquence etc*); réglage *m* (*de puissance, d'intensité*); **to lose c. of one's car,** perdre le contrôle de sa voiture; **the driver/pilot lost c.,** le conducteur/pilote a perdu le contrôle; **the truck went out of c.,** on a perdu le contrôle du camion; **ship out of c.,** navire qui n'est plus maître de sa manœuvre; **temperature c.,** régulation *f* thermique; **automatic c.,** réglage automatique; **dual c.,** double commande; **remote c.,** télécommande *f*, commande à distance; *Comptr* **c. key,** touche *f* contrôle; **c. lever/mechanism,** levier *m*/appareil *m* de commande; *Av* **c. column,** levier de commande; *Sp Aut* **c. point,** contrôle (*du passage de voitures etc*); *Av* **c. tower,** tour *f* de contrôle;

(f) *Tech* (*means*) (organe *m* de) commande *f*; **the controls,** les commandes; **to be at the controls,** (*of person*) être aux commandes; *Av* **flying controls,** commandes de vol; *Rad etc* **volume c.,** bouton *m* de (réglage de) volume;

(g) (*at seance*) contrôleur, -euse (*d'un médium*).

control² *vt* **(a)** (*direct*) diriger; réglementer (*des affaires, la production*); régler (*la dépense*); commander (*le mouvement d'une machine*); diriger, être à la tête de (*une entreprise*); *Mil* contrôler (*une région stratégique*); **he cannot c. his pupils,** il ne sait pas tenir ses élèves; **to c. the traffic,** réglementer la circulation; **(b)** (*bring under control*) maîtriser (*un cheval*); réprimer (*un soulèvement*); dompter (*ses passions*); contrôler (*ses réactions etc*); contenir, enrayer (*la hausse des prix, l'inflation*); retenir (*ses larmes*); *Med* équilibrer (*un diabète etc*); **to c. oneself,** se contrôler, se maîtriser; **c. yourself!,** retenez-vous!; **to try to c. oneself,** faire un effort sur soi-même.

controlled [kən'trəʊld] *adj* (*person*) qui sait se contenir; (bien) équilibré; *Econ* (*économie*) dirigé; (*marché*) réglementé; *Med* (*diabète etc*) équilibré; **the transition to democracy must take place in a c. manner,** le passage à la démocratie doit se faire dans l'ordre; *Journ* **c. circulation magazine,** revue *f* à diffusion restreinte; *Admin* **c. crossing,** passage réglementé; *Mil* **c. explosion,** (*of car bomb etc*) explosion contrôlée.

controller [kən'trəʊlər] *n* **(a)** (*person*) contrôleur, -euse; *Av* **air traffic c.,** contrôleur de la navigation aérienne, aiguilleur *m* du ciel; **(b)** *Fin* contrôleur *m*; **(c)** (*apparatus*) contrôleur *m*; commande *f*; *Av* **flight c.,** contrôleur de vol; **(d)** *Comptr* contrôleur *m*; **disk c.,** contrôleur de disques.

controlling [kən'trəʊlɪŋ] *adj* qui gouverne; (*puissance*) dirigeant; *Fin Com* **c. interest,** (*in company*) participation *f* majoritaire.

controversial [kɒntrə'vɜːʃəl] *adj* controversé.

controversy ['kɒntrəvɜːsɪ, kən'trɒvəsɪ] *n* controverse *f*; **to be the subject of c.,** être sujet à controverse; **question that has given rise to much c.,** question fort controversée.

contumacious [kɒntjʊ'meɪʃəs] *adj Fml* (*disobedient*) désobéissant; (*resistant*) rebelle.

contumacy ['kɒntjʊməsɪ, kɒn'tjuː-] *n* **(a)** *Jur* contumace *f*; **(b)** *Fml* (*disobedience*) désobéissance *f*; **(c)** (*resistance*) rébellion *f*.

contumely ['kɒntjuːmlɪ] *n Fml* **(a)** (*insolence*) insolence *f*; **to treat s.o. with c.,** traiter qn avec mépris; **(b)** (*shame*) honte *f*; **to cover s.o. with c.,** couvrir qn de honte.

contusion [kən'tjuːʒən] *n Med* contusion *f*.

conundrum [kə'nʌndrəm] *n* **(a)** (*riddle*) devinette *f*; **(b)** (*mystery*) énigme *f*.

conurbation [kɒnɜː'beɪʃən] *n* conurbation *f*.

convalesce [kɒnvə'les] *vi Med* relever de maladie, se remettre (d'une maladie); (*rest*) être en convalescence; **he is convalescing in Brighton,** il est en convalescence à Brighton.

convalescence [kɒnvə'lesəns] *n Med* convalescence *f*.

convalescent¹ [kɒnvə'lesənt] *n Med* convalescent, -ente; **c. home,** maison *f* de convalescence.

convalescent² *adj Med* convalescent.

convection [kən'vekʃən] *n Phys El etc* convection *f*; **c. drying,** séchage *m* par convection; **c. drier,** séchoir *m* à convection; **c. heater,** radiateur *m* à convection.

convector [kən'vektər] *n* appareil *m* de chauffage par onvection, radiateur *m* à convection.

onvene [kən'viːn] **1** *vt* convoquer, réunir (*une assemblée*); **the Chairman convenes extraordinary general meetings,** le président convoque les assemblées générales extraordinaires; *Jur* **to c. s.o. before a court,** citer qn devant un tribunal. **2** *vi* s'assembler.

convener [kən'viːnər] *n* secrétaire *m*.

convenience [kən'viːnɪəns] *n* **(a)** commodité *f*, convenance *f*; **for c. I use canned fruit,** j'utilise des fruits en conserves pour des raisons de commodité; **a bus service is provided for our customers' c.,** un service d'autobus est proposé pour l'agrément de nos clients; **marriage of c.,** mariage *m* de convenance; **at your c.,** à votre bon plaisir; **at your earliest c.,** dans les meilleurs délais; *Com* **c. foods,** aliments *mpl* tout prêts; *Nau* **flag of c.,** pavillon *m* de complaisance; *Am* **c. store,** magasin *m* de voisinage; **(b)** (*installation*) **(public) c.,** w.c. *mpl* (publics), toilettes *fpl*; **rooms fitted with all modern conveniences,** chambres installées avec tout (le) confort moderne.

convenient [kən'viːnɪənt] *adj* commode, pratique; (*time*) opportun; **if it is c. for you,** si cela vous convient, si vous n'y voyez pas d'inconvénient; **2 o'clock isn't very c.,** 14 heures ne m'arrange pas; **to find a c. opportunity to do sth,** trouver l'occasion de faire qch; **we climbed through a c. hole in the fence,** nous avons escaladé la clôture en passant par un trou bien situé; **the ticket collector wasn't there — how very c.!,** le contrôleur n'était pas là — c'est très pratique ça!; **the flat is very c. for the shops,** l'appartement est bien situé pour les commerçants.

conveniently [kən'viːnɪəntlɪ] *adv* commodément; (*to arrive*) opportunément, à propos; **the house is c. situated near the town centre,** la maison est commodément située près du centre ville; **someone c. forgot to lock the door,** (*accidentally*) quelqu'un a oublié de fermer la porte, ce qui est bien pratique; (*deliberately*) comme par hasard, quelqu'un a oublié de fermer la porte.

convent ['kɒnvənt] *n Rel* couvent *m*; **to enter a c.,** entrer au couvent; **c. (school),** couvent; **she goes to the c.,** elle fait ses études au couvent *ou F* chez les bonnes sœurs.

convention [kən'venʃən] *n* **(a)** (*meeting*) assemblée *f*, convention *f*; *US Pol* convention; *Fr Hist* **the C.,** la Convention; **medical c.,** congrès médical; **c. centre,** palais *m* des congrès; **(b)** (*agreement*) accord *m*, contrat *m*; (*international*) convention *f* (**on,** relative à); **the Hague Conventions,** les conventions de la Haye; **(c)** (*established practice*) usage *m*; **the c. is that ....,** (*in science*) la convention consiste à ...; **a c. used in musical notation,** une convention utilisée dans la notation musicale; **(d)** (*custom*) *usu pl* **conventions,** convenances *fpl*; **to observe the conventions,** respecter les convenances; **social conventions,** les conventions sociales.

conventional [kən'venʃən(ə)l] *adj* **(a)** (*accepted*) conventionnel; *Pej* sans originalité; **c. propriety,** les convenances admises; **(b)** (*established, traditional*) classique, traditionnel; **the c. wisdom is that ...,** la sagesse populaire veut que ...; *Mil* **c. warfare/weapon,** guerre *f*/arme *f* classique; *Constr* **c. material,** matériau traditionnel.

conventionality [kənvenʃə'nælɪtɪ] *n* **(a)** (*established practice*) convention *f*; usage admis; **(b) conventionalities,** les conventions *fpl* (sociales); **(c)** (*quality*) caractère conventionnel *ou* ordinaire (*de qch*).

conventionally [kən'venʃən(ə)lɪ] *adv* **(a)** (*in an accepted fashion*) conventionnellement; *Pej* sans originalité; **(b)** (*traditionally*) d'une manière classique.

conventioneer [kənvenʃə'nɪər] *n esp Am* congressiste *mf*.

converge [kən'vɜːdʒ] **1** *vi* converger (**on,** sur); **three armies were converging on Paris,** trois armées convergeaient sur Paris; **the two lines c. at this point,** les deux lignes convergent à ce point. **2** *vt* faire converger (*des rayons lumineux etc*).

convergence [kən'vɜːdʒəns] *n* convergence *f* (*de lignes, d'opinions*); *Math* focalisation *f*; **c. surface,** (*on cathode ray tube*) surface *f* de convergence.

convergent [kən'vɜːdʒənt] *adj* convergent; *Opt* **c. lens,** lentille convexe *ou* convergente.

conversant [kən'vɜːsənt] *adj* **to be c. with sth,** (*with French grammar, the law etc*) s'y connaître en qch; (*with type of engine etc*) connaître qch; (*with recent developments etc*) être au courant de qch.

conversation [kɒnvə'seɪʃən] *n* **(a)** conversation *f*, entretien *m*; **to hold** *or* **have a c. with s.o.,** s'entretenir avec qn; **to get into c. (with s.o.),** entamer une conversation (avec qn); **to change the c.,** changer de conversation; détourner la conversation; **she was just making c.,** elle parlait pour ne rien dire; **his c. was very dull,** sa conversation était sans aucun intérêt; **I'm not good at c.,** je ne suis pas très doué pour faire la conversation; **c. skills,** l'art de la conversation; *Art* **c. piece,** tableau *m* de genre; **the vase is quite a c. piece,** le vase alimente bien des conversations; **c. stopper,** une remarque *ou* un sujet qui arrête net les conversations; **that was a c. stopper,** cela a arrêté net la conversation; **(b)** *Comptr* dialogue *m*.

conversational [kɒnvə'seɪʃən(ə)l] *adj* **(a)** de (la) conversation; **in a c. tone,** sur le ton de la conversation; **c. style,** style familier; **(b)** *Comptr* (*mode*) dialogue.

conversationalist [kɒnvə'seɪʃənəlɪst] *n* **to be a c.,** (*to like talking*) bien parler; (*to be a good talker*) aimer la conversation; **I'm not much of a c.,** je ne suis pas brillant causeur.

conversationally [kɒnvə'seɪʃən(ə)lɪ] *adv* sur le ton de la conversation.

converse[1] [kən'vɜːs] *vi Fml* parler; **to c. with s.o. on** *or* **about sth,** converser avec qn sur qch.

converse[2] ['kɒnvɜːs] **1** *adj* (*in logic*) converse; *Math* réciproque. **2** *n* (*in logic*) proposition *f* converse; *Math* proposition réciproque.

conversely ['kɒnvɜːslɪ, kən'vɜːslɪ] *adv* réciproquement; vice versa; inversement.

conversion [kən'vɜːʃən] *n* **(a)** *Rel & Fig* conversion *f*; **their c. to Christianity,** leur conversion au christianisme; *Fig* **his c. to their way of thinking,** sa conversion à leur manière de penser;

(b) (*adaptation, alteration*) conversion *f* (**of sth into sth,** de qch en qch); **c. of water into steam,** conversion de l'eau en vapeur; **c. of iron into steel,** conversion du fer en acier; **the c. of a house into flats,** la transformation d'une maison pour en faire des appartements; l'aménagement *m* *ou* la transformation d'une maison en appartements; *Fin* **c. loan/order/right,** emprunt *m*/ordre *m*/droit *m* de conversion; **c. of securities,** conversion de titres; *Tech* **c. factor,** facteur *m* de conversion; **c. plant,** usine *f* de transformation; **c. table,** (*of currency, measurements etc*) table *f* de conversion;

(c) (*result*) adaptation *f*; **the car is a c. from a standard model,** la voiture est un modèle standard adapté;

(d) *Rugby US Fb* transformation *f*;

(e) *Jur* **c. of funds to one's own use, improper c. of funds,** détournement *m* de fonds.

convert[1] ['kɒnvɜːt] *n* converti, -ie; **to become a c. to sth,** se convertir à qch; **to make a c. of s.o.,** convertir qn; **she's made another c.,** elle a encore converti quelqu'un.

convert[2] [kən'vɜːt] **1** *vt* **(a)** *Rel* convertir (*qn*) (*à une religion*); **to be converted to Christianity,** se convertir au christianisme; *Fig* **she converted them to her way of thinking,** elle les a amenés à voir les choses à sa manière; *Fig* **you're preaching to the converted,** tu prêches un converti;

(b) (*alter, adapt*) transformer, convertir (**sth into sth,** qch en qch); **to c. iron into steel,** convertir le fer en acier; **the car has been converted to run on unleaded petrol,** la voiture a été modifiée pour rouler à l'essence sans plomb; **her studio was a converted cowshed,** son studio était une étable aménagée; **to c. miles into kilometres,** convertir les mil(l)es en kilomètres; *Fin* **converted share,** action convertie;

(c) *Rugby US Fb* **to c. a try,** transformer un essai; **converted goal,** transformation *f*;

(d) *Jur* **to c. funds to another purpose,** affecter des fonds à un autre usage; **to c. funds to one's own use,** détourner des fonds.

2 *vi* (*of settee etc*) se transformer (**into a bed,** en lit); **we've converted to electricity,** nous sommes passés à l'électricité.

converter [kən'vɜːtər] *n* **(a)** *Metal* **steel c., Bessemer c.,** convertisseur *m* Bessemer; **(b)** *El Rad etc* convertisseur *m*; **(c)** (*person*) convertisseur, -euse (*des infidèles etc*).

convertibility [kənvɜːtə'bɪlɪtɪ] *n* convertibilité *f*.

convertible [kən'vɜːtəb(ə)l] **1** *adj* **(a)** (*thing*) convertible (**into,** en); (*divan etc*) transformable; **(b)** *Aut* décapotable; **(c)** *Fin* (*loan, security*) convertible; **c. currency,** monnaies *fpl* convertibles; **(d)** (*person*) que l'on peut convertir (**to,** à). **2** *n Aut* (voiture *f*) décapotable *f*.

convex ['kɒnveks] *adj* **(a)** *Phys etc* convexe; **(b)** *US* (*route, chaussée*) bombé.

convexity [kən'veksɪtɪ] *n Phys etc* convexité *f*.

convey [kən'veɪ] *vt* **(a)** (*communicate*) transmettre (*un ordre*); donner (*une idée*); communiquer (*une nouvelle*) (**to,** à); **please c. my good wishes to the young couple,**

veuillez transmettre tous mes vœux aux jeunes époux; **to c. one's meaning,** communiquer sa pensée; **his writing conveys the mood of the country,** sa manière d'écrire évoque l'atmosphère du pays; **(b)** *(transport)* transporter, porter *(qch, qn)*; (a)mener *(qn)*; *(of air etc)* transmettre *(le son, une odeur)*; **(c)** *Jur* faire cession de *(un bien)*; transférer, céder *(un bien)* **(to,** à); *(of solicitor)* dresser l'acte de cession de *(une terre etc)*.

conveyance [kən'veɪəns] *n* **(a)** *(communication)* transmission *f*, communication *f* *(de qch à qn)*; *Phys* transmission *(du son, de la chaleur)*; **(b)** *(transport)* transport *m*; moyen *m* de transport; **(c)** *(vehicle)* véhicule *m (de transport)*; voiture *f*; *Jur* **public c.,** véhicule de transport(s) en commun; **(d)** *Jur* transfert *m*, cession *f*, disposition *f* *(de biens)*; *(document)* acte translatif de propriété; acte de cession.

conveyancing [kən'veɪənsɪŋ] *n Jur* **(a)** procédure translative de propriété; **(b)** *(drawing up documents)* rédaction *f* des actes de cession *ou* des actes translatifs de propriété.

conveyor, conveyer [kən'veɪər] *n* **(a)** *Ind* (appareil *m*) transporteur *m*; *Min* convoyeur *m*; **roller c.,** transporteur à rouleaux; **c. (belt),** convoyeur, tapis roulant; **belt c.,** transporteur (à bande); **bucket c.,** transporteur à godets; **(b)** *Fml (person)* porteur, -euse *(d'une lettre, d'un paquet)*; *(carrier)* voiturier *m*.

convict¹ ['kɒnvɪkt] *n (convicted person)* détenu, -ue; *Old-fashioned (prisoner)* forçat *m*, bagnard *m*; **former c.,** repris *m* de justice.

convict² [kən'vɪkt] *vt* **to c. s.o. of a crime,** déclarer qn coupable d'un crime; **he was convicted,** il fut reconnu coupable; il fut condamné; **there wasn't enough evidence to c. them,** il n'y avait pas assez de preuves pour les déclarer coupables; **you stand convicted by your own words,** vos propres paroles vous condamnent.

conviction [kən'vɪkʃən] *n* **(a)** *Jur* condamnation *f*; **previous convictions,** condamnations antérieures; **c. for murder,** condamnation pour meurtre; **(b)** *(belief)* conviction *f*; **to act from c.,** agir par conviction; **to have the courage of one's convictions,** avoir le courage de ses opinions; **to carry c.,** *(of evidence etc)* être convaincant; **his voice/argument lacked c.,** sa voix/son argument manquait de conviction; **(c)** *(persuasion)* conviction *f*; **to be open to c.,** être accessible à la persuasion.

convince [kən'vɪns] *vt* convaincre, persuader *(qn)* **(of,** de; **that ...,** que ...); **to allow oneself to be convinced,** se laisser convaincre.

convinced [kən'vɪnsd] *adj* convaincu, de conviction; **a c. monetarist,** un monétariste convaincu; **she's c. (that) they know,** elle est convaincue qu'ils étaient au courant; **I'm not c.,** je ne suis pas convaincu.

convincing [kən'vɪnsɪŋ] *adj (argument)* convaincant; *(language)* persuasif; *(performance etc)* qui emporte conviction; **she wasn't very c. as Juliet,** *(of actress)* elle n'était pas convaincante dans le rôle de Juliette; **the explosion was very c.,** *(of special effect)* l'explosion était très réaliste.

convincingly [kən'vɪnsɪŋlɪ] *adv* d'une manière convaincante.

convivial [kən'vɪvɪəl] *adj (person)* bon convive, bon vivant; *(atmosphere)* convivial, joyeux; **to have a c. evening,** passer une soirée conviviale.

conviviality [kənvɪvɪ'ælɪtɪ] *n* franche gaieté *(dans un repas)*; convivialité *f*, esprit *m* de société.

convocation [kɒnvə'keɪʃən] *n* **(a)** convocation *f* *(d'une assemblée)*; **(b)** *Rel* assemblée *f*, synode *m*.

convoke [kən'vəʊk] *vt* convoquer *(une assemblée)*.

convoluted ['kɒnvəluːtɪd] *adj* **(a)** *(complicated)* *(plot)* compliqué; **(b)** *Biol* convoluté.

convolution [kɒnvə'luːʃən] *n* **(a)** *(complication)* circonvolution *f*; **the convolutions of her argument,** les circonvolutions de son argumentation; **(b)** *(twist)* repli *m*, sinuosité *f*; *Anat* **cerebral convolutions,** circonvolutions cérébrales.

convolvulus, *pl* **-uses** [kən'vɒlvjʊləs, -əsɪz] *n (plant)* volubilis *m*, belle-de-jour *f*, *pl* belles-de-jour.

convoy¹ ['kɒnvɔɪ] *n Mil Nau* convoi *m*; **ship under** *or* **in c.,** bâtiment convoyé *ou* en convoi; **to be on c. duty,** *(of ship)* assurer un convoi.

convoy² *vt Mil Nau* convoyer, escorter.

convulse [kən'vʌls] **1** *vt* **(a)** bouleverser *(qn, qch, la vie de qn)*; **to be convulsed with laughter/pain,** se tordre de rire/douleur; **scene that convulses the audience,** scène qui fait tordre de rire toute la salle; **(b)** *Med* convulsionner *(un muscle)*. **2** *vi* se contracter; **his body convulsed and he died,** son corps s'est contracté et il est mort.

convulsion [kən'vʌlʃən] *n Med* *(usu pl)* **convulsions,** convulsions *fpl*; **infantile convulsions,** convulsions des enfants; **to be seized with convulsions of laughter,** *F* **to be in convulsions,** se tordre de rire; *Fig* **political convulsions,** bouleversements *mpl* politiques.

convulsive [kən'vʌlsɪv] *adj (mouvement etc)* convulsif.

convulsively [kən'vʌlsɪvlɪ] *adv* convulsivement.

coo¹ [kuː] *int Eng Sl* tiens!, ça alors!

coo² *vi (of dove, F of person)* roucouler; *(of baby)* gazouiller; **what a beautiful baby, he cooed,** quel beau bébé, a-t-il roucoulé.

cooing ['kuːɪŋ] *n* roucoulement *m*.

cook¹ [kʊk] *n* cuisinier, -ère; *Nau* coq *m*; **to be a good/bad c.,** être bon/mauvais cuisinier; **head c.,** chef *m* (de cuisine); *Fig* **head c. and bottlewasher,** factotum *m*; *Prov* **too many cooks spoil the broth,** trop de cuisinières gâtent la sauce.

cook² **1** *vt* faire, préparer *(un repas)*; (faire) cuire *(de la viande etc)*; **half-cooked,** demi-cuit, à moitié cuit; **the meat should be cooked all the way through,** la viande doit être cuite à cœur; *Fig F* **to c. s.o.'s goose,** *(upset plans)* renverser les projets de qn; *(beat up, kill, ruin)* faire son affaire à qn; *Fig F* **to c. the accounts** *or* **the books,** falsifier *ou* truquer les comptes. **2** *vi (of food)* cuire; *(of person)* faire la cuisine, cuisiner; **can you c.?,** tu sais faire la cuisine?; **I have to c. for six,** je dois cuisiner pour six; *F* **what's cooking?,** qu'est-ce qui se passe?

►cook up *vtsep F (fabricate)* inventer, imaginer *(une excuse etc)*.

cookbook ['kʊkbʊk] *n* livre *m* de cuisine.

cooked [kʊkt] *adj* cuit; **this isn't c.!,** ce n'est pas cuit!; **a c. breakfast,** un petit déjeuner à l'anglaise.

cooker ['kʊkər] *n* **(a)** *(stove)* cuisinière *f*; **gas c.,** cuisinière à gaz; **pressure c.,** cocotte minute *f* ®; **(b)** *Br F (apple)* pomme *f* à cuire.

cookery ['kʊkərɪ] *n* (l'art *m* de la) cuisine *f*; **c. book/classes,** livre *m*/leçons *fpl* de cuisine; **c. programme,** émission *f* sur la cuisine.

cookhouse ['kʊkhaʊs] *n* cuisine *f*.

cookie ['kʊkɪ] *n* **(a)** *esp Am (sweet biscuit)* biscuit *m*; *F* **that's the way the c. crumbles!,** c'est la vie (que veux-tu)!; **(b)** *Am F (person)* **a tough c.,** un dur à cuire; *F* **a smart c.,** un petit malin; **(c)** *Scot* petit pain au lait.

cooking ['kʊkɪŋ] *n* **(a)** *(process)* cuisson *f* *(de la viande etc)*; **c. fat,** matière grasse pour la cuisine; **c. time,** temps *m* de cuisson; **(b)** *(style, activity)* cuisine *f*; **plain** *or* **home c.,** cuisine bourgeoise; **my mother's c.,** la cuisine de ma mère; **do you like c.?,** est-ce que tu aimes faire la cuisine?; **to do the c.,** faire la cuisine; **c. apples,** pommes à cuire; **c. utensils,** batterie *f* de cuisine; **(c)** *(falsification)* *F* **c. of accounts,** falsification *f* des comptes.

cool¹ [kuːl] **1** *adj* **(a)** *(vent, temps etc)* frais; *(lukewarm)* tiède; *(boisson)* rafraîchissant; **it's c.,** il fait frais; **it's getting c.,** le temps se rafraîchit; *Com etc* **to be kept in a c. place,** tenir au frais;

(b) *(calm)* calme; **to keep c. and collected,** garder son sang-froid; **keep c.!,** du calme!; **to keep a c. head,** garder la tête froide, garder son sang-froid;

(c) *(unfriendly)* *(person, reception etc)* froid;

(d) *F (bold, impudent)* sans gêne; **I call that c.!** ça, c'est du toupet!; **well, you're a c. customer!,** eh bien, vous avez du culot *ou* du toupet!;

(e) *F (of money)* **I lost a c. thousand,** j'ai perdu mille livres bien comptées;

(f) *esp Am Sl (elegant)* super *inv*; **you look c. in that jacket,** tu es super avec cette veste; **he thinks he's so c.,** il se croit vraiment super;

(g) *esp Am Sl (acceptable)* sympa *inv*, cool *inv*; **my sister's c.,** ma sœur est sympa *ou* cool; **it's not c. to smoke,** ce n'est pas cool de fumer; **is it c. to smoke dope here?,** *(will anyone object?)* est-ce que c'est OK de fumer de l'herbe ici?

2 *n* **(a)** fraîcheur *f*; **in the c. of the evening,** dans la fraîcheur du soir;

(b) *F (calm)* **to keep/lose one's c.,** garder/perdre son sang-froid.

3 *adv F* **to play it c.,** *(act calm)* jouer (en) décontracté; *(be calm)* être décontracté.

cool² **1** *vt* rafraîchir, refroidir *(l'eau, l'air)*; refroidir *(le zèle de qn)*; *F* **c. it!,** calme-toi!, on se calme!; **to c. one's heels,** faire le pied de grue. **2** *vi (of liquid)* se rafraîchir, (se) refroidir; *(of anger, friendship etc)* se refroidir; s'attiédir; **his anger soon cooled,** sa colère a vite passé.

►cool down **1** *vi* **(a)** *(become calm)* s'apaiser, se calmer; **we'll talk about it when you've cooled down,** nous en parlerons quand tu te seras calmé; **(b)** (*of weather*) se rafraîchir; *Fig* **things have cooled down between them,** les relations se sont refroidies entre eux. **2** *vtsep* **(a)** (*make calm*) apaiser (*qn*); **(b)** (*of cold drink*) rafraîchir (*qn*).

►**cool off** *vi* (*of affection, enthusiasm*) se refroidir.

coolant ['ku:lənt] *n Tech* agent *m* de refroidissement.

cooler ['ku:lər] *n* **(a)** *Tech* (appareil *m*) refroidisseur *m*; *Ind* réfrigérant *m*, refroidisseur *m*; **butter c.,** beurrier refroidisseur; **oil c.,** radiateur *m* d'huile; **(b)** *Sl* (*prison*) taule *f*, tôle *f*.

cool-headed ['ku:l'hedɪd] *adj* (*personne*) de sang-froid, calme, imperturbable.

coolie ['ku:lɪ] *n Pej* coolie *m*.

cooling ['ku:lɪŋ] **1** *adj* (*breeze*) rafraîchissant; *Ind etc* réfrigérant, refroidissant. **2** *n* rafraîchissement *m*, refroidissement *m* (*de la température etc*); *Ind* réfrigération *f*; **air c.,** refroidissement par air; *Tech* **c. jacket,** chemise *f* d'eau; **c. off period** *Ind* période *f* de réflexion; *Ind* **c. tower,** tour *f* de réfrigération, refroidisseur *m*; **c. system,** système *m* de refroidissement.

coolly ['ku:lɪ] *adv* (*see adj*) **(a)** fraîchement; **(b)** (*agir*) avec calme; **she walked c. out of the room,** elle a calmement quitté la pièce; **(c)** (*recevoir qn*) froidement; **(d)** *F* effrontément.

coolness ['ku:lnɪs] *n* **(a)** fraîcheur *f* (*de l'air*); **(b)** (*calm*) calme *m*, sang-froid *m*; **(c)** froideur *f* (*d'un accueil*); **(d)** *F* (*impudence*) culot *m*.

coon [ku:n] *n* **(a)** *US F* (*raccoon*) raton laveur; **(b)** *Offensive Sl* nègre *m*.

coop [ku:p] *n* **(hen) c.,** cage *f* à poules, poulailler *m*; **chicken c.,** poussinière *f*.

►**coop up** *vtsep* (*usu passive*) **to c. s.o. up,** tenir qn enfermé; **we were cooped up for hours in a tiny room,** nous étions enfermés pendant des heures dans une pièce minuscule; **to feel cooped up,** se sentir à l'étroit.

co(-)op ['kəʊɒp] *n* (*shop*) coop *f*.

cooper ['ku:pər] *n* tonnelier *m*.

cooperage ['ku:pərɪdʒ] *n* tonnellerie *f*.

co(-)operate [kəʊ'ɒpəreɪt] *vi* (*of person*) coopérer (**with s.o. in sth,** avec qn à qch); **the two governments are co-operating in the drug war,** les deux gouvernements coopèrent dans la lutte contre la drogue; **the horse wouldn't c. when we tried to put the saddle on,** le cheval n'a pas voulu coopérer quand nous avons essayé de lui mettre la selle; **if you c. your sentence may be reduced,** si vous coopériez, votre peine pourrait être réduite.

co(-)operation [kəʊɒpə'reɪʃən] *n* coopération *f*; **your c. would be appreciated,** nous vous serions reconnaissants de votre coopération.

co(-)operative [kəʊ'ɒp(ə)rətɪv] **1** *adj* **(a)** *Com* coopératif; **c. society,** société coopérative; **c. dairy,** coopérative laitière; **(b) to be c.,** prêter son aide; **you're not being very c.,** vous ne m'aidez guère. **2** *n Com* coopérative *f* (*agricole, vinicole etc*).

co(-)opt [kəʊ'ɒpt] *vt* **(a)** (*onto a committee*) coopter (*qn*); **(b)** *F* (*commandeer*) réquisitionner (*qn*); **I've been co-opted to help with the spring cleaning,** j'ai été réquisitionné pour le nettoyage de printemps.

co(-)ordinate¹ [kəʊ'ɔ:dɪnət] **1** *adj* égal, -aux (**with,** à); *Gram* **c. clauses,** propositions coordonnées. **2** *n* **(a)** *Math Astron etc* coordonnée *f*; **(b)** *Com* **co-ordinates,** (*clothes*) coordonnées *fpl*.

co(-)ordinate² [kəʊ'ɔ:dɪneɪt] *vt* coordonner (*un projet*) (**with,** à, avec); **co-ordinated movement,** mouvement *m* d'ensemble.

co(-)ordinating [kəʊ'ɔ:dɪneɪtɪŋ] *adj* **(a)** coordinateur, -trice; **(b)** *Gram* (*conjuction*) coordonnant.

co(-)ordination [kəʊɔ:dɪ'neɪʃən] *n* coordination *f*; **you need good c. to play tennis,** il faut avoir une bonne coordination pour jouer au tennis; **the c. of the invasion,** la coordination de l'invasion.

co(-)ordinator [kəʊ'ɔ:dɪneɪtər] *n* coordinateur, -trice.

coot [ku:t] *n* **(a)** (*bird*) **(common, bald) c.,** foulque *f* (macroule), *Can* foulque noire; **(b)** *F Pej* (*person*) idiot, -ote.

co-owner ['kəʊ'əʊnər] *n* (*of building etc*) copropriétaire *mf*.

co-ownership ['kəʊ'əʊnəʃɪp] *n* copropriété *f*.

cop¹ [kɒp] *n F* **(a)** (*policeman*) flic *m*; **speed c.,** motard *m*; **to play cops and robbers,** jouer aux gendarmes et aux voleurs; **(b)** *Br Sl* (*arrest*) **it's a fair c.!,** je suis fait; **(c)** *Br Sl* **it's not much c.,** ça ne vaut pas grand-chose.

cop² *vt Sl* (*catch*) attraper, pincer (*qn*); **to get copped,** se faire pincer (*par la police etc*); *Br* **to c. it,** (*get caught*) se faire pincer; (*get injured*) recevoir une blessure; (*die*) mourir.

►**cop out** *vi Sl* (*avoid responsibility*) se défiler; (*choose easy solution*) choisir la solution de facilité.

cope¹ [kəʊp] *n Rel* chape *f*.

cope² *vt* **(a)** *Constr* chaperonner, mettre un couronnement à (*un mur*); **(b)** *Rel* mettre la chape à (*un évêque*).

cope³ *vi* se débrouiller, s'en tirer; **to c. with,** faire face à (*une situation, un danger*); venir à bout de (*une difficulté*); **to be able to c. with a job,** être à la hauteur d'une tâche; **I can't c. with her when she gets angry,** je ne peux pas la supporter quand elle se met en colère; **the engine couldn't c. with all that extra weight,** le moteur ne pouvait pas faire face à tout ce poids supplémentaire; **I just can't c.,** je n'y arrive plus; **I'll c. with it,** je m'en chargerai; **I'll c.,** je me débrouillerai; **he seems to be coping,** il a l'air de se débrouiller.

Copenhagen [kəʊpən'heɪg(ə)n] *n* Copenhague *f*.

copier ['kɒpɪər] *n* **(a)** (*person*) copiste *mf*; **(b)** *Pej* (*imitator*) copiste *mf*, imitateur, -trice; **(c)** *F* (*device*) duplicateur *m*, copieur *m*; (*photocopying machine*) copieur.

copilot ['kəʊpaɪlət] *n Av* copilote *m*.

coping ['kəʊpɪŋ] *n Constr* chaperon *m* (*d'un mur etc*); **c. stone,** pierre *f* de couronnement.

copious ['kəʊpɪəs] *adj* copieux, abondant; **c. notes,** des notes abondantes; **c. amounts,** de grandes quantités (*de bière etc*).

copiously ['kəʊpɪəslɪ] *adv* (*to weep*) copieusement.

co-plaintiff ['kəʊ'pleɪntɪf] *n Jur* codemandeur, -eresse.

cop-out ['kɒpaʊt] *n Sl* **(a)** (*act*) solution *f* de facilité; **that's a bit of a c.-o.,** c'est la solution de facilité; **(b)** *Am* (*person*) personne qui se défile.

copper¹ ['kɒpər] *n* **(a)** (*metal*) cuivre *m* (rouge); **c. wire,** fil *m* de cuivre; **(b)** *Br F* sou *m*; **coppers,** petite monnaie; **to give a beggar a few coppers,** donner des sous à un mendiant; **(c)** (*receptacle*) cuve *f* à lessive; **(d) c.(-coloured),** cuivré; *Bot* **c. beech,** hêtre *m* rouge.

copper² *n F* (*policeman*) flic *m*.

copper³ *vt* (*in metalwork*) cuivrer (*un métal*).

copperhead ['kɒpəhed] *n* (*snake*) trigonocéphale *m*.

copperplate ['kɒpəpleɪt] *n* **(a) c. (writing),** écriture moulée; **written in c.,** calligraphié; **(b)** (*in engraving*) taille-douce *f*; **c. printing,** impression *f* en creux *ou* en taille-douce; **c. engraving,** chalcographie *f*.

coppersmith ['kɒpəsmɪθ] *n* chaudronnier *m* en *ou* de cuivre.

copperware ['kɒpəweər] *n* dinanderie *f*.

coppery ['kɒpərɪ] *adj* (*colour*) cuivré.

coppice ['kɒpɪs] *n* taillis *m*, hallier *m*.

copra ['kɒprə] *n Com* copra(h) *m*.

co-processor [kəʊ'prəʊsesər] *n Comptr* coprocesseur *m*; **maths c.,** coprocesseur arithmétique.

coproduction [kəʊprə'dʌkʃən] *n Cin etc* coproduction *f*.

copse [kɒps] *n* taillis *n*.

copter ['kɒptər] *n Av F* hélico *m*.

Coptic ['kɒptɪk] **1** *adj* coptique, copte. **2** *n Ling* copte *m*.

copula ['kɒpjʊlə] *n Gram etc* copule *f*.

copulate ['kɒpjʊleɪt] *vi* copuler, s'accoupler.

copulation [kɒpjʊ'leɪʃən] *n Physiol* copulation *f*, coït *m*.

copulative ['kɒpjʊlətɪv] *adj Gram etc* copulatif; *Physiol Anat* copulateur, -trice.

copy¹ ['kɒpɪ] *n* **(a)** copie *f*, reproduction *f*; **this picture is only a c.,** ce tableau n'est qu'une copie;

(b) (*written*) copie *f*, transcription *f* (*d'une lettre, d'un texte*); (*of typewritten letter etc*) double *m*; *Jur* expédition *f* (*d'un acte, d'un titre*); **rough c.,** brouillon *m*; *Jur etc* **fair c.,** copie (au net); **certified c.,** copie authentique; **true c.,** copie conforme; **file c.,** exemplaire *m* des archives; **c. typist,** dactylographe *f*;

(c) exemplaire *m* (*d'un livre*); numéro *m* (*d'un journal*); **500 copies of the book were printed,** le livre a été tiré à 500 exemplaires; **review/press c.,** exemplaire de publicité/de service de presse;

(d) *Typ* (*written material for printing*) manuscrit *m*, copie *f*; *Journ* matière *f* à reportage; **c. editor,** correcteur, -trice d'épreuves; **this would make good c.,** voilà un bon sujet d'article;

(e) *Comptr* **c. check,** contrôle *m* par duplication;

(f) *Old-fashioned* (*model*) modèle *m* (*de dessin*); exemple *m* (*d'écriture*).

copy² **1** *vt* **(a)** imiter, reproduire (*une œuvre d'art etc*); suivre (*un dessin*); **(b)** (*model oneself on*) se modeler sur (*qn*); imiter (*la démarche de qn*); *Art Liter Mus* copier, pasticher (*le style de qn*); **(c)** (*write out*) copier (*une lettre etc*); **(d)**

Sch (*cheat*) copier; **(e)** *Ling* calquer (*qch*) (**from,** sur); **expression copied from the English,** expression calquée sur l'anglais; **(f)** *Comptr* copier; **(g)** (*send c. to*) envoyer une copie à. **2** *vi Sch* copier (*sur un autre élève*).
►**copy out** *vtsep* recopier; **to c. out a passage from a book,** transcrire *ou* recopier un passage d'un livre.
copybook ['kɒpɪbʊk] *n* cahier *m* d'écriture; *Fig* **to blot one's c.,** ternir sa réputation; **a c. example,** un exemple classique.
copycat ['kɒpɪkæt] *n Sch F* copieur, -euse; **they're just copycats,** ils nous *ou* les singent; **c. crime,** crime inspiré par un autre.
copy-edit ['kɒpɪedɪt] *Typ* **1** *vi* corriger les épreuves. **2** *vt* corriger (*les épreuves*).
copy-editing ['kɒpɪ'edɪtəŋ] *n Typ* correction *f* d'épreuves.
copying ['kɒpɪɪŋ] *n* transcription *f*, imitation *f*; *Sch* copiage *m*; **c. machine,** duplicateur *m*; copieur *m*; **c. ink,** encre *f* à copier.
copyist ['kɒpɪɪst] *n* copiste *mf*, scribe *m*.
copy-protected ['kɒpɪprə'tektɪd] *adj Comptr* protégé contre la copie.
copyright¹ ['kɒpɪraɪt] **1** *n* droit *m* d'auteur (*sur son œuvre*), copyright *m*; **it's still subject to c.,** c'est toujours soumis au droit d'auteur; **breach** *or* **infringement of c.,** violation *f* du droit d'auteur; **to hold the c. on sth,** avoir le droit d'auteur sur qch; **out of c.,** (tombé) dans le domaine public; **c. reserved,** tous droits réservés; **c. notice,** mention *f* de réserve. **2** *adj* (*livre*) qui est protégé par des droits d'auteur; (*article*) dont le droit de reproduction est réservé; **c. (in all countries),** tous droits de reproduction et de traduction réservés (pour tous pays).
copyright² *vt* réserver les droits de (*un livre*).
copywriter ['kɒpɪraɪtər] *n* (concepteur-)rédacteur *m* publicitaire.
coquetry ['kəʊkɪtrɪ, kɒk-] *n* coquetterie *f*.
coquette [kəʊ'ket, kɒk-] *n* coquette *f*.
coquettish [kə'ketɪʃ, kɒk-] *adj* **(a)** (*woman*) flirteuse; **(b)** (*smile etc*) provocant, *F* aguichant.
cor¹ [kɔːr] *n Mus* **c. anglais,** cor anglais.
cor² *int Eng Sl* ça alors!
coracle ['kɒrək(ə)l] *n* (*boat*) coracle *m*.
coral ['kɒr(ə)l] **1** *adj* **(a) c. island,** île corallienne *ou* de corail; **c. necklace,** collier *m* de corail; **c. reef,** récif corallien; **c. red,** corallin; **(b)** (*colour*) de corail. **2** *n* **(a)** corail *m*, -aux; **(b)** (*colour*) corail *m*.
corbel ['kɔːb(ə)l] *n Archit* corbeau *m*, console *f*.
cord¹ [kɔːd] *n* **(a)** (*string*) corde *f* (mince); (*for curtains*) cordon *m*; (*string*) ficelle *f*; nerf *m* (*de dos de livre*); **(b)** *Anat* **the vocal cords,** les cordes vocales; **the spinal c.,** le cordon médullaire; **the umbilical c.,** le cordon ombilical; **(c)** *Tex* (*corduroy*) velours *m* à côtes; **cords,** pantalon *m* de velours côtelé; **(d)** *US El* cordon *m*, fil *m*.
cord² *vt* corder; ligoter (*un fagot etc*).
cordage ['kɔːdɪdʒ] *n Nau* cordage *m*.
corded ['kɔːdɪd] *adj Tex* côtelé, à côtes.
cordial ['kɔːdɪəl] **1** *adj* (*accueil*) cordial, chaleureux. **2** *n* (*drink*) cordial *m*.
cordiality [kɔːdɪ'ælɪtɪ] *n* cordialité *f*; **exchange of cordialities,** échange *m* de cordialités.
cordially ['kɔːdɪəlɪ] *adv* cordialement; *Am* **c. yours,** (*at end of letter*) bien cordialement.
cordite ['kɔːdaɪt] *n* cordite *f*.
cordless ['kɔːdlɪs] *adj* **c. telephone,** téléphone *m* sans fil.
cordon ['kɔːd(ə)n] *n* **(a)** (*of troops, ships etc*) cordon *m*; **a police c.,** un cordon de police; **sanitary c.,** cordon sanitaire; **(b)** *Sewing* cordon *m*, tresse *f*; **(c) c. (tree),** cordon *m*; **(d)** (*of order*) cordon *m*; **c. bleu** ['kɒrdɒn'bluː] cordon(-)bleu.
►**cordon off** *vtsep* (*close*) barrer (*une rue*); **the street was cordoned off by the police,** (*they ordered it closed*) la police a barré la rue; (*they acted as a barrier*) on a isolé la rue par un cordon de police.
corduroy ['kɔːdərɔɪ] *n Tex* velours à côtes *ou* côtelé; **c. trousers, corduroys,** pantalon *m* de velours côtelé; **c. road,** chemin *m* de rondins.
core¹ [kɔːr] *n* **(a)** centre *m*, partie centrale (*d'une masse*); cœur *m* (*du bois, d'un argument etc*); trognon *m* (*d'une pomme etc*); **hard c.,** noyau *m*; **selfish to the c.,** d'un égoïsme foncier; *F* **he's rotten to the c.,** il est corrompu jusqu'à la moelle; **c. issue,** question centrale; **c. time** *or* **hours,** (*in flexitime scheme*) plage *f* fixe; *Ling* **c. vocabulary,** vocabulaire *m* de base; **(b)** *Geol etc* noyau *m*; (*of the earth*) nifé *m*; *Min* **c. sample,** carotte *f*, témoin *m*, échantillon carotté; **(c)** *Tech* (*of mould*) noyau *m*; **c. box,** boîte *f* à noyau(x); *El* noyau (*d'un aimant*); mèche *f* (*d'un câble*); *Nucl* cœur *m* (*d'une pile atomique*); *Comptr* noyau; *Constr etc* **watertight c.,** noyau d'étanchéité; *Comptr* **c. memory,** mémoire *f* à tores (magnétiques); **(d)** *Med* bourbillon *m* (*d'un abcès*); cornillon *m* (*d'un cor*).
core² *vt* enlever le cœur de (*une pomme*).
►**core out** *vtsep Metal* enlever le noyau (*d'une pièce de fonte etc*); noyauter, évider (*un moule*).
coreligionist [kəʊrɪ'lɪdʒ(ə)nɪst] *n Rel* coreligionnaire *mf*.
corer ['kɔːrər] *n Min etc* perforateur creux; **apple c.,** vide-pomme *m*, *pl* vide-pommes.
co-respondent [kəʊrɪ'spɒndənt] *n* complice *mf* (*en adultère*); *Jur* codéfendeur *m* (*en adultère*).
coriander [kɒrɪ'ændər] *n Bot Culin* coriandre *f*; **c. (seed),** graines *fpl* de coriandre.
Corinthian [kə'rɪnθɪən] **1** *adj* **(a)** *Geog* corinthien; **(b)** *Arch* corinthien; **C. column,** colonne corinthienne. **2** *n Geog* Corinthien, -ienne.
cork¹ [kɔːk] *n* **(a)** (*material*) liège *m*; **c. oak,** chêne-liège *m*, *pl* chênes-lièges; **c. sole,** semelle *f* de *ou* en liège; **(b)** (*stopper*) bouchon *m* (*de liège*); *Br F* **put a c. in it!,** la ferme!; **crown c.,** capsule *f* (métallique) de bouteille.
cork² *vt* **(a)** boucher (*une bouteille*); **(b)** (*blacken*) **to c. one's face,** se grimer avec un bouchon brûlé; **(c)** (*attach cork floats to*) garnir (*un filet etc*) de bouchons.
corkage ['kɔːkɪdʒ] *n* (*in restaurant*) = droit *m* (de débouchage) sur un vin qui a été apporté par les consommateurs.
corked [kɔːkt] *adj* (*vin*) qui sent le bouchon.
corker ['kɔːkər] *n Old-fashioned Br Sl* **(a)** (*thing, action*) chose *f ou* action *f* qui vous en bouche un coin; **that joke was a c.,** c'était une plaisanterie à vous en boucher un coin; **(b)** (*man*) type épatant; (*pretty woman*) canon *m*.
corking [kɔːkɪŋ] *adj Old-fashioned Br Sl* épatant, fameux.
corkscrew¹ ['kɔːkskruː] *n* tire-bouchon *m*, *pl* tire-bouchons; **c. curl,** (*in hair*) tire-bouchon; boudin *m*.
corkscrew² **1** *vi* (*of wire*) vriller; (*of stair*) tourner en vrille. **2** *vt* tracer (*une ligne*) en spirale.
cork-tipped ['kɔːktɪpt] *adj* (*cigarette*) à bout de liège.
corkwood ['kɔːkwʊd] *n* bois *m* de liège.
corm [kɔːm] *n Bot* bulbe *m* (solide).
cormorant ['kɔːmərənt] *n* (*bird*) cormoran *m*.
corn¹ [kɔːn] *n* **(a)** *esp Am* **(Indian) c.,** maïs *m*; **c. on the cob,** maïs en épi; **c. belt,** région *f* du maïs; **c. bread,** *Am Culin* pain *m* de farine de maïs; **c. meal,** farine *f* de maïs; **c. oil,** huile *f* de maïs; **c. silk,** barbe *f*; **c. whiskey,** whisky *m* de maïs; **(b)** (*grain*) *no pl* blé(s) *m(pl)*; **winter c.,** semis *m* d'hiver; **C. Exchange,** halle *f* aux blés; **c. bunting,** (*bird*) (bruant *m*) proyer *m*; **c. chandler** *or* **merchant,** marchand *m* de blé *ou* de grains; **c. dolly,** poupée fabriquée avec des épis de blé; **c. poppy,** coquelicot *m*; **c. salad,** mâche *f*; **(c)** (*seed*) grain *m* (*de blé etc*); **(d)** *F* (*sentimentality, banality*) banalité *f*; **that film was pure c.,** ce film n'était que banalités; **(e)** *esp Scot* avoine *f*; **to give one's horse a feed of c.,** donner un picotin à son cheval.
corn² *n Med* cor *m* (*à l'orteil etc*); **c. plaster,** coricide *m*; *Fig F* **to tread on s.o.'s corns,** froisser qn.
Corn *abbr* **Cornwall.**
corncob ['kɔːnkɒb] *n* épi *m* de maïs; **c. (pipe),** pipe *f* en épi de maïs.
corncockle ['kɔːnkɒk(ə)l] *n* (*plant*) nielle *f* des blés.
corncrake ['kɔːnkreɪk] *n* (*bird*) râle *m* des genêts; *F* **a voice like a c.,** une voix de crécelle.
cornea ['kɔːnɪə] *n Anat* cornée *f* (*de l'œil*).
corneal ['kɔːnɪəl] *adj Anat* cornéen; *Med* **c. graft,** greffe *f* de la cornée.
corned [kɔːnd] *adj Culin* **c. beef,** bœuf *m* de conserve, corned beef *m*, *Mil F* singe *m*; **c. beef sandwich,** sandwich au bœuf de conserve *ou* au corned beef.
cornelian [kɒ'niːlɪən] *n* (*gem*) cornaline *f*.
corner¹ ['kɔːnər] *n* **(a)** coin *m*; **to turn down the c. of a page,** faire une corne à une page; **the bottom left-hand c.,** (*of page, photograph etc*) coin en bas à gauche; *Constr* **c. post,** poteau *m* d'angle;
(b) (*interior*) coin *m* (*d'une pièce etc*); **c. cupboard,** armoire *f* de coin; **chimney c.,** coin de feu; **to put a child in the c.,** mettre un enfant au coin; *Fig* **to drive s.o. into a c.,** acculer qn, mettre qn au pied du mur; *Fig* **driven into a c.,** acculé, au pied du mur; *Fig* **in a tight c.,** en mauvaise passe; **the four corners of the earth,** les quatre coins du monde; **to search every c. of the house,** chercher dans tous les coins et recoins de la maison;
(c) (*on street*) coin *m*, angle *m*; **situated at the c.,** situé au coin; **the house on the c., the c. house,** la maison qui fait l'angle, la maison au coin; **at** *or* **on the c. of A Street**

and B Street, au coin *ou* à l'angle de la rue A et de la rue B; **you'll find the grocer's round the c.,** vous trouverez l'épicerie en tournant le coin; **spring is just around the c.,** ce sera bientôt le printemps; **with the elections just round the c.,** avec les élections qui approchent; **another rise in mortgage rates is just round the c.,** une autre augmentation des taux de prêt se prépare; **you never know what's around the c.,** on ne sait jamais ce qui peut se produire; **to turn the c.,** tourner le coin; (*pass critical point*) passer le moment critique; (*of sick person*) surmonter la crise; **c. shop,** magasin *m* de quartier; *Can* dépanneur *m*; **c. site,** emplacement *m* en coin;

(d) (*bend in road*) tournant *m*; *Aut etc* virage *m*; **sharp c.,** tournant brusque; *Aut etc* **to take a c.,** prendre un virage, virer; **to cut a c. (close),** virer court; *Fig* **to cut corners,** (*economize excessively*) faire des économies exagérées (*d'argent, de temps*); (*break rules*) contourner les règlements;

(e) *Fb* **c. (kick),** corner *m*; **to take a c.,** faire un corner; **c. flag,** piquet *m* de coin;

(f) (*of lips*) commissure *f*; **to look out of the c. of one's eye,** regarder du coin de l'œil;

(g) *Com* monopole *m*; **to have a c. in sth,** avoir un monopole dans qch;

(h) a little c. of Normandy, un petit coin de Normandie.

corner[2] **1** *vt* **(a)** (*drive into a corner*) acculer, coincer (*qn*); *Fig* mettre (*qn*) au pied du mur; **we've got him cornered,** (*of criminal etc*) nous l'avons coincé; **(b)** *Com* accaparer (*le marché*) **(in,** de); **they've cornered the market,** ils se sont accaparé le marché; **(c)** (*place in a corner*) mettre (*qch*) dans un coin; **(d)** *Carp* biseauter (*le bois*). **2** *vi Aut etc* prendre un virage; **this car corners well,** cette voiture prend bien les virages.

cornered ['kɔːnəd] *adj* (*driven into a corner*) acculé, coincé; *Fig* au pied du mur.

cornering ['kɔːnərɪŋ] *n* **(a)** acculement *m* (*d'un animal etc*); **(b)** *Com* accaparement *m* (*du marché*); **(c)** *Aut* **the car is good at c.,** la voiture prend bien les virages.

cornerstone ['kɔːnəstəʊn] *n Constr & Fig* pierre *f* angulaire, pierre d'angle; *Fig* **the c. of civilization,** la pierre angulaire de la civilisation.

cornet ['kɔːnɪt, *Am* kɔː'net] *n* **(a)** *Mus* (*instrument*) cornet *m* à pistons; (*player*) cornettiste *m*; **(b)** (*of paper*) cornet *m* (en papier); **(c)** *Br* **(ice-cream) c.,** cornet *m* de glace.

cornet(t)ist [kɔː'netɪst] *n Mus* cornettiste *mf*.

cornfield ['kɔːnfiːld] *n* champ *m* de blé *ou Am* de maïs.

cornflakes ['kɔːnfleɪks] *npl Culin* flocons *mpl* de maïs, cornflakes *mpl*.

cornflour ['kɔːnflaʊər] *n Br* farine *f* de maïs.

cornflower ['kɔːnflaʊər] *n* (*plant*) bleuet *m*, bluet *m*, barbeau *m*; **c. blue,** bleu barbeau *inv*.

cornice ['kɔːnɪs] *n* **(a)** *Archit* corniche *f*; **(b)** (*of wardrobe*) chapiteau *m*; **(c)** (*of snow*) corniche *f*.

Cornish ['kɔːnɪʃ] **1** *adj Geog* cornouaillais; *Br Culin* **C. pasty,** = chausson *m* de viande. **2** *n Ling* cornique *m*.

Cornishman, -woman, *pl* **-men, -women** ['kɔːnɪʃmən, -wʊmən, -mən, -wɪmɪn] *n* Cornouaillais, -aise (*du sud-ouest de l'Angleterre*).

cornstarch ['kɔːnstɑːtʃ] *n Am Culin* farine *f* de maïs.

cornucopia, *pl* **-as** [kɔːnjʊ'kəʊpɪə, -əz] *n Myth & Fig* corne *f* d'abondance.

Cornwall ['kɔːnw(ə)l] *n* Cornouailles *f*.

corny ['kɔːnɪ] *adj F* (*joke, story*) bateau *inv*; (*film, novel*) banal; **don't be so c.,** arrête de dire des bêtises.

corolla [kə'rɒlə] *n Bot* corolle *f*.

corollary [kə'rɒlərɪ] *n* corollaire *m* **(to,** à).

corona, *pl* **-ae** [kə'rəʊnə, -iː] *n Astron Bot El etc* couronne *f*; *Astron* **solar c.,** couronne solaire; *El* **c. discharge,** effluve *f* électrique; **c. shielding,** dispositif *m* anti-effluves.

coronary ['kɒrən(ə)rɪ] **1** *adj Med* coronarien; **c. (artery),** artère *f* coronaire; **c. thrombosis,** infarctus *m* du myocarde; **c. cushion** *or* **ring,** bourrelet *m* (*de pied de cheval*). **2** *n* **to have a c.,** avoir un infarctus du myocarde.

coronation [kɒrə'neɪʃən] *n* couronnement *m*; **c. mug,** tasse commémorative du couronnement.

coroner ['kɒrənər] *n Jur* coroner *m* (= *officier civil chargé d'instruire, assisté d'un jury, en cas de mort violente ou subite*); **c.'s inquest,** enquête *f* du coroner.

coronet ['kɒrənɪt] *n* (petite) couronne *f*; (*lady's*) diadème *m*.

corp, Corp (a) (*abbr* **corporation**) Cie; **(b)** *Mil abbr* **corporal.**

corporal[1] ['kɔːpər(ə)l] *adj* corporel; (*défectuosité*) physique; **c. punishment,** punition corporelle.

corporal[2] *n Mil* (*of infantry*) caporal *m*, -aux; (*of cavalry, artillery*) brigadier *m*; *Mil Av* caporal-chef *m*.

corporate ['kɔːp(ə)rət] *adj* **(a)** *Com* corporatif, de société; **c. budget,** budget *m* de la société; **c. culture,** culture *f* de société; **c. image,** image *f* de la société; **the company cares about its c. image,** la société se préoccupe de son image; **our c. image demands that ...,** notre image en tant que société exige que ...; **I mean 'we' in the c. sense,** par "nous" j'entends la société; **to be a good c. citizen,** (*of company*) avoir le sens des responsabilités civiques; *Am* **c. apartments,** appartements destinés au personnel d'une société; **c. law,** droit *m* des sociétés; **c. lawyer,** juriste spécialisé dans le droit des sociétés; **c. literature,** brochures décrivant une société; **c. member,** (*of association*) société-membre *f*; **c. name,** raison sociale; **c. strategy,** stratégie *f* de la société;

(b) (*forming a single body*) constitué (en corps), formant (un) corps; *Jur* **body c., c. body,** corps constitué, corporation *f*; (*considered as an individual*) personne morale;

(c) (*of a group of people*) de corporation, de corps; **c. feeling,** esprit *m* de corps.

corporation [kɔːpə'reɪʃən] *n* **(a)** *Am Com* société enregistrée; compagnie *f*; **public c.,** entreprise publique; *Br Admin* **c. tax,** impôt sur les sociétés; **(b)** *Br* (*council*) **municipal c.,** conseil municipal, municipalité *f*; **(c)** *F* (*paunch*) bedaine *f*, bedon *m*; **(d)** *Jur* personne morale.

corporeal [kɔː'pɔːrɪəl] *adj* corporel, matériel.

corps [kɔːr, *pl* kɔːz] *n inv* corps *m*; *Mil* corps d'armée; **the diplomatic c.,** le corps diplomatique; **tank c.,** blindés *mpl*; **c. d'élite,** corps d'élite; **c. de ballet,** corps de ballet.

corpse[1] [kɔːps] *n* cadavre *m*, corps *m* (mort).

corpse[2] *vi Th* (*of actor, actress*) avoir le fou rire sur scène.

corpulence ['kɔːpjʊləns] *n* corpulence *f*, obésité *f*.

corpulent ['kɔːpjʊlənt] *adj* corpulent, obèse.

corpus ['kɔːpəs] *n* **(a)** (*writings*) corpus *m*, recueil *m* (*d'inscriptions etc*); **(b)** *Jur* **c. delicti,** le corps du délit; **(c)** *Cathol* **Corpus Christi,** la Fête-Dieu.

corpuscle ['kɔːpʌs(ə)l] *n* corpuscule *m*; **red/white blood corpuscles,** globules rouges/blancs.

corral[1] [kɒ'rɑːl] *n* corral *m*, *pl* -als.

corral[2] *vt* renfermer (*des bestiaux, chevaux etc*) dans un corral; *Fig* encercler (*des manifestants*).

correct[1] [kə'rekt] *vt* **(a)** (*remove errors from*) corriger les fautes de (*un thème etc*); corriger (*une épreuve d'imprimerie, un thème*); **(b)** (*rectify*) rectifier (*une erreur*); modifier (*le réglage d'un instrument*); *Com* **corrected invoice,** facture rectificative; **to c. a squint,** (*of glasses*) corriger un strabisme; **(c)** (*find fault with*) reprendre (*qn*); **he had the nerve to c. my grammar/English/pronunciation,** il a eu le culot de me reprendre sur ma grammaire/mon anglais/ma prononciation; **I said it was 2 o'clock but someone corrected me,** j'ai dit qu'il était 2 heures mais quelqu'un m'a corrigé; **c. me if I'm wrong, but ...,** corrigez-moi si je me trompe, mais ...; **to c. oneself,** se reprendre; **(d)** (*punish*) punir, infliger une correction à (*un coupable etc*); **(e)** (*compensate for*) contrebalancer (*une influence, un goût*).

correct[2] *adj* **(a)** correct, exact; **c. answer,** réponse *f* juste; **the c. time,** l'heure exacte; **c. to a millimetre,** exact à un millimètre près; **his prediction proved c.,** sa prédiction s'est vérifiée; **you must be Mr Jones — that's c.,** vous devez être M. Jones — c'est exact; **if my memory is c.,** si j'ai bonne mémoire, si ma mémoire est bonne; **figures c. at time of going to press,** les chiffres sont exacts au moment de mettre sous presse; **(b)** (*behaviour etc*) bienséant, correct; (*person*) comme il faut; **it's the c. thing to ...,** la politesse veut que ... .

correction [kə'rekʃən] *n* **(a)** correction *f* (*d'une épreuve, d'un devoir etc*); redressement *m* (*d'un compte*); **to make corrections to a text,** apporter des corrections à un texte; **subject to c.,** sous toutes réserves; **(b)** (*punishment*) correction *f*, punition *f*; *Arch* **house of c.,** maison *f* de correction *ou* de redressement; **(c)** *Phys Mil MecE etc* (*compensation*) correction *f*; *Opt* **c. for astigmatism/***etc*, correction de l'astigmatisme/*etc*.

corrective [kə'rektɪv] **1** *n Med* correctif *m*. **2** *adj* correctif, rectifiant; (*verre*) correcteur; **c. exercises,** gymnastique médicale *ou* corrective.

correctly [kə'rektlɪ] *adv* **(a)** (*answer, report*) correctement; **or (to put it) more c.,** ou pour mieux dire; **(b)** (*behave*) correctement; **to speak c.,** parler correctement *ou* comme il faut.

correctness [kə'rektnɪs] *n* **(a)** correction *f*, convenance *f* (*de tenue etc*); **(b)** exactitude *f*, justesse *f* (*d'une description*); rectitude *f* (*de jugement*).

corrector [kə'rektər] *n* **(a)** (*person*) correcteur, -trice; **(b)** *Tech* (appareil *m*, dispositif *m*) correcteur *m*.
correlate ['kɒrɪleɪt] **1** *vi* correspondre (**with, to,** à), être en corrélation (**with,** avec); (*in statistics*) corréler. **2** *vt* mettre (*qch*) en corrélation (**with,** avec); **poverty and ill-health are closely correlated,** il y a une corrélation étroite entre la pauvreté et la maladie.
correlation [kɒrɪ'leɪʃən] *n* corrélation *f* (**with,** avec; **between,** entre).
correlative [kɒ'relətɪv] **1** *adj* corrélatif. **2** *n* corrélatif *m*.
correspond [kɒrɪs'pɒnd] *vi* **(a)** correspondre, être conforme (**with, to,** à); *Com* **to c. to sample,** être conforme à l'échantillon; **(b)** (*be equivalent to*) correspondre (**to,** avec); **the gendarmes roughly c. to our motorway police,** les gendarmes sont à peu près l'équivalent de notre motorway police; **(c)** (*write letters*) correspondre, échanger des lettres (**with,** avec); **they corresponded for many years,** ils ont correspondu *ou* ils se sont écrit pendant des années.
correspondence [kɒrɪs'pɒndəns] *n* **(a)** (*relationship*) correspondance *f* (**with, to,** avec); **the c. between cause and effect,** le rapport entre la cause et l'effet; **(b)** (*letter writing*) correspondance *f*; **to be in c. with s.o.,** être en correspondance avec qn; **they kept up a c. for many years,** ils sont restés en correspondance pendant des années; *Journ* **c. column,** courrier *m* des lecteurs; *Sch* **c. course,** cours *m* par correspondance; **(c)** (*mail*) courrier *m*; **I don't get much c.,** je ne reçois pas beaucoup de courrier; **to do one's c.,** faire sa correspondance.
correspondent [kɒrɪs'pɒndənt] *n* correspondant, -ante; **regular c.,** correspondant régulier; *Journ TV* **parliamentary c.,** rédacteur *m* parlementaire; **war c.,** correspondant de guerre; **special c.,** envoyé spécial.
corresponding [kɒrɪ'spɒndɪŋ] *adj* **(a)** correspondant (**to,** à), conforme (**to,** à); **than in the c. period last year,** par rapport à la même période l'année dernière; **(b) c. member,** membre correspondant (*d'une société*).
correspondingly [kɒrɪ'spɒndɪŋlɪ] *adv* également, à l'avenant.
corridor ['kɒrɪdɔːr] *n* couloir *m*, corridor *m*; *Av* **air c.,** couloir aérien; *Hist* **the Polish C.,** le couloir de Dantzig; **the news had reached the corridors of power,** la nouvelle avait fait son chemin jusqu'aux allées du pouvoir; **c. train,** train *m* à couloir.
corroborate [kə'rɒbəreɪt] *vt* corroborer, confirmer (*une déclaration*).
corroboration [kərɒbə'reɪʃən] *n* corroboration *f*, confirmation *f*; **in c. of ...,** à l'appui de ... .
corroborative [kə'rɒb(ə)rətɪv] *adj* (*evidence, statement*) qui confirme, corroborant.
corrode [kə'rəʊd] **1** *vt* corroder, attaquer (*le métal*); *Fig* user (*un amour etc*). **2** *vi* se corroder.
corroded [kə'rəʊdɪd] *adj* corrodé, attaqué; **badly c. metal,** métal très corrodé *ou* attaqué.
corrosion [kə'rəʊʒən] *n* corrosion *f*.
corrosive [kə'rəʊsɪv] *adj & n* corrosif *m*, corrodant *m*.
corrugated ['kɒrʊgeɪtɪd] *adj* **c. iron,** tôle ondulée; **c. iron roof,** toit en tôle ondulée; **c. cardboard,** carton ondulé.
corrupt¹ [kə'rʌpt] *adj* **(a)** (*official etc*) corrompu; (*press*) vénal; **(b)** (*depraved*) corrompu, dépravé; **the c. cinema of today,** la corruption du cinéma d'aujourd'hui; **(c)** *Comptr* (*disk, file*) corrompu; **(d)** *Liter* (*text*) corrompu, altéré.
corrupt² *vt* **(a)** (*deprave*) corrompre (*la jeunesse*); **(b)** *Comptr* corrompre; **(c)** *Liter* corrompre, altérer (*un texte etc*).
corruptible [kə'rʌptəb(ə)l] *adj* corruptible; (*financially*) vénal, -aux.
corrupting [kə'rʌptɪŋ] *adj* dépravant, corrupteur, -trice; **c. influence,** influence corruptrice.
corruption [kə'rʌpʃən] *n* **(a)** (*giving and taking bribes*) action *f* de corrompre, corruption *f*; **bribery and c.,** corruption; **c. is endemic here,** ici la corruption est endémique; **(b)** (*moral*) corruption *f*, dépravation *f*; **(c)** *Comptr* corruption *f*; **(d)** *Liter* corruption *f*.
corruptive [kə'rʌptɪv] *adj* corrupteur, -trice.
corruptly [kə'rʌptlɪ] *adv* d'une manière corrompue; par corruption.
corsage [kɔː'sɑːʒ] *n* **(a)** *esp Am* fleur *f* (*portée au corsage, à la taille ou au poignet*); **(b)** (*bodice of dress*) corsage *m*.
corsair ['kɔːseər] *n Hist* corsaire *m*.
corset ['kɔːsɪt] *n* corset *m*; **orthopaedic** *or* **surgical c.,** corset orthopédique.
Corsica ['kɔːsɪkə] *n* Corse *f*.
Corsican ['kɔːsɪkən] **1** *adj* corse. **2** *n* Corse *mf*.
cortège [kɔː'teʒ] *n* cortège *m*; **funeral c.,** convoi *m ou* cortège funèbre.
cortex, *pl* **-ices** ['kɔːteks, -ɪsiːz] *n Bot Anat* cortex *m*.
cortisone ['kɔːtɪzəʊn] *n Bio Ch Med* cortisone *f*.
corundum [kə'rʌndəm] *n Miner* corindon *m*.
corvette [kɔː'vet] *n Nau* corvette *f*.
cos *abbr* **(a)** *Math* **cosine**; **(b)** *Com* **companies**.
cos [kɒs] *n Br* **c. (lettuce),** (laitue *f*) romaine *f*.
cosh¹ [kɒʃ] *n Br F* matraque *f*.
cosh² *vt Br F* assommer, matraquer (*qn*).
cosignatory ['kəʊ'sɪgnətərɪ] **1** *n* cosignataire *mf* (**to,** de). **2** *adj* cosignataire.
cosily ['kəʊzɪlɪ] *adv* confortablement, douillettement.
cosine ['kəʊsaɪn] *n Math* cosinus *m*.
cosiness ['kəʊzɪnɪs] *n* confort *m* (*d'un fauteuil, d'un petit coin intime*); chaleur *f* agréable (*du coin du feu etc*).
cosmetic [kɒz'metɪk] **1** *n* cosmétique *m*; **cosmetics,** produits *mpl* de beauté; **the cosmetics industry,** l'industrie *f* des cosmétiques; **cosmetics counter,** (*in shop*) rayon *m* des produits de beauté. **2** *adj* **(a)** cosmétique; **c. surgery,** chirurgie *f* esthétique; **to have c. surgery,** se faire faire une opération de chirurgie esthétique; **(b)** (*superficial*) superficiel; **the policy change is c. rather than real,** le changement de politique est plutôt un changement de forme que de fond; **the alterations they made on the translation are purely c.,** les changements qu'ils ont apportés à la traduction sont de pure forme.
cosmetician [kɒzmɪ'tɪʃən] *n* esthéticien, -ienne.
cosmic ['kɒzmɪk] *adj* (*rayon etc*) *& Fig* cosmique.
cosmology [kɒz'mɒlədʒɪ] *n* cosmologie *f*.
cosmonaut ['kɒzmənɔːt] *n* cosmonaute *mf*.
cosmopolitan [kɒzmə'pɒlɪt(ə)n] **1** *n* cosmopolite *mf*. **2** *adj* (*city etc*) cosmopolite.
cosmos ['kɒzmɒs] *n* cosmos *m*.
Cossack ['kɒsæk] **1** *adj* cosaque. **2** *n* Cosaque *mf*.
cosset ['kɒsɪt] *vt* dorloter, choyer, câliner (*qn*).
cossie ['kɒzɪ] *n Austr F* maillot *m* de bain.
cost¹ [kɒst] *n* (*price etc*) coût *m*, frais *mpl*; *Jur* **costs,** frais d'instance, dépens *mpl*; *Jur* **they were ordered to pay costs,** ils ont été condamnés aux dépens; **c. of living,** coût de la vie; **c.-of-living allowance** *or US* **adjustment,** indemnité *f* de cherté de vie *ou* de vie chère; **c.-of-living index,** indice *m* du coût de la vie; **at the c. of one's life,** au prix de sa vie; **at little/great c.,** à peu de/à grands frais; **for the c. of a room in a hotel you could ...,** pour le prix d'une chambre à l'hôtel, vous pourriez ...; *Fig* **to count the cost(s) of sth,** calculer le coût de qch; **at any c., at all costs,** à tout prix, à n'importe quel prix, coûte que coûte; **I learnt it to my c.,** je l'ai appris à mes dépens *ou* pour mon malheur; **as I know to my c.,** comme je l'ai appris à mes dépens; **the c. in human life,** (*of disaster etc*) le prix en vies humaines; *Ind Com* **c. price,** prix de revient; **to sell at c.,** vendre au prix coûtant; **c. accounting,** comptabilité *f* de prix de revient; **c. analysis,** analyse *f* des coûts; **c. benefit analysis,** analyse coûts-bénéfices; **c. conscious,** (*company*) qui contrôle les dépenses; **c., insurance and freight,** coût, assurance, fret; **c.-cutting measures,** mesures visant à réduire les coûts.
cost² *vt* **(a)** (*pt & pp* **cost**) coûter; **it costs $25,** ça coûte 25 dollars; **it cost me £30 a night to stay here,** ça m'a coûté 30 livres par nuit de séjourner ici; **how much does it c.?,** combien cela coûte-t-il?; **it costs nothing to join the library,** l'inscription à la bibliothèque est gratuite; **that will c. him a great deal of money/trouble,** cela lui coûtera beaucoup d'argent/de peine; **to c. a fortune** *or* **the earth,** coûter un argent fou, coûter les yeux de la tête; *Br F* **if you go by air it'll c. you,** si tu y vas par avion, tu vas le sentir passer; **the attempt cost him his life,** cette tentative lui a coûté la vie; **it must have cost her something to admit that,** il a dû lui en coûter de l'avouer;
(b) (*pt & pp* **costed**) *Com Ind* établir le prix de revient de (*un article*); évaluer le coût de (*un travail*); **how much was it costed at?,** (*of work*) à combien est-ce que le coût a été évalué?
▶**cost out** *vtsep* = **COST² (b)**.
co-star¹ ['kəʊstɑːr] *n Cin etc* acteur *ou* actrice qui partage la vedette avec un(e) autre.
co-star² *vi Cin etc* partager la vedette (**with,** avec).
Costa Rican ['kɒstə'riːkən] **1** *adj* costaricain. **2** *n* Costaricain, -aine.
cost-effective [kɒstɪ'fektɪv] *adj Com* rentable; **the project must be made c.-e.,** il faut rentabiliser le projet.
cost-effectiveness [kɒstɪ'fektɪvnɪs] *n Com* rentabilité *f*.
coster(monger) ['kɒstər, 'kɒstəmʌŋgər] *n Old-fashioned Br* marchand *m* des quatre saisons.
costing ['kɒstɪŋ] *n Ind Com* établissement *m* du *ou* des prix

de revient (*d'un article*); évaluation *f* du coût (*d'un travail*); **the c. of translations depends on their technical difficulty,** l'évaluation du coût des traductions dépend de leur difficulté sur le plan technique.

costive ['kɒstɪv] *adj Med* constipé.

costliness ['kɒstlɪnɪs] *n* **(a)** (*high price*) cherté *f*; **(b)** (*quality*) richesse *f*, somptuosité *f* (*de l'ameublement etc*).

costly ['kɒstlɪ] *adj* **(a)** (*expensive*) coûteux, cher; *Fig* **it was a c. mistake,** c'était une erreur qui a coûté cher; **(b)** (*valuable*) précieux; (*ameublement etc*) riche, somptueux.

costume ['kɒstjʊm] *n* **(a)** costume *m*; **national c.,** costume national; **bathing** *or* **swimming c.,** maillot *m* de bain; **c. jewellery,** bijoux *mpl* fantaisie; *Cin TV Th* **c. drama,** film *ou* programme *ou* pièce historique; *esp Am* **c. party,** bal costumé; **(b)** *Old-fashioned* (*woman's suit*) tailleur *m*.

costum(i)er [kɒs'tjʊmər, -ɪər] *n* costumier *m*; **theatrical c.,** costumier de théâtre.

cosy ['kəʊzɪ] **1** *adj* (*place, thing*) douillet; (*person*) bien au chaud; **c. room,** pièce confortable; **it's c. here,** il fait bon ici; *Fig* **a c. little job,** (*undemanding*) un travail pépère; **at university it's all very c. — the real world is different,** à l'université, on est bien au chaud —le monde réel est bien différent. **2** *n* **egg c.,** couvre-œuf *m*, *pl* couvre-œufs; **tea c.,** couvre-théière *m*, *pl* couvre-théières.

►**cosy up to** *vipo esp Am* (*ingratiate oneself with*) se mettre dans les petits papiers de (*qn*).

cot [kɒt] *n* (*for child*) lit *m* d'enfant; *esp Am* (*folding bed*) petit lit (pliant); (*camp bed*) lit de camp; *Nau* cadre *m* à l'anglaise; *Med* **c. death,** mort subite du nourrisson.

cotangent ['kəʊ'tændʒ(ə)nt] *n Math* cotangente *f*.

cote [kəʊt] *n* (*for doves*) colombier *m*; (*for sheep*) abri *m*.

coterie ['kəʊtərɪ] *n* coterie *f*.

cottage ['kɒtɪdʒ] *n* **(a)** *Br* petite maison (*à la campagne*), cottage *m*; **thatched c.,** chaumière *f*; **c. industry,** travail *m* à domicile; *F Fig* entreprise mal organisée; **c. cheese,** fromage blanc; **c. hospital,** hôpital *m* de médecine générale en zone rurale (*où on ne traite pas les cas sérieux*); **c. flat,** = appartement situé dans un pavillon; **c. pie,** hachis parmentier; **(b)** (*for holidays*) *Am* chalet *m*; **(c)** (*for homosexuals*) lieu *m* de drague.

cottager ['kɒtɪdʒər] *n* **(a)** *Br* habitant, -ante de cottage; **(b)** *Am* propriétaire *mf ou* locataire *mf* de chalet.

cotter ['kɒtər] *n MecE* goupille *f*; **c. (pin),** clavette *f* d'arrêt.

cotton ['kɒt(ə)n] *n* **(a)** (*crop*) coton *m*; **to pick c.,** cueillir le coton; **c. (plant, bush),** cotonnier *m*; **c. field,** champ *m* de coton; **c. plantation,** plantation *f* de coton; **c. growing,** culture *f* du coton; *US* **c. belt,** région *f* du coton; **c. mill,** filature *f* de coton; **c. picker,** ramasseur, -euse de coton; *Pharm* **c. wool,** *US* **absorbent c.,** ouate *f*, coton hydrophile; **my legs feel like c. wool,** j'ai les jambes en coton; *Fig* **to wrap s.o. in c. wool,** mettre qn dans du coton; *Am Culin* **c. candy,** barbe *f* à papa; **c. grass,** (*plant*) linaigrette *f*, lin *m* des marais; **(b)** *Tex* **c. (cloth),** (toile *f* de) coton *m*; percale *f*; **coarse c.,** rouennerie *f*; **printed c.,** coton imprimé; **c. yarn,** coton filé; fil *m* de coton; **c. goods,** cotonnades *fpl*; **a c. shirt,** une chemise en coton; **(c)** (*for sewing*) fil *m* à coudre, fil de coton; **embroidery c.,** coton à broder.

►**cotton on** *vi F* (*understand*) piger; **to c. on to sth,** piger qch.

►**cotton to** *vipo Am F* **(a)** (*take a liking to*) se prendre d'amitié pour (*qn*); **(b)** (*approve of*) avoir (*qn*) à la bonne; **I don't c. to that kind of behaviour,** je n'approuve pas ce genre de comportement.

cotton-picking ['kɒt(ə)n'pɪkɪŋ] *adj Am F* (*intensifier*) sacré.

cottonseed ['kɒt(ə)nsiːd] *n* graine *f* de coton; **c. oil,** huile *f* de coton.

cottontail ['kɒt(ə)nteɪl] *n US* lapin *m* (de garenne).

cotyledon [kɒtɪ'liːd(ə)n] *n Bot* cotylédon *m*.

couch¹ [kaʊtʃ] *n* divan *m*; **studio c.,** divan-lit *m*, *pl* divans-lits; **c. grass,** (*weed*) chiendent *m*; *F* **c. potato,** mollasson, -onne.

couch² *vt* **(a)** (*phrase*) formuler, rédiger; **their reply was couched in insulting language,** leur réponse était exprimée en termes injurieux; **(b)** *Tech* (*in brewing*) coucher (*le grain*); (*in papermaking*) coucher (*une feuille*) sur les feutres; **(c)** *Lit* (*of animal*) **to be couched on the ground,** être couché par terre.

couchette [kʊ'ʃet] *n Rail etc* couchette *f*.

cougar ['kuːgər] *n* (*animal*) coug(o)uar *m*, puma *m*.

cough¹ [kɒf] *n* toux *f*; **I've got a c.,** je tousse; **he gave a c. to warn me,** il toussota pour m'avertir; **dry/loose c.,** toux sèche/grasse; **whooping c.,** coqueluche *f*; **c. drop** *or* **lozenge** *or* **sweet,** pastille contre *ou* pour la toux; **c. mixture** *or* **syrup,** sirop *m* contre la toux.

cough² *vi* (*of person, animal, F engine*) tousser.

►**cough up 1** *vtsep* **(a)** (*produce by coughing*) cracher (en toussant); **to c. up phlegm/blood,** cracher des glaires/du sang; **(b)** *F* (*pay*) sortir; **I had to c. up £50 for the meal,** j'ai dû sortir 50 livres pour le repas. **2** *vi F* (*pay*) raquer, casper, casquer; **she coughed up in the end,** elle a fini par casquer; **come on — c. up!,** file-moi mon argent!

coughing ['kɒfɪŋ] *n* toux *f*; **fit of c.,** quinte *f* de toux; **your c. woke me up,** tu m'as réveillé en toussant.

could *see* **CAN**.

couldn't-care-less ['kʊd(ə)ntkeə'les] *adj* **c.-c.-l. attitude,** je-m'en-fichisme *m*, je-m'en-foutisme *m*.

coulomb [kuːlɒmb] *n El* coulomb *m*, ampère-seconde *m*.

coulter ['kəʊltər] *n Agr* coutre *m* (*de charrue*).

council ['kaʊnsəl] *n* **(a)** *Admin* conseil *m*; **city c.,** (*people*) conseil municipal; (*government*) municipalité *f*; *Br* **district c.,** (*people*) = conseil municipal; (*government*) = municipalité; *Br* **county c.,** = conseil général; *Br* **the c. sent a repairman,** la municipalité a envoyé un réparateur; *Br* **to be on the c.,** être au conseil municipal; **the Privy C.,** le Conseil privé (du souverain); **C. of Europe,** Conseil de l'Europe; *Mil & Fig* **to hold a c. of war,** tenir un conseil de guerre; *Econ* **consumer c.,** comité (consultatif) des consommateurs; *Br* **c. house** *or* **flat,** = habitation *f* à loyer modéré, H.L.M. *f*; **c. offices,** les bureaux de la municipalité; **c. estate,** cité *f* de H.L.M.; **c. meeting,** réunion du conseil municipal; **(b)** *Rel* concile *m* (*œcuménique etc*).

councillor ['kaʊnsɪlər] *n* conseiller *m*, membre *m* du conseil; **county c.,** = conseiller général; **C. John Smith,** M. John Smith, membre du conseil.

counsel¹ ['kaʊns(ə)l] *n* **(a)** (*discussion*) délibération *f*, consultation *f*; **to take c. with s.o.,** se consulter avec qn (**about,** sur); **(b)** (*advice*) conseil *m*, avis *m*; **(c) to keep one's (own) c.,** (*about one's plans, intentions*) garder ses projets pour soi; (*about one's opinions*) garder son opinion pour soi; **(d)** *Br Jur* (*no pl*) avocat *m*, conseil *m*; **to be represented by c.,** être représenté par un avocat; **c. for the defence,** défenseur *m*; (*in criminal law*) avocat de la défense; **King's/Queen's c.,** conseiller *m* du Roi/de la Reine, conseiller de la Couronne.

counsel² *vt* (-**ll**-, *US* -**l**-) conseiller (*la patience, la prudence*); **to c. s.o. to do sth,** conseiller à qn de faire qch.

counselling [kaʊns(ə)lɪŋ] *n* activité *f* de conseil; **to offer c. for alcoholics,** offrir un service de conseil aux alcooliques.

counsellor, *US* **counselor** ['kaʊns(ə)lər] *n* **(a)** (*diplomatic*) conseiller *m* d'ambassade; **(b)** (*moral*) conseiller *m*; **marriage guidance c.,** conseiller conjugal; **(c)** *US Jur* avocat, -ate.

count¹ [kaʊnt] *n* **(a)** compte *m*; (*of votes*) dépouillement *m*; (*of people*) dénombrement *m*, comptage *m*; (*total*) total *m*; *Comptr* comptage *m*; **to keep c.,** tenir le compte (**of,** de); **to lose c.,** perdre le compte; **I've lost c. of how many times I've asked you to ...,** je ne sais pas combien de fois je t'ai demandé de ...; **to lose c. of time,** perdre la notion du temps; **a quick c. revealed that half were car owners,** un comptage rapide a révélé que la moitié étaient propriétaires de voitures; **at the last c.,** au dernier comptage; **this is short of the c.,** cela ne fait pas le compte; *Med* **blood c.,** numération *f* globulaire; **c. noun,** nom dénombrable;

(b) *Boxing* compte *m* (de dix seconds); **to take the c.,** rester au tapis pour le compte, être knock-out; *Boxing & Fig* **to be out for the c.,** être K.O.;

(c) *Jur* chef *m* (*d'accusation*); **not guilty on the first c.,** non coupable au premier chef; *Fig* **I'm angry with them on both counts,** je suis fâché avec eux pour les deux raisons; **to fail on a number of counts,** (*of project etc*) échouer à plusieurs égards;

(d) *Parl* **c. out,** ajournement *m* (*quand il y a moins de quarante membres présents*).

count² 1 *vt* **(a)** compter (*des personnes, la dépense*); dénombrer (*des personnes, ses troupeaux etc*); (*at election*) **to c. the votes,** dépouiller le scrutin; **I counted three wrecked cars,** j'ai compté trois voitures démolies;

(b) (*include*) compter; **counting the dog there were four of us,** nous étions quatre en comptant le chien; **without** *or* **not counting ...,** sans compter ...;

(c) (*consider*) compter (**as,** comme); **I don't c. him as a friend,** je ne le considère pas comme un ami; **to c. s.o. among one's friends,** compter qn parmi ses amis; **to c.**

s.o./sth (to be) sth, tenir qn/qch pour qch; **c. yourself lucky you weren't killed,** estime-toi heureux de n'avoir pas été tué; **to be counted as a member,** être compté au nombre des membres.

2 *vi* **(a)** compter; **to c. on one's fingers,** compter sur ses doigts; **to c. (up) to 100,** compter jusqu'à 100; **to c. from 1 to 100,** compter de 1 à 100; **counting from tomorrow,** à compter de demain;

(b) (*be considered*) compter (**among,** parmi, au nombre de); **he counts among my best friends,** il compte parmi *ou* au nombre de mes meilleurs amis; *Cards* **card that counts,** (carte) marquante *f*; **two children c. as one adult,** deux enfants comptent comme un adulte; **he's under five so he doesn't c.,** il a moins de cinq ans donc il ne compte pas; **marks in this exam c. towards your degree,** les notes de cet examen comptent pour votre licence; **his weight will c. against him in the race,** son poids va jouer contre lui dans la course;

(c) (*be of importance*) avoir de l'importance, compter; **I don't c. around here,** je ne compte pas ici; **every vote counts,** chaque voix compte *ou* a son importance; **every minute counts,** il n'y a pas une minute à perdre; **experience counts for more than qualifications,** l'expérience compte plus que les diplômes.

count³ *n* (*title*) comte *m*; **the C. of Monte Cristo,** le comte de Monte Cristo.

►**count against** *vipo* jouer contre (*qn*).

►**count down** *vi Astronaut* compter à rebours.

►**count in** *vtsep* (*include*) **c. me in!,** compte-moi!

►**count on** *vipo* **(a)** (*depend on*) compter sur (*qn, qch*); **we're counting on you to give a speech,** nous comptons sur vous pour faire ce discours; **you can always c. on him to be late,** tu peux compter sur lui pour être en retard; **I wouldn't c. on the train arriving on time,** je ne compterais pas sur le fait que le train soit à l'heure; **can I c. on your vote?,** puis-je compter sur votre voix?; **(b)** (*expect*) compter; **I didn't c. on seeing you,** je ne comptais pas te voir.

►**count out** *vtsep* **(a)** (*add up*) compter (*l'argent*); **he counted me out twenty £1 notes,** il m'a compté vingt billets de 1 livre; **(b)** (*exclude*) ne pas compter sur (*qn*); **he's teetotal, so you can c. him out,** il ne boit pas, donc ne le compte pas; **no thanks, c. me out!,** non merci, ne comptez pas sur moi; **(c)** *Boxing* **to be counted out,** rester au tapis pour le compte, être (mis) knock-out; **(d)** *Parl* **to c. out the House,** ajourner la Chambre faute d'un quorum.

►**count up** *vtsep* (*add up*) compter.

countable ['kaʊntəb(ə)l] *adj Gram* **c. noun,** nom *m* dénombrable.

countdown ['kaʊntdaʊn] *n* (*for rocket launch etc*) compte *m* à rebours; *Fig* **the c. to Christmas has begun,** on commence à compter les jours qui nous séparent de Noël.

countenance¹ ['kaʊntɪnəns] *n esp Lit* **(a)** (*expression*) (expression *f* du) visage *m*; (*bearing*) contenance *f*; **to lose c.,** se décontenancer, perdre contenance; **to be out of c.,** avoir perdu contenance, être décontenancé; **(b)** (*support*) appui *m;* **to give** *or* **lend c. to s.o./sth,** appuyer qn/qch.

countenance² *vt* approuver, sanctionner (*une action*); **she wouldn't c. borrowing money,** elle n'approuverait pas le fait d'emprunter de l'argent; **I only countenanced the plan on the understanding that ...,** je n'ai approuvé le projet qu'à condition que ... .

counter¹ ['kaʊntər] *n* **(a)** (*in shop*) comptoir *m*; (*in supermarket*) rayon *m*; (*in bank etc*) guichet *m*; **payable over the c.,** payable au guichet; **you can get** *or* **buy these drugs over the c.,** on peut acheter ces médicaments sans ordonnance; *Fin* **to buy shares over the c.,** acheter des actions sur le marché hors cote; *Fin* **over-the-c. market,** marché *m* hors cote; **sold over the c.,** vendu (au) comptant; **to sell under the c.,** vendre en cachette; **c. hand,** vendeur, -euse; **c. staff,** vendeurs *mpl*; **(b)** (*token in games*) (*square*) fiche *f*; (*round*) jeton *m*; *Ind* jeton; **the hostage was being used as a bargaining c.,** l'otage a été utilisé comme monnaie d'échange; **(c)** (*device*) compteur *m*; *Comptr* compteur; *Nucl* **Geiger c.,** compteur (de) Geiger.

counter² **1** *n Fencing* contre *m*; *Boxing* coup *m* d'arrêt, contre. **2** *adj* **(a)** contraire, opposé (**to,** à); **(b)** contre-; **c. declaration,** contre-déclaration *f*; *Med* **c. indication,** contre-indication *f*; **c. reaction,** contre-réaction *f*. **3** *adv* en sens inverse; **to act c. to one's orders,** agir contrairement aux ordres que l'on a reçus; **to run c. to sth,** aller à l'encontre de qch.

counter³ *vt* aller à l'encontre de (*qn, qch*); contrecarrer (*les desseins de qn*); **measures have been taken to c. the threat of the disease,** des mesures ont été prises pour lutter contre la menace que représente la maladie; *Boxing* **to c. (a blow),** parer *ou* bloquer (un coup) et riposter en même temps.

counteract [kaʊntə'rækt] *vt* contrarier, contrecarrer (*un projet*); neutraliser (*une influence*); parer à (*un résultat*); riposter à, contrecarrer (*un effet*); **to c. the effects of a drug,** neutraliser les effets d'un médicament.

counterattack¹ ['kaʊntərətæk] *n Mil & Fig* contre-attaque *f*.

counterattack² *Mil & Fig vt & vi* contre-attaquer.

counterattraction ['kaʊntərə'trækʃən] *n* = attraction destinée à faire concurrence au clou de la fête etc.

counterbalance¹ ['kaʊntəbæləns] *n* contrepoids *m*.

counterbalance² [kaʊntə'bæləns] *vt* contrebalancer, faire contrepoids à (*qch*).

countercharge ['kaʊntətʃɑːdʒ] *n Jur* contre-accusation *f*; contre-plainte *f*.

countercheck ['kaʊntətʃek] *vt* vérifier (une seconde fois).

counterclaim¹ ['kaʊntəkleɪm] *n Jur etc* demande reconventionnelle.

counterclaim² *vt Jur* faire une demande reconventionnelle (*en dommages-intérêts*).

counterclockwise [kaʊntə'klɒkwaɪz] *adv esp Am* dans le sens contraire de celui des aiguilles d'une montre.

counterculture ['kaʊntəkʌltʃər] *n* culture alternative.

counterespionage [kaʊntə'respɪənɑːʒ] *n* contre-espionnage *m*.

counterfeit¹ ['kaʊntəfɪt] **1** *adj* faux; **c. coin,** fausse monnaie. **2** *n* contrefaçon *f*, faux *m*; **the note was a c.,** le billet était un faux.

counterfeit² *vt* contrefaire (*la monnaie etc*).

counterfeiter ['kaʊntəfɪtər] *n* faux monnayeur.

counterfoil ['kaʊntəfɔɪl] *n* souche *f*, talon *m* (*de chèque, de quittance*).

counterintelligence ['kaʊntərɪn'telɪdʒəns] *n* contre-espionnage *m*.

countermand ['kaʊntəmɑːnd] *vt* annuler (*un ordre*); *Com* **to c. the order for sth,** décommander qch.

countermeasure ['kaʊntəmeʒər] *n* contre-mesure *f*, *pl* contre-mesures.

countermove ['kaʊntəmuːv] *n* contre-mesure *f*, *pl* contre-mesures.

counteroffensive ['kaʊntərə'fensɪv] *n Mil* contre-offensive *f*.

counterorder ['kaʊntərɔːdər] *n* contrordre *m*.

counterpane ['kaʊntəpeɪn] *n* courtepointe *f*.

counterpart ['kaʊntəpɑːt] *n* **(a)** (*person*) homologue *mf*; pendant *m* (*d'un tableau etc*); **to be the c. of ...,** aller de pair avec ...; **the Foreign Minister met her Spanish c.,** le ministre des affaires étrangères a rencontré son homologue espagnol; **(b)** (*of document*) double *m*.

counterplot ['kaʊntəplɒt] *n* contre-ruse *f*.

counterpoint ['kaʊntəpɔɪnt] *n Mus* contrepoint *m*.

counterpoise¹ ['kaʊntəpɔɪz] *n* **(a)** (*weight*) contrepoids *m*; **c. bridge,** pont *m* à bascule; **(b)** (*balance*) équilibre *m*; **in c.,** en équilibre.

counterpoise² *vt* contrebalancer, faire contrepoids à (*qch*).

counterproductive ['kaʊntəprə'dʌktɪv] *adj* qui a des effets contraires; **that would be c.,** cela irait à l'encontre du but recherché, cela serait absurde.

counterproposal ['kaʊntəprə'pəʊz(ə)l] *n* contre-proposition *f*.

Counter-Reformation ['kaʊntərefə'meɪʃən] *n Rel Hist* **the C.-R.,** la Contre-Réforme.

counter-revolution ['kaʊntərevə'luːʃən] *n Pol* contre-révolution *f*.

counter-revolutionary [kaʊntərevə'luːʃənərɪ] *Pol* **1** *n* contre-révolutionnaire *mf*. **2** *adj* contre-révolutionnaire.

countersign¹ ['kaʊntəsaɪn] *n Mil etc* mot *m* de passe.

countersign² *vt* contresigner, signer en second, viser (*un ordre etc*); ratifier (*un ordre*).

countersignature ['kaʊntə'sɪgnətjər] *n* **(a)** *Jur* (*authentication*) contreseing *m*; **(b)** (*approval*) approuvé *m*.

countersink¹ ['kaʊntəsɪŋk] *n* **(a)** (*tool*) **c. bit,** fraise *f*; **(b)** noyure *f* (*pour tête de vis*); fraisure *f* (*d'un trou*).

countersink² *vt* (*pt & pp* **countersunk**) noyer (*la tête d'une vis*); *Carp MecE etc* fraiser.

counterstroke ['kaʊntəstrəʊk] *n Mil* retour offensif.

countersunk ['kaʊntəsʌŋk] *adj* (*screw*) fraisé, noyé.

countertenor ['kaʊntətenər] *n Mus* (*person*) haute-contre *m*, *pl* hautes-contre.

countertrade ['kaʊntətreɪd] *n* contre-achat *m*.

counterweight ['kaʊntəweɪt] *n* contrepoids *m*.

countess ['kaʊntɪs] *n* (*title*) comtesse *f*.
counting ['kaʊntɪŋ] *n* compte *m*; dépouillement *m* (*du scrutin*); dénombrement *m* (*des personnes*).
countless ['kaʊntlɪs] *adj* innombrable, sans nombre.
countrified ['kʌntrɪfaɪd] *adj* aux allures campagnardes *ou* provinciales; **it's very c. here,** c'est comme la campagne ici.
country ['kʌntrɪ] *n* **(a)** (*political entity*) pays *m*; **the countries of Europe,** les pays de l'Europe; *esp Br Pol* **to go to the c.,** aller devant le pays; **in this c.,** (*that we come from*) dans notre pays; (*where we are at the moment*) dans ce pays; **the criminals have left the c.,** les criminels ont quitté le pays; **the Prime Minister isn't in the c.,** le premier ministre est à l'étranger; **the smallest village in the c.,** le plus petit village du pays; **to die for/love one's c.,** mourir pour/aimer sa patrie;
(b) (*opposed to town*) campagne *f*; **in the c.,** à la campagne; **to spend a day in the c.,** passer une journée à la campagne; **c. and western (music),** country *m*; **c. club,** = club sportif ou de loisirs situé dans un site campagnard; **c. dancing,** danse *f* folklorique; **c. gentleman,** gentilhomme campagnard; **c. house,** maison *f* de campagne; (*of aristocrat etc*) manoir *m*; **c. life,** vie *f* de *ou* à la campagne;
(c) (*opposed to capital*) la province; **a quiet little c. town,** une petite ville tranquille de province; **c. cousin,** cousin de province;
(d) (*region*) pays *m*, région *f*; **rough c.,** terrain accidenté; **open c.,** rase campagne; **flat c.,** pays *ou* terrain plat; **rich/fertile c.,** pays riche/fertile; **we're in wheat-growing c.,** nous sommes dans une région à blé; **this is Proust c.,** c'est le pays de Proust.
countryfolk ['kʌntrɪfəʊk] *npl* gens *mpl* de la campagne.
countryman, *pl* **-men** ['kʌntrɪmən, -men] *n* **(a)** campagnard *m*; **(b) fellow c.,** compatriote *m*.
countryside ['kʌntrɪsaɪd] *n* la campagne; (*region*) pays *m*; **beautiful c.,** beau paysage; **voters in the c.,** les électeurs des régions rurales; **refugees have left the c. for the towns,** les réfugiés ont quitté la campagne pour aller dans les villes.
countrystyle ['kʌntrɪstaɪl] *adj* **c. cooking,** cuisine campagnarde.
countrywoman, *pl* **-women** ['kʌntrɪwʊmən, -wɪmɪn] *n* **(a)** campagnarde *f*; **(b) fellow c.,** compatriote *f*.
county ['kaʊntɪ] *n* **(a)** comté *m*; *Br* = division territoriale et administrative de la Grande-Bretagne et de l'Irlande; *US* = d'un État; *Br* **the c. of Kent,** le comté du Kent; *US* **New York C.,** le comté de New York; *US* **c. line,** frontière *f* délimitant un comté; *Br* **c. town,** chef-lieu *m* de comté, *pl* chefs-lieux; *Br* **c. society,** l'aristocratie et la haute bourgeoisie du comté; *Cr* **c. cricket,** = les grands matchs entre les équipes de comté; **(b)** (*population*) les habitants *mpl* du comté.
coup [ku:] *n* coup *m* (audacieux); **to bring off a c.,** réussir un coup; **c. (d'état),** coup d'état.
coupé ['ku:peɪ] *n Aut* **sports c.,** coupé *m* sport.
couple¹ ['kʌp(ə)l] *n* **(a)** *F* (*two*) deux; **a c. of seconds,** deux secondes; **in a c. of days,** dans deux jours; **(b)** couple *m* (*d'époux, d'amants, de danseurs*); **the married c.,** les (deux) époux *mpl*; **the newly married c.,** les nouveaux mariés; **they make a lovely c.,** ils font un beau couple; **a married c.,** un couple marié.
couple² **1** *vt* **(a)** (*bring together*) (ac)coupler (*des bœufs, deux idées*); accoupler (*le mâle et la femelle*); associer (*des noms etc*); relier (*des personnes, des objets*); **common sense coupled with intelligence,** le bon sens joint à l'intelligence; **the course couples theory with practical work,** le cours allie la théorie à la pratique; **(b)** *MecE etc* engrener, embrayer (*une machine*); raccorder (*des tuyaux*); *El* associer, accoupler (*des piles*); *Rail* **to c. up a carriage,** atteler *ou* accrocher un wagon. **2** *vi* (*of male and female*) s'accoupler.
coupler ['kʌplər] *n* **(a)** *Mus* (*organ*) tirant *m* à accoupler; pédale *f* d'accouplement; **(b)** *Rail* attelage *m*.
couplet ['kʌplɪt] *n Liter* distique *m*; **rhyming couplets,** couplets *mpl* qui riment.
coupling ['kʌp(ə)lɪŋ] *n* **(a)** accouplement *m*, appariement *m* (*des animaux*); association *f* (*d'idées, de deux noms*); **(b)** *Tech* accouplement *m*, raccordement *m* (*de deux roues etc*); *Rail* attelage *m* (*des wagons*); *El etc* couplage *m*, association *f* (*d'éléments de pile etc*); **(c)** (*static device*) raccord *m*, joint *m*; *Rail* attelage *m*; (*device for transmitting motion*) accouplement *m*, embrayage *m*.
coupon ['ku:pɒn] *n* coupon *m*; **international reply c.,** coupon-réponse international, *pl* coupons-réponse; *Com* **(free) gift c.,** bon-prime *m*, *pl* bons-primes; *Admin* **petrol c.,** bon *m* d'essence; *Br Sp* **football** *or* **pools c.,** = formulaire de concours de pronostics de football; *Fin* **interest c.,** coupon d'intérêts.
courage ['kʌrɪdʒ] *n* courage *m*; **to have the c. to do sth,** avoir le courage de faire qch; **to pluck up** *or* **muster c., to take one's c. in both hands,** prendre son courage à deux mains; **to restore s.o.'s c.,** redonner du courage à qn; **he didn't have the moral c. to face them,** il n'a pas eu le courage moral de leur faire face; **physical c.,** courage physique.
courageous [kə'reɪdʒəs] *adj* courageux.
courageously [kə'reɪdʒəslɪ] *adv* courageusement, avec courage.
courgette [kʊə'ʒət] *n Br* courgette *f*.
courier ['kʊrɪər] *n* **(a)** (*messenger*) courrier *m*, messager *m*; **to send sth/to arrive by c.,** envoyer qch/arriver par messagerie; **motorcycle c.,** messager en moto; **she was a c. for drug dealers,** elle servait de messager à des trafiquants de drogue; **(b)** (*in tourism*) accompagnateur, -trice.
course¹ [kɔ:s] *n* **(a)** cours *m* (*d'un fleuve, du temps, des affaires etc*); cours, ordre *m* (*des événements*); cours, trajet *m* (*d'une balle etc*); évolution *f* (*d'une maladie*); **in the c. of conversation,** au cours de la conversation; **in the c. of the evening he got very drunk,** au cours de la soirée, il s'est beaucoup enivré; **in the c. of the next year,** au cours de l'année prochaine; **in the c. of time,** dans la suite *ou* le cours des temps; **in the ordinary** *or* **normal c. of things** *or* **events,** normalement; **in due c.,** en temps utile; **to let nature take its c.,** laisser la nature faire les choses; **let things take their c.,** laisser les choses se faire *ou* suivre leur évolution *ou* suivre leur cours; **it's best to let the fever run its c.,** il vaut mieux laisser la fièvre évoluer normalement; **that is a matter of c.,** cela va sans dire; **as a matter of c.,** tout naturellement, automatiquement; **blood tests are carried out as a matter of c.,** des examens sanguins sont effectués automatiquement;
(b) of c., bien entendu, naturellement; **of c. ... but,** bien sûr ... mais; **of c. not!,** bien sûr que non!; **of c. she was angry!,** bien sûr qu'elle était fâchée!; **he forgot of c.,** bien entendu, il a oublié;
(c) (*route*) route *f*, direction *f*; **to keep one's c.,** ne pas dévier de sa route; *Nau* maintenir son cap; **to change (one's) c.,** changer de direction; *Nau* changer le cap; *Nau & Fig* **to be on c.,** suivre le cap fixé; **to be driven off c.,** (*of ship*) dévier de son cap; *MecE* **upward/downward c. of a piston,** course ascendante/descendante d'un piston;
(d) c. (of action) ligne *f* de conduite, chose *f* à faire; **to take a c. of action,** adopter une ligne de conduite; **it is the only c. open to me,** c'est ma seule ressource; **the best c. would be to ...,** la meilleure chose à faire *ou* le mieux serait de ...; **his best c. would be to ...,** le mieux pour lui serait de ...; **the right c.,** la bonne voie;
(e) *Sch Univ* cours *m*; **to give a c. of lectures,** donner un cours; **to take** *or* **follow** *or F* **do a c.,** suivre un cours; **a degree c.,** un cours de licence; **he has published a French c.,** il a publié une méthode de français;
(f) *Med* **c. (of treatment),** traitement *m*; **a c. of injections,** une série de piqûres;
(g) (*of meal*) plat *m*; **aren't you having a first c.?,** tu ne prends pas d'entrée?; **four-c. dinner,** dîner *m* à quatre plats; **three courses and a sweet,** trois plats et un dessert; **main c.,** plat principal *ou* de résistance;
(h) *Sp etc* champ *m*, terrain *m* (*de courses*); *Horseriding* parcours *m*; **golf c.,** terrain *m* de golf, golf *m*;
(i) *Constr* assise *f* (*de briques, de charpente*); **damp c.,** couche isolante *ou* hydrofuge *ou* d'isolement;
(j) *Nau* basse voile, voile basse;
(k) *HydE* canal *m*, bief *m*;
(l) *Min* galerie *f*.
course² **1** *vi* **(a)** (*of liquids*) courir, couler; **the blood courses through the veins,** le sang circule *ou* coule dans les veines; **tears were coursing down my face,** j'avais le visage ruisselant de larmes; **(b)** (*in hunting*) courir le lièvre. **2** *vt* courir (*un lièvre*).
coursing ['kɔ:sɪŋ] *n* **(a)** (*hunting*) chasse *f* à courre au lièvre; **(b)** = concours de vitesse entre lévriers lâchés sur un lièvre en champ clos.
court¹ [kɔ:t] *n* **(a)** *Jur* cour *f*, tribunal *m*; (*courtroom*) auditoire *m* de tribunal; **law c., c. of law,** tribunal; **civil/criminal c.,** tribunal civil/criminel; **magistrate's c.,** = tribunal d'instance; *Br* **county c.,** tribunal de grande instance; **c. of appeal,** cour d'appel; **International C. of Justice,** Cour internationale de justice; **to go to c.,** aller en justice; **to take s.o. to c.,** faire un procès à qn; **are you**

prepared to say that in c. *or* **in a c. of law?,** est-ce que vous seriez prêt à le jurer devant le tribunal?; **in open c.,** en plein tribunal; **case before the c.,** affaire *f* en cause; **to come before the c.,** comparaître devant le tribunal; **to settle a case out of c.,** arranger une affaire à l'amiable; **we've decided to settle out of c.,** nous avons décidé d'arranger ça à l'amiable; **tell the c. what you saw,** veuillez dire à la cour ce que vous avez vu; **sale by order of the c.,** vente *f* judiciaire; **this is a matter for the courts, not the government,** c'est à la justice d'en décider, pas au gouvernement; *Mil Nau* **c. of inquiry,** commission *f* d'enquête (*sur une question de discipline*); **c. case,** affaire *f*; *Mil* **c. martial,** (*pl* **courts martial**) tribunal militaire;

(b) *Sp* **(tennis) c.,** court *m* (de tennis), tennis *m*; **grass c.,** court sur gazon; **hard c.,** court en dur; *US* **c. tennis,** jeu *m* de paume;

(c) (*royal etc*) cour *f*; **to pay c. to s.o.,** faire la cour à qn; **to hold c.,** (*of celebrity etc*) se faire faire la cour (par ses admirateurs); *Cards* **c. card,** figure *f*; *Journ* **c. circular,** = rubrique décrivant les engagements officiels des membres de la famille royale; **c. shoe,** escarpin *m*;

(d) (*courtyard*) cour *f*; (*in names of blocks of flats*) = résidence *f*; (*in names of palaces*) château *m*; palais *m*.

court² **1** *vt* **(a)** (*seek*) rechercher (*une alliance etc*); (re)chercher, solliciter (*l'amitié de qn*); briguer (*la faveur de qn*); aller au-devant de (*un échec*); braver (*la mort*); **to c. popularity,** chercher à se faire bien voir (**with,** auprès de); **the government seems to be courting disaster,** on dirait que le gouvernement cherche le désastre; **to c. the electorate,** chercher à gagner les voix des électeurs; **(b)** *Old-fashioned* (*seek in marriage*) courtiser, faire la cour à (*une femme*); **when I was courting your mother,** lorsque je faisais la cour à ta mère. **2** *vi Old-fashioned* **to be courting,** (*of individual*) avoir un petit ami *ou* une petite amie; (*of couple*) sortir ensemble, se fréquenter; **courting couple,** couple *m* d'amoureux.

courteous ['kɜːtɪəs] *adj* courtois, poli (**to, towards,** envers).

courteously ['kɜːtɪəslɪ] *adv* courtoisement, poliment.

courtesan [kɔːtɪ'zæn] *n* courtisane *f*.

courtesy ['kɜːtəsɪ] *n* courtoisie *f*, politesse *f*; **common c.,** la politesse la plus élémentaire; **he didn't have the c. to reply to my letter,** il n'a pas eu la politesse de répondre à ma lettre; **by c. of ...,** avec la gracieuse permission de ...; **exchange of courtesies,** échange *m* de politesses; *Aut* **c. car,** (*provided by garage*) voiture prêtée gratuitement; *Am* (*provided by airline*) voiture mise à la disposition des passagers; **c. bus,** autobus gratuit; *Aut* **c. light,** plafonnier *m*; **c. title,** titre *m* de courtoisie.

courthouse ['kɔːthaʊs] *n esp Am* palais *m* de justice, tribunal *m*.

courtier ['kɔːtɪər] *n* courtisan *m*.

courtly ['kɔːtlɪ] *adj* (*polite*) courtois, d'une politesse raffinée; (*dignified*) élégant, à l'air digne et aristocratique; **c. love,** l'amour courtois.

court-martial ['kɔːt'mɑːʃ(ə)l] *vt* (**-ll-,** *US* **-l-**) traduire (*qn*) devant le tribunal militaire; **to be court-martialled,** passer devant le tribunal militaire.

courtroom ['kɔːtruːm] *n Jur* salle *f* d'audience; (*people*) auditoire *m* d'un tribunal.

courtship ['kɔːtʃɪp] *n* cour *f* (*faite à une femme*); **their c. was a stormy affair,** la période pendant laquelle ils se sont fréquentés a été assez mouvementée; *Zool* **c. display,** parade nuptiale.

courtyard ['kɔːtjɑːd] *n* cour *f* (*de maison etc*).

couscous ['kuːskuːs] *n* couscous *m*.

cousin ['kʌz(ə)n] *n* cousin, -ine; **first c., full c.,** cousin germain; **second c.,** cousin issu de germain; **our American cousins,** nos cousins américains; **a distant c. of the sparrow,** un cousin éloigné du moineau.

couth [kuːθ] *adj Br Hum* **he's not very c.,** il n'est pas très raffiné.

couture ['kuː'tʊər] *n Sewing* **haute c.,** haute couture.

couturier, *f* **-ière** [kuː'tjʊərɪeɪ, -ɪeər] *n Sewing* grand couturier, grande couturière; (*head of company*) directeur, -trice d'une maison de haute couture.

covalent ['kəʊ'veɪlənt] *adj Ch* covalent.

cove¹ [kəʊv] *n Geog* anse *f*, petite baie.

cove² *n Old-fashioned Br F* type *m*; **a queer c.,** un drôle de pistolet.

coven ['kʌv(ə)n] *n* bande *f ou* réunion *f* de sorcières.

covenant¹ ['kʌvənənt] *n* **(a)** *Jur* convention *f*, contrat *m*; **(b)** *Pol* pacte *m*, traité *m*; **(c)** *Rel Hist* pacte *m*, covenant *m*.

covenant² *Jur* **1** *vt* promettre (*qch*) par contrat; stipuler (*une somme*); **to c. to do sth,** convenir de *ou* s'engager à faire qch. **2** *vi* **to c. with s.o. for sth,** convenir (par contrat) de qch avec qn.

Coventry ['kʌvəntrɪ, 'kɒv-] *n Br F* **to send s.o. to C.,** mettre qn en quarantaine.

cover¹ ['kʌvər] *n* **(a)** (*soft covering*) couverture *f* (*de lit etc*); fourreau *m* (*de parapluie*); *Nau* étui *m* (*de canot*); **loose c.,** (*for chair*) housse *f*; *Aut* **car c.,** housse; *Met* **heavy cloud c.,** forte nébulosité;

(b) (*lid etc*) couvercle *m* (*de marmite etc*); cloche *f* (*pour plat*); capuchon *m* (*de ventilateur*); calotte *f* (*d'une pompe*); plaque *f* (*d'égout*); *Nau* capot *m* (*de cabestan*); *MecE etc* **c. plate,** plaque de couverture;

(c) (*of book, magazine*) couverture *f*; (*in bookbinding*) les plats *mpl*; **to read a book from c. to c.,** lire un livre d'un bout à l'autre; **the picture on the (front) c.,** la photographie se trouvant sur la première page de couverture; **c. girl,** cover-girl *f*, *pl* cover-girls; *Journ* **c. story,** article principal (*illustré en couverture*);

(d) (*envelope*) enveloppe *f*, pli *m*; **under separate c.,** sous pli séparé; **first-day c.,** (*for philatelists*) enveloppe premier jour;

(e) (*shelter from weather*) abri *m*; **to take c.,** (*from the rain etc*) se mettre à l'abri; **they took c. under a tree,** ils se sont mis à l'abri sous un arbre; **take c.!,** garez-vous!; **the rocks gave us some c.,** les rochers nous ont fourni un abri; **to be under c.,** être à couvert *ou* à l'abri;

(f) *Mil etc* (*from gunfire etc*) couvert *m*, abri; (*firing*) tir *m* de soutien *ou* de protection; **under c.,** à couvert, à l'abri; **to take c.,** se mettre à couvert, s'abriter; **the rocks provided c. for snipers,** les rochers ont fourni des abris pour les tireurs isolés; **without c.,** (à) découvert; **air/radar c.,** couverture aérienne/radar;

(g) (*in hunting*) couvert *m*, fourré *m*; gîte *m*, remise *f*; **to take c.,** se remiser; **to break c.,** sortir de son terrier; *Fig* (*of person*) sortir de sa retraite;

(h) (*something that conceals*) voile *m*, masque *m*; **under (the) c. of,** sous le couvert de (*la nuit etc*); sous le masque de (*l'amitié etc*); **to blow s.o.'s c.,** (*in espionage, undercover police work*) démasquer qn;

(i) (*in insurance*) couverture *f*, provision *f*; **with/without c.,** (*opérer*) avec couverture/à découvert; **full c.,** garantie totale; **c. note,** garantie *f*;

(j) (*in restaurant*) couvert *m*; **c. charge,** couvert;

(k) *Mus* **c. (version)** nouvelle version.

cover² *vt* **(a)** couvrir (*qn, qch*) (**with,** de); **covered in** *or* **with snow,** couvert de neige *ou* par la neige; **to c. one's head,** se couvrir (la tête); **to c. one's ears,** (*so as not to hear*) se boucher les oreilles; **writing covered the page,** une écriture couvrait la page; **the scarf covered her mouth,** l'écharpe lui couvrait la bouche; **the car drove past, covering us with dust,** la voiture nous a dépassés en nous couvrant de poussière; **to be well covered,** (*warmly dressed*) être chaudement vêtu; *F* (*plump, fat*) être bien en chair; **to c. s.o. with ridicule,** couvrir qn de ridicule; **covered with shame,** couvert de honte; **to c. oneself with glory,** se couvrir de gloire;

(b) *Tech* (*coat etc*) couvrir, recouvrir; tapisser (*un mur*) (**with,** de); (*in bookbinding*) couvrir (*un livre*); *El etc* recouvrir (*un fil conducteur*);

(c) (*hide*) couvrir, dissimuler (*son inquiétude, sa confusion etc*); **to c. one's tracks,** dépister ses adversaires;

(d) *Mil etc* protéger (*une frontière etc*); couvrir (*qn*); **to c. s.o. with a pistol,** mettre *ou* tenir qn en joue; *F* **I've got you covered,** (*I have a gun aimed at you*) je te tiens!;

(e) (*deal with, take into account*) couvrir; **the course covers the first half of the century,** le cours couvre la première moitié du siècle; **to c. all eventualites,** parer à toute éventualité; **that's not covered,** ce n'est pas traité; **it's covered in some detail,** c'est traité en détail;

(f) (*travel*) couvrir, parcourir (*une distance*); **we covered 100 kilometres before breakfast,** nous avons fait cent kilomètres avant le petit déjeuner; **to c. a great deal** *or* **a lot of ground,** (*travel great distance*) faire beaucoup de chemin; (*travel, search etc over a wide area*) parcourir un champ très vaste; *Fig* (*of book, author etc*) couvrir de nombreux domaines;

(g) (*in insurance etc*) couvrir (*un risque*); *Fin* **to be covered,** (*of creditor*) être à couvert; **we're not covered against** *or* **for theft,** nous ne sommes pas couverts contre *ou* pour le vol; **to c. oneself,** se couvrir (**against a risk,** d'un risque); *Fig* **the president covered himself by saying that it was not his responsibility,** le président s'est couvert en disant que cela ne relevait pas de sa responsabilité.

(h) (*of money*) couvrir; **£100 won't c. the cost of a new carpet,** 100 livres ne couvriront pas le coût d'une moquette neuve; **that should c. the cost of your ticket,** cela devrait couvrir le coût de votre billet; **to c. (one's) expenses,** couvrir *ou* rentrer dans ses frais; **to c. a deficit,** combler un déficit; **will that c. it?,** est-ce que ça suffira?;

(i) *Journ* couvrir (*un événement sportif etc*);

(j) (*in breeding*) couvrir, saillir (*la femelle*);

(k) *Mus* **to c. a song,** faire une nouvelle version d'une chanson.

►**cover for** *vipo* (*replace*) remplacer (*qn*).

►**cover in** *vtsep* (*fill in*) recouvrir (*une canalisation sous terre etc*); remplir (*une tranchée*).

►**cover up 1** *vtsep* **(a)** (*conceal*) recouvrir; dissimuler (*la vérité, des illégalités*); **(b)** (*cover*) couvrir, recouvrir; **keep the baby covered up,** garde le bébé bien couvert; **they covered up the bodies,** ils ont recouvert les corps; **that dress is a bit too low — c. yourself up a bit,** cette robe est trop décolletée — couvre-toi un peu. **2** *vi* **(a)** (*conceal something*) cacher la vérité; **don't try to c. up — I know it was you,** n'essaye pas de me cacher la vérité — je sais que c'était toi; **to c. up for s.o.,** servir de couverture à qn; **architects and builders are covering up for each other,** les architectes et les entrepreneurs se protègent les uns les autres; **(b)** *Boxing* se couvrir.

coverage ['kʌvərɪdʒ] *n* **(a)** *Journ etc* compte-rendu *m* sur un sujet; **news c.,** (ensemble *m* des) informations *fpl*; **some people objected to XTV's c. of these events,** certaines personnes ont protesté contre la manière dont XTV a traité ces événements; **there was no c. of this match,** il n'y a pas eu de programme consacré à ce match; **the c. given to the elections was biased,** le compte-rendu des élections était partial; **the book gives good c. of the coup,** le livre fournit un bon récit du coup; **sports get too much c. on TV,** on voit trop de sport à la télé; **(b)** (*in insurance*) couverture *f*, provision *f*.

coverall(s) ['kʌvərɔːl, -z] *n*(*pl*) *Am* bleu(s) *m*(*pl*) (de travail).

covered ['kʌvəd] *adj* **(a)** couvert; **c. market,** marché couvert; **c. way,** chemin couvert; *esp US* **c. wagon,** charrette *f* à bâche; **(b)** (*by insurance policy*) (*risk*) couvert; (*person*) assuré.

covering ['kʌvərɪŋ] **1** *adj* **(a) c. letter,** lettre explicative; *Com* **c. note,** garantie *f*; **(b)** *Mil* (*forces, troupes*) de couverture; **c. fire,** tir *m* de soutien *ou* de protection. **2** *n* **(a)** (*act*) action *f* de couvrir (*qch*); (*in breeding*) action de couvrir (*la femelle*); **(b)** (*for protection*) enveloppe *f*, revêtement *m*, recouvrement *m*; (*of chocolate*) couche *f*; (*on furniture*) housse *f*; **(c)** (*of snow, dust*) couche *f*.

coverlet ['kʌvəlɪt] *n* dessus *m* de lit.

covert¹ ['kʌvət] *adj* (*threat etc*) caché, voilé; (*action etc*) clandestin.

covert² *n* **(a)** (*in hunting*) couvert *m*; fourré *m*; **(b)** *Orn* **coverts,** plumes tectrices (*de la queue, des ailes*).

covertly ['kʌvətlɪ] *adv* secrètement.

cover-up ['kʌvərʌp] *n* dissimulation *f* (*d'une irrégularité etc*); **the president denied there had been a c.-up,** le président a nié le fait qu'il y ait eu une dissimulation.

covet ['kʌvɪt] *vt* **(-t-)** convoiter (*les biens, la femme etc d'autrui*); ambitionner, aspirer à (*qch*), **to c. a title/honour** *etc*, convoiter un titre/un honneur/*etc*; **a highly coveted prize,** un prix très convoité.

covetous ['kʌvɪtəs] *adj* (*person*) avide (**of gain,** de gain); (*regard*) de convoitise; **to be c. of s.o.'s property,** convoiter les biens d'autrui.

covetously [kʌvɪtəslɪ] *adv* avec convoitise.

covetousness ['kʌvɪtəsnɪs] *n* **(a)** (*greed*) cupidité *f*, avidité *f*; **(b)** (*for particular thing*) convoitise *f*.

covey ['kʌvɪ] *n* compagnie *f*, vol *m* (*de perdrix etc*).

cow¹ [kaʊ] *n* **(a)** vache *f*; **milch** *or* **milking c.,** vache laitière; *Fig* **milch c.,** (*person*) vache à lait; **c. in** *or* **with calf,** vache pleine; **till the cows come home,** (*attendre*) jusqu'à la semaine des quatre jeudis; (*disputer, parler*) à n'en plus finir; **sacred c.,** *Rel* vache sacrée; *Fig* institution *f* intouchable; **c. parsley,** (*plant*) cerfeuil *m* sauvage; **(b)** *Sl* (*woman*) peau *f* de vache; **she wouldn't let me in the house, the c.!,** elle n'a pas voulu me laisser entrer dans la maison, la peau de vache!; **old c.,** vache *f*, vieille bique; **silly c.,** idiote; **(c)** (*of seal etc*) femelle *f*; **c. elephant,** éléphant *m* femelle.

cow² *vt* intimider, dompter (*qn*); **to look cowed,** avoir l'air d'un chien battu.

coward ['kaʊəd] *n* lâche *mf*, poltron, -onne; **I'm a terrible c. in the dark,** j'ai bien peur quand il fait noir; **he's a moral c.,** c'est un lâche, *F* il n'aime pas se mouiller.

cowardice ['kaʊədɪs] **, cowardliness** ['kaʊədlɪnəs] *n* lâcheté *f*, poltronnerie *f*.

cowardly ['kaʊədlɪ] *adj* lâche.

cowbell ['kaʊbel] *n* clochette *f* (*pour bétail*).

cowboy ['kaʊbɔɪ] *n* **(a)** cowboy *m*; **to play cowboys and indians,** jouer aux cowboys et aux indiens; **c. film,** film *m* de cowboys; **(b)** *Br F Pej* (*careless or dishonest workman*) petit rigolo; **a bunch of cowboys,** des petits rigolos.

cowcatcher ['kaʊkætʃər] *n US Rail* chasse-bestiaux *m*.

cower ['kaʊər] *vi* se tapir (à terre); **to c. before s.o.,** (*show fear*) trembler devant qn.

cowhand ['kaʊhænd] *n* vacher *m*, cowboy *m*.

cowherd ['kaʊhɜːd] *n* vacher *m*, bouvier *m*.

cowhide ['kaʊhaɪd] *n* peau *f* ou cuir *m* de vache.

cowl¹ [kaʊl] *n* **(a)** *Rel* (*hood*) capuchon *m*; (*habit*) habit *m* à capuchon; **c. neck,** (*on sweater*) col *m* cagoule *ou* boule; **(b)** *Tech* (*of chimney*) capuchon *m*, abat-vent *m inv*; *Av Nau* capot *m* (*de moteur, de cheminée*).

cowl² *vt* capuchonner (*une cheminée*).

cowled [kaʊld] *adj* (en)capuchonné.

cowlick ['kaʊlɪk] *n F* épi *m* (*de cheveux*).

cowling ['kaʊlɪŋ] *n* **(a)** (*of chimney*) capuchonnement *m*; **(b)** *Av* (*of engine*) capot *m*.

cowman, *pl* **-men** ['kaʊmæn, -men] *n* vacher *m*; *US* (*rancher*) propriétaire *m* d'un ranch.

co-worker ['kəʊ'wɜːkər] *n* collègue *mf*.

cowpat ['kaʊpæt] *n* bouse *f* de vache.

cowpoke ['kaʊpəʊk] *n US Sl* cowboy *m*.

cowpox ['kaʊpɒks] *n Vet* cowpox *m*, vaccine *f*.

cowpuncher ['kaʊpʌntʃər] *n US F* cowboy *m*.

cowrie ['kaʊərɪ] *n* (*mollusc*) porcelaine *f*.

cowshed ['kaʊʃed] *n* étable *f*.

cowslip ['kaʊslɪp] *n* (fleur *f* de) coucou *m*, primevère commune.

cox¹ [kɒks] *n Sp* (*in rowing*) barreur *m*.

cox² *vt & vi Sp* (*in rowing*) gouverner (*un canot*), barrer.

coxswain ['kɒks(ə)n] *n* barreur *m*.

coy [kɔɪ] *adj* (*shy*) timide; *Pej* qui fait la sainte-nitouche; **to go all c.,** (*of child*) *& Pej* faire son *ou* sa timide; **with a c. little smile,** (*seductive*) avec un petit sourire séducteur; **why be so c. about accepting?,** pourquoi faire semblant d'hésiter?; **he was rather c. about the price,** il était plutôt évasif quant au prix.

Coy *Mil abbr* **company**.

coyly ['kɔɪlɪ] *adv* timidement; *Pej* en faisant son *ou* sa timide.

coyness ['kɔɪnɪs] *n* (*shyness*) timidité *f*; *Pej* fausse timidité; (*evasiveness*) réserve *m*.

coyote [kɔɪ'jəʊtɪ] *n* (*animal*) coyote *m*.

coypu ['kɔɪpuː] *n* (*animal*) coypou *m*, vagondin *m*.

coziness ['kəʊzɪnɪs] *n Am* = **COSINESS**.

cozy ['kəʊzɪ] *adj Am* = **COSY**.

cp (*abbr* **compare**) comparer.

Cpl *Mil abbr* **Corporal**.

CPU [siːpiː'juː] *n Compt abbr* **central processing unit**.

crab¹ [kræb] *n* **(a)** (*crustacean*) crabe *m*; **fiddler c.,** crabe appelant; *Culin* **c. paste,** pâte *f* de crabe; **c. pot,** casier *m* à crabes; **(b)** *Sl* **c. (louse),** morpion *m*; **to have crabs,** avoir des morpions; **(c)** *Astron* **the C.,** (*constellation*) le Cancer; (*nebula*) le Crabe; **(d)** *Ind etc* chariot *m* (*de pont roulant*).

crab² *n Bot* **c. (apple),** pomme *f* sauvage; **c. (apple tree),** pommier *m* sauvage.

crab³ *vi F* être critique (**about sth/s.o.** à propos de qch/qn).

crabbed ['kræbɪd] *adj* **(a)** (*person*) maussade, grincheux; **(b)** (*style*) entortillé; (*writing*) en pattes de mouche.

crabby ['kræbɪ] *adj* = **CRABBED (a)**.

crack¹ [kræk] **1** *n* **(a)** (*split*) fente *f*, fissure *f*; (*in skin, wood*) gerçure *f*; (*in wrought steel etc*) tapure *f*; (*in wall, ground*) crevasse *f*, lézarde *f*; (*in varnish, enamel*) craquelure *f*; (*in glass, pottery, bell etc*) fêlure *f*; *Fig* **to paper over the cracks,** masquer les défauts;

(b) (*of door etc*) entrebâillement *m*; **open the window a c.,** ouvrez la fenêtre un petit peu; *Fig* **at the c. of dawn,** à la pointe du jour;

(c) (*sound*) craquement *m* (*de branches, de glace etc*); claquement *m* (*de fouet*); détonation *f*, claquement sec (*d'une arme à feu*); crépitement *m* (*d'une fusillade*); *Fig F* **to have a c. at sth,** essayer de faire qch; **to give s.o.** *or* **let s.o. have a c. at sth,** laisser qn tenter le coup; *Fig F* **to get a fair c. of the whip,** avoir toutes ses chances; **to give s.o. a fair c. of the whip,** donner toutes ses chances à qn;

(d) *F* (*blow*) **c. on the head,** coup sec sur la tête;

(e) (*gibe*) *F* saillie *f*; **to make a c.,** lancer une blague; **a**

cheap c. about short people, une plaisanterie facile sur les gens de petite taille; **nasty c.,** plaisanterie acérée;
(f) *(illegal drug)* crack *m*; **c. house,** = établissement où a lieu le trafic de crack.
2 *adj F* d'élite; **c. shot,** fin tireur, tireur d'élite; **c. regiment,** régiment *m* d'élite; *Sp* **c. player,** as *m* crack.

crack² *int* clac!, crac!, pan!

crack³ 1 *vt* **(a)** *(damage, break etc)* fêler *(une cloche, un verre)*; gercer *(la peau)*; lézarder, crevasser *(un mur, la terre)*; fendre *(une pierre etc)*; fracturer *(un os)*; **to c. a nut,** *(with nutcrackers)* casser une noisette; *(with teeth)* croquer une noisette sous la dent; **to c. a bottle of wine (with s.o.),** vider une bouteille de vin (avec qn);
(b) *(make sound)* faire claquer *(un fouet)*; faire craquer *(ses doigts)*;
(c) *F* **to c. s.o. over the head,** assommer qn;
(d) *(solve)* résoudre *(un problème)*; décrypter *(un chiffre)*; percer *(un coffre-fort)*; **I think I've cracked it,** je crois que j'y suis arrivé;
(e) *(make)* **to c. a joke,** faire *ou* lâcher une plaisanterie; **to c. jokes,** raconter des blagues; **'where are you going, the North Pole?', he cracked,** 'où est-ce que tu vas, au Pôle Nord?', a-t-il plaisanté;
(f) *Ind* fractionner *(une huile lourde)*.
2 *vi* **(a)** *(become cracked)* se fêler; *(of wall)* se lézarder; *(of skin)* se gercer; *(of steel)* s'égrener; *(of paint, varnish)* se fendiller;
(b) *(of voice)* se casser; *(at puberty)* muer;
(c) *(of person, health)* s'effondrer; *F* **she cracked under the strain of the work,** *(had a nervous breakdown)* elle a craqué sous la pression du travail; *F* **the boss has finally cracked,** le patron est devenu fou;
(d) *(make sound)* craquer; *(of whip)* claquer; **a rifle cracked,** un coup de fusil a retenti.

►crack down *vi (become stricter)* devenir plus strict; *(inflict punishment)* sévir.

►crack down on *vipo (become stricter)* prendre des mesures plus sévères *ou* énergiques contre *(qch)*; *(punish)* sévir contre *(l'alcool au volant)*.

►crack up 1 *vi* **(a)** *(break)* se mettre en morceaux, se briser; **the ice is cracking up,** la glace se brise; **(b)** *(collapse)* craquer; **she cracked up under the strain,** elle a craqué sous la pression; **our marriage is cracking up,** notre mariage s'écroule; **(c)** *F (be helpless with laughter)* s'écrouler; **I cracked up when she said that,** je me suis écroulé quand elle a dit ça. **2** *vtsep F (praise)* **it's not all it's cracked up to be,** ce n'est pas tout ce qu'on en dit; **to c. s.o./sth up,** vanter *ou* prôner qn/qch.

crackbrained ['krækbreɪnd] *adj F (person)* au cerveau fêlé; **c. idea,** idée folle.

crack-down ['krækdaʊn] *n* mesures *fpl* énergiques (**on sth,** contre un abus); **a government c.-d. on reporting,** restrictions gouvernementales concernant les reportages.

cracked [krækt] *adj F (crazy)* cinglé.

cracker ['krækər] *n* **(a)** *(biscuit)* biscuit sec, cracker *m*; *Am* **c. barrel,** boîte *f* à biscuits; **(b)** *Br F (excellent thing)* merveille *f*; *(pretty woman)* canon *m*; **that joke was a c.!,** cette plaisanterie était une merveille!; **(c)** *(noisemaker)* pétard *m*; **Christmas c.,** diablotin *m*; **jumping c.,** crapaud *m*; **(d) (pair of) nut crackers,** casse-noisette(s) *m inv*, casse-noix *m inv*.

crackerjack ['krækədʒæk] **1** *n Am F* = **CRACKER (b). 2** *adj* rupin, chouette.

crackers ['krækəz] *adj Br F* **he's c.,** il est cinglé *ou* loufoque; **to go c.,** perdre la raison *ou F* la boule.

crackhead ['krækhed] *n (drug addict)* consommateur, -trice de crack.

cracking ['krækɪŋ] **1** *adj F* **(a)** excellent, épatant; **to be in c. (good) form,** être en pleine forme; **at a c. pace,** à fond de train; **(b) to get c.,** s'y mettre; **they got c. with their work,** ils se sont mis au travail; **get c.!,** grouille-toi! **2** *n* **(a)** *(sound)* claquement *m*, craquement *m*; **(b)** *(of paint)* craquelure *f*, craquelage *m*; **(c)** *Ind (of oil)* fractionnement *m*, craquage *m*.

crackle¹ ['kræk(ə)l] *n* **(a)** *(sound)* craquement *m*; crépitement *m*, crépitation *f*; *Rad* crachements *mpl*; **(b)** *(finish)* craquelure *f (de peinture, de porcelaine)*; *Cer* **c. finish,** craquelage *m*; **(c)** *Cer* craquelé *m*.

crackle² **1** *vi* **(a)** *(of dried leaves etc)* craquer; *(of shots)* crépiter; *(of snow, something frying)* grésiller; *(of fire)* pétiller; *Rad* crachoter; **(b)** *(form cracks)* se fendiller; se craqueler. **2** *vt* fendiller; *Cer* craqueler.

crackleware ['kræk(ə)lweər] *n Cer* craquelé *m*.

crackling ['kræklɪŋ] **1** *adj* pétillant, crépitant. **2** *n* **(a)** = **CRACKLE¹ (a)**; **(b)** *Cer (process)* craquelage *m*; **(c)** *Br Culin* peau croquante *(du porc rôti)*, couenne *f*; **(d)** *Old-fashioned Br Sl* **a nice bit of c.,** une belle pépée.

crackpot ['krækpɒt] *F* **1** *n* cerveau fêlé; **he's a c.,** il est cinglé. **2** *adj (idea, scheme)* fou.

crackup ['krækʌp] *n* débâcle *f (d'un système)*; effondrement *m (de la raison, de la santé)*.

cradle¹ ['kreɪd(ə)l] *n* **(a)** berceau *m (d'un enfant, d'une civilisation)*; *Nau* cadre *m (d'hôpital)*; **wicker c.,** moïse *m*; **from the c.,** dès le berceau; **from the c. to the grave,** du berceau au tombeau; **to have c. cap,** *(of baby)* avoir des croûtes de lait; *F* **to rob the c.,** les prendre au berceau *ou* au biberon; *F* **I don't go in for robbing the c.** *or* **c. robbing** *or* **snatching,** je ne les prends pas au berceau *ou* au biberon; *F* **he's/she's a c. snatcher,** il/elle les prend au berceau *ou* au biberon; **(b)** *Ind etc* berceau *m (d'une machine etc)*; cadre *m*; *Constr Min* pont volant; sellette *f (de peintre)*; *Min* **c. (rocker),** *(for gold)* berceau; *Cin* **c. head,** trépied *m* à bascule *(pour prise de vues)*; **(c)** *Agr (of scythe)* râteau *m*, crochets *mpl*; **(d)** *Med (splint)* gouttière *f*; *(over bed)* cerceau *m*, arceau *m*; **(e)** *Tel* support *m (de combiné)*.

cradle² *vt* **(a)** mettre *ou* coucher *(qn)* dans un berceau; **cradled in luxury,** bercé dans le luxe; **(b)** *(in one's arms)* bercer *(qn)*; tenir *(qch)* délicatement; **to c. a child in one's arms,** bercer un enfant dans ses bras; **he cradled the rifle in his arms,** il serrait le fusil dans ses bras.

cradlesong ['kreɪd(ə)lsɒŋ] *n Mus* berceuse *f*.

craft [krɑːft] *n* **(a)** *(profession)* profession *f*; *(art)* art *m*; *(activity)* métier manuel; *Sch* travaux manuels; **the c. of weaving,** l'art du tissage; **arts and crafts,** artisanat *m* d'expression; **painter who is master of his c.,** peintre qui a du métier; *Sch* **c. class,** classe *f* de travaux manuels; **c. teacher,** professeur *m* de travaux manuels; **(b)** *(skill)* habileté *f*, adresse *f*; *Pej* ruse *f*, artifice *m*; **(c)** *(craftsmen, -women)* corps *m* de métier; **(d)** *Nau (pl* **craft)** embarcation *f*, petit navire; **small c.,** canots *mpl*, petits bateaux.

craftily ['krɑːftɪlɪ] *adv* astucieusement.

craftiness ['krɑːftɪnɪs] *n* ruse *f*, *F* roublardise *f*.

craftsman, *pl* **-men** ['krɑːftsmən] *n* **(a)** *(artisan)* artisan *m*, ouvrier qualifié; **(b)** *(artist)* artiste *m* dans son métier; **this is the work of a c.,** c'est l'œuvre d'un spécialiste *ou* de quelqu'un qui s'y connaît.

craftsmanship ['krɑːftsmənʃɪp] *n (skill)* dextérité manuelle; *(knowledge, experience)* (connaissance *f* du) métier *m*; **a wonderful piece of c.,** un chef-d'œuvre merveilleux; **think of the c. that has gone into making this table!,** songe à la dextérité qu'il a fallu pour faire cette table!

craftswoman, *pl* **-women** ['krɑːftswʊmən, -wɪmɪn] *n* artiste *f* dans son métier.

crafty ['krɑːftɪ] *adj* astucieux, rusé, malin, *F* roublard.

crag [kræg] *n* rocher *ou* flanc de montagne escarpé, rocher à pic; **overhanging c.,** rocher en surplomb.

craggy ['krægɪ] *adj* **(a)** *(rocky)* rocailleux; **(b)** *(face)* anguleux, taillé à coups de serpe.

cram [kræm] *v* **(-mm-) 1** *vt* **(a)** fourrer (**sth into sth,** qch dans qch); **they crammed 60 people into the bus,** ils ont entassé 60 personnes dans le bus; **cupboards crammed with linen,** armoires bourrées de linge; **at school they crammed our heads with facts,** à l'école, ils nous ont bourré le crâne (d'informations); **to c. s.o. with food,** bourrer qn de nourriture; **to c. food into one's mouth,** s'empiffrer, se bâfrer; **(b)** *Sch* faire bachoter *(un candidat pour un examen)*; **to c. maths,** *(of student)* potasser ferme les maths; **(c)** *Agr* appâter, gaver *(de la volaille)*. **2** *vi F* **(a)** s'entasser; **we all crammed into the car,** nous nous sommes tous entassés dans la voiture; **(b)** *Sch F* potasser, se bourrer le crâne; **to c. for an exam,** = bachoter; **(c)** se gorger de nourriture; se gaver (**with,** de).

►cram in 1 *vtsep (force in)* entasser; **they crammed in more clothes,** ils ont entassé encore d'autres vêtements. **2** *vi (enter)* s'entasser; **100 people crammed in,** 100 personnes se sont entassées.

cram-full ['kræm'fʊl] *adj (train, room etc)* bondé; **the streets were c.-f. of people,** les rues grouillaient de monde.

crammer ['kræmər] *n Sch F (person)* = bachoteur *m*; *(school)* boîte *f* à bac.

cramming ['kræmɪŋ] *n* **(a)** *(forcing in)* entassement *m*; **(b)** *Sch F* bachotage *m*, bourrage *m* de crâne *(pour un examen)*; **(c)** *Agr (of poultry)* gavage *m*.

cramp¹ [kræmp] *n Med* crampe *f*; **writer's c.,** crampe des écrivains; **to have c.** *or Am* **cramps,** être pris d'une crampe.

cramp² *n Carp* serre-joint(s) *m inv*; *(on printing press)*

cornière *f*; *Constr etc* **c. (iron),** crampon *m*.
cramp³ *vt* **(a)** gêner (*les mouvements, l'esprit etc*); **to be cramped up in a small space,** être à l'étroit; *F* **to c. s.o.'s style,** priver qn de ses moyens; **(b)** *Constr* cramponner, agrafer (*des pierres etc*); *Carp etc* serrer (*au serre-joint*).
cramped [kræmpt] *adj* (*pièce*) étriqué; (*écriture*) gêné; (*style*) contraint; **it's very c. in this office,** on est très à l'étroit dans ce bureau; **to live/work in c. conditions,** vivre/travailler dans un espace restreint; **to be c. for space,** être *ou* se sentir à l'étroit.
crampon ['kræmpən] *n* crampon *m* à glace.
cranberry ['krænbərɪ] *n* canneberge *f*; *Culin* **c. sauce,** sauce *f* à la canneberge; **c. juice,** jus *m* de canneberge.
crane¹ [kreɪn] *n* **(a)** *MecE etc* grue *f*; *Cin* grue de prise de vue; **jib c.,** grue à volée *ou* à flèche; *Aut* **breakdown c.,** grue de dépannage, grue dépanneuse; **c. driver** *or* **operator,** conducteur *m* de grue, grutier *m*; **c. fly,** tipule *f*; **(b)** (*bird*) grue *f*; **crowned c.,** grue couronnée.
crane² **1** *vt* tendre, allonger (*le cou*); **to c. one's neck to see sth,** se hausser pour voir qch. **2** *vi* **to c. forward,** allonger le cou *ou* la tête en avant.
crane's-bill, cranesbill ['kreɪnzbɪl] *n* bec-de-grue *m*, *pl* becs-de-grue; géranium *m*.
cranial ['kreɪnɪəl] *adj Anat* (*nerf etc*) crânien.
craniology [kreɪnɪ'ɒlədʒɪ] *n* craniologie *f*.
cranium, *pl* **-ia** ['kreɪnɪəm, -ɪə] *n Anat* crâne *m*.
crank¹ [kræŋk] *n MecE Aut* manivelle *f*; cigogne *f* (*de meule à aiguiser*); **c. axle,** essieu coudé.
crank² *vt MecE* couder (*un essieu*).
crank³ *n* **(a)** *F* (*eccentric*) maniaque *mf*, excentrique *mf*; **health food c.,** fanatique *mf* des aliments naturels; **(b)** *Am F* (*ill-tempered person*) personne *f* d'une humeur difficile.
►**crank up** *vtsep* lancer (*le moteur*) à la manivelle.
crankcase ['kræŋk'keɪs] *n Aut* carter *m*.
cranked [kræŋkt] *adj MecE* (*essieu*) coudé.
crankiness ['kræŋkɪnɪs] *n F* **(a)** (*eccentricity*) excentricité *f*; (*whimsicalness*) humeur capricieuse; **(b)** *Am* (*ill-temper*) humeur *f* difficile.
crankshaft ['kræŋkʃɑːft] *n* vilebrequin *m*.
cranky ['kræŋkɪ] *adj F* **(a)** (*eccentric*) excentrique, maniaque; (*whimsical*) capricieux; **(b)** *Am* (*ill-tempered*) d'une humeur difficile.
cranny ['krænɪ] *n* **(a)** fente *f*, lézarde *f*; **(b)** niche *f*; **nooks and crannies,** coins *mpl* et recoins *mpl*.
crap¹ [kræp] *n Sl* **(a)** merde *f*; *Vulg* **to have a c.,** chier; **(b)** *Fig* (*worthless things*) camelote *f*, saloperie *f*; (*nonsense*) foutaise(s) *f(pl)*, connerie(s) *f(pl)*; (*dirty, disgusting substance*) saloperie; **he's listening to that classical c. again,** il est encore en train d'écouter ces conneries classiques; **he eats c. all day long,** il bouffe des saloperies toute la journée; **these books are c.,** ces bouquins, c'est de la connerie *ou* de la merde; **you don't believe all that c. about witches, do you?,** tu ne crois quand même pas à toutes ces conneries sur les sorcières, hein?; **that's c.!, she never said that!,** c'est de la connerie!, elle n'a jamais dit ça!
crap² *adj Sl* (*bad*) merdique; (*stupid*) con; **what a c. programme!,** (*bad*) quelle émission merdique!; (*stupid*) quelle émission conne!
crap³ *vi Vulg* chier.
crap⁴ *n Am* **c. game,** jeu *m* de dés, craps *m*.
crape [kreɪp] *n* **(a)** *Tex* (*material*) crêpe noir (de deuil); **c. band,** brassard *m* de deuil; **(b)** *Med* **c. bandage,** bande *f* Velpeau ®.
crapper ['kræpər] *n Sl* (*toilet*) chiottes *fpl*.
crappy ['kræpɪ] *adj Sl* **(a)** (*dirty*) sale; **(b)** (*bad, stupid*) = **CRAP²**.
craps [kræps] *npl* (*often with sing verb*) *Am* jeu *m* de dés, craps *m*; **to shoot c.,** jouer aux dés.
crapshooter ['kræpʃuːtər] *n Am* joueur, -euse de dés.
crash¹ [kræʃ] **1** *n* **(a)** (*noise*) fracas *m*; **there was a c. as the vase hit the ground,** un fracas s'est fait entendre quand le vase est tombé par terre; **the c. of thunder,** le fracas du tonnerre; **to fall with a c.,** tomber avec fracas;
(b) (*impact*) écrasement *m*; chute *f* (*accidentelle*); *Aut Rail Av* accident *m*; **car/train/plane c.,** accident de voiture/ferroviaire/d'avion; **we were in a c.,** (*car accident*) nous avons eu un accident de voiture; *Aut Admin* **c. barrier,** glissière *f*; *Nau* **c. dive,** plongée *f* raide (*d'un sous-marin*); **c. helmet,** casque protecteur; *Av* **c. landing,** atterrissage brutal;
(c) (*disaster*) catastrophe *f*, débâcle *f*; **financial c.,** débâcle financière, krach *m*; *Fin Hist* **the Wall Street C.,** le krach de Wall Street;
(d) *Sl* **c. pad,** logement *m* temporaire.
2 *int* patatras!; **c. went the vase,** le vase tomba avec un grand fracas; **he drove c. into the wall,** il est allé s'emboutir contre le mur.
crash² **1** *vi* **(a)** (*make sound*) retentir; éclater avec fracas; **the thunder crashed,** (*once*) il y eut un violent coup de tonnerre; (*repeatedly*) le tonnerre retentissait;
(b) (*move*) **to c. (down),** tomber avec fracas; **the bottle crashed against the wall,** la bouteille s'est écrasée contre le mur; **the bookcase came crashing down,** la bibliothèque s'est écroulée avec fracas; **the vase crashed to the ground,** le vase tomba et se brisa avec fracas; **the mast came crashing down,** le mât s'abattit; **to c. through sth,** passer à travers qch avec fracas;
(c) *Aut* entrer en collision; *Av* s'écraser au sol; *Comptr* tomber en panne; **the two cars crashed head on,** les deux voitures se sont tamponnées de front; **to c. into a tree,** s'emboutir sur un arbre, *F* tamponner *ou* entrer dans un arbre;
(d) (*of business, government etc*) sauter.
2 *vt* **(a)** briser, fracasser; *Av* écraser (*son appareil*) au sol; *Comptr* faire tomber en panne; *Aut* **to c. one's car,** avoir un accident avec sa voiture; **to c. the gears,** faire grincer la boîte de vitesses;
(b) *F* **to c. a party,** s'incruster (dans une soirée);
(c) *esp Am Sl* (*sleep*) roupiller, pioncer; (*go to sleep*) se mettre à roupiller; **can I c. at your place tonight?,** je peux pioncer chez toi ce soir?; **he crashed on the floor,** il a roupillé par terre.
crash³ *adj F* **c. course,** cours (*d'instruction*) accéléré; *Admin* **c. programme,** programme *m* choc *ou* d'urgence; **c. diet,** régime *m* choc.
►**crash out** *vi Sl* **(a)** (*go to sleep*) se mettre à roupiller; **I crashed out on the train,** je me suis mis à roupiller dans le train; **(b)** (*spend night*) pioncer (*chez qn*).
crash-dive ['kræʃdaɪv] *v Nau* **1** *vt* faire plonger raide (*un sous-marin*). **2** *vi* plonger raide.
crashing ['kræʃɪŋ] *adj* **a c. bore,** une personne *ou* une besogne *ou* une soirée *etc* assommante.
crash-land ['kræʃ'lænd] *v Av* **1** *vi* atterrir brutalement. **2** *vt* faire atterrir brutalement (*un avion etc*).
crash-proof ['kræʃpruːf] *adj Aut* antichoc *inv*, résistant aux chocs.
crashworthiness ['kræʃwɜːðɪnɪs] *n* (*of vehicle, helicopter*) résistance *f* aux chocs.
crass [kræs] *adj* grossier; **c. stupidity,** stupidité grossière; **c. ignorance,** ignorance *f* crasse.
crate¹ [kreɪt] *n* **(a)** caisse *f* à claire-voie *ou* en voliges; (*for food*) cageot *m*; (*for glass etc*) harasse *f*; (*for bottles*) casier *m*; **wicker c.,** mannequin *m*; **(b)** *Old-fashioned F* (*aircraft*) coucou *m*; (*car*) caisse *f*.
crate² *vt* emballer (*des marchandises*) dans une caisse à claire-voie.
crater¹ ['kreɪtər] *n Geol* cratère *m* (*volcanique, lunaire*); (*shell hole*) entonnoir *m*, cratère; **the explosion had left a c. 20 feet wide,** l'explosion avait laissé un cratère de 6 mètres de large; **c. lake,** lac *m* de cratère; **bomb c.,** cratère formé par une bombe.
cravat [krə'væt] *n* foulard *m*.
crave [kreɪv] **1** *vt* **(a)** (*long for, need*) désirer ardemment, réclamer (*qch*); **child that craves affection,** enfant affamé d'affection; **she craves tobacco,** elle a une envie furieuse de fumer; **(b)** *Lit* (*beg*) **to c. s.o.'s pardon,** demander pardon à qn; **to c. indulgence,** solliciter l'indulgence. **2** *vi* **to c. for sth,** désirer ardemment qch, réclamer qch.
craven ['kreɪv(ə)n] *Lit* **1** *adj* lâche. **2** *n* lâche *mf*.
craving ['kreɪvɪŋ] *n* désir ardent, appétit *m* insatiable (**for,** de); **c. for alcohol,** passion *f* de l'alcool; (*need*) besoin *m* d'alcool; **I have a c. for chocolate,** (*at this moment*) j'ai envie de chocolat.
craw [krɔː] *n* (*of bird*) jabot *m*; *Fig* **it sticks in my c.,** ça me reste en travers de la gorge.
crawfish ['krɔːfɪʃ] *n esp US* = **CRAYFISH**.
crawl¹ [krɔːl] *n* **(a)** (*action*) reptation *f* (*d'un serpent*); *Br F* **pub c.,** tournée *f* des bars; **(b)** (*slow pace*) **to go along at a c.,** (*on foot*) traîner les pieds; (*in vehicle*) avancer très lentement; **the traffic had slowed to a c.,** la circulation avait ralenti et on roulait au pas; **(c)** *Swimming* crawl *m*; **to do the c.,** faire *ou* nager le crawl, crawler.
crawl² *vi* **(a)** (*of person*) marcher à quatre pattes; (*of snake, worm, baby*) ramper; **he crawled to the ditch,** il se traîna jusqu'au fossé; **to c. on one's hands and knees,** aller à quatre pattes; **to c. into a hole,** se glisser dans un trou; **to c. to the door,** gagner la porte en rampant; **(b)** (*move slowly*) avancer lentement; *Aut F* faire du surplace;

(c) (*be infested*) **to be crawling with vermin,** grouiller de vermine; *F* **the streets were crawling with troops,** les rues fourmillaient *ou* grouillaient de militaires; **(d)** *F* (*be obsequious*) **to c. to s.o.,** s'aplatir devant qn, lécher les bottes à qn; **I refuse to c.,** je refuse de m'aplatir; **(e)** *Swimming* crawler, faire le crawl.

crawler ['krɔːlər] *n* **(a)** reptile *m*; animal *m* qui rampe; *Br F* **pub c.,** pilier *m* de cabarets *ou* de bars; *Aut* **c. lane,** voie *f* pour véhicules lents; **(b)** *F* lèche-bottes *m inv*; **(c)** *Swimming* crawleur, -euse; **(d)** (*baby's overalls*) **crawlers,** grenouillère *f*.

crawling ['krɔːlɪŋ] **1** *adj* **(a)** (*baby, snake*) rampant; **(b)** grouillant (**with,** de); **cheese c. with maggots,** fromage qui grouille de vers; **(c)** (*obsequious*) lèche-bottes, lèche-cul. **2** *n* **(a)** (*movement*) reptation *f*; **(b)** (*obsequiousness*) léchage *m* de bottes.

crayfish ['kreɪfɪʃ] *n* **(freshwater) c.,** écrevisse *f*; **(sea) c.,** langouste *f*.

crayon¹ ['kreɪɒn, -ən] *n Art* **(a)** crayon *m* pastel; **(coloured) c.,** crayon de couleur; **(b)** (*drawing*) (dessin *m* au) pastel *m*.

crayon² *vt Art* **(a)** (*draw*) dessiner (*qch*) au pastel; **(b)** (*colour in*) crayonner (*une esquisse*).

craze¹ [kreɪz] *n* manie *f* (**for sth,** de qch); **discotheques are all the c.,** les discothèques font fureur; **this is the latest dance c.,** c'est la dernière danse à la mode.

craze² **1** *vt* **(a)** (*drive insane*) rendre (*qn*) fou; (*unbalance*) déranger (*l'esprit*); **(b)** *Cer* craqueler (*la porcelaine*). **2** *vi Cer* se craqueler.

crazed [kreɪzd] *adj* **(a)** fou, *f* folle (**with grief,** de douleur); affolé (**with fear,** de terreur); **(b)** *Cer etc* craquelé.

-crazed [kreɪzd] *suff* rendu fou par; **drug/power-c.,** rendu fou par la drogue/le pouvoir; **he was half-c. with grief,** la douleur l'avait rendu à moitié fou.

crazily ['kreɪzɪlɪ] *adv* follement; (*to lean*) bizarrement.

craziness ['kreɪzɪnɪs] *n* (*of person*) folie *f*, démence *f*.

crazy ['kreɪzɪ] *adj* **(a)** (*person*) fou, *f* folle (à lier), *F* toqué; (*idea etc*) saugrenu, insensé, *F* dingue; **c. with fear,** fou de terreur; *F* **to go c.,** devenir fou (**with anger,** de colère); **to drive** *or* **send s.o. c.,** rendre qn fou; **you're c.!,** vous êtes fou!; **but that's c. — we've only just arrived!,** mais c'est dingue – nous venons juste d'arriver!; **to be c. about** *or* **over s.o./sth,** être fou de qn/qch; **like c.,** comme un enragé; *US* **c. bone,** le petit juif; **(b)** *F* (*dress, building, angle etc*) bizarre; **c. paving,** = dallage irrégulier en pierres plates; **(c)** *esp Am Sl* (*very good*) fou, dément; **2** *n esp Am Sl* (*person*) original, -ale; **c. house,** asile *f ou* maison *f* de fous.

CRE [siːɑːr'iː] *n Br Admin* (*abbr* **Commission for Racial Equality**) = commission pour l'égalité raciale.

creak¹ [kriːk] *n* cri *m*, grincement *m* (*de gonds etc*); craquement *m* (*du bois, de chaussures neuves etc*).

creak² *vi* (*of hinge etc*) grincer; (*of timber, shoes*) craquer; **the chair creaked under his weight,** la chaise grinçait *ou* craquait sous son poids.

creaking ['kriːkɪŋ] **1** *adj* (*hinge etc*) qui crie, qui grince; (*timber, shoes*) qui craque. **2** *n* (*of hinge*) cri(s) *m(pl)*, grincement *m*; (*of timber, shoes*) craquement *m*.

creaky ['kriːkɪ] *adj* (*hinge*) qui grince; (*timber*) qui craque.

cream¹ [kriːm] **1** *n* **(a)** (*of milk*) crème *f*; (*used in cakes etc*) crème fraîche; **single/double c.,** crème fleurette/épaisse; **strawberries and c.,** fraises *fpl* à la crème; **clotted c.,** crème caillée; **whipped c.,** crème fouettée *ou* Chantilly; **c. cake,** gâteau *m* à la crème; **c. puff,** chou *m* à la crème; **c. jug,** pot *m* à crème; **c. sherry,** sherry doux; **c. cheese,** fromage frais; *Br F* **c. cracker,** biscuit sec; *Br* **c. tea,** = repas se composant de thé et de scones servis avec de la crème et de la confiture;
(b) *Fig* (*best part etc*) (le) meilleur, (le) dessus du panier; **they're the c. of the crop,** (*of students, job applicants etc*) c'est le dessus du panier, c'est la crème; **the c. of society,** la crème de la société;
(c) (*filling for chocolate*) fondant *m*; (*individual chocolate*) boule *f* de crème;
(d) (*soup*) **c. of tomato/asparagus soup,** crème *f* de tomate/d'asperges;
(e) (*sauce*) **c. of horseradish,** crème *f* au raifort;
(f) (*lotion etc*) crème *f* (*de toilette, de beauté*); **shoe c.,** crème pour chaussures;
(g) **c. of tartar,** crème *f* de tartre;
(h) (*colour*) crème *f*.
2 *adj* **c.(-coloured),** crème *inv*.

cream² **1** *vt* **(a)** (*remove cream from*) écrémer (*le lait*); **(b)** (*add cream to*) ajouter de la crème à (*son café etc*); **(c)** (*beat*) battre (*du beurre*) en crème; **to c. potatoes,** réduire les pommes de terre en purée; **c. the butter and sugar,** (*in recipe*) battre le beurre et le sucre jusqu'à ce qu'ils forment un mélange mousseux *ou* crémeux; **(d)** *Am Fig* (*beat up*) casser la figure à (*qn*); (*defeat*) battre (*un adversaire*) à plate couture, mettre la pâtée à (*un adversaire*). **2** *vi* (*of milk*) se couvrir de crème, crémer.

►**cream off** *vtsep* (*remove*) **to c. off the best part of sth,** prélever la meilleure partie de qch; **the universities c. off the best students,** les universités écrèment toujours les meilleurs étudiants.

creamed [kriːmd] *adj* **(a)** (*lait*) écrémé; **(b)** *Culin* (*poulet etc*) à la crème; **c. potatoes,** pommes *fpl* de terre en purée.

creamer ['kriːmər] *n Am* **(a)** (*jug*) pot *m* à crème; **(b)** (*for coffee*) succédané *m*.

creamery ['kriːmərɪ] *n* **(a)** (*shop*) crémerie *f*; **(b)** *Agr Ind* coopérative laitière; **c. butter,** beurre laitier.

creamy ['kriːmɪ] *adj* **(a)** (*containing cream*) crémeux; **(b)** (*resembling cream*) crémeux; (*teint*) velouté; **rich c. voice,** voix veloutée; **rich c. sauce,** sauce onctueuse.

crease¹ [kriːs] *n* **(a)** pli *m* (*d'un pantalon etc*); (*accidental*) faux pli, **to remove the creases from sth,** enlever les faux plis de qch; **to put a c. in a pair of trousers,** faire le pli d'un pantalon; **(b)** *Cr* **(batting) c.,** ligne *f* du batteur.

crease² **1** *vt* **(a)** plisser, faire des plis à (*qch*); (*accidentally*) faire des faux plis à, froisser (*une robe etc*); **well-creased trousers,** pantalon avec un pli impeccable; **to be all creased,** (*of dress etc*) être chiffonné; **to c. one's brow,** froncer les sourcils; **(b)** (*of bullet*) frôler (*qn*). **2** *vi* **(a)** (*become creased*) prendre un (faux) pli; se froisser; **(b)** = **CREASE UP 1**.

►**crease up** *Br Sl* **1** *vi* (*laugh uncontrollably*) se tordre (de rire); **I creased up when she said that,** je me suis tordu (de rire) quand elle a dit ça. **2** *vtsep* (*make laugh uncontrollably*) faire rire (*qn*) à se tordre; **he creases me up,** il me fait rire à me tordre.

crease-resistant ['kriːsrɪ'zɪstənt] *adj* infroissable.

create [krɪ'eɪt] **1** *vt* créer (*le monde, un pair, Th un rôle*); créer, susciter (*une difficulté*); faire, produire (*une impression*); **she created a studio out of an old shed,** elle a créé un studio à partir d'une cabane; **if opportunities do not exist you must c. them,** si les occasions n'existent pas, il faut les créer; **the government must c. jobs,** le gouvernement doit créer des emplois; **to c. a scene,** faire une scène; **to c. a disturbance,** troubler l'ordre public. **2** *vi* **(a)** (*be creative*) créer; **(b)** *Br Sl* faire du tapage, faire une scène, rouspéter (**about,** à propos de).

creation [krɪ'eɪʃən] *n* **(a)** (*action*) création *f* (*du monde, d'un titre*); **job c.,** création d'emplois; **(b)** (*product*) création *f*, produit *m*, œuvre *f*; **the latest creations,** les dernières modes; **(c)** (*the universe*) création *f*; *Rel* **(the) C.,** la Création.

creative [krɪ'eɪtɪv] *adj* (*professional artist, designer etc*) créateur, -trice; (*activity, child, amateur artist etc*) créatif, -ive; **c. drive,** impulsion créatrice; **I don't do anything c.,** je ne fais rien de créatif.

creativeness [krɪ'eɪtɪvnɪs], **creativity** [kriə'tɪvɪtɪ] *n* créativité *f*.

creator [krɪ'eɪtər] *n* créateur, -trice (*d'une mode, Th d'un rôle etc*); **the C.,** le Créateur.

creature ['kriːtʃər] *n* **(a)** (*living being*) créature *f*, être *m* (vivant); **creatures from outer space,** extra-terrestres *mpl*; **(b)** (*animal*) animal *m*, bête *f*; **dumb creatures,** les bêtes; **(c)** (*person*) **pretty c.,** jolie créature; **poor c.!,** le *ou* la pauvre!; **c. comforts,** aisance matérielle; **to like one's c. comforts,** aimer ses aises; *Pej* **c. of the government,** homme vendu au gouvernement, instrument *m* du gouvernement; **man is the c. of circumstances,** l'homme dépend des circonstances; **I am a c. of habit,** je suis un homme *ou* une femme d'habitude.

crèche [kreɪʃ, kreʃ] *n Br* (*for children*) crèche *f*; **c. facilities,** garderie *f*; **the centre has c. facilities,** le centre dispose d'une garderie; **(b)** *Rel* crèche *f*.

cred [kred] *n F see* **street cred(ibility)**.

credence ['kriːdəns] *n* croyance *f*, foi *f*; **to give** *or* **attach c. to sth,** ajouter foi à qch; **letter of c.,** lettre *f* de créance.

credentials [krɪ'denʃəlz] *npl* **(a)** (*proof of identity*) pièces justificatives d'identité; (*of a diplomat etc*) lettres *fpl* de créance; **(b)** (*proof of ability*) références *fpl*; **what are your c.?,** quelles sont vos références?; *Fig* **a film director with excellent c.,** un metteur en scène aux excellents antécédents.

credibility [kredɪ'bɪlɪtɪ] *n* (*of person, policy*) crédibilité *f*; **the government has lost c. in the eyes of** *or* **with the**

public, le gouvernement a perdu sa crédibilité aux yeux du public; **the president's actions gave him some c.**, les actions du président lui ont conféré une certaine crédibilité; **c. gap,** manque *m* de crédibilité.

credible ['kredɪb(ə)l] *adj* crédible; **it is hardly c. that ...,** il n'est pas vraisemblable que + *sub* ... .

credit¹ ['kredɪt] *n* **(a)** *Com Fin* crédit *m*; **to be in c.**, avoir de l'argent sur son compte; **to give s.o. c.**, faire crédit à qn; **we do not give c.**, (*of shop*) la maison ne fait pas crédit; **to sell on c.**, vendre à crédit; **to live on c.**, vivre à crédit; **debit and c.**, débit *m* et crédit; **to enter a sum to s.o.'s c.**, porter une somme au crédit *ou* à l'actif de qn, créditer qn d'une somme; **his c. is good,** *Fin* il a une bonne réputation de solvabilité; *Fig* (*is trusted*) on lui fait toute confiance; *Br Banking* **c. account,** compte créditeur; **to open a c. account with s.o.**, ouvrir un crédit chez qn; **c. agency,** institution *f* de crédit; **c. bank,** banque *f* de crédit; **c. balance,** solde créditeur; **c. card,** carte *f* de crédit; *Am* **c. line, line of c.**, ligne *f* de crédit; **c. note,** note *f* de crédit; **c. rating,** degré *m* de solvabilité; **c. squeeze,** resserrement *m* du crédit;
(b) (*influence*) crédit *m*, influence *f* (**with,** auprès de); **he has lost c. with the public,** son crédit a décliné auprès du public; **to gain c.**, (*of theory etc*) acquérir du crédit;
(c) (*belief*) croyance *f*, créance *f*; **to give c. to** *or* **place c. in a rumour,** ajouter foi à un bruit; **facts that lend c. to a rumour,** faits qui accréditent un bruit;
(d) (*merit*) mérite *m*, honneur *m*; **to take c. for an action,** s'attribuer le mérite d'une action; **they took the c., but she did all the work,** ils se sont attribué le mérite, mais c'est elle qui a fait tout le travail; **I can't claim much of the c. for the project's success,** je ne peux pas m'attribuer grand mérite pour la réussite du projet; **most of the c. should go to the actors,** c'est aux acteurs que devrait revenir le plus grand mérite; **with c.**, honorablement; *Sch* (*in an examination*) avec mention assez bien; **I gave him c. for more sense,** je lui supposais plus de jugement; **she's shrewder than most people give her c. for,** elle est plus perspicace que la plupart des gens ne le pensent; **it must be said to her c. that ...,** il faut porter à son crédit que ...; **the team have three wins to their c.**, l'équipe compte trois victoires à son actif; **it does him c.**, cela lui fait (grand) honneur; **your children do you c.** *or* **are a c. to you,** vos enfants vous font honneur; **she is a c. to the school,** elle fait honneur à l'école; **on the c. side, it must be said he was honest enough to own up,** il faut dire en sa faveur qu'il a eu l'honnêteté d'avouer; *Cin* **c. titles, credits,** générique *m*; *Th* crédits, remerciements *mpl*;
(e) *esp US Univ* unité *f* de valeur.

credit² *vt* **(a)** *Com Fin* **to c. s.o./an account with a sum,** créditer qn/un compte d'une somme; **to c. a sum to an account,** porter une somme au crédit d'un compte; **(b)** (*attribute*) attribuer, prêter (**s.o. with a quality,** une qualité à qn); **to c. s.o. with superior intelligence,** créditer qn d'une intelligence supérieure; **I credited you with more sense,** je vous croyais *ou* supposais plus de jugement; **to be credited with having done sth,** passer pour avoir fait qch; **(c)** (*accept as true*) **to c. s.o. with a quality,** reconnaître une qualité à qn; **(d)** (*believe*) ajouter foi à, croire (*un bruit, qn*); *F* **I wouldn't have credited it,** je ne l'aurais pas cru possible; **you wouldn't c. it,** c'est à ne pas croire; *F* **would you c. it?,** tu te rends compte?

creditable ['kredɪtəb(ə)l] *adj* (*action*) estimable, digne d'éloges.

creditably ['kredɪtəblɪ] *adv* honorablement, avec honneur.

creditor ['kredɪtər] *n* créancier, -ière; *Econ* **c. nation,** nation créditrice; **c. account,** compte créditeur.

credo, *pl* **-os** ['kriːdəʊ, 'kreɪ-, -əʊz] *n Rel Mus* credo *m inv*.

credulity [krɪ'djuːlɪtɪ] *n* crédulité *f*; **his story stretched c.**, son histoire était vraiment difficile à croire.

credulous ['kredjʊləs] *adj* crédule.

creed [kriːd] *n* **(a)** *Rel* credo *m inv*; **the (Apostles') C.**, le symbole des Apôtres, le credo; **(b)** (*beliefs*) croyance *f*, foi (confessionnelle); **political c.**, credo politique; **(c)** (*expression of beliefs*) profession *f* de foi.

creek [kriːk] *n esp Br* (*small bay*) crique *f*, anse *f*; *Am Austr New Zealand* (*stream*) ruisseau *m*, petit cours d'eau; *Sl* **to be up the c. (without a paddle),** (*of person*) être dans de beaux draps, être dans le pétrin; (*of plan*) être mal parti.

creel [kriːl] *n* (*fishing basket*) panier *m* de pêche.

creep¹ [kriːp] *n F* **(a) the creeps,** la chair de poule; **to give s.o. the creeps,** (*scare*) donner la chair de poule à qn; (*annoy*) horripiler qn; **(b)** *Sl* (*disgusting person*) personnage répugnant, saligaud *m*; **(c)** *Sl* (*obsequious person*) lèche-bottes *m inv*, lèche-cul *m inv*; **(d)** (*act*) action *f* de ramper; **(e)** (*of metal*) fluage *m*.

creep² *vi* (*pt & pp* **crept** [krept]) **(a)** (*of insect, animal*) ramper; (*of roots*) tracer; (*of person*) se traîner; **to c. into bed,** se glisser dans son lit; **he crept into the room,** il entra furtivement *ou* à pas de loup dans la chambre; *Fig* **a moralizing tone has crept into her writing,** un ton moralisateur s'est insidieusement glissé dans ses écrits; **a feeling of uneasiness crept over me,** un sentiment de gêne commençait à me gagner; **to make s.o.'s flesh c.**, donner la chair de poule à qn; **(b)** *F* (*be obsequious*) ramper (*devant les grands*); **she's always creeping to the teacher,** elle est toujours en train de ramper devant le professeur; **(c)** (*of plant*) ramper; (*upwards*) grimper; **(d)** (*of metal*) subir un fluage.

▶**creep along** *vi* s'avancer en rampant; (*stealthily*) s'avancer furtivement, *F* marcher à pas de loup.

▶**creep away** *vi* s'éloigner en rampant; (*stealthily*) s'éloigner à pas de loup.

▶**creep by** *vi* (*go past stealthily*) passer furtivement; **time** *or* **the hours crept slowly by,** les heures passaient lentement.

▶**creep up** *vi* **(a)** (*approach stealthily*) approcher furtivement, s'approcher furtivement; **she crept up behind me,** elle est arrivée derrière moi tout doucement; **the speedometer crept up to 120,** l'aiguille de l'indicateur de vitesse a avancé lentement *ou* est montée tout doucement jusqu'à 120; **(b)** (*climb*) se traîner jusqu'en haut.

▶**creep up on** *vipo* (*approach stealthily*) surprendre (*qn*), prendre (*qn*) à l'improviste; **old age has crept up on me,** j'ai vieilli sans m'en rendre compte.

creeper ['kriːpər] *n* **(a)** (*plant*) plante rampante; (*climbing*) plante grimpante; **(b) creepers,** (*shoes*) souliers *mpl* à semelles de crêpe; *US* (*crampons*) crampons *mpl* à verglas; **(c)** *Am* **creepers,** (*child's garment*) barboteuse *f*.

creeping ['kriːpɪŋ] **1** *adj* **(a)** (*animal*) rampant; *Med* **c. paralysis,** paralysie progressive; **(b)** *Pej* (*obsequious*) servile, rampant; *Sl* **c. Jesus,** lèche-bottes *m*; **(c)** (*plant*) rampant; (*upwards*) grimpant. **2** *n* **(a)** (*movement*) reptation *f*; **(b)** (*obsequiousness*) servilité *f*.

creepy ['kriːpɪ] *adj F* **(a)** (*film, story*) qui donne la chair de poule; **it was c.**, c'était à vous donner la chair de poule; **a c. old house,** une vieille maison sinistre; **(b)** (*like an insect*) **I could feel c. things on my leg,** je sentais quelque chose qui rampait sur ma jambe.

creepy-crawly ['kriːpɪ'krɔːlɪ] *F* **1** *n* insecte rampant, bestiole rampante; **I hate c.-crawlies,** je déteste les insectes rampants. **2** *adj* **c.-c. feeling,** (sensation *f* de) fourmillement *m*.

cremate [krɪ'meɪt] *vt* incinérer (*un mort*).

cremation [krɪ'meɪʃən] *n* incinération *f*, crémation *f*.

crematorium, *pl* **-ia** [kremə'tɔːrɪəm, -ɪə] *n* crématorium *m*.

crème [krem, kreɪm] *n Culin* crème *f*; **c. caramel,** crème (renversée) au caramel, crème caramel; **c. de menthe,** crème de menthe.

crenellated, *Am* **crenelated** ['krenəleɪtɪd] *adj* (*wall etc*) crénelé.

creole ['kriːəʊl] *Ling* **1** *n* créole *m*. **2** *adj* créole.

Creole ['kriːəʊl] **1** *n* créole *mf*; *US* = descendant, -ante des colons français ou espagnols de la Louisiane. **2** *adj* créole; *US* = qui descend des colons français ou espagnols de la Louisiane.

creosote¹ ['krɪəsəʊt] *n Ch* créosote *f*.

creosote² *vt* créosoter (*le bois*).

crêpe [kreɪp, krep] *n* **(a)** *Tex* crêpe *m*; **c. de Chine,** crêpe de Chine; *Med* **c. bandage,** bande *f* Velpeau ®; **c. skirt,** jupe *f* en crêpe; **(b) c. (rubber),** crêpe *m*; **c.(-rubber) soles,** semelles *fpl* (de) crêpe; **(c) c. paper,** papier *m* crépon; **(d)** *Culin* crêpe *f*; **c. Suzette,** crêpe Suzette.

Cres (*abbr* **Crescent**) rue.

crescendo [krɪ'ʃendəʊ] **1** *n Mus* crescendo *m inv*; **to reach a c.**, atteindre un crescendo. **2** *adv* crescendo.

crescent ['kresənt] **1** *n* (*shape*) croissant *m*; (*street*) rue *f ou* côté *m* de rue en arc de cercle. **2** *adj* **c.(-shaped),** en forme de croissant *ou* de demi-lune; **the c. moon,** le croissant de la lune.

cress [kres] *n Bot Culin* cresson *m*; **garden c.**, cresson alénois, passerage cultivé; **c. soup,** soupe *f* au cresson.

crest [krest] *n* **(a)** crête *f* (*de coq, reptile*); huppe *f* (*d'alouette*); aigrette *f* (*de paon*); (*on animal's neck*) crête du cou; **(b)** cimier *m*, crête *f* (*de casque*); **(c)** crête *f*, sommet *m* (*de colline, d'une vague*); *Phys* crête, point haut

(*d'une onde*); **(d)** *Archit* crête *f*, faîte *m*, faîtage *m*; **(e)** *Anat* crête *f*, arête *f* (*d'un os*); **(f)** *Her* (*on helmet*) cimier *m*; (*on escutcheon*) timbre *m*; (*coat of arms*) armoiries *fpl*; (*insignia*) écusson *m*.
crested ['krestɪd] *adj* **(a)** (*bird*) à crête, à huppe, huppé; (*animal*) à crête, crêté; **white-c. waves,** vagues *fpl* aux crêtes blanches; **(b)** (*helmet*) orné d'un cimier; (*plumed*) panaché; **(c)** *F* (*aristocratic*) armorié; orné d'un écusson.
crestfallen ['krestfɔːl(ə)n] *adj* (*person*) abattu, découragé; (*look*) déconfit; **to look c.,** baisser l'oreille.
cretaceous [krɪ'teɪʃəs] **1** *adj* crétacé. **2** *n Geol* **the C.,** le crétacé.
Cretan ['kriːt(ə)n] **1** *adj* crétois. **2** *n* Crétois, -oise.
Crete [kriːt] *n* Crète *f*.
cretin ['kretɪn] *n Pej & Med* crétin *m*.
cretinism ['kretɪnɪz(ə)m] *n Med* crétinisme *m*.
cretinous ['kretɪnəs] *adj Pej & Med* crétin.
cretonne [kre'tɒn, 'kretɒn] *n Tex* cretonne *f*; **c. curtains,** rideaux *mpl* de cretonne.
crevasse [krɪ'væs] *n* crevasse *f* (glaciaire).
crevice ['krevɪs] *n* fente *f*; lézarde *f* (*de mur*); crevasse *f*, fissure *f* (*de rocher*).
crew¹ [kruː] *n* **(a)** *Nau* équipage *m*; (*in rowing*) équipe *f*; **c. neck,** (*of sweater*) col ras du cou; (*sweater*) pull *m* ras du cou; **c. cut,** (*hairstyle*) cheveux (coupés) en brosse; **(b)** (*gang, team*) équipe *f*; **ambulance/camera c.,** équipe d'ambulanciers/de cameramen; *Av* **air** *or* **flight c.,** équipage *m* (d'avion); *Av* **ground c.,** équipe au sol; *Ind* **maintenance c.,** équipe d'entretien; **c. member,** membre *m* d'équipage *ou* d'équipe (*d'avion, de char etc*); **(c)** (*group of people*) bande *f*, troupe *f*; **sorry c.,** triste engeance *f*; **they're a good c. to work with,** c'est une bonne équipe avec qui travailler.
crew² **1** *vt* armer (*un navire*) d'un équipage; fournir (*un avion etc*) d'un équipage; **yacht that can't be crewed by less than six,** (*operated*) yacht qui exige un équipage de six au moins. **2** *vi* **to c. for s.o.,** servir d'équipier à qn.
crewel ['kruːəl] *n* laine *f* à broder *ou* à tapisserie.
crib¹ [krɪb] *n* **(a)** (*for child*) lit *m* d'enfant; *Rel* (*in Nativity*) crèche *f*; *Am* **c. death,** mort subite du nourrisson; **(b)** *Agr* (*for feeding animals*) mangeoire *f*, râtelier *m*; *Am* huche *f*, coffre *m* (*pour le maïs, le sel etc*); armoire *f* (*à outils*); **(c)** *Br F* (*plagiarism*) plagiat *m*; *Sch* = traduction d'auteur ou corrigé de thèmes etc employés subrepticement; **(d)** = **CRIBBAGE**.
crib² *vt* (-bb-) **1** *vt* reproduire, copier (*un passage d'un auteur*); *Sch* **to c. an exercise from s.o.,** copier un devoir sur qn. **2** *vi Sch* = se servir de traductions ou de corrigés; **to c. from an author,** plagier un auteur.
cribbage ['krɪbɪdʒ] *n Cards* cribbage *m*.
crick¹ [krɪk] *n* foulure *f*; **c. in the back,** tour *m* de reins; **c. in the neck,** torticolis *m*.
crick² *vt* **to c. one's neck,** attraper le torticolis.
cricket¹ ['krɪkɪt] *n* (*insect*) grillon *m*.
cricket² *n Sp* cricket *m*; **to play c.,** jouer au cricket; *Old-fashioned Br Fig* **that's not c.,** cela n'est pas de jeu *ou* ne se fait pas; **c. bat,** batte *f* de cricket; **c. field** *or* **pitch,** terrain *m* de cricket.
cricketer ['krɪkɪtər] *n* joueur, -euse de cricket.
crier ['kraɪər] *n* **town c.,** crieur public *ou* municipal.
crikey ['kraɪkɪ] *int Br Sl* mince alors!
crime [kraɪm] *n* crime *m*; *Jur* délit *m*; **capital c.,** crime capital; *Fig* **it's a c. to cut down this tree,** c'est un crime d'abattre cet arbre; *Fig* **it's not a c. to ...,** ce n'est pas un crime de ...; **to make a study of c.,** étudier le crime *ou* la criminalité; **c. figures,** chiffres *mpl* concernant la criminalité; **c. reporter,** chroniqueur, -euse judiciaire; *Mil* **c. sheet,** feuille *f* de punitions; **c. story,** roman noir; (*detective novel*) roman policier; **c. wave,** vague *f* de criminalité; **c. writer,** auteur *m* de romans noirs; (*of detective novels*) auteur de romans policiers.
Crimea (the) [ðəkraɪ'mɪə] *n* la Crimée.
Crimean [kraɪ'mɪən] *adj Hist* **the C. War,** la guerre de Crimée.
criminal ['krɪmɪn(ə)l] **1** *adj Jur* criminel; **c. act,** action criminelle; **to take c. proceedings against s.o.,** poursuivre qn criminellement; *Br* **the C. Investigation Department,** = la Police Judiciaire, *F* la P.J.; *Fig* **it would be c. to cut down these trees,** ce serait un crime d'abattre ces arbres; **c. action** *or* **case,** action *f ou* cas *m* au criminel; *Jur* **c. conversation,** adultère *m*; **c. court,** cour pénale; **c. law,** droit pénal; **c. lawyer,** avocat *m* au pénal; **c. offence,** délit *m*; (*serious*) crime *m*; **c. record,** casier *m* judiciaire. **2** *n* criminel, -elle.
criminalize ['krɪmɪnəlaɪz] *vt* criminaliser.
criminally ['krɪmɪn(ə)lɪ] *adv* criminellement.
criminologist [krɪmɪ'nɒlədʒɪst] *n* criminologiste *mf*.
criminology [krɪmɪ'nɒlədʒɪ] *n* criminologie *f*.
crimp¹ [krɪmp] *n* frisure *f* (*des cheveux*); sertissage *m* (*d'une cartouche etc*); gaufrage *m*; pli *m* (*d'un drap*).
crimp² *vt* friser (*les cheveux*); gaufrer (à la paille); plisser, crêper (*de l'étoffe etc*); **crimped hair,** cheveux crêpelés à gaufrures.
crimson¹ ['krɪmz(ə)n] *n* cramoisi *m*; **to blush c.,** devenir cramoisi; **c. with rage,** rouge de colère.
crimson² *vi* (*of person, face*) devenir cramoisi.
cringe [krɪndʒ] *vi* **(a)** (*flinch*) se faire tout petit; se blottir (*de peur*); se dérober (*par crainte d'un coup*); **he did not c.,** il n'a pas bronché; **(b)** (*be servile*) s'humilier, ramper, s'aplatir (**to, before s.o.,** devant qn); **(c)** *F* (*be embarrassed*) avoir envie de rentrer sous terre; **her singing makes me c.,** quand elle chante, ça me donne envie de rentrer sous terre.
cringe-making ['krɪndʒmeɪkɪŋ] *adj Br F* qui donne envie de rentrer sous terre.
cringing ['krɪndʒɪŋ] *adj* **(a)** (*afraid*) craintif; **(b)** (*servile*) servile, obséquieux.
crinkle¹ ['krɪŋk(ə)l] *n* pli *m*, ride *f*.
crinkle² **1** *vt* (*usu passive*) froisser, chiffonner (*du papier*); **to c. one's nose,** froncer le nez; **crinkled paper,** papier plissé *ou* gaufré; (*for decoration*) papier crépon. **2** *vi* se froisser; (*of apples, potatoes*) se rider.
crinkly ['krɪŋklɪ] *adj* plein de rides.
crinoline ['krɪn(ə)lɪn] *n Hist* crinoline *f*.
cripes [kraɪps] *int Old-fashioned Br Sl* mince alors!
cripple¹ ['krɪp(ə)l] *n* estropié, -ée, infirme *mf*, invalide *mf*; *Fig* **an emotional c.,** un handicapé sur le plan affectif.
cripple² *vt* **(a)** estropier (*qn*); **the men who were crippled in the war,** les mutilés de guerre; **(b)** *Fig* disloquer (*une machine, un système*); désemparer (*un navire*); paralyser (*l'industrie, la volonté*).
crippled ['krɪp(ə)ld] *adj* **(a)** (*person*) estropié; infirme; **c. with rheumatism,** perclus de rhumatismes; **a c. arm,** un bras malade; **(b)** *Fig* (*vaisseau*) désemparé; (*machine*) hors de fonctionnement; **the country is c. with debt,** le pays est criblé par les dettes.
crippling ['krɪplɪŋ] *adj* **(a)** (*disease etc*) estropiant; **(b)** *Fig* (*taxation, strike etc*) paralysant; **the c. effect of the blockade,** l'effet paralysant du blocus.
crisis, *pl* **-es** ['kraɪsɪs, -iːz] *n* crise *f* (*dans les affaires etc*); **things are coming to a c.,** le moment décisif approche; **to go through a c.,** passer par une crise; **an economy in c.,** une économie en crise; **c. management,** gestion *f* de crises; **c. point,** point *m* critique.
crisp¹ [krɪsp] **1** *adj* (*biscuit, pastry etc*) croquant, croustillant; (*apple, lettuce*) croquant; (*bacon*) croustillant; (*curls*) crépu, frisé; (*air*) vif; (*style*) nerveux; (*tone*) tranchant; **the snow was c. underfoot,** la neige craquait sous mes *ou* nos *etc* pas; **a c. five pound note,** un billet de 5 livres flambant neuf *ou* tout frais. **2** *n* **cooked to a c.,** rôti à point pour croquer sous la dent; **burnt to a c.,** carbonisé; *Br* **(potato) crisps,** (pommes *fpl*) chips *mpl*.
crisp² *vt* froncer (*du crêpe*); donner du croustillant *ou* du croquant à (*des biscuits etc*).
crispbread ['krɪspbred] *n* = biscotte *f* scandinave.
crisper ['krɪspər] *n* (*in refrigerator*) tiroir *m ou* casier *m* à légumes.
crisply ['krɪsplɪ] *adv* (*parler*) d'un ton tranchant; (*écrire*) d'un style nerveux *ou* net.
crispness ['krɪspnɪs] *n* qualité croustillante (*d'un gâteau etc*); dureté *f* (*de la neige*); état parcheminé (*du papier etc*); froid vif (*de l'air*); netteté *f* (*de style etc*); **to lose its c.,** (*of fabric etc*) se défraîchir.
crispy ['krɪspɪ] *adj* **c. bacon,** bacon croustillant.
criss-cross¹ ['krɪskrɒs] **1** *adj* (*pattern etc*) entrecroisé. **2** *n* entrecroisement *m*.
criss-cross² **1** *vt* entrecroiser (*des fils etc*); **brow criss-crossed with wrinkles,** front craquelé de rides; **a network of streets criss-crosses the town,** un réseau de rues parcourt la ville dans tous les sens. **2** *vi* s'entrecroiser.
criterion, *pl* **-ia** [kraɪ'tɪərɪən, -ɪə] *n* critère *m*; **what criteria do you apply** *or* **what are your criteria when selecting candidates?,** sur quels critères vous fondez-vous *ou* quels sont vos critères lorsque vous sélectionnez des candidats?
critic ['krɪtɪk] *n* **(a)** (*critical person*) censeur *m* (*de la conduite d'autrui*), critiqueur *m*; **she has her critics,** il y en a qui la critiquent; **there are few critics of the policy,** peu de gens critiquent la politique; **(b)** *Art Cin Liter Mus TV Journ* critique *m*; **music/drama/literary c.,** critique

musical/dramatique/littéraire; **film c.**, critique de cinéma; **the critics loved the play**, les critiques ont adoré la pièce.

critical ['krɪtɪk(ə)l] *adj* **(a)** critique; **a c. audience**, un public exigeant; **to be c. of s.o./sth**, se montrer critique à l'égard de qn/qch; **she is very c. of her parents' behaviour**, elle se montre très critique à l'égard du comportement de ses parents; **the report was c. of the police**, le rapport était critique à l'égard de la police; **stop being so c.**, arrête de critiquer;
(b) *Art Cin Liter Mus TV Journ* (*dissertation, étude*) critique; **the film received c. acclaim**, le film a été salué unanimement par les critiques, le film a fait l'unanimité de la critique;
(c) (*decisive*) (*situation, moment, âge etc*) critique; *Med* **she is in a c. condition**, elle est dans un état critique; **c. success**, film *etc* acclamé par les critiques; **she is going through a c. time**, elle subit *ou* traverse une crise en ce moment; **the size of the incision is c.**, la taille de l'incision est critique; *Opt* **c. angle**, angle *m* limite *ou* critique; *Nucl Phys* **c. mass**, masse *f* critique; **c. path analysis/method**, analyse *f*/méthode *f* du chemin critique; **the next few days will be c.**, les prochains jours seront décisifs.

critically ['krɪtɪklɪ] *adv* **(a)** (*considérer qch*) en critique; (*regarder qch*) d'un œil critique; **(b)** (*acclaimed etc*) par les critiques; **(c)** *Med* **c. ill**, dangereusement malade; **the c. ill**, les grands malades.

criticism ['krɪtɪsɪz(ə)m] *n* **(a)** (*action, act of criticizing*) critique *f*; **it wasn't meant as a c.**, ce n'était pas une critique; **to lay oneself open to c.**, s'exposer à la critique; **the report contained strong c. of this department**, le rapport contenait de graves critiques de ce service; **(b)** *Cin Liter Mus Journ Art* critique *f*; **textual c.**, critique textuelle; **to write a c. of a book/***etc*, écrire la critique d'un livre/*etc*.

criticize ['krɪtɪsaɪz] **1** *vt* **(a)** (*disapprove of*) censurer, blâmer (*qn*); **to c. sth severely**, se répandre en critiques sur qch; **to c. the defects of a work**, relever les fautes d'un ouvrage; **(b)** (*judge*) critiquer, faire la critique de (*qch*). **2** *vi* (*disapprove*) critiquer; **it's easy to c.**, c'est facile de critiquer; **stop criticizing**, arrête de faire des critiques.

critique [krɪ'tiːk] *n* critique *f*; article *m* critique (*sur une œuvre littéraire etc*).

critter ['krɪtər] *n US Dial* = **CREATURE**.

croak¹ [krəʊk] *n* (*of frog*) coassement *m*; (*of raven*) croassement *m*.

croak² *vi* **(a)** (*of frog*) coasser; (*of raven*) croasser; **(b)** (*of person*) parler d'une voix enrouée *ou* rauque; **(c)** *Sl* (*die*) crever, claquer.

croaking [krəʊkɪŋ] *n* (*of frog*) coassement *m*; (*of raven*) croassement *m*.

croaky ['krəʊkɪ] *adj* (*voice*) enroué, rauque.

Croat ['krəʊæt] **1** *adj* croate. **2** *n* Croate *mf*.

Croatian [krəʊ'eɪʃən] **1** *adj* croate. **2** *n* **(a)** Croate *mf*; **(b)** *Ling* croate *m*.

crochet¹ ['krəʊʃeɪ, -ʃɪ] *n* (travail *m* au) crochet *m*; **c. hook**, crochet; **c. work**, ouvrage *m* ou travail au crochet.

crochet² *v* (**crocheted** ['krəʊʃeɪd, -ʃɪd]) **1** *vt* faire (*qch*) au crochet; **crocheted sweater**, pull *m* au crochet. **2** *vi* faire du crochet.

crocheting ['krəʊʃeɪɪŋ, -ʃɪ-] *n* (travail *m* au) crochet *m*.

crock¹ [krɒk] *n* (*pot*) pot *m* de terre; (*jug*) cruche *f*; **(b)** (*in gardening*) tesson *m* (*pour couvrir le trou d'un pot de fleurs*).

crock² *n F* **old c.**, (*person*) vieux bonhomme fini, croulant *m*; (*car*) vieux clou, vieille bagnole.

crockery ['krɒkərɪ] *n* (*no pl*) (*earthenware, chinaware*) faïence *f*, poterie *f*; (*tableware*) vaisselle *f* de table *ou* de cuisine.

crocodile ['krɒkədaɪl] *n* **(a)** (*animal*) crocodile *m*; *El* **c. clip**, pince *f* crocodile; **c. tears**, larmes *fpl* de crocodile; **(b) c. (skin)**, peau *f* de crocodile, *F* croco *m*; **c. handbag**, sac *m* à main en crocodile, *ou* en croco; **(c)** *Br F* élèves d'un pensionnat marchant deux à deux.

crocus, *pl* **-uses** ['krəʊkəs, -əsɪz] *n* (*plant*) crocus *m*; **autumn c.**, safran cultivé.

croft [krɒft] *n esp Scot* petite ferme.

crofter ['krɒftər] *n esp Scot* petit fermier.

crone [krəʊn] *n* vieille bique.

crony ['krəʊnɪ] *n* **(old) c.**, (vieil) ami, (vieille) amie, (vieux) copain, (vieille) copine.

crook¹ [krʊk] *n* **(a)** *F* (*criminal*) escroc *m*; **that second-hand car salesman is a c.**, ce vendeur de voitures d'occasion est un voleur; **(b)** (*of shepherd*) houlette *f*; (*of bishop*) crosse *f*; **(c)** (*curve*) angle *m*, courbure *f*; (*of river, path etc*) détour *m*, coude *m*; **she held the bottle in the c. of her arm**, elle tenait la bouteille dans son bras replié.

crook² *vt* courber, recourber; **to c. one's finger**, recourber son doigt.

crook³ *adj Austr F* **(a)** (*ill*) malade; (*furious*) furieux; **to go c.**, se mettre en colère (**at s.o.**, contre qn); **to feel a bit c.**, ne pas se sentir dans son assiette; **(b)** (*machinery etc*) en panne; (*thing, place etc*) moche.

crooked ['krʊkɪd] **(a)** *F* (*criminal*) malhonnête, déshonnête; **a c. policeman**, un policier malhonnête; **c. means**, moyens *mpl* obliques; **(b)** courbé (*en crosse*); (*path*) tortueux; (*limb, tree*) contourné, déjeté; (*nose*) crochu, de travers; (*leg*) torse; **the painting was c.**, le tableau était de travers; **a c. smile**, un sourire forcé; **(c)** [krʊkt] (*stick etc*) à béquille.

crookedly ['krʊkɪdlɪ] *adj* **(a)** (*to deal*) malhonnêtement; **(b)** (*to hang*) de travers.

crookedness ['krʊkɪdnɪs] *n* **(a)** (*dishonesty*) malhonnêteté *f*; **(b)** irrégularité *f* (*des contours etc*).

croon [kruːn] **1** *vt* **(a)** (*sing*) chantonner, fredonner (*une chanson*); **(b)** (*say*) dire (*qch*) d'une voix charmeuse. **2** *vi* chantonner.

crooner ['kruːnər] *n* fredonneur, -euse; (*ballad singer*) chanteur *m* de charme.

crop¹ [krɒp] *n* **(a)** *Agr etc* récolte *f*, moisson *f*; (*of fruit etc*) cueillette *f*; (*in forestry*) peuplement *m*; **cash c.**, culture commerciale; **food crops**, récoltes alimentaires; **a poor/good c.**, une mauvaise/bonne récolte; **the potato c.**, la récolte de pommes de terre; **to harvest the crops**, faire la récolte *ou* la moisson; **a fine c. of hair**, une belle chevelure; **this year's c. of films**, les films de cette année; **c. rotation**, alternance *f* des cultures; **(b)** (*haircut*) coupe *f* (des cheveux); **to give s.o. a close c.**, tondre les cheveux de qn; **(c)** (*handle of whip*) manche *m*; **riding c.**, cravache *f*; **hunting c.**, stick *m* de chasse; **(d)** (*of bird etc*) jabot *m*.

crop² *v* (-pp-) **1** *vt* **(a)** (*cut*) tondre, tailler (*une haie, les cheveux etc*); émarger (*un livre*); écourter, couper (*les oreilles, la queue*); **hair cropped close**, cheveux coupés ras; **(b)** (*of cattle*) brouter (*l'herbe*); **(c)** cultiver (*les pommes de terre etc*); **to c. land with corn**, mettre une terre en blé. **2** *vi* (*of land*) donner une récolte.

▶**crop up** *vi* (*arise*) se présenter, surgir; **her name cropped up in the conversation**, son nom a surgi dans la conversation; **did anything c. up while I was away?**, est-ce qu'il s'est passé quelque chose pendant mon absence?; **something has cropped up**, (*I'll be late etc*) j'ai eu un empêchement.

cropper ['krɒpər] *n* **(a)** *F* **to come a c.**, (*fall*) faire une chute, *F* ramasser une pelle; (*encounter disaster*) se heurter à un obstacle imprévu; (*fail*) se planter; **he's so arrogant he'll come a c. one day**, il est tellement arrogant qu'il va se planter un de ces jours; **to come a c. over sth**, se casser les dents sur qch; **(b)** (*person*) cultivateur *m*; **(c) good/bad c.**, (*plant*) plante *f* qui donne de bonnes/de mauvaises récoltes *ou* qui donne bien/mal.

croquet ['krəʊkeɪ, -kɪ] *n Sp* (jeu *m* de) croquet *m*; **to play c.**, jouer au croquet; **c. mallet**, maillet *m*; **c. player**, joueur, -euse de croquet.

croquette [krɒ'ket] *n Culin* croquette *f*; **potato c.**, croquette de pomme de terre.

crosier ['krəʊzɪər] *n Rel* crosse *f* (*d'évêque*).

cross¹ [krɒs] *n* **(a)** (*sign, shape*) croix *f*; **the stations of the C.**, le chemin de Croix; *Fig* **everyone has a c. to bear**, chacun a sa croix à porter; **to make the sign of the c.**, faire le signe de la croix; **processional c.**, croix processionnelle; **market c.**, croix de la place du marché; **St Andrew's c.**, croix de Saint-André; **the Red C.**, la Croix rouge; **C. of the Legion of Honour**, croix de la Légion d'Honneur; **Military C.**, Croix de Guerre; **to sign with a c.**, signer d'une croix; **c. bearer**, porte-croix *m inv*; **c. hairs**, (*on gunsight*) mire *f*; **(b)** (*of animals, plants etc*) (*different species*) croisement *m*; (**between ... and ...**, entre ... et ...); (*same species*) métis, -isse; **to be a c. between sth and sth**, être un mélange de qch et de qch; **it's a c. between a car and a van**, c'est un compromis entre une voiture et une camionnette; **(c)** *Boxing* cross *m*, coup croisé.

cross² **1** *vt* **(a)** (*form a cross etc*) croiser (*deux bâtons etc*); (*in writing*) barrer (*un chèque*); **to c. one's t's**, mettre les barres à ses t; **to c. swords**, croiser le fer (**with**, avec); **to c. one's legs/arms**, (se) croiser les jambes/les bras; **let's keep our fingers crossed**, croisons les doigts; **I've got my fingers crossed for you**, je serre les pouces pour toi; *Rel* **to c. oneself**, faire le signe de croix, se signer; *F* **c. my**

heart (and hope to die), croix de bois croix de fer (si je mens je vais en enfer); **(b)** (*go across*) passer (*la mer, un fleuve*); traverser (*la rue, la frontière etc*); franchir (*le seuil, la frontière*); passer (sur), traverser (*un pont*); **the bridge that crosses the river,** le pont qui traverse la rivière; **to c. s.o.'s path,** se trouver sur le chemin de qn; *Br Pol* **to c. the floor (of the House),** changer de parti (politique); *Nau* **to c. the line,** passer l'équateur; **to c. s.o.'s mind,** (*of thought*) traverser l'esprit de qn, venir à l'esprit *ou* à l'idée de qn; **didn't it c. your mind that she might have been lying?,** est-ce qu'il ne t'est pas venu à l'idée qu'elle ait pu mentir?; **(c)** (*oppose*) contrarier, contrecarrer (*qn, les desseins de qn*); (*go against*) se mettre en travers de la volonté de qn; **to be crossed in love,** avoir une déception amoureuse; **(d)** (*in breeding etc*) (*different species*) croiser; (*same species*) métisser (*des races*); **he crossed a detective movie with a comedy,** il a fait un compromis entre un film policier et une comédie.

2 *vi* **(a)** (*of roads, letters etc*) se croiser; (*of lines*) se croiser, s'entrecroiser; **(b)** (*go across*) passer (d'un lieu à un autre); **to c. from Dover to Calais,** faire la traversée de Douvres à Calais.

cross³ *adj* **(a)** (*annoyed*) maussade, de mauvaise humeur; (*angry*) fâché; **to get c.,** se fâcher (**with,** contre; **about,** de); **he looks c.,** il a l'air fâché; **don't be c. with me,** il ne faut pas m'en vouloir; **you never hear a c. word,** on n'entend jamais un mot plus haut que l'autre; **we've never had a c. word,** nous n'avons jamais échangé un mot plus haut que l'autre; **(b)** (*transverse*) transversal, -aux; oblique; mis en travers; *Am* **c. street,** rue transversale; **c. section,** coupe *f* en travers, coupe *ou* section transversale; **in c. section,** en coupe transversale; *Fig* **a c. section of life,** une tranche de vie; *Fig* **a c. section of the population,** un groupe représentatif de la population; **(c)** (*crossing*) (entre)croisé; **c. lines,** lignes *fpl* qui se croisent; **(d)** (*opposed*) contraire, opposé (**to,** à).

►**cross off** *vtsep* (*remove*) rayer (*un nom*); **to c. a name off a list,** rayer un nom sur une liste; *Fig* **you can c. me off — I'm working tomorrow night,** ne compte pas sur moi – je travaille demain soir.

►**cross out** *vtsep* biffer, barrer, rayer (*un mot, une phrase etc*).

►**cross over** *vi* traverser (*une rue, la mer, une frontière etc*); **they crossed over to Cherbourg in their yacht,** ils ont fait la traversée jusqu'à Cherbourg dans leur yacht.

crossbar ['krɒsbɑːr] *n* (barre *f* de) traverse *f*, entretoise *f*; (*of window*) croisillon *m*; (*of door*) épar(t) *m*; (*on man's bike*) barre *f*; *Aut* barre d'accouplement (*des roues avant*); *Fb etc* barre transversale.

crossbeam ['krɒsbiːm] *n Constr* sommier *m*, traverse *f*; *Constr* (*on piles*) chapeau *m*; *Gym* portique *m*; *Nau* barrotin *m*.

cross-bencher ['krɒsbentʃər] *n Br Parl* = député indépendant.

crossbill ['krɒsbɪl] *n* (*bird*) bec-croisé *m*, *pl* becs-croisés.

crossbones ['krɒsbəʊnz] *npl* **skull and c.,** tête *f* de mort et tibias croisés (*du pavillon des pirates*).

crossbow ['krɒsbəʊ] *n* arbalète *f*.

crossbred ['krɒsbred] *adj* (*from different species*) croisé; (*from same species*) métis, -isse.

crossbreed¹ ['krɒsbriːd] *n* race croisée; produit *m* d'un croisement.

crossbreed² [krɒs'briːd] *vt* (*pt & pp* **crossbred**) (*different species*) croiser; (*same species*) métisser.

crosscheck¹ ['krɒs'tʃek] *n* contre-vérification *f*, vérification par recoupement.

crosscheck² *vt* contre-vérifier, vérifier par recoupement.

cross-country¹ ['krɒs'kʌntrɪ] *adj* (*promenade*) à travers champs; (*véhicule*) tout-terrain; *Sp* **c.-c. running,** le cross; **c.-c. runner,** crossman *m*, *pl* crossmen.

cross-country² *n Sp* **(a)** (*race, racing*) cross *m*; **there's a c.-c. in the park on Sunday,** il y a un cross dans le parc dimanche; **(b)** **c.-c. (skiing),** ski *m* de fond.

crosscut ['krɒskʌt] *n* coupe *f* en travers; **c. saw,** scie *f* passe-partout; **c. file,** lime *f* à taille croisée.

cross-dressing ['krɒs'dresɪŋ] *n* travestisme *m*.

crosse [krɒs] *n Sp* crosse *f* (*du jeu de la crosse*).

crossed [krɒst] *adj Tel* **c. line,** ligne embrouillée; *Fin* **c. cheque,** chèque barré; **the regimental badge is c. rifles,** le badge du régiment représente deux fusils croisés.

cross-examination ['krɒsɪgzæmɪ'neɪʃən] *n Jur* interrogatoire *m* contradictoire; *Fig* interrogatoire serré.

cross-examine ['krɒsɪg'zæmɪn] *vt Jur* interroger (*qn*) contradictoirement; *Fig* soumettre (*qn*) à un interrogatoire serré.

cross-eyed ['krɒsaɪd] *adj* louche, qui louche; **to be c.-e.,** loucher.

cross-fertilization ['krɒsfɜːtɪlaɪ'zeɪʃən] *n* hybridation *f*, *F* pollinisation croisée; *Fig* osmose *F*.

crossfire ['krɒsfaɪər] *n Mil etc* feu croisé; **to be caught in the c.,** *Mil* être pris dans le feu croisé; *Fig* (*of argument*) se retrouver au milieu.

cross-grained ['krɒsgreɪnd] *adj* **(a)** (*wood*) aux fibres irrégulières; à fibres torses; **(b)** *Fig* (*bad tempered*) revêche; (*quarrelsome*) querelleur, -euse; (*perverse*) difficile.

crosshatch ['krɒshætʃ] *vt* (*in drawing*) hachurer en croisillons.

crosshatching ['krɒshætʃɪŋ] *n* (système *m* de) hachures croisées *ou* en croisillons.

cross-headed ['krɒs'hedɪd] *adj Tech* **c. screw/screwdriver,** vis *f*/tournevis *m* cruciforme.

cross-holding ['krɒs'həʊldɪŋ] *n Fin* participation croisée.

crossing ['krɒsɪŋ] *n* **(a)** traversée *f* (*de la mer*); passage *m* (*d'un fleuve, des Alpes*); *Mil* franchissement *m* (*d'un fleuve*); **we had a fine** *or* **good c.,** nous avons eu *ou* fait une belle traversée; **a sea c.,** une traversée maritime; **(b)** (*in street*) passage *m* pour piétons, passage clouté; **(c)** (*of wires, telephone lines etc*) croisement *m*, entrecroisement *m*; **(d)** (*of roads*) croisement *m*, intersection *f*, carrefour *m*; *Rail* **level** *or Am* **grade c.,** passage *m* à niveau; **(e)** croisement *m*, mélange *m* (*de deux espèces*).

cross-legged ['krɒs'leg(ɪ)d] *adj* les jambes croisées; **to sit c.-l.,** être assis en tailleur *ou* à la Turque.

crossly ['krɒslɪ] *adv* (*with annoyance*) avec mauvaise humeur; (*angrily*) d'un air *ou* d'un ton fâché.

crossover ['krɒsəʊvər] *n* **(a)** croisement *m*; *MecE* coude *m* de croisement (*d'un tube*); *Rail* voie *f* de croisement; **(b)** (*of clothing*) croisure *f* (*d'un habit*); **(c)** *Mus* = chanteur qui est passé d'un style de musique à un autre.

crosspatch ['krɒspætʃ] *n F* ronchon *m*.

crosspiece ['krɒspiːs] *n* (barre *f* de) traverse *f*.

cross-purpose ['krɒs'pɜːpəs] *n* **to be (talking) at c. purposes,** (*of two people*) ne pas parler de la même chose.

cross-question ['krɒs'kwestʃən] *vt* = **CROSS-EXAMINE.**

cross-refer ['krɒs'rɪfɜːr] *vt* (**-rr-**) renvoyer; **this entry is cross-referred to another,** cette rubrique renvoie à une autre.

cross-reference¹ ['krɒs'ref(ə)rəns] *n* renvoi *m*.

cross-reference² *vt* établir les renvois (*d'un livre*); **to c.-r. X to Y,** renvoyer de X à Y.

crossroad ['krɒsrəʊd] *n Am* (*across a road*) route *f* perpendiculaire; (*between main roads*) route secondaire, route départementale.

crossroads ['krɒsrəʊdz] *n* (*with sing verb*) carrefour *m*, croisement *m* (*de routes*); *Fig* **the city is at the c. of Europe,** la ville est au carrefour de l'Europe; *Fig* **we are now at the c.,** c'est l'heure des décisions irrévocables.

cross-stitch ['krɒs'stɪtʃ] *n Sewing* point croisé.

crosstalk ['krɒstɔːk] *n* **(a)** *Br* répliques *fpl*; **(b)** *Telecom* diaphonie *f*.

cross-town [krɒs'taʊn] *adj Am* (*bus, trolley*) qui traverse la ville.

cross-trees ['krɒs'triːz] *npl Nau* barres (de hune) traversières.

crosswalk ['krɒswɔːk] *n Am* passage clouté.

crossway ['krɒsweɪ] *n Am* = **CROSSROAD.**

crosswind ['krɒswɪnd] *n* vent *m* de travers.

crosswise ['krɒswaɪz] *adv* en travers.

crossword ['krɒswɜːd] *n* **c. (puzzle),** mots croisés; **have you finished the c.?,** est-ce que tu as fini les mots croisés?

crotch [krɒtʃ] *n* entrecuisse *m*; (*of trousers*) fourche *f*.

crotchet ['krɒtʃɪt] *n Mus* noire *f*.

crotchety ['krɒtʃətɪ] *adj* grognon; (*humeur*) difficile.

croton ['krəʊt(ə)n] *n* (*plant*) croton *m*.

crouch¹ [kraʊtʃ] *n* accroupissement *m*.

crouch² *vi* (*of animal*) se tapir; (*of person*) s'accroupir; **tiger crouching for a spring,** tigre tapi avant de sauter.

►**crouch down** *vi* = **CROUCH².**

croup¹ [kruːp] *n* croupe *f* (*de cheval etc*).

croup² *n Med* croup *m*; **false c.,** faux croup; **to have c.,** avoir le croup.

croupier ['kruːpɪər] *n* croupier *m*.

crow¹ [krəʊ] *n* (*bird*) corneille *f*; *Am Fig* **to eat c.,** s'humilier; **c.'s nest,** nid *m* de corneille; *Nau* nid *m* de pie; **as the c. flies,** à vol d'oiseau.

crow² *n* **(a)** (*of cock*) chant *m* du coq, *F* cocorico *m*; **(b)** (*of baby*) gazouillis *m*.

crow³ *vi* **(a)** (*of cock*) chanter; *Fig* faire cocorico (**about,** à propos de); *Fig* **to c. over s.o.,** chanter victoire sur qn; **(b)** (*of baby*) gazouiller.

crowbar ['krəʊbɑːr] *n* pince *f* (à levier).

crowd¹ [kraʊd] *n* **(a)** (*large number of people*) foule *f*; (*in building*) foule, affluence *f*; **to come in a c.** *or* **in crowds,** venir en foule; **to draw crowds,** attirer la foule; **that's what happens when you get a c. of boys together,** c'est ce qui se produit quand tout un groupe de garçons se trouve rassemblé; **the thief disappeared into the c.,** le voleur a disparu dans la foule; **there wasn't much of a c. at the game,** il n'y avait pas grand monde au match; **there was quite a c. in the square,** il y avait pas mal de monde dans le square; **a football c.,** une foule d'amateurs de football; **the c.,** la foule; **to stand out from the c.,** se distinguer (de la foule); *Fig* **to follow the c.,** suivre le mouvement; *Th Cin* **the c.,** les figurants *mpl*; **c. puller,** clou *m*; **c. scene,** scène *f* de masses; **(b)** *F* (*group*) bande *f*, clique *f*; **they're a good c.,** ce sont de bons types; **they stick to their own c.,** ils font bande à part.

crowd² 1 *vt* **(a)** (*force in, on*) serrer, (en)tasser (*des personnes, des choses*); (*fill*) remplir, bourrer (**with,** de); **they crowded 10,000 people into the square,** ils ont entassé 10000 personnes sur la place; **too many books had been crowded onto the shelf,** on avait entassé trop de livres sur l'étagère; **crowded together,** pressés *ou* serrés l'un contre l'autre; **we are too crowded here,** on est gêné ici; **(b)** (*come too close to*) *Sp* tasser (*un concurrent*); serrer (*une autre voiture*); *US* importuner (*un débiteur*); **don't c. me!,** (*don't pressure me*) ne me pousse pas!; **to be crowded off the pavement,** être forcé de quitter le trottoir. **2** *vi* **to c. (together),** se presser en foule; se serrer; **they all crowded into the room,** ils se sont tous entassés dans la pièce; **to c. round s.o.,** se presser autour de qn; **they all crowded round,** ils se sont tous amassés.

▶**crowd in on** *vipo* assaillir; **here memories c. in on me,** ici des souvenirs m'assaillent en foule.

▶**crowd out** *vtsep* (*force out*) ne pas laisser de place à (*qn, qch*).

crowded ['kraʊdɪd] *adj* (*train, cinema, restaurant etc*) bondé; (*rue, profession*) encombré; (*journée*) chargé; **room c. with furniture,** pièce encombrée de meubles; **the hall was c. with people,** la salle était bondée; **the streets were c.,** il y avait foule dans les rues; **it's a bit c. in here,** il y a un peu trop de monde; **the c. events of that day,** les nombreux événements de cette journée.

crowding ['kraʊdɪŋ] *n* **(a)** encombrement *m*; entassement *m*; **(b)** *Sp* tassage *m* (*d'un concurrent*).

crowfoot ['krəʊfʊt] *n* (*pl usu* **crowfoots**) (*plant*) renoncule *f* (âcre).

crowing ['krəʊɪŋ] *n* **(a)** (*of cock*) chant *m*; **(b)** (*of baby*) gazouillis *m*.

crown¹ [kraʊn] *n* **(a)** couronne *f* (*de fleurs, d'or*); **the martyr's c.,** la couronne du martyre; **the c. of thorns,** la couronne d'épines; **royal c.,** couronne royale; **to wear the c.,** porter la couronne;

(b) **the C.** *or* **c.,** la Couronne (*symbole de l'État monarchique*); **c. lands** *or* **estates,** terres domaniales *ou* appartenant à la Couronne; **c. prince,** prince héritier; **the c. jewels,** les joyaux *mpl* de la Couronne; **c. colony,** colonie *f* de la Couronne; *Can* **C. corporation,** société *f* d'État; *Jur* **c. witness,** témoin *m* à charge; **c. court,** = tribunal *m* de grande instance;

(c) *Fig* couronnement *m* (*de la vie*); comble *m* (*des bonheurs, des malheurs*);

(d) (*of tooth, natural and artificial*) couronne *f*;

(e) *Arch* couronne *f* (*de cinq shillings*); *Br* **half a c.,** une demi-couronne;

(f) (*highest part*) clef *f* (*d'une voûte*); bombement *m* (*d'un pont, d'une chaussée*); cime *f* (*d'un arbre*); crête *f* (*de colline*); faîte *m* (*de toit*); diamant *m* (*d'ancre*); voûte *f* (*de fourneau*); *Aut* **to drive on the c. of the road,** conduire sur l'axe de la route; *MecE* **c. wheel** *or* **gear,** roue dentée sur une surface latérale; *Aut* **c. wheel and pinion,** pignon *m* et couronne d'entraînement; *Br Com* **c. cap,** capsule *f* (métallique) de bouteille;

(g) (*of hat*) fond *m*.

crown² 1 *vt* **(a)** couronner (*qn, la tête de qn*) (**with,** de); **to c. s.o. king,** couronner qn roi; **they crowned her head with a garland of flowers,** ils lui ont couronné la tête d'une guirlande de fleurs; **the crowned heads of Europe,** les têtes couronnées d'Europe; *Br F* **I'll c. you!,** je vais te flanquer un de ces coups sur la tête!; **(b)** *Fig* combler, couronner (*le bonheur etc de qn*); récompenser (*les efforts de qn*); *Br F* **to c. it all,** pour comble de malheur; **(c)** (*be at summit of*) couronner; **the woods that c. the hill,** les bois qui couronnent la colline; **(d)** (*in dentistry*) couronner (*une dent etc*); **(e)** (*in roadbuilding*) bomber (*une route*); **(f)** (*at draughts*) **to be crowned,** aller à dame. **2** *vi* (*of road etc*) bomber.

crowning ['kraʊnɪŋ] **1** *adj Fig* (*ambition, achievement*) suprême; **c. glory,** (*of career*) couronnement *m*; *Hum* (*hair*) chevelure *f* (*de qn*). **2** *n* **(a)** (*of prince etc*) couronnement *m*; **(b)** (*of road*) bombement *m*.

crow's(-)foot, *pl* **-feet** ['krəʊzfʊt, -fiːt] *n* patte *f* d'oie (*au coin de l'œil*).

crozier ['krəʊzɪər] *n Rel* crosse *f* (*d'évêque*).

CRT [siːɑː'tiː] *n abbr* **cathode ray tube.**

crucial ['kruːʃ(ə)l] *adj* (*point etc*) décisif, critique, crucial, -aux; **the c. test,** l'épreuve décisive; **to be c. to sth,** être crucial pour qch.

crucible ['kruːsɪb(ə)l] *n Metal Ch Ind* creuset *m*.

crucifix ['kruːsɪfɪks] *n* crucifix *m*, christ *m*; **roadside c.,** calvaire *m*.

crucifixion [kruːsɪ'fɪkʃən] *n* crucifixion *f*, crucifiement *m*.

cruciform ['kruːsɪfɔːm] *adj* cruciforme.

crucify ['kruːsɪfaɪ] *vt* **(a)** crucifier (*qn, la chair etc*); **Christ Crucified,** le Crucifié; **(b)** *Sl* (*defeat*) flanquer la pâtée à (*qn*); (*criticize*) mettre (*qn*) au pilori.

cruddy ['krʌdɪ] *adj Sl* merdique.

crude [kruːd] **1** *adj* **(a)** (*method, idea, style etc*) informe, grossier; (*tool etc*) primitif; **c. oil,** pétrole brut; **(b)** (*language, joke*) grossier; **c. statement of the facts,** exposé brutal des faits. **2** *n Petr* pétrole brut.

crudely ['kruːdlɪ] *adv* (*see adj*) **(a)** d'une manière fruste; **a c. constructed canoe,** un canoë construit sommairement; **(b)** crûment, grossièrement.

crudeness ['kruːdnɪs] **, crudity** ['kruːdɪtɪ] *n* **(a)** nature grossière *ou* informe (*du style*); caractère primitif (*d'un outil etc*); **(b)** crudité *f* (*d'expression etc*); grossièreté *f* (*de manières etc*).

cruel ['krʊəl] *adj* (*winter, joke, treatment*) cruel; **to be c. to s.o.,** être cruel envers qn; **it was a c. blow,** c'était un coup dur; **you have to be c. to be kind,** qui aime bien châtie bien.

cruelly ['krʊəlɪ] *adv* cruellement.

cruelty ['krʊəltɪ] *n* cruauté *f* (**to** envers); *Jur* sévices *mpl* (**to one's wife,** envers sa femme); **an act of c.,** une cruauté; **mental c.,** cruauté mentale.

cruet ['krʊɪt] *n Culin* **c. (stand),** = huilier *m*.

cruise¹ [kruːz] *n* **(a)** *Nau* croisière *f*; **pleasure c.,** excursion *f ou* voyage *m* d'agrément (*en mer*); **to go on a c.,** partir en croisière; **c. ship,** bateau *m* de croisière; **(b)** *Mil* **c.(-type) missile,** missile *m* de croisière.

cruise² 1 *vi* **(a)** *Nau* (*of yacht, liner*) croiser, être en croisière; **(b)** (*of taxi*) marauder, faire la maraude; **(c)** *Av Aut etc* (*maintain constant speed*) aller à une vitesse de croisière; **they were cruising at 60,** ils faisaient une vitesse de croisière de 60; **(d)** *Sl* (*look for sexual partner*) draguer. **2** *vt* **to c. the bars,** draguer dans les bars.

cruiser ['kruːzər] *n* **(a)** *Nau* **(battle) c.,** croiseur *m* de bataille; **(cabin) c.,** yacht *m* de croisière (*à moteur*); **(b)** = **CRUISERWEIGHT.**

cruiserweight ['kruːzəweɪt] *n Br Boxing* poids lourd.

cruising ['kruːzɪŋ] **1** *adj* **(a)** (*ship*) en croisière; **(b)** (*taxi*) en maraude. **2** *n* **(a)** *Nau* croisière(s) *f(pl)*; **c. holiday,** croisière; **(b)** (*of taxi*) maraude *f*; **(c)** *Av* **c. speed/altitude,** vitesse *f*/altitude *f* de croisière.

crumb¹ [krʌm] *n* **(a)** (*small piece*) miette *f* (*de pain*); **cake crumbs,** miettes de gâteau; **they make the profit and we get the crumbs from their table,** ils réalisent les bénéfices et nous récupérons les miettes; **c. of comfort,** brin *m* de consolation; **crumbs of news,** fragments *mpl* d'information; **(b)** (*opposed to crust*) mie *f* (de pain).

crumb² *vt Culin* paner (*des côtelettes etc*), couvrir de chapelure.

crumble¹ ['krʌmb(ə)l] **1** *vi* (*of stone etc*) s'effriter; (*of masonry*) s'écrouler; (*of earth*) s'ébouler; (*of bread*) s'émietter; (*of empire, opposition, resistance, prices*) s'effondrer; **everything is crumbling to dust,** tout tombe en poussière. **2** *vt* émietter (*du pain*); désagréger (*les pierres*).

crumble² *n Br Culin* **apple c.,** = dessert aux pommes recouvert de pâte sablée.

crumbling ['krʌmblɪŋ] **1** *adj* qui s'écroule, qui s'effrite; (*mur*) croulant; (*empire, opposition, resistance*) qui s'écroule. **2** *n* effritement *m*; éboulement *m*, écroulement *m*; (*of bread*) émiettement *m*.

crumbly ['krʌmblɪ] *adj* (*cake, bread*) qui s'émiette trop; (*cheese*) qui s'émiette; (*stone, brick*) qui se désagrège.

crumbs [krʌmz] *int Eng F* ça alors!, zut!

crummy ['krʌmɪ] *adj Sl* (*film, job, idea etc*) minable; **what a c. joint!,** quelle sale boîte!; **to feel c.,** (*ill*) ne pas se sentir dans son assiette; (*unhappy, upset*) ne pas se sentir fier (**about doing,** d'avoir fait).

crumpet ['krʌmpɪt] *n* **(a)** *Culin* = sorte de crêpe servie rôtie et beurrée; **(b)** (*no pl*) *Br Sl* nanas *fpl*; **a nice bit of c.,** une belle pépée.

crumple ['krʌmp(ə)l] **1** *vt* friper, froisser (*du drap etc*); **to c. paper,** chiffonner du papier; (*make into a ball*) faire une boule avec du papier. **2** *vi* (*of cloth*) se friper, se froisser; (*of leaves, parchment*) se ratatiner; *Sp etc* (*of opposition*) s'effondrer; (*of mudguard, car*) se mettre en accordéon; (*of face*) se décomposer; **he crumpled as the bullet hit him,** il s'est écroulé quand la balle l'a atteint; *Aut* **c. zone,** zone *f* de déformation.

►**crumple up** *vtsep* (*screw up into a ball*) faire une boule avec (*du papier*).

crumpled ['krʌmp(ə)ld] *adj* (*paper*) froissé, chiffonné; (*skirt etc*) froissé, fripé, chiffonné; (*car*) à la tôle froissée.

crunch¹ [krʌntʃ] *n* **(a)** (*bite*) coup *m* de dents; **(b)** (*sound*) bruit *m* de craquement; crissement *m* (*du sable*); **(c)** *Fig* (*critical moment*) **when it comes to the c.,** au moment critique; **when it came to the c. he let them down,** il les a laissés tomber au moment crucial; **if it comes to the c. we can sell the car,** si les choses se corsent nous pouvons vendre la voiture.

crunch² **1** *vt* croquer, broyer (*qch avec les dents*); écraser (*la neige durcie*); *Comptr* **to c. numbers,** exécuter des calculs. **2** *vi* craquer, crisser; **hard snow crunches underfoot,** la neige durcie craque sous les pieds.

►**crunch up** *vtsep* (*crush*) broyer; **the car had been crunched up,** la voiture s'était trouvée broyée.

crunching ['krʌntʃɪŋ] *n* = **CRUNCH¹ (b)**.

crunchy ['krʌntʃɪ] *adj* **(a)** (*food*) croquant, croustillant; **(b)** (*snow*) qui craque (sous les pas).

crupper ['krʌpər] *n* **(a)** (*part of harness*) croupière *f*, culière *f*; **(b)** *Anat* croupe *f* (*de cheval*).

crusade¹ [kruː'seɪd] *n Hist & Fig* croisade *f*; **to go on a c.,** partir en croisade; **a one-man c. against drug-dealing,** une croisade menée par un seul homme contre la drogue; **to start a c.,** lancer une croisade (**against,** contre).

crusade² *vi* **(a)** *Hist* aller *ou* être en croisade; **(b)** *Fig* mener une campagne (**against,** contre; **for,** pour); **she spent her life crusading against injustice/for woman's rights,** elle a passé sa vie à se battre contre l'injustice/pour les droits de la femme.

crusader [kruː'seɪdər] *n* **(a)** *Hist* croisé *m*; **c. castle,** château *m* de croisé; **(b)** *Fig* champion, -ionne (**for sth,** de qch); **a c. against injustice,** un champion de la lutte contre l'injustice.

crush¹ [krʌʃ] *n* **(a)** (*action*) écrasement *m*; **(b)** (*crowd*) presse *f*, foule *f*; **there was a terrible c.,** il y avait un monde fou; **two people were injured in the c.,** deux personnes ont été blessées dans la bousculade; **c. barrier,** barrière *f* pour contenir la foule; *Th* **c. bar,** bar *m* des spectateurs; **(c)** (*drink*) **orange c.,** orangeade *f*; **lemon c.,** citronnade *f*; **(d)** *F* (*infatuation*) béguin *m*; **to have a c. on s.o.,** avoir un béguin pour qn, en pincer pour qn.

crush² **1** *vt* **(a)** écraser (*qn, qch*); exprimer le jus de (*raisins etc*); (*of boa constrictor*) enserrer (*sa victime*); froisser (*une robe*); *Min etc* broyer, concasser (*du minerai*); piler (*de la glace*); **crushed together,** (*of people*) tassés, serrés; **we were nearly crushed to death,** on a failli être écrasés; **(b)** (*destroy*) écraser (*l'ennemi*); étouffer, écraser (*une révolte*); **to c. s.o.'s hopes,** réduire les espoirs de qn à néant; **this remark crushed her,** (*humiliated her*) cette remarque l'a écrasée. **2** *vi* se presser en foule, se bousculer (*pour entrer dans un endroit*); s'entasser (*dans un endroit*).

crusher ['krʌʃər] *n* broyeur *m*, concasseur *m*.

crushing ['krʌʃɪŋ] **1** *adj* **(a)** (*news, defeat etc*) écrasant; (*reply etc*) cinglant, humiliant; **to be dealt a c. blow,** (*of army, hopes etc*) en prendre un sacré coup; **to treat s.o. with c. contempt,** écraser qn de son mépris; **(b)** *Tech* (*roller etc*) concasseur. **2** *n* aplatissage *m*, écrasement *m*; broyage *m*, concassage *m* (*du minerai*).

crust¹ [krʌst] *n* **(a)** (*of bread, pie*) croûte *f*; **not a c. to eat,** pas une croûte à manger; **piece of c.,** croûton *m*; *F* **we manage to earn a c.,** nous arrivons à gagner notre croûte; **(b)** (*of the earth etc*) écorce *f*, croûte *f* (terrestre); couche *f* (*de glace*); *F* **the upper c.,** la fine fleur de la société, le dessus du panier, la crème; **(c)** (*of wine*) dépôt *m*; **(d)** croûte *f* (*d'une plaie*).

crust² **1** *vt* encroûter; couvrir d'une croûte (*de glace etc*). **2** *vi* **(a)** (*become covered with a crust*) se couvrir d'une croûte; **(b)** (*of wound etc*) faire croûte.

crustacean [krʌs'teɪʃən] **1** *adj* crustacéen. **2** *n* crustacé *m*.

crusty ['krʌstɪ] *adj* **(a)** *Culin* (*bread, roll*) qui a une forte croûte, croustillant; **(b)** (*surly*) bourru.

crutch [krʌtʃ] *n* **(a)** (*support*) béquille *f*; *Fig* soutien *m*; **a c. to lean on,** un soutien; **to go about** *or* **walk on crutches,** marcher avec des béquilles; **(b)** *Constr etc* étai *m*; support *m* arrière (*de motocyclette*); **(c)** = **CROTCH**.

crux, *pl* **cruxes** [krʌks, 'krʌksɪz] *n* point capital *ou* crucial (*d'une discussion etc*); **the c. of the matter,** le nœud de la question.

cry¹ [kraɪ] *n* **(a)** cri *m* (*d'une personne, d'un animal*); **to give** *or* **utter a c.,** pousser un cri; **a c. of pain,** un cri de douleur; **no one heard their cries,** personne n'a entendu leurs cris; **there were cries of 'down with the king!',** on criait 'à bas le roi!'; **their c. was 'one man, one vote',** leur slogan était 'un homme, une voix'; **battle c.,** cri de bataille; *Fig* cri de ralliement; **to be in full c.,** (*of hounds etc*) être acharné à la poursuite (**after,** de); *Fig* pousser les hauts cris; **it is a far c. from ...,** il y a loin de ...; **(b)** (*weeping*) **to have a good c.,** pleurer un bon coup.

cry² *v* (*pt & pp* **cried** [kraɪd]) **1** *vi* **(a)** (*weep*) pleurer; **you mustn't c.,** il ne faut pas pleurer; **big girls don't c.,** les grandes filles ne pleurent pas, on ne pleure pas quand on est une grande fille; **to c. over sth,** pleurer *ou* verser des larmes sur qch; **to c. for joy,** pleurer de joie; **(b)** (*shout, call*) crier, pousser un cri *ou* des cris; **to c. aloud,** pousser de grands cris; **to c. for help,** crier au secours; **to c. for mercy,** demander grâce. **2** *vt* **(a)** (*exclaim*) s'écrier; **'that is untrue!' he cried,** 'c'est faux!' s'écria-t-il; **to c. one's wares,** crier sa marchandise; **(b) to c. one's eyes** *or* **one's heart out,** (*weep*) pleurer à chaudes larmes; **she cried herself to sleep,** elle s'est endormie à force de pleurer.

►**cry down** *vtsep* décrier, déprécier (*qn, qch*).

►**cry off** *vi* (*cancel acceptance of invitation*) se dédire, se faire excuser; **two of the guest speakers cried off at the last moment,** deux des conférenciers invités se sont faits excuser au dernier moment.

►**cry out** *vi* (*shout*) pousser des cris, s'écrier; **the pain made her c. out,** la douleur lui a fait pousser des cris; *F* **for crying out loud!,** nom de nom!

►**cry out for** *vipo* (*need desperately*) réclamer (*qch*); *Fig* **that wall is crying out for a coat of paint,** ce mur a bien besoin d'un coup de peinture.

crybaby ['kraɪbeɪbɪ] *n F* pleurnicheur, -euse.

crying ['kraɪɪŋ] **1** *adj* **(a)** (*injustice, need etc*) criant; (*abuse etc*) scandaleux; **it's a c. shame that ...,** il est scandaleux que + *sub* ...; **(b)** (*child*) pleurant, qui pleure. **2** *n* **(a)** (*weeping*) pleurs *mpl*, larmes *fpl*; **(b)** (*shouting, calling*) cri(s) *m(pl)*.

cryogenics [kraɪə'dʒenɪks] *n* (*with sing verb*) cryogénie *f*.

crypt [krɪpt] *n* (*in church architecture*) & *Anat* crypte *f*.

cryptic ['krɪptɪk] *adj* (*person, remark*) sibyllin; (*person, message*) mystérieux, énigmatique, obscur; **a c. silence,** un silence énigmatique; **c. clue,** (*in crossword*) définition obscure.

cryptically ['krɪptɪklɪ] *adv* énigmatiquement, mystérieusement; (*parler*) à mots couverts.

crypto- ['krɪptəʊ] *pref* crypto-; **c.-communist,** cryptocommuniste.

cryptogram ['krɪptəʊgræm] *n* cryptogramme *m*.

cryptographer [krɪp'tɒgrəfər] *n* cryptographe *mf*.

crystal ['krɪst(ə)l] **1** *n* **(a)** *Ch Miner* cristal *m*, -aux; **rock c.,** cristal de roche; **salt crystals,** cristaux de sel; **in c. form,** sous forme cristalline; **(b) c. (glass),** cristal *m*; **as clear as c.,** clair comme le jour *ou* comme de l'eau de roche; **c. factory,** cristallerie *f*; **c. (ball),** boule *f* de cristal; **c. gazing,** divination *f* par la boule de cristal; **(c)** (*on watch*) verre *m* de montre; **(d)** *Electron etc* quartz *m*, cristal *m*; *Old-fashioned Rad* **c. set,** récepteur *m* à cristal, récepteur à galène. **2** *adj* clair, limpide, cristallin; **he gazed into the c. water,** il a regardé dans l'eau limpide.

crystal-clear ['krɪst(ə)l'klɪər] *adj* **(a)** = **CRYSTAL 2**; **(b)** (*argument*) clair comme le jour, clair comme de l'eau de roche; **it's all c.-c. to me now,** ça me paraît clair comme de l'eau de roche maintenant; **to make sth c.-c.,** rendre qch bien clair.

crystalline ['krɪstəlaɪn] *adj* cristallin; *Anat* **c. lens,** (*of the eye*) cristallin *m*.

crystallization [krɪstəlaɪ'zeɪʃən] *n* cristallisation *f*.

crystallize ['krɪstəlaɪz] **1** *vt Ch & Fig* cristalliser; faire candir (*du sucre*); **crystallized fruits,** fruits confits. **2** *vi Ch & Fig* se cristalliser; (*of sugar*) se candir.

crystallography [krɪstə'lɒgrəfɪ] *n* cristallographie *f*.

CS ['siː'es] *n* **CS gas,** gaz *m* CS.

CSE [siːesˈiː] *n Br Sch* (*abbr* **Certificate of Secondary Education**) = certificat de fin d'études secondaires; **I've got seven CSEs,** j'ai le certificat de fin d'études secondaires dans sept matières; **CSE maths,** mathématiques du certificat de fin d'études secondaires.

cub¹ [kʌb] *n* **(a)** (*of fox*) renardeau *m*; (*of bear*) ourson *m*; (*of lion*) lionceau *m*; (*of wolf*) louveteau *m*; *Fig* jeune homme mal appris; *Journ* **c. reporter,** journaliste en herbe; **(b) C. (scout),** louveteau *m*.

cub² *vi* (**-bb-**) **(a)** (*of fox, bear etc*) mettre bas (*des petits*); (*of wolf*) louveter; **(b)** (*in hunting*) chasser le renardeau.

Cuba [ˈkjuːbə] *n* (l'île *f* de) Cuba *m*; **in C.,** à Cuba.

Cuban [ˈkjuːbən] **1** *adj* cubain; **C. heel,** (*on shoe*) talon cubain. **2** *n* Cubain, -aine.

cubbyhole [ˈkʌbɪhəʊl] *n* (*room*) (toute) petite pièce; (*cupboard*) placard *m*; (*pigeonhole*) petit compartiment.

cube¹ [kjuːb] *n* **(a)** *Math* cube *m*; **27 is the c. of three,** 27 est le cube de trois; **c. root,** racine *f* cubique; **(b)** (*piece*) dé *m* (*de pain, de viande etc*); morceau *m* (*de sucre*); **cut the meat into cubes,** coupez la viande en dés; **stock c.,** bouillon-cube *m*.

cube² *vt* **(a)** *Math* élever au cube; **27 cubed,** 27 au cube; **(b)** couper (*la viande etc*) en dés; **(c)** (*measure*) cuber (*du bois etc*).

cubic [ˈkjuːbɪk] *adj* **(a)** *Math* **c. metre,** mètre *m* cube; **c. measurement,** cubage *m*; **c. capacity,** volume *m*; (*of engine*) cylindrée *f*; **c. measures,** mesures *fpl* de volume; **(b)** (*cube-shaped*) cubique.

cubicle [ˈkjuːbɪk(ə)l] *n* (*in swimming pool*) cabine *f*; (*for trying on clothes*) cabine d'essayage; (*in dormitory*) compartiment *m*, alcôve *f*.

cubism [ˈkjuːbɪz(ə)m] *n Art* cubisme *m*.

cubist [ˈkjuːbɪst] *adj & n Art* cubiste *mf*.

cuckold¹ [ˈkʌkəld] *n* cocu *m*.

cuckold² *vt* cocufier, faire cocu.

cuckoo¹ [ˈkʊkuː] **1** *n* (*bird*) coucou *m*; **c. clock,** (pendule *f* à) coucou; *Ent* **c. spit,** crachat *m* de coucou. **2** *adj* (*foolish*) niais *m*; **to go c.,** devenir loufoque. **3** *int* coucou!

cuckoo² *vi* faire coucou.

cuckoopint [ˈkʊkuːpaɪnt] *n* (*plant*) pied-de-veau *m*.

cucumber [ˈkjuːkʌmbər] *n* concombre *m*; *Fig* **to be cool as a c.,** (*in a crisis etc*) être d'un calme imperturbable; **you'll look as cool as a c. in this dress,** vous aurez toujours l'air fraîche dans cette robe; **..., she said cool as a c.,** dit-elle avec un calme imperturbable *ou* comme si de rien n'était; *Zool* **sea c.,** concombre de mer; **c. sandwich,** sandwich *m* au concombre.

cud [kʌd] *n* bol *m* alimentaire (*d'un ruminant*); **to chew the c.,** (*of cow etc*) ruminer; *Fig* (*of person*) ruminer une idée, méditer.

cuddle¹ [ˈkʌd(ə)l] *n* câlin *m*; **to give s.o. a c.,** faire un câlin à qn; **do you want a c.?,** tu veux un câlin?

cuddle² **1** *vt* serrer (*qn*) dans ses bras, câliner (*qn*); **children need lots of cuddling,** les enfants ont besoin d'être beaucoup câlinés. **2** *vi* (*of two people*) se serrer (*l'un l'autre*), se câliner, se faire des câlins; **two young people kissing and cuddling,** deux jeunes gens serrés l'un contre l'autre en train de s'embrasser; **c. down and go to sleep,** (*to child*) enfonce-toi bien sous la couverture et fais dodo.

▶**cuddle up** *vi* (*lie, sit etc closely*) se pelotonner; **they cuddled up for warmth,** ils se sont pelotonnés pour se tenir chaud; **c. up if you're cold,** (*to me*) pelotonne-toi si tu as froid; (*to each other*) serrez-vous *ou* pelotonnez-vous l'un contre l'autre si vous avez froid; **to c. up to s.o.,** se blottir *ou* se pelotonner contre qn.

cuddly [ˈkʌdlɪ] *adj F* (*enfant, animal etc*) qu'on a envie de câliner, qu'on a envie de caresser; (*ours etc*) en peluche; *Hum* (*person*) dodu.

cudgel¹ [ˈkʌdʒ(ə)l] *n* gourdin *m*, trique *f*; *Fig* **to take up the cudgels on s.o.'s behalf,** prendre fait et cause pour qn.

cudgel² *vt* (**-ll-**, *US* **-l-**) donner des coups de bâton à (*qn*); *Fig* **to c. one's brains,** se creuser le cerveau.

cue¹ [kjuː] *n Th* réplique *f*; *Mus* indication *f* de rentrée (*d'un instrument*); *Comptr* caractère indicateur; **to take/miss one's c.,** donner/manquer la réplique; **to give s.o. his c.,** donner la réplique à qn; **I was late for my c.,** j'ai donné la réplique trop tard; **he nodded — that was my c. to make the coffee,** il a hoché la tête pour me faire signe de faire le café; **to take one's c. from s.o.,** prendre exemple sur qn; **(right) on c.,** au bon moment.

cue² *vt* donner la réplique à (*qn*).

cue³ *n* queue *f* (*de billard*); **c. rack,** porte-queues *m inv*.

▶**cue in** *vtsep* **(a)** *Th Cin etc* donner le signal pour (*qch*); **(b)** (*inform*) mettre (*qn*) à la page.

cuff¹ [kʌf] *n* **(a)** poignet *m* (*de chemise*); (*that takes cuff links*) manchette *f*; (*of coat sleeve*) parement *m*; **double c.,** poignet mousquetaire; **c. links,** boutons *mpl* de manchette; *F* **off the c.,** (*discours etc*) impromptu; **to do sth off the c.,** faire qch au pied levé; **I can't tell you off the c.,** je ne peux pas te le dire comme ça *ou* tout de suite; **(b)** *Am* **cuffs,** (*of trousers*) revers *mpl* de pantalon; **(c)** *F* **cuffs,** = **HANDCUFFS.**

cuff² *n* taloche *f*, calotte *f*; **he gave me a c. on the head,** il m'a mis une taloche sur la tête.

cuff³ *vt* talocher, calotter (*qn*).

cuisine [kwɪˈziːn] *n* (l'art *m* de la) cuisine *f*.

cuke [kjuːk] *n F* concombre *m*.

cul-de-sac [ˈkʌldəsæk] *n* (*pl* **culs-de-sac, cul-de-sacs**) cul-de-sac *m*, *pl* culs-de-sac, impasse *f*; *Fig* **to be in a c.-de-s.,** être dans une impasse.

culinary [ˈkʌlɪnərɪ] *adj* de cuisine; (*skill*) culinaire; (*herb*) pour la cuisine; **the c. art,** l'art *m* culinaire.

cull¹ [kʌl] *n* **(a)** (*killing*) élimination *f* des sujets malsains d'un troupeau; **(b)** (*animal*) bête *f* à éliminer du troupeau.

cull² *vt* **(a)** (*reduce by killing*) débarrasser (*un troupeau*) des sujets malsains ou trop nombreux; (*kill*) éliminer (*les sujets malsains ou trop nombreux*) d'un troupeau; **(b)** (*collect*) cueillir (*des fleurs*); (*choose*) choisir (**from,** dans); **the poems have been culled from her early work,** les poèmes ont été choisis parmi ses premières œuvres.

culminate [ˈkʌlmɪneɪt] *vi* **(a)** atteindre son plus haut point; **to c. in sth,** se terminer en qch; aboutir à *ou* dans *ou* en qch; **these protests culminated in a battle with the police,** ces manifestations se sont terminées par un affrontement avec la police; **her excavations culminated in the discovery of a Roman temple,** les fouilles ont abouti à la découverte d'un temple romain; **(b)** *Astron* (*of star*) culminer.

culminating [ˈkʌlmɪneɪtɪŋ] *adj* (*point, moment*) culminant.

culmination [kʌlmɪˈneɪʃən] *n* **(a)** point culminant; apogée *m* (*de la gloire etc*); **the c. of these events was the overthrow of the monarch,** le point culminant de ces événements a été le renversement de la monarchie; **(b)** *Astron* culmination *f*.

culotte [kuːˈlɒt] *n* (*garment*) jupe-culotte *f*, *pl* jupes-culottes.

culpability [kʌlpəˈbɪlɪtɪ] *n* culpabilité *f*.

culpable [ˈkʌlpəb(ə)l] *adj Fml & Jur* (*négligence etc*) coupable.

culprit [ˈkʌlprɪt] *n* **(a)** (*guilty person & Fig*) coupable *mf*, responsable *mf*; (*event*) cause *f*; **I'm the c.,** c'est moi le coupable; **ice on the roads is the main c.,** la glace sur les routes est la cause principale; **(b)** *Jur* accusé, -ée; (*for petty offence*) prévenu, -ue.

cult [kʌlt] *n* **(a)** *Rel* culte *m* (**of,** de); *Fig* culte (*de qn, qch*); **to make a c. of sth,** avoir un culte pour qch; **a personality c., a c. of personality,** un culte de la personnalité; **c. figure,** idole *f*; **c. movie,** film-légende *m*; **(b)** (*sect*) culte *m*.

cultivate [ˈkʌltɪveɪt] *vt* **(a)** cultiver (*la terre, un champ, des légumes etc*); **(b)** *Biol* faire une culture (*d'un bacille*); **(c)** (*form*) cultiver (*ses amis, l'amitié de qn*); **(d)** (*develop*) cultiver (*un art*); **try to c. a more open approach,** essaye de cultiver une démarche plus ouverte; **to c. an easy manner,** arrondir ses manières.

cultivated [ˈkʌltɪveɪtɪd] *adj* **(a)** *Agr* (*land, plant*) cultivé; **(b)** (*educated*) (*voix etc*) qui témoigne d'une bonne éducation; (*esprit*) cultivé.

cultivation [kʌltɪˈveɪʃən] *n* culture *f*; **field under c.,** champ cultivé.

cultivator [ˈkʌltɪveɪtər] *n Agr* **(a)** (*machine*) cultivateur *m* motoculteur *m*; **(b)** (*person*) cultivateur, -trice.

cultural [ˈkʌltʃər(ə)l] *adj* **(a)** (*institut, développement*) culturel; **(b)** *Agr* de culture.

culture¹ [ˈkʌltʃər] *n* **(a)** (*artistic activity*) culture *f*; *F* **c. vulture,** = grand consommateur de culture; **(b)** (*society*) culture *f*; **in Polynesian cultures,** dans les cultures polynésiennes; **c. shock,** choc culturel, dépaysement culturel; **(c)** (*refinement*) culture *f*; **he lacks c.,** il n'a aucune culture; **(d)** *Agr* culture *f* (*des champs, des abeilles etc*); **(e)** *Biol* culture *f*; **c. medium,** milieu *m* de culture.

culture² *vt* (*in bacteriology*) faire une culture de (*un bacille*).

cultured [ˈkʌltʃəd] *adj* **(a)** (*educated*) cultivé, lettré; **his c. mind,** son esprit cultivé; **highly c. woman,** femme hautement cultivée; **(b)** (*pearl*) de culture.

culvert [ˈkʌlvət] *n* **(a)** *Constr* canal *m*, -aux; **(b)** *El* conduit souterrain.

cum [kʌm] **(a)** *prep* qui sert aussi de; **spare room-c.-study,** chambre d'ami qui sert aussi de bureau; **(b)** *St Exch* **c. dividend,** coupon attaché.
Cumb *abbr* **Cumberland**.
cumbersome ['kʌmbəsəm] *adj* (*clothing, luggage*) encombrant, gênant; (*system*) lourd, gênant; (*sentence*) lourd.
cumin ['kʌmɪn, 'kju:-] *n Bot Culin* cumin *m*.
cummerbund ['kʌməbʌnd] *n* large ceinture *f*.
cumulative ['kju:mjʊlətɪv] *adj* cumulatif; *Com etc* (*erreur*) cumulé; *Jur* **c. evidence,** accumulation *f* de témoignages; **c. total,** cumul *m*; *Fin* **c. interest,** intérêts cumulatifs.
cumulonimbus ['kju:mjʊləʊ'nɪmbəs] *n Met* cumulonimbus *m inv*.
cumulus, *pl* **-li** ['kju:mjʊləs, -laɪ] *n Met* cumulus *m*.
cuneiform [kjʊ'neɪɪfɔ:m] **1** *n* (écriture *f*) cunéiforme *m*. **2** *adj* cunéiforme.
cunnilingus [kʌnɪ'lɪŋgəs] *n* cunnilingus *m*.
cunning¹ ['kʌnɪŋ] *n* **(a)** (*deviousness*) ruse *f*, finesse *f*, *F* roublardise *f*; **(b)** (*ingenuity*) astuce *f*, ingéniosité *f*.
cunning² *adj* **(a)** (*devious*) rusé, fin, *F* roublard; (*look*) sournois; **c. as a fox,** malin comme un renard; **(b)** (*ingenious*) (*dispositif*) ingénieux, astucieux.
cunningly ['kʌnɪŋlɪ] *adv* (*see adj*) **(a)** avec ruse; astucieusement; **(b)** ingénieusement.
cunt [kʌnt] *n* **(a)** *Vulg* (*vagina*) con *m*, chatte *f*; **(b)** *Offensive Vulg* (*unpleasant person, thing*) salaud *m*, salope *f*.
cup¹ [kʌp] *n* **(a)** tasse *f*; **coffee/tea c.,** tasse à café/à thé; **c. of coffee/of tea,** tasse de café/de thé; *Fig* **that's just my c. of tea,** c'est tout à fait dans mes cordes; *Fig* **that's not everyone's c. of tea,** ce n'est pas au goût de tout le monde; *Fig* **they're not my c. of tea,** ils ne sont pas mon genre; **(metal) c.,** gobelet *m*, timbale *f*; **paper/plastic c.,** gobelet en carton/plastique; *Culin* **cider c.,** boisson glacée au cidre (*avec des fruits*);
(b) (*measurement*) tasse *f*; (*of soap powder*) mesure *f*, verre *m*; **two cups of flour,** deux tasses de farine;
(c) *Sp* coupe *f*; **to win a c.,** remporter une coupe; *Tennis* **the Davis C.,** la coupe Davis; *Fb* **c. tie,** match *m* éliminatoire de coupe; **c. final,** finale *f* du championnat *ou* de coupe;
(d) *Lit* coupe *f*; *Rel* calice *m* (*du saint Sacrement*); **to drink a bitter c.,** vider un calice amer; **my c. of joy is overflowing,** je déborde de joie; *Old-fashioned* **to be in one's cups,** être gris;
(e) *Bot* calice *f* (*d'une fleur*); *Anat* emboîture *f* (*d'un os*); *Tech* godet *m*; (*of bra, swimming costume*) bonnet *m*; **what size c. do you take?,** (*in bra etc*) quelle profondeur de bonnet est-ce que vous prenez?; **c. valve,** soupape *f* à cloche.
cup² *vt* (**-pp-**) **with one's chin cupped in one's hand,** le menton dans le creux de la main; **to c. one's hand behind one's ear,** mettre sa main en cornet; **to c. one's hands round one's mouth,** mettre les mains en porte-voix; **she scooped up the water with her cupped hands,** elle a recueilli l'eau dans ses mains jointes.
cup-and-ball [kʌpən'bɔ:l] *adj MecE* **c.-a.-b. joint,** joint *m* à rotule.
cupbearer ['kʌpbeərər] *n* échanson *m*.
cupboard ['kʌbəd] *n* armoire *f*; (*in wall*) placard *m*; **c. under the stairs,** placard sous l'escalier; **store c.,** armoire à provisions; **airing c.,** chauffe-linge *m inv*; *Fig* **c. love,** amour intéressé.
cupcake ['kʌpkeɪk] *n Culin* petit four dans une caissette en papier.
cupful ['kʌpfʊl] *n* pleine tasse, pleine coupe (**of,** de); **add two cupfuls of milk,** ajouter deux tasses de lait.
Cupid ['kju:pɪd] *n* Cupidon *m*; *Art etc* Amour *m*.
cupidity [kju:'pɪdɪtɪ] *n* cupidité *f*.
cupola ['kju:pələ] *n Archit* coupole *f*, dôme *m*; *Nau* coupole; *Metal* **c. (furnace),** cubilot *m*.
cuppa ['kʌpə] *n Br F* tasse *f* de thé.
cupric ['kju:prɪk] *adj Ch* (*acide*) cuprique.
cup-shaped ['kʌpʃeɪpt] *adj Bot* cupulaire.
cur [kɜ:r] *n Old-fashioned* **(a)** (*dog*) sale cabot *m*; **(b)** (*despicable man*) homme *m* méprisable, mufle *m*.
curable ['kjʊərəb(ə)l] *adj* guérissable; (*mal*) curable.
curacy ['kjʊərəsɪ] *n Rel* vicariat *m*.
curare [kjʊə'rɑ:rɪ] *n* curare *m*.
curate ['kjʊərət] *n Rel* vicaire *m*; **c. in charge,** desservant *m*.
curative ['kjʊərətɪv] **1** *adj* curatif. **2** *n* remède *m*.
curator [kjʊə'reɪtər] *n* **(a)** (*of museum, gallery*) conservateur *m*; **(b)** *Jur Scot* tuteur, -trice; curateur *m* (*d'un dément*).
curb¹ [kɜ:b] *n* **(a) c. (chain),** gourmette *f*; **c. bit,** mors *m* à gourmette; **c. reins,** rênes *fpl* de mors; **to put a c. on one's passions,** refréner *ou* mettre un frein à ses passions; **(b)** *Am* bordure *f*, rebord *m* (*de trottoir etc*).
curb² *vt* mettre la gourmette à (*un cheval*); réprimer, refréner (*sa colère*); maîtriser, brider (*ses passions*); modérer (*son impatience*); freiner (*l'inflation etc*); **you must learn to c. your tongue!,** vous devez apprendre à tenir votre langue!
curbstone ['kɜ:bstəʊn] *n Am* pierre *f* de rebord (*de trottoir*).
curd [kɜ:d] *n* (lait *m*) caillé *m*; **curds and whey,** lait caillé sucré; **lemon c.,** = pâte composée d'œufs, de beurre et de jus de citron.
curdle ['kɜ:d(ə)l] **1** *vi* (*of milk*) se cailler; *Fig* **my blood curdled,** mon sang s'est glacé. **2** *vt* cailler (*le lait*); coaguler (*un liquide*); *Fig* glacer, figer (*le sang*).
cure¹ ['kjʊər] *n* **(a)** (*treatment*) cure *f*; (*remedy*) & *Fig* remède *m* (**for,** contre); **rest c.,** cure de repos; **to take a c.,** faire une cure; **past c.,** (*of person*) incurable; (*of thing*) irrémédiable, irréparable; **the c. is worse than the disease,** le remède est pire que le mal; **(c)** *Rel* **c. of souls,** cure *f ou* charge *f* d'âmes; **(b)** (*recovery*) guérison *f*.
cure² *vt* **(a)** guérir (*qn*) (**of,** de); corriger (*qn*) (*d'une mauvaise habitude*); remédier à (*un mal*); **this experience cured him of his infatuation,** cette expérience l'a guéri de son engouement; **they were completely cured,** ils ont été complètement guéris; *Prov* **what can't be cured must be endured,** où il n'y a pas de remède il faut se résigner; **(b)** (*prepare*) saler, fumer (*la viande etc*); confire (*des sardines*); saurer (*des harengs*); saler (*les peaux*).
cure-all ['kjʊərɔ:l] *n* panacée *f*.
curettage [kjʊə'retɪdʒ] *n Med* curet(t)age *m*.
curfew ['kɜ:fju:] *n* couvre-feu *m*; **to ring the c. (bell),** sonner le couvre-feu; *esp Am Fig* **to be on c.,** (*of teenager*) devoir rentrer à une heure précise.
curing ['kjʊərɪŋ] *n* **(a)** (*of patient*) guérison *f*; **(b)** (*preparation*) salaison *f* (*de la viande*).
curio ['kjʊərɪəʊ] *n* bibelot *m*, petit objet d'art.
curiosity [kjʊərɪ'ɒsɪtɪ] *n* **(a)** curiosité *f*; **out of** *or* **from c.,** par curiosité; **I was dying of c.,** je mourais de curiosité; *Prov* **c. killed the cat,** = la curiosité est un vilain défaut; **(b)** (*object*) curiosité *f*, rareté *f*.
curious ['kjʊərɪəs] *adj* **(a)** curieux; *Pej* indiscret, -ète; **to be c. to see sth,** être curieux de voir qch; **he was c. to know why,** il était curieux de savoir pourquoi; **they didn't seem at all c. as to** *or* **about how it had happened,** ils n'avaient pas du tout l'air curieux de savoir comment cela s'était produit; **(b)** (*strange*) curieux, singulier; **c. sight,** chose curieuse à voir; **a c.-looking object,** un objet d'un aspect bizarre.
curiously ['kjʊərɪəslɪ] *adv* (*see adj*) **(a)** avec curiosité; *Pej* indiscrètement; **(b)** curieusement, singulièrement; **c. enough ...,** chose curieuse *ou* singulière ... .
curl¹ [kɜ:l] *n* **(a)** boucle *f* (*de cheveux*); spirale *f* (*de fumée*); crête recourbée (*d'une vague*); ronce *f* (*dans le grain du bois*); *Metal* bordure *f* (*d'une tôle etc*); **in curls,** (*of hair*) bouclé, frisé; **to fall in curls,** (*of hair*) tomber en boucles; **(b)** (*action*) action *f* de se recourber; **with a c. of the lips,** avec une moue dédaigneuse; **(c)** *Agr etc* **leaf c.,** enroulement *m* des feuilles.
curl² **1** *vt* boucler, friser (*les cheveux*); *Metal* border (*une tôle etc*); **to c. one's lip,** faire une moue dédaigneuse; **to c. sth round sth,** enrouler qch autour de qch. **2** *vi* **(a)** (*of hair*) boucler, friser; (*of paper*) se recroqueviller; (*of smoke*) s'élever en spirales; (*of waves*) onduler, déferler; (*of lip*) se relever avec dédain; *Fig* **stories that make your hair c.,** histoires qui font dresser les cheveux; **to c. round sth,** (*of plant etc*) s'enrouler autour de qch; **(b)** *Sp* jouer au curling.
►**curl up** **1** *vi* **(a)** (*lie, sit comfortably*) se blottir, se pelotonner; **to c. up in an armchair,** se pelotonner dans un fauteuil; **I like to c. up in bed with a good book,** j'aime me blottir au lit avec un bon livre;
(b) (*form a curl*) se recroqueviller; **hedgehogs c. up into a ball for protection,** les hérissons se recroquevillent en boule pour se protéger;
(c) (*of leaves, paper etc*) s'enrouler; (*of thread, rope*) vriller;
(d) *F* (*be embarrassed*) avoir envie de disparaître *ou* de devenir invisible; (*writhe*) se tortiller *ou* se crisper sous un sarcasme; **it made me c. up,** ça m'a donné envie de disparaître *ou* de devenir invisible; **I wanted to c. up and die,** j'avais envie de me recroqueviller dans un coin et de

me laisser mourir.

2 *vtsep* (*form into a curl*) **to c. (oneself) up,** se rouler en boule, se pelotonner; **curled up in bed,** couché en chien de fusil; **to c. itself up,** (*of cat etc*) se mettre en rond; se mettre en boule.

curled [kɜːld] *adj* (*hair*) frisé; (*leaf*) crépu; *Metal* (*tôle*) bordé.

curler ['kɜːlər] *n* **(a)** (*for hair*) bigoudi *m;* **(b)** *Sp* joueur *m* de curling.

curlew ['kɜːljuː] *n* (*bird*) courlis *m*.

curlicue ['kɜːlɪkjuː] *n* trait *m* de plume en parafe.

curliness ['kɜːlɪnɪs] *n* **(a)** (*of hair*) frisure *f*; **(b)** sinuosité *f*.

curling ['kɜːlɪŋ] *n* **(a)** frisure *f* (*des cheveux*); *Metal* bordage *m* (*des tôles etc*); **c. irons** *or* **tongs,** fer *m* à friser; **(b)** *Sp* curling *m*; **c. stone,** pierre *f*.

curly ['kɜːlɪ] *adj* **(a)** (*hair etc*) bouclé, frisé; (*long piece of paper etc*) en spirale; (*lettuce*) frisé; **she had short c. hair,** elle avait les cheveux courts et bouclés; **the dried leaves had gone c.,** les feuilles séchées s'étaient enroulées sur elles-mêmes; **(b)** (*wood*) à grain ondulé.

curly-headed, -haired ['kɜːlɪhedɪd, -heəd] *adj* à la tête bouclée, aux cheveux frisés; (*African*) crépu.

currant ['kʌrənt] *n* **(a)** (*dried grape*) raisin *m* de Corinthe, raisin sec; **c. bun,** petit pain aux raisins; **(b)** (*soft fruit*) groseille *f*; **c. bush,** groseillier *m*.

currency ['kʌrənsɪ] *n* **(a)** *Fin* (*unit*) unité *f* monétaire (*d'un pays*); (*specie*) numéraire *m*; (*coins, notes*) monnaie *f*; **this coin is no longer legal currency,** cette pièce n'a plus cours; **foreign c.,** devise étrangère; (*coins, notes*) monnaie étrangère; **hard/soft c.,** devise forte/faible; **the world's major currencies,** les principales monnaies du monde; **to buy currency,** acheter des devises; **c. speculation,** spéculation *f* sur les devises; **c. speculator,** spéculateur *m* sur devises; **c. unit,** unité *f* monétaire;

(b) (*circulation*) circulation *f*, cours *m* (*de l'argent, des idées*); **to give c. to a rumour,** mettre un bruit en circulation, répandre un bruit; **to gain c.,** (*of news*) s'accréditer; (*of expression, habit*) devenir de plus en plus courant; **the expression is common c.,** l'expression est monnaie courante; **this view had some c. at one time,** cette opinion était accréditée à un moment donné;

(c) (*period*) (terme *m* d')échéance *f* (*d'une lettre de change*).

current¹ ['kʌrənt] *adj* **(a)** (*existing, present*) courant, en cours, actuel; **c. month,** mois *m* en cours; **the c. theory is that ...,** la théorie actuelle est que ...; **c. affairs,** actualités *fpl*; *TV Rad* **c. affairs programme,** programme *m* d'actualités; **c. number,** dernier numéro (*d'une revue*); **the c. treasurer,** l'actuel trésorier (de l'association); *Br Fin etc* **c. account,** compte courant; **c. assets,** actif *m* réalisable et disponible; **c. price,** prix courant; **(b)** (*accepted, used*) courant, admis, reçu; **to be c.,** avoir cours; **in c. use,** d'usage courant; **the word is in c. use,** le mot s'emploie couramment.

current² *n* **(a)** (*of river, tide etc*) courant *m*; *Met* **air c.,** courant d'air; *Fig* **the c. of public opinion,** la tendance de l'opinion publique; **to drift with the c.,** se laisser aller au fil de l'eau; *Fig* suivre le courant; **to swim against the c.,** nager contre le courant; *Fig* **to go against the c.,** aller à contre-courant; **(b)** *El* courant *m*; **direct/alternating c.,** courant continu/alternatif.

currently ['kʌrəntlɪ] *adv* **(a)** (*at present*) actuellement, en ce moment; **she is c. appearing in Othello,** elle apparaît en ce moment dans Othello; **(b)** (*commonly*) couramment, généralement.

curriculum, *pl* **-a** [kə'rɪkjʊləm, -ə] *n Sch* programme *m* d'études; *esp Br* **c. vitae,** curriculum vitae *m*.

curry¹ ['kʌrɪ] *n Culin* (*spices, dish*) cari *m*, curry *m*; **beef/chicken c.,** bœuf *m*/poulet *m* au curry; **c. powder,** poudre *f* de curry, curry en poudre.

curry² *vt Culin* apprêter (*du poulet etc*) au cari *ou* au curry; **curried eggs,** œufs *mpl* à l'indienne.

curry³ *vt* **(a) to c. favour with s.o.,** s'insinuer dans les bonnes grâces de qn; **(b)** (*groom*) étriller (*un cheval*).

currycomb ['kʌrɪkəʊm] *n* étrille *f*.

curse¹ [kɜːs] *n* **(a)** malédiction *f*, mauvais sort; **a c. on ...!,** maudit soit ...!; *Fig* **the country is under a c.,** un mauvais sort a été jeté sur le pays; **to put a c. on s.o.,** jeter un sort à qn; **(b)** *Old-fashioned* (*swearword*) imprécation *f*, juron *m*; **to let out a c.,** lâcher un juron; **curses!,** zut!; **(c)** (*scourge*) fléau *m*; **here the rabbits are a c.,** ici les lapins sont un fléau; *F* **to have the c.,** (*of woman*) avoir ses règles *ou F* ses anglais.

curse² **1** *vt* maudire (*qn, qch*); **he is cursed with a violent temper,** il est affligé d'un mauvais caractère; **c. (it)!,** le diable l'emporte!; **he cursed his luck,** il a maudit son sort; **you'll c. the day you came here,** tu maudiras le jour où tu es venu ici. **2** *vi* (*blaspheme*) blasphémer; (*swear*) sacrer, jurer; **to c. and swear,** jurer et sacrer; **to c. at s.o.,** injurier qn.

cursed *adj* **(a)** [kɜːst] (*under a curse*) maudit; **the place is c.,** ce lieu est maudit; **(b)** ['kɜːsɪd] *F* sacré, satané; **it's a c. nuisance,** c'est bigrement embêtant.

cursing ['kɜːsɪŋ] *n* jurons *mpl*.

cursive ['kɜːsɪv] **1** *adj* cursif; **c. handwriting,** écriture courante *ou* cursive. **2** *n* écriture courante *ou* cursive.

cursor ['kɜːsər] *n* (*on slide rule*) & *Comptr* curseur *m*; *Comptr* **c. key,** touche *f* de curseur; *Comptr* **move the c. to the right/left,** déplacez le curseur vers la droite/gauche.

cursorily ['kɜːsərɪlɪ] *adv* (*examine*) à la hâte; (*look at*) superficiellement.

cursory ['kɜːsərɪ] *adj* (*coup d'œil*) rapide, superficiel; (*examen*) fait à la hâte.

curt [kɜːt] *adj* (*manner*) brusque; (*tone*) cassant; **c. reply,** réponse sèche.

curtail [kɜː'teɪl] *vt* **(a)** (*shorten*) raccourcir, abréger, écourter (*une visite*); **(b)** (*limit*) diminuer, restreindre (*la liberté de qn*); amoindrir (*l'autorité de qn*); réduire (*ses dépenses*).

curtailment [kɜː'teɪlmənt] *n* restriction *f*, diminution *f* (*d'autorité etc*); réduction *f* (*de dépenses*).

curtain¹ ['kɜːt(ə)n] *n* **(a)** *Br* (*on window etc*) rideau *m*; **to draw the c.,** (*open*) tirer *ou* ouvrir le rideau; (*close*) fermer le rideau; *Pol* **the Iron C.,** le rideau de fer; **c. ring,** anneau *m* de rideau; **c. rail** *or* **rod,** tringle *f* de rideau; **c. hook,** crochet *m* de rideau; **c. wall,** (*of castle*) mur *m* d'enceinte; *Constr* enceinte *f*; **(b)** *Th* rideau *m*; **safety c.,** rideau de fer; *Sl* **it's curtains for him,** il est fichu; *Sl* **it'll be curtains for you if ...,** vous y laisserez votre peau si ...; **c. call,** rappel *m*; **to take three c. calls,** être rappelé trois fois.

curtain² *vt* garnir (*une alcôve etc*) de rideaux.

▶**curtain off** *vtsep* (*conceal*) masquer (*une partie d'une pièce*) par un rideau.

curtain-raiser ['kɜːt(ə)nreɪzər] *n Th* lever *m* de rideau; *Fig* préambule *m*.

curtly [kɜːtlɪ] *adv* (*to say*) brusquement, d'un ton cassant.

curtness ['kɜːtnɪs] *n* brusquerie *f* (*de paroles*), ton cassant.

curts(e)y¹ ['kɜːtsɪ] *n* révérence *f* (*que fait une femme en pliant le genou*); **to make a c. to s.o.,** faire une révérence à qn.

curts(e)y² *vi* (*of woman, girl*) faire une révérence (**to,** à).

curvaceous [kɜː'veɪʃəs] *adj F* (*woman*) bien roulée, bien carrossée, qui a des formes.

curvature ['kɜːvətʃər] *n* sphéricité *f* (*de la terre etc*); *Phys Opt* courbure *f* (*de l'espace*); *Med* **c. of the spine,** déviation *f* de la colonne vertébrale.

curve¹ [kɜːv] *n* courbe *f*; (*in road*) tournant *m*, virage *m*; **the c. of the bay,** la courbe de la baie; **curves,** (*of woman*) rondeurs *fpl*, formes *fpl*; *Math etc* **to plot a c.,** tracer une courbe.

curve² **1** *vi* se courber; **the road curves round the castle,** la route décrit une (ligne) courbe autour du château; **to c. down/up(wards),** monter/descendre en courbe. **2** *vt* courber, recourber; cintrer (*une porte, un tuyau*).

curved [kɜːvd] *adj* (*bent out of shape*) courbé, cintré; (*nose*) busqué; **c. blade,** (*intentionally bent*) lame *f* courbe.

curvilinear [kɜːvɪ'lɪnɪər] *adj* curviligne.

curvy [kɜːvɪ] *adj* **(a)** (*curved*) courbé, cintré; **(b)** *F* (*woman*) qui a des formes.

cushion¹ ['kʊʃən] *n* **(a)** coussin *m*; **scatter c.,** petit coussin décoratif; *Fig* **muscle provides a c. against blows,** les muscles constituent un coussin qui amortit les chocs; **the annual increase in salary acts as a c. against inflation,** l'augmentation annuelle des salaires amortit les effets de l'inflation; **(b)** *Billiards* bande *f*; **off the c.,** par la bande; **stroke off the c.,** doublé *m*; **(c)** *Tech* coussin *m* (*d'air etc*); **steam c.,** matelas *m* de vapeur (*dans le cylindre*); vapeur *f*.

cushion² *vt* **(a)** (*reduce effect of*) amortir (*un coup, un choc, une chute etc*); *MecE* matelasser (*le piston*); **they have been cushioned from unemployment,** ils ont été protégés contre le chômage; **(b)** (*provide with cushions*) garnir de coussins; **(c)** *Billiards* acculer (*une bille*) à la bande.

cushioned ['kʊʃənd] *adj* **(a)** (*blow, shock*) amorti; **(b)** (*covered in cushions*) garni de coussins.

cushioning ['kʊʃənɪŋ] *n MecE* matelassage *m*.

cushy ['kʊʃɪ] *adj F* (*vie etc*) facile, pépère, peinard; **c. job**

or **number,** boulot peinard.

cusp [kʌsp] *n* **(a)** *Astron* corne *f* (*de la lune*); **(b)** *Math* sommet *m* (*d'une courbe*); **(c)** *Anat* cuspide *f*.

cuspidor ['kʌspɪdɔːr] *n esp US* crachoir *m*.

cuss [kʌs] *n F* **(a)** (*swear word*) juron *m*; **it isn't worth a (tinker's) c.,** ça ne vaut pas un clou; **(b)** (*person*) individu *m*, type *m*; **an awkward c.,** un mauvais coucheur.

cussed ['kʌsɪd] *adj F* sacré; (*person*) entêté; **it's a c. nuisance,** c'est bigrement embêtant.

cussedness ['kʌsɪdnɪs] *n F* entêtement *m*; **out of sheer c.,** par esprit de contradiction.

custard ['kʌstəd] *n* **(a)** *Culin* crème anglaise; **baked c.,** crème cuite au four; **c. powder,** poudre *f* pour faire la crème anglaise; **c. tart,** flan *m*; *Cin etc* **c. pie,** tarte *f* à la crème (*utilisée comme projectile*); **(b)** (*fruit*) **c. apple,** anone réticulée.

custodial [kʌ'stəʊdɪəl] *adj Jur* **c. sentence,** peine *f* de détention.

custodian [kʌs'təʊdɪən] *n* gardien, -ienne; (*of museum etc*) conservateur *m*; **the police are the custodians of law and order,** la police est la garante de l'ordre public.

custody ['kʌstədɪ] *n* **(a)** (*guardianship*) garde *f* (*d'enfants etc*); **to have c. of s.o./sth,** avoir la garde de qn/qch; **in safe c.,** sous bonne garde; **(b)** *Jur* détention *f*; **to take s.o. into c.,** arrêter qn, mettre qn en état d'arrestation; **to be in c.,** être en détention préventive.

custom ['kʌstəm] **1** *n* **(a)** (*practice*) coutume *f*, usage *m*; (*of individual*) habitude *f*; **according to c.,** selon l'usage; **it is the c. of the country,** c'est la pratique du pays; **it is their c. to fast on that day,** (*habit*) c'est leur habitude de jeûner ce jour-là; (*tradition*) c'est leur coutume de jeûner ce jour-là; **it was a c. with him to ...,** il avait l'habitude de ...; **the manners and customs,** les us *mpl* et coutumes (*d'un pays*); **(b)** *Jur* droit coutumier, coutume *f* (*d'un pays*); **(c)** *Com* (*of a company, shop*) clientèle *f*; **to lose s.o.'s c.,** perdre un client; **I'll take my c. elsewhere,** je vais aller voir ailleurs, je vais changer de crèmerie. **2** *adj* **c. car,** voiture *f* à carrosserie spéciale.

customarily [kʌstə'mərɪlɪ] *adv* habituellement, d'habitude; (*normally*) ordinairement.

customary ['kʌstəm(ə)rɪ] *adj* **(a)** accoutumé, habituel, d'usage, coutumier; **at the c. hour,** à l'heure accoutumée; **it is c. to ...,** il est de coutume *ou* d'usage de ...; **as is c.,** comme il est d'usage; **her c. politeness,** sa politesse habituelle *ou* coutumière; **(b)** *Jur* **c. law,** droit coutumier; **c. right,** droit *m* d'usage.

custom-built ['kʌstəmbɪlt] *adj* fait *ou* fabriqué sur commande; *Aut* **c.-b. body,** carrosserie spéciale.

customer ['kʌstəmər] *n* **(a)** (*of shop etc*) client, -ente; (*of public house etc*) consommateur *m*; **regular c.,** (*of restaurant etc*) habitué, -ée; **the c. is always right,** le client a toujours raison, le client est roi; **c. service (department),** service *m* clientèle; **(b)** *F* (*person*) individu *m*, type *m*; **a queer c.,** un drôle de type; **a very cool c.,** un type qui ne s'en fait pas *ou* qui ne se gêne pas; **an ugly c.,** un sale type; **an awkward c.,** un type pas commode.

customization [kʌstəmaɪ'zeɪʃən] *n* adaptation *f* aux besoins du client; personnalisation *f*.

customize ['kʌstəmaɪz] *vt* (*make*) faire sur commande; (*adapt*) personnaliser.

custom-made ['kʌstəm'meɪd] *adj* fait *ou* fabriqué sur commande; **his clothes are c.-m.,** ses vêtements sont faits sur mesure.

customs ['kʌstəmz] *n Admin* douane *f*; **c. officer,** douanier *m*; **c. duties,** droits *mpl* de douane; **c. declaration,** déclaration *f* de *ou* en douane; **c. union,** union douanière; **to go through (the) c.,** passer la douane *ou* par la douane; **c. examination/formalities,** examen *m* de la douane/formalités douanières; **c. clearance,** dédouanement *m*.

cut¹ [kʌt] *n* **(a)** (*incision*) coupe *f*; *Com etc* réduction *f* (*de prix, de dépenses*); *Cin TV* coupure *f* (*dans un film etc*); **to make a clean c.,** trancher net; **the first c.,** l'entame *f*; **power** *or* **electricity c.,** coupure *f* de courant; *Cin* **c. from one shot to another,** raccord *m* de deux plans; **to make a c. in a text,** faire une coupure dans un texte; **a two-hundred word c.,** une réduction de deux cents mots; **wage cuts,** réductions de salaires; **we were asked to take a c. in our wages,** on nous a demandé de supporter une réduction de salaire;

(b) (*blow*) coup *m* (*de couteau, d'épée*); *Cr Tennis* coup tranchant; coup, revers *m* (*de fortune*); (*remark*) sarcasme blessant; **c. with a whip,** coup de fouet; **the unkindest c. of all,** le coup le plus dur; **she revels in the c. and thrust of debate,** elle prend plaisir aux joutes oratoires;

(c) *Tech etc* (*of file*) taille *f*, entaille *f*; (*of machine tool*) passe *f*; **saw c.,** trait *m* de scie;

(d) (*wound*) coupure *f*, estafilade *f*; (*gash*) balafre *f*; *Surg* incision *f*; **c. across the cheek,** balafre à la joue;

(e) (*style*) coupe *f* (*d'un vêtement, des cheveux*); taille *f* (*d'une pierre précieuse*); **crew c.,** cheveux (coupés) en brosse;

(f) *Culin* **c. off the joint,** tranche *f* de rôti; **prime c.,** morceau *m* de (premier) choix; **cheap cuts,** bas morceaux; *Am* **cold cuts,** assiette anglaise;

(g) *F Fig* commission *f*, *F* gratte *f*; **he gets his c.,** il a part au gâteau;

(h) **short c.,** raccourci *m*; *Fig* solution *f* de facilité; **to take a short c.,** couper au plus court, prendre (par) un raccourci; *Fig* utiliser la solution de facilité;

(i) *Cards* coupe *f*; **c. for partners,** tirage *m* pour les places;

(j) *F* **to be a c. above s.o./sth,** être supérieur à qn/qch;

cut² *v* (*pt & pp* **cut**; *prp* **cutting**) **1** *vt & vi* **(a)** couper, tailler; (*in slices*) trancher; couper, sectionner (*une corde*); hacher (*le tabac etc*); faucher (*les foins*); tondre (*le gazon*); (*of wind*) couper, cingler (*le visage*); (*in bookbinding*) rogner (*les bords*); **to c. one's finger,** se couper le *ou* au doigt; **to c. one's nails,** se couper les ongles; **to have one's hair cut,** se faire couper les cheveux; *Fig* **this remark cut him to the quick,** cette parole l'a piqué au vif; **fog you could c. with a knife,** brouillard à couper au couteau; **atmosphere you could c. with a knife,** atmosphère à couper au couteau; **to c. like a knife,** (*of wind*) couper comme un couteau; **to c. into a cake,** entamer un gâteau; **to c. into the bark,** inciser l'écorce; **the string is cutting (into) me,** le cordon me coupe la chair.

(b) (*separate*) **to c. sth in two** *or* **in half,** couper qch en deux; **to c. a slice of cake/***etc*, couper une tranche de gâteau/*etc*; **to c. to pieces,** couper (*qch*) en morceaux; tailler en pièces (*une armée*); **to c. one's way through the wood,** se frayer un chemin à travers le bois; **to c. an animal loose,** délier une bête; **to c. oneself loose from sth,** se libérer de qch;

(c) (*shorten, reduce*) faire des coupures dans (*un film etc*); abréger, raccourcir (*un discours*); couper, réduire (*les nombres, ses dépenses*); diminuer (*la production*); **the film was cut to 100 minutes,** le film a été raccourci à 100 minutes; **prices/wages have been cut by 10%,** les prix/salaires ont été réduits de 10%; **this cuts their journey time by 20 minutes,** ça réduit la durée de leur trajet de 20 minutes; **shopping at the supermarket helps to c. costs,** faire ses achats au supermarché permet de réduire les frais; **to c. a speech/a visit short,** écourter un discours/une visite; **to c. s.o. short,** couper la parole à qn; **to c. a long story short,** bref, pour dire la chose en deux mots; *F* **c. it short!,** soyez bref!;

(d) (*omit, remove*) supprimer; **this scene/chapter was later cut,** cette scène/ce chapitre a été supprimé(e) par la suite; *Sl* **c. the crap,** arrête tes conneries;

(e) *Cin* (*edit*) procéder au montage de (*un film*);

(f) *Tech etc* couper, tailler (*une pierre, du verre etc*); percer, creuser (*un canal*); graver, ciseler (*des caractères sur le métal ou la pierre*); tailler (*un habit*); fileter (*une vis*); *Mus* faire (*un disque*);

(g) **to c. a tooth,** (*of child*) faire une dent;

(h) *Cards* **to c. the cards,** tirer pour les places *ou* pour la donne;

(i) *Cr Tennis* trancher, couper (*la balle*);

(j) *El etc* (*turn off*) couper;

(k) **to c. s.o. (dead),** (*ignore*) faire semblant de ne pas voir qn; **he cut me dead,** il m'a complètement ignoré;

(l) *Sch F* sécher (*un cours, une classe*).

2 *vi* **(a)** (*of knife*) couper; **those scissors don't c. very well,** ces ciseaux ne coupent pas très bien; **cloth that cuts easily,** tissu qui se coupe facilement; *Lit* **to c. through the waves,** fendre les eaux; **that's an argument that cuts both ways,** c'est un argument à deux tranchants; *US* **to c. loose,** (*free oneself*) s'émanciper; (*escape*) s'évader; *F* **to c. and run,** filer (en vitesse), décamper, se sauver;

(b) *Cin TV Th* (*change scene*) **the action cuts to the street,** l'action passe à la rue; *Cin etc* **C.!,** coupez!;

(c) *Cards* couper.

cut³ *adj* **(a)** (*crystal, diamond*) taillé; **a c. glass jug,** une cruche en cristal taillé; **well c. suit,** complet de bonne coupe *ou* bien coupé; **c. and dried,** (*opinions*) tout fait; **(b)** (*reduced, shortened*) réduit; **the c. version of the film,** la version raccourcie du film.

▶**cut across** *vipo* couper à travers (*un terrain de jeu, la forêt etc*) *Fig* **concern for the environment cuts across party lines,** le souci de l'environnement dépasse les affiliations politiques.

▶**cut along** *vi Old-fashioned Br F* se sauver, filer.

▶**cut away** *vtsep (remove)* couper, ôter, retrancher; **they had to c. away wreckage to reach the victim,** ils on dû découper l'épave pour atteindre la victime; **c. away the fat,** ôtez le gras.

▶**cut back 1** *vtsep* **(a)** *(prune)* tailler *(un rosier, un framboisier)*; élaguer *(un arbre)*; **they cut back the undergrowth to widen the path,** ils ont taillé les broussailles pour élargir le sentier; **(b)** *(reduce)* baisser *(les prix)*; diminuer *(la production etc)*; **arms spending has been cut right back,** les dépenses d'armement ont été nettement réduites. **2** *vi* **(a)** *(reduce)* réduire *(la production)*; *(reduce spending)* économiser **(on,** sur); **you'll have to c. back on the cream cakes,** *(eat fewer of them)* il faudra que vous mangiez moins de gâteaux à la crème; **(b)** *(go back)* s'en retourner, rebrousser chemin; *Cin (of action)* revenir en arrière.

▶**cut down 1** *vtsep* **(a)** *(fell)* couper, abattre *(un arbre)*; couper *(le blé)*; **(b)** *(kill)* abattre; faucher *(des troupes ennemies)*; *Lit* **to be cut down in one's prime,** être fauché à la fleur de l'âge; **(c)** *(shorten)* abréger *(un discours etc)*; tronquer *(un ouvrage)*; couper, réduire *(les dépenses)*; **to c. trousers down,** *(to make shorts)* raccourcir un pantalon; **(d)** *(cut through ropes etc)* couper; **to c. down a hanged man,** couper la corde d'un pendu; **the parachutist had to be c. down from the tree,** il a fallu couper les cordes du parachutiste pour le décrocher de l'arbre. **2** *vi (reduce sth)* faire des réductions **(on sth,** de qch); **start by cutting down,** commence par réduire; **we had to c. down on our holidays abroad,** il a fallu que nous prenions moins de vacances à l'étranger.

▶**cut in 1** *vi* **(a)** *(interrupt conversation)* intervenir dans une conversation; *Tel* faire intrusion (dans une conversation); *(interrupt speaker)* couper la parole à qn; **(b)** *Aut* faire une queue de poisson; **he cut in in front of me,** il m'a fait une queue de poisson; **(c)** *Cards* (r)entrer dans le jeu *(à la place du joueur écarté au sort)*; **(d)** *(at a dance)* enlever la danseuse *ou* le danseur de qn. **2** *vtsep* **(a)** *F (include in a deal)* **to c. s.o. in (on a deal),** donner à qn sa part du gâteau; **(b)** *(say)* intervenir; **'you're wrong', she cut in,** 'tu as tort' est-elle intervenue; **(c)** *El* intercaler *(une résistance)*.

▶**cut into** *vipo* **(a)** *(interrupt)* **to c. into a conversation,** intervenir dans *ou* interrompre brusquement la conversation; **(b)** *(use)* **to c. into one's savings,** entamer ses économies; **this work cuts into my free time,** ce travail empiète sur mes heures de loisir.

▶**cut off** *vtsep* **(a)** *(remove by cutting)* couper, découper *(un morceau)*; **pages with the corners cut off,** pages dont les coins ont été découpés; **take these trousers and c. the legs off (them),** prends ce pantalon et coupes-en les jambes; **he's had all his hair cut off,** il s'est fait couper les cheveux tout court; **to c. off s.o.'s head,** trancher la tête à qn; *Lit* **to be cut off in one's prime,** être emporté *ou* fauché à la fleur de l'âge;

(b) *(isolate)* couper *(qn)* (du monde); **to c. off the enemy,** couper la ligne de retraite de l'ennemi; **to c. off s.o.'s retreat,** couper la retraite à qn; **to be cut off,** se trouver isolé; **I feel cut off,** je me sens coupé du monde; **there was heavy snow and many villages were cut off,** il y avait beaucoup de neige et de nombreux villages se sont trouvés isolés; **to c. oneself off from the world,** se retirer du monde; **she c. herself off from the family,** elle s'est coupée de sa famille;

(c) *(disconnect) Tel* couper *(qn)*; couper, supprimer *(la vapeur etc)*; *El* couper, interrompre *(le courant)*; *Aut* couper *(l'allumage)*; **I've been cut off,** on m'a coupé; **to c. off s.o.'s water/supplies,** couper *ou* supprimer l'eau/les vivres à qn;

(d) *(disinherit)* déshériter *(qn)*; **the old man cut his son off without a penny,** le vieillard n'a pas laissé un sou à son fils.

▶**cut out 1** *vtsep* **(a)** *(remove by cutting)* couper, enlever *(qch)*; retrancher *(un passage d'un livre)*; *Surg* exciser *(une tumeur etc)*; **to c. a picture out of a magazine,** découper une photo dans un magazine;

(b) *(shape by cutting)* découper *(des images)*; couper, tailler, découper *(un vêtement)*; échancrer *(une robe etc)*; **to c. a statue out of wood,** tailler une statue dans le bois; *Fig* **to be cut out for sth,** être fait pour qch, avoir des dispositions pour qch; **he's not cut out to be a leader,** il n'est pas de l'étoffe dont on fait les chefs; *Fig* **to have one's work cut out,** avoir largement de quoi faire *ou* de quoi s'occuper; **she's got her work cut out looking after those kids,** elle a largement de quoi faire à s'occuper de ces gamins;

(c) *(eliminate)* supprimer *(qch)*; **to c. out luxuries,** se priver de tout luxe; **to c. out smoking,** renoncer à fumer; **I wish he'd c. out the jokes,** j'aimerais bien qu'il arrête ses plaisanteries; *F* **c. it out!,** ça suffit maintenant!, ça va comme ça!; **the new building cuts out a lot of the light,** le nouveau bâtiment coupe une bonne partie de la lumière;

(d) *(oust)* **to c. s.o. out of a deal,** évincer qn dans une affaire.

2 *vi (stop) El (of cutout)* s'ouvrir; *(of engine)* caler; *(of sound etc)* s'arrêter.

▶**cut up 1** *vtsep* **(a)** *(chop up)* couper, débiter *(le bois, la viande)*; détailler *(une carcasse)*; découper, dépecer *(une volaille etc)*; hacher *(des légumes etc)*; **onions cut up small,** oignons émincés; **to c. sth up into small pieces,** couper qch en petits morceaux; **(b)** *F usu passive (upset)* **to be very cut up,** être profondément affecté *ou* affligé **(about sth,** par qch). **2** *vi Br F* **to c. up rough,** devenir violent

cutaneous [kjʊ'teɪnɪəs] *adj* cutané.

cutaway ['kʌtəweɪ] **1** *adj* entaillé; évidé; **c. coat,** jaquette *f*. **2** *n* **(a)** *(coat)* jaquette *f*; **(b)** *Tech (drawing)* vue *f* en coupe; **c. model,** maquette *f* en coupe.

cutback ['kʌtbæk] *n* réduction *f (de la production, d'un budget)*.

cute [kjuːt] *adj F* **(a)** *(attractive)* mignon; **what a c. little kitten,** quel mignon petit chaton; **(b)** *(clever)* malin, *f* -igne; *(idea)* original; **don't get c. with me!,** ne fais pas le malin avec moi!

cuteness ['kjuːtnɪs] *n esp Am F* **(a)** *(attractiveness)* charme *m*; **(b)** *(cleverness)* finesse *f*.

cuticle ['kjuːtɪk(ə)l] *n Anat* peau *f (à la base d'un ongle)*; cuticule *f*; **c. pen,** repousse-peaux *m inv*, repoussoir *m*.

cutlass ['kʌtləs] *n Nau* sabre *m* d'abordage.

cutler ['kʌtlər] *n* coutelier *m*.

cutlery ['kʌtlərɪ] *n esp Br* coutellerie *f* (et argenterie *f* de table); **c. drawer,** tiroir *m* à couverts; **canteen of c.,** ménagère *f*.

cutlet ['kʌtlɪt] *n Culin* **(a)** côtelette *f (d'agneau, de veau)*; **(b)** *(croquette)* croquette *f (de volaille etc)*.

cutoff ['kʌtɒf] *n* **(a)** *US (short cut)* raccourci *m*; **(b)** *MecE* obturateur *m (du cylindre)*; **(c)** *Electron* déconnexion *f*, mise *f* hors de contact, mise hors circuit; **(d)** *(limit)* limite *f*; **c. point,** point *m* de coupure; **(e) cutoffs,** *(shorts)* = jean dont on a coupé les jambes pour en faire un short.

cutout ['kʌtaʊt] *n* **(a)** *(picture)* image découpée; *Th Cin* décor découpé; **a cardboard c. of Humphrey Bogart,** une silhouette en carton de Humphrey Bogart; **(b)** *El* coupe-circuit *m inv*; disjoncteur *m*; fusible *m* (de sûreté); **(c)** *Aut* (soupape *f* d')échappement *m* libre *(du silencieux)*.

cut-price ['kʌtpraɪs] **,** *Am* **cut-rate** ['kʌtreɪt] *adj Com* à prix réduit; **c.-p. goods,** des marchandises à prix réduits; **c.-p. shop,** magasin où on vend des marchandises à prix réduits.

cutter ['kʌtər] *n* **(a)** coupeur *m (de vêtements)*; tailleur *m (de pierre, de diamants)*; *Cin* monteur, -euse; **coal c.,** haveur *m*; **(b)** *(tool, device)* coupoir *m*, lame *f*, couteau *m*; **rotary c.,** roue *f* à couteaux; **coal c.,** haveuse *f*; **milling c.,** fraise *f*; *Culin* **pastry c.,** emporte-pièce *m inv*; **(c)** *Nau* canot *m (d'un bâtiment de guerre)*; **revenue c.,** vedette *f* de la douane.

cutthroat ['kʌtθrəʊt] **1** *n* assassin *m*; *Cards* **c. (bridge),** bridge *m* à trois; **c. (razor),** rasoir *m* à manche. **2** *adj* **c. competition,** concurrence acharnée.

cutting ['kʌtɪŋ] **1** *adj* **(a) c. edge,** arête tranchante, tranchant *m*;

(b) *(wind)* cinglant, glacial;

(c) *(remark etc)* mordant, blessant; *(criticism)* incisif; **that was a bit c.,** c'était plutôt blessant; **she was rather c. about them,** elle a dit des choses blessantes à leur égard.

2 *n* **(a)** *(act of cutting)* coupe *f*, coupage *m (d'une branche, des foins etc)*; *Tech* cisaillage *m (d'une barre de fer etc)*; taille *f (d'un diamant, d'une haie etc)*; découpage *m (de la viande etc)*; *Cin* montage *m*; réduction *f (des salaires, des prix)*; rabais *m (des prix)*; *(in bookbinding)* rognage *m (des bords)*; *Surg* **c. out,** excision *f*; *MecE* **c. action,** cisaillement *m*; **c. angle,** angle *m* de coupe; **c. tool,** outil tranchant; *Cin* **c. room,** salle *f* de montage; **my best scenes ended up on the c. room floor,** mes meilleures scènes ont été coupées;

(b) *(piece cut off)* coupon *m*, bout *m (d'étoffe etc)*; *(of plant)* bouture *f*; *(of vine)* sarment *m*; **to grow a plant from a c.,** faire pousser une plante à partir d'une bouture; **to take a c.,** faire une bouture; **(newspaper) c.,** coupure *f* de journal; **c. from a newspaper,** coupure prise dans un journal; **cuttings,** copeaux *mpl*, rognures *fpl*, recoupe *f* (*de bois, de métal etc*);

(c) *Constr etc* tranchée *f*, déblai *m*; (*in forest*) percée *f*, tranchée; **railway c.,** (voie *f* en) déblai.

cutting away *n* enlèvement *m*, retranchement *m*.

cutting back *n* ravalement *m* d'un arbre; réduction *f* (*de la production, d'un budget*).

cutting down *n* abattage *m* (*des arbres*).

cuttingly ['kʌtɪŋlɪ] *adv* (*to say*) caustiquement, d'un ton piquant.

cutting off *n* suppression *f* (*des vivres etc*).

cutting out *n Surg* excision *f*; *Sewing* découpage *m*.

cutting up *n* **c. up of timber,** débit *m* du bois.

cuttlebone ['kʌt(ə)lbəʊn] *n* os *m* de seiche.

cuttlefish ['kʌt(ə)lfɪʃ] *n* seiche *f*.

cutwork ['kʌtwɜːk] *n Sewing* broderie ajourée.

CV [siː'viː] *n abbr* **curriculum vitae**.

cwt *abbr* **hundredweight**.

cyanide ['saɪənaɪd] *n Ch* cyanure *m*; **potassium c.,** cyanure de potassium.

cyanosis [saɪə'nəʊsɪs] *n Med* cyanose *f*.

cybernetics [saɪbə'netɪks] *n* (*with sing verb*) cybernétique *f*.

cyclamen ['sɪkləmən] *n Bot* cyclamen *m*.

cycle¹ ['saɪk(ə)l] *n* **(a)** (*pattern*) cycle *m* (*de mouvements etc*); **trade c.,** cycle économique; *Astron* **lunar c.,** cycle lunaire; *Aut* **four-stroke c.,** cycle à quatre temps; *Physiol* **menstrual c.,** cycle menstruel; **(b)** (*bicycle*) bicyclette *f*, vélo *m*; **c. shop,** magasin *m* de bicyclettes; **c. track,** piste *f* cyclable; **c. lane,** voie *f* pour les deux roues; **c. racing,** courses *fpl* cyclistes; **c. racing track,** vélodrome *m*; **(c)** *Am* = **MOTORCYCLE**.

cycle² *vi* faire de la bicyclette *ou* du vélo; aller à bicyclette.

cycler ['saɪklər] *n US* cycliste *mf*.

cyclic(al) ['sɪklɪk, -ɪk(ə)l] *adj* (*of movement etc*) cyclique; **c. unemployment,** chômage conjoncturel.

cycling ['saɪklɪŋ] *n* cyclisme *m*; **c. club,** club *m* de cyclisme; **c. track,** piste *f* cyclable.

cyclist ['saɪklɪst] *n* cycliste *mf*.

cyclone ['saɪkləʊn] *n Met* cyclone *m*; **eye of a c.,** œil *m* de cyclone.

cyclonic [saɪ'klɒnɪk] *adj* cyclonique; cyclonal, -aux.

cyclostyle ['saɪkləʊstaɪl] *vt Old-fashioned* polycopier (*au moyen d'un stencil*).

cyclotron ['saɪkləʊtrɒn] *n Nucl Phys* cyclotron *m*.

cyder ['saɪdər] *n* = **CIDER**.

cygnet ['sɪgnɪt] *n* (*bird*) jeune cygne *m*.

cylinder ['sɪlɪndər] *n* **(a)** *Math* cylindre *m*; **(b)** *Tech Comptr etc* cylindre *m*; barillet *m* (*de pompe etc*); barillet (*de revolver*); *Typ* rouleau *m* porte-papier; *MecE Aut* **piston c.,** cylindre de piston; **c. block,** bloc *m* de culasse; **c. head,** culasse *f*, calotte *f*; **c. head gasket,** joint *m* de culasse; **four-c. engine,** moteur *m* à quatre cylindres; *Typ* **c. press,** presse *f* à cylindre(s).

cylindrical [sɪ'lɪndrɪk(ə)l] *adj* cylindrique.

cymbal ['sɪmb(ə)l] *n* cymbale *f*.

cynic ['sɪnɪk] **1** *adj* cynique. **2** *n* personne *f* cynique; *Antiq Phil* Cynique *m*.

cynical ['sɪnɪk(ə)l] *adj* cynique.

cynically ['sɪnɪklɪ] *adv* cyniquement.

cynicism ['sɪnɪsɪz(ə)m] *n* **(a)** cynisme *m*; **(b)** (*remark*) mot *m* caustique.

cypher ['saɪfər] *n & v* = **CIPHER¹,²**.

cypress ['saɪprəs] *n* (*tree*) cyprès *m*.

Cypriot(e) ['sɪprɪət] **1** *adj* chypriote, cypriote. **2** *n* Chypriote *mf*, Cypriote *mf*.

Cyprus ['saɪprəs] *n* Chypre *f*.

Cyrillic [sɪ'rɪlɪk] **1** *adj* cyrillique. **2** *n* **in C.,** en caractères cyrilliques.

cyst [sɪst] *n* **(a)** *Biol Anat* sac *m*; **(b)** *Med* kyste *m*.

cystitis [sɪs'taɪtɪs] *n Med* cystite *f*; **to have c.,** faire une cystite.

cytology [saɪ'tɒlədʒɪ] *n Biol* cytologie *f*.

czar [zɑːr] *n* = **TSAR**.

czarevitch ['zɑːrəvɪtʃ] *n* = **TSAREVITCH**.

czarina [zɑː'riːnə] *n* = **TSARINA**.

czarist ['zɑːrɪst] *adj & n* = **TSARIST 1, 2**.

Czech [tʃek] **1** *adj* tchèque. **2** *n* **(a)** Tchèque *mf*; **(b)** *Ling* tchèque *m*.

Czechoslovak [tʃekəʊ'sləʊvæk], **Czechoslovakian** [-'vækɪən] **1** *adj* tchécoslovaque. **2** *n* Tchécoslovaque *mf*.

Czechoslovakia [tʃekəʊslə'vækɪə] *n* Tchécoslovaquie *f*.

D

D, d [diː] *n* **(a)** (la lettre) D, d *m*; *Mil etc* **D day,** le jour J; *Br Pol* **D notice,** = avis envoyé aux journaux par le gouvernement pour leur interdire de publier un article; **(b)** *Mus* ré *m*.
d (a) (*abbr* **deceased**) m.; **(b)** *Arch* (*abbr* **denarius**) pence.
D *US Pol abbr* **democrat.**
DA [diː'eɪ] *n US Jur abbr* **district attorney.**
dab¹ [dæb] *n* **(a)** (*touch*) coup léger, tape *f*; **(b)** (*portion*) tache *f* (*d'encre, de peinture*); petit morceau (*de beurre*); touche *f* (*de couleur*); **just give it a d. of paint,** mets-y un coup de peinture; **(c)** *Old-fashioned F* **dabs,** empreintes digitales.
dab² *vt* (**-bb-**) **(a)** (*touch*) donner un petit coup *ou* une tape à (*qn*); **(b)** (*daub*) tapoter; (*with pad*) tamponner; **to d. one's eyes (with a handkerchief),** se tamponner les yeux; **to d. paint on sth,** donner un coup de peinture à qch.
dab³ *n* (*fish*) limande *f*.
dab⁴ *adj & n F* **to be a d. (hand) at (doing) sth,** être passé maître en (l'art de faire) qch; *F* être calé en qch.
►dab off *vtsep* ôter en tamponnant.
dabble ['dæb(ə)l] **1** *vt* tremper (*ses mains*) dans l'eau. **2** *vi F* **to d. on the Stock Exchange,** boursicoter; **to d. in politics,** se mêler de politique; **to d. in art/music,** toucher un peu à l'art/à la musique.
dabbler ['dæblər] *n* (*amateur, dilettante*) amateur *m*; **d. on the Stock Exchange,** boursicoteur *m*, boursicotier *m*.
dace [deɪs] *n* (*fish*) vandoise *f*; dard *m*.
dachshund ['dækshʊnd] *n* (*dog*) teckel *m*.
dactyl ['dæktɪl] *n* dactyle *m*.
dad [dæd] *n F* papa *m*.
Dada ['dɑːdɑː] *n Art Lit* dada *m*, dadaïsme *m*.
Dadaism ['dɑːdɑːɪz(ə)m] *n Art Lit* dadaïsme *m*.
daddy ['dædɪ] *n F* papa *m*; **sugar d.,** papa gâteau.
daddy-longlegs ['dædɪ'lɒŋlegz] *n F* (*insect*) cousin *m*.
dado ['deɪdəʊ] *n Archit* **(a)** dé *m* (*de piédestal*); **(b)** lambris *m* (d'appui) (*d'une salle*).
daff [dæf] *n Br F* = **DAFFODIL.**
daffodil ['dæfədɪl] **1** *n* (*flower*) (narcisse *m*) jonquille *f*. **2** *adj* **d. (yellow),** jonquille *inv*.
daffy ['dæfɪ] *adj F* timbré, toqué.
daft [dɑːft] *adj Br F* timbré, toqué, cinglé, maboul(e); **to be d. about s.o./sth,** être fou de qn/qch; **don't talk d.!,** ne dis pas de bêtises!
daftness ['dɑːftnɪs] *n Br F* stupidité *f*, bêtise *f*.
dagger ['dægər] *n* **(a)** poignard *m*, dague *f*; *F* **to be at daggers drawn,** être à couteaux tirés (**with,** avec); **to look daggers at s.o.,** foudroyer qn du regard; **(b)** *Typ* croix *f*.
dago ['deɪgəʊ] *n Offensive Sl* métèque *m*.
dahlia ['deɪlɪə] *n* (*flower*) dahlia *m*.
daily ['deɪlɪ] **1** *adj* journalier, quotidien, de tous les jours; **to earn one's d. bread,** gagner son pain quotidien; *Rel* **give us this day our d. bread,** donne-nous aujourd'hui notre pain de ce jour; **d. paper,** (journal *m*) quotidien *m*; *Br* **d. help** *or* **woman,** femme *f* de ménage; *F* **d. dozen,** gymnastique quotidienne. **2** *adv* (*téléphoner etc*) quotidiennement, tous les jours; (*attendre qch*) d'un jour à l'autre. **3** *n* **(a)** *Journ* quotidien *m*; **(b)** *Br F* femme *f* de ménage.
daintily ['deɪntɪlɪ] *adv* délicatement; **to eat d.,** manger d'une manière délicate.
daintiness ['deɪntɪnɪs] *n* délicatesse *f* (*de goût etc*).
dainty¹ ['deɪntɪ] *adj* **(a)** (*dish, food*) friand, délicat; **(b)** (*person*) (*in health, in manners*) délicat; (*in build*) menu; **(c)** (*choosy*) délicat, difficile; **these animals are d. feeders,** ces animaux sont délicats sur la nourriture; **(d)** (*fragile*) fragile.
dainty² *n Lit* (*sweet*) friandise *f*; mets délicat.
dairy ['deərɪ] *n* **(a)** (*on farm*) laiterie *f*; **d. butter,** beurre laitier; **d. farm,** ferme laitière; **d. farming,** industrie laitière; **d. herd,** (troupeau *m* de) vaches laitières; **d. ice cream,** glace *f* à la crème; **d. produce,** produits laitiers; **(b)** (*shop*) laiterie *f*, crémerie *f*.
dairymaid ['deərɪmeɪd] *n* fille *f* de laiterie.
dairyman, *pl* **-men** ['deərɪmən] *n* **(a)** (*on farm*) nourrisseur *m*; **(b)** (*milkman*) laitier *m*.
dais ['deɪɪs] *n* estrade *f* (d'honneur).
daisy ['deɪzɪ] *n* (*flower*) pâquerette *f*; (*bigger*) marguerite *f*; **Michaelmas d.,** aster *m* œil-du-Christ; **as fresh as a d.,** frais comme une rose; *Sl* **he's pushing up the daisies,** il mange les pissenlits par les racines; **d. chain,** guirlande *f* de pâquerettes.
daisy wheel ['deɪzɪwiːl] *n* (*on printer*) marguerite *f*; **d.-w. printer,** imprimante à marguerite.
Dak *abbr* **Dakota.**
Dalai Lama ['dælaɪ'lɑːmə] *n* Dalaï-lama *m*.
dale [deɪl] *n* vallée *f*; (*smaller*) vallon *m*.
dalliance ['dælɪəns] *n Lit* badinage *m*.
dally ['dælɪ] *vi esp Lit* **(a)** (*trifle*) folâtrer, folichonner (**with s.o.,** avec qn); (*flirt*) badiner, flirter (**with,** avec); **to d. with an idea,** caresser une idée; **(b)** (*dawdle*) tarder, lambiner, traînasser; **to d. over sth,** s'attarder à qch.
Dalmatian [dæl'meɪʃən] *adj & n* **D. (dog),** dalmatien *m*.
dam¹ [dæm] *n HydE* barrage *m* (*de retenue*); digue *f* (*de canal*); **storage d.,** barrage-réservoir *m*.
dam² *vt* (**-mm-**) **to d. (up),** construire un barrage en aval de (*une vallée*); endiguer (*un cours d'eau, un lac*); obstruer (*un caniveau etc*); *Fig* contenir (*ses émotions*).
dam³ *n* mère *f* (*en parlant des animaux*).
damage¹ ['dæmɪdʒ] *n* **(a)** (*physical*) dommage(s) *m*(*pl*), dégâts *mpl*; (*to engine, ship etc*) avarie(s) *f* (*pl*); **storm d.,** dégâts causés par un orage; **to pay for the d.,** payer les dégâts; *Br F* **what's the d.?,** (*how much do I owe?*) ça se monte à combien?; **there's no great d. done,** il n'y a pas grand mal; **(b)** (*harm*) préjudice *m*; **to cause s.o. d.,** porter préjudice à qn; **to do d. to a cause,** faire du tort à une cause; **d. control,** fait *m* de limiter les dégâts; **(c)** *Jur* **damages,** dommages-intérêts *mpl*, indemnité *f*; **to be liable for damages,** être tenu au versement de dommages-intérêts.
damage² *vt* **(a)** endommager; avarier (*une marchandise, une machine*); abîmer (*qch*); accidenter (*une voiture*); **(b)** faire tort à (*qn*); léser (*des intérêts*); porter atteinte à, ternir (*la réputation de qn etc*).
damaged ['dæmɪdʒd] *adj* endommagé, abîmé; (*goods*) avarié; (*car*) accidenté.
damaging ['dæmɪdʒɪŋ] *adj* préjudiciable; **d. admission,** aveu *m* préjudiciable.
Damascus [də'mɑːskəs] *n* Damas *m*.
damask ['dæməsk] *n* **(a)** *Tex* damas *m*; **d. silk,** soie damassée; **(b)** *Metal* **d. steel,** acier damassé; **(c) d. rose,** rose *f* de Damas; **(d) d. (colour),** rose foncé *m inv*.
dame [deɪm] *n* **(a)** *Arch & Am F* femme *f*; (*in pantomime*) vieille femme comique (*rôle joué par un homme*); **an old d.,** une vieille femme; **(b)** *Br* dame *f* (*titre accordé aux femmes titulaires de certaines décorations*); **D. Margot Fonteyn,** Dame Margot Fonteyn.
dammit ['dæmɪt] *int F* sacristi!, sacrebleu!; **it was as near as d.,** il était moins une.
damn¹ [dæm] *n F* **I don't give** *or* **care a d.,** je m'en fiche éperdument; **it's not worth a d.,** ça ne vaut rien.
damn² *vt* **(a)** condamner (*un livre etc*); éreinter (*une pièce de théâtre*); **to d. sth with faint praise,** faire un commentaire peu enthousiaste sur qch, faire des éloges tièdes sur qch; **(b)** *Rel* damner; *F* **well I'll be damned!,** ça alors!; **I'm** *or* **I'll be damned if I'll do it,** si tu crois que je vais le faire!; **(c)** *F* jurer après (*qn*); envoyer (*qn*) au diable; **d. you!,** que le diable t'emporte!, va te faire fiche!; **d. (it)!,** zut!; **d. and blast (it)!,** sacré nom d'un chien!
damn³ *F* **1** *adj* = **DAMNED 1 (b)**. **2** *adv* = **DAMNED 3; he's doing d. all,** il n'en fout pas une (rame); **she knows d. all about it,** elle y connaît que dal(l)e.
damnable ['dæmnəb(ə)l] *adj* **(a)** *Rel* damnable; **(b)** *F*

maudit.
damnably ['dæmnəblı] *adv* **(a)** *Rel* damnablement; **(b)** *F* diablement, rudement (*difficile etc*).
damnation [dæm'neıʃən] **1** *n* damnation *f*; *Rel* **eternal d.**, la peine du dam. **2** *int F* zut!
damned [dæmd] **1** *adj* **(a)** damné; **(b)** *F* sacré; **you d. fool!**, sacré imbécile!, espèce d'idiot!; **he's a d. nuisance!**, ce qu'il est embêtant *ou* casse-pieds!; **well I'm d.!**, elle est bien bonne celle-là! **2** *n* **the d.**, (*used as pl*) les damnés *mpl*; **to suffer the tortures of the d.**, souffrir comme un damné. **3** *adv* diablement, vachement; **it's d. hot**, il fait rudement chaud; **I should d. well hope so**, ah, ben j'espère bien!; **you can do what you d. well like!**, fais ce que tu veux, je m'en fiche!
damnedest ['dæmdest] *n F* **to do one's d.**, faire tout son possible.
damning ['dæmıŋ] *adj* (*fait etc*) accablant.
Damocles ['dæməkli:z] *n* **the sword of D.**, l'épée *f* de Damoclès.
damp¹ [dæmp] *n* humidité *f* (*de l'air etc*); moiteur *f* (*de la peau*); **d. mark**, tache *f* d'humidité.
damp² *vt* **(a)** (*wet*) humecter (*le linge etc*); **(b)** (*diminish*) étouffer (*le feu, un son*); **to d. down a furnace**, boucher un haut fourneau; **(c)** abattre (*le courage de qn*); rabattre (*la joie de qn*); **to d. s.o.'s spirits**, décourager qn; **that damped his ardour**, cela a freiné son ardeur; **to d. the appetite**, (*of unpleasant sight etc*) couper l'appétit.
damp³ *adj* humide; (*skin*) moite; **his hands are always d.**, il a toujours les mains moites; **the house is very d.**, la maison est très humide; **d. heat**, chaleur *f* humide; *Fig* **d. squib**, affaire ratée.
dampcourse ['dæmpkɔ:s] *n Constr* matériau isolant contre l'humidité.
dampen [dæmp(ə)n] *vt* = **DAMP² (a), (c)**.
damper ['dæmpər] *n* **(a)** *Fig* événement décourageant; douche froide (*sur l'enthousiasme etc*); **the news put rather a d. on the celebrations/the company**, la nouvelle a jeté un froid sur les réjouissances/la compagnie; **(b)** *Mus* (*of piano, sound*) étouffoir *m*; **d. pedal**, grande pédale (*du piano*); **(c)** *Tech* registre *m* (*de foyer, de cheminée, de fourneau*); soupape *f* de réglage *ou* à papillon (*d'un tuyau de poêle*); *El* amortisseur *m*; *Rad* sourdine *f*; **(d)** mouilleur *m* (*pour timbres, enveloppes*).
dampish ['dæmpıʃ] *adj* un peu humide.
dampness ['dæmpnıs] *n* humidité *f*; moiteur *f*.
damp-proof ['dæmppru:f] *adj* hydrofuge.
damp-proofing ['dæmppru:fıŋ] *n* isolation *f* contre l'humidité.
damsel ['dæmz(ə)l] *n* **(a)** *Arch & Lit* demoiselle *f*; **(b)** (*insect*) **d. fly**, demoiselle *f*.
damson ['dæmz(ə)n] *n* prune *f* de Damas; **d. tree**, prunier *m* de Damas.
dance¹ [dɑ:ns] *n* **(a)** danse *f*; *Mus* (air *m* de) danse; **to lead** *or* **begin the d.**, mener la danse; *F* **to lead s.o. a (merry) d.**, donner du fil à retordre à qn; **folk d.**, danse folklorique; **d. music**, musique *f* de danse; **d. band**, orchestre *m* de musique de danse; **d. hall**, salle *f* de danse; (*not permanent*) dancing *m*; **(b)** (*ball*) (*for teenagers*) boum *f*; (*for older people*) soirée dansante; (*formal*) bal *m*, *pl* bals; **her parents are giving a d. for her birthday**, ses parents organisent une soirée pour son anniversaire.
dance² **1** *vi* danser; **are you dancing?**, vous dansez?; **to d. with s.o.**, danser avec qn; **to d. for joy**, danser de joie; **to d. about**, gambader. **2** *vt* danser (*une valse etc*); **to d. attendance on s.o.**, faire l'empressé auprès de qn.
dancer ['dɑ:nsər] *n* danseur, -euse.
dancing ['dɑ:nsıŋ] **1** *adj* dansant; **d. dervish**, derviche tourneur. **2** *n* danse *f*; **to go d.**, aller danser; **d. school**, école *f* de danse; **d. partner**, cavalier *m*, dame *f*; partenaire *mf*.
D & C [di:ən'si:] *n Med* dilatation *f* et curetage.
dandelion ['dændılaıən] *n* (*weed*) pissenlit *m*.
dander ['dændər] *n esp Am F* **to get s.o.'s/one's d. up**, mettre qn/se mettre en colère.
dandle ['dænd(ə)l] *vt* **(a)** (*on knees*) faire sauter (*un enfant*); **(b)** (*in arms*) bercer (*un enfant*).
dandruff ['dændrəf] *n* pellicules *fpl* (*du cuir chevelu*); **he has very bad d.**, il a beaucoup de pellicules; **d. shampoo**, shampooing *m* contre les pellicules *ou* anti-pelliculaire.
dandy ['dændı] **1** *n* dandy *m*, élégant *m*. **2** *adj Am F* épatant, chouette; **everything's just d.**, tout marche à merveille.
Dane [deın] *n* Danois, -oise.
danger ['deındʒər] *n* danger *m*, péril *m*; **out of d.**, hors de danger; **to keep out of d.**, rester à l'abri du danger; **to be in d. of falling**, courir le risque *ou* être en danger de tomber; **in d. of (losing) his life**, en danger de mort; *Med* **to be on the d. list**, être dans un état critique; **to be off the d. list**, être hors de danger; **there is some d. that ...**, il y a quelque danger que ... (ne) + *sub*; **there is no d. that ...**, il n'y a pas de danger que ... + *sub*; **he's a d. to society**, c'est un danger public; *Rail etc* **d. signal**, signal *m* à l'arrêt; *Ind etc* **d. money**, prime *f* de risque.
dangerous ['deındʒərəs] *adj* **(a)** dangereux, périlleux; (*maladie*) grave; **you are on d. ground**, vous êtes sur un terrain brûlant; **(b)** (*example, maxim*) pernicieux.
dangerously ['deındʒərəslı] *adv* dangereusement; **d. ill**, gravement malade.
dangle ['dæŋg(ə)l] **1** *vi* pendiller; **with one's legs dangling**, les jambes ballantes. **2** *vt* balancer (*qch au bout d'un cordon etc*).
Danish ['deınıʃ] **1** *adj* danois; **D. blue (cheese)**, bleu *m* du Danemark; **D. (pastry)**, = sorte de chausson fourré aux fruits. **2** *n Ling* danois *m*.
dank [dæŋk] *adj* (*temps, cachot*) humide (et froid).
Danube (the) [ðə'dænju:b] *n* le Danube.
dapper ['dæpər] *adj* pimpant, coquet.
dapple¹ ['dæp(ə)l] *n* **(a)** tache *f* de couleur (*sur la robe d'un cheval etc*); **(b)** (*horse*) cheval pommelé; **d. grey**, (*cheval*) gris pommelé.
dapple² *vt* tacheter; **a wall dappled with sunlight**, un mur sur lequel le soleil vient se refléter par endroits.
dapple-grey [dæp(ə)l'greı] *n* (*horse*) cheval gris pommelé.
Darby ['dɑ:bı] *n* **D. and Joan**, = Philémon et Baucis; **D. and Joan club**, club *m* des vieux *ou* du troisième âge.
dare¹ ['deər] **1** *modal v aux* (*third sg pr* **dare**; *pt* **dared**; *no pp*; **d. not** *often contracted to* **daren't**) oser; **I d. not** *or* **daren't speak to him**, je n'ose pas lui parler; **don't you d. touch him!**, ne touchez pas un cheveu de sa tête!; **don't you d. (do that)!**, ne t'avise pas de faire ça!; **I d. say that ...**, je suppose que ...; **I d. say**, sans doute, c'est bien possible. **2** *vt* (*third sg pr* **dares**; *pt, pp* **dared**) oser; braver, affronter (*le danger, la mort etc*); **to d. to do sth**, oser faire qch; **how d. you!**, vous avez cette audace!; **let him do it if he dare(s)!**, qu'il le fasse s'il l'ose!; **to d. s.o. to do sth**, défier qn de faire qch; **I d. you!**, chiche!
dare² *n* défi *m*; **to do sth for a d.**, faire qch pour relever un défi.
daredevil ['deədev(ə)l] **1** *n* casse-cou *m inv*, risque-tout *m inv*. **2** *adj* audacieux, -euse.
daring ['deərıŋ] **1** *adj* audacieux, hardi; (*foolhardy*) téméraire; (*robe*) provocant; **greatly d.**, bien osé, fort osé. **2** *n* audace *f*; (*foolhardiness*) témérité *f*; **to lose one's d.**, perdre de son audace.
daringly ['deərıŋlı] *adv* (*see adj*) audacieusement; témérairement; **a d. low dress**, une robe au décolleté audacieux.
dark¹ [dɑ:k] *adj* **(a)** sombre, obscur; **d. glasses**, lunettes noires *ou* de soleil; **it's d.**, (*outside*) il fait nuit, il fait noir; il fait sombre (*dans la pièce*); **it is getting** *or* **growing d.**, il commence à faire sombre *ou* à faire nuit; **everything became d.**, tout s'assombrit;
(b) (*colour*) foncé, sombre; **d. blue dresses**, robes *fpl* bleu foncé;
(c) (*person*) brun; (*complexion*) basané; **she has d. hair**, elle est brune;
(d) (*unhappy*) (*pensée etc*) triste; (*avenir etc*) sombre; (*sinister*) sinistre; **to look on the d. side of things**, voir tout en noir; **to harbour d. designs**, nourrir de noirs desseins;
(e) (*secret*) mystérieux, secret, -ète; **to keep sth d.**, tenir qch secret; *Fig* **a d. horse**, (*stranger*) un concurrent inconnu; (*unexpected competition*) un concurrent que l'on ne croyait pas dangereux; **he's a d. horse**, (*a stranger*) on ne sait rien de lui; (*gave nothing away*) il a bien caché son jeu;
(f) *Hist* **the D. Ages**, le haut moyen âge; **the D. Continent**, le Continent noir, l'Afrique *f*.
dark² *n* ténèbres *fpl*, obscurité *f*; **in the d.**, dans le noir; **the child is afraid of the d.**, l'enfant a peur du noir; **after d.**, à *ou* après la tombée de la nuit; *Fig* **to be (kept) in the d.**, être (laissé) dans l'ignorance; **we kept her in the d. about it**, on l'a laissé dans l'ignorance de cela, on ne lui en a rien dit.
darken ['dɑ:k(ə)n] **1** *vt* obscurcir (*une chambre etc*); assombrir (*le ciel, l'avenir*); foncer (*une couleur*); attrister (*la vie de qn*); troubler (*la raison*); **never d. my door again!**, ne remettez plus les pieds chez moi! **2** *vi* s'obscurcir; (*of sky, brow*) s'assombrir; (*of colour*) se foncer.

darkening ['dɑːk(ə)nɪŋ] *n* assombrissement *m* (*du ciel etc*); noircissement *m* (*d'un tableau etc*).
dark-eyed ['dɑːk'aɪd] *adj* aux yeux foncés.
dark-haired ['dɑːk'heəd] *adj* aux cheveux foncés.
darkish ['dɑːkɪʃ] *adj* un peu sombre.
darkly ['dɑːklɪ] *adv* **(a)** obscurément; **(b)** (*regarder qn*) d'un air menaçant.
darkness ['dɑːknɪs] *n* **(a)** obscurité *f*; **the room was in complete d.,** il faisait tout à fait noir dans la pièce; **the house was in d.,** (*no lights were on*) la maison était dans l'obscurité; **(b)** (*of colour*) teinte foncée; **(c)** ignorance *f*.
darkroom ['dɑːkruːm] *n Phot* cabinet noir, chambre noire.
dark-skinned ['dɑːk'skɪnd] *adj* à peau brune, qui a la peau brune.
darling ['dɑːlɪŋ] *n* chéri, -ie; (*favourite*) favori, -ite; **(my) d.!,** mon chéri!, ma chérie!, mon chou!; **she's a little d.,** c'est un petit amour; **a mother's d.,** *F* le chouchou de sa maman; **the d. of the people,** l'idole *f* du peuple; **a d. little place,** un petit endroit charmant; **be a d. and ...,** tu serais un amour si ... .
darn¹ [dɑːn] *n* reprise *f* (*dans un bas etc*).
darn² *vt* repriser.
darn³ *vt & vi F* **d. (it)!,** zut!
darn⁴, darned [dɑːnd] *adj F* sacré; **it's a d. nuisance,** c'est vachement embêtant.
darning ['dɑːnɪŋ] *n* reprise *f*; **invisible d.,** reprise perdue; **d. egg/wool/needle,** œuf *m*/laine *f*/aiguille *f* à repriser.
dart¹ [dɑːt] *n* **(a)** (*weapon*) dard *m*, trait *m*; **paper d.,** avion *m* en papier; **(b)** (*in games*) fléchette *f*; **game of darts,** jeu *m* de fléchettes; **do you want a game of darts?,** tu veux faire une partie de fléchettes?; **(c)** *Sewing* pince *f*; **(d)** (*movement*) mouvement soudain; **to make a sudden d.,** foncer, se précipiter (**for, towards,** sur, vers).
dart² **1** *vt* lancer, darder (*un regard etc*). **2** *vi* se précipiter, s'élancer, foncer (**at s.o./sth,** sur qn/qch); **he darted across the road,** il a traversé la rue comme une flèche; **to d. in/out,** entrer/sortir comme une flèche.
dartboard ['dɑːtbɔːd] *n* cible *f* (*de jeu de fléchettes*).
dash¹ [dæʃ] *n* **(a)** (*drop*) goutte *f*, larme *f* (*de cognac etc*); filet *m*, goutte (*de vinaigre*); **add a d. of lemon,** ajoutez-y un filet de citron; **d. of colour,** touche *f* de couleur (*dans un tableau*); **(b)** trait *m* (*de plume, de l'alphabet Morse*); *Typ* tiret *m*; (*minus sign*) moins *m*; **(c)** (*movement*) course *f* à toute vitesse; *US Sp* sprint *m*; **to make a d. forward,** s'élancer en avant; **a quick d. across to Paris,** un petit saut à Paris; **to make a d. at sth,** se précipiter sur qch; **to make a d. at s.o.,** foncer sur qn; **to make a d. for it,** saisir l'occasion de s'enfuir; **(d)** (*style*) élan *m*, entrain *m*; **to cut a d.,** faire de l'épate; **(e)** *Aut F* tableau *m* de bord.
dash² **1** *vt* **(a)** (*throw*) heurter violemment (*qch contre qch*); **to d. sth to the ground,** jeter qch par terre; **the ship was dashed against a rock,** le navire a été jeté sur un écueil; **to d. sth to pieces,** fracasser qch, briser qch en morceaux; **(b)** *Fig* déconcerter (*qn*); détruire (*les espérances*); refroidir (*l'enthousiasme*); **to d. s.o.'s spirits,** abattre le courage de qn; **he saw his hopes dashed,** il a vu tomber à l'eau ses espérances; **(c)** *F* **d. (it)!,** zut! **2** *vi* **I must d.,** il faut que je file; **to come dashing up/in,** arriver/entrer comme un bolide; **to d. up/down the stairs,** monter/descendre l'escalier quatre à quatre; **to d. into the room,** entrer précipitamment *ou* en coup de vent dans la salle.
►**dash away** *vi* partir en coup de vent, filer à toute vitesse.
►**dash off** **1** *vi* partir en coup de vent, filer à toute vitesse. **2** *vtsep* faire (*qch*) en vitesse; dessiner *ou* faire (*un croquis*) rapidement; écrire (*une lettre*) en vitesse.
►**dash out** *vi* sortir en coup de vent *ou* en trombe.
dashboard ['dæʃbɔːd] *n Aut* tableau *m* de bord.
dashed [dæʃd] *Old-fashioned Br F* **1** *adj* sacré; **what a d. nuisance!,** quel empoisonnement! **2** *adv* vachement; **it's d. hot,** il fait vachement chaud.
dashing ['dæʃɪŋ] *adj* (*person*) impétueux; (*looks*) fringant, qui a belle allure; **d. young man,** beau jeune homme.
dashingly ['dæʃɪŋlɪ] *adv* (*se conduire*) avec fougue, avec brio.
dastardly ['dæstədlɪ] *adj Lit* **(a)** (*personne*) lâche; **(b)** (*crime etc*) infâme, ignoble.
DAT [diːeɪ'tiː] *n* (*abbr* **digital audio tape**) cassette *f* numérique; **DAT recorder,** magnétophone *m* numérique.
data ['deɪtə, 'dɑːtə] *n Comptr etc* données *fpl*, renseignements *mpl*; *Comptr* **d. processing,** (*science*) informatique *f*; (*handling*) traitement *m* de l'information; **d. protection act,** = Loi Informatique et Libertés; **d. bank,** banque *f* de données; **d. base,** base *f* de données; **to have/put sth in a d. base,** avoir/mettre qch dans une base de données; **d. base management,** gestion *f* de base(s) de données; **d. block,** bloc *m* de données; **d. buffer,** mémoire *f* tampon; **d. bus,** bus *m* de données; **d. capture,** saisie *f* de données; **d. carrier,** support *m* de données; **d. flow,** flux *m* de données; **d. pen,** crayon *m* électronique; **d. stream,** flot *m* de données; **d. switch,** commutateur *m* de données.
date¹ [deɪt] *n* (*fruit*) datte *f*; **d. palm,** dattier *m*.
date² *n* **(a)** date *f*; (*on coins, books etc*) millésime *m*; (*of month*) quantième *m*; **d. of birth,** date de naissance; **what's the d. (today)?,** le combien sommes-nous aujourd'hui?; **to fix a d. for sth,** prendre date *ou* fixer une date pour qch; **shall we fix a d. now?,** est-ce que nous prenons date *ou* fixons une date maintenant?; **have you set a d. yet?,** (*for wedding*) est-ce que vous avez déjà décidé de la date du mariage?; **I'm not free on that d.,** je ne suis pas libre à cette date; **what dates are you free?,** à quelles dates êtes-vous libre?; **d. stamp,** dateur *m*, timbre *m* à date; *Geog* **d. line,** ligne *f* de changement de date (*le méridien 180°*); **to cross the (international) d. line,** passer la ligne de changement de date; **up to d.,** à jour; **to be up to d.,** (*with work, reading*) être à jour; (*with what's happening*) être au courant; (*in fashion*) être à la page; **to bring a diary/etc up to d.,** mettre à jour son journal/*etc*; **to d.,** à ce jour; **out of d.,** périmé; **this style is out of d.,** ce style est démodé;
(b) *Com Fin* terme *m*, échéance *f* (*d'un billet*); **d. of maturity, due d.,** (date *f* d')échéance;
(c) *F* (*appointment*) rendez-vous *m inv*; (*boyfriend, girlfriend*) ami, -e; **blind d.,** = rendez-vous avec quelqu'un qu'on ne connaît pas; *US* **double d.,** rendez-vous entre deux couples; **to make a d.,** fixer un rendez-vous; **I have a d. tonight,** j'ai un rendez-vous ce soir; (*with boyfriend etc*) je sors avec quelqu'un ce soir; *Am* **I don't have a d. for the prom,** je n'ai pas de cavalier *ou* de cavalière pour le bal de fin d'année; **where's your d.?,** où est la personne qui t'accompagne?; **my d. didn't show up,** on m'a posé un lapin.
date³ **1** *vt* **(a)** dater (*une lettre etc*); millésimer (*une bouteille de vin etc*); composter (*un billet*); **to d. back,** antidater; **work of art that is difficult to d.,** œuvre d'art à laquelle il est difficile d'assigner une date; **his clothes d. him,** ses vêtements démodés montrent qu'il n'est pas jeune; **that dates you,** (*shows how old you are*) ça montre ton âge; **(b)** sortir avec (*un homme, une femme*), fréquenter (*qn*). **2** *vi* **(a)** dater (**from,** de); **church dating from** *or* **back to the XIIIth century,** église qui remonte au *ou* qui date du XIIIe siècle; **friendship dating back to the days of their youth,** amitié qui remonte à leur jeunesse; **his style is beginning to d.,** son style commence à dater; **(b)** *F* (*of couple*) se fréquenter; **they've been dating for years,** cela fait des années qu'ils se fréquentent.
dated ['deɪtɪd] *adj* **(a)** démodé; **his style is rather d.,** son style commence à dater; **(b)** *Fin* **long-/short-d.,** à longue/courte échéance.
dateless ['deɪtlɪs] *adj* (*dress, style etc*) intemporel.
dateline [deɪtlaɪn] *n Journ* date *f* (*d'un communiqué etc*).
dating¹ ['deɪtɪŋ] *n* **(a)** datage *m* (*d'un document etc*); compostage *m* (*de billets*); **(b)** *Archeol etc* datation *f*.
dating² *n* **d. agency** agence matrimoniale.
dative ['deɪtɪv] *adj & n Gram* **d. (case),** (cas *m*) datif *m*; **in the d.,** au datif.
datum ['deɪtəm] *n Fml* (*pl* **data**) donnée *f*, élément *m* (*d'information*); **d. point,** (*in robotics*) point *m* de référence.
daub¹ [dɔːb] *n* **(a)** *Pej* (*picture*) croûte *f*, barbouillage *m*; **(b)** *Constr* torchis *m*.
daub² *vt* **(a)** *Pej Art* barbouiller (*une toile*); **(b)** barbouiller (**with,** de).
daughter ['dɔːtər] *n* fille *f*.
daughterboard ['dɔːtəbɔːd] *n Comptr* carte *f* fille.
daughter-in-law ['dɔːtərɪnlɔː] *n* belle-fille *f*, *pl* belles-filles; (*wife of son*) bru *f*, belle-fille.
daunt [dɔːnt] *vt* intimider (*qn*); **nothing daunted,** intrépide(ment).
daunting [dɔːntɪŋ] *adj* (*task etc*) intimidant.
dauntless ['dɔːntlɪs] *adj* intrépide, sans peur.
dauntlessly ['dɔːntlɪslɪ] *adv* intrépidement.
davenport ['dævənpɔːt] *n Am* canapé(-lit) *m*.
davit ['dævɪt] *n Nau* bossoir *m* (*d'embarcation*).
Davy ['deɪvɪ] *n* (*dimin of* **David**) = David *m*; *Nau F* **to go to D. Jones's locker,** boire à la grande tasse.
dawdle ['dɔːd(ə)l] *vi* flâner, traînasser, lambiner.
dawdler ['dɔːdlər] *n* flâneur, -euse, traînard, -arde.
dawdling [dɔːdlɪŋ] *n* flânerie *f*.

dawn¹ [dɔːn] *n* aube *f*, aurore *f*; *Fig* aurore, aube (*de la vie*); *Fig* commencement *m* (*de la civilisation*); **at d.**, à l'aube; **at (the) crack of d.**, à la pointe du jour; **the d. chorus,** le chant des oiseaux à l'aube; *St Exch* **d. raider,** raider *m*.

dawn² *vi* (*of day, morning*) poindre; *Fig* (commencer à) paraître; **day is dawning,** le jour se lève; *Fig* **when the truth dawned on him,** quand il a compris la vérité; *Fig* **it dawned on me that ...,** j'ai commencé à me rendre compte que ... .

dawning [dɔːnɪŋ] *adj* (*jour*) naissant.

day [deɪ] *n* **(a)** jour *m*; (*referring to duration*) journée *f*; **it's been a sunny d.,** il a fait une journée de soleil; **to work d. and night,** travailler nuit et jour; **all d. (long),** toute la journée; **to work/to be paid by the d.,** travailler/être payé à la journée; **it's all in a d.'s work,** ça fait partie de la routine; **eight-hour d.,** journée de huit heures; **in the course of the d.,** dans la journée; **at the end of the d.,** à la fin de la journée; *Fig* en fin de compte, au bout du compte; **twice a d.,** deux fois par jour; **I remember it to this (very) d.,** je m'en souviens encore aujourd'hui; **a year ago to the d.,** il y a un an jour pour jour; **the d. before/after he came,** la veille/le lendemain de son arrivée; **two days before/after his wedding,** l'avant-veille *f*/le surlendemain de son mariage; **two days later,** deux jours après *ou* plus tard, le surlendemain; **every other d.,** tous les deux jours, un jour sur deux; **d. after d., d. in d. out,** jour après jour; **d. by d.,** jour par jour; **from d. to d.,** de jour en jour, d'un jour à l'autre; **to live from d. to d.,** vivre au jour le jour; *F* **from d. one,** dès le début; **he's sixty if he's a d.,** il a soixante ans bien sonnés; *Mil etc* **officer of the d.,** officier *m* de jour; *Fig* **let's call it a d.,** (*finish work*) ça suffit pour aujourd'hui; (*end relationship*) finissons-en, rompons; **to carry** *or* **win the d.,** gagner la journée *ou* la bataille; *F* **that'll be the d.!,** j'aimerais voir ça!; **pay d.,** jour de paie; *Mil* jour de solde; *St Exch* jour de liquidation *ou* de règlement; **Friday is pay d.,** vendredi c'est le jour de paie; **d. bed,** lit *m* de repos; *Fin* **d. bill,** effet *m* à date fixe; **d. labourer,** journalier *m*, ouvrier *m* à la journée; *Med* **d. nurse,** infirmier, -ière qui est de service de jour; **d. nursery,** crèche *f*; **d. pupil,** externe *mf*; *Rail etc* **d. return,** (billet *m* d')aller *m* et retour valable pour la journée; *Sch* **d. school,** externat *m*; *Ind* **d. shift,** équipe *f* de jour; **to be on d. shift** *or F* **days,** (*of worker*) être de jour; *Met* **d. temperature,** température *f* diurne; **d. trip,** excursion *f ou* voyage *m* d'une journée; **a d. trip to Paris,** une excursion d'une journée à Paris; **d. tripper,** excursionniste *mf*;

(b) (*dawn*) jour *m*; **before d.,** avant le jour; **at break of d.,** au point du jour; **in the full light of d.,** (*daylight*) en plein midi; **to travel by d.,** voyager de jour;

(c) (*24 hours*) jour *m*; *Jur etc* **ten clear days' notice,** préavis *m* de dix jours francs;

(d) d. of the month, quantième *m* du mois; **what d. (of the week) is it (today)?,** quel jour (de la semaine) sommes-nous?; **to pass the time of d. with s.o.,** échanger quelques paroles de politesse avec qn; **I met him one d.,** je l'ai rencontré un jour; **one d., some d., one of these days,** un jour (ou l'autre), un de ces jours; **the baby's due any d. now,** le bébé va naître d'un jour à l'autre; **the other d.,** l'autre jour; **open d.,** (*at school, office etc*) journée *f* portes ouvertes; **to take/get a d. off,** prendre/obtenir un jour de congé; *Fig* **to name the d.,** fixer le jour du mariage; *Rel* **the d. of judgement,** le jour du jugement;

(e) (*anniversary, celebration*) fête *f*; **Mother's/Father's D.,** la fête des Mères/des Pères; **Saint David's D.,** Saint-David *f*; = fête nationale galloise; **All Saints' D.,** la Toussaint; **All Souls' D.,** le Jour des Morts; **Christmas D.,** le jour de Noël; *F* **let's make a d. of it!,** allons faire la fête!;

(f) (*time*) **the good old days,** le bon vieux temps; **in the days of ...,** au *ou* du temps de ...; **in my young days,** au *ou* du temps de ma jeunesse; **in those days,** en ce temps-là, à cette époque, alors; **these days,** de notre temps; **in this d. and age,** de nos jours; **those were the days,** c'était la belle vie (alors); **in his d.,** (*when he was young*) en son temps; (*when he was alive*) de son vivant; **she was a great actress in her d.,** c'était une grande actrice à son époque; **he ended his days in poverty,** il a fini ses jours pauvre; **in days to come,** à l'avenir; **to have had its d.,** (*of theory, fashion etc*) être démodé; *Prov* **everything has its d.,** chaque chose a son heure de gloire; **every dog has its d.,** tout le monde a sa chance un jour ou l'autre; **it's early days (yet),** ce n'est que le début.

daybook ['deɪbʊk] *n Com* (livre *m*) journal *m*, -aux.

dayboy ['deɪbɔɪ] *n Sch* externe *m*.

daybreak ['deɪbreɪk] *n* point *m* du jour, lever *m* du jour; **at d.,** au lever du jour, au point du jour.

daycare ['deɪkeər] *n* **the children go to d.,** les enfants vont à la garderie; **d. centre,** (*for children*) garderie *f*; **d. facilities,** service *m* de garderie.

daydream¹ ['deɪdriːm] *n* rêverie *f*, songerie *f*.

daydream² *vi* rêvasser, songer; **to d. about the future,** fantasmer sur le futur; **she spends all her time daydreaming,** elle passe tout son temps à rêvasser.

daydreaming ['deɪdriːmɪŋ] *n* rêverie *f*, songerie *f*, rêvasserie *f*; **d. will get you nowhere,** les rêveries ne te mèneront nulle part.

daygirl ['deɪgɜːl] *n Sch* externe *f*.

daylight ['deɪlaɪt] *n* **(a)** jour *m*, lumière *f* du jour; **d. hours,** heures durant lesquelles il fait jour; **in broad d.,** en plein jour; *Fig* au grand jour; **(b)** (*dawn*) l'aube *f*, le point du jour; **before d.,** avant le jour; **(c)** *Fig* **to (begin to) see d.,** (*come to the end of a task*) apercevoir la fin; (*understand*) (commencer à) voir clair; **(d)** *F* **to beat the living daylights out of s.o.,** rosser qn, tabasser qn; **to scare the living daylights out of s.o.,** flanquer la trouille *ou* une peur bleue à qn.

daylight-saving ['deɪlaɪt'seɪvɪŋ] *n* **d.-s. time,** heure avancée d'été.

daytime ['deɪtaɪm] *n* jour *m*, journée *f*; **in the d.,** pendant la journée, de jour.

day-to-day ['deɪtə'deɪ] *adj* (*task*) de routine; **d.-to-d. management of a company,** administration courante d'une entreprise.

daze¹ [deɪz] *n* étourdissement *m*, ahurissement *m*; **to be in a d.,** être hébété *ou* ahuri.

daze² *vt* **(a)** (*of drug etc*) stupéfier, hébéter; (*of blow*) étourdir; **(b)** (*bewilder*) abasourdir, ahurir (*qn*).

dazed [deɪzd] *adj* **(a)** stupéfié, hébété; tout étourdi (*par un coup*); **(b)** (*bewildered*) abasourdi, sidéré; **she had a d. look on her face, she looked d.,** elle avait l'air abasourdi, elle paraissait abasourdie.

dazzle¹ ['dæz(ə)l] *n* éblouissement *m*.

dazzle² *vt* éblouir, aveugler; **dazzled with** *or* **by the light,** aveuglé par la lumière; **she was quite dazzled by him,** elle a été vraiment éblouie par lui.

dazzling ['dæzlɪŋ] *adj* (*light, beauty*) éblouissant; (*light*) aveuglant; (*success*) éclatant.

dazzlingly ['dæz(ə)lɪŋlɪ] *adv* **d. beautiful,** d'une beauté éblouissante.

DBS [diːbiː'es] *n Telecom abbr* **direct broadcasting satellite.**

DC [diː'siː] *n* **(a)** *El abbr* **direct current**; **(b)** *Am F* (*abbr* **District of Columbia**) = Washington.

DDT [diːdiː'tiː] *n Ch* DDT *m*.

deacon ['diːkən] *n Rel* diacre *m*.

deaconess ['diːkənɪs] *n* diaconesse *f*.

dead [ded] **1** *adj* **(a)** (*person, tree, flower*) mort; (*doigt*) mort, engourdi par le froid; **he is d.,** il est mort *ou* décédé; **the d. man/woman,** le mort/la morte; *Fig* **d. man,** (*empty bottle*) cadavre *m*; **d. man's fingers,** (*coral*) alcyon *m*; **d. man's handle,** (*on train controls*) manette *f*, homme mort; **to drop** *or* **fall (down) d.,** tomber (raide) mort; *Sl* **drop d.!,** va te faire voir!; **to shoot s.o. d.,** tuer qn net (d'un coup de revolver); *F* **d. as a doornail, d. as mutton,** mort et bien mort; **d. and gone, d. and buried,** mort et enterré; **half d. with fright,** à moitié mort de peur; **more d. than alive,** plus mort que vif; **to leave s.o. for d.,** laisser qn pour mort; *Fig* **I wouldn't be seen d. wearing it,** je ne porterais ça pour rien au monde; *Fig* **I wouldn't be seen d. there,** je n'y irais pour rien au monde; **to be d. to the world,** (*asleep*) être profondément endormi; **to go d.,** (*of limb*) s'engourdir; *F* **to be d. from the neck up,** être idiot; *F* **if Dad finds out, you're a d. duck,** si Papa l'apprend, gare à toi!; **to make a d. set at s.o.,** (*of woman*) chercher à tout prix à mettre le grappin sur qn; **d. water,** eau stagnante; *Nau* remous *m* de sillage; *Geog* **the D. Sea,** la Mer Morte; **to become a d. letter,** (*of regulation*) tomber en désuétude; **d. letters,** lettres *fpl* de rebut; **d.-letter office,** bureau *m* des rebuts; **d. language,** langue morte;

(b) (*hardened*) **d. to all sense of honour,** insensible à tout sentiment d'honneur;

(c) (*lacking power, energy etc*) (*feu*) mort; (*charbon*) éteint; (*couleur*) terne; (*son*) mat; *El* (*fil*) hors *ou* sans tension; (*pile*) épuisé; *Tel* **the line** *or* **phone is d.,** il n'y a pas de tonalité;

(d) (*ville*) mort; **d. season,** morte-saison *f*, *pl* mortes-saisons; **this place is d. in winter,** cet endroit est mort l'hiver; **d. centre,** point mort (*du piston*); (*of lathe*) centre *m* fixe; **d. end,** (*street etc*) cul-de sac *m*, *pl* culs-de sac, impasse *f*; (*of pipe*) bout *m* aveugle; **d. end job,** emploi *m* sans avenir; *Fig* **to reach** *or* **come to a d. end,** arriver à une impasse; *Constr* **d. load** *or* **weight,** poids mort; *Aut* poids utile; *Fig* **he's a d. weight,** c'est un poids mort; *Fb* **d. ball,** ballon mort; *Mil* **d. angle,** angle mort;

(e) d. stop, arrêt complet; *Nau* **d. calm,** calme plat; **d. silence,** silence *m* de mort; **d. secret,** profond secret; **d. level,** niveau parfait; **d. loss,** perte sèche; *F* (*person*) propre *m* à rien; **d. heat,** arrivée *f* ex-aequo; **it was a d. heat,** il y a eu une arrivée ex-aequo.

2 *n* **(a) the d.,** les morts *mpl*; **to rise from the d.,** ressusciter des morts; **d. march,** marche *f* funèbre; **(b)** (*depths*) **at d. of night,** au plus profond de la nuit; **in the d. of winter,** au plus fort de l'hiver.

3 *adv* (*completely*) absolument; **d. drunk,** ivre mort; **d. tired,** mort de fatigue; **d. sure,** absolument certain; **d. on the hour,** à l'heure tapante; **he was d. right,** il avait absolument raison; **he was d. set on doing it,** il voulait le faire à tout prix; *F* **d. broke,** fauché; *F* **d. beat,** crevé; *Nau* **wind d. ahead,** vent droit debout; **d. slow,** aussi lentement que possible; (*road sign*) au pas; *Hum* **he has two speeds — d. slow and stop,** il a deux vitesses — la première et le point mort; **with the tide running d. against us,** avec le courant en plein contre nous; **to be d. (set) against sth,** être absolument opposé à qch; **d. smooth surface,** surface parfaitement plane; **to stop d.,** s'arrêter net.

dead-and-alive ['ded(ə)ndə'laɪv] *adj* mort, triste; **a d.-and-a. hole,** un trou perdu, *Sl* un bled.

deadbeat ['ded'biːt] *n esp Am F* (*sponger*) pique-assiette *m inv*.

deaden ['ded(ə)n] *vt* amortir (*un coup*); assourdir, étouffer, feutrer (*un son*); émousser (*les sens*); calmer (*les nerfs*).

deadening ['ded(ə)nɪŋ] *n* amortissement *m* (*d'un coup*); assourdissement *m* (*du bruit, d'un son*).

deadhead[1] ['dedhed] *n F* **(a)** (*dullard*) nullité *f*; **(b)** *Th* personne *f* en possession d'un billet de faveur; *Rail* personne en possession d'un titre de transport gratuit.

deadhead[2] *vt* **to d. flowers,** (*in garden*) enlever les fleurs fanées.

deadline ['dedlaɪn] *n* (*day*) date *f* limite; (*time*) heure *f* limite; (*of journalist*) délai *m* de remise; **the d. for returning your essays,** la date limite *ou* la dernière limite pour rendre vos dissertations; **to meet a d.,** faire qch dans le délai prescrit, respecter un délai.

deadliness ['dedlɪnɪs] *n* **(a)** nature mortelle (*d'un poison etc*); **(b)** *F* (*boredom*) ennui mortel.

deadlock[1] ['dedlɒk] *n* serrure *f* à pêne dormant; *Fig* impasse *f*; **to reach d.,** arriver à une impasse.

deadlock[2] *vt* **talks are deadlocked,** les discussions ont atteint une impasse, les discussions en sont au point mort.

deadly ['dedlɪ] **1** *adj* **(a)** (*poison, blow etc*) mortel; (*arme*) meurtrier; (*haine*) implacable, mortel; (*combat*) à mort; *Fig* (*pâleur, silence etc*) de mort; **the seven d. sins,** les sept péchés capitaux; **d. nightshade,** (*plant*) belladone *f*; **(b)** *F* (*boring*) ennuyeux, rasant. **2** *adv* **(a)** comme la mort; **d. pale,** d'une pâleur mortelle; *F* **d. dull,** rasant; **(b)** (*completely*) **to be d. serious,** être tout à fait sérieux.

deadpan ['dedpæn] *adj* (*visage*) impassible, figé; (*humour*) de pince-sans-rire.

deadwood ['dedwʊd] *n Fig* personne improductive; (*thing*) chose *f* inutile; **there is too much d. in this office,** il y a trop de gens payés à ne rien faire dans ce bureau.

deaf [def] **1** *adj* sourd; **d. in one ear,** sourd d'une oreille; **d. and dumb,** sourd-muet, *f* sourde-muette; **d. as a (door)post,** sourd comme un pot; **d. to entreaties,** sourd aux supplications; *Prov* **there are none so d. as those that will not hear,** il n'y a pire sourd que celui qui ne veut (pas) entendre; **to turn a d. ear to,** refuser d'écouter (*qn*); rester sourd à (*les prières*). **2** *n* **the d.,** (*used as pl*) les sourds *mpl*.

deaf-aid ['defeɪd] *n* appareil *m* acoustique; **she wears a d.-a.,** elle porte un appareil acoustique.

deafen ['def(ə)n] *vt* assourdir (*qn*); **you're deafening me,** vous me percez les oreilles.

deafening ['def(ə)nɪŋ] *adj* (*bruit*) assourdissant.

deaf-mute ['def'mjuːt] *n* sourd-muet, *f* sourde-muette, *pl* sourds-muets, sourdes-muettes.

deafness ['defnɪs] *n* surdité *f*.

deal[1] [diːl] *n* **a good d.,** (*a lot*) beaucoup; **I have a great/good d. to do,** j'ai beaucoup de/bien des choses à faire; **there's a great d. of truth in that,** il y a beaucoup de vrai là-dedans; **I think a great d. of him,** je l'estime beaucoup; **he is a good d. better,** il va beaucoup mieux.

deal[2] *n* **(a)** *Cards* donne *f*; **whose d. is it?,** à qui de donner?; **your d.!,** à vous la donne!; **(b)** *Com etc* affaire *f*, marché *m*; **d. on the Stock Exchange,** coup *m* de Bourse; *US Hist* **the New D.,** le New Deal; **cash d.,** transaction *f* au comptant; **package d.,** contrat global; **big d.,** grosse affaire; *F Iron* la belle affaire!; **it's a d.!,** d'accord!, entendu!; *Pol* **d. between parties,** accord *m* entre partis; **to give s.o. a fair d.,** agir loyalement envers qn; **to give s.o. a raw d.,** en faire voir de dures à qn.

deal[3] *v* (*pt & pp* **dealt** [delt]) **1** *vt* **(a)** donner, distribuer (*les cartes*); **(b) to d. s.o. a blow,** porter un coup à qn. **2** *vi* **(a)** (*trade*) traiter; **to d. in leather/in options,** faire le commerce des cuirs/des primes; **(b)** *Cards* faire la donne, donner, *F* faire.

deal[4] *n* **(a)** (*plank*) madrier *m*; **(b)** (*sawn wood*) (bois *m* de) pin *m*, sapin *m*.

▶**deal out** *vtsep* distribuer (*des vivres, des dons*) (**to, among,** entre); donner, distribuer (*les cartes*); **to d. out justice,** rendre la justice.

▶**deal with** *vipo* **(a)** (*do business with*) avoir affaire à *ou* avec (*qn*); *Com* traiter *ou* négocier *ou* commercer avec (*qn*); se fournir chez (*un épicier etc*); **man easy/difficult to d. with,** homme commode/pas commode; **I refuse to d. with him,** je refuse de traiter avec lui; **(b)** (*be about*) traiter de, s'occuper de (*un sujet*); **(c)** (*handle*) conclure, terminer (*une affaire*); aviser à (*une situation*); *Com* donner suite à (*une commande*); **I know how to d. with him,** je sais m'y prendre avec lui; **I'll d. with this,** je m'en occupe.

dealer ['diːlər] *n* **(a)** *Cards* donneur, -euse; **(b)** *Com* négociant *m* (**in,** en); (*supplier*) fournisseur *m* (**in,** de); *St Exch* marchand *m* de titres; *Aut etc* concessionnaire *m*; (*in drugs*) dealer *m*, trafiquant, -ante; **secondhand d.,** brocanteur, -euse; **double d.,** filou *m*.

dealership ['diːləʃɪp] *n Aut* concession *f*.

dealing out *n* distribution *f* (*de dons etc*); distribution, donne *f* (*de cartes*).

dealings ['diːlɪŋz] *npl* relations *fpl*, rapports *mpl*; *Pej* tractations *fpl* (**with,** avec); *Com* transactions *fpl*; **to have d. with s.o.,** avoir des rapports avec qn; *Com* faire des affaires *ou* traiter des affaires avec qn; **underhand d.,** menées sourdes.

dean [diːn] *n Rel Univ* doyen *m*.

deanery ['diːnərɪ] *n Rel* résidence *f* du doyen.

dear [dɪər] **1** *adj* **(a)** (*loved*) cher, chère (**to,** à); **he is d. to me,** il m'est cher; **all that I hold d.,** tout ce qui m'est cher; **what a d. little child!,** quel amour d'enfant!; **a d. little house,** une petite maison coquette; **to run for d. life,** courir aussi vite que possible; **D. Sir,** (*in letter*) Monsieur; **D. Madam,** Madame, Mademoiselle; **D. Mr Thomas,** Cher Monsieur; **D. Alice,** (Ma) chère Alice; *esp Am* **a d. John letter,** une lettre de séparation;

(b) (*costly*) cher, coûteux; **these cigars are too d.,** ces cigares sont trop chers.

2 *n* (*friend*) cher, *f* chère; (*darling*) chéri, chérie; **my d.,** (*adult*) cher ami, chère amie; (*child*) mon petit chou; **you're a d.!,** tu es un amour!; **be a d. and ...,** sois gentil *ou* gentille et ... .

3 *adv* **(a)** (*vendre, acheter, coûter, payer*) cher;

(b) he sold his life d., il vendit chèrement sa vie.

4 *int* **d. d.!, d. me!,** mon Dieu, mon Dieu!; **oh d.!,** (*what have I done*) oh là là!; (*that's a pity*) hélas!; **oh d. no!,** (oh) que non!

dearie ['dɪərɪ] *F* **1** *n* mon (petit) chéri, ma (petite) chérie. **2** *int* **d. me!,** mon Dieu!

dearly ['dɪəlɪ] *adv* **(a)** (*very much*) **I love him d.,** je l'aime tendrement *ou* de tout mon cœur; **he d. loves to play jokes on people,** il trouve tout son plaisir à jouer des tours aux gens; **I would d. like to meet her,** je souhaite de tout mon cœur la rencontrer; **(b)** (*at great cost*) cher, chèrement; **you shall pay d. for this,** cela vous coûtera cher.

dearness ['dɪənɪs] *n* cherté *f* (*des vivres etc*).

dearth [dɜːθ] *n Fml* disette *f*, pénurie *f* (*de vivres, d'idées, de livres etc*); pauvreté *f* (*d'idées*).

death [deθ] *n* mort *f*; *Jur Admin* décès *m*; *Fig* **the d. of one's hopes/plans/***etc*, la fin de ses espoirs/projets/*etc*; *Hist* **the Black D.,** la peste noire; **to be at d.'s door** *or* **on the verge of d.,** être sur le point de mourir; **to die a violent d.,** mourir de mort violente; **at (the time of) his d.,** à sa mort; **until d.,** pour la vie; **till d. do us part,** (*in marriage ceremony*) jusqu'à ce que la mort nous sépare; *F* **to be sick to d. of sth,** en avoir marre de qch; **six food-poisoning deaths have been reported,** on a signalé six décès par intoxication alimentaire; **there has been a d. in the family,** il y a eu un décès dans la famille; **he fell to his**

d., il a fait une chute mortelle; **you'll catch your d. of cold if you go out in this weather,** vous allez crever de froid si vous sortez par ce temps; **that play has been done to d.**, cette pièce a été jouée beaucoup trop souvent; *F* **he'll be the d. of me,** il me fera mourir; **that car will be the d. of her,** cette voiture va l'achever; **it would be the d. of him,** ce serait sa mort; **to put s.o. to d.**, mettre qn à mort, exécuter qn; **condemned to d., under sentence of d.**, condamné à mort; **to drink/smoke oneself to d.**, se tuer à force de boire/fumer; **to starve s.o. to d.**, faire mourir qn de faim; **to beat s.o. to d.**, battre qn à mort; **one false move could mean d.**, (*for trapeze artist etc*) un faux mouvement pourrait entraîner la mort; **to die the d.**, se faire massacrer; (*be embarrassed*) être mortellement embarrassé; **to die a thousand deaths,** souffrir mille morts; **d. to traitors!**, à mort les traîtres!; *Fig* **to be in at the d.**, assister au dénouement (*d'une affaire*); *F* **to look like d. (warmed up),** avoir une figure de cadavre; **register of births, marriages and deaths,** registre *m* de l'état civil; *Journ* **deaths,** nécrologie *f*; **d. adder,** (*snake*) acanthopis *m*; **d. cap,** (*toadstool*) amanite *f* phalloïde; **d. cell,** cellule *f* de condamné à mort; **d. certificate,** extrait *m* (d'acte) de décès; **d. duties,** *US* **d. taxes,** droits *mpl* de succession; **d. knell,** glas *m*; **d. mask,** masque *m* mortuaire; **d. penalty,** peine *f* de mort; **d. rate,** taux *m* de mortalité; **d. rattle,** râle *m* de la mort; *US* **d. row,** quartier d'une prison où les condamnés attendent leur exécution; *Am Aut* **d. seat,** place *f* du mort; **d. toll,** bilan *m*; *US Geog* **D. Valley,** Vallée *f* de la mort; **d. warrant,** ordre *m* d'exécution; *Fig* **you've just signed your own d. warrant,** tu viens de signer ta condamnation à mort; *Psy* **d. wish,** pulsion *f* de mort; *Fig* **to have a d. wish,** (*of government etc*) courir à sa perte.

deathbed ['deθbed] *n* lit *m* de mort; **d. confession,** confession faite sur le lit de mort.

deathblow ['deθbləʊ] *n* coup mortel *ou* fatal; *Fig* **marriage was** *or* **dealt a d. to her career,** le mariage a asséné un coup mortel à sa carrière.

deathless ['deθlɪs] *adj* impérissable, immortel; *Hum* **d. prose,** prose impérissable.

deathlike ['deθlaɪk] *adj* (*pâleur etc*) de mort.

deathly ['deθlɪ] **1** *adj* de mort, cadavérique; **d. silence,** silence *m* de mort. **2** *adv* comme la mort; **d. pale,** d'une pâleur mortelle.

death's-head ['deθshed] *n* tête *f* de mort; **d.-h. moth,** (sphinx *m*) atropos *m*.

deathtrap ['deθtræp] *n* endroit *ou* véhicule dangereux; **the house is a d.**, cette maison est dangereuse.

deathwatch ['deθwɒtʃ] *n* **d. beetle,** vrillette *f*, *F* horloge *f* de la mort.

deb [deb] *n Br F* débutante *f*; **d.'s delight,** un beau parti.

debacle ['deɪbɑːk(ə)l] *n* débâcle *f*.

debag [diː'bæg] *vt* **(-gg-)** *Old-fashioned Br F* déculotter (*qn*).

debar [diː'bɑːr] *vt* **(-rr-)** **to d. s.o. from sth,** exclure qn de qch, interdire qch à qn; **to d. s.o. from doing sth,** interdire à qn de faire qch.

debase [dɪ'beɪs] *vt* **(a)** (*degrade*) avilir, dégrader (*qn*); rabaisser (*son style*); **(b)** (*make less valuable*) altérer (*le métal*); **to d. the currency,** déprécier la monnaie.

debasement [dɪ'beɪsmənt] *n* **(a)** avilissement *m* (*de qn*); **(b)** dépréciation *f* (*des monnaies*).

debatable [dɪ'beɪtəb(ə)l] *adj* contestable, discutable; **it's d. whether he is to blame or she is,** il est difficile de dire si c'est lui ou elle qui est à blâmer.

debate¹ [dɪ'beɪt] *n* débat *m*, discussion *f*; **after much d.**, après bien des discussions.

debate² **1** *vt* débattre contradictoirement, discuter, agiter (*une question etc*); mettre (*un sujet*) en discussion; **a much debated question,** une question fort controversée; **I was debating (with myself** *or* **in my mind) whether to go or not,** je délibérais si j'irais ou non. **2** *vi* discuter, disputer (**with s.o. on sth,** avec qn sur qch).

debater [dɪ'beɪtər] *n* spécialiste *mf* des débats contradictoires.

debating [dɪ'beɪtɪŋ] *n* **d. society,** société *f* de débats contradictoires.

debauch¹ [dɪ'bɔːtʃ] *n* débauche *f*.

debauch² *vt* débaucher, corrompre (*qn*).

debauched [dɪ'bɔːtʃt] *adj* débauché, corrompu.

debauchery [dɪ'bɔːtʃərɪ] *n* débauche *f*, dérèglement *m* de(s) mœurs.

debenture [dɪ'bentʃər] *n Fin* obligation *f*; **d. bond,** titre *m* d'obligation; **d. stock,** obligations sans garantie; **d. holder,** obligataire *mf*.

debilitate [dɪ'bɪlɪteɪt] *vt* débiliter; **a debilitating illness,** une maladie affaiblissante.

debility [dɪ'bɪlɪtɪ] *n Med* débilité *f*, asthénie *f*.

debit¹ ['debɪt] *n Fin* débit *m*; **d. and credit,** doit *m* et avoir *m*; **to enter sth on the d. side of an account,** porter qch au débit d'un compte; **d. account,** compte débiteur; **d. card,** = carte de paiement électronique sur les points de vente avec transaction en ligne; **d. entry,** article *m* au débit; **d. note,** bordereau *m* de débit; **d. side,** (*of account*) débit *m*; *Fig* **on the d. side,** sur le plan négatif.

debit² *vt* débiter (*un article, un compte*); **to d. s.o. with a sum,** porter une somme au débit de qn, débiter qn d'une somme.

debonair [debə'neər] *adj Lit* **(a)** (*suave*) doucereux, mielleux; **(b)** (*cheerful*) jovial, -aux.

debouch [dɪ'baʊtʃ] *vi* (*of stream, street etc*) déboucher (**into,** dans).

debrief [diː'briːf] *vt Mil Av etc* faire faire un compte-rendu (de fin de mission) à (*un pilote etc*); **to be debriefed,** faire rapport.

debriefing [diː'briːfɪŋ] *n* rapport *m* (de fin de mission), debriefing *m*.

debris ['debriː] *n* débris *mpl*.

debt [det] *n* dette *f*; **bad d.**, mauvaise créance; **d. of honour,** dette d'honneur; **to be in d.**, être endetté, avoir des dettes; **to be in d. to s.o.**, être en dette envers qn; **to be out of d.**, n'avoir plus de dettes, être quitte; **he has a great many debts,** il a beaucoup de dettes; *F* **to be up to the** *or* **one's ears in d.**, être criblé de dettes; **I shall always be in your d.**, je vous serai toujours redevable; **to get** *or* **run into d.**, s'endetter, faire des dettes; **d. collector,** agent *m* de recouvrement; **d. collection agency,** agence *f* de recouvrement de dettes; **d. rescheduling,** rééchelonnement *m* des dettes; **d. servicing,** service *m* de la dette.

debtor ['detər] *n* débiteur, -trice.

debug [diː'bʌg] *vt* **(a)** (*remove faults in*) *Comptr* déboguer, mettre au point (*un programme*); éliminer les erreurs de prototype *etc*; dépanner (*une machine*); **(b)** (*remove microphones from*) éliminer les microphones clandestins dans (*une pièce*).

debugger [diː'bʌgər] *n Comptr* (programme *m*) débogueur *m*.

debunk [diː'bʌŋk] *vt F* déboulonner (*qn*); démentir (*qch*); **to d. a myth,** détruire un mythe.

début¹ ['deɪbjuː] *n* début *m*; (*in society*) entrée *f* dans le monde; **to make one's d.**, (*of actor etc*) débuter, faire ses débuts (**as,** dans le rôle de).

début² *vi esp Am* débuter; **she début'd** ['deɪbjuːd] **in the role of ...**, elle a fait ses débuts *ou* a débuté dans le rôle de ... .

débutante ['debjutɑːnt, tænt] *n Br* débutante *f*.

decade ['dekeɪd] *n* **(a)** (*ten years*) décennie *f*; *Fr Hist* décade (*du calendrier républicain*); **(b)** *Rel* dizaine *f* (*d'un chapelet*).

decadence ['dekədəns] *n* **(a)** (*of morals*) décadence *f*; **(b)** *Lit Art* décadentisme *m*.

decadent ['dekədənt] **1** *adj* décadent. **2** *n Lit Art* décadent *m*.

decaffeinate [diː'kæfineɪt] *vt* décaféiner.

decagram(me) ['dekəgræm] *n* (*unit of measurement*) décagramme *m*.

decal [dɪ'kæl, diː-] *n F* décalcomanie *f*.

decalcification [diːkælsɪfɪ'keɪʃən] *n* décalcification *f*.

decalcify [diː'kælsɪfaɪ] *vt* décalcifier (*les os etc*).

Decalogue ['dekəlɒg] *n Bible* Décalogue *m*.

decamp [diː'kæmp] *vi Mil* lever le camp; *F* décamper, filer, ficher le camp.

decant [dɪ'kænt] *vt* transvaser (*un liquide*); décanter (*une bouteille de vin*) dans une carafe.

decanter [dɪ'kæntər] *n* carafe *f* (*à liqueur, à vin*).

decapitate [dɪ'kæpɪteɪt] *vt* décapiter.

decapitation [dɪkæpɪ'teɪʃən] *n* décapitation *f*.

decapod ['dekəpɒd] *n* (*crustacean*) décapode *m*.

decarbonize [diː'kɑːbənaɪz] *vt* **(a)** décarburer, décarboniser (*l'acier etc*); **(b)** *Aut* décalaminer (*une culasse*).

decathlete [dɪ'kæθliːt] *n Sp* décathlonien *m*.

decathlon [dɪ'kæθlɒn] *n Sp* décathlon *m*.

decay¹ [dɪ'keɪ] *n* **(a)** (*decline*) décadence *f*, déchéance *f* (*d'une famille, d'un pays etc*); déclin *m* (*de la beauté etc*); délabrement *m* (*d'un bâtiment*); **moral d.**, déchéance morale; **senile d.**, affaiblissement sénile; **to fall into d.**, (*of house*) tomber en ruine, se délabrer; (*of state*) tomber en décadence; **(b)** (*rot*) pourriture *f*, corruption *f*, décomposition *f* (*du bois etc*); carie *f* (*des dents*); *Phys* **d.**

time, période *f* d'extinction.

decay[2] **1** *vi* **(a)** (*of nation, family*) tomber en décadence; (*of building*) tomber en ruine, se délabrer; (*of empire*) décliner; (*of beauty, flowers*) (se) passer, se flétrir; **(b)** (*of meat, fruit*) se gâter, pourrir; (*of timber*) pourrir; (*of teeth*) se carier. **2** *vt* carier (*les dents*).

decayed [dɪ'keɪd] *adj* **(a)** (*building*) en ruines; **(b)** (*bois*) pourri; (*dent*) carié.

decaying [dɪ'keɪɪŋ] *adj* **(a)** (*in decline*) en décadence; **(b)** (*rotting*) en pourriture.

decease[1] [dɪ'siːs] *n Jur Admin* décès *m*.

decease[2] *vi Jur Admin* décéder.

deceased [dɪ'siːst] **1** *adj* décédé; **son of Robert Martin, d.,** fils de feu M. Robert Martin. **2** *n* **the d.,** le défunt, la défunte.

deceit [dɪ'siːt] *n* **(a)** (*action*) supercherie *f*, tromperie *f*; *Jur* fraude *f*; **(b)** = **DECEITFULNESS**.

deceitful [dɪ'siːtfʊl] *adj* trompeur, -euse, fourbe; **to be d.,** (*of person*) être faux; **it was very d. of her,** c'était très faux de sa part.

deceitfully [dɪ'siːtfʊlɪ] *adv* avec duplicité.

deceitfulness [dɪ'siːtfʊlnɪs] *n* fausseté *f*, duplicité *f*.

deceive [dɪ'siːv] *vt* tromper, abuser (*qn*); tromper (*son mari, sa femme*); tromper, décevoir (*les espérances de qn*); **to d. oneself,** s'abuser; **I thought my eyes were deceiving me,** je ne pouvais pas en croire mes yeux.

deceiver [dɪ'siːvər] *n* trompeur, -euse.

decelerate [diː'seləreɪt] *vi* décélérer, ralentir.

deceleration [diːselə'reɪʃən] *n* décélération *f*, ralentissement *m*.

December [dɪ'sembər] *n* décembre *m*; **in D.,** en *ou* au mois de décembre; **(on) the third of D.,** le trois décembre.

decency ['diːsənsɪ] *n* **(a)** décence *f* (*de costume etc*); **(b)** (*convention*) bienséance *f*, convenance(s) *f(pl)*; **common d.,** les convenances (sociales); **he didn't even have the (common) d. to let us know,** il n'a pas eu la bienséance élémentaire de nous informer; **the decencies,** les convenances; **to observe the decencies,** observer les convenances.

decent ['diːsənt] *adj* **(a)** (*suitable*) bienséant, convenable; (*respectable*) décent, honnête; **are you d.?,** es-tu habillé (convenablement)?; **I'm not d.,** je ne suis pas dans une tenue convenable; **(b)** (*acceptable*) passable; **this wine is quite d.,** ce vin est très buvable *ou* se laisse boire; **the flat is quite a d. size,** l'appartement est d'une taille raisonnable; **I earn a d. wage,** je gagne un salaire décent; **(c)** *F* (*kind*) **a d. (sort of) chap,** un bon type; **it's very d. of you,** c'est très gentil de votre part.

decently ['diːsəntlɪ] *adv* (*see adj*) **(a)** décemment, convenablement; avec bienséance, avec décence; **(b)** *F* passablement; **he pays quite d.,** il ne paie pas mal; **(c)** de façon correcte, correctement, avec gentillesse; **he's treated me really d.,** il m'a traité de façon vraiment correcte.

decentralization [diːsentrəlaɪ'zeɪʃən] *n* décentralisation *f* (*administrative etc*).

decentralize [diː'sentrəlaɪz] *vt* décentraliser (*l'administration etc*); *Comptr* **decentralized processing,** traitement décentralisé.

decent-sized ['diːsənt'saɪzd] *adj* (*house etc*) d'une taille raisonnable.

deception [dɪ'sepʃən] *n* tromperie *f*, supercherie *f*, fraude *f*.

deceptive [dɪ'septɪv] *adj* (*thing, appearance*) trompeur, -euse; **appearances are d.,** les apparences sont trompeuses; **he** *or* **his manner is very d.,** on ne peut jamais deviner ce qu'il va faire *ou* dire.

deceptively [dɪ'septɪvlɪ] *adv* **he has a d. quiet manner,** il a un air tranquille (bien) trompeur; **the flat is d. small,** l'appartement est plus grand qu'il n'y paraît; **she is d. thin,** c'est une fausse maigre.

deceptiveness [dɪ'septɪvnɪs] *n* caractère trompeur (*de qch*).

decibel ['desɪbel] *n Phys* décibel *m*.

decide [dɪ'saɪd] **1** *vt* trancher (*une question*); juger (*un différend*); décider de (*qch*); **to d. s.o.'s fate,** décider du sort de qn; **event that decided his career,** événement *m* qui décida de sa carrière; **nothing has been** *or* **is decided yet,** il n'y a encore rien de décidé; **that decided me (to leave),** cela me décida (à partir); **to d. to do sth,** se décider *ou* se résoudre à faire qch, décider *ou* résoudre de faire qch; **it was decided to wait for his reply,** on a décidé d'attendre sa réponse. **2** *vi* **to d. on,** se décider à, décider de (*qch*); arrêter (*un plan de conduite*); déterminer (*une méthode de travail*); fixer (*un jour*); **to d. against sth,** se prononcer contre qch; **we've decided against a holiday this year,** nous avons décidé de ne pas prendre de vacances cette année; **have you decided?,** êtes-vous décidé?; **have you decided on a date/a name?,** vous êtes-vous décidés sur une date/un nom?

decided [dɪ'saɪdɪd] *adj* **(a)** (*ton*) net, résolu; (*refus*) catégorique; **they are quite d. about it,** ils sont tout à fait décidés; **(b)** (*distinct*) (*différence*) marqué, prononcé; (*changement*) sensible; (*succès*) incontestable.

decidedly [dɪ'saɪdɪdlɪ] *adv* **(a)** (*agir*) résolument; **(b)** décidément; (*réussir*) incontestablement; **he is d. better,** il va décidément mieux.

decider [dɪ'saɪdər] *n* facteur décisif; *Sp* but *ou* point décisif; (*game, match*) la belle.

deciding [dɪ'saɪdɪŋ] *adj* (*factor, vote*) décisif; *Sp* **the d. game** *or* **set,** la belle; **the chairman has the d. vote,** le président a voix prépondérante.

deciduous [dɪ'sɪdjʊəs] *adj Bot* à feuilles caduques; *Zool* (*antlers etc*) caduc.

decilitre, *US* **deciliter** ['desɪliːtər] *n* (*unit of measurement*) décilitre *m*.

decimal ['desɪm(ə)l] **1** *adj* (*fraction, system, coinage etc*) décimal, -aux; *Math* **d. point,** virgule *f* (décimale); **d. place,** décimale *f*, chiffre *m* après la virgule; *Comptr* position décimale; *F* **to go d.,** adopter le système décimal; **correct to five d. places,** exact jusqu'à la cinquième décimale. **2** *n* fraction décimale.

decimalization [desɪməlaɪ'zeɪʃən] *n* décimalisation *f*.

decimate ['desɪmeɪt] *vt* (*of disease etc*) décimer (*la population etc*).

decimation [desɪ'meɪʃən] *n* décimation *f*.

decimetre, *US* **decimeter** ['desɪmiːtər] *n* (*unit of measurement*) décimètre *m*.

decipher [dɪ'saɪfər] *vt* déchiffrer (*des hiéroglyphes, une écriture difficile*); déchiffrer, décoder (*une dépêche chiffrée*).

decipherable [dɪ'saɪf(ə)rəb(ə)l] *adj* déchiffrable.

decision [dɪ'sɪʒən] *n* **(a)** décision *f* (*d'une question, de faire qch*); vote *m* (*sur une question*); **to give a d. on a case,** décider *ou* statuer sur un cas; **the judge's d. is final,** (*in competition etc*) la décision du juge est irrévocable; **to come to** *or* **arrive at** *or* **reach a d.,** arriver à une décision (**about,** quant à, touchant), se décider; **d. maker,** décideur *m*; **d. making,** prise *f* de décisions; **(b)** (*resolution*) résolution *f*, fermeté *f*; **..., he said with d.,** ... dit-il fermement.

decisive [dɪ'saɪsɪv] *adj* **(a)** (*question, battle etc*) décisif; (*experiment etc*) concluant; (*preuve*) victorieux; **(b)** (*manner etc*) décidé; (*tone*) tranchant, net.

decisively [dɪ'saɪsɪvlɪ] *adv* (*see adj*) **(a)** d'une façon décisive; **(b)** (*to act*) d'un air décidé; (*to say*) d'un ton tranchant.

decisiveness [dɪ'saɪsɪvnɪs] *n* **(a)** caractère décisif *ou* concluant (*d'une expérience etc*); **(b)** = **DECISION (b)**.

deck[1] [dek] *n* **(a)** *Nau* pont *m*; **on d.,** sur le pont; **below deck(s),** dans l'entrepont; **after d.,** pont arrière; **lower/upper d.,** pont inférieur/supérieur; **promenade d.,** pont promenade; **boat d.,** pont des embarcations; **mess d.,** poste *m* d'équipage; **to come** *or* **go on d.,** monter sur le pont; **to clear the decks (for action),** faire le branle-bas de combat; *Fig* se préparer à agir; *F* **to hit the d.,** (*to avoid injury*) tomber à plat ventre; (*get out of bed*) se lever; **hit the d.!,** (*fall to the ground*) mettez-vous à plat ventre par terre!; (*get out of bed*) debout!; **d. cargo** *or* **load,** pontée *f*; **d. chair,** transat *m*; **d. hand,** matelot *m* de pont; **d. officer,** officier *m* de pont;

(b) (*of vehicle*) plate-forme *f*, *pl* plates-formes; **top d.,** (*of bus*) impériale *f*; **single-d. bus,** autobus *m* sans impériale;

(c) *Constr* tablier *m*; plancher *m* (*d'un pont*); *Am* terrasse *f*;

(d) *Am* **d. of cards,** jeu *m* de cartes; *Am F* **not to have** *or* **not to play with a full d.,** (*not be very bright*) avoir quelques cases de vides;

(e) (*for records etc*) platine *f*; **cassette d.,** platine à cassette; **tape d.,** platine à bande magnétique;

(f) *US Aut* (*space behind back seat*) coffre *m*; (*cover of space*) couvercle *m* du coffre.

deck[2] *vt* **(a)** (*decorate*) parer, orner (**sth with sth,** qch de qch); **to d. oneself out,** s'endimancher; **they were decked out in their best clothes,** ils étaient sur leur trente et un; **(b)** *Nau* ponter (*un navire*); **(c)** *esp Am F* (*knock to the ground*) flanquer (*qn*) par terre.

-decker ['dekər] *suff* **single-d. (bus),** autobus *m* sans impériale; **double-d. (bus),** autobus à impériale; **double-d. sandwich,** sandwich *m* double.

deckhouse ['dekhaʊs] *n Nau* rouf *m*.

deckle ['dek(ə)l] *n* (*in paper*) cadre volant, rebord *m* (*de la forme*); **d. edge,** barbes *fpl* (*du papier*).
deckle-edged ['dek(ə)ledʒd] *adj* (*paper*) à barbes.
declaim [dɪ'kleɪm] **1** *vi* déclamer (**against,** contre). **2** *vt* déclamer (*des vers etc*).
declamation [deklə'meɪʃən] *n* déclamation *f*.
declamatory [dɪ'klæmətərɪ, -trɪ] *adj* (*style etc*) déclamatoire.
declaration [deklə'reɪʃən] *n* **(a)** déclaration *f* (*de guerre etc*); **statutory d.,** attestation *f*; **customs d.,** déclaration de *ou* en douane; **d. of income,** déclaration de revenu; *US Hist* **D. of Independence,** Déclaration d'Indépendance; **(b)** *Cards* annonce *f*.
declare [dɪ'kleər] **1** *vt* **(a)** déclarer (**sth to s.o.,** qch à qn); **to d. war,** déclarer la guerre (**on, against,** à); **the two countries have declared war,** (*on each other*) les deux pays se sont déclaré la guerre; **have you anything to d.?,** avez-vous quelque chose à déclarer?; **to d. a strike,** proclamer la grève; **she was declared the winner,** elle a été déclarée vainqueur; *Fin* **to d. a dividend of ten per cent,** déclarer un dividende de dix pour cent; **to d. s.o. guilty,** déclarer qn coupable; **(b)** *Cards* appeler (*l'atout, une couleur*); *Fig* **to d. one's hand,** avouer ses intentions; **to d. oneself,** prendre parti; (*of lover*) faire sa déclaration; **to d. itself,** (*of disease*) se déclarer. **2** *vi Cr* fermer son jeu (avant la chute des dix guichets); *Cards* annoncer son jeu; **well I d.!,** ciel!, ça alors!; **to d. for/against sth,** déclarer pour/contre qch.
declared [dɪ'kleəd] *adj* avoué, déclaré.
declassification [di:klæsɪfɪ'keɪʃən] *n* (*of information, document*) remise *f* en circulation.
declassify [di:'klæsɪfaɪ] *vt* remettre en circulation (*un document secret etc*).
declension [dɪ'klenʃən] *n Gram* déclinaison *f*.
declinable [dɪ'klaɪnəb(ə)l] *adj Gram* déclinable.
declination [deklɪ'neɪʃən] *n* **(a)** *Astron* déclinaison *f*; **(b)** *Am* refus courtois *ou* formel.
decline[1] [dɪ'klaɪn] *n* déclin *m* (*du jour, d'un empire*); baisse *f* (*de prix*); ralentissement *m* (*des affaires*); **to be on the d.,** (*of crime, birth rate*) être sur le déclin, décliner, être en baisse; (*of prices*) être en baisse, être en diminution; (*of patient*) décliner.
decline[2] **1** *vt* **(a)** refuser courtoisement (*une invitation*); décliner (*un honneur*); refuser; repousser (*l'intervention de qn*); **to d. to do sth,** refuser de faire qch; **(b)** *Gram* décliner (*un nom etc*). **2** *vi* **(a)** (*refuse*) s'excuser; se faire excuser; (*of day, sun etc*) décliner; (*of day*) tirer à sa fin; baisser; **(b)** (*of health, influence etc*) décliner, baisser; *Com* (*of prices, business*) être en baisse.
declining [dɪ'klaɪnɪŋ] *adj* **(a)** (*soleil*) couchant, baissant; *Lit* **in one's d. years,** au déclin de la vie; **she spent her d. years in a nursing home,** elle a passé le déclin de sa vie *ou* la fin de ses jours dans une maison de retraite; **(b)** *Econ* (*industrie*) déclinant; (*marché*) en baisse.
declivity [dɪ'klɪvɪtɪ] *n* déclivité *f*, pente *f*.
declutch [di:'klʌtʃ] *vi Aut* débrayer.
decoction [dɪ'kɒkʃən] *n* décoction *f*.
decode [di:'kəʊd] *vt* déchiffrer, décoder, transcrire en clair (*une dépêche*); *Comptr* décoder; **decoded message,** message transcrit en clair.
decoder [di:'kəʊdər] *n* (*person, machine*) décodeur *m*; déchiffreur *m*; *Comptr TV* décodeur.
decoding [di:'kəʊdɪŋ] *n* (*of message*) déchiffrement *m*, décodage *m*, transcription *f* en clair; *Comptr* décodage.
decoke [di:'kəʊk] *n Aut F* **d. machine,** machine *f* de décalaminage; **the car needs a d.,** la voiture a besoin d'un décalaminage *ou* d'être décalaminée.
décolleté [deɪ'kɒlteɪ] **1** *adj* (*dress, woman*) décolleté. **2** *n* décolletage *m*.
decommission [di:kə'mɪʃən] *vt* mettre hors-service (*un réacteur nucléaire, une usine*).
decommissioning [di:kə'mɪʃənɪŋ] *n* (*of nuclear reactor, plant*) mise *f* hors-service.
decompose [di:kəm'pəʊz] **1** *vi* (*of organic matter*) se décomposer, entrer en décomposition. **2** *vt* décomposer (*la matière, un composé, la lumière etc*); *Ch* dédoubler (*un sel double*).
decomposition [di:kɒmpə'zɪʃən] *n* décomposition *f*.
decompress [di:kəm'pres] *vt Tech* décomprimer (*un gaz etc*); *Med* faire séjourner (*un plongeur*) dans une chambre de décompression.
decompression [di:kəm'preʃən] *n Tech* décompression *f*; *Med* séjour *m* dans une chambre de décompression; **d. chamber,** chambre *f* de décompression; *Med* **d. sickness** *or* **illness,** maladie *f* des caissons (*dont souffrent les plongeurs*).
decongestant [di:kən'dʒestənt] *Med* **1** *n* décongestionnant *m*. **2** *adj* (*tablets, syrup etc*) décongestionnant.
decongestion [di:kən'dʒestjən] *n Med* décongestion *f*.
deconsecrate [di:'kɒnsəkreɪt] *vt Rel* désaffecter (*une église*).
decontaminate [di:kən'tæmɪneɪt] *vt* décontaminer (*qn, une région*).
decontamination [di:kəntæmɪ'neɪʃən] *n* décontamination *f*.
decontrol[1] [di:kən'trəʊl] *vt* libérer (*le commerce*) des contraintes du gouvernement; **to d. prices,** mettre fin au contrôle des prix.
decontrol[2] *n Am* libération *f* (*des prix etc*).
décor ['deɪkɔ:r] *n Th etc* décor *m*; *F* **he's part of the d.,** (*has been here for a long time*) il fait partie des meubles.
decorate ['dekəreɪt] *vt* **(a)** décorer, orner (**sth with sth,** qch de qch); pavoiser (*une rue*); **to d. a Christmas tree,** décorer un arbre de Noël; **(b)** peindre et tapisser, décorer (*un appartement*); **(c)** (*with medal*) décorer, remettre une décoration à (*qn*); **she was decorated for bravery,** elle a été décorée pour son courage.
decorating ['dekəreɪtɪŋ] *n* décoration *f* (*de qch*).
decoration [dekə'reɪʃən] *n* **(a)** décoration *f*; pavoisement *m* (*des rues etc*); **decorations,** décorations (*d'une ville en fête etc*); **interior d.,** décoration d'intérieur; **(b)** peinture *f* et pose *f* de la tapisserie, décoration *f* (*d'une pièce*); **(c)** remise *f* d'une décoration (*à qn*); (*medal*) décoration, médaille *f*.
decorative ['dek(ə)rətɪv] *adj* (*art, ornement, F femme*) décoratif; (*dessin*) d'ornement; **the house is in excellent d. order,** la décoration de la maison est en excellent état.
decoratively ['dek(ə)rətɪvlɪ] *adv* décorativement.
decorator ['dekəreɪtər] *n* décorateur *m*; *Br* **(painter and) d.,** peintre décorateur; *Br* **we're having the decorators in next week,** les peintres viennent la semaine prochaine; **interior d.,** décorateur-ensemblier *m*, *pl* décorateurs-ensembliers.
decorous ['dekərəs] *adj* bienséant, convenable.
decorously ['dekərəslɪ] *adv* avec bienséance, convenablement.
decorticate [di:'kɔ:tɪkeɪt] *vt* décortiquer (*le riz etc*).
decorum [dɪ'kɔ:rəm] *n* décorum *m*, bienséance *f*; **a breach of d.,** une inconvenance; **to have a sense of d.,** avoir de la tenue.
decouple [dɪ'kʌp(ə)l] *vt El* découpler.
decoupling [dɪ'kʌplɪŋ] *n El* découplage *m*.
decoy[1] ['di:kɔɪ] *n* **(a)** (*in hunting*) appât *m*, leurre *m*; **d. (bird),** moquette *f*; (oiseau *m*) appelant *m*; **(b)** *Fig* compère *m*; **police d.,** policier *m* en civil (*pour tromper un criminel*).
decoy[2] [dɪ'kɔɪ] *vt* leurrer (*des oiseaux, qn*); **to d. s.o. into a trap,** attirer qn dans un piège.
decrease[1] ['di:kri:s] *n* diminution *f*, décroissement *m*, décroissance *f*, amoindrissement *m*; **d. in price,** baisse *f* de prix; **d. in speed,** ralentissement *m*; **to be on the d.,** (*of crime etc*) être en diminution.
decrease[2] [dɪ'kri:s] **1** *vt* diminuer; *Knitting* **d. three stitches,** diminuer de trois mailles, faire trois diminutions. **2** *vi* diminuer, décroître; *Knitting* diminuer, faire des diminutions.
decreasing [dɪ'kri:sɪŋ] *adj* décroissant; **in d. order of importance,** par ordre d'importance décroissante.
decreasingly [dɪ'kri:sɪŋlɪ] *adv* de moins en moins.
decree[1] [dɪ'kri:] *n* **(a)** *Admin* décret *m*, édit *m*, arrêté *m*; **to issue a d.,** promulguer un décret; **(b)** *Rel* décret *m*; **(c)** *Jur* décision *f*, arrêt *m*, jugement *m*; **d. nisi** ['naɪsaɪ], jugement provisoire (*en matière de divorce*); **d. absolute,** jugement irrévocable.
decree[2] *vt* (*order*) décréter, ordonner; *Jur* arrêter (**that,** que).
decrepit [dɪ'krepɪt] *adj* **(a)** (*person*) décrépit; **(b)** (*car, house etc*) délabré; (*furniture*) vermoulu.
decrepitude [dɪ'krepɪtju:d] *n* **(a)** (*of person*) décrépitude *f*; **(b)** (*of car, house etc*) état délabré.
decriminalization [di:krɪmɪnəlaɪ'zeɪʃən] *n* (*of drug*) dépénalisation *f*.
decriminalize [di:'krɪmɪnəlaɪz] *vt Jur* dépénaliser (*la possession de drogues*).
decry [dɪ'kraɪ] *vt* décrier, dénigrer (*qn, qch*).
dedicate ['dedɪkeɪt] *vt* **(a)** (*assign*) dédier, consacrer (*une église*); **to d. oneself** *or* **one's life to s.o.,** se vouer à qn; **to d. oneself** *or* **one's life to sth,** se vouer à qch, se consacrer à qch; **(b)** dédicacer (*un livre, un disque*) (**to,** à).

dedicated ['dedɪkeɪtɪd] *adj* dédié (*à sa profession etc*); (*médecin, professeur*) par vocation; *Comptr* (*terminal*) spécialisé; **d. word processor,** machine *f* servant uniquement au traitement de texte.

dedication [dedɪ'keɪʃən] *n* **(a)** consécration *f* (*d'une église*); *Am* inauguration *f* (*d'un édifice*); **(b)** dédicace *f* (*d'un livre*); **to write a d. in a book,** dédicacer un livre; **to read out the dedications,** (*of disc jockey*) lire les dédicaces; **(c)** (*devotion*) attachement *m* (**to,** à); **a life of d.,** une vie de dévouement; **I admire your d. (to your work),** j'admire ton dévouement à ton travail.

deduce [dɪ'djuːs] *vt* déduire, conclure (**from,** de); **to d. sth from a fact,** arguer qch d'un fait; **I d. therefore that you will not be there,** j'en conclus donc que vous ne serez pas là.

deduct [dɪ'dʌkt] *vt* déduire (**from,** de); **to d. sth from the price,** rabattre qch sur le prix; **to be deducted,** à déduire; **tax is deducted at source,** l'impôt est prélevé à la source.

deductible [dɪ'dʌktɪb(ə)l] *adj* déductible; **charitable donations are d.,** (*from income tax*) les dons au profit d'œuvres de bienfaisance sont déductibles.

deduction [dɪ'dʌkʃən] *n* **(a)** (*subtraction*) déduction *f* (**from a quantity,** sur une quantité); (*from pay*) retenue *f*; **d. from wages,** prélèvement *m* sur le salaire; **(b)** (*conclusion*) déduction *f*, conclusion *f* (**from,** tirée de); **by a process of d.,** par déduction.

deductive [dɪ'dʌktɪv] *adj* (*raisonnement*) déductif, par déduction.

deed¹ [diːd] *n* **(a)** (*action*) action *f*, acte *m*; **to do one's good d. for the day,** faire sa bonne action *ou* sa B.A. quotidienne; *Lit* **d. of valour,** haut fait; **foul d.,** forfait *m*; **(b)** *Jur* acte notarié; **d. of covenant,** = document par lequel on s'engage à verser une certaine somme à quelqu'un ou à un organisme; **mortgage d.,** acte hypothécaire; **to change one's name by d. poll,** changer légalement son nom; **d. box,** coffre *m* à documents.

deed² *vt esp Am Jur* (*transfer by deed*) transférer qch par un acte.

deejay ['diːdʒeɪ] *n Mus F* disk jockey *m*, présentateur *m* de disques.

deem [diːm] *vt Arch & Lit* **I do not d. it necessary/proper to ...,** je ne juge pas *ou* ne crois pas *ou* ne considère pas nécessaire/convenable de ...; **it is deemed necessary/proper to ...,** on juge *ou* croit nécessaire/convenable de ...; **if it is deemed necessary,** si c'est jugé nécessaire; **I d. it a great honour,** je considère cela comme un grand honneur; **he was deemed (to be) the winner,** il a été considéré comme étant le vainqueur.

deep [diːp] **1** *adj* **(a)** (*water, wound, sleep, despair etc*) profond; **to be ten metres d.,** avoir dix mètres de profondeur, avoir une profondeur de dix mètres; **d. end,** bout le plus profond (*d'une piscine*); *Fig* **to go off the d. end,** (*get angry*) s'emporter; (*panic*) s'affoler; *Fig* **to be thrown in at the d. end,** subir le baptême du feu; **to be in d. water,** (*in serious difficulties*) être dans de mauvais draps; **d. in debt,** criblé de dettes; **d. in thought,** plongé dans ses pensées; **to inflict a d. wound,** (*of weapon*) pénétrer très avant *ou* très profondément; **d. shelves,** rayons *mpl* larges; *Mil* **two/four d.,** sur deux/quatre rangs; **d. thinker,** penseur profond; **his d. learning,** ses connaissances profondes; **d. concern,** vive préoccupation; **the D. South,** (*of the United States*) le sud profond;

(b) (*colour*) foncé, sombre; (*sound*) grave; **d. blue,** bleu foncé; **in a d. voice,** d'une voix profonde;

(c) (*conduct*) difficile à pénétrer; (*person*) malin, astucieux.

2 *adv* profondément; **d.-lying causes,** causes profondes; **d. down he's very kind,** au fond il est très gentil; *Prov* **still waters run d.,** il faut se méfier de l'eau qui dort; **the harpoon sank d. into the flesh,** le harpon a pénétré très avant *ou* très profondément dans la chair; **to work d. into the night,** travailler tard dans la nuit.

3 *n* **the d.,** l'océan *m*; **to commit a body to the d.,** immerger un mort.

deep-dish ['diːpdɪʃ] *adj Am Culin* **d.-d. pie,** tourte *f*.

deepen ['diːp(ə)n] **1** *vt* **(a)** approfondir, creuser (*un puits etc*); rendre (*un sentiment*) plus intense; **this only deepened his resentment,** cela n'a fait qu'augmenter son ressentiment; **(b)** foncer (*une couleur*); rendre (*un son*) plus grave. **2** *vi* **(a)** (*of river, silence etc*) devenir plus profond; **(b)** (*of colour*) devenir plus foncé; (*of sound*) devenir plus grave; (*of shadows*) s'épaissir.

deepfreeze¹ ['diːp'friːz] *vt* congeler, surgeler (*des aliments*).

deepfreeze² *n* congélateur *m*; *Fig* **to put sth in the d.,** mettre qch en attente (permanente).

deep-fry ['diːp'fraɪ] *vt* faire cuire (*du poisson etc*) dans la friture.

deep-fryer ['diːp'fraɪər] *n* friteuse *f*.

deep-laid ['diːp'leɪd] *adj* (*plan, scheme*) habilement comploté.

deeply ['diːplɪ] *adv* profondément; **to go d. into sth,** pénétrer *ou* entrer fort avant dans qch, approfondir qch; **to fall d. in love with s.o.,** tomber profondément amoureux de qn; **d. interesting,** fort intéressant; **d. offended,** gravement offensé.

deepness ['diːpnɪs] *n* profondeur *f* (*de la voix etc*); *Mus* gravité *f* (*d'un son*).

deep-rooted ['diːp'ruːtɪd] *adj* (*arbre*) à enracinement profond; (*affection*) profond; (*préjugé*) vivace.

deep-sea ['diːp'siː] *adj* (*plante, animal*) pélagique; **d.-s. fishery** *or* **fishing,** pêche hauturière; **d.-s. diver,** plongeur *m* sous-marin.

deep-seated ['diːp'siːtɪd] *adj* (*aversion*) profond, bien enraciné; (*affection*) profond; (*conviction*) intime.

deep-set ['diːp'set] *adj* (*eyes*) enfoncé, creux.

deer ['dɪər] *n inv* cerf *m*; **d. park,** chasse gardée pour le cerf.

deerhound ['dɪəhaʊnd] *n* (*dog*) lévrier *m* d'Écosse.

deerskin ['dɪəskɪn] *n* peau *f* de daim; *Com* daim *m*; **d. gloves,** gants *mpl* en daim.

deerstalker ['dɪəstɔːkər] *n* **(a)** chasseur *m* (de cerf) à l'approche; **(b)** (*hat*) chapeau *m* de chasse (à la Sherlock Holmes).

deerstalking ['dɪəstɔːkɪŋ] *n* chasse *f* (au cerf) à l'approche.

de-escalate [diː'eskəleɪt] *vt* faire diminuer (*une crise, la tension, des bombardements*).

deface [dɪ'feɪs] *vt* défigurer (*qch*); mutiler (*une statue*); barbouiller (*une affiche*).

de facto [diː'fæktəʊ] *adv Lit & Jur* de facto; *Jur* **de f. and de jure,** de droit et de fait.

defamation [defə'meɪʃən] *n* diffamation *f*; **to sue for d. of character,** poursuivre en diffamation, faire un procès en diffamation.

defamatory [dɪ'fæmət(ə)rɪ] *adj* (*remark etc*) diffamatoire, diffamant.

defame [dɪ'feɪm] *vt* diffamer (*qn*).

default¹ [dɪ'fɔːlt] *n* **(a)** *Jur* défaut *m*, non-comparution *f*; (*criminal law*) contumace *f*; **judgment by d.,** jugement *m* par contumace; **by d.,** (*if not otherwise specified*) implicitement; *Tech* par défaut; *Comptr* **d. drive/font,** lecteur *m*/police *f* par défaut; *Sp* **match won by d.,** match gagné par forfait; **the machine sets itself to 1 by d.,** la machine se réglera à 1 par défaut; **(b)** *Com* **d. in paying,** défaut *m* de paiement; **in d. of ...,** à défaut de ..., faute de ...; **(c)** *Tennis* disqualification *f*.

default² **1** *vi Jur* être en état de contumace; ne pas comparaître; *St Exch* manquer à ses engagements; **to d. on alimony payments,** manquer aux versements de pension alimentaire. **2** *vt Tennis* disqualifier (*qn*).

defaulter [dɪ'fɔːltər] *n* **(a)** *Jur* défaillant, -ante; (*criminal law*) contumace *mf*; *St Exch* défaillant *m*, failli *m*; **(b)** *Mil Nau* retardataire *m*, réfractaire *m*; (*undergoing punishment*) consigné *m*.

defeat¹ [dɪ'fiːt] *n* **(a)** défaite *f* (*d'une armée*); **to suffer a d.,** essuyer une défaite; **(b)** renversement *m* (*d'un projet*); *Parl etc* échec *m* (*d'une mesure*); défaite *f* (*du gouvernement*).

defeat² *vt* **(a)** battre, vaincre (*une armée, un adversaire*); **this defeats me,** (*I don't understand*) cela me dépasse; *Tennis* **she was defeated by three sets to love,** elle a été battue par trois sets à zéro; **(b)** déjouer, faire échouer (*un projet*); frustrer (*une espérance*); *Parl etc* mettre en minorité (*le gouvernement etc*); faire échouer (*une mesure*); **to d. the ends of justice,** contrarier la justice; **to d. one's own object,** aller à l'encontre de ses propres intentions; **that does rather d. the object of the exercise,** cela va plutôt à l'encontre du but de l'exercice.

defeatism [dɪ'fiːtɪz(ə)m] *n* défaitisme *m*.

defeatist [dɪ'fiːtɪst] *adj & n* défaitiste *mf*.

defecate ['defəkeɪt] *vi* déféquer.

defecation [defə'keɪʃən] *n* défécation *f*.

defect¹ ['diːfekt] *n* défaut *m*, imperfection *f* (*de construction*); **this plate has a d.,** cette assiette a un défaut; **d. in pronunciation,** défaut de prononciation.

defect² [dɪ'fekt] *vi Mil etc* passer à l'ennemi; **she has defected,** elle est passée à l'ennemi.

defection [dɪ'fekʃən] *n Mil etc* défection *f*; **there have been a number of defections to the West,** il y a eu une certain nombre de défections vers l'ouest.

defective [dɪ'fektɪv] **1** *adj* **(a)** défectueux, imparfait; (*développement*) vicieux; (*enfant*) anormal; (*mémoire*) infidèle; (*freins*) en mauvais état; *Ind* **d. part,** (pièce *f*) défectueuse *f*; **to be d. in sth,** manquer de qch; **(b)** *Gram* (*verbe etc*) défectif. **2** *n* **mental d.,** arriéré, -ée.

defector [dɪ'fektər] *n Mil etc* transfuge *mf*.

defence, *US* **defense** [dɪ'fens] *n* **(a)** (*action*) défense *f*, protection *f*; **to put up a stubborn d.,** se défendre avec acharnement; **self d.,** autodéfense *f*; *Mil etc* **civil d.,** = défense passive, protection civile; **air d.,** défense aérienne; **(b)** (*means*) dispositif défensif; *Mil Sp etc* **the d.,** les défenseurs *mpl*; **seaward defences,** (*of port*) ouvrages *mpl* de défense face à la mer; **d. spending,** dépenses *fpl* pour la défense; **d. electronics,** électronique *f* de défense; **d. mechanism,** (*of body*) système *m* immunitaire; (*of subconscious*) mécanisme *m* défense; **(c)** (*argument*) défense *f*, justification *f*; *Jur* défense; **to speak in d. of s.o.,** défendre qn; **I must say, in my own d., that ...,** je dois dire pour ma propre défense que ...; **counsel for the d.,** défenseur *m*; (*in civil law*) avocat *m* de la défense; **to appear for the d.,** (*of barrister*) représenter la défense; **witness for the d.,** témoin *m* à décharge; **to conduct one's own d.,** défendre soi-même sa cause.

defenceless, *US* **defenseless** [dɪ'fenslɪs] *adj* sans défense.

defend [dɪ'fend] **1** *vt* **(a)** défendre, protéger (**from, against,** contre); **(b)** défendre, justifier (*une opinion*); **(c)** *Jur* défendre (*un accusé*); assumer *ou* soutenir la défense de (*qn*); **to d. one's actions,** justifier ses actions. **2** *vi* **(a)** *Jur* assumer *ou* soutenir la défense; **(b)** *Sp* défendre.

defendant [dɪ'fendənt] *adj & n Jur* défendeur, -eresse; (*on appeal*) intimé, -ée; (*in criminal case*) accusé, -ée.

defender [dɪ'fendər] *n* défenseur *m*; **D. of the Faith,** défenseur de la foi.

defending [dɪ'fendɪŋ] *adj* **(a) d. champion,** champion, -ionne en titre; **(b)** *Jur* **d. counsel,** défenseur *m*.

defense, defenseless *US* = **DEFENCE, DEFENCELESS**.

defensible [dɪ'fensəb(ə)l] *adj* **(a)** (*cause*) défendable; (*position*) tenable; **(b)** (*opinion*) justifiable, soutenable.

defensive [dɪ'fensɪv] **1** *adj* défensif, de défense; **don't be so d.,** ne sois pas tant sur la défensive; *Mil etc* **d. action,** action défensive; **d. position,** position *f* de défense. **2** *n* défensive *f*; **to be/go on the d.,** se tenir/se mettre sur la défensive.

defer[1] [dɪ'fɜːr] *vt* (**-rr-**) **(a)** (*delay, postpone*) différer, ajourner, remettre (*une affaire*); reculer (*un paiement*); suspendre (*un jugement*); **to d. sth to a later date,** remettre *ou* reporter qch à plus tard; **(b)** *Mil etc* mettre (*qn*) en sursis (d'appel); **to d. s.o. on medical grounds,** réformer qn.

defer[2] *vi* se ranger (*à l'opinion de qn*); se soumettre (*à la volonté de qn*).

deference ['defərəns] *n* déférence *f*; **to pay** *or* **show d. to s.o., to treat s.o. with d.,** témoigner de la déférence à *ou* envers qn; **in** *or* **out of d. to ...,** par déférence pour ... .

deferential [defə'renʃəl] *adj* (*air, ton*) de déférence, respectueux; **to be d. to s.o.,** se montrer plein de déférence *ou* de respect pour *ou* envers qn, se montrer respectueux envers qn.

deferentially [defə'renʃəlɪ] *adv* avec déférence, avec respect.

deferment [dɪ'fɜːmənt] *n* **(a)** ajournement *m*, remise *f* (*d'une affaire*); **(b)** *Mil etc* réforme *f* (*pour raison de santé*); **to apply for d. (of call up),** faire une demande de sursis (d'appel).

deferred [dɪ'fɜːd] *adj* (*share etc*) différé; **d. payment,** (*postponed*) paiement différé; (*in instalments*) paiement par versements échelonnés; *Jur* **d. sentence,** = jugement dont le prononcé est suspendu.

defiance [dɪ'faɪəns] *n* défi *m*; **a gesture of d.,** un geste de défi; **in d. of,** au mépris de (*la loi, un ordre*).

defiant [dɪ'faɪənt] *adj* (*geste, regard, parole*) de défi, provocant; (*person*) intraitable.

defiantly [dɪ'faɪəntlɪ] *adv* (*to say, look at*) d'un ton *ou* d'un air provocant; (*to look at*) d'un air de défi.

defibrillation [dɪfaɪbrɪ'leɪʃən] *n Med* défibrillation *f*.

defibrillator [dɪfaɪbrɪ'leɪtər] *n Med* défibrillateur *m*.

deficiency [dɪ'fɪʃənsɪ] *n* **(a)** (*lack*) manque *m*, insuffisance *f* (**of,** de); *Med* (*of minerals, vitamins*) carence *f* (**in, of,** de); (*of function, organ*) déficience *f*; **d. disease,** maladie *f* de carence; **(b)** (*flaw, defect*) défaut *m*, imperfection *f*; **(c)** (*deficit*) manquant *m*, déficit *m*; *Com* découvert *m*; *Pol* déficit budgétaire.

deficient [dɪ'fɪʃənt] *adj* (*faulty*) défectueux; (*lacking*) insuffisant, incomplet; **to be d. in sth,** manquer de qch, être dépourvu de qch; **mentally d.,** arriéré.

deficit ['defɪsɪt] *n Fin Com* déficit *m*; **to be in d.,** être en déficit; **budget that shows a d.,** budget déficitaire; **to make up the d.,** combler le déficit.

defile[1] ['diːfaɪl] *n* (*passage*) défilé *m*.

defile[2] [dɪ'faɪl] *vi Mil etc* (*of troops etc*) défiler.

defile[3] *vt* souiller (*qch*); salir (*la mémoire de qn,qch*); profaner (*un lieu saint, une tombe*).

defilement [dɪ'faɪlmənt] *n* fait *m* de salir (*la mémoire de qn*); souillure *f*, salissure *f* (*de qch*); profanation *f* (*d'un lieu saint, d'une tombe*).

definable [dɪ'faɪnəb(ə)l] *adj* définissable; déterminable.

define [dɪ'faɪn] *vt* **(a)** définir (*un mot, un objet*); **(b)** préciser (*son attitude politique, sa position etc*); formuler (*des objectifs, etc*); **(c)** déterminer (*l'étendue ou les limites de qch*); délimiter (*des pouvoirs*); **well-defined limits,** limites bien déterminées; **(d) well-defined outlines,** contours nettement dessinés *ou* dégagés.

definite ['defɪnɪt] *adj* **(a)** (*certain*) défini, bien déterminé; (*date*) définitif, certain; (*réponse*) précis, catégorique; *Com* (*commande*) ferme; **there has been a d. improvement in her condition/work,** il y a eu une amélioration certaine de son état/travail; **to have very d. views about sth,** avoir une opinion bien arrêtée sur qch; **at a d. time,** à une heure déterminée; **and that's d.!,** et c'est sûr!; **you are not d. enough,** vous ne précisez pas assez; **she is very d. about it,** elle est tout à fait sûre de cela; **I'm d. it was him,** je suis certain *ou* sûr que c'était lui; **(b)** *Gram* (*article*) défini; **past d.,** passé défini.

definitely ['defɪnɪtlɪ] *adv* précisément; nettement; catégoriquement; **d. superieur,** nettement supérieur; **she is d. better,** elle va décidément mieux; **he is d. mad,** il n'y a pas de doute qu'il est fou; **are you going? — d.!,** est-ce que vous y allez? — bien sûr que oui!; **d. not!,** certainement pas!

definition [defɪ'nɪʃən] *n* **(a)** (*meaning*) définition *f*; **by d.,** par définition; **to give the d. of sth,** donner la définition de qch, définir qch; **(b)** *Opt* netteté *f* (*de l'image*); *TV* définition *f*.

definitive [dɪ'fɪnɪtɪv] *adj* (*verdict, result*) définitif; (*authoritative*) qui fait autorité; **d. biography/edition,** biographic *f*/édition *f* qui fait autorité.

definitively [dɪ'fɪnɪtɪvlɪ] *adv* définitivement; en définitive.

deflate [diː'fleɪt] **1** *vt* **(a)** dégonfler (*un ballon, un pneu*); *Fig* remettre (*qn*) à sa place; **(b)** *Econ* **to d. the currency,** amener la déflation de la monnaie. **2** *vi* **(a)** (*of tyre etc*) se dégonfler; **(b)** *Econ* amener la déflation de la monnaie.

deflation [diː'fleɪʃən] *n* **(a)** dégonflement *m* (*d'un ballon, d'un pneu*); *Fig* fait *m* de se dégonfler; **(b)** *Fin* déflation *f*.

deflationary [diː'fleɪʃən(ə)rɪ] *adj Econ* (*politique etc*) de déflation; (*budget, measure*) déflationniste.

deflect [dɪ'flekt] **1** *vt* (faire) dévier, détourner; défléchir (*la lumière*); *Fig* **to d. criticism,** détourner la critique; *Fig* **the government will not be deflected from its aims,** le gouvernement ne se laissera pas détourner de ses objectifs; *Mil* **to be deflected,** (*of projectile*) dériver. **2** *vi* (se) dévier, se détourner, défléchir.

deflection [dɪ'flekʃən] *n* **(a)** déflexion *f* (*de la lumière*); déviation *f* (*de l'aiguille du compas*); **(b)** *El Electron* (*of voltmeter etc*) déviation *f*, déflexion *f*.

deflector [dɪ'flektər] *n Tech* déflecteur *m*; **sound d.,** abat-son *m inv*.

deflexion [dɪ'flekʃən] *n* = **DEFLECTION**.

defloration [deflə'reɪʃən] *n* (*de vierge*) défloration *f*.

deflower [diː'flauər] *vt* **(a)** déflorer (*une vierge*); **(b)** défleurir (*une plante etc*).

defoliant [diː'fəulɪənt] *n* défoliant *m*.

defoliate [diː'fəulɪeɪt] *vt* défeuiller (*des arbres etc*).

defoliation [diːfəulɪ'eɪʃən] *n* défoliation *f*.

deforest [diː'fɒrɪst] *vt* déboiser (*une région*).

deforestation [diːfɒrɪs'teɪʃən] *n* (*of region*) déboisement *m*.

deform [dɪ'fɔːm] *vt* déformer; *MecE* fausser (*une poutre etc*); **shoes that d. the feet,** chaussures qui déforment les pieds; **the baby was born deformed,** le bébé est né avec une malformation.

deformation [diːfɔː'meɪʃən] *n* déformation *f* (*d'un os etc*).

deformity [dɪ'fɔːmɪtɪ] *n* difformité *f*.

defraud [dɪ'frɔːd] **1** *vt* frauder (*le fisc etc*); *Jur* léser (*qn*); **to d. s.o. of sth,** frustrer qn de qch, escroquer qch à qn; **to**

d. a bank/one's employer, escroquer une banque/son employeur. **2** *vi Jur* **conspiracy to d.**, entente délictueuse dans le but de frauder.

defrauder [dɪ'frɔːdər] *n* fraudeur, -euse.

defray [dɪ'freɪ] *vt* **to d. s.o.'s expenses,** rembourser les frais de qn; **to d. the cost of sth,** couvrir les frais de qch.

defreeze [diː'friːz] *vt* décongeler.

defrock [diː'frɒk] *vt Rel* défroquer (*un curé*).

defrost [diː'frɒst] **1** *vt* **(a)** dégivrer (*un réfrigérateur etc*); **(b)** décongeler (*la viande etc*). **2** *vi* **(a)** (*of refrigerator*) dégivrer; **(b)** (*of meat*) se décongeler.

deft [deft] *adj* (*naturally*) adroit; **with a d. hand,** d'une main exercée.

deftly ['deftlɪ] *adv* adroitement; d'une main exercée.

deftness ['deftnɪs] *n* adresse *f*, habileté *f*, dextérité *f*.

defunct [dɪ'fʌŋkt] **1** *adj* (*person*) défunt, -e, décédé, -ée; *Fig* (*project, industry*) qui a périclité; (*company*) dissous, *f* dissoute. **2** *n* **the d.**, le défunt, la défunte.

defuse [diː'fjuːz] *vt* désamorcer (*une bombe, Fig une crise*).

defy [dɪ'faɪ] *vt* défier (*qn*); mettre (*qn*) au défi; braver (*qn, un ordre, la loi*); **to d. description,** échapper à toute description; **I d. him to prove it,** je le défie de le prouver.

degenerate[1] [dɪ'dʒen(ə)rət] *adj & n* dégénéré, -ée.

degenerate[2] [dɪ'dʒenəreɪt] *vi* dégénérer (**from,** de; **into,** en); **the discussion degenerated into a fight,** la discussion à dégénéré en bagarre.

degeneration [dɪdʒenə'reɪʃən] *n* dégénérescence *f*, dégénération *f*; *Med* **fatty d.**, dégénérescence graisseuse.

degenerative [dɪ'genərətɪv] *adj* (*disease*) qui empire, qui s'aggrave; **she has a d. heart condition,** elle a des troubles cardiaques qui s'aggravent.

degradation [degrə'deɪʃən] *n* **(a)** avilissement *m*, dégradation *f*; **to live a life of d.**, vivre dans la dégradation; **(b)** *Geol* désagrégation *f*; *Phys* dégradation *f*; **(c)** *Mil* dégradation *f*.

degrade [dɪ'greɪd] *vt* **(a)** avilir, dégrader (*qn*); **porn magazines d. women,** les magazines pornographiques avilissent les femmes; **I won't d. myself by answering that,** je ne m'abaisserai pas à répondre à ça; **(b)** *Phys* dégrader (*l'énergie*); *Geol* désagréger (*des roches*); **(c)** dégrader, casser (*un officier etc*).

degrading [dɪ'greɪdɪŋ] *adj* (*experience*) avilissant, dégradant.

degree [dɪ'griː] *n* **(a)** (*extent*) & *Phys Geog etc* degré *m*; **to some** *or* **a (certain) d.**, à un certain degré, (jusqu')à un certain point; **she's right to a d.**, elle a raison jusqu'à un certain point *ou* dans une certaine mesure; **to** *or* **in a high d.**, éminemment; **in the highest d.**, au plus haut *ou* au dernier degré; **to such a d. that ...**, à tel point que ...; **by degrees,** petit à petit, graduellement; *Gram* **d. of comparison,** degré de comparaison; *Phys* **d. of humidity,** titre *m* d'eau *ou* d'humidité; **to feel a d. of optimism,** ressentir quelque optimisme; *Jur* **marriage within the prohibited** *or* **forbidden degrees,** mariage entre parents ou alliés au degré prohibé; **angle of 30 degrees,** angle *m* de 30 degrés; **we can expect temperatures of 15 to 20 degrees,** nous pouvons nous attendre à des températures de 15 à 20 degrés; **it's 25 degrees,** il fait 25 degrés; **ten degrees of frost,** dix degrés au-dessous de zéro; *Math* **equation of the second/third d.**, équation *f* du second/troisième degré;

(b) *Univ* grade *m* (universitaire); **bachelor's d.**, = licence *f* (*ès lettres etc*); **to take** *or* **do a d.**, passer *ou* faire une licence (**in,** en); **when did you do** *or* **take your d.?**, quand est-ce que tu as passé ta licence?

-degree [də'griː] *suff* **first/second/***etc***-d. burn,** brûlure *f* du premier/deuxième/*etc* degré; *US* **first/second-d. murder,** meurtre *m* avec/sans préméditation.

dehire [diː'haɪər] *vt US Euph* remercier (*qn*).

dehumanize [diː'hjuːmənaɪz] *vt* déshumaniser; **it was a dehumanizing experience,** c'était une expérience déshumanisante.

dehumidifier [diːhjuː'mɪdɪfaɪər] *n* déshumidificateur *m*.

dehumidify [diːhjuː'mɪdɪfaɪ] *vt* déshumidifier.

dehydrate [diː'haɪdreɪt] **1** *vt* déshydrater; **to become dehydrated,** se déshydrater; **she's dehydrated,** elle est déshydratée. **2** *vi* (*of person*) se déshydrater.

dehydration [diːhaɪ'dreɪʃən] *n* déshydratation *f*.

de-ice [diː'aɪs] *vt* dégivrer (*un avion*).

de-icer [diː'aɪsər] *n* dégivreur *m*.

de-icing [diː'aɪsɪŋ] *n* (*of plane etc*) dégivrage *m*.

deification [diːɪfɪ'keɪʃən, deɪ-] *n* déification *f*.

deify ['diːɪfaɪ, deɪ-] *vt* déifier (*qn*).

deign [deɪn] *vt* **to d. to do sth,** daigner faire qch; condescendre à faire qch; **without deigning to look at me,** sans daigner me regarder.

deindex [diː'ɪndeks] *vt Fin* désindexer (*les salaires*) par rapport au coût de la vie.

deindustrialization [diːɪndʌstrɪəlaɪ'zeɪʃən] *n* désindustrialisation *f*.

deity ['diːɪtɪ, deɪ-] *n* **(a)** (*god*) dieu *m*, déesse *f*, déité *f*, divinité *f*; *Rel* **the D.**, la Divinité; Dieu *m*; **(b)** (*divinity*) divinité *f* (*de Jésus-Christ etc*).

déjà vu ['deɪʒæ'vuː] *n* **I had a feeling of d. v.**, j'ai eu une impression de déjà vu.

deject [dɪ'dʒekt] *vt* abattre, décourager (*qn*).

dejected [dɪ'dʒektɪd] *adj* abattu, découragé; **she looks thoroughly d.**, elle a l'air complètement découragée; **to become d.**, se décourager.

dejectedly [dɪdʒektɪdlɪ] *adv* d'un air abattu *ou* découragé.

dejection [dɪ'dʒekʃən] *n* découragement *m*.

de jure ['diː'dʒʊərɪ] *adv Lit Jur* de jure.

dekko ['dekəʊ] *n Br Sl* coup *m* d'œil; **let's have a d.**, fais *ou* faites voir; **to take a d.**, jeter un (coup d')œil.

Del *abbr* **Delaware.**

delay[1] [dɪ'leɪ] *n* retard *m*; **without d.**, sans retard *ou* délai; **without (any) further d.**, sans plus tarder; **an hour's d.**, une heure de retard; **all flights are subject to d.**, tous les vols ont du retard; **delays of four hours can be expected,** on peut s'attendre à des retards de quatre heures; **the road works caused traffic delays,** les travaux ont retardé *ou* entravé la circulation.

delay[2] **1** *vt* **(a)** retarder, remettre (*son départ*); différer, arriérer (*un paiement*); **delayed-action fuse,** fusée *f* à retardement; **(b)** retenir, retarder (*qn*); entraver, retarder (*le progrès, la circulation*); **they've been delayed by fog,** ils ont été retardés par le brouillard; **she's suffering from delayed shock,** elle souffre d'un choc après coup *ou* a posteriori. **2** *vi* **(a)** tarder (**in doing sth,** à faire qch); *Mil* **delaying action,** action retardatrice, combat retardateur; **don't d., book your holiday now,** ne tardez pas, réservez vos vacances maintenant; **(b)** (*linger*) s'attarder.

delectable [dɪ'lektəb(ə)l] *adj* délectable, délicieux.

delectation [diːlek'teɪʃən] *n* délectation *f*.

delegate[1] ['delɪgət] *n* délégué, -ée.

delegate[2] ['delɪgeɪt] **1** *vt* **(a)** (*appoint*) déléguer (*qn*) (**to do sth,** pour faire qch); **(b)** déléguer (*des pouvoirs*). **2** *vi* déléguer; **she's not very good at delegating,** elle ne sait pas bien déléguer; **he must learn how to d.**, il faut qu'il apprenne à déléguer.

delegation [delɪ'geɪʃən] *n* (*act, state, representatives*) délégation *f*; **to send a d.**, envoyer une délégation.

delete [dɪ'liːt] **1** *vt* effacer, rayer (*un mot etc*) (**from,** de); *Comptr* effacer; **d. where inapplicable,** (*on form*) rayer les mentions inutiles. **2** *vi Comptr* effacer.

deleterious [delɪ'tɪərɪəs] *adj* nuisible (*à la santé*).

deletion [dɪ'liːʃən] *n* **(a)** (*action*) suppression *f* (*d'un mot, d'un passage*); **(b)** (*what has been deleted*) passage *ou* mot effacé *ou* supprimé.

delft [delft] *n Cer* faïence *f* de Delft; **d. blue,** bleu *m* de faïence.

deli ['delɪ] *n F* = **DELICATESSEN (a)**.

deliberate[1] [dɪ'lɪb(ə)rət] *adj* **(a)** (*intentional*) délibéré, réfléchi, intentionnel, voulu; (*insolence*) calculé; (*insult*) prémédité; **(b)** (*unhurried*) (*person*) circonspect, avisé; (*movement etc*) lent, sans hâte.

deliberate[2] [dɪ'lɪbəreɪt] *vt & vi* délibérer (**on,** sur), réfléchir (**on,** sur); **to d. over** *or* **on a question,** délibérer (d')une question.

deliberately [dɪ'lɪb(ə)rətlɪ] *adv* (*see adj*) **(a)** de propos délibéré, à dessein, intentionnellement, exprès; **to do sth d.**, faire qch exprès *ou* intentionnellement; **you d. disobeyed me,** tu m'as désobéi intentionnellement; **(b)** sans hâte.

deliberation [dɪlɪbə'reɪʃən] *n* **(a)** (*thought, discussion*) délibération *f*; **after due d.**, après mûre délibération; **the deliberations of an assembly,** les débats *mpl* d'une assemblée; **(b)** (*lack of haste*) sage lenteur *f*, mesure *f*; **with d.**, posément, sans hâte; **to act with d.**, agir avec circonspection *ou* après réflexion.

deliberative [dɪ'lɪbərətɪv] *adj* (*function*) délibératif; (*assemblée*) délibérant.

delicacy ['delɪkəsɪ] *n* **(a)** délicatesse *f*; finesse *f* (*de l'ouïe*); sensibilité *f* (*d'un instrument de précision*); légèreté *f* (*de touche*); **(b)** fragilité *f* (*de santé*); **(c)** (*tactfulness*) tact *m*; **(d) negotiations of the utmost d.**, négociations très délicates; **(e)** (*food*) mets délicat.

delicate ['delɪkət] *adj* **(a)** (*glass, person etc*) délicat; (*trait*) fin, délicat; **to have a d. touch,** (*of painter*) avoir une touche délicate; (*of pianist*) avoir un toucher délicat; **d. piece of machinery,** mécanisme délicat; **(b)** (*health*) fragile, délicat; **(c)** (*sentiments*) de délicatesse; **(d)** (*situation*) délicat, difficile; (*question*) épineux; **we're at a very d. stage in our negotiations,** nous en sommes à une étape très délicate de nos négociations; **to tread on d. ground,** toucher à des questions délicates.

delicately ['delɪkətli] *adv* délicatement; avec délicatesse.

delicatessen [delɪkə'tesən] *n* **(a)** (*shop*) épicerie fine; **(b)** (*food*) plats cuisinés; = charcuterie *f*.

delicious [dɪ'lɪʃəs] *adj* exquis; (*mets, odeur*) délicieux.

delight[1] [dɪ'laɪt] *n* **(a)** (*source of pleasure*) délices *fpl*, délice *m*; **the film is a d.,** le film est un délice; **he is a d. to work with,** c'est un plaisir de travailler avec lui; **it is such a d. to ...,** c'est si bon de ...; **to be s.o.'s d.,** faire le bonheur de qn; **(b)** (*pleasure*) joie *f*; **much to the d. of ..., to the great d. of ...,** au grand plaisir de ..., à la grande joie de ...; **it gives me great d. to welcome you here,** c'est pour moi un grand plaisir que de vous accueillir ici; **to take d. in (doing) sth,** prendre grand plaisir à faire qch.

delight[2] *vt* enchanter, ravir (*qn*); (*of music*) charmer (*les oreilles*); **I'm delighted with it,** j'en suis ravi *ou* enchanté.

delighted [dɪ'laɪtɪd] *adj* ravi, enchanté; **I'm d. to make your acquaintance,** je suis ravi *ou* enchanté de faire votre connaissance; **I am d. for you,** je suis ravi pour vous; **I'd be d. to!,** j'en serais ravi!

►**delight in** *vipo* se délecter de, aimer beaucoup (*qch*); **to d. in doing sth,** se délecter à *ou* aimer beaucoup faire qch.

delightful [dɪ'laɪtfʊl] *adj* délicieux, ravissant, charmant; **she has a d. sense of humour,** elle a un sens de l'humour délicieux; **a d. child,** un enfant charmant; **they have a d. home,** ils ont une maison ravissante.

delightfully [dɪ'laɪtfʊlɪ] *adv* délicieusement; **he sings d.,** il chante à ravir.

delimit [diː'lɪmɪt] *vt* délimiter.

delimitation [dɪlɪmɪ'teɪʃən] *n* délimitation *f*.

delimiter [diː'lɪmɪtər] *n Comptr* séparateur *m*.

delineate [dɪ'lɪnɪeɪt] *vt* **(a)** tracer (*un triangle etc*); **(b)** dessiner (*les traits de qn*); délinéer (*un profil*).

delinquency [dɪ'lɪŋkwənsɪ] *n* délinquance *f*.

delinquent [dɪ'lɪŋkwənt] *adj & n* délinquant, -ante.

delirious [dɪ'lɪrɪəs] *adj* (*malade*) en délire, dans le délire, délirant; **to be d.,** avoir *ou* être dans le délire, délirer; *Fig* **to be d. with joy,** délirer de joie, être délirant de joie; *Fig* **I'm d.,** je suis dans le délire; *Fig* **I'm d. at** *or* **about the prospect,** cette perspective me fait délirer.

deliriously [dɪ'lɪrɪəslɪ] *adv* frénétiquement; **d. happy,** délirant de joie.

delirium [dɪ'lɪrɪəm] *n* délire *m*; **to be in a d.,** être en plein délire; *Fig Lit* **to be in a d. of joy,** être transporté de joie; **d. tremens,** delirium *m* tremens.

deliver [dɪ'lɪvər] **1** *vt* **(a)** remettre, délivrer (*un paquet, un télégramme etc*); distribuer (*des lettres*); livrer (*des marchandises*); *Jur* signifier (*un acte*); **do you want your newspaper (to be) delivered?,** est-ce que vous voulez qu'on vous livre votre journal?, est-ce que vous voulez que votre journal vous soit livré?; **do you have your milk delivered?,** est-ce que vous vous faites livrer votre lait?, est-ce qu'on vous livre votre lait?; **to d. a message,** faire une commission; **to d. sth at s.o.'s house,** livrer qch à domicile; *Com* **delivered free,** livraison franco; **to d. the goods,** livrer les marchandises; *Fig* remplir ses engagements; **to d. sth to s.o.,** livrer qch à qn;

(b) *Obst* **to d. a woman (of a child),** (faire) accoucher une femme; **to be delivered of a child,** accoucher d'un enfant;

(c) porter, donner (*un coup*); lancer (*la balle etc*); *Nau* lâcher (*une bordée*);

(d) faire, prononcer, délivrer (*un discours*); faire (*une conférence*); *Jur* prononcer, rendre (*un jugement*);

(e) (*of machine, dynamo etc*) débiter, fournir (*du courant*);

(f) *Fml* (*rescue*) délivrer (*qn*) (**from his enemies,** de ses ennemis); **to d. s.o. from death,** sauver qn de la mort; *Rel* **d. us from evil,** délivre-nous du mal.

2 *vi* (*of store*) livrer; *Fig* **to d. (on one's promise),** tenir sa promesse.

►**deliver over** *vtsep* (*give*) céder, transférer, transmettre (*un bien etc*) (**to,** à).

►**deliver up** *vtsep* (*surrender*) restituer, rendre (*une ville*) (**to,** à).

deliverance [dɪ'lɪv(ə)rəns] *n Fml* délivrance *f* (**from,** de).

deliverer [dɪ'lɪvərər] *n* **(a)** *Fml* (*saviour*) libérateur, -trice, sauveur *m*; **(b)** livreur *m* (*de marchandises*).

delivery [dɪ'lɪv(ə)rɪ] *n* **(a)** livraison *f* (*d'un paquet etc*); remise *f* (*d'une lettre*); distribution *f* (*des lettres*); *Jur* signification *f* (*d'un acte*); **to take d. of sth,** prendre livraison de qch; **charge for d.,** (frais *mpl* de) port *m*; *US* **general d.,** poste restante; **parcels awaiting d.,** colis *mpl* en souffrance; **d. note/schedule/time,** bulletin *m*/calendrier *m*/délai *m* de livraison; **free d.,** livraison franco; **d. man** *or* **boy/girl,** livreur/livreuse; **to pay on d.,** payer à *ou* sur livraison; **d. date,** date *f* de livraison; **d. van,** camion *m* de livraison;

(b) *Obst* accouchement *m* (*d'une femme*); **it was an easy d.,** ça a été un accouchement facile;

(c) prononciation *f* (*d'un discours*); diction *f* (*d'un orateur*); **to have a good d.,** avoir un bon débit;

(d) *Sp* lancement *m*, envoi *m* (*de la balle*); (*of player*) manière *f* de lancer (*la balle*); *Mil* lancement (*d'une fusée etc*);

(e) débit *m* (*d'eau, de courant etc*); refoulement *m* (*d'une pompe*);

(f) reddition *f* (*d'un prisonnier*); *Fin* cession *f*, remise *f* (*de titres*); *Jur* tradition *f* (*d'un bien*); délivrance *f* (*d'un legs etc*) (**to,** à); **for d.,** (*of stocks*) au comptant.

dell [del] *n* vallon *m*.

delouse [diː'laʊs] *vt* ôter les poux de (*qch, qn*); épouiller (*qn*).

delphinium [del'fɪnɪəm] *n* (*flower*) pied-d'alouette *m*, *pl* pieds-d'alouette.

delta ['deltə] *n* **(a)** (*in Greek Alphabet*) delta *m inv*; **(b)** (*of river*) delta *m*, *pl* deltas; *Av* **d. wing,** aile *f* (en) delta.

delude [dɪ'luːd] *vt* tromper (*qn*), induire (*qn*) en erreur; **to d. oneself,** se faire des illusions.

deluge[1] ['deljuːdʒ] *n* **(a)** (*flood*) déluge *m*; **a d. of rain,** une pluie diluvienne; **(b)** *Fig* déluge *m* (*de paroles*); avalanche *f* (*de lettres, de questions etc*).

deluge[2] *vt* (*flood*) *& Fig* inonder (**with,** de).

delusion [dɪ'luːʒən] *n* illusion *f*; **to be under a d.,** se faire des illusions, s'abuser; **to suffer from delusions,** être sujet à des hallucinations; **delusions of grandeur,** folie *f* des grandeurs.

de luxe [dɪ'lʌks] *adj* de luxe; (*appartement*) (de) grand standing.

delve [delv] *vi* fouiller; **to d. in(to) one's pocket,** fouiller dans sa poche; **to d. into the past,** remonter dans le passé.

Dem [dem] *n US Pol abbr* **democrat.**

demagnetize [diː'mægnɪtaɪz] *vt* démagnétiser.

demagogic [demə'gɒgɪk] *adj* démagogique.

demagogue ['deməgɒg] *n* démagogue *m*.

demand[1] [dɪ'mɑːnd] *n* **(a)** demande *f*, réclamation *f*; **d. for payment,** demande de paiement; **final d. (notice),** dernier rappel; **payable on d.,** payable sur demande; **d. note,** avertissement *m*; **(b)** *Econ* demande *f*; **supply and d.,** l'offre *f* et la demande; **to be in (great/little) d.,** être (très/peu) demandé *ou* recherché; **to be much in d. as ...,** (*of person*) être très demandé en tant que ...; **there's not much d. for it,** ce n'est pas très demandé, ce n'est pas très recherché; **(c) demands,** (*of workers, kidnappers*) exigences *fpl*; (*of a situation, job etc*) nécessités *fpl*, exigences *fpl*; **to give in to s.o.'s demands,** céder aux exigences de qn; **to make great demands on s.o.'s patience,** exiger de qn beaucoup de patience; **I have many demands on my time,** je suis très pris.

demand[2] *vt* **(a)** réclamer (*qch*) (**of, from,** à); **they're demanding payment,** ils réclament le paiement; **to d. an apology/explanation,** exiger des excuses/une explication; **I d. to speak to the manager,** j'exige de parler au directeur; **to d. to know whether ...,** insister pour savoir si ...; **to d. that ...,** exiger que ... + *sub*; **(b)** (*of situation, job etc*) demander, exiger; **the matter demands great care,** l'affaire exige *ou* réclame beaucoup de soin.

demanding [dɪ'mɑːndɪŋ] *adj* (*job, person*) exigeant; (*job, task*) astreignant; **she's very d.,** (*of boss, child*) elle est très exigeante; **being a physiotherapist is physically d.,** être kinésithérapeute est physiquement astreignant.

demarcation [diːmɑː'keɪʃən] *n* démarcation *f*, délimitation *f*; **d. line,** ligne *f* de démarcation; *Ind* **d. dispute,** conflit *m* sur la répartition des tâches.

demean [dɪ'miːn] *vt* **to d. oneself,** s'abaisser, s'avilir; **it was very demeaning having to ...,** c'était très avilissant de devoir ... .

demeanour, *US* **demeanor** [dɪ'miːnər] *n* comportement *m*, attitude *f*, conduite *f*.

demented [dɪ'mentɪd] *adj* fou, *f* folle; *Med* dément; **to become d.,** tomber en démence; *Fig* **like one d.,** (*hurler etc*) comme un fou.

dementia [dɪ'menʃɪə] *n Med* démence *f*; **senile d.,** démence sénile.

demerara [demə'reərə] *n* **d. (sugar),** = cassonade *f*.
demerit [diː'merɪt] *n* **(a)** *Fml* (*fault*) démérite *m*, tort *m*; **(b)** *Am Sch* blâme *m*.
demesne [də'meɪn] *n* **(a)** *Jur* possession *f*; **(b)** *Fml* domaine *m*.
demigod ['demɪgɒd] *n* demi-dieu *m*, *pl* demi-dieux.
demijohn ['demɪdʒɒn] *n Ind etc* dame-jeanne *f*, *pl* dames-jeannes, bonbonne *f*.
demilitarization [diːmɪlɪt(ə)raɪ'zeɪʃən] *n* démilitarisation *f*.
demilitarize [diː'mɪlɪtəraɪz] *vt* démilitariser.
demise¹ [dɪ'maɪz] *n* **(a)** *Admin* décès *m*, mort *f* (*de qn*); *Fig* (*of hopes, newspaper etc*) fin *f*; **(b)** *Jur* (*by lease*) cession *f* à bail; (*by will*) cession par testament; transfert *m* (*d'un titre etc*).
demise² *vt Jur* céder à bail *ou* par testament; transmettre (*un titre etc*).
demisemiquaver ['demɪsemɪkweɪvər] *n Mus* triple croche *f*.
demist [diː'mɪst] *vt* désembuer.
demister [diː'mɪstər] *n Aut* (dispositif *m*) antibuée *m*.
demo ['deməʊ] *n F* **(a)** (*protest*) manif *f*; **(b)** (*of singer etc*) disque *m ou* cassette *f* de démonstration; *Comptr* **d. disk,** disquette *f* de démonstration *ou* d'évaluation.
demob¹ [diː'mɒb] *vt* **(-bb-)** *Old-fashioned Br Mil F* démobiliser.
demob² *n Old-fashioned Br Mil F* démobilisation *f*.
demobilization [diːməʊbɪlaɪ'zeɪʃən] *n Mil* démobilisation *f*.
demobilize [diː'məʊbɪlaɪz] *vt & vi Mil* démobiliser.
democracy [dɪ'mɒkrəsɪ] *n* démocratie *f*; **people's d.,** démocratie populaire; **social d.,** social-démocratie *f*.
democrat ['deməkræt] *n* démocrate *mf*; **social d.,** social-démocrate *mf*, *mpl* sociaux-démocrates; *US Pol* **the Democrats,** le parti démocrate.
democratic [demə'krætɪk] *adj* démocratique; *US Pol* **D. Party,** parti *m* démocrate.
democratically [demə'krætɪklɪ] *adv* (*elected etc*) démocratiquement.
democratize [dɪ'mɒkrətaɪz] **1** *vt* démocratiser. **2** *vi* se démocratiser.
demodulation [diːmɒdjʊ'leɪʃən] *n Electron* (*of signal etc*) démodulation *f*.
demographer [dɪ'mɒgrəfər] *n* démographe *mf*.
demographic [deməʊ'græfɪk] *adj* démographique.
demographics [deməʊ'græfɪks] *npl* statistiques *fpl* démographiques; **the d. show that ...,** selon les statistiques démographiques ... .
demography [dɪ'mɒgrəfɪ] *n* démographie *f*.
demolish [dɪ'mɒlɪʃ] *vt* démolir (*un édifice*); démanteler (*des fortifications etc*); *Fig* **he had soon demolished most of the cake,** il avait bientôt dévoré les trois-quarts du gâteau; *Fig* **to d. s.o.,** (*in an argument*) démolir qn; (*in competition, fight*) mettre la pâtée à qn; **to d. an argument,** démolir un argument.
demolition [demə'lɪʃən, diː-] *n* démolition *f*; **d. contractor,** démolisseur *m*; **d. work,** travail *m* de démolition.
demon ['diːmən] *n* démon *m*, diable *m*; **the D.,** le Démon; *Fig* **that child's a little d.,** cet enfant est un petit démon; *Fig* **he's a d. for work,** c'est un monstre de travail.
demonetize [dɪ'mʌnɪtaɪz] *vt* démonétiser (*une monnaie*).
demoniac [dɪ'məʊnɪæk] **1** *adj* démoniaque. **2** *n* démoniaque *mf*.
demoniacal [diːmə'naɪək(ə)l] *adj* démoniaque.
demonic [dɪ'mɒnɪk] *adj* démoniaque.
demonology [diːmə'nɒlədʒɪ] *n* démonologie *f*.
demonstrable [dɪ'mɒnstrəb(ə)l, 'demən-] *adj* (*fact*) démontrable.
demonstrably [dɪ'mɒnstrəblɪ, 'demən-] *adv* **d. true/false statement,** affirmation *f* dont la vérité/la fausseté peut être prouvée; **that's d. false,** c'est faux de toute évidence.
demonstrate ['demənstreɪt] **1** *vt* **(a)** (*prove*) démontrer (*une vérité*); **that just demonstrates how stupid he is,** ça ne fait que démontrer à quel point il est stupide; **(b)** (*show, explain*) décrire, expliquer (*un système*); donner une démonstration pratique du fonctionnement de (*un appareil*); **the stewardess demonstrated the use of life jackets,** l'hôtesse de l'air a fait une démonstration de l'utilisation des gilets de sauvetage. **2** *vi Pol etc* manifester, faire une manifestation (**against,** contre).
demonstration [demən'streɪʃən] *n* **(a)** démonstration *f* (*d'une vérité*); **(b)** démonstration *f* pratique (*d'un appareil*); **would you like a d.?,** est-ce que vous voulez que je vous fasse une démonstration?; **d. car,** voiture *f* de démonstration; *Sch* **d. (class, lecture),** (séance *f* de) démonstration; **(c)** manifestation *f* (*politique etc*); **to hold** *or* **stage a d.,** manifester; **d. march,** marche *f* de protestation; **to go on a d. march,** (*take part*) prendre part à une marche de protestation.
demonstrative [dɪ'mɒnstrətɪv] *adj* **(a)** (*argument etc*) démonstratif; **(b)** (*person*) démonstratif; **(c)** *Gram* (*adjectif etc*) démonstratif.
demonstrator ['demənstreɪtər] *n* **(a)** (*of machine etc*) démonstrateur, -trice; **(b)** *US Aut* voiture *f* de démonstration; **(c)** manifestant, -ante (*politique etc*).
demoralization [dɪmɒrəlaɪ'zeɪʃən] *n* démoralisation *f*.
demoralize [dɪ'mɒrəlaɪz] *vt* démoraliser (*les troupes etc*).
demoralizing [dɪ'mɒrəlaɪzɪŋ] *adj* (*échec etc*) démoralisant.
demote [dɪ'məʊt] *vt* réduire (*qn*) à un grade inférieur *ou* à une classe inférieure, rétrograder (*qn*); *Mil* **he's been demoted to private,** il a été rétrogradé au grade de simple soldat; **she's been demoted to assistant manager,** elle a été rétrogradée au poste de directeur-adjoint.
demotic [dɪ'mɒtɪk] *adj* populaire, du peuple; (*Greek*) démotique.
demotion [dɪ'məʊʃən] *n* réduction *f* à un grade inférieur *ou* à une classe inférieure, rétrogradation *f*.
demulsify [dɪ'mʌlsɪfaɪ] *vi* désémulsionner.
demur¹ [dɪ'mɜːr] *n* objection *f*; **without d.,** sans faire d'objection.
demur² *vi* **(-rr-) (a)** soulever des objections (**at, to,** contre); **(b)** *Jur* opposer une exception.
demure [dɪ'mjʊər] *adj* modeste, réservé; *Pej* d'une modestie affectée.
demurely [dɪ'mjʊəlɪ] *adv* d'un air modeste *ou* réservé; *Pej* avec une modestie affectée.
demureness [dɪ'mjʊənɪs] *n* modestie *f*, réserve *f* (*d'une jeune fille*); *Pej* modestie affectée.
demystify [diː'mɪstɪfaɪ] *vt* démystifier.
demythologize [diːmɪ'θɒlədʒaɪz] *vt* démythifier.
den [den] *n* **(a)** tanière *f*, antre *m*, repaire *m* (*de bêtes féroces*); *Fig* nid *m* (*de brigands*); *Fig* **d. of thieves,** retraite *f* de voleurs; **(b)** *esp Am* (*in home*) cabinet *m* de travail; fumoir *m*; **(c)** (*site, centre*) bouge *m*; **gambling d.,** maison *f* de jeu; **d. of vice,** lieu *m* de débauche.
denationalization [diːnæʃənəlaɪ'zeɪʃən] *n* dénationalisation *f*.
denationalize [diː'næʃənəlaɪz] *vt* dénationaliser.
denature [diː'neɪtʃər] *vt* dénaturer (*un produit*).
dengue ['deŋgɪ] *n Med* **d. (fever),** dengue *f*.
denial [dɪ'naɪəl] *n* **(a)** refus *m* (*d'un droit, d'une demande*); **d. of justice,** déni *m* de justice; **(b)** démenti *m* (*de la vérité de qch*); **absolute** *or* **flat d.,** dénégation absolue; **to issue a d.,** publier un démenti; **(c)** *Bible* **Peter's d.,** le reniement de Pierre.
denier ['denɪər] *n Tex* (*of hosiery*) denier *m*; **a 30-d. stocking,** un bas 30 deniers.
denigrate ['denɪgreɪt] *vt Lit* dénigrer (*qn, un projet*).
denim ['denɪm] *n* **(a)** *Tex* (toile *f* de) jean *m*; **d. skirt,** jupe *f* en jean; **(b) denims,** bleus *mpl* (*de travail*); (*jeans*) (blue-)jean *m*.
denizen ['denɪzən] *n Lit* habitant, -ante.
Denmark ['denmɑːk] *n* Danemark *m*.
denominate [dɪ'nɒmɪneɪt] *vtr* dénommer.
denomination [dɪnɒmɪ'neɪʃən] *n* **(a)** *Rel* culte *m*, confession *f*; **(b)** *Fin* valeur *f*; **coins of all denominations,** pièces *fpl* de toutes valeurs; **(notes of) small denominations,** petites coupures; **(c)** *Fml* (*name*) dénomination *f*.
denominator [dɪ'nɒmɪneɪtər] *n Math* dénominateur *m*; **lowest common d.,** plus petit dénominateur commun; *Math & Fig* **to have a common d.,** avoir un dénominateur commun.
denote [dɪ'nəʊt] *vt* **(a)** (*indicate*) dénoter, montrer, indiquer (**sth,** qch; **that,** que); **(b)** (*mean*) signifier; *Ling* dénoter.
denouement [deɪ'nuːmɒn] *n* (*of play, situation*) dénouement *m*.
denounce [dɪ'naʊns] *vt* **(a)** (*betray*) dénoncer (*un criminel, un crime*); **to d. s.o. to the authorities,** signaler qn à la justice; **to d. s.o. as an impostor,** taxer qn d'imposture; **(b)** (*protest about*) s'élever contre (*un abus*); condamner (*l'art moderne etc*); **(c)** dénoncer (*un traité*).
dense [dens] *adj* **(a)** *Phys* (*body, metal etc*) dense; **(b)** (*smoke, fog etc*) épais, *f* -aisse; (*coward*) compact; (*population*) nombreux; **(c)** *F* (*stupid*) stupide, bête.
densely ['denslɪ] *adv* **d. wooded country,** pays couvert de forêts épaisses; **d. populated region,** région très peu-

plée.

denseness ['densnɪs] *n* **(a)** épaisseur *f* (*du brouillard*); **(b)** *F* (*of person*) stupidité *f*.

density ['densɪtɪ] *n* **(a)** *Phys Ch El etc* densité *f*; *Nucl Phys* **ion/neutron d.**, densité ionique/neutronique; **(b)** densité *f* (*de la population, de la circulation routière*).

dent¹ [dent] *n* bosse *f* (*d'une théière etc*); (*in surface of moon etc*) trou *m*; **there's a d. in the car,** la voiture a une bosse; *Fig* **to make a d. in one's fortune,** faire une brèche à sa fortune; *Fig* **to make** *or* **put a d. in s.o.'s self-confidence,** entamer la confiance en soi *ou* l'assurance de qn.

dent² *vt* bosseler, bossuer, cabosser; *Fig* **to d. s.o.'s self-confidence,** entamer la confiance en soi *ou* l'assurance de qn; **my self-confidence has been dented,** mon assurance en a pris un coup.

dental ['dent(ə)l] *adj* **(a)** dentaire; **d. appointment,** rendez-vous *m* chez le dentiste; **d. floss,** soie *f* dentaire; **d. hygiene,** hygiène *f* dentaire; **your d. hygiene is poor,** vous avez une mauvaise hygiène dentaire; **d. hygienist,** spécialiste *mf* de l'hygiène dentaire; **d. practice** *or* **surgery** *or Am* **office,** cabinet *m* de dentiste; **d. surgeon,** chirurgien *m* dentiste; **(b)** *Ling* dental, -aux; **d. consonant,** (consonne *f*) dentale *f*.

dented ['dentɪd] *adj* bosselé, cabossé; *Aut* **d. wing,** aile bosselée *ou* faussée.

dentifrice ['dentɪfrɪs] *n* dentifrice *m*.

dentist ['dentɪst] *n* dentiste *mf*; **to go to the d.'s,** aller chez le dentiste.

dentistry ['dentɪstrɪ] *n* dentisterie *f*.

dentition [den'tɪʃən] *n* dentition *f*.

dentures ['dentʃəz] *npl* dentier *m*, prothèse *f* dentaire; **to wear d.,** porter un dentier.

denude [dɪ'nju:d] *vt* dénuder, dépouiller (*qch*).

denunciation [dɪnʌnsɪ'eɪʃən] *n* **(a)** dénonciation *f* (*d'un complice etc*); accusation publique (*de qn*); **(b)** condamnation *f* (*d'un abus, de l'art moderne etc*); **(c)** dénonciation *f* (*d'un traité*).

Denver ['denvər] *n Aut F* **D. boot,** sabot *m*.

deny [dɪ'naɪ] *vt* **(a)** nier (*un fait, une vérité*); démentir (*une nouvelle*); repousser (*une accusation*); opposer un démenti à (*une déclaration*); **the accused denies the charge,** l'accusé nie; **to d. having done sth,** nier avoir fait qch; **there is no denying the fact,** c'est un fait indéniable; **there's no denying that ...,** on ne saurait nier que ...; **(b)** renier (*qn, sa foi*); **(c)** refuser (*une prière etc*); **to d. s.o. sth** *or* **sth to s.o.,** refuser qch à qn; **to be denied one's request, to have one's request denied,** se voir refuser sa demande; **(d) to d. oneself sth,** se priver de qch; **to d. oneself for one's children,** se priver pour ses enfants.

deodorant [di:'əʊdərənt] *n* (*for body*) déodorant *m*; (*for room*) désodorisant *m*.

deodorize [di:'əʊdəraɪz] *vt* désodoriser.

deontology [di:ɒn'tɒlədʒɪ] *n Phil* déontologie *f*.

deoxidize [di:'ɒksɪdaɪz] *vt Ch Ind* désoxyder.

deoxyribonucleic [di:'ɒksɪraɪbəʊnju:'kleɪɪk] *adj* **d. acid,** acide *m* désoxyribonucléique.

depart [dɪ'pɑ:t] **1** *vi* **(a)** (*leave*) partir; **to d. from a place,** quitter un lieu; **(b)** (*differ, deviate*) **to d. from,** se départir de, s'écarter de (*son devoir*); déroger à (*un usage*); sortir de, s'écarter de (*son sujet*); manquer à (*la vérité*). **2** *vt* **to d. this life,** quitter cette vie *ou* ce monde.

departed [dɪ'pɑ:tɪd] **1** *adj* **(a)** (*glory etc*) passé, évanoui; **(b)** (*dead*) mort, défunt, décédé. **2** *n* **the d.,** le mort, la morte.

department [dɪ'pɑ:tmənt] *n* **(a)** (*in company, organization*) département *m*, service *m*; (*in shop*) rayon *m*; (*in school, university*) département, U.F.R. *f* (= unité de formation et de recherche); **personnel/accounts d.,** service du personnel/de la comptabilité; **out-patient's d.,** (*in hospital*) service des consultations externes; **head of d.,** chef *m* de service; **glove d.,** rayon des gants; **d. store,** grand magasin; *Fig* **that's not (really) my d.,** ce n'est pas mon rayon; **(b)** (*of government*) ministère *m*; **D. of Education and Science,** = Ministère de l'Éducation; *US* **War D.,** Ministère de la Guerre; **(c)** *Geog* (*in France*) département *m*.

departmental [di:pɑ:t'ment(ə)l] *adj* départemental, -aux; **d. manager,** chef *m* de service.

departure [dɪ'pɑ:tʃər] *n* **(a)** départ *m* (*de qn, d'un train etc*); *Av* **there's only one d. a day for Montreal,** il n'y a qu'un départ par jour pour Montréal; *Fml* **to take one's d.,** prendre congé; **her unexpected d. from politics,** son départ inattendu de la scène politique; **d. time,** heure *f* de départ; *Av* **d. lounge,** salle *f* de départ; **(b)** déviation *f* (**from a principle,** d'un principe); exception *f* (*à la règle générale*); manquement *m* (*à la vérité*); **a d. from his usual habits,** une action contraire à ses habitudes; **a new d.,** une nouvelle tendance *ou* direction *ou* orientation; **politics is a new d. for her,** la politique constitue un nouveau départ pour elle.

depend [dɪ'pend] *vi* (*be decided by*) dépendre (**on,** de); **that depends, it all depends,** ça dépend; **that depends entirely on you,** cela ne tient qu'à vous; **it depends on the weather,** ça dépend du temps; **it depends on how much money I have,** ça dépend de combien d'argent j'ai; **depending on whether ...,** suivant que ...; **it depends on whether she accepts,** ça dépend si elle accepte.

▶**depend on** *vipo* (*rely on*) compter sur (*qn, qch*); **you can d. on him,** vous pouvez avoir confiance en lui; **you can never d. on what he says,** on ne peut pas se fier à ce qu'il dit; **you can't d. on the weather in Britain,** on ne peut pas compter sur le temps en Grande-Bretagne; **you can d. on it,** tu peux compter dessus; **to d. on imports from abroad,** être tributaire de l'étranger; **to d. financially/emotionally on s.o.,** dépendre de quelqu'un financièrement/sur le plan affectif.

dependability [dɪpendə'bɪlɪtɪ] *n* (*of person*) confiance *f* que l'on inspire; (*of information*) véracité *f*; (*of machine*) sécurité *f* (de fonctionnement).

dependable [dɪ'pendəb(ə)l] *adj* (*person*) digne de confiance, sur qui l'on peut compter; (*information*) sûr; (*machine*) d'un fonctionnement sûr; **he is not d.,** on ne peut pas compter sur lui.

dependant [dɪ'pendənt] *n* personne *f* à charge; **dependants,** charges *fpl* de famille.

dependence [dɪ'pendəns] *n* **(a)** dépendance *f* (**on,** de); **(b)** (*trust*) confiance *f* (**on,** en); **(c)** *Med* (état *m* de) dépendance *f* (*d'une drogue*).

dependency [dɪ'pendənsɪ] *n* **(a)** *esp Am* = **DEPENDENCE**; **(b)** dépendance *f* (*d'une ville, d'un État*).

dependent [dɪ'pendənt] *adj* **(a)** dépendant (**on,** de); *Jur* relevant (**on,** de); **to be d. on s.o./sth,** dépendre de qn/qch; **institution d. on voluntary contributions,** institution soutenue par des contributions bénévoles; **(b)** *Gram* (*proposition*) subordonné; **(c) to be d. on s.o.,** être à la charge de qn; **two d. children,** deux enfants à charge; **(d)** *Med* adonné (**on a drug,** à une drogue).

depict [dɪ'pɪkt] *vt* dépeindre, représenter.

depiction [dɪ'pɪkʃən] *n* peinture *f*, description *f*.

depilatory [dɪ'pɪlət(ə)rɪ] *adj & n* (crème *f etc*) dépilatoire *m*.

deplane [di:'pleɪn] *vi* descendre d'avion.

deplete [dɪ'pli:t] *vt* **(a)** épuiser (*des provisions etc*); **stocks are very depleted,** les stocks sont très bas; **(b)** démunir (*une garnison de ses troupes*).

depletion [dɪ'pli:ʃən] *n* épuisement *m*, diminution *f*.

deplorable [dɪ'plɔ:rəb(ə)l] *adj* déplorable, lamentable.

deplorably [dɪ'plɔ:rəblɪ] *adv* déplorablement, lamentablement.

deplore [dɪ'plɔ:r] *vt* déplorer, regretter vivement.

deploy [dɪ'plɔɪ] **1** *vt Mil & Fig* déployer (*une unité, ses ressources*). **2** *vi* se déployer; (*of troops*) s'articuler (sur le terrain).

deployment [dɪ'plɔɪmənt] *n Mil & Fig* déploiement *m* (*d'une unité, de ses ressources*); *Mil* articulation *f* (*de troupes sur le terrain*).

depolarization [di:pəʊləraɪ'zeɪʃən] *n Opt El* dépolarisation *f*.

depolarize [di:'pəʊləraɪz] *vt Opt El* dépolariser.

deponent [dɪ'pəʊnənt] **1** *n* **(a)** *Gram* verbe déponent; **(b)** *Jur* témoin déposant. **2** *adj Gram* (*verb*) déponent.

depopulate [di:'pɒpjʊleɪt] *vt* dépeupler (*un pays*).

depopulation [di:pɒpjʊ'leɪʃən] *n* dépopulation *f*, dépeuplement *m* (*d'un pays*).

deport [dɪ'pɔ:t] *vt* expulser (*un étranger*); déporter (*un condamné politique etc*).

deportation [di:pɒ'teɪʃən] *n* expulsion *f* (*d'un étranger*); déportation *f* (*d'un condamné politique etc*); **d. order,** arrêté *m* d'expulsion.

deportee [di:pɔ:'ti:] *n* expulsé, -ée; déporté, -ée.

deportment [dɪ'pɔ:tmənt] *n* tenue *f*, maintien *m*.

depose [dɪ'pəʊz] **1** *vt* **(a)** déposer (*un roi etc*); **(b)** *Jur* déposer, attester (**that,** que). **2** *vi Jur* faire une déposition.

deposit¹ [dɪ'pɒzɪt] *n* **(a)** *Banking* dépôt *m*; **to make a d.,** déposer de l'argent; **to make a d. of £500,** déposer 500 livres en banque; **bank d.,** dépôt bancaire *ou* en banque; **on d.,** en dépôt; **d. account,** compte *m* à terme; **safe d.,** dépôt en coffre-fort; **(b)** (*returnable*) caution *f*; (*first payment*) acompte *m*; (*not returnable but no obligation to continue* *payments*) arrhes *fpl*; **we require a d. of £500,** nous exigeons une caution de 500 livres; **to leave** *or* **put down a d. on sth,** verser une somme *ou* un acompte en garantie de qch; **to pay a d.,** verser des arrhes; *Pol* **to lose one's d.,** (*of candidate*) = perdre sa caution; **(c)** (*material*) dépôt(s) *m*(*pl*), précipité *m*; **alluvial deposits,** alluvions *fpl*; **(d)** (*of gold etc*) gisement *m*, couche *f*; **coal d.,** gisement houiller; **(e)** *Tech* (*coating*) apport *m*; **d. of silver,** précipité d'argent.

deposit² *vt* **(a)** déposer (*de l'argent à la banque*); mettre (*des documents*) en dépôt (**with a bank,** dans une banque); **(b)** déposer, poser (**sth on sth,** qch sur qch); **(c)** (*of liquid*) déposer (*un sédiment*); **the flood waters deposited a layer of mud,** les inondations ont laissé un dépôt de boue.

deposition [diːpəˈzɪʃən] *n* **(a)** déposition *f* (*d'un roi etc*); **(b)** *Jur* déposition *f*, témoignage *m*.

depositor [dɪˈpɒzɪtər] *n Banking* déposant, -ante.

depository [dɪˈpɒzɪt(ə)rɪ] *n* dépôt *m*, magasin *m*, entrepôt *m*; **furniture d.,** garde-meubles *m inv*.

depot [ˈdepəʊ] *n* **(a)** *Mil* dépôt *m*; *Com etc* dépôt, entrepôt *m*; **supply/ammunition d.,** dépôt de ravitaillement/munitions; **goods d.,** dépôt des marchandises; **(b)** *US* **(railroad) d.,** gare *f* (de chemin de fer); **freight d.,** gare des marchandises; **bus d.,** gare routière.

depravation [deprəˈveɪʃən] *n* dépravation *f*.

deprave [dɪˈpreɪv] *vt* dépraver.

depraved [dɪˈpreɪvd] *adj* (*homme, goût*) dépravé.

depravity [dɪˈprævɪtɪ] *n* dépravation *f*.

deprecate [ˈdeprɪkeɪt] *vt* désapprouver (*une action*).

deprecating [ˈdeprɪkeɪtɪŋ] *adj* désapprobateur, -trice.

deprecatory [ˈdeprɪkeɪtərɪ] *adj* **(a)** (*smile etc*) d'excuse; **(b)** (*disapproving*) désapprobateur, -trice.

depreciate [dɪˈpriːʃɪeɪt] **1** *vt* **(a)** déprécier, rabaisser (*la valeur de qch*); dévaloriser (*la monnaie*); *Com Ind* amortir (*le mobilier, l'outillage etc*); **(b)** dénigrer (*qn, une bonne action*). **2** *vi* (*of property etc*) se déprécier, diminuer de valeur; (*of prices, shares etc*) baisser; **the tractor depreciated by £200,** la valeur du tracteur a baissé de 200 livres.

depreciation [dɪpriːʃɪˈeɪʃən] *n* **(a)** dépréciation *f* (*de l'argent, Ind du matériel etc*); dévalorisation *f* (*de la monnaie*); (*margin*) moins-value *f*; **annual d.,** (*of machinery etc*) dépréciation annuelle; **(b)** dénigrement *m* (*d'une bonne action, de qn*).

depreciatory [dɪˈpriːʃɪət(ə)rɪ] *adj* (*remark etc*) de dénigrement, critique.

depredation [deprɪˈdeɪʃən] *n* (*usu pl*) (*of war*) déprédation(s) *f*(*pl*); (*by soldiers, looters etc*) pillage *m*.

depress [dɪˈpres] *vt* **(a)** (*press down*) (a)baisser (*qch*); *Aut etc* appuyer sur (*la pédale*); **(b)** (*cause to fall*) faire languir (*le commerce*); faire baisser (*le prix de qch*); **(c)** (*sadden, dishearten*) déprimer, décourager (*qn*).

depressant [dɪˈpresənt] *n Med* (*drug*) calmant *m*.

depressed [dɪˈprest] *adj* **(a)** *Com* (*marché*) languissant, déprimé; **d. area,** région touchée par la crise; **(b)** (*person*) déprimé; **to feel d.,** être déprimé, *F* avoir le cafard; **(c)** *Archit* (*arc*) surbaissé.

depressing [dɪˈpresɪŋ] *adj* déprimant; (*paysage*) triste.

depressingly [dɪˈpresɪŋlɪ] *adv* d'une manière déprimante.

depression [dɪˈpreʃən] *n* **(a)** abaissement *m* (*de qch*); *Aut* enfoncement *m* (*d'une pédale*); *Astron* dépression *f* (*d'un astre*); *Mil* **angle of d.,** angle *m* de dépression; **(b)** *Com* crise *f*, affaissement *m* (*des affaires*); **economic d.,** dépression économique; *Hist* **the (Great) D.,** la crise de 29; **(c)** dépression *f*, *F* le cafard; *Med* **state of d.,** état dépressif; *Med* **to suffer (from) acute d.,** être en pleine dépression; **(d)** *Met* dépression *f*; **a d. over the Atlantic,** une dépression au-dessus de l'Atlantique; **(e)** dépression *f*, enfoncement *m*, creux *m* (*de terrain*).

depressive [dɪˈpresɪv] *adj* dépressif.

depressor [dɪˈpresər] *n Med* (*for tongue*) abaisse-langue *m inv*.

depressurize [diːˈpreʃəraɪz] *vt & vi Av* dépressuriser.

deprivation [deprɪˈveɪʃən] *n* **(a)** (*removal*) privation *f* (*de droits etc*); destitution *f* (*de fonction*); **(b)** (*hardship*) privation *f*; **to suffer deprivations,** souffrir de privations.

deprive [dɪˈpraɪv] *vt* **(a) to d. s.o. of sth,** priver qn de qch, enlever qch à qn; **to d. oneself,** s'infliger des privations; **(b)** déposséder (*qn*) d'une charge.

deprived [dɪˈpraɪvd] *adj* (*enfant*) déshérité; **she had a d. childhood,** elle a eu une enfance défavorisée; **are you feeling d.?,** vous vous sentez frustré?

dept *n* **(a)** *abbr* **department**; **(b)** *abbr* **departure**.

depth [depθ] *n* **(a)** profondeur *f* (*d'une rivière, de la pensée etc*); **in d.,** en profondeur; (*étudier qch*) à fond; **a study in d. of ...,** une étude approfondie *ou* très poussée de ...; **at a d. of 50 fathoms,** par 50 brasses de fond; **to dive to a d. of 50 fathoms,** descendre *ou* plonger à 50 brasses de fond; **I hadn't realised the d. of her feelings,** je ne m'étais pas rendu compte que ses sentiments étaient aussi profonds; *Nau* **d. charge,** grenade sous-marine; **d. finder,** sondeur *m*; **(b) to go** *or* **get out of one's d.,** perdre pied; *Fig* sortir de sa compétence; **to be out of one's d.,** avoir perdu pied; *Fig* ne plus être sur son terrain;

(c) hauteur *f* (*d'un piston etc*); épaisseur *f* (*d'une couche*);

(d) gravité *f* (*d'un son*); portée *f* (*de l'intelligence*); vigueur *f*, intensité *f* (*de coloris*);

(e) fond *m* (*d'une forêt etc*); milieu *m* (*de la nuit*); **in the depths of winter,** en plein hiver;

(f) *MecE* **d. of cut,** profondeur *f* de passe *ou* de coupe (*d'une machine-outil*); *Opt* **d. of field/focus,** profondeur de champ/de foyer;

(g) the depths, *Lit* l'abîme *m*; les profondeurs *fpl* (*de l'océan etc*); les ténèbres *fpl* (*de l'ignorance etc*); **in the depths of despair,** dans le plus profond désespoir; **the lowest depths,** le dernier degré (*de la honte etc*).

deputation [depjʊˈteɪʃən] *n* **(a)** (*representatives*) députation *f*; **(b)** députation *f*, délégation *f* (*de qn*).

depute¹ [dɪˈpjuːt] *vt* **(a)** députer, déléguer (*qn*) (**to do sth,** pour faire qch); **(b)** déléguer (*des pouvoirs*) (**to,** à).

depute² [ˈdepjuːt] *n Scot* = **DEPUTY**.

deputize [ˈdepjʊtaɪz] *vi* **to d. for s.o.,** faire l'intérim de qn, remplacer qn.

deputy [ˈdepjʊtɪ] *n* fondé *m* de pouvoir; substitut *m*, suppléant *m* (*d'un juge etc*); délégué *m* (*d'un fonctionnaire*); (*of sheriff*) adjoint *m*; **to act as d. for s.o.,** suppléer qn; **d. director,** directeur adjoint; **d. governor,** sous-gouverneur *m*; *Sch* **d. head,** directeur-adjoint; **d. judge,** juge suppléant; **d. manager,** sous-directeur *m*; *Can Admin* **D. Minister,** Sous-Ministre *m*; **D. Prime Minister,** vice-Premier-Ministre *m*.

derail [dɪˈreɪl] *vt* faire dérailler (*un train*); *Fig* faire avorter (*un projet*); **to be derailed,** dérailler.

derailment [dɪˈreɪlmənt] *n* (*of train*) déraillement *m*.

derange [dɪˈreɪndʒ] *vt* aliéner (*l'esprit*); déranger le cerveau de (*qn*); **he** *or* **his mind is deranged,** il a le cerveau détraqué, c'est un détraqué.

derangement [dɪˈreɪndʒmənt] *n* **d. of mind,** dérangement *m* d'esprit; aliénation mentale.

Derby *n* **(a)** *Br Horseracing* [ˈdɑːbɪ] **the D.,** le derby d'Epsom; **donkey D.,** course *f* d'ânes; *Fb* **local d.,** derby; **(b)** *US* [ˈdɜːbɪ] (*hat*) chapeau *m* melon.

deregulate [diːˈregjʊleɪt] *vt* déréglementer (*une industrie*).

deregulation [diːregjʊˈleɪʃən] *n* (*of an industry*) déréglementation *f*.

derelict [ˈderəlɪkt] **1** *adj* **(a)** (*car, house*) abandonné; (*house*) (tombé) en ruines; **(b)** *US* **to be d. (in one's duty),** être négligent de son devoir. **2** *n* **(a)** *Jur* épave *f*; *esp Nau* navire abandonné (*en mer*); **(b)** (*person*) délaissé, -ée, épave humaine.

dereliction [derɪˈlɪkʃən] *n* **(a) d. of duty,** négligence *m* dans le service; **(b)** (*abandonment*) abandon *m*, délaissement *m*.

derestricted [diːrɪˈstrɪktɪd] *adj* (*route*) sans limitation de vitesse.

deride [dɪˈraɪd] *vt* tourner (*qn, qch*) en dérision, railler, ridiculiser (*qn*).

derision [dɪˈrɪʒən] *n* dérision *f*; **object of d.,** objet *m* de dérision.

derisive [dɪˈraɪsɪv] *adj* (*laughter*) moqueur.

derisively [dɪˈraɪsɪvlɪ] *adv* (*to look at*) d'un air moqueur; (*to look at, say*) d'un air *ou* d'un ton de dérision.

derisory [dɪˈraɪsərɪ] **(a)** (*offre*) dérisoire; **(b)** = **DERISIVE**.

derivation [derɪˈveɪʃən] *n* **(a)** dérivation *f*; **d. of a word from Latin,** dérivation d'un mot du latin; **what is the d. of ...?,** quelle est l'origine de ...?; **(b)** *Math* dérivation *f* (*d'une fonction*).

derivative [dɪˈrɪvətɪv] **1** *adj Gram* (*mot*) dérivé; **his work is very d.,** (*of author*) il n'a pas encore trouvé son style propre, il emprunte beaucoup aux autres. **2** *n Gram Ch Ind* dérivé *m*; *Math* dérivée *f*; **petroleum d.,** dérivé du pétrole; **to be a d. of sth,** être un dérivé de qch.

derive [dɪˈraɪv] *vt* tirer (*son origine etc*) (**from,** de); tirer (*des revenus etc*) (**from,** de); prendre (*du plaisir*) (**from,** à); **income derived from an investment,** revenu provenant d'un placement; *Ch* **to d. one compound from another,** dériver un composé d'un autre; **word derived**

from Latin, mot qui vient du latin; **to be derived from,** dériver de, (pro)venir de.
▶**derive from** *vipo* (pro)venir de (*qch*).
dermatitis [dɜːmə'taɪtɪs] *n Med* dermite *f*, dermatite *f*.
dermatologist [dɜːmə'tɒlədʒɪst] *n* dermatologue *mf*, dermatologiste *mf*.
dermatology [dɜːmə'tɒlədʒɪ] *n* dermatologie *f*.
derogate ['derəgeɪt] *vi* déroger (**from one's position/one's dignity/***etc*, à son rang/à sa dignité/*etc*).
derogation [derə'geɪʃən] *n* **(a)** dérogation *f* (**of a law,** à une loi); **(b) d. from a right,** atteinte portée à un droit.
derogatory [dɪ'rɒgət(ə)rɪ] *adj* **(a)** (*disrespectful*) qui abaisse (**to s.o.,** qn); (*sens*) péjoratif (*d'un mot*); **d. remark,** remarque désobligeante; **(b)** dérogeant, qui déroge (**to,** à).
derrick ['derɪk] *n* **(a)** *Petr* derrick *m*; tour *f* de forage; **(b)** *Nau* mât *m* de charge.
derring-do ['derɪŋ'duː] *n Arch* bravoure *f*; **deeds of d.-do,** hauts faits.
derv [dɜːv] *n Br Aut* gazole *m*.
dervish ['dɜːvɪʃ] *n* derviche *m*; **whirling** *or* **dancing d.,** derviche tourneur.
desalinate [diː'sælɪneɪt] *vt* dessaler.
desalination [diːsælɪ'neɪʃən] *n Ind* dessalaison *f*; dessalement *m* (*de l'eau de mer*).
descale [diː'skeɪl] *vt* détartrer (*une bouilloire*).
descant ['deskænt] *n Mus* déchant *m*.
descend [dɪ'send] **1** *vi* descendre; (*of rain*) tomber; **a feeling of sadness descended upon him,** un sentiment de tristesse s'empara de lui; **to d. on s.o.,** (*attack*) s'abattre sur qn; *Fig* (*intrude on*) faire irruption chez qn; **to d. to s.o's level/to doing sth,** s'abaisser au niveau de qn/(jusqu')à faire qch; **to d.** *or* **be descended from s.o.,** descendre de qn; **to d. from s.o. to s.o.,** (*of property, privilege*) passer de qn à qn. **2** *vt* descendre (*une colline, un escalier*).
descendant, -ent [dɪ'sendənt] *n* descendant, -ante.
descending [dɪ'sendɪŋ] **(a)** (*scale etc*) descendant; *Math* (*progression*) décroissant; **in d. order,** en ordre décroissant; **(b)** (*mouvement*) de descente.
descent [dɪ'sent] *n* **(a)** descente *f* (*d'un alpiniste, d'un aéronaute etc*); **(b)** (*path, road etc*) descente *f*, pente *f*; **(c)** *Fig* irruption *f* (**on,** dans, à, sur); **(d)** (*origins*) descendance *f*; **to trace one's d. back to ...,** faire remonter sa famille à ...; **to be of Norman d.,** descendre des Normands; **(e)** *Jur* transmission *f* (*d'un bien*) par droit de succession *ou* par héritage.
describe [dɪs'kraɪb] *vt* **(a)** décrire, dépeindre (*qn, qch*); *Com* désigner (*des marchandises etc*); donner le signalement de (*un homme recherché par la police*); **can you d. the man?,** pouvez-vous nous décrire cet homme?; **she described him as being tall and in his 40s,** d'après sa description, il était grand et avait environ 40 ans; **the book describes how they escaped,** le livre décrit la façon dont ils se sont évadés; **to d. s.o./sth as ...,** qualifier qn/qch de ...; *Pej* **to d. oneself as an actor,** se représenter comme acteur; **(b)** (*draw*) décrire (*une courbe, un cercle*); tracer (*un triangle*).
description [dɪs'krɪpʃən] *n* **(a)** description *f* (*de qn, de qch*); *Com* désignation *f* (*de marchandises*); (*for police purposes*) signalement *m*; (*in a card index*) fiche *f* signalétique; (*on passport etc*) profession *f*; **to be beyond d.,** être indescriptible; **to give a d. of s.o./sth,** décrire qn/qch; **to answer (to) the d.,** répondre au signalement; **(b)** (*sort, kind*) sorte *f*, espèce *f*; **people of this d.,** les gens *mpl* de cette espèce; **people of all descriptions,** les gens de toutes sortes.
descriptive [dɪs'krɪptɪv] *adj* (*style*) descriptif.
descry [dɪs'kraɪ] *vt Lit* discerner.
desecrate ['desɪkreɪt] *vt* profaner, souiller.
desecration [desɪ'kreɪʃən] *n* profanation *f*.
desegregate [diː'segrɪgeɪt] *vt* mettre fin à la ségrégation raciale (*dans un pays, une école etc*).
desegregation [diːsegrɪ'geɪʃən] *n* déségrégation *f*.
deselect [diːse'lekt] *vt Br Pol* retirer à (*qn*) l'investiture du parti.
desensitize [diː'sensɪtaɪz] *vt Phot Med* désensibiliser.
desert¹ [dɪ'zɜːt] *n* (*usu pl*) **deserts,** mérites *mpl*, dû *m*; **he has got his (just) deserts,** il n'a que ce qu'il mérite.
desert² ['dezət] **1** *adj* (*région, flore*) désertique. **2** *n* désert *m*; **the Sahara D.,** le désert du Sahara; **d. rat,** (*animal*) gerboise *f*; *Mil F* (*World War II*) militaire qui a fait la campagne de l'Afrique du Nord; **d. boots,** bottines lacées; **d. island,** île déserte.
desert³ [dɪ'zɜːt] **1** *vt* déserter, quitter (*un lieu*); déserter, abandonner (*son poste*); abandonner (*qn*); **to d. one's party,** tourner casaque; **to d. s.o.,** (*of courage*) abandonner qn; **her sense of humour has deserted her,** elle a perdu son sens de l'humour. **2** *vi Mil* déserter; **to d. from the army,** déserter l'armée.
deserted [dɪ'zɜːtɪd] *adj* (*person*) abandonné; (*place*) désert; **the streets were d.,** les rues étaient désertes.
deserter [dɪ'zɜːtər] *n Mil* déserteur *m*.
desertification [dɪzɜːtɪfɪ'keɪʃən] *n* (*of land*) désertification *f*.
desertion [dɪ'zɜːʃən] *n* **(a)** abandon *m*, délaissement *m* (*de qn*); *Jur* abandon de famille; **he divorced her for desertion,** il a demandé le divorce parce qu'elle avait abandonné le domicile conjugal; **(b)** *Mil* désertion *f*; abandon *m* de poste.
deserve [dɪ'zɜːv] *vt* mériter (*qch*); être digne de (*éloges etc*); **he deserves to be punished,** il mérite qu'on le punisse; **she thoroughly deserves it!,** elle ne l'a pas volé!; **she deserves better,** elle mérite mieux que ça; **he deserved to win,** (*and did*) il méritait de gagner; (*and did not*) il aurait mérité de gagner.
deserved [dɪ'zɜːvd] *adj* (*bien*) mérité.
deservedly [dɪ'zɜːvɪdlɪ] *adv* justement, à juste titre.
deserving [dɪ'zɜːvɪŋ] *adj* (*person*) méritant, de mérite; (*action, cause*) méritoire.
desiccate ['desɪkeɪt] *vt* dessécher; **desiccated coconut,** noix de coco déshydratée.
design¹ [dɪ'zaɪn] *n* **(a)** (*intention*) dessein *m*, intention *f*; **by d.,** à dessein; **to have designs on s.o./sth,** avoir des desseins sur qn/qch; **(b)** (*pattern*) (*on sweater, carpet*) motif *m*, dessin *m* (*d'ornement*); (*in embroidery*) modèle *m*; **(c)** (*plan*) plan *m* (*d'un roman etc*); grandes lignes, ébauche *f* (*d'un tableau etc*); *Ind etc* étude *f*, avant-projet *m* (*d'une machine etc*); **industrial d.,** esthétique industrielle; **d. engineer,** ingénieur *m* d'études; **d. office** *or* **department,** service *m* d'études; **d. team,** équipe *f* des concepteurs; **to study d.,** étudier le design; **(d)** (*arrangement of parts*) dessin *m* (*d'une machine etc*); **machine of faulty d.,** machine *f* de construction; *Com* **our latest d.,** notre dernier modèle; **d. centre,** centre *m* d'exposition (de modèles) défectueuse.
design² *vt* **(a)** destiner (**for,** à); **boats designed for river traffic,** bateaux destinés à la navigation fluviale; **machine designed for a special purpose,** machine construite dans un but spécial; **(b)** préparer (*un projet*); **(c)** étudier, concevoir; établir le plan de (*un bâtiment, un avion etc*); créer (*une robe*); établir (*un mécanisme etc*); **well-designed furniture,** meubles *mpl* aux lignes étudiées.
designate¹ ['dezɪgnət] *adj* (*évêque etc*) désigné.
designate² ['dezɪgneɪt] *vt* désigner, nommer (**s.o. to an office,** qn à une fonction); **to d. s.o. as** *or* **for one's successor,** désigner qn pour *ou* comme son successeur.
designation [dezɪg'neɪʃən] *n* **(a)** *Admin* désignation *f* (*d'une personne*); **(b)** désignation *f*, nomination *f* (*d'un successeur*); **d. to a post,** nomination à un emploi; **(c)** (*title, name*) désignation *f*, nom *m*.
designedly [dɪ'zaɪnɪdlɪ] *adv* à dessein, exprès.
designer [dɪ'zaɪnər] *n* **(a)** *Art Ind* dessinateur, -trice; (*of clothes*) styliste *mf*, créateur, -trice; *Th Cin* décorateur, -trice; **d. jeans/bedlinen/***etc*, jean *m*/literie *f*/*etc* de marque; *Hum* **d. stubble,** barbe *f* de trois jours; **(b)** auteur *m*, inventeur, -trice (*d'un projet*).
designing [dɪ'zaɪnɪŋ] *adj Pej* intrigant.
desirability [dɪzaɪərə'bɪlɪtɪ] *n* **(a)** caractère *m* désirable; avantage *m* (*d'une ligne de conduite*); **(b)** attrait *m* (*d'une femme*).
desirable [dɪ'zaɪərəb(ə)l] *adj* **(a)** (*worth having*) souhaitable; (*change, improvement*) désirable; **a knowledge of French is d.,** connaissance du français souhaitée; *Com* **d. property,** belle maison, bel appartement; **(b)** (*sexually*) attrayant, désirable.
desire¹ [dɪ'zaɪər] *n* **(a)** désir *m*, souhait *m* (**for,** de); **to have a d. for sth,** désirer qch; **to have one's heart's d.,** obtenir ce que l'on désire le plus (au monde); **to have a d. to do sth,** avoir le désir *ou* avoir envie de faire qch; **to express the** *or* **a d.,** exprimer le désir (**that,** que; **to do,** de faire); **I feel no d. to ...,** je n'éprouve aucune envie de ...; **the d. for a cigarette was overwhelming,** mon *ou* ton *ou* son *etc* envie de fumer une cigarette était irrésistible; **(b)** (*sexual*) appétit *m* (charnel), désir *m* (**for,** de); **to feel d.,** éprouver du désir.
desire² *vt* **(a)** désirer (*qch*), avoir envie de (*qch*); **to d. to do sth,** désirer faire qch; **it is to be desired that ...,** il est souhaitable que ... + *sub*; **it leaves much/nothing to be desired,** cela laisse beaucoup/ne laisse rien à désirer; **(b)** désirer (*un homme, une femme*); **(c)** *Lit* **to d. sth of s.o.,**

(*request*) demander qch à qn; (*want*) désirer qch de qn; **to d. s.o. to do sth,** prier qn de faire qch.
desirous [dɪ'zaɪərəs] *adj Fml* désireux (**of,** de).
desist [dɪ'zɪst] *vi Lit* cesser (**from doing,** de faire).
desk [desk] *n* **(a)** (*in office*) bureau *m*; (*for writing at*) secrétaire *m*; *Sch* bureau *m* (*de professeur*); pupitre *m* (*d'écolier*); **to have a d. job,** avoir un travail de bureau; **reading d.,** pupitre; *Rel* lutrin *m*; *Comptr etc* **control d.,** pupitre de commande; **d. diary,** agenda *m* de bureau; **(b)** (*in shop*) caisse *f*; (*in hotel*) réception *f*; **please leave your keys 'at the d.,** (*in hotel*) prière de laisser les clefs à la réception; **pay at the d.,** (*in shop*) payez à la caisse; *Am* **d. clerk,** (*in hotel*) réceptionniste *mf*.
deskill [diː'skɪl] *vt* déqualifier (*qn*).
desktop ['desktɒp] *n* **on my d.,** sur mon bureau; **d. (computer),** ordinateur *m* de bureau; **d. publishing,** publication assistée par ordinateur, microédition *f*, *Can* éditique *f*.
desolate¹ ['desələt] *adj* **(a)** (*house*) abandonné; **(b)** (*place*) désert, vide; **(c)** (*person*) affligé, désolé; (*cry*) de désolation.
desolate² ['desəleɪt] *vt* **(a)** ravager (*un pays etc*); (*of epidemic etc*) dépeupler (*une ville*); **(b)** affliger, désoler (*qn*).
desolately ['desələtlɪ] *adv* **(a)** dans la solitude; **(b)** (*to say, look at*) d'un ton *ou* d'un air désolé.
desolation [desə'leɪʃən] *n* **(a)** désolation *f*, dévastation *f* (*d'un pays vaincu etc*); **(b)** désolation *f* (*d'un paysage etc*); **(c)** (*of person*) désolation *f*, chagrin *m*.
despair¹ [dɪs'peər] *n* désespoir *m*; **to be in d.,** être au désespoir; **to drive s.o. to d.,** réduire qn au désespoir; **child who is the d. of his parents,** enfant qui fait le désespoir de ses parents.
despair² *vi* perdre espoir, (se) désespérer; **I d. of you,** tu me désespères; **don't d.,** ne désespère pas; **to d. of doing sth,** désespérer de faire qch; **his life is despaired of,** on craint pour sa vie.
despairing [dɪ'speərɪŋ] *adj* désespéré.
despairingly [dɪ'speərɪŋlɪ] *adv* désespérément, avec désespoir.
despatch [dɪs'pætʃ] *n & v* = **DISPATCH¹,²**.
desperado [despə'rɑːdəʊ] *n* desperado *m*, hors-la-loi *m*.
desperate ['desp(ə)rət] *adj* **(a)** (*condition, maladie etc*) désespéré; (*remède*) désespéré; **(b)** (*lutte*) désespéré; (*résistance, lutte*) acharné; **a d. man,** un désespéré; **to do something d.,** faire un malheur; **she made a d. attempt to save him,** elle a tenté désespérément de lui sauver la vie; **to be d. for money/a job,** avoir un besoin désespéré d'argent/de travail; **I'm d., it's d.,** c'est urgent; *F* **I'm d. for a cup of tea,** je meurs d'envie de boire une tasse de thé; **(c)** (*very bad*) terrible, affreux.
desperately ['desp(ə)rətlɪ] *adv* **(a) d. ill,** gravement malade; **(b)** (*lutter, supplier etc*) désespérément; **(c)** (*extremely*) extrêmement; (*in love*) éperdument; **to be d. in love with s.o.,** aimer qn à la folie; **to be d. sorry,** être navré.
desperation [despə'reɪʃən] *n* désespoir *m*; **to drive s.o. to d.,** pousser qn à bout, réduire qn au désespoir; **in d.,** en désespoir de cause; **to do sth out of d.,** faire qch par désespoir; **an act of d.,** un acte de désespoir.
despicable [dɪ'spɪkəb(ə)l] *adj* méprisable.
despicably [dɪ'spɪkəblɪ] *adv* bassement.
despise [dɪ'spaɪz] *vt* mépriser (*qn, qch*); dédaigner (*qch*); **these things are not to be despised,** cela n'est pas à dédaigner.
despite [dɪs'paɪt] *prep* en dépit de, malgré (*qch*); **d. what she says,** quoi qu'elle en dise.
despoil [dɪs'pɔɪl] *vt Fml* dépouiller, piller, spolier.
despondency [dɪs'pɒndənsɪ] *n* découragement *m*, abattement *m*.
despondent [dɪ'spɒndənt] *adj* découragé, abattu; **to become d.,** se laisser abattre; **to feel d.,** se sentir déprimé.
despondently [dɪ'spɒndəntlɪ] *adv* d'un air découragé *ou* abattu.
despot ['despɒt] *n* despote *m*, tyran *m*.
despotic [dɪs'pɒtɪk] *adj* **(a)** (*gouvernement, pouvoir*) despotique; **(b)** *Fig* arbitraire, despote.
despotically [dɪs'pɒtɪklɪ] *adv* (*see adj*) **(a)** despotiquement; **(b)** arbitrairement, despotiquement.
despotism ['despətɪz(ə)m] *n* despotisme *m*.
des res ['dezrez] *n F* jolie petite maison; joli petit appartement.
dessert [dɪ'zɜːt] *n* dessert *m*; **what did you have for d.?,** qu'est-ce que tu as eu comme dessert?; **d. knife/plate,** couteau *m*/assiette *f* à dessert; **d. wine,** vin *m* de liqueur.
dessertspoon [dɪ'zɜːtspuːn] *n* cuillère *f* (à dessert).
destabilization [diːsteɪbəlaɪ'zeɪʃən] *n* (*of government, economy*) déstabilisation *f*.
destabilize [diː'steɪbəlaɪz] *vt* déstabiliser (*un gouvernement, une économie*).
destination [destɪ'neɪʃən] *n* destination *f*; **to reach one's d.,** arriver à sa destination; *Comptr* **d. disk,** disquette *f* cible.
destine ['destɪn] *vt* destiner (*qn, qch*) (**for,** à; **to a calling,** à une carrière).
destined ['destɪnd] *adj* **(a)** (*meant*) destiné; **he was d. for the Church,** il était destiné à l'église; **she is d. to be successful,** elle est destinée au succès; **he was d. never to see her again,** il ne devait plus la revoir; **(b)** (*of plane etc*) **d. for,** à destination de.
destiny ['destɪnɪ] *n* destin *m*, sort *m*; **such was his d.,** tel fut son destin.
destitute ['destɪtjuːt] **1** *adj* **(a)** (*lacking*) dépourvu, dénué (**of,** de); **(b)** (*needy*) indigent, sans ressources; **to be utterly d.,** être dans la misère. **2** *n* **the d.,** (*used as pl*) les pauvres *mpl*.
destitution [destɪ'tjuːʃən] *n* **(a)** (*lack*) dénuement *m*; **(b)** (*need*) indigence *f*, misère *f*.
destroy [dɪs'trɔɪ] *vt* **(a)** détruire, annihiler (*qch*); anéantir (*des espérances etc*); **(b)** tuer, abattre (*un animal*); **to d. oneself,** se suicider.
destroyer [dɪs'trɔɪər] *n* **(a)** *Nau* contre-torpilleur *m*, destroyer *m*; **(b)** destructeur, -trice.
destruct [dɪs'trʌkt] **1** *vt* détruire. **2** *vi* s'autodétruire.
destructible [dɪs'trʌktɪb(ə)l] *adj* destructible.
destruction [dɪs'trʌkʃən] *n* **(a)** destruction *f*, anéantissement *m* (*de qch*); consomption *f* (*par le feu*); **(b)** (*damage*) ravages *mpl*; **the d. caused by the fire/storm,** les ravages du feu/de la tempête.
destructive [dɪs'trʌktɪv] *adj* destructeur, -trice; **d. child,** enfant qui détruit tout; **d. criticism,** critique négative *ou* non constructive.
destructively [dɪs'trʌktɪvlɪ] *adv* d'une manière destructrice.
destructiveness [dɪs'trʌktɪvnɪs] *n* effet *ou* pouvoir destructeur *ou* destructif (*d'un explosif etc*); (*of child etc*) penchant *m* à détruire.
destructor [dɪs'trʌktər] *n* incinérateur *m* (*à ordures*).
desuetude [dɪ'sjuːɪtjuːd] *n Fml* désuétude *f*.
desultorily ['desəltrɪlɪ] *adv* d'une manière décousue.
desultory ['desəlt(ə)rɪ] *adj* (*conversation*) décousu, sans suite; (*attempt*) peu convaincant; (*manner*) désinvolte.
detach [dɪ'tætʃ] *vt* **(a)** détacher, séparer (*qch*) (**from,** de); dételer (*des wagons*); décoller (*un timbre etc*); **(b)** *Mil Nau* détacher (*des troupes, un navire etc*).
detachable [dɪ'tætʃəb(ə)l] *adj* (*component, lining*) amovible.
detached [dɪ'tætʃt] *adj* **(a)** détaché, séparé (**from,** de); *Med* **d. retina,** rétine décollée; **d. house,** maison séparée; **(b)** *Mil* (*officier*) en affectation spéciale; **(c)** (*person*) désintéressé; (*manière*) désinvolte; (*air*) détaché, indifférent.
detachment [dɪ'tætʃmənt] *n* **(a)** action *f* de détacher, séparation *f* (**from,** de); dételage *m* (*de wagons*); décollement *m* (*d'un timbre, Med de la rétine*); **(b)** *Mil* détachement *m*; **gun d.,** peloton *m* (*des servants*); **on d.,** détaché; **(c)** détachement *m* (*de l'esprit*) (**from,** de); (*of person*) désintéressement *m*; indifférence *f* (**from,** envers); insouciance *f*.
detail¹ ['diːteɪl] *n* **(a)** détail *m*; **to go** *or* **enter into all the details,** entrer dans *ou* donner tous les détails; **in d.,** en détail; **in every d.,** dans le moindre détail; **in the fullest d.,** dans le plus grand détail; **points** *or* **questions of d.,** questions de détail; **minor details,** l'accessoire *m*; **that's just a minor d.,** ça n'a pas d'importance; **I can't give you any details,** je ne peux vous donner aucune précision; **I'll send you the details of the property,** je vous enverrai les informations concernant la propriété; **for further details, please contact ...,** pour plus de renseignements, veuillez contacter ...; **(b)** *Mil* extrait *m* de l'ordre du jour; **details,** l'ordre *m* du jour; **(c)** détachement *m* (*Mil de corvée etc, surtout US de policiers*).
detail² *vt* **(a)** détailler, raconter en détail; énumérer (*les faits*); **(b)** *Mil etc* **to d. s.o. for a duty,** désigner qn pour un service, affecter qn à un service.
detailed ['diːteɪld] *adj* détaillé; (*récit*) circonstancié, détaillé; (*travail*) minutieux; **to give a d. account of sth,** raconter qch en détail.
detain [dɪ'teɪn] *vt* **(a)** détenir (*qn en prison*); garder (*qn à l'hôpital*); **(b)** retenir, arrêter (*qn*); empêcher (*qn*) de

partir; *Sch* consigner (*un élève*); **this question need not d. us,** cette question ne nous retiendra pas; **police have detained a man for questioning,** la police a mis un homme en garde à vue.

detainee [diːteɪ'niː] *n* détenu, -ue; prisonnier, -ière.

detect [dɪ'tekt] *vt* **(a)** (*notice*) percevoir (*un son*); apercevoir (*un mouvement etc*); **(b)** (*find*) dépister (*une maladie*).

detectable [dɪ'tektəb(ə)l] *adj* perceptible, discernable.

detection [dɪ'tekʃən] *n* **(a)** (*discovery*) découverte *f*; **to escape d.,** se dérober aux recherches; (*of mistake etc*) passer inaperçu; **(b)** *Mil etc* détection *f* (*des mines, des avions etc*); **radar d.,** détection radar; **sound d.,** détection par le son; **(c)** (*by detective*) travail *m* de détective.

detective [dɪ'tektɪv] *n* (*police officer*) agent *m* de la police judiciaire; (*private investigator*) détective *m* (privé); **d. story,** roman policier.

detector [dɪ'tektər] *n* (*device*) détecteur *m*; **smoke d.,** détecteur de fumée; **sound d.,** détecteur (*d'armes, d'engins*) par le son.

détente ['deɪtɒnt] *n Pol* détente *f*.

detention [dɪ'tenʃən] *n* **(a)** détention *f* (*en prison*); **d. without trial,** (*of political activist*) détention arbitraire; *Mil* **six week's d.,** six semaines de prison; *Mil* **d. barracks,** locaux *mpl* disciplinaires; **d. centre,** (*for young persons*) maison *f* de redressement; *Jur* **d. order,** ordre *m* de détention; **(b)** *Sch* retenue *f*; **to give a boy d.,** consigner un élève; **to be in d.,** être consigné *ou* en retenue; **(c)** *Nau* arrêt *m* (*d'un navire*); **(d)** *Jur* détention *f* (*d'une somme due etc*).

deter [dɪ'tɜːr] *vt* (-rr-) décourager (*qn*); dissuader (*l'ennemi*) (**from doing sth,** de faire qch).

detergent [dɪ'tɜːdʒənt] **1** *adj* détersif. **2** *n* détergent *m*, lessive *f*.

deteriorate [dɪ'tɪərɪəreɪt] *vi* (*of relations, weather, health*) se détériorer; (*of product, health*) s'altérer; (*of person*) dépérir; **her condition has deteriorated,** (*of patient*) son état s'est aggravé; **the house has been allowed to d.,** on a laissé la maison se détériorer.

deterioration [dɪtɪərɪə'reɪʃən] *n* (*of relations, weather, health*) détérioration *f*; (*of product, health*) altération *f*; (*of person*) dépérissement *m*; **d. in quality,** baisse *f* de qualité.

determinant [dɪ'tɜːmɪnənt] *n Fml* facteur déterminant.

determination [dɪtɜːmɪ'neɪʃən] *n* **(a)** (*of person*) détermination *f*, résolution *f*; **air of d.,** air résolu *ou* décidé *ou* déterminé; **(b)** détermination *f* (*d'une date, de la position d'un astre*); **(c)** *Jur* (*decision, finding*) décision *f*; **(d)** *Jur* (*termination*) résolution *f*, résiliation *f* (*d'un contrat etc*).

determine [dɪ'tɜːmɪn] **1** *vt* **(a)** (*of person*) se décider, se déterminer, se résoudre (**to do,** à faire); **to be determined to do sth,** être résolu à faire qch; **(b)** déterminer, fixer (*une date, des règles etc*); délimiter (*une frontière*); déterminer, constater (*la nature ou les dimensions de qch*); **to d. the cost/value of sth,** établir le coût/la valeur de qch; **(c)** décider, résoudre (*une question etc*); régler (*un point en litige*); **the magistrate determined that they were guilty,** le magistrat les a déclarés coupables; **to d. s.o.'s fate,** décider du sort de qn; **this set will d. the outcome of the match,** cette manche va déterminer le résultat du match; **(d)** *Jur* résoudre, résilier (*un contrat, un bail*). **2** *vi* (*of person*) se décider, se déterminer, se résoudre (**on doing,** à faire).

determined [dɪ'tɜːmɪnd] *adj* **(a)** (*person*) résolu; **to be d. to do sth,** être résolu à faire qch; **(b)** (*price, limit*) déterminé.

determiner [dɪ'tɜːmɪnər] *n Gram* déterminant *m*.

determining [dɪ'tɜːmɪnɪŋ] *adj* (*facteur*) déterminant.

deterrent [dɪ'terənt] **1** *adj* dissuasif (*effet d'une bombe nucléaire, effet d'une politique*). **2** *n* **(a) to act as a d. (to crime),** (*of penalty etc*) exercer un effet dissuasif contre le crime; **(b)** *Mil Pol* arme *f* de dissuasion; **the nuclear d.,** la dissuasion nucléaire.

detest [dɪ'test] *vt* détester, *Fml* abhorrer; **I d. being interrupted,** je déteste être dérangé; **I d. having to wait,** je déteste attendre.

detestable [dɪ'testəb(ə)l] *adj* détestable.

detestably [dɪ'testəblɪ] *adv* détestablement.

detestation [diːtes'teɪʃən] *n* **(a)** (*hatred*) haine *f*; **(b)** (*object of hatred*) chose *f* détestable, abomination *f*.

dethrone [dɪ'θrəʊn] *vt* détrôner.

dethronement [dɪ'θrəʊnmənt] *n* détrônement *m*.

detonate ['detəneɪt] **1** *vt* faire détoner (*un explosif*); faire exploser (*une bombe*); faire sauter (*une mine*). **2** *vi* détoner.

detonation [detə'neɪʃən] *n* détonation *f*, explosion *f*.

detonator ['detəneɪtər] *n* **(a)** (*for explosive*) détonateur *m*, amorce *f*; **percussion d.,** détonateur à percussion; **(b)** *Rail* (*fog signal*) détonateur *m*.

detour[1] ['diːtʊər] *n* détour *m*; *Am* déviation *f* (*d'itinéraire etc*); **to make a d.,** faire un détour.

detour[2] **1** *vi* faire un détour. **2** *vt* faire faire un détour à (*qn*).

detoxification [diːtɒksɪfɪ'keɪʃən], *F* **detox** ['diːtɒks] *n esp Am* désintoxication *f*; **d. centre,** (*for addicts*) centre *m* de désintoxication; **to take part in a d. programme,** suivre une cure de désintoxication.

►**detract from** *vipo* diminuer (*le plaisir de qn*); rabaisser, amoindrir (*le mérite de qn*).

detractor [dɪ'træktər] *n* détracteur, -trice.

detrain [diː'treɪn] **1** *vt* débarquer (*des troupes*) d'un train. **2** *vi* (*of troops*) débarquer (du train).

detriment ['detrɪmənt] *n* détriment *m*, préjudice *m*; **to the d. of ...,** au détriment de ...; **without d. to ...,** sans nuire à ... .

detrimental [detrɪ'ment(ə)l] *adj* nuisible, préjudiciable (**to,** à); **it would be d. to my interests,** cela desservirait mes intérêts; **smoking is d. to your health,** fumer est mauvais pour la santé.

detritus [dɪ'traɪtəs] *n Geol* détritus *m*(*pl*).

deuce[1] [djuːs] *n* **(a)** (*of dice, dominoes, cards*) deux *m*; **(b)** *Tennis* égalité *f*, quarante à, quarante partout.

deuce[2] *n Old-fashioned F* diable *m*; **what the d. does he mean?,** que diable veut-il dire?; **what the d. are you doing here?,** que diable faites-vous ici?

deuced ['djuːsɪd] *adj Old-fashioned Br F* sacré; **it's d. annoying,** c'est sacrément embêtant.

devaluation [diːvæljʊ'eɪʃən] *n Econ* dévaluation *f*.

devalue [diː'væljuː] *vt Econ* dévaluer.

devastate ['devəsteɪt] *vt* dévaster, ravager; *Fig* terrasser, foudroyer (*qn*).

devastating ['devəsteɪtɪŋ] *adj* (*storm etc*) dévastateur, -trice, ravageur, -euse; *Fig* (*argument*) accablant; (*charme*) irrésistible; (*choc etc*) foudroyant.

devastatingly ['devəsteɪtɪŋlɪ] *adv* **d. beautiful,** d'une beauté incomparable.

devastation [devəs'teɪʃən] *n* dévastation *f*.

develop [dɪ'veləp] *v* (**-p-** [dɪ'veləpt]) **1** *vt* **(a)** (*expand, improve*) développer (*les facultés etc*); développer, élargir (*une pensée etc*); *Chess* déployer (*son jeu*); **to d. one's muscles,** se muscler;

(b) *Econ* exploiter, mettre en valeur (*une région*); développer les ressources de (*une région*); *Tech* réaliser (*un nouveau dessin etc*); **to d. a site,** (re)construire; **less developed countries,** pays moins avancés;

(c) (*acquire*) contracter (*une maladie, une mauvaise habitude*); faire (*de la fièvre*); manifester (*une tendance*); **to d. a dislike for/an interest in sth,** se mettre à détester/apprécier qch;

(d) *Phot* développer (*une épreuve*);

(e) *Math* développer (*une surface, une fonction*);

(f) *Phys etc* engendrer (*de la chaleur*).

2 *vi* **(a)** (*of the body, the faculties etc*) se développer;

(b) *Econ* (*of country, region*) se développer;

(c) se manifester, se révéler; (*of argument, crisis*) se produire; (*of fever*) se déclarer.

developer [dɪ'veləpər] *n* **(a)** *Econ* promoteur *m*; **late d.,** enfant *mf* qui se développe tard; **(b)** *Phot* développeur *m*; (*chemical*) (agent *m*) révélateur *m*.

developing [dɪ'veləpɪŋ] **1** *adj* qui se développe, qui fait des progrès; (*pays*) en voie de développement. **2** *n* **(a)** *Econ* exploitation *f*, mise *f* en valeur (*d'une région*); **(b)** *Phot* développement *m*; **d. bath,** (bain *m*) révélateur *m*; **d. tray,** cuvette *f*.

development [dɪ'veləpmənt] *n* **(a)** développement *m* (*du corps, des facultés*); développement, amplification *f* (*d'un sujet*); élargissement *m* (*d'une idée*); *Mus* développement;

(b) *Econ* exploitation *f*, mise *f* en valeur (*d'une région etc*); aménagement *m*, (re)construction *f* (*d'un terrain*); *Tech* réalisation *f*, mise au point (*d'un nouveau dessin etc*); *Br Admin* **d. area,** zone *f ou* région *f* à développer; **d. grant,** subvention *f* pour le développement;

(c) (*progress, change*) développement *m*, progrès *m*; déroulement *m* (*des événements etc*); évolution *f* (*des événements, de la pensée*); **to await further developments,** attendre les événements; **the latest developments in Poland,** les derniers événements survenus en Pologne; **the latest developments in medical research,** les dernières découvertes médicales;

(d) *Phot* développement *m*;

(e) *Math* développement *m* (*d'une surface, d'une*

fonction); développée *f* (*d'une spirale*).

deviant ['di:vɪənt] *adj & n Psy* déviant, -ante.

deviate ['di:vɪeɪt] *vi* dévier, s'écarter (**from,** de); **to d. from one's original intentions/plans,** s'écarter de ses premières intentions/premiers plans.

deviation [di:vɪ'eɪʃən] *n* déviation *f* (*d'une aiguille aimantée etc*); écart *m* (*de la norme etc*).

deviationism [di:vɪ'eɪʃənɪz(ə)m] *n Pol* déviationnisme *m*.

deviationist [di:vɪ'eɪʃənɪst] *adj & n Pol* déviationniste *mf*.

device [dɪ'vaɪs] *n* **(a)** (*item of equipment*) dispositif *m*, appareil *m*, mécanisme *m*; **locking d.,** système *m* de verrouillage; **safety d.,** dispositif de sécurité; **(b)** (*plan*) stratagème *m*; **to leave s.o. to their own devices,** (*alone*) laisser qn s'occuper comme bon lui semble; (*without help*) laisser qn se débrouiller; **(c)** (*on shield, flag etc*) emblème *m*, devise *f*.

devil¹ ['dev(ə)l] *n* **(a)** (*Satan*) diable *m*; **d.'s advocate,** avocat *m* du diable; **to play d.'s advocate,** être l'avocat du diable; **to be between the d. and the deep (blue) sea,** être pris entre deux feux; **talk of the d. (and he's sure to appear),** quand on parle du loup (, on en voit la queue); *Old-fashioned* **d. take it!,** que le diable l'emporte!; *F* **go to the d.!,** allez au diable!; **to play the d. with sth,** mettre la confusion dans qch; *Fig* **to give the d. his due ...,** pour être honnête, il faut admettre que ...; **(and) d. take the hindmost,** sauve qui peut; *F* **what the d. are you doing?,** que diable faites-vous là?; **how the d. ...?,** comment diable ...?; **like the d.,** (*travailler*) avec acharnement; **to have the d. of a job** *or* **the d.'s own job (to do sth),** avoir un mal de chien *ou* un mal de tous les diables (à faire qch); **he's got the d. of a temper,** il a un fichu caractère; **there'll be the d. to pay,** ça va barder; *Culin Am* **d.'s food cake,** = gâteau *m* au chocolat;
(b) (*demon*) démon *m*; **she-d.,** diablesse *f*, *Fig* mégère *f*; *Fig* **that child's a little d.,** cet enfant est un petit démon; **he's a bit of a d.,** il est quelque peu rageur; **poor d.!,** pauvre diable!; **the silly d.!,** quelle espèce d'idiot!; **the d. finds work for idle hands to do,** = l'oisiveté est la mère de tous les vices.

devil² *v* (**-ll-**, *US* **-l-**) **1** *vi F* **to d. for s.o.,** servir de nègre à (*un avocat etc*). **2** *vt Culin* faire griller et poivrer fortement (*de la viande*); **devilled eggs,** œufs durs au curry.

devilfish ['dev(ə)lfɪʃ] *n* **(a)** (*fish*) raie *f* manta; **(b)** (*octopus*) pieuvre *f*.

devilish ['dev(ə)lɪʃ] **1** *adj* diabolique; *Fig* (*problem etc*) sacré; de diable, du diable. **2** *adv Old-fashioned F* **it's d. hot!,** il fait rudement chaud!

devil-may-care ['dev(ə)lmeɪ'keər] *adj* insouciant, je-m'en-foutiste; **d.-m.-c. spirit,** (*reckless*) esprit *m* téméraire; (*carefree*) esprit insouciant.

devilment ['dev(ə)lmənt] , **devilry** ['dev(ə)lrɪ] *n* **(a)** méchanceté *f*; **(b)** (*mischief*) diablerie *f*, espièglerie *f*; **what d. is he up to now?,** qu'est-ce qu'il nous prépare comme sottise?

devious ['di:vɪəs] *adj* **(a)** (*course, way*) détourné, tortueux; **(b)** (*person*) retors; **that was a bit d. of you,** c'était un peu sournois de ta part; **to achieve one's ends by d. means,** prendre des voies détournées pour arriver à son but.

deviously [di:vɪəslɪ] *adv* d'une façon détournée.

deviousness ['di:vɪəsnɪs] *n* **(a)** (*actions*) détours *mpl*; **(b)** caractère retors (*d'une personne*).

devise¹ [dɪ'vaɪz] *n Jur* legs *m* (immobilier).

devise² *vt* **(a)** combiner (*un projet*); inventer, imaginer (*un appareil*); tramer (*un complot*); **(b)** *Jur* léguer (*des biens immobiliers*).

devitalize [di:'vaɪtəlaɪz] *vt* affaiblir (*l'économie*).

devoid [dɪ'vɔɪd] *adj* dénué, dépourvu (**of,** de).

devolution [di:və'lu:ʃən] *n* **(a)** *Pol* décentralisation administrative; **(b)** *Biol* dégénérescence *f*; **(c)** *Jur* dévolution *f*, transmission *f* par succession.

devolve [dɪ'vɒlv] *vt* déléguer, transmettre (*des fonctions, des pouvoirs*) (**to s.o.,** à qn).

▶**devolve on** *vipo* **(a)** (*of responsibility, duty etc*) revenir, incomber à (*qn*); **(b)** *Jur* (*of property*) être dévolu à (*qn*).

▶**devolve to** *vipo Jur* (*of property*) être dévolu à (*qn*).

▶**devolve upon** *vipo* = **DEVOLVE ON**.

devote [dɪ'vəʊt] *vt* consacrer, dévouer (*son temps, son argent*) (**to,** à); accorder (*du temps*) (**to,** à); **review specially devoted to history,** revue entièrement consacrée à l'histoire; **to d. oneself to sth,** se vouer à, se consacrer à (*une occupation*); s'adonner à, se livrer à (*l'étude etc*).

devoted [dɪ'vəʊtɪd] *adj* dévoué, attaché (**to,** à); **they are d. to each other,** ils sont dévoués l'un à l'autre.

devotedly [dɪ'vəʊtɪdlɪ] *adv* avec dévouement; **to serve s.o. d.,** servir qn avec dévouement.

devotee [devəʊ'ti:] *n* fervent, -ente; **a d. of Haydn,** un fervent *ou* un grand amateur de Haydn; **a d. of classical music,** un passionné de musique classique.

devotion [dɪ'vəʊʃən] *n* **(a)** dévotion *f* (*à Dieu, à un saint*); **(b)** (*prayers*) **devotions,** dévotions *fpl*, prières *fpl*; **(c)** *Fig* dévouement *m* (**to s.o.,** à, pour qn); **d. to duty,** dévouement; **d. to work,** assiduité *f* au travail.

devotional [dɪ'vəʊʃən(ə)l] *adj Rel* (*livre etc*) de dévotion; **d. articles,** articles *mpl* de piété.

devour [dɪ'vaʊər] *vt* dévorer; *Fig* **to d. s.o. with one's eyes,** dévorer qn des yeux; *Fig* **to d. a book,** dévorer un livre; *Fig* **to be devoured by curiosity/hatred,** être dévoré par la curiosité/la haine.

devouring [dɪ'vaʊərɪŋ] *adj Fig* **a d. passion,** une passion dévorante *ou* dévoratrice.

devout [dɪ'vaʊt] *adj* **(a)** (*person*) dévot; **a d. Catholic,** un catholique fervent; **(b)** (*wish etc*) fervent, sincère; **it is my d. wish that ...,** c'est mon vœu le plus sincère que ... .

devoutly [dɪ'vaʊtlɪ] *adv* (*see adj*) **(a)** dévotement, avec dévotion; **(b)** sincèrement.

devoutness [dɪ'vaʊtnɪs] *n* dévotion *f*, piété *f*.

dew [dju:] *n* **(morning) d.,** rosée *f*; **evening d.,** serein *m*; **d. is falling,** il tombe de la rosée; *Tech* **d. point,** point *m* de rosée *ou* de condensation.

dewclaw ['dju:klɔ:] *n Zool* ergot *m* (*des chiens etc*).

dewdrop ['dju:drɒp] *n* goutte *f* de rosée.

dewlap ['dju:læp] *n* **(a)** fanon *m* (*de la vache*); **(b)** *Fig* peau flasque et pendante (*sous le menton de qn*).

dewy ['dju:ɪ] *adj* couvert de rosée; humecté de rosée; *Fig* **d. complexion,** teint frais.

dewy-eyed [dju:ɪ'aɪd] *adj* **(a)** (*with tears*) les yeux brillants de larmes; **(b)** (*trusting*) naïf, -ve, ingénu; **don't act the d.-e. innocent with me,** ne fais pas l'ingénu avec moi.

dexterity [deks'terɪtɪ] *n* (*mental*) dextérité *f*, doigté *m*; (*physical*) habileté *f*; **manual d.,** habileté manuelle.

dext(e)rous ['dekstrəs] *adj* adroit, habile (**in doing sth,** à faire qch).

dextrin ['dekstrɪn] *n Ch Ind* dextrine *f*.

dextrose ['dekstrəʊs] *n Ch* dextrose *m*.

dextrously ['dekstrəslɪ] *adv* adroitement, avec dextérité.

DFC [di:ef'si:] *n abbr* **Distinguished Flying Cross.**

DFM [di:ef'em] *n abbr* **Distinguished Flying Medal.**

DHSS [di:eɪtʃes'es] *n Br Admin* (*abbr* **Department of Health and Social Security**) = Ministère *m* de la Santé.

diabetes [daɪə'bi:ti:z] *n Med* diabète *m*; **to have d.,** avoir du diabète.

diabetic [daɪə'betɪk] *Med* **1** *n* diabétique *mf*. **2** *adj* diabétique; **to be in a d. coma,** faire un *ou* être en coma diabétique; **d. biscuits/jam/***etc*, biscuits/confiture/*etc* pour diabétiques.

diabolic [daɪə'bɒlɪk] *adj* (*cruauté etc*) diabolique, atroce; (*complot*) infernal; (*ricanement*) satanique.

diabolical [daɪə'bɒlɪk(ə)l] *adj Br F* **(a)** (*very bad*) nul; **(b)** (*intensifier*) **what a d. liberty,** quel culot!

diabolically [daɪə'bɒlɪklɪ] *adv* diaboliquement.

diacritic [daɪə'krɪtɪk] *Gram* **1** *n* (signe *m*) diacritique *m*. **2** *adj* (*signe*) diacritique.

diacritical [daɪə'krɪtɪk(ə)l] *adj Gram* (*signe*) diacritique.

diadem ['daɪədem] *n* diadème *m*.

diaeresis, *US* **dieresis,** *pl* **-eses** [daɪ'erəsɪs, -əsi:z] *n Gram* tréma *m*.

diagnose ['daɪəgnəʊz] *vt* diagnostiquer (*une maladie, une panne du moteur etc*); faire le diagnostic (*d'une maladie*); **she has been diagnosed as a schizophrenic,** d'après le diagnostic, elle est schizophrène.

diagnosis, *pl* **-ses** [daɪəg'nəʊsɪs, -si:z] *n Med* **(a)** diagnostic *m* (*d'une maladie*); *Med & Fig* **what's the d.?,** quel est le diagnostic?; **to make** *or* **give a d.,** faire un diagnostic; **(b)** (*art*) diagnose *f*.

diagnostic [daɪəg'nɒstɪk] *adj* diagnostique; *Comptr* **d. disk/program,** disquette *f*/programme *m* de diagnostic; *Med* **d. kit,** trousse *f* diagnostique; *Med Comptr* **d. test,** test *m* de diagnostic.

diagnostician [daɪəgnɒs'tɪʃən] *n* personne *f* qui fait un diagnostic; **she's an excellent d.,** elle fait de très bons diagnostics.

diagnostics [daɪəg'nɒstɪks] *npl Med* diagnostique *f*.

diagonal [daɪ'ægən(ə)l] **1** *adj Math* diagonal, -aux; *Constr* (*beam etc*) en écharpe. **2** *n Math* diagonale *f*.

diagonally [daɪ'ægən(ə)lɪ] *adv* diagonalement, en diagonale.

diagram ['daɪəgræm] *n* diagramme *m*, schéma *m*; *Phys etc* graphique *m*, courbe *f* (*de température etc*); *MecE* diagramme, caractéristique *f* (*du moteur etc*); **geometrical d.,**

figure *f* géométrique; *Fig* **do I need to draw you a d.?,** est-ce que je dois te faire un dessin?

diagrammatic [daɪəgrə'mætɪk] *adj* schématique.

dial[1] ['daɪəl] *n* cadran *m* (*d'horloge, de baromètre, d'un instrument scientifique etc*); *Tel* cadran (d'appel); *Rad F* **don't touch that d.,** (*don't change channels*) restez avec nous; *Nau* **compass d.,** rose *f* des vents; *Am Tel* **d. tone,** tonalité *f*.

dial[2] *vt* (**-ll-**, *US* **-l-**) *Tel* composer, faire (*un numéro*); *Comptr* composer (*un cadran*); **to d.** *Br* **999** *or Am* **911,** = appeler Police Secours.

dialect ['daɪəlekt] *n* dialecte *m*; **provincial d.,** patois *m*.

dialectic(al) [daɪə'lektɪk, -ɪk(ə)l] *adj Phil* dialectique; **d. materialism,** matérialisme *m* dialectique.

dialectic(s) [daɪə'lektɪk, -s] *n Phil* dialectique *f*.

dialling, *US* **dialing** ['daɪəlɪŋ] *n Tel* composition *f* du numéro; **d. code,** indicatif *m* (départemental); **d. tone,** tonalité *f*; **I can't get a d. tone,** je n'arrive pas à avoir la tonalité.

dialogue, *US* **dialog** ['daɪəlɒg] *n* dialogue *m*; *Pol* **to enter into a d.,** entamer le dialogue; *Cin etc* **d. writer,** dialoguiste *mf*.

dialyse ['daɪəlaɪz] *vt Ch* dialyser.

dialysis, *pl* **-es** [daɪ'ælɪsɪs, -iːz] *n Ch Surg* dialyse *f*; **she's in d.,** elle est sous dialyse; **to have d. (treatment),** être sous dialyse; **d. machine,** dialyseur *m*.

diamanté [daɪə'mænteɪ, dɪə-] *n* broderie diamantée.

diameter [daɪ'æmɪtər] *n* diamètre *m*; **the wheel is 60 cm in d.,** la roue a 60 cm de diamètre; **internal d.,** calibre *m* (*d'un tube*); alésage *m* (*d'un cylindre etc*).

diametric(al) [daɪə'metrɪk, -ɪk(ə)l] *adj* **in d. opposition,** (*opinion etc*) diamétralement opposé (**to,** à).

diametrically [daɪə'metrɪklɪ] *adv* **d. opposed,** (*opinion etc*) diamétralement opposé; **to be d. opposed to sth,** être diamétralement opposé à qn.

diamond ['daɪəmənd] *n* **(a)** (*gem*) diamant *m*; *Tech* **(cutting) d.,** diamant de vitrier; **rough/cut d.,** diamant brut/taillé; *Fig* **he's a rough d.,** ses manières frustes cachent beaucoup de qualités; **d. mine,** mine *f* de diamants; **d. necklace/ring,** collier *m*/bague *f* de diamants; **d. cutting,** taille *f* du diamant; **d. cutter,** (*person*) tailleur *m* de diamants; **d. jubilee,** (*of monarch, company*) soixantième anniversaire *m*; **d. wedding,** noces *fpl* de diamant; **(b)** (*shape*) losange *m*; **d. pattern,** dessin *m* en losanges; **(c)** *Cards* carreau *m*; **the six of diamonds,** le six de carreau; **(d)** *Baseball* terrain *m* de baseball.

diamond-shaped ['daɪəməndʃeɪpt] *adj* en losange.

diapason [daɪə'peɪsən] *n Mus* **(a)** principaux jeux de fond (*d'un orgue*); **(b)** (*tuning fork*) diapason *m*.

diaper ['daɪəpər] *n Am* couche *f*, lange *m* (*de bébé*).

diaphanous [daɪ'æfənəs] *adj* diaphane.

diaphragm ['daɪəfræm] *n* **(a)** *Anat* diaphragme *m*; **(b)** (*membrane*) diaphragme *m*, membrane *f*; *Phot* diaphragme; **(c)** *Med* diaphragme *m* (contraceptif).

diarist ['daɪərɪst] *n* auteur *m* d'un journal (intime).

diarrhoea [daɪə'rɪə] *n Med* diarrhée *f*; **to have d.,** avoir la diarrhée.

diary ['daɪərɪ] *n* **(a)** journal *m* (intime); **to keep a d.,** tenir un journal (intime); **(b)** (*for appointments*) agenda *m*; **I'll just check my d.,** je vais vérifier sur mon agenda; **desk d.,** (*loose leaf*) bloc *m* calendrier; (*bound*) agenda.

Diaspora (the) [ðədaɪ'æspərə] *n Jewish Rel* la Diaspora.

diastole [daɪ'æstəlɪ] *n Med* diastole *f*.

diatom ['daɪətəm] *n Biol* diatomée *f*.

diatribe ['daɪətraɪb] *n* diatribe *f* (**against,** contre).

dibber ['dɪbər], **dibble[1]** ['dɪb(ə)l] *n* (*for bulbs etc*) plantoir *m*.

dibble[2] **1** *vt* semer (*des graines*) au plantoir; repiquer (*des plantes*) au plantoir. **2** *vi* semer *ou* repiquer au plantoir.

dibs [dɪbz] *npl* **(a)** (*game*) osselets *m*; **(b)** *Old-fashioned F* argent *m*, fric *m*.

dice[1] [daɪs] *npl* (*pl of* **die[1]**) **(a)** (*in game*) dés *mpl*; **to throw the d.,** lancer les dés; *Am Fig F* **no d.,** pas question.

dice[2] **1** *vi* jouer aux dés; **to d. with death,** risquer sa vie. **2** *vt Culin* couper (*des légumes*) en cubes.

dicey ['daɪsɪ] *adj esp Br F* hasardeux; (*dangerous*) risqué.

dichotomy [daɪ'kɒtəmɪ] *n* dichotomie *f*.

dicing ['daɪsɪŋ] *n* **(a)** le jeu des dés; **(b)** (*gambling*) les dés *mpl*, le jeu.

dick [dɪk] *n F* **(a)** *esp US* détective *m*, flic *m*; **(b)** *esp Br* (*fellow*) individu *m*, type *m*; **clever d.,** petit malin; **(c)** *Vulg* (*penis*) verge *f*.

Dick [dɪk] *n* (*dimin of* **Richard**) = Richard *m*.

dickens ['dɪkɪnz] *n F* **what the d. are you doing?,** que diable fais-tu?; **the d. of a row,** un bruit de tous les diables.

Dickensian [dɪ'kenzɪən] *adj* (*scene etc*) digne de figurer dans un roman de Dickens.

dicker ['dɪkər] *vi* marchander; **to d. for sth,** marchander qch.

dickhead ['dɪkhed] *n Br Sl* tête *f* de nœud.

dicky[1] ['dɪkɪ] *n F* **(a)** (*in children's language*) **d. (bird),** (petit) oiseau *m*, zoziau *m*; *Br* **did you hear anything? — not a d. bird,** est-ce que tu as entendu? – non, rien du tout; **they haven't heard a d. bird from her,** elle n'a pas fait signe de vie; **(b)** faux plastron (*de chemise*); **(c)** *Old-fashioned Aut* spider *m*.

dicky[2] *adj Br F* défectueux; (*heart*) malade, qui flanche; **to feel d.,** se sentir tout chose.

Dictaphone ® ['dɪktəfəʊn] *n* Dictaphone ® *m*.

dictate[1] ['dɪkteɪt] *n* ordre *m*; **to follow the dictates of one's conscience,** écouter sa conscience; **the dictates of fashion,** les exigences de la mode.

dictate[2] [dɪk'teɪt] **1** *vt* **(a)** dicter (*une lettre, un passage*); **(b)** dicter (*des conditions de paix etc*); **(c)** (*determine*) déterminer (*qch*); **the size of the harvest will be dictated by the weather,** l'importance de la moisson dépendra du temps. **2** *vi* faire la loi; **I won't be dictated to,** on ne me donne pas d'ordres; **we shouldn't let fashion designers d. to us,** on ne devrait pas laisser les créateurs de mode nous faire la loi.

dictating [dɪk'teɪtɪŋ] *n* **d. machine,** machine *f* à dicter.

dictation [dɪk'teɪʃən] *n* dictée *f*; **to take d. from s.o.,** écrire sous la dictée de qn; **to give d.,** dicter; *Sch* **to do d.,** faire la dictée.

dictator [dɪk'teɪtər] *n Pol etc* dictateur *m*.

dictatorial [dɪktə'tɔːrɪəl] *adj* **(a)** (*pouvoir*) dictatorial, -aux; **(b)** (*ton*) impérieux; (*personne, ton*) autoritaire.

dictatorially [dɪktə'tɔːrɪəlɪ] *adv* (*see adj*) **(a)** dictatorialement; **(b)** impérieusement, autoritairement.

dictatorship [dɪk'teɪtəʃɪp] *n* dictature *f*.

diction ['dɪkʃən] *n* **(a)** (*pronunciation*) diction *f*; **(b)** style *m* (*d'un orateur*).

dictionary ['dɪkʃən(ə)rɪ] *n* dictionnaire *m*; **English-French d.,** dictionnaire anglais-français; **d. of quotations,** dictionnaire de citations.

dictum, *pl* **-ums, -a** ['dɪktəm, -əmz, -ə] *n* **(a)** (*statement*) affirmation *f*, dire *m*; **(b)** (*saying*) maxime *f*, dicton *m*.

didactic [dɪ'dæktɪk] *adj* didactique.

didactically [dɪ'dæktɪklɪ] *adv* didactiquement.

diddle ['dɪd(ə)l] *vt F* duper, refaire, rouler (*qn*); **he diddled me out of £500,** il m'a refait *ou* roulé de 500 livres.

diddler ['dɪdlər] *n F* carotteur, -euse.

didn't ['dɪd(ə)nt] = **did not,** *see* **DO.**

die[1] [daɪ] *n* **(a)** (*pl* **dice**) dé *m* (*à jouer*); **the d. is cast,** le sort est jeté, les dés sont jetés; **(b)** (*pl* **dies** [daɪz]) *Metal* matrice *f*; coquille *f* (*de moulage*); (*in minting*) coin *m*; **stamping** *or* **embossing d.,** matrice *ou* machine *f* à estamper; **screw-cutting d.,** mère *f* (de filet de vis); **d. casting,** moulage *m* en coquille; **d. stamping,** matriçage *m*; **d. sinker,** graveur *m* d'étampes *ou* de matrices; **(c)** *Metal* (*tool*) poinçonneuse *f* (à main).

die[2] *v* (*pt & pp* **died** [daɪd]; *prp* **dying** ['daɪɪŋ]) **1** *vi* mourir; **to be dying,** mourir; **he died yesterday,** il est mort hier; **to d. in one's sleep,** mourir pendant son sommeil; *Aut F* **the engine died on me,** le moteur a calé; **to d. rich/a millionaire,** mourir riche/millionnaire; **they died like heroes,** ils sont morts en héros; **to d. of grief/starvation,** mourir de chagrin/faim; **to d. from** *or* **of a wound,** mourir des suites d'une blessure; **old superstitions d. hard,** les vieilles superstitions ont la vie dure; **never say d.!,** (*don't give up*) il ne faut jamais désespérer; (*stay cheerful*) courage!, tenez bon!; **I thought I would d. of boredom/curiosity,** j'ai cru mourir d'ennui/de curiosité; **I nearly died laughing,** je mourais de rire; *F* **we were dying of cold,** nous mourions de froid; **to be dying to do sth,** brûler *ou* mourir d'envie de faire qch; **I'm dying for a drink/cigarette,** je meurs de soif/d'envie de fumer une cigarette; **day is dying,** le jour s'en va; **his secret died with him,** il a emporté son secret dans le tombeau.

2 *vt* **to d. a natural death,** (*not be murdered*) mourir de mort naturelle; (*of old age*) mourir de sa belle mort; (*of fashion etc*) passer de mode.

▶**die away** *vi* (*of sound*) s'affaiblir; (*of voice*) s'éteindre; (*of wind*) tomber; *Mus* **to let the sound d. away,** éteindre le son.

▶**die back** *vi* (*of plant*) se faner.

▶**die down** *vi* (*of fire etc*) baisser; (*of wind*) tomber; (*of sound*) s'éteindre; (*of excitement, storm*) se calmer; (*of ap-*

plause) mourir.

▶**die off** *vi* mourir; *F* **they're dying off like flies,** ils meurent les uns après les autres *ou* comme des mouches.

▶**die out** *vi* (*of family etc*) s'éteindre; (*of species*) disparaître.

die-hard ['daɪhɑːd] *n* immobiliste *m*; *Pol* conservateur *m* à outrance; **d. policy,** (politique *f* d')immobilisme *m*; politique outrancière.

dieresis [daɪ'erəsɪs] *n US* = **DIAERESIS.**

diesel ['diːz(ə)l] **1** *adj* (*moteur, locomotive*) diesel; **d. oil** *or* **fuel,** gazole *m*. **2** *n* diesel *m*.

diesel-electric [diːzəlɪ'lektrɪk] *adj* diesel-électrique, *pl* diesel-électriques.

diet¹ ['daɪət] *n* **(a)** (*what is eaten*) alimentation *f*; **their d. consists mainly of fish,** leur nourriture se compose essentiellement de poisson; **(b)** *Med* régime *m*; (*to lose weight*) régime, diète *f*; **to be on a d.,** être au régime; **to go on a d.,** se mettre au régime; **to put s.o. on a diet,** mettre qn au régime; **milk d.,** régime lacté; **starvation d.,** régime draconien.

diet² *vi* se mettre *ou* être au régime.

diet³ *n Pol* diète *f*.

dietary ['daɪət(ə)rɪ] **1** *adj* diététique; **d. fibre,** fibres *fpl* (alimentaires). **2** *n* régime *m* (alimentaire) (*d'un malade, d'une prison etc*).

dietetic [daɪə'tetɪk] *adj* diététique.

dietetics [daɪə'tetɪks] *npl* (*usu with sing verb*) diététique *f*.

dietician, dietitian [daɪə'tɪʃən] *n* diététicien, -ienne.

differ ['dɪfər] *vi* **(a)** différer (**from,** de), être différent (**from,** de); **to d. in size/shape/colour/***etc*, être de tailles/de formes/de couleurs/*etc* différentes; **(b)** (*disagree*) être d'opinion différente *ou* d'avis différent; **I beg to d.,** permettez-moi d'être d'un autre avis; **to agree to d.,** garder chacun son opinion; **that's where we d.,** (*disagree*) c'est sur ce point que nous sommes en désaccord; (*are different*) c'est ce qui nous différencie; **I d. with her about** *or* **on the diagnosis,** je ne suis pas d'accord avec elle sur le diagnostic.

difference ['dɪf(ə)rəns] *n* **(a)** différence *f*, écart *m* (**between,** entre); différence (*entre deux nombres etc*); **d. in age/in altitude,** différence d'âge/d'altitude; **d. in temperature,** écart de température; **the d. in you is amazing,** c'est incroyable à quel point tu as changé; **I don't quite see the d.,** je ne saisis pas la nuance; **she doesn't make any d. between the children,** (*of schoolmistress etc*) elle ne fait pas de distinction entre les enfants; **it doesn't make any d.,** cela ne fait aucune différence; **it makes no d. (to me),** cela ne (me) fait rien, cela m'est parfaitement égal; **to make a d.,** (*improve society*) faire avancer les choses; **the new colour scheme makes a big** *or* **all the d.,** les nouvelles couleurs font toute la différence; **that makes all the d.,** voilà qui change complètement les choses; **he's a businessman, but with a d.,** c'est bien un homme d'affaires, mais pas comme les autres; **differences in price,** écarts de prix; **to split the d.,** *Com* partager la différence; (*settle argument*) faire un compromis; **(b)** (*disagreement*) désaccord *m*, différend *m* (**about sth,** au sujet de qch); **to have a d. of opinion with s.o.,** se disputer avec qn; **to settle a d.,** (*of two people*) régler un différend, se mettre d'accord; **we have our differences,** nous ne sommes pas toujours d'accord.

different ['dɪf(ə)rənt] *adj* **(a)** différent (**from,** *Am also* **than,** de); **entirely d. ideas,** des idées tout à fait différentes; **I feel a d. man,** je ne me sens plus le même; **that dress makes you look d.,** cette robe vous change; **I do it in a d. way,** je m'y prends tout autrement; **that's quite a d. matter,** ça c'est une autre affaire; **(b)** (*various*) divers; **d. colours,** couleurs diverses *ou* variées; **d. kinds of...,** diverses *ou* différentes espèces de...; **at d. times,** à différentes *ou* diverses reprises; **(c)** (*unusual*) au-dessus de l'ordinaire; **he just wants to be d.,** il cherche à se faire remarquer; **it's certainly d.,** c'est original.

differential [dɪfə'renʃəl] **1** *adj* différentiel; *Math* **d. calculus,** calcul différentiel; *Aut etc* **d. gear,** engrenage différentiel. **2** *n Math* différentielle *f*; *Aut* différentiel *m*; écart *m* (*des prix, des salaires*); **weight d.,** différence *f* de poids; **wage** *or* **pay differentials,** hiérarchie salariale.

differentiate [dɪfə'renʃɪeɪt] **1** *vt* différencier (**sth from sth,** qch de qch); *Math* différencier (*une fonction*). **2** *vi* faire la différence (**between two things,** entre deux choses); **to d. between male and female employees,** traiter les employés hommes différemment des employées femmes.

differentiation [dɪferenʃɪ'eɪʃən] *n* différenciation *f*.

differently ['dɪf(ə)rəntlɪ] *adv* différemment.

difficult ['dɪfɪkəlt] *adj* **(a)** (*tâche, problème*) difficile; **this question is d. to answer,** il est difficile de répondre à cette question; **I find it d.** *or* **it is d. for me to ...,** j'ai de la peine à ..., j'ai du mal à ...; **it is d. to believe that ...,** on a peine à croire que ...+*sub*; **why do you have to make life d. for people?,** quel besoin as-tu de compliquer la vie aux gens?; **it makes life d. not knowing how long they'll be staying for,** cela n'arrange pas les choses de ne pas savoir s'ils vont rester longtemps; **it's been a d. time for all of us,** ça a été une période dure pour nous tous; **(b)** (*person*) difficile, peu commode; **he's d. to get on with,** il est peu commode; **don't be so d.!,** ne fais pas le *ou* la difficile!; **you're just being d.,** tu fais le *ou* la difficile.

difficulty ['dɪfɪkəltɪ] *n* **(a)** difficulté *f*; **to have d. in doing sth,** avoir du mal *ou* des difficultés à faire qch; **to have d. (in) breathing,** avoir du mal à respirer; **there will be no d. about that,** cela ne fera pas de difficultés; **the d. is to ...,** le difficile, c'est de ...; **with d.,** avec difficulté, difficilement; **(b)** (*obstacle*) obstacle *m*, difficulté *f*; **I see no d. about it,** je n'y vois pas d'inconvénient; **to raise** *or* **make difficulties,** soulever des objections; **there's the d.!** voilà la difficulté!; **(c)** (*difficult situation*) embarras *m*, ennui *m*; **to be in d.** *or* **difficulties,** (*of swimmer*) être en difficulté; *Fig* (*of company, marriage*) connaître des difficultés; **ship in difficulties,** navire *m* en difficulté; **financial difficulties,** embarras pécuniaire; **to get into difficulties,** se mettre dans un mauvais pas; **to get out of one's difficulties,** se tirer d'affaire.

diffidence ['dɪfɪdəns] *n* manque *m* de confiance en soi, manque d'assurance.

diffident ['dɪfɪdənt] *adj* qui manque d'assurance *ou* de confiance en soi; (*sourire*) timide; **to be d. about doing sth,** être hésitant à faire qch.

diffidently [dɪfɪdəntlɪ] *adv* timidement.

diffract [dɪ'frækt] *vt Opt* diffracter (*de la lumière*).

diffraction [dɪ'frækʃən] *n Opt* (*of light*) diffraction *f*.

diffuse¹ [dɪ'fjuːs] *adj* (*light, style etc*) diffus.

diffuse² [dɪ'fjuːz] **1** *vt* répandre (*la lumière, une nouvelle etc*); diffuser (*la lumière*). **2** *vi* se répandre; (*of light, gas etc*) se diffuser.

diffused [dɪ'fjuːsd] *adj* **d. lighting,** éclairage tamisé.

diffuseness [dɪ'fjuːsnɪs] *n* prolixité *f*, caractère diffus (*du style*).

diffuser [dɪ'fjuːsər] *n* (*for hairdryer*) diffuseur *m*.

diffusion [dɪ'fjuːʒən] *n* diffusion *f* (*d'un fluide, du style, etc*); rayonnement *m* (*des idées*); *Phys* dispersion *f* (*des rayons*); *Rad etc* diffusion (*de nouvelles*).

diffusive [dɪ'fjuːsɪv] *adj* **(a)** diffusif; **(b)** (*style*) diffus, prolixe.

dig¹ [dɪg] *n* **(a)** coup *m* de bêche (*au jardin etc*); *Archeol* fouille *f*; **give the ground a good d.,** remuez bien le sol; *Archeol* **to go on a d.,** faire des fouilles; **a d. in the ribs,** un coup de coude dans les côtes; **(b)** remarque déplaisante (**at s.o.,** à qn); **to get a d. in at s.o.,** lancer un coup de patte à qn; **that's a d. at you,** cette remarque est à votre intention.

dig² *v* (*pt & pp* **dug** [dʌg]; *prp* **digging** ['dɪgɪŋ]) **1** *vt* **(a)** bêcher (*la terre*); (*with tractor etc*) labourer (*la terre*); arracher (*des pommes de terre*); creuser (*la tourbe*); **to d. a grave,** creuser une tombe; *Fig* **to d. one's own grave,** creuser sa propre tombe; **(b)** enfoncer (*qch*) (**in,** dans); *F* **to d. s.o. in the ribs,** donner un coup de coude à qn; **(c)** *Old-fashioned Sl* (*understand*) comprendre, piger (*qch*); (*like*) aimer (*qn, qch*); **I d. that,** ça me plaît *ou* me botte. **2** *vi* travailler la terre; *Archeol* faire des fouilles; **to d. for gold,** faire des fouilles pour trouver de l'or.

▶**dig in 1** *vtsep* enterrer (*le fumier etc*); **to d. one's toes** *or* **heels in,** s'entêter; *F* **to d. oneself in,** s'incruster. **2** *vi* **(a)** *Mil* s'établir (*en creusant des tranchées*); **(b)** *F* manger.

▶**dig into** *vipo F* **(a)** manger (*une tarte*); **(b)** fouiller dans (*le passé de qn, des dossiers*).

▶**dig out** *vtsep* **(a)** (*remove*) extraire, déterrer (*qch*); dégager (*qn*); **(b)** (*find*) déterrer (*de vieux manuscrits etc*).

▶**dig up** *vtsep* déraciner (*une plante etc*); mettre à jour (*un trésor*); piocher (*la rue etc*); déterrer, exhumer (*un corps*); *F* **where did you d. that up?,** où as-tu déniché ça?

digest¹ ['daɪdʒest] *n* **(a)** abrégé *m*, résumé *m* (*d'une science*); **(b)** digeste *m*; recueil *m* de lois; **(c)** *Journ* condensé *m*, *F* digest *m*.

digest² [dɪ'dʒest, daɪ-] *vt Physiol* digérer (*les aliments*); *Fig* digérer (*une insulte, ce qu'on lit*).

digestible [dɪ'dʒestəb(ə)l] *adj* digestible; **easily d.,** d'une digestion facile, digeste.

digestion [dɪ'dʒestʃən, daɪ-] *n* **(a)** *Physiol* digestion *f*; *Fig* digestion, assimilation *f* (*de ce qu'on a lu*); **sluggish d.,** digestion laborieuse; **to have a good d.,** ne pas avoir de problèmes de digestion.

digestive [dɪ'dʒestɪv, daɪ-] **1** *adj* (*appareil, suc etc*) digestif; **d. troubles,** troubles digestifs *ou* de digestion. **2** *n* **(a)** *Pharm etc* digestif *m*; **(b)** *Br* **d. (biscuit),** = sorte de sablé.

digger ['dɪgər] *n* **(a)** (*tool*) truelle *f*; *Constr* **(mechanical) d.,** excavateur *m*; **(b)** (*with spade*) bêcheur *m*; (*for gold etc*) chercheur *m*; **(c) d. (wasp),** guêpe fouisseuse.

Digger [dɪgər] *n F* (*Australian*) australien; **hey D.!,** ohé l'australien!

digging ['dɪgɪŋ] *n* bêchage *m* (*de la terre*), labour *m* à la bêche; creusement *m* (*de fossés etc*); excavation *f* (*d'un puits etc*); *Archeol* fouilles *fpl*.

digit ['dɪdʒɪt] *n* **(a)** *Math* chiffre *m* (arabe); **the ten digits,** les neuf chiffres et le zéro; **double d. inflation,** taux *m* d'inflation à deux chiffres; *Comptr* **binary d.,** chiffre binaire, bit *m*; **d. selector,** sélecteur *m* d'indice; **(b)** (*on hand*) doigt *m*; (*on foot*) orteil *m*; *Br Hum* **extract the d.!,** grouille-toi!

digital ['dɪdʒɪt(ə)l] *adj Anat etc* digital, -aux; *Comptr etc* (*calculateur etc*) numérique; **d. watch/clock,** montre *f*/horloge *f* à affichage digital; **d. recording,** (*of music*) enregistrement *m* numérique, numériser.

digitalis [dɪdʒɪ'teɪlɪs] *n* **(a)** *Bot* digitale *f*; **(b)** *Pharm* digitaline *f*.

digitize ['dɪdʒɪtaɪz] *vt Comptr* convertir (*des données*) en numérique, numériser.

digitizer ['dɪdʒɪtaɪzər] *n Comptr* numériseur *m*.

dignified ['dɪgnɪfaɪd] *adj* plein de dignité; (*air*) digne; **to have a d. manner,** avoir de la dignité.

dignify ['dɪgnɪfaɪ] *vt* donner de la dignité à (*qch*); **to d. s.o. with the name of ...,** honorer qn du nom de ... .

dignitary ['dɪgnɪt(ə)rɪ] *n* dignitaire *m*.

dignity ['dɪgnɪtɪ] *n* dignité *f*; **a woman of great d.,** une femme d'une grande dignité; **to preserve one's d.,** garder sa dignité; **to be** *or* **stand on one's d.,** se retrancher derrière sa dignité; **the d. of labour,** la dignité du travail.

digress [daɪ'gres] *vi* faire une digression *ou* des digressions (**from,** de); s'écarter du sujet; **I'd like to d. for a moment,** j'aimerais faire une parenthèse.

digression [daɪ'greʃən] *n* digression *f*, écart *m* (*du sujet*).

digs [dɪgz] *npl Br F* logement *m*; **to live in d.,** loger en meublé; **where are your d.?,** où est-ce que tu crèches?

dihedral [daɪ'hiːdrəl] **1** *n* dièdre *m*. **2** *adj* (*angle*) dièdre.

dike [daɪk] *n & vtr* = **DYKE**[1,2].

dilapidated [dɪ'læpɪdeɪtɪd] *adj* (*building etc*) délabré, dans un état de délabrement; *Hum* (*chapeau*) dépenaillé.

dilapidation [dɪlæpɪ'deɪʃən] *n* délabrement *m*, dégradation *f* (*d'un bâtiment etc*).

dilate [daɪ'leɪt] **1** *vt* dilater. **2** *vi* (*of eyes etc*) se dilater.

►**dilate on** *vipo* s'étendre sur (*un sujet*).

dilation [daɪ'leɪʃən] *n* dilatation *f*; *Med* **d. and curettage,** dilatation et curetage.

dilatoriness ['dɪlət(ə)rɪnɪs] *n* lenteur *f* (à agir).

dilatory ['dɪlət(ə)rɪ] *adj* (*person*) lent (à agir); (*action*) tardif; *Jur etc* **d. means,** moyens dilatoires.

dildo ['dɪldəʊ] *n* godemiché *m*.

dilemma [daɪ'lemə] *n* embarras *m*; (*in logic*) dilemme *m*; **to be on the horns of a d.,** être pris dans un dilemme; **to be in a d.,** être fort embarrassé; **you place** *or* **put me in a d.,** tu me mets dans l'embarras.

dilettante, *pl* **-ti** [dɪlɪ'tɑːntɪ] **1** *n* dilettante *m*. **2** *adj* **in a d. manner,** (*faire qch*) en dilettante.

dilettantism [dɪlɪ'tɑːntɪz(ə)m] *n* dilettantisme *m*.

diligence ['dɪlɪdʒ(ə)ns] *n* assiduité *f*, application *f*, zèle *m*.

diligent ['dɪlɪdʒ(ə)nt] *adj* (*person, work*) assidu, appliqué.

diligently ['dɪlɪdʒ(ə)ntlɪ] *adv* avec assiduité, assidûment.

dill [dɪl] *n* (*herb*) aneth *m*.

dilly-dally ['dɪlɪdælɪ] *vi* (**dilly-dallied**) **(a)** (*loiter*) traîner, traînasser, lambiner; **(b)** (*vacillate*) hésiter, tergiverser.

dilute[1] [daɪ'luːt, dɪ-] *adj* (*acid etc*) dilué, étendu.

dilute[2] **1** *vt* **(a)** diluer (*un acide, de la peinture, du jus d'orange*); allonger (*une sauce*) (**with,** de); **to d. wine with water,** couper du vin avec de l'eau; **to become diluted,** se diluer; **(b)** *Fig* atténuer (*une doctrine etc*); **diluted radicalism,** radicalisme *m* à l'eau de rose. **2** *vi* diluer; **d. to taste,** (*notice on bottle*) diluer à votre convenance.

dilution [daɪ'luːʃən, dɪ-] *n* dilution *f*; réduction *f* (*d'un acide*).

dim[1] [dɪm] *adj* (**dimmer, dimmest**) (*light*) faible, pâle; (*colour*) effacé; (*sight*) faible, trouble; (*forest, room, lighting*) sombre; (*outline, memory*) vague, faible, estompé; (*intelligence*) vague, confus; *F* (*person*) bête; **to grow d.,** (*of light, faculties*) baisser, s'éteindre; (*of recollection*) s'effacer; (*of sight*) se troubler; (*of outline*) s'effacer, s'estomper; **their chances of winning the championship are d.,** leurs chances de gagner le championnat sont faibles; **prospects for an end to the strike are d.,** les chances de voir la grève finir sont minces; *F* **to take a d. view of sth,** avoir une piètre opinion de qch; *F* **don't be so d.!** sois pas si bête!

dim[2] *v* (**-mm-**) **1** *vt* atténuer, réduire (*la lumière*); obscurcir (*la vue*); troubler (*la mémoire, l'intelligence*); ternir (*la beauté de qn, la surface d'un miroir*); *Fig* éclipser (*la gloire de qn*); **to d. the lights,** baisser les lumières; *Am Aut* **to d. one's headlights,** se mettre en code; **dimmed headlights,** phares *mpl* code. **2** *vi* (*of light*) baisser; (*of eyes*) s'obscurcir; (*of outline*) s'effacer, s'estomper.

dime [daɪm] *n US* dime *f* (= un dixième de dollar); *Am Fig* **arts graduates are a d. a dozen,** les licenciés ès lettres courent les rues; **d. store,** magasin *m* bon marché.

dimension [daɪ'menʃən, dɪ-] *n* dimension *f*; **what are the dimensions of the room?,** quelles sont les dimensions de la pièce?; **of large dimensions,** de grandes dimensions; *Math* **the fourth d.,** la quatrième dimension; *Fig* **there's another d. to the problem,** le problème a une autre dimension.

dimensional [daɪ'menʃən(ə)l, dɪ-] *adj* dimensionnel.

-dimensional [-daɪ'menʃən(ə)l] *suff* **two/three-d.,** à deux/trois dimensions; *Cin* **three-d.** (*also* **3D** ['θriːdiː]) **film,** film *m* en relief.

diminish [dɪ'mɪnɪʃ] **1** *vt* diminuer, réduire; **to d. the importance of sth,** diminuer l'importance de qch. **2** *vi* diminuer, s'atténuer.

diminished [dɪ'mɪnɪʃt] *adj* diminué; *Mus* (*intervalle*) diminué; *Jur* **d. responsibility,** responsabilité diminuée.

diminishing [dɪ'mɪnɪʃɪŋ] *adj* décroissant, qui diminue; (*value*) à la baisse; (*popularity*) qui baisse; *Econ* **law of d. returns,** loi *f* des rendements non-proportionnels *ou* décroissants.

diminution [dɪmɪ'njuːʃən] *n* diminution *f*, réduction *f*.

diminutive [dɪ'mɪnjʊtɪv] **1** *n Gram* diminutif *m*. **2** *adj* **(a)** (*tiny*) tout petit, minuscule; **(b)** *Gram* diminutif.

dimly ['dɪmlɪ] *adv* (*voir*) indistinctement; (*sentir, se souvenir*) vaguement; **d. lit room,** pièce mal éclairée.

dimmer ['dɪmər] *n El* interrupteur *m* à gradation de lumière; *Cin* obscurateur *m* de salle; **d. bulb,** ampoule *f* veilleuse.

dimness ['dɪmnɪs] *n* faiblesse *f* (*d'éclairage, de la vue*); obscurité *f* (*d'une pièce*); imprécision *f*, vague *m* (*d'un souvenir*); *F* stupidité *f*, bêtise *f* (*de qn*).

dimple[1] ['dɪmp(ə)l] *n* **(a)** (*on cheek, chin*) fossette *f*; **(b)** (*on water, ground*) ride *f*.

dimple[2] **1** *vt* **(a)** (*of smile*) former des fossettes dans (*les joues de qn*); **(b)** (*of wind*) rider (*la surface de l'eau*). **2** *vi* **(a)** (*of cheeks*) former des fossettes; **(b)** (*of water*) onduler.

dimpled ['dɪmp(ə)ld] *adj* (*joues*) à fossettes.

dimwit ['dɪmwɪt] *n F* idiot, -ote; **you d.!,** imbécile!

dimwitted [dɪm'wɪtɪd] *adj F* idiot, bête.

din [dɪn] *n* tapage *m*, vacarme *m*, chahut *m*; **what a d.!,** quel boucan!

►**din into** *vtaspo* **to d. sth into s.o.,** seriner qch à qn; **you have to d. it into him,** il faut le lui enfoncer à coups répétés dans la tête.

dinar ['diːnɑːr] *n* (*monetary unit*) dinar *m*.

dine [daɪn] *vi* dîner.

►**dine off, dine on** *vipo* manger (*qch*) au dîner.

►**dine out** *vi* (*in restaurant*) dîner en ville *ou* dans un restaurant; (*at friends' home*) dîner chez des amis; **to d. out on a story,** raconter souvent la même histoire à table; **you'll be dining out on that for years,** ça te fera une bonne histoire à raconter pendant des années.

diner ['daɪnər] *n* **(a)** (*person*) dîneur, -euse; **(b)** *Am* petit restaurant (*au bord d'une route*); *Am Rail* wagon-restaurant *m*, *pl* wagons-restaurants.

dinette [daɪ'net] *n* coin-repas *m*.

ding-dong ['dɪŋ'dɒŋ] **1** *n* tintement *m* (*des cloches*); digue-din-don *m inv*. **2** *adj* **to have a d.-d. argument,** (*of two people*) se disputer violemment; **d.-d. match,** partie vivement disputée.

dinghy ['dɪŋ(g)ɪ] *n Nau* dinghy *m*, *pl* dinghies; **sailing d.,** dinghy à voile; **(ship's) d.,** youyou *m*; **rubber** *or* **inflatable d.,** canot *m* pneumatique.

dinginess ['dɪndʒɪnɪs] *n* (*dirtiness*) aspect miteux; (*darkness*) aspect sombre.

dingo ['dɪŋgəʊ] *n* (*animal*) dingo *m* (de l'Australie).

dingy ['dɪndʒɪ] *adj* (*room, furniture etc*) défraîchi; (*colour*) terne; (*hôtel*) peu confortable.

dining ['daɪnɪŋ] *n Rail* **d. car,** wagon-restaurant *m*, *pl* wagons-restaurants; *Sch etc* **d. hall,** réfectoire *m*; **d. room,** salle *f* à manger; **d.(-room) table,** table *f* de salle à manger.

dink [dɪŋk] *n Hum* (*abbr* **double income, no kids**) = couple sans enfants, qui touche deux salaires.

dinkum ['dɪŋkəm] *adj Austr F* (*person*) sincère; authentique; **fair d.,** régulier, vrai de vrai.

dinky ['dɪŋkɪ] *adj Old-fashioned F* mignon, gentil.

dinner ['dɪnər] *n* **(a)** (*evening meal*) dîner *m*; *Can* souper *m*; **what's for d.?,** qu'y a-t-il au dîner?; **(it's) d. time!,** à table!; **to go out to d.,** (*in restaurant*) dîner en ville *ou* dans un restaurant; (*at friends' home*) dîner chez des amis; **to invite s.o. to d.,** (*in restaurant*) inviter qn à dîner au restaurant; (*in one's home*) inviter qn à dîner; **to give a d. party,** donner un dîner; **to have** *or* **give a d. (party) for s.o.,** organiser un dîner pour qn; **after-d. speech,** discours *m* d'après-dîner; **public d.,** banquet *m*; *Mil* **regimental d.,** repas *m* de corps; **d. jacket,** (*for man*) smoking *m*; **d. service,** service *m* de table; **d. table,** table *f* de salle à manger; **(b)** *F* (*midday meal*) déjeuner *m*; *Can* dîner *m*; **to give the dog his d.,** donner à manger au chien; *Sl* **to be got up like a dog's d.,** être tout fringué; *Sch* **d. hour,** l'heure du déjeuner; *Br Sch* **d. lady,** = femme de service dans une cantine scolaire.

dinner-dance ['dɪnədɑːns] *n* dîner-dansant *m*, *pl* dîners-dansants.

dinosaur ['daɪnəsɔːr] *n* dinosaure *m*.

dint [dɪnt] *n* **by d. of (doing) sth,** à force de (faire) qch.

diocese ['daɪəsɪs] *n Rel* diocèse *m*.

diode ['daɪəʊd] *n Electron* (lampe *f*) diode *f*.

dioptre, *US* **diopter** [daɪ'ɒptər] *n Opt* dioptrie *f*.

dioxide [daɪ'ɒksaɪd] *n Ch* dioxyde *m*, bioxyde *m*.

dip¹ [dɪp] *n* **(a)** inclinaison *f*, dépression *f* (*du terrain*); (*in road*) caniveau *m*; baisse *f* (*dans les prix etc*); dépression (*de l'horizon*); inclinaison (*d'une aiguille aimantée*); *Br Aut* **d. switch,** basculeur *m* de phares; **(b)** baignade *f*; **I'm going for a d.,** je vais me baigner; **(c)** *Culin* = sauce dans laquelle on trempe les crudités etc; *Ind* solution *f*, bain *m* (*de dorure etc*); *Agr* **(sheep) d.,** bain parasiticide (pour moutons); **(d)** plongement *m*, immersion *f* (*de qch dans un liquide etc*); **(e)** *Nau* salut *m* (*avec le pavillon*); **(f)** *Sl* (*pickpocket*) pickpocket *m*.

dip² *v* (-pp-) **1** *vt* **(a)** plonger, tremper (*les mains etc*) (**into,** dans); **(b)** *Ind* immerger, décaper (*un métal*); teindre (*la laine, un tissu*); confire (*les peaux*); plonger (*des chandelles*); **to d. sheep,** baigner les moutons (*dans un bain parasiticide*); **(c)** baisser (*qch*) subitement; *Br Aut* **to d. one's headlights,** se mettre en code; *Nau* **to d. a flag,** (faire) marquer un pavillon. **2** *vi* **(a)** plonger (*dans l'eau etc*); **(b)** (*of compass needle*) incliner; (*of scale*) pencher; (*of ground*) s'abaisser, descendre; (*of prices etc*) baisser; **the road dips sharply,** la route descend brusquement; **the sun dipped below the horizon,** le soleil est descendu derrière l'horizon; **(c)** (*of bird in flight*) piquer.

►**dip into** *vipo* **(a)** (*use part of*) prendre dans (*son capital*); **I'm always dipping into my pocket,** je suis toujours à débourser; **(b)** (*read or study parts of*) feuilleter (*un livre*); effleurer (*un sujet*).

diphtheria [dɪf'θɪərɪə] *n Med* diphtérie *f*; **to have d.,** être atteint de la diphtérie; **to die of d.,** mourir de la diphtérie.

diphthong ['dɪfθɒŋ] *n Ling* diphtongue *f*.

diploid ['dɪplɔɪd] *adj Biol* diploïde.

diploma [dɪ'pləʊmə] *n* diplôme *m* (**in,** de, en); **D. in Education** (*usu* **Dip Ed** ['dɪp'ed]), = C.A.P.E.S. *m* (Certificat d'aptitude au professorat de l'enseignement secondaire).

diplomacy [dɪ'pləʊməsɪ] *n* **(a)** *Pol* diplomatie *f*; **(b)** (*tactfulness*) diplomatie *f*, tact *m*; **to attain one's ends by d.,** user d'adresse pour atteindre son but; *F* **he doesn't go in much for d.,** la diplomatie n'est pas son fort.

diplomat ['dɪpləmæt] *n* diplomate *mf*.

diplomatic [dɪplə'mætɪk] *adj* **(a)** (*corps etc*) diplomatique; **to enter the d. service,** entrer dans la diplomatie *ou F* dans la carrière; **d. bag,** valise *f* diplomatique; **d. immunity,** immunité *f* diplomatique; **(b)** (*tactful*) politique, diplomatique; **d. answer,** réponse *f* politique; **you should have been more d.,** tu aurais dû être plus diplomate; **he knows how to be d.,** il a beaucoup de souplesse.

diplomatically [dɪplə'mætɪklɪ] *adv* diplomatiquement.

diplomatist [dɪ'pləʊmətɪst] *n* diplomate *mf*.

dipole ['daɪpəʊl] *n El* dipôle *m*.

dipped [dɪpt] *adj* incliné; *Br Aut* **d. headlights,** codes *mpl*.

dipper ['dɪpər] *n* **(a)** (*bird*) *F* cincle plongeur; *esp Am* martin-pêcheur *m*, *pl* martins-pêcheurs; **(b)** *Astron Am* **the Great** *or* **Big D.,** la Grande Ourse; **big d.,** (*at fairground*) le grand huit; **(c)** *Aut* **d. (switch),** basculeur *m* de phares; **(d)** (*ladle*) cuillère *f* à pot, louche *f*.

dipping ['dɪpɪŋ] **1** *adj* incliné; **steeply d.,** plongeant. **2** *n* **(a)** plongée *f*, immersion *f*; *Metal* décapage *m*; **sheep d.,** baignage *m* des moutons; **d. net,** épuisette *f*; **(b)** *Br Aut* (*of headlights*) mise *f* en code.

dippy ['dɪpɪ] *adj Old-fashioned F* toqué.

dipso ['dɪpsəʊ] *n Sl* (*drinker*) poivrot, -ote.

dipsomania [dɪpsə'meɪnɪə] *n* dipsomanie *f*.

dipsomaniac [dɪpsə'meɪnɪæk] *n* dipsomane *mf*.

dipstick ['dɪpstɪk] *n Aut* jauge *f* (de niveau) d'huile.

Dir *n abbr* **director**.

dire ['daɪər] *adj* néfaste, affreux; (*pressentiment*) lugubre; **d. necessity,** dure nécessité; **to be in d. need of sth,** avoir un besoin urgent de qch; **to be in d. straits,** se trouver dans la plus grande détresse; **this decision will have d. consequences,** cette décision aura des conséquences néfastes.

direct¹ [dɪ'rekt, daɪ-] *vt* **(a)** (*send, aim*) adresser (*une lettre, des observations etc*) (**to s.o.,** à qn); **to d. s.o.'s attention to sth,** appeler *ou* attirer l'attention de qn sur qch; **accusation directed against s.o.,** accusation visant *ou* qui vise qn; **to d. one's steps towards ...,** diriger ses pas *ou* se diriger vers...; **can you d. me to the station?,** pouvez-vous m'indiquer le chemin de la gare?; **(b)** (*manage*) diriger, mener, gérer (*une entreprise*); conduire (*une armée, ses affaires*); *Th Cin* mettre (*une pièce, un film*) en scène; diriger (*un film, des acteurs etc*); **who directed it?,** (*the play*) qui est le metteur en scène?; (*the film*) de qui est la mise en scène?, de qui est ce film?;

(c) (*instruct*) ordonner à, dire à (*qn*) (**to do,** de faire); **to d. traffic,** régler la circulation; **as directed** (*as ordered*) conformément aux ordres; (*as instructed*) selon les instructions; *Jur* **to d. the jury,** (*of judge*) instruire le jury (sur un point de droit).

direct² **1** *adj* (*straight, immediate*) direct; (*cause*) immédiat; **to be a d. descendant of s.o.,** descendre de qn en ligne directe; **in d. contradiction,** en contradiction directe; *Tel* **d. broadcast satellite,** satellite *f* de télédiffusion directe; **d. mail advertising,** publicité directe; *Br Banking* **to pay by d. debit,** payer par prélèvement automatique; *Gram* **d. object/speech,** complément *m* d'objet/discours direct; *Mil etc* **d. hit,** coup *m* au but; *Av* **d. flight,** vol direct; *Econ* **d. tax,** impôt direct; *El* **d. current,** courant continu; *Tel* **d. dialling,** automatique *m*; **(b)** (*person*) franc, *f* franche. **2** *adv* (*aller*) directement, tout droit; **to dispatch goods d. to s.o.,** expédier des marchandises directement à qn; *Rad TV* **the concert will be broadcast d. from Paris,** ce concert sera transmis en direct de Paris.

direction [dɪ'rekʃən, daɪ-] *n* **(a)** (*management*) direction *f*, administration *f* (*d'une société etc*); réglementation *f* (*de la circulation*); *Th Cin* mise *f* en scène; **under the d. of ...,** (*of orchestra*) sous la direction de ...; (*of company*) dirigé par;

(b) (*course*) direction *f*, sens *m*; **in the d. of ...,** dans la direction de ...; **I'm going in your d.,** je vais dans la même direction que toi; **we were going in the d. of Paris,** nous nous dirigions vers Paris; **in every d.,** dans tous les sens; **in the opposite d.,** en sens inverse; **in which d.?,** de quel côté?; **you are not looking in the right d.,** vous ne regardez pas du bon côté; **to lose one's sense of d.,** perdre le sens de l'orientation; **to have a good/bad sense of d.,** avoir un bon/mauvais sens de l'orientation; *Fig* **a step in the right d.,** un pas dans la bonne direction; **to lack d.,** manquer de suite dans les idées; (*in life*) manquer de buts; **change of d.,** changement *m* de direction; *Av Nau* changement de cap; *Fig* **improvements in many directions,** améliorations sous bien des rapports; *Electron* **d. finder,** radiogoniomètre *m*; *Aut* **d. sign,** panneau *m* de signalisation;

(c) **directions,** (*instructions*) instructions *fpl*; **you have been given the wrong directions,** on vous a mal renseigné; **to give s.o. directions to a place,** indiquer à qn comment aller à un endroit; **to ask for directions,** (*to a place*) demander son chemin; **stage directions,** indications *fpl* scéniques; **directions (for use),** notice *f* (explicative); *Jur* **d. to the jury,** exposé de la loi fait par le juge au jury.

directional [dɪ'rekʃən(ə)l, daɪ-] *adj Electron* directionnel.

directive [dɪ'rektɪv, daɪ-] *n Mil etc* directive *f*.

directly [dɪ'rektlɪ, daɪ-] **1** *adv* **(a)** (*aller*) directement, tout droit; (*descendre de qn*) en ligne directe; **to come d. to the point,** aller droit au fait; **I am not d. concerned,** je ne suis pas directement concerné; **d. opposite the church,**

juste en face de l'église; **(b)** *(answer)* franchement; **(c)** *(soon)* tout à l'heure; **I'm coming d.,** je viens tout de suite. **2** *conj* aussitôt que, dès que; **I'll come d. I've finished,** je viendrai dès que j'aurai fini.

directness [dɪ'rektnɪs, daɪ-] *n* franchise *f* *(d'une réponse etc)*; *Pej* franchise bourrue; **his d. of speech,** son franc-parler.

director [dɪ'rektər, daɪ-] *n* directeur -trice *(d'une société etc)*; gérant *m* *(d'une entreprise)*; *Cin Th* metteur *m* en scène; *Cathol* directeur de conscience; **managing d.,** administrateur délégué, gérant; **d. of music,** *Rel* maître *m* de chapelle; *Mil etc* chef *m* de musique; *Cin* **d. of photography,** directeur, -trice de la photographie; *Jur* **d. of public prosecutions,** = chef de parquet; **d.'s chair,** régisseur *m*.

directorate [dɪ'rektər(e)ɪt, daɪ-] *n* conseil *m* d'administration.

directorship [dɪ'rektəʃɪp, daɪ-] *n* **(a)** *(position)* poste *m* *ou* fonctions *fpl* de directeur *ou* d'administrateur; **she holds directorships in several companies,** elle fait partie du conseil d'administration de plusieurs entreprises; **(b)** *(term of office)* **during my d.,** *(in past)* pendant que j'étais directeur; *(in present)* depuis que je suis directeur.

directory [dɪ'rektərɪ, daɪ-] *n Tel* annuaire *m*; *(of addresses)* répertoire *m* d'adresses; *(in France)* = le Bottin; *Comptr* répertoire; **street d.,** guide *m* des rues; **commercial d.,** annuaire du commerce.

dirge [dɜːdʒ] *n* hymne *m ou* chant *m* funèbre.

dirigible ['dɪrɪdʒɪb(ə)l] **1** *n* (ballon *m*) dirigeable *m*. **2** *adj* *(balloon)* dirigeable.

dirk [dɜːk] *n* poignard *m* (des Écossais).

dirt [dɜːt] *n* **(a)** saleté *f*; *(mud)* boue *f*, crotte *f*; *(unwashed)* crasse *f*; *(excrement)* crotte *f*; corps étranger(s), saletés *(dans une machine, une solution etc)*; **hands ingrained with d.,** mains encrassées; **to show the d.,** *(of material)* être salissant; *Fig* **to treat s.o. like d.,** traiter qn comme le dernier des derniers; *Am F* **to be d. poor,** être vachement pauvre; *Ind etc* **d. money,** indemnité *f ou* prime *f* de salissure; **d. road,** chemin *m* en terre, chemin de terre battue; *Am* **d. farmer/farming,** exploitant *m*/exploitation *f* agricole; *Sp* **d. track,** piste *f* en cendrée; **d.-track racing,** courses *fpl* (motocyclistes) sur cendrée;
(b) *(condition)* saleté *f*, malpropreté *f*;
(c) *F* obscénités *fpl*; **to talk d.,** raconter des cochonneries; *Sl* **to do d. on s.o.,** faire un sale coup à qn;
(d) *Am* *(gossip)* ragot *m*; **what's the latest d.?,** quel est le dernier ragot?

dirt-cheap ['dɜːt'tʃiːp] *adj* à vil prix; **I got it d.-c.,** je l'ai eu pour trois fois rien.

dirtily ['dɜːtɪlɪ] *adv* *(see adj)* **(a)** salement; **(b)** grossièrement.

dirtiness ['dɜːtɪnɪs] *n* saleté *f*, malpropreté *f*.

dirty¹ ['dɜːtɪ] **1** *adj* **(a)** sale, malpropre, souillé, crasseux; *(with mud)* crotté; *(valve, piston etc)* encrassé; **to get d.,** *(of child, clothes etc)* se salir; **to get one's hands d.,** se salir les mains; **d. clothes,** linge *m* sale; **d. dishes,** vaisselle *f* sale; **d. weather,** sale temps; *Nau* gros temps; *Typ* **d. copy,** manuscrit brouillé *ou* peu clair; **d. money,** *Ind etc* indemnité *f* de salissure; *F* argent sale; *Fig* **to do s.o.'s d. work for them,** *F* faire le sale boulot pour qn;
(b) *(esprit)* cochon; *(histoire etc)* sale; *(livre, film)* pornographique; **d. joke,** cochonnerie *f*, blague obscène; **d. word,** mot grossier; **work is a d. word nowadays,** personne ne veut plus travailler de nos jours; *F* **d. old man,** vieux cochon; **to tell d. stories,** raconter des cochonneries *ou* des obscénités; *F* **d. trick,** sale tour *m*; **to play a d. trick on s.o.,** jouer un sale tour *ou* un sale coup à qn; **it's a d. business,** c'est une sale affaire *ou* une affaire louche; **d. look,** sale coup *m* d'œil; **to give s.o. a d. look,** regarder qn d'un sale œil.
2 *n* **to do the d. on s.o.,** jouer un sale tour *ou* coup à qn.
3 *adv F (intensive)* **a d. great lorry,** un camion monstre.

dirty² **1** *vt* salir *(ses habits etc)*; **to d. one's hands,** se salir les mains. **2** *vi* se souiller, se salir; **to d. easily,** *(of material)* se salir facilement.

disability [dɪsə'bɪlɪtɪ] *n* **(a)** *(handicap)* infirmité *f*; *Admin* invalidité *f*; **d. pension,** pension *f* d'invalidité; **(b)** *Jur* incapacité légale; inhabilité *f* *(à faire qch)*.

disable [dɪ'seɪb(ə)l] *vt* mettre *(qn)* hors de combat; estropier *(qn)*; désemparer *(un navire)*; mettre *(une machine)* hors de service; **to be disabled,** *(of ship)* être avarié *ou* désemparé.

disabled [dɪ'seɪb(ə)ld] **1** *adj* infirme; *(as result of accident etc)* handicapé, estropié; **d. ex-serviceman,** mutilé *m* de guerre. **2** *n* **the badly d.,** *(used as pl)* les grands infirmes; les grands mutilés; **facilities for the d.,** aménagements *mpl* pour les handicapés.

disablement [dɪ'seɪblmənt] *n* **(a)** *(handicap)* invalidité *f*; *Admin* **degree of d.,** coefficient *m* d'invalidité; **(b)** *(action)* mise *f* hors de combat; *(of machine)* mise hors service.

disabuse [dɪsə'bjuːz] *vt* désabuser *(qn)*; **they disabused him of this idea,** on lui a ôté cette idée de la tête.

disadvantage¹ [dɪsəd'vɑːntɪdʒ] *n* désavantage *m*; inconvénient *m*; **the d. of the plan is that ...,** l'inconvénient de ce projet est que ...; **to take s.o. at a d.,** prendre qn au dépourvu; **to be at a d. owing to sth,** être désavantagé par qch; **if you don't speak Italian, you'll be at a d.,** si tu ne parles pas italien, tu seras désavantagé; **to be seen at a d.,** être vu sous un jour désavantageux.

disadvantage² *vt* désavantager *(qn)*.

disadvantaged [dɪsəd'vɑːntɪdʒd] *adj* désavantagé.

disadvantageous [dɪsædvən'teɪdʒəs] *adj* désavantageux, défavorable (**to,** à).

disaffected [dɪsə'fektɪd] *adj* *(supporters, troops etc)* mécontent.

disaffection [dɪsə'fekʃən] *n* désaffection *f*, mécontentement *m*; **d. among the troops is growing,** le mécontentement grandit au sein des troupes.

disagree [dɪsə'griː] *vi* **(a)** *(not correspond)* être en désaccord, ne pas être d'accord (**with,** avec); *(of accounts)* différer, ne pas concorder; **to d. with s.o.,** ne pas être du même avis que qn; **I d.,** je ne suis pas de cet avis; **(b)** *(quarrel)* se brouiller (**with,** avec); être en mésintelligence (**with s.o.,** avec qn); **(c)** *(not suitable)* ne pas convenir (**with,** à); **the climate disagrees with him,** le climat ne lui convient pas *ou* ne lui va pas; **wine disagrees with him,** le vin lui est contraire.

disagreeable [dɪsə'griːəb(ə)l] *adj* *(person, job)* désagréable; *(remark)* désobligeant.

disagreeableness [dɪsə'griːəblnɪs] *n* *(of person)* mauvaise humeur; *(of job)* désagrément *m*; *(of remark)* désobligeance *f* (**to,** envers).

disagreeably [dɪsə'grɪəblɪ] *adv* désagréablement; fâcheusement.

disagreement [dɪsə'griːmənt] *n* **(a)** *(of figures)* différence *f* (**between,** entre); **(b)** *(failure to agree)* désaccord *m* (**with s.o. about sth,** avec qn sur qch); conflit *m* d'opinions; **we are in d.,** nous sommes en désaccord; **to be in d. with s.o.,** ne pas partager l'avis de qn; **(c)** *(quarrel)* brouille *f*, différend *m*; **to have a d.,** *(of two people)* se disputer; **to have a d. with s.o.,** se disputer avec qn.

disallow [dɪsə'laʊ] *vt* **(a)** *(reject)* ne pas admettre, ne pas reconnaître *(une hypothèse etc)*; *Jur* rejeter *(un témoignage)*; **(b)** *(cancel)* *Fb etc* annuler *(un but, une victoire)*.

disappear [dɪsə'pɪər] *vi* disparaître (**from a place,** d'un endroit); **to d. in** *or* **into the crowd,** se perdre dans la foule; **since she disappeared,** depuis sa disparition.

disappearance [dɪsə'pɪərəns] *n* disparition *f*.

disappearing [dɪsə'pɪərɪŋ] *n* disparition *f*; **to do a d. act,** *(of conjurer)* faire disparaître qn *ou* qch; *Fig F* *(of person)* partir, s'esquiver; **the scissors have done a d. act,** les ciseaux ont disparu.

disappoint [dɪsə'pɔɪnt] *vt* décevoir, désappointer *(qn)*; *(after promising)* manquer de parole à *(qn)*; tromper *(les espérances de qn)*; **he was bitterly disappointed,** il a eu une grave déception; **to be disappointed in love,** avoir des chagrins d'amour; **we were all disappointed that you couldn't come,** nous avons tous été très déçus que tu ne puisses pas venir; **he was disappointed at** *or* **about not being invited,** il a été déçu de ne pas être invité; **I am disappointed in** *or* **with you,** vous avez trompé *ou* démenti mes espérances; **I was very much disappointed in it** *or* **with it,** cela m'a beaucoup déçu.

disappointed [dɪsə'pɔɪntɪd] *adj* déçu; *(candidat)* refusé; **d. customers,** clients mal satisfaits.

disappointing [dɪsə'pɔɪntɪŋ] *adj* décevant; **the film was rather d.,** ce film était plutôt décevant; **how d.!,** quelle déception!; *(what a nuisance)* quel contretemps!

disappointment [dɪsə'pɔɪntmənt] *n* déception *f*; **it was a bit of a d.,** *(of film, holiday etc)* c'était un peu décevant; **bitter d.,** vive contrariété; **to suffer many disappointments,** essuyer bien des déboires; **you've been a great d. to your parents,** tu as beaucoup déçu tes parents; **to their great d., she did not come,** à leur grande déception, elle n'est pas venue.

disapprobation [dɪsæprəʊ'beɪʃən] *n Fml* désapprobation *f* (**of,** de).

disapproval [dɪsə'pruːv(ə)l] *n* désapprobation *f* (**of,** de); **look of d.,** regard désapprobateur; **to look at s.o. with d.,** regarder qn avec désapprobation; **much to our d.,** bien que nous n'approuvions pas.

disapprove [dɪsə'pruːv] **1** *vi* **I d.,** je le désapprouve, je n'approuve pas; **to d. of sth,** désapprouver qch; **to d. of sth being done,** désapprouver que l'on fasse qch; **she disapproves of her son-in-law,** son gendre n'est pas à son goût; **your mother disapproves of me,** ta mère ne m'aime pas. **2** *vt* désapprouver, réprouver (*qn*); trouver mauvais (*un usage etc*).

disapproving [dɪsə'pruːvɪŋ] *adj* (*look, tone etc*) désapprobateur, -trice.

disapprovingly [dɪsə'pruːvɪŋlɪ] *adv* avec désapprobation, d'un air *ou* d'un ton désapprobateur.

disarm [dɪs'ɑːm] **1** *vt* désarmer (*un prisonnier etc*); désamorcer (*une bombe etc*); *Fig* **she quite disarmed us,** elle nous a désarmés. **2** *vi* désarmer.

disarmament [dɪs'ɑːməmənt] *n* désarmement *m*.

disarming [dɪs'ɑːmɪŋ] *adj* (*sourire etc*) désarmant.

disarmingly [dɪs'ɑːmɪŋlɪ] *adv* **he was d. frank,** il montrait une franchise désarmante; **to smile d.,** sourire de façon désarmante.

disarrange [dɪsə'reɪndʒ] *vt* déranger (*qch*), mettre (*qch*) en désordre; **to d. s.o.'s hair,** décoiffer qn; **to d. s.o.'s plans,** déranger *ou* bouleverser les projets de qn.

disarrangement [dɪsə'reɪndʒmənt] *n* dérangement *m*, désajustement *m*.

disarray [dɪsə'reɪ] *n* désarroi *m*, désordre *m*; **in complete d.,** en plein désarroi; (*of troops*) en déroute; **the news threw the company into complete d.,** cette nouvelle a semé la panique dans l'entreprise.

disassociate [dɪsə'səʊʃɪeɪt] *vt* dissocier.

disaster [dɪ'zɑːstər] *n* désastre *m*; (*by shipwreck, fire*) sinistre *m*; **d. area,** région sinistrée; **the president has declared the town a d. area,** le président a déclaré la ville zone sinistrée; *Fig* **the party was an absolute d.,** la soirée était un vrai désastre; **railway d.,** catastrophe *f* ferroviaire; **our journey was a series of disasters,** notre voyage n'a été qu'une suite de malheurs; **they were near the summit when d. struck,** ils avaient presque atteint le sommet quand la catastrophe a eu lieu; **he is heading for d.,** il court à sa perte; **it would be a d.!,** ce serait le désastre!; **d. movie,** film-catastrophe *m*, *pl* films-catastrophes.

disastrous [dɪ'zɑːstrəs] *adj* désastreux.

disastrously [dɪ'zɑːstrəslɪ] *adv* désastreusement.

disavow [dɪsə'vaʊ] *vt* désavouer, renier.

disband [dɪs'bænd] **1** *vt* licencier (*des troupes etc*); dissoudre (*un comité etc*). **2** *vi* (*of troops*) se débander; (*on instructions*) être licencié; (*of committee*) être dissout.

disbar [dɪs'bɑːr] *vt* (**-rr-**) rayer (*un avocat*) du barreau *ou* du tableau de l'ordre.

disbarment [dɪs'bɑːmənt] *n* radiation *f* (*d'un avocat*) du tableau de l'ordre *ou* de la liste du barreau.

disbelief [dɪsbɪ'liːf] *n* incrédulité *f* (**in sth,** à l'égard de qch); **she looked at him in d.,** elle l'a regardé incrédule; **she shook her head in d.,** elle secouait la tête car elle ne pouvait pas y croire.

disbelieve [dɪsbɪ'liːv] *Fml* **1** *vt* ne pas croire, refuser de croire (*qn, qch*). **2** *vi* **to d. in s.o./sth,** ne pas croire à qn/qch.

disbeliever [dɪsbɪ'liːvər] *n* incrédule *mf*.

disbelieving [dɪsbɪ'liːvɪŋ] *adj* (*look*) incrédule.

disbud [dɪs'bʌd] *vt* ébourgeonner (*un arbre fruitier*).

disburse [dɪs'bɜːs] *vt* débourser (*de l'argent*).

disbursement [dɪs'bɜːsmənt] *n* **(a)** (*of money*) déboursement *m*; **(b) disbursements,** (*expenditure*) débours *m*.

disc, *US* **disk** [dɪsk] *n* **(a)** (*record*) disque *m*; *Rad* **d. jockey,** disc-jockey *m*; **(b)** *Comptr* = **DISK**; **(c)** disque *m* (*de la lune etc*); *Tech* disque, plateau *m*; rondelle *f* (*en carton etc*); *Mil etc* **identity** *or* **identification d.,** plaque *f* d'identité; *Aut* **parking d.,** disque de stationnement; *Aut* **d. brakes,** freins *mpl* à disque; *Phot* **d. camera,** appareil *m* photo à disque; **d. film,** disque; **d. wheel,** roue pleine *ou* à voile plein; *Agr* **d. harrow,** pulvériseur *m*; *Agr* **d. plough,** charrue *f* à disques; **(d)** *Anat* disque *m*; **intervertebral d.,** disque intervertébral; *Med* **slipped d.,** hernie discale; **to slip a d.,** se faire une hernie discale.

discard¹ ['dɪskɑːd] *n* **(a)** *Cards* (*at cribbage*) écart *m* (*action ou carte*); (*at bridge*) défausse *f*; **(b)** (*rejected part*) pièce *f* de rebut.

discard² [dɪs'kɑːd] **1** *vt* **(a)** se débarrasser de (*qch*); abandonner (*qn, un projet*); mettre au rebut (*un vêtement*); **(b)** *Cards* (*at cribbage*) écarter (*une carte*); (*at bridge etc*) se défausser de (*une couleur*). **2** *vi* (*at bridge*) se défausser.

discern [dɪ'sɜːn] *vt* distinguer, discerner, percevoir (*qch, qn*); **to d. a distant object,** discerner *ou* reconnaître un objet dans le lointain; **to d. good from bad,** discerner le bien du mal.

discernible [dɪ'sɜːnɪb(ə)l] *adj* perceptible.

discernibly [dɪ'sɜːnɪblɪ] *adv* perceptiblement.

discerning [dɪ'sɜːnɪŋ] *adj* (*person*) éclairé, plein de discernement; (*intelligence*) pénétrant; (*taste*) délicat; **a house/car for the d. buyer,** une maison/une voiture pour celui qui fait la différence *ou* pour l'acheteur avisé.

discernment [dɪ'sɜːnmənt] *n* **(a)** (*ability to distinguish*) discernement *m* (**between ... and ...,** de ... et de ...); **(b)** (*judgment*) discernement *m*, jugement *m*.

discharge¹ ['dɪstʃɑːdʒ] *n* **(a)** *Med* (*release*) renvoi *m* (*d'un malade*); *Jur* mise *f* en liberté, libération *f* (*d'un prisonnier*); acquittement *m* (*d'un accusé*); **d. in bankruptcy,** réhabilitation *f* (d'un failli); **to apply for one's d.,** demander *ou* obtenir sa réhabilitation;

(b) (*dismissal*) renvoi *m* (*d'un employé*); congé *m* (*d'un domestique*); *Mil* (*after active service*) démobilisation *f*; *Mil Nau* (*for unfitness*) réforme *f*; *Mil Nau* **to take one's d.,** prendre son congé;

(c) décharge *f* (*d'artillerie*); départ *m* (*d'une arme à feu*);

(d) (*emission*) décharge *f*, évacuation *f* (*d'eau etc*); décharge, dégagement *m* (*de gaz*); échappement *m* (*de vapeur*); débit *m* (*d'une pompe*); *El* décharge (*d'électricité, d'une pile*); *Med* (*of blood*) perte *f*; (*of pus*) suppuration *f*; (*from factory etc*) eaux usées; **d. pipe,** tuyau *m* de décharge *ou* de débit; **d. pump,** pompe *f* d'extraction *ou* d'épuisement;

(e) (*performance, fulfilment*) accomplissement *m* (*d'un devoir*); paiement *m* (*d'une dette*); **in the d. of his duties,** dans l'exercice de ses fonctions;

(f) déchargement *m* (*d'un navire, d'une cargaison*).

discharge² [dɪs'tʃɑːdʒ] **1** *vt* **(a)** (*release*) renvoyer (*un malade guéri*); libérer, mettre en liberté (*un prisonnier*); acquitter (*un accusé*); décharger, libérer, acquitter (*qn*) (**of an obligation,** d'une obligation); *Jur* réhabiliter, décharger (*un failli*); **he was discharged from hospital yesterday,** il est sorti de l'hôpital hier; **to d. oneself from hospital,** signer sa propre décharge; *Jur* **to d. the jury,** congédier les jurés; **discharged bankrupt,** failli réhabilité;

(b) (*dismiss*) congédier, renvoyer (*un employé*); débaucher (*un ouvrier*); destituer (*un fonctionnaire*); licencier (*des troupes*); congédier, mettre en congé, donner son congé à, désenrôler (*un militaire*); *Mil Nau* (*for unfitness*) réformer (*un homme*); **to be discharged from the force,** être congédié;

(c) décharger, tirer, faire partir (*une arme à feu*); lancer (*un projectile*); *El* décharger (*une pile etc*); **discharged battery,** accu *m* à vide;

(d) (*emit*) dégager (*de la vapeur*); (*of chemical reaction*) dégager (*un gaz*); (*of gland*) sécréter (*des hormones*); (*of reservoir etc*) déverser (*de l'eau*); (*of pump*) débiter (*de l'eau*); **to d. pus,** (*of abscess*) suppurer; **river that discharges its water into a lake,** rivière qui déverse ses eaux dans un lac;

(e) (*perform, fulfil*) accomplir (*un devoir*); s'acquitter de (*son devoir*); liquider, solder (*une dette*); payer (*une amende*); apurer (*un compte, une obligation*);

(f) décharger (*un navire, un réservoir etc*); décharger, débarquer (*une cargaison*); (*of vehicle*) déposer (*des voyageurs*).

2 *vi* **(a)** (*of gun*) partir, se décharger;

(b) (*of abscess, wound*) suppurer; (*of river*) se jeter, déboucher (**into a lake,** dans un lac);

(c) (*of battery*) se décharger.

disciple [dɪ'saɪp(ə)l] *n Rel & Fig* disciple *m*.

disciplinarian [dɪsɪplɪ'neərɪən] *n* **(a)** (*practitioner*) disciplinaire *m*; **he is a strict d.,** il est strict en matière de discipline; **(b)** partisan, -ane d'une forte discipline.

disciplinary ['dɪsɪplɪnərɪ] *adj* disciplinaire; **to take d. action,** (*of an employer*) prendre des mesures disciplinaires.

discipline¹ ['dɪsɪplɪn] *n* **(a)** discipline *f*; **iron d.,** discipline de fer; **to keep d.** (*of teacher*) maintenir la discipline; **to keep children under d.,** soumettre les enfants à la discipline; **(b)** (*branch of learning*) discipline *f*.

discipline² *vt* **(a)** discipliner (*des élèves, des troupes*); (*punish*) punir; **to d. oneself,** se discipliner; **(b)** former (*le caractère*).

disclaim [dɪs'kleɪm] *vt* **(a)** désavouer, dénier (*qch*); **to d. all knowledge of/responsibility for sth,** nier toute connaissance/responsabilité de qch; **(b)** rejeter, renier (*l'autorité de qn*); **(c)** *Jur* se désister de, renoncer à (*un droit etc*).

disclaimer [dɪs'kleɪmər] *n* (a) dénégation *f* (*de responsabilité*); **d. of authorship** (**of a work**), désaveu *m* (d'une œuvre); **to issue a d.**, publier un démenti; (b) *Jur* désistement *m*; renonciation *f* (**of a right**, à un droit).

disclose [dɪs'kləʊz] *vt* (a) (*make known*) divulguer, révéler, dévoiler (*un secret etc*); **she disclosed that she had an illegitimate child**, elle a révélé qu'elle avait un enfant illégitime; (b) (*show*) révéler (*qch*).

disclosure [dɪs'kləʊʒər] *n* (a) révélation *f* (*de sa pensée etc*); divulgation *f* (*d'un secret*); (b) (*fact disclosed*) révélation *f*; (c) mise *f* à découvert (*d'un trésor etc*).

disco ['dɪskəʊ] *n F* discothèque *f*; **d. dancing**, disco *m*.

discolour, *US* **discolor** [dɪs'kʌlər] 1 *vt* ternir, délaver (*un tissu etc*); **to become discoloured**, se décolorer; (*of fabric*) se ternir. 2 *vi* (*of fabric*) se ternir.

discolouration, *US* **discoloration** [dɪskʌlə'reɪʃən] *n* (*of fabric*) ternissure *f*.

discombobulate [dɪskəm'bɒbjʊleɪt] *vt Am F* déconcerter, confondre (*qn*).

discomfit [dɪs'kʌmfɪt] *vt* embarrasser, déconcerter (*qn*).

discomfiture [dɪs'kʌmfɪtʃər] *n* deconfiture *f* (*de qn*), embarras *m*, trouble *m*; **he showed signs of d.**, il avait l'air embarrassé; **much to his d.**, à sa grande déconfiture.

discomfort [dɪs'kʌmfət] *n* (a) manque *m* de confort, inconfort *m*; (b) malaise *m*, gêne *f*; **to be in some d.**, (*of patient*) ne pas être bien; **to cause d.**, (*of stitches, wound etc*) gêner.

discomposure [dɪskəm'pəʊʒər] *n* trouble *m*, agitation *f*; perturbation *f* (*d'esprit*).

disconcert [dɪskən'sɜːt] *vt* déconcerter, troubler (*qn*).

disconcerting [dɪskən'sɜːtɪŋ] *adj* (*news etc*) déconcertant, troublant.

disconcertingly [dɪskən'sɜːtɪŋlɪ] *adv* d'une manière déconcertante.

disconnect [dɪskə'nekt] *vt* (a) *El* déconnecter, débrancher (*un accu, un appareil etc*); mettre (*un accumulateur etc*) hors circuit; *Tel* couper (*la ligne*); *Tel* **I've been disconnected**, (*I cannot continue the call*) on a coupé la communication; (*because I haven't paid the bill*) ils m'ont coupé le téléphone *ou* la ligne; (b) (*separate*) disjoindre, séparer, détacher (**sth from sth**, qch de qch); décrocher (*des wagons*); débrayer, désembrayer (*une machine etc*); **to d. a waterpipe from the main supply**, isoler un tuyau d'eau de l'arrivée.

disconnected [dɪskə'nektɪd] *adj* (a) *El* débranché; *MecE* débrayé; (b) (*speech, style etc*) décousu, sans suite; (*histoire*) sans queue ni tête; (c) détaché, isolé.

disconnecting [dɪskə'nektɪŋ] *n* (a) *El* mise *f* (*d'un accu etc*) hors circuit; débranchement (*d'un appareil*); (b) désunion *f* (*des parties d'une machine*); décrochage *m* (*d'un wagon etc*); débrayage *m*, désembrayage *m* (*d'une machine etc*).

disconnection, disconnexion [dɪskə'nekʃən] *n* (a) = **DISCONNECTING**; (b) séparation *f* (**between**, entre).

disconsolate [dɪs'kɒnsələt] *adj* tout triste; inconsolable.

disconsolately [dɪs'kɒnsələtlɪ] *adv* tristement.

discontent [dɪskən'tent] *n* mécontentement *m*; **general d.**, mécontentement général.

discontented [dɪskən'tentɪd] *adj* mécontent (**with**, de); peu satisfait (*de son sort etc*).

discontinue [dɪskən'tɪnjuː] *vt* (a) **to d. (doing) sth**, discontinuer (de faire) qch; *Com* **that item has been discontinued**, cet article n'est plus suivi; (b) *Jur* abandonner (*un procès*).

discontinuity [dɪskɒntɪ'njuːɪtɪ] *n* discontinuité *f*; manque *m* de suite (*dans les idées*).

discontinuous [dɪskən'tɪnjʊəs] *adj* (*with interruptions*) discontinu; (*intermittent*) intermittent.

discord ['dɪskɔːd] *n* (a) (*disagreement*) discorde *f*, désaccord *m*; (b) (*noise*) bruit discordant; discordance *f*, désaccord *m* (*des voix etc*); (c) *Mus* dissonance *f* (*de deux notes*); accord dissonant.

discordance [dɪs'kɔːdəns] *n* (a) désaccord *m* (*d'opinions etc*); (b) discordance *f* (*des sons*).

discordant [dɪs'kɔːdənt] *adj* (a) **d. opinions**, opinions opposées; (b) (*sound*) discordant; (*voice*) criard; (c) *Mus* dissonant.

discotheque ['dɪskətek] *n* discothèque *f*.

discount¹ ['dɪskaʊnt] *n* (a) *Com* remise *f*; **to sell sth at a d.**, vendre qch au rabais; **cash d.**, escompte *m* de caisse; **trade d.**, remise d'usage; **to allow a d. of 10%**, consentir un rabais de 10%; **d. price**, prix *m* faible; **d. store**, magasin *m* de demi-gros; (b) *Fin* escompte *m*; **d. bank**, banque *f* d'escompte; **to be at a d.**, (*of shares*) être en perte; se trouver en moins-value; *Fig* (*of politeness etc*) être en défaveur.

discount² [dɪs'kaʊnt, 'dɪskaʊnt] *vt* (a) *Fin* escompter; prendre (*un effet*) à l'escompte; (b) (*not consider*) ne pas tenir compte de (*qn, qch*); (*ignore*) faire peu de cas de (*l'avis de qn, un avertissement*); **you must d. half of what he says**, il faut rabattre la moitié de ce qu'il dit; **police have discounted the possibility of suicide**, la police a écarté la thèse du suicide.

discourage [dɪs'kʌrɪdʒ] *vt* (a) (*cause to lose heart*) décourager, abattre (*qn*); **to become discouraged**, se décourager; **don't get discouraged**, ne te décourage pas; (b) (*put difficulties in the way of*) décourager (*un projet, un soupirant etc*); **to d. s.o. from (doing) sth**, décourager qn de (faire) qch; **the hospital discourages smoking in the wards**, l'hôpital n'encourage pas les gens à fumer dans les salles.

discouragement [dɪs'kʌrɪdʒmənt] *n* (a) découragement *m* (*de qn*); (b) désapprobation *f* (*d'un projet*).

discouraging [dɪs'kʌrɪdʒɪŋ] *adj* décourageant; **he was very d. about my chances**, il n'était pas du tout encourageant quant à mes chances.

discourse ['dɪskɔːs] *n Lit* (a) (*conversation*) discours *m*; (b) (*dissertation*) dissertation *f* (**on**, sur).

►**discourse on, discourse upon** *vipo Lit* (a) (*speak of*) discourir sur (*qch*); (b) (*discuss*) parler de, s'entretenir de (*qch*).

discourteous [dɪs'kɜːtɪəs] *adj* discourtois, impoli.

discourteously [dɪs'kɜːtɪəslɪ] *adv* impoliment, d'une façon impolie.

discourtesy [dɪs'kɜːtəsɪ] *n* incivilité *f*, impolitesse *f*.

discover [dɪs'kʌvər] *vt* découvrir (*la vérité, une planète, la cause d'une maladie etc*); découvrir, révéler (*un acteur, une vedette*); **we have discovered a good gardener**, nous avons déniché un bon jardinier; **I discovered too late that ...**, je me suis rendu compte trop tard que ... .

discoverer [dɪs'kʌvərər] *n* découvreur *m* (*de l'Amérique etc*).

discovery [dɪs'kʌvərɪ] *n* découverte *f* (*d'une planète etc*); **the discoveries of Marie Curie**, les découvertes de Marie Curie; **voyage of d.**, voyage *m* d'exploration; **to make a d.**, faire une découverte; **great d.**, grande découverte; (*a find*) trouvaille *f*.

discredit¹ [dɪs'kredɪt] *n* (a) (*suspicion*) doute *m*; **to throw d. on a statement**, mettre en doute une affirmation; (b) discrédit *m* (*de qn, de qch*); **to bring d. on s.o./sth**, jeter le discrédit sur qn/qch, discréditer qn/qch; **to bring sth into d.**, discréditer qch; **to bring d. on oneself**, se discréditer.

discredit² *vt* (a) (*not believe*) ne pas croire (*un bruit*); (*not trust*) mettre en doute (*un bruit*); (b) discréditer (*qn, une opinion*), déconsidérer (*qn*); **his conduct has discredited him with the public**, sa conduite lui a fait perdre la considération du public.

discreditable [dɪs'kredɪtəb(ə)l] *adj* peu digne, peu honorable; **conduct d. to a barrister**, conduite *f* indigne d'un avocat.

discreet [dɪs'kriːt] *adj* discret, -ète; **we have to be d.**, il faut que nous soyons discrets; **she's very d. about her private life**, elle est très discrète sur sa vie privée; **to maintain a d. silence**, observer un silence discret; **a d. smile**, un petit sourire contenu.

discreetly [dɪs'kriːtlɪ] *adv* discrètement, avec discrétion.

discrepancy [dɪs'krepənsɪ] *n* désaccord *m*; **there is a d. between the two stories**, les deux récits ne cadrent pas; *Fin* **there is a d. in the accounts**, les comptes ne sont pas justes; **how do you explain the d.?**, (*in statements, accounts*) comment expliquez-vous la différence?

discrete [dɪs'kriːt] *adj Math etc* discret, ète.

discretion [dɪs'kreʃən] *n* (a) (*liberty of action*) discrétion *f*; **I shall use my own d.**, je ferai comme je jugerai à propos; **to leave sth to s.o.'s d.**, laisser qch à la discrétion de qn; **at the manager's d.**, comme le directeur le décidera; **at your d.**, comme vous voudrez; *Jur* **fine at** *or* **left to the d. of the judge**, amende *f* laissée à l'appréciation du juge; (b) (*good sense*) jugement *m*, prudence *f*; **the age of d.**, l'âge *m* de raison; **d. is the better part of valour**, l'essentiel du courage c'est la prudence; (c) (*tact*) discrétion *f*, réserve *f*; **he is the soul of d.**, il est la discrétion même.

discretionary [dɪs'kreʃən(ə)rɪ] *adj Jur* (*pouvoir*) discrétionnaire.

discriminate [dɪs'krɪmɪneɪt] 1 *vi* distinguer, établir une distinction (**between**, entre); faire la différence (*entre deux choses*); **to d. in favour of s.o.**, faire des distinctions en faveur de qn. 2 *vt* distinguer (**from**, de, d'avec).

▶**discriminate against** *vipo* faire de la discrimination envers (*les moins payés*); **to be (sexually/racially) discriminated against,** être victime de discrimination (sexuelle/raciale).

discriminating [dɪs'krɪmɪneɪtɪŋ] *adj* **(a)** (*person*) plein de discernement, capable de juger; (*buyer*) avisé, averti; (*ear*) fin; **(b)** *Admin* (*duty, tariff*) différentiel.

discrimination [dɪskrɪmɪnɪ'neɪʃən] *n* **(a)** discrimination *f*, distinction *f*; mesures *fpl* discriminatoires; **without d.,** sans discrimination; **race** *or* **racial/sexual d.,** discrimination raciale/sexuelle; **(b)** (*in matters of taste*) jugement *m*, discernement *m*; **(c)** (*of differences etc*) discrimination *f*, discernement *m* (**between ... and ...,** entre ... et) ... .

discriminatory [dɪs'krɪmɪnət(ə)rɪ] *adj Pej* (*loi etc*) discriminatoire.

discursive [dɪs'kɜːsɪv] *adj* (*style etc*) décousu.

discus ['dɪskəs] *n Sp* disque *m*; **d. thrower,** lanceur, -euse de disque; **the d.,** (*event*) le lancer du disque.

discuss [dɪs'kʌs] *vt* discuter, débattre (*un problème etc*); délibérer de (*une question*); (*of book*) traiter de (*un sujet*); **I know they were discussing me,** je sais qu'on parlait de moi; **I refuse to d. it,** je refuse d'en parler; **have you discussed it with your parents?,** est-ce que tu en as discuté avec tes parents?

discussion [dɪs'kʌʃən] *n* discussion *f*; **a subject for d.,** un sujet de discussion; **question under d.,** question en discussion; **after much d. of sth,** après avoir longtemps discuté qch.

disdain[1] [dɪs'deɪn] *n* dédain *m* (**of,** de).

disdain[2] *vt* dédaigner (*qn, qch*); **to d. to do sth,** dédaigner de faire qch.

disdainful [dɪs'deɪnfʊl] *adj* dédaigneux (**of,** de).

disdainfully [dɪs'deɪnfʊlɪ] *adv* dédaigneusement.

disease [dɪ'ziːz] *n* maladie *f*; **to die of a d.,** mourir d'une maladie; **skin d.,** maladie de la peau; **Parkinson's d.,** maladie de Parkinson; *Vet* **foot and mouth d.,** fièvre aphteuse.

diseased [dɪ'ziːzd] *adj* malade; *Fig* (*mind*) défaillant.

disembark [dɪsem'bɑːk] *vt & vi* débarquer (**from,** de).

disembarkation [dɪsembɑː'keɪʃən] *n* débarquement *m*.

disembodied [dɪsɪm'bɒdɪd] *adj* (*esprit*) désincarné.

disembowel [dɪsɪm'baʊəl] *vt* éventrer, éviscérer.

disenchant [dɪsɪn'tʃɑːnt] *vt* désillusionner (*qn*).

disenchanted [dɪsɪn'tʃɑːntɪd] *adj* désillusionné; **she's d. with her job,** son travail la déçoit beaucoup, elle n'a plus d'illusions quant à son travail.

disenchantment [dɪsɪn'tʃɑːntmənt] *n* désillusion *f*.

disengage [dɪsɪn'geɪdʒ] **1** *vt* dégager, débarrasser (**s.o./sth from sth,** qn/qch de qch); *MecE* désengrener (*une roue dentée*); débrayer, désembrayer (*un organe*). **2** *vi* (*of person*) se dégager; *MecE* (*of catch etc*) se déclencher, se défaire; *Mil* (*of troops*) se retirer.

disengaged [dɪsɪn'geɪdʒd] *adj MecE etc* débrayé.

disengagement [dɪsɪn'geɪdʒmənt] *n* **(a)** (*of person*) détachement *m*, dégagement *m* (**from,** de); *MecE* débrayage *m* (*d'un organe*); **(b)** *Pol Mil* désengagement *m*.

disentangle [dɪsɪn'tæŋg(ə)l] *vt* débarrasser (**s.o./sth from sth,** qn/qch de qch); débrouiller (*une ficelle*); dénouer (*une intrigue*); **to d. itself,** (*of rope etc*) se démêler; **to d. oneself from sth,** se libérer de qch; *Fig* (*from scandal etc*) se sortir de qch.

disestablish [dɪsɪs'tæblɪʃ] *vt* séparer (*l'Église*) de l'État.

disestablishment [dɪsɪs'tæblɪʃmənt] *n* **d. of the Church,** séparation *f* de l'Église et de l'État.

disfavour, *US* **disfavor** [dɪs'feɪvər] *n* défaveur *f*; **to regard sth with d.,** être défavorable à qch; **to fall into d.,** tomber en disgrâce; **to fall into d. with s.o.,** perdre le soutien *ou* les faveurs de qn; **at the risk of incurring s.o.'s d.,** au risque de déplaire à qn.

disfigure [dɪs'fɪgər] *vt* défigurer (*qn, une statue etc*); (*of buildings etc*) gâter, abîmer (*le paysage*); **a disfiguring disease,** une maladie qui défigure.

disfigured [dɪs'fɪgəd] *adj* défiguré.

disfigurement [dɪs'fɪgəmənt] *n* défiguration *f* (*de qn, d'une statue*); enlaidissement *m* (*d'un paysage*).

disfranchise [dɪs'fræntʃaɪz] *vt* priver (*qn*) du droit électoral *ou* de ses droits civiques; priver (*un bourg*) de ses droits de représentation.

disgorge [dɪs'gɔːdʒ] **1** *vt* dégorger, rendre (*la nourriture*). **2** *vi* **river that disgorges into ...,** rivière qui se déverse dans ... .

disgrace[1] [dɪs'greɪs] *n* **(a)** disgrâce *f*, défaveur *f*; **to be in d.,** (*out of favour*) être en disgrâce; (*of child*) être en pénitence; **she is in d. with the party,** elle n'est pas en faveur auprès du parti; **(b)** (*shame*) honte *f*, déshonneur *m*; **there is no d. in doing that,** il n'y a pas honte à faire cela; **to bring d. on one's family,** déshonorer sa famille; **to be a d. to one's family,** être la honte de sa famille; faire honte à sa famille; *F* **it's a d.!,** c'est une honte *ou* un scandale!; *F* **you're a d.,** tu me fais honte!; *F* **house prices are a d.,** c'est une honte de vendre les maisons si cher.

disgrace[2] *vt* **(a)** (*esp in passive*) **to be disgraced,** être disgrâcié (**for,** pour); **(b)** (*shame*) déshonorer, faire déshonneur à (*qn*); **to d. oneself,** se couvrir de honte; **you disgraced me in front of all those people,** tu m'as couvert de honte devant tous ces gens.

disgraceful [dɪs'greɪsfʊl] *adj* honteux, infâme; **it's d.,** c'est scandaleux.

disgracefully [dɪs'greɪsfʊlɪ] *adv* honteusement; (*late, rude, expensive*) scandaleusement.

disgruntled [dɪs'grʌnt(ə)ld] *adj* (*discontented*) contrarié, mécontent (**at,** de); (*sulky*) maussade; **what are you looking so d. about?,** pourquoi cet air mécontent?, pourquoi est-ce que tu fais la tête?

disguise[1] [dɪs'gaɪz] *n* **(a)** (*costume*) déguisement *m*; **put this on as a d.,** déguise-toi avec ça; **in d.,** déguisé; **(b)** (*pretence*) feinte *f*; **to throw off all d.,** laisser tomber le masque, lever le masque.

disguise[2] *vt* **(a)** (*change appearance of*) déguiser, travestir (*qn*); déguiser (*la vérité, sa pensée, ses sentiments*); déguiser, contrefaire (*sa voix, son écriture*); **to d. oneself as a clown,** se déguiser en clown; **there is no disguising the fact that ...,** il faut avouer que ...; **(b)** (*hide*) dissimuler (*ses sentiments*); masquer (*une odeur*); **to d. one's disappointment,** cacher sa déception.

disgust[1] [dɪs'gʌst] *n* **(a)** (*loathing*) dégoût profond, répugnance *f* (**at, for, towards,** pour); **(b)** (*distaste*) dégoût *m* (moral); **that kind of attitude fills me with d.,** ce genre d'attitude me dégoûte; **she turned away from him in d.,** dégoûtée, elle s'est détournée de lui.

disgust[2] *vt* **(a)** (*make sick*) dégoûter, donner la nausée à (*qn*); **(b)** (*offend*) indigner; **to be disgusted at** *or* **with** *or* **by sth,** être écœuré de qch; **he is disgusted that ...,** il est indigné *ou* révolté *ou* scandalisé que ... + *sub ou* de ce que ... + *ind*.

disgusting [dɪs'gʌstɪŋ] *adj* dégoûtant, *F* dégueulasse; (*wine etc*) répugnant, *F* dégueulasse; (*noise etc*) épouvantable; **it's d.!,** c'est dégoûtant *ou F* dégueulasse!

disgustingly [dɪs'gʌstɪŋlɪ] *adv* **d. dirty,** d'une saleté répugnante; **d. sweet/bad,** épouvantablement sucré/mauvais; **d. rich/underpaid,** scandaleusement riche/sous-payé; **a joke in d. bad taste,** une blague d'un mauvais goût détestable.

dish[1] [dɪʃ] *n* **(a)** (*for food*) plat *m*; (*earthenware*) terrine *f*; **vegetable d.,** légumier *m*; **butter d.,** beurrier *m*; **to wash** *or* **do the dishes,** faire la vaisselle; **a d. of strawberries,** un plat de fraises; **(b)** *Culin* plat *m* (*de viande, de légumes etc*); mets *m*; **it's not a d. I often make,** ce n'est pas une recette *ou* un plat que je prépare souvent; **(c)** *TV etc* **d. (antenna),** antenne *f* parabolique; **(d)** *F* (*female*) belle fille; (*male*) beau mec; **she's/he's a real d.,** ce qu'elle est belle/ce qu'il est beau; **(e)** (*container*) récipient *m*; *Phot* cuvette *f*; **(f)** (*depression*) creux *m*, dénivellement *m* (*de terrain etc*).

dish[2] *vt F* **to d. s.o.'s chances,** gâcher les chances de qn.

▶**dish out** *vtsep* **(a)** servir (*la viande etc*); **(b)** (*give*) distribuer (*des bonbons*); **to d. out punishment,** (*of boxer*) assener des coups (*à son adversaire*); (*of schoolmaster etc*) punir (*ses élèves*); **to d. out advice,** prodiguer des conseils.

▶**dish up 1** *vtsep* mettre (*la viande etc*) sur un plat; servir (*un plat, un repas*). **2** *vi* servir; **shall I d. up?,** je peux servir?, je sers?

disharmony [dɪs'hɑːmənɪ] *n* **(a)** (*disagreement*) désaccord *m*, manque *m* d'harmonie; **(b)** (*of sound*) dissonance *f*.

dishcloth ['dɪʃklɒθ] *n* (*for washing*) lavette *f*; (*for drying*) torchon à (essuyer la) vaisselle.

dishearten [dɪs'hɑːt(ə)n] *vt* décourager, abattre, rebuter (*qn*); **to become disheartened,** perdre courage.

disheartening [dɪs'hɑːt(ə)nɪŋ] *adj* décourageant.

dishevelled [dɪ'ʃev(ə)ld] *adj* (*person*) échevelé, dépeigné; (avec) les cheveux ébouriffés; **d. hair,** cheveux ébouriffés.

dishmop ['dɪʃmɒp] *n* lavette *f* (à vaisselle).

dishonest [dɪs'ɒnɪst] *adj* malhonnête, peu honnête.

dishonestly [dɪs'ɒnɪstlɪ] *adv* malhonnêtement.

dishonesty [dɪs'ɒnɪstɪ] *n* (*characteristic*) improbité *f*; (*characteristic, action*) malhonnêteté *f*.

dishonour¹, *US* **dishonor** [dɪs'ɒnər] *n* **(a)** (*shame*) déshonneur *m*; **to bring d. on one's family,** déshonorer sa famille; **(b)** (*source of shame*) chose déshonorante; **(c)** *Fin* non-paiement *m* (*d'un chèque*); non-acceptation *f* (*d'un effet de commerce*).
dishonour², *US* **dishonor** *vt* **(a)** (*shame*) déshonorer (*sa famille*); **(b)** *Com* ne pas accepter (*un effet*); refuser de payer (*un effet*); **dishonoured cheque,** chèque impayé.
dishonourable, *US* **dishonorable** [dɪs'ɒnərəb(ə)l] *adj* **(a)** (*person*) sans honneur; **(b)** (*action, conduct*) honteux, indigne; *Mil* **to receive a d. discharge,** être renvoyé de l'armée pour manquement à l'honneur.
dishonourably, *US* **dishonorably** [dɪs'ɒnərəblɪ] *adv* avec déshonneur, de façon déshonorante; *Mil* **to be d. discharged,** être renvoyé de l'armée pour manquement à l'honneur.
dishrag ['dɪʃræg] *n* lavette *f*.
dishtowel ['dɪʃtaʊ(ə)l] *n* torchon à (essuyer la) vaisselle.
dishwasher ['dɪʃwɒʃər] *n* **(a)** (*person*) plongeur, -euse; **(b)** (*machine*) lave-vaisselle *m inv*; *Can* laveuse *f* à vaisselle; **d. safe,** (*glass, plate etc*) garanti lave-vaisselle.
dishwater ['dɪʃwɔːtər] *n* **(a)** eau *f* de vaisselle; **(b)** *Fig F* (*tasteless soup, coffee etc*) lavasse *f*.
dishy ['dɪʃɪ] *adj F* séduisant, sexy; **he's/she's very d.,** ce qu'il est beau/ce qu'elle est belle.
disillusion [dɪsɪ'luːʒən] *vt* désillusionner, désabuser, désenchanter.
disillusioned [dɪsɪ'luːʒənd] *adj* désillusionné, désenchanté; **I'm very d. with her,** elle me déçoit beaucoup; **to become d.,** perdre ses illusions.
disillusionment [dɪsɪ'luːʒənmənt] *n* désillusionnement *m*, désenchantement *m*.
disincentive [dɪsɪn'sentɪv] *n Econ etc* facteur décourageant; **heavy taxation is a d. to expansion,** les taxes élevées découragent toute expansion.
disinclination [dɪsɪŋklɪ'neɪʃən] *n* répugnance *f*, aversion *f* (**for, to,** pour); **to have** *or* **show a d. to do sth,** montrer peu d'empressement à faire qch.
disinclined [dɪsɪn'klaɪnd] *adj* peu disposé, peu enclin (*à faire qch*).
disinfect [dɪsɪn'fekt] *vt* désinfecter (*une plaie*).
disinfectant [dɪsɪn'fektənt] *n* désinfectant *m*.
disinfection [dɪsɪn'fekʃən] *n* désinfection *f*.
disinflation [dɪsɪn'fleɪʃən] *n Econ* désinflation *f*, déflation *f*.
disinformation [dɪsɪnfə'meɪʃən] *n* désinformation *f*; **d. campaign,** campagne *f* de désinformation.
disingenuous [dɪsɪn'dʒenjʊəs] *adj* (*person*) qui manque de franchise, insincère.
disingenuousness [dɪsɪn'dʒenjʊəsnɪs] *n* manque *m* de franchise.
disinherit [dɪsɪn'herɪt] *vt* déshériter (*son fils*).
disintegrate [dɪs'ɪntɪgreɪt] **1** *vi* (*of stone etc*) se désagréger, se désintégrer, s'effriter; *Nucl Phys* se désintégrer. **2** *vt* désagréger.
disintegration [dɪsɪntɪ'greɪʃən] *n* désagrégation *f*, désintégration *f*, effritement *m* (*de la pierre*); *Nucl Phys* désintégration *f*.
disinter [dɪsɪn'tɜːr] *vt* (**-rr-**) déterrer, exhumer (*un mort, des antiquités*).
disinterest [dɪs'ɪnt(ə)rɪst] *n* = **DISINTERESTEDNESS**.
disinterested [dɪs'ɪnt(ə)rɪstɪd] *adj* **(a)** (*unbiassed*) désintéressé; **(b)** *F* (*indifferent*) indifférent (**in,** à).
disinterestedness [dɪs'ɪnt(ə)rɪstɪdnɪs] *n* **(a)** (*of action, observer etc*) désintéressement *m*; **(b)** *F* (*indifference*) indifférence *f* (**in,** à).
disinterment [dɪsɪn'tɜːmənt] *n* déterrement *m*, exhumation *f*.
disinvest [dɪsɪn'vest] *vi* désinvestir (**from, in,** de).
disinvestment [dɪsɪn'vestmənt] *n* (*from a country*) désinvestissement *m*.
disjointed [dɪs'dʒɔɪntɪd] *adj* (*discours*) sans suite, incohérent; (*style*) haché, décousu.
disk [dɪsk] *n* **(a)** Comptr disque *m*; (*floppy*) disquette *f*; **to get sth on d.,** enregistrer qch sur disque *ou* disquette; **d. drive,** lecteur *m* de disques *ou de* disquettes; **d. operating system,** système *m* d'exploitation de disques; **d. controller,** contrôleur *m* de disques; **(b)** *US* = **DISC**.
diskette [dɪs'ket] *n Comptr* disquette *f*.
diskless ['dɪsklɪs] *adj Comptr* sans disque.
dislike¹ [dɪs'laɪk] *n* aversion *f*, dégoût *m*, répugnance *f* (**of, for,** pour); **to take** *or* **conceive a d. to s.o.,** prendre qn en grippe; **to take** *or* **conceive a d. for sth,** prendre qch en horreur.
dislike² *vt* ne pas aimer; **I don't d. him,** il ne me déplaît pas; **to d. doing sth,** détester faire qch.
dislocate ['dɪsləkeɪt] *vt* **(a)** *Med* luxer, démettre, disloquer (*un membre*); **to d. one's jaw,** se décrocher la mâchoire; **(b)** désorganiser (*les affaires*); bouleverser (*un projet*).
dislocation [dɪslə'keɪʃən] *n* **(a)** *Med* luxation *f*, déboîtement *m*, dislocation *f* (*d'un membre*); **(b)** désorganisation *f* (*des affaires*); bouleversement *m* (*d'un projet etc*).
dislodge [dɪs'lɒdʒ] *vt* **(a)** (*remove*) déloger, débusquer (*l'ennemi*) (**from,** de); **(b)** (*move*) détacher; **several bricks had become dislodged,** plusieurs briques s'étaient détachées.
disloyal [dɪs'lɔɪəl] *adj* infidèle (*à son roi, à l'amitié*); (*behaviour*) déloyal, -aux.
disloyalty [dɪs'lɔɪəltɪ] *n* infidélité *f*, déloyauté *f*.
dismal ['dɪzməl] *adj* lugubre, sombre, triste; (*paysage, avenir*) morne; (*échec*) lamentable; **what d. weather,** quel temps maussade; **my prospects look d.,** (*of doing sth*) mes chances sont maigres.
dismally ['dɪzməlɪ] *adv* tristement; **to fail d.,** échouer lamentablement.
dismantle [dɪs'mænt(ə)l] *vt* démonter (*une machine, un fusil etc*); démanteler (*une forteresse*).
dismast [dɪs'mɑːst] *vt Nau* démâter (*un navire*).
dismay¹ [dɪs'meɪ] *n* consternation *f*; **in d.,** consterné, atterré; **to my d.,** à ma grande consternation; **to be filled with d.,** être consterné *ou* effaré.
dismay² *vt* consterner; **we were dismayed at** *or* **by the news,** cette nouvelle nous jeta dans la consternation.
dismember [dɪs'membər] *vt* démembrer.
dismemberment [dɪs'membəmənt] *n* démembrement *m*.
dismiss [dɪs'mɪs] *vt* **(a)** congédier, renvoyer (*un employé*); chasser (*un domestique*); révoquer (*un fonctionnaire*); **to be dismissed,** recevoir son congé; *Mil* **to d. s.o. from the service,** (*pour un militaire de carrière*) rayer qn des cadres de l'armée; (*pour le service militaire*) réformer qn;
(b) (*send away*) congédier (aimablement) (*qn*); donner à (*qn*) la permission de se retirer; congédier, éconduire (*un importun etc*); dissoudre (*une assemblée*); *Mil* **to d. a parade,** faire rompre les rangs (aux troupes); *Mil* **d.!,** rompez (les rangs)!; *Cr* **dismissed for ten,** (*of batsman*) mis hors jeu quand il n'a marqué que dix points;
(c) (*cease or refuse to consider*) quitter, abandonner (*un sujet de conversation etc*); **to d. sth from one's mind,** chasser *ou* éloigner qch de ses pensées; **to d. a threat,** ne tenir aucun compte d'une menace;
(d) (*reject*) écarter (*une proposition*); *Jur* rejeter (*une demande, un appel*); **to d. a case,** (*of judge*) rendre une fin de non-recevoir; **to d. a charge,** rendre une ordonnance de non-lieu.
dismissal [dɪs'mɪs(ə)l] *n* **(a)** congédiement *m*, renvoi *m* (*d'un employé*); révocation *f* (*d'un fonctionnaire*); **(b)** *Jur* fin *f* de non-recevoir; rejet *m* (*d'une demande, d'un appel*).
dismount [dɪs'maʊnt] **1** *vi* descendre (*de cheval, de bicyclette*). **2** *vt* **(a)** démonter, désarçonner (*un cavalier*); **(b)** démonter (*un canon, une machine*).
disobedience [dɪsə'biːdɪəns] *n* désobéissance *f* (**to s.o.,** à qn); **civil d.,** résistance passive.
disobedient [dɪsə'biːdɪənt] *adj* (*dog, child*) désobéissant; **to be d. to s.o.,** désobéir à qn; **that was very d. of you,** c'était très désobéissant de ta part.
disobey [dɪsə'beɪ] *vt* désobéir (*à qn, à un ordre*); enfreindre (*un ordre, la loi*).
disobliging [dɪsə'blaɪdʒɪŋ] *adj* désobligeant (**to,** envers).
disorder¹ [dɪs'ɔːdər] *n* **(a)** (*confusion*) désordre *m*, confusion *f*; **in d.,** en désordre; **they fled in d.,** ils se sont enfuis en débandade; **(b)** (*unrest*) désordre *m*, trouble *m*; **serious disorders have broken out,** de graves désordres ont éclaté; **(c)** *Med* trouble(s) *m(pl)*; **heart d.,** troubles cardiaques; **nervous d.,** troubles nerveux, affection nerveuse; **personality d.,** trouble caractériel *ou* de la personnalité.
disorder² *vt* déranger; mettre (*qch*) en désordre.
disordered [dɪs'ɔːdəd] *adj* (*esprit*) malade; (*intestin*) dérangé.
disorderliness [dɪs'ɔːdəlɪnɪs] *n* **(a)** (*untidiness*) désordre *m*; **(b)** (*of mob*) turbulence *f*; **(c)** *Jur* conduite *f* contraire aux bonnes mœurs.
disorderly [dɪs'ɔːdəlɪ] *adj* **(a)** (*untidy*) (*person*) qui manque d'ordre; (*person, work etc*) désordonné; (*room etc*) en désordre; **(b)** (*mob etc*) turbulent, tumultueux; **(c)** (*person, behaviour*) désordonné, déréglé; **to lead a d. life,** vivre dans le dérèglement; *Jur* **d. conduct,** conduite *f* contraire aux bonnes mœurs; *Jur* **to charge s.o. with being drunk and d.,** inculper qn pour ivresse et conduite

contraire aux bonnes mœurs; *Jur* **d. house,** (*brothel*) maison *f* de débauche; (*gaming house*) maison de jeu.
disorganization [dɪsɔːgənaɪ'zeɪʃən] *n* désorganisation *f*.
disorganize [dɪs'ɔːgənaɪz] *vt* désorganiser; **to become disorganized,** se désorganiser; **he's very disorganized,** il est très désorganisé.
disorientate [dɪs'ɔːrɪənteɪt] , *US* **disorient** [dɪs'ɔːrɪənt] *vt* désorienter; **to be disorient(at)ed,** être désorienté.
disorientation [dɪsɔːrɪən'teɪʃən] *n* désorientation *f*.
disown [dɪs'əʊn] *vt* désavouer (*une œuvre*); renier (*qn*); **to d. a child,** refuser de reconnaître la paternité.
disparage [dɪs'pærɪdʒ] *vt* déprécier, décrier, dénigrer (*qn, qch*).
disparagement [dɪs'pærɪdʒmənt] *n* dénigrement *m*, dépréciation *f*.
disparaging [dɪs'pærɪdʒɪŋ] *adj* (*terme*) de dénigrement; **d. remark,** remarque désobligeante.
disparagingly [dɪs'pærɪdʒɪŋlɪ] *adv* (*to say, look at*) d'un ton *ou* d'un air méprisant; **to speak d. of s.o.,** parler de qn en termes de mépris.
disparate ['dɪspərɪt] *adj* disparate.
disparity [dɪs'pærɪtɪ] *n* **(a)** (*difference*) inégalité *f*, disconvenance *f* (**of,** de); **d. of age,** différence *f* d'âge; **the d. in their ages,** la différence d'âge entre eux; **(b)** (*dissimilarity*) disparité *f*, écart *m* (**between,** entre).
dispassionate [dɪs'pæʃənət] *adj* **(a)** (*calm*) sans passion, dépassionné, calme; **(b)** (*impartial*) impartial, -aux; **to take a d. view of things,** juger impartialement les choses.
dispassionately [dɪs'pæʃənətlɪ] *adv* (*see adj*) **(a)** sans passion; **(b)** sans parti pris, impartialement.
dispatch¹ [dɪs'pætʃ] *n* **(a)** expédition *f*, envoi *m* (*de qch*); **d. note,** bulletin *m ou* bordereau *m* d'expédition; **(b)** (*speed*) promptitude *f*; **with d.,** promptement; **(c)** (*message*) dépêche *f* (*diplomatique etc*); *Admin etc* **d. box,** boîte *f* à documents; **d. case,** serviette *f* (en cuir); *Mil* **d. rider,** estafette *f*; *Mil etc* **to be mentioned in dispatches,** être cité à l'ordre (du jour); **(d)** expédition *f* (*d'une affaire*); **(e)** exécution *f* (*d'un condamné*).
dispatch² *vt* **(a)** dépêcher (*un courrier*); expédier (*une lettre*); envoyer (*qn*); **(b)** *F* expédier (*un repas*); **(c)** (*kill*) achever (*un animal*); expédier (*qn*) dans l'autre monde.
dispatcher [dɪs'pætʃər] *n* **(a)** *Com etc* expéditeur, -trice; **(b)** régulateur *m*, contrôleur *m* (*du mouvement des trains, des avions etc*).
dispel [dɪs'pel] *vt* **(-ll-)** chasser, dissiper (*un doute, les nuages, une peur*).
dispensable [dɪs'pensəb(ə)l] *adj* **(a)** dont on peut se passer; **(b)** *Rel* (*vœu etc*) dispensable.
dispensary [dɪs'pensərɪ] *n* **(a)** officine *f* (*d'une pharmacie*); **(b)** pharmacie *f*.
dispensation [dɪspen'seɪʃən] *n* **(a)** *Jur Rel* **d. from sth,** dispense *f* de qch; **d. from fasting,** dispense du jeûne; **(b)** dispensation *f*, distribution *f* (*des récompenses, des aumônes*); **(c)** décret *m*, arrêt *m* (*de la Providence*); **under the present d.,** étant donné le règlement actuel.
dispense [dɪs'pens] *vt* **(a)** (*distribute, give out*) dispenser, distribuer (*des aumônes*); administrer, rendre (*la justice*); **(b)** *Pharm* préparer (*des médicaments*); exécuter (*une ordonnance*); **dispensing chemist,** pharmacien diplômé; **d. optician,** = opticien ne pouvant fournir que des lunettes (et non pas des lentilles de contact); **d. machine,** distributeur *m*; **(c)** dispenser, exempter (*qn*) (**from doing,** de faire); *Rel* **to d. s.o. from fasting,** dispenser qn du jeûne.
▶**dispense with** *vipo* se passer de (*qn, qch*); *Euph* **we've dispensed with her services,** nous nous sommes passés de ses services.
dispenser [dɪs'pensər] *n* **(a)** *Pharm* pharmacien, -ienne; **(b)** (*machine*) distributeur *m* (*de cigarettes, de bonbons etc*); **(c)** *Rel* dispensateur, -trice, distributeur, -trice (*d'aumônes etc*).
dispensing [dɪs'pensɪŋ] *n* **(a)** dispensation *f*, distribution *f* (*des aumônes etc*); **(b)** *Pharm* préparation *f* (*des médicaments*); *Br* **d. chemist,** pharmacie *f*.
dispersal [dɪs'pɜːs(ə)l] *n* dispersion *f* (*de troupes, de la foule, de la pollution etc*).
dispersant [dɪs'pɜːsənt] *n* dispersant *m*.
disperse¹ [dɪs'pɜːs] **1** *vt* **(a)** (*scatter*) disperser, éparpiller (*une foule*); dissiper, chasser (*les nuages*); *Med* résoudre, dissoudre (*une tumeur*); (*of prism etc*) disperser (*la lumière*); **(b)** (*arrange*) disperser (*ses troupes etc*). **2** *vi* (*of crowd*) se disperser, s'éparpiller; (*of light*) se disperser; (*of darkness, clouds*) se dissiper.
dispersion [dɪs'pɜːʃən] *n* dispersion *f*.
Dispersion [dɪs'pɜːʃən] *n Jew Rel* **the D.,** la Diaspora.
dispirit [dɪs'pɪrɪt] *vt* décourager, abattre (*qn*).
dispirited [dɪs'pɪrɪtɪd] *adj* découragé, abattu.
displace [dɪs'pleɪs] *vt* **(a)** (*shift*) déplacer (*qch*); **weight of water displaced by a body,** poids de l'eau déplacée par un corps; *Pol* **displaced persons,** personnes déplacées; **to d. a bone,** se déplacer un os; **(b)** (*supplant*) remplacer (**by,** par); évincer (*qn*); **to d. s.o. (in s.o.'s affections),** supplanter qn.
displacement [dɪs'pleɪsmənt] *n* **(a)** (*of water*) déplacement *m*; *Nau* déplacement (*d'un navire*); **volumetric d.,** déplacement volumétrique; *Nau* **ship of 5,000 tons d.,** navire *m* d'un déplacement de 5 000 tonnes; **(b) d. of A by B,** remplacement *m* de A par B.
display¹ [dɪs'pleɪ] *n* **(a)** étalage *m*, exposition *f* (*de marchandises*); **for d. only,** (*on book etc*) en présentation uniquement; **the treasures are on d. in the local museum,** les trésors sont exposés dans le musée local; **on d. is merchandise from all over the world,** des produits du monde entier sont exposés; **you'll have a fine d. of flowers by next year,** vous aurez un beau déploiement de fleurs d'ici l'année prochaine; **d. copy,** (*of book etc*) exemplaire *m* de présentation; *Com* **d. rack** *or* **unit,** présentoir *m*; **d. pack,** présentoir *m*; **d. staff,** étalagistes *mpl*; **(b)** *esp Pej* affichage *m*, étalage *m* (*de sentiments, d'opinions etc*); démonstration *f* (*de force*); étalage (*de luxe*); **to be fond of d.,** aimer l'ostentation; **(c)** (*event*) manifestation *f* (*artistique etc*); **air d.,** fête *f* aéronautique; **(d)** *Typ* lignes *fpl* en vedette; **d. ad(vertisement),** grande annonce; **(e)** *Electron etc* écran *m*; (*text appearing*) affichage *m*; **(f)** (*of bird*) parade *f*.
display² **1** *vt* **(a)** étaler, exposer (*des marchandises*); afficher (*un avis*); **(b)** (*show*) afficher, déployer, étaler, manifester (*un sentiment, une opinion etc*); **to d. courage,** faire preuve de courage; **(c)** *Typ* mettre (*une ligne etc*) en vedette; **(d)** *Electron etc* afficher, visualiser. **2** *vi* (*of bird*) parader.
displease [dɪs'pliːz] *vt* fâcher, contrarier (*qn*); **to be displeased at** *or* **with s.o./sth,** être mécontent de qn/de qch; être fâché contre qn/de qch.
displeasing [dɪs'pliːzɪŋ] *adj* déplaisant, désagréable (**to,** à).
displeasure [dɪs'pleʒər] *n* déplaisir *m*; **to incur s.o.'s d.,** s'attirer le mécontentement de qn.
disport [dɪs'pɔːt] *vt & vi Old-fashioned* **to d. (oneself),** s'amuser, s'ébattre, folâtrer.
disposable [dɪs'pəʊzəb(ə)l] **1** *adj* (a) (*serviettes, briquet etc*) à jeter, jetable; (*bottle*) nonconsigné; **d.** *Br* **nappy** *or* *Am* **diaper,** couche *f* jetable; **d. wrapping,** emballage perdu; **(b)** (*fonds, revenu etc*) disponible. **2** *n F* couche *f* jetable.
disposal [dɪs'pəʊz(ə)l] *n* **(a)** mise *f* au rebut; évacuation *f* (*des ordures etc*); **(refuse) d. plant,** dépotoir *m*; **(b) to be at s.o.'s d.,** être à la disposition de qn; **I am entirely at your d.,** je suis à votre entière disposition; **to put sth at s.o.'s d.,** mettre qch à la disposition de qn; **to have a boat at one's d.,** avoir un bateau à sa disposition; **(c)** vente *f* (*de biens*); **for d.,** à vendre; *Jur* **d. of property,** dispositions *fpl* testamentaires; **(d)** arrangement *m* (*des objets*).
dispose [dɪs'pəʊz] **1** *vt* **(a)** (*make willing*) disposer, porter (**s.o. to (do) sth,** qn à (faire) qch); **I am not disposed to help him,** je ne suis pas disposé à l'aider; **(b)** disposer, arranger (*des objets*). **2** *vi Prov* **man proposes, God disposes,** l'homme propose et Dieu dispose.
▶**dispose of** *vipo* **(a)** (*get rid of*) se débarrasser de (*qch, qn*); mettre (*qch*) au rebut; **(b)** *Com* écouler (*des marchandises*); vendre (*un article*); céder (*son fonds, un bail*); **(c)** (*settle*) régler (*une affaire*); **(d)** *F* (*kill*) liquider (*qn*); (*beat*) mettre la pâtée à (*un adversaire*); **(e)** (*use*) employer (*son temps*); **(f)** (*have at one's disposal*) disposer de.
disposed [dɪ'spəʊzd] *adj* **d. to sth,** enclin *ou* porté à qch.
-disposed [dɪ'spəʊzd] *suff* **well/ill-d.,** bien/mal intentionné (**to, towards,** envers, pour).
disposition [dɪspə'zɪʃən] *n* **(a)** (*temperament*) nature *f*, humeur *f*; **child of a pleasant d.,** enfant *mf* d'un bon naturel; **she is of a kindly d.,** c'est une bonne nature; **(b)** (*arrangement*) disposition *f*, arrangement *m*; **(c)** *Jur* disposition *f* (*testamentaire*); **(d)** (*inclination*) désir *m*, intention *f* (*de faire qch*); inclination *f* (*à faire qch*); (*tendency*) penchant *m*, tendance *f* (**to sth,** à qch; **to do sth,** à faire qch).
dispossess [dɪspə'zes] *vt* déposséder (*qn*); (*of house, land*) exproprier (*qn*); **to d. s.o. of sth,** déposséder *ou Jur* dessaisir qn de qch.
dispossession [dɪspə'zeʃən] *n* dépossession *f*; *Jur* dessaisissement *m*; (*of house, land*) expropriation *f*.
disproportion [dɪsprə'pɔːʃən] *n* disproportion *f*.

disproportionate [dɪsprəˈpɔːʃənət] *adj* disproportionné (**to,** à).
disproportionately [dɪsprəˈpɔːʃənətlɪ] *adv* d'une façon disproportionnée.
disprove [dɪsˈpruːv] *vt* (*pp* **disproved,** *Jur* **disproven** [dɪsˈprəʊv(ə)n]) réfuter (*un dire*); démontrer la fausseté de (*un dire, un hypothèse*).
disputable [dɪsˈpjuːtəb(ə)l] *adj* contestable, discutable.
disputation [dɪspjʊˈteɪʃən] *n* **(a)** (*debate*) discussion *f* (*d'un sujet*); **(b)** (*argument*) controverse *f*, débat *m*.
dispute[1] [ˈdɪspjʊt, dɪsˈpjuːt] *n* **(a)** (*debate*) contestation *f*, controverse *f*; **the matter in d.,** l'affaire contestée *ou* en contestation; **the fact is beyond d.,** le fait est incontestable; **(b)** (*argument*) querelle *f*, dispute *f* (**as to,** relative à); **to settle a d.,** régler une querelle; **industrial d.,** conflit *m* du travail; **to be in d.,** être en conflit.
dispute[2] [dɪsˈpjuːt] **1** *vi* se disputer, se quereller. **2** *vt* discuter (*une question*); contester (*une affirmation etc*); **to d. (the possession of) sth with s.o.,** disputer qch à qn; **I'm not disputing that,** je ne conteste pas cela, je ne dis pas le contraire.
disqualification [dɪskwɒlɪfɪˈkeɪʃən] *n* **(a)** mise *f* en état d'incapacité; *Sp* disqualification *f* (*d'un concours*); **that resulted in his immediate d.,** cela a eu pour conséquence sa disqualification immédiate; **(b)** (*disqualifying factor*) cause *f* d'incapacité (**for,** à); **(c)** *Jur* inhabilité *f* (**to act,** à agir).
disqualify [dɪsˈkwɒlɪfaɪ] *vt* **(a)** rendre incapable (**for sth,** de faire qch); *Sp* disqualifier (*un joueur*); **(b)** *Jur* frapper (*qn*) d'incapacité; **disqualified from making a will,** inhabile à tester; **to be disqualified from a competition,** être exclu d'un concours; **to d. s.o. from driving,** retirer le permis de conduire à qn.
disquiet[1] [dɪsˈkwaɪət] *n Lit* inquiétude *f*; **his absence caused me some d.,** son absence m'a causé de l'inquiétude.
disquiet[2] *vt* inquiéter, troubler.
disquieting [dɪsˈkwaɪətɪŋ] *adj* (*news, development etc*) inquiétant, troublant.
disregard[1] [dɪsrɪˈgɑːd] *n* indifférence *f* (**of, for,** a l'égard de); inobservation *f* (*de la loi*).
disregard[2] *vt* ne tenir aucun compte de, ne pas faire attention à (*qn, qch*); négliger (*qn, qch*); enfreindre (*un ordre*); *Mil* manquer à (*la consigne*); **to d. a warning,** ne pas tenir compte d'un avertissement; **I'll d. what you just said,** je ne tiendrai pas compte de ce que vous venez de dire.
disremember [dɪsrɪˈmembər] *vt US* ne pas se souvenir de (*qn, qch*).
disrepair [dɪsrɪˈpeər] *n* (*no pl*) délabrement *m*; **to fall into d.,** tomber en ruine, se délabrer; **the building is in d.,** le bâtiment est délabré.
disreputable [dɪsˈrepjʊtəb(ə)l] *adj* **(a)** (*action*) déshonorant, peu honorable; **(b)** (*person*) de mauvaise réputation; **d. neighbourhood,** (*run-down*) quartier sordide; (*with a bad reputation*) quartier mal famé; **she has some d. friends,** elle a des amis pas très fréquentables; **a d. old jacket/hat/***etc*, une vieille veste/vieux chapeau minable.
disreputably [dɪsˈrepjʊtəblɪ] *adv* honteusement; d'une façon peu honorable.
disrepute [dɪsrɪˈpjuːt] *n* déshonneur *m*; mauvaise réputation; **to bring s.o. into d.,** ruiner la réputation de qn; **to bring the law into d.,** discréditer la loi.
disrespect [dɪsrɪˈspekt] *n* irrévérence *f*, irrespect *m*, manque *m* de respect (**for,** envers); **to treat s.o./sth with d.,** manquer de respect à qn/pour qch; **I mean no d.,** je ne veux pas paraître irrespectueux.
disrespectful [dɪsrɪˈspektfʊl] *adj* irrespectueux, irrévérencieux; **to be d. to s.o.,** manquer de respect à qn.
disrespectfully [dɪsrɪˈspektfʊlɪ] *adv* (*parler de qn*) sans respect.
disrobe [dɪsˈrəʊb] **1** *vt* aider (*un magistrat, un prêtre*) à se dévêtir de sa robe. **2** *vi* (*of judge, clergyman etc*) se dévêtir de sa robe; (*of person*) se déshabiller.
disrupt [dɪsˈrʌpt] *vt* désorganiser (*une administration, un plan etc*); interrompre (*une séance, la circulation etc*).
disruption [dɪsˈrʌpʃən] *n* rupture *f*; interruption *f* (*d'une séance, de la circulation etc*).
disruptive [dɪsˈrʌptɪv] *adj* (*élément*) perturbateur; (*élève*) turbulent; **d. strike,** grève paralysante.
dissatisfaction [dɪsætɪsˈfækʃən] *n* insatisfaction *f*, mécontentement *m* (**with,** de).
dissatisfied [dɪˈsætɪsfaɪd] *adj* mécontent, peu satisfait (**with,** de); **I am very d. with the service I received,** je suis très mécontent *ou* je ne suis pas du tout satisfait du service que j'ai reçu.
dissatisfy [dɪˈsætɪsfaɪ] *vt* mécontenter.
dissect [dɪˈsekt, daɪ-] *vt* disséquer (*un animal, une plante*); éplucher (*un livre*).
dissecting [dɪˈsektɪŋ, daɪ-] *n* **d. knife,** scalpel *m*.
dissection [dɪˈsekʃən, daɪ-] *n* dissection *f*.
dissemble [dɪˈsemb(ə)l] **1** *vt* dissimuler, cacher (*ses sentiments etc*). **2** *vi* agir avec dissimulation; déguiser sa pensée.
disseminate [dɪˈsemɪneɪt] *vt* disséminer, propager, répandre (*des opinions etc*); diffuser (*l'information*).
disseminated [dɪˈsemɪneɪtɪd] *adj Med* **d. sclerosis,** sclérose *f* en plaques.
dissemination [dɪsemɪˈneɪʃən] *n* (*of opinions*) dissémination *f*, propagation *f*; (*of information*) diffusion *f*.
dissension [dɪˈsenʃən] *n* dissension *f*; **to sow d.,** semer la dissension *ou* le désaccord.
dissent[1] [dɪˈsent] *n* **(a)** (*opposition*) dissentiment *m*; avis *m* contraire; **(b)** *Rel* dissidence *f*.
dissent[2] *vi* **(a)** différer (**from s.o. about sth,** de qn sur qch); **to d. from a report,** avoir une opinion contraire à celle exprimée dans un rapport; **(b)** *Rel* être dissident.
dissenter [dɪˈsentər] *n* **(a)** dissident, -ente; **(b)** *Rel* personne *f* qui n'appartient pas à l'Église anglicane.
dissenting [dɪˈsentɪŋ] *adj* (*opinion, voice*) dissident.
dissertation [dɪsəˈteɪʃən] *n* dissertation *f*.
disservice [dɪˈsɜːvɪs] *n* mauvais service rendu; **to do s.o. a d.,** rendre un mauvais service à qn; **to do oneself a d.,** se faire du tort.
dissidence [ˈdɪsɪdəns] *n Pol* dissidence *f*; (*disagreement*) désaccord *m*.
dissident [ˈdɪsɪdənt] *adj & n* dissident, -ente.
dissimilar [dɪˈsɪmɪlər] *adj* dissemblable (**to,** à, de); **they are not d.,** ils se ressemblent (beaucoup).
dissimilarity [dɪsɪmɪˈlærɪtɪ] *n* dissemblance *f*, dissimilarité *f* (**to,** de; **between,** entre).
dissimulate [dɪˈsɪmjʊleɪt] **1** *vt* dissimuler. **2** *vi* dissimuler, feindre; cacher ses pensées.
dissimulation [dɪsɪmjʊˈleɪʃən] *n* dissimulation *f*.
dissipate [ˈdɪsɪpeɪt] **1** *vt* dissiper (*les nuages etc*); gaspiller (*une fortune*). **2** *vi* (*of cloud, heat etc*) se dissiper; *Phys* (*of energy*) se dégrader.
dissipated [ˈdɪsɪpeɪtɪd] *adj* (*vie*) dissipé; **to be d.,** vivre dans la dissipation.
dissipation [dɪsɪˈpeɪʃən] *n* **(a)** dissipation *f* (*du brouillard, de ses biens*); gaspillage *m* (*d'une fortune*); **(b)** (*of person*) vie désordonnée.
dissociate [dɪˈsəʊsɪeɪt] **1** *vt* **(a)** dissocier (**from,** de); **to d. oneself from s.o./a policy,** se désolidariser de qn/d'une politique; **(b)** *Ch* dissocier (*un composé etc*). **2** *vi Ch* se dissocier.
dissociation [dɪsəʊsɪˈeɪʃən] *n* dissociation *f*.
dissolute [ˈdɪsəluːt] *adj* (*person*) dissolu, débauché; (*conduite*) licencieux; (*vie*) déréglé; **to lead a d. life,** vivre dans la débauche.
dissoluteness [ˈdɪsəluːtnɪs] *n* débauche *f*.
dissolution [dɪsəˈluːʃən] *n* dissolution *f* (*d'un mariage etc*).
dissolve[1] [dɪˈzɒlv] *n Cin TV* fondu *m*, enchaîné *m*.
dissolve[2] **1** *vt* (faire) dissoudre, faire fondre (*du sucre*); dissiper (*un nuage, une illusion*); dissoudre (*un mariage, une association, un parlement*). **2** *vi* **(a)** (*of sugar*) se dissoudre, fondre; (*of cloud, illusion, opposition*) se dissiper; (*of crowd*) se disperser; (*of Parliament*) se dissoudre; **to d. into tears,** fondre en larmes; **to d. into thin air,** partir *ou* s'en aller en fumée; **(b)** *Cin TV* enchaîner.
dissonance [ˈdɪsənəns] *n Mus* dissonance *f*.
dissonant [ˈdɪsənənt] *adj Mus* dissonant.
dissuade [dɪˈsweɪd] *vt* **to d. s.o. from (doing) sth,** dissuader qn de (faire) qch.
dissuasion [dɪˈsweɪʒən] *n* dissuasion *f* (**from,** de).
distaff [ˈdɪstɑːf] *n* quenouille *f*; *Fig* **the d. side,** le côté maternel (*d'une famille*).
distance[1] [ˈdɪstəns] *n* **(a)** distance *f*; **at a d. of ...,** à une distance de ...; **within five minutes walking d.,** à cinq minutes de marche; **a short d. away,** tout près, à deux pas; **it is quite a d. (away),** (*of house etc*) ce n'est pas tout près; **to see sth from a d.,** voir qch de loin; **to see sth in the d.,** voir qch au loin; *Mil* **within striking d.,** (*of target*) à portée de fusil *ou* de canon *etc*; (*of own forces*) à portée de l'ennemi; **in the middle d.,** au second plan; **(b)** distance *f* (*entre deux endroits*); distance, intervalle *m* (*qui sépare deux choses*); **to go part of the d. on foot,** faire une partie du trajet à pied; **to keep s.o. at a d.,** tenir qn à distance; **at this d. in time,** à cet intervalle de temps; **(c)** *Sp* parcours *m*; durée *f* (*d'un match de boxe*); **long-/medium-d. race/runner,** course *f*/coureur *m* de fond/de

demi-fond; *Sp Boxing Fig* **to go** *or* **last** *or* **stay the d.,** tenir la distance; **the fight went the d.,** le combat est allé jusqu'à la limite;

(d) (*of person*) réserve *f*, air distant; **to keep one's d., to keep at a d.,** (*from sth dangerous, infectious*) garder ses distances, ne pas s'approcher; *Fig* se tenir sur la réserve, garder ses distances; **to keep s.o. at a d.,** se tenir sur la réserve avec qn, garder la distance avec qn.

distance² *vt* distancer (*un concurrent*); **to d. oneself from s.o.,** prendre ses distances à l'égard de qn.

distant ['dɪstənt] *adj* **(a)** (*endroit, objet, parent*) éloigné; (*pays*) lointain; (*in time*) éloigné; (*souvenir*) lointain; (*ressemblance etc*) faible, vague; *Rail* **d. signal,** signal *m* à distance; **d. look,** regard perdu dans le vague; **in the d. future,** dans un avenir lointain; **in the not too d. future,** dans un futur proche; **in the dim and d. past,** dans le temps, il y a bien longtemps; **(b)** (*person, manner*) réservé, distant; **to be d. with s.o.,** tenir qn à distance, se montrer réservé avec qn; **(c)** *Old-fashioned* **three miles d.,** à trois mil(l)es de distance; **not far d. from ...,** à peu de distance de ... .

distantly ['dɪstəntlɪ] *adv* **(a)** de loin; **d. related,** d'une parenté éloignée; **(b)** (*to treat s.o.*) avec réserve.

distaste [dɪs'teɪst] *n* dégoût *m* (**for,** de), répugnance *f* (**for,** pour).

distasteful [dɪs'teɪstfʊl] *adj* (*task etc*) désagréable, déplaisant; (*joke*) de mauvais goût.

distastefulness [dɪs'teɪstfʊlnɪs] *n* caractère désagréable *ou* répugnant (*d'une tâche etc*); (*of joke*) mauvais goût.

distemper¹ [dɪs'tempər] *n Vet* maladie *f* des jeunes chiens.

distemper² *n Art etc* détrempe *f*.

distemper³ *vt* badigeonner (*un mur*) en couleur; *Art* peindre (*un tableau, un mur*).

distend [dɪs'tend] **1** *vt* gonfler (*les joues*); dilater (*les narines*); distendre, ballonner (*l'estomac*). **2** *vi* (*of cheeks*) se gonfler; (*of nostrils*) se dilater; (*of stomach*) se ballonner, se distendre.

distension [dɪs'tenʃən] *n* dilatation *f*, distension *f*.

distich ['dɪstɪk] *n* (*couplet*) distique *m*.

distil, *US* **distill** [dɪs'tɪl] *v* **(-ll-) 1** *vt Ch Ind* distiller (*de l'eau etc*). **2** *vi Ch Ind* se distiller, passer; (*of liquid, secretion etc*) distiller (**from,** de).

►**distil off, distil out** *vtsep Ch Ind* chasser (*qch*) par la distillation.

distillate ['dɪstɪleɪt] *n Ch Ind* produit *m* de la distillation.

distillation [dɪstɪ'leɪʃən] *n Ch Ind* **(a)** (*process*) distillation *f*; **fractional d.,** distillation fractionnée; **(b)** (*result*) produit *m* de la distillation.

distiller [dɪs'tɪlər] *n Ind* distillateur *m*.

distillery [dɪs'tɪlərɪ] *n Ind* distillerie *f*.

distinct [dɪs'tɪŋkt] *adj* **(a)** (*different*) distinct, différent (**from,** de); **to keep two things d.,** distinguer entre deux choses; **women, as d. from men,** les femmes, par opposition aux hommes; **(b)** (*clear*) distinct, net, *f* nette, clair; (*memory*) clair, net, précis; (*orders*) formel, précis; (*promise*) formel; (*preference*) marqué; **the coast becomes more d.,** la côte se précise.

distinction [dɪs'tɪŋkʃən] *n* **(a)** (*difference*) distinction *f* (**between,** entre); **to make** *or* **draw a d. between two things,** faire une distinction entre deux choses; **without d. of age,** sans distinction d'âge; **class d.,** distinction de classes; **(b)** (*honour*) distinction *f*; **academic distinctions,** distinctions académiques; **(c)** (*excellence*) distinction *f*; **to gain d.,** se distinguer; **man of d.,** homme distingué; *Univ* **with d.,** (*thesis etc*) avec mention.

distinctive [dɪs'tɪŋktɪv] *adj* distinctif.

distinctively [dɪs'tɪŋktɪvlɪ] *adv* distinctivement.

distinctly [dɪs'tɪŋktlɪ] *adv* **(a)** (*parler, entendre, voir*) distinctement, clairement; **I d. remember telling you,** je me rappelle clairement te l'avoir dit; **I told him d.,** je le lui ai dit expressément; **(b)** (*definitely*) décidément; **she is d. better,** elle va sensiblement mieux.

distinctness [dɪs'tɪŋktnɪs] *n* clarté *f*, netteté *f*.

distinguish [dɪs'tɪŋgwɪʃ] **1** *vt* **(a)** (*recognize*) discerner (*un objet, un son*); **I could not d. him among the crowd,** je n'ai pu le distinguer dans la foule; **(b)** (*characterize*) distinguer, différencier (**from,** de); **reason distinguishes man from the other animals,** la raison sépare l'homme des autres animaux; **distinguishing mark,** signe distinctif; **to d. oneself by ...,** se distinguer *ou* se signaler *ou* se faire remarquer par ... . **2** *vi* **to d. between two things,** faire une distinction entre deux choses.

distinguishable [dɪs'tɪŋgwɪʃəb(ə)l] *adj* **(a)** (*recognizable*) reconnaissable; **hardly d. sound,** son à peine perceptible; **the coast was hardly d.,** c'est à peine si l'on distinguait la côte; **(b)** que l'on peut distinguer, qui se distingue (**from,** de).

distinguished [dɪs'tɪŋgwɪʃd] *adj* distingué; (*écrivain etc*) de distinction; **to look d.,** avoir l'air distingué.

distort [dɪs'tɔːt] **1** *vt* **(a)** tordre (*qch*); décomposer, déformer (*les traits, le visage*); distordre (*les membres*); fausser, déjeter (*une surface*); **(b)** déformer (*la vérité*); fausser, dénaturer (*les faits, des paroles*); **to d. the meaning of a text,** dénaturer un texte; **(c)** *Electron Rad* déformer (*la réception radiophonique etc*). **2** *vi* se déformer, se fausser.

distorted [dɪs'tɔːtɪd] *adj* tordu; (*features, face*) déformé; *El* (*champ*) tors, déformé; **face d. by rage,** visage convulsé de fureur.

distorting [dɪs'tɔːtɪŋ] *adj* déformant.

distortion [dɪs'tɔːʃən] *n* **(a)** distorsion *f*; altération *f* (*des traits*); contorsion *f* (*du corps*); **(b)** altération *f* (*d'un texte*); déformation *f* (*des faits, de la vérité*); **(c)** *Electron Rad etc* distorsion *f*, déformation *f* (*de la transmission*); (*of sound*) distorsion sonore; déviation *f* (*du champ magnétique*); *Opt* déformation, distorsion; *MecE* distorsion (*d'un organe*); torsion *f*, déformation.

distract [dɪs'trækt] *vt* **(a)** distraire, détourner (*l'esprit, l'attention*) (**from,** de); diviser (*l'attention*); **go away!, you're distracting me!,** va-t'en!, tu me déranges!; **(b)** troubler, affoler (*qn*).

distracted [dɪs'træktɪd] *adj* affolé, bouleversé; (*look*) éperdu.

distractedly [dɪs'træktɪdlɪ] *adv* comme un affolé, comme un fou, (*aimer qn*) follement, éperdument.

distracting [dɪs'træktɪŋ] *adj* qui distrait l'attention; **I find noise d. when I'm working,** le bruit me dérange quand je travaille.

distraction [dɪs'trækʃən] *n* **(a)** (*amusement*) divertissement *m*; **he's seeking d.,** il cherche à se distraire; **(b)** (*interruption*) interruption *f* (*au milieu du travail etc*); **(c) to drive s.o. to d.,** rendre qn fou, faire perdre la tête à qn; **to love s.o. to d.,** aimer qn éperdument *ou* à la folie.

distrain [dɪs'treɪn] *vi Jur* **to d. upon s.o.,** contraindre qn par saisie de biens; **to d. upon a debtor,** exécuter une saisie sur un débiteur.

distraint [dɪs'treɪnt] *n Jur* saisie *f*, (saisie-)exécution *f*, *pl* (saisies-)exécutions.

distraught [dɪs'trɔːt] *adj* angoissé; **to look d.,** avoir l'air affolé; **he is d. over his wife's illness,** la maladie de sa femme l'angoisse; **d. with grief,** fou de douleur.

distress¹ [dɪs'tres] *n* **(a)** (*mental suffering*) angoisse *f*; **to cause s.o. d.,** faire de la peine à qn; **(b)** (*difficulty*) détresse *f*, embarras *m*; **companions in d.,** compagnons d'infortune; *Nau* **ship in d.,** navire en détresse; **d. signal,** signal *m* de détresse; *US* **d. merchandise,** marchandise liquidée *ou* sacrifiée *ou* bradée; **(c)** *Jur* (*action*) saisie *f*; (*goods*) biens saisis; **d. warrant,** mandat *m* de saisie.

distress² *vt* **(a)** affliger, angoisser; faire de la peine à (*qn*); **(b)** vieillir (*un meuble*).

distressed [dɪs'trest] *adj* **(a)** (*suffering*) affligé, désolé; **to be d. about sth,** être angoissé par qch; **(b)** (*in difficulty*) dans la détresse; **(c)** (*meuble*) vieilli; **(d)** *Jur* saisi.

distressing [dɪs'tresɪŋ] *adj* affligeant, pénible.

distribute [dɪs'trɪbjuːt] *vt* **(a)** distribuer, répartir; faire la distribution de (*qch*); *Com* être concessionnaire de (*un produit*); *Fin* répartir (*un dividende*); **(b)** disperser, répartir (*qch*) (*sur une surface etc*); **evenly distributed load,** charge uniformément répartie.

distribution [dɪstrɪ'bjuːʃən] *n* **(a)** (mise *f* en) distribution *f*; (*of film*) distribution *f*; *Com* **d. channel/network,** circuit *m*/réseau *m* de distribution; *Cin* **d. rights,** (*to a film*) droits *mpl* de distribution; *El etc* **d. (switch)board,** tableau *m* de distribution; **d. box,** boîte *f* de dérivation *ou* de jonction; **(b)** répartition *f* (*de la population, de la main-d'œuvre etc*); **d. of wealth,** distribution *f* des richesses.

distributive [dɪs'trɪbjʊtɪv] *adj & n* distributif *m*.

distributor [dɪs'trɪbjʊtər] *n* distributeur,-trice; concessionnaire *m* (*d'une marque d'automobiles etc*); *El Aut etc* distributeur; *El* **d. box,** boîte *f* de dérivation *ou* de jonction.

distributorship [dɪs'trɪbjʊtəʃɪp] *n* **to have the d. for ...,** distribuer ... .

district ['dɪstrɪkt] *n* **(a)** (*of country*) région *f*, territoire *m*; *Admin* district *m*, secteur *m*; **mining d.,** région minière; *Com etc* **d. manager,** directeur régional; **urban d.,** district urbain; **postal d.,** secteur postal; **electoral d.,** *US* **congressional d.,** circonscription électorale; *US Jur* **d. court,** = tribunal *m* d'instance; *US Jur* **d. attorney,** = procureur *m* de la République; *Br* **d. nurse,** infirmière visiteuse; **(b)** quartier *m* (*d'une ville*); *Admin* = arrondissement *m* (*d'une grande ville*).

distrust[1] [dɪs'trʌst] *n* méfiance *f*, défiance *f* (**of,** de); **to have a d. of sth,** se méfier *ou* se défier de qch.

distrust[2] *vt* se méfier de, se défier de (*qn, qch*); **to d. one's own eyes,** n'en pas croire ses propres yeux.

distrustful [dɪs'trʌstfʊl] *adj* défiant, méfiant (**of,** de); **he was d. of his own capabilities,** il manquait de foi en ses propres capacités.

disturb [dɪs'tɜːb] *vt* **(a)** (*interrupt*) déranger (*qn*); troubler (*le repos etc*); *Phys* perturber (*le champs magnétique*); affoler (*l'aiguille aimantée*); **don't d. him,** ne le dérangez pas; **he was arrested for disturbing the peace,** il a été arrêté parce qu'il troublait l'ordre public; **(b)** (*disarrange*) déranger (*des papiers*); agiter, remuer (*une surface, la terre*); **(c)** (*worry*) inquiéter, troubler (*qn*); *Jur* inquiéter, troubler (*qn*) dans la jouissance d'un droit.

disturbance [dɪs'tɜːbəns] *n* **(a)** (*interruption*) dérangement *m*; **(b)** (*disarrangement*) trouble *m*; **atmospheric d.,** perturbation *f* atmosphérique; **emotional disturbances,** troubles émotifs; **(c)** (*noise*) bruit *m*, tumulte *m*; (*fight*) bagarre *f*; (*riot*) émeute *f*; **political disturbances,** troubles *mpl* politiques; **to make** *or* **create a d.,** troubler l'ordre public; **(d)** *Jur* trouble *m* de jouissance.

disturbed [dɪs'tɜːbd] *adj* (*mentally, emotionally*) perturbé.

disturbing [dɪs'tɜːbɪŋ] *adj* (*news, development etc*) inquiétant, troublant.

disunite [dɪsjʊ'naɪt] **1** *vt* désunir, jeter la désunion dans (*une famille*). **2** *vi* se désunir.

disunity [dɪs'juːnɪtɪ] *n* désunion *f*.

disuse [dɪs'juːs] *n* désuétude *f* (*d'un terme etc*); abandon *m*, mise *f* au rancart (*d'une machine etc*); **to fall into d.,** (*of word, custom*) tomber en désuétude.

disused [dɪs'juːzd] *adj* mis au rancart; (*public building*) désaffecté; (*mine, well, railway line*) abandonné.

disyllabic [dɪsɪ'læbɪk] *adj* dissyllabe, dissyllabique.

ditch[1] [dɪtʃ] *n* fossé *m*; (*along roadside*) caniveau *m*; (*between fields*) douve *f*; *Av Sl* (*sea*) baille *f*; **drainage d.,** rigole *f* d'écoulement; *Sp* **open d.,** douve.

ditch[2] **1** *vt* **(a)** *F* jeter (*qch*), se débarrasser de (*qch*); abandonner (*un projet etc*); plaquer (*qn*); **(b)** entourer (*un champ*) de fossés; creuser des fossés dans (*un champ*). **2** *vi Av* faire un amerrissage forcé.

ditching ['dɪtʃɪŋ] *n* **(a)** *Av* amerrissage forcé; **(b)** **hedging and d.,** entretien *m* des haies et fossés.

ditchwater ['dɪtʃwɔːtər] *n* eaux stagnantes (*d'un fossé*); *F* **it's as clear as d.,** c'est la bouteille à l'encre; **as dull as d.,** ennuyeux comme la pluie *ou* un jour de pluie.

dither[1] ['dɪðər] *n F* **to be all of** *or* **in a d.,** ne plus savoir où donner de la tête, paniquer.

dither[2] *vi F* hésiter, tergiverser; **stop dithering!,** décide-toi!

dithery ['dɪðərɪ] *adj F* **to feel d.,** se sentir nerveux.

ditto ['dɪtəʊ] **1** *n Com* dito *m inv*. **2** *adv* idem, de même; *F* **I'm hungry — d.,** j'ai faim — moi aussi *ou* moi pareil *ou* moi de même.

ditty ['dɪtɪ] *n* chanson *f*, chansonnette *f*.

diuretic [daɪjʊ'retɪk] *adj & n Med* diurétique *m*.

diurnal [daɪ'ɜːn(ə)l] **1** *adj Astron Biol* diurne. **2** *n Rel* diurnal *m*, -aux.

divan [dɪ'væn] *n* divan *m*; **d. bed,** divan-lit *m*.

dive[1] [daɪv] *n* **(a)** *Swimming* plongeon *m*; *Nau* plongée *f* (*d'un sous-marin, d'un scaphandrier*); *Swimming* **high d.,** plongeon de haut vol; *Av* **vertical d., nose d.,** piqué *m*; *Av* **to pull out of a d.,** effectuer un rétablissement; *Av* **d. bombing/bomber,** bombardement *m*/bombardier *m* en piqué; **he made a d. for the shelter,** il s'est précipité vers l'abri; **the goalie made a d. for the ball,** le goal a plongé pour attraper la balle; **(b)** *F Pej* (*place*) bouge *m*.

dive[2] *vi* (*pt* **dived,** *US F* **dove** [dəʊv]; *pp* **dived**) plonger (**into,** dans); (*of submarine*) plonger, effectuer une plongée; **to d. for pearls,** pêcher des perles; *Av* **to d. down on an enemy,** piquer de haut sur un ennemi; **to d. into one's pocket,** plonger la main dans sa poche; **to d. into a doorway for shelter,** se précipiter dans une entrée pour s'abriter; *F* **they all dived into the pub,** ils se sont précipités dans le pub.

▶**dive in** *vi* **(a)** (*to water*) plonger; **(b)** *F* (*start eating*) **d. in!,** attaquons!

dive-bomb ['daɪvbɒm] *vt Av* attaquer en piqué.

diver ['daɪvər] *n* **(a)** plongeur, -euse; (*in deep sea*) scaphandrier *m*; **pearl d.,** pêcheur *m* de perles; **skin d.,** plongeur sous-marin autonome; **(b)** (*bird*) plongeon *m*, plongeur *m*.

diverge [daɪ'vɜːdʒ] **1** *vi* (*of roads, lines etc*) diverger, s'écarter; (*of opinions*) diverger. **2** *vt* faire diverger (*des rayons etc*).

divergence [daɪ'vɜːdʒəns] *n* divergence *f*.

divergent [daɪ'vɜːdʒənt] **, diverging** [daɪ'vɜːdʒɪŋ] *adj* divergent; **we take d. views on certain points,** nos opinions divergent *ou* diffèrent sur certains points.

divers ['daɪvəz] *adj Arch* (*several*) divers, plusieurs.

diverse [daɪ'vɜːs] *adj* **(a)** (*different*) divers, différent; **(b)** (*varied*) divers, varié, changeant.

diversely [daɪ'vɜːslɪ] *adv* diversement.

diversification [daɪvɜːsɪfɪ'keɪʃən] *n* **(a)** (*of company etc*) diversification *f*; **(b)** diversité *f* (*de goûts etc*).

diversify [daɪ'vɜːsɪfaɪ] **1** *vi* (*of company etc*) se diversifier; **to d. into furniture,** se diversifier et commencer à fabriquer *ou* produire *ou* vendre *etc* des meubles. **2** *vt* diversifier, varier.

diversion [daɪ'vɜːʃən] *n* **(a)** déviation *f*, détournement *m* (*de la circulation etc*); *HydE El* dérivation *f*; **to create** *or* **make a d.,** (*to distract attention*) faire diversion; **(b)** (*amusement*) divertissement *m*, distraction *f*; **to seek d. from sth,** chercher à se distraire de qch; **(c)** *Mil* diversion *f*.

diversionary [daɪ'vɜːʃən(ə)rɪ] *adj* **(a)** (*activité*) destiné à faire diversion; **(b)** *Mil* (*manœuvre*) de diversion.

diversity [daɪ'vɜːsɪtɪ] *n* diversité *f*, variété *f*.

divert [daɪ'vɜːt, dɪ-] *vt* **(a)** détourner, dériver (*un cours d'eau, la circulation*); parer, écarter (*un coup*); détourner (*l'attention, la conversation*) (**from,** de); distraire l'attention de (*qn*); *El* dévier (*le courant*); *Nau* dérouter; **(b)** divertir, amuser (*qn*); **to d. oneself by doing sth,** faire qch pour se distraire.

diverting [daɪ'vɜːtɪŋ] *adj* divertissant, amusant.

divest [daɪ'vest] *vt* **(a)** *Fml* priver, dénuer (*qn*) (**of,** de); **to d. oneself of,** enlever (*son manteau*); se dévêtir de (*son autorité*); se désinvestir de (*une fonction*); renoncer à (*un droit*); **(b)** *Jur* déposséder (*qn*) (**of,** de).

divestment [daɪ'vestmənt] *n Am* = **DISINVESTMENT**.

divide[1] [dɪ'vaɪd] *n Geog* ligne *f* de partage des eaux; *Fig* faille *f*.

divide[2] **1** *vt* **(a)** (*split*) diviser (*un héritage etc*); démembrer (*un royaume*); détailler (*de la viande etc*); morceler (*un terrain*); mettre le désaccord dans (*une famille*); **to d. sth in two,** couper *ou* diviser qch en deux; **to d. sth into parts,** diviser qch en parties; **house divided against itself,** maison désunie; **opinions are divided,** les avis sont partagés; **we are divided on this issue,** nous sommes partagés sur ce sujet; **the issue has divided the party,** la question a divisé le parti; *Pol* **to d. the House,** faire voter la Chambre;

(b) (*distribute*) partager, répartir (**among,** entre); **we d. the work among us,** nous nous partageons le travail;

(c) *Math* diviser;

(d) (*separate*) séparer (**from,** de); **the mountains that d. France from Spain,** les montagnes qui séparent la France d'avec l'Espagne.

2 *vi* **(a)** se diviser, se partager (**into,** en); se séparer; (*of political party*) se scinder; (*of road*) bifurquer;

(b) *Pol* (*of House*) aller aux voix;

(c) *Math* **twelve divides by three,** douze est divisible par trois.

▶**divide out** *vtsep* = **DIVIDE[2] 1(a)**.

▶**divide up** *vtsep* = **DIVIDE[2] 1(b)**.

divided [dɪ'vaɪdɪd] *adj* **(a)** (*inheritance*) divisé; (*attention*) distrait; **to have divided loyalties,** être partagé *ou* déchiré (entre deux causes); *Am* **d. highway,** = autoroute *f* à deux chaussées (séparées par un rail); **d. skirt,** jupe-culotte *f*, *pl* jupes-culottes; *El* **d. circuit,** circuit partagé; réseau *m* multiple; **(b)** (*work*) partagé; **(c)** (*scale, thermometer etc*) gradué.

dividend ['dɪvɪdend] *n Math & Fin* dividende *m*; *Fin* **d. on shares,** dividende d'actions; *Fin* **d. paid to each creditor,** (*in insolvency*) dividende payé à chaque créancier; *Fig* **to pay dividends,** (*of action etc*) porter des fruits.

divider [dɪ'vaɪdər] *n* (*in room*) cloison *f ou* meuble *m* de séparation.

dividers [dɪ'vaɪdəz] *npl* compas *m* à pointes sèches.

dividing [dɪ'vaɪdɪŋ] *adj* (*ligne etc*) de démarcation; *Fig* **d. line,** séparation *f*, distinction *f*; **d. wall,** mur mitoyen; mur de séparation, cloison *f*; *El* **d. box,** boîte *f* de dérivation.

divination [dɪvɪ'neɪʃən] *n* divination *f*.

divine[1] [dɪ'vaɪn] **1** *adj* (*judgment, worship etc & Fig*) divin; **to attend d. service,** aller à l'église; *Hist* **the d. right of kings,** la monarchie de droit divin; *Fig* **you look d. in that dress,** vous êtes divine *ou* adorable dans cette

robe. 2 *n* théologien *m*.
divine² 1 *vt* deviner (*l'avenir*); pressentir (*un malheur*). 2 *vi* prédire.
divinely [dɪ'vaɪnlɪ] *adv* divinement.
diviner [dɪ'vaɪnər] *n* devin *m*, devineresse *f*; **water d.**, radiesthésiste *m*, sourcier *m*.
diving ['daɪvɪŋ] *n* (*underwater*) plongée *f* (sous-marine); (*from d. board*) plongeon *m*; **skin d., scuba d.**, plongée sous-marine autonome; **d. bell**, cloche *f* à plongeurs; *Swimming* **d. board**, plongeoir *m*; *Nau* **d. rudder**, gouvernail *m* de profondeur (*de sous-marin*); **d. suit**, tenue *f* de plongée.
divining [dɪ'vaɪnɪŋ] *n* divination *f*; **water d.**, radiesthésie *f*; **d. rod**, baguette *f* divinatoire *ou* de sourcier.
divinity [dɪ'vɪnɪtɪ] *n* **(a)** (*divine nature*) divinité *f* (**of**, de); **the D.**, la Divinité; **(b)** *Rel* **Doctor of D.**, docteur *m* en théologie; **(c)** *Sch* catéchisme *m*.
divisible [dɪ'vɪzɪb(ə)l] *adj* divisible (**by**, par).
division [dɪ'vɪʒən] *n* **(a)** division *f*, partage *m* (**into**, en); scission *f* (*d'un parti*); morcellement *m* (*des terres*); graduation *f* (*d'une échelle etc*);
(b) (*distribution*) répartition *f*, partage *m* (*des bénéfices etc*); **d. of labour**, division *f* du travail;
(c) (*discord*) division *f*, désunion *f*; **to bring d. into a family**, amener la désunion dans une famille;
(d) *Math* division *f*; **d. sign**, signe *m* de division;
(e) *Parl* vote *m*; **to come to a d.**, voter; **without a d.**, sans aller aux voix; sans scrutin; *Br Pol* **d. lobby**, = pièces dans lesquelles se rendent les députés selon qu'ils ont voté oui ou non; *Br Pol* **d. bell**, = signal sonore qui avertit les députés qu'ils vont être appelés à voter;
(f) (*section*) division *f* (*d'un livre, d'un pays*); subdivision *f* (*d'un casier etc*); *Biol* groupe *m*, classe *f*; *Jur* section *f* (*de la cour*); *Mil etc* division; *esp US Rail* section de ligne; degré *m* (*d'une échelle, d'un thermomètre etc*); **airborne/armoured d.**, division aéroportée/blindée; *Pol* **parliamentary d.**, circonscription électorale;
(g) *Constr etc* cloison *f*, séparation *f*.
divisive [dɪ'vaɪsɪv] *adj* qui sème la discorde.
divisor [dɪ'vaɪzər] *n Math* diviseur *m*.
divorce¹ [dɪ'vɔːs] *n* **(a)** *Jur* divorce *m*; **I want a d.**, je veux divorcer; **they're getting a d.**, ils ont demandé le divorce; **why don't you ask him** *or* **her for a d.?**, pourquoi est-ce que tu ne lui demandes pas de divorcer?; **why don't you get a d.?**, (*from husband or wife*) pourquoi est-ce que tu ne divorces pas?; **to specialize in d. (cases)**, (*of lawyer*) se spécialiser dans les cas de divorce; **to sue for (a) d., to file a petition for d.**, demander le divorce; **their marriage ended in d.**, ils ont divorcé; **one in three marriages ends in d.**, un couple sur trois divorce; **to take** *or* **start d. proceedings**, intenter une action en divorce; **(b)** *Fig* divorce *m*, séparation *f* (**between sth and sth**, de qch et de qch).
divorce² 1 *vt* **(a)** *Jur* (*of judge*) prononcer le divorce de (*les époux*); **to get divorced from s.o., to d. s.o.**, (*of husband or wife*) divorcer d'avec qn; **she is divorced from him**, elle est divorcée d'avec lui; **she is divorced**, elle est divorcée; **they are divorced**, ils sont divorcés; **(b)** *Fig* **you cannot d. form from content**, on ne peut pas séparer le fond et la forme; **an idea divorced from reality**, une idée irréelle *ou* loin de la réalité; **passage divorced from the context**, passage isolé du contexte. 2 *vi* (*of husband and wife*) divorcer.
divorcé [dɪvɔː'siː] *n* divorcé *m*.
divorcée [dɪvɔː'siː] *n* divorcée *f*.
divot ['dɪvət] *n* motte *f* (*de terre*).
divulge [daɪ'vʌldʒ] *vt* divulguer; **he refused to d. her whereabouts**, il a refusé de divulguer l'endroit où elle se trouvait.
divvy ['dɪvɪ] *n F* dividende *m*.
►**divvy up** *vtsep F* partager.
dixie, dixy ['dɪksɪ] *n esp Mil F* gamelle *f*.
dixieland ['dɪksɪlænd] *n* **d. (jazz)**, dixieland *m*.
DIY [diːaɪ'waɪ] *adj Br abbr* **do-it-yourself**.
dizzily ['dɪzɪlɪ] *adv* **(a)** avec une sensation de vertige; **(b)** vertigineusement.
dizziness ['dɪzɪnɪs] *n* étourdissement *m*, vertige(s) *m(pl)*; **fit of d.**, éblouissement *m*.
dizzy ['dɪzɪ] *adj* **(a)** pris de vertige; **d. spell**, éblouissement *m*; **to feel d.**, avoir le vertige; **to make s.o. d.**, donner le vertige à qn; **(b)** *Fig* (*height, speed etc*) vertigineux; **(c)** *Fig* (*scatterbrained*) écervelé; **d. blonde**, blonde évaporée.
DJ ['diːdʒeɪ] *n* **(a)** *abbr* **disc jockey**; **(b)** *abbr* **dinner jacket**.
D Lit(t) [diː'lɪt] *n abbr* **Doctor of Letters**.
DNA [diːen'eɪ] *n* (*abbr* **deoxyribonucleic acid**) ADN *m*.

do¹ [duː] *v* (**he does** [dʌz]; *pt* **did** [dɪd]; *pr sub sg & pl* **do**; *pp* **done** [dʌn]; *in the aux use* **don't** [dəʊnt], **didn't** [dɪd(ə)nt] *are common for* **do not, did not**; **doesn't** [dʌz(ə)nt] *for* **does not**) 1 *vt* **(a)** faire (*une bonne action, son devoir, le ménage, une traduction*); *Math* faire (*un calcul*); *Math* résoudre (*un problème*); *Th* faire (*Hamlet etc*); *F* visiter, faire (*une ville, un musée*); **what do you do (for a living)?**, qu'est-ce que vous faites (dans la vie)?; **what are you doing?**, qu'est-ce que vous faites?; **to do right/wrong**, bien/mal faire; bien/mal agir; **he did brilliantly (in his exam)**, il a réussi brillamment (son examen); **you would do well to ...**, vous feriez bien de ...; **do as you're told**, fais ce qu'on te dit; **she's doing medicine**, elle fait médecine; **to do the interpreting**, faire l'interprète; **the car was doing sixty**, la voiture faisait du soixante; **to do ten years (in prison)**, faire dix ans de prison; **it isn't done**, cela ne se fait pas; **it is quite commonly done**, c'est de pratique courante; **it's as good as done**, c'est une affaire faite; *F* **that's done it!**, ça y est!; **it gives me something to do**, cela me donne de l'occupation; **don't do it again!**, ne recommencez pas!; **what is to be done?**, que faire?; **it can't be done**, cela n'est pas possible, c'est (chose) impossible; **there's nothing to be done**, il n'y a rien à faire; **she did nothing but cry**, elle n'a fait que pleurer; **I don't know what to do**, je ne sais que faire, je ne sais pas quoi faire; *F* **this music doesn't do anything for me**, cette musique ne me dit rien, je n'aime pas cette musique; **what can I do for you?**, que puis-je faire pour vous?; **what are you going to do about it?**, que proposez-vous de faire?; **what would he do without you?**, que deviendrait-il sans vous?; **it was all I could do to lift it**, c'est à peine si j'ai pu le soulever; **it was all I could do not to laugh**, j'ai eu du mal à ne pas rire; **well done!**, très bien!, bravo!; **to do s.o.'s/one's hair**, coiffer qn/se coiffer; **to do one's teeth**, se faire les dents; **he does repairs**, il fait des réparations; **to be done**, (*of meat, vegetable*) être prêt *ou* cuit; **meat well done**, viande bien cuite; **done to a turn**, cuit à point; *F* **to do s.o. (down)**, (*cheat*) refaire qn, faire qn; **I've been done!**, j'ai été roulé!, on m'a eu!; *F* **they do you very well at this hotel**, on est très bien servi à cet hôtel; *Com F* **we can do you this article at ...**, nous pouvons vous faire cet article à ...; **that dress/hairstyle does something/nothing for you**, cette robe/coiffure t'arrange *ou* te met en valeur/ne t'arrange pas *ou* ne te met pas du tout en valeur; *F* **they did three other houses in the neighbourhood**, (*burgled them, visited them*) ils sont passés dans trois autres maisons dans le quartier; *F* **to do drugs**, (*take them*) se droguer; **I don't do drugs**, je ne prends pas de drogues; *F* **to do s.o.**, (*beat*) frapper qn;
(b) (*in perfect tenses and past participle*) **to have done**, avoir fini; *Lit* **the day is done**, la journée tire à sa fin; *F* **have you done?**, as-tu fini?; **have you done shouting?**, as-tu fini de crier?; **done!**, (*after a bargain made*) entendu!, d'accord!;
(c) (*replacing vtr or vi*) **they work in the fields as their fathers did**, ils travaillent aux champs comme le faisaient leurs pères; **he writes better than I do**, il écrit mieux que moi;
(d) (*replacing vtr and taking its construction*) **he envies me as much as I do him**, il me porte autant d'envie que je lui en porte;
(e) (*replacing vtr and obj*) **if you understood the question as well as I do**, si vous compreniez la question aussi bien que moi;
(f) (*elliptical auxiliary*) **may I open these letters? — (please) do**, puis-je ouvrir ces lettres? — je vous en prie!; **did you see him? — I did**, l'avez-vous vu? — oui(, je l'ai vu); **do you like her?, — no I don't**, l'aimez-vous? — non(, je ne l'aime pas); **you don't like it — yes, I do**, vous ne l'aimez pas — mais si; **you like him, don't you?**, vous l'aimez, n'est-ce pas?; **she lives here, doesn't she?**, elle habite ici, n'est-ce pas?; **that does you good, doesn't it?**, ça fait du bien, hein?; **don't!**, ne faites pas ça!; **you like Paris? so do I**, vous aimez Paris? moi aussi; **they have always existed and still do**, ils ont toujours existé et existent encore; **if you want to speak to him, do it now**, si vous désirez lui parler, faites-le maintenant;
(g) (*aux used for emphasis*) **he DID go**, il y est bien allé; **I DO believe he is a thief**, je crois vraiment que c'est un voleur; **it doesn't matter — it DOES (matter)!**, ça ne fait rien — si, ça fait quelque chose!; **why don't you work? — I DO (work)!**, pourquoi ne travaillez-vous pas? — mais si, je travaille!; **do you remember him? — DO I** *or* **do I remember him!**, vous souvenez-vous de lui? — si je m'en

souviens!; DO **sit down,** asseyez-vous donc!; **yes, people** DID **live there,** oui, des gens ont vécu là; **I don't like coffee, but I** DO **like tea,** je n'aime pas le café, mais j'aime bien le thé; **rarely does it happen that ...,** il arrive rarement que ...;

(h) *Jur* **charged that he did on the 15th of August utter threats,** accusé d'avoir proféré des menaces le 15 août;

(i) (*usual form in questions and negative statements except with* **have** *but see* **have, be,** *and modal verbs; also in negative commands*) **did you see him?,** l'avez-vous vu?; **we do not know,** nous ne le savons pas; **do not speak!,** ne parlez pas!; **don't do it!,** n'en faites rien!; **don't be afraid,** n'ayez pas peur; **do you mind?,** ça ne vous fait rien?; *Iron* vous permettez?

2 *vi* **(a) how do you do?,** (*on first introduction*) enchanté (de faire votre connaissance); **to be doing well,** (*of patient*) être sur la voie de la guérison; (*in business*) être en bonne voie, faire de bonnes affaires; (*of business*) bien aller, réussir; (*of plant*) bien pousser; **that young man will do well,** c'est un garçon qui réussira;

(b) (*serve, suffice*) **that will do,** (*is satisfactory*) c'est bien (comme cela), c'est bon; (*stop it*) ça suffit, c'est assez; **tea will do,** (*if you haven't got coffee*) du thé fera l'affaire; **this room will do for the office,** cette pièce ira bien pour le bureau; **will this one do?,** ceci fera l'affaire?; **that will never do,** cela n'ira jamais, ça n'ira pas du tout; **to make do with what one has,** s'arranger avec ce qu'on a; **we'll just have to make do,** il faudra faire avec; **that will do me,** cela fera mon affaire; **it would never do for them to see me,** il ne faudrait pas qu'ils me voient; **there's nothing doing,** (*business is bad*) les affaires vont mal; tout va mal; (*it's the off season*) c'est la morte-saison; **there's never anything doing at this time of year,** il ne se passe jamais rien à cette période de l'année; **nothing doing!,** (*I, she etc won't*) rien à faire!, ça ne prend pas!

do² *n* **(a) the do's and don'ts,** ce qu'il faut faire et ce qu'il ne faut pas faire; **the do's and don'ts of society,** ce qui se fait et ce qui ne se fait pas dans le monde; *F* **come on, fair do's!,** (*I want my share*) dis donc, donne-moi ma part!; (*be fair*) dis donc, sois juste!; **(b)** *F* (*party etc*) réception *f*; soirée *f*.

do³ [dəʊ] *n Mus* (*fixed*) do *m*, ut *m*.

▶do away with *vipo* **(a)** (*abolish*) abolir, abandonner (*un usage*); *F* **they should do away with school,** ils devraient supprimer l'école; **(b)** *F* (*kill*) supprimer (*qn*); *Iron* se défaire de (*qn*); **she has threatened to do away with herself,** elle a menacé de se supprimer.

▶do by *vipo F* (*treat*) **to do well/badly by s.o.,** bien/mal agir *ou* se bien/mal conduire envers qn; **he has been hard done by,** il a été traité durement; **she did very well by her grand-daughter at Christmas,** (*gave her lots of gifts*) elle a gâté sa petite-fille à Noël; **he'll feel very hard done by if you don't at least send him a birthday card,** il se sentira vraiment lésé si tu ne lui envoies même pas de carte d'anniversaire.

▶do down *vtsep* **(a)** (*cheat*) estamper (*qn*); **why did you let the seller do you down?,** pourquoi as-tu laissé le vendeur t'estamper?; **(b)** (*say bad things about*) dire du mal de (*qn*); **there's always someone ready to do you down,** il y a toujours des gens prêts à dire du mal des autres.

▶do for *vipo F* **(a)** (*murder*) tuer (*qn*); faire son affaire à (*qn*); **he's done for,** (*is dead*) c'est un homme mort; (*is ruined*) il est fini *ou F* fichu; **if he keeps on treating her this way, she'll do for him,** s'il continue à la traiter de cette façon, elle va le descendre; **(b)** (*exhaust*) épuiser (*qn*); **it was that last hill that did it for me,** c'est la dernière colline qui m'a épuisé; **(c)** (*clean house for*) faire *ou* tenir le ménage de (*qn*); **who does for you?,** qui fait votre ménage?; **(d)** (*convict of*) condamner (*qn*); **she was done for shoplifting,** elle a été condamnée pour vol à l'étalage.

▶do in *vtsep F* **(a)** (*murder*) faire son affaire à (*qn*); **somebody on our street was done in last night,** quelqu'un de notre rue a été descendu cette nuit; **(b)** (*exhaust*) crever (*qn*); **I'm absolutely done in,** je suis fourbu *ou* vanné; **Christmas shopping always does me in,** les achats de Noël me crèvent chaque année.

▶do out *vtsep* (*clean*) faire, nettoyer (*la cuisine, une chambre*).

▶do out of *vtaspo F* (*cheat*) soutirer *ou* carotter (*qch*) à (*qn*); refaire *ou* escroquer (*qn*) de (*l'argent*); **to do s.o. out of a job,** supplanter qn; **she has been done out of her share of money,** elle s'est fait escroquer de sa part de l'argent.

▶do over *vtsep* **(a)** (*redecorate*) refaire la décoration de (*une maison*); **(b)** *F* (*beat up*) frapper (*qn*); **(c)** *Am* (*repeat*) refaire (*un travail*).

▶do up 1 *vi* (*of clothes*) s'agrafer. **2** *vtsep* **(a)** (*fasten*) fermer, boutonner, agrafer (*un vêtement*); **(b)** (*wrap*) faire, envelopper, ficeler (*un paquet*); emballer, empaqueter (*des marchandises*); **(c)** (*improve appearance of*) réparer (*qch*); remettre (*qch*) à neuf; décorer (*une maison etc*); *F* **to do oneself up,** faire sa toilette.

▶do with *vipo* **(a) what did you do with my umbrella?,** qu'avez-vous fait de mon parapluie?; **she didn't know what to do with herself,** (*to keep busy*) elle ne savait que faire *ou* à quoi s'occuper; (*for joy*) elle ne se tenait pas de joie; (*for awkwardness*) elle était gênée;

(b) (*need*) (*usually formed with* **could**) **I could do with a cup of tea,** je prendrais bien une tasse de thé; **we can do with your help,** vous n'êtes pas de trop; **I can do with little,** je sais me contenter de peu; **you could do with a haircut,** une coupe de cheveux ne te ferait pas de mal;

(c) (*be connected with*) **she's something to do with insurance,** elle est dans les assurances; **it has to do with your mother, I'm afraid,** j'ai bien peur que ça concerne ta mère; **I want nothing to do with him,** je ne veux pas avoir affaire à lui; **to have nothing to do with sth,** (*not be involved in or responsible for*) n'être pour rien dans qch, n'avoir rien à voir avec qch; (*not be connected with*) n'avoir rien à faire avec qch, n'avoir pas de rapport à *ou* avec qch; **you should have nothing to do with it,** (*don't get involved*) tu ne devrais pas t'en mêler; **I had nothing to do with it,** je n'y suis pour rien; **it's nothing to do with you,** vous n'avez rien à voir là-dedans;

(d) (*finish*) **to have done with sth,** en avoir fini avec qch; **I've done with trying to help people,** j'en ai fini d'aider les gens; **let's have done with it!,** finissons-en!; **to have done with s.o.,** (*terminated relationship with lover, girlfriend etc*) avoir rompu avec qn; (*with lover etc, friend*) en avoir fini avec qn; **I haven't done with him yet!,** (*haven't finished scolding him*) je n'en ai pas encore fini avec lui!; **that's all over and done with!,** c'est fini, tout ça!;

(e) *F* (*finish using*) finir avec (*le journal, les ciseaux*);

(f) *F* (*with negative*) (*not like*) **I can't be doing with getting up early,** je ne peux pas me faire à me lever tôt; **I can't be doing with television,** je n'aime pas la télévision; **I can't be doing with her,** je ne l'aime pas.

▶do without *vipo* (*manage without*) se passer de (*qch*); **to do without food,** se passer de nourriture; *F* **I could do without him,** je me passerais bien de lui; **we can do without the sarcasm,** on n'a pas besoin de ces sarcasmes; **you'll just have to do without,** il faudra s'en passer.

DOA [diːəʊ'eɪ] *adj Med* (*abbr* **dead on arrival**) **to be DOA,** être mort avant son arrivée à l'hôpital.

doc [dɒk] *n* (= **doctor**) **(a)** *F* toubib *m*; **thanks d.,** merci docteur; **(b) D. Martens** ®, (*shoes*) Doc Martens *fpl*.

docile ['dəʊsaɪl] *adj* docile; (*animal*) sage.

docility [dəʊ'sɪlɪtɪ] *n* docilité *f*.

dock¹ [dɒk] *n* **(a)** *Nau* bassin *m* (*d'un port*); **to go into d.,** entrer au bassin; **the docks,** les docks *mpl*; *F* **in d.,** (*of car, plane*) en réparation; **dry d., graving d.,** cale sèche; **ship in dry d.,** navire *m* en radoub; **floating d.,** dock flottant; chantier *m* à flot; **naval docks,** = **DOCKYARD**; **(b)** *Th* **scene d.,** remise *f* à décors.

dock² 1 *vt* **(a)** *Nau* faire entrer (*un navire*) au bassin *ou* à quai; (*for repairs*) faire entrer (*un navire*) en cale sèche; (*on canal, river*) garer (*une péniche etc*); **(b)** arrimer (*deux engins spatiaux*). **2** *vi* **(a)** (*of ship*) entrer *ou* arriver au bassin *ou* aux docks *ou* à quai; (*for repair*) entrer en cale sèche; **when do we d.?,** quand arrivons-nous à quai?; **we'll be docking at New York,** nous entrerons à quai à New York; **(b)** (*of two spacecraft*) s'arrimer.

dock³ *n Jur* banc *m* des accusés *ou* des prévenus; **prisoner in the d. Martin,** accusé Martin.

dock⁴ *n* tronçon *m*, partie charnue (*de la queue d'un cheval ou d'un chien*); **d. (piece),** (*on harness*) culeron *m*, trousse-queue *m inv*.

dock⁵ *vt* **(a)** diminuer (*le traitement de qn*); **to d. two pounds from s.o.'s wages,** supprimer deux livres du salaire de qn; **(b) to d. a horse('s tail)/a dog('s tail),** couper la queue à un cheval/un chien.

dock⁶ *n* (*weed*) patience *f*.

docker ['dɒkər] *n Br* docker *m*, débardeur *m*.

docket¹ ['dɒkɪt] *n* **(a)** *Jur* registre *m* des jugements rendus; *US* rôle *m* des causes; bordereau *m* (*des pièces d'un dossier*); **(b)** étiquette *f*, fiche *f* (*d'un document, d'une lettre*); **wages d.,** bordereau *m* de paye; **(c)** *Admin*

récépissé *m* de douane.
docket² *vt* **(a)** *Jur* enregistrer (*un jugement rendu*); *US* porter (*une cause*) sur le rôle des causes; **(b)** étiqueter, classer (*des papiers*).
docking ['dɒkɪŋ] *n* **(a)** mise *f* au bassin; (*for repairs*) radoub *m*; **(b)** arrimage *m* (*de deux engins spatiaux*); **d. manœuvre,** manœuvre *f* d'abordage.
dockland ['dɒklænd] *n* les quartiers *mpl* des docks.
dockyard ['dɒkjɑːd] *n* chantier naval *ou* de constructions navales; **naval d.,** arsenal *m* maritime.
doctor¹ ['dɒktər] *n* **(a)** *Med* médecin *m*, docteur *m*; **to go to the d.('s),** aller chez le docteur; **the d. will see you now,** le docteur va vous recevoir maintenant; **good morning d.,** bonjour docteur; *Br F* **to be under the d. for sth,** être suivi par le docteur pour qch; **I would like to see D. Brown,** j'aimerais voir le Docteur Brown; **I am a d.,** je suis médecin; **woman d.,** femme *f* médecin; **family d.,** médecin de famille; **ship's d.,** médecin de bord; **army d.,** médecin militaire; *Br* **National Health (Service) d.,** = médecin conventionné; *F* **just what the d. ordered,** la bonne formule; **(b)** *Univ* docteur *m*; **D. of Divinity/Laws/Medicine,** docteur en théologie/droit/médecine; **D. of Literature/Science,** docteur ès lettres/sciences; **d.'s degree,** doctorat *m*.
doctor² *vt* **(a)** *Pej F* falsifier, fausser (*des comptes, un texte*); piper (*un dé, des cartes*); frelater (*du vin etc*); *Horseracing* doper (*un cheval*); châtrer (*un chat etc*); **to d. s.o.'s drink,** ajouter de la drogue dans le verre de qn à son insu; **(b)** soigner (*un malade*).
doctoral ['dɒktər(ə)l] *adj* (*thesis etc*) de doctorat.
doctorate ['dɒktərɪt] *n Univ* doctorat *m*; **to have a d. in history,** avoir un doctorat en histoire.
doctoring [dɒktərɪŋ] *n* **(a)** *Pej F* falsification *f* (*d'un texte etc*); doping *m* (*d'un cheval*); castration *f* (*d'un chat*); **(b)** *F* profession *f* de médecin; **(c)** soins *mpl* (**of s.o.,** donnés à qn).
doctrinaire [dɒktrɪ'neər] *adj & n Pej* doctrinaire *mf*.
doctrinal [dɒk'traɪn(ə)l] *adj* doctrinal, -aux.
doctrine ['dɒktrɪn] *n* doctrine *f*.
docudrama ['dɒkjʊdrɑːmə] *n TV* docudrame *m*.
document¹ ['dɒkjʊmənt] *n* document *m*, pièce *f*; **legal d.,** acte *m* authentique; *Jur* **documents relating to a case,** dossier *m* d'une affaire; **to draw up a d.,** rédiger un acte; **d. case,** porte-documents *m inv*.
document² *vt* documenter; **the film documents the lives of the long term unemployed,** le film montre en détail la vie des chômeurs de longue durée; **well-documented book,** livre bien documenté; **the first documented case of ...,** le premier cas établi de ....
documentary [dɒkjʊ'ment(ə)rɪ] **1** *adj* (*evidence, film*) documentaire; *Com* **d. credit,** crédit *m* documentaire. **2** *n Cin TV* documentaire *m*.
documentation [dɒkjʊmen'teɪʃən] *n* documentation *f*.
dodder ['dɒdər] *vi* (*of person*) trembloter; marcher d'un pas branlant.
dodderer ['dɒdərər] *n* croulant, -ante.
doddering [dɒdərɪŋ] *adj* **(a)** (*démarche*) branlant; **(b)** (*person*) gaga *inv*, gâteux; **d. old fool,** un vieux gâteux.
doddery ['dɒdərɪ] *adj F* branlant, tremblotant; **I still feel a bit d.,** (*after illness*) je ne me sens pas encore d'aplomb.
doddle ['dɒd(ə)l] *n Br F* **it's a d.,** (*easy*) c'est simple comme bonjour.
dodge¹ [dɒdʒ] *n* **(a)** (*to avoid sth, s.o.*) mouvement *m ou* saut *m* de côté; **she made a d. to the left,** elle a fait un saut vers la gauche; **(b)** *Pej F* ruse *f*, truc *m*, combine *f*; **he's up to all the dodges,** il connaît toutes les combines; **tax dodge,** combine pour payer moins d'impôts.
dodge² **1** *vi* **(a)** se jeter de côté; **to d. behind a tree,** sauter *ou* se glisser derrière un arbre; **(b)** *Boxing Fb* esquiver, éviter; **(c)** *F Pej* biaiser, ruser, user d'artifices. **2** *vt* **(a)** esquiver (*un coup*); éviter (*qn*); **(b)** *F Pej* esquiver, tourner, éluder (*une difficulté*); escamoter (*une question*); **to d. military service,** couper au service militaire; **stop dodging the issue,** arrête d'éluder le problème.
dodgem ['dɒdʒəm] *adj & n* **d. cars, dodgems,** autos tamponneuses.
dodger ['dɒdʒər] *n F* tire-au-flanc *m*; *Old-fashioned* **an artful d.,** un fin matois; *US* **draft d.,** réfractaire *m*; **fare d.,** voyageur, -euse sans billet; **tax d.,** personne *f* qui essaye de payer le moins d'impôts possible.
dodgy ['dɒdʒɪ] *adj F* **(a)** (*situation*) délicat; (*translation, contract*) douteux; **to be a bit d.,** (*not work properly*) ne pas marcher très bien; **the ceiling looks a bit d.,** le plafond n'a pas l'air en très bon état, le plafond a l'air un peu suspect; **(b)** (*person*) roublard.
dodo, *pl* **-oes, -os** ['dəʊdəʊ, -z] *n* **(a)** (*bird*) dronte *m*, dodo *m*; *Fig* **(as) dead as a d.,** mort et enterré; **(b)** *F* (*person*) andouille *f*.
doe [dəʊ] *n* **(a)** (*deer*) daine *f*; biche *f*; **d.-eyed,** aux yeux de biche; **(b)** (*of rabbit*) lapine *f*; (*of wild rabbit and hare*) hase *f*.
DOE [diːəʊ'iː] *n* (*Br Admin* **Department of the Environment**) = ministère *m* de l'Environnement.
doer ['duːər] *n* **(a)** personne *f* dynamique; **she's a d.,** c'est une femme très active; **(b)** auteur *m* (*d'une action*).
doeskin ['dəʊskɪn] *n* peau *f* de daim; *Tex* simili-daim *m*; **d. glove,** gant *m* en peau de daim.
doesn't ['dʌz(ə)nt] = **does not**, *see* **DO¹**.
doff [dɒf] *vt Lit* enlever, ôter (*son chapeau*).
dog¹ [dɒg] *n* **(a)** chien *m*; *Fig* **he's a d. in a manger,** il fait l'empêcheur de tourner en rond; **don't be such a d. in the manger,** arrête de faire l'empêcheur de tourner en rond; **beware of the d.,** (attention) chien méchant; **to lead a d.'s life,** mener une vie de chien; **to lead s.o. a d.'s life,** faire mener une vie de chien à qn; **it's a d.'s life being a lexicographer,** c'est une vie de chien que d'être lexicographe; **to die like a d.,** mourir comme un chien; **to treat s.o. like a d.,** traiter qn comme un chien; **to follow s.o. about like a d.,** suivre qn comme un petit chien; **you can't teach an old d. new tricks,** = on ne peut pas apprendre un nouveau métier etc à quelqu'un qui a dépassé un certain âge; **every d. has his day,** à chacun vient sa chance; *F* **what a d.'s breakfast** *or* **dinner!,** quel gâchis!; (*of text*) quel torchon!; *F* **to make a d.'s breakfast** *or* **dinner of sth,** gâcher qch; *Br F* **to be dressed up like a d.'s dinner,** être habillé comme un clown; *esp Am* **to put on the d.,** faire des frais; **the d. days (of summer),** la canicule; *F* **he doesn't stand a d.'s chance,** il n'a pas l'ombre d'une chance; *F* **I'm going to see a man about a d.,** = réponse que l'on donne pour éviter de préciser où l'on va; **give a d. a bad name,** qui veut noyer son chien l'accuse de la rage; **let sleeping dogs lie,** ne réveillez pas le chat qui dort; **it's a case of d. eat d.,** c'est un cas où les loups se mangent entre eux; **it's a d.-eat-d. world,** c'est un monde où les loups se mangent entre eux, c'est une jungle; **(Cape) hunting d.,** lycaon *m*; **prairie d.,** cynomys *m*; **sporting d.,** chien de chasse; **sheep d.,** chien de berger; **police d.,** chien policier; **guide d.,** chien d'aveugle; **hot d.,** hot dog *m*; *Astron* **the D. Star,** Sirius *m*; **d. racing,** courses *fpl* de lévriers; **d. biscuit,** biscuit *m* pour chien; *Swimming* **d. paddle,** nage *f* à la chien; **d. rose,** (*flower*) églantine *f*, rose *f* sauvage; (*bush*) églantier *m*, rosier *m* sauvage; **d. show,** exposition canine; **d. collar,** collier *m* de chien; *F* faux col (*d'ecclésiastique*); *Mil etc* **d. handler,** maître-chien *m*; *US* **d. tag,** plaque *f* d'identité (*de chien, F de militaire*); *F* **d. Latin,** latin *m* de cuisine;
(b) mâle *m* (*de certains animaux*); **d. fox,** renard *m* mâle;
(c) *Old-fashioned* **you lucky d.!,** veinard! *m*; **sly d.,** rusé coquin, fin renard; **gay d.,** coureur *m* (de femmes); **dirty d.,** salaud *m*, sale type *m*;
(d) *Am Sl* (*film, party etc*) fiasco *m*; *Pej* (*woman*) cageot *m*;
(e) *Tech* (*pawl*) cliquet *m*; (*of lathe*) toc *m* (*d'entraînement*); *MecE* crabot *m*; *Metal* agrafe *f* (*de châssis de moulage*); sergent *m* (*de tonnelier*);
(f) **(fire) d.,** chenet *m*.
dog² *vt* (**-gg-** [dɒgd]) suivre (*qn*) à la piste; **to d. s.o.'s footsteps,** marcher sur les talons de qn; **he is dogged by misfortune,** il est poursuivi par la malchance; **she has been dogged by injury for the last year,** elle a eu blessure sur blessure au cours de l'année passée.
dogcart ['dɒgkɑːt] *n* (*vehicle*) dog-cart *m*, *pl* dog-carts.
dog-catcher ['dɒgkætʃər] *n* = employé municipal qui est chargé d'attraper les chiens errants.
doge [dəʊdʒ] *n Hist* doge *m*.
dog-eared ['dɒgɪəd] *adj* (*book*) aux pages cornées; (*page*) corné.
dogfight ['dɒgfaɪt] *n* combat *m* de chiens; *Mil Av* combat aérien; *Fig* bagarre *f*.
dogfish ['dɒgfɪʃ] *n* chien *m* de mer, roussette *f*.
dogfood ['dɒgfuːd] *n* pâtée *f* (pour chiens).
dogged ['dɒgɪd] *adj* résolu, tenace; *Pej* obstiné, entêté; (*attachment*) inébranlable.
doggedly ['dɒgɪdlɪ] *adv* avec ténacité; *Pej* obstinément; **to work d.,** travailler sans relâche.
doggedness ['dɒgɪdnɪs] *n* ténacité *f*; *Pej* obstination *f*, entêtement *m*.
doggerel ['dɒgərəl] *n* **d. (verse),** (*silly and comical*) poésie *f* burlesque; (*worthless, mediocre*) vers *mpl* de

mirliton.
doggie ['dɒgɪ] *n F* toutou *m*, chienchien *m*; **d. bag,** = petit sac fourni par certains restaurants pour emporter les restes.
doggo ['dɒgəʊ] *adv* **to lie d.,** se tenir coi.
doggone ['dɒgɒn] *adj US F* sacré; **d. it!,** zut!, nom d'un chien!
doggy ['dɒgɪ] **1** *adj* **(a)** *(devotion etc)* de chien; **(b)** *F (person)* qui se connaît en chiens; qui adore les chiens. **2** *n F* = **DOGGIE**; **d. paddle,** nage *f* à la chien.
doghouse ['dɒghaʊs] *n esp Am* chenil *m*; *Fig* **to be in the d.,** être en défaveur *ou* en disgrâce; **you're in the d. with Mum,** tu n'es pas en odeur de sainteté avec Maman.
dogleg[1] ['dɒgleg] *n* coude *m (dans un tuyau, un chemin etc)*.
dogleg[2] *vi (of pipe, road)* former un angle.
doglike ['dɒglaɪk] *adj (fidélité)* de chien.
dogma, *pl* **-as** ['dɒgmə, -əz] *n* dogme *m*.
dogmatic [dɒg'mætɪk] *adj* **(a)** *(opinion etc)* dogmatique; **(b)** *(person)* dogmatique, autoritaire, tranchant; **to be very d.,** trancher sur tout, être très dogmatique.
dogmatically [dɒg'mætɪklɪ] *adv* dogmatiquement, d'un ton autoritaire *ou* tranchant *ou* dogmatique.
dogmatism ['dɒgmətɪz(ə)m] *n* **(a)** *(of opinion etc)* dogmatisme *m*; **(b)** *(of person)* tour *m* d'esprit autoritaire *ou* positif.
dogmatist ['dɒgmətɪst] *n* dogmatique *mf*.
dogmeat ['dɒgmiːt] *n* viande *f* pour chiens.
do-gooder [duː'gʊdər] *n F Pej* âme *f* charitable, faiseur, -euse de bonnes œuvres.
dog-paddle ['dɒgpæd(ə)l] *vi* nager comme un chien.
dogs [dɒgz] *npl Br F* **(a) the d.,** courses *fpl* de lévriers; **to go to the d.,** aller aux courses de lévriers; *Fig (of person)* gâcher sa vie; *(of business)* aller à la ruine; **this country's going to the d.,** ce pays va à la ruine; **(b)** *(feet)* panards *mpl*, ripatons *mpl*.
dogsbody ['dɒgzbɒdɪ] *n F* factotum *m*; **she's the general d.,** elle est la bonne à tout faire.
dogsled ['dɒgsled] *n* luge tirée par des chiens.
dog-tired ['dɒg'taɪəd] *adj F* claqué, crevé, mort de fatigue.
dogtooth ['dɒgtuːθ] *n Archit* dent-de-chien *f*, *pl* dents-de-chien; **d. violet,** *(flower)* érythrone *m*, dent-de-chien.
dogtrot ['dɒgtrɒt] *n* petit trot; **to go somewhere at a d.,** aller quelque part au petit trot.
dogwatch ['dɒgwɒtʃ] *n Nau* petit quart.
dogwood ['dɒgwʊd] *n (shrub)* cornouiller *m*.
doh [dəʊ] *n* = **DO[3]**.
doily ['dɔɪlɪ] *n* **(a)** *(underneath plate etc)* petit napperon; **(b)** *(on plate)* dessus *m* d'assiette.
doing ['duːɪŋ] *n* **talking is one thing, d. is another,** c'est bien beau de parler, encore faudrait-il agir; **that takes some d.,** ça ne se fait pas en un tour de main; **this is his d.,** c'est son ouvrage; **all this is your d.,** c'est vous qui êtes la cause de tout cela; **it was none of my d.,** ce n'est pas à moi qu'il faut s'en prendre.
doing away with *n* suppression *f* de, abandon *m* de *(qch)*.
doing up *n* remise *f* à neuf.
doings ['duːɪŋz] *npl* **(a)** *(of person)* ce qu'on fait; *Pej* agissements *mpl (de qn)*; **to be informed of s.o.'s d.,** être au courant des faits et gestes de qn; **(b)** *F (events)* événements *mpl*; **there have been great d. at their house,** il y a eu bien du mouvement chez eux; **(c)** *F (equipment etc)* les machins *mpl*, les trucs *mpl*.
do-it-yourself [duːɪtjə'self] *n* bricolage *m*; **do-it-y. enthusiast,** passionné *m* de bricolage; **do-it-y. kit,** panoplie *f* de construction; **do-it-y. shop,** magasin *m* de bricolage.
do-it-yourselfer [duːɪtjə'selfər] *n* bricoleur, -euse.
dol *(abbr* **dollar***)* dol(l)..
Dolby ['dɒlbɪ] *n* dolby *m*.
doldrums (the) [ðə'dɒldrəmz] *npl Nau* zone *f* calme; *Fig* le cafard, les idées noires; **to be in the d.,** *(of person)* avoir le moral à zéro, être aux trente-sixième dessous; *(of business, market)* être dans le marasme.
dole [dəʊl] *n Br F* **d. (money),** indemnité *f* de chômage; **to go on the d.,** s'inscrire au chômage; **to be on the d.,** être au chômage; **d. queues are lengthening,** le nombre des chômeurs s'accroît.
▶**dole out** *vtsep* distribuer *(qch)*.
doleful ['dəʊlfʊl] *adj (mine)* lugubre; *(cri)* plaintif; *(person)* triste, affligé.
dolefully ['dəʊlfʊlɪ] *adv* plaintivement; tristement.
doll [dɒl] *n* **(a)** *(for child)* poupée *f*; marionnette *f (de ventriloque)*; **baby d.,** baigneur *m*; **to play with a d.,** jouer à la poupée; **d.'s house,** maison *f* de poupée; *Fig* jolie petite maisonnette; **(b)** *F (woman)* femme *f*, jeune fille *f*; **(c)** *F* jolie femme; **(d)** *Am F* amour *m*; **be a d. (and do),** sois un amour (et fais).
▶**doll up** *vtsep* bichonner *(qn)*; **to d. oneself up,** *(of woman)* se pomponner; *(of man)* se faire beau; **to be all dolled up,** être sur son trente et un; **they've dolled their place up,** ils ont retapé leur maison.
dollar ['dɒlər] *n (currency)* dollar *m*; *F* **I bet my bottom d. that ...,** je parie jusqu'à mon dernier sou que ...; *Econ* **d. area,** zone *f* dollar.
dollop ['dɒləp] *n F* **a d. of butter,** un gros morceau de beurre; **a good d. of cream,** une bonne cuillerée de crème.
dolly ['dɒlɪ] *n* **(a)** *F (for child)* poupée *f*; **(b)** *F (young woman)* **d.(-bird),** poupée *f*; **(c)** *Cin* travelling *m*; chariot *m*; **(d)** agitateur *m (pour le linge)*; **d. tub,** *(for laundry)* baquet *m* à lessive; *Min* cuve *f* à rincer (l'or); **(e)** *Metal* tas *m* à river *(de riveur)*; **(f)** *Constr* avant-pieu *m*, *pl* avant-pieux; **(g)** *Rail (shunting engine)* diabolo *m*.
dolman [dɒlmən] *n* **d. sleeve,** *(on sweater etc)* manche *f* chauve-souris.
dolmen ['dɒlmen] *n Archeol* dolmen *m*.
dolomite ['dɒləmaɪt] *n Miner* dolomite *f*; *Geol (rock)* dolomie *f*.
Dolomites (the) [ðə'dɒləmaɪts] *npl* les Dolomites *fpl*.
dolphin ['dɒlfɪn] *n (mammal) & Her* dauphin *m*.
dolphinarium [dɒlfɪ'neərɪəm] *n* aquarium *m* pour dauphins.
dolt [dəʊlt] *n* sot *m*, lourdaud *m*, nigaud *m*, gourde *f*.
doltish ['dəʊltɪʃ] *adj* sot, lourdaud, bête.
domain [də'meɪn] *n* **(a)** *(property & Fig)* domaine *m*; terres *fpl*; **(b)** *Math Phys* domaine *m (d'une fonction)*.
dome [dəʊm] *n* **(a)** *Archit* dôme *m*, coupole *f*; *Can* **d. fastener,** bouton-pression *m*, pression *mf*; **(b)** *Fig* dôme *m*, calotte *f (des cieux)*; sommet arrondi *(d'une colline)*; calotte *f (du crâne)*; *F* tête *f*; **(c)** *Metal* dôme *m*, voûte *f (de fourneau)*.
domed [dəʊmd] *adj* **(a)** *(édifice)* à dôme, à coupole; **(b)** en forme de dôme.
Domesday ['duːmzdeɪ] *n Hist* **D. Book,** = (livre *m* du) cadastre *m* de l'Angleterre *(établi en 1086 par Guillaume le Conquérant)*.
domestic [də'mestɪk] **1** *adj* **(a)** *(vertu, malheur)* domestique; *(charbon)* de ménage; **she does d. work,** *(to earn a living)* elle fait des ménages; **to be in d. service,** être employé de maison; **to have d. problems,** avoir des problèmes domestiques; **water for d. use,** eau ménagère; **d. animal,** animal domestique; **d. appliances,** appareils ménagers; **d. duties,** les affaires *fpl ou* les soins *mpl* de ménage; **d. life,** la vie de famille; **d. servant,** domestique *mf*; bonne *f*; *Br Sch* **d. science,** enseignement ménager; **(b)** *(commerce, dissension, vol etc)* intérieur; *(production)* national; **d. products,** denrées *fpl* du pays; *US* **d. mail,** correspondance *f* à destination de l'intérieur; **(c)** *(person)* casanier; *(femme)* d'intérieur. **2** *n Br Fml* domestique *mf*; bonne *f*; *Am* femme *f* de ménage.
domesticate [də'mestɪkeɪt] *vt* **(a)** *(tame)* domestiquer, apprivoiser *(un animal)*; **(b)** *(naturalize)* acclimater *(un animal, une plante)*; **(c) to be domesticated,** *(of person)* aimer la vie d'intérieur; **to become domesticated,** prendre goût à la vie d'intérieur; **her husband is quite domesticated,** son mari l'aide pas mal à faire les travaux ménagers.
domesticity [dəʊmes'tɪsɪtɪ] *n* **(a)** *(liking for home)* attachement *m* au foyer; goûts *mpl* domestiques; **(b)** *(home life)* vie *f* de famille; **(c)** simplicité *f (d'un intérieur)*.
domicile[1] ['dɒmɪsaɪl] *n Com Jur* domicile *m*.
domicile[2] *vt* **(a)** établir *(qn)* (dans un pays); **domiciled at Leeds,** domicilié *ou* demeurant à Leeds; **(b)** *Com* domicilier *(un effet)*; **bills domiciled in France,** traites *fpl* payables en France.
domiciliary [dɒmɪ'sɪlɪərɪ] *adj (visite etc)* domiciliaire; *(assistance)* à domicile.
dominance ['dɒmɪnəns] *n* **(a)** dominance *f (d'une maladie etc)*; prédominance *f (d'une race)*; **(b)** *Biol* dominance *f (d'un gène)*.
dominant ['dɒmɪnənt] **1** *adj (character, gene)* dominant; *(person)* dominateur, -trice; *(hauteur)* qui domine le paysage. **2** *n Mus* dominante *f*; **d. chord,** accord *m* de dominante; **d. seventh,** septième *f* de dominante.
dominantly ['dɒmɪnəntlɪ] *adv* d'une manière dominante.
dominate ['dɒmɪneɪt] *vt* **(a)** dominer (sur) *(qn, un peuple)*; **to d. a match/game/etc,** *(of player, team)* dominer un match/un jeu/*etc*; **to be dominated by s.o.,** subir la loi de qn; **man dominated by ambition,** homme en proie à l'ambition; **(b)** *(of mountain etc)* dominer *(le paysage)*; **the**

fortress dominates the town, la forteresse commande la ville.

dominating ['dɒmɪneɪtɪŋ] *adj* (*feature, colour etc*) dominant; (*personality*) dominateur, -trice.

domination [dɒmɪ'neɪʃən] *n* domination *f* (**over,** sur); **to be under s.o.'s d.,** être dominé par qn.

domineer [dɒmɪ'nɪər] *vi* se montrer autoritaire.

▶**domineer over** *vipo* tyranniser (*qn*).

domineering [dɒmɪ'nɪərɪŋ] *adj* (*person, character etc*) dominateur, -trice, autoritaire.

dominical [də'mɪnɪk(ə)l] *adj Rel* dominical, -aux.

Dominican¹ [də'mɪnɪkən] *adj & n Rel* dominicain, -aine.

Dominican² **1** *adj* dominicain; **the D. Republic,** la République Dominicaine. **2** *n* Dominicain, -aine.

dominion [də'mɪnjən] *n* **(a)** (*rule*) autorité *f*, empire *m*; **to have** *or* **hold d. over ...,** exercer son empire *ou* dominer sur ...; **(b)** (*land*) dominion *m*.

domino, *pl* **-oes** ['dɒmɪnəʊ, -əʊz] *n* **(a)** domino *m*; **dominoes,** (*game*) (*usu with sing verb*) (jeu *m* de) dominos; **to play dominoes,** jouer aux dominos; **game of dominoes,** partie *f* de dominos; *Pol Fig* **the d. theory,** la théorie des dominos; *Pol Fig* **d. effect,** effet *m* d'entraînement; **(b)** domino *m* (*de bal masqué*).

don¹ [dɒn] *n* **(a)** *Univ* professeur *m* (*d'université*); **(b)** (*Spanish title*) Don *m*.

don² *vt* (**-nn-**) revêtir, endosser (*un uniforme*); mettre, coiffer (*un chapeau*).

donate [də'neɪt] **1** *vt* faire un don de (*qch*); *Med* **to d. blood,** donner du *ou* son sang; **how much did you d.?,** combien est-ce que tu as donné? **2** *vi* faire un don.

donation [də'neɪʃən] *n* donation *f*, don *m*; **all donations are tax-deductible,** tous les dons sont déductibles des impôts; **to make a d. to a charity,** faire un don *ou* une donation à une œuvre de bienfaisance.

donator [də'neɪtər] *n* donateur, -trice.

done *see* **DO¹**.

donkey ['dɒŋkɪ] *n* **(a)** (*animal*) âne *m*, *f* ânesse; *F* baudet *m*; **he would talk the hind legs off a d.,** il est bavard comme une pie; **it happened d.'s years ago,** ça s'est passé il y a des années; **I haven't seen him for d.'s years,** je ne l'ai pas vu depuis une éternité; *Nau* **d. boiler,** chaudière *f* auxiliaire; **d. engine,** petit-cheval *m*, *pl* petits-chevaux; **d. jacket,** grosse veste; **d. race,** course *f* d'ânes; **(b)** *Fig* imbécile *mf*.

donkey-work ['dɒŋkɪwɜːk] *n* **(a)** (*drudgery*) gros travail; **(b)** (*groundwork*) le plus gros d'un travail.

donnish ['dɒnɪʃ] *adj* (*person*) pédant; (*air, ton*) d'érudit; **he's a bit d.,** il a un petit air professoral.

donor ['dəʊnər] *n* **(a)** *Med* donneur, -euse (*de sang, d'organe etc*); **d. card,** carte *f* de donneur; **(b)** *Jur* donateur, -trice.

don't *see* **DO¹**.

don't know [dəʊnt'nəʊ] *n F* votant indécis.

donut ['dəʊnʌt] *n esp Am Culin* = sorte de beignet; *Can* beigne *f*.

doodah ['duːdɑː] *n F* truc *m*, machin *m*.

doodle¹ ['duːd(ə)l] *n F* crayonnage *m*, griffonnage *m*; **the paper was covered with doodles,** la feuille était toute griffonnée.

doodle² **1** *vt F* crayonner, griffonner (distraitement) (*qch*). **2** *vi* crayonner, griffonner distraitement; (*on piano*) pianoter.

doodlebug ['duːd(ə)lbʌg] *n Hist F* bombe volante.

doolally [duː'lælɪ] *adj Sl* (*crazy, confused*) timbré.

doom¹ [duːm] *n* destin *m* (funeste), sort *m* (malheureux); **he met his d.,** il trouva la mort; *Fig* **to be full of** *or* **all d. and gloom,** (*of person, forecast etc*) être pessimiste; **the situation's not all d. and gloom,** la situation n'est pas aussi sombre qu'il y paraît.

doom² *vt* condamner (**to,** à); **doomed,** (*town*) condamné; (*person*) perdu; **attempt doomed to failure,** tentative condamnée à l'insuccès *ou* vouée à l'échec.

doom-laden ['duːmleɪd(ə)n] *adj* (*forecast, words etc*) lugubre, peu réjouissant.

doomsday ['duːmzdeɪ] *n* le (jour du) jugement dernier; *F* **till d.,** indéfiniment; **to put off sth till d.,** renvoyer qch aux calendes grecques.

Doomsday ['duːmzdeɪ] *n* **D. Book,** *see* **DOMESDAY**.

door [dɔːr] *n* **(a)** porte *f* (*de maison etc*); **doors of a wardrobe,** portes *ou* battants *mpl* d'une armoire; **front d.,** porte d'entrée; **back d.,** porte de service; **folding d.,** porte pliante; **sliding d.,** porte coulissante; **revolving d.,** porte tournante, tambour *m*; **two doors away,** deux portes plus loin; **the house next d.,** la maison à côté; **I live next d.,** j'habite à côté; **the journey takes twenty-five minutes d. to d.,** le voyage prend vingt-cinq minutes de porte à porte; **to answer the d.,** aller ouvrir la porte; **to show s.o. the d.,** éconduire qn; **to show s.o. to the d.,** conduire qn à la porte, reconduire qn; **out of doors,** dehors, en plein air; **to shut the d. in s.o.'s face,** fermer la porte au nez de qn; **to leave the d. open to** *or* **for negotiations,** laisser la porte ouverte à des négociations; **to close** *or* **shut the d. on any discussion,** rendre impossible toute discussion; **behind closed doors,** (*discussions etc*) entre quatre murs, à huis-clos; **to meet behind closed doors,** se rencontrer à huis-clos; **to lay a charge at s.o.'s d.,** imputer qch à qn; **d.-to-d. canvassing** *or* **selling,** porte-à-porte *m*; **to do d.-to-d. canvassing** *or* **selling, to canvas** *or* **sell d.-to-d.,** faire du porte-à-porte; **to be a d.-to-d. salesman,** être V.R.P., faire du porte-à-porte; **the foot in the d. technique,** (*of salesman*) = la vente (en porte-à-porte) forcée; **to put one's foot in the d.,** mettre le pied dans l'embrasure de la porte; **d. chain,** chaîne *f* de sûreté; **d. curtain,** portière *f*; **d. handle,** poignée *f ou* bouton *m* de porte; **d. knocker,** marteau *m* de porte, heurtoir *m*; **(b)** portière *f*, porte *f* (*de wagon, de voiture etc*); porte (*de réfrigérateur etc*).

doorbell ['dɔːbel] *n* sonnette *f*.

do-or-die [duːɔː'daɪ] *adj* (*effort, attempt etc*) acharné; **this do-or-d. attitude,** cette attitude de détermination inébranlable.

doorframe ['dɔːfreɪm] *n* chambranle *m ou* châssis *m* de porte.

doorjamb ['dɔːdʒæm] *n* montant *m* de porte.

doorkeeper ['dɔːkiːpər] *n* portier *m*, concierge *mf*.

doorknob ['dɔːnɒb] *n* poignée *f* (ronde) de porte.

doorman, *pl* **-men** ['dɔːmən] *n* portier *m*.

doormat ['dɔːmæt] *n* **(a)** paillasson *m* (*d'entrée*); **(b)** *Fig* (*person*) lavette *f*, chiffe molle; **don't be such a d.,** ne te laisse pas marcher sur les pieds comme ça; **to treat s.o. like a d.,** traiter qn comme une chose insignifiante.

doornail ['dɔːneɪl] *n F* **(as) dead as a d.,** mort et bien mort.

doorpost ['dɔːpəʊst] *n* montant *m* de porte.

doorstep¹ ['dɔːstep] *n* **(a)** seuil *m*, pas *m* (de la porte); **don't leave him standing on the d.,** ne le laisse pas sur le pas de la porte; *Fig* **there are shops and a library on your d.,** tu as des boutiques et une bibliothèque à ta porte; **(b)** *Br F* grosse tranche de pain.

doorstep² *vi* (*of canvasser*) faire du porte-à-porte.

doorstepping ['dɔːstepɪŋ] *n Journ F* technique des journalistes qui importunent les gens à leur domicile.

doorstop ['dɔːstɒp] *n* **(a)** (*fixed*) butoir *m*; **(b)** (*wedge*) cale-porte *m*, *pl* cale-portes.

doorway ['dɔːweɪ] *n* (baie *f* de) porte *f*; (*frame*) encadrement *m* de la porte; **in the d.,** sous la porte.

dope¹ [dəʊp] *n* **(a)** drogue *f*; *Sp* doping *m*, stimulant *m*; **(b)** *Sl* crétin *m*; **what a d.!,** quelle nouille!, quel andouille!; **(c)** *Old-fashioned Sl* rencard *m*, tuyau *m*; **to give s.o. the d. on sth,** rencarder qn sur qch; **(d)** *Av Aut* enduit *m*; **(e)** *Petr* additif *m*, dopant *m*; **(f)** (*for explosives*) absorbant *m*.

dope² *vt* **(a)** doper (*qn, un cheval*); verser une drogue dans (*une boisson*); **(b)** *Av Aut* enduire; **(c)** *Petr* **doped fuel,** carburant dopé, additionné d'anti-détonant.

dopehead ['dəʊphed] *n Sl* camé, -ée.

dopey ['dəʊpɪ] *adj F* **(a)** drogué, dopé; (*from sleep*) endormi; **(b)** (*stupid*) abruti, stupide; **what a d. thing to say,** que c'était stupide de dire une chose pareille.

doping ['dəʊpɪŋ] *n* **(a)** administration *f* d'un narcotique (**of s.o.,** à qn); doping *m* (*d'un cheval etc*); **(b)** *Av Aut* enduisage *m*; **(c)** *Petr* dopage *m* (*d'un combustible*).

Doric ['dɒrɪk] *adj & n Archit* dorique *m*.

dorm [dɔːm] *n Sch F* dortoir *m*.

dormant ['dɔːmənt] *adj* **(a)** (*passion etc*) assoupi, endormi; **to lie d.,** être en sommeil; **(b)** (*plant, bud*) dormant; **(c)** (*volcan*) en repos.

dormer ['dɔːmər] *n* **d. (window),** lucarne *f*, (fenêtre *f* en) mansarde *f*.

dormitory ['dɔːmɪt(ə)rɪ] *n* **(a)** dortoir *m*; **d. town,** cité-dortoir *f*, *pl* cités-dortoirs; **(b)** *Am* maison *f ou* foyer *m* d'étudiants.

dormouse, *pl* **-mice** ['dɔːmaʊs, -maɪs] *n* loir *m*.

dorsal ['dɔːs(ə)l] *adj Biol* dorsal, -aux; **d. fin,** nageoire dorsale (*d'un poisson*).

dory ['dɔːrɪ] *n* **(a)** (*fish*) **(John) D.,** dorée *f*, saint-pierre *m inv*; **(b)** (*boat*) doris *m*.

DOS [dɒs] *n Comptr* (*abbr* **disk operating system**) DOS *m*.

dosage ['dəʊsɪdʒ] *n* **(a)** dosage *m*, posologie *f* (*d'un médicament*); **(b)** administration *f* d'un médicament (**of**

s.o., à qn).

dose¹ [dəʊs] *n* **(a)** *Med Nucl Phys* dose *f*; *F* **to get through sth like a d. of salts,** faire qch en deux temps trois mouvements, faire qch en deux coups de cuillère à pot; **(b)** *F* attaque *f* (*de grippe etc*); **(c)** *Sl* (*of veneral disease*) vérole *f*.

dose² *vt* **(a)** administrer un médicament à (*qn*); **to d. oneself with quinine,** se bourrer de quinine; **(b)** doser (*un médicament, le champagne*).

dosh [dɒʃ] *n Sl* (*money*) fric *m*.

doss¹ [dɒs] *n Br Sl* **(a)** (*bed*) lit *m*, pieu *m*; **(b)** (*sleep*) somme *m*, roupillon *m*; **to have a d.,** faire un somme.

doss² *vi Br Sl* coucher à l'asile de nuit.

▶**doss down** *vi Br Sl* se coucher, se pieuter; **do you mind dossing down on the floor?,** est-ce que ça t'embête de coucher par terre?

dosser ['dɒsər] *n Br* **(a)** (*person*) clochard, -arde; **(b)** (*place*) asile *m* de nuit.

dossier ['dɒsɪeɪ, -ɪər] *n* dossier *m* (*d'une affaire*).

doss-house ['dɒshaʊs] *n Br Sl* asile *m* de nuit.

dot¹ [dɒt] *n* **(a)** point *m* (*d'un trait pointillé, d'un i, de ponctuation etc*); *Telecom* **dots and dashes,** points et traits; **on the d.,** (*arriver*) à l'heure tapante; **on the d. of three o'clock, three o'clock on the d.,** trois heures pile; *F* **since the year d.,** il y a des siècles; *F* **that was in the year d.,** c'était il y a une éternité; **three dots,** trois points, points de suspension; *Comptr* **d. matrix printer,** imprimante *f* matricielle; **(b)** *Mus* point *m* d'augmentation.

dot² *vt* (-tt-) **(a)** mettre un point sur (*un i*); *F* **to d. one's i's (and cross one's t's),** mettre les points sur les i; **(b)** marquer (*une surface*) avec des points; pointiller (*une ligne, un dessin*); **dotted with,** (*of surface etc*) parsemé de (*fleurs etc*); **the islands are dotted all round the coast,** les îles sont éparpillées tout autour de la côte; **(c)** *Mus* pointer (*une note*); **(d)** *F* **to d. and carry one,** boiter (*en marchant*); **(e)** *Sl* **to d. s.o. one,** flanquer un gnon à qn.

dotage ['dəʊtɪdʒ] *n* gâtisme *m*; **to be in one's d.,** être gâteux.

dote [dəʊt] *vi* être gâteux.

▶**dote on, dote upon** *vipo* aimer (*qn*) à la folie, être fou *ou* folle de (*qn*).

doting ['dəʊtɪŋ] *adj* qui montre une tendresse *ou* une indulgence ridicule; qui aime follement.

dotted ['dɒtɪd] *adj* **(a)** (*contour*) pointillé; **d. line,** (ligne *f* en) pointillé *m*, ligne pointillée; **to sign on the d. line,** signer à l'endroit indiqué (*sur une formule*); *Fig* donner son consentement; **tear along the d. line,** déchirer en suivant les pointillés; **(b)** *Mus* (*note*) pointé.

dottle ['dɒt(ə)l] *n F* culot *m* (*de pipe*).

dotty ['dɒtɪ] *adj F* toqué, piqué; **he's d. about her,** il est toqué *ou* fou d'elle.

double¹ ['dʌb(ə)l] **1** *adj* **(a)** (*having two, two together*) double; *F* **to be caught in a d. bind** *or Am* **whammy,** être dans une impasse; **to do a d. take,** marquer une pause; *Br Univ* **she took a d. first in English and History,** elle a deux licences avec mention très bien, une en anglais et l'autre en histoire; **to apply a d. standard,** utiliser deux poids, deux mesures; *Am* **to go on a d. date,** sortir à deux couples; **with a d. meaning,** à deux *ou* double sens; (*ambiguous*) ambigu, -uë; **'all' is spelt 'a, d. l',** 'all' s'écrit 'a, deux l'; **to reach d. figures,** (*of inflation etc*) atteindre les deux chiffres; **to play a d. game,** jouer double jeu; **to lead a d. life,** mener une vie double; **d. ace,** (*in dicing, dominoes*) double-as *m*, *pl* doubles-as; **d. agent,** agent *m* double; *Mus* **d. bass,** double basse *f*; *Mus* **d. bassoon,** contrebasson *m*; **d. bed,** grand lit, lit pour deux personnes; **d. bedroom,** chambre *f* pour deux personnes; *Cin* **d. bill** *or* **feature,** double programme *m*; **d. boiler** *or* **saucepan,** bain-marie *m*, *pl* bains-marie; **d. chin,** double menton *m*; *Br* **d. cream,** *Can* crème *f* à fouetter; **d. daffodil,** narcisse *m* double; *Comptr* **d. density (disk),** disquette *f* (à) double densité; **d. entendre,** *Pej* ambiguïté *f*, double entente *f*; *Tennis* **d. fault,** double faute *f*; **to d. fault,** faire une double faute; *Biol* **d. helix,** double hélice *f*; *Am* **d. indemnity,** (*in insurance*) indemnité double; **d. knitting (wool),** grosse laine; *Journ* **d. page spread,** page centrale; **d. pneumonia,** pneumonie *f* double; **to have d. pneumonia,** faire une pneumonie double; *Comptr* **d. sided diskette,** disquette à double face; **d. sink,** évier *m* à deux bacs; **d. strike printing,** imprimerie *f* à double frappe; **d. suicide,** suicide *m* double; **d. talk,** propos *mpl* nègre-blanc; **d. time,** = multiplication par deux du salaire horaire (des employés travaillant pendant le week-end etc); **d. whisky, d. Scotch,** double (dose *f* de) whisky *m*;

(b) *Mil etc* **d. time,** pas redoublé, pas de course; **in d. time,** au pas de gymnastique, au pas de course, en moins de deux.

2 *adv* **to see d.,** voir double; **to fold a sheet (of paper) d.,** plier une feuille en deux; **bent d.,** (*of person*) courbé en deux; **bent d. with pain/laughter,** plié en deux de douleur/rire; **d. the number,** le double, deux fois autant; **to pay d. the value,** payer le double de la valeur; **I am d. your age,** je suis deux fois plus âgé que vous, j'ai deux fois votre âge.

3 *n* **(a)** (*of person*) double *m*, *F* sosie *m* (*de qn*); *Th Cin* doublure *f*;

(b) *F* chambre *f* à deux personnes;

(c) *Tennis* **men's/women's/mixed doubles,** double *m* messieurs/dames/mixte;

(d) *Mil etc* **at the d.,** au pas de gymnastique, au pas de course; *Fig* en moins de deux;

(e) *Horseracing* pari couplé; **to bring off a d.,** réussir un double;

(f) *Cards* (*at bridge*) contre *m*; (*dominoes*) double *m*; *Billiards* doublé *m*;

(g) double *m*; **to toss d. or quits,** jouer (à) quitte ou double.

double² **1** *vt* **(a)** doubler (*un nombre etc*); porter (*un chiffre*) au double; *Tex* doubler (*le fil*); **to d. the stakes,** doubler la mise; **he doubled my salary,** il a doublé mon salaire; **(b)** plier en deux, replier (*du papier etc*); **(c)** *Cards* (*at bridge*) contrer; **(d)** *Billiards* **to d. the red,** doubler la rouge; **(e)** *Nau* doubler (*un cap*). **2** *vi* **(a)** (*of population, salary etc*) (se) doubler; **to d. in value,** doubler de valeur; **(b)** *Mil etc* prendre le pas de gymnastique.

▶**double as** *vipo* servir de (*qch*); *Th* **to d. as s.o.,** jouer un personnage en plus d'un rôle principal.

▶**double back** **1** *vtsep* replier, rabattre (*une couverture etc*). **2** *vi* (*of person, hunted animal etc*) revenir sur ses pas.

▶**double for** *vipo* remplacer (*qn*); *Th* doubler (*qn*); *Cin* (*of stuntman*) être la doublure de (*qn*).

▶**double over** **1** *vi* se plier; **to d. over with pain,** se plier en deux de douleur, se tordre de douleur. **2** *vtsep* replier, rabattre.

▶**double up** **1** *vi* **(a)** se plier (en deux); se courber (en deux); **to d. up with laughter,** se tordre de rire; **(b)** (*share room*) partager une chambre; **to d. up with s.o.,** partager une chambre avec qn; **do you mind doubling up with me?,** est-ce que ça te dérange de partager une chambre avec moi? **2** *vtsep* **(a)** replier (*du papier, de l'étoffe etc*); **(b)** (*of blow etc*) faire plier (*qn*) en deux; asseoir (*qn*) par terre.

double-acting ['dʌb(ə)l'æktɪŋ] *adj MecE* (*cylindre, machine à vapeur*) à double effet.

double-barrelled ['dʌb(ə)l'bærəld] *adj* (*fusil*) à deux coups; **d.-b. name,** patronymique *m* double (*par exemple* Mr J. Wynn-Jones).

double-bass ['dʌb(ə)l'beɪs] *n Mus* contrebasse *f* à cordes.

double-blind ['dʌb(ə)l'blaɪnd] *adj Med* **d.-b. test,** = test dans lequel ni les patients ni les docteurs ne savent à qui est administré le médicament ou le placebo.

double-bottomed ['dʌb(ə)l'bɒtəmd] *adj* (*casserole etc*) à double fond; (*canot etc*) à double coque.

double-breasted ['dʌb(ə)l'brestɪd] *adj* (*veston*) croisé.

double-check ['dʌb(ə)l'tʃek] *vt* revérifier.

double-clutch ['dʌb(ə)l'klʌtʃ] *vi US Aut* faire un double débrayage.

double-cross¹ ['dʌb(ə)l'krɒs] *vt F* duper (*qn*).

double-cross² *n F* duperie *f* (*d'un associé*).

double-crosser ['dʌb(ə)l'krɒsər] *n* traître *m*.

double-dealing ['dʌb(ə)l'diːlɪŋ] *n* duplicité *f*.

double-decker ['dʌb(ə)l'dekər] *n* **(a)** *Br* autobus *m* à impériale; **(b)** *esp Am* sandwich *m* double.

double-declutch ['dʌb(ə)l'diːklʌtʃ] *vi Br Aut* faire un double débrayage.

double-edged ['dʌb(ə)l'edʒd] *adj* (*épée, compliment, argument*) à deux tranchants.

double-faced ['dʌb(ə)l'feɪst] *adj* **(a)** *Pej* (*person*) à double face, à deux visages; hypocrite; **(b)** *Tex* réversible.

double-glazed ['dʌb(ə)l'gleɪzd] *adj* à double vitrage.

double-glazing ['dʌb(ə)l'gleɪzɪŋ] *n* double vitrage *m*; **to put in d.-g.,** installer du double vitrage.

double-headed ['dʌb(ə)l'hedɪd] *adj* à deux têtes; bicéphale; *Her* **d.-h. eagle,** aigle *f* à deux têtes; **d.-h. coin,** pièce *f* de monnaie à deux faces.

double-header [dʌb(ə)l'hedər] *n Am Sp* = deux matchs disputés l'un après l'autre.

double-jointed ['dʌb(ə)l'dʒɔɪntɪd] *adj* (*person, limb*) désarticulé.

double-lock ['dʌb(ə)l'lɒk] *vt* fermer (*une porte etc*) à double tour.

double-park ['dʌb(ə)l'pɑːk] *vt & vi Aut* stationner en double file.

double parking ['dʌb(ə)l'pɑːkɪŋ] *n* stationnement *m* en double file.

double-pointed ['dʌb(ə)l'pɔɪntɪd] *adj Knitting* **d.-p. needle,** aiguille *f* à deux empointements *ou* empointée aux deux extrémités.

double-quick ['dʌb(ə)l'kwɪk] *adj & adv* **in d.-q. time, d.-q.,** *Mil* au pas de gymnastique; *F* en moins de rien; **call an ambulance d.-q.,** appelle une ambulance tout de suite *ou* en moins de deux.

double-space ['dʌb(ə)l'speɪs] *vt* écrire *ou* taper (*un texte*) en double interligne; **d.-spaced,** à double interligne.

double-stop ['dʌb(ə)l'stɒp] *vi* (**-pp-**) *Mus* (*on violin*) faire des doubles-cordes.

double-stopping ['dʌb(ə)l'stɒpɪŋ] *n* double-corde *f*.

doublet ['dʌblɪt] *n* **(a)** *Ling* doublet *m*; **(b)** *Arch* pourpoint *m*, justaucorps *m*.

doubling ['dʌblɪŋ] *n* doublement *m* (*d'un nombre etc*).

doubly ['dʌb(ə)lɪ] *adv* doublement; **to be d. careful,** redoubler de prudence.

doubt¹ [daʊt] *n* doute *m*; **to be in d.,** être en *ou* dans le doute; **when in d.,** dans le doute; **to cast doubts on sth,** mettre qch en doute; **to have one's doubts about sth,** avoir des doutes sur *ou* au sujet de qch; **I have my doubts whether this is true,** je doute que cela soit vrai; **beyond (a shadow of a) d.,** hors de doute; **facts beyond d.,** faits avérés; **no d. he will come,** il viendra sans doute; **there is** *or* **seems to be no d. that ...,** il ne semble faire aucun doute que ...; **there is no d. about her guilt,** il n'y a aucun doute sur sa culpabilité; **there is some d. about her guilt,** il y a des doutes quant à sa culpabilité; **is there any d. in your mind?,** est-ce qu'il y a un doute dans votre esprit?; **do you have any doubts?,** est-ce que vous avez des doutes?; (*about getting married etc*) est-ce que vous hésitez?; **I have no doubts,** je n'ai aucun doute; **without (a, any) d.,** sans aucun doute.

doubt² *vt* douter de (*qn, la parole de qn*); mettre en doute (*la parole de qn*); **I d. it,** j'en doute; **I d. whether** *or* **if he will come,** je doute qu'il vienne.

doubtful ['daʊtfʊl] *adj* **(a)** (*person*) indécis, incertain; (*future*) incertain; **I'm d. about going,** j'hésite à y aller; **I was still d. about speaking to him,** j'hésitais encore à lui parler; **it is d. whether ...,** il est douteux *ou* à douter que ...; **to be d. of** *or* **about sth,** avoir des doutes sur qch; **(b)** (*caractère*) équivoque, suspect; (*question*) discutable; **in d. taste,** d'un goût douteux.

doubtfully ['daʊtfʊlɪ] *adv* **(a)** (*to say*) d'un air de doute; **(b)** (*to stand etc*) en hésitant, d'une façon indécise.

doubting ['daʊtɪŋ] *adj* incrédule, sceptique; **d. Thomas,** Thomas l'incrédule; **you're always such a d. Thomas,** tu es toujours tellement sceptique.

doubtless ['daʊtlɪs] *adv* **(a)** (*certainly*) sans aucun doute; **(b)** (*probably*) sans doute, très probablement.

douche [duːʃ] *n* **(a)** douche *f*; *Med* lavage *m* interne; (*as contraceptive*) douche vaginale; **(b)** *Med* (*instrument*) poire *f* à injection.

dough [dəʊ] *n* **(a)** pâte *f* (à pain); **(b)** *Old-fashioned Sl* fric *m*, pognon *m*.

doughnut ['dəʊnʌt] *n Culin* = sorte de beignet; *Can* beigne *f*.

doughty ['daʊtɪ] *adj Arch & Lit* vaillant.

doughy ['dəʊɪ] *adj* **(a)** (*pain*) pâteux; **(b)** *Fig* (*visage*) terreux.

dour [dʊər] *adj* austère, sévère.

douse [daʊs] *vt* **(a)** plonger *ou* tremper (*qch*) dans l'eau; **(b)** arroser *ou* asperger (*qn*) d'eau; **(c)** *F* éteindre (*la lumière, le feu*).

dove [dʌv] **1** *n* (*bird*) colombe *f*; **ring d.,** (pigeon *m*) ramier *m*, palombe *f*; *Pol* **the doves and the hawks,** les colombes et les faucons. **2** *adj* **d.(-coloured** *or* **-grey),** colombin, gorge-de-pigeon *inv*.

dovecote ['dʌvkɒt] *n* colombier *m*, pigeonnier *m*.

Dover ['dəʊvər] *n* Douvres; **the Straits of D.,** le Pas de Calais.

dovetail¹ ['dʌvteɪl] *n Carp* **(a)** queue-d'aronde *f*, *pl* queues-d'aronde; **(b) d. (joint),** assemblage *m* à queue-d'aronde.

dovetail² **1** *vt* assembler à queue-d'aronde; **dovetailed joint,** assemblage *m* à queue-d'aronde; **to d. two schemes (together, into each other),** harmoniser deux projets. **2** *vi* (*of schemes etc*) se rejoindre, se raccorder.

dowager ['daʊədʒər] *n* douairière *f*; **d. duchess,** duchesse douairière; *F* **d.'s hump,** = la bosse qui se développe chez les femmes d'un certain âge suite à une carence de calcium.

dowdiness ['daʊdɪnɪs] *n* manque *m* d'élégance *ou* de chic.

dowdy ['daʊdɪ] *adj* peu élégant; (*dress, image*) démodé.

dowel¹ ['daʊəl] *n Carp* **(a) d. (pin),** goujon *m* (*d'assemblage*); cheville *f* (*en bois*); **(b) d. (wood),** fenton *m*.

dowel² *vt* (**-ll-**, *US* **-l-**) *Carp* goujonner (*des planches*); enlacer (*un joint*); **dowelled joint,** enlaçure *f*.

dower ['daʊər] *n* douaire *m* (*de veuve*); **d. house,** maison assignée en douaire.

down¹ [daʊn] **1** *adv* **(a)** (*motion*) vers le bas; (de haut) en bas; **I'll be d. in a minute,** je descends dans une minute; **to lay d. one's arms,** mettre bas les armes; **to shoot** *or* **bring d. an aircraft,** abattre *ou F* descendre un avion; **to fall d.,** tomber à terre *ou* par terre; **money d., cash d.,** argent *m* (au) comptant *ou* sur table; **d. to the ground,** jusqu'à terre; **it suits me d. to the ground,** ça me va parfaitement; **d. with traitors!,** à bas les traîtres!; **d. with it!,** (*of medicine etc*) avalez!; **d.!,** (*to dog*) couché!;

(b) (*in crossword*) verticalement;

(c) (*position*) **d. below,** en bas, en contre-bas; **d. there,** là-bas; **further d.,** plus bas; **d. under,** aux antipodes; *US* **d. South,** dans les États du sud; **the blinds were d.,** les stores étaient baissés; **to lay sth face d.,** placer qch face en dessous *ou* à l'envers; **head d.,** la tête en bas; *Fig* **to hit a man when he's d.,** frapper un homme à terre; **to put sth d.,** (*in writing*) coucher qch par écrit; écrire qch; **she's d. for 20,** elle est inscrite pour (une cotisation de) 20; **he's 20 d.,** il a un déficit de 20; **I've got you d. to present the bouquet,** je t'ai désigné pour offrir le bouquet; **she's d. with flu,** elle est grippée; *F* **that gets me d.,** ça me déprime; *Tel* **the lines are d.,** les lignes sont coupées; **the wind is d.,** le vent est tombé *ou* s'est apaisé; **the river is d.,** la rivière est basse; **the price of gold is d.,** le prix de l'or a baissé; **bookings are d. on last week's,** les réservations sont en baisse par rapport à la semaine dernière; **you can have it for £50 d.,** c'est à vous pour 50 livres au comptant; *Comptr* **to be d.,** être en panne; **your team is five-two d.,** ton équipe est en train de perdre par cinq à deux; **to go d. by the bows,** (*of ship*) piquer de l'avant; **d. by the stern,** enfoncé par l'arrière;

(d) (*order, time*) **everyone from the boss d.,** tout le monde, y compris le patron; **from prince d. to beggar,** du prince jusqu'au mendiant; **I'm d. to my last cigarette/cheque,** j'en suis à ma dernière cigarette/mon dernier chèque; **d. to recent times,** jusqu'au temps présent; **d. to here,** (en descendant) jusqu'ici; **it's d. to you whether or not we go,** (*it's your decision*) c'est à toi de décider si nous y allons ou pas; **our lack of cash is all d. to the repairs to the roof,** (*is attributable to*) notre manque d'argent est entièrement dû aux réparations du toit;

(e) (*phrases*) **to be d. on s.o.,** en vouloir à qn; *F* **to come d. on s.o. like a ton of bricks,** tomber sur qn à bras raccourcis; **to be d. (in the mouth),** être découragé *ou* déprimé; **you look very d.,** tu as l'air très déprimé; *F* **to be d. and out,** être sans le sou, être sur la paille.

2 *prep* **to slide d. the wall,** se laisser couler le long du mur; **the tears ran d. his face,** les larmes lui coulaient le long des joues; **to go d. the street/a hill,** descendre la rue/une colline; **to go d. the river,** descendre le fleuve; **to fall d. the stairs,** tomber en bas de l'escalier; *F* **he's gone d. the pub,** il est allé au pub; *Rail* **d. the line,** en aval.

3 *adj* **(a)** (*depressed*) découragé, déprimé;

(b) *Rail* **d. train,** train descendant; *Rad* **d. lead** [liːd], descente *f* d'antenne; *Mus* **d. bow,** (*on violin*) tirez; **with the d. bow,** en tirant; **d. payment,** acompte *m*, versement *m* à la commande; *Comptr etc* **d. time,** (*of machine*) temps *m* de non-disponibilité; (*unproductive time*) perte *f* de temps.

4 *n F* **to have a d. on s.o.,** en vouloir à qn.

down² *vt* **(a)** terrasser, abattre (*qn*); descendre (*un avion*); *Boxing etc* abattre (*un adversaire*); **(b)** *Ind* **to d. tools,** débrayer; cesser le travail; **(c)** *F* **to d. a drink,** s'envoyer un verre.

down³ *n* **(a)** (*on bird, person*) duvet *m*; **(b)** (*on plants*) poil *m*, coton *m*, duvet *m*; (*on fruit*) duvet.

down⁴ *n Geog* (*usu pl*) **downs,** chaîne *f* de collines crétacées; *Br* **the (North** *or* **South) Downs,** les Downs *mpl*.

Down [daʊn] *n Med* **D.'s syndrome,** mongolisme *m*; *Med* trisomie *f*; **a D.'s syndrome baby,** bébé mongolien *ou Med* trisomique.

down-and-out ['daʊnən'aʊt] **1** *adj* **to be d.-and-o.,** être sans le sou. **2** *n* clochard *m*.

down-at-heel ['daʊnət'hiːl] *adj* **(a)** (*shoe*) éculé; **(b)** (*person*) râpé, *F* miteux.

downbeat ['daʊnbiːt] **1** *n Mus* (temps *m*) frappé *m*. **2** *adj*

F triste, déprimé; (*speech*) pessimiste.
downcast ['daʊnkɑːst] *adj* **(a)** (*person*) abattu, déprimé; **to look d.**, avoir l'air découragé; **(b)** (*look, eyes etc*) baissé.
downer [daʊnər] *n Sl* **(a)** (*drug*) tranquillisant *m*; **(b)** (*depressing situation, experience*) **to be on a d.**, avoir le moral à zéro, être aux trente-sixième dessous; **she's a real d.**, elle vous met le moral à zéro.
downfall ['daʊnfɔːl] *n* ruine *f* (*d'une personne*); écroulement *m*, effondrement *m* (*d'un ministère etc*); **drink was** *or* **brought about his d.**, la boisson l'a perdu.
downgrade¹ ['daʊngreɪd] *n* **(a)** *Rail etc* pente descendante; descente *f*, déclivité *f*; **(b)** décadence *f*; **to be on the d.**, baisser, être sur le déclin *ou F* sur le retour; (*of business*) péricliter.
downgrade² *vt* (*move to lower position*) rétrograder (*un employé*); déclasser (*un employé*) à une échelle de salaire inférieure; classer (*des marchandises*) dans une catégorie inférieure; **he was downgraded to area manager**, il a été rétrogradé au rang de responsable régional; **the hurricane has been downgraded to a storm**, l'ouragan n'est maintenant plus qu'une tempête.
downgrading ['daʊngreɪdɪŋ] *n* déclassement *m* (*d'un employé*) à une échelle de salaire inférieure; (*to lower position*) rétrogradation *f*; classement *m* (*des marchandises*) dans une catégorie inférieure.
downhearted [daʊn'hɑːtɪd] *adj* découragé, déprimé; **to become d.**, se décourager.
downhill ['daʊn'hɪl] **1** *n* **(a)** descente *f*, pente *f*; **(b)** *Ski* descente *f*. **2** *adj* en pente, incliné; **d. skiing**, ski alpin. **3** *adv* **to go d.**, (*of road*) aller en descendant; (*of car etc*) descendre (*la côte*); *F* (*of person*) être sur le déclin; (*of business etc*) péricliter; (*of s.o.'s work*) devenir moins bon; *Hum* **it's d. all the way after you're 40**, après 40 ans, c'est le déclin.
download [daʊn'ləʊd] *Comptr* **1** *vt* télécharger; **d. font**, police *f* téléchargeable. **2** *vi* se télécharger.
downloadable [daʊn'ləʊdəb(ə)l] *Comptr adj* téléchargeable.
down-market [daʊn'mɑːkɪt] **1** *adj* (*car, house etc*) bas de gamme; (*person*) ordinaire; (*district, accent*) populaire. **2** *adv* **to move d.-m.**, passer au bas de gamme; (*go to a cheap restaurant etc*) donner dans le populaire.
downpipe ['daʊnpaɪp] *n* tuyau *m* de descente.
downplay [daʊn'pleɪ] *vt* minimiser (*l'importance de qch*).
downpour ['daʊnpɔːr] *n* forte pluie, averse *f*.
downright ['daʊnraɪt] **1** *adv* **(a)** (*idiotic etc*) tout à fait, complètement; **(b)** nettement, carrément; (*nier, refuser*) catégoriquement. **2** *adj* **(a)** (*person, language*) direct; franc, *f* franche; **(b)** complet, absolu; (*mensonge*) éclatant; **d. fool**, franc imbécile; **a d. no**, un non catégorique.
downside ['daʊnsaɪd] *n esp Am* côté négatif (*de qch*).
downsize [daʊn'saɪz] *esp Am* **1** *vt* réduire les dimensions de (*une voiture*); **downsized car**, voiture *f* aux dimensions réduites. **2** *vi* (*of company*) réduire ses effectifs.
downstage ['daʊnsteɪdʒ] *Th* **1** *adv & adj* sur le devant (de la scène), à l'avant-scène. **2** *n* avant-scène *f*.
downstairs **1** [daʊn'steəz] *adv* **(a)** (*down the stairs*) en bas (*de l'escalier*); **to come** *or* **go d.**, descendre (l'escalier); **(b)** (*on a lower floor*) en bas; **our neighbours d.**, nos voisins d'en-dessous. **2** ['daʊnsteəz] *adj* **the d. rooms**, les pièces *fpl* d'en bas *ou* du bas *ou* du rez-de-chaussée. **3** ['daʊnsteəz] *n* rez-de-chaussée *m inv*.
downstream **1** *adv* [daʊn'striːm] en aval, à l'aval (**from**, de). **2** *adj* ['daʊnstriːm] d'aval; *Petr* **d. operations**, opérations *fpl* en aval.
downstroke ['daʊnstrəʊk] *n* **(a)** (*in writing*) plein *m*; **(b)** *MecE* course descendante; mouvement *m* de descente (*du piston*); **(c)** *Orn* abaissée *f* (*d'ailes*).
downswept ['daʊnswept] *adj* (*wings*) surbaissé.
downswing ['daʊnswɪŋ] *n* (*in economy etc*) tendance *f* à la baisse.
down-to-earth ['daʊntə'ɜːθ] *adj* (*person, approach, attitude*) terre(-)à(-)terre *inv*, réaliste.
downtown ['daʊn'taʊn] *Am* **1** *adv* vers (le centre de) la ville; **he gave me a lift d.**, il m'a descendu en ville; **to live d.**, habiter en ville. **2** *adj* **d. New York**, le centre de New York; **d. theatres**, théâtres *mpl* du centre. **3** *n* centre *m* (*d'une ville*); quartier *m* des affaires.
downtrodden ['daʊntrɒd(ə)n] *adj* **(a)** *Fig* (*people*) opprimé, tyrannisé; **(b)** (*grass etc*) piétiné.
downturn ['daʊntɜːn] *n* (*in economy etc*) baisse *f*.
downward ['daʊnwəd] **1** *adj* (*mouvement, sentier*) descendant; (*regard*) dirigé en bas; **d. trend**, (*in prices etc*) tendance *f* à la baisse. **2** *adv* = **DOWNWARDS**.
downwards ['daʊnwədz] *adv* de haut en bas; vers le bas, en descendant; (*on river*) en aval; (*regarder*) en bas; **to lay sth face d.**, placer qch face en dessous; **from the twelfth century d.**, à partir du *ou* depuis le douzième siècle; **children of five and d.**, enfants de cinq ans et au-dessous.
downwind **1** *adv* [daʊn'wɪnd] *Av* (*atterrir*) vent arrière; **to move d. of an animal**, se déplacer sous le vent d'un animal. **2** *adj* ['daʊnwɪnd] *Av* (*atterrissage*) vent arrière.
downy ['daʊnɪ] *adj* duveteux, duveté; (*fruit*) velouté.
dowry ['daʊrɪ] *n* dot *f*.
dowse¹ [daʊz] *vi* employer une baguette de sourcier, faire de la radiesthésie.
dowse² [daʊs] *vt* = **DOUSE (a),(b)**.
dowser ['daʊzər] *n* sourcier *m*, radiesthésiste *mf*.
dowsing ['daʊzɪŋ] *n* radiesthésie *f*; **d. rod**, baguette *f* divinatoire de sourcier.
doyen ['dɔɪjən] *n* doyen *m* (d'âge).
doyenne ['dɔɪjen] *n* doyenne *f* (d'âge).
doz *n* (*abbr* **dozen**) d(ou)z..
doze¹ [dəʊz] *n* petit somme; **to have a d.**, faire un petit somme.
doze² *vi* sommeiller, somnoler.
►**doze off** *vi* s'assoupir.
dozen ['dʌz(ə)n] *n* **(a)** (*inv*) douzaine *f*; **a d. eggs**, une douzaine d'œufs; **half a d., a half d.**, une demi-douzaine; **six d. bottles of wine**, six douzaines de bouteilles de vin; **by the d.**, à la douzaine; **(b)** (*pl* **dozens**) **they arrived in their dozens**, ils arrivèrent par douzaines; **dozens of people think as I do**, des douzaines de gens pensent comme moi; **to have dozens of things to do**, avoir des tas de choses à faire; **dozens and dozens of times**, maintes et maintes fois; **a baker's d., thirteen to the d.**, treize à la douzaine; *F* **to talk nineteen to the d.**, bavarder comme une pie.
dozenth ['dʌz(ə)nθ] *adj* douzième.
doziness ['dəʊzɪnɪs] *n* somnolence *f*.
dozing ['dəʊzɪŋ] *n* assoupissement *m*.
dozy ['dəʊzɪ] *adj* **(a)** somnolent, assoupi; **(b)** *Br F* (*not very bright*) nunuche.
D Phil [diː'fɪl] *n abbr* **Doctor of Philosophy**.
DPP [diːpiː'piː] *n* (*abbr* **Director of Public Prosecutions**) ≈ Procureur de la République.
dpt *n abbr* **department**.
Dr *n* **(a)** (*abbr* **doctor**) Dr.; **(b)** (*abbr* **Drive**) av..
drab [dræb] **1** *adj* **(a)** (*couleur*) terne; (*vêtement*) de couleur terne; **(b)** *Fig* morne, monotone; (*existence*) terne, décoloré. **2** *n* (*grey*) gris *m*; (*brown*) beige *m*.
drachm [dræm] *n* (*measurement*) drachme *f*.
drachma, *pl* **-mas** ['drækmə, -məz] *n* drachme *f*.
draconian [drə'kəʊnɪən] *adj* (*law etc*) draconien.
draft¹ [drɑːft] *n* **(a)** brouillon *m* (*de lettre*); projet *m* (*de loi*); avant-projet *m*, *pl* avant-projets (*de traité*); *Archit MecE etc* dessin *m* schématique, tracé *m*; **rough d.**, (*of map etc*) ébauche *f*; **do you want it in d.?**, tu le veux au brouillon?; **first d. of a novel**, premier jet d'un roman; **d. contract**, projet *m* de contrat; *Comptr* **d. mode**, mode *m* rapide; *Comptr* **d. quality**, (*of printout*) qualité *f* ordinateur *ou* listing; **(b)** *Com* traite *f*; lettre *f* de change; **banker's d.**, chèque *m* bancaire; **(c)** *US Mil* conscription *f*; **to be d. age**, être en âge de faire son service; *F* **d. dodger** *or* **evader**, réfractaire *m*; **d. board**, = conseil *m* de révision; **(d)** *Mil* détachement *m* (*de troupes*); contingent *m* (*de recrues*).
draft² *vt* **(a)** faire le brouillon de (*une lettre*); rédiger (*un acte, un projet*); **to d. a bill**, établir un projet de loi; **(b)** *US Mil* appeler (*des soldats*) sous les drapeaux; **(c)** *Mil* détacher, envoyer en détachement (*des troupes*); affecter (*un militaire*) (**to**, à); **to d. troops into ...**, faire passer des troupes dans ...; *Fig* **could we d. in some outside help?**, est-ce que nous pourrions obtenir de l'aide à l'extérieur?; **to d. s.o. to a post**, désigner qn pour *ou* à un poste.
draft³ *n US* = **DRAUGHT¹**.
draftsman, draftsmanship *etc US* = **DRAUGHTSMAN, DRAUGHTSMANSHIP** *etc*.
drafty ['drɑːftɪ] *adj US* = **DRAUGHTY**.
drag¹ [dræg] *n* **(a)** tirage *m*, résistance *f* (*à l'avancement*), frottement excessif; *Av* traînée *f*; *Billiards* effet *m* rétrograde; ralentissement *m* (*d'un moteur à ressort etc*); **uphill d.**, montée fatigante; **there's a long d. ahead**, il y a encore toute une tirée; *Aut Av* **d. factor**, coefficient *m* de traînée;
(b) *F* ennui *m*; (*person*) raseur, -euse; **it's an awful d.**, c'est la barbe; **the party was a d.**, la soirée était rasante;
(c) *Sl* **to have a d.**, tirer une taffe (*d'une cigarette*);
(d) *Sl* costume féminin (porté par un homme); **he was in d.**, il portait des vêtements de femme; **d. artist**, artiste *m* de travesti; **d. queen**, travelo *m*; **d. show**, spectacle *m* de travesti;
(e) *esp US Sl* **the (main) d.**, la rue principale; *Am Aut* **d.**

(race), concours *m* d'accélération;

(f) *Am F* **to have d.,** (*influence*) avoir du piston;

(g) (*in hunting*) voie artificielle; **d. (hunt),** chasse *f* à courre où la meute suit une piste artificielle; drag *m*;

(h) *Agr* herse *f*; traîneau (grossier);

(i) enrayure *f*; **d. (shoe),** sabot *m*; **to put a d. on a wheel,** enrayer une roue;

(j) (*for dredging*) drague *f*; (*for retrieving lost object*) araignée *f*; *Nau* grappin *m* à main; (*for helping drowning person*) gaffe *f* de sauvetage.

drag² *v* (**-gg-** [drægd]) **1** *vt* **(a)** traîner, tirer (*qn, qch*); entraîner (*qn*) (contre sa volonté); **to d. one's feet,** traîner les pieds; *Fig* **to d. one's feet** *or* **heels,** montrer peu d'empressement (*à faire qch*); **he dragged himself to the door,** il se traîna jusqu'à la porte; **to d. its anchor,** (*of ship*) déraper; **(b)** draguer (*un étang, un fleuve*); **(c)** *Agr* herser (*le terrain*). **2** *vi* **(a)** (*of skirt etc*) traîner (*à terre*); (*of lawsuit, Th of scene etc*) traîner en longueur; (*of conversation, action*) traîner, languir; **time is dragging,** les heures traînent; **(b)** offrir de la résistance; (*of brakes*) frotter (*sur les roues*); **(c)** *F* **to d. on** *or* **at a cigarette,** tirer des bouffées d'une cigarette; **(d)** draguer (**for sth,** à la recherche de qch); **(e)** *Fishing* pêcher à la drague; **to d. for oysters,** pêcher les huîtres à la drague.

▶**drag along** *vtsep* traîner, entraîner (*qn, qch*).

▶**drag away** *vtsep* entraîner, emmener (*qn*) de force; arracher (*qn, qch*) (**from,** de); **I couldn't d. myself away,** j'étais cloué sur place; **if you could d. yourself away from the television,** si tu pouvais t'arracher de devant la télévision.

▶**drag behind** **1** *vtsep* traîner (*qch*) derrière (*soi*). **2** *vi* (*lag*) être à la traîne.

▶**drag down** *vtsep* **(a)** entraîner (*qn, qch*) en bas; faire descendre (*qn*) de force; **he dragged me down with him,** il m'a entraîné dans sa chute; **(b)** (*of illness etc*) déprimer (*qn*).

▶**drag in** *vtsep* **(a)** traîner (*un colis etc*) (dans une pièce *etc*); faire entrer (*qn*) de force; **(b)** *F* (*refer to*) faire allusion à (*qch*); **why do you always have to d. in my one mistake?,** pourquoi est-ce que tu te crois obligé de faire sans arrêt allusion à ma seule erreur?; **he keeps dragging her name in (to the conversation),** il n'arrête pas de glisser son nom dans le conversation.

▶**drag off** *vtsep* = **DRAG AWAY**.

▶**drag on** *vi* (*of affair etc*) s'éterniser; **to let a matter d. on,** laisser traîner une affaire; **the play dragged on and on,** la pièce n'en finissait pas.

▶**drag out** *vtsep* **(a)** traîner (*un colis*); faire sortir (*qn*) de force; **to d. s.o. out of bed,** tirer qn de son lit; **to d. the truth out of s.o.,** arracher la vérité à qn; **(b)** faire traîner (*une affaire*); **I had to d. out my presentation to fill the time,** il a fallu que je fasse traîner mon exposé pour gagner du temps; **(c) to d. out a wretched existence,** traîner une existence misérable.

▶**drag up** *vt* **(a)** entraîner *ou* tirer (*qn, qch*) jusqu'en haut; *F* **you dragged me up to London for this?,** et c'est pour ça que tu m'as fait venir à Londres?; **(b)** (*refer to*) faire allusion à, évoquer (*qch*); *F* **why do you d. up that old story?,** pourquoi déterrer cette vieille histoire?; **there's no need to d. up the past,** ça ne sert à rien de déterrer le passé; **(c)** *F* (*raise badly*) **those children are being dragged up,** ces enfants sont élevés n'importe comment; **where were YOU dragged up?,** où as-tu été élevé?

dragging ['drægɪŋ] **1** *adj* **d. step,** pas traînant. **2** *n* **(a)** traînage *m*, traînement *m* (*d'un fardeau derrière soi etc*); *Nau* **d. of the anchor,** dérapage *m*; **(b)** dragage *m* (*d'un étang etc*); **(c)** *Fishing* pêche *f* à la drague *ou* au traîneau.

draggy ['drægɪ] *adj F* **(a)** (*evening, party*) ennuyeux, chiant; **(b)** (*listless*) pas dans son assiette; **to feel a bit d.,** ne pas être dans son assiette.

dragnet ['drægnet] *n* **(a)** cordon *m* de police; **twenty suspects were picked up in the d.,** vingt personnes suspectes furent arrêtées dans la rafle; **(b)** *Fishing* seine *f*, drège *f*.

dragon ['drægən] *n* **(a)** *Myth & F* dragon *m*; *Mil* **d.'s teeth,** rangées *fpl* de tétraèdres de béton (*comme défense antichar*); *Sl* **to chase the d.,** se shooter; **(b)** (*lizard*) dragon *m*; draco *m*.

dragonfly ['drægənflaɪ] *n* (*insect*) libellule *f*.

dragoon¹ [drə'guːn] *n Mil* dragon *m*.

dragoon² *vt F* **to d. s.o. into doing sth,** forcer qn à faire qch.

dragrope ['drægrəʊp] *n* **(a)** *Mil* bricole *f*, combleau *m*; **(b)** *Av* guide-rope *m*, *pl* guide-ropes (*d'un ballon*).

drain¹ [dreɪn] *n* **(a)** égout *m*; canalisation *f* sanitaire (*d'une maison*); **smell of drains,** odeur *f* d'égout; **the drains are overflowing,** les égouts débordent; **to pour sth down the drain,** (dé)verser qch dans les égouts; *Fig* **to throw money down the d.,** jeter son argent par la fenêtre; *Fig* **that's five years' work down the d.,** voilà cinq années de travail perdues; **to laugh like a d.,** rire à gorge déployée;

(b) perte *f*, fuite *f* (*d'énergie etc*); drainage *m* (*de capitaux etc*); **constant d. on the resources,** hémorragie continuelle; **the car is a continual d. on our resources,** la voiture nous cause de constantes dépenses; **the brain d.,** l'exode *m ou* le drainage *ou* la fuite des cerveaux;

(c) *Med* drain *m*; *MecE etc* tuyau *m* d'écoulement; **overflow d.,** (tube *m* de) trop-plein *m*, *pl* trop-pleins;

(d) canal *m*, -aux (*de décharge*); caniveau *m*, rigole *f*; *Agr* fossé *m* d'assainissement.

drain² **1** *vt* **(a)** évacuer, faire écouler (*des eaux*); (*from vegetables etc*) faire égoutter (*l'eau*); **to d. the wealth of a country,** épuiser les richesses d'un pays;

(b) boire (*un liquide*) jusqu'à la dernière goutte; vider (*une coupe*);

(c) (*remove liquid from*) assécher, drainer (*un terrain*); mettre à sec, vider (*un étang*); assainir (*un champ*); saigner (*un fossé*); désamorcer (*une pompe*); (faire) égoutter (*des bouteilles, des légumes*); vidanger (*le carter*); *Med* vider, drainer (*un abcès*);

(d) épuiser (*qn, la bourse*); **to d. s.o.'s energy,** épuiser qn; **to feel drained,** (*of energy*) être épuisé; (*of emotions*) être vidé; **to be drained of emotion,** ne plus ressentir aucune émotion; **to d. s.o. of their strength,** épuiser les forces de qn; **the company is being drained of its top executives,** la société perd ses cadres supérieurs;

(e) creuser des rigoles d'assèchement dans (*une prairie etc*).

2 *vi* (*of dishes etc*) (s')égoutter.

▶**drain away** **1** *vtsep* (*remove*) faire couler (*de l'huile etc*). **2** *vi* (*of water*) s'écouler; (*of strength, enthusiasm, energy etc*) s'épuiser.

▶**drain off** **1** *vtsep* faire couler (*de l'eau, de l'huile*). **2** *vi* (*of water*) s'écouler.

drainage ['dreɪnɪdʒ] *n* **(a)** = **DRAINING**; **d. ditch,** rigole *f* d'écoulement; *Geog* **d. area** *or* **basin,** bassin *m* hydrographique; *Med* **d. tube,** drain *m*; **(b)** *Constr* (*from land etc*) système *m* d'écoulement des eaux; (*drains*) système d'égouts; **main d.,** tout-à-l'égout *m inv*; **soil with good d.,** sol *m* perméable; **to improve the d. of soil,** rendre le sol plus perméable; **(c)** (*water*) eaux *fpl* de surface; (*sewage*) eaux d'égout.

drainer ['dreɪnər] *n* égouttoir *m*.

draining ['dreɪnɪŋ] *n* **(a)** écoulement *m* (*des eaux*); assèchement *m* (*d'un marais*); drainage *m*, assainissement *m* (*d'un terrain*); égouttement *m* (*des bouteilles etc*); vidange *f* (*d'un carter etc*); *Med* drainage (*d'une plaie*); **d. board,** égouttoir *m* (d'évier); **(b)** creusage *m* des rigoles d'assèchement (*dans une prairie etc*).

drainpipe ['dreɪnpaɪp] *n* tuyau *m* d'écoulement *ou* de drainage; *F* **d. trousers,** pantalon étroit *ou* en tuyau de poêle.

drake [dreɪk] *n* (*bird*) canard *m* mâle; **wild d.,** malard *m*.

dram [dræm] *n* **(a)** *Pharm* drachme *f* (= un seizième d'once = 1,77 grammes); **(b)** *F* goutte *f* (*de whisky*); **to take a d.,** prendre un petit verre (de whisky).

DRAM [dræm] *n Comptr* (*abbr* **dynamic random access memory**) mémoire *f* RAM dynamique.

drama ['drɑːmə] *n* **(a)** *Th & Fig* drame *m*; **to make a d. out of a trivial incident,** faire un drame d'un incident sans importance; **(b)** (*art form*) l'art *m* dramatique, le théâtre; **the masterpieces of French d.,** les chefs-d'œuvre du théâtre français; **d. student,** étudiant, -ante en art dramatique; **d. school,** cours *m* d'art dramatique *ou* de théâtre.

dramatic [drə'mætɪk] *adj* **(a)** (*ouvrage, situation*) dramatique; **the d. works of Corneille,** le théâtre de Corneille; **d. effect(s),** dramaturgie *f*; **(b)** (*geste, effet*) théâtral.

dramatically [drə'mætɪklɪ] *adv* (*see adj*) **(a)** dramatiquement; **(b)** théâtralement.

dramatics [drə'mætɪks] *npl* (*usu with sing verb*) le théâtre; *Pej* **this is no time for d.,** ce n'est pas le moment de faire un drame *ou* de dramatiser.

dramatist ['dræmətɪst] *n* auteur *m* dramatique, dramaturge *m*.

dramatization [dræmətaɪ'zeɪʃən] *n* dramatisation *f* (*d'un événement*); adaptation *f* (*d'un roman etc*).

dramatize ['dræmətaɪz] **1** *vt* dramatiser (*un événement*); adapter (*un roman*); **there's no need to d. it,** il ne faut pas en faire un drame. **2** *vi* **novel that would d. well,**

roman qui s'adapterait bien à la scène *ou* à l'écran *ou* à la radio; **there's no need to d.,** il ne faut pas en faire un drame.

drape¹ [dreɪp] **1** *vt* draper, tendre (**with, in,** de); draper (*une encolure, une étoffe*); **to d. sth over sth,** draper qch autour de qch *ou* sur qch; **the hall was draped in black,** la salle était tendue de noir; **she was draped over the sofa,** elle s'était étalée sur le canapé; **she draped herself round him,** elle l'a enlacé; **he had a coat draped over his arm,** il avait un manteau sur le bras. **2** *vi* (*of material*) se draper.

drape² *n* **(a)** drapé *m* (*d'une robe etc*); **(b) drapes,** tentures *fpl*; *Am* (*curtains*) rideaux *mpl*.

draper ['dreɪpər] *n Old-fashioned Br* marchand, -ande de tissus.

drapery ['dreɪpərɪ] *n* **(a)** *Old-fashioned Br* (*trade*) commerce *m* des tissus; (*shop*) magasin *m* de tissus; **linen d.,** (articles *mpl* de) blanc *m*; **(b)** tentures *fpl*.

drastic ['dræstɪk] *adj* (*action*) énergique; (*measures, solution, change*) radical, -aux, drastique; (*cuts*) draconien; (*remedy*) drastique; (*shortage*) dramatique, critique; (*need*) urgent; **things are getting d.,** la situation devient critique; **that's quite a d. haircut,** il a *ou* tu as *etc* la boule à zéro; **that's a bit d.,** c'est un peu exagéré; **to make d. cuts,** faire des coupes sombres; **d. reductions,** (*notice in shop*) soldes monstres.

drastically ['dræstɪklɪ] *adv* (*to act*) énergiquement; (*shortened, improved etc*) radicalement; **to be d. short of sth,** manquer dramatiquement de qch; **they're not d. different,** ils ne sont pas fondamentalement différents; **d. reduced prices,** prix cassés.

drat [dræt] *int Old-fashioned F* **d. (it)!,** sacristi!, nom de nom!; **d. the child!,** au diable cet enfant!

dratted ['drætɪd] *adj Old-fashioned F* maudit (*garçon etc*).

draught¹, *US* **draft** [drɑːft] *n* **(a)** courant *m* d'air; **I'm in a d., I feel a d.,** je suis dans un courant d'air; **d. excluder,** bourrelet *m*; **d.-proof,** à l'épreuve des courants d'air; *F* **we're feeling the d.,** (*of firm etc*) les affaires vont mal; **(b)** tirage *m* (*d'une cheminée*); *Ind etc* entrée *f* d'air; venue *f* du vent; **(c)** (*drinking*) trait *m*, gorgée *f*; **(d)** *Arch Med* potion *f*; **poisoned d.,** potion empoisonnée; **(e)** *Nau* tirant *m* d'eau (*d'un navire*); **(f) beer on d.,** bière *f* à la pression; **d. beer,** bière au tonneau; **(g)** traction *f*, tirage *m*; **d. animal,** bête *f* de trait.

draught² *n & vt* = **DRAFT¹·²**.

draughtboard ['drɑːftbɔːd] *n* damier *m*.

draughts ['drɑːfts] *n Br* (jeu *m* de) dames *fpl*.

draughtsman, *US* **draftsman,** *pl* **-men** ['drɑːftsmən] *n* **(a)** *Ind* dessinateur *m*, traceur *m* (*de plans, d'épures etc*); **(b)** *Art* dessinateur *m*.

draughtsmanship, *US* **draftsmanship** ['drɑːftsmənʃɪp] *n* **(a)** l'art *m* du dessin industriel; *Ind* le dessin; **(b)** talent *m* de dessinateur.

draughtswoman, *US* **draftswoman,** *pl* **-women** [drɑːftswʊmən, -wɪmɪn] **(a)** *Ind* dessinatrice *f* (*de plans, d'épures etc*); **(b)** *Art* dessinatrice *f*.

draughty, *US* **drafty** ['drɑːftɪ] *adj* (*room*) plein de courants d'air; (*coin de rue etc*) exposé à tous les vents.

draw¹ [drɔː] *n* **(a)** *Sp* partie nulle, match nul; **the game ended in a d.,** ils ont fait partie nulle; **(b)** (*action*) tirage *m* au sort; (*lottery*) loterie *f*; tombola *f*; *Sp* tableau *m* des concurrents à chaque tour d'une série d'épreuves de championnat *etc*; *F* **that's just the luck of the d.,** ça c'est la vie!; **(c)** attraction *f*; clou *m* (*de la fête etc*); *Th* pièce *f* qui fait recette; **(d) to take a d. at one's pipe,** tirer une bouffée de sa pipe; *F* **to be quick on the d.,** (*with gun*) avoir la gâchette facile; (*with answers*) avoir la répartie facile; **to be a fast d.,** avoir la gâchette facile; **the fastest d. in the West,** le tireur le plus rapide de l'Ouest.

draw² *v* (**drew** [druː], **drawn** [drɔːn]) **1** *vt* **(a)** *Art* dessiner (*un paysage, une figure*); tracer (*un cercle, un plan*); tirer, mener (*une ligne*); construire (*des figures géométriques*); **to d. a map,** dessiner une carte; (*of surveyor*) dresser une carte; **to d. s.o.'s picture,** faire le portrait de qn; **the author has drawn the characters skilfully,** l'auteur a tracé les personnages avec adresse; **to d. a comparison,** faire *ou* établir une comparaison (**between two things,** entre deux choses);

(b) (*pull*) tirer (*une charrette*); hâler (*un filet*) à bord; tendre (*un arc*); baisser (*un store*); **to d. the curtains,** tirer les rideaux; **drawn by a locomotive,** remorqué par une locomotive; **to d. breath,** souffler; *Fig* **I haven't drawn breath all day,** (*I've been very busy*) je n'ai pas arrêté de la journée;

(c) (*extract*) retirer, ôter (**sth from** *or* **out of sth,** qch de qch); ôter (*une vis*); retirer, tirer, faire sauter (*un bouchon*); arracher (*un clou, une dent etc*); **to d. one's sword,** tirer l'épée, dégainer; **to d. one's revolver,** sortir son revolver de l'étui *ou* de sa poche, dégainer; **to d. a knife,** sortir un couteau; **to d. a card (from the pack),** tirer une carte; **to d. money from the bank,** retirer *ou* sortir de l'argent de la banque; **to d. blood,** (*of weapon*) faire couler le sang; **to d. (from the pool),** (*in dominoes*) piocher; **to d. lots for sth,** tirer qch au sort; **number five was drawn,** le numéro cinq sortit au tirage; **to d. a prize at a lottery,** gagner un lot à une loterie; *Fin* **to be drawn,** (*of bonds*) sortir au tirage; **to d. straws,** tirer à la courte paille; **to d. a confession from s.o.,** arracher un aveu à qn; **to d. water from the river,** puiser *ou* tirer de l'eau à la rivière; **to d. wine (from a barrel),** tirer du vin (d'un tonneau); **to d. consolation from sth,** tirer consolation de qch; **to d. a conclusion from sth,** tirer *ou* déduire une conclusion de qch;

(d) *Sp* **to d. a game with s.o.,** faire partie nulle *ou* match nul avec qn;

(e) (*receive*) toucher (*un salaire, Mil des rations*); **to d. (one's) supplies from s.o.,** s'approvisionner chez qn; *Cards* **to d. trumps,** faire tomber les atouts;

(f) (*attract*) attirer (*une foule etc*); **a pretty girl drew his eye,** une jolie fille attira son regard; **to d. a crowd,** (*of incident*) créer un attroupement; (*of play*) attirer le public; **to d. s.o. into conversation,** entamer une conversation avec qn; **to d. s.o. into the conversation,** faire entrer qn dans la conversation; **to feel drawn to s.o.,** se sentir attiré par qn ; **to d. the enemy's fire,** *Mil* attirer sur soi le feu de l'ennemi; *Fig* provoquer une attaque sur soi-même; **his accusation drew an instant denial,** son accusation provoqua un démenti immédiat; **the government refused to be drawn,** le gouvernement refusa de se commettre;

(g) libeller, rédiger (*un chèque*); **to d. a cheque on a bank,** tirer un chèque sur une banque;

(h) vider (*une volaille etc*);

(i) *Nau* **to d. twenty feet of water,** (*of ship*) tirer *ou* jauger vingt pieds d'eau, avoir vingt pieds de tirant d'eau;

(j) *Med* faire aboutir (*un abcès*);

(k) *Metal* étirer, tirer (*du fil, des tubes etc*).

2 *vi* **(a)** dessiner; **he draws extremely well,** c'est un dessinateur de premier ordre;

(b) être à égalité, faire match nul; **they drew two all,** ils ont fait deux partout;

(c) (*move*) s'approcher; **to d. near** *or* **close to s.o.,** se rapprocher de qn, s'approcher de qn; **when they drew near ...,** à leur approche ...; **the train drew into the station,** le train entra en gare; **to d. level with a competitor,** arriver à (la) hauteur d'un concurrent; **to d. to an end,** tirer *ou* toucher à sa fin;

(d) (*of chimney, pipe etc*) tirer; (*of pump*) aspirer; *Med* (*of plaster*) tirer;

(e) *Nau* **the sails were drawing well,** les voiles portaient plein.

▶**draw alongside** *vi* (*of vehicle*) rouler à côté de.

▶**draw apart 1** *vtsep* séparer, écarter. **2** *vi* (*of people*) se séparer, s'écarter.

▶**draw aside** *vtsep* tirer *ou* prendre (*qn*) à l'écart; détourner, écarter (*qch*); tirer, écarter (*les rideaux*).

▶**draw away 1** *vtsep* entraîner (*qn*); détourner (**s.o. from sth,** qn de qch); **she drew us away from the other guests,** elle nous a entraîné à l'écart des autres invités. **2** *vi* **(a)** (*of car etc*) s'éloigner; *Sp* **the first half-dozen runners are now beginning to d. away,** les six premiers coureurs prennent de la distance sur les autres; *Sp* **to d. away from a competitor,** prendre de l'avance sur un concurrent; **(b)** (*recoil*) reculer, avoir un mouvement de recul.

▶**draw back 1** *vtsep* **(a)** tirer (*qch, qn*) en arrière; **(b)** tirer, ouvrir (*les rideaux*); **(c)** (*attract back*) **what drew you back to your home town?,** qu'est-ce qui t'a poussé à revenir dans ta ville natale?; **I'm increasingly being drawn back to folk music,** je reviens de plus en plus à la musique folk. **2** *vi* **(a)** reculer; **(b)** (*from commitment etc*) se dédire; **it is too late to d. back now,** quand le vin est tiré, il faut le boire.

▶**draw in 1** *vtsep* **(a)** (*of cat etc*) rentrer, rétracter (*ses griffes*); (*of horseman*) serrer (*les rennes, la bride*); *Fig F* **to d. in one's horns,** faire des économies; **(b)** aspirer (*l'air*); **(c)** (*involve*) impliquer (*qn*); **they're arguing and I don't want to be drawn in,** ils se disputent mais je ne veux pas y être mêlé. **2** *vi* **(a)** (*of days, nights*) diminuer, raccourcir; **(b)** (*of train, bus etc*) arriver; **a car drew in to the kerb,** une voiture s'est rangée le long du trottoir.

▶**draw off** *vtsep* soutirer (*un liquide*).

▶**draw on 1** *vi* **(a)** (*approach*) approcher; **evening was**

drawing on, la nuit approchait; **as time drew on his health improved,** avec le temps sa santé s'améliora; **(b)** (*go past slowly*) s'avancer; **as the day gradually drew on,** au fur et à mesure que la journée s'écoulait. **2** *vipo* **(a)** (*use*) se servir de (*qch*); **to d. on one's savings,** prendre sur ses économies; **to d. on the reserves,** puiser dans les réserves; **to d. on s.o.'s experiences for a novel,** s'inspirer des expériences de qn pour un roman; **(b)** tirer sur (*une pipe, une cigarette*). **3** *vtsep* (*put on*) mettre (*qch*); **she drew on a pair of white gloves,** elle a enfilé une paire de gants.

►**draw out 1** *vtsep* **(a)** sortir, retirer (*qch de qch*); arracher (*un clou*); **to d. out money from the bank,** retirer de l'argent de la banque; **(b)** encourager (*qn*) à sortir de sa réserve; faire parler (*qn*); **(c)** (*prolong*) prolonger (*un repas, un discours*); tirer (*une affaire*) en longueur, (faire) traîner (*une affaire*); **long drawn out tale,** récit prolongé *ou* à n'en plus finir; **they drew the meeting out on purpose,** ils ont fait exprès de faire traîner la réunion; **(d)** (*stretch*) allonger (*un cordage*); étirer (*le fer*); étendre (*l'or*). **2** *vi* **(a)** (*of bus, train etc*) partir; **(b)** (*of days*) se prolonger.

►**draw to** *vtsep* tirer, fermer (*les rideaux*).

►**draw together 1** *vt* rassembler, réunir (*des personnes, des choses*); **the child's illness had drawn them together,** la maladie de l'enfant les avait rapprochés. **2** *vi* se rassembler, se mettre en groupe.

►**draw up 1** *vtsep* **(a)** tirer (*qch*) vers le haut; tirer, aspirer (*de l'eau*); **he drew the blankets up to his chin,** il ramena les couvertures jusqu'à son menton; **to d. oneself up,** se (re)dresser; **she drew herself up to her full height,** elle s'est dressée de toute sa hauteur; *Nau* **to d. up a boat (on the beach),** tirer un bateau à sec; **to d. up a chair,** approcher une chaise (*de la table*);

(b) dresser, rédiger (*un document*); établir (*un compte, un budget, un itinéraire*); dresser, rédiger, arrêter (*un programme*); indiquer (*une procédure*); élaborer (*un projet*); **document drawn up before a lawyer,** acte passé devant (un) notaire; **to d. up a will,** faire un testament;

(c) ranger, aligner (*des troupes*).

2 *vi* **(a)** (*of car etc*) s'arrêter, stopper; **to d. up at the kerb,** ranger la voiture le long du trottoir;

(b) (*of troops*) se mettre en rang, s'aligner; **to d. up in line,** se mettre en ligne;

(c) to d. up to the table, s'approcher de la table; **to d. up with s.o.,** arriver à la hauteur de qn.

drawback ['drɔːbæk] *n* **(a)** inconvénient *m*, désavantage *m*; **(b)** *Admin* remboursement *m* (à la sortie) des droits d'importation.

drawbridge ['drɔːbrɪdʒ] *n* **(a)** (*over moat*) pont-levis *m*, *pl* ponts-levis; **(b)** *Constr* pont basculant *ou* à bascule.

drawcard ['drɔːkɑːd] *n US* attraction *f*, *F* clou *m* (*d'une fête etc*).

drawcord ['drɔːkɔːd] *n* cordon *m* (*de rideaux etc*).

drawee [drɔː'iː] *n Com* tiré *m*, payeur *m* (*d'une lettre de change*).

drawer ['drɔːər] *n* **(a)** *Art* dessinateur *m*, traceur *m*; **she's a good d.,** elle dessine bien; **(b)** [drɔːr] tiroir *m*; **chest of drawers,** commode *f*; **bottom d.,** trousseau *m* (de mariage); *Old-fashioned F* **they're not really (out of the) top d.,** ils n'appartiennent pas vraiment à l'élite; *Com* **cash d.,** tiroir-caisse *m*, *pl* tiroirs-caisses; **(c)** *Com* tireur *m* (*d'une lettre de change*); **(d)** (*of water*) puiseur, -euse.

drawers [drɔː(ə)z] *npl Arch* **(pair of) drawers,** (*for men*) caleçon *m*; (*for women*) culotte *f*.

drawing ['drɔːɪŋ] *n* **(a)** *Art* dessin *m*; **to make a d. of sth,** tracer qch; **line d.,** dessin au trait; **rough d.,** ébauche *f*, croquis *m*; **pencil d.,** dessin au crayon; *Ind MecE* **engineering d.,** dessin industriel; **sectional d.,** (vue *f* en) coupe *f*; **d. board,** planche *f* à dessin; **still on the d. board,** (*avion, projet*) encore à l'étude; **d. book,** cahier *m* de dessin; **d. paper,** papier *m* à dessin; *Br* **d. pin,** punaise *f*; **d. office,** atelier *m ou* bureau *m* d'études; **(b) d. room,** salon *m*; *Am Rail* voiture *f ou* compartiment *m* salon; **(c)** (*of cart*) tirage *m*; **(d)** (*of water*) puisage *m*; (*of teeth*) extraction *f*; (*of lots*) tirage *m*; **(e)** attraction *f* (**towards,** vers); **d. power,** pouvoir attractif *ou* attirant; *Am* **d. card,** attraction, clou *m* (*d'une fête etc*); **(f)** *Com Fin* **drawings,** prélèvements *mpl*, levées *fpl*; **(g)** vidage *m* (*d'une volaille*); **(h)** *Metal* étirage *m* (*des métaux*).

drawing off *n* soutirage *m* (*du vin*).

drawing up *n* rédaction *f*, dressement *m* (*d'un acte*); **(b)** élaboration *f* (*d'une constitution*).

drawl¹ [drɔːl] *n* voix traînante; ton traînant; **to speak with a d.,** parler d'une voix traînante; **to speak with an affected d.,** traîner la voix avec affectation.

drawl² *vi* traîner la voix en parlant, parler d'une voix traînante, traîner ses paroles.

►**drawl out** *vtsep* dire *ou* prononcer (*qch*) avec une voix traînante *ou* une nonchalance affectée.

drawling ['drɔːlɪŋ] **1** *adj* (*voice, tone*) traînant. **2** *n* affectation *f* de langueur dans le débit.

drawn [drɔːn] *adj* **(a)** (*visage*) hagard, abattu; **d. features,** traits tirés; **(b) with d. sword(s),** sabre *m* au clair; *Sewing* **d.(-thread) work,** ouvrage *m ou* travail *m* à jour(s); **(c)** (*bataille*) indécis; **d. match,** partie nulle *ou* remise.

drawsheet ['drɔːʃiːt] *n Med* alaise *f*, alèse *f*.

drawstring ['drɔːstrɪŋ] *n* cordon *m*.

dray [dreɪ] *n* (*cart*) camion *m*, haquet *m* (*de brasseur*).

drayhorse ['dreɪhɔːs] *n* cheval *m* de roulage.

dread¹ [dred] *n* crainte *f*; terreur *f*, épouvante *f*; **to be** *or* **stand in d. of s.o./sth,** craindre *ou* redouter qn/qch.

dread² *vt* redouter, appréhender, craindre (*qn, qch*); **I'm dreading Monday,** je redoute la journée de lundi; **I'm dreading my driving test,** j'appréhende de passer le permis de conduire; **to d. that ...,** redouter que (ne) ... + *sub*; **I d. to think of it,** j'ai horreur d'y penser; **I d. having them both here,** j'appréhende de les avoir tous les deux en même temps; **the dreaded Monday finally arrived,** le lundi si redouté est finalement arrivé.

dreadful ['dredfʊl] **1** *adj* **(a)** (*douleur, bruit etc*) atroce, épouvantable; **it is d. that nothing can be done,** c'est affreux qu'on ne puisse rien faire; **(b)** *F* (*intensive*) terrible; **it's a d. bore!,** c'est assommant!; **(c)** *Fml* (*causing dread*) terrible, redoutable. **2** *n Arch* **penny d.,** roman *m* à deux sous.

dreadfully ['dredfʊlɪ] *adv* **(a)** terriblement, horriblement; **I was d. frightened,** j'avais horriblement peur; **(b)** *F* (*intensive*) **d. ugly,** affreusement laid; **our neighbours are d. noisy,** nos voisins sont terriblement bruyants; **I am d. sorry,** je regrette infiniment.

dreadlocks ['dredlɒks] *npl* coiffure *f* rasta.

dream¹ [driːm] *n* rêve *m*, *Lit* songe *m*; **to have a d.,** faire un rêve; **to have a d. about s.o./sth,** rêver de qn/qch; **to have beautiful/bad dreams,** faire de beaux/mauvais rêves; **sweet dreams!,** faites de beaux rêves!; **to see sth in a d.,** voir qch en songe; **to cherish a d.,** caresser un rêve; **to be in a d.,** être dans un rêve; **my d. house, the house of my dreams,** la maison de mes rêves; **it is my d. to go to Australia,** je rêve d'aller en Australie; *F* **a d. of a car,** la voiture rêvée; **it's a d.,** c'est le rêve; **it's a d. come true,** c'est un rêve devenu réalité, mon rêve s'est réalisé; **it worked like a d.,** cela a réussi à merveille; **d. sequence,** (*in film*) scène *f* de rêve; **d. world,** monde *m* imaginaire; *Austr* **in the d. time,** (*of native people*) = époque avant l'arrivée de l'homme sur la terre; *F* il y a des siècles.

dream² *v* (*pt & pp* **dreamt** [dremt], **dreamed** [driːmd, dremt]) **1** *vi* **(a)** (*in sleep*) rêver; **to d. of** *or* **about s.o./sth,** rêver de qn/qch; **you must have been dreaming!,** vous l'avez rêvé!; **to d. of one's youth,** rêver à sa jeunesse; **(b)** (*consider*) **I shouldn't d. of doing it,** jamais je ne m'aviserais de faire cela; **no one would have dreamt of suspecting him,** personne n'aurait songé à le soupçonner. **2** *vt* **I dreamt (that) you were ill,** j'ai rêvé que vous étiez malade; **little did I d. that ...,** je ne songeais guère que ...; **you must have dreamt it!,** vous l'avez rêvé!

►**dream away** *vtsep* passer (*son temps*) à rêver; **he'll d. his whole life away,** il passera sa vie à rêver.

►**dream up** *vt F* inventer, imaginer (*une idée etc*); **what have you dreamed up now?,** qu'est-ce que tu as encore inventé?

dreamboat ['driːmbəʊt] *n F* (*attractive man, woman*) canon *m*.

dreamer ['driːmər] *n* rêveur, -euse; *Pej* songe-creux *m inv*.

dreamily ['driːmɪlɪ] *adv* (*to look at, say*) d'un air *ou* d'un ton rêveur; (*to wander*) comme dans un rêve; **to think d. of the future,** rêvasser à l'avenir.

dreaming ['driːmɪŋ] *n* rêves *mpl*.

dreamland ['driːmlænd] *n* le pays *ou* le monde des rêves, le pays des songes.

dreamless ['driːmlɪs] *adj* (*sommeil*) sans rêves.

dreamy ['driːmɪ] *adj* **(a)** (*person, mood*) rêveur, -euse, songeur, -euse; **d. look,** air rêveur; *Pej* air distrait; **(b)** *Sl* magnifique, superbe.

drearily ['drɪərɪlɪ] *adv* tristement; (*to look at, say*) d'un air *ou* d'un ton morne.

dreariness ['drɪərɪnɪs] *n* tristesse *f* (*de l'existence etc*); grisaille *f* (*du temps*); aspect *m* morne (*d'un paysage etc*); manque *m* d'éclat (*d'un livre, d'un discours etc*).

dreary ['drɪərɪ] *adj* (*temps, paysage*) triste, morne; (*dis-*

cours etc) morne, ennuyeux; (*régime*) monotone.
dredge¹ [dredʒ] *n* **(a)** (bateau *m*) dragueur *m*; **(b)** (*machine*) drague *f*; **d. bucket,** godet *m* de drague; **(c)** *Fishing* **d. (net),** (filet *m* de) drague *f*.
dredge² **1** *vt* draguer, dévaser (*un canal*); **to d. away mud,** enlever la vase avec une drague. **2** *vi* **to d. for sth,** draguer à la recherche de qch.
dredge³ *vt Culin* saupoudrer; **to d. flour over meat,** saupoudrer la viande de farine.
►**dredge up** *vt* enlever (*la vase*) avec une drague; pêcher *ou* recueillir (*un objet submergé*) avec une drague; *Fig* déterrer (*un scandale*).
dredger¹ ['dredʒər] *n* **(a)** (bateau *m*) dragueur *m*; **(b)** (*machine*) drague *f*; **bucket d.,** drague à godets; **grab d.,** drague à benne piocheuse; **(c)** (ouvrier *m*) dragueur *m*; **oyster d.,** dragueur d'huîtres.
dredger² *n Culin* saupoudroir *m* (*à sucre etc*).
dredging ['dredʒɪŋ] *n* (*of canal etc*) dragage *m*.
dregs [dregz] *npl* lie *f*, fond *m* (*de la coupe*); *Fig* **the d. of society,** les bas-fonds *mpl* de la société.
drench¹ [drentʃ] *n Vet* breuvage *m*, purge *f*.
drench² *vt* **(a)** tremper, mouiller (**with,** de); **to get drenched (with rain),** se faire tremper, *F* se faire saucer; **drenched to the skin,** trempé jusqu'aux os; **to be drenched with sweat,** être en nage; **(b)** arroser abondamment (*le sol*); **(c)** *Vet* administrer un breuvage à (*une bête*).
drenching ['drentʃɪŋ] **1** *adj* (*rain*) battant, diluvien. **2** *n* **(a) we got a d.,** nous avons été trempés, *F* nous avons pris la sauce; **(b)** *Vet* administration *f* d'un breuvage (*à une bête*).
Dresden ['drezdən] *n* Dresde; **D. (china),** porcelaine *f* de Saxe.
dress¹ [dres] *n* **(a)** (*for woman*) robe *f*; **ball d.,** robe de bal; **d. designer,** styliste *mf*, modéliste *mf*; **d. materials,** tissus *mpl* pour robes; **d. preserver** *or* **shield,** dessous-de-bras *m inv*; **(b)** (*attire*) costume *m*; (*appearance*) toilette *f*, mise *f*; **in full d.,** (*of men*) en grande tenue; (*of women*) en grande toilette; **evening d.,** tenue de soirée; **it's a d. affair,** il faudra se mettre en tenue de soirée; **bird in its winter d.,** oiseau *m* dans son plumage d'hiver; *Mil* **fatigue d.,** tenue de corvée; (jeu *m* de) treillis *m*; *Mil* **mess d., formal d.,** uniforme *m* de cérémonie *ou* de soirée; *Mil* **full d.,** grande tenue; uniforme de parade; *Mil* **(full) d. parade,** parade *f* en grande tenue; *Mil* **walking-out d.,** tenue de ville; *Th* **d. circle,** premier balcon; *Th* **d. rehearsal,** générale *f*; **d. shirt,** chemise *f* de soirée; **d. suit,** habit *m* (*de soirée*).
dress² *v* (**dressed** [drest]) **1** *vt* **(a)** (*put clothes on*) habiller, vêtir (*qn*); *Th* costumer (*une pièce*); **to be dressed in black/silk,** être vêtu de noir/soie; **well/badly dressed,** bien/mal habillé; **to be plainly dressed,** avoir une mise simple; **dressed as a clown/a witch/***etc*, (*for a party*) déguisé en clown/en sorcière/*etc*; **dressed to kill,** sur son trente et un; **to d. oneself, to get dressed,** s'habiller;
(b) (*decorate*) orner, parer (**sth with sth,** qch de qch); *Nau* pavoiser (*un navire*); *Com* **to d. the window,** faire la vitrine; **dressed over all,** (*of ship*) sous le grand pavois;
(c) *Mil* aligner (*des troupes, des tentes etc*);
(d) *Med* panser (*une blessure, un blessé*); faire un pansement à (*un blessé*);
(e) *Tech* apprêter (*une surface*); corroyer (*le cuir*); apprêter (*les peaux*); dresser, tailler (*des pierres*); dresser, corroyer (*le bois*); trier (*le minerai*); préparer (*une matière première, le coton etc*); *Metal* nettoyer (*une pièce coulée*); *Culin* habiller (*une volaille, la viande*); *Culin* accommoder (*des plats*); *Culin* garnir, assaisonner, garnir (*une salade*); **dressed poultry,** volaille prête à cuire *ou* parée; **to d. timber roughly,** dégrossir le bois; **to d. s.o.'s hair,** coiffer qn.
2 *vi* s'habiller; **she's dressing,** elle est en train de s'habiller *ou* de se préparer; **to d. in black,** s'habiller de noir; **to d. (for dinner),** (*of man*) se mettre en habit; (*of woman*) se mettre en robe du soir; **they always d. for dinner,** ils s'habillent toujours pour le dîner.
►**dress down** *vtsep F* (*reprimand*) passer un savon à (*qn*).
►**dress up** **1** *vtsep* **(a)** (*put elegant clothes on*) **to d. oneself up,** se faire beau *ou* belle; **to be dressed up to the nines,** être sur son trente et un; **(b)** (*put on fancy dress*) se déguiser; **you could d. yourself up as Pierrot,** tu pourrais te déguiser en Pierrot; **to d. s.o. up,** costumer qn, déguiser qn (**as sth,** en qch). **2** *vi* **(a)** (*wear elegant clothes*) se faire beau *ou* belle; **(b)** (*wear fancy dress*) se déguiser; **children love to d. up,** les enfants aiment se déguiser.
dressage ['dresɑːʒ] *n Horseriding* dressage *m* (supérieur).
dresser¹ ['dresər] *n* **(a)** (*for plates etc*) buffet *m*; (*Welsh dresser*) vaisselier *m*; **(b)** *Am* (table *f* de) toilette *f*, coiffeuse *f*.
dresser² *n* **(a) to be a smart d.,** s'habiller avec chic; **(b)** *Th* habilleur, -euse; **(c)** (*tool*) (*for wood*) raboteuse *f*; (*for stone*) rabotin *m*; **(d)** *Br Med Surg* panseur, -euse; **(e) window d.,** étalagiste *mf*; **(f)** *Ind* apprêteur, -euse.
dressing ['dresɪŋ] *n* **(a)** habillement *m*, toilette *f*; **d. case,** nécessaire *m*, trousse *f* de toilette; **d. gown,** robe *f* de chambre; (*for women*) peignoir *m*; **d. room,** (*in home*) cabinet *m* de toilette; *Th Cin* loge *f* (*d'acteur, d'actrice*); *Sp* vestiaire *m*; **d. table,** (table *f* de) toilette *f*, coiffeuse *f*; **d.-table set,** garniture *f* de toilette;
(b) *Nau* pavoisement *m* (*d'un navire*);
(c) *Mil* alignement *m* (*des troupes*);
(d) *Med* pansement *m* (*d'une blessure*); **to apply a d.,** mettre *ou* faire un pansement; **surgical d. case,** trousse *f* de pansement; *Mil* **d. station,** poste *m* de secours;
(e) *Agr* engrais *m*; **a heavy d. of manure,** un gros apport de fumier; **surface d., top d.,** engrais en couverture, couche *f* d'engrais;
(f) *Culin* **(salad) d.,** assaisonnement *m* (*pour la salade*); **French d.,** vinaigrette *f*;
(g) *Tech* apprêt *m*, habillage *m* (*des peaux*); apprêtage *m* (*des étoffes*); dressage *m*, taille *f* (*des pierres*); dressage, corroyage *m* (*du bois*); préparation *f* mécanique (*du minerai*); rhabillage *m* (*d'une meule*); *Metal* nettoyage *m* (*d'une pièce coulée*); *Fishing* montage *m* (*d'une mouche*); *Tex* apprêt, empois *m*; *Culin* habillage *m* (*d'une volaille*); *Culin* accommodage *m*, assaisonnement *m* (*des plats*); *Constr* **surface d.,** enduisage *m* de surface;
(h) *Archit* **dressings,** moulures *fpl*;
(i) *Am Culin* farce *f*.
dressing down *n F* verte semonce, savon *m*; **to give s.o. a d. down,** passer un savon à qn; **to get a d. down,** se faire passer un savon.
dressing up *n* **an occasion for d. up,** une occasion pour sortir en grande toilette; **(b)** déguisement *m*; **d. up clothes,** vêtements *mpl* de mascarade.
dressmaker ['dresmeɪkər] *n* (*female*) couturière *f*; (*male*) couturier *m*.
dressmaking ['dresmeɪkɪŋ] *n* (*by tailor, dress designer*) couture *f*; *Ind* confection *f* de robes.
dressy ['dresɪ] *adj* **(a)** (*clothes etc*) chic, élégant; (*dress*) habillé; **(b)** *Pej* (*person*) trop habillé.
drib [drɪb] *n only used in* **in dribs and drabs,** petit à petit, peu à peu.
dribble¹ ['drɪb(ə)l] *n* **(a)** petite(s) goutte(s) (*d'eau etc*); *Fig* **supplies are coming through in dribbles,** les approvisionnements sont délivrés au compte-gouttes; **(b)** (*of person*) bave *f*; **(c)** *Fb etc* dribble *m*.
dribble² **1** *vi* **(a)** (*of person*) baver; **(b)** (*of water etc*) dégoutter, tomber goutte à goutte; **(c)** *Billiards* **to d. into the pocket,** (*of ball*) rouler doucement dans la blouse. **2** *vt* **(a) to d. (out),** laisser couler (*un liquide*) goutte à goutte; **(b)** *Fb etc* dribbler (*le ballon*); **(c)** *Billiards* **to d. the ball into the pocket,** faire rouler tout doucement la bille dans la blouse.
dribbler ['drɪblər] *n Fb etc* dribbleur *m*.
dribbling ['drɪblɪŋ] *n* **(a)** (*of person*) écoulement *m* de bave; **(b)** *Fb etc* dribbling *m*.
driblet ['drɪblɪt] *n* **(a)** *Fig* petite somme d'argent; **(b)** gouttelette *f*, petite goutte (*d'eau etc*); **in driblets,** goutte à goutte, au compte-gouttes.
drier ['draɪər] *n* = **DRYER**.
drift¹ [drɪft] *n* **(a)** mouvement *m*; direction *f*, sens *m* (*d'un courant*); cours *m* (*des affaires, des événements*); dérive *f* (*d'un avion, d'un navire*); dérivation *f* (*d'un projectile etc*); *Constr* déviation *f* (*d'un trou de sonde*); *Electron* glissement *m*; **policy of d.,** politique *f* de laisser-faire; **d. current,** courant *m* de surface; **d. ice,** glaces flottantes; *Fishing* **d. (net),** filet traînant; **d. transistor,** drift *m*; **continental d.,** dérive des continents; **the d. from the land,** la lente désertification des campagnes;
(b) (*meaning*) sens général, portée *f* (*des paroles de qn*); **I see his d.,** je vois où il veut en venir; *F* **I get the d.,** je pige;
(c) amoncellement *m* (*de sable etc*); *Geog* apport(s) *m(pl)* (*de sable*); congère *f* (*de neige*);
(d) *Min* direction *f* (*d'une galerie*); (*passage*) (galerie *f* de) chassage *m*; (*exploratory*) galerie d'exploration;
(e) *Tech* **d. (punch),** chasse-clef *m*, *pl* chasse-clefs; **d. (pin),** (*for rivet holes*) broche *f* (d'assemblage).
drift² **1** *vi* **(a)** être entraîné; (*of boat*) dériver, aller à la dérive; *Av* déporter; (*of questions, events*) tendre (**towards**

sth, vers un but); **to d. with the current,** se laisser aller au fil de l'eau; **wisps of smoke are drifting across the sky,** des fumées se traînent dans le ciel; **she's been drifting,** elle ne s'est pas fixée; **conversation drifted from one subject to another,** la conversation passait d'un sujet à un autre; **to d. apart,** (*of friends*) se perdre de vue; (*of married couple*) se séparer peu à peu; **the audience started to d. towards the exit,** les spectateurs se dirigeaient lentement vers la sortie; **to d. into war,** être entraîné dans la guerre; **to d. into crime,** être entraîné vers le crime; **to let things d.,** laisser aller les choses;

(b) (*of sand etc*) s'amonceler, s'amasser; (*of snow*) se former en congères, s'amasser;

(c) *Min* chasser; percer en direction.

2 *vt* **(a)** flotter (*du bois*); (*of current*) entraîner (*qch*);

(b) (*of wind*) amonceler, entasser (*la neige, le sable*);

(c) *MecE* brocher, mandriner (*un trou de rivet*).

drifter ['drɪftər] *n* **(a)** *Fishing* bateau *m* de pêche à filets traînants; **(b)** *Fig* personne *f* qui se laisse aller; **he's been a d. all his life,** il ne s'est jamais fixé.

drifting ['drɪftɪŋ] **1** *adj* (*navire etc*) à la dérive; (*nuage*) traînant. **2** *n* **(a)** entraînement *m* par le courant *ou* par le vent; **(b)** amoncellement *m* (*des neiges*); **(c)** *MecE* brochage *m*, mandrinage *m*.

driftwood ['drɪftwʊd] *n* bois flottant *ou* flotté.

drill¹ [drɪl] *n* **(a)** *Metal Carp* (*for wood, metal*) foret *m*, mèche *f*; (*for metal*) foreuse *f*, drille *f*; (*power-driven*) perceuse *f*; **spoon d.,** cuiller *f*, cuillère *f*; **electric d.,** perceuse électrique; **percussion d.,** perceuse à percussion; **d. chuck,** mandrin *m* (de tour) porte-mèche;

(b) (*of dentist*) fraise *f*;

(c) *Min Constr* perforateur *m*, perforatrice *f*; (*for taking borings*) sondeuse *f*, sonde *f*; **pneumatic d.,** marteau-piqueur *m* (à air comprimé), *pl* marteaux-piqueurs; **d. (bit),** burin *m*;

(d) (*training*) exercice(s) *m(pl)*; *Mil* **to do punishment d.,** faire la pelote; *Fig* **to know the d.,** savoir ce qu'il faut faire *ou* comment s'y prendre; **fire d.,** exercices de sauvetage (en cas d'incendie); *Mil* **recruit d.,** école *f* du soldat; *Mil* **firing d.,** instruction *f* du tir; *Mil* **rifle d.,** maniement *m* du fusil; *Sch* **verb d.,** exercices oraux sur les verbes; *Mil* **d. ground,** terrain *m* d'exercice *ou* de manœuvres; **d. sergeant,** sergent instructeur.

drill² **1** *vt* **(a)** forer (*un puits etc*); perforer (*une plaque*); percer (*un trou*); **(b)** fraiser (*une dent*); **(c)** *Min* (per)forer (*la roche etc*); **(d)** *Gym etc* faire faire l'exercice à (*des hommes*); *Mil* instruire, exercer (*des soldats*); *Nau* **well-drilled crew,** équipage bien exercé; *F* **to d. s.o. (in what to do/say),** faire la leçon à qn (sur ce qu'il faut faire/dire); **I can't d. (it) into him that ...,** je ne peux pas lui faire comprendre que ...; *Sch* **to d. pupils in French verbs,** faire faire aux élèves des exercices oraux sur les verbes français. **2** *vi* **(a) to d. for oil,** forer pour rechercher du pétrole; **(b)** (*of troops etc*) faire l'exercice.

drill³ *n Agr* **(a)** (*row*) rayon *m*, sillon *m*; **to sow the grain in drills,** semer la graine en rayons; **(b)** (*machine*) semoir *m* (à cuillers); **d. harrow,** herse *f* à semer; **d. hoe,** rigoleur *m*.

drill⁴ *vt Agr* semer en rayons.

drill⁵ *n Tex* coutil *m*; (*for denims etc*) treillis *m*.

drilling ['drɪlɪŋ] *n* **(a)** *Metal* forage *m*, perçage *m*; *Min* perforation *f* (*des roches etc*); *Min* forage *m*, sondage *m* (*d'un puits*); **d. machine,** sondeuse *f*, sonde *f*; *Petr* **oil d.,** forage pétrolier; **d. rig,** installation *f* de forage; **offshore d. rig,** île *f* de forage; **d. mud,** boue *f* (de forage); **d. platform,** plate-forme *f* de forage; **(b)** (*of tooth*) fraisage *m*; **(c)** *Mil* exercices *mpl*, manœuvres *fpl*.

drily ['draɪlɪ] *adv* = **DRYLY**.

drink¹ [drɪŋk] *n* boisson *f*; (*in bar, café*) consommation *f*; (*alcohol*) verre *m*, *F* pot *m*; **to give s.o. food and d.,** donner à boire et à manger à qn; **to give s.o. a d.,** donner à boire à qn; **to have a d.,** (*non-alcoholic*) boire *ou* prendre quelque chose; (*alcoholic*) prendre un verre *ou F* un pot; **I'd love a d. of water,** je voudrais bien un verre d'eau; **will you join me in a d.?,** tu prends un verre avec moi?; **we're going for a d.,** nous allons prendre un verre *ou F* un pot; **how about a d. after work?,** on prend un verre après le travail?; **to pay for the drinks,** payer les consommations; **long d.,** = gin, vodka etc allongé de jus d'orange, de limonade etc; **short d.,** = gin, whisky etc non dilué; *F* **the d.,** *Nau* la mer; l'eau *f* (*d'un lac, d'une rivière*); **to fall into the d.,** *Nau* tomber à la mer *ou* à la baille; (*into lake, river*) tomber dans l'eau; **strong d.,** spiritueux *mpl*; **soft drinks,** boissons sans alcool; **come round for a d.,** venez prendre un verre; **to take to d.,** s'adonner à la boisson, se mettre à boire; **to have a d. problem,** (trop) boire; **to be under the influence of d.,** avoir trop bu; *Jur* **to drive a car while under the influence of d.,** conduire en état d'ébriété; **to drive s.o. to d.,** pousser qn à l'ivrognerie; **don't d. and drive,** ≈ boire ou conduire, il faut choisir.

drink² *v* (*pt* **drank** [dræŋk]; *pp* **drunk** [drʌŋk], *Arch* **drunken** ['drʌŋkən]) **1** *vt* boire (*de l'eau etc*); **will you have something to d.?,** voulez-vous boire *ou* prendre quelque chose?; **to d. s.o.'s health,** boire à la santé de qn; **to d. s.o. under the table,** faire rouler qn sous la table. **2** *vi* être adonné à la boisson; **I don't d.,** je ne bois pas; **I'm worried about the amount he drinks,** je m'inquiète de la quantité qu'il boit; **to d. heavily,** s'alcooliser; **to d. like a fish,** boire comme un trou; **fit to d.,** bon à boire, potable.

▸**drink away** *vtsep* boire (*sa paie*).

▸**drink down** *vtsep* boire, avaler (*une boisson*).

▸**drink in** *vtsep Fig* boire (*les paroles de qn*).

▸**drink off** *vt* boire (*un verre*) d'un coup; avaler (*une coupe de champagne*).

▸**drink up** **1** *vtsep* achever de boire (*qch*). **2** *vi* **d. up!,** videz vos verres!

drinkable ['drɪŋkəb(ə)l] *adj* buvable; (*eau*) potable; **the wine's very d.,** ce vin se laisse boire.

drink-driving ['drɪŋk'draɪvɪŋ] *n Br F* **he was arrested for d.-d.,** il a été arrêté pour conduite en état d'ébriété.

drinker ['drɪŋkər] *n* buveur, -euse; **I'm not much of a d.,** je ne bois pas beaucoup; **wine/beer/tea/***etc* **drinkers,** buveurs de vin/de bière/de thé/*etc*; **he's a heavy** *or* **hard d.,** il boit beaucoup; **she's a social d.,** elle ne boit que pour les grandes occasions.

drinking ['drɪŋkɪŋ] **1** *adj* **I'm not a d. man,** je n'ai pas l'habitude de boire. **2** *n* **(a)** boire *m*; **d. fountain,** fontaine publique; *Ind etc* poste *m* d'eau potable; **d. glass,** verre *m* à boire; **d. trough,** abreuvoir *m*; **d. water,** eau *f* potable; **d. song,** chanson *f* à boire; **(b)** (*to excess*) ivrognerie *f*, alcoolisme *m*; **it was her d. that destroyed the marriage,** c'est son alcoolisme qui a détruit leur mariage; **d. bout,** beuverie *f*.

drip¹ [drɪp] *n* **(a)** (*sound*) bruit *m* de l'eau qui tombe *ou* qui s'écoule; bruit d'un robinet qui goutte; **(b)** (*drop*) goutte *f*; **the drips from the trees,** l'égoutture *f* des arbres; **d. cup,** cuvette *f* d'égouttage; **d. feed,** distributeur *m* compte-gouttes (*d'huile*); **d.-feed lubricator,** (graisseur *m*) compte-gouttes *m inv*; **d. mat,** dessous *m* de bouteille *ou* de verre; **(c)** *Med* goutte-à-goutte *m inv*; **he's on a d.,** il est sous perfusion; **(d)** *Sl* **he's/she's a d.,** c'est un mou/une molle.

drip² *v* (**-pp-**) **1** *vi* dégoutter, s'égoutter; (*of rain, water*) tomber goutte à goutte; **the perspiration was dripping from his forehead,** la sueur lui dégouttait du front, son front était ruisselant de sueur; **just leave it to d.,** (*of shirt etc*) laisse-le s'égoutter; **the tap has been dripping all night,** le robinet a fui toute la nuit; *Fig* **to be dripping with jewels,** être couvert de bijoux. **2** *vt* faire dégoutter (*du liquide*); laisser tomber (*du liquide*) goutte à goutte.

drip-dry ['drɪpdraɪ] *adj* (*shirt etc*) ne nécessitant aucun repassage.

drip-feed ['drɪpfiːd] *vt* (**drip-fed**) *Med* nourrir, alimenter (*un malade*) par perfusion.

drip-feeding ['drɪpfiːdɪŋ] *n* alimentation *f* par perfusion, drip-feeding *m*.

dripping ['drɪpɪŋ] **1** *adj* ruisselant; (*robinet*) qui goutte; **to be d. wet,** être trempé; **d. with perspiration/blood,** ruisselant de sueur/sang. **2** *n* **(a)** égouttement *m*; **(b)** *Br Culin* graisse *f* de rôti; **bread and d.,** tartine *f* à la graisse.

drippy ['drɪpɪ] *adj F* (*person*) mou, *f* molle; (*film, novel*) fade.

drive¹ [draɪv] *n* **(a)** *Aut* promenade *f* en voiture; (*in taxi*) course *f*; **a 50-km d.,** un parcours *ou* un trajet de 50 km; **it's an hour's d. away,** c'est à une heure en voiture; **to go for** *or* **take a d.,** aller faire une promenade *ou F* un (petit) tour en voiture; **it's a very pleasant d. to the coast,** la route est très belle jusqu'à la côte; *Aut* **test d.,** conduite *f* d'essai; **(b)** conduite *f* (*du bétail*); battue *f* (*du gibier*); *Am* (*action*) (transport *m* du bois par le) flottage *m*; *Can* drave *f*; (*logs*) train *m* (*de bois flotté*).

(c) *MecE* (mouvement *m* de) propulsion *f*; commande *f* (*par un organe*); transmission *f*, actionnement *m*; *Comptr* entraînement *m*; (*for disk*) lecteur *m*; **belt/chain d.,** entraînement *ou* transmission par courroie/chaîne; **gear d.,** commande par engrenages; *Aut* **direct d.,** prise directe; **front-wheel d.,** traction *f* avant; **vehicle with four-wheel d.,** véhicule *m* à quatre roues motrices;

(d) *Aut* conduite *f*; **left-hand d.,** conduite à gauche; **car with left-hand d.,** voiture avec conduite à gauche;

(e) *Golf Tennis* drive *m*; *Cr* coup droit long et appuyé; **(forearm) d.,** (drive de) coup droit;
(f) *Fig* (*initiative*) énergie *f*, dynamisme *m*; **to have plenty of d.,** être énergique *ou* entreprenant;
(g) (*campaign*) offensive *f* (*contre une place forte, un abus*); campagne *f* (*de vente etc*); **membership d.,** campagne *f* pour attirer des membres;
(h) *Psy* pulsion *f* (*sexuelle etc*);
(i) (*of house*) allée *f*; avenue *f* (*d'un château etc*); **the car's sitting in the d.,** la voiture est garée dans l'allée;
(j) *Cards* tournoi *m* (*de bridge, de whist*);
(k) *Min* galerie *f* en direction.

drive² *v* (*pt* **drove** [drəʊv]; *pp* **driven** ['drɪvn]) **1** *vt* **(a)** conduire (*une voiture, une locomotive*); piloter (*une voiture de course*); faire marcher (*une machine*); *Sp* driver (*un trotteur*); **can you d. a car?,** savez-vous conduire?; **to d. s.o. to a place,** conduire qn en voiture quelque part;
(b) chasser, faire aller (devant soi); conduire, mener (*le bétail*); rabattre (*le gibier*); diriger (*un flottage de bois*); **to d. the enemy from his positions,** déloger l'ennemi; **the wind is driving the rain against the window panes,** le vent chasse la pluie contre les vitres; **the waves drove the ship onto the rocks,** les vagues ont poussé le navire contre les rochers; **to d. the country (for game),** battre la campagne;
(c) pousser (*qn à une action*); réduire (*qn au désespoir etc*); **I was driven to resign,** j'ai été forcé de démissionner; **he won't be driven,** on ne le mène pas comme on veut; **to d. s.o. mad** *or* **out of their mind,** rendre qn fou; **to d. s.o. wild,** pousser qn à bout; **she drove me to it,** c'est elle qui m'y a poussé;
(d) surmener (*ses employés*); **to d. oneself too hard,** se surmener; **she drives herself as hard as she drives us,** elle se surmène autant qu'elle nous surmène;
(e) enfoncer (*un clou, un pieu*); serrer (*une vis*);
(f) percer, forer (*un tunnel*); pratiquer (*une galerie*); **to d. a railway through the desert,** tracer *ou* construire une ligne de chemin de fer à travers le désert;
(g) to d. a bargain, conclure un marché; **to d. a hard bargain,** chercher à gagner le dernier centime;
(h) to d. the ball, *Cr* chasser la balle; *Tennis* jouer un drive, driver; *Golf* driver;
(i) *MecE* actionner, faire marcher (*une machine*); (*of part*) actionner (*un organe*); *Comptr* (*of program*) commander; **driven by compressed air,** commandé par air comprimé.
2 *vi* **(a)** *Aut* conduire; **can you d.?,** savez-vous conduire?; **I don't d.,** (*I never learned*) je n'ai pas mon permis; (*any more*) je ne conduis plus; **to d. to the airport,** conduire jusqu'à l'aéroport; **who was driving?,** qui était au volant?; **to d. to a place,** se rendre en voiture à un endroit; **to d. slowly,** rouler à petite allure *ou* lentement; **to d. on the right (of the road),** circuler à droite, tenir la droite; **car that drives well,** voiture facile à conduire;
(b) to d. before the wind, (*of clouds etc*) chasser devant le vent; **the rain driving against the window panes,** la pluie qui fouette les vitres.

►**drive along** *vi* rouler (en voiture); **I was driving along slowly,** je roulais lentement; **to d. along the road,** rouler sur la route.

►**drive at** *vi* **what are you driving at?,** où voulez-vous en venir?; **what do you think she was driving at?,** où croyez-vous qu'elle voulait en venir?

►**drive away 1** *vtsep* **(a)** chasser, éloigner, écarter (*qn, qch*); **(b)** *Aut* emmener (*qn*) en voiture; **the men came in a car and drove her away,** des hommes sont arrivés et l'ont emmenée en voiture; **they were driven away in a taxi,** ils ont été conduits en taxi. **2** *vi* partir *ou* s'en aller en voiture; (*of car, driver*) démarrer.

►**drive back 1** *vtsep* **(a)** (*repel*) repousser, faire reculer (*qn, qch*); **(b)** *Aut* reconduire *ou* ramener (*qn*) en voiture. **2** *vi Aut* rentrer *ou* revenir en voiture.

►**drive down 1** *vtsep* **(a)** faire baisser (*des prix*); **(b)** *Aut* **to d. s.o. down to** *or* **into the country,** conduire qn (en voiture) à la campagne. **2** *vi Aut* se rendre en voiture (*de la ville à la campagne, de Londres en province*); **we drove down,** nous sommes allés *ou* venus en voiture.

►**drive home** *vtsep* **(a)** enfoncer, renfoncer (*un clou*); visser (*une vis*); **(b)** (*make understand*) faire comprendre à, *F* faire rentrer dans la tête de (*qn*); **d. it home to them that they mustn't speak to strangers,** fais-leur comprendre qu'ils ne doivent pas parler à des inconnus; **(c)** *Aut* reconduire (*qn*) chez lui (en voiture).

►**drive in 1** *vtsep* = **DRIVE HOME (a)**. **2** *vi Aut* entrer (en voiture).

►**drive off** = **DRIVE AWAY**.

►**drive on 1** *vi Aut* continuer (sa route); **d. on!,** continuez! **2** *vtsep* pousser (*qn*) (**to do sth,** à faire qch); **her friends drove her on to sue,** ses amis l'ont poussée à intenter un procès.

►**drive out** *vtsep* chasser (*qn, qch*); faire sortir (*qn*).

►**drive through 1** *vtaspo* **to d. one's sword through s.o.'s body,** passer son sabre à travers le corps à qn. **2** *vi Aut* passer en voiture; **we'll just d. through,** (*not stop*) nous ne ferons que passer en voiture. **3** *vipo Aut* passer par (*une ville*) en voiture.

►**drive up 1** *vi Aut* s'approcher; **they've just driven up,** ils viennent de s'approcher; **a car drove up to the door,** une voiture vint s'arrêter devant la porte. **2** *vtsep* augmenter (*des prix*).

drive-in ['draɪvɪn] *n Am Aut* (*cinema*) cinéma en plein air auquel on assiste en voiture, drive-in *m inv*; *Can* ciné-parc *m, pl* cinés-parcs; (*restaurant*) restaurant où les clients sont servis dans leurs voitures; **d.-in bank,** banque dont les guichets sont accessibles aux clients dans leurs voitures.

drivel¹ ['drɪv(ə)l] *n F* radotage *m*, bêtises *fpl*, balivernes *fpl*; **to talk d.,** radoter.

drivel² *vi* (**-ll-**, *US* **-l-**) *F* radoter; **what are you drivelling about?,** qu'est-ce que tu radotes?

drivelling, *US* **driveling** ['drɪv(ə)lɪŋ] *adj F* radoteur, -euse; **you d. imbecile!,** espèce d'idiot!

driven ['drɪv(ə)n] *adj* **(a) d. snow,** neige *f* vierge; **(b) electrically d.,** actionné par l'électricité; à commande électrique.

driver ['draɪvər] *n* **(a)** conducteur, -trice (*d'automobile*); chauffeur, -euse (*de taxi*); mécanicien *m* (*de locomotive*); conducteur *m* (*d'autobus*); mécanicien, wattman *m* (*de tramway*); (*of horse-drawn vehicle*) conducteur, - trice; cocher *m* (*de fiacre etc*); *Sp* driver *m* (*de sulky*); **racing d.,** coureur *m* (automobile); *Am* **d.'s license,** permis *m* de conduire; **d.'s seat,** siège *m* du conducteur; *Fig* **to be in the d.'s seat,** mener l'affaire;
(b) *Comptr* (*software*) programme *m* de gestion;
(c) conducteur *m* (*de bestiaux*);
(d) log d., flotteur *m*, driver *m*; *Can* draveur *m*;
(e) slave d., surveillant *m* d'esclaves; *Fig* homme *ou* femme qui fait marcher *ou* trimer son personnel; **she's a real slave d.,** c'est un véritable négrier;
(f) (*tool*) poinçon *m*; chassoir *m*;
(g) *Golf* driver *m*.

driveway ['draɪvweɪ] *n* entrée *f* (*d'une demeure etc*).

driving ['draɪvɪŋ] **1** *adj* **(a)** *MecE* (*wheel etc*) moteur, -trice; menant; **d. belt,** courroie *f* de commande; **d. force,** force motrice; *Fig* **the d. force behind the scheme,** le moteur d'un projet; **d. gear,** (engrenage *m* de) transmission *f*; **d. shaft,** arbre *m* de transmission; **d. wheel,** roue motrice (*de locomotive etc*); roue de transmission;
(b) (*rain*) battant; **d. snow,** neige fouettée par le vent.
2 *n* **(a)** conduite *f* (*d'une voiture etc*); **d. is fun,** c'est amusant de conduire; *Aut* **d. lessons,** leçons *fpl* de conduite; *Br* **d. licence,** permis *m* de conduire; **d. school,** auto-école *f, pl* auto-écoles; **d. seat,** siège *m* du conducteur; *Fig* **to be in the d. seat,** mener l'affaire; **d. test,** (examen *m* pour) permis de conduire; **to pass one's d. test,** avoir son permis (de conduire);
(b) log d., flottage *m* du bois; *Can* drave *f*;
(c) *MecE* commande *f*, transmission *f*;
(d) enfoncement *m* (*d'un clou, d'un pieu*); serrage *m* (*d'une vis*);
(e) *Min* percement *m* (*d'une galerie*);
(f) *Golf* **d. iron,** grand fer, driver *m*.

drizzle¹ ['drɪz(ə)l] *n* bruine *f*, crachin *m*; **the rain came down in a steady d.,** il pleuvait dru et menu.

drizzle² *vi* bruiner; **it was drizzling,** il bruinait, il faisait de la bruine.

drizzly ['drɪz(ə)lɪ] *adj* (*jour*) bruineux.

drogue [drəʊg] *n* **(a)** *Nau* cône-ancre *m, pl* cônes-ancres; **(b)** *Av* parachute *m* de queue (*pour freinage rapide*).

droll [drəʊl] *adj* drôle, comique; (*odd*) bizarre, curieux.

dromedary ['drɒməd(ə)rɪ] *n* dromadaire *m*.

drone¹ [drəʊn] *n* **(a)** (*bee*) abeille *f* mâle, faux-bourdon *m, pl* faux-bourdons; *Fig* fainéant *m*, parasite *m*; **(b)** (*noise*) bourdonnement *m* (*des abeilles*); *Mus* bourdon *m* (*de cornemuse*); *Fig* débit *m* monotone (*d'un pasteur etc*); ronronnement *m*, vrombissement *m* (*d'un avion*); **(c)** *Mil Av* avion téléguidé, drone *m*.

drone² 1 *vi* (*of bee etc*) bourdonner; *Fig* (*of person*) parler d'un ton monotone. **2** *vt* dire (*qch*) d'un ton monotone.

►**drone on** *vi* **he droned on for hours,** il n'a pas cessé de parler de sa voix monotone.

▶drone out *vtsep* = **DRONE² 2.**

drool [druːl] *vi* **(a)** baver; **(b)** (*talk nonsense*) radoter; *Fig* (*gloat*) s'extasier.

▶drool over *vipo* s'extasier sur (*qch*).

droop¹ [druːp] *n* attitude penchée (*de la tête*).

droop² **1** *vi* (*of head etc*) (se) pencher; (*of shoulders*) tomber; (*of eyelids*) s'abaisser; (*of feathers*) pendre; (*of flower*) pencher; (*of person*) languir. **2** *vt* baisser, pencher (*la tête*).

drooping ['druːpɪŋ] *adj* (*shoulders, moustache*) tombant; (*head*) baissé, penché; (*eyelids*) abaissé; (*flower*) qui commence à faner; (*person*) languissant; **to revive s.o.'s d. spirits,** remonter le moral à qn.

drop¹ [drɒp] *n* **(a)** goutte *f* (*d'eau, de sang*); doigt *m*, larme *f* (*de vin*); *Culin* filet *m* (*de vinaigre*); (*of necklace, chandelier etc*) pendant *m*, pendeloque *f*; **d. by d.,** goutte à goutte; *Fig* **it's only a d. in the ocean** *or* **bucket,** ce n'est qu'une goutte d'eau dans la mer; *Pharm* **drops,** gouttes; **nasal drops,** gouttes pour le nez; *F* **to take a d.,** boire un verre; **you've had a d. too much (to drink),** tu as bu un verre de trop; **he likes a wee d.,** il aime bien prendre la goutte; **acid d.,** bonbon acidulé; **chocolate d.,** pastille *f* de chocolat;

(b) (*fall*) chute *f*, baisse *f* (*de prix etc*); **a d. of a hundred metres,** un à-pic de cent mètres; **careful, it's a long d.,** attention, c'est haut; *Fig* **at the d. of a hat,** sans hésiter, sans hésitation; **sales show a d. of 10%,** les ventes accusent une régression de 10%; **d. in value** *or* **in takings,** moins-value *f*; **d. in voltage/pressure,** perte *f* de charge/pression; **there's been a big d. in enrolment,** il y a eu une forte chute *ou* baisse des inscriptions; **d. in the ground,** dénivellation *f* du terrain;

(c) *Av* parachutage *m*, droppage *m*; **delayed d.,** ouverture retardée (*d'un parachute*);

(d) (*of lock*) cache-entrée *m inv*; (*of gallows*) bascule *f*, trappe *f*; *F* **the d.,** la potence;

(e) *Th* **d. (curtain),** rideau *m* d'entr'acte;

(f) *Rugby* **d. kick,** coup tombé, coup de pied à ras de terre; **d. goal,** drop-goal *m*, *pl* drop-goals, drop *m*; *Tennis* **d. shot** *or* **stroke,** volée amortie, amorti *m*;

(g) *Archit* **d. arch,** arc-ogive surbaissé, *pl* arcs-ogives; **d.-leaf table,** table *f* à battants; *Metal* **d. forge** *or* **hammer,** marteau-pilon *m*, *pl* marteaux-pilons; mouton *m*; **d. stamp,** martinet *m*; *Nau* **d. keel,** dériveur *m*; aile *f* de dérive; *Th* **d. scene,** (*scenery*) toile *f* de fond; (*curtain*) rideau *m* d'entr'acte; **d. handlebars,** (*on bicycle*) guidon renversé;

(h) (*for spies to leave letters etc*) boîte-aux-lettres *f*;

(i) *F* **to have the d. on s.o.,** (*of cowboy etc*) avoir tiré plus vite que qn; (*have advantage*) avoir pris un avantage sur qn.

drop² *v* (**-pp-** [drɒpt]) **1** *vi* **(a)** (*of liquid*) tomber goutte à goutte, dégoutter (**from,** de);

(b) tomber; (*of person*) se laisser tomber; (*of ground*) s'abaisser; *Med* (*of womb etc*) descendre; **the book dropped from** *or* **out of her hands,** le livre lui tomba des mains; **his jaw dropped,** il en est resté bouche bée; **to d. into a chair,** s'affaler dans un fauteil; **I am ready to d.,** (*with fatigue*) je tombe de fatigue, je ne tiens plus sur mes jambes; (*with sleep*) je tombe de sommeil; **people are dropping like flies,** (*succumbing quickly to flu etc*) les gens tombent comme des mouches; **to d. (down) dead,** tomber (raide) mort; *Sl* **d. dead!,** allez au diable!;

(c) (*of prices, temperature etc*) baisser; (*of wind*) tomber;

(d) **there the matter dropped,** l'affaire en resta là; *F* **let it d.!,** n'en parlons plus!;

(e) **to d. to the rear,** passer à l'arrière; **to d. downstream,** (*of boat*) naviguer en aval; **to d. into the habit** *or* **the way of ...,** prendre l'habitude de ... .

2 *vt* **(a)** laisser tomber (*qch*); lâcher (*qch*); baisser (*un voile, un rideau*); lancer (*une bombe*); lâcher (*un parachutiste*); *Nau* débarquer (*le pilote*); jeter, mouiller (*l'ancre*); sauter (*une maille*); (*of sheep etc*) mettre bas (*des petits*); **d. it!,** (*to dog*) lâche ça!; **to d. a word in s.o.'s ear,** couler *ou* glisser un mot à l'oreille de qn; **to d. a letter into the pillar box,** jeter une lettre à la poste; **to d. s.o. a line/a card,** envoyer *ou* écrire un mot/une carte à qn; **to d. everything,** laisser tout tomber;

(b) verser (*une larme etc*);

(c) (*lose*) perdre (*de l'argent*) (**over sth,** sur qch); *Sp* perdre (*un point*);

(d) (*lower*) baisser, laisser tomber (*les yeux, le bras, la voix etc*); **to d. a curtsey,** faire une révérence; **to d. the folding seat (of a taxi),** rabattre le strapontin; **to d. the hem of a dress,** allonger un robe; *Av* **to d. a wing,** piquer de l'aile;

(e) (*set down*) déposer, descendre (*qn*) (de voiture);

(f) (*omit*) omettre, supprimer (*une lettre, une syllabe*); ne pas prononcer (*les r etc*); **cases in which the article is dropped,** cas où l'on supprime l'article;

(g) (*give up, stop*) abandonner, délaisser (*un travail*); cesser, lâcher (*une poursuite*); quitter (*une habitude*); **to d. the idea of doing sth,** renoncer à (l'idée de) faire qch; **I've dropped the idea,** j'y ai renoncé; **let's d. the subject,** ne parlons plus de cela!, brisons là!; *F* **d. it!,** cessez donc!, en voilà assez!; *Sch* **to d. maths,** arrêter les maths; **to d. s.o.,** cesser de voir qn, laisser tomber qn; *F* **to d. s.o. like a hot brick** *or* **potato,** laisser tomber qn du jour au lendemain; *Sp* **to d. a player,** laisser tomber un équipier; **she's been dropped from the team,** elle a été écartée de l'équipe.

▶drop back *vi* = **DROP BEHIND 1.**

▶drop behind **1** *vi* se laisser distancer *ou* dépasser. **2** *vipo* se laisser distancer *ou* dépasser par (*qn*).

▶drop by *vi* passer chez qn.

▶drop down *vi* **(a)** tomber par terre; **to d. down dead,** tomber (raide) mort; **(b)** (*of flap etc*) s'abaisser.

▶drop in **1** *vtsep* ajouter (*qch*) goutte à goutte; laisser tomber (*qch*) dedans; **d. this letter in the box for me,** mets cette lettre à la boîte; *F* **you dropped me right in it,** tu m'as mis dans la merde. **2** *vi* **to d. in at the butcher's,** passer chez le boucher; **to d. in on s.o.,** (*for a few minutes*) faire une petite visite à qn; (*arrive unexpectedly*) venir en visite chez qn (sans être attendu); **I'll d. in on my way home,** (*to see you*) je passerai (chez toi) en rentrant; **they're always dropping in on us,** ils nous tombent toujours dessus à l'improviste.

▶drop off **1** *vi* **(a)** (*of leaves etc*) tomber, se détacher; **I feel as if my arm is going to d. off,** (*because this case is so heavy*) j'ai l'impression que mon bras va lâcher; **(b)** *F* (*to sleep*) s'assoupir, s'endormir; **it was two o'clock before I finally dropped off,** je ne me suis pas endormi avant deux heures du matin; **(c)** (*of membership, attendance etc*) diminuer. **2** *vtsep* **(a)** (*deposit*) déposer (*qch*); **d. these books off at the library,** dépose ces livres à la bibliothèque; **(b)** (*let out of car*) déposer (*qn*); **where do you want to be dropped off?,** où veux-tu que je te dépose?; **d. me off at the corner,** déposez-moi au coin de la rue.

▶drop out **1** *vtsep* laisser tomber (*qch*) dehors. **2** *vi* **(a)** tomber dehors; **(b)** (*from school*) abandonner (ses études); (*of a contest*) se retirer; (*of a class*) abandonner un cours; (*from society*) refuser la société; vivre en marge de la société; **he dropped out at the age of 14,** il a abandonné ses études à 14 ans; **(c)** *Typ etc* **the letter s has dropped out,** la lettre s a disparu.

drop-forge ['drɒpfɔːdʒ] *vt Metal* étamper, estamper.

drop-forging ['drɒpfɔːdʒɪŋ] *n* **(a)** (*process*) estampage *m*; **(b)** (*result*) pièce *f* emboutie *ou* étampée.

drophead ['drɒphed] *n Aut* capote *f* rabattable; **d. coupé,** coupé décapotable.

droplet ['drɒplɪt] *n* gouttelette *f*.

dropout ['drɒpaʊt] *n Sch Univ F* étudiant, -ante qui abandonne ses études; (*from society*) marginal, -ale.

dropped [drɒpt] *adj* **(a)** *Aut etc* (*essieu etc*) surbaissé; **(b)** *Rugby* **d. goal,** drop-goal *m*, *pl* drop-goals; **(c)** *Med* **d. eyelid,** chute *f* de la paupière.

dropper ['drɒpər] *n* compte-gouttes *m inv*.

dropping ['drɒpɪŋ] *n* **(a)** descente *f*, chute *f* (*d'un objet*); *Av* lâchage *m* (*d'un parachutiste, de colis*); *Av* **d. zone,** zone *f* de largage *ou* de droppage; **d. (of young),** mise *f* bas; agnelage *m*, vêlage *m etc*; **(b)** baisse *f*, chute (*des prix*); **(c)** égouttement *m* (*d'un liquide*); **d. tube,** pipette *f*, compte-gouttes *m inv*; **(d)** suppression *f* (*d'un mot*); abandon *m* (*d'un projet*); **(e)** *Aut etc* surbaissement *m* (*du châssis*).

dropping off *n* diminution *f* (*de l'assistance etc*).

dropping out *n Sch Univ F* abandon *m* (*d'un cours etc*); (*from society*) désinsertion sociale.

droppings ['drɒpɪŋs] *npl* (*of animals, birds*) fiente *f*; (*of sheep*) crottes *fpl*; (*of stags*) fumées *fpl*.

dropsical ['drɒpsɪk(ə)l] *adj Med* hydropique.

dropsy ['drɒpsɪ] *n Med* hydropisie *f*.

dross [drɒs] *n* **(a)** *Metal* scories *fpl*, crasse *f* (*du métal en fusion*); **(b)** (*waste*) impuretés *fpl*, déchets *mpl*; *F* rebut *m*.

drought [draʊt] *n* sécheresse *f*.

drove [drəʊv] *n* **(a)** troupeau *m* (*de bœufs etc*) en marche; **(b)** foule *f* (de personnes en marche); **they walk about in droves,** ils se promènent en grandes bandes; **to arrive** *or* **come in droves,** (*of sightseers, tourists etc*) arriver en foule.

drover ['drəʊvər] *n* conducteur *m ou* toucheur *m* de bestiaux.

drown [draʊn] **1** *vt* **(a)** noyer; **to d. oneself,** se noyer; **to be drowned (by accident),** se noyer, être noyé; **drowned at sea,** noyé en mer; **to d. one's sorrows (in drink),** noyer son chagrin dans la boisson; **(b)** *(flood)* inonder, submerger *(une prairie)*; **eyes drowned in tears,** yeux noyés de larmes; **don't d. it!,** *(when adding water etc to alcoholic drink)* ne le noie pas!; **(c)** *(make inaudible)* étouffer *(un son)*; **the noise of the waterfall drowns the voice,** le bruit de la cascade couvre la voix. **2** *vi* se noyer, être noyé.

drowned [draʊnd] *adj* **(a)** noyé; **a d. man/woman,** un noyé/une noyée; *Fig* **he came home like a d. rat,** il est rentré trempé comme une soupe; **(b)** *(terrain)* inondé.

▶**drown out** *vtsep* = **DROWN 1 (c).**

drowning ['draʊnɪŋ] **1** *adj* **a d. man,** un homme qui se noie. **2** *n* **(a) (case of) d.,** noyade *f*; **to save s.o. from d.,** sauver qn qui se noie; **(b)** inondation *f (des champs)*.

drowse [draʊz] *vi* somnoler, s'assoupir.

drowsily ['draʊzɪlɪ] *adv (to look at, say)* d'un air *ou* d'un ton somnolent, à demi endormi.

drowsiness ['draʊzɪnɪs] *n* somnolence *f*, assoupissement *m*; **may cause d.,** *(notice on bottle of cough mixture etc)* peut entraîner une somnolence.

drowsy ['draʊzɪ] *adj* assoupi, somnolent; **to be** *or* **feel d.,** avoir envie de dormir, avoir sommeil.

drub [drʌb] *vt* **(-bb-)** battre, rosser *(qn, l'ennemi)*.

▶**drub into** *vtaspo* faire entrer *(qch)* de force dans la tête de *(qn)*.

drubbing ['drʌbɪŋ] *n* volée *f* de coups *(de bâton, de poing)*; *Fig* défaite *f*; **to give an opponent a d.,** battre un adversaire à plates coutures.

drudge¹ [drʌdʒ] *n* femme *f ou* homme *m* de peine; **the household d.,** la cendrillon.

drudge² *vi* trimer, peiner.

drudgery ['drʌdʒərɪ] *n* travail pénible *ou* ingrat, corvée(s) *f(pl)*.

drug¹ [drʌg] *n* **(a)** *(medication)* produit *m* pharmaceutique, drogue *f*; **(b)** *(narcotic)* narcotique *m*, stupéfiant *m*; **to take** *or* **be on** *or F* **do drugs,** se droguer; **to be arrested on d. charges,** être arrêté pour utilisation *ou* possession *ou* trafic de stupéfiants; **athletes who take drugs,** les athlètes qui se dopent; *Fig* **a d. on the market,** article *m* invendable; **truth d.,** sérum *m* de vérité; **d. abuse,** consommation *f* de stupéfiants; **d. addict,** toxicomane *mf*; **d. addiction,** toxicomanie *f*; **d. baron,** nabab *m* de la drogue; **d. money,** narco-dollars *mpl*; **d. taking,** toxicomanie *f*; *Sp* dopage *m*; **d. traffic** *or F* **pushing** *or* **peddling,** trafic *m* des stupéfiants; **d. trafficker,** narco-traffiquant, -ante.

drug² *v* **(-gg-)** *vt* donner *ou* administrer un narcotique *ou* des stupéfiants à *(qn)*; doper *(un cheval)*; **to d. oneself,** prendre un narcotique; *(habitually)* se droguer; **they had drugged his wine,** on avait mis un narcotique dans son vin.

druggist ['drʌgɪst] *n Am* pharmacien *m*; **wholesale d.,** pharmacien en gros, droguiste *m*.

drugstore ['drʌgstɔːr] *n Am* drugstore *m*.

druid ['druːɪd] *n* druide *mf*.

drum¹ [drʌm] *n* **(a)** *Mus* tambour *m*; **to beat the d.,** battre du tambour; *Fig* **to bang the big d.,** battre la (grosse) caisse; *Fig* **to bang** *or* **beat the d. for s.o./sth,** battre le tambour pour qn/qch; **big d., bass d.,** grosse caisse; *Mil* **the drums,** la batterie; *Mil* **d. major,** tambour-major *m*, *pl* tambours-majors; *US* **d. majorette,** majorette *f*; **(b)** *Anat* tympan *m (de l'oreille)*; **(c)** *(container)* tonneau *m* en fer, fût *m*; bidon *m*, tambour *m (à huile)*; **air d.,** réservoir *m* d'air comprimé; **(d)** *Archit* tambour *m (d'une colonne)*; **(e)** *MecE etc* tambour *m*, barillet *m*; *Constr etc* tambour, cylindre *m (pour malaxage etc)*; cylindre *(de treuil)*; tambour *(de moulinet)*; **concrete mixing d.,** mélangeur *m* à béton, bétonnière *f*; **cable d.,** tambour, dévidoir *m (pour câble électrique)*.

drum² *v* **(-mm-) 1** *vi* battre du tambour; **to d. on the window panes,** *(of person, rain)* tambouriner sur les vitres; **her fingers were drumming on the table,** elle battait le rappel sur la table. **2** *vt* **to d. a tune on sth,** tambouriner un air sur qch.

▶**drum into** *vtaspo* enfoncer *(qch)* dans la tête de *(qn)*; **d. it into them that they mustn't take sweets from strangers,** mets-leur bien dans la tête qu'ils ne doivent pas accepter de bonbons offerts par des inconnus.

▶**drum out** *vt* **(a)** *Mil* renvoyer *(un militaire)* **(of,** de); **(b)** expulser *(qn) (d'un club etc)* avec ignominie.

▶**drum up** *vt* racoler *(des partisans)*; battre le rappel de *(ses amis)*; **to d. up customers,** rechercher de la clientèle; **to d. up support for sth,** rechercher du soutien pour qch.

drumbeat ['drʌmbiːt] *n* coup *m ou* roulement *m* de tambour.

drumhead ['drʌmhed] *n* dessus *m* de tambour; *Mil* **d. service,** office divin en plein air.

drummer ['drʌmər] *n* tambour *m (qui joue du tambour)*; *(of kettle-drum)* timbalier *m*; *(jazz)* batteur *m*.

drumming ['drʌmɪŋ] *n* **(a)** tambourinage *m*, bruit *m* de tambour; **(b)** *Orn* tambourinage *m (du pic)*.

drumstick ['drʌmstɪk] *n* **(a)** *Mus* baguette *f* de tambour *ou* de timbale; **(b)** *Culin* pilon *m*, (bas *m* de la) cuisse *f (d'une volaille)*.

drunk [drʌŋk] **1** *adj* ivre, gris, soûl **(with,** de); *Fig* enivré **(with success,** par le succès); **to get d.,** se soûler; **to make s.o. d.,** soûler qn; **d. as a lord,** soûl comme un Polonais; *Jur* **d. and disorderly,** = en état d'ivresse manifeste dans un lieu public; *Fig* **d. with joy/power,** ivre de joie/puissance; **he is d. with power,** le pouvoir lui a monté à la tête; **blind d.,** soûl perdu; **dead d.,** ivre mort. **2** *n* ivrogne *m*.

drunkard ['drʌŋkəd] *n* ivrogne *m*.

drunken ['drʌŋk(ə)n] *adj* ivre; **d. brawl,** querelle *f* d'ivrognes; **d. state,** état *m* d'ivresse; *Jur* **d. driving,** conduite *f* en état d'ébriété.

drunkenly ['drʌŋk(ə)nlɪ] *adv* en ivrogne; comme un ivrogne.

drunkenness ['drʌŋk(ə)nnɪs] *n* **(a)** ivresse *f*; **(b)** *(habitual)* ivrognerie *f*.

drunkometer [drʌŋ'kɒmɪtər] *n US* alcootest *m*.

drupe [druːp] *n Bot* drupe *m*.

dry¹ [draɪ] **1** *adj* **(drier, driest) (a)** *(weather, cold)* sec; *(well etc)* tari, à sec; *(country)* aride; *Ind Ch etc (procédé, analyse)* par voie sèche; **to be** *or* **feel d.,** *(of person)* avoir la gorge sèche; **to pump a well d.,** épuiser l'eau d'un puits; **to run** *or* **go d.,** *(of channel)* se dessécher; *(of spring, well)* s'épuiser, (se) tarir; *(of pump)* se désamorcer; **at the end of five minutes he had run d.,** au bout de cinq minutes il était à sec; **to be kept d.,** *(notice on container)* garder au sec; *F* **d. as a bone, bone d.,** sec comme une allumette; **d. battery** *or* **cell,** pile sèche; **d. bread,** pain sec; **d. clothing,** vêtements secs; *Fig* **d. country,** pays sec *(où les boissons alcooliques sont prohibées)*; *Fig* **to go d.,** prohiber la consommation des boissons alcooliques; *Nau* **d. dock,** cale sèche; **to be in d. dock,** *(of ship)* être en cale sèche; **there wasn't a d. eye in the house,** tout le monde pleurait; *Fishing* **d. fly,** mouche sèche; **d. goods,** marchandises sèches; *Am* articles *mpl* de nouveauté; étoffes *fpl*, tissus *mpl*; **d. goods store,** magasin *m* de nouveautés; **d. land,** *(as opposed to sea)* terre *f* ferme; **d. martini,** martini *m* bianco; **d. rot,** pourriture sèche *(du bois)*; **d. run,** *Mil* exercices *mpl* d'entraînement avec munitions à blanc; *Fig* coup *m* d'essai; **to have d. skin,** avoir la peau sèche; **d. walling,** murs *mpl* en pierres sèches; *(process)* construction *f* en pierres sèches; **d. wine,** vin sec; **medium d. wine,** vin demi-sec, *pl* vins demi-secs; **extra d. champagne,** champagne brut; **d. work,** travail *m* qui donne soif;

(b) *(subject etc)* aride, sans intérêt; **to be as d. as dust,** *(of book etc)* être ennuyeux comme la pluie;

(c) *(lacking warmth)* sec; *(wit etc)* teinté d'ironie; **he has a d. manner,** il est d'une approche froide; **to answer with d. sarcasm,** répondre d'un air de pince-sans-rire; **d. humour,** esprit caustique; **a man of d. humour,** un pince-sans-rire.

2 *n* **(a)** *Br Pol F* dur, dure;

(b) *Austr F* la saison sèche;

(c) to stay in the d., rester au sec *ou* à couvert.

dry² *v* **(dried** [draɪd]) **1** *vt* sécher *(qch)*; faire sécher *(le linge)*; *(with spin drier)* essorer *(le linge)*; étancher *(le terrain)*; *(of wind)* sécher *(les chemins)*; dessécher *(la peau)*; **to d. the dishes,** essuyer la vaisselle; **to d. one's eyes,** s'essuyer les yeux; **to d. one's tears,** sécher ses larmes. **2** *vi* **(a)** se sécher, se dessécher; **to put sth out to d.,** mettre qch à sécher dehors; **it's my turn to d.,** c'est à moi d'essuyer la vaisselle; **ink that dries black,** encre qui vire au noir en séchant; **(b)** *(of cow)* tarir, se sécher.

▶**dry off 1** *vi (of varnish, paint etc)* sécher. **2** *vtsep* sécher *(qn)*; **come and d. yourself off in front of the fire,** viens te sécher devant le feu.

▶**dry out 1** *vi* **(a)** *F (of alcoholic, drug addict)* se faire désintoxiquer; **(b)** *(of moisture)* s'évaporer, sécher; **leave your wet things in the bathroom to d. out,** laisse tes affaires à sécher dans la salle de bain. **2** *vtsep* **(a)** désintoxiquer *(un alcoolique)*; **(b)** faire évaporer *(l'eau etc)*.

▶**dry up 1** *vi* **(a)** *(of well, pool etc)* se dessécher, tarir; **the well has dried up,** le puits est à sec; **(b)** *(of author etc)* épuiser son inspiration; (*of speaker, actor etc*) oublier son texte; *Sl* **d. up!**, la ferme!, ta gueule! **2** *vtsep* essuyer (*la vaisselle*); étancher (*le terrain*); (*of wind*) sécher (*les chemins*); dessécher (*la peau*).

dryad ['draɪæd] *n Myth* dryade *f*.

dry-clean ['draɪ'kliːn] *vt* nettoyer à sec.

dry-cleaner ['draɪ'kliːnər] *n* nettoyeur *m* à sec, teinturier *m*; **take it to the d.-c.'s,** portez-le à la teinturerie *ou* au pressing.

dry-cleaning ['draɪ'kliːnɪŋ] *n* **(a)** nettoyage *m* à sec; **d.-c. is not recommended,** le nettoyage à sec n'est pas recommandé; **(b)** (*clothes*) vêtements laissés chez le teinturier; **pick up the d.-c. for me,** va me chercher les vêtements chez le teinturier.

dry-dock ['draɪ'dɒk] **1** *vt* mettre (*un navire*) en cale sèche. **2** *vi* (*of ship*) entrer en cale sèche.

dryer ['draɪər] *n* **(a)** (*device*) *Ind* sécheur *m*, séchoir *m*; **hair d.,** (*held in hand*) séchoir (*à cheveux*), sèche-cheveux *m inv*; (*on stand*) casque *m* sèche-cheveux; **clothes-d.,** séchoir (*de plafond, pliant etc*); **spin d.,** essoreuse *f* (*centrifuge*); **tumble(r) d.,** séchoir rotatif (*à air chaud*); *Phot* **plate d.,** sèche-cliché *m*, *pl* sèche-clichés; **(b)** (*in paint etc*) siccatif *m*.

dry-eyed ['draɪ'aɪd] *adj* les yeux secs, à l'œil sec.

drying ['draɪɪŋ] **1** *adj* **(a)** (*vent etc*) desséchant; **(b) quick-d.,** (*oil, varnish*) siccatif. **2** *n* séchage *m*; (*of skin*) dessèchement *m*; (*with a cloth*) essuyage *m*; **d. rack,** châssis *m* de séchage, séchoir *m*; **d. barn,** (*for tobacco*) suerie *f*.

drying out **(a)** désintoxication *f* (*d'un alcoolique*); **(b)** assèchement *m*, dessèchement *m*.

drying up **(a)** tarissement *m* (*d'un cours d'eau etc*); **(b)** essuyage *m* (*de la vaisselle*).

dryly ['draɪlɪ] *adv* **(a)** (*without warmth*) d'un ton sec; sèchement; **(b)** avec une pointe d'ironie; (*répondre*) d'un air de pince-sans-rire.

dryness ['draɪnɪs] *n* **(a)** sécheresse *f* (*d'une région, du temps*); aridité *f* (*du sol*); **(b)** aridité *f* (*d'un discours*); **(c)** sévérité *f* (*de ton*); causticité *f* (*de l'esprit*).

dry-roasted [draɪ'rəʊstɪd] *adj* (*peanuts*) grillé à sec.

DSC [diːes'siː] *n abbr* **Distinguished Service Cross**.

DSM [diːe'sem] *n abbr* **Distinguished Service Medal**.

DSO [diːe'səʊ] *n abbr* **Distinguished Service Order**.

DST [diːes'tiː] *n* (*abbr* **daylight saving time**) HAE *f*.

DTI [diːtiː'aɪ] *n Br Admin* (*abbr* **Department of Trade and Industry**) = Ministère de l'Industrie et du Commerce.

DTP [diːtiː'piː] *n Comptr* (*abbr* **desktop publishing**) PAO *f*.

DTs [diː'tiːz] *npl F* (*abbr* **delirium tremens**) **to have the DTs,** (*of alcoholic*) avoir une crise de delirium tremens.

dual ['djuːəl] *adj* **(a)** double; **to have d. nationality,** avoir la double nationalité; **to have a d. function** *or* **purpose,** avoir une double fonction; *Br Aut* **d. carriageway,** route *f* à deux chaussées (séparées par un rail); *Aut* **d.-control car,** voiture *f* à double commande; *Psy* **d. personality,** dédoublement *m* de la personnalité; **d. wheels,** roues jumelées; *Av* **d. wheel (assembly),** diabolo *m*; **(b)** *Math* dual.

dualism ['djuːəlɪz(ə)m] *n* dualité *f*; *Phil* dualisme *m*.

duality [djuː'ælɪtɪ] *n* dualité *f*; dédoublement *m* (*de la personnalité etc*).

dual-purpose ['duːəl'pɜːpəs] *adj* à double emploi.

dub¹ [dʌb] *vt* (**-bb-**) *Cin* doubler (*un film*); **it has been dubbed into French,** ça a été doublé en français.

dub² *vt* (**-bb-**) **(a) to d. s.o. (a) knight,** armer *ou* adouber qn chevalier; *Fig* **he was dubbed the king of tennis,** on l'a surnommé le roi du tennis; **(b)** préparer (*le cuir*) avec le dégras.

dubbin¹ ['dʌbɪn] *n* (*for leather*) dégras *m*.

dubbin² *vt* enduire (*des chaussures*) de dégras.

dubbing ['dʌbɪŋ] *n Cin* doublage *m*.

dubious ['djuːbɪəs] *adj* **(a)** qui doute; **d. expression,** air *m* de doute; **she looked d.,** elle avait l'air d'avoir des doutes; **d. as to what he should do,** ne sachant trop ce qu'il devait faire; **I'm still a bit d.,** j'ai encore quelques doutes; **we were d. about the scheme,** nous avions des doutes sur le projet; **(b)** (*résultat*) incertain; (*lumière*) douteux, vague; (*avantage*) contestable; **(c)** *Pej* (*honneur*) équivoque; (*compagnie*) douteux, louche; **financiers of d. character,** financiers véreux.

dubiously ['djuːbɪəslɪ] *adv* (*to say, look at*) d'un ton *ou* d'un air de doute.

dubiousness ['djuːbɪəsnɪs] *n* **(a)** incertitude *f* (*du résultat etc*); **(b)** équivoque *f* (*d'un compliment etc*).

ducal ['djuːk(ə)l] *adj* ducal, -aux.

ducat ['dʌkət] *n Arch* (*coin*) ducat *m*.

duchess ['dʌtʃɪs] *n* duchesse *f*.

duchesse ['duːʃes] *n Culin* **d. potatoes,** pommes *fpl* (de terre) duchesse.

duchy ['dʌtʃɪ] *n* duché *m*.

duck¹ [dʌk] *n* **(a)** canard *m*; (*female*) cane *f*; **wild d.,** canard sauvage; *Fig F* **to look like a dying d. (in a thunderstorm),** avoir l'air pitoyable; **to take to sth like a d. to water,** mordre à qch; **criticism runs off him like water off a duck's back,** il est imperméable à la critique; **to play at ducks and drakes,** faire des ricochets (sur l'eau); *Fig* **a sitting d.,** une cible facile; *Eng Dial* **what do you want, ducks?,** et pour vous, ma petite dame?; et pour le monsieur?; *Culin* **Peking d.,** canard à la Pékinoise; *Culin* **Bombay d.,** poisson sec assaisonné de cari; *F* **dead d.,** (*person*) raté, -ée; (*plan etc*) fiasco *m*; *Fig* **lame d.,** malheureux, -euse; *Com* canard boiteux; *St Exch* spéculateur *m* insolvable; **d. pond,** mare *f* aux canards;
(b) *Cr* zéro *m*; **to make a d.,** faire chou blanc; **to break one's d.,** marquer son premier point.

duck² **1** *vi* **(a)** baisser la tête, se baisser (*pour se dérober à un coup etc*); *Boxing* esquiver de la tête; **to d. behind a tree/car/***etc*, se cacher derrière un arbre/une voiture/*etc*; **(b)** plonger dans l'eau. **2** *vt* **(a)** baisser subitement (*la tête*); **to d. a blow,** esquiver un coup; **(b)** *Fig* se dérober à (*ses obligations etc*); **to d. an embarrassing question,** se dérober à une question embarrassante; **to d. the issue,** s'esquiver; (*in reply*) user de faux-fuyants; **(c)** plonger (*qn*) dans l'eau, faire faire le plongeon à (*qn*).

duck³ *n* **(a)** mouvement instinctif de la tête (*pour se dérober à un coup etc*); *Boxing* esquive *f*; **(b)** plongeon *m*, bain *m* (*inattendu, involontaire*).

duck⁴ *n Tex* coutil *m*, toile fine; **ducks,** (*trousers*) pantalon *m* de coutil *ou* de toile; (*clothes*) complet *m* de coutil *ou* de toile.

►**duck out** *vi* se défiler; **to d. out of doing sth,** arriver à couper à qch, arriver à éviter de faire qch.

duck-billed ['dʌkbɪld] *adj* **d.-b. platypus,** (*animal*) ornithorynque *m*.

duckboards ['dʌkbɔːdz] *npl* caillebotis *m*.

ducking ['dʌkɪŋ] *n* plongeon *m* (involontaire); **to give s.o. a d.,** faire boire une tasse à qn; **to get** *or* **take a d.,** boire la tasse.

duckling ['dʌklɪŋ] *n* canardeau *m*; (*male*) caneton *m*; (*female*) canette *f*; **the Ugly D.,** le vilain petit Canard.

duckweed ['dʌkwiːd] *n* (*plant*) lentille *f* d'eau.

ducky ['dʌkɪ] **1** *n Br F* mon petit chou; ma cocotte. **2** *adj US F* tout mignon.

duct¹ [dʌkt] *n* **(a)** (*tube*) conduit *m*; *Constr etc* caniveau *m*, -aux (*pour câbles etc*); **air d.,** manche *f* à air, gaine *f* (d'installation de ventilation); **(b)** *Anat* canal *m*, -aux, vaisseau *m*, -aux; **auditory d.,** conduit auditif; **(c)** *Bot* trachée *f*.

ductile ['dʌktaɪl] *adj* (*métal*) ductile; *Fig* (*caractère*) docile, malléable, souple.

ductility [dʌk'tɪlɪtɪ] *n* ductilité *f* (*d'un métal*); *Fig* docilité *f*, souplesse *f* (*de caractère*).

dud [dʌd] **1** *n F* (*person*) incapable *mf*; *Mil* obus non éclaté; **I'm a d. at history,** je suis nul en histoire; **the note was a d.,** le billet était faux. **2** *adj Mil* **d. shell,** obus non éclaté; *Fin* **d. cheque,** chèque *m* sans provision *ou* en bois.

dude [djuːd] *n US F* **(a)** (*fashion plate*) gommeux *m*; **(b)** (*man*) type *m*; **(c)** hôte *m* d'un ranch-hôtel; **d. ranch,** ranch-hôtel.

dudgeon ['dʌdʒən] *n* **in high d.,** fort en colère, fort indigné.

due [djuː] **1** *adj* **(a)** *Com Fin* (*debt*) exigible; (*bill*) échu; **bill d. on 1st May,** effet *m* payable le premier mai; **balance d.,** solde dû; **debts d. to us,** dettes actives; **debts d. by us,** dettes passives; **bond d. for repayment,** obligation amortie; **to fall** *or* **become d.,** (*of bill etc*) échoir, devenir payable; **falling d.,** échéance *f*; **redemption before d. date,** remboursement anticipé; **are you d. any money from him?,** est-ce qu'il te doit de l'argent?; **the money d. to you,** l'argent qui vous est dû; **you're d. an apology,** je vous dois *ou* il vous doit *etc* une excuse; **they are d. our thanks,** ils méritent nos remerciements;
(b) (*merited, proper*) dû, juste, mérité; **the first place is d. to Milton,** la première place revient à Milton; **to give s.o. d. warning,** avertir qn dans les formes; **with d. care,** avec tout le soin requis; **he was received with d. ceremony,** il fut reçu avec tout le cérémonial qui lui était dû; **in d. form,** en bonne et due forme; **after d. consideration,** après mûre réflexion; **with all d. respect,** avec tout le respect que je vous dois; **to treat s.o. with d. respect** *or* **the respect d. to them,** traiter qn avec le respect qui lui est dû; **in d. course,** (*eventually*) en temps voulu.

(c) d. to, (*caused by*) causé par, attribuable à; (*as a result of*) par suite de; **it is d. to his negligence,** c'est sa négligence qui en est (la) cause, c'est dû à sa négligence; **what is it d. to?,** à quoi cela tient-il?, à quoi est-ce que c'est dû?; **d. to fog the boat arrived late,** par suite du brouillard, le bateau est arrivé en retard;
(d) (*expected*) **the train is d. (to arrive) at two o'clock,** le train doit arriver à deux heures; **there's a bus d. now,** un bus doit arriver d'un moment à l'autre; **he is d. to arrive this evening,** il doit arriver ce soir; **when is the baby d.?,** pour quand la naissance est-elle prévue?, quand le bébé doit-il naître?; **I'm d. (for) a rise,** j'attends une augmentation de salaire.
2 *adv* **d. north,** droit vers le nord, plein nord.
3 *n* **(a)** (*what is owed*) dû *m*; **to give s.o. their d.,** donner à qn ce qui lui est dû *ou* ce qui lui revient; **one must give the devil his d.,** il faut faire la part du diable;
(b) dues, (*for membership*) droits *mpl*, frais *mpl*; (*club subscription*) cotisation annuelle; *Am Fig* **she's paid her dues,** (*merits respect*) elle mérite le respect; (*has worked hard*) elle a peiné pour en arriver où elle en est; **market dues,** hallage *m*; *Nau* **harbour dues,** droits de port.
duel¹ ['djʊəl] *n* **(a)** duel *m*; **to fight a d.,** se battre en duel; **(b)** *Fig* lutte *f*, contestation *f*.
duel² *vi* (**-ll-**, *US* **-l-**) se battre en duel.
duelling, *US* **dueling** ['djʊəlɪŋ] *n* le duel; **d. pistols,** pistolets *mpl* de combat.
duellist, *US* **duelist** ['djʊəlɪst] *n* duelliste *m*.
duet [djuː'et] *n* duo *m*; (*for piano*) morceau *m* à quatre mains.
duettist [djuː'etɪst] *n Mus* duettiste *mf*.
duff¹ [dʌf] *n* **(plum) d.,** pudding *m* aux raisins.
duff² *adj F* (*bad quality*) de mauvaise qualité; (*not functioning properly*) qui marche mal.
▶**duff up** *vtsep Br Sl* rosser (*qn*).
duffel ['dʌf(ə)l] *n* = **DUFFLE**.
duffer ['dʌfər] *n F* **(a)** (*person*) bousilleur, euse; *Sch* cancre *m*; **to be a d. at,** être nul en (*histoire etc*); **(b)** (*worthless object*) cruche *f*, gourde *f*; **(c) some old d.,** (*old man*) un vieux croulant.
duffle ['dʌf(ə)l] *n* **d. coat,** duffle-coat *m*, *pl* duffle-coats; *Can* corvette *f*; **d. bag,** sac marin *ou* de campeur.
dug [dʌg] *n* mamelle *f*, tétine *f*; pis *m* (*de vache*).
dugout ['dʌgaʊt] *n* **(a)** (*canoe*) canot creusé dans un tronc d'arbre; pirogue *f*; **(b)** *Mil etc* tranchée-abri *f*, *pl* tranchées-abris.
duke [djuːk] *n* **(a)** duc *m*; **(b)** *Sl* **dukes,** (*fists*) poings *mpl*.
▶**duke out** *vtsep US* **to d. it out,** se bagarrer (**with,** avec).
dukedom ['djuːkdəm] *n* **(a)** (*territory*) duché *m*; **(b)** (*title*) titre *m* de duc; (*rank*) dignité *f* de duc.
dulcet ['dʌlsɪt] *adj Lit* (*son*) doux, suave, agréable; **to say sth in d. tones,** dire qch d'un ton suave.
dulcimer ['dʌlsɪmər] *n Mus* tympanon *m*.
dull¹ [dʌl] *adj* **(a)** (*person*) lent, lourd; **to be d.-witted,** avoir l'esprit lourd *ou* engourdi; *Prov* **all work and no play makes Jack a d. boy,** on s'abrutit à toujours travailler; **(b)** (*pain*) sourd; (*bruit*) sourd, étouffé; **(c)** *Com Fin* (*marché*) calme, inactif; **business is d.,** les affaires ne marchent pas fort; **(d)** (*depressed*) triste, morne; **(e)** (*tedious*) triste, ennuyeux; (*vie*) monotone; (*soirée*) assommant; (*style*) terne; **he's a very d. speaker,** c'est un orateur ennuyeux; **as d. as ditchwater,** ennuyeux comme la pluie; **deadly d.,** abrutissant, assommant; **it's deadly d. here,** on s'ennuie à mourir ici; **(f)** (*blunt*) émoussé; **to become d.,** (*of tool etc*) s'émousser; **(g)** (*colour, surface*) terne, mat; (*yeux*) sans éclat; **paper with a d. finish,** papier mat *ou* non satiné; **(h)** (*weather*) triste, sombre.
dull² **1** *vt* **(a)** engourdir, alourdir (*l'esprit*); émousser (*les sens*); **(b)** amortir (*une douleur*); rendre moins vif (*le plaisir*); amortir, assourdir (*le son*); **sorrow is dulled by the passage of time,** le temps émousse la douleur; **(c)** ternir (*les couleurs*); dépolir (*une surface*); mater (*un métal*); **(d)** émousser (*un outil*). **2** *vi* **(a)** (*of senses etc*) s'hébéter, s'engourdir; **(b)** (*of colour*) se ternir; (*of metal etc*) se dépolir.
dullard ['dʌləd] *n* lourdaud *m*; *Sch* cancre *m*.
dul(l)ness ['dʌlnɪs] *n* **(a)** (*of mind*) lourdeur *f* d'esprit; émoussement *m* (*des sens*); **(b)** ennui *m*, tristesse *f*; monotonie *f* (*de la vie, d'un discours*); **(c)** *Com Fin* stagnation *f* (*des affaires*); inactivité *f* (*du marché*); **(d)** manque *m* de tranchant (*d'une lame etc*); émoussement *m* (*d'une pointe*); **(e)** manque *m* d'éclat (*d'une couleur*); **(f)** faiblesse *f* (*d'un son, d'une lumière*); bruit sourd (*d'un coup*).
dully ['dʌllɪ] *adv* **(a)** (*stupidly*) lourdement, lentement; **(b)** (*boringly*) d'une manière ennuyeuse; tristement; **(c)** sourdement, faiblement; sans éclat.
duly ['djuːlɪ] *adv* **(a)** (*properly*) dûment; justement; **d. appointed,** (*membre*) régulièrement désigné; **(b)** (*as expected*) en temps voulu; **rent d. paid,** loyer payé exactement; **and all the shops were d. shut,** et tous les magasins étaient bien entendu fermés.
dumb [dʌm] *adj* **(a)** (*unable to speak*) muet, *f* muette; **deaf and d.,** sourd-muet, *f* sourde-muette; **d. animals,** les bêtes *fpl*; **I was struck d. with astonishment,** la stupeur m'a rendu muet; **d. show,** pantomime *f*; jeu muet; **(b)** (*stupid*) *F* bête, sot, *f* sotte; **to play** *or* **act d.,** faire le niais; **d. blonde,** blonde évaporée; **d. cluck,** imbécile *mf*.
dumbbell ['dʌmbel] *n* **(a)** (*weight*) haltère *m*; **(b)** *esp Am Sl* (*idiot*) sot *m*.
dumbfound [dʌm'faʊnd] *vt* abasourdir, ahurir, ébahir (*qn*).
dumbfounded [dʌm'faʊndɪd] *adj* abasourdi, ahuri, ébahi (**at,** de); **I am d.,** je n'en reviens pas; **we were d. at the news,** la nouvelle nous frappa de stupeur.
dumbly ['dʌmlɪ] *adv* (*to follow, stare*) sans rien dire.
dumbness ['dʌmnɪs] *n* **(a)** mutisme *m*; **deaf and d.,** surdi-mutité *f*; **(b)** *F* (*stupidity*) sottise *f*, bêtise *f*.
dumbo ['dʌmbəʊ] *n F* andouille *f*, imbécile *mf*.
dumbstruck ['dʌmstrʌk] *adj* = **DUMBFOUNDED**.
dumbwaiter ['dʌmweɪtər] *n* (*revolving*) plateau tournant; (*lift*) monte-plats *m inv*.
dumdum ['dʌmdʌm] *n* **(a)** *Mil* **d. (bullet),** (balle *f*) dumdum *f*, *pl* dum-dums; **(b)** *F* (*idiot*) idiot, -ote.
dummy ['dʌmɪ] *n* **(a)** (*in shop window*) & *Sewing* mannequin *m*; marionnette *f* (*de ventriloque*); *F* **standing there like a stuffed d.,** planté comme un piquet; **(b)** chose *f* factice, faux paquet; *Mil* simulacre *m* (*de grenade etc*); maquette *f* (*d'un livre*); **d. run,** *Nau* évolution *f* d'entraînement; *Mil Av* incursion aérienne sans bombardement; *F* coup *m* d'essai. **(c)** *Pej* muet *m*; (*idiot*) sot *m*, lourdaud *m*; **(d)** (*representative*) homme *m* de paille; prête-nom *m inv;* **(e)** *Br* (*for baby*) tétine *f*; **(f)** *Cards* (*player or hand at bridge, whist*) mort *m*; **to be** *or* **play d.,** faire le mort; **d. bridge,** bridge *m* à trois personnes; **d. whist,** whist *m* avec un mort.
dump¹ [dʌmp] *n* **(a)** (lieu *m* de) décharge *f*; **refuse** *or* **rubbish d.,** décharge; **(b)** *F* taudis *m*; **what a d.!,** (*of place*) quel trou!, quel bled!; (*of office etc*) quelle saloperie de boîte!; **(c)** tas *m*, amas *m* (*de déchets etc*); **(d)** *Mil* **ammunition d.,** dépôt *m* de munitions; parc *m* à munitions; **(e)** *Comptr* **memory** *or* **storage d.,** vidage *m* (de) mémoire; **(f)** *Constr etc* basculeur *m*, culbuteur *m*; **d. truck,** tombereau *m*, dumper *m*.
dump² **1** *vt* **(a)** décharger, déverser (*une charretée de sable etc*); jeter (*les ordures*) à la voirie; déverser (*des déchets dans l'océan*); laisser tomber lourdement (*un ballot etc*); déposer (*qn*) rudement (*sur une chaise etc*); *Av* se délester de (*la cargaison*); *F* **to d. s.o.,** (*get rid of*) se débarrasser de qn; (*leave*) plaquer qn; **(b)** faire un dépôt de (*vivres etc*); **(c)** *Com* **to d. goods on a foreign market,** faire du dumping; = écouler à perte des marchandises à l'étranger; **(d)** *Comptr* vider (*une mémoire*). **2** *vi Com* faire du dumping.
▶**dump on** *vipo Am F* **(a)** (*criticize*) s'en prendre à (*qn, qch*); **(b)** (*tell one's problems to*) se décharger de ses problèmes sur (*qn*).
dumper ['dʌmpər] *n Constr etc* **d. (truck),** tombereau *m*, dumper *m*.
dumping ['dʌmpɪŋ] *n* **(a) d. bucket,** benne basculante; **d. ground,** (lieu *m* de) décharge *f*; *Fig* **people use the home as a d. ground for their elderly parents,** les gens utilisent la maison de retraite pour se débarrasser de leurs parents âgés; **(b)** *Com* dumping *m* (*du trop-plein de la production*); **(c)** *Comptr* vidage *m* (*d'une mémoire*).
dumpling ['dʌmplɪŋ] *n* **(a)** *Culin* boulette *f* de pâte (*servie avec un ragoût etc*); **apple d.,** pomme enrobée (*dans de la pâte et cuite au four*); **(b)** *Fig* (*plump person*) boulot, -otte, petit gros, petite grosse.
dumps [dʌmps] *npl F* cafard *m*, idées noires; **to be down in the d.,** broyer du noir, avoir le cafard.
dumpster ['dʌmpstər] *n Am* benne *f* à ordures.
dumpy ['dʌmpɪ] *adj* (*person etc*) trapu, boulot.
dun¹ [dʌn] **1** *adj* brun grisâtre; (*horse*) gris louvet. **2** *n* cheval *m* gris louvet.
dun² *vt* (**-nn-**) importuner, harceler (*un débiteur*); **dunned by his creditors,** pressé par ses créanciers.
dunce [dʌns] *n Sch* cancre *m*; **d.'s cap,** bonnet *m* d'âne.
dunderhead ['dʌndəhed] *n F* imbécile *mf*.
dune [djuːn] *n* **(sand) d.,** dune *f*; **d. buggy,** buggy *m*.

dung [dʌŋ] *n* **(a)** fiente *f*, crotte *f*; (*of wild animal*) fumées *fpl*; bouse *f* (*de vache*); crottin *m* (*de cheval*); **d. beetle,** bousier *m*; **(b)** *Agr* fumier *m*, engrais *m*.
dungaree [dʌŋgə'riː] *n* **(a) dungarees,** (*with sleeves*) combinaison *f*; (*with bib*) salopette *f*; bleus *mpl* (*de mécanicien*); **(b)** *Tex* treillis *m*.
dungeon ['dʌndʒ(ə)n] *n* **(a)** cachot *m* (*d'un château du moyen âge*); **(b)** (*tower*) donjon *m*.
dunghill ['dʌŋhɪl] *n* tas *m* de fumier, fumier *m*.
dunk [dʌŋk] **1** *vt* tremper (*du pain, un croissant*) (*dans son café etc*). **2** *vi* faire trempette.
Dunkirk [dʌn'kɜːk] *n* Dunkerque *f*.
dunlin ['dʌnlɪn] *n* (*bird*) bécasseau *m* variable.
dunno [dʌ'nəʊ] *Sl* (= **don't know**) sais pas!
dunnock ['dʌnək] *n* (*bird*) accenteur *m* mouchet.
duo ['djuːəʊ] *n* **(a)** *Mus* duo *m*; **(b)** (*two people*) couple *m*.
duodecimal [djuːəʊ'desɪm(ə)l] **1** *adj* duodécimal, -aux. **2** *npl Math* **duodecimals,** multiplication duodécimale; calcul *m* par le système duodécimal.
duodenal [djuːəʊ'diːn(ə)l] *adj Anat Med* (*ulcère etc*) duodénal, -aux.
duodenum, *pl* **-na, -nums** [djuːəʊ'diːnəm, -nə, -nəmz] *n Anat* duodénum *m*.
dupe[1] [djuːp] *n* dupe *f*.
dupe[2] *vt* duper, tromper; **to be duped,** se laisser duper; **to d. s.o. into doing sth,** convaincre qn de faire qch en le dupant.
duple ['djuːp(ə)l] *adj Mus* **d. time,** mesure *f* à deux temps.
duplex ['djuːpleks] **1** *adj* double; duplex *inv*; *El Tel* (*ligne, voie*) duplex; (*exploitation etc*) en duplex; *MecE* **d. lathe,** tour *m* à double outil; **d. crank,** manivelle *f* double. **2** *adj & n Am* **d. (house),** maison jumelée; *Can* duplex *m*; **d. (apartment),** (appartement *m*) duplex *m*.
duplicate[1] ['djuːplɪkət] **1** *adj* (en) double; *Jur* (*document*) ampliatif; **d. set of tools,** outils *mpl* de rechange; **d. receipt,** duplicata *m* d'un. **2** *n* **(a)** double *m*, répétition *f* (*d'une œuvre d'art etc*); **(b)** duplicata *m* (*d'un chèque etc*); double *m*, contrepartie *f* (*d'un écrit*); ampliation *f* (*d'un acte*); **in d.,** (en) double; en duplicata; en double exemplaire.
duplicate[2] ['djuːplɪkeɪt] *vt* **(a)** faire le double de (*qch*); copier (*un document*); reproduire (*un document*) en double exemplaire; **(b)** tirer plusieurs exemplaires de (*une lettre circulaire*) au duplicateur, polycopier (*une lettre circulaire*).
duplicating ['djuːplɪkeɪtɪŋ] *n* **(a)** duplication *f*; **(b)** tirage *m* de plusieurs exemplaires (*d'une lettre etc*) au duplicateur; **d. machine,** duplicateur *m*, machine *f* à polycopier.
duplication [djuːplɪ'keɪʃən] *n* duplication *f*, reproduction *f*; **unnecessary d. of work,** double emploi *m*.
duplicator ['djuːplɪkeɪtər] *n* duplicateur *m*, machine *f* à polycopier.
duplicity [djuː'plɪsɪtɪ] *n* duplicité *f*; mauvaise foi.
durability [djʊərə'bɪlɪtɪ] *n* durabilité *f*; *Ind* résistance *f* (*des matériaux etc*).
durable ['djʊərəb(ə)l] **1** *adj* (*peace*) durable; (*tissu*) résistant; *Com* **d. goods,** biens *mpl* d'équipement. **2** *npl* **(consumer) durables,** biens *mpl* d'équipement.
duration [djʊ'reɪʃən] *n* durée *f*; étendue *f* (*de la vie*); **the peace was of short d.,** la paix fut de courte durée; **for the d.,** *Mil* (*s'engager*) pour la durée de la guerre; *Fig* jusqu'à la Saint-Glinglin.
duress [djʊ'res] *n* **(a)** *Jur* contrainte *f*, coercition *f*; **to act under d.,** agir sous la contrainte; **(b)** (*imprisonment*) emprisonnement *m*.
Durex ® ['djʊəreks] *n* préservatif *m*.
during ['djʊərɪŋ] *prep* pendant, durant; **d. his life,** sa vie durant; **d. the whole week,** toute la semaine; **d. the winter,** au cours de l'hiver; **d. the journey,** en cours de route; **d. the last year,** dans le courant de l'année dernière; **killed d. a brawl,** tué au cours d'une rixe; **d. that time,** pendant ce temps.
durum ['djʊərəm] *n* **d. wheat,** blé dur.
dusk [dʌsk] *n* crépuscule *m*; **at d.,** à la nuit tombante, à la tombée de la nuit.
duskiness ['dʌskɪnɪs] *n* **(a)** (*swarthiness*) teint brun *ou* bistré; (*darkness of skin*) teint noiraud; **(b)** demi-jour *m*.
dusky ['dʌskɪ] *adj* **(a)** sombre, obscur; **(b)** (*complexion*) brun foncé *inv*; mat; (*dark-skinned*) noirâtre.
dust[1] [dʌst] *n* **(a)** (*dirt, powder*) poussière *f*; sciure *f* (*de marbre*); **to cover sth with d.,** couvrir qch de poussière; **to raise a cloud of d.,** soulever un nuage de poussière; *Fig* **once the dust has settled,** une fois que les choses seront revenues à la normale, une fois que la situation se sera apaisée; **to reduce sth to d.,** réduire qch en poussière; **to trample s.o. in the d.,** fouler qn aux pieds; *Fig* **to bite the d.,** (*die, fail*) mordre la poussière; **to shake the d. off one's feet,** secouer la poussière de ses pieds; **to throw d. in s.o.'s eyes,** jeter de la poudre aux yeux de qn; *F* **to kick up** *or* **raise a d.,** faire du foin; **brick d.,** poussière de brique; *Phys* **cosmic d.,** poussière cosmique; **d. bag,** (*for vacuum cleaner*) (*disposable*) sac papier; (*fixed*) sac tissu; *Am* **d. ball** *or* **bunny** *or* **kitten** *etc*, mouton *m*; **to take a d. bath,** (*of bird*) s'ébrouer dans la poussière; *Geog* **d. bowl,** zone *f* semi-aride *ou* semi-désertique; *US* **the D. Bowl,** le désert de poussière; *Old-fashioned* **d. coat,** cache-poussière *m inv*; *Am* **d. cloth,** torchon *m* (à épousseter); *MecE* **d. collector,** capteur *m* de poussières; **d. cover,** housse *f* (*pour fauteuil etc*); **d. cover** *or* **jacket** *or* **wrapper,** chemise *f*, jaquette *f* (*d'un livre*); couverture *f* (*en papier*); *Met* **d. devil,** tourbillon *m* de poussière; **d. storm,** tempête *f* de poussière; **d. trap,** nid *m* à poussière; *Ind* attrape-poussières *m inv*;
(b) cendres *fpl* (*d'un mort*); **all their hopes had turned to d. and ashes,** tous leurs espoirs s'étaient anéantis;
(c) give the table a d., donner un coup de chiffon à la table (pour enlever la poussière).
dust[2] *vt* **(a)** épousseter (*une pièce, un meuble*); **(b)** saupoudrer (*un gâteau etc*) (**with,** de); **sugar-dusted doughnuts,** beignets saupoudrés de sucre.
►**dust down, dust off** *vtsep* épousseter (*qch*); **to d. oneself off** *or* **down,** se brosser (pour enlever la poussière); *Fig* **to d. off legislation/a lecture/***etc*, réactualiser *ou* dépoussiérer une législation/un cours/*etc* abandonné(e) depuis longtemps.
dustbin ['dʌstbɪn] *n Br* poubelle *f*.
dustcart ['dʌstkɑːt] *n Br* camion *m* d'enlèvement des ordures ménagères, camion des boueux.
dustcloud ['dʌstklaʊd] *n* nuage *m* de poussière.
duster ['dʌstər] *n* **(a)** chiffon *m* (à épousseter); **feather d.,** plumeau *m*; *Sch* **blackboard d.,** chiffon (à effacer); **(b)** *Nau Sl* pavillon *m*; **red d.,** = pavillon marchand; **(c)** *Am* **d. (coat),** manteau léger; *Old-fashioned* cache-poussière *m inv*.
dustiness ['dʌstɪnɪs] *n* état poudreux *ou* poussiéreux.
dusting ['dʌstɪŋ] *n* **(a)** époussetage *m* (*d'une pièce, d'un meuble etc*); **(b)** saupoudrage *m* (*d'un gâteau etc*); *Phot* poudrage *m*; **d. powder,** (*talc*) (poudre *f* de) talc *m*; *Med* poudre *f* antiseptique.
dustman, *pl* **-men** ['dʌstmən] *n Br* boueur *m*, boueux *m*, éboueur *m*.
dustpan ['dʌstpæn] *n* pelle *f* à poussière.
dustsheet ['dʌstʃiːt] *n* housse *f* (*pour meubles*).
dust-up ['dʌstʌp] *n F* coup *m* de torchon; **to have a d.-up with s.o.,** se quereller avec qn; **they've had a bit of a d.-up,** le torchon a brûlé entre eux.
dusty ['dʌstɪ] *adj* poussiéreux, poudreux; recouvert de poussière; **to get d.,** se couvrir de poussière; *Old-fashioned Sl* **it's not so d.,** c'est pas mal du tout; *Old-fashioned F* **d. answer,** réponse décevante; **I gave him a d. answer,** je l'ai envoyé promener.
dutch [dʌtʃ] *n Br Sl* **my old d.,** ma femme, ma vieille.
Dutch [dʌtʃ] **1** *adj* **(a)** (*costume etc*) hollandais; (*fromage etc*) de Hollande; (*gouvernement*) néerlandais; *Fig* **to talk to s.o. like a D. uncle,** faire la morale à qn; **D. auction,** enchères *fpl* au rabais; **D. barn,** hangar *m* à récoltes; **D. cap,** diaphragme *m*; **D. courage,** bravoure *f* après boive; **I'll need a little D. courage,** il faut que je boive un peu pour me donner du courage; *Am* **D. door,** porte *f* à double vantail; **D. elm disease,** maladie *f* des ormes; *Am* **D. oven,** cocotte *f*; **D. treat,** régal où chacun paie son écot; **(b)** *US* **(Pennsylvania) D.,** allemand de Pennsylvanie.
2 *n* **(a) the D. (people),** les Hollandais *mpl*;
(b) *Ling* le hollandais; **Cape D.,** afrikaans *m*; *Fig* **to talk double D.,** baragouiner; *Fig* **it's all double D. to me,** (*what they're saying*) je ne peux rien comprendre à ce baragouin; (*this topic*) c'est de l'hébreu pour moi.
3 *adv* **to go D.,** payer son écot; **let's go D.,** payons chacun notre part.
Dutchman, *pl* **-men** ['dʌtʃmən] *n* Hollandais *m*; *F* **if that's a real diamond (then) I'm a D.,** si c'est un vrai diamant je mange mon chapeau.
dutiable ['djuːtɪəb(ə)l] *adj* (*goods purchased abroad*) soumis aux droits de douane, soumis à des droits, imposable, taxable.
dutiful ['djuːtɪfʊl] *adj* (*child etc*) respectueux, soumis; **a d. husband,** un mari plein d'égards pour sa femme.
dutifully ['djuːtɪfʊlɪ] *adv* avec soumission, respectueusement.
duty ['djuːtɪ] *n* **(a)** devoir *m* (**to,** envers); **to do one's d.,** faire son devoir; **to fail in one's d.,** manquer à son devoir;

to do one's d. by s.o., remplir son devoir envers qn; **I shall make it my d. to ...,** je considérerai de mon devoir de ...; **it is your d. to ...,** il est de ton devoir de ...; **you are (in) d. bound to do it,** votre devoir vous y oblige; **I feel d. bound to ...,** je me sens obligé par le devoir de ...; **from a sense of d.,** par devoir; **to pay a d. call,** faire une visite de politesse;

(b) (*task*) *usu pl* **duties,** fonction(s) *f(pl)*, attributions *fpl*; *Mil* mission *f*; **public duties,** fonctions publiques; **to take up one's duties,** entrer en fonctions *ou* en charge; **to hand over one's duties,** (*resign*) résigner ses fonctions; (*transfer them*) remettre ses fonctions (**to,** à); **to be on detached** *or US* **temporary d.,** être en mission;

(c) to be on d., être de service; (*in factory, playground etc*) être de surveillance; *Nau* être de service *ou* de corvée; *Mil Nau etc* **while on d.,** dans l'exécution du service; **to be off d.,** ne pas être de service; **to do d. for s.o.,** remplacer qn (dans son service); **to do d. for sth,** servir de qch; **d. chart** *or* **roster,** tableau *m* de service; **on guard d.,** de service de garde; **tour of d.,** tour *m* de service; *US* **active d.,** service actif; **fatigue d.,** corvée *f*; **d. officer/N.C.O.,** officier *m*/sous-officier *m* de service.

(d) (*tax*) droit *m*; **customs d.,** droit(s) de douane; **liable to d.,** passible de droits; **d. paid,** franc de douane; **stamp d.,** droit de timbre;

(e) *MecE etc* **heavy-d.,** (*machine*) à grand rendement, à fort débit; (*appareil*) soumis à un travail très dur; (*cric etc*) pour poids lourds.

duty-free ['djuːtɪ'friː] **1** *adj* exempt de droit; **how much wine can I bring back d.-f.?,** quelle quantité de vin est-ce que j'ai le droit de ramener hors taxe?; **d.-f. shop,** magasin *m* hors taxe. **2** *n* (*purchase*) achat *m* hors taxe.

duvet ['duːveɪ] *n* couette *f*; *Swiss* duvet *m*; **d. cover,** housse *f* de couette.

dux [dʌks] *n esp Scot Sch* premier *m* de la classe.

DV [diː'viː] *adv* (*abbr* **deo volente**) si Dieu le veut.

dwarf¹ [dwɔːf] **1** *n* (*person*) *& Myth* nain, *f* naine. **2** *adj* (*plant, tree*) nain.

dwarf² *vt* **(a)** empêcher (*qn, qch*) de croître; rabougrir (*une plante*); **(b)** rapetisser (*par contraste*); **tower that dwarfs the main building,** tour dont la hauteur écrase le corps de bâtiment; **the church is dwarfed by the skyscraper,** l'église est écrasée par le gratte-ciel.

dwarfish ['dwɔːfɪʃ] *adj* (de) nain.

dwell [dwel] *vi* (*pt & pp* **dwelt** [dwelt]) **(a)** rester; **this hope dwells within our hearts,** cet espoir repose dans notre cœur; **to let one's eye d. on s.o.,** arrêter son regard sur qn; **(b)** *Lit* **to d. in a place,** habiter (dans) un lieu.

►dwell on, dwell upon *vipo* (*think about, spend time on*) insister sur, s'étendre sur (*un sujet, un problème*); faire ressortir (*les difficultés*); appuyer sur (*une syllabe etc*).

dweller ['dwelər] *n* habitant, -ante (**in, on,** de); **cave-d.,** troglodyte *mf*; **city-d.,** citadin *m*.

dwelling ['dwelɪŋ] *n* **d. (place),** domicile *m*, demeure *f*; *Lit* lieu *m* de séjour; **d. house,** maison *f* d'habitation.

dwindle ['dwɪnd(ə)l] *vi* **to d. (away),** diminuer, dépérir; (*of political party*) s'amenuiser; **to d. to nothing,** se réduire à rien.

dwindling ['dwɪnd(ə)lɪŋ] **1** *adj* diminuant, faiblissant. **2** *n* diminution *f*, dépérissement *m*; amenuisement *m* (*d'un parti politique*); *Fin* déperdition *f* (*de capital*).

dye¹ [daɪ] *n* (*for clothes, hair*) teinture *f*; **fast d.,** bon teint; *Lit* **villain of the deepest d.,** coquin fieffé; *Phot* **d. solution,** bain colorant.

dye² *v* (*prp* **dyeing**) **1** *vt* teindre; **to d. sth black/red,** teindre qch en noir/rouge; **to have a dress dyed,** faire teindre une robe; **to d. one's hair,** se teindre les cheveux. **2** *vi* (se) teindre; **material that dyes well,** tissu qui prend bien la teinture.

dyed-in-the-wool ['daɪdɪnðə'wʊl] *adj Tex* (*drap*) teint en laine; *Fig* invétéré, inébranlable; *Fig* **a d.-in-the-wool Englishman/conservative,** un Anglais/conservateur bon teint.

dyeing ['daɪɪŋ] *n* **(a)** teinture *f* (*d'étoffes, des cheveux*); **(b)** (*trade*) teinturerie *f*.

dyer ['daɪər] *n* teinturier *m*; **d. and cleaner,** teinturier dégraisseur.

dyestuff ['daɪstʌf] *n* matière colorante, colorant *m*.

dyeworks ['daɪwɜːks] *npl* (*usu with sing verb*) teinturerie *f*.

dying ['daɪɪŋ] **1** *adj* mourant, agonisant; **in a d. voice,** d'une voix éteinte; **d. words,** dernières paroles; **with his d. breath,** de sa voix agonisante; **it was my mother's d. wish that ...,** c'était les dernières volontés de ma mère que ...; **I shall remember it to my d. day,** je m'en souviendrai jusqu'à la mort. **2** *n* **(a)** (*death throes*) agonie *f*; (*death*) mort *f*; **(b) the dead and the d.,** les morts *mpl* et les moribonds *mpl*; **prayers for the d.,** prières *fpl* des agonisants.

dyke¹ [daɪk] *n* **(a)** *HydE* digue *f*, levée *f*; (*embankment*) chaussée surélevée *ou* en remblai; **(b)** (*ditch*) fossé *m*, chenal *m*, -aux.

dyke² *vt* endiguer (*un cours d'eau*); protéger (*un terrain*) par des digues.

dyke³ *n F* (*lesbian*) gouine *f*.

dynamic [daɪ'næmɪk] *adj Fig & Phys* dynamique; *Phys* **to become d.,** (*of force etc*) se dynamiser; *Fig* **d. personality** *or* **character,** caractère *m* dynamique; *Mus* **d. range,** dynamique *f* (*d'un instrument*); *Comptr* **d. RAM,** mémoire RAM dynamique.

dynamically [daɪ'næmɪklɪ] *adv* dynamiquement.

dynamics [daɪ'næmɪks] *npl* (*usu with sing verb*) dynamique *f*.

dynamism ['daɪnəmɪz(ə)m] *n Fig & Phys* dynamisme *m*.

dynamite¹ ['daɪnəmaɪt] *n* dynamite *f*; *F* **subject that is political d.,** sujet explosif sur le plan politique; *F* **this information is d.,** cette information c'est de la dynamite; *F* **it's d.!,** c'est du tonnerre!; *F* **this new band is d.,** ce nouveau groupe déménage vraiment.

dynamite² *vt* faire sauter (*des roches etc*) à la dynamite; dynamiter (*un édifice etc*).

dynamo, *pl* **-os** ['daɪnəmoʊ, -əʊz] *n* dynamo *f*; génératrice *f*, générateur *m* (*de courant*); *Fig* **she's a human d.,** elle a une énergie extraordinaire.

dynastic [dɪ'næstɪk] *adj* dynastique.

dynasty ['dɪnəstɪ] *n* dynastie *f*.

dyne [daɪn] *n* (*unit of force*) dyne *f*.

dysentery ['dɪsəntrɪ] *n Med* dysenterie *f*; **amoebic d.,** dysenterie amibienne; **to have d.,** avoir la dysenterie.

dyslectic [dɪs'lektɪk] **, dyslexic** [dɪs'leksɪk] *adj & n Med* dyslexique *mf*.

dyslexia [dɪs'leksɪə] *n Med* dyslexie *f*; **to have d.,** faire de la dyslexie.

dysmenorrhoea, *US* **dysmenorrhea** [dɪsmenə'rɪə] *n Med* dysménorrhée *f*.

dyspepsia [dɪs'pepsɪə] *n Med* dyspepsie *f*; **acid d.,** aigreurs *fpl ou F* brûlures *fpl* d'estomac.

dyspeptic [dɪs'peptɪk] **1** *n Med* dyspepsique *mf*, dyspeptique *mf*. **2** *adj* **(a)** *Med* dyspepsique, dyspeptique; **(b)** *F* ronchon, grognon.

dysphasia [dɪs'feɪzɪə] *n Med* dysphasie *f*.

dystrophy ['dɪstrəfɪ] *n Med* dystrophie *f*; **muscular d.,** dystrophie musculaire progressive, myopathie *f*.

E

E, e [iː] *n* **(a)** (la lettre) E, e *m*; **E number,** (*on processed food package*) additif *m* dont le code commence par E; **(b)** *Mus* mi *m*; **key of E flat,** clef *f* de mi bémol; **(c)** *F* (*rejection*) **to give s.o. the big E.,** virer qn.

e (*abbr* **east**) E.

each [iːtʃ] **1** *adj* chaque; **e. day,** chaque jour, tous les jours; **e. elector has two votes,** chaque électeur a deux voix; **e. one of us,** chacun *ou* chacune de nous *ou* d'entre nous. **2** *pron* chacun, -une; **e. of us,** chacun *ou* chacune d'entre nous; **we e. earn £10, we earn £10 e.,** nous gagnons 10 livres chacun; **peaches at 25p e.,** pêches à 25 pence chacune *ou* 25 pence pièce; **a little of e.,** un peu de chaque; **e. other,** l'un l'autre, l'une l'autre; les uns les autres, les unes les autres; **separated from e. other,** séparés l'un de l'autre; **to fight e. other,** se battre; **we can help e. other,** nous pouvons nous aider l'un l'autre, nous pouvons nous aider mutuellement, nous pouvons nous entraider; **they flatter e. other,** ils se flattent réciproquement.

eager [ˈiːɡər] *adj* passionné; vif (*désir, espoir*); (*regard*) avide; **to be e. to do sth,** être impatient de faire qch; **they were e. to learn,** ils étaient avides d'apprendre; **he was e. to disassociate himself from them,** il était impatient de se séparer d'eux; **I didn't want to seem too e.,** (*in relationship etc*) je ne voulais pas sembler trop empressé; *F* **an e. beaver,** un(e) zélé(e).

eagerly [ˈiːɡəlɪ] *adv* passionnément, avidement; **to desire sth e.,** désirer qch passionnément; **to listen e.,** écouter avidement *ou* avec empressement; **her e. awaited second album,** son deuxième album impatiemment attendu.

eagerness [ˈiːɡənɪs] *n* impatience *f* (*de voir qn*); empressement *m* (*à se rendre utile etc*); vif désir (*d'apprendre qch etc*); **to show e. in doing sth,** montrer un intérêt très vif à faire qch; **e. to succeed,** ardent désir de réussir.

eagle [ˈiːɡ(ə)l] *n* **(a)** (*bird*) aigle *m*; *Rel* **e. lectern,** aigle; **(b)** *Her* aigle *f*; **double-headed e.,** aigle à deux têtes; **(c)** *Mil US* aigle *m* (= *insigne de grade de colonel*); **(d)** *Golf* deux coups sous la normale; eagle *m*, *Can* aiglon *m*.

eagle-eyed [iːɡ(ə)ˈlaɪd] *adj* aux yeux d'aigle.

eaglet [ˈiːɡlɪt] *n* (*bird*) aiglon *m*.

E & OE [iːəndˈəʊiː] *Com* (*abbr* **errors and omissions excepted**) s.e. & o..

ear[1] [ˈɪər] *n* **(a)** oreille *f*; *Anat* **the external e.,** l'oreille externe; **the middle e.,** l'oreille moyenne; **the internal e.,** l'oreille interne; *Med* **e., nose and throat specialist,** oto-rhino-laryngologiste *mf*; **a smile from e. to e.,** un sourire épanoui jusqu'aux deux oreilles; **to go in (at) one e. and out (at) the other,** (*of words*) entrer par une oreille et sortir par l'autre; **your ears must have been burning,** les oreilles ont dû vous siffler; **up to one's ears in work,** accablé de travail; *F* **to be (thrown) out on one's e.,** se faire sortir; **e. trumpet,** cornet *m* acoustique; **e. lobe,** lobe *m* de l'oreille; **e. protector,** protège-tympan *m inv*; *Rugby* protège-oreilles *m inv*;

(b) (*hearing*) **to have sharp ears,** avoir l'ouïe fine; **deaf in one e.,** sourd d'une oreille; *Mus* **to have a good/poor e.,** avoir de l'oreille ne pas avoir d'oreille; **to have an e. for music,** avoir l'oreille musicale; **to play by e.,** jouer sans notes; *Fig* **to play it by e.,** aller au pifomètre; **to have an e. for poetry,** avoir le sens de la poésie; **to keep one's ears open** *or* **one's e. to the ground,** se tenir aux écoutes; **I'm all ears,** je suis tout ouïe; **to lend an e.** *or* **lend one's e. to s.o.,** prêter l'oreille à qn; **to close one's ears to the truth,** fermer l'oreille à la vérité; **you might drop this hint in his e.,** glissez-lui cet avis à l'oreille; **word reached their e. of the enemy's plan,** les projets de l'ennemi leur sont venus à l'oreille;

(c) *Tech* (*of vase*) anse *f*, oreille *f*; (*of bell*) anse;

(d) (*of seashell*) oreillette *f*.

ear[2] *n* (*of wheat etc*) épi *m*; **wheat in the e.,** blé *m* en épi.

earache [ˈiːəreɪk] *n* mal *m* d'oreille(s); *Med* otalgie *f*; **to have e.,** avoir mal à l'oreille *ou* aux oreilles.

eardrops [ˈɪədrɒps] *npl Med* gouttes *fpl* pour les oreilles.

eardrum [ˈɪədrʌm] *n Anat* tympan *m* (*de l'oreille*).

-eared [ˈɪəd] *suff* **long/short/***etc***-e.,** aux oreilles longues/courtes/*etc*.

earflap [ˈɪəflæp] *n* oreillette *f* (de casquette).

earful [ˈɪəfʊl] *n* **I got an e. of water,** j'ai pris de l'eau plein l'oreille; *F* **to give s.o. an e.,** donner une verte semonce *ou* dire son fait à qn.

earhole [ˈɪəhəʊl] *n Br F* trou *m* de l'oreille.

earl [ɜːl] *n* comte *m*.

earldom [ˈɜːldəm] *n* **(a)** (*land*) comté *m*; **(b)** (*title*) titre *m* de comte.

early [ˈɜːlɪ] (**earlier, earliest**) **1** *adj* **(a)** (*in the day*) matinal; **in the e. morning,** de bon matin; **e. morning walk,** promenade matinale; **you're e.,** (*in morning*) tu es matinal; (*ahead of time*) tu es en avance; **I am half an hour e.,** je suis en avance d'une demi-heure; **in the e. afternoon,** au commencement de l'après-midi; **to have an e. dinner,** dîner de bonne heure; **e. rising,** l'habitude de se lever de bonne heure; **to be an e. riser,** être matinal, se lever de bon matin; **I'm going to have an e. night,** je vais me coucher de bonne heure; *Prov* **the e. bird catches the worm,** l'avenir appartient à ceux qui se lèvent tôt; **an e. bird,** un lève-tôt, un matinal; *Br Com etc* **e. closing,** (*practice*) fermeture *f* l'après-midi; (*day*) jour où les magasins sont fermés l'après- midi; **it's e. days yet,** il est encore trop tôt (**to,** pour);

(b) (*first etc*) **the earliest times,** les temps les plus reculés; **the e. Church,** l'Église primitive; **e. Christians,** les premiers chrétiens; **in (the) e. summer, in the e. part of summer,** dans les *ou* aux premiers jours de l'été, au commencement de l'été; **in the e. nineteenth century,** au début du XIXe siècle; **in the e. sixties,** au début des années soixante; **from the earliest times,** depuis les temps les plus reculés; **the earliest legends,** les premières légendes; *Art* **the e. masters,** les primitifs; **e. radios didn't have loudspeakers,** les premières radios n'avaient pas de haut-parleurs; **e. youth,** première jeunesse; **e. age,** âge *m* tendre; **at an e. age,** tout jeune; **from the earliest age,** dès la plus tendre enfance; **my earliest recollections,** mes souvenirs les plus lointains; **he received his e. education at ...,** il reçut sa première éducation à ...;

(c) (*premature*) précoce, hâtif; (*death*) prématuré; **e. beans,** (*earlier than normal*) haricots *mpl* précoces; (*first*) haricots de primeur; **e. vegetables** *or* **fruit** *or* **produce,** primeurs *fpl*; **we're having an e. winter,** l'hiver est précoce; **Easter is e. this year,** Pâques est tôt cette année; **to take e. retirement,** prendre la retraite anticipée;

(d) at an e. date, prochainement; à une date prochaine; **at an earlier date,** (*previous*) à une date antérieure; (*sooner*) à une date plus rapprochée; **to take an e. opportunity to do sth,** faire qch à la première occasion; **at the earliest possible moment,** dans le plus bref délai possible; **at your earliest convenience,** dès que possible; *Mil* **e. warning system,** réseau *m* de radars de guet *ou* de pré-alerte.

2 *adv* **(a)** de bonne heure, tôt; **earlier,** plus tôt; **as I mentioned earlier,** (*in time*) comme je l'ai mentionné plus tôt; (*in writing*) comme je l'ai mentionné ci-dessus *ou* plus haut; **too e.,** trop tôt; **to arrive five minutes (too) e.,** arriver avec cinq minutes d'avance; **e. in the morning,** le matin de bonne heure, de grand matin; **e. in the evening,** très tôt dans la soirée; **to get up e.,** se lever de bonne heure; **they left the party e.,** ils ont quitté la soirée tôt; **e. in the winter,** à l'entrée de l'hiver; **e. in the year,** au début de l'année; **e. on it was apparent that ...,** dès l'abord il est apparu que ...; **e. in (his) life,** dans ses jeunes années, dans sa jeunesse; **e. in his career,** au début de sa carrière; **as e. as the tenth century,** dès le dixième siècle; **as e. as possible,** le plus tôt possible; **next week at the earliest,** la semaine prochaine au plus tôt;

(b) (*prematurely*) **to die e.**, (*young*) mourir jeune; (*sooner than expected*) mourir prématurément; **this flower blooms very e.**, cette fleur s'épanouit très précocement;

(c) (*near the beginning*) **e. in the list**, tout au commencement de la liste.

early-closing ['ɜːlɪ'kləʊzɪŋ] *adj Br Com* **e.-c. day**, jour où les magasins ferment tôt.

earmark[1] ['ɪəmɑːk] *n Agr* marque *f* à l'oreille (*d'un mouton etc*).

earmark[2] *vt* **(a)** (*assign*) donner à (*des fonds*) une affectation spéciale; **to e. funds for a project**, assigner des fonds à un projet; **the land has been earmarked for a new school**, le terrain a été affecté à la construction d'une nouvelle école; *F* **to e. sth for oneself**, se réserver qch; **(b)** (*mark the corner of*) faire une marque au coin de (*un document, un chèque*); **(c)** *Agr* marquer (*les moutons etc*) à l'oreille.

earmuff ['ɪəmʌf] *n* protège-oreilles *m inv*, cache-oreilles *m inv*.

earn [ɜːn] *vt* **(a)** (*make*) gagner (*de l'argent*); **how much do you e.?**, combien gagnez-vous?; **to e. one's living by writing**, gagner sa vie de sa plume; *Fin* **to e. interest**, (*of money*) produire des intérêts; *Ind* **earning capacity**, rapport *m* (*d'une entreprise*); **(b)** (*deserve*) mériter, gagner (*l'affection de qn*); **she earned their respect**, elle a gagné leur respect; **you've earned it**, (*this break, rise etc*) tu l'as bien mérité; **his conduct earned him universal praise**, sa conduite lui valut les éloges de tous; **this action earned her many enemies**, cette action lui a valu de nombreux ennemis, par cette action elle s'est attirée de nombreux ennemis.

earned [ɜːnd] *adj* **e. income**, revenu salarial.

earner ['ɜːnər] *n* **(a)** (*person*) **(wage) e.**, salarié, -ée; **she's not a big e.**, elle ne gagne pas beaucoup; **(b)** *Br F* (*activity, business*) **a nice little e.**, une activité lucrative *ou* rémunératrice; **that garage/window-cleaning round must be a nice little e.**, ce garage/cette tournée de nettoyage de vitres doit être une activité bien lucrative.

earnest[1] ['ɜːnɪst] **1** *adj* (*person*) sérieux; (*expression*) pénétré, grave; (*demand*) pressant; (*request*) fervent; (*effort*) sérieux; (*desire*) profond. **2** *n* **in e.**, sérieusement; pour de bon; **to be in e.**, être sérieux; **are you in e.?**, parlez-vous sérieusement?; **to speak in e.**, parler sérieusement; **I thought you were in e.**, je vous ai pris au sérieux; **to set to work in e.**, se mettre sérieusement à l'ouvrage; **half in jest, half in e.**, moitié plaisantant, moitié sérieux, mi-figue, mi-raisin.

earnest[2] *n Old-fashioned Com etc* arrhes *fpl*.

earnestly ['ɜːnɪstlɪ] *adv* (*speak*) sérieusement; **we e. hope that ...**, nous espérons bien sincèrement que ....

earnestness ['ɜːnɪstnɪs] *n* caractère sérieux (*d'une discussion*); gravité *f*, sérieux *m* (*de ton*); ferveur *f* (*d'une prière*).

earning ['ɜːnɪŋ] *n* (*act*) gain *m*; **e. capacity**, (*of company etc*) rapport *m* (*d'une entreprise*).

earnings ['ɜːnɪŋz] *npl* **(a)** (*salary*) salaire *m*; **my e.**, ce que je gagne; *Jur* **living on immoral e.**, vagabondage spécial; **(b)** (*profits*) profits *mpl*, bénéfices *mpl* (*d'une entreprise*).

earphone ['ɪəfəʊn] *n Rad Tel* écouteur *m*.

earpiece ['ɪəpiːs] *n Tel* écouteur *m* (*de récepteur*).

ear-piercing ['ɪəpiːəsɪŋ] *adj* (*cri*) qui vous perce les tympans.

earplug ['ɪəplʌg] *n* (*for sleeping*) boule *f* Quiès ®; (*for protection from noise*) protège-tympan *m inv*.

earring ['ɪərɪŋ] *n* boucle *f* d'oreille; **stud e.**, dormeuse *f*; **drop e.**, pendant *m* d'oreille.

earshot ['ɪəʃɒt] *n* **within/out of e.**, à portée de voix/hors de portée de la voix.

ear-splitting ['ɪəsplɪtɪŋ] *adj* (*scream*) qui vous déchire les tympans; (*noise*) à crever les tympans; **the noise was e.-s.**, le bruit était à vous déchirer les oreilles.

earth[1] [ɜːθ] *n* **(a)** (*the planet*) terre *f*; (*the world*) le monde; **the e.'s crust**, l'écorce *f* terrestre; **the e.'s atmosphere**, l'atmosphère *f* terrestre; **on e.**, sur terre; *Bible* **on e. as it is in heaven**, sur la terre comme au ciel; *F* **where/why on e. ...?**, où/pourquoi diable ...?; **there's no reason on e.**, il n'y a absolument aucune raison; **it wouldn't cost the e.**, ça ne coûterait pas les yeux de la tête; **he promised people the e.**, il a promis la lune aux gens; **e. creature**, (*in science fiction*) créature terrienne; **e. observation satellite**, satellite *f* d'observation de la Terre; **e. orbit**, (*of satellite*) orbite *f* terrestre; **e. sciences**, sciences *fpl* de la terre;

(b) (*the ground*) le sol; *Fig* **to come back to e. (with a bump)**, revenir (brutalement) sur terre; **down to e.**, (*practical*) réaliste, qui a les pieds sur terre; (*mundane*) terre à terre; **the e. moved**, la terre a tremblé; (*while making love*) *& Hum* c'était fantastique;

(c) *Agr etc* (*soil*) terre *f*; **loose/heavy e.**, terre(s) meuble(s)/lourde(s); *Ch* **fuller's e.**, terre à foulon; **e. floor**, (*of hut etc*) sol *m* en terre battue;

(d) *Br El* terre *f*, masse *f*; (*terminal*) mise *f* à terre; **dead e.**, contact parfait avec le sol; **e. to frame**, (*of car etc*) contact à la masse; **e. cable/wire**, câble *m*/fil *m* de terre; **e. connection**, prise *f* de terre;

(e) (*of fox*) terrier *m*, tanière *f*; **to go to e.**, (*of fox, fugitive*) se terrer; **to run to e.**, chasser (*un renard*) jusqu'à son terrier; dénicher (*qn*); découvrir la retraite de (*qn*); découvrir la source de (*une erreur de calcul etc*).

earth[2] **1** *vt* **(a)** *El* mettre (*le courant*) à la terre; **(b)** (*in hunting*) poursuivre (*un renard*) jusqu'à son terrier; **(c)** = **EARTH UP**. **2** *vi* (*of fox*) se terrer.

►**earth up** *vtsep* (*in gardening*) butter, chausser (*une plante*).

earthbound ['ɜːθbaʊnd] *adj* **(a)** (*mundane*) terre à terre *inv*; **(b) e. spirit**, esprit qui ne peut pas quitter le monde des vivants; **(c)** (*heading towards earth*) qui se dirige vers la terre.

earthen ['ɜːθ(ə)n] *adj* **(a)** (*crockery etc*) en *ou* de terre (cuite); **(b)** (*floor*) en terre battue.

earthenware ['ɜːθ(ə)nweər] *n* poterie *f* (de terre); **glazed e.**, faïence *f*; (*stoneware*) grès flambé; **e. jug**, cruche *f* en *ou* de terre (cuite).

earthfall ['ɜːθfɔːl] *n* éboulement *m* de terres.

earthlight ['ɜːθlaɪt] *n Astron* lumière cendrée (*de la lune*).

earthling ['ɜːθlɪŋ] *n* (*in science fiction*) habitant, -ante de la terre.

earthly[1] ['ɜːθlɪ] *adj* terrestre; **the E. Paradise**, le Paradis terrestre; *F* **there's no e. reason for ...**, il n'y a pas la moindre raison du monde pour ...; **it's of no e. use to me**, ça ne me sert *ou* ne me servirait à rien; **he hasn't got an e. chance**, il n'a pas la moindre chance (*de réussir*).

earthly[2] *n Br F* **he hasn't got an e.**, il n'a pas la moindre chance (*de réussir*).

earthman ['ɜːθmæn] *n* (*science fiction*) terrien *m*.

earthmover ['ɜːθmuːvər] *n* bulldozer *m*.

earthmoving ['ɜːθmuːvɪŋ] *n* **e. equipment**, engins *m* de terrassement.

earthquake ['ɜːθkweɪk] *n* tremblement *m* de terre, séisme *m*; **e. survivor**, survivant *m* d'un tremblement de terre.

earth-shaking ['ɜːθʃeɪkɪŋ], **earth-shattering** ['ɜːθʃætərɪŋ] *adj F* stupéfiant.

earthwoman ['ɜːθwʊmən] *n* (*in science fiction*) terrienne *f*.

earthwork ['ɜːθwɜːk] *n* (travaux *mpl* de) terrassement *m*; **e. embankment**, terrassement en remblai; **earthworks**, *Constr etc* travaux *mpl* en terre *ou* de terrassement; (*prehistoric*) *& Mil* fortifications *fpl* en terre.

earthworm ['ɜːθwɜːm] *n* lombric *m*, ver *m* de terre.

earthy ['ɜːθɪ] *adj* **(a)** terreux; **to have an e. smell**, sentir la terre; **(b)** (*person*) vert; (*humour*) truculent, vert.

earwax ['ɪəwæks] *n* cire secrétée par les oreilles, *Fml* cérumen *f*.

earwig ['ɪəwɪg] *n* (*insect*) perce-oreille *m*, *pl* perce-oreilles.

ease[1] [iːz] *n* **(a)** (*facility*) aisance *f* (*de manières etc*); moelleux *m* (*des mouvements*); facilité *f* (*d'élocution etc*); simplicité *f* (*de réglage*); douceur *f*, facilité (*de manœuvre*); **with e.**, facilement; aisément; **with the utmost** *or* **the greatest of e.**, avec la plus grande facilité; **the e. with which we entered the building**, la facilité avec laquelle nous sommes entrés dans le bâtiment;

(b) (*peace*) tranquillité *f* (*d'esprit*); repos *m*, bien-être *m* (*du corps*); **to be at e.**, avoir l'esprit tranquille; **to be** *or* **feel ill at e.**, être mal à l'aise; (*worried*) être inquiet (**about**, au sujet de); **to be at one's e.**, (*relaxed*) être à son aise; (*calm*) être tranquille; **to put s.o. at e.**, (*help to relax*) mettre qn à l'aise; (*calm*) tranquilliser qn; **set your mind at e.**, rassurez-vous, soyez tranquille; **to take one's e.**, se mettre à l'aise; *Mil etc* **to stand at e.**, se mettre *ou* se tenir au repos; **(stand) at e.!**, repos!; **e. from pain**, soulagement *m*;

(c) (*leisure*) loisir *m*; (*idleness*) oisiveté *f*; **a life of e.**, une vie d'oisiveté.

ease[2] **1** *vt* **(a)** (*alleviate*) adoucir, calmer, alléger (*la souffrance*); soulager, apporter du soulagement à (*un malade*); tranquilliser (*l'esprit*); **to e. s.o.'s anxiety**, calmer les inquiétudes de qn;

(b) débarrasser, délivrer (**s.o. of** *or* **from sth**, qn de qch); **to e. oneself of a burden,** se soulager d'un fardeau; **(c)** (*relax*) détendre, relâcher (*un cordage, un ressort*); desserrer (*une vis*); modérer, soulager (*la pression*); **to e. the congestion in a street,** décongestionner la circulation d'une rue;

(d) (*move carefully, slowly*) déplacer doucement; **to e. a box open,** ouvrir doucement une boîte; **to e. one's way through a crowd,** se faufiler à travers la foule;

(e) *Sewing* donner plus d'ampleur à (*une robe*); *MecE* donner du jeu à (*un organe*); *Constr* ajuster (*une porte*).

2 *vi* (*of pain, rain etc*) s'atténuer; (*of tension, St Exch market etc*) se détendre; **the wind has eased,** le vent s'est calmé; **the situation has eased,** la situation s'est détendue.

►**ease off 1** *vtsep* **(a)** (*release*) enlever doucement; **she eased the lid off the jar,** elle a doucement enlevé le couvercle de sur le pot; **(b)** *Nau* (*let out*) filer, choquer (*un cordage*). **2** *vi* **(a)** (*work less*) se relâcher; moins travailler; **he's been told to e. off if he doesn't want a heart attack,** on lui a dit de moins travailler s'il ne veut pas avoir une crise cardiaque; **(b)** (*diminish*) (*of pain, rain*) s'atténuer; *St Exch* (*of rates*) se détendre; **(c)** *Nau* s'éloigner un peu du rivage.

►**ease up 1** *vi* **(a)** = **EASE OFF 2 (a),(b)**; **(b)** (*slow down*) ralentir. **2** *vtsep Nau* soulager (*un palan*).

easel ['iːz(ə)l] *n* chevalet *m* (*de peintre etc*).

easily ['iːzɪlɪ] *adv* **(a)** (*without difficulty*) facilement, sans difficulté; **you can e. imagine my disappointment,** vous concevez sans peine ma déception; **he is not e. satisfied,** il n'est pas facile à satisfaire; **e. moved,** facile à émouvoir; **he came in e. first,** il est arrivé bon premier; **he is e. forty,** il a bien quarante ans; **the information could e. be wrong,** les informations pourraient très bien être fausses; **the door shuts e.,** la porte se ferme sans effort; **the car holds six people e.,** six personnes tiennent à l'aise dans cette voiture; **that's e. said,** c'est vite dit; **(b)** (*in a relaxed manner*) à son aise; **to take things** *or* **life e.,** prendre les choses comme elles viennent, prendre la vie comme elle vient; *Pej* se laisser vivre, se la couler douce.

easiness ['iːzɪnɪs] *n* **(a)** (*of task*) facilité *f*; **(b)** (*easy-going nature*) complaisance *f*, humeur *f* facile (*de qn*); (*indifference*) indifférence *f*, insouciance *f*; **(c)** (*grace*) grâce *f* (*du style etc*); **(d)** (*ease of operation*) jeu *m* facile (*d'une machine*); **(e)** (*well-being*) bien-être *m*; **(f)** *Econ* aisance *f*, facilité *f*.

easing ['iːzɪŋ] *n* **(a)** soulagement *m* (*de la souffrance*); allègement *m* (*d'une poutre etc*); **(b)** *Constr* adoucissement *m* (*d'une courbe*); **(c)** (*relaxation*) **e. of tension,** détente *f* (politique *etc*); **e. of the market,** détente du marché.

easing off *n* **(a)** atténuation *f* (*de la douleur etc*); **(b)** (*of person*) relâchement *m* (**from work,** du travail); **(c)** *St Exch* détente *f*.

east [iːst] **1** *n* est *m*; **house facing (the) e.,** maison exposée à l'est; **on the e., to the e.,** à l'est **(of,** de); **the E.,** (*the Orient*) l'Orient *m*; (*Eastern Europe*) l'Est; **the Middle E.,** le Moyen-Orient; **the Far E.,** l'Extrême-Orient; **the e. of England,** l'est de l'Angleterre. **2** *adv* à l'est; **to travel e.,** voyager vers l'est; **e. of the Rhine,** à l'est du Rhin. **3** *adj* (*coast etc*) est; (*wind*) d'est; (*country*) de l'est; (*wall, window*) qui fait face à l'est; **e. end,** chevet *m* (*d'une église*); **the E. End,** = les quartiers pauvres et populeux de la partie est (*de Londres, de Glasgow*); **the E. Side,** = les quartiers est (*de New York*); *esp Am* **E. Europe,** Europe *f* de l'Est; **E. Germany,** Allemagne *f* de l'Est; **the E. Indies,** les Indes orientales; *Hist* **the E. India Company,** la compagnie des Indes orientales.

eastbound ['iːstbaʊnd] *adj* (*train etc*) allant vers l'est; *Rail* (*on station*) qui va vers l'est; (*in large city*) en direction de la banlieue est.

Easter ['iːstər] *n* Pâques *m*; **E. Day, E. Sunday,** le jour *ou* le dimanche de Pâques; **E. Monday,** le lundi de Pâques; **E. week,** (*following Easter*) la semaine de Pâques; (*Holy Week*) la semaine sainte; **E. egg,** œuf *m* de Pâques; **E. Island,** l'île *f* de Pâques.

easterly ['iːstəlɪ] **1** *adj* (*vent*) d'est, qui vient de l'est; (*courant*) qui se dirige vers l'est; (*point*) situé à *ou* vers l'est; **in an e. direction,** (*of wind*) qui souffle vers l'est. **2** *adv* vers l'est. **3** *n* vent *m* d'est.

eastern ['iːstən] *adj* est, de l'est; (*of Far East*) oriental, -aux; **the E. Church,** l'Église *f* d'Orient; **E. Europe,** Europe *f* de l'Est; *Am* **E. Standard Time,** heure normale de l'est; *Can* **the E. Townships,** les Cantons *mpl* de l'Est.

Easterner ['iːstənər] *n* oriental, -ale; *Am* habitant, -ante des *US* États *ou Can* provinces de l'est.

Eastertide ['iːstətaɪd] *n* Pâques *m*.

eastward ['iːstwəd] **1** *adj* **(a)** (*in the east*) à l'est, dans l'est; **(b)** (*in an eastward direction*) du côté de l'est. **2** *adv* = **EASTWARDS**.

eastwards ['iːstwədz] *adv* à l'est; (*with motion*) vers l'est.

easy ['iːzɪ] **(easier, easiest) 1** *adj* **(a)** (*not difficult*) (*work*) facile, aisé; (*question, test*) facile; (*method, solution*) simple; **that is e. to see,** cela se voit; **it is e. for him to ...,** il lui est facile de ...; **it's e. to say ...,** on a vite fait de dire ...; **this will make your job easier,** ceci facilitera votre tâche; *Fig* **it makes life much easier not having to fill in these forms,** ça facilite bien les choses de ne pas avoir à remplir ces formulaires; **within e. reach of ...,** à distance commode de ...; **it's within e. walking distance,** on peut facilement y aller à pied; *F* **as e. as ABC** *or* **as falling off a log,** simple comme bonjour; **it isn't e.,** ce n'est pas facile; **it isn't e. being a mother,** il n'est pas facile d'être une mère; **the e. way out** *or* **option,** la solution de facilité; *F* **e. money,** argent gagné sans peine; **by e. stages,** (*travel*) à petites étapes; **at an e. pace,** à petite vitesse; **the film is very e. on the eye,** le film est reposant à regarder; **he's/she's e. on the eye,** il/elle n'est pas mal du tout; *Com* **by e. payments, on e. terms,** avec facilités de paiement; *Sp etc* **to come in an e. first,** arriver bon premier; **to have an e. time,** se la couler douce;

(b) (*easy-going*) facile, accommodant; **e. to get on with,** d'un commerce facile; **e. to live with,** facile à vivre; *F* **I'm e.!,** ça m'est égal!; **woman of e. virtue,** femme *f* de mœurs faciles *ou* légères;

(c) (*manners etc*) libre, dégagé; (*style*) facile, naturel;

(d) (*movement*) moelleux; **e. fit,** *MecE* ajustage *m* lâche; (*jeans, clothes*) lâche, de coupe confortable; **my coat is an e. fit,** mon manteau est de coupe confortable;

(e) (*comfortable*) à l'aise; (*without worries*) sans inquiétude; (*life*) sans souci; **to be e. in one's mind,** avoir l'esprit tranquille; **with an e. conscience,** la conscience tranquille; *F* **to be on e. street,** ne pas avoir de problèmes financiers;

(f) *Com* (*market*) tranquille; **prices are (getting) easier,** on accuse une détente dans les prix; **cotton was easier,** le coton a accusé une détente.

2 *adv* **(a)** (*in a relaxed manner*) **to take things** *or* **it e.,** prendre les choses en douceur; **to take things** *or* **life e.,** prendre les choses comme elles viennent *ou* la vie comme elle vient; *Pej* se laisser vivre, se la couler douce; **take it e.!,** ne vous en faites pas!; **you'll have to go e. for a bit,** il va falloir freiner un peu; **to go e. with sth/s.o.,** ménager qch/qn; **e. does it!,** (allez-y) doucement!; **go e. on the electricity/the curry powder,** allez-y doucement avec l'électricité/le curry; **e. (ahead)!,** (*in rowing*) (en avant) doucement!; *Mil* **stand e.!,** repos!;

(b) *F* (*without difficulty*) **I can do it e.,** cela me sera facile; **easier said than done,** c'est plus facile à dire qu'à faire; *Prov* **e. come e. go,** ce qui vient de la flûte s'en va par le tambour.

easy-going ['iːzɪ'gəʊɪŋ] *adj* **(a)** (*not given to anger*) qui prend les choses tranquillement; (*not worrying*) qui ne se fait pas de bile; (*undemanding*) accommodant, coulant, peu exigeant; (*unprincipled*) qui a la conscience élastique; **an e.-g. man,** un homme facile à vivre; **(b)** (*horse*) à l'allure douce.

eat [iːt] *v* **(ate** [et, *esp Am* eɪt]; **eaten** ['iːt(ə)n]) **1** *vt* **(a)** manger (*du pain, de la soupe etc*); **to e. one's breakfast/dinner/supper,** déjeuner/dîner/souper; **to e. a good dinner,** faire un bon dîner; **fit to e.,** bon à manger, mangeable; **I don't e. meat,** je ne mange pas de viande; **to e. one's fill,** manger à sa faim; **he won't e. you,** il ne vous mangera pas; *F* **we e. teams like you for breakfast,** nous ne faisons qu'une seule bouchée d'équipes comme la vôtre; **to e. one's words,** se rétracter; *Fig* **to e. humble pie,** s'humilier (devant qn); **if it comes off, I'll e. my hat,** si ça réussit, je mange mon chapeau; **to e. s.o. out of house and home,** ruiner qn en nourriture; **she ate her way through six packets of biscuits,** elle a réussi à engloutir six paquets de biscuits;

(b) *F* (*trouble*) **what's eating you?,** qu'est-ce qui vous inquiète *ou* tracasse?

2 *vi* **(a)** manger; **I haven't eaten since yesterday,** je n'ai pas mangé depuis hier; **to e. like a horse,** manger comme un ogre; **to e. like a bird,** avoir un appétit d'oiseau, manger trois fois rien; **he eats out of my hand,** (*of bird*) il vient manger dans ma main; (*of person*) il fait tout ce que je veux; **treat them right and you'll have them eating out of your hand,** traite-les bien et tu en feras ce que tu voudras;

(b) (*have a meal*) dîner; **we e. at seven,** nous dînons à sept heures; **let's e.!,** à table!; **have you eaten?,** est-ce que tu as mangé?

►eat away *vtsep* (*erode*) éroder, miner (*des roches, une falaise*); saper (*des fondations*); (*of acid*) dissoudre (*un métal*).

►eat away at *vipo* = **EAT AWAY, EAT INTO.**

►eat into *vipo* **(a)** (*attack*) ronger; **rust had eaten into the metal,** la rouille avait rongé le métal; **to e. into wood,** (*of insect, worm*) ronger le bois; **(b)** (*diminish*) entamer; **these expenses had eaten into their savings,** ces dépenses avaient entamé leurs économies.

►eat off *vtsep* **to e. one's head off,** s'empiffrer; **that horse eats its head off,** ce cheval coûte plus à nourrir qu'il ne vaut.

►eat out 1 *vi* (*eat in restaurant*) manger au restaurant; **we don't e. out much,** nous ne mangeons pas souvent au restaurant. **2** *vtsep F* **to e. one's heart out,** se ronger le cœur; **e. your heart out, USA!,** = dommage pour les États-Unis!

►eat up 1 *vtsep* **(a)** (*eat completely*) manger jusqu'à la dernière miette (*un gâteau etc*); **e. up your bread!,** finis ton pain!; **(b)** (*consume*) consumer (*qch*) sans profit; *F* **stove that eats up the coal,** poêle qui mange beaucoup de charbon; **to e. up the miles,** (*of car etc*) dévorer la route; **jealousy is eating him up,** la jalousie le dévore; **to be eaten up with,** être dévoré de (*orgueil*); être consumé par (*l'ambition*); **(c)** (*exhaust*) épuiser (*les provisions*). **2** *vi* (*eat everything*) finir son assiette; **e. up!,** (*there's lots more*) vas-y, mange!

eatable ['iːtəb(ə)l] **1** *adj* comestible; (*fit to eat*) mangeable, bon à manger; **fruit that is quite e.,** fruit qui se laisse manger. **2** *npl esp Hum* **eatables,** provisions *fpl* de bouche, comestibles *mpl*.

eater ['iːtər] *n* **(a)** (*person*) mangeur, -euse; **small/big e.,** petit/gros mangeur; **(b)** (*apple*) pomme *f* à couteau *ou* de dessert.

eatery ['iːtəri] *n F* café-restaurant *m*.

eating ['iːtɪŋ] *n* manger *m*; **healthy e.,** alimentation saine; **these birds make poor/good e.,** ces oiseaux sont mauvais/bons à manger; **e. habits,** habitudes *fpl* alimentaires; **e. apple,** pomme *f* à couteau *ou* de dessert; **e. house,** restaurant *m*; **cheap e. house,** gargote *f*.

eating away *n* corrosion *f* (*du métal etc*); érosion *f* (*du littoral*).

eats [iːts] *npl F* le manger; **plenty of e.,** amplement de quoi manger.

eau-de-Cologne ['əudəkə'ləun] *n* eau *f* de Cologne.

eaves [iːvz] *npl Constr* avant-toit *m*.

eavesdrop ['iːvzdrɒp] *vi* (**-pp-**) écouter aux portes; **to e. on a conversation,** tendre l'oreille pour écouter une conversation privée.

eavesdropper ['iːvzdrɒpər] *n* oreille indiscrète.

ebb¹ [eb] *n* **(a)** (*of tide*) reflux *m*; baisse *f* (*de la marée*); **the e. and flow,** le flux et le reflux; **the tide is on the e.,** la marée baisse; **e. tide,** marée descendante, marée de jusant; **(b)** déclin *m* (*de la fortune, de la vie*); **the patient is at a low e.,** le malade est très bas; **to be at one's lowest e.,** (*weak, depressed*) être dans un très grand abattement; (*in financial trouble*) être à bout de ressources.

ebb² *vi* **(a)** (*of tide*) baisser; **to e. and flow,** monter et baisser; **(b)** = **EBB AWAY.**

►ebb away *vi* (*decline, disappear*) s'écouler; **his life was ebbing away,** il baissait d'heure en heure.

ebbing ['ebɪŋ] *adj* **(a)** (*water*) qui reflue; **(b)** (*fortune etc*) sur le déclin; **e. strength,** forces diminuantes.

ebonite ['ebənaɪt] *n* ébonite *f*.

ebony ['ebəni] *n* **(a)** (*wood*) (bois *m* d')ébène *f*; **e. box,** boîte *f* en bois d'ébène; **(b) e. (tree),** ébénier *m*; **(c)** (*colour*) ébène *f*; **e. hair,** des cheveux ébène.

ebullience [ɪ'bʌliəns] *n* bouillonnement *m*, effervescence *f* (*de la colère, de la jeunesse etc*).

ebullient [ɪ'bʌliənt] *adj* enthousiaste, exubérant.

EC [iː'siː] *n Admin* **(a)** (*abbr* **European Commission**) Commission européenne; **(b)** (*abbr* **European Community**) CEE *f*.

eccentric [ek'sentrɪk] **1** *adj* **(a)** (*person, behaviour*) excentrique; **(b)** *Math Astron* (*cercle etc*) excentrique; *MecE* (*came*) désaxé; (*arbre*) excentré. **2** *n* **(a)** (*person*) excentrique *mf*, original, -ale; **(b)** *MecE* excentrique *m*.

eccentrically [ek'sentrɪkli] *adv* excentriquement.

eccentricity [eksen'trɪsɪti] *n* **(a)** excentricité *f* (*de caractère*); originalité *f* (**in,** de); **eccentricities,** excentricités (*de qn*); **(b)** *Math* excentricité *f* (*d'une ellipse*); *MecE* excentricité, désaxage *m*.

ecclesiastic [ɪkliːzɪ'æstɪk] **1** *n* ecclésiastique *m*. **2** *adj* ecclésiastique.

ecclesiastical [ɪkliːzɪ'æstɪk(ə)l] *adj* (*habit etc*) ecclésiastique.

ECG [iːsiː'dʒiː] *n Med* **(a)** (*abbr* **electrocardiogram**) électrocardiogramme *m*; **(b)** (*abbr* **electrocardiograph**) électrocardiographe *m*.

echelon ['eʃəlɒn] *n* **(a)** (*level*) **the higher echelons of industry/***etc*, les niveaux supérieurs de l'industrie/*etc*; **(b)** *Mil* échelon *m*; **in e.,** en échelon.

echo¹, *pl* **-oes** ['ekəu, -əuz] *n* écho *m*; *Fig* **there are echoes of the 18th century in this novel,** il y a des accents du XVIIIe siècle dans ce roman; **e. sounding,** sondage *m* par ultra-sons; **e. chamber,** chambre *f* sonore; **e. sounder,** écho-sondeur *m*, *pl* écho-sondeurs.

echo² 1 *vt* répéter (en écho); **to e. s.o.'s opinions,** se faire l'écho des opinions de qn; *Fig* **the yellow of the walls is echoed in the curtains,** le jaune des murs se trouve rappelé dans les rideaux. **2** *vi* faire écho; **the woods echoed with the songs of birds,** les bois retentissaient des chants des oiseaux; **room that does not e.,** pièce sourde; **his voice echoes through the room,** sa voix résonne dans la salle.

éclair [eɪ'kleər] *n Culin* éclair *m*; **chocolate e.,** éclair au chocolat.

eclectic [e'klektɪk] *adj & n* éclectique *mf*.

eclecticism [e'klektɪsɪz(ə)m] *n* éclectisme *m*.

eclipse¹ [ɪ'klɪps] *n* **(a)** *Astron* éclipse *f*; **solar/lunar e.,** éclipse de soleil/de lune; **total/partial e.,** éclipse totale/partielle; **(b)** *Nau* éclipse *f* (*d'un phare*); **(c)** *Fig* (*overshadowing*) éclipse *f*; **the e. of this team by a younger one,** l'éclipse de cette équipe par une équipe plus jeune; **to suffer an e.,** être éclipsé.

eclipse² *vt* **(a)** *Astron etc* éclipser (*la lune, la lumière d'un phare etc*); **(b)** *Fig* (*overshadow, supersede*) éclipser, surpasser (*qn*).

ecliptic [ɪ'klɪptɪk] *adj Astron* écliptique.

eco-friendly ['iːkəufrendli] *adj* (*product*) qui ne nuit pas à l'environnement.

ecological [iːkə'lɒdʒɪk(ə)l] *adj* écologique.

ecologist [ɪ'kɒlədʒɪst] *n* écologiste *mf*.

ecology [ɪ'kɒlədʒi] *n* écologie *f*.

econometrics [ɪkɒnə'metrɪks] *n* économétrie *f*.

economic [iːkə'nɒmɪk] *adj* **(a)** *Econ* économique; **e. geography,** géographie *f* économique; **(b)** *Br* (*profitable*) (*loyer*) rentable; **(c)** *F* (*inexpensive*) économique.

economical [iːkə'nɒmɪk(ə)l] *adj* (*person*) économe; (*apparatus etc*) économique; **to be e. with sth,** économiser qch; **to be e. with the truth,** dire la vérité avec parcimonie; **it is more e. to buy larger packets,** c'est plus économique d'acheter des paquets plus grands; **e. speed,** vitesse *f* économique (*d'un navire etc*).

economically [iːkə'nɒmɪkli] *adv* économiquement; **to use sth e.,** ménager qch.

economics [iːkə'nɒmɪks] *npl* (*usu with sing verb*) **(a)** *Econ* les sciences *fpl* économiques; **(b)** (*financial pros and cons*) aspects économiques *ou* financiers; **the e. of town planning,** les aspects financiers de l'urbanisme.

economist [ɪ'kɒnəmɪst] *n Econ* économiste *mf*; *Arch* personne *f* économe (**of,** de).

economize [ɪ'kɒnəmaɪz] **1** *vi* économiser, faire des économies; **to e. on sth,** économiser sur qch. **2** *vt* économiser, ménager (*le temps, l'argent etc*).

economy [ɪ'kɒnəmi] *n* **(a)** (*careful use*) économie *f* (*d'argent etc*); **e. in fuel consumption,** économie de combustible; **to practise e.,** économiser; *Nau Av* **e. class,** classe *f* économique; *Com* **e. pack,** paquet *m* économique; **e. size,** format *m* économique; **(b)** (*saving*) économie *f*; **to make economies,** faire des économies; **economies of scale,** économies d'échelle; **(c)** *Econ* (*of a country*) économie *f*, régime *m* économique; **political e.,** économie politique; **planned e.,** économie planifiée; **(d)** *Old-fashioned* **(domestic) e.,** économie *f* domestique.

ecosystem ['iːkəusɪstəm] *n* écosystème *m*.

ECSC [iːsiːes'siː] *n Admin* (*abbr* **European Coal and Steel Community**) CECA *f*.

ecstasy ['ekstəsi] *n* **(a)** transport *m* (de joie), joie délirante, ravissement *m*; **to be in an e. of joy,** se pâmer de joie; **to go into ecstasies over sth,** s'extasier devant qch; **(b)** *Rel etc* extase *f*.

ecstatic [ek'stætɪk] *adj* extatique.

ecstatically [ek'stætɪkli] *adv* avec extase; (*to look at*) d'un air extasié; **e. happy,** heureux jusqu'au ravissement.

ectopic [ek'tɒpɪk] *adj Obst* **e. pregnancy,** grossesse extra-utérine.

ectoplasm ['ektəuplæz(ə)m] *n* ectoplasme *m*.

ECU ['eɪkjuː, *occ* iːsiː'juː] *n* (*abbr* **European Currency Unit**) ECU *m inv*.

Ecuador ['ekwədɔːr] *n* (la République de) l'Équateur *m*.

Ecuadoran ['ekwədɔːrən] **, Ecuadorian** [ekwə'dɔːrɪən] **1** *adj* écuadorien, équatorien. **2** *n* Écuadorien, -ienne, Équatorien, -ienne.

ecumenical [iːkjʊ'menɪk(ə)l] *adj Rel* (*conseil*) œcuménique.

eczema ['eksɪmə] *n Med* eczéma *m*; **to have e.,** avoir *ou* faire de l'eczéma.

ed (a) (*abbr* **edition**) éd(it); **(b)** *abbr* **editor**; **(c)** *abbr* **edited.**

Eddie ['edɪ] *n* (*dimin of* **Edward**) Eddie *m*.

eddy¹ ['edɪ] *n* (*of water, wind*) remous *m*, tourbillon *m*; *El* **e. currents,** courants *mpl* de Foucault; courants parasites.

eddy² *vi* (*of water*) faire des remous; (*of wind*) tourbillonner, tournoyer.

edelweiss ['eɪd(ə)lvaɪs] *n* (*plant*) édelweiss *m*.

edema [ɪ'diːmə] *n US* œdème *m*.

Eden ['iːd(ə)n] *n Bible* **(the Garden of) E.,** l'Éden *m*, le Paradis terrestre.

edge¹ [edʒ] *n* **(a)** (*of blade*) fil *m*, tranchant *m*; (*of tool*) angle *m*; (*of skate*) carre *f*; **to give s.o. the rough e. of one's tongue,** dire son fait à qn; **knife with a keen e. on it,** couteau *m* à tranchant aigu; **to put an e. on a tool,** aiguiser *ou* affiler un outil; **to take the e. off,** émousser (*l'appétit*); gâter (*le plaisir*); couper tout l'effet de (*un argument*); **e. tool,** outil tranchant;
(b) (*of stone etc*) arête *f*, angle *m*; **sharp/rounded e.,** arête vive/mousse; **feather e.,** biseau *m*; **inside/outside e.,** dedans *m*/dehors *m*; *Carp* **straight e.,** limande *f*;
(c) (*rim*) bord *m*, rebord *m* (*de table, de vase*); tranche *f* (*d'une planche, d'une médaille, d'un livre*); **gilt edges,** tranches dorées; **with gilt edges,** doré sur tranches; **milled e.,** crénelage *m*, grènetis *m*; *Av* **leading/trailing e.,** bord d'attaque/de fuite (*de l'aile*); **on e.,** (*of brick*) de chant, de can; (*of person*) énervé, nerveux; **to set sth on e.,** (*tilt*) mettre qch de chant *ou* de can; **to set s.o. on e.,** crisper qn, énerver qn; **to set s.o.'s teeth on e.,** faire grincer des dents à qn; **to set s.o.'s nerves on e.,** agacer les nerfs de qn; **she is on e. today,** elle est nerveuse aujourd'hui; **a movie that will have you on the e. of your seat,** un film au suspens insoutenable; *F* **to have an** *or* **the e. on s.o.,** être avantagé par rapport à qn;
(d) (*border*) lisière *f*, bordure *f*, orée *f* (*d'un bois*); bord *m*, rive *f* (*d'une rivière*); bordure *f* (*d'une route*); marge *f* (*d'un chemin*); limite *f* (*d'une plaine*); liséré *m*, bord (*d'une étoffe etc*); lèvre *f* (*d'une plaie*); *Phot etc* **white e.,** (*of a print*) liséré blanc; **e. trimmer** *or* **cutter,** coupe-bordure *m*, *pl* coupe-bordure(s); **at the water's e.,** au bord de l'eau; **at the e. of a precipice,** au bord d'un précipice.

edge² 1 *vt* **(a)** (*sharpen*) affiler, aiguiser (*un couteau*); affûter (*un outil*); repiquer (*une meule*); **(b)** (*put an edge on*) tomber (*un bord de tôle*); **(c)** *Sewing etc* (*border*) border (*une étoffe, la route*) (**with,** de); lisérer (*une jupe*); **(d)** (*move slowly*) **to e. one's way into a room,** se faufiler *ou* se glisser dans une pièce; **to e. one's chair nearer,** rapprocher *ou* avancer sa chaise peu à peu. **2** *vi* (*move slowly*) bouger doucement; **to e. towards s.o./sth,** s'approcher tout doucement de qn/qch; **the driver edged forwards,** le conducteur a avancé doucement.

►edge away *vi* (*move away slowly*) s'éloigner *ou* s'écarter tout doucement (**from s.o.,** de qn).

►edge out 1 *vi* (*leave cautiously*) **I opened the window and edged out,** j'ai ouvert la fenêtre et je me suis glissé dehors; **the driver/car edged out,** le conducteur/la voiture se dégagea lentement. **2** *vtsep* **(a) to e. one's way out,** se frayer un chemin; **she edged her way out on to the ledge,** elle gagna le rebord de la fenêtre avec précaution; **(b)** (*supplant*) évincer; **some people are trying to e. her out of the chairmanship,** certains essayent de l'évincer de la présidence.

►edge past 1 *vi* (*move past cautiously*) passer prudemment. **2** *vipo* **I edged past her,** je suis passé discrètement à côté d'elle.

►edge up 1 *vi* (*climb slowly*) (*of prices*) grimper petit à petit. **2** *vtsep* **they edged their way up the cliff,** ils ont escaladé péniblement la falaise.

edged [edʒd] *adj* (*tool, weapon etc*) tranchant, acéré.

-edged [edʒd] *suff* **double-e.,** à double tranchant; **sharp-e.,** au tranchant affilé *ou* bien aiguisé.

edgeways ['edʒweɪz] **, edgewise** ['edʒwaɪz] *adv* **(a)** (*on its edge*) de chant; **to lay** *or* **set a plank e.,** placer une planche de chant; *F* **I can't get a word in e.,** impossible de placer un mot (dans la conversation); **(b)** (*from the side*) (*vu*) latéralement, de côté; **(c)** (*of two things*) côte à côte; (*of two boards*) affronté.

edginess ['edʒɪnɪs] *n* nervosité *f*.

edging ['edʒɪŋ] *n* **(a)** (*action*) pose *f* d'un liséré *ou* d'une ganse (*à une robe etc*); entretien *m* de la bordure (*d'une pelouse etc*); **e. shears,** cisaille *f* à bordures; **e. tool,** coupe-gazon *m inv*, tranche-gazon *m inv*, molette *f*; **(b)** *Sewing etc* liséré *m*, passement *m*, ganse *f*; *Mil* contour *m* (*d'épaulette*); (*in gardening*) bordure *f* (*de parterre etc*).

edgy ['edʒɪ] *adj* (*person*) énervé; **to get e.,** s'énerver.

edible ['edɪb(ə)l] **1** *adj* comestible; (*fit to eat*) bon à manger, mangeable; **it's very e.,** c'est très bon; **e. oil,** huile *f* comestible. **2** *npl* **edibles,** comestibles *mpl*.

edict ['iːdɪkt] *n* édit *m*; *Hist* **the E. of Nantes,** l'Édit de Nantes.

edification [edɪfɪ'keɪʃən] *n* instruction *f*; **a film show had been provided for the e. of the children,** un film a été projeté pour instruire les enfants.

edifice ['edɪfɪs] *n* édifice *m*.

edify ['edɪfaɪ] *vt* édifier (*qn*).

edifying ['edɪfaɪɪŋ] *adj* (*spectacle, livre etc*) édifiant.

Edinburgh ['edɪnbrə] *n* Édimbourg.

edit ['edɪt] *vt* **(a)** (*prepare*) préparer (*un texte*) pour la publication; annoter (*le texte d'un auteur*); donner une édition annotée de (*une œuvre*); diriger (*une série de textes etc*); **(b)** (*be in charge of*) rédiger, diriger (*un journal, une revue*); **edited by ...,** (*série, journal etc*) sous la direction de ...; **(c)** *Cin* monter (*un film*); **(d)** *Cin etc* (*remove*) couper; **this sentence was edited from the broadcast of the interview,** cette phrase a été coupée dans la diffusion de l'interview; **(e)** *Comptr* éditer.

►edit out *vtsep Cin etc* (*remove*) couper (*une scène*).

editing ['edɪtɪŋ] *n* **(a)** préparation *f*, annotation *f* (*d'un texte*); **(b)** (*of newspaper etc*) rédaction *f*, direction *f*; **(c)** *Cin* (*of film*) montage *m*; **(d)** *Cin etc* suppression *f* (*d'une scène, d'un passage etc*).

edition [ɪ'dɪʃən] *n* édition *f* (*d'un ouvrage*); **limited e.,** édition à tirage limité; **school e.,** édition scolaire; **cheap e.,** édition populaire; **book in its fourth e.,** livre à sa quatrième édition; **first e.,** édition originale.

editor ['edɪtər] *n* **(a)** (*of a text*) éditeur *m*; (*of a critical edition*) auteur *m*; **(b)** (*in charge of publication*) surveillant *m* de la publication; (*of a series, a dictionary*) directeur *m*; (*of a magazine, a newspaper*) rédacteur *m* en chef, directeur; **news e.,** rédacteur au service des informations; **sports e.,** rédacteur sportif; **(c)** *TV Rad* **programme e.,** éditorialiste *mf*; **(d)** *Cin* (*of a film*) monteur *m*.

editorial [edɪ'tɔːrɪəl] **1** *adj* de rédaction; **e. office,** (salle *f* de) rédaction *f*; **the e. staff,** la rédaction; **e. freedom,** liberté *f* des rédacteurs. **2** *n Journ* éditorial *m*.

editorialist [edɪ'tɔːrɪəlɪst] *n* éditorialiste *mf*.

EDP [iːdiː'piː] *n abbr* **electronic data processing.**

educable ['edjʊkəb(ə)l] *adj* éducable.

educate ['edjʊkeɪt] *vt* **(a)** donner de l'instruction à, instruire (*qn*); **he was educated in France/at Oxford,** il a fait ses études en France/à Oxford; **to have one's child educated,** faire faire des études à son enfant; **(b)** (*train, instruct*) former (*qn, le goût de qn*).

educated ['edjʊkeɪtɪd] *adj* (*person*) instruit, lettré; **an e. guess,** une supposition éclairée; **self-e.,** autodidacte.

education [edjʊ'keɪʃən] *n* **(a)** enseignement *m*, instruction *f*; **the e. of young people in the use of birth control methods,** l'éducation des jeunes pour l'utilisation des méthodes contraceptives; **it was an e. working there,** c'était instructif de travailler là-bas; **compulsory e.,** enseignement obligatoire; **primary/secondary e.,** enseignement primaire/secondaire; **higher** *or* **university e.,** (*system*) enseignement supérieur; (*of person*) études supérieures; **further e.,** enseignement post-scolaire; **adult e.,** enseignement des adultes; *Br* **Department of E. and Science,** = Ministère *m* de l'Éducation nationale; **he has had a good e.,** il a reçu une bonne instruction; *Br* **e. authority,** = Direction *f* de l'enseignement; **(b)** (*learning*) éducation *f*; **a man without e.,** un homme sans éducation; **gaps in one's e.,** des lacunes dans son éducation.

educational [edjʊ'keɪʃən(ə)l] *adj* (*maison, ouvrage*) d'éducation, d'enseignement; (*ouvrage*) éducateur; (*programme*) scolaire; (*procédé*) éducatif, pédagogique; **e. film,** film éducatif; **for e. purposes,** dans un but pédagogique; **working there was very e.,** c'était très instructif de travailler là-bas.

education(al)ist [edjʊ'keɪʃənɪst, -əlɪst] *n* éducateur, -trice, pédagogue *mf*.

educationally [edjʊ'keɪʃən(ə)lɪ] *adv* **e. subnormal,** (*child*) arriéré.

educator ['edjʊkeɪtər] *n* éducateur, -trice.
Edward ['edwəd] *n* Édouard *m*.
Edwardian [ed'wɔːdɪən] *adj* qui a rapport à l'époque du roi Édouard VII; **the E. era,** la belle époque.
EEC [iːiː'siː] *n* (*abbr* **European Economic Community**) CEE *f*.
EEG [iːiː'dʒiː] *n Med* **(a)** (*abbr* **electroencephalogram**) EEG *m*; **(b)** (*abbr* **electroencephalograph**) = appareil *m* à EEG.
eel [iːl] *n* anguille *f*; **e. basket** *or* **pot,** nasse *f* à anguilles; *Br Culin* **jellied eels,** anguilles en gelée; **he's as slippery as an e.,** il vous glisse entre les doigts; **conger e.,** congre *m*, anguille de mer; **electric e.,** anguille électrique.
eelworm ['iːlwɜːm] *n* anguillule *f*.
eerie ['ɪərɪ] *adj* surnaturel; qui donne des frissons; **an e. silence,** un silence surnaturel.
eerily ['ɪərɪlɪ] *adv* étrangement; à donner des frissons; **e. quiet,** (*house etc*) d'un calme inquiétant.
eeriness ['ɪərɪnɪs] *n* étrangeté surnaturelle (*d'un lieu, d'un son etc*).
eery ['ɪərɪ] *adj* = **EERIE**.
eff [ef] *vi Br Sl* **he's always effing and blinding,** il n'arrête pas de jurer.
►**eff off** *vi Br Sl* **e. off!,** va te faire foutre!; *F* **she told him to e. off,** elle lui a dit d'aller se faire foutre.
efface [ɪ'feɪs] *vt* effacer; oblitérer (*une inscription, la mémoire de qch etc*); **to e. oneself,** s'effacer; se tenir à l'écart.
effacement [ɪ'feɪsmənt] *n* effacement *m*.
effect¹ [ɪ'fekt] *n* **(a)** (*result*) effet *m*; résultat *m*, conséquence *f* (*d'un fait*); **the e. of heat on metals,** l'action de la chaleur sur les métaux; **the e. of this action was to bring prices down,** cette action a eu pour effet de faire baisser les prix; **cause and e.,** la cause et l'effet; **the effects of the economic crisis,** les effets de la crise économique; **side effects,** réactions *fpl* secondaires; *Ch etc* réactions latérales; **to have an e. on s.o./sth,** faire *ou* produire de l'effet sur qn/qch, affecter qn/qch; **to have no e.,** ne faire *ou* ne produire aucun effet; **let's see what e. the addition of hydrogen has,** voyons l'effet que produit l'addition d'hydrogène; **to take e.,** faire (son) effet; (*of regulation, law etc*) entrer en vigueur; (*of drug*) agir, opérer; (*of vaccination*) prendre; **law that comes into e. today,** loi qui entre en vigueur à partir d'aujourd'hui; **to no e.,** en vain, sans résultat; **to bring** *or* **carry into e.,** mettre (*qch*) à exécution; exécuter, effectuer, réaliser (*qch*); donner suite à (*une décision etc*);
(b) (*purpose, meaning*) sens *m*, teneur *f* (*d'un document*); **to the e. that ...,** (*clause*) portant que ...; **we have made provisions to this e.,** nous avons pris des dispositions dans ce sens; **that is what he said, or words to that e.,** voilà ce qu'il a dit, ou quelque chose d'approchant;
(c) *Electron etc* **flicker e.,** effet *m* de scintillation; *Phys* **Joule e.,** effet Joule;
(d) (*simulation*) **moonlight e.,** effet *m* de lune; **clever use of lighting created the e. of a thunderstorm,** une utilisation adroite de la lumière donnait l'impression qu'il y avait un orage; *Th etc* **stage effects,** jeux *mpl* scéniques; **sound effects,** bruitage *m*; *Cin TV etc* **special effects,** trucage *m*;
(e) (*impression*) effet *m*, impression *f*; **the combination of colours creates** *or* **has a pleasing e.,** le mélange des couleurs laisse une impression agréable; **for effect,** (*to impress*) pour faire de l'effet; **words meant for e.,** phrases à effet;
(f) in e., en fait, en réalité; **that is in e. a refusal,** c'est de fait un refus;
(g) (*belongings*) **personal effects,** effets *ou* biens personnels; **household effects,** *Jur* **movable effects,** biens mobiliers.
effect² *vt* effectuer, réaliser, exécuter (*qch*); *Mil* opérer (*une retraite*); **to e. a payment,** effectuer un paiement.
effective [ɪ'fektɪv] **1** *adj* **(a)** (*moyen, remède etc*) efficace; **the medicine was e.,** le médicament a produit son effet; **(b)** *Econ etc* (*real*) (*rendement*) effectif; *El* (*charge*) efficace; (*fréquence*) utile; **the e. silencing of all opposition,** le fait de faire taire pour de bon les opposants; *MecE* **e. power,** rendement *m*; **e. range,** (*of firearm*) portée *f* utile; *Av* rayon *m* d'action; *Electron* étendue *f* de mesure; **(c)** (*striking*) (*contraste*) frappant, saisissant; (*réponse*) plein d'à-propos; (*discours*) qui fait de l'effet; (*orateur*) dont les paroles portent; **(d)** *Admin* **e. date,** date *f* d'entrée en vigueur; **to become e.,** (*of decree etc*) entrer en vigueur; **e. as from October 10,** applicable à partir du 10 octobre. **2** *npl Mil* **effectives,** effectifs *mpl*.
effectively [ɪ'fektɪvlɪ] *adv* **(a)** efficacement, utilement; **(b)** (*really, in effect*) effectivement, en réalité; **the country was e. ruled by the military,** en réalité, le pays était dirigé par les militaires; **(c)** (*strikingly*) d'une façon frappante.
effectiveness [ɪ'fektɪvnɪs] *n* efficacité *f*.
effectual [ɪ'fektjʊəl] *adj* **(a)** efficace; **(b)** *Jur* (*contrat*) valide; (*règlement*) en vigueur.
effectually [ɪ'fektjʊəlɪ] *adv* efficacement.
effeminacy [ɪ'femɪnəsɪ] *n* caractère efféminé.
effeminate [ɪ'femɪnət] *adj* efféminé.
effervesce [efə'ves] *vi* **(a)** être *ou* entrer en effervescence; (*of drinks*) mousser; **(b)** (*of person*) pétiller de joie *ou* d'animation.
effervescence [efə'vesəns] *n* **(a)** (*of a liquid*) effervescence *f*; **(b)** (*of youth etc*) pétillement *m*.
effervescent [efə'vesənt] *adj* **(a)** effervescent; (*drink*) gazeux; **(b)** (*person*) effervescent.
effete [ɪ'fiːt] *adj* (*civilization, method etc*) caduc, -uque; (*person*) mou, veule.
efficacious [efɪ'keɪʃəs] *adj* efficace.
efficaciousness [efɪ'keɪʃəsnɪs], **efficacy** ['efɪkəsɪ] *n* efficacité *f*.
efficiency [ɪ'fɪʃənsɪ] *n* (*of method, organization*) efficacité *f*; (*of machine etc*) (*output*) rendement *m*; (*functioning*) bon fonctionnement; *MecE* effet *m* utile; (*of person*) capacité *f*, compétence *f*; **e. expert,** expert *m* en organisation.
efficient [ɪ'fɪʃənt] *adj* (*method, work, organization*) efficace; (*machine*) (*productive*) à bon rendement; (*functioning well*) d'un fonctionnement sûr; (*person*) capable, compétent; **to be e. in one's work,** se montrer capable dans son travail; **e. use of one's time,** utilisation rationnelle de son temps; **energy e.,** (*machine*) qui ne consomme pas beaucoup d'énergie.
efficiently [ɪ'fɪʃəntlɪ] *adv* (*effectively*) efficacement; (*competently*) avec compétence; **the company is now run more e.,** l'entreprise est désormais dirigée plus efficacement.
effigy ['efɪdʒɪ] *n* effigie *f*; **to burn/hang s.o. in e.,** brûler/pendre qn en effigie.
effing ['efɪŋ] *Br Sl* **1** *adj* foutu; **this e. weather,** ce temps de merde. **2** *adv* **how e. stupid!,** quelle connerie! **3** *n* (*swearing*) **there's too much e. and blinding,** on entend trop de grossièretés.
efflorescence [eflə'resəns] *n* **(a)** *Bot* floraison *f*; **(b)** *Ch Med etc* efflorescence *f*.
efflorescent [eflə'resənt] *adj Bot* efflorescent.
effluence ['efluəns] *n* émanation *f*, effluence *f*.
effluent ['efluənt] *n* **1** *adj* effluent; **e. drain,** canalisation *f* de sortie (*d'un collecteur d'eaux d'égout etc*). **2** *n* effluent *m* (*de collecteur d'eaux d'égout*).
effluvium, *pl* **-ia** [e'fluːvɪəm, -ɪə] *n* effluve *m*, émanation *f*; *Pej* émanation désagréable *ou* fétide.
effort ['efət] *n* **(a)** effort *m*; **physical e.,** effort physique; **without e.,** sans effort; **to make an e. to do sth,** faire (un) effort pour faire qch; **he made no e. to contact us,** il n'a fait aucun effort pour nous joindre; **put some e. into it!,** fais un effort!; **she put all her e. into her work,** elle s'est jetée corps et âme dans son travail; **their efforts were rewarded,** leurs efforts ont été récompensés; *Fml* **we make every e. to ensure our products reach you in perfect condition,** nous faisons tout ce qui est en notre pouvoir pour que nos produits vous parviennent en bon état; *F* **it's an e. to get up so early,** il faut vraiment faire un effort pour se lever si tôt; **wasted e.,** peine perdue;
(b) *F* (*attempt*) tentative *f*; **that's not a bad e.,** ce n'est pas mal réussi; **some of my first efforts at making pots were pretty awful,** certains de mes premiers essais en poterie étaient plutôt ratés; **literary/artistic e.,** œuvre *f* littéraire/artistique; *F* **what do you think of his latest e.?,** qu'est-ce que vous pensez de ce qu'il vient de faire?;
(c) *Phys* effort *m* (*de traction etc*); poussée *f*, travail *m*.
effortless ['efətlɪs] *adj* (*skill etc*) facile.
effortlessly ['efətlɪslɪ] *adv* sans effort; **her voice soars e. to the high notes,** elle peut chanter très haut sans aucun effort.
effrontery [ɪ'frʌntərɪ] *n* effronterie *f*; **she had the e. to correct me!,** elle a eu l'audace de me corriger!
effusion [ɪ'fjuːʒən] *n* effusion *f*.
effusive [ɪ'fjuːsɪv] *adj* démonstratif, expansif; (*style*) exubérant; (*compliments*) sans fin; **to be e. in one's thanks,** se confondre en remerciements.
effusively [ɪ'fjuːsɪvlɪ] *adv* avec effusion; **to thank s.o. e.,** se confondre en remerciements.
effusiveness [ɪ'fjuːsɪvnɪs] *n* effusion *f*.

EFL [iːeˈfel] *n Sch* (*abbr* **English as a Foreign Language**) = anglais langue étrangère; **to have an EFL qualification,** = avoir une qualification en anglais langue étrangère.
EFT [iːefˈtiː] *n Comptr abbr* **electronic funds transfer**.
EFTA [ˈeftə] *n* (*abbr* **European Free Trade Association**) AELE *f*.
EFTPOS [ˈeftpɒs] *n Comptr abbr* **electronic funds transfer at point of sale**.
eg [iːˈdʒiː] (*abbr* **exempli gratia**) ex.
egalitarian [ɪgælɪˈteərɪən] *adj & n* égalitaire *mf*.
egalitarianism [ɪgælɪˈteərɪənɪz(ə)m] *n* égalitarisme *m*.
egg [eg] *n* **(a)** œuf *m* (*de poule, d'insecte etc*); lente *f* (*de pou*); **eggs and bacon,** œufs au jambon *ou* au bacon; *F* **as sure as eggs is eggs,** aussi sûr que deux et deux font quatre; *F* **to have e. on one's face,** être couvert de ridicule; **you can't teach your grandmother to suck eggs,** ce n'est pas aux vieux singes qu'on apprend à faire des grimaces; *Old-fashioned F* **a bad e.,** un vaurien; *Old-fashioned F* **a good e.,** un type épatant; *Prov* **don't put all your eggs into one basket,** il ne faut pas mettre tous ses œufs dans le même panier; **e. cup,** coquetier *m*; **e. custard,** crème anglaise; **e. flip,** = lait *m* de poule; **e. mayonnaise,** œuf mayonnaise; **e. sandwich,** sandwich *m* à l'œuf; **e. spoon,** cuillère *f* à œufs; **e. timer,** sablier *m*; **e. tooth,** (*of bird*) dent *f* d'éclosion; **e. white,** blanc *m* d'œuf; **e. yolk,** jaune *m* d'œuf; **(b) darning e.,** œuf *m* à repriser; **tea e.,** boule *f* à thé.
►**egg on** *vtsep* (*incite*) encourager; **the crowd egged the boxers on,** la foule encourageait les boxeurs; **to e. s.o. on (to do sth),** pousser *ou* inciter qn (à faire qch).
egg-and-spoon [ˈegənˈspuːn] *adj* **e.-and-s. race,** = course dans laquelle les coureurs doivent porter un œuf dans une cuillère.
eggbeater [ˈegbiːtər] *n Culin* batteur *m ou* fouet *m* à œufs.
egghead [ˈeghed] *n F* intellectuel, -elle, cerveau *m*.
egg-laying [ˈegleɪɪŋ] **1** *adj* ovipare. **2** *n* ponte *f*.
eggnog [ˈegnɒg] *n Culin* lait *m* de poule.
eggplant [ˈegplɑːnt] *n esp Am* aubergine *f*.
egg-shaped [ˈegʃeɪpt] *adj* ovoïde; ovoïdal, -aux.
eggshell [ˈegʃel] *n* **(a)** coquille *f* (d'œuf); *Cer* **e. china,** coquille d'œuf; **e. finish,** (*on paint*) fini *m* coquille d'œuf; **e. blue/***etc*, (*paint*) bleu *m/etc* semi-mat; **(b)** (*colour*) (couleur *f*) coquille *f* d'œuf, blanc cassé.
eggwhisk [ˈegwɪsk] *n* = **EGGBEATER**.
eggy [ˈegɪ] *adj F* taché *ou* souillé de jaune d'œuf.
egis [ˈiːdʒɪs] *n US* = **AEGIS**.
eglantine [ˈegləntaɪn] *n* (*plant*) églantier *m*.
ego [ˈiːgəʊ, ˈegəʊ] *n* **the e.,** le moi, l'ego *m*; **you've got an enormous e.,** tu as un ego démesuré; **it gave my e. a boost,** mon ego en est ressorti gonflé; **his bruised e.,** son ego blessé; *F* **e. trip,** autosatisfaction *f*; **it was a real e. trip for her,** c'était une occasion pour elle de donner libre cours à sa vanité.
egocentric [iːgəʊˈsentrɪk] *adj Psy* égocentrique.
egocentricity [iːgəʊsenˈtrɪsɪtɪ] *n* égocentrisme *m*.
egoism [ˈiːgəʊɪz(ə)m] *n* égoïsme *m*.
egoist [ˈiːgəʊɪst] *n* egoïste *mf*.
egoistic(al) [iːgəʊˈɪstɪk, -ɪk(ə)l] *adj* égoïste.
egoistically [iːgəʊˈɪstɪklɪ] *adv* égoïstement.
egomania [iːgəʊˈmeɪnɪə] *n* manie *f* égocentrique.
egotism [ˈiːgəʊtɪz(ə)m] *n* égotisme *m*.
egotist [ˈiːgəʊtɪst] *n* égotiste *mf*.
egotistic(al) [iːgəʊˈtɪstɪk, -ɪk(ə)l] *adj* égotiste.
egregious [ɪˈgriːdʒəs] *adj Pej* fameux (*sot*); **e. blunder,** maladresse *f* insigne.
egress [ˈiːgres] *n* **(a)** *Fml* (*exit*) sortie *f*, issue *f*; **(b)** *Astron* émersion *f*.
egret [ˈiːgrɪt] *n* (*bird*) aigrette *f*.
Egypt [ˈiːdʒɪpt] *n* Égypte *f*.
Egyptian [ɪˈdʒɪpʃən] **1** *adj* égyptien, d'Égypte. **2** *n* Égyptien, -ienne.
eh [eɪ, e] *int* eh!, hé!, hein?
eider [ˈaɪdər] *n* (*bird*) **e. (duck),** eider *m* à duvet.
eiderdown [ˈaɪdədaʊn] *n* **(a)** (*feathers*) duvet *m* d'eider; **(b)** (*quilt*) édredon *m*.
eight [eɪt] *n* **(a)** (*numeral*) huit *m*; **at e. (o'clock),** à huit heures; **at the age of e., at e. (years old),** à huit ans; **at e.-thirty,** à huit heures et demie; **a boy of e.,** un garçon de huit ans; **a mother of e.,** la mère de huit enfants; *Cards* **the e. of spades,** le huit de pique; **to take an e. in gloves,** avoir une pointure de huit (pour les gants); *F* **to have had one over the e.,** avoir bu un coup de trop; **to cut figures of e.,** (*in skating*) faire des huit; **(b)** *Sp* (*in rowing*) (*team*) équipe *f* de huit rameurs; (*boat*) canot *m* à huit rameurs; **to be in the last e.,** être en huitième de finale; *Am* **e. ball,** (*in pool*) bille noire (qui porte le numéro huit); *Fig* **to be behind the e. ball,** être dans une situation délicate.
eight-day [ˈeɪtˈdeɪ] *adj* **e.-d. clock,** huitaine *f*.
eighteen [eɪˈtiːn] *n* dix-huit *m*; **she is e. (years old),** elle a dix-huit ans; **at e. thirty (hours),** à dix-huit heures trente.
eighteenth [eɪˈtiːnθ] **1** *adj* dix-huitième; **(on) the e. of May,** le dix-huit mai; **Louis the E.,** Louis Dix-huit. **2** *n* **(a)** (*of month*) dix-huit *m*; **on the e.,** le dix-huit; **(b)** (*fraction*) dix-huitième *m*.
eightfold [ˈeɪtfəʊld] **1** *adj* octuple. **2** *adv* huit fois autant; **to increase e.,** octupler.
eighth [eɪtθ] **1** *adj* huitième; **in the e. place,** huitièmement; **(on) the e. of April,** le huit avril; **Henry the E.,** Henri Huit; *esp Am Mus* **e. note,** croche *f*. **2** *n* **(a)** (*of month*) huit *m*; **on the e.,** le huit; **(b)** (*fraction*) huitième *m*; **three eighths,** trois huitièmes.
eightieth [ˈeɪtɪɪθ] *adj & n* quatre-vingtième *m*; *Swiss Belg* huitantième *m*; *Swiss Can* octantième *m*.
eighty [ˈeɪtɪ] *n* quatre-vingts *m*; *Swiss Belg* huitante *m*; *Swiss Can* octante *m*; **e.-one,** quatre-vingt-un; **page e.,** page quatre-vingt; **in the eighties,** (*decade*) dans les années quatre-vingt; **she is in her eighties,** elle a quatre-vingts ans passés; **it** *or* **the temperature was in the eighties,** (*degrees Fahrenheit*) il faisait environ 80 degrés Fahrenheit.
Eire [ˈeərə] *n* Eire *f*.
either [ˈaɪðər, *esp Am* ˈiːðər] **1** *adj & pron* **(a)** (*each of the two*) l'un(e) et l'autre; **on e. side,** de chaque côté, des deux côtés;
(b) (*one or other*) l'un(e) ou l'autre; **e. of them,** soit l'un(e), soit l'autre; **I don't believe e. of you,** je ne vous crois ni l'un ni l'autre; **e. candidate may win,** l'un ou l'autre candidat pourra l'emporter; **there is no evidence e. way,** les preuves manquent de part et d'autre; **I do not want e. of them,** je ne veux ni l'un(e) ni l'autre.
2 *conj & adv* **(a) e. ..., or ...,** ou ..., ou ...; **e. you or your brother,** (ou) vous ou votre frère, soit vous, soit votre frère; **it's e. that motorbike or me!,** c'est cette moto ou moi!; **e. come in or go out!,** entrez ou sortez!; **you may pay e. by cheque or by credit card,** tu peux payer par chèque ou par carte de crédit;
(b) not ... e., ne ... non plus; **if you don't go, I won't go e.,** si vous n'y allez pas je n'irai pas non plus; **she's caught cold, and she isn't very strong e.,** elle s'est enrhumée, elle qui n'est déjà pas si forte.
either-or [ˈaɪðərɔːr] *adj* **an e.-or situation,** = situation dans laquelle il faut choisir entre deux maux le moindre.
ejaculate [ɪˈdʒækjʊleɪt] **1** *vi* **(a)** s'écrier; **(b)** *Physiol* éjaculer. **2** *vt* pousser (*un cri*).
ejaculation [ɪdʒækjʊˈleɪʃən] *n* **(a)** (*exclamation*) cri *m*, exclamation *f* (*de joie etc*); **(b)** *Physiol* éjaculation *f*.
eject [ɪˈdʒekt] **1** *vt* **(a)** (*of person*) expulser (*un agitateur etc*) (**from,** de); *Jur* évincer (*un locataire*); **(b)** (*of volcano etc*) projeter (*des cendres etc*); jeter, émettre (*des flammes etc*). **2** *vi Av* (*of pilot*) s'éjecter.
ejection [ɪˈdʒekʃən] *n* **(a)** expulsion *f* (*de qn*); *Jur* évincement *m*, éviction *f* (*d'un locataire*); *Av* éjection *f* (*du pilote*); **e. seat,** siège *m* éjectable; **(b)** (*by volcano*) jet *m* (*de flammes*); rejet *m* (*de lave*).
ejector [ɪˈdʒektər] *n* **(a)** *Av* **e. seat,** siège *m* éjectable; **to use the e. seat,** s'éjecter; **(b)** (*on firearm*) éjecteur *m*.
►**eke out** [iːk] *vtsep* **(a) to e. out a living,** gagner péniblement sa vie; **they eked out a miserable existence on the barren land,** ils tiraient leur maigre subsistance du sol aride; **(b)** (*supplement*) suppléer à l'insuffisance de (*ses revenus etc*); **(c)** (*make last*) économiser, faire durer (*les vivres*).
El [el] *n US* (*abbr* **elevated railroad**) chemin de fer *ou* métro aérien.
elaborate¹ [ɪˈlæbərət] *adj* (*style*) travaillé; (*inspection, research etc*) minutieux; (*dress etc*) recherché; (*hairstyle*) compliqué; (*work*) soigné; (*tool etc*) compliqué; **the security arrangements were very e.,** les consignes de sécurité étaient très élaborées; **the cake was a very e. affair,** c'était un gâteau très élaboré.
elaborate² [ɪˈlæbəreɪt] **1** *vi* donner plus de détails (**on sth,** sur qch); **could you e.?,** est-ce que tu peux être plus précis? **2** *vt* (*formulate*) élaborer (*un plan*).
elaboration [ɪlæbəˈreɪʃən] *n* élaboration *f*.
élan [eɪˈlɑn] *n* élan *m*, impétuosité *f*.
eland [ˈiːlənd] *n* (*animal*) **common e.,** éland *m* du Cap.
elapse [ɪˈlæps] *vi* (*of time*) s'écouler, passer; **years have elapsed since then,** des années ont passé depuis.
elastic [ɪˈlæstɪk] **1** *adj Phys* (*corps*) élastique; (*bois etc*)

flexible; (*pas*) élastique; *Anat* (*tissu*) élastique; **to be e.,** faire ressort; *Econ* **e. supply/demand,** offre *f*/demande *f* élastique; *Pej* **e. conscience,** conscience *f* élastique. **2** *n* **(a)** élastique *m*; **e. band,** élastique *m*, (bande *f* en) caoutchouc *m*; **(b)** *esp Am* (*rubber band*) (bande *f* en) caoutchouc *m*.

elasticated [ɪ'læstɪkeɪtɪd] *adj* (*clothing*) extensible.

elasticity [iːlæs'tɪsɪtɪ] *n Phys* élasticité *f* (*d'un corps*); flexibilité *f* (*du bois, d'un métal*); souplesse *f* (*de corps*); *Med* tonicité *f* (*des muscles*); (*of person*) élasticité; **coefficient of e.,** coefficient *m* d'élasticité; **e. of interpretation,** (*of a law*) élasticité; *Econ* **the e. of supply and demand,** l'élasticité de l'offre et de la demande.

elastomer [ɪ'læstəmər] *n* élastomère *m*.

Elastoplast ® [ɪ'læstəplɑːst] *n* sparadrap *m*.

elate [ɪ'leɪt] *vt* exalter; **to be elated with success,** être enivré de succès.

elated [ɪ'leɪtɪd] *adj* transporté, exalté; **to feel e.,** se sentir plein de joie.

elation [ɪ'leɪʃən] *n* (*joy*) joie *f*, gaieté *f*; (*intoxication*) exaltation *f*; ivresse *f* (*du succès*).

Elba ['elbə] *n* **the island of E.,** l'île *f* d'Elbe.

elbow¹ ['elbəʊ] *n* **(a)** (*of arm, sleeve*) coude *m*; **e. joint,** articulation *f* du coude; **to lean one's e. on sth,** s'accouder sur qch; **e. to e.,** (*se tenir*) coude à coude; **to be at s.o.'s e.,** être *ou* se tenir aux côtés de qn; **to be out at the elbows,** (*of person*) être déguenillé; (*of jacket etc*) être troué aux coudes; **I'm up to my elbows in work,** je suis submergé de travail; **to rub elbows with all sorts of people,** fréquenter *ou* coudoyer toutes sortes de gens; *F* **to give s.o. the e.,** virer qn; *F* **to get the e.,** se faire jeter *ou* virer; **to bend the e.,** lever le coude; *F* **e. grease,** huile *f* de coude; **(b)** (*of a pipe etc*) coude *m*, genou *m*; *MecE* **e. joint,** raccord coudé; **(c)** (*of a road etc*) coude *m*, tournant *m*.

elbow² *vt* pousser (*qn*) du coude; **to e. s.o. aside,** écarter qn d'un coup de coude; **to e. one's way through the crowd,** se frayer un passage à travers la foule en jouant des coudes.

►**elbow out** *vtsep* (*remove*) évincer (*qn*); **there have been attempts to e. him out as chairman,** on a essayé de l'évincer de la présidence.

elbow-length ['elbəʊleŋθ] *adj* **e.-l. gloves,** gants longs (*montant jusqu'au coude*).

elbowroom ['elbəʊrʊm] *n* **to have (enough) e.,** avoir ses coudées franches; **give me some more e.,** laisse-moi les coudées franches.

elder¹ ['eldər] **1** *adj* aîné, plus âgé (*de deux personnes*); **my e. brother,** mon frère aîné; **Pliny the E.,** Pline l'Ancien; **e. statesman,** doyen *m* des hommes politiques. **2** *n* **(a)** aîné, -ée; plus âgé, -ée (*de deux personnes*); **he is my e. by two years,** il est de deux ans mon aîné; **children should obey their elders,** les enfants devraient obéir à leurs aînés; **(b)** *Hist Rel* (*of a tribe*) ancien *m*.

elder² *n* **e. (tree),** sureau *m*.

elderberry ['eldəberɪ] *n* (*fruit*) baie *f* de sureau; **e. wine,** vin *m* de sureau.

elderflower ['eldəflaʊər] *n* fleur *f* de sureau.

elderly ['eldəlɪ] **1** *adj* d'un certain âge, assez âgé; *Fig* **an e. typewriter,** une machine à écrire qui a fait son temps. **2** *n* **the e.,** (*used as pl*) les personnes âgées.

eldest ['eldɪst] **1** *adj* aîné; **my e. daughter,** ma fille aînée, mon aînée; **their e. son,** leur fils aîné. **2** *n* aîné, -ée.

elect¹ [ɪ'lekt] **1** *adj* élu; **the president e.,** le président élu. **2** *n Rel* **the e.,** (*used as pl*) les élus *mpl*.

elect² *vt* **(a)** *Pol* élire (*qn*); **to e. s.o. to the presidency,** élire qn à la présidence; **to get elected,** être élu; **she was elected president,** elle a été élue présidente; **(b)** *Jur* **to e. domicile,** élire domicile; **(c)** *Fml* (*choose*) choisir (**to do,** de faire).

election [ɪ'lekʃən] *n Pol* élection *f* (*d'un candidat etc*); **to stand for e.,** poser sa candidature, se porter candidat; **the party did well in the recent elections,** le parti a obtenu de bons résultats aux dernières élections; **e. campaign/promise,** campagne/promesse électorale; **e. committee,** comité électoral; **e. results,** résultat *m* des élections.

electioneer [ɪlekʃə'nɪər] *vi* faire de la propagande électorale.

electioneering [ɪlekʃə'nɪərɪŋ] *n* propagande électorale.

elective [ɪ'lektɪv] *adj* **(a)** *Pol* (*office etc*) électif; (*body etc*) électoral, -aux; **(b)** *Am Sch* (*subject*) facultatif.

elector [ɪ'lektər] *n* électeur, -trice, votant, -ante; *Hist* (*of Holy Roman Empire*) électeur.

electoral [ɪ'lektər(ə)l] *adj* électoral, -aux; **e. body,** corps électoral; **e. college,** collège électoral; **e. roll,** liste électorale.

electorate [ɪ'lektərət] *n Pol* le corps électoral, les électeurs *mpl*.

electric [ɪ'lektrɪk] *adj* (*lumière, cuisinière, voiture etc*) électrique; *Fig* **the atmosphere of the meeting was e.,** l'atmosphère de la réunion était électrique; **e. blanket,** couverture chauffante; **e. blue,** bleu *m* électrique; *US Jur* **e. chair,** chaise *f* électrique; **e. charge,** charge *f* électrique; **e. eel,** anguille *f* électrique, gymnote *m*; **e. fence,** clôture électrifiée; **e. field,** champ *m* électrique; **e. generator,** générateur *ou* génératrice d'électricité; **e. guitar,** guitare *f* électrique; **e. heater,** radiateur *m* électrique; **e. motor,** moteur *m* électrique; **e. power station,** centrale *f* électrique; **e. shock,** décharge *f* électrique; **to get an e. shock from sth,** recevoir une décharge électrique; **e. wave,** onde *f* électrique.

electrical [ɪ'lektrɪk(ə)l] *adj* électrique; **e. appliance,** appareil *m* électrique; **e. fault,** défaut *m* dans le système électrique; **e. engineering,** électrotechnique *f*; (*industry*) industrie *f* de l'équipement électrique; **e. engineer,** électrotechnicien, -enne, ingénieur *m* en électricité.

electrician [ɪlek'trɪʃən] *n* électricien, -ienne.

electricity [ɪlek'trɪsɪtɪ] *n* électricité *f*; **the e. hasn't been connected,** l'électricité n'a pas été branchée; **lit by e.,** éclairé à l'électricité; **many homes are without e.,** (*temporarily*) de nombreux foyers sont privés d'électricité; (*not installed*) de nombreux foyers n'ont pas l'électricité; *Fig* **you could feel the e. in the air,** il y avait de l'électricité dans l'air.

electrics [ɪ'lektrɪks] *npl Br F* (*of machine*) système *m* électrique.

electrification [ɪlektrɪfɪ'keɪʃən] *n* **(a)** (*of railways etc*) électrification *f*; **(b)** électrisation *f* (*d'un corps etc*).

electrify [ɪ'lektrɪfaɪ] *vt* **(a)** (*convert*) électrifier (*une ligne de chemin de fer etc*); **(b)** (*charge with electricity*) électriser (*un corps, Fig un auditoire*).

electrifying [ɪ'lektrɪfaɪɪŋ] *adj* (*effect etc*) électrisant.

electrocardiogram [ɪlektrəʊ'kɑːdɪəʊgræm] *n Med* électrocardiogramme *m*.

electrocardiograph [ɪlektrəʊ'kɑːdɪəʊgræf] *n Med* électrocardiographe *m*.

electrocardiography [ɪlektrəʊkɑːdɪ'ɒgrəfɪ] *n Med* électrocardiographie *f*.

electrochemistry [ɪlektrəʊ'kemɪstrɪ] *n* électro-chimie *f*.

electroconvulsive [ɪlektrəʊkən'vʌlsɪv] *adj Med* **e. therapy,** électrothérapie *f*.

electrocute [ɪ'lektrəkjuːt] *vt* électrocuter.

electrocution [ɪlektrə'kjuːʃən] *n* électrocution *f*.

electrode [ɪ'lektrəʊd] *n* électrode *f*; **e. holder,** porte-électrodes *m inv*.

electrodynamics [ɪlektrəʊdaɪ'næmɪks] *n* (*usu with sing verb*) électrodynamique *f*.

electroencephalogram [ɪlektrəʊen'sefələʊgræm] *n Med* électroencéphalogramme *m*.

electroencephalograph [ɪlektrəʊen'sefələʊgræf] *n Med* appareil *m* à EEG.

electrolysis [ɪlek'trɒlɪsɪs] *n* électrolyse *f*.

electrolyte [ɪ'lektrəʊlaɪt] *n El* électrolyte *m*.

electrolytic [ɪlektrəʊ'lɪtɪk] *adj* électrolytique.

electromagnet [ɪlektrəʊ'mægnɪt] *n* électro-aimant *m*, *pl* électro-aimants.

electromagnetic [ɪlektrəʊmæg'netɪk] *adj* (*champ, onde etc*) électromagnétique.

electromagnetism [ɪlektrəʊ'mægnɪtɪz(ə)m] *n* électromagnétisme *m*.

electromotive [ɪlektrəʊ'məʊtɪv] *adj* électromoteur, -trice; **e. force,** force électromotrice.

electron [ɪ'lektrɒn] *n Phys* électron *m*; **positive e.,** électron positif; **negative e.,** électron négatif; **e. microscope,** microscope *m* électronique.

electronic [ɪlek'trɒnɪk] *adj* électronique; **e. banking,** gestion *f* électronique des opérations bancaires; **e. computer,** calculateur *m* électronique; **e. brain,** cerveau *m* électronique; **e. mail,** courrier *m* électronique; **e. organ,** orgue *m* électronique; **e. data processing,** traitement *m* électronique de l'information; **e. funds transfer,** transfert *m* électronique de fonds; **e. funds transfer at point of sale,** transfert électronique de fonds au point de vente.

electronically [ɪlek'trɒnɪklɪ] *adv* électroniquement.

electronics [ɪlek'trɒnɪks] *npl* (*usu with sing verb*) **(a)** électronique *f*; **e. company,** électronicien *m*; **e. engineer,** ingénieur électronicien, électronicien, -ienne; **e. industry,** industrie *f* électronique; **(b)** (*of machine*) système *m* électronique.

electroplate¹ [ɪ'lektrəʊpleɪt] *n* **(a)** (métal *m*) plaqué *m*;

(b) *(no pl)* articles plaqués; *(plated with silver)* articles argentés.

electroplate² *vt* plaquer *(un métal)*; *(with silver)* argenter.

electroshock [ɪlektrəʊ'ʃɒk] *n Med* **e. (therapy),** électrothérapie *f*.

electrostatic [ɪlektrəʊ'stætɪk] *adj (générateur etc)* électrostatique.

electrostatics [ɪlektrəʊ'stætɪks] *npl (usu with sing verb)* électrostatique *f*.

electrotechnic(al) [ɪlektrəʊ'teknɪk,-ɪk(ə)l] *adj* électrotechnique.

electrotherapy [ɪlektrəʊ'θerəpɪ] *n Med* électro-thérapie *f*.

electrotype¹ [ɪ'lektrəʊtaɪp] *n Typ* galvanotype *m*.

electrotype² *vt Typ* galvanotyper.

elegance ['elɪgəns] *n* élégance *f*.

elegant ['elɪgənt] *adj* **(a)** *(appearance, person)* élégant; **e. furniture,** meubles *mpl* d'un goût raffiné; **(b)** *Am F (excellent)* excellent, de premier ordre.

elegantly ['elɪgəntlɪ] *adv* élégamment, avec élégance; **e. dressed,** habillé avec élégance.

elegiac [elɪ'dʒaɪək] **1** *adj* élégiaque. **2** *npl* **elegiacs,** vers *mpl* élégiaques.

elegy ['elɪdʒɪ] *n* élégie *f*.

element ['elɪmənt] *n* **(a)** *(aspect)* **e. of uncertainty,** part *f* d'incertitude; **there is an e. of risk involved,** cela comporte un risque; **disturbing e.,** élément *m* d'instabilité; **the personal e.,** le facteur humain; **(b)** *(part of a whole)* élément *m*, partie *f*; *El (of kettle etc)* élément; *Comptr* **data e.,** élément d'information; *Nucl Phys* **fuel e.,** *(for charging reactor)* charge *f*; **the hooligan e. (in our society/in a football crowd),** les hooligans (dans notre société/parmi les spectateurs d'un match de football); **(c)** *Ch* corps *m* simple; **(d) the four elements,** les quatre éléments *mpl*; **to brave the elements,** braver les éléments; **exposed to the elements,** exposé aux intempéries; **to be in one's e.,** être dans son élément; **(e) elements,** rudiments *mpl (d'une science)*.

elemental¹ [elɪ'ment(ə)l] *adj* **(a)** *(belonging to the elements)* qui appartient aux éléments *ou* aux forces de la nature; *(esprit)* élémentaire; **(b)** *(primitive)* élémentaire, primitif; **(c)** *Ch* élémentaire; **(d)** *(basic)* fondamental, essentiel.

elemental² *n* esprit *m*.

elementary [elɪ'ment(ə)rɪ] *adj* élémentaire; **e. body,** *Ch* corps *m* simple; *Med* corps élémentaire; *Sch* **e. algebra,** rudiments *mpl* d'algèbre; *Am Sch* **e. school,** école *f* primaire.

elephant ['elɪfənt] *n* éléphant *m*; **e. calf,** *F* **baby e.,** éléphanteau *m*; **e. seal,** éléphant de mer.

elephantiasis [elɪfæn'taɪəsɪs] *n Med* éléphantiasis *f*.

elephantine [elɪ'fæntaɪn] *adj* **(a)** *(movement etc)* éléphantin; *(proportions etc)* éléphantesque; *Fig* gauche; **e. wit,** esprit lourd.

elevate ['elɪveɪt] *vt* **(a)** *(raise)* élever, hausser; *Mil* pointer *(un canon)* en hauteur; *Rel* élever *(l'hostie, l'esprit)*; **to e. s.o. to a high rank,** élever qn à un haut rang; **(b)** *(exalt)* exalter *(qn)*; élever *(l'âme de qn)*.

elevated ['elɪveɪtɪd] *adj* **(a)** *(raised, exalted)* élevé; **e. position,** position élevée; **e. thoughts,** hautes pensées; **he has an e. opinion of himself,** il a une très haute opinion de lui-même; **(b)** *(overhead)* surélevé; **e. highway,** route surélevée; **e. railway** *or US* **railroad,** chemin de fer *ou* métro aérien.

elevating ['elɪveɪtɪŋ] **1** *adj* **(a)** *(discourse etc)* édifiant; **e. principles,** principes moralisateurs; **(b)** *Av (force)* ascensionnel. **2** *n* élévation *f*, levage *m*.

elevation [elɪ'veɪʃən] *n* **(a)** élévation *f (de qch à une certaine hauteur, de qn à un rang supérieur)*; *Rel* **the E. (of the Host),** l'Élévation; **(b)** *Geog* **e. above sea level,** altitude *f ou* hauteur *f* au-dessus du niveau de la mer; **(c)** *(hill)* élévation *f*, éminence *f*; **(d)** *Astron* élévation *f (d'un astre etc)*; **(e)** *Mil* hausse *f*; pointage *m* en hauteur; **angle of e.,** angle *m* de hausse; **e. mechanism,** dispositif *m* de pointage en hauteur; **(f)** *Archit etc* élévation *f (d'un édifice etc)*; **front e.,** façade *f (d'un édifice)*; **(g)** *(nobility, refinement)* élévation *f*, dignité *f (du style)*; noblesse *f*, grandeur *f (du caractère)*.

elevator ['elɪveɪtər] *n* **(a)** élévateur *m*; *US (for goods)* monte-charge *m inv*; **bucket e.,** élévateur à godets; **(b)** *Am (lift)* ascenseur *m*; **grain e.,** élévateur *m* à grains; *(silo)* silo *m*; **(c)** *Av* gouvernail *m* de profondeur *ou* d'altitude; **e. angle,** angle *m* de braquage.

eleven [ɪ'lev(ə)n] *n* **(a)** *(numeral)* onze *m*; **the e. o'clock train,** le train de onze heures; **(b)** *Sp* le onze; **the French e.,** le onze de France.

elevenses [ɪ'lev(ə)nzɪz] *npl Br F* collation *f ou* casse-croûte *m inv* de onze heures (du matin).

eleventh [ɪ'lev(ə)nθ] **1** *adj* onzième; **on the e. of May,** le onze mai; **at the e. hour,** au dernier moment, à la dernière heure. **2** *n* **(a)** *(of month)* onze *m*; **on the e.,** le onze; **(b)** *(fraction)* onzième *m*.

eleventh-hour [ɪ'lev(ə)nθ'aʊər] *adj* de la dernière heure *ou* chance, de dernière minute; **an e.-h. rescue attempt,** une tentative de sauvetage de dernière heure.

elf, *pl* **elves** [elf, elvz] *n Myth* elfe *m*, lutin *m*, lutine *f*.

elfin ['elfɪn] *adj* d'elfe, de lutin; *(paysage)* féerique.

elfish ['elfɪʃ] *adj* **(a) = ELFIN; (b)** *(mischievous)* espiègle; **e. smile,** sourire *m* espiègle.

elicit [ɪ'lɪsɪt] *vt* **(a)** *(extract, draw out)* découvrir *(la vérité)*; tirer *(les faits)* au clair; obtenir *(une réponse de qn)*; **(b)** *(give rise to)* provoquer *(une réponse)*.

elide [ɪ'laɪd] *vt* élider *(une voyelle etc)*.

eligibility [elɪdʒɪ'bɪlɪtɪ] *n* **(a)** *(entitlement)* éligibilité *f (en droit)*; **(b)** *(of a suitor etc)* acceptabilité *f*.

eligible ['elɪdʒɪb(ə)l] *adj* **(a)** *(entitled)* éligible *(en droit)* **(to,** à); **to be e.,** avoir droit **(for,** à); **she wasn't e. for a tax rebate,** elle n'avait pas droit à une réduction d'impôts; **(b)** digne d'être élu *ou* choisi; acceptable; **e. young man,** bon parti.

eliminate [ɪ'lɪmɪneɪt] *vt* éliminer *(des matières toxiques, des noms d'une liste etc)*; supprimer, écarter *(des possibilités d'erreur etc)*; *Sl (kill)* supprimer *(qn)*; *Math* **to e. x** *or* **y,** éliminer x *ou* y; **the police have eliminated him from their enquiries,** la police l'a écarté de son enquête; *Sp* **they were eliminated in the first round,** ils ont été éliminés au premier round.

eliminating [ɪ'lɪmɪneɪtɪŋ] *adj* éliminateur, -trice; *Sp* **e. heats,** épreuves *fpl* éliminatoires.

elimination [ɪlɪmɪ'neɪʃən] *n* élimination *f*; **by process of e.,** en procédant par élimination.

eliminator [ɪ'lɪmɪneɪtər] *n* éliminateur *m*.

elision [ɪ'lɪʒən] *n (of a vowel etc)* élision *f*.

élite [eɪ'li:t] *n* élite *f*; **the é. of society,** l'élite de la société; *Mil* **é. regiment,** corps *m* d'élite.

elitism [eɪ'li:tɪz(ə)m] *n* élitisme *m*.

elitist [eɪ'li:tɪst] *adj & n* élitiste *mf*.

elixir [ɪ'lɪksər] *n* élixir *m*; **the e. of life,** l'élixir de longue vie.

Elizabeth [ɪ'lɪzəbəθ] *n* Élisabeth *f*.

Elizabethan [ɪlɪzə'bi:θ(ə)n] *adj (house etc)* élisabéthain.

elk [elk] *n* **(Scandinavian) e.,** élan *m*; **(American) e.,** wapiti *m*.

ell [el] *n Arch (measurement)* aune *f*.

ellipse [ɪ'lɪps] *n Math* ellipse *f*.

ellipsis, *pl* **-ipses** [ɪ'lɪpsɪs, -si:z] *n Gram* ellipse *f*.

ellipsoid [ɪ'lɪpsɔɪd] *n Math* ellipsoïde *m*.

elliptic(al) [ɪ'lɪptɪk, -ɪk(ə)l] *adj Gram Math* elliptique.

elliptically [ɪ'lɪptɪklɪ] *adv* elliptiquement.

elm [elm] *n (tree)* orme *m*; **e. grove,** ormaie *f*.

elocution [elə'kju:ʃən] *n* élocution *f*, diction *f*; **e. lessons,** cours *mpl* de diction.

elocutionist [elə'kju:ʃənɪst] *n (teacher)* professeur *m* de diction.

elongate ['i:lɒŋgeɪt] **1** *vt* allonger, étendre. **2** *vi* s'allonger, s'étendre.

elongated ['i:lɒŋgeɪtɪd] *adj* allongé, prolongé.

elongation [i:lɒŋ'geɪʃən] *n* **(a)** allongement *m*; *(of a line)* prolongement *m*; **(b)** *Astron* élongation *f*.

elope [ɪ'ləʊp] *vi* s'enfuir (pour se marier).

elopement [ɪ'ləʊpmənt] *n* fuite *f*.

eloquence ['eləkwəns] *n* éloquence *f*.

eloquent ['eləkwənt] *adj* éloquent; **to be an e. speaker,** être éloquent, avoir de l'éloquence; *Fig* **an e. gesture,** un geste éloquent; **the state of the economy is an e. indictment of this policy,** la situation économique en dit long sur cette politique.

eloquently ['eləkwəntlɪ] *adv* éloquemment.

else [els] **1** *adv* **or e.,** *(otherwise)* autrement; *(if not, then)* ou bien; **come tomorrow or e. it will be too late,** venez demain, autrement il sera trop tard; **he must be joking or e. he's mad,** il plaisante, ou bien alors il est fou; **do what I tell you or e. ...!,** fais ce que je te dis, sinon ...!

2 *adj & adv (with indef or interr pron or adv)* **anyone** *or* **anybody e.,** toute autre personne, n'importe qui d'autre; **he is no more stupid than anyone e.,** il n'est pas plus bête qu'un autre; **can I speak to anyone e.?,** y a-t-il quelqu'un d'autre à qui je puisse parler?; **it couldn't be anyone e.'s,** ça ne pouvait être celui de personne d'autre; **anything e.,**

n'importe quoi d'autre; **have you anything e. to do?,** avez-vous autre chose à faire?; *Com* **anything e., madam?,** et avec cela, madame?; **someone** *or* **somebody e.,** quelqu'un d'autre, un autre; **you are taking me for someone e.,** vous me prenez pour quelqu'un d'autre; **something e.,** quelque chose d'autre, autre chose; **I was thinking of something e.,** je pensais à autre chose; **no one e., nobody e.,** personne d'autre, aucun autre; **no one e. could do it,** il n'y a que lui *ou* elle *etc* qui puisse le faire; **nothing e.,** rien d'autre; **nothing e., thank you,** c'est tout, merci; **who e.?,** qui d'autre?, qui encore?; **what e.?,** quoi encore?, quoi de plus?; **what e. can I say?,** qu'est-ce que je peux dire de plus?; **everything e.,** tout le reste; **everyone** *or* **everybody e. knows it,** tous les autres le savent; **little e.,** pas grand-chose d'autre; **he eats bread but little e.,** il ne mange guère que du pain; **there isn't much e. to be done,** il ne reste pas beaucoup à faire; (*we've no choice*) il n'y a pas grand chose d'autre à faire; **where e.?,** (*did you go, look etc*) où encore?; (*did you think you would find it, her etc*) où est-ce que tu pensais le *ou* la *etc* trouver sinon là?; **everywhere e.,** partout ailleurs; **somewhere e.,** autre part, ailleurs; **nowhere e.,** nulle part ailleurs; **anywhere e.,** n'importe où (ailleurs); **can I find some anywhere e.?,** puis-je en trouver ailleurs?

elsewhere ['elsweər] *adv* ailleurs, autre part; **e. the weather will be fine,** ailleurs, il fera beau; **her ambitions lie e.,** ses ambitions se situent à un autre niveau.

ELT [iːel'tiː] *n Sch* (*abbr* **English Language Teaching**) = enseignement de l'anglais à des étudiants étrangers.

elucidate [ɪ'luːsɪdeɪt] **1** *vt* élucider, éclaircir, tirer au clair (*un fait, une question*); dégager le sens de (*un passage*). **2** *vi* s'expliquer, être plus clair; **can you e.?,** peux-tu être plus clair?

elucidation [ɪluːsɪ'deɪʃən] *n* élucidation *f*, éclaircissement *m* (**of,** de).

elude [ɪ'luːd] *vt* éluder (*une question*); esquiver, éviter (*un coup*); échapper à (*la mort*); se soustraire à (*la justice*); **to e. s.o.'s grasp,** échapper aux mains de qn.

elusive [ɪ'luːsɪv] *adj* insaisissable, intangible; (*personality*) fuyant, flottant.

elusiveness [ɪ'luːsɪvnɪs] *n* nature *f* insaisissable.

elver ['elvər] *n* (*young eel*) civelle *f*.

elvish ['elvɪʃ] *adj* = **ELFISH**.

Elysian [ɪ'lɪzɪən] *adj Myth* élyséen.

'em [əm] *pron F* = **THEM**.

emaciate [ɪ'meɪsɪeɪt] *vt* amaigrir, émacier, dessécher (*le corps*).

emaciated [ɪ'meɪsɪeɪtɪd] *adj* émacié, décharné.

emaciation [ɪmeɪsɪ'eɪʃən] *n* amaigrissement *m*, émaciation *f*, dessèchement *m* (*du corps*).

e-mail ['iːmeɪl] *n* courrier *m* électronique.

emanate ['eməneɪt] *vi* émaner, découler (**from,** de).

emanation [emə'neɪʃən] *n* émanation *f*.

emancipate [ɪ'mænsɪpeɪt] *vt* émanciper (*un mineur, les femmes etc*); affranchir (*un esclave*).

emancipated [ɪ'mænsɪpeɪtɪd] *adj* émancipé; (*slave*) affranchi.

emancipation [ɪmænsɪ'peɪʃən] *n* émancipation *f*; affranchissement *m* (*d'un esclave etc*).

emasculate [ɪ'mæskjʊleɪt] *vt* émasculer, châtrer.

emasculation [ɪmæskjʊ'leɪʃən] *n* émasculation *f*, castration *f*.

embalm [ɪm'bɑːm] *vt* embaumer.

embalmer [ɪm'bɑːmər] *n* embaumeur *m*.

embalming [ɪm'bɑːmɪŋ] *n* embaumement *m*.

embankment [ɪm'bæŋkmənt] *n Rail etc* talus *m*, remblai *m*; (*to contain a river*) digue *f*; (*alongside a river etc*) berge *f*, quai *m*.

embargo¹, *pl* **-oes** [em'bɑːgəʊ, -əʊz] *n* embargo *m*, séquestre *m*; **to be under an e.,** être séquestré; **to put an e. on,** mettre un embargo sur (*des marchandises etc*).

embargo² *vt* mettre l'embargo sur, séquestrer.

embark [em'bɑːk] **1** *vt* embarquer (*des troupes etc*); (*of ship*) prendre à bord (*des troupes etc*). **2** *vi* s'embarquer (*à bord d'un navire*); *Fig* **to e. (up)on,** s'embarquer dans (*une aventure etc*).

embarkation [embɑː'keɪʃən] *n Nau* embarquement *m*; **e. card,** carte *f* d'accès à bord.

embarrass [ɪm'bærəs] *vt* embarrasser, gêner (*qn*).

embarrassed [ɪm'bærəst] *adj* embarrassé, gêné; **to be/feel e.,** être/se sentir gêné; **an e. silence,** un silence embarrassé.

embarrassing [ɪm'bærəsɪŋ] *adj* embarrassant, gênant.

embarrassingly [ɪm'bærəsɪŋlɪ] *adv* d'une manière embarrassante *ou* gênante.

embarrassment [ɪm'bærəsmənt] *n* embarras *m*, gêne *f*; **blushing with e.,** rouge de confusion; **to be in a state of financial e.,** avoir des embarras d'argent.

embassy ['embəsɪ] *n* **(a)** (*building*) ambassade *f*; **the French E.,** l'ambassade de France; **e. staff,** personnel *m* d'ambassade; **(b)** (*mission*) **special e.,** mission spéciale.

embattled [ɪm'bæt(ə)ld] *adj* (*prepared for battle*) rangé *ou* formé en bataille; (*engaged in battle*) engagé dans la bataille.

embed [ɪm'bed] *vt* (**-dd-**) **(a)** enfoncer (*un clou dans un mur*); poser (*un câble dans le sable*); encastrer (*un châssis dans un mur*); **embedded in concrete,** noyé dans le béton; **(b)** *Comptr* intégrer.

embedded [ɪm'bedɪd] *adj Comptr* **e. command,** commande intégrée.

embellish [ɪm'belɪʃ] *vt* embellir, orner (*qch*); enjoliver (*un récit*); colorier (*son style*).

embellishment [ɪm'belɪʃmənt] *n* embellissement *m*, ornement *m*; enjolivure *f*.

ember ['embər] *n* (*usu pl*) **embers,** braise *f*, charbons ardents.

Ember ['embər] *adj Rel* **E. days,** les Quatre-Temps *mpl*.

embezzle [ɪm'bez(ə)l] **1** *vt* détourner, distraire, s'approprier (*des fonds*). **2** *vi* commettre des détournements.

embezzlement [ɪm'bezəlm(ə)nt] *n* détournement *m* de fonds, appropriation *f* de fonds.

embezzler [ɪm'bezlər] *n* détourneur *m* de fonds.

embitter [ɪm'bɪtər] *vt* remplir d'amertume; aigrir (*le caractère*); empoisonner (*les plaisirs*); envenimer (*une querelle etc*).

embittered [ɪm'bɪtəd] *adj* aigri (**by,** par).

emblazon [ɪm'bleɪz(ə)n] *vt* blasonner, décorer d'armoiries; **emblazoned with the arms of the town,** peint aux armes de la ville.

emblazoned [ɪm'bleɪz(ə)nd] *adj* blasonné.

emblem ['embləm] *n* (*symbol*) emblème *m*; *Her* emblème, devise *f*; *Aut* (*on radiator*) écusson *m*; **sporting e.,** insigne sportif.

emblematic [emblə'mætɪk] *adj* emblématique.

embodied [ɪm'bɒdɪd] *adj* concrétisé; (*art*) mis en pratique.

embodiment [ɪm'bɒdɪmənt] *n* incarnation *f*; personnification *f*; **he is the e. of kindness,** il est la bonté même.

embody [ɪm'bɒdɪ] *vt* (**embodied**; **embodying**) **(a)** (*give form to*) incarner; **(b)** (*personify*) personnifier (*une qualité*); **(c)** (*incorporate*) incorporer (*un article dans une loi*); renfermer, rédiger (*ses principes dans un traité*).

embolden [ɪm'bəʊldən] *vt* enhardir (**s.o. to do sth,** qn à faire qch).

embolism ['embəlɪz(ə)m] *n Med* embolie *f*.

embonpoint [ɒmbɒn'pwæn] *n* embonpoint *m*, rondeurs *fpl*.

emboss [ɪm'bɒs] *vt* travailler en relief; bosseler (*le métal*); repousser, estamper (*le métal, le cuir*).

embossed [ɪm'bɒst] *adj* (*métal*) gravé en relief, travaillé en bosse; (*métal, cuir*) estampé, repoussé; **e. work,** travail *m* en relief *ou* en repoussé.

embossing [ɪm'bɒsɪŋ] *n* **(a)** (*technique, activity*) bosselage *m* (*du métal*); estampage *m*, repoussage *m* (*du cuir*); **e. punch,** repoussoir *m*; **e. press,** (*in paper making*) presse *f* à imprimer en relief; **(b)** (*result*) relief *m*, repoussé *m*, bosselure *f*.

embrace¹ [ɪm'breɪs] *n* étreinte *f*; (*of lovers*) étreinte amoureuse; **iron e.,** étreinte de fer.

embrace² **1** *vt* **(a)** embrasser, étreindre; donner une accolade à (*qn*); **(b)** (*adopt*) embrasser (*une religion*); adopter (*une cause*); **(c)** (*include*) embrasser (**in,** dans); contenir (**in,** dans); comprendre (*des sujets*); **(d)** (*take in*) **the view from the terrace embraces the whole valley,** de la terrasse, la vue s'étend sur toute la vallée *ou* embrasse toute la vallée. **2** *vi* (*of two people*) s'embrasser; **they embraced,** ils s'embrassèrent.

embracing [ɪm'breɪsɪŋ] *adj* qui embrasse, qui renferme; (*geste*) ample, compréhensif.

embrasure [ɪm'breɪʒər] *n* **(a)** *Archit* embrasure *f*, ébrasement *m*; **(b)** *Mil* embrasure *f*, sabord *m*.

embrocation [embrə'keɪʃən] *n Med* embrocation *f*.

embroider [ɪm'brɔɪdər] **1** *vt* **(a)** *Sewing* broder; **(b)** (*exaggerate*) enjoliver (*un récit*). **2** *vi* **(a)** *Sewing* faire de la broderie; **(b)** (*exaggerate*) broder, enjoliver, *F* en rajouter.

embroidering [ɪm'brɔɪdərɪŋ] *n* **(a)** = **EMBROIDERY (a)**; **(b)** (*exaggeration*) enjolivement *m* (*d'un récit*).

embroidery [ɪm'brɔɪdərɪ] *n* **(a)** *Sewing* broderie *f*; **e. frame,** métier *m* à broder; **(b)** (*added details*) fioriture *f*

(*d'un récit*).
embroil [ɪm'brɔɪl] *vt* **(a)** (*usu pass*) (*involve*) **embroiled in a quarrel,** entraîné dans une querelle; **to become embroiled in sth,** se trouver mêlé à qch; **(b)** (*put into confusion*) brouiller, embrouiller (*une affaire*).
embroilment [ɪm'brɔɪlmənt] *n* **(a)** (*involvement*) implication *f*; **(b)** (*confusion*) embrouillement *m* (*d'une affaire*).
embryo, *pl* **-os** ['embrɪəʊ, -əʊz] *n Biol & Fig* embryon *m*; **in e.,** (*foetus, plan*) à l'état embryonnaire; (*artist*) en herbe; **e. research,** recherche *f* portant sur les embryons.
embryology [embrɪ'ɒlədʒɪ] *n* embryologie *f*.
embryonic [embrɪ'ɒnɪk] *adj Biol* embryonnaire; *Fig* en germe.
embus [ɪm'bʌs] *Mil etc* **1** *vt* embarquer (*des troupes*) dans un autocar. **2** *vi* monter dans un autocar.
emcee ['em'siː] *n F* maître *m* de cérémonies; *Rad TV* animateur, -trice.
emend [ɪ'mend] , **emendate** ['iːmendeɪt] *vt* corriger, apporter des amendements à (*un texte*).
emendation [iːmen'deɪʃən] *n* **(a)** (*action*) amendement *m*, correction *f* (*d'un texte*); **(b)** (*proposed alteration*) variante proposée.
emerald ['em(ə)rəld] **1** *n Miner* émeraude *f*. **2** *adj & n* (*colour*) **e. (green),** (vert *m* d')émeraude *f*; *Lit* **the E. Isle,** la verte Irlande.
emerge [ɪ'mɜːdʒ] *vi* **(a)** (*from liquid*) émerger (**from,** de); surgir (*de l'eau etc*); **(b)** (*from hole, from behind sth etc*) déboucher (**from,** de); sortir (*d'un trou, de l'obscurité*); émerger (*de l'ombre, du brouillard*); **the moon is emerging from behind the clouds,** la lune se dégage des nuages; **she emerged as an important politician in the 1960s,** c'est dans les années 60 qu'elle a émergée en tant que personnalité politique importante; **(c)** (*arise*) (*of difficulty etc*) se dresser, surgir; **from these facts it emerges that ...,** de ces faits il ressort que ...; **it later emerged that ...,** il est apparu par la suite que ... .
emergence [ɪ'mɜːdʒəns] *n* émergence *f* (*d'une théorie etc*); apparition *f* (*d'un nouvel État, d'un nouveau leader*).
emergency [ɪ'mɜːdʒənsɪ] *n* **(a)** circonstance *f* critique, cas urgent; **to provide for emergencies,** parer aux éventualités *ou* à l'imprévu; **this is an e.,** c'est une urgence; **to meet an e.,** faire face à une situation critique; **a telephone number you can call in an e.,** un numéro de téléphone que l'on peut appeler en cas d'urgence; **in case of e.,** en cas d'urgence; **state of e.,** état *m* d'urgence; **national e.,** catastrophe nationale; **e. brake,** frein *m* de secours; **e. exit,** sortie *f* de secours; *Cin etc* **e. light** *or* **lighting,** éclairage *m* de sécurité; **e. rations,** vivres *mpl* de réserve; **e. regulations,** mesures *fpl* d'exception; **e. repairs,** réparations *fpl* d'urgence; **e. services,** services *mpl* d'urgence; **e. supply,** en-cas *m inv*; **e. tank,** réservoir *m* auxiliaire; **(b)** *Med* **an e.,** une urgence; **e. operation,** opération *f* à chaud; **e. ward,** salle *f* d'urgence.
emergent [ɪ'mɜːdʒənt] *adj* émergent; **e. nations,** nations *fpl* en voie de développement.
emery ['emərɪ] *n* émeri *m*; **e. board,** lime *f* émeri; **e. paper,** papier *m* d'émeri; **e. powder,** poudre *f* d'émeri; **e. wheel,** meule *f* (en) émeri.
emetic [ɪ'metɪk] *adj & n Med* émétique *m*.
emf, EMF [iːe'mef] *n El abbr* **electromotive force.**
emigrant ['emɪgrənt] *adj & n* émigrant, -ante.
emigrate ['emɪgreɪt] *vi* émigrer.
emigrating ['emɪgreɪtɪŋ] *adj* émigrant.
emigration [emɪ'greɪʃən] *n* émigration *f*.
emigré ['emɪgreɪ] *n* émigré, -ée; **e. writer,** écrivain émigré.
eminence ['emɪnəns] *n* **(a)** (*position of importance*) grandeur *f*, distinction *f* (*d'une charge*); position éminente; **to rise to e.,** parvenir à une haute position; **(b)** (*raised ground*) éminence *f*, élévation *f* (*de terrain*); **(c)** *Anat* éminence *f*, saillie *f*; **(d)** *Rel* (*title of cardinal*) Eminence *f*; **your E.,** votre Eminence.
eminent ['emɪnənt] *adj* éminent; (*docteur etc*) distingué.
eminently ['emɪnəntlɪ] *adv* éminemment; **an e. respectable family,** une famille des plus honorables; **an e. suitable place,** un endroit *ou* une place parfaitement adapté(e) (**for,** à); **what an e. sensible idea!,** quelle sage idée!
emir [e'mɪər] *n* émir *m*.
emirate ['emɪreɪt] *n* émirat *m*.
emissary ['emɪsərɪ] *n* émissaire *m*.
emission [ɪ'mɪʃən] *n* **(a)** émission *f*, dégagement *m* (*de gaz, de chaleur etc*); (*of pollutant*) émission; **e. current,** courant *m* d'émission; **e. efficiency,** efficacité *f* (*d'une cathode thermo-électronique*); **(b)** *Banking etc* émission *f* (*de billets de banque etc*).
emit [ɪ'mɪt] *vt* **(a)** dégager (*de la chaleur etc*); exhaler, dégager (*une odeur*); lancer, jeter (*des étincelles*); rendre (*un son*); **(b)** *Banking* émettre (*du papier-monnaie*).
emitter [ɪ'mɪtər] *n Nucl Phys* émetteur *m*.
Emmy ['emɪ] *n US TV* ≈ Sept *m* d'Or.
emollient [ɪ'mɒlɪənt] *adj & n Med* émollient *m*.
emolument [ɪ'mɒljʊmənt] *n* (*usu pl*) **emoluments,** émoluments *mpl*, appointements *mpl*, honoraires *fpl*.
emotion [ɪ'məʊʃən] *n* émotion *f*; **to appeal to the emotions,** faire appel aux sentiments; **to be in control of one's emotions,** maîtriser ses émotions; **without showing the least e.,** sans montrer le moindre signe d'émotion; **voice touched with e.,** voix émue.
emotional [ɪ'məʊʃən(ə)l] *adj* **(a)** (*trouble etc*) émotif; **for e. reasons,** pour des raisons émotives; **(b)** (*liable to emotion*) émotif; **to be e.,** s'attendrir facilement; **he got very e.,** (*tearful*) il a pris ça très à cœur; (*tearfully angry*) il a pris ça très mal; **(c)** (*full of emotion*) émouvant; **she made an e. plea for the hostages' release,** elle a lancé un appel très émouvant pour que les otages soient libérés.
emotionally [ɪ'məʊʃən(ə)lɪ] *adv* **(a)** émotionnellement; **I am too e. involved,** cela me concerne de trop près; **I don't want to get e. involved,** je ne veux pas m'attacher; **to be e. involved with s.o.,** avoir des liens affectifs avec qn; **e. disturbed,** troublé sur le plan émotionnel; **(b)** (*with strong emotion*) avec beaucoup d'émotion.
emotionless [ɪ'məʊʃənlɪs] *adj* indifférent; (*face, look*) impassible; (*style*) sobre.
emotive [ɪ'məʊtɪv] *adj* (*personne*) émotif; (*débat*) passionnel; **race is a very e. issue,** le racisme est un sujet qui déchaîne les passions.
empanel [ɪm'pæn(ə)l] *vt* (**-ll-**, *US* **-l-**) *Jur* **to e. a jury,** constituer le jury; **to e. a juror,** inscrire un juré sur la liste du jury.
empathize ['empəθaɪz] *vi* s'identifier (**with s.o.,** avec qn).
empathy ['empəθɪ] *n Psy* empathie *f*.
emperor ['empərər] *n* empereur *m*; **e. moth,** saturnie *f*, *F* paon *m* de nuit; **e. penguin,** manchot *m* empereur.
emphasis ['emfəsɪs] *n* **(a)** (*insistence*) insistance *f*; **to lay e. on,** appuyer *ou* insister sur (*un fait*); souligner (*un mot*); **too much e. is placed on individualism,** l'individualisme l'emporte trop souvent; **the e. is on written work,** l'accent est mis sur le travail écrit; **(b)** (*in words*) force *f*, accentuation *f*; **oratorical e.,** accent *m* oratoire; **(c)** *Gram* mise *f* en relief; *Ling* accent *m* (*sur un mot ou une syllabe*).
emphasize ['emfəsaɪz] *vt* accentuer, appuyer sur (*un mot, un fait*); attirer l'attention sur (*un fait*); faire ressortir, mettre en relief (*une qualité etc*); **she emphasized the need for caution,** elle a bien insisté sur la nécessité d'être prudent.
emphatic [ɪm'fætɪk] *adj* **(a)** (*manière, geste*) énergique; (*orateur*) vigoureux; (*refus*) positif, net; **(b)** *Ling* (*syllabe*) accentué.
emphatically [ɪm'fætɪk(e)lɪ] *adv* **(a)** (*to say*) avec emphase; (*to gesture*) énergiquement; (*to refuse*) carrément, catégoriquement; (*to deny*) catégoriquement; **(b)** (*insistently*) en termes pressants; **(c)** (*intensive*) **he is most e. a leader,** c'est un chef s'il en fut jamais.
empire ['empaɪər] *n* empire *m*; *Hist* **the Holy Roman E.,** le Saint Empire Romain Germanique; *Br Hist* **the (British) E.,** l'Empire britannique; *Fig* **a shipbuilding e.,** un empire dans le monde de la construction navale; *Archit* **E. style,** style *m* Empire; **E. furniture,** meubles *mpl* Empire; *Br Hist* **E. troops,** (*of British Empire*) armée coloniale.
empire-builder ['empaɪəbɪldər] *n Fig* constructeur *m* d'empires.
empire-building ['empaɪəbɪldɪŋ] *n Fig* construction *f* d'empires.
empiric [em'pɪrɪk] **1** *adj* empirique. **2** *n* empiriste *m*.
empirical [em'pɪrɪk(ə)l] *adj* empirique; **e. formula,** formule *f* empirique.
empiricism [em'pɪrɪsɪz(ə)m] *n* empirisme *m*.
emplacement [ɪm'pleɪsmənt] *n Mil* emplacement *m* (*d'un canon*).
emplane [ɪm'pleɪn] **1** *vi* monter en avion. **2** *vt* faire monter (*qn, des troupes*) en avion.
employ¹ [ɪm'plɔɪ] *n Fml* emploi *m*; **to be in s.o.'s e.,** être au service de qn, être employé par qn.
employ² *vt* **(a)** (*give work to*) employer (*qn*) à son service; **who would e. someone with a criminal record?,** qui emploierait quelqu'un dont le casier (judiciaire) n'est pas vierge?; **to e. s.o. as secretary,** employer qn comme secrétaire; **(b)** (*occupy*) **to e. oneself, to be employed,**

s'occuper, être occupé (**in doing sth,** à faire qch); **(c)** (*use*) employer (*des moyens etc*); se servir de (*la force etc*).

employable [ɪm'plɔɪəb(ə)l] *adj* susceptible d'être employé; **qualifications make you more e.,** il est plus facile de se faire embaucher quand on a des qualifications.

employed [ɪm'plɔɪd] **1** *adj* employé; **gainfully e.,** rémunéré. **2** *n* **employers and e.,** (*used as pl*) le patronat et le salariat.

employee [ɪmplɔɪ'iː, em'plɔiː] *n* employé, -ée; **a Smith Co e., an e. of Smith Co,** un(e) employé(e) de Smith & Co; **relations between management and employees,** relations entre la direction et le personnel.

employer [ɪm'plɔɪər] *n* patron, patronne, *Fml* employeur, -euse; **she's a good e. (to work for),** c'est une bonne patronne; **body of employers,** patronat *m*; **employers' association,** organisation patronale, syndicat patronal; **this company is the town's largest e.,** c'est cette entreprise qui emploie le plus de gens dans la ville.

employment [ɪm'plɔɪmənt] *n* **(a)** (*work*) emploi *m*, travail *m*; **to be looking for e.,** chercher un emploi *ou* du travail; **to be without e.,** être sans emploi *ou* sans travail; **to be in e.,** avoir un emploi; **the firm gives e. to 2,000 (people),** l'entreprise emploie 2 000 personnes; **e. agency** *or* **bureau,** bureau *m ou* agence *f* de placement; (*for manual workers*) service *m* d'embauche; **(b)** (*act of giving work*) embauche *f*; **the e. of 200 more staff,** l'embauche de 200 employés supplémentaires; **(c)** (*use*) emploi *m* (*de l'argent etc*).

emporium [ɪm'pɔːrɪəm] *n* (*shop*) grand magasin.

empower [ɪm'paʊər] *vt* **(a)** *Jur* donner pouvoir *ou* procuration à (*qn*); **(b)** (*authorize*) **to e. s.o. to do sth,** autoriser qn à faire qch, donner *ou* conférer plein(s) pouvoir(s) à qn pour faire qch.

empress ['emprɪs] *n* impératrice *f*.

emptiness ['emptɪnɪs] *n* vide *m* (*d'une chambre etc*); *F* **to feel an e.,** (*hungry*) se sentir l'estomac creux; (*after bereavement etc*) sentir un vide.

empty¹ ['emptɪ] **1** *adj* **(a)** vide (**of,** de); (*rue*) désert; (*bourse*) vide; (*immeuble*) inoccupé; (*estomac*) creux; (*wagon*) sans chargement; **to come back e.,** (*of lorry etc*) revenir à vide; **you shouldn't run on an e. stomach,** tu ne devrais pas courir à jeun; **to feel e.,** (*hungry*) se sentir l'estomac creux; (*after bereavement etc*) sentir un vide; **(b)** *Fig* (*head*) vide; (*mind*) nul; (*words, threats*) vain; **word e. of meaning,** mot *m* vide de sens. **2** *n Com* caisse *f* vide; bouteille *f* vide; **returnable empties,** bouteilles consignées.

empty² **1** *vt* vider (*un verre etc*) (**into,** dans); décharger, *Min* verser (*un wagon*); dépeupler (*les rues*); vidanger (*une fosse d'aisance, un carter*). **2** *vi* (*of river etc*) se déverser (**into,** dans); (*of theatre*) se vider.

►**empty out** *vtsep* (*empty*) vider (*ses poches*); **he emptied the contents of his pockets out on to the table,** il a vidé le contenu de ses poches sur la table.

empty-handed ['emptɪ'hændɪd] *adv* les mains vides.

empty-headed ['emptɪ'hedɪd] *adj* sans cervelle.

emptying *n* vidage *m* (*d'un verre etc*); vidange *f* (*d'un tonneau etc*); déchargement *m* (*d'un wagon*); dépeuplement *m* (*des rues*).

EMS [iːe'mes] *n* (*abbr* **European Monetary System**) SME *m*.

emu ['iːmjuː] *n* (*bird*) émeu *m*.

emulate ['emjʊleɪt] *vt* (*imitate*) imiter (*qn, qch*); (*try to equal, surpass*) être l'émule de (*qn*); *Comptr* émuler.

emulation [emjʊ'leɪʃən] *n* émulation *f*; *Comptr* émulation.

emulator ['emjʊleɪtər] *n* émulateur *m*; *Comptr* émulateur.

emulsifier [ɪ'mʌlsɪfaɪər] *n* émulsifiant *m*.

emulsify [ɪ'mʌlsɪfaɪ] *vt* émulsionner.

emulsion [ɪ'mʌlʃən] *n* **(a)** émulsion *f*; *Phot* **plate e.,** émulsion pour plaques; **(b) e. (paint),** peinture mate.

enable [ɪ'neɪb(ə)l] *vt* **to e. s.o. to do sth,** mettre qn à même *ou* en état de faire qch; *Jur* habiliter qn à faire qch; **this legacy enabled him to retire,** cet héritage lui permit de prendre sa retraite.

enabling [ɪ'neɪb(ə)lɪŋ] *adj Jur* habilitant; **e. act,** loi *f* qui habilite une personne juridique.

enact [ɪ'nækt] *vt* **(a)** (*act out*) jouer, représenter (*une tragédie*); **(b)** *Jur* décréter (*une loi*); ordonner, décréter (*une mesure*).

enactment [ɪ'næktmənt] *n* **(a)** (*of a play*) représentation *f*; **(b)** *Jur* (*of a law*) établissement *m*, promulgation *f*; **(c)** (*decree*) ordonnance *f*, décret *m*; **by legislative e.,** par un texte législatif.

enamel [ɪ'næm(ə)l] *n* **(a)** *Art etc* émail *m*, *pl* émaux; **e. saucepan,** casserole émaillée; **e. work,** émaillure *f*; (*painting on enamel*) peinture *f* sur émail; **e. ware,** ustensiles *mpl* en fer émaillé; **(b)** *Anat* émail *m* (*des dents*); **(c)** (*varnish*) vernis *m*, émail *m*, *pl* émails; **e. paint,** peinture *f* au vernis; **to finish a bicycle in baked e.,** émailler une bicyclette à chaud *ou* au four.

enamel² *vt* (-ll-, *US* -l-) **(a)** (*cover with enamel*) émailler (*la porcelaine etc*); **(b)** (*paint, varnish*) ripoliner (*une porte etc*); vernir (*le fer, le cuir*).

enamelled [ɪ'næm(ə)ld] *adj* **(a)** (*covered with enamel*) (*brique etc*) émaillé; (*carreau*) vernissé; **e. saucepan,** casserole émaillée; **(b)** (*painted*) peint en émail.

enamelling [ɪ'næm(ə)lɪŋ] *n* **(a)** émaillage *m*; **(b)** (*art*) émaillure *f*; (*painting*) peinture *f* en émail.

enamoured [ɪ'næməd] *adj* passionné (**of sth,** pour qch); *Lit* amoureux (**of s.o.,** de qn); **to become e. of s.o.,** s'éprendre de qn.

encage [ɪn'keɪdʒ] *vt* encager (*un animal*), mettre (*un animal*) en cage.

encamp [ɪn'kæmp] **1** *vt* (faire) camper (*une armée*). **2** *vi* camper.

encampment [ɪn'kæmpmənt] *n* campement *m*, camp *m*.

encapsulate [ɪn'kæpsjʊleɪt] *vt* **(a)** (*summarize*) résumer; **(b)** *Pharm* capsuler.

encase [ɪn'keɪs] *vt* **(a)** (*provide with a covering*) envelopper (*qch*); (*coat, cover*) revêtir (**s.o. in sth,** qn de qch); **(b)** encaisser, enfermer (**in,** dans); mettre (*un objet*) dans un étui.

encash [ɪn'kæʃ] *vt Br Banking* encaisser (*un chèque*).

encashment [ɪn'kæʃmənt] *n Br Banking* encaissement *m* (*d'un chèque*).

encaustic [en'kɔːstɪk] **1** *adj Art* (*tableau etc*) à l'encaustique; (*peinture*) encaustique; *Cer* **e. tile,** carreau *m* céramique. **2** *n Art* encaustique *f*.

encephalitis [ensefə'laɪtɪs] *n Med* encéphalite *f*.

enchant [ɪn'tʃɑːnt] *vt* **(a)** (*delight*) enchanter, ravir; **(b)** (*put under a spell*) ensorceler.

enchanted [ɪn'tʃɑːntɪd] *adj* **(a)** (*delighted*) enchanté (**with,** de); **(b)** (*under a spell, magic*) enchanté, ensorcelé; **an e. forest,** une forêt enchantée.

enchanting [ɪn'tʃɑːntɪŋ] *adj* enchanteur, -eresse, ravissant, charmant; **an e. little cottage,** une charmante petite maison de campagne.

enchantingly [ɪn'tʃɑːntɪŋlɪ] *adv* à ravir.

enchantment [ɪn'tʃɑːntmənt] *n* **(a)** (*delight*) ravissement *m*, enchantement *m*; **he professed his e.,** il a déclaré qu'il était enchanté; *Lit* **distance lends e. (to the view),** tout paraît beau (vu) de loin; **(b)** (*placing under a spell*) enchantement *m*, ensorcellement *m*.

enchantress [ɪn'tʃɑːntrɪs] *n* enchanteresse *f*.

encircle [ɪn'sɜːk(ə)l] *vt* ceindre, encercler; cerner, entourer (*une armée*).

encirclement [ɪn'sɜːkəlmənt] *n* encerclement *m*.

encircling [ɪn'sɜːk(ə)lɪŋ] *n* encerclement *m*; *Mil* **e. movement,** manœuvre *f* de débordement.

encl *n* (*abbr* **enclosure**) p.j.

enclave ['enkleɪv] *n* enclave *f*.

enclose [ɪn'kləʊz] *vt* **(a)** (*include*) inclure, (r)enfermer (**in,** dans); **to e. sth in a letter,** joindre qch à une lettre; **letter enclosing a cheque,** lettre contenant un chèque; **enclosed herewith,** sous ce pli; **enclosed please find ...,** veuillez trouver ci-inclus *ou* ci-joint ...; **(b)** (*surround*) clôturer (*un champ*) (**with,** de); entourer, investir (*l'ennemi, une ville*); **garden enclosed with** *or* **in** *or* **by high walls,** jardin entouré de hauts murs; **(c)** (*cover*) blinder (*un moteur électrique etc*); enfermer (*un mécanisme*) dans un carter.

enclosed [ɪn'kləʊzd] *adj* **(a)** (*in letter*) joint, ci-joint, ci-inclus; **the e. documents,** les pièces jointes; **(b)** (*field etc*) clos, enclos; (*army*) entouré, cerné; (*city*) investi; *Rel* (*order, monk etc*) cloîtré; **e. space,** espace clos; **(c)** *MecE etc* (*covered*) recouvert, enfermé; en carter.

enclosure [ɪn'kləʊʒər] *n* **(a)** (*area*) enclos *m*, clos *m*, enceinte *f*; *Horseracing* le pesage; **the public enclosures,** la pelouse; **(b)** (*fence, wall etc*) enceinte *f*, clôture *f*; **(c)** *Com* (*in letter*) pièce annexée *ou* incluse, annexe *f*; **enclosures,** pièces jointes.

encode [en'kəʊd] *vt* chiffrer (*un texte etc*); *Comptr* encoder.

encompass [ɪn'kʌmpəs] *vt* **(a)** (*surround*) entourer (**with,** de); **(b)** (*include*) englober, envelopper, renfermer (**with, within,** dans); **their repertoire encompasses most musical styles,** leur répertoire englobe la plupart des genres musicaux.

encore¹ [ɒŋ'kɔːr] **1** *n* **(a)** = chanson ou morceau etc exécuté à la fin d'un spectacle ou d'un concert etc par un artiste que l'on a bissé; **to call for an e.,** (*of audience*) bisser; **to give an e.,** (*of pianist, singer etc*) bisser; **(b)**

(*shout*) bis *m*. **2** *int* **e.!**, bis!

encore² **1** *vt* bisser (*un passage, un acteur*). **2** *vi* crier bis, bisser.

encounter¹ [ɪn'kaʊntər] *n* **(a)** (*meeting*) rencontre *f* (*d'amis etc*); **a brief e. on a train,** une brève rencontre dans le train (**with,** avec); **(b)** (*confrontation*) rencontre *f* (hostile); (*fight*) combat *m*; (*duel*) duel *m*; *Sp Journ* confrontation *f*.

encounter² *vt* rencontrer (*qn, un obstacle*); éprouver (*des difficultés*); affronter (*l'ennemi*); trouver (*de la résistance*); essuyer (*une tempête*).

encourage [ɪn'kʌrɪdʒ] *vt* **(a)** encourager, inciter (**s.o. to do sth,** qn à faire qch); **the new law will e. people to drink more,** la nouvelle loi encouragera les gens à boire plus; **she encouraged me to go to drama school,** elle m'a incité à m'inscrire à un cours de théâtre; **don't e. him!,** ne l'encourage pas!; **(b)** (*support*) appuyer (*une bonne œuvre*); favoriser (*les arts, le commerce*); encourager (*une croyance*); **they encouraged their daughter's ambition,** ils ont encouragé leur fille à réaliser ses ambitions.

encouraged [ɪn'kʌrɪdʒd] *adj* encouragé, soutenu; **to feel e.,** se sentir soutenu.

encouragement [ɪn'kʌrɪdʒmənt] *n* encouragement *m*; **to give s.o. e.,** encourager qn; **to get** *or* **receive e. from s.o.,** être encouragé par qn; **her success was a great e. to us,** sa réussite nous a beaucoup encouragés; *Iron* **he doesn't need any e.,** il n'a pas besoin qu'on l'aide.

encouraging [ɪn'kʌrɪdʒɪŋ] *adj* (*news, person*) encourageant; **it is e. to see the progress that has been made,** c'est encourageant de constater les progrès qui ont été faits.

encouragingly [ɪn'kʌrɪdʒɪŋlɪ] *adv* d'une manière encourageante.

encroach [ɪn'krəʊtʃ] *vi* **the sea is encroaching,** la mer gagne du terrain.

►**encroach on, encroach upon** *vipo* empiéter sur (*une terre etc*); usurper, *Jur* léser (*les droits de qn*); **the sea is encroaching on the land,** la mer gagne du terrain.

encroachment [ɪn'krəʊtʃmənt] *n* **(a)** *Jur etc* **e. upon s.o.'s rights,** usurpation *f* des droits de qn, empiètement *m* sur les droits de qn; **(b)** (*of the sea etc*) ingression *f*.

encrust [ɪn'krʌst] *vt* **(a)** (*decorate*) incruster; **the crown was encrusted with diamonds,** la couronne était incrustée de diamants; **(b)** (*cover with hard outer layer*) couvrir (d'une croûte), incruster (**with,** de); **shoes encrusted with mud,** des chaussures couvertes de boue.

encumber [ɪn'kʌmbər] *vt* **(a)** encombrer (**with,** de); gêner (*qn, le mouvement*); **(b)** *Jur* **encumbered estate,** (*with debts*) propriété grevée de dettes; (*with mortgage*) propriété grevée d'hypothèques.

encumbrance [ɪn'kʌmbrəns] *n* **(a)** embarras *m*, charge *f*; **to be an e. to s.o.,** être à charge de qn; **man without family encumbrances,** homme sans charges de famille; **(b)** *Jur* charges *fpl* (*d'une succession*); **to free an estate from encumbrances,** dégrever une propriété.

encyclic [ɪn'sɪklɪk] *adj Cathol* encyclique.

encyclical [ɪn'sɪklɪk(ə)l] *Cathol* **1** *n* encyclique *f*. **2** *adj* (*letter*) encyclique.

encyclopaedia, *US* **encyclopedia** [ɪnsaɪklə'piːdɪə] *n* encyclopédie *f*; **an e. entry,** une entrée d'encyclopédie; **e. salesman,** représentant *m* en encyclopédies.

encyclopaedic, *US* **encyclopedic** [ɪnsaɪklə'piːdɪk] *adj* encyclopédique.

end¹ [end] *n* **(a)** (*extremity*) bout *m*, extrémité *f* (*d'un bâton, d'une rue etc*); fin *f* (*d'un livre*); queue *f* (*d'une procession etc*); about *m* (*d'une poutre*); tronçon *m* (*de mât etc*); tronche *f* (*de câble*); bout (*de chandelle*); bout, *F* mégot *m* (*de cigarette*); **the e. of the table,** le bout de la table; *Rail* **e. of line,** tête *f* de ligne; **to come to the e. of the road,** arriver au bout de la route; (*in one's career*) arriver au bout de sa carrière; (*in one's life*) arriver au bout de sa vie; (*be unable to make progress*) être dans une impasse; **east e.,** (*in church architecture*) chevet *m* (*d'une église*); *Fig* **to get hold of the wrong e. of the stick,** prendre quelque chose à contre-sens; *Fig* **I don't know one e. of a tennis racket/a computer/***etc* **from the other,** je ne sais même pas à quoi ressemble une raquette de tennis/un ordinateur/*etc*; *F Tel* **at the other e. of the line,** à l'autre bout de la ligne, au bout du fil; **what's the weather like at your e.?,** quel temps fait-il chez vous?; **the problem's at the supplier's e.,** le problème est chez le fournisseur; **it's at the other e. of town,** c'est à l'autre bout de la ville; *Fb etc* **to change ends,** changer de camp; **the deep/shallow e.,** (*of swimming pool*) le grand/le petit fond; **to keep one's e. up,** (*stay cheerful*) ne pas se laisser démonter; (*contribute*) y mettre du sien; **e. to e.,** bout à bout; **to make (both) ends meet,** joindre les deux bouts; **from e. to e.,** d'un bout à l'autre; **on e.,** (*barrel etc*) debout, sur bout; **to stand a box (up) on e.,** dresser une boîte debout; **his hair was standing on e.,** ses cheveux se dressaient sur sa tête *ou* se hérissaient; **five hours on e.,** cinq heures de suite *ou* d'affilée; **e. on,** bout à bout; *Aut* **big e.,** tête *f* de bielle; **small e.,** pied *m* de bielle; *Rail* **the e. carriage,** le wagon de queue; *Tech* **e. piece,** embout *m*;

(b) (*limit*) limite *f*, borne *f*; **to the ends of the earth,** jusqu'au bout du monde; **from one e. of the country to the other,** d'un bout à l'autre du pays;

(c) (*of time, quantity etc*) bout *m*, fin *f* (*du mois*); fin (*de travail*); issue *f* (*d'une réunion*); terme *m* (*d'un procès etc*); **the third from the e.,** le troisième avant la fin; **we shall never hear the e. of it,** on n'entendra jamais la fin; **and that's the e. of it!,** et voilà tout!; **there's no e. to it,** cela n'en finit pas; *Sl* **no e. of ...,** infiniment de ...; **it'll do you no e. of good,** ça te fera énormément de bien; **it helped me no e.,** ça m'a énormément aidé; *F* **you're the e.!,** tu es impossible!; **to make an e. of, to put an e. to,** en finir avec (*qch*); mettre fin à (*un abus etc*); supprimer (*la concurrence*); **to draw to an e.,** tirer *ou* toucher à sa fin; **to come to an e.,** prendre fin; (*of meeting etc*) se clore; **to bring sth to an e.,** mettre fin à qch; **the war was at an e.,** la guerre était terminée; **to be at the e. of one's resources,** être au bout de ses ressources; **I am at the e. of my patience,** je suis à bout de patience; **at the e. of,** à la fin de (*le mois, l'hiver*); à l'expiration de (*cette période*); au bout de (*six mois*); **at the e. of the day,** à la fin de la journée; *Fig* en fin de compte, au bout du compte; **in the e.,** à la longue, à la fin; **you'll get used to it in the e.,** tu t'y habitueras à la longue; **she gave me the money back in the e.,** elle m'a rendu l'argent à la fin, elle a fini par me rendre l'argent; **he always pays me back in the e.,** il finit toujours par me rendre ce qu'il me doit; **e. of the world,** fin du monde; **until the e. of time,** jusqu'à la fin des temps; *Rel* **world without e.,** pour les siècles des siècles; **it's not the e. of the world,** ce n'est pas la fin du monde; **the e. of one's life,** la fin *ou* le terme de la vie; **to come to a bad e.,** mal finir; **to meet one's e.,** trouver la mort; **e. product,** produit fini; *Fig* (*consequence*) suite *f*, résultat *m*; **e. result,** résultat final; *Comptr* **e. user,** utilisateur final;

(d) (*aim, purpose*) fin *f*, but *m*, dessein *m*; **to attain** *or* **achieve one's end(s),** en arriver *ou* parvenir à ses fins, atteindre son but; **to this e.,** dans cette intention; **with this e. in view,** avec cet objectif en vue; *Prov* **the e. justifies the means,** la fin justifie les moyens.

end² **1** *vt* **(a)** finir, terminer, achever (*un ouvrage etc*); conclure (*un discours*); clore (*une séance*); **to e. one's days peacefully,** terminer ses jours en paix; **to e. a speech with a quotation,** terminer un discours avec une citation; *F* **to e. it all,** en finir; **the war to e. all wars,** la dernière des dernières (guerres), la der des ders; **it's the x to e. all xs,** ce x, c'est le tout dernier cri;

(b) (*fit an end on*) embouter (*une canne etc*).

2 *vi* finir, se terminer (**at, in,** dans, en); (*of word*) se terminer (**in,** en); (*of subscription*) expirer; **the path ends at the lakeside,** le chemin aboutit au bord du lac; **to e. in a point,** (*of stick*) se terminer en pointe; **to e. happily,** (*of story*) avoir une fin heureuse, bien se terminer; **it ended in a fight,** ça a fini en bagarre, ça s'est terminé par une bagarre; **this will e. in tears!,** ça va se finir par des larmes; **his extravagance will e. by ruining him,** son extravagance aboutira à sa ruine; **the film ends with her saying ...,** le film se termine sur elle disant ...; **the story ends on a happy note,** l'histoire se termine sur une note gaie; **how will it all e.?,** (*what is the world coming to?*) comment tout cela va-t-il se terminer?; *Prov* **all's well that ends well,** tout est bien qui finit bien; **I must e. by thanking Mr Brown,** pour conclure je dois remercier M. Brown; **let us e. with a song,** finissons par une chanson; **a word ending in 's',** un mot qui se termine par 's'.

►**end up** *vi* (*finish*) finir; **no one thought she'd e. up in prison,** personne ne pensait qu'elle finirait en prison; **we ended up going to see a movie,** en fin de compte nous sommes allés voir un film; **he ended up dead,** il a fini par se faire tuer.

end-all ['endɔːl] *n see* **BE-ALL**.

endanger [ɪn'deɪndʒər] *vt* mettre (*qn, qch*) en danger; exposer, risquer (*sa vie etc*); compromettre (*des intérêts*).

endangered [ɪn'deɪndʒəd] *adj* en danger, en péril, menacé; **e. species,** espèce menacée.

endear [ɪn'dɪər] *vt* rendre (*qn, qch*) cher (**to,** à); **he has**

endeared himself to all, il s'est fait universellement aimer; **her outspokenness did not e. her to the régime,** sa franchise ne l'a pas rendue populaire auprès du régime.
endearing [ɪn'dɪərɪŋ] *adj* qui inspire l'affection; (*qualité*) qui rend qn sympathique; (*mot*) tendre.
endearment [ɪn'dɪəmənt] *n* **term of e.,** expression *f* de tendresse; **endearments,** mots *mpl* tendres.
endeavour[1] [ɪn'devər] *n* effort *m*, tentative *f*; **to use** *or* **make every e. to ...,** faire tout son possible *ou* tous les efforts possibles pour ...; **in an e. to persuade them,** dans une tentative pour les persuader.
endeavour[2] *vt* **to e. to do sth,** s'efforcer *ou* tenter *ou* essayer de faire qch, chercher à faire qch.
endemic [en'demɪk] **1** *adj Bot Med & Fig* endémique. **2** *n Med* endémie *f*.
endemically [en'demɪklɪ] *adv* endémiquement.
endgame ['endgeɪm] *n Chess* fin *f* de partie.
ending ['endɪŋ] *n* **(a)** terminaison *f*, achèvement *m*; **(b)** (*of a story etc*) fin *f*, conclusion *f*; **happy e.,** dénouement heureux; **a surprise e.,** une fin surprenante; **to come to an abrupt e.,** terminer abruptement; **(c)** *Gram* (*of a word*) désinence *f*, terminaison *f*; **case e.,** flexion casuelle.
endive ['endaɪv] *n* (*plant*) **(a) (curled) e.,** chicorée frisée; **(b)** *Am* endive *f*.
endless ['endlɪs] *adj* **(a)** (*in space*) sans bornes, infini; (*voyage etc*) sans fin, interminable; (*câble, vis*) sans fin; **e. space,** l'infini *m*; **(b)** (*in time*) sans fin; (*discussion*) à n'en plus finir, interminable; (*pain*) continuel, incessant; (*chatter*) intarissable; **it's an e. task, it's e.,** cela n'en finit pas; **(c)** (*in number*) innombrable; **to take e. pains to do** *or* **over sth,** se donner une peine infinie à faire qch; **the possibilities are e., there are e. possibilities,** les possibilités sont innombrables.
endlessly ['endlɪslɪ] *adv* sans fin, sans cesse; éternellement.
endocardium [endəʊ'kɑːdɪəm] *n Anat* endocarde *m*.
endocarp ['endəʊkɑːp] *n* endocarpe *m*.
endocrine ['endəʊkraɪn] *Physiol* **1** *adj* (*glande*) endocrine. **2** *n* (glande *f*) endocrine *f*.
endocrinology [endəʊkraɪ'nɒlədʒɪ] *n Med* endocrinologie *f*.
endorse [ɪn'dɔːs] *vt* **(a)** *Admin Fin etc* endosser (*un document, un chèque*); viser (*un passeport*); avaliser (*un effet*); **(b)** *Br Admin* **to e. a driving licence,** = décompter des points sur un permis de conduire; **(c)** (*approve*) appuyer, sanctionner (*une opinion, une action*); souscrire à (*une décision, une opinion*); *Jur* approuver (*un appel*); **I e. all you have done,** j'approuve tout ce que vous avez fait; *esp Am Com* **our products are endorsed by leading athletes,** nos produits sont signés par les plus grands athlètes.
endorsement [ɪn'dɔːsmənt] *n* **(a)** *Admin Fin etc* endossement *m*, endos *m* (*d'un chèque*); aval *m* (*d'un effet*); (*on passport*) mention spéciale; (*in insurance*) avenant *m*; **(b)** *Br Admin* contravention inscrite sur le permis de conduire; **(c)** (*approval*) approbation *f* (*d'une action*); adhésion *f* (*à une opinion*).
endorser [ɪn'dɔːsər] *n Fin* endosseur *m*.
endoscope ['endəʊskəʊp] *n Med* endoscope *m*.
endosperm ['endəʊspɜːm] *n Bot* endosperme *m*.
endow [ɪn'daʊ] *vt* **(a)** doter; **endowed with great talents,** doué de grands talents; **woman endowed with great beauty,** femme dotée d'une grande beauté; *F* **to be well endowed,** (*of man, woman*) avoir tout ce qu'il faut; **(b)** *Fin* doter (*qn, une société*) **(with,** de); assurer un revenu à (*sa fille etc*); fonder (*un lit dans un hôpital, une chaire dans une université etc*).
endowment [ɪn'daʊmənt] *n* **(a)** *Fin* dotation *f* (*l'action ou le fonds*); fondation *f* (*léguée à un hospice*); (*in insurance*) **(pure) e. assurance** *or* **policy,** assurance *f* en cas de vie, assurance à capital différé; **(ordinary) e. assurance,** assurance mixte; **e. mortgage,** hypothèque associée à une assurance-vie; **(b)** (*talent*) don *m* (naturel), talent *m*.
endpaper ['endpeɪpər] *n* page *f* de garde.
endue [ɪn'djuː] *vt Lit* revêtir (**with,** de).
endurable [ɪn'djuːərəb(ə)l] *adj* supportable.
endurance [ɪn'djuːrəns] *n* résistance *f*; **physical e.,** endurance *f* (physique); **beyond e.,** insupportable, intolérable; **e. test,** *MecE* essai *m* de durée; *Sp* épreuve *f* d'endurance.
endure [ɪn'djuːər] **1** *vt* supporter, endurer, souffrir avec patience (*des insultes etc*); soutenir (*des reproches etc*); *Prov* **what can't be cured must be endured,** où il n'y a pas de remède il faut se résigner. **2** *vi* durer, rester; **work that will e.,** ouvrage *m* qui restera *ou* durera.
enduring [ɪn'djuːərɪŋ] *adj* durable, qui dure, permanent; (*peace*) stable; (*evil*) persistant, qui persiste.
endways ['endweɪz] **, endwise** ['endwaɪz] *adv* **(a)** (*end up*) de chant, debout; **e. on,** avec le bout en avant; **(b)** (*end to end*) bout à bout; **(c)** (*lengthways*) longitudinalement.
enema ['enəmə] *n Med* lavement *m*; **they gave him an e.,** ils lui ont administré un lavement.
enemy ['enəmɪ] **1** *n* **(a)** ennemi, -e; **man without an e.,** homme sans ennemis; **to be one's own (worst) e.,** se desservir soi-même; **(b)** *Mil etc* (*no pl*) **the e.,** l'ennemi *m*, l'adversaire *m*. **2** *adj* (*pays, navire etc*) ennemi; **e. alien,** ressortissant, -ante d'un pays ennemi.
enemy-occupied ['enəmɪ'ɒkjʊpaɪd] *adj Mil* **e.-o. territory,** territoire occupé par l'ennemi.
energetic [enə'dʒetɪk] *adj* (*person, action*) énergique; **I'm not feeling very e.,** je ne me sens pas beaucoup d'énergie.
energetically [enə'dʒetɪklɪ] *adv* énergiquement, avec énergie; (*to deny, reply etc*) énergiquement.
energetics [enə'dʒetɪks] *npl* (*usu with sing verb*) énergétique *f*.
energize ['enədʒaɪz] *vt* **(a)** donner de l'énergie à (*qn*); stimuler (*qn*); **(b)** *El* alimenter; amorcer (*une dynamo*); aimanter (*l'âme d'une bobine*).
energy ['enədʒɪ] *n* **(a)** (*vitality*) énergie *f*, vigueur *f* ; **to have no e.,** ne pas avoir d'énergie; **I don't have the e.,** (*to do it, go out etc*) l'énergie me manque; **man of e.,** homme *m* énergique; **to devote** *or* **apply all one's energies to a task,** consacrer *ou* apporter *ou* appliquer tous ses efforts *ou* toute son énergie à une tâche; **(b)** *Phys* énergie *f*, travail *m*; **e. consumed,** puissance absorbée; **kinetic e.,** énergie cinétique; **to store up e.,** emmagasiner du travail; **atomic e.,** énergie atomique; *Electron* **e. band,** bande *f* d'énergie; *Pol* **E. Minister,** *Br* **E. Secretary,** ministre *m* de l'Énergie; **the e. crisis,** la crise de l'énergie.
energy-saving ['enədʒɪseɪvɪŋ] *adj* (*device*) d'économie d'énergie, pour économiser l'énergie, qui économise l'énergie.
enervate ['enəveɪt] *vt* affaiblir (*le corps, la volonté*).
enervating ['enəveɪtɪŋ] *adj* (*climate*) débilitant.
enervation [enə'veɪʃən] *n* **(a)** (*action*) affaiblissement *m*; **(b)** (*result*) mollesse *f*.
enfeeble [ɪn'fiːb(ə)l] *vt* (*of pain, age*) affaiblir.
enfilade[1] ['enfɪleɪd] *n Mil* tir *m* d'enfilade.
enfilade[2] *vt Mil* enfiler, prendre en enfilade.
enfold [ɪn'fəʊld] *vt* envelopper (**sth in sth,** qch dans qch); **to e. s.o. in one's arms,** étreindre qn, embrasser qn.
enforce [ɪn'fɔːs] *vt* **(a)** (*put into effect*) mettre en vigueur (*une loi etc*); faire valoir (*ses droits*); faire respecter, faire obéir (*la loi*); appliquer (*la loi*); imposer, faire observer (*un règlement*); **such a law would be impossible to e.,** une telle loi serait impossible à appliquer; **to e. obedience,** se faire obéir; **(b)** *Fml* (*reinforce*) donner de la force à, faire valoir (*un argument*); appuyer (*une demande*).
enforceable [ɪn'fɔːsəb(ə)l] *adj* (*contrat*) exécutoire.
enforced [ɪn'fɔːst] *adj* (*silence etc*) forcé.
enforcement [ɪn'fɔːsmənt] *n Jur* exécution *f*, mise *f* en vigueur, application *f* (*d'une loi*); **law e. officers,** fonctionnaires chargés de l'application de la loi.
enfranchise [ɪn'fræntʃaɪz] *vt* **(a)** *Pol* admettre (*un citoyen*) au suffrage, accorder le droit de vote à (*qn*); **(b)** affranchir (*un esclave*).
enfranchisement [ɪn'fræntʃɪzmənt] *n* **(a)** *Pol* admission *f* (*d'un citoyen*) au suffrage; **(b)** affranchissement *m* (*d'un esclave*).
engage [ɪn'geɪdʒ] **1** *vt* **(a)** (*employ, hire*) engager (*un domestique etc*); embaucher (*des ouvriers*); *Nau* recruter (*des hommes*); louer (*un taxi*);
(b) (*occupy*) occuper (*qn*); fixer (*l'attention*); attirer, gagner (*l'affection de qn*); **to e. s.o. in conversation,** entrer en conversation avec qn, engager la conversation avec qn; **I can't come tonight as I am (otherwise) engaged,** je ne peux pas venir ce soir parce que je suis pris; **to be engaged in writing a novel,** être occupé à écrire un roman;
(c) *Mil* **to e. the enemy,** attaquer l'ennemi; **to e. an enemy aircraft,** ouvrir le feu sur un appareil ennemi;
(d) *MecE* mettre en prise (*un engrenage, une vitesse*); **to e. first (gear),** mettre en première (vitesse); **to e. the clutch,** embrayer;
(e) *Fml* (*pledge*) engager (*sa parole, son honneur*); **to e. oneself to do sth,** s'engager à faire qch.
2 *vi* **(a)** (*take part*) **to e. in,** s'adonner à (*des sports*); **to e. in conversation,** commencer une conversation;
(b) *Mil* attaquer; **we engaged at 4 o'clock,** nous avons attaqué à 4 heures; **to e. in an action,** se lancer dans une action;
(c) *MecE* (*of cog wheel*) (s')engrener, (s')engager (**with,**

avec); (*of clutch*) s'embrayer;

(d) *Fml* (*pledge*) s'engager.

engaged [ɪn'geɪdʒd] *adj* **(a) to be e. (to be married),** être fiancé(e); **they're e.,** ils sont fiancés; **to become** *or* **get e.,** se fiancer; **the e. couple,** les fiancés; **(b)** (*busy*) **heavily e.,** très occupé; **(c)** *Br Tel* **the number is e.,** la ligne est occupée; **to get the e. tone,** entendre le signal de ligne occupée; **(d)** (*taken*) occupé; *Fml* **this seat is e.,** cette place est retenue *ou* occupée *ou* prise; **'e'.,** (*on lavatory*) occupé; **(e)** *MecE* (*gear wheels*) en prise.

engagement [ɪn'geɪdʒmənt] *n* **(a)** (*to be married*) fiançailles *fpl*; **e. ring,** anneau *m ou* bague *f* de fiançailles; **(b)** (*meeting etc*) rendez-vous *m*; **owing to a previous e.,** à cause d'une promesse antérieure; **public e.,** engagement *m* à paraître en public; **she has many social engagements,** elle est très demandée; **to have an e.,** être pris, être occupé; **e. book,** agenda *m*; **(c)** (*obligation*) engagement *m*, promesse *f*, obligation *f*; *Com* **to carry out** *or* **meet one's engagements,** faire face à ses engagements, remplir ses engagements; **(d)** *Mil* (*action*) combat *m*, engagement *m*; (*of a unit*) intervention *f*; **(e)** *MecE* mise *f* en prise; (*of clutch*) embrayage *m*; prise *f* (*d'un pignon avec une roue etc*); **(f)** (*employment*) engagement *m* (*de domestiques*); recrutement *m*.

engaging [ɪn'geɪdʒɪŋ] *adj* (*sourire, ton*) engageant, attrayant, attirant; (*ton*) liant; **to have an e. manner,** être liant.

engagingly [ɪn'geɪdʒɪŋlɪ] *adv* d'une manière engageante; (*sourire*) gentiment.

engender [ɪn'dʒendər] *vt* faire naître, produire (*un effet*); engendrer (*une maladie, un sentiment*).

engine ['endʒɪn] *n* **(a)** *MecE etc* moteur *m*; (*for ship*) machine *f*; **car e.,** moteur de voiture; **petrol** *or US* **gas e.,** moteur à essence; **steam e.,** machine à vapeur; **internal combustion e.,** moteur à combustion interne *ou* à explosion; **jet e.,** moteur à réaction; **traction e.,** locomobile *f*, tracteur *m*; **e. house,** bâtiment *m* des machines *ou* des moteurs; dépôt *m* (*de pompes à incendie etc*); **e. room,** salle *f* des machines; *Nau* chambre *f* des machines; **e. trouble,** problème *m* de moteur; **(b)** *esp Br Rail* **(railway) e.,** locomotive *f*; **e. driver,** conducteur *m*, mécanicien *m* (*de locomotive*); **e. shed,** garage *m ou* dépôt *m ou* remise *f* des locomotives; **circular e. shed,** rotonde *f*; **(c)** (*machine, device*) machine *f*, appareil *m*; **fire e.,** pompe *f* à incendie.

engineer[1] [endʒɪ'nɪər] *n* **(a)** ingénieur *m*; **civil e.,** ingénieur civil; **marine e.,** ingénieur du génie maritime; **mechanical/electrical e.,** ingénieur mécanicien/électricien; **mining e.,** ingénieur des mines; **consulting e.,** ingénieur conseil; **production e.,** ingénieur (chargé) de la production;

(b) *Nau* ingénieur *m*, mécanicien *m*; **chief e.,** chef mécanicien; *Nau* **e. officer,** ingénieur mécanicien; **second e.,** officier mécanicien en second;

(c) *Av* **flight e.,** (*on military aircraft*) mécanicien navigant; (*on civil aircraft*) mécanicien de bord; **aircraft e.,** mécanicien de piste;

(d) *Mil* soldat *m* du génie, sapeur *m*; **the engineers,** le génie, l'arme *f* du génie; **the Royal Engineers,** *US* **the Corps of Engineers,** = le Génie; **electrical/mechanical e.,** sapeur électricien/mécanicien;

(e) *Am Rail* conducteur *m*, mécanicien *m* (*de locomotive*);

(f) *Fig* (*instigator*) l'âme *f*, l'instigateur *m* (*d'un projet, d'un complot*).

engineer[2] *vt* **(a)** *usu Pej* (*cause, bring about*) machiner (*un coup*); manigancer (*une affaire*); *Sp* amener (*un but*); **she engineered his escape,** elle a organisé son évasion; **(b)** (*build*) construire (en qualité d'ingénieur) (*des ponts, des routes*).

engineering [endʒɪ'nɪərɪŋ] *n* **(a)** technique *f ou* science *f* de l'ingénieur, ingénierie *f*; **a degree in e.,** une licence en ingénierie; **the pipeline was a tremendous feat of e.,** le pipeline était une remarquable prouesse technique; **civil e.,** génie civil; **marine e.,** génie maritime; **electrical e.,** électrotechnique *f*; **agricultural e.,** génie agricole *ou* rural; **mechanical e.,** mécanique *f*; **precision e.,** mécanique de précision; **light e.,** petite mécanique; **production e.,** technique de la production; **electrical e. industry,** industrie *f* de l'équipement électrique; **industrial e.,** organisation industrielle; **e. department,** service *m* technique; **e. and design department,** bureau *m* d'études; **e. consultant,** ingénieur *m* conseil; **e. works,** atelier *m* de constructions mécaniques; **(b)** *usu Pej* machinations *fpl*, manœuvres *fpl*.

engineman, *pl* **-men** ['endʒɪnmæn, -men] *n Am Rail* mécanicien *m*.

engine-room ['endʒɪnruːm] *adj* **e.-r. telegraph,** chadburn *m*.

England ['ɪŋglənd] *n* l'Angleterre *f*; **in E.,** en Angleterre; **to go to E.,** aller en Angleterre; *Sp* **the E. team,** l'équipe d'Angleterre; **an E. player,** un joueur de l'équipe d'Angleterre.

English ['ɪŋglɪʃ] **1** *adj* anglais; **E. born** *or* **by birth,** de naissance anglaise; *Culin* **E. breakfast,** petit déjeuner à l'anglaise; **E. history,** histoire *f* d'Angleterre; **the E. Channel,** la Manche; *Archit* **early E. (style),** premier style gothique; *Am* **E. muffin,** muffin *m*; *Fig* **an E. rose,** = femme ou jeune fille à la beauté typiquement anglaise.

2 *n* **(a) the E.,** (*used as pl*) les Anglais *mpl*;

(b) *Ling* anglais *m*, la langue anglaise; **her E. is excellent,** son anglais est excellent; **E. E., British E.,** l'anglais d'Angleterre; **American/Australian E.,** l'anglais américain/australien; **the King's** *or* **Queen's E.,** l'anglais correct; **E. speaking,** anglophone, de langue anglaise; **to study E.,** étudier l'anglais; **to speak E.,** parler anglais; **in E.,** en anglais; **E. teacher,** professeur d'anglais; **in plain E.,** en bon anglais; **let me tell you in plain E. that ...,** je vais vous dire clairement que ... .

Englishman, *pl* **-men** ['ɪŋglɪʃmən] *n* Anglais *m*; *Prov* **an E.'s home is his castle,** tout homme est maître chez lui.

Englishwoman, *pl* **-women** ['ɪŋglɪʃwʊmən, -wɪmɪn] *n* Anglaise *f*.

engrave [ɪn'greɪv] *vt* graver; **to e. on wood,** graver sur bois; **engraved on the memory,** gravé dans la mémoire.

engraver [ɪn'greɪvər] *n* (*person*) graveur *m*.

engraving [ɪn'greɪvɪŋ] *n* (*process, print*) gravure *f*; (*print*) estampe *f*; **line e.,** gravure au burin.

engross [ɪn'grəʊs] *vt* **(a)** absorber, occuper (*qn*); **engrossed in her reading,** toute à sa lecture; **to become engrossed in sth,** s'abstraire *ou* s'absorber dans qch; **(b)** *Jur* (*draw up*) rédiger (*un document*); (*copy*) grossoyer (*un document*).

engrossing [ɪn'grəʊsɪŋ] *adj* (*study, article etc*) absorbant.

engrossment [ɪn'grəʊsmənt] *n* **(a)** (*absorption*) absorption *f* (*de l'attention*) (**in,** dans); **(b)** *Jur* rédaction *f* de la grosse.

engulf [ɪn'gʌlf] *vt* engloutir, engouffrer; **to be engulfed by the waves,** sombrer dans les flots.

enhance [ɪn'hɑːns, -'hæns] *vt* rehausser (*le mérite de qch*); accroître (*le plaisir*); mettre en valeur (*la beauté de qn*); agrandir (*la réputation*); **our heating system can e. the quality of your life,** notre système de chauffage peut améliorer la qualité de votre vie.

enhancement [ɪn'hɑːnsmənt, -'hæns-] *n* renchérissement *m*, rehaussement *m* (*de prix*); augmentation *f* (*de plaisir etc*).

enharmonic [enhɑː'mɒnɪk] *adj* enharmonique.

enigma [ɪ'nɪgmə] *n* énigme *f*; (*person*) personne énigmatique *ou* mystérieuse.

enigmatic [enɪg'mætɪk] *adj* énigmatique, mystérieux.

enigmatically [enɪg'mætɪklɪ] *adv* énigmatiquement, mystérieusement.

enjoin [ɪn'dʒɔɪn] *vt* enjoindre (**sth on s.o.,** qch à qn); **to e. s.o. to do sth,** enjoindre à qn de faire qch.

enjoy [ɪn'dʒɔɪ] **1** *vt* **(a)** (*take pleasure from*) aimer, prendre plaisir à (*qch*); savourer (*une pipe, un repas*); goûter (*la musique etc*); **to e. the fine weather,** jouir du beau temps; **to e. oneself,** s'amuser, se divertir; **e. yourself!,** amusez-vous bien!; **to e. doing sth,** aimer *ou* trouver du plaisir à faire qch; **I e. cooking,** j'aime (bien) faire la cuisine; **I don't e. being woken up in the middle of the night,** je n'aime pas qu'on me réveille en plein milieu de la nuit; **if you're tense you won't e. the party,** si tu es tendu, tu ne t'amuseras pas à la soirée; **(b)** (*benefit from*) jouir de, posséder (*une fortune, la confiance de qn*); **to e. good health,** jouir d'une bonne santé; *Hum* **to e. bad health,** se complaire dans ses maux. **2** *vi Am* **e.!,** bon appétit!

enjoyable [ɪn'dʒɔɪəb(ə)l] *adj* (*séjour, excursion*) agréable; **we had a most e. evening,** nous avons passé une soirée des plus agréables.

enjoyably [ɪn'dʒɔɪəblɪ] *adv* agréablement.

enjoyment [ɪn'dʒɔɪmənt] *n* **(a)** (*pleasure*) plaisir *m*; **to get e. out of sth,** retirer du plaisir de qch; **the noise spoiled our e. of the music,** le bruit nous a empêchés de profiter pleinement de la musique; **(b)** (*benefit*) jouissance *f* (*d'un droit etc*).

enlarge [ɪn'lɑːdʒ] **1** *vt* **(a)** (*increase in size*) agrandir; étendre (*une propriété*); accroître, augmenter (*sa fortune*); élargir (*un trou*); *Med* hypertrophier (*le cœur, le foie*); *Phot* agrandir (*un cliché etc*); **to have** *or* **get a photograph**

enlarged, faire agrandir une photo; **enlarged edition,** (*of reference book*) édition augmentée; *Med* **enlarged tonsils,** amygdales hypertrophiées; **(b)** (*develop*) développer (*une idée*). **2** *vi* **(a)** (*increase in size*) s'agrandir, s'étendre, s'élargir; **(b)** (*speak at greater length*) **to e. on,** s'étendre sur, discourir longuement sur (*un sujet, l'importance de qch*).

enlargement [ɪn'lɑːdʒmənt] *n* **(a)** (*increase*) agrandissement *m*; extension *f* (*d'une propriété*); accroissement *m* (*d'une fortune*); élargissement *m* (*d'un trou*); augmentation *f*; **(b)** *Phot* agrandissement *m*; **(c)** *Med* hypertrophie *f* (*du cœur, de la rate*).

enlarger [ɪn'lɑːdʒər] *n Phot* agrandisseur *m*.

enlighten [ɪn'laɪt(ə)n] *vt* éclairer; **can you e. me?,** est-ce que tu peux m'éclairer?; **to e. s.o. on a subject** *or* **as to sth,** éclairer qn sur un sujet.

enlightened [ɪn'laɪt(ə)nd] *adj* (*person*) éclairé; **nowadays teachers are more e.,** de nos jours les enseignants sont plus éclairés *ou* mieux informés; **e. criticism,** critique éclairée; **e. despot,** despote éclairé.

enlightenment [ɪn'laɪtənmənt] *n* **(a)** éclaircissement *m* **(on,** sur); **for your e.,** pour votre édification; **(b)** *Hist* **the (age of) E.,** le siècle des lumières.

enlist [ɪn'lɪst] **1** *vt* recruter (*des partisans*); s'assurer (*le concours de qn*); *Mil* enrôler, engager (*un soldat*); **to e. s.o.'s support for a cause,** rallier qn à une cause; **she enlisted the help of two bystanders,** elle a obtenu de l'aide de la part de deux spectateurs. **2** *vi Mil* (*of soldier*) s'engager.

enlisted [ɪn'lɪstɪd] *adj* enrôlé, engagé, appelé (*sous les drapeaux*); *US Mil* **e. man,** simple soldat; **e. men,** les hommes de troupe et les gradés.

enlistment [ɪn'lɪstmənt] *n Mil* engagement *m*.

enliven [ɪn'laɪv(ə)n] *vt* animer (*qn, qch*); égayer (*une fête*); **to e. business,** stimuler les affaires.

en masse ['ɒn'mæs] *adv* en masse, tous ensemble.

enmesh [ɪn'meʃ] *vt* prendre (*qn*) dans un piège; (*in net*) prendre au filet; *Fig* **to be enmeshed in a situation,** être pris au piège dans une situation.

enmity ['enmɪtɪ] *n* inimitié *f*, haine *f*, hostilité *f*.

ennoble [ɪ'nəʊb(ə)l] *vt* **(a)** (*raise to the nobility*) anoblir (*un roturier*); **(b)** (*make nobler*) ennoblir (*qn, le caractère*).

ennoblement [ɪ'nəʊb(ə)lmənt] *n* **(a)** (*of commoner*) anoblissement *m*; **(b)** (*of character etc*) ennoblissement *m*.

enormity [ɪ'nɔːmɪtɪ] *n* énormité *f* (*d'un crime etc*); **enormities,** énormités, atrocités *fpl*.

enormous [ɪ'nɔːməs] *adj* (*building, hands, sum, difference, improvement*) énorme; (*gratitude, patience, whisky*) immense; (*power, intelligence*) colossal, -aux; (*loss*) gigantesque; (*idiot, stupidity*) monumental, -aux.

enormously [ɪ'nɔːməslɪ] *adv* énormément; **I was e. grateful,** j'étais infiniment reconnaissant.

enormousness [ɪ'nɔːməsnɪs] *n* grandeur démesurée.

enough [ɪ'nʌf] **1** *adj & n* assez; **(not) e. money,** (pas) assez d'argent; **will this be e.?,** est-ce que ça suffira?; *F* **I've had e. of it** *or* **them** *etc*, j'en ai assez; **I've had e. to drink,** j'ai assez bu; **that's e. for me,** cela me suffit; **that's e.,** (*to eat, drink, of your behaviour*) c'est assez, ça suffit; (*of your behaviour*) en voilà assez!; **more than e.,** plus qu'il n'en faut, plus que suffisant; **there was more than e.,** il y en avait de reste; **have you e. to pay the bill?,** avez-vous de quoi payer?; **wages that are not e. to live on,** salaire qui ne suffit pas pour vivre; **he has e. to live on,** il a de quoi vivre; **e. said!,** assez parlé!; **e. of this nonsense!,** assez de ces bêtises!; **one word was e. to prove that ...,** il a suffi d'un mot pour prouver que ...; **it was e. to drive you crazy,** c'était à vous rendre fou; *Prov* **e. is as good as a feast,** assez vaut (un) festin.

2 *adv* **good e.,** assez bon; **fair e.!,** ça va!, d'accord!; **it's a good e. reason,** c'est une raison comme une autre; **she is not strong e.,** elle n'est pas assez forte; **to be near e. to see,** être assez près pour voir; **I haven't been here long e. to say,** cela ne fait pas assez longtemps que je suis ici pour le savoir; (*intensive*) **you know well e. what I mean,** vous savez très bien ce que je veux dire; **curiously** *or* **oddly e., nobody knew anything about it,** chose curieuse, personne n'en savait rien; **well e.,** assez bien, pas mal; **the house is comfortable e.,** la maison est assez confortable.

en passant [ɒnpæ'sɒn] *adv* en passant.

enquire [ɪŋ'kwaɪər] *vt & vi* = **INQUIRE**.

enquiry [ɪn'kwaɪ(ə)rɪ] *n* = **INQUIRY**.

enrage [ɪn'reɪdʒ] *vt* rendre furieux, exaspérer (*qn*).

enrapture [ɪn'ræptʃər] *vt* ravir, enchanter (*un auditoire etc*).

enraptured [ɪn'ræptʃəd] *adj* ravi, enchanté (d'admiration).

enrich [ɪn'rɪtʃ] *vt* enrichir (*qn, une langue etc*); fertiliser, amender (*la terre*); *Aut* **to e. the mixture,** enrichir le mélange; **this experience enriched my life,** cette expérience a beaucoup apporté à ma vie.

enriched [ɪn'rɪtʃd] *adj* **e. with gold,** rehaussé d'or; **e. with vitamin C,** enrichi à la vitamine C; *Nucl Phys* **e. uranium,** uranium enrichi.

enrichment [ɪn'rɪtʃmənt] *n* enrichissement *m*.

enrol, *US* **enroll** [ɪn'rəʊl] *v* (*Br* **enrols**, *US* **enrolls**, *Br & US* **enrolled, enrolling**) **1** *vt Mil* enrôler, encadrer (*des recrues*); embaucher (*des ouvriers*); immatriculer (*des étudiants*); **to e. oneself,** s'enrôler, s'engager **(in the army,** dans l'armée); s'inscrire **(in a society,** à une société). **2** *vi* s'enrôler, s'engager **(in the army,** dans l'armée); s'inscrire **(in a society,** dans une société); **to e. for a course of lectures,** s'inscrire pour une série de conférences.

enrolment, *US* **enrollment** [ɪn'rəʊlmənt] *n* enrôlement *m* (*de soldats etc*); embauche *f* (*d'ouvriers etc*); immatriculation *f* (*d'étudiants*).

ensconce [ɪn'skɒns] *vt* **to e. oneself,** se blottir, se nicher **(in a corner,** dans un coin); se camper **(in an armchair,** dans un fauteuil); **she was ensconced in front of the television,** elle était campée devant la télévision.

ensemble [ɒn'sɒnb(ə)l] *n* (*clothing etc*) *& Mus* ensemble *m*.

enshrine [ɪn'ʃraɪn] *vt* enchâsser **(in,** dans); **this right is enshrined in the constitution,** ce droit fait partie intégrante de la constitution.

ensign ['ensaɪn] *n* **(a)** (*flag*) drapeau *m*; *Nau* pavillon national; *Br Nau* **white e.,** = pavillon de la Marine anglaise et du Royal Yacht Squadron; *Br Nau* **red e.,** = pavillon marchand; **(b)** *US Nau* (*officer*) enseigne *m* (*de vaisseau de deuxième classe*).

ensilage [en'sɪlɪdʒ] *n Agr* ensilage *m*, silotage *m*.

enslave [ɪn'sleɪv] *vt* réduire à l'esclavage, asservir, rendre (*qn*) esclave.

enslavement [ɪn'sleɪvmənt] *n* réduction *f* (*d'une nation etc*) à l'esclavage, asservissement *m*.

ensnare [ɪn'sneər] *vt* prendre (*qn*) au piège; *Pej* (*of woman*) attraper, séduire (*un homme*).

ensue [ɪn'sjuː] *vi* s'ensuivre; **a long silence ensued,** il se fit un long silence.

ensuing [ɪn'sjuːɪŋ] *adj* (*année*) qui suit; (*événement*) subséquent; **in the e. years,** au cours des années qui suivirent.

en suite ['ɒn'swiːt] **1** *n* = salle de bain qui communique avec une chambre. **2** *adv* **with a bathroom en s.,** (*of bedroom*) avec salle de bain communiquante. **3** *adj* (*bathroom*) communiquant.

ensure [ɪn'ʃʊər] *vt* assurer (*le succès*); réaliser (*la guérison*); **I have taken steps to e. that ...,** j'ai pris des mesures pour que ... + *sub*.

ENT [iːen'tiː] *adj Med* (*abbr* **ear, nose and throat**) O.R.L. *f*.

entail[1] ['enteɪl] *n* **(a)** *Jur* (*act*) substitution *f*; **(b)** (*property*) bien substitué; **(c)** (*inheritance*) héritage *m* inéluctable.

entail[2] [en'teɪl] *vt* **(a)** (*involve*) entraîner, occasionner (*des dépenses*); (*in logic*) entraîner; imposer (*beaucoup de travail*) **(on,** à); comporter (*des difficultés*); **(b)** *Jur* **to e. an estate,** substituer un bien **(on s.o.,** au profit de qn); **entailed estate,** bien substitué.

entangle [ɪn'tæŋg(ə)l] *vt* **(a)** (*catch*) empêtrer; **to get** *or* **become entangled in the seaweed,** s'empêtrer dans les algues; **(b)** (*mix up*) emmêler (*les cheveux, du fil*); enchevêtrer (*du fil de fer*); **to get entangled,** s'emmêler, s'embrouiller; **(c)** *Fig* embarrasser, empêtrer (*qn*); **to get entangled with s.o.,** (*emotionally*) avoir une liaison avec qn.

entanglement [ɪn'tæŋg(ə)lmənt] *n* **(a)** embrouillement *m*, enchevêtrement *m*; **barbed wire e.,** réseau(x) *m(pl)* de fil de fer barbelé; **(b)** *Fig* **emotional entanglements,** complications sentimentales; **an e. with a woman,** une liaison avec une femme.

entente [ɒn'tɒnt] *n* entente *f*; **e. cordiale,** entente cordiale.

enter ['entər] *v* **(-r-) 1** *vt* **(a)** (*go into*) entrer dans (*une maison, un pays*); **to e. a war,** entrer en guerre; **the bullet had entered his heart,** la balle lui avait pénétré dans le cœur; **it never entered my head that ...,** il ne m'est pas venu à l'esprit que ...;

(b) (*join*) **to e. the Army/Navy,** se faire soldat/marin; **to e. the Church,** entrer dans les ordres; **to e. a**

university/convent, entrer à une université/dans un couvent; **to e. s.o.'s service,** entrer au service de qn;

(c) (*begin*) **to e. one's sixtieth year,** entrer dans sa soixantième année;

(d) (*include, register*) **to e. a name on a list,** inscrire *ou* porter un nom sur une liste; **to e. a student at a university,** admettre un étudiant à une université; **to e. s.o. for a race,** inscrire qn au nombre des participants d'une course; **to e. a horse for a race,** engager un cheval dans une course; **to e. goods,** (*in customs*) déclarer des marchandises en douane; *Com* **to e. an item in the ledger,** inscrire *ou* porter un article au grand livre; **to e. sth to** *or* **against s.o.,** porter *ou* inscrire qch au compte de qn; *Jur etc* **to e. an action against s.o.,** intenter un procès à qn; **to e. a protest,** protester formellement;

(e) (*take part in*) participer à (*une course, une compétition*);

(f) *Comptr* entrer, introduire (*des données*).

2 *vi* **(a)** entrer (**through,** par); *Th* **e. Hamlet,** entre Hamlet;

(b) (*take part*) **to e. for a race,** se faire inscrire pour une course; **to e. for an examination,** se présenter à un examen; **are you going to e.?,** (*for competition, exam*) est-ce que tu vas te présenter?

►**enter into** *vipo* **(a)** (*begin*) entrer en (*service*); entrer dans (*les affaires*); entrer en (*relations*) (**with,** avec); engager (*des négociations*) (**with,** avec); conclure (*un engagement*) (**with,** avec); passer (*un contrat*) (**with,** avec); **to e. into partnership with s.o.,** s'associer avec qn; **to e. into holy matrimony,** se marier; **to e. into (a) conversation with s.o.,** engager une conversation avec qn; **(b)** (*have a part in*) entrer en ligne de compte, entrer en jeu; **factors that do not e. into the question,** facteurs qui ne rentrent pas en ligne de compte; **(c) to e. into the spirit of the game,** entrer dans le jeu.

►**enter on** *vipo* **(a)** (*commence*) débuter (dans), commencer, entamer; **she has entered on a new career,** elle a commencé une nouvelle carrière; **(b)** *Jur* entrer en possession de, prendre possession de (*un bien*).

►**enter up** *vtsep Com* **to e. up an item in the ledger,** inscrire *ou* porter un article au grand livre.

►**enter upon** *vipo* = **ENTER ON.**

enteric [en'terɪk] **1** *adj Med* entérique; **e. fever,** fièvre *f* typhoïde. **2** *n* fièvre *f* typhoïde.

entering ['entərɪŋ] *n* **(a)** entrée *f* (*dans un endroit*); **(b)** admission *f* (*d'un étudiant*); inscription *f* (*d'un nom etc*); *Com* inscription *f*, enregistrement *m*.

enteritis [entə'raɪtɪs] *n Med* entérite *f*.

enterprise ['entəpraɪz] *n* **(a)** (*undertaking*) entreprise *f* difficile; **(b)** *Com* **free e.,** la libre entreprise; **private e.,** l'entreprise privée; le secteur privé; **(c)** (*initiative*) **to show e.,** faire preuve d'un esprit entreprenant; **man of great e.,** homme entreprenant.

enterprising ['entəpraɪzɪŋ] *adj* entreprenant; (*imaginative*) plein d'imagination; (*bold*) aventureux.

enterprisingly ['entəpraɪzɪŋlɪ] *adv* d'une façon entreprenante; (*boldly*) hardiment.

entertain [entə'teɪn] **1** *vt* **(a)** (*amuse*) amuser, divertir (*qn*); **she entertained us with stories of her travels,** elle nous a divertis en nous racontant ses histoires de voyages; **(b)** (*invite to party etc*) régaler, fêter (*qn*); **to e. s.o. to dinner,** donner à dîner *ou* offrir un dîner à qn; **(c)** (*accept*) admettre, accueillir (*une proposition, une opinion*); faire un accueil favorable à (*une demande*); **(d)** (*harbour etc*) concevoir (*une idée, des doutes*); éprouver (*des craintes, des soupçons*); nourrir (*un espoir, une idée*); chérir (*une illusion*). **2** *vi* offrir une réception; **they e. a great deal,** ils reçoivent beaucoup (de monde).

entertainer [entə'teɪnər] *n* artiste *mf* de cabaret, fantaisiste *mf*; (*comedian*) comique *mf*.

entertaining [entə'teɪnɪŋ] **1** *adj* amusant, divertissant. **2** *n* **(a)** (*of guests*) réception *f*; **(b)** (*of suggestion, idea*) admission *f*.

entertainingly [entə'teɪnɪŋlɪ] *adv* (*parler*) d'une manière amusante *ou* divertissante.

entertainment [entə'teɪnmənt] *n* **(a)** (*amusement*) divertissement *m*, amusement *m*; **much to the e. of the crowd,** au grand amusement de la foule; **(b)** *Th etc* spectacle *m*, divertissement *m*; **the e. business,** l'industrie *f* du spectacle; **entertainments guide,** guide *m* des spectacles; **entertainments officer,** (*on ship*) = officier chargé des spectacles; **e. tax,** taxe *f* sur les spectacles; **(c)** (*hospitality*) hospitalité *f*; (*reception*) réception *f*, fête *f*; *Admin Com* **e. expenses,** frais *mpl* de représentation.

enthral, *US* **enthrall** [ɪn'θrɔːl] *vt* (*Br* **enthrals,** *US* **enthralls,** *Br & US* **enthralled, enthralling**) captiver, passionner; **we were enthralled by his stories,** nous étions captivés par ses histoires.

enthralling [ɪn'θrɔːlɪŋ] *adj* (*spectacle etc*) captivant, passionnant.

enthrone [ɪn'θrəʊn] *vt* mettre (*un roi*) sur le trône; introniser (*un évêque*).

enthronement [ɪn'θrəʊnmənt] *n* intronisation *f*.

enthuse [ɪn'θjuːz] **1** *vi* s'enthousiasmer (**over, about,** pour), se passionner (**over, about,** de, pour). **2** *vt* enthousiasmer.

enthusiasm [ɪn'θjuːzɪæz(ə)m] *n* enthousiasme *m* (**for, about,** pour); **she showed little e. for the idea,** elle a témoigné peu d'enthousiasme à l'égard de cette idée.

enthusiast [ɪn'θjuːzɪæst] *n* enthousiaste *mf*; fanatique *mf* (*de golf*); passionné, -ée (*de musique*).

enthusiastic [ɪnθjuːzɪ'æstɪk] *adj* enthousiaste; (*pêcheur*) passionné; **to become e. about sth,** s'enthousiasmer pour qch; *Iron* **don't sound so e.!,** tu pourrais te montrer un peu plus enthousiaste!

enthusiastically [ɪnθjuːzɪ'æstɪklɪ] *adv* avec enthousiasme; **to accept e.,** accepter d'enthousiasme; **they greeted us e.,** ils nous ont salués avec enthousiasme.

entice [ɪn'taɪs] *vt* attirer, séduire (*qn*); **to e. s.o. away,** entraîner qn à sa suite; **to e. s.o. into a place,** attirer qn dans un endroit; **to e. s.o. to do sth,** convaincre qn de faire qch à force de cajoleries.

enticement [ɪn'taɪsmənt] *n* **(a)** (*act*) séduction *f*; **(b)** (*charm*) attrait *m*, charme *m*; **(c)** (*lure*) appât *m*.

enticing [ɪn'taɪsɪŋ] **1** *adj* (*offer etc*) séduisant, tentant, attrayant; (*dish*) alléchant; **the water doesn't look very e.,** l'eau n'a pas l'air très tentante. **2** *n Jur* séduction *f*.

enticingly [ɪn'taɪsɪŋlɪ] *adv* d'une manière séduisante *ou* attrayante.

entire [ɪn'taɪər] *adj* **(a)** (*whole*) entier, tout; **the e. population,** la population (tout) entière; **the e. day,** toute la journée; **she read the e. book in an afternoon,** elle a lu le livre en entier en l'espace d'un après-midi; **(b)** (*complete*) entier, complet; **to enjoy s.o.'s e. confidence,** jouir de l'entière confiance de qn.

entirely [ɪn'taɪəlɪ] *adv* entièrement, tout à fait, complètement; **to agree e. with s.o.,** être entièrement *ou* tout à fait d'accord avec qn; **e. unnecessary,** absolument inutile; **you are e. mistaken,** vous vous trompez du tout au tout.

entirety [ɪn'taɪərətɪ] *n* intégralité *f*, intégrité *f*; totalité *f* (*d'un domaine etc*); **in its e.,** en entier, intégralement, dans son entier; **to tell a story in its e.,** raconter une histoire dans son entier.

entitle [ɪn'taɪt(ə)l] *vt* **(a)** (*give a right to*) donner à (*qn*) le droit (**to,** à); **to e. s.o. to do sth,** donner (le) droit à qn de faire qch; **to be entitled to sth,** avoir droit à qch; **to be entitled to do sth,** avoir le droit de faire qch; **that doesn't e. you to criticize me,** ça ne te donne pas le droit de me critiquer; *Jur* **to be entitled,** être apte, avoir habilité (*à hériter*); **(b)** (*give title to*) intituler (*un livre, un chapitre, une chanson etc*); **(c)** (*give artistocratic title to*) donner à (*qn*) le titre de (*duc, prince etc*).

entitlement [ɪn'taɪt(ə)lmənt] *n* ce qui revient de droit à qn; (*esp money*) allocation *f* (à laquelle on a droit); **(annual) holiday e.,** congé annuel (auquel on a droit).

entity ['entɪtɪ] *n* entité *f*.

entomb [ɪn'tuːm] *vt* (*bury*) mettre dans la tombe, mettre au tombeau; (*of ruins etc*) ensevelir (*qn*).

entombment [ɪn'tuːmmənt] *n* mise *f* au tombeau; (*by ruins*) ensevelissement *m*.

entomological [entəmə'lɒdʒɪk(ə)l] *adj* entomologique.

entomologist [entə'mɒlədʒɪst] *n* entomologiste *mf*.

entomology [entə'mɒlədʒɪ] *n* entomologie *f*.

entourage [ɒntuː'rɑːʒ] *n* entourage *m*.

entr'acte [ɒn'trækt] *n Th* entracte *m*.

entrails ['entreɪlz] *npl* entrailles *fpl* (*d'un animal*).

entrain [ɪn'treɪn] **1** *vt* embarquer, faire embarquer (*des troupes etc*) en train. **2** *vi* s'embarquer (*en train*).

entrance[1] ['entrəns] *n* **(a)** (*way in*) entrée *f*; **wide/narrow e.,** entrée large/étroite; **main e.,** entrée principale; **the e. is at the rear,** (*of bus etc*) l'entrée s'effectue par l'arrière; **e. gate,** grille *f* d'entrée; **e. hall,** vestibule *m* (*d'une maison*); hall *m* (*d'un grand hôtel*); **(b)** (*act of entering*) entrée *f*; *Th & Fig* **to make one's e.,** faire son entrée (*dans une salle etc*); **actor's e. on the stage,** entrée en scène d'un acteur; **to force an e. into a house,** forcer l'entrée d'une maison; **(c)** (*to association, club etc*) admission *f*, accès *m*; **to give e. to sth,** donner accès à qch; **e. fee,** (*to club*) droit *m* d'inscription; **e. examination,** examen *m* d'entrée.

entrance² [ɪn'trɑːns] *vt* extasier, ravir, transporter *(qn)*; **to be entranced by ...,** s'extasier sur ..., être en extase devant ...; **I was entranced with the music,** j'étais enchanté par la musique.
entrancing [ɪn'trɑːnsɪŋ] *adj (rêve)* enchanteur; *(conte)* passionnant; *(mélodie)* ravissant.
entrancingly [ɪn'trɑːnsɪŋlɪ] *adv* à ravir.
entrant ['entrənt] *n (in race)* inscrit, -ite; *(in examination)* candidat, -ate; *(in profession)* débutant, -ante.
entrap [ɪn'træp] *vt* **(-pp-)** prendre *(qn)* au piège.
entreat [ɪn'triːt] *vt* **to e. s.o. to do sth,** prier *ou* implorer *ou* supplier qn de faire qch; **they entreated him to stay,** ils lui demandèrent avec instance de rester; *Lit & Fml* **be merciful, I e. you,** avez pitié, je vous en implore.
entreating [ɪn'triːtɪŋ] *adj (ton, regard)* suppliant, implorant.
entreaty [ɪn'triːtɪ] *n* prière *f*, supplication *f*; **at s.o.'s urgent e.,** sur les vives instances de qn; **look of e.,** regard suppliant.
entrée ['ɒntreɪ] *n* **(a)** *Culin* entrée *f*; *(as main course)* plat *m* de résistance; **(b)** entrée *f* **(to, into,** dans).
entrench [ɪn'trentʃ] *vt Mil* retrancher *(un camp, une ville)*; *Fig* **to e. oneself behind** *or* **in sth,** se retrancher *ou* se terrer derrière qch.
entrenched [ɪn'trentʃd] *adj Mil* retranché; *Fig* **the two sides are more e. than ever,** les deux camps sont plus retranchés que jamais; *Fig* **to be e. in one's beliefs,** être retranché derrière ses croyances.
entrenchment [ɪn'trentʃmənt] *n Mil & Fig* retranchement *m*.
entrepôt ['ɒntrəpəʊ] *n* entrepôt *m*.
entrepreneur [ɒntrəprə'nɜːr] *n* entrepreneur *m*.
entrepreneurial [ɒntrəprə'nɜːrɪəl] *adj* d'un entrepreneur, qui a l'esprit d'entreprise; **an e. class,** une classe qui a l'esprit d'entreprise.
entrepreneurship [ɒntrəprə'nɜːʃɪp] *n* esprit *m* d'entreprise.
entropy ['entrəpɪ] *n* entropie *f*.
entrust [ɪn'trʌst] *vt* **to e. s.o. with,** charger qn de *(une tâche etc)*; investir qn de *(une mission)*; **to e. a secret/child to s.o.,** confier un secret/un enfant à qn; **to e. s.o. with the care of sth,** commettre qch à la garde de qn; **to be entrusted with the sale of sth,** être chargé de la vente de qch.
entry ['entrɪ] *n* **(a)** *(act of entering)* entrée *f*; **to gain e. to a house,** pénétrer dans une maison; **right of free e.,** droit *m* de passer librement les frontières; **'no e.',** passage interdit (au public); *(in one way street)* sens interdit; **to make one's e.,** faire son entrée; *(of actor)* entrer en scène;
(b) *(beginning)* début *m (dans la politique etc)*; *Mus (of an instrument)* entrée *f*; *(in a fugue)* prise *f (d'un sujet)*;
(c) *Jur* prise *f* de possession; **illegal e. (of a dwelling),** violation *f* de domicile;
(d) *(way in)* entrée *f* **(to a mine,** d'une mine);
(e) *(writing down)* enregistrement *m (d'un acte etc)*; inscription *f (d'un nom sur une liste)*; *(in bookkeeping)* inscription *(dans un livre de commerce)*; *(item)* article *m*, poste *m*, écriture *f*; **single/double e.,** comptabilité *f* en partie simple/double; **to make an e.,** *(in bookkeeping)* porter un article à compte; *(in journal etc)* inscrire quelque chose; **to make an e. against s.o.,** débiter qn; **author/subject entries,** *(in cataloguing)* fiches *fpl* auteur/sujet; *Nau* **e. in the log,** élément *m* du journal de bord; **the e. for 5th January 1945,** *(in journal)* ce qui a été inscrit le 5 janvier 1945;
(f) *Sp etc (of competitor)* inscription *f*; *(list of competitors)* liste *f* de concurrents; **there are twenty entries,** *(in race)* il y a vingt coureurs; *(in contest)* il y a vingt candidats; **e. form,** feuille *f* d'inscription.
entry-level ['entrɪlev(ə)l] *adj (car, computer)* d'entrée de gamme.
entwine [ɪn'twaɪn] **1** *vt* enlacer **(with,** de); entrelacer *(des rameaux etc)*; **with arms entwined,** les bras entrelacés. **2** *vi* s'enlacer **(round,** autour de); *(of two or more things)* s'entrelacer.
enumerate [ɪ'njuːməreɪt] *vt* énumérer, détailler, dénombrer *(les raisons, ses services)*.
enumeration [ɪnjuːmə'reɪʃən] *n* enumération *f*, dénombrement *m*, recensement *m*.
enunciate [ɪ'nʌnsɪeɪt] **1** *vt* **(a)** *(pronounce clearly)* prononcer, articuler *(des sons)*; **(b)** *(state clearly)* énoncer, déclarer *(une opinion etc)*. **2** *vi* **to e. clearly,** articuler distinctement.
enunciation [ɪnʌnsɪ'eɪʃən] *n* **(a)** *(pronunciation)* articulation *f*; pronunciation *f (d'un mot)*; **(b)** *(of opinion etc)* énonciation *f*; *Math* énoncé *m (d'un problème)*.
enuresis [enjʊ'riːsɪs] *n Med* énurésie *f*.
envelop [ɪn'veləp] *vt* **(-p-)** envelopper **(in,** dans, de); **enveloped in mist,** *(paysage)* enveloppé *ou* voilé de brume.
envelope ['envələʊp, *occ* 'ɒnvələʊp] *n* **(a)** *(for letter)* enveloppe *f*; **adhesive e.,** enveloppe gommée; **window e.,** enveloppe à fenêtre; **to put a letter in an e.,** mettre une lettre sous enveloppe; **in a sealed e.,** sous pli cacheté; **e. file,** chemise *f* (de carton); **(b)** *(covering)* enveloppe *f*; *Biol* enveloppe, tunique *f (d'un organe)*.
envelopment [ɪn'veləpmənt] *n* enveloppement *m*.
envenom [ɪn'venəm] *vt* envenimer.
enviable ['envɪəb(ə)l] *adj* enviable, digne d'envie; **in the e. position of being offered two jobs,** dans la position enviable de se voir proposer deux emplois.
enviably ['envɪəblɪ] *adv* d'une manière enviable.
envious ['envɪəs] *adj* envieux; **my sister's got a big house, but I'm not e.,** ma sœur a une grande maison, mais je ne l'envie pas; **e. glances,** regards *mpl* d'envie; **to be e. of s.o.,** envier qn; **to look at s.o. with e. eyes,** regarder qn d'un œil jaloux; **to make s.o. e.,** rendre qn jaloux.
enviously ['envɪəslɪ] *adv (parler)* avec envie; *(regarder qch)* d'un œil jaloux.
environment [ɪn'vaɪrənmənt] *n* **(a)** *(surroundings)* milieu *m*; **in an office/a hospital e.,** dans un bureau/milieu hospitalier; **they work in a noisy e.,** ils travaillent dans un milieu bruyant; **(b) the e.,** l'environnement *m*; *Pol* **Department** *or* **Ministry of the E.,** = ministère *m* de (la Protection de la Nature et de) l'Environnement.
environmental [ɪnvaɪrən'ment(ə)l] *adj (conditions)* qui ont rapport à l'environnement; *(change)* de l'environnement; *(brought about by the environment)* produit par l'environnement; **chemicals that cause e. damage,** produits chimiques nuisibles à l'environnement; **the company must improve its e. performance,** la société doit améliorer ses performances en matière d'environnement; **e. group,** un groupe écologiste, un groupe de protection de l'environnement.
environmentalist [ɪnvaɪrən'mentəlɪst] **1** *n* écologiste *mf*. **2** *adj (issues, politics)* écologique.
environment-friendly [ɪn'vaɪrənmənt'frendlɪ] *adj (product)* qui ne nuit pas à l'environnement; **to be e.-f.,** ne pas nuire à l'environnement.
environs [ɪn'vaɪrənz] *npl* environs *mpl*, alentours *mpl (d'une ville)*; **New York and its e.,** New York et ses environs.
envisage [ɪn'vɪzɪdʒ] *vt* envisager *(une difficulté)*.
envision [en'vɪʒən] *vt Am* envisager.
envoy ['envɔɪ] *n (person)* envoyé, -ée (diplomatique).
envy¹ ['envɪ] *n* **(a)** envie *f*, jalousie *f*; **to be green with e.,** être dévoré d'envie; **(b)** *(object)* objet *m* d'envie; **to be the e. of s.o.,** être un objet d'envie pour qn.
envy² *vt* envier, porter envie à *(qn)*; **I don't e. you,** je ne t'envie pas; **to e. s.o. sth,** envier qch à qn.
enzyme ['enzaɪm] *n Biol Ch* enzyme *f*, diastase *f*.
EOC [iːəʊ'siː] *n Br Admin* (*abbr* **Equal Opportunities Commission**) = organisme désigné par le gouvernement pour veiller à l'application des dispositions relatives aux droits des femmes au travail.
Eocene ['iːəʊsiːn] *adj & n Geol* éocène *m*.
EOE [iːəʊ'iː] *abbr* **errors and omissions excepted.**
eon ['iːən] *n US* = **AEON.**
EP [iː'piː] *n abbr* **extended-play.**
epaulette, *US* **epaulet** ['epɒlet] *n Mil* épaulette *f*.
ephedrine ['efɪdrin] *n Pharm* éphédrine *f*.
ephemera, *pl* **-ae, -as** [ɪ'femərə, -iː, -əz] *n* **(a)** chose *f* éphémère; **(b)** *(insect)* éphémère *m*.
ephemeral [ɪ'femərəl] *adj* éphémère; *(passion)* fugitif; *(beauty)* passager.
ephemerid [ɪ'femərɪd] *n (insect)* éphémère *m*.
epic ['epɪk] **1** *adj* épique; *(flight, moment etc)* légendaire. **2** *n (poem)* poème *m* épique, épopée *f*; *(film)* film *m* à grand spectacle.
epicarp ['epɪkɑːp] *n Bot* épicarpe *m*.
epicentre, *US* **epicenter** ['epɪsentər] *n* épicentre *m (d'une séisme)*.
epicure ['epɪkjʊər] *n* **(a)** épicurien, -ienne; **(b)** *(gourmet)* gourmet *m*, gastronome *mf*.
epicurean [epɪkjʊ'rɪən] *adj & n* épicurien, -ienne.
epidemic [epɪ'demɪk] **1** *adj (maladie)* épidémique; *Fig* **corruption has reached e. proportions,** la corruption prend des allures d'épidémie. **2** *n Med & Fig* épidémie *f*.
epidemiological [epɪdiːmɪə'lɒdʒɪk(ə)l] *adj (evidence, research, study)* épidémiologique.
epidemiologist [epɪdiːmɪ'ɒlədʒɪst] *n* épidémiologiste *mf*.

epidemiology [epɪdiːmɪ'ɒlədʒɪ] *n* épidémiologie *f*.
epidermis [epɪ'dɜːmɪs] *n Anat* épiderme *m*.
epidural [epɪ'djuːr(ə)l] **1** *adj Anat* épidural, -aux. **2** *n Obst* péridurale *f*; **she had an e.,** on lui a fait une péridurale.
epiglottis [epɪ'glɒtɪs] *n* épiglotte *f*.
epigram ['epɪgræm] *n* épigramme *f*.
epigrammatic [epɪgrə'mætɪk] *adj* épigrammatique.
epigrammatically [epɪgrə'mætɪklɪ] *adv* épigrammatiquement.
epigraph ['epɪgræf] *n* épigraphe *f*.
epilepsy ['epɪlepsɪ] *n* épilepsie *f*.
epileptic [epɪ'leptɪk] **1** *n* épileptique *mf*. **2** *adj* épileptique; **e. fit,** crise *f* épileptique.
epilogue ['epɪlɒg] *n Liter & Fig* épilogue *m*.
Epiphany [ɪ'pɪfənɪ] *n Rel* l'Épiphanie *f*.
epiphyte ['epɪfaɪt] *n Bot* (plante *f*) épiphyte *m*.
episcopacy [ɪ'pɪskəpəsɪ] *n* épiscopat *m*.
episcopal [ɪ'pɪskəp(ə)l] *adj* épiscopal, -aux; **e. palace,** évêché *m*; **e. ring,** anneau pastoral.
Episcopal [ɪ'pɪskəp(ə)l] *adj Am Scot* **the E. Church,** l'Église épiscopale.
episcopalian [ɪpɪskə'peɪlɪən] *adj & n* épiscopalien, -ienne.
Episcopalian [ɪpɪskə'peɪlɪən] **1** *n Am Scot* membre *m* de l'Église épiscopale. **2** *adj* de l'Eglise épiscopale.
episcopate [ɪ'pɪskəpeɪt] *n* épiscopat *m*.
episiotomy [əpiːzɪ'ɒtəmɪ] *n Obst* épisiotomie *f*.
episode ['epɪsəʊd] *n* (*of story etc*) épisode *m*; (*incident*) incident *m*.
episodic(al) [epɪ'sɒdɪk, -ɪk(ə)l] *adj* épisodique.
epistemic [epɪ'stiːmɪk] *adj* épistémique.
epistemology [ɪpɪstɪ'mɒlədʒɪ] *n* épistémologie *f*.
epistle [ɪ'pɪs(ə)l] *n* **(a)** *Rel* épître *f* ; **e. side (of altar),** côté *m* de l'épître; **(b)** *Fml* (*letter*) épître *f*, lettre *f*.
epistolary [ɪ'pɪstələrɪ] *adj* (*style*) épistolaire.
epitaph ['epɪtæf] *n* épitaphe *f*.
epithelium [epɪ'θiːlɪəm] *n Anat* épithélium *m*.
epithet ['epɪθet] *n* épithète *f*.
epithetic(al) [epɪ'θetɪk, -ɪk(ə)l] *adj* épithétique.
epitome [ɪ'pɪtəmɪ] *n* **(a)** (*typical example*) **to be the e. of sth,** incarner qch; **he is the e. of elegance,** il est l'élégance même; **(b)** (*summary*) épitomé *m*, abrégé *m*.
epitomize [ɪ'pɪtəmaɪz] *vt* **(a)** (*embody*) incarner (*qch*); **he epitomizes everything that is wrong with our society,** il incarne tout ce qui ne va pas dans notre société; **(b)** (*summarize*) abréger, résumer (*un discours etc*).
epizootic [epɪzəʊ'ɒtɪk] *Vet* **1** *adj* (*maladie*) épizootique. **2** *n* épizootie *f*.
epoch ['iːpɒk] *n* époque *f*, âge *m*; **to mark an e.,** faire époque, faire date.
epoch-making ['iːpɒkmeɪkɪŋ] *adj* (*découverte, événement*) qui fait époque, qui fait date.
eponym ['epənɪm] *n* éponyme *m*.
eponymous [ɪ'pɒnɪməs] *adj* éponyme.
epoxy [ɪ'pɒksɪ] *Ch* **1** *adj* **e. resin,** résine *f* époxyde. **2** *n* époxyde *m*.
EPROM ['iːprɒm] *n Comptr* (*abbr* **erasable programme read only memory**) mémoire morte programmable et effaçable.
Epsom ['epsəm] *n Pharm* **E. salts,** sel *m* d'Epsom.
equability [ekwə'bɪlɪtɪ, iːk-] *n* uniformité *f* (*de climat, de température etc*); égalité *f* (*d'humeur*).
equable ['ekwəb(ə)l] *adj* (*climate, temperature*) uniforme, régulier; **e. temperament,** humeur égale.
equably ['ekwəblɪ] *adv* d'humeur égale.
equal¹ ['iːkwəl] **1** *adj* **(a)** égal, -aux (**to, with,** à); **e. numbers of boys and girls,** un nombre égal de garçons et de filles; **on e. terms,** à conditions égales; **to be on e. terms** *or* **on an e. footing with s.o.,** être sur un pied d'égalité avec qn; **e. distribution of taxes,** péréquation *f* de l'impôt; **cinema e. to any in London,** cinéma à l'instar des cinémas de Londres; **all things being e.,** si tout se déroule normalement, si tout va bien; **e. pay for e. work,** à travail égal, salaire égal; **the constitution guarantees e. rights to all citizens,** la constitution garantit des droits égaux à tous les citoyens; **to be an e. opportunity employer,** offrir des chances égales d'emploi à tous; *Math* **e.** *or* **equals sign,** signe *m* d'égalité;

(b) to be e. to (doing) sth, être à la hauteur de *ou* à même de (faire) qch; **I don't feel e. to (doing) it,** (*I'm too tired etc*) je ne m'en sens pas le courage *ou* la force; (*I'm not good enough*) je ne m'en sens pas à la hauteur; **to be e. to the occasion,** être à la hauteur d'une situation; **not to be e. to a task,** ne pas être à la hauteur d'une tâche.

2 *n* égal, -ale, pair *m*; **your equals,** vos pareils, vos égaux; **you won't find her e.,** vous ne trouverez pas son semblable; **to treat s.o. as an e.,** traiter qn d'égal à égal.
equal² *vt* (**-ll-**, *US* **-l-**) **(a)** (*be equal to*) égaler, être égal à (*qn, qch*) (**in,** en); **nothing can e. this splendour,** rien ne saurait égaler cette splendeur; **no one has equalled her record,** personne n'a égalé son record; **not to be equalled,** sans égal, qui n'a pas son égal; **(b)** (*total*) faire; **four fives** *or* **four times five equals twenty,** quatre fois cinq font vingt.
equality [ɪ'kwɒlɪtɪ] *n* égalité *f*; (**with s.o.,** avec qn); **e. of opportunity,** égalité des chances.
equalization [iːkwəlaɪ'zeɪʃən] *n* **(a)** égalisation *f*; *Admin* péréquation *f* (*de contributions*); **(b)** compensation *f*; compensation (*de terrassements*); *MecE* équilibrage *m*.
equalize ['iːkwəlaɪz] **1** *vt* égaliser (**sth with sth,** qch avec qch); faire la péréquation de (*les salaires*); compenser, équilibrer (*des forces etc*). **2** *vi* (*become equal*) s'égaliser; (*become balanced*) se compenser, s'équilibrer; *Sp* égaliser.
equalizer ['iːkwəlaɪzər] *n El* égaliseur *m* de potentiel; *MecE* compensateur *m*; *Sp* point égalisateur; (*in football, hockey*) but égalisateur.
equalizing ['iːkwəlaɪzɪŋ] *adj* (*courant etc*) compensateur; (*pression*) de compensation.
equally ['iːkwəlɪ] *adv* également, pareillement; **e. exhausted,** tout aussi fatigué; **she worked e. hard,** elle a travaillé tout aussi dur; **to contribute e. to the expenses,** contribuer pour une part égale à la dépense; **the money was divided e. between the children,** l'argent a été partagé de façon égale entre les enfants; **e., they may be telling the truth,** il se pourrait tout aussi bien qu'ils disent la vérité.
equanimity [iːkwə'nɪmɪtɪ, ek-] *n* égalité *f* d'âme, équanimité *f*; **to disturb s.o.'s e.,** troubler la sérénité de qn; **to recover one's e.,** se ressaisir; **with e.,** d'une âme égale.
equate [ɪ'kweɪt] *vt* **(a)** (*make equal*) égaler (**to, with,** à); *Math* mettre (*deux expressions etc*) en équation; **(b)** (*think of as equal*) **I e. communism with the Soviet Union,** j'assimile le communisme à l'Union Soviétique; **to e. Jupiter with Zeus,** donner Jupiter comme l'équivalent de Zeus.
equating [ɪ'kweɪtɪŋ] *n* **(a)** (*making equal*) égalisation *f*; *Math* mise *f* en équation; **(b)** (*thinking of as equal*) assimilation *f*.
equation [ɪ'kweɪʃən] *n* **(a)** *Math Ch Astron* équation *f*; *Math* **simple/quadratic e.,** équation du premier/deuxième degré; **(b)** (*making equal*) égalisation *f* (*des dépenses au revenu etc*); **(c)** (*thinking of as equal*) assimilation *f*; **the e. of fame with success,** l'assimilation de la célébrité au succès.
equator [ɪ'kweɪtər] *n* équateur *m* (de la terre); **at the e.,** sous l'équateur.
equatorial [ekwə'tɔːrɪəl] *adj* équatorial, -aux.
equerry ['ekwərɪ] *n* écuyer *m*.
equestrian [ɪ'kwestrɪən] **1** *adj* (*statue etc*) équestre; **e. performances,** exercices *mpl* d'équitation. **2** *n* cavalier *m*; (*in circus*) écuyer *m*.
equestrienne [ɪkwestrɪ'en] *n* cavalière *f*; (*in circus*) écuyère *f*.
equidistant [iːkwɪ'dɪstənt] *adj* équidistant (**from,** de).
equilateral [iːkwɪ'læt(ə)rəl] *adj* équilatéral, -aux.
equilibrate [ɪ'kwɪlɪbreɪt] **1** *vt* équilibrer, faire contrepoids à (*une force etc*). **2** *vi* s'équilibrer, se faire contrepoids.
equilibration [ɪkwɪlɪ'breɪʃən] *n* équilibration *f*.
equilibrium [iːkwɪ'lɪbrɪəm] *n* équilibre *m*, aplomb *m*; **stable/unstable e.,** équilibre stable/instable; **to lose one's e.,** perdre l'équilibre.
equine ['iːkwaɪn, 'ekwaɪn] **1** *adj* équin; (*race*) chevalin. **2** *n* équidé *m*.
equinoctial [iːkwɪ'nɒkʃəl, ek-] *adj* **(a)** (*line, year etc*) équinoxial; (*storm etc*) d'équinoxe; **e. tides,** marées d'équinoxe, les grandes marées.
equinox ['iːkwɪnɒks, 'ek-] *n* équinoxe *m*; **spring** *or* **vernal e.,** équinoxe du printemps, point vernal; **autumn(al) e.,** équinoxe d'automne.
equip [ɪ'kwɪp] *vt* (**-pp-**) **(a)** (*provide with equipment*) équiper (*un soldat*); meubler, monter (*une maison*); outiller, monter (*une usine*); **to e. s.o. with sth,** munir *ou* équiper qn de qch; **to e. oneself with sth,** s'équiper *ou* se munir de qch; **(b)** (*prepare*) préparer (*qn*) (**to do sth,** pour faire qch); **her training had not equipped her for such an eventuality,** sa formation ne l'avait pas parée à une telle éventualité.
equipage ['ekwɪpɪdʒ] *n* (*vehicle*) équipage *m*.
equipment [ɪ'kwɪpmənt] *n* **(a)** (*act*) équipement *m* (*d'une expédition*); aménagement *m* (*d'une maison*); outillage *m* (*d'une usine etc*); installation *f* (*d'un laboratoire etc*); **(b)**

(*result*) équipement *m*; (*in house*) appareils *mpl*; (*in factory*) installations *fpl*, matériel *m*; **heavy e.,** matériel lourd; **emergency e.,** matériel *ou* installations de secours; **electrical e.,** équipement électrique; *Sp* **sports e.,** équipement sportif; **camping e.,** matériel de camping; *Mil* **regulation** *or* **standard e.,** matériel réglementaire; **surplus e.,** matériel en excédent; **(c)** *Fig* **intellectual e.,** capacité intellectuelle.

equipoise ['ekwɪpɔɪz] *n* (*equilibrium*) équilibre *m*.

equipped [ɪ'kwɪpt] *adj* **(a)** (*soldier, expedition etc*) équipé; **e. with,** équipé *ou* doté de; **the aircraft is e. to take aerial photographs** *or* **for aerial photography,** l'avion est équipé pour prendre des photos aériennes; **(b)** (*prepared*) préparé.

equitable ['ekwɪtəb(ə)l] *adj* équitable, juste.

equitably ['ekwɪt(ə)blɪ] *adv* équitablement; avec justice.

equitation [ekwɪ'teɪʃən] *n* équitation *f*.

equity ['ekwɪtɪ] *n* **(a)** (*fairness*) équité *f*, justice *f*; **(b)** *Jur* équité *f*; recours *m* aux principes mêmes de la justice (*lorsque celle-ci se trouve en conflit avec le droit commun ou écrit*); **(c)** (*of shareholders*) capitaux *mpl ou* fonds *mpl* propres; avoir *m* des actionnaires; (*of company*) capital *m* actions; *Fin* **equities,** actions *fpl* ordinaires; **the equities market,** le marché des actions ordinaires; **(d)** *Br Th* **E.,** (*actors' union*) le syndicat des artistes de la scène.

equivalence [ɪ'kwɪvələns] *n* équivalence *f*.

equivalent [ɪ'kwɪvələnt] **1** *adj* équivalent; **to be e. to sth,** être équivalent *ou* équivaloir à qch. **2** *n* équivalent *m*; **to drink the e. of one glass of wine,** boire la valeur d'un verre de vin; **the Soviet e. of the FBI,** l'équivalent soviétique du FBI; **there is no e. in our culture,** il n'y a pas d'équivalent dans notre culture.

equivocal [ɪ'kwɪvək(ə)l] *adj* **(a)** (*ambiguous*) équivoque; ambigu, -uë; (*mot*) à double sens, équivoque; (*réponse*) équivoque; **(b)** (*uncertain*) incertain, douteux; **(c)** (*doubtful*) suspect, douteux, équivoque.

equivocally [ɪ'kwɪvəklɪ] *adv* d'une manière équivoque.

equivocate [ɪ'kwɪvəkeɪt] *vi* user d'équivoque, tergiverser.

equivocation [ɪkwɪvə'keɪʃən] *n* tergiversation *f*; **to resort to equivocations,** user d'équivoque, tergiverser.

er [ə, ɜː] *int* euh.

ER [iː'ɑːr] *n Br* (*abbr* **Elizabeth Regina**) la Reine Elizabeth.

era ['ɪərə] *n* ère *f* (*géologique etc*); **to mark an e.,** faire date.

ERA [iːɑː'rɑɪ] *n US* (*abbr* **Equal Rights Amendment**) = modification proposée à la constitution relative aux droits de la femme.

eradicate [ɪ'rædɪkeɪt] *vt* (*prejudice, evil*) extirper, déraciner; (*disease*) éradiquer, faire disparaître.

eradication [ɪrædɪ'keɪʃən] *n* éradication *f*, extirpation *f* (*d'un préjugé, d'un abus etc*); (*of disease*) éradication *f*.

erase [ɪ'reɪz] *vt* effacer (*un mot, un enregistrement sur bande*); raturer, gommer (*un mot*); oblitérer (*un souvenir*); *Comptr* **to e. a file/disk/***etc*, effacer un fichier/un disque/*etc*.

eraser [ɪ'reɪzər] *n* gomme *f* (à effacer); **ink e.,** gomme à encre.

erasing [ɪ'reɪzɪŋ] *n* effacement *m*.

erasure [ɪ'reɪʒər] *n* **(a)** (*act*) effacement *m*; **(b)** (*what is erased*) mot *ou* chiffre effacé.

ere [eər] *Arch & Lit* **1** *prep* avant; **e. now,** auparavant; déjà; **e. long,** bientôt. **2** *conj* avant que + *sub*; **e. you forget,** avant que tu (n')oublies.

erect¹ [ɪ'rekt] *adj* (*person*) droit, debout; (*penis*) en érection, dressé; **with head e.,** la tête haute *ou* relevée; **to stand e.,** se tenir droit.

erect² *vt* (*construct, put up*) ériger, construire (*un édifice*); élever (*une statue*) (**to,** à); dresser (*un échafaudage, un autel*); dresser (*un mât*); installer (*une machine*); **to e. a tent,** monter une tente.

erectile [ɪ'rektaɪl] *adj Physiol* (*tissue*) érectile.

erection [ɪ'rekʃən] *n* **(a)** construction *f*, érection *f* (*d'un édifice*); érection (*d'une statue*); dressage *m* (*d'un mât*); installation *f* (*d'une machine*); **(b)** *Physiol* érection *f* (*d'un organe*); **to have an e.,** (*of male*) avoir une érection; **(c)** (*act of straightening*) redressement *m* (*du corps*); **(d)** (*building, structure*) bâtisse *f*, construction *f*, édifice *m*.

erectness [ɪ'rektnɪs] *n* attitude droite.

erector [ɪ'rektər] *n* **(a)** (*person*) constructeur *m* (*de bâtiments*); **(b)** *Anat* **e. (muscle),** (muscle *m*) érecteur *m*.

erg [ɜːg] *n Phys* erg *m*.

ergo ['ɜːgəʊ, 'eəgəʊ] *adv* (*in logic*) ergo, donc.

ergonomic [ɜːgə'nɒmɪk] *adj* ergonomique.

ergonomically [ɜːgə'nɒmɪklɪ] *adv* **e. designed,** (*chair etc*) d'une conception ergonomique.

ergonomics [ɜːgə'nɒmɪks] *npl* (*usu with sing verb*) ergonomie *f*.

ergot ['ɜːgɒt] *n Agr Pharm* ergot *m*.

ergotism ['ɜːgətɪz(ə)m] *n Med* ergotisme *m*.

Erie ['ɪərɪ] *n* **Lake E.,** le lac Érié.

erigeron [ɪ'rɪdʒərən] *n* (*plant*) érigéron *m*.

Erin ['erɪn] *n Arch & Lit* l'Irlande *f*.

Eritrea [erɪ'treɪə] *n* Erythrée *f*.

Eritrean [erɪ'treɪən] *n* Erythréen, -enne.

ermine ['ɜːmɪn] *n* hermine *f*.

erode [ɪ'rəʊd] *vt* (*of elements*) éroder; (*of acid, corrosive substance*) ronger; corroder; *Fig* **the power of the church has been eroded,** le pouvoir de l'église a été miné; **our savings have been eroded by inflation,** nos économies se sont trouvées grignotées par l'inflation.

erogenous [ɪ'rɒdʒɪnəs] *adj* (*zone etc*) érogène.

Eros ['ɪərɒs] *n* Eros *m*.

erosion [ɪ'rəʊʒən] *n* érosion *f* (*marine etc*); *Fig* détérioration *f*; **wind e.,** érosion éolienne; **soil e.,** érosion du sol; *Fig* **the e. of real earnings by inflation,** la diminution du salaire réel causée par l'inflation.

erotic [ɪ'rɒtɪk] *adj* (*art, book, film etc*) érotique.

erotica [ɪ'rɒtɪkə] *npl* écrits *ou* dessins *etc* érotiques.

erotically [ɪ'rɒtɪklɪ] *adv* érotiquement.

eroticism [ɪ'rɒtɪsɪz(ə)m] *n* érotisme *m*.

err [ɜːr] *vi* **(a)** (*make mistake(s)*) errer, faire erreur; **to e. is human,** tout le monde peut se tromper, l'erreur est humaine; **(b)** (*sin*) pécher; **he does not e. on the side of modesty,** il ne pèche pas par la modestie; **let's e. on the side of caution and do ...,** mesure de prudence, faisons ...; **it's better to e. on the side of being too generous,** il vaut mieux pécher par générosité, il vaut mieux être trop généreux que pas assez; **(c)** (*stray*) s'égarer, s'écarter (**from,** de); **to e. from the straight and narrow,** s'égarer du droit chemin.

errand ['erənd] *n* commission *f*, course *f*; **to go on** *or* **run errands,** (aller) faire des commissions *ou* des courses; *Old-fashioned Com* **e. boy,** garçon *m* de courses.

errant ['erənt] *adj* **(a)** (*straying*) dévoyé; **e. husband,** mari infidèle; **(b)** *Arch* errant; **knight e.,** chevalier errant.

errata [ɪ'rɑːtə] *npl* errata *mpl*.

erratic [ɪ'rætɪk] *adj* **(a)** (*irregular*) irrégulier; **e. working,** irrégularité *f* de marche (*d'une machine*); *Aut* **e. driving,** conduite mal assurée; **(b)** (*person*) capricieux, bizarre, velléitaire; (*life*) désordonné; **her playing is e.,** (*of sportswoman, musician etc*) son jeu est inégal; **the road/river follows an e. course,** la route/rivière suit un cours irrégulier; **(c)** *Med* (*pain*) erratique.

erratically [ɪ'rætɪklɪ] *adv* sans méthode, sans règle; **to work e.,** (*person*) travailler irrégulièrement; (*of machine*) fonctionner irrégulièrement *ou* par à-coups; *Aut* **to drive e.,** conduire d'une façon mal assurée.

erratum, *pl* **-ta** [ɪ'rɑːtəm, -tə] *n* erratum *m*, *pl* errata.

erring ['ɜːrɪŋ] *adj* dévoyé, égaré; tombé dans l'erreur; (*mari, femme*) infidèle.

erroneous [ɪ'rəʊnɪəs] *adj* (*calcul*) erroné, faux; (*supposition*) faux; **arguments resting on e. premises,** arguments reposant sur des prémisses fausses *ou* erronées.

erroneously [ɪ'rəʊnɪəslɪ] *adv* par erreur.

erroneousness [ɪ'rəʊnɪəsnɪs] *n* erreur *f*, fausseté *f*.

error ['erər] *n* **(a)** (*error*) erreur *f*, faute *f*; **e. of judgement,** erreur de jugement; **human e.,** défaillance humaine; **printing** *or* **printer's e.,** faute d'impression; *Com* **errors and omissions excepted,** sauf erreur ou omission; **in e.,** par erreur;

(b) *Tech* erreur *f*, écart *m*, aberration *f*, déviation *f*; *Comptr* erreur *f*; **allowable e.,** erreur permise, tolérance *f*; **vertical e.,** écart en hauteur; **compass e.,** déviation du compas; *Comptr* **e. code,** code *m* indiquant une erreur; **e. correction,** correction *f* d'erreurs; *Comptr* **e. message,** message *m* d'erreur; *Comptr* **e. routine,** sous-programme *m* de correction d'erreurs;

(c) (*being wrong*) **to be in e.,** être dans l'erreur, avoir tort; **to fall into e.,** tomber dans l'erreur; **he has seen the e. of his ways,** il est revenu de ses égarements;

(d) (*wrongdoing*) écart *m* (*de conduite*); **errors of youth,** erreurs *fpl ou* écarts de jeunesse.

ersatz [eə'zæts, 'ɜːzæts] **1** *n* ersatz *m*, succédané *m*. **2** *adj* **the coffee is e.,** le café n'est qu'un ersatz *ou* un succédané.

Erse [ɜːs] *Ling* **1** *n* **(a)** (*gaelic*) erse *m*, gaélique *m*; **(b)** (*Irish gaelic*) irlandais *m*. **2** *adj* **(a)** gaélique; **(b)** irlandais.

erstwhile ['ɜːstwaɪl] *Arch & Lit* **1** *adv* autrefois, jadis. **2** *adj* ancien (*élève etc*).

eructate ['iːrʌkteɪt] *vi Fml* éructer.

eructation [iːrʌk'teɪʃən] *n Fml* éructation *f*.

erudite [ˈerʊdaɪt] *adj* érudit, savant.
erudition [erʊˈdɪʃən] *n* érudition *f*; **work of monumental e.,** vrai monument d'érudition.
erupt [ɪˈrʌpt] *vi* **(a)** (*of volcano*) entrer en éruption; **(b)** (*of violence, anger*) éclater; (*of person*) exploser; **(c)** (*of teeth*) percer; (*of spot*) sortie.
eruption [ɪˈrʌpʃən] *n* **(a)** éruption *f*; **volcano in e.,** volcan *m* en éruption; **(b)** (*of anger, joy etc*) éclat *m*, accès *m*; **(c)** (*of teeth*) éruption *f*; *Med* éruption, poussée *f* (*de boutons*).
erysipelas [erɪˈsɪpɪləs] *n Med* érysipèle *m*.
erythrocyte [eˈrɪθrəʊsaɪt] *n Physiol* érythrocyte *m*.
ESA [iːeˈseɪ] *n* (*abbr* **European Space Agency**) ASE *f*.
escalate [ˈeskəleɪt] **1** *vi* **(a)** (*of prices etc*) monter (en flèche); **(b)** (*of conflict etc*) s'aggraver; **small incidents can easily e. into a world war,** de simples incidents (militaires) peuvent facilement mener à une guerre mondiale. **2** *vt* intensifier, aggraver; **strikers accused the management of escalating the situation,** les grévistes ont accusé la direction d'aggraver la situation.
escalation [eskəˈleɪʃən] *n* **(a)** (*of prices etc*) augmentation *f* (rapide); (*of interest rates*) escalade *f*; **(b)** (*of war, situation*) escalade *f*.
escalator [ˈeskəleɪtər] *n* **(a)** (*moving stairway*) escalier *m* mécanique, escalator *m*; **(b)** *Econ* **e. (clause),** échelle *f* mobile.
escalope [ˈeskəlɒp] *n Culin* escalope *f*.
escapade [ˈeskəpeɪd] *n* escapade *f*, frasque *f*, fredaine *f*.
escape¹ [ɪsˈkeɪp] *n* **(a)** (*flight*) fuite *f*, évasion *f*; **to make one's e.,** s'échapper, se sauver; **to make good one's e.,** réussir à s'échapper; **to have a narrow e.,** l'échapper belle; **to have a miraculous e.,** échapper comme par miracle; *Fig* **the cinema provided an e. from their daily routine,** le cinéma leur offrait un moyen de s'évader de leur routine quotidienne; *Com etc* **e. clause,** clause *f* échappatoire; **e. hatch,** trappe *f* de secours; *Comptr* **e. key,** touche *f* d'échappement; **e. route,** (*from fire etc*) itinéraire *m* de sortie de secours; (*of criminal*) itinéraire ménagé pour s'échapper; *Astronaut* **e. velocity,** vitesse *f* de libération de l'attraction terrestre; **(b)** (*of gas, water etc*) échappement *m*, fuite *f*, dégagement *m*; **(c) fire e.,** échelle *f* de sauvetage; **(d)** *HydE* déversoir *m*; *MecE etc* **e. valve,** soupape *f* d'échappement *ou* de trop-plein; **e. wheel,** (*in clock*) roue *f* d'échappement.
escape² **1** *vi* **(a)** (*of person*) échapper, s'échapper, prendre la fuite; **to e. from prison,** s'évader de prison; **escaped prisoner,** évadé, -ée; **to e. by the skin of one's teeth,** échapper tout juste; **to e. uninjured,** s'en tirer indemne; **he escaped with a fright,** il en a été quitte pour la peur; **(b)** (*of gases, fluids*) s'échapper, fuir.
2 *vt* **(a)** (*of person*) échapper à (*un danger*); **he narrowly escaped death,** il a échappé tout juste à la mort; **he just escaped being killed,** il a bien failli être tué, il a manqué (de) se faire tuer; **they escaped punishment,** ils ont échappé à la punition;
(b) (*go unnoticed by*) échapper à (*qn*); **nothing escapes her eagle eye,** rien n'échappe à son regard perçant; **to e. notice,** échapper à l'attention, passer inaperçu;
(c) (*of name, date etc*) échapper à (*qn*); **his name escapes me,** son nom m'échappe;
(d) (*of sound*) **a cry escaped him,** un cri lui a échappé.
escapee [eskeɪˈpiː] *n* évadé, -ée.
escapement [ɪsˈkeɪpmənt] *n* échappement *m* (*d'une pendule, d'un piano etc*).
escaper [ɪsˈkeɪpər] *n* fugitif, -ive.
escapism [ɪsˈkeɪpɪz(ə)m] *n* évasion *f* (*de la réalité*); **the movie is pure e.,** le film constitue de la pure évasion.
escapist [ɪsˈkeɪpɪst] *n* = personne qui cherche à fuir la réalité; **e. literature,** littérature *f* d'évasion.
escapologist [eskəˈpɒlədʒɪst] *n* prestidigitateur *m* spécialiste de l'évasion.
escarpment [ɪsˈkɑːpmənt] *n* escarpement *m*.
eschatology [eskəˈtɒlədʒɪ] *n Rel* eschatologie *f*.
escheat [ɪsˈtʃiːt] *vi Jur* (*of estate*) tomber en déshérence; revenir à l'État *ou* à la Couronne.
eschew [ɪsˈtʃuː] *vt Arch & Lit* renoncer à (*qch*).
escort¹ [ˈeskɔːt] *n* **(a)** escorte *f*; (*for tourists etc*) guide *m*; (*to a woman*) cavalier *m*; (*to a man*) cavalière *f*; *Nau* (*ship*) escorteur *m*, bâtiment *m* d'escorte; **the police provided an e.,** la police a fourni une escorte; **a police e.,** une escorte de police; *Mil Av* **e. fighter,** chasseur *m* d'escorte; **e. agency,** agence *f* d'hôtesses; **(b)** (*act of escorting*) escorte *f*; **under the e. of ...,** sous l'escorte de ...; **to conduct a prisoner under e.,** conduire un prisonnier sous escorte.
escort² [ɪsˈkɔːt] *vt* escorter, faire escorte à, servir d'escorte à (*un convoi*); servir de cavalier à (*une dame*); conduire (*un prisonnier*) sous escorte.
escrow [ˈeskrəʊ] *n Jur* argent *ou* biens placé(s) en dépôt légal; **to put money in e.,** placer de l'argent en dépôt légal.
escutcheon [ɪsˈkʌtʃ(ə)n] *n* écu *m*, écusson *m*; *Hum* **a blot on s.o.'s e.,** une tache de la réputation de qn.
Eskimo, *pl* **-os, -o** [ˈeskɪməʊ, -əʊz] **1** *adj* esquimau, (*occ* -aude *in feminine*), -aux, eskimo *inv*; **an E. woman,** une femme esquimau *ou* eskimo *ou* esquimaude; **E. dog,** chien esquimau. **2** *n* Esquimau, -aude.
esophagus [ɪˈsɒfəgəs] *n US Anat* œsophage *m*.
esoteric [esəʊˈterɪk] *adj* ésotérique, secret.
ESP [iːesˈpiː] *n abbr* **extrasensory perception.**
espadrille [espəˈdrɪl] *n* espadrille *f*.
espalier [ɪsˈpælɪər, -ɪeɪ] *n* espalier *m*.
esparto [esˈpɑːtəʊ] *n* **e. (grass),** sparte *m*; alfa *m*.
especial [ɪsˈpeʃəl] *adj* spécial, -aux, particulier; **of e. importance,** d'une importance toute particulière.
especially [ɪsˈpeʃəlɪ] *adv* surtout; **we were e. lucky with the weather,** le temps nous était particulièrement favorable; **he likes birds, e. parrots,** il aime les oiseaux, spécialement les perroquets; **I did it e. for you,** je l'ai fait spécialement *ou* exprès pour vous.
Esperanto [espəˈræntəʊ] *n Ling* espéranto *m*.
espionage [ˈespɪənɑːʒ] *n* espionnage *m*; **industrial e.,** espionnage industriel.
esplanade [espləˈneɪd] *n* esplanade *f*; (*in seaside town*) digue *f*.
espousal [ɪsˈpaʊz(ə)l] *n* **the e. of a cause,** l'adhésion *f* à une cause.
espouse [ɪsˈpaʊz] *vt* épouser, embrasser (*une cause, un parti etc*).
espresso [esˈpresəʊ] **1** *n* (café *m*) expresso *m*; **e. machine,** machine *f* à expresso. **2** *adj* expresso.
espy [ɪsˈpaɪ] *vt Arch & Lit* apercevoir, aviser.
Esq *Old-fashioned abbr* **Esquire.**
esquire [ɪsˈkwaɪər] *n Old-fashioned* (*titre honorifique*) **David Thomas, E.,** = Monsieur David Thomas.
essay [ˈeseɪ] *n* **(a)** (*piece of writing*) *Lit* essai *m*; *Sch* composition *f*; (*for younger students*) rédaction *f*; **(b)** (*attempt*) essai *m*, tentative *f* **(at,** de).
essayist [ˈeseɪɪst] *n Lit* essayiste *mf*, auteur *m* d'essais.
essence [ˈesəns] *n* **(a)** *Phil Rel etc* essence *f*; fond *m* (*d'une affaire*); **the very e. of authority,** l'autorité même; **in e.,** essentiellement; **speed is of the e.,** la vitesse est essentielle; **(b)** *Ch Culin etc* essence *f*, extrait *m*; **meat e.,** extrait de viande; **vanilla e.,** extrait de vanille.
essential [ɪˈsenʃəl] **1** *adj* **(a)** (*difference etc*) essentiel; **(b)** (*indispensable*) essentiel, indispensable; **e. foodstuffs,** denrées *fpl* de première nécessité; **e. part,** essence *f* (*d'une doctrine etc*); **e. feature,** fond *m* (*d'une politique etc*); **it is e. to do that,** il est essentiel *ou* absolument nécessaire de faire cela; **the e. thing,** l'essentiel *m*; **prudence is e.,** la prudence s'impose; **waterproof clothing is e.,** des vêtements imperméables sont indispensables; **(c)** (*oil*) essentiel. **2** *n* (*usu pl*) **reduced to its essentials,** dépouillé; **to concentrate on essentials,** s'attacher à l'essentiel; **one of the essentials of a business man,** une des qualités indispensables à un homme d'affaires.
essentially [ɪˈsenʃ(ə)lɪ] *adv* essentiellement.
est (a) *Com* (*abbr* **established**) établi, fondé; **A. Jones, est. 1885,** A. Jones, établi en 1885; **(b)** (*abbr* **estimated**) estimatif.
EST [iːesˈtiː] *n Am* (*abbr* **Eastern Standard Time**) HNE *f*.
establish [ɪsˈtæblɪʃ] *vt* **(a)** (*make firm*) affermir (*sa foi*); asseoir (*son pouvoir*); instaurer (*le règne de la justice*); *Jur* confirmer, ratifier (*un testament*); **to e. one's right,** faire apparaître son bon droit; **the troops established a beachhead,** les troupes ont établi une tête de pont;
(b) (*set up*) établir (*un gouvernement*); édifier (*un système*); fonder (*une maison de commerce*); créer (*une agence*); constituer (*une société*); mettre sur pied (*une paix*); **to e. close relations with s.o.,** nouer des relations avec qn; **to e. s.o.'s reputation as an author,** faire la réputation de qn comme auteur; **the film established her as an important director,** le film a établi sa réputation de metteur en scène important; **to e. oneself in business,** s'établir dans les affaires; *Pej* **to e. oneself in s.o.'s house,** s'installer *ou* s'incruster chez qn; *Com* **established 1885,** établi en 1885;
(c) (*prove, become clear about*) établir (*un fait*); démontrer (*l'identité de qn*); constater (*la réalité d'un fait*); établir (*l'innocence de qn*); **research has established links between the two diseases,** la recherche a permis d'éta-

blir des liens entre les deux maladies; **the facts established by the inquiry,** les faits qui résultent des informations;
(d) *Rel Pol* ériger (*une Église*) en Église d'État.

established [ɪs'tæblɪʃt] *adj* établi; (*maison, amitié*) solide; (*fait*) avéré; **e. reputation,** réputation solide *ou* bien établie; **e. scientific fact,** fait acquis à la science; **the E. Church,** (*organization*) l'Église établie; (*religion*) la religion d'État; **the e. order,** l'ordre établi.

establishment [ɪs'tæblɪʃmənt] *n* **(a)** affermissement *m* (*de sa foi*); *Jur* homologation *f* (*d'un testament*);
(b) établissement *m* (*d'un gouvernement, d'une Église*); création *f* (*d'un système*); fondation *f* (*d'une maison de commerce*); constitution *f* (*d'une société*); assiette *f* (*d'un impôt*);
(c) (*of fact etc*) constatation *f*;
(d) (*company etc*) établissement *m*, maison *f*; **business e.,** maison de commerce; **private e.,** maison particulière;
(e) (*staff*) personnel *m* d'une maison; *Mil etc* effectif *m* (*d'une unité etc*); **to be on the e.,** faire partie du personnel; *Mil* **peacetime e.,** effectifs de paix;
(f) the (Church) E., l'Église établie;
(g) (*established order*) **the E.,** (*national institutions*) les institutions *fpl* (d'un pays); (*dominant group*) le groupe dirigeant; (*prevailing values*) l'ordre établi; **e. person,** traditionaliste *mf*; **to be against the E., to be anti-E.,** être anticonformiste; **to revolt against the E.,** se révolter contre l'ordre établi; **a playwright who was seen as an E. figure,** un dramaturge qui était considéré comme un conformiste.

estate [ɪs'teɪt] *n* **(a)** *Jur* (*property*) bien *m*, domaine *m*, immeuble *m*; (*of deceased person*) succession *f*, biens; (*of bankrupt*) actif *m*; **e. duty,** droits *mpl* de succession; **real e.,** biens immobiliers; **landed e.,** propriété foncière; **(b)** (*land*) terre *f*, propriété *f*; **country house and e. for sale,** à vendre château et domaine; *Br* **housing e.,** cité ouvrière; groupe *m* de H.L.M.; *Br* **industrial e.,** zone industrielle; **trading e.,** zone commerciale; *Br* **e. agent/agency,** agent immobilier/agence immobilière; *Br Aut* **e. car,** familiale *f*, break *m*; **(c)** (*state*) état *m*, condition *f*; **man's e.,** l'âge d'homme; **(d)** *Lit* (*social condition*) **of high/low e.,** de haut rang/d'humble condition; **(e)** *Fr Hist* **the Estates (of the Realm),** les états *mpl*, les ordres *mpl* (de l'ancien régime); **the Third E.,** le Tiers (État).

esteem¹ [ɪs'tiːm] *n* estime *f*, considération *f*; **to hold s.o. in high e.,** avoir qn en haute estime; **to go up/down in s.o.'s e.,** monter/baisser dans l'estime de qn.

esteem² *vt* **(a)** (*regard*) estimer (*qn*); priser (*qch*); **to e. sth lightly,** faire peu de cas de qch; **highly esteemed,** (*person*) fort estimé; **(b)** (*consider*) estimer, regarder (**sth as sth,** qch comme qch); **to e. it an honour that ....** se sentir honoré que ... .

ester ['estər] *n Biol Ch* ester *m*.

esthete, esthetic *etc US see* **AESTHETE, AESTHETIC** *etc*.

estimable ['estɪməb(ə)l] *adj* estimable, digne d'estime.

estimate¹ ['estɪmət] *n* **(a)** (*rough calculation*) appréciation *f*, évaluation *f*, calcul *m* (*du contenu de qch, de la force de qch*); **it's only an e.,** ce n'est qu'une estimation; **rough e.,** approximation grossière; **at a rough e.,** à vue de nez; **at the lowest e.,** au bas mot; **(b)** *Com* devis *m* (estimatif); **free e.,** devis gratuit; **building e.,** devis de construction; **preliminary e.,** devis de prévision; **to put in an e.,** donner un devis, soumissionner; *Pol* **the Estimates,** les prévisions *fpl* budgétaires.

estimate² ['estɪmeɪt] *vt* estimer, évaluer (*les frais etc*); **to e. sth at so much,** estimer *ou* calculer qch à tant; **his fortune is estimated at ...,** on évalue sa fortune à ...; **I e. that it will take three years,** j'estime que cela prendra trois ans.

estimated ['estɪmeɪtɪd] *adj* (*coût*) estimatif; (*valeur*) estimé; **it will cost an e. £500,000,** on estime que cela coûtera 500 000 livres; **it is only an e. figure,** ce n'est qu'une estimation; **e. time of arrival,** heure d'arrivée prévue.

estimation [estɪ'meɪʃən] *n* **(a)** (*rough calculation*) estimation *f*, appréciation *f*, évaluation *f*; calcul *m* (*des frais etc*); **(b)** (*judgement*) jugement *m*; **in my e.,** d'après moi, à mon avis; **(c)** (*regard*) estime *f*, considération *f*; **she is rising in the e. of the public,** elle remonte dans l'estime du public; **he's gone down in my e.,** il est descendu dans mon estime.

Estonia [es'təʊnɪə] *n* Estonie *f*.

Estonian [es'təʊnɪən] **1** *adj* estonien. **2** *n* Estonien, -ienne.

estrange [ɪs'treɪndʒ] *vt* s'aliéner l'affection de (*qn*); **to become estranged from s.o.,** se détacher de qn; **to be estranged,** (*of married couple*) être séparés.

estranged [ɪs'treɪndʒd] *adj* **an e. couple,** des époux séparés; **her e. husband,** son mari dont elle est séparée.

estrangement [ɪs'treɪn(d)ʒmənt] *n* aliénation *f* (*de qn*); (*of two people*) éloignement *m*, brouille *f* (**between,** entre); (*of married couple*) séparation *f*.

estrogen ['iːstrədʒen] *n US Bio Ch* œstrogène *m*.

estrous ['iːstrəs] *adj US Biol* (*cycle*) œstral, -aux.

estrus ['iːstrəs] *n US Biol* œstrus *m*.

estuary ['estjʊ(ə)rɪ] *n* estuaire *m*; **the Thames e.,** l'estuaire de la Tamise.

ETA [iːtiː'eɪ] *n Av* (*abbr* **estimated time of arrival**) = heure d'arrivée prévue.

et al [et'æl] (*abbr* **et alii**) et autres.

etc [et'setrə] *adv* (*abbr* **et cetera**) etc.; **they sell milk, bread etc.,** ils vendent du lait, du pain etc.; *F* **you have to fill in the form in duplicate etc. etc.,** il faut remplir le formulaire en deux exemplaires et cætera, et cætera.

et cetera [et'setrə] *adv* et cætera.

etceteras [et'setrəs] *npl* extras *mpl*; **roast turkey with all the e.,** dinde rôtie avec tout ce qui s'ensuit.

etch [etʃ] **1** *vt* graver (*un dessin etc*) à l'eau-forte; graver (*une planche*); **to e. away the metal,** enlever le métal à l'eau-forte; *Fig* **the scene was etched in his memory,** la scène était gravée dans sa mémoire. **2** *vi* faire de la gravure à l'eau-forte.

etcher ['etʃər] *n* graveur *m* à l'eau-forte.

etching ['etʃɪŋ] *n* **(a)** (*art*) art *m* de graver à l'eau-forte; **(b)** (*individual work*) gravure *f* à l'eau-forte, eau-forte *f*, *pl* eaux-fortes.

eternal [ɪ'tɜːn(ə)l] **1** *adj* **(a)** éternel; **e. life,** la vie éternelle; *Fig* **the e. triangle,** l'éternel triangle; **(b)** (*continual*) continuel, sans fin; **e. quarrelling,** querelles incessantes. **2** *n* **the E.,** l'Éternel *m*.

eternally [ɪ'tɜːn(ə)lɪ] *adv* éternellement; **I shall be e. grateful to you,** je vous serai éternellement reconnaissant.

eternity [ɪ'tɜːnɪtɪ] *n* éternité *f*; *F* **I waited an e.,** j'ai attendu pendant une éternité; *Br* **e. ring,** bague entièrement sertie de pierres symbolisant l'éternité du mariage.

ethane ['iːθeɪn] *n Ch* éthane *m*.

ether ['iːθər] *n* **(a)** éther *m*; **methyl e.,** éther méthylique; **e. addict,** éthéromane *mf*; **(b)** *Phys* **waves in the e.,** ondes *fpl* de l'éther; **(c)** *Arch & Lit* **the e.,** la voûte éthérée.

ethereal [ɪ'θɪərɪəl] *adj* (*region etc*) éthéré; (*form*) léger, impalpable.

ethereally [ɪ'θɪərɪəlɪ] *adv* **e. beautiful,** d'une beauté éthérée.

etherize ['iːθəraɪz] *vt Med* éthériser.

ethic ['eθɪk] *adj Gram* **e. dative,** datif *m* éthique.

ethical ['eθɪk(ə)l] *adj* moral, -aux; **e. writer,** moraliste *m*; *Pharm* **e. drug,** = remède vendu uniquement sur l'ordonnance d'un médecin; **the doctor's behaviour was not e.,** le comportement du médecin n'était pas conforme au code déontologique.

ethically ['eθɪklɪ] *adv* d'après (les doctrines de) l'éthique.

ethics ['eθɪks] *npl* (*usu with sing verb*) éthique *f*, morale *f*; (*of profession*) déontologie *f*; **e. code, code of e.,** code *m* déontologique.

Ethiopia [iːθɪ'əʊpɪə] *n* Éthiopie *f*.

Ethiopian [iːθɪ'əʊpɪən] **1** *adj* éthiopien. **2** *n* Éthiopien, -ienne.

ethnic(al) ['eθnɪk, -ɪk(ə)l] *adj* ethnique.

ethnically ['eθnɪklɪ] *adv* du point de vue ethnique.

ethnographer [eθ'nɒgrəfər] *n* ethnographe *mf*.

ethnography [eθ'nɒgrəfɪ] *n* ethnographie *f*.

ethnological [eθnə'lɒdʒɪk(ə)l] *adj* ethnologique.

ethnologically [eθnə'lɒdʒɪklɪ] *adv* ethnologiquement.

ethnologist [eθ'nɒlədʒɪst] *n* ethnologue *mf*.

ethnology [eθ'nɒlədʒɪ] *n* ethnologie *f*.

ethological [iːθə'lɒdʒɪk(ə)l] *adj* éthologique.

ethology [ɪ'θɒlədʒɪ] *n* éthologie *f*.

ethos ['iːθɒs] *n* génie *m* (*d'un peuple etc*).

ethyl ['eθɪl] *n Ch* éthyle *m*; **e. alcohol,** alcool *m* éthylique.

ethylene ['eθɪliːn] *n Ch* éthylène *m*.

etiolate ['iːtɪəʊleɪt] *vt* étioler (*une plante*).

etiology [iːtɪ'ɒlədʒɪ] *n US* étiologie *f*.

etiquette ['etɪket] *n* étiquette *f*; **court e.,** le cérémonial de cour; **the e. of the Bar,** les règles *fpl* du Barreau.

Etonian [iː'təʊnɪən] *n Sch* élève *m* (du collège) d'Eton; **Old E.,** ancien élève d'Eton.

Etruscan [ɪ'trʌskən] **1** *adj* étrusque. **2** *n* Étrusque *mf*.

etymological [etɪmə'lɒdʒɪk(ə)l] *adj* (*dictionary etc*) étymologique.

etymologically [etɪmə'lɒdʒɪklɪ] *adv* étymologiquement.

etymologist [etɪ'mɒlədʒɪst] *n* étymologiste *mf*.
etymology [etɪ'mɒlədʒɪ] *n* étymologie *f*.
eucalyptus, *pl* **-ti, -tuses** [juːkə'lɪptəs, -taɪ, -təsɪz] *n* (*tree*) eucalyptus *m*; *Pharm* **e. oil,** essence *f* d'eucalyptus.
Eucharist (the) [ðə'juːkərɪst] *n Rel* l'eucharistie *f*; **to receive the E.**, recevoir l'eucharistie.
Euclidean [juː'klɪdɪən] *adj* (*géométrie*) euclidien.
eugenics [juː'dʒenɪks] *npl* (*usu with sing verb*) eugénique *f*, eugénisme *m*.
eulogize ['juːlədʒaɪz] *vt* faire l'éloge *ou* le panégyrique de (*qn, qch*).
eulogy ['juːlədʒɪ] *n* panégyrique *m*; **to pronounce a e. on s.o.**, faire l'éloge *ou* le panégyrique de qn.
eunuch ['juːnək] *n* eunuque *m*.
euphemism ['juːfɪmɪz(ə)m] *n* euphémisme *m*.
euphemistic [juːfɪ'mɪstɪk] *adj* euphémique.
euphemistically [juːfɪ'mɪstɪklɪ] *adv* euphémiquement; par euphémisme.
euphonious [juː'fəʊnɪəs] *adj* euphonique.
euphonium [juː'fəʊnɪəm] *n Mus* saxhorn *m* basse; basse *f* (des cuivres); **e. player,** bassiste *m*.
euphony ['juːfənɪ] *n* euphonie *f*; **for the sake of e.**, par euphonie.
euphorbia [juː'fɔːbɪə] *n* (*plant*) euphorbe *f*.
euphoria [juː'fɔːrɪə] *n* euphorie *f*.
euphoric [juː'fɔːrɪk] *adj* euphorique.
Eurasia [jʊə'reɪʃə, -ʒə] *n* Eurasie *f*.
Eurasian [jʊə'reɪʃən, -ʒən] **1** *adj* eurasien; (*faune etc*) eurasiatique. **2** *n* Eurasien, -ienne.
eureka [juː'riːkə] *int* euréka.
eurhythmics [juː'rɪðmɪks] *npl* (*usu with sing verb*) gymnastique *f* rythmique.
Euro ['jʊərəʊ] *adj F* européen; **a E. M.P.**, un membre du parlement européen.
Eurocheque ['jʊərəʊtʃek] *n* eurochèque *m*.
Eurocrat ['jʊərəʊkræt] *n* eurocrate *mf*.
Eurodollar ['jʊərəʊdɒlər] *n Fin* Eurodollar *m*.
Europe ['jʊərəp] *n* Europe *f*; **Council of E.**, Conseil *m* de l'Europe; **in E.**, en Europe.
European [jʊərə'piːən] **1** *adj* européen; **E. Commission,** Commission européenne; **E. Economic Community,** Communauté économique européenne; *US* **E. plan,** = tarif d'hôtel qui n'inclut pas les repas; **E. Free Trade Association,** Association européenne de libre échange. **2** *n* Européen, -éenne; *F* (*white person*) blanc, blanche.
Eustachian [juːs'teɪʃən] *adj Anat* **E. tube,** trompe *f* d'Eustache.
eutectic [juː'tektɪk] *adj & n Ch* eutectique *m*.
euthanasia [juːθə'neɪzɪə] *n* euthanasie *f*.
eutrophic [juː'trɒfɪk] *adj* (*lake*) eutrophe.
eutrophication [juːtrɒfɪ'keɪʃən] *n* (*of lake*) eutrophisation *f*.
evacuate [ɪ'vækjʊeɪt] *vt* évacuer (*un lieu, la population*); *MecE* refouler (*les gaz brûlés d'un moteur etc*); *Phys* faire le vide dans (*un tube*); *Physiol* **to e. the bowels,** vider les intestins; **children were evacuated to the countryside,** les enfants ont été évacués vers la campagne.
evacuation [ɪvækjʊ'eɪʃən] *n* évacuation *f* (*d'un lieu, des gens*); *Physiol* évacuation (*du ventre*); *MecE* refoulement *m* (*des gaz brûlés d'un moteur etc*); *Phys* production *f* du vide (*dans un tube*).
evacuee [ɪvækjʊ'iː] *n* évacué, -ée; **e. children,** enfants évacués.
evade [ɪ'veɪd] *vt* éviter (*un coup, un danger*); esquiver (*un coup, ses créanciers*); se soustraire à (*la justice*); éluder, tourner (*un obstacle, la loi*); déjouer (*la vigilance de qn*); **to e. customs duty (on sth),** passer qch en fraude; **to e. tax,** frauder le fisc; **to e. a question,** éluder une question.
evader [ɪ'veɪdər] *n* éludeur *m* (**of,** de); **tax e.**, fraudeur, -euse du fisc.
evaluate [ɪ'væljʊeɪt] *vt* évaluer (*les dommages*), estimer le montant de (*les dommages*).
evaluation [ɪvæljʊ'eɪʃən] *n* évaluation *f* (*du dommage*); *Mil* **e. of information,** critique *f* du renseignement.
evanescent [evə'nesənt] *adj* évanescent, éphémère.
evangelical [iːvæn'dʒelɪk(ə)l] *Rel* **1** *adj* **(a)** qui appartient à la religion réformée; **the E. Church,** l'Église évangélique; **(b)** (*relating to the Gospels*) évangélique; (*conforming to the Gospel*) conforme à l'Évangile; **e. preacher,** évangéliste *mf*. **2** *n* protestant, -ante évangélique.
evangelicalism [iːvæn'dʒelɪkəlɪz(ə)m] *n Rel* évangélisme *m*; doctrine *f* de l'Église évangélique.
evangelism [ɪ'vændʒɪlɪz(ə)m] *n Rel* évangélisme *m*, prédication *f* de l'Évangile.
evangelist [ɪ'væn(d)ʒɪlɪst] *n* évangéliste *mf*.
evangelize [ɪ'væn(d)ʒɪlaɪz] **1** *vt* évangéliser; prêcher l'Évangile à (*qn*). **2** *vi* prêcher l'Évangile; *Fig* **he has been evangelizing about jazz for years,** il prêche les mérites du jazz depuis des années.
evaporate [ɪ'væpəreɪt] **1** *vt* (faire) évaporer (*un liquide*); **evaporated milk,** lait condensé (non sucré). **2** *vi* (*of liquid etc*) s'évaporer, se vaporiser; (*of acid*) se volatiliser; *Fig* (*of money*) disparaître comme par enchantement; **her enthusiasm suddenly evaporated,** son enthousiasme s'est soudainement envolé.
evaporation [ɪvæpə'reɪʃən] *n* évaporation *f*, vaporisation *f* (*d'un liquide, d'un parfum*); volatilisation *f* (*d'un acide etc*).
evaporator [ɪ'væpəreɪtər] *n Ind* évaporateur *m*.
evasion [ɪ'veɪʒən] *n* **(a)** (*escape*) évasion *f*, fuite *f*; (*act of dodging a commitment*) dérobade *f*; **tax e.**, fraude fiscale; **(b)** (*subterfuge*) subterfuge *m*, échappatoire *f*, faux-fuyant *m*, *pl* faux-fuyants; **without e.**, sans détours.
evasive [ɪ'veɪsɪv] *adj* (*person*) évasif; (*personnalité*) fuyant; **to give an e. answer,** faire une réponse évasive, répondre évasivement; *Mil etc* **to take e. action,** faire une manœuvre d'évitement.
evasively [ɪ'veɪsɪvlɪ] *adv* (*to answer*) évasivement.
evasiveness [ɪ'veɪsɪvnɪs] *n* caractère évasif.
eve [iːv] *n* **(a)** (*day before*) veille *f*; **Christmas E.**, la veille de Noël; **New Year's E.**, la Saint-Sylvestre; **on the e. of ...**, à la veille de ...; *Fig* **to be on the e. of success,** être à la veille du succès; **(b)** *Arch & Lit* soir *m*.
Eve [iːv] *n* Ève *f*; *F* **a daughter of E.**, une fille d'Ève; *Br Culin* **E.'s pudding,** compote de pommes recouverte de génoise.
even¹ ['iːv(ə)n] *adj* **(a)** (*surface, ground etc*) uni, égal, -aux; **to be e. with sth,** être au niveau de *ou* à ras de qch; **to make e.**, araser (*les assises d'une construction*); aplanir (*une surface*); affleurer (*les bords de deux planches etc*); égaliser (*des entre-deux etc*);
(b) (*regular*) (*pulse*) égal, régulier; **e. temperature,** température égale; **e. temper,** caractère *m* calme;
(c) (*in equal amounts*) *Horseracing* **e. money,** pari *m* avec enjeu égal; *Horseracing* **at e. money,** cheval coté à égalité; **to break e.**, ne faire ni pertes ni profits; **to break e. on a deal,** rentrer dans ses frais dans une affaire; **he has an e. chance of succeeding,** il a une chance sur deux de réussir; *Sp* **to be e.**, être à égalité; **e. match,** partie égale; *Fig* **to get e. with s.o.**, prendre sa revanche sur qn; **to be e. with s.o.**, être quitte avec qn; **I'll be e. with him yet,** je la lui rendrai;
(d) (*fair*) **with an e. hand,** impartialement; **e. bargain,** marché *m* équitable *ou* juste;
(e) (*number*) pair; **odd or e.**, pair ou impair; *Comptr* **e. parity,** parité *f*.
even² *adv* **(a)** même; (*with comparative*) encore; (*with negative*) même; **or e. ...**, ou même ...; **e. the cleverest,** même les plus habiles; **e. the children knew,** même les enfants savaient; **I never e. saw it,** je ne l'ai même pas vu; **e. supposing that ...**, même en supposant que ...; **that would be e. worse/better,** ce serait encore pis/mieux; **e. more/less,** encore plus/moins; **he seemed e. sadder than usual,** il paraissait encore plus triste que d'habitude; **this would be sad, tragic e.**, ça serait triste, tragique même; **without e. speaking,** sans dire un mot; **e. if she failed,** même si elle échouait; **he always goes by bus, e. though he has a car,** il prend toujours l'autobus, bien qu'il ait une voiture; **e. with a computer the work would take months,** même avec un ordinateur, le travail prendrait des mois; **e. so,** mais cependant, quand même; **e. then she wouldn't believe me,** même alors elle ne voulait pas me croire;
(b) (*with time*) **e. as I speak,** au moment même où je parle; **e. now,** à l'instant même; **e. then,** déjà (à cette époque).
even³ *vt* **(a)** (*make smooth*) aplanir, niveler, égaliser (*une surface etc*); affleurer (*deux planches etc*); araser (*les assises d'un mur*); **(b)** (*make equal*) rendre égal; *Typ* **to e. the spacing,** égaliser l'espacement.
►**even out 1** *vi* (*become smooth, flat*) s'aplanir, s'égaliser, se niveler; (*of curve on graph*) s'aplanir; **the road goes uphill and then evens out,** la route monte puis s'aplanit; **prices finally evened out,** les prix ont fini par s'égaliser. **2** *vtsep* (*make equal, fairer*) répartir également; **taxation has been evened out,** l'imposition a été répartie également; **that evens things out,** on est quitte(s).
►**even up** *vtsep* **(a)** (*make equal*) égaliser; **that last goal evened up the score,** le dernier but a égalisé le score; **that will e. things up,** (*if you pay for this*) on sera

quittes; **(b)** *(increase)* arrondir au chiffre supérieur; **let's e. it up to a pound,** arrondissons la somme à une livre.

even-handed ['iːv(ə)n'hændɪd] *adj* équitable, juste, impartial.

evening ['iːvnɪŋ] *n* **(a)** soir *m*; *(duration)* soirée *f*; **tomorrow e.**, demain soir; **yesterday e.**, hier (au) soir; **in the e.**, le soir, au soir; **what do you do in the evenings?**, qu'est-ce que vous faites le soir?; **at nine o'clock in the e.**, à neuf heures du soir; **I'm going out this e.**, je sors ce soir; **(on) that e.**, ce soir-là; **(on) the e. before, (on) the previous e.**, la veille au soir; **the next e.**, le lendemain soir; **one** *or* **on a fine summer e.**, (par) un beau soir d'été; **every e.**, tous les soirs; **every Monday e.**, tous les lundis soir; **on the e. of Monday, 29th March,** dans la soirée du lundi 29 mars; **all (the) e.**, toute la soirée; **during the e.**, pendant la soirée; *Fig Lit* **in the e. of life,** au déclin de la vie; **e. class,** cours *m* du soir; **e. paper,** journal *m* du soir; *Th* **e. performance,** représentation *f* de soirée; *Astron* **e. star,** étoile *f* du soir;

(b) *(evening party)* soirée *f*; **musical e.**, soirée musicale; **e. dress** *or* **wear,** *(for men)* tenue *f* de soirée; *(for women)* robe *f* du soir; **in e. dress,** en tenue de soirée; **e. gown,** robe de soirée *ou* du soir.

evenly ['iːv(ə)nlɪ] *adv* **(a)** *(étendre, filer)* uniment; **spread the glue e.**, étaler la colle régulièrement; **(b)** *(respirer, tourner)* régulièrement; **(c)** *(fairly)* *(diviser)* également; **e. matched,** *(of equal size)* de grandeur égale; *(of equal strength)* de force égale; **the (two) teams/boxers were e. matched,** les (deux) équipes/boxeurs étaient de force égale.

evenness ['iːvənnɪs] *n* **(a)** *(smoothness)* caractère plat *ou* égal *ou* nivelé; **(b)** *(regularity)* égalité *f*; régularité *f* *(de mouvement)*; **(c)** *(calm)* calme *m* *(d'esprit)*; égalité *f* *(d'humeur)*.

even-numbered ['iːvən'nʌmbəd] *adj* (portant un nombre) pair.

evens ['iːv(ə)nz] *npl* *(in betting)* **to lay e.**, parier à l'égalité; **horses quoted at e.**, cheval coté à égalité.

evensong ['iːv(ə)nsɒŋ] *n Church of Eng* office *m* du soir; *Cathol* vêpres *fpl* et salut *m*.

event [ɪ'vent] *n* **(a)** *(occurrence)* événement *m*; **it's quite an e.**, c'est un véritable événement; *Com* **great coat e.!**, grands soldes de manteaux!; *F* **a happy e.**, un heureux événement; **in the course of events,** par la suite; **as recent events have shown,** comme l'ont montré de récents événements;

(b) *(outcome)* issue *f*, résultat *m*; **in either e.**, dans l'un ou l'autre cas; **wise after the e.**, sage après coup; **at all events, in any e.**, en tout cas; **in the e. of his refusing,** au *ou* dans le cas où il refuserait, pour le cas où il refuserait; **in the e. of his death,** en cas de décès; **in the e. of rain,** au cas où il pleuvrait, en cas de pluie;

(c) *Sp* *(meeting)* réunion sportive; *(individual category, contest)* épreuve *f*; *Boxing Fencing etc* rencontre *f*; **sporting e.**, manifestation sportive; **field events,** *(athletics)* épreuves *fpl* sur terrain; **track events,** courses *fpl* *ou* épreuves sur piste.

even-tempered ['iːv(ə)n'tempəd] *adj* d'humeur égale.

eventer [ɪ'ventər] *n Horseriding* participant, -ante au concours complet.

eventful [ɪ'ventfʊl] *adj* *(life)* plein d'incidents, mouvementé; *(day, year)* mémorable.

eventide ['iːv(ə)ntaɪd] *n Lit* soir *m*.

eventing [ɪ'ventɪŋ] *n Horseriding* concours complet d'obstacles.

eventual [ɪ'ventjʊəl] *adj* **(a)** *(final)* définitif; **his prodigality and his e. ruin,** sa prodigalité et sa ruine finale; **(b)** *(possible)* éventuel; **the e. profits from his new deal,** les profits éventuels de sa nouvelle affaire.

eventuality [ɪventjʊ'ælɪtɪ] *n* éventualité *f*; **in that e.**, dans cette éventualité.

eventually [ɪ'ventjʊəlɪ] *adv* en fin de compte; par la suite; **he e. became a judge,** il finit par être nommé juge; **they e. reached the castle,** ils ont fini par arriver au château; **I'll get round to mending that door e.**, je finirai par réparer cette porte un de ces jours.

ever ['evər] *adv* **(a)** jamais; **the best mother that e. was,** la meilleure mère qui fût jamais; **I read seldom if e.**, je lis rarement, pour ne pas dire jamais; **if e. I catch him,** si jamais je l'attrape; **nothing e. happens,** il n'arrive jamais rien; **hardly e., scarcely e.**, presque jamais; **he's a liar if e. there was one,** c'est un menteur s'il en fût jamais; **it started to rain faster than e.**, il s'est mis à pleuvoir de plus belle; **without e. having thought of it,** sans jamais y avoir pensé; **worst e., best e.**, sans précédent; *Sl* **did you e.!**, par exemple!; **they lived happily e. after,** ils vécurent heureux à tout jamais; **e. since (then),** dès lors, depuis; **I have been here e. since lunch,** je suis là depuis le déjeuner; **he came to Scotland in 1960 and he's been here e. since,** il est arrivé en Écosse en 1960 et il y est toujours resté;

(b) *(always)* toujours; **e.-increasing influence,** influence toujours plus étendue; *Old-fashioned* **yours e., e. yours,** *(letter ending)* bien cordialement à vous, tout(e) à vous; **e. the gentleman, he opened the door for her,** en gentleman, comme toujours, il lui a ouvert la porte; **she was as cheerful as e.**, elle était aussi gaie qu'à l'habitude; **for e.**, pour toujours, à jamais; **to go away for e.**, partir sans retour; **for e. and e.**, à tout jamais; **Scotland for e.!**, vive l'Écosse!; **to live for e.**, vivre éternellement; **he's for e. grumbling,** il ne cesse pas de se plaindre;

(c) *(intensive)* **as quickly as e. you can,** aussi vite que possible; **as soon as e. he comes home,** aussitôt qu'il rentrera; **it was the funniest sight e.**, c'était à se tordre; *F* **e. so pretty,** joli comme tout; *F* **it was e. so long ago,** ça fait tellement longtemps; *F* **e. so many times,** je ne sais combien de fois; **thank you e. so much,** merci mille fois; **I'm e. so pleased,** j'en suis tellement content; *F* **e. such a lot of money,** une somme d'argent tellement importante; **how e. you manage I don't know,** je me demande comment vous faites; **what e. shall we do?**, qu'est-ce que nous allons bien faire?; **what ever's the matter with you?**, mais qu'est-ce que vous avez donc?; **what e. can it be?**, qu'est-ce que ça peut bien être?; **when e. will he come?**, quand donc viendra-t-il?; **where e. have you been?**, mais d'où venez-vous?; **who e. told you that?**, qui est-ce qui a bien pu vous dire cela?; **why e. not?**, mais pourquoi pas?; *Am Sl* **is he** *or* **she** *or* **it** *etc* **e.!**, *(generous, stupid, a beautiful day etc)* et comment!

evergreen ['evəgriːn] **1** *adj* toujours vert; *Bot* à feuilles persistantes; **e. oak,** chêne vert; *Fig* **e. topic,** question *f* toujours d'actualité; *Fin* **e. facility,** = possibilité *f* de prêt permanent. **2** *n* arbre *m* à feuilles persistantes.

everlasting [evə'lɑːstɪŋ] **1** *adj* **(a)** *(eternal)* éternel; *Bible* **the mighty God, the e. Father,** le Dieu tout-puissant, le Père éternel; **e. flower,** immortelle *f*; **e. pea,** pois *m* vivace; **(b)** *(material)* inusable, solide; **(c)** *(continual)* perpétuel, continuel; **I am tired of her e. complaints,** je suis las de ses plaintes sans fin. **2** *n* **the E.**, l'Éternel *m*.

everlastingly [evə'lɑːstɪŋlɪ] *adv* **(a)** *(eternally)* éternellement; **(b)** *(continually)* perpétuellement.

evermore [evə'mɔːr] *adv* toujours; **for e.**, à jamais.

every ['evrɪ] *adj* **(a)** chaque; tout; tous les ...; **e. week,** toutes les semaines, chaque semaine; **e. word he says is a lie,** tout ce qu'il dit est mensonge; **I have copied e. word of it,** je l'ai copié mot pour mot; **his desire to meet your e. wish,** son désir d'aller au-devant de chacun de vos désirs; **e. action of hers,** *Lit* **her e. action,** chacune de ses actions; **e. day,** chaque jour, tous les jours; **it's not e. day you get married,** ce n'est pas tous les jours qu'on se marie; **confidence is increasing e. day,** la confiance s'accroît de jour en jour; **e. other** *or* **second day,** tous les deux jours, un jour sur deux; **e. other Sunday,** un dimanche sur deux; **e. second or third day,** tous les deux ou trois jours; **e. third man was chosen,** on choisissait un homme sur trois; **at e. quarter past the hour,** toutes les heures, au quart; **e. few minutes,** toutes les cinq minutes; **e. so often, e. now and again** *or* **then,** de temps en temps, de temps à autre; **e. time that she comes,** chaque fois qu'elle vient; **perseverance wins e. time,** la persévérance l'emporte toujours;

(b) *(intensive)* **he was e. inch a republican,** il était républicain jusqu'au bout des ongles; **I have e. reason to believe that ...**, j'ai tout lieu de croire que ...; **you have e. right to be angry,** tu as tout à fait le droit d'être en colère; **e. bit as good/intelligent as ...**, tout aussi bon/intelligent que ...; **I shall give you e. assistance,** je vous aiderai de tout mon pouvoir; **I look forward with e. confidence to the future,** j'envisage l'avenir avec une pleine confiance; *Am* **e. which way I look,** où que je regarde; *Am* **to look e. which way for s.o.**, chercher qn partout; *Am* **(from) e. which way,** de tous les côtés;

(c) **e. one,** chacun, chacune; **e. one of us was there,** nous étions tous là; **they are my friends, e. one of them,** ils sont tous mes amis; **e. man for himself,** chacun pour soi; *(in danger)* sauve qui peut!; **e. person has this right,** chacun a ce droit; **e. man Jack of them,** tous sans exception.

everybody ['evrɪbɒdɪ] *indef pron* tout le monde; **e. has his** *or* **her** *or* *F* **their own way of doing things,** chacun *ou* chacune a sa manière de faire les choses; **e. else,** tous les autres; **e. knows that,** tout le monde *ou* n'importe qui sait cela; **not e. can do it,** ce n'est pas tout le monde qui pourrait le faire; **e. else knows it,** tous les autres le savent; **e. in the room was smoking,** tout le monde dans la pièce fumait.

everyday ['evrɪdeɪ] *adj* **(a)** (*daily*) journalier, quotidien; **e. occurrence,** (*happening every day*) fait journalier; (*ordinary*) fait banal; **e. life,** la vie quotidienne; **(b)** (*used every day*) de tous les jours; **(c)** (*ordinary*) usuel, ordinaire; **e. expression,** expression courante; **e. English,** l'anglais de tous les jours; **words in e. use,** mots d'usage courant.

everyone ['evrɪwʌn] *indef pron* = **EVERYBODY.**

everyplace ['evrɪpleɪs] *adv Am F* = **EVERYWHERE.**

everything ['evrɪθɪŋ] *indef pron* tout; **he has eaten e.,** il a tout mangé; **(a place for e., and) e. in its place,** chaque chose à sa place; **e. good,** tout ce qu'il y a de bon; **they sell e.,** on y vend de tout; *Com* **e. for cyclists,** tout ce qui concerne le cyclisme; *F* **we're in a bad way with strikes and e.,** ça marche mal à cause des grèves et de tout ça; **money is not e.,** l'argent n'est pas tout; **beauty isn't e.,** il n'y a pas que la beauté (qui compte); **she's e. to me,** elle est tout pour moi.

everywhere ['evrɪweər] *adv* partout, en tous lieux; **to look e. for s.o.,** chercher qn partout; **e. you go,** partout où vous allez, où que vous alliez; **e. you look there is poverty,** de quelque côté que l'on se tourne, on voit la pauvreté; **e. in France,** partout en France.

evict [ɪ'vɪkt] *vt* évincer, expulser (*un locataire*) (**from,** de); **evicted tenant,** locataire évincé.

eviction [ɪ'vɪkʃən] *n Jur* éviction *f*, expulsion *f* (*d'un locataire*); **e. notice,** avis *m* d'expulsion.

evidence¹ ['evɪdəns] *n* **(a)** (*non-legal use*) évidence *f*; **to fly in the face of the e.,** se refuser à l'évidence; **if you can't believe the e. of your eyes!,** si vous n'êtes pas convaincu par ce que vous voyez devant vous!; **on the e. of their past performances,** si l'on en juge par leurs performances passées; **to be in e.,** (*of person etc*) être en évidence; **the army was much in e. on the streets,** l'armée était très fortement présente dans les rues;
(b) (*indication*) signe *m*, marque *f*; **to bear** *or* **give e. of sth,** porter la marque de qch; **there was no e. of his stay in the house,** rien ne montrait qu'il eût séjourné dans la maison; **there is no evidence to suggest a link between the two diseases,** il n'y a aucune preuve suggérant qu'il y ait un lien entre les deux maladies; **books were e. of her interest in the subject,** les livres constituaient une preuve de son intérêt pour le sujet;
(c) *Jur* preuve *f*; (*testimony*) témoignage *m*; **internal e.,** preuves intrinsèques; **external e.,** preuves extrinsèques; **oral e.,** preuve orale; **written/documentary e.,** preuve littérale/documentaire; **to give e.,** témoigner, déposer (en justice); **to give e. in s.o.'s favour,** témoigner en faveur de qn; **to call s.o. in e.,** appeler qn en témoignage; **the e. was strongly against him,** les témoignages pesaient contre lui;
(d) *Jur* (*witness*) témoin(s) *m(pl)*; **to turn King's** *or* **Queen's** *or* **US State's e.,** témoigner contre ses complices (*sous promesse de pardon*).

evidence² *vt Fml* témoigner de (*qch*).

evident ['evɪdənt] *adj* évident; (*fact, truth*) patent; **it was e. that ...,** il était évident *ou* clair que ... .

evidently ['evɪdəntlɪ] *adv* évidemment, manifestement; **he was e. afraid,** il était évident *ou* clair qu'il avait peur; **the government, e. worried, put off the elections,** le gouvernement, manifestement inquiet, a remis les élections à plus tard.

evil ['iːv(ə)l] **1** *adj* **(a)** (*person*) mauvais, malveillant; (*spirit*) malfaisant, malin; (*day*) malheureux; (*moment*) funeste; **the E. One,** le Malin; **e. influence,** influence *f* néfaste; **e. eye,** mauvais œil; **e. tongue,** mauvaise langue; **to silence e. tongues,** faire taire la médisance; **house of e. repute,** lieu mal famé; **e. omen,** présage *m* de malheur; **to fall on e. days,** tomber dans l'infortune *ou* dans le malheur; *F* **to put off the e. hour,** (*of visit to dentist etc*) repousser le moment fatal; **(b)** (*smell*) mauvais, nauséabond. **2** *n* mal *m*, *pl* maux; **a social e.,** une plaie sociale; **to speak e. of s.o.,** dire du mal de qn.

evildoer ['iːv(ə)lduːər] *n* malfaiteur *m*.

evil-looking ['iːv(ə)llʊkɪŋ] *adj* de mauvaise mine; (*homme*) louche; **he drew an e.-l. knife,** il tira un vilain couteau.

evilly ['iːvɪlɪ] *adv* avec malveillance; (*regarder qn*) d'un mauvais œil, d'un air méchant.

evil-minded ['iːv(ə)l'maɪndɪd] *adj* malintentionné, malveillant.

evil-smelling ['iːv(ə)l'smelɪŋ] *adj* nauséabond.

evince [ɪ'vɪns] *vt Fml* montrer, témoigner (*une qualité etc*); manifester (*de la curiosité etc*).

eviscerate [ɪ'vɪsəreɪt] *vt* **(a)** éviscérer, éventrer; **(b)** *Fig* émasculer (*un ouvrage littéraire etc*).

evisceration [ɪvɪsə'reɪʃən] *n* éviscération *f*.

evocation [evə'keɪʃən] *n* évocation *f*.

evocative [ɪ'vɒkətɪv] *adj* évocateur, -trice (**of,** de).

evoke [ɪ'vəʊk] *vt* **(a)** (*conjure up*) évoquer (*un souvenir*); **(b)** (*provoke*) **this remark evoked a smile,** cette observation a provoqué *ou* suscité un sourire.

evolution [iːvə'luːʃən] *n* **(a)** *Biol etc* évolution *f*, développement *m* (*d'une espèce, d'un projet etc*); **the theory of e.,** la théorie de l'évolution des espèces; *Fig* **the e. of events,** le déroulement des événements; **her e. from journalist to revolutionary leader,** son passage de la carrière de journaliste à celle de dirigeante d'un groupe révolutionnaire; **(b)** (*manoeuvre*) évolution *f* (*d'un acrobate, de troupes etc*).

evolutionary [iːvə'luːʃən(ə)rɪ] *adj Biol* (*character, symptom, disease*) évolutif.

evolutionism [iːvə'luːʃənɪz(ə)m] *n Biol* évolutionnisme *m*.

evolutionist [iːvə'luːʃənɪst] *n Biol* évolutionniste *mf*.

evolve [ɪ'vɒlv] **1** *vt* dérouler, développer (*un projet*); développer, déduire (*une théorie, une vérité*) (**from,** de); développer (*par évolution*). **2** *vi* (*of events*) se dérouler; (*of gas etc*) se dégager; (*of race*) se développer, évoluer; **medicine has evolved into a sophisticated science,** la médecine est devenue une science sophistiquée.

ewe [juː] *n* brebis *f*.

ewer ['jʊər] *n Old-fashioned* pot *m* à eau; broc *m* de toilette.

ex¹ [eks] *prep* **(a)** *Com* (*out of*) **price ex works,** prix *m* départ usine, prix sortie d'usine; **(b)** (*without*) *Fin* **shares quoted ex dividend/ex coupon,** actions cotées dividende détachée/coupon détaché.

ex² *n F* (*former husband or wife*) **my ex,** mon ex.

ex- [eks] *prep* (*former*) ancien; ex-; **ex-minister,** ex-ministre; **an ex-teacher,** un ancien professeur; **ex-wife,** ex-femme; **all her ex-boyfriends,** tous ses ex.

exacerbate [eg'zæsəbeɪt] *vt* exacerber, aggraver (*une douleur etc*); irriter, exaspérer (*qn*).

exact¹ [ɪg'zækt] *adj* **(a)** exact, précis; **to give e. details,** donner des détails précis *ou* des précisions, préciser; **the e. sciences,** les sciences exactes; **an e. replica,** une réplique exacte; **those were her e. words,** c'est ce qu'elle a dit mot pour mot; **the e. quantity/length/***etc*, la quantité/longueur/*etc* exacte; **the e. word,** le mot juste; **to tender the e. amount,** (*on bus*) faire l'appoint; **(b)** (*discipline*) strict, rigoureux; **(c)** (*person*) **to be e.,** être exact (*dans ses paiements*); être strict (*en affaires*); **she was very e. in her reporting of events,** elle a été très précise dans son compte-rendu des événements.

exact² *vt* **(a)** (*take*) exiger (*un impôt*) (**from,** de); extorquer (*une rançon à qn*); **(b)** (*insist on*) exiger, réclamer (*l'obéissance*) (**from,** de).

exacting [ɪg'zæktɪŋ] *adj* (*person*) exigeant; (*work*) astreignant; **to be too e.,** se montrer trop exigeant.

exaction [ɪg'zækʃən] *n* exaction *f*.

exactitude [ɪg'zæktɪtjuːd] *n* exactitude *f*, précision *f*; justesse *f* (*d'un raisonnement, d'un calcul*).

exactly [ɪg'zæktlɪ] *adv* **(a)** exactement, précisément; (*of time*) juste; **I don't know e. what happened,** je ne sais pas au juste ce qui est arrivé; **but that's e. what I mean!,** mais c'est précisément ce que je veux dire!; **e.!,** précisément!, parfaitement!; **it is e. five,** il est cinq heures juste; **not e.,** pas precisément; **she didn't e. agree, but ...,** elle n'était pas vraiment d'accord, mais ...; **he is not e. a scholar,** ce n'est pas precisément un savant; **(b)** (*with precision*) précisément, exactement; **e. calibrated,** précisément étalonné.

exaggerate [ɪg'zædʒəreɪt] **1** *vt* exagérer; agrandir, amplifier (*les fautes etc*); grandir (*un incident*); charger (*un récit*); **the importance of this incident has been exaggerated in the press,** l'importance de cet incident a été exagérée dans la presse; *Fig* **the shoes exaggerated the size of his feet,** les chaussures exagéraient la taille de ses pieds. **2** *vi* exagérer; **let's not e.!,** n'exagérons rien!

exaggerated [ɪg'zædʒəreɪtɪd] *adj* exagéré; (*praise*) outré; **e. behaviour,** comportement excessif; **to have an e. opinion of oneself,** avoir une trop haute opinion de soi-même; **to attach e. importance to sth,** prêter une importance excessive à qch.

exaggeratedly [ɪg'zædʒərəɪtɪdlɪ] *adv* exagérément.

exaggeration [ɪgzædʒə'reɪʃən] *n* exagération *f*; **without e.,** sans exagération; **that's an e.!,** vous exagérez!

exalt [ɪg'zɔːlt] *vt* **(a)** *(praise)* exalter, vanter *(les vertus de qn)*; **to e. s.o. to the skies,** porter qn jusqu'aux nues; **(b)** *(raise in rank)* élever *(qn en rang etc)*.

exalted [ɪg'zɔːltɪd] **(a)** *(noble)* exalté; *(ton)* élevé; **(b)** *(rank)* élevé; *(person)* haut placé.

exam [ɪg'zæm] *n* = **EXAMINATION (b)**.

examination [ɪgzæmɪ'neɪʃən] *n* **(a)** *(inspection)* examen *m*; inspection *f*, visite *f* *(des machines etc)*; vérification *f* *(de comptes)*; dépouillement *m* *(d'un rapport)*; *Jur* compulsation *f* *(de dossiers etc)*; **on e.,** après examen, examen fait; **on further e.,** après un examen plus approfondi; *Jur* **the case is under e.,** l'affaire est soumise à la vérification; **to undergo a medical e.,** passer une visite médicale; **(b)** *Sch etc* examen *m*; **entrance e.,** examen d'entrée; **competitive e.,** concours *m*; **written/oral e.,** épreuves écrites/orales; **to take** *or* **sit an e.,** passer *ou* subir un examen; **to pass/fail an e.,** être reçu/refusé à un examen; **e. paper,** sujet *m* d'examen, questions *fpl* d'examen; **e. result,** résultat *m* d'examen; **(c)** *Jur* interrogatoire *m* *(d'un accusé etc)*; audition *f* *(de témoins)*; instruction *f* *(d'une cause)*.

examine [ɪg'zæmɪn] *vt* **(a)** *(inspect)* examiner, inspecter *(une machine)*; *(in Customs)* examiner, fouiller *(les bagages)*; vérifier *(des comptes)*; contrôler *(un passeport)*; compulser, étudier, examiner *(des dossiers etc)*; dépouiller *(un inventaire, un compte)*; *Med* examiner *(un malade)*; **to e. one's conscience,** faire son examen de conscience; **to e. a question thoroughly,** examiner une question à fond; **to get examined,** se faire examiner; *Nau* **to stop and e. a ship,** arraisonner un navire; **(b)** *Sch etc* examiner, faire passer un examen à *(qn)*; **to e. a candidate in Latin,** examiner un candidat en latin; **(c)** *Jur etc* interroger, faire subir un interrogatoire à *(un prévenu, un témoin)*; instruire *(une cause)*.

examinee [ɪgzæmɪ'niː] *n Sch* candidat, -ate.

examiner [ɪg'zæmɪnər] *n* **(a)** inspecteur, -trice *(de bagages etc)*; compulseur *m* *(de dossiers etc)*; **(b)** *Sch* examinateur, -trice; **the examiners,** le jury (d'examen).

examining [ɪg'zæmɪnɪŋ] *adj* examinateur, -trice; **e. body,** jury *m* d'examen; **e. magistrate,** = juge *m* d'instruction.

example [ɪg'zɑːmp(ə)l] *n* **(a)** exemple *m*; **to give an e.,** donner un exemple; **to quote sth as an e.,** citer qch à titre d'exemple; **she showed me some examples of her work,** elle m'a montré des spécimens de son travail; *Iron* **a perfect e. of what NOT to do in a crisis,** un exemple parfait de ce qu'il ne faut pas faire dans une crise; **for e., by way of e.,** par exemple, en guise d'exemple; **large towns, as for e. London,** les grandes villes, telles que Londres (par exemple);

(b) *(model)* **to set an e.,** donner l'exemple; **let that be an e. to you!,** que ça te serve d'exemple!; **to make an e. of s.o.,** faire un exemple de qn; punir qn pour l'exemple; **to take s.o. as an e.,** prendre exemple sur qn; **to follow s.o.'s e.,** suivre l'exemple de qn; **to be an e.** *or* **a good e. to s.o.,** être un exemple *ou* un bon exemple pour qn; **their father wasn't a very good e.,** leur père n'a pas été un très bon exemple;

(c) *(precedent)* précédent *m*; **without e.,** sans exemple, sans précédent.

exasperate [ɪg'zɑːspəreɪt] *vt* exaspérer, irriter; **exasperated at** *or* **by his insolence,** exaspéré par son insolence.

exasperating [ɪg'zɑːspəreɪtɪŋ] *adj* exaspérant, irritant.

exasperatingly [ɪg'zɑːspəreɪtɪŋlɪ] *adv* d'une manière exaspérante *ou* irritante; **to be e. slow,** être d'une lenteur exaspérante.

exasperation [ɪgzɑːspə'reɪʃən] *n* exaspération *f*; **to drive s.o. to e.,** pousser qn à bout.

excavate ['ekskəveɪt] *vt* excaver, creuser *(un tunnel)*; fouiller *(la terre)*; approfondir *(un canal)*; déterrer *(des ruines etc)*; *Archeol* **to e. a site,** faire des fouilles.

excavation [ekskə'veɪʃən] *n* **(a)** excavation *f* *(de la terre etc)*; approfondissement *m* *(d'un canal)*; **(b)** *(site)* terrain excavé; *Archeol etc* fouille *f*; **the excavations at Pompeii,** les fouilles de Pompéi.

excavator ['ekskəveɪtər] *n* **(a)** *Constr* *(machine)* excavateur, -trice, pelleteuse *f*; **(b)** *Archeol* *(person)* personne *f* qui fait des fouilles.

exceed [ɪk'siːd] *vt* **(a)** *(go beyond)* excéder, dépasser *(des limites etc)*; **not exceeding ten pounds,** ne dépassant pas dix livres; **not exceeding 250 gr.,** *(parcels etc)* jusqu'à 250 g.; **do not expose to temperatures exceeding 50°C,** ne pas exposer à des températures excédant 50°C; **to e. one's instructions,** aller au-delà des instructions reçues; **to e. one's rights** *or* **one's powers,** outrepasser ses droits *ou* sa compétence; *Aut* **to e. the speed limit,** dépasser *ou* excéder la limitation de vitesse; **he was fined for exceeding the speed limit,** il a eu une contravention pour excès de vitesse; **(b)** *(surpass)* surpasser *(qn, qch)* **(in,** en**)**; **the outcome exceeded all our hopes,** le résultat a dépassé toutes nos espérances; **demand exceeded supply,** la demande a excédé l'offre.

exceedingly [ɪk'siːdɪŋlɪ] *adv* extrêmement.

excel [ɪk'sel] *v* **(-ll-) 1** *vi* exceller **(in doing sth,** à faire qch); **to e. at a game,** exceller à un jeu; **at school she excelled in chemistry,** à l'école, elle excellait en chimie. **2** *vt* surpasser *(qn)*; **to e. oneself,** se surpasser; *Iron* **he's excelled himself this time,** il s'est surpassé cette fois-ci.

excellence ['eksələns] *n* excellence *f*; mérite *m*, qualité *f*, supériorité *f* *(de qn, de qch)*; **students are expected to strive for e.,** on demande aux étudiants de s'efforcer à atteindre l'excellence; **centre of e.,** centre *m* d'excellence.

excellency ['eksələnsɪ] *n* *(title)* **Your E.,** votre Excellence *f*; **his E. the French Ambassador,** son Excellence l'ambassadeur de France.

excellent ['eksələnt] *adj* excellent, parfait; **e.!,** excellent!

excellently ['eksələntlɪ] *adv* admirablement, d'une manière excellente.

except[1] [ɪk'sept] **1** *prep* excepté, à l'exception de, sauf; **nobody e. him,** personne excepté *ou* sauf lui; **all e. the doctor,** tous, à l'exception du docteur, tous, sauf le docteur; **nobody heard it e. me,** personne ne l'a entendu sauf moi; **e. by agreement between the parties,** sauf accord entre les parties; **e. when/if,** sauf quand/si; **e. for,** à part, si ce n'est; **the dress is ready e. for the buttons,** la robe est prête, à l'exception des boutons. **2** *conj* **e. (that),** excepté que, si ce n'est que; **he came out of it unscathed, e. that he lost his hat,** il en est sorti indemne, si ce n'est qu'il a perdu son chapeau.

except[2] *vt* excepter, exclure **(from,** de**)**; **present company excepted,** les présents exceptés; **errors and omissions excepted,** sauf erreur ou omission.

excepting [ɪk'septɪŋ] *prep & conj* = **EXCEPT**[1]; **not e. my wife,** sans excepter ma femme.

exception [ɪk'sepʃən] *n* **(a)** exception *f*; **to make an e. to a rule,** faire une exception à une règle; **an e. was made in view of the circumstances,** une exception a été faite étant données les circonstances; **the e. proves the rule,** l'exception confirme la règle; **without e.,** sans (aucune) exception; **with the e. of ...,** à l'exception de ..., exception faite de ...; **with a few exceptions,** sauf de rares exceptions, à quelques exceptions près; **with certain exceptions,** sauf exceptions; **(b)** *(objection)* objection *f*; **to take e. to sth,** *(object)* trouver à redire à qch; *(take offence)* se formaliser *ou* s'offenser de qch; **to take e. to s.o.'s doing sth,** trouver mauvais que qn fasse qch; **I take great e. to that remark,** je trouve cette remarque très offensante.

exceptionable [ɪk'sepʃənəb(ə)l] *adj* *(usu with a negative)* critiquable; **nothing e.,** rien de critiquable; **to find nothing e. in sth,** ne rien trouver à redire à qch.

exceptional [ɪk'sepʃən(ə)l] *adj* **(a)** *(case, circumstances etc)* exceptionnel; *Jur.* **jurisdiction of an e. court,** juridiction *f* d'exception; **(b)** *(outstanding)* exceptionnel; **an e. woman,** une femme exceptionnelle *ou* remarquable; **a man of e. good looks,** un homme d'une beauté exceptionnelle.

exceptionally [ɪk'sepʃən(ə)lɪ] *adv* **(a)** *(unusually)* exceptionnellement, extraordinairement; **an e. fine day,** un jour exceptionnellement beau; **e. cheap,** d'un bon marché exceptionnel; **e., no bail was granted,** à titre exceptionnel, il n'a pas été accordé de remise en liberté sous caution; **(b)** *(outstandingly)* **e. gifted child,** enfant remarquablement doué.

excerpt ['ɪksɜːpt] *n* extrait *m*, citation *f*; *Mus* **excerpts from Carmen,** extraits de Carmen.

excess [ɪk'ses] *n* **(a)** excès *m* *(de lumière, de zèle etc)*; **to eat/drink to e.,** manger/boire à l'excès; **indulgence carried to e.,** indulgence poussée trop loin; **(b)** *(excessive action)* excès *m*; **to commit excesses,** commettre des excès; *(cruel acts)* commettre des cruautés; **(c)** *(quantity, sum etc)* excédent *m* *(de dépenses etc)*; **to pay the e. (on one's ticket),** prendre un supplément; **sum in e.,** somme *f* en surplus; **sum in e. of 50,** somme au-dessus de 50; *Rail* **e. fare,** supplément *m*; **e. luggage** *or* **baggage,** excédent de bagages; **e. weight,** excédent de poids; **(d)** *(in insurance)* franchise *f*.

excessive [ɪk'sesɪv] *adj* *(heat etc)* excessif; *(zeal)* immodéré; *(virtue etc)* outré, exagéré; *(ambition)* démesuré; **to be an e. drinker/smoker,** boire/fumer à l'excès; **e. expenses,** dépenses exagérées; **I thought the fine was e.,** j'ai trouvé l'amende excessive.

excessively [ɪk'sesɪvlɪ] *adv* (*souffrir etc*) excessivement, extrêmement; (*manger*) à l'excès; **to be e. generous,** être (par) trop généreux; **he's not e. intelligent,** il n'est pas particulièrement intelligent.

exchange¹ [ɪks'tʃeɪndʒ] *n* **(a)** échange *m* (*de prisonniers, de coups etc*); *Sch* **e. (visit),** échange; **the conference was a useful opportunity for an e. of views,** la conférence a constitué une occasion utile pour un échange de vues; **we had an angry** *or* **heated e.,** nous avons eu des mots; **in e. (for sth),** en échange (de qch); **car taken in part e.,** reprise *f*; *Sch* **e. student,** étudiant qui participe à un échange; *Admin* **e. of posts,** permutation *f* (*de deux fonctionnaires*); *Nucl Phys* **e. reaction,** réaction *f* d'échange.

(b) *Fin* (*of currency*) change *m*; **foreign e.,** change *m*; **dollar e.,** change du dollar *ou* en dollars; **bill of e.,** effet *m*, traite *f*, lettre *f* de change; *US* **exchanges,** lettres de change, traites; **e. bank,** banque *f* s'occupant d'opérations de change; **(foreign) e. broker,** cambiste *m ou* agent *m* de change; **e. control,** contrôle *m* des changes; **(foreign) e. office,** bureau *m* de change; **e. rate, rate of e.,** cours *m ou* taux *m* du change; **at the current rate of e.,** au cours du jour, au taux du change du jour;

(c) *Fin* **(Stock) E.,** bourse *f* (des valeurs); **commodities e.,** bourse de commerce; **corn e.,** bourse des céréales; *US Mil* **post e.,** économat *m* de l'armée;

(d) *Tel* **(telephone) e.,** central *m* téléphonique; **local e. area,** = réseau urbain; **e. office,** bureau central (téléphonique).

exchange² *vt* échanger (*des coups, des paroles, des prisonniers*); troquer (*des denrées etc*); **to e. sth for sth,** échanger *ou* troquer qch pour *ou* contre qch, faire un échange de qch pour *ou* contre qch; **to e. glances,** échanger un regard; échanger des regards; *Admin* **to e. posts with s.o.,** permuter avec qn.

exchangeable [ɪks'tʃeɪndʒəb(ə)l] *adj* échangeable **(for,** pour, contre).

exchequer [eks'tʃekər] *n* **(a)** *Br Admin* **the E.,** (*money*) le Trésor public; (*government department*) ≈ le Ministère des Finances; **the Chancellor of the E.,** ≈ le Ministre des Finances; **(b)** *F* budget *m* (*d'un particulier*).

excise¹ ['eksaɪz] *n Admin* **(a)** (*tax*) contributions indirectes; *Belg* accise *f*; **(b)** (*service*) service *m* des contributions indirectes, la régie; *Br* **Customs and E.,** la Régie; **e. duties,** droits *mpl* de régie.

excise² [ɪk'saɪz] *vt Surg* exciser, couper (*un organe*); couper (*un passage d'un livre*).

exciseman, *pl* **-men** ['eksaɪz(ə)mən] *n Br Hist* employé de l'excise *ou* de la régie.

excision [ɪk'sɪʒən] *n* excision *f*, coupure *f*; *Surg* excision, abscission *f*, ablation *f*.

excitable [ɪk'saɪtəb(ə)l] *adj* **(a)** (*person, temperament*) émotionnable, émotif; **(b)** *El Physiol* excitable.

excite [ɪk'saɪt] *vt* **(a)** (*arouse emotion in*) agiter, énerver, surexciter (*qn*); mettre (*qn*) en émoi; **don't e. him,** ne l'énerve pas; **easily excited,** surexcitable, émotionnable; **the idea clearly excited them,** il était évident que l'idée les intéressait beaucoup; **(b)** (*stimulate*) exciter, animer (*un sentiment, une passion*); stimuler (*l'appétit*); *Physiol* exciter, stimuler (*un nerf*); **(c)** (*give rise to*) provoquer, exciter, soulever; inspirer (*un sentiment*); susciter (*de l'intérêt*); piquer (*la curiosité de qn*); **(d)** *El* exciter, amorcer (*une dynamo, un relais etc*).

excited [ɪk'saɪtɪd] *adj* **(a)** (*person*) énervé, surexcité; (*impatient*) impatient; (*upset*) troublé; **e. children,** enfants excités; **e. crowd,** foule surexcitée *ou* en émoi; (*impatient*) foule impatiente; **she was very e. about her trip to Canada,** elle était très excitée à l'idée de son voyage au Canada; **doctors are e. by this discovery,** les médecins sont enthousiasmés par cette découverte; **to get e.,** s'exciter; (*to get angry*) s'énerver; **don't get e.!,** ne vous énervez pas!, du calme!; **he gets e. over nothing,** il s'emballe pour un rien; **it's nothing to get e. about,** (*it's not interesting*) il n'y a pas de quoi en faire toute une histoire; (*don't get upset*) il n'y a pas de quoi s'inquiéter; **(b)** *El Physiol* excité; **e. state,** *Nucl Phys* état excité *ou* d'excitation; *El* état d'amorçage.

excitedly [ɪk'saɪtɪdlɪ] *adv* d'une manière agitée; avec agitation.

excitement [ɪk'saɪtmənt] *n* **(a)** agitation *f*, vive émotion; surexcitation *f*; **the thirst for e.,** la soif des sensations fortes; **the e. of departure,** l'émoi *m* du départ; **to cause great e.,** faire (grande) sensation; **there is some e. in the city at the prospect of an official visit,** il y a un certain émoi dans la ville à la perspective d'une visite officielle; **to be in a state of e.,** être dans tous ses états; **in the e. of the moment,** dans l'excitation du moment; **(b)** *Physiol* surexcitation *f* (*d'un organe*).

exciting [ɪk'saɪtɪŋ] *adj* **(a)** passionnant; (*situation, scene*) sensationnel; (*full of suspense*) plein de suspense; **e. developments in medical research,** développements passionnants dans la recherche médicale; *Sp* **e. finish,** arrivée palpitante; **an e. game,** une partie mouvementée; **(b)** *Med* (*cause*) excitateur; **(c)** *El* **e. dynamo,** dynamo *f* d'excitation; **e. coil,** bobine inductrice.

excitingly [ɪk'saɪtɪŋlɪ] *adv* d'une manière sensationnelle.

exclaim [ɪks'kleɪm] **1** *vi* s'écrier, s'exclamer. **2** *vt* **'leave me alone,' he exclaimed,** 'laissez-moi,' s'est-il écrié.

exclamation [ekskla'meɪʃən] *n* exclamation *f*; **e. mark** *or US* **point,** point *m* d'exclamation.

exclamatory [eks'klæmət(ə)rɪ] *adj* exclamatif.

exclude [ɪks'kluːd] *vt* exclure **(from,** de); empêcher (*l'air*) d'entrer; écarter (*le doute, les soupçons*); **to e. s.o. from a society,** (*expel*) exclure qn d'une société; (*not allow to join*) refuser à qn l'entrée d'une société; **excluding ...,** à l'exclusion de ...; **this excludes all possibility of doubt,** le doute n'est plus permis.

exclusion [ɪks'kluːʒən] *n* **(a)** exclusion *f* **(from,** de); **to the e. of ...,** à l'exclusion de ...; **(b)** (*refusal to allow to join*) refus *m* d'admission **(from,** à).

exclusive [ɪks'kluːsɪv] **1** *adj* **(a)** (*right etc*) exclusif; **to have e. rights in a production,** avoir l'exclusivité d'une production; *Journ* **e. interview,** interview exclusive;

(b) (*only*) seul, unique; **it has been his e. occupation for ten years,** ç'a été son occupation unique pendant dix ans;

(c) (*expensive, upper-class*) exclusif;

(d) (*club etc*) très fermé;

(e) (*in logic*) exclusif; **two qualities that are mutually e.,** deux qualités qui s'excluent.

2 *adv* **(a)** (*with numbers*) exclusivement; **chapters one to twenty e.,** chapitres un à vingt exclusivement;

(b) (*not including extras*) sans compter les extras; **rent (of a flat), £6000 a year e.,** loyer (d'un appartement) 6 000 livres par an, contributions et charges en plus;

(c) (*not including*) **e. of,** non compris; **e. of wrappings,** sans compter l'emballage, l'emballage non compris; **price of dinner e. of wine,** prix du dîner, vin non compris.

3 *n Journ* article *m* en exclusivité; **a Times e.,** une exclusivité du Times.

exclusively [ɪks'kluːsɪvlɪ] *adv* exclusivement.

exclusivity [eksklu:'sɪvɪtɪ] *n* **(a)** exclusivité *f*; **(b)** *Com* (*of dealership etc*) exclusivité *f*.

excommunicate¹ [ekskə'mjuːnɪkeɪt] *vt* excommunier.

excommunicate² [ekskə'mjuːnɪkət] *adj & n* excommunié, -ée.

excommunication [ekskəmjuːnɪ'keɪʃən] *n* excommunication *f*.

excrement ['ekskrɪmənt] *n* excrément *m*.

excrescence [eks'kresəns] *n* excroissance *f*.

excrescent [eks'kresənt] *adj Fml* **(a)** (*outward-growing*) qui forme une excroissance; **(b)** (*superfluous*) superflu, redondant.

excreta [ɪks'kriːtə] *npl* excrétions *fpl*.

excrete [ɪks'kriːt] *vt* excréter; (*of plant*) sécréter.

excretion [ɪks'kriːʃən] *n* excrétion *f*; sécrétion *f* (*d'une plante*).

excruciating [ɪks'kruːʃɪeɪtɪŋ] *adj* (*pain*) atroce, horrible; *F* **e. music,** musique *f* atroce.

excruciatingly [ɪks'kruːʃɪeɪtɪŋlɪ] *adv* atrocement; **e. painful,** atrocement douloureux; *F* **e. funny,** (*story*) tordant; *F* **e. boring,** à en mourir d'ennui.

exculpate ['ekskʌlpeɪt] *vt* disculper, exonérer **(from,** de); justifier (*qn*).

exculpation [ekskʌl'peɪʃən] *n* disculpation *f*, exonération *f* **(from,** de); justification *f* (*de qn*).

excursion [ɪks'kɜːʃən] *n* **(a)** (*journey*) excursion *f*; *Aut Cycling etc* randonnée *f*; **to make an e.,** faire une excursion; *Rail* **e. ticket,** billet *m* d'excursion; **(b)** (*digression*) digression *f* (*dans un discours*); **after a brief e. into sculpture she returned to painting,** après une brève incursion dans la sculpture, elle est retournée à la peinture.

excursionist [ɪks'kɜːʃənɪst] *n* excursionniste *mf*.

excusable [ɪks'kjuːzəb(ə)l] *adj* (*erreur etc*) excusable, pardonnable.

excusably [ɪks'kjuːzəblɪ] *adv* de manière excusable.

excuse¹ [ɪks'kjuːs] *n* **(a)** (*justification*) excuse *f*; **there is no e. for his behaviour,** sa conduite est inexcusable; **there was no e. for (doing) that,** il n'y avait aucun prétexte à (faire) cela; **ignorance of the law is no e.,** nul n'est censé ignorer la loi; **that's no e.!,** ce n'est pas une excuse!;

(b) (*pretext*) excuse *f*, prétexte *m*; **poor** *or* **feeble e.,** faible excuse; **their e. was that they'd forgotten,** leur prétexte était qu'ils avaient oublié; **to make excuses,** s'excuser; **I make no excuses (for these views/***etc***),** je ne ressens pas le besoin de justifier (ces opinions/*etc*); **stop making excuses for him,** arrête de lui trouver des excuses; **to look for an e.,** chercher des excuses; (*in order not to do sth*) chercher des faux-fuyants *ou* une échappatoire; **to find an e. for sth,** trouver une excuse à qch; **any e. to get out of the house!,** tout prétexte est bon pour sortir de la maison; **he's just using his broken leg as an e. to ...,** il se sert du fait qu'il a une jambe cassée comme excuse pour ...;

(c) (*example*) **a poor e. for a letter,** un semblant de lettre; **a poor e. for a car,** un vieux tacot délabré.

excuse² [ɪks'kjuːz] *vt* **(a)** (*forgive*) excuser, pardonner; **to e. s.o.'s laziness, to e. s.o.'s being lazy,** excuser la paresse de qn; **e. my being late,** excusez-moi d'être en retard; **e. me yawning,** je vous demande pardon si je bâille; **to e. the absence of s.o.,** excuser l'absence de qn; **he may be excused for laughing,** il est excusable d'avoir ri; **you could be excused for thinking it was spring,** on aurait pu facilement penser que c'était le printemps; **if you will e. the expression,** si vous voulez me pardonner l'expression; **if you will e. me I have to finish my work,** si vous voulez bien m'excuser, il faut que je finisse mon travail; **e. me!,** (*let me past, sorry*) pardon!, excusez-moi!; **e. me?,** (*what did you say?*) pardon?; **e. me, it was yesterday that ...,** (*expressing contradiction*) pardon, c'était hier que ...;

(b) (*exempt*) exempter, dispenser (*qn*) (**from doing sth,** de faire qch); **to e. s.o. from attendance,** excuser qn; *Mil Nau* **to be excused a fatigue,** être exempté d'une corvée; *Sch* **may I be excused?,** est-ce que je peux sortir?;

(c) (*justify*) **his youth excuses him,** sa jeunesse l'excuse *ou* peut lui servir d'excuse; **I know they were angry, but that doesn't e. their behaviour,** je sais qu'ils étaient en colère, mais ça n'excuse pas leur comportement;

(d) (*give an excuse*) **to e. oneself,** s'excuser; **I excused myself,** (*apologized for leaving*) je me suis excusé de devoir partir.

excuse-me [ɪks'kjuːzmiː] *n* = danse où on change de partenaire lorsque quelqu'un s'approche en disant 'excusez-moi'.

ex-directory [eksdɪ'rektərɪ, -daɪ-] *adj Br Tel* **ex-d. number,** numéro *m* ne figurant pas dans l'annuaire, numéro se trouvant sur la liste rouge; **they** *or* **their number must be ex-d.,** ils doivent être sur la liste rouge; **to go ex-d.,** (*of subscriber*) (demander à) être mis sur la liste rouge.

execrable ['eksɪkrəb(ə)l] *adj* exécrable, abominable.

execrably ['eksɪkrəblɪ] *adv* exécrablement, abominablement.

execrate ['eksɪkreɪt] *vt* **(a)** (*abhor*) exécrer; **(b)** (*curse*) maudire.

execration [eksɪ'kreɪʃən] *n* **(a)** (*abhorrence*) exécration *f* (**of,** de); **(b)** (*cursing*) malédiction *f*.

execute ['eksɪkjuːt] *vt* **(a)** (*carry out*) exécuter (*un travail, un ordre*); mettre à exécution (*un projet*); accomplir (*une opération*); *Fin* effectuer (*un transfert*); *Jur* exécuter (*un testament*); souscrire, signer (*un acte*); *Mus* exécuter, jouer (*un morceau*); **(b)** (*put to death*) exécuter; **(c)** *Comptr* exécuter.

execution [eksɪ'kjuːʃən] *n* **(a)** exécution *f* (*d'un projet, d'un ordre*); accomplissement *m* (*d'un dessein etc*); *Jur* souscription *f* (*d'un acte*); exécution (*d'un testament*); *Mus* exécution (*d'un morceau de musique*); jeu *m* (*d'un musicien*); **to put** *or* **carry a plan into e.,** mettre un projet à exécution; **in the e. of one's duty,** dans l'exercice de ses fonctions; **(b)** *Jur* saisie-exécution *f*, *pl* saisies-exécutions; **(c)** exécution *f* (*d'un criminel*); **e. by firing squad,** exécution par un peloton d'exécution; **(d)** *Comptr* exécution *f*.

executioner [eksɪ'kjuːʃənər] *n* bourreau *m*.

executive [ɪg'zekjʊtɪv] **1** *adj* exécutif; **e. briefcase,** attaché-case *m*; **e. powers,** pouvoirs exécutifs; **e. suite,** (*in hotel*) suite *f* de luxe; **e. officer,** cadre supérieur; **chief e. officer,** président-directeur général; *Cin* **e. producer,** producteur délégué; *Mil* **e. duties,** service *m* de détail; **e. jet,** avion *m* de société; *Pol US* **e. session,** séance *f* à huis clos; **e. model** *or* **version,** (*of car etc*) modèle *m ou* version *f* de (grand) luxe. **2** *n* **(a)** (*in business*) cadre *m*; **sales e.,** directeur commercial; *Admin* **e. (officer),** haut fonctionnaire; **(b)** (*of a government*) (pouvoir *m*) exécutif *m*; **(c)** (*of political party, union*) bureau *m*, comité central; **the union's national e.,** le bureau national du syndicat.

executor [ɪg'zekjʊtər] *n Jur* exécuteur, -trice testamentaire; **literary e.,** exécuteur littéraire.

executrix, *pl* **-trices** [ɪg'zekjʊtrɪks, -trɪsiːz] *n Jur* exécutrice testamentaire.

exegesis [eksɪ'dʒiːsɪs] *n* exégèse *f*.

exemplarily [ɪg'zemplərɪlɪ] *adv* exemplairement.

exemplary [ɪg'zemplərɪ] *adj* **(a)** (*outstanding*) (*conduct*) exemplaire; (*husband*) modèle; **(b)** (*serving as example*) (*punishment*) exemplaire; *Jur* **e. damages,** dommages-intérêts *m* exemplaires; **(c)** (*typical*) typique.

exemplify [ɪg'zemplɪfaɪ] *vt* **(a)** (*show by example*) démontrer par des exemples, illustrer; **(b)** (*serve as example of*) servir d'exemple à (*une règle*).

exempt¹ [ɪg'zempt] *adj* exempt, dispensé, exempté (**from,** de); franc, *f* franche (*d'impôts*); *Mil* **to be e. from fatigues,** être dispensé des corvées.

exempt² *vt* exempter, dispenser (*qn*) (**from,** de); **to e. s.o. from doing sth,** exempter qn de faire qch; *Mil* **exempted from military service,** dispensé du service militaire.

exemption [ɪg'zem(p)ʃən] *n* exemption *f*, dispense *f* (*d'un impôt, du service militaire*).

exercise¹ ['eksəsaɪz] *n* **(a)** (*physical, mental*) exercice *m*; **outdoor e.,** exercice au grand air; **to take e.,** prendre de l'exercice; **I don't get much e.,** je ne fais pas beaucoup d'exercice; **school e.,** exercice scolaire; **piano exercises,** exercices pour piano; *Gym* **physical exercises,** exercices physiques; **breathing exercises,** gymnastique *f* respiratoire, exercices respiratoires; **e. book,** cahier *m*; **e. bike,** vélo *m* d'appartement; **e. class,** cours *m* de gymnastique; **e. yard,** préau *m* (*de prison*);

(b) *Mil Nau* exercice *m*; **tactical exercises,** évolutions *fpl* tactiques;

(c) (*activity*) **religious exercises,** pratiques religieuses; **it was an interesting e.,** c'était une expérience intéressante; **sending an ambassador would be a pointless e.,** envoyer un ambassadeur ne servirait à rien;

(d) (*use, practice*) exercice *m* (*d'une faculté, de ses fonctions*); pratique *f* (*d'un métier, d'une religion*); **in the e. of one's duties/rights,** dans l'exercice de ses fonctions/droits; *St Exch* **e. of an option,** levée *f* d'une prime.

exercise² **1** *vt* **(a)** (*train etc*) exercer (*le corps, l'esprit*); faire faire l'exercice à (*des troupes*); **to e. a horse,** exercer un cheval; (*take for a walk*) promener un cheval; **(b)** (*practise*) exercer (*un droit, ses fonctions*); exercer, pratiquer (*un métier*); user de (*un droit*); **to e. one's will/authority,** faire acte de volonté/d'autorité; **we must e. caution,** nous devons user de prudence; *Fin* **to e. an option,** lever une prime; **(c)** (*bother*) tracasser; mettre à l'épreuve (*la patience de qn*). **2** *vi* prendre de l'exercice; (*train*) s'entraîner.

exert [ɪg'zɜːt] *vt* **(a)** (*use*) employer, faire usage de (*la force*); exercer (*une influence, une pression*); déployer (*son talent*); **(b) to e. oneself,** se remuer, se donner du mal; **to e. oneself to do sth,** s'efforcer de faire qch, faire des efforts pour faire qch.

exertion [ɪg'zɜːʃən] *n* **(a)** usage *m*, emploi *m* (*de la force, d'un talent*); **(b)** (*effort*) effort *m*; **without great e.,** sans grand effort.

exeunt ['eksɪənt] *vi Th* **e. Romeo and Juliet,** Roméo et Juliette sortent.

exfoliate [eks'fəʊlɪeɪt] *vi* s'exfolier.

exfoliating [eks'fəʊlɪeɪtɪŋ] *adj* exfoliant; **e. cream,** crème exfoliante.

exfoliation [eksfəʊlɪ'eɪʃən] *n* exfoliation *f*.

ex gratia [eks'greɪʃɪə] *adj & adv* à titre de faveur, à titre gracieux; **ex g. payment,** paiement *m* à titre gracieux.

exhalation [eksə'leɪʃən] *n* **(a)** (*of breath*) expiration *f*; (*of smell*) exhalation *f*; **(b)** (*thing exhaled*) effluve *m*, exhalaison *f*.

exhale [eks'heɪl] **1** *vt* expirer (*l'air des poumons*); exhaler (*son dernier souffle etc*); exhaler, émettre (*un gaz, des odeurs*). **2** *vi* **(a)** expirer; **(b)** (*of vapour etc*) s'exhaler.

exhaust¹ [ɪg'zɔːst] *n Aut MecE* **(a)** échappement *m* (*des gaz*); (*what is ejected*) gaz *m* d'échappement; **e. fumes,** gaz *mpl* d'échappement; **e. pipe,** (tuyau *m* d')échappement; **e. stroke,** course *f* d'échappement; **(b)** (*pipe*) (tuyau *m* d') échappement *m*.

exhaust² *vt* **(a)** (*tire*) épuiser, éreinter, exténuer (*qn*); **to e. oneself in useless efforts,** se consumer en efforts inutiles; **(b)** (*use up*) épuiser (*les réserves, un sujet de conversation*); **to e. s.o.'s patience,** venir à bout de la patience de qn; **(c)** (*remove*) aspirer (*l'air, un gaz*).

exhausted [ɪg'zɔːstɪd] *adj* **(a)** (*person*) épuisé, exténué, éreinté; **I'm e.,** je n'en peux plus; **(b)** (*land, resources*) épuisé; **my patience is e.,** je suis à bout de patience.

exhausting [ɪg'zɔːstɪŋ] *adj* (*effort, climat*) épuisant; (*travail*) épuisant éreintant.

exhaustion [ɪg'zɔːstʃən] *n* **(a)** (*of person, animal*) **(state of) e.,** épuisement *m*; **to be in a state of complete e.,** être complètement à bout de forces; **I was ready to drop with e.,** je tombais de fatigue; **(b)** (*of resources, earth*) épuisement *m*; **(c)** *Phys* (*of gas*) aspiration *f*.

exhaustive [ɪg'zɔːstɪv] *adj* (*list*) exhaustif; **e. investigation,** enquête approfondie; **to make an e. study of a subject,** traiter un sujet à fond; **to make e. enquiries,** faire des recherches approfondies.

exhaustively [ɪg'zɔːstɪvlɪ] *adv* exhaustivement; (*to study*) à fond.

exhibit[1] [ɪg'zɪbɪt] *n* **(a)** *Art etc* (*in museum, exhibition etc*) objet exposé (*à une exposition, en vitrine*); **(b)** *Jur* pièce *f* à conviction (*en procédure criminelle*); pièce *ou* document *m* à l'appui.

exhibit[2] **1** *vt* **(a)** *Art etc* (*of artist*) exposer (*des tableaux etc*); **(b)** *Jur* exhiber, produire (*des pièces à l'appui*); **(c)** (*show*) exhiber, montrer, faire voir (*un objet*); faire preuve de (*courage, mauvaise volonté*); offrir, présenter (*qch*) (à la vue); **he exhibited no remorse,** il n'a manifesté aucun remords. **2** *vi* (*of artist*) exposer.

exhibition [eksɪ'bɪʃən] *n* **(a)** (*event*) exposition *f*; **great international e.,** grande exposition internationale; **Ideal Home E.,** = Salon *m* des Arts ménagers; *Com* **e. room,** salon d'exposition (*d'automobiles etc*); **(b)** exposition *f*, étalage *m* (*de marchandises etc*); manifestation *f* (*d'un talent*); démonstration *f* (*d'un procédé etc*); *Jur* production *f* (*des pièces*); *F* **to make an e. of oneself,** se donner en spectacle; **(c)** *US Sch* = séance musicale etc donnée par les élèves, et à laquelle sont invités les parents; **(d)** *Br Univ* (*award*) bourse *f*.

exhibitionism [eksɪ'bɪʃənɪz(ə)m] *n* **(a)** désir *m* de se faire remarquer; **(b)** *Psy* exhibitionnisme *m*.

exhibitionist [eksɪ'bɪʃənɪst] *n* **(a) he's an e.,** il aime se faire remarquer; **(b)** *Psy* exhibitionniste *mf*.

exhibitor [ɪg'zɪbɪtər] *n* **(a)** *Art* (*at exhibition*) exposant, -ante; **(b)** *Br Cin* exploitant, -ante.

exhilarate [ɪg'zɪləreɪt] *vt* (*of mountain air*) vivifier; (*of experience, news etc*) faire exulter.

exhilarated [ɪg'zɪləreɪtɪd] *adj* exultant.

exhilarating [ɪg'zɪləreɪtɪŋ] *adj* (*air, wind, walk etc*) vivifiant; (*experience*) grisant, passionnant; (*news*) qui vous réchauffe le cœur; **the ride on the motorbike was e.,** le tour de moto était grisant.

exhilaration [ɪgzɪlə'reɪʃən] *n* gaieté *f* de cœur, joie *f* de vivre.

exhort [ɪg'zɔːt] *vt* exhorter, encourager (*qn*) (**to do,** à faire).

exhortation [ɪgzɔː'teɪʃən] *n* exhortation *f* (**to do,** à faire).

exhumation [ekshjuː'meɪʃən] *n* exhumation *f*.

exhume [eks'hjuːm] *vt* exhumer, déterrer.

exigence ['eksɪdʒəns] , **exigency** ['eksɪdʒənsɪ] *n* **(a)** (*necessity*) exigence *f*, nécessité *f*; **(b)** (*situation*) situation *f* critique; cas pressant; **in this e.,** dans cette situation urgente.

exigent ['eksɪdʒənt] *adj Lit* **(a)** (*urgent*) urgent, pressant; **(b)** (*demanding*) exigeant.

exiguity [eksɪ'gjuːɪtɪ] *n Fml* exiguïté *f* (*d'un logement etc*); modicité *f* (*d'un revenu etc*).

exiguous [ɪg'zɪgjʊəs] *adj Fml* exigu, -uë, fort petit; (*revenu*) modique.

exile[1] ['eksaɪl] *n* exil *m*, bannissement *m*; **to send s.o. into e.,** envoyer qn en exil, bannir qn; **to go into e.,** partir en exil *ou* pour l'exil; (*voluntarily*) s'exiler; **he lives in e. in Madrid,** il vit en exil à Madrid; **government in e.,** gouvernement *m* en exil.

exile[2] *n* (*person*) exilé, -ée, banni, -ie; *Fig* **tax e.,** = personne vivant à l'étranger pour éviter de payer les impôts dans son propre pays.

exile[3] *vt* exiler, bannir (*qn*) (**from,** de).

exist [ɪg'zɪst] *vi* **(a)** exister; (*of conditions etc*) régner; **fairies don't e.,** les fées n'existent pas; **to cease to e.,** cesser d'exister; **to continue to e.,** subsister; **these old shops still e. in a few places,** ces vieilles boutiques existent encore dans quelques endroits; *F* **as far as you're concerned I don't e., do I?,** en ce qui te concerne, c'est comme si je n'existais pas, hein?; **(b)** (*live*) se maintenir en vie; **I can't e. on that,** cela ne me suffit pas pour vivre.

existence [ɪg'zɪstəns] *n* **(a)** (*state of existing*) existence *f*; **the e. of these laws is not enough,** l'existence de ces lois ne suffit pas; **to be in e.,** exister; **the oldest manuscript in e.,** le plus ancien manuscrit existant; **the firm has been in e. for fifty years,** la maison existe depuis cinquante ans; **to come into e.,** naître; **to spring into e.,** naître soudainement; **to go out of e.,** disparaître, cesser d'exister; **(b)** (*life*) existence *f*, vie *f*; **to lead a pleasant e.,** mener une existence agréable.

existent [ɪg'zɪstənt] *adj* **(a)** (*that exists*) existant; **(b)** (*current*) d'aujourd'hui.

existential [egzɪs'tenʃəl] *adj* existentiel, -elle.

existentialism [egzɪs'tenʃəlɪz(ə)m] *n Phil* existentialisme *m*.

existentialist [egzɪs'tenʃəlɪst] *Phil* **1** *n* existentialiste *mf*. **2** *adj* (*theory, writing*) existentialiste.

existing [ɪg'zɪstɪŋ] *adj* existant; actuel, présent; **in e. circumstances,** dans les circonstances actuelles; **we are upgrading our e. equipment,** nous sommes en train de moderniser notre matériel existant.

exit[1] ['eksɪt] *n* **(a)** (*way out*) sortie *f*, issue *f* (*d'un théâtre etc*); (*from highway*) sortie; (*roadway*) bretelle *f* de sortie; **emergency e.,** sortie *ou* issue de secours; **e. only,** (*passage etc*) strictement réservé à la sortie; **(b)** (*act of going out*) sortie *f*; *Th* **to make one's e.,** sortir, quitter la scène; **the audience must have free e. at all times,** le public doit pouvoir sortir librement à tout moment; *Admin* **e. visa/permit,** visa *m*/permis *m* de sortie; *Pol* **e. poll,** = sondage effectué lorsque les électeurs viennent de voter; **e. sign,** panneau *m* indiquant une sortie; **e. staircase,** escalier *m* de sortie; **(c)** *Comptr* sortie *f*; **e. routine,** routine *f* de sortie.

exit[2] *v* (**-t-**) **1** *vi* **(a)** *Th* faire sa sortie; **e. Macbeth,** Macbeth sort; **(b)** *F* (*leave*) sortir; **(c)** *Comptr* sortir. **2** *vt Comptr* sortir de (*un programme, une séance etc*).

exocrine ['eksəʊkraɪn] *adj* (*glande*) exocrine.

exodus ['eksədəs] *n* **(a)** *Bible* exode *m* (*des Hébreux etc*); **(the Book of) Exodus,** l'Exode; **(b)** (*departure*) départ *m*, sortie *f* (*d'un groupe de gens etc*); **there was a general e.,** il y eut une sortie générale; **e. of capital,** évasion *f ou* fuite *f* des capitaux.

ex officio ['eksə'fɪʃɪəʊ] *adj & adv* (*membre*) de droit, à titre d'office; **to act ex o.,** agir d'office.

exonerate [ɪg'zɒnəreɪt] *vt* **(a)** (*absolve*) **to e. s.o. (from blame),** disculper *ou* justifier qn; **(b)** (*exempt*) exonérer, décharger (**s.o. from an obligation,** qn d'une obligation).

exoneration [ɪgzɒnə'reɪʃən] *n* **(a) e. from blame,** disculpation *f*, justification *f*; **(b)** (*exemption*) exonération *f*, décharge *f* (**from,** de).

exorbitance [ɪg'zɔːbɪt(ə)ns] *n* énormité *f* (*des prix*).

exorbitant [ɪg'zɔːbɪt(ə)nt] *adj* exorbitant, exagéré, excessif; (*intérêt*) usuraire; **e. price,** prix exorbitant.

exorbitantly [ɪg'zɔːbɪt(ə)ntlɪ] *adv* (*priced*) d'une manière exorbitante; excessivement.

exorcism ['eksɔːsɪz(ə)m] *n* exorcisme *m*.

exorcist ['eksɔːsɪst] *n* exorciste *m*.

exorcize ['eksɔːsaɪz] *vt* exorciser (*un démon, un possédé etc*); conjurer (*un esprit*).

exotic [ɪg'zɒtɪk] **1** *adj* exotique; **a taste for the e.,** le goût de l'exotique. **2** *n Bot* plante *f* exotique.

exotically [ɪg'zɒtɪklɪ] *adv* exotiquement.

expand [ɪks'pænd] **1** *vt* dilater (*un gaz*); étendre (*les limites d'un empire*); développer (*une idée, une formule algébrique, la poitrine*); élargir (*l'esprit*); déployer (*les ailes etc*); **the police force is to be expanded,** les effectifs de la police doivent être augmentés; **we are expanding our range of cosmetics,** nous sommes en train d'élargir notre gamme de produits de beauté. **2** *vi* **(a)** (*of solid, air, gas*) se dilater; (*of balloon*) se gonfler; (*of steam*) se détendre; (*of chest*) se développer; (*of sail etc*) s'étendre, se déployer; *MecE* (*of belt*) s'allonger; (*of company*) s'agrandir; **as the Empire expanded,** à mesure que l'Empire grandissait *ou* s'étendait; **(b)** (*talk, write at greater length*) préciser sa pensée; **could you e.?,** est-ce que vous pourriez préciser ce que vous voulez dire par là?

►**expand on, expand upon** *vipo* (*talk, write at greater length about*) développer; **he would not e. on his earlier statement,** il ne voulait pas développer davantage la déclaration qu'il avait faite plus tôt.

expandable [ɪks'pændɪb(ə)l] *adj Comptr* extensible.

expanded [ɪks'pændɪd] *adj* allongé; étendu; (*metal*) déployé; **e. polystyrene,** polystyrène expansé.

expander [ɪks'pændər] *n Gym* **(chest) e.,** extenseur *m*.

expanding [ɪks'pændɪŋ] *adj* **(a)** en expansion; (*gaz*) qui se dilate; (*ballon etc*) qui se gonfle, qui enfle; (*commerce*) qui se développe, qui prend de l'extension; **the e. universe,** l'univers *m* en expansion; **(b)** (*watch strap*) extensible; (*suitcase*) à soufflets.

expanse [eks'pæns] *n* étendue *f* (*de pays, d'eau etc*); **a vast e.,** une vaste étendue (*d'eau, de neige etc*); une mer (*de sable etc*).

expansion [ɪks'pænʃən] *n* **(a)** (*making larger*) dilatation *f* (*d'un gaz*); développement *m* (*d'un sujet, de la poitrine etc*); *Comptr* **e. card,** carte *f* d'extension; *Comptr* **e. slot,** emplacement *m* pour extension; **(b)** (*becoming larger*) expansion *f* (*d'un solide, d'un liquide, d'un commerce etc*); dilatation *f* (*d'un gaz, d'un métal etc*); épanouissement *m* (*d'une fleur, du cœur*); *Econ* relance *f*; **colonial e.,** expansion coloniale; **(c)** *MecE* **e. joint,** fourreau compensateur; (joint *m*) compensateur *m*; (*in concrete work*) joint de dilatation; **e. bit,** foret *m ou* mèche *f* extensible.

expansionism [ɪks'pænʃənɪz(ə)m] *n* expansionnisme *m*.

expansionist [ɪks'pænʃənɪst] *adj & n* expansionniste *mf*.

expansive [ɪks'pænsɪv] *adj* **(a)** (*force*) expansif; (*gas*) expansible, dilatable; **(b)** (*person*) expansif; **in an e. mood,** en veine d'épanchement.

expansiveness [ɪks'pænsɪvnɪs] *n* **(a)** expansibilité *f*; **(b)** (*of person*) expansivité *f*, nature expansive.

expat [eks'pæt] *adj & n Br F* expatrié, -ée.

expatiate [eks'peɪʃɪeɪt] *vi* discourir (longuement) (**on,** sur).

expatriate¹ [eks'pætrɪət] *n* expatrié, -ée; **an e. Scot,** un Ecossais expatrié.

expatriate² [eks'pætrɪeɪt] *vt* expatrier (*qn*); **to e. oneself,** s'expatrier; (*renounce one's nationality*) renoncer à sa nationalité.

expatriation [ekspætrɪ'eɪʃən] *n* **(a)** expatriation *f*; **(b)** (*renunciation of nationality*) renonciation *f* à sa nationalité.

expect [ɪks'pekt] **1** *vt* **(a)** attendre (*qn, une lettre, un coup de téléphone etc*); s'attendre à (*un événement*); compter sur (*l'arrivée de qn etc*); **to e. s.o. to dinner,** attendre qn à dîner; **the delivery isn't expected until Thursday,** on n'attend pas la livraison avant jeudi; **I expected as much,** je m'y attendais; **I knew what to e.,** je savais à quoi m'attendre; **to e. the worst,** s'attendre au pire; **as one might e., as might be expected,** comme on doit s'y attendre, comme de raison; **she played with the brilliance (which) we have come to e. (from her),** elle a joué avec le brio auquel elle nous a maintenant habitués; **to e. that s.o. will do sth/that sth will happen,** s'attendre à ce que qn fasse qch/à ce que qch arrive; **to e. to do sth,** compter *ou* espérer faire qch; **I don't e. them to be pleased,** je ne m'attends pas à ce qu'ils soient contents; **the movie was better than I expected (it to be),** le film était meilleur que je ne m'y attendais; **she was angry — well, what did you e.?,** elle était en colère — et alors, ça t'étonne?; **he is not expected to recover,** on ne s'attend pas à ce qu'il se rétablisse; **they arrived later than expected,** ils sont arrivés plus tard que prévu; **she's expecting a baby,** elle attend un bébé;

(b) (*require*) **to e. sth from s.o.,** exiger qch de qn; **I e. you to be punctual,** je vous demande d'arriver à l'heure; **I don't e. you to be perfect,** je ne te demande pas d'être parfait; **how do you e. me to do it?,** comment voulez-vous que je le fasse?; **is it too much to e. a little courtesy?,** est-ce qu'un peu de courtoisie est trop demander?; **it's too much to e. of a child,** c'est trop attendre d'un enfant; **I know what is expected of me,** je sais ce qu'on attend de moi; **people e. too much from marriage,** les gens attendent trop du mariage;

(c) (*think*) penser, croire (que); **I e. he'll pay,** je pense qu'il payera; **I e. so,** je crois bien que oui; **I e. they knew already,** je pense qu'ils savaient déjà.

2 *vi Br F* **she's expecting,** elle attend un bébé.

expectancy [ɪks'pektənsɪ] *n* **(a)** (*expectation*) attente *f*; **eager e.,** vive impatience; **life e.,** espérance *f* de vie; **(b)** *Jur* expectative *f* (*d'un héritage etc*).

expectant [ɪks'pekt(ə)nt] *adj* **(a)** (*expecting*) (qui est) dans l'attente (**of sth,** de qch); **e. mother,** femme enceinte, future mère; **(b)** *Jur* (*bien, héritier etc*) en expectative.

expectantly [ɪks'pekt(ə)ntlɪ] *adv* dans l'expectative, dans l'attente; **he looked at me e.,** il m'a regardé comme s'il attendait quelque chose.

expectation [ekspek'teɪʃən] *n* **(a)** attente *f*, espérance *f*; **to come up to/fall short of (s.o.'s) expectations,** remplir *ou* répondre à/tromper l'attente de qn; **to succeed beyond one's expectations,** réussir au delà de ses espérances; **contrary to all expectations,** contrairement à *ou* contre toute attente; **to have high expectations of s.o./sth,** attendre beaucoup de qn/qch; **in (the) e. of,** dans l'attente de; **(b)** (*anticipation*) **with eager e.,** avec une vive impatience; **to live in e.,** vivre dans l'expectative; **(c)** *Jur* expectative *f* d'héritage; **expectations,** espérances *fpl*; **uncle from whom one has expectations,** oncle *m* à héritage; **(d)** (*probability*) probabilité *f* (*d'un événement*); **e. of life,** espérance *f* de vie.

expected [ɪks'pektɪd] *adj* attendu; (*hoped for*) espéré; **the e. disaster never happened,** le désastre attendu ne s'est jamais produit.

expectorant [ɪks'pektərənt] *adj & n Med* expectorant *m*.

expectorate [eks'pektəreɪt] **1** *vt* expectorer (*des mucosités etc*). **2** *vi* cracher.

expedience [ɪks'piːdɪəns], **expediency** [ɪks'piːdɪənsɪ] *n* **(a)** (*convenience*) convenance *f*, opportunité *f* (*d'une mesure etc*); **on grounds of e.,** pour des raisons de convenance; **(b)** *Pej* (*opportunism*) opportunisme *m*.

expedient [ɪks'piːdɪənt] **1** *adj* **(a)** expédient convenable; **do what you think e.,** faites ce que vous jugerez à propos; **(b)** *Pej* opportun. **2** *n* expédient *m*, moyen *m*.

expedite ['ekspɪdaɪt] *vt* **(a)** *Fml* (*hasten*) activer, pousser, hâter (*une mesure*); accélérer (*un procédé*); **I'll do what I can to e. matters,** je ferai ce que je pourrai pour accélérer les choses; **(b)** *Old-fashioned* (*despatch*) expédier, dépêcher (*une affaire*).

expedition [ekspə'dɪʃən] *n* **(a)** (*trip*) expédition *f*; **an e. to the North Pole,** un expédition au pôle nord; *F* **a shopping e.,** une expédition dans les magasins; **(b)** *Old-fashioned* (*promptness*) promptitude *f*.

expeditionary [ekspə'dɪʃ(ə)nərɪ] *adj Mil* (*corps etc*) expéditionnaire.

expeditious [ekspə'dɪʃəs] *adj Fml* (*procédé*) expéditif; (*réponse*) prompt.

expeditiously [ekspə'dɪʃəslɪ] *adv Fml* promptement.

expel [ɪks'pel] *vt* (**-ll-**) expulser (*qn*); chasser, expulser (*un corps étranger, l'ennemi etc*); chasser, refouler (*un liquide, un gaz*); *Admin* expulser *ou* refouler un étranger; **to e. a pupil from school,** renvoyer un élève (*de l'école*).

expendable [ɪks'pendəb(ə)l] *adj* **he** *or* **it is e.,** il n'est pas irremplaçable *ou* indispensable; **the general considered these troops to be e.,** le général considérait qu'on pouvait sacrifier ces troupes.

expenditure [ɪks'pendɪtʃər] *n* **(a)** dépense *f* (*d'argent etc*); consommation *f* (*de munitions*); **(b)** (*amount*) dépense(s) *f(pl)*; **heavy e.,** une forte dépense, de fortes dépenses; **e. on arms exceeded that on housing,** les dépenses pour l'armement ont dépassé celles consacrées au logement.

expense [ɪks'pens] *n* **(a)** (*cost*) dépense *f*, frais *mpl*; **regardless of e.,** sans regarder à la dépense; **at great/little e.,** à grands/peu de frais; **at my own e.,** à mes propres frais; **book published at author's e.,** livre édité à compte d'auteur; **to go to great e.,** faire beaucoup de dépenses; **to put s.o. to e.,** faire faire des dépenses à qn; **don't go to any e. over ...,** ne faites pas de frais pour ...; **they went to considerable e./no e. was spared to ...,** ils ont dépensé des sommes considérables/on n'a pas regardé à la dépense pour ...; *Fig* **a joke at my e.,** une plaisanterie à mes dépens; **at the e. of the poor/his social life,** aux dépens des pauvres/de sa vie sociale;

(b) (*Com*) **expenses,** frais *mpl*, dépenses *fpl*; **it's on expenses,** c'est la société qui paie; **to offer s.o. £100 and expenses,** offrir à qn 100 livres, plus les frais; **e. account,** indemnité pour frais professionnels; **travelling expenses,** frais de déplacement, indemnité *f* de voyage; **living expenses,** frais de séjour; **general expenses,** frais généraux; **incidental expenses,** faux frais; **to incur expenses,** faire des dépenses; **to have all expenses paid,** être défrayé de tout; **an all expenses-paid trip to Paris,** un voyage à Paris tous frais payés;

(c) (*financial burden*) **to be a great e. to s.o.,** être une grande charge pour qn.

expensive [ɪks'pensɪv] *adj* (*objet*) coûteux, cher; (*procédé*) dispendieux; (*passe-temps*) onéreux; **he has e. tastes,** il a des goûts de luxe; **an e. shop/restaurant,** un magasin/restaurant cher; **that butcher's very e.,** ce boucher est très cher; **to be** *or* **come e.,** revenir cher; **that can be e.,** ça peut être cher; **travelling is e.,** les voyages coûtent cher.

expensively [ɪks'pensɪvlɪ] *adv* (*s'habiller*) coûteusement; **to live e.,** mener la vie large.

expensiveness [ɪks'pensɪvnɪs] *n* cherté *f* (*d'une denrée, de la vie etc*); prix élevé (*de qch*).

experience¹ [ɪks'pɪərɪəns] *n* **(a)** expérience *f*; **to gain e. of life,** faire l'apprentissage de la vie; **practical e.,** la pratique; **to have much e.,** avoir beaucoup d'expérience; **driving e.,** expérience de la route; **he still lacks e.,** il manque encore de pratique; **she has several years e.,** elle

a plusieurs années d'expérience; **a man of e.**, un homme d'expérience; **e. shows that ...**, l'expérience démontre que ...; **to know sth from e.**, savoir qch par expérience; **I know from bitter e. that ...**, je sais, pour l'avoir éprouvé cruellement, que ...; **he was clearly speaking from e.**, de toute évidence, il parlait en connaissance de cause *ou* il parlait d'expérience; **in my e.**, d'après mon expérience; **my e. has been that** *or* **in my e. people appreciate politeness,** j'en ai fait l'expérience, les gens apprécient la politesse; **have you had any previous e.?**, avez-vous déjà travaillé dans ce métier?; **she is not without e.**, (*sexually*) elle n'est pas innocente; **I had no e. of looking after disabled people,** je ne m'étais jamais occupé de personnes handicapées; **I have enough business e. to ...**, j'ai assez de pratique des affaires pour ...; **the black e. in this country,** la condition des noirs dans ce pays; **I lost a lot of money but I'll just have to put it down to e.**, j'ai perdu beaucoup d'argent mais au moins ça me servira de leçon; **well, it's all e.**, voilà qui est à mettre au compte de l'expérience;
(b) (*individual event*) expérience *f*; **to have a nasty e.**, faire une mauvaise expérience; **the journey was an e.**, ce voyage a été enrichissant; *Pej* ce voyage a été une drôle d'expérience; **it was his first e. of love,** c'était la première fois qu'il tombait amoureux.

experience² *vt* (*emotions, feeling, pain*) ressentir; (*real hunger, poverty*) connaître, faire l'expérience de; (*difficulties, problems*) avoir; **the problems we experienced with this machine,** les problèmes que nous avons eus *ou* connus avec cette machine.

experienced [ɪks'pɪərɪənst] *adj* qui a de l'expérience, expérimenté; (*observateur*) averti; (*œil*) exercé (**in,** à); **to be e. in sth,** avoir l'expérience de qch, s'y connaître en qch; **e. in business,** rompu aux affaires; **a more e. doctor,** un médecin plus expérimenté.

experiment¹ [ɪks'perɪmənt] *n* expérience *f*; **to make** *or* **carry out an e.**, faire *ou* procéder à une expérience; **as an e., by way of e.**, à titre d'essai *ou* d'expérience.

experiment² *vi* expérimenter, faire une expérience *ou* des expériences (**on,** sur; **with,** avec); **an artist should be prepared to e.**, un artiste devrait être prêt à toutes les expériences; **to e. on dogs,** expérimenter sur les chiens.

experimental [ɪksperɪ'ment(ə)l] *adj* **(a)** (*sujet*) d'expérience; (*physique*) expérimental; **this new reactor is at the e. stage,** ce nouveau réacteur est à l'essai *ou* en cours d'expérimentation; **e. research,** recherche *f* (expérimentale); **e. rocket,** fusée expérimentale; **(b)** (*based on experiment*) (*savoir*) expérimental, -aux, fondé sur l'expérience.

experimentally [ɪksperɪ'ment(ə)lɪ] *adv* (*see adj*) **(a)** à titre d'essai; **(b)** (*découvrir qch*) expérimentalement.

experimentation [ɪksperɪmen'teɪʃən] *n* expérimentation *f*.

expert ['ekspɜːt] **1** *adj* expert, habile; **to be e. in** *or* **at sth,** être expert en qch; connaître à fond qch. **2** *n* expert *m*; spécialiste *mf*; **I'm no e.**, je ne suis pas un expert; *Jur* **medical e.**, médecin légiste; **the experts,** les spécialistes; **according to the experts,** selon les experts; **she is an e. in this field,** elle est expert en la matière; **the eye of an e.**, un œil expert; **e. panel,** jury *m* d'experts; **e.'s report,** expertise *f*; **e. advice,** avis autorisé; **an e. opinion,** une opinion avisée; *Jur* **e. witness,** expert cité comme témoin.

expertise [ekspɜː'tiːz] *n* connaissances *fpl* (techniques, financières *etc*); (*as a cook, carpenter etc*) savoir-faire *m*; adresse *f*, habileté *f* (**in,** à).

expertly ['ekspɜːtlɪ] *adv* habilement, en expert.

expiate ['ekspɪeɪt] *vt* expier (*un péché, une faute*).

expiation [ekspɪ'eɪʃən] *n* expiation *f*; **in e. of his crime,** pour expier *ou* en expiation de son crime.

expiration [ekspɪ'reɪʃən] *n* **(a)** (*expiry*) cessation *f*, expiration *f* (*d'un bail*); échéance *f* (*d'un marché à prime*); fin *f* (*d'un terme*); expiration, déchéance *f* (*d'une police d'assurance*); **date of e.**, date *f* d'expiration (*d'une garantie etc*); **(b)** *Physiol* expiration *f* (*de l'air des poumons*).

expire [ɪks'paɪər] **1** *vi* **(a)** (*of law, treaty etc*) expirer, venir à expiration; **expired policy,** (*in insurance*) police déchue; **this passport expires on ...**, ce passeport expire le ...; **expired passport,** passeport périmé; **(b)** (*die*) expirer, mourir; (*of hope*) s'évanouir. **2** *vt Physiol* expirer, exhaler (*l'air des poumons*).

expiring [ɪks'paɪərɪŋ] *adj* **(a)** (*lease, contract*) qui expire, qui est à son terme; **(b)** (*dying*) expirant, qui se meurt; **with an e. voice,** d'une voix mourante.

expiry [ɪks'paɪərɪ] *n* expiration *f*, fin *f* (*d'un terme*); terme *m* (*d'une période*); **e. date,** date *f* d'expiration.

explain [ɪks'pleɪn] **1** *vt* **(a)** expliquer (*une règle etc*); **that explains everything,** voilà qui explique tout; **I can e. everything,** je peux tout expliquer; **that is easily explained,** cela s'explique facilement; **that explains his embarrassment,** cela explique son embarras; **she explained to us how the system works,** elle nous a expliqué comment le système fonctionne; **I explained that we were tourists,** j'ai expliqué que nous étions des touristes; **(b)** (*justify*) justifier (*sa conduite etc*); **(c) to e. oneself,** s'expliquer; (*justify oneself*) se justifier. **2** *vi* donner des explications; **you'd better e.**, allons, expliquez-vous.

►**explain away** *vtsep* (*give plausible explanation for*) donner une explication satisfaisante de (*qch*); **the government can't e. away the inflation figures,** le gouvernement ne peut fournir aucune explication satisfaisante des chiffres de l'inflation; **he tried to e. away his absence from the meeting,** il a essayé de justifier son absence à la réunion.

explainable [ɪks'pleɪnəb(ə)l] *adj* (*conduite etc*) explicable; **it's easily e.**, cela s'explique facilement.

explanation [eksplə'neɪʃən] *n* explication *f*, éclaircissement *m*; **to give explanations,** fournir des explications; **to give an e. of one's behaviour,** justifier sa conduite; **one e. is that ...**, l'une des explications est que ...; **the e. is that ...**, cela s'explique par le fait que ... .

explanatory [ɪks'plænət(ə)rɪ] *adj* explicatif; **e. notes,** commentaires *mpl*.

expletive [ɪks'pliːtɪv] **1** *n* **(a)** (*swear word*) juron *m*; **(b)** *Gram etc* particule explétive, explétif *m*. **2** *adj Gram etc* explétif.

explicable [eks'plɪkəb(ə)l] *adj* explicable.

explicit [eks'plɪsɪt] *adj* explicite; **to be more e. (in one's statements),** préciser (ses affirmations); **e. sex and violence,** (*on television etc*) de la violence et du sexe montrés de façon explicite.

explicitly [eks'plɪsɪtlɪ] *adv* explicitement.

explode [ɪks'pləʊd] **1** *vt* **(a)** (*detonate etc*) faire éclater (*un obus*); faire sauter (*une mine*); faire exploser (*un gaz*); **(b)** (*to show to be false*) démontrer la fausseté de (*qch*); discréditer (*une théorie*). **2** *vi* faire explosion; (*of boiler, shell etc*) éclater; (*of mine*) sauter; (*of gas, dynamite etc*) exploser, détoner; **the car exploded,** la voiture a explosé; *Fig* **to e. with laughter,** (*of person*) éclater de rire; *Fig* **he'll e.**, (*with anger*) il explosera, il va sortir de ses gonds; (*with repressed feeling*) il va craquer; *Fig* **the population exploded after the war,** il y a eu une explosion démographique après la guerre.

exploded [ɪks'pləʊdɪd] *adj* **(a)** (*obus*) éclaté; (*mine*) qui a sauté; **(b)** (*théorie*) abandonné, reconnu pour faux; **(c)** (*technical drawing*) *& Phot* **e. view,** vue éclatée.

exploit¹ ['eksplɔɪt] *n* exploit *m*, haut fait.

exploit² [eks'plɔɪt] *vt* **(a)** (*take advantage of*) exploiter (*qn, les talents de qn, un scandale*); **immigrant workers are being exploited,** les travailleurs immigrés se font exploiter; **(b)** (*use*) exploiter (*une mine, une forêt etc*).

exploitation [eksplɔɪ'teɪʃən] *n* exploitation *f*.

exploration [eksplə'reɪʃən] *n* **(a)** (*trip*) exploration *f*; **voyage of e.**, voyage *m* de découverte; **Magellan called here on his explorations,** au cours de ses explorations, Magellan est passé par ici; **(b)** (*act*) exploration *f*, reconnaissance *f* (*du terrain*); **e. work,** travaux *mpl* de recherches; **the e. of a possibility,** l'étude *f* d'une possibilité; **(c)** *Med* exploration *f* (*d'une plaie*).

explorative [ɪks'plɒrətɪv] *adj* explorateur, -trice.

exploratory [ɪks'plɒrət(ə)rɪ] *adj* **(a)** (*well, poll*) d'exploration; **(b)** (*voyage*) de découverte; **(c)** (*dialogue*) préliminaire; **(d)** *Med* **e. surgery,** opération *f* exploratoire.

explore [ɪks'plɔːr] *vt* **(a)** explorer (*une région, une ville*); aller à la découverte dans (*un continent*); faire l'exploration de (*un pays*); tâter (*le terrain*); **we are exploring the possibility of further disarmament,** nous étudions la possibilité d'un désarmement plus important; **(b)** *Med* explorer, sonder (*une plaie*).

explorer [ɪks'plɒrər] *n* **(a)** (*person*) explorateur, -trice; **(b)** (*apparatus*) instrument explorateur; *esp Med* sonde *f*.

explosion [ɪks'pləʊʒən] *n* **(a)** explosion *f* (*d'un mélange gazeux, d'un obus etc*); déflagration *f* (*d'un gaz*); *Fig* débordement *m* (*de fureur*); explosion (*de rires*); **there was an e.**, il y a eu une explosion; **to cause an e.**, provoquer une explosion; **(b)** (*noise*) détonation; *Fig* **population e.**, explosion *f* démographique.

explosive [ɪks'pləʊsɪv] **1** *adj* **(a)** explosif, détonant; **e. device,** engin explosif; **e. mixture,** mélange détonant; *Nucl Phys* **e. fission,** fission explosive; *Fig* **an e. situation,** une situation explosive; **(b)** *Ling* (*consonant*) explosif. **2** *n* **(a)** explosif *m*; **high e.,** explosif à grande puissance; **(b)** *Ling* (consonne *f*) explosive *f*.

exponent [ɪks'pəʊnənt] *n* **(a)** interprète *mf* (*d'un système etc*); *Mus* interprète, exécutant, -ante (*d'une œuvre*); protagoniste *mf* (*d'un sport*); **the leading exponents of this genre,** les principaux représentants de ce genre; **(b)** *Math* exposant *m* (*d'une quantité*).

exponential [ekspəʊ'nenʃəl] *adj* exponentiel; *Math* **e. curve,** courbe exponentielle.

export¹ ['ekspɔːt] *n* **(a)** (*product*) marchandise exportée; article *m* d'exportation; **coffee is an important e.,** on exporte beaucoup de café; **exports,** exportations *fpl* (*d'un pays*); **exports are up by 20%,** les exportations ont augmenté de 20%; **visible/invisible exports,** exportations visibles/invisibles; **(b)** (*trade*) exportation *f*; **the e. of coal,** l'exportation de charbon; **for e. only,** réservé à l'exportation; **e. duty,** droit(s) *m(pl)* de sortie; **e. earnings,** recettes *fpl* d'exportation; **e. licence,** licence *f* d'exportation; **e. trade,** commerce *m* d'exportation; **a flourishing e. trade,** une exportation florissante.

export² [eks'pɔːt] **1** *vt* **(a)** exporter (*des marchandises*); *Fig* **Europeans exported their way of life,** les Européens ont exporté leur mode de vie; **(b)** *Comptr* exporter. **2** *vi* exporter.

exportation [ekspɔː'teɪʃən] *n* exportation *f*.

exporter [eks'pɔːtər] *n* exportateur, -trice; **the country is a major e. of technology,** ce pays est un des grands exportateurs de technologie.

expose [ɪks'pəʊz] *vt* **(a)** (*put in unprotected position*) laisser sans abri; abandonner (*un nouveau-né*); **to e. oneself,** faire de l'exhibitionnisme; *Phot* exposer (*un film*); **to e. s.o./oneself to danger,** exposer qn/s'exposer au danger; **to e. one's flank to the enemy,** prêter le flanc à l'ennemi; **to e. oneself to ridicule,** s'exposer à la risée publique; **(b)** (*lay bare*) mettre (*qch*) à découvert *ou* à nu *ou* à jour; afficher (*son ignorance*); étaler (*des marchandises à vendre*); *Rel* exposer (*le saint Sacrement*); **to e. oneself,** faire de l'exhibitionnisme; **a man exposed himself to her,** un exhibitionniste l'a approchée; **(c)** (*reveal*) éventer (*un secret*); dévoiler (*un crime*); dénoncer (*qn, un vice*).

exposé [eks'pəʊzeɪ] *n* **(a)** (*article, documentary, book etc*) exposé *m*; **(b)** révélation *f* (*d'un scandale etc*).

exposed [ɪks'pəʊzd] *adj* **(a)** exposé (*à la vue, aux éléments*); (*engrenages*) à découvert; *Phot* (*film*) exposé, impressionné; *Mil* **e. position,** endroit exposé; *Fig* **this leaves the Prime Minister in an e. position,** cela laisse le premier ministre dans une position fragile; **to be e.,** (*of troops*) être en l'air; **(b)** (*laid bare*) à nu.

exposition [ekspə'zɪʃən] *n* **(a)** (*explanation*) exposé *m*, exposition *f*, présentation *f*; (*in novel*) exposition; *Mus* exposition; **(b)** *Am* exposition *f* (*de peinture etc*); **(c)** *Rel* exposition *f*.

expostulate [ɪks'pɒstjʊleɪt] *vi* faire des remontrances (**with,** à; **about,** sur, au sujet de).

expostulation [ɪkspɒstjʊ'leɪʃən] *n* remontrance(s) *f(pl)*.

exposure [ɪks'pəʊʒər] *n* **(a)** exposition *f* (*à l'air, au froid, à un danger*); abandon *m* (*d'un nouveau-né*); **to die of e.,** mourir de froid; *Nucl Phys* **e. (to radiation),** irradiation *f*; **(b)** exposition *f*, étalage *m* (*de marchandises à vendre*); *Min etc* mise *f* à nu *ou* à découvert (*du minerai etc*); *Jur* **indecent e.,** outrage public à la pudeur; **(c)** dévoilement *m* (*d'un crime etc*); dénonciation *f* (*d'un escroc*); **to threaten s.o. with e.,** menacer qn d'un scandale; **(d)** *Phot* prise *f* de vue; **time e.,** pose *f*; **e. time,** temps *m* de pose; **e. meter,** posemètre *m*; **e. counter,** compteur *m* de prises de vue; **(e)** (*of building, place*) exposition *f*, orientation *f*.

expound [ɪks'paʊnd] *vt* exposer (*une doctrine, ses principes*); interpréter (*les Écritures saintes*).

express¹ [ɪks'pres] **1** *adj* **(a)** (*law, stipulation etc*) exprès, *f* expresse; (*order*) formel, explicite; **for this e. purpose,** dans ce but même; **(b)** (*rapid*) **e. train,** (train *m*) express *m*, rapide *m*; **e. delivery,** envoi *m* par exprès; **e. letter/messenger,** lettre *f*/messager *m* exprès; **by e. messenger,** par exprès; *US* **e. company,** compagnie *f* de messageries; **(c)** (*image*) exact, fidèle (**of,** de). **2** *adv* sans arrêt; **lift that goes e. to the twentieth floor,** ascenseur qui monte directement au vingtième étage. **3** *n* **(a)** *Rail* express *m*, rapide *m*; **(b)** *US F* (*freight company*) **the e.,** compagnie *f* de messageries.

express² *vt* **(a)** exprimer (*ses sentiments*); dire (*son sentiment*); manifester (*sa volonté*); émettre (*une opinion*); formuler (*un souhait*); témoigner (*sa reconnaissance*); **a millionaire has expressed an interest in (buying) the castle,** un millionnaire s'est déclaré intéressé par le château; **well/badly expressed,** bien/mal rendu; **to e. oneself,** s'exprimer; **he has difficulty in expressing himself,** il a du mal à s'exprimer; **(b)** *Math* exprimer; **to e. sth as an equation,** exprimer qch sous forme d'équation; **(c)** (*remove*) exprimer (*l'huile etc*) (**out of, from,** de).

express³ *vt* envoyer (*une lettre*) par exprès; *US* envoyer *ou* expédier (*un colis*) par les messageries.

expression [ɪks'preʃən] *n* **(a)** (*of face, eyes*) expression *f*; **he had a strange e. (on his face),** il avait une drôle d'expression; *Mus* **with e.,** (*chanter, jouer*) avec expression; **(b)** (*phrase*) expression *f*, locution *f*; *Math* **algebraical e.,** expression *ou* formule *f* algébrique; **(c)** (*act of expressing*) expression *f*, manifestation *f* (*d'une pensée, de la joie etc*); **beyond e.,** au delà de toute expression, inexprimable; **freedom of e.,** liberté *f* d'expression; **these feelings found e. in her poetry,** sa poésie a su exprimer ces sentiments; **he raised his fist in an e. of defiance,** il brandit le poing en signe de défi.

expressionism [ɪks'preʃənɪz(ə)m] *n* *Art etc* expressionnisme *m*.

expressionist [ɪks'preʃənɪst] *adj & n* expressionniste *mf*.

expressionless [ɪks'preʃənlɪs] *adj* (*figure, voix*) sans expression; (*visage*) impassible.

expressive [ɪks'presɪv] *adj* expressif, plein d'expression; (*geste, silence*) éloquent; **attitude e. of disdain,** attitude qui exprime le dédain.

expressively [ɪks'presɪvlɪ] *adv* avec expression.

expressiveness [ɪks'presɪvnɪs] *n* caractère expressif, force *f* d'expression (*d'un visage etc*).

expressly [ɪks'preslɪ] *adv* **(a)** (*clearly*) expressément, formellement (*défendu*); **(b)** (*with a clear purpose*) (*faire qch*) dans le seul but (**to,** de).

expressway [ɪks'presweɪ] *n* autoroute *f*, voie *f* rapide.

expropriate [eks'prəʊprɪeɪt] *vt* exproprier (*un propriétaire, une propriété*).

expropriation [eksprəʊprɪ'eɪʃən] *n* expropriation *f* (*d'un propriétaire, d'une propriété*).

expulsion [ɪks'pʌlʃən] *n* expulsion *f* (*d'un étranger etc*); renvoi *m* (*d'un élève*).

expunge [ɪks'pʌndʒ] *vt* effacer, rayer (*un nom d'une liste, un passage dans un livre*).

expurgate ['ekspɜːgeɪt] *vt* expurger (*un livre*); épurer (*un texte*); supprimer (*un passage etc*); **expurgated edition,** édition expurgée.

expurgation [ekspɜː'geɪʃən] *n* expurgation *f* (*d'un livre*); épuration *f* (*d'un texte, d'une association*); suppression *f* (*d'un passage*).

exquisite ['ekskwɪzɪt] **(a)** *adj* (*food, wine*) exquis; (*pleasure etc*) vif; (*torture*) raffiné; **(b)** (*delicate*) très sensible, délicat, subtil.

exquisitely [eks'kwɪzɪtlɪ] *adv* **(a)** (*delicately*) d'une manière exquise; **e. done,** (*of needlework etc*) perlé; **(b)** (*extremely*) excessivement, extrêmement (*petit, sensible etc*).

exquisiteness [eks'kwɪzɪtnɪs] *n* **(a)** (*delicacy, subtlety*) perfection délicate (*d'une œuvre d'art*); finesse *f* (*de l'oreille*); **(b)** (*extreme degree*) caractère vif (*du plaisir etc*); acuité *f* (*de la douleur*).

ex-serviceman, *pl* **-men** [eks'sɜːvɪsmən] *n* militaire *m* en retraite.

ex-servicewoman, *pl* **-women** [eks'sɜːvɪswʊmən, -wɪmɪn] *n* militaire féminine en retraite.

ext *abbr* **extension.**

extant [eks'tænt] *adj* existant encore, qui existe encore.

extemporaneous [ɪkstempə'reɪnɪəs] *adj* improvisé, impromptu.

extemporaneously [ɪkstempə'reɪnɪəslɪ] *adv* (*parler etc*) impromptu.

extempore [ɪks'tempərɪ] **1** *adv* (*parler*) impromptu, sans préparation; **to speak e.,** improviser (un discours). **2** *adj* (*discours*) improvisé, impromptu; (*orateur*) qui parle sans préparation.

extemporization [ɪkstempəraɪ'zeɪʃən] *n* improvisation *f*.

extemporize [ɪks'tempəraɪz] **1** *vt* improviser (*un discours*); faire (*une prière*) à l'impromptu. **2** *vi* improviser, parler à l'impromptu; *Mus* improviser (**on the organ/***etc*, à l'orgue/*etc*).

extend [ɪks'tend] **1** *vt* **(a)** (*stretch*) étendre, allonger (*le corps*); prolonger (*une ligne*); **to e. an aerial/telescope,** développer une antenne/un télescope;

(b) (*prolong*) prolonger (*une période de temps, Rail un billet*); *Com* proroger (*l'échéance d'un billet*); continuer (*des recherches*); **the deadline has been extended until 25th May,** la date limite a été repoussée au 25 mai;

(c) (*broaden, increase*) étendre, porter plus loin (*les *limites*); étendre (*la signification d'un mot*); accroître (*des connaissances*); agrandir, augmenter (*son pouvoir, ses terres*); reculer (*les frontières d'un État*); **we are going to e. our premises,** nous allons nous agrandir; **the scope of the law was extended,** le champ d'action de cette loi a été élargi;

(d) (*hold out*) tendre (*la main*); **to e. a welcome to s.o.,** souhaiter la bienvenue à qn; *Banking* **to e. credit to s.o.,** accorder un crédit à qn;

(e) *Sp etc* (*push to the limit*) faire rendre son maximum à, pousser (*un cheval, un coureur etc*); **to e. oneself,** donner son maximum.

2 *vi* **(a)** s'étendre, s'allonger (**to, over, across,** jusqu'à, au delà de); **to e. beyond the wall,** s'avancer au-delà du mur; **the government's concern with austerity does not e. to its own departments,** la volonté du gouvernement de mener une politique d'austérité ne s'étend pas jusqu'à ses propres départements;

(b) (*of period of time*) se prolonger, continuer; **enquiries extending over a number of years,** investigations prolongées pendant un grand nombre d'années.

extended [ɪks'tendɪd] *adj* **(a)** (*corps, bras*) étendu, allongé; *Mil* (*troupes*) déployé; *Horseriding* **e. trot,** trot allongé; *Mil* **in e. order,** en ordre dispersé; **(b)** (*long*) long, prolongé; (*prolonged*) prolongé; (*voyage*) de quelque durée; **(c)** (*increased*) augmenté, agrandi; **e. family,** famille au sens large.

extended-play [ɪks'tendɪd'pleɪ] *n* **e.-p. record,** disque *m* double durée.

extending [ɪks'tendɪŋ] **1** *adj* (*table*) à rallonges; (*échelle*) à coulisse. **2** *n* extension *f*, allongement *m*; (*in time*) prolongation *f*.

extension [ɪks'tenʃən] *n* **(a)** (*act of stretching out*) extension *f* (*du bras*); prolongement *m* (*d'un canal, d'un chemin de fer etc*); agrandissement *m*, extension (*d'une usine etc*); (r)allonge *f* (*de table, de cric etc*); *Surg* extension (*d'une jambe cassée*); *Av* sortie *f* (*du train d'atterrissage etc*); *MecE* **e. piece,** pièce *f* formant prolongement; **e. ladder,** échelle *f* à coulisse;

(b) (*growing*) extension *f*, accroissement *m* (*des affaires etc*); **there has been a considerable e. of his business,** son commerce a pris une extension considérable;

(c) (*extra part*) (r)allonge *f* (*de table etc*); allonge *f* (*de câble*); *Tel* poste *m* supplémentaire; *Tel* **e. 35,** poste 35; *El* **e. light,** baladeuse *f*; **e. loudspeaker,** haut-parleur séparé;

(d) (*on building*) annexe *f*; **we're having an e. built,** nous faisons agrandir la maison; **an e. is being added to the museum,** on construit une annexe au musée;

(e) *Gram* complément *m* (*du sujet, de l'attribut*);

(f) (*of period of time*) prolongation *f* (*de congé, d'un billet de chemin de fer*); **to get an e.,** (*of a deadline*) obtenir un délai; **arrangement for an e.,** (*postponement*) atermoiement *m*;

(g) *Sch* **e. courses,** formation continue.

extensive [ɪks'tensɪv] *adj* **(a)** étendu, vaste, ample; **e. knowledge,** vastes connaissances; **e. researches,** travaux approfondis; **there was e. damage to both wings,** les deux ailes ont été très endommagées; **to make e. use of sth,** faire un usage considérable de qch; **(b)** (*agriculture*) extensif.

extensively [ɪks'tensɪvlɪ] *adv* (*to travel, read etc*) beaucoup; (*rewritten etc*) largement; **to use sth e.,** se servir beaucoup de qch, faire un usage considérable de qch; **it was e. damaged,** il a subi des dommages considérables.

extent [ɪks'tent] *n* étendue *f* (*d'un terrain, des connaissances etc*); importance *f* (*du dommage etc*); **vast e. of ground,** grande superficie de terrain; **credit to the e. of £500,** crédit jusqu'à concurrence de 500 livres; **to an e., to a certain e., to some e.,** jusqu'à un certain point, dans une certaine mesure; **to a great e., to a large e.,** en grande partie, dans une large mesure; **to such an e. that ...,** à tel point que ...; **to what e. is this true?,** jusqu'à quel point est-ce vrai?; **to the e. that he can play a few tunes, he is a musician,** dans la mesure où il peut jouer quelques airs, c'est un musicien; **the e. to which the strike affected production is unclear,** les conséquences de la grève sur la production sont mal définies.

extenuate [ɪks'tenjʊeɪt] *vt* atténuer, amoindrir (*la faute de qn*).

extenuating [ɪks'tenjʊeɪtɪŋ] *adj* (*circonstance*) atténuant.

extenuation [ɪkstenjʊ'eɪʃən] *n* atténuation *f* (*d'une faute*); **circumstances in e. of his fault,** circonstances qui atténuent sa faute.

exterior [ɪks'tɪərɪər] **1** *adj* extérieur (**to,** à), en dehors (**to,** de); *Math* **e. angle,** angle *m* externe; **e. wall,** mur extérieur. **2** *n* **(a)** extérieur *m*, dehors *mpl*; **on the e.,** à l'extérieur; **house with an imposing e.,** maison aux dehors imposants; **despite her stern e. she is very likeable,** malgré un extérieur sévère elle est très sympathique; **(b)** *Th Cin* extérieur *m*.

exteriorize [ɪks'tɪərɪəraɪz] *vt* extérioriser.

exterminate [ɪks'tɜːmɪneɪt] *vt* exterminer (*des insectes, une population etc*).

extermination [ɪkstɜːmɪ'neɪʃən] *n* extermination *f* (*d'une population etc*).

exterminator [ɪks'tɜːmɪneɪtər] *n* (*person*) exterminateur, -trice.

extern [eks'tɜːn] *n US Med* externe *mf*.

external [ɪks'tɜːn(ə)l] **1** *adj* (*médicament, angle*) externe; (*mur*) extérieur; (*affaires*) du dehors, de l'extérieur; (*commerce*) extérieur; étranger, -ère; (*étudiant*) libre; *Med* **for e. use only,** à usage externe; *Comptr* **e. device,** dispositif *m* externe, périphérique *m*; (*printer*) imprimante *f*; *Fin* **e. financing,** fonds extérieurs. **2** *n* (*usu pl*) **(a)** (*appearance*) **externals,** extérieur *m*, formes extérieures, dehors *mpl*; **to judge by externals,** juger les choses selon les apparences; **(b)** (*inessential things*) **externals,** choses *fpl* secondaires.

externalize [ɪks'tɜːnəlaɪz] *vt* exprimer (*ses sentiments*).

externally [ɪks'tɜːn(ə)lɪ] *adv* extérieurement, à l'extérieur.

extinct [ɪks'tɪŋkt] *adj* (*animal, plant*) disparu, qui n'existe plus; (*office, title*) aboli, tombé en désuétude; (*volcano, passion*) éteint; **to become e.,** (*of race*) s'éteindre, disparaître.

extinction [ɪks'tɪŋkʃən] *n* extinction *f* (*d'un incendie, d'une race*); anéantissement *m* (*d'une espérance*); **race threatened with e.,** race en passe de disparaître.

extinguish [ɪks'tɪŋgwɪʃ] *vt* éteindre (*le feu, un incendie, une race*); souffler (*la chandelle*); anéantir (*une espérance*).

extinguisher [ɪks'tɪŋgwɪʃər] *n* **(a)** (*for fire*) appareil *m* d'extinction; (appareil) extincteur *m* (d'incendie); **foam e.,** extincteur à mousse; **(b)** (*for candle*) éteignoir *m*.

extirpate ['ekstɜːpeɪt] *vt Fml* extirper, déraciner (*un arbre, un abus*).

extirpation [ekstɜː'peɪʃən] *n Fml* extirpation *f*, éradication *f* (*d'un arbre, d'un vice*).

extol, *US* **extoll** [ɪks'təʊl] *vt* (*Br* **extols**, *US* **extolls**, *Br & US* **extolled**, **extolling**) exalter, vanter, prôner; célébrer, chanter (*la beauté de qch*); **she was extolling the virtues of central heating,** elle vantait les vertus du chauffage central; **to e. s.o. to the skies,** porter qn aux nues.

extort [ɪks'tɔːt] *vt* extorquer (*de l'argent etc*) (**from s.o.,** à qn); arracher (*une promesse, un aveu*) (**from s.o.,** à qn).

extortion [ɪks'tɔːʃən] *n* extorsion *f* (*d'argent etc*); arrachement *m* (*d'une promesse, d'un aveu*).

extortionate [ɪks'tɔːʃənɪt] *adj* **(a)** (*price*) exorbitant; **(b)** (*person*) extorsionnaire, rapace.

extortioner [ɪks'tɔːʃənər], **extortionist** [ɪks'tɔːʃənɪst] *n* extorqueur, -euse.

extra ['ekstrə] **1** *adj* **(a)** (*additional*) en sus, de plus, supplémentaire; **e. trains are being laid on for the festival,** des trains supplémentaires seront mis en circulation pour le festival; **the commissioner is asking for 500 e. police officers,** le préfet réclame 500 officiers de police supplémentaires; **e. charge,** prix *m* en sus; supplément *m* de prix; **at no e. cost,** sans supplément; **e. pay,** prime *f*, supplément *m* de salaire; *Mil Nau* supplément de solde; **e. work,** (*hours*) heures *fpl* supplémentaires; (*work*) surcroît *m* de travail; **e. time,** *Ind etc* heures supplémentaires; *Br Sp* prolongation *f*; *Br Sp* **to go into e. time,** jouer les prolongations; **as an e. precaution,** pour plus de précaution; *Sch* **e. subject,** matière facultative; **to make an e. effort,** faire un surcroît d'effort;

(b) (*spare*) de réserve, de rechange; **bring some e. batteries,** prends des piles de rechange.

2 *adv* **(a)** (*more than usual*) plus que d'ordinaire, extra-; *F* **an e. special wine for those e. special occasions,** un grand vin pour les grandes occasions; **this is an e. special cake for your birthday,** voici un gâteau exceptionnel pour ton anniversaire; **e. strong binding/rope,** reliure *f*/corde *f* extra-solide; **e. white/fast,** extra-blanc/-rapide; **e. smart,** ultra-chic; **e. large,** (*clothing*) grand patron;

(b) (*in addition*) en plus; **meals taken in the bedroom are charged (for) e.,** il y a un supplément pour les repas servis dans la chambre; **I had to pay e. for the sun roof,** il a fallu que je paye un supplément pour le toit ouvrant; **packing e.,** emballage en sus.

3 *n* **(a)** supplément *m* (*de menu*); édition spéciale (*d'un journal*); (*on car*) option *f*;

(b) (*person*) extra *m*; *Th Cin* figurant, -ante; **to be** *or* **work as an e.,** faire de la figuration;
(c) (*expenses*) **extras,** frais *mpl ou* dépenses *fpl* supplémentaires; suppléments *mpl*; *Typ* surcharge *f*;
(d) (*luxuries*) **little extras,** les petits à côtés, les extras *mpl*.

extra(-) ['ekstrə] *pref* (*outside*) extra; **extragalactic,** extragalactique; **extravascular,** extravasculaire.

extract¹ ['ekstrækt] *n* (a) (*of substance*) extrait *m*, concentré *m*; **malt/beef e.,** extrait de malt/de bœuf; **meat e.,** concentré de viande; (b) *Liter etc* extrait *m*; **extracts,** (*of novel etc*) morceaux choisis.

extract² [ɪks'trækt] *vt* extraire, arracher (*une dent*); extraire (*de l'huile, du métal etc*); **to e. a passage from a book,** extraire un passage d'un livre; **to e. a bullet from a wound,** retirer une balle d'une plaie; **to e. money/a confession from s.o.,** arracher de l'argent/un aveu à qn, tirer de l'argent/un aveu de qn.

extraction [ɪks'trækʃən] *n* (a) (*removal*) extraction *f* (*du jus d'un citron etc*); arrachage *m* (*d'un clou*); extraction (*d'une dent*); **e. of stone from a quarry,** extraction de la pierre d'une carrière; (b) (*origin*) extraction *f*; origine *f*; **of humble e.,** de basse extraction; **of Italian e.,** d'origine italienne.

extractor [ɪks'træktər] *n* (a) (*tool*) pince *f*; (*in dentistry*) davier *m*; *Surg* extracteur *m* (*de calculs etc*); **e. (fan),** aérateur *m*; **e. hood,** (*for stove*) hotte *f* (*d'aération*); **juice e.,** presse-fruit *m*, *pl* presse-fruits; (b) (*person*) extracteur *m* (*de dents etc*).

extracurricular ['ekstrəkə'rɪkjʊlər] *adj Sch* hors-programme *inv*; **e. activities,** activités *fpl* périscolaires.

extraditable [ekstrə'daɪtəb(ə)l] *adj* (*person*) passible d'extradition; (*crime, offence*) qui justifie l'extradition.

extradite ['ekstrədaɪt] *vt Jur* (a) (*hand over*) extrader (*un criminel*); (b) (*obtain extradition of*) obtenir l'extradition de (*un criminel*).

extradition [ekstrə'dɪʃən] *n* extradition *f*; **the Spanish government is seeking/has obtained his e.,** le gouvernement espagnol a demandé/obtenu son extradition; **e. treaty,** accord *m* d'extradition.

extra-dry ['ekstrə'draɪ] *adj* (*vin*) très sec.

extra-fine ['ekstrə'faɪn] *adj* extra-fin.

extrajudicial ['ekstrədʒuː'dɪʃəl] *adj* extrajudiciaire.

extramarital ['ekstrə'mærɪt(ə)l] *adj* extra-conjugal, -aux.

extramural ['ekstrə'mjʊər(ə)l] *adj* (a) *Sch* **e. lecturer,** = conférencier en dehors de la Faculté accrédité pour certains cours; **e. course,** cours *m* supplémentaire; (b) (*quartier*) extra-muros *inv*.

extraneous [ɪks'treɪnɪəs] *adj* étranger (**to,** à); (*considérations*) en dehors de la question.

extraordinarily [ɪks'trɔːd(ə)nərɪlɪ] *adv* extraordinairement; **it was an e. brave/foolish action,** c'était un acte particulièrement courageux/inconscient.

extraordinariness [ɪks'trɔːdənrɪnɪs] *n* caractère *m ou* nature *f* extraordinaire.

extraordinary [ɪks'trɔːd(ə)nrɪ] *adj* (a) (*remarkable*) (*conduite*) extraordinaire; **the e. thing is that ...,** ce qu'il y a d'étrange *ou* de singulier c'est que ...; **that's e., he was here only an hour ago!,** c'est incroyable, il était là il y a une heure à peine!; **I find it e. that you did not inform the police,** je trouve incroyable que vous n'ayez pas prévenu la police; **they went to e. lengths to conceal the truth,** ils se sont donné un mal fou pour cacher la vérité; (b) (*special*) extraordinaire; **ambassador e.,** ambassadeur *m* extraordinaire; **to call an e. general meeting of the shareholders,** convoquer une assemblée générale extraordinaire.

extrapolate [ek'stræpəleɪt] *vt* extrapoler.

extrasensory ['ekstrə'sensərɪ] *adj* extra-sensoriel; **e. perception,** perception extra-sensorielle; **to have e. perception,** avoir des dons de perception extra-sensorielle.

extraterrestrial ['ekstrətɪ'restrɪəl] *adj & n* extraterrestre *mf*.

extraterritorial ['ekstrəterɪ'tɔːrɪəl] *adj* (*privilège*) d'exterritorialité.

extraterritoriality [ekstrəterɪtɔːrɪ'ælɪtɪ] *n* exterritorialité *f*.

extravagance [ɪks'trævəgəns] *n* (a) (*excessive, wasteful expenditure*) folles dépenses, prodigalités *fpl*; **she accused the government of e.,** elle a accusé le gouvernement de dilapider le trésor public; **a piece of e., an e.,** une dépense inutile, une folie; (b) (*exaggeration*) extravagance *f*, exagération *f*.

extravagant [ɪks'trævəgənt] *adj* (a) (*person*) dépensier, gaspilleur; (*tastes*) dispendieux; **don't be so e. with the butter,** ne gaspillez pas le beurre; **he considered two baths a week (to be) e.,** il trouvait que deux bains par semaine, c'était du gaspillage; (b) (*exaggerated*) extravagant; (*claim*) exagéré, déraisonnable; (*praise*) outré; (*style*) exagéré (*price*) exorbitant, prohibitif; **e. claims have been made for the drug,** des propriétés abusives ont été attribuées à ce médicament.

extravagantly [ɪks'trævəgəntlɪ] *adv* (a) (*excessively*) **he spent money e.,** il jetait l'argent par la fenêtre; **to live e.,** vivre sur un grand pied, dépenser sans compter; **e. furnished house,** maison meublée avec un luxe exagéré; (b) (*exaggeratedly*) d'une façon extravagante; **to talk/act e.,** dire/faire des folies *ou* des extravagances.

extravaganza [ekstrævə'gænzə] *n* œuvre *f* (musicale, littéraire) d'une extravagance bouffonne, œuvre fantaisiste.

extravert ['ekstrəvɜːt] *adj & n Psy* = **EXTROVERT**.

extreme [ɪks'triːm] **1** *adj* (a) (*heat, difficulty etc*) extrême; *Pol* (*nationalism*) outrancier; (*opinions*) extrémiste; **to be in e. peril,** être en (très) grand danger; **to behave with e. awkwardness,** se conduire avec la dernière gaucherie; **an e. case,** un cas exceptionnel; **the question is one of e. delicacy,** le problème est délicat entre tous;
(b) (*far*) extrême; **at the e. end of the quay,** tout au bout du quai; *Pol* **the e. left,** l'extrême gauche; **on the e. left of the photograph,** à l'extrême gauche de la photo;
(c) (*final*) **the e. penalty,** le dernier supplice; *Cathol* **e. unction,** extrême-onction *f*.
2 *n* extrême *m*; **they were rude in the e.,** ils étaient mal polis à l'extrême; **to go from one e. to the other,** passer d'un extrême à l'autre; **now he's going to the other e. and ...,** il est passé d'un extrême à l'autre et maintenant ...; **in the e.,** au dernier degré; **to go to extremes,** pousser les choses à l'extrême; **extremes of temperature,** extrêmes de température.

extremely [ɪks'triːmlɪ] *adv* extrêmement; **to be e. witty,** avoir énormément d'esprit; **the map is e. useful,** la carte est extrêmement utile.

extremism [ɪks'triːmɪz(ə)m] *n Pol* extrémisme *m*.

extremist [ɪks'triːmɪst] *adj & n Pol* extrémiste *mf*.

extremity [ɪks'tremɪtɪ] *n* (a) (*end*) extrémité *f*, point *m* extrême; bout *m* (*d'une corde, d'une rue*); sommité *f* (*d'une plante, d'une branche*); **the extremities,** (*of the body*) les extrémités *fpl*; (b) (*need*) gêne *f*; **to be reduced to the last e.,** en être réduit à la dernière extrémité.

extricate ['ekstrɪkeɪt] *vt* dégager, tirer (**s.o. from a critical position,** qn d'un mauvais pas); **to e. oneself from a danger,** se tirer d'un danger; **I managed to e. myself from this conversation,** j'ai réussi à me dégager de cette conversation; **to e. oneself from difficulties,** se débrouiller, se tirer d'affaire.

extrinsic [eks'trɪnsɪk] *adj* extrinsèque.

extrovert ['ekstrəvɜːt] *Psy* **1** *n* extraverti, -ie, extroverti, -ie; **she's much more of an e. than her sister,** elle est bien plus extravertie que sa sœur, c'est une extravertie bien plus que sa sœur. **2** *adj* extroverti; **to have e. tendencies,** être d'un naturel extraverti.

extrude [eks'truːd] **1** *vt* expulser, faire jaillir (**from,** de); *Metal* filer, profiler; *Ind* (*plastics*) boudiner (à chaud); **extruded section** *or* **shape,** profilé *m*. **2** *vi Geol* (*of rock etc*) s'épancher.

extrusion [eks'truːʒən] *n* expulsion *f* (*de qch*); émission *f* (*d'une sécrétion*); *Geol* épanchement *m* (*volcanique*); *Metal* extrusion *f*; filage *m* (à chaud); *Ind* (*of plastics*) boudinage *m*, extrusion.

exuberance [ɪg'zjuːb(ə)rəns] *n* exubérance *f*; (*of person*) gaieté débordante; (*of vegetation*) richesse *f*.

exuberant [ɪg'zjuːb(ə)rənt] *adj* exubérant; (*person*) débordant de vie; (*vegetation*) riche; (*health, vitality*) débordant.

exuberantly [ɪg'zjuːb(ə)rəntlɪ] *adv* avec exubérance; **e. healthy,** débordant de santé.

exude [ɪg'zjuːd] **1** *vt* exsuder; *Fig* **she exudes health,** elle respire la santé. **2** *vi* exsuder, suinter; (*of sap*) couler, s'écouler.

exult [ɪg'zʌlt] *vi* (a) (*rejoice*) exulter, se réjouir (**at, in,** de); (b) (*triumph*) **to e. over s.o.,** triompher de qn.

exultant [ɪg'zʌltənt] *adj* (*sentiment*) joyeux; (*cri*) de triomphe; **to be e.,** exulter.

exultantly [ɪg'zʌltəntlɪ] *adv* (*parler etc*) d'un air de triomphe.

exultation [egzʌl'teɪʃən] *n* exultation *f*.

ex voto [eks'vəʊtəʊ] *n Rel* **ex v. (offering),** ex-voto *m inv*.

eye¹ [aɪ] *n* (a) œil *m*, *pl* yeux; *Zool* **simple e.,** œil simple, ocelle *m*; *Zool* **compound e.,** œil composé *ou* à facettes; **to have good eyes,** avoir de bons yeux; **to have blue eyes,**

avoir les yeux bleus; *Bible* **an e. for an e., a tooth for a tooth,** œil pour œil, dent pour dent; **to open/close one's eyes,** ouvrir/fermer les yeux; **to open one's eyes wide,** ouvrir les yeux tout grands; *Fig* **to do sth with one's eyes open,** faire qch en connaissance de cause; **she went into the partnership with her eyes open,** elle est devenue leur *ou* son partenaire en connaissance de cause; **to keep one's eyes and ears open,** avoir l'œil et l'oreille aux aguêts; **to keep one's eyes open** *or F* **peeled** *or* **skinned,** avoir l'œil; **he could not keep his eyes open,** il dormait debout; **to open s.o.'s eyes,** ouvrir les yeux à qn, dessiller les yeux à qn; **working for the government opened my eyes to the level of corruption,** travailler pour le gouvernement m'a ouvert les yeux sur l'importance de la corruption; **to shut** *or* **close one's eyes to s.o.'s faults,** fermer les yeux sur les défauts de qn; **to have the sun/the light in one's eyes,** avoir le soleil/la lumière dans les yeux; **to be up to the** *or* **one's eyes in work/debt,** avoir du travail/des dettes par-dessus la tête; **I've got something in my e.,** j'ai quelque chose dans l'œil; **with tears in one's eyes,** les larmes aux yeux; **dry your eyes,** essuyez vos larmes; *F* **that's one in the e. for him!,** ça lui fait les pieds!; *F* **my e.!,** mon œil!; *F* **that's all my e. (and Betty Martin),** tout ça c'est de la blague *ou* des histoires; **to strike/catch the e.,** frapper/attirer l'œil *ou* les regards; **to catch s.o.'s e.,** (*of person, thing*) attirer l'attention de qn; *Parl* **to catch the Speaker's e.,** obtenir la parole; **it pleases/delights the e.,** cela charme/réjouit les yeux *ou* les regards; **he has eyes in** *or* **at the back of his head,** il a des yeux d'Argus; **he has eyes for nobody but her,** il n'a d'yeux que pour elle; **to set** *or* **lay eyes on sth,** poser les yeux sur qch, apercevoir qch, voir qch; **it was the biggest fish I'd ever laid eyes on,** c'était le plus gros poisson que j'aie jamais vu; **to see sth with one's own eyes,** voir qch de ses propres yeux; **it took place before my (very) eyes,** cela s'est passé sous mes yeux; **to see sth in one's mind's e.,** voir qch en imagination *ou* en idée; *Fig* **where are your eyes?,** êtes-vous aveugle?; **with jealous eyes,** d'un œil jaloux; **to make eyes at s.o.,** *F* **to give s.o. the (glad) e.,** lancer des œillades *ou* faire de l'œil à qn; *F* **to make sheep's eyes at s.o.,** lancer des œillades amoureuses à qn; **to see e. to e. with s.o.,** voir les choses du même œil que qn; **you can see that with half an e.,** cela saute aux yeux; **anyone with half an e. can see it's a fake,** du premier coup d'œil n'importe qui verrait que c'est un faux; **with half an e. on the weather,** sans quitter le ciel des yeux; **to run** *or* **cast one's e. over sth,** jeter un coup d'œil sur qch; *Mil* **eyes right/left!,** tête (à) droite/(à) gauche!; **eyes front!,** fixe!; **to keep an e. on sth/s.o.,** surveiller qch/qn; **the police have had their e. on him for some time,** cela fait un certain temps que la police l'a à l'œil; **keep your e. on him!,** ne le quittez pas des yeux!; **keep an e. on the weather,** surveille le temps; **to keep one's e. on the ball,** suivre *ou Golf* fixer la balle; **keep your eyes on the road,** regarde la route; **under the e. of ...,** sous la surveillance de ...; **with an e. to ...,** en vue de ...; **to be all eyes,** être tout yeux; **all eyes were upon her,** elle était au centre de tous les regards, tous les regards étaient posés sur elle; **everyone is equal in the eye(s) of the law,** tout le monde est égal devant la loi; **in the eyes of all he is guilty,** aux yeux de tous il est coupable; **to be very much in the public e.,** occuper une position très en vue; **to have an e. for a horse,** s'y connaître en chevaux, être bon juge des chevaux; **with the e. of a painter,** d'un œil de peintre; **e. bank,** banque *f* des yeux; **e. contact,** échange *m* de regards; **to make e. contact with s.o.,** regarder qn (droit) dans les yeux; *Med* **e. drops,** gouttes *fpl* pour les yeux; **e. hospital,** clinique *f ou* centre *m* ophtalmologique; **at e. level,** à la hauteur des yeux; **e. shadow,** ombre *f* à paupières; **e. socket,** orbite *f*;

(b) (*markings*) (*usu pl*) **eyes,** yeux *mpl*, miroirs *mpl* (*de la queue d'un paon*); **bird's eyes,** (*in mahogany etc*) tourbillons *mpl*;

(c) (*bud*) œil *m*, bourgeon *m*; (*on potato*) germe *m*; (*in grafting*) œilleton *m*;

(d) œil *m*, *pl* œils, trou *m* (*d'une aiguille*); œil, boucle *f* (*d'un cordage*); collet *m*, œillet *m* (*d'un étai*); anneau *m* (*pour tringle etc*); **to pass through the e. of a needle,** passer par le trou d'une aiguille;

(e) (*with screw thread*) piton *m*; **e. end,** œil *m*, piton (*de câble*);

(f) *Electron* **electric** *or* **magic e.,** cellule *f* photoélectrique, œil *m* magique;

(g) *Met* œil *m* (*d'un typhon*); *Fig* **at the e. of the hurricane,** dans un havre de paix *ou* un îlot préservé;

(h) *F* (*private detective*) détective *ou* enquêteur privé.

eye² *vt* (**eyed, eyeing**) **(a)** (*look at*) regarder, observer (**with suspicion,** d'un air soupçonneux); **(b)** (*weigh up*) mesurer (*qn, un obstacle etc*) des yeux.

▶**eye up** *vtsep* **(a)** (*with sexual interest*) **to e. up the girls/boys,** reluquer les filles/les garçons; **he eyed her up,** il l'a déshabillée du regard; **(b)** (*estimate strength etc of*) jauger (d'un coup d'œil); **they eyed up their opponents,** ils ont jaugé leurs adversaires (d'un coup d'œil).

eyeball ['aɪbɔːl] *n* globe *m* oculaire; *Fig* **to come e. to e.,** s'affronter.

eyebath ['aɪbɑːθ] *n Med* œillère *f*; (*liquid*) bain *m* d'œil.

eyebrow ['aɪbraʊ] *n* sourcil *m*; **to knit one's eyebrows,** froncer le(s) sourcil(s); *Fig* **he never raised an e.,** (*in disapproval*) il n'a pas sourcillé; *Fig* **(some) eyebrows were raised at this suggestion,** (*in disapproval*) cette proposition a suscité des grimaces de désapprobation; (*in astonishment*) cette proposition a suscité de l'étonnement; **e. pencil,** crayon *m* pour les sourcils.

eye-catching ['aɪkætʃɪŋ] *adj* (*design, dress*) accrocheur, -euse; (*publicité*) tapageur; **an e.-c. title,** un titre accrocheur.

eyecup ['aɪkʌp] *n* = **EYEBATH**.

-eyed [aɪd] *suff* **blue-e.,** aux yeux bleus; **wide-e.,** aux grands yeux.

eyeful ['aɪfʊl] *n F* **to get an e.,** se rincer l'œil; **she's quite an e.,** elle vaut le coup d'œil.

eyeglass ['aɪglɑːs] *n* (*monocle*) monocle *m*; **watchmaker's e.,** loupe *f* d'horloger.

eyeglasses ['aɪglɑːsɪz] *npl US* (*spectacles*) lunettes *fpl*.

eyehole ['aɪhəʊl] *n* **(a)** (*in mask*) **eyeholes,** ouvertures *fpl* pour les yeux; **(b)** (*small opening*) petite ouverture; judas *m* (*d'une porte etc*); *Tech* trou *m* de regard *ou* de visite.

eyelash ['aɪlæʃ] *n* cil *m*.

eyelet ['aɪlɪt] *n* œillet *m*.

eyelevel ['aɪlev(ə)l] *adj* **e.-l. grill,** gril *m* à la hauteur des yeux.

eyelid ['aɪlɪd] *n* paupière *f*; **he didn't bat an e.,** il n'a pas sourcillé.

eyeliner ['aɪlaɪnər] *n* eye-liner *m*.

eye-opener ['aɪəʊp(ə)nər] *n* **(a) that was an e.-o. for him,** cela lui a ouvert les yeux, ça a été une révélation pour lui; **(b)** *Am* (*drink*) petit verre du matin.

eye-opening ['aɪəʊp(ə)nɪŋ] *adj* qui ouvre les yeux; **e.-o. experience,** une expérience révélatrice *ou* qui ouvre les yeux.

eyepiece ['aɪpiːs] *n* **(a)** *Opt* oculaire *m* (*de microscope etc*); viseur *m* (*de théodolite etc*); **(b)** *Metal* lunette *f* de regard (*d'un fourneau*); **(c)** (*of gas mask*) lunette *f*.

eyeshade ['aɪʃeɪd] *n* visière *f*.

eyesight ['aɪsaɪt] *n* vue *f*; **to have good e.,** avoir une bonne vue *ou* de bons yeux; **my e. is failing,** ma vue baisse.

eyesore ['aɪsɔːr] *n* **the building is an e.,** le bâtiment est une horreur *ou* blesse la vue.

eyespot ['aɪspɒt] *n* ocelle *f* (*de papillon etc*).

eyestrain ['aɪstreɪn] *n* **to suffer from e.,** avoir les yeux fatigués.

eyetooth, *pl* **-teeth** ['aɪtuːθ, -tiːθ] *n* dent canine; **to cut one's eyeteeth,** faire ses canines; *F* (*come to end of childhood*) sortir de sa première enfance; **I'd give my eyeteeth to go with them,** je donnerais n'importe quoi pour aller avec eux.

eyewash ['aɪwɒʃ] *n Pharm* collyre *m*; *Fig* **that's all e.,** (*nonsense*) tout ça c'est du boniment.

eyewitness ['aɪwɪtnɪs] *n* témoin *m* oculaire (**of,** de); **an e. account,** le récit d'un témoin oculaire.

eyrie ['ɪərɪ] *n* aire *f* (*d'un aigle*).

F

F, f [ef] *n* **(a)** (la lettre) F, f *mf*; *Br F* **the F word,** ≈ le mot de Cambronne; **(b)** *Mus* fa *m*; **F clef,** clef *f* de fa.

fa [fɑː] *n Mus* fa *m*.

FA [eˈfeɪ] *n* **(a)** *Eng Sp* (*abbr* **Football Association**) = fédération anglaise de football; **FA Cup,** coupe *f* de la fédération anglaise de football; **FA Cup match,** match *m* de coupe de la fédération anglaise de football; **(b)** *Sl* **sweet FA,** rien du tout, nib de nib.

fab [fæb] *adj Old-fashioned F* sensass.

fable [ˈfeɪb(ə)l] *n* fable *f*, conte *m*.

fabled [ˈfeɪb(ə)ld] *adj* célèbre dans la fable; légendaire.

fabric [ˈfæbrɪk] *n* **(a)** *Tex etc* tissu *m*, étoffe *f*; **dress fabrics,** tissus pour robes; **silk, woollen and cotton fabrics,** soieries *fpl*, lainages *mpl* et cotonnades *fpl*; **(b)** structure *f* (*d'un édifice, d'un système*); gros œuvre (*d'un bâtiment*); **the f. of society,** l'édifice social.

fabricate [ˈfæbrɪkeɪt] *vt* inventer, fabriquer (*une nouvelle*); forger (*un document*).

fabrication [fæbrɪˈkeɪʃən] *n* invention *f* (*d'une nouvelle*); contrefaçon *f* (*d'un document*); **it's pure f.,** c'est de la pure fabrication; **a pure f.,** une histoire inventée de toute pièce.

fabulous [ˈfæbjʊləs] *adj* **(a)** (*conte*) fabuleux; (*personnage*) légendaire; **(b)** *F* prodigieux; (*prix*) fou; **we had a f. evening,** on a passé une soirée merveilleuse.

fabulously [ˈfæbjʊləslɪ] *adv* fabuleusement; prodigieusement (*riche etc*).

façade [fæˈsɑːd] *n* façade *f*.

face¹ [feɪs] *n* **(a)** figure *f*, visage *m*; **what a f.!,** quelle tête!, *Sl* quelle gueule!; *Fig* **I'm just going to put my f. on,** je vais me maquiller; **I shall never be able to look her in the f. again,** je ne pourrai jamais plus la regarder en face; **he won't show his f. here again!,** il ne remettra pas les pieds ici!; **the f. of Britain is changing,** le visage de la Grande-Bretagne est en train de changer; **her f. doesn't fit,** (*in job, company etc*) sa tête ne nous *ou* leur *etc* revient pas; **the unacceptable f. of capitalism,** le visage inacceptable du capitalisme; **Communism with a human f.,** le communisme à visage humain; **to hide one's f. in shame,** se cacher le visage de honte; **to set one's f. against sth,** s'opposer résolument à qch; **in the f. of danger,** devant le danger; **I told him so to his f.,** je le lui ai dit au nez *ou* à sa barbe; *F* **shut your f.!,** ferme-la!, la ferme!; **full-f. portrait,** portrait *m* de face; **f. to f.,** face à face; **to bring s.o. f. to f. with s.o.,** confronter qn avec qn; **to come f. to f. with s.o.,** se trouver face à face avec qn; **to meet s.o. f. to f.,** rencontrer qn face-à-face; **f. cream,** crème *f* pour le visage; **f. pack,** masque *m*; **to give oneself a f. pack,** se faire un masque; **f. cloth** *or* **flannel,** = gant *m* de toilette; **f. powder,** poudre *f* pour le visage; *Sp* **f. mask** *or* **guard,** masque protecteur; *Cards Am* **f. card,** figure *f*; **f. scrub,** (*cosmetic*) exfoliant *m* (*pour le visage*);

(b) (*expression*) mine *f*, physionomie *f*; **to pull a long f.,** tirer une tête longue comme ça; **to make** *or* **pull faces,** faire des grimaces (**at,** à); **to keep a straight f.,** garder son sérieux; **to put a good f. on it,** faire contre mauvaise fortune bon cœur;

(c) (*appearance*) apparence *f*, aspect *m* (*de qch*); **on the f. of it,** au premier aspect, à première vue; **f. value,** valeur nominale; **I took him at (his) f. value,** je l'ai jugé sur les apparences; **to take what s.o. says at f. value,** prendre ce que qn dit pour argent comptant; **to save f.,** sauver la face; **the agreement saved f. all round,** l'accord a sauvé la face à tout point de vue; **to lose f.,** perdre la face; **loss of f.,** humiliation *f*;

(d) *F* (*cheek*) front *m*, toupet *m*; **he had the f. to tell me so,** il a eu le culot de me le dire;

(e) (*surface*) surface *f* (*de la terre*); **they disappeared from** *or* **off the f. of the earth,** ils ont disparu de la surface du globe;

(f) (*main side*) face *f* (*d'une pièce de monnaie, une falaise, d'un polyèdre etc*); endroit *m* (*d'un tissu*); recto *m* (*d'un document*); devant *m*, façade *f* (*d'un immeuble*); facette *f*, plan *m* (*d'un cristal*); plat *m* (*d'un marteau*); table *f* (*d'une enclume*); tranche *f* (*d'une meule*); semelle *f* (*d'un rabot*); *Sp* face (*d'une crosse de golf*); *MecE* plateau *m* (*de tour*); *Constr MecE* surface *f*; **bearing f.,** (sur)face portante; **the north f. of the Eiger,** la face nord de l'Eiger; **f. up/down,** face en dessus/en dessous; *Min* **coal f., working f.,** front *m* de taille (du charbon);

(g) cadran *m* (*d'une horloge, d'une montre*);

(h) *Typ* œil *m* (*d'un caractère*); **bold/light f.,** (caractère *m*) gras *m*/maigre *m*.

face² **1** *vt* **(a)** (*confront*) affronter, braver, faire face à (*un danger, un ennemi*); **to f. facts,** regarder les choses en face; **let's f. it,** voyons les choses comme elles sont; **f. it,** (*you haven't a chance*) sois réaliste; **the problem that faces us,** le problème qui se pose; **to be faced with a difficulty,** se heurter à une difficulté; **to be faced with a decision,** être confronté à une décision; **to f.** *or* **be faced with a crisis/a grim future,** être confronté à une crise/un avenir lugubre; **he dared not f. me,** il n'a pas osé me rencontrer face à face; *Fig* **to f. the music,** faire front;

(b) (*look towards*) faire face à, se tenir devant (*qn, qch*); se présenter de face devant (*qn*); **to f. the front,** regarder devant soi; **sunflowers always f. the sun,** le tournesol est toujours tourné vers le soleil; **hotel facing the square,** hôtel en façade sur la place; **the picture facing page 10,** la gravure en regard de la page 10; **facing each other,** l'un en face de l'autre; *Rail* **seat facing the engine,** place dans le sens de la marche;

(c) *Cards* retourner (*une carte*);

(d) *Metal etc* dresser, planer, surfacer; *Constr* revêtir (*un mur etc*) (**with,** de).

2 *vi* **the house faces north,** la maison est exposée au nord *ou* regarde le nord; **terrace facing south,** terrasse orientée au sud; **to f. both ways,** faire face des deux côtés; *Fig* ménager la chèvre et le chou; *Mil* **right f./left f.!,** face à droite/à gauche!

►**face about** *vi Mil* faire demi-tour.

►**face down** *vtsep esp Am* (*confront*) faire face à (*un ennemi, un critique*).

►**face on to** *vipo* donner sur (*un jardin, une rue*).

►**face out** *vtsep* **(a)** (*deal with, confront*) faire face à; surmonter par soi-même (*une situation difficile*); **to f. it out,** ne pas broncher; **(b)** (*oppose, resist*) résister à (*qn*); **to f. out opposition,** résister à l'opposition; **her fellow directors faced her out on her plans for the company,** ses collègues directeurs lui ont résisté quant à ses projets pour la société.

►**face up to** *vipo* **(a)** (*confront*) affronter (*qn, un danger*); **to f. up to one's fears,** faire face à ses craintes; **(b)** (*accept*) regarder en face, faire face à (*qch*); **to f. up to one's responsibilities,** faire face à ses responsabilités.

►**face with** *vtaspo* (*confront with*) confronter (*qn*) à (*qch*); **why don't you f. them with it?,** (*what they said or did*) pourquoi est-ce que tu ne le leur dit pas en face?; **he confessed when faced with the evidence/the dead man's wife,** il a avoué lorsqu'il a été confronté aux preuves/à la femme du défunt.

faceless [ˈfeɪslɪs] *adj Fig* anonyme; non identifiable; **f. men in government offices,** fonctionnaires anonymes.

face-lift [ˈfeɪslɪft] *n* **(a)** lifting *m*; **to have a f.-l.,** se faire faire un lifting; **(b)** restauration *f* (*de la façade d'un bâtiment*); rénovation *f*, retapage *m*; **Glasgow's had a f.-l.,** Glasgow a été remis à neuf.

facer [ˈfeɪsər] *n Br F* **that's a f.!,** quelle tuile!

face-saving [ˈfeɪsseɪvɪŋ] *adj* (*agreement, compromise etc*) qui sauve la face.

facet¹ [ˈfæsɪt] *n* **(a)** facette *f* (*d'un diamant, Ent de l'œil etc*); **(b)** *Fig* aspect *m* (*d'une situation etc*).

facet² *vt* (**-tt-**, *US* **-t-**) facetter (*une pierre précieuse*).

facetious [fəˈsiːʃəs] *adj* facétieux, plaisant, gouailleur;

(*style*) bouffon; **I was being f.,** je plaisantais.

facetiously [fə'siːʃəslɪ] *adv* facétieusement.

facetiousness [fə'siːʃəsnɪs] *n* caractère facétieux, bouffonnerie *f*; humeur facétieuse.

face-to-face ['feɪstə'feɪs] *adj* (*meeting etc*) face-à-face.

facetted ['fæsɪtɪd] *adj* à facettes.

facial ['feɪʃ(ə)l] **1** *adj* facial, -aux; (*expression*) du visage. **2** *n* soins *mpl* du visage; **to have a f.,** se faire faire des soins du visage.

facile ['fæsaɪl, -ɪl] *adj Pej* facile; **to be a f. liar,** être habile à controuver des mensonges.

facilitate [fə'sɪlɪteɪt] *vt* faciliter (*une action*).

facility [fə'sɪlɪtɪ] *n* **(a)** (*ease*) facilité *f*; **f. in speaking/writing,** facilité à parler/écrire; **to do sth with great f.,** faire qch avec une grande facilité; **facilities for payment,** facilités de paiement; **they are given every f. for improving their French,** on leur accorde toutes facilités de se perfectionner en français; **(b)** (*means*) (*usu pl*) **facilities,** aménagements *mpl*; **the building has limited facilities for the handicapped,** le bâtiment est doté d'aménagements limités pour les handicapés; **storage/cooking facilities,** installations *fpl* de stockage/cuisine; **we have no facilities for it,** nous ne sommes pas équipés pour cela; *Av* **ground facilities,** installations au sol; *Euph* **can I use the facilities?,** est-ce que je peux utiliser les toilettes?; **(c)** *esp Am* établissement *m*; (*hotel*) hôtel *m*; **training/research f.,** établissement de formation/recherche.

facing ['feɪsɪŋ] **1** *n* **(a)** revers *m* (*d'un habit etc*); (*on outside*) parement *m*; (*on inside*) parementure *f*; *Constr* revêtement *m* (*d'un mur etc*); perré *m* (*d'un talus, d'une tranchée*); *Constr MecE* surface *f* de portée; *Aut* garniture *f* (*de frein, d'embrayage*); *Mil* **regimental facings,** parements (de la manche ou du col) servant à distinguer les différents corps; *Constr* **f. brick,** brique *f* de parement; **(b)** *Carp Metal etc* dressage *m* (*d'une surface*); **f. tool,** outil *m* à surfacer; **(c)** *Mil etc* mouvement *m* de front; **f. about,** volte-face *f*. **2** *adj* (*page*) ci-contre.

facsimile [fæk'sɪmɪlɪ] *n* **(a)** (*copy*) fac-similé *m*, *pl* fac-similés; *Jur* copie figurée (*d'un testament etc*); **to reproduce sth in f., to make a f. of sth,** faire un fac-similé de qch; **f. signature,** signature autographiée; **(b)** *Telecom* télécopie *f*; **f. machine,** télécopieur *m*.

fact [fækt] *n* fait *m*; **an accomplished f.,** un fait accompli; **f. and fiction,** le réel et l'imaginaire; **scientific facts,** les vérités *fpl* scientifiques; **to stick to the facts,** s'en tenir aux faits; **just give me the facts,** donnez-moi simplement les faits; **the facts of a case,** les faits d'une cause; **the f. that you're a woman,** le fait que vous soyez une femme; **the f. (of the matter) is ...,** le fait est que ...; **owing to the f. that ...,** du fait que ...; **it's a f. that ...,** il est de fait que ...; **to know for a f. that ...,** savoir pertinemment que ...; **apart from the f. that ...,** hormis que ...; **in f.,** de fait; **in point of f.,** en fait; **as a matter of f.,** (*really*) en réalité; (*actually*) en effet; *Jur* **the jury only decides issues of f.,** les jurés ne sont juges que du fait; **the facts of life,** les choses de la vie; **it's a f. of life,** c'est une réalité.

fact-finding ['fæktfaɪndɪŋ] *adj* (*mission etc*) d'information, d'enquête.

faction¹ ['fækʃən] *n* faction *f*, cabale *f*.

faction² *n Cin TV* docudrame *m*.

factious [fækʃəs] *adj* factieux.

factitious [fæk'tɪʃəs] *adj* factice, artificiel.

factor ['fæktər] *n* **(a)** facteur *m* (*concourant à un résultat*); *Math* diviseur *m*, facteur; *Tech* (*of drag, amplification etc*) coefficient *m*; **the highest common f.,** le plus grand commun diviseur; **f. of production,** intrant *m*, input *m*; **demand f.,** facteur de consommation *f*; **f. of safety, safety f.,** marge *f* de sécurité; **load f.,** coefficient de charge; **an important f. in the life of a nation,** un facteur important dans la vie d'une nation; **the human f.,** l'élément humain; **(b)** *Com* agent *m* (*dépositaire*); commissionnaire *m* en gros; *Scot* intendant *m* (*d'un domaine*).

factoring ['fæktərɪŋ] *n Com* affacturage *m*.

factory ['fækt(ə)rɪ] *n Br Ind* usine *f*; **munitions f.,** fabrique *f* de munitions; **biscuit f.,** biscuiterie *f*; *Fishing etc* **f. ship,** navire-usine *m*, *pl* navires-usines; **f. farm,** exploitation *f* d'élevage industriel; **f. farming,** élevage industriel; **f. workers,** ouvriers *mpl* en usine; **f. manager,** directeur *m* d'usine.

factotum [fæk'təʊtəm] *n* factotum *m*, homme *m ou* femme *f* à tout faire.

factual ['fæktʃʊəl] *adj* (*account*) factuel, reposant sur les faits; (*connaissance*) des faits; (*considération*) pratique.

factually ['fæktʃʊəlɪ] *adv* en ce qui concerne les faits; (*to report etc*) objectivement.

facultative ['fækəltətɪv] *adj* facultatif, -ive.

faculty ['fækəltɪ] *n* **(a)** (*of mind, body*) faculté *f*, pouvoir *m*; **the f. of speech,** le don de la parole; **to be in possession of all one's faculties,** jouir de toutes ses facultés; **(b)** (*ability*) facilité *f*, talent *m*; **to have a f. for doing sth,** avoir des facilités pour faire qch; **to have the f. of observation,** être observateur; **(c)** *Univ* faculté *f* (*des lettres, de droit etc*); *Am* professorat *m*, corps enseignant (*d'une université, d'un collège*); **the medical f.,** les physiciens et les chirurgiens.

fad [fæd] *n* manie *f*, lubie *f*, dada *m*; **it's only a passing f.,** c'est un caprice dont on reviendra; **the f. for macrobiotic food,** la lubie pour les aliments macrobiotiques: **to have fads about sth,** avoir des lubies à propos de qch.

faddiness ['fædɪnɪs] *n* maniaquerie *f*.

faddist ['fædɪst] *n F* **food f.,** maniaque *mf* en fait de nourriture.

faddy ['fædɪ] *adj* capricieux, maniaque; **he's f. about his food, he's a f. eater,** il est difficile sur la nourriture.

fade [feɪd] **1** *vi* (*of flowers, colour etc*) se faner, se flétrir; (*of material*) se décolorer, déteindre; (*of hope*) s'éteindre; (*of light, sound*) s'affaiblir; **the light is fading,** le jour baisse; **colours that f. into each other,** couleurs qui se fondent; **summer fades into autumn,** peu à peu l'automne succède à l'été; **to f. from memory,** s'effacer de la mémoire. **2** *vt* faner, décolorer; **curtains faded by the sun,** rideaux décolorés par le soleil; *Cin* **to f. one scene into another,** enchaîner deux scènes.

▶**fade away** *vi* (*of light, sound*) s'affaiblir; *Fig* (*of person*) dépérir.

▶**fade in 1** *vi* (*of scene*) arriver dans un fondu; (*of music*) arriver dans un fondu sonore. **2** *vtsep* faire arriver (*une scène*) dans un fondu; faire arriver (*la musique*) dans un fondu sonore.

▶**fade out 1** *vi* (*of scene*) s'effacer dans un fondu; (*of music*) disparaître dans un fondu sonore. **2** *vtsep* faire partir (*une scène*) dans un fondu; faire disparaître (*la musique etc*) dans un fondu sonore.

faded ['feɪdɪd] *adj* (*flower, colour etc*) fané, flétri; (*material*) décoloré; (*beauty etc*) défraîchi, passé; (*photograph*) jauni.

fade-in ['feɪdɪn] *n* (*of scene, music*) ouverture *f* en fondu.

fade-out ['feɪdaʊt] *n* (*of scene, music*) fermeture *f* en fondu.

fading ['feɪdɪŋ] **1** *adj* (*fleur*) qui se fane; (*lumière*) pâlissant. **2** *n* **(a)** flétrissure *f* (*d'une plante*); décoloration *f* (*d'une étoffe*); **(b)** *Rad* fading *m*; **(c)** *Cin* fondu *m*.

faecal, *US* **fecal** ['fiːk(ə)l] *adj* fécal, -aux; **f. matter,** matières fécales, déjections *fpl*.

faeces, *US* **feces** ['fiːsiːz] *npl Physiol* fèces *fpl*, matières fécales.

▶**faff about, faff around** [fæf] *vi Br F* perdre son temps à des bricoles.

fag¹ [fæg] *n* **(a)** *Br F* (*unpleasant job*) corvée *f*; **(b)** *Am Pej Sl* (*homosexual*) pédé *m*, pédale *f*; **(c)** *Br F* (*cigarette*) sèche *f*, clope *m*; **f. end,** bout *m* (*d'un morceau d'étoffe, de l'hiver etc*); *Br F* mégot *m* (*d'une cigarette*), clope; **(d)** *Eng Sch* jeune élève attaché au service d'un grand.

fag² *vi* (**-gg-**) **(a)** *Eng Sch* (*of pupil*) **to f. for a senior,** faire les corvées d'un grand; **(b)** *Old-fashioned F* travailler dur, s'échiner.

▶**fag out** *vtsep F* (*of work etc*) éreinter (*qn*); **fagged out,** épuisé, éreinté.

faggot¹ ['fægət] *n* **(a)** *Am Pej Sl* (*homosexual*) pédé *m*, pédale *f*; **(b)** *Br Culin* boulette *f* (de viande); **(c)** fagot *m*; bourrée *f* (*de bois*); *Metal* faisceau *m* (*de fer en barres*).

faggot² *vt* (**-t-**) mettre en fagots (*du bois*); *Metal* mettre en faisceaux (*le fer, l'acier*).

fah [fɑː] *n Mus* = **FA**.

Fahrenheit ['færənhaɪt] *adj Phys* (*échelle, thermomètre*) Fahrenheit; **ten degrees F.,** dix degrés Fahrenheit.

faience [faɪ'jɑːns] *n* faïence *f*, poterie vernissée *ou* émaillée.

fail¹ [feɪl] *n* **(a)** (*in exam*) échec *m*; **(b) without f.,** à coup sûr.

fail² 1 *vi* **(a)** (*not succeed*) ne pas réussir; manquer son coup; (*in exam*) échouer; (*of negotiations etc*) ne pas aboutir; (*of play*) faire fiasco; *Com* faire faillite; **enterprise which failed,** entreprise qui a échoué; **I f. to see why ...,** je ne vois pas pourquoi ...; *Sch* **to f. in an examination,** être refusé *ou* recalé à un examen;

(b) (*be inadequate*) manquer, faillir, faire défaut; (*of light*) s'éteindre; (*of health, patient*) décliner; (*of health, light, memory*) baisser; **when all else failed,** en désespoir de cause; **to f. in one's duty,** manquer à son devoir; **to f.**

to do sth, négliger de faire qch; **she was charged with failing to report an accident,** elle a été inculpée pour avoir manqué de signaler un accident; **he failed to mention that ...,** il a omis de faire remarquer que ...; **the cheque failed to arrive,** le chèque n'est pas arrivé; **the engine failed to start,** le moteur a refusé de démarrer; **the brakes failed,** les freins ont lâché; **it never fails,** (*it always happens*) ça ne manque jamais; (*of remedy*) ça ne rate jamais; **she never fails to visit me on Sundays,** elle ne manque jamais de me rendre visite le dimanche; **his sight is beginning to f.,** sa vue commence à faiblir; **his heart failed,** son cœur a lâché.

2 *vt Sch* refuser, recaler (*un candidat*); être refusé à (*un examen*); **to f. a drugs test,** être positif au contrôle antidopage; **words f. me,** les mots me manquent; **words f. me to express my thanks,** je ne sais comment vous exprimer mes remerciements; **his courage failed him,** le courage lui a fait défaut; **I won't f. you,** vous pouvez compter sur moi.

failed [feɪld] *adj* (*candidat*) refusé, recalé; *Com* (*maison*) en faillite; (*artiste*) raté.

failing ['feɪlɪŋ] **1** *adj* (*sight etc*) défaillant, baissant; **to be in f. health,** avoir une santé défaillante. **2** *n* (*fault*) faiblesse *f*, défaut *m*; **with all her failings,** avec tous ses défauts. **3** *prep* à *ou* au défaut de; **f. a satisfactory reply,** faute de réponse satisfaisante; **f. which,** faute de quoi; **f. all else,** en désespoir de cause; **call me at home or f. that at the office,** appelle-moi à la maison ou, à défaut, au bureau.

fail-safe ['feɪlseɪf] *adj* **f.-s. device** *or* **system,** dispositif *m* de sécurité positive.

failure ['feɪljər] *n* **(a)** (*lack of success*) insuccès *m*, non-réussite *f*; échec *m* (*à un examen, d'une pièce*); (*person*) raté, -ée; *Com* faillite *f*; *Th etc* four *m*, fiasco *m*; **I'm a complete f. as a lexicographer,** en tant que lexicographe, je suis complètement raté; *Sch* **there are too many failures,** trop de candidats ont été recalés; **the experiment was** *or* **proved** *or* **turned out a f.,** l'expérience n'a pas réussi *ou* a raté; **the expedition ended in f.,** l'expédition s'est soldée par un échec; **(b)** (*inadequacy*) manque *m*; **f. to keep a promise,** manquement *m* à une promesse; **f. to pay a bill,** défaut *m* de paiement d'un effet; **(c)** (*of machine*) panne *f*; **mechanical f.,** défaillance *f* mécanique; *El* **power f.,** panne *f* de courant; *Med* **heart f.,** syncope *f* (mortelle).

fain [feɪn] *adv Arch & Lit* volontiers.

faint¹ [feɪnt] *adj* **(a)** (*weak*) (*hope etc*) faible; (*praise*) tiède; (*colour*) pâle, délavé; (*sound, touch etc*) léger; (*idea*) vague, peu précis; (*mark etc*) à peine visible; (*inscription*) indistinct; **to give a f. smile,** sourire du bout des lèvres; **a f. tinge of blue,** une légère nuance bleuâtre; **I haven't the faintest (idea),** je n'en ai pas la moindre idée; **the sound of the footsteps grew fainter,** le bruit des pas s'affaiblit; **(b)** *Med* **to feel f.,** se sentir mal; **(c)** *Arch & Lit* (*timid*) timide; *Prov* **f. heart never won fair lady,** jamais honteux n'eut belle amie.

faint² *n* évanouissement *m*, défaillance *f*; **to fall down in a f.,** tomber évanoui.

faint³ *vi* **to f. (away),** s'évanouir, défaillir.

faint-hearted ['feɪnt'hɑːtɪd] *adj* pusillanime.

fainting ['feɪntɪŋ] *n* évanouissement *m*; **f. fit,** syncope *f*.

faintly ['feɪntlɪ] *adv* (*weakly*) faiblement, mollement; légèrement; **f. visible,** à peine visible; **to smile f.,** esquisser un sourire.

faintness ['feɪntnɪs] *n* (*of voice etc*) faiblesse *f*; (*of breeze etc*) légèreté *f*.

fair¹ ['feər] *n* foire *f*; **world f.,** exposition universelle; **fun f.,** fête foraine; **village f.,** kermesse *f*.

fair² **1** *adj* **(a)** (*just*) juste, équitable; (*prix*) raisonnable; (*salaire*) équitable; **to get a f. trial,** être jugé de façon équitable; **f. play,** jeu loyal, franc jeu, fair-play *m inv*; **fair's f.,** il faut être juste; **that's only f.,** ce n'est que juste; **it's not f.,** ce n'est pas juste; **it isn't f. to expect children to ...,** ce n'est pas raisonnable de demander à des enfants de ...; **f. enough!,** ça va!, d'accord!; **it's all f. and above board** *or* **all f. and square,** c'est de bonne guerre; **he is strict but f.,** il est sévère mais sans parti pris; **it is only f. to say that ...,** il faut dire que ...; **but, to be f.,** (*honest, reasonable*) mais, pour être honnête; **by f. means or foul,** d'une manière ou d'une autre; *Prov* **all's f. in love and war,** en amour la ruse est de bonne guerre;

(b) (*quite good*) assez bon; **in f. condition,** acceptable; **a f. number of ...,** un nombre respectable de ...; **he has a f. chance of success,** il a des chances de réussir; **f. to middling,** comme ci comme ça; **in a f. way to recovering,** en bonne voie pour se rétablir;

(c) (*wind etc*) propice, favorable; **f. weather,** beau temps; **the barometer is at set f.,** le baromètre est au beau fixe;

(d) *esp Lit & Arch* (*attractive*) beau, belle; **the f. sex,** le beau sexe;

(e) (*specious*) spécieux; **f. promises,** de belles promesses;

(f) (*light-coloured*) (*person, hair*) blond; (*skin*) blanc, blanche;

(g) (*clean, unmarked*) net, sans tache; **f. copy,** copie *f* au propre;

(h) (*intensive*) *Sl* **it's a f. old do,** c'est une pure escroquerie.

2 *adv* **(a)** (*agir*) loyalement; **to play f.,** jouer franc jeu; **to fight f.,** se battre loyalement; **you can't say fairer than that,** il n'y a pas plus équitable;

(b) *F* (*completely*) complètement; (*almost*) pratiquement; **struck f. (and square) on the chin,** frappé en plein menton.

fairground ['feəgraʊnd] *n* champ *m* de foire.

fair-haired ['feə'heəd] *adj* blond, aux cheveux blonds; *US Fig* **f.-h. boy,** chouchou *m*.

fairing ['feərɪŋ] *n Av Aut* carénage *m*.

fairish ['feərɪʃ] *adj* **(a)** (*hair*) plutôt blond; **(b)** (*quite good*) assez bon.

fairly ['feəlɪ] *adv* **(a)** (*juger etc*) équitablement, avec justice; **to treat s.o. f.,** traiter qn avec impartialité; **(b)** (*agir, jouer etc*) honnêtement; **to come by sth f.,** obtenir qch par des moyens honnêtes; **(c)** (*quite*) assez (*riche, habile etc*); **f. good wine,** vin passablement bon; **it is f. certain that ...,** il est à peu près certain que ...; **to do sth f. well,** faire qch d'une façon passable; **(d)** (*well*) bien; **once the ship was f. under way,** une fois le navire en bonne route; **(e)** *F* (*completely*) complètement, absolument.

fair-minded ['feə'maɪndɪd] *adj* équitable, juste.

fairness ['feənɪs] *n* **(a)** (*of decision*) impartialité *f*; (*of person*) intégrité *f*, équité *f*, honnêteté *f*; équité (*d'une loi, d'un partage*); **in all f.,** en toute justice; **(b)** *Arch & Lit* (*beauty*) beauté *f*; **(c)** couleur blonde (*des cheveux*); blancheur *f* (*de la peau*).

fair-sized ['feə'saɪzd] *adj* assez grand.

fairway ['feəweɪ] *n* **(a)** *Golf* fairway *m*; **(b)** *Nau* chenal *m*, passe *f*, passage *m*.

fair-weather ['feə'weðər] *adj* (*bateau*) qui convient seulement pour le beau temps; **f.-w. friends,** amis des beaux jours.

fairy ['feərɪ] **1** *n* **(a)** fée *f*; **the wicked f.,** la fée Carabosse; **(b)** *Pej* (*homosexual man*) pédé *m*, tapette *f*, tante *f*. **2** *adj* féerique; **f. footsteps,** pas légers; **f. queen,** reine *f* des fées; **f. godmother,** marraine *f* fée; *Fig* marraine gâteau; **f. light,** lampion *m*; **f. lights,** guirlande lumineuse (pour sapin de Noël); **f. story** *or* **tale,** conte *m* de fées; *Fig* (*lie*) histoires *fpl* à dormir debout.

fairyland ['feərɪlænd] *n* le pays *ou* le royaume des fées; (*imaginary world*) féerie *f*; **at night the garden became a f.,** le soir, le jardin se transforma en pays enchanté.

faith [feɪθ] *n* **(a)** foi *f*; **to have (every) f. in s.o./sth,** avoir (entièrement) confiance en qn/qch; **I don't have much f. in doctors,** je ne fais pas beaucoup confiance aux médecins; **to have f. in God,** avoir foi en Dieu; **to put one's f. in s.o.,** accorder toute sa confiance à qn; **f. healer,** guérisseur *m* par la prière; **f. healing,** guérison *f* par la prière; **(b)** (*religion*) religion *f*, foi *f*, croyance *f*; **what f. are you?,** de quelle religion êtes-vous?; **to be of the Catholic/Jewish f.,** être de religion catholique/juive; **the Christian f.,** la foi chrétienne; **(c)** (*loyalty*) **to keep f. with s.o.,** tenir ses engagements envers qn; **to break f. with s.o.,** manquer de foi *ou* de parole à qn; **good faith,** bonne foi; **to say sth in good f.,** dire qch en toute bonne foi; **to do sth in all good f.,** faire qch en tout honneur; **bad f.,** perfidie *f*.

faithful ['feɪθful] **1** *adj* fidèle; (*friend etc*) loyal, -aux; (*copy*) exact, juste; (*traduction*) fidèle; **to remain f. to s.o.,** rester fidèle à qn; **f. promise,** promesse formelle; **f. in every detail,** exact jusqu'au moindre détail. **2** *n Rel* **the f.,** (*used as pl*) les fidèles *mpl*; (*Islam*) les croyants *mpl*; *Pol* **the party f.,** les fidèles du parti.

faithfully ['feɪθfulɪ] *adv* **(a)** (*loyally*) fidèlement, loyalement; **yours f.,** *Old-fashioned* **we remain yours f.,** (*in letter*) recevez l'expression de nos sentiments distingués; **he promised f. to come tomorrow,** il a promis formellement de venir demain; **(b)** (*traduire, copier etc*) exactement.

faithfulness ['feɪθfulnɪs] *n* **(a)** (*loyalty*) fidélité *f*, loyauté *f* (**to,** envers); **(b)** (*accuracy*) fidélité *f*, exactitude *f* (*d'un récit etc*).

faithless ['feɪθlɪs] *adj* **(a)** (*lacking faith*) infidèle, sans foi; **(b)** (*disloyal*) infidèle (**to,** à); **(c)** (*treacherous*) déloyal, -aux; perfide.

faithlessness ['feɪθlɪsnɪs] *n* **(a)** (*lack of faith*) manque *m* de confiance; **(b)** (*disloyalty*) infidélité *f* (**to,** à); **(c)** (*treacherousness*) déloyauté *f*.

fake¹ [feɪk] **1** *n* article faux *ou* truqué; **it's a f.,** c'est un faux; **he's a f.,** c'est un bluffeur. **2** *adj* faux.

fake² *vt* truquer (*des calculs etc*); **faked balance sheet,** bilan truqué; **to f. a story,** inventer une histoire; **she faked her own death,** elle a fait croire à sa propre mort; **it's all faked,** (*in cinema etc*) c'est du trucage.

faker ['feɪkər] *n* comédien, -ienne.

faking ['feɪkɪŋ] *n* **it's just f.,** c'est de la comédie.

fakir ['feɪkɪər, fə'kɪər] *n* fakir *m*.

falcon ['fɔːlkən] *n* (*bird*) faucon *m*; **peregrine f.,** faucon pèlerin.

falconer ['fɔːlkənər] *n* fauconnier *m*.

falconry ['fɔːlkənrɪ] *n* fauconnerie *f*.

Falkland ['fɔːklənd] *n* **the F. Islands, the Falklands,** les (îles *fpl*) Malouines *fpl*, les îles Falkland.

fall¹ [fɔːl] *n* **(a)** chute *f* (*d'un corps etc*); (*in wrestling*) tomber *m*; *Th* baisser *m* (*du rideau*); précipitations *fpl* (*de neige, de pluie*); **free f.,** chute libre; **to have a f.,** faire une chute; **a bad f.,** une mauvaise chute; **there has been a heavy f. of snow,** il est tombé beaucoup de neige; *esp Am F* **f. guy,** (*dupe*) pigeon *m*; (*scapegoat*) bouc *m* émissaire, souffre-douleur *m inv*;
(b) *Am* **the f.,** l'automne *m*;
(c) (*waterfall*) (*usu pl*) **falls,** chute *f* (d'eau); *HydE* hauteur *f* de chute (*d'un barrage*); **the Victoria Falls,** les Chutes Victoria; **the Niagara Falls,** les Chutes du Niagara;
(d) décrue *f*, baisse *f* (*des eaux*); reflux *m*, jusant *m* (*de la marée*); cadence *f* (*de la voix*);
(e) (*decrease*) diminution *f* (*de poids etc*); chute *f* (*du baromètre etc*); baisse *f* (*de la température*); *Com Fin* baisse (*des prix, des actions*); dépréciation *f* (*de la monnaie*); **heavy f.,** forte baisse; **f. in prices,** chute de prix;
(f) (*slope*) pente *f* (*d'une route etc*);
(g) (*ruin*) perte *f*, ruine *f* (*de qn*);
(h) (*capture*) chute *f* (*d'une ville*); déchéance *f* (*d'un empire etc*); renversement *m* (*d'un gouvernement etc*);
(i) (*subsidence*) éboulement *m*;
(j) *Rel* **the F.,** la chute.

fall² *vi* (*pt* **fell** [fel]; *pp* **fallen** ['fɔːlən]) **(a)** (*from a height*) tomber; *Astron* (*of star*) filer; **to f. to the ground,** tomber à terre; **she fell to her death,** elle a fait une chute mortelle; **to f. off a ladder,** tomber d'une échelle; **to f. 20 feet,** tomber de 20 pieds; **to f. out of the window,** tomber par la fenêtre; **to f. on one's feet,** retomber sur ses pieds; *Fig* avoir de la chance; **to f. into a trap,** donner dans un piège; **to f. into s.o.'s hands,** tomber entre les mains de qn; **night is falling,** la nuit tombe; **his hair fell to his shoulders,** (*hung down*) ses cheveux lui descendaient jusqu'aux épaules;
(b) (*from standing or perpendicular position*) **to f. to the ground,** tomber par terre; **to f. on one's knees,** tomber à genoux; **to f. (in battle),** tomber au champ d'honneur;
(c) (*collapse*) (*of building*) s'écrouler, s'effondrer; **to f. to pieces,** tomber en morceaux; **when Liège fell,** lorsque Liège capitula; **the government has fallen,** le gouvernement a été renversé;
(d) (*diminish*) (*of price etc*) diminuer; (*of price, exchange etc*) baisser, se déprécier; (*of wind*) tomber; *Fig* **his stock is falling,** son crédit est en baisse; **the thermometer has fallen ten degrees,** le thermomètre a baissé de dix degrés;
(e) (*become lower*) (*of ground*) aller en pente, s'incliner; (*of tide etc*) baisser; *Math* (*of curve*) décroître; **her eyes fell,** elle a baissé les yeux; **his face fell,** sa figure s'allongea; **my spirits fell,** j'ai perdu tout courage; **to f. from one's position,** déchoir de sa position; **to f. in s.o.'s estimation,** perdre dans l'estime de qn;
(f) (*alight*) **a shadow fell on the wall,** une ombre se projeta sur le mur;
(g) (*occur*) tomber; **Christmas falls on a Thursday,** Noël tombe un jeudi; **the accent falls on the last syllable,** l'accent tombe sur la dernière syllabe; **to f. to s.o.'s share,** (*be assigned to etc*) échoir (en partage) à qn; **these facts f. under another category,** ces faits entrent dans une autre catégorie;
(h) (*enter into given state*) **to f. under suspicion,** (*of person*) devenir l'objet des soupçons, devenir suspect; **to f. on evil days,** connaître de mauvais jours; **I soon fell into their ways,** (*became used to their way of doing things*) je me suis vite accoutumé à leur manière de faire; (*learnt routine*) j'ai bientôt appris la routine; **to f. into a habit,** contracter une habitude; **to f. into error,** être induit en erreur;
(i) (*become*) **to f. ill** *or* **sick,** tomber malade; **to f. asleep,** s'endormir; **to f. vacant,** (*of post*) se trouver vacant; **to f. a victim to ...,** être victime de ...;
(j) (*begin*) **they fell to work (again),** ils se (re)mirent au travail;
(k) *Rel* tomber, pêcher;
(l) *Nau* **to f. to leeward,** (*of ship*) tomber sous le vent.

►**fall about** *vi* (*fall in different directions*) tomber de côté et d'autre; **to f. about (laughing),** se tordre de rire.

►**fall apart** *vi* (*fall to pieces*) se désintégrer, tomber en morceaux; *Fig* **opposition to the law was falling apart,** l'opposition à cette loi perdait peu à peu de sa virulence.

►**fall away** *vi* **(a)** (*of ground*) s'affaisser; **(b)** (*of attendance*) diminuer; (*of followers etc*) déserter; **(c)** (*of prejudice etc*) disparaître.

►**fall back** *vi* **(a)** (*fall*) tomber à la renverse *ou* en arrière; **to f. back on the cushions,** retomber sur les coussins; **(b)** (*of troops*) se replier, reculer; **to f. back a pace,** reculer d'un pas; **(c)** *St Exch Fin* se replier.

►**fall back on** *vipo* (*resort to*) avoir recours à; **she fell back on the usual clichés,** elle a eu recours aux clichés habituels; **to have some money to f. back on,** avoir de l'argent en réserve comme en-cas; **you can always f. back on me,** en dernière ressource vous pouvez compter sur moi.

►**fall behind** *vi* (*of runner, political party etc*) être à la traîne, se faire distancer, rester en arrière; **to f. behind with the rent/payments/***etc*, être en retard pour payer son loyer/des traites/*etc*.

►**fall down** *vi* **(a)** (*fall to ground*) tomber à terre *ou* par terre; **(b)** (*of building etc*) s'écrouler, s'effondrer; **(c)** (*fail*) échouer; **that's where their argument falls down,** c'est sur ce point que leurs arguments ne tiennent plus debout; **I fell down badly on the first question,** j'ai complètement raté la première question; **to f. down on the job,** louper le travail.

►**fall for** *vipo F* **(a)** (*fall in love with*) tomber amoureux de (*qn*); **I've fallen for that antique chair,** j'ai eu le coup de foudre pour cette vieille chaise; **(b)** (*be deceived by*) se laisser prendre *ou* piéger; **you didn't f. for that old story, did you?,** tu ne t'es pas laissé prendre à cette vieille histoire?; **to f. for a trick,** s'y laisser prendre.

►**fall in** *vi* **(a)** (*of building, roof etc*) s'écrouler, s'effondrer; (*of trench etc*) s'ébouler; (*of cheeks*) se creuser; **(b)** *Mil* former les rangs; **f. in!,** rassemblement!

►**fall in with** *vipo* **(a)** (*meet up with*) rencontrer (*qn*) par hasard; (*associate with*) fréquenter (*qn*); **my son fell in with a bad crowd,** mon fils s'est mis à avoir de mauvaises fréquentations; **(b)** accepter (*une proposition*); accéder à (*une requête*); **I fell in with the plans for a picnic,** j'ai accepté le projet d'un pique-nique.

►**fall off** *vi* **(a)** (*fall from something*) tomber; **I picked the violin up and the neck fell off,** j'ai pris le violon et le manche est tombé; **(b)** (*of followers etc*) faire défection; (*of profits*) diminuer; (*of speed*) ralentir; (*of zeal*) se relâcher; **his popularity is falling off,** sa popularité baisse; **(c)** (*deteriorate*) décliner; (*of skill*) baisser; **(d)** *Nau* abattre sous le vent.

►**fall on** *vipo* **(a)** (*of blame, responsibility, suspicion*) retomber sur (*qn*); **(b)** (*attack*) attaquer (*l'ennemi*).

►**fall out** *vi* **(a)** (*fall from*) tomber dehors; (*of hair*) tomber; **(b)** *Mil* rompre les rangs; **f. out!,** rompez!; **(c)** (*quarrel*) se brouiller, se fâcher (**with,** avec); **they have fallen out,** ils sont fâchés.

►**fall over 1** *vi* (*of person*) tomber (par terre); (*of thing*) se renverser, être renversé. **2** *vipo* (*stumble on*) trébucher sur (*un obstacle*); **move that suitcase before someone falls over it,** déplace cette valise avant que quelqu'un ne se prenne les pieds dedans; *F* **publishers were falling over each other for her new book,** les éditeurs se disputaient avec acharnement son nouveau livre; **he was falling over himself in his anxiety to please her,** il se mettait en quatre pour lui plaire.

►**fall through** *vi* (*of scheme etc*) ne pas aboutir, échouer, *F* tomber à l'eau.

►**fall to** *vi Old-fashioned F* (*begin eating*) s'attaquer au repas.

►**fall upon** *vipo* = **FALL ON.**

fallacious [fə'leɪʃəs] *adj* trompeur, -euse; (*espoir, paix*) illusoire.

fallacy ['fæləsɪ] *n* erreur *f*; (*in logic*) sophisme *m*; **it is a f. that ...,** ce serait une erreur de croire que ...; **the f. of this argument is that ...,** ce qui est faux dans ce raisonnement, c'est que ... .

fallen ['fɔːlən] **1** *adj* (*leaf*) tombé; *Old-fashioned* **f. woman,** femme déchue; fille perdue. **2** *n* **the f.,** (*used as pl*) les morts *mpl* (*sur le champ de bataille*).

fallibility [fælɪ'bɪlɪtɪ] *n* faillibilité *f*.

fallible ['fælɪb(ə)l] *adj* faillible.

falling ['fɔːlɪŋ] **1** *adj* (*darkness etc*) tombant; (*température*) en baisse; *Com* (*prix*) qui baisse; (*marché*) avec tendance à la baisse; *Astron* **f. star,** étoile filante. **2** *n* **(a)** chute *f*; **(b)** baisse *f* (*de prix, du baromètre etc*).

falling away *n* **(a)** (*of ground*) affaissement *m*; **(b)** (*of support*) affaiblissement *m*; (*of supporters*) défection *f*, désertion *f*.

falling in *n* acquiescement *m*, acceptation *f* (**with sth,** de qch).

falling off *n* (*of support*) affaiblissement *m*; désertion *f*, défection *f* (*de partisans*); diminution *f* (*de chiffres, de taux etc*); déclin *m* (*de pouvoir, de popularité*); relâchement *m* (*de zèle*); ralentissement *m* (*de commandes, des affaires*).

Fallopian [fə'ləʊpɪən] *adj* **F. tubes,** trompes *fpl* de Fallope.

fallout ['fɔːlaʊt] *n* retombées *fpl* (radioactives); *Fig* **the political f. from the scandal,** les retombées politiques du scandale.

fallow¹ ['fæləʊ] *Agr* **1** *n* jachère *f* (*volontaire*); friche *f* (*à l'abandon*). **2** *adj* (*land*) en friche; en jachère; **to lie f.,** être en jachère *ou* en friche.

fallow² *adj* **f. deer,** daim *m*.

false [fɔːls] **1** *adj* **(a)** (*incorrect*) faux, *f* fausse; (*idea*) erroné; **to give s.o. a f. impression of sth,** donner à qn une fausse impression sur qch; **f. report,** fausse nouvelle, *F* canard *m*; **f. modesty,** fausse modestie; (*about sexual matters*) fausse pudeur; **f. alarm,** fausse alerte; *Ling* **f. friend,** faux ami; **one f. move and he would have killed me,** si j'avais fait un faux mouvement, il m'aurait tué; **f. start,** faux départ; *Sp* **to get off to a f. start,** faire un faux départ; *Mus* **f. note,** fausse note;

(b) (*dishonest*) hypocrite; (*unfaithful*) infidèle; (*promise etc*) mensonger; **he turns on the charm for them — it's all so f.,** il veut leur faire du charme – quelle hypocrisie!; **to be in a f. position,** être dans une situation délicate; **under f. pretences,** par des moyens frauduleux; (*by lying*) sous des prétextes fallacieux; **f. witness,** faux témoin; **to bear f. witness,** rendre faux témoignage;

(c) (*not real*) (*hair etc*) artificiel, postiche; (*action etc*) feint, prétendu; (*document etc*) forgé; (*coin, seal etc*) faux, contrefait; **f. bottom,** double fond (*d'une boîte etc*); **f. name,** faux nom; **(a set of) f. teeth,** fausses dents, dentier *m*.

2 *adv* **to play s.o. f.,** trahir qn; **his memory played him f.,** sa mémoire l'a trahi *ou* lui a joué des tours.

false-hearted [fɔːls'hɑːtɪd] *adj* fourbe.

falsehood ['fɔːlshʊd] *n* **(a) to distinguish truth from f.,** distinguer le vrai du faux; **(b)** (*lie*) **to tell a f.,** dire un mensonge.

falsely ['fɔːlslɪ] *adv* faussement.

falseness ['fɔːlsnɪs] *n* **(a)** fausseté *f* (*d'un rapport etc*); **(b)** *Old-fashioned* infidélité *f* (*d'un amant etc*).

falsetto [fɔːl'setəʊ] *Mus* **1** *n* **(a)** (*voice*) voix *f* de fausset; **(b)** (*singer*) fausset *m*. **2** *adj* (*voice*) de fausset.

falsies ['fɔːlsɪz] *npl F* (*padding*) (bonnet *m* à) base rembourrée, coussinet *m*.

falsification [fɔːlsɪfɪ'keɪʃən] *n* falsification *f*.

falsify ['fɔːlsɪfaɪ] *vt* (**falsified; falsifying**) **(a)** falsifier (*un document*); fausser (*un bilan*); dénaturer (*des faits etc*); **(b)** (*disprove*) prouver la fausseté de (*qch*).

falsity ['fɔːlsɪtɪ] *n* fausseté *f* (*d'une doctrine etc*).

falter ['fɔːltər] **1** *vi* (*of voice*) hésiter, trembler; (*of person*) chanceler; (*of person, courage*) défaillir; **he faltered in his speech,** il eut un moment d'hésitation. **2** *vt* dire (*qch*) d'une voix hésitante.

▶**falter out** *vtsep* balbutier (*une excuse etc*).

faltering ['fɔːltərɪŋ] *adj* (*voice etc*) hésitant; (*courage, memory etc*) défaillant; (*legs*) chancelant; **to speak in a f. voice,** parler d'une voix mal assurée; **with f. steps,** d'un pas mal assuré; **a child's first f. steps,** les premiers pas hésitants d'un enfant.

fame [feɪm] *n* renom *m*, renommée *f*, réputation *f*; **to win f.,** se faire un grand nom; **to seek f. and fortune,** rechercher la gloire et la fortune; **house of ill f.,** maison mal famée.

famed [feɪmd] *adj* célèbre, bien connu (**for,** pour).

familiar [fə'mɪlɪər] **1** *adj* **(a)** (*well-known*) familier, bien connu; **a f. face,** une figure de connaissance; **she looks f.,** je l'ai déjà vue quelque part; **it strikes one as f.,** (*seen before*) cela laisse une impression de déjà vu; (*heard before*) cela laisse une impression de déjà entendu; **to be on f. ground,** être sur son terrain; **an all too f. story of drug addiction and homelessness,** (c'est) toujours ce même problème de drogue et de sans-abris; **his voice sounded f. to me,** il me sembla reconnaître sa voix; **(b)** (*acquainted*) **to be f. with sth/s.o.,** bien connaître qch/qn; **to be f. with the customs,** être au courant des usages; **(c)** (*intimate*) familier, intime; *Ling* familier; **to be on f. terms with s.o.,** avoir des rapports d'intimité avec qn; **you are rather too f.,** vous prenez trop de privautés; **f. spirit,** démon familier. **2** *n* **(a)** (*in witchcraft*) démon familier; **(b)** *Old-fashioned* (*friend*) familier *m*, intime *m*.

familiarity [fəmɪlɪ'ærɪtɪ] *n* **(a)** (*intimacy*) familiarité *f*; intimité *f*; *Prov* **f. breeds contempt,** la familiarité engendre *ou* fait naître le mépris; **(b)** (*acquaintance*) connaissance *f* (**with,** de); **her f. with French,** sa connaissance du français.

familiarization [fəmɪlɪəraɪ'zeɪʃən] *n* accoutumance *f* (**with,** à); habitude *f* (**with,** de).

familiarize [fə'mɪlɪəraɪz] *vt* **(a)** (*acquaint*) **to f. s.o. with sth,** faire connaître qch à qn; **to f. oneself with a language,** se familiariser avec une langue; **(b)** (*make known*) rendre (*qch*) familier.

familiarly [fə'mɪlɪəlɪ] *adv* familièrement; **f. known as ...,** communément connu comme ... .

family ['fæmlɪ, -ɪlɪ] *n* **(a)** famille *f*; **large f.,** famille nombreuse; **a friend of the f., a f. friend,** un ami de la famille; **they don't want (to have** *or* **start) a f. yet,** ils ne veulent pas encore avoir un enfant *ou* fonder de famille; **to be one of the f.,** être de la maison; *F* **we've got f. coming to stay,** nous allons avoir de la famille en visite; *F* **she's like f.,** c'est comme si elle était de la famille; **it runs in the f.,** cela tient de famille; **disease that runs in the f.,** maladie *f* héréditaire; **the painting has been in the f. for generations,** ce tableau est dans la famille depuis des générations; **we will keep it in the f.,** (*of heirloom, land etc*) ça restera dans la famille; (*of scandal*) ça ne sortira pas de la famille; **you can see the f. resemblance** *or* **likeness,** on ne peut pas ne pas remarquer un air de famille; *Sl* **she's in the f. way,** elle est enceinte; *Br Arch* **f. allowance,** allocation familiale; **f. butcher,** boucher *m* du coin; **a f. dinner,** un dîner en famille; **f. doctor,** médecin *m* de famille; **f. hotel,** hôtel *m* de famille; **f. income supplement,** ≈ allocations familiales; **f. life,** vie familiale; **f. likeness,** air *m* de famille; **f. man,** père *m* de famille; (*man who takes interest in his family*) = homme attaché à sa famille; **f. name,** nom *m* de famille; **f. planning,** limitation *f* des naissances, planning familial; **f. planning clinic,** clinique *f* du planning familial; **f. portraits,** portraits *mpl* d'ancêtres; **f.-size(d) jar,** en pot familial; **f. tree,** arbre *m* généalogique;

(b) *Biol* famille *f* (*de plantes, de mots etc*).

famine ['fæmɪn] *n* **(a)** (*food shortage*) famine *f*; **to die of f.,** mourir de faim; **(b)** (*shortage*) disette *f* (*d'eau etc*).

famished ['fæmɪʃd] *adj* affamé; *F* **to be** *or* **feel f.,** mourir de faim.

famishing ['fæmɪʃɪŋ] *adj Old-fashioned F* **to be f.,** mourir de faim.

famous ['feɪməs] **1** *adj* **(a)** célèbre, renommé (**for,** pour, par); **many f. names have stayed here,** beaucoup de personnages célèbres ont séjourné ici; **f. in history,** célèbre dans l'histoire; **town f. for its monuments,** ville célèbre par ses monuments; **(b)** *F Old-fashioned* (*excellent*) parfait, fameux. **2** *n* **the f.,** (*used as pl*) les célébrités *fpl*; **she associates with the rich and f.,** elle fréquente les riches et les célébrités.

famously ['feɪməslɪ] *adv F* fameusement, à merveille; **I get on f. with him,** on s'entend à merveille.

fan¹ [fæn] *n* **(a)** (*hand-held*) éventail *m*; *Geog* **alluvial f.,** cône *m* d'alluvions; *Archit* **f. vaulting,** voûte(s) *f* (*pl*) en éventail; *Av* **f. marker,** radiobalise *f* à faisceau en éventail; *Bot* **f. palm,** palmier-éventail *m*; **(b)** (*machine*) ventilateur *m* (*rotatif, à ailes, soufflant*); *Ind* soufflet *m*; *Sl* **when the shit** *or* **it hits the f.,** quand la merde me *ou* nous *etc* tombera dessus; **extractor f.,** aérateur *m*; *Aut* **radiator f.,** ventilateur; **f. belt,** courroie *f* de ventilateur; **f. heater,** radiateur soufflant; **f.(-assisted) oven,** four *m* à chaleur pulsée; **f.-cooled,** refroidi par ventilateur; **(c)** *Agr* (*winnowing machine*) tarare *m*.

fan² *vt* (**-nn-**) **(a)** (*blow air on*) éventer (*qn*); souffler sur (*le feu*); *Fig* attiser, exciter (*les passions*); *Fig* attiser, envenimer (*une querelle*); **these remarks had fanned the flames of nationalist feeling,** ces remarques avaient exacerbé le sentiment nationaliste; **terraces fanned by cool sea breezes,** terrasses rafraîchies par les brises de mer; **(b)** *Agr* (*winnow*) vanner (*le grain*).

fan³ *n F* fanatique *mf*, fana *m* (*de la télévision, du sport etc*); **a f. of s.o./sth,** un fana de qn/qch; **I'm a big f. (of hers),** je suis un de ses fans; **football f.,** fana de football; **f. club,** club *m* de fans, fan-club *m*; *F* **f. mail,** courrier *m* des admirateurs et admiratrices (*d'une vedette etc*).

►**fan out 1** *vi* (*spread out*) se déployer *ou* s'étaler en éventail. **2** *vtsep* (*spread out*) étaler (en éventail).

fanatic [fə'nætɪk] *adj & n* fanatique *mf*.

fanatical [fə'nætɪk(ə)l] *adj* fanatique.

fanatically [fə'nætɪklɪ] *adv* fanatiquement.

fanaticism [fə'nætɪsɪzəm] *n* fanatisme *m*.

fancied ['fænsɪd] *adj* imaginaire, imaginé.

fancier ['fænsɪər] *n* connaisseur, -euse (*en chiens etc*).

fanciful ['fænsɪfʊl] *adj* **(a)** (*person*) capricieux, fantasque; (*travail etc*) fantaisiste; (*portrait*) de fantaisie; **(b)** (*projet*) chimérique.

fancifully ['fænsɪfʊlɪ] *adv* d'une manière fantasque.

fancy¹ ['fænsɪ] **1** *n* **(a)** (*imagination*) imagination *f*, fantaisie *f*; (*imagined thing*) chose *f* imaginaire; **the realm of f.,** le domaine de l'imagination; **it's only f.!,** c'est pure imagination!; **idle fancies,** vaines imaginations;

(b) (*whim*) fantaisie *f*, caprice *m*; **just as the f. takes me,** comme l'idée me prend, *F* comme ça me chante; **to take a f. to sth,** prendre goût à qch; **to take a f. to s.o.,** (*become fond of*) prendre qn en affection; (*become sexually attached to*) s'éprendre *ou* s'enticher de qn; **it took** *or* **caught my f. at once,** cela m'a séduit du premier coup.

2 *adj* (*jewels, gadget, hat*) de fantaisie; (*prose*) recherché; (*footwork*) très habile; **just a bottle of ordinary wine, nothing f.,** juste une bouteille de vin ordinaire, rien de spécial; **f. biscuits,** biscuits assortis; **f. goods,** nouveautés *fpl*; **f. dress,** travesti *m*, déguisement *m*; **f. dress ball,** bal travesti; *F* **to cut out the f. stuff,** élaguer; **f. price,** prix trop élevé; *Sl Pej* **f. man,** amant *m*, jules *m*; *Sl Pej* **f. woman,** maîtresse *f*.

fancy² *vt* **(a)** (*imagine*) s'imaginer, se figurer (*qch*); *F* **f. now!, just f.!, f. (that)!,** qui l'aurait dit?, figurez-vous ça!; **f. meeting you!,** toi ici!; **f. him not knowing that!,** il ne sait pas ça! incroyable!;

(b) (*have impression*) croire, penser; **I f. I have seen her before,** j'ai l'impression de l'avoir déjà vue; **he fancied he heard footsteps,** il a cru entendre des pas;

(c) *esp Br F* (*feel desire for*) **to f. sth,** se sentir attiré vers qch; **I don't f. his offer,** son offre ne me dit rien; **I f. a bit of chicken,** je mangerais volontiers un morceau de poulet; *Horseracing* **strongly fancied horse,** cheval très coté; **to f. s.o.,** se sentir attiré vers qn; **he fancies you,** tu lui plais;

(d) (*have good opinion*) **to f. oneself,** être infatué de sa petite personne, se gober; **he fancies himself as a speaker,** il se croit orateur; **I don't f. their chances of winning,** je ne crois pas qu'ils aient des chances de gagner;

(e) *Br F* (*want*) **I wouldn't f. being in her shoes,** je ne voudrais pas être à sa place.

fancy-free ['fænsɪ'friː] *adj* **to be f.-f.,** avoir le cœur libre.

fancywork ['fænsɪwɜːk] *n Sewing* ouvrage(s) *m(pl)* d'agrément; broderie *f*.

fanfare ['fænfeər] *n* fanfare *f* (*exécutée par des cors de chasse*); sonnerie *f* (*de trompettes*).

fanfold ['fænfəʊld] *adj Comptr* **f. paper,** papier continu plié en accordéon.

fang [fæŋ] *n* croc *m* (*de chien etc*); crochet *m* (*de vipère*); dent *f* à venin.

fanlight ['fænlaɪt] *n* imposte *f*.

fanny ['fænɪ] *n* **(a)** *Br Sl* **sweet f. adams,** rien du tout, nib de nib; **(b)** *Am Sl* (*buttocks*) derrière *m*, fesses *fpl*; **f. pack** banane *f*; **(c)** *Br Vulg* (*vagina*) chatte *f*.

fan-shaped ['fænʃeɪpt] *adj* en éventail.

fantail ['fænteɪl] *n* (*bird*) pigeon *m* paon.

fantailed ['fænteɪld] *adj* **f. pigeon,** pigeon *m* paon.

fantasia [fæn'teɪzɪə] *n Mus* fantaisie *f*.

fantasize ['fæntəsaɪz] **1** *vi* fantasmer (**about,** sur). **2** *vt* **to f. that ...,** imaginer que ... .

fantastic [fæn'tæstɪk] *adj* **(a)** (*strange*) fantasque, bizarre; (*person*) original, -aux; (*thing*) fantastique, grotesque; **it sounds f., but it's true,** (*unbelievable*) ça paraît inouï mais c'est vrai; **it's f. to suppose that ...,** (*absurd*) c'est absurde de penser que ...; **a f. sum,** une somme faramineuse; *Com* **f. reductions,** baisses phénoménales; **(b)** *F* (*excellent*) formidable.

fantastically [fæn'tæstɪklɪ] *adv* (*see adj*) **(a)** d'une manière fantasque; *F* **f. beautiful,** incroyablement beau; **(b)** *F* formidablement.

fantasy ['fæntəzɪ] *n* **(a)** (*imagined event*) vision *f*, idée *f* bizarre; (*idea*) idée fantasque; **sexual f.,** fantasme sexuel; **his f. was to own a house in the country,** son rêve était d'avoir une maison à la campagne; **(b)** (*imagination*) fantaisie *f*; **you live in a f. world!,** tu vis dans un monde imaginaire!; **(c)** *Art* (*work*) œuvre *f* fantastique; *Archit* édifice *m* fantastique; *Mus* fantaisie *f*.

fanzine ['fænziːn] *n* fanzine *m*.

far¹ [fɑːr] *adv* (**farther, -est** ['fɑːðər, -ɪst]; **further, -est** ['fɜːðər, -ɪst]) **(a)** (*distance*) loin; **to go f.,** aller loin, faire du chemin; **how f. did you go?,** jusqu'où êtes-vous allé?; **this young man will go f.,** ce jeune homme ira loin; **to go too f.,** aller trop loin; **is it f. from here?,** est-ce loin d'ici?; **as f. as the eye can see,** à perte de vue; **to live f. away,** demeurer au loin; **her thoughts were f. away,** sa pensée était ailleurs; **it isn't f. off,** ce n'est pas loin, ça approche; **f. out at sea,** au (grand) large; **f. beneath/above us,** loin au-dessous/au-dessus de nous; **f. and wide,** de tous côtés; **f. and near,** partout; **f. from ...,** loin de ...; **not f. from ...,** à peu de distance de ...; **the story so f.,** = résumé des chapitres précédents; *Fig* **a pound does not go very f. nowadays,** on ne va pas loin avec une livre de nos jours; **to go so f. as to do sth,** aller jusqu'à faire qch; **I'll go so f. as to say that ...,** j'irai jusqu'à dire que ..., je dirai même que ...; **things went so f. that ...,** les choses sont allées si loin que ...; **that is going too f.,** cela passe la mesure; **how f. have you got?,** où en êtes-vous? (*de votre lecture etc*); **as f. as I can judge ...,** pour autant que je puisse en juger ...; **as f. as I know,** autant que je sache; **I will help you as f. as I can** *or* **as f. as possible,** je vous aiderai de mon mieux; **so f. so good,** jusqu'ici ça va bien; **in so f. as ...,** dans la mesure où ...; **f. from admiring him I loathe him,** bien loin de l'admirer je le déteste; **f. from it,** loin de là; **not f. from it,** peu s'en faut; **f. be it from me to,** loin de moi l'idée de faire; **she is not f. off sixty,** elle approche de la soixantaine; **by f.,** de loin; **by f. the best,** de beaucoup le meilleur;

(b) (*time*) **so f.,** jusqu'ici; **have you seen him? — not so f.,** l'avez-vous vu? – pas encore; **as f. back as I can remember,** aussi loin que je puisse me rappeler; **as f. back as 1900,** déjà en 1900; **as f. as I can see,** autant que je puisse prévoir; **to work f. into the night,** travailler bien avant dans la nuit;

(c) (*much*) beaucoup; **it is f. better,** c'est beaucoup mieux; **she's f. too intelligent to do that,** elle est bien trop intelligente pour faire ça; **f. too many/little/***etc*, beaucoup trop nombreux/petit/*etc*; **f. and away the best,** de beaucoup le meilleur; **the night was f. advanced,** la nuit était fort avancée.

far² *adj* (**farther, -est** ['fɑːðər, -ɪst]; **further, -est** ['fɜːðər, -ɪst]) **(a)** (*distant*) lointain, éloigné; **a f. country,** un pays lointain; **in the f. distance,** tout au loin; **the F. East,** l'Extrême-Orient *m*; **(b)** (*other*) **the f. end,** le bout le plus éloigné (*d'une planche etc*); **the f. bank of the river,** la rive opposée de la rivière.

farad ['færæd] *n El* farad *m*.

faraway ['fɑːrəweɪ] *adj* lointain, éloigné; **his eyes had a f. look,** il avait le regard perdu dans le vague.

farce [fɑːs] *n Th* farce *f*; **knockabout f.,** grosse farce; **the trial was a f.,** le procès a été grotesque.

farcical ['fɑːsɪk(ə)l] *adj Th* bouffon, burlesque; (*incident*) absurde, grotesque; **this accusation is f.,** cette accusation est grotesque.

farcically ['fɑːsɪklɪ] *adv* d'une manière absurde *ou* grotesque.

fare¹ [feər] *n* **(a)** *Rail etc* prix *m* du voyage; (*in taxi*) prix de la course; **half f.,** demi-place *f*, *pl* demi-places; **single f.,** aller *m* (simple), (prix d')aller; **return f.,** aller et retour *m*; **excess f.,** supplément *m*; **to pay one's f.,** payer son billet *ou* sa course; **fares, please!,** (*in bus*) = tickets, s'il vous plaît!; **rail/bus fares are going up,** les billets de train/les tickets de bus augmentent; **(b)** (*taxi passenger*) client, -ente; voyageur, -euse; **(c)** *esp Fml* (*food*) chère *f*, manger *m*; **good f.,** bonne chère; **prison f.,** régime *m* de prison; **bill of f.,** carte *f* du jour.

fare² *vi* **to f. well,** aller bien; **he went out to see how the lambs were faring,** il est sorti pour voir ce que devenaient les agneaux.

farewell [feə'wel] *int & n* adieu *m*; **to bid s.o. f.,** dire adieu à qn; **to say one's farewells,** faire ses adieux; **a f. dinner,** un dîner d'adieu.

far-fetched ['fɑː'fetʃt] *adj* (*idea, example, story*) tiré par les cheveux.

far-flung ['fɑːflʌŋ] *adj* (*empire etc*) très étendu.

farinaceous [færɪ'neɪʃəs] *adj* farineux, farinacé.

farm¹ [fɑːm] *n* **(a)** *Agr* ferme *f*, exploitation *f* agricole; **I**

work on a f., je travaille dans une ferme; **sheep/trout f.,** élevage *m* de moutons/truites; **dairy f.,** ferme laitière; **poultry f.,** exploitation avicole; **stud f.,** haras *m*; **f. animals,** animaux *mpl* de ferme; **f. buildings,** dépendances *mpl* (d'une ferme); **f. hand** *or* **labourer** *or* **worker,** ouvrier *m* agricole; **f. horse,** cheval *m* de ferme; **f. machinery,** machines *fpl* agricoles; **(b)** (*installation*) **sewage f.,** champs *mpl* d'épandage; **(c)** (*centre*) **health f.,** établissement *m* de cure.

farm² **1** *vt* cultiver, exploiter (*une propriété*); **to f. 400 acres,** = exploiter 160 hectares. **2** *vi* être cultivateur.

►farm out *vtsep* (*send to other people*) confier (*des enfants*) à l'extérieur; **to f. out work,** faire appel à des collaborateurs extérieurs; (*subcontract*) sous-traiter.

farmer ['fɑːmər] *n* agriculteur, -trice, cultivateur, -trice; **(tenant) f.,** fermier, -ière; **sheep f.,** éleveur, -euse de moutons; **poultry f.,** aviculteur, -trice.

farmhouse ['fɑːmhaʊs] *n* (maison *f* de) ferme *f*.

farming ['fɑːmɪŋ] **1** *adj* **f. communities,** agglomérations rurales. **2** *n* exploitation *f* agricole; agriculture *f*; **mixed f.,** polyculture *f*; **sheep f.,** élevage *m* de moutons; **poultry f.,** aviculture *f*.

farmstead ['fɑːmsted] *n* ferme *f*.

farmyard ['fɑːmjɑːd] *n* cour *f* de ferme.

Faroe ['feərəʊ] *n* **the F. Islands, the Faroes,** les îles *fpl* Féroé.

far-off ['fɑːrɒf] *adj* lointain, éloigné, reculé; **a f.-o. time,** un temps reculé.

far-out ['fɑːraʊt] *adj F* d'avant-garde; (*fantastic*) super.

far-reaching ['fɑː'riːtʃɪŋ] *adj* de grande envergure, d'une grande portée; **to have a f.-r. influence,** avoir une grande portée.

farrier ['færɪər] *n* maréchal-ferrant *m*, *pl* maréchaux-ferrants.

farrow¹ ['færəʊ] *n* (*piglets*) portée *f* de cochons.

farrow² **1** *vt* (*of sow*) mettre bas (*des cochons*). **2** *vi* (*of sow*) **to f. (down),** faire des petits, cochonner.

far-seeing ['fɑː'siːɪŋ] *adj* prévoyant, clairvoyant, perspicace; **to be f.-s.,** voir loin, *F* avoir bon nez.

far-sighted ['fɑː'saɪtɪd] *adj* **(a)** = **FAR-SEEING**; **(b)** (*long-sighted*) hypermétrope; (*because of age*) presbyte.

far-sightedness ['fɑː'saɪtɪdnɪs] *n* **(a)** prévoyance *f*, perspicacité *f*; **(b)** (*long-sightedness*) hypermétropie *f*; (*because of old age*) presbytie *f*.

fart¹ [fɑːt] *n Sl* pet *m*; *Fig* (*person*) merdeux, -euse.

fart² *vi Sl* péter, lâcher un pet.

►fart about, fart around *vi Sl* **(a)** (*play the fool*) déconner; **(b)** (*waste time*) glander.

farther ['fɑːðər] (*comp of* **far**) **1** *adv* **(a)** (*place*) plus loin (**than, que**); **f. off,** plus éloigné, plus loin; **they stopped a little f. on,** ils se sont arrêtés un peu plus loin; **f. on in the book,** plus loin dans le livre; **I can go no f.,** je ne saurais aller plus loin; (*exhausted*) je n'en peux plus!; **f. west/down,** plus à l'ouest/bas; **before she could get any f. with her story ...,** avant qu'elle ne puisse continuer son histoire ...; **(b)** (*time*) **f. (back),** plus en arrière; **f. back than 1500,** avant 1500. **2** *adj* plus lointain; **at the f. end of the room,** à l'autre bout de la salle; au fond de la salle.

farthest ['fɑːðɪst] (*superl of* **far**) **1** *adv* le plus loin; **this is the f. east they reached,** voici le point le plus à l'est qu'ils ont atteint. **2** *adj* **(a)** (*distant*) **f. (off),** le plus éloigné, le plus reculé; **(b)** (*distance etc*) le plus long.

farthing ['fɑːðɪŋ] *n Br Arch* (*coin*) quart *m* d'un penny; *F* **not to have a f.,** n'avoir pas le sou; *F* **I don't care a brass f.,** je m'en moque éperdument.

fascia, *pl* **-s** ['feɪʃə, -z] *n* **(a)** *Archit* bandelette *f*, bande *f*; **(b)** (*on shop front*) enseigne *f* en forme d'entablement; **(c)** *Aut* tableau *m* de bord.

fascicle ['fæsɪk(ə)l] **, fascicule** ['fæsɪkjuːl] *n* fascicule *m*.

fascinate ['fæsɪneɪt] *vt* fasciner, charmer, séduire (*qn*); **insects f. him,** les insectes le fascinent; **to be fascinated by sth,** être fasciné par qch.

fascinating ['fæsɪneɪtɪŋ] *adj* fascinant, séduisant.

fascination [fæsɪ'neɪʃən] *n* fascination *f*, attrait *m*; **I don't understand the f. of tennis,** je ne comprends pas l'attrait que peut avoir le tennis; **the sport has** *or* **holds a f. for millions,** ce sport fascine des millions de gens.

fascism ['fæʃɪz(ə)m] *n Pol* fascisme *m*.

fascist ['fæʃɪst] *adj & n Pol* fasciste *mf*.

fash [fæʃ] *vt Scot* agacer, ennuyer (*qn*); **dinna f. yourself,** ne te fais pas de bile.

fashion¹ ['fæʃən] *n* **(a)** (*in clothes etc*) mode *f*, vogue *f*; **in f.,** à la mode, en vogue; **out of f.,** passé de mode, démodé; **in the latest f.,** à la dernière mode; **to set the f.,** fixer *ou* mener la mode; **to become the f., to come into f.,** devenir à la mode; **go out of f.,** se démoder; **it's all the f.,** c'est la grande vogue; **it's the latest f.,** c'est la dernière mode; *Com* **f. house,** maison *f* de haute couture; **f. show,** présentation *f* de collections; **f. magazine,** journal *m* de modes; **(b)** manière *f* (*de faire qch*); **crabs walk in a peculiar f.,** les crabes marchent d'une façon étrange; **we rubbed noses, Eskimo f.,** nous nous sommes frotté le nez à la manière des esquimaux; **after a f.,** tant bien que mal.

fashion² *vt* façonner, former; confectionner (*une robe etc*); **fully fashioned,** bien ajusté.

fashionable ['fæʃənəb(ə)l] *adj* à la mode, en vogue; **blue is very f. this year,** le bleu se porte beaucoup cette année; **a f. film director,** un metteur en scène en vogue; **a f. part of town,** un quartier très en vogue *ou* à la mode *ou* branché.

fashionably ['fæʃənəblɪ] *adv* (*habillé*) à la mode.

fast¹ [fɑːst] **1** *adj* **(a)** (*rapid*) rapide; *Phot* (*pellicule*) rapide; **you're a f. walker,** vous marchez vite; **he likes f. cars,** il aime les voitures qui vont vite; *Rail* **f. train,** rapide *m*; express *m*; **the f. lane,** (*on motorway*) la voie rapide; *Fig* **life in the f. lane,** la vie à cent à l'heure; **f. food,** restauration *f* rapide; **f. food restaurant,** fast-food *m*, sandwicherie *f*, brasserie *f*; **f. food chain,** chaîne *f* de restauration rapide; **f. forward (button),** (*on tape recorder*) avance *f* rapide; *Sp* **a f. time,** (*in race etc*) un bon temps *ou* chrono; *F* **he pulled a f. one on me,** il m'a joué un mauvais tour; **he's a f. worker,** il travaille vite; (*with women*) il va vite en besogne;

(b) (*clock, watch*) en avance; **my watch is five minutes f.,** *F* **I'm five minutes f.,** ma montre avance de cinq minutes;

(c) (*secure*) (*stake etc*) ferme, fixe, solide; (*grip etc*) tenace; (*door, lid etc*) bien fermé; (*colour*) solide, résistant; **these colours are not f.,** ces couleurs ne résistent pas; *Nau* **to make f. (to a buoy),** prendre le corps-mort; **to make f. (alongside),** s'amarrer;

(d) (*immoral*) dissolu; **f. living,** la débauche; **f. woman,** femme légère.

2 *adv* **(a)** (*rapidly*) vite, rapidement; **to run f.,** courir vite; **she was walking faster than me,** elle marchait plus rapidement que moi; **not so f.!,** pas si vite!, doucement!; **bad news travels f.,** les mauvaises nouvelles courent vite;

(b) (*securely*) ferme, solidement; **to hold f.,** tenir ferme; tenir bon; **to stand f.,** tenir bon; ne pas bouger; **to stick f.,** bien tenir; (*be stuck*) rester pris, rester collé; *Tex* **f. dyed,** grand teint *inv*; **to be f. asleep,** dormir d'un profond sommeil; *F* **to play f. and loose,** jouer double jeu (**with s.o.,** avec qn).

fast² *n* jeûne *m*; *Rel* **f. day,** jour *m* de jeûne; **to break one's f.,** rompre le jeûne.

fast³ *vi* jeûner; *Med* être à la diète.

fastback ['fɑːstbæk] *n Aut* arrière profilé; (*car*) voiture *f* à l'arrière profilé.

fasten ['fɑːs(ə)n] **1** *vt* **(a)** (*attach*) attacher (**to, on,** à); **to f. papers together with a clip,** attacher des papiers (ensemble) avec une agrafe; **to f. one's eyes on s.o.,** fixer le regard sur qn; **(b)** (*hold securely*) fixer, assurer; **to f. a door with a bolt,** fermer une porte au verrou. **2** *vi* s'attacher, se fixer; (*of garment*) s'agrafer, se boutonner (**at the back,** par derrière); (*of door etc*) se fermer; **door that fastens with a bolt,** porte qui se ferme au verrou; **the crab fastened on to his leg,** le crabe s'accrocha à sa jambe.

►fasten down *vtsep* fixer (*qch*) à terre *ou* en place.

►fasten up **1** *vtsep* agrafer, boutonner (*sa robe etc*). **2** *vi* **this dress fastens up at the back,** cette robe se boutonne *ou* s'agrafe dans le dos.

fastener ['fɑːs(ə)nər] *n* attache *f*; (*of garment*) agrafe *f*; (*of purse*) fermoir *m*; (*of window etc*) fermeture *f*; (*of French window*) espagnolette *f*; **zip f.,** fermeture à glissière, fermeture éclair ®; **snap f.,** bouton *m* (fermoir) à pression.

fastening ['fɑːs(ə)nɪŋ] *n* **(a)** (*action*) action *f* d'attacher; fixage *m*, fixation *f* (*de qch sur qch*); (*with bolts*) boulonnage *m*; agrafage *m* (*d'un vêtement*); **(b)** (*device*) = **FASTENER**; **fastenings,** attaches *fpl*.

fast-forward [fɑːst'fɔːwəd] **1** *vt* mettre (*une cassette*) en avance rapide. **2** *vi* se dérouler en avance rapide.

fastidious [fæ'stɪdɪəs] *adj* difficile, délicat (**about sth,** sur qch); **to be f.,** être difficile à contenter.

fastidiously [fæ'stɪdɪəslɪ] *adv* avec une délicatesse exagérée.

fastidiousness [fæ'stɪdɪəsnɪs] *n* goût *m* difficile.

fasting ['fɑːstɪŋ] *n* jeûne *m*; *Med* diète *f* (absolue).

fast-moving ['fɑːst'muːvɪŋ] *adj* rapide.

fastness ['fɑːstnɪs] *n* **(a)** (*of colour, dye*) solidité *f*; **(b)** (*of moorings etc*) sûreté *f*; fiabilité *f*; **(c)** *Lit* (*stronghold*)

mountain f., forteresse *f*.

fat¹ [fæt] *adj* (**fatter**; **fattest**) **(a)** (*person*) gros, grosse, gras, grasse, corpulent; (*meat*) gras; (*tissue*) adipeux; *F* (*cheque, salary*) gros; **to get f.**, engraisser; *Fig* **to grow f. at the expense of others**, s'engraisser aux dépens d'autrui; **f. volume**, gros tome; **f. wallet**, portefeuille bien garni; *US F* **f. cat**, (*rich person*) richard *m*; *F* **a f. lot of good that'll do you!**, cela vous fera une belle jambe!; *F* **that was a f. lot of good** *or* **use!**, on est bien aidé avec ça!; **a f. lot you know about it!**, comme si vous en saviez quelque chose!; *F* **f. chance he's got!**, il est mal barré!; **(b)** (*land*) riche, fertile, gras; (*clay, lime etc*) gras.

fat² *n* **(a)** graisse *f*; **fats**, matières grasses; **animal/vegetable f.**, graisse animale/végétale; *F* **the fat's in the fire!**, ça va chauffer; **f. content**, teneur *f* en graisse *ou* en lipides; **f. intake**, ration *f* de corps gras; **(b)** gras *m* (*de viande*); **to live off the f. of the land**, vivre comme un coq en pâte.

fatal ['feɪt(ə)l] *adj* **(a)** (*blow, accident*) mortel; **this condition can prove f.**, cela peut être mortel; **(b)** (*disastrous*) **f. decision**, décision *f* funeste; **f. error** *or* **mistake**, erreur fatale, faute capitale; **(c)** (*ordained by fate*) fatal, -als; **the f. hour**, l'heure fatale.

fatalism ['feɪtəlɪzəm] *n* fatalisme *m*.

fatalist ['feɪtəlɪst] *n* fataliste *mf*.

fatalistic [feɪtə'lɪstɪk] *adj* fataliste.

fatality [fə'tælɪtɪ] *n* **(a)** (*fatal accident*) accident mortel; **there were no fatalities**, il n'y a pas eu de mort; **(b)** caractère *m* funeste (**of**, de).

fatally ['feɪt(ə)lɪ] *adv* **(a)** mortellement (*blessé*); **(b)** (*according to fate*) fatalement.

fate [feɪt] *n* destin *m*, sort *m*; **stroke of f.**, coup *m* du destin *ou* du sort; **f. had decreed that ...**, le sort a voulu que ...; *Myth* **the Fates**, les Parques *fpl*; **to leave s.o. to their f.**, abandonner qn à son sort; **to meet one's f.**, trouver la mort; **a f. worse than death**, un destin pire que la mort.

fated ['feɪtɪd] *adj* **(a)** (*destined*) destiné, condamné (**to do sth**, à faire qch); **(b)** (*doomed*) voué à la destruction.

fateful ['feɪtfʊl] *adj* **(a)** (*voix etc*) prophétique; (*parole*) fatidique; **(b)** (*jour etc*) décisif, fatal, -als; **(c)** (*événement etc*) fatal, -als, inévitable.

fathead ['fæthed] *n F* imbécile *mf*.

father¹ ['fɑːðər] *n* **(a)** père *m*; **from f. to son**, de père en fils; **he's his f.'s son**, c'est bien le fils de son père; **on the f.'s side**, du côté paternel; **like a f.**, paternellement; **yes, F.**, oui, (mon) père; **like f. like son**, tel père tel fils; **F. Christmas**, le père Noël; **F. Time**, le Temps; *F* **we had the f. and mother of a row**, nous avons eu une de ces empoignades!; **F.'s Day**, la fête des pères; **f. figure**, = personne qui tient le rôle du père;
(b) (*ancestor*) **our fathers**, nos ancêtres *mpl*, nos aïeux *mpl*;
(c) (*founder*) père *m*, fondateur *m* (*d'une science, d'un art etc*); **the Fathers of the Church**, les Pères de l'Église;
(d) (*God*) Père *m*; **God the F.**, Dieu le Père; **Our F. which** *or* **who art in Heaven**, notre Père qui est aux cieux;
(e) *Rel* (*priest*) père *m*; **the Holy F.**, (*Pope*) le Saint-Père; **f. confessor**, père spirituel, directeur *m* (de conscience); **F. Martin**, (*in monastic order*) le Père Martin; (*priest*) l'abbé Martin; **yes, F.**, (*in address*) oui, mon Père;
(f) (*senior*) doyen *m* (*de la Chambre etc*); *Typ etc* **f. of the chapel**, chef *m* de l'atelier.

father² *vt* engendrer (*un enfant*); inventer, produire (*qch*); concevoir (*un projet*).

fatherhood ['fɑːðəhʊd] *n* paternité *f*.

father-in-law, *pl* **fathers-in-law** ['fɑːðərɪnlɔː, 'fɑːðəzɪnlɔː] *n* beau-père, *pl* beaux-pères.

fatherland ['fɑːðəlænd] *n* patrie *f*.

fatherless ['fɑːðəlɪs] *adj* sans père, orphelin, -ine de père.

fatherly ['fɑːðəlɪ] *adj* (*person, tone, manner etc*) paternel; **to behave in a f. way towards s.o.**, se montrer paternel envers qn; être un père pour qn.

fathom¹ ['fæðəm] *n Nau* (*measurement*) brasse *f*.

fathom² *vt* sonder; *Fig* pénétrer, sonder (*un mystère*); **I can't f. him (out)**, je ne le comprends pas.

fatigue¹ [fə'tiːg] *n* **(a)** (*tiredness*) fatigue *f*; **to be suffering from f.**, être épuisé; **mental f.**, fatigue cérébrale; **to be dropping with f.**, tomber de fatigue; *Tech* **metal f.**, fatigue des métaux; **(b)** *Mil* **f. (duty)**, corvée *f*; **cookhouse f.**, corvée de cuisine(s); **f. dress, fatigues**, tenue *f* de corvée, treillis *m*; **f. party**, (détachement *m* de) corvée.

fatigue² *vt* fatiguer (*qn, Tech un métal etc*); **to f. oneself doing sth**, se fatiguer à faire qch.

fatiguing [fə'tiːgɪŋ] *adj* fatigant.

fatness ['fætnɪs] *n* embonpoint *m*, corpulence *f* (*de qn*); adiposité *f* (*de la chair etc*).

fatso ['fætsəʊ] *n Pej F* gros lard.

fatted ['fætɪd] *adj* **to kill the f. calf**, tuer le veau gras.

fatten ['fæt(ə)n] **1** *vt* engraisser (*des moutons, des veaux etc*). **2** *vi* engraisser, devenir gras.

►**fatten up** *vtsep* **(a)** = **FATTEN 1**; **(b)** *F* faire grossir, engraisser (*qn*); **we'll have to f. you up a bit**, il va falloir qu'on t'engraisse un peu.

fattening ['fæt(ə)nɪŋ] **1** *adj* (*food*) qui fait grossir. **2** *n* (*of animals*) engraissement *m*, engraissage *m*.

fatty ['fætɪ] **1** *adj* graisseux; (*tissue etc*) adipeux; **f. foods**, aliments gras; *Ch* **f. acid**, acide gras. **2** *n F* (*child*) gros enfant; (*man*) gros (bonhomme), patapouf *m*; (*woman*) grosse (bonne femme), dondon *f*; **hi, f.!**, ohé, mon gros!

fatuity [fæ'tjuːɪtɪ] *n* sottise *f*, imbécillité *f*.

fatuous ['fætjʊəs] *adj* imbécile, idiot; (*sourire*) béat.

fatuously ['fætjʊəslɪ] *adv* sottement, d'un air imbécile.

fatuousness ['fætjʊəsnɪs] *n* = **FATUITY**.

faucet ['fɔːsɪt] *n Am* robinet *m*.

fault¹ [fɔːlt] *n* **(a)** (*flaw*) défaut *m*; **to shut one's eyes to s.o.'s faults**, fermer les yeux sur les défauts de qn; **in spite of all his faults**, malgré tous ses travers; **scrupulous to a f.**, scrupuleux à l'excès; **to find f. with s.o./sth**, trouver à redire contre qn/à qch; **(b)** *Tech* défaut *m*, vice *f* (*de construction*); **(c)** (*guilt*) faute *f*; **to be at f.**, être en faute, être coupable; **whose f. is it?**, à qui la faute?; **I am afraid it was my f.**, je crains bien que ce ne soit de ma faute; **through no f. of mine**, sans que je sois en cause; **(d)** (*error*) **spelling f.**, faute *f* d'orthographe; **(e)** *Tennis* faute *f*; **double f.**, double faute; **foot f.**, faute de pied; **(f)** *Geol* faille *f*; **f. line/plane**, ligne *f*/plan *m* de faille.

fault² *vt* prendre (*qn*) en défaut; trouver un défaut dans (*qch*); **I can't f. her research**, je ne trouve aucune erreur dans ses recherches.

fault-finder ['fɔːltfaɪndər] *n* (*person*) critiqueur, -euse; (*device*) détecteur *m* de fuites.

fault-finding ['fɔːltfaɪndɪŋ] **1** *adj* censeur, -euse. **2** *n* **(a)** (*criticism*) disposition *f* à critiquer; **(b)** *Tech* localisation *f* des défauts.

faultiness ['fɔːltɪnɪs] *n* défectuosité *f*, imperfection *f*.

faultless ['fɔːltlɪs] *adj* (*work etc*) sans défaut, sans faute; parfait; (*dress*) impeccable, irréprochable.

faultlessly ['fɔːltlɪslɪ] *adv* parfaitement; (*dressed*) d'une manière impeccable.

faultlessness ['fɔːltlɪsnɪs] *n* perfection *f*.

fault-tolerant ['fɔːlt'tɒlərənt] *adj Comptr* quasi insensible aux défaillances.

faulty ['fɔːltɪ] *adj* (*work etc*) défectueux, imparfait; (*style etc*) incorrect; (*reasoning etc*) erroné; *Gram* (*construction etc*) vicieux; **f. workmanship**, mauvaise construction.

faun [fɔːn] *n Myth* faune *m*.

fauna ['fɔːnə] *n* faune *f* (*d'une région, d'un pays*).

faux pas ['fəʊ'pɑː] *n* faux pas, gaffe *f*.

favour¹, *US* **favor** ['feɪvər] *n* **(a)** (*approval*) faveur *f*, approbation *f*; **to find f. with s.o.**, trouver grâce aux yeux de qn; **to gain s.o.'s f.**, gagner la faveur de qn; **to be restored** *or* **to return to f.**, rentrer en grâce; **to be in/out of f.**, (*of person*) être bien/mal vu, *F* avoir/ne pas avoir la cote; (*of style*) être à la mode/démodé; **to fall out of f. with s.o.**, perdre les bonnes grâces de qn;
(b) (*service*) service *m*; **to ask s.o. a f., to ask a f. of s.o.**, solliciter un service *ou* une faveur de qn; **as a f.**, à titre gracieux; **to do s.o. a f.**, faire une faveur à qn, obliger qn; **will you do me a great f.?**, voulez-vous me rendre un grand service?; *Br Sl* **do me a f.!**, (*it's worth much more!*) tu te fous de moi!; **she's not doing herself any favours by being so arrogant**, son arrogance la dessert;
(c) (*preference*) partialité *f*, préférence *f*; **to show f. towards s.o.**, favoriser qn; **without fear or f.**, sans distinction de personnes; **to speak in s.o.'s f.**, parler en faveur de qn *ou* pour qn; **he has everything in his f.**, tout lui sourit; **in f. of ...**, en faveur de ...; **this route was abandoned in f. of a more direct one**, cette route a été abandonnée pour une autre qui était plus directe; **to be in f. of sth**, être partisan de qch, préconiser qch; **he's in f. of (introducing) subsidies**, il est favorable à *ou* partisan de la mise en place de subventions; **to write a cheque in f. of s.o.**, faire un chèque à l'ordre de qn;
(d) *Arch* (*ribbon etc*) faveur *f*, cocarde *f*;
(e) *Lit Hum* **favours**, (*of woman*) faveurs *fpl*; **she was not free with her favours**, elle n'était pas prodigue de ses faveurs.

favour², *US* **favor** *vt* **(a)** (*approve of*) approuver, préférer (*qch*); accorder une préférence à (*qn*); être pour (*un projet*); **(b)** (*bestow favour on*) favoriser (*qn*); accorder une grâce à *(qn)*; **to f. s.o. with a smile,** gratifier qn d'un sourire; **(c)** *(give advantage to)* avantager *(qn)*; montrer de la partialité pour *(qn)*; faciliter *(qch)*; **to be favoured by circumstances,** avoir les circonstances en sa faveur; **(d)** *(of fact etc)* soutenir *(une théorie etc)*.

favourable, *US* **favorable** ['feɪv(ə)rəb(ə)l] *adj* favorable; *(weather, wind etc)* propice; *(reception etc)* bienveillant; *(terms etc)* bon, avantageux; *(report etc)* bon, rassurant; **in a f. light,** sous un jour favorable; *Com* **on f. terms,** à bon compte.

favourably, *US* **favorably** ['feɪv(ə)rəblɪ] *adv* favorablement; **I was f. impressed,** j'ai été favorablement impressionné.

favoured, *US* **favored** ['feɪvəd] *adj* **(a)** *(person)* favorisé, avantagé; **the most-f. nation,** la nation la plus favorisée; **the f. few,** les élus *(du patron etc)*; **(b)** *Old-fashioned* **ill-f.,** laid, de mauvaise mine.

favourite, *US* **favorite** ['feɪv(ə)rɪt] **1** *n* favori, *f* favorite; **the youngest daughter is his f.,** c'est la plus jeune qui est sa préférée; *Sp* **to back the f.,** jouer le favori; **chocolate cake is a firm f. with children,** c'est vraiment le gâteau au chocolat que les enfants préfèrent. **2** *adj (fils, auteur)* favori, préféré; **my f. opera,** mon opéra de prédilection.

favouritism, *US* **favoritism** ['feɪv(ə)rɪtɪz(ə)m] *n* favoritisme *m*.

fawn¹ [fɔːn] *n* **(a)** *(deer)* faon *m*; **(b) f. (colour),** couleur *f* fauve; **f.(-coloured),** fauve *m*; **f. jacket,** une veste (couleur) fauve.

fawn² *vi* **to f. on s.o.,** *(of dog)* caresser qn, faire des caresses à qn; *(of person)* se mettre à plat ventre devant qn.

fawning ['fɔːnɪŋ] **1** *adj (flattering)* adulateur, -trice; *(servile)* servile. **2** *n* adulation *f*.

fax¹ [fæks] *n* **(a) f. (machine),** télécopieur *m*, fax *m*; **to send sth by f.,** envoyer qch par fax *ou* par télécopie; **f. shot,** publicité directe par télécopie; **(b)** *(copy)* fax *m*; **to send s.o. a f.,** envoyer un fax à qn; **f. message,** (message *m* par) fax; **f. number,** numéro *m* de fax.

fax² *vt (send)* faxer.

►fax back *vtsep (return by fax)* renvoyer par fax *ou* par télécopie; **we'll f. it back to you,** nous vous le renverrons par fax; **I'll f. you back,** je vous réponds par fax.

faze [feɪz] *vt F* déconcerter *(qn)*.

FBI [efbiː'aɪ] *n US (abbr* **Federal Bureau of Investigation***)* ≈ Police Judiciaire; **FBI agent,** un agent du FBI.

FC [ef'siː] *abbr* **Football Club.**

FDA [efdiː'eɪ] *n US (abbr* **Food and Drug Administration***)* = office *f* du contrôle pharmaceutique et alimentaire.

fealty ['fɪəltɪ] *n Hist* féauté *f*; fidélité *f*.

fear¹ [fɪər] *n* **(a)** crainte *f*, peur *f*; **a sudden f.,** une alarme; **my greatest f. was that they would forget,** ce que je craignais le plus, c'est qu'ils oublient; **she was a stranger to f.,** elle ignorait ce qu'était la peur; **deadly f.,** effroi *m*; **to be overcome by** *or* **with f.,** être en proie à la frayeur; **to be** *or* **stand** *or* **go in f. of s.o./sth,** avoir peur de *ou* redouter *ou* craindre qn/qch; **to go in f. of one's life,** craindre pour sa vie; **for f. of making a mistake,** de crainte d'erreur; **there is no f. that he will come back,** il n'y a pas de danger qu'il revienne; *F* **no f.!,** pas de danger!, jamais de la vie!; **(b)** *(respect)* respect *m*, crainte *f (de Dieu, des lois etc)*; *F* **to put the f. of God into s.o.,** faire à qn une semonce dont il se souviendra longtemps.

fear² **1** *vt* **(a)** craindre, avoir peur de *(qn, qch)*; appréhender, craindre *(un événement)*; **what they most feared,** ce qu'ils craignaient le plus; **I f. it is too late,** j'ai peur *ou* je crains qu'il ne soit trop tard; **I f. he will not come,** je crains qu'il ne vienne pas; **I f. he's out,** je crains qu'il ne soit pas là; **I f. I'm late,** je crois bien être en retard; **(b)** *(respect)* craindre *(Dieu etc)*. **2** *vi* avoir peur; **we'll be here tomorrow, never f.,** nous serons là demain, n'aie pas peur; *Old-fashioned* **f. not, help is at hand,** n'ayez crainte, l'assistance ne saurait tarder; **to f. for s.o./sth,** s'inquiéter au sujet de qn/qch; **I was beginning to f. for her sanity,** je commençais à m'inquièter pour son état mental; **we feared for our lives,** nous craignions pour nos vies.

feared [fɪəd] *adj (person etc)* redouté.

fearful ['fɪəfʊl] *adj* **(a)** *(noise etc)* affreux, effrayant; *F* **a f. mess,** un désordre effrayant *ou* formidable; **(b)** *(person)* peureux, craintif; **f. of ...,** qui craint de ...; **f. of what would happen ...,** par crainte de ce qui arriverait ... .

fearfully ['fɪəfʊlɪ] *adv* **(a)** *(frighteningly)* affreusement, terriblement; *F* **f. expensive/***etc*, horriblement cher/*etc*; **(b)** *(out of fear)* peureusement.

fearfulness ['fɪəfʊlnɪs] *n* **(a)** *(of noise etc)* caractère terrifiant *(de qch)*; **(b)** *(of person) (fear)* crainte *f*; *(concern)* appréhension *f*.

fearless ['fɪəlɪs] *adj* intrépide, courageux, sans peur (**of,** de); **he was f. of danger,** il ne reculait devant aucun danger.

fearlessly ['fɪəlɪslɪ] *adv* intrépidement, sans peur.

fearlessness ['fɪəlɪsnɪs] *n* intrépidité *f*, courage *m*.

fearsome ['fɪəsəm] *adj* effrayant, redoutable.

feasibility [fiːzə'bɪlɪtɪ] *n* **(a)** praticabilité *f*, faisabilité *f (d'un plan etc)*; **f. study,** étude *f* de faisabilité; **(b)** plausibilité *f*, vraisemblance *f (d'une histoire etc)*.

feasible ['fiːzəb(ə)l] *adj* **(a)** *(plan etc)* faisable, réalisable, praticable; **(b)** *(story etc)* vraisemblable.

feast¹ [fiːst] *n* **(a)** *(large meal)* festin *m*, banquet *m*; **(b)** *Rel etc* **f. (day),** (jour *m* de) fête *f*; **moveable f.,** fête mobile.

feast² **1** *vi* faire festin, festoyer; **to f. (up)on sth,** se régaler de qch. **2** *vt* régaler, fêter *(qn)*; **to f. one's eyes on sth,** repaître ses yeux de qch.

feasting ['fiːstɪŋ] *n* festoiement *m*.

feat [fiːt] *n* **(a)** *(exploit)* exploit *m*; **f. of arms,** fait *m* d'armes; **(b)** *(achievement)* tour *m* de force; **feats of engineering,** triomphes *mpl* de l'ingénieur; **f. of skill,** tour d'adresse.

feather¹ ['feðər] *n* **(a)** plume *f*; *(of tail, wing)* penne *f*; **as light as a f.,** léger comme une plume; **feathers of an arrow,** (em)pennes *fpl* d'une flèche; *Fig* **to show the white f.,** manquer de courage; **you could have knocked me down with a f.,** je n'en revenais pas; *Fig* **that's a f. in her cap,** elle peut en être fière; **f. bed,** lit *m* de plume; *Fig* sinécure *f*; **f. duster,** plumeau *m*; **(b)** *(in gem)* paillette *f*, crapaud *m*; **(c)** *MecE* languette *f*; clavette plate; **(d)** *(in rowing)* nage plate.

feather² **1** *vt* **(a)** empenner *(une flèche)*; **to tar and f. s.o.,** emplumer qn; *Fig* **to f. one's nest,** faire sa pelote *ou* son beurre; **(b)** *(in rowing)* ramener *(l'aviron)* à plat; **f. your oars!,** avirons à plat!; **(c)** *Av* mettre *(une hélice)* en drapeau. **2** *vi* **(a)** *(in rowing)* nager plat; **(b)** = **FEATHER OUT.**

►feather out *vi (of young bird)* s'emplumer.

featherbed ['feðəbed] *vt F* subventionner (excessivement).

featherbedding ['feðəbedɪŋ] *n* subventionnement excessif.

featherbrained ['feðəbreɪnd] *adj F* étourdi.

feather-edge ['feðəredʒ] *n Carp etc* biseau *m*.

feather-edged ['feðəredʒd] *adj* taillé en biseau.

feathering ['feðərɪŋ] *n* **(a)** *(of birds)* plumage *m*; **(b)** *(of arrow)* empennage *m*; **(c)** *(in rowing)* nage plate; **(d)** *Av* mise *f* en drapeau *(de l'hélice)*.

featherstitch ['feðəstɪtʃ] *n Sewing* point *m* d'épines.

featherweight ['feðəweɪt] *n Boxing* poids *m* plume.

feathery ['feðərɪ] *adj (snow, wheat etc)* plumeux.

feature¹ ['fiːtʃər] *n* **(a)** trait *m (du visage)*; **prominent features,** traits accusés; **(b)** *(characteristic)* trait *m*, caractéristique *f (d'un paysage etc)*; *(of car, machine)* caractéristique; **main features,** grands traits; **physical features of a country,** topographie *f* d'un pays; **special f.,** particularité *f*; **prominent f.,** trait saillant; **the redeeming f.,** le beau côté *(de qch)*; **a f. of the course is ...,** un des aspects de la formation est ...; **paper that makes a f. of sports,** journal qui fait une large place aux sports; **(c)** *Cin* **f. (film),** long métrage; **double-f. programme,** programme à deux longs métrages; **(d)** *Journ* article *m* vedette; *(news report etc)* grand reportage; *Rad etc* numéro *m* vedette; *Com* article *m* réclame.

feature² **1** *vt* **(a)** *Cin* représenter *(qn)*; **film featuring John Smith,** film avec John Smith en vedette; **(b)** *Journ* mettre *(une nouvelle)* en manchette; **(c)** *(have as special feature)* présenter, comporter; **the new model features four-wheel drive,** le nouveau modèle comporte quatre roues motrices; **(d)** *(characterize)* caractériser, marquer, distinguer *(qch)*. **2** *vi Cin (of actor)* faire une apparition.

feature-length ['fiːtʃəleŋθ] *adj Cin (cartoon etc)* long métrage *inv*.

featureless ['fiːtʃəlɪs] *adj* sans traits bien marqués.

febrile ['fiːbraɪl] *adj (pouls etc)* fébrile, fiévreux.

February ['febrʊərɪ] *n* février *m*; **in F.,** au mois de février, en février; **(on) the first/the seventh of F.,** le premier/le sept février.

fecal, feces *US* = **FAECAL, FAECES.**

feckless ['feklɪs] *adj* **(a)** *(weak, ineffectual)* propre à rien, incapable; **(b)** *(irresponsible)* étourdi, irréfléchi.

fecklessness ['feklɪsnɪs] *n (see adj)* **(a)** incapacité *f*; **(b)** étourderie *f*.

fecundity [fɪ'kʌndɪtɪ] *n* fécondité *f*, productivité *f*.

fed¹ [fed] *n US F* flic *m*.
fed² *see* **FEED²**.
Fed *abbr* **Federal**.
federal ['fedərəl] **1** *adj* (*government etc*) fédéral, -aux. **2** *n US Hist* fédéral *m*, nordiste *m*.
federalism ['fedərəlɪz(ə)m] *n* fédéralisme *m*.
federalist ['fedərəlɪst] *n* fédéraliste *mf*.
federalize ['fedərəlaɪz] *vt* **(a)** fédéraliser; **(b)** *US* charger le gouvernement fédéral du contrôle de (*qch*).
federate¹ ['fedərət] *adj* (*state etc*) fédéré.
federate² ['fedəreɪt] **1** *vt* fédérer. **2** *vi* se fédérer.
federation [fedə'reɪʃən] *n* fédération *f*; **employers' f.**, association patronale.
fed up ['fedʌp] *adj F* **to be f. up**, en avoir assez, en avoir plein le dos; **she sounded pretty f. up**, elle avait l'air d'en avoir marre; **I'm f. up with it**, j'en ai marre.
fee [fiː] *n* **(a)** honoraires *mpl* (*d'un médecin consultant, d'un avocat etc*); cachet *m* (*d'un acteur*); jeton *m* de présence (*d'un administrateur*); **school fees**, frais *mpl* de scolarité; **boarding-school fees**, pension *f*; **entrance f.**, droit *m* d'entrée; **registration f.**, (*for conference etc*) droit d'inscription; (*for letter*) taxe *f* de recommandation; **for a small f.**, moyennant une légère redevance; **(b)** *Jur* propriété *f* héréditaire; *Jur* **property held in f. simple**, propriété sans conditions *ou* libre; **(c)** *Hist* fief *m*.
feeble ['fiːb(ə)l] *adj* **(a)** (*weak*) (*person*) faible, infirme, débile; (*action, light etc*) faible, *F* **that's pretty f.**, (*as an excuse, attempt*) c'est un peu léger; (*as a joke*) ce n'est pas très drôle; **(b)** *F* (*ineffectual*) mou, peu capable.
feeble-minded ['fiːb(ə)l'maɪndɪd] **1** *adj* d'esprit faible, arriéré. **2** *n* **the f.-m.**, (*used as pl*) les débiles mentaux.
feeble-mindedness ['fiːb(ə)l'maɪndɪdnɪs] *n* faiblesse *f* d'esprit, arriération *f*.
feebleness ['fiːb(ə)lnɪs] (*of person*) faiblesse *f*, débilité *f*.
feebly ['fiːblɪ] *adv* faiblement.
feed¹ [fiːd] *n* **(a)** nourriture *f*, pâture *f* (*pour les animaux*); fourrage *m* (*pour les chevaux etc*); *F* (*meal*) repas *m*; **to have a good f.**, bien manger; **horse off his f.**, cheval qui boude sur son avoine; *F* **to be off one's f.**, (*of baby*) bouder sur la nourriture; **it's time for baby's f.**, il faut donner à manger au bébé;
(b) mesure *f*, ration *f* (*de nourriture pour les animaux*); **f. of oats**, picotin *m* d'avoine;
(c) *Th etc* acteur, -trice qui donne la réplique; (*of comedian*) faire-valoir *m*; **f. line**, réplique *f*;
(d) *Tech* alimentation *f* (*d'une machine etc*); (*device*) appareil *m ou* système *m* d'alimentation; (*pipe*) conduit *m* d'alimentation; **f. belt**, (*of machine gun*) bande-chargeur *f* (souple), *pl* bandes-chargeurs; **f. pump**, pompe *f* d'alimentation; **f. pipe**, tuyau *m* d'alimentation.
feed² *v* (*pt & pp* **fed** [fed]) **1** *vt* **(a)** nourrir, donner à manger à (*qn*); nourrir (*une famille etc*); approvisionner (*un pays etc*); ravitailler (*une armée*); faire manger (*un chien etc*); affourrager (*des bestiaux*); allaiter (*un bébé*); (*of mother bird*) donner la becquée à (*ses petits*); **to f. the birds**, donner à manger aux oiseaux, nourrir les oiseaux; **we were well fed**, nous étions bien nourris; **the animals are fed a diet of nuts and fruit**, les animaux sont nourris de noisettes et de fruits; **we were fed bread and water**, on nous donnait de l'eau et du pain; **field that feeds three cows**, champ qui nourrit trois vaches; **manure feeds the ground**, le fumier nourrit la terre; **to f. the mind**, nourrir l'esprit;
(b) *Tech* alimenter (*une machine, le feu etc*); charger (*un fourneau etc*); *Comptr* faire avancer, alimenter (*une feuille*); *Fb etc* **to f. the forwards**, alimenter les avants;
(c) *Th* donner la réplique à (*un acteur*).
2 *vi* manger; (*of cattle, sheep*) paître, brouter; **to f. on sth**, se nourrir *ou* vivre de qch.
►**feed back** *vtsep* (*information*) envoyer.
►**feed in** *vtsep Comptr* introduire en machine *ou* en mémoire; **to f. sth into the computer**, entrer qch dans l'ordinateur, mettre qch en mémoire.
►**feed up** *vtsep* **(a)** engraisser (*les animaux*); **(b)** *see* **FED UP**
feedback ['fiːdbæk] *n Electron etc* réaction *f*, rétroaction *f*, *F* feed-back *m inv*; *Comptr* réaction, rétroaction; *Fig* (*reaction*) écho *m*; **we haven't had much f.**, nous n'avons pas eu beaucoup d'écho.
feeder ['fiːdər] *n* **(a)** (*person*) nourrisseur *m* (*de bestiaux*); *Ind* alimenteur, -euse (*d'une machine etc*); chargeur, -euse (*d'un fourneau etc*); (*eater*) mangeur, -euse; **heavy f.**, gros mangeur; **(b)** bavette *f*, bavoir *m* (*d'enfant*); **(c)** *Geog* affluent *m* (*d'un cours d'eau*); *HydE* canal *m* d'alimentation *ou* d'amenée; (*road*) route *f* de raccordement; *Rail* embranchement *m*; canalisation *f* (*de gaz etc*); *El* câble *m ou* ligne *f* d'alimentation.
feeding ['fiːdɪŋ] *n* **(a)** alimentation *f* (*de qn, d'une machine etc*); affourragement *m* (*des bestiaux*); **force(d) f.**, gavage *m*; *Med* **f. cup**, biberon *m*, canard *m*; **f. frenzy**, (*of sharks*) = frénésie causée par la présence de nourriture; *Ind* **f. mechanism**, mécanisme alimentateur; **f. time**, (*at zoo etc*) (heure *f* des) repas *mpl*; **(b)** *MecE* avance *f*, avancement *m* (*du travail à l'outil, de l'outil au travail etc*).
feel¹ [fiːl] **(a)** (*act of touching*) toucher *m*; **rough to the f.**, rude au toucher; **to have a f. of sth**, toucher qch, tâter qch; **to have a f. in a drawer for sth**, chercher qch à tâtons dans un tiroir; **(b)** (*texture*) toucher *m*, manier *m* (*du papier etc*); **to recognize sth by the f. of it**, reconnaître qch au toucher; **(c)** (*sensation*) sensation *f*; **the f. of a collar round my neck**, la sensation d'un faux-col autour de mon cou; **(d)** (*knack*) **he has the f. of his car**, il a sa voiture bien en main; **you'll soon get the f. of the work**, vous allez bientôt vous habituer au travail; **to have a f. for translation**, avoir le sens de la traduction; **you need to have a f. for it**, il faut l'avoir en soi.
feel² *v* (*pt & pp* **felt** [felt]) **1** *vt* **(a)** (*touch*) toucher (*qch avec la main*); tâter (*le pouls etc*); palper (*un organe*); **to f. one's way**, (*in darkness*) avancer *ou* marcher à tâtons; *Fig* explorer le terrain, y aller doucement; **to f. one's way towards sth**, avancer vers qch à tâtons;
(b) (*be conscious of, experience*) sentir (*qch*); éprouver (*de l'amertume, de la douleur etc*); ressentir (*une injure, de la pitié, de la joie*); **I felt the floor trembling**, j'ai senti trembler le sol; **she felt his arms around her**, elle sentait ses bras l'entourant; **f. the weight of that!**, (*how light it is*) vois comment c'est léger!; (*how heavy it is*) vois comment c'est lourd!; **to f. the heat**, être sensible à la chaleur; **to f. the cold**, être sensible au froid, être frileux; **to make one's authority felt**, affirmer son autorité, faire sentir son autorité; **she felt nothing, only emptiness**, elle ne ressentait rien, seulement un vide; **do you f. anything for her?**, est-ce que tu éprouves *ou* ressens quelque chose à son égard?; **I f. it in my bones that I shall succeed**, quelque chose me dit que je réussirai; **I felt it necessary to intervene**, j'ai jugé nécessaire d'intervenir; **what do you f. about ...?**, qu'est-ce que vous pensez de ...?; **what I f. about it is ...**, mon sentiment là-dessus, c'est que ...; **I felt that he could have tried harder**, j'avais le sentiment qu'il aurait pu faire plus d'efforts; **to f. a fool**, se sentir bête *ou* stupide; **to f. a new woman/man**, se sentir comme neuve/neuf;
2 *vi* **(a)** (*of person*) **to f. hot/cold**, avoir chaud/froid; **to f. ill/tired**, se sentir malade/fatigué; **I f. really stupid**, je me sens vraiment stupide; **to f. sick**, *Br* avoir envie de vomir; *Am* ne pas se sentir bien, se sentir malade; **they felt betrayed**, ils se sont sentis trahis; **my foot feels better**, mon pied va mieux; **how do you f.?, how are you feeling?**, comment te sens-tu?; **to f. all the better for it**, s'en trouver mieux; **I f. ten years younger**, je me sens dix ans de moins; **not to f. oneself**, ne pas être dans son assiette; **I f. quite myself again**, je me sens tout à fait rétabli; **to f. up to doing sth**, (*well enough*) se sentir assez bien pour faire qch; (*competent enough*) se sentir de taille à faire qch; **to f. certain that ...**, être certain que ...; **how would you f. if I were to offer you a job in Japan?**, qu'est-ce que vous diriez si je vous offrais un emploi au Japon?; **how would you f. if she left you?**, qu'est-ce que tu ressentirais si elle te quittait?; **how do you think I f.?**, (*that's a stupid question*) qu'est-ce que tu crois?; **how would YOU f.?**, (*if s.o. did that to you*) qu'est-ce que tu ressentirais?; **she feels strongly about fox-hunting**, elle est fortement opposée à la chasse au renard; **I f. as if ...**, j'ai l'impression que ...; **I felt as if I'd seen him before**, j'avais l'impression de l'avoir déjà vu; **I felt as if** *or F* **like I was wasting my time**, j'avais l'impression de perdre mon temps; **to f. like doing sth**, se sentir d'humeur à faire qch; **I felt like crying**, j'avais envie de pleurer; **if you f. like it**, si le cœur vous en dit; **I don't f. like it**, ça ne me dit rien; **I f. like a cup of tea**, j'ai envie d'une tasse de thé; **I f. like going home**, j'ai envie de rentrer à la maison; **to f. like a fool**, se sentir bête *ou* stupide; **to f. like a new man/woman**, se sentir comme neuf/neuve;
(b) (*of things*) **to f. hard/soft**, être dur/doux au toucher; **the wall/her forehead felt hot**, le mur/son front était chaud au toucher; **my hands f. cold**, j'ai froid aux mains; **my arm feels as if it's broken**, j'ai l'impression que je me suis cassé le bras; **the room feels damp**, la pièce (me) paraît humide; **it feels like ...**, cela donne la sensation de ...; **it felt good to be alive**, c'était bon d'être en vie; **what**

did it f. like when you won?, qu'est-ce que vous avez ressenti en gagnant?
(c) *(explore, touch with fingers)* **to f. in one's pockets for sth,** chercher qch dans ses poches; **in the dark he felt on the ground for the key,** il cherchait ses clefs à tâtons sur le sol.

►feel about, feel around *vi (search by touching)* chercher à tâtons; **to f. about** *or* **around for sth,** chercher qch à tâtons.

►feel for *vipo* **(a)** *(feel sympathy for)* éprouver de la compassion à l'égard de *(qn)*; **I f. for her,** elle a toute ma sympathie; **to feel for s.o. in their sorrow,** partager la douleur de qn; **(b)** *(search for by touch)* chercher *(qch)* à tâtons.

►feel up *vtsep Sl (touch sexually)* peloter *(qn)*.

feeler ['fiːlər] *n* **(a)** *Biol* antenne *f (d'un insecte etc)*; corne *f (d'escargot)*; tentacule *m (d'un mollusque etc)*; **(b)** *Fig (tentative enquiry etc)* ballon *m* d'essai; **to put out feelers,** lancer un ballon d'essai, tâter le terrain; **peace feelers,** sondages *mpl* de paix; **(c)** *MecE* **f. (gauge),** calibre *m* d'épaisseur (à lames).

feeling ['fiːlɪŋ] **1** *adj (person)* sensible.
2 *n* **(a)** *(act of touching)* fait *m* de tâter;
(b) *(sense)* **(sense of) f.,** toucher *m*; **to have no f. in one's arm,** avoir le bras mort;
(c) *(sensation)* sensation *f (douloureuse, de froid etc)*;
(d) *(emotion)* sentiment *m*; **his feelings towards me,** ses sentiments envers moi; **public f. ran high against the proposal,** le sentiment populaire s'élevait contre cette proposition; **feelings are running very high,** les esprits sont très échauffés; **what are your feelings about fox-hunting?,** qu'est-ce que vous pensez de la chasse au renard?; **I don't have any strong feelings about it,** ça m'est plus ou moins égal; **no hard feelings!,** sans rancune!; **to have no feelings,** n'avoir aucun cœur; **to suppress one's feelings,** refouler ses sentiments; **with f.,** *(parler etc) (emotionally)* avec émotion; *(angrily)* avec emportement; *(chanter etc)* avec âme; **I had a f. I might find you here,** je pensais bien vous trouver ici; **I've got a nasty** *or* **unpleasant f. that ...,** j'ai la désagréable impression que ...; **I had a f. of danger,** j'avais le sentiment d'être en danger; **she had a f. of elation,** elle éprouvait un sentiment d'allégresse; **I know the f.!,** je sais ce que c'est!; **I've got that Monday morning f.,** je suis dans cet état d'âme propre à lundi matin; **there is a general f. that ...,** l'impression règne (dans le public) que ...;
(e) *(sensitivity)* sensibilité *f*; **to have a f. for music/nature,** être sensible à la musique/la nature; **to have a f. for sth,** *(do well)* avoir qch en soi.

feelingly ['fiːlɪŋlɪ] *adv* avec émotion.

feet *see* **FOOT**[1].

feign [feɪn] *vt* feindre, simuler *(une maladie etc)*; affecter *(la surprise)*; **to f. sleep,** faire semblant de dormir.

feigned [feɪnd] *adj (illness)* simulé; *(surprise)* feint.

feint[1] [feɪnt] *n Mil* fausse attaque; *Boxing Fencing etc* feinte *f*; **his anger is only a f.,** sa colère n'est qu'une simulation.

feint[2] *vi Mil* faire une fausse attaque; *Boxing etc* feinter; *Boxing* **to f. with the right,** feinter du droit.

feint[3] *n (narrow rule)* **f.-ruled paper,** papier réglé.

feistiness ['faɪstɪnəs] *n esp Am (of person)* caractère plein d'entrain.

feisty ['faɪstɪ] *adj esp Am (person)* plein d'entrain.

feldspar ['feldspɑːr] *n Miner* feldspath *m*.

felicitous [fɪ'lɪsɪtəs] *adj* heureux; *(word etc)* bien trouvé, à propos; **f. in one's choice of words,** heureux dans le choix de ses mots.

felicity [fɪ'lɪsɪtɪ] *n* **(a)** *Fml & Lit* félicité *f*, bonheur *m*; **(b)** à-propos *m*, bien-trouvé *m (d'une observation etc)*.

feline ['fiːlaɪn] **1** *adj* félin; **f. grace,** grâce féline, grâce de chat. **2** *n* félin *m*.

fell[1] [fel] *vt* abattre, terrasser *(un adversaire etc)*; abattre, couper *(un arbre)*; **felled wood** *or* **timber,** abattis *m*, bois gisant, vente *f*.

fell[2] *see* **FALL**[2].

fell[3] *adj Arch & Lit (person etc)* féroce; *(thing)* sinistre; **at one f. swoop,** d'un seul coup.

fell[4] *n Eng Scot Dial* colline *ou* montagne rocheuse.

fell[5] *n* peau *f (de bête)*.

fella, feller ['felə, -ər] *n F* mec *m*, type *m*; *Br Dial (boyfriend)* copain *m*, *Can* chum *m*.

felling ['felɪŋ] *n* abattage *m (d'un bœuf)*; abattage, coupe *f (de bois)*.

fellow ['feləʊ] *n* **(a)** *(comrade)* camarade *m*, compagnon *m*; **f. being** *or* **creature,** semblable *mf*; **f. citizen,** concitoyen, -enne; **f. countryman** *or* **countrywoman,** compatriote *mf*; **f. feeling,** sympathie *f*; **f. passenger/sufferer,** compagnon de voyage/misère; **f. soldier,** compagnon d'armes, camarade de régiment; **f. student,** camarade *mf* d'études; **f. traveller,** *(on train etc) & Pol* compagnon *m* de route;
(b) *(colleague)* semblable *m*, pareil *m*; *(one of a pair)* pendant *m*; **a vase and its f.,** un vase et son pendant;
(c) *(at university) (professor)* = professeur permanent; *(postgraduate student)* chargé, -ée de cours; *(of learned society)* membre *m*; **F. of the Royal Society,** = membre de la Société royale (de Londres);
(d) *F (boyfriend)* copain *m*, *Can* chum *m*;
(e) *Old-fashioned F* homme *m*; **a good f.,** un brave garçon; **a decent f.,** un bon gars; **he's a queer f.,** c'est un drôle de type; **the poor little f.,** le pauvre petit.

fellowship ['feləʊʃɪp] *n* **(a)** *(friendship)* **(good) f.,** amitié *f*, camaraderie *f*; **(b)** *(association)* association *f*, corporation *f*; **(c)** *(at university)* bourse *f* universitaire *(avec obligation de faire un cours, des recherches)*; *(of learned society)* titre *m* de membre.

felon ['felən] *n Jur Arch* criminel, -elle.

felonious [fe'ləʊnɪəs] *adj Jur Arch* criminel; **f. act,** action qui constitue un crime.

felony ['felənɪ] *n Jur Arch* crime *m*; **to compound a f.,** pactiser avec un crime.

felspar ['felspɑːr] *n* = **FELDSPAR**.

felt[1] [felt] *n Tex etc* feutre *m*; **roofing f., tarred f.,** feutre bitumé.

felt[2] *vt Tex* feutrer *(de la laine, des poils)*; *Constr* couvrir *(un toit etc)* de feutre bitumé.

felt[3] *see* **FEEL**[2].

felt-tip ['felt'tɪp] *n* **f.-t. (pen),** crayon *m* feutre.

female ['fiːmeɪl] **1** *adj (person)* féminin; *(voix etc)* de femme; *(animal, plant etc)* femelle; *Tech* femelle; *Tech* **male-f. coupling/connection/adapter,** accouplement *m*/accordement *m*/adaptateur *m* mâle-femelle; **male and f. patients,** malades hommes et femmes; *Jur* **male and f. heirs,** héritiers *mpl* mâles et femelles; **f. screw,** écrou *m*. **2** *n* **(a)** *Jur (person)* femme *f*; *F Pej* gonzesse *f*; **f. impersonator,** travesti *m*; **(b)** *(animal, plant)* femelle *f*.

feminine ['femɪnɪn] **1** *adj* féminin; **this word is f.,** ce mot est féminin. **2** *n Gram* féminin *m*; **in the f.,** au féminin.

femininity [femɪ'nɪnɪtɪ] *n* féminité *f*.

feminism ['femɪnɪzəm] *n* féminisme *m*.

feminist ['femɪnɪst] *adj & n* féministe *mf*.

femoral ['femərəl] *adj Anat* fémoral, -aux.

femur, *pl* **femurs, femora** ['fiːmər, -əz, 'femərə] *n Anat* fémur *m*.

fen [fen] *n* marais *m*, marécage *m*; **the Fens,** = les plaines marécageuses de l'Angleterre de l'est.

fence[1] [fens] *n* **(a)** *(for delimiting an area)* clôture *f*; *(more solid, for preventing entry)* barrière *f*; **wire f.,** clôture en fil métallique; **electric f.,** clôture électrique; **sunk f.,** saut *m* de loup; *Fig* **to sit on the f.,** ménager la chèvre et le chou; **to be on the other side of the f.,** être de l'autre côté de la barricade; *Pol* être du parti opposé; *esp Am Fig* **to mend one's fences,** *(of politician)* regagner la confiance des gens; *Am Fig* **to mend one's fences with s.o.,** *(of individual)* se remettre en bons termes avec qn; **f. post,** poteau *m* de clôture; **(b)** *Horseriding (in steeplechasing)* obstacle *m*, haie *f*; *(in showjumping)* obstacle, barrière *f*; **to put a horse over the fences,** mettre un cheval sur les obstacles; **(c)** *Tech* guide *m (d'une scie circulaire etc)*; garde *f (d'une machine-outil etc)*; **(d)** *Sl (receiver of stolen property)* receleur, -euse *(d'objets volés)*.

fence[2] **1** *vt* clôturer *(un jardin)*. **2** *vi* **(a)** *Sp* faire de l'escrime; *Fig* **to f. with a counsel,** répondre en éludant les questions d'un avocat; *Fig* **stop fencing!,** arrête d'éluder la question!; **(b)** *Sl (receive stolen property)* faire du recel.

►fence in *vtsep* clôturer *(un terrain etc)*.

►fence off *vtsep* séparer par une clôture; **to f. off one corner of a field,** séparer un coin d'un champ par une clôture.

fence-mending ['fensmendɪŋ] *n esp Am Fig* reprise *f* des relations.

fencer ['fensər] *n Sp* escrimeur *m*.

fencing ['fensɪŋ] *n* **(a)** *(barrier etc)* clôture *f*, barrière *f*; *(material)* matériaux *mpl* pour clôture; **wire f.,** treillage *m* en fil de fer; **(b)** action *f* de clôturer *(un terrain etc)*; **(c)** *Sp* escrime *f*; **f. bout,** assaut *m* d'armes; **f. school,** école *f* d'escrime; **(d)** *Sl (receiving)* recel *m*.

fend [fend] *vi* **to f. for oneself,** se débrouiller.

►fend off *vtsep* parer, détourner *(un coup etc)*; parer (*une attaque*).

fender ['fendər] *n Nau* bourrelet *m* de défense; *Am Aut* garde-boue *m inv*; (*protecting wall, door, post etc*) bouteroue *f*; *Am Rail* pare-choc(s) *m inv* (*de locomotive, de tramway*); (*for clearing track*) chasse-pierres *m inv*; (*for fireplace*) garde-cendre *m inv*; *Am Aut F* **it was just a f. bender,** (*minor accident*) il y a eu de la tôle froissée.

fenland ['fenlænd] *n* pays marécageux.

fennel ['fen(ə)l] *n Bot Culin* fenouil *m*; **sweet f.,** fenouil officinal.

feral ['ferəl] *adj Fml* (*cat, dog etc*) devenu sauvage.

ferment¹ ['fɜːment] *n* **(a)** (*yeast etc*) ferment *m*; **(b)** fermentation *f* (*des liquides*); *Fig* (*commotion*) effervescence *f*, agitation *f*; **the whole town was in a (state of) f.,** toute la ville était en effervescence *ou* dans un état d'agitation.

ferment² [fə'ment] **1** *vi* (*of liquids etc, Fig of sedition*) fermenter; (*of wine*) travailler. **2** *vt* fermenter (*un liquide etc*).

fermentation [fɜːmen'teɪʃən] *n* fermentation *f* (*d'un liquide etc*); travail *m* (*du vin*); *Fig* agitation *f*.

fern [fɜːn] *n* (*plant*) fougère *f*; **hillside covered with f.,** coteau couvert de fougères.

ferocious [fə'rəʊʃəs] *adj* (*animal, person, look etc*) féroce.

ferociously [fə'rəʊʃəslɪ] *adv* férocement, avec férocité.

ferocity [fə'rɒsɪtɪ] *n* férocité *f*.

ferret¹ ['ferɪt] *n* (*animal*) furet *m*.

ferret² *v* (-t-) **1** *vi* **(a)** chasser au furet; **(b)** *F* **to f. (about) in one's pockets,** fureter *ou* fouiller dans ses poches (**for sth,** pour trouver qch). **2** *vt* chasser (*les lapins etc*) au furet.

▶**ferret out** *vtsep* (*dislodge*) dénicher (*qn, qch*); déterrer (*un secret*).

ferreting ['ferɪtɪŋ] *n* chasse *f* au furet.

ferrety ['ferɪtɪ] *adj* de furet; *Pej* **f. eyes,** yeux *mpl* de fouine.

ferric ['ferɪk] *adj Ch* ferrique; **f. ammonium salt,** sel *m* ferrico-ammonique.

Ferris wheel ['ferɪswiːl] *n* grande roue (*dans les parcs d'attractions*).

ferrite ['feraɪt] *n* ferrite *m*.

ferroconcrete ['ferəʊ'kɒŋkriːt] *n* béton armé.

ferromagnetic ['ferəʊmæg'netɪk] *adj* ferromagnétique.

ferrous ['ferəs] *adj Ch* (*oxyde etc*) ferreux; **f. sulphide,** pyrite *f* de fer.

ferrule ['ferəl, -uːl] *n* bout ferré, embout *m* (*de canne*); frette *f* (*d'un manche d'outil etc*).

ferry¹ ['ferɪ] *n* (*boat*) bac *m*, ferry *m*; **to take the f.,** prendre le bac; **passenger/car f.,** bac à piétons/à voitures; **train f.,** bac transbordeur; **air f.,** avion transbordeur; *Jur* **f. (right),** droit *m* de bac; **f. service,** ligne *f* de bac *ou* de ferry.

ferry² *vt* **to f. s.o./a car across a river,** passer qn/une voiture en bac *ou* en ferry de l'autre côté de la rivière; **he spent the day ferrying voters to the polls,** il a passé la journée à transporter des électeurs aux urnes.

ferryboat ['ferɪbəʊt] *n* bac *m*, ferry *m*.

ferrying ['ferɪɪŋ] *n* transport *m* en *ou* par bac *ou* ferry; **f. across,** passage *m* en bac *ou* en ferry.

ferryman, *pl* **-men** ['ferɪmən] *n* passeur *m*.

fertile ['fɜːtaɪl] *adj* (*sol, femme etc*) fertile, fécond (**in,** en); (*man*) fécond; (*œuf*) fécondé; productif (**of,** de); **f. imagination,** imagination *f* fertile.

fertility [fɜː'tɪlɪtɪ] *n* fertilité *f*, fécondité *f* (*du sol, de l'imagination de qn, d'une femme etc*); productivité *f* (*du sol*); **f. drug,** médicament *m* de traitement de la stérilité; **f. symbol,** symbole *m* de fertilité.

fertilization [fɜːtɪlaɪ'zeɪʃən] *n* fertilisation *f*, fécondation *f* (*d'un œuf etc*); *Biol* **self f.,** autofécondation *f*.

fertilize ['fɜːtɪlaɪz] *vt* **(a)** fertiliser, féconder (*un œuf, une plante etc*); *Bot* **to cross-f.,** hybrider (*deux espèces*); **(b)** fertiliser, engraisser (*le sol*).

fertilizer ['fɜːtɪlaɪzər] *n Agr* engrais *m*; **artificial fertilizers,** engrais chimiques.

fervent ['fɜːvənt] *adj* (*prayer, supporter*) ardent, fervent; (*wish*) ardent.

fervently ['fɜːvəntlɪ] *adv* (*prier etc*) avec ferveur; (*désirer etc*) avec ardeur.

fervour, *US* **fervor** ['fɜːvər] *n* (*of prayer, supporter*) ferveur *f*, ardeur *f*; (*of wish*) ardeur.

fescue ['feskjuː] *n Bot* **f. (grass),** fétuque *f*.

fess(e) [fes] *n Her* fasce *f*.

fester ['festər] *vi* (*of wound etc*) suppurer, s'envenimer; (*of resentment etc*) couver.

festering ['festərɪŋ] **1** *adj* (*wound etc*) ulcéreux, suppurant; (*resentment*) qui couve. **2** *n* suppuration *f*, ulcération *f* (*d'une blessure etc*).

festival ['festɪv(ə)l] *n* (*of music, drama etc*) festival *m*, -als; fête *f*; *esp Rel* **harvest f.,** = office d'action de grâces (célébré après la rentrée des récoltes); **film f.,** festival du film; **street f.,** fête de quartier.

festive ['festɪv] *adj* (*jour etc*) de fête; (*table etc*) de festin; **the f. season,** l'époque *f* des fêtes; **to be in f. mood,** (*person*) avoir le cœur en fête.

festivity [fes'tɪvɪtɪ] *n* fête *f*, réjouissance *f*, festivité *f*; **festivities,** festivités, réjouissances.

festoon¹ [fes'tuːn] *n* feston *m*, guirlande *f*.

festoon² *vt* festonner (*qch*) (**with,** de); disposer (*des fleurs etc*) en festons.

feta ['feta] *n* **f. (cheese),** feta *f*.

fetal ['fiːt(ə)l] *adj* = **FOETAL.**

fetch [fetʃ] **1** *vt* **(a)** (*go to get*) aller chercher (*qn, qch*); **to f. water from the river,** aller puiser de l'eau dans la rivière; **to f. s.o. from the airport,** aller chercher qn à l'aéroport; **I'll f. you,** je viendrai te chercher; **(b)** *Com etc* rapporter; atteindre (*un certain prix*); **it fetched a high price,** cela s'est vendu cher; **(c)** (*hit*) **to f. s.o. a blow,** flanquer un coup à qn; **(d)** (*utter*) pousser (*un soupir, un gémissement*). **2** *vi* **f.!,** (*to dog*) va chercher!; **I'm not going to f. and carry for you!,** je ne vais pas être ta bonne à tout faire!

▶**fetch back** *vtsep* (*bring back*) ramener (*qn*); rapporter (*qch*).

▶**fetch up 1** *vi Nau* (*reach*) **to f. up at a port,** parvenir *ou* arriver à un port; *F* **they finally fetched up at our house,** ils ont finalement abouti chez nous; **the car fetched up against a wall,** la voiture s'est (finalement) arrêtée en heurtant un mur. **2** *vtsep* **(a)** (*bring from lower place*) faire monter (*qn, qch*); **(b)** *F* (*vomit*) dégueuler.

fetching ['fetʃɪŋ] *adj* (*sourire, air*) séduisant, attrayant; (*chapeau*) ravissant.

fête¹ [feɪt] *n* fête *f*; **village f.,** fête communale.

fête² *vt* fêter (*qn, un événement*); faire fête à (*qn*).

fetid ['fetɪd, 'fiːtɪd] *adj* fétide, puant.

fetish ['fetɪʃ] *n Psy* fétiche *m*; *F* **he has a f. for black silk,** il est obsédé par la soie noire; *F* **to make a f. of sth,** être obsédé par qch.

fetishism ['fetɪʃɪzəm] *n Psy* fétichisme *m*.

fetishist ['fetɪʃɪst] *n Psy* fétichiste *mf*.

fetishistic [fetɪ'ʃɪstɪk] *adj Psy* fétichiste.

fetlock ['fetlɒk] *n* fanon *m* (*du cheval*); **f. joint,** boulet *m*.

fetter¹ ['fetər] *n usu pl* **fetters,** chaînes *fpl*, fers *mpl* (*d'un prisonnier etc*); **in fetters,** enchaîné, dans les fers; **to burst one's fetters,** rompre ses liens *ou* ses fers.

fetter² *vt* enchaîner (*qn*); entraver (*un cheval*).

fettle¹ ['fet(ə)l] *n* **to be in fine** *or* **good f.,** être en condition *ou* en forme.

fettle² *vt Metal Cer etc* ébarber, ébavurer.

fetus ['fiːtəs] *n* = **FOETUS.**

feud¹ [fjuːd] *n* inimitié *f* (*entre familles, clans etc*); **family** *or* **blood f.,** vendetta *f*.

feud² *vi* se quereller (**over,** au sujet de).

feudal ['fjuːd(ə)l] *adj Hist* (*régime, service etc*) féodal, -aux; *Pej* (*attitude, approach to sth*) moyenâgeux.

feudalism ['fjuːdəlɪz(ə)m] *n* le système féodal.

feudally ['fjuːd(ə)lɪ] *adv* féodalement.

fever ['fiːvər] *n Med* (*high temperature, disease*) fièvre *f*; **high f.,** forte fièvre; **she's got a f.,** elle a de la fièvre; **yellow f.,** fièvre jaune; **hay f.,** rhume *m* des foins; **scarlet f.,** scarlatine *f*; *Vet* **swine f.,** rouget *m* du porc; *Fig* **f. of joy/excitement,** joie/excitation fébrile *ou* fiévreuse; **expectation had reached f. pitch,** l'attente était fiévreuse; **things are at f. pitch,** l'atmosphère est enfiévrée; **gold f.,** fièvre de l'or.

fevered ['fiːvəd] *adj* enfiévré, fiévreux; **a f. imagination,** une imagination enfiévrée.

feverish ['fiːvərɪʃ] *adj Med* fiévreux, fébrile; **to feel f.,** se sentir fiévreux; *Fig* **f. activity,** activité fébrile *ou* fiévreuse.

feverishly ['fiːvərɪʃlɪ] *adv* fiévreusement, fébrilement.

feverishness ['fiːvərɪʃnɪs] *n* état *m* fébrile.

few [fjuː] **1** *adj* **(a)** (*not many*) peu de (*personnes, choses*); **to have f. friends,** avoir peu d'amis; **very f. opportunities,** très peu d'occasions; **with f. exceptions,** à de rares exceptions près; **on the f. occasions I've spoken to her,** les rares fois où je lui ai parlé; **his visits are f. and far between,** ses visites sont rarissimes; **trains every f. minutes,** trains toutes les deux ou trois minutes; **every f. days,** tous les deux ou trois jours; **too f. points,** pas suffisamment de points; **those that met him are f.,** peu sont ceux qui l'ont rencontré; **f. in number,** peu nombreux;

f. novelists have equalled her, peu de romanciers l'ont égalée;

(b) (*some*) **a f.,** quelques; **I have only a f. pounds,** je n'ai que quelques livres; **he had a good f. enemies,** il avait pas mal d'ennemis; **in a f. minutes,** dans quelques minutes; **quite a f. minutes passed,** plusieurs minutes se sont écoulées; **in the next f. days,** dans les jours qui suivent *ou* suivaient.

2 *pron* **(a)** (*not many*) peu (*de gens etc*); **there are very/too f. of us,** nous sommes peu/trop peu nombreux; **f. (of them) could speak French,** peu parmi eux parlaient français; **there are so f. of them,** ils sont tellement peu nombreux;

(b) (*some*) **a f. of these cakes/oranges,** quelques-uns de ces gâteaux/quelques-unes de ces oranges; **a f. of the survivors,** quelques-uns des survivants; **I know a f. of them,** j'en connais quelques-uns; **a f. of us,** quelques-uns d'entre nous; **I've seen/read a f.,** j'en ai vu/lu quelques-uns; *F* **you've had a f. too many,** tu as bu un peu trop; **she only knew a f. (of them),** elle ne connaissait que quelques-uns d'entre eux.

3 *n* **the f.,** (*used as pl*) la minorité; **the fortunate f.,** les heureux élus.

fewer ['fjuːər] **1** *adj* (*comp of* **few**) moins (de); **there are f. trees here,** il y a moins d'arbres ici; **no f. than thirty,** pas moins de trente; **the houses became f.,** les maisons devenaient plus rares *ou* moins nombreuses; **f. and f. people,** de moins en moins de gens. **2** *pron* moins; **there are f. (of them) than I thought,** il y en a moins que je n'avais pensé.

fewest ['fjuːɪst] **1** *adj* (*superl of* **few**) le moins (de); **the f. people possible,** le moins de gens possible; **the area where there are the f. houses,** la région où il y a moins de maisons. **2** *pron* **the region where the f. live,** la région où vit le moins grand nombre de gens.

fey [feɪ] *adj* **(a)** *Scot* (*foreseeing death*) qui a des pressentiments de mort *ou* des visions de l'au-delà; (*having second sight*) qui est doué de seconde vue; **(b)** (*silly*) un peu idiot.

fez [fez] *n* (*hat*) fez *m*.

fiancé, *f* **fiancée** [fɪ'ɒnseɪ] *n* fiancé, -ée.

fiasco [fɪ'æskəʊ] *n* fiasco *m*; **to be a f.,** (*of play*) faire un four, être un fiasco.

fib¹ [fɪb] *n F* petit mensonge; **you're telling me fibs,** tu me racontes des histoires.

fib² *vi* **(-bb-)** *F* (*lie*) dire des petits mensonges *ou* des mensonges sans conséquence; **you're fibbing to me again,** tu es encore en train de me raconter des histoires.

fibber ['fɪbər] *n F* menteur, -euse.

fibre, *US* **fiber** ['faɪbər] *n* fibre *f*; *Metal* fibre, nerf *m* (*de l'acier*); **moral/muscle f.,** fibre musculaire/morale; **every f. of his being revolted at the idea,** chaque fibre de son être se révoltait à cette idée; *Tex* **man-made** *or* **synthetic f.,** fibre synthétique; **(dietary) f.,** fibres (alimentaires); **vegetable f.,** crin végétal; **wood f.,** fibre de bois; **glass f.,** fibre de verre; **a high-f. diet,** une alimentation riche en fibres; **f. optics,** technologie *f* des fibres optiques; **f. optic cable,** câble *m* en fibres optiques.

fibreboard, *US* **fiberboard** ['faɪbəbɔːd] *n* panneau *m* de fibres agglomérées.

fibreglass, *US* **fiberglass** ['faɪbəglɑːs] *n* fibre *f* de verre; **f. canoe,** canoë *m* en fibre de verre.

fibrescope, *US* **fiberscope** ['faɪbəskəʊp] *n Med Opt* fibroscope *m*.

fibrillation [faɪbrɪ'leɪʃən] *n* fibrillation *f*.

fibroid ['faɪbrɔɪd] **1** *adj* (*tumeur etc*) fibroïde. **2** *n Med* fibrome *m*.

fibroma, *pl* **-mata** [faɪ'brəʊmə, -mətə] *n Med* fibrome *m*.

fibrositis [faɪbrəʊ'saɪtɪs] *n Med* fibrosite *f*.

fibrous ['faɪbrəs] *adj* (*tissu etc*) fibreux.

fickle ['fɪk(ə)l] *adj* inconstant, volage, capricieux; (*caractère*) changeant, versatile.

fickleness ['fɪk(ə)lnɪs] *n* inconstance *f*, humeur *f* volage; **the f. of luck,** les caprices *mpl* de la chance.

fiction ['fɪkʃən] *n* **(a)** (*creation of imagination*) fiction *f*, création *f* de l'imagination; *Jur* **legal f.,** fiction légale; **these tales are pure f.,** tous ces contes sont totalement imaginaires; **(b)** (*in library, bookshop*) romans *mpl*; **light f.,** romans de lecture facile.

fictional ['fɪkʃən(ə)l] *adj* fictif.

fictionalize ['fɪkʃənəlaɪz] *vt* romancer.

fictitious [fɪk'tɪʃəs] *adj* **(a)** fictif; *Com* **f. assets,** actif fictif; **(b)** (*récit*) inventé.

fictitiously [fɪk'tɪʃəslɪ] *adv* fictivement.

fiddle¹ ['fɪd(ə)l] *n F* **(a)** (*violin*) violon *m*; (*musician*) (joueur, -euse de) violon; **bass f.,** contrebasse *f*; *Fig* **to play second f.,** jouer un rôle secondaire (**to s.o.,** auprès de qn); **(b)** (*swindle*) combine *f*; **to be on the f.,** faire du fricotage.

fiddle² **1** *vi* **(a)** (*play violin*) jouer du violon; *Pej* racler du violon; *Fig* **to f. while Rome burns,** = s'occuper de choses futiles au lieu de lutter contre une calamité; **(b)** (*play, fidget*) jouer avec, tripoter, trifouiller; **to f. with one's watch,** jouer avec sa montre; **don't f. with the switch,** laissez l'interrupteur tranquille, ne tripotez pas l'interrupteur; **she fiddled with a few knobs,** elle a manipulé quelques boutons; **(c)** *F* (*swindle*) combiner, fricoter. **2** *vt F* **(a)** (*tamper with*) bricoler (*un compteur etc*); **to f. the accounts,** truquer les comptes; **(b)** (*obtain dishonestly*) carotter; **he fiddled a week's leave,** il a carotté huit jours de permission.

fiddlededee [fɪd(ə)ldɪ'diː] *int Old-fashioned F* bah!, turlututu!

fiddle-faddle ['fɪd(ə)lfæd(ə)l] *F* **1** *n* bagatelles *fpl*, balivernes *fpl*, fadaises *fpl*. **2** *int* = **FIDDLEDEDEE**.

fiddler ['fɪdlər] *n F* **(a)** joueur *m* de violon, *Pej* violoneux *m*; **strolling f.,** violoneux *m*; **(b)** *Pej* (*swindler*) combinard, -arde.

fiddlesticks ['fɪd(ə)lstɪks] *int Old-fashioned* balivernes!, quelle blague!

fiddling ['fɪdlɪŋ] **1** *adj* **(a)** (*insignificant*) futile, insignifiant; **(b)** (*awkward*) (*task*) agaçant. **2** *n* **(a)** *F* raclage *m* (*de violon*); **(b)** (*fidgeting*) trifouillage *m*, tripotage *m*; **(c)** *F* (*dishonest dealing*) combines *fpl*, fricotage *m*.

fiddly ['fɪdlɪ] *adj* (*travail*) délicat, minutieux; **it was f. getting this nut off,** ça a été délicat d'enlever cet écrou.

fidelity [fɪ'delɪtɪ] *n* **(a)** fidélité *f* (*d'un ami etc*); loyauté *f* (*de qn*); **(b)** (*accuracy*) fidélité *f*, exactitude *f* (*d'une traduction*); **high f.,** haute fidélité.

fidget¹ ['fɪdʒɪt] *n* **(a)** (*usu pl*) **the fidgets,** l'agitation nerveuse; **to have the fidgets,** ne pas tenir en place; **(b)** (*person*) **he's a f.,** il ne tient pas en place; **what a f. you are!,** mais tiens-toi donc tranquille!

fidget² *vi* **(-t-)** remuer continuellement, ne pas tenir en place; (*become excited*) s'énerver; **don't f.!,** (*to child*) tiens-toi tranquille!

fidgetiness ['fɪdʒɪtɪnɪs] *n* agitation nerveuse.

fidgety ['fɪdʒɪtɪ] *adj* qui ne tient pas en place, qui remue continuellement; (*excited*) nerveux, impatient.

fiduciary [fɪ'djuːʃərɪ] **1** *adj Jur Fin* fiduciaire. **2** *n* héritier *m* fiduciaire; (*trustee*) dépositaire *m*.

fief [fiːf] *n Hist & Fig* fief *m*.

field¹ [fiːld] *n* **(a)** *Agr* champ *m*; *Agr* (*under pasture*) pré *m*; (*of oil, gas, coal, diamonds etc*) gisement *m*; **to work in the fields,** travailler dans les champs; **f. of wheat,** champ de blé; **strawberry f.,** plantation *f* de fraisiers; **in the open f.,** en plein champ; *Av* **landing f.,** terrain *m* d'atterrissage; *Am* **f. hockey,** hockey *m* sur gazon;

(b) *Mil* **f. (of battle),** champ *m* de bataille; **in the f.,** en campagne; **to hold the f.,** *Mil* (*of army*) se maintenir sur ses positions; (*of theory etc*) faire autorité; **to take the f.,** entrer en campagne; **f. of honour,** champ d'honneur; **f. artillery,** artillerie *f* de campagne; **f. battery,** batterie *f* de campagne; **f. day,** *Mil* jour *m* de grandes manœuvres *ou* de revue; *esp Am Sp* réunion *f* athlétique; *Fig* **to have a f. day,** (*enjoy oneself*) s'en donner à cœur joie; **f. exercise,** exercice *m* en campagne, manœuvre *f*; **f. glasses,** jumelles *mpl*; **f. gun,** canon *m* de campagne; **f. hospital,** ambulance *f* divisionnaire; **f. marshal,** maréchal *m*; **f. officer,** officier *m* supérieur; **f. rations,** ration *f* de guerre; **f. service,** service *m* en campagne; **f. telegraph,** télégraphe *m* militaire;

(c) *Sp* (*ground*) *Fb Cr etc* terrain *m*; (*baseball*) champ *m*; *Cr* (*bowlers*) les chasseurs *mpl*; **f. events,** (*in athletics*) concours *mpl*;

(d) (*in race*) *& Horseracing* **the f.,** les partants *mpl*; **big f.,** champ fourni; *Fig* **there are three candidates in the f.,** trois candidatures ont été déposées; **to lead the f.,** *Sp* mener le peloton; *Fig* (*of theory, ideas etc*) faire autorité; *F* **to play the f.,** (*in relationships*) ne pas mettre tous ses œufs dans le même panier;

(e) (*domain*) théâtre *m*, champ *m* (*d'opération etc*); domaine *m* (*d'une science*); *Com* marché *m* (*pour un produit*); **in the political f.,** sur le plan politique; **she is the leading artist in her f.,** elle est la plus grande artiste dans son domaine; **that's not my f.,** ce n'est pas mon domaine; **to work in the f.,** travailler sur le terrain; **to test a product in the f.,** essayer un produit sur le terrain; **f. engineer,** ingénieur *m* de chantier *ou* sur le terrain; **f. study,** étude *f* sur le terrain *ou* sur les lieux; **f. worker,**

travailleur *m* sur le terrain; **f. trials,** (*of vehicle*) essais *mpl* sur le terrain; *Sch etc* **f. trip,** voyage *m* d'étude (sur le terrain); **f. work,** (*research etc*) travaux *mpl ou* recherches *fpl* sur le terrain *ou* sur les lieux; *Min etc* exploration *f*; *Com* démarchage *m* auprès de la clientèle;

(f) *Opt Phot etc* champ *m*; **f. of view** *or* **of vision,** champ visuel; *Phys* **f. of force,** champ de force; **magnetic f.,** champ magnétique; **f. coil,** bobine *f* d'excitation *ou* d'inducteur, bobine inductrice;

(g) *Her* champ *m*, sol *m*; *Art* champ, fond *m* (*d'un tableau etc*); champ (*d'une médaille*);

(h) *Comptr* (*in database*) champ *m*.

field² **1** *vt* **(a)** *Sp* réunir (*une équipe*); *Mil etc* **to be able to f. 50,000 men,** pouvoir mettre 50 000 hommes en ligne; *Pol* **to f. 500 candidates,** présenter 500 candidats; **(b)** *Cr* **to f. a ball,** arrêter (et relancer) une balle (dans le champ). **2** *vi* *Cr* tenir le champ (pour relancer la balle).

fielder ['fiːldər] *n Cr etc* chasseur *m*.

fieldmouse, *pl* **-mice** ['fiːldmaʊs, -maɪs] *n* mulot *m*.

fiend [fiːnd] *n* **(a)** (*demon*) démon *m*, diable *m*; **(b)** (*evil person*) monstre *m* (de cruauté); **(c)** *F* (*fanatic*) **fresh-air f.,** maniaque *mf ou* fanatique *mf* du plein air; **dope f.,** toxicomane *mf*.

fiendish ['fiːndɪʃ] *adj* diabolique, satanique; *Fig* diabolique; **to take a f. pleasure in sth,** prendre un plaisir diabolique à qch.

fiendishly ['fiːndɪʃlɪ] *adv* diaboliquement; *F* **f. difficult,** d'une difficulté infernale; *F* **it was f. cold,** il faisait un froid de tous les diables.

fierce ['fɪəs] *adj* **(a)** (*person*) redoutable; (*animal*) féroce; (*fire etc*) ardent; (*battle, competition*) acharné; (*wind etc*) furieux, violent; **f. encounter,** rencontre violente; **there was f. criticism of the policy,** la politique a suscité des critiques violentes; **she was f. in her defence of him,** elle le défendait avec acharnement; **f. fighting,** lutte acharnée; *Aut etc* **f. brake,** frein brutal; **(b)** *Am F* (*unpleasant*) désagréable; **the weather has been f.,** il a fait un temps de chien.

fiercely ['fɪəslɪ] *adv* violemment; (*to defend, fight, criticize*) avec acharnement; **the sun beat down f.,** le soleil frappait très fort.

fierceness ['fɪəsnɪs] *n* violence *f*, véhémence *f* (*de qn*); férocité *f* (*d'un animal*); ardeur *f* (*du feu etc*); acharnement *m* (*d'une bataille*); fureur *f* (*du vent etc*); *Aut etc* brutalité *f* (*des freins*).

fieriness ['faɪərɪnɪs] *n* **(a)** ardeur *f* (*du soleil*); saveur cuisante (*d'une boisson spiritueuse*); **(b)** (*of character*) ardeur *f*, fougue *f*, impétuosité *f*, emportement *m*.

fiery ['faɪərɪ] *adj* **(a)** ardent, brûlant, enflammé; *esp US* **f. cross,** = symbole du Ku Klux Klan; **f. furnace,** fournaise ardente; **f. red,** rouge ardent, rouge feu; **f. sky,** ciel embrasé; **f. taste,** saveur cuisante; **(b)** (*person, character*) fougueux, emporté, impétueux, colérique; **to make f. speeches against s.o.,** vomir feu et flamme contre qn.

FIFA ['fiːfə] *n abbr* **Federation of International Football Associations.**

fife [faɪf] *n Mus* fifre *m*.

fifteen [fɪf'tiːn, 'fɪftiːn] *n* **(a)** quinze *m*; **she is f. (years old),** elle a quinze ans; **the plane will land at f. thirty (hours),** l'avion va atterrir à quinze heures trente; **(b)** *Rugby* **the French f.,** le quinze de France.

fifteenth [fɪf'tiːnθ, 'fɪftiːnθ] **1** *adj* quinzième; **Louis the F.,** Louis Quinze; **(on) the f. (of the month),** le quinze du mois. **2** *n* quinzième *m*.

fifth [fɪfθ] **1** *adj* cinquième; **Henry the F.,** Henri Cinq; *US Jur & Hum* **to plead the F. Amendment, to take the F. (Amendment),** = refuser de répondre pour ne pas dire quelque chose pouvant être utilisé contre soi; *Am* **to feel like a f. wheel,** avoir l'impression d'être la cinquième roue du carrosse; *Br Sch* **f. form,** = classe *f* de seconde; *Pol* **f. column,** cinquième colonne; **f. columnist,** personne affiliée à la cinquième colonne. **2** *n* **(a)** (*of month*) cinq *m*; **on the f.,** le cinq; **(b)** (*fraction*) cinquième *m*; **two fifths,** deux cinquièmes; **(c)** *Mus* quinte *f*.

fifth-generation ['fɪfθdʒenə'reɪʃən] *adj Comptr* de la cinquième génération.

fifthly ['fɪfθlɪ] *adv* cinquièmement.

fifth-rate ['fɪfθreɪt] *adj* médiocre.

fiftieth ['fɪftɪəθ] *adj & n* cinquantième *m*.

fifty ['fɪftɪ] *n* cinquante *m*; **f.-one,** cinquante et un; **f.-two,** cinquante-deux; **about f. books,** une cinquantaine de livres; **the fifties,** les années cinquante; **to be f.,** avoir cinquante ans; **to be in one's fifties,** avoir passé la cinquantaine.

fifty-fifty [fɪftɪ'fɪftɪ] *adj* (*partnership*) à parts égales; **to split the profits f.-f.,** partager les bénéfices à parts égales; **to go f.-f. on sth,** partager le coût de quelque chose à parts égales; **her chances are f.-f.,** (*of surviving*) elle a cinquante pour cent de chances de s'en tirer; (*of winning*) elle a cinquante pour cent de chances de gagner.

fig¹ [fɪg] *n* **(a)** (*fruit*) figue *f*; **green figs,** figues fraîches; **dried figs,** figues sèches; *Old-fashioned F* **he doesn't give** *or* **care a f. what you think,** il se fiche éperdument de ce que tu penses; *Old-fashioned F* **a f. for him!,** zut pour lui!; **f. leaf,** feuille *f* de figuier; *Art* feuille de vigne; **(b) f. (tree),** figuier *m*.

fig² *n* (*in book etc*) (*abbr* **figure**) fig; **see f. 21b,** voir fig 21b.

fight¹ [faɪt] *n Boxing Mil etc* combat *m*; (*argument*) dispute *f*; **hand to hand f.,** (lutte *f*) corps à corps *m*; **f. to the death,** lutte à mort; **they had a f.,** (*in which they hit each other*) ils se sont battus; (*they argued*) ils se sont disputés; **to get into a f. with s.o.,** se battre avec qn; (*argue*) se disputer avec qn; **do you want a f.?,** est-ce que tu veux te battre?; **the f. for life,** la lutte pour la vie; **her f. against cancer,** sa lutte contre le cancer; **to carry on a stubborn f. against s.o.,** soutenir une lutte opiniâtre contre qn; **to show f.,** résister, offrir de la résistance; **I won't give in without a f.,** je ne vais pas me laisser faire sans me battre; *Sp etc* **to put up a good f.,** bien se défendre; **there was no f. left in him,** il n'avait plus le cœur à se battre; *Boxing* **are you going to the f. tomorrow?,** est-ce que tu vas au combat demain?; **he still has a lot of f. left in him,** il n'a pas dit son dernier mot; **you'll have a f. on your hands,** (*it will be difficult*) tu vas avoir du mal; **the f. for the leadership of the party,** la lutte pour la tête du parti.

fight² *v* (*pt & pp* **fought** [fɔːt]) **1** *vi* (*physically*) se battre; (*struggle*) lutter; (*argue*) se disputer; *Mil* **he fought in Russia,** il s'est battu en Russie; **to f. against the enemy,** combattre l'ennemi; **to f. against adversity,** lutter contre l'adversité; **to f. against sleep,** lutter contre le sommeil; **to f. for s.o.,** se battre pour qn; **to f. for sth,** (*on behalf of*) se battre pour qch; (*to get something*) se battre pour avoir qch; **to f. for breath,** lutter pour reprendre souffle; **to f. for one's rights,** se battre pour ses droits; **she fought to clear her name,** elle s'est battue pour prouver son innocence; **two dogs fighting over a bone,** deux chiens qui se disputent un os; **to f. fair,** faire la bonne guerre; **they were fighting over some islands/who would sleep where,** ils se battaient pour des îles/pour décider qui allait dormir où; **to be fighting for one's life,** (*of someone seriously ill, competitor*) lutter pour sa vie; **to go down fighting,** se battre jusqu'au bout.

2 *vt* se battre avec *ou* contre (*qn*); combattre (*qn, un incendie, une maladie*); *Boxing* **to f. the champion,** affronter le champion; **I'll f. you in the courts,** je vous traînerai en justice; **I'll f. you for custody,** je ferai tout ce que je peux contre toi pour obtenir la garde des enfants; **to f. a battle,** livrer (une) bataille; **to f. the good fight,** combattre pour la bonne cause; **the match was fought yesterday,** le match s'est disputé hier; **to f. s.o.'s battles,** prendre le parti de qn; **I'm not going to f. your battles for you,** c'est à vous de vous débrouiller; **he fought his way through the crowd,** il se fraya un chemin à travers la foule; **to f. one's way (out),** se frayer un passage (pour sortir); **to f. one's way to the top,** (*of one's profession*) se battre pour atteindre le sommet; **to f. an action (at law),** se défendre dans un procès; **to f. an election,** se présenter à une élection; **she will be fighting a popular businessman,** (*in election*) elle s'opposera à un homme d'affaires populaire; **to f. an emotion,** lutter contre une émotion.

▶**fight back** **1** *vtsep* (*suppress*) lutter contre (*une émotion etc*); refouler (*ses larmes*); **to f. one's way back again,** remonter le courant. **2** *vi* (*retaliate*) résister; **to f. back against an illness,** lutter contre une maladie.

▶**fight down** *vtsep* (*suppress*) vaincre (*une passion, la résistance etc*).

▶**fight off** *vtsep* (*repel*) repousser (*l'ennemi, une attaque, les avances de quelqu'un*); résister (avec effort) à (*une maladie etc*); **to f. off one's fear,** lutter contre sa peur; **the singer had to f. off over-eager fans,** le chanteur a dû repousser des fans trop enthousiastes; **to f. off a cold with aspirin,** juguler un rhume à force d'aspirine.

▶**fight out** *vtas* **to f. it out,** se mesurer l'un à l'autre; **you'll have to f. that out with him,** tu régleras ça avec lui.

fighter ['faɪtər] *n* **(a)** (*person who fights*) combattant *m*; (*boxer*) boxeur *m*; *Fig* **she's a f.,** c'est une battante; **(b)** *Mil Av* **f. aircraft** *or* **plane,** chasseur *m*, avion *m* de chasse; **f.**

squadron/pilot, escadron *m*/pilote *m* de chasse.
fighter-bomber ['faɪtəbɒmər] *n* chasseur-bombardier *m*, *pl* chasseurs-bombardiers.
fighting ['faɪtɪŋ] **1** *adj* militant, de combat; *Mil* **f. men,** combattants *mpl*; **f. forces,** effectifs *mpl* sous les armes; **f. cock,** coq *m* de combat; *Mil* **f. unit,** unité combattante; **f. strength,** effectif *m* de combat; *F* **I still have a f. chance,** j'ai encore une chance si je résiste jusqu'au bout; **f. drunk,** dans un état d'ivresse agressive. **2** *n* combat *m*; *Boxing* pugilat *m*, boxe *f*; **close f.,** (lutte *f*) corps à corps *m*; **there was a lot of f. at my school,** il y avait beaucoup de bagarre dans mon école; **the f. on the eastern front,** les combats sur le front est; **to be f. fit,** être dans une forme éblouissante.
figment ['fɪgmənt] *n* fiction *f*, invention *f*; **figments of the imagination,** imaginations *fpl*; **it was a f. of your imagination,** tu l'as imaginé.
figuration [fɪgə'reɪʃən] *n* **(a)** figuration *f* (*d'une idée etc*); **(b)** (*representation*) représentation figurative; **(c)** *Mus* contrepoint fleuri.
figurative ['fɪgərətɪv] *adj* **(a)** (*language etc*) figuré, métaphorique; **in the f. sense,** au (sens) figuré; **(b)** (*art*) figuratif; **f. writing,** écriture *f* en images.
figuratively ['fɪgərətɪvlɪ] *adv* **(a)** (*to speak*) au figuré, métaphoriquement; **(b)** *Art Liter* figurativement.
figure¹ ['fɪgər, *Am* 'fɪgjər] *n* **(a)** (*number*) *Math etc* chiffre *m*; **it's difficult to give an exact f.,** il est difficile de donner un chiffre exact; **in round figures,** en chiffres ronds; **to carry a f.,** retenir un chiffre; **to be good at figures,** être bon en calcul; **f. of eight,** (*shape*) (figure *f* en forme de) huit *m*; **to draw figures of eight,** décrire des huits; **to fetch a high f.,** se vendre cher; **his score barely managed to get into double figures,** son score s'élevait tout juste à un nombre à deux chiffres; **our takings have reached four figures,** nous avons décroché les quatre chiffres; **figures,** détails chiffrés (*d'un projet etc*); (*statistics*) statistiques *fpl*; **the figures for 1975,** les statistiques de 1975; *Com* **sales figures,** chiffres de vente;
(b) (*shape*) figure *f*; (*of person*) taille *f*, silhouette *f*; **to have a good f.,** être bien fait de sa personne; (*of woman*) avoir une jolie silhouette; **to look after/keep one's f.,** soigner/garder sa ligne;
(c) (*human form*) forme humaine; **a fine f. of a man,** un bel homme; **a fine f. of a woman,** une belle femme;
(d) (*person, character*) personnage *m*; **a distinguished f.,** une personnalité; **a f. of fun,** un objet de ridicule; **he was a father f. to me,** il m'a tenu lieu de père;
(e) (*appearance*) figure *f*, apparence *f*, air *m*; **to cut a sorry f.,** faire piètre figure;
(f) *Art etc* image *f*, représentation *f* (*de la forme humaine*); **the central f. of a painting,** le personnage principal d'un tableau;
(g) (*illustration*) illustration *f* (*dans un livre*); **see f. 21b,** voir figure 21b; **geometrical f.,** figure *f* géométrique;
(h) (*pattern*) figure *f*; dessin *m* (*sur un tissu*); **the figures of a dance,** les figures d'une danse; **f. skating/skater,** patinage *m*/patineur, -euse artistique;
(i) f. of speech, (*expression*) façon *f* de parler; (*in rhetoric*) figure *f* de rhétorique; **it's just a f. of speech,** ce n'est qu'une façon de parler.
figure² **1** *vi* **(a)** (*appear*) figurer; **his name figures on the list,** son nom figure sur la liste; **(b)** (*calculate*) calculer; **(c)** *Am F* (*make sense*) sembler logique *ou* normal; **that figures,** ça colle. **2** *vt* **(a)** *Am* (*think*) penser; **I figured that she might be feeling lonely,** je me suis dit qu'elle se sentait peut-être seule; **(b)** *Am* (*estimate*) estimer, évaluer; **I f. that it will take three years,** j'estime que cela prendra trois ans; **(c)** (*put pattern on*) brocher, gaufrer (*la soie etc*); imprimer (*le coton etc*); **(d)** *Mus* chiffrer (*la basse*); **(e)** (*imagine*) figurer, représenter (*qn, un paysage etc*); **f. to yourself a happy family,** imaginez une famille heureuse.
►**figure on** *vipo Am F* compter sur, s'attendre à (*qch*); (*plan on*) compter sur (*qn*); **to f. on doing sth,** avoir l'intention de *ou* compter faire qch; **I didn't f. on this happening,** je ne m'attendais pas à ce que cela se produise; **he didn't f. on a woman for the position,** (*did not consider hiring one*) il ne pensait pas à une femme pour le poste; (*did not think one would get it*) il ne s'attendait pas à ce qu'une femme obtienne le poste.
►**figure out** *F* **1** *vtsep* (*work out*) calculer (*une somme*); résoudre (*un problème*); **he couldn't f. out what she meant,** il n'arrivait pas à comprendre ce qu'elle voulait dire; **we figured out that they must have paid more than we did,** nous avons réalisé qu'ils avaient dû payer plus que nous; **she can't f. you out at all,** elle n'arrive pas du tout à te comprendre. **2** *vi Am* **it will f. out at about $100,** cela coûtera une centaine de dollars.
►**figure up** *vi Am* (*amount*) **to f. up to sth,** s'élever à qch.
-figure ['fɪgər] *suff* **three/four/five/***etc***-f.,** à trois/quatre/cinq chiffres; **four-f. number,** nombre *m* à quatre chiffres.
figured ['fɪgəd] *adj* **(a)** (*material, velvet etc*) façonné; (*silk etc*) broché; **(b)** (*wood*) ronceux; **(c)** *Mus* (*contrepoint*) figuré; (*basse*) chiffré.
figurehead ['fɪgəhed] *n* (*on ship*) figure *f* de proue; *Fig Pej* (*man*) homme *m* de paille; **she's just a f.,** elle inaugure les chrysanthèmes.
figurine ['fɪgəriːn] *n Art etc* figurine *f*.
Fiji ['fiːdʒiː] *n* **F., the F. Islands,** les îles *fpl* Fidji.
Fijian [fiː'dʒiːən] **1** *adj* fidjien. **2** *n* Fidjien, -ienne.
filament ['fɪləmənt] *n* **(a)** *El* filament *m*; **f. lamp,** lampe *f* à incandescence; **(b)** *Biol* filament *m*, filet *m*.
filbert ['fɪlbət] *n* aveline *f*; (*hazelnut*) grosse noisette.
filch [fɪltʃ] *vt* chiper (**sth from s.o.,** qch à qn).
file¹ [faɪl] *n* (*tool*) lime *f*; **nail f.,** lime à ongles.
file² *vt* limer (*le métal etc*); **to f. one's nails,** se limer les ongles.
file³ *n* **(a)** (*folder*) classeur *m*; (*documents*) dossier *m*; **give me the f. on James Brown,** passez-moi le dossier James Brown; **have we got anything on f. about it?,** y-a-t'il quelque chose là-dessus dans les dossiers?; **cardboard f.,** chemise *f*; **we have placed your report on our files,** nous avons classé votre rapport dans nos dossiers; **card-index f.,** fichier *m*; **card f.,** fichier sur cartes; **master f.,** fichier permanent; *Am* **f. cabinet,** classeur; **f. card,** fiche *f* (de classeur); *esp Am* **f. clerk,** documentaliste *mf*; **files,** archives *fpl*; **f. copy,** exemplaire *m* d'archives; **f. number,** cote *f* (*d'un document dans un dossier*); **(b)** *Comptr* fichier *m*; **f. management system,** système *m* de gestion de fichiers; **f. server,** serveur *m* de fichiers.
file⁴ *vt* **(a)** (*classify*) classer (*des fiches, des lettres etc*); **it was filed under 'jazz',** c'était classé dans la catégorie 'jazz'; **(b)** *Jur* **to f. a petition,** (*of court official*) déposer une requête; (*of plaintiff*) enregister une requête; **to f. one's petition (in bankruptcy),** déposer son bilan; **(c)** *esp US Admin* déposer (*un document, une plainte*) (**with,** auprès de qn).
file⁵ *n* (*line*) file *f*; **in single** *or* **Indian f.,** en file indienne; **to walk in single f.,** marcher à la file *ou* en file indienne; *Mil* **in f.,** (en rang) par deux.
file⁶ *vi* (*walk in line*) marcher à la file *ou* en ligne de file; **to f. off,** défiler; **to f. past,** défiler; **to f. past a catafalque,** défiler devant un catafalque; **to f. in/out,** entrer/sortir un à un.
►**file away** *vtsep* = **FILE DOWN (a).**
►**file down** *vtsep* (*metalwork*) & *Carp* **(a)** (*remove by filing*) enlever (*une saillie etc*) à la lime; **(b)** (*smooth by filing*) polir (*une surface*) à la lime; (*of blacksmith etc*) raboter (*le sabot d'un cheval*).
►**file off** *vtsep* = **FILE DOWN (a).**
filial ['fɪlɪəl] *adj* filial, -aux.
filially ['fɪlɪəlɪ] *adv* filialement.
filibuster¹ ['fɪlɪbʌstər] *n* **(a)** *Parl* obstruction *f*; **(b)** *Hist* (*pirate*) flibustier *m*.
filibuster² *vi* **(a)** *Parl* faire de l'obstruction; **filibustering tactics,** manœuvres obstructionnistes; **(b)** *Hist* (*of pirate*) flibuster.
filibustering ['fɪlɪbʌstərɪŋ] *n Parl* obstruction *f*.
filigree ['fɪlɪgriː] *n* filigrane *m*; **f. work,** (travail *m* en) filigrane.
filing¹ ['faɪlɪŋ] *n* **(a)** (*of metal etc*) limage *m*; **(b)** (*small pieces of metal etc*) (*usu pl*) **filings,** limaille *f*.
filing² *n* **(a)** classement *m* (*de documents, de fiches etc*); **f. cabinet,** classeur *m*; **f. clerk,** documentaliste *mf*; **f. system,** méthode *f* de classement; **f. tray,** corbeille *f* pour correspondance à classer; **(b)** *Jur* (*by court official*) enregistrement *m* (*d'une requête*); (*by plaintiff*) dépôt *m* (*d'une demande*).
filing down *n* polissage *m* à la lime; rabotage *m* (*des sabots de cheval*).
Filipino [fɪlɪ'piːnəʊ] **1** *adj* philippin. **2** *n* Philippin, -ine.
fill¹ [fɪl] *n* **(a) to have one's f. of sth,** en avoir assez de qch; **to eat one's f.,** manger à sa faim; **(b)** charge *f*, plein *m*; *Tech* matériau *m* de remplissage; *Constr* remblai *m*; **a f. of tobacco,** une pipée de tabac.
fill² **1** *vt* **(a)** remplir, emplir (*une cruche etc*) (**with,** de); bourrer (*sa pipe*); charger (*un wagon etc*); **to f. s.o.'s glass,** servir à boire à qn; (*to the brim*) verser une rasade à qn; **to f. the air with one's cries,** remplir l'air de ses cris; **a smell of cooking filled the house,** une odeur de cuisine

envahissait la maison; **to f. one's head with useless things,** se farcir la tête de choses inutiles; **to be filled with admiration,** être rempli d'admiration;

(b) (*plug*) combler (*une brèche, une lacune etc*); plomber (*une dent*); pourvoir à (*une vacance*); **to f. woodwork,** mastiquer les boiseries (*avant de les peindre*); **I'm having two teeth filled tomorrow,** on va me faire deux plombages demain; **two places remain to be filled,** deux postes restent à pourvoir; **the position has already been filled,** le poste a déjà été pourvu;

(c) (*occupy*) occuper; **a position she has filled for some time,** un poste qu'elle occupe depuis quelque temps; **to f. s.o.'s shoes,** (*succeed*) succéder à qn; (*take on someone's responsibilities*) prendre les fonctions de qn; **the thoughts that filled his mind,** les pensées qui occupaient son esprit; **reading fills my evenings,** la lecture remplit mes soirées;

(d) (*fulfil*) exécuter (*une commande, une ordonnance*); **to f. every requirement,** répondre à tous les besoins;

(e) (*pour*) verser; **to f. concrete into a coffering,** remplir un coffrage de béton, verser du béton dans un coffrage.

2 *vi* **(a)** (*of tank, bath, container*) se remplir; (*of hole*) se combler; **her eyes filled with tears,** ses yeux se sont remplis de larmes; **the hall is beginning to f.,** la salle commence à se remplir;

(b) *Nau* (*of sails*) se gonfler.

►fill in 1 *vtsep* **(a)** (*make level*) combler, boucher (*un trou*); remblayer (*un fossé*); (*block*) condamner (*une porte*); **(b)** (*complete*) remplir (*un formulaire*); **to f. in a gap in one's knowledge,** combler un vide *ou* une lacune dans ses connaissances; **f. in the blanks,** remplir les espaces vides; **(c)** (*insert*) insérer (*la date*); **(d)** *F* **to f. s.o. in on the details,** mettre qn au courant des détails (*d'une affaire*); **she quickly filled us in on what had been happening,** elle nous a rapidement mis au courant de ce qui s'était passé; **(e)** (*use up*) **to f. in time,** occuper son temps; **she's filling in time before going to university by working in a shop,** avant d'aller à l'université elle occupe son temps en travaillant dans un magasin. **2** *vi* (*of person*) remplacer (*qn*); **to f. in for s.o.,** remplacer qn; **I'm filling in while she's on holiday,** je la remplace pendant ses vacances.

►fill out 1 *vtsep* **(a)** (*pad out*) étoffer (*un discours etc*); **(b)** (*complete*) remplir (*un formulaire*). **2** *vi Nau* (*of sails*) se gonfler; (*of person*) engraisser, grossir; (*of adolescent female*) prendre des formes; **her cheeks are filling out,** ses joues se remplissent, elle prend des joues.

►fill up 1 *vtsep* **(a)** (*fill*) remplir (*un verre*) jusqu'au bord; *Aut F* **f. her up,** (faites) le plein; **(b)** (*plug*) boucher (*un trou avec du mastic etc*); **(c)** (*make level*) remblayer (*un fossé etc*); **(d)** (*complete*) remplir (*un formulaire*). **2** *vi* **(a)** (*become full*) (*of tank, container etc*) se remplir; (*of hole*) se combler; **the bucket was filling up with water,** le seau se remplissait d'eau; **(b)** (*fill tank etc*) **to f. up with petrol/water,** faire le plein d'essence/d'eau.

filler ['fɪlər] *n* **(a)** (*person*) remplisseur, -euse; (*thing*) remplisseuse *f*; **shelf f.,** (*in supermarket etc*) réassortisseur, -euse; **oil f.,** entonnoir *m*; **(b)** (*substance*) (matière *f* de) remplissage *m*; tripe *f* (*d'un cigare*); (*for wood etc*) bouche-pores *m inv*; (*in painting*) mastic *m*; **(c)** *Ling* **f. (word),** mot *m* de remplissage.

fillet¹ ['fɪlɪt] *n* **(a)** *Culin* filet *m* (*de bœuf, de sole*); rouelle *f* (*de veau*); **f. steak,** filet de bœuf; **(b)** *Archit etc* filet *m*; (*on column*) bande *f*; *Carp* baguette *f*, listel *m* (*de panneau*); *MecE* collet *m*, boudin *m* (*sur un tuyau etc*); **(c)** (*for hair*) ruban *m*; **(d)** *Her* filet *m*; **(e)** (*in bookbinding*) *& Typ* filet *m*.

fillet² *vt* **(-tt-) (a)** *Culin* détacher les filets de (*poisson*); désosser (*un poisson*); **filleted sole,** filets *mpl* de sole; **(b)** *Archit* orner (*qch*) d'un filet; *Carp* orner (*qch*) d'une baguette.

filling ['fɪlɪŋ] **1** *adj* (*food*) nourrissant.

2 *n* **(a)** (r)emplissage *m* (*d'un verre*); chargement *m* (*d'un wagon etc*); bourrage *m* (*d'une pipe à tabac*); mise *f* en eau (*d'un réservoir*); peuplement *m* (*d'un étang*); *Aut* **f. station,** station-service *f*, *pl* stations-service; (*small*) poste *m* d'essence;

(b) (*act of plugging, blocking*) comblement *m* (*d'un vide*); remblayage *m* (*d'un fossé etc*); *Constr* remplissage *m*; (*in dentistry*) plombage *m* (*d'une dent*); **f. of a vacancy,** nomination *f* de quelqu'un à un poste;

(c) (*occupancy*) occupation *f* (*d'une poste etc*);

(d) (*substance*) (matière *f* de) remplissage *m*; tripe *f* (*d'un cigare*); (*in dentistry*) plombage *m*; *Carp* mastic *m*; *Constr* remplissage *m*; (*rubble*) blocage *m*; (*liquid*) coulis *m*; *Culin* (*for pie, sandwich*) garniture *f*; **I've got two fillings,** (*in my teeth*) j'ai deux plombages; **cake with a chocolate f.,** gâteau fourré au chocolat.

filling in *n* comblement *m* (*d'un trou*); remblayage *m* (*d'un fossé etc*); rédaction *f* (*d'un formulaire*).

filling out *n* gonflement *m* (*d'un ballon etc*).

filling up *n* remplissage *m* (*d'un tonneau etc*); comblement *m* (*d'une lacune*); bouchage *m* (*d'un trou etc*); remblayage *m* (*d'un fossé etc*).

fillip ['fɪlɪp] *n* **(a)** stimulant *m*, encouragement *m*; **to give a f. to business,** stimuler les affaires; **(b)** (*with finger*) chiquenaude *f*.

fill-up ['fɪlʌp] *n Aut* plein *m*; **do you want a f.-up?,** (*I'll buy you a drink*) tu prends un autre verre?; (*shall I fill your glass?*) je te remplis ton verre?

filly ['fɪlɪ] *n* **(a)** (*horse*) pouliche *f*; **(b)** *Old-fashioned F* jeune fille *f*.

film¹ [fɪlm] *n* **(a)** *Cin* film *m*; (*celluloid strip*) bande *f*; **silent f.,** film muet; **full/short-length f.,** long/court métrage; **supporting f.,** film en première partie; **news f.,** actualités *fpl*; **to act** *or* **play in a f.,** jouer dans un film; **to shoot a f.,** tourner un film; **the films,** le cinéma; **I've seen her in films,** je l'ai vue dans des films; **to be in films,** faire du cinéma; **to have a f. test,** tourner une bande *ou* un bout d'essai; **f. actor/actress,** acteur/actrice de cinéma; **f. clip,** séquence *f* de film; **f. club,** ciné-club *m*; **f. critic,** critique *m* de cinéma; **f. library,** cinémathèque *f*; **the f. industry,** l'industrie *f* cinématographique *ou* du cinéma; **f. maker,** réalisateur *m* de films; **f. producer,** producteur *m* de cinéma; **f. director,** réalisateur *m*, metteur *m* en scène; **f. studio,** studio cinématographique *ou* de cinéma; **f. script,** scénario *m*, script *m*; **f. set,** plateau *m* de cinéma; **f. star,** vedette *f* de cinéma; **f. strip,** film fixe (*d'enseignement*);

(b) *Phot* pellicule *f*, film *m*; **I've run out of f.,** ma pellicule est finie; **a (roll of) f.,** un rouleau de pellicule, une pellicule; **colour f.,** film (en) couleur(s); **f. cassette,** cartouche *f* de pellicule *ou* de film;

(c) (*layer*) pellicule *f*, couche *f* (*de glace, d'huile*); *Med* taie *f* (*sur l'œil*); voile *m* (*de brume, de fumée etc*); **wrapped in plastic f.,** emballé dans un film en plastique.

film² 1 *vt* **(a)** *Cin* filmer, tourner (*une scène etc*); porter (*un roman*) à l'écran; filmer (*qn*); **(b)** *Lit* recouvrir (*qch*) d'une pellicule; (*cover with mist etc*) recouvrir (*qch*) d'un voile. **2** *vi* = **FILM OVER**.

►film over *vi* se couvrir d'une pellicule; (*of the eyes*) se couvrir d'une taie.

filming ['fɪlmɪŋ] *n Cin* tournage *m*.

filmy ['fɪlmɪ] *adj* (*substance*) qui forme une pellicule; (*eye*) couvert d'une taie; (*lace, cloud etc*) léger.

filter¹ ['fɪltər] *n* **(a)** filtre *m*; épurateur *m* (*d'essence etc*); **air f.,** filtre à air; épurateur d'air; **coffee f.,** filtre à café; *HydE* **f. bed,** bassin *m* de filtration; **f. coffee,** (*as opposed to espresso etc*) café-filtre *m*, *pl* cafés-filtre; **f. paper,** papier *m* filtre; **f. tip,** bout *m* filtre; (*cigarette*) cigarette *f* à filtre; *Br* **a packet of Gauloise ® f.,** un paquet de Gauloise ® filtres; **(b)** *Opt Phot* **colour f.,** filtre *m* de couleur; écran *m* filtre; **(c)** *El Electron etc* **frequency f.,** filtre *m* de fréquences; **f. circuit,** circuit *m* de filtrage; **(d)** *Br* (*on traffic light*) = flèche verte qui s'allume lorsque la circulation est possible pour une voie particulière.

filter² 1 *vt* filtrer (*l'eau*); épurer (*l'air etc*). **2** *vi* **(a)** (*of water etc*) filtrer (**through,** à travers); (*seep*) suinter; **(b)** *Br Aut etc* changer de file; **to f. to the right/left,** glisser à droite/à gauche; **(c)** *F* **to f. into/out of a building,** entrer dans/quitter lentement un édifice.

►filter out 1 *vtsep* (*remove with filter*) séparer (*des impuretés*) par filtrage; **f. out the solids,** retenir les solides par filtrage. **2** *vi* (*leave slowly*) quitter lentement; **information is beginning to f. out that ...,** des informations commencent à filtrer selo lesquelles ... .

►filter through 1 *vi* (*pass slowly*) passer lentement; **the news soon filtered through,** les nouvelles filtrèrent rapidement. **2** *vipo* filtrer à travers; **the light filtered through the branches,** la lumière filtrait à travers les branches.

filterable ['fɪltərəb(ə)l] *adj Med* (*virus*) filtrant.

filtering ['fɪltərɪŋ] *n* filtrage *m*, filtration *f*.

filth [fɪlθ] *n* **(a)** (*dirt*) immondices *mpl*; (*excreta*) ordure *f*; **to live in f.,** vivre dans la saleté; **(b)** (*obscenity*) **to talk f.,** dire des obscénités; **what are you reading that f. for?,** pourquoi est-ce que tu lis ces cochonneries?

filthy ['fɪlθɪ] **1** *adj* **(a)** (*very dirty*) sale, immonde; **you're f.!,** tu es dégoutant!; *esp Br F* **f. weather,** temps *m* de chien; *F* **in a f. temper,** d'une humeur massacrante; *F* **he gave me a f. look,** il m'a jeté un sale regard; **(b)** (*book, talk etc*) ordurier, obscène; (*person*) crapuleux; **you've got a f. mind!,** tu as l'esprit mal tourné! **2** *adv F* **f. dirty,**

crasseux; **f. rich,** pourri de fric.

filtration [fɪl'treɪʃən] *n* filtration *f*, filtrage *m*.

fin [fɪn] *n* **(a)** (*of fish etc*) nageoire *f* (*d'un poisson, d'une baleine*); aileron *m* (*d'un requin*); **fins,** (*for swimmer, diver*) palmes *fpl*; **(b)** (*of boat*) dérive *f*; *Av* (*of plane*) empennage *m*; (*of bomb etc*) ailette *f*; *Aut etc* (*of radiator etc*) ailette *f*; **cooling fins,** ailettes de refroidissement; **stabilizer f.,** aileron stabilisateur.

finagle [fɪ'neɪg(ə)l] *v F* = **WANGLE**.

final ['faɪn(ə)l] **1** *adj* **(a)** (*last*) final, -als, dernier; **f. details,** derniers détails; **f. preparations,** derniers préparatifs; **to make a f. effort,** faire un dernier effort; **to put the f. touches to sth,** mettre la dernière main à qch; *Com Fin* **f. date (for payment),** terme fatal; **f. demand,** (*for payment*) dernier avis; **f. instalment,** dernier versement, versement de libération;

(b) (*beyond recall*) définitif; **f. text,** texte définitif; *Jur* **f. judgment,** jugement définitif *ou* sans appel; **the umpire's decision is f.,** la décision de l'arbitre est sans appel; **take this as f.,** tenez-le-vous pour dit; **this is the f. warning,** c'est le dernier avertissement;

(c) *Gram* (*proposition*) final; *Phil* (*cause*) final.

2 *n* **(a)** *Sp* **the f.** *or* **finals,** la finale; **to be through to the finals,** être en finale; *Fb* **cup f.,** finale de coupe;

(b) *Univ* **to sit** *or* **take one's finals,** = passer son dernier examen de licence;

(c) (*lettre*) finale *f* (*d'un mot*).

finale [fɪ'nɑːlɪ] *n* **(a)** *Mus* finale *m;* **(b)** *Th etc* conclusion *f*; **grand f.,** apothéose *f*.

finalist ['faɪnəlɪst] *n Sp* finaliste *mf*.

finality [faɪ'nælɪtɪ] *n* **(a)** (*of decision*) caractère définitif, irrévocabilité *f*; **(b)** *Phil* finalité *f*.

finalization [faɪnəlaɪ'zeɪʃən] *n* (*of details, plans etc*) mise *f* au point.

finalize ['faɪnəlaɪz] *vt* mener (*qch*) à bonne fin; (*details, plans etc*) mettre au point; **details of the president's visit have yet to be finalized,** les détails de la visite du président restent à préciser.

finally ['faɪn(ə)lɪ] *adv* **(a)** (*at last*) finalement, enfin; **(b)** (*irrevocably*) définitivement; **(c)** (*lastly*) à la fin, en dernier.

finance[1] [faɪ'næns, fɪ-] *n* **(a)** finance *f*; **high f.,** la haute finance; **f. company,** société *f* de crédits; **(b)** (*funds*) **his finances are low,** ses fonds sont bas.

finance[2] *vt* financer (*un projet*); financer, commanditer (*qn, une entreprise etc*).

financial [faɪ'nænʃəl, fɪ-] *adj* (*difficulty, planning etc*) financier; *Rad TV* **f. news,** informations financières; **f. year,** exercice financier, année *f* budgétaire.

financially [faɪ'næʃəlɪ, fɪ-] *adv* financièrement.

financier [faɪ'nænsɪər, fɪ-] *n* financier *m*.

financing [faɪ'nænsɪŋ, fɪ-] *n* (*of project etc*) financement *m*.

finch [fɪntʃ] *n* (*bird*) fringillidé *m*.

find[1] [faɪnd] *n* découverte *f*, trouvaille *f*.

find[2] *v* (*pt & pp* **found** [faʊnd]) **1** *vt* **(a)** (*discover by chance*) trouver, découvrir; **to f. happiness with s.o.,** rencontrer le bonheur auprès de qn; **to f. s.o. at home** *or* **in,** trouver qn chez lui; **they found him dead,** on l'a trouvé mort; **we must leave everything as we f. it,** il faut tout laisser tel quel; **I found her waiting in the hall,** je l'ai trouvée qui m'attendait dans le vestibule; **I often f. myself smiling,** je me surprends souvent à sourire; **I found myself in London,** (*instead of Manchester etc*) je me suis retrouvé à Londres; **they found an unexpected supporter in Mr Smith,** ils ont trouvé en M. Smith un partisan inattendu;

(b) (*discover by searching*) **the (lost) key has been found,** la clef s'est retrouvée; (*at last*) **to try to f. sth,** chercher qch; **I ran to f. a doctor,** j'ai couru chercher un médecin; **f. some paper,** allez chercher du papier; **she was nowhere to be found,** elle était introuvable; **you won't f. a better bike at this price,** vous ne trouverez pas une meilleure moto à ce prix; **to f. a job for s.o.,** trouver un emploi à qn; **to f. a leak in a main,** localiser une fuite dans une conduite; **the bullet found its mark,** la balle a atteint son but; **I can f. no reason for ...,** je ne vois pas de raison pour ...; **he keeps finding excuses,** il arrive toujours à trouver des excuses; **to f. a way to do sth,** trouver le moyen de faire qch; **to f. it in one's heart to do sth,** avoir le cœur de faire qch; **to f. favour with s.o.,** gagner la faveur de qn; **to f. one's balance,** trouver son équilibre; **to f. oneself,** se trouver;

(c) (*learn*) constater; **you will f. that I am right,** vous verrez que j'ai raison; **I was surprised to f. that ...,** j'ai été surpris de constater que ...; **I found that she had left the house,** j'ai appris qu'elle avait quitté la maison;

(d) (*experience*) **to f. some difficulty in doing sth,** éprouver quelque difficulté à faire qch; **they will f. it easy/difficult,** cela leur sera facile/difficile; **to f. it impossible/necessary to do sth,** se trouver dans l'impossibilité/la nécessité de faire qch; **how do you f. this wine?,** comment trouvez-vous ce vin?; **I f. her rather offhand,** je la trouve plutôt désinvolte;

(e) *Jur* **to f. s.o. guilty,** déclarer qn coupable;

(f) (*provide*) **to f. the money for an undertaking,** procurer les capitaux *ou* fournir l'argent pour une entreprise; **wages £20, all found,** gages 20 livres, tout fourni.

2 *vi Jur* **to f. for s.o.,** prononcer *ou* rendre un verdict en faveur de qn.

►**find out 1** *vtsep* **(a)** (*discover*) se rendre compte de (*les faits*); découvrir (*la vérité*); **we found out that she was French,** nous avons découvert qu'elle était française; **did you f. anything out?,** est-ce que vous avez découvert quoi que ce soit?; **(b) to f. s.o. out,** (*learn truth about*) découvrir le vrai caractère de qn; (*catch someone doing wrong*) prendre qn en défaut; **we've been found out,** nous nous sommes faits prendre. **2** *vi* (*discover something*) apprendre; **I'll f. out,** je le saurai; **your mother had better not f. out!,** j'espère pour toi que ta mère ne l'apprendra pas; **to f. out about sth,** se renseigner sur qch; **I have found out all about it,** j'ai pu établir tous les faits.

finder ['faɪndər] *n* **(a)** (*person*) trouveur, -euse; *Jur* inventeur, -trice (*d'un objet perdu*); *Prov* **finders keepers (, losers weepers),** ce qui tombe dans le fossé est pour le soldat; **(b)** (*of telescope*) chercheur *m*.

finding ['faɪndɪŋ] *n* **(a)** (*discovery of scientist, inquiry etc*) résultat *m*, découverte *f*; **he published his findings in a scientific journal,** il a fait publier les résultats de ses recherches dans un journal scientifique; **(b)** *Jur* conclusion *f* (*du tribunal, du jury*) sur un point de fait; **his f. is that ...,** il est arrivé à la conclusion que ... .

fine[1] [faɪn] *n* amende *f*; **to impose a f. on s.o.,** infliger une amende à qn; **to pay a f.,** payer une amende; **parking f.,** amende pour stationnement illégal.

fine[2] *vt Jur* condamner (*qn*) à une amende; **to f. s.o. £20,** frapper qn d'une amende de 20 livres.

fine[3] *adj* **(a)** (*excellent*) excellent, magnifique; **meat of the finest quality,** viande de premier choix; **a f. athlete,** un excellent athlète; **f. display,** étalage *m* superbe; **we had a f. time,** nous nous sommes bien amusés; **that's f.!,** voilà qui est parfait!; *Iron* **you're a f. one, you are!,** vous êtes joli, vous!; *Iron* **you're a f. one to talk!,** vous pouvez bien parler!; **that's f. by** *or* **with me,** ça me va; **she's/everything is f.,** elle/tout va bien;

(b) *F* (*intensive*) **he was in a f. (old) temper!,** ce qu'il rageait!;

(c) (*beautiful*) beau, bel, belle; **a f. statue,** une belle statue; **a f. piece of writing,** un bon écrit; **a particularly f. example of marquetry,** un particulièrement bel exemple de marqueterie; **the f. arts,** les beaux-arts *mpl*;

(d) (*weather*) beau; **when the weather is f.,** quand il fait beau; **a f. day,** une belle journée; **one of these f. days,** un de ces (beaux) jours; **it's turned out f. again,** aujourd'hui encore il fait beau;

(e) (*noble, admirable*) **to appeal to s.o.'s finer feelings,** faire appel aux sentiments élevés de qn; **she's a f. woman,** c'est une femme admirable;

(f) (*socially refined*) **a f. lady,** (*elegant*) une dame élégante; (*of high rank*) une grande dame;

(g) (*texture, dust*) fin; (*gravel etc*) menu, fin; **f. rain,** pluie fine; **to chop meat f.,** hacher menu la viande; **to have f. hair,** avoir les cheveux fins;

(h) (*pointed*) effilé; (*writing*) délié, mince; (*needle*) fin; (*blade*) affilé, aigu; (*pen*) pointu; **f. print,** petits caractères; **not to put too f. a point on it,** pour parler carrément;

(i) (*subtle*) fin; **f. distinction,** distinction subtile; **she's got washing the car down to a f. art,** elle est passée maître dans l'art de laver la voiture; **there's a f. line between eccentricity and madness,** il n'y a qu'un pas de l'excentricité à la folie; **to cut it f.,** (*arrive just in time*) arriver de justesse; (*pay just in time*) payer juste à temps; (*decide just in time*) décider au dernier moment; *Billiards* **to cut the ball too f.,** prendre la bille trop fin *ou* trop fine;

(j) (*metals, oil etc*) fin; **gold twenty-two carats f.,** or à vingt-deux carats de fin.

fine[4] *int* bon!, entendu!, d'accord!

fine[5] *adv* **to get on** *or* **do f.,** (*in new job etc*) se débrouiller très bien; (*be well*) aller bien; **to get on f.,** (*of two people*) bien s'entendre.

fine[6] 1 *vt* **(a)** affiner (*l'or etc*); **(b)** = **FINE DOWN**. **2** *vi* (*of liquid*) se clarifier, devenir clair.

►**fine down** *vtsep* **(a)** (*refine*) clarifier (*la bière*); **(b)** (*make thinner*) amincir (*qch*); (*make smoother*) alléger (*une planche etc*).

▶**fine off** *vtsep* = **FINE DOWN (b)**.

fine-cut ['faɪn'kʌt] *adj* **(a)** (*features*) finement *ou* délicatement ciselé; **(b)** (*tabac*) haché fin.

fine-draw ['faɪn'drɔː] *vt* (**fine-drew**; **fine-drawn**) *Sewing* rentraire, faire une reprise perdue à (*une déchirure*).

fine-drawn ['faɪn'drɔːn] *adj* **(a)** (*features etc*) fin; **(b)** (*distinction*) subtil; **(c)** (*wire*) finement étiré; (*thread*) délié; **(d)** *Sewing* **f.-d. mend,** reprise perdue; **f.-d. seam,** rentraiture *f*.

fine-grained ['faɪn'greɪnd] *adj* (*wood, leather*) à grain fin.

fine-looking ['faɪn'lʊkɪŋ] *adj* beau, bel, belle.

finely ['faɪnlɪ] *adv* **(a)** (*excellently*) magnifiquement; **(b)** (*skilfully*) habilement; **(c)** (*delicately*) délicatement; **(d)** (*in small size*) **f. powdered,** finement pulvérisé; **f. chopped,** haché fin; **f. ground,** moulu très fin.

fineness ['faɪnnɪs] *n* **(a)** (*excellence*) qualité supérieure, excellence *f*; **(b)** (*splendour*) splendeur *f*, magnificence *f* (*d'un costume etc*); **(c)** finesse *f* (*des cheveux, d'un tissu etc*); délicatesse *f*, subtilité *f* (*des sentiments etc*); **(d)** titre *m*, aloi *m* (*de l'or*); pureté *f* (*du vin etc*).

finery ['faɪnərɪ] *n* parure *f*; *Pej* fanfreluches *fpl*; **decked out in all his f.,** paré de ses plus beaux atours.

fine-spun ['faɪn'spʌn] *adj* **(a)** *Tex* au fil ténu *ou* délié; **(b)** (*raisonnement etc*) subtil.

finesse [fɪ'nes] *n* **(a)** (*skill*) finesse *f*, délicatesse *f*, subtilité *f* (*du style etc*); **(b)** (*ruse*) finesse *f*, ruse *f*; **(c)** *Cards* impasse *f*.

fine-tooth ['faɪn'tuːθ] *adj* (*peigne*) fin; **to go through sth with a f.-t. comb,** passer qch au peigne fin.

fine-tune ['faɪntjuːn] *vt* (*radio, engine etc*) régler avec précision; *Fig* (*plan*) peaufiner.

finger[1] ['fɪŋgər] *n* **(a)** doigt *m* (*de la main*); **first f.,** index *m*; **middle f.,** médius *m*, doigt du milieu; **ring f.,** annulaire *m*; **little f.,** auriculaire *m*; **he's got them wrapped round his little f.,** il fait d'eux ce qu'il veut; **to eat sth with one's fingers,** manger qch avec les doigts; **to lay** *or* **put one's f. on the source of the trouble,** mettre le doigt sur la source du mal; **I can't quite put my f. on it,** je n'arrive pas à mettre le doigt dessus; *F* **don't you dare lay a f. on him,** je vous défends de le toucher; **she wouldn't lift a f. to help you,** elle ne remuerait pas le petit doigt pour vous aider; **I've been working my fingers to the bone,** j'ai travaillé jusqu'à l'épuisement; **they could be counted on the fingers of one hand,** on pourrait les compter sur les doigts de la main; **to keep one's fingers crossed,** croiser les doigts; *Br Sl* **get** *or* **pull** *or* **take your f. out!,** grouille-toi!, *Sl* bouge ton cul!; **the f. (of suspicion) was pointed at him,** on le montre d'un doigt suspicieux; *Sl* **to put the f. on s.o.,** (*inform on*) balancer qn; **to give s.o. the f.,** = faire un bras d'honneur à qn; **he has a f. in every pie,** il est mêlé à tout; *Culin* **f. biscuit,** biscuit *m* à la cuiller; **f. board,** touche *f* (*de violon etc*); **f. bowl,** rince-doigts *m inv*; **f. exercises,** exercices *mpl* de doigté; *Mus* **f. hole,** trou *m* (*de flûte etc*); **f. plate,** (*on door etc*) plaque *f* de propreté;
(b) (*measure etc*) **f. of brandy,** doigt *m* de cognac; **f. of bread,** mouillette *f*;
(c) (*of glove*) doigt *m*;
(d) *Tech* doigt *m* (*de guidage*).

finger[2] *vt* **(a)** (*feel*) toucher, tâter, *F* tripoter (*qch*); **(b)** *Mus* doigter (*un morceau*); **to f. the piano,** tapoter sur le piano; **(c)** *Sl* (*inform on*) balancer (*qn*).

fingering ['fɪŋgərɪŋ] *n* **(a)** (*act of feeling*) maniement *m*; **(b)** *Mus* doigté *m*.

fingermark ['fɪŋgəmɑːk] *n* trace *f* de doigt.

fingernail ['fɪŋgəneɪl] *n* ongle *m* (de la main).

fingerprint[1] ['fɪŋgəprɪnt] *n* empreinte digitale; **f. identification,** dactyloscopie *f*; **to take s.o.'s fingerprints,** prendre les empreintes digitales de qn; **f. expert,** expert *m* en empreintes digitales.

fingerprint[2] *vt* prendre les empreintes digitales de (*qn*).

fingerstall ['fɪŋgəstɔːl] *n Med* doigtier *m*.

fingertip ['fɪŋgətɪp] *n* bout *m* du doigt; **he is a Frenchman to his fingertips,** il est Français jusqu'au bout des ongles; **to have sth at one's fingertips,** savoir qch sur le bout des doigts; **f. control,** commande *f* au doigté.

finicky ['fɪnɪkɪ] *adj* (*person, style etc*) méticuleux, vétilleux.

finish[1] ['fɪnɪʃ] *n* **(a)** (*end*) fin *f* (*de la vie etc*); *Sp* arrivée *f* (*d'une course*); *Sp* **he has a fast f.,** il a un bon finish; *F* **that was the f. (of him),** ce fut le coup de grâce; **to fight to the f.,** se battre jusqu'au dernier moment; **(b)** (*workmanship*) fini *m*, finesse *f* de l'exécution (*d'un travail etc*); **(c)** (*surface*) apprêt *m*; **paint with a gloss/matt f.,** peinture vernie/mate; **(d)** *Tech* finition *f*.

finish[2] **1** *vt* **(a)** finir, terminer, achever; mettre fin à (*une affaire etc*); compléter (*un ouvrage etc*); **to f. doing sth,** achever de faire qch; **to f. what one was saying,** finir ce qu'on avait à dire; **f. your soup!,** finis ta soupe!;
(b) (*ruin*) achever (*qn*); **he's finished!,** il est fini *ou* achevé!; **this defeat has finished the team's chances,** cette défaite a mis un terme aux chances de l'équipe; **she was finished as a singer/an actress,** sa carrière de chanteuse/d'actrice était finie; **you're finished here,** (*I'm sacking you*) tu es viré;
(c) (*put finishing touches to*) perfectionner, donner du fini à (*un ouvrage etc*); *Tex* apprêter (*un tissu*); *Metal* usiner (*une pièce*); *Sewing* **to f. a buttonhole,** brider une boutonnière.
2 *vi* finir, cesser, se terminer, s'achever; **the meeting finished in a brawl,** le meeting se termina par des coups; **when do you f.?,** (*leave work*) quand est-ce que tu finis?; **have you finished?,** (*eating etc*) tu as terminé?; **to f. in a point,** (*of blade, shape etc*) se terminer en pointe; **he finished by calling me a liar,** il a fini par me traiter de menteur; *Sp* **to f. fourth,** finir *ou* arriver quatrième; *Sp* **where did she f.?,** à quelle place est-ce qu'elle a fini?

▶**finish off 1** *vtsep* **(a)** (*complete*) terminer (*une tâche*); *Sewing* **to f. off a buttonhole,** brider une boutonnière; **(b)** (*have the last of*) finir (*le gâteau, le ragoût*); **(c)** *F* (*exhaust*) achever, épuiser (*qn*); **(d)** *F* (*defeat, ruin*) faire la ruine de (*une société, une industrie*); **(e)** *F* (*kill*) achever (*qn*); **to f. off a wounded animal,** donner le coup de grâce à une bête; **this fly killer will soon f. them off!,** ce tue-mouches aura bientôt raison d'elles; **cirrhosis of the liver finally finished him off,** une cirrhose du foie a fini par avoir raison de lui. **2** *vi* (*end*) finir; **they finished off with some fruit/a song,** ils ont fini avec des fruits/une chanson.

▶**finish up 1** *vtsep* **(a)** (*complete*) finir, terminer; **f. up your soup!,** finis ta soupe!; **(b)** (*have the last of*) finir; **don't f. up the pie,** ne finis pas la tourte, ne mange pas toute la tourte. **2** *vi* (*end up*) finir; **we finished up in a ditch,** nous avons fini dans un fossé; **I'm going to f. up a nervous wreck!,** je vais finir par m'user les nerfs.

▶**finish with** *vipo* **(a)** (*stop using*) ne plus avoir besoin de; **have you finished with the dictionary/mustard?,** est-ce que tu as fini avec le dictionnaire/la moutarde?; **I've finished with it,** je n'en ai plus besoin; **(b)** (*stop doing*) en avoir fini avec; **I've finished with acting,** j'en ai fini avec le théâtre; **I've finished with trying to help people,** plus jamais je n'essaierai d'aider les gens; **(c)** (*finish dealing with*) **I haven't finished with you!,** je n'en ai pas fini avec toi!; **wait until I've finished with him!,** attendez que je lui aie réglé son compte!; **(d)** (*end relationship with*) rompre avec (*qn*); **I've finished with you,** tout est fini entre nous.

finished ['fɪnɪʃt] *adj* **(a)** (*article etc*) fini, apprêté; (*produit*) ouvré; **machine f.,** apprêté à la machine; **badly f. goods,** marchandises mal finies; **(b)** (*person, appearance etc*) soigné, parfait.

finisher ['fɪnɪʃər] *n* (*person*) *Ind* finisseur, -euse; *Sp* finisseur, -euse; **he's a fast f.,** c'est un bon finisseur, il a un bon finish.

finishing ['fɪnɪʃɪŋ] **1** *adj* dernier; **the f. stroke,** le coup de grâce; **f. touches,** finitions *fpl*; **to put the f. touches to sth,** mettre la dernière main à qch. **2** *n* **(a)** (*completion*) achèvement *m* (*d'une tâche etc*); *Sp* **f. line,** ligne *f* d'arrivée; **f. school,** = école d'arts d'agrément pour les jeunes filles; **(b)** *Tech* finition *f*; apprêtage *m* (*du cuir, du papier*); **f. coat,** dernière couche (*de peinture etc*); *Metal* **f. pass,** passe *f* de finissage; dernier enduit (*de chaux etc*); *Ind* **f. shop,** atelier *m* de finitions; **(c)** *Constr* (*usu pl*) **finishings,** menuiserie *f* (*d'une maison etc*).

finite ['faɪnaɪt] **1** *adj* (*nature etc*) fini, limité; *Gram* (*verbe*) à un mode fini; **a f. number of possibilities,** un nombre limité de possibilités. **2** *n* **the f. and the infinite,** le fini et l'infini.

fink [fɪŋk] *n esp Am F* **(a)** (*unpleasant person*) salaud *m*; **(b)** (*strikebreaker*) jaune *m*; **(c)** (*informer*) balance *f*, indic *m*.

Finland ['fɪnlənd] *n* Finlande *f*.

Finn [fɪn] *n* Finlandais, -aise, Finnois, -oise.

finnan ['fɪnən] *n Culin* **f. haddie,** haddock *m*.

Finnish ['fɪnɪʃ] **1** *adj* finlandais, finnois. **2** *n Ling* finlandais *m*, finnois *m*.

fiord [fjɔːd] *n Geog* fjord *m*, fiord *m*.

fir [fɜːr] *n* **(a) f. (tree),** sapin *m*; **Douglas f.,** sapin de Douglas; **Scots f.,** pin *m* d'Écosse; **f. cone,** pomme *f* de pin; **(b)** (*wood*) (bois *m* de) sapin *m*; (*pine*) (bois de) pin *m*.

fire[1] ['faɪər] *n* **(a)** feu *m*; **to make** *or* **light a f.,** faire du feu; **to set** *or* **lay a f.,** préparer un feu; **wolves are afraid**

of f., les loups ont peur du feu; *Fig* **to go through f. and water,** subir des épreuves; *Fig* **to play with f.**, jouer avec le feu; **open f.**, feu de cheminée; **camp f.**, feu de camp; **wood f.**, feu de bois; **gas/electric f.**, radiateur *m* à gaz/électrique; **to throw sth into the f.**, jeter qch au feu; **a roaring f.**, une belle flambée; **blacksmith's f.**, feu de forge; *Cer* **f. clay,** argile *f* réfractaire; **f. irons,** garniture *f* de foyer; **f. screen,** devant *m* de cheminée, écran *m* pare-étincelles, garde-feu *m*; **f. worship,** culte *m* du feu;

(b) (*destructive*) incendie *m*; **bush f.**, feu *m* de brousse; **to cause** *or* **start a f.**, provoquer un incendie; **to set f. to sth, to set sth on f.**, mettre le feu à qch; **to catch f.**, prendre feu; **f.!**, au feu!; **on f.**, en feu; *F* **my singing isn't going to set the world** *or Br* **the Thames on f.**, la façon dont je chante n'a rien de fantastique; *F* **to get on like a house on f.**, (*of work etc*) marcher rondement; (*of two people*) s'entendre à merveille; **f. alarm,** sirène *f* d'incendie; **f. brigade,** *Am* **f. department,** (corps *m* de) sapeurs-pompiers *mpl*, *F* les pompiers *mpl*; *Nau Av* **f. bulkhead,** cloison *f* pare-feu; *Am* **f. chief,** capitaine *m* des pompiers; **f. door,** porte *f* coupe-feu; **f. drill,** exercice *m* de sauvetage en cas d'incendie; **f. engine,** *Am* **f. truck** *or* **tender,** voiture *f* de pompiers; **f. escape,** (*ladder*) échelle *f* à incendie; (*staircase*) escalier *m* de secours; **f. fighter,** pompier *m*; **f. fighting,** lutte *f* contre l'incendie; **f. hazard,** risque *m* d'incendie; **that old gas cooker must be a f. hazard,** cette vieille cuisinière à gaz doit présenter un risque d'incendie; **f. hose,** tuyau *m* de pompe à incendie; **f. hydrant,** bouche *f* d'incendie; **f. insurance,** assurance *f* contre l'incendie; *US* **f. marshal,** capitaine *m* des pompiers; (*investigator, enforcer*) = préposé à l'enquête des incendies et à la mise en vigueur des règlements relatifs à la prévention des incendies; **f. raiser,** incendiaire *mf*; **f. station,** poste *m* d'incendie; (*with living quarters*) caserne *f* de (sapeurs-)pompiers; **f. wall,** cloison *f* pare-feu; *Old-fashioned Br* **f. watcher,** guetteur *m* d'incendies;

(c) *Mil etc* feu *m*, tir *m*; (*shots*) coups *mpl* de feu; **individual f., f. at will,** tir à volonté; **to open f.**, ouvrir *ou* commencer le feu; **to cease f.**, cesser le feu; **under enemy f.**, sous le feu de l'ennemi; **we are under f.**, on tire sur nous; **to come under f.**, être exposé aux tirs (**from s.o.**, de qn); *Fig* **to be** *or* **come under f.**, être exposé à de sévères critiques (**from**, de la part de); **to draw s.o.'s f.**, s'attirer les tirs sur soi-même; **between two fires,** entre deux feux; *Fig* **to hang f.**, (*of project etc*) être en attente; **f. power,** puissance *f* de tir;

(d) (*of diamond*) lumière *f*, éclat *m*;

(e) (*enthusiasm*) enthousiasme *m*; (*ardour*) fougue *f*; **the f. of youth,** l'enthousiasme de la jeunesse.

fire[2] **1** *vt* **(a)** *Fml & Lit* (*set on fire*) mettre le feu à (*une maison etc*);

(b) (*fill with enthusiasm*) animer, enthousiasmer (*qn*); exciter (*l'imagination*); **to be fired with enthusiasm for sth,** brûler d'enthousiasme pour qch;

(c) *Cer* cuire (*de la poterie etc*);

(d) (*heat*) chauffer (*une locomotive etc*); allumer (*une chaudière*); **oil-fired/gas-fired central heating,** chauffage *m* au mazout/au gaz;

(e) (*in engine*) enflammer (*le mélange*);

(f) *Mil etc* décharger (*un fusil, un pistolet*); lancer (*une fusée, une torpille*); tirer un coup de (*canon*); **to f. a gun at s.o.**, lâcher un coup de fusil à qn; **without firing a shot,** sans tirer un coup; *Fig* **to f. a question at s.o.**, poser une question à qn à brûle-pourpoint;

(g) *F* (*dismiss*) virer, saquer (*un employé etc*); **you're fired!**, vous êtes viré!

2 *vi* **(a)** (*of engine*) tourner;

(b) *Mil etc* (*of person*) tirer; (*of shot*) partir; **the revolver failed to f.**, le revolver a fait long feu; **to f. at** *or* **on s.o./sth,** tirer sur qn/qch; **to f. at s.o. with a revolver,** tirer un coup de revolver sur qn; **f.!**, feu!; **to f. at will,** tirer à volonté; **we were fired on,** nous avons reçu des coups de feu, on nous a tiré dessus.

▶**fire away** *vi Mil etc* tirer à feu continu (**at**, sur); *Fig* **f. away!**, allez y!, commencez!

▶**fire off** *vtsep Mil etc* tirer (*un coup de fusil etc*); *Fig* poser (*des questions*) à brûle-pourpoint.

fire-and-brimstone ['faɪərən(d)'brɪmstəʊn] *adj* (*sermon, preacher*) annonçant les feux de l'enfer.

firearm ['faɪərɑːm] *n* arme *f* à feu; **firearms training,** formation *f* en vue de l'utilisation des armes à feu.

fireball ['faɪəbɔːl] *n* **(a)** *Met* éclair *m* en boule; **(b)** *Astron* bolide *m*.

fireboat ['faɪəbəʊt] *n* bateau-pompe *m*, *pl* bateaux-pompes.

firebox ['faɪəbɒks] *n Rail* foyer *m*, boîte *f* à feu.

firebrand ['faɪəbrænd] *n* **(a)** (*burning wood*) tison *m*, brandon *m*; **(b)** (*person*) brandon *m* de discorde.

firebreak ['faɪəbreɪk] *n* (*in forest etc*) coupe-feu *m inv*.

firebrick ['faɪəbrɪk] *n* brique *f* réfractaire.

firebug ['faɪəbʌg] *n F* incendiaire *mf*, pyromane *mf*.

firecracker ['faɪəkrækər] *n* pétard *m*.

firedamp ['faɪədæmp] *n Min* grisou *m*; **f. explosion,** coup *m* de grisou.

firedog ['faɪədɒg] *n* (*in fireplace*) chenet *m*.

fire-eater ['faɪəriːtər] *n* **(a)** (*in fair etc*) avaleur *m* de feu; **(b)** *F* (*aggressive person*) batailleur, -euse, exalté *m*.

fire-extinguisher ['faɪərɪkstɪŋgwɪʃər] *n* extincteur *m* d'incendie.

fire-fighting ['faɪəfaɪtɪŋ] *adj* **f.-f. equipment,** matériel *m* de lutte contre l'incendie.

firefly ['faɪəflaɪ] *n* (*insect*) luciole *f*.

fireguard ['faɪəgɑːd] *n* **(a)** (*in front of open fire*) écran *m* pare-étincelles, garde-feu *m inv*, devant *m* de cheminée; **(b)** = **FIREBREAK**.

firehouse ['faɪəhaʊs] *n US* poste *m* d'incendie; (*with living quarters*) caserne *f* de (sapeurs-)pompiers.

firelight ['faɪəlaɪt] *n* lumière *f* du feu; **by** *or* **in the f.**, à la lumière du feu.

firelighter ['faɪəlaɪtər] *n* allume-feu *m inv*.

fireman, *pl* **-men** ['faɪəmən] *n* **(a)** (*firefighter*) (sapeur-)pompier *m*; **(b)** *Rail etc* chauffeur *m* (*d'une machine à vapeur etc*).

fireplace ['faɪəpleɪs] *n* cheminée *f*.

fireplug ['faɪəplʌg] *n esp US* bouche *f* d'incendie.

fireproof[1] ['faɪəpruːf] *adj* incombustible, ignifuge; **f. material,** matière ignifugée; **f. vault,** salle blindée; **f. door,** porte *f* coupe-feu; **f. dish,** plat *m* allant au feu.

fireproof[2] *vt* ignifuger (*un tissu etc*); rendre (*qch*) ininflammable.

fireside ['faɪəsaɪd] *n* coin *m* du feu; **sitting by the f.**, assis au coin du feu; **f. chair,** chaise *f* de coin du feu; **f. chat,** (*of politician etc*) causerie *f* au coin du feu.

firetrap ['faɪətræp] *n* **this building's a real f.**, ce bâtiment est un véritable piège (en cas d'incendie).

firewarden ['faɪəwɔːdən] *n Am* guetteur *m* d'incendies.

firewatcher ['faɪəwɔːtʃər] *n* guetteur, -euse d'incendies.

firewatching ['faɪəwɔːtʃɪŋ] *n Br* surveillance *f* contre les incendies.

firewater ['faɪəwɔːtər] *n F* gnole *f*, gnôle *f*, gniole *f*, gnaule *f*, niôle *f*.

firewood ['faɪəwʊd] *n* bois *m* de chauffage, bois à brûler; **bundle of f.**, margotin *m*.

firework ['faɪəwɜːk] *n esp Br* **(a)** (*device*) pièce *f* d'artifice; **f. display,** feu *m* d'artifice; **(b)** (*effect*) (*usu pl*) **fireworks,** feu *m* d'artifice; **grand display of fireworks,** grand feu d'artifice; *F* **whenever they get together there's fireworks,** (*they argue*) chaque fois qu'ils se rencontrent il y a du grabuge; **there'll be fireworks,** il va y avoir du grabuge.

firing ['faɪərɪŋ] *n* **(a)** *Mil etc* (*of firearm, rocket*) tir *m*; (*shooting*) tir, feu *m*; **heavy f. could be heard,** on entendait une vive fusillade; **f. party** *or* **squad,** (*for execution*) peloton *m* d'exécution; (*for ceremonial duties*) peloton chargé de tirer la salve d'honneur; **f. pin,** percuteur *m*; **f. position,** (*of weapon*) position *f* de tir; (*of person*) position du tireur; **f. practice,** exercice *m* de tir; **f. range,** (*distance*) distance *f* de tir; (*place*) stand *m ou* travée *f* de tir; **(b)** chauffage *m*, chauffe *f* (*d'un four, d'une locomotive etc*); **coal/oil f.**, chauffe au charbon/mazout; **(c)** *Cer* cuisson *f* (*des briques, de la poterie etc*); **(d)** (*of engine*) allumage *m*; **f. order** *or* **sequence,** ordre *m* d'allumage (*des cylindres*).

firm[1] [fɜːm] *n Com* maison *f* (de commerce), entreprise *f*, firme *f*; **the firm's giving us a rise,** la firme nous accorde une augmentation; **a large f.**, une grosse entreprise; **f. of solicitors,** étude *f* de notaires.

firm[2] **1** *adj* **(a)** (*flesh etc*) ferme; (*post, nail etc*) solide, fixe; (*tread etc*) assuré; **as f. as a rock,** inébranlable; **to rule with a f. hand,** gouverner d'une main ferme; **to walk with a f. step,** marcher d'un pas assuré; **(b)** (*friendship, intention, person etc*) ferme; (*voice*) ferme, assuré; (*date*) fixe; (*evidence*) convaincant; **to be f. about sth,** tenir bon sur qch; **she was polite but f.**, elle a été polie mais ferme; **to have a f. belief that ...**, avoir la ferme conviction que ...; **(c)** *Com Fin etc* (*offer, sale*) ferme; **these shares remain f. at ...**, ces actions se maintiennent à ...; **there has been no f. news,** il n'y a aucune nouvelle certaine. **2** *adv* **to stand f.**, tenir bon *ou* ferme; **to stand f. about sth,** tenir bon sur qch.

firm[3] **1** *vt* **to f. the soil,** affermir *ou* tasser le sol. **2** *vi* =

FIRM UP 2.

▶**firm up 1** *vtsep* (*make firm*) raffermir. **2** *vi* (*become firm*) (*of price, muscles etc*) se raffermir.

firmly ['fɜːmlɪ] *adv* **(a)** (*solidly*) fermement; (*marcher*) d'un pas assuré; **I f. believe that ...,** j'ai la ferme conviction que ...; **to deal f. with s.o.,** traiter qn fermement *ou* avec fermeté; **she remains f. entrenched in her views,** elle demeure fermement retranchée derrière ses opinions; **(b)** (*to say*) d'un ton ferme.

firmness ['fɜːmnɪs] *n* **(a)** (*solidity*) fermeté *f*; force *f* (*de caractère etc*); (*of tread*) assurance *f*; **(b)** (*of friendship, intention, person, voice etc*) fermeté *f*; (*of voice*) assurance *f*; **(c)** *Com Fin etc* raffermissement *m* (*des valeurs etc*).

firmware ['fɜːmweər] *n Comptr* microprogramme *m*.

first [fɜːst] **1** *adj* (*in time, order*) premier; **the f. (day) of the month,** le premier (jour) du mois; **twenty-f.,** vingt et unième; **eighty-f.,** quatre-vingt-unième; **ninety-f.,** quatre-vingt-onzième; **one hundred and f.,** cent unième; **the f. of April,** le premier avril; **the f. three years,** les trois premières années; **on the f. floor,** au premier étage; *Am* au rez-de-chaussée; **Charles the F.,** Charles Premier; **at f. sight,** à première vue; **at the f. attempt,** au premier *ou* de prime abord; **to use** *or* **wear sth for the f. time,** étrenner qch; **it was my f. flight,** c'était mon baptême de l'air; **to fall head f.,** tomber la tête la première; **to be the f. person to do sth,** être le premier *ou* la première à faire qch; **to come out f. in an examination,** être reçu premier à un examen; **English is my f. language,** l'anglais est ma langue maternelle; **English is my f. foreign language,** l'anglais est ma première langue; **at f. light,** aux premières lueurs du jour; **f. name,** prénom *m*; **to be on f.-name terms with s.o.,** appeler qn par son prénom; **f. cousin,** cousin(e) germain(e); *Th etc* **f. night, f. performance,** première *f*; *Med* **f. aid,** secourisme *m*, premiers secours; **to give/receive f.-aid,** donner/recevoir les premiers secours; **f. aider,** secouriste *mf*; *Gram* **in the f. person,** à la première personne; *Br Sch* **f. year** *or* **form,** = (classe de) sixième *f*; *Aut* **f. gear,** première (vitesse); **f. edition,** (*of book*) édition princeps *ou* originale; **America's f. lady,** l'épouse du Président des Etats-Unis; **the f. lady of British cinema,** la plus grande dame du cinéma britannique; **the F. World War,** la première guerre mondiale; **to put f. things f.,** mettre en avant les choses essentielles; **f. things f.!,** chaque chose en son temps; **I don't know the f. thing** *or* **have the f. idea about motorbikes,** je ne connais absolument rien aux motos; **f. thing in the morning,** (*as soon as I get up*) dès que je me lève; (*as soon as I arrive at the office etc*) dès que j'arrive; (*immediately the shop etc opens*) à l'ouverture; **to travel f. class,** voyager en première (classe); *Mus* **f. violin/trombone,** premier violon/trombone; **f. lieutenant,** lieutenant *m* en premier; *Nau* **f. mate,** second *m*; **f. offender,** personne qui commet un délit pour la première fois; **f. officer,** *Nau* second; *Av* co-pilote *m*; **to have news at f. hand,** tenir une nouvelle de première main; *Parl* **f. reading,** (*of bill*) première lecture.

2 *n* **(a)** (*person, thing*) (le) premier, (la) première; **we were the very f. to arrive,** nous sommes arrivés les tout premiers; *Sp etc* **to come in an easy f.,** arriver bon premier; **to be the f. to do sth,** être le premier à faire qch; *Univ* **to get a f.,** avoir une licence avec mention très bien; **the inflatable life jacket was a Scottish f.,** (*it was invented there*) le gilet de sauvetage est une invention écossaise; **this is a f. for France,** (*the first time it has won the competition*) c'est une première pour la France;

(b) (*beginning*) commencement *m*; **from f. to last,** depuis le début jusqu'à la fin; **from the f.,** dès le commencement; **at f.,** d'abord;

(c) *Aut* première *f* (vitesse); **to climb a hill in f.,** monter une côte en première (vitesse).

3 *adv* **(a)** premièrement, d'abord; **I shall f. have to give it careful consideration,** il faudra d'abord que j'examine cela soigneusement; **f. and foremost,** surtout et avant tout; **f. of all,** pour commencer, en premier lieu; *F* **f. off, why did you do it?,** pour commencer, pourquoi est-ce que vous avez fait cela?; **f. forget that ...,** commencez par oublier que ...;

(b) (*for the first time*) pour la première fois; **when did you f. see him?,** quand l'avez-vous vu pour la première fois?;

(c) (*rather*) plutôt; *F* **I'll see him damned f.,** qu'il aille plutôt au diable;

(d) (*before others*) le premier, la première; **do this f.,** (*before anything else*) commence par ça; **what should I do f.?,** par quoi est-ce que je dois commencer?; **he arrived f.,** il arriva le premier; **to claim the right to speak f.,** réclamer la priorité de parole; **you go f.!,** passez devant!; **f. come f. served,** premier arrivé, premier servi; **it's a case of f. come f. served,** les premiers arrivés sont les premiers servis; **tickets were handed out on a f. come f. served basis,** les billets ont été distribués par ordre d'arrivée; **ladies f.!,** place aux dames!; **women and children f.!,** les femmes et les enfants d'abord!; *Comptr & Ind* **f.-in f.-out,** premier entré, premier sorti;

(e) (*first class*) **to travel f.,** voyager en première (classe).

first-aid [fɜːst'eɪd] *adj Med* **f.-a. kit,** trousse *f* de secours; **f.-a. post,** poste *m* de (premier) secours; **f.-a. dressing,** paquet individuel de pansement; **f.-a. class,** cours *m* de secourisme.

first-born ['fɜːstbɔːn] **1** *adj* (*enfant*) premier-né, *pl* premiers-nés. **2** *n* (*enfant*) premier-né(e), *pl* premiers-né(e)s.

first(-)class ['fɜːstklɑːs] **1** *adj* **(a)** (*wagon*) de première classe; (*article*) de première qualité; (*hôtel etc*) de premier ordre; *Univ* **f.-c. honours (degree),** licence *f* avec mention très bien; *F* **the food was f.-c.,** la nourriture était excellente; **(b)** (*postal service*) à tarif normal; **f.-c. mail,** lettres *etc* envoyées au tarif normal; *Am* lettre close; **f.-c. stamp,** timbre pour tarif normal. **2** *adv* **to travel f.-c.,** voyager en première; **to send a letter f.-c.,** envoyer une lettre au tarif normal.

first-day ['fɜːstdeɪ] *adj* **f.-d. cover,** (enveloppe *f* de) premier jour (d'émission).

first-degree ['fɜːstdɪ'griː] *adj* (*brûlure*) au premier degré; *US* **f.-d. murder,** assassinat *m*.

first-foot¹ ['fɜːst'fʊt] *n Scot* = première personne à se rendre chez quelqu'un pour souhaiter la bonne année.

first-foot² *vi Scot* = être le premier à se rendre chez quelqu'un pour souhaiter la bonne année.

first-hand ['fɜːsthænd] *adj* (*nouvelle*) de première main; **she had the news f.-h.,** elle a reçu la nouvelle directement.

firstly ['fɜːstlɪ] *adv* premièrement, en premier lieu.

first-nighter [fɜːst'naɪtər] *n Th* habitué, -e des premières.

first-past-the-post ['fɜːstpɑːstðə'pəʊst] *adj Pol* **f.-p.-the-p. system,** scrutin *m* à un tour.

first(-)rate ['fɜːst'reɪt] *adj* excellent, de première classe; **of f.-r. quality,** de toute première qualité; **f.-r. idea,** fameuse idée.

first-strike ['fɜːst'straɪk] *adj* (*missile*) de première frappe.

first-time ['fɜːst'taɪm] *adj Com* **f.-t. buyer,** (*of property*) personne *f* achetant une propriété pour la première fois.

firth [fɜːθ] *n Geog Scot* estuaire *m*; **the F. of Forth,** le golfe du Forth.

fiscal ['fɪsk(ə)l] **1** *adj Fin* fiscal, -aux; *Am* **f. year,** année *f* budgétaire, année d'exercice. **2** *n Scot* **procurator f.,** = procureur général.

fish¹, *pl* **fishes** *or* **fish** [fɪʃ, 'fɪʃɪz] *n* **(a)** poisson *m*; **I don't like f.,** (*as food*) je n'aime pas le poisson; *Culin* **fried f.,** poisson frit; *Br* **f. and chips,** poisson frit avec des frites; *F* **I've other f. to fry,** j'ai d'autres chats à fouetter; **there are plenty more f. in the sea,** un(e) de perdu(e), dix de retrouvé(e)s; **to feel like a f. out of water,** ne pas se sentir dans son élément; **at university she was a small f. in a big pond,** à l'université, elle se sentait complètement perdue; **neither f., flesh nor good red herring,** ni chair ni poisson; **f. bone,** arête *f* (de poisson); **f. cake,** croquette *f* de poisson; *Culin* **f. course** *or* **dish,** plat *m* de poisson; **f. farm,** établissement *m* piscicole; **f. farmer,** pisciculteur *m*; **f. farming,** pisciculture *f*; *Br* **f. fingers,** *Am* **f. sticks,** bâtonnets *mpl* de poisson; **f. kettle,** poissonnière *f*; *Culin* **f. knife and fork,** couverts *mpl* à poisson; **f. market,** marché *m* au poisson; **f. meal,** farine *f* de poisson; **f. pond,** étang *m*; (*for breeding fish*) vivier *m*; **f. shop,** (*fishmonger's*) poissonnerie *f*; *Br F* (*fish-and-chip shop*) boutique *f* vendant du poisson et des frites à emporter; *Culin* **f. slice,** spatule *f* large; **f. tank,** vivier *m*;

(b) *Astron* **the Fish(es),** les Poissons *mpl*.

fish² **1** *vi* pêcher; **to f. for trout/pearls,** pêcher la truite/des perles; *F* **to f. for compliments,** chercher des compliments. **2** *vt* **(a)** pêcher (*un saumon etc*); **(b)** pêcher dans (*une rivière*).

fish³, *pl* **fishes** *n Rail* éclisse *f*.

▶**fish out** *vtsep* (*remove from water*) repêcher (*qn, qch*); **to f. out a dead body,** (re)pêcher un cadavre; **she put her hand in the drawer and fished out a twenty-dollar bill,** elle a mis la main dans le tiroir et en a sorti un billet de vingt dollars; **he fished a pencil out of his pocket,** il a fouillé dans sa poche et en a tiré un crayon.

▶**fish up** *vtsep* (*bring up from water*) repêcher; **to f. up a dead body,** (re)pêcher un cadavre; **to f. up a mine,**

relever une mine.
fish-and-chip [fɪʃən'tʃɪp] *adj Br Culin Com* **f.-and-c. shop,** = boutique qui vend du poisson frit et des frites.
fisherman, *pl* **-men** ['fɪʃəmən] *n* pêcheur *m*; **f.'s bend,** (*knot*) nœud *m* de grappin.
fishery ['fɪʃərɪ] *n* **(a)** (*fishing industry*) pêche *f*; **f.-protection vessel,** garde-pêche *m inv*; **(b)** (*fishing ground*) pêcherie *f*.
fish-eye ['fɪʃaɪ] *Phot* **1** *adj* **f.-e. lens,** objectif *m* à grand-angle extrême. **2** *n F* grand-angle *m*.
fish-hook ['fɪʃhʊk] *n* hameçon *m*.
fishing ['fɪʃɪŋ] *n* pêche *f*; **there's good f. to be had here,** il y a du poisson par ici; **trout f.,** pêche à la truite; **pearl f.,** pêche des perles; **fly f.,** pêche à la mouche; **f. boat** *or* **smack,** bateau *m* de pêche; **f. ground,** pêcherie *f*; **f. line,** ligne *f* (de pêche); **f. net,** filet *m* de pêche; **f. port,** port *m* de pêche; **f. rights,** droits *mpl* de pêche; **f. rod,** canne *f* à pêche; **f. tackle,** articles *mpl* de pêche; **f. trip,** partie *f* de pêche; **f. vessel,** navire *m* de pêche, pêcheur *m*; **f. village,** village *m* de pêcheurs.
fishmonger ['fɪʃmʌŋgər] *n esp Br* poissonnier *m*; **f.'s (shop),** poissonnerie *f*.
fishnet ['fɪʃnet] **1** *n esp Am* filet *m* de pêche. **2** *adj* **f. stockings,** bas *mpl* résille.
fishplate ['fɪʃpleɪt] *n Rail* éclisse *f*.
fishtail ['fɪʃteɪl] *n* queue *f* de poisson.
fishwife, *pl* **-wives** ['fɪʃwaɪf, -waɪvz] *n* marchande *f* de poisson; **she swears like a f.,** elle jure comme un charretier.
fishy ['fɪʃɪ] *adj* **(a)** (*odeur, goût*) de poisson; **(b)** *F* (*business etc*) douteux, louche; **f. story,** histoire qui ne tient pas debout.
fissile ['fɪsaɪl] *adj* fissile.
fission ['fɪʃən] *n* **(a)** *Phys* fission *f*; **nuclear/thermal f.,** fission nucléaire/thermique; **(b)** *Biol* scissiparité *f*.
fissure[1] ['fɪʃər] *n* fissure *f*, fente *f* (*dans un mur etc*).
fissure[2] **1** *vt* fissurer, fendre (*un rocher etc*). **2** *vi* (*of rock etc*) se fissurer, se fendre.
fist [fɪst] *n* **(a)** poing *m*; **he went for them with his fists,** il tomba sur eux à coups de poing; **to clench one's f., to make a f.,** serrer le poing; **to shake one's f.** *or* **fists at s.o.,** menacer qn du poing; **(b)** *Sl* main *f*.
fistful ['fɪstfʊl] *n F* poignée *f* (*d'argent etc*).
fisticuffs ['fɪstɪkʌfs] *npl Old-fashioned F* coups *mpl* de poing.
fistula ['fɪstjʊlə] *n Med* fistule *f*.
fit[1] [fɪt] *n* accès *m* (*de folie etc*); quinte *f* (*de toux*); (*apoplexy*) crise *f* d'apoplexie; **(epileptic) f.,** crise *f* d'épilepsie; **fainting f.,** évanouissement *m*; **to have** *or F* **throw a f.,** piquer une crise; *F* **he'll have a f. when he finds out,** il en aura une congestion quand il le saura; **in a f. of temper,** dans un mouvement de colère; **f. of crying,** crise de larmes; **f. of laughter,** accès *m* de rire; **to be in fits (of laughter),** avoir le fou rire; **in a f. of idleness,** dans un moment de paresse; **to have sudden fits of energy,** avoir des élans d'énergie; **to work by fits and starts,** travailler par à-coups.
fit[2] *adj* (**fitter; fittest**) **(a)** (*appropriate*) bon, propre (**for sth,** à qch); **f. to eat,** bon à manger, mangeable; **f. to drink,** buvable, potable; **I've nothing f. to wear,** je n'ai rien à me mettre; **story that is not f. to be repeated,** histoire qu'il ne serait pas convenable de répéter; **a meal f. for a king,** un repas digne d'un roi; **I'm not f. to be seen,** je ne suis pas présentable; **to think f.** *or* **see f. to do sth,** juger convenable *ou* trouver bon de faire qch; **do as you see** *or* **think f.,** faites comme bon vous semble; **she cried f. to break her heart,** elle pleurait à gros sanglots;
(b) (*capable*) capable; **f. for sth,** en état de faire qch; **f. for duty,** bon pour le service; *Mil* valide; **f. to do sth,** capable de faire qch; **that's all he's f. for,** il n'est bon qu'à cela; **she's not a f. mother,** c'est une mère indigne;
(c) (*ready*) disposé (à faire qch); **I felt f. to drop,** je me sentais prêt à tomber (de fatigue);
(d) (*healthy*) en forme; **to get f.,** retrouver la forme; **I'm a lot fitter,** je suis bien plus en forme; **to be (fighting) f.,** être en forme; **to keep f.,** se maintenir en forme; **he is not yet f. to go back to work,** il n'est pas encore en état de reprendre son travail; *F* **to be as f. as a fiddle,** être en parfaite santé.
fit[3] *n* ajustement *m*; *MecE* ajustage *m* (*d'un assemblage etc*); **your coat is a perfect/poor f.,** votre manteau vous va parfaitement/ne vous va pas très bien; **it was a tight f. but everyone squeezed in,** il n'y avait pas beaucoup de place mais tout le monde a tenu.
fit[4] *v* (**-tt-**) **1** *vt* **(a)** (*be suitable for*) s'accorder avec (*qch*); **to make the punishment f. the crime,** proportionner la peine au délit;
(b) (*of clothes*) être à la taille de (*qn*); **key that fits the lock,** clef qui va à la serrure;
(c) (*install*) adapter, ajuster (**sth to sth,** qch à qch); **to f. a nozzle on the end of a pipe,** adapter un ajutage à l'extrémité d'un tuyau; **to f. a handle to a broom,** emmancher un balai; **to f. one part into another,** emboîter une pièce dans une autre; **to f. a carpet,** poser une moquette; **I'm going to be fitted for my new dress,** je vais faire l'essayage de ma nouvelle robe;
(d) (*assemble*) **to f. parts together,** monter *ou* assembler des pièces; **to f. a machine together,** assembler une machine;
(e) (*equip*) munir, pourvoir (**sth with sth,** qch de qch); **fitted with two propellers,** pourvu de deux hélices;
(f) (*insert*) **to f. sth/s.o. into/onto sth,** mettre *ou* rentrer *ou F* caser qch/qn dans/sur qch; **we can f. another two (people) inside,** il y a de la place pour deux personnes de plus.
2 *vi* aller, tenir; **the lid doesn't f.,** ce n'est pas le bon couvercle; **to f. (together),** s'ajuster, s'adapter; **pieces that f. together,** pièces *fpl* rapportables; **to f. on sth,** s'adapter sur qch; **to f. into sth,** s'emboîter dans qch; **piece that fits into another,** pièce qui entre dans une autre; **your dress fits well/badly,** votre robe vous va/ne vous va pas bien; **all her tools easily fitted into the bag,** tous ses outils tenaient largement dans son sac; **we won't all f. into the car,** nous ne tiendrons pas tous dans la voiture; **the photos just f. onto the page,** les photos tiennent juste sur la page.
►**fit in 1** *vtsep* (*find room, time for*) emboîter (*des tubes etc*); faire cadrer (*des projets etc*); **I can't f. any more clothes in,** (*the drawer etc*) je ne peux plus mettre aucun vêtement; **the hairdresser says she can f. me in tomorrow,** la coiffeuse dit qu'elle peut s'arranger pour me prendre demain. **2** *vi* **(a)** (*go into place*) tenir; **these clothes won't f. in,** ces vêtements ne tiendront pas; **(b)** (*harmonize*) **to f. in between two things,** s'emboîter entre deux choses; **to f. in with sth,** être en harmonie avec qch; **your plans don't f. in with mine,** vos projets ne cadrent pas avec les miens; **he doesn't f. in there,** il n'y est pas dans son élément; **(c)** (*agree*) correspondre; **that doesn't f. in with what I was told,** ça ne correspond pas à ce qu'on m'a dit.
►**fit out** *vtsep* équiper (**sth with sth,** qch de qch); armer (*un navire*); équiper (*un navire neuf*); **to f. s.o. out,** équiper qn de (*vêtements etc*).
►**fit up** *vtsep* **(a)** (*provide*) doter, pourvoir, munir; **they fitted me up with an artificial leg,** ils m'ont doté d'une jambe artificielle; **(b)** (*equip*) aménager (**sth for sth,** qch pour qch).
fitful ['fɪtfʊl] *adj* (*sleep*) agité.
fitment ['fɪtmənt] *n* **(a)** *Br* (*piece of furniture*) élément *m*; **(b)** (*of machine*) accessoire *m*.
fitness ['fɪtnɪs] *n* **(a)** (*health*) forme *f* (physique); **f. freak,** fana *mf* de la forme; **(b)** (*suitability*) (*of person*) aptitude *f* (**for a job**/*etc*, à un emploi/*etc*); (*of remark*) justesse *f*, à-propos *m*; **her f. for government,** son aptitude à gouverner.
fitted ['fɪtɪd] *adj* **(a)** ajusté; *Sewing* ajusté; **f. carpet,** moquette *f*; **f. sheet,** drap *m* housse; **f. wardrobe/cooker,** garde-robe/four encastré(e); **(b)** (*equipped*) **f. kitchen,** cuisine encastrée; **(c)** (*person, thing*) **to be f. for sth/to do sth,** être fait pour qch/pour faire qch.
fitter ['fɪtər] *n* **(a)** *MecE Aut etc* ajusteur *m*, assembleur, -euse; **electrical f.,** installateur *m* d'appareils électriques; **(b)** *Sewing* essayeur, -euse.
fitting ['fɪtɪŋ] **1** *adj* convenable, approprié (**to,** à); (*remarque*) à propos; **it was a f. tribute to a great athlete,** c'était un hommage mérité rendu à un grand athlète; **a f. end for a murderer,** une fin appropriée pour un meurtrier.
2 *n* **(a)** ajustement *m* (*d'une pièce etc*); emboîtement *m* (*d'un pignon etc*); installation *f* (*d'appareils*); **f. of sth on sth,** adaptation *f* de qch à qch; *Ind* **f. shop,** atelier *m* d'ajustage;
(b) (*of clothes*) essayage *m*, ajustage *m*; *Com* **made in three fittings,** fabriqué en trois tailles; (*of shoes*) fabriqué en trois largeurs; **f. room,** cabine *f* d'essayage;
(c) (*installations*) (*usu pl*) **fittings,** agencements *mpl*, installations *fpl* (*d'un bureau etc*); accessoires *mpl* (*sanitaires etc*); **door fittings,** ferrures *fpl* de porte; **brass fittings,** garnitures *fpl* en cuivre; *El* **light f.,** appareil *m* d'éclairage; **ceiling f.,** plafonnier *m*; **wall f.,** applique *f*.
fitting out *n* équipement *m* (*d'une expédition etc*); armement *m* (*d'un navire*).
fittingly ['fɪtɪŋlɪ] *adv* convenablement, à propos; **f., he was buried in his home town,** comme il convenait, il a été enterré dans sa ville natale.
five [faɪv] *n* **(a)** (*numeral*) cinq *m*; **f.-o'clock shadow,** barbe *f* d'un jour; *Br* **a f.-pound note,** un billet de cinq li-

vres; *Br* **it costs f. pence,** ça coûte cinq pence; **he leaves his office at f.,** il quitte son bureau à cinq heures; *Econ* **F.-Year Plan,** Plan quinquennal; **(b)** *Sp* **fives,** (*game*) = balle *f* au mur.

five-finger ['faɪv'fɪŋgər] *adj Mus* **f.-f. exercises,** exercices *mpl* de doigté.

fivefold ['faɪvfəʊld] **1** *adj* quintuple. **2** *adv* cinq fois autant; au quintuple; **to increase f.,** quintupler.

fiver ['faɪvər] *n F Br* billet *m* de cinq livres; *US* billet de cinq dollars; *Br* **it'll cost you a f.,** ça te coûtera cinq livres.

fivespot ['faɪvspɒt] *n US* billet *m* de cinq dollars.

five-star ['faɪv'stɑːr] *adj* (*hotel*) cinq étoiles.

fix¹ [fɪks] *n* **(a)** *F* (*difficulty*) embarras *m*, difficulté *f*; **to be in a f.,** être dans une situation embarrassante; **to get into a f.,** se mettre dans l'embarras; **(b)** *Sl* (*of drug*) piqûre *f* de drogue; **to give oneself a f.,** se piquer; *F Fig* **my daily f. of television news,** ma dose quotidienne de journaux télévisés; **(c)** *Av Nau* position *f*; **to get a f. on a ship/***etc*, déterminer la position d'un navire/*etc*.

fix² *vt* **(a)** (*attach securely*) fixer; caler, monter (*une roue sur l'essieu, une poulie etc*); assurer (*une planche avec des clous etc*); attacher (*un hameçon à une ligne etc*); **to f. sth in one's memory,** se graver qch dans la mémoire; **to f. one's attention on sth,** fixer son attention sur qch; **to f. one's eye(s) on s.o.,** fixer qn (du regard);

(b) fixer, établir (*une limite, le taux de l'intérêt etc*); désigner (*l'endroit pour un rendez-vous*); régler (*l'itinéraire d'un voyage etc*); **the date is not yet fixed,** la date n'est pas encore certaine; **there's nothing fixed yet, nothing is fixed yet,** il n'y a encore rien de décidé;

(c) (*arrange*) arranger (*une réunion etc*); (*repair*) réparer, retaper (*qch*); préparer (*un repas etc*); **to f. sth with s.o.,** arranger qch avec qn; **I've fixed it with her,** je me suis arrangé avec elle; *F* **how are you fixed for money/for time?,** tu as assez d'argent/de temps?; **I'll f. him!,** je lui ferai son affaire!; **just wait while I f. my hair,** attends que je me coiffe;

(d) (*set up*) établir (*un camp*);

(e) (*bribe*) graisser la patte à (*qn*); (*rig*) truquer (*un match etc*);

(f) *Ch Phot etc* fixer (*le mercure, une teinture etc*);

(g) *Med* stériliser (*à la formaline etc*);

(h) *US Dial* **to be fixing to do sth,** être décidé *ou* déterminé de faire qch.

►**fix on 1** *vtsep* (*attach*) fixer; **I fixed the handle on with glue,** j'ai fixé la poignée avec de la colle. **2** *vipo* (*choose, decide*) se décider pour (*qch*); **have you fixed on a date?,** avez-vous fixé une date?

►**fix up** *F vtsep* **(a)** (*assemble, put up*) monter (*une tente*); **they fixed up a temporary telephone,** ils ont installé une ligne de téléphone provisoire; **to f. up a room as a study,** transformer une pièce en bureau; **(b)** (*arrange*) arranger (*une affaire*); **it's all fixed up,** c'est une affaire réglée; **I've already fixed up to go out tonight,** j'ai déjà prévu de sortir ce soir; **(c)** (*improve*) réparer, retaper (*qch*); **they're fixing up the house,** ils retapent leur maison; **you should f. yourself up a bit,** tu devrais t'arranger un peu; **(d)** (*provide*) **to f. s.o. up with,** trouver (*un travail, une chambre*) pour qn; **I've fixed you up with a blind date,** je t'ai arrangé un rendez-vous.

fixation [fɪk'seɪʃən] *n* **(a)** *Psy* fixation *f*; **to have a mother f.,** faire une fixation sur sa mère; **(b)** fixation *f* (*de l'impôt, du mercure etc*).

fixative ['fɪksətɪv] *adj & n Art* fixatif *m*.

fixed [fɪkst] *adj* **(a)** (*immobile*) fixe, immobile, stationnaire; *Comptr* **f. disk,** disque *m* fixe; **f. pulley,** poulie *f* fixe; **(b)** (*unchanging*) fixe, constant, invariable; (*règle*) établi, absolu; (*idée*) fixe; **of f. length,** de longueur constante; **f. price,** prix *m* fixe *ou* forfaitaire; **f. income,** revenu fixe; **to have f. ideas,** avoir des idées (bien) arrêtées; **to have no f. plans,** ne pas avoir de projets bien déterminés; **f. point,** point *m* fixe, point de repère; *Fin* **f. assets,** immobilisations *fpl*; **f. costs,** frais *mpl* fixes; **(c)** (*regard*) fixe; (*sourire*) figé; **(d)** *Ch* (*huile, sel*) fixe; **(e)** *F Pej* (*match etc*) truqué.

fixedly ['fɪksɪdlɪ] *adv* fixement.

fixer ['fɪksər] *n* **(a)** *F Pej* combinard *m*; (*drug seller*) pourvoyeur *m* de drogues; **(b)** *Art* fixatif *m*; *Phot* fixateur *m*.

fixing ['fɪksɪŋ] *n* **(a)** fixation *f*, mise *f* en place (*d'un appareil etc*); fixage *m* (*d'une épreuve photographique*); ancrage *m* (*de crampons etc*); pose *f* (*d'une serrure*); *Phot* **f. solution/bath,** solution *f*/bain *m* de fixage; **(b)** *Av Nau* relevé *m*, relèvement *m* (*d'une position*); **(c)** *Com* établissement *m* (*des prix etc*); **(d)** *usu pl esp Am* (*trimmings*) **fixings,** accessoires *mpl*; *Culin* **roast turkey with all the fixings,** dinde rôtie avec tout ce qui s'ensuit.

fixity ['fɪksɪtɪ] *n* fixité *f*; **f. of purpose,** détermination *f*.

fixture ['fɪkstʃər] *n* **(a)** (*installation*) appareil *m* fixe; **to make sth a f.,** fixer qch (à demeure); *F* **he's become a f. here,** il s'est bien ancré chez nous; il fait partie des meubles; **fixtures,** aménagements *mpl* (*d'une maison etc*); appareils (*électriques etc*); **£3000 for fixtures and fittings,** 3 000 livres de reprise; **bathroom fixtures and fittings,** installations et accessoires de salles de bain; **(b)** *Br Sp* rencontre *f* (prévue); match *m* (prévu); **list of fixtures, f. list,** calendrier *m* (de la saison).

fizz¹ [fɪz] *n* **(a)** (*sound*) pétillement *m* (*du champagne etc*); sifflement *m* (*de la vapeur*); **(b)** *F* (*soft drink*) boisson gazeuse; (*champagne*) champagne *m*.

fizz² *vi* (*of champagne*) pétiller; (*of steam*) siffler.

fizzle ['fɪz(ə)l] *vi* (*of wine*) pétiller; (*of gas burner etc*) siffler.

►**fizzle out** *vi F* (*of plan*) ne pas aboutir; (*of enthusiasm, interest*) tomber; (*of story*) finir en queue de poisson.

fizzy ['fɪzɪ] *adj esp Br F* (*mineral water, drink*) gazeux; (*wine*) mousseux.

fjord [fjɔːd] *n Geog* fjord *m*, fiord *m*.

Fla *abbr* **Florida.**

flab [flæb] *n F* (*fat*) lard *m*, graisse *f*.

flabbergast ['flæbəgɑːst] *vt F* abasourdir, ahurir (*qn*); **I was flabbergasted,** j'en étais sidéré.

flabbiness ['flæbɪnɪs] *n* flaccidité *f*, manque *m* de fermeté (*de la chair etc*); *Fig* mollesse *f* (*de qn*).

flabby ['flæbɪ] *adj* (*muscles etc*) flasque, mou, molle; (*cheeks*) pendant; *Fig* (*person*) mollasse; (*prose*) qui manque de vigueur.

flaccid ['flæksɪd] *adj* mou, molle; (*chair*) flasque.

flag¹ [flæg] *n* **(a)** *Mil etc* drapeau *m*; *Nau* pavillon *m*; **I like to show the f. when I'm abroad,** je m'emploie à défendre les couleurs de mon pays quand je suis à l'étranger; **the 6th fleet is showing the f. in the Mediterranean,** la 6ème flotte fait acte de présence en Méditerranée; **white f.,** drapeau blanc; **yellow f.,** pavillon de quarantaine; **pilot f.,** pavillon (de) pilote; **black f.,** pavillon noir; *Ski* **pair of flags,** porte *f*; **f. of convenience,** pavillon de complaisance; *Nau* **f. captain,** commandant *m* du navire amiral; *Nau* **f. officer, officer of f. rank,** officier général; **f. signals,** signalisation *f* par fanions; **f. day,** (*for charity*) jour de quête pour une œuvre de bienfaisance; **F. Day,** (*in United States*) le 14 juin; **(b)** drapeau *m* (*de taximètre*); **taxi with the f. up,** taxi libre; **(c)** *Comptr* (*marker*) drapeau *m*, indicateur *m*.

flag² *vt* **(a)** (*hang flags on*) pavoiser (*un édifice*); **(b)** (*signal to*) transmettre des signaux à (*qn*) au moyen de fanions; héler, faire signe à (*un taxi*); **(c)** (*mark*) **to f. a file,** marquer des papiers dans un dossier; *Comptr* **to f. an error,** marquer une erreur (d'un indicateur).

flag³ *vi* (*of thing*) pendre mollement; (*of sail*) battre; (*of plant*) languir; (*of person*) s'alanguir; (*of conversation*) traîner, languir; (*of attention*) faiblir, fléchir; (*of courage*) s'amollir; **our spirits were flagging,** notre moral faiblissait; **his strength was flagging,** ses forces baissaient.

flag⁴ *n Constr* carreau *m*, dalle *f*.

flag⁵ *vt* (*pave*) daller (*un trottoir etc*); paver de carreaux.

flag⁶ *n* (*plant*) iris *m*.

►**flag down** *vtsep* (*stop*) arrêter, stopper (*un automobiliste, une voiture*).

►**flag out** *vtsep Sp* jalonner (*un champ de course*).

►**flag up** *vtsep* (*mark, indicate*) marquer.

flagellate¹ ['flædʒəleɪt] *adj & n* flagellé *m*.

flagellate² *vt* flageller, fouetter.

flagellation [flædʒə'leɪʃən] *n* flagellation *f*.

flageolet ['flædʒəlet, flædʒə'let] *n Mus* flageolet *m*.

flagged [flægd] *adj* (*floor*) carrelé, dallé.

flagging¹ ['flægɪŋ] **1** *adj* (*conversation etc*) languissant; **to revive s.o.'s f. spirits,** remonter le moral à qn. **2** *n* amollissement *m* (*du courage*); ralentissement *m* (*du zèle*).

flagging² *n* (*paving*) carrelage *m*, dallage *m*.

flagon ['flægən] *n* **(a)** (*large bottle*) grosse bouteille (ventrue), bonbonne *f*; **(b)** (*jug*) pot *m* (à anse).

flagpole ['flægpəʊl] *n* mât *m* de drapeau; *Fig F* **to run sth up the f.,** proposer qch pour voir les réactions.

flagrant ['fleɪgrənt] *adj* (*offence*) flagrant, scandaleux; (*offender*) notoire; **a f. injustice,** une injustice criante.

flagrante delicto (in) [ɪnflə'græntɪdɪ'lɪktəʊ] *adv Jur* en flagrant délit.

flagrantly ['fleɪgrəntlɪ] *adv* d'une manière flagrante.

flagship ['flægʃɪp] *n Nau* (*navire m*) amiral *m*; *Fig* **the London store is the f. of the chain,** le magasin de Londres est le plus important de la chaîne; **the rail company's f. service,** le service le plus prestigieux de la compagnie des chemins de fer.

flagstaff ['flægstɑːf] *n* mât *m* de drapeau; *Nau* mât de pavillon.

flagstone ['flægstəʊn] *n* dalle *f*; **f. pavement,** dallage *m* en pierre.

flag-waving ['flægweɪvɪŋ] *n F* déclarations cocardières; **f.-w. speech,** discours cocardier.

flail¹ [fleɪl] *n Agr* fléau *m*.

flail² 1 *vt Agr* battre au fléau; *Fig* (*strike wildly*) battre violemment. 2 *vi* (*of rope, cable*) se balancer violemment; **I dodged my assailant's flailing arms,** j'ai esquivé les coups de mon assaillant.

►**flail about, flail around** *vi* (*wave wildly*) s'agiter; se débattre des mains et des pieds.

flair [fleər] *n* (*skill*) aptitude *f* (**for,** à); (*skill in detecting things etc*) flair *m*; (*energy etc*) dynamisme *m*; **to have a f. for languages,** avoir le don des langues; **to dress/write with f.,** (*stylishness*) s'habiller/écrire avec style.

flak [flæk] *n* **(a)** (*artillery*) artillerie anti-aérienne; (*fire*) tir *m* contre-avions; **f. jacket,** gilet *m* de protection; **(b)** *F* (*criticism*) critique *f*; **she got a lot of f. for this decision,** on l'a beaucoup critiquée pour cette décision.

flake¹ [fleɪk] *n* **(a)** flocon *m* (*de neige*); écaille *f*, éclat *m*, paillette *f* (*de métal etc*); **soap flakes,** savon *m* en paillettes; **(b)** *Am F* barjo *mf*.

flake² *vi* (*of metal, paint etc*) s'écailler; **my skin was flaking,** ma peau pelait.

►**flake away, flake off** *vi* (*of metal, paint etc*) s'écailler; (*of skin*) peler.

►**flake out** *vi F* (*fall asleep*) s'endormir; **I just want to f. out on the sofa,** j'ai envie de m'effondrer sur le canapé; **to be flaked out,** être vidé *ou* crevé.

flaking ['fleɪkɪŋ] 1 *adj* (*peinture*) qui s'écaille; (*peau*) qui pèle. 2 *n* écaillement *m* (*de la peinture*).

flaky ['fleɪkɪ] *adj* **(a)** (*snow etc*) floconneux; **(b)** (*mineral etc*) écailleux; *Culin* **f. pastry,** pâte feuilletée; **(c)** *Am F* (*crazy*) barjo.

flamboyance [flæm'bɔɪəns] *n* qualité flamboyante.

flamboyant [flæm'bɔɪənt] *adj* flamboyant.

flame¹ [fleɪm] *n* **(a)** flamme *f*; **in flames,** en flammes, en feu; **to burst into flame(s), to go up in flames,** s'enflammer brusquement, se mettre à flamber; **f. cutter,** (*in metalworking*) chalumeau *m* à découper; **f. gun,** agriflamme *m*; **f. red,** rouge feu; **f. red hair,** chevelure flamboyante; **f. tree,** flamboyant *m*; **(b)** (*light*) éclat *m* (*d'une pierre précieuse*); **(c)** *Lit* passion *f*, ardeur *f*; *F* (*person*) béguin *m*; **he is an old f. of mine,** c'est un de mes anciens amoureux.

flame² 1 *vi* **(a)** (*of fire etc*) flamber, flamboyer; *Lit* (*of passions etc*) flamber; **(b)** (*of diamond etc*) briller. 2 *vt Med etc* flamber (*un instrument*).

►**flame up** *vi* (*blaze*) s'enflammer; *F* (*of person*) se mettre en colère.

flame-coloured ['fleɪmkʌləd] *adj* ponceau *inv*, couleur de feu *inv*.

flamenco [flə'meŋkəʊ] *n Mus* flamenco *m*.

flameproof ['fleɪmpruːf] *adj* **(a)** ininflammable; (*material*) ignifuge; **(b)** *El* antidéflagrant.

flamethrower ['fleɪmθrəʊər] *n Mil etc* lance-flammes *m inv*.

flaming ['fleɪmɪŋ] 1 *adj* **(a)** (*feu*) flambant, flamboyant; **(b)** (*soleil*) ardent; **f. red,** rouge feu *inv*; *F* **in a f. temper,** d'une humeur massacrante; **(c)** *Br F* sacré; **you f. idiot!,** sacré imbécile! 2 *adv Br Sl* complètement, carrément; **he's so f. stupid,** il est complètement stupide.

flamingo, *pl* **-o(e)s** [flə'mɪŋgəʊ, -əʊz] *n* (*bird*) flamant *m*.

flammable ['flæməb(ə)l] *adj* inflammable.

flan [flæn] *n Culin* tarte *f*; **f. case,** fond *m* de tarte.

Flanders ['flɑːndəz] *n* la Flandre.

flange¹ [flændʒ] *n* bourrelet *m*, collerette *f* (*d'un tube, d'un tuyau*); collet *m*, rebord *m* (*d'une tôle*); boudin *m*, rebord (*d'une roue*); aile *f* (*d'une poutre*); *Rail* patin *m* (*de rail*); **cooling f.,** ailette *f* de refroidissement; **f. coupling,** raccordement *m* à bride.

flange² *vt Tech* brider (*qch*); border (*une tôle*); bourreler (*une roue*).

flanged [flændʒd] *adj* (*tube*) à bride(s); (*roue*) à boudin; (*rail*) à patin; (*poutre*) à aile; (*tôle*) à bord tombé; *Aut* (*radiateur*) à ailettes.

flank¹ [flæŋk] *n* **(a)** flanc *m* (*d'une personne, d'un animal*); *Culin* flanchet *m* (*de bœuf*); **(b)** côté *m*, flanc *m* (*d'une montagne etc*); *Mil* flanc (*d'une armée etc*); **left/right f.,** aile gauche/droite; **to protect one's flanks,** se couvrir sur les flancs.

flank² *vt* **(a)** flanquer; **to f. sth with** *or* **by sth,** flanquer qch de qch; **flanked by two policemen,** encadré de deux gendarmes; **(b)** *Mil* prendre (*l'ennemi etc*) de flanc; enfiler (*une tranchée etc*).

flanker ['flæŋkər] *n Rugby* avant-aile *m*, *pl* avant-ailes.

flannel ['flæn(ə)l] 1 *n* **(a)** *Tex* (*material*) flanelle *f*; **flannels,** un pantalon de flanelle; **(b)** *Br* **(face) f.,** = gant *m* de toilette. 2 *adj* (*trousers etc*) de flanelle.

flannelette [flænə'let] *n Tex* pilou *m*, veloutine *f*.

flap¹ [flæp] *n* **(a)** battement *m*, coup *m* (*d'aile*); clapotement *m*, claquement *m* (*d'une voile*); **(b)** rabat *m* (*d'une enveloppe*); patte *f* (*d'une poche*); pan *m* (*d'un vêtement*); rabat *m* (*de la jaquette d'un livre etc*); *MecE* clapet *m* (à charnière); abattant *m* (*de table*); trappe *f* (*de cave*); *Av* volet *m*; *Surg* lambeau *m*; **desk with a writing f.,** secrétaire *m*; *Av* **landing f.,** volet d'atterrissage; **(c)** *F* (*panic*) affolement *m*; **to get into a f.,** s'agiter, s'affoler; **to be in a f.,** ne plus savoir où donner de la tête; **there's a big f. on,** c'est la panique, c'est l'effolement total.

flap² *v* (-pp-) 1 *vt* battre; **the bird flaps its wings,** l'oiseau bat des ailes; **to f. one's arms about,** agiter les bras. 2 *vi* **(a)** (*of sail*) battre, claquer; (*of wings*) battre; **(b)** *F* (*panic*) s'agiter, s'affoler.

flapjack ['flæpdʒæk] *n Culin* **(a)** *Am* (*pancake*) crêpe *f*; **(b)** *Br* (*biscuit*) biscuit *m* à l'avoine.

flapper ['flæpər] *n* = jeune femme (des années 20).

flapping ['flæpɪŋ] *n* **(a)** battement *m* (*des ailes*); clapotement *m*, claquement *m* (*d'une voile*); **(b)** *F* (*panic*) agitation *f*, affolement *m*.

flare¹ [fleər] *n* **(a)** (*bright flame*) flamboiement; (*of jet engine etc*) flammes *fpl*; **(b)** *Mil Av* feu *m* de signal; (*rocket*) fusée éclairante; **f. pistol,** pistolet *m* de signalisation; **f. path,** piste éclairée; **(c)** *Phot* **f. (spot),** spectre *m* secondaire; **(d)** (*of tube etc*) évasement *m*; (*of skirt*) godet *m*; **(a pair of) flares,** un pantalon (à) pattes d'éléphant.

flare² 1 *vi* **(a)** (*of lamp etc*) flamboyer; **(b)** (*of skirt etc*) s'évaser; **(c)** (*of temper*) s'échauffer; **tempers flared at the council meeting,** le ton est monté pendant la réunion du conseil. 2 *vt* évaser (*un tube, une jupe etc*).

►**flare up** *vi* **(a)** (*of candle etc*) s'enflammer brusquement; **(b)** (*of anger, fighting etc*) éclater; (*of person*) s'emporter; **to f. up again,** éclater de nouveau, reprendre; **he flares up at the slightest thing,** il monte comme une soupe au lait.

flared [fleəd] *adj* (*jupe, tube etc*) evasé.

flare-up ['fleərʌp] *n* **(a)** flambée soudaine; **(b)** déclenchement *m* (*de la guerre*); éruption *f* (*de la colère*); (*renewal*) recrudescence *f* (*de la colère, d'une guerre*); (*argument*) altercation *f*; (*of person*) flambée *f ou* éclat *m* de colère; **there have been several f.-ups of ethnic violence lately,** on a assisté récemment à des explosions de violences raciales.

flash¹ [flæʃ] *n* **(a)** éclair *m*; (*of diamond etc*) éclat *m*; lueur *f*, éclair (*d'une arme à feu*); *Petr* détente *f*; **a f. of lightning,** un éclair; **f. of wit,** saillie *f*; **f. of inspiration,** éclair de génie; **f. of hope,** rayon *m* d'espoir; **(as) quick as a f.,** vif comme l'éclair; **in a f.,** en un rien de temps, en un clin d'œil; *Fig* **a f. in the pan,** un feu de paille; *Nucl Phys* **f. burn,** brûlure *f* par irradiation; **f. flood,** crue subite; **f. point,** (*of oil etc*) point *m* d'inflammabilité; *Fig* situation explosive *ou* critique; **f. welding,** (*in metalwork*) soudure *f* par étincelage; **(b)** *Phot* flash *m*, *pl* flashes; **f. gun,** flash *m*; **f. photography,** photographie *f* au flash; **(c)** *Am F* (*torch*) torche *f* (électrique); **(d)** *Journ* flash *m*; **news f.,** flash d'information; **(e)** *Cin* scène *f* de raccord (très courte); **(f)** (*no pl*) (*on moulding*) bavure *f*; **(g)** *Br Mil* (*badge*) écusson *m*.

flash² 1 *vi* **(a)** (*of light, diamonds*) briller; (*on police car etc*) clignoter; (*of eyes etc*) jeter des éclairs; (*with enthusiasm*) briller; (*of lake etc*) miroiter; **his eyes flashed with anger,** ses yeux lançaient des éclairs de colère;

(b) (*move fast*) **to f. past,** passer comme un éclair; **she flashed past me on a skateboard,** elle m'a doublé en skateboard à la vitesse de l'éclair; **it flashed across my mind that ...,** l'idée m'est venue tout d'un coup que ...; **my life flashed before me,** ma vie a défilé devant mes yeux;

(c) *Br* (*expose oneself*) s'exhiber.

2 *vt* **(a)** faire étinceler (*ses bijoux*); étaler (*son argent*); projeter (*une image sur l'écran etc*); lancer (*un sourire, un regard*) (**at s.o.,** à qn); **to f. a light in s.o.'s eyes,** diriger une lumière dans les yeux de qn; **she flashed her headlights at us,** elle a braqué ses phares sur nous; **he flashed a grin at me,** il m'a adressé un grand sourire; **to f. a piece of news all over Europe,** répandre une nouvelle en éclair à travers l'Europe;

(b) (*show quickly*) montrer (*qch*) rapidement; **he flashed a photo in front of me,** il m'a passé une photo sous les yeux.

flash[3] *adj Br F* (*showy*) tape-à-l'œil *inv*, voyant, extravagant; **in all his f. clothes,** dans ses vêtements tape-à-l'œil.

▶**flash around** *vtas F* (*show off*) étaler; **he likes flashing his money around,** il aime étaler sa richesse; **don't f. your money around here!,** ne montre pas ton argent ici!

▶**flash back** *vi* **(a)** (*of gas stove etc*) avoir un retour de flamme; **(b)** (*of film*) revenir en arrière; (*of mind*) remonter (dans le passé).

▶**flash over** *vi El* (*of conductor etc*) cracher des étincelles.

flashback ['flæʃbæk] *n Cin* retour *m* en arrière, flash-back *m*; **a f. to prewar days,** un coup d'œil rétrospectif sur les années d'avant-guerre.

flashbulb ['flæʃbʌlb] *n Phot* ampoule *f* (de) flash.

flashcube ['flæʃkjuːb] *n Phot* flash *m* cube.

flasher ['flæʃər] *n* **(a)** *Br F* exhibitionniste *m*; **(b)** *Aut F* clignotant *m*.

flashily ['flæʃɪlɪ] *adv* **f. dressed,** à toilette tapageuse.

flashing ['flæʃɪŋ] **1** *adj* (*torch etc*) éclatant; (*feu, signal*) clignotant; (*phare*) à éclats; **f. eyes,** yeux étincelants. **2** *n* flamboiement *m* (*du feu*); éclat *m* (*d'un diamant*); miroitement *m* (*d'un miroir*); clignotement *m* (*d'un signal*); projection *f* (*d'un rayon de lumière*).

flashlamp ['flæʃlæmp] *n* torche *f* (électrique).

flashlight ['flæʃlaɪt] *n* **(a)** *Phot* ampoule *f* de flash; **f. photography,** photographie *f* au flash; **(b)** *esp Am* torche *f* (électrique); **(c)** (*of lighthouse etc*) feu *m* à éclats.

flashover ['flæʃəʊvər] *n El* étincelle *f* de rupture.

flashy ['flæʃɪ] *adj* voyant, tapageur, -euse; **f. young man,** jeune homme à toilette tapageuse.

flask [flɑːsk] *n* flacon *m*; *Ch* fiole *f*; (*spherical*) ballon *m*; **brandy f.,** flacon à cognac; **(vacuum) f.,** bouteille isolante, thermos ® *m ou f*; **a f. of tea,** un(e) thermos ® de thé.

flat[1] [flæt] **1** *adj* **(a)** plat; (*toit*) plat, en terrasse; *Med* (*pied*) plat; (*curve etc*) aplati; *Archit* (*voûte*) plat; (*arc*) déprimé; (*surface*) plat, uni; (*nez*) camus; (*picture*) sans relief; (*in painting*) (*couleur*) mat; **to beat sth f.,** aplatir qch; **as f. as a pancake,** plat comme une galette; *F* **to go into a f. spin,** (*of person*) s'affoler; **f. bed,** (*of lorry*) plateau *m*; **f. cap,** casquette *f*; **f. chest,** poitrine plate; **f. country,** pays plat, pays de plaine; **f. race,** course plate *ou* de plat; *Horseracing* **f. racing,** le plat; *Comptr TV* **f. screen,** écran plat; **f. screen tube,** tube *m* cathodique plat; **f. sheets,** (*in bookbinding*) feuilles *fpl* à plat; **f. tyre,** pneu à plat; (*deflated*) pneu dégonflé; (*punctured*) pneu crevé;

(b) (*absolute*) net, nette; (*démenti*) formel, absolu; (*refus*) net, catégorique; **to give a f. refusal,** refuser net; *F* **that's f.!,** voilà qui est net!;

(c) (*existence etc*) monotone, ennuyeux; (*style etc*) terne; (*voix*) terne, blanc; (*drink*) éventé, plat; (*vin*) mou; (*battery*) à plat; **to go flat,** (*of drink*) s'éventer; *Nau* **f. calm,** calme plat;

(d) (*unchanging*) invariable, uniforme; **f. rate,** taux *m ou* tarif *m* uniforme; **f. fare, f.-rate fare,** (*on bus etc*) tarif unique; **f.-rate subscription,** abonnement *m* à forfait;

(e) (*sound*) sourd; *Mus* bémol *inv*; **symphony in D f.,** symphonie en ré bémol; **you're f.,** (*singing*) vous chantez en dessous du ton; (*playing*) vous jouez en dessous du ton.

2 *adv* **(a)** à plat; dans une position horizontale; **to fall f. on one's face,** tomber à plat ventre; *F* (*be humiliated*) essuyer une humiliation; **to fall f.,** (*of joke etc*) manquer son effet, tomber à plat; (*of play etc*) faire un four; **stretched out f. on the ground,** étendu à plat sur le sol;

(b) (*absolutely*) nettement, positivement; *F* **he told me f. that ...,** il m'a dit carrément que ...; **to be f. broke,** être à sec; **to work f. out,** travailler d'arrache-pied; **to go f. out,** filer à toute allure;

(c) *Mus* (*chanter etc*) en dessous du ton.

3 *n* **(a)** plat *m* (*d'un sabre etc*); **blow with the f. of the hand,** coup donné avec le plat de la main;

(b) (*land*) plaine *f*; (*left exposed at low tide*) sèche *f*;

(c) on the f., (*horizontally*) horizontalement; *Rail* (*voie*) en palier; *Sp* sur le plat;

(d) *Horseracing* **the f.,** la saison du plat;

(e) *esp Br* appartement *m*; **furnished/unfurnished f.,** appartement meublé/non meublé; **service f.,** appartement avec service; **block of flats,** immeuble (divisé en appartements);

(f) (*shoe*) **flats,** chaussures plates.

(g) *Th* ferme *f*;

(h) *Mus* bémol *m*;

(i) *F* (*flat tyre*) pneu à plat; (*deflated*) pneu dégonflé; (*punctured*) pneu crevé.

flat-bed ['flætbed] *adj* **f.-b. truck** *or Br* **lorry,** semi-remorque *m* plateau.

flat-bottomed ['flæt'bɒtəmd] *adj* à fond plat.

flatcar ['flætkɑːr] *n Am* wagon *m* en plateforme.

flat-chested ['flæt'tʃestɪd] *adj* plat.

flatfish, -fishes *or* **-fish** ['flætfɪʃ, -fɪʃɪz] *n* poisson plat.

flatfoot ['flætfʊt] *n* **(a)** *Med* pied plat; **(b)** *Old-fashioned Br F* (*policeman*) agent *m* de police.

flat-footed ['flæt'fʊtɪd] *adj* **(a)** *Med* à pied plat, aux pieds plats; **(b)** *Br F* (*uncompromising*) franc, franche; (*refus*) absolu; **(c)** *Br F* (*awkward*) gauche.

flatiron ['flætaɪən] *n Arch* fer *m* à repasser.

flatlet ['flætlɪt] *n esp Br* petit appartement, studio *m*.

flatly ['flætlɪ] *adv* **(a)** (*absolutely*) nettement, carrément; (*refuser*) net; (*nier*) absolument; **(b)** (*monotonously*) d'une façon monotone.

flatmate ['flætmeɪt] *n Br* colocataire *mf* (d'un appartement).

flatness ['flætnɪs] *n* **(a)** égalité *f*, nature plate (*d'une surface etc*); manque *m* de relief; aplatissement *m* (*d'une courbe etc*); **(b)** netteté *f* (*d'un refus*); **(c)** monotonie *f* (*de l'existence etc*); insipidité *f* (*du style etc*); (*of beer etc*) évent *m*.

flatten ['flæt(ə)n] *v* **(-n-) 1** *vt* **(a)** aplatir, aplanir (*qch*); (*of wind, rain*) coucher (*le blé etc*); **to f. oneself against a wall,** se plaquer *ou* se coller contre un mur; *F* **to f. s.o.,** (*in fight*) mettre la pâtée à qn; (*humiliate*) écraser qn; (*put in place*) remettre qn à sa place; **(b)** (*make dull*) rendre (*qch*) fade *ou* insipide; **(c)** *Mus* bémoliser (*une note*). **2** *vi* **(a)** s'aplatir, s'aplanir; **(b)** (*become dull*) devenir fade *ou* insipide.

▶**flatten out** *vi* **(a)** *Av* reprendre le vol horizontal; (*after dive*) se redresser; **(b)** (*of terrain*) devenir (plus) plat.

flattened ['flæt(ə)nd] *adj* **(a)** aplati, aplani; (*nez*) épaté; (*voûte*) surbaissé; **(b)** *Mus* (*note*) bémolisé.

flatter ['flætər] **1** *vt* flatter; **the portrait flatters her,** ce portrait la flatte *ou* l'avantage; **he flatters himself that he will succeed,** il est persuadé de sa réussite. **2** *vi* être flatteur.

flatterer ['flætərər] *n* flatteur, -euse, flagorneur, -euse.

flattering ['flætərɪŋ] *adj* (*words etc*) flatteur, -euse; (*exaggerated*) adulatoire; **it is f. to be asked to give this speech,** c'est flatteur d'être sollicité pour faire ce discours; **to speak in f. terms of s.o., to make f. remarks about s.o.,** parler de qn en termes flatteurs.

flatteringly ['flætərɪŋlɪ] *adv* en termes flatteurs.

flattery ['flætərɪ] *n* flatterie *f*; (*exaggerated*) flagornerie *f*; **f. will get you nowhere!,** ça ne vous apportera rien de flatter les gens!

flat top ['flæt'tɒp] *n US F* porte-avions *m inv*.

flatulence ['flætjʊləns] *n* **(a)** *Med* flatuosité *f*; **to suffer from f.,** avoir des vents; **(b)** *Fig* emphase *f* (*de style etc*).

flatulent ['flætjʊlənt] *adj* **(a)** *Med* (*person etc*) flatulent; **(b)** *Fig* (*style*) boursouflé.

flatware ['flætweər] *n Am* vaisselle plate.

flaunt [flɔːnt] *vt* étaler, afficher, faire parade de (*sa richesse*).

flautist ['flɔːtɪst] *n Mus* flûtiste *mf*.

flavour[1], *US* **flavor** ['fleɪvər] *n* saveur *f*, goût *m*; (*of tea etc*) arôme *m*; (*of ice cream etc*) parfum *m*; **what f. (of) ice cream did you want?,** quel parfum tu voulais?, *F* à quoi tu voulais ta glace?; **her stories have a Mediterranean f.,** ses histoires sentent bon la Méditerranée; *F* **I'm not f. of the month,** je ne suis pas en odeur de sainteté.

flavour[2], *US* **flavor** *vt* assaisonner, parfumer (*un mets etc*); **to f. a sauce with garlic,** relever une sauce avec de l'ail; **vanilla flavoured,** (parfumé) à la vanille.

flavouring, *US* **flavoring** ['fleɪvərɪŋ] *n* (*savoury*) assaisonnement *m*; (*sweet*) parfum *m*.

flavourless, *US* **flavorless** ['fleɪvəlɪs] *adj* (*food etc*) sans saveur, fade, insipide; (*wine*) plat.

flaw[1] [flɔː] *n* **(a)** défaut *m*, défectuosité *f*, imperfection *f*; point *m* faible (*d'un projet*); (*crack*) (*in glass etc*) fêlure *f*; (*in wood etc*) fente *f*; (*in metal*) brisure *f*; **there is one f. in their argument,** il y a une faille dans leur argument; **(b)** *Jur* (*in document etc*) vice *m* de forme (*entraînant la nullité*).

flaw[2] *vt* endommager, défigurer.

flawed [flɔːd] *adj* défectueux; (*bois*) gercé; (*diamant*) qui a un crapaud.

flawless ['flɔːlɪs] *adj* sans défaut, parfait; (*technique*) impeccable.

flawlessly ['flɔːlɪslɪ] *adv* parfaitement.

flawlessness ['flɔːlɪsnɪs] *n* perfection *f*.

flax [flæks] *n* (*plant*) lin *m*; **f. field,** linière *f*.

flax-coloured ['flækskʌləd] *adj* couleur de lin *inv*.
flaxen ['flæksən] *adj* **(a)** (*toile etc*) de lin; **(b)** (*hair*) blond de lin *inv*, blond filasse *inv*.
flay [fleɪ] *vt* **(a)** écorcher (*un animal*); **to be flayed alive,** être écorché vif; **(b)** *F* (*criticize*) fouetter, étriller (*qn*); **the critics flayed him,** les critiques l'ont éreinté.
flea [fliː] *n* (*insect*) puce *f*; *Fig F* **she sent him away with a f. in his ear,** elle l'a envoyé promener; **to have fleas,** avoir des puces; **sand f.,** (*crustacean*) crevettine *f*; **f. collar,** collier *m* anti-puces; *F* **f. market,** marché *m* aux puces.
fleabag ['fliːbæg] *n Sl* **(a)** *Br* (*person*) pouilleux, -euse; (*animal*) sac *m* à puces; **(b)** *US* (*hotel*) hôtel pouilleux.
fleabite ['fliːbaɪt] *n* **(a)** morsure *f* de puce; **(b)** *Fig* (*trifle*) vétille *f*, bagatelle *f*.
flea-bitten ['fliːbɪt(ə)n] *adj* (*person*) mordu par les puces.
fleapit ['fliːpɪt] *n Br Sl* cinéma *etc* pouilleux.
fleck¹ [flek] *n* **(a)** (*mark*) petite tache (*de lumière etc*); moucheture *f* (*de couleur*); **(b)** (*particle*) particule *f* (*de poussière*).
fleck² *vt* tacheter; **hair flecked with grey,** cheveux qui grisonnent; **flecked material,** tissu moucheté.
fled *see* **FLEE.**
fledged [fledʒd] *adj* (*oiseau*) qui a toutes ses plumes; *see* **FULLY-FLEDGED.**
fledgling ['fledʒlɪŋ] *n* **(a)** (*young bird*) oisillon *m*; **(b)** (*beginner*) novice *mf*; **f. lawyer,** avocat novice.
flee [fliː] *v* (*pt & pp* **fled** [fled]) **1** *vi* (*of person*) s'enfuir, prendre la fuite; (*of time etc*) fuir; **to f. from a place,** s'enfuir d'un endroit; **to f. to America,** s'enfuir en Amérique. **2** *vt* s'enfuir de (*qn, un pays etc*); fuir (*la tentation etc*).
fleece¹ [fliːs] *n* **(a)** (*of sheep*) toison *f*; *Liter* **the Golden F.,** la Toison d'or; **(b)** *Tex* (*material*) molleton *m*; **f. lining,** doublure *f* de molleton; **(c)** (*cloud formation*) moutonnement *m* de nuages.
fleece² *vt F* (*cheat, overcharge*) écorcher (*qn*); **I've been fleeced,** je me suis fait estamper.
fleecing ['fliːsɪŋ] *n F* écorcherie *f*.
fleecy ['fliːsɪ] *adj* (*wool*) floconneux; (*material etc*) laineux; (*cloud*) moutonné; **f.-lined,** doublé de molleton.
fleeing ['fliːɪŋ] **1** *adj* (*army etc*) en fuite. **2** *n* fuite *f*.
fleet¹ [fliːt] *n* **(a)** *Nau* flotte *f*; (*naval unit*) escadre *f*; **the F.,** = la Marine nationale; **the Atlantic F.,** l'escadre de l'Atlantique; **battle f.,** flotte de ligne; **merchant f.,** flotte de commerce; **fishing f.,** flottille *f* de pêche; **the F. Air Arm,** = l'Aéronavale *f*; *US* **f. admiral,** amiral *m*; **(b)** parc *m* (*de voitures, de taxis*); **air f.,** flotte aérienne; **a f. of coaches took the tourists to their hotel,** une caravane de cars a amené les touristes à leur hôtel.
fleet² *adj Lit* vite, leste; **f. of foot,** au pied léger.
Fleet [fliːt] *n Br Journ* **F. Street,** = rue où se trouvait le siège des principaux journaux britanniques; **F. Street gave the event little coverage,** la presse britannique n'a quasiment pas couvert cet événement; **the F. Street papers,** les journaux britanniques; **F. Street journalist,** un journaliste de Fleet Street.
fleet-footed ['fliːt'fʊtɪd] *adj Lit* au pied léger.
fleeting ['fliːtɪŋ] *adj* (*time*) fugitif, fugace; (*beauty*) passager; (*happiness*) éphémère; **to pay s.o. a f. visit,** faire une courte visite à qn; **to catch a f. glimpse of sth,** entrevoir qch, apercevoir qch.
Fleming ['flemɪŋ] *n* Flamand, -ande.
Flemish ['flemɪʃ] **1** *adj* flamand. **2** *n Ling* flamand *m*.
flense [flens] *vt* dépecer (*une baleine*).
flesh¹ [fleʃ] *n* **(a)** (*of person, fruit*) chair *f*; **to make s.o.'s f. creep,** donner la chair de poule à qn; **to put on f.,** (*of animal*) prendre chair; (*of person*) grossir, prendre de l'embonpoint; **f. wound,** blessure légère *ou* en séton; **he exacts his pound of f. from his debtors,** il traite ses débiteurs en usurier; **to mortify the f.,** châtier son corps; **it was he in the f.,** c'était lui en chair et en os; **his own f. and blood,** la chair de sa chair; **it is more than f. and blood can stand** *or* **bear,** c'est plus que la nature humaine ne saurait endurer; *F* **to press the f.,** serrer des mains; **the spirit is willing but the f. is weak,** l'esprit est prompt, mais la chair est faible; **to go the way of all f.,** payer sa dette à la nature; **the sins of the f.,** le péché de la chair; **(b)** (*colour*) **f. colour,** couleur *f* chair; *Th etc* **f. tights,** collants *mpl* chair; *Art* **f. tints,** carnations *fpl*; **(c)** (*rare*) (*meat*) viande *f*; *Rel* **to eat f.,** faire gras.
▶**flesh out 1** *vtsep* (*add details to*) étoffer (*un projet*). **2** *vi* (*become fatter*) engraisser, prendre de l'embonpoint.
flesh-coloured ['fleʃkʌləd] *adj* (*tights etc*) (couleur) chair.
fleshpots ['fleʃpɒts] *npl* **the f.,** la bonne chère.
fleshy ['fleʃɪ] *adj* (*limb, fruit etc*) charnu; (*leaf*) succulent.
fleur-de-lis, *pl* **fleurs-de-lis** ['flɜːdə'liː] *n Her* fleur *f* de lis.
flew *see* **FLY³.**
flex¹ [fleks] **1** *vt* fléchir (*le bras etc*); faire jouer (*ses muscles*). **2** *vi* (*of spring*) fléchir.
flex² *n Br El* cordon *m*, câble *m*.
flexibility [fleksɪ'bɪlɪtɪ] *n* (*of material, plans*) flexibilité *f*, élasticité *f*, souplesse *f*; (*of character*) souplesse *f*.
flexible ['fleksɪb(ə)l] *adj* (*material, plans*) flexible, souple; (*character*) souple; **f. working hours,** horaire *m* à la carte, *Can* horaire flexible.
flexion ['flekʃən] *n* **(a)** flexion *f*, courbure *f* (*d'un ressort etc*); **(b)** (*bend*) courbe *f*.
flexitime ['fleksɪtaɪm] **, flextime** ['flekstaɪm] *n Ind etc* horaire *m* à la carte, *Can* horaire flexible; **we're on f.,** nous avons des horaires à la carte.
flibbertigibbet [flɪbətɪ'dʒɪbɪt] *n F* écervelé, -ée, évaporé, -ée, hurluberlu *m*.
flick¹ [flɪk] *n* **(a)** petit coup (*de fouet, de queue etc*); (*with finger*) chiquenaude *f*; **a f. of the wrist,** un tour de main; **at the f. of a switch,** juste en appuyant sur un bouton; *Br* **f. knife,** (*with folding blade*) couteau *m* à cran (d'arrêt); (*with retractable blade*) couteau à lame rentrable; **(b)** *Old-fashioned Br* **the flicks,** (*cinema*) le ciné, le cinoche; **to go to the flicks,** aller au ciné *ou* au cinoche.
flick² *vt* (*with whip etc*) effleurer (*un cheval etc*); (*with finger*) donner une chiquenaude à (*qch*); **to f. a duster over sth,** donner un coup de torchon à qch.
▶**flick away** *vtsep* (*with fingers*) repousser (*qch*) d'une chiquenaude.
▶**flick off** *vtsep* (*with fingers*) enlever (*qch*) d'une chiquenaude; **to f. sth off with a duster,** faire envoler qch d'un coup de torchon.
▶**flick on** *vtsep* **to f. on the lights,** allumer; *Aut* allumer les phares.
▶**flick through** *vipo* feuilleter (*un livre*).
flicker¹ ['flɪkər] *n* petit mouvement vacillant; battement *m* (*des paupières*); *Cin* scintillement *m* (*de la reproduction*); *TV* papillotement *m*; **without a f.,** sans un battement de cil; **a f. of light,** une petite lueur tremblotante.
flicker² *vi* (*of flame etc*) trembloter, vaciller; (*of eyelids*) cligner; (*of light*) clignoter; (*of snake's tongue*) onduler; (*of needle etc*) osciller; *Cin* (*of reproduction*) scintiller; **the candle flickered out,** la bougie vacilla et s'éteignit; **a smile flickered on his lips,** un sourire erra sur ses lèvres.
flickering ['flɪkərɪŋ] **1** *adj* (*light*) clignotant. **2** *n* tremblotement *m*, clignotement *m*; *Cin* scintillement *m*; *TV* papillotement *m*.
flier ['flaɪər] *n* **(a)** (*pilot etc*) aviateur, -trice; **(b)** (*fall*) **to take a f. over the handlebars,** se trouver projeté par-dessus le guidon; **(c)** (*leaflet*) feuille volante, prospectus *m*.
flight¹ [flaɪt] *n* **(a)** vol *m* (*d'un oiseau, d'un avion etc*); course *f* (*d'un projectile, d'un astre etc*); **these birds are not capable of f.,** ces oiseaux ne peuvent pas voler; *Av* **blind/instruments f.,** vol sans visibilité/aux instruments; **level f.,** vol horizontal *ou* en palier; **f. of fancy,** essor *m* de l'imagination; **f. attendant,** (*male*) steward *m*; (*female*) hôtesse *f* de l'air; **f. crew,** équipage *m*; **f. deck,** (*on aircraft*) poste *m* de pilotage; (*on aircraft carrier*) pont *m* d'envol; **f. engineer,** mécanicien *m* de bord; **f. feather,** (*of bird*) penne *f*; *Br Mil Av* **f. lieutenant,** capitaine aviateur; **f. path,** trajectoire *f* de vol; **f. personnel,** personnel navigant; **f. simulator,** simulateur *m* de vol; **f. trainer,** appareil *m* d'entraînement au vol;
(b) (*distance*) volée *f*, distance parcourue (*par un oiseau etc*); migration *f* (*d'oiseaux etc*); trajectoire *f* (*d'un projectile*); **time of f.,** durée *f* du trajet (*d'un projectile etc*); *Av* **it's an hour's f. from London,** c'est à une heure de vol de Londres;
(c) (*specific trip*) **maiden f.,** vol inaugural, premier vol (*d'un avion*); **first f.,** (*of person*) baptême *m* de l'air; **solo f.,** vol en solo; **f. A200 to Brussels,** vol A200 pour Bruxelles; **I don't want to miss my f.,** je ne veux pas rater mon avion; **my f. is at 2.15,** mon avion est à 2h15; **how was your f.?,** comment s'est passé le vol?; **connecting f.,** (vol de) correspondance *f*; *Mil Av* **reconnaissance f.,** vol de reconnaissance; **f. clearance,** autorisation *f* de vol; **f. control,** (*of individual aircraft*) conduite *f*; (*from ground*) contrôle *m* de la navigation aérienne; *Mil* contrôle des missions aériennes; **f. formation,** *US* **f. pattern,** formation *f* de vol; **f. log,** journal *m* de vol; **f. plan,** plan *m* de vol; **f. recorder,** enregistreur *m* de vol;
(d) (*group*) vol *m*, volée *f* (*d'oiseaux etc*); escadrille *f*

(*d'avions*); *Fig* **in the top f.,** parmi les tout premiers; **the Queen's** *or* **King's F.,** = avions au service de la famille royale;

(e) f. (of stairs), escalier *m*; **you go up two flights,** tu montes de deux étages *ou* de deux volées d'escalier; *Sp* **f. of hurdles,** série *f* de haies (*dans une course d'obstacles*); *HydE etc* **f. of locks,** suite *f* de biefs;

(f) (*on arrow, dart*) plume *f*.

flight² *n* (*escape*) fuite *f*; **headlong f.,** sauve-qui-peut *m inv*; **to take (to) f.,** prendre la fuite; **to put the enemy to f.,** mettre l'ennemi en fuite; **in full f.,** en pleine déroute; *Fin* **the f. of capital,** l'exode *m ou* la fuite des capitaux.

flightiness ['flaɪtɪnɪs] *n* inconstance *f*.

flightless ['flaɪtlɪs] *adj* (*bird*) coureur.

flighty ['flaɪtɪ] *adj* **(a)** (*person*) frivole, étourdi; **(b)** (*conduite*) instable.

flimsily ['flɪmzɪlɪ] *adv* d'une manière peu solide; **f. constructed,** d'une construction peu solide.

flimsiness ['flɪmzɪnɪs] *n* **(a)** manque *m* de consistance (*d'un tissu etc*); **(b)** faiblesse *f*, pauvreté *f* (*d'une excuse etc*).

flimsy ['flɪmzɪ] **1** *adj* **(a)** fragile, peu solide; (*paper etc*) léger; **(b)** (*excuse*) faible, pauvre; (*evidence*) peu convaincant; **to condemn s.o. on the flimsiest evidence,** condamner qn sur les preuves les plus faibles. **2** *n* **(a)** papier *m* pelure; **(b)** *Journ* copie *f* (de reporter).

flinch [flɪntʃ] *vi* **(a)** (*shy away*) fléchir; **she didn't f. from carrying out her duty,** elle ne s'est pas dérobée à l'accomplissement de son devoir; **(b)** tressaillir, sursauter (*de douleur*); **to bear pain without flinching,** supporter la douleur sans broncher; **I flinched at the thought of it,** d'y penser m'a fait tressaillir.

fling¹ [flɪŋ] *n* **(a)** (*throw*) jet *m*, coup *m*; **(b)** *F* (*attempt*) **I'll have a f. at it,** je vais essayer; **(c)** (*dance*) **(highland) f.,** = pas seul écossais; **(d)** *F* (*impulsive behaviour*) **to have one's f.,** faire la fête; **youth will have its f.,** il faut que jeunesse se passe; **(e)** (*affair*) **to have a f.,** avoir une aventure (**with s.o.,** avec qn).

fling² *v* (*pt & pp* **flung** [flʌŋ]) **1** *vt* jeter (*qch*); lancer (*une balle etc*); **to f. s.o. into prison,** jeter qn en prison; **to f. oneself into s.o.'s arms/an armchair,** se jeter dans les bras de qn/un fauteuil; **to f. oneself into a task,** se lancer dans une tâche; **to f. one's arms around s.o.,** jeter ses bras autour de qn. **2** *vi* se précipiter; **she flung out of the house,** elle est sortie brusquement de la maison.

►**fling about** *vtsep* jeter (*des objets*) de côté et d'autre; **to f. one's arms about,** gesticuler violemment; **to f. one's money about,** gaspiller son argent.

►**fling away** *vtsep* (*throw*) jeter (*qch*) de côté; (*get rid of*) jeter (*qch*), se débarrasser de (*qch*); **to f. one's money away,** gaspiller son argent.

►**fling down** *vtsep* jeter (*qch*) à terre; **he flung the books down on the table,** il a jeté les livres sur la table.

►**fling off** *vtsep* **(a)** (*rid oneself of*) secouer (*le joug*); **(b)** (*take off*) retirer brusquement (*son manteau etc*).

►**fling open** *vtsep* ouvrir toute grande (*la fenêtre etc*); **to f. open the door,** ouvrir la porte d'un mouvement brusque.

►**fling out** *vtsep* **(a)** (*throw*) jeter (*qch*) dehors; (*get rid of*) jeter (*qch*), se débarrasser de (*qch*); *F* **to f. s.o. out,** flanquer qn à la porte; **(b)** (*extend*) **to f. out one's arm,** étendre le bras d'un grand geste.

►**fling up** *vtsep* **(a)** (*throw in air*) jeter (*qch*) en l'air; **(b)** *F* (*abandon*) abandonner, renoncer à (*un projet*); démissionner de (*son travail*).

flint [flɪnt] *n Miner* silex *m*; (*for making fire*) pierre *f* à feu; (*for cigarette lighter*) pierre à briquet; **f. glass,** flint(-glass) *m*; *Hist* **f. implements,** outils *mpl* en silex taillés.

flinty ['flɪntɪ] *adj* **(a)** (*of, resembling flint*) de silex; **(b)** *Fig* (*cœur*) de pierre, dur.

flip¹ [flɪp] *n* **(a)** (*flick*) chiquenaude *f*, pichenette *f*; *F* **f. side,** revers *m* (*d'un disque*); **(b)** (*jerking movement*) petite secousse vive; **f. of the tail,** coup *m* de queue; **(c)** (*of opinion, policy*) revers *m*.

flip² *v* (**-pp-**) **1** *vt* **(a)** (*flick*) donner une chiquenaude *ou* une pichenette à (*une boulette de papier etc*); **to f. a coin,** jouer à pile ou face; *Sl* **to f. one's lid,** sortir de ses gonds; (*go crazy*) perdre la boule; **(b)** *El* basculer (*un interrupteur*); **(c)** (*jerk*) donner une secousse vive à (*sa ligne en pêchant etc*); **(d)** *F* (*turn over*) retourner (*un disque*). **2** *vi Sl* **(a)** (*get very angry*) sortir de ses gonds; (*go crazy*) perdre la boule; **(b)** (*become ecstatic*) flasher, flipper (**over,** sur).

flip³ *n* (*drink*) flip *m*.

flip⁴ *adj F* (*flippant*) léger, désinvolte, cavalier.

►**flip open** *vtsep* ouvrir.

►**flip out** *vi esp Am Sl* (*get very angry*) sortir de ses gonds.

►**flip over 1** *vtsep* (*turn over*) retourner (*un disque*); **to f. over the pages of a magazine,** feuilleter les pages d'un magazine. **2** *vi* (*turn over*) se retourner, faire des tours sur soi-même; **the plane just seemed to f. over,** l'avion semblait se retourner.

►**flip through** *vipo* (*turn pages quickly*) feuilleter (*un livre*).

flip-flop ['flɪpflɒp] *n* **(a)** (*sandals*) (*usu pl*) **flip-flops,** tongs *fpl*; **(b)** (*jump*) saut périlleux; **(c)** *Electron* **f.-f. (circuit),** (circuit *m*) basculeur *m* monostable.

flippancy ['flɪpənsɪ] *n* légèreté *f*, désinvolture *f*.

flippant ['flɪpənt] *adj* léger, désinvolte, cavalier.

flippantly ['flɪpəntlɪ] *adv* d'un ton *ou* d'une manière désinvolte.

flipper ['flɪpər] *n* **(a)** palme *f* (*de nageur sous-marin etc*); nageoire *f* (*de cétacé, de phoque*); aileron *m* (*de requin*); **(b)** *Sl* (*hand*) main *f*, patte *f*.

flipping ['flɪpɪŋ] *Br F* **1** *adj* fichu; **a f. nuisance,** un fichu embêtement. **2** *adv* sacrément; **it's f. hot,** il fait sacrément chaud.

flip-top ['flɪp'tɒp] *adj* **f.-t. pack,** paquet dur.

flirt¹ [flɜːt] *n* (*man*) flirteur *m*; (*woman*) flirteuse *f*.

flirt² *vi* flirter; **to f. with an idea,** flirter avec une idée.

flirtation [flɜː'teɪʃən] *n* flirt *m* (**with s.o./sth,** avec qn/qch).

flirtatious [flɜː'teɪʃəs] *adj F* flirteur; (*look, smile*) enjôleur.

flirtatiously [flɜː'teɪʃəslɪ] *adv* en flirtant.

flit¹ [flɪt] *n Br F* **to do a (moonlight) f.,** déménager à la cloche de bois.

flit² *vi* (**-tt-**) **(a)** (*of bird etc*) **to f. by,** passer légèrement; **to f. about,** aller et venir d'un pas léger; *Fig* **to f. from one thing to another,** passer d'une chose à l'autre; **(b)** *Scot North Eng* (*move house*) déménager; **(c)** *F Pej* déménager à la cloche de bois.

flitch [flɪtʃ] *n* flèche *f* (*de lard*).

float¹ [fləʊt] *n* **(a)** flotteur *m* (*de chaudière, de carburateur etc*); **f. chamber,** *US* **f. bowl,** (*in engine*) chambre *f* du flotteur; **(b)** *Fishing* flotteur *m*, bouchon *m* (*d'une ligne, d'un filet de pêche*); galet *m* (*de filet*); **(c)** *Biol* flotteur *m* (*de plante aquatique*); vessie *f* natatoire (*de poisson*); **(d)** (*raft*) radeau *m*; (*floating logs*) train *m* (de bois); (*swimming aid*) bouée *f*; **(e)** *Th Cin* portant *m* mobile; *Th* **the floats,** (*footlights*) la rampe; **(f)** (*vehicle*) (*in carnival etc*) char *m* de carnaval; **milk f.,** voiture *f* de livraison du lait; **(g)** *Com esp Am* (*petty cash*) petite caisse; *esp Br* (*in cash till etc*) fond *m* de caisse; (*advance*) avance *f*; **they gave me a f. of £200 for the trip,** (*advance*) ils m'ont donné un viatique de 200 livres, ils m'ont donné 200 livres pour le voyage; **(h)** *US Culin* (*drink*) = soda, jus de fruit ou milk-shake dans lequel on ajoute une boule de glace.

float² **1** *vi* **(a)** flotter, surnager; (*of boat*) être à flot; *Swimming* faire la planche; **metal doesn't f.,** le métal ne flotte pas; **a cork was floating on the surface of the pond,** un bouchon de liège flottait à la surface de la mare; **to f. down the stream,** descendre le courant; **(b)** (*move as if in water*) **to f. to the surface,** revenir à la surface; **to f. in the air,** planer dans l'air; **she floated out of the room,** elle est sortie de la pièce d'un pas léger; **(c)** *MecE* (*of part of machine*) avoir du jeu; **(d)** *Pol* (*of voter*) être indécis. **2** *vt* **(a)** flotter (*des bois etc*); (*launch*) mettre (*un navire*) à flot *ou* à l'eau; (*refloat*) renflouer (*un navire*); **(b)** *Com* lancer (*une compagnie etc*); *Fin* émettre, lancer (*un emprunt*); **to f. an idea/a rumour,** lancer une idée/une rumeur.

►**float about, float around** *vi* (*circulate*) circuler, courir; **there were rumours floating about that ...,** le bruit courait que ...; *F* **he's floating around somewhere,** il est dans les parages; *F* **he just floats around all day,** il traîne sans rien faire toute la journée.

►**float off 1** *vi* (*of ship etc*) se déséchouer. **2** *vipo* (*of ship etc*) **the boat floated off the sandbank at high tide,** à marée haute, le bateau s'est dégagé du banc de sable. **3** *vtsep* renflouer (*une épave etc*); **they floated the boat off the sandbank,** ils ont remis à flot le bateau échoué sur un banc de sable.

floater ['fləʊtər] *n* **(a)** (*swimmer*) baigneur, -euse qui fait la planche; **(b)** *Fin* lanceur *m* (*d'une compagnie etc*); **(c)** *Tech* flotteur *m*.

floating ['fləʊtɪŋ] **1** *adj* **(a)** flottant, à flot; **the ship is, in effect, a f. hotel,** en fait, ce bateau est un hôtel flottant; **f. light,** veilleuses *f* (*à flotteur, à huile*); **f. bridge,** pont *m* de bateaux *ou* de radeaux; **f. crane,** ponton-grue *m*, *pl* pontons-grues; *Com* **f. cargo,** cargaison *f* sur mer; *Culin* **f. islands,**

île flottante; **(b)** *(population)* flottant; *Fin* *(exchange rate)* flottant; *(capital)* circulant, mobile; *MecE etc* *(bearing)* flottant; *Pol* *(voteur)* indécis; *Comptr* **f. point,** virgule flottante; *Anat* **f. ribs,** côtes flottantes; *Med* **f. kidney,** rein mobile *ou* flottant. **2** *n* flottement *m* *(d'un bâtiment)*; *Swimming* la planche; mise *f* à flot *(d'un navire)*; renflouage *m* *(d'une épave etc)*; flottage *m* *(du bois)*; *Com* lancement *m* *(d'une société commerciale etc)*; *Fin* émission *f* *(d'un emprunt)*.

floating off *n* renflouage *m* *(d'une épave etc)*.

flocculent ['flɒkjʊlənt] *adj* floconneux.

flock[1] [flɒk] *n* bande *f* *(d'animaux)*; troupeau *m* *(de moutons, d'oies)*; volée *f* *(d'oiseaux)*; **a pastor and his f.,** un pasteur et ses ouailles *fpl*; **a f. of visitors,** une foule de visiteurs.

flock[2] *vi* *(gather)* s'attrouper, s'assembler; **everybody is flocking to see the exhibition,** tout le monde se précipite pour voir l'exposition; **in summer people f. to the sea,** en été les gens vont en foule au bord de la mer.

flock[3] *n* bourre *f* *(de laine)*; **f. mattress,** matelas *m* en bourre de laine; **f. wallpaper,** papier *m* tontisse.

►**flock together** *vi* *(gather)* s'attrouper, s'assembler.

floe [fləʊ] *n* **(ice) f.,** masse *f* de glaces flottantes, banquise *f*.

flog [flɒg] *vt* (-gg-) **(a)** flageller, battre *(qn)* à coups de fouet; **to f. a horse,** cravacher un cheval; *F* **to f. a dead horse,** se dépenser en pure perte; *Fig* **to f. a subject to death,** ne pas savoir se taire sur une question; **(b)** *Br F* *(sell)* vendre, bazarder *(qch)*.

►**flog off** *vtsep Br F* *(sell off)* liquider.

flood[1] [flʌd] *n* **(a)** inondation *f*; **the river was in f.,** la rivière débordait; **crops ruined by the floods,** récoltes perdues à cause des inondations; **the victims of the f.,** les inondés; *Bible* **the F.,** le Déluge; **the floods of the Nile,** les crues du Nil; **a f. of light,** des flots *mpl* de lumière; **floods of tears/abuse,** un torrent de larmes/d'injures; **f. plain,** plaine *f* d'inondation; **f. water,** inondation *f*; **the f. waters receded,** les inondations ont diminué; **(b) f. (tide),** flux *m*, marée montante.

flood[2] **1** *vt* inonder *(un terrain etc)*; *Nau* noyer *(les soutes)*; *Agr* irriguer *(un champ etc)*; noyer *(le carburateur)*; étouffer *(le moteur)*; **to be flooded,** *(of house, ship etc)* être envahi par l'eau; **to f. a (cigarette) lighter,** noyer la mèche d'un briquet; **to f. the market with ...,** inonder le marché de ...; **to be flooded with letters,** être inondé *ou* submergé de lettres; **flooded with light,** *(room)* inondé de lumière. **2** *vi* *(of river etc)* *(overflow)* déborder; *(be in flood)* être en crue; *Fig* **the sun's rays came flooding through the window,** les rayons du soleil entraient à flots par la fenêtre; **spectators were flooding into the stadium,** les spectateurs affluaient dans le stade.

►**flood back** *vi* *(return to memory)* revenir (à l'esprit); **it all came flooding back,** tout m'est *ou* leur est *etc* revenu brutalement.

►**flood in** *vi* *(of light, water)* arriver à flots; *(of correspondence, people)* affluer.

►**flood out 1** *vtsep* *(force to leave)* forcer à partir; **many families have been flooded out,** les inondations ont forcé beaucoup de familles à évacuer leur maison. **2** *vi* *(of people)* sortir à flots.

flooded ['flʌdɪd] *adj* *(terrain)* inondé; *(carburateur)* noyé.

floodgate ['flʌdgeɪt] *n* vanne *f* (de décharge); porte *f* d'écluse; **to open/close the floodgates,** lever/mettre les vannes; *Fig* **to open the floodgates to immigration/immorality/***etc*, ouvrir les vannes de l'immigration/l'immoralité/*etc*; *Fig* **to open the floodgates of one's passions,** donner *ou* laisser libre cours à ses passions.

flooding ['flʌdɪŋ] *n* inondation *f* *(d'un terrain etc)*; débordement *m* *(d'une rivière etc)*; *Agr* irrigation *f* *(d'un champ etc)*; *Nau etc* noyage *m* *(des soutes etc)*; **road liable to f.,** *(road sign)* route inondable; **there has been f. in many parts of the country,** il y a eu des inondations dans de nombreuses régions.

floodlight[1] ['flʌdlaɪt] *n* lumière *f* de grande intensité; projecteur *m* *(pour l'illumination des monuments)*; *Phot* (lampe *f*) flood *f*.

floodlight[2] *vt* (*pt & pp* **floodlighted** *or* **floodlit**) illuminer par projecteurs.

floodlighting ['flʌdlaɪtɪŋ] *n* illumination *f* par projecteurs.

floodlit ['flʌdlɪt] *adj* illuminé (par des projecteurs).

floor[1] [flɔːr] *n* **(a)** plancher *m*; parquet *m* *(de la Bourse, d'une assemblée législative)*; **parquet f.,** parquet *m*; **tiled f.,** carrelage *m*; *F* **to wipe the f. with s.o.,** battre qn à plate(s) couture(s); **to take the f.,** *(at meeting)* prendre la parole; *(at dance)* se joindre aux danseurs; **Mr Taylor has the f.,** la parole est à M. Taylor; **questions from the f.,** *(at meeting)* questions du public; **dance f.,** piste *f* de danse; *Ind* **the factory** *or* **shop f.,** l'atelier *m*; **f. polish,** cire *f* à parquet; **f. tile,** dalle *f* de sol; **f. show,** spectacle *m* de cabaret;

(b) *(storey)* étage *m*; palier *m*; **house on two floors,** maison avec étage; *Br* **ground f.,** rez-de-chaussée *m*; **first f.,** *Br* premier étage; *Am* rez-de-chaussée; **to live on the fifth f.,** *Br* habiter au cinquième; *Am* habiter au quatrième; **we live on the same f.,** nous habitons sur le même palier, nous sommes voisins de palier; **on the f. above/below,** à l'étage du dessus/dessous; **we're ten floors up,** nous sommes au dixième étage; **their offices are two floors down,** leurs bureaux sont deux étages plus bas; *F* **to get in on the ground f.,** *(join project at beginning)* être là depuis le début; *Fin* acheter des actions dès leur émission *ou* au plus bas prix; **f. manager,** *(in department store)* chef *m* de rayon; **f. waiter,** garçon *m* d'étage *(dans un hôtel)*;

(c) fond *m* *(de l'océan)*; *Min* sole *f* *(d'une galerie de mine)*; **the forest f.,** le sol de la forêt; **threshing f.,** aire *f* *(d'une grange)*.

floor[2] *vt* **(a)** *Constr* *(with floorboards)* planchéier *(une pièce)*; *(with wooden blocks)* parqueter *(une pièce)*; *(with tiles)* carreler *(une pièce)*; **(b)** terrasser *(un adversaire)*, envoyer *(un adversaire)* au tapis; **(c)** *F* *(of problem, question)* réduire *(qn)* à quia, clouer le bec à *(qn)*.

floorboard ['flɔːbɔːd] *n* planche *f* *(du plancher, à planchéier)*.

floorcloth ['flɔːklɒθ] *n* serpillière *f*.

flooring ['flɔːrɪŋ] *n* **(a)** *Constr* *(with floorboards)* planchéiage *m*; *(with wooden blocks)* parquetage *m*; *(with tiles)* carrelage *m*, dallage *m*; **(b)** *(floor)* plancher *m* *(d'une voiture, d'un avion etc)*; **parquet f.,** parquet *m*.

floorspace ['flɔːspeɪs] *n* surface *f* (couverte), superficie *f* *(d'une pièce etc)*; *(of vehicle)* surface du plancher.

floorwalker ['flɔːwɔːkər] *n* *US* inspecteur, -trice, surveillant, -ante (de magasin).

floozie, floozy ['fluːzɪ] *n Sl* pouffiasse *f*.

flop[1] [flɒp] *n* **(a)** *(sound)* coup mat, bruit sourd; **(b)** *F* *(failure)* four *m*, fiasco *m*, bide *m*; *(person)* raté, -ée; **it was a f.,** ça a fait un four *ou* un bide, c'était un fiasco.

flop[2] **1** *int* plouf!, patapouf!, floc! **2** *adv* **to fall f.,** faire patapouf.

flop[3] *vi* (-pp-) **(a)** faire plouf, faire floc; *(of person)* se laisser tomber, s'affaler; *(into water)* tomber; **the cushion flopped onto the floor,** le coussin est tombé sur le sol; **to f. down on(to) a seat,** tomber lourdement sur un siège, se laisser tomber comme un sac sur un siège; **(b)** *F* *(fail)* échouer; *(of play etc)* faire un four.

flophouse ['flɒphaʊs] *n Am* asile *m* de nuit.

floppy ['flɒpɪ] **1** *adj* *(hat etc)* pendant, souple; *(garment)* lâche, trop large; **with f. ears,** à oreilles pendantes; *Comptr* **f. disk,** disquette *f*, disque *m* souple. **2** *n Comptr* disquette *f*, disque *m* souple.

flora ['flɔːrə] *n* **the f. and fauna of a region,** la flore et la faune d'une région.

floral ['flɔːrəl] *adj* floral, -aux; **dress with a bold f. design,** robe *f* à grands ramages.

floret ['flɔːrɪt] *n* fleuron *m*.

floribunda [flɒrɪ'bʌndə] *n* *(flower)* (rose *f*, rosier *m*) floribunda *inv*.

florid ['flɒrɪd] *adj* *(style etc)* fleuri, orné à l'excès; *(dress etc)* à fleurs; *(complexion)* coloré.

Florida ['flɒrɪdə] *n* Floride *f*.

florin ['flɒrɪn] *n Br Arch* *(coin)* (pièce *f* de) deux shillings.

florist ['flɒrɪst] *n* fleuriste *mf*; **f.'s (shop),** magasin *m* de fleurs; **to go to the f.'s,** aller chez le fleuriste.

floss [flɒs] *n Tex* **f. silk,** bourre *f* de soie; **(dental) f.,** fil *m* (de soie) dentaire.

flotation [fləʊ'teɪʃən] *n* **(a)** *Com* lancement *m* *(d'une compagnie)*; *Fin* émission *f* *(d'un emprunt)*; **(b)** *Nau* flottaison *f*; flottage *m* *(du bois etc)*.

flotilla [flə'tɪlə] *n Nau* flottille *f*; *(of small boats)* escadrille *f*.

flotsam ['flɒtsəm] *n* épave(s) flottante(s); **f. and jetsam,** choses refoulées par la mer; *Fig* **the f. of the war/of society,** *(people)* les laissés-pour-compte de la guerre/de la société.

flounce[1] [flaʊns] *n* mouvement vif *(d'indignation, d'impatience)*.

flounce[2] *vi* s'élancer, se jeter *(avec un mouvement d'indignation, d'impatience)*; **to f. in/out/off,** entrer/sortir/partir brusquement.

flounce[3] *n Sewing* volant *m*.

flounce[4] *vt Sewing* garnir de volants; **flounced skirt,** jupe *f* à volants.
flounder[1] ['flaʊndər] *n* (*fish*) flet *m*, carrelet *m*.
flounder[2] *vi* (*in water, mud etc*) patauger, barboter; **to f. about in the water,** se débattre dans l'eau; **to f. along,** avancer en trébuchant; **to f. in a speech,** patauger dans un discours.
floundering ['flaʊndərɪŋ] **1** *adj* qui patauge *ou* barbote (*dans la boue etc*). **2** *n* barbotement *m*, pataugeage *m*.
flour[1] ['flaʊər] *n* farine *f*; fleur *f* (*de soufre*); **to dust sth with f.,** (en)fariner qch; **potato f.,** fécule *f* de pommes de terre; **f. dredger,** saupoudroir *m* à farine; **f. mill,** minoterie *f*.
flour[2] *vt Culin* saupoudrer (*une pâte etc*) de farine; (en)fariner (*qn, qch*).
flourbin ['flaʊəbɪn] *n* farinière *f*, huche *f*, maie *f*.
flourish[1] ['flʌrɪʃ] *n* **(a)** (*in writing*) trait *m* de plume; (*after signature*) parafe *m*; fioriture *f* (*de style*); **(b)** (*gesture*) grand geste; brandissement *m* (*d'épée*); **to take off one's hat with a f.,** saluer d'un grand coup de chapeau; **to carry things off with a f.,** y mettre du panache; **(c)** *Mus* fioriture(s) *f(pl)*, ornement *m*; fanfare *f* (*de trompettes*).
flourish[2] **1** *vi* **(a)** (*of plant*) croître, se développer; (*of person, business etc*) être florissant, prospérer; (*of arts*) fleurir; **to f. in a sandy soil,** se plaire dans un terrain sablonneux; **trade is flourishing,** le commerce est prospère; **(b)** *Mus* faire des fioritures; (*of trumpets*) sonner une fanfare. **2** *vt* brandir (*une épée, un bâton, un journal etc*).
flourishing ['flʌrɪʃɪŋ] *adj* (*plant, industry etc*) florissant; (*commerce*) prospère.
floury ['flaʊərɪ] *adj* **(a)** (*hands etc*) enfariné, couvert de farine; **(b)** (*potatoes etc*) farineux.
flout [flaʊt] *vt* railler (*qn*); narguer (*ses ennemis*); faire fi de (*l'autorité de qn, les conventions etc*).
flow[1] [fləʊ] *n* **(a)** coulée *f* (*d'un liquide*); courant *m*, flux *m* (*de vapeur*); *Metal etc* fluage *m*; *Geog Geol* écoulement *m* (*d'un cours d'eau, d'une couche*); *El* passage *m* (*d'un courant*); passage, arrivée *f* (*d'air, d'essence etc*); flot *m*, flux (*de la marée*); *Med* écoulement (*du sang*); *Fin* mouvement *m* (*de capital*); circulation *f* (*de l'information*); **a steady f. of immigrants,** un courant ininterrompu d'immigration; **ebb and f.,** flux et reflux; **f. of money,** flux monétaire; **cash f.,** cash-flow *m*; **the speaker was interrupted in full f.,** l'orateur a été interrompu en plein discours; **f. chart, f. diagram,** diagramme *m* des opérations successives; *Comptr* organigramme *m*; **f. path,** branche *f* de traitement; **f. point,** point *m* de fluage; limite *f* d'écoulement;
(b) volume *m* (*de liquide débité*); débit *m* (*d'une rivière, d'une pompe, d'un courant électrique*); **the f. of traffic,** le flux de la circulation; **there was a heavy f. of traffic,** il y avait beaucoup de circulation;
(c) (*stream*) courant *m*, cours *m* (*d'eau*); coulée *f* (*de lave*); flot *m* (*de sang etc*); *Physiol* **menstrual f.,** règles *fpl*;
(d) *Sewing* lignes tombantes (*d'une robe*); drapé *m* (*d'un vêtement*).
flow[2] *vi* **(a)** (*of water, river*) couler, s'écouler; (*of electric current, blood in veins*) circuler; **to f. into the sea,** se verser dans la mer; **lava that flows down the mountain,** lave qui dévale la montagne; **the tears flowed down her cheeks,** les larmes coulaient sur ses joues; **blood flowed from the wound,** le sang s'écoulait de la blessure; **blood flowing to the head,** sang qui afflue à la tête; **you can feel the energy f.,** on sent circuler l'énergie; **the work is flowing nicely,** le travail suit bien son cours; **the ideas are really flowing today,** les idées affluent aujourd'hui;
(b) (*of traffic, people*) s'écouler;
(c) (*of literary style, prose*) couler; **to keep the conversation flowing,** entretenir la conversation; **these two paragraphs don't f.,** ces deux paragraphes ne s'enchaînent pas bien;
(d) (*of hair etc*) flotter;
(e) (*result*) dériver, découler (**from,** de); **God from whom all blessings f.,** Dieu, de qui découlent toutes les grâces; **land flowing with milk and honey,** pays où coulent le lait et le miel;
(f) (*of tide*) monter, remonter.
►**flow away** *vi* (*of liquid*) s'écouler.
►**flow back** *vi* refluer; (*of water*) regorger (*dans un tuyau etc*).
►**flow in** *vi* (*of liquid*) entrer; (*of people, money*) affluer.
►**flow out** *vi* (*leave*) sortir, s'écouler.
flower[1] ['flaʊər] *n* **(a)** fleur *f*; **wild flowers,** fleurs sauvages *ou* des champs; **bunch of flowers,** bouquet *m* (de fleurs); **cut flowers,** fleurs coupées; **to put flowers on a grave,** fleurir une tombe; **no flowers by request,** ni fleurs ni couronnes; **in f.,** (*of plant*) en fleur; **in full f.,** en plein épanouissement; **to burst into f.,** fleurir; **in the f. of youth,** dans la première fleur de la jeunesse; **f. arrangement,** composition florale; **f. arranging,** art *m* de composer les bouquets; **f. garden,** jardin *m* d'agrément; **f. girl,** marchande *f* de fleurs (*dans la rue*); (*at wedding*) = jeune fille qui porte les fleurs dans un cortège; **f. head,** capitule *m*; **f. market,** marché *m* aux fleurs; **f. seller,** marchand, -e de fleurs (*dans la rue*); **f. show,** exposition *f* horticole, floralies *fpl*; **f. vase,** vase *m* à fleurs;
(b) *Ch etc* **flowers of sulphur,** fleurs *fpl* de soufre;
(c) *Typ* (*ornament*) fleuron *m*;
(d) *Fig* fine fleur, crème *f* (*de l'armée etc*).
flower[2] *vi* (*of plant*) fleurir, être en fleur; (*of art etc*) fleurir, s'épanouir.
flowerbed ['flaʊəbed] *n* plate-bande *f*, *pl* plates-bandes; (*round*) corbeille *f*.
flowered ['flaʊəd] *adj* (*jardin, talus etc*) fleuri; *Tex* (*tissu*) à fleurs.
-flowered ['flaʊəd] *suff* **white/yellow/**etc**-f.,** à fleurs blanches/jaunes/*etc*; **many-f.,** multiflore.
flowering ['flaʊərɪŋ] **1** *adj* **(a)** (*garden, plant*) fleuri, en fleur; **(b)** (*shrub*) à fleurs. **2** *n* fleuraison *f* (*d'une plante*); *Fig* **her late f. as an artist,** son épanouissement tardif en tant qu'artiste.
flowerpot ['flaʊəpɒt] *n* pot *m* de fleurs; (*ornamental*) cache-pot *m inv*.
flowery ['flaʊərɪ] *adj* **(a)** (*pré, tapis etc*) fleuri; **(b)** *Pej* (*style etc*) fleuri; **f. phrases,** fleurs *fpl* de rhétorique.
flowing ['fləʊɪŋ] **1** *adj* (*stream etc*) coulant; (*style etc*) coulant, fluide; (*movement*) gracieux; (*hair*) tombant (dans le cou); (*beard*) long. **2** *n* écoulement *m* (*de l'eau*).
flowline ['fləʊlaɪn] *n* ligne *f* de jonction de symboles (*sur un organigramme*).
flowmeter ['fləʊmiːtər] *n* débitmètre *m*, indicateur *m* d'écoulement *ou* de débit (*des liquides etc*).
flown *see* **FLY**[3].
flu [fluː] *n Med F* grippe *f*; **Asian f.,** grippe asiatique; **I've got (the) f.,** j'ai la grippe; **f. epidemic,** épidémie *f* de grippe.
flub[1] [flʌb] *n Am F* gaffe *f*, bourde *f*.
flub[2] *vt & vi* (**-bb-**) *Am F* faire une gaffe.
fluctuate ['flʌktjʊeɪt] *vi* **(a)** fluctuer; (*of conditions etc*) varier; **prices f. between ... and ...,** les prix oscillent entre ... et ...; **(b)** (*of person*) vaciller (*dans ses opinions etc*).
fluctuating ['flʌktjʊeɪtɪŋ] *adj* (*temperature etc*) variable; (*prices etc*) oscillant.
fluctuation [flʌktjʊ'eɪʃən] *n* variations *fpl* (*de température etc*); **exchange f.,** fluctuation(s) *f(pl)* du change.
flue [fluː] *n* **(a)** *Constr* tuyau *m* de cheminée, conduit *m* de fumée; **f. boiler,** chaudière *f* à tubes-foyers; **f. brush,** torche-tubes *m inv*, hérisson *m*; **(b)** *Mus* bouche *f* (de tuyau d'orgue); **f. pipe,** tuyau *m* à bouche; **f. stop,** jeu *m* de flûte.
fluency ['fluːənsɪ] *n* facilité *f* (*de parole, de style*); **her f. in French,** son aisance à s'exprimer en français.
fluent ['fluːənt] *adj* (*speech etc*) coulant, facile; **to be a f. speaker,** avoir la parole facile; **he is a f. speaker of French, he speaks f. French, he is f. in French,** il parle le français couramment.
fluently ['fluːəntlɪ] *adv* (*parler, lire*) couramment; (*s'exprimer*) avec facilité.
fluff[1] [flʌf] *n* **(a)** duvet *m* (*d'étoffe*); coton *m* (*de laine*); **a bit of f.,** une peluche; *Old-fashioned Br F* (*girl*) une poule; **(pieces of) f.,** (*under bed etc*) moutons *mpl*; **(b)** (*of rabbit etc*) fourrure douce; **(c)** *Th F* (*mistake*) raté *m*.
fluff[2] *vt* **(a)** lainer (*un drap etc*); **(b)** = **FLUFF OUT, FLUFF UP**; **(c)** *Th F* rater, louper (*son entrée*); *Sp* **to f. a shot,** rater un coup.
►**fluff out, fluff up** *vtsep* faire bouffer (*les cheveux*); **to f. up its feathers,** (*of bird*) hérisser ses plumes; **f. up the potatoes with a fork,** fouetter la purée avec une fourchette.
fluffy ['flʌfɪ] *adj* (*drap*) pelucheux; (*poussin etc*) duveteux; **f. hair,** cheveux flous; **a light f. cake,** un gâteau léger et mousseux.
fluid ['fluːɪd] **1** *adj* fluide, liquide; *MecE* (*embrayage*) hydraulique; (*transmission*) fluide; (*style etc*) coulant, facile; (*opinions etc*) changeant, inconstant; **industry in a f. state,** industrie en voie de transformation rapide; **f. situation,** situation *f* fluide; **f. ounce,** = 0,03 litres. **2** *n* fluide *m*, liquide *m*, solution *f*; *Aut* **brake f.,** liquide pour freins; *Med* **sterilizing f.,** solution stérilisante; **body fluids,** sécrétions *fpl*; *Med* **fluids only,** liquides uniquement.

fluidify [fluːˈɪdɪfaɪ] *vt* liquéfier (*un solide*).
fluidity [fluːˈɪdɪtɪ] *n* fluidité *f*, facilité *f* (*de style etc*); caractère changeant (*des opinions etc*).
fluidize [ˈfluːɪdaɪz] *vt* rendre fluide.
fluke¹ [fluːk] *n* **(a)** (*fish*) flet *m*; **(b) f. (worm),** douve *f* (*du foie*).
fluke² *n* **(a)** *Nau* patte *f*, aile *f* (*d'ancre*); **(b)** (*of whale*) **flukes,** nageoires *fpl*.
fluke³ *n* **(a)** *Billiards* point volé; **by a f.,** par raccroc; **(b)** *Fig F* (*stroke of luck*) coup *m* de veine, chance *f*; **his success was due to a f.,** c'est un hasard qu'il ait réussi; **it was a pure f.,** c'était un véritable coup de chance; (*just coincidence*) c'était un pur hasard.
fluke⁴ *vt Billiards* raccrocher (*la boule*).
fluky [ˈfluːkɪ] *adj F* **f. shot,** coup de chance.
flume [fluːm] *n* **(a)** buse *f* (*d'un moulin à eau*); **(b)** (*for logs etc*) canal *m* d'amenée; **(c)** *US Geog* ravin *m*.
flummox [ˈflʌməks] *vt F* réduire (*qn*) à quia.
flung *see* **FLING².**
flunk [flʌŋk] *esp Am F* **1** *vi* se faire recaler, se faire coller (*à un examen*). **2** *vt* **(a)** (*of teacher*) recaler, coller (*qn à un examen*); **(b)** (*of student*) rater, se faire coller à (*un examen*).
flunkey [ˈflʌŋkɪ] *n Pej* laquais *m*.
fluoresce [fluəˈres] *vi* entrer en fluorescence.
fluorescence [fluəˈresəns] *n* fluorescence *f*.
fluorescent [fluəˈresənt] *adj* fluorescent; **f. lighting,** éclairage fluorescent *ou* par fluorescence.
fluoridation [fluərɪˈdeɪʃən] *n Ch* fluoration *f*.
fluoride [ˈfluəraɪd] *n Ch* fluorure *f*.
fluorine [ˈfluəriːn] *n Ch* fluor *m*.
fluoroscope [ˈfluərəskəʊp] *n* fluoroscope *m*.
flurry¹ [ˈflʌrɪ] *n* **(a)** rafale *f* (*de neige*); **(b)** (*agitation*) agitation *f*, bouleversement *m*, émoi *m*; **f. of excitement,** vague *f* d'excitation.
flurry² *vt* **to get flurried,** perdre la tête.
flush¹ [flʌʃ] *n* (*in hunting*) envolée *f* (*d'oiseaux*).
flush² *vt* (*in hunting*) (faire) lever, faire partir (*des perdrix etc*).
flush³ *n* **(a)** (*of lavatory*) chasse *f* (d'eau); curage *m* (*d'un égout*); **to pull the f.,** tirer la chasse (d'eau); **(b)** accès *m*, élan *m* (*d'émotion etc*); **in the first f. of victory,** dans l'ivresse de la victoire; **(c)** éclat *m* (*de lumière, de la beauté etc*); **in the first f. of youth,** dans le premier éclat de la jeunesse; **(d)** rougeur *f*, flot *m* de sang (*au visage*); *Med* suffusion *f*; **hot f.,** bouffée *f* de chaleur; **the words brought a f. to her cheeks,** ces mots l'ont fait rougir.
flush⁴ **1** *vt* **(a)** faire jaillir (*l'eau*); **to f. a drain,** donner une chasse à un égout; **to f. the lavatory,** tirer la chasse d'eau; **to f. sth down the lavatory,** jeter qch dans les toilettes (et tirer la chasse d'eau); **(b)** (*redden*) faire rougir; **the exercise had flushed their cheeks,** l'exercice leur avait fait monter le sang au visage. **2** *vi* **(a)** (*of person*) rougir; **he** *or* **his face flushed,** il a rougi; **she flushed crimson,** elle est devenue écarlate; **(b)** (*in lavatory*) tirer la chasse d'eau; **the lavatory isn't flushing properly,** la chasse d'eau (des toilettes) ne fonctionne pas bien.
flush⁵ *n Cards* (*poker*) flush *m*; longue couleur; **straight f.,** séquence *f* flush.
flush⁶ **1** *adj* **(a)** (*surface etc*) ras; de niveau; (*door, lock etc*) encastré; (*screw, nail*) noyé; (*rivet*) à tête noyée *ou* perdue; **f. mounted,** monté à fleur; **to be f. with sth,** être à fleur de qch, être de niveau avec qch; **f. with the ground,** à ras de sol; **(b)** *F* **to be f. (with money),** (*of person*) être en fonds. **2** *adv Typ* **f. left/right,** justifié à gauche/droite.
flush⁷ *vt* (*make level*) affleurer (*deux surfaces etc*).
▶**flush away** *vtsep* (*dispose of in lavatory*) jeter (*qch*) dans les toilettes (et tirer la chasse d'eau).
▶**flush out** *vtsep* **(a)** (*force to emerge*) forcer à sortir, faire sortir de force; (*force to reveal oneself*) faire se trahir; **they used tear gas to f. the students out,** ils ont utilisé des gaz lacrymogènes pour faire sortir les étudiants; **(b)** (*clean*) rincer par circulation d'eau; **to f. out a drain,** donner une chasse à un égout.
flushed [flʌʃd] *adj* (*visage*) empourpré, congestionné; **f. with anger,** rouge de colère; **f. with success,** exalté par le succès.
fluster¹ [ˈflʌstər] *n* agitation *f*, trouble *m*; **in a f.,** tout en émoi, déconcerté.
fluster² **1** *vt* (*cause to panic*) faire perdre la tête à (*qn*); (*make nervous*) rendre (*qn*) nerveux; **to be** *or* **get flustered,** se troubler. **2** *vi* s'agiter, s'énerver.
flute¹ [fluːt] *n* **(a)** *Mus* flûte *f*; **transverse f.,** flûte traversière; *Th* **the Magic F.,** la Flûte Enchantée; **f. (player),** (joueur, -euse de) flûte; **f. stop,** (*on organ*) jeu *m* de flûte; **(b)** (*groove*) cannelure *f* (*de colonne*); **f. (glass),** flûte *f*.
flute² **1** *vt* **(a)** (*decorate with grooves*) canneler (*une colonne*); **(b)** jouer (*un air*) sur la flûte. **2** *vi* (*of birds*) flûter; *Mus* jouer de la flûte.
fluted [ˈfluːtɪd] *adj* (*wood etc*) à cannelures; (*column*) cannelé.
fluting [ˈfluːtɪŋ] *n* **(a)** (*action*) façonnage *m* des cannelures; **(b)** (*no pl*) (*result*) cannelures *fpl*.
flutist [ˈfluːtɪst] *n esp Am Mus* flûtiste *mf*.
flutter¹ [ˈflʌtər] *n* **(a)** volettement *m*, trémoussement *m* (*d'un oiseau*); battement *m* (*des ailes, des paupières*); palpitation *f* (*du cœur*); flottement *m* (*d'un drapeau etc*); pulsation *f* (*du son*); *TV* scintillation *f*; **(b)** (*agitation*) agitation *f*, trouble *m*; **to be in a f. of excitement** *or F* **all in a f.,** être tout en émoi; **(b)** *Br F* (*bet*) petite spéculation; **to have a little f.,** faire un ou deux petits paris; (*in gambling house etc*) risquer de petites sommes au jeu; **to have a f. on the horses,** risquer de petites sommes au tiercé.
flutter² **1** *vi* (*of birds, insects*) (*fly*) voleter; (*flap wings*) battre des ailes; (*of flag etc*) flotter, s'agiter (au vent); (*of heart*) palpiter; (*of pulse*) battre irrégulièrement; **to make s.o.'s heart f.,** faire tressaillir le cœur de qn; **the letter fluttered to the ground,** la lettre a volé par terre. **2** *vt* **to f. its wings,** (*of bird*) battre des ailes; **she fluttered her eyelashes at him,** elle l'a regardé en battant des cils.
fluvial [ˈfluːvɪəl] *adj* fluvial, -aux.
flux¹ [flʌks] *n* **(a)** *Med* flux *m* (*de sang etc*); (*in oceanography*) flux, montant *m* (*de la marée*); courant *m* (*d'eau etc*); **f. and reflux,** flux et reflux, flot *m* et jusant; **(b)** (*constant change*) changement continuel; **to be in a state of f.,** être sujet à des changements fréquents; **(c)** *Phys* flux *m* (*magnétique etc*); **(d)** *Metal* fondant *m*, flux *m*; **gold f.,** (*in glassmaking*) aventurine *f*.
flux² **1** *vi* (*of metal*) fondre, devenir liquide. **2** *vt Metal* fondre, mettre en fusion (*un métal*).
fluxion [ˈflʌkʃən] *n Med* fluxion *f* (*de sang etc*).
fluxmeter [ˈflʌksmiːtər] *n Phys* fluxmètre *m*.
fly¹, *pl* **flies** [flaɪ, -z] *n* **(a)** (*insect*) mouche *f*; **Spanish f.,** mouche d'Espagne, cantharide *f*; **horse f.,** taon *m*; **tsetse f.,** (mouche) tsé-tsé *f*; **they were dying** *or* **dropping like flies,** ils tombaient comme des mouches; **he wouldn't hurt a f.,** il ne ferait pas de mal à une mouche; *F* **a f. in the ointment,** un cheveu (sur la soupe); *Fig* **to catch flies,** bayer aux corneilles; **there are** *or F* **there's no flies on her,** elle n'est pas bête; **I wish I could be a f. on the wall,** (*at that interview, meeting etc*) si je pouvais être une petite souris; **f. orchid,** (*plant*) ophrys *f* mouche; **f. agaric,** (*fungus*) fausse oronge; **f. spray,** produit *m* tue-mouches à vaporiser; **f. swat(ter),** tapette *f* à mouches; **f. whisk,** chasse-mouches *m inv*; **(b)** *Fishing* mouche *f* (*artificielle, naturelle*); **wet f.,** mouche mouillée *ou* noyée; **wet/dry-f. fishing,** pêche *f* à la mouche noyée/sèche; **(c)** *Typ* receveur *m* mécanique.
fly² *n* **(a)** (*often in pl*) **flies,** braguette *f* (*de pantalon*); **your flies are** *or* **f. is undone** *or* **open,** ta braguette est ouverte; **f. front closing** *or* **closure,** (*of coat etc*) boutonnage *m ou* fermeture *f* sous patte; **(b) f. (sheet),** (*of tent*) (*flap*) auvent *m*; (*roof*) double toit *m*; **f. sheet,** (*circular*) prospectus *m*; **(c)** *Th* **the flies,** les cintres *mpl*; **(d)** *Tech* régulateur *m*, contrepoids *m* (*de sonnerie d'horloge etc*); *Tex* **f. shuttle,** navette volante; *Ind* **f. ash,** cendres volantes.
fly³ *v* (*pt* **flew** [fluː]; *pp* **flown** [fləʊn]) **1** *vi* **(a)** (*of bird etc*) voler; *F* **the bird has flown,** l'oiseau s'est envolé; **to f. high,** voler haut; (*of person*) avoir de l'ambition; **as the crow flies,** à vol d'oiseau;

(b) *Av* (*of aircraft*) voler; (*of pilot*) effectuer un vol, voler; (*of passenger*) prendre l'avion, voyager en avion; **he flew for** *or* **with the RAF,** il volait pour la RAF; **I've never flown before,** c'est la première fois que je prends l'avion; **it's cheaper to f.,** il est moins cher de prendre l'avion; **I've never flown in a 747,** je n'ai jamais voyagé en 747; **to f. blind,** voler sans visibilité; **to f. over London,** survoler Londres; **we flew 400 miles,** nous avons parcouru 640 kilomètres en avion; **who did you f. with?,** (*which airline*) avec quelle compagnie est-ce que tu as voyagé?; *Fig* **to f. in the face of the evidence,** se refuser à admettre l'évidence;

(c) (*of hair etc*) flotter; (*of flag*) se déployer, flotter, battre; **the American flag flew above the building,** le drapeau américain flottait au-dessus du bâtiment;

(d) (*move quickly etc*) (*of person etc*) courir *ou* aller à toute vitesse; (*of time*) fuir, filer; (*of cork etc*) voler, sauter en l'air; (*of sparks*) jaillir; **to f. to s.o.'s help,** courir à l'aide de qn; *F* **it's late, I must f.,** il se fait tard, il faut que je me sauve; *F* **I flew home and changed,** j'ai filé à la maison pour me changer; **time is flying,** le temps s'envole; **to f. into a temper,** se mettre en colère; **to f. at s.o.,** (*attack them*) se jeter sur qn; **the door flew open,** la porte s'ouvrit en coup de vent; **to f. into a rage** *or F* **off the handle,** s'emporter, sortir de ses gonds; *F* **to send s.o. flying,** envoyer rouler qn; **to f. to pieces** *or* **to bits,** éclater, voler en éclats; **to let f.,** (*lose one's temper*) s'emporter; lancer (*une flèche*); décocher (*un trait*); lâcher (*une volée d'injures*); **to let f. at s.o.,** (*abuse, reprimand*) s'en prendre à qn; (*hit*) flanquer un coup à qn.

2 *vt* **(a)** *Av* piloter (*un avion*); emmener (*qn, qch*) en avion; transporter (*qn, qch*) par avion; **we were flown to Norway,** on nous a emmenés en Norvège en avion; **f. ABC airlines,** voyager avec la compagnie aérienne ABC; **several airlines f. this route,** plusieurs compagnies aériennes empruntent cette route; **he had flown three missions,** il avait effectué trois missions en vol; **her employers flew her to the States,** ses employeurs l'ont envoyée aux États-Unis en avion;

(b) *Nau* battre (*un pavillon*); **the ship was flying the Italian flag,** le bateau arborait le pavillon italien;

(c) **to f. pigeons,** lancer des pigeons voyageurs; **to f. a kite,** faire voler un cerf-volant; *Fig* lancer un ballon d'essai; *esp Am* **go f. a kite!,** (*go away*) fiche-moi le camp; (*I'm not going to do it*) va te faire voir;

(d) (*flee*) s'enfuir; **to f. the country,** s'enfuir du pays; *esp Am* **to f. the coop,** disparaître; **to f. the nest,** (*of fledgling, child*) quitter le nid.

fly⁴ *adj Br F Sl* malin, -igne; **he's very f.,** c'est un malin.

▶fly about, fly around *vi* (*of bird*) voler çà et là; (*of butterfly etc*) voltiger.

▶fly away *vi* (*of bird etc*) s'envoler.

▶fly by *vi* **(a)** (*of time*) passer à toute vitesse; **the time has flown by!,** comme le temps a passé!; **as the days flew by,** à mesure que les jours s'enfuyaient; **(b)** *Av* (*of aircraft*) passer.

▶fly in 1 *vi* **(a)** (*arrive by aircraft*) arriver en avion; **(b)** (*approach*) (*of pilot, aircraft*) arriver; **the planes flew in over the coast,** les avions sont arrivés en survolant la côte. **2** *vtsep* (*transport by aircraft*) amener (*qn, qch*) en avion; **the air force flew in supplies,** les forces aériennes ont amené des ravitaillements.

▶fly off 1 *vi* (*of bird, aircraft etc*) s'envoler; (*leave in aircraft*) partir en avion; (*of button etc*) sauter. **2** *vtsep* (*transport by aircraft*) envoyer par avion.

▶fly out 1 *vi* **(a)** (*of bird*) sortir en volant; **(b)** (*leave in aircraft*) partir en avion; **a medical team flew out to the disaster area,** une équipe médicale s'est rendue en avion sur la région sinistrée; **(c)** (*be ejected*) être éjecté; **the lorry turned sharply and some boxes flew out,** le camion a pris un virage raide et des boîtes se sont trouvées éjectées. **2** *vtsep* (*transport by aircraft*) emmener (*qn, qch*) en avion; **her husband's employer flew her out to be with him,** l'employeur de son mari l'a envoyée le retrouver par avion.

▶fly past *vi* **(a)** (*of bird, aircraft*) passer (en volant); *Mil Av* (*in formation*) exécuter un défilé aérien; *Fig* **he flew past on a bicycle,** il est passé à toute vitesse en bicyclette; **(b)** (*of time*) passer vite.

▶fly up *vi* **(a)** (*of bird etc*) s'envoler; **(b)** (*become vertical*) s'élever; **his arm flew up,** son bras s'est élevé; **the other end of the broom flew up,** l'autre extrémité du balai s'est relevée.

flyaway ['flaɪəweɪ] *adj* **(a)** (*bow etc*) flottant, négligé; **f. hair,** cheveux légers et indisciplinés; **(b)** (*person*) léger, étourdi.

flyblown ['flaɪbləʊn] *adj* (*meat*) plein *ou* couvert d'œufs de mouches.

flyby ['flaɪbaɪ] *n Mil Av* défilé aérien.

fly-by-night ['flaɪbaɪnaɪt] *F* **1** *adj* (*company etc*) douteux, véreux. **2** *n* **(a)** *Pej* personne qui file à l'anglaise pour éviter de payer une note; (*firm*) entreprise douteuse *ou* véreuse; **(b)** (*who goes out at night*) oiseau *m* de nuit.

fly-by-wire ['flaɪbaɪwaɪər] *n Mil Av* commandes informatisées.

flycatcher ['flaɪkætʃər] *n* (*bird*) gobe-mouches *m inv*; *Am* moucherolle *f*; **spotted f.,** gobe-mouches gris.

fly-drive ['flaɪdraɪv] *adj Com* **f.-d. holiday,** vacances en formule avion-voiture.

flyer ['flaɪər] *n* = **FLIER.**

fly-half ['flaɪhɑːf] *n Rugby* demi *m* d'ouverture.

flying ['flaɪɪŋ] **1** *adj* **(a)** (*oiseau, poisson etc*) volant; (*ribbon, hair etc*) volant, léger; *Hist* **f. bomb,** bombe volante; *US Av* **f. corps,** corps *m* d'armée aérien; **f. fox,** roussette *f*; **unidentified f. object,** objet volant non identifié; **f. saucer,** soucoupe volante;

(b) (*rapid*) (*course etc*) rapide; (*camp*) temporaire; **f. column,** *Mil* colonne *f* mobile, groupement *m* mobile; *Ind* **f. picket,** piquet *m* de grève volant; **f. squad,** brigade volante; **to take a f. leap over sth,** franchir qch d'un saut; *Sp* **f. start,** départ *m* en flèche; **we got off to a f. start,** nous nous sommes lancés (*dans ce projet etc*) sans anicroche; **to pay a f. visit to London,** faire une visite éclair à Londres; *Fig F* **to take a f. jump,** aller se faire voir;

(c) **to pass an exam with f. colours,** réussir un examen haut la main;

(d) *Constr etc* (*échafaudage*) à bascule; **f. bridge,** pont volant; **f. buttress,** arc-boutant *m, pl* arcs-boutants;

(e) (*fleeing*) en fuite; *Liter Mus* **the F. Dutchman,** le Vaisseau fantôme.

2 *n* **(a)** vol *m* (*d'un oiseau, d'une flèche etc*); *Av* aviation *f*; pilotage *m* (*d'un avion*); **I don't like f.,** je n'aime pas prendre l'avion; **I haven't done much f.,** (*as pilot*) je n'ai pas beaucoup volé; (*as passenger*) je n'ai pas pris l'avion très souvent; **blind f.,** vol *m* sans visibilité; **instrument f.,** navigation *f* aux instruments; **f. boat,** hydravion *m* monocoque; **he is interested in anything connected with f.,** il s'intéresse à tout ce qui a trait à l'aviation; **night f.,** vol *m* de nuit; **f. club,** aéro-club *m, pl* aéro-clubs; **f. lessons,** leçons *fpl* de pilotage aérien;

(b) jaillissement *m* (*d'étincelles*);

(c) (*escape*) fuite *f* (*de qn*);

(d) lancement *m* (*des pigeons, d'un cerf-volant*);

(e) déploiement *m* (*d'un drapeau*).

fly-kick ['flaɪkɪk] *n Rugby* coup *m* de pied à suivre.

flyleaf ['flaɪliːf] *n* (*of book*) (feuille *f* de) garde *f*.

flyover ['flaɪəʊvər] *n* **(a)** *Br* (*elevated road*) saut-de-mouton *m, pl* sauts-de-mouton; **f. crossing,** croisement *m* à niveaux différents; **(b)** *Am Av* survol *m*; (*ceremonial*) défilé aérien.

flypaper ['flaɪpeɪpər] *n* papier *m* tue-mouches.

fly-past ['flaɪpɑːst] *n Mil Av* défilé aérien.

flypost ['flaɪpəʊst] *vt* coller illicitement des affiches.

flyposting ['flaɪpəʊstɪŋ] *n* affichage illégal.

fly-tipping ['flaɪtɪpɪŋ] *n Br* dépôt *m* d'ordures illégal.

flyweight ['flaɪweɪt] *n Boxing* (*boxer*) boxeur *m* poids mouche; **f. (boxing),** poids *m* mouche; **f. champion,** champion *m* poids mouche.

flywheel ['flaɪwiːl] *n MecE etc* volant *m* (*d'entraînement, de commande*).

FM [e'fem] *n Rad* (*abbr* **frequency modulation**) FM *f*; **a station on FM, an FM station,** une station FM.

f-number ['efnʌmbər] *n Phot* échelle *f* d'ouverture.

FO [e'fəʊ] *n Br Admin* (*abbr* **Foreign Office**) ministère *m* des affaires étrangères.

foal¹ [fəʊl] *n* poulain *m*, pouliche *f*; (*of donkey*) ânon *m*, bourriquet *m*; **mare in** *or* **with f.,** jument pleine.

foal² **1** *vi* pouliner. **2** *vt* mettre bas (*un poulain*).

foam¹ [fəʊm] *n* **(a)** écume *f*; (*on beer*) mousse *f*; **waves white with f.,** vagues moutonneuses; **to break into f.,** (*of wave*) déferler; **f.-flecked,** moucheté d'écume; **f. bath,** bain *m* de mousse; **(b)** (*from mouth*) bave *f*, écume *f*; **(c)** (*artificial substance*) mousse *f*; **f. fire extinguisher,** extincteur *m* à mousse carbonique; **polystyrene f.,** mousse *f* en polystyrène; **f. rubber,** caoutchouc *m* mousse.

foam² *vi* (*of sea etc*) écumer; (*of beer etc*) mousser; **to f. at the mouth,** avoir l'écume aux lèvres; (*of dog etc*) baver; *F Fig* (*be furious*) écumer (de rage); **he was foaming at the mouth about the latest price rises,** il écumait de rage en évoquant les dernières hausses de prix.

foaming ['fəʊmɪŋ] *adj* (*sea, horse etc*) écumant; (*sea*) moutonnant; (*beer etc*) moussant; (*blood, saliva*) spumeux.

foamy ['fəʊmɪ] *adj* (*sea*) écumant; (*drink*) mousseux.

fob [fɒb] *n* **(a)** **f. (pocket),** gousset *m* (de pantalon); **(b)** (*chain*) chaîne *f*; **f. (watch),** montre *f* de gousset.

▶fob off *vtsep* **to f. s.o. off with sth,** se débarrasser de qn en lui racontant *ou* donnant *etc* qch; **they fobbed him off with some excuse,** ils lui ont donné la première excuse venue.

f.o.b., FOB [efəʊ'biː] *adj Com* (*abbr* **free on board**) f. à b., FOB.

focal ['fəʊk(ə)l] *adj* **(a)** *Phys Opt Math* focal, -aux; **f. length,** distance *ou* longueur focale; **f. point,** (*of mirror etc*) foyer *m*; *Fig* (*of discussion etc*) point central; (*of room*) point de mire; **(b)** *Med* (*infection*) focal.

focalization [fəʊkəlaɪ'zeɪʃən] *n* **(a)** focalisation *f*; **(b)** *Med* localisation *f* (*d'une maladie*) à son foyer.

focalize ['fəʊkəlaɪz] **1** *vt* **(a)** = **FOCUS²**; **(b)** mettre au point (*l'œil*); **(c)** *Med* localiser (*une maladie*) à son foyer. **2** *vi* (*of illness*) se localiser à son foyer.

fo'c'sle ['fəʊks(ə)l] *n* = **FORECASTLE**.

focus¹, *pl* **foci, focuses** ['fəʊkəs, 'fəʊsaɪ, 'fəʊkəsɪz] *n* **(a)** *Math Opt etc* foyer *m* (*de lentille etc*); *Opt Phot* **depth of f.**, profondeur *f* de foyer; **in f.**, (*of image*) au point; (*of instrument*) réglé; **out of f.**, (*of image*) pas au point; (*of instrument*) non réglé, déréglé; (*of headlamp, bulb etc*) mal réglé; **to bring sth into f.**, mettre qch au point; *Phot* **fixed-f. camera**, appareil *m* à mise au point fixe; **(b)** centre *m* (*d'un tremblement de terre etc*); *Med* siège *m* (*d'une maladie*); **she was the f. of attention**, elle était le centre d'attention; *Med* **f. of infection**, foyer *m* d'infection.

focus² *v* (**-s-**) **1** *vt* **(a)** concentrer (*les rayons de lumière etc*) (**in, on,** dans, sur); faire converger (*des rayons*); **all eyes were focused on him**, il était le point de mire de tous les regards; **(b)** mettre au point (*un microscope etc*). **2** *vi* **(a)** (*with eyes*) fixer; **to f. on sth**, (*with eyes*) fixer qch; (*of debate, speaker etc*) se concentrer sur qch; **to f. one's attention on sth**, concentrer son attention sur qch; **to f. attention on sth**, attirer l'attention des gens sur qch; *Phot* **to f. on an object**, mettre au point sur un objet; **(b)** (*of light, sound etc*) converger (**on**, sur).

focusing ['fəʊkəsɪŋ] *n* **(a)** convergence *f* (*de rayons etc*); **(b)** focalisation *f*, mise *f* au point (*d'une jumelle etc*).

fodder¹ ['fɒdər] *n* fourrage *m*; **green/dry f.**, fourrage (en) vert/(en) sec; *F* **cannon f.**, chair *f* à canon.

fodder² *vt* donner le fourrage à (*une bête*).

foe [fəʊ] *n Lit* ennemi *m*, adversaire *m*.

foetal ['fiːt(ə)l] *adj Biol* fœtal, -aux; **f. heartbeat**, rythme *m* cardiaque du fœtus.

foetid ['fiːtɪd] *adj* = **FETID**.

foetus *pl* **-uses** ['fiːtəs, -əsɪz] *n Biol* fœtus *m*.

fog¹ [fɒg] *n* **(a)** brouillard *m*; **in the f.**, dans le brouillard; *Fig* **I'm in a f.**, je ne sais plus où j'en suis; **f. bank**, nappe *m* de brouillard; *Av etc* **f. dispersal**, dénébulation *f*; **f. light**, projecteur *m* pour le brouillard; *Aut* (phare *m*) antibrouillard *m*; **f. signal**, *Nau* signal *m*, -aux de brume; *Rail* pétard *m*; **(b)** *Phot* (*on negative*) voile *m*; **(c)** (*condensation*) buée *f* (*sur les vitres etc*).

fog² *v* (**-gg-**) **1** *vt* **(a)** embrumer (*un endroit*); *F* brouiller (*les idées*); embrouiller (*qn*); **I am a bit fogged**, je ne sais plus très bien où j'en suis; **(b)** *Phot* voiler (*un cliché*); **(c)** embuer (*une glace etc*). **2** *vi* **(a)** (*of spectacles, windows*) se couvrir de buée, s'embuer; **(b)** *Phot* (*of negative*) se voiler.

►fog up *vi* = **FOG² 2 (a)**.

fogbound ['fɒgbaʊnd] *adj* (*airport*) bloqué par le brouillard.

fogey ['fəʊgɪ] *n F* **old f.**, vieille baderne; **young f.**, pépère *m*.

fogginess ['fɒgɪnɪs] *n* **(a)** état brumeux (*du temps*); **(b)** confusion *f* (*des idées de qn*); *Phot* voile *m*.

fogging ['fɒgɪŋ] *n* **(a)** ternissement *m* (*d'une glace*); **(b)** *Phot* voile *m*.

foggy ['fɒgɪ] *adj* **(a)** brumeux; **f. weather**, temps brumeux; **on a f. day**, par un jour de brouillard; **it's f.**, il y a où il fait du brouillard; **(b)** (*photograph etc*) voilé; **to have only a f. idea of sth**, n'avoir qu'une vague idée de qch; *F* **I haven't the foggiest (idea)!**, je n'en ai pas la moindre idée!

foghorn ['fɒghɔːn] *n Nau* corne *f* de brume, sirène *f*; *F* **voice like a f.**, voix *f* de stentor.

foglamp ['fɒglæmp] *n* (phare *m*) antibrouillard *m*.

foible ['fɔɪb(ə)l] *n* (*idiosyncrasy*) particularité *f*; (*weakness*) côté *m* faible, point *m* faible.

foil¹ [fɔɪl] *n* **(a)** (*metal sheet*) feuille *f* (*d'or etc*); tain *m* (*d'une glace*); **silver f.**, feuille d'argent; *Culin* **household f., cooking f.**, papier *m* aluminium; **sandwiches wrapped in f.**, sandwiches enveloppés dans du papier aluminium; **(b)** (*person, thing*) repoussoir *m*; **to serve as a f. to s.o.'s beauty**, servir de repoussoir à la beauté de qn; **(c)** *Av Nau* patin *m*, aile *f* (*d'un hydrofoil*); **(d)** *Archit* lobe *m* (*d'un arc etc*).

foil² *n Fencing* **(a)** fleuret *m*; **(b) foils**, escrime *f* au fleuret.

foil³ *vt* (*thwart*) faire échouer, faire manquer (*une tentative etc*); contrecarrer (*un plan, un complot*); **to be foiled at all points**, (*of person*) échouer sur toute la ligne; **foiled again!**, encore raté!

foist [fɔɪst] *vt* refiler (**sth on s.o.**, qch à qn); **to f. oneself on s.o.**, s'imposer à qn *ou* chez qn.

fold¹ [fəʊld] *n* **(a)** (*crease*) pli *m*, repli *m* (*du papier etc*); *Sewing* **box folds**, plis rentrés; **folds of fat**, bourrelets *mpl* de graisse; **(b)** *Geol* pli *m*, plissement *m*.

fold² **1** *vt* **(a)** plier (*une feuille de papier etc*); **to f. sth in two** *or* **in half**, plier qch en deux; **to f. sth in paper**, envelopper qch dans du papier; **to f. s.o. in one's arms**, enlacer qn, serrer qn dans ses bras; **to f. one's arms**, (se) croiser les bras; **with folded arms**, les bras croisés; **to f. one's hands**, joindre les mains; **(b)** *Culin* **f. the whites into the mixture**, incorporer petit à petit les blancs dans le mélange. **2** *vi* **(a)** (*of screen etc*) se (re)plier; **(b)** *F* (*of business*) cesser les affaires; *Th* **the play folded after a week**, la pièce a été retirée au bout d'une semaine.

fold³ *n* **(a)** *Agr* **sheep f.**, parc *m* à moutons; **(b)** *Fig* sein *m* (*de l'Église, de la famille*); **to bring back a lost sheep to the f.**, ramener au bercail une brebis égarée; **to return to the f.**, (*of member of family*) rentrer au bercail; (*of politician etc*) rentrer dans les rangs.

fold⁴ *vt Agr* (em)parquer (*les moutons*).

►fold away **1** *vi* (*of table etc*) se replier, être escamotable. **2** *vtsep* (*store*) plier (*qch*) pour le ranger; **f. your clothes away neatly**, plie tes affaires et range-les.

►fold back **1** *vtsep* (*turn*) rabattre (*un col etc*); retourner (*les couvertures d'un lit*). **2** *vi* (*of door etc*) se rabattre.

►fold down **1** *vtsep* retourner (*les couvertures d'un lit*). **2** *vi* (*of seat etc*) se rabattre.

►fold in *vtsep* **(a)** (*turn in*) replier (*les bords*) en dedans; **(b)** (*insert*) encarter, insérer; **literary supplement folded in with each number**, supplément littéraire encarté dans chaque numéro; **(c)** *Culin* **to f. in the whites of the eggs**, incorporer les blancs d'œufs.

►fold under *vtsep* (*turn under*) replier (*les bords*) en dessous.

►fold up **1** *vtsep* (re)plier (*un siège, une table*); replier, fermer (*un paravent*). **2** *vi* **(a)** se replier; **seat that folds up**, siège pliant; **(b)** = **FOLD² 2 (b)**.

-fold [fəʊld] *suff* **three/eleven/twenty/*etc*-f.**, (*in three/eleven/etc parts*) en trois/onze/vingt/*etc* parties; (*to increase*) par un facteur de trois/de onze/de vingt/*etc*.

foldaway ['fəʊldəweɪ] *adj* repliable, escamotable; (*siège*) pliant, rabattable; **f. bed**, lit *m* escamotable.

folder ['fəʊldər] *n* **(a)** (*for papers etc*) chemise *f*, dossier *m*; **(b)** *Com* (*leaflet*) prospectus *m* (plié); **(c)** (*device*) plioir *m*; **(d)** (*person*) plieur, -euse (*de journaux etc*).

folding ['fəʊldɪŋ] **1** *adj* (*seat*) pliant, rabattable; (*bed*) pliant, rabattant; (*joint, volet*) brisé; **f. camera**, appareil *m* à soufflet; **f. door**, porte brisée; *esp Am F* **f. money**, billet *m*; **f. screen**, paravent *m*; **f. stool**, pliant *m*; **f. table**, table pliante *ou* escamotable; (*with extending sections*) table à battants; **car with a f. top**, voiture *f* décapotable. **2** *n* **(a)** pliage *m* (*de l'étoffe etc*); (*in bookbinding*) pliure *f* (*de feuilles*); croisement *m* (*des bras*); **(b)** (*act of wrapping*) enveloppement *m* (**of sth in sth**, de qch dans qch); **(c)** *Geol* plissement *m* (*du terrain*).

foldout ['fəʊldaʊt] *n* dépliant *m*.

foliage ['fəʊlɪɪdʒ] *n* feuillage *m*, frondaison *f*; **f. plant**, plante *f* à feuillage.

foliate ['fəʊlɪeɪt] *adj Bot* feuillu.

foliation [fəʊlɪ'eɪʃən] *n* **(a)** foliation *f*, feuillaison *f* (*d'une plante*); **(b)** *Archit* (ornementation *f* en) rinceaux *mpl*; **(c)** *Geol* foliation *f* (*d'une roche*); **(d)** foliotage *m* (*d'un livre*).

folic ['fəʊlɪk] *adj* **f. acid**, acide *m* folique.

folio, *pl* **-os** ['fəʊlɪəʊ, -əʊz] **1** *n* (*in bookbinding*) folio *m*, feuille *f* (*de manuscrit*); *Typ etc* numéro *m* (*d'une page*); **(book in) f.**, (livre *m*) in-folio *m*. **2** *adj* **f. book**, (livre *m*) in-folio *m*.

folk [fəʊk] *n F & Dial* (*pl* **folk**, *esp Am* **folks**) gens *mfpl*; **I don't care what f. think**, je me moque de ce que les gens pensent; **country f.**, campagnards *mpl*; **my/your f.**, les miens, ma famille/les vôtres, votre famille; *esp Am F* **hi, folks!**, salut, tout le monde!; **f. medicine**, médecine *f* populaire; **f. music**, musique *f* folk *ou* folklorique; **f. museum**, musée *m* folklorique; **Welsh F. Museum**, musée du folklore gallois, musée populaire gallois; **f. singer**, chanteur, -euse de chansons folkloriques; (*modern*) folk-singer *m*, *pl* folk-singers; **f. song**, chanson traditionnelle *ou* folklorique; (*modern*) folk-song *m*, *pl* folk-songs; **f. tale**, conte *m* folklorique.

folklore ['fəʊklɔːr] *n* folklore *m*.

folkloric ['fəʊklɔːrɪk] *adj* folklorique.

folksy ['fəʊksɪ] *adj F* **(a)** (*folkloric*) folklorique; **(b)** (*friendly*) sociable.

foll (*abbr* **following**) suiv.

follicle ['fɒlɪk(ə)l] *n Anat Bot etc* follicule *m*.

follow ['fɒləʊ] **1** *vt* **(a)** suivre (*qn etc*); poursuivre (*l'ennemi etc*); **to f. s.o. about**, suivre qn partout; **a man followed by his dog**, un homme suivi de son chien; **f. that car!**, suivez cette voiture!; *F* **to f. one's nose**, aller tout droit devant soi;

(b) (*go along*) suivre (*un chemin*); **boat that follows the coast,** bateau qui longe la côte; **we followed the route taken by Columbus,** nous avons suivi la route empruntée par Christophe Colomb;

(c) (*succeed*) succéder à (*qn, qch*); **the years f. one another,** les années se succèdent *ou* se suivent; **as sure as day follows night,** aussi sûr que deux et deux font quatre; **in the months that followed his resignation,** dans les mois qui ont suivi sa démission; **George IV was followed by William IV,** Guillaume IV a succédé à Georges IV; **dinner followed by a dance,** dîner suivi d'un bal; **to f. a tragedy with a light comedy,** faire suivre une tragédie d'une comédie légère; **she is a hard act to f.,** il est difficile de prendre sa relève *ou* sa suite; **how do you expect me to f. that?,** comment veux-tu que je prenne la suite?; **following our correspondence,** (comme) suite à notre échange de lettres;

(d) (*imitate*) imiter (*les anciens maîtres*); être le disciple de (*qn*); suivre (*l'exemple de qn*); **to f. suit,** (*do the same*) faire de même;

(e) (*practise, carry out*) exercer, suivre (*une profession*); poursuivre (*une carrière*); s'assujetir à (*un régime*); suivre (*la mode etc*); **to f. instructions,** suivre des consignes; **you're not following the music,** vous ne suivez pas la musique;

(f) (*keep up with*) aller aussi vite que (*qn*);

(g) (*understand*) suivre, comprendre (*une explication etc*); **I don't quite f. you,** je ne vous comprends pas très bien;

(h) (*pay attention to*) prêter attention à (*un discours, un sermon*); **we are following events there very closely,** nous suivons de très près les événements qui se déroulent là-bas; **I don't f. the tennis any more,** je ne suis plus le tennis; **have you been following that programme?,** est-ce que vous avez suivi cette émission?

2 *vi* **(a)** (*of person, event*) suivre, venir à la suite de, venir après; **my husband is following later,** mon mari viendra plus tard; **to f. close behind s.o.,** emboîter le pas à qn; **in the days that followed,** dans les jours qui ont suivi; **a very long silence followed,** il s'ensuivit un très long silence; **roast beef with strawberries to f.,** du rosbif suivi par des fraises; **as follows,** comme suit; **our method is as follows,** notre méthode est la suivante; **what follows is a brief account,** ce qui suit est un bref compte-rendu;

(b) (*result*) s'ensuivre, résulter (**from,** de); **it follows that ...,** il s'ensuit que ...; **it does not f. that ...,** ça ne veut pas nécessairement dire que ... + *ind*;

(c) (*keep up*) suivre; **he went too fast for me to f.,** il allait trop vite pour que je puisse le suivre;

(d) (*understand*) suivre; **I don't f.,** je ne suis pas.

▶**follow on** *vi* **(a)** (*come after*) suivre; **you go ahead, we'll f. on,** partez en avant, nous vous suivons; **(b)** continuer, se poursuivre; (*result*) **it follows on from this that ...,** il en résulte que ...; **(c)** *Cr* = reprendre la garde du guichet au commencement de la seconde partie du match (au lieu d'alterner avec l'autre équipe).

▶**follow out** *vtsep* (*execute*) exécuter (*des ordres*).

▶**follow through 1** *vtsep* (*execute*) **to f. a project through (to the end),** poursuivre un projet jusqu'à sa conclusion. **2** *vi Sp* suivre le coup.

▶**follow up 1** *vtsep* (*take further*) poursuivre (*avec énergie*); *Com* faire suivre (*une lettre*) d'une seconde lettre; poursuivre (*un avantage*); exploiter (*un succès*); donner suite immédiate à (*une victoire etc*); **to f. up a clue,** suivre une piste. **2** *vi* (*add to previous action*) continuer; **he followed up with a right to the jaw,** il a continué avec un droit à la mâchoire.

follower ['fɒləʊər] *n* **(a)** (*supporter*) partisan, -ane, disciple *mf*; **(b)** (*servant*) serviteur *m* (*d'un prince etc*); **the King and his followers,** le roi et sa suite.

following ['fɒləʊɪŋ] **1** *adj* **(a)** qui suit, suivant; **on the f. day,** le jour suivant, le jour d'après, le lendemain; **the f. Monday was a holiday,** le lundi suivant était férié; **the f. resolution,** la résolution que voici *ou* suivante; **the f. persons,** les personnes dont les noms suivent, les personnes suivantes; **two days f.,** deux jours de suite; **(b)** *Nau* **f. wind,** vent *m* arrière. **2** *n* **(a)** *Pol etc* parti *m* (*d'un chef*); suite *f* (*d'un prince*); **to have a big f.,** avoir un grand nombre de partisans *ou* de disciples; **television programme that commands a wide f.,** émission télévisée très suivie; **(b) the f.,** ce qui suit; les personnes suivantes *ou* dont les noms suivent; **the f. is the full list,** voici la liste complète. **3** *prep* après, à la suite de; **f. the election defeat ...,** après la défaite aux élections ... .

follow-my-leader [fɒləʊmɪ'liːdər] *n Br* jeu *m* de la queue leu leu.

follow-on ['fɒləʊ'ɒn] *n* continuation *f*, suite *f*; *Cr* **to try to avoid** *or* **save the f.-on,** = s'efforcer de marquer le nombre de points requis pour ne pas avoir à reprendre la garde du guichet.

follow-the-leader ['fɒləʊðə'liːdər] *n Am* = **FOLLOW-MY-LEADER**.

follow-through ['fɒləʊ'θruː] *n Sp* fin *f* du coup.

follow-up ['fɒləʊ'ʌp] *n* suite *f*; *Com etc* relance *f* (*de la publicité etc*); *Med* examens *mpl* de contrôles à long terme; **f.-up action,** suite; *Mil* action *f* de soutien; **to take f.-up action on sth,** donner suite à qch; **f.-up letter,** lettre *f* de rappel; *Med* **f.-up care,** soins post-hospitaliers; **f.-up interview,** (*for job*) deuxième entretien.

folly ['fɒlɪ] *n* **(a)** folie *f*, sottise *f*; **an act of f., a f.,** une folie; **it would be the height of f. to ...,** ce serait la plus grande folie de ...; **(b)** *Archit* folie *f*.

foment [fə'ment] *vt* **(a)** fomenter (*la discorde, des troubles*); **(b)** *Med* fomenter (*une plaie*).

fomentation [fəʊmen'teɪʃən] *n* **(a)** fomentation *f* (*de la discorde etc*); **(b)** *Med* fomentation *f*.

fond [fɒnd] *adj* **(a) to be f. of s.o./sth,** (*to like*) bien aimer qn/qch; **they are f. of each other,** ils s'aiment bien; **I'm f. of you but I don't love you,** je t'aime bien mais c'est tout; **he was very f. of me,** il me portait beaucoup d'affection; **to become f. of s.o.,** s'attacher à qn; **to be f. of music,** être amateur de musique; **f. of sweets,** friand de sucreries; **to be passionately f. of reading,** adorer la lecture; **I'm not f. of being told I'm an idiot,** je n'apprécie pas qu'on me traite d'idiot; **(b)** (*indulgent*) indulgent; **(c)** (*person*) affectueux, tendre; (*sourire*) attendri; **with f. regards,** (*in letter*) bien amicalement; **(d)** (*souvenir etc*) doux; (*espoir*) dont on se flatte; **in the f. hope of catching a glimpse of my idol,** dans le doux espoir d'apercevoir mon idole.

fondant ['fɒndənt] *n* fondant *m*.

fondle ['fɒnd(ə)l] *vt* caresser, câliner (*qn*); (*of lover, mother*) faire des câlins *ou* mamours à (*qn, son enfant*); caresser (*un chien, un chat etc*).

fondly ['fɒndlɪ] *adv* **(a)** (*to smile etc*) tendrement, affectueusement; **(b)** (*to hope etc*) crédulement; naïvement; **I f. believed that ...,** j'ai naïvement cru que ... .

fondness ['fɒndnɪs] *n* **(a)** (*affection*) affection *f*, tendresse *f* (**for,** pour, envers); **(b)** (*liking*) penchant *m*, prédilection *f*, goût *m* (**for sth,** pour qch); (*strong liking*) amour *m* (**for sth,** de qch); **(c)** (*indulgence*) indulgence excessive (*d'une mère etc*).

fondue ['fɒnduː] *n Culin* fondue *f*; **beef/cheese f.,** fondue bourguignonne/savoyarde.

font[1] [fɒnt] *n* fonts baptismaux.

font[2] *n Comptr* police *f*; *Typ* police, fonte *f*.

fontanel(le) [fɒntə'nel] *n Anat* fontanelle *f*.

food [fuːd] *n* **(a)** (*no pl*) nourriture *f*; (*for expedition*) vivres *mpl*; *Agr* pâture *f* (*d'animaux*); mangeaille *f* (*de volaille*); **there's some f. in the fridge,** il y a à manger dans le frigidaire; **f. is expensive here,** la nourriture est chère ici; **take some f. for the journey,** prenez de quoi manger pendant le voyage; **f. and clothing,** le vivre et le vêtement; **hotel where the f. is good,** hôtel où la cuisine *ou* la table est bonne; **to be off one's f.,** ne pas avoir d'appétit; **to hunt** *or* **search for f.,** (*of animal*) chercher sa nourriture; **plant f.,** *Bot* aliments *mpl* des plantes; (*in gardening*) engrais *m*; **f. for the mind,** nourriture de l'esprit; **to give s.o. f. for thought,** donner à penser à qn; **f. allergy,** allergie *f* alimentaire; *Biol* **f. chain,** chaîne *f* alimentaire; **f. counter,** (*in large store*) **f. hall** *or* **department,** rayon *m* d'alimentation; **f. industry,** l'industrie *f* alimentaire; **f. mixer,** mixer *m*; **f. poisoning,** intoxication *f* alimentaire; **f. processor,** robot *m* de cuisine; *US* **f. stamp,** ticket *m* alimentaire; **f. value,** valeur nutritive;

(b) (*type of food*) aliment *m*; **canned** *or* **tinned foods,** aliments de conserve (en boîte); **health foods,** (*for special diet*) produits *mpl* diététiques; (*natural foods*) produits alimentaires naturels; **skin f.,** aliment pour la peau;

(c) (*as opposed to drink*) manger *m*; **f. and drink,** le boire et le manger.

foodie ['fuːdɪ] *n F* fana *mf* de bouffe; (*stress on cooking*) fana de cuisine.

foodstore ['fuːdstɔːr] *n* magasin *m* d'alimentation.

foodstuff ['fuːdstʌf] *n* (*usu pl*) **foodstuffs,** produits *mpl* alimentaires *ou* d'alimentation.

fool[1] [fuːl] **1** *n* imbécile *mf*, idiot, -ote; **to play** *or* **act the f.,** faire l'idiot; **to make a f. of oneself,** se couvrir de ridicule; **no one likes being made a f. of,** personne n'aime être ridiculisé; **I felt such a f.,** je me sentais vraiment idiot; **you'd be a f. to buy it,** tu serais bête de l'acheter; *F* **silly f.!**, espèce d'idiot!; **what a f.!**, quel idiot!; **he's no f.**, il n'est pas bête; **he's a bigger f. than I thought**, il est plus bête que je ne le pensais; **(the) more f. you!**, (*for believing them, buying it etc*) ce que tu es bête!; **like a f., I agreed**, comme un idiot, j'ai accepté; **any f. knows that**, le premier imbécile venu sait cela; **some f. (of a) doctor**, un imbécile de docteur; *Prov* **there's no f. like an old f.**, un vieux fou est le pire des fous; **to make a f. of s.o.**, (*tease*) se moquer de qn; *F* mettre qn en boîte; (*make look ridiculous*) exposer qn au ridicule; **she's nobody's** *or* **no one's f.**, c'est une maline *ou* une rusée; **to go on a f.'s errand**, y aller pour des prunes *ou* pour le roi de Prusse; **to send s.o. on a f.'s errand**, envoyer qn décrocher la lune; **All Fools' Day, April Fools' Day**, le premier avril; **f.'s gold**, pyrite *f* de fer; **they're living in a f.'s paradise**, ils rêvent tout éveillés *ou* debout; *Bot* **f.'s parsley**, petite ciguë.

2 *adj esp Am* stupide; **what a damn f. idea!**, quelle idée stupide!

fool² 1 *vi* **(a)** (*act foolishly*) faire l'idiot; **stop fooling!**, assez de bêtises!; **(b)** (*not be serious*) dire des blagues; **I was only fooling**, je plaisantais. 2 *vt* (*deceive*) duper (*qn*); (*tease*) faire marcher (*qn*); **you can't f. me**, on ne m'a pas comme ça; *Iron* **her? — a socialist? — you could've fooled me!**, elle? — une socialiste? — je ne l'aurais pas cru; **to (allow oneself to) be fooled**, se laisser duper; **to be fooled into doing sth**, être amené par duperie à faire qch; **they had me fooled**, ils m'ont eu.

fool³ *n Br Culin* marmelade *f* à la crème; **gooseberry f.**, marmelade de groseilles (à maquereau) à la crème.

▶fool about, fool around *vi* **(a)** (*act foolishly*) faire l'imbécile; (*with undesirable companion*) courir la ville (**with**, avec); **stop fooling around!**, arrête de faire l'imbécile!; **to f. about** *or* **around with**, tripoter (*un appareil etc*); jouer avec (*un fusil etc*); **she fooled around with drugs**, elle a touché à la drogue; **(b)** (*have affair*) être infidèle; **if I thought my husband/wife was fooling around ...**, si je pensais que mon mari/ma femme me trompait ...; **to f. around with s.o.**, coucher avec qn.

▶fool with *vipo Am* (*handle or play with carelessly*) tripoter (*un appareil etc*); jouer avec (*un fusil*); **to f. with drugs**, toucher à la drogue; **that girl you're fooling with**, cette fille avec laquelle tu couches.

foolery ['fuːlərɪ] *n* **(a)** (*stupidity*) **(piece of) f.**, sottise *f*, folie *f*; **(b)** (*playing the fool*) bouffonnerie *f*, pitrerie *f*.

foolhardiness ['fuːlhɑːdɪnɪs] *n* témérité *f*, imprudence *f*.

foolhardy ['fuːlhɑːdɪ] *adj* téméraire, imprudent.

foolish ['fuːlɪʃ] *adj* (*stupid*) bête; (*imprudent*) insensé; **it is f. of him to ...**, c'est fou de sa part de ...; **a f. hope**, un fol espoir; **to do something f.**, faire une bêtise; **to look f.**, avoir l'air penaud; **to make s.o. look f.**, tourner qn en ridicule, ridiculiser qn; **to feel f.**, se sentir idiot.

foolishly ['fuːlɪʃlɪ] *adv* bêtement.

foolishness ['fuːlɪʃnɪs] *n* bêtise *f*; *Old-fashioned* **what f. is this?**, qu'est-ce que c'est que ces bêtises?

foolproof ['fuːlpruːf] *adj* (*mécanisme*) indéréglable, indétraquable, de sûreté, à toute épreuve; (*scheme*) à toute épreuve, sûr; **it's f.**, il n'y a aucun risque, ça marche à tous les coups.

foolscap ['fuːlskæp] *n esp Br* papier *m* ministre; **a sheet of f.**, une feuille de papier ministre.

foot¹, *pl* **feet** [fʊt, fiːt] *n* **(a)** (*of human*) pied *m*; **to put one's best f. forward**, (*get on with task*) abattre la besogne; (*make rapid progress*) avancer vite *ou* à toute allure; *Fig* **to sit at s.o.'s feet**, être le disciple de qn; **to set f. on an island**, mettre pied sur une île; **I shall never set f. in his house again**, jamais je ne remettrai les pieds chez lui; **to put one's feet up**, (*raise*) surélever les pieds; (*have a rest*) se reposer; *F* **to sweep s.o. off their feet**, enthousiasmer qn; (*in love affair*) faire perdre la tête à qn; **to rise to one's feet**, (*stand*) se lever; (*in debate*) prendre la parole; **he jumped to his feet**, d'un bond il fut debout; **to be on one's feet**, se tenir debout; **she is on her feet all day**, elle est sur ses jambes du matin au soir; **to be on one's feet again**, être de nouveau sur pied; **to set s.o. on their feet**, (re)mettre qn sur pied, (r)établir qn; **to begin to find one's feet**, (*in new job, situation etc*) commencer à s'adapter; **to put one's f. down**, (*of parent etc*) mettre le holà (*à qch*); *Aut F* accélérer; *Fig* **to get a f. in the door**, établir un premier contact; **the main thing is to get a f. in the door**, le principal est d'établir le contact; **it's not much of a job but it's a f. in the door**, ce n'est pas terrible comme travail, mais ça fait un contact; **to put one's f. in the door**, (*of salesperson etc*) coincer son pied dans la porte; *F* **to put one's f. in it**, mettre les pieds dans le plat, faire une gaffe; **idol with feet of clay**, statue *f* aux pieds d'argile; *F* **to have** *or* **get cold feet**, avoir la frousse; **to have one's feet firmly on the ground**, avoir les pieds sur terre; **not to put a f. wrong**, ne faire aucune erreur; **to catch s.o. on the wrong f.**, prendre qn au dépourvu; *Tennis etc* prendre qn à contre-pied; **to start** *or* **get off on the wrong f.**, (*of two people*) faire un mauvais départ; **he's constantly getting under my feet**, je l'ai toujours dans les pattes; *F* **my f.!**, mon œil!; **on f.**, à pied; **to go on f.**, aller à pied; **under f.**, sous les pieds; **to trample** *or* **tread sth under f.**, fouler qch aux pieds; **f. brake**, frein *m* (à pédale *ou* à pied); **f. control**, commande *f* au pied; *Tennis* **f. fault**, faute *f* de pied; **f. passenger**, voyageur *m* à pied; **f. pump**, pompe *f* à pied; **f. scraper**, gratte-pieds *m inv*; **f. soldier**, soldat *m* d'infanterie, fantassin *m*;

(b) (*of animal*) pied *m* (*d'animaux à sabot*); patte *f* (*de chien etc*); **the fore/hind feet**, le bipède antérieur/postérieur (*du cheval*); *Vet* **f. rot**, fourchet *m*, piétin *m*;

(c) (*no pl*) *Arch Mil* (*infantry*) fantassins *mpl*, soldats *mpl* d'infanterie; **2,000 f.**, 2 000 fantassins; **a regiment of f.**, un régiment d'infanterie; **the 42nd F.**, le 42ème d'infanterie;

(d) (*lower part*) pied *m*, semelle *f* (*d'un bas*); bout *m* (*d'une table*); pied (*d'un lit, d'une tombe, de verre à boire*); extrémité inférieure (*d'un lac*); base *f* (*de colonne etc*); pied, bas *m* (*de montagne, d'échelle*); *Typ* pied (*d'une lettre*); **at the f. of the stairs**, au bas *ou* en bas de l'escalier; **at the f. of the page**, au bas de la page; **at the f. of the list/class**, à la queue de la liste/classe;

(e) *Liter* (*in poetry*) pied *m*;

(f) (*measurement*) pied anglais (= 30 cm 48); **square f.**, pied carré; **cubic f.**, pied cube; **to be five f.** *or* **feet high**, avoir cinq pieds de haut(eur); **three f.** *or* **feet six (inches)**, trois pieds six pouces; **a f. of water**, un pied d'eau; **at 2,000 feet (above sea level)**, à 2 000 pieds (au dessus du niveau de la mer).

foot² *vt* **(a)** *F* **to f. it**, (*walk*) marcher (à pied); **(b)** *F* (*pay*) **to f. the bill**, payer la note *ou* les dépenses; **(c)** *Am F* = **FOOT UP**.

▶foot up *vtsep Am F* (*add up*) additionner (*un compte*).

footage ['fʊtɪdʒ] *n* **(a)** (*length*) longueur *f* (*en pieds*); **(b)** *Cin* métrage *m* (*d'un film etc*); **they had some f. of the rioting**, ils avaient des séquences sur les émeutes.

foot-and-mouth [fʊtən'maʊθ] *adj Vet* **f.-and-m. disease**, fièvre aphteuse.

football ['fʊtbɔːl] *n* **(a)** (*soccer*) football *m*, *F* foot *m*; *Am* football; **did you watch the f.?**, tu as regardé le football?; **f. fan** *or* **supporter**, supporteur, -trice d'une équipe de football; **f. ground**, terrain *m* de football; **f. hooligan**, hooligan *m*, houligan *m* (de football); **f. hooliganism**, hooliganisme commis lors de match(e)s de football; **f. player**, joueur *m* de football, **(b)** (*ball*) ballon *m* (de football).

footballer ['fʊtbɔːlər] *n* footballe(u)r *m*.

footbath ['fʊtbɑːθ] *n* bain *m* de pieds.

footbridge ['fʊtbrɪdʒ] *n* pont *m* pour piétons; (*narrow*) passerelle *f*.

-footed ['fʊtɪd] *suff* **two/four/***etc* **-f.**, à deux/quatre/*etc* pieds.

footer ['fʊtər] *n* **(a)** *Comptr* bas *m* de page; **(b)** *Old-fashioned Br F* (*soccer*) football *m*.

footfall ['fʊtfɔːl] *n* (bruit *m* de) pas *m*; **I heard a light f.**, j'ai entendu un pas léger.

foot-fault ['fʊtfɔːlt] *Tennis* **1** *vi* faire une faute de pied. **2** *vt* (*of umpire*) **to f. a player**, décider qu'un joueur a fait une faute de pied.

footgear ['fʊtgɪər] *n* chaussures *fpl*.

foothills ['fʊthɪlz] *npl* collines basses *ou* avancées (*d'une chaîne*), avant-monts *mpl*.

foothold ['fʊthəʊld] *n* prise *f ou* assiette *f* pour le pied; **to get a f.**, prendre pied; **to keep one's f.**, préserver l'équilibre; **to lose one's f.**, perdre pied; *Fig* **enemy troops gained a f. on the island**, les troupes ennemies ont pris pied sur l'île.

footing ['fʊtɪŋ] *n* **(a)** (*dancing*) & *Fencing etc* pose *f* des pieds; **(b)** = **FOOTHOLD**; **to lose one's f.**, (*in bathing etc*) perdre pied, perdre terre; **to miss one's f.**, poser le pied à faux (*en descendant etc*); **to gain a f.**, s'implanter, prendre pied (*quelque part*); **(c)** (*situation*) position *f*, condition *f* (*d'une personne*); condition, état *m* (*d'une institution etc*); **on a war f.**, (*of troops*) sur le pied de guerre; (*of country, economy*) en état de guerre; **to be on a sound f.**, (*of company, economy*) être sain *ou* ferme *ou* bien établi; **to place (two people) on the same f.**, mettre (deux personnes) sur le même rang; **to be on an equal f.**, être de pair *ou* sur un pied d'égalité (**with**, avec); **(d)** *Constr* empattement *m*, socle *m* (*d'un mur*).

►**footle about, footle around** ['fu:t(ə)l] *vi F* (*waste time*) perdre son temps à des futilités.
footlights ['fʊtlaɪts] *npl Th* rampe *f*.
footling ['fu:tlɪŋ] *adj F* insignifiant.
footloose ['fʊtlu:s] *adj* (*personne*) libre; **to be f. and fancy-free,** être libre comme l'air.
footman, *pl* **-men** ['fʊtmən] *n* valet *m* de pied.
footnote ['fʊtnəʊt] *n* note *f ou* renvoi *m* en bas de page.
footpath ['fʊtpɑ:θ] *n* sentier *m* pour piétons; (*alongside canal, railway*) banquette *f*, accotement *m*; (*in street*) trottoir *m*.
footplate ['fʊtpleɪt] *n Rail* plate-forme *f*, *pl* plates-formes, tablier *m* (*de locomotive*).
footplateman, *pl* **-men** ['fʊtpleɪtmən] *n Rail* mécanicien *m* de locomotive.
foot-pound ['fʊtpaʊnd] *n* (*pl* **foot-pounds**) *Phys* (*measurement*) pied-livre *m*, *pl* pieds-livres.
footprint ['fʊtprɪnt] *n* **(a)** empreinte *f* de pas; **footprints on the sand,** pas *mpl* sur le sable; **(b)** *Comptr* encombrement *m*.
footrest ['fʊtrest] *n* **(a)** (*on chair*) repose-pied(s) *m inv*; *Med* porte-pieds *m inv*; (*on motorcycle*) repose-pied(s); (*on bicycle*) cale-pied(s) *m inv*; **(b)** (*on footscraper*) sellette *f*.
foot-second ['fʊt'sekənd] *n* (*pl* **foot-seconds**) *Phys* (*measurement*) pied *m* par seconde.
footsie ['fʊtsɪ] *n F* **to play f. with s.o.,** faire du pied à qn.
footslog ['fʊtslɒg] *vi* (**-gg-**) marcher, faire la route à pied.
footsore ['fʊtsɔ:r] *n* qui a mal aux pieds.
footstall ['fʊtstɔ:l] *n Archit* socle *m*.
footstep ['fʊtstep] *n* **(a)** pas *m*; **I hear footsteps,** j'entends un bruit de pas; **(b)** (*footprint*) (empreinte *f* de) pied *m*; *Fig* **to follow** *or* **tread** *or* **walk in s.o.'s footsteps,** marcher sur les traces *ou* pas de qn; *Fig* **to follow in one's father's footsteps,** suivre les traces de son père.
footstool ['fʊtstu:l] *n* tabouret *m* (pour les pieds).
footwarmer ['fʊtwɔ:mər] *n* chancelière *f*.
footway ['fʊtweɪ] *n* chemin *m* pour piétons.
footwear ['fʊtweər] *n* chaussures *fpl*.
footwork ['fʊtwɜ:k] *n* (*in dancing, sports etc*) jeu *m* de pieds *ou* de jambes; **getting out of the animal's way involved some pretty fancy f.,** se retirer du chemin de l'animal a demandé un jeu de jambes plutôt élaboré.
fop [fɒp] *n Arch* bellâtre *m*, fat *m*, dandy *m*.
foppish ['fɒpɪʃ] *adj* (*man*) qui met trop de recherche à sa toilette; (*clothes*) d'une élégance affectée.
for [fɔ:r, *unstressed* fər] **1** *prep* **(a)** (*representing*) **A f. Andrew,** A comme André; **what's the Russian f. 'book'?,** comment dit-on 'livre' en russe?;
(b) (*instead of*) **to act f. s.o.,** agir pour qn *ou* au nom de qn; **he took me f. my brother,** il m'a pris pour mon frère;
(c) (*as*) **to have s.o. f. a teacher,** avoir qn comme professeur; **they left him f. dead,** on le laissa pour mort; **f. example,** par exemple; **f. the first time,** pour la première fois;
(d) (*in return for*) **you can hire a car f. five pounds a day,** on peut louer une voiture pour cinq livres par jour; **to exchange one thing f. another,** échanger une chose contre une autre; **to sell sth f. ten francs,** vendre qch dix francs; **three f. £5,** trois pour 5 livres; **to be paid f. one's services,** recevoir un paiement pour ses services; **claim f. loss of ...,** réclamation résultant de la perte de ...; **oh, f. some peace and quiet!,** que ne donnerais-je pour la paix!; **too stupid f. words,** d'une bêtise indicible; **to get sth f. free,** obtenir qch gratis;
(e) (*in favour of*) **he is f. free trade,** il est partisan du libre-échange, il est pour le libre-échange; **I'm all f. it,** je suis tout à fait pour; **judgment f. the plaintiff,** arrêt *m* en faveur du demandeur;
(f) (*purpose*) **what f.?,** pourquoi (faire)?; **what's that gadget f.?,** à quoi sert ce truc-là?; **garments f. men,** vêtements pour hommes; **f. sale,** à vendre; **a cure f. indigestion,** un remède contre l'indigestion; **can you give me something f. the pain?,** est-ce que vous pouvez me donner quelque chose pour *ou* contre la douleur?; **f. books on gardening try Jackson's bookshop,** pour trouver des livres sur le jardinage, essayez la librairie Jackson; **it is f. your own good,** c'est pour votre bien; **fit f. eating,** bon à manger; **eager f. praise,** avide d'éloges; **it's time f. school,** c'est l'heure de la classe; **to come f. dinner,** venir dîner; *F* **he's f. it!** ['fɔ:rɪt], **he's in f. it!** ['ɪnfərɪt], qu'est-ce qu'il va prendre!; **now f. it!,** allons-y!; **and now f. some music,** et maintenant, un peu de musique; **now f. the flour,** et maintenant, la farine;
(g) (*because of*) **to marry s.o. f. her** *or* **his money,** épouser qn pour son argent; **to choose s.o. f. his** *or* **her ability,** choisir qn en raison de sa compétence; **to die f. one's country,** mourir pour la patrie; **art f. art's sake,** l'art pour l'art; **f. God's sake!, f. the love of God!,** pour l'amour de dieu!; **he's well known f. his views on taxation,** il est célèbre pour ses opinions sur l'impôt; **to jump f. joy,** sauter de joie; **to criticize s.o. f. doing sth,** critiquer qn d'avoir fait qch; **she couldn't sleep f. the pain,** elle ne pouvait pas dormir à cause de la douleur; **if you owned millions, would you be any (the) happier f. it?,** si vous aviez des millions en seriez-vous plus heureux?;
(h) (*considering*) **f. all the use he is he might as well go and play,** pour ce qu'il fait d'utile il peut aussi bien aller jouer;
(i) (*direction*) **ship (bound) f. America,** navire à destination de l'Amérique; **the train f. London,** le train pour *ou* à destination de *ou* en direction de Londres; **I'm leaving f. France,** je pars pour la France; **his feelings f. you,** ses sentiments envers vous *ou* à votre égard; **to swim f. sth,** nager vers qch;
(j) (*extent*) **the road is lined with trees f. two miles,** la route est bordée d'arbres pendant deux mil(l)es; **bends f. one mile,** (*on sign*) virages sur un mil(l)e; **I'm going away f. a fortnight,** je pars pour quinze jours; **he will be away f. a year,** il sera absent pendant un an; **she won't be back f. a month,** elle ne sera pas de retour avant un mois; **we have food f. three days,** nous avons des vivres pour trois jours; **I lived there f. five years,** j'y ai vécu (pendant) cinq ans; **I have not seen him f. three years,** il y a trois ans que je ne l'ai vu; **I have been here f. three days,** il y a trois jours que je suis ici, je suis ici depuis trois jours; **I had known him f. years,** je le connaissais depuis des années, il y avait des années que je le connaissais; **f. now, f. the time being,** pour l'instant, pour le moment;
(k) (*intention, destination*) **this box is f. you,** cette boîte est pour vous; **I'll come f. you tomorrow,** je viendrai vous prendre demain; **to make a name f. oneself,** se faire un nom; **to act f. the best,** agir pour le mieux; **your job f. tomorrow,** votre travail pour demain; **can you give him an appointment f. three o'clock?,** pouvez-vous lui donner un rendez-vous pour trois heures?; **to care f. s.o./sth,** aimer qn/qch; **you are the man f. me,** vous êtes l'homme qu'il me faut; **that is just the thing f. you,** c'est juste ce qu'il vous faut; **there's no time f. that,** il n'y a pas de temps pour ça;
(l) (*to the amount of*) **a cheque f. £50,** un chèque de 50 livres; **put me down f. £5,** inscrivez-moi pour 5 livres;
(m) (*with regard to*) **he is big f. his age,** il est grand pour son âge; **not bad f. a beginner!,** pour un débutant ce n'est pas si mal!; **f. sheer impudence his remarks are hard to beat,** pour ce qui est de l'effronterie, ses commentaires sont imbattables; **as f. him,** quant à lui; **as f. that,** pour ce qui est de cela; **f. myself, f. my part,** pour moi, quant à moi, pour ma part; **the same goes f. you,** ça s'applique à vous aussi; **this shop is better f. books,** ce magasin est mieux pour les livres; **see f. yourself!,** voyez (par) vous-même!;
(n) (*in spite of*) **f. all that,** malgré tout, malgré cela, tout de même; **she loved him, f. all his faults,** elle l'aimait malgré tous ses défauts;
(o) (*owing to*) **were it not f. her** *or* **but f. her, I should have died,** sans elle, je serais mort;
(p) (*corresponding to, in opposition to*) **word f. word,** mot pour mot; (*traduire*) mot à mot; **they sell twenty red bikes f. every black one,** pour chaque vélo noir vendu, il y en a vingt rouges;
(q) (*introducing an infinitive clause*) **it is easy/difficult/impossible f. him to come,** il lui est facile/difficile/impossible de venir; **it is too late f. us to start,** il est trop tard pour que nous partions; **they made way f. him to pass,** on se rangea pour le laisser passer; **I have brought it f. you to see,** je l'ai apporté pour que vous le voyiez; **it is not f. me to decide/to criticize him,** ce n'est pas à moi de décider/de le critiquer; **it is usual f. the mother to accompany her daughter,** il est d'usage que la mère accompagne sa fille; **it's no good f. Mr Wilson to talk,** M. Wilson a beau dire; (*because he is similarly guilty etc*) M. Wilson peut bien dire; **I am delighted f. Miss Brown to know,** je suis enchanté que Mlle Brown le sache; **he gave orders f. the trunks to be packed,** il donna l'ordre de faire les malles; **to arrange f. sth to be done,** prendre des dispositions pour que qch se fasse; **to wait f. sth to be done,** attendre que qch se fasse; **f. that to be done,** pour que ça soit fait; **it took an hour f. the taxi to get to the station,** le taxi a mis une heure pour aller jusqu'à la gare; **the best plan will be f. you to go away for a time,** le mieux sera que vous vous absentiez pour quelque temps; **it**

would be a disgrace f. you to back out now, vous retirer maintenant serait honteux.

2 *conj* car; **f. it was then too late,** car alors il était trop tard.

forage[1] ['fɒrɪdʒ] *n* **(a)** (*provisions*) fourrage(s) *m(pl)*, affouragement *m*; **(b)** (*act of searching for provisions*) fourragement *m*; **to go on the f.,** aller au fourrage; *Mil* **f. cap,** bonnet *m* de police, calot *m*.

forage[2] *vi* fourrager, aller au fourrage; *F* **to f. for sth,** fourrager *ou* fouiller pour trouver qch; **never mind me, I'll f. for myself,** ne t'occupe pas de moi, je me débrouillerai.

▶**forage about, forage around** *vi* (*rummage*) fourrager, fouiller; **to f. about in a drawer,** fourrager *ou* fouiller dans un tiroir.

foray[1] ['fɒreɪ] *n* razzia *f*, incursion *f*, raid *m*; **to make a brief f. into the business world,** faire une courte incursion dans le monde des affaires.

foray[2] *vi* faire des incursions *ou* des raids.

forbear[1] ['fɔːbeər] *n* aïeul *m*, -eux, ancêtre *m*.

forbear[2] [fɔː'beər] *v* (*pt* **forbore** [fɔː'bɔːr]; *pp* **forborne** [fɔː'bɔːn]) *Lit* **1** *vt* s'abstenir de (*qch*). **2** *vi* **to f. from doing sth,** s'abstenir de *ou* se garder de faire qch; **to f. from mentioning sth,** se taire sur qch.

forbearance [fɔː'beərəns] *n* **(a)** patience *f*; *Lit* longanimité *f*; **to show f. towards s.o.,** montrer de l'indulgence envers qn; **(b) f. from doing sth,** abstention *f* de faire qch.

forbearing ['fɔːbeərɪŋ] *adj* patient, indulgent.

forbid [fə'bɪd] *vt* (*pt* **forbade** [fə'bæd, -'beɪd]; *pp* **forbidden** [fə'bɪd(ə)n]) **(a)** (*prohibit*) défendre, interdire; proscrire (*un usage etc*); *Jur* prohiber (*qch*); **to f. s.o. sth,** défendre qch à qn; **I am forbidden (to drink) tea,** le thé m'est défendu; **I f. it!,** je l'interdis!; **(b)** (*prevent*) empêcher (*qch*); **Heaven f. that I should do such a thing!,** Dieu me préserve de faire une telle chose!; **God f.!,** à Dieu ne plaise! **(that,** que + *sub*).

forbidden [fə'bɪd(ə)n] *adj* défendu, interdit; **cycling on the grass is strictly f.,** il est formellement interdit de rouler à bicyclette sur la pelouse; **f. fruit,** fruit défendu; **tread on f. ground,** empiéter sur un terrain défendu; *Fig* toucher à un sujet tabou.

forbidding [fə'bɪdɪŋ] *adj* (*visage, aspect*) sinistre; (*caractère*) mal avenant; (*ciel, temps*) sombre; (*rocher, bâtiment*) menaçant.

force[1] [fɔːs] *n* **(a)** force *f*; **by sheer** *or* **brute f.,** de vive force; **by sheer f. of will,** à force de volonté; **owing to the f. of circumstances,** par la force des choses; **to use f. against the strikers,** avoir recours à la force contre les grévistes; **to resort to f.,** (*of nation etc*) avoir recours à la force; (*of individual*) se porter à des voies de fait;

(b) (*authority*) influence *f*, autorité *f*; **f. of example,** influence de l'exemple; **moral f.,** force morale;

(c) (*effort*) énergie *f*; effort *m* (*d'un choc etc*); intensité *f* (*du vent*); vigueur *f* (*de l'imagination etc*); **a blow with plenty of f. behind it,** un coup bien appuyé *ou* bien asséné; **considerable f. would be needed to break the door down,** il faudrait une force considérable pour défoncer la porte; **the full f. of the explosion,** toute la force de l'explosion;

(d) *Phys* force *f*, effort *m*; **f. exerted by an engine,** effort d'un moteur; **f. of gravity,** (force de la) pesanteur *f*; *Nucl Phys* **nuclear f.,** force nucléaire; *Met* **f. ten on the Beaufort scale,** force dix sur l'échelle de Beaufort;

(e) *Mil etc* force *f*, troupe *f*, élément(s) *m(pl)*; **a f. of 20,000 men,** une troupe de 20 000 hommes; **an armed f.,** une force (armée); **the armoured forces,** les blindés *mpl*; **the land forces,** l'armée *f* de terre; **strike f.,** *Av* force de frappe; *Nau* force d'intervention; **task f.,** *Mil* groupement opérationnel *ou* tactique; *Nau* force (navale) opérationnelle *ou* tactique; **the (armed) forces,** les forces armées; **he was in the forces,** il était dans l'armée; **the naval forces,** l'armée de mer, la marine de guerre; **the police f.,** *F* **the F.,** la Police; **a strong f. of police,** un fort détachement de police; **two different police forces,** deux forces de police différentes; **to join forces with s.o. in doing sth,** se joindre à qn pour faire qch; **we turned out in (full) f.,** nous étions là en masse; **forces slang,** argot *m* militaire;

(f) (*value*) vertu *f*, valeur *f*, efficacité *f* (*d'un remède, d'un argument etc*);

(g) (*sense*) signification *f* (*d'un mot, d'un document*); valeur *f* (*d'un mot, d'une expression*); **verb used with passive f.,** verbe employé avec la valeur d'un passif;

(h) (*of law, rule etc*) **to be in f.,** être en vigueur; **to put the law into f.,** appliquer la loi; **to come into f.,** entrer en vigueur.

force[2] *vt* **(a)** (*compel*) **to f. s.o. to do sth** *or* **into doing sth,** forcer *ou* contraindre qn à faire qch; **no one's forcing you!,** (*to go etc*) personne ne t'y force!; **I am forced to conclude that ...,** je suis forcé de conclure que ...; **to be forced to give way,** céder à la force; **that forced me to think,** cela m'a obligé à réfléchir; **to f. s.o. into/out of the room,** faire entrer/sortir qn de force; **to f. sth on s.o.,** imposer qch à qn; **to f. drink on s.o.,** contraindre qn à boire; **to f. from s.o.,** arracher (*une promesse etc*) à qn;

(b) (*obtain, produce etc by effort*) prendre (*qn, qch*) par force *ou* de force; forcer, enfoncer (*une porte, une fenêtre*); forcer (*une serrure*); **to f. s.o.'s hand,** forcer la main à qn; **to f. the pace,** forcer l'allure *ou* le pas; **she forced a smile,** elle s'est forcée à sourire; **to f. (the meaning of) a word,** forcer le sens d'un mot; **to f. a plant,** forcer une plante; *Aut* **to f. the engine,** trop pousser le moteur; **to f. one's way into a house,** pénétrer de force dans une maison; **to f. sth into sth,** faire entrer qch de force dans qch; **to f. air into the carburettor,** refouler l'air dans le carburateur.

▶**force back** *vtsep* repousser, faire reculer (*l'ennemi etc*); refouler (*l'air, l'eau etc*).

▶**force down** *vtsep* faire descendre (*qch*) de force; **to f. air down into a mine shaft,** refouler de l'air dans un puits de mine; **to f. prices down,** faire baisser les prix; *Av* **the plane was forced down,** on a forcé l'avion à atterrir; **to f. down food/medicine/***etc*, avaler un aliment/un médicament/*etc* à contre-cœur; **to f. food/medicine/***etc* **down s.o.,** faire avaler un aliment/un médicament/*etc* de force à qn.

▶**force open** *vtsep* (*une porte, une fenêtre*) ouvrir de force; forcer (*une serrure*).

▶**force out** *vtsep* pousser (*qn, qch*) dehors; faire sortir (*qn, qch*) de force; (*in engine*) refouler au dehors (*les gaz brûlés*); **to f. out a few words of congratulation,** féliciter qn du bout des lèvres.

▶**force up** *vtsep* faire monter (*qch*) de force; **to f. prices up,** faire monter (*les prix*).

forced [fɔːst] *adj* forcé; (*rire*) forcé, faux; **to give a f. laugh,** rire du bout des lèvres, avoir un rire forcé; *MecE* **f. circulation,** circulation forcée (*d'une chaudière*); **f. draught,** tirage forcé; **f. feed (of oil),** graissage *m* sous pression; **f. feeding,** gavage *m*; **f. labour,** travail forcé; *Av* **f. landing,** atterrissage forcé; *Mil* **f. march,** marche forcée; **f. sale,** vente forcée; **f. vegetables/fruit,** légumes *mpl*/fruits *mpl* forcés, primeurs *fpl*.

force-feed[1] ['fɔːs'fiːd] *adj MecE etc* **f.-f. oiler,** burette *f* à pompe *ou* à piston; **f.-f. lubrication,** graissage *m* sous pression.

force-feed[2] *vt* (*pt & pp* **-fed** [-fed]) gaver (*une oie*); nourrir (*qn*) de force.

forceful ['fɔːsful] *adj* (*personality*) énergique; (*argument*) puissant.

forcefully ['fɔːsfulɪ] *adv* (*to speak*) énergiquement; (*to argue*) énergiquement, avec force.

force-land ['fɔːs'lænd] *vi Av* faire un atterrissage forcé.

forcemeat ['fɔːsmiːt] *n Culin* farce *f*, hachis *m*.

forceps ['fɔːseps] *npl* **(a pair of) f.,** une pince; *Surg* forceps *m*; (*in dentistry*) davier *m*; *Obst* **f. delivery,** accouchement *m* au forceps.

forcible ['fɔːsɪb(ə)l] *adj* **(a)** (*entrée etc*) de force; *Jur* **f. entry,** prise de possession illégale et par la violence; **(b)** (*argument*) vigoureux, plein de force.

forcibly ['fɔːsɪblɪ] *adv* **(a)** (*by force*) de force; **to detain s.o. f.,** retenir qn de force; **(b)** (*convincingly*) vigoureusement; **she argued f. for their release,** elle a argumenté énergiquement *ou* avec force en faveur de leur libération; **they put their case very f.,** ils se sont défendus avec force.

forcing ['fɔːsɪŋ] *n* **(a)** forcement *m* (*d'une serrure*); enfoncement *m* (*d'une porte*); *Culin* **f. bag,** poche *f* à douille; **(b)** (*in gardening*) forçage *m*, culture forcée; **f. frame,** châssis *m*.

ford[1] [fɔːd] *n* gué *m* (*d'une rivière*).

ford[2] *vt* guéer, traverser à gué (*une rivière*).

fordable ['fɔːdəb(ə)l] *adj* (*river*) guéable.

fore [fɔːr] **1** *adj* **(a)** antérieur; de devant; **the f. side of sth,** la partie antérieure *ou* le devant de qch; **(b)** *Nau* (de l')avant; **f. hatch,** panneau *m* avant; *Nau* **f. and aft,** de bout en bout; *Nau* de l'avant à l'arrière; **f.-and-aft sail,** voile *f* aurique; **f.-and-aft bulkhead,** cloison médiane; *Mil* **f.-and-aft cap,** calot *m*. **2** *n Nau* avant *m*; **at the f.,** au mât de misaine; *Fig* **to the f.,** (*prominent*) en vue, en évidence, en vedette; **this question has been very much to the f. in the talks,** cette question a vraiment été au premier plan au cours des discussions; **to come to the f.**, commencer à être connu. 3 *int Golf* gare devant!

forearm¹ ['fɔːrɑːm] *n* avant-bras *m inv*.

forearm² [fɔːr'ɑːm] *vt* prémunir (*qn*).

forebear ['fɔːbeər] *n* = **FORBEAR¹**.

forebode [fɔː'bəʊd] *vt* **(a)** (*of thing*) présager (*le malheur*); **policy that forebodes disaster,** politique qui laisse prévoir le désastre; **(b)** (*of person*) pressentir (*un malheur*).

foreboding [fɔː'bəʊdɪŋ] *n* **(a)** (*bad omen*) mauvais augure; **(b)** (*intuition*) (mauvais) pressentiment *m*; **she was filled with (a sense of) f.**, elle était envahie par un mauvais pressentiment.

forecast¹ ['fɔːkɑːst] *n* prévision *f*; **his f. was wrong,** ses prévisions étaient fausses; **there have been forecasts of higher interest rates,** il y a eu des prévisions d'augmentation des taux d'intérêts; **gloomy economic forecasts,** prévisions économiques peu réjouissantes; **racing f.**, pronostic *m* des courses; **weather f.**, prévisions météorologiques; **long/short-range f.**, prévision à longue échéance/sur période courte; **did you hear the (weather) f. this morning?**, est-ce que tu as entendu les prévisions météorologiques *ou F* la météo ce matin?

forecast² *vt* (*pt & pp* **forecast(ed)**) prévoir (*les événements etc*); *Met* pronostiquer (*le temps*); prévoir (*un orage etc*); *Sp* pronostiquer (*le résultat*); **it's difficult to f. what will happen,** il est difficile de prévoir ce qui va se passer.

forecaster ['fɔːkɑːstər] *n* pronostiqueur, -euse; **weather f.**, météorologiste *mf*.

forecasting ['fɔːkɑːstɪŋ] *n* pronostication *f* (*d'un résultat etc*); prévision *f* (*du temps*).

forecastle ['fəʊks(ə)l] *n Nau* gaillard *m*; (*in merchant vessel*) poste *m* de l'équipage.

foreclose [fɔː'kləʊz] *Jur* **1** *vt* **to f. the mortgage,** saisir l'immeuble hypothéqué. **2** *vi* saisir l'immeuble hypothéqué; (*on a loan*) récupérer le prêt; **the bank has foreclosed on us,** la banque nous a saisi l'immeuble hypothéqué *ou* a décidé de récupérer le prêt.

foreclosure [fɔː'kləʊʒər] *n Jur* saisie *f* (d'une hypothèque).

forecourt ['fɔːkɔːt] *n* avant-cour *f*, *pl* avant-cours; (*of garage, station*) devant *m*.

foredoomed [fɔː'duːmd] *adj* condamné d'avance (**to,** à).

forefather ['fɔːfɑːðər] *n* aïeul *m*, *pl* aïeux.

forefinger ['fɔːfɪŋgər] *n* index *m*.

forefoot, *pl* **-feet** ['fɔːfʊt, -fiːt] *n* (*of animal*) pied antérieur, patte *f* de devant.

forefront ['fɔːfrʌnt] *n* premier rang; **this question is still in the f.**, cette question occupe toujours le premier plan.

foregather [fɔː'gæðər] *vi* = **FORGATHER**.

forego [fɔː'gəʊ] *vt* = **FORGO**.

foregoing ['fɔːgəʊɪŋ] *adj* précédent, antérieur; (*previously cited*) déjà cité; **the f.**, ce qui précède.

foregone ['fɔːgɒn] *adj* décidé d'avance; **it was a f. conclusion,** c'était prévu.

foreground ['fɔːgraʊnd] *n Art Phot etc* premier plan; **in the f.**, au premier plan.

forehand ['fɔːhænd] *Tennis* **1** *adj* **f. stroke,** coup droit; **f. drive,** drive *m* de coup droit. **2** *n* coup droit; **to serve to one's opponent's f.**, servir sur le coup droit adverse; **to take a ball on the f.**, jouer le coup droit.

forehead ['fɒrɪd, 'fɔːhed] *n Anat* front *m*; **wide/receding f.**, front large/fuyant.

foreign ['fɒrɪn] *adj* **(a)** (*from different country, countries*) étranger, qui n'est pas du pays; **she looked f.**, elle paraissait étrangère; **a f.-sounding name,** un nom aux consonances étrangères; **f. aid,** aide *f* aux pays étrangers; (*from point of view of recipient*) aide de l'étranger; *Pol* **f. affairs,** les affaires étrangères; **f. correspondent,** correspondant *m* à l'étranger; **our relations with f. countries,** nos rapports avec l'extérieur; **f. countries, f. parts,** pays étrangers, l'étranger *m*; **I don't like f. food,** je n'aime pas la cuisine étrangère; *Mil* **the (French) F. Legion,** la Légion étrangère; **f. minister,** (*of certain countries*) ministre *m* des affaires étrangères; *Br* **the F. Office,** = le Ministère des Affaires étrangères; *Br* **the F. Secretary,** = le Ministre des Affaires étrangères; *esp US* **the f. service,** le corps diplomatique; **f. trade,** commerce extérieur; **f. travel,** voyages *mpl* à l'étranger; **(b)** (*not belonging*) étranger; **f. to (sth),** qui n'appartient pas à (qch); **such feelings are f. to his nature,** de tels sentiments lui sont étrangers; **to be f. to the discussion,** (*of point, subject etc*) être étranger à la discussion, ne rien avoir à voir avec la discussion; *Med etc* **f. body,** corps étranger.

foreign-built ['fɒrɪn'bɪlt] *adj* (*voiture*) de marque étrangère; (*navire*) construit à l'étranger.

foreigner ['fɒrɪnər] *n* étranger, -ère; **I feel like a f. here,** je me sens étranger ici.

foreignness ['fɒrɪnnɪs] *n* air étranger; (*exotic nature*) exotisme *m*.

foreknowledge [fɔː'nɒlɪdʒ] *n* connaissance anticipée; **to have f. of sth,** avoir connaissance à l'avance de qch.

foreland ['fɔːlənd] *n* cap *m*, promontoire *m*.

foreleg ['fɔːleg] *n* jambe *f ou* patte *f* de devant.

forelock ['fɔːlɒk] *n* (*of person*) mèche *f* (de cheveux) sur le front; *Lit* **to take time by the f.**, saisir l'occasion par les cheveux; **to touch one's f.**, = porter la main à son front (pour saluer qn).

foreman, *pl* **-men** ['fɔːmən] *n* **(a)** *Ind etc* contremaître *m*; **f. of a gang of workmen,** chef *m* d'équipe *ou* de brigade; **works f.**, conducteur *m* de travaux; *Typ* **printer's f.**, prote *m*; **(b)** *Jur* président *m*.

foremast ['fɔːmɑːst] *n Nau* mât *m* de misaine; (*on lateen rigged vessel*) (arbre *m* de) trinquet *m*.

forementioned ['fɔː'menʃənd] *adj* dont il a déjà été fait mention; *Jur Admin* précité.

foremost ['fɔːməʊst] **1** *adj* (*in time*) premier; (*in rank*) le plus avancé; (*in place*) le plus en avant; **in the f. rank,** au tout premier rang. **2** *adv* **first and f.**, tout d'abord, en premier lieu; **I shall only leave this room feet f.**, je ne quitterai cette pièce que les pieds devant.

forename ['fɔːneɪm] *n* prénom *m*.

forenoon ['fɔːnuːn] *n esp Scot & Irish* matinée *f*; **in the f.**, dans *ou* pendant la matinée.

forensic [fə'rensɪk, fɒ-] **1** *adj* (*médecine, chimie*) légal; **f. scientist,** expert *m* légiste. **2** *n F* (*department*) service *m* médico-légal; **did f. come up with anything?**, est-ce que le service médico-légal a trouvé quelque chose?

foreordain ['fɔːrɔː'deɪn] *vt* prédestiner (**s.o. to sth,** qn à qch; **s.o. to do sth,** qn à faire qch).

forepart ['fɔːpɑːt] *n* avant *m*, devant *m*.

foreplay ['fɔːpleɪ] *n* (*sexual*) préliminaires *mpl*; **he doesn't go in much for f.**, il n'est pas très porté sur les préliminaires.

forequarter ['fɔːkwɔːtər] *n* quartier *m* de devant (*de bœuf etc*); **forequarters of a horse,** avant-main *m ou* avant-train *m* d'un cheval.

forerunner ['fɔːrʌnər] *n* avant-coureur *m*, *pl* avant-coureurs, précurseur *m*.

foresail ['fɔːseɪl, 'fɔːs(ə)l] *n* (voile *f* de) misaine *f*.

foresee [fɔː'siː] *vt* (*pt* **foresaw** [fɔː'sɒ] ; *pp* **foreseen** [fɔː'siːn]) prévoir, entrevoir (*un malheur*); **I f. difficult times ahead,** j'entrevois des moments difficiles; **it was an accident which should have been foreseen,** c'était un accident qu'on aurait dû prévoir.

foreseeable [fɔː'siːəb(ə)l] *adj* (*conséquence etc*) que l'on peut prévoir; (*l'avenir etc*) prévisible; **not in the f. future,** pas dans un avenir prévisible.

foreshadow [fɔː'ʃædəʊ] *vt* présager, annoncer, faire pressentir (*un événement etc*).

foreshore ['fɔːʃɔːr] *n* laisse *f* de mer; (*beach*) plage *f*.

foreshorten [fɔː'ʃɔːt(ə)n] *vt* (*of pointer*) dessiner (*un objet*) en raccourci *ou* en perspective; **foreshortened figure,** figure vue en raccourci; **the distances are foreshortened,** les distances sont réduites (par la perspective).

foreshortening ['fɔːʃɔːt(ə)nɪŋ] *n* raccourci *m*.

foresight ['fɔːsaɪt] *n* **(a)** prévoyance *f*; **lack of f.**, imprévoyance *f*, imprévision *f*; **(b)** (*on gun*) guidon *m*, bouton *m* de mire.

foreskin ['fɔːskɪn] *n Anat* prépuce *m*.

forest¹ ['fɒrɪst] *n* **(a)** forêt *f*; **deciduous/coniferous f.**, forêt à feuilles caduques/de conifères; **tropical rain f.**, forêt tropicale humide; **f.-covered hills,** collines boisées; *Geog* **the Black F.**, la Forêt Noire; *Fig* **a f. of masts/telegraph poles,** une forêt de mâts/poteaux télégraphiques; **f. fire,** feu *m* de forêt; *esp Am* **f. ranger,** garde forestier; **(b)** (*land for hunting*) (*for monarch*) chasse royale; (*for lord*) chasse seigneuriale.

forest² *vt* boiser (*une région*).

forestall [fɔː'stɔːl] *vt* anticiper, devancer, prévenir.

forestay ['fɔːsteɪ] *n Nau* étai *m* de misaine.

forested ['fɒrɪstɪd] *adj* boisé.

forester ['fɒrɪstər] *n* (garde *m*) forestier *m*.

forestry ['fɒrɪstrɪ] *n* sylviculture *f*; *Br Admin* **F. Commission,** ≈ service des Eaux et Forêts.

foretaste ['fɔːteɪst] *n* avant-goût *m*, *pl* avant-goûts.

foretell [fɔː'tel] *vt* (*pt & pp* **foretold** [fɔː'təʊld]) **(a)** (*of person*) prédire; **(b)** (*of thing*) présager; **the sky foretells fine weather,** le ciel annonce du beau temps.

forethought ['fɔːθɔːt] *n* prévoyance *f*, prudence *f*.

foretoken [fɔːˈtəʊkən] *vt* présager, annoncer (*une tempête etc*).
foretop [ˈfɔːtɒp] *n Nau* hune *f* de misaine.
fore-topsail [ˈfɔːtɒpseɪl, -s(ə)l] *n Nau* petit hunier.
forever [fəˈrevər] **1** *adv* **(a)** (*until end of time*) pour toujours, à jamais; **a good bike should last f.**, un vélo de bonne qualité devrait durer pour toujours; **to live f.**, vivre éternellement *ou* pour toujours; **(b)** (*ceaselessly*) éternellement, sans cesse; **he was f. changing his mind,** il changeait d'avis sans arrêt. **2** *n F* **to take f. to do sth,** prendre une éternité à faire qch.
forewarn [fɔːˈwɔːn] *vt* prévenir; **to f. s.o. of sth,** avertir qn de qch; *Prov* **forewarned is forearmed,** un homme averti en vaut deux.
forewoman, *pl* **-women** [ˈfɔːwʊmən, -wɪmɪn] *n* **(a)** *Ind etc* contremaîtresse *f*, *F* première *f*; **(b)** *Jur* président *m*, présidente *f* (*d'un jury*).
foreword [ˈfɔːwɜːd] *n* (*to book*) avant-propos *m inv*, préface *f*.
forfeit¹ [ˈfɔːfɪt] *adj Hist Jur* confisqué; **his lands were f.,** on lui a confisqué ses terres.
forfeit² *n* **(a)** amende *f*; (*for non-performance of contract*) dédit *m*; *Sp esp Horseracing* forfait *m*; **f. clause (of a contract),** clause *f* de dédit; **to have to pay a f.,** être mis à l'amende; **(b)** (*in game*) gage *m*; **to play forfeits,** jouer aux gages.
forfeit³ *vt* **(a)** (*have confiscated*) perdre (*qch*) par confiscation; être déchu de (*un droit*); **(b)** (*lose*) perdre (*qch*); **to f. one's life,** payer de sa vie; **to f. one's honour,** forfaire à l'honneur.
forfeiture [ˈfɔːfɪtʃər] *n* **(a)** (*act of having confiscated*) perte *f* (*de biens*) par confiscation; *Jur Fin* déchéance *f*, forfaiture *f* (*de titres, d'un droit*); **(b)** (*loss*) perte *f* (*de la vie, de l'honneur etc*).
forgather, foregather [fɔːˈgæðər] *vi* s'assembler, se réunir; **to f. with s.o.,** rencontrer qn.
forge¹ [fɔːdʒ] *n* atelier *m* de forgeron, forge *f*; *Metal* **f. (shop),** atelier de forge; forge; **f. hammer,** marteau-pilon *m*, *pl* marteaux-pilons.
forge² **1** *vt* **(a)** (*of blacksmith etc*) forger (*un fer à cheval etc*); *Metal* forger, cingler (*le fer*); *Fig* **to f. an alliance,** forger une alliance; **(b)** (*counterfeit*) contrefaire (*une signature, des billets de banque*); fabriquer, inventer (*une calomnie etc*). **2** *vi* commettre *ou* faire un faux.
▶**forge ahead** *vi* **(a)** (*press forward*) avancer à toute vitesse; *Nau* courir de l'avant; (*of person*) (*in business*) pousser de l'avant; *Sp* foncer; **(b)** (*outstrip competitors*) dépasser tous ses concurrents.
forged [fɔːdʒd] *adj* **(a)** *Metal* (*fer*) forgé; **(b)** (*document, billet de banque etc*) faux, contrefait; **f. document,** faux *m*; (*identity paper*) faux papier.
forger [ˈfɔːdʒər] *n* contrefacteur *m* (*de billets de banque*); (*of signature etc*) faussaire *mf*.
forgery [ˈfɔːdʒərɪ] *n* **(a)** (*activity*) contrefaçon *f*; falsification *f* (*de documents*); *Jur* **to be guilty of f.,** être coupable de faux; **(b)** faux document, faux *m*; **the signature was a f.,** la signature était contrefaite; **it's a f.,** (*of document, work of art*) c'est un faux; (*of signature*) c'est une fausse signature.
forget [fəˈget] *v* (*pt* **forgot** [fəˈgɒt]; *pp* **forgotten** [fəˈgɒt(ə)n]; *prp* **forgetting**) **1** *vt* **(a)** oublier (*un fait, une personne*); désapprendre (*son français*); **f. it!,** (*in reply to apology*) il n'y a pas de quoi!; **f. it, it wasn't important,** (*what I said*) non, non, ça n'a pas d'importance; **look, f. it will you?,** (*stop talking about it*) écoute, laisse tomber, d'accord?; **tell them they can f. it,** (*they're being unreasonable*) dis-leur d'aller se faire voir; **you can f. the holiday,** (*we can't afford it*) tu peux laisser tomber l'idée d'aller en vacances; **I had forgotten it,** j'en avais perdu le souvenir; **to f. s.o.'s birthday,** oublier (de souhaiter) l'anniversaire de qn; **I'll never f. what you've done for me,** je n'oublierai jamais ce que tu as fait pour moi; **don't f. that he's only ten years old, he's only ten years old, don't f.,** n'oubliez pas qu'il n'a que dix ans; **to f. how to do sth,** oublier comment on fait qch, ne plus savoir faire qch; **don't f. your friends,** n'oubliez pas vos amis; **to be forgotten,** tomber dans l'oubli; **it's best forgotten,** il vaut mieux ne plus en parler; **things best forgotten,** choses qu'il vaut mieux oublier; **never to be forgotten,** (*person*) inoubliable; (*event*) mémorable; **a never-to-be-forgotten day,** un jour mémorable;
(b) (*omit*) omettre, oublier (*un nom sur une liste etc*); **have I forgotten anyone?,** est-ce que j'ai oublié quelqu'un?; **to f. to do sth,** oublier *ou* omettre de faire qch; **don't f. to ...,** ne manquez pas de ...;
(c) (*leave by mistake*) oublier (*son mouchoir, ses gants etc*); **I forgot my umbrella on the train,** j'ai oublié mon parapluie dans le train;
(d) (*neglect*) négliger (*son devoir etc*); **to f. one's manners,** manquer de savoir-vivre; *F* **to f. oneself,** s'oublier; **to f. oneself so far as to do sth,** s'oublier au point de faire qch.
2 *vi* oublier; **before I f.,** (*can you do sth?*) avant que j'oublie *ou* que je n'oublie; **to f. about sth/s.o.,** oublier qch/qn; **he warned me of the danger but I forgot (all) about it,** il m'a averti du danger mais je n'y ai plus pensé; **and you can f. about going to London!,** et ce n'est pas la peine de songer à aller à Londres!
forgetful [fəˈgetfʊl] *adj* **(a)** oublieux (**of,** de); **to be very f.,** avoir très mauvaise mémoire; **(b)** (*negligent*) négligent; **to be f. of one's duty,** négliger son devoir.
forgetfulness [fəˈgetfʊlnɪs] *n* **(a)** manque *m* (habituel) de mémoire; **a moment of f.,** un moment d'oubli; **(b)** (*negligence*) négligence *f*.
forget-me-not [fəˈgetmɪnɒt] *n* (*plant*) myosotis *m*.
forging [ˈfɔːdʒɪŋ] *n* **(a)** *Metal* (*activity*) travail *m* de forge; (*forged item*) pièce forgée; **f. mill,** forge *f*; **f. press,** marteau-pilon *m*, *pl* marteaux-pilons; **(b)** (*counterfeiting*) contrefaçon *f* (*de documents etc*).
forgivable [fəˈgɪvəb(ə)l] *adj* excusable, pardonnable.
forgivably [fəˈgɪvəblɪ] *adv* de façon excusable *ou* pardonnable.
forgive [fəˈgɪv] *v* (*pt* **forgave** [fəˈgeɪv]; *pp* **forgiven** [fəˈgɪv(ə)n]) **1** *vt* **(a)** pardonner; *Arch & Rel* remettre (*une faute, une injure*); **to f. s.o. sth,** pardonner qch à qn; **to f. s.o. a debt,** faire grâce d'une dette à qn; **if you'll f. the pun,** pardonnez-moi ce jeu de mots; **(b) to f. s.o.,** pardonner à qn; **he asked me to f. him,** il m'a demandé pardon, il m'a demandé de le pardonner; **am I forgiven?,** est-ce que tu me pardonnes?; **one might perhaps be forgiven for thinking that ...,** il n'est pas interdit de penser que ...; **f. me for intruding,** excusez-moi de vous déranger. **2** *vi* pardonner; **f. and forget,** il faut oublier et pardonner.
forgiveness [fəˈgɪvnɪs] *n* **(a)** (*act*) pardon *m*, rémission *f* (*d'une faute etc*); remise *f* (*d'une dette*); **to ask s.o.'s f.,** demander pardon à qn; **(b)** (*quality*) indulgence *f*.
forgiving [fəˈgɪvɪŋ] *adj* indulgent, peu rancunier.
forgo, forego [fɔːˈgəʊ] *vt* (*pt* **forwent** [fɔːˈwent]; *pp* **forgone** [fɔːˈgɒn]) renoncer à (*qch*), s'abstenir de (*qch*).
forgotten [fəˈgɒt(ə)n] *adj* oublié.
fork¹ [fɔːk] *n* **(a)** fourchette *f*; **carving f.,** fourchette à découper; **f. lunch** *or* **buffet,** repas *m* à la fourchette; **(b)** *Agr* fourche *f*; **garden f.,** fourche à bêcher; **(c)** branche fourchue *ou* bifurquée (*d'un arbre*); (*of water diviner*) baguette *f* divinatoire; (*to support branch etc*) poteau fourchu; **(d)** *Cycling* **front fork(s),** fourche *f* avant *ou* de direction; **(e)** *Mus* **tuning f.,** diapason *m*; **(f)** (*in road*) bifurcation *f*, jonction *f*; fourche *f* (*de branches, des jambes, de pantalon*); **take the left f.,** prenez la route *ou* le sentier à gauche; **f. of lightning,** zigzag *m* (d'éclair).
fork² **1** *vi* (*of tree etc*) fourcher; (*of road*) fourcher, faire la fourche, (se) bifurquer; **f. right for York,** (*on sign*) prenez à droite pour York. **2** *vt* fourcher (*le sol*); remuer (*le sol, le foin*) à la fourche; **they were forking hay onto the truck,** ils chargeaient du foin à la fourche dans le camion.
▶**fork in** *vtsep* enfouir (*du fumier*) en fourchant.
▶**fork off** *vi* bifurquer.
▶**fork out** **1** *vtsep* (*provide, often unwillingly*) **to f. out money,** allonger *ou* abouler de l'argent. **2** *vi* (*pay out money*) **he had to f. out,** il a dû casquer *ou* allonger la monnaie; **come on, f. out,** (*what you owe me*) allez, donne.
▶**fork over** *vtsep* retourner légèrement (*un parterre*) à la fourche.
forked [fɔːkt] *adj* (*branch, pipe*) fourchu, bifurqué, en fourche; (*road*) bifurqué, à bifurcation; (*tongue*) fourchu; (*lightning*) ramifié.
forkful [ˈfɔːkfʊl] *n* **(a)** (*of food etc*) fourchetée *f*; **(b)** (*of hay etc*) fourchée *f*.
forking [fɔːkɪŋ] *n* bifurcation *f*, fourche *f* (*d'un arbre, d'une route etc*).
fork-lift [ˈfɔːklɪft] *n* **f.-l. (truck),** chariot *m* (élévateur) à fourche; **f.-l. driver,** conducteur *m* de chariot (élévateur) à fourche.
forlorn [fəˈlɔːn] *adj Lit* **(a)** (*endroit*) abandonné, délaissé; (*mine*) triste; *Am* **f. of hope,** privé de tout espoir; **to look f.,** avoir l'air triste; **(b)** (*desperate*) désespéré, perdu; **f. hope,** aventure désespérée.
form¹ [fɔːm] *n* **(a)** (*shape*) forme *f*, configuration *f* (*d'un objet*); figure *f*, silhouette *f* (*d'un homme, d'un animal*); **to take f.,** prendre forme;

(b) (*manifestation*) forme *f*, nature *f*; *Biol* forme (spéciale) (*d'une variété*); *Gram Liter Mus* forme; **tonic taken in the f. of pills,** remontant pris sous (la) forme de pilules; **what f. did the lesson take?,** quelle forme la leçon a-t-elle pris?; **f. and content,** (*of book etc*) la forme et le fond; **poverty in every f.,** la misère sous toutes ses formes; **it's a f. of disease,** c'est une forme spéciale de maladie; **the different forms of worship,** les différentes pratiques religieuses; **work that lacks f.,** œuvre qui manque de forme;

(c) (*formality*) forme *f*, formalité *f*; *Jur etc* **in due** *or* **proper f.,** en bonne (et due) forme; **receipt in due f.,** quittance régulière; **to go through the f. of refusing,** faire semblant de refuser; **for f.'s sake,** pour la forme; **as a matter of f.,** par manière d'acquit; **it is a mere matter of f.,** c'est une pure formalité; *F* **to know the f.,** savoir ce qu'il faut faire;

(d) (*etiquette*) les convenances *fpl*, l'étiquette *f*; **it is good f.,** c'est de bon ton; **good f. demands that ...,** la politesse exige que ...; **it is not good f., it's bad f.,** c'est de mauvais ton *ou* de mauvais genre;

(e) (*formula*) formule *f*, forme *f* (*d'un acte etc*); **correct f. of words,** tournure correcte de phrase; **forms of address,** (*when writing*) formules *fpl* de politesse; (*when speaking*) titres *mpl* de politesse;

(f) (*printed document with spaces*) formule *f*, formulaire *m*; **printed f.,** imprimé *m*; **f. 20,** modèle *m* numéro 20; **application f.,** bulletin *m* de demande; (*for shares*) bulletin de souscription; (*for job*) demande *f* d'emploi; **order f.,** bulletin de commande; **to fill in** *or* **up a f.,** remplir une formule *ou* un formulaire; **f. letter,** lettre *f* type; *Comptr* **f. feed,** avancement *m* du papier;

(g) *esp Sp* (*condition*) forme *f*, condition *f* (d'entraînement); **to be in/out of f.,** être/ne pas être en forme; **to be in good f.,** (*at a party etc*) être en train *ou* en forme; **in excellent f.,** dans une forme excellente; **he felt in good f.,** il se sentait en forme; **on present f.,** (*the company will make a profit etc*) si l'on en juge par la situation actuelle;

(h) *Horseracing* performances *fpl* (*d'un cheval*); (*in newspaper etc*) tableau *m* des performances (*des chevaux*);

(i) *Br F* **he's got f.,** (*of person*) son casier judiciaire n'est pas vierge; **has he got f.?,** est-ce qu'il a un casier judiciaire?;

(j) *Br Sch* classe *f*; **first f.,** (classe *f* de) sixième *f*; **sixth f.,** (classe de) première; **f. master,** = professeur principal; **f. room,** salle *f* de classe, la classe;

(k) *Comptr* imprimé *m*; **f. feed,** avancement *m* de l'imprimé;

(l) *Br* (*bench*) banc *m*, banquette *f*; (*in amphitheatre*) gradin *m*;

(m) *Metal* forme *f*, moule *m*; *Constr etc* coffrage *m*, coffre *m* (*pour béton armé*); *Typ* forme; *Typ* **to lock up a f.,** serrer une forme;

(n) (*of hare*) gîte *m*, forme *f*.

form² **1** *vt* **(a)** (*shape*) former, faire, façonner (*qch*); développer (*l'esprit*); *Metal* former, emboutir (*une pièce*); former, organiser (*une société etc*); instituer, établir (*une république etc*); former, faire (*un nouveau mot etc*); se former, se faire (*une idée etc*); concevoir (*des doutes*); contracter (*une liaison etc*); arrêter (*un plan*); **to f. the impression that ...,** avoir l'impression que ...; **to f. a friendship,** (*of two people*) devenir amis; **to f. a friendship with s.o.,** devenir ami avec qn; **they formed themselves into a committee,** ils se constituèrent en comité; **the past tense is formed by the addition of -ed,** le passé se forme par l'addition de -ed; **he had formed a plan to ...,** il avait projeté de ...;

(b) (*constitute*) former, faire; constituer (*un gouvernement*); **the walls f. a square,** les murs forment un carré; **to f. part of sth,** faire partie de qch; **the ministers who f. the cabinet,** les ministres qui composent *ou* constituent le gouvernement.

2 *vi* **(a)** prendre forme, se former, se produire; **his style is forming,** son style se fait;

(b) *Mil* se former en rangs; **to f. into line,** se mettre en ligne.

▶**form up** *vi Mil* se former en rangs.

formal ['fɔːm(ə)l] **1** *adj* **(a)** (*occasion etc*) cérémonieux, solennel; (*garden*) à la française; **f. dinner,** grand dîner; **f. dress,** (*ceremonial dress*) tenue *f* de cérémonie; (*evening dress*) tenue de soirée; **is it f.?,** (*the party, dance etc*) est-ce que c'est habillé?; **she had no f. schooling,** elle n'a pas fait d'études conventionnelles; **(b)** *esp Pej* (*person*) pointilleux, formaliste; **he's always very f.,** il est toujours très compassé; **f. style,** style empesé; **(c)** (*procedure*) formel, en règle; (*order*) positif, explicite; (*contrat*) en due forme; **to give s.o. a f. warning,** avertir qn dans les formes; **(d)** (*logic*) *& Rel* formel. **2** *n Am* (*dress*) robe *f* de soirée; (*occasion*) soirée *f* de cérémonie; (*with dancing*) bal *m* de cérémonie.

formaldehyde [fɔː'mældɪhaɪd] *n Ch* formaldéhyde *m*, aldéhyde *m* formique.

formalin ['fɔːməlɪn] *n Ch* formol *m*.

formalism ['fɔːməlɪz(ə)m] *n* formalisme *m*.

formality [fɔː'mælɪtɪ] *n* **(a)** (*procedure*) formalité *f*; **legal formalities,** formes *fpl* juridiques; **a mere f.,** une pure formalité; **(b)** raideur *f* (*de maintien*); compassement *m* (*d'un discours*); **the f. of the dance,** le caractère cérémonieux du bal; **(c)** (*ceremony*) cérémonie *f*, formalité(s) *f(pl)*.

formalize ['fɔːməlaɪz] *vt* **(a)** donner une forme exacte à (*un contrat etc*); **(b)** donner une forme conventionnelle à (*son art etc*).

formally ['fɔːməlɪ] *adv* **(a)** (*with formality*) cérémonieusement; **they greeted her f.,** ils l'ont accueillie cérémonieusement; **(b)** (*openly, officially*) officiellement; **the organization f. renounced violence,** l'organisation a officiellement renoncé à la violence; **(c)** (*procedurally*) **f. correct,** correct quant à la forme.

format¹ ['fɔːmæt] *n* **(a)** format *m* (*d'un livre etc*); **(b)** *Comptr* format *m*.

format² *vt* **(-tt-)** *Comptr* formater (*une page, une disquette*).

formation [fɔː'meɪʃən] *n* **(a)** (*act of creating*) formation *f* (*du pluriel, de la houille etc*); développement *m* (*de l'esprit d'un enfant*); constitution *f* (*d'une société etc*); établissement *m* (*d'une république etc*); **(b)** *Mil etc* (*arrangement*) formation *f*, dispositif *m* (*des troupes*); **battle f.,** *US* **combat f.,** formation de combat; **close f.,** ordre serré; **to break f.,** décrocher; *Av* **f. flying,** vol *m* de groupe; **(c)** (*unit*) unité *f*; **armoured f.,** formation blindée; **(d)** *Geol* **granite f.,** formation *f* granitique.

formative ['fɔːmətɪv] **1** *adj* (*experience etc*) formateur, -trice; **the f. years,** les années de formation. **2** *n Ling* élément formateur.

formatting ['fɔːmætɪŋ] *n Comptr* formatage *m*; **f. instructions,** instructions *fpl* pour le formatage.

forme [fɔːm] *n Typ* forme *f*.

former¹ ['fɔːmər] **1** *adj* **(a)** (*previous*) antérieur, -eure, précédent; (*pupil, servant, colleague etc*) ancien; **my f. pupils,** mes anciens élèves; **a f. convict,** un repris de justice; **in f. times,** autrefois; **he is a mere shadow of his f. self,** il n'est plus que l'ombre de ce qu'il était autrefois; **(b)** (*as opposed to the latter*) premier; **I prefer the f. alternative to the latter,** je préfère la première alternative à la dernière. **2** *pron* celui-là, celle-là, ceux-là, celles-là; **of the two methods I prefer the f.,** des deux méthodes je préfère celle-là.

former² *n* **(a)** (*person*) fondateur, -trice (*d'une alliance etc*); **(b)** *MecE* gabarit *m*, calibre *m* (de forme).

-former ['fɔːmər] *suff Br Sch* **first/second/***etc***-f.,** élève *mf* de sixième/cinquième/*etc*.

formerly ['fɔːməlɪ] *adv* autrefois, jadis; **Mr Martin, f. a liberal,** M. Martin, autrefois libéral; **Mrs Boyle, f. Miss Reid,** Madame Boyle, auparavant Mademoiselle Reid.

formic ['fɔːmɪk] *adj Ch* (*acide*) formique.

Formica ® [fɔː'maɪkə] *n* Formica ® *m*; **F. work top,** plan *m* de travail en Formica ®.

formidable ['fɔːmɪdəb(ə)l] *adj* formidable, redoutable; **a f. adversary,** un rude adversaire; **a f. weapon,** une arme redoutable.

forming ['fɔːmɪŋ] *n* **(a)** formation *f* (*d'une lettre*); formation, développement *m* (*du caractère*); (*metal*) formage *m*, façonnage *m* (*d'une pièce*); **(b)** constitution *f* (*d'une société etc*).

forming up *n Mil* rassemblement *m*.

formless ['fɔːmlɪs] *adj* informe, sans forme.

Formosa [fɔː'məʊsə] *n Arch* Formose *f*.

formula, *pl* **-as, -ae** ['fɔːmjʊlə, -əz, -iː] *n* **(a)** formule *f*; **hackneyed formulas,** formules stéréotypées; **to find a f. acceptable to all parties,** découvrir une formule qui soit acceptable à tous les partis; *Aut* **F. 1,** Formule 1; **(b)** *Ch etc* (*pl usu* **formulae**) formule *f*; **(c)** *Am* (*for feeding baby*) lait *m* en poudre; **gentle f.,** (*shampoo, make-up remover etc*) formule douce.

formulate ['fɔːmjʊleɪt] *vt* **(a)** formuler (*une loi, une doctrine etc*); élaborer (*un projet*); **(b)** formuler, exprimer (*son opinion, des objections*).

formulation [fɔːmjʊ'leɪʃən] *n* **(a)** formulation *f*, élaboration *f* (*d'un projet*); **(b)** expression *f* (*d'une opinion*).

formwork ['fɔːmwɜːk] *n* coffrage *m* (*pour béton armé*).
fornicate ['fɔːnɪkeɪt] *vi* forniquer.
fornication [fɔːnɪ'keɪʃən] *n* fornication *f*.
fornicator ['fɔːnɪkeɪtər] *n* fornicateur *m*, *F* coureur *m* de jupons; coureuse *f*.
forsake [fə'seɪk] *vt* (*pt* **forsook** [fə'sʊk]; *pp* **forsaken** [fə'seɪk(ə)n]) **(a)** (*abandon*) abandonner, délaisser (*qn*); **(b)** (*renounce*) renoncer à, abandonner (*une croyance etc*).
forsaking [fə'seɪkɪŋ] *n* **(a)** abandon(nement *m*) *m*; **(b)** (*of belief etc*) renoncement *m* (**of,** à).
forsooth [fə'suːθ] *adv Arch & Lit* **(a)** (*in truth*) en vérité; **(b)** *Iron* par exemple!, ma foi!
forswear [fɔː'sweər] *vt* (*pt* **forswore** [fɔː'swɔːr]; *pp* **forsworn** [fɔː'swɔːn]) **(a)** renoncer à (*qch*); *Rel* abjurer, renier (*qch*); **(b) to f. oneself,** se parjurer.
forsythia [fɔː'saɪθɪə] *n* (*shrub*) forsythia *m*.
fort [fɔːt] *n Mil* fort *m*, forteresse *f*; *F* **to hold the f.**, (*look after house etc*) garder la maison; (*look after office, shop etc*) tenir la boutique (*en l'absence des chefs*).
forte¹ [fɔːt, 'fɔːtɪ] *n* fort *m*; **singing is not his f.**, le chant n'est pas son fort.
forte² ['fɔːtɪ] *Mus* **1** *adj & adv* forte *inv*. **2** *n* forte *m*.
forth [fɔːθ] *adv* **(a)** (*forwards*) en avant; **to walk back and f.**, marcher de long en large, faire les cent pas; **to venture f.**, (*after illness, from hiding etc*) s'aventurer à sortir; **(b) and so f.**, (*etcetera*) et ainsi de suite, et cetera; **(c)** *Arch* (*time*) **from this time f.**, désormais, dorénavant.
forthcoming [fɔːθ'kʌmɪŋ] *adj* **(a)** prochain, à venir; (*book*) qui va sortir; **help is f.**, des secours sont en route; **the f. session,** la prochaine session; **(b)** (*available*) **to be f.**, ne pas se faire attendre; **the money will be f.**, on trouvera l'argent nécessaire; **no answer was f.**, aucune réponse n'est venue (**from,** de); **the promised help was not f.**, les secours promis ont fait défaut; **(c)** (*person*) (*sociable*) sociable, expansif; (*frank*) ouvert, franc, *f* franche; **not (very) f.**, réservé, renfermé (**about,** au sujet de).
forthright ['fɔːθraɪt] *adj* (*person*) franc, franche.
forthrightness ['fɔːθraɪtnɪs] *n* franchise *f*.
forthwith [fɔːθ'wɪθ] *adv Fml* tout de suite, immédiatement, aussitôt; **the council must be summoned f.**, il faut convoquer le conseil d'urgence.
fortieth ['fɔːtɪɪθ] *adj & n* quarantième *m*.
fortification [fɔːtɪfɪ'keɪʃən] *n* fortification *f*.
fortified ['fɔːtɪfaɪd] *adj* **(a)** (*wine*) viné; **(b)** *Mil* fortifié; **f. town,** ville fortifiée, place forte.
fortify ['fɔːtɪfaɪ] *vt* **(a)** fortifier (*qn*); affermir, fortifier (*qn, la résolution de qn*); renforcer, fortifier (*un navire etc*); **fortified with the rites of the Church,** muni des sacrements de l'Église; **to f. oneself against the cold,** se garantir contre le froid; (*with alcohol*) boire la goutte pour se prémunir contre le froid; **(b)** viner (*un vin*); augmenter la valeur nutritive de (*un aliment*); **(c)** *Mil* fortifier (*une place*).
fortifying ['fɔːtɪfaɪɪŋ] **1** *adj* fortifiant; (*drink etc*) remontant. **2** *n* **(a)** affermissement *m* (*du courage etc*); renforcement *m* (*d'un navire etc*); **(b)** (*of wine*) vinage *m*; (*of food*) augmentation *f* de la valeur nutritive; **(c)** *Mil* fortification *f* (*d'une ville*).
fortissimo [fɔː'tɪsɪməʊ] *Mus* **1** *adv* fortissimo. **2** *n* fortissimo *m inv*.
fortitude ['fɔːtɪtjuːd] *n* force morale.
fortnight ['fɔːtnaɪt] *n esp Br* quinzaine *f*, quinze jours *mpl*; **today f.**, (d')aujourd'hui en quinze; **a f. tomorrow,** demain en quinze; **in a f.'s time,** dans une quinzaine (de jours); **a f. ago,** il y a quinze jours; **to adjourn a case for a f.**, remettre une cause à quinzaine; **to take a f.'s holiday,** prendre quinze jours de vacances.
fortnightly ['fɔːtnaɪtlɪ] *esp Br* **1** *adj* bimensuel, semimensuel. **2** *adv* bimensuellement, tous les quinze jours.
FORTRAN ['fɔːtræn] *n Comptr* FORTRAN *m*.
fortress ['fɔːtrɪs] *n* forteresse *f*; (*town*) place forte; **the place was built like a f.**, l'endroit était construit comme une forteresse; **a f. city,** ville *f* à fortifications.
fortuitous [fɔː'tjuːɪtəs] *adj* fortuit, imprévu.
fortuitously [fɔː'tjuːɪtəslɪ] *adv* fortuitement, par hasard.
fortunate ['fɔːtjənət, -tʃ-] *adj* **(a)** (*person etc*) heureux; **to be f.**, avoir de la chance; **to be f. enough to ...**, avoir la chance de ...; **(b)** (*occasion etc*) propice, favorable, heureux; **it was f. that you remembered,** encore heureux que tu t'en sois souvenu; **how f.!**, quel bonheur!, quelle chance!
fortunately ['fɔːtjənətlɪ] *adv* heureusement, par bonheur; **f. we had brought an umbrella,** heureusement, nous avions apporté un parapluie.
fortune ['fɔːtʃən] *n* **(a)** (*good luck*) fortune *f*, bonne chance; (*prosperity*) prospérité *f*, richesse *f*; (*riches*) richesses *fpl*, biens *mpl*; **a man of f.**, un homme riche; **to make a** *or* **one's f.**, faire fortune; **to come into a f.**, hériter une fortune; **her jewels are worth a f.**, ses bijoux valent une fortune; *F* **it cost me a (small) f.**, cela m'a coûté un argent fou *ou* une fortune *ou* les yeux de la tête *ou* la peau des fesses; **her face is her f.**, son visage fait sa richesse; **(b)** (*luck*) fortune *f*; (*chance*) hasard *m*, chance *f*; (*destiny*) destinée *f*, sort *m*; *Myth* le Sort, le Destin; **piece of good f.**, coup *m* de bonheur; **by good f.**, par bonheur; **f. favours him,** la fortune lui sourit; **the fortunes of war,** le sort des armes; **to tell fortunes,** dire la bonne aventure; **to tell s.o.'s f. by the cards,** tirer les cartes à qn; **f. cookie,** = friandise chinoise avec un message à l'intérieur.
fortune-hunter ['fɔːtʃənhʌntər] *n* coureur *m* de dot.
fortune-teller ['fɔːtʃəntelər] *n* diseur, -euse de bonne aventure; (*with cards*) tireur, -euse de cartes.
fortune-telling ['fɔːtʃəntelɪŋ] *n* la bonne aventure; (*with cards*) cartomancie *f*.
forty ['fɔːtɪ] *n* quarante *m*; **f.-one,** quarante et un; **f.-two,** quarante-deux; **about f. guests,** une quarantaine d'invités; **to be f. (years old),** avoir quarante ans; **life begins at f.**, la vie commence à quarante ans; **the forties,** les années quarante; **to be in one's forties,** avoir passé la quarantaine; **the Roaring Forties,** les quarantièmes rugissants; *F* **to have f. winks,** piquer *ou* faire un petit somme.
forty-five ['fɔːtɪ'faɪv] *n* (*record*) disque *m* quarante-cinq tours.
fortyish ['fɔːtɪɪʃ] *adj* d'une quarantaine d'années.
forum ['fɔːrəm] *n* tribune *f* libre, forum *m*; **a f. in which workers can put forward their views,** un forum permettant aux ouvriers d'exprimer leurs opinions.
forward¹ ['fɔːwəd, *Nau* 'fɒrəd] **1** *adj* **(a)** (*of place*) de devant, situé en avant; *Nau* (de l')avant, sur l'avant; (*mouvement etc*) progressif, en avant; **f. motion,** marche *f* (en) avant; **f. and backward movement,** mouvement *m* d'avant en arrière; *Rugby* **f. pass,** passe *f* en avant, en-avant *m*; *Mil* **f. positions,** premières positions; *Nau* **f. turret,** tourelle *f* avant;

(b) (*of time*) (*plants, child etc*) avancé, précoce; (*opinions etc*) avancé;

(c) (*impudent, bold*) effronté, hardi; **it would have been thought f. of a woman to ...**, cela aurait été considéré comme effronté de la part d'une femme de ...;

(d) *Com* (*price etc*) à terme; *St Exch* **f. deals,** opérations *fpl* à terme.

2 *adv* (*occ* **forwards** ['fɔːwədz]) **(a)** (*of time*) **from that day f.**, à partir de ce jour-là; **to look f. to sth** *or* **to doing sth,** attendre qch avec plaisir *ou* avec impatience; **I look f. to your visit,** je me réjouis de votre visite; *Com* **to date f. a cheque,** postdater un chèque; **carriage f.**, (en) port dû; **charges f.**, frais *mpl* à percevoir à la livraison; *Com Fin* **to sell f.**, vendre à terme;

(b) (*of direction*) en avant; **to go** *or* **move f.**, (s')avancer; **to rush f.**, se précipiter (en avant); **to come** *or* **step f.**, faire un pas en avant; **f.!**, en avant!;

(c) (*of position*) à l'avant; **the seat is too far f.**, la banquette est trop avancée *ou* trop en avant; *Nau* **f. of the beam,** sur l'avant du travers; **the crew's quarters are f.**, le logement de l'équipage est à l'avant; *Com* **to carry the balance f.**, (*in bookkeeping*) reporter le solde à nouveau; **(carried) f.**, report *m*; **new doctrines were put** *or* **brought f.**, on mit en avant de nouvelles doctrines; **to come f.**, se proposer (*pour un emploi etc*); se présenter (**as a candidate/witness,** comme candidat/témoin).

3 *n Fb etc* (*player*) avant *m*.
forward² *vt* **(a)** (*send*) faire suivre (*une lettre*); expédier, envoyer, *Com* transiter (*des marchandises etc*); **please f.**, prière de faire suivre, à faire suivre; **to f. sth to s.o.**, faire parvenir qch à qn; **to f. goods to Paris,** faire parvenir des marchandises sur Paris; **(b)** avancer, favoriser (*les intérêts de qn etc*).
forwarding ['fɔːwədɪŋ] *n* **(a)** expédition *f*, envoi *m*; **f. address,** nouvelle adresse (*pour faire suivre une lettre*); **f. agent,** (agent *m*) transitaire *m*; **f. house,** maison *f* d'expédition, maison de transit; **f. instructions,** indications *fpl* concernant l'expédition; **(b)** avancement *m* (*d'une affaire etc*).
forward-looking ['fɔːwədlʊkɪŋ] *adj* progressiste.
forwardness ['fɔːwədnɪs] *n* **(a)** avancement *m*, progrès *m* (*d'un travail etc*); **(b)** état avancé, précocité *f* (*de la saison, d'un élève etc*); **(c)** (*eagerness*) empressement *m*, ardeur *f*; **(d)** (*boldness*) hardiesse *f*, présomption *f*.
forwards ['fɔːwədz] *adv see* **FORWARD¹ 2**.
forwent *see* **FORGO**.

fossil ['fɒs(ɔ)l] **1** *n* fossile *m*; *Fig* **an old f.,** une vieille croûte, un vieux fossile. **2** *adj* (*flore etc*) fossile; **f. fuel,** combustible *m* fossile.

fossilization [fɒsɪlaɪ'zeɪʃən] *n* fossilisation *f*.

fossilize ['fɒsɪlaɪz] **1** *vt* fossiliser. **2** *vi* se fossiliser; *Fig* (*of person*) s'encroûter, se fossiliser.

fossilized ['fɒsɪlaɪzd] *adj* fossilisé; (*ideas etc*) fossile.

foster¹ ['fɒstər] *vt* **(a)** prendre (*un enfant*) en famille d'accueil; **(b)** (*promote*) entretenir, nourrir (*une idée etc*); encourager, favoriser (*les plans de qn*); protéger (*les arts etc*); **to f. friendship between peoples,** stimuler l'amitié entre les peuples.

foster² *adj* **f. child,** *Admin* = enfant placé dans une famille d'accueil; **f. home,** famille *f* d'accueil; **placing of children in f. homes,** placement familial des enfants; **f. father,** père nourricier; *Admin* = assistant familial; **f. mother,** (mère) nourricière *f*; *Admin* = assistante familiale; **f. parents,** famille *f* d'accueil.

fostering ['fɒstərɪŋ] *n* **(a)** prise *f* (*d'un enfant*) en famille d'accueil; *Admin* parrainage *m* (*d'un enfant*); **(b)** (*promotion, encouragement*) entretien *m* (*d'une idée etc*); patronage *m*, encouragement *m* (*des arts etc*).

fought *see* **FIGHT²**.

foul¹ [faʊl] **1** *adj* **(a)** (*smell*) infect, nauséabond; (*thoughts*) immonde, impur, corrompu; (*language*) grossier, ordurier; (*deed etc*) noir, infâme, odieux; **that soup was f.!,** cette soupe était infecte!; **what f. weather!,** quel sale temps!, quel temps infect!; *Nau* **f. weather,** gros temps; **f. air,** air vicié; **f. breath,** mauvaise haleine; **f. deed,** infamie *f*; **f.-smelling/-tasting,** qui a une odeur/un goût infect(e);

(b) (*linge etc*) sale, souillé; (*eau*) croupi; (*gun, spark plug*) encrassé; (*pump*) engorgé; (*tongue*) chargé; *Typ* (*copie*) peu clair, illisible; *Nau* **f. bottom,** mauvais fond (*pour mouiller*); (*of ship*) carène *f* sale;

(c) *Sp etc* déloyal, -aux, illicite; **f. play,** *Sp* jeu déloyal; tricherie *f*; (*criminal behaviour*) action criminelle; (*underhand dealings*) intrigue *f*; **f. play is not suspected,** on ne croit pas à un crime; **f. shot,** (*in basketball*) coup franc.

2 *n* **(a)** *Sp* coup illicite *ou* déloyal; *Fb Rugby* faute *f*;

(b) *Nau* collision *f*, entrechoquement *m*.

3 *adv* **(a) it smells f.!,** ça pue!; *F* **to feel f.,** ne pas se sentir bien;

(b) irrégulièrement, déloyalement; **to fight f.,** se battre déloyalement; **to play s.o. f.,** faire une crasse à qn; *Nau* **to run f. of another ship,** (*collide with*) aborder *ou* heurter *ou* entrer en collision avec un autre navire; **to fall f. of the law,** avoir des démêlés avec la justice.

foul² **1** *vt* **(a)** salir, souiller (*un endroit, sa réputation etc*); encrasser (*un canon de fusil, les bougies*); **(b)** embarrasser, obstruer (*une ligne de chemin de fer etc*); *Nau* surjaler (*une ancre*); engager (*un cordage etc*); (*of ship etc*) entrer en collision avec, (se) heurter contre (*un autre navire etc*); **(c)** *Sp* commettre une faute contre (*qn*); *Horseracing* couper (*un cheval*). **2** *vi* **(a)** (*of gun barrel etc*) s'encrasser; (*of pump*) s'engorger; **(b)** *Nau* (*of anchor, rope etc*) s'engager; (*of anchor*) surjaler; *MecE* (*of moving part*) toucher.

►**foul up** **1** *vtsep* **(a)** (*put out of order*) déranger, dérégler (*une machine*); mettre (*une machine*) en panne; **(b)** *F* (*ruin*) gâcher (*un projet*); **it will f. things up if he finds out,** ça va tout gâcher s'il l'apprend. **2** *vi* **(a)** *Sl* (*of person*) merder; **(b)** (*of gun barrel etc*) s'encrasser; (*of pump*) s'engorger.

foulbrood ['faʊlbruːd] *n* (*in beekeeping*) loque *f*.

fouler ['faʊlər] *n Sp* **he's a persistent f.,** il commet des fautes sans arrêt.

fouling ['faʊlɪŋ] *n* **(a)** encrassement *m* (*d'un fusil, des bougies*); engorgement *m* (*d'une pompe*); **(b)** engagement *m* (*d'une ancre, d'une hélice etc*); abordage *m* (*de deux navires etc*); **(c)** (*in rifle barrel etc*) crasse *f*.

foully ['faʊlɪ] *adv* **(a)** (*dirtily*) salement; **(b)** (*parler etc*) grossièrement; **(c)** (*ignobly*) bassement; **he was f. murdered,** il fut ignoblement assassiné.

foul-mouthed ['faʊl'maʊðd] *adj* (*person*) au langage ordurier, grossier, -ière.

foulness ['faʊlnɪs] *n* **(a)** saleté *f*; (*of smell*) infection *f*; impureté *f*, fétidité *f* (*de l'air etc*); **(b)** grossièreté *f*, obscénité *f* (*de langage etc*); **(c)** infamie *f* (*d'un acte*).

foul-up ['faʊlʌp] *n F* **(a)** dérèglement *m*, dérangement *m* (*d'un instrument etc*); **(b)** (*mistake*) cafouillage *m*; **there's been a f.-up,** quelque chose a cloché *ou* cafouillé.

found¹ [faʊnd] *vt* **(a)** fonder (*un édifice, une ville*); fonder, créer (*un collège etc*); établir (*une maison de commerce etc*); fonder (*une famille*); **to f. a fortune,** (*lay foundations of fortune*) établir les bases d'une fortune; (*make fortune*) bâtir une fortune (**on,** sur); **(b)** baser, fonder (*ses soupçons etc*) (**on,** sur); **founded on fact,** (*of novel etc*) reposant sur des faits véridiques; **ill-founded,** (*bruit*) mal fondé; **well-founded,** (*bruit*) bien fondé; (*peur*) légitime.

found² **1** *see* **FIND²**. **2** *adj* (*with adv prefixed*) (*ship etc*) **well-f.,** bien équipé (**in,** de).

found³ *vt Metal* fondre (*les métaux*); mouler (*la fonte*).

foundation [faʊn'deɪʃən] *n* **(a)** fondation *f* (*d'un édifice, d'une ville etc*); établissement *m*, institution *f* (*d'un empire, d'une maison de commerce*); fondation et dotation *f* (*d'un hôpital*);

(b) *Constr* massif *m* de base, soubassement *m*; fondement *m*, fondation *f* (*d'un édifice*); assiette *f* (*d'une chaussée*); assise *f* (*d'une machine etc*); **to lay the f. of an alliance,** jeter les bases d'une alliance; **the foundations of modern society,** les assises *ou* fondations de la société moderne; *Constr* **to lay the f. stone,** poser la première pierre; *Sch* **f. course,** année *f* préparatoire;

(c) fondement *m*, base *f* (*d'une théorie etc*); motif *m*, cause *f* (*d'un doute*); **rumour without f.,** bruit dénué de fondement;

(d) (*institution*) institution dotée, fondation *f*; (*legacy*) capital légué pour œuvres de bienfaisance, fondation; **f. school,** école dotée; **f. scholar,** élève boursier;

(e) fond *m* (*d'une robe etc*); fond *m* de teint (*d'une toile*); **embroidery on a silk f.,** broderie *f* sur fond de soie; **f. (cream),** base *f* (de maquillage), fond de teint; **f. garment,** gaine *f*; (*top and bottom*) combiné *m*.

founder¹ ['faʊndər] *n* fondateur *m* (*d'un hôpital etc*); **f. member,** membre *m* fondateur.

founder² *n Metal* fondeur *m*.

founder³ **1** *vi* (*of hopes, horse*) s'effondrer; *Nau* (*of ship*) sombrer, couler. **2** *vt* courbaturer (*un cheval*).

foundering ['faʊndərɪŋ] *n* effondrement *m*.

founding¹ ['faʊndɪŋ] **1** *adj* (*member*) fondateur, -trice; *US Hist* **F. Father,** = membre de la Convention constituante de 1787. **2** *n* = **FOUNDATION (a)**.

founding² *n Metal* fonderie *f*, moulage *m*.

foundling ['faʊndlɪŋ] *n* enfant trouvé, -ée; *Hist* **f. hospital,** hospice *m* des enfants trouvés.

foundry ['faʊndrɪ] *n Metal* fonderie *f* (*de fer etc*); **f. iron,** fonte *f* de moulage.

fount¹ [faʊnt] *n Lit* source *f* (d'eau); source, cause *f*, principe *m* (*du bonheur etc*); **the f. of all knowledge,** la source de toute science.

fount² [faʊnt, fɒnt] *n Typ* fonte *f*; **wrong f.,** lettre *f* d'un autre œil.

fountain ['faʊntɪn] *n* fontaine *f*; jet *m* d'eau (*de jardin public etc*); *Arch & Lit* source *f* (d'eau); **f. of wisdom,** source de sagesse; *Am* **soda f.,** = bar pour glaces et rafraîchissements non alcoolisées; **drinking f.,** distributeur *m* d'eau potable; **f. pen,** stylo *m* à plume.

fountainhead ['faʊntɪnhed] *n* **the f. of all knowledge,** la source de toute science.

four [fɔːr] *n* **(a)** quatre *m*; **twenty-f.,** vingt-quatre; **f. fives** *or* **five fours are twenty, f. times five is twenty,** quatre fois cinq *ou* cinq fois quatre font vingt; **we have tea at f. thirty,** nous prenons le thé à quatre heures et demie; **to be f. (years old),** avoir quatre ans; **scattered to the f. corners of the earth,** éparpillé aux quatre coins du monde; **to get down/run on all fours,** se mettre/courir à quatre pattes; **(b)** *Sp* **a f.,** (*in rowing*) un quatre; *Cr* **to hit a f.,** marquer quatre points; *Golf* **a f.-ball (match),** une partie à quatre joueurs et quatre balles.

four-colour ['fɔː'kʌlər] *adj Typ etc* à quatre couleurs; **f.-c. work,** quadrichromie *f*.

four-cornered ['fɔː'kɔːnəd] *adj* à quatre coins; (*quadrangular*) quadrangulaire.

four-cycle ['fɔː'saɪk(ə)l] *adj Am* (*engine, cylinder etc*) à quatre temps.

four-engined ['fɔːr'endʒɪnd] *adj Av* (*avion*) quadrimoteur.

four-eyed [fɔː'raɪd] *adj F* binoclard.

four-eyes ['fɔːraɪz] *n F* binoclard, -e.

four-figure ['fɔː'fɪgər] *adj Math* (*nombre*) à quatre chiffres; (*logarithme*) à quatre décimales.

fourfold ['fɔːfəʊld] **1** *adj* quadruple. **2** *adv* quatre fois autant, au quadruple; **to increase f.,** quadrupler.

four-footed ['fɔː'fʊtɪd] *adj* (*animal*) quadrupède, à quatre pattes.

four-handed ['fɔː'hændɪd] *adj* **(a)** *Cards* (*jeu*) à quatre (personnes); **(b)** *Mus* (*morceau*) à quatre mains; **(c)** (*singe*) à quatre mains, quadrumane.

four-in-hand ['fɔːrɪn'hænd] **1** *n* **(a)** (*carriage*) véhicule *m* à quatre chevaux; **(b)** *Arch* (*necktie*) cravate-plastron *f*, *pl* cravates-plastrons. **2** *adv* **to drive f.-in-h.,** conduire à quatre (chevaux).

four-leaf ['fɔː'liːf] *adj* **f.-l. clover,** trèfle *m* à quatre feuilles.

four-leaved ['fɔː'liːvd] *adj* (*plant*) quadrifolié; **f.-l. clover,** trèfle *m* à quatre feuilles.

four-legged ['fɔː'legɪd] *adj* (*animal*) quadrupède; (*table*) à quatre pieds; **our f.-l. friends,** nos amis les bêtes.

four-letter ['fɔː'letər] *adj F* **f.-l. word,** obscénité *f*; *Iron* **life is a f.-l. word,** la vie est une connerie.

four-master ['fɔː'mɑːstər] *n Nau* quatre-mâts *m inv.*

four-part ['fɔː'pɑːt] *adj Mus* à quatre parties; (*singing*) à quatre voix.

fourpenny ['fɔːp(ə)nɪ] *adj Old-fashioned Br Sl* **to give s.o. a f. one,** flanquer un gnon *ou* une beigne à qn.

four-phase ['fɔː'feɪz] *adj El* (*système*) tétraphasé.

four-poster ['fɔː'pəʊstər] **1** *n* lit *m* à colonnes. **2** *adj* (*bed*) à colonnes.

fourscore [fɔː'skɔːr] *adj Arch & Lit* quatre-vingt.

four-seater [fɔː'siːtər] *n Aut* voiture *f* à quatre places.

foursome ['fɔːsəm] *n* groupe *m* de quatre personnes; (*two couples*) deux couples; *Golf* partie (de) double *ou* à deux contre deux; **to go out in a f.,** (*of four people*) sortir à quatre; (*of two couples*) sortir à deux couples; **to make up a f.,** (*of four people*) former un groupe de quatre personnes; (*of two couples*) former deux couples; (*be the fourth person*) faire le quatrième.

four-speed ['fɔː'spiːd] *adj Aut* à quatre vitesses.

foursquare ['fɔː'skweər] **1** *adj* **(a)** (*refusal*) carré; **(b)** (*building*) solide. **2** *adv* (*to decide, refuse*) carrément; (*to build*) solidement.

four-stroke ['fɔːstrəʊk] *adj MecE* (*moteur*) à quatre temps.

fourteen ['fɔːtiːn] *n* quatorze *m*; **she is f.,** elle a quatorze ans; **the plane will arrive at f. thirty (hours),** l'avion arrivera à quatorze heures trente.

fourteenth [fɔː'tiːnθ] **1** *adj* quatorzième; **Louis the F.,** Louis Quatorze; **(on) the f. of May,** le quatorze mai. **2** *n* **(a)** (*of month*) quatorze *m*; **(b)** (*fraction*) quatorzième *m*.

fourth [fɔːθ] **1** *adj* quatrième; **Henry the F.,** Henri Quatre; **he's f. in his class,** il est le quatrième de sa classe; *Aut* **in f. (gear),** en quatrième (vitesse); **the f. of January, January the f.,** le quatre janvier; *US* **the F. of July,** = l'anniversaire du jour de l'indépendance; *Br Sch* **the f. year** *or* **form,** = la classe de troisième; *Cards etc* **to make a f.,** faire le quatrième; **the F. World,** le quart-monde. **2** *n* **(a)** (*of month*) quatre *m*; **on the f.,** le quatre; **(b)** (*fraction*) quart *m*; **three-fourths of the globe,** les trois quarts du globe; **(c)** *Mus* quarte *f*.

fourthly ['fɔːθlɪ] *adv* quatrièmement, en quatrième lieu.

four-wheel ['fɔː'wiːl] *adj* (*véhicule*) à quatre roues; **tractor with f.-w. drive,** tracteur à quatre roues motrices; **does it have f.-w. drive?,** est-ce qu'il a quatre roues motrices?; **it's a f.-w. drive,** c'est un quatre-quatre.

four-wheeled ['fɔː'wiːld] *adj* à quatre roues.

four-wheeler ['fɔː'wiːlər] *n* voiture *f* à quatre roues.

fowl¹ [faʊl] *n* **(a)** (*domesticated bird*) poule *f*, coq *m*, volaille *f*; *Culin* volaille; **to keep fowls,** élever des poules; *Culin* **boiling f.,** poule (au pot); *Vet* **f. pest,** peste *f* aviaire *ou* des poules; **f. pox,** diphtérie *f* aviaire; **(b)** (*pl* **fowl**) oiseau *m*; **water f.,** gibier *m* d'eau; **(c)** *Lit* oiseau *m*.

fowl² *vi* faire la chasse au gibier ailé.

fowling ['faʊlɪŋ] *n* chasse *f* aux oiseaux; **f. piece,** fusil *m* de chasse (à petit plomb).

fox¹ [fɒks] *n* renard *m*; **red f.,** renard commun; **Arctic f.,** renard bleu; **silver f.,** renard argenté; **f.'s earth,** renardière *f*, terrier *m* de renard, *F* **an old f.,** un vieux madré; *F* **a sly f.,** un fin renard, un roublard; **f. brush,** queue *f* de renard; **f. hunt,** chasse *f* au renard; **f. cub,** renardeau *m*; **f. fur,** (fourrure *f*) renard; **f. fur coat,** manteau *m* en renard.

fox² *vt* **(a)** (*mystify*) mystifier, tromper (*qn*); **you've got me foxed,** je suis perplexe; **(b)** (*discolour*) tacher de roux (*les feuilles d'un livre*); maculer (*une gravure*).

foxglove ['fɒksglʌv] *n* (*plant*) digitale *f* (pourprée).

foxhole ['fɒkshəʊl] *n* **(a)** renardière *f*, terrier *m* de renard; **(b)** *Mil* abri individuel; (*for sniper*) trou *m* de tirailleur.

foxhound ['fɒkshaʊnd] *n* fox-hound *m*, *pl* fox-hounds.

fox-hunting ['fɒkshʌntɪŋ] *n* chasse *f* au renard.

foxiness ['fɒksɪnɪs] *n* **(a)** *Pej* (*of person*) roublardise *f*; **(b)** état maculé (*des pages*); **(c)** goût foxé (*du vin*); **(d)** *Am Sl* (*of woman*) air *m* sexy.

foxmark ['fɒksmɑːk] *n* tache *f* de roux (*sur une feuille d'un livre*).

foxtail ['fɒksteɪl] *n* **(a)** queue *f* de renard; **(b)** (*plant*) **f. (grass),** vulpin *m*.

fox-terrier ['fɒks'terɪər] *n* fox-terrier *m*, *pl* fox-terriers, *F* fox *m*.

foxtrot¹ ['fɒkstrɒt] *n* (*dance*) fox-trot *m inv.*

foxtrot² *vi* (-tt-) danser le fox-trot.

foxy ['fɒksɪ] *adj* **(a)** (*visage etc*) qui ressemble à un renard; **(b)** (*crafty*) rusé, astucieux; **(c)** (*hair, complexion*) roux, rousse; **(d)** (*wine, beer*) foxé; **(e)** *Am Sl* (*woman*) sexy.

foyer ['fɔɪeɪ, 'fwæjeɪ] *n Th* foyer *m* du public; *Cin* (hall *m* d')entrée *f*.

FPA [efpiː'eɪ] *n abbr* **Family Planning Association.**

fraction ['frækʃən] *n* **(a)** *Math* fraction *f*; **vulgar** *or* **common f.,** fraction ordinaire; **decimal f.,** fraction décimale; **compound f.,** fraction de fraction; **(b)** (*small part*) petite portion, petite partie (*de qch*); **the new method takes only a f. of the time,** la nouvelle méthode prend bien moins de temps; **he escaped death by a f. of a second,** il a été à deux doigts de la mort; **a f. too small,** un tout petit peu trop petit; **(c)** *Fin* fraction *f*, rompu *m* (*d'action, d'obligation*); **(d)** *Ch* fraction *f* (*de distillation*); **(e)** *Pol* fraction *f*, groupe *m* fractionnaire (*d'un parti*).

fractional ['frækʃən(ə)l] *adj* **(a)** *Math* fractionnaire; *F* **the difference is only f.,** la différence est minime; **(b)** *Ch* fractionné; **f. distillation,** distillation fractionnée, fractionnement *m*.

fractionally ['frækʃən(ə)lɪ] *adv* **f. larger/heavier,** plus grand/lourd d'un tout petit peu.

fractionate ['frækʃəneɪt] *vt Ch Ind* fractionner (*le pétrole etc*).

fractionize ['frækʃənaɪz] *vt Math* fractionner.

fractious ['frækʃəs] *adj* de mauvaise humeur; (*bébé*) pleurnicheur.

fractiousness ['frækʃəsnɪs] *n* mauvaise humeur; (*of baby*) pleurnicherie *f*, pleurnichage *m*.

fracture¹ ['fræktʃər] *n* **(a)** *Med* (*of bone*) fracture *f*; **simple f.,** fracture simple; **compound f.,** fracture multiple; **to set a f.,** réduire une fracture; **(b)** fracture *f*, rupture *f* (*d'un essieu etc*); **(c)** *Geol* cassure *f*, fracture *f*; **(d)** *Ling* fracture *f* (*d'une voyelle*).

fracture² **1** *vt* **(a)** *Med* fracturer (*un os*); **fractured skull,** crâne fracturé; **fractured ribs,** côtes enfoncées; **(b)** (*break*) casser, briser (*qch*). **2** *vi* **(a)** *Med* (*of bone, limb*) se fracturer; **(b)** (*break*) se casser, se briser.

fragile ['frædʒaɪl] *adj* **(a)** (*cup etc*) fragile; **(b)** (*person*) (*weak*) faible; (*delicate*) délicat; *F* **I'm feeling a bit f. this morning,** (*hung over*) j'ai mal aux cheveux ce matin.

fragilely ['frædʒaɪllɪ] *adv* fragilement.

fragility [frə'dʒɪlɪtɪ] *n* **(a)** (*of ornament etc*) fragilité *f*; *Metal* frangibilité *f*; **(b)** (*of person*) (*weakness*) faiblesse *f*; (*delicateness*) délicatesse *f*.

fragment¹ ['frægmənt] *n* **(a)** fragment *m*, morceau *m* (*de porcelaine etc*); éclat *m* (*d'obus*); morceau (*de papier*); **(b)** *Liter* fragment *m*; extrait *m* (*d'un livre*); œuvre inachevée (*d'un auteur*).

fragment² [fræg'ment] **1** *vi* se fragmenter. **2** *vt* réduire en fragments, briser en morceaux.

fragmentary ['frægmənt(ə)rɪ] *adj* fragmentaire.

fragmentation [frægmən'teɪʃən] *n* fragmentation *f*; *Mil* **f. bomb,** bombe *f ou* grenade *f* à fragmentation.

fragrance ['freɪgrəns] *n* parfum *m*.

fragrant ['freɪgrənt] *adj* parfumé, odorant, fragrant; (*scent*) embaumé; **to be f.,** sentir bon; **woods f. with wild strawberries,** bois qui embaument les fraises sauvages.

frail [freɪl] *adj* **(a)** (*person*) faible, frêle; **a f. old gentleman,** un vieil homme frêle *ou* fragile; **(b)** (*object*) peu solide, fragile; (*beauté, bonheur*) éphémère.

frailness ['freɪlnɪs] *n* **(a)** (*of person*) faiblesse *f*, débilité *f*, *esp* faiblesse de l'âge; (*of character*) faiblesse morale; **(b)** fragilité *f* (*du verre etc*); caractère *m* éphémère (*de la beauté etc*).

frailty ['freɪltɪ] *n* **(a)** = **FRAILNESS (a)**; **(b)** (*moral flaw*) faible *m*, défaut *m*.

frame¹ [freɪm] *n* **(a)** cadre *m*, encadrement *m* (*d'un tableau, miroir etc*); chambranle *m*, châssis dormant (*d'une fenêtre, d'une porte*); *TV* trame *f* (double); *Cin* image *f* (*de film*); (*of comic strip*) case *f*; **gilded f.,** cadre doré; *Cin* **frames per second,** images par seconde; *TV* **f. frequency,** fréquence *f* des trames; *US* fréquence des images;

(b) (*framework*) ossature *f* (*d'une personne, d'un animal, de l'aile d'un avion*); charpente *f* (*d'un bâtiment, d'un pont etc*); cadre *m* (*d'une bicyclette etc*); châssis *m* (*d'une locomotive, d'une automobile*); bâti *m* (*d'une machine*); monture *f* (*d'un parapluie*); armature *f* (*d'une raquette*); *Nau Archit* membrure *f*, carcasse *f* (*d'un navire*); **man of gigantic f.,** homme bâti comme un colosse; *Am* **f. house,** maison *f* en bois; **f. of a bed,** châlit *m*; **f. saw,** scie montée *ou* à châssis; **(spectacle) frames,** monture; **glasses with metal frames,** lunettes à monture de métal; *Math* **f. of reference, reference f.**, système *m* de coordonnées; référentiel *m*;

(c) (*system*) construction *f*, structure *f*, disposition *f*; système *m*, forme *f* (*de gouvernement*); ordre *m* (*de la société*); plan *m* (*de l'univers*); **f. of mind,** état *m ou* disposition d'esprit; **he is in a bad f. of mind,** il est mal disposé;

(d) *Sewing* (*floor standing*) métier *m* (*à broder*); (*handheld*) tambour *m* (*à broder*); *Tex* métier (*à filer*);

(e) (*in gardening*) châssis *m*;

(f) *Sp* reprise *f*, coup *m* (*de jeu de quilles*); (*in snooker*) (*wooden device*) triangle *m*; (*game*) partie *f*.

(g) *Sl* (*false incrimination*) coup monté (*contre qn*).

frame² *vt* **(a)** encadrer (*un tableau etc*); *TV* cadrer, centrer (*l'image*); **to have a picture/photo/document framed,** faire encadrer un tableau/une photo/un document; **black hair framed her face,** des cheveux noirs encadraient son visage; **(b)** faire la charpente de (*un toit*); *Nau Archit* construire la carcasse de (*un navire*); charpenter (*un roman etc*); composer (*un poème, une réponse etc*); *Jur* rédiger (*une loi*); former, régler (*ses pensées etc*); se faire (*une opinion*); **(c)** *Sl* (*falsely incriminate*) monter une accusation *ou* un coup contre (*qn*); **I've been framed,** c'est un coup monté (contre moi).

framemaker ['freɪmmeɪkər] *n* carcassier *m* (*de parapluies etc*).

framer ['freɪmər] *n* (*of pictures*) encadreur *m*.

frame-up ['freɪmʌp] *n Sl* (*false incrimination*) coup monté.

framework ['freɪmwɜːk] *n see* **FRAME¹ (b)**; charpente *f*, bâti *m*, carcasse *f*; charpente (*d'un roman etc*); coffrage *m* (*de travaux en béton*); **open f.,** treillis *m*; **it comes within the f. of the U.N.,** cela entre dans le cadre de l'O.N.U.

framing ['freɪmɪŋ] *n* **(a)** encadrement *m* (*d'un tableau etc*); *TV* cadrage *m*, centrage *m* (*de l'image*); **(b)** construction *f* (*de qch*); composition *f* (*d'un poème etc*); *Jur* rédaction *f* (*d'une loi*); **(c)** invention *f*, fabrication *f* (*d'une accusation*); **(d)** *Sl* (*false incrimination*) accusation *f* à tort; **(e) metal f. (for window),** vitrière *f*.

franc [fræŋk] *n* (*currency*) franc *m*.

France [frɑːns] *n* France *f*, *F* l'Hexagone; **in F.,** en France.

Frances ['frɑːnsɪs] *n* Françoise *f*.

franchise ['fræntʃaɪz] *n* **(a)** concession *f* (*octroyée à une compagnie d'utilité publique*); *Com* franchise *f*, contrat *m* de franchisage; **to have the** *or* **a f. for sth in a given territory,** avoir le droit de vendre qch dans un territoire déterminé; **(b)** *Pol* droit *m* de vote.

franchisee [fræntʃaɪ'ziː] *n Com* franchisé, -ée.

franchising ['fræntʃaɪzɪŋ] *n* franchisage *m*.

franchisor ['fræntʃaɪzər] *n Com* franchiseur, -euse.

Francis ['frɑːnsɪs] *n* François *m*.

Franciscan [fræn'sɪskən] *n & adj* franciscain *m*.

francophile ['fræŋkəʊfaɪl] *adj & n* francophile *mf*.

francophobe ['fræŋkəʊfəʊb] *adj & n* francophobe *mf*.

francophone ['fræŋkəʊfəʊn] *adj & n* francophone *mf*.

frangible ['frændʒɪb(ə)l] *adj* frangible, cassant, fragile.

frank¹ [fræŋk] *adj* (*person, feelings*) franc, *f* franche; sincère; (*speech*) direct, ouvert; **to be f.,** être franc; **to be quite f. with you,** pour être franc avec vous; **I don't think you're being f. with me,** je ne crois pas que tu me dises la vérité.

frank² *vt* affranchir (*une lettre*) (*esp à la machine*).

Frank¹ [fræŋk] *n Hist* Franc, Franque.

Frank² *n* (*dimin of* **Francis**) = François *m*.

frankfurter ['fræŋkfɜːtər] *n* saucisse *f* de Francfort.

frankincense ['fræŋkɪnsens] *n* encens *m* (mâle).

franking ['fræŋkɪŋ] *n* affranchissement *m* (*esp à la machine*); **f. machine,** machine *f* à affranchir.

Frankish ['fræŋkɪʃ] *adj Hist* franc, *f* franque.

frankly ['fræŋklɪ] *adv* franchement; (*parler*) franchement, à cœur ouvert; **f. incredible,** tout bonnement incroyable; **I tell you f. that ...,** je vous dis carrément que ...; **(quite) f., no!,** franchement, non!

frankness ['fræŋknɪs] *n* franchise *f*, sincérité *f*.

frantic ['fræntɪk] *adj* **(a)** frénétique, forcené; **f. efforts,** efforts effrénés; **f. with pain,** fou de douleur; **it drives him f.,** cela le met hors de lui; **I'm f.,** je suis hors de moi; **I was f. when I heard she'd had an accident,** j'ai paniqué en apprenant qu'elle avait eu un accident; **(b)** *F* (*terrible*) affreux, terrible.

frantically, *esp US* **franticly** ['fræntɪklɪ] *adv* (*see adj*) **(a)** frénétiquement, avec frénésie; **to rush f. around,** courir frénétiquement dans tous les sens; **(b)** *F* affreusement, terriblement; **I'm f. busy,** j'ai tellement à faire que je ne sais où donner de la tête.

fraternal [frə'tɜːn(ə)l] *adj* fraternel.

fraternally [frə'tɜːn(ə)lɪ] *adv* fraternellement.

fraternity [frə'tɜːnɪtɪ] *n* **(a)** (*brotherhood*) fraternité *f*; **(b)** (*group engaged in same activity*) confrérie *f*; **the sporting f.,** la grande famille du sport; **(c)** *Am Univ* = association de camarades de classe.

fraternization [frætənaɪ'zeɪʃən] *n* fraternisation *f* (**with,** avec).

fraternize ['frætənaɪz] *vi* fraterniser (**with,** avec).

fraternizing ['frætənaɪzɪŋ] *n* fraternisation *f* (**with,** avec).

fraud [frɔːd] *n* **(a)** supercherie *f*, tromperie *f*; *Jur* fraude *f*, dol *m*; **to obtain sth by f.,** obtenir qch par fraude *ou* frauduleusement; **guilty of f.,** coupable de manœuvres frauduleuses; **the f. squad,** la brigade de (la police chargée de) la répression des fraudes; **(b)** (*person*) imposteur *m*; **he's a f.,** c'est un imposteur; **(c)** (*thing, place*) attrape *f*; **this place is a f.,** cet endroit ne répond pas à la réputation qu'on lui a faite.

fraudulence ['frɔːdjʊləns] *n* caractère frauduleux (*d'une transaction*); infidélité *f* (*d'un dépositaire etc*).

fraudulent ['frɔːdjʊlənt] *adj Jur* frauduleux; **f. bankrupt,** banqueroutier frauduleux.

fraudulently ['frɔːdjʊləntlɪ] *adv* frauduleusement, par fraude.

fraught [frɔːt] *adj* **(a)** plein (**with problems,** de problèmes); **the voyage was f. with danger,** la traversée a été remplie *ou* pleine d'embûches; **f. with risks,** plein de risques; **an atmosphere f. with ...,** une atmosphère chargée de ...; **it's a f. subject,** c'est un thème ardu; **(b)** (*thing*) désolant, pénible; (*person*) désolé.

fray¹ [freɪ] *n* (*brawl*) bagarre *f*, échauffourée *f*, mêlée *f*; (*quarrel*) rixe *f*; **the thick of the f.,** au plus épais de la mêlée; **to enter the f.,** descendre dans l'arène; **to return to the f.,** rentrer en lice.

fray² **1** *vt* érailler, effiler (*un tissu etc*). **2** *vi* (*of material*) s'érailler, s'effiler; **my collar is fraying,** mon col s'effrange.

frayed [freɪd] *adj* **(a)** (*cloth, garment etc*) éraillé, frangé; (*rope*) usé; **shirt f. at the cuffs,** chemise élimée aux manchettes; **(b)** (*nerves*) à vif; **my nerves are f.,** je suis à bout de nerfs; **tempers were getting a little f.,** on commençait à se fâcher.

frazzle ['fræz(ə)l] *n F* **to be worn to a f.,** (*of person*) être complètement éreinté; **to beat s.o. to a f.,** battre qn à plate(s) couture(s); **a joint cooked** *or* **burnt to a f.,** un rôti calciné.

freak¹ [friːk] *n* **(a) f. (of nature),** monstre *m*, phénomène *m*; **he's a f.,** c'est un excentrique; **people treat me as some kind of f.,** (*because of what I think, do etc*) les gens me trouvent anormal; **drugs f.,** toxicomane *mf*; **jazz f.,** fana *mf* de jazz; **f. show,** exhibition *f* de monstres; **f. accident,** accident *m* bizarre; **f. storm,** orage inattendu; **f. weather,** temps anormal; **(b)** (*whim*) caprice *m*, fantaisie *f*, lubie *f*; **f. of fortune,** jeu *m* de la fortune.

freak² *vi* = **FREAK OUT 1.**

►**freak out** **1** *vi* **(a)** (*become angry*) se mettre en colère; (*be shocked, scared*) paniquer; (*become mentally unbalanced*) être déboussolé; (*be ecstatic*) ne plus se sentir; **Mum'll f. out when she sees that mess,** Maman va être furieuse quand elle verra tout ce désordre; **(b)** (*of drug taker*) se défoncer, être du voyage; (*dance etc with abandon*) s'éclater; **people were freaking out to the music,** les gens s'éclataient sur la musique. **2** *vtsep* (*shock, scare*) bouleverser (*qn*); (*mentally unbalance*) rendre (*qn*) fou.

freakish ['friːkɪʃ] *adj* **(a)** (*weather etc*) insolite, anormal; **(b)** (*whimsical*) capricieux, fantasque, bizarre; (*imagination*) libertin; **f. notion,** fantaisie *f*.

freckle¹ ['frek(ə)l] *n* tache *f* de rousseur; **she's got freckles,** elle a des taches de rousseur.

freckle² **1** *vt* marquer (*qn, la peau*) de taches de rousseur. **2** *vi* (*of skin*) se couvrir de taches de rousseur.

freckled ['frek(ə)ld] *adj* **(a)** (*person, face, arm etc*) couvert de taches de rousseur; **(b)** (*animal's coat*) tacheté.

Fred [fred] **, Freddy** ['fredɪ] *n* (*dimin of* **Frederick**) = Frédéric *m*.

Frederic(k) ['fred(ə)rɪk] *n* Frédéric *m*.

free¹ [friː] **1** *adj* **(a)** libre; *Nau* (*port*) franc; **to set f.,** mettre (*qn*) en liberté; affranchir (*un esclave*); laisser s'envoler (*un oiseau*); délivrer, libérer (*un prisonnier*); **to break f.,** (*from bonds*) se dégager de ses liens; (*escape*) s'échapper; **to be allowed to go f.,** être mis en liberté, être relâché; **man is a f. agent,** l'homme est libre; *F* **you're a f. agent,** vous êtes libre; *F* **it's a f. country,** on est en démocratie; **of**

one's own f. will, de (son) propre gré; *Hist* **F. France,** la France libre; **the F. French,** les Français *mpl* libres; *Br* **f. house,** = débit de boissons qui est libre de vendre les produits de n'importe quelle brasserie; *Jur* **f. pardon,** grâce *f*; **f. spirit,** esprit *m* libre; *Pol* **the f. world,** le monde libre; **(b)** (*unoccupied*) libre; *Tel* (*line*) libre; **is this table f.?,** est-ce que cette table est libre?; **I am f. tomorrow,** je suis libre demain; **to have some f. time,** avoir du temps de libre; **f. time,** temps *m* libre, loisir *m*; **(c)** (*unrestricted*) libre, sans entraves; (*amour*) libre; (*style etc*) franc, *f* franche; aisé; **she's f. and graceful in all her actions,** elle fait tout avec aisance et grâce; **as f. as the air** *or* **a bird,** libre comme l'air; **to be (entirely) f. to do sth,** être (entièrement) libre de faire qch; **I am f. to do what I please,** je suis libre de mes mouvements; **with his f. hand,** avec sa main libre; **to have a f. hand,** avoir pleine liberté d'action, avoir ses coudées franches (**to do,** pour faire); **to give** *or* **allow s.o. a f. hand,** donner carte blanche à qn; **f. from** *or* **of sth,** débarrassé de qch; **to be f. from care** *or* **worry** *or* **anxiety,** être sans souci; **wood f. from knots,** bois exempt de nœuds; **style f. from affectation,** style dénué de toute recherche; **at last I am f. of him,** enfin je suis débarrassé de lui; **right of f. entry,** droit *m* de passer librement les frontières; **interest f. of tax,** intérêts nets *ou* exempts d'impôt; **f. of duty,** (*in customs*) exempt de droits d'entrée; **to import sth f. of duty,** faire entrer qch en franchise; **you are allowed to bring in half a litre f.,** il y a une tolérance d'un demi-litre; **f. climbing,** escalade *f* libre, libre *m*; **f. diving,** plongée sous-marine autonome; **f. end,** brin *m* libre (*d'un cordage*); **f. enterprise,** libre entreprise *f*; **f. fall,** chute *f* libre (*d'un poids, d'un parachutiste*); **f. market economy,** économie *f* de marché; **f. port,** port franc; **f. speech,** libre parole *f*; *Econ* **f. trade,** libre-échange *m*; *Cycling* **f. wheel,** roue *f* libre; **f. zone,** zone franche; **(d)** (*spontaneous*) (*action etc*) libre, spontané, volontaire; (*choix*) arbitraire; **as a f. gift,** en pur don; *Psy* **f. association,** association *f* d'idées; *Sch* **f. composition,** composition *f* libre (*en langue étrangère*); **f. translation,** traduction *f* libre; **f. verse,** (*in poetry*) vers *mpl* libres; **(e)** (*generous*) (*person*) libéral, généreux; (*supply*) abondant, copieux; **to be f. with one's money,** être prodigue de son argent; **he was very f. with his advice,** il a été très prodigue en conseils; **(f)** (*uninhibited*) (*person, speech*) franc, *f* franche, ouvert, sans réserve; (*language*) libre, licencieux; **f. and easy,** désinvolte, sans gêne; **things are f. and easy here,** ici on ne fait pas de façons; **to make f. with sth,** se servir de qch sans se gêner; **he made very f. with my whisky,** il ne se gênait pas pour boire mon whisky; **to be rather f. in one's conversation,** tenir des propos peu convenables; *F* **feel f.,** faites comme chez vous; **feel f. to speak your mind,** n'hésitez pas à dire ce que vous pensez; **may I take another? — feel f.,** puis-j'en reprendre? – je vous en prie; **(g)** (*without charge*) (*concert, échantillon*) gratuit; *Th* (*billet*) de faveur; **it came f. with the magazine,** c'était une prime offerte pour l'achat du magazine; *Fig* **there's no such thing as a f. lunch,** tout se paie; **f. demonstration in the home,** démonstration gracieuse à domicile; **admission f.,** entrée gratuite *ou* gratis; *Com* **delivery f.,** livré franco *inv*; **post f.,** franco de port; **f. on board,** franco à bord; **f. copy,** (*in publishing*) spécimen *m*; **f. gift,** offre gratuite, prime *f*; *Fb* **f. kick,** coup franc; **f. luggage allowance,** bagage(s) *m(pl)* en franchise; **(h)** *Ch* (*gas etc*) (à l'état) libre, non-combiné; (*power, energy*) libre, disponible; **f. gold,** or *m* à l'état natif. **2** *adv* **(a)** (*without charge*) franco, gratuitement; **catalogue sent f. on request,** catalogue gratuit sur demande; **the museum is open f. on Saturdays,** l'entrée du musée est gratuite le samedi; **for f.,** *F* **f. gratis and for nothing,** gratis; **to get sth for f.,** obtenir qch pour rien; **(b)** *Nau* **vessel running f.,** navire *m* courant largue; **(c)** (*followed by a present participle*) **f. flowing,** qui coule abondamment; **f. flowering,** qui fleurit abondamment.

free² *vt* (**freed; freeing**) **(a)** affranchir (*un esclave etc*); libérer, élargir (*un prisonnier etc*); **to f. oneself from s.o.'s grasp,** se dégager des mains de qn; **I couldn't f. my foot,** je ne pouvais pas dégager mon pied; **to f. s.o.'s hands,** (*untie*) détacher les mains de qn; **to f. s.o. from an obligation,** libérer qn d'une obligation; **to f. oneself from one's commitments,** se délier de tous ses engagements; **(b)** (*clear obstructions from*) débarrasser (**from, of,** de); dégager (*un sentier etc*); déblayer (*le terrain*); *MecE etc* dégager (*une pièce*); désobstruer (*un filtre engorgé*); dégorger (*une pompe*); *Admin* mettre (*des denrées réglementées*) en vente libre; détaxer (*des denrées taxées*); **to f. a property (from mortgage),** déshypothéquer une propriété.

-free [friː] *suff* sans; **sugar/gluten/***etc***-f.,** sans sucre/gluten/*etc*; **knot-f. timber,** bois *m* sans nœuds; **accident-f. driving record,** passé de chauffeur vierge d'accidents; **our journey was trouble-f.,** notre voyage s'est déroulé sans encombres.

freebase ['friːbeɪs] *vi Sl* purifier de la cocaïne; (*of drug addict*) utiliser de la cocaïne pure.

freebie, freebee ['friːbiː] *n F* cadeau *m* (*accordé à un client etc*); **it was a f. with the magazine,** c'était un cadeau offert avec le magazine.

freeboard ['friːbɔːd] *n Nau* (franc-)bord *m*.

freeborn ['friːbɔːn] *adj* libre de naissance, né libre.

freedom ['friːdəm] *n* **(a)** liberté *f*, indépendance *f*; **in f.,** en liberté; **f. of information/speech,** liberté d'information/d'expression; **we have less f. now,** nous sommes moins libres maintenant; **f. to do sth,** liberté de faire qch; **f. fighter,** guérillero *m*, révolutionnaire *mf*; **(b)** franchise *f*, familiarité *f* (*d'une conversation etc*); (*boldness*) hardiesse *f*; (*uninhibitedness*) sans-gêne *m*; **(c)** (*of action etc*) facilité *f*, liberté *f*; **(d)** (*exemption*) exemption *f*, franchise *f*; **f. from tax,** exemption d'impôts; **f. of a city,** droit *m* de cité; (*honorary citizenship*) citoyenneté *f* d'honneur d'une ville; **to receive the f. of a town,** être nommé citoyen, -enne d'honneur d'une ville; **(e)** libre usage *m* (*de qch*); **the f. of the seas,** la liberté de la haute mer; **to give s.o. the f. of one's library,** mettre sa bibliothèque à la disposition de qn.

Freefone ® ['friːfəʊn] *n Br Tel* appel gratuit, numéro vert; **call F. 123,** composez le numéro vert 123.

free-for-all ['friːfərɔːl] *n F* **f.-f.-a. (race** *or* **competition),** concours auquel tout le monde peut participer; **f.-f.-a. (fight),** rixe *f*, bagarre *f*, mêlée *f*; **the queue turned into a f.-f.-a.,** la file d'attente s'est transformée en pagaille générale.

free-form ['friːfɔːm] *adj Art* spontané.

freehand ['friːhænd] **1** *adj* (*dessin*) à main levée. **2** *adv* (*dessiner*) à main levée.

free-handed [friː'hændɪd] *adj* généreux.

freehold ['friːhəʊld] **1** *adj* tenu en propriété perpétuelle et libre. **2** *n* propriété foncière perpétuelle et libre.

freeholder ['friːhəʊldər] *n* propriétaire foncier (à perpétuité).

freeing ['friːɪŋ] *n* **(a)** libération *f*, délivrance *f* (*d'un prisonnier*); affranchissement *m* (*d'un esclave*); exemption *f* (*de qn, d'un impôt*); **(b)** dégagement *m* (*d'un cordage*); débarrassement *m* (*d'un passage etc*); dégorgement *m* (*d'un tuyau etc*).

freelance¹ ['friːlɑːns] **1** *n* (*journaliste etc*) indépendant, -ante, pigiste *mf*. **2** *adj* (*journaliste etc*) indépendant; *Journ* **f. work,** travail indépendant *ou* à la pige *ou* en free-lance. **3** *adv* **to work f.,** faire du travail indépendant, travailler à la pige *ou* en free-lance.

freelance² *vi* être un journaliste *ou* acteur *etc* indépendant, faire de la pige, travailler à la pige *ou* en free-lance.

freeload ['friːləʊd] *vi esp Am F* parasiter.

freeloader [friː'ləʊdər] *n esp Am F* pique-assiette *mf inv*, écornifleur, -euse.

freely ['friːlɪ] *adv* **(a)** (*donner, faire qch*) librement; **to give f. to s.o.,** faire des libéralités à qn; **(b)** (*parler, agir etc*) franchement, en toute liberté; **to speak f. to s.o.,** parler à qn à cœur ouvert; **(c)** (*couler etc*) abondamment, copieusement; **(d) to see that a mechanism works f.,** s'assurer du bon fonctionnement d'un mécanisme.

freeman, *pl* **-men** ['friːmən] *n* **(a)** homme *m* libre; **(b)** citoyen *m* d'honneur; **to be made a f. of the city,** être nommé citoyen d'honneur.

freemason ['friːmeɪs(ə)n] *n* franc-maçon, *pl* francs-maçons.

freemasonry ['friːmeɪs(ə)nrɪ] *n* franc-maçonnerie *f*.

Freepost ® ['friːpəʊst] *n Br* correspondance-réponse *f*.

free-range ['friː'reɪndʒ] *adj* (*œufs, poulet*) de ferme.

freesia ['friːʒə] *n* (*plant*) freesia *m*.

free-spoken ['friː'spəʊk(ə)n] *adj* (*person*) franc, *f* franche, qui parle ouvertement.

freestanding ['friː'stændɪŋ] *adj* (*mur etc*) autoportant; *Archit* (*column*) isolé; (*clinic, restaurant, machine*) autonome.

freestyle ['friːstaɪl] *n Swimming* nage *f* libre; (*wrestling*) lutte *f* libre.

freethinker ['friːθɪŋkər] *n* libre penseur, -euse.

free-trader ['friːtreɪdər] *n Econ* libre-échangiste *mf*, *pl* libre-échangistes.

freeway ['fri:weɪ] *n US* autoroute *f* (gratuite).
freewheel¹ ['fri:wi:l] *vi* **(a)** *Cycling* faire roue libre; *Aut* marcher *ou* rouler en roue libre; **to f. down a hill,** descendre une côte en roue libre; **(b)** *esp Am* (*travel in carefree fashion*) se laisser aller.
freewheel² *n* roue *f* libre.
freewheeling ['fri:wi:lɪŋ] *adj F* (*discussion*) libre.
freeze¹ [fri:z] *n* **(a)** *Met* gel *m*, gelée *f*; **the big f.**, la grande gelée; **(b)** (*act of fixing*) **price and wage f.**, blocage *m* des prix et des salaires.
freeze² *v* (*pt* **froze** [frəʊz]; *pp* **frozen** [frəʊz(ə)n]) **1** *v impers* **it's freezing,** il gèle; **it's freezing hard,** il gèle ferme.
2 *vi* **(a)** (*of liquid*) (se) geler, se congeler; **the river has frozen,** la rivière est prise; **the earth had frozen hard,** la terre avait gelé; **to f. to death,** mourir de froid; *F* **I'm freezing,** j'ai très froid, je gèle; *F* **we froze in our thin clothes,** on n'était pas assez couvert, on s'est caillé; **the smile froze on his lips,** le sourire se figea sur ses lèvres;
(b) (*of person*) rester cloué sur place, se figer; (*stiffen*) se raidir, se guinder; **f.!,** ne bougez pas!; **I froze at the sound of his voice,** je me suis immobilisé au son de sa voix.
3 *vt* **(a)** geler, congeler (*qch*); congeler (*la viande*); **to f. the blood (in one's veins),** glacer le sang *ou* le cœur; **to be frozen to death,** mourir de froid;
(b) geler (*des crédits, des devises*); bloquer (*les salaires*);
(c) *Med* insensibiliser avec une anesthésie locale.
►**freeze out** *vtsep F* **(a)** (*exclude*) évincer (*qn*); supplanter (*un rival*); **(b)** (*boycott*) boycotter (*qn*).
►**freeze over** *vi & vt* **the pond has/is frozen over,** l'étang a/est gelé d'un bout à l'autre.
►**freeze up** *vi* (*become frozen*) geler; **the river has frozen up,** la rivière est prise; **the radiator froze up,** le radiateur a gelé.
freeze-dry ['fri:z'draɪ] *vt* lyophiliser (*un sérum etc*).
freeze-drying ['fri:z'draɪɪŋ] *n* lyophilisation *f*.
freeze-frame ['fri:zfreɪm] *n Cin* arrêt *m* sur image.
freezer ['fri:zər] *n* congélateur *m*; **upright f.**, congélateur vertical; **chest f.**, congélateur bahut; **f. (compartment),** congélateur, freezer *m* (*d'un réfrigérateur*).
freezer-fridge ['fri:zəfrɪdʒ] *n F* congélateur *m* avec réfrigérateur.
freeze-up ['fri:zʌp] *n* gelée *f*.
freezing ['fri:zɪŋ] **1** *adj* réfrigérant, congelant; (*temps etc*) glacial, -als; *F* **it's f. in here!,** ça gèle ici! **2** *adv* **f. cold,** très froid; *F* **a f. cold shower,** une douche glacée. **3** *n* **(a)** (*becoming frozen*) congélation *f*, gel *m*; *Phys* **f. point,** point *m* de congélation; **the thermometer is at f. point,** le thermomètre est à zéro; **the temperature was below f.,** la température était inférieure à zéro; **(b)** (*making frozen*) réfrigération *f* (*d'un liquide etc*); congélation *f* (*de la viande etc*); **f. compartment,** congélateur *m*, freezer *m* (*d'un réfrigérateur*); **f. instructions,** (*for food*) consignes *fpl* pour la congélation; **f. mixture,** mélange réfrigérant; **(c)** blocage *m* (*des salaires etc*).
freight¹ [freɪt] *n* **(a)** (*transport*) fret *m*; transport *m* (*de marchandises*); **air f.**, transport par air; **(b)** (*cargo*) fret *m*, cargaison *f*, chargement *m* (*d'un navire*); marchandises *fpl* (transportées); **to take in f.**, prendre du fret; *Am Rail* **f. car,** wagon *m* à *ou* de marchandises; *Av* **f. plane,** avion-cargo *m*, *pl* avions-cargos; **f. train,** train *m* de marchandises; **(c)** (*price of transport*) fret *m*; **to pay the f.,** payer le fret.
freight² *vt* **(a)** (*load*) charger (*un vaisseau*); **(b)** (*hire*) (af)fréter (*un navire*); (*of owner*) donner (*un navire*) à fret; **(c)** *esp Am* (*transport*) transporter.
freightage ['freɪtɪdʒ] *n* **(a)** (af)frètement *m* (*d'un vaisseau*); **(b)** (*cargo*) fret *m*, cargaison *f*; **(c)** (*transport*) transport *m* des marchandises.
freighter ['freɪtər] *n* **(a)** (*ship*) cargo *m*, navire *m* de charge; *Am Rail* wagon *m* de marchandises; *Av* avion-cargo *m*, *pl* avions-cargos; **(b)** affréteur *m* (*d'un vaisseau*); **(c)** *Am* consignateur, -trice (*de marchandises pour transport par voie de terre*); **(d)** (*operator of transport company*) entrepreneur *m* de transports; exportateur *m*.
freightliner ['freɪtlaɪnər] *n Rail* train *m* de marchandises en conteneurs.
French [frentʃ] **1** *adj* français; (*dish, fashion etc*) à la française; (*lesson, teacher*) de français; **to take F. leave,** filer à l'anglaise; **of F. make,** de fabrication française; **the F. Ambassador,** l'ambassadeur, -drice de France; **F. bean,** haricot vert; **F. bread,** pain *m* à la française; **F. Canada,** le Canada français; **F. Canadian,** (*person*) Canadien, -ienne français(e); (*language*) le français canadien; **F. chalk,** craie *f* de tailleur; *Culin* **F. dressing,** vinaigrette *f*; *Culin esp Am* **F. fried potatoes,** *F* **F. fries,** frites *fpl*; *Mus* **F. horn,** cor *m* d'harmonie; **F. kiss,** patin *m*; *Sl* **F. letter,** capote anglaise; **F. loaf** *or* **stick,** baguette *f*; **F. pleat,** (*hairstyle*) chignon *m*; **F. polish,** vernis *m* au tampon; **F. Switzerland,** la Suisse Romande; *Culin* **F. toast,** = pain perdu; **the F. West Indies,** les Antilles Françaises; **F. windows,** *Am* **F. doors,** porte-fenêtre *f*, *pl* portes-fenêtres.
2 *n* **(a)** *Ling* français *m*, la langue française; **to speak F.,** parler français; **to learn/know F.,** apprendre/savoir parler le français; **say it in F.,** dites-le en français; **her F. is excellent,** elle parle très bien français; **Canadian F.,** le français canadien *ou* du Canada; *Hum* **excuse my F.,** passez-moi l'expression;
(b) the F., (*used as pl*) les Français *mpl*.
Frenchify ['frentʃɪfaɪ] *vt Pej* franciser (*son style etc*).
Frenchman, *pl* **-men** ['frentʃmən] *n* Français *m*.
French-polish ['frentʃ'pɒlɪʃ] *vt* vernir (*un meuble etc*) au tampon.
French-speaking ['frentʃ'spi:kɪŋ] *adj* francophone.
Frenchwoman, *pl* **-women** ['frentʃwʊmən,-wɪmɪn] *n* Française *f*.
Frenchy ['frentʃɪ] *n F* Français, -aise.
frenetic [frə'netɪk] *adj* (*person, action etc*) frénétique.
frenetically [frə'netɪklɪ] *adv* frénétiquement.
frenzied ['frenzɪd] *adj* (*person*) affolé, forcené; (*rage*) fou, *f* folle; (*applause*) frénétique, délirant.
frenzy ['frenzɪ] *n* frénésie *f*, folie *f* (*du désespoir etc*); **in a f. of excitement,** dans un accès d'excitation.
frequency ['fri:kwənsɪ] *n* **(a)** (*of letters etc*) fréquence *f*; *Math* **f. of errors,** répartition *f* des erreurs; **I was surprised by the f. of his visits to the library,** j'étais surpris d'apprendre qu'il allait si souvent à la bibliothèque; **(b)** *Phys* fréquence *f*; *El* **high/low f.,** haute/basse fréquence; **very high f.,** très haute fréquence; *TV Rad* **radio f.,** fréquence radio(électrique); **f. band,** bande *f* de fréquences; **f. modulation,** modulation *f* de fréquence; **f. range,** gamme *f* de fréquences.
frequent¹ ['fri:kwənt] *adj* **(a)** (*visits etc*) fréquent; qui arrive souvent; (*visitor*) assidu; (*customer*) habituel; **f. visits to the theatre,** sorties fréquentes au théâtre; **f. theatregoers,** des gens qui vont souvent au théâtre; **(b)** *Med* (*pulse*) rapide; **(c)** (*widespread*) très répandu; **it's quite a f. practice,** c'est une coutume assez répandue.
frequent² [frɪ'kwent] *vt* fréquenter, hanter (*les théâtres, les cafés etc*); **to f. s.o.,** fréquenter qn.
frequentation [fri:kwen'teɪʃən] *n* fréquentation *f*.
frequenter [frɪ'kwentər] *n* habitué, -ée, familier *m* (*d'une maison etc*).
frequently ['fri:kwəntlɪ] *adv* fréquemment.
fresco, *pl* **-o(e)s** ['freskəʊ, -əʊz] *n Art* **(a)** (*style*) fresque *f*; **to paint in f.,** peindre à fresque; **f. painter,** fresquiste *mf*; **(b)** (*painting*) (peinture *f* à) fresque *f*; **the frescoes of Raphael,** les fresques de Raphaël.
fresh [freʃ] **1** *adj* **(a)** (*fruit, eggs, fish*) frais, *f* fraîche; **f. or tinned peas,** pois frais ou en boîte; **f. vegetables,** légumes frais;
(b) (*new*) nouveau, -el, -elle; (*news etc*) frais, *f* fraîche; récent; **f. paragraph,** nouveau paragraphe; **f. dangers to face,** de nouveaux dangers à affronter; **to put f. courage into s.o.,** ranimer le courage de qn; **to let f. air into a room,** aérer une pièce; **to put f. water in the fish tank,** changer l'eau d'un aquarium; **f. outbreak of fire,** reprise *f* du feu; **it is still f. in my mind,** je l'ai encore frais à la mémoire; **the wound was f.,** la plaie était récente; **f. from London,** nouvellement arrivé de Londres; **the bread was f. from the oven,** le pain sortait du four;
(c) (*air*) frais, *f* fraîche, pur; (*cool*) frais; **it's f. this morning,** il fait frais ce matin; **in the f. air,** au grand air, en plein air; *F* **f.-air fiend,** fanatique *mf* d'air frais; (*outdoor person*) fanatique du grand air; *Nau* **f. breeze,** bonne brise; **f. water,** eau douce;
(d) (*full of vigour*) vigoureux, alerte; (*refreshed*) dispos; (*horse etc*) fougueux, animé; **f. troops,** troupes fraîches; **as f. as a daisy,** frais et dispos;
(e) (*complexion*) frais, fleuri; (*colour*) frais; **a f.-faced youth,** un jeune homme au teint frais;
(f) (*inexperienced*) inexpérimenté; **to be a f. hand at sth,** être novice dans qch;
(g) *F* (*impudent*) effronté; **to get f. with a girl,** prendre des libertés avec une jeune fille; **don't (you) get f. with me!,** ne te fiche pas de moi!
2 *adv* fraîchement, nouvellement, récemment (*arrivé, peint etc*); **f.-cut flowers,** fleurs nouvellement cueillies; **f.-killed poultry,** volaille fraîchement tuée.

3 *n* fraîcheur *f* (*du matin etc*); fraîche *f* (*du soir*).

freshen ['freʃən] **1** *vi* **(a)** (*of temperature*) (se) rafraîchir; (*of wind, weather*) fraîchir; **(b)** (*of person*) = **FRESHEN UP 1**. **2** *vt* rafraîchir (*l'air, la mémoire etc*); *Nau* rafraîchir (*une amarre, les remorques*).

►**freshen up 1** *vi* (*wash*) faire un bout de toilette. **2** *vtsep* (*renew*) **to f. up paint,** (r)aviver la couleur.

fresher ['freʃər] *n* = **FRESHMAN**.

freshly [freʃlɪ] *adv* (*with pp only*) fraîchement, de frais; **f. picked peaches,** des pêches fraîchement cueillies.

freshman, *pl* **-men** ['freʃmən] *n Sch F* étudiant, -ante de première année.

freshness ['freʃnɪs] *n* **(a)** (*of fruit, fish etc*) fraîcheur *f*; **(b)** (*of event*) caractère récent; (*of impression etc*) fraîcheur *f*; **(c)** (*of wind etc*) fraîcheur *f*, froideur *f*; **(d)** (*liveliness*) vigueur *f*, vivacité *f*; **(e)** (*inexperience*) naïveté *f*, inexpérience *f*; **(f)** *F* (*impudence*) effronterie *f*.

freshwater ['freʃwɔːtər] *adj* (*poisson etc*) d'eau douce; *F* **f. sailor,** marin *m* d'eau douce.

fret¹ [fret] *n* (*agitation*) agitation *f*; (*irritation*) irritation *f*; état *m* d'agacement; **to be in a f.,** se faire du mauvais sang *ou* de la bile.

fret² *v* (**-tt-**) **1** *vi* se tourmenter, s'inquiéter; (*get upset from worrying*) se faire du mauvais sang; **don't f.!,** (*don't worry*) ne vous inquiétez pas!; (*don't upset yourself*) ne vous faites pas de bile!, ne vous faites pas de mauvais sang!; **child fretting for his mother,** enfant qui réclame sa mère (*en pleurnichant*); **to f. over** *or* **about trifles,** s'irriter pour des sujets futiles. **2** *vt* **(a)** (*worry*) inquiéter, tracasser (*qn*); **don't f. yourself!,** ne te tracasse pas!; **(b)** (*wear away*) ronger (*qch*); **to f. a rope,** érailler un cordage.

fret³ *n Mus* touchette *f*, touche *f* (*de guitare etc*).

fret⁴ *n Archit* frette *f*; **(Greek) f.,** grecque *f*.

fret⁵ *vt* **(a)** découper (*le bois*); **f. saw,** scie *f* à découper; **(b)** *Archit* sculpter, orner (*un plafond etc*).

fretful ['fretfʊl] *adj* (*person*) qui se fait du mauvais sang; **f. baby,** bébé agité.

fretfully ['fretfʊlɪ] *adv* (*to speak*) d'un ton maussade; (*to look*) d'un air chagrin.

fretfulness ['fretfʊlnɪs] *n* irritabilité *f*.

fretting ['fretɪŋ] *n* **(a)** (*worrying*) inquiétude *f*; (*being upset*) agitation *f*; **I wish he'd stop his f.!,** si seulement il pouvait arrêter de se faire du mauvais sang!; **(b)** (*of rope etc*) usure *f*.

fretwork ['fretwɜːk] *n* **(a)** (*of ceilings etc*) ornementation *f*, sculpture *f*; **(b)** *Carp* (*technique*) découpage *m*; (*finished work*) travail ajouré, bois découpé.

Freudian ['frɔɪdɪən] *adj Psy* freudien; **F. slip,** lapsus *m*.

FRG [efɑː'dʒiː] *n* (*abbr* **Federal Republic of Germany**) RFA *f*.

friable ['fraɪəb(ə)l] *adj* (*terre etc*) friable.

friar ['fraɪər] *n Cathol* moine *m*, frère *m*, religieux *m*; **Grey Friars,** Franciscains *mpl*; **Black Friars,** Dominicains *mpl*; **White Friars,** Carmes *mpl*; *Pharm* **f.'s balsam,** baume *m* de benjoin.

friary ['fraɪərɪ] *n* monastère *m*.

fricassee¹ [frɪkə'siː] *n Culin* fricassée *f*; (*of rabbit or hare*) gibelotte *f*.

fricassee² *vt Culin* fricasser.

fricative ['frɪkətɪv] *Ling* **1** *adj* (*consonant*) fricatif, sifflant. **2** *n* fricative *f*, sifflante *f*.

friction ['frɪkʃən] *n* **(a)** *Phys* frottement *m*, friction *f*; **f. brake,** frein *m* à friction; **f. drive,** entraînement *m* par friction; *Comptr* **f. feed,** avancement *m* par friction; **(b)** frottement *m* (*de deux corps*); **f. surface,** frottoir *m* (*d'une boîte d'allumettes*); *Am* **f. tape,** chatterton *m*; **(c)** (*disagreement*) friction *f*, désaccord *m*; **there's f. between them,** il y a du tirage entre eux; **(d)** (*of scalp etc*) friction *f*; **f. gloves,** gants *mpl* de crin.

frictional ['frɪkʃən(ə)l] *adj Phys* à *ou* de friction.

Friday ['fraɪdɪ] *n* vendredi *m*; **he's coming (on) F.,** il viendra vendredi; **he comes every F.,** il vient tous les vendredis; **Good F.,** (le) Vendredi saint; **(Man) F.,** *Liter* Vendredi; *F* factotum *m*, homme *m* à tout faire; *F* **girl F.,** aide *f* de bureau.

fridge [frɪdʒ] *n F* frigo *m*.

fridge-freezer ['frɪdʒ'friːzər] *n F* frigo *m* avec congélateur.

fried [fraɪd] **1** *adj* frit; **they eat a lot of f. food,** ils mangent beaucoup de friture; **f. eggs,** œufs *mpl* sur le plat; **f. potatoes,** pommes de terre sautées. **2** *see* **FRY¹**.

friend [frend] *n* **(a)** ami, *f* amie; **I am speaking to you as a f.,** je vous parle en ami(e); **that's what friends are for,** c'est à ça que servent les amis; **they made friends,** ils sont devenus amis; **she's been a good f. to us,** elle nous a prouvé que son amitié est sincère; **we're just good friends,** nous sommes bons amis, c'est tout!; **bosom f.,** ami(e) intime; **a school f.,** un ami *ou* camarade d'école; **man f.** (*pl* **men friends**), ami homme, *pl* amis hommes; **woman f.** (*pl* **women friends**), amie femme, *pl* amies femmes; *Old-fashioned* **lady f.,** petite amie; **to be friends with s.o.,** être ami avec qn; **they've been friends for years,** ils sont amis depuis des années; **to be more than friends,** être plus qu'amis; **to make friends,** se faire des amis; **they made friends,** ils sont devenus amis; **to make friends with s.o.,** se lier d'amitié avec qn; **I made friends with them,** nous sommes devenus amis; *Prov* **a f. in need is a f. indeed,** au besoin on connaît l'ami; *F* **you'd better be** *or* **stay friends with them,** vous feriez bien de ne pas vous brouiller avec eux; **let us part friends,** séparons-nous (en) bons amis; **he's no f. of mine,** (*he's an enemy*) il n'est nullement mon ami; (*he means me no good*) il ne me veut pas de bien;

(b) (*acquaintance*) connaissance *f*; *F* **to have friends in high places** *or* **at court,** avoir des protections *ou* des relations *ou* des amis influents; **a f. at court,** un ami en haut lieu *ou* bien placé; **to dine with a few friends,** dîner en petit comité; *Parl* **my honourable f.,** *Jur* **my learned f.,** mon (cher) confrère; **I'm offering you a bargain, my f.,** (*to stranger*) cher ami, c'est une affaire que je vous propose;

(c) (*supporter*) ami, *f* amie, partisan *m* (*de l'ordre etc*); patron, -onne (*des arts etc*); **f. of the poor,** bienfaiteur, -trice des pauvres; **she's no f. of trade unionism,** elle n'est pas favorable au syndicalisme; **the Friends of Canterbury Cathedral,** la Société des Amis *ou* les Amis de la Cathédrale de Cantorbéry;

(d) *Rel* **F.,** Quaker, -eresse, Ami, -ie; **the Society of Friends,** la Société des Amis, les Quakers.

friendless ['frendlɪs] *adj* sans amis, sans appui.

friendliness ['frendlɪnɪs] *n* bienveillance *f*, bonté *f*, dispositions amicales (**to, towards,** envers).

friendly ['frendlɪ] **1** *adj* **(a)** amical, -aux; sympathique; **he gave me a f. wave,** il m'a fait un signe amical de la main; **piece of f. advice,** avis amical; **f. gathering,** réunion *f* d'amis; **to be f. with s.o.,** être ami avec qn; **she's very f. with the boss all of a sudden,** elle est très copine avec le patron tout d'un coup; **they became very f.,** ils se sont pris d'amitié l'un pour l'autre; **in a f. manner,** amicalement; **to be on f. terms with s.o.,** être en bons termes *ou* en relations d'amitié avec qn; **f. nation,** pays ami; *Sp* **f. match,** match amical; **(b)** (*well disposed*) bienveillant, favorablement disposé; **(c)** *Br Fin* **f. society,** société *f* de mutualité; **(d)** (*software etc*) convivial, -aux. **2** *n Sp* match amical.

-friendly ['frendlɪ] *suff* **ozone-f.,** qui préserve la couche d'ozone; **environment-f.,** qui respecte l'environnement.

Friendly Islands (the) [ðə'frendlɪaɪləndz] *npl* Tonga *m*, les îles *fpl* des Amis.

friendship ['frendʃɪp] *n* amitié *f*; **to form a f. with s.o.,** se lier (d'amitié) avec qn.

fries [fraɪz] *npl esp Am F* **(French) f.,** frites *fpl*.

frieze¹ [friːz] *n Tex* ratine *f*.

frieze² *n* **(a)** *Archit* frise *f*; **(b)** bordure *f* (*de papier peint*).

frigate ['frɪgət] *n* **(a)** *Nau* frégate *f*, escorteur *m*; **(b)** (*bird*) **f. (bird),** frégate *f*.

fright [fraɪt] *n* **(a)** peur *f*, effroi *m*; **he was seized with f.,** l'effroi l'a saisi; **to take f.,** s'effrayer (**at,** de); **to give s.o. a f.,** faire peur à qn; *F* **I got an awful f.,** j'ai eu une peur bleue; **(b)** *F* (*grotesque looking person*) personne laide *ou* grotesque; (*badly dressed person*) personne mal fagotée; **what a f. you look!,** comme vous voilà fagoté!

frighten ['fraɪt(ə)n] **1** *vt* effrayer (*qn*), faire peur à (*qn*); **it frightens him** *or* **her,** cela lui fait peur; **it frightens me that so many people believe him,** ça m'effraie que tant de personnes le croient; **these animals are easily frightened,** ces animaux s'effarouchent d'un rien; **you f. me to death,** vous me faites mourir de peur. **2** *vi* **I don't f. easily,** c'est difficile de me faire peur.

►**frighten away** *vtsep* (*scare*) effaroucher (*qn, un animal*); **don't f. away the birds,** n'effarouchez pas les oiseaux.

►**frighten off** *vtsep* (*scare*) effaroucher (*qn, un animal*); (*of dog etc*) chasser (*des voleurs etc*).

frightened ['fraɪt(ə)nd] *adj* (*person etc*) apeuré; **I wasn't as f. as you were,** je n'avais pas aussi peur que vous; **to feel f.,** avoir peur; **f. out of one's wits,** terrifié; **f. to death,** mort de peur.

frightening ['fraɪt(ə)nɪŋ] *adj* effrayant.

frighteningly ['fraɪt(ə)nɪŋlɪ] *adv* à faire peur.
frightful ['fraɪtfʊl] *adj* effroyable, épouvantable; *F* **to have a f. headache,** avoir un mal de tête affreux.
frightfully ['fraɪtfʊlɪ] *adv* affreusement; **he is f. ugly,** il est laid à faire peur; *F* **I am f. sorry,** je regrette énormément; *F* **f. rich,** colossalement riche.
frightfulness ['fraɪtfʊlnɪs] *n* atrocité *f*.
frigid ['frɪdʒɪd] *adj* **(a)** glacial, -als; (très) froid; (*style*) glacial, -als; (*answer*) glacé; **(b)** *Med* (*sexually*) frigide.
frigidity [frɪ'dʒɪdɪtɪ] *n* **(a)** frigidité *f*; froideur *f* (*de style*); **(b)** froideur *f* (sexuelle); *Med* frigidité *f*.
frigidly ['frɪdʒɪdlɪ] *adv* glacialement; **f. polite,** d'une politesse glaciale.
frill[1] [frɪl] *n* (*on clothing etc*) volant *m*, ruche *f*; *Culin* (*on ham etc*) papillote *f*; **shirt f.,** jabot *m*; *Fig* **a plain meal without frills,** un repas simple sans présentation compliquée; *Fig* **a sturdy, no frills touring bike,** un vélo de randonnée solide, sans gadgets.
frill[2] *vt* plisser, froncer, rucher (*le linge etc*).
frilled [frɪld] *adj* (*ribbon etc*) froncé, ruché; (*shirt*) à jabots; **f. lizard,** iguane australien.
frilly ['frɪlɪ] *adj* froncé, ruché.
fringe[1] [frɪndʒ] *n* **(a)** *Tex* frange *f*; **(b)** (*edge*) bordure *f*, bord *m*; **the outer fringe(s) of London,** la banlieue excentrique de Londres; **to live on the f. of society,** vivre en marge de la société; **f. benefits,** avantages *mpl* accessoires; (*for employees*) compléments *mpl* de salaire en nature; **f. theatre,** petit théâtre expérimental; *TV* **f. area,** zone *f* limitrophe; **(c)** *esp Br* (*of hair*) frange *f*; **to wear a f.,** avoir une frange, être coiffé à la chien.
fringe[2] *vt* franger (*un tapis etc*); **eyes fringed with black lashes,** yeux bordés de cils noirs.
►**fringe on, fringe upon** *vipo* (*come close to*) friser (*qch*); **boldness that fringes on insolence,** hardiesse qui frise l'insolence.
fringing ['frɪndʒɪŋ] *adj* marginal, -aux; (*récif*) frangeant.
frippery ['frɪpərɪ] *n* (*clothing, ornaments*) parure *f* sans valeur.
Frisco ['frɪskəʊ] *n F* San Francisco.
frisk[1] [frɪsk] *n* **(a)** (*movement*) **with a f. of its tail,** en donnant un coup de queue; **(b)** *F* (*search*) fouille *f*.
frisk[2] **1** *vi* (*of lambs etc*) s'ébattre, gambader, folâtrer; (*of horse*) cabrioler. **2** *vt* **(a)** (*of dog etc*) **to f. its tail,** frétiller de la queue; **(b)** fouiller (*un suspect etc*).
►**frisk about** *vi* = **FRISK[2] 1.**
friskiness ['frɪskɪnɪs] *n* vivacité *f*.
frisking ['frɪskɪŋ] *n* fouille *f* (*d'un suspect, d'un voyageur*).
frisky ['frɪskɪ] *adj* vif; (*cheval*) qui fait des cabrioles; **to feel f.,** (*of person*) se sentir plein d'entrain.
fritillary [frɪ'tɪlərɪ] *n* **(a)** (*plant*) fritillaire *f*; **(b)** (*butterfly*) damier *m*.
fritter ['frɪtər] *n Culin* beignet *m*; **apple f.,** beignet aux pommes.
►**fritter away** *vtsep* dissiper (*sa fortune*); gaspiller (*son argent, son temps*) (**on records/***etc*, à *ou* pour acheter des disques/*etc*).
frivolity [frɪ'vɒlɪtɪ] *n* **(a)** (*of person*) frivolité *f*; **(b)** (*object*) frivolité *f*, chose *f* frivole.
frivolous ['frɪvələs] *adj* **(a)** (*person etc*) frivole; **(b)** (*complaint etc*) vain, futile.
frivolously ['frɪvələslɪ] *adv* (*see adj*) **(a)** frivolement; **(b)** futilement.
frivolousness ['frɪvələsnɪs] *n* **(a)** (*of person*) frivolité *f*; **(b)** futilité *f* (*d'une objection etc*).
frizz[1] [frɪz] *n* (*curly hair*) cheveux crêpelés; crêpelure *f* (*des cheveux*).
frizz[2] **1** *vt* crêper, frisotter (*les cheveux*). **2** *vi* (*of hair*) frisotter.
frizziness ['frɪzɪnɪs] *n* crêpelure *f* (*des cheveux*).
frizzle ['frɪz(ə)l] **1** *vi* grésiller (*dans la poêle*). **2** *vt Culin* faire frire (*le lard*).
frizzy ['frɪzɪ] *adj* (*hair*) crêpelé, crêpelu, frisotté.
fro [frəʊ] *adv* **to go to and f.,** aller et venir.
frock [frɒk] *n* **(a)** robe *f* (*d'enfant, de femme*); **(b)** froc *m*, bure *f* (*de moine*); **(c) f. coat,** redingote *f*.
frog[1] [frɒg] *n* **(a)** (*animal*) grenouille *f*; **tree f.,** rainette *f* (verte); *F* **to have a f. in one's throat,** avoir un chat dans la gorge; **(b)** *Offensive Sl* **F.,** Français, -aise.
frog[2] *n Mil etc* **(a)** (*for sword*) porte-epée *m inv*; (*for bayonet*) porte-baïonnette *m inv*; **(b)** (*braid*) brandebourg *m*.
frogged [frɒgd] *adj* (*uniform, tunic etc*) orné de brandebourgs.
froggie ['frɒgɪ] *n Hum F* Français, -aise.
frogging ['frɒgɪŋ] *n* (*on uniform etc*) brandebourgs *mpl*.
frogman, *pl* **-men** ['frɒgmən] *n* homme-grenouille *m*, *pl* hommes-grenouilles.
frogmarch ['frɒgmɑːtʃ] *vt* porter (*qn*) à quatre *ou* le derrière en l'air.
frogspawn ['frɒgspɔːn] *n inv* œufs *mpl* de grenouille; *Br Sl* tapioca *m* au lait.
froing ['frəʊɪŋ] *n F* **toing and f.,** va-et-vient *m*.
frolic[1] ['frɒlɪk] *n* **(a)** (*of young animal, child etc*) ébats *mpl*, gambades *fpl*; **(b)** (*entertainment*) fredaine *f*, divertissement *m*.
frolic[2] *vi* (**frolicked**) s'ébattre, gambader.
from [frɒm, *unstressed* frəm] *prep* **(a)** (*place*) de; **he returned f. London,** il est revenu de Londres; **f. Paris to London,** de Paris à Londres; **f. Milan she went to Turin,** de Milan, elle est allée à Turin; **f. town to town,** de ville en ville; **f. side to side,** d'un côté à l'autre; **a nail protruded f. the wood,** un clou dépassait du bois; **you can see France f. here,** d'ici, on peut voir la France; **f. your point of view,** selon votre point de vue;
(b) (*indicating range*) **the bird lays f. four to six eggs,** l'oiseau pond de quatre à six œufs; **wine f. four francs a bottle,** vins à partir de quatre francs la bouteille; **every flavour of ice-cream f. vanilla to pistachio,** tous les parfums de glace de la vanille à la pistache;
(c) (*time*) depuis, dès, à partir de; **f. that day,** depuis ce jour, à partir de ce jour; **f. tomorrow on,** à partir de demain; **house let f. June 1st,** maison louée à compter du premier juin; **f. his childhood,** depuis *ou* dès son enfance; **f. morning till night,** du matin au soir; **f. time to time,** de temps en temps;
(d) (*distance*) **he is away f. home,** il est en voyage; **not far f. ...,** pas loin de ...; **ten kilometres f. Paris,** à dix kilomètres de Paris;
(e) (*separation*) de, à; **separation f. s.o.,** séparation d'avec qn; **he stole a pound f. her,** il lui a volé une livre; **she removed the dust f. the lens,** elle a enlevé la poussière de l'objectif; **police cleared the demonstrators f. the square,** la police a évacué les manifestants du square; **to dissuade s.o. f. doing sth,** dissuader qn de faire qch;
(f) (*protection*) contre; **to shelter f. the rain,** s'abriter contre la pluie;
(g) (*change*) **f. bad to worse,** de mal en pis; **the price has been increased f. fifty pence to sixty pence,** on a augmenté le prix de cinquante pence à soixante pence;
(h) (*difference*) d'avec, de; **he can't distinguish the good f. the bad,** il ne sait pas distinguer le bon d'avec le mauvais;
(i) (*origin*) **a train/plane f. Manchester,** un train/avion en provenance de Manchester; **where do you come f.?, where are you f.?,** d'où viens-tu?; **wheat f. Russia,** blé venant de Russie; **a quotation f. Shakespeare,** une citation tirée de Shakespeare; **to draw a conclusion f. sth,** tirer une conclusion de qch; **Inspector Lestrade f. Scotland Yard,** l'inspecteur Lestrade de Scotland Yard; **made f.,** fait de; **he grabbed a revolver f. the table,** il saisit un revolver sur la table; **to drink f. the stream,** boire au ruisseau; **to drink f. the bottle,** boire à la bouteille; **to take sth f. one's pocket,** prendre qch dans sa poche;
(j) (*sender*) **a letter f. my father,** une lettre de mon père; **I have brought it to you f. a friend,** je vous l'apporte de la part d'un ami; **tell her that f. me,** dites-lui cela de ma part; **f. ...,** (*on parcel*) expéditeur, -trice ...;
(k) (*model*) d'après; **painted f. nature,** peint d'après nature;
(l) (*as a result of*) **to act f. conviction,** agir par conviction; **I know him f. seeing him at the club,** je le reconnais pour l'avoir vu au cercle; **f. his looks you might suppose that ...,** à le voir on dirait que ...; **f. what I heard ...,** d'après ce que j'ai entendu dire ...; **f. what I can see ...,** à ce que je vois ...;
(m) (*with adv prep*) **f. above,** d'en haut; **I saw him f. a long way off,** je l'ai vu de loin; **f. among the trees ...,** de parmi les arbres ...; **take one f. among ...,** prenez-en un parmi ...;
(n) (*after adv*) **to come down f. one's room,** descendre de sa chambre; **to move away f. s.o.,** s'éloigner de qn.
frond [frɒnd] *n* fronde *f* (*de fougère*); feuille *f* (*de palmier*).
front[1] [frʌnt] **1** *n* **(a)** devant *m*; façade *f* (*d'un bâtiment*); (*drawing*) *& Archit* élévation *f*; devanture *f* (*d'un magasin*); avant *m* (*d'une voiture*); devant (*de chemise*); **carriage in the f. of the train,** voiture en tête du train; **I spilled soup all down my f.,** je me suis renversé de la soupe dessus; *Th* **f. of house,** salle *f*; **f. of house manager,** directeur administratif; *Th* **out f.,** dans la salle; *Br* **the f.,** (*at*

seaside) la promenade; *Br* **house on the f.**, maison faisant face à la mer;

(b) (*first row etc*) premier rang; **to push one's way to the f.**, se frayer un chemin jusqu'au premier rang; se pousser (en avant);

(c) (*outward appearance*) contenance *f*, face *f*; **to put a bold f. on it**, faire bonne contenance; *Br F* **to have the f. to do sth**, (*nerve*) avoir l'effronterie *ou* le front de faire qch; **it's only a f. on his part**, ce n'est qu'une façade de sa part; **the company was just a f. for their arms dealing operation**, la société n'était qu'une couverture pour leur trafic d'armes; *Pej* **f. (man)**, prête-nom *m*, *pl* prête-noms; *Pej* **f. organization**, couverture *f*, façade *f*;

(d) *Mil etc* front *m*; **to be sent to the f.**, être envoyé au front; *Pol* **common f.**, front commun; **popular f.**, front populaire; *Fig* **to make progress on all fronts**, faire des progrès sur tous les fronts; *Met* **warm/cold f.**, front chaud/froid;

(e) (*phrases*) **in f.**, devant, en avant; **to send s.o. on in f.**, envoyer qn devant; **in f. of**, *US* **f. of**, devant; (*opposite*) en face de; **he stood right in f. of me**, (*faced me*) il se trouvait juste en face de moi; (*had his back to me*) il s'est mis juste devant moi; *F* **I want the money up f.**, je veux mon argent avant; **he was very up f. about it**, il a été franc sur ce point; **it's right in f. of you**, (*what you are looking for*) c'est juste devant vous.

2 *adj* antérieur, de devant, d'avant; *Parl* **f. bench**, = le banc des ministres et celui des membres du cabinet fantôme; **f. carriage**, (*of train*) voiture *f* de tête; **f. door**, porte *f* d'entrée (principale); *esp Br* **f. garden**, jardin *m* de devant; *Mil* **f. line**, ligne *f* de contact *ou* de feu; **f.-line troops**, troupes *fpl* du front; **f.-loader, f.-loading washing machine**, machine *f* à laver avec chargement en façade; **f. office**, réception *f*, bureau *m* d'accueil; *Journ* **the f. page**, la première page, *F* la une; **to make the f. page, to be f.-page news**, (*of person, incident*) faire la une; **f.-page news**, nouvelles sensationnelles; **artists in the f. rank**, artistes de premier plan; **f. room**, chambre *f* sur la rue; **in the f. row**, au premier rang; *Rugby* **f.-row forward**, avant *m* de première ligne; *Th* **f.-row seat**, siège *m* de premier rang; *Aut* **f. seat**, siège avant; *Th & Fig* **to have a f.(-row) seat**, être aux premières loges; **f. view**, vue *f* de face; *Archit* élévation *f*; **f. wheel**, (*of car, bicycle*) roue *f* avant; *Aut* **f.-wheel drive**, traction *f* avant.

front² **1** *vi* **(a)** (*of building*) **the house fronts north**, la maison est exposée *ou* orientée au nord; **(b)** *Mil* faire front; **left f.!**, à gauche front!, à gauche, gauche! **2** *vt* **(a)** donner une (nouvelle) façade à (*un édifice*); **(b)** *Mus* **to f. a band**, (*lead it*) diriger un orchestre.

►**front on, front onto** *vipo* (*of building*) (*be opposite*) faire face à (*qch*); (*point towards*) être tourné vers (*qch*); **the river and the houses fronting on it**, le fleuve et les maisons donnant dessus.

frontage ['frʌntɪdʒ] *n* **(a)** longueur *f* de façade (*d'un édifice*); devanture *f* (*d'un magasin*); **premises with frontages on two streets**, local avec façades sur deux rues; **(b)** terrain *m* en bordure (*d'un fleuve etc*).

frontal¹ ['frʌnt(ə)l] *n* **(a)** *Rel* devant *m* d'autel, fronteau *m*; **(b)** façade *f* (*d'un bâtiment*).

frontal² *adj Anat* frontal, -aux; *Archit* (*vue etc*) de face; *Mil* (*attaque etc*) de front; **full f. nudity**, nudité vue de face.

front-bench ['frʌnt'bentʃ] *adj esp Br Parl* **f.-b. MP**, = **FRONTBENCHER**.

frontbencher ['frʌnt'bentʃər] *n esp Br Parl* = membre de la Chambre siégeant aux premières banquettes (réservées aux ministres).

front-end ['frʌntend] *adj Comptr* **f.-e. processor**, (ordinateur *m*) frontal *m*.

frontier ['frʌntɪər] *n* frontière *f*; **natural frontiers**, frontières naturelles; **the frontiers of human knowledge**, les bornes *fpl* des connaissances humaines; **f. guard**, garde-frontière *m*, *pl* gardes-frontière; **f. town**, ville *f* frontière.

frontispiece ['frʌntɪspiːs] *n Typ* frontispice *m*.

frontrunner ['frʌntrʌnər] *n* (*in election*) favori *m*.

frosh [frɒʃ] *n US Univ F* étudiant, -ante de première année.

frost¹ [frɒst] *n Met* gelée *f*, gel *m*; **there was a f.**, il y avait du gel; **ground f.**, gelée blanche; **ten degrees of f.**, dix degrés au-dessous de zéro; **hoar f.**, givre *m*; *Lit* frimas *m*.

frost² **1** *vt* **(a)** givrer (*les vitres etc*); **(b)** *esp Am Culin* glacer (*un gâteau etc*); **(c)** (*damage by frost*) geler (*un arbre fruitier*); **(d)** (*in glassmaking*) dépolir (*le verre*). **2** *vi* = **FROST OVER, FROST UP**.

►**frost over, frost up** *vi* (*of windscreen etc*) se givrer, se couvrir de givre.

frostbite ['frɒstbaɪt] *n Med* (*of feet etc*) gelure *f*; **to have f.**, avoir des gelures.

frostbitten ['frɒstbɪt(ə)n] *adj* **(a)** (*nose etc*) gelé; **(b)** (*plant*) brûlé par le froid, grillé (par la gelée).

frostbound ['frɒstbaʊnd] *adj* (*sol*) gelé.

frosted ['frɒstɪd] *adj* **(a)** (*window panes*) givré; **(b)** *esp Am Culin* (*gâteau*) glacé; **(c)** (*glass*) dépoli.

frost-free ['frɒstfriː] *adj* (*refrigerator, freezer*) à dégivrage automatique.

frostily ['frɒstɪlɪ] *adv* (*to say*) d'une manière glaciale.

frostiness ['frɒstɪnɪs] *n* **(a)** froid glacial (*du temps*); **(b)** manière glaciale (*de qn*).

frosting ['frɒstɪŋ] *n* **(a)** (*of window panes*) givrage *m*; **(b)** *esp Am Culin* (*on cake*) glace *f*; (*action*) glaçage *m*; *Fig* **the f. on the cake**, la cerise sur le gâteau; **(c)** dépolissage *m* (*du verre*).

frostproof ['frɒstpruːf] *adj* résistant à la gelée.

frosty ['frɒstɪ] *adj* **(a)** glacial, -als; (*temps*) de gelée; **(b)** (*accueil*) glacial; **f. answer**, réponse glacée; **(c)** (*window*) couvert de givre; (*ground*) gelé.

froth¹ [frɒθ] *n* **(a)** (*foam*) écume *f*; mousse *f* (*de la bière etc*); **(b)** *Pej* (*empty words*) paroles creuses.

froth² *vi* écumer, mousser; (*of waves*) moutonner; **he was frothing at the mouth**, il avait l'écume aux lèvres; **the frothing water**, les eaux écumantes.

►**froth up** *vi* mousser fortement.

frothy ['frɒθɪ] *adj* **(a)** écumeux, mousseux; (*waves*) moutonneux; (*dress etc*) léger, bouffant; **(b)** *Pej* (*speech*) vide, creux.

frown¹ [fraʊn] *n* froncement *m* de sourcils; (*disapproving look*) air désapprobateur; (*stern look*) regard sévère; **to say sth with a f.**, dire qch en fronçant les sourcils *ou* d'un air désapprobateur.

the frown² *vi* (*of person*) froncer les sourcils; se renfrogner; **to f. at s.o.**, regarder qn en fronçant les sourcils.

►**frown on, frown upon** *vipo* (*disapprove*) désapprouver (*une suggestion etc*).

frowning ['fraʊnɪŋ] *adj* (*looks, face etc*) renfrogné, rechigné; (*brow*) sourcilleux.

frowsty ['fraʊstɪ] *adj F* qui sent le renfermé.

frowzy ['fraʊzɪ] *adj* **(a)** (*salle*) qui sent le renfermé; **(b)** (*person, clothes etc*) mal tenu, peu soigné.

froze *see* **FREEZE²**.

frozen ['frəʊz(ə)n] **1** *adj* **(a)** gelé, glacé; (*meat, peas etc*) congelé, surgelé; **f. foods**, (produits *mpl*) surgelés *mpl*, congelés *mpl*; *F* **my hands are f.**, j'ai les mains gelées *ou* glacées; **I've got f. waiting for you**, je me suis gelé à vous attendre; **(b)** (*assets etc*) non liquide, gelé. **2** *see* **FREEZE²**.

fructify ['frʌktɪfaɪ] **1** *vi* fructifier; *Fig* produire des bénéfices. **2** *vt* faire fructifier.

fructose ['frʌktəʊs] *n Ch* fructose *m*.

frugal ['fruːg(ə)l] *adj* **(a)** (*person, life*) frugal, -aux; (*thrifty*) économe; **to be f. of** *or* **with sth**, ménager qch; **(b)** (*meal etc*) frugal, -aux, sobre; **f. eater**, petit mangeur, petite mangeuse.

frugality [fruː'gælɪtɪ] *n* **(a)** (*of person, life*) frugalité *f*; (*thriftiness*) économie *f*; **(b)** (*of meal*) sobriété *f*.

frugally ['fruːg(ə)lɪ] *adv* frugalement.

fruit¹ [fruːt] *n* **(a)** fruit *m*; **would you like some f.?**, prendrez-vous un fruit?; **apples and other fruit(s)**, les pommes et autres fruits; **a stone f.**, un fruit à noyau; **eat more f.**, mangez plus de fruits; **soft f.**, *Am* **small f.**, petits fruits; **dried f.**, fruits secs; **stewed f.**, compote *f* de fruits; **to bear f.**, (*of tree*) donner des fruits, porter fruit; *Fig* (*of labour*) porter fruit; **my enquiries bore f.**, mes recherches furent couronnées de succès; **f. basket**, (*for display etc*) corbeille *f* à fruits; (*for carrying*) panier *m* à fruits; **f. bat**, chauve-souris *f* frugivore; **f. bowl**, (*for display etc*) coupe *f* à fruits; **f. bud**, bourgeon *m* à fruit; **f. cup**, boisson glacée avec fruits; **f. dish**, compotier *m*; (*for display*) coupe à fruits; **f. drop**, bonbon acidulé; **f. farmer** *or* **grower**, fruiticulteur *m*; **f. farming**, culture fruitière; **f. fly**, (*insect*) mouche *f* à fruits; **f. juice**, jus *m* de fruit; **f. knife**, couteau *m* à fruit(s); *Br* **f. machine**, machine *f* à sous, *Sl* tire-pognon *m*, *pl* tire-pognons; **f. salad** *or* **cocktail**, macédoine *f* *ou* salade *f* de fruits; **f. shop**, fruiterie *f*; **f. stall**, étalage *m* de fruit; **f. tree**, arbre fruitier *ou* à fruit;

(b) *Fig* fruit *m*; **the fruits of the earth**, les fruits *ou* les biens *mpl* de la terre; **the f. of her womb**, le fruit de ses entrailles; **the fruits of industry**, les fruits *ou* les produits *mpl* de l'industrie; **his knowledge is the f. of much study**, son savoir est le fruit de longues études;

(c) *F* **yes, my old f.**, oui, mon vieux *ou* ma vieille;

(d) *Am Offensive Sl* (*homosexuel*) pédé *m*.

fruit² *vi* (*of tree*) porter des fruits.
fruit-bearing ['fruːtbeərɪŋ] *adj* (*tree etc*) frugifère, fructifère.
fruitcake ['fruːtkeɪk] *n* **(a)** *Culin* cake *m*; **(b)** *esp Br F* (*eccentric, mad person*) cinglé, -ée, fou, *f* folle; **to be as nutty as a f.,** être complètement cinglé.
fruit-eating ['fruːtiːtɪŋ] *adj* (*animal*) frugivore.
fruiterer ['fruːtərər] *n esp Br* fruitier, -ière; **f.'s (shop),** fruiterie *f*.
fruitful ['fruːtfʊl] *adj* **(a)** (*work, discussion etc*) fructueux, profitable; **(b)** (*tree etc*) fructueux, productif; (*soil etc*) fertile, fécond; **(c)** *Arch* (*prolific*) fécond, prolifique.
fruitfully ['fruːtfʊlɪ] *adv* fructueusement, à profit.
fruitfulness ['fruːtfʊlnɪs] *n* **(a)** *Fig* caractère fructueux, utilité *f* (*d'un travail etc*); **(b)** productivité *f* (*d'un arbre etc*); fertilité *f* (*du sol etc*).
fruiting ['fruːtɪŋ] *adj* (*tree etc*) frugifère, fructifère.
fruition [fruː'ɪʃən] *n* réalisation *f* (*d'un projet, d'un espoir*); **to come to f.,** porter fruit; **to bring sth to f.,** réaliser qch.
fruitless ['fruːtlɪs] *adj* sans fruit, stérile, infructueux; **f. efforts,** efforts sans résultat.
fruity ['fruːtɪ] *adj* **(a)** (*goût etc*) de fruit; (*vin*) fruité, fruiteux; **(b)** *F* **f. voice,** voix (trop) étoffée; **(c)** *esp Br* (*roman, scandale etc*) corsé; **(d)** *Am Offensive Sl* (*homosexual*) de pédé; **(e)** *US* (*crazy*) toqué, cinglé.
frump [frʌmp] *n F* femme mal attifée; **she's a f.,** elle est ficelée comme l'as de pique.
frumpish ['frʌmpɪʃ] **, frumpy** ['frʌmpɪ] *adj* **f. woman,** femme mal attifée *ou F* mal fagotée.
frustrate [frʌs'treɪt] *vt* **(a)** (*upset, annoy*) décevoir, frustrer (*qn*); **(b)** (*thwart*) contrecarrer (*qn*); faire échouer (*un projet*); **to f. s.o.'s hopes,** frustrer qn dans son espoir, frustrer l'espoir de qn.
frustrated [frʌs'treɪtɪd] *adj* (*writer etc*) frustré; **(sexually) f.,** frustré.
frustrating [frʌs'treɪtɪŋ] *adj* (*experience etc*) frustrant.
frustration [frʌs'treɪʃən] *n* **(a)** *Psy etc* frustration *f*; **(b)** anéantissement *m* (*des projets de qn*); frustration *f* (*d'un espoir*).
fry¹ [fraɪ] *v* **(fried) 1** *vt Culin* (faire) frire, (faire) cuire en friteuse (*du poisson etc*); **to f. sth in butter/oil/*etc*,** faire frire qch dans du beurre/de l'huile/*etc*; **to f. an egg,** faire cuire un œuf sur le plat. **2** *vi* **(a)** (*of food*) frire; **(b)** *esp US Sl* (*of convict*) mourir *ou* finir sur la chaise électrique.
fry² *n* (*no pl*) (*of fish*) frai *m*, fretin *m*, alevin *m*; **small f.,** menu fretin; *Fig* (*insignificant people*) le menu fretin, les gens insignifiants; (*children*) les gosses *mpl*; **salmon f.,** saumoneaux *mpl* dans la deuxième année.
fry³ *n* (*offal*) issues *fpl*; fressure *f* (*d'agneau, de porc*).
fryer ['fraɪər] *n Culin* **(a)** (*person*) = personne qui fait de la friture; **(b)** (*frying pan*) poêle *f* à frire; **(deep) f.,** friteuse *f*; **(c)** (*chicken*) poulet *m* à frire.
frying ['fraɪɪŋ] *n* friture *f*; *esp Br* **f. pan,** poêle *f* à frire; *F* **to jump out of the f. pan into the fire,** échanger un mal contre un pis.
fry-pan ['fraɪpæn] *n Am* poêle *f* à frire.
fry-up ['fraɪʌp] *n Br Culin F* pommes de terre, bacon, saucisses *etc* frits ensemble.
ft (*abbr* **foot** *or* **feet**) p., pd..
fuchsia ['fjuːʃə] *n* (*plant*) fuchsia *m*.
fuck¹ [fʌk] *Vulg* **1** *n* baise *f*; **to be a good f.,** bien baiser; **to not care** *or* **give a f.,** n'en avoir rien à foutre; **what the f. is that?,** qu'est-ce que c'est que ça, bordel de merde?; **for f.'s sake!,** bordel!; **like f. they are,** qu'ils aillent se faire foutre. **2** *int* merde!, bordel!
fuck² *Vulg* **1** *vt* foutre, baiser (*qn*); **f. it!,** merde!; **f. you!,** va te faire foutre!, je t'emmerde!; **f. him!, f. what he says!,** qu'il aille se faire foutre!; **f. me!,** putain!; **f. all,** que dalle; **she does f. all work,** elle en fout pas une rame; **I'm fucked!,** (*exhausted*) je suis vanné!; **the car's fucked!,** la voiture est foutue! **2** *vi* baiser.
▸**fuck about, fuck around** *Vulg* **1** *vi* **(a)** (*play the fool*) déconner; **(b)** (*waste time*) glander. **2** *vtas* (*treat badly*) emmerder (*qn*).
▸**fuck off** *Vulg* **1** *vi* (*go away*) aller se faire foutre; **f. off!,** va te faire foutre! **2** *vtsep* (*annoy*) emmerder (*qn*).
▸**fuck up** *Vulg* **1** *vtsep* (*ruin*) foutre (*qch*) en l'air, foirer; **her parents have really fucked her up,** ses parents lui ont foutu des complexes pas possibles. **2** *vi* (*bungle sth*) foirer, déconner.
fucker ['fʌkər] *n Vulg* **stupid f.,** connard *m*; **old f.,** vieux mec.
fucking ['fʌkɪŋ] *Vulg* **1** *adj* foutu, de mes deux; **this f. car,** cette voiture de mes deux, cette putain de voiture; **a f. good film,** un vachement bon film; **he's a f. idiot!,** c'est un connard!; *Br* **f. hell!,** bordel de merde!; **who the f. hell does she think she is?,** mais merde, pour qui elle se prend? **2** *adv* bougrement (*froid etc*); **you're f. out of your mind!,** bordel, ça va vraiment pas! **3** *n* baise *f*.
fuck-up ['fʌkʌp] *n Vulg* gâchis *m*.
fuddled ['fʌd(ə)ld] *adj F* **(a)** (*drunk*) soûl; **to get f.,** s'enivrer; **slightly f.,** un peu gris; **(b)** (*confused*) brouillé (*dans ses idées*).
fuddy-duddy ['fʌdɪdʌdɪ] *F* **1** *n* vieil encroûté. **2** *adj* vieux jeu *inv*.
fudge¹ [fʌdʒ] *n* **(a)** *Culin* fondant américain; **(b)** (*foolishness*) bêtise(s) *f(pl)*; **(c)** *Journ* dernières nouvelles; **(d) his answer was a f.,** sa réponse n'était qu'une dérobade.
fudge² *vt* **(a)** (*botch*) bousiller (*un travail etc*); **(b)** (*falsify*) truquer (*des comptes etc*); **(c)** (*avoid*) **to f. an issue,** éluder une question.
fuel¹ ['fjʊəl] *n* combustible *m*; (*for engine*) carburant *m*; **domestic** *or* **household f.,** combustible de ménage; **solid f.,** combustible solide; *Fig* **to add f. to the flames,** jeter de l'huile sur le feu; *Fig* **to add fresh f. to a quarrel,** alimenter une querelle; **jet f.,** carburéacteur *m*; *Nucl Phys* **nuclear f.,** combustible nucléaire; *Nucl Phys* **f. element,** élément *m* combustible; **f. gauge,** jauge *f* d'essence; *MecE* **f. injection,** injection *f*; **f. oil,** fuel(-oil) *m*, mazout *m*; **f. tank,** réservoir *m* à carburant *ou* d'essence; *Nucl Phys* **f. rod,** assemblage *m* d'éléments combustibles.
fuel² *v* **(-ll-,** *US* **-l-) 1** *vt* alimenter, charger (*un fourneau etc*); ravitailler *ou* alimenter (*un véhicule, une machine etc*) en combustible *ou* en carburant; *Fig* nourrir (*les spéculations*). **2** *vi* se ravitailler en combustible *ou* en carburant *ou* en essence.
fuel-injected ['fjʊəlɪndʒektɪd] *adj Aut etc* à injection.
fuelling, *US* **fueling** ['fjʊəlɪŋ] *n* ravitaillement *m* en combustible *ou* en carburant *ou* en essence.
fug [fʌg] *n esp Br F* forte odeur de renfermé; (*in smoke-filled room*) air empesté de tabac.
fuggy ['fʌgɪ] *adj esp Br F* (*salle etc*) qui sent le renfermé.
fugitive ['fjuːdʒɪtɪv] **1** *n* fugitif, -ive, fuyard, -arde; (*refugee*) réfugié, -ée; **f. from justice,** fugitif recherché par la justice. **2** *adj* **(a)** (*prisoner*) fugitif, fuyard; **(b)** (*happiness*) fugitif, fugace, éphémère.
fugue [fjuːg] *n Mus Psy* fugue *f*.
fulcrum, *pl* **-cra, -crums** ['fʌlkrəm, -krə, -krəmz] *n* pivot *m* (*d'un levier*); couteau *m* (*de balance*).
fulfil, *US* **fulfill** [fʊl'fɪl] *vt* (*Br* **fulfils,** *US* **fulfills,** *Br & US* **fulfilled, fulfilling) (a)** accomplir (*une prophétie*); répondre à, remplir (*l'attente de qn*); satisfaire (*un désir*); exaucer (*une prière*); accomplir (*une tâche*); remplir, s'acquitter de (*une obligation*); remplir (*les conditions requises*); obéir à (*un commandement*); remplir (*les instructions de qn*); **to f. oneself,** se réaliser; **to feel fulfilled,** (*of person*) sentir qu'on s'est réalisé; **to f. one's potential,** réaliser son potentiel; **to f. the purpose in view,** répondre au but envisagé; **(b)** (*complete*) achever, compléter (*une période de temps*).
fulfilling [fʊl'fɪlɪŋ] *adj* (*travail etc*) satisfaisant.
fulfilment, *US* **fulfillment** [fʊl'fɪlmənt] *n* accomplissement *m* (*d'une prophétie, d'un devoir, d'un désir etc*); exaucement *m* (*d'une prière*); exécution *f* (*d'un projet, d'un contrat*); *Jur* accomplissement (*d'une condition*); **to find f.,** se réaliser; **to have a feeling of f.,** avoir un sentiment de plénitude.
full¹ [fʊl] **1** *adj* **(a)** (*receptacle*) plein, rempli; (*house, cupboard*) comble; (*bus etc*) plein, complet; (*day*) chargé; **f. to the brim,** rempli jusqu'au bord; **f. to overflowing,** plein à déborder; **don't speak with your mouth f.,** ne parle pas la bouche pleine; **to be f. (up),** (*of person*) être repu *ou* rassasié; **the bus is f. up,** l'autobus est au complet; **f. up!,** complet!; **to be f. of sth,** être plein de qch; **to have one's pockets f. of money,** avoir les poches pleines d'argent; **her eyes were f. of tears,** elle avait les yeux pleins de larmes; **f. of holes,** plein de trous; **look f. of hatred,** regard chargé de haine; **to be f. of hope,** être rempli d'espoir; **to be f. of praise for s.o.,** ne pas tarir d'éloges sur qn; **to be f. of ideas,** être plein d'idées; **to be f. of one's own importance,** être pénétré de sa propre importance; **f. of oneself,** plein de soi-même; *Cards* (*poker*) **f. hand** *or* **house,** main pleine; *Th etc* **f. house,** salle *f* comble; **f. session** (*of a committee etc*), réunion plénière;
(b) (*notes etc*) ample, copieux; **she received her f. share of the money,** elle a eu sa bonne part de l'argent; **in the fullest detail,** dans le plus grand détail; **to ask for full-**

er information, demander des précisions sur qch;
(c) (*complete*) complet, entier; **in f. flower,** en pleine fleur; **roses in f. bloom,** roses épanouies; **f. board,** pension complète; **f. brother/sister,** frère/sœur germain(e); **f. cargo,** plein chargement; **in f. flight/retreat,** en pleine déroute/retraite; **to lead a f. life,** mener une vie bien remplie; **I waited two f. hours** *or* **a f. two hours,** j'ai attendu deux bonnes heures; **we were under f. sail,** nous avions toutes voiles dehors; **to give f. scope to s.o.,** donner libre carrière à qn; **in f. uniform,** en grande tenue; **to be in f. swing,** (*of party, sales etc*) battre son plein; **f. meal,** repas complet; **f. measure,** mesure *f* comble; **f. member,** membre *m* titulaire; **f. moon,** pleine lune; **f. name,** (*on form*) nom *m* en toutes lettres; **what is your f. name?,** quels sont vos nom et prénoms?; **f. pay,** paie entière; **leave on f. pay,** congé *m* à solde entière; **f. price,** prix fort; **to pay the f. price for sth,** payer le prix fort pour qch; **to pay f.** *Th* **price** *or Rail etc* **fare,** payer place entière; **f. professor,** professeur *m* titulaire; **f. stop** *or* **point,** (*in punctuation*) point *m* (final); *F* **to come to a f. stop,** s'arrêter net; **f. text,** texte intégral; *Sp Fb etc* **f. time,** fin *f* de match; **f. weight,** poids *m* juste;
(d) (*face*) plein, rond; (*sleeve etc*) large, bouffant; **too f.,** trop large; **to have a f. figure,** (*of woman*) avoir une silhouette généreuse; **f. lips,** lèvres grosses *ou* fortes; **f. voice,** voix pleine *ou* ronde;
(e) *Nau* (*sail*) plein, gonflé; **the sails are f.,** les voiles portent bien.
2 *n* **to publish a letter in f.,** publier une lettre intégralement; **money refunded in f.,** on rembourse intégralement l'argent *ou* l'argent en totalité; **to pay in f.,** payer intégralement; **name in f.,** nom et prénoms; **to write out a word in f.,** écrire un mot en toutes lettres; **to the f.,** tout à fait; **to live life to the f.,** vivre sa vie pleinement; **to indulge one's tastes to the f.,** donner libre cours à ses goûts.
3 *adv* **(a)** (*completely*) **to turn a tap f. on,** ouvrir un robinet en grand; **to turn the radio f. on,** mettre la radio à fond; **to drive a car f. out,** conduire à toute vitesse; **to make a f.-out effort to do sth,** faire tout son possible pour faire qch; **I know it f. well,** je le sais bien *ou* parfaitement;
(b) (*right*) **lying f. in the sun,** couché en plein (au) soleil; **f. in the centre,** en plein (dans le) centre; **hit f. in the face,** atteint en pleine figure.

full² *vt Tex* fouler (*l'étoffe*).

fullback ['fʊlbæk] *n Sp* arrière *m*.

full-blooded ['fʊl'blʌdɪd] *adj* **(a)** de race pure; (*cheval*) de sang, pur-sang *inv*; **f.-b. Indians,** Indiens de race pure; **(b)** (*vigorous*) vigoureux; **(c)** (*fiery*) (*tempérament*) sanguin.

full-blown ['fʊl'bləʊn] *adj* **(a)** (*rose etc*) épanoui, en pleine fleur; **(b)** *Fig* (*doctor*) qualifié; **she is a f.-b. lawyer,** elle a (obtenu) tous ses diplômes; **to have f.-b. AIDS,** avoir le sida (à son stade symptomatique).

full-bodied ['fʊl'bɒdɪd] *adj* **(a)** (*vin*) corsé, qui a du corps; **(b)** (*person*) replet, corpulent.

fullbred ['fʊl'bred] *adj* de race pure.

full-cream ['fʊlkriːm] *adj* **f.-c. milk,** lait entier.

full-dress ['fʊl'dres] *adj* (*tenue*) de cérémonie, de parade; *Mil Nau* **f.-d. uniform,** tenue numéro un; *F* **f.-d. debate,** débat solennel.

fuller ['fʊlər] *n Tex* fouleur, -euse; **f.'s earth,** terre *f* à foulon; **f.'s teasel,** (*plant*) cardère *f* à foulon.

full-faced ['fʊl'feɪst] *adj* **(a)** (*person*) à la figure ronde, au visage plein; **(b)** (*portrait*) de face.

full-fledged ['fʊl'fledʒd] *adj* = **FULLY-FLEDGED**.

full-frontal ['fʊl'frʌnt(ə)l] *adj F* **f.-f. nudity,** de nudité vue de face.

full-grown ['fʊl'grəʊn] *adj* (*arbre*) qui a atteint son développement complet; (*person*) adulte.

fulling ['fʊlɪŋ] *n Tex* foulage *m*.

full-length ['fʊl'leŋθ] *adj* (*portrait*) en pied; (*miroir*) qui permet de se voir en pied; (*fenêtre*) qui occupe toute la hauteur du plafond au sol; (*robe de soirée*) long; **f.-l. film,** long métrage.

ful(l)ness ['fʊlnɪs] *n* **(a)** état plein (*d'un récipient*); **out of the f. of his heart,** comme son cœur débordait; **(b)** plénitude *f*, perfection *f*, totalité *f* (*de la force etc*); **in the f. of time,** avec le temps; **(c)** ampleur *f* (*d'un vêtement, d'un compte rendu etc*); abondance *f* (*de détail*); rondeur *f* (*de la forme*); richesse *f* (*du style etc*).

full-page ['fʊl'peɪdʒ] *adj* (*illustration*) hors texte; (*réclame*) d'une page entière.

full-scale ['fʊl'skeɪl] *adj* **(a)** = **FULL-SIZE(D)**; **(b)** (*reform*) complet, intégral; (*attack*) de grande envergure; **f.-s. panic,** panique totale.

full-size(d) ['fʊl'saɪz, -aɪzd] *adj* (*dessin etc*) grandeur nature; *Ind* à la dimension exacte; **a f.-s. model,** un modèle grandeur nature.

full-time ['fʊl'taɪm] **1** *adv* **to work f.-t.,** travailler à plein temps *ou* à temps complet. **2** *adj* (*work, employee*) à temps complet, à plein temps; *Fig* **looking after the baby is a f.-t. job,** s'occuper du bébé ne laisse pas une minute de libre.

fully ['fʊlɪ] *adv* **(a)** pleinement, entièrement; **to be f. satisfied,** être pleinement satisfait; **f. paid,** payé intégralement; **capital f. paid (up),** capital entièrement versé; **f. paid-up policy,** = police dont les primes sont à jour; **f. paid-up member,** membre qui s'est totalement acquitté de sa contribution; **to treat a subject f.,** traiter un sujet à fond; **I will write you more f.,** je vous écrirai plus longuement; **(b)** (*at least*) **it takes f. two hours,** cela prend bien *ou* au moins deux heures.

fully-fashioned ['fʊlɪ'fæʃənd] *adj* (*stockings, sweater*) bien ajusté.

fully-fledged ['fʊlɪ'fledʒd] *adj* (*bird*) qui a toutes ses plumes; *F* (*doctor etc*) qualifié; **now you're a f.-f. actor!,** maintenant tu es un acteur pour de bon!

fulmar ['fʊlmər] *n* (*bird*) pétrel glacial.

fulminate ['fʌlmɪneɪt] *vi* fulminer (**against,** contre).

fulmination [fʌlmɪ'neɪʃən] *n* fulmination *f*.

fulsome ['fʊlsəm] *adj* (*praise etc*) excessif; **f. flattery,** flagornerie *f*, adulation *f*.

fulsomely ['fʊlsəmlɪ] *adv* à l'excès.

fumarole ['fjuːmərəʊl] *n Geol* fumerolle *f*.

fumble ['fʌmb(ə)l] **1** *vi* (*in enclosed space*) fouiller (au hasard); (*on floor, in dark etc*) tâtonner; **to f. in a dark room for sth,** chercher qch à tâtons dans une pièce obscure; **to f. for words,** chercher ses mots; **to f. with sth,** manier qch maladroitement. **2** *vt* manier (*qch*) maladroitement; *Sp* **to f. the ball,** mal attraper la balle.

fumbling ['fʌmblɪŋ] **1** *adj* maladroit, gauche. **2** *n* (*with keys etc*) maniement maladroit; (*in drawer etc*) tâtonnement *m*.

fume¹ [fjuːm] *n* (*vapour*) vapeur *f*; (*gas*) gaz *m*; **petrol fumes,** vapeurs d'essence; *Aut* **exhaust fumes,** gaz d'échappement.

fume² **1** *vi* fumer, émettre de la fumée *ou* des vapeurs; *Fig* rager; fumer (**with rage,** de colère); **I was fuming,** j'étais exaspéré (**at,** de). **2** *vt* exposer (*qch*) à la fumée; **fumed oak,** chêne patiné.

fumigate ['fjuːmɪgeɪt] *vt* fumiger (*qch*); désinfecter (*un appartement etc*) par fumigation.

fumigation [fjuːmɪ'geɪʃən] *n* fumigation *f*; désinfection *f* (*d'une chambre*).

fumigator ['fjuːmɪgeɪtər] *n* **(a)** (*person*) fumigateur *m*; **(b)** (*device*) appareil *m* fumigatoire.

fumitory ['fjuːmɪtərɪ] *n* (*plant*) fumeterre *f*.

fun [fʌn] *n* amusement *m*, gaieté *f*; (*joking*) plaisanterie *f*; **to make f. of** *or* **poke f. at s.o./sth,** se moquer de qn/qch, rire de qn/qch; **a figure** *or* **object of f.,** un objet de plaisanterie; **to say sth in f.,** dire qch en plaisantant; **for f., in f.,** (*as a joke*) par plaisanterie; (*for enjoyment*) pour se distraire; **I did it for the f. of the thing** *or* **of it,** (*for amusement*) je l'ai fait histoire de rire; (*for enjoyment*) je l'ai fait pour le plaisir; **they beat up prisoners for the f. of it,** ils tabassent les prisonniers pour le plaisir; **he is great f.** *or* **full of f.,** il est très drôle; **she's f. to be with,** on s'amuse avec elle; **it was great f.,** c'était très amusant; **it wasn't much f. walking home in the rain,** rentrer à pied sous la pluie n'avait rien d'une partie de plaisir; **to have f.,** s'amuser, se divertir; *F* **a f. party,** une soirée où l'on s'amuse bien; **we had lots of f. and games,** on s'est bien amusé; *Iron* on a eu bien des ennuis; **I don't want to spoil your f.,** je ne veux pas vous empêcher de vous amuser; **to join in the f.,** s'amuser avec tout le monde; **that's when the f. began,** c'est là que ça a commencé à barder; **all the f. of the fair,** toutes les attractions de la foire; **what f.!,** comme c'est amusant!; *Iron* très amusant!; **f. fur,** fourrure *f* synthétique; **a f.-packed** *or* **-filled holiday,** des vacances pendant lesquelles on n'a pas le temps de s'ennuyer; **f. run,** = course organisée au profit d'une œuvre de bienfaisance.

function¹ ['fʌŋkʃən] *n* **(a)** (*of body, machine*) fonction *f*; **vital functions,** fonctions vitales; **the spring performs the f. of a shock absorber,** le ressort joue le rôle d'(un) amortisseur; *Comptr* **f. key,** touche *f* de fonction; **(b)** (*of person*) fonction *f*, charge *f*; **in his f. as a magistrate,** en sa qualité de magistrat; **he combines the functions of servant and gardener,** il tient le double emploi de domestique et de jardinier; **to discharge one's functions,**

s'acquitter de ses fonctions; **(c)** *(occasion) (reception)* réception *f*, réunion *f*; *(public ceremony)* cérémonie *f* publique; **society f.**, réception mondaine; **(d)** *Math etc* fonction *f*; **the resistance is a f. of the pressure,** la résistance est fonction de la pression.

function² *vi (operate, work)* fonctionner; **to f. as sth,** *(fill a role)* faire fonction de qch.

functional ['fʌŋkʃən(ə)l] *adj* **(a)** *(mobilier etc)* fonctionnel, utilitaire; **f. illiterate,** = personne dont l'analphabétisme l'empêche de faire face aux situations courantes; **(b)** *Math* fonctionnel.

functionally ['fʌŋkʃən(ə)lɪ] *adv* **to be f. illiterate,** = être analphabète au point de ne pas pouvoir faire face aux situations courantes.

functionary ['fʌŋkʃənərɪ] *n Pej* fonctionnaire *m*.

functioning ['fʌŋkʃənɪŋ] *n (of machine etc)* fonctionnement *m*.

fund¹ [fʌnd] *n* **(a)** *Fin etc* fonds *m*, caisse *f*; **International Monetary F.,** Fonds monétaire international; **old-age pension f., retirement f.,** caisse de retraite pour la vieillesse; **fighting f.,** caisse de défense *(d'un syndicat etc)*; **strike f.,** *(of union)* caisse à utiliser en cas de grève; **slush f.,** caisse noire; **to start a f.,** lancer une souscription; **(b) funds,** fonds *mpl*, ressources *fpl* pécuniaires; *(of government)* les fonds publics; **to be in funds,** être en fonds; **funds are low,** les fonds sont bas; *Banking* **'no funds',** 'défaut de provision,' 'manque de fonds'; *Admin* **to buy funds,** acheter de la rente; **f.-holder,** rentier, -ière; **(c)** *(supply)* fonds *m*, capacité *f (d'esprit)*; **unfailing f. of humour,** des ressources d'humour intarissables; **she had an enormous f. of anecdotes,** elle avait un énorme stock d'anecdotes.

fund² *vt Fin* **(a)** financer *(un projet)*; pourvoir *(une société etc)* de fonds; **(b)** consolider *(une dette publique)*; **(c) to f. money,** placer de l'argent dans les fonds publics.

fundamental [fʌndə'ment(ə)l] **1** *adj* **(a)** fondamental, -aux, essentiel; *(question)* principal, de fond; **of f. importance,** d'une importance capitale; **(b)** *(colour etc)* primitif; **(c)** *Mus* **f. note,** note fondamentale. **2** *n* **(a) fundamentals,** principe(s) *m(pl)*; notions fondamentales, fondements *mpl (d'une science etc)*; partie essentielle *(d'un système etc)*; **fundamentals of arithmetic,** notions fondamentales d'arithmétique; **to reach agreement on fundamentals,** réaliser un accord sur les points essentiels; **(b)** *Mus* son fondamental.

fundamentalism [fʌndə'mentəlɪzəm] *n Rel* intégrisme *m*.

fundamentalist [fʌndə'mentəlɪst] *n Rel* intégriste *mf*.

fundamentally [fʌndə'mentəlɪ] *adv* fondamentalement.

funded ['fʌndɪd] *adj (biens)* en rentes; **f. capital,** capitaux investis; **f. debt,** dette consolidée.

funding ['fʌndɪŋ] *n* **(a)** *(for project)* financement *m*; **(b)** consolidation *f (d'une dette)*; assiette *f (d'une rente)*.

fund-raiser ['fʌndreɪzər] *n* **(a)** *(professional)* = personne employée par une œuvre de bienfaisance pour amasser des fonds; **(b)** *(event)* = match ou concert etc au profit d'une œuvre de bienfaisance.

fund-raising ['fʌndreɪzɪŋ] **1** *n* collecte *f* de fonds pour une œuvre de bienfaisance. **2** *adj* **f.-r. scheme,** projet *m (d'un hôpital etc)* pour se procurer des fonds.

funeral ['fju:nərəl] *n* funérailles *fpl*, obsèques *fpl*; *(burial)* enterrement *m*; **to attend s.o.'s f.,** assister à l'enterrement de qn; *F* **that's your f.!,** ça c'est votre problème!; **f. ceremony,** cérémonie *f* funèbre; **f. director,** entrepreneur *m* de pompes funèbres; **f. parlour** *or US* **home,** établissement *m* de pompes funèbres; **f. procession,** convoi *m* (funèbre); **f. service,** office *m* des morts.

funereal [fju:'nɪərɪəl] *adj F* lugubre, funèbre, triste; *(voice)* lugubre, sépulcral, -aux; *(pace)* lent; **to proceed at a f. pace,** avancer à un pas d'enterrement.

funfair ['fʌn'feər] *n (travelling)* fête foraine, foire *f*; *(fixed)* parc *m* d'attractions.

fungicide ['fʌndʒɪsaɪd] *n* fongicide *m*.

fungoid ['fʌŋgɔɪd] *adj* **(a)** *Bot* fongoïde; **(b)** *Med* fongueux.

fungous ['fʌŋgəs] *adj* fongueux.

fungus, *pl* **-uses, -i** ['fʌŋgəs, -əsɪz, -gaɪ, -dʒaɪ] *n* **(a)** champignon *m*; **edible/poisonous f.,** champignon comestible/vénéneux; **(b)** *Med* fongus *m*.

funicular [fju:'nɪkjʊlər] **1** *adj (railway)* funiculaire. **2** *n* funiculaire *m*.

funk¹ [fʌŋk] *n Old-fashioned esp Br Sl* **(a)** *(fright)* frousse *f*; **to be in a (blue) f.,** avoir une peur bleue, avoir une frousse de tous les diables; **to get into a f.,** caner; *Mil F* **f. hole,** abri *m*, planque *f*; **(b)** *(coward)* froussard, -arde.

funk² *Old-fashioned esp Br Sl* **1** *vt* **to f. sth/doing sth,** avoir peur de qch/de faire qch; **to f. it,** caner, se dégonfler. **2** *vi* caner, se dégonfler.

funk³ *n Mus* funky *m*, funk *m*; **f. band,** groupe *m* funk.

funky ['fʌŋkɪ] *adj* **(a)** *Mus* funky, funk; **(b)** *Old-fashioned esp Br Sl* froussard.

funnel¹ ['fʌn(ə)l] *n* **(a)** entonnoir *m*; *Ind* **(loading) f.,** trémie *f*, hotte *f*; **(b)** *(of locomotive, steamship)* cheminée *f*; **(c)** *(for ventilation)* tuyau *m ou* cheminée *f* d'aération.

funnel² *v* **(-ll-) 1** *vi* **the crowd funnelled into a narrow passage,** la foule s'est engouffrée dans un passage étroit. **2** *vt* canaliser; **complaints are funnelled to the head office,** les réclamations sont canalisées vers le bureau central.

funnily ['fʌnɪlɪ] *adv* **(a)** *(amusingly)* drôlement, comiquement; **(b)** *(curiously)* curieusement; **f. enough ...,** chose curieuse ... .

funniness ['fʌnɪnɪs] *n* **(a)** *(of person)* drôlerie *f*; caractère amusant *ou* comique *(de qch)*; **(b)** *(strangeness)* bizarrerie *f*.

funny ['fʌnɪ] **1** *adj* **(a)** *(amusing)* drôle, comique, amusant; **it was really too f.!, it was too f. for words!,** c'était vraiment trop drôle!, c'était tordant!; **she's a very f. woman,** *(comic, actress)* elle est très drôle; **none of your f. tricks!, don't try to be f.!,** pas de farces!; **the f. thing about it is ...,** le comique de la chose c'est que ...; **f. bone,** le petit Juif *(à l'articulation du coude)*; *Cin* **f. film,** film *m* comique;

(b) *(strange)* curieux, bizarre; **he is a f. person,** c'est un drôle d'homme; **he was f. that way,** il était comme ça; **a f. idea,** une drôle d'idée; **well, that's f.!,** voilà qui est curieux *ou* étrange; **(it's) f. you should say that ...,** c'est drôle que vous disiez cela ...; **it's a f. thing but ...,** c'est drôle, mais ...; **there's something f. about it,** il y a quelque chose de louche dans cette affaire; *F* **no f. business!,** pas de blagues!, pas de bêtises!; **this butter tastes f.,** ce beurre a un drôle de goût; *F* **I came over all f.,** je me suis senti(e) tout(e) drôle; **he went a bit f. in his old age,** il devint un peu bizarre dans sa vieillesse; *Sl* **f. farm,** maison *f* de fous; *F* **f. money,** des sommes mirobolantes *ou* astronomiques; **her paintings sell for f. money,** ses peintures vont chercher des sommes mirobolantes *ou* astronomiques.

2 *npl esp Am* **the funnies,** bandes dessinées, pages *fpl* comiques *(d'un périodique)*.

fur¹ [fɜ:r] *n* **(a)** fourrure *f*; poil *m (de lapin etc)*; **to line a garment with f.,** doubler un vêtement de fourrure; *F* **to make the f. fly,** *(make a scene)* faire une scène violente; *(fight)* se battre avec acharnement; **f. and feather,** *(in hunting)* gibier *m* à poil et à plume; **furs,** peaux *fpl (d'animaux)*; **f. coat,** manteau *m* de fourrure; **f. fabric,** fourrure synthétique; **f. farm,** élevage *m* d'animaux à fourrure; **f.-lined coat,** manteau doublé de fourrure; **f. skins,** pelleterie *f*; **f. trade,** commerce *m* de fourrures, pelleterie; **(b)** *(deposit) (in bottles)* dépôts *mpl*; *(in kettle)* tartre *m*; *Med (on tongue)* enduit *m*; **(c)** *Her* fourrure *f*.

fur² *v* **(-rr-) 1** *vt* entartrer, incruster *(une chaudière etc)*; *Med* charger *(la langue)*. **2** *vi* = **FUR UP**.

►**fur up** *vi (of boiler etc)* s'incruster, s'entartrer; *Med (of tongue)* se charger, s'empâter.

furbish ['fɜ:bɪʃ] *vt* **(a)** *(polish)* fourbir, polir, astiquer *(une pièce de métal)*; **(b)** *(renovate)* remettre à neuf *(des meubles)*; revoir *(son français)*.

furious ['fjʊərɪəs] **1** *adj* furieux; *(look)* furibond; *(battle etc)* acharné, forcené; **to drive at a f. speed,** conduire à une allure folle; **to get f.,** entrer en fureur; **to be f. with s.o.,** être furieux contre qn. **2** *adv* **he was going at it fast and f.,** il y allait frénétiquement.

furiously ['fjʊərɪəslɪ] *adv* furieusement; *(combattre)* avec acharnement, avec furie; *(conduire)* à une allure folle; **the fire was blazing f.,** l'incendie faisait rage.

furl [fɜ:l] **1** *vt* rouler *(un parapluie etc)*; fermer *(un éventail)*; *Nau* serrer, ferler *(une voile)*. **2** *vi (of umbrella)* se rouler.

furlong ['fɜ:lɒŋ] *n (measurement)* furlong *m* (=201 mètres).

furlough ['fɜ:ləʊ] *n Mil etc* congé *m*, permission *f*; **to be/go on f.,** être/aller en permission.

furnace ['fɜ:nɪs] *n* **(a)** fourneau *m*, four *m*; *Fig* fournaise *f*; **this room is like a f.,** cette chambre est une (vraie) fournaise; **(b) (central-heating) f.,** calorifère *m*.

furnish ['fɜ:nɪʃ] *vt* **(a)** meubler *(une maison etc)*; **to f. one's room** *or* **one's home,** se meubler; **(b)** *(provide)* fournir, donner *(des renseignements)*; pourvoir *(les fonds nécessaires)*; produire, alléguer *(des raisons)*; offrir, présenter, fournir *(une occasion)*; **to f. s.o. with sth,** fournir *ou* pourvoir *ou* munir qn de qch.

furnished ['fɜːnɪʃd] *adj* **(a)** (*flat, room*) meublé; **to live in f. rooms,** loger en meublé; **(b)** (*provided*) pourvu, fourni, équipé (**with,** de); **well f. shop,** magasin bien achalandé.

furnisher ['fɜːnɪʃər] *n* **(a)** *Com* (*furniture seller*) marchand *m* d'ameublement; **(b)** (*provider*) fournisseur *m* (**of,** de).

furnishing ['fɜːnɪʃɪŋ] *n* **(a)** action *f* de meubler (*une maison etc*); **f. fabrics,** tissus *mpl* d'ameublement; **(b)** fourniture *f*, provision *f* (*des choses nécessaires etc*); prestation *f* (*de capitaux*); allégation *f* (*d'une raison etc*).

furnishings ['fɜːnɪʃɪŋz] *npl* (*furniture*) ameublement *m* (*d'une maison*); **soft f.,** (*fabrics*) tissus *mpl* d'ameublement; (*carpets and curtains*) tapis *mpl* et rideaux *mpl*.

furniture ['fɜːnɪtʃər] *n* **(a)** meubles *mpl*, mobilier *m* (*d'une maison etc*); **piece of f.,** meuble; **set of dining-room f.,** mobilier *ou* meubles de salle à manger; **f. polish,** encaustique *f* pour les meubles; **f. remover,** déménageur *m*; **f. shop,** magasin *m* d'ameublement; **f. van,** camion *m* de déménagement; **(b)** ferrures *fpl* (*d'une porte, d'un cercueil etc*).

furore [fjʊ'rɔːrɪ] , *US* **furor** ['fjʊərɔːr] *n* (*uproar*) tumulte *m* (**over,** au sujet de); (*enthusiasm*) enthousiasme démesuré; **to create a f.,** (*cause uproar*) provoquer un tumulte; (*be very popular*) faire fureur.

furred [fɜːd] *adj* **(a)** (*animal*) à poil; **(b)** (*boiler etc*) entartré, encrusté; **f. tongue,** langue chargée.

furrier ['fʌrɪər] *n* pelletier, -ière, fourreur *m*.

furriery ['fʌrɪərɪ] *n* pelleterie *f*.

furring ['fɜːrɪŋ] *n* **(a)** incrustation *f* (*d'une chaudière etc*); chargement *m* (*de la langue*); **(b)** (*in boiler etc*) tartre *m*.

furrow[1] ['fʌrəʊ] *n* **(a)** *Agr* **(open) f.,** sillon *m*; *Fig* **to plough a lonely f.,** (*of inventor, reformer etc*) poursuivre seul une idée; (*keep oneself to oneself*) faire bande à part; **(b)** (*on face*) ride profonde, sillon *m*.

furrow[2] *vt* **(a)** creuser des sillons dans (*la terre*); **(b)** rider profondément (*le front etc*); **his brow is furrowed with wrinkles,** des rides profondes lui sillonnent le front.

furrowed ['fʌrəʊd] *adj* (*front, visage*) coupé de rides profondes.

furry ['fɜːrɪ] *adj* **(a)** (*animal*) à poil; (*insecte etc*) velu; (*mousse etc*) qui ressemble à (de) la fourrure; **(b)** (*boiler, kettle*) entartré; **f. tongue,** langue chargée.

further[1] ['fɜːðər] (*comp of* **far**) **1** *adv* **(a)** (*distance*) plus loin (**than,** que); (*extent*) davantage, plus; **to penetrate f. into the country,** pénétrer plus avant dans le pays; **I can go no f.,** je ne peux pas aller plus loin; (*I'm exhausted*) je n'en peux plus; **to move f. away,** s'éloigner; **I didn't question him any f.,** je ne l'ai pas interrogé davantage; **until you hear f.,** jusqu'à nouvel avis; **I've nothing f. to say,** je n'ai rien d'autre à dire; **to go no f. into the matter,** en rester là; **to add water to the wine to make it go f.,** allonger le vin d'eau; **that doesn't get us much f.,** cela ne nous avance pas beaucoup; **f. back,** (*in time*) à une période plus reculée; **f. back than the last century,** antérieurement au siècle dernier;
(b) (*moreover*) d'ailleurs, de plus; **we would f. add that ...,** nous nous permettons d'ajouter en outre que ...;
(c) *Fml* **f. to,** (*following*) suite à.
2 *adj* **(a)** (*of two*) **at the f. end of the room,** à l'autre bout *ou* au fond de la salle; **the f. bank of the river,** la rive opposée de la rivière;
(b) (*additional*) additionnel, supplémentaire; **without f. ado,** (*fuss*) sans plus de cérémonie; (*delay*) sans plus attendre; **upon f. consideration,** après plus ample(s) réflexion(s); **do you have any f. instructions?,** est-ce que vous avez d'autres consignes?; **one or two f. details,** encore un ou deux détails; **without f. loss of time,** sans perdre plus de temps; **to await f. news,** attendre de plus amples nouvelles; *Br* **f. education,** enseignement *m* postscolaire; **f. information,** renseignements complémentaires (**about,** au sujet de); *Com* **f. orders,** commandes ultérieures; nouvelles commandes.

further[2] *vt* avancer (*les intérêts de qn*); seconder (*un dessein*).

furtherance ['fɜːðərəns] *n* avancement *m* (*d'un travail etc*); **for the f.** *or* **in f. of sth,** pour avancer qch.

furthermore [fɜːðə'mɔːr] *adv* en outre, au surplus, de plus, du reste, par ailleurs.

furthermost ['fɜːðəməʊst] *adj* (*endroit etc*) le plus lointain, le plus reculé, le plus éloigné; **to the f. ends of the earth,** jusqu'au bout du monde.

furthest ['fɜːðɪst] (*superl of* **far**) **1** *adv* **he went f.,** il est allé le plus loin. **2** *adj* **the f. part of the cave,** la partie la plus reculée de la caverne.

furtive ['fɜːtɪv] *adj* (*manner, person*) sournois, cachottier; (*smile etc*) furtif, dérobé.

furtively ['fɜːtɪvlɪ] *adv* (*see adj*) sournoisement; furtivement.

fury ['fjʊərɪ] *n* **(a)** (*of person*) furie *f*, fureur *f*; déchaînement *m*, violence *f* (*du vent etc*); **to get into a f.,** entrer en fureur, s'emporter; *F* **to work like f.,** travailler avec acharnement; **(b)** *Myth* **the Furies,** les Furies *fpl*.

furze [fɜːz] *n* (*plant*) ajonc *m*.

fuse[1], *US* **fuze** [fjuːz] *n* **(a)** *Mil etc* fusée *f* (*d'obus etc*); (*for bomb*) amorce *f*; **time f.,** fusée à retard(ement); **to set a f.,** régler une fusée; *Fig F* **to have a short f.,** démarrer au quart de tour; **(b)** *Min etc* étoupille *f*, mèche *f*; **safety f.,** cordeau *m* (bickford).

fuse[2], *US* **fuze** *vt* **(a)** *Mil etc* amorcer (*une bombe*); **(b)** *Min etc* étoupiller (*un trou de mine*).

fuse[3] *n El* **(safety) f.,** fusible *m* (de sécurité); *F* plomb *m*; **to blow a f.,** faire sauter un plomb; *Fig F* (*of person*) sortir de ses gonds; **the f. has blown** *or F* **gone,** le plomb a sauté; **f. box,** boîte *f* à fusibles; **f. wire,** fil *m* à fusible.

fuse[4] **1** *vt* **(a)** (*melt*) fondre, mettre en fusion (*un métal etc*); **to f. two pieces together,** réunir deux pièces par fusion; **(b)** (*join*) fusionner, amalgamer (*deux partis etc*); **(c)** *El* faire sauter les plombs de (*un circuit*). **2** *vi* **(a)** (*of metals etc*) fondre; **(b)** (*of parties etc*) fusionner, s'amalgamer; **(c)** *El* **the lights have fused,** les plombs ont sauté.

fused [fjuːzd] *adj El* muni d'un fusible.

fusee, *US* **fuzee** [fjuː'ziː] *n* fusée *f* (*d'une montre etc*).

fuselage ['fjuːzəlɑːʒ] *n Av* fuselage *m*.

fusilier [fjuːzɪ'lɪər] *n Mil* fusilier *m*.

fusillade [fjuːzɪ'leɪd] *n Mil* fusillade *f*.

fusion ['fjuːʒən] *n* **(a)** fusion *f*; fonte *f* (*d'un métal*); *Nucl Phys* **controlled f.,** fusion contrôlée; *Mil* **f. bomb,** bombe *f* thermonucléaire; **(b)** (*amalgamation*) fusionnement *m* (*de plusieurs banques etc*); *Pol* fusion *f* (*de deux partis etc*).

fuss[1] [fʌs] *n* **(a)** (*exaggeration*) histoires *fpl*; **what's all the f. about?,** qu'est-ce que c'est que toutes ces histoires?; (*what's wrong*) qu'est-ce qui cloche?; **without any f.,** sans bruit; **a lot of f. about nothing,** beaucoup de bruit pour rien; **to make** *or F* **kick up a f.,** (*complain loudly*) faire un tas d'histoires; **(b)** (*excessive attention etc*) façons *fpl*; **a great f.,** bien des cérémonies; **without (any) f.,** sans cérémonies; **don't make such a f. about it,** ne faites pas tant d'embarras *ou* d'histoires; **to make a f. of s.o.,** être aux petits soins pour qn; (*talk about with excessive admiration*) mettre qn en avant, faire grand cas de qn; **he likes to be made a f. of,** (*of person*) il aime qu'on fasse grand cas de lui; (*of dog*) il aime qu'on le caresse.

fuss[2] **1** *vi* faire des embarras *ou* des histoires; **stop fussing!,** arrête de faire des histoires!; **she never stops fussing with her hair,** elle ne cesse pas d'arranger nerveusement ses cheveux. **2** *vt* tracasser, agiter (*qn*); *F* **I'm not fussed,** ça ne me fait rien.

▶**fuss about, fuss around** *vi* (*be busy*) s'affairer.

▶**fuss over** *vipo* (*pay excessive attention to*) être aux petits soins pour (*qn*).

fussily ['fʌsɪlɪ] *adv* **(a)** en faisant des embarras; d'une manière tatillonne; (*self-importantly*) d'un air important; **(b) f. dressed,** vêtu avec trop de recherche.

fussiness ['fʌsɪnɪs] *n* **(a)** (*of person*) (*behaviour*) tendance *f* à faire beaucoup d'embarras; (*character*) esprit tracassier; **(b)** (*of dress, decor etc*) manque *m* de simplicité.

fusspot ['fʌspɒt] *n Br F* (*about food, cleanliness etc*) chichiteux, -euse; (*finicky person*) tatillon, -onne; (*worrier*) tracassier, -ière.

fussy ['fʌsɪ] *adj* **(a)** (*person*) tracassier, méticuleux; (*finicky*) tatillon, -onne; **to be f.,** faire des difficultés à propos de rien, *F* faire des embarras; **I'm not f.,** je ne suis pas difficile; (*I don't mind*) cela m'est égal; **to be f. about one's food,** être difficile sur la nourriture; **I'm very f. about what I eat,** je suis très difficile sur la nourriture; **(b)** (*dress*) trop pomponné; (*style*) qui manque de simplicité.

fustian ['fʌstɪən] *n Tex* futaine *f*; *Fig* (*pompousness*) grandiloquence *f*, emphase *f*.

fustiness ['fʌstɪnɪs] *n* **(a)** (*smell*) odeur *f* de renfermé *ou* de moisi; **(b)** *Fig* caractère démodé (*d'une théorie*).

fusty ['fʌstɪ] *adj* **(a)** (*pain*) qui sent le moisi; (*maison, vêtement*) qui sent le renfermé; (*odeur*) de renfermé; **(b)** *Fig* (*ideas etc*) suranné, démodé.

futile ['fjuːtaɪl] *adj* **(a)** (*vain*) vain; **f. attempt,** vaine tentative; **it's f., give up,** c'est inutile, laisse tomber; **(b)** (*prétexte etc*) puéril, futile; **f. ideas,** idées creuses.

futility [fjuː'tɪlɪtɪ] *n* futilité *f*; impuissance *f* (*des efforts de qn*).

futon [fuː'tɒn] *n* futon *m*.

future ['fjuːtʃər] **1** *adj* futur; (*events*) à venir; **my f. wife,**

ma future épouse; **at some f. date,** dans l'avenir; *Com* **goods for f. delivery,** marchandises livrables ultérieurement; *Fin* **to sell for f. delivery,** vendre livrable à terme; *Gram* **f. tense,** temps futur.

2 *n* **(a)** avenir *m*; **in (the) f., for the f.,** à l'avenir; **in the near f.,** dans un proche avenir, sous peu; **in the distant f.,** dans un avenir lointain; **to think of the f.,** songer à l'avenir; **the public transport of the f.,** les transports en commun de l'avenir; **you're looking at the f.,** (*when you look at this car/computer/etc*) voilà la voiture/l'ordinateur/*etc* de demain *ou* de l'avenir;

(b) avenir *m* (*de qn*); **job with a (good) f.,** situation d'avenir; **to ruin one's f.,** briser son avenir; **she has a brilliant f. (before her),** elle a devant elle un bel avenir;

(c) *Fin St Exch* **futures,** opérations *fpl* à terme; **futures market,** marché *m* à terme;

(d) *Gram* (temps *m*) futur *m*; **f. perfect,** futur antérieur; **verb in the f.,** verbe au futur.

futurism ['fjuːtʃərɪz(ə)m] *n Art* futurisme *m*.

futurist ['fjuːtʃərɪst] *n Art* futuriste *mf*.

futuristic ['fjuːtʃə'rɪstɪk] *adj Art* futuriste.

futurologist [fjuːtʃə'rɒlədʒɪst] *n* futurologue *m*.

futurology [fjuːtʃə'rɒlədʒɪ] *n* futurologie *f*.

fuze [fjuːz] *n & vt US* = **FUSE**[1,2].

fuzee [fjuː'ziː] *n US* = **FUSEE**.

fuzz[1] [fʌz] *n* **(a)** (*on blankets etc*) peluches *fpl*, bourre *f*; **(b)** (*on peach*) duvet *m*.

fuzz[2] *n Sl* (*police officer*) flic *m*; **the f.,** (*the police*) les flics.

fuzziness ['fʌzɪnɪs] *n* **(a)** manque *m* de netteté (*d'un contour*); *Art Phot* flou *m* (*d'un cliché etc*); **(b)** crêpelure *f* (*des cheveux*); aspect duveté.

fuzzy ['fʌzɪ] *adj* **(a)** (*outline etc*) sans netteté; (*enregistrement*) qui manque de netteté; *Art Phot* flou; **everything looks f. to me,** j'ai une vue confuse de tout; **(b)** (*hair*) crêpu; (*softer*) duveté; (*cloth etc*) floconneux.

fwd *abbr* **forward**.

G

G, g [dʒiː] *n* **(a)** (la lettre) G, g *m*; **(b)** *Mus* sol *m*; **G clef,** clef *f* de sol; **in G minor,** en sol mineur; **(c) G-string,** *Mus* corde *f* de sol; (*of stripper*) cache-sexe *m inv*; **(d)** *US* = mille dollars; **G-man,** agent *m* de la police fédérale; **(e) G-suit,** combinaison spatiale; **(f)** *Phys* **G,** conductance *f*; **(g)** *Cin* **G.,** visible par tous.
g (*abbr* **gramme**) gr..
Ga *abbr* **Georgia.**
gab¹ [gæb] *n F* bagou(t) *m*; **to have the gift of the g.,** avoir du bagou(t).
gab² *vi* (**-bb-**) *F Pej* (*chat*) bavarder; (*gossip*) caqueter, jaser.
gabardine [gæbə'diːn, 'gæbədiːn] *n* gabardine *f*.
gabble¹ ['gæb(ə)l] *n* bredouillement *m* (*de paroles prononcées trop vite*).
gabble² **1** *vi* bredouiller, manger ses mots. **2** *vt* débiter (*un discours*) à toute vitesse.
▶gabble away *vi* baragouiner; **two foreigners were gabbling away to each other,** deux étrangers baragouinaient dans leur langue.
▶gabble out *vtsep* = **GABBLE² 2.**
gaberdine [gæbə'diːn, 'gæbədiːn] *n* garbardine *f*.
gable ['geɪb(ə)l] *n Archit Constr* **g. (end),** pignon *m*; **g. roof,** comble *m* sur pignon(s); **g. window,** faîtière *f*.
gabled ['geɪb(ə)ld] *adj* (*house*) à pignon(s); (*wall*) en pignon; (*roof*) sur pignon(s).
Gabon ['gæbən] *n* le Gabon.
Gabonese [gæbə'niːz] **1** *adj* gabonais. **2** *n* Gabonais, -aise.
▶gad about [gæd] *vi* courir le monde; **he spent a year gadding about Europe,** il a passé un an à s'amuser dans toute l'Europe; **she's been out gadding about (town) all night,** elle a passé toute la nuit à faire la fête (en ville).
gadfly ['gædflaɪ] *n* (*insect*) taon *m*; *Fig* casse-pieds *mf inv*.
gadget ['gædʒɪt] *n* gadget *m*; *F* chose *m*, machin *m*; **it's just another g.,** c'est un gadget de plus.
gadgetry ['gædʒɪtrɪ] *n* gadgets *mpl*.
Gaelic ['geɪlɪk] **1** *adj* gaélique. **2** *n Ling* gaélique *m*.
gaff¹ [gæf] *n* **(a)** *Fishing* gaffe *f*; **(b)** *Nau* corne *f*; **g. topsail,** voile *f* de flèche.
gaff² *vt Fishing* gaffer (*un saumon etc*).
gaff³ *n F* **to blow the g.,** vendre la mèche; **to blow the g. on s.o.,** dénoncer qn, vendre qn.
gaffe [gæf] *n* (*blunder*) gaffe *f*, bourde *f*.
gaffer ['gæfər] *n* **(a)** *Br F* (*foreman*) contremaître *m*, chef *m* d'équipe; (*boss, owner*) le patron, le singe; **(b)** *F* (*old man*) vieux *m*; **(c)** *Cin TV* chef *m* électricien.
gag¹ [gæg] *n* **(a)** (*on mouth*) bâillon *m*; *Surg* ouvre-bouche *m inv*; *Fig* **the law was used as a g. on the freedom of the press,** la loi bâillonnait la presse; **(b)** *Parl* clôture *f* (*des débats*); **(c)** *Th Cin F* (*joke*) blague *f*; (*visual*) gag *m*; **to do sth for a g.,** faire qch pour rire *ou* pour s'amuser.
gag² *v* (**-gg-**) **1** *vt* **(a)** (*tie a gag on*) bâillonner (*qn, la presse*); **(b)** *Parl* clôturer (*un débat*). **2** *vi* **(a)** *Th Cin F* faire des gags; **(b)** *F* (*retch*) avoir des haut-le-cœur.
gaga ['gɑːgɑː] *adj F* gaga *inv*, gâteux; **to go g.,** devenir gaga *ou* gâteux.
gage¹ [geɪdʒ] *n* gage *m*, garantie *f*.
gage² *n & vt* = **GAUGE¹·².**
gage³ *n* = **GREENGAGE.**
gagging ['gægɪŋ] *n* **(a)** (*of person*) bâillonnement *m*; **(b)** *Parl* clôture *f* (*d'un débat*); **(c)** *Th Cin* (*jokes*) blagues *fpl*; (*visual*) gags *mpl*; improvisations *fpl* comiques (*dans un rôle*); **(d)** (*retching*) haut-le-cœur *m*.
gaggle¹ ['gæg(ə)l] *n* troupeau *m* (*d'oies*); *Fig* **a g. of young schoolgirls,** un troupeau de jeunes élèves.
gaggle² *vi* (*of goose*) cacarder.
gagman ['gægmən] *n Am Cin Th* auteur *m* de gags, gagman *m*, *pl* gagmen.
gaiety ['geɪətɪ] *n* **(a)** (*cheerfulness*) gaieté *f*; **(b)** (*festivities*) (*usu pl*) **gaieties,** amusement *m*, réjouissances *fpl*.
gaily ['geɪlɪ] *adv* **(a)** (*happily*) gaiement, allègrement; **(b)** (*brightly*) de couleurs gaies; **g. coloured,** aux couleurs vives.
gain¹ [geɪn] *n* **(a)** (*profit*) gain *m*, profit *m*, avantage *m*; **eager for g.,** âpre au gain; **my g. is your loss,** le profit de l'un est le dommage de l'autre; **(b)** (*increase*) augmentation *f*; hausse *f* (*de valeur*); **g. in weight,** accroissement *m* de poids; **there has been a net g. in their income,** leurs revenus ont été nettement augmentés; **(c)** *Electron* gain *m*.
gain² **1** *vt* **(a)** (*acquire*) acquérir (*une réputation*); obtenir (*des renseignements*); s'acquérir (*la sympathie*); **you will g. nothing by it,** vous n'y gagnerez rien; **to g. permission,** obtenir une permission; **we have lost a daughter but gained a son,** nous avons perdu une fille mais gagné un fils; **to g. s.o.'s affection,** gagner l'affection de qn; **to g. experience,** acquérir de l'expérience;

(b) (*acquire more of*) gagner, prendre; gagner (*du temps*); (re)prendre (*des forces*); **to g. weight,** prendre du poids; **to g. popularity,** gagner de la popularité; **he has gained prestige through this action,** cette action a rehaussé son prestige; **the party has gained support,** le parti a gagné des voix; **to g. ground,** (*of racer, pursuer*) gagner du terrain (**on,** sur); (*of a custom*) se répandre, se développer;

(c) (*win*) **to g. a victory,** remporter une victoire; **they gained two points,** ils ont gagné deux points; **to g. the upper hand,** prendre le dessus;

(d) (*of clock*) **to g. five minutes a day,** avancer de cinq minutes par jour.

2 *vi* **(a)** (*benefit*) bénéficier (de), être aidé (par); **we have gained by having her in the team,** cela nous a aidés de la compter dans l'équipe; **I had a good teacher and I think I gained by that,** j'ai eu un bon professeur et je crois que ça m'a servi;

(b) (*increase*) **to g. in popularity/experience,** gagner en popularité/acquérir de l'expérience;

(c) (*of clock*) prendre de l'avance;

(d) (*of racer, pursuer*) gagner du terrain; **they're gaining!,** ils gagnent du terrain!
▶gain on *vipo* (*of racer, pursuer*) gagner du terrain sur (*un adversaire, un concurrent*); **to g. on a competitor,** gagner du terrain.
gainful ['geɪnfʊl] *adj* profitable, rémunérateur, -trice; (*emploi*) rémunéré.
gainfully ['geɪnfʊlɪ] *adv* **g. employed,** actif.
gainsay [geɪn'seɪ] *vt* (*pp & pt* **gainsaid** [geɪn'sed]) *usu Lit* contredire, démentir (*qn, qch*).
gait [geɪt] *n* allure *f*, démarche *f*; (*of horse*) train *m*; **unsteady g.,** pas mal assuré.
gaiter ['geɪtər] *n* guêtre *f*.
gal [gæl] *n F* girl *f*.
gala ['gɑːlə] *n* gala *m*; **swimming g.,** grand concours de natation; **in g. dress,** en habit de gala; **g. evening,** soirée *f* de gala; **g. performance,** représentation *f* de gala.
galactic [gə'læktɪk] *adj Astron* (*pôle etc*) galactique.
Galahad ['gæləhæd] *n Myth* **Sir G.,** Galaad *m*; *Fig* personne noble et généreuse, seigneur *m*.
Galapagos [gə'læpəgəs] *n* **the G. (Islands),** les îles *fpl* Galapagos.
galaxy ['gæləksɪ] *n* **(a)** *Astron* galaxie *f*; **the G.,** la Voie Lactée; **(b)** *Fig* brillante assemblée (*de femmes*); constellation *f* (*d'hommes illustres etc*); **a g. of stars,** une flopée de stars.
gale [geɪl] *n* grand (coup de) vent, vent fort; **the roof was blown off in a g.,** un grand coup de vent a emporté le toit; **it's blowing a g.,** le vent souffle en tempête; **there were gales of laughter from the dining room,** il y avait de grands éclats de rire dans la salle à manger; **g. force winds,** vents forts; **g. warning,** avis *m ou* signal *m* de tempête.
galena [gə'liːnə] *n Miner* galène *f*.

Galilean [gælɪ'liːən] *Bible* **1** *adj* galiléen. **2** *n* Galiléen, -éenne.
Galilee ['gælɪliː] *n* Galilée *f*; **the Sea of G.**, la mer *ou* le lac de Galilée.
Galileo [gælɪ'leɪəʊ] *n* Galilée *m*.
gal(l) *abbr* **gallon(s)**.
gall¹ [gɔːl] *n* **(a)** effronterie *f*, culot *m*, toupet *m*; **she had the g. to ...**, elle a eu le culot *ou* le toupet de ...; **(b)** *Physiol* fiel *m*, bile *f* (*d'animal*); **g. bladder**, vésicule *f* biliaire.
gall² *n Bot* galle *f*, cécidie *f*; **g. nut**, noix *f* de galle; **g. wasp**, cynips *m*.
gall³ *n* **(a)** écorchure *f*, excoriation *f* (*causée par le frottement*); **(b)** *Fig* humiliation *f*; blessure *f* (*faite à l'amour-propre*).
gall⁴ *vt* **(a)** (*make sore*) écorcher (*par le frottement*), excorier; **(b)** *Fig* (*annoy*) irriter (*qn*).
gallant ['gælənt] *adj* **(a)** (*brave*) brave, vaillant; **the ship and her g. crew**, le navire et son valeureux équipage; **g. deed**, acte *m* de bravoure; **(b)** (*horse etc*) noble; **(c)** [gə'lænt] (*with women*) galant.
gallantly *adv* **(a)** ['gæləntlɪ] (*bravely*) bravement, vaillamment; **(b)** [gə'læntlɪ, 'gæləntlɪ] (*with women*) en homme galant.
gallantry ['gæləntrɪ] *n* **(a)** (*bravery*) vaillance *f*, valeur *f*, bravoure *f*; **a medal for g.**, une médaille de bravoure; **(b)** (*with women*) galanterie *f*.
galleon ['gælɪən] *n Nau Hist* galion *m*.
gallery ['gælərɪ] *n* **(a)** galerie *f* (*d'une salle etc*); **strangers'** *or* **public g.**, (*in Houses of Parliament*) tribune *f* du public; **press g.**, tribune de la presse; *Th* **the g.**, (*seats*) la (troisième) galerie; *F* le paradis; **to play to the g.**, jouer pour la galerie; **(b) (art) g.**, galerie *f*; (*museum*) musée *m* (d'art); **portrait g.**, galerie *ou* musée de portraits; **(c)** *Min* galerie *f*; **(d) shooting g.**, stand *m* de tir; **(e)** *Am* (*balcony*) balcon *m*; (*veranda*) véranda *f*.
galley ['gælɪ] *n* **(a)** *Nau Arch* galère *f*; (*rowing boat*) yole *f*; **g. slave**, galérien *m*; *Fig* **I'm nothing but a g. slave**, c'est à moi de faire toutes les sales besognes; **(b)** *Nau Av* (*kitchen*) cuisine *f*; **(c)** *Typ* galée *f*; **g. (proof)**, (épreuve *f* en) placard *m*.
Gallic ['gælɪk] *adj* français; *Hist* gaulois.
gallicism ['gælɪsɪz(ə)m] *n Ling* gallicisme *m*.
gallicize ['gælɪsaɪz] **1** *vt* franciser. **2** *vi* se franciser.
galling ['gɔːlɪŋ] *adj* irritant, exaspérant; **it was g. to reflect that ...**, ça me *ou* la *etc* rendait malade de penser que ... .
►gallivant about *F* **1** *vi* (*travel*) **she's always gallivanting about**, elle est toujours en voyage *ou* en visite. **2** *vipo* (*travel around*) **you can't go gallivanting about the country**, tu ne peux pas aller par monts et par vaux.
gallon ['gælən] *n* gallon *m* (= 4 lit. 54; *US* = 3 lit. 78); *Aut* **miles per g.**, = consommation d'essence aux cent kilomètres; *F* **they drink gallons of beer**, ils boivent de la bière à tire-larigot.
gallop¹ ['gæləp] *n* **(a)** (*pace*) galop *m*; **at a g.**, au galop (allongé); **(at) full g.**, au grand galop; **(b)** (*ride*) galopade *f*; **to have** *or* **go for a g.**, faire une galopade.
gallop² *v* (**-p-**) **1** *vi* **(a)** (*of horse*) galoper; (*of horse, rider*) aller au galop; **to g. away** *or* **off**, s'éloigner au galop; *Fig* **to g. through prayers**, réciter les prières au grand galop. **2** *vt* faire galoper (*un cheval*).
galloping ['gæləpɪŋ] *adj* au galop; *Fig* **at a g. pace**, à la vitesse grand V; **g. inflation**, inflation galopante.
Gallo-Roman ['gæləʊ'rəʊmən] *adj* gallo-romain, *pl* gallo-romains.
gallows ['gæləʊz] *npl* (*often with sing verb*) potence *f*, gibet *m*; *F* **g. bird**, gibier *m* de potence; **g. humour**, humour noir.
gallstone ['gɔːlstəʊn] *n Med* calcul *m* biliaire; **to have gallstones**, avoir des calculs.
Gallup ['gæləp] *n* **G. poll**, sondage *m* Gallup.
galore [gə'lɔːr] *adv F* à gogo; **children g.**, une flopée d'enfants; **books g.**, des livres en masse; **money g.**, de l'argent à gogo.
galoshes [gə'lɒʃɪz] *npl* bottes *fpl* en caoutchouc.
galumph [gə'lʌmf] *vi F* galoper lourdement (et avec bruit).
galvanic [gæl'vænɪk] *adj El* galvanique.
galvanism ['gælvənɪz(ə)m] *n El* galvanisme *m*.
galvanization [gælvənaɪ'zeɪʃən] *n* galvanisation *f*.
galvanize ['gælvənaɪz] *vt* galvaniser; *Fig* **to g. s.o./sth into life**, galvaniser qn/qch.
galvanized ['gælvənaɪzd] *adj* **g. iron**, fer galvanisé.
galvanizing ['gælvənaɪzɪŋ] **1** *n* galvanisation *f*. **2** *adj* **g. effect**, effet *m* de galvanisation; **the imminent danger had a g. effect on us**, la confrontation au danger nous a galvanisés.
galvanometer [gælvə'nɒmɪtər] *n* galvanomètre *m*.
Gambia (the) [ðə'gæmbɪə] *n* la Gambie; **the G. (River)**, la Gambie.
gambit ['gæmbɪt] *n Chess* gambit *m*; *Fig* tour *m*; **opening g.**, manœuvre *f* d'approche; **a g. to get their sympathy**, un stratagème pour gagner leur sympathie.
gamble¹ ['gæmb(ə)l] *n* jeu *m* de hasard; (*risk*) affaire *f* où l'on risque fort de perdre; **it's a g. but it may pay off**, c'est un risque *ou* c'est risqué mais ça peut être payant; **pure g.**, pure spéculation, affaire de chance.
gamble² **1** *vi* jouer de l'argent; **I don't g.**, je ne joue pas pour de l'argent; **to g. on a throw of the dice**, miser sur un coup de dé(s); **to g. on the Stock Exchange**, jouer en bourse, spéculer; **to g. on a rise in prices**, jouer à la hausse; **they're gambling on there not being an inspector on the train**, ils misent sur le fait qu'il n'y aura pas de contrôleur dans le train; **she's gambling on getting home by 8 o'clock**, elle compte rentrer avant 8 heures; **Napoleon gambled and lost**, Napoléon a joué et perdu. **2** *vt* **to g. one's money on horses**, jouer aux courses.
►gamble away *vtsep* perdre (*sa fortune etc*) au jeu.
gambler ['gæmblər] *n* joueur, -euse (pour de l'argent); **g. on the Stock Exchange**, spéculateur, -trice.
gambling ['gæmblɪŋ] *n* le jeu, jeux d'argent; **g. on the Stock Exchange**, spéculation *f*; **g. debts**, dettes *fpl* de jeu; *Pej* **g. den** *or* **house** *or US* **joint**, tripot *m*.
gambol¹ ['gæmb(ə)l] *n* gambade *f*, cabriole *f*.
gambol² *vi* (**-ll-**, *US* **-l-**) gambader, cabrioler, faire des gambades.
gambrel ['gæmbrəl] *n Archit* toit *m* en croupe.
game¹ [geɪm] *n* **(a)** jeu *m*; **g. of skill/chance**, jeu d'adresse/de hasard; **card games**, jeux de cartes; **ball g.**, jeu de ballon; *Am Sp* le baseball; *Am Sp* (*individual game*) match *m* de baseball; **outdoor games**, jeux de plein air; **Olympic Games**, Jeux Olympiques; *Br Sch* **games**, sports *mpl*; **games teacher**, professeur d'éducation physique; **he's good at games**, c'est un sportif;

(b) *Fig* **to play the g.**, jouer le jeu, jouer selon les règles; **that's not playing the g.**, ce n'est pas loyal; **to play a dangerous g.**, jouer un jeu dangereux; **to beat s.o. at his own g.**, battre qn avec ses propres armes; **two can play at that g.**, on peut jouer à deux à ce petit jeu-là; *F* **what's his g.?**, où veut-il en venir?; **I know your (little) g.!**, je sais bien où vous voulez en venir!; **so that's your g.!**, voilà donc ce que vous manigancez!; **he's at his old games again**, voilà qu'il refait des siennes; **I've been in this g. a long time**, j'ai été de la partie pendant longtemps; **that's a dirty g. you're playing!**, vous faites là un vilain métier; *Br Sl* **to be on the g.**, (*be a prostitute*) faire le trottoir; **to spoil s.o.'s g.**, déjouer les plans de qn; **the game's up**, l'affaire est à l'eau;

(c) (*individual game*) partie *f* (*de cartes, d'échecs etc*); manche *f* (*d'une partie de cartes*); **how's the g. going?**, comment marche la partie?; (*what is the score?*) où en est la partie?; **anyone for darts/tennis? — I'll give you a g.**, quelqu'un veut faire une partie de fléchettes/de tennis? — oui, moi; **you might get a g.**, (*if someone is absent*) tu pourras peut-être jouer; **we had a good g.**, nous avons bien joué; **he plays a good g. of cards/billiards**, il joue bien aux cartes/au billard; *Tennis* **g., set, and match**, jeu, set et match; *Chess etc* **opening/end g.**, début *m*/fin *f* de partie; *Tennis* **g. point**, balle *f* de jeu;

(d) (*amusement*) divertissement *m*, jeu *m*; *F* **what a g.!**, quelle farce!; **the children were playing a g. of cowboys and indians**, les enfants jouaient aux cowboys et aux indiens; **they were just playing a g., pretending to be angry**, ils faisaient semblant d'être en colère pour jouer *ou* pour plaisanter; **let's stop playing games and come to the point**, trêve de plaisanteries, passons aux choses sérieuses; **politics is just a g. to them**, ils ne prennent pas la politique au sérieux; **it isn't a g.!**, (*it's serious*) ce n'est pas un jeu!;

(e) (*in hunting*) gibier *m*; **big g.**, les grands fauves; **big-g. hunting**, la chasse aux grands fauves; *Fig* **he's fair g.**, c'est une bonne proie; **he regards married women as fair g.**, pour lui, les femmes mariées sont de bonnes proies; **small g.**, menu gibier; **g. birds**, gibier à plumes; **g. licence**, permis *m* de chasse; **g. preserve**, parc *m* à gibier;

(f) *Culin* gibier *m*; **g. pie**, pâté *m* de gibier en croûte.
game² *vi* jouer (de l'argent).
game³ *adj F* courageux, résolu; **a g. little child**, un petit enfant courageux; **to be g.**, (*courageux*) avoir du cran; (*prêt*) être d'attaque; **I'm g.!**, d'accord (j'en suis)!; **he's g.**

for anything, il est toujours partant, *Pej* il est prêt à tout *ou* capable de tout.

game[4] *adj* (*leg*) boiteux, perclus.

gamecock [ˈgeɪmkɒk] *n* coq *m* de combat.

gamekeeper [ˈgeɪmkiːpər] *n* garde-chasse *m*, *pl* gardes-chasse(s); (*in state-owned forest*) garde forestier.

gamely [ˈgeɪmlɪ] *adv* courageusement.

gameness [ˈgeɪmnɪs] *n* courage *m*.

gameshow [ˈgeɪmʃəʊ] *n TV Rad* jeu télévisé *ou* radiophonique.

gamesmanship [ˈgeɪmzmənʃɪp] *n* l'art *m* de gagner (*sans enfreindre les règles du jeu*).

gamete [ˈgæmiːt, gæˈmiːt] *n Biol* gamète *m*.

gaming [ˈgeɪmɪŋ] *n* le jeu; **g. house/table,** maison *f*/table *f* de jeu.

gamma [ˈgæmə] *n* (*in Greek alphabet*) gamma *m*; **g. globulin,** gammaglobuline *f*; **g. rays,** rayons *mpl* gamma.

gamma-ray [ˈgæməreɪ] *adj Med* **g.-r. therapy,** gammathérapie *f*.

gammon [ˈgæmən] *n* quartier *m* (*du porc*); (*meat*) jambon fumé; **g. steak,** tranche épaisse de jambon fumé.

gammy [ˈgæmɪ] *adj F* = **GAME**[4].

gamp [gæmp] *n Br F* parapluie *m*, pépin *m*.

gamut [ˈgæmət] *n* (*of colours*) & *Mus* gamme *f*; *Fig* **this character runs the whole g. of emotions from despair to ecstasy,** ce personnage passe par toute la gamme d'émotions, du désespoir à l'extase.

gander [ˈgændər] *n* **(a)** (*male goose*) jars *m*; **(b)** *Br Sl* (*look*) coup *m* d'œil; **just take a g.!,** mate-moi ça!

gang [gæŋ] *n* (*of criminals*) bande *f*, *F* gang *m*; (*of children*) bande; *Ind* équipe *f*; convoi *m* (*de prisonniers*); **can I join your g.?,** (*of children*) je peux faire partie de votre bande?; **the whole g.,** (*of friends, colleagues*) toute la bande; **g. war(fare),** guerre *f* des gangs; *Pol Hist* **the G. of Four,** la Bande des Quatre.

▶**gang up** *vi F* former un gang; **to g. up with s.o.,** s'allier avec qn; **to g. up on s.o.,** se liguer contre qn.

ganger [ˈgæŋər] *n Br Rail* chef *m* d'équipe.

Ganges (the) [ðəˈgændʒiːz] *n* le Gange.

gangland [ˈgæŋlænd] *n* (*area*) la zone des gangsters (*dans une grande ville*); (*underworld*) le monde criminel, le milieu; **a g. killing,** un règlement de compte (entre gangsters); **g. warfare,** guerre *f* des gangsters.

gangling [ˈgæŋglɪŋ] *adj* dégingandé; **a g. youth,** un jeune dégingandé.

ganglion, -ia [ˈgæŋglɪən, -ɪə] *n Anat* ganglion *m*.

gangplank [ˈgæŋplæŋk] *n Nau* passerelle *f;* (*between two ships*) traversine *f*.

gangrene [ˈgæŋgriːn] *n Med* gangrène *f*, nécrose *f*; **to have g.,** avoir la gangrène.

gangrenous [ˈgæŋgrɪnəs] *adj* gangreneux, gangrené; **to go g.,** (*of wound*) se gangrener.

gangster [ˈgæŋstər] *n* gangster *m*; **g. film,** film *m* de gangsters.

gangsterism [ˈgæŋstərɪz(ə)m] *n* gangstérisme *m*.

gangway [ˈgæŋweɪ] *n* **(a)** (*passage*) passage *m*; couloir central (*d'autobus etc*); **central g.,** allée centrale; **when you set the chairs out leave a g.,** en installant les chaises, laissez un passage; **g. please!,** dégagez, s'il vous plaît!; **(b)** *Nau* (*gangplank*) passerelle *f* de service; (*opening for gangplank*) coupée *f* (*dans la muraille*); *Av* (*for plane*) passerelle; **(c)** (*over mud etc*) passage *m*.

gannet [ˈgænɪt] *n* (*bird*) fou *m* (de Bassan); *Hum Fig* (*person*) goinfre *mf*.

gantry [ˈgæntrɪ] *n* **(a)** *Ind* (*for travelling crane*) pont roulant; (*for rocket*) portique *m* de lancement; *Rail* **signal g.,** portique de signalisation; **g. crane,** grue *f* à portique; **travelling g.,** portique roulant; **(b)** (*for barrel*) chantier *m*.

gaol[1] [dʒeɪl] *n* prison *f*; **six months' g.,** six mois de prison; **to be in g.,** être en prison.

gaol[2] *vt* mettre (*qn*) en prison, écrouer (*qn*).

gaolbird [ˈdʒeɪlbɜːd] *n* (*prisoner*) prisonnier *m*; (*habitual criminal*) récidiviste *m*.

gaolbreak [ˈdʒeɪlbreɪk] *n* évasion *f* de prison.

gaolbreaker [ˈdʒeɪlbreɪkər] *n* évadé *m* de prison.

gaoler [ˈdʒeɪlər] *n* gardien *m* de prison; **his g.,** son gardien.

gap [gæp] *n* **(a)** (*opening*) trou *m*; (*in a hedge etc*) trouée *f*, ouverture *f*, vide *m*; (*in a wall etc*) brèche *f*; (*in a surface*) discontinuité *f*; **to fill (in, up)** *or* **to stop a g.,** boucher *ou* colmater un trou; combler un vide; **gaps between the planks,** des jours entre les planches; **there's a g. in the curtains,** les rideaux bâillent; **the shelling had opened great gaps in the ranks,** le bombardement avait créé des vides dans les rangs; **(b)** (*interval*) écart *m*; distance *f* (*entre deux convois*); (*which shouldn't be there*) interstice *m*; **a g. of 2 cm,** un intervalle de 2 cm; **age g.,** différence *f* d'âge; **there is an age g. between them,** il y a une différence d'âge entre eux; **the g. between us and our competitors has narrowed,** l'écart entre nos concurrents et nous a diminué; **to close a g.,** réduire l'écart; **leave a g. of six inches between the chairs,** laissez un espace de six pouces entre les chaises; **a g. of over twenty years,** un intervalle de plus de vingt ans; *Aut* **spark g.,** intervalle d'allumage; **(c)** (*empty space*) trou *m*, lacune *f*, vide *m* (*dans des souvenirs etc*); **his death leaves a g. in the family circle,** sa mort laisse un vide dans la famille; **there were gaps in his teeth,** il avait les dents écartées; **to fill the gaps in one's education,** combler les lacunes de son éducation; **there is a g. of two years in the records,** il y a un trou de deux ans dans les archives; **there are a lot of gaps in her account of the event,** il y a beaucoup d'omissions dans sa version des événements; **to bridge the g.,** combler le fossé *ou* le déficit; *Com* **g. in the market,** créneau *m*; *Econ* **trade g.,** déficit commercial; **(d)** *Geog* (*in hills, mountains*) trouée *f*; *esp US* col *m*; **(e)** (*in recording*) blanc *m* sonore; (*in recorded tape*) plage *f* de silence; **(f)** *MecE* coupure *f*, rompu *m* (*d'un banc de tour*).

gape[1] [geɪp] *n* bâillement *m*.

gape[2] *vi* **(a)** (*stare*) être *ou* rester bouche bée; **to g. at s.o./sth,** regarder qn/qch bouche bée; **what are you gaping at?,** qu'est-ce que tu regardes bouche bée?; **stop gaping!,** *F* remets-toi!; **(b)** (*open one's mouth*) ouvrir la bouche toute grande; (*yawn*) bâiller (*d'ennui*); **to g. (open),** (*of thing*) s'ouvrir (tout grand); (*of hole*) être béant; (*of seam etc*) bâiller; **these boards g.,** ces planches ne joignent pas.

gaping [ˈgeɪpɪŋ] **1** *adj* (*hole etc*) béant. **2** *n* **(a)** (*staring*) contemplation *f* bouche bée; **(b)** (*opening, yawning*) bâillement *m*.

gap-toothed [ˈgæptuːθt] *adj* aux dents écartées.

garage[1] [ˈgærɑːʒ, -rɪdʒ] *n Aut* garage *m*; **lock-up g.,** box *m*, *pl* boxes; **g. proprietor** *or* **owner,** garagiste *m*; **g. mechanic,** mécanicien *m* de garage, *F* garagiste; *Am* **g. sale,** = brocante *f* chez un particulier.

garage[2] *vt* garer, remiser (*une voiture*).

garageman, *pl* **-men** [ˈgærɑːʒmæn, -rɪdʒ, -men] *n* mécanicien *m* de garage, *F* garagiste *m*.

garb[1] [gɑːb] *n Lit* costume *m*, habit *m*; **in clerical g.,** en habit ecclésiastique.

garb[2] *vt Lit* habiller, vêtir (**in,** de); **garbed all in black,** vêtu tout de noir.

garbage [ˈgɑːbɪdʒ] *n* **(a)** *esp Am* ordures ménagères; **g. heap,** tas *m* d'ordures; **g. can,** poubelle *f*; **g. disposal unit,** broyeur *m* à ordures; **g. man** *or* **collector,** (é)boueur *m*; *Comptr* **g. in, g. out,** mauvaise entrée égale mauvais résultats; **(b)** *Fig* bêtises *fpl*; **he's talking g.,** il dit n'importe quoi.

garble [ˈgɑːb(ə)l] *vt* fausser (*des nouvelles, une citation*); dénaturer (*les faits*); altérer (*un texte*); **garbled account,** compte rendu trompeur *ou* mensonger; **garbled message,** message embrouillé.

garden[1] [ˈgɑːd(ə)n] *n* jardin *m*; **flower g.,** jardin d'agrément; **kitchen g., vegetable g.,** (jardin) potager *m*; **back/front g.,** jardin de derrière/de devant; **market g.,** *Am* **truck g.,** jardin maraîcher; **rock g.,** jardin alpin; **g. of remembrance,** = cimetière *m* d'un crématorium; **botanical g.,** jardin botanique; **zoological gardens,** jardin zoologique; **public garden(s),** jardin public, parc *m*; **beer g.,** = café *m* en plein air; **g. furniture/chair,** meubles *mpl*/chaise *f* de jardin; **g. centre,** jardinerie *f*; *F* **to lead s.o. up the g. path,** duper *ou* faire marcher qn; **g. plants,** plantes *fpl* de jardin; **g. produce,** produits maraîchers; **g. tools,** outils *mpl* de jardinage; **g. party,** réception *f* en plein air, garden-party *f*, *pl* garden-parties; **g. city,** cité-jardin *f*, *pl* cités-jardins; **g. suburb,** = banlieue résidentielle.

garden[2] *vi* jardiner, faire du jardinage.

gardener [ˈgɑːdnər] *n* jardinier *m*; **he's a keen g.,** c'est un adepte du jardinage; **landscape g.,** jardinier paysagiste; **market g.,** *Am* **truck g.,** maraîcher, -ère; **nursery g.,** pépiniériste *mf*.

gardenia [gɑːˈdiːnɪə] *n* (*flower*) gardénia *m*.

gardening [gɑːdnɪŋ] *n* jardinage *m*; **landscape g.,** l'art *m* de dessiner les jardins; **market g.,** *Am* **truck g.,** maraîchage *m*; **g. book,** livre *m* de jardinage; **g. expert,** spécialiste *mf* du jardinage; **g. tools,** outils *mpl* de jardinage.

gargantuan [gɑːˈgæntjʊən] *adj* gargantuesque.

gargle[1] [ˈgɑːg(ə)l] *n Med* gargarisme *m*.

gargle² **1** *vi Med* se gargariser. **2** *vt Med* **to g. one's throat,** se gargariser la gorge.
gargoyle ['gɑːgɔɪl] *n Archit etc* gargouille *f*.
garish ['geərɪʃ] *adj* **(a)** (*clothes, wallpaper etc*) voyant; (*taste*) vulgaire; **(b)** (*light, colour*) cru.
garishness ['geərɪʃnɪs] *n* **(a)** (*of clothes, wallpaper etc*) luxe criard; (*of taste*) vulgarité *f*; **(b)** (*of light, colour*) crudité *f*.
garland¹ ['gɑːlənd] *n* guirlande *f*, couronne *f* (de fleurs).
garland² *vt* enguirlander; **garlanded with flowers,** paré de guirlandes de fleurs.
garlic ['gɑːlɪk] *n* ail *m*, *pl* ails *or* aulx; **clove of g.,** gousse *f* d'ail; **g. bread,** = pain au beurre et à l'ail, servi chaud; **g. sausage,** saucisson *m* à l'ail.
garlicky ['gɑːlɪkɪ] *adj F* qui sent l'ail.
garment ['gɑːmənt] *n* vêtement *m*.
garner ['gɑːnər] *vt* **(a)** (*collect*) recueillir (*des informations*); **(b)** (*store*) stocker (*des renseignements*); *Am & Lit* mettre (*le grain*) en grenier *ou* en grange.
garnet ['gɑːnɪt] *n Miner* grenat *m*; **g. necklace,** collier *m* de grenat.
garnish¹ ['gɑːnɪʃ] *n Culin etc* garniture *f*.
garnish² *vt* garnir, orner, embellir (**with,** de); *Culin* garnir (*un plat*).
garnishee [gɑːnɪ'ʃiː] *n Jur* tiers-saisi *m*, *pl* tiers-saisis; **g. order,** ordonnance *f* de saisie-arrêt.
garnishing ['gɑːnɪʃɪŋ] *n* garnissage *m*; *Culin* garniture *f*.
garret ['gærət] *n* mansarde *f*; **to live in a g.,** habiter sous les combles.
garrison¹ ['gærɪs(ə)n] *n Mil* garnison *f*; **g. duty,** service *m* de place *ou* de garnison; **g. town,** ville *f* de garnison.
garrison² *vt Mil* **(a)** (*station*) mettre (*des troupes*) en garnison; **troops garrisoned at Lille,** troupes *fpl* en garnison à Lille; **(b)** **to g. a town,** (*provide with a garrison*) mettre une garnison dans une ville; (*be stationed in*) être en garnison dans une ville.
garrotte¹, *US* **garrote** [gə'rɒt] *n* **(a)** strangulation *f*; **(b)** (*execution*) supplice *m* du garrot.
garrotte², *US* **garrote** *vt* **(a)** étrangler (*qn*); **(b)** (*execute*) faire subir le supplice du garrot à (*qn*).
garrotting, *US* **garroting** [gə'rɒtɪŋ] *n* **(a)** strangulation *f*; **(b)** (*execution*) supplice *m* du garrot.
garrulity [gæ'ruːlɪtɪ] , **garrulousness** ['gærʊləsnɪs] *n* loquacité *f*.
garrulous ['gærʊləs] *adj* loquace, bavard.
garrulously [gærʊləslɪ] *adv* avec volubilité.
garter ['gɑːtər] *n* jarretière *f*; *Am* (*for stockings*) jarretelle *f*; *Am* (*for socks*) fixe-chaussettes *mpl*; **the Order of the G.,** l'Ordre *m* de la Jarretière; **Knight of the G.,** chevalier *m* de l'Ordre de la Jarretière; *Am* **g. belt,** porte-jarretelles *m inv*; *Knitting* **g. stitch,** point *m* mousse.
gas¹, *pl* **gases** [gæs, 'gæsɪz] *n* **(a)** gaz *m*; **to pay the g. bill** *or* **for the g.,** payer le gaz; **to cook by g.,** faire la cuisine au gaz; *Ind* **the g. industry,** l'industrie *f* du gaz; **laughing g.,** (*anaesthetic*) gaz hilarant; **to have g.,** (*at dentist's*) se faire anesthésier; **marsh g.,** méthane *m*; **natural g.,** gaz naturel; **town g.,** gaz de ville; **g. burner,** bec *m* de gaz; **g. cooker** *or* **stove,** cuisinière *f* à gaz; **g. cylinder,** bouteille *f* de gaz; **g. fire,** radiateur *m* à gaz; **g. fitter,** poseur *m ou* ajusteur *m* d'appareils à gaz; **g. furnace,** fourneau *m* à gaz; **g. holder** *or* **tank,** gazomètre *m*, réservoir *m* à gaz; **g. lamp,** (*in street*) réverbère *m*; **g. lighter,** (*for fire, cooker*) allume-gaz *m inv*; (*for cigarettes etc*) briquet *m* (à gaz); **g. main** *or* **pipe,** tuyau *m* à gaz, conduite *f* de gaz; (*big*) gazoduc *m*; **g. meter,** compteur *m* à gaz; **to read the g. meter,** relever le compteur à gaz; **g. oven,** four *m* à gaz; *Comptr* **g. plasma screen,** écran *m* à plasma; **g. ring,** (*for cooking*) réchaud *m* à gaz (à un feu); (*on a cooker*) brûleur *m* à couronne;
(b) *Mil etc* gaz *m* de combat; **blister g.,** gaz vésicant; **mustard g.,** ypérite *f*; **tear g.,** gaz lacrymogène; **g. attack,** attaque *f* aux gaz; **g. chamber,** chambre *f* à gaz; **g. mask,** masque *m* à gaz; **g. warfare,** guerre *f* chimique;
(c) *Min* grisou *m*;
(d) *Am* (*gasoline*) essence *f*; **to fill up with g.,** faire le plein d'essence; **to step on the g.,** *Aut* (*press on accelerator*) appuyer sur le champignon; (*hurry*) se presser, *F* se grouiller; **a bit more g.!,** un peu plus d'accélération!; *F* **g. guzzler,** voiture *f* qui bouffe de l'essence; **g. station,** station-service, *pl* stations-service; **g. tank,** réservoir *m*;
(e) *F* (*worthless talk*) bavardage *m*, verbiage *m*;
(f) *Am* **what a g.!,** (*situation, activity*) c'est bien rigolo!
gas² *v* (**-ss-**) **1** *vt* asphyxier, intoxiquer (*par un gaz*); (*deliberately*) gazer; **to g. oneself,** s'asphyxier. **2** *vi F* jaser, bavarder.
gasbag ['gæsbæg] *n F* bavard, -arde; (*boaster*) vantard *m*.
Gascony ['gæskənɪ] *n* la Gascogne.
gaseous ['gæsɪəs, 'geɪsɪəs, geɪʃɪəs] *adj* gazeux.
gash¹ [gæʃ] *n* (*on person*) coupure *f*, entaille *f*; (*on face*) balafre *f*; (*in earth's surface etc*) fente *f*; **she had a nasty g. on her leg,** elle avait une vilaine entaille à la jambe; **the explosion had ripped a great g. in the ship's side,** l'explosion avait fait une grande déchirure sur le côté du bateau.
gash² *vt* entailler, couper; balafrer (*le visage*); **to g. one's chin,** se faire une entaille au menton.
gasholder ['gæshəʊldər] *n* réservoir *m* à gaz.
gasification [gæsɪfɪ'keɪʃən] *n* gazéification *f*.
gasify ['gæsɪfaɪ] **1** *vt* gazéifier. **2** *vi* se gazéifier.
gasket ['gæskɪt] *n* **(a)** *MecE* joint *m* d'étanchéité, garniture *f* (*de joint*); **to blow a g.,** *Aut* faire sauter un joint de culasse; *Fig* se mettre en rage, piquer une colère; **(b)** *Nau* raban *m* (*de ferlage*).
gaslight ['gæslaɪt] *n* lumière *f* du gaz; **by g.,** à la lumière du gaz.
gasman, *pl* **-men** ['gæsmæn, -men] *n F* contrôleur *m ou* employé *m* du gaz, gazier *m*.
gasoline ['gæsəliːn] *n Am* essence *f*.
gasometer [gæ'sɒmɪtər] *n* gazomètre *m*, réservoir *m* à gaz.
gasp¹ [gɑːsp] *n* hoquet *m*, sursaut *m* (*de surprise*); **there were gasps of admiration from the audience,** il y a eu des sursauts d'admiration dans le public; **to be at one's last g.,** agoniser, être à l'agonie; *Fig F* être sur le point de rendre son dernier soupir; **to give one's last g.,** rendre le dernier soupir; **to defend sth to the last g.,** défendre qch jusqu'à son dernier souffle.
gasp² **1** *vi* avoir un hoquet (*de surprise*); sursauter (*de terreur*); **to make s.o. g.,** couper le souffle à qn; **to g. for breath** *or* **for air,** haleter, suffoquer; *F* **I'm gasping (for a drink),** je meurs de soif. **2** *vt* dire (*qch*) d'une voix entrecoupée; **she managed to g. her name,** elle a réussi à dire son nom d'une voix entrecoupée.
►**gasp out** *vtsep* = **GASP² 2.**
gassed [gæsd] *adj* atteint par les gaz asphyxiants; (*deliberately*) gazé.
gassing ['gæsɪŋ] *n* **(a)** (*asphyxiation*) asphyxie *f ou* intoxication *f* par les gaz d'éclairage; (*deliberate*) gazage *m*; **(b)** *F* (*talk*) bavardage *m*.
gassy ['gæsɪ] *adj* gazeux; (*wine etc*) mousseux, crémant; *Min* grisouteux.
gastric ['gæstrɪk] *adj* gastrique; **g. ulcer,** ulcère *m* simple de l'estomac; **g. flu,** grippe gastro-intestinale; **g. juice,** suc *m* gastrique.
gastritis [gæs'traɪtɪs] *n Med* gastrite *f*; **to have g.,** faire une gastrite.
gastro-enteritis [gæstrəʊəntə'raɪtɪs] *n Med* gastro-entérite *f*.
gastronome ['gæstrənəʊm] *n* gastronome *m*.
gastronomic(al) [gæstrə'nɒmɪk, -ɪk(ə)l] *adj* gastronomique.
gastronomy [gæs'trɒnəmɪ] *n* gastronomie *f*.
gastropod ['gæstrəʊpɒd] *adj & n* (*mollusc*) gastéropode *m*.
gasworks ['gæswɜːks] *npl* (*usu with sing verb*) usine *f* à gaz.
gate¹ [geɪt] *n* **(a)** (*of castle, city etc*) porte *f*; **the gate(s) of hell,** les portes de l'enfer; **(b)** (*at garden, field etc*) barrière *f*, porte *f* à claire-voie; (*metal*) grille *f* (*d'entrée*); *Ski* porte; *Rail* **level-crossing** *or Am* **grade-crossing g.,** barrière du passage à niveau; *Av* **g. no. 15,** (*in airport*) porte 15; *Sp* **(starting) g.,** starting-gate *m*; **toll g.,** barrière *f* (de péage); **(c)** (*at stadium*) entrée *f*; **to pay at the g.,** payer à l'entrée; *Sp* **the g.,** (*spectators*) le public; (*also* **g. money**) la recette, les entrées; **(d)** *HydE* **(lock) g.,** vanne *f* (d'écluse); **(e)** *Aut* **g. (quadrant),** grille *f* (*de changement de vitesse*); **(f)** *Electron* porte *f*; **(logic) g.,** porte logique.
gate² *vt* **(a)** *Br Univ* **to be gated,** se faire consigner; **(b)** *HydE* vanner (*une écluse*).
gâteau ['gætəʊ] *n* gros gâteau à la crème.
gate-crash ['geɪtkræʃ] *F* **1** *vi* resquiller. **2** *vt* **to g.-c. a party,** entrer dans une soirée sans y être invité.
gate-crasher ['geɪtkræʃər] *n F* resquilleur, -euse.
gate-crashing ['geɪtkræʃɪŋ] *n F* resquillage *m*.
gatehouse ['geɪthaʊs] *n* **(a)** (*of an estate*) loge *f*; **(b)** (*of a castle*) corps-de-garde *m inv*.
gatekeeper ['geɪtkiːpər] *n* **(a)** portier, -ière; **(b)** *Rail* garde-barrière *mf*, *pl* gardes-barrière(s).
gate-leg(ged) ['geɪtleg, -d] *adj* (*table*) à abattants.
gatepost ['geɪtpəʊst] *n* montant *m* (de barrière); *F* **between you and me and the g.,** entre nous soit dit.

gateway ['geɪtweɪ] *n* porte *f*, entrée *f*, passage *m*; **the g. to the Continent,** la porte du Continent.

gather ['gæðər] **1** *vt* **(a)** assembler, rassembler (*des personnes*); rassembler, recueillir (*des choses*); cueillir (*des fleurs*); récolter (*du blé*); recueillir (*des informations*); ramasser (*du bois, des papiers*); faire la cueillette de (*fraises etc*); retrousser (*ses jupes*); (*in bookbinding*) rassembler (*les feuilles d'un livre*); *Horseriding* rassembler (*un cheval*); **to g. the harvest,** rentrer la moisson; **to g. honey from the flowers,** (*of bees*) butiner les fleurs; **we are gathered here today ...,** nous sommes rassemblés ici aujourd'hui ...; **to g. one's thoughts,** rassembler ses pensées; **to g. all one's strength (in order) to do sth,** rassembler *ou* ramasser toutes ses forces pour faire qch; **to g. one's hair into a knot,** tordre ses cheveux en chignon; **tiger gathered for a spring,** tigre accroupi avant de sauter;
(b) (*accumulate*) **to g. speed,** acquérir *ou* prendre de la vitesse; **to g. momentum,** prendre de la vitesse; **to g. strength,** (*of person*) reprendre des forces; **to g. dirt,** s'encrasser; **to g. dust,** ramasser la poussière;
(c) (*wrap*) serrer; *Sewing* froncer (*une jupe etc*); **to g. the blankets round one,** se serrer dans les couvertures; **he gathered her in his arms,** il l'a serrée dans ses bras;
(d) (*conclude, understand*) conclure; **so far as I can g.,** à ce que je comprends; **I g. from the papers that ...,** à en croire les journaux ...; **I g. he has been ill,** on me dit qu'il a été malade; **I g. from the evidence that ...,** je déduis *ou* j'infère de ces témoignages que ...; **prices have gone up — so I g.,** les prix ont augmenté — c'est bien ce qu'il me semble.
2 *vi* **(a)** (*of people*) se réunir, s'assembler, se rassembler; **a crowd gathered,** une foule se forma;
(b) (*of things*) s'accumuler, s'amonceler, s'amasser; **the clouds are gathering,** les nuages s'amoncellent *ou* s'amassent; **a storm is gathering,** un orage se prépare; **in the gathering darkness,** dans la nuit grandissante; **with gathering force,** avec une force croissante;
(c) *Med* (*of wound*) abcéder; (*of abscess*) aboutir, mûrir; **the pus gathers,** le pus s'accumule.

►**gather in** *vtsep* **(a)** (*collect*) rentrer; **the harvest had been safely gathered in,** la moisson a été rentrée sans problème; **she gathered in the sheep,** elle a fait rentrer les mentons; **(b)** *Sewing* froncer.

►**gather round 1** *vipo* se rassembler autour de (*qn*). **2** *vi* s'approcher; **g. round!,** approchez-vous!; **they gathered round,** ils se sont approchés.

►**gather together 1** *vtsep* (*collect*) rassembler (*ses affaires, ses enfants*). **2** *vi* (*assemble*) se rassembler.

►**gather up** *vtsep* (*collect*) ramasser (*ses affaires*); **she gathered up her skirts and ran,** elle a rassemblé les plis de sa jupe et a couru; **to g. up one's hair,** attacher ses cheveux; **he gathered her up in his arms,** il l'a serrée dans ses bras.

gathered [gæðəd] *adj Sewing* (*volant etc*) froncé, à fronces; **g. pages,** (*in bookbinding*) feuilles assemblées.

gathering ['gæðərɪŋ] *n* **(a)** (*people*) (*in a hall etc*) assemblée *f*, réunion *f*; (*in a street*) rassemblement *m*; (*threatening*) attroupement *m*; (*act of gathering*) rassemblement; attroupement (*d'une foule*); **the g. of the clans,** le rassemblement des clans; **family g.,** réunion de famille; **a small g. was listening to him,** quelques personnes attroupées l'écoutaient; **(b)** (*of things*) accumulation *f*; cueillette *f* (*des fruits etc*); (*of crops*) récolte *f*; accumulation, amoncellement *m* (*de nuages*); **(c)** fain *m*, augmentation *f* (*de vitesse*); reprise *f* (*de forces*); **(d)** *Sewing* (*act*) action *f* de faire des fronces; (*pleats*) fronces *fpl*; **(e)** *Med* (*act*) collection *f* (*du pus*); (*abscess*) abcès *m*; **(f)** (*in bookbinding*) (*act*) assemblage *m* (*des feuilles*); (*sheets*) cahier *m*.

gathers ['gæðəz] *npl Sewing* fronces *fpl*.

GATT [gæt] *n* (*abbr* **General Agreement on Tariffs and Trade**) G.A.T.T. *m*.

gauche [gəʊʃ] *adj* gauche, maladroit.

gaucheness ['gəʊʃnɪs] *n* gaucherie *f*, maladresse *f*.

gaudily [gɔːdɪlɪ] *adv* d'une manière voyante; (*peint*) en couleurs criardes.

gaudiness ['gɔːdɪnɪs] *n* éclat criard (*d'une couleur etc*).

gaudy ['gɔːdɪ] *adj* (*colour*) voyant, criard; (*display*) de mauvais goût.

gauge[1] [geɪdʒ] *n* **(a)** (*size*) calibre *m* (*d'un écrou etc*); *Aut etc* espacement *m* (*des roues*); *Rail* écartement *m*, largeur *f* (*de la voie*); *Cin* pas *m* (*de l'image, de la perforation*); *Tex* **fine/heavy g.,** (*of stockings*) de jauge fine/de grosse jauge; *Rail* **narrow-g. track,** voie étroite;
(b) (*device*) indicateur *m*; (*for liquid*) jauge *f*; **standard g.,** calibre *m* étalon; **cal(l)iper g.,** jauge à coulisse; calibre de précision; **wire g.,** calibre pour fils métalliques;
(c) (*measuring instrument*) indicateur *m*, contrôleur *m*; *Phys* **vacuum g.,** indicateur *ou* jauge *f* du vide; *MecE* **water/oil g.,** indicateur de niveau d'eau/d'huile; **pressure g.,** manomètre *m*; *Aut* **petrol** *or* **fuel g.,** jauge d'essence; **tyre(-pressure) g.,** manomètre (pour pneus); *Fig* **an opinion poll is a useful g. of public opinion,** un sondage constitue un indicateur utile de l'opinion publique;
(d) *Nau* tirant *m* d'eau (*d'un navire*); **weather g.,** avantage *m* du vent.

gauge[2] *vt* calibrer (*un écrou etc*); jauger, mesurer (*l'huile*); **to g. sth by the eye,** mesurer qch à l'œil; *Fig* **to g. a situation,** évaluer une situation; **it was difficult to g. how interested they were/their enthusiasm,** il était difficile de juger dans quelle mesure ils étaient intéressés/de leur enthousiasme.

gauging ['geɪdʒɪŋ] *n* calibrage *m*; jaugeage *m*; **g. rod** *or* **stick,** jauge *f*.

Gaul [gɔːl] *Antiq n* **(a)** (*region*) Gaule *f*; **(b)** (*inhabitant*) Gaulois, -oise.

Gaullist ['gəʊlɪst] *adj & n Pol* gaulliste *mf*.

gaunt [gɔːnt] *adj* **(a)** (*person, face*) maigre, décharné; **(b)** (*place*) désolé.

gauntlet[1] ['gɔːntlɪt] *n* **(a)** (*part of armour*) gantelet *m*, gant *m*; *Fig* **to throw** *or* **fling down the g.,** jeter le gant; *Fig* **to take up the g.,** relever le gant; **(b) g. (glove),** gant *m* à crispins *ou* à manchette.

gauntlet[2] *n* **to run the g.,** *Mil* passer par les baguettes; *Nau* courir la bouline; *Fig* soutenir un feu roulant (de critiques adverses); **they had to run the g. of enemy artillery,** ils ont dû soutenir le feu roulant de l'artillerie de l'ennemi; **he had to run the g. of their abuse,** il a dû soutenir le feu roulant de leurs injures.

gauntness ['gɔːntnɪs] *n* (*of person, face*) maigreur *f*, *Lit* aspect *m* hâve; (*of place*) désolation *f*.

gauze [gɔːz] *n* gaze *f*; *Med* **antiseptic g.,** gaze aseptique; **wire g.,** toile *f* métallique; *Med* **g. bandage,** bande *f* de gaze.

gave *see* **GIVE[2]**.

gavel ['gæv(ə)l] *n* marteau *m* (*de commissaire-priseur, Am de juge*).

gavotte [gə'vɒt] *n Mus* gavotte *f*.

gawk[1] [gɔːk] *n F* godiche *mf*; **big g.,** grand dadais.

gawk[2] *vi F* = **GAWP**.

gawker ['gɔːkər] *n Am* badaud *m*, curieux, -euse.

gawkiness ['gɔːkɪnɪs] *n* gaucherie *f*; *F* air empoté.

gawky ['gɔːkɪ] *adj* gauche; *F* empoté.

gawp [gɔːp] *vi F* rester bouche bée, gober des mouches; **stop gawping!,** ne reste pas la bouche ouverte!

gay [geɪ] **1** *adj* **(gayer, gayest) (a)** (*homosexual*) homosexuel; **g. club/magazine,** club *m*/magazine *m* pour homosexuels; **(b)** *Old-fashioned* (*happy*) gai, allègre; (*laugh*) enjoué; (*colour*) vif, gai; **to lead a g. life,** mener une vie de plaisir(s). **2** *n Sl* homosexuel *m*.

gaze[1] [geɪz] *n* regard *m* fixe; **she turned her g. to the dog,** elle a tourné son regard vers le chien; **exposed to the public g.,** exposé aux regards inquisiteurs de tous.

gaze[2] *vi* regarder fixement; **they gazed around them,** ils ont regardé autour d'eux; **to g. at** *or* **on s.o./sth,** fixer *ou* contempler *ou* considérer qn/qch.

gazebo [gə'ziːbəʊ] *n* belvédère *m*.

gazelle [gə'zel] *n* (*animal*) gazelle *f*.

gazette[1] [gə'zet] *n* journal officiel; **the Police G.,** ≈ la Gazette des tribunaux.

gazette[2] *vt* annoncer, publier (*une faillite, une nomination etc*) dans un journal officiel.

gazetteer [gæzɪ'tɪər] *n* répertoire *m* géographique.

gazump [gə'zʌmp] *vt Br F* = revenir sur une promesse de vente faite à qn pour accepter une offre plus élevée; **we were gazumped,** le propriétaire est revenu sur la promesse de vente qu'il nous avait faite.

gazumping [gə'zʌmpɪŋ] *n Br F* = le fait de revenir sur une promesse de vente pour accepter une offre plus élevée.

GB ['dʒiːbiː] *n abbr* **Great Britain**.

GBH [dʒiːbiː'eɪtʃ] *n Jur* (*abbr* **grievous bodily harm**) = coups et blessures graves.

GCE [dʒiːsiː'iː] *n Br Sch* (*before 1988*) (*abbr* **General Certificate of Education**) **1** *adj* **GCE examination,** = examen *m* du diplôme général d'enseignement; **GCE O level,** = brevet élémentaire du premier cycle; **GCE A level,** = baccalauréat *m*. **2** *n* **GCE in Maths,** = diplôme général d'enseignement en maths.

GCSE [dʒiːsiːes'iː] *n Eng Sch abbr* **General Certificate**

of Secondary Education.

GDP [dʒiːdiː'piː] *n Econ* (*abbr* **gross domestic product**) P.I.B. *m.*

GDR [dʒiːdiː'ɑːr] *n* (*abbr* **German Democratic Republic**) RDA *f.*

Gds (*abbr* **Gardens**) = rue.

gear[1] [gɪər] *n* **(a)** (*of car, bike etc*) vitesse *f*; *MecE etc* (*gearwheel*) engrenage *m*; (*mechanism*) appareil *m*, mécanisme *m*; **control g.**, appareils *ou* organes *mpl* de commande; *Av* dispositif *m ou* organe(s) de manœuvre; *Av* **landing g.**, train *m* d'atterrissage; **driving** *or* **transmission g.**, transmission *f*, commande *f*; **g. drive**, transmission par engrenages; **in g.**, embrayé, engagé, en prise; (*functioning*) en action, en marche; **the car's still in g.**, la voiture est encore embrayée; *esp Am Sl* **get your ass in g.**, grouille-toi; **out of g.**, débrayé, désengrené, hors de prise; (*not functioning*) au repos; **to throw** *or* **put out of g.**, débrayer, désengrener; (*stop functioning*) mettre (*une machine*) au repos; *Fig* désorganiser, perturber (*une organisation etc*); **a ten-g. racing bike**, un vélo de course à dix vitesses; *Aut* **neutral g.**, point mort; **first/bottom g.**, première vitesse; **top g.**, quatrième *ou* cinquième vitesse; *Fig* **I'm not in top g. at the moment**, je marche un peu au ralenti en ce moment; **to change** *or Am* **shift g.**, *Aut & Fig* changer de vitesse; *Cycling* changer de braquet; **g. changes**, changements *mpl* de vitesse; *Br Aut* **g. lever**, levier *m* de (changement de) vitesse; **g. ratio**, rapport *m* d'engrenages *ou* des dentures;

(b) (*equipment*) attirail *m*, équipement *m*, appareil *m*; *Nau* apparaux *mpl*; attirail (*de pêche*); matériel *m* (*de camping*); **photographic g.**, équipement photographique; **lifting g.**, matériel de levage; *Fig F* **he arrived with all his g.**, (*his belongings*) il est arrivé avec tout son attirail *ou* tous ses bagages;

(c) *F* (*clothes*) fringues *fpl*; **where do you get your g.?**, où est-ce que tu trouves tes fringues?;

(d) (*harness*) harnais *m*, harnachement *m* (*de cheval de trait*).

gear[2] **1** *vi* s'embrayer, s'engrener. **2** *vt MecE* engrener, embrayer.

▶**gear down 1** *vi* (*of factory etc*) ralentir la production. **2** *vtsep* **(a)** (*decrease*) ralentir; **to g. down production**, ralentir la production; **(b)** *MecE* démultiplier (*la vitesse de révolution*).

▶**gear to** *vtaspo* (*intend for*) adapter (*qch*) en fonction de (*qch*); **wages geared to the cost of living**, salaires indexés au coût de la vie; **this book is geared to the needs of students**, ce livre est spécialement adapté aux besoins des étudiants.

▶**gear up 1** *vi* (*prepare*) se préparer; **the shops are gearing up for Christmas**, les magasins se préparent pour Noël. **2** *vtsep* **(a)** (*prepare*) préparer; **businesses are getting geared up for a single European market**, les entreprises se préparent en vue du marché unique européen; **(b)** *MecE* multiplier (*la vitesse de révolution*).

gearbox ['gɪəbɒks] *n Aut* boîte *f* de vitesses; *MecE* boîte *ou* carter *m* d'engrenage *ou* de transmission.

gearing ['gɪərɪŋ] **(a)** *MecE etc* (*gears*) engrenage *m*, embrayage *m*; système *m ou* jeu *m* d'engrenages; (*drive*) transmission *f*, commande *f*; **(b)** *Fin* ratio *m* d'endettement.

gearing down *n MecE* démultiplication *f.*

gearing up *n MecE* multiplication *f*; *Cycling* développement *m.*

gearshift ['gɪəʃɪft] *n Am Aut* (*lever*) levier *m* de vitesse; (*action*) changement *m* de vitesse; **automatic g.**, changement de vitesse automatique.

gearwheel ['gɪəwiːl] *n MecE* (roue *f* d')engrenage *m*; *Cycling* pignon *m.*

gecko, *pl* **-os, -oes** ['gekəʊ, -əʊz] *n* gecko *m.*

gee[1] [dʒiː] *int* (*to horse*) **g.-up!**, hue!

gee[2] *int Am* **g. (whiz(z))!**, ça alors!, mince alors!

gee-gee ['dʒiːdʒiː] *n F* (*in children's language*) cheval *m.*

geese [giːs] *npl see* **GOOSE**.

geezer ['giːzər] *n Br F* type *m*; **old g.**, vieux type; **funny old g.**, drôle *m* de bonhomme.

Geiger ['gaɪgər] *n Nucl Phys* **G. counter**, compteur *m* Geiger.

geisha ['geɪʃə] *n* geisha *f.*

gel[1] [dʒel] *n Ch* colloïde *m* (coagulé); (*for hair, eyes*) gel *m.*

gel[2] *vi* (**-ll-**) *Ch* se coaguler; *Fig* (*of ideas, plans*) prendre corps *ou* forme; *Fig F* **the musicians didn't g.**, la cohésion ne s'est pas faite entre les musiciens.

gelatine [dʒelə'tiːn] *n* gélatine *f*; *Phot* **g. paper**, papier *m* gélatiné; **explosive g.**, plastic *m.*

gelatinize [dʒɪ'lætɪnaɪz] **1** *vt* gélatiniser. **2** *vi* se gélatiniser.

gelatinous [dʒɪ'lætɪnəs] *adj* gélatineux.

geld [geld] *vt* châtrer (*un animal*); hongrer (*un cheval*).

gelding ['geldɪŋ] *n* animal châtré; (*horse*) (cheval *m*) hongre *m.*

gelignite ['dʒelɪgnaɪt] *n* gélignite *f.*

gem [dʒem] *n* **(a)** (*precious stone*) pierre précieuse; **g. stone**, pierre gemme; **(b)** *Fig* perle *f*; **that joke was a g.**, cette plaisanterie était une perle; **he's a g. of a husband**, c'est la perle des maris; **the g. of the collection**, le joyau de la collection; **(c)** *Typ* diamant *m.*

Gemini ['dʒemɪnaɪ] *npl Astron* les Gémeaux *mpl*; **I'm a G.**, je suis Gémeaux.

gen [dʒen] *n Br F* renseignements *mpl*, tuyaux *mpl* (**on sth**, sur qch).

▶**gen up** *vtsep F* (*provide with information*) rencarder (*qn*) (**on**, sur).

▶**gen up on** *vipo F* se rencarder sur (*qch*).

Gen (*abbr* **General**) gal.

gender ['dʒendər] *n* **(a)** *Gram* genre *m*; **to agree in g.**, s'accorder en genre (**with**, avec); **(b)** (*sex*) sexe *m*; **the male/female g.**, le sexe masculin/féminin; **it is not a question of race or g.**, ce n'est pas une question de race ou de sexe.

gender-bender ['dʒendə'bendər] *n F* **(a)** *Comptr* commutateur *m*; **(b)** personne *f* qui imite les habitudes vestimentaires du sexe opposé.

gene [dʒiːn] *n Biol* gène *m*; **dominant/recessive g.**, gène dominant/récessif; *F* **music's in his genes**, il a la musique dans les gènes.

genealogical [dʒiːnɪə'lɒdʒɪk(ə)l] *adj* (*tableau, arbre*) généalogique.

genealogist [dʒiːnɪ'ælədʒɪst] *n* généalogiste *mf.*

genealogy [dʒiːnɪ'ælədʒɪ] *n* généalogie *f.*

genera ['dʒenərə] *npl see* **GENUS**.

general ['dʒen(ə)r(ə)l] **1** *adj* **(a)** (*strike, paralysis*) général, -aux; **the rain has been pretty g.**, il a plu un peu partout; **g. effect**, effet *m* d'ensemble; **there has been a g. improvement in educational standards**, il y a eu une amélioration générale du niveau de l'enseignement; **the g. tone of her remarks was that ...**, ce qui ressortait de ses remarques c'est que ...; **g. meeting**, assemblée générale; **g. business**, (*in agenda*) questions diverses; **he made himself a g. nuisance**, il a été embêtant à tout point de vue; **I had a g. tidy-up**, j'ai fait du rangement un peu partout; *Pol* **g. election**, élections générales; *Rel* **g. confession**, confession *f* en commun; **word in g. use**, mot généralement *ou* couramment employé; **to come into g. use**, se généraliser; **as a g. rule**, en règle générale; **speaking in a g. way**, (parlant) d'une manière générale; **G. Agreement on Tariffs and Trade**, Accord général sur les tarifs douaniers et le commerce; **the g. public**, le grand public; **g. knowledge**, culture générale; *Med* **g. practitioner**, médecin *m* généraliste; *Med* **g. hospital**, hôpital général; **in g. terms**, en termes généraux; *Med* **g. anaesthetic**, anesthésie générale; **G. Assembly**, (*of United Nations*) Assemblée générale; *Am* **g. delivery**, poste restante;

(b) *Mil* **g. officer**, (officier *m*) général *m*;

(c) (*in titles*) **inspector g.**, inspecteur général *ou* en chef; (*Channel Isles*) *& Fr Hist* **States G.**, États généraux.

2 *n* **(a) to argue from the g. to the particular**, arguer du général au particulier;

(b) in g., en général, généralement;

(c) *Mil* général *m*; (*rank*) général d'armée; *Rel* général (*d'un ordre religieux*); **major g.**, général de division; **g. staff**, état-major *m*, *pl* états-majors.

generality [dʒenə'rælɪtɪ] *n* **(a)** (*statement*) **to confine oneself to generalities**, s'en tenir aux généralités; **(b)** (*quality*) caractère général; **(c) the g. of mankind**, la plupart des hommes.

generalization [dʒen(ə)rəlaɪ'zeɪʃən] *n* généralisation *f*; **to make generalizations**, généraliser.

generalize ['dʒen(ə)rəlaɪz] **1** *vi* **(a)** généraliser, faire des généralisations; **I don't like generalizing, but ...**, je n'aime pas faire des généralisations, mais ...; **(b)** *Med* (*of disease*) se répandre. **2** *vt* **(a)** généraliser (*des faits etc*); **(b)** (*make widespread*) répandre (*un usage etc*); **to become generalized**, (*of practice*) se généraliser.

generally ['dʒenrəlɪ] *adv* **(a)** (*widely*) généralement, universellement; **the word is g. understood to mean ...**, le mot veut généralement dire ...; **(b)** (*taken overall*) généralement; **to make oneself g. useful**, se rendre généralement utile; **g. speaking**, (parlant) d'une façon générale; **she behaved in a g. antisocial manner**, d'une manière générale, elle s'est comportée de façon antisociale; **(c)** *(as a general rule)* en règle générale, généralement, en général; **the roads are g. crowded at this time,** en général, les routes sont très encombrées à cette heure-ci.

general-purpose ['dʒen(ə)r(ə)l'pɜːpəs] *adj* (à) toutes fins, (pour) tous usages, (d'usage) universel.

generalship ['dʒen(ə)rəlʃɪp] *n Mil (skill)* l'art d'être général; **his g.**, la compétence de général dont il a fait preuve.

generate ['dʒenəreɪt] *vt* amener, produire *(un résultat)*; provoquer *(un sentiment)*; *Comptr* créer, générer; *El Phys etc* produire *(un courant électrique, de la chaleur etc)*; *Math* engendrer *(une surface etc)*; **environment that generates crime,** ambiance génératrice de crime; **newspaper articles generated some interest in Soviet cinema,** les articles de journaux ont fait naître un certain intérêt à l'égard du cinéma russe.

generating ['dʒenəreɪtɪŋ] **1** *adj* générateur, -trice; *El* **g. station,** centrale *f* électrique. **2** *n* génération *f*.

generation [dʒenə'reɪʃən] *n* **(a)** *(period, people)* génération *f*; **from g. to g.**, de génération en génération; de père en fils; **for generations there had always been a doctor in the family,** ils étaient médecins de père en fils; **people of my g. will remember ...,** les gens de ma génération se souviendront ...; **the g. born in the early 1940s,** la génération née au début des années 1940; **he's my g.**, il est de ma génération; **the younger/older g.**, la jeune/l'ancienne génération; **the present g.**, la génération actuelle; **the g. gap,** l'écart *m ou* le fossé entre les générations; **(b)** *El Phys etc* génération *f*, production *f (de la chaleur etc)*; *Math* génération *(d'une surface etc)*; *Comptr* création *f*, génération; *Comptr* **data g.**, élaboration *f* des données; **(c)** génération *f*, formation *f (des idées etc)*.

-generation [dʒenə'reɪʃən] *suff* **second-g. immigrant,** immigrant *m* de la deuxième génération; **third-g. fax machines,** télécopieurs de la troisième génération.

generator ['dʒenəreɪtər] *n El* génératrice *f*, dynamo *m*; *Comptr* (programme *m*) générateur *m*; *Tech* générateur, appareil producteur *(de chaleur etc)*; **electric g.**, générateur électrique.

generatrix, *pl* **-ices** ['dʒenəreɪtrɪks, -ɪsiːz] *n Math* génératrice *f (d'une surface etc)*.

generic [dʒɪ'nerɪk] *adj (nom etc)* générique.

generically [dʒɪ'nerɪklɪ] *adv* génériquement.

generosity [dʒenə'rɒsɪtɪ] *n* **(a)** *(with money, gifts)* générosité *f*, libéralité *f*; **thanks to the g. of Mr Jones,** grâce à la générosité de M. Jones; **(b)** *(of spirit)* magnanimité *f*; **in a spirit of g.**, *(agir)* par générosité.

generous ['dʒen(ə)rəs] *adj* **(a)** *(with money, gifts)* généreux, libéral, -aux; **g. gift,** don généreux; **g. mark,** *(for homework etc)* note généreuse; **she's g. with her money,** elle n'est pas avare de son argent; **he took a g. helping of the stew,** il s'est servi amplement de ragoût; *F* **she's built on g. lines,** elle a des formes généreuses; **g. head,** *(on beer)* mousse généreuse; **(b)** *(big-hearted)* magnanime; **he has a g. nature,** c'est une âme généreuse.

generously ['dʒen(ə)rəslɪ] *adv (see adj)* **(a)** généreusement, libéralement; **they g. donated $50,000,** ils ont généreusement fait don de 50 000 dollars; **he helped himself g. to the stew,** il s'est servi libéralement de ragoût; **(b)** magnanimement; **she g. offered to help,** elle a généreusement proposé son aide.

genesis ['dʒenɪsɪs] *n* genèse *f*, origine *f*; *Bible* **(the Book of) G.**, la Genèse.

genetic [dʒɪ'netɪk] *adj Biol* génétique; **g. code,** code *m* génétique; **g. engineering,** manipulation *f* génétique; **g. fingerprint,** empreinte *f* génétique; **g. fingerprinting,** détermination *f* de l'empreinte génétique.

genetically [dʒɪ'netɪklɪ] *adv Biol* génétiquement; **to g. alter a mouse,** manipuler génétiquement une souris.

geneticist [dʒɪ'netɪsɪst] *n Biol* généticien, -ienne.

genetics [dʒɪ'netɪks] *npl (usu with sing verb) Biol* génétique *f*.

Geneva [dʒɪ'niːvə] *n* Genève *f*; **Lake G.**, le lac Léman; *Hist* **the G. Convention,** la Convention de Genève.

genial ['dʒiːnɪəl] *adj* **(a)** *(person)* plein de bienveillance, affable; plein de bonne humeur; **(b)** *(climate)* doux, *f* douce, clément; *(fire)* réconfortant.

geniality [dʒiːnɪ'ælɪtɪ] *n* **(a)** *(of person)* bienveillance *f*; bonne humeur; **(b)** *(of climate)* douceur *f*, clémence *f*.

genially ['dʒiːnɪəlɪ] *adv* affablement.

genie, *pl* **genii** ['dʒiːnɪ, 'dʒiːnɪaɪ] *n Myth* djinn *m*.

genital ['dʒenɪt(ə)l] **1** *adj* génital, -aux. **2** *npl* **genitals,** organes génitaux externes.

genitive ['dʒenɪtɪv] **1** *n Gram* génitif *m*; **in the g.**, au génitif. **2** *adj* génitif; **g. case,** génitif *m*.

genius ['dʒiːnɪəs] *n* **(a)** *(pl* **geniuses** ['dʒiːnɪəsɪz]) *(person)* génie *m*; **she's a mathematical g.**, c'est un génie en mathématiques; **(b)** *(no pl) (talent)* génie *m*; **man of g.**, homme *m* de génie; **work of g.**, œuvre *f* de génie; **to show g.**, faire preuve de génie; *F* **that goal was pure g.**, ce goal était du génie pur et simple; **(c)** *(no pl) (aptitude)* aptitudes naturelles; **to have a g. for business,** avoir le génie des affaires; **to have a g. for doing sth,** avoir le don de faire qch; **(d)** *(no pl) (of a nation, era)* génie particulier, esprit *m*; **(e)** *(spirit) (pl* **genii** ['dʒiːnɪaɪ]) génie *m ou* esprit *m* tutélaire *(d'un lieu etc)*; **she is his good/evil g.**, c'est son bon/mauvais génie; **(f)** *(pl* **genii** ['dʒiːnɪaɪ]) *(genie)* démon *m*, djinn *m*.

Genoa ['dʒenəʊə] *n* **(a)** Gênes *f*; **(b) G. (jib),** génois *m*, grand foc.

genocidal [dʒenə'saɪd(ə)l] *adj (guerre etc)* génocide.

genocide ['dʒenəsaɪd] *n* génocide *m*.

Genoese [dʒenəʊ'iːz] **1** *adj* génois. **2** *n* Génois, -oise.

genotype ['dʒenəʊtaɪp] *n Biol* génotype *m*.

genre ['ʒɒnrə] *n* genre *m*; **g. painting,** tableau *m* de genre.

gent [dʒent] *n Br F* monsieur *m*; **gents' footwear,** chaussures *fpl* pour hommes; **gents,** toilettes pour hommes; **where's the gents?,** où sont les toilettes?

genteel [dʒen'tiːl] *adj* **(a)** *Pej (affected)* maniéré; **(b)** *Old-fashioned* comme il faut; **g. society,** société *f* comme il faut; **g. poverty,** pauvreté *f* digne.

gentian ['dʒenʃɪən] *n (plant)* gentiane *f*; **g. bitter,** (amer *m* de) gentiane; **g. blue,** bleu *m* gentiane.

Gentile ['dʒentaɪl] *adj & n* gentil, -ile; **the Gentiles,** les Gentils *mpl*.

gentility [dʒen'tɪlɪtɪ] *n* **(a)** *Pej (affectation)* prétention *f* au bon ton; manières affectées; **(b)** *(nobility)* bonne famille; *(people)* la haute bourgeoisie; **shabby g.**, la misère en habit noir.

gentle ['dʒent(ə)l] *adj* (**gentler**, **gentlest**) **(a)** *(delicate, kind)* doux, *f* douce; *(reprimand)* peu sévère; *(tap on shoulder etc)* léger; *(exercise)* modéré; *(slope)* doux, faible; **to be g. with s.o.**, être doux avec qn; **g. as a lamb,** doux comme un agneau; **the gentle(r) sex,** le sexe faible; **a g. giant,** un bon géant; **g. breeze,** petite brise; **(b)** *Old-fashioned (noble)* **of g. birth,** bien né; *Lit* **the g. art,** la pêche à la ligne; *Iron* **the g. art of smuggling,** le noble art de la contrebande.

gentlefolk ['dʒent(ə)l'fəʊk] *npl Old-fashioned* personnes *fpl* de bonne famille *ou* de la meilleure bourgeoisie.

gentleman, *pl* **-men** ['dʒent(ə)lmən] *n* **(a)** *(well-bred man)* homme bien élevé, gentleman *m*; **g.'s agreement,** = convention verbale, où n'est engagée que la parole d'honneur entre les deux parties; **to act** *or* **behave like a g.**, se conduire en gentleman; **he's no g.**, il est mal élevé; **thank you, you're a g.**, merci, vous êtes un gentleman;

(b) *(man)* monsieur *m*, homme *m*; **Ladies and Gentlemen!**, *(to audience)* mesdames et messieurs!; **there's a g. to see you,** il y a un monsieur qui voudrait vous parler; **this young gentleman's lost,** ce petit jeune homme est perdu; *Com* **gentlemen's hairdresser,** coiffeur *m* pour hommes; **gentlemen,** *(on toilet)* messieurs; **g.'s g.**, valet *m* de chambre; *Hum* **g. of the road,** clochard *m*; *Old-fashioned* **g. friend,** *(of woman)* ami *m*;

(c) *(nobleman etc)* gentilhomme *m*, *pl* gentilshommes; **G. in waiting,** gentilhomme de service *(près du roi)*; *Jur* **g. (of independent means),** rentier *m*; **gentlemen's club,** club *m* dont l'accès est réservé aux hommes;

(d) *Old-fashioned Sp* amateur *m*.

gentleman-farmer ['dʒent(ə)lmən'fɑːmər] *n* gentleman-farmer *m*, *pl* gentlemen-farmers.

gentlemanly ['dʒent(ə)lmənlɪ] *adj* bien élevé; **it would have been more g. to say nothing,** un homme bien élevé *ou* un gentleman n'aurait rien dit.

gentleness ['dʒent(ə)lnɪs] *n* douceur *f*.

gently ['dʒentlɪ] *adv* doucement; **to speak g.**, parler d'un ton doux *ou* avec douceur; **to deal g. with s.o.**, traiter qn avec indulgence; **g. (does it)!**, allez-y doucement!; **the road slopes g.**, la route est en pente douce.

gentrification [dʒentrɪfɪ'keɪʃən] *n Br* = fait d'accroître le standing d'un quartier d'habitation.

gentrified ['dʒentrɪfaɪd] *adj Br (area, street)* = dont on a accru le standing.

gentry ['dʒentrɪ] *n (no pl)* petite noblesse; **landed g.**, aristocratie terrienne.

genuflect ['dʒenjʊflekt] *vi* faire une génuflexion.

genuflection, genuflexion [dʒenjʊ'flekʃən] *n* génuflexion *f*.

genuine ['dʒenjʊɪn] *adj* **(a)** *(manuscript etc)* authentique, véritable; *Com* (*article*) garanti d'origine; (*Burgundy*) authentique; (*diamond*) véritable; **(b)** (*sincere*) sincère, franc, *f* franche; (*belief*) sincère; (*friend*) loyal; (*person*) sans affectation; (*buyer*) sérieux; **I think he's being g.**, je crois qu'il est sincère; **she comes across as a g. person**, elle donne l'impression d'être une personne sincère; **g. surprise**, véritable surprise *f*.

genuinely ['dʒenjʊɪnlɪ] *adv* (*see adj*) **(a)** authentiquement; **(b)** sincèrement; **I g. believed that ...**, je croyais sincèrement que ...; **g. surprised**, sincèrement surpris.

genuineness ['dʒenjʊɪnnɪs] *n* **(a)** authenticité *f* (*d'un manuscrit etc*); **(b)** (*sincerity*) sincérité *f*.

genus, *pl* **genera** ['dʒiːnəs, 'dʒenərə] *n Biol* genre *m*.

geo- ['dʒiːəʊ] *pref* géo(-).

geode ['dʒiːəʊd] *n Geol* géode *f*.

geodesic [dʒiːəʊ'diːsɪk] *adj* géodésique; **g. dome**, dôme *m* géodésique.

geodesy [dʒɪ'ɒdɪsɪ] *n* géodésie *f*.

geographer [dʒɪ'ɒgrəfər] *n* géographe *mf*.

geographic(al) [dʒɪə'græfɪk, -ɪk(ə)l] *adj* géographique.

geographically [dʒɪə'græfɪklɪ] *adv* géographiquement.

geography [dʒɪ'ɒgrəfɪ] *n* géographie *f*; **physical g.**, géographie physique; *Euph* **I'll show you the g. of the house**, je vais vous montrer où sont les toilettes; **g. (book)**, (livre *m* de) géographie.

geologic(al) [dʒɪə'lɒdʒɪk, -ɪk(ə)l] *adj* géologique.

geologically [dʒɪə'lɒdʒɪklɪ] *adv* géologiquement.

geologist [dʒɪ'ɒlədʒɪst] *n* géologue *mf*.

geology [dʒɪ'ɒlədʒɪ] *n* géologie *f*; **g. (book)**, (livre *m* de) géologie.

geometer [dʒɪ'ɒmɪtər] *n* **(a)** géomètre *m*; **(b)** *Ent* (*caterpillar*) arpenteuse *f*; (*moth*) géomètre *f*.

geometric(al) [dʒɪə'metrɪk, -ɪk(ə)l] *adj* géométrique; **g. design**, dessin *m* géométrique; **g. progression**, progression *f* géométrique.

geometrically [dʒɪə'metrɪklɪ] *adv* géométriquement.

geometry [dʒɪ'ɒmɪtrɪ] *n* géométrie *f*; **plane g.**, géométrie plane; **g. (book)**, (livre *m* de) géométrie.

geomorphologic(al) [dʒɪəʊmɔːfə'lɒdʒɪk, -ɪk(ə)l] *adj* géomorphologique.

geomorphology [dʒɪəʊmɔː'fɒlədʒɪ] *n* géomorphologie *f*.

geophysical [dʒɪəʊ'fɪzɪk(ə)l] *adj* géophysique.

geophysicist [dʒiːəʊ'fɪzɪsɪst] *n* géophysicien, -ienne.

geophysics [dʒɪəʊ'fɪzɪks] *npl* (*usu with sing verb*) géophysique *f*.

geopolitics [dʒɪəʊ'pɒlɪtɪks] *npl* (*usu with sing verb*) géopolitique *f*.

Geordie ['dʒɔːdɪ] *Br F* **1** *n* habitant, -ante du Tyneside; (*by birth*) originaire *mf* du Tyneside. **2** *adj* (*customs, dialect etc*) qui est originaire du Tyneside.

George [dʒɔːdʒ] *n* **(a)** Georges *m*; *Old-fashioned F* **by G.!**, sapristi!; **(b)** *Av F* George *m*.

georgette [dʒɔː'dʒet] *n Tex* crêpe *m* georgette.

Georgia ['dʒɔːdʒɪə] *n* Géorgie *f*.

Georgian¹ ['dʒɔːdʒɪən] *adj Eng Hist* **(a)** du règne des quatre rois Georges; **a G. house**, une maison datant de l'époque 1720-1830; **(b)** (*of George V*) du règne de Georges V.

Georgian² **1** *adj* géorgien. **2** *n* Géorgien, -ienne.

geoscience [dʒiːəʊ'saɪəns] *n* géoscience *f*.

geostationary [dʒiːəʊ'steɪʃənərɪ] *adj* (*satellite*) géostationnaire; **to be in g. orbit**, (*of satellite*) être en orbite géostationnaire.

geothermal [dʒiːəʊ'θɜːməl] *adj* (*energy etc*) géothermique.

geotropism [dʒɪ'ɒtrəpɪz(ə)m] *n* géotropisme *m*.

geranium [dʒə'reɪnɪəm] **1** *n* **(a)** (*plant*) géranium *m*; **(b)** (*colour*) **g. (red)**, vermeil *m*. **2** *adj* **g. (red)**, vermeil.

gerbil ['dʒɜːbɪl] *n* (*rodent*) gerbille *f*.

geriatric¹ [dʒerɪ'ætrɪk] *n Med* malade *m* gériatrique; *Pej* croulant *m*.

geriatric² *adj* des vieillards; **g. medicine**, gériatrie *f*; **g. ward**, service *m* de gériatrie.

geriatrician [dʒerɪə'trɪʃən] *n* gériatre *mf*.

geriatrics [dʒerɪ'ætrɪks] *npl Med* (*usu with sing verb*) gériatrie *f*.

germ [dʒɜːm] *n* **(a)** *Med* germe *m*, microbe *m* (*d'une maladie*); **I don't want your germs!**, je ne veux pas de tes microbes!; **g. warfare**, guerre *f* bactériologique; **(b)** *Biol* germe *m* (*d'un organisme*); **g. cell**, cellule *f*; (*male*) spermatozoïde *m*; (*female*) ovule *m*; *Fig* **the g. of an idea**, le germe d'une idée.

German ['dʒɜːmən] **1** *adj* allemand; **West/East G.**, ouest-/est-allemand; *Med* **G. measles**, rubéole *f*; *esp Am* **G. shepherd**, (*dog*) berger allemand. **2** *n* **(a)** Allemand, -ande; **(b)** *Ling* allemand *m*; **High/Low G.**, haut/bas allemand.

germander [dʒɜː'mændər] *n* (*plant*) germandrée *f*.

germane [dʒɜː'meɪn] *adj Fml* se rapportant (**to**, à).

Germanic [dʒɜː'mænɪk] **1** *adj* allemand; *Hist* germanique, germain. **2** *n Ling* germanique *m*.

Germanist ['dʒɜːmənɪst] *n Ling* germaniste *mf*.

Germanize ['dʒɜːmənaɪz] *vt* germaniser.

Germany ['dʒɜːmənɪ] *n* Allemagne *f*; **West/East G.**, l'Allemagne de l'ouest/de l'est; **the two Germanies**, les deux Allemagnes.

germ-free ['dʒɜːmfriː] *adj* (*milieu etc*) stérile.

germicidal [dʒɜːmɪ'saɪd(ə)l] *adj* germicide.

germicide ['dʒɜːmɪsaɪd] *n* germicide *m*.

germinate ['dʒɜːmɪneɪt] **1** *vi* (*of seed, Fig of idea*) germer. **2** *vt* faire germer (*des graines etc*).

germination [dʒɜːmɪ'neɪʃən] *n* germination *f*.

gerontocracy [dʒerɒn'tɒkrəsɪ] *n* gérontocracie *f*.

gerontologist [dʒerɒn'tɒlədʒɪst] *n* gérontologue *mf*.

gerontology [dʒerɒn'tɒlədʒɪ] *n* gérontologie *f*.

gerrymander ['dʒerɪmændər] *vt Pol* **to g. constituencies**, faire du charcutage électoral.

gerrymandering [dʒerɪ'mændərɪŋ] *n Pol* charcutage électoral.

gerund ['dʒerənd] *n Gram* gérondif *m*; nom verbal; **in the g.**, au gérondif.

gerundive [dʒɪ'rʌndɪv] *Gram* **1** *adj* du gérondif. **2** *n* adjectif verbal.

gesso ['dʒesəʊ] *n Art* enduit *m* de plâtre (*pour les fresques*); (*substance*) plâtre *m* de Paris, gypse *m*.

gestate [dʒes'teɪt] *vi* être en gestation.

gestation [dʒes'teɪʃən] *n Physiol* gestation *f*; **g. period**, période *f* de gestation.

gesticulate [dʒes'tɪkjʊleɪt] *vi* gesticuler.

gesticulation [dʒestɪkjʊ'leɪʃən] *n* gesticulation *f*.

gesture¹ ['dʒestʃər] *n* geste *m*; **to make a g.**, faire un geste; **with a sweeping g.**, d'un geste large; **g. of defiance**, geste de défi; *Fig* **as a g. of friendship**, en témoignage d'amitié; **a g. towards peace**, un geste vers la paix.

gesture² **1** *vi* faire des gestes; **she gestured to them to be silent**, elle leur a fait signe de se taire. **2** *vt* exprimer (*qch*) par gestes; **he gestured us over**, il nous a fait signe d'approcher.

get [get] *v* (*pt* **got** [gɒt]; *pp* **got**, *Arch & Am also* **gotten** ['gɒt(ə)n]; *prp* **getting** ['getɪŋ]) **1** *vt* **(a)** (*obtain*) procurer, obtenir; **to g. sth for s.o.**, procurer qch à qn; (*buy*) acheter qch pour qn; **where did you g. that?**, où avez-vous trouvé *ou* acheté cela?; **where can we g. some information?**, où est-ce que nous pouvons obtenir des informations?; **to g. sth to eat**, (*find*) trouver de quoi manger; (*eat*) manger qch (*au restaurant etc*); **I got this car cheap**, j'ai eu *ou* j'ai acheté cette voiture (à) bon marché; **if you're going to buy shoes, g. good ones**, si tu vas acheter des chaussures, prends-en de bonnes; **to g. a job**, (*obtain*) obtenir un travail; (*find*) trouver un travail; **I don't think I've got the right answer**, je n'ai pas trouvé la solution; **to g. s.o.'s permission to do sth**, obtenir la permission de qn de faire qch; **to g. one's own way**, faire valoir sa volonté; **I'll do it if I g. the time/a moment**, je le ferai si j'ai le temps/si je trouve un moment; **you g. a fine view from the top of the mountain**, il y a une vue magnifique du sommet de la montagne; **we don't g. many accidents here**, nous n'avons pas beaucoup d'accidents par ici; **you g. a lot of people marrying young here**, il y a beaucoup de gens qui se marient jeunes par ici; **I finally got her on her own** *or* **alone**, j'ai fini par la trouver seule;

(b) (*receive etc*) recevoir (*un cadeau etc*); gagner, remporter (*un prix*); **what did you g. for your birthday?**, qu'est-ce que tu as eu pour ton anniversaire?; **I got your letter last week**, j'ai eu ta lettre la semaine dernière; **I didn't g. a reply**, je n'ai pas eu de réponse; **room that gets no sun**, pièce où le soleil ne donne pas; **he gets his shyness from his mother**, il tient sa timidité de sa mère; **I got the idea from a book**, j'ai trouvé l'idée dans un livre; **I need all the advice I can g.**, j'ai besoin de tous les conseils qu'on peut me donner; **to g. a medal**, recevoir une médaille; **she got a telling off**, elle s'est fait passer un savon; **to g. ten years**, prendre dix ans de prison; **to g. the sack**, être congédié *ou* mis à la porte; **to g. £5,000 a year**, gagner 5 000 livres par an; **to g. 10% interest**, recevoir 10% d'intérêt; **to g. a good price for sth**, obtenir un bon prix pour qch; **what did you g. for your car?**, combien on t'a donné pour ta voiture?; **to g. nothing by it** *or* **out of it**, n'y rien gagner; **she got very little from her lessons**, elle a très peu tiré *ou* appris de ses leçons;

(c) *Rad TV* **we can't g. Moscow,** nous ne pouvons pas avoir Moscou; **we can only g. three channels here,** nous ne pouvons recevoir que trois chaînes ici; *Tel* **I had a job to g. you,** j'ai eu du mal à vous joindre; *Tel* **I couldn't g. her at the office,** je n'ai pas pu l'avoir au bureau; *Tel* **g. me Washington 330 330,** (*to operator*) appelez-moi Washington 330 330;

(d) (*catch*) prendre, attraper; (*train, bus*) prendre; attraper (*un rhume, une maladie*); *F* **we'll g. them yet!,** on les aura!; **I'll g. you for that,** je te le revaudrai; **you've got me this time,** (*caught me*) cette fois-ci vous m'avez eu; (*I don't know the answer*) je donne ma langue au chat; **the piranhas got him in the end,** les piranhas ont fini par l'avoir;

(e) (*hit*) (*with fist, foot*) atteindre; (*with stick etc*) atteindre, frapper; (*with bullet, arrow, stone etc*) toucher; **he got a bullet in his shoulder,** il a reçu une balle dans l'épaule; **where did they g. you?,** (*of bullet, stab wound*) où est-ce qu'ils t'ont touché?;

(f) *F* (*move emotionally*) émouvoir (*qn*); **the play didn't really g. me,** la pièce ne m'a pas fait grand-chose, la pièce ne m'a fait ni chaud ni froid;

(g) (*annoy*) mettre en boule; **that gets me** *or* **gets my goat,** ça me met en boule; **it gets me the way she's blaming them,** ça me met en boule la façon dont elle les blâme; **what gets me is that ...,** ce qui me met en boule, c'est que ...;

(h) *F* (*understand*) comprendre; **I don't g. your meaning,** je ne vous comprends pas; **g. me?,** tu y es?, tu piges?; **oh, I g. you!,** ah! j'ai pigé!; **I don't g. it,** je ne comprends pas; **to g. a joke,** comprendre une blague; **g. it?,** (*do you understand the joke?*) tu piges?;

(i) *Sl* (*consider*) **g. a load of this!,** (*listen*) écoute un peu ça!; **g. him!,** (*he looks outrageous*) regarde-le, celui-là!; (*he made an outrageous remark*) écoute-le, celui-là!; **g. him riding around in a Rolls when he's on the dole!,** tu te rends compte! il roule en Rolls alors qu'il touche le chômage!;

(j) (*fetch*) aller chercher; **he went and got a book from the library,** il est allé chercher un livre dans la bibliothèque; **go and g. a doctor,** allez chercher un médecin; **g. me the big screwdriver,** allez me chercher le gros tournevis; **can I g. you anything?,** (*to s.o. ill etc*) est-ce que je peux aller vous chercher quelque chose?; **get him a chair, someone,** que quelqu'un aille lui chercher une chaise;

(k) (*prepare*) faire, préparer; **can I g. you an omelette?,** est-ce que je peux vous faire une omelette?; **g. me a sandwich,** fais-moi un sandwich; **she got herself some breakfast,** elle s'est préparé le petit déjeuner; **to g. lunch (ready),** préparer le déjeuner;

(l) (*move, send*) faire parvenir, faire transporter; **you'll never g. that box through the door,** tu n'arriveras jamais à faire passer cette boîte par la porte; **they got her to the airport on time,** ils l'ont amenée à l'aéroport à l'heure; **I got a message to them,** je leur ai fait parvenir un message; **how can I g. it to you?,** comment vous le faire parvenir?; **how am I to g. this parcel home?,** (*by myself*) comment vais-je faire pour transporter ce paquet chez moi?; **to g. the children to bed,** faire coucher les enfants, mettre les enfants au lit; *Fig* **where has all this got us?,** (*our hard work, arguing*) où est-ce que tout ça nous a menés?; **this is getting us nowhere,** (*of method, argument*) ça ne nous mène nulle part, ça ne nous mène à rien; **to g. s.o. on (to) a subject,** amener qn à parler de qch;

(m) (*cause to be*) **to g. sth dry/wet,** sécher/mouiller qch; **to g. sth clean/dirty,** nettoyer/salir qch; **I couldn't get the drawer open,** je n'arrivais pas à ouvrir le tiroir; **to g. sth ready,** préparer qch; **to g. the answer right,** trouver la bonne réponse; **I got his name wrong,** j'ai fait erreur sur son nom; **you've got him worried,** tu l'as fait s'inquiéter;

(n) (*with pp or inf or prp*) (*cause*) **to g. sth done by s.o., to g. s.o. to do sth (for one),** faire faire qch à *ou* par qn; **to g. sth mended,** faire réparer qch; **to g. oneself noticed,** se faire remarquer; **g. him to read it,** faites-le-lui lire; **to g. s.o. to agree,** décider qn à consentir; **you'll never g. him to admit to it,** tu ne le lui feras jamais admettre; **we must g. him to come and see us,** il faut le persuader de venir nous voir; **I can't g. the door to shut,** je n'arrive pas à fermer la porte; **to g. one's work finished,** venir à bout de son travail; **to g. one's dress torn,** déchirer sa robe; *Aut* **to g. the engine running,** mettre le moteur en marche; **that got him guessing,** ça l'a intrigué;

(o) (*do eventually*) **to g. to do sth,** finir par faire qch; **you'll g. to like him,** vous finirez par l'aimer; **to g. to know sth,** apprendre qch; **when you g. to know him,** quand on le connaît mieux; **they got to be friends,** ils sont devenus amis; **she got to be very rich,** elle est devenue très riche;

(p) (*have opportunity to do*) **to g. to do sth,** avoir l'occasion de faire qch; **as a diplomat she got to visit many countries,** en tant que diplomate elle a pu *ou* a eu l'occasion de visiter de nombreux pays; **I didn't g. to speak to him in person,** je n'ai pas pu lui parler en personne; **I finally got to see the Taj Mahal,** j'ai finalement réussi à voir le Taj Mahal;

(q) (*have*) **have got,** avoir; **what have you got there?,** qu'avez-vous là?; **what's that got to do with it!,** qu'est-ce que cela a à voir?; **he's got measles,** il a la rougeole; *F* **you've got it!,** vous y êtes!; **have you got any children?,** avez-vous des enfants?; **I haven't got any,** je n'en ai pas; **have you got a light?,** avez-vous du feu?;

(r) (*must*) **have got,** être obligé (*de faire qch*); **it has got to be done,** il faut que cela se fasse; **have you really got to work on Sundays?,** est-ce que vous êtes vraiment obligé de travailler le dimanche?

2 *vi* **(a)** (*reach, make one's way*) arriver, se rendre (**to,** à); **how does one g. there?,** comment fait-on pour y aller?; **when I got home,** quand je suis arrivé à la maison; **how do I g. to the station?,** (*asking one's way*) le chemin de la gare, s'il vous plaît?; *F* **to g. there,** (*reach a place*) arriver; (*reach a goal*) arriver, réussir; **we're not getting anywhere, we're getting nowhere,** nous n'aboutissons à rien, nous n'arrivons à rien, nous n'allons nulle part; **to g. to the top of a tree/ladder,** monter jusqu'au haut d'un arbre/d'une échelle; **where has he got to?,** qu'est-ce qu'il est devenu?; **where have you got to?,** où en êtes-vous? (*dans votre travail etc*); **she got to the door and turned round,** elle est arrivée à la porte et s'est retournée; **to g. to one's feet,** se lever; **to g. to university,** aller à l'université; *Sl* **g. the hell out of here!,** fiche(-moi) le camp!; **they only got as far as Marseilles,** ils ne sont pas allés plus loin que Marseille; **he got as far as saying ...,** il a été jusqu'à dire ...; **we got on to (the subject of) divorce,** nous en sommes venus à parler du divorce; **he gets on my nerves,** il m'agace; **it's getting beyond a joke,** ça dépasse la plaisanterie; **it got to the point where they weren't speaking to one another,** c'en est venu au point qu'ils ne se parlaient pas; **eventually we got to talking about politics,** nous avons fini par en venir à parler de politique;

(b) to g. behind a tree, se mettre derrière un arbre; **she got inside the barrel,** elle est rentrée dans le fût;

(c) to g. to work, (*start working*) se mettre au travail; (*reach workplace*) arriver à son (lieu de) travail;

(d) (*with adj complement*) (*become*) devenir; **to g. old,** devenir vieux, vieillir; **I'm getting used to it,** je commence à m'y habituer; **to g. angry,** se mettre en colère; **to g. better,** (*improve*) s'améliorer; (*after illness*) se remettre; **it's getting late,** il se fait tard; **it's getting dark,** il commence à faire nuit;

(e) (*with pp*) **to g. dressed,** s'habiller; **to g. married,** se marier; **to g. shaved,** (*by self*) se raser; (*by barber*) se faire raser; **to g. killed,** se faire tuer; **to g. drowned,** se noyer; **to g. caught,** (*by police etc*) se faire prendre; (*by rain etc*) être surpris; **he got dismissed,** il s'est fait renvoyer; **to g. started,** commencer;

(f) (*with prp*) (*start*) **to g. going,** (*leave*) partir, se mettre en route; (*start work*) se mettre au travail; (*hurry*) se dépêcher; **let's g. going** *or F* **cracking,** allons-y!, en route!; **to g. talking with s.o.,** entrer en conversation avec qn.

►**get about** *vi* **(a)** (*move around*) circuler; **he gets about a great deal,** il se déplace beaucoup; **she can't g. about,** (*of invalid*) elle ne peut pas encore sortir; **I don't g. about so much these days,** (*of old person*) je ne sors plus tellement ces temps-ci; **(b)** (*spread*) se répandre, circuler; **it got about that she was planning to resign,** le bruit s'est répandu qu'elle projetait de démissionner.

►**get across 1** *vi* **(a)** (*succeed in crossing*) traverser; **(b)** *F* (*communicate with*) communiquer; **she can't g. across to her audience,** elle ne peut pas communiquer avec son public; *Th* **the play failed to g. across,** la pièce n'a pas passé la rampe. **2** *vtas* **(a)** (*over water, over street*) faire traverser (*qn*); **we had no boat and we couldn't get the supplies across,** nous n'avions pas de bateau et nous ne pouvions pas faire passer les vivres; **the border wasn't**

guarded so it was easy to g. the people across, la frontière n'était pas gardée et il était donc facile de faire passer les gens; **(b)** *F* (*communicate*) **I couldn't g. it across to him,** je n'ai pas réussi à le lui faire comprendre.

►**get ahead** *vi* **(a)** (*make progress*) avancer; **you'll never g. ahead unless you work hard,** tu n'arriveras à rien si tu ne travailles pas dur; **(b)** (*move in front*) prendre la tête.

►**get along** *vi* **(a)** (*leave*) s'en aller, partir; **it's time for me to be getting along,** il est temps que je parte; *F* **g. along with you!,** (*go away*) allez-vous-en!; (*that's silly, not true*) allons donc!, vous plaisantez!; **(b)** (*progress*) **how are you getting along in your new job?,** comment ça va, ton nouveau travail?; **how are you getting along in the new house?,** comment ça va, dans la nouvelle maison?; **we've got along all right without their help,** nous nous sommes bien débrouillés sans leur aide; **I can g. along without you,** je peux me débrouiller sans toi; **(c)** (*be on good terms*) (bien) s'entendre (**with,** avec); **I wish I got along better with my neighbours,** j'aimerais bien m'entendre mieux avec mes voisins.

►**get around** *vi* **(a)** (*be active, move around*) circuler, voyager; (*gain experience*) rouler sa bosse; **old people find it hard to g. around,** les personnes âgées ont du mal à se déplacer; **she gets around a great deal,** elle est toujours par ci, par là; **you g. around, don't you!,** tu sors beaucoup hein!; **(b)** (*spread*) se répandre; **the word got around that he had some information,** on a raconté qu'il avait des informations; **(c)** (*avoid, circumvent*) couper à, échapper à (*des difficultés*); **there's no getting around it — we'll have to tell her,** il n'y a pas d'autre moyen — il va falloir que nous le lui disions.

►**get around to** *vipo* **to g. around to (doing) sth,** trouver le temps de faire qch; **I'll g. around to it one day,** je trouverai le temps de le faire un de ces jours.

►**get at** *vipo* **(a)** (*reach, have access to*) atteindre (*un endroit, qn*); **the study is locked and I can't g. at my books,** le bureau est fermé à clef et je ne peux pas prendre mes livres; **it's on the top shelf where the children can't g. at it,** c'est sur l'étagère du haut où les enfants ne peuvent pas l'atteindre; **to g. at the truth,** découvrir la vérité; *F* **just let me g. at him!,** si jamais il me tombe sous la main!;

(b) (*imply*) **what are you getting at?,** où voulez-vous en venir?;

(c) *F* (*suborn*) suborner (*un témoin*);

(d) *F* (*criticize unfairly*) attaquer (*qn*); **she's always getting at her husband,** elle est toujours à dénigrer son mari; **you're not being got at, no one's getting at you,** on ne s'en prend pas à toi, personne ne s'en prend à toi; **he keeps getting at me to get my hair cut,** il est toujours sur mon dos pour que je me fasse couper les cheveux; **you'll have to really g. at her if you want her to do something,** il va falloir que tu sois vraiment sur son dos si tu veux qu'elle fasse quelque chose.

►**get away 1** *vi* (*leave*) partir; (*escape*) s'échapper, se sauver; **to g. away for a few days,** (parvenir à) s'absenter pendant quelques jours; **g. away!,** allez-vous-en!; *F* **g. away (with you)!,** tu plaisantes!, ça ne prend pas!; **car that gets away quickly,** voiture qui a une bonne reprise. **2** *vtas* (*remove*) emmener (*qn*) de force d'un endroit; se saisir de (*qch*); **she wanted to go into the burning building but they managed to g. her away,** elle voulait entrer dans le bâtiment en feu mais ils ont réussi à l'emmener.

►**get away from 1** *vipo* (*manage to leave, escape*) quitter (*un endroit*); **to g. away early from the office,** quitter le bureau de bonne heure; **I couldn't g. away from him,** (*he wouldn't stop talking*) je ne pouvais pas m'en défaire; **how wonderful to g. away from it all!,** quel plaisir de tout quitter!; **there's no getting away from it,** il faut bien l'admettre. **2** *vtas* (*remove*) faire partir, faire sortir, emmener; **g. your dog away from my garden!,** faites sortir votre chien de mon jardin!; **they managed to g. him away from the TV,** ils ont fini par l'arracher de devant *ou* à la télévision; **to g. sth away from s.o.,** prendre qch à qn.

►**get away with** *vipo* **(a)** (*escape with*) **the burglars got away with £10,000,** les cambrioleurs ont raflé 10 000 livres; **(b)** (*be let off with*) s'en tirer avec; **he got away with a small fine,** il s'en est tiré avec une petite amende; **(c)** (*not be punished for*) **that child gets away with murder,** on laisse tout faire à ce gamin; **criminals must not be allowed to g. away with it,** on ne doit pas laisser les criminels s'en tirer; **she pretended she was a policewoman and she got away with it,** elle a fait semblant d'être femme policier et ça a marché; **her skirt is really tiny but she gets away with it,** sa jupe est vraiment très courte mais elle peut se le permettre.

►**get back 1** *vi* **(a)** (*return*) revenir, retourner; **when did you g. back?,** quand est-ce que tu es rentré?; **I got back from Italy yesterday,** je suis rentré d'Italie hier; **to g. back to London,** rentrer à Londres; **to g. back home,** rentrer chez soi; **to g. back into bed,** se recoucher; **to g. back to nature,** retourner à la nature;

(b) (*move away, step back*) reculer (**from,** de); **g. back or I'll shoot!,** reculez ou je tire!

2 *vtsep* **(a)** (*recover*) se faire rendre (*qch*); recouvrer (*ses biens*); reprendre (*ses forces*); **I'll g. the book back from her tomorrow,** je lui demanderai de rendre le livre demain; **to g. one's money back,** (*loan returned*) récuper son argent; (*reimbursed*) se faire rembourser;

(b) (*return*) faire revenir (*qch*); **g. the file back to me as soon as possible,** rendez-moi le dossier dès que possible;

(c) (*put back*) remettre (*qch*); **to g. sth back into its box,** faire rentrer qch dans sa boîte.

►**get back at** *vipo* (*have revenge*) prendre sa revanche sur (*qn*).

►**get back to** *vipo* **(a)** (*return*) retourner à; **to g. back to work,** (*after illness*) reprendre le travail; (*after short break*) se remettre au travail; **(b)** (*contact*) recontacter; **can we g. back to you on that later?,** est-ce que nous pouvons vous recontacter à ce sujet plus tard?

►**get behind 1** *vi* (*become delayed*) prendre du retard; **to g. behind with one's work,** prendre du retard dans son travail. **2** *vipo* **(a)** (*move to the back of*) se mettre derrière (*qch*); **g. behind that tree,** mets-toi derrière cet arbre; **(b)** (*persuade, nag*) être sur le dos de (*qn*).

►**get by 1** *vi* **(a)** (*succeed in passing*) passer; **there wasn't enough room to g. by,** il n'y avait pas assez de place pour passer; **(b)** *F* (*manage*) se débrouiller; **we just g. by,** on s'en tire, sans plus; **he thinks he'll g. by without studying,** il croit qu'il va s'en tirer sans étudier; **you can g. by on a few dollars a day,** vous pouvez vous en tirer avec quelques dollars par jour. **2** *vipo* **(a)** (*move past*) **can you g. by the washing machine?,** la machine à laver vous laisse assez de place pour passer?; **(b)** (*escape attention of*) échapper à (*la censure, le rédacteur*).

►**get down 1** *vi* **(a)** (*from wall, tree etc*) descendre (**from, off,** de); **(b)** (*lower one's body*) **g. down or she'll see us!,** baisse-toi! sinon elle va nous voir; **to g. down on one's knees,** se mettre à genoux; **g. down!,** (*to dog*) couché!; **(c)** (*leave table*) quitter la table, sortir de table; **may I g. down?,** est-ce que je peux quitter la table? **2** *vtsep* **(a)** (*bring, fetch down*) descendre (*un livre d'un rayon etc*); **(b)** (*reduce*) faire baisser; **the doctors got his temperature down,** les docteurs ont fait baisser sa température; **to g. one's weight down,** perdre du poids; **(c)** (*make a note of*) noter (*qch*) (**in writing, on paper,** par écrit). **3** *vtas* **(a)** (*depress*) déprimer; **this rain is getting me down,** cette pluie me déprime; **(b)** (*swallow*) avaler; **g. this soup down,** avale cette soupe.

►**get down to** *vipo* (*tackle*) se mettre à; **to g. down to work,** se mettre au travail; **we'd better g. down to the facts,** il faut en venir aux faits; **we eventually got down to details,** nous avons fini par en arriver aux détails.

►**get in 1** *vi* **(a)** (*gain entrance*) entrer; **how did the thieves g. in?,** comment est-ce que les voleurs sont entrés?; **water had got in everywhere,** l'eau avait pénétré partout;

(b) (*arrive*) arriver; **if the train gets in on time,** si le train arrive à l'heure; **we got in at about eleven,** nous sommes rentrés (chez nous) vers onze heures;

(c) (*be elected*) être élu; **the Conservatives didn't g. in,** les conservateurs n'ont pas été élus.

2 *vipo* (*enter*) **g. in the car!,** entre dans la voiture!, monte en voiture!; **the smoke got in our eyes,** la fumée nous est rentrée dans les yeux.

3 *vtsep* **(a)** (*summon*) faire venir (*le médecin*);

(b) (*bring inside*) rentrer (*la lessive, la moisson etc*);

(c) (*plant in the ground*) planter, mettre en terre;

(d) (*manage to do*) réussir à faire; **she got in some last-minute revision before the exam,** elle a réussi à faire des révisions de dernière minute avant l'examen;

(e) (*insert*) glisser, placer; **I couldn't g. a word in,** je n'ai pas pu placer un mot, je n'ai pas pu en placer une;

(f) (*stock up with*) faire provision de; **to g. coal in for the winter,** faire une provision de charbon pour l'hiver.

4 *vtas* **(a)** (*ensure admission to*) permettre d'entrer; **a press card should g. you in,** une carte de presse devrait vous permettre d'entrer; **these exam results will g. you in,** (*to university*) ces résultats d'examens vous permettront d'être admis;

(b) (*ensure election of*) assurer l'élection de (*qn, un parti*); **her reputation for integrity got her in,** sa réputation d'intégrité a assuré son élection.

►get into 1 *vipo* **(a)** (*gain entrance*) entrer dans (*une maison, un bois etc*); monter dans (*une voiture, un train etc*); **to g. into parliament,** être élu député; **to g. into a university,** entrer en faculté;

(b) (*put on*) mettre (*ses vêtements*); endosser (*un pardessus etc*); **I can't g. into this dress any more,** je n'entre plus dans cette robe;

(c) (*affect*) **I don't know what's got into her these days,** je ne sais pas ce qu'elle a *ou* ce qui lui prend en ce moment;

(d) (*phrases*) **to g. into a panic,** être pris de panique; **to g. into a rage,** se mettre en rage; **to g. into a bad habit,** acquérir *ou* prendre une mauvaise habitude; **to g. into trouble,** se mettre dans de mauvais draps; **to g. into debt,** s'endetter;

(e) (*learn*) **to g. into the way of doing sth,** (*learn*) apprendre à faire qch; (*get used to*) prendre l'habitude de faire qch; **the system may seem difficult but you'll soon g. into it,** le système peut sembler difficile mais tu t'y feras vite;

(f) *F* (*become interested in*) commencer à s'intéresser à (*qch*); **it's a hard book to g. into,** c'est un livre dans lequel il est difficile de rentrer; **I've really got into African music recently,** j'ai vraiment commencé à m'intéresser à la musique africaine dernièrement.

2 *vtaspo* **(a)** (*insert*) **to g. sth into sth,** (faire) (r)entrer qch dans qch; **to g. the key into the lock,** mettre *ou* introduire la clef dans la serrure; **to g. an article into a paper,** faire accepter un article par un journal;

(b) (*involve*) **you got me into this mess,** tu m'as mis dans ce pétrin; **to g. s.o. into trouble,** attirer des ennuis à qn; **to g. a girl into trouble,** mettre une fille enceinte;

(c) (*cause to be*) mettre (*qn*) dans; **to g. s.o. into a rage,** mettre quelqu'un en rage; **to g. s.o. into a good mood,** mettre quelqu'un de bonne humeur.

►get in with *vipo* **(a)** (*ingratiate oneself with*) s'insinuer dans les bonnes grâces de qn, se mettre bien avec qn; **if you want to g. in with him ...,** si tu veux te mettre bien avec lui ...; **(b)** (*associate with*) fréquenter (*qn, un groupe etc*); **she got in with the wrong crowd at school,** elle s'est mise à avoir de mauvaises fréquentations à l'école.

►get off 1 *vi* **(a)** (*descend from vehicle*) descendre; *Sl* **I told him where to g. off,** je lui ai dit ses quatre vérités;

(b) (*let go of sth*) laisser qch; **hey! g. off! that's MY book,** hé! laisse ça! c'est mon livre;

(c) (*go unpunished*) s'en tirer; **to g. off lightly,** s'en tirer à bon compte;

(d) (*leave, especially referring to work*) quitter, sortir; *Av* décoller; **I'd like to g. off early tomorrow,** j'aimerais bien quitter (le travail) tôt *ou* sortir tôt (du travail) demain.

(e) to g. off (to sleep), s'endormir;

(f) to g. off to a late start, (*start late*) commencer avec du retard; **to g. off to a good start,** (*start well*) bien commencer.

2 *vipo* **(a)** (*descend from*) descendre de; **g. off that wall!,** descends de ce mur!;

(b) (*let go of*) laisser; **g. off my books,** laisse mes livres;

(c) (*be exempted from*) couper à, échapper à; **he managed to g. off military service,** il s'est débrouillé pour couper au service militaire.

3 *vtas* **(a)** (*remove*) enlever (*un couvercle etc*); **g. your feet off the table!,** enlève tes pieds de sur la table!; **g. your hands off me/that baby/that cake/***etc*, ne me touche pas/ne touche pas ce bébé/ce gâteau/*etc*; **you'll never g. that stain off,** tu n'arriveras jamais à faire partir cette tache; **we got his clothes off,** nous lui avons enlevé ses vêtements;

(b) (*send*) expédier, envoyer (*une lettre*); **to g. the children off to bed,** envoyer les enfants au lit; *Nau* **to g. a ship off,** (*a sandbank etc*) renflouer *ou* déséchouer *ou* remettre à flot un bateau;

(c) (*save from punishment*) tirer (*qn*) d'affaire; *Jur* faire acquitter un prévenu; **it'll take a good lawyer to g. her off,** il va falloir un bon avocat pour la tirer d'affaire;

(d) (*have as holiday*) prendre (*une journée, une semaine etc*) de congé; **can you g. tomorrow afternoon/next week off?,** est-ce que tu peux prendre un congé demain après-midi/la semaine prochaine?;

(e) (*obtain*) tenir (*qch de qn*); **I got that story off the woman next door,** je tiens cette histoire de la voisine; **I got this cold off the woman next door,** la voisine m'a passé ce rhume;

(f) (*free from*) se faire dispenser (*de faire qch*); **those burns got him off work,** ces brûlures le dispensent d'aller travailler;

(g) to g. a baby off, (*to sleep*) endormir un bébé; **that got us off to a late start,** nous sommes partis avec du retard à cause de ça.

►get off with *vipo F* **(a)** (*be punished lightly*) en être quitte pour, s'en tirer avec (*une amende*); **(b) to g. off with s.o.,** (*establish sexual relationship with*) draguer qn; (*have sex with*) coucher avec qn; **to g. off with each other,** (*kiss etc*) se peloter.

►get on 1 *vi* **(a)** (*board*) monter sur (*une échelle*); monter dans (*un train*);

(b) (*progress*) réussir, arriver, progresser; **to g. on in life,** arriver dans la vie;

(c) (*continue with work, journey*) continuer; **right, let's g. on, shall we?,** bien, si on continuait?;

(d) (*cope, manage*) aller; **how are you getting on?,** comment allez-vous?; (*at work*) comment va votre travail?; **how did you g. on?,** (*in exam, at dentist's*) comment ça s'est passé?; **I'll let you know how he's getting on,** je vous donnerai de ses nouvelles; **I can't g. on without her,** je ne peux pas me passer d'elle;

(e) (*have good relationship*) s'entendre;

(f) (*become late*) se faire tard; **time's getting on,** l'heure avance;

(g) (*age*) **to be getting on (in years),** prendre de l'âge.

2 *vtas* (*put on*) mettre (*ses chaussures etc*); enfiler (*ses bas etc*); **I can't g. these trousers on any more,** je n'entre plus dans ce pantalon; **she's just getting her coat on,** elle est en train de mettre son manteau; **I can't g. the lid on,** je n'arrive pas à mettre le couvercle.

3 *vipo* **(a)** (*board, enter*) monter dans (*un bus, un train, un avion etc*);

(b) (*climb onto*) grimper sur (*le toit*); monter sur (*une chaise, une échelle*);

(c) (*be put on*) se retrouver sur; **how did these papers g. on my desk?,** comment est-ce que ces papiers se sont retrouvés *ou* sont arrivés sur mon bureau?

►get on for *vipo* (*approach*) **to be getting on for forty,** approcher de *ou* friser la quarantaine; **it's getting on for midnight,** il est presque minuit; **there were getting on for 200 people at the wedding,** il y avait près de 200 personnes au mariage.

►get onto *vipo* **(a)** (*contact*) contacter, se mettre en contact avec, se mettre en rapport avec; **I'll g. onto the bank about it,** je vais contacter la banque à ce sujet; **I'll g. on to him to finish the work,** je vais le contacter pour lui dire de finir le travail; **(b)** (*locate, find name of*) trouver le nom *ou* les coordonnées de (*qn*); **how did you g. onto me?,** comment est-ce que vous avez trouvé mon nom?; **(c)** (*move forward*) en arriver à; **they eventually got onto money,** ils ont fini par en arriver à parler d'argent.

►get on with *vipo* **(a)** (*have good relationship with*) s'entendre bien avec; **I don't g. on with my parents,** je ne m'entends pas avec mes parents; **(b)** (*progress*) avancer; **how are you getting on with the painting?,** alors, ça avance la peinture?; **(c)** (*continue with*) continuer; **just g. on with what you are supposed to be doing,** (*said by teacher etc*) continuez ce que vous avez à faire; **let Dad g. on with his work,** laissez Papa travailler en paix; **I wish the press would let me g. on with my life,** si la presse pouvait me laisser vivre en paix; **I've got enough work to be getting on with,** j'ai assez de travail à faire, j'ai assez de pain sur la planche.

►get out 1 *vi* **(a)** (*leave*) sortir; *F* **g. out!,** fiche(-moi) le camp!;

(b) *F* (*be released from prison, hospital*) sortir; (*escape*) s'évader; **when does she g. out?,** quand est-ce qu'elle sort?;

(c) (*leave one's house, flat*) sortir de chez soi; **he ought to g. out more,** il devrait sortir plus de chez lui;

(d) (*leak*) être éventé, s'ébruiter; **how did the news g. out?,** comment la nouvelle s'est-elle répandue?; **the secret got out,** le secret a transpiré.

2 *vtsep* **(a)** (*bring out*) sortir (*ses outils, ses livres etc*); **to g. out one's car,** (*from garage*) sortir sa voiture; **to g. a book out from the library,** emprunter un livre à la bibliothèque; **he could hardly g. a word out,** c'est à peine s'il a pu sortir un mot; **we have to g. this report out by Monday,** nous devons sortir ce rapport pour lundi;

(b) (*free*) faire sortir (*les otages etc*);
(c) (*remove*) arracher (*un clou etc*); retirer (*un bouchon*); faire disparaître (*une tache*);
(d) *Cr* renverser le guichet à (*qn*).

▶get out of 1 *vipo* **(a)** (*leave*) sortir de; descendre de (*une voiture*); **let's g. out of here,** partons d'ici; **he managed to g. out of the country,** (*of criminal, refugee*) il a réussi à quitter le pays; **to g. out of bed,** se lever; **to g. out of prison/the army,** sortir de prison/quitter l'armée;
(b) (*extricate oneself from*) se tirer de, se faire exempter de; **to g. out of doing sth,** se faire exempter de faire qch; **he always gets out of doing the washing up,** il arrive toujours à se tirer de la corvée de vaisselle; **to g. out of a difficulty,** se tirer d'une position difficile; **I'd like to see her g. out of this one,** j'aimerais bien voir comment elle va s'en tirer cette fois; **to g. out of s.o.'s way,** faire place à qn;
(c) (*become unaccustomed to*) perdre l'habitude de; **to g. out of the habit of doing sth,** perdre l'habitude de faire qch.
2 *vtaspo* **(a)** (*bring out*) sortir (*qch*) de; **g. the phone book out of the drawer,** sors l'annuaire téléphonique du tiroir; **she got the nail out of her shoe,** elle a retiré le clou de sa chaussure; **I couldn't g. the key out of the lock,** je n'arrivais pas à sortir la clef de la serrure; **to g. a secret out of s.o.,** arracher un secret à qn; **I can't g. anything out of him,** je ne peux rien tirer de lui; **we finally got the truth out of her,** nous avons fini par lui arracher la vérité; **I can't g. the idea out of my mind,** je ne peux pas me débarrasser de l'idée; **to g. money out of s.o.,** soutirer de l'argent à qn; **to g. s.o. out of a difficulty,** tirer qn de difficulté; **the firemen got us out of the building,** les pompiers nous ont fait sortir du bâtiment: **to g. a stain out of a carpet,** enlever *ou* ôter une tache d'un tapis;
(b) (*derive*) retirer de; **I didn't g. much out of my lessons,** je n'ai pas tiré grand-chose de mes leçons.

▶get over 1 *vi* **(a)** (*cross*) passer par-dessus, franchir; **the wall was low so it was easy to g. over,** le mur était bas donc il a été facile de le franchir;
(b) (*communicate*) **to g. over to s.o.,** se faire comprendre de qn.
2 *vipo* **(a)** (*cross*) escalader, passer par-dessus; **to g. over a wall,** passer par-dessus un mur;
(b) (*recover from*) se remettre de (*une maladie*); venir à bout de (*ses difficultés*); revenir de (*sa surprise*); **she can't g. over it,** (*illness, emotional shock, trauma*) elle ne s'en remet pas; (*surprise, shock etc*) elle n'en revient pas; (*loss*) elle est inconsolable; **it will take her a long time to g. over it,** elle s'en ressentira longtemps, ça lui prendra longtemps pour s'en remettre;
(c) (*overcome*) surmonter (*la peur etc*);
(d) (*communicate*) faire passer; **she got her point over very well,** elle a très bien fait passer ce qu'elle voulait dire.
3 *vtas* faire traverser; (*across water*) faire passer (*qch*); **we got the children over the road,** nous avons fait traverser la route aux enfants.

▶get over with *vtas* (*complete*) terminer, finir, en finir avec (*qch*); **she got her work over with as quickly as possible,** elle a fini son travail aussi vite que possible; **when I g. my exams over with I'll be able to relax,** quand j'aurai terminé mes examens, je pourrai me détendre.

▶get round 1 *vi* **(a)** (*travel around*) faire le tour de; **it would take a day to g. round,** (*the exhibition, museum*) ça prendrait une journée pour en faire le tour;
(b) (*arrive*) venir; **the doctor said she'd g. round as soon as she can,** le docteur a dit qu'elle viendrait dès qu'elle pourrait;
(c) (*of news, rumour*) se répandre.
2 *vipo* **(a)** faire le tour de (*une exposititon, un musée*); tourner (*un coin*);
(b) (*circumvent*) contourner (*une difficulté*); **there's no getting round it,** (*you'll have to own up*) il n'y a pas moyen d'y couper; **how did they g. round the export regulations?,** comment est-ce qu'ils ont réussi à contourner les réglementations concernant l'exportation?;
(c) (*cajole*) embobiner (*qn*), faire ce qu'on veut de (*qn*).
3 *vtas* **(a)** (*bring, take*) **I'll g. the books round (to you) as soon as I can,** je t'apporterai les livres dès que je le pourrai;
(b) (*persuade*) **you've got me round to your way of thinking,** tu m'as convaincu.

▶get round to *vipo* trouver le temps de faire qch; **I'll g. round to mending that tap eventually,** je finirai par trouver le temps de réparer ce robinet.

▶get through 1 *vi* **(a)** (*arrive*) parvenir à franchir un obstacle; **the road was blocked and no one could g. through,** la route était bloquée et personne ne pouvait passer; **the message didn't g. through,** le message n'est pas passé; **only a few trains got through to the besieged city,** seuls quelques trains sont arrivés jusqu'à la ville assiégée; **the news got through to them,** la nouvelle leur est parvenue;
(b) *Tel* obtenir la communication (**to s.o.,** avec qn); *Fig* (*communicate*) se faire comprendre (de qn); **I'm not getting through (to you), am I?,** je ne me fais pas bien comprendre, hein?;
(c) *Am* (*finish*) finir, terminer; **the class doesn't usually g. through until six o'clock,** la leçon ne se termine généralement pas avant six heures;
(d) (*pass exam*) être reçu (à un examen).
2 *vipo* **(a)** (*negotiate successfully*) **you won't g. through the roadblock,** tu n'arriveras pas à franchir le barrage routier; **to g. through the day,** faire passer la journée;
(b) (*pass through*) passer à travers (*un trou etc*);
(c) (*succeed in*) réussir; **to g. through an exam,** être reçu à un examen;
(d) (*finish*) achever, arriver au bout de (*son travail etc*); **to g. through a lot of work,** abattre du travail;
(e) (*use up*) utiliser; **he gets through eight shirts a week,** il salit huit chemises par semaine; **we'll never g. through all this food,** nous ne viendrons jamais à bout de toute cette nourriture.
3 *vtas* **(a)** (*transport, send successfully*) faire parvenir; **they got the food supplies through,** ils ont réussi à faire parvenir les provisions alimentaires (à destination); **to g. sth through customs,** (faire) passer qch à la douane; **they got a message through,** ils ont fait passer un message; *Parl* **to g. a bill through,** faire adopter un projet de loi;
(b) (*make comprehensible*) faire comprendre; **I finally got it through to him that I wasn't interested,** j'ai fini par lui faire comprendre que je n'étais pas intéressé;
(c) (*cause to succeed*) **it was your essay that got you through the exam,** c'est ta dissertation qui t'a permis de réussir l'examen;
(d) (*enable to endure*) **I need four cups of coffee to g. me through the day,** il me faut quatre tasses de café pour passer la journée.

▶get together 1 *vi* **(a)** (*of people*) se réunir, se rassembler (**to do,** pour faire); **(b)** (*co-operate*) s'entendre, travailler en collaboration; **the two countries got together to deal with coastal pollution,** les deux pays ont collaboré pour s'attaquer au problème de la pollution côtière. **2** *vtsep* (*collect*) rassembler, ramasser (*des objets*); réunir (*des amis etc*); **g. your things together, we're going,** rassemble tes affaires, nous partons; **to g. some money together,** réunir une somme d'argent; **let me g. my thoughts together,** laissez-moi rassembler mes idées.

▶get under 1 *vipo* (*go beneath*) se mettre sous (*la table etc*). **2** *vtas* (*place beneath*) mettre *ou* placer sous; **I can't g. the carpet under the table,** je n'arrive pas à placer le tapis sous la table.

▶get up 1 *vi* **(a)** (*get out of bed*) se lever;
(b) (*stand up*) se lever, se mettre debout; **g. up!,** levez-vous!; **to g. up from a chair/the table,** se lever de sa chaise/de table;
(c) *Met* **the wind/a storm was getting up,** le vent/une tempête se levait.
2 *vipo* (*get on top of, climb onto*) monter sur, monter à; **to g. up a ladder,** monter à une échelle.
3 *vtsep* **(a) to g. up speed,** donner de la vitesse;
(b) (*organize*) organiser (*une fête, une pétition etc*).
4 *vtas* **(a)** (*move up*) monter jusque; **how are we going to g. this desk up to the fifth floor?,** comment allons-nous monter ce bureau jusqu'au cinquième étage?; **to g. s.o. up the stairs,** aider qn à monter l'escalier;
(b) (*rouse*) faire (se) lever; **I need that alarm clock to g. me up in the morning,** il me faut ce réveil pour me faire (me) lever le matin;
(c) to g. oneself up as s.o./sth, (*dress up*) se déguiser en qn/qch;
(d) *Vulg* **to g. it up,** (*of man*) bander, avoir la trique.

▶get up to *vipo* **(a)** (*reach*) arriver; **it took ages to g. up to the top of the hill,** ça a pris une éternité pour arriver en haut de la colline; **I've got up to chapter 5,** j'en suis au chapitre 5; **where have you got up to?,** où en êtes-vous?; **(b)** (*create*) **those children are always**

getting up to something *or* **to some mischief,** ces enfants sont toujours en train de faire des bêtises; **the dog's been getting up to his usual tricks,** le chien a fait ses bêtises habituelles.

getatable, get-at-able [get'ætəb(ə)l] *adj F* accessible, d'accès facile.

getaway ['getəweɪ] *n* **(a)** (*of criminal*) fuite *f*; **g. car,** voiture *f* pour fuire; **to make one's g.,** s'enfuir; **(b)** *Aut* démarrage *m*; **smart g.,** bonne accélération; **(c)** *Sp* démarrage *m* (*d'un coureur*).

Gethsemane [geθ'semənɪ] *n* Gethsémani *m*.

get-rich-quick ['get'rɪtʃ'kwɪk] *adj F* (*projet*) qui promet une fortune; (*developer, contractor*) qui veut faire fortune rapidement.

get-together ['get'təgeðər] *n F* réunion *f*; **I'm having a g.-t. with some friends,** je rencontre *ou* vois quelques amis; **you and I must have a little g.-t. one day,** il faut qu'on se voie un de ces jours tous les deux.

get-up ['getʌp] *n F* **(a)** (*clothes*) habillement *m*, tenue *f*, toilette *f*; (*fancy dress*) déguisement *m*; **what a g.-up!,** quel costume!; **(b)** *Com* présentation *f* (*des marchandises*).

get-up-and-go ['getʌpən'gəʊ] *n F* allant *m*, entrain *m*; **she's full of g.-up-and-go today,** elle est pleine d'entrain aujourd'hui; **where's your g.-up-and-go?,** où est ton entrain?

gewgaw ['gjuːgɔː] *n* babiole *f*.

geyser ['giːzər] *n* **(a)** *Geol* geyser *m*; **(b)** *Br* (*water heater*) chauffe-eau *m inv* à gaz; **(c)** *Br Sl* (*man*) mec *m*.

Ghana ['gɑːnə] *n* Ghana *m*.

Ghanaian, Ghanian [gɑː'neɪən, 'gɑːnɪən] **1** *adj* ghanéen. **2** *n* Ghanéen, -enne.

ghastliness ['gɑːstlɪnɪs] *n* horreur *f* (*d'un crime*); aspect *m* sinistre (*de qch*).

ghastly ['gɑːstlɪ] **1** *adj* **(a)** (*experience*) horrible, affreux, épouvantable; *F* **what g. weather!,** quel temps abominable!; **a g. mistake,** une erreur monstrueuse; **(b)** (*pale*) blême; (*pâleur*) mortel; (*lumière*) blafard; **he looked g.,** il avait l'air d'un déterré. **2** *adv* **g. pale,** pâle comme un mort.

Ghent [gent] *n* Gand *m*.

gherkin ['gɜːkɪn] *n* cornichon *m*; *Culin* **pickled gherkins,** cornichons confits (au vinaigre).

ghetto ['getəʊ] *n* ghetto *m*; *F* **g. blaster,** mini-stéréo *f* portable.

ghost¹ [gəʊst] *n* **(a)** fantôme *m*, spectre *m*; **to believe in ghosts,** croire aux revenants; **you look as if you'd seen a g.,** vous avez l'air d'un déterré; **to be the mere g. of one's former self,** n'être plus que l'ombre de soi-même; **not the g. of a chance,** pas la moindre chance; **g. of a smile,** sourire *m* vague; **g. ship,** vaisseau-fantôme *m*; **g. story,** histoire *f* de revenants; **g. town,** ville-fantôme *f*; **(b)** *Rel* **the Holy G.,** l'Esprit Saint, le Saint-Esprit; **(c)** *Arch* (*soul*) âme *f*; (*still used in*) **to give up the g.,** rendre l'âme, expirer; *Fig* **the car finally gave up the g. yesterday,** la voiture a rendu l'âme hier; **(d)** nègre *m* (*d'un auteur*); **(e)** *Opt* spectre *m* secondaire; image blanche; *TV* écho *m*; *TV* **g. image,** image fantôme.

ghost² *Liter* **1** *vi* servir de nègre (**for an author,** à un écrivain). **2** *vt* écrire (*les discours de qn*); **to g. a book,** servir de nègre à l'auteur d'un livre; **ghosted work,** ouvrage écrit par un nègre.

ghosting ['gəʊstɪŋ] *n TV* images *fpl* fantôme.

ghostly ['gəʊstlɪ] *adj* spectral, -aux, de fantôme.

ghostwrite ['gəʊstraɪt] *vi & vt* = **GHOST²**.

ghostwriter ['gəʊstraɪtər] *n* = **GHOST¹ (d)**.

ghoul [guːl] *n* **(a)** (*ghost*) vampire *m*; **(b)** *F* (*person*) personne qui a des goûts macabres *ou* morbides; **a crowd of ghouls had gathered at the scene of the accident,** une foule d'amateurs de spectacles macabres s'était amassée sur la scène de l'accident; **(c)** (*grave robber*) déterreur *m* de cadavre; **(d)** *Myth* goule *f*.

ghoulish ['guːlɪʃ] *adj* **(a)** (*humour etc*) macabre; **(b)** *Myth* de goule.

GHQ [dʒiːeɪtʃ'kjuː] *n Mil* (*abbr* **General Headquarters**) = Q.G. *m inv*.

GHz *n abbr* **gigahertz**.

GI [dʒiː'aɪ] *n F* **GI (Joe),** soldat américain, G.I. *m inv*; **GI bride,** = femme étrangère ayant épousé un G.I.

giant ['dʒaɪənt] **1** *n Myth & Fig* géant *m*; *esp Sp* **g. killer,** = équipe etc qui remporte la victoire sur une équipe etc adverse habituellement victorieuse. **2** *adj* (*chêne, carton*) géant; **with g. strides,** à pas de géant.

giantess [dʒaɪən'tes] *n* géante *f*.

Gib [dʒɪb] *n F* Gibraltar *m*.

gibber ['dʒɪbər] *vi* produire des sons inarticulés (*comme un singe, un idiot*); (*of foreigners speaking amongst themselves*) baragouiner; **he was gibbering with rage/fear,** il bégayait de rage/frayeur.

gibberish ['dʒɪbərɪʃ] *n* baragouin *m*, charabia *m*; **to talk g.,** raconter du charabia.

gibbet ['dʒɪbɪt] *n* gibet *m*, potence *f*.

gibbon ['gɪbən] *n* (*monkey*) gibbon *m*.

gibbous ['gɪbəs] *adj* gibbeux; *Astron* **g. moon,** lune *f* au troisième *ou* dernier quartier.

gibe¹ [dʒaɪb] *n* raillerie *f*, moquerie *f*, quolibet *m*; **to make a g.,** lancer une raillerie *ou* une moquerie *ou* un quolibet (**at,** à).

gibe² *vt & vi* **to g. (at) s.o.,** railler qn, se moquer de qn.

giblets ['dʒɪblɪts] *npl* abattis *mpl* (*de volaille*).

Gibraltar [dʒɪ'brɔːltər] *n* Gibraltar *m*; **the Straits of G.,** le détroit de Gibraltar.

giddily ['gɪdɪlɪ] *adv* **(a)** d'une manière vertigineuse; **(b)** (*frivolously*) étourdiment.

giddiness ['gɪdɪnɪs] *n* **(a)** (*vertigo*) étourdissement *m*, vertige *m*; **fits of g.,** des étourdissements, des vertiges; **(b)** (*frivolousness*) frivolité *f*.

giddy ['gɪdɪ] *adj* **(a)** (*person*) étourdi; **to be** *or* **feel g.,** avoir le vertige; **I feel g.,** la tête me tourne; **it makes me (feel) g.,** cela me donne le vertige; **(b)** (*height*) vertigineux, qui donne le vertige; **(c)** (*frivolous*) frivole; *Fig* **g. round of pleasures,** tourbillon *m* de plaisirs.

gift [gɪft] *n* **(a)** (*to individual*) cadeau *m*; **Christmas g.,** cadeau de Noël; **it was a g.,** c'était un cadeau; (*of bargain*) c'était donné; (*easy victory*) c'était un jeu d'enfants; *F* **he thinks he's God's g. to women,** il croit que toutes les femmes vont tomber à ses pieds; **I wouldn't have it as a g.,** je n'en voudrais pas quand bien même on me le donnerait; *Prov* **never look a g. horse in the mouth,** à cheval donné on ne regarde pas à la bride; **g. shop,** magasin *m* de nouveautés; **g. voucher,** bon-cadeau *m*; **(b)** (*donation*) don *m*; **a g. of £2,000,** un don de 2 000 livres; **to make a g. of sth to s.o.,** faire don de qch à qn; *Jur* **as a g.,** à titre d'avantage; **(c)** *Com* (*on presentation of coupons*) prime *f*; **free g.,** cadeau *m*; **(d)** (*talent*) talent *m*; **to have a g. for mathematics,** avoir le don *ou F* la bosse des mathématiques.

giftbook ['gɪftbʊk] *n* livre *m* d'étrennes.

gifted ['gɪftɪd] *adj* bien doué; (*artiste*) de talent.

giftwrap ['gɪftræp] *vt* faire un paquet-cadeau de (*qch*).

giftwrapped ['gɪftræpt] *adj Com* (*article*) emballé en paquet-cadeau; **would you like it g.?,** c'est pour offrir?, je vous fais un paquet-cadeau?

giftwrapping ['gɪftræpɪŋ] *n* **(a)** (*of parcel*) emballage *m*; **(b)** (*paper, ribbons etc*) emballage-cadeau *m*.

gig¹ [gɪg] *n* **(a)** (*carriage*) cabriolet *m*; **(b)** *Nau* yole *f*.

gig² *n Mus* engagement *m* d'un soir.

gig³ *vi Mus* jouer un soir.

giga- ['gaɪgə] *pref* giga-.

gigabyte ['gaɪgəbaɪt] *n Comptr* gigaoctet *m*.

gigahertz ['gaɪgəhɜːts] *n* gigahertz *m*.

gigantic [dʒaɪ'gæntɪk] *adj* géant, gigantesque; (*bâtiment etc*) colossal, -aux.

gigantically [dʒaɪ'gæntɪklɪ] *adv* gigantesquement.

giggle¹ ['gɪg(ə)l] *n* petit rire; **to have (a fit of) the giggles,** avoir le fou rire; *F* **to do sth for a g.,** faire qch pour se marrer *ou* pour rigoler.

giggle² *vi* rire, glousser; **what are you giggling about?,** qu'est-ce qui vous fait rire?

giggling ['gɪg(ə)lɪŋ] **1** *adj* qui rit *ou* glousse. **2** *n* rires *mpl* bêbêtes, fou rire.

giggly ['gɪg(ə)lɪ] *adj* qui pousse des petits rires; **to be in a g. mood,** être d'humeur joyeuse.

GIGO [dʒiːaɪdʒiː'əʊ] *Comptr Sl abbr* **garbage in, garbage out.**

gigolo ['dʒɪgələʊ] *n* gigolo *m*.

gild [gɪld] *vt* (*pt* **gilded**; *pp* **gilded**, *occ* **gilt** [gɪlt]) dorer; **to g. the lily,** renchérir sur la perfection; **to g. the pill,** dorer la pilule.

gilding ['gɪldɪŋ] *n* dorure *f*.

gill¹ [gɪl] *n* (*usu pl*) **(a)** (*of fish*) **gills,** ouïe(s) *f(pl)*, branchie(s) *f(pl)*; **(b) gills,** (*of mushroom*) lames *fpl*, lamelles *fpl*; *F* **to be** *or* **look green about the gills,** (*look ill*) avoir le teint verdâtre *ou* jaune.

gill² [dʒɪl] *n* (*measure*) (0.142 l.) = canon *m* (*de vin*).

gillie ['gɪlɪ] *n Scot* serviteur *m* (*d'un chasseur, d'un pêcheur*).

gillyflower ['dʒɪlɪflaʊər] *n* **(a)** *F* (*wallflower*) giroflée *f* jaune *ou* des murailles; **(b) (clove) g.,** œillet *m* giroflée.

gilt¹ [gɪlt] *see* **GILD**.

gilt² *adj* (*cadre etc*) doré.

gilt³ *n* dorure *f*, doré *m*; *St Exch* **gilts,** fonds *mpl* d'État;

valeurs *fpl* de tout repos *ou* de premier ordre *ou* *F* de père de famille; *F* **that takes the g. off the gingerbread,** voilà qui enlève le charme *ou* l'attrait.

gilt[4] *n* (*pig*) jeune truie *f.*

gilt-edged ['gɪlt'edʒd] *adj* **(a)** (*book*) doré sur tranche; **(b)** *St Exch* **g.-edge(d) stock(s),** fonds *mpl* d'État; valeurs *fpl* de tout repos *ou* de premier ordre *ou* *F* de père de famille.

gimbals ['dʒɪmb(ə)lz] *npl Av Nau etc* (suspension *f* à) cardan *m.*

gimcrack ['dʒɪmkræk] *adj* (*meubles*) de pacotille, de camelote; (*maison*) de carton; (*bijoux*) en toc.

gimlet ['gɪmlɪt] *n* **(a)** (*tool*) vrille *f;* foret *m* à bois; *Fig* **g. eyes,** yeux perçants; **(b)** (*cocktail*) = mélange de gin ou de vodka et de jus de citron vert.

gimme ['gɪmiː] *Sl* = **give me.**

gimmick ['gɪmɪk] *n F* truc *m,* astuce *f;* **advertising g.,** artifice *m ou* astuce *ou* truc publicitaire.

gimmickry ['gɪmɪkrɪ] *n F* astuces *fpl;* combinaisons *fpl* (*pour attirer l'attention du public*).

gimmicky ['gɪmɪkɪ] *adj F* plein d'astuces; **a bit too g.,** trop artificiel.

gin[1] [dʒɪn] *n* **(a)** (*drink*) gin *m;* (*made in Holland*) genièvre *m;* **(b)** *Cards* **g. (rummy),** rami *m.*

gin[2] *n* **(a)** (*trap*) piège *m;* **(b)** *Tex* **(cotton) g.,** égreneuse *f* de coton.

ginger ['dʒɪndʒər] **1** *n* **(a)** *Bot Culin* gingembre *m;* **preserved g.,** gingembre confit; **g. ale** *or* **beer,** boisson gazeuse au gingembre; **g. biscuit** *or* **nut** *or* **snap,** biscuit *m* au gingembre; **g. wine,** vin *m* de gingembre; **(b)** *F* (*liveliness*) énergie *f; Pol* **g. group,** groupe *m* de pression; les militants *mpl* (*d'un parti*); **(c)** *F* (*redhead*) **hi, g.!,** ohé, poil de carotte! **2** *adj F* (*hair*) roux, *f* rousse.

►**ginger up** *vtsep F* mettre du cœur au ventre de (*qn*); activer (*la production etc*); **we need something to g. up the party,** il nous faut quelque chose pour mettre un peu d'animation dans la soirée.

gingerbread ['dʒɪndʒəbred] **1** *n Culin* pain *m* d'épice. **2** *adj* **(a)** *Culin* **g. man,** bonhomme *m* de *ou* en pain d'épice; **(b)** *F* (*architecture*) prétentieux et peu solide.

gingerly ['dʒɪndʒəlɪ] **1** *adv* **g., in a g. fashion,** doucement, avec précaution; **he stepped g. between the cowpats,** il a avancé avec précaution entre les bouses de vache. **2** *adj* doux, *f* douce, léger.

gingery ['dʒɪndʒərɪ] *adj* **(a)** (*taste*) de gingembre; **(b)** *F* (*hair, colour*) roux, *f* rousse; **(c)** (*lively*) animé; **(d)** (*temperament*) irascible, coléreux.

gingham ['gɪŋəm] *n Tex* guingan *m;* **g. curtains/dress/** *etc,* rideaux *mpl*/robe *f*/*etc* en guingan.

gingivitis [dʒɪndʒɪ'vaɪtɪs] *n Med* gingivite *f.*

ginseng ['dʒɪnseŋ] *n* ginseng *m.*

gippo ['dʒɪpəʊ] *n Br Offensive Sl* romanichel, -elle.

gipsy ['dʒɪpsɪ] *n* **(a)** bohémien, -ienne, romanichel, -elle; (*Spanish*) gitan, -ane; **g. music,** musique *f* tzigane; **(b)** *Ent* **g. moth,** zigzag *m.*

gipsyish ['dʒɪpsɪɪʃ] *adj* comme un bohémien *ou* un romanichel; (*swarthy*) noiraud.

giraffe [dʒɪ'ræf, -'rɑːf] *n* girafe *f.*

gird [gɜːd] *vt* (*pt & pp* **girded, girt** [gɜːt]) *Arch & Lit* **(a)** (*wrap around with a belt*) ceindre; **to g. up one's loins,** se ceindre les reins; **to g. (on) one's sword,** ceindre son épée; **(b)** (*surround*) ceindre (**with,** de).

girder ['gɜːdər] *n Constr* poutre *f* (métallique).

girdle[1] ['gɜːd(ə)l] *n* (*corset*) gaine *f;* (*belt*) ceinture *f; Anat* **pelvic/pectoral g.,** ceinture pelvienne/scapulaire.

girdle[2] *vt Lit* ceindre, entourer.

girdle[3] *n Culin* tôle *f* (*sur laquelle on cuit des galettes*); **g. cake,** galette *f.*

girl [gɜːl] *n* fille *f;* (*young woman*) jeune fille, jeune femme *f;* **little g.,** petite fille, fillette *f;* **when I was a g.,** quand j'étais petite; **g.'s name,** prénom féminin; **girls' school,** école *f* de filles; **old g.,** ancienne élève; **a French/an Indian g.,** une jeune Française/Indienne; **a blind g.,** une jeune aveugle; **his g.,** (*daughter*) sa fille; (*girlfriend*) sa petite amie; **that's my g.!,** (*well done*) bravo!, très bien!; **my dear g.!,** ma chère!; *Sl* **the old g.,** (*wife*) ma femme, la bourgeoise; (*mother*) ma mère; (*boss*) la patronne; (*car*) *F* ma vieille voiture *ou* bagnole; *Old-fashioned* **hello, old g.!,** salut ma vieille!; **my eldest/youngest g.,** ma fille aînée/cadette; *Br* **G. Guide,** (*aged 11-16*) guide *f;* (*over 16*) guide aînée.

girlfriend ['gɜːlfrend] *n* (*of boy, man*) (petite) amie *f;* (*of girl, woman*) amie, copine *f;* **his g.,** son amie, sa petite amie.

girlhood ['gɜːlhʊd] *n* enfance *f,* première jeunesse.

girlie ['gɜːlɪ] *n F* **g. magazines,** = revues qui contiennent de nombreuses photos de femmes nues, revue *f* érotique.

girlish ['gɜːlɪʃ] *adj* **(a)** (*behaviour, figure etc*) de petite fille, de jeune fille; **(b)** (*boy*) mou, efféminé; **g. good looks,** air enfantin *ou* de très jeune fille.

giro ['dʒaɪrəʊ] *n Br Banking* **National G.,** = service *m* de chèques postaux; **g. account,** compte *m* chèque postal; **bank g.,** virement *m* bancaire.

girt *see* **GIRD.**

-girt [gɜːt] *suff* **sea-g. Britain,** la Grande-Bretagne encerclée par les mers.

girth [gɜːθ] *n* **(a)** (*on harness*) sangle *f;* **saddle g.,** sangle de selle; **(b)** (*circumference*) circonférence *f* (*d'un arbre etc*); tour *m* (*de poitrine, de taille*); **of considerable g.,** (*of person*) d'une belle corpulence.

gismo ['gɪzməʊ] *n esp Am F* machin *m,* truc *m,* gadget *m.*

gist [dʒɪst] *n* fond *m,* substance *f,* essence *f* (*d'une conversation*); point essentiel (*d'une question*); **to get the g. (of the matter),** saisir l'essentiel; **I think I got the g. of what she was saying,** je crois que j'ai compris l'essentiel de ce qu'elle disait.

git [gɪt] *n Br Sl* con, conne.

give[1] [gɪv] *n* élasticité *f;* jeu *m* (*dans un mécanisme etc*).

give[2] *v* (*pt* **gave** [geɪv]; *pp* **given** ['gɪv(ə)n]) **1** *vt* **(a)** (*present*) donner; **to g. sth to s.o., to g. s.o. sth,** donner qch à qn; **to g. s.o. a present,** faire *ou* donner un cadeau à qn; **to g. alms,** faire l'aumône; **to g. a dinner,** donner un dîner; **to g. s.o. one's hand,** donner *ou* tendre la main à qn; **to g. s.o. a note from s.o.,** remettre à qn un petit mot de qn; **g. me the good old days!,** parlez-moi du bon vieux temps!; **g. me British weather any day!,** rien ne vaut le climat de la Grande Bretagne!; **married? those two? I'd g. it two weeks at the outside,** mariés? ces deux-là? je leur donne deux semaines au grand maximum;

(b) (*bestow, pledge*) donner; **to g. s.o. sth to eat/drink,** donner à manger/à boire à qn; **to g. s.o. six month's imprisonment,** condamner qn à six mois de prison; **he was given life,** il a été condamné à perpétuité; **to g. a child a name,** donner un nom à un enfant; **to g. s.o. a job to do,** assigner une tâche *ou* un rôle à qn; **g. her my love,** embrasse-la pour moi; **to g. s.o. one's support,** prêter son appui à qn; **to g. one's word,** donner sa parole; **she gave herself to him,** elle s'est donnée à lui;

(c) (*in exchange*) donner; **to g. a good price for sth,** donner *ou* payer un bon prix pour qch; **I'll g. you £10 for it,** je vous en donnerai 10 livres; **to g. sth in exchange for sth,** donner qch contre qch; **I would g. a lot** *or* **a great deal to know ...,** je donnerais beaucoup pour savoir ...;

(d) (*sacrifice*) **to g. one's life for one's beliefs,** donner sa vie pour ses convictions; **I've given you six years of my life,** je t'ai donné six ans de ma vie; **she gave this job the best years of her life,** elle a consacré ses plus belles années à ce travail;

(e) (*devote*) **to g. one's mind** *or* **oneself to one's studies,** s'adonner *ou* s'appliquer à ses études; **to g. one's attention to s.o.,** faire attention à qn; **he gave it considerable thought,** il y a beaucoup réfléchi; **I can g. you 10 minutes,** je peux te consacrer 10 minutes;

(f) (*do*) **to g. a laugh,** rire, laisser échapper un rire; **to g. a sigh,** soupirer, pousser un soupir; **to g. a jump,** sauter, faire un saut; (*with surprise*) tressauter; **to g. s.o.'s hand a squeeze,** serrer la main à qn; **to g. s.o. a smile,** adresser un sourire à qn; **he gave me an odd look,** il m'a lancé un regard singulier;

(g) (*say, impart*) faire (*une réponse*); donner (*une raison, une explication, son avis*); donner, fournir (*des détails*); **he gave his age as twenty,** il a déclaré avoir vingt ans; **to g. a description of sth,** faire une description de qch, décrire qch; **to g. an order,** donner un ordre; (*in shop*) faire une commande; **to g. a decision,** faire connaître sa décision; *Jur* rendre un arrêt; **don't g. me that!,** (*don't try to fool me*) ne me raconte pas d'histoires!; **don't g. me that stuff about how hard your life is,** ne va pas me raconter que tu as la vie dure.

(h) (*grant*) **she gave him her hand (in marriage),** elle lui a accordé sa main; **to g. s.o. an interview,** accorder une interview à qn; **we were given a choice,** on nous a fait choisir; **g. me a chance!,** donne-moi une chance!; **g. me five minutes,** accorde-moi cinq minutes; **we'll get there in two hours, g. or take a few minutes,** on fera le trajet en deux heures, à quelques minutes près; **g. us a song!,** chante-nous quelque chose; **aren't you going to g. me a kiss?,** tu ne vas pas m'embrasser?;

(i) (*provide*) donner (*un exemple*); **given these facts, explain why ...,** à partir de ces données, expliquez pourquoi ...; **given her age,** (*considering it*) étant donné son âge;

given a triangle ABC, soit un triangle ABC; **to g. no sign of life,** ne donner aucun signe de vie;

(j) (*perform, execute*) donner (*un concert etc*); **to g. a recitation,** réciter, dire des vers; *Th* **they're giving Macbeth this week,** on joue Macbeth cette semaine; **she gave an outstanding performance,** (*of actress*) son interprétation était formidable; **to g. a toast,** proposer un toast; **I g. you our host,** je bois à la santé de notre hôte;

(k) (*be origin of*) **he gave me his cold,** il m'a donné *ou* passé son rhume; **that gave me the idea of travelling,** cela m'a donné l'idée de voyager;

(l) (*cause*) faire, causer (*de la peine, du plaisir*); **to g. oneself trouble,** se donner du mal; **to g. s.o. to believe** *or* **understand that ...,** faire croire *ou* donner à entendre à qn que ...;

(m) (*yield*) rendre; **investment that gives 10%,** placement qui rend *ou* rapporte 10%; **this lamp gives a poor light,** cette lampe éclaire mal; **to g. an average of ...,** donner une moyenne de ...;

(n) *F* (*hit etc*) **to g. it (to) s.o.,** (*beat up*) rosser qn; (*reprimand*) laver la tête à qn; **g. it to them!,** allez-y!; **I gave him what for!,** (*reprimanded him*) je lui ai passé un bon savon!; **to g. as good as one gets,** rendre coup pour coup.

2 *vi* **(a)** (*give gift etc*) donner, offrir; **it is better to g. than to receive,** donner vaut mieux que recevoir; **please g. generously,** soyez généreux; **to g. of one's time,** donner (un peu de) son temps; **to g. and take,** faire des concessions mutuelles;

(b) (*of cloth, elastic*) se détendre; *Fig* (*of person*) céder; **the springs don't g. enough,** les ressorts manquent de souplesse; **the door will g. if you push hard enough,** la porte cédera si vous la poussez assez fort;

(c) *F* **what gives?,** (*hi!*) salut!; (*what's going on?*) qu'est-ce qui se fricote?; (*what's the news?*) quoi de neuf?;

(d) *Sl* **g.!,** (*tell me etc*) vide ton sac!

►**give away** *vtsep* **(a)** (*give for nothing*) donner, faire cadeau de; **I'm practically giving them away!,** (*said by salesman*) c'est pratiquement donné!; **(b)** (*at ceremony*) **to g. away the prizes,** distribuer les prix; **to g. the bride away,** conduire la mariée à l'autel; **(c)** (*betray, reveal*) (*of person*) trahir, vendre (*qn*); (*of accent, clothes etc*) trahir (*qn*); **to g. oneself away,** (*show one's feelings*) se trahir; (*of criminal*) se trahir; **to g. the game** *or* **show away,** vendre la mèche; **I'm not going to g. anything away,** (*that might help you to answer*) je ne veux rien vous révéler.

►**give back** *vtsep* rendre, restituer (*qch*); renvoyer (*un écho*); refléter (*une image*); **I'll g. it back to you tomorrow,** je te le rendrai demain; **to g. s.o. back his liberty,** rendre la liberté à qn.

►**give in 1** *vtsep* (*hand over*) donner, remettre (*qch*); **I gave the wallet in to the police,** j'ai remis le portefeuille à la police; **to g. in one's name,** donner son nom; **to g. in one's examination paper,** remettre sa copie d'examen. **2** *vi* (*under pressure in battle*) céder; (*in fight, battle*) se rendre; (*of rebel*) se soumettre; (*not know the answer*) renoncer, abandonner; **to g. in to intimidation,** se laisser intimider; **you g. in too easily,** tu abandonnes trop facilement; **to g. in to s.o.,** céder à qn.

►**give off** *vtsep* (*emit*) dégager, émettre (*une odeur*); répandre (*la chaleur*); *Ch* dégager (*un gaz*).

►**give onto** *vipo* (*of window, door etc*) donner sur (*un jardin, la rue*).

►**give out 1** *vtsep* **(a)** (*distribute*) distribuer (*du ravitaillement, des livres etc*); **(b)** (*emit*) dégager (*une odeur*); répandre (*la chaleur*); **(c)** (*make known*) **it was given out that ...,** on a annoncé *ou* dit que ... . **2** *vi* **(a)** (*become used up*) manquer, faire défaut; (*of supplies*) s'épuiser; **my strength/patience was giving out,** j'étais à bout de forces/patience; **(b)** (*of radio, car etc*) tomber en panne.

►**give over 1** *vtsep* **(a)** (*transfer*) remettre (*qch*) **(to s.o.,** entre les mains de qn); **(b)** (*devote*) consacrer (*l'après midi, le reste de la soirée etc*) **(to,** à); **(c)** (*usu passive*) (*abandon*) **given over to despair,** abandonné *ou* en proie au désespoir. **2** *vi Sl* (*stop*) **g. over, will you?,** c'est vraiment assez!, est-ce fini, par exemple!

►**give up 1** *vtsep* **(a)** (*abandon*) abandonner (*ses biens, ses prétentions*); renoncer à (*un projet etc*); **to g. up the idea of doing sth,** renoncer à (l'idée de) faire qch; **he gave up all hope of being promoted,** il a abandonné tout espoir d'avoir une promotion; **to g. up smoking,** cesser de fumer; **to g. up one's job,** résigner son emploi *ou* ses fonctions; **to g. up the game/struggle,** abandonner la partie/renoncer à la lutte; **to g. s.o. up (for lost),** considérer qn comme perdu; **the doctors have given him up,** les médecins l'ont condamné; **I'd given you up!,** je ne vous attendais plus!; **he gave himself up to grief,** il s'est laissé aller au désespoir;

(b) (*surrender*) livrer (*qn à la justice etc*); rendre (*sa proie*); **to g. up one's seat to s.o.,** céder sa place à qn; **to g. oneself up,** se constituer prisonnier; **I g. myself up,** je me rends; **she gave herself up to her studies,** elle s'est consacrée entièrement à ses études; **his mornings were given up to business,** ses matinées étaient consacrées aux affaires.

2 *vi* **(a)** (*surrender*) se rendre; **I g. up,** (*what's the answer?*) j'abandonne, je donne ma langue au chat;

(b) (*abandon a course of action, struggle etc*) abandonner, laisser tomber; **you mustn't g. up now,** tu ne peux pas abandonner maintenant; **I g. up!,** (*you're or it's etc hopeless*) j'abandonne!

►**give up on** *vipo* (*stop hoping for*) **his mother gave up on him,** sa mère a perdu toutes ses illusions à son sujet; **don't g. up on me,** ne me laisse pas tomber.

►**give way** *vi* **(a)** (*collapse*) succomber; (*of ladder*) se casser, se rompre; (*of cable*) partir; **the ground gave way under our feet,** le sol s'est affaissé *ou* s'est dérobé sous nos pieds; **my legs are giving way (under me),** mes jambes fléchissent *ou* mollissent *ou* se dérobent sous moi; **his health is giving way,** sa santé s'affaiblit;

(b) (*yield*) **to g. way to s.o.,** (*in argument*) céder à qn; (*give one's place to*) céder la place à qn; **to g. way to despair/grief,** s'abandonner au désespoir/à la douleur; **to g. way to temptation,** céder à la tentation; **to g. way to a car,** céder le passage à une voiture; *Aut* **g. way,** cédez le passage;

(c) (*be superseded by*) **her tears gave way to laughter,** ses rires l'ont emporté sur ses larmes; **natural fibres have given way to synthetics,** les fibres naturelles ont été remplacées par les synthétiques.

give-and-take ['gɪvən'teɪk] *n* (*mutual concession*) concessions *fpl* (mutuelles); **there has to be some g.-and-t.,** il faut que chacun fasse des concessions.

giveaway ['gɪvəweɪ] *n F* **(a)** révélation *f* involontaire; (*clue*) indice *m*; **her remark about inflation was the g.,** sa remarque sur l'inflation l'a trahie; **it was a dead g.,** c'était un geste *ou* un mot qui en disait long; **(b)** *Com* prime *f*, cadeau *m*; **g. price,** prix défiant toute concurrence.

given ['gɪv(ə)n] *adj* **(a)** donné, déterminé; **in a g. time,** dans une période donnée; **at any g. time,** à tout moment; **at a g. point,** à un point donné; **g. name,** prénom *m*, nom *m* de baptême; **(b)** (*apt, likely*) **to be g. to forgetfulness,** être enclin à la distraction; **I'm g. to losing my temper,** c'est dans ma nature de me mettre en colère.

giver ['gɪvər] *n* (*of blood, organ*) donneur, -euse; (*of money*) donateur, -trice.

giving ['gɪvɪŋ] **1** *adj* (*person*) généreux, -euse; **of a g. nature,** généreux. **2** *n* don *m*, donation *f*; *Sch* **prize g.,** distribution *f* des prix.

gizmo ['gɪzməʊ] *n esp Am F* machin *m*, truc *m*, gadget *m*.

gizzard ['gɪzəd] *n* gésier *m*; *F* **that sticks in my g.,** je ne peux pas avaler *ou* digérer ça.

glacé ['glæsɪ] *adj* **(a)** *Culin* **g. fruits,** fruits glacés; **(b)** (*leather*) glacé.

glacial ['gleɪsɪəl, -ʃəl] *adj* **(a)** *Geol* (*érosion, vallée etc*) glaciaire; **(b)** (*wind*) & *Fig* glacial, -als.

glaciation [gleɪsɪ'eɪʃən, -ʃɪ'eɪ-] *n* glaciation *f*.

glacier ['glæsɪər, gleɪs-, *Am* 'gleɪʃər] *n Geol* glacier *m*.

glad [glæd] *adj* (**gladder, gladdest**) **(a)** (*person*) heureux, content; **to be g. to hear sth,** apprendre qch avec plaisir, être heureux *ou* bien content d'apprendre qch; **I'm g. you like him,** je suis content que vous l'aimiez; **I'm g.,** (*to know that you're better etc*) ça me fait plaisir (de l'apprendre); **he is only too g. to help you,** il ne demande pas mieux que de vous aider; **they would be g. of your help,** ils seraient bien heureux d'avoir votre aide; **to be g. of an opportunity to do sth,** se réjouir de l'occasion de faire qch; **it makes my heart g. to hear him,** cela me réjouit le cœur de l'entendre; **(b)** (*smile*) de contentement; (*shout*) de plaisir; **g. news,** *Lit* **g. tidings,** bonne nouvelle; *F* **to give s.o. the g. eye,** faire de l'œil à qn; *US* **to give s.o. the g. hand,** = faire un accueil chaleureux à qn (*souvent dans un but intéressé*); *F* **to put on one's g. rags,** se mettre sur son trente-et-un.

gladden ['glæd(ə)n] *vt* réjouir; rendre (*qn*) heureux; **it gladdens my heart to see them,** cela me réjouit le cœur de les voir.

glade [gleɪd] *n* clairière *f* (*dans une forêt*).

glad-hand ['glædhænd] *vt & vi US* (*welcome warmly*) faire un accueil chaleureux (à qn); (*of politician etc*) =

serrer la main à tout le monde (*souvent dans un but intéressé*).
gladiator ['glædieitər] *n* gladiateur *m*.
gladiatorial [glædiə'tɔːriəl] *adj* (*combats*) de gladiateurs.
gladiolus, *pl* **-li** [glædi'əuləs, -lai] *n* (*plant*) glaïeul *m*.
gladly ['glædli] *adv* avec plaisir, volontiers; **I accept g.,** j'accepte avec grand plaisir.
gladness ['glædnis] *n* joie *f*, allégresse *f*.
Gladstone ['glædstən] *n* **G. bag,** = type de petit sac de voyage.
glam [glæm] *adj F* = **GLAMOROUS.**
Glam *abbr* **Glamorganshire.**
glamorize ['glæməraiz] *vt* rendre séduisant *ou* attrayant; **to g. war,** peindre la guerre sous de belles couleurs; **a TV programme that glamorizes violence,** une émission de télé qui rend la violence attrayante; **an advertising campaign that seeks to g. smoking,** une campagne publicitaire qui cherche à valoriser l'image des fumeurs.
glamorous ['glæmərəs] *adj* (*person*) séduisant; (*woman*) ravissant et élégant; (*career etc*) prestigieux, -euse; **a g. grandmother,** une grand-mère élégante; **working in the film industry is not always g.,** ce n'est pas toujours prestigieux de travailler dans le cinéma.
glamour, *US also* **glamor** ['glæmər] *n* fascination *f* (*d'une personne*); prestige *m* (*d'un nom, d'un style de vie*); éclat *m* (*d'une cérémonie etc*); **the false g. of war,** le faux éclat de la guerre; **g. is back in fashion,** l'élégance revient à la mode; *F* **g. boy,** beau mâle; **g. girl,** belle fille séduisante, pin up *f*.
glance¹ [glɑːns] *n* **(a)** (*quick look*) regard *m*, coup *m* d'œil; **at a g.,** d'un coup d'œil; **at first g.,** à première vue, au premier coup d'œil; **to give sth a g., to have a g. at sth,** jeter un coup d'œil sur qch; **(b)** (*flash*) trait *m* de lumière, éclat *m*.
glance² *vi* **(a)** (*look quickly*) **to g. at s.o./sth,** jeter un regard sur qn/qch, lancer un coup d'œil à qn/sur qch; **to g. around,** jeter un regard autour de soi; **to g. through** *or* **over sth,** examiner rapidement qch; **to g. through a book,** parcourir *ou* feuilleter un livre; **(b)** (*of steel, weapons*) étinceler, jeter des lueurs.
►glance off 1 *vi* (*of bullet etc*) dévier, ricocher. **2** *vipo* dévier de, ricocher sur; **the blow glanced off his helmet,** le coup a ricoché sur son casque.
glancing ['glɑːnsiŋ] *adj* (*blow*) oblique.
gland¹ [glænd] *n* glande *f*; **lymphatic glands,** ganglions *mpl* lymphatiques; **poison g.,** (*of snake*) glande à venin.
gland² *n MecE* **packing g.,** bague *f* de presse-étoupe.
glanders ['glændəz] *npl* (*with sing verb*) *Vet* morve *f*.
glandular ['glændjulər] *adj Physiol Med* glandulaire; *Med* **g. fever,** mononucléose infectieuse.
glare¹ [gleər] *n* **(a)** (*angry stare*) regard fixe et irrité; **(b)** (*of sun etc*) éclat *m*, éblouissement *m*, lumière éblouissante; (*of headlight etc*) éblouissement, aveuglement *m*; **in the full g. of publicity,** sous les feux de la rampe.
glare² *vi* **(a)** (*stare angrily*) lancer un regard furieux *ou* furibond (**at s.o.,** à qn); **(b)** (*of sun etc*) briller d'un éclat éblouissant.
glaring ['gleəriŋ] *adj* **(a)** (*eyes*) furieux; **(b)** (*light*) éblouissant, éclatant; (*sun*) aveuglant; (*colour etc*) voyant; **(c)** (*fact*) manifeste, patent, qui saute aux yeux; (*error, injustice, omission*) flagrant; (*abuse*) scandaleux, choquant.
glaringly ['gleəriŋli] *adv* **it's g. obvious,** ça saute aux yeux.
glasnost ['glɑːznɒst] *n Pol* glasnost *f*.
glass [glɑːs] *n* **(a)** (*material*) verre *m*; **the g. industry,** l'industrie *f* du verre; **cut g.,** verre taillé; **plate g.,** glace *f* de vitrage; **broken g.,** éclats *mpl* de verre; **Bohemian g.,** verre de Bohême; **clear/frosted g.,** verre clair/dépoli; **the stained g. of a church,** les vitraux *mpl ou* les verrières *fpl* d'une église; *Prov* **people who live in g. houses shouldn't throw stones,** il faut être sans défauts pour critiquer autrui; **g. with care,** (*notice on parcel*) fragile; **g. bottle,** bouteille *f* de *ou* en verre; **g. case,** vitrine *f*; **to keep/display sth in a g. case** *or* **under g.,** garder/exposer qch sous verre; **g. cutter,** (*person*) coupeur *m* de verre, vitrier *m*; (*tool*) coupe-verre *m inv*, diamant *m* (*de vitrier*); **g. cutting,** taille *f* du verre; **g. door,** porte vitrée, porte de *ou* en verre; **g. eye,** œil *m* de verre; *Boxing etc F* **g. jaw,** mâchoire *f* fragile; **g. partition,** cloison *m* de *ou* en verre; **g. roof,** verrière (*de gare etc*); **g. manufacture,** verrerie *f*; **g. wool,** laine *f* de verre;
(b) (*single piece*) vitre *f* (*de fenêtre*); glace *f* (*de voiture*); verre *m* (*de montre, de lampe*); **pane of g.,** vitre; **(c)** (*cup*) verre *m*; **wine g.,** verre à vin; **g. of wine,** verre de vin; **liqueur g.,** verre à liqueur; **stem g.,** verre à pied; **to sell wine by the g.,** vendre le vin au verre;
(d) (*no pl*) (*glassware*) **table g.,** verrerie *f* de table; **oven g.,** verrerie allant au four;
(e) (*lens*) lentille *f* (*d'un instrument d'optique*); **magnifying g.,** (*instrument*) loupe *f*; (*in instrument*) verre grossissant;
(f) (*telescope*) **(field) g.,** lunette *f* d'approche, longue-vue *f, pl* longues-vues;
(g) (*mirror*) **(looking) g.,** glace *f*, miroir *m*;
(h) (*barometer*) baromètre *m* (à cadran); **the g. is falling,** le baromètre baisse;
(i) (*in gardening*) châssis *m*; (*glasshouse*) serre *f*; **grown under g.,** (*in cold frame*) cultivé sous verre *ou* sous châssis; (*in glasshouse*) cultivé en serre.
►glass in *vtsep* vitrer (*un balcon etc*).
glass-blower ['glɑːsbləuər] *n* souffleur *m* de verre.
glass-blowing ['glɑːsbləuiŋ] *n* soufflage *m* de verre.
glasscloth ['glɑːsklɒθ] *n* torchon *m* (pour essuyer les verres).
glasses ['glɑːsiz] *npl* lunettes *fpl*, verres *mpl*; **dark** *or* **sun g.,** lunettes de soleil; **to wear g.,** porter des lunettes; **field g.,** jumelles *fpl*; **opera g.,** jumelles de théâtre.
glassful ['glɑːsful] *n* (plein) verre *m* (*d'eau etc*).
glasshouse ['glɑːshaus] *n* **(a)** (*in garden*) serre *f*; **(b)** *Br Mil F* prison *f* militaire, trou *m*; **(c)** *US* (*factory*) verrerie *f*.
glasspaper ['glɑːspeipər] *n* papier *m* de verre.
glassware ['glɑːsweər] *n* articles *mpl* de verre; (*crystal*) cristaux *mpl*.
glassworks ['glɑːswɜːks] *npl* (*usu with sing verb*) verrerie *f*; (*for crystal*) cristallerie *f*.
glassy ['glɑːsi] *adj* (*smooth*) vitreux; **g. look/eye,** regard/œil vitreux.
Glaswegian [glæs'wiːdʒiən] **1** *n* habitant, -ante de Glasgow; (*by birth*) originaire *mf* de Glasgow. **2** *adj* de Glasgow.
Glauber ['glaubər] *n Pharm* **G.'s salt(s),** sel *m* (admirable) de Glauber; sulfate *m* de soude.
glaucoma [glɔː'kəumə] *n Med* glaucome *m*; **to have g.,** avoir un glaucome.
glaucous ['glɔːkəs] *adj* glauque.
glaze¹ [gleiz] *n* **(a)** *Cer* vernis *m* (luisant); **(b)** *Culin* glaçage *m*; (*on pastry*) dorure *f*; **(c)** (*of leather, cloth*) lustre *m*, glacé *m*; **(d)** *Art* vernis *m*; **(e)** *US* (*ice*) verglas *m*.
glaze² *vt* **(a)** vitrer (*une fenêtre, une maison*); **(b)** *Cer* glacer, vernisser, émailler (*la poterie*); vitrifier (*les tuiles etc*); **(c)** *Culin* glacer; **(d)** *Ind* glacer, lustrer (*un tissu*); vernir, vernisser, glacer (*le cuir*); lisser (*le papier*); **(e)** *Art* glacer (*un tableau*); *Phot* émailler (*une épreuve*).
►glaze over *vi* (*of eyes*) devenir vitreux.
glazed [gleizd] *adj* **(a)** (*roof, door*) vitré; **(b)** *Cer* glacé, émaillé; (*brick*) vitrifié; **(c)** *Culin* glacé; **(d)** *Ind* (*fabric*) glacé, lustré; (*leather*) glacé, verni, vernissé; (*paper*) brillant, satiné; **(e)** (*eye, look*) vitreux.
glazed-in [gleizd'in] *adj* **g.-in light,** verrine *f*.
glazier ['gleiziər] *n* vitrier *m*.
glazing ['gleiziŋ] *n* **(a)** (*fitting of windows etc*) pose *f* des vitres; **(b)** (*no pl*) (*windows*) vitrerie *f*; **double g.,** double vitrage *m*; **(c)** *Cer Phot* émaillage *m*; **(d)** *Ind* glaçage *m*, lustrage *m* (*de tissu, cuir*); vernissage *m* (*de cuir*); satinage *m* (*de papier*).
GLC [dʒiːel'siː] *n abbr* **Greater London Council.**
gleam¹ [gliːm] *n* rayon *m*, lueur *f*, trait *m* (*de lumière*); reflet *m* (*d'un couteau etc*); miroitement *m* (*d'un lac etc*); **there's a strange g. in his eye,** il y a une drôle de lueur dans son regard; *Hum* **when you were just a g. in your father's eye,** bien avant ta naissance; **g. of hope,** lueur d'espoir.
gleam² *vi* luire, reluire; (*of water*) miroiter, brasiller; (*of eyes*) briller.
gleaming ['gliːmiŋ] **1** *adj* luisant, miroitant; **g. eyes,** yeux luisants. **2** *n* miroitement *m*.
glean [gliːn] **1** *vt* glaner (*du blé, des renseignements etc*); **I couldn't g. much from the brochure,** je n'ai pas pu tirer grand-chose de la brochure. **2** *vi* faire la glane.
gleaner ['gliːnər] *n* glaneur, -euse.
gleaning ['gliːniŋ] *n* **(a) gleanings,** (*of crops*) glanes *fpl*; **gleanings from the newspapers,** informations glanées dans les journaux; **(b)** (*act of gleaning*) glanage *m*, glane *f*.
glebe [gliːb] *n Rel* terre assignée à un bénéfice.
glee [gliː] *n* **(a)** (*delight*) joie *f*, allégresse *f*; **the children gave shouts of g.,** les enfants ont crié de joie; **she announced it with some g.,** elle l'a annoncé avec un malin plaisir; **in high g.,** tout joyeux; **(b)** *Mus* petit chant à trois ou quatre parties (*pour voix d'hommes*); *esp Am* **g. club,** chorale *f*.

gleeful ['gli:fol] *adj* joyeux, allègre.
gleefully ['gli:folı] *adv* allègrement, plein de joie.
glen [glen] *n* vallée étroite; gorge *f* (*de montagne*).
glengarry [glen'gærı] *n Scot* **g. (bonnet),** = béret écossais.
glib [glıb] *adj* (*answer*) spécieux; (*speaker*) qui a de la faconde; **his explanation was a bit too g.,** son explication était un peu trop facile; **to have a g. tongue,** avoir la langue bien pendue.
glibly ['glıblı] *adv* (*to reply*) spécieusement; (*to speak*) avec aisance.
glibness ['glıbnıs] *n* (*of excuse, reply*) spéciosité *f*; (*of speaker*) faconde *f*; facilité *f* (*de parole*), bagou *m*.
glide¹ [glaıd] *n* **(a)** (*movement*) glissement *m*; (*in dancing*) glissade *f*, glissé *m*; **(b)** (*of glider*) vol plané; (*of aircraft*) descente *f* en (vol) plané; **g. path,** (*of glider*) trajectoire *f* de (vol) plané; (*of aircraft*) trajectoire de descente *ou* d'atterrissage; **(c)** *Mus* port *m* de voix; **(d)** *Ling* son *m* transitoire.
glide² *vi* **(a)** (*slide*) (se) glisser, couler; **to g. (along) over the water,** glisser sur l'eau; **(b)** (*of birds*) planer (dans l'air); (*of aircraft*) planer, faire un vol plané; (*in glider*) faire du vol à voile.
glider ['glaıdər] *n Av* (*machine*) planeur *m*; (*person*) spécialiste *mf* du vol à voile; **g. pilot,** pilote *m* de planeur.
gliding ['glaıdıŋ] *n* **(a)** (*movement*) glissement *m*; **(b)** *Av* (vol *m*) plané *m*; vol à voile; **g. club,** club *m* de vol à voile.
glimmer¹ ['glımər] *n* faible lueur *f* (*d'une chandelle etc*); reflet *m* (*de l'eau etc*); **g. of hope,** rayon *m ou* lueur d'espoir; **not the slightest g. of intelligence,** pas la moindre trace d'intelligence.
glimmer² *vi* jeter une faible lueur; (*of water*) miroiter; (*of sea*) brasiller.
glimmering ['glımərıŋ] **1** *adj* (*light*) faible; (*water*) miroitant. **2** *n* émission *f* d'une faible lueur; miroitement *m*.
glimpse¹ [glımps] *n* vision momentanée (*de qch*); **to catch a g. of s.o./sth,** entrevoir qn/qch; **a g. of the future,** un aperçu de ce que sera le futur.
glimpse² *vt* avoir une vision fugitive de (*qch*); entrevoir (*qn, qch*).
glint¹ [glınt] *n* trait *m*, lueur *f*, éclair *m* (*de lumière*); reflet *m* (*d'un couteau etc*); **hair with glints of gold,** chevelure à *ou* aux reflets d'or.
glint² *vi* étinceler; (*of lights*) miroiter (dans l'eau); **the blade glinted in the sunlight,** la lame miroitait au soleil; **his eyes were glinting with fury,** ses yeux étincelaient de fureur.
glisten ['glıs(ə)n] *vi* (re)luire, scintiller; (*of sea*) miroiter; **his forehead glistened with sweat,** la sueur perlait sur son front.
glistening ['glıs(ə)nıŋ] *adj* luisant, scintillant; miroitant.
glitch [glıtʃ] *n F* (*problem etc*) pépin *m*.
glitter¹ ['glıtər] *n* scintillement *m*; *Fig* (*of occasion etc*) éclat *m*.
glitter² *vi* briller, scintiller, (re)luire; *Prov* **all that glitters is not gold,** tout ce qui brille n'est pas or.
glitterati [glıtə'rɑ:ti:] *npl F* le beau monde.
glittering ['glıtərıŋ] *adj* scintillant; (*occasion*) brillant; (*jewel*) qui lance des éclairs; *Fig* **the g. world of showbusiness,** le monde de lumière du showbizness.
glitz [glıts] *n F* (*of show business etc*) brillant *m*, éclat *m*.
glitzy ['glıtsı] *adj F* (*party etc*) brillant.
gloaming ['gləʊmıŋ] *n* crépuscule *m*; **in the g.,** au crépuscule.
gloat [gləʊt] *vi* jubiler; **don't g.,** ne te réjouis pas.
▶**gloat over** *vipo* (*what one has*) couver *ou* dévorer qch des yeux; (*with malice*) contempler qch avec un malin plaisir; **to g. over s.o.'s misfortune,** se réjouir du malheur de qn.
gloating ['gləʊtıŋ] *adj* (*œil*) avide; (*sourire, regard*) d'exultation méchante.
glob [glɒb] *n F* (*of cream etc*) petite boule.
global ['gləʊb(ə)l] *adj* **(a)** mondial, -aux; planétaire; **g. war(fare),** guerre mondiale; *Met* **g. warming,** réchauffement *m* de la planète; **(b)** (*comprehensive*) global, -aux.
globalization [gləʊb(ə)laı'zeıʃən] *n* mondialisation *f*.
globe [gləʊb] *n* sphère *f*; (*of the earth*) globe *m* terrestre; (*lampshade*) globe (de lampe); (*fish bowl*) bocal *m*, -aux; *Anat* globe (*de l'œil*); **to go round the g.,** faire le tour du globe; **g. artichoke,** artichaut *m*; *Met* **g. lightning,** éclair *m* en boule.
globeflower ['gləʊbflaʊər] *n* (*plant*) trolle *m*.
globetrotter ['gləʊbtrɒtər] *n F* globe-trotter *m*, *pl* globe-trotters.
globetrotting ['gləʊbtrɒtıŋ] *n F* parcours *m* du monde (en globe-trotter).
globular ['glɒbjʊlər] *adj* globulaire, globuleux.
globule ['glɒbju:l] *n* globule *m*, gouttelette *f* (*d'eau etc*).
globulin ['glɒbjʊlın] *n Biol Ch* globuline *f*.
glockenspiel ['glɒkənʃpi:l] *n Mus* carillon *m*, glockenspiel *m*.
gloom [glu:m] *n* **(a)** (*darkness*) obscurité *f*, ténèbres *fpl*; **shrouded in g.,** (*of landscape*) enténébré; **(b)** (*melancholy*) assombrissement *m*, mélancolie *f*; tristesse *f* pessimiste; **to cast** *or* **throw a g. over** *or* **on the company,** jeter une ombre *ou* un voile de tristesse sur l'assemblée; **there is g. in the City,** la Bourse de Londres est pessimiste.
gloomily ['glu:mılı] *adv* mélancoliquement.
gloominess ['glu:mınıs] *n* **(a)** (*darkness*) assombrissement *m*; obscurité *f* (*du temps etc*); **(b)** (*melancholy*) tristesse *f*, air *m* sombre, mélancolie *f*.
gloomy ['glu:mı] *adj* **(a)** (*dark*) sombre, ténébreux; **the weather is g.,** il fait sombre; **(b)** (*melancholy*) lugubre, morne, sombre; (*prediction etc*) sombre; **g. thoughts,** pensées noires; **g. picture,** tableau poussé au noir; **to paint a g. picture,** (*of article, speaker etc*) donner une image très noire; **to become g.,** (*of person*) se rembrunir.
glorification [glɔ:rıfı'keıʃən] *n* glorification *f*.
glorified ['glɔ:rıfaıd] *adj* **(a)** *Rel* glorifié; (*corps*) glorieux; **(b)** (*exalted*) en plus grand, en mieux, embelli; *Br F* **it's just a g. motor scooter,** ce n'est qu'un scooter amélioré.
glorify ['glɔ:rıfaı] *vt Rel* glorifier; rendre gloire à (*Dieu*); (*extol*) exalter, célébrer; chanter les louanges de (*qn*); **the book glorifies war,** ce livre glorifie la guerre.
glorious ['glɔ:rıəs] *adj* **(a)** (*reign, martyr*) glorieux; (*action, victory*) éclatant; *Br Hist* **the G. Revolution,** la (seconde) Révolution d'Angleterre; **(b)** (*splendid, beautiful*) resplendissant, radieux; **g. in her youth and beauty,** resplendissante de jeunesse et de beauté; **(c)** *F* (*excellent*) magnifique, splendide; **what g. weather!,** quel temps superbe!
gloriously ['glɔ:rıəslı] *adv* **(a)** glorieusement; **(b)** *F* **g. drunk,** superbement ivre.
glory ['glɔ:rı] *n* **(a)** (*honour*) gloire *f*; **to cover oneself with g.,** se couvrir de gloire; **the athletes get all the g.,** ce sont les athlètes qui remportent toute la gloire; **to give g. to God,** rendre gloire à Dieu; **g. be to God!,** gloire à Dieu!; *F* **g. be!,** Dieu merci!;
(b) (*thing*) sujet *m* de gloire; **to be the g. of the age,** faire la gloire du siècle; *esp Br F* **g. hole,** (*room, cupboard*) capharnaüm *m*, (chambre *f* de) débarras *m*; *Nau* (*locker*) casier *m*; (*stokers' quarters*) poste *m* des chauffeurs; (*cabin boys' quarters*) poste des garçons de cabine;
(c) *Rel* **eternal g.,** gloire éternelle; **the saints in g.,** les glorieux *mpl*;
(d) (*splendour*) splendeur *f*, éclat *m* (*d'un spectacle etc*); *F* **in all her g.,** parée de ses plus beaux atours; **Spain, in the days of her g.,** l'Espagne, au temps de sa splendeur; **the glories of the Irish countryside,** les splendeurs de la campagne irlandaise;
(e) (*halo*) gloire *f* (*d'un saint etc*).
▶**glory in** *vipo* (*rejoice*) se glorifier de (*qch*), se faire gloire de (*qch*); **to g. in one's freedom,** profiter pleinement de sa liberté; **the dog, who gloried in the name of Marmaduke, ...,** le chien, qui portait le nom ronflant de Marmaduke, ...
Glos *abbr* **Gloucestershire.**
gloss¹ [glɒs] *n Liter* (*in text*) glose *f*, commentaire *m*; (*translation*) traduction *f* interlinéaire.
gloss² *vt Liter* gloser sur, annoter (*un texte*).
gloss³ *n* **(a)** lustre *m*, vernis *m*, poli *m*, brillant *m*; *Tex* cati *m*; **to take the g. off,** délustrer (*qch*); *Tex* décatir (*une étoffe*); **g. paint,** peinture *f* vernis; **(b)** *Fig* (*veneer*) vernis *m* (*de légalité etc*).
gloss⁴ *vt* **(a)** lustrer, glacer; *Tex* catir (*l'étoffe*); brillanter (*le fil*); **(b)** *Fig* farder, déguiser (*la vérité*).
▶**gloss over** *vipo* **(a)** (*make light of*) farder (*les faits*); glisser *ou* passer sur (*les défauts de qn*); **she very kindly glossed over my mistakes,** elle est très gentiment passée sur mes erreurs; **(b)** (*ignore*) passer (*un fait*) sous silence; **he glossed over his past,** il a passé son passé sous silence; **(c)** (*conceal, cover up*) dissimuler.
glossary ['glɒsərı] *n* glossaire *m*, lexique *m*.
glossiness ['glɒsınıs] *n* lustre *m*, vernis *m*.
glossy ['glɒsı] *adj* lustré, glacé, brillant; (*poil*) lustré, (re)luisant; *Phot* (*papier*) brillant; **g. magazine,** journal *m* sur papier glacé; *Phot* **g. print,** épreuve sur papier brillant. **2** *n* (*pl* **glossies**) journal *m* sur papier glacé.
glottal ['glɒt(ə)l] *adj Anat Ling* glottal, -aux, glottique; *Ling* **g. stop,** coup *m* de glotte.
glottis ['glɒtıs] *n Anat* glotte *f*.

glove¹ [glʌv] *n* gant *m*; **to put on one's gloves,** mettre ses gants, se ganter; **to take off one's gloves,** se déganter; **it fits like a g.!,** ça me *ou* te *ou* lui *etc* va comme un gant; *Fig* **the gloves were off,** on y allait carrément *ou* sans ménagement; *Sp* **boxing gloves,** gants de boxe; **rubber gloves,** gants en caoutchouc; *Aut* **g. compartment,** boîte *f* à gants; **g. counter** *or* **department,** (*in large store*) rayon *m* des gants; **g. maker** *or* **manufacturer,** gantier, -ière; **g. puppet,** marionnette *f* (à gaine), pupazzo *m*.
glove² *vt* ganter.
glover ['glʌvər] *n* gantier, -ière.
glow¹ [gləʊ] *n* **(a)** (*light*) lueur *f*; (*of hot metal*) incandescence *f*; **the g. of the setting sun,** l'embrasement *m* du soleil couchant; **(b)** (*complexion*) teint *m* rouge (*de qn*); vermeil *m* (*des joues etc*); **g. of health,** éclat *m* du teint dû à la santé; **(c)** *Physiol* sensation *f* de douce chaleur; (*of passion*) ardeur *f*, chaleur *f*; **he felt a warm g. spread over him as the whisky went down,** il sentit une sensation de chaleur dans tout le corps après avoir bu le whisky; *Fig* **it gives you a warm g.,** (*of news, scene etc*) ça vous fait chaud au cœur.
glow² *vi* **(a)** (*of light, fire*) luire rouge, rougeoyer; **(b)** (*of person, face*) rayonner; **her face was glowing with pleasure,** son visage rayonnait de plaisir; **to g. with colour,** (*of painting*) rayonner de couleur; **to be glowing with health,** éclater de santé; **his cheeks were glowing,** il avait les joues en feu; **to g. with enthusiasm,** brûler d'enthousiasme.
glower ['glaʊər] *vi* braquer *ou* fixer les yeux (**at s.o.,** sur qn) (d'un air maussade, menaçant).
glowering ['glaʊərɪŋ] *adj* (*air*) maussade; (*regard*) farouche.
glowing ['gləʊɪŋ] *adj* **(a)** (*metal*) (chauffé au) rouge, incandescent, rougeoyant; **(b)** (*coal, embers, cigarette*) luisant; (*eyes*) de braise; **(c)** (*complexion*) rayonnant; (*cheeks*) rouge; **(d)** (*colours, words*) chaleureux; (*person*) ardent, enthousiaste; (*description*) en termes chaleureux; **to paint sth in g. colours,** présenter qch sous un jour des plus favorables; **the reviews were g.,** les critiques étaient très élogieuses; **to speak in g. terms of s.o.,** faire les louanges de qn.
glow-worm ['gləʊwɜːm] *n* (*firefly*) ver luisant.
gloxinia [glɒk'sɪnɪə] *n* (*plant*) gloxinia *m*.
glucose ['gluːkəʊs] *n* glucose *m*.
glue¹ [gluː] *n* colle *f* (forte), glu *f*; **fish g.,** colle de poisson; *F* **he sticks to me like g.,** il me suit partout; **to sniff g.,** (*of drug addict*) sniffer de la colle.
glue² *v* (**glued; gluing**) **1** *vt* coller (à la colle forte); **to g. sth on to sth,** coller qch sur qch; **I glued it on,** je l'ai collé dessus; **to g. two things together,** coller deux choses (ensemble); *Fig* **she watched the crowds passing, her face glued to the window,** le visage collé à la fenêtre, elle regardait passer la foule; **they were glued to the television,** ils étaient rivés à la télévision; **keep your eyes glued to the road,** gardez les yeux rivés *ou* fixés sur la route. **2** *vi* **wood that glues well,** bois qui colle bien.
gluepot ['gluːpɒt] *n* pot *m* à colle.
glue-sniffer ['gluːsnɪfər] *n* sniffeur, -euse (de colle).
glue-sniffing ['gluːsnɪfɪŋ] *n* inhalation *f* de colle.
gluey ['gluːɪ] *adj* gluant, poisseux.
glug¹ [glʌg] *n* **g. (g.),** glouglou *m*.
glug² *vi* (**-gg-**) faire glouglou.
glum [glʌm] *adj* (*visage*) renfrogné, maussade; (*air*) morne; **to look g.,** se renfrogner, *F* faire une tête.
glumly ['glʌmlɪ] *adv* d'un air maussade.
glumness ['glʌmnɪs] *n* air *m* maussade.
glut¹ [glʌt] *n* *Com* encombrement *m* (*du marché*); surabondance *f* (*d'une denrée etc*); **it's a g. on the market,** c'est un article dont tout le monde est pourvu *ou* dont personne ne veut plus; **there is a g. of pears,** le marché regorge de poires; **I've had a g. of pears,** (*from my garden*) j'ai eu un tas de poires.
glut² *vt* (**-tt-**) **(a)** *Com* encombrer, inonder (*le marché*); **the market is glutted with this article,** le marché regorge de cet article; **(b)** (*feed excessively*) rassasier, assouvir (*qn, sa faim etc*); **to g. oneself,** se rassasier, se gorger (**on,** de).
glutamine ['gluːtəmaɪn] *n Ch* glutamine *f*.
gluten ['gluːtən] *n* gluten *m*.
glutinous ['gluːtɪnəs] *adj* glutineux.
glutton ['glʌt(ə)n] *n* **(a)** (*person*) glouton, -onne, *F* goinfre *m*, bâfreur, -euse; **she's a g. for work,** c'est un bourreau de travail; **you're a g. for punishment,** tu cherches les complications; **(b)** (*wolverine*) glouton *m*.
gluttonous ['glʌtənəs] *adj* glouton.
gluttonously [glʌtənəslɪ] *adv* gloutonnement.
gluttony ['glʌtənɪ] *n* gloutonnerie *f*, *F* goinfrerie *f*.
glycerin(e) ['glɪsərɪn, -iːn] **, glycerol** ['glɪsərɒl] *n Ch etc* glycérine *f*, glycérol *m* .
glycol ['glaɪkɒl] *n Ch* glycol *m*.
G-man, -men ['dʒiːmæn, -men] *n US F* = agent du F.B.I..
GMT [dʒiːem'tiː] *n* (*abbr* **Greenwich Mean Time**) G.M.T..
gnarled [nɑːld] *adj* **(a)** (*tree*) (*knotty*) noueux, rugueux; (*twisted*) tordu; **(b)** (*hands, fingers*) noueux, déformé; (*old man, woman*) fripé.
gnash [næʃ] *vt* **to g. one's teeth,** grincer des dents.
gnashing ['næʃɪŋ] *n* grincement *m* (*des dents*).
gnat [næt] *n* (*insect*) moucheron *m*.
gnaw [nɔː] *vt* (*pt* **gnawed**; *pp* **gnawed, gnawn**) (*of rodent*) ronger (*qch*); **to g. a bone,** (*of dog*) ronger un os; **gnawed by hunger,** tenaillé par la faim; **gnawed by remorse,** rongé par le remords.
▶gnaw at, gnaw into, gnaw through *vipo* ronger (*qch*).
gnawing ['nɔːwɪŋ] *adj* (*animal*) rongeur, -euse; (*hunger*) dévorant, tenaillant; (*anxiety*) rongeant; **the g. pains of hunger,** les tiraillements de la faim.
gneiss [naɪs] *n Geol* gneiss *m*.
gnome [nəʊm] *n Myth* gnome *m*; **(garden) g.,** = statue de nain qui décore un jardin; *F Pej* **the gnomes of Zurich,** les banquiers internationaux de Zurich.
gnosis ['nəʊsɪs] *n Rel* gnose *f*.
gnostic ['nɒstɪk] *adj & n Rel Hist* gnostique *mf*.
gnosticism ['nɒstɪsɪz(ə)m] *n Rel Hist* gnosticisme *m*.
GNP [dʒiːen'piː] *n Econ* (*abbr* **Gross National Product**) P.N.B. *m*.
gnu [nuː] *n* (*animal*) gnou *m*.
go¹ [gəʊ] **1** *n* (*pl* **goes**) **(a)** (*activity*) aller *m*; **to be always on the go,** être toujours à trotter *ou* à courir; **to keep s.o. on the go,** faire trimer qn; **it's all go,** on n'a pas une minute à soi, ça n'arrête pas;
(b) (*energy*) **to be full of** *or* **have plenty of go,** avoir de l'allant; **music full of go,** musique pleine de vie;
(c) (*try*) coup *m*, essai *m*; **to make a go of it,** (*succeed*) y réussir; **(it's) your go!,** (*in game*) à vous de jouer!; **to have a go at,** (*try*) essayer de faire (*qch*); (*start eating*) s'attaquer à (*un rôti, un pâté etc*); **let's have a go!,** tentons le coup!, allons-y!; (*let me try*) laisse-moi essayer; **she had a go at me,** (*abused me verbally*) elle s'en est pris à moi; **(it's) no go!,** rien à faire!; **at one go,** d'un (seul) coup; **£1 a go,** (*at fair etc*) une livre la partie *ou* le tour; **to have a go on the dodgems,** faire un tour d'auto-tamponneuses; **he wouldn't let me have** *or* **give me a go,** (*on his bicycle etc*) il ne me laisserait pas l'essayer;
(d) *F* (*of fever etc*) accès *m*; (*of flu*) attaque *f*;
(e) *Old-fashioned* **it's all the go,** ça fait fureur *ou* rage.
2 *adj Astronaut* **all systems are go,** tout est paré et en ordre de marche (pour le départ).
go² *v* (**he goes;** *pt* **went** [went]; *pp* **gone** [gɒn]) (*the aux is usu* **have,** *occ* **be**) **1** *vi* **(a)** aller; **to go to a place,** aller *ou* se rendre à un endroit; **to go to Paris/to the country,** aller à Paris/à la campagne; **to go to France/Japan,** aller en France/au Japon; **to go home,** aller *ou* rentrer chez soi; **to go to church/Mass,** aller à l'église/à la messe; **to go to the doctor's,** aller chez le médecin; **to go to prison,** être mis en prison; **to go to the lavatory,** aller aux toilettes; **to come and go,** aller et venir; **to go to s.o.'s house,** aller chez qn; **to go on a journey,** faire un voyage; **to go for a walk,** aller se promener, faire une promenade; **to go on foot/by train/by car,** aller à pied/par le train/en voiture; **there he goes!,** le voilà (qui passe)!; **who goes there?,** qui va là?; **the car was going very slowly/fast,** la voiture allait très lentement/vite; **to go at 100 km an hour,** faire 100 km *ou* du cent à l'heure; **to go at full speed,** se lancer à toute vitesse; **you go first,** (*after you*) à vous d'abord; (*you leave first*) partez le premier *ou* devant; **to go up/down/across/along a street,** remonter/descendre/traverser/passer par une rue; **to go into a room,** entrer dans une pièce; **to go behind s.o.'s back,** faire qch derrière le dos de qn; **to go over** *or* **across a bridge,** traverser un pont; **the ball went over the wall,** la balle a passé par-dessus le mur; **to go forward,** avancer; **to go ahead of s.o.,** devancer qn; **which road goes to London?,** quel est le chemin qui va à Londres?; **to go to school,** aller à l'école; **to go to sea,** se faire marin; **to go into the army,** s'engager (dans l'armée); (*be called up*) partir au régiment; **to go hungry/thirsty,** avoir faim/soif; **to go under** *or* **by a false name,** être connu sous un faux nom; **wine that goes to the head,** vin qui monte à la tête; *F* **to be six months gone,** (*of woman*) être enceinte de six

mois; **to go one's own way,** faire à sa guise; **there you go!,** (*handing sth to s.o.*) voilà!; **it's expensive, but there you go,** (*that's how it is*) c'est cher mais c'est comme ça; **there you go again!,** vous voilà reparti!; **promotion goes by seniority,** l'avancement se fait à l'ancienneté; **to go riding,** (aller) se promener à cheval; **to go hunting/fishing,** aller à la chasse/à la pêche; **to go looking for sth,** partir à la recherche de qch;

(b) (*be active, function*) marcher; **to set** *or* **get a piece of machinery going,** mettre une machine en marche *ou* en mouvement; *F* **get going!,** file!, vas-y!; **my watch won't go,** ma montre ne marche pas; **the bell went 10 minutes ago,** la cloche a sonné il y a dix minutes; **enough timber to keep three sawmills going,** assez de bois pour alimenter trois scieries; **to keep the conversation going,** entretenir la conversation; **when he gets going he never stops,** quand il est lancé *ou* une fois lancé il ne sait pas s'arrêter;

(c) (*progress*) **everything's going well,** tout marche bien; **things are going badly,** cela va mal; **how are things going?, how is it going?,** comment ça va?; **if all goes well,** si tout va bien; **the rehearsal went well/badly,** la répétition a bien/mal marché; **the way things are going,** au train où vont les choses; **I forget how the tune goes,** l'air m'échappe; **how does the chorus go?,** quelles sont les paroles du refrain?; **the story goes that ...,** à ce que l'on raconte ...; **as the saying goes,** selon le dicton; **as things go today,** par le temps qui court; **that's not dear as things go today,** ce n'est pas cher au prix où sont les choses; **which way will the decision go?,** comment décidera-t-on?; **I don't know how things will go,** je ne sais pas comment cela tournera; **judgement went for/against the plaintiff,** l'arrêt fut prononcé en faveur du/contre le demandeur;

(d) (*of time*) passer; **there were only five minutes to go before ...,** il ne restait que cinq minutes avant ...; **how's the time going?,** combien de temps nous reste-t-il?; **it has just gone eight,** il est un peu plus de huit heures;

(e) (*happen*) **what she says goes,** c'est elle qui commande;

(f) (*be accepted*) **anything goes,** (*do, wear etc whatever you like*) on fait ce qu'on veut; **it goes without saying that ...,** il va de soi que ...; **that goes without saying,** cela va sans dire;

(g) *F* (*make sound, perform action*) **to go crack/bang,** faire crac/pan; **go like this with your left foot,** fais comme ça du pied gauche; **and then he went, 'oh, I forgot',** et alors il a dit 'oh, j'ai oublié';

(h) (*match*) **these colours don't go,** ces couleurs jurent;

(i) (*leave*) partir; s'en aller; **after** *or* **when I had gone,** après mon départ; **we must go** *or* **must be going,** il est temps de partir; **let me go,** laissez-moi partir; **go!,** (*go away*) allez vous-en!; *Sp* (*in race etc*) partez!; **from the word go,** dès le commencement; **that old chair will have to go,** il va falloir se débarrasser de cette vieille chaise; **a hundred employees will have to go,** il va falloir mettre cent employés à la porte; *Euph* **his wife went first,** (*died*) sa femme s'en est allée avant lui; *Euph* **when I am gone, after I have gone,** quand je ne serai plus là;

(j) (*disappear*) disparaître; **my hat has gone,** mon chapeau a disparu; **it's all gone,** il n'y en a plus; **that's the way the money goes,** voilà comme l'argent file; **most of my money goes on food,** la plupart de mon argent passe dans la nourriture; **her sight is going,** elle est en train de perdre la vue;

(k) (*break*) (se) casser; **the spring went,** le ressort s'est cassé; **the batteries are going,** les piles sont presque mortes; *El* **a fuse went,** un plomb a sauté; **my dress is going at the seams,** ma robe s'use aux coutures;

(l) (*be on sale, available*) **to be going cheap,** se vendre (à) bon marché; **they are going at ten francs each,** ils sont en vente *ou* en solde à dix francs pièce; **the lot went for £20,** le lot fut adjugé à 20 livres; **going! going! gone!,** (*at auction*) une fois! deux fois! adjugé!; **let's see if there's any lunch going,** allons voir si le déjeuner est prêt; **there are drinks going in the drawing room,** on sert l'apéritif dans le salon; **there's a job going at the factory,** il y a une place à l'usine;

(m) (*introducing an action*) **to go and do sth,** aller faire qch; **to go to dinner with s.o.,** aller dîner avec qn *ou* (*at their place*) chez qn; **to go to** *or* **and see s.o.,** aller voir qn; **go and see** *or esp Am* **go see what's happening,** va voir ce qui se passe; **to go and look for sth,** aller chercher qch; *F* **and then he went and got married!,** et puis il a eu l'idée de se marier!; *Sl* **now you've (been and) gone and done it!,** vous en avez fait une belle!, ça y est cette fois-ci!; **he went (forward) to help her, but ...,** il est allé *ou* a fait un mouvement pour l'aider, mais ...;

(n) (*aux forming an immediate future*) **I'm going to tell you a story,** je vais vous raconter une histoire; **the shortage is not going to last,** la disette ne durera pas; **I'm going to have my own way,** je veux faire comme je l'entends; **I'm not going to be cheated,** je ne me laisserai pas abuser; **I was going to walk,** (*intention*) j'avais l'intention d'y aller à pied; **I'm going to go to France for my holiday,** je compte passer mes vacances en France;

(o) (*have recourse to*) **to go to law,** avoir recours à la justice; **to go to war,** entrer en guerre; **to go to press,** mettre sous presse; **I will go up to £100,** je veux bien payer jusqu'à 100 livres;

(p) (*fit*) **too big to go into the basket,** trop grand pour entrer dans le panier; **the key won't go in(to) the lock,** la clef n'entre pas dans la serrure; *Math F* **six into twelve goes twice,** douze divisé par six fait deux; **four into three won't go,** trois n'est pas divisible par quatre;

(q) (*belong*) **where does this book go?,** où faut-il mettre *ou* où est la place de ce livre?; **the scissors go in the drawer,** les ciseaux vont dans le tiroir;

(r) (*be given*) **the proceeds will go to charity,** les bénéfices seront distribués *ou* iront à des œuvres charitables; **his estate will go to his eldest son,** la propriété va revenir à son fils aîné;

(s) (*contribute*) contribuer (*à qch*); **the qualities that go to make a great man,** les qualités qui font un grand homme; **ingredients that go to make a good dish,** ingrédients qui contribuent à faire un bon plat; **these reforms go some way to(wards) improving the situation,** ces réformes contribuent à améliorer la situation; **the money will go to(wards) a new community centre,** cet argent servira à un nouveau centre social; **to go to prove sth,** servir à prouver qch; **it only goes to show that you can't be too careful,** cela montre qu'on ne peut jamais prendre trop de précautions;

(t) (*extend*) s'étendre; **the garden goes down to the river,** le jardin s'étend jusqu'à la rivière; **the difference goes deep,** il y a une profonde différence; **as far as the style goes,** quant au style, pour ce qui est du style;

(u) (*become*) devenir; **to go mad,** devenir fou; **to go Communist,** devenir communiste; **he went cold all over,** son sang s'est glacé; **this tea's gone cold,** le thé a refroidi; **to go red,** rougir; **to go white,** blanchir; **my hair is going grey,** mes cheveux grisonnent *ou* deviennent gris; **to go to the bad,** mal tourner;

(v) **to let go,** lâcher prise; **let me go!, let go of me!,** lâchez-moi!; **let go of my arm!,** lâche-moi le bras!; **let go of that child!,** lâche cet enfant!; *Nau* **to let a rope go,** laisser aller *ou* lâcher un cordage; **to let a prisoner/animal g.,** relâcher un prisonnier/animal; **to let oneself go,** (*relax*) se décontracter; (*stop taking care of oneself*) se laisser aller; **we'll let it go at that,** tenons-nous-en là, cela ira comme ça; **well, let it go at that!,** passons!

2 *vt F* **that's really going it!,** (*that's fast*) ça, c'est de la vitesse!; **to go it alone,** agir tout seul; (*in business*) se lancer tout seul; *F* **I could really go a beer,** je me paierais bien une bière; **to go 10,** risquer 10; *Cards* **to go no/two/three trumps,** annoncer sans/deux/trois atout(s); **to go one better,** surenchérir (**than s.o.,** sur qn).

►**go about 1** *vi* (*move*) circuler; (*of rumour*) courir; *Nau* virer de bord; *Mil etc* faire demi-tour; **policemen usually go about in pairs,** en général, les policiers circulent par deux; **you can't go about saying things like that!,** arrête de dire ce genre de choses!; **she's been going about with that Smith boy,** on l'a vue traîner avec le fils Smith. **2** *vipo* **(a)** parcourir (*le pays*); **to go about the streets,** circuler dans les rues; **(b)** (*tackle*) **how to go about it,** comment s'y prendre; **how do I go about getting a licence?,** que dois-je faire pour obtenir un permis?; **(c)** vaquer à (*son travail, ses occupations*).

►**go after** *vipo* (*pursue*) essayer d'obtenir; courir après (*qn*); **she really goes after what she wants,** elle essaye vraiment d'obtenir ce qu'elle veut.

►**go ahead** *vi* **(a)** (*proceed*) continuer, poursuivre; **may I say something? — go ahead,** puis-je dire quelque chose? — allez-y; **to go ahead with sth,** commencer qch; **he went ahead and did it,** (*without hesitating*) il l'a fait sans l'ombre d'une hésitation; (*despite warnings*) rien ne l'a arrêté; **the building work was finally able to go ahead,** la construction a pu commencer; **(b)** (*go in front*) avancer; **you go ahead,** (*I'll follow later*) partez devant.

▶**go along** *vi* **(a)** (*walk, ride, drive etc*) suivre son chemin; **we were going along quite slowly when ...,** nous avancions plutôt lentement quand ...; **(b)** (*proceed*) **I check the figures as I go along,** je vérifie les chiffres au fur et à mesure; **(c)** (*agree*) suivre.

▶**go along with** *vipo* coopérer avec (*qn*); approuver, accepter (*qch*); **she wouldn't go along with it,** elle n'était pas d'accord.

▶**go around** *vi* = **GO ABOUT 1.**

▶**go at** *vipo* s'attaquer à (*qn, qch*); **to go at it hard,** ne pas y aller de main morte.

▶**go away** *vi* (*leave*) s'en aller, partir; **go away!,** va t'en!; **to go away on business/for the weekend,** s'absenter pour affaires/pour le week-end; **to go away with sth,** emporter qch.

▶**go back** *vi* **(a)** (*return*) s'en retourner; (*turn back*) retourner en arrière; rebrousser chemin; (*move back*) reculer; **to go back home,** retourner chez soi; **to go back to Paris,** retourner à Paris; **he's never gone back,** (*to that place*) il n'y est jamais retourné; **let's go back the way we came,** reprenons le même chemin qu'à l'aller; **to go back two paces,** faire deux pas en arrière; **to go back to the beginning,** recommencer; **he went back to his reading,** il s'est replongé dans sa lecture; **to go back to sleep,** se rendormir; **to go back to one's old ways,** retomber dans ses anciennes habitudes; **(b)** (*date back*) remonter à (*l'origine de qch*); **there are records going back to 1700,** il y a des récits qui remontent à 1700; **we go back a long way,** ça fait longtemps qu'on se connaît.

▶**go back on** *vipo* (*abandon, alter*) revenir sur; **he never goes back on a decision,** il ne revient jamais sur une décision.

▶**go by 1** *vi* **(a)** (*pass*) passer; **to watch people going by,** regarder passer les gens; *Fig* **to let an opportunity go by,** laisser passer une occasion; **(b)** (*elapse*) s'écouler; **half an hour went by,** une demi-heure s'est écoulée; **as the years go by,** à mesure que les années passent. **2** *vipo* **(a)** (*judge on the basis of*) juger; **don't go by what he says/his opinion,** ne juge pas d'après ce qu'il dit/ne tiens pas compte de ses opinions; **to go by appearances,** juger d'après les apparences; **(b)** (*follow*) **to go by the rules,** suivre *ou* respecter les règles; **go by your sister's example,** suis l'exemple de ta sœur; **(c)** (*be known as*) être connu comme; **to go by a different/false name,** être connu sous un nom différent/un faux nom; **this carpet goes by the name of Texpile,** ce tapis est vendu sous le nom de Texpile.

▶**go down 1** *vi* **(a)** (*descend*) descendre; (*of sun*) se coucher; (*of ship*) sombrer; **going down!,** (*in lift*) on descend!, pour descendre!; **go down and answer the door,** descends ouvrir; **to go down on one's knees,** se mettre *ou* se jeter à genoux; *F* **to go d. with flu,** attraper la grippe; **to go down in the world,** avoir connu des jours meilleurs; **the captain went down with his ship,** le capitaine a sombré avec son navire; **I'm not going to go down without a fight,** (*be defeated*) je me battrai jusqu'à la fin; *Br Univ* **to go down (from the university),** (*at end of studies*) quitter l'université; (*at end of term*) partir en vacances;

(b) (*decrease*) (*of floods, temperature*) baisser, s'abaisser; (*of wind*) baisser, tomber; (*of prices, value*) baisser; **to go d. in s.o.'s estimation,** baisser dans l'estime de qn;

(c) (*be received*) **to go down well,** (*of drink*) se laisser boire; (*of food*) se laisser manger; (*of entertainment, speech, suggestion*) plaire, être bien reçu; **he went down in history as a tyrant,** l'histoire a retenu de lui l'image d'un tyran;

(d) (*lose air*) (*of swelling*) se désenfler, se dégonfler; (*of tyre, balloon*) se dégonfler;

(e) (*extend*) continuer (*jusqu'à la fin de la page etc*);

(f) *Cards* (*bridge*) perdre le coup; ne pas faire autant de levées qu'on en a annoncé;

(g) *US F* **what's going down?,** qu'est-ce qui se passe?

2 *vipo* (*descend*) descendre de (*une colline, une échelle*).

▶**go for** *vipo* **(a)** (*attack*) attaquer, tomber sur (*qn*); **go for him!,** (*to dog*) pille! pille!; **they went for each other in court,** (*physically*) ils se sont empoignés devant le tribunal; (*verbally*) ils se sont engueulés devant le tribunal; **(b)** (*strive to attain*) essayer d'obtenir; **if you really want the job, go for it!,** si tu veux vraiment le poste, mets-y le paquet; **with his next jump, he's going for the gold,** avec son prochain saut, il vise la médaille d'or; **(c)** (*like*) être porté sur, être attiré par; **I don't go for him much,** (*don't like him*) je ne l'aime pas tellement; (*don't think him attractive*) il ne m'attire pas spécialement, il ne me fait ni chaud ni froid; **she's always gone for the Scandinavian type,** elle a toujours été attirée par le type scandinave, elle a toujours été portée sur le type scandinave.

▶**go in 1** *vi* **(a)** (*enter*) entrer; rentrer; **let's go in!,** entrons!; **(b)** (*of sun*) se cacher; **(c)** *Cr* prendre son tour au guichet; **(d)** *Mil etc F* (*attack*) attaquer. **2** *vipo F* (*enter*) entrer dans, rentrer dans; **to go in a house/room,** entrer dans une maison/une pièce.

▶**go in for** *vipo* **(a)** (*use, produce, show interest in*) **they don't go in for injections so much nowadays,** ils ne sont pas tellement pour les piqûres de nos jours; **why do scientists go in for all that jargon?,** pourquoi est-ce que les scientifiques utilisent tout ce jargon?; **this publisher doesn't really go in for fiction,** cet éditeur ne fait pas tellement dans le roman; **we don't go in for pop music,** nous ne sommes pas très musique pop; **(b)** (*pursue*) s'adonner à, se consacrer à; **he doesn't go in for team sports,** il n'est pas très porté sur les sports d'équipe; **to go in for painting,** (*as hobby*) faire de la peinture; **to go in for teaching,** (*as career*) entrer dans l'enseignement; **(c)** (*enter*) **to go in for an examination,** se présenter à un examen; **to go in for a competition,** prendre part à un concours.

▶**go into** *vipo* **(a)** (*enter*) entrer dans; rentrer dans; **they went into the house,** ils sont entrés dans la maison; **she's gone into hospital,** elle est entrée à l'hôpital; **to go into mourning,** prendre le deuil; **to go into hysterics,** avoir une crise de nerfs; **to go into fits of laughter,** avoir des crises de fou rire; **to go into teaching,** (*as career*) entrer dans l'enseignement; **(b)** (*examine*) examiner, étudier (*une question*), mettre (*une question*) à l'étude; **I shall go into the matter,** je vais m'occuper de l'affaire; **to go into the reasons for sth,** rechercher les raisons de qch; **(c)** (*explain, provide*) expliquer; **he wasn't prepared to go into the reasons for his behaviour,** il n'était pas disposé à expliquer les raisons de son comportement; **to go into details,** entrer dans les détails; **(d)** (*embark on*) s'embarquer dans, se lancer dans (*une description*).

▶**go in with** *vipo* se joindre à (*qn*) (*dans une entreprise etc*).

▶**go off 1** *vi* **(a)** (*leave*) partir, s'en aller, s'éloigner; *Th* quitter la scène; *F* **she's gone off and left him,** elle l'a quitté; **he went off with the woman next door,** il a fichu le camp avec la voisine, il s'est tiré avec la voisine; **to go off with sth,** emporter qch, enlever qch;

(b) (*deteriorate*) (*of food, work*) se détériorer; (*of wine*) perdre de son arôme; (*of milk*) tourner; (*of butter*) rancir; (*of fish, meat*) se gâter; (*of feeling*) passer; (*of tennis player*) perdre sa forme; (*of woman*) perdre de sa beauté;

(c) (*proceed*) **everything went off well,** tout a bien marché, tout s'est bien passé; **how did the concert go off?,** comment le concert s'est-il passé?;

(d) (*cease working, be disconnected*) **the power/light went off,** l'électricité a été coupée/la lumière s'est éteinte;

(e) (*of gun*) partir, se décharger; (*of bomb*) éclater; **the pistol didn't go off,** le pistolet a raté; **the firework went off in my face,** le feu d'artifice m'a explosé dans la figure;

(f) (*of alarm*) se déclencher; (*of alarm clock*) sonner;

(g) (*go to sleep*) s'endormir.

2 *vipo* (*lose liking for*) perdre le goût de (*qch*); **I've gone off cheese,** je n'aime plus le fromage; **I've completely gone off him,** j'ai commencé à le prendre en grippe; **I've gone off the idea,** cette idée ne me dit plus rien.

▶**go on 1** *vi* **(a)** (*continue*) continuer; **'and that's not all,' he went on,** 'et ce n'est pas tout', a-t-il poursuivi; **go on with what you were doing,** continuez ce que vous étiez en train de faire; **I must go on with my work,** il me faut continuer mon travail; **go on looking!,** cherchez toujours!; **the lecture went on rather a long time,** le cours a duré plutôt longtemps; **I have enough to be going on with,** j'en ai assez pour le moment; **to go on to another question,** passer à une autre question; *Sl* **go on (with you)!,** allons donc!; **you mustn't go on like that,** (*get upset*) il ne faut pas vous laisser aller comme ça;

(b) (*of time*) passer;

(c) (*talk excessively, unreasonably*) parler à n'en plus finir; **how he goes on!,** impossible de l'arrêter!; **once he starts he goes on and on,** une fois qu'il est parti, il n'y a plus moyen de l'arrêter; **they were going on about the ozone layer,** ils parlaient à n'en plus finir de la couche d'ozone; **what are you going on about now?,** qu'est-ce que vous racontez?; **she went on a bit,** (*even though what she said was interesting*) elle s'est un peu étendue sur la question; **he's always going on at me,** il est toujours à me gronder;

(d) (*happen*) **this has been going on for years,** cela fait des années que ça dure; **what's going on here?,** qu'est-ce qui se passe ici?;
(e) (*begin to operate, be connected*) se mettre en marche; **the streetlights go on when it gets dark,** les réverbères s'allument quand il commence à faire nuit;
(f) *Th* (*walk on stage*) entrer en scène; **the band went on at 10 o'clock,** le groupe est entré en scène à 10 heures;
(g) (*fit*) **I can't get the lid to go on,** je n'arrive pas à mettre le couvercle; **these shoes won't go on,** ces chaussures ne vont pas; **these jeans won't go on any more,** je ne rentre plus dans ce jean.
2 *vipo* **(a)** *F* (*enter*) monter dans (*un bateau, un train*);
(b) (*embark on*) **to go on a journey,** partir en voyage; **to go on a diet,** se mettre au régime; **to go on social security,** s'inscrire au chômage;
(c) (*approach*) aller sur; **she's two going on three,** elle va sur les trois ans;
(d) (*be guided by*) se fonder sur (*qch*); **the police have nothing to go on,** la police n'a rien sur quoi se fonder.

►**go on for** *vipo* (*approach*) approcher de, aller sur; **he's going on for forty,** il va sur la quarantaine.

►**go out** *vi* **(a)** sortir; **I haven't been out all day,** je ne suis pas sorti de la journée; **she's gone out to get a paper,** elle est sortie pour acheter un journal; **to go out for a walk,** sortir se promener; **she was dressed to go out,** elle était en tenue de ville; **she's decided to go out to work,** elle a décidé de travailler à l'extérieur; *Ind* **to go out (on strike),** se mettre en grève; *Fig* **the magic seemed to have gone out of their relationship,** la magie semblait avoir disparu de leur relation; *Fig* **her heart went out to them,** elle a ressenti de la pitié pour eux; **we don't go out much in the evenings,** nous ne sortons pas beaucoup le soir; **to go out for a meal,** aller au restaurant;
(b) (*date*) sortir (*avec qn*); **they've been going out (together) for a month,** ils sortent ensemble depuis un mois; **to go out with s.o.,** sortir avec qn, fréquenter qn; **he went out with her for two years before they got married,** il l'a fréquentée pendant deux ans avant de l'épouser;
(c) (*of fire, light*) s'éteindre; **the lights go out at midnight,** on éteint les lumières à minuit; *Fig* **I went out like a light,** (*fell asleep*) je me suis endormi tout de suite;
(d) (*of tide*) baisser, se retirer;
(e) (*become unfashionable*) passer de mode, se démoder;
(f) *Sp* (*be eliminated*) être éliminé; **I bet they go out in the next round,** je parie qu'ils vont être éliminés à la prochaine manche;
(g) (*of letter*) être envoyé;
(h) *TV Rad* être diffusé; **the programme goes out at peak viewing time,** l'émission est diffusée aux heures de grande écoute.

►**go over 1** *vi* **(a)** (*cross*) **I went over and tapped him on the shoulder,** je suis allé vers lui et je lui ai tapé sur l'épaule; **(b)** (*transfer allegiance*) **to go over to the enemy,** passer à l'ennemi; **to go over to the other side,** changer de parti; **he's thinking of going over to cigars,** il songe à passer aux cigares; **(c)** (*be received*) (*of suggestion, joke*) passer; (*of play*) faire son petit effet, passer la rampe; *F* **to go over big,** décrocher le grand succès. **2** *vipo* **(a)** (*examine*) examiner, revoir (*un compte, un rapport etc*); passer (*des papiers etc*) en revue; relire (*un document*); repasser, revoir (*une leçon*); **to go over sth in one's mind,** repasser qch dans son esprit; **(b)** (*discuss*) parler de (*qch*); **we must have gone over this point a dozen times!,** nous avons dû parler de cette question une douzaine de fois!; **(c)** (*rehearse*) revoir.

►**go round 1** *vi* **(a)** (*make a detour*) faire un détour; **to go a long way round,** faire un grand détour;
(b) (*spin*) tourner; **my head's going round,** la tête me tourne;
(c) (*visit*) aller voir; **I said I'd go round (and see her),** j'ai dit que j'irais la voir; **he's gone round to a friend's,** il est allé chez un ami;
(d) (*circulate*) (*of rumour*) circuler, courir; (*of bottle*) circuler;
(e) (*suffice*) suffire; **the food only just went round,** il y avait juste assez de nourriture pour tout le monde; **to make the food go round,** ménager la nourriture; **there isn't enough to go round,** il n'y en a pas assez pour tout le monde.
2 *vipo* **(a)** (*detour*) **to go round the long way,** faire un long détour;
(b) (*tour*) faire le tour de (*un musée*); **I hate going round the shops,** j'ai horreur de faire les boutiques; **they went round the neighbourhood looking for their cat,** ils ont fait le tour du quartier pour chercher leur chat;
(c) (*be sufficient for*) suffire pour; **will the soup go round twenty?,** est-ce qu'il y aura assez de soupe pour vingt?, est-ce que la soupe suffira pour vingt?

►**go through 1** *vi* **(a)** (*travel through, penetrate*) passer, traverser; **the gates were open and we went through,** les barrières étaient ouvertes et nous sommes passés;
(b) (*be completed, accepted*) **the bill has gone through,** la loi a passé; **the deal didn't go through,** le marché n'a pas été conclu; **when does the divorce go through?,** quand est-ce que le divorce va être prononcé?
2 *vipo* **(a)** (*suffer*) subir, essuyer (*de rudes épreuves*); **he went through agony,** (*wondering what had happened*) il a été au supplice; **she was still cheerful in spite of all she had gone through,** elle était toujours pleine d'entrain malgré tout ce qu'elle avait enduré;
(b) (*complete*) remplir (*des formalités*);
(c) (*examine*) examiner (*des documents*); revoir (*une leçon, des comptes*); trier (*sa garde-robe*);
(d) (*search*) visiter, fouiller (*des valises*); **to go through s.o.'s pockets,** fouiller dans les poches de qn;
(e) (*use up*) (*money*) dépenser; (*goods*) utiliser, consommer; **to go through all one's money,** dépenser tout son argent; **we've gone through six bottles of milk,** nous avons consommé six bouteilles de lait.

►**go through with** *vipo* (*carry out*) réaliser, exécuter, aller jusqu'au bout de; **she decided that she couldn't go through with the wedding,** elle a décidé qu'elle ne pouvait pas se marier; **I mean to go through with it,** j'irai jusqu'au bout.

►**go together** *vi* **(a)** (*harmonize*) aller ensemble; **(b)** (*date*) sortir ensemble; **they've been going together for a long time,** ils sortent ensemble depuis longtemps.

►**go under 1** *vi* **(a)** (*of drowning man*) couler, s'enfoncer; **(b)** (*fail*) succomber, sombrer; (*go bankrupt*) faire faillite; **a lot of businesses have gone under,** de nombreuses entreprises ont fait faillite. **2** *vipo* **to go under a false/different name,** utiliser *ou* prendre un faux nom/un nom différent; **since the divorce she's been going under her old name,** depuis le divorce elle utilise son nom de jeune fille; **a glue that goes under the name of Stikit,** une colle qui s'appelle Stikit.

►**go up** *vi* **(a)** (*climb, rise*) monter; **to go up to bed,** monter se coucher; **to go up in an aircraft,** monter en avion; **going up!,** (*in lift*) on monte!, pour monter!; *Th* **before the curtain goes up,** avant le lever du rideau; **a shout went up from the crowd,** un cri s'éleva de la foule; *Br Univ* **to go up (to Oxford),** entrer à l'université (d'Oxford); **to go up in the world,** faire son chemin; **(b)** (*of prices, temperature etc*) monter; **bread is going up,** (*in price*) le pain augmente; **to go up in s.o.'s estimation,** monter dans l'estime de qn; **(c)** (*explode, be destroyed*) sauter; **to go up in flames,** se mettre à flamber; *Fig* **their plans went up in smoke,** leurs projets sont partis en fumée.

►**go with** *vipo* **(a)** (*accompany*) marcher *ou* aller de pair avec (*qch*); **mathematical ability usually goes with skill at chess,** des capacités en mathématiques vont souvent de pair avec une habileté aux échecs; **a company car goes with the job,** une voiture de société va de pair avec le poste; **(b)** (*harmonize*) s'accorder avec (*qch*); (*of colours*) se marier avec (*une teinte*); **the carpet doesn't go with the furniture,** le tapis n'est pas assorti aux meubles; **(c)** (*date*) fréquenter (*qn*); **is she going with someone?,** est-ce qu'elle fréquente (un garçon *ou* un homme)?; **(d)** (*have sex with*) coucher avec (*qn*); **to go with a prostitute,** coucher avec une prostituée.

►**go without 1** *vi* (*not have sth*) se passer de qch, se priver de qch; **I'd rather go without,** je préfère m'en passer; **as children they often went without,** lorsqu'ils étaient enfants ils ont souvent été privés; **they went without so that the children got enough to eat,** ils ont dû se priver pour que les enfants aient assez à manger. **2** *vipo* (*not have*) se passer de (*qch*); **I went without breakfast so I wouldn't be late,** je me suis passé de petit déjeuner pour ne pas être en retard; **I went without television for a week,** je me suis passé de télévision pendant une semaine.

goad[1] [gəʊd] *n* aiguillon *m*; pique-bœuf *m*, *pl* pique-bœufs.

goad[2] *vt* aiguillonner, piquer (*les bœufs*); piquer, stimuler (*la curiosité de qn*); **to g. s.o. into doing sth,** talonner qn jusqu'à ce qu'il fasse qch.

►**goad on** *vtsep* aiguillonner, inciter (*qn*).

go-ahead ['gəʊəhed] *F* **1** *adj* **(a)** (*enterprising*) plein d'allant, entreprenant; **go-a. business woman,** femme d'affaires entreprenante; **(b)** (*forward-looking*) tourné vers l'avenir; **we're very go-a. here,** nous sommes très tournés vers l'avenir ici. **2** *n* **to give s.o. the go-a.,** donner à qn le feu vert; **to give sth the go.-a.,** donner le feu vert pour qch.

goal [gəʊl] *n* **(a)** (*aim*) but *m*; **to achieve a g.,** atteindre un but, réaliser un objectif; **my g. is in sight,** j'approche de mon but *ou* du but; **(b)** *Fb etc* but *m*; **to score a g.,** marquer un but; **the team's highest g. scorer,** le meilleur buteur de l'équipe; **to keep g.,** garder le but; **Macleod was in g. for Rangers,** Macleod était dans les buts des Rangers; **g. kick,** coup *m* de pied de but; **g. line,** ligne *f* de but.

goalkeeper ['gəʊlki:pər] , *F* **goalie** ['gəʊlɪ] *n Fb etc* gardien *m* de but, *F* goal *m*.

goalless ['gəʊllɪs] *adj Fb etc* **g. draw,** match *m* sans but marqué, match nul.

goalmouth ['gəʊlmaʊθ] *n* entrée *f* du but.

goalpost ['gəʊlpəʊst] *n* montant *m ou* poteau *m* de but; *Fig* **to move the goalposts,** changer les règles du jeu.

goat [gəʊt] *n* chèvre *f*; **she g.,** bique *f*; **he g.,** bouc *m*; **g.'s milk,** lait *m* de chèvre; *Fig F* **it gets my g.,** ça me met en boule *ou* me tape sur les nerfs; *Astron* **the G.,** le Capricorne; *Pej* **a silly old g.,** (*old man*) imbécile *m*; *F* **a randy old g.,** un obsédé sexuel; **g. cheese, g.'s milk cheese,** fromage *m* de chèvre.

goatee [gəʊ'ti:] *n* (*beard*) barbiche *f*, bouc *m*.

goatherd ['gəʊthз:d] *n* chevrier, -ière.

goatskin ['gəʊtskɪn] *n* **(a)** peau *f* de chèvre; peau de bique; **(b)** (*bottle*) outre *f* (en peau de bouc).

goatsucker ['gəʊtsʌkər] *n* (*bird*) engoulevent *m*.

gob¹ [gɒb] *n F* **(a)** (*piece*) gros morceau (*de qch*); **(b)** *Br Sl* (*spittle*) mollard *m*; **(c)** *esp Br Sl* (*mouth*) gueule *f*; **shut your g.!,** ferme-la!, ta gueule!

gob² *vi Br Sl* (*spit*) mollarder.

gobble¹ ['gɒb(ə)l] **1** *vt* avaler (*qch*) gloutonnement, dévorer, *F* bâfrer, *F* bouffer (*qch*). **2** *vi* **don't g.!,** (*to child*) mange plus lentement!

gobble² *n* (*of turkey*) glouglou *m*.

gobble³ *vi* (*of turkey*) glouglouter.

▶**gobble down** *vtsep* (*eat quickly*) avaler (*qch*) gloutonnement.

▶**gobble up** *vtsep* (*eat quickly*) engloutir, engouffrer; *Fig* (*money*) engloutir; *Fig* **the empire gobbled up these territories,** l'empire a absorbé ces territoires.

gobbledegook, gobbledygook ['gɒb(ə)ldɪgu:k] *n F* charabia *m*.

go-between ['gəʊbɪtwi:n] *n* intermédiaire *mf*; **to act** *or* **serve as a go-b.,** servir d'intermédiaire (**to,** à).

goblet ['gɒblɪt] *n* **(a)** verre *m* à pied; **(b)** *Lit* coupe *f*.

goblin ['gɒblɪn] *n* gobelin *m*, lutin *m*.

gob-smacked ['gɒbsmækt] *adj F* **I was g.-s.,** j'en suis resté abasourdi.

gobstopper ['gɒbstɒpər] *n Br F* gros bonbon en boule.

go-by ['gəʊbaɪ] *n F* **to give s.o. the go-by,** snober qn.

GOC [dʒi:əʊ'si:] *n Mil abbr* **general officer commanding**.

go-cart ['gəʊkɑ:t] *n* **(a)** *esp Am* (*child's toy*) petit chariot; **(b)** *esp Am* (*baby-walker*) poussette *f*; **(c)** *Sp* kart *m*.

god [gɒd] *n* dieu *m*; **the g. of war,** le dieu de la guerre; **a river g.,** une divinité de la rivière; **feast (fit) for the gods,** festin digne des dieux; *F* **little tin g.,** petit dieu en toc; **to make a g. of money,** diviniser l'argent; *Th F* **the gods,** le poulailler, le paradis.

God [gɒd] *n* Dieu *m*; **a man of G.,** un homme de Dieu; **to play G.,** se prendre pour Dieu; **G. willing,** s'il plaît à Dieu; **I wish to G. ...,** plût à Dieu ...; **in G.'s name, in the name of G.,** au nom de Dieu; *F* **what in G.'s name are you doing?,** que faites-vous là, grand Dieu!; **G. knows,** Dieu seul le sait; **she's G. knows where,** elle est Dieu sait où; **thank G.!,** Dieu merci!; *Sl* **oh G.!, my G.!,** mon Dieu!, grand Dieu!; **G. forbid,** à Dieu ne plaise!

god-awful ['gɒdɔ:fʊl] *adj Sl* dégueulasse.

godchild, *pl* **-children** ['gɒdtʃaɪld, -tʃɪldrən] *n* filleul *m*, filleule *f*.

goddamn ['gɒd'dæm] *esp US* **1** *int Arch* sapristi!, nom de Dieu! **2** *adj* (*more often* **god-damned**) *Sl* sacré; **this g. idiot,** ce sacré imbécile.

goddaughter ['gɒddɔ:tər] *n* filleule *f*.

goddess ['gɒdɪs] *n* déesse *f*; *Fig* **a g. of the screen, a screen g.,** une déesse de l'écran.

godfather ['gɒdfɑ:ðər] *n* parrain *m*.

god-fearing ['gɒdfi:rɪŋ] *adj* (*person*) craignant Dieu; **decent g.-f. folk,** les gens décents et croyants.

godforsaken ['gɒdfəseɪk(ə)n] *adj* misérable; *Fig* (*endroit*) perdu; **what a g. country!,** quel bled!

godhead ['gɒdhed] *n* divinité *f*.

godless ['gɒdlɪs] *adj* (*person, action etc*) impie.

godlike ['gɒdlaɪk] *adj* de Dieu; d'un dieu; divin.

godliness ['gɒdlɪnɪs] *n* piété *f*.

godly ['gɒdlɪ] *adj* dévot, pieux, saint; **to lead a g. life,** vivre pieusement *ou* saintement.

godmother ['gɒdmʌðər] *n* marraine *f*.

godparent ['gɒdpeərənt] *n* parent spirituel; **my godparents,** mon parrain et ma marraine.

godsend ['gɒdsend] *n* aubaine *f*; **this money is a g. to him,** cet argent lui tombe du ciel; **the president's gaffe was a g. to the opposition,** la gaffe du président a été une aubaine pour l'opposition.

godson ['gɒdsʌn] *n* filleul *m*.

goer ['gəʊər] *n* **(a) to be a good/bad g.,** (*of horse*) courir bien/mal; (*of car*) marcher bien/mal; **(b)** personne active; **he's a g.,** il est plein d'allant.

-goer ['gəʊər] *suff* **church/cinema/theatre/***etc* **g.,** personne qui va souvent à l'église/au cinéma/au théâtre/*etc*.

gofer, gopher ['gəʊfər] *n esp Am Sl* (*male*) homme *m* à tout faire; (*female*) bonne *f* à tout faire.

goffer [*Br* 'gəʊfər, *Am* 'gɒfər] *n* (*pleat, iron*) godron *m*.

go-getter ['gəʊgetər] *n F* battant, -ante; **to be a go-g.,** avoir une personnalité de battant, être un battant.

goggle ['gɒg(ə)l] *vi* (*of person*) rouler de gros yeux; (*of eyes*) être saillant; **to g. at s.o.,** regarder qn en roulant de gros yeux.

gogglebox ['gɒg(ə)lbɒks] *n Br F* la télé.

goggle-eyed ['gɒg(ə)laɪd] *adj F* qui a des yeux à fleur de tête *ou* en boules de loto; **they watched g.-e.,** ils regardaient les yeux écarquillés.

goggles ['gɒg(ə)lz] *npl* lunettes *fpl* (protectrices); *Ind* lunettes de travail; **snow g.,** lunettes d'alpiniste *ou* de skieur.

go-go ['gəʊgəʊ] *n* **go-go dancer,** danseuse *f* (*dans une boîte de nuit etc*).

going ['gəʊɪŋ] **1** *adj* **(a)** (*functioning*) qui marche; **to start** *or* **set sth g.,** mettre qch en marche; **the business is a g. concern,** la maison est en pleine activité; **to be sold as a g. concern,** à vendre avec fonds; **(b)** (*current*) **the g. price** *or* **rate,** le prix courant *ou* actuel. **2** *n* **(a)** (*activity*) **comings and goings,** allées *fpl* et venues *fpl*; **that's very good g.!,** voilà qui n'est pas mal du tout!; *Typ* **g. to press,** mise *f* sous presse; **g. to law/to war,** recours *m* à la justice/à la guerre; **theatre g.,** visites *fpl* au théâtre; **(b)** (*leaving*) départ *m*; **(c)** (*terrain*) état *m* du sol; **the g. is rough,** le chemin est rude; *Horseracing* **good/heavy g.,** terrain bon/lourd; *Fig* **to get out while the going's good,** partir pendant que la voie est libre; *Fig* **it's heavy g. getting him to talk,** on a du mal à le faire parler.

-going ['gəʊɪŋ] *suff* **(a) theatre/cinema/***etc***-g,** fréquentation *f* des théâtres/des cinémas/*etc*; **(b) slow/fast-g.,** qui marche lentement/vite.

going-away ['gəʊɪŋə'weɪ] *adj* **g.-a. dress,** robe *f* de voyage de noce.

going back *n* (*return*) retour *m*; (*retreat*) recul *m*; **g. back on one's word,** manque *m* de parole.

going out *n* sorties *f(pl)*.

going-over ['gəʊɪŋ'əʊvər] *n F* **to give s.o. a g.-o.,** (*search*) fouiller qn; (*beating*) battre qn.

goings-on ['gəʊɪŋzɒn] *npl F* **g.-on,** (*events*) événements *mpl*; (*activities*) activités *fpl*; **strange g.-on,** des choses étranges qui se passent; **what extraordinary g.-on!,** quelles histoires extraordinaires!; (*behaviour*) voilà une conduite extraordinaire!;

goitre, *US* **goiter** ['gɔɪtər] *n Med* goitre *m*.

go-kart ['gəʊkɑ:t] *n Sp* kart *m*; **go-k. racing,** karting *m*.

gold [gəʊld] **1** *n* **(a)** or *m*; **pure g.,** or pur; *F* **fool's g.,** pyrite *f* de fer; **to pay s.o. in g.,** payer qn en or; *Hist* **the Field of the Cloth of G.,** le camp du Drap d'or; **g. brooch/necklace,** broche *f*/collier *m* d'or *ou* en or; **g. braid,** (*on uniform etc*) galon doré; **g. bullion,** or en barres *ou* en lingots; **g. coin,** pièce *f* d'or; **g. content,** teneur *f* en or; **g. crown,** couronne *f* en or; **g. currency** *or* **money,** monnaie *f* d'or; **g. dust,** poussière *f* d'or; *Fig* **to be g. dust,** valoir de l'or; **g. filling,** obturation *f* à l'or *ou* en or; **g. lamé dress,** robe lamée d'or; **g. leaf** *or* **foil,** feuille *f* d'or, or en feuille; **g. mine,** mine *f* d'or; *F* **a regular g. mine,** une vraie mine d'or; **g. plate,** plaqué-or; *Mus* **g. record,** disque *m* d'or; **g. reserve,** réserve *f* d'or; *Hist* **g. rush,** la ruée vers l'or; **the g. standard,** l'étalon-or *m*;

(b) *Sp* **g. (medal),** médaille *f* d'or;

(c) (*colour*) (couleur *f* de l')or *m*; **the reds and golds of autumn,** les rouges et les ors de l'automne; **old g.,** vieil or *inv.*

2 *adj* **g. dress,** robe *f* couleur d'or; **g. paint,** peinture dorée.

goldbeater ['gəʊldbiːtər] *n* batteur, -euse d'or.

goldcrest ['gəʊldkrest] *n* (*bird*) roitelet huppé.

gold-digger ['gəʊld'dɪgər] *n* chercheur *m* d'or; *Pej Fig* (*woman*) croqueuse *f* de diamants.

golden ['gəʊld(ə)n] *adj* **(a)** (*made of gold*) d'or; *Myth* **the G. Fleece,** la Toison d'or; **to worship the g. calf,** adorer le veau d'or; *Fig* **g. handshake,** (grosse) indemnité *f* de départ; *Fig* **g. hello,** pont *m* d'or; **(b)** (*gold-coloured*) **g. hair,** cheveux *mpl* d'or; **the G. Horn,** la Corne d'Or; **g. eagle,** aigle royal; **g. pheasant,** faisan doré; **(c)** (*excellent, best*) **the g. age,** l'âge *m* d'or; **g. boy** *or* **girl,** (*of tennis etc*) enfant chéri; **g. rule,** règle *f* d'or; **g. opportunity,** occasion *f* en or; **the g. mean,** le juste milieu; **(d)** (*commemorating 50 years*) **g. wedding,** noces *fpl* d'or.

goldeneye ['gəʊldənaɪ] *n* (*bird*) garrot *m* à œil d'or, canard *m* garrot.

goldenrod ['gəʊld(ə)nrɒd] *n* (*plant*) verge *f* d'or.

goldfield ['gəʊldfiːld] *n* champ *m ou* région *f* aurifère.

goldfinch ['gəʊldfɪntʃ] *n* (*bird*) chardonneret *m*.

goldfish ['gəʊldfɪʃ] *n* poisson *m* rouge; **g. bowl,** bocal *m* à poisson rouge.

gold-plated ['gəʊld'pleɪtɪd] *adj* plaqué or.

gold-rimmed ['gəʊld'rɪmd] *adj* **g.-r. spectacles,** lunettes *fpl* à monture dorée.

goldsmith ['gəʊldsmɪθ] *n* orfèvre *m*; **g.'s work,** orfèvrerie *f*.

gold-tipped ['gəʊld'tɪpt] *adj* à bout doré.

golf¹ [gɒlf] *n Sp* golf *m*; **to play g.,** jouer au golf; **clock g.,** golf miniature; **g. ball,** balle *f* de golf; (*on typewriter*) boule *f*; **g. ball (typewriter),** machine *f* à écrire à boule; **g. club,** (*for hitting ball*) crosse *f* de golf, club *m*; (*association*) club de golf; **g. course** *or* **links,** terrain *m ou* parcours *m* de golf, un golf; **g. umbrella,** parapluie *m* de golf.

golf² *vi* jouer au golf; **I went golfing yesterday,** hier j'ai fait du golf.

golfer ['gɒlfər] *n* golfeur, -euse, joueur, -euse de golf.

Goliath [gə'laɪəθ] *n Bible* Goliath *m*.

golliwog ['gɒlɪwɒg] *n* = poupée *f* en étoffe représentant un Noir.

golly ['gɒlɪ] *int F Old-fashioned* fichtre!, mince (alors)!

goloshes [gə'lɒʃɪz] *npl* = **GALOSHES**.

gonad ['gɒnæd, 'gəʊ-] *n Biol* gonade *f*.

gondola ['gɒndələ] *n* **(a)** (*boat*) gondole *f*; **(b)** *Av* (*of airship*) gondole *f*, nacelle *f* (*d'un ballon*); *Am* (*cable car*) nacelle *ou* cabine *f* de téléphérique; **(c)** *Am Rail* **g. (car),** wagon plat; **(d)** (*in supermarket etc*) gondole *f*.

gondolier [gɒndə'lɪər] *n* gondolier *m*.

gone [gɒn] *adj F* **to be g.,** (*dead*) être mort; **oh well, that's that g.!,** (*of broken machine etc*) bon, ben c'est foutu!; **to be pretty far g.,** (*drunk*) être dans un état avancé, être bien parti; *Sl* **g. on s.o.,** amoureux *ou* toqué de qn.

goner ['gɒnər] *n F* **(a)** (*person about to die*) mourant, -ante; **I thought she was a g.,** je pensais qu'elle allait mourir *ou* crever; **(b)** (*person facing disaster*) type fini *ou* fichu; **he's a g.,** il est fichu *ou* foutu.

gong [gɒŋ] *n* **(a)** *Mus etc* gong *m*; **to sound the g.,** faire retentir le gong; **(b)** *Br Sl* (*medal*) médaille *f*; **he was wearing all his gongs,** il exhibait toute sa batterie de cuisine.

gonna ['gənə] *Sl* = **going to.**

gonorrhoea, *US* **gonorrhea** [gɒnə'rɪə] *n Med* gonorrhée *f*; **to have g.,** avoir de la gonorrhée.

goo [guː] *n F* **(a)** (*sticky substance*) substance collante; **(b)** (*sentimentality*) sentimentalité excessive *ou* à l'eau de rose.

good [gʊd] **1** *adj* (**better, best**) **(a)** bon, bonne; **g. wine,** bon vin; **g. handwriting,** belle écriture; **g. weather,** beau temps; **g. to eat,** bon à manger; **this is g. enough for me,** cela fera mon affaire; **that's a g. one,** (*of story, joke*) en voilà une bonne; **to have a g. time,** s'amuser (bien); **he's too g. for that job,** il mérite une meilleure situation; **she thinks he's too g. for her,** elle croit qu'il est trop bien pour elle; **if it's g. enough for you, it's g. enough for me,** si c'est assez bien pour vous c'est assez bien pour moi; **this isn't g. enough!,** (*you will have to do better*) ça ne va pas, ça!; **to have g. sight,** avoir une bonne vue *ou* de bons yeux; **g. living,** bonne chère; **the g. old days,** le bon vieux temps; **it's as g. a way as any other,** c'est une façon qui en vaut une autre; **to give s.o. as g. as one gets,** rendre coup pour coup à qn; **this method is as g. if not better,** cette méthode est aussi bonne, pour ne pas dire meilleure; **it's as g. as new,** c'est comme neuf, c'est pour ainsi dire neuf, c'est quasi neuf; **to make sth as g. as new,** remettre qch à neuf; **it's as g. as settled,** c'est comme si c'était fait; **are you married? — as g. as,** (*I'm living with s.o.*) tu es marié? — non mais c'est comme si; **it is as g. as saying that ...,** ça revient à dire que ...; **very g.!,** (*well done, congratulations etc*) très bien!, parfait!; (*all right*) très bien, je m'en charge;

(b) (*advantageous*) avantageux; **g. opportunity,** bonne occasion; **to be in a g. position to do sth,** être bien placé pour faire qch; **it is not always g. to ...,** il n'est pas toujours bon de ...;

(c) (*pleasant*) heureux; **g. news,** bonnes *ou* heureuses nouvelles; **too g. to be true,** trop beau pour y croire *ou* pour être vrai; **g. for you!, g. show!,** *Austr* **g. on you!,** tant mieux pour toi *ou* pour vous!; **it's g. to be alive!,** il fait bon vivre!; **it's g. to know you've got friends,** il est bon de savoir qu'on a des amis; **it's g. to see you,** je suis *ou* nous sommes content(s) de te voir; **g. morning!, g. afternoon!,** bonjour! (monsieur *etc*); *Fml* **g. day,** (*hello*) bonjour; (*goodbye*) au revoir; **g. night!,** (*when going to bed*) bonne nuit!; (*when leaving*) bonsoir!; **to wish s.o. a g. night,** souhaiter une bonne nuit à qn;

(d) (*attractive*) **she looks g. in that hat,** ce chapeau lui va bien; **that pizza looks g.,** cette pizza a l'air bonne; **(that) sounds g.!,** bonne idée!; **g. looks,** beauté *f*;

(e) to make g., (*of person*) prospérer, faire son chemin; **an immigrant made g.,** un immigrant qui a fait son chemin; **to make g. a loss,** combler une perte; **to make g. one's losses,** se rattraper de ses pertes; **to make g. an injustice/damage,** réparer une injustice/des dégâts; **to make g. one's promise,** remplir sa promesse;

(f) (*beneficial*) **this medicine is very g. for coughs,** ce remède est très bon pour la toux; **beer is not g. for me,** la bière ne me vaut rien; **to drink more than is g. for one,** boire plus que de raison; **it will be g. for them to have some company,** ça leur fera du bien d'avoir de la compagnie; **it isn't g. for people to live alone,** il n'est pas bon de vivre seul;

(g) (*skilful*) **to be g. with one's hands,** être adroit *ou* habile de ses mains; **to be g. with children,** savoir y faire avec les enfants; **to be g. at maths,** être bon *ou* fort en math; **g. for nothing,** bon à rien;

(h) (*morally good*) **g. Christian,** bon chrétien, bonne chrétienne; **to lead a g. life,** vivre en homme de bien; **g. conduct** *or* **behaviour,** bonne conduite; **he proved to be a g. friend,** il s'est montré un véritable ami; **g. nature,** bon naturel; *F* **there's g. and bad everywhere,** il y a du bien et du mal partout; **G. Friday,** le vendredi saint; *Bible & Fig* **G. Samaritan,** bon Samaritain;

(i) (*well-behaved*) sage; **answer would you, there's a g. boy,** sois gentil, réponds; **be g.!,** (*to child*) sois sage!; **as g. as gold,** sage comme une image;

(j) (*kind*) aimable; **that's very g. of you,** c'est bien aimable *ou* gentil de votre part; **would you be g. enough to ...?,** auriez-vous l'amabilité *ou* la gentillesse de ...?; **she has always been g. to me,** elle s'est toujours montrée bonne pour moi; **he's a g. sort,** c'est un bon type; **to do s.o. a g. turn,** rendre service à qn; **g. old Anne, I knew she wouldn't let us down!,** cette brave Anne, je savais bien qu'elle ne nous laisserait pas tomber!; **g. old London,** bon vieux Londres; *F* **g. Lord!, g. heavens!, g. gracious!,** grand Dieu!, par exemple!; **g. grief!,** fichtre alors!;

(k) *Old-fashioned* **his g. lady,** sa femme; **take this suitcase, my g. man,** prenez cette valise mon brave (homme);

(l) (*happy*) **the sunshine/exercise made me feel g.,** le soleil/l'exercice m'a fait du bien; **her smile made him feel better,** son sourire l'a réconforté; **I don't feel g. about behaving like that,** je ne me sens pas très fier de m'être conduit comme ça;

(m) (*well, healthy*) **to feel g.,** se sentir en bonne forme *ou* bien en train; **I don't feel too f.,** je ne suis pas dans mon assiette;

(n) (*substantial*) **it makes a g. meal for four,** ça fait un bon repas pour quatre; **to earn g. money,** gagner largement sa vie; **you've got a g. chance,** tu as une bonne chance; **of a g. size,** de bonne taille;

(o) (*with quantity, number*) **a g. half,** une bonne moitié; **a g. two hours,** deux bonnes heures; **a g. while, a g. time,** pas mal de temps; **a g. round sum,** une somme rondelette; **a g. twenty years ago,** il y a bien vingt ans, vingt ans bien comptés; **a g. deal, a g. many,** beaucoup; **a g. few,** pas mal; **to come in a g. third,** arriver bon troisième;

(p) (*food*) bon (à manger), en bon état; **is the meat still g.?,** est-ce que la viande est encore bonne?;

(q) *(valid)* **g. reason,** bonne raison, raison valable; **he** *or* **his credit is g. for £25,000,** il peut payer jusqu'à 25 000 livres, il est bon pour 25 000 livres; **this car ought to be g. for another five years,** cette voiture devrait me faire encore bien cinq ans; *F* **she's g. for another ten years,** elle est bonne pour encore dix ans.

2 *adv* **(a)** *F* **they beat us g. and proper,** ils nous ont battus à plate(s) couture(s); **he was g. and mad,** il était absolument furieux; **she was g. and sorry,** elle le regrettait amèrement; **put the paint on g. and thick,** appliquer la peinture en couches bien épaisses;

(b) *F esp Am* *(well)* bien; **she sure sings g.,** elle chante bien, c'est sûr; **how are you? — g. thanks,** comment allez-vous? — bien merci.

3 *n* **(a)** *(morally good behaviour)* bien *m*; **to return g. for evil,** rendre le bien pour le mal; **to do g.,** faire du *ou* le bien; **that will do more harm than g.,** cela fera plus de mal que de bien; **he's up to no g.,** il prépare quelque mauvais coup;

(b) *(benefit)* **I did it for your g.,** je l'ai fait pour votre bien; **for the g. of one's health,** en vue de sa santé; **to act for the common g.,** agir dans l'intérêt commun; **it will do you g. to spend a week in the country,** cela vous fera du bien de passer une semaine à la campagne; **what g. will that do you?, what g. will it be to you?,** à quoi cela vous avancera-t-il?; **that won't be much g.,** ça ne servira pas à grand-chose; **what's the g. of that?,** à quoi bon (faire) cela?; **(it's) no g. talking about it,** inutile d'en parler; **that's no g.,** *(pointless)* cela ne sert à rien; *(worthless)* ça ne vaut rien; **he's no g.,** il est nul; **it's no g. complaining,** il ne sert à rien de se plaindre;

(c) *(profit)* **to be five pounds to the g.,** avoir cinq livres de gagné *ou* de profit; **it is all to the g.,** c'est autant de gagné;

(d) for g. (and) all, *(permanently)* pour de bon; **he is gone for g.,** il est parti pour de bon; **to settle down for g.,** se fixer définitivement;

(e) the g. and the bad, *(used as pl)* les bons et les méchants.

4 *int* bien; **I feel better today — g.,** je me sens mieux aujourd'hui — tant mieux; **g., that's settled then,** bien, c'est arrangé alors.

goodbye ['gʊd'baɪ] *int & n* au revoir; **g. for now!,** à bientôt!; **to say g. to s.o.,** dire au revoir à qn; **she said her goodbyes,** elle a dit au revoir; *(for good)* elle a fait ses adieux; **it was g. to Paris for the time being,** c'était au revoir Paris pour le moment; **that was g. to £5000,** j'ai dû dire adieu à mes cinq mille livres.

good-for-nothing ['gʊdfənʌθɪŋ] **1** *adj (person)* qui n'est bon à rien. **2** *n* vaurien, -ienne.

good-hearted [gʊd'hɑːtɪd] *adj* qui a bon cœur.

good-humoured, *US* **-humored** [gʊd'hjuːməd] *adj (personne)* d'un caractère facile; *(sourire etc)* de bonne humeur; *(plaisanterie etc)* sans malice; **he is always g.-h.,** il a bon caractère.

good-humouredly, *US* **-humoredly** [gʊd'hjuːmədlɪ] *adv* avec bonhomie; *(rire)* avec bonne humeur.

goodish ['gʊdɪʃ] *adj* **(a)** *(quite good)* assez bon, passable; **(b)** assez grand *(nombre etc)*; **it's a g. step from here,** c'est à un bon bout de chemin d'ici; **a g. size,** assez grand.

good-looker ['gʊd'lʊkər] *n F* **he's/she's a g.-l.,** il/elle est beau/belle.

good-looking ['gʊdlʊkɪŋ] *adj* (**better-looking, best-looking**) beau, *f* belle; **he's very g.-l.,** il est beau garçon; **she's quite g.-l.,** elle n'est pas mal.

goodly ['gʊdlɪ] *adj* large, ample *(portion etc)*; *(nombre)* considérable.

good-natured [gʊd'neɪtʃəd] *adj (person)* au bon naturel, accommodant, de bon caractère; *(laugh)* jovial.

goodnaturedly [gʊd'neɪtʃədlɪ] *adv* avec bonhomie.

goodness ['gʊdnɪs] *n* **(a)** *(of person)* bonté *f*; **(b)** *(of thing)* bonne qualité; **contains all the g. of full cream milk,** *(in advertising)* contient toutes les bonnes choses se trouvant dans le lait entier; **to extract all the g. out of sth,** extraire de qch tout ce qu'il y a de bon; **(c)** *(as euphemism)* **g. gracious!,** bonté divine!, mon Dieu!; **thank g.!,** Dieu merci!; **for goodness' sake, be quiet!,** taisez-vous, pour l'amour de Dieu!; **g. (only) knows what I must do,** Dieu seul sait ce que je dois faire.

goodnight [gʊd'naɪt] *n* **after they had said their goodnights,** *(and gone to bed)* après s'être dit bonne nuit; *(and left)* après s'être dit bonsoir.

goods [gʊdz] *npl Jur* biens *mpl*, effets *mpl*; *Com Econ* marchandises *fpl*, articles *mpl*; **manufactured g.,** produits fabriqués; **leather g.,** articles en cuir, maroquinerie *f*; **knit(ted) g.,** bonneterie *f*; **consumer g.,** biens de consommation; **stolen g.,** objets volés; **to deliver the g.,** livrer la marchandise *ou* les marchandises; *Fig (keep one's promise)* remplir ses engagements, tenir parole; **a cassette player that can deliver the g.,** un lecteur de cassettes qui tient ses promesses; *Sl* **a nice bit of g.,** un beau brin de fille, une jolie poupée; *Rail* **g. train/station/depot,** train *m*/gare *f*/dépôt *m* de marchandises.

good-tempered [gʊd'tempəd] *adj* de caractère facile *ou* égal, qui a bon caractère.

good-time ['gʊdtaɪm] *adj F* qui ne pense qu'à s'amuser.

goodwill ['gʊd'wɪl] *n* **(a)** bonne volonté, bienveillance *f*, bon vouloir (**towards,** pour, envers); **to retain s.o.'s g.,** conserver les bonnes grâces de qn; **(b)** *(willingness)* bon cœur; **to set to work with g.,** se mettre à l'œuvre de bon cœur; **(c)** *Com* clientèle *f*; actif incorporel.

goody ['gʊdɪ] *F* **1** *n* **(a)** *(person)* bon type; **the goodies and the baddies,** les bons et les méchants; **(b) goodies,** friandises *fpl*. **2** *int* **(g.) g.!,** chouette!

goody-goody ['gʊdɪgʊdɪ] *F Pej* **1** *n* personne *f* d'une piété affectée. **2** *adj* d'une piété affectée; **she's awfully g.-g.,** elle fait la prude *ou* la sainte nitouche.

gooey ['guːɪ] *adj F* **(a)** *(sticky)* gluant, collant; **(b)** *(sentimental)* à l'eau de rose.

goof¹ [guːf] *n F* gaffe *f*.

goof² *vi F* gaffer, faire une gaffe.

▶**goof about, goof around** *vi* faire l'idiot.

▶**goof off** *vi US (evade work, waste time)* glander, glandouiller.

goofball ['guːfbɔːl] *n Am Sl* **(a)** *(fool)* idiot, -iote; **(b)** *(drug)* somnifère *m*.

goofy ['guːfɪ] *adj F* **(a)** *(stupid)* loufoque; **(b)** *Br (teeth)* en avant.

gook [guːk] *n US* **(a)** *Offensive Sl* Chinetoque *mf*; **(b)** *(muck)* saleté *f*.

goon [guːn] *n F* **(a)** *(stupid person)* imbécile *mf*; **(b)** *F (criminal)* gorille *m*.

goosander [guː'sændər] *n (bird)* harle *m* bièvre.

goose¹, *pl* **geese** [guːs, giːs] *n* **(a)** *(bird)* oie *f*; **wild g.,** oie sauvage; **flock of geese,** troupeau *m* d'oies; *Fig* **all his geese are swans,** d'après lui, tout ce qu'il fait tient du prodige; **their g. is cooked,** les voilà dans de beaux draps; *Prov* **to kill the g. that lays the golden egg,** tuer la poule aux œufs d'or; **goose('s) egg,** œuf *m* d'oie; **g. fat,** graisse *f* d'oie; **g. pimples, g. flesh,** *Am* **g. bumps,** chair *f* de poule; *Mil* **g. step,** pas *m* de l'oie; **(b)** *Fig F (person)* niais, *f* niaise, bêbête *f*; *Old-fashioned* **I'm not such a g.,** je ne suis pas si bête que ça.

goose² *vt Sl* donner un coup de doigt dans le derrière de *(qn)*.

gooseberry ['gʊzb(ə)rɪ] *n* **(a)** groseille *f* à maquereau, groseille verte; *Br F* **to play g.,** tenir la chandelle; **g. bush,** groseillier *m* (à maquereau); **where do children come from? — they're found under a g. bush,** d'où viennent les enfants? — les petites filles naissent dans les roses et les petits garçons naissent dans les choux; *Culin* **g. fool,** crème *f* de groseilles (à maquereau); **(b) Cape g.,** coqueret *m* du Pérou; **Chinese g.,** souris végétale.

goosefoot ['guːsfʊt] *n* (*pl* **goosefoots**) *Bot* chénopode *m*.

goosegog ['gʊzgɒg] *n Br F* groseille *f* à maquereau.

goose-step ['guːsstep] *vi* **(-pp-)** *Mil* faire le pas de l'oie.

goos(e)y ['guːsɪ] *adj F* **to go g.,** avoir la chair de poule.

GOP [dʒiːəʊ'piː] *n US Pol* (*abbr* **Grand Old Party**) = le Parti républicain.

gopher ['gəʊfər] *n* **(a) (pocket) g.,** géomys *m*; **(b)** *(ground squirrel)* spermophile *m*; **(c)** *esp Am Sl* = **GOFER**.

gorblimey ['gɔːblaɪmɪ] *int Eng Dial* nom d'un chien!

Gordian ['gɔːdɪən] *adj Fig* **to cut the G. knot,** trancher le nœud gordien.

gore¹ [gɔːr] *n* sang versé; **there's plenty of g. in this movie,** ce film est sanglant à souhait; *Lit* **he lay in his g.,** il baignait dans son sang.

gore² *vt (of bull)* blesser *(qn)* avec les cornes, encorner *(qn)*; **gored to death,** tué d'un coup de corne.

gore³ *n Sewing* godet *m*; *Nau* pointe *f* (de voile); *Archit* pan *m (d'un dôme)*; *Av* fuseau *m*.

gore⁴ *vt Sewing* faire *ou* mettre des godets à *(une robe etc)*; **gored skirt,** jupe à godets.

gorge¹ [gɔːdʒ] *n* **(a)** *Geog* gorge *f*, défilé *m*; **(b)** *Arch & Lit (throat)* gosier *m*; **it makes my g. rise,** cela me soulève le cœur; **(c)** *MecE* gorge *f (de poulie)*.

gorge² **1** *vi* se gorger, se repaître, se rassasier (**on,** de); *F* s'empiffrer (**on,** de). **2** *vt* rassasier *(qn)*; avaler, engloutir *(sa nourriture)*; gaver *(une oie)*; **to g. oneself,** se gaver, *F* s'empiffrer.

gorgeous ['gɔːdʒəs] *adj* magnifique, fastueux, *F* épatant; (*weather*) superbe, magnifique; (*repas*) somptueux; **a. g. sunset,** un coucher de soleil splendide; **hello g.!,** (*to girl*) bonjour ma belle!
gorgeously ['gɔːdʒəslɪ] *adv* magnifiquement, splendidement; somptueusement.
gorgon ['gɔːgən] *n Myth* gorgone *f*.
gorilla [gə'rɪlə] *n* (*animal*) & *F* gorille *m*.
gormandize ['gɔːməndaɪz] **1** *vt* bâfrer, manger goulûment. **2** *vi* goinfrer, *F* s'empiffrer.
gormandizer ['gɔːməndaɪzər] *n* glouton, -onne.
gormandizing ['gɔːməndaɪzɪŋ] *n* goinfrerie *f*.
gormless ['gɔːmlɪs] *adj Br F* idiot, bête; **he's g.,** c'est une nouille.
gorse [gɔːs] *n* (*shrub*) ajonc *m*.
gory ['gɔːrɪ] *adj* sanglant, ensanglanté.
gosh [gɒʃ] *int F* sapristi!, mince (alors)!
goshawk ['gɒshɔːk] *n* (*bird*) autour *m*.
gosling ['gɒzlɪŋ] *n* oison *m*.
go-slow ['gəʊ'sləʊ] *n Ind* **go-s. (strike),** grève *f* du zèle.
gospel ['gɒsp(ə)l] *n* **(a)** évangile *m*; **St Mark's G., the G. according to St Mark,** l'Évangile selon saint Marc; *Fig* **to take sth for g.,** accepter qch comme parole d'évangile; *Fig* **it's the g. truth,** c'est parole d'évangile; *Rel* **the g. for the day,** l'évangile du jour; **to preach the g.,** prêcher l'évangile; *Fig* **to preach the g. of economy,** prêcher l'économie; **g. oath,** serment prêté sur l'évangile; **(b)** *Mus* **g. (music),** gospel *m*; **g. singer,** chanteur, -euse de gospel.
gospeller ['gɒspələr] *n* **(hot) g.,** évangélisateur *m*.
gossamer ['gɒsəmər] **1** *n* **(a)** (*spider's web*) fils *mpl* de la Vierge, filandres *fpl*; **g. thread,** freluche *f*, filandre *f*; **(b)** *Tex* gaze légère. **2** *adj* (*tissu*) très léger, arachnéen.
gossip¹ ['gɒsɪp] *n* **(a)** (*person*) bavard, -arde; (*ill-natured*) commère *f*, cancanier, -ière; **(b)** (*talk*) bavardage *m*; (*ill-natured*) commérage(s) *m(pl)*, cancans *mpl*, potins *mpl*; *Journ* **g. column,** chronique mondaine, échos *mpl*; **g. columnist** *or* **writer,** échotier *m*.
gossip² *vi* bavarder, caqueter; (*ill-naturedly*) cancaner, potiner; **to g. about s.o.,** faire des commérages sur qn.
gossiping ['gɒsɪpɪŋ] *n* bavardage *m*; commérage *m*.
gossipmonger ['gɒsɪpmʌŋgər] *n* commère *f*, cancanier, -ière.
gossipy ['gɒsɪpɪ] *adj* (*style*) anecdotique; (*person*) cancanier, -ière; **g. letter,** lettre pleine de racontars.
got *see* **GET**.
Gothic ['gɒθɪk] **1** *adj Archit Art Ling etc* gothique; *Liter* **g. novel,** roman *m* gothique; **g. film,** film *m* d'horreur. **2** *n* **(a)** *Art* gothique *m*; **(b)** *Ling* gotique *m*, gothique *m*.
gotta ['gɒtə, 'gɒdə] *Sl* = **got to.**
gotten *Am see* **GET**.
gouache [gʊ'ɑːʃ] *n Art* gouache *f*.
gouge¹ [gaʊdʒ] *n Carp Surg* gouge *f*.
gouge² *vt* gouger (*le bois*).
▸**gouge out** *vtsep* creuser (*une cannelure etc*) à la gouge; **to g. s.o.'s eye out,** faire sauter un œil à qn.
goulash ['guːlæʃ] *n Culin* goulache *f*.
gourd ['gʊəd] *n* **(a)** (*plant*) gourde *f*; **(b)** (*bottle*) gourde *f*, calebasse *f*.
gourmand ['gʊəmənd] **1** *adj* (*gluttonous*) glouton; (*also discerning*) gourmand. **2** *n* (*glutton*) glouton *m*; (*gourmet*) gourmet *m*.
gourmandise [gʊəmən'diːz] *n* gourmandise *f*.
gourmet ['gʊəmeɪ] *n* gourmet *m*, gastronome *m*; **g. cooking,** cuisine *f* gastronomique.
gout [gaʊt] *n Med* goutte *f*; **to have g.,** avoir de la goutte.
gouty ['gaʊtɪ] *adj* (*person, joint etc*) goutteux.
Gov (a) *abbr* **government**; **(b)** *abbr* **governor**.
govern ['gʌvən] **1** *vt* **(a)** gouverner, régir (*un État etc*); administrer (*une province etc*); *MecE* gouverner; *Gram* se construire avec, gouverner, régir (*l'accusatif etc*); **laws that g. chemical reactions,** lois qui régissent les réactions chimiques; **(b)** (*restrain*) maîtriser, gouverner, contenir (*ses passions etc*). **2** *vi* (*rule*) gouverner.
governance ['gʌvənəns] *n* **(a)** gouvernement *m* (*d'une province etc*); **(b)** (*control*) maîtrise *f*, empire *m*.
governess ['gʌvənɪs] *n* gouvernante *f*; institutrice *f* (privée).
governing ['gʌvənɪŋ] **1** *adj* gouvernant; **g. body,** conseil *m* d'administration. **2** *n* gouvernement *m*.
government ['gʌv(ə)nmənt] *n* **(a)** *Pol* gouvernement *m*; **form of g.,** régime *m*; **local g.,** gouvernement local; **self-g.,** autonomie *f* (*d'un État*); **the British G.,** le Gouvernement britannique; **g. offices,** bureaux *mpl* du Gouvernement; **g. loan,** emprunt public; **g. action,** action gouvernementale; **g. intervention,** intervention *f* du gouvernement; **g. monopoly,** monopole *m* d'État; **(b)** (*cabinet*) ministère *m*; **to form a g.,** former un ministère *ou* un gouvernement; **the G. party,** le parti gouvernemental; **(c) G. house,** (*governor's residence*) résidence officielle d'un gouverneur.
governmental [gʌvən'ment(ə)l] *adj* gouvernemental, -aux.
governor ['gʌv(ə)nər] *n* **(a)** (*of colony, prison, bank, US state*) gouverneur *m*; (*of a reform school etc*) directeur *m*; (*member of board of governors of a school etc*) membre *m* du conseil d'administration; **g. general,** gouverneur général; *Br F* **the g.,** (*boss*) le patron, le singe; **(b)** (*device*) *MecE* régulateur *m*; modérateur *m* (*de vitesse*).
governorship ['gʌvənəʃɪp] *n* (*post*) poste *m* de gouverneur; (*function*) fonctions *fpl* de gouverneur.
Govt *abbr* **government**.
gown¹ [gaʊn] *n* **(a)** robe *f* (*de femme*); **dinner g.,** robe de soirée; **dressing g.,** robe de chambre; **towelling g.,** peignoir *m*, sortie *f* de bain; **(b)** robe *f*, toge *f* (*de magistrat, d'universitaire etc*); blouse *f* (*de chirurgien*).
gown² *vt* revêtir (*qn*) d'une robe *ou* d'une toge.
GP [dʒiː'piː] *n Br Med abbr* **general practitioner**.
gr (*abbr* **gramme(s)**) g..
grab¹ [græb] *n* **(a)** (*movement*) **to make a g. at sth,** faire un mouvement vif pour saisir qch; *F* **to be up for grabs,** être à prendre; (*be on market, for sale*) être à vendre; **we're getting rid of the chairs, so they're all up for grabs,** on se débarrasse des chaises, alors servez-vous si vous voulez *ou* vous n'avez qu'à vous servir; **is that last chocolate cake up for grabs?,** le chocolat qui reste là, on peut le prendre?; **you can take it if you like, it's up for grabs,** vous pouvez le prendre si vous voulez, il est là pour ça; **(b)** *Constr* **g. (bucket),** benne preneuse *ou* piocheuse.
grab² *v* **(-bb-) 1** *vt* **to g. (hold of) sth/s.o.,** saisir qch (d'un geste brusque), empoigner qch/qn; **he grabbed a revolver from the table,** il a saisi un revolver sur la table; **he grabbed me by the lapels,** il m'a empoigné par le revers; **to save oneself by grabbing a rope,** se raccrocher à un cordage; **(b)** *F Fig* **how does that g. you?,** (*my suggestion*) ça te dit?; **the idea doesn't g. me,** ça ne me dit rien. **2** *vi* **to g. at s.o.,** s'agripper à qn; **don't g.!,** (*esp to children*) ne m'arrache *ou* ne lui *etc* arrache pas les choses *ou* la nourriture *etc* des mains!
grabby ['græbɪ] *adj F* **(a)** (*greedy*) accapareur, -euse; **to be g.,** avoir les doigts crochus; **(b) he's very g.,** (*of child*) il touche à tout.
grace¹ [greɪs] *n* **(a)** (*of movement, dancer etc*) grâce *f*; (*of language*) élégance *f*; *Mus* **g. note,** note *f* d'agrément;
(b) (*of manners*) grâce *f*; **to do sth with good/bad g.,** faire qch de bonne/mauvaise grâce; **to have the g. to apologize,** avoir la bonne grâce de faire des excuses; **at school they taught us the social graces,** à l'école on nous a enseigné le savoir-vivre;
(c) (*favour*) faveur *f*, gracieuseté *f*; **to be in/get into s.o.'s good graces,** être dans/entrer dans les bonnes grâces de qn; *Rel* **the g. of God,** la grâce de Dieu; **in a state of g.,** en état de grâce; **to fall from g.,** perdre la grâce; **it has the saving g. that ...,** cela a au moins ce mérite que ...; **in the year of g. 1066,** en l'an de grâce 1066;
(d) *Fin* **days of g.,** délai *m* (*accordé pour le paiement d'un effet*); **to give a creditor seven days' g.,** accorder à un créancier sept jours de grâce *ou* de faveur;
(e) (*prayer*) (*before meal*) bénédicité *m*; (*after meal*) grâces *fpl*; **to say g.,** réciter la bénédicité;
(f) (*address*) **His G.,** (*the duke*) Monsieur (le duc de ...); (*the archbishop*) Monseigneur (l'archevêque de ...); **Her G.** (*the duchess*) Madame (la duchesse de ...);
(g) *Myth* **the Graces,** les Grâces *fpl*;
(h) *Arch* (*pardon*) grâce *f*, pardon *m*; (*still used in*) **act of g.,** loi *f* d'amnistie.
grace² *vt* **(a)** (*honour*) honorer (**with,** de); **to g. a meeting with one's presence,** honorer une réunion de sa présence; **(b)** (*ornament*) embellir, orner.
grace-and-favour ['greɪsən'feɪvər] *adj* (*residence etc*) prêté gratuitement par le souverain à un sujet qui lui a rendu service.
graceful ['greɪsful] *adj* **(a)** (*person, movement*) gracieux, élégant; **g. figure,** taille élégante; **she is a g. dancer,** elle danse avec grâce; **(b)** (*speech*) gracieux, poli, bien tourné.
gracefully ['greɪsfulɪ] *adv* avec grâce, avec élégance.
gracefulness ['greɪsfulnɪs] *n* grâce *f*, élégance *f*.
graceless ['greɪslɪs] *adj* **(a)** (*inelegant*) gauche, inélégant; **(b)** *F* (*rude*) effronté; **(c)** *Rel* impie.
gracious ['greɪʃəs] **1** *adj* **(a)** (*kind, polite*) gracieux, indulgent; **to be g. to s.o.,** être affable avec *ou* envers qn;

our g. King *or* **Queen,** notre gracieux souverain; **(b)** (*of God*) plein de grâce *ou* de compassion (**to,** envers); **(c)** (*living etc*) élégant. **2** *int* **g. (me)!, good(ness) g.!,** miséricorde!, mon Dieu!; **good g. no!,** jamais de la vie!

graciously [ˈgreɪʃəslɪ] *adv* gracieusement; **to be g. pleased to do sth,** daigner faire qch.

graciousness [ˈgreɪʃəsnɪs] *n* **(a)** (*kindness, politeness*) gracieuseté *f*, bienveillance *f* (**to, towards,** envers); **(b)** (*of God*) bonté *f*, miséricorde *f*; **(c)** (*of life, house etc*) élégance *f*; **(d)** (*of style*) grâce *f*, aménité *f*.

grad [græd] *n Univ F abbr* **graduate.**

gradate [grəˈdeɪt] **1** *vi* (*of colours*) se dégrader. **2** *vt* graduer (*qch*); dégrader (*des teintes*).

gradation [grəˈdeɪʃən] *n* **(a)** (*act of changing*) gradation *f*, progression *f*; (*classification*) classification *f* par degrés; *Art* (dé)gradation *f* (*des teintes*); **(b)** (*degree*) degré *m*; **(c)** *Ling* **(vowel) g.,** mutation *f* vocalique.

grade[1] [greɪd] *n* **(a)** grade *m*, rang *m*, degré *m* (*d'une hiérarchie etc*); échelon *m* (*d'une administration*); **(b)** (*quality*) qualité *f*; classe *f*; (*of oil*) grade *m*; *Com etc* **high/low-g.,** de qualité supérieure/inférieure; *Aut* **high-g. petrol,** = supercarburant *m*, *F* super *m*; **(c)** *esp Am* (*gradient*) pente *f*, rampe *f*; montée *f*; descente *f* (*d'une voie ferrée etc*); *Fig* **to make the g.,** se montrer à la hauteur; **(d)** *Am* (*level*) niveau *m*; **g. level,** palier *m*; *Rail* **g. crossing,** passage *m* à niveau; **(e)** *Am Sch* (*mark*) note *f*; (*year at school*) classe *f* (*esp dans une école primaire*); **to get high grades,** avoir de bonnes notes; *US* **g. school, the grades,** = école primaire; **(f)** *Agr* **g. cattle, grades,** bétail amélioré par croisement.

grade[2] *vt* **(a)** (*classify*) classer, trier (*des marchandises etc selon leurs qualités*); *Am Sch* **to g. essays,** = corriger des dissertations (et leur donner une note); **(b)** graduer (*des exercices etc*); *Art* fondre (*des teintes*); **graded tax,** (*upwards*) impôt progressif; (*downwards*) impôt dégressif; **(c)** *Am Constr Rail* ménager ou régulariser la pente de (*la voie etc*); *Constr* niveler (*un terrain*); **(d)** *Agr* améliorer (*une race etc*).

▶grade down *vtsep* (*move to lower category*) classer (*qch*) dans une catégorie inférieure.

▶grade up *vtsep* **(a)** (*move to higher category*) classer (*qch*) dans une catégorie supérieure; **(b)** *Agr* améliorer (*une race etc*).

gradient [ˈgreɪdɪənt] *n* **(a)** *Constr etc* inclinaison *f*; (*of ground*) dénivellation *f*; **downward g.,** pente *f*, déclivité *f*; **upward g.,** rampe *f*, montée *f*; **angle of g.,** angle *m* de gradient; **a g. of 1 in 6,** une dénivellation d'un sixième; **steep/low g.,** forte/faible pente; **(b)** *Math Phys* gradient *m* (*de température etc*).

grading [ˈgreɪdɪŋ] *n* **(a)** (*classification*) classement *m*, gradation *f*; triage *m* (*du minerai etc*); *Am Sch* correction *f* (*des dissertations etc avec notes*); **(b)** *Art* (dé)gradation *f* (*des teintes*); **(c)** *Am Constr Rail* (a)ménagement *m* (*d'une pente*); **(d)** *Agr* amélioration *f* par croisement.

gradual [ˈgrædjʊ(ə)l] **1** *adj* progressif, graduel; **g. slope,** pente douce; **g. transition,** transition ménagée (**from ... to ...,** de ... à ...); **g. process,** gradation *f*. **2** *n Rel* graduel *m*.

gradually [ˈgrædjʊ(ə)lɪ] *adv* par degrés, petit à petit; **it happened very g.,** ça s'est produit très progressivement.

graduate[1] [ˈgrædjʊət] *n Univ* diplômé, -ée; = licencié, -ée; **biology g.,** licencié en biologie; *Am Sch* **high school g.,** = titulaire du baccalauréat.

graduate[2] [ˈgrædjʊeɪt] **1** *vi* **(a)** *Univ* recevoir ses diplômes; = être reçu licencié, -ée; **he graduated from Oxford,** il a fait ses études à Oxford; **I graduated in 1989,** j'ai eu ma licence en 1989; *Am Sch* **to g. from high school,** terminer ses études au lycée; *Fig* **she learnt on a cheap violin before graduating to a better instrument,** elle a appris à jouer avec un violon bon marché avant de passer à un meilleur instrument; **(b)** (*change*) **to g. into sth,** se changer graduellement en ... . **2** *vt* **(a)** graduer (*une échelle, un thermomètre etc*); **graduated in centimetres,** gradué en centimètres; **(b)** graduer (*des exercises etc*).

graduated [ˈgrædʊeɪtɪd] *adj* **g. income tax,** impôt progressif.

graduation [grædjʊˈeɪʃən] *n* **(a)** *Univ* remise *f* des diplômes; (*by student*) réception *f* d'un diplôme; *Fig* **my g. from driving vans to driving trucks,** mon passage progressif de la conduite de camionnettes à la conduite de camions; **g. ceremony,** cérémonie *f* de la remise des diplômes; **(b)** graduation *f* (*d'un thermomètre etc*); **graduations,** degrés *mpl*, grades *mpl*.

graffiti [græˈfiːtiː] *npl* graffiti *mpl*; **a piece of g.,** un graffiti; **there's some g. on the wall,** il y a des graffiti sur le mur; **obscene g.,** graffiti obscènes.

graft[1] [grɑːft] *n* (*from a plant*) greffon *m*; (*from a tree*) ente *f*; (*operation*) greffe *f*; *Surg* **bone/skin g.,** greffe osseuse/épidermique; **I had to have a skin g.,** j'ai dû subir une greffe épidermique; **skin g. operation,** greffe épidermique.

graft[2] *vt* (*onto a plant*) greffer; (*onto a tree*) enter (*un greffon, une souche*); *Surg* greffer, implanter (**onto,** sur); *Fig* **this piece was grafted onto the symphony later,** ce morceau est venu se greffer sur la symphonie plus tard.

graft[3] *n F* **(a)** *Am* (*bribery etc*) gratte *f*, graissage *m* de patte, pots-de-vin *mpl*; **(b)** *Br* (*work*) **hard g.,** travail *m*, boulot *m*.

graft[4] *vi F* **(a)** *Am* gratter, faire de la gratte; donner *ou* recevoir des pots-de-vin; **(b)** *Br* (*work hard*) travailler dur.

grafting [ˈgrɑːftɪŋ] *n* (*in horticulture, arboriculture*) greffe *f*, greffage *m*; *Surg* greffe (humaine); **skin g.,** greffe épidermique.

Grail [greɪl] *n Lit* **the Holy G.,** le Saint-Graal.

grain[1] [greɪn] *n* **(a)** (*of wheat etc*) grain *m*; **(b)** (*no pl*) (*cereals*) céréales *fpl*; **a shipment of g.,** une cargaison de céréales; **g. crop,** récolte *f* de grains *ou* de céréales; **g. alcohol,** alcool *m* de grain; **g. elevator,** élévateur *m* pour le grain; **g. market,** marché *m* aux grains; **(c)** (*of pepper, salt, sand*) grain *m*; **not a g. of common sense,** pas un grain *ou* deux sous de bon sens, pas une once de bon sens; **(d)** (*measurement*) grain *m* (= 0,0648 g.); **(e)** (*of wood, photo etc*) grain *m*; (*of wood, meat*) fil *m*; (*of leather*) grain, grenure *f*; **close g.,** grain fin; *Phot* **coarse g.,** gros grain; **fine g.,** grain fin; **against** *or* **across the g.,** contre le fil; à contre-fil; **it goes against the g. for me to do it,** c'est à contrecœur que je le fais.

grain[2] *vt* **(a)** grener (*le sel etc*); granuler (*la poudre*); **(b)** greneler, (*le cuir, le papier etc*); **(c)** (*paint a grain on*) veiner (*une surface*) façon bois; marbrer (*une surface*).

graining [ˈgreɪnɪŋ] *n* **(a)** (*of leather*) grenure *f*; **(b)** veinage *m* (*de la peinture*); décor *m* imitant le bois *ou* le marbre; décor en bois *ou* en marbre.

grainy [ˈgreɪnɪ] *adj Phot* granuleux.

gram [græm] *n* (*measurement*) gramme *m*.

grammar [ˈgræmər] *n* **(a)** grammaire *f*; **to write bad g.,** écrire de façon peu grammaticale; **that's not (good) g.,** ce que vous dites là n'est pas grammatical; *Sch* **g. school,** *Br* = lycée *m*; *US* = école *f* primaire; **(b) g. (book),** grammaire *f*; **a French g.,** une grammaire française.

grammarian [grəˈmeərɪən] *n* grammairien, -ienne.

grammatical [grəˈmætɪk(ə)l] *adj* (*sentence etc*) grammatical, -aux.

grammatically [grəˈmætɪklɪ] *adv* grammaticalement.

gramme [græm] *n* (*measurement*) gramme *m*.

gramophone [ˈgræməfəʊn] *n Old-fashioned Br* gramophone *m*; **g. record,** disque *m*.

grampus [ˈgræmpəs] *n* (*killer whale*) épaulard *m*, orque *f*.

gran [græn] *n esp Br F* mamie *f*, mémé *f*.

granary [ˈgrænərɪ] *n* grenier *m*; *Com* entrepôt *m* de grain; **Egypt was the g. of the ancient world,** l'Égypte était le grenier de l'antiquité; *Br Culin* **g. bread** *or* **loaf,** pain complet incorporant des morceaux de grains.

grand [grænd] **1** *adj* **(a)** (*imposing*) grandiose, imposant, magnifique; **the g. manner,** la grande manière; **the mayor looked very g. in her robes and chain,** madame le maire avait un air très imposant avec ses vêtements de cérémonie et ses colliers; **g. old man of trade unionism,** vétéran *m* du syndicalisme; **a g. lady,** une grande dame; **lexicographer is a rather g. name for someone who writes dictionaries,** lexicographe est un nom plutôt impressionnant pour quelqu'un qui écrit des dictionnaires; *US Jur* **g. larceny,** vol qualifié; *Cards & Tennis* **g. slam,** grand chelem; *Br Horseracing* **the G. National,** le Grand National; **g. concert,** grand concert; **g. display of fireworks,** grand feu d'artifice; **g. finale,** apothéose *f*; **g. piano,** piano *m* à queue;

(b) *F* (*excellent*) excellent, splendide; (*meal*) magnifique; **he's g.,** c'est un type épatant; **I'm not feeling too g.,** je ne suis pas dans mon assiette;

(c) (*overall*) **a g. total of £21.52,** une somme totale de 21 livres 52 pence;

(d) (*in titles*) **g. duke,** grand-duc *m*, *pl* grands-ducs; **g. duchess,** grande-duchesse *f*, *pl* grandes-duchesses; **G. Hotel,** le Grand Hôtel; **g. master,** (*of order*) grand maître; (*of freemasons*) vénérable *m*; *Chess* champion *m*.

2 *n* **(a)** *F Am* mille dollars; *Br* mille livres;

(b) *Mus* piano *m* à queue; **concert g.,** piano à queue de concert; **baby g.,** (piano) quart *m* de queue.

grandchild, *pl* **-children** [ˈgræntʃaɪld, -tʃɪldrən] *n* petit-fils *m*, petite-fille *f*, *pl* petits-enfants; **that will be some-**

thing to tell your grandchildren, voilà quelque chose que tu pourras raconter à tes petits-enfants.

gran(d)dad ['grændæd] *n F* papi *m*, pépé *m*.

grandaddy ['grændædɪ] *n Fig* **the g. of them all,** (*of car, locomotive etc*) l'ancêtre de toutes.

granddaughter ['grændɔːtər] *n* petite-fille *f*, *pl* petites-filles.

grandee [græn'diː] *n* grand *m* (*d'Espagne*).

grandeur ['grændjər] *n* **(a)** grandeur *f*; (*of person*) noblesse *f*, éminence *f*; **to have delusions of g.,** avoir la folie des grandeurs; **(b)** (*magnificence*) splendeur *f*, magnificence *f*; **the g. of the landscape,** la majesté du paysage; **(c)** (*pomp*) pompe *f*, éclat *m* (*d'une cérémonie, d'un train de vie*).

grandfather ['grænfɑːðər, 'grænd-] *n* grand-père, *pl* grands-pères; **g. clock,** horloge comtoise.

grandiloquence [græn'dɪləkwəns] *n* grandiloquence *f*, emphase *f*.

grandiloquent [græn'dɪləkwənt] *adj* grandiloquent.

grandiose ['grændɪəʊs, -əʊz] *adj* **(a)** (*magnificent*) grandiose, magnifique; **(b)** (*pretentious*) pompeux; **g. plans,** projets pompeux.

grandly ['grændlɪ] *adv* **(a)** (*imposingly*) de façon grandiose *ou* impressionnante; **(b)** *F* (*excellently*) splendidement, magnifiquement.

grandma ['grænmɑː, 'grænd-, 'græm-] *n F* mamie *f*, mémé *f*.

grandmother ['grænmʌðər, 'grænd-] *n* grand-mère *f*, *pl* grands-mères.

grandnephew ['græn'nefjʊ, grænd-] *n* petit-neveu *m*, *pl* petits-neveux.

grandness ['grændnɪs] *n* grandeur *f*; *Pej* affectation *f* de grandeur; air important.

grandniece ['græn'niːs, 'grænd-] *n* petite-nièce *f*, *pl* petites-nièces.

grandpa ['grænpɑː] *n F* papi *m*, pépé *m*.

grandparent ['grænpeərənt, 'grænd-] *n* grand-père *m*, grand-mère *f*, *pl* grands-parents *mpl*.

grandson ['grænsʌn, 'grænd-] *n* petit-fils *m*, *pl* petits-fils.

grandstand¹ ['grænstænd, grænd-] *n Sp* tribune *f* (d'honneur), grande tribune; *Sp* **g. finish,** arrivée palpitante; **to have a g. view of sth,** être bien placé pour voir qch.

grandstand² *vi esp Am Fig* jouer pour la galerie.

grange [greɪndʒ] *n* **(a)** *Br* (*farm*) manoir *m* (avec ferme); château *m*; **(b)** *Arch* (*granary*) grange *f*.

granite ['grænɪt] *n* granit(e) *m*; **g. building,** édifice en granit(e).

granitic [græ'nɪtɪk] *adj* granitique, graniteux.

grannie, granny ['grænɪ] *n F* mamie *f*, mémé *f*; **an old g.,** une vieille mémé; **g. knot,** nœud *m* de ménagère *ou* de soldat; **g. flat** *or* **annexe,** = partie d'une maison aménagée indépendamment pour héberger un parent âgé.

grant¹ [grɑːnt] *n* **(a)** (*financial aid*) subvention *f*; *Univ* allocation *f* d'études; **to make a g. to s.o.,** accorder une subvention à qn; **to receive a State g.,** être subventionné par l'État; **(b)** concession *f*, octroi *m* (*d'une permission etc*); délivrance *f* (*d'un brevet*); *Jur* don *m*; cession *f* (*d'un bien etc*); *Jur* (*document*) acte *m* de donation.

grant² *vt* **(a)** accorder, concéder, octroyer (*une permission etc*); délivrer (*une autorisation, un brevet*); exaucer (*une prière*); accéder à (*une requête*); *Jur* faire cession de (*qch*); **he was granted permission to ...,** il reçut la permission de ...; **the countries that have been granted autonomy,** les pays qui se sont vus accorder l'autonomie; **God g. that ...,** Dieu veuille que ...; **to take sth for granted,** considérer qch comme admis *ou* comme convenu; **you take too much for granted,** vous présumez trop; **he takes it for granted that he can borrow my books,** il se croit permis d'emprunter mes livres; **we take all this for granted,** tout cela nous semble normal; **she felt that she was being taken for granted,** il lui semblait que ses mérites n'étaient pas assez reconnus; **you shouldn't take people for granted,** il ne faut pas faire comme si les gens n'existaient pas; **don't take me for granted,** ne fais pas comme si je n'existais pas;
(b) accorder, allouer (*une subvention à qn*);
(c) (*admit*) admettre (*un argument*); **it must be granted that ...,** il faut reconnaître que ...; **I g. you that he is lazy, he is lazy, granted,** il est paresseux, je vous l'accorde.

grant-in-aid [græntɪn'eɪd] *n* subvention *f*.

granular ['grænjʊlər] *adj* (*surface, texture*) granulaire, granuleux.

granulate ['grænjʊleɪt] **1** *vt* granuler; grener, grainer (*la poudre etc*); cristalliser (*le sucre*); grenailler (*un métal etc*). **2** *vi* **(a)** (*take on the form of grains*) se former en grains; (*of sugar etc*) se cristalliser; **(b)** *Med* (*of wound*) bourgeonner.

granulated ['grænjʊleɪtɪd] *adj Culin* **g. sugar,** sucre cristallisé.

granulation [grænjʊ'leɪʃən] *n* granulation *f*; granulage *m* (*de la poudre etc*); grenaillement *m* (*d'un métal*).

granule ['grænjʊl] *n* granule *m*.

grape [greɪp] *n* (grain *m* de) raisin *m*; **a (variety of) g.,** un raisin; **bunch of grapes,** grappe *f* de raisin; **I'll have grapes,** je prendrai du raisin; **to gather the grapes,** faire les vendanges; *F* **sour grapes!,** ils sont trop verts!; **g. harvest,** vendange(s) *f(pl)*; **g. hyacinth,** (*plant*) muscari *m*; **g. juice,** jus *m* de raisin; **g. picker,** vendangeur, -euse.

grapefruit ['greɪpfruːt] *n* pamplemousse *m*; **g. tree,** pamplemoussier *m*.

grapeshot ['greɪpʃɒt] *n* (*ammunition*) mitraille *f*.

grapevine ['greɪpvaɪn] *n* **(a)** vigne *f*, treille *f*; **(b)** *Fig* téléphone *m* arabe; **I heard on the g. that ...,** la rumeur publique voudrait que ... .

graph¹ [grɑːf] *n* graphique *m*, graphe *m*, diagramme *m*, courbe *f*, tracé *m* (*d'une équation etc*); **g. paper,** papier *m* pour graphique, papier millimétré.

graph² *vt* graphiquer (*une courbe*); tracer (*une courbe*) graphiquement.

graphic ['græfɪk] *adj* **(a)** *Math* (*also* **graphical**) (*représentation etc*) graphique; **(b)** (*vivid*) pittoresque, vivant; **she gave a g. description of his injuries,** elle a fait une description pittoresque de ses blessures; **g. art,** art *m* graphique; **g. artist,** graphiste *mf*; **(c)** *Art* (*design etc*) graphique; **(d) g. equalizer,** (*on hi-fi*) égaliseur *m* graphique.

graphically ['græfɪklɪ] *adv* **(a)** *Math* (*résoudre un problème*) graphiquement; **(b)** (*vividly*) d'une manière pittoresque.

graphics ['græfɪks] *npl* (*usu with sing verb*) graphique *f*; *Comptr* graphisme *m*, graphiques *fpl*; *Comptr* **g. card,** carte *f* graphique *ou* pour graphisme; **g. mode,** mode *m* graphique; **g. software,** logiciel *m* graphique *ou* de graphisme; **the g. are tremendous,** les graphismes *ou* les graphiques sont formidables.

graphite ['græfaɪt] *n* graphite *m*, mine *f* de plomb.

graphologist [græ'fɒlədʒɪst] *n* graphologue *mf*.

graphology [græ'fɒlədʒɪ] *n* graphologie *f*.

grapnel ['græpnəl] *n Nau* grappin *m*, crochet *m*; *HydE* araignée *f*; *Av* ancre *f* (*de ballon*).

grapple¹ ['græp(ə)l] *n* = **GRAPNEL**.

grapple² **1** *vi* lutter corps à corps; **the two men grappled in the darkness,** les deux hommes ont lutté corps à corps dans le noir; **to g. with s.o./a difficulty,** en venir aux prises avec qn/une difficulté; **I've been grappling with this problem for weeks,** je me collette avec ce problème depuis des semaines; **to g. with inflation,** être aux prises avec l'inflation. **2** *vt* accrocher, agripper (*qn, qch*).

grappling ['græp(ə)lɪŋ] *n* **(a)** (*struggle*) (lutte *f*) corps à corps *m* (**with,** avec); **(b)** (*with hook*) accrochage *m*; *Nau* **g. iron** *or* **hook,** grappin *m*, crochet *m*.

grasp¹ [grɑːsp] *n* **(a)** (*of hand*) poigne *f*; **to have a strong g.,** avoir de la poigne; **(b)** (*hold*) prise *f*; **to wrest sth from s.o.'s g.,** arracher qch des mains de qn; *Fig* **to have within one's g.,** avoir (*qch*) à sa portée; tenir (*le succès*) entre ses mains; *Fig* **it is now within everyone's g.,** (*financially etc*) c'est maintenant à la portée de tout le monde; **(c)** (*understanding*) compréhension *f*; **to have a good g. of modern history,** avoir une bonne connaissance de l'histoire moderne; **he has no g. of the importance of this contract,** il ne comprend absolument pas l'importance de ce contrat; **their g. of the situation was poor,** leur compréhension de la situation n'était pas bonne.

grasp² *vt* **(a)** (*hold firmly*) saisir; empoigner (*un outil etc*); serrer (*qch*) dans sa main; **to g. s.o.'s hand,** serrer la main à qn; **I grasped his arm,** je lui ai saisi le bras; **(b)** (*seize*) s'emparer de, se saisir de (*qch*); **to g. the opportunity,** saisir l'occasion (*de faire qch*); **(c)** (*understand*) comprendre (*une difficulté etc*); se rendre compte de (*l'importance de qch*); **I did not quite g. what he said,** je n'ai pas tout à fait saisi ce qu'il disait.

▶**grasp at** *vipo* (*attempt to take hold of*) tâcher de saisir *ou* d'atteindre (*qch*); (*seize*) saisir avidement (*une occasion, une offre*).

grasping ['grɑːspɪŋ] *adj* avide, cupide.

grass¹ [grɑːs] *n* **(a)** (*plant*) herbe *f*; **blade of g.,** brin *m* d'herbe; **she doesn't let the g. grow under her feet,** elle ne perd pas son temps; **the g. roots,** (*of political party etc*) la base; **to attack a problem at the g. roots,** remonter à la source d'un problème; **the feeling at the g. roots is that ...,** le sentiment à la base est que ...; **quaking g.,** (*plant*) brize *f*; **g. seed,** (*for lawn*) graine *f* pour gazon; (*as feed*) graine fourragère; **g. snake,** couleuvre *f* à collier, serpent *m* d'eau; *F* **g. widow,** (*whose husband is away*) femme dont le mari est absent *ou* en voyage; (*who is divorced or separated*) femme divorcée *ou* séparée (de son mari); **g. box,** (*on lawn mower*) panier *m* à herbes; *Tex* **g. cloth,** (toile *f* de) ramie *f*;

(b) (*lawn*) gazon *m*; **keep off the g.,** défense de marcher sur le gazon *ou* sur les pelouses; *F* n'empiétez pas sur mes plates-bandes; *Fig* **the g. is always greener (on the other side of the fence),** c'est toujours mieux ailleurs; *Tennis* **she plays well on g.,** elle joue bien sur gazon; *Tennis* **g. court,** court *m* en gazon;

(c) (*pasture*) herbage *m*, pâture *f*, fourrage *m* en vert; **to put** *or* **turn a horse out to g.,** mettre un cheval à l'herbe; *Fig* **to put s.o. out to g.,** mettre qn à la retraite; **to be (out) at g.,** (*of animal*) être au vert; **to put land under g.,** enherber une terre, mettre une terre en herbe;

(d) *F* (*marijuana*) herbe *f*;

(e) *Br Sl* (*informer*) dénonciateur, -trice.

grass² **1** *vt* mettre en herbe, enherber (*un champ*); gazonner (*un jardin*). **2** *vi Br Sl* (*inform*) chanter; **to g. on s.o.,** dénoncer qn.

grass(-)green ['grɑːs'griːn] *adj* (*colour*) vert pré *inv*.

grasshopper ['grɑːshɒpər] *n* (*insect*) sauterelle *f*.

grassland ['grɑːslænd] *n* prairies *fpl*, prés *mpl*.

grass-root(s) ['grɑːsruːt, -s] *adj* de base, qui émane de la base; **there is no g.-r. support for their policy,** il n'y a pas de soutien de la base pour leur politique; **the g.-r. feeling is that ...,** le sentiment à la base est que ... .

grassy ['grɑːsɪ] *adj* herbu, herbeux; (*lane*) vert; (*plain*) verdoyant.

grate¹ [greɪt] *n* grille *f* (*de foyer*); (*fireplace*) foyer *m*, âtre *m*; **let's have a fire in the g.!,** faisons un feu dans la cheminée!

grate² **1** *vt* **(a)** *Culin* râper (*du fromage*); **(b)** (*scrape*) **to g. sth on sth,** frotter qch contre qch (avec un grincement); **to g. one's teeth,** grincer des dents. **2** *vi* **(a)** (*of machinery*) grincer; (*of chalk on blackboard*) crisser; **the door grated on its hinges,** la porte grinçait *ou* criait sur ses gonds; **(b)** (*irritate*) taper sur les nerfs; **it really grates (on me),** ça me tape vraiment sur les nerfs; **his pretentiousness grated on her,** sa prétention lui tapait sur les nerfs; **to g. on the ear,** écorcher *ou* affliger l'oreille.

grateful ['greɪtfʊl] *adj* **(a)** (*person*) reconnaissant (**to s.o. for sth,** à, envers qn de qch); **to be g. to s.o. for sth,** savoir (bon) gré à qn de qch; **I'm g. for all you've done,** je vous suis reconnaissant de tout ce que vous avez fait, je vous sais gré de tout ce que vous avez fait; **they weren't at all g.,** ils n'étaient pas du tout reconnaissants; **he gave her a g. smile,** il lui a adressé un sourire reconnaissant; **I would be g. if you could let me know as soon as possible,** je vous serais reconnaissant de m'informer dès que possible; **(b)** (*opportunity etc*) bienvenu, heureux.

gratefully ['greɪtfʊlɪ] *adv* avec reconnaissance.

grater ['greɪtər] *n* râpe *f*; **cheese g.,** râpe à fromage.

gratification [grætɪfɪ'keɪʃən] *n* **(a)** (*pleasure*) satisfaction *f*, plaisir *m*; **to do sth for one's own g.,** faire qch pour son propre contentement; **she had the g. of knowing that ...,** elle avait la satisfaction de savoir que ...; **(b)** satisfaction *f*, assouvissement *m* (*des passions*).

gratified ['grætɪfaɪd] *adj* satisfait, content (**with,** de); (*sourire*) de satisfaction.

gratify ['grætɪfaɪ] *vt* **(a)** (*please*) faire plaisir à (*qn*); **(b)** (*satisfy*) satisfaire, contenter (*une passion etc*); **to g. s.o.'s whims,** satisfaire aux caprices de qn.

gratifying ['grætɪfaɪɪŋ] *adj* agréable; (*perspective etc*) qui donne de la satisfaction (**to s.o.,** à qn).

grating¹ ['greɪtɪŋ] **1** *adj* **(a)** (*bruit*) discordant, grinçant; **g. sound,** grincement *m*; crissement *m*; **(b)** (*voice*) rude; **g. laugh,** ricanement *m*. **2** *n* **(a)** *Culin* râpage *m*; **gratings,** râpure(s) *f(pl)*; **(b)** (*of a hinge*) grincement *m*, crissement *m*.

grating² *n* grille *f*, grillage *m* (*de fenêtre*).

gratis ['grɑːtɪs] **1** *adj* gratis, gratuit. **2** *adv* gratis, gratuitement, à titre gratuit.

gratitude ['grætɪtjuːd] *n* gratitude *f*, reconnaissance *f* (**to,** envers); **to show one's g.,** témoigner de sa reconnaissance.

gratuitous [grə'tjuːɪtəs] *adj* **(a)** (*free*) gratuit; (*service etc*) bénévole; **(b)** (*unnecessary*) gratuit, sans motif, sans raison; **g. violence,** violence gratuite.

gratuitously [grə'tjuːɪtəslɪ] *adv* (*see adj*) **(a)** gratuitement, à titre gratuit; **(b)** gratuitement, sans motif, sans raison.

gratuity [grə'tjuːɪtɪ] *n* **(a)** gratification *f*, pourboire *m*; **no gratuities,** défense de donner des pourboires; **(b)** *Mil* prime *f* de démobilisation.

grave¹ [greɪv] *n* tombe *f*, tombeau *m*; **mass g.,** fosse commune; **to be in one's g.,** être enterré; **she worked herself into an early g.,** elle s'est tuée au travail; *Fig* **he must have turned in his g.,** il a dû se retourner dans sa tombe; **to make s.o. turn in their g.,** faire retourner qn dans sa tombe; **someone's walking over my g.,** j'ai le frisson; **to have one foot in the g.,** avoir un pied dans la tombe; **from beyond the g.,** d'outre-tombe; **g. robber,** déterreur *m* de cadavres.

grave² *vt* (*pt* **graved**; *pp* **graven, graved**) *Arch* graver (*une inscription*); **graven on his memory,** gravé dans sa mémoire; *Bible* **graven image,** image taillée.

grave³ *adj* grave, sérieux; (*tone*) solennel; (*situation*) grave; (*error*) lourd; **to make a g. mistake,** se tromper lourdement; **g. news,** de graves nouvelles; **she looked very g.,** elle avait l'air très grave.

grave⁴ [grɑːv] *adj Ling* **g. accent,** accent *m* grave.

grave⁵ [greɪv] *vt Nau* radouber (*un navire*).

gravedigger ['greɪvdɪgər] *n* fossoyeur *m*.

gravel¹ ['græv(ə)l] *n* **(a)** gravier *m*; **g. pit,** carrière *f* de gravier; **g. path,** allée couverte de gravier; **(b)** *Med* gravelle *f*, *F* graviers *mpl*, sable *m*.

gravel² *vt* **(-ll-,** *US* **-l-)** **(a)** (*cover with gravel*) couvrir de gravier; **gravelled path,** allée couverte de gravier; **(b)** *esp US F* embarrasser (*qn*).

gravelly ['græv(ə)lɪ] *adj* **(a)** (*containing gravel*) graveleux; (*lit de rivière*) pierreux; (*chemin*) couvert de gravier; *F* **g. voice,** voix râpeuse; **(b)** *Med* (*urine etc*) graveleux.

gravely ['greɪvlɪ] *adv* (*to say*) gravement, solennellement; **g. ill,** gravement malade; **g. wounded,** grièvement blessé.

graven *see* **GRAVE²**.

graveness ['greɪvnɪs] *n* gravité *f* (*du maintien etc*).

gravestone ['greɪvstəʊn] *n* pierre tombale.

graveyard ['greɪvjɑːd] *n* (*for people, Fig for cars*) cimetière *m*; **this firm is the g. of personal initiative,** cette maison est le tombeau *ou* la fin de toute initiative individuelle.

graving ['greɪvɪŋ] *n Nau* radoub *m*; **g. dock,** bassin *m* de radoub.

gravitate ['grævɪteɪt] *vi Phys* graviter (**towards,** vers; **round,** autour de); *Fig* **most of the guests had gravitated to the bar,** la plupart des invités s'étaient dirigés vers le bar.

gravitation [grævɪ'teɪʃən] *n Phys* gravitation *f*; *Fig* mouvement *m*; **law of g.,** loi *f* de la pesanteur.

gravitational [grævɪ'teɪʃən(ə)l] *adj Phys* gravitationnel; (*champ*) de gravitation; **g. pull,** gravitation *f*.

gravity ['grævɪtɪ] *n* **(a)** *Phys* gravité *f*, pesanteur *f*; (force *f* de) gravitation *f*; **law of g.,** loi *f* de la pesanteur; **centre of g.,** centre *m* de gravité; **force of g.,** force de gravitation; **specific g.,** poids *m* *ou* gravité spécifique; *Tech* **g. feed,** alimentation *f* en charge *ou* par gravité; **(b)** (*of person*) gravité *f*, sérieux *m*; (*of situation, injury*) gravité; **to lose one's g.,** perdre son sérieux.

gravy ['greɪvɪ] *n* **(a)** *Culin* jus *m* (*qui sort de la viande*); (*sauce*) sauce *f* (au jus); **g. boat,** saucière *f*; **(b)** *US Sl* (*money*) (*gained easily*) gratte *f*; (*gained illegally*) profit *m* illicite; **the g. train,** (*easy source of income*) l'assiette *f* au beurre; (*illegal source of income*) un bon filon.

gray [greɪ] *adj & n esp US* = **GREY**.

grayling ['greɪlɪŋ] *n* **(a)** (*fish*) ombre *m* (de rivière); **(b)** (*butterfly*) (papillon *m*) agreste *m*.

graze¹ [greɪz] *Agr* **1** *vi* (*of cattle etc*) paître, brouter, pâturer; **to g. on a field,** pâturer un champ. **2** *vt* (faire) paître (*un troupeau*); pacager, mettre en pacage (*un champ*); (*of cattle etc*) pâturer (*un champ*); paître (*l'herbe*).

graze² *n* écorchure *f*; (*slighter*) éraflure *f*.

graze³ *vt* **(a)** (*scrape*) écorcher *ou* (*slighter*) érafler (*ses genoux etc*); **(b)** (*brush past*) effleurer; **the bullet grazed his shoulder,** la balle lui rasa l'épaule.

grazing ['greɪzɪŋ] *n Agr* **(a)** pâturage *m* (*de troupeaux etc*); **g. rights,** droit *m* de pâturage *ou* de pacage; **(b) g. (land, ground),** pâture *f*, pacage *m*.

grease¹ [griːs] *n Culin MecE etc* graisse *f*; *MecE* (*dirty*) cambouis *m*; **axle g.,** graisse pour essieux; **g. box,** boîte *f* à graisse *ou* de graissage; **g. gun,** pistolet *m* graisseur; *Av Aut* **g. monkey,** mécano *m*; **g. stain,** (*on clothing*) tache *f* de graisse; (*in arboriculture*) glu *f* horticole; **g. band,** bande enduite de glu horticole.

grease² *vt Tech* graisser, lubrifier (*une machine*); suiffer (*un mât*); *Culin* beurrer (*un moule à gâteau*); *F* **to g. s.o.'s palm,** graisser la patte à qn.

►**grease back** *vtsep* **to g. back one's hair,** coiffer ses cheveux vers l'arrière avec de la brillantine.

greased [griːsd] *adj F* **like g. lightning,** en quatrième vitesse.

greasepaint ['griːspeɪnt] *n* fard *m*; *Th* **stick of g.,** crayon gras (de maquillage); **white g.,** blanc gras.

greaseproof ['griːspruːf] *adj* (*papier*) gras.

greaser ['griːsər] *n* **(a)** *Br esp Aut Sl* mécano *m*; **(b)** *Old-fashioned Br Sl* (*motorcyclist*) motard *m*; **(c)** *US Offensive Sl* = Mexicain.

greasiness ['griːsɪnɪs] *n* **(a)** état graisseux *ou* gras; **(b)** *F* (*of manner*) onctuosité *f*.

greasy ['griːsɪ] *adj* **(a)** (*containing, covered in grease*) graisseux, huileux; (*sausage etc*) gras; (*grease-stained*) taché de graisse; **to taste g.,** sentir le graillon; **to make one's clothes g.,** graisser ses habits; **g. hair,** cheveux gras; **g. pole,** mât *m* de cocagne (*de fête villageoise etc*); *Sl* **g. spoon,** boui-boui *m*; **(b)** (*slippery*) gras, *f* grasse, glissant; **g. road,** chemin gras *ou* glissant; **(c)** (*manner*) onctueux, patelin.

great [greɪt] **1** *adj* **(a)** (*large, important*) grand; **a g. crowd,** une grande foule, une foule énorme; **the G. Lakes,** les Grands Lacs; **Greater London,** le grand Londres, l'agglomération londonienne; *Zool* **the g. apes,** les grands singes; **a g. deal,** beaucoup (**of,** de); une grande quantité; **a g. many,** beaucoup (de + *pl*); **a g. many people,** beaucoup de gens, beaucoup de monde; **the g. majority, the greater part,** la plupart, la majeure partie (**of,** de); **to a g. extent,** en grande partie; **to reach a g. age,** parvenir à un âge avancé; **his greatest fault,** son plus grand défaut, son défaut capital; **to take g. care,** prendre grand soin (**of,** de); **g. difference,** grande *ou* forte différence; **with g./with the greatest of pleasure,** avec grand/avec le plus grand plaisir; **g. scoundrel,** grand fripon; **they are g. friends,** ce sont de grands amis; **it is no g. matter,** ce n'est pas une grosse affaire; **to have no g. opinion of s.o.,** tenir qn en médiocre estime; **the g. thing is that ...,** le grand avantage *ou* le principal, c'est que ...; **g. artist,** grand artiste; **a g. man,** un grand homme; **Alexander the G.,** Alexandre le Grand; **the G. War,** la Grande Guerre; *F* **G. Scott!,** grands dieux!;

(b) *F* (*very good*) **to have a g. time,** s'amuser bien; **(that's) g!,** fameux!, magnifique!; **a g. idea,** une idée géniale; **isn't he g.!,** qu'est-ce qu'il est bien!; *F* **to be g. at tennis,** être fort au tennis; **I'm not g. on Roman history,** je ne suis pas très fort *ou* calé en histoire romaine; *Iron* **that's g.!,** zut alors!

2 *adv F* très bien; **I feel g.!,** je me sens en super forme!, **I don't feel g. about what I did,** je ne me sens pas très fier de ce que j'ai fait; **he's doing g.,** (*in health*) il se porte à merveille.

3 *n* (*person*) grand, -e; **one of the greats of world cinema,** un des grands du cinéma mondial.

great-aunt ['greɪt'ɑːnt] *n* grand-tante *f*, *pl* grands-tantes.

greatcoat ['greɪtkəʊt] *n* **(a)** pardessus *m*; **(b)** *Mil* (*worn by cavalry*) manteau *m*; (*worn by infantry*) capote *f*.

greatest ['greɪtɪst] *n* **to be the g.,** être le meilleur.

great-grandchild, *pl* **-children** ['greɪt'græntʃaɪld, -grænd-, -tʃɪldrən] *n* arrière-petits-fils *m*, arrière-petite-fille *f*, *pl* arrière-petits-enfants *m*.

great-granddaughter ['greɪt'grændɔːtər, -'grænd-] *n* arrière-petite-fille *f*, *pl* arrière-petites-filles.

great-grandfather ['greɪt'grænfɑːðər, -'grænd-] *n* arrière- grand-père *m*, *pl* arrière-grands-pères, bisaïeul *m*, *pl* bisaïeuls.

great-grandmother ['greɪt'grænmʌðər, -'grænd-] *n* arrière- grand-mère *f*, *pl* arrière-grand-mères, bisaïeule *f*.

great-grandparents ['greɪt'grænpeərənts, -'grænd-] *npl* arrière-grands-parents *mpl*.

great-grandson ['greɪt'grænsʌn, -'grænd-] *n* arrière-petit-fils *m*, *pl* arrière-petits-fils.

great-greatgrandfather ['greɪt'greɪt'grænfɑːðər, -'grænd-] *n* trisaïeul *m*, *pl* trisaïeuls.

great-greatgrandmother ['greɪt'greɪt'grænmʌðər, -'grænd-] *n* trisaïeule *f*.

greatly ['greɪtlɪ] *adv* grandement; **g. irritated,** très *ou* fortement irrité; **I would g. prefer ...,** je préférerais (de) beaucoup ...; **to contribute g. to a result,** contribuer puissamment à un résultat.

great-nephew ['greɪt'nefjuː] *n* petit-neveu *m*, *pl* petits-neveux.

greatness ['greɪtnɪs] *n* **(a)** (*of person, action etc*) grandeur *f*; élévation *f*, noblesse *f* (*de pensée*); **g. of soul,** grandeur d'âme; **(b)** (*extent, size*) grandeur *f*; importance *f*.

great-niece ['greɪt'niːs] *n* petite-nièce *f*, *pl* petites-nièces.

great-uncle ['greɪt'ʌŋk(ə)l] *n* grand-oncle *m*, *pl* grands-oncles.

grebe [griːb] *n* grèbe *m*; **great crested g.,** grèbe huppé.

Grecian ['griːʃən] *adj* grec, *f* grecque; **in the G. style,** à la grecque.

Greece [griːs] *n* Grèce *f*.

greed [griːd] *n* **(a)** (*for material things*) avidité *f*, cupidité *f*, âpreté *f* au gain; **it's sheer g.!,** c'est de l'avidité pure et simple; **(b)** (*gluttony*) gourmandise *f*, gloutonnerie *f*.

greedily ['griːdɪlɪ] *adv* **(a)** avidement, cupidement; **(b)** (*eat*) goulûment, gloutonnement; (*to look, say*) avec gourmandise.

greediness ['griːdɪnɪs] *n* = **GREED.**

greedy ['griːdɪ] *adj* **(a)** (*for material things*) avide, cupide, âpre (au gain); **(b)** (*gluttonous*) gourmand, glouton, -onne; *Sl* **g. guts,** goinfre *m*, bâfreur *m*.

Greek [griːk] **1** *adj* grec, *f* grecque; **the G. Church,** l'Église grecque, l'Église orthodoxe. **2** *n* **(a)** (*person*) Grec, Grecque; **(b)** *Ling* grec *m*; **modern G.,** le grec moderne; *F* **it's all G. to me,** c'est de l'hébreu pour moi.

green [griːn] **1** *adj* **(a)** vert; *F* (*young, inexperienced*) jeune, inexpérimenté; (*naive*) naïf; **he's not as g. as he looks,** il n'est pas si niais qu'il en a l'air; **as g. as grass,** vert comme pré; *F* (*person*) naïf; **to grow g.,** verdir; (*of grass*) verdoyer; **she has g. fingers** *or Am* **a g. thumb,** elle a la main verte; *Agr* **g. crop,** récolte *f* de fourrages verts; **g. old age,** verte vieillesse; **to keep s.o.'s memory g.,** entretenir la mémoire de qn; **g. belt,** ceinture *ou* zone verte; **to give s.o. the g. light (to do sth),** donner le feu vert à qn (pour faire qch); *Agr* **the g. revolution,** la révolution verte; **to go** *or* **turn g.,** verdir; (*feeling sick*) blêmir; **to make s.o. g. with envy,** faire pâlir qn d'envie; **g. bean,** haricot vert; **g. pepper,** poivron vert;

(b) *Pol* (*consumer, policy etc*) vert, écologiste; **the G. Party,** (*in UK*) le parti écologiste.

2 *n* **(a)** (*colour*) vert *m*; **the greens of a picture,** les verts d'un tableau;

(b) (*of trees, plants etc*) verdure *f*;

(c) (*vegetables*) **greens,** légumes verts;

(d) (*grassy area*) pelouse *f*, gazon *m*; **village g.,** pelouse communale, pré communal; = place *f* du village; **the g.,** la pelouse; *Golf* le vert; **bowling g.,** (terrain *m* pour) jeu *m* de boules; **g. keeper,** (*of bowling green, golf course*) préposé à l'entretien des pelouses;

(e) *Pol* vert, -e.

greenback ['griːnbæk] *n US F* billet vert.

greenery ['griːnərɪ] *n* verdure *f*.

green-eyed ['griːnaɪd] *adj* aux yeux verts; *Lit* **the g.-e. monster,** la sombre jalousie.

greenfield ['griːnfiːld] *n* **g. site,** (*for factory etc*) terrain jamais construit.

greenfinch ['griːnfɪntʃ] *n* (*bird*) verdier *m*.

greenfly ['griːnflaɪ] *n* (*insect*) puceron *m* (*du rosier*); **to have g.,** (*of plant*) avoir des pucerons; **g. spray,** produit *m* à vaporiser contre les pucerons.

greengage ['griːngeɪdʒ] *n* reine-claude *f*, *pl* reines-claudes.

greengrocer ['griːngrəʊsər] *n esp Br* (*selling vegetables*) marchand, -ande de fruits et légumes; **g.'s (shop),** magasin *m* de fruits et légumes.

greenhorn ['griːnhɔːn] *n F* blanc-bec *m*, *pl* blancs-becs; *Mil* bleu *m*.

greenhouse ['griːnhaʊs] *n* serre *f*; **the g. effect,** l'effet *m* de serre; **g. gas,** gaz *m* à effet de serre.

greening ['griːnɪŋ] *n* **the recent g. of the Labour Party,** la récente conversion du Parti Travailliste à l'écologie.

greenish ['griːnɪʃ] *adj* verdâtre.

Greenland ['griːnlənd] *n* Groenland *m*; **in G.,** au Groenland.

Greenlander ['griːnləndər] *n* Groenlandais, -aise.

greenness ['griːnnɪs] *n* (*of fruit etc*) immaturité *f*; (*inexperience*) inexpérience *f*; (*naivety*) naïveté *f*, simplicité *f*; (*of countryside etc*) vert *m*, verdure *f*.

greenroom ['griːnruːm] *n Th* foyer *m* des artistes.

greenstuff ['griːnstʌf] *n* **(a)** *Br* (*vegetables*) légumes verts; **(b)** *US Sl* (*paper money*) billets *mpl*.

greensward ['griːnswɔːd] *n Lit* pelouse *f*, (tapis *m* de) gazon *m*.

Greenwich ['grɪnɪdʒ, -ɪtʃ, gren-] *n* Greenwich; **G. Mean Time,** temps moyen de Greenwich.

greenwood ['griːnwʊd] *n* bois *m*, forêt *f* (*en été*).

greet [griːt] *vt* saluer; (*welcome*) accueillir (*qn*) avec quelques paroles aimables; **to g. a speech with cheers,** acclamer un discours; **the announcement was greeted with cheers,** l'annonce a été saluée par des acclamations; **to g. the ear,** frapper l'oreille; **to g. the eyes,** s'offrir à l'œil.

greeting ['griːtɪŋ] *n* salutation *f*, salut *m*; **to send greetings to s.o.,** envoyer ses salutations à qn; **New Year greetings,** compliments *mpl* du jour de l'an; **greetings card,** carte *f* de vœux.

gregarious [grɪ'geərɪəs] *adj* (*person*) sociable; *Zool Bot* grégaire; **the g. instinct,** l'instinct grégaire.

gregariously [grɪ'geərɪəslɪ] *adv Zool* (*vivre*) en troupes, par bandes.

gregariousness [grɪ'geərɪəsnɪs] *n* (*of person*) sociabilité *f*; *Zool Bot* grégarisme *m*.

Gregorian [grɪ'gɔːrɪən] *adj Rel* (*chant etc*) grégorien.

gremlin ['gremlɪn] *n F* lutin *m*.

grenade [grə'neɪd] *n Mil* grenade *f*.

grenadier [grenə'dɪər] *n Mil* grenadier *m*.

grenadine ['grenədiːn] *n* **(a)** *Tex* grenadine *f*; **(b)** (*syrup*) grenadine *f*.

grew *see* **GROW**.

grey¹, *US* **gray** [greɪ] **1** *adj* **(a)** gris; **g. squirrel,** écureuil gris; **g. wolf,** loup gris; **g. matter,** substance grise (du cerveau); **a g. area,** une zone incertaine; **to turn** *or* **go g.,** grisonner; *esp US* **g. power,** = pouvoir (économique, social etc) de personnes âgées; *esp US* **G. Panthers,** = groupe de pression composé de personnes âgées; **(b)** (*complexion*) blême; **to turn g.,** blêmir; **(c)** (*outlook etc*) sombre, morne; **a g. dismal morning,** un matin gris et triste; **a g. life,** une vie grise. **2** *n* **(a)** (*colour*) gris *m*; **hair touched with g.,** cheveux grisonnants; *Comptr* **shades of g.,** niveaux *mpl* de gris; **(b)** (*horse*) cheval gris.

grey², *US* **gray** *vi* (*of hair*) grisonner.

greybeard ['greɪbɪəd] *n* (*old husband*) vieux barbon.

grey-eyed ['greɪ'aɪd] *adj* aux yeux gris.

grey-haired, -headed ['greɪ'heəd, -'hedɪd] *adj* aux cheveux gris; (*greying*) grisonnant.

greyhound ['greɪhaʊnd] *n* lévrier *m*; **g. racing,** courses *fpl* de lévriers; **g.(-racing) track,** cynodrome *m*.

greying ['greɪɪŋ] *adj* grisonnant.

greyish ['greɪɪʃ] *adj* grisâtre.

greylag ['greɪlæg] *n* (*bird*) **g. (goose),** oie cendrée.

greyness ['greɪnɪs] *n* **(a)** (*colour*) teinte grise; **the g. of London,** la grisaille de Londres; **(b)** (*depressing quality*) caractère *m* morne *ou* sombre, tristesse *f*.

grid [grɪd] *n* **(a)** (*framework*) grille *f*, grillage *m*; *El* grille, grillage (*d'accumulateur*); grille (*d'un tube électronique etc*); **g. valve,** tube *m* à grille; **cattle g.,** grille sur la route permettant aux voitures mais non au bétail de passer; **(b)** = **GRIDIRON**; **(c)** (*on map*) quadrillage *m*; **g. reference,** coordonnées *fpl*; **g. system,** réseau *m* de quadrillage; **g. lines,** droites *fpl* du quadrillage; *El* **the g.,** le réseau électrique national; **g. layout,** (*of town*) quadrillage, damier *m*; **(d)** *Sp* **(starting) g.,** ligne *f* de départ (*d'une piste automobile*).

griddle ['grɪd(ə)l] *n Culin* tôle *f* (*sur laquelle on cuit des galettes*); **g. cake,** galette *f*.

gridiron ['grɪdaɪən] *n* **(a)** *Culin* gril *m*; *Nau* gril de carénage; *Th* gril (*pour la manœuvre des décors*); **(b)** *Am Fb* terrain *m* de football.

gridlock ['grɪdlɒk] *n Am* (*on road*) embouteillage *m*; *Fig* impasse *f*.

grief [griːf] *n* chagrin *m*, douleur *f*, peine *f* ; **to die of g.,** mourir de chagrin; **to come to g.,** (*experience disaster, disappointment*) se voir accablé de malheurs; (*of plan etc*) échouer, mal tourner; (*have an accident*) avoir un accident; (*of rider*) faire une chute; *F* **good g.!,** mon Dieu!

grief-stricken ['griːfstrɪk(ə)n] *adj* pénétré *ou* accablé de douleur, en proie à la douleur.

grievance ['griːvəns] *n* **(a)** (*feeling of having been wronged*) grief *m*; **to have a g. against s.o.,** avoir un grief contre qn; **to air** *or* **state one's grievances,** conter *ou* exprimer ses doléances; **(b)** (*wrong*) injustice *f*; **to redress a g.,** réparer un tort.

grieve [griːv] **1** *vi* se chagriner, s'affliger (**over, about sth,** de qch); **the whole nation grieved at his death,** la nation entière pleura sa mort; **he was grieving for his lost daughter,** il pleurait sa fille perdue; **she is still grieving,** elle a encore de la peine. **2** *vt* chagriner, affliger, peiner (*qn*); **we are grieved to learn ...,** nous apprenons avec peine ...; **it grieves me to ...,** cela me peine de ... .

grieved [griːvd] *adj* chagriné, affligé, désolé (**at,** de); **deeply g.,** navré (**at,** de).

grievous ['griːvəs] *adj* **(a)** (*causing grief*) douloureux, pénible; (*loss*) cruel; **(b)** (*wound etc*) grave; **g. bodily harm,** coups et blessures graves; *Jur* **to cause g. bodily harm,** causer de graves blessures; **(c)** *Lit* (*news*) affligeant, douloureux.

grievously ['griːvəslɪ] *adv* **(a)** douloureusement, péniblement, cruellement; **(b)** (*seriously*) gravement; grièvement (*blessé*).

griffin ['grɪfɪn] *n Myth* griffon *m*.

griffon ['grɪfən] *n* **(a)** (*dog*) griffon *m*; **(b)** *Myth* griffon *m*; **(c)** (*bird*) **g. (vulture),** vautour *m* griffon.

grift [grɪft] *vi Am Sl* escroquer.

grifter ['grɪftər] *n Am Sl* escroc *m*.

grill¹ [grɪl] *n Br Culin* **(a)** (*food*) grillade *f*; **I'll have a mixed g.,** je vais prendre un assortiment de grillades; **(b)** (*in restaurant*) grill-room *m*, *pl* grill-rooms; (*restaurant*) rôtisserie *f*.

grill² *n Br Culin* (*on cooker*) gril *m*; (*in oven*) grilloir *m*; **to cook sth under the g.,** cuire qch sur le *ou* au gril.

grill³ **1** *vt* **(a)** *Br* (*cook*) griller (*la viande*); faire cuire (*qch*) sur le *ou* au gril; **(b)** *F* (*interrogate*) cuisiner (*un détenu etc*). **2** *vi* griller, être grillé; cuire sur le *ou* au gril.

grill(e) [grɪl] *n* grille *f* (*de porte*); **(counter) g.,** grille de comptoir (*d'un bureau de banque etc*); *Aut* **radiator g.,** calandre *f*.

grilled¹ [grɪld] *adj Culin* grillé; **g. meat,** viande grillée, grillade *f*.

grilled² *adj* (*door*) grillagé, à grille.

grilling ['grɪlɪŋ] *n* **(a)** (*of food*) cuisson *f* sur le *ou* au gril; **(b)** *F* cuisinage *m* (*d'un détenu etc*); **to give s.o. a g.,** cuisiner qn.

grillroom ['grɪlrʊm] *n* (*in restaurant*) grill-room *m*, *pl* grill-rooms; (*restaurant*) rôtisserie *f*.

grim [grɪm] *adj* menaçant, sinistre; (*paysage*) lugubre; (*sourire*) sardonique; (*humour*) macabre; **to hold on like g. death,** se cramponner désespérément; **g. determination,** volonté *f* inflexible; **to look g.,** (*of person*) avoir une mine sévère; **her face was g. as she announced the death toll,** son visage était sévère lorsqu'elle a annoncé le nombre de morts; **the g. prospect of another famine,** la perspective sinistre d'une autre famine; *F* **how do you feel? — pretty g.!,** comment ça va? — plutôt mal; **things are looking g.,** ça s'annonce mal.

grimace¹ [grɪ'meɪs] *n* grimace *f*; **to make a g.,** faire la grimace.

grimace² *vi* grimacer, faire la grimace.

grime [graɪm] *n* saleté *f*; (*dust*) poussière *f* de charbon *ou* de suie (*qui vous entre dans la peau*).

griminess ['graɪmɪnɪs] *n* saleté *f*, noirceur *f*.

grimly ['grɪmlɪ] *adv* sinistrement; sévèrement; (*fight, hold on*) avec acharnement.

grimness ['grɪmnɪs] *n* caractère *m* sinistre, aspect *m* redoutable (*de qch*); (*of face*) sévérité *f*; (*of struggle*) acharnement *m*.

grimy ['graɪmɪ] *adj* sale, encrassé, noirci; (*with soot*) noir (de suie).

grin¹ [grɪn] *n* **(a)** (*smile*) large sourire *m*; **to give a broad g.,** se fendre la bouche en un large sourire; **(b)** (*grimace*) grimace *f* qui découvre les dents.

grin² *vi* **(-nn-)** **(a)** (*smile*) sourire; (*broadly*) sourire d'une oreille à l'autre; **he grinned broadly,** son visage s'est épanoui en un large sourire; **to g. like a Cheshire cat,** sourire jusqu'aux oreilles; **to g. and bear it,** (tâcher de) garder le sourire; *F* encaisser (sans broncher); **(b)** (*grimace*) grimacer en montrant les dents; **grinning savages,** sauvages grimaçants.

grind¹ [graɪnd] *n* **(a)** *F* (*work*) labeur monotone et continu; **the daily g.,** le boulot journalier; **what a g.!,** quelle corvée!; **(b)** (*erotic dance*) déhanchement *m*; **(c)** (*sound*) grincement *m*, crissement *m*.

grind² *v* (*pt & pp* **ground** [graʊnd]) **1** *vt* **(a)** (*pulverize*) moudre (*du blé, du café*); concasser (*du poivre*); broyer (*des couleurs*); piler (*qch dans un mortier*); **to g. sth to dust,** pulvériser qch; **to g. sth under one's heel,** écraser qch sous ses pieds; *Fig* **to g. the faces of the poor,** opprimer les pauvres; **(b)** (*polish*) meuler (*une pièce coulée*); dépolir (*le verre, un bouchon*); **(c)** (*sharpen*) aiguiser, affûter (*un outil*); passer (*un couteau etc*) à la meule; mettre le tranchant à (*une lame*); **to g. one's teeth,** grincer des dents; **(d)** *Mus* jouer de (*un orgue de Barbarie*). **2** *vi* **(a)** (*of wheels*) grincer, crisser; **(b)** *F* (*work hard*) bûcher, turbiner; *Sch* bachoter.

▶grind down **1** *vtsep* (*opposition*) grignoter; **a people ground down by poverty,** un peuple accablé par une pauvreté extrême; *see also* **GRIND² 1 (a)**. **2** *vi* (*of substance*) se moudre.

►**grind into** *vtaspo* **to g. nuts into a powder,** moudre des noisettes finement.
►**grind on** *vi* (*proceed relentlessly*) traîner; **the negotiations ground on all summer,** les négociations ont traîné tout l'été.
►**grind out** *vtsep* (*produce without originality*) pondre (*des articles, des poèmes*); **to g. out a tune,** tourner un air; **he ground out the same jokes night after night,** il a ressassé les mêmes plaisanteries soir après soir.
►**grind up** *vtsep* (*pulverise*) pulvériser; **to g. sth up small,** moudre qch fin.
grinder ['graɪndər] *n* **(a)** (*device*) appareil broyeur, broyeuse *f*; (*of a mill*) meule courante; *MecE* rectifieuse *f*, machine *f* à rectifier; (*for sharpening*) machine *f* à aiguiser *ou* à affûter, affûteuse *f*; **coffee g.,** moulin *m* à café; *Fig* **to put s.o. through the g.,** faire passer un mauvais quart d'heure à qn; **(b)** (*person*) broyeur, -euse; rémouleur *m* (*de couteaux, de ciseaux*); **organ g.,** joueur, -euse d'orgue de Barbarie; **(c)** (*molar*) (dent *f*) molaire *f*; **(d)** *US F* (*sandwich*) gros sandwich.
grinding ['graɪndɪŋ] **1** *adj* (*pain*) déchirant; (*worry*) rongeant; **g. sound,** grincement *m*, crissement *m*; **g. poverty,** misère écrasante. **2** *n* **(a)** mouture *f* (*du blé*); broyage *m*, broiement *m* (*des couleurs*); pilage *m* (*dans un mortier*); *Ind* **g. mill,** broyeur *m*; **(b)** (*polishing*) meulage *m*; rodage *m*; polissage *m* à la meule; **(c)** (*sharpening*) aiguisage *m*, affûtage *m*; **(d)** (*sound*) grincement *m*, crissement *m*.
grindstone ['graɪndstəʊn] *n* meule *f* (en grès) à aiguiser; *Fig* **he keeps our noses to the g.,** il ne nous laisse aucun répit.
gringo ['grɪŋgəʊ] *n usu Pej* (*in Latin America*) gringo *m*.
grip¹ [grɪp] *n* **(a)** (*hold, grasp*) prise *f*, serrage *m*; (*in wrestling*) prise; serrement *m* (*d'un outil*); adhérence *f* (*des roues sur la route*); **to have a strong g.,** avoir une bonne poigne; **your g. is wrong,** (*on tennis racket, golf club etc*) la manière dont tu tiens la raquette *ou* le club *etc* est mauvaise; **to come** *or* **get to grips,** en venir aux prises (**with,** avec); *Fig F* **I can't get to grips with Shakespeare,** je n'arrive pas à comprendre Shakespeare; **these tyres give a better g. in wet weather,** ces pneus donnent une meilleure adhérence par temps humide; **to get a g. on sth,** prendre une prise sur qch; **to get** *or* **take** *or* **keep a g. on oneself,** se maîtriser, se contrôler; *Br Sl* **get a g.!,** (*don't panic!*) pas de panique!; **to lose one's g.,** (*on rope etc*) lâcher prise; *F* baisser (*du point de vue mental*); **he was beginning to lose his g. on the situation,** il commençait à perdre le contrôle de la situation; **I must be losing my g.,** je vieillis; **in the g. of a disease,** en proie à une maladie; **the country was in the g. of the worst winter for years,** le pays connaissait le pire hiver depuis des années; **to have a firm g. on sth,** tenir qch bien en main;
(b) (*of oar, handlebars*) poignée *f*; (*of pistol*) poignée, crosse *f*; *Tennis* (*of racket*) manchon *m*;
(c) *MecE etc* pince *f*; griffe *f*;
(d) **(hair) g.,** pince *f* (à cheveux);
(e) *Old-fashioned Am* (*bag*) valise *f*; mallette *f*.
grip² *v* (-pp-) **1** *vt* (*seize*) saisir, prendre (*qch*); (*hold*) empoigner, agripper (*qch*); **to g. sth in a vice,** serrer *ou* pincer qch dans un étau; **fear gripped her,** la peur la saisit; **play that grips the audience,** pièce qui passionne les spectateurs. **2** *vi* (*of wheel*) adhérer; **the wheels are not gripping,** les roues n'adhèrent pas.
gripe¹ [graɪp] *n* **(a)** *F* (*complaint*) ronchonnerie *f*, rouspétance *f*; **what's your g.?,** de quoi est-ce que tu te plains?; **(b)** *F* (*pain*) **gripes,** colique *f*; **g. water,** médicament *m* contre les coliques.
gripe² **1** *vt* **(a)** (*cause pain*) donner la colique à (*qn*); **(b)** *Arch* (*afflict*) affliger (*qn*). **2** *vi F* ronchonner, rouspéter.
griping ['graɪpɪŋ] **1** *adj* **g. pains,** coliques *fpl*. **2** *n F* (*complaining*) ronchonnerie *f*, rouspétance *f*.
gripping ['grɪpɪŋ] *adj* (*book, story*) passionnant.
grisly ['grɪzlɪ] *adj* macabre, sinistre; (*story, sight*) effrayant, épouvantable.
grist [grɪst] *n* blé *m* à moudre; **it's all g. to the mill,** ça fait venir l'eau au moulin; **all is g. that comes to his mill,** il fait profit de tout.
gristle ['grɪs(ə)l] *n* (*in meat*) nerfs *mpl*.
gristly ['grɪslɪ] *adj* (*meat*) nerveux.
grit¹ [grɪt] *n* **(a)** (*small particles*) grès *m*, sable *m*; *MecE etc* corps étrangers; impuretés *fpl*; **(b)** *Fig* (*courage*) cran *m*, courage *m*; **man of g.** *or* **who has plenty of g.,** homme qui a du cran; **(c)** (*stone*) grès *m* (dur); **millstone g.,** grès à meule(s); **(d)** (*texture of stone*) grain *m*.
grit² *v* (-tt-) **1** *vt* **(a)** (*put grit on*) sabler (*un pavé glissant etc*); **(b)** **to g. one's teeth,** grincer des dents; *Fig* **you'll just have to g. your teeth,** il va falloir que tu prennes ton mal en patience. **2** *vi* (*put grit on roads*) sabler les routes.
grits [grɪts] *npl Am* gruau *m* d'avoine; grosse farine d'avoine.
gritstone ['grɪtstəʊn] *n* grès *m* (dur).
gritter ['grɪtər] *n Br* camion *m* de sablage.
gritting ['grɪtɪŋ] *n Br* (*of roads*) sablage; **g. lorry,** camion *m* de sablage.
gritty ['grɪtɪ] *adj* **(a)** (*sol*) cendreux; (*fruit, texture*) graveleux; **(b)** *F* (*brave*) qui a du cran, résolu.
grizzle ['grɪz(ə)l] *vi* (*complain*) ronchonner; *esp Br* (*whine*) pleurnicher, geindre.
grizzled ['grɪz(ə)ld] *adj* (*hair, person*) grisonnant.
grizzling ['grɪzlɪŋ] *n esp Br* (*whining*) pleurnicherie *f*, pleurnichement *m*; (*complaining*) ronchonnement *m*.
grizzly ['grɪzlɪ] **1** *adj* **(a)** (*hair, person*) grisonnant; **(b)** **g. bear,** grizzli *m*, grizzly *m*. **2** *n* grizzli *m*, grizzly *m*.
groan¹ [grəʊn] *n* (*of pain*) gémissement *m*; (*at boring story, bad joke*) grognement désapprobateur; (*of tree, timber*) grincement *m*; **to give** *or* **utter a deep g.,** pousser un profond gémissement.
groan² **1** *vi* gémir, pousser un gémissement; (*of tree, timber*) grincer; (*at bad joke*) émettre des grognements désapprobateurs; **stop groaning!,** (*complaining*) arrête de gémir!; **to g. inwardly,** étouffer une plainte *ou* un gémissement; **the cart is groaning under the load,** la charrette gémit sous le fardeau. **2** *vt* (*say*) gémir.
groats [grəʊts] *npl* gruau *m* d'avoine *ou* de froment.
grocer ['grəʊsər] *n* épicier, -ière; **the g.'s will be closed,** l'épicerie sera fermée; **to go to the g.'s,** aller à l'épicerie *ou* chez l'épicier.
groceries ['grəʊsərɪz] *npl* (articles *mpl* d') épicerie *f*.
grocery ['grəʊsərɪ] *n* (*shop*) épicerie *f*; **to be in the g. business,** être dans l'épicerie.
grog [grɒg] *n* (*drink*) grog *m*.
groggy ['grɒgɪ] *adj F* chancelant, titubant; (*boxeur*) groggy; **to feel g.,** avoir les jambes en coton; **I'm feeling a bit g.,** je ne suis pas dans mon assiette.
grogshop ['grɒgʃɒp] *n Austr F* = débit où on vend les boissons à emporter.
groin [grɔɪn] *n* **(a)** *Anat* aine *f*; **g. injury,** blessure *f* à l'aine; **she kicked him in the g.,** elle lui a donné un coup de pied dans les parties; **(b)** *Archit* arête *f* (*de voûte*).
grommet ['grɒmɪt] *n MecE* bague *f* d'étoupe; *Nau* erse *f*, erseau *m*.
groom¹ [gruːm] *n* **(a)** (*of horse*) palefrenier *m*; garçon *m* d'écurie; **(b)** (*at wedding*) le marié; **(c)** gentilhomme *m*, valet *m* (*de la Chambre du Roi etc*).
groom² *vt* **(a)** panser (*un cheval*); **(b)** *Fig* préparer, former (*un candidat*) (en vue d'un poste *ou* d'une fonction dans la politique); **the dictator groomed his successor for power,** le dictateur a formé son successeur au pouvoir.
groomed [gruːmd] *adj* **well-g.,** (*horse*) bien entretenu; (*person*) bien soigné, soigné de sa personne.
grooming ['gruːmɪŋ] *n* **(a)** (*of horse*) entretien *m*; **(b)** (*of person*) **good g. is very important,** une bonne présentation est très importante; **(c)** *Fig* (*of candidate*) préparation *f*.
groove¹ [gruːv] *n* **(a)** (*slot*) rainure *f*; rayure *f* (*d'un canon etc*); cannelure *f* (*d'une colonne etc*); *Carp MecE* rainure; *MecE* creux *m* (*d'une vis*); (*for sliding shutter etc*) coulisse *f*, glissière *f*; cannelure (*d'une poulie*); **(sound) g.,** (*on record*) sillon *m* sonore; **thumbnail g.,** (*of penknife etc*) onglet *m*; **(b)** *F* routine *f*; **to get into a g.,** s'encroûter, devenir routinier.
groove² *vt* rainer; rayer (*un canon etc*); canneler (*une colonne*).
groovy ['gruːvɪ] *adj Old-fashioned F* formidable, épatant.
grope¹ [grəʊp] *n* **(a)** tâtonnement *m*; **(b)** *Sl* (*sexual*) pelotage *m*.
grope² **1** *vi* tâtonner; marcher à tâtons; **to g. for sth,** chercher qch à tâtons *ou* à l'aveuglette; **to g. for a word,** chercher un mot. **2** *vt* **(a)** **to g. one's way,** avancer à tâtons, se diriger en tâtonnant (**towards sth,** vers qch); **(b)** *Sl* (*sexually*) peloter (*qn*).
groper ['grəʊpər] *n* (*fish*) mérou *m*.
groping ['greʊpɪŋ] **1** *adj* tâtonnant. **2** *n* tâtonnement *m*.
grosbeak ['grəʊsbiːk] *n* (*bird*) gros-bec *m*.
grosgrain ['grəʊgreɪn] *n Tex* gros-grain *m*.
gross¹ [grəʊs] *n inv* (*quantity*) douze douzaines *fpl*, grosse *f*.
gross² *adj* **(a)** (*fat*) gras, *f* grasse, gros, *f* grosse, obèse; **(b)** (*blatant*) grossier; (*ignorance*) crasse; (*injustice*) flagrant; (*abuse*) choquant; **(c)** (*vulgar*) (*joke*) grossier; **g.**

pleasures, plaisirs grossiers; **g. feeder,** goulu, -ue; **(d)** *esp Am Sl (excessive)* **that's g.,** c'est trop; **(e)** *Com Fin (bénéfice, revenu)* brut; *Econ* **g. domestic product,** produit intérieur brut; **g. national product,** produit national brut; **g. weight,** poids brut, brut *m*; **g. margin,** marge brute; **(f)** *Nau (déplacement)* global, total; **g. (register) tonnage,** (tonnage *m* de) jauge brute, tonnage brut.

gross³ *vt Com etc (company)* gagner *(tant de francs)* brut; *(sale)* produire *(tant de francs)* brut; **they grossed £10 million,** cela leur a rapporté 10 millions de livres brut.

grossly ['grəʊslɪ] *adv* grossièrement; *(exaggerated)* énormément; **to be g. mistaken,** se tromper grossièrement.

grossness ['grəʊsnɪs] *n* **(a)** *(obesity)* obésité *f*; **(b)** *(of abuse etc)* énormité *f*; **(c)** *(vulgarity)* grossièreté *f*.

grotesque [grəʊ'tesk] **1** *adj (bizarre)* grotesque; *(absurd)* absurde. **2** *n* grotesque *m*.

grotesquely [grəʊ'tesklɪ] *adv* grotesquement.

grotto, *pl* **-oes, -os** ['grɒtəʊ, -əʊz] *n* grotte *f*.

grotty ['grɒtɪ] *n Br Sl* moche, dégueulasse.

grouch¹ [graʊtʃ] *n* **(a)** *(person)* grogneur, euse; **(b)** maussaderie *f*; **to have a g. against s.o.,** en vouloir à qn.

grouch² *vi* grogner, grommeler, ronchonner.

grouchy ['graʊtʃɪ] *adj* maussade, grognon.

ground¹ [graʊnd] *adj* **(a)** *(coffee, wheat)* moulu; **g. rice,** semoule *f* de riz; *Am* **g. beef,** bœuf hâché; **(b)** *(steel)* meulé; *(glass)* dépoli.

ground² *n* **(a)** sol *m*, terre *f*; **sitting on the g.,** assis par terre; **to pick sth up off the g.,** ramasser qch par terre; **to fall to the g.,** tomber à *ou* par terre; *(of scheme)* tomber à l'eau; **above g.,** sur terre; *Min* au jour, à la surface; **under g.,** sous terre; **at g. level,** au niveau du sol; **curtains down to the g.,** rideaux qui pendent jusqu'à terre; **burnt (down) to the g.,** brûlé de fond en comble; *F* **that suits me down to the g.** *or US* **from the g. up,** *(of arrangement etc)* ça m'arrange le mieux du monde; *(of clothing etc)* cela me va à merveille; **to cut the g. from under s.o.'s feet,** couper l'herbe sous le pied à qn; **the plane didn't get off the g.,** l'avion n'a pas décollé, l'avion n'a pas quitté le sol; **the idea never got off the g.,** l'idée n'a jamais abouti à rien; **to work oneself into the g.,** se tuer au travail; **he's driven this car into the g.,** il a usé cette voiture jusqu'à la corde; **it is excellent g. cover,** *(of plant)* c'est une excellente plante pour recouvrir le sol; **to run** *or* **go to g.,** *(of fox) & Fig* se terrer; **to run a fox to g.,** poursuivre un renard jusqu'à son terrier; *Mil* **g. attack,** attaque *f* terrestre; *Aut* **g. clearance,** hauteur *f* du châssis au-dessus du sol; *Av Astronaut* **g. control,** contrôle *m* au sol; **g. crew** *or* **personnel,** personnel *m* au sol, personnel non navigant; *Br* **g. floor,** rez-de-chaussée *m*; *Fig* **to get in on the g. floor,** *(of a project)* participer dès le début; *Mil* **g. forces,** forces *fpl* terrestres; *Met* **g. frost,** gelée blanche; *Constr* **g. plan,** plan horizontal, projection horizontale; **g. rule,** règle *f* de base; **g. staff,** *(of football ground etc)* préposés à l'entretien du terrain;

(b) *(land)* terrain *m*; **rocky** *or* **rough g.,** terrain rocheux *ou* raboteux; **open g.,** terrain découvert; **country house with extensive grounds,** château avec domaine; *Br* **football g.,** terrain de football; *Mil* **parade g.,** terrain d'exercice *ou* de manœuvre; *Fig* **to find a common g. for negotiations,** trouver un terrain d'entente en vue de négocier; **to be on sure** *or* **firm g., to be sure of one's g.,** connaître le terrain; être sûr de son fait; **to be on shaky g.,** être en terrain peu sûr; **to change** *or* **shift one's g.,** changer d'arguments; *Fig* **to break new g.,** faire une nouvelle découverte, faire une percée, faire œuvre de pionnier; **to cover a lot of g.,** *(travel a great distance)* faire beaucoup de chemin; *(travel, search over a wide area)* parcourir un champ très vaste; *(deal with many subjects)* couvrir de très nombreux domaines; **to gain g.,** gagner du terrain, progresser; *(of idea)* faire son chemin; *(of news)* se répandre; **to give** *or* **lose g.,** céder *ou* perdre du terrain; *(of troops)* se replier; **to stand** *or* **hold one's g.,** tenir bon, tenir ferme; **g. rent,** loyer *m* de la terre; *(as source of income)* rente foncière;

(c) fond *m (de la mer)*; *Nau* **to touch g.,** *(of ship)* talonner; *Fishing* **g. line,** ligne *f* de fond;

(d) *(background)* fond *m*, champ *m (d'un tableau)*; **light colour on a dark g.,** couleur claire sur un fond sombre; *Art* **the middle g.,** le second plan *(d'un tableau)*;

(e) *(reason)* raison *f*, cause *f*, motif *m*; base *f (de soupçons etc)*; **g. for complaint,** grief *m*; **what grounds have you for saying that?,** sur quoi vous fondez-vous pour affirmer cela?; **on what grounds?,** à quel titre?; **on personal grounds,** pour des raisons personnelles; *Jur* **grounds for divorce,** motifs de divorce; **grounds for appeal,** voies *fpl* de recours;

(f) *Am El* terre *f*, masse *f*; **to connect to g.,** mettre *(un pôle)* à la masse; **g. connection,** prise *f* de terre;

(g) **grounds,** *(of coffee etc)* marc *m*; *(of wine)* lie *f*;

(h) *Mus* **g. note,** son fondamental; **g. bass,** basse contrainte.

ground³ **1** *vt* **(a)** *(base)* fonder, baser, appuyer **(on, in sth,** sur qch); asseoir *(sa conviction)* **(on,** sur); **(b)** *Am El* mettre *(le courant)* à la terre *ou* à la masse; **(c)** *Nau* jeter *(un navire)* à la côte; *Av* interdire de vol *(un avion)*; *Am F* **to be grounded,** *(of teenager)* ne pas avoir le droit de sortir; *Mil* **g. arms!,** l'arme au pied!, reposez armes! **2** *vi Nau (of ship)* échouer, s'échouer **(on,** sur); *(of balloon)* atterrir.

groundbait ['graʊndbeɪt] *n Fishing* amorce *f* de fond.

grounded ['graʊndɪd] *adj* **(a)** *(based)* **well/ill g.,** *(croyance)* bien/mal fondé; **well g. rumour,** bruit consistant; **(b)** *Am El* (mis) à la terre, (mis) à la masse.

groundhog ['graʊndhɒg] *n* marmotte *f* d'Amérique; *Am* **g. day,** = jour où la marmotte d'Amérique, sortant de son terrier, indique que le printemps est arrivé.

grounding ['graʊndɪŋ] *n* **(a)** assise *f (d'un argument sur qch)*; **(b)** *Am El* mise *f (du courant)* à la terre *ou* à la masse; **(c)** *Nau* échouage *m*; *Av* interdiction *f* de vol; atterrissage *m (d'un ballon)*; **(d) to have a good g. in Latin,** avoir une connaissance solide des rudiments du latin.

groundless ['graʊndlɪs] *adj (soupçon etc)* mal fondé, sans fondement.

groundnut ['graʊndnʌt] *n* arachide *f*.

groundsel ['graʊndsəl] *n (weed)* séneçon *m*.

groundsheet ['graʊndʃiːt] *n (of tent)* tapis *m* de sol.

groundsman, *pl* **-men** ['graʊndzmən] *n Sp* préposé (à l'entretien d'un terrain de jeux).

groundspeed ['graʊndspiːd] *n Av* vitesse *f* par rapport au sol.

groundswell ['graʊndswel] *n Nau* houle *f ou* lame *f* de fond; *Fig* **g. of public opinion,** grand mouvement d'opinion publique.

ground-to-air ['graʊndtʊ'eər] *adj Mil (missile etc)* sol-air *inv*.

ground-to-ground ['graʊndtʊ'graʊnd] *adj Mil (missile etc)* sol-sol *inv*.

groundwork ['graʊndwɜːk] *n* **(a)** *(initial work)* travaux préparatifs; plan *m*, canevas *m (d'un roman etc)*; *Fig* **to do the g.,** préparer le terrain; **(b)** *Art* couleur *f* de fond *(d'un tableau etc)*.

group¹ [gruːp] *n* **(a)** *(of people, companies) & Mus* groupe *m*; *(of things)* groupe, ensemble *m*; *MecE* ensemble; **to form a g.,** se grouper; **(arranged) in groups of three,** *(objects etc)* disposés en groupes de trois; *Pol* **political g.,** groupe(ment) politique; *Mus* **pop/rock g.,** groupe pop/rock; **pressure g.,** groupe de pression; **blood g.,** groupe sanguin; **g. action/decision,** action/décision collective; **g. photograph,** photographie *f* de groupe; **g. practice,** cabinet *m* de groupe; *Psy* **g. therapy/dynamics,** psychothérapie *f*/dynamique *f* de groupe; **(b)** *Mil Av (command)* commandement aérien tactique; *(area)* zone *f* de défense aérienne; *US* escadre aérienne; **g. captain,** colonel *m*.

group² **1** *vt* grouper, disposer en groupes; combiner *(des idées)*. **2** *vi* se grouper **(round,** autour de).

grouper ['gruːpər] *n (fish)* mérou *m*.

groupie ['gruːpɪ] *n F* groupie *f*.

grouping ['gruːpɪŋ] *n* groupage *m (de colis etc)*; groupement *m (de figures etc)*; **political g.,** groupement politique.

grouse¹ [graʊs] *n inv (bird)* tétras *m*, grouse *mf*; **red g.,** lagopède *m* (rouge) d'Écosse; **black g.,** tétras lyre; **g. shooting,** chasse *f* à la grouse.

grouse² *n* **(a)** *(grumble)* grogne *f*; **he enjoys a good g.,** il aime à grogner; **(b)** *(grievance)* **to have a g. against s.o.,** avoir un grief contre qn.

grouse³ *vi* ronchonner, grogner **(at, about,** contre).

grouser ['graʊsər] *n* grognon *mf*.

grousing ['graʊsɪŋ] *n* grognonnerie *f*.

grout¹ [graʊt] *n Constr* coulis *m*; mortier clair *ou* liquide; **cement g.,** lait *m ou* laitance *f* de ciment.

grout² *vt Constr* jointoyer *(des pierres)*.

grove [grəʊv] *n* futaie *f*, bosquet *m*; **beech g.,** hêtraie *f*; **orange g.,** orangeraie *f*; **olive g.,** oliveraie *f*.

grovel ['grɒv(ə)l] *vi* **(-ll-,** *US* **-l-)** ramper; **to g. in the dirt,** se vautrer *ou* se traîner dans la boue; **to g. to** *or* **before s.o.,** ramper *ou* se prosterner devant qn.

grovelling, *US* **groveling** ['grɒv(ə)lɪŋ] **1** *adj* rampant; *Fig* servile. **2** *n* servilité *f*; prosternation *f (devant qn)*.

grow [grəʊ] *v* (*pt* **grew** [gruː]; *pp* **grown** [grəʊn]) **1** *vi* **(a)** *(of plants)* croître, pousser; *(of seeds)* germer; **to g. again,**

repousser; (*of plants, hair*) revenir; **she let her hair g. long,** elle a laissé pousser ses cheveux, elle s'est laissé pousser les cheveux; **olives do not g. in England,** l'olivier ne pousse pas en Angleterre; *F* **it doesn't g. on trees,** (*esp of money*) ça ne pousse pas sur les arbres;

(b) (*of person*) grandir; (*of company*) s'agrandir; **you've grown,** tu as grandi; **to g. tall,** devenir grand, grandir; **she has grown two inches,** elle a grandi de 5 cm;

(c) (*increase*) croître, s'accroître, grandir, s'agrandir; **the crowd grew,** la foule augmentait *ou* grossissait; **his influence grew,** son influence a grandi; **support for the strike is growing,** le soutien en faveur de la grève s'accroît; **the rumour was growing,** la rumeur grandissait; **to g. in wisdom/beauty,** croître en sagesse/beauté;

(d) (*become*) devenir; **to g. old,** devenir vieux, vieillir; **to g. younger,** rajeunir; **to g. big** *or* **bigger,** grandir; (*swell*) grossir; (*increase*) augmenter; **to g. smaller,** rapetisser; (*diminish*) diminuer; **the noise grew louder,** le bruit a augmenté; **to g. alarmed/excited,** s'alarmer/s'exciter; **to g. angry,** se fâcher; **to g. less,** diminuer; **it is growing dark,** il commence à faire sombre;

(e) (*reach point*) **I have grown to think that ...,** j'en suis venu à penser que ...; **they grew to like the house,** ils en sont venus à aimer la maison;

(f) (*to become more mature*) mûrir.

2 *vt* **(a)** cultiver (*des roses, des légumes*); planter (*des choux*); **soil that will not g. asparagus,** sol qui se refuse aux asperges;

(b) se laisser pousser (*la barbe*); **to g. one's hair (long),** se laisser pousser les cheveux, laisser pousser ses cheveux; **the stag grows fresh antlers every year,** de nouveaux andouillers poussent au cerf chaque année.

►grow apart *vi* (*of people*) devenir de plus en plus distant.

►grow in *vi* (*of hair*) repousser; (*of nail*) s'incarner.

►grow into *vi* **(a)** (*become*) devenir; **she had grown into a woman,** elle était devenue femme; **the company grew into a huge organization,** la société s'était développée jusqu'à devenir une énorme organisation; **(b)** (*become big enough for*) devenir assez grand pour porter (*un vêtement*); **he grew into his brother's shirts,** il est devenu assez grand pour porter les chemises de son frère.

►grow on *vipo F* **that picture grows on me,** plus je regarde ce tableau plus il me plaît; **this music grows on you,** plus on écoute cette musique plus on l'aime; **habit that grows on you,** habitude qui vous gagne; **it's grown on me,** je me suis mis à l'aimer petit à petit; **it will g. on you,** tu finiras par l'aimer.

►grow out *vi* **she let the dye grow out,** elle a laissé pousser ses cheveux jusqu'à ce que les traces de teinture aient disparu.

►grow out of *vipo* **(a)** (*become too large for*) devenir trop grand pour (*porter, faire qch*); **he's grown out of his shoes,** ses chaussures sont devenues trop petites pour lui; **(b)** (*become too old for*) **to g. out of (doing) sth,** passer l'âge de faire qch; **she grew out of her dolls,** elle a passé l'âge de jouer à la poupée; **it's just a phase — he'll g. out of it,** ce n'est qu'une phase — ça lui passera; **to g. out of one's friends,** ne plus avoir grand-chose en commun avec ses amis.

►grow up *vi* **(a)** (*become adult*) grandir; **I want to be a doctor when I g. up,** je veux être docteur quand je serai grand; **we didn't have television when I was growing up,** nous n'avions pas la télévision quand j'étais enfant; **(b)** (*behave like adult*) **he never grew up,** il est toujours resté enfant; **I wish you'd g. up!,** j'aimerais bien que tu mûrisses!; **(c)** (*develop*) se développer, se faire jour; **a theory has grown up that ...,** une théorie s'est fait jour selon laquelle ...; **a custom has grown up,** la coutume s'est établie; **a legend grew up around these events,** une légende s'est développée autour de ces événements.

grower ['grəʊər] *n* **(a)** (*person*) cultivateur, -trice; **rose g.,** rosiériste *mf*; **(b)** (*plant*) **fast g./slow g.,** plante *f* qui croît vite/lentement.

growing ['grəʊɪŋ] **1** *adj* **(a)** (*plant*) croissant, qui pousse; **(b)** (*child*) en cours de croissance; **(c)** (*increasing*) (*debt*) qui augmente; (*opinion*) de plus en plus répandu; (*discontent*) grandissant; **there was a g. fear that ...,** on craignait de plus en plus que ... . **2** *n* **(a)** croissance *f*; **g. pains,** douleurs *fpl* de croissance; **(b)** culture *f* (*de légumes etc*).

-growing ['grəʊɪŋ] *suff* culture *f* de ...; **wheat/potato/**
etc-**g.,** culture du blé/de la pomme de terre/*etc*; **a potato-g. region,** une région à pommes de terre.

growl¹ [graʊl] *n* grondement *m*, grognement *m*.

growl² *vi & vtr* **(a)** (*of animal*) grogner; (*of cat*) feuler; gronder (**at,** contre); **(b)** (*of person*) gronder, grogner, grommeler.

growling ['graʊlɪŋ] *n* grognement *m*, grondement *m*; (*of cat*) feulement *m*.

grown¹ [grəʊn] *adj* grand; **a g. woman,** une femme adulte; **when fully g. these animals can ...,** lorsqu'ils ont atteint l'âge adulte, ces animaux peuvent ... .

grown² *see* **GROW**.

grown-up 1 ['grəʊnʌp] *n* grand, grande personne; **the g.-ups,** les grands, les grandes personnes. **2** [grəʊn'ʌp] *adj* adulte; **you're 12 years old now, you ought to be a little more g.-up,** tu as 12 ans maintenant, tu devrais être un peu plus adulte.

growth [grəʊθ] *n* **(a)** croissance *f*; *Med* **(human) g. hormone,** hormone *f* somatotrope *ou* de croissance, somatotrophine *f*;

(b) (*increase*) accroissement *m*; croissance *f* (*des affaires*); extension *f* (*des affaires, d'une maison de commerce*); expansion *f* (*de la population*); **economic g.,** croissance *f* économique; **rate of g.,** taux *m* d'expansion *ou* de croissance; **the recent g. of small businesses,** la croissance récente des petites entreprises; **g. industry,** industrie *f* en expansion; **g. shares** *or* **stock,** actions susceptibles d'une hausse rapide, valeurs *fpl* d'avenir, valeurs de croissance;

(c) (*something that has grown*) **yearly g.,** pousse annuelle; **g. of hair,** poussée *f* de cheveux; **a week's g. on his chin,** le menton couvert d'une barbe de huit jours;

(d) *Med* tumeur *f*, excroissance *f*; *F* grosseur *f*; **benign/malignant g.,** tumeur bénigne/maligne; **I have a g. on my neck,** (*I don't know what it is*) j'ai une grosseur au cou.

groyne [grɔɪn] *n* brise-lames *m inv*.

grub¹ [grʌb] *n* **(a)** (*larva*) larve *f*; (*maggot*) asticot *m*, *F* ver (blanc); **(b)** *Sl* (*food*) boustifaille *f*; **grub's up!,** à la soupe!; **(c)** *Rugby* **g. kick,** coup *m* de pied (bas) à suivre.

grub² 1 *vt* **(a)** fouir, travailler superficiellement (*la terre*); **(b)** défricher (*un terrain*). **2** *vi* fouiller (*dans la terre*).

►grub about *vi* (*search*) fouiller, farfouiller; **I was grubbing about in the dirt looking for my key,** j'étais en train de farfouiller par terre à chercher ma clef.

►grub out *vtsep* extirper (*des racines etc*).

►grub up *vtsep* **(a)** (*dig out*) extirper (*une racine*); déraciner (*une plante*); **(b)** défricher (*un terrain*).

grubber ['grʌbər] *n Agr* (*small hoe*) hoyau *m*; (*for pulling up roots*) arrachoir *m*.

grubbiness ['grʌbɪnɪs] *n* saleté *f*, malpropreté *f*.

grubby ['grʌbɪ] *adj* sale, crasseux, malpropre.

grubstake ['grʌbsteɪk] *n Am* = provisions données à un prospecteur (*contre un pourcentage de ses profits*).

grudge¹ [grʌdʒ] *n* rancune *f*; **to bear s.o. a g., to have a g. against s.o.,** tenir rancune à qn; **she's not one to bear a g.,** elle n'est pas du genre rancunier.

grudge² *vt* **(a)** (*give unwillingly*) donner (*qch à qn*) à contrecœur *ou* à regret; **to g. s.o. the food they eat,** lésiner sur la nourriture de qn; **(b)** (*resent*) **to g. s.o. their pleasures,** voir d'un mauvais œil les plaisirs de qn; **she grudges him his success,** elle lui en veut à cause de son succès; **I don't g. spending the money but ...,** je ne répugne pas à dépenser mais ... .

grudging ['grʌdʒɪŋ] *adj* (*praise, gift*) fait *ou* donné à contrecœur.

grudgingly ['grʌdʒɪŋlɪ] *adv* (*faire qch*) à contrecœur, de mauvaise grâce.

gruel ['gru:əl] *n* gruau *m* (d'avoine); (*thin*) brouet *m*.

gruelling, *US* **grueling** ['gru:əlɪŋ] *adj* (*race*) éreintant, épuisant; (*interview*) difficile; (*match*) âprement disputé; **we had a g. time,** ç'a été tout ce qu'il y a de plus dur.

gruesome ['gru:səm] *adj* horrible, affreux, macabre; *Hum* **the g. twosome,** les deux terreurs.

gruesomely ['gru:səmlɪ] *adv* horriblement, affreusement.

gruff [grʌf] *adj* (*ton*) bourru, rébarbatif, brusque; **g. voice,** grosse voix.

gruffly ['grʌflɪ] *adv* d'un ton bourru.

gruffness ['grʌfnɪs] *n* ton bourru; brusquerie *f*.

grumble¹ ['grʌmb(ə)l] *n* grommellement *m*, grognement *m*, grondement *m*; murmure *m* (de mécontentement); **to obey without a g.,** obéir sans murmurer; *F* **to have a good old g.,** rouspéter.

grumble² 1 *vi* grommeler, grogner, *F* rouspéter; **(we) mustn't g.,** il ne faut pas se plaindre; **to g. about the food,** se plaindre de la nourriture, trouver à redire à la nourriture; **to g. at s.o.,** grommeler *ou* rouspéter contre qn.

2 *vt* **'I do all the work here', he grumbled,** 'c'est moi qui fait tout ici', a-t-il grommelé.

grumbler ['grʌmblər] *n* **(a)** grognon *m*, grommeleur, -euse, *F* rouspéteur, -euse; **(b)** (*malcontent*) mécontent, -ente.

grumbling ['grʌmblɪŋ] **1** *adj* grognon; **g. appendix,** appendicite *f* chronique. **2** *n* **(a)** *F* rouspétance *f*; **(b)** (*discontent*) mécontentement *m*.

grummet ['grʌmɪt] *n* = **GROMMET**.

grump [grʌmp] *n* **(a)** grincheux, -euse; **(b) to have the grumps,** être grincheux.

grumpily ['grʌmpɪlɪ] *adv* maussadement; (*to say, look at*) d'un ton *ou* d'un air maussade.

grumpiness ['grʌmpɪnɪs] *n* mauvaise humeur, maussaderie *f*.

grumpy ['grʌmpɪ] *adj* maussade, renfrogné; **a g. old man,** un vieux grincheux.

grungy ['grʌndʒɪ] *adj esp Am F* nul; (*ugly*) moche; (*mood*) désagréable.

grunt¹ [grʌnt] *n* grognement *m* (*de porc, de qn*); **to give a g.,** pousser *ou* faire entendre un grognement.

grunt² **1** *vi* (*of pig, person*) grogner, pousser un grognement. **2** *vt* **to g. an answer,** grogner une réponse.

grunt³ *n US Mil Sl* (*private*) bidasse *m*.

grunting ['grʌntɪŋ] *n* grognement(s) *m(pl)*.

gruntled ['grʌnt(ə)ld] *adj Br Hum F* content.

GST [dʒiːesˈtiː] *n Can Fin* (*abbr* **goods and services tax**) TPS *f* (*taxe sur les produits et services*).

gt (*abbr* **great**) grand.

Guadeloupe [gwɑːdəˈluːp] *n* Guadeloupe *f*.

guano ['gwɑːnəʊ] *n* guano *m*.

guarantee¹ [gærənˈtiː] *n* **(a)** (*document*) garantie *f* (**against,** contre); **a clock with a 12-month g.,** une horloge garantie 12 mois; **this camera's still got two months' g. left,** il y a encore deux mois de garantie sur cet appareil-photo; **it's still under g.,** c'est encore sous garantie; **(b)** (*security*) garantie *f*, caution *f*, gage *m*; **to leave sth as a g.,** laisser qch en gage; **(c)** (*person*) (*guarantor*) garant, -ante, caution *f*.

guarantee² *vt* garantir, cautionner (*qn, qch*); se porter garant *ou* caution pour (*qn, qch*); garantir (*une dette*); **watch guaranteed for two years,** montre garantie deux ans; **it's guaranteed not to rust,** c'est garanti anti-rouille; **I can't g. that she'll come,** je ne garantis pas qu'elle viendra; **to g. s.o. against loss,** garantir qn contre les pertes.

guaranteed [gærənˈtiːd] *adj* **a g. success,** un succès garanti.

guarantor [gærənˈtɔːr] *n* garant, -ante, caution *f*; **to stand as g. for s.o.,** appuyer qn de sa garantie.

guaranty ['gærəntɪ] *n* = **GUARANTEE¹(a),(b)**.

guard¹ [gɑːd] *n* **(a)** (*readiness*) garde *f*; **to be on one's g.,** être *ou* se tenir sur ses gardes; **to be on one's g. against sth,** être sur ses gardes contre qch; **to put s.o. on his g.,** mettre qn en garde; **to be caught off one's g.,** être pris au dépourvu; *Fencing Boxing* **on g.!,** en garde!;

(b) (*of sentry etc*) **to be on g. (duty),** être en *ou* de faction, être de garde; **to go on g., to mount g.,** monter la garde; **to come off g.,** descendre de garde; **to keep g.,** monter la garde, être de garde; **to keep a prisoner under g.,** garder un prisonnier à vue; **he was marched off under g.,** il fut emmené sous escorte; **g. dog,** chien *m* de garde;

(c) (*no pl*) *Mil* garde *f*; **main g.,** gros *m* d'avant-garde; **mounting of the g.,** parade *f*; **one of the old g.,** un vieux de la vieille; **g. of honour,** garde d'honneur; **to form a g. of honour,** faire la haie; **to set a g. on a bridge,** faire surveiller un pont;

(d) (*person*) *Mil* soldat *m* de garde; *Br Rail* chef *m* de train; *US* **prison g.,** gardien *m* de prison; *Br Mil* **the Guards,** les Gardes *mpl* du corps; *Br Mil* **a Guards officer,** un officier de la garde; *Br Rail* **g.'s van,** wagon *m* du chef de train; (*for luggage etc*) fourgon *m*;

(e) (*device*) dispositif protecteur; protecteur *m* (*d'une machine*); carter *m* (*d'engrenages etc*); garde-fou *m*, *pl* garde-fous (*de passerelle etc*); **fire g.,** garde-feu *m inv*;

(f) *Fencing* garde *f* (*d'un fleuret*).

guard² *vt* **(a)** garder (*une entrée*); **to g. s.o. from** *or* **against a danger,** garder *ou* protéger qn d'un danger; **(b)** surveiller (*sa langue*); mesurer (*ses paroles*); **(c)** *Tech* protéger (*un engrenage etc*); mettre un carter à (*un mécanisme*).

▶**guard against** *vipo* (*be careful to avoid*) se garder de (*qch*), parer à (*qch*); **to g. against colds,** se protéger contre les rhumes; **to g. against an error,** se méfier d'une erreur.

guarded ['gɑːdɪd] *adj* **(a)** (*speech*) prudent, circonspect; (*reply*) qui n'engage à rien; **(b)** (*mechanism*) protégé; **(c)** (*prisoner*) gardé à vue; (*building*) gardé, surveillé.

guardedly ['gɑːdɪdlɪ] *adv* avec circonspection, avec précaution.

guardhouse ['gɑːdhaʊs] *n* corps-de-garde *m inv*.

guardian ['gɑːdɪən] *n* **(a)** gardien, -ienne; **(b)** *Jur* tuteur, -trice (*de mineur*); conseil *m* judiciaire (*d'une personne prodigue*); **(c) g. angel,** ange gardien.

guardianship ['gɑːdɪənʃɪp] *n* **(a)** garde *f*; **(b)** *Jur* gestion *f* tutélaire; tutelle *f*.

guarding ['gɑːdɪŋ] *n* garde *f* (*de qn, qch*).

guardrail ['gɑːdreɪl] *n* garde-corps *m inv*, garde-fou *m*, *pl* garde-fous; *Rail* contre-rail *m*, *pl* contre-rails; (*balustrade*) balustrade *f*.

guardroom ['gɑːdruːm] *n Mil* **(a)** (*for guards*) corps-de-garde *m inv*; **(b)** (*for prisoners*) salle *f ou* poste *m* de police.

guardsman, *pl* **-men** ['gɑːdzmən] *n Mil* **(a)** *Br* (*soldier*) soldat *m* de la Garde; (*officer*) officier *m* de la Garde; **(b)** *US* **(National) G.,** soldat *m* de la Garde Nationale.

Guatemala [gwætɪˈmɑːlə] *n* Guatemala *m*.

Guatemalan [gwætɪˈmɑːlən] **1** *adj* guatémaltèque. **2** *n* Guatémaltèque *mf*.

guava ['gwɑːvə] *n* **(a)** (*fruit*) goyave *f*; **(b) g. (tree),** goyavier *m*.

gubernatorial [guːbənəˈtɔːrɪəl] *adj esp US* (*election, residence*) du gouverneur.

gudgeon¹ ['gʌdʒən] *n* (*fish*) goujon *m*.

gudgeon² *n MecE* goujon *m*, tourillon *m*, axe *m*; **g. pin,** *Br* (*in engine*) axe de pied de bielle; (*in machine*) tourillon de la crosse.

guelder-rose ['geldəˈrəʊz] *n* (*shrub*) boule-de-neige *f*.

Guernsey ['gɜːnzɪ] *n* **(a)** *Geog* Guernesey; **(b)** (*sweater*) tricot *m*; jersey *m*; **(c)** (*cow*) vache *f* de Guernesey.

guer(r)illa [gəˈrɪlə] *n Mil* guérillero *m*; **troop** *or* **band of guer(r)illas,** guérilla *f*; **g. leader,** dirigeant *m* de la guérilla; **g. warfare,** guérilla.

guess¹ [ges] *n* conjecture *f*, estimation *f*; **to have** *or* **make a g.,** tâcher de deviner; (*conjecture*) hasarder une conjecture; **you've made a lucky g.,** vous êtes bien tombé; **it was just a lucky g.,** c'était un coup de chance; **your g. is as good as mine,** j'en sais autant que toi; **it's anybody's g.,** qui sait?, Dieu seul le sait; **I give you three guesses,** tu devines?; **at a g.,** au jugé.

guess² **1** *vt* **(a)** deviner (*qch*); **to g. the length of sth,** estimer la longueur de qch; **g. who did it!,** devinez qui l'a fait!; **I guessed him to be twenty-five,** je lui ai donné vingt-cinq ans; **to g. sth from s.o.'s manner,** deviner qch d'après l'attitude de qn; **g. what! I saw Ian yesterday,** tu ne sais pas quoi? j'ai vu Ian hier; **you've guessed it!,** vous l'avez deviné!; **(b)** *esp Am* (*think*) croire, penser; **I g. you're right,** je suppose que vous avez raison. **2** *vi* **(a)** deviner; **to g. right/wrong,** bien/mal deviner; **you've guessed right,** vous l'avez deviné; **they kept the press guessing as to the date of the wedding,** ils ont laissé la presse dans l'ignorance de la date du mariage; **to g. at sth,** (tâcher de) deviner qch; **we could only g. at their plans,** nous ne pouvions qu'essayer de deviner leurs intentions; **I couldn't begin to g.,** je n'en ai pas la moindre idée; **(b)** *esp Am* **I g.,** à ce que je pense.

guessing ['gesɪŋ] *n* estimation *f*; **g. games,** devinettes *fpl*.

guesstimate¹ ['gestɪmɪt] *n* calcul *m* au pif.

guesstimate² ['gestɪmeɪt] **1** *vt* calculer (*qch*) au pif. **2** *vi* faire un calcul au pif.

guesswork ['geswɜːk] *n* estimation *f*, conjecture *f*; **it's pure g.,** c'est de la pure conjecture; **by g.,** au jugé; **by sheer g.,** à vue de nez.

guest¹ [gest] *n* **(a)** invité, -ée; (*at meal*) convive *mf*; **be my g.!,** (*also Iron*) faites comme chez vous!; **g. artist,** artiste invité(e); **g. room,** chambre *f* d'ami(s); **g. speaker,** conférencier invité; *Cin TV* **g. star,** invité-vedette, invitée-vedette; **(b)** (*at hotel*) client; **the landlord and his guests,** l'hôtelier et ses hôtes; **paying g.,** pensionnaire *mf*; **g. book,** registre *m*.

guest² *vi TV Rad Mus* **to g. on s.o.'s show,** faire une apparition à une émission; **another guitarist guested on one of the numbers,** un autre guitariste a participé à l'un des morceaux.

guesthouse ['gesthaʊs] *n* **(a)** (*hotel*) pension *f* de famille; **(b)** (*of monastery etc*) hôtellerie *f*.

guff [gʌf] *n F* bêtises *fpl*, âneries *fpl*.

guffaw¹ [gʌˈfɔː] *n* gros rire (bruyant).

guffaw² *vi* s'esclaffer.

Guiana [gaɪˈɑːnə] *n Hist* Guyane *f*.

guidance ['gaɪdəns] *n* **(a)** direction *f*, conduite *f*; **under the g. of ...,** sous la direction de ...; **sent for your g.,** envoyé à titre d'indication; *Sch* **vocational g.,** orientation professionnelle; **(b)** (*of missile*) guidage *m*; **radio g.,** radioguidage *m*.

guide[1] [gaɪd] *n* **(a)** (*person*) guide *m*; **museum g.,** guide de musée; **to take sth as a g.,** prendre qch pour règle; **(girl) g.,** guide *f*, éclaireuse *f*; *Cathol* guide *f*; **g. dog,** chien *m* d'aveugle; **(b)** (*book*) guide *m*; livret *m* (*de musée*); indicateur *m* (*des chemins de fer*); **g. to Switzerland,** guide de la Suisse; **the book is a useful g. to the world of finance,** le livre constitue un guide utile du monde de la finance; **(c)** (*indication*) indication *f*, exemple *m*; **as a g.,** à titre indicatif; **(d)** *MecE etc* guide *m* (*d'ascenseur etc*); **g. rope,** câble *m* de guidage; *Av* guiderope *m*; *Rail* **g. rail,** contre-rail *m*, *pl* contre-rails; **g. (card),** (*in card index*) intercalaire *m*.

guide[2] *vt* guider, conduire, diriger; **to g. a child's first steps,** guider les premiers pas d'un enfant; **I will be guided by your advice,** je suivrai vos conseils.

guidebook ['gaɪdbʊk] *n* guide *m*.

guided ['gaɪdɪd] *adj* **(a)** (*tour etc*) guidé; sous la conduite d'un guide; **(b)** *Mil* (*missile*) guidé; **radio-g.,** radioguidé.

guideline ['gaɪdlaɪn] *n* **(a)** *Pol etc* (*indication*) directive *f*; **as a general g.,** comme indication générale; **there are clear guidelines for** *or* **on the use of firearms,** il y a des directives claires concernant l'utilisation d'armes à feu; **(b)** (*in printing*) ligne *f* pour guider la main (*en écrivant*).

guidepost ['gaɪdpəʊst] *n* poteau indicateur.

guiding ['gaɪdɪŋ] *adj* qui sert de guide; (*principe*) directeur; **the g. principles of his life,** les principes sur lesquels se guide sa vie; **g. star,** guide *m*.

guild [gɪld] *n* **(a)** *Hist* corporation *f*; **merchant g.,** guilde *f* de commerçants; **(b)** (*organization*) association *f*, confrérie *f*; **church g.,** cercle paroissial.

guilder ['gɪldər] *n* florin *m*.

guildhall ['gɪldhɔːl] *n* **(a)** (*of a guild*) salle *f* de réunion d'une guilde; **(b)** (*town hall*) hôtel *m* de ville.

guile [gaɪl] *n* artifice *m*, ruse *f*, astuce *f*; **she is without g.,** elle est sans artifice.

guileless ['gaɪllɪs] *adj* **(a)** (*sincere*) franc, *f* franche, sincère; **(b)** (*naive*) candide, naïf.

guillemot ['gɪlɪmɒt] *n* (*bird*) guillemot *m*.

guillotine[1] ['gɪlətiːn] *n* **(a)** (*for execution*) guillotine *f*; **to go to the g.,** aller à la guillotine, être mené à la guillotine; **(b)** (*for cutting paper*) guillotine *f*, massicot *m*; **(c)** *Parl* clôture *f* par tranches.

guillotine[2] *vt* **(a)** (*execute*) guillotiner (*qn*); **(b)** (*cut*) guillotiner, massicoter (*du papier etc*); **(c)** *Parl* appliquer la clôture par tranches à (*un projet de loi*).

guilt [gɪlt] *n* **(a)** culpabilité *f* (**for sth,** pour qch); **the g. does not lie with him alone,** il n'y a pas que lui de coupable; **(b)** (*feeling*) culpabilité *f*; **to feel g.,** ressentir de la culpabilité; **she felt no g.,** elle n'a ressenti aucune culpabilité; **feelings of g.,** sentiments *mpl* de culpabilité; **g. complex,** complexe *m* de culpabilité.

guiltily ['gɪltɪlɪ] *adv* coupablement; d'un air coupable; **she looked away g.,** elle a détourné les yeux d'un air coupable.

guiltless ['gɪltlɪs] *adj* innocent (**of sth,** de qch).

guilty ['gɪltɪ] *adj* **(a)** coupable (**of,** de); **g. person,** coupable *mf*; **he is not the only g. party,** il n'y a pas que lui de coupable; *Jur* **to plead g./not g.,** plaider coupable/non coupable; **to find s.o. g./not g.,** déclarer qn coupable/innocent; **verdict of g./not g.,** verdict *m* de culpabilité/d'acquittement; **(b)** (*feeling guilt*) qui se sent coupable; **I feel g. about not telling them,** je me sens coupable de ne pas le leur avoir dit; **you're making me feel g.,** tu me fais me sentir coupable; **she looked very g.,** elle avait l'air très coupable; **g. conscience,** mauvaise conscience; (*more serious*) conscience chargée; **(c)** (*act*) coupable.

guinea ['gɪnɪ] *n* (*bird*) pintade *f*; *Culin* pintadon *m*.

Guinea ['gɪnɪ] *n* **(a)** Guinée *f*; **g. cock,** pintade *f* mâle; **g. hen,** pintade; **g. pig,** cobaye *m*, cochon *m* d'Inde; *Fig* **to be a g. pig,** servir de cobaye; **(b)** *Br Arch* **g.,** (pièce *f* d'or d'une) guinée *f* (= 21 shillings).

guise [gaɪz] *n* dehors *m*, apparence *f*; **under** *or* **in the g. of friendship,** sous l'apparence *ou* sous le masque de l'amitié; **under the g. of religion,** sous le manteau *ou* le couvert de la religion.

guitar [gɪ'tɑːr, *Am also* 'gɪtɑːr] *n Mus* guitare *f*; **to play the g.,** jouer de la guitare; **(electric) g.,** guitare électrique; **g. player,** guitariste *mf*; **bass g.,** basse *f*.

guitarist [gɪ'tɑːrɪst] *n Mus* guitariste *mf*.

gulch [gʌltʃ] *n Am* ravin *m*.

gulf [gʌlf] *n* **(a)** *Geog* golfe *m*; **the G. Stream,** le Gulf-Stream; **the G.,** le Golf; **(b)** (*abyss*) gouffre *m*, abîme *m*; **there is a g. between the two ideologies,** un abîme sépare les deux idéologies.

gull[1] [gʌl] *n* (*bird*) mouette *f*; (*bigger*) goéland *m*; **black-headed g.,** mouette rieuse; **herring g.,** goéland argenté; *Aut* **g. wing doors,** portes qui se soulèvent.

gull[2] *n Arch F* gogo *m*, jobard *m*.

gull[3] *vt Arch F* duper, rouler (*qn*).

gullet ['gʌlɪt] *n Anat* œsophage *m*; *F* gosier *m*.

gulley ['gʌlɪ] *n & vi* = **GULLY**[1,2].

gullibility [gʌlɪ'bɪlɪtɪ] *n* crédulité *f*.

gullible ['gʌlɪb(ə)l] *adj* facile à duper, crédule.

gully ['gʌlɪ] *n Geol* petit ravin.

gulp[1] [gʌlp] *n* **(a)** (*act of gulping*) coup *m* de gosier; **to swallow sth at one g.,** avaler qch d'un coup; **he confessed with a g. that ...,** il admit, la gorge serrée, que ...; **(b)** (*mouthful*) grosse bouchée.

gulp[2] **1** *vt* **(a)** (*swallow*) = **GULP DOWN**; **(b)** (*say nervously, with shock*) dire (*qch*) la gorge serrée *ou* nouée. **2** *vi* essayer d'avaler; **he gulped,** sa gorge se serra.

▶**gulp back** *vtsep* **to g. back one's tears,** avaler *ou* refouler ses larmes.

▶**gulp down** *vtsep* (*swallow*) avaler (*qch*) à grosses bouchées; ingurgiter (*une huître*); **he gulped it down,** il n'en fit qu'une bouchée; (*drinking*) il n'en fit qu'une gorgée.

gum[1] [gʌm] *n* **(a)** gomme *f*; (*adhesive*) gomme, colle *f*; **(b) g. arabic,** gomme *f* arabique; **(c) (chewing) g.,** chewing-gum *m*; **bubble g.,** chewing-gum qui fait des bulles; **(wine/fruit/etc) g.,** boule *f* de gomme; **(d)** (*disease of fruit trees*) gomme *f*; **(e) g. tree,** gommier *m*; *F* **to be up a g. tree,** être dans le pétrin.

gum[2] *v* (-mm-) *vt* **(a)** (*coat with adhesive*) gommer, encoller (*le papier, la toile*); **(b)** (*stick with adhesive*) coller (*une page dans un livre etc*); **to g. two pages together,** réunir deux feuilles avec de la colle; **(c)** = **GUM UP 1**.

gum[3] *n Anat* gencive *f*; **g. disease,** maladie *f* des gencives.

gum[4] *int Old-fashioned Br F* **by g.!,** fichtre!, mazette!

▶**gum up** *vtsep* gommer (*un piston*); encrasser (*une lime*); *F* **to g. up the works,** mettre des bâtons dans les roues.

gumboil ['gʌmbɔɪl] *n* abcès *m* à la gencive; *Med* parulie *f*.

gumboot ['gʌmbuːt] *n* botte *f* de caoutchouc.

gumdrop ['gʌmdrɒp] *n* (*sweet*) boule *f* de gomme.

gummed [gʌmd] *adj* (*label*) gommé.

gummed up ['gʌm'dʌp] *adj* (*piston*) gommé; *F* (*projet*) qui ne marche plus.

gummy ['gʌmɪ] *adj* gommeux; (*sticky*) gluant.

gumption ['gʌmʃən, gʌmp-] *n F* jugeotte *f*, sens *m* pratique; **she's got plenty of g.,** c'est une débrouillarde.

gumshield ['gʌmʃiːld] *n Boxing* protège-dents *m inv*.

gumshoe ['gʌmʃuː] *n* **(a)** (*rubber overshoe*) caoutchouc *m*; **(b)** *Am F* détective privé.

gun[1] [gʌn] *n* **(a)** *Mil* (*artillery*) canon *m*, bouche *f* à feu, pièce *f* (d'artillerie); **the guns,** l'artillerie *f*, le canon; **the big guns,** la grosse artillerie, les grosses pièces; **do you hear the guns?,** entendez-vous le canon?; *Br Nau* **g. room,** poste *m* des aspirants; **21-g. salute,** salve de 21 coups de canon; **g. carriage,** affût *m* de canon; (*at military funeral*) prolonge *f* d'artillerie; *F* **big g.,** (*important person*) gros manitou, grosse légume; **it was blowing great guns,** il faisait un vent à décorner les bœufs; **to be going great guns,** (*of work, sale*) marcher très fort; *Am F* **son of a g.,** coquin *m*;

(b) (*rifle*) fusil *m*; (*handgun*) revolver *m*, pistolet *m*; **air g.,** fusil *ou* carabine *f* à air comprimé; **machine g.,** mitrailleuse *f*; **harpoon g.,** fusil harpon; *Fig* **to stick to one's guns,** ne pas en démordre; **a party of six guns,** (*hunters*) une bande de six chasseurs; **g. barrel,** canon *m* de fusil; **g. dog,** chien *m* d'arrêt; **g. room,** salle *f* aux fusils; *F* **to jump the g.,** agir prématurément; **hired g.,** (*in Westerns etc*) mercenaire *m*;

(c) *Tech etc* **(grease) g.,** seringue *f*, injecteur *m* (à graisse); **(spray) g.,** pistolet *m* (à peinture); *Electron* **(electron) g.,** canon *m* à électrons.

gun[2] *vt* (-nn-) *Aut* (faire) emballer (*son moteur*).

▶**gun down** *vtsep* (*kill*) abattre; **he was gunned down in cold blood,** il a été abattu de sang froid.

▶**gun for** *vipo* **(a)** (*want to reprimand, punish*) en avoir après qn; **he's gunning for us,** c'est à nous qu'il en veut; **(b)** (*try to get*) pourchasser; **he's gunning for the heavyweight title,** il a le titre poids lourd en vue; **(c)** (*in hunting*) **to g. for game,** chasser le gibier au tir.

gunboat ['gʌnbəʊt] *n* aviso-torpilleur *m*, *pl* avisos-torpilleurs.

guncotton ['gʌnkɒt(ə)n] *n* fulmicoton *m*.

gundeck ['gʌndek] *n Nau* batterie *f*.

gunfight ['gʌnfaɪt] *n* combat *m* avec des armes à feu.

gunfighter ['gʌnfaɪtər] *n* bandit armé.

gunfire ['gʌnfaɪər] *n Mil* (*of artillery*) canonnade *f*, feu *m* (des pièces); (*of smaller guns*) coups *mpl* de feu; **we heard g.,** nous avons entendu des coups de feu.
gunge [gʌndʒ] , **gunk** [gʌŋk] *n* (*no pl*) *F* magma *m*.
gung-ho [gʌŋhəʊ] *adj* **to be g.-ho about sth,** être trop enthousiaste à l'égard de qch.
gunmaker ['gʌnmeɪkər] *n* armurier *m*.
gunman, *pl* **-men** ['gʌnmən] *n* **(a)** (*terrorist*) terroriste *m*; (*robber*) voleur armé, bandit *m*; **(b)** *US* = **GUNMAKER**.
gunmetal ['gʌnmet(ə)l] *n* **(a)** (*bronze*) bronze *m* à canon; **(b)** *Com F* métal oxydé; **(c) g. (grey),** gris acier (foncé).
gunnel ['gʌn(ə)l] *n* = **GUNWALE**.
gunner ['gʌnər] *n* artilleur *m*; *Nau* (*warrant officer*) canonnier *m*; **(machine) g.,** mitrailleur *m*.
gunnery ['gʌnərɪ] *n* artillerie *f*.
gunny ['gʌnɪ] *n esp US* **(a)** (*material*) toile *f* de jute; **(b) g. (sack),** sac *m* en jute.
gunplay ['gʌnpleɪ] *n esp US* coups *mpl* de revolver.
gunpoint ['gʌnpɔɪnt] *n* **at g.,** sous la menace d'un pistolet *ou* d'un fusil; **to hold s.o. at g.,** menacer qn d'un pistolet *ou* d'un fusil.
gunport ['gʌnpɔːt] *n Nau* sabord *m* de batterie.
gunpowder ['gʌnpaʊdər] *n* poudre *f* (à canon); *Br Hist* **the G. Plot,** la Conspiration des Poudres.
gunrunner ['gʌnrʌnər] *n* contrebandier *m* d'armes.
gunrunning ['gʌnrʌnɪŋ] *n* contrebande *f* d'armes.
gunship ['gʌnʃɪp] *n* **(helicopter) g.,** hélicoptère *m* de combat.
gunshot ['gʌnʃɒt] *n* coup *m* de feu; (*of rifle*) coup de fusil; (*of cannon*) coup de canon; **g. wound,** blessure *f* par balle; **to receive a g. wound,** recevoir un coup de feu; **within/out of g.,** à/hors de portée de fusil.
gun-shy ['gʌnʃaɪ] *adj* (*dog*) qui a peur des coups de feu.
gunslinger ['gʌnslɪŋər] *n US F* bandit armé.
gunsmith ['gʌnsmɪθ] *n* armurier *m*; **g.'s shop,** armurerie *f*.
gunstock ['gʌnstɒk] *n* fût *m* (de fusil).
gunwale ['gʌn(ə)l] *n Nau* plat-bord *m*, *pl* plats-bords; **gunwales,** fargues *fpl* (*de canot*).
guppy ['gʌpɪ] *n* (*fish*) guppy *m*.
gurgle¹ ['gɜːg(ə)l] *n* (*of liquid*) glouglou *m*; (*of falling water*) gargouillis *m*; (*of stream*) murmure *m*; *Fig* (*of person*) gloussement *m*, roucoulement *m*; *Fig* **gurgles of laughter,** des roucoulements de rire.
gurgle² **1** *vi* (*of liquid*) glouglouter, faire glouglou (*en sortant de la bouteille*); (*of stream*) murmurer, gargouiller; (*of person*) glousser, roucouler; **he gurgled with laughter,** il a gloussé de rire. **2** *vt* **she gurgled her delight,** elle a roucoulé de plaisir.
gurgling ['gɜːg(ə)lɪŋ] **1** *adj* (*liquid in bottle*) glougloutant, qui fait glouglou; (*stream*) murmurant; **a g. laugh,** un gloussement de rire. **2** *n* (*of liquid*) glouglou *m*; (*of stream*) gargouillement *m*; (*of person*) roucoulement *m*.
Gurkha ['gɜːkə] *n* Go(u)rkha *m*; *Br Mil* **G. regiment,** régiment *m* de Go(u)rkhas.
gurnard ['gɜːnəd] , **gurnet** ['gɜːnɪt] *n* (*fish*) grondin *m*.
guru ['gʊruː] *n Rel & Fig* gourou *m*.
gush¹ [gʌʃ] *n* **(a)** jaillissement *m* (*d'une source*); effusion *f* (*de larmes*); bouillonnement *m* (*d'un torrent*); **(b)** jet *m*, flot *m* (*de sang*); **(c)** épanchement *m* de sentiments, débordement sentimental.
gush² **1** *vi* **(a)** (*spurt, pour*) jaillir, couler à flots; (*of torrent*) bouillonner; **tears gushed from her eyes,** des larmes jaillirent de ses yeux; **(b)** (*talk effusively*) faire de longs discours sentimentaux, *F* la faire au sentiment; **she gushed over their baby,** elle s'attendrissait sur leur bébé. **2** *vt* **to g. water/oil,** lancer des jets d'eau/un jet de pétrole.
►gush forth, gush out *vi* = **GUSH² 1 (a)**.
gusher ['gʌʃər] *n* **(a)** (*person*) personne exubérante; **(b)** *Petr* source (de pétrole) jaillissante, puits jaillissant.
gushing ['gʌʃɪŋ] *adj* **(a)** (*water*) jaillissant, vif; (*torrent*) bouillonnant; **(b)** (*person*) (trop) exubérant; (*compliments*) chaleureux; **she's rather g.,** elle se jette à votre tête.
gushy ['gʌʃɪ] *adj* = **GUSHING (b)**.
gusset ['gʌsɪt] *n* pièce *f* triangulaire (*d'étoffe etc*); *Sewing* soufflet *m*; gousset *m* (*de manche etc*).
gust¹ [gʌst] *n* **(a) g. (of wind),** coup *m* de vent, rafale *f*, bourrasque *f*, *Nau* grain *m*; **g. of rain,** ondée *f*, giboulée *f*; **(b)** bouffée *f* (*de fumée, de colère etc*).
gust² *vi* (*of wind*) souffler par rafales.
gusto ['gʌstəʊ] *n* délectation *f*, goût *m*; **to eat sth with g.,** manger qch en savourant; *F* **to do sth with g.,** faire qch avec plaisir.
gusty ['gʌstɪ] *adj* (*weather, place*) venteux; (*wind*) soufflant en rafales; (*day*) de grand vent.
gut¹ [gʌt] *n* **(a)** *Anat* (*of animal*) boyau *m*; (*of human*) intestin *m*; **small g.,** intestin grêle; *Sl* **to sweat** *or* **work one's guts out,** se casser les reins; *F* **she hates my guts,** elle ne peut pas me saquer, elle ne peut pas me voir en peinture; **I'll have his guts for garters,** je vais le réduire en chair à pâté; *Fig* **it's just a g. feeling,** c'est une intuition; *Fig* **g. reaction,** réaction viscérale;
(b) *F* (*courage*) **to have guts,** avoir du cran, avoir du cœur au ventre; **I didn't have the guts to tell them,** je n'ai pas eu le courage de le leur dire; **he hasn't any guts,** il manque de cran;
(c) *Sl* (*stomach*) bide *m*; **pull in your g.,** rentre ton bide; **a beer g.,** = estomac distendu par la consommation excessive de bière; **g. ache,** mal *m* au bide;
(d) (*for violins etc*) corde *f* de boyau.
gut² *vt* **(-tt-)** **(a)** étriper (*un animal*); vider (*un poisson, une volaille*); **(b)** (*of fire*) ne laisser que les quatre murs de (*une maison*).
gutless ['gʌtlɪs] *adj Sl* qui manque de cran.
gutsy ['gʌtsɪ] *adj Sl* **(a)** (*brave*) qui a du cran; (*prose*) vigoureux; **(b)** (*greedy*) goinfre.
gutter¹ ['gʌtər] *n* **(a)** (*in street*) ruisseau *m* (de rue), caniveau *m*; **open g.,** cassis *m*; *Fig* **to end up in the g.,** finir sous les ponts; **g. language,** langage *m* des rues; *Journ F* **g. press,** presse *f* de bas étage; **(b)** *Constr* gouttière *f*, chéneau *m* (de toit); **g. pipe,** tuyau *m* de descente; **g. tile,** tuile creuse; **(c)** *Typ* les petits fonds (*de deux pages en vis-à-vis*).
gutter² *vi* (*of candle*) couler.
guttering ['gʌtərɪŋ] *n* **(a)** *Constr* (*on building*) gouttières *fpl*; **(b)** (*of candle*) coulage *m*.
guttersnipe ['gʌtəsnaɪp] *n* gamin, -ine des rues.
guttural ['gʌtərəl] **1** *adj* guttural, -aux. **2** *n Ling* gutturale *f*.
guv [gʌv] , **guv'nor** ['gʌvnər] *n Br Sl* **the g.,** (*boss*) le patron, le singe; (*father*) le vieux, le paternel; **all right, g.,** d'accord, chef.
guy¹ [gaɪ] *n* **(a)** *F* (*man*) type *m*, individu *m*; **who's that g.?,** qu'est-ce que c'est que ce type-là?; **a great g.,** un chic type; **a tough g.,** un dur; **come on, you guys,** allez les gars *ou* les mecs; *esp Am* (*people*) allez tout le monde; *esp Am* **do you guys want to go out?,** vous voulez sortir?; *esp Am* **hi guys!,** salut les copains!; **(b)** *Br* = effigie burlesque de Guy Fawkes, le chef de la Conspiration des Poudres (1605); *Fig F* (*person*) épouvantail *m*.
guy² *vt* **(guyed; guying)** se moquer de (*qn*), *F* charrier (*qn*), mettre (*qn*) en boîte; *Th* charger (*un rôle*).
guy³ *n* **g. (rope),** corde *f* de tente.
Guyana [gaɪ'ænə] *n* Guyane *f*.
Guyanese [gaɪə'niːz] **1** *adj* guyanais. **2** *n* Guyanais, -aise.
guzzle ['gʌz(ə)l] *F* **1** *vt* bâfrer, bouffer (*la nourriture*); lamper (*la boisson*); *esp Am* **to g. gas,** (*of car*) bouffer de l'essence. **2** *vi* (*of eater*) s'empiffrer, goinfrer; (*of drinker*) boire avidement.
guzzler ['gʌzlər] *n F* (*of food*) bâfreur, -euse, goinfre *m*; (*of drink*) buveur, -euse, pochard, -arde.
gym [dʒɪm] *n F* **(a)** = **GYMNASIUM**; **(b)** = **GYMNASTICS**; **g. shoes,** (chaussures *fpl* de) tennis *mpl*.
gymkhana [dʒɪm'kɑːnə] *n* gymkhana *m* équestre; *esp Am* gymkhana automobile.
gymnasium, *pl* **-iums, -ia** [dʒɪm'neɪzɪəm, -ɪəmz, -ɪə] *n Sp* gymnase *m*.
gymnast ['dʒɪmnæst] *n* gymnaste *mf*.
gymnastic [dʒɪm'næstɪk] *adj* gymnastique.
gymnastics [dʒɪm'næstɪks] *npl* (*usu with sing verb*) gymnastique *f*; **to do g.,** faire de la gymnastique; **mental g.,** gymnastique intellectuelle; **g. teacher,** professeur *m* de gymnastique.
gymslip ['dʒɪmslɪp] *n esp Br Sch* tunique *f*.
gynaecologic(al), *US* **gynecologic(al)** [gaɪnɪkɒ'lɒdʒɪk, -ɪk(ə)l] *adj* gynécologique.
gynaecologist, *US* **gynecologist** [gaɪnɪ'kɒlədʒɪst] *n* gynécologue *mf*.
gynaecology, *US* **gynecology** [gaɪnɪ'kɒlədʒɪ] *n* gynécologie *f*.
gyp [dʒɪp] *n Br F* **to give s.o. g.,** (*of aching tooth etc*) faire souffrir qn.
gypsum ['dʒɪpsəm] *n Miner* gypse *m*.
gypsy ['dʒɪpsɪ] *n* = **GIPSY**.
gyrate [dʒaɪ'reɪt] *vi* tourner; (*less regularly*) tournoyer.
gyration [dʒaɪ'reɪʃən] *n* giration *f*.
gyratory ['dʒaɪrətrɪ, -ərɪ, dʒaɪ'reɪtərɪ] *adj* giratoire; *Admin* **g. (traffic) system,** (système *m* de circulation en) sens *m* giratoire.
gyrfalcon ['dʒɜːfɔːlkən] *n* (*bird*) gerfaut *m*.

gyro ['dʒaɪrəʊ] **1** *adj* gyroscopique; **g. control,** commande *f* gyroscopique. **2** *n* **(a)** = **GYROSCOPE**; **(b)** = **GYROCOMPASS**.

gyrocompass [dʒaɪrəʊ'kʌmpəs] *n Nau* gyrocompas *m*, compas *m* gyroscopique.

gyromagnetic [dʒaɪrəʊmæg'netɪk] *adj* gyromagnétique.

gyropilot ['dʒaɪrəʊpaɪlət] *n Av* pilote *m* automatique, gyropilote *m*; *Nau* (*compass*) gyropilote.

gyroplane ['dʒaɪrəpleɪn] *n Av* autogyre *m*.

gyroscope ['dʒaɪrəskəʊp] *n* gyroscope *m*, gyro *m*.

gyroscopic [dʒaɪrə'skɒpɪk] *adj* gyroscopique.

gyrostat ['dʒaɪrəstæt] *n* gyrostat *m*.

H

H, h [eɪtʃ] *n* (la lettre) H, h *mf*; **to drop one's h's** [ˈeɪtʃɪz], ne pas aspirer les h; *Mil* **H bomb,** bombe *f* H.

ha [hɑː] *int* ha!, ah!

habeas corpus [ˈheɪbɪəsˈkɔːpəs] *n Jur* **(writ of) h.c.,** habeas corpus *m*.

haberdasher [ˈhæbədæʃər] *n Com* **(a)** *Br* mercier *m*; **(b)** *Am* chemisier *m*.

haberdashery [ˈhæbədæʃərɪ] *n Com* **(a)** *Br* mercerie *f*; **(b)** *Am* chemiserie *f*.

habit [ˈhæbɪt] *n* **(a)** (*custom, practice*) habitude *f*, coutume *f*; **to be in the** *or* **make a h. of doing sth,** avoir l'habitude de faire qch; **I try not to make a h. of working late,** j'essaye de ne pas prendre l'habitude de travailler tard; **don't make a h. of it,** fais attention à ne pas répéter ça; **it's a h. with him,** c'est une habitude chez lui; **to get into the h. of doing sth,** prendre l'habitude de faire qch; **to get s.o. into the h. of doing sth,** habituer qn à faire qch; **to get into bad habits,** prendre de mauvaises habitudes; **to get out of a h.,** perdre une habitude; **from force of h.,** poussé par l'habitude; **to do sth by sheer force of h.,** faire qch par pure habitude; **(b)** *F* (*addiction*) accoutumance *f*; **that's when I knew I had a h.,** c'est à ce moment-là que je me suis rendu compte que j'étais accro; **a cocaine h.,** une accoutumance à la cocaïne; **(c)** (*of monk, nun*) habit *m*; **riding h.,** tenue *f* d'équitation.

habitable [ˈhæbɪtəb(ə)l] *adj* habitable; **to make a room/** *etc* **h.,** rendre une pièce/*etc* habitable.

habitat [ˈhæbɪtæt] *n* habitat *m*.

habitation [hæbɪˈteɪʃən] *n* **(a)** habitation *f* (*d'une maison*); **fit for h.,** habitable; **(b)** (*dwelling place*) habitation *f*, demeure *f*.

habit-forming [ˈhæbɪtfɔːmɪŋ] *adj* (*drug*) qui cause *ou* crée une accoutumance.

habitual [həˈbɪtjʊəl] *adj* **(a)** (*customary*) habituel, d'usage; **(b)** (*liar, drunk*) invétéré; **h. criminal** *or* **offender,** récidiviste *mf*.

habitually [həˈbɪtjʊəlɪ] *adv* habituellement, d'habitude; par habitude.

habituate [həˈbɪtjʊeɪt] *vt* **to h. s.o. to sth/to doing sth,** habituer *ou* accoutumer qn à qch/à faire qch.

hack¹ [hæk] *n* **(a)** (*cut*) taillade *f*, entaille *f*; **(b)** (*blow*) coup *m*; *Fb* coup *m* de pied (sur le tibia); **(c)** (*tool*) pic *m*, pioche *f* (*de mineur etc*).

hack² **1** *vt* **(a)** hacher; **to h. sth to pieces,** couper *ou* tailler qch en pièces; **to h. one's way through the jungle,** se frayer un chemin à coups de hache dans la jungle; **to h. s.o. to death,** lacérer qn à mort; *Fig* **to h. an argument to death,** ressasser *ou* rabâcher un argument; **(b)** *Fb etc* **to h. s.o.'s shins,** donner délibérément à un adversaire un coup de pied sur le tibia; **(c)** *esp Am Sl* (*cope*) **he can't h. it,** il ne s'en sort pas, il est complètement dépassé. **2** *vi* **(a)** (*cut*) taillader, entailler; **to h. (away) at a tree,** entailler un arbre à coups de hache; **(b)** (*cough*) émettre une toux sèche.

hack³ *n* **(a)** (*horse for hire*) cheval *m*, -aux de louage; (*for riding*) cheval de selle; *F* (*nag*) rosse *f*; **(b)** *Am F* (*taxi*) taxi *m*; (*taxi driver*) chauffeur *m* de taxi; **(c)** **h. writer, literary h.,** nègre *m*.

hack⁴ **1** *vt Br* (*ride*) **to h. a horse along the road,** se promener à cheval. **2** *vi* **(a)** *Br* se promener à cheval; **(b)** *Comptr* **to h. into a database,** s'introduire en fraude dans une base de données, *F* pirater une base de données.

▶**hack about** *vtsep* (*often passive*) mutiler (*un corps*); **the piece of wood had been hacked about,** ce morceau de bois avait été mis en pièces; *Fig* **my article has been hacked about,** mon article a été massacré.

▶**hack down** *vtsep* abattre (*un arbre*).

▶**hack off** *vtsep* (*chop off*) trancher.

▶**hack up** *vtsep* (*chop up*) hacher.

hacker [ˈhækər] *n Comptr Sl* pirate *m*.

hacking¹ [ˈhækɪŋ] **1** *adj* **h. cough,** toux sèche et pénible. **2** *n* **(a)** (*with axe etc*) hachage *m*, hachement *m*; **(b)** *Fb etc* coups *mpl* de pied (sur le tibia); **(c)** *Comptr Sl* piratage *m* informatique.

hacking² *n Br* promenade(s) *f(pl)* à cheval; **h. jacket,** veste *f* d'équitation.

hackle [ˈhæk(ə)l] *n* (*of bird*) plume *f* du cou (*des gallinacés*); **hackles,** camail *m*; **his hackles rose,** (*of dog, person*) il s'est hérissé; *Fig* **to get one's hackles up,** se hérisser, monter sur ses ergots; *Fig* **to make s.o.'s hackles rise,** hérisser qn.

hackney [ˈhæknɪ] *n* **(a)** (*carriage for hire*) cabriolet *m* de louage; **(b)** (*horse*) cheval *m* de selle; (*trotter*) (cheval) trotteur *m* (de course); **(c)** (*taxi*) **h. carriage,** taxi *m*.

hackneyed [ˈhæknɪd] *adj* (*language*) rebattu, usé, banal; **h. phrase,** formule stéréotypée, cliché *m*.

hacksaw [ˈhæksɔː] *n* scie *f* à métaux.

hackwork [ˈhækwɜːk] *n* (*paid literary work*) travail *m* de nègre; (*badly done*) travail d'écriture bâclé; (*routine etc*) travail alimentaire.

had *see* **HAVE².**

haddock [ˈhædək] *n* (*fish*) aiglefin *m*, eglefin *m*; *Culin* **smoked h.,** haddock *m* (fumé).

Hades [ˈheɪdiːz] *n Myth* Hadès *m*, les Enfers *mpl*.

hadn't [hæd(ə)nt] = **had not**; *see* **HAVE².**

Hadrian [ˈheɪdrɪən] *n Antiq* Adrien *m*, Hadrien *m*; **H.'s Wall,** le Mur d'Adrien.

haema- [ˈhiːmə] *pref Med etc* héma-.

haemato- [ˈhiːməˈtɒ, -təʊ] *pref Med etc* hémato-.

haematology, *US* **hematology** [hiːməˈtɒlədʒɪ] *n Physiol* hématologie *f*.

haematoma, *US* **hematoma,** *pl* **-omas, -omata** [hiːməˈtəʊmə, -əʊməz, -əʊmətə] *n Med* hématome *m*.

haemo- [hiːməʊ, -mə] *pref Med etc* hémo-.

haemoglobin, *US* **hemoglobin** [hiːməʊˈgləʊbɪn] *n Physiol* hémoglobine *f*.

haemophilia, *US* **hemophilia** [hiːməʊˈfɪlɪə] *n Med* hémophilie *f*.

haemophiliac, *US* **hemophiliac** [hiːməʊˈfɪlɪæk] *n Med* hémophile *mf*.

haemophilic, *US* **hemophilic** [hiːməʊˈfɪlɪk] *adj Med* hémophile.

haemorrhage¹, *US* **hemorrhage** [ˈhemərɪdʒ] *n Med* hémorragie *f*.

haemorrhage², *US* **hemorrhage** *vi* faire (une) hémorragie.

haemorrhoids, *US* **hemorrhoids** [ˈhemərɔɪdz] *npl Med* hémorroïdes *fpl*; **to have h.,** avoir des hémorroïdes.

haemostat, *US* **hemostat** [ˈhiːməʊstæt] *n Med* pince(s) *f(pl)* hémostatique(s).

haft [hɑːft] *n* manche *m*, poignée *f* (*d'un outil etc*).

hag [hæg] *n* (vieille) sorcière *f*; *F* **she's an old h.,** c'est une vieille taupe.

haggard [ˈhægəd] *adj* **(a)** (*gaunt*) hâve; (*face*) décharné; **(b)** (*wild*) (*face*) égaré, hagard.

haggis [ˈhægɪs] *n Scot Culin* = panse de brebis farcie d'un hachis d'abats et de farine d'avoine très épicé.

haggle [ˈhæg(ə)l] *vi* marchander, *F* chipoter; **I'm not going to h.,** je ne vais pas chipoter; **to h. about** *or* **over the price of sth,** chicaner sur le prix de qch.

haggling [ˈhæg(ə)lɪŋ] *n* marchandage *m*.

hagiographer [hægɪˈɒgrəfər] *n* hagiographe *mf*.

hagiography [hægɪˈɒgrəfɪ] *n* hagiographie *f*.

hag-ridden [ˈhægrɪd(ə)n] *adj* (*by nightmares*) tourmenté de cauchemars; (*by an idea etc*) obsédé, tourmenté.

Hague (the) [ðəˈheɪg] *n* la Haye.

hah [hɑː] *int* ha!, ah!

ha-ha¹ [hɑːˈhɑː] *int* ha, ha!

ha-ha² [ˈhɑːhɑː] *n* saut-de-loup *m*, *pl* sauts-de-loup.

hail¹ [heɪl] *n Met* grêle *f*; *Fig* **h. of blows/stones,** grêle *ou* volée *f* de coups/de pierres; *Fig* **a h. of abuse,** une flopée d'injures.

hail² **1** *v impers Met* grêler; **it's hailing,** il grêle. **2** *vt* **to h. blows on s.o.,** donner une volée de coups à qn.

hail³ **1** *int* salut!; *Cathol* **h., Mary, full of grace!,** je te salue, Marie, pleine de grâce!. **2** *n* **(a)** appel *m*; **within h.,** à portée de (la) voix; **(b)** *Cathol* **the H. Mary,** l'Ave Maria *m inv*; **to say two H. Marys,** dire deux Ave Maria.

hail⁴ **1** *vt* **(a)** (*greet*) saluer (*qn*); **(b)** (*attract attention*) héler (*qn, un navire*); *Nau* arraisonner (*un navire*); **to h. a taxi,** appeler *ou* héler un taxi (qui passe); **within hailing distance,** à portée de (la) voix; **(c)** (*acclaim*) acclamer; **to h. s.o. (as) king,** acclamer qn roi; **the bridge was hailed as an engineering marvel,** le pont a été acclamé comme une merveille de technicité. **2** *vi Nau* (*of ship*) **to h. from a port,** (*be based at*) dépendre d'un port; (*come from*) venir d'un port; **where does she h. from?,** d'où vient-il?

▶**hail down** **1** *vi* **blows/missiles hailed down on our heads,** nous avons reçu une volée de coups/une pluie de missiles; **criticism hailed down on him,** il a subi une avalanche de critiques. **2** *vtsep* (*throw*) **they hailed stones down on us,** ils ont lancé des pierres sur nous.

hail-fellow-well-met ['heɪlfeləʊwel'met] *adj* **to be h.-f.-w.-m. with everyone,** être à tu et à toi avec tout le monde.

hailstone ['heɪlstəʊn] *n* grêlon *m*.

hailstorm ['heɪlstɔːm] *n* averse *f* de grêle.

hair [heər] *n* **(a)** (*of human head*) cheveux *mpl*; (*single*) cheveu *m*; **if you harm** *or* **touch a h. on that child's head ...,** si tu touches un cheveu de cet enfant ...; **to split hairs,** ergoter, couper les cheveux en quatre; **h. crack,** (*in metal*) gerçure *f*; *Typ* **h. stroke,** empattement *m* (*de lettre*); (*in handwriting*) délié *m*; **h. trigger,** détente *f* (*d'une arme à feu*); **the h.,** les cheveux, la chevelure; **long fair h.,** de longs cheveux blonds; **to comb one's h.,** se peigner; **to have** *or* **get one's h. cut,** se faire couper les cheveux; **to do one's h.,** se coiffer; **I like your h.,** j'aime bien ta coiffure; **to wash one's h.,** se laver la tête; **to have one's h. set** *or F* **done,** se faire faire une mise en plis; **to let down one's h.,** défaire *ou* laisser tomber ses cheveux; *F* **to let one's h. down,** (*relax*) se mettre à son aise; s'amuser follement; **to tear one's h.,** s'arracher les cheveux; **it was enough to make your h. stand on end,** c'était à faire dresser les cheveux (sur la tête); *F* **keep your h. on!,** calmez-vous!; *F* **to get in s.o.'s h.,** taper sur les nerfs de qn, enquiquiner qn; **h. tonic** *or* **lotion,** lotion *f* capillaire; **h. cream,** crème *f* pour les cheveux; **h. oil,** brillantine *f*; *Br* **h. slide,** barrette *f*; **h. lacquer** *or* **spray,** laque *f*; **h. dryer,** séchoir *m* à cheveux, sèche-cheveux *m inv*; **h. gel,** gel *m*; **h. restorer,** lotion capillaire contre la calvitie;

(b) (*individual hair, of human face and body, animals, plants*) poil *m*; *Fig* **a h. of the dog,** (*for hangover*) antidote *m*; **(body) h.,** (*of human*) poil; **(facial) h.,** (*of human*) poil du visage, duvet *m*; **removal of unwanted h.,** épilation *f*, dépilation *f*; *F* **that'll put hairs on your chest,** ça te rendra plus viril;

(c) (*coat*) (*of animal*) poil *m*, pelage *m*; (*of horse*) crin *m*; (*of pig*) soie *f*; **h. mattress,** matelas *m* de crin; **h. shirt,** haire *f*, cilice *m*;

(d) *Opt* cheveu *m*, fil *m* (*de réticule d'appareil de visée*); **cross hairs,** réticule *m*.

hairball ['heəbɔːl] *n* (*in cat's stomach*) boule *f* de poils.

hairbrush ['heəbrʌʃ] *n* brosse *f* à cheveux.

haircut ['heəkʌt] *n* **(a)** (*act*) coupe *f* de cheveux; **to have a h.,** se faire couper les cheveux; **(b)** (*hairstyle*) coupe *f* de cheveux, coiffure *f*.

hairdo ['heəduː] *n F* coiffure *f*.

hairdresser ['heədresər] *n* coiffeur, -euse; **to go to the h.'s,** aller chez le coiffeur.

hairdressing ['heədresɪŋ] *n* coiffure *f*; **h. salon,** salon *m* de coiffure.

-haired [heəd] *suff* **short/grey/***etc***-h.,** aux cheveux courts/gris/*etc*.

hairgrip ['heəgrɪp] *n esp Br* pince *f* (à cheveux).

hairless ['heəlɪs] *adj* (*person*) sans cheveux; (*bald*) chauve; (*face*) glabre, nu; (*animal*) sans poils.

hairline ['heəlaɪn] *n* **(a)** (*of person*) racine *f* des cheveux; **his h. is receding,** son front commence à se dégarnir; **(b)** *Typ* délié *m*; **h. type,** capillaires *fpl*; **(c)** *Tech* (*in metal*) gerçure *f*; **(d)** *Opt* cheveu *m*, fil *m* (*de réticule d'appareil de visée*); **hairlines,** réticule *m*.

hairnet ['heənet] *n* filet *m* (*pour cheveux*).

hairpiece ['heəpiːs] *n* mèche *f* postiche.

hairpin ['heəpɪn] *n* épingle *f* à cheveux; **h. bend,** (*on road*) lacet *m*, virage *m* en épingle à cheveux.

hair-raising ['heəreɪzɪŋ] *adj* effrayant; (*aventure*) effroyable; (*récit*) à vous faire dresser les cheveux sur la tête.

hair's-breadth ['heəzbredθ] *n* épaisseur *f* d'un cheveu; **he escaped death by a h.-b.,** il a été à deux doigts de la mort, il a frisé la mort; **to be within a h.-b. of disaster,** être à un cheveu de la ruine.

hair-splitting ['heəsplɪtɪŋ] **1** *n* ergotage *m*, ergoterie *f*; (*dispute*) chicane(rie) *f*. **2** *adj* (*argument etc*) (trop) subtil.

hairspring ['heəsprɪŋ] *n* (*of watch, clock etc*) spiral *m*, *pl* spiraux.

hairstyle ['heəstaɪl] *n* coiffure *f*.

hairstylist ['heəstaɪlɪst] *n* coiffeur, -euse.

hairy ['heərɪ] *adj* **(a)** (*hands, chest etc*) velu, poilu; (*scalp*) chevelu; (*person*) hirsute; **(b)** *F* (*dangerous*) périlleux; (*frightening*) effrayant; **things are getting rather h.,** la situation devient assez désespérée.

Haiti ['heɪtɪ, 'haɪ-] *n* Haïti *m or f*.

Haitian ['heɪʃən, 'heɪtɪən] **1** *adj* haïtien. **2** *n* Haïtien, -ienne.

hake [heɪk] *n* (*fish*) merluche *f*, colin *m*.

halberd ['hælbəd] *n Mil Hist* hallebarde *f*.

halcyon ['hælsɪən] *n* **(a)** *Myth* alcyon *m*; **h. days,** bons vieux jours; **(b)** (*bird*) halcyon *m*.

hale [heɪl] *adj* vigoureux, robuste, encore gaillard; **to be h. and hearty,** être frais et gaillard.

half, *pl* **halves** [hɑːf, hɑːvz] **1** *n* **(a)** moitié *f*; (*of beer, hour*) demi *m*; **what is h. of twelve?,** quelle est la moitié de douze?; **h. the time he isn't there,** la moitié du temps, il n'est pas là; **h. of them were students,** la moitié d'entre eux étaient étudiants; **the first h. of the year,** la première moitié de l'année; **she gave each of us h.,** elle nous en a donné la moitié à chacun; *F* **my better h.,** ma (chère) moitié; **to fold/cut sth in h.** *or* **in halves,** plier/couper qch en deux; **they don't do things by halves,** ils ne font pas les choses à moitié; **to go halves with s.o.,** partager avec qn; se mettre de moitié avec qn; **chicken halves,** (*portions*) demi-poulets *mpl*; **bigger by h.,** plus grand de moitié; *F* **she is too clever by h.,** elle est beaucoup trop mali(g)ne; **two halves,** deux demis; **three and a h.,** trois et demi; **I waited for two and a h. hours,** j'ai attendu pendant deux heures et demie; *Br* **one and two halves,** (*on bus, train*) un tarif normal, deux tarifs enfant; *Rail* **outward/return h.,** (*of ticket*) coupon *m* d'aller/de retour;

(b) *Sp* (*player*) demi *m*; **wing h.,** demi aile; **scrum h.,** demi de mêlée; **centre h.,** demi centre; **the first h. (of the game),** la première mi-temps; **the second h.,** la seconde mi-temps; **in our h. (of the ground),** dans notre camp.

2 *adj* demi; **h. an hour,** une demi-heure; **I'll be with you in h. a second** *or Br F* **h. a tick,** je suis à vous dans une seconde; **h. a dozen,** une demi-douzaine; **I've got h. a mind to complain,** j'ai bien envie de faire une réclamation; **h. board,** demi-pension *f*; **at h. price,** à moitié prix; *Mil* **h. right/left,** demi-à-droite/à-gauche *m*; **h. day,** demi-journée *f*; *Fb etc* **h. time,** (la) mi-temps; *Fb* **the h.-time results,** le score à la mi-temps; *Br F* **h. seas over,** gris, soûl, ivre; *Tennis* **h. volley,** demi-volée *f*.

3 *adv* à moitié; **she only h. understands,** elle ne comprend qu'à moitié; **he h. opened the door,** il entrouvrit la porte; **the bottle was h. full/empty,** la bouteille était à moitié *ou* à demi pleine/vide; **h. dressed,** à demi vêtu; **h. naked,** à moitié nu; **h. asleep,** à moitié endormi; **h. dead,** à moitié mort; **h. done,** (*work*) à moitié fait; (*cooked meat etc*) à moitié cuit; **you're h. right,** tu n'as pas tout à fait tort; **h. laughing, h. crying,** moitié riant, moitié pleurant; **I was h. afraid that you wouldn't come,** j'avais quelque crainte que vous ne veniez pas; **it is h. past two** *or F* **h. two,** il est deux heures et demie; **h. past twelve,** midi *ou* minuit et demi; **h. as big,** moitié aussi grand; **he gets h. as much money as you,** il reçoit moitié moins d'argent que vous; **h. as big again,** plus grand de moitié; *F* **it isn't h. bad,** ce n'est pas mauvais du tout, ce n'est pas si mal; *Br Sl* **it isn't h. cold!,** il fait rudement froid!; *Br Sl* **he doesn't h. say some stupid things!,** il dit vraiment n'importe quoi *ou* des conneries!; *Br Sl* **not h.!,** tu parles!, et comment!

half-a-crown [hɑːfə'kraʊn] *n Br Arch* demi-couronne *f*.

half-and-half ['hɑːfən(d)'hɑːf] **1** *adj & adv* moitié l'un moitié l'autre, *F* moitié-moitié; **how shall I mix them? — h.-and-h.,** comment faut-il les mélanger? – à doses égales; **how do you like your coffee? — h.-and-h.,** comment prenez-vous le café? – moitié café, moitié lait. **2** *n* **(a)** mélange *m*; **(b)** *Am* = mélange de lait et de crème liquide.

halfback ['hɑːfbæk] *n Fb* demi-arrière *m*, *pl* demi-arrières.

half-baked [hɑːf'beɪkt] *adj F* **(a)** (*poorly planned*) insuffisamment étudié; (*scheme*) qui ne tient pas debout; **(b)** (*inexperienced*) inexpérimenté; (*foolish*) niais.

half-blood ['hɑːfblʌd] *n* = **HALFBREED**.

halfbreed ['hɑːfbriːd] *n* **(a)** *Offensive Sl* (*person*) métis, -isse; **(b)** (*horse*) cheval *m* demi-sang, *pl* chevaux demi-sang.

half-brother ['hɑːfbrʌðər] *n* demi-frère *m*, *pl* demi-frères; (*through mother*) frère utérin; (*through father*) frère consanguin.

half-caste ['hɑːfkɑːst] *adj & n* métis, -isse.

half-circle ['hɑːf'sɜːk(ə)l] *n* demi-cercle *m*, *pl* demi-cercles; *Nau* **to turn a h.-c.,** faire demi-tour.

half(-)cock ['hɑːf'kɒk] *n* **(gun) at h. c.,** (*rifle etc*) à moitié armé, sur le cran de sûreté; **h.-c. notch,** cran *m* de sûreté; *F* **to go off at h. c.,** mal partir, mal démarrer; (*of person*) monter sur ses grands chevaux.

half-crown [hɑːf'kraʊn] *n* = **HALF-A-CROWN**.

halfhearted ['hɑːf'hɑːtɪd] *adj* sans enthousiasme; (*effort*) timide, hésitant.

halfheartedly ['hɑːf'hɑːtɪdlɪ] *adv* sans enthousiasme.

halfheartedness ['hɑːf'hɑːtɪdnɪs] *n* tiédeur *f*, manque *m* d'enthousiasme.

half-hourly [hɑːf'aʊəlɪ] **1** *adv* toutes les demi-heures. **2** *adj* de toutes les demi-heures, de trente minutes; **at h.-h. intervals,** toutes les demi-heures.

half-length ['hɑf'leŋθ] *n* demi-longueur *f*, *pl* demi-longueurs; **h.-l. portrait,** portrait *m* en buste.

half-life ['hɑːflaɪf] *n Nucl Phys etc* demi-vie *f* (*d'un isotope etc*), *pl* demi-vies.

half-light ['hɑːf'laɪt] *n* demi-jour *m*, *pl* demi-jours.

half-mast ['hɑːf'mɑːst] *n Br* **at h.-m.,** à mi-mât; **flag at h.-m.,** pavillon *m* en berne; *Hum* **to be at h.-m.,** (*of trousers*) arriver à mi-mollet; (*of socks*) descendre.

half-moon ['hɑːf'muːn] *n* **(a)** demi-lune *f*, *pl* demi-lunes; **(b)** *Anat* lunule *f* (*des ongles*).

half-nelson ['hɑːf'nels(ə)n] *n* (*in wrestling*) simple prise *f* de tête à terre.

half-note ['hɑːfnəʊt] *n esp Am Mus* blanche *f*.

half-pay ['hɑːf'peɪ] *n* demi-salaire *m*; (*in civil service*) demi-traitement *m*; Mil demi-solde *f*; **on h.-p.,** à mi-salaire; à demi-traitement; en demi-solde.

halfpenny ['heɪpnɪ, 'hɑːfpenɪ] *n Arch Br* demi-penny *m*; *F* = sou *m*.

half-price ['hɑːf'praɪs] **1** *adj* (*ticket*) demi-tarif. **2** *adv* (à) demi-tarif; **children get in h.-p.,** les enfants payent demi-tarif.

half-sister ['hɑːf'sɪstər] *n* demi-sœur *f*, *pl* demi-sœurs; (*through mother*) sœur utérine; (*through father*) sœur consanguine.

half-size ['hɑːf'saɪz] *n Com* (*in dress*) demi-taille *f*; (*in shoes*) demi-pointure *f*; **we don't stock h.-sizes of that shoe,** nous n'avons pas les demi-pointures de ce modèle en stock.

half-staff ['hɑːf'stɑːf] *n Am* = **HALF-MAST**.

half-term ['hɑːf'tɜːm] *n Br Sch* congé *m* de mi-trimestre.

half-timbered ['hɑːf'tɪmbəd] *adj Archit* (*maison*) à colombage.

half-title ['hɑːf'taɪt(ə)l] *n Typ* avant-titre *m* (*d'un livre*), *pl* avant-titres.

halftone [hɑːf'təʊn] *n* **(a)** *Art* demi-teinte *f*, *pl* demi-teintes; *Phot* similigravure *f* (tramée); **(b)** *Mus* demi-ton *m*, *pl* demi-tons.

half-track ['hɑːf'træk] *n Aut* (auto)chenille *f*, half-track *m*.

half-truth ['hɑːf'truːθ] *n* demi-vérité *f*, *pl* demi-vérités.

halfway [hɑːf'weɪ] **1** *adv* **(a)** à moitié chemin, à mi-chemin; (*of piston*) à mi-course; **h. between the two towns,** à mi-chemin entre les deux villes; **h. to Paris,** à mi-chemin de Paris; **we're h. there,** nous avons fait la moitié du chemin; (*in project etc*) nous sommes à mi-chemin; **h. up (the hill),** à mi-côte, à mi-pente; **I was h. up** *or* **down the stairs,** j'étais à mi-hauteur de l'escalier; **the lift got stuck h. up,** l'ascenseur s'est bloqué à mi-hauteur; **h. through (a period of time),** à mi-terme; **we're h. through the work,** nous avons fait la moitié du travail; **to meet s.o. h.,** (*of distance*) rencontrer qn à mi-distance; **I'll meet you h.,** (*in price*) faisons moitié-moitié; (*in the concessions you're asking for*) faisons un arrangement;

(b) (*partly*) à peu près; **haven't you got a h. acceptable shirt?,** tu n'as pas une chemise à peu près convenable?

2 *adj* **h. house,** maison *f ou* auberge *f* à mi-chemin; (*rehabilitation centre*) centre *m* de réadaptation (*pour drogués etc*); (*compromise*) juste milieu *m*; *Fb* **h. line,** ligne *f* des cinquante mètres.

3 *n* **there's no h. with him,** avec lui il n'y a pas de demi-mesures.

halfwit ['hɑːfwɪt] *n* faible *mf* d'esprit, simple *mf*.

halfwitted [hɑːf'wɪtɪd] *adj* faible d'esprit, simple.

half-yearly ['hɑːf'jɪəlɪ] **1** *adv* par semestre; tous les six mois. **2** *adj* semestriel.

halibut ['hælɪbət] *n* (*fish*) flétan *m*.

halitosis [hælɪ'təʊsɪs] *n Med* mauvaise haleine.

hall [hɔːl] *n* **(a) (entrance) h.,** entrée *f* (*d'une maison*); hall *m* (*d'un grand hôtel*); **h. porter,** concierge *m*; **h. stand,** portemanteau *m*;

(b) *Am* (*corridor*) couloir *m*, corridor *m*;

(c) (*room, building*) salle *f*; **(dining) h.,** (*of stately home*) salle à manger; *Univ* (*of college etc*) réfectoire *m*; **the servants' h.,** l'office *f*; **lecture h.,** salle de conférences; **assembly h.,** salle d'assemblée; **concert h.,** salle de concert; **music h.,** music-hall *m*; *Am* salle de concert; *Br* **parish h.,** salle paroissiale; **town h.,** hôtel *m* de ville; *Br Univ* **h. (of residence),** résidence *f* universitaire, maison *f* d'étudiants; *esp Am* **H. of Fame,** = Panthéon *m*; **she was inducted into the Country Music H. of Fame,** elle a été admise parmi les grands de la musique country; *Br Univ* **to eat in h.,** = manger au restaurant universitaire; **to live in h.,** loger en résidence universitaire;

(d) (*manor house*) manoir *m*; **she works up at the h.,** elle travaille au château; **Ludgely H.,** (*in name*) le château de Ludgely;

(e) (*of guild etc*) maison *f*.

hallelujah [hælɪ'luːjə] *int & n* alléluia *m*.

hallmark¹ ['hɔːlmɑːk] *n* (cachet *m* de) contrôle *m* (*sur les objets d'orfèvrerie*); *Fig* **the h. of genius,** l'empreinte *f* du génie.

hallmark² *vt* contrôler, poinçonner (*l'orfèvrerie*).

hallo [hə'ləʊ] *int* = **HELLO**.

hallow¹ ['hæləʊ] *n Rel* **All Hallows' (Day),** (le jour de) la Toussaint.

hallow² *vt* sanctifier, consacrer; **hallowed** ['hæləʊd, *occ* 'hæləʊɪd] **be Thy name,** que Ton nom soit sanctifié.

hallowed ['hæləʊd] *adj* béni, sanctifié; **h. ground,** terre sainte.

Hallowe'en [hæləʊ'iːn] *n* = veille *f* de la Toussaint.

hallucinate [hə'luːsɪneɪt] **1** *vt* halluciner. **2** *vi* avoir des hallucinations.

hallucination [həluːsɪ'neɪʃən] *n* hallucination *f*.

hallucinatory [hə'luːsɪnət(ə)rɪ] *adj* hallucinatoire.

hallucinogen [hə'luːsɪnədʒen] *n* hallucinogène *m*.

hallucinogenic [həluːsɪnəʊ'dʒenɪk] *adj* hallucinogène.

hallway ['hɔːlweɪ] *n* **(a)** vestibule *m*, entrée *f*; **(b)** *Am* (*corridor*) couloir *m*.

halo, *pl* **-os, -oes** ['heɪləʊ, -əʊz] *n* **(a)** (*of saint*) auréole *f*, nimbe *m*; *Hum* **your halo's slipping!,** tu descends de ton piédestal; **(b)** *Astron Opt Phot* halo *m*; auréole *f* (*de la lune*).

halogen ['hælədʒən] *adj & n Ch* halogène *m*.

halt¹ [hɒlt] *n* **(a)** (*act of stopping*) arrêt *m*, temps *m* d'arrêt; interruption *f* (momentanée); halte *f*, pause *f*; **a brief h. at an inn,** une brève halte dans une auberge; **to bring to a h.,** faire marquer un temps d'arrêt *ou* une pause à (*un processus etc*); provoquer l'interruption momentanée de (*un mouvement, une action*); arrêter, faire stopper (*un véhicule, une foule etc*); **to come to a h.,** marquer un temps d'arrêt, s'interrompre momentanément; s'arrêter, stopper; (*on journey*) faire halte; (*in a speech*) rester sans pouvoir rien dire; **to call a h. to sth,** arrêter qch; *Aut* **h. sign,** stop *m*; *Mil* **at the h.,** de pied ferme, sur place; **(b)** stationnement *m* (*d'un véhicule, d'une troupe etc*); **(c)** *Rail* (*small station*) halte *f*.

halt² **1** *vi* faire halte, s'arrêter; **to h. at ...,** faire un arrêt à ..., s'arrêter à ...; *Mil* **company h.!,** compagnie halte! **2** *vt* faire faire une halte à (*qn*); (*for good*) arrêter (*qch*); (*temporarily*) interrompre (*qch*).

halt³ **1** *adj Arch & Bible* boiteux. **2** *n* **the h.,** (*used as pl*) les estropiés *mpl*.

halter¹ ['hɔːltər] *n* **(a)** (*for horse*) licou *m*; **(b)** (*clothing*) **h. (top),** (corsage *m ou* haut *m*) bain-de-soleil *m inv*; **h.-neck dress/***etc*, robe *f*/*etc* dos nu; **(c)** corde *f* (*de pendaison*).

halter² *vt* **to h. a horse,** mettre un licou à un cheval.

halting ['hɔːltɪŋ] **1** *adj* (*words, speech etc*) hésitant; (*style*) heurté. **2** *n* hésitation *f*.

haltingly ['hɔːltɪŋlɪ] *adv* en hésitant.

halve [hɑːv] *vt* **(a)** diviser en deux, couper en deux moitiés; **(b)** (*share*) partager (*qch*) en deux; **(c)** (*reduce*) réduire (*les dépenses etc*) de moitié.

halves [hɑːvz] *npl see* **HALF**.

halving ['hɑːvɪŋ] *n* partage *m* en deux, division *f* en deux, bipartition *f*.

halyard ['hæljəd] *n Nau* drisse *f*.

ham¹ [hæm] *n* **(a)** *Culin* jambon *m*; **h. and eggs,** œufs *mpl* au jambon; **h. sandwich,** sandwich *m* au jambon; **(b)** *F* (*buttocks*) **the hams,** les fesses *fpl*, le derrière; **(c)** *Th Cin* *etc F* **h. actor,** cabotin *m*; **(d)** *Rad F* (*enthusiast*) **radio h.,** amateur *m* de radio.

ham² *v* (**-mm-**) *Th Cin etc F* **1** *vi* jouer comme un pied. **2** *vt* **he hams all his parts,** il charge tous ses rôles.

►**ham up** *vtsep Th Cin etc F* **to h. it up,** jouer comme un pied.

Hamburg ['hæmbɜːg] *n* Hambourg.

hamburger ['hæmbɜːgər] *n Culin* hamburger *m*.

Hamburger ['hæmbɜːgər] *n* Hambourgeois, -oise.

ham-fisted ['hæm'fɪstɪd] *adj F* maladroit.

Hamitic [hə'mɪtɪk] *adj* chamitique.

hamlet ['hæmlɪt] *n* hameau *m*.

hammer¹ ['hæmər] *n* **(a)** (*tool*) marteau *m*; (*heavy*) masse *f*; **wooden h.,** maillet *m*; *Constr* **bush h.,** boucharde *f*; **the h. and sickle,** la faucille et le marteau; **to go at it h. and tongs,** (*work etc energetically*) y aller de bon cœur, ne pas y aller de main morte; (*quarrel*) se quereller; (*fight*) se bagarrer; *Sp* **throwing the h., h. throwing,** lancement *m* du marteau; **h. thrower,** lanceur *m* de marteau; **(b)** (*of auctioneer*) marteau *m*; **to come under the h.,** être mis aux enchères; **(c)** (*in clock, alarm, piano etc*) marteau *m*; *Mus* **tuning h.,** accordoir *m*, clef *f* d'accordeur; **(d)** *Anat* marteau *m* (*de l'oreille interne*); **(e)** (*of firearm*) chien *m*.

hammer² **1** *vt* marteler; *F* (*beat*) bourrer (*qn*) de coups; (*of boxer etc*) cogner dur sur (*son adversaire*); (*defeat*) battre (*son adversaire*) à plate(s) couture(s); (*criticize*) massacrer, descendre (*qn, un livre etc*); **to h. into shape,** façonner (*un pot etc*) à coups de marteau; *Fig F* perfectionner (*un projet etc*); *F* **to h. sth into s.o.,** faire entrer qch dans la tête de qn; **I'll h. it into her,** je veux lui faire entrer ça dans la tête; **to h. prices,** écraser les prix. **2** *vi* travailler avec le marteau; **to h. at** *or* **on the door,** frapper à la porte à coups redoublés.

►**hammer home** *vtsep* **(a)** enfoncer (*qch*) (à l'aide d'un marteau); **make sure you h. the nails home,** assure-toi que tu as bien enfoncé les clous; **(b)** *Fig* (*insist on*) insister sur (*qch*).

►**hammer in** *vtsep* enfoncer (*un clou*) à coups de marteau.

►**hammer out** *vtsep* **(a)** (*in metalwork*) étendre (*l'or etc*) sous le marteau; panner (*le cuivre*); **to h. out a dent in sth,** débosseler qch; **(b)** *Fig F* (*draw up*) élaborer, mettre au point; **unions and management hammered out an agreement,** les syndicats et le patronat sont parvenus à un accord.

hammerhead ['hæməhed] *n* **(a) h. (shark),** requin *m* marteau; **(b)** (*bird*) ombrette *f* (du Sénégal); **(c)** *Constr* **h. crane,** grue *f* marteau.

hammering ['hæmərɪŋ] *n* martelage *m*; (*noise*) martèlement *m*; battage *m* (*du fer*); *F* (*with fists*) dégelée *f* (de coups); **to give a h.,** (*hit*) cogner dur sur (*qn*), bourrer (*qn*) de coups; (*defeat*) battre (*qn*) à plate(s) couture(s); (*criticize*) descendre (*qn, un livre etc*); **our team got a h.,** notre équipe a été battue à plate(s) couture(s).

hammertoe ['hæmətəʊ] *n Med* orteil *m* en marteau.

hammock ['hæmək] *n* hamac *m*.

hammy ['hæmɪ] *adj Th Cin etc F* (*acting*) outrancier; **h. actor,** cabotin *m*, acteur qui en fait trop.

hamper¹ ['hæmpər] *n* panier *m* (*à provisions etc*), manne *f*; bourriche *f* (*d'huîtres etc*); **Christmas h.,** panier *m* de Noël.

hamper² *vt* embarrasser, gêner, empêtrer (*qn*); **to h. the progress of business,** entraver la marche des affaires; **high winds hampered the rescue work,** les sauveteurs ont été gênés dans leur travail par la force des vents; **she was hampered by her long cloak,** elle était empêtrée dans son grand manteau.

hamster ['hæmstər] *n* hamster *m*.

hamstring¹ ['hæmstrɪŋ] *n Anat* tendon *m* du jarret; **h. injury,** lésion *f* du tendon du jarret.

hamstring² *vt* (*pt & pp* **hamstringed** *or* **-strung**) **(a)** (*cut hamstrings of*) couper le(s) jarret(s) à (*qn, un cheval*); **(b)** *Fig* paralyser; (*financially*) couper les moyens à (*qn*); **we are hamstrung by a lack of funds,** nous sommes paralysés par l'absence de fonds suffisants.

hand¹ [hænd] *n* **(a)** main *f*; **he writes with his left h.,** il écrit de la main gauche; **the h. of God,** le doigt de Dieu; **on one's hands and knees,** à quatre pattes; **to vote by show of hands,** voter à main levée; *Fig* **to have one's hands tied,** avoir les mains liées; **I could beat you at tennis with one h. tied behind my back,** je pourrais te battre au tennis même avec une main dans le dos; **to be bound h. and foot,** être pieds et poings liés; **to hold in one's h.,** tenir (*une épée, son chapeau*) à la main; tenir (*des graines*) dans la main; tenir (*le succès*) entre les mains; **to take s.o. by the h.,** prendre qn par la main; **give me your h.,** donnez-moi la main; **he asked for her h. in marriage,** il lui a demandé sa main; *F* **to put** *or* **dip one's h. in the till,** puiser dans la caisse; **I can't put my h. on it,** je n'arrive pas à mettre la main dessus; **to lay hands on sth,** mettre la main sur qch, s'emparer de qch; **to lay hands on s.o.,** faire violence à qn; **hands off!,** n'y touchez pas!; (*off me*) bas les pattes!; **hands up!,** haut les mains!; **to rule with a firm h.,** gouverner d'une main ferme; *Fb* **hands,** (faute *f* de) main; **these birds will eat out of your h.,** ces oiseaux te mangeront dans la main; *Fig* **I'll soon have him eating out of my h.,** bientôt, il me mangera dans la main, je l'amènerai bientôt à faire exactement ce que je veux; **to try one's h. at sth,** essayer (de faire) qch, y mettre la main; **to get one's h. in,** se faire la main; **to keep one's h. in,** garder la main; **she can turn** *or* **set her h. to anything,** c'est une femme qui peut tout faire; **to have a h. in sth,** être impliqué dans qch, se mêler de qch; **I had no h. in this crime,** je ne suis absolument pas responsable de ce crime; **to give** *or* **lend s.o. a (helping) h.,** aider qn; **to lend a h.,** mettre la main à la pâte; **to have one's hands full,** avoir les mains prises; *Fig* (*be busy*) avoir du pain sur la planche; **to have s.o./sth on one's hands,** avoir qn/qch à sa charge *ou* sur les bras; **to have an hour on one's hands,** avoir une heure à tuer; **to have time on one's hands,** avoir du temps libre; **she's got a lot on her hands at the moment,** elle est très occupée en ce moment; **the case is off our hands,** l'affaire ne dépend plus de nous; **to change hands,** (*of goods etc*) changer de mains; (*of business etc*) changer de propriétaire; **to fall into enemy hands,** tomber entre les mains de l'ennemi; **in the wrong hands this knowledge could be very dangerous,** s'il tombait aux mains de personnes malintentionnées, ce savoir pourrait être très dangereux; **to be in good hands,** être en bonnes mains; **to put oneself in s.o.'s hands,** se confier à qn; *Jur* **to put a matter in the hands of a lawyer,** confier une affaire à un avocat; **the matter's in their hands now,** désormais, l'affaire est entre leurs mains; **it's out of my hands,** je ne peux (plus) rien y faire; **he never does a h.'s turn,** il ne fait jamais rien de ses dix doigts; *F* **to give s.o. a big h.,** (*applaud*) applaudir vivement qn; **I only have one pair of hands!,** je n'ai que deux mains!; **h. basin,** lavabo *m*; **h. luggage,** bagages *mpl* à main; **h. glass,** loupe *f* à main (*pour la lecture*); (*mirror*) miroir *m* à main; (*in gardening*) cloche *f*; **h. grenade,** grenade *f* (à main);

(b) (*phrases*) **to be (near) at h.,** (*of object etc*) être sous la main *ou* à portée de la main; (*of event etc*) approcher, être proche; **the hour is at h.,** l'heure est proche; **there is always a doctor at h.,** il y a toujours un médecin de service; **made** *or* **done by h.,** fait à la main; **to wash clothes by h.,** laver du linge à la main; **to send/deliver a letter by h.,** envoyer/distribuer une lettre par porteur; **sword in h.,** sabre au poing; **to have so much money in h.,** avoir tant d'argent disponible; **stock in h.,** marchandises en magasin; **I've five minutes in h.,** j'ai encore cinq minutes; **the matter in h.,** la chose en question; **work in h.,** travail *m* en cours *ou* en chantier; **to have one's car well in h.,** avoir sa voiture bien en main; **the situation is well in h.,** la situation est bien en main; **to take s.o. in h.,** prendre qn en main; **work on h.,** travail en cours *ou* à faire; **I'm on h. if you need me,** je suis à votre disposition si vous avez besoin de moi; **on (the) one h.,** d'une part; **on the other h.,** d'autre part; **to do sth out of h.,** faire qch sur-le-champ; **to shoot s.o. out of h.,** abattre qn sans autre forme de procès; **to get out of h.,** (*of situation, inflation etc*) échapper à notre *ou* leur *etc* contrôle; (*of children, class etc*) perdre toute discipline; (*of garden*) revenir à l'état sauvage; **to come to h.,** arriver à destination; **your parcel came to h. this morning,** votre paquet m'est parvenu ce matin; **use whatever is to h.,** utilisez ce que vous avez sous la main; **the first excuse to h.,** le premier prétexte venu; **to be h. in glove with s.o.,** être d'intelligence *ou Pej* de mèche avec qn; **to wait on s.o. h. and foot,** être aux petits soins avec qn; **to walk h. in h. with s.o.,** marcher avec qn la main dans la main; **to work h. in h. with s.o.,** agir de concert avec qn; **h. over h., h. over fist,** main sur main (*en grimpant etc*); *F* **to make money h. over fist,** s'enrichir rapidement; **to pass sth from h. to h.,** passer qch de main en main; **to be living from h. to mouth,** vivre au jour le jour; *Sp etc* **to win hands down,** gagner haut la main; **to beat s.o. hands down,** battre qn à plate(s) couture(s);

(c) (*worker*) ouvrier, -ière; *Nau* matelot *m*; **(the ship's) hands,** l'équipage *m*; *Ind etc* **to take on hands,** embaucher de la main-d'œuvre; *Nau* **all hands on deck!**, tout le monde sur le pont!; **to be lost with all hands,** (*of ship*) périr corps et biens; **to be a good** *or F* **dab h. at sth/at doing sth,** être adroit *ou* avoir de l'habileté à qch/à faire qch; **an old h.**, un expert, un spécialiste;

(d) (*handwriting*) écriture *f*; **round/running h.**, écriture ronde/cursive; **he writes a very good h.**, il a une belle écriture; **in one's own h.**, (*écrire une lettre*) de sa propre main;

(e) (*signature*) signature *f*; *Jur* **to set one's h. to a deed,** apposer sa signature à un acte; **note of h.**, billet *m* à ordre;

(f) *Cards* (*player*) joueur, -euse; (*round*) partie *f*; **to have a good h.**, avoir un beau jeu, avoir du jeu; **to win the h.**, gagner la main; **first/fourth h.**, premier/dernier en cartes; **to finish the h.**, finir la partie; **to show one's h.**, faire voir son jeu;

(g) (*measurement*) paume *f*; **horse fifteen hands high,** cheval de quinze paumes;

(h) *Typ* index *m*; (*of signpost, barometer*) indicateur *m*; (*of clock, watch*) aiguille *f*; **the little h. is pointing to three,** la petite aiguille est sur le trois;

(i) *Culin* (*of bananas*) régime *m*; **h. of pork,** jambon *m* d'épaule.

hand² *vt* **(a)** passer, remettre, donner (*qch à qn*); **he handed her the letter to read,** il lui a donné la lettre à lire; *F* **to h. it to s.o.**, reconnaître la supériorité de qn; **you've got to h. it to him,** devant lui, chapeau!; **you've got to h. it to these Russians, they know how to dance!**, il faut reconnaître que ces Russes savent danser!; **(b)** *Nau* serrer (*une voile*).

►**hand around** *vtsep* = **HAND ROUND**.

►**hand back** *vtsep* (*return*) repasser; **she handed me back the bottle,** elle m'a repassé la bouteille.

►**hand down** *vtsep* **(a)** descendre (*qch*) (et le remettre à qn); **h. me down that bottle,** descends-moi cette bouteille; **(b)** (*help someone down*) donner la main à (*qn*) pour l'aider à descendre; **(c)** (*usu passive*) (*bequeath etc*) transmettre (*un collier, une tradition*) (**from,** de; **to,** en); **all her clothes had been handed down from her older sisters,** tous ses vêtements venaient de ses sœurs aînées; **(d)** *Jur* **to h. down a sentence,** prononcer une sentence.

►**hand in** *vtsep* **(a)** remettre, déposer (*un paquet, un télégramme*); **to h. in one's resignation,** démissionner; **to h. in homework,** rendre un devoir; **to h. lost property in (to the police),** remettre un objet trouvé (à la police); **(b)** *Nau* **to h. in the sail,** crocher dans la toile.

►**hand off** *vtsep Rugby* repousser (*qn*) du plat de la main.

►**hand on** *vtsep* transmettre (*une coutume*); passer (*une nouvelle*) (**to,** à).

►**hand out** *vtsep* **(a)** (*distribute*) distribuer (*des tracts, des biscuits*); **(b)** (*give*) donner; **he's always handing out advice,** il se permet de donner des conseils.

►**hand over 1** *vtsep* **(a)** (*give*) donner, remettre; **(b)** (*deliver*) remettre, livrer; **she handed over the documents to a lawyer,** elle a remis les documents à un avocat; **(c)** (*surrender*) céder (*son bien*); **h. over your wallet!**, donne ton portefeuille!; **to h. s.o. over to justice,** livrer *ou* remettre qn aux mains de la justice; **(d)** (*transfer*) transmettre (*des pouvoirs*); **we now h. you over to our foreign affairs correspondent,** nous passons maintenant la parole au responsable des affaires étrangères; **to h. over the command to ...**, remettre le commandement à .... **2** *vi* **(a)** (*transfer*) **I now h. over to the weatherman,** je passe maintenant la parole au responsable météo; **when will she h. over to the new president?**, quand va-t-elle laisser la place au nouveau président?; **(b)** (*give*) **I know you have it, so h. over!**, passe-le moi, je sais que tu l'as!

►**hand round** *vtsep* (*circulate*) faire passer, faire circuler (*la bouteille etc*).

hand- [hænd] *pref* à la main; **h. sewn/***etc*, cousu/*etc* (à la) main; **h.-operated,** à commande manuelle.

handbag ['hændbæg] *n Br* sac *m* à main; *Can* sacoche *m*.

handball ['hændbɔːl] *n Sp* hand-ball *m*.

handbell ['hændbel] *n* sonnette *f*, clochette *f*.

handbill ['hændbɪl] *n* prospectus *m*.

handbook ['hændbʊk] *n* **(a)** guide *m* (*du voyageur, du touriste*); livret *m* (*d'un musée etc*); **(b)** *Sch etc* manuel *m* (*de sciences etc*).

handbrake ['hændbreɪk] *n Aut* frein *m* à main.

h & c (*abbr* **hot and cold**) eau courante chaude et froide.

handcart ['hændkɑːt] *n* charrette *f* à bras.

handcuff ['hændkʌf] *vt* mettre *ou* passer les menottes à, menotter (*qn*); **to h. s.o. to s.o.**, attacher deux personnes ensemble avec des menottes; **to h. s.o. to sth,** attacher qn à qch avec des menottes.

handcuffs ['hændkʌfs] *npl* menottes *fpl*.

-handed [hændɪd] *suff* **left-h.**, (*person*) gaucher; **right-h.**, (*person*) droitier; **two-h.**, (*sword etc*) à deux mains; (*card game*) à deux; (*ambidextrous*) ambidextre.

handful ['hændfʊl] *n* **(a)** poignée *f* (*de sable etc*); **(b)** (*small number*) petit nombre; **there was** *or F* **were only a h. of people there,** il n'y avait là que quelques personnes; **(c)** *F* (*difficult person*) **that child is a h.**, cet enfant-là me donne du fil à retordre.

handgrip ['hændgrɪp] *n* **(a)** (*grip*) prise *f*; **(b)** (*handshake*) poignée *f* de main; **(c)** *Cycling* poignée *f*.

handgun ['hændgʌn] *n Am* revolver *m*, pistolet *m*.

hand-held ['hænd'held] *adj Cin TV* **h.-h. camera,** caméra *f* portable.

handhold ['hændhəʊld] *n* prise *f*.

handicap¹ ['hændɪkæp] *n* **(a)** *Med* handicap *m*; (*disadvantage*) handicap, désavantage *m*; **to have a severe h.**, avoir un lourd handicap; **(b)** *Sp* handicap *m*; rendement *m* (*accordé à un concurrent*); *Horseracing* (*race*) handicap; **(weight) h.**, (*of racehorse*) surcharge *f*; **time/distance h.**, rendement *m* de temps/distance.

handicap² *vt* (**-pp-**) **(a)** (*disadvantage*) handicaper, désavantager; **their lack of preparation handicapped them,** ils ont été désavantagés par leur manque de préparation; **(b)** *Sp* handicaper.

handicapped ['hændɪkæpt] **1** *adj* handicapé, désavantagé. **2** *n* **the (physically/mentally) h.**, (*used as pl*) les handicapés (physiques/mentaux).

handicraft ['hændɪkrɑːft] *n* **(a)** (*trade*) artisanat *m*, métier manuel; **(b)** (*result*) artisanat *m*, produit artisanal.

handiness ['hændɪnɪs] *n* **(a)** commodité *f* (*d'un outil etc*); maniabilité *f* (*d'un navire etc*); **(b)** (*skill with hands*) adresse *f*, dextérité *f*, habileté *f* (manuelle).

handing ['hændɪŋ] *n* remise *f* (*de qch*) (**to s.o.**, à qn)

handing down, handing on *n* transmission *f* (*d'une tradition*).

handing over *n* remise *f* (*de qch*) entre les mains de qn; *Jur* cession *f* (*de biens*); *Admin* transmission *f* (*de pouvoirs*).

handiwork ['hændɪwɜːk] *n* **(a)** (*action*) travail *m* manuel; **(b)** (*result*) ouvrage *m*, travail *m*, œuvre *f*; **the repair/fruit bowl is Jenny's h.**, c'est Jenny qui a fait la réparation/la corbeille à fruits; **this quarrel (of theirs) is your h.**, c'est de ta faute s'ils se disputent.

handkerchief ['hæŋkətʃɪf] *n* mouchoir *m*; **garden the size of a pocket h.**, jardin grand comme un mouchoir de poche.

hand-knit(ted) ['hændnɪt, -nɪtəd] *adj* (*sweater etc*) tricoté (à la) main.

handle¹ ['hænd(ə)l] *n* **(a)** manche *m* (*de balai, de couteau, d'outil etc*); bras *m*, balancier *m* (*de pompe*); bras (*de brouette*); brancard *m* (*de civière*); queue *f* (*de poêle*); poignée *f* (*d'épée, de levier, de boîte, de valise etc*); clef *f* (*de robinet*); anse *f* (*de corbeille, de seau etc*); **(door) h.**, poignée *f*; *F* **to fly off the h.**, s'emporter, s'emballer; **you're giving him a h. against you,** vous lui donnez des armes *ou* un avantage contre vous; **(b)** *F* (*title*) titre *m*; **to have a h. to one's name,** avoir un titre (*de noblesse*).

handle² 1 *vt* **(a)** (*touch, hold*) tâter, toucher; **to h. a material,** tâter un tissu; **h. with care,** (*on package*) = fragile;

(b) (*operate*) manier, manipuler (*qch*); manœuvrer (*un navire, les voiles etc*); gouverner (*un navire*); conduire (*une voiture*); **how to h. a gun,** comment se servir d'un fusil;

(c) (*treat*) traiter; **to h. s.o. roughly,** malmener qn, rudoyer qn; **the author handles the subject well,** l'auteur traite bien le sujet;

(d) (*manage*) **to h. a situation,** prendre en main une situation; **to h. a crisis,** prendre une crise en main; **I can't h. interviews,** je n'arrive pas à affronter les interviews; **he can't h. it when people get aggressive,** il n'arrive pas à faire face aux gens qui deviennent agressifs; **she can h. bullies,** elle sait s'occuper des petites brutes; **to h. a lot of money,** brasser beaucoup d'argent;

(e) (*deal with*) **to h. a lot of business,** brasser beaucoup d'affaires; **to h. large orders,** s'occuper de grandes commandes; **who handles your products in France?**, qui distribue vos produits en France?

2 *vi Aut* (*of car*) **to h. well,** bien conduire.

handlebar ['hænd(ə)lbɑːr] *n* (*usu pl*) **handlebars,** guidon *m* (de bicyclette); *F* **h. moustache,** moustaches *fpl* en guidon (de bicyclette).

handler ['hændlər] *n Com* manutentionnaire *mf*; **(dog) h.**, maître *m* (de) chien.

handling ['hændlɪŋ] *n* **(a)** (*touching, holding*) manipulation *f*, action *f* de toucher; **(b)** (*of tool*) maniement *m*; (*of explosives*) manipulation *f*; (*of a ship*) manœuvre *f*; (*of a car*) conduite *f*; **(c)** (*treatment*) traitement *m* (*de qn, d'un sujet etc*); **rough h.,** traitement brutal; **(d)** (*of crisis, situation*) prise *f* en main; (*of funds*) maniement *m*; **(e)** *Com* manutention *f*; distribution *f*; **(f)** *Fb* (faute *f* de) main *f*.

handmade ['hænd'meɪd] *adj* fait *ou* fabriqué à la main.

hand-me-down ['hændmɪdaʊn] *n F* **h.-me-downs,** vêtements usagés *ou* d'occasion, frusques *fpl*; **I used to wear my brother's h.-me-downs,** je récupérais les vêtements usagés de mon frère; **h.-me-d. clothes,** vêtements usagés, frusques.

hand-out ['hændaʊt] *n F* **(a)** *Pej* aumône *f*; (*food*) = nourriture distribuée aux mendiants; **I don't want to live off h.-outs,** je ne veux pas vivre de la charité des autres; **state h.-o.,** = allocation d'aide publique; **(b)** *Journ* compte rendu communiqué à la presse; *Sch etc* notes *fpl* (polycopiées) (*données aux élèves*); **(c)** *Com* (*brochure*) prospectus *m*, circulaire *m* publicitaire; (*sample*) cadeau *m* publicitaire.

hand-pick ['hænd'pɪk] *vt* trier (*le charbon etc*) à la main; éplucher (*la laine etc*) à la main; **the volunteers have been hand-picked,** les volontaires ont été triés sur le volet.

hand-picked ['hænd'pɪkd] *adj* (*réunion*) très sélect; (*personne*) trié sur le volet.

handrail ['hændreɪl] *n* garde-fou *m*, *pl* garde-fous, garde-corps *m inv*; *Nau Rail* rambarde *f*; (*of staircase etc*) rampe *f*, main courante.

handsaw ['hændsɔː] *n* scie *f* à main.

handset ['hændset] *n Tel* combiné *m*.

handshake ['hændʃeɪk] *n* **(a)** poignée *f ou* serrement *m* de main; **(b)** *Comptr* = **HANDSHAKING**; **h. message,** message *m* d'établissement de liaison.

handshaking ['hændʃeɪkɪŋ] *n Comptr* établissement *m* d'une liaison.

hands-off ['hæn'zɒf] *adj Pol* non-interventionniste; **the director has a h.-off style of management,** le directeur est partisan de laisser de l'autonomie à son personnel, *Pej* la direction est trop lointaine.

handsome ['hænsəm] *adj* **(a)** (*good-looking*) beau, *f* belle; **a h. man,** un bel homme; **she was still a h. woman,** elle était toujours belle; **a h. building,** une belle construction; **(b)** (*conduct etc*) gracieux, généreux; **he received very h. treatment,** on l'a traité d'une façon très généreuse; **(c)** (*considerable*) bon (*prix*); (*cadeau*) généreux; **h. fortune,** belle fortune; **to make a h. profit,** faire *ou* réaliser de beaux bénéfices.

handsomely ['hænsəmlɪ] *adv* **(a)** bien (*habillé, meublé etc*); **(b)** (*agir*) généreusement; (*payer*) libéralement.

handsomeness ['hænsəmnɪs] *n* **(a)** beauté *f* (*d'une personne, d'un monument etc*); **(b)** générosité *f* (*d'une action*); libéralité *f* (*d'une récompense*).

hands-on ['hæn'zɒn] *adj* (*training*) pratique; **h.-on exhibition,** (*at museum*) = exposition où les gens sont encouragés à toucher aux objets; **the director has a h.-on style of management,** le directeur s'implique vraiment.

handspring ['hændsprɪŋ] *n Gym* saut *m* de mains.

handstand ['hændstænd] *n Gym* **to do a h.,** faire le poirier.

hand-to-hand ['hæntə'hænd] **1** *adj* (*fighting*) corps-à-corps. **2** *adv* **to fight h.-to-h.,** se battre au corps-à-corps.

hand-to-mouth ['hæntə'maʊθ] *adj & adv* **to live h.-to-m., to have a h.-to-m. existence,** tirer le diable par la queue.

hand-tooling ['hændtuːlɪŋ] *n* **(a)** *Ind* (*on a lathe etc*) travail *m* à la main; **(b)** (*in bookbinding*) dorure à froid faite à la main.

handwork ['hændwɜːk] *n* travail *m* à la main, travail manuel.

handwriting ['hændraɪtɪŋ] *n* écriture *f*; **this letter is in the h. of ...,** cette lettre a été écrite par ... *ou* est de la main de ...; **h. expert,** expert *m* en écritures.

handwritten ['hændrɪt(ə)n] *adj* (*letter etc*) manuscrit.

handy ['hændɪ] *adj* **(a)** (*tool etc*) pratique; (*ship*) maniable; **that would come in very h.,** cela serait très utile *ou* ferait bien l'affaire; **a h. tip,** un bon conseil; **(b)** (*convenient*) commode; **your new flat's h. for the shops,** il y a toutes les commodités à proximité de ton nouvel appartement; **(c)** (*within reach*) à portée (de la main); **I always keep my tools h.,** j'ai toujours mes outils sous la main; **(d)** adroit (*de ses mains*); habile; **he's very h. about the house,** (*good at making, repairing things*) c'est un bon bricoleur; **h. at sth/at doing sth,** adroit à qch/à faire qch; **to be h. with one's fists,** savoir se servir de ses poings.

handyman, *pl* **-men** ['hændɪmæn, -men] *n* (*employee*) homme *m* à tout faire *ou* à toute main; (*DIY expert etc*) bricoleur *m*; *Am* **h.'s special,** = maison qui a besoin de beaucoup de travaux.

hang¹ [hæŋ] *n* **(a)** (*of a cliff etc*) pente *f*, inclinaison *f*; (*of clothing*) ajustement *m*; (*of material*) drapé *m*; *F* **to get the h. of sth,** (*acquire knack*) attraper le coup *ou* saisir le truc de *ou* pour faire qch; (*understand*) comprendre qch, piger qch; **when you've got the h. of things,** quand vous serez au courant; **(b)** *F* **I don't give** *or* **care a h.,** je m'en moque *ou* m'en fiche.

hang² *v* (*pt & pp* **hung** [hʌŋ]) **1** *vt* **(a)** (*suspend*) pendre, accrocher, suspendre (**on, from,** à); monter (*une porte*); **to h. a coat on a hook,** pendre un manteau à une patère; **they hung banners from their windows,** ils ont accroché des bannières à leurs fenêtres; **to h. sth on the wall,** pendre qch au mur; **to h. a picture,** suspendre un tableau; (*exhibit*) exposer un tableau (*au Salon etc*); *Aut etc* **low-hung,** (*essieu etc*) surbaissé;

(b) (*droop*) **to h. one's head,** baisser la tête;

(c) coller (*du papier à tapisser*); **to h. a room with tapestries,** tendre une salle de tapisseries; **hall hung with flags,** salle ornée de drapeaux;

(d) *Culin* faire faisander (*la viande, le gibier*);

(e) to h. fire, (*of troops etc*) suspendre le feu; *Fig* (*of undertaking*) traîner (en longueur);

(f) (*pt & pp* **hanged** [hæŋd]) pendre (*un criminel*); **he hanged himself,** il s'est pendu; *F* **I'm hanged if I know!,** je n'en sais fichtre rien!; **h. it!,** zut!, mince alors!; *Prov* **you might as well be hanged for a sheep as for a lamb,** autant vaut être pendu pour un mouton que pour un agneau.

2 *vi* **(a)** (*be suspended*) pendre, être suspendu; *Culin* (*of game*) se faisander; **picture hanging on the wall,** tableau pendu *ou* accroché au mur; **the boy was hanging by his arms from the tree,** le garçon était suspendu à l'arbre par les bras; **to h. out of the window,** (*of person*) se pencher par la fenêtre, (*of thing*) pendre à la fenêtre; **time hangs heavy (on my hands),** le temps me pèse *ou* me semble long;

(b) (*of drapery, clothes etc*) tomber, se draper; **to h. loose** *or* **limply,** pendiller; **his clothes h. loosely on him,** il flotte dans ses vêtements; **this door hangs badly,** cette porte est mal suspendue (sur ses gonds); *esp Am Sl* **h. loose!,** relax, Max!;

(c) (*of criminal*) être pendu; *Fig F* **if he doesn't like it he can go h.,** si ça ne lui plaît pas, qu'il aille se faire pendre; *Old-fashioned* **you'll h. for this!,** tu seras pendu pour ça!

▶**hang about 1** *vi F* **(a)** (*wait*) poireauter; **to keep s.o. hanging about,** faire poireauter qn; **h. about, that's not what I said!,** eh, minute! ce n'est pas ce que j'ai dit!; **(b)** (*waste time*) traîner, flâner; **to h. about the house doing nothing,** traîner à la maison sans rien faire; **young men hanging about on street corners,** jeunes qui traînent dans la rue; **don't h. about or we'll never finish!,** ne perds pas de temps ou nous n'aurons jamais fini!; *F* **you don't h. about, do you!,** vous êtes un *ou* une rapide, vous!; *F* **this car doesn't h. about,** cette voiture est un vrai bolide. **2** *vipo* (*frequent*) fréquenter, traîner dans (*un endroit*).

▶**hang around 1** *vi* **(a)** = **HANG ABOUT 1**; **(b)** (*associate*) **to h. around with s.o.,** traîner avec qn. **2** *vipo* = **HANG ABOUT 2.**

▶**hang back** *vi* (*not go forward*) rester en arrière; (*hesitate*) hésiter; (*be reluctant*) renâcler.

▶**hang in** *vi esp Am Sl* (*persevere, not lose heart*) tenir bon; **just h. in there,** courage, tenez bon.

▶**hang on 1** *vi* **(a)** (*hold*) se cramponner, s'accrocher; **h. on tight!,** cramponne-toi bien!; **(b)** *F* (*wait*) patienter, attendre; *Tel* **h. on!,** ne quittez pas!; **h. on for a moment,** attendez un moment; **(c)** (*endure*) supporter, *F* tenir le coup. **2** *vipo* **(a)** (*hold*) **to h. on s.o.'s arm,** (*of thing*) pendre au bras de qn; (*of person*) se pendre au bras de qn; **(b)** (*lean*) **a horse that hangs on the bit,** un cheval qui s'appuie sur le mors; **(c)** (*be attentive to*) **to h. on s.o.'s lips** *or* **words,** être pendu aux lèvres de qn; **the children hung on his every word,** les enfants l'écoutaient avidement; **(d)** (*depend*) dépendre de, tenir à; **everything hangs on his answer,** tout dépend de sa réponse.

▶**hang on to** *vipo* **(a)** (*hold tightly*) se cramponner à, ne pas lâcher; **he hung on to the cliff face,** il s'est agrippé à la paroi de la falaise; **(b)** (*keep*) garder; **I'd h. on to those documents if I were you,** si j'étais toi, je garderais précieusement ces documents; **he hung on to these outdated ideas,** il se cramponnait à des idées démodées.

▶**hang out 1** *vtsep* (*suspend*) pendre *ou* mettre (*qch*) au dehors; **to h. out the washing,** étendre le linge; **to h. out a flag,** arborer un pavillon. **2** *vi* **(a)** (*be suspended*) pendre (au dehors); **the rocks h. out over the gully,** les rochers surplombent le ravin; **his shirt was hanging out,** sa chemise dépassait; *Sl* **to let it all h. out,** se défouler; **(b)** *F* (*live*) crécher; (*frequent*) traîner; **where do you h. out?,** (*live*) où créchez-vous?

▶**hang over** *vipo* planer *ou* peser sur; **a thick fog hangs over the town,** un épais brouillard plane sur la ville; *Fig* **a heavy silence hung over the meeting,** un silence pesait sur l'assemblée; **a question mark is hanging over the outcome of the debate,** un point d'interrogation plane sur l'issue du débat; **I have an appointment with the dentist hanging over me,** je vais me retrouver chez le dentiste sous peu; **we've got the threat of eviction hanging over us,** nous risquons d'être expulsés d'une minute à l'autre.

▶**hang together** *vi* **(a)** (*of people*) rester unis; **(b)** (*of statements etc*) s'accorder, *F* tenir debout.

▶**hang up 1** *vtsep* (*suspend*) accrocher, pendre (*son chapeau, un tableau etc*); *Fig* **to h. up one's dancing shoes/racket/***etc*, (*of dancer/tennis player/etc*) quitter la scène. **2** *vi Tel* raccrocher (l'appareil); **to h. up on s.o.,** raccrocher au nez de qn.

hangar ['hæŋər] *n esp Av* hangar *m*.

hangdog ['hæŋdɒg] *adj* **h. look,** air *m* de chien battu.

hanger ['hæŋər] *n* (*hook*) crochet *m* (de suspension); (*loop on coat etc*) attache *f*; *MecE* suspenseur *m*; **(coat) h.,** cintre *m*; **bearing h.,** chaise suspendue.

hanger-on, *pl* **hangers-on** [hæŋə'rɒn, hæŋə'zɒn] *n* parasite *m*, pique-assiette *m inv*.

hang-glide ['hæŋglaɪd] *vi* faire du deltaplane.

hang-glider ['hæŋglaɪdər] *n* (*craft*) deltaplane *m*; (*person*) deltaplaneur *m*.

hang-gliding ['hæŋglaɪdɪŋ] *n* (sport *m* du) deltaplane *m*.

hanging ['hæŋɪŋ] **1** *adj* **(a)** (*hook etc*) pendant; (*bridge*) suspendu; (*scaffolding*) volant; *Geog* (*valley*) suspendu; **h. cupboard,** armoire murale; **h. wardrobe,** penderie *f*; **the H. Gardens of Babylon,** les jardins suspendus de Babylone; **(b)** *F* **h. judge,** = juge féroce, qui condamne les accusés à la potence. **2** *n* **(a)** (*suspending*) suspension *f* (*d'une lampe, d'un tableau etc*); montage *m*, accrochage *m* (*d'une porte*); tenture *f*, pose *f* (*d'une tapisserie*); pendaison *f* (*d'un criminel*); *Culin* faisandage *m* (*du gibier*); **h. committee,** = comité de réception ou jury d'admission des tableaux; **(b) (wall) hangings,** tenture(s) *f*(*pl*) tapisserie(s) *f*(*pl*).

hangman, *pl* **-men** ['hæŋmən] *n* bourreau *m*.

hangnail ['hæŋneɪl] *n* envie *f* (de l'ongle).

hang-out ['hæŋaʊt] *n F* (*home*) logement *m*; (*haunt*) repaire *m*, nid *m*.

hangover ['hæŋəʊvər] *n F* **(a)** (*from drinking*) **to have a h.,** avoir la gueule de bois, avoir mal aux cheveux; **(b)** (*practice, belief etc*) reliquat *m*; **a h. from the past,** un reliquat du passé.

hang-up ['hæŋʌp] *n* **(a)** *F* (*complex*) complexe *m*; **he's got a h.-up about driving,** il fait un blocage, il ne veut pas conduire; **you've got a lot of h.-ups,** tu es très complexé; **(b)** *Comptr* arrêt imprévu (*de la machine*).

hank [hæŋk] *n* (*of wool etc*) écheveau *m*; (*of thread*) torchette *f*, peignée *f*.

hanker ['hæŋkər] *vi* **to h. after** *or* **for sth,** avoir bien envie de qch, soupirer après qch, convoiter qch.

hankering ['hæŋkərɪŋ] *n* vif désir, grande envie (**after, for,** de); **to have a h. for sth,** avoir grande envie de qch.

hankie, hanky ['hæŋkɪ] *n F* mouchoir *m*.

hanky-panky ['hæŋkɪ'pæŋkɪ] *n F* **(a)** (*sexual activity*) batifolage *m*, galipettes *fpl*; **(b)** (*underhand behaviour*) coup fourré, entourloupette *f*.

Hanoverian [hænə'vɪərɪən] **1** *adj* hanovrien. **2** *n* Hanovrien, -ienne.

Hansard ['hænsɑːd] *n Parl* = compte rendu officiel des débats parlementaires.

Hanseatic [hænsɪ'ætɪk] *adj Hist* **the H. League,** la Ligue hanséatique.

hansom ['hænsəm] *n Hist* **h. (cab),** cabriolet *m*.

Hants *abbr* **Hampshire.**

ha'penny, *pl* **ha'pence** ['heɪpənɪ, -pəns] *n Br F* = **HALFPENNY.**

haphazard [hæp'hæzəd] *adj* (*attempt*) au petit bonheur; (*arrangement*) fortuit; **to choose in a h. way,** choisir à l'aveuglette.

haphazardly [hæp'hæzədlɪ] *adv* au petit bonheur, à l'aveuglette.

hapless ['hæplɪs] *adj Arch & Lit* infortuné, malheureux.

happen¹ ['hæp(ə)n] **1** *vi* (*take place*) arriver, se passer; **it happened ten years ago,** cela s'est passé il y a dix ans; **did someone see what happened?,** (*of accident, incident*) quelqu'un a-t-il vu ce qui s'est passé *ou* est arrivé?; **it happens over and over again,** c'est toujours la même chose; **don't let it h. again!,** que cela n'arrive plus!; **it couldn't h. here,** ce n'est pas ici que ça arriverait; **I don't like what's happening in this country,** je n'aime pas ce qui se passe dans ce pays; **just as if nothing had happened,** comme si de rien n'était; **whatever happens,** quoi qu'il arrive; **as it happens,** justement, précisément; **as often happens,** comme il est fréquent; **what has happened to him?,** (*what has occurred?*) qu'est-ce qui lui est arrivé?; (*what has become of him?*) qu'est-ce qu'il est devenu?; **if anything happens to me,** (*if I die*) s'il m'arrive quelque chose; **what's happened to my pen?,** (*where is it?*) qu'est-ce qu'on a fait de mon stylo?; (*what's wrong with it?*) qu'est-il arrivé à mon stylo?

2 *vt* (*chance*) **he happened to pass that way,** il s'est trouvé à passer par là; **a taxi happened to be passing,** par hasard *ou* par bonheur un taxi passait; **I h. to know that ...,** il se trouve que je sais que ...; **do you h. to know whether ...?,** sauriez-vous par hasard si ...?; **it just so happens that ...,** il se trouve justement que ...; **if you h. to find it,** s'il arrive que vous le trouviez; **she happens to be my sister,** il se trouve qu'elle est ma sœur.

▶**happen along, happen by** *vi* (*arrive by chance*) arriver par hasard.

▶**happen on** *vipo* (*come across*) tomber sur (*qn, qch*).

happening ['hæp(ə)nɪŋ] *n* événement *m*; *Th* happening *m*.

happenstance ['hæp(ə)nstæns] *n esp Am* **it was h.,** c'était le hasard.

happily ['hæpɪlɪ] *adv* **(a)** heureusement; **they laughed h.,** ils rirent de bon cœur; **we were sitting there quite h. watching television,** nous étions installés tranquillement devant la télévision; **to live h.,** vivre heureux; **a h. married couple,** un ménage heureux; **they lived h. ever after,** (*at end of fairy story*) = ils furent heureux et eurent beaucoup d'enfants; **he'll quite h. say one thing and do the opposite,** ça ne le gêne pas de dire une chose et de faire exactement le contraire; **(b)** (*fortunately*) heureusement.

happiness ['hæpɪnɪs] *n* bonheur *m*, félicité *f*.

happy ['hæpɪ] *adj* **(a)** heureux; **to make s.o. h.,** rendre qn heureux, faire la joie de qn; **his money hasn't made him h.,** l'argent n'a pas fait son bonheur; **h. life,** vie heureuse; **to be as h. as the day is long,** être heureux comme un poisson dans l'eau; **h. to oblige,** ravi de rendre service; **to be h. to do sth,** être heureux *ou* content de faire qch; **h. birthday!,** joyeux *ou* bon anniversaire!; **h. Christmas!,** joyeux Noël!; *F* **h. days,** (*as toast*) à votre santé!; *Cards* **h. families,** jeu *m* des sept familles; **in happier circumstances,** dans des circonstances plus favorables; **in happier times,** en des jours meilleurs; **I'm very h. with his work,** je suis très satisfait *ou* content de son travail; **I'm not at all h. about it,** cela ne me plaît pas du tout; **give me a good book and I'm h.,** un bon livre suffit à me satisfaire; **this game keeps the children h. for hours,** avec ce jeu, les enfants sont contents pendant des heures; *Old-fashioned F* **to be h.,** (*drunk*) être un peu gris; **h. hour,** (*in bar*) = moment pendant lequel les boissons sont moins chères; **h. medium,** juste milieu *m*;

(b) (*wording*) bien choisi, à propos; (*coincidence*) heureux.

happy-go-lucky ['hæpɪgəʊ'lʌkɪ] *adj* sans souci, insouciant; **to do sth in a h.-go-l. fashion,** faire qch au petit bonheur.

Hapsburg ['hæpsbɜːg] *n Hist* Habsbourg.

harangue¹ [hə'ræŋ] *n* harangue *f*.

harangue² 1 *vt* haranguer (*la foule etc*). **2** *vi* prononcer *ou* faire une harangue.

harass ['hærəs, hə'ræs] *vt* **(a)** *Mil* harceler, tenir en alerte (*l'ennemi*); **(b)** tracasser, tourmenter (*qn*); (*sexually*) harceler; **to be looking harassed,** avoir l'air tracassé *ou* tourmenté; **to h. s.o. to do sth,** harceler qn pour qu'il fasse qch; **he was harassing me for money,** il me harcelait pour que je lui donne de l'argent.

harassment ['hærəsmənt, hə'ræs-] *n* **(a)** *Mil* harcèlement *m*; **(b)** (*of person*) tracasserie *f*, tourment *m*; (*for money etc*) harcèlement *m*; **police h.,** tracasseries policières; **sexual h.,** harcèlement sexuel.

harbinger ['hɑːbɪndʒər] *n Lit* avant-coureur *m*, *pl* avant-coureurs; messager, -ère; (*precursor*) précurseur *m*; **the riot was a h. of things to come,** la bagarre annonçait ce qui allait arriver.

harbour¹, *US* **harbor** ['hɑːbər] *n Nau* port *m*; **tidal h.,** port à *ou* de marée; **h. dues,** droits *mpl* de mouillage; **h. master,** capitaine *m ou* officier *m* de port; (*of small port*) lieutenant *m* de port.

harbour², *US* **harbor 1** *vt* héberger; donner asile à (*qn*); receler (*un criminel*); retenir (*la saleté*); entretenir, nourrir (*des soupçons*); **to h. a grudge against s.o.,** garder rancune à qn. **2** *vi* chercher asile, se réfugier (**in,** dans).

hard [hɑːd] **1** *adj* **(a)** (*firm*) dur; (*stock, rates etc*) tendu, tenu, soutenu; **h. substance,** substance dure; **to become** *or* **get h.,** (*of cement etc*) durcir; **to become harder,** se rendurcir; *Fig* **h. facts,** la dure réalité; **there's no h. evidence,** il n'y a pas de preuve tangible; *Comptr* **h. copy,** copie *f* sur papier; **h. core,** *Constr* empierrement *m*; (*of people*) noyau dur; **there is a h. core of resistance to the reforms,** il y a une résistance farouche à ces réformes; *Tennis* **h. court,** court *m* en dur; *Comptr* **h. disk,** disque dur; *Constr* **h. hat,** (*hat*) casque *m*; (*worker*) ouvrier *m* de construction; *Metal* **h. lead,** plomb *m* aigre; **h. line,** position *f* ferme; **the president takes a h. line on drugs,** la position du président vis-à-vis de la drogue est très ferme; *Culin* **h. sauce,** = sauce au beurre, au sucre et au brandy ou au rhum servie avec le pudding; **h. shoulder,** bande *f* d'arrêt d'urgence; **h. snow,** neige durcie; **h. and fast,** (*of ship*) à sec; bien pris; **h.-and-fast rule,** règle absolue *ou* rigoureuse;

(b) (*difficult*) difficile; (*tâche, chemin*) pénible; **to be h. to please,** être exigeant *ou* difficile à contenter; **to be h. of hearing,** être dur d'oreille; **the h. of hearing,** les malentendants *mpl*; **article that is h. to sell,** article difficile à vendre; **the laws make it h. to leave the country,** à cause des lois, il est difficile de quitter le pays; **I find it h. to believe that ...,** j'ai peine à croire que ... + *sub*; **it is h. to understand,** c'est difficile à comprendre; **it's h. to say,** c'est difficile à dire; **the hardest part of the job is done,** le plus dur est fait;

(c) (*severe, harsh*) (*person, manner etc*) dur, sévère (**to, towards,** envers); (*maître*) sévère, exigeant; (*cœur*) dur; *Phot* (*épreuve*) heurté, contrasté; **to be h. on s.o.,** être sévère envers qn; **it's hardest on the children,** le plus dur, c'est pour les enfants; **it's h. to lose a child,** c'est une dure épreuve de perdre un enfant; **to say h. things to s.o.,** dire des choses dures à qn; **to be as h. as nails,** ne pas avoir de cœur; (*physically*) avoir des muscles d'acier; être résistant; **h. fact,** fait brutal; **a h. life,** une vie difficile; **times are h.,** les temps sont durs *ou* difficiles; **to have a h. time of it,** en voir de dures; *F* **h. luck!, h. lines!,** *Br Sl* **h. cheese!,** pas de chance!, quelle guigne!; **no h. feelings?,** tu ne m'en veux pas?; **h. liquor,** spiritueux *mpl*; *F* **a drop of the h. stuff,** une goutte d'alcool *ou* d'eau-de-vie; **h. drugs,** drogues dures; *Ling* **h. consonant,** consonne dure; *Tech* **h. light,** lumière crue; **h. water,** eau *f* calcaire; *Tech* eau dure;

(d) (*strenuous*) **h. work,** (*working hard*) travail assidu; (*hard task*) travail ingrat; **it was h. work to convince him,** j'ai eu fort à faire pour le convaincre; **it is h. work for me to ..., I find it h. work to ...,** j'ai beaucoup de peine *ou* bien du mal à ...; **h. gallop,** galop soutenu; **h. drinker,** grand buveur; **h. fight,** rude combat *m*; **the h. sell,** méthode *f* de vente agressive; (*publicity*) battage *m* publicitaire; **it's a h. blow for him,** c'est un rude coup pour lui; **to try one's hardest,** faire tout son possible; **h. labour,** travaux forcés;

(e) (*extreme*) (*winter*) rigoureux; **h. frost,** forte gelée;

(f) (*tough*) **a h. man,** un dur; *Br Sl* **he's h.,** c'est un dur.

(g) *Comptr Typ* **h. hyphen,** trait *m* d'union (qui fait partie du mot); **h. return,** retour *m* de chariot qui marque la fin d'une ligne.

2 *adv* **(a)** (*vigorously*) fort; **as h. as one can,** de toutes ses forces; **to hit** *or* **strike h.,** cogner dur; **to jam on the brakes h.,** serrer les freins à bloc; **to look** *or* **gaze** *or* **stare h. at s.o.,** regarder fixement qn; **we can't find it — well, look harder!,** nous ne le trouvons pas — et bien cherchez mieux!; **to think h.,** réfléchir profondément; **to try h.,** faire de son mieux; **to try harder,** faire plus d'efforts; **to drink h.,** boire beaucoup; **to play h.,** jouer de son mieux; (*roughly*) avoir un jeu dur; **to swim h. for the shore,** nager de toutes ses forces vers le rivage; **to work h. at sth,** travailler dur *ou* ferme à qch; **she works too h.,** elle se surmène; **to be h. at work,** être en plein travail; **it's raining h.,** il pleut à verse; **it will go h. with him if ...,** cela sera sérieux (pour lui) si...; *Nau* **h. over!,** la barre toute!; *F* **to be h. up (for money),** être fauché *ou* à sec; *F* **to be h. up for volunteers/suggestions/*etc*,** manquer de bénévoles/suggestions/*etc*;

(b) (*with difficulty*) difficilement, avec peine; **you'd be h. pushed to find a shop open at this time,** tu vas avoir du mal à trouver une boutique ouverte à cette heure-ci;

(c) (*near*) **h. by,** tout près, tout contre; **to follow h. (up)on** *or* **after** *or* **behind s.o.,** suivre qn de près;

(d) (*harshly*) *F* **to feel h. done by,** se sentir traité de façon injuste.

3 *n* **(a)** *Br Sl* (*hard labour*) **fifteen years' h.,** quinze ans de travaux forcés;

(b) *Br Nau* cale *f* (*de débarquement*);

(c) *Tex* **hards,** déchets *mpl* de chanvre *ou* de lin.

hardback ['hɑːdbæk] **1** *n* livre cartonné; **the book is only available in h.,** ce livre n'est disponible qu'en version cartonnée. **2** *adj* cartonné.

hard-bitten ['hɑːd'bɪt(ə)n] *adj F* (*person*) dur à cuire.

hardboard ['hɑːdbɔːd] *n Constr* carton dur, Isorel ® *m*.

hard-boiled [hɑːd'bɔɪld] *adj* **(a)** *Culin* **h.-b. egg,** œuf dur; **(b)** *F* = **HARD-BITTEN.**

hard-core ['hɑːdkɔːr] *adj* convaincu, inconditionnel; **h.-c. reactionaries,** des réactionnaires convaincus; **h.-c. pornography,** pornographie *f* hard.

hardcover ['hɑːdkʌvər] *n esp Am* = **HARDBACK.**

hard-earned [hɑːd'ɜːnd] *adj* (*money etc*) péniblement gagné; (*prize etc*) bien mérité; **don't waste your h.-e. wages,** ne gaspille pas l'argent que tu as péniblement gagné.

harden ['hɑːd(ə)n] **1** *vt* **(a)** durcir, (r)endurcir (*qch*); tremper (*l'acier etc*); *Med* scléroser (*les muscles etc*); **to h. oneself** *or* **to become hardened to the cold,** s'endurcir *ou* s'aguerrir au froid; **to h. s.o.'s heart,** endurcir le cœur de qn; **(b)** *Metal* = **CASE-HARDEN**; **(c)** = **HARDEN OFF. 2** *vi* **(a)** (*of substance*) (se) durcir, s'endurcir; (*of person, constitution*) s'endurcir, s'aguerrir; **attitudes have hardened,** les attitudes se sont durcies; **scientific opinion has hardened to the view that ...,** le monde savant est de plus en plus d'avis que ...; **(b)** *Fin* (*of shares etc*) se raffermir; **prices are hardening,** les prix sont en hausse.

▶**harden off** *vtsep* **to h. off seedlings,** fortifier de jeunes plants.

▶**harden up** *vi Fin* (*of shares etc*) se raffermir.

hardened ['hɑːd(ə)nd] *adj* (*substance*) durci, endurci; (*steel, glass*) trempé; (*criminal*) endurci.

hardener ['hɑːd(ə)nər] *n* (*for paint, glue*) durcisseur *m*.

hardening ['hɑːd(ə)nɪŋ] *n* **(a)** durcissement *m*, (r)endurcissement *m*, affermissement *m*; *Metal* trempe *f* (*de l'acier*); *Med* **h. of the arteries,** durcissement des artères; **(b)** *Metal* = **CASE-HARDENING.**

hard-faced, -featured [hɑːd'feɪst, -'fiːtʃəd] *adj* (*person*) aux traits durs *ou* sévères.

hard-fought ['hɑːd'fɔːt] *adj* vivement *ou* chaudement contesté, *Fml* âprement disputé.

hard-hat ['hɑːdhæt] *adj esp US* = caractéristique des attitudes conservatrices et des préjugés attribués aux ouvriers de la construction.

hard-headed ['hɑːd'hedɪd] *adj* **(a)** (*tough*) positif, pratique; **h.-h. business man,** homme d'affaires réaliste; **(b)** *esp Am* (*stubborn*) obstiné, têtu.

hardhearted ['hɑːd'hɑːtɪd] *adj* (*person*) impitoyable, au cœur dur; (*père*) dénaturé.

hard-hit ['hɑːd'hɪt] *adj* gravement atteint *ou* touché; **one particularly h.-h. village,** un village touché de façon particulièrement grave.

hard-hitting [hɑːd'hɪtɪŋ] *adj* qui frappe dur; **the speech was a h.-h. attack on this policy,** le discours était une attaque franche contre cette politique; *Boxing etc* **h.-h. opponent,** adversaire cogneur.

hardiness ['hɑːdɪnɪs] *n* robustesse *f*, vigueur *f*.

hardline ['hɑːdlaɪn] *adj Pol etc* (*conservative*) convaincu; (*policy*) intransigeant.

hardliner [hɑːd'laɪnər] *n Pol etc* faucon *m*, épervier *m*.

hardly ['hɑːdlɪ] *adv* (*scarcely*) à peine, ne ... guère; **she can h. read,** c'est à peine si elle sait lire; **I need h. say ...,** il va sans dire ...; **h. anyone/anything,** presque personne/rien; **h. ever,** presque jamais; **she would h. set her own house on fire,** elle n'aurait sûrement pas mis le feu à sa propre maison; **he could h. have said that,** il n'aurait sûrement pas dit cela.

hardness ['hɑːdnɪs] *n* **(a)** dureté *f* (*d'une substance*); trempe *f* (*de l'acier*); tons heurtés (*d'un cliché, d'un tableau*); crudité *f* (*de l'eau*); **(b)** difficulté *f* (*d'un travail, d'un problème*); **h. of hearing,** dureté *f* d'oreille; **(c)** sévérité *f*, rigueur *f* (*d'une règle etc*); caractère *m* insensible (*de qn*); dureté *f*, brutalité *f*; **(d)** *Fin* tension *f* (*du marché, des actions*).

hard-nosed ['hɑːdnəʊzd] *adj esp Am F* = **HARD-**

HEADED.
hard-on ['hɑːdɒn] *n Sl* **to have a h.-on,** bander.
hard-pressed, -pushed [hɑːd'prest, -'pʊʃt] *adj* acculé; (*debtor*) aux abois, fort embarrassé.
hardship ['hɑːdʃɪp] *n* privation *f*; (dure) épreuve *f*; tribulation *f*; **he has suffered great hardships,** il en a vu de dures.
hardtack ['hɑːdtæk] *n Nau* biscuit *m* de mer.
hardtop ['hɑːdtɒp] *n Aut* hard-top *m*.
hardware ['hɑːdweər] *n* (*no pl*) **(a)** *Com* quincaillerie *f*; **h. dealer,** quincaillier, -ière; **h. shop** *or* **store,** quincaillerie *f*; **(b)** éléments *mpl ou* parties *fpl* métalliques (*d'un appareil, d'une installation*); ferrures *fpl*; **(c)** *Comptr* matériel *m*, hardware *m*; **(d)** *Sl* (*weapons*) armes *fpl*.
hard-wearing [hɑːd'weərɪŋ] *adj* (*vêtement etc*) de bon usage, de bon service; (*tissu*) durable.
hard-won [hɑːd'wʌn] *adj* (*trophy, victory*) chaudement disputé, remporté de haute lutte.
hardwood ['hɑːdwʊd] *n* bois dur.
hard-working ['hɑːd'wɜːkɪŋ] *adj* laborieux, travailleur, -euse, assidu.
hardy ['hɑːdɪ] *adj* **(a)** (*robust*) robuste; endurci (*à la fatigue etc*); *Bot* résistant; (*arbuste*) vivace; (*plante*) de pleine terre; **h. annual,** *Bot* plante annuelle de pleine terre; *Fig F* question qui revient régulièrement sur le tapis; **(b)** (*courageous*) hardi, courageux, audacieux.
hare¹ [heər] *n* lièvre *m*; **doe h.,** hase *f*; *Culin* **jugged h.,** civet *m* de lièvre; **to run with the h. and hunt with the hounds,** ménager la chèvre et le chou; jouer double jeu; **to start a h.,** (*in hunting*) lever un lièvre; (*in conversation*) donner un nouveau tour à la conversation; *Sp* **h. and hounds,** = jeu *m* de piste, rallye *m*.
hare² *vi F* (*of person*) courir comme un lièvre *ou* à toutes jambes; **to h. off after s.o.,** s'élancer à la poursuite de qn.
harebell ['heəbel] *n* (*plant*) campanule *f*.
harebrained ['heəbreɪnd] *adj* écervelé, étourdi; **h. scheme,** projet insensé.
harelip ['heəlɪp] *n Med* bec-de-lièvre *m*, *pl* becs-de-lièvre.
harem [hɑː'riːm] *n* harem *m*.
haricot ['hærɪkəʊ] *n* **h. (bean),** haricot blanc.
hark [hɑːk] *vi esp Arch Lit* prêter l'oreille (**at, to,** à); **h.!,** écoutez!; *F* **h. at him!,** ta, ta, ta, comme il y va!
►**hark back** *vi* (*recall*) **to h. back (to the past),** ressasser le passé; **to h. back to sth,** ramener la conversation sur un sujet.
harlequin ['hɑːlɪkwɪn] *n Th* arlequin *m*; **h. coat,** habit bigarré *ou* mi-parti.
harlot ['hɑːlət] *n Arch* prostituée *f*.
harm¹ [hɑːm] *n* mal *m*, tort *m*; **to do h. to s.o.,** faire du tort à qn; **what h. has she done you?,** quel mal vous a-t-elle fait?; **to see no h. in sth,** ne pas voir de mal à qch; **you will come to no h.,** il ne vous arrivera pas de mal; **out of h.'s way,** (*of fragile object etc*) à l'abri du danger, en sûreté; (*of dangerous object etc*) mis dans l'impossibilité de nuire à personne; **they put the china in a cupboard, out of h.'s way,** ils ont mis la porcelaine à l'abri dans un placard; **put these chemicals where they'll be out of h.'s way,** mets ces produits chimiques en lieu sûr; **it will do more h. than good,** cela fera plus de mal que de bien; **that won't do any h.,** cela ne gâtera rien; **it won't do him any h.,** cela ne lui fera pas de mal; **there's no h. in saying so,** il n'y a pas de mal à le dire; **there's no h. in trying,** on peut toujours essayer.
harm² *vt* faire du mal *ou* du tort à (*qn*), causer du tort à (*qn*), nuire à (*qn*); léser (*les intérêts de qn*); (*physically*) faire du mal à; nuire à (*la santé*)
harmful ['hɑːmfʊl] *adj* (*substances*) nocif; (*remarks*) nuisible; (*ideas, influence*) malfaisant, pernicieux; **it's h. to your health,** cela nuit à votre santé; **in small doses the drug is not h.,** à petites doses, ce médicament n'est pas dangereux; **it had a h. effect on her education,** cela a eu des conséquences fâcheuses sur son éducation.
harmfully ['hɑːmfʊlɪ] *adv* de façon nuisible, dangereusement.
harmfulness ['hɑːmfʊlnɪs] *n* nocivité *f*; nature *f* nuisible (**of,** de).
harmless ['hɑːmlɪs] *adj* (*animal*) inoffensif; (*person*) sans malice; (*pastime*) innocent; (*drug*) anodin; **h. talk,** conversation anodine.
harmlessly ['hɑːmlɪslɪ] *adv* sans faire de mal; (*s'amuser*) innocemment; (*taquiner*) gentiment; **to gossip h.,** faire des commérages sans méchanceté.
harmonic [hɑː'mɒnɪk] **1** *adj* harmonique; **h. series,** *Mus* échelle *f* harmonique; *Math* série *f* harmonique; *Math Phys* **h. motion,** mouvement sinusoïdal. **2** *n* **(a)** *Mus* harmonique *m* (*d'un son fondamental*); (*on stringed instrument*) harmonique, son flûté; **harmonics,** sons harmoniques; **(b)** *Math Phys* harmonique *m* (*d'un mouvement ondulatoire*).
harmonica [hɑː'mɒnɪkə] *n* harmonica *m*.
harmonious [hɑː'məʊnɪəs] *adj* **(a)** (*combination, relationship*) harmonieux; **(b)** (*music*) mélodieux.
harmoniously [hɑː'məʊnɪəslɪ] *adv* harmonieusement; (*travailler, vivre*) en harmonie.
harmonium [hɑː'məʊnɪəm] *n* harmonium *m*.
harmonization [hɑːmənaɪ'zeɪʃən] *n* harmonisation *f*.
harmonize ['hɑːmənaɪz] **1** *vt* **(a)** *Mus* harmoniser (*une mélodie*); **(b)** harmoniser (*des idées etc*); faire accorder (*des textes etc*); allier (*des couleurs etc*) (**with,** avec). **2** *vi* **(a)** *Mus* (*of singer*) chanter en harmonie; (*of musician*) jouer en harmonie; **(b)** (*of sounds, colours etc*) s'harmoniser; (*of facts, things*) s'accorder; (*of people, ideas etc*) se mettre en harmonie, s'accorder; **colours that h. well,** couleurs qui vont bien ensemble; **to h. with sth,** s'adapter harmonieusement à qch.
harmony ['hɑːmənɪ] *n* **(a)** *Mus* harmonie *f*; **to study h.,** étudier l'harmonie; **songs full of h.,** chants mélodieux; **(b)** (*of people, ideas etc*) harmonie *f*, accord *m*; (*of voices, instruments*) concert *m*; (*of texts*) concordance *f*; **to live in perfect h.,** vivre en parfaite intelligence; **in h. with ...,** qui s'harmonise *ou* qui s'accorde avec ... .
harness¹ ['hɑːnɪs] *n* **(a)** (*of horse*) harnais *m*, harnachement *m*; **draught h.,** harnais d'attelage; *Fig* **to get back into h. (again),** (*of person*) reprendre le collier; *Fig* **to die in h.,** mourir à la peine; **h. horse,** cheval *m* d'attelage; *US Horseracing* **h. race,** course *f* au trot; **h. room,** sellerie *f*; **(b)** *Tech Av etc* **(parachute) h.,** ceinture *f ou* harnais *m* de parachutiste; *Ind Aut etc* **(safety) h.,** harnais de sécurité; **(c)** *Tex* harnais *m* (*de métier à tisser*).
harness² *vt* **(a)** harnacher (*un cheval*); **to h. a horse to a cart,** atteler un cheval à une charrette; **(b)** aménager (*une chute d'eau etc*); **to h. atomic energy for industrial purposes,** mettre l'énergie nucléaire au service de l'industrie.
harnessing ['hɑːnɪsɪŋ] *n* **(a)** (*of a horse*) harnachement *m*; attelage *m*; **(b)** (*of waterfall etc*) aménagement *m*; (*of energy*) exploitation *f*.
harp¹ [hɑːp] *n Mus* harpe *f*.
harp² *vi* (*play the harp*) jouer de la harpe.
►**harp on** *vi* (*talk insistently*) revenir sans arrêt sur la même chose; **he's always harping on about inflation,** il est toujours en train de nous rebattre les oreilles avec l'inflation.
harpist ['hɑːpɪst] *n Mus* harpiste *mf*.
harpoon¹ [hɑː'puːn] *n* harpon *m*, lance *f*; **pronged h.,** foëne *f*; **h. gun,** (*on deck of ship*) canon *m* lance-harpon; (*small*) fusil *m* à harpon.
harpoon² *vt* harponner.
harpooner [hɑː'puːnər] *n* harponneur *m*.
harpsichord ['hɑːpsɪkɔːd] *n Mus* clavecin *m*.
harpsichordist ['hɑːpsɪkɔːdɪst] *n Mus* claveciniste *mf*.
harpy ['hɑːpɪ] *n Myth* harpie *f*; *F* **old h.,** vieille mégère; **h. eagle,** (*bird*) harpie.
harridan ['hærɪd(ə)n] *n Old-fashioned F* vieille sorcière.
harrier¹ ['hærɪər] *n* **(a)** (*person*) pilleur *m*, pillard *m*; **(b)** (*bird*) busard *m*.
harrier² *n* **(a)** (*dog*) harrier *m*; **harriers,** meute *f* (*de chiens pour la chasse au lièvre*); **(b)** *Sp* (*runner*) coureur *m*; **harriers,** club *m* de course à pied *ou* de cross.
harrow¹ ['hærəʊ] *n Agr* herse *f*.
harrow² *vt Agr* herser (*un terrain*); *Fig* **to h. s.o.'s feelings, to h. s.o.,** déchirer le cœur à qn.
harrowing ['hærəʊɪŋ] *adj* (*story etc*) poignant, navrant; (*cry*) déchirant.
harry ['hærɪ] *vt* attaquer, harceler (*l'ennemi*); pourchasser, harceler (*un débiteur*).
Harry ['hærɪ] *n* (*dimin of* **Henry**) = Henri *m*; *Old-fashioned Br F* **to play old H. with s.o.,** en faire voir des vertes et des pas mûres à qn.
harsh [hɑːʃ] *adj* **(a)** (*rough*) dur, rêche, rude (*au toucher*); âpre (*au goût*); strident (*à l'oreille*); (*bruit*) désagréable; (*voix*) rude, rauque; (*vin*) âpre; **(b)** (*severe, brutal*) (*caractère*) bourru; (*traitement*) dur; (*maître, réponse*) rude; (*punishment*) sévère; (*climate, winter*) rude; (*light*) cru; **to say h. things to s.o.,** en dire de dures à qn; **she was very h. about them,** elle a été très dure à leur égard; **h. words,** mots durs.
harshly ['hɑːʃlɪ] *adv* (*répondre etc*) durement, rudement; (*traiter qn*) sévèrement.
harshness ['hɑːʃnɪs] *n* **(a)** dureté *f*, rudesse *f* (*au toucher*); stridence *f* (*d'un son*); aspérité *f* (*du style, de la voix*); **(b)**

sévérité *f* (*d'une punition, d'une loi*).

hart [hɑːt] *n* cerf *m*; (*in hunting*) cerf âgé de plus de cinq ans.

harum-scarum ['heərəm'skeərəm] *F* **1** *adj* étourdi, écervelé. **2** *adv* étourdiment. **3** *n* écervelé, -ée; **she's a h.-s.,** c'est une évaporée.

harvest[1] ['hɑːvɪst] *n* **(a)** moisson *f* (*du blé*); récolte *f* (*des fruits*); fenaison *f* (*du foin*); vendange *f* (*du vin*); **a good/poor h.,** une bonne/mauvaise récolte; **to get in the h.,** faire la moisson; **to help with the h.,** aider à la moisson; **h. thanksgiving** *or* **festival,** action *f* de grâces (*après la rentrée des récoltes*); **h. home,** fête *f* de la moisson; **h. moon,** lune *f* de la moisson; **h. mouse,** souris *f* des moissons; **(b)** (*time of year*) (temps *m ou* époque *f* de) la moisson; **at h. (time),** à l'époque de la moisson.

harvest[2] **1** *vt* moissonner (*les blés*); récolter (*les fruits*). **2** *vi* rentrer *ou* faire la moisson.

harvester ['hɑːvɪstər] *n* **(a)** (*person*) moissonneur, -euse; **(b)** (*machine*) moissonneuse *f*.

harvesting ['hɑːvɪstɪŋ] *n* (rentrée *f* de la) moisson *f*.

has-been ['hæzbiːn] *n F* (*person*) ringard *m*, ringarde *f*.

hash[1] [hæʃ] *n* **(a)** *Culin* hachis *m*; *Am* **h. browns,** pommes de terre sautées; **(b)** *F* (*mess*) **to make a h. of sth,** gâcher *ou* gâter un travail; faire un beau gâchis de qch; **he made a h. of it,** il a tout bousillé *ou* saboté; **to settle s.o.'s h.,** régler son compte à qn; **(c)** *F* (*rehash*) réchauffé *m* (*de vieilles idées etc*); compilation *f* (*de l'œuvre d'autrui*); **(d)** *Sl* = **HASHISH**.

hash[2] *vt* **(a)** *Culin* **to h. meat,** hacher de la viande (en petits morceaux); **(b)** *F* (*mess up*) bousiller.

▶hash over *vtsep F* (*discuss*) discuter (*qch*).

▶hash up *vtsep* bousiller (*qch*).

hashish ['hæʃiːʃ] *n* hachisch *m*.

hasn't ['hæz(ə)nt] = **has not,** *see* **HAVE[2]**.

hasp [hɑːsp] *n* **(a)** (*for padlocking*) **(staple) h.,** moraillon *m*; **(b)** (*on door*) loquet *m*; (*on French window*) espagnolette *f*; (*on book etc*) fermoir *m*.

hassle[1] ['hæs(ə)l] *n F* **(a)** (*inconvenience*) problème *m*, embêtement *m*; **it's too much h. going by train,** c'est trop d'embêtements d'aller par le train; **all the h. of filling out the form,** tous les embêtements pour remplir le formulaire; **(b)** (*argument*) dispute *f*, chamaillerie *f*; (*aggressive behaviour, talk*) chamaillerie *f*; **the police give us a lot of h.,** la police nous fait des tas d'histoires.

hassle[2] *F* **1** *vt* ennuyer, embêter (*qn*); **he keeps hassling me for money,** il n'arrête pas de m'embêter pour que je lui donne de l'argent. **2** *vi* se quereller; se disputer, se chamailler.

hassock ['hæsək] *n Rel* agenouilloir *m*.

haste [heɪst] *n* hâte *f*, célérité *f*; **to do sth in h.,** faire qch à la hâte *ou* en hâte; **a note written in h.,** un billet écrit à la hâte; **to make h.,** se hâter, se presser, se dépêcher (**to do sth,** de faire qch); *Prov* **more h. less speed,** plus on se hâte moins on avance.

hasten ['heɪs(ə)n] *esp Lit & Fml* **1** *vt* accélérer, hâter, presser (*le pas etc*); avancer (*le départ de qn*). **2** *vi* se hâter, se dépêcher, se presser (**to do sth,** de faire qch); **I don't agree with him, I h. to add,** je m'empresse d'ajouter que je ne suis pas d'accord avec lui.

hastily ['heɪstɪlɪ] *adv* **(a)** (*quickly*) à la hâte, précipitamment; **(b)** (*rashly*) de façon irréfléchie; (*parler*) sans réflechir; (*juger qch*) à la légère; (*out of temper*) brusquement.

hastiness ['heɪstɪnɪs] *n* **(a)** (*speed*) précipitation *f*, hâte *f*; **(b)** (*rashness*) irréflexion *f*; **(c)** (*quick temper*) emportement *m*, brusquerie *f*.

hasty ['heɪstɪ] *adj* **(a)** (*départ, adieu*) précipité; (*croquis*) fait à la hâte; (*repas*) sommaire; **I sent him a h. note,** je lui ai envoyé un billet écrit à la hâte; **to be too h. in doing sth,** mettre trop de hâte à faire qch; **(b)** (*aveu*) irréfléchi; **to jump to a h. conclusion,** conclure à la légère; **(c)** (*short-tempered*) (*person*) vif; **to have a h. temper,** s'emporter facilement.

hat [hæt] *n* chapeau *m*; **top h.,** chapeau haut de forme; **straw h.,** chapeau de paille; **paper h.,** chapeau de papier, coiffure *f* de cotillon; *F* **I'm saying that with my lawyer's h. on,** je dis ça en ma qualité de juriste; *F* **she wears several different hats in the company,** elle remplit plusieurs rôles dans la société; **to put on/take off one's h.,** mettre/enlever son chapeau; *Fig* **I take my h. off to him** *or* **you!,** chapeau!; **hats off!,** chapeaux bas!; *F* **to pass the h. round,** faire passer le chapeau, faire la quête (**for s.o./sth,** pour qn/qch); **to throw one's h. in the ring,** jeter son chapeau dans l'arène; *F* **my h.!,** mon Dieu!; **to talk through one's h.,** parler à tort et à travers; **to keep sth under one's h.,** garder qch pour soi; **if that comes off I'll eat my h.,** si ça réussit, je mange mon chapeau; **that's old h.,** ça c'est vieux jeu; **h. trick,** (*by conjuror*) tour *m ou* coup *m* du chapeau; *Fb etc* trois buts marqués de suite par le même joueur; *Cr* mise *f* hors jeu de trois batteurs avec trois balles de suite; *Fig* **that's my h. trick,** jamais deux sans trois.

hatband ['hætbænd] *n* ruban *m* de chapeau.

hatbox ['hætbɒks] *n* boîte *f ou* carton *m* à chapeau.

hatch[1] [hætʃ] *n* **(a)** *Nau* descente *f*, écoutille *f*; **cargo h.,** panneau *m* de chargement *ou* de déchargement; **h. (cover),** panneau de descente, panneau (d'écoutille); **to batten down the hatches,** condamner les descentes; *F* **down the h.!,** (*when drinking*) cul sec!; **(b)** (*trap door etc*) trappe *f*; panneau *m* d'accès; **(service** *or* **serving) h.,** passe-plats *m inv*; *Av etc* **(escape) h.,** panneau d'évacuation; **(c)** (*lower half of door*) partie basse d'une porte coupée; demi-porte *f*, *pl* demi-portes; **(d)** *HydE* vanne *f* d'écluse.

hatch[2] *n Agr* **(a)** (*of an egg, clutch*) éclosion *f*; **(b)** (*clutch*) couvée *f*.

hatch[3] **1** *vt* faire éclore (*des poussins*); incuber, (faire) couver (*des œufs*); (*in fish farming, of fish*) incuber (*les œufs*); *Fig* **to h. a plot,** ourdir *ou* tramer un complot. **2** *vi* (*of young birds, eggs*) éclore; **newly hatched chickens,** poussins qui sortent de la coquille.

hatch[4] *n* (*in technical drawing etc*) hachure *f*.

hatch[5] *vt* (*in technical drawing*) hacher, hachurer (*un dessin*).

▶hatch out *vi* = **HATCH[3] 2.**

hatchback ['hætʃbæk] *n Aut* **(a)** (*car*) voiture *f* à hayon (arrière); **(b)** (*part, door*) hayon *m* (arrière).

hatchery ['hætʃərɪ] *n Agr* couvoir *m*, couveuse *f*; (*in fish farming*) appareil *m* à éclosion.

hatchet ['hætʃɪt] *n* hachette *f*; *Fig* **to bury the h.,** enterrer la hache de guerre; *Journ F etc* **h. job,** démolissage *m*; **to do a h. job on sth/s.o.,** démolir qch/qn; **h. face,** visage *m* en lame de couteau; **h. man,** (*hired killer*) tueur *m* (à gages); *Pol etc* homme *m* de main.

hatching ['hætʃɪŋ] *n* (*in technical drawing*) hachure(s) *f(pl)*.

hatchway ['hætʃweɪ] *n Nau* descente *f*, écoutille *f*.

hate[1] [heɪt] *n* **(a)** (*hatred*) haine *f*; **h. mail,** lettres *fpl* d'injures; **(b)** (*object of dislike*) objet *m* d'aversion; **her pet h.,** sa bête noire.

hate[2] *vt* haïr, détester, exécrer (*qn, qch*); **I h. him,** il m'est odieux; **I h. classical music,** je déteste la musique classique; **I h. myself for agreeing to it,** je m'en veux d'y avoir consenti; **I h. it when he's in a bad mood,** je déteste quand il est de mauvaise humeur; **to h. to do sth,** détester (de) faire qch; **she hates to be contradicted,** elle ne peut pas souffrir qu'on la contredise; **she hates being kissed,** elle a horreur qu'on l'embrasse; **I'd h. anyone to find out,** je ne supporterais pas que quelqu'un l'apprenne; *F* **I h. to tell you, but I think you've missed your train,** je regrette de devoir te dire que je pense que tu as raté ton train.

hateful ['heɪtfʊl] *adj* (*person, thing*) odieux, détestable.

hatefully ['heɪtfʊlɪ] *adv* odieusement, détestablement.

hater ['heɪtər] *n* ennemi *m* (**of,** de); **to be an animal-h.,** détester les animaux.

hatless ['hætlɪs] *adj* (*person*) sans chapeau, tête nue.

hatpeg ['hætpeg] *n* patère *f*.

hatpin ['hætpɪn] *n* épingle *f* à chapeau.

hatrack ['hætræk] *n* porte-chapeaux *m inv*.

hatred ['heɪtrɪd] *n* haine *f* (**of s.o.,** de, contre qn); **to incur s.o.'s h.,** s'attirer la haine de qn.

hatshop ['hætʃɒp] *n* (*for men*) chapellerie *f*; (*for women*) boutique *f* de modiste.

hatstand ['hætstænd] *n* porte-chapeaux *m inv*.

hatter ['hætər] *n* chapelier, -ière.

haughtily ['hɔːtɪlɪ] *adv* hautainement; d'une manière hautaine *ou* arrogante.

haughtiness ['hɔːtɪnɪs] *n* hauteur *f*, arrogance *f*.

haughty ['hɔːtɪ] *adj* hautain, arrogant, altier.

haul[1] [hɔːl] *n* **(a)** (*effort*) amenée *f*; effort *m* (*pour tirer, haler, amener qch*); **(b)** (*in fishing*) prise *f*, pêche *f*; **to make** *or* **get a good h.,** faire (une) bonne pêche; *Fig* (*of financier etc*) faire son butin; **at one h.,** d'un seul coup de filet; **(c)** (*distance, journey*) parcours *m*, trajet *m*; *Av* **long-h. aircraft,** (avion *m*) long-courrier *m*; *Av etc* **short/long h.,** étape *ou* distance courte/longue; **there's still a long h. ahead,** il y a encore toute une tirée; **it's a long h. from Glasgow to Naples,** (*by road*) c'est un long trajet de Glasgow à Naples.

haul[2] **1** *vt* **(a)** tirer; traîner (*une charge*); remorquer (*un *bateau, un train*); *F* **to h. s.o. over the coals,** réprimander qn, *F* passer un savon à qn; **(b)** *Com* (*transport by road*) transporter (*des marchandises*) par camions. **2** *vi* **(a)** (*pull*) tirer, traîner; **they all hauled together,** ils ont tous tiré ensemble: **to h. on a rope,** haler sur une manœuvre; **(b)** *Nau* (*sail, move etc*) **to h. alongside,** accoster.

▶**haul down** *vtsep* (*bring down*) descendre (*qch*); *Nau* haler bas, affaler (*les voiles etc*); rentrer (*un pavillon*).

▶**haul in** *vtsep* (*bring in*) tirer (*qch*) en dedans; *Nau* haler en dedans; *F* **they hauled in some experts to back up their case,** ils ont amené des experts pour les soutenir.

▶**haul up** *vtsep* **(a)** (*hoist*) monter (*qch*): *Nau* hisser (*un pavillon*); **to h. up a boat,** rentrer une embarcation; (*on the beach*) haler un bateau à sec; **(b)** *F* (*call to account*) **to h. s.o. up,** demander des comptes à qn (**for sth,** de qch); **to be hauled up before the court,** être sommé de comparaître.

haulage ['hɔːlɪdʒ] *n* **(a)** *Com* (*transportation*) (transport *m* par) roulage *m*, charriage *m*, camionnage *m*; **road h.,** transports routiers; **h. contractor,** entrepreneur *m* de transports; **(b)** (*towing*) traction *f*, remorquage *m*; **(c)** *Com* (*costs*) frais *mpl* de roulage *ou* de transport.

haulier ['hɔːlɪər], *US* **hauler** ['hɔːlər] *n Com* camionneur *m*, entrepreneur *m* de transports; (*driver*) routier *m*.

hauling ['hɔːlɪŋ] *n* **(a)** traction *f*, remorquage *m*; **(b)** *Nau* halage *m*; **h. rope,** câble *m* de halage.

haunch [hɔːntʃ] *n* **(a)** *Anat* hanche *f*; **haunches,** arrière-train *m*; **sitting on his haunches,** (*person*) accroupi; (*dog*) assis; **(b)** *Culin* cuissot *m* (*de chevreuil*).

haunt¹ [hɔːnt] *n* retraite *f*, repaire *m*; rendez-vous *m* (*de bons compagnons*); **this pub was one of his haunts,** ce pub était l'un des ses repaires; **the h. of existentialists,** le lieu de rendez-vous des existentialistes.

haunt² *vt* **(a)** (*of ghost*) hanter (*une maison etc*); **(b)** (*of person, animal*) fréquenter, hanter (*un endroit, qn*); **(c)** (*of thoughts etc*) obséder, poursuivre (*qn*); troubler, hanter (*l'esprit, le sommeil*); **to be haunted by memories,** être obsédé par des souvenirs.

haunted ['hɔːntɪd] *adj* (*château etc*) hanté; **the red room is h.,** il y des revenants dans la chambre rouge; **he has a h. look,** il a l'air égaré.

haunting ['hɔːntɪŋ] **1** *adj* (*mélodie, souvenir etc*) qui vous hante; (*souvenir etc*) obsédant; **h. memory,** hantise *f*. **2** *n* hantement *m* (*d'un lieu etc*).

Havana [hə'vænə, -'vɑː-] *n* **(a)** la Havane; **(b) a H. (cigar),** un havane.

have¹ [hæv] *n F* **the haves and the h.-nots,** les riches *mpl* et les pauvres *mpl*.

have² *vt* (*pr* **have**; *3rd person* **has** [hæz]; *pl* **have**; *pr sub sing & pl* **have**; *past & past sub* **had** [hæd]; *pl* **had**; *prp* **having**; *pp* **had**; **have not, has not, had not** *are frequently shortened into* **haven't, hasn't, hadn't**; **I have, he has, we have** *etc into* **I've, he's, we've** *etc*; **I had** *etc into* **I'd** *etc*) **(a)** avoir; **a week has seven days,** une semaine a sept jours; **he had no friends,** il n'avait pas d'amis; **all I h.,** tout ce que je possède *ou* que j'ai; **she has a shop,** elle tient une boutique; **he has big hands,** il a de grosses mains; **my bag has no name on it,** ma valise ne porte pas de nom; **she had the pen in her desk all the time,** le stylo était dans son bureau tout ce temps-là; **I h. nothing to do,** je n'ai rien à faire; **I h. work to do,** j'ai à travailler; **to h. a right,** jouir d'un droit; **I h. it!,** j'y suis!; *Br F* **come on!, let's be having you!,** (*come forward*) allez, par ici!; (*hurry up!*) allez!, dépêche-toi; *F* **he had it coming to him,** c'est bien fait pour lui, il l'a bien mérité; *F* **I'm not having any,** (*I don't believe it*) ça ne prend pas avec moi; (*I'm not getting involved*) je ne vais pas m'en mêler;

(b) (*invite etc*) **we're having visitors tomorrow,** nous attendons des invités demain; **to h. friends to dinner,** avoir des amis à dîner;

(c) (*obtain*) **there was no work to be had,** on ne pouvait pas obtenir de travail; **the only potatoes to be had,** (*at this moment*) les seules pommes de terre qu'il y a, les seules pommes de terre que l'on puisse trouver; **to h. one's wish,** obtenir ce que l'on désire;

(d) (*receive etc*) **to h. news from s.o.,** recevoir des nouvelles de qn; **I h. it on good authority,** je l'ai appris de bonne source; **I will let you h. it for £5,** je vous le céderai pour cinq livres; **let me h. your keys,** donnez-moi vos clefs; **you shall h. it back tomorrow,** je vous le rendrai demain; *F* **I let him h. it,** (*verbally*) je lui ai dit son fait; (*physically*) je lui ai flanqué une raclée; *F* **I've had it!,** (*if s.o. finds out*) je suis foutu!; (*I'm exhausted*) je suis crevé! *F* **this coat has had it,** (*is worn out*) ce manteau est foutu; *F* **the car has just about had it,** la voiture est prête à rendre l'âme; *F* **he's had it,** (*dead, dying*) il a sa dose; *F* **I've had it up to here with you,** j'en ai jusque-là de toi;

(e) (*take*) prendre (*un repas*); **to h. tea with s.o.,** prendre le thé avec qn; **what will you h., sir? — I'll h. a chop,** que prendra monsieur? — donnez-moi une côtelette; **to h. a cigarette,** fumer une cigarette;

(f) (*in numerous verbal phrases*) **to h. measles,** avoir la rougeole, *F* faire une rougeole; **to h. a cold,** être enrhumé; **to h. dealings with s.o.,** avoir affaire à qn; **to h. the choice,** avoir le choix; **to h. an idea,** avoir une idée; **to h. a dream,** faire un rêve; **to h. a game,** faire une partie; **to h. a fall,** faire une chute; **to h. a lesson,** prendre une leçon; **to h. a bath,** prendre un bain; **to h. a wash,** se laver; **to h. a shave,** se raser;

(g) (*experience*) **I had a pleasant evening,** j'ai passé une soirée agréable; **I didn't h. any trouble in finding it,** je n'ai eu aucune peine à le trouver; **we had a rather strange adventure,** il nous est arrivé une aventure assez étrange; **to h. fine/wet weather,** avoir du beau temps/de la pluie;

(h) (*claim*) prétendre, soutenir, affirmer; **rumour has it that ...,** le bruit court que ...; **as Plato has it,** comme dit Platon;

(i) (*hold*) **to h. s.o. in one's power,** avoir qn en son pouvoir; **he had me by the throat,** il me tenait à la gorge;

(j) *F* (*outwit*) avoir, attraper (*qn*); **to be had,** donner dans le panneau; *F* donner dedans; **you've been had!,** on vous a eu!; (*for a purchase*) on vous a refilé un rossignol; **you h. me there!,** (*in guessing game*) là, je donne ma langue au chat!;

(k) (*give birth to*) **how many children has she had?,** combien d'enfants a-t-elle eus?; **our cat has had kittens,** notre chatte a fait des petits;

(l) (*beget*) **he had two children by her,** il a eu d'elle deux enfants;

(m) (*have sexual intercourse with*) *F* prendre, coucher avec (*qn*);

(n) (*causative*) **to h. sth done,** faire faire qch; **to h. s.o. do sth,** faire faire qch à qn; **to h. one's hair cut,** se faire couper les cheveux; **three houses had their windows shattered,** trois maisons ont eu leurs fenêtres brisées; **I had my watch stolen,** je me suis fait voler ma montre; **to h. a tooth out,** se faire arracher une dent; **I shall h. everything ready,** je veillerai à ce que tout soit prêt;

(o) (*want*) **which one will you h.?,** lequel voulez-vous?; **she won't h. him,** elle ne veut pas de lui; **as luck would h. it he arrived too late,** la malchance voulut qu'il arrivât trop tard; **what would you h. me do?,** que voulez-vous que je fasse?; **I would h. you know that ...,** sachez que ...;

(p) (*allow*) **I will not h. such conduct,** je ne supporterai pas une pareille conduite; **I won't h. you coming in here,** je ne veux pas que vous entriez ici; *F* **he wouldn't h. it,** (*that he was wrong*) il n'a pas voulu me *ou* nous *etc* écouter; *F* **we tried to give the dog a bath but he wasn't having any of it!,** nous avons essayé de faire prendre un bain au chien, mais il n'était pas décidé à se laisser faire;

(q) (*place*) mettre; **I'll h. the television in that corner,** (*when I get one*) je mettrai la télé dans ce coin; (*to person holding it*) mettez la télé dans ce coin; *Horseracing* **to h. sth on a horse,** (*a bet*) miser sur un cheval;

(r) (*be compelled*) **to h. to do sth,** devoir faire qch, être obligé *ou* forcé de faire qch; **I had to go away,** j'ai dû m'en aller; **I don't h. to work,** moi je n'ai pas besoin de travailler; *Iron* **of course you HAD to go and tell him!,** bien sûr, il a fallu que tu ailles le lui dire!; **the clock will h. to be mended,** la pendule a besoin d'être réparée; **I don't like housework but it has to be done,** je n'aime pas faire le ménage mais il faut bien que quelqu'un le fasse; **first the potatoes have to be washed,** il faut d'abord laver les pommes de terre;

(s) (*as auxiliary*) **to h. been/given/done,** avoir été/donné/fait; **to h. hurt oneself,** s'être blessé; **I h. lived in London for three years,** j'habite Londres depuis trois ans; **well, you HAVE grown!,** ce que tu as grandi!; **you h. forgotten your gloves — so I h.!,** vous avez oublié vos gants — en effet! *ou* tiens, c'est vrai!; **you h. been in prison before — I haven't!,** vous avez déjà fait de la prison — c'est faux!;

(t) (*with* **better, sooner** *etc*) **I had better say nothing,** je ferais mieux de ne rien dire; **I'd sooner start at once,** j'aimerais bien mieux partir tout de suite.

▶**have around** *vtas* **(a)** (*keep available*) garder *ou* avoir sous la main; **(b)** (*invite*) inviter; **we must h. them around for dinner,** il faudra qu'on les invite à dîner.

▶**have away** *vtas Br Sl* (*have sexual intercourse*) **to h. it away (with s.o.),** s'envoyer en l'air (avec qn).
▶**have back** *vtas* **(a)** (*invite in return*) rendre une invitation; **we're having them back on Saturday,** nous leur rendons leur invitation samedi prochain; **(b)** (*invite after an event*) **after the movie we had them back for coffee,** après le cinéma, nous les avons invités à venir prendre le café chez nous.
▶**have down** *vtas* (*invite from upstairs*) inviter.
▶**have in** *vtas* **(a)** (*summon*) appeler, faire venir; **we had to h. the doctor in,** nous avons dû appeler le médecin; **we're having the painters in next week,** les peintres viennent la semaine prochaine; **(b)** (*invite*) inviter, recevoir; **she had friends in for tea,** elle a reçu quelques amis pour le thé; **(c) to h. it in for s.o.,** (*have a grudge against*) garder à qn un chien de sa chienne, en avoir après qn; **they had it in for me from the day I arrived,** ils en ont eu après moi dès mon arrivée.
▶**have off** *vtas* **(a)** (*remove*) retirer; **the doctor had the plaster off in no time,** le médecin a retiré le plâtre sans perdre de temps; **the barber nearly had my ear off,** le coiffeur a failli me couper l'oreille; **(b)** (*have removed*) faire retirer; **she's having the plaster off next week,** on lui retire son plâtre la semaine prochaine; **(c)** *Br Sl* **to h. it off (with s.o.),** s'envoyer en l'air (avec qn); **I reckon those two are having it off,** j'ai bien l'impression qu'il y a quelque chose entre eux.
▶**have on 1** *vtsep* (*wear*) porter; **they had nothing on,** ils étaient nus; **she had her black dress on,** elle avait *ou* portait sa robe noire. **2** *vtas* **(a)** *F* (*fool*) faire marcher qn; **I was only having you on,** c'était juste pour te faire marcher; **(b)** (*have arranged*) avoir qch de prévu *ou* des projets; **he has a lot on this week,** il est très occupé cette semaine; **I h. something else on tonight,** j'ai d'autres projets pour ce soir; **(c)** (*have information about*) avoir des informations sur (*qn*); **the police h. nothing on him,** la police n'a rien sur lui; **(d)** (*install, put on*) installer, mettre; **they soon had the roof-rack on,** très vite, ils ont installé *ou* mis la galerie; **she had her coat on in no time,** en un clin d'œil, elle a mis son manteau.
▶**have out** *vtas* **(a)** (*remove*) sortir (*qn*); retirer (*qch*); (*of dentist*) extraire, arracher (*une dent*); **(b)** (*have extracted*) se faire arracher (*une dent*); **(c)** (*resolve*) sortir, mettre les choses au point; **let's h. this out once and for all,** mettons les choses au point une fois pour toutes; **I intend to h. it out with him,** j'ai l'intention de mettre les choses au point avec lui.
▶**have over** *vtas* (*invite*) inviter (*qn*).
▶**have up** *vtas* **(a)** (*usu passive*) (*bring to court*) **to be had up for vagrancy,** passer devant le tribunal pour vagabondage; **(b)** (*erect, install*) installer, mettre en place; **they had the decorations up in a few hours,** ils ont installé les décorations en quelques heures; **(c)** (*invite*) (*from downstairs*) faire monter *ou* venir (*les voisins etc*); **he had them up to his flat for tea,** il les a invités à venir prendre le thé.
haven ['heɪv(ə)n] *n* (*shelter*) abri *m*, asile *m*, refuge *m*; *Lit* havre *m*, port *m*.
have-not ['hæv'nɒt] *n* démuni, -e; **the have-nots of our society,** les (plus) démunis de notre société.
haven't ['hæv(ə)nt] = **have not,** *see* **HAVE².**
haversack ['hævəsæk] *n* **(a)** *Mil* musette *f*; **(b)** havresac *m* (de camping).
havoc ['hævək] *n* ravage *m*, dégâts *mpl*, dévastation *f*; **to cause** *or* **wreak h.,** faire de grands dégâts *ou* de grands ravages (*dans un pays etc*); **to play h. with,** ravager (*les récoltes etc*); déranger, détraquer (*la santé etc*); désorganiser complètement (*les plans de qn etc*).
haw¹ [hɔː] *n Bot* cenelle *f*.
haw² *vi* bégayer; **to hum and h.,** (*hesitate when speaking*) bafouiller; (*be evasive*) tourner autour du pot.
Hawaii [hə'waiː] *n* Hawaï.
Hawaiian [hə'waɪən] **1** *adj* hawaïen; *Mus* **H. guitar,** guitare hawaïenne. **2** *n* Hawaïen, -ïenne.
hawk¹ [hɔːk] *n* **(a)** (*bird*) faucon *m*; **to have eyes like a h.,** avoir des yeux d'aigle; **to watch s.o./sth like a h.,** ne pas lâcher qn/qch des yeux; **(b)** *Pol* faucon *m*; **(c)** (*predatory person*) vautour *m*, rapace *m*; **(d)** *Ent* **h. moth,** sphinx *m*; crépusculaire *m*, smérinthe *m*.
hawk² *vi* (*hunt*) chasser au faucon.
hawk³ *vt* (*sell*) colporter (*des marchandises*); (*spread*) colporter, répandre (*une rumeur etc*).
▶**hawk up** *vtsep* expectorer.
hawker¹ ['hɔːkər] *n* (*in hunting etc*) fauconnier *m*.
hawker² *n* (*seller*) colporteur *m*, démarcheur, -euse.
hawk-eyed ['hɔːkaɪd] *adj* (*person*) aux yeux d'aigle.
hawking¹ ['hɔːkɪŋ] *n* (*hunting*) chasse *f* au faucon, fauconnerie *f*.
hawking² *n* (*selling*) colportage *m*.
hawkish ['hɔːkɪʃ] *adj Pol etc* belliciste; **h. politician,** faucon *m*.
hawknosed ['hɔːknəʊzd] *adj* (*person*) au nez aquilin.
hawser ['hɔːzər, 'hɔːs-] *n Nau* haussière *f*, aussière *f*; (*for mooring only*) amarre *f*; **steel h.,** aussière *ou* amarre en fil d'acier.
hawthorn ['hɔːθɔːn] *n* (*shrub*) aubépine *f*.
hay¹ [heɪ] *n* foin *m*; **to make h.,** faire le(s) foin(s), faner; *Prov* **to make h. while the sun shines,** battre le fer pendant qu'il est chaud; *F* **to hit the h.,** se coucher; *Med* **h. fever,** rhume *m* des foins; **h. rake,** râteau *m*, fauchet *m*.
hay² *vi* faire les foins.
haycart ['heɪkɑːt] *n* fourragère *f* de foin.
haycock ['heɪkɒk] *n* tas *m ou* meulette *f* de foin.
hayfork ['heɪfɔːk] *n* fourche *f* à foin.
haying ['heɪɪŋ] *n* fenaison *f*.
hayloft ['heɪlɒft] *n* fenil *m*.
haymaker ['heɪmeɪkər] *n* **(a)** (*person*) faneur, -euse; **(b)** (*machine*) faneuse *f*, tourne-foin *m inv*; **(c)** *F* (*punch*) uppercut *m*; swing *m*.
haymaking ['heɪmeɪkɪŋ] *n* fenaison *f*.
hayrack ['heɪræk] *n* râtelier *m* d'écurie.
hayrick ['heɪrɪk] *n* meule *f* de foin; (*square*) barge *f*.
hayseed ['heɪsiːd] *n Am F* péquenaud *m*.
haystack ['heɪstæk] *n* = **HAYRICK.**
haywire ['heɪwaɪər] *adj F* confus, embrouillé; (*of person*) emballé, excité; **to go h.,** (*of plan*) louper, finir en queue de poisson; (*of mechanism etc*) se détraquer; **he's gone h.,** il déménage.
hazard¹ ['hæzəd] *n* **(a)** (*danger*) risque *m*, danger *m*, péril *m*; *Aut etc* point dangereux; **ice presents another h. for drivers,** le verglas est un danger supplémentaire pour les conducteurs; *Aut* **h. lights,** feux *mpl* de détresse; **(b)** *Golf* accident *m* de terrain.
hazard² *vt* risquer, hasarder (*sa vie, sa fortune*); hasarder (*une opinion*); **to h. a guess,** tenter de deviner.
hazardous ['hæzədəs] *adj* (*coup, commerce*) hasardeux, chanceux, hasardé; (*profit etc*) aléatoire; (*projet*) aventureux.
haze¹ [heɪz] *n* (*mist*) brume légère; obscurité *f*, incertitude *f* (*de l'esprit*); **her mind was in a h.,** son esprit était embrouillé; **to see everything through an alcohol-induced h.,** voir tout sous l'emprise de l'alcool.
haze² *vt* tourmenter (*qn*); *Am Univ* brimer (*un nouvel étudiant etc*).
hazel ['heɪz(ə)l] **1** *n* **(a) h. (tree),** noisetier *m*, coudrier *m*, avelinier *m*; **(b)** (*colour*) (couleur *f* de) noisette *f*. **2** *adj* noisette; **h. eyes,** yeux *mpl* (couleur) noisette.
hazelnut ['heɪz(ə)lnʌt] *n Bot* noisette *f*, aveline *f*.
hazily ['heɪzɪlɪ] *adv* vaguement.
haziness ['heɪzɪnɪs] *n* (*of atmosphere, mind*) état brumeux *ou* nébuleux; (*of memory*) imprécision *f*.
hazy ['heɪzɪ] *adj* (*air etc*) brumeux, embrumé; (*outline*) flou, estompé; (*idea etc*) vaporeux, nébuleux; (*memory, knowledge*) vague; **to be h. about,** n'avoir qu'une connaissance imprécise de (*qch*); n'avoir qu'un souvenir vague de (*un événement*).
HDTV ['eɪtʃdiːtiːviː] *n TV* (*abbr* **high definition television**) TVHD *f*.
he [hiː] **1** *pers pron* (*of person, male animal, Lit of certain things personified*) **(a)** (*unstressed*) il; **he loves her,** il l'aime; **what is he saying?,** que dit-il?; **here he comes,** le voici qui vient; **he's a strange man,** c'est un homme étrange; **(b)** (*stressed*) lui; **he and I,** lui et moi; **I am as tall as he (is),** je suis aussi grand que lui; *esp Lit* **he who believes,** celui qui croit. **2** *n* **(a)** *F* (*male*) mâle *m*; **it's a he,** (*of newborn child*) c'est un garçon; (*of animal*) c'est un mâle; **(b)** (*in children's game*) (jeu *m* de) chat *m*; **you're he!,** c'est toi le chat!
he- [hiː] *pref* **he-bear,** ours mâle; **he-goat,** bouc *m*.
head¹ [hed] *n* **(a)** tête *f*; **bald h.,** tête chauve; **from h. to foot,** de la tête aux pieds, des pieds à la tête; **he gave orders over my h.,** il a donné des ordres sans me consulter; *Fig* **to be in over one's h.,** (*in water, difficult situation*) ne pas avoir pied; **h. down,** la tête baissée; **h. first,** la tête la première; **to stand on one's h.,** faire le poirier; *F* **I could do it standing on my h.,** c'est simple comme bonjour; **to stand** *or* **turn sth on its h.,** poser qch la tête en bas; *Fig* retourner qch; **recent events have turned the situation on its h.,** les événements récents ont retourné la situation; **to turn h. over heels,** faire la

culbute; (*fall backwards*) tomber à la renverse; **to fall h. over heels in love with s.o.,** tomber follement amoureux de qn; **she stands h. and shoulders above me,** elle fait une tête de plus que moi; *Fig* **she's h. and shoulders above the other athletes,** elle est bien supérieure aux autres athlètes; *Horseracing* **to win by a h.,** (*of horse*) gagner d'une tête; **to win by a short h.,** gagner de justesse; **to let s.o. have their h.,** lâcher les rênes à qn, donner (libre) carrière à qn; **his blood will be upon your h.,** son sang retombera sur votre tête; **on your own h. be it,** assumez-en la responsabilité; **to cut off s.o.'s h.,** décapiter qn, couper la tête à qn; *F* **to shout one's h. off,** crier à tue-tête *ou* à pleins poumons; *F* **to talk one's h. off,** bavarder comme une pie; **to bite** *or* **snap s.o.'s h. off,** rembarrer qn; **a fine h. of hair,** une belle chevelure; *Art etc* **coin bearing the h. of George III,** pièce (frappée) à l'effigie de Georges III; **I haven't got a h. for heights,** j'ai le vertige; **to have a good** *or* **strong h. for drink,** bien tenir l'alcool; **wine that goes to one's h.,** vin qui décoiffe; vin qui monte à la tête; **all the praise went to his h.,** toutes les louanges lui sont montées à la tête; *Med* **h. cold,** rhume *m* de cerveau; **h. louse,** pou *m*; **h. start,** (*in race*) avantage *m* dès le départ; **to give s.o. a h. start,** (*in race*) laisser partir qn devant; *Fig* **to have a h. start,** avoir un avantage dès le départ; *Mus* **h. voice, h. register,** voix *f* de tête; **h. restraint,** (*in car*) repose-tête *m inv*, appuie-tête *m inv*;

(b) (*intellect, mind*) **to have a good h. for business,** avoir le sens des affaires, s'entendre aux affaires; **to get sth into one's h.,** se mettre qch dans la tête; **I can't get that into his h.,** je ne peux pas lui enfoncer ça dans la tête; **he has taken it into his h. that ...,** il s'est mis dans la tête *ou* en tête que ...; **it never entered my h. that ...,** je n'aurais jamais pensé que ...; **to put ideas into s.o.'s h.,** donner des idées à qn; **his name has gone right** *or* **clean out of my h.,** j'ai complètement oublié son nom; **the girl's got a good h. on her shoulders,** cette fille a la tête sur les épaules; **we put our heads together,** nous avons conféré ensemble; *Prov* **two heads are better than one,** deux conseils valent mieux qu'un; **I think he made it up out of his own h.,** je crois que c'est lui qui a inventé ça; **not off the top of my h.,** (*I'd have to check*) pas au pied levé; **she made some figures up off the top of her h.,** elle a inventé des chiffres; **off the top of my h. I'd say somewhere like Paris,** à tout hasard je dirais un endroit comme Paris; **to be over the heads of the audience,** (*of speech, lecture etc*) dépasser l'entendement de l'auditoire; **to lose one's h.,** perdre la tête *ou F* la boule *ou* la boussole; **to keep one's h.,** (*in crisis*) garder la tête sur les épaules; **to be off one's h.,** être fou *ou F* timbré *ou* toqué; **to go off one's h.,** devenir fou; **he's not quite right in the h., he's a bit weak in the h.,** il est faible d'esprit *ou* un peu timbré;

(c) *F* (*headache*) **I've got a bad h.** *or* **an awful h.,** j'ai mal à la tête *ou* un de ces maux de tête; (*after drinking*) j'ai mal aux cheveux;

(d) *Culin* **sheep's h.,** tête *f* de mouton; **calf's h.,** tête de veau; **potted h.,** fromage *m* de tête;

(e) (*antlers*) bois *mpl*, tête *f* (*de cerf*); **deer of the first/second h.,** cerf *m* à la première/deuxième tête;

(f) (*top part, end*) tête *f* (*d'arbre, de fleur etc*); pomme *f* (*de chou*); pointe *f* (*d'asperge*); pied *m* (*de céleri*); épi *m* (*de blé*); tête (*de violon, d'épingle etc*); pomme (*de canne*); tête (*de marteau*); fer *m* (*de lance etc*); tête (*de volcan etc*); haut *m* (*de page*); chapiteau *m* (*de colonne etc*); haut (*de l'escalier etc*); *Min* carreau *m* (*de carrière*); bouche *f* (*de puits de mine*); tête, culasse *f* (*de cylindre*); chapiteau (*d'alambic, de fusée etc*); cône *m* (*de torpille*); tête (*de piston*); fond *m* (*de barrique etc*); peau *f* (*de tambour*); chevet *m*, tête (*de lit*); haut bout (*de la table*); source *f* (*d'une rivière*); *Med* tête (*d'un furoncle*); *Typ* tête, intitulé *m* (*d'un chapitre etc*); en-tête *m*, *pl* en-têtes (*d'une page etc*); (*in bookkeeping*) rubrique *f*; *Tennis* tête (*d'une raquette*); (*on fermenting liquid*) chapeau *m*; **to come to a h.,** mûrir, aboutir; **to bring matters to a h.,** forcer une décision; **things are coming to a h.,** une crise est proche; **at the h. of the lake,** à l'extrémité du lac; **rivet h.,** rivure *f*; **h. on beer,** mousse *f*, *F* faux-col *m*, *pl* faux-cols; **beer with no h.,** bière éventée; *HydE* **h. gate,** porte *f* d'amont (*d'une écluse*); *Min* **h. frame,** chevalement *m*;

(g) *Nau F* (*latrine*) latrines *fpl*;

(h) *Cycling* colonne *f* de direction (*du cadre*);

(i) = **HEADLAND**;

(j) (*front or chief place*) **at the h. of a procession,** à la tête d'un cortège; **to be at the h. of the list,** venir en tête de liste; **at the h. of the queue,** en tête de file; **to sit at the h. of the table,** présider la table;

(k) (*person in charge*) chef *m* (*de famille, de l'Église, d'une entreprise*); **h. of state,** chef d'État; *Br Sch* **h. (teacher),** directeur, -trice; **h. (of department),** *Sch* chef de département; (*in company*) chef de service; (*in store*) chef de rayon; *Br Sch* **h. boy** *or* **girl,** = élève choisi(e) parmi les grand(e)s pour maintenir la discipline etc; **h. clerk,** premier commis; chef de bureau; **h. foreman,** chef d'atelier; **h. gardener,** jardinier *m* en chef; **h. office,** (*of company, organization*) siège social; **h. post office,** bureau central (des postes); **h. waiter,** maître *m* d'hôtel;

(l) (*in genealogy*) souche *f* (*d'une famille*);

(m) (*no pl*) (*unit*) **six h. of cattle,** six têtes de bétail; **thirty h. of oxen,** trente bœufs;

(n) (*person*) **to pay so much per h.** *or* **a h.,** payer tant par tête *ou* par personne;

(o) (*of coin*) face *f*; **heads or tails?,** pile ou face?; **heads I win, tails you lose,** je gagne de toutes les façons *ou* de toute façon; *F* **I can't make h. or tail of this,** je n'y comprends rien; ça n'a ni queue ni tête;

(p) *Phys HydE MecE* charge *f*, pression *f* (*d'un fluide, gaz etc*); **h. of water,** (*pressure*) charge *ou* pression d'eau; **full h. of steam,** charge *ou* pression de vapeur; *Phys* **loss of h.,** perte *f* de pression;

(q) (*on tape recorder*) tête *f*; *Comptr* tête *f*; **h. crash,** crash *m* de tête.

head² **1** *vt* **(a)** (*lead*) conduire, mener (*un cortège*); être à la tête de (*un parti*); venir en tête de (*un cortège, le scrutin*); **to h. the list,** (*be the first on it*) être *ou* venir en tête de (la) liste; (*sign first*) s'inscrire en tête de la liste (*de souscriptions etc*);

(b) (*direct*) diriger (*une voiture*); **just h. me towards the nearest bar,** dirigez-moi vers le bar le plus proche; *Nau* **to h. the ship for Southampton,** mettre le cap sur Southampton;

(c) (*put a head on*) mettre une tête à (*une épingle, un clou etc*); **the article is headed ...,** l'article est intitulé ...;

(d) (*skirt around*) contourner (*un lac*) par l'amont; contourner (*une rivière*) par sa source;

(e) *Fb* jouer (*le ballon*) de la tête; marquer (*un but*) de la tête;

(f) (*cut top, end off*) étêter, écimer (*un arbre, une branche*).

2 *vi* **(a)** (*go*) **to h. to the East,** (*of ship*) aller vers l'Est; **where are you heading** *or* **headed?,** où allez-vous?;

(b) *Min* avancer;

(c) (*form a head*) (*of cabbage etc*) pommer; (*of grain*) monter en épi, épier; (*of abscess*) aboutir, mûrir.

▶**head back** *vi* rentrer, retourner; **it's time we were heading back,** il est temps que nous rentrions.

▶**head for** *vipo* (*go towards*) **to h. for a place,** s'avancer *ou* se diriger vers un endroit; *Nau* piquer *ou* avoir le cap sur un endroit; **we were heading for ...,** nous étions en route pour ...; **let's h. for home,** rentrons; **where are you headed for?,** vers où *ou* dans quelle direction allez-vous?; **you're heading in the right direction,** vous allez dans la bonne direction; **the country is heading for civil war,** le pays va droit à la guerre civile; **you're heading for trouble,** vous allez avoir des ennuis.

▶**head in** *vtsep Fb* **to h. the ball in,** marquer (un but) de la tête.

▶**head off** *vtsep* (*divert*) barrer la route à (*qn*); intercepter (*des fugitifs*); rabattre (*le gibier*); faire rebrousser chemin à (*qn*); couper la retraite à (*l'ennemi*); parer à (*une question*); **I'll h. them off at the pass,** je leur couperai la retraite au col.

▶**head up** *vtsep* (*team etc*) diriger.

headache ['hedeɪk] *n* **(a)** mal *m* de tête, *pl* maux de tête; **to have a h.,** avoir mal à la tête; *F* **you give me a h.,** vous me cassez la tête; **(b)** *F* (*worry, problem*) embêtement *m*, casse-tête *m*, plaie *f*; **it can be a h. finding somewhere to park,** ça peut être la plaie pour trouver un endroit où se garer; **this injury is another h. for the team's manager,** cette blessure représente un autre casse-tête pour le manager de l'équipe.

headband ['hedbænd] *n* bandeau *m*.

headboard ['hedbɔːd] *n* dosseret *m*.

headbutt¹ ['hedbʌt] *n* coup *m* de tête; **to give s.o. a h.,** donner un coup de tête à qn.

headbutt² *vt* donner un coup de tête à.

headcase ['hedkeɪs] *n Br F* cinglé, -ée.

headcheese ['hedtʃiːz] *n Am Culin* fromage *m* de tête.

headdress ['heddres] *n* coiffe *f*; (*of Red Indians*) coiffure *f*.

headed ['hedɪd] *adj* **h. (note) paper,** papier *m* à en-tête.

-headed ['hedɪd] *suff* **big/two/***etc***-h.**, qui a la grosse tête/qui a deux têtes/*etc*.

header ['hedər] *n* **(a)** *Typ Comptr* en-tête *m*; **(b)** *Fb F* coup *m* de tête; **(c)** *F* (*fall*) **to take a h.**, piquer une tête; (*into water*) plonger (dans l'eau) la tête la première; (*on to ground*) tomber (par terre) la tête la première; **(d)** *Br F* (*crazy person*) cinglé, -ée; **(e)** *Constr* boutisse *f*.

headfirst ['hed'fɜːst] *adv* (*to fall*) la tête la première.

headgear ['hedgɪər] *n* (*no pl*) couvre-chef *m*; **the guerillas wore all kinds of h.**, les guérilleros portaient toutes sortes de couvre-chefs.

head-hunt ['hed'hʌnt] **1** *vt Fig* **to be h.-hunted**, être recruté par un chasseur de têtes. **2** *vi* (*of savage*) *& Fig* chasser des têtes.

head-hunter ['hedhʌntər] *n* (*savage*) *& Fig* chasseur *m* de têtes.

head-hunting ['hedhʌntɪŋ] *n* recrutement *m* de cadres par approche directe.

headiness ['hedɪnɪs] *n* **(a)** (*of wine etc*) qualité capiteuse; **(b)** (*rashness*) impétuosité *f*.

heading ['hedɪŋ] *n* **(a)** (*in book etc*) tête *f* (*d'un chapitre, d'un article*); rubrique *f* (*d'un article*); chapeau *m* (*de passage cité, d'un rapport*); en-tête *m*, *pl* en-têtes (*d'une page etc*); (*in bookkeeping*) poste *m*, rubrique; **this subject comes under the h. of rhetoric,** cette discipline fait partie de la rhétorique; **(b)** *Fb* jeu *m* de tête; **(c)** *Min* (*head of tunnel*) avancée *f*, avancement *m*; (*tunnel*) galerie *f* d'avancement; **(d)** *Constr* **h. (course),** assise *f* de boutisses.

headlamp ['hedlæmp] *n* = **HEADLIGHT**.

headland ['hedlənd] *n Geog* cap *m*, promontoire *m*.

headless ['hedlɪs] *adj* **(a)** sans tête; (*corps*) décapité; **(b)** *Biol* (*animal etc*) acéphale.

headlight ['hedlaɪt] *n* phare *m* (*d'automobile*); feu *m* d'avant (*de locomotive*).

headline¹ ['hedlaɪn] *n* **(a)** *Journ* titre *m*, gros titre; **to get into** *or* **hit the headlines,** faire la une, faire les gros titres; **pollution has been in the headlines a lot recently,** la pollution a beaucoup fait la une récemment; *Rad TV* **... and here are the headlines,** ... et voici les grands titres (de l'actualité); **the disappearance of a dog isn't normally h. news,** la disparition d'un chien ne fait pas normalement la une de l'actualité; **(b)** *Typ* en-tête *m*, *pl* en-têtes; ligne *f* de tête.

headline² **1** *vt Journ* mettre en vedette *ou* en première page. **2** *vi Mus etc* (*be chief attraction of a show*) être en vedette (d'un spectacle).

headliner ['hedlaɪnər] *n Mus etc* vedette *f*; **the headliners are a jazz band,** le groupe-vedette est un groupe de jazz.

headlong ['hedlɒŋ] **1** *adv* **to fall h.**, tomber la tête la première; **to rush h. to one's ruin,** courir à corps perdu à sa ruine; **they rushed h. into the deal,** ils se sont jetés à corps perdu dans cette affaire. **2** *adj* (*fall*) la tête la première; **to take a h. dive,** piquer une tête; **there was a h. rush to buy the shares,** tout le monde s'est précipité pour acheter les actions; **h. flight,** sauve-qui-peut *m inv*.

headman, *pl* **-men** ['hedmən] *n* chef *m* (*d'une tribu etc*).

headmaster [hed'mɑːstər] *n Sch* directeur *m* (*d'une école*); principal *m* (*d'un collège*); proviseur *m* (*d'un lycée*).

headmistress [hed'mɪstrɪs] *n Sch* directrice *f* (*d'une école*); principale *f* (*d'un collège*); proviseur *m* (*d'un lycée*).

head-on ['he'dɒn] *adj & adv* de front; **h.-on collision,** collision frontale *ou* de plein fouet; **they met h.-on,** ils se sont abordés de front; **h.-on confrontation,** confrontation *f* en face à face.

headphones ['hedfəunz] *npl Tel Rad* casque *m* (téléphonique, d'écoute), écouteurs *mpl*.

headquarter ['hedkwɔːtər] **1** *vi* (*of company*) **to h. in Glasgow,** établir son siège à Glasgow. **2** *vt* **to be headquartered in Glasgow,** avoir son siège à Glasgow.

headquarters [hed'kwɔːtəz] *npl* (*often with sing verb*) **(a)** *Admin Com etc* siège social, résidence *f* (*administrative*), bureau principal; administration centrale (*de l'O.N.U. etc*); **to have its h. at ...,** siéger *ou* avoir son siège à ...; **(b)** *Mil* (*of lower units*) poste *m* de commandement; (*of higher units*) quartier général; (*staff*) état-major *m*, *pl* états-major; **company/platoon h.**, groupe *m* de commandement de la compagnie/de la section.

headrest ['hedrest] *n* appui-tête *m*, *pl* appuis-tête.

headroom ['hedruːm] *n* hauteur *f* libre; (*of an arch*) échappée *f*; **there wasn't enough h. for the bus,** il n'y avait pas un dégagement suffisant au-dessus du bus.

headscarf ['hedskɑːf] *n* foulard *m*.

headset ['hedset] *n Rad TV* casque *m* (radio, téléphonique).

headship ['hedʃɪp] *n Br Sch* direction *f* (*d'un collège etc*).

headshrinker ['hedʃrɪŋkər] *n* réducteur *m* de têtes; *F* (*psychiatrist*) psychiatre *mf*.

headstall ['hedstɔːl] *n* (*for horse*) têtière *f*, licou *m*.

headstand ['hedstænd] *n Gym* poirier *m*, arbre fourchu; **to do a h.**, faire le poirier.

headstock ['hedstɒk] *n MecE* (*on lathe*) poupée *f* fixe.

headstone ['hedstəun] *n* **(a)** (*on grave*) pierre tombale; **(b)** *Archit Constr* clef *f* de voûte.

headstrong ['hedstrɒŋ] *adj* volontaire, têtu, entêté.

head-up ['he'dʌp] *adj Mil Av* **h.-up display,** affichage *m* en hauteur.

headway ['hedweɪ] *n* progrès *m*; **to make h.**, avancer, faire des progrès; (*of ship*) faire de la route; **to make no h.**, ne pas avancer; **the two sides have made some h. in their negotiations,** les deux parties ont avancé dans leurs négociations.

headwind ['hedwɪnd] *n Nau* vent *m* contraire; vent debout.

headword ['hedwɜːd] *n* (mot *m*) en-tête *m*, *pl* en-têtes; entrée *f* (*dans un dictionnaire*).

heady ['hedɪ] *adj* **(a)** (*wine, perfume*) capiteux; (*perfume*) troublant; (*height etc*) vertigineux; **the h. times during the revolution,** les moments grisants pendant la révolution; **(b)** (*person, action*) impétueux, emporté, violent.

heal [hiːl] **1** *vt* guérir (**s.o. of a disease,** qn d'une maladie); *Med & Fig* guérir, cicatriser (*une blessure*); *Fig* **to h. the breach (between two people),** amener une réconciliation (entre deux personnes). **2** *vi* (*of wound*) se cicatriser, se refermer; **the wound hasn't healed properly,** la blessure ne s'est pas bien cicatrisée.

►heal over, heal up *vi* = **HEAL 2**.

healer ['hiːlər] *n* guérisseur, -euse.

healing ['hiːlɪŋ] **1** *adj* (*remedy etc*) curatif; (*ointment*) cicatrisant; (*plant, remedy*) vulnéraire; (*wound*) qui se cicatrise. **2** *n* guérison *f*; (*of a wound*) cicatrisation *f*.

health [helθ] *n* santé *f*; **to restore s.o. to h.**, rendre la santé à qn; **to regain one's h.**, recouvrer la santé; **exercise is good for the** *or* **one's h.**, l'exercice est bon pour la santé; **good h.**, bonne santé; **ill** *or* **poor h.**, mauvaise santé; **chronic ill h.**, invalidité *f*; **to be in good h.**, être en bonne santé *ou* bien portant; *Fig* **the economy is in good h.**, l'économie se porte bien; **to be in bad** *or* **poor h.**, se porter mal, être mal portant; **public h.**, santé *ou* hygiène publique; **the Department of H. and Social Security** = le Ministère de la Santé et de la Sécurité Sociale; **to drink to s.o.'s h.**, boire à la santé de qn; **(your very) good h.!**, (à votre) santé!; **h. foods,** aliments *mpl* diététiques; **h. food shop,** magasin *m* de produits diététiques; **(public) h. officer** *or* **inspector,** inspecteur *m* de la santé publique; *Br* **h. visitor,** infirmière visiteuse.

health-giving ['helθgɪvɪŋ] *adj* (*effet etc*) bienfaisant, salutaire; (*air etc*) tonifiant, vivifiant.

healthily ['helθɪlɪ] *adv* sainement; salubrement.

healthiness ['helθɪnɪs] *n* (*of place, climate*) salubrité *f*; (*of person*) bonne santé.

healthy ['helθɪ] *adj* (*person, animal*) en bonne santé, bien portant; (*skin, lungs etc*) sain; (*plant*) robuste; (*climate, food etc*) salubre, sain; (*appetite*) robuste; **h. eating,** alimentation saine; **to look healthier,** avoir meilleure mine; **h. living,** vie saine; **a h. interest in the opposite sex,** un grand intérêt à l'égard du sexe opposé; **it isn't h. for a child to spend so much time reading,** il n'est pas sain pour un enfant de passer tant de temps à lire; **a h. democracy,** une démocratie qui se porte bien; **a h. economy,** une économie saine *ou* prospère; **to make a h. profit,** faire de bons bénéfices; **it is a h. sign that ...,** il est encourageant que ... + *sub*.

heap¹ [hiːp] *n* **(a)** (*pile*) tas *m*, monceau *m*, amas *m*, amoncellement *m* (*de bois, de pierres*); **the books were in a h. on the floor,** les livres étaient en tas sur le sol; **h. of junk,** tas de ferraille; **(b)** *F* (*large number*) *usu pl* **she had heaps of children,** elle avait une ribambelle d'enfants; **I've got heaps of things to do,** j'ai un tas de choses à faire **you've got heaps of time,** vous avez largement le temps; **to have heaps of room/money,** avoir plein de place/d'argent; **to fall in a h.**, (*of person*) s'affaisser (*sur soi-même*); **to be struck all of a h.**, en rester abasourdi *ou* stupéfait; **(c)** *Sl* (*car*) **this old h.**, cette vieille bagnole, ce vieux tas de ferraille.

heap² *vt* **(a)** (*pile*) entasser, amonceler, mettre en tas (*des pierres, du bois*); amasser (*des richesses*); **to h. insults on s.o.**, accabler qn d'injures; **(b)** (*cover, fill*) **to h. sth/s.o. with sth,** combler qch/qn de qch; **she heaped my plate**

with cherries, elle a rempli mon assiette de cerises.

►**heap up** *vtsep* (*make pile of*) empiler, entasser.

heaped ['hi:pt] *adj* entassé, amoncelé; *Culin* **a h. teaspoonful/tablespoonful/***etc*, (*in recipe*) une bonne cuillère à café/à soupe/*etc*.

heaps [hi:ps] *adv F* **to be h. better,** se porter beaucoup mieux.

hear [hɪər] *v* (*pt & pp* **heard** [hɜ:d]) **1** *vt* **(a)** (*perceive*) entendre; **I heard a ring,** j'ai entendu sonner; **let's h. it,** dites (donc); racontez-nous ça; **I heard my name (mentioned),** j'ai entendu dire mon nom; **to h. s.o. speak,** entendre parler qn; **I could hardly make myself heard,** je pouvais à peine me faire entendre; *F* **I've heard that one before!,** j'ai déjà entendu ça (quelque part)!; **you heard!,** ne faites pas celui *ou* celle qui n'a pas entendu!;

(b) (*listen to*) écouter; **they refused to h. me,** on n'a pas voulu m'écouter; **h. me out,** écoutez-moi jusqu'au bout; **h.! h.!,** (*at meeting*) très bien! très bien!; *Rel* **to h. Mass,** assister à la messe; *Jur* **to h. a case,** connaître d'une affaire; entendre une cause; **to h. a prayer,** exaucer *ou* écouter une prière;

(c) (*learn*) apprendre (*une nouvelle*); apprendre, savoir (*la vérité*); **I heard it from a friend,** je l'ai su par un ami, je l'ai appris par un ami; **I heard a rumour that she was in Spain,** j'ai entendu une rumeur selon laquelle elle serait en Espagne; **I have heard that...,** j'ai appris *ou* on m'a appris que ...; **I h. you're getting married,** j'apprends que tu vas te marier; **for six months we heard nothing,** (*received no news*) pendant six mois nous n'avons pas eu de nouvelles; **she was very famous for a while then we heard no more about her,** elle a été célèbre pendant un moment puis on n'a plus entendu parler d'elle; **I have heard a great deal about him,** on m'a beaucoup parlé de lui; **to h. tell of (s.o., sth),** entendu parler de (qn, qch).

2 *vi* **(a)** (*have hearing*) entendre (bien); **I can't h. properly,** je n'entends pas bien;

(b) (*receive news, word*) **to h. from s.o.,** recevoir des nouvelles *ou* une lettre de qn; **let me h. how you get on,** donnez-moi de vos nouvelles; **you'll h. from me!,** (*as threat*) vous aurez de mes nouvelles!; **you'll be hearing from my lawyers!,** mon avocat vous contactera!; on en reparlera devant les tribunaux!; **to h. about s.o./sth,** avoir des nouvelles de qn/sur qch, entendre parler de qn/qch; **I don't want to h. any more about it,** je ne veux plus en entendre parler.

►**hear of** *vipo* **(a)** (*learn about*) entendre parler de (*qn*); **he has not been heard of since,** depuis on n'en a plus entendu parler; **this is the first I have heard of it,** c'est la première fois que j'en entends parler; **I only heard of it yesterday,** je n'en ai eu connaissance qu'hier; **I never heard of such a thing!,** a-t-on jamais entendu une chose pareille!, je n'ai jamais vu une chose pareille!; **(b)** (*in neg*) (*allow*) **I won't h. of you going to a hotel,** il est hors de question que vous alliez à l'hôtel; **I won't h. of it,** je ne veux pas en entendre parler.

hearer ['hɪərər] *n* auditeur, -trice; **hearers,** auditoire *m*.

hearing ['hɪərɪŋ] *n* **(a)** (*ability to hear*) ouïe *f*; **he has very little h.,** son ouïe est très défaillante; **my h. is very bad,** mon ouïe est très faible; **loud noise can permanently damage your h.,** trop de bruit peut endommager l'ouïe de façon irréversible; **the h. impaired,** les malentendants *mpl*; *Med* **h. aid,** audiophone *m*; **(b)** (*range*) portée *f* de voix; **within h.,** à portée d'oreille; **out of h.,** hors de portée de la voix; **it was said in my h.,** on l'a dit devant moi *ou* en ma présence; **(c)** (*act of listening*) audition *f*, audience *f*; **he was refused a h.,** on a refusé de l'entendre; **to condemn s.o. without a h.,** condamner qn sans connaissance de cause; **(d)** *Jur* **h. of witnesses,** audition *f* des témoins; **h. of the case,** l'audience *f*; (*by judge alone*) l'audition de la cause par le juge; **the case comes up for h. tomorrow,** l'affaire passera en jugement demain.

hearken ['hɑ:k(ə)n] *vi Arch & Lit* écouter.

hearsay ['hɪəseɪ] *n* ouï-dire *m inv*; **that's only h.,** ce ne sont que des ouï-dire; **I know it** *or* **have it only from h.,** je ne le sais que par ouï-dire; *Jur* **h. evidence,** déposition *f* sur la foi d'autrui.

hearse [hɜ:s] *n* corbillard *m*, fourgon *m* mortuaire.

heart [hɑ:t] *n* **(a)** *Anat* cœur *m*; *Cathol* **the Sacred H.,** le Sacré-Cœur; *Med* **to have h. trouble** *or* **a weak h.,** être cardiaque; **h. attack,** crise *f* cardiaque; **h. disease,** maladie *f* de cœur; **h. failure,** arrêt *m* cardiaque; **h. murmur,** souffle *m* au cœur; **h. surgery,** opération *f* du cœur; **h. transplant,** greffe *f* du cœur;

(b) (*phrases*) **to have a big h.,** avoir très bon cœur; **h. of gold,** cœur d'or; **h. of stone,** cœur de pierre; **you've got no h.,** tu n'as pas de cœur; **have a h.!,** ayez un peu de cœur!; **her h.'s in the right place,** (*she is kind*) elle a bon cœur; (*have good intentions*) elle a de bonnes intentions; **his h. was full** *or* **heavy,** il avait le cœur gros; **with a heavy h.,** le cœur serré *ou* gros; **to have one's h. in one's mouth,** avoir un serrement de cœur; **to press** *or* **clasp s.o. to one's h.,** serrer *ou* presser qn sur son cœur; **to break s.o.'s h.,** briser le cœur à qn; **it was enough to break your h.,** c'était à fendre le cœur *ou* l'âme; **in my h. of hearts,** au plus profond de mon cœur; **from the bottom of one's h.,** (*remercier qn, féliciter qn*) de tout son cœur; **to be sick at h.,** avoir le cœur gros *ou* serré; **to learn/know sth by h.,** apprendre/savoir qch par cœur; **to cry one's h. out,** pleurer à s'en briser le cœur; **to love s.o. with all one's h.,** aimer qn de tout son cœur; **to win s.o.'s h.,** gagner le cœur de qn; **matters of the h.,** affaires *fpl* de cœur; **to have s.o.'s welfare at h.,** avoir à cœur le bonheur de qn; **she's a socialist at h.,** au fond, elle est socialiste; **a cause close to my h.,** une cause qui me tient à cœur; **to take sth to h.,** prendre qch à cœur; **to have set one's h. on sth/on doing sth,** avoir qch à cœur/avoir *ou* prendre à cœur de faire qch; **I have set my h. on it,** j'y tiens; **he's a man after my own h.,** c'est un homme selon mon cœur; **to one's h.'s content,** à cœur joie, à souhait; **to eat/drink to one's h.'s content,** manger/boire tout son soûl; **to put (all) one's h. into sth,** y aller de tout son cœur; **his** *or* **my** *etc* **h. isn't in it,** le cœur n'y est pas; **to put one's h. and soul** *or* **to throw oneself h. and soul into sth,** se donner corps et âme à une affaire; **to put new h. into s.o.,** donner du courage *ou* du cœur à qn; **to take h.,** (re)prendre courage; **to lose h.,** se décourager; **to lose one's h. to s.o.,** tomber amoureux de qn; **my h. sank at the news,** à cette nouvelle mon courage s'évanouit; **she didn't have the h. to tell him,** elle n'a pas eu le cœur de le lui dire;

(c) (*centre*) cœur *m* (*d'un chou*); cœur, vif *m* (*d'un arbre*); âme *f*, mèche *f* (*d'un câble*); **h. of oak,** homme courageux; **the h. of the matter,** le fond du problème; **in the h. of ...,** au cœur de ... (*une ville, d'un pays*); au (beau) milieu de (*une forêt*); au (fin) fond de (*un désert*);

(d) *Cards* **heart(s),** cœur *m*; **to play a h.** *or* **hearts,** jouer du cœur *ou* cœur; **king/queen of hearts,** roi *m*/dame *f* de cœur;

(e) *Her* **h. (point),** cœur *m*, abîme *m* (*de l'écu*).

heartache ['hɑ:teɪk] *n* chagrin *m ou* peine *f* de cœur.

heartbeat ['hɑ:tbi:t] *n* battement *m ou* pulsation *f* du cœur.

heartbreak ['hɑ:tbreɪk] *n* déchirement *m* de cœur.

heartbreaker ['hɑ:tbreɪkər] *n* (*man*) bourreau *m* des cœurs; (*woman*) croqueuse *f* d'hommes.

heartbreaking ['hɑ:tbreɪkɪŋ] *adj* navrant, accablant, déchirant; **it was h.,** c'était à fendre l'âme.

heartbroken ['hɑ:tbrəʊk(ə)n] *adj* **to be h.,** avoir le cœur brisé.

heartburn ['hɑ:tbɜ:n] *n Med* brûlures *fpl* d'estomac.

hearten ['hɑ:t(ə)n] *vt* encourager (*qn*), donner du courage à (*qn*).

heartening ['hɑ:t(ə)nɪŋ] *adj* (*conseil, mot*) encourageant.

heartfelt ['hɑ:tfelt] *adj* (*émotion, vœu*) sincère; qui vient *ou* part du cœur; **to express one's h. thanks to s.o.,** exprimer ses remerciements sincères à qn.

hearth, *pl* **hearths** [hɑ:θ, hɑ:θs] *n* **(a)** foyer *m*, âtre *m*; **without h. or home,** sans feu ni lieu; **h. rug,** devant *m* de foyer; **(b)** *Metal* aire *f*, foyer *m*, sole *f* (*de four à réverbère*); creuset *m* (*de haut fourneau*); **smith's h.,** forge *f*.

hearthstone ['hɑ:θstəʊn] *n* pierre *f* de la cheminée, (marbre *m* du) foyer *m*.

heartily ['hɑ:tɪlɪ] *adv* **(a)** (*cordially*) (*greet*) cordialement; (*welcome, applaud*) chaleureusement; (*work, laugh*) de bon cœur; (*se réjouir*) sincèrement; *F* **to be h. sick of sth,** être profondément dégoûté de qch; **(b)** (*dîner*) copieusement; (*manger*) de bon appétit, avec appétit.

heartiness ['hɑ:tɪnɪs] *n* **(a)** (*cordiality*) cordialité *f*, chaleur *f* (*d'un accueil*); sincérité *f* (*d'un consentement*); **(b)** (*vigour*) vigueur *f* (*de l'appétit*); ardeur *f*, empressement *m*.

heartland ['hɑ:tlænd] *n Pol Econ etc* centre *m*, cœur *m*; **the country's industrial h.,** le centre industriel du pays.

heartless ['hɑ:tlɪs] *adj* (*person*) sans cœur, insensible; (*action, remark*) dur, cruel; **it was h. of you to say that,** c'était cruel de ta part de dire ça.

heartlessly ['hɑ:tlɪslɪ] *adv* sans cœur, sans pitié; (*cruelly*) cruellement.

heartlessness ['hɑ:tlɪsnɪs] *n* manque *m* de cœur, insensibilité *f*; (*cruelty*) cruauté *f*.

heart-lung ['hɑ:t'lʌŋ] *adj Med* **h.-l. machine,** cœur-poumon artificiel; **h.-l. transplant,** greffe *f* cœur-poumon.

heart-rending ['hɑːtrendɪŋ] *adj* (*soupir, nouvelle*) à fendre le cœur; (*spectacle*) navrant; **h. cries,** cris déchirants.
heart-searching ['hɑːtsɜːtʃɪŋ] *n* **after much h.-s.,** après avoir longuement réfléchi.
heartsick ['hɑːtsɪk] *adj* écœuré; **to be** *or* **feel h.,** avoir le cœur serré *ou* gros.
heartstrings ['hɑːtstrɪŋz] *npl Fig* **to tug at s.o.'s h.,** serrer le cœur de qn.
heart-throb ['hɑːtθrɒb] *n Br F* idole *f*, coqueluche *f*.
heart-to-heart [hɑːtə'hɑːt] **1** *adj* (*conversation*) intime, à cœur ouvert; **to have a h.-to-h. talk with s.o.,** parler avec qn à cœur ouvert. **2** *n* conversation *f* intime *ou* à cœur ouvert.
heart-warming ['hɑːtwɔːmɪŋ] *adj* réconfortant, qui réchauffe le cœur; **it was h.-w. to see father and child getting on so well,** c'était à vous réchauffer le cœur de voir le père et l'enfant s'entendre si bien.
hearty ['hɑːtɪ] *adj* **(a)** (*cordial*) cordial, -aux; (*sentiment*) sincère, qui part du cœur; (*rire*) jovial; **my heartiest congratulations,** mes félicitations les plus chaleureuses; **h. cheers,** acclamations nourries; **she has a h. dislike of hypocrisy,** elle a une sainte horreur de l'hypocrisie; **(b)** (*vigorous*) vigoureux, robuste, bien portant; **he is still (hale and) h.,** il est encore gaillard; **(c)** (*substantial*) (*repas*) copieux, abondant; **h. appetite,** gros *ou* rude appétit; **he's a h. eater,** c'est un gros mangeur.
heat¹ [hiːt] *n* **(a)** chaleur; ardeur *f* (*du soleil, d'un foyer*); *Phys Ch etc* chaleur; *Metal* (*temperature*) chaleur, chaude *f*; **in the h. of the day,** au plus chaud de la journée; *Med* **h. exhaustion** *or* **prostration,** épuisement dû à la chaleur; **h. haze,** brume *f* de chaleur; **h. wave,** vague *f* de chaleur, canicule *f*; *Culin* **cook at a low h.,** cuire à faible température; **h. of combustion,** chaleur de combustion; **blood h.,** température *f* du sang; **latent h.,** chaleur latente; **radiant h.,** chaleur radiante; **h. constant,** constante *f* calorifique; *Tech* **h. engine,** machine *f ou* moteur *m* thermique; **h. loss,** déperdition *f* de chaleur; **h. shield,** bouclier *m* thermique (*d'un véhicule spatial etc*); **h. treatment,** *Ind* traitement *m* thermique; *Med* thermothérapie *f*; **h. exchanger,** échangeur *m* de chaleur; **h. pump,** pompe *f* à chaleur; **h. sink,** dissipateur thermique *ou* de chaleur;
(b) (*passion*) **to get into a h.,** s'échauffer, s'emporter; **to reply with some h.,** répondre avec une certaine vivacité; **h. of a discussion,** feu *m* d'une discussion; **to take the h. out of the situation,** dédramatiser la situation; **the h. of passion,** la fougue des passions; **in the h. of the moment,** dans la chaleur du moment;
(c) *Sl* (*pressure*) **to turn on the h.,** (*in interrogation etc*) faire pression sur qn; **until the h. is off,** jusqu'à ce que les choses se calment;
(d) (*of animal*) chaleur *f*, rut *m*; **to be on** *or* **in h.,** être en chaleur;
(e) *Med* (*rash*) rougeur *f* (*sur la peau*); **h. rash,** boutons *mpl* de chaleur;
(f) *Sp* épreuve *f*, manche *f*; **qualifying** *or* **eliminating h.,** (épreuve *f*, série *f*) éliminatoire *f*; **dead h.,** course *f* à égalité.
heat² **1** *vt* **(a)** chauffer (*l'eau, une maison etc*); **to h. sth to (a temperature of) 80°,** porter qch à 80°; **to h. a house with gas,** chauffer une maison au gaz; **(b)** (*arouse*) échauffer (*le sang etc*); échauffer, enflammer (*l'imagination, les passions*). **2** *vi* (*of water etc*) chauffer; (*of bearing etc*) chauffer, s'échauffer.
►heat up 1 *vtsep* (*warm*) (faire) réchauffer (*un plat etc*). **2** *vi* (*of water*) chauffer; (*of room*) se réchauffer; (*of discussion etc*) s'échauffer.
heat-conducting ['hiːtkəndʌktɪŋ] *adj* thermoconducteur, -trice.
heated ['hiːtɪd] *adj* **(a)** chaud, chauffé; *MecE* (*palier*) échauffé, qui chauffe; **(b)** (*passionate, angry*) (*discussion*) chaud, animé; **to become h.,** (*of discussion, person*) s'échauffer.
heatedly ['hiːtɪdlɪ] *adv* avec chaleur, avec emportement.
heater ['hiːtər] *n* **(a)** (*for room etc*) radiateur *m*; **(electric) h.,** radiateur électrique; **(fan) h.,** radiateur soufflant; **(water) h.,** chauffe-eau *m inv*; **(immersion) h.,** thermoplongeur *m*; **(b)** *Tech* réchauffeur *m*; **(c)** *Electron* filament incandescent; **(d)** *US Sl* (*pistol etc*) revolver *m*.
heath [hiːθ] *n* **(a)** (*tract of land*) bruyère *f*, lande *f*; **(b)** (*heather*) bruyère *f*.
heathen ['hiːð(ə)n] **1** *adj* (*pagan*) païen, -ïenne; (*barbarian*) sauvage, barbare. **2** *n* **the h.,** (*used as pl*) les païens *mpl*.
heathenish ['hiːðənɪʃ] *adj* (*pagan*) païen; (*barbarian*) barbare.
heathenism ['hiːðənɪz(ə)m] *n* paganisme *m*.
heather ['heðər] *n* (*shrub*) bruyère *f*, brande *f*.
heating ['hiːtɪŋ] **1** *adj* **h. bill,** facture *f* de chauffage; **h. power,** puissance *f ou* pouvoir *m* calorifique; rendement *m* calorique; *El* puissance de chauffage; *Tech* **h. apparatus,** appareil *m* de chauffage; *MecE etc* **h. coil,** serpentin *m* de chauffage, réchauffeur *m*; *El etc* **h. element** *or* **unit,** élément chauffant. **2** *n* **(a)** (*system*) chauffage *m*; **there's no h. in the bathroom,** il n'y a pas de chauffage dans la salle de bain; **electric h.,** chauffage électrique; **oil h.,** chauffage au mazout; **(b)** (*of a meal etc*) réchauffage *m*; **(c)** (*becoming hot*) échauffement *m* (*d'un outil etc*).
heatproof ['hiːtpruːf] *adj* calorifuge; (*vernis etc*) allant au feu.
heat-resistant, -resisting ['hiːtrɪzɪstənt, -rɪzɪstɪŋ] *adj* résistant à la chaleur; (*Tech*) thermorésistant.
heat-seeking ['hiːtsiːkɪŋ] *adj* (*missile*) guidé par la chaleur.
heatstroke ['hiːtstrəʊk] *n Med Vet* coup *m* de chaleur.
heave¹ [hiːv] *n* **(a)** effort *m* (*pour soulever etc*); **with a mighty h.,** avec un énorme effort; *Nau* **h. of the sea,** poussée *f ou* entraînement *m* des lames; houle *f*; **(b)** (*retch*) haut-le-cœur *m inv*.
heave² *v* (*pt & pp* **heaved** *or esp Nau* **hove** [həʊv]) **1** *vt* **(a)** (*lift*) faire un effort pour lever, soulever (*un fardeau*); (*pull*) faire un effort pour tirer (*qch*); (*push*) faire un effort pour pousser (*qch*); (*drag*) faire un effort pour traîner (*qch*); (*throw*) faire un effort pour lancer (*qch*); **he heaved the sacks of coal onto the truck,** il a lancé les sacs de charbon dans le camion avec effort; **she heaved herself out of her chair,** elle s'est soulevée de la chaise avec effort; *Nau* **to h. the anchor,** lever l'ancre;
(b) (*utter*) pousser (*un soupir etc*);
(c) *Nau* **to h. the ship ahead/astern/***etc*, virer le navire de l'avant/de l'arrière/*etc*.
2 *vi* **(a) h.!,** (*push*) poussez!; (*pull*) tirez!; (*lift*) soulevez!; **they heaved on the rope,** ils ont tiré sur la corde avec effort;
(b) (*swell*) (se) gonfler, se soulever; (*of sea*) s'agiter, se soulever; (*of ship*) se soulever sur la lame; (*of bosom*) palpiter;
(c) (*retch*) (*of person*) avoir des haut-le-cœur; (*of the stomach*) se soulever;
(d) *Nau* (*of land, ship*) **to h. in sight,** paraître (à l'horizon).
►heave to *vi & vtas Nau* (se) mettre en panne *ou* à la cape; (*in gale*) caranguer.
heave-ho ['hiːv'həʊ] **1** *int Nau* oh hisse! **2** *n Sl* **to give s.o. the h.-ho,** sacquer qn, virer qn.
heaven ['hev(ə)n] *n* ciel *m*, *pl* cieux; **in h.,** au ciel; **to go to h.,** aller au ciel *ou* en paradis; **it's h. on earth,** c'est le paradis sur terre; **to move h. and earth to do sth,** remuer ciel et terre pour faire qch; **the heavens opened,** il a commencé à pleuvoir à torrents; *F* **it stinks to high h.,** ça pue; **(good) heavens!, heavens above!,** juste ciel!, bonté divine!; **thank h. (for that)!,** Dieu merci!; **h. (alone) knows!,** Dieu seul le sait!; **for h.'s sake!,** pour l'amour de Dieu!, pour l'amour du ciel!; **where in the name of h.** *or* **in h.'s name is he?,** où diable est-il?; **this is h.!,** c'est merveilleux!
heavenly ['hev(ə)nlɪ] *adj* (*musique etc*) céleste; (*don*) du ciel; **h. body,** astre *m*; **our h. Father,** notre Père céleste; *F* **what h. peaches!,** quelles pêches délicieuses!; *F* **to have a h. evening,** passer une soirée merveilleuse.
heaven-sent ['hev(ə)nsent] *adj* providentiel.
heavily ['hevɪlɪ] *adv* **(a)** (*marcher, tomber, appuyer*) lourdement; **time hangs h. on his hands,** le temps lui pèse; **she walked h.,** elle avançait d'un pas pesant; **(b)** (*to a considerable extent*) fortement, fort; **h. underlined,** fortement souligné; **to drink h.,** boire beaucoup; **it was raining h.,** il pleuvait fort, il pleuvait beaucoup; **to rely h. on sth,** dépendre beaucoup de qch; **to lose h.,** perdre gros; **h. indebted,** fortement endetté; **the secret service was h. involved in training guerillas,** les services secrets étaient lourdement impliqués dans la formation des guérilleros; **to be h. hit,** (*by financial misfortune etc*) être gravement atteint; **to be h. taxed,** être fortement imposé; **(c)** (*to sigh*) profondément; **to sleep h.,** dormir profondément; **(d)** (*to breathe*) péniblement.
heaviness ['hevɪnɪs] *n* **(a)** lourdeur *f*, pesanteur *f* (*d'un corps, de l'allure*); poids *m* (*d'un fardeau*); lourdeur (*d'un aliment*); **(b)** engourdissement *m*, lassitude *f*, abattement *m* (*des membres, de l'esprit*); **h. of heart,** serrement *m* de cœur.
heavy ['hevɪ] **1** *adj* **(a)** (*parcel etc*) lourd, pesant; (*step*)

pesant, lourd, alourdi; (*style*) lourd, monotone; *Phys* (*body*) grave; *Atom Phys* (*atom*) lourd; **h. blow,** coup violent; (*dealt by fate etc*) rude coup; **h. meal,** repas lourd à digérer; **h. water,** eau lourde;

(b) (*large, thick*) (*luggage, coat, shoes*) gros, *f* grosse; **h. wire,** fil *m* (de) grosse épaisseur; **h. industry,** industrie lourde; *Nau* **h. armament,** artillerie de gros calibre; **h. losses,** lourdes *ou* fortes pertes; **h. features,** gros traits; **h. beard,** forte barbe;

(c) (*intense*) **h. rain,** pluie battante; **h. shower,** grosse averse; *Mil* **h. fire,** feu nourri, feu intense; **h. cold,** gros rhume; **h. sleep,** profond sommeil, sommeil de plomb;

(d) (*oppressive*) (*odeur*) lourd; (*ciel*) sombre, morne; **air h. with scent,** air chargé de parfums; **h. responsibility,** lourde responsabilité; **h. fine,** lourde amende; **to rule with a h. hand,** gouverner d'une main rude *ou* sévère;

(e) (*with sleep*) **h. eyes,** yeux battus; **h. with sleep,** accablé de sommeil;

(f) (*hard*) (*work*) pénible, difficile, dur, laborieux; (*breathing*) pénible; (*task*) lourd; (*day*) chargé; *F* **to be h. on electricity/petrol/***etc*, consommer beaucoup d'électricité/d'essence/*etc*; **she did the h. work,** c'est elle qui a fait le gros travail; **this book is h. reading,** ce livre est indigeste; **to find it h. going,** avancer avec difficulté; **h. soil,** sol gras; **h. weather,** gros temps; **he made h. weather of it,** il s'est compliqué la tâche; **h. sea,** forte mer, grosse mer;

(g) *Th* **h. parts,** rôles sombres *ou* sérieux; **h. father,** père noble; *F* **to come the h. father,** prendre un ton de père autoritaire;

(h) (*eater, drinker*) gros; **to be a h. sleeper,** avoir le sommeil dur;

(i) *Sl* (*tense, frightening*) difficile, menaçant; **the situation got really h.,** la situation est devenue vraiment menaçante;

(j) *Mus* **h. metal,** heavy metal *m*; **h. metal band,** groupe *m* de heavy metal.

2 *adv* **to weigh h.,** peser lourd; **food that lies h. on the stomach,** nourriture lourde *ou* indigeste *ou* qui pèse lourd sur l'estomac.

3 *n* **(a)** *F* (*tough man*) dur *m*;

(b) *Th* (*serious part*) rôle *m* sérieux *ou* sombre; (*villain*) rôle de scélérat *ou* de traître;

(c) *Journ* **heavies,** journaux sérieux.

heavy-duty [hevɪ'djuːtɪ] *adj* (*machine*) à grand *ou* fort rendement, de grande puissance; (*clothing*) résistant; (*boots*) solide, robuste; *Aut* (*tyre*) tous-terrains; *Aut* (*jack*) pour poids lourds; (*oil*) à haute teneur.

heavy-eyed [hevɪ'aɪd] *adj* aux yeux battus.

heavy-handed [hevɪ'hændɪd] *adj* **(a)** (*clumsy*) maladroit, gauche; **(b)** (*harsh*) oppressif, cruel.

heavy-headed [hevɪ'hedɪd] *adj* **to feel h.-h.,** se sentir la tête lourde; (*tired*) avoir envie de dormir.

heavy-hearted [hevɪ'hɑːtɪd] *adj* qui a le cœur lourd *ou* gros.

heavy-laden [hevɪ'leɪd(ə)n] *adj* **(a)** lourdement chargé; **(b)** (*with cares*) accablé de soucis.

heavyweight ['hevɪweɪt] **1** *n* **(a)** *Boxing* poids lourds; **(b)** (*serious, important person*) personne *f* de poids; **he is not a literary h.,** ce n'est pas un grand de la littérature. **2** *adj* **(a)** *Boxing* (catégorie (des)) poids lourd(s); **h. champion,** champion *m* (de la catégorie (des)) poids lourd(s); **(b)** (*serious, important*) sérieux; **(c)** *Tex* lourd.

Hebrew ['hiːbruː] **1** *adj Bible* hébreu, *f* hébraïque. **2** *n* **(a)** *Bible* Hébreu *m*; **(b)** *Ling* hébreu *m*.

Hebridean [hebrɪ'diːən] *adj* des Hébrides.

Hebrides (the) [ðə'hebrɪdiːz] *n* les Hébrides *fpl*.

heck [hek] *F* **1** *int* sapristi!, zut! **2** *n* **what the h. are you doing here?,** que diable fais-tu là?; **a h. of a lot,** tout un tas; **not a h. of a lot,** pas tellement, pas beaucoup.

heckle ['hek(ə)l] *vt* (*at public meetings*) interpeller (*qn*), poser des questions embarrassantes à (*qn*).

heckler ['heklər] *n Pol etc* interpellateur, -trice, adversaire *m* qui cherche à embarrasser le candidat.

heckling ['hek(ə)lɪŋ] *n* interpellation(s) *f(pl)*.

hectare ['hektɑːr] *n* (*measurement*) hectare *m*.

hectic ['hektɪk] *adj* **(a)** (*busy*) agité, fiévreux; (*existence, morning*) mouvementé; **it gets very h. in the post office at Christmas,** c'est la bousculade à la poste à Noël; **we had a h. time,** nous ne savions où donner de la tête; **(b)** *Med* (*fièvre*) hectique.

hectically ['hektɪklɪ] *adv* fiévreusement.

hectolitre ['hektəliːtər] *n* hectolitre *m*, *F* hecto *m*.

hector ['hektər] **1** *vt* rudoyer (*qn*). **2** *vi* prendre des tons autoritaires.

hectoring ['hektərɪŋ] *adj* (*tone etc*) autoritaire, impérieux.

he'd [hiːd] **(a)** = **he had**, *see* **HAVE[2]**; **(b)** = **he would**, *see* **WILL[3]**.

hedge[1] [hedʒ] *n* **(a)** *Bot* haie *f*; **to buy sth as a h. against inflation,** acheter qch pour se mettre à l'abri de l'inflation; **h. clippers** *or* **shears,** taille-haies *m inv*; **(b)** *St Exch* arbitrage *m*, couverture *f*.

hedge[2] **1** *vt* mettre une haie autour de (*un terrain*); **to h. one's bets,** (*in betting*) répartir les risques; *Fig* (*cover oneself*) se couvrir; éviter de se compromettre. **2** *vi* **(a)** *Horseracing* parier pour et contre; **(b)** *St Exch* arbitrer, se couvrir; **(c)** (*in discussion*) se réserver; éviter de se compromettre; **(d) the laws are hedged about with exceptions,** les lois sont remplies d'exceptions.

►**hedge in** *vtsep* (*surround*) entourer (*un terrain*) d'une haie; entourer (*qn*); **hedged in with difficulties,** entouré de difficultés.

►**hedge off** *vtsep* (*separate with a hedge*) séparer (*un terrain*) par une haie (**from,** de).

hedgehog ['hedʒhɒg] *n* **(a)** *Br* hérisson *m*; **to curl up like a h.,** se pelotonner en rond; **(b)** *Am* porc-épic *m*, porcs-épics.

hedgehop ['hedʒhɒp] *vi* (**-pp-**) *Av F* voler en rase-mottes, faire du rase-mottes.

hedgerow ['hedʒrəʊ] *n* bordure *f* d'arbres *ou* d'arbustes formant une haie; **animals of the hedgerows,** animaux qui vivent dans les haies.

hedging ['hedʒɪŋ] *n* **(a)** (*care of hedges*) entretien *m* des haies; **(b)** (*hedges*) bordure *f*; **(c)** *Horseracing* répartition *f* des risques; **(d)** *St Exch* arbitrage *m*; *US* contrepartie *f*; **(e)** (*in discussion etc*) hésitation *f* à prendre des décisions.

hedonism ['hiːdənɪz(ə)m, 'hed-] *n Phil* hédonisme *m*.

hedonist ['hiːdənɪst, 'hed-] *n Phil* hédoniste *mf*.

hedonistic ['hiːdənɪstɪk, 'hed-] *adj* hédoniste.

heeby-jeebies ['hiːbɪ'dʒiːbɪz] *npl Sl* **to have the h.-j.,** (*be nervous*) avoir la frousse.

heed[1] [hiːd] *n esp Lit* **to give** *or* **pay h. to sth/s.o.,** faire attention à qch/qn; **to take h.,** prendre garde; **to take h. of a warning,** tenir compte d'un avertissement.

heed[2] *vt esp Lit* tenir compte de (*qch*); **his advice was not heeded,** on n'a tenu aucun compte de ses conseils.

heedful ['hiːdfʊl] *adj Lit* vigilant, prudent, circonspect; **h. of advice,** attentif aux conseils.

heedless ['hiːdlɪs] *adj* **(a)** (*thoughtless*) étourdi, insouciant, imprudent; **(b)** (*not paying attention*) **to be h. of,** être inattentif à (*ce qui se passe*); être peu soucieux de (*l'avenir etc*); **they continued, h. of her warning/the danger,** ils ont continué sans se soucier de son avertissement/du danger.

heedlessly ['hiːdlɪslɪ] *adv* étourdiment, avec insouciance.

hee-haw[1] ['hiːhɔː] *n* hi-han *m*.

hee-haw[2] *vi* braire; faire hi-han.

heel[1] [hiːl] *n* **(a)** (*of foot*) talon *m*; **to have the police at one's heels,** avoir la police à ses trousses; **to tread on s.o.'s heels,** marcher sur les talons de qn; **to follow close on s.o.'s heels,** suivre qn de près, emboîter le pas à qn; **to take to one's heels,** prendre ses jambes à son cou; *F* **to cool** *or* **kick one's heels,** poireauter; **to kick up one's heels,** sauter de joie; **to turn on one's h.,** tourner les talons; **to come to h.,** (*of dog*) venir derrière à l'ordre; *F* (*of person*) se soumettre; **h.!,** (*to dog*) au pied!; **to bring s.o. to h.,** rappeler qn à l'ordre;

(b) (*of shoe*) talon *m*; **high** *or* **low heels,** talons hauts *ou* bas; **down at h.,** (*shoe*) éculé; *F* **to be down at h.,** (*of person*) être dans la dèche; (*of building, district*) être dans un état lamentable; **h. bar,** talon-minute *m*;

(c) (*of bread*) croûton *m*;

(d) *Sl* (*person*) chameau *m*, salaud *m*;

(e) *Tech etc* (*of tool*) talon *m*; (*of spine of book*) queue *f*; *Nau* (*of mast*) pied *m*, caisse *f*; (*of rudder*) talon;

(f) (*of hoof of horse etc*) derrière *m* du sabot.

heel[2] *vt* **(a)** (*fit with a heel*) mettre un talon à (*une chaussure*); (*repair*) réparer le talon de (*une chaussure*); refaire le talon de (*un bas*); **(b)** *Rugby Fb* talonner (*le ballon*) pour le sortir de la mêlée.

heel[3] *n Nau* bande *f*, gîte *f*, inclinaison *f* (*d'un navire*).

heel[4] *vi Nau* (*of ship*) avoir *ou* donner de la bande, prendre de la gîte.

►**heel over** *vi* = **HEEL[4]**.

heelcap ['hiːlkæp] *n* contrefort *m* du talon (*d'une chaussure*).

heeling ['hiːlɪŋ] *n* **(a)** (*fitting of a heel*) pose *f* du talon (*à une chaussure etc*); (*mending*) réparation *f* du talon; **soling and h.,** ressemelage complet; **(b)** *Rugby Fb* talonnage *m*.

heeltap ['hiːltæp] *n* (*in shoe*) rondelle *f* en cuir (*pour talon*).

heft [heft] *vt Am F Br Dial* **(a)** (*guess weight of*) soupeser (*qch*); **(b)** (*lift*) soulever (*qch*).

hefty ['heftɪ] *adj F* **(a)** (*person*) fort, solide, costaud; **(b)** (*heavy*) lourd, pesant; **a h. blow,** un coup violent; **(c)** (*substantial*) gros, important; **a h. bill,** une note de taille.

Hegelian [he'geɪlɪən] *adj & n* hégélien, -ienne.

hegemony [hɪ'gemənɪ] *n* hégémonie *f*.

hegira [hɪ'dʒaɪrə] *n* hégire *f*.

heifer ['hefər] *n Agr* génisse *f*.

heigh-ho ['heɪ'həʊ] *int* eh bien!

height [haɪt] *n* **(a)** (*of person*) taille *f*, grandeur *f*, stature *f* (*de qn*); **what's your h.?, what h. are you?,** combien mesurez-vous?; **of average h.,** de taille moyenne;
(b) (*of object*) hauteur *f*, élévation *f*; **wall two metres in h.,** mur qui a deux mètres de haut; **a h. of 20 feet,** une hauteur de 20 pieds; **overall h.,** (*of vehicle*) hauteur totale;
(c) (*of an arch*) flèche *f*, montée *f*; **maximum h. (of bridge),** hauteur *f* libre (d'un pont);
(d) (*altitude*) altitude *f*; **h. above sea level,** altitude au-dessus du niveau de la mer; *Av* **cruising h.,** altitude de croisière; **the plane was gaining/losing h.,** l'avion prenait/perdait de l'altitude; **h. indicator,** altimètre *m*; **to have a good head for heights,** ne pas avoir le vertige; **I'm scared of heights,** j'ai le vertige;
(e) (*hill, mountain*) hauteur *f*; éminence *f* (*de terrain*);
(f) (*highest point*) apogée *m* (*de la gloire etc*); faîte *m* (*des grandeurs*); comble *m* (*de la folie etc*); sommet *m* (*de l'éloquence*); **this is the h. of insolence!,** c'est de la plus haute insolence!; **at the h. of the storm,** au plus fort de l'orage; **an actress at the h. of her career,** une actrice à l'apogée de sa carrière; **in the h. of summer,** en plein été; **the season is at its h.,** la saison bat son plein; **it's the h. of fashion,** c'est la dernière mode *ou* le dernier cri.

heighten ['haɪt(ə)n] **1** *vt* **(a)** (*increase etc*) augmenter (*un prix*); accroître, augmenter (*un plaisir*); aggraver (*un mal*); accentuer (*un contraste*); relever, faire ressortir (*une couleur etc*); renchérir sur (*une histoire*); renforcer (*une impression, des spéculations*); **to h. the interest in sth,** augmenter l'intérêt pour qch; **the riots have heightened racial tensions in the city,** les émeutes ont accentué *ou* aggravé les tensions raciales dans la ville; **(b)** (*increase height of*) surélever, rehausser (*un mur etc*). **2** *vi* (*of tension*) s'accroître.

heightened ['haɪt(ə)nd] *adj* accru, exacerbé; **there is a h. awareness of the dangers of pollution,** il y a une sensibilisation accrue *ou* exacerbée aux dangers de la pollution, il y a une prise de conscience accrue des dangers de la pollution.

heightening ['haɪt(ə)nɪŋ] *n* **(a)** (*increase etc*) augmentation *f* (*des prix*); accroissement *m* (*d'un plaisir*); aggravation *f* (*d'un mal*); rehaussement *m* (*d'une couleur*); **there has been a h. of speculation,** il y a eu un renforcement de la spéculation; **(b)** (*raising of height*) surélévation *f*, rehaussement *m* (*d'un mur etc*).

heinous ['heɪnəs] *adj* (*crime*) odieux, atroce, abominable.

heir [eər] *n* héritier *m*; **to be h. to an estate,** être le légataire d'une propriété; **the h. to the throne,** l'héritier du trône; **h. apparent,** héritier présomptif; **h. presumptive,** héritier présomptif (*sauf naissance d'un héritier en ligne directe*).

heir-at-law, *pl* **heirs-at-law** ['eərætlɔː, 'eəz-] *n Jur* héritier *m* légitime.

heiress ['eərɪs] *n* héritière *f*.

heirloom ['eəluːm] *n* héritage *m*; meuble *m ou* bijou *m* de famille.

heist [haɪst] *n esp Am Sl* fric-frac *m*.

Helen ['helɪn] *n* Hélène *f*.

helianthus [hiːlɪ'ænθəs] *n* (*flower*) hélianthe *m*, tournesol *m*.

helical ['helɪk(ə)l] *adj* **(a) h. shell,** hélice *f*, coquille contournée; **(b)** *MecE* (*gear etc*) hélicoïdal, -aux; (*spring*) hélicoïde, en hélice.

helicopter ['helɪkɒptər] *n Av* hélicoptère *m*; **h. pilot,** pilote *m* d'hélicoptère; *Mil* **h. gunship,** hélicoptère *m* de combat.

►**helicopter in** *vtsep* (*troops, supplies*) amener en hélicoptère, héliporter.

►**helicopter out** *vtsep* (*people*) emmener en hélicoptère, héliporter.

heliograph ['hiːlɪəgræf] *n* **(a)** (*for sending signals*) héliographe *m*; **(b)** *Phot* héliogravure *f*.

heliotrope ['hiːlɪətrəʊp] **1** *n* (*flower*) héliotrope *m*. **2** *adj* héliotrope *inv*.

helipad ['helɪpæd] *n* zone *f* d'atterrissage pour hélicoptère.

heliport ['helɪpɔːt] *n Av* héliport *m*.

helium ['hiːlɪəm] *n Ch* hélium *m*; **h. balloon,** ballon gonflé à l'hélium.

helix, *pl* **helices** ['hiːlɪks, 'hiːlɪsiːz] *n* **(a)** *Math* hélice *f*; *Archit etc* spirale *f*; **(b)** *Anat* (*of the ear*) hélix *m*; **(c)** (*snail*) hélice *f*, colimaçon *m*.

hell [hel] **1** *n* **(a)** enfer *m*;
(b) *F* (*in phrases*) **it was h. working in the mine,** c'était l'enfer de travailler dans la mine; **it can be h. trying to park here,** quelquefois c'est l'enfer pour se garer ici; **it was all h. let loose,** c'était infernal; **all h. broke loose,** ça a bardé; **to make s.o.'s life h.** *or* **a h. on earth,** faire un enfer de la vie de qn; **these shoes are giving me h.,** ces chaussures me font un mal de chien; **to give s.o. h.,** passer un savon à qn; *Br* **it's as cold as h.,** il fait un froid de canard; **go to h.!,** va(-t-en) au diable!; **to h. with him!,** qu'il aille au diable!; **get the h. out of here!,** fiche-moi le camp d'ici!; **to work like h.,** travailler comme un malade; **to run like h.,** courir comme un dératé; **like h. (I will)!, the h. I will!,** jamais de la vie!; **I feel like h.,** je me sens au trente-sixième dessous; **I wish to h. I could remember,** si seulement je pouvais me souvenir; **come h. or high water,** contre vents et marées; **there'll be h. to pay if your mother finds out,** ça va barder si ta mère l'apprend; **to go h. for leather,** galoper ventre à terre; **a h. of a price,** un prix salé; **you've got a h. of a nerve!,** tu as un culot du diable!; **there was a** *or* **one h. of a fight,** il y a eu une bagarre de tous les diables; **he's a h. of a guy,** c'est un type formidable; **it was a h. of a good film,** c'était un film super; **what the h. do you think you're doing?,** que diable es-tu en train de fabriquer?; **what the hell's going on?,** que diable se passe-t-il?, qu'est-ce qui se passe nom de Dieu?; **who the h. are you?,** qui diable êtes-vous?; **what the h., you only live once,** que diable, on ne vit qu'une fois; **to do sth for the h. of it,** faire qch sans raison particulière; **to play merry h. with sth,** foutre qch en l'air; **to raise h.,** (*make noise*) faire un foin d'enfer, faire un boucan de tous les diables; (*react unfavourably*) faire une scène terrible *ou* de tous les diables;
(c) *Myth* les enfers *mpl*.
2 *int F* **(oh) h.!,** zut alors!; (*stronger*) merde alors!; *F* **h.'s bells!, h.'s teeth, h. and damnation,** (sacré) nom de nom!

he'll [hiːl] = **he will,** *see* **WILL**[3].

hellbender ['helbendər] *n US F* (séance *f* de) beuverie *f*.

hellbent ['helbent] *adj F* d'une détermination féroce *ou* têtue; **to be h. on doing sth,** vouloir à tout prix faire qch; **the human race seems h. on self-destruction,** la race humaine semble vouloir s'autodétruire à tout prix.

hellcat ['helkæt] *n F* sorcière *f*, mégère *f*.

hellebore ['helɪbɔːr] *n* (*plant*) ellébore *m*, varaire *mf*.

Hellene ['heliːn] *n* Hellène *mf*.

Hellenic [he'liːnɪk] *adj* (*people*) hellène; (*language, history*) hellénique.

hellfire ['hel'faɪər] *n* feu *m* de l'enfer; **a h. preacher,** prédicateur annonçant les feux de l'enfer.

hellhole ['helhəʊl] *n* enfer *m*; *F* (*bar, club etc*) bouge *m*.

hellish ['helɪʃ] *F* **1** *adj* infernal, -aux; **it was (simply) h.,** c'était infernal. **2** *adv* terriblement.

hellishly ['helɪʃlɪ] *adv* infernalement; diaboliquement.

hello [he'ləʊ] *int* bonjour!; *Tel* allô; **h. there, wake up!,** (*calling attention*) holà! debout!, hé, là-bas, debout!; **h., is that you?,** (*indicating surprise*) tiens!, c'est vous!; **to say h.,** dire bonjour; **say h. to him for me,** dis-lui bonjour de ma part; **she gave them a cheery 'h.',** elle leur a lancé un 'bonjour' joyeux.

hell-raiser ['helreɪzər] *n F* chahuteur *m*.

hell-raising ['helreɪzɪŋ] *n* vie *f* de patachon, vie de bâton de chaise.

helluva ['heləvə] *F* = **hell of a,** *see* **HELL 1**.

helm [helm] *n Nau* barre *f* (*du gouvernail*); gouvernail *m*, timon *m*; **the man at the h.,** *Nau* l'homme de barre; *Fig* l'homme qui tient le gouvernail *ou* qui dirige l'entreprise; **to be at the h.,** être à la barre; **to take the h.,** prendre la direction des affaires.

helmet ['helmɪt] *n* casque *m* (*de soldat, de pompier etc*); **(crash) h.,** casque protecteur.

helmsman, *pl* **-men** ['helmzmən] *n Nau* homme *m* de barre, timonier *m*.

help[1] [help] *n* **(a)** aide *f*, assistance *f*, (*when in danger etc*) secours *m*; **with God's h.,** Dieu aidant; grâce à Dieu; **to shout for h.,** crier au secours, appeler à l'aide; **he's past h.,** il est perdu; **can I be of (any) h.?,** puis-je vous aider?; **some students need h. to decide which course to take,** certains étudiants ont besoin qu'on les aide à décider quel cursus choisir; **she needs h.,** (*from a psychiatrist etc*) elle a besoin d'aide; **to give h. to s.o.,** apporter de l'aide à qn;

the government provides some financial h., le gouvernement offre une aide financière; **the map wasn't much h.,** la carte n'a pas servi à grand-chose; **I had h.,** (*I didn't do it on my own*) on m'a aidé; *F* **a fat lot of h. you are,** tu parles d'une aide!; **to come to s.o.'s h.,** venir au secours de qn;

(b) to be a h. to s.o., être d'un grand secours à qn; rendre service à qn; **my daughter's been a great h.,** ma fille m'a bien rendu service; **that was a big h.,** ça a beaucoup aidé;

(c) (*person*) aide *mf*; *esp Br* **daily h.,** femme *f* de ménage; *esp Br* **home h.,** aide ménagère; **mother's h.,** aide familiale;

(d) *esp Am* (*pl* **help**) ouvrier, -ière; employé, -ée;

(e) (*alternative*) **there was no h. for it,** il n'y avait rien d'autre à faire.

help² **1** *vt* **(a)** aider, secourir, assister (*qn*); **can I** *or* **may I h. you?,** puis-je vous aider?; (*in shop, restaurant*) que désirez-vous?; (*on telephone*) que puis-je faire pour vous?; **so h. me God!,** que Dieu me juge si je ne dis pas la vérité!; *F* **so h. me,** (*no matter what*) je jure; **come and h. me,** venez m'aider *ou* me donner un coup de main; **he helped me with my homework,** il m'a aidé à faire mes devoirs; **to h. s.o. to do sth,** aider qn à faire qch; **he helped the old lady up the stairs,** il a aidé la vieille dame à monter l'escalier; **to h. s.o. on/off with their coat,** aider qn à mettre/enlever son manteau; **to h. s.o. out of a difficulty,** aider qn à se tirer d'une difficulté; **he helped the ball into the goal,** il a donné un petit coup de pouce au ballon pour le faire entrer dans les buts; **to h. one another,** s'entraider; *Prov* **God helps those who help themselves,** aide-toi et le ciel t'aidera; **it helped me knowing that someone was waiting for me,** ça m'a aidé de savoir que quelqu'un m'attendait; **h.!,** au secours!; **h.!, I'm late!,** mon Dieu!, je suis en retard!;

(b) (*aid*) faciliter (*la digestion, le progrès*); **that doesn't h. the situation, that doesn't h. much,** cela ne nous avance pas; *Iron* **to h. matters, we had a puncture,** ce qui n'était pas pour arranger les choses, nous avons eu une crevaison;

(c) (*at table*) servir (*qn*); **to h. s.o. to soup/wine,** servir du potage/verser du vin à qn; **h. yourself,** servez-vous; *F* **to h. oneself to sth,** (*serve*) se servir en *ou* de qch; *Iron* (*steal*) voler *ou* prendre *ou* chiper qch;

(d) (*prevent*) (*with negation expressed or implied*) empêcher; **it can't be helped!,** tant pis!, il n'y a rien à faire *ou* on n'y peut rien; **I can't h. laughing,** je ne peux pas m'empêcher de rire; **I couldn't h. overhearing,** je n'ai pu m'empêcher de surprendre la conversation; **I can't h. it,** c'est plus fort que moi, je ne peux pas m'en empêcher; (*it can't be helped*) je n'y peux rien; **they can't h. being born there,** ils n'ont pas demandé à naître là; **I'm not going back if I can h. it,** je ne vais pas y retourner si j'ai le choix.

2 *vi* **(a)** aider; **can I h.?,** est-ce que je peux faire quelque chose?; **I was only trying to h.!,** je voulais seulement aider!; **he offered to h. with the clearing up,** il a proposé d'aider à ranger; **it helps if you can speak the language,** c'est plus facile si on parle la langue; **forgetting the map didn't h. much,** le fait d'avoir oublié la carte n'a pas arrangé les choses; **it's near the post office if that helps,** (*of information*) c'est près du bureau de poste si ça peut vous aider; **every little helps,** tous les dons sont les bienvenus;

(b) (*avoid*) **don't be away longer than you can h.,** tâchez d'être absent le moins de temps possible.

▶help out **1** *vi* (*help*) aider; **everyone helped out with the cleaning up,** tout le monde a aidé à nettoyer. **2** *vtas* (*help*) aider; **I need £20 — can you h. me out?,** j'ai besoin de 20 livres — est-ce que tu peux me les prêter?; **they helped him out with food and money,** ils l'ont aidé en lui donnant de la nourriture et de l'argent.

helper ['helpər] *n* aide *mf*; assistant, -ante.

helpful ['helpfʊl] *adj* **(a)** (*person*) secourable, serviable; **he always tries to be h.,** il essaie toujours de rendre service; **(b)** (*book*) utile; (*advice*) utile, salutaire; **the dictionary is not a bit h.,** le dictionnaire ne sert pas à grand-chose.

helpfully ['helpfʊlɪ] *adv* utilement.

helpfulness ['helpfʊlnɪs] *n* **(a)** (*of person*) serviabilité *f*; **(b)** (*of book etc*) utilité *f*, aide *f*.

helping ['helpɪŋ] **1** *adj* **to lend a h. hand,** prêter son aide; **to give s.o. a h. hand,** prêter la main à qn. **2** *n* portion *f* (*de nourriture*); **two helpings of soup,** deux assiettées *fpl* de soupe; **I had two helpings** *or* **a second h.,** j'en ai repris, je me suis resservi.

helpless ['helplɪs] *adj* **(a)** (*powerless*) faible, impuissant; (*ship*) désemparé; **I am h. in the matter,** je n'y puis rien; **a h. onlooker,** un spectateur impuissant; **we were h. to prevent what was happening,** nous ne pouvions rien faire contre ce qui se passait; **I was h. with laughter,** je n'en pouvais plus de rire; *F* **he's one of the h. sort,** il n'a aucune initiative; **(b)** (*orphan etc*) sans appui, délaissé.

helplessly ['helplɪslɪ] *adv* faiblement; sans faire preuve d'aucune initiative; **to watch h.,** regarder en spectateur impuissant.

helplessness ['helplɪsnɪs] *n* **(a)** (*powerlessness*) faiblesse *f*, impuissance *f*; **(b)** (*of orphan etc*) abandon *m*, délaissement *m*.

helpline [helplaɪn] *n Tel* (*for information on household appliances etc*) = numéro vert; (*for battered women*) = SOS femmes battues; (*for victims of child abuse*) = SOS enfants martyrs.

helter-skelter ['heltə'skeltər] **1** *adv* (*courir, fuir*) pêle-mêle, à la débandade. **2** *adj* **h.-s. flight,** fuite désordonnée, débandade *f*. **3** *n* **(a)** *Br* toboggan *m* (*dans une foire*); **(b)** (*disorder*) tohu-bohu *m*.

hem¹ [hem] *n* **(a)** *Sewing* (*of a garment*) bord *m*; (*of a handkerchief etc*) ourlet *m*; **(b)** = **HEMLINE**.

hem² *vt Sewing* border, mettre un bord à (*un vêtement*); ourler (*un mouchoir etc*); *Nau* gainer (*une voile*).

hem³ *int* hem!

hem⁴ *vi* faire hem *ou* hum; toussoter; **to h. and haw,** (*mumble*) bredouiller, bafouiller; hésiter (*à prendre une décision etc*).

▶hem in *vtsep* (*surround*) entourer, cerner (*l'ennemi*); investir (*une place*); **hemmed in by high mountains,** enserré entre de hautes montagnes.

hema- ['hiːmə] *pref US Med* = **HAEMA-**.

he-man, *pl* **-men** ['hiːmæn, -men] *n F* homme viril.

hemato- [hiːmə'təʊ] *pref US Med* = **HAEMATO-**.

hematology [hiːmə'tɒlədʒɪ] *n US Med* = **HAEMATOLOGY**.

hemicycle ['hemɪsaɪk(ə)l] *n Archit* hémicycle *m*.

hemiplegia [hemɪ'pliːdʒɪə] *n Med* hémiplégie *f*.

hemisphere ['hemɪsfɪər] *n* hémisphère *m*; *Geog* **the northern/southern h.,** l'hémisphère nord *ou* boréal/ l'hémisphère sud *ou* austral.

hemispheric(al) [hemɪ'sferɪk, -ɪk(ə)l] *adj* hémisphérique.

hemline ['hemlaɪn] *n Sewing* hauteur *f* de l'ourlet; **hemlines are coming down,** la mode rallonge.

hemlock ['hemlɒk] *n* (*plant*) ciguë *f*.

hemo- ['himəʊ] *pref US Med* = **HAEMO-**.

hemp [hemp] *n* **(a)** (*plant*) chanvre *m*; *Tex* chanvre, filasse *f*; **(b)** *Pharm etc* **Indian h.,** chanvre indien, hachisch *m*.

hemstitch¹ ['hemstɪtʃ] *n Sewing* ourlet *m* à jour.

hemstitch² *vt* ourler (*un mouchoir etc*) à jour.

hen [hen] *n* **(a)** (*chicken*) poule *f*; *Culin* **boiling h.,** poule au pot; *F* **h. party,** réunion *f* de femmes seules; **(b)** femelle *f* (*d'oiseau etc*); **h. bird,** oiseau *m* femelle; **h. pheasant,** (poule *f*) faisane *f*.

henbane ['henbeɪn] *n* (*plant*) jusquiame *f*, herbe *f* aux poules.

hence [hens] *adv* **(a)** (*of issue, consequence*) de là, en conséquence; **h. his anger,** de là sa fureur; **(b)** (*of time*) dorénavant, désormais; à partir d'aujourd'hui; **five years h.,** dans cinq ans (d'ici); **(c)** *Arch & Lit* (*of place*) **(from) h.,** d'ici; **five miles h.,** à deux lieues d'ici.

henceforth [hens'fɔːθ], **henceforward** [hens'fɔːwəd] *adv* désormais, dorénavant, à l'avenir.

henchman, *pl* **-men** ['henʃmən] *n* **(a)** *Pej Pol etc* acolyte *m*; **(b)** *Hist* écuyer *m*.

hencoop ['henkuːp] *n* cage *f* à poules.

henhouse ['henhaʊs] *n* poulailler *m*.

henna ['henə] *n* (*shrub, dye*) henné *m*.

henpeck ['henpek] *vt F* (*of wife*) mener (*son mari*) par le bout du nez.

henpecked ['henpekt] *adj* **h. husband,** mari mené par le bout du nez.

henroost ['henruːst] *n* **(a)** (*perch*) juchoir *m*, perchoir *m*; **(b)** *F* = **HENHOUSE**.

Henry ['henrɪ] *n* Henri *m*.

hep [hep] *adj Old-fashioned F* à la page, dans le vent.

hepatic [he'pætɪk] *adj Anat etc* hépatique.

hepatitis [hepə'taɪtɪs] *n Med* hépatite *f*.

heptagon ['heptəgən] *n Math* heptagone *m*.

her¹ [*unstressed* hər, *stressed* hɜːr] *pers pron* (*of person, female animal, certain things personified*) **(a)** (*unstressed*) (*direct*) la, (*before a vowel sound*) l'; (*indirect*) lui; (*reflexive, after preposition*) elle; **I hate h.,** je la déteste; **have you seen h.?,** l'avez-vous vue?; **I shall tell h. so,** je le lui

dirai; **look at h.**, regardez-la; **tell h.**, dites-lui; **I am thinking of h.**, je pense à elle; **I remember h.**, je me souviens d'elle; **she closed the door behind h.**, elle referma la porte derrière elle; *Fml* **Poland's friends deserted h.**, (*country*) la Pologne a été abandonnée par ses amis; **the enemy sank h.**, (*ship*) il a été coulé par l'ennemi; *F* **I'll get h. started,** (*car etc*) je vais la faire démarrer;
(b) (*stressed*) elle; *Lit* (*with dem force*) celle; **I can forgive her parents but not HER,** je peux pardonner à ses parents, mais pas à elle; **to h. who should take offence at this I would say ...,** à celle qui s'en offenserait je dirais ...;
(c) (*complement of verb* **to be**) **it's h.!**, c'est elle!; **that's h.!**, la voilà!

her² *poss adj* son, *f* sa, *pl* ses; **h. hat,** son chapeau; **h. dress/dresses,** sa robe/ses robes; **h. father and mother,** son père et sa mère; *Admin* ses père et mère; **h. eyes are blue,** elle a les yeux bleus; **she has hurt h. hand,** elle s'est fait mal à la main; **H. Majesty,** sa Majesté; *Fml* **France reassured h. allies,** la France rassura ses alliés; **the ship and h. crew,** le navire et son équipage.

her³ *n F* **it's a h., not a him,** (*of baby*) c'est une fille, pas un garçon; (*of animal*) c'est une femelle, pas un mâle.

herald¹ ['herəld] *n* **(a)** héraut *m*; **the Heralds' College,** le Collège héraldique (*à Londres*); **(b)** *Fig* (*of spring etc*) présage *m*.

herald² *vt* annoncer, proclamer (*l'arrivée etc de qn, de qch*); **these negotiations h. a new era for world peace,** ces négociations marquent le début d'une nouvelle ère pour la paix mondiale; **to h. the dawn,** annoncer l'aube du jour.

heraldic [hɪ'rældɪk] *adj* héraldique; **h. bearing,** armoirie *f*, blason *m*.

heraldry ['herəldrɪ] *n* l'héraldique *f*; (*coat of arms*) le blason; **book of h.,** armorial *m*, -aux.

herb [hɜːb, *US* ɜːrb] *n* (*plant*) herbe *f*; *Culin* **(sweet) herbs,** (fines) herbes; **medicinal herbs,** plantes médicinales; **h. tea,** infusion *f*, tisane *f* (d'herbes); **h. garden,** = carré où poussent les herbes fines.

herbaceous [hɜː'beɪʃəs] *adj Bot* herbacé; **h. border,** bordure *f* de plantes herbacées.

herbage ['hɜːbɪdʒ, *US* ɜːrb-] *n* **(a)** (*plants*) herbes *fpl*, herbage(s) *m(pl)*; **(b)** *Jur* droit(s) *m(pl)* de pacage.

herbal ['hɜːb(ə)l, *US* 'ɜːrb(ɔ)l] **1** *n* (*book*) herbier *m*. **2** *adj* (*drink*) fait avec des herbes; (*infusion*) d'herbes; (*remedy*) à base d'herbes *ou* de plantes; **h. medicine,** médecine *f* par les plantes, phytothérapie *f*.

herbalist ['hɜːbəlɪst] *n* herboriste *mf*.

herbarium [hɜː'beərɪəm] *n* herbier *m*.

herbicide ['hɜːbɪsaɪd] *n* herbicide *m*.

herbivorous [hɜː'bɪvərəs] *adj* (*animal*) herbivore.

Herculean [hɜːkjʊ'lɪən] *adj* (*effort*) herculéen; (*strength*) d'Hercule.

Hercules ['hɜːkjʊliːz] *n Myth Astron* Hercule *m*; *Fig* hercule.

herd¹ [hɜːd] *n* (*of livestock, buffalo*) troupeau *m*; (*of deer*) harde *f*; (*of horses etc*) troupe *f*, bande *f*; (*of people*) troupeau, foule *f*; **the h. instinct,** (*in animals, people*) l'instinct grégaire; **the common h.,** le populaire, le peuple.

herd² *vt* garder, surveiller (*le bétail etc*); *F* diriger (*un groupe de touristes etc*); **the candidates were all herded into the waiting room,** on avait entassé les candidats dans la salle d'attente; **the prisoners were herded onto trucks,** les prisonniers étaient entassés dans des camions.

►**herd together 1** *vi* (*of animals*) (*live in herds*) vivre en troupeaux; (*form a herd*) s'assembler en troupeau; *F* (*of people*) s'associer *ou* se déplacer en grands groupes. **2** *vtsep* (r)assembler (*le bétail etc*) en troupeau.

herder ['hɜːdər] *n esp US* = **HERDSMAN**.

herdsman, *pl* **-men** ['hɜːdzmən] *n esp Br* gardien *m* de troupeau.

here [hɪər] **1** *adv* **(a)** ici; **come h.!**, (venez) ici!; **in h., please,** par ici, s'il vous plaît; **near h.**, près d'ici; **over h.**, ici; **from h. to there,** d'ici à là; **Mr Green's not h. today,** M. Green n'est pas là aujourd'hui; **it's h. to stay,** (*of fashion*) cela restera; **h. and now,** immédiatement, tout de suite; **h. goes!**, allons-y!; **h. in Scotland,** ici, en Écosse; **h. I am referring to taxation,** (*at this point*) c'est aux impôts que je fais allusion; **we disagree h.**, c'est là que nous ne sommes pas d'accord; **h. lies ...,** (*on tombstone*) ci-gît ...; *Lit* **h. below,** (*on this earth*) ici-bas;
(b) here's your hat!, voici *ou* voilà votre chapeau!; **h. you are!**, (*on seeing, finding s.o.*) vous voici!, vous voilà!; (*giving sth*) tenez!; **h. she comes!**, la voici (qui vient)!; **h. I am!**, me voici!, me voilà!; **here's what you have to do,** voilà ce que tu as à faire; **h. is** *or* **h. we have a woman who has spent ten years in prison,** voici une femme qui a passé dix ans en prison;
(c) (*esp over drink etc*) **here's to you!**, à votre santé;
(d) my friend h. will tell you, mon ami que voici vous le dira;
(e) h. and there, partout, *Lit* par-ci, par-là, ça et là; **h., there and everywhere,** (un peu) partout; **neither h. nor there,** ni ici ni ailleurs; **that's neither h. nor there,** cela n'a aucun rapport.
2 *int* **(a)** (*at roll call*) présent!;
(b) (*to attract s.o.'s attention*) **h.! come and look at this,** eh! viens voir ça!; **h., take this,** tiens, prends ça.
3 *n* **the h. and now,** le présent.

hereabout(s) ['hɪərəbaʊt, -s] *adv* près d'ici, par ici.

hereafter [hɪər'ɑːftər] **1** *adv* **(a)** (*of position*) (*in book, writings etc*) ci-après, ci-dessous; **(b)** *esp Jur* (*of time*) dorénavant, désormais; ultérieurement; **(c)** (*after death*) dans la vie à venir, dans l'autre monde. **2** *n Lit* l'au-delà *m*; **in the h.,** dans l'autre monde.

hereby [hɪə'baɪ, hɪəbaɪ] *adv* par ceci, par ce moyen, par là; *Jur* par ces présentes; **the council h. declares that ...,** le conseil déclare par le présent acte que ... .

hereditary [hɪ'redɪt(ə)rɪ] *adj* (*disease etc*) héréditaire.

heredity [hɪ'redɪtɪ] *n* hérédité *f*.

herein [hɪər'ɪn] *adv Lit & Jur* **(a)** (*of place, position*) ici, dans ce livre, dans ce lieu; **the letter enclosed h.,** la lettre ci-incluse; **(b)** (*in this matter*) sur ce point.

heresy ['herəsɪ] *n* hérésie *f*; **to smack of h.,** (*of opinion*) sentir l'hérésie *ou* le brûlé *ou* le fagot.

heretic ['herətɪk] *n* hérétique *mf*.

heretical [hɪ'retɪk(ə)l] *adj* hérétique.

hereto [hɪə'tuː, 'hɪətuː] *adv Jur* **annexed h., h. annexed,** ci-joint.

heretofore ['hɪətʊ'fɔːr] *adv Arch & Lit* jusqu'ici; **as h.,** comme par le passé.

hereunder [hɪər'ʌndər] *adv Jur etc* ci-dessous.

hereupon ['hɪərəpɒn] *adv Jur etc* là-dessus; **h. he left,** sur ce *ou* là-dessus, il partit.

herewith [hɪə'wɪθ] *adv* **(a)** = **HEREBY**; **(b)** *Com* **price list h. enclosed,** prix-courant ci-inclus *ou* sous ce pli.

heritable ['herɪtəb(ə)l] *adj* **(a)** *Biol* (*maladie, vice*) héréditaire; **(b)** *Jur* (*droit*) héréditaire; (*propriété*) = dont on peut hériter; (*person*) capable d'hériter.

heritage ['herɪtɪdʒ] *n* héritage *m*, patrimoine *m*; (*of nation, humanity*) patrimoine.

hermaphrodite [hɜː'mæfrədaɪt] *adj & n Zool Bot* hermaphrodite *m*.

hermetic [hɜː'metɪk] *adj* hermétique; **h. sealing,** scellement *m* hermétique; *Fig* **the university was a h. world,** l'université était un monde très fermé *ou* hermétique.

hermetically [hɜː'metɪklɪ] *adv* (*sealed*) hermétiquement.

hermit ['hɜːmɪt] *n* ermite *m*; **to live like a h.,** vivre en solitaire *ou* en ermite; **h. crab,** bernard-l'ermite *m*.

hermitage ['hɜːmɪtɪdʒ] *n* ermitage *m*.

hernia ['hɜːnɪə] *n Med* hernie *f*; **to have a h.,** avoir une hernie; **strangulated h.,** hernie étranglée.

hero, *pl* **-oes** ['hɪərəʊ, -əʊz] *n* héros *m*; **a sporting h.,** un champion sportif; **h. worship,** culte *m* des héros.

Herod ['herəd] *n Hist* Hérode *m*.

heroic [hɪ'rəʊɪk] *adj* héroïque; **h. deed,** action *f* d'éclat; *Liter* **h. poem,** poème *m* épique; *Liter* **h. verse/couplet,** vers *m* décasyllabe/distique *m* héroïque.

heroically [hɪ'rəʊɪklɪ] *adv* héroïquement.

heroics [hɪ'rəʊɪks] *npl Pej* (*behaviour*) coup *m* d'éclat; (*style*) grandiloquence *f*, emphase *f*.

heroin ['herəʊɪn] *n Ch Pharm* héroïne *f*; **h. addict,** héroïnomane *mf*.

heroine ['herəʊɪn] *n* héroïne *f*.

heroism ['herəʊɪz(ə)m] *n* héroïsme *m*.

heron ['herən] *n* (*bird*) héron *m*.

hero-worship ['hɪərəʊwɜːʃɪp] *vt* idolâtrer (*qn*).

herpes ['hɜːpiːz] *n Med* herpès *m*; **to have h.,** avoir de l'herpès; **h. virus,** virus *m* de l'herpès.

herring ['herɪŋ] *n* (*fish*) hareng *m*; *Com* **salted h.,** hareng salé; **h. boat,** harenguier *m*.

herringbone ['herɪŋbəʊn] *n* **(a) h. (pattern),** dessin *m* à chevrons; **(b)** *Sewing* **h. (stitch),** point croisé; point d'épine; **(c)** *Ski* montée *f* en ciseaux *ou* en pas de canard.

hers [hɜːz] *poss pron* le sien, la sienne, les siens, les siennes; **this book is h.,** ce livre est à elle *ou* lui appartient; **a friend of h.,** un(e) de ses ami(e)s, un(e) ami(e) à elle; **it's no business of h.,** ce n'est pas son affaire.

herself [hɜː'self] *pers pron* **(a)** (*emphatic*) elle-même; **she**

did all the work h., elle a fait tout le travail elle-même *ou* toute seule; **she's looking (quite) h. again,** (*after illness*) elle paraît complètement remise; **she's not h. today,** elle n'est pas elle-même aujourd'hui; **(b)** (*reflexive*) se; **she hurt h.,** elle s'est fait mal; **she was living by h.,** elle vivait seule.

Herts *abbr* **Hertfordshire**.

hertz [hɜːts] *n El* hertz *m*.

he's [hiːz] **(a)** = **he is,** *see* **BE**; **(b)** = **he has,** *see* **HAVE²**.

hesitancy ['hezɪtənsɪ] *n* hésitation *f*.

hesitant ['hezɪtənt] *adj* hésitant, irrésolu; **I would be h. to ...,** j'hésiterais à ...; **he's a very h. speaker,** il hésite beaucoup en parlant.

hesitantly ['hezɪtəntlɪ] *adv* avec hésitation.

hesitate ['hezɪteɪt] **1** *vi* hésiter (*en parlant, en agissant*); **to h. before taking a decision,** hésiter avant de prendre une décision; **she didn't h. for a moment,** elle n'a pas hésité un instant; **without hesitating,** sans hésiter. **2** *vt* **to h. to do sth,** hésiter à faire qch.

hesitation [hezɪ'teɪʃən] *n* hésitation *f*; **without (the slightest) h.,** sans (la moindre) hésitation; **he has no h. about it,** il n'hésite pas du tout.

hessian ['hesɪən] *n Tex* toile *f* de jute.

het [het] *adj Br F* **h. up,** (*annoyed*) fâché; (*upset, tense*) à cran; **don't get h. up about it,** ne t'en fais pas pour cela.

hetero ['hetərəʊ] *adj & n F* = **HETEROSEXUAL**.

heterodox ['hetərəʊdɒks] *adj* hétérodoxe.

heterogeneous [hetərə'dʒiːnɪəs] *adj* hétérogène.

heterosexual [hetərəʊ'seksjʊəl] *adj & n* hétérosexuel, -elle.

heuristic [hjʊ'rɪstɪk] **1** *adj* heuristique. **2** *npl* **heuristics,** heuristique *f*.

hew [hjuː] *vt* (*pt* **hewed** [hjuːd]; *pp* **hewed, hewn** [hjuːn]) couper, tailler (*avec une hache, un ciseau etc*); tailler, dresser, équarrir (*une pierre*).

►**hew down** *vtsep* (*cut down*) abattre (*un arbre*).

►**hew off** *vtsep* abattre *ou* élaguer (*une branche*).

►**hew out** *vtsep* creuser; **the cavern had been hewn out of the rock,** la caverne a été creusée dans la pierre.

hewer ['hjuːər] *n* tailleur *m*, coupeur *m* (*de pierres etc*).

hex¹ [heks] *n Am F* (*spell*) sortilège *m*, sort *m*; **to put a h. on s.o./sth,** jeter un sort à qn/qch.

hex² *vt Am F* jeter un sort à (*qn, qch*).

hex³ *adj Comptr* **h. code,** code hexadécimal.

hexadecimal [heksə'desəm(ə)l] *adj Comptr* hexadécimal, -aux.

hexagon ['heksəgən] *n Math* hexagone *m*.

hexagonal [hek'sægən(ə)l] *adj* hexagonal, -aux.

hexameter [hek'sæmɪtər] *n Liter* hexamètre *m*.

hey [heɪ] *int* **(a)** (*to attract attention*) hé!, holà!; **(b)** (*scepticism*) hein?; **(c) h. presto!,** passez muscade!

heyday ['heɪdeɪ] *n* apogée *m* (*de ses forces, de la gloire etc*); **in its h. it was one of the busiest ports in the world,** à son heure de gloire, c'était l'un des ports les plus importants du monde; **to be in the h. of youth,** être dans *ou* à la fleur de l'âge.

HGH ['eɪtʃdʒiːeɪtʃ] *n Biol abbr* **human growth hormone**.

HGV [eɪtʃdʒiː'viː] *n Br Admin* (*abbr* **heavy goods vehicle**) poids lourd; **HGV licence,** permis *m* poids lourd.

hi [haɪ] *int* **(a)** *F* salut!; **(b)** (*to attract attention*) hé!, là-bas!, ohé!

hiatus, *pl* **-uses** [haɪ'eɪtəs, -əsɪz] *n* **(a)** (*gap*) lacune *f*; **(b)** *Gram* hiatus *m*.

hibernate ['haɪbəneɪt] *vi* hiberner.

hibernation [haɪbə'neɪʃən] *n* hibernation *f*; **to go into h.,** hiberner.

hibiscus [hɪ'bɪskəs] *n* (*plant*) ketmie *f*, hibiscus *m*.

hiccough¹, hiccup ['hɪkʌp] *n* **(a)** hoquet *m*; **to have (the) hiccoughs,** avoir le hoquet; **(b)** *Fig* (*problem*) problème *m*, *F* hic *m*; **there's been some sort of h. with the delivery,** il y a un hic dans la livraison.

hiccough², hiccup 1 *vi* hoqueter. **2** *vt* dire (*qch*) en hoquetant.

hick [hɪk] *Am F* **1** *n* paysan *m*, rustaud *m*. **2** *adj* **a h. town,** un bled.

hickey ['hɪkɪ] *n Am F* **(a)** (*spot*) bouton *m*; (*love bite*) suçon *m*; **(b)** (*gadget*) machin *m*, truc *m*.

hickory ['hɪkərɪ] *n* (*tree or wood*) noyer *m* (blanc) d'Amérique, hickory *m*.

hid *see* **HIDE²**.

hidden ['hɪd(ə)n] *adj* (*difficulty, treasure etc*) caché; *Fin* **h. reserves,** réserve latente; **you may have h. talents,** il se peut que tu aies des dons cachés; *Fig* **h. hand,** influence *f* occulte.

hide¹ [haɪd] *n* (*of hunter etc*) affût *m*, cachette *f*.

hide² *v* (*pt* **hid** [hɪd]; *pp* **hidden** ['hɪd(ə)n]) **1** *vt* cacher (**from** à); enfouir (*qch dans la terre*); **where has she hidden herself?,** où est-elle allée se cacher *ou F* se fourrer?; **to h. one's face,** se cacher la figure, se voiler la face; **to h. one's light under a bushel,** cacher son talent; **he doesn't h. his feelings,** il ne dissimule pas ses sentiments; **to h. sth from s.o.,** cacher qch à qn; (*not divulge information*) taire qch à qn; **they hid him from the police,** ils l'ont caché pour que la police ne le trouve pas; **to h. sth from sight,** soustraire qch aux regards; **clouds hid the sun,** des nuages voilaient le soleil; **trees h. the house from sight,** les arbres cachent la maison.

2 *vi* se cacher; (*stay hidden*) se tenir caché; (*go to hide*) aller se cacher; **I didn't know where to h.,** je ne savais où me cacher; **she was hiding in a corner,** (*of shy person*) elle restait dans un coin; **to h. from s.o.,** se cacher de qn.

hide³ *n* peau *f*, dépouille *f* (*d'un animal*); *Com* cuir *m*; *F* **to save one's h.,** sauver sa peau; **I haven't seen h. nor hair of her,** je ne l'ai pas vue du tout.

►**hide away 1** *vi* = **HIDE² 2**. **2** *vtas* = **HIDE² 1**.

►**hide out** *vi* (*be in hiding*) se cacher, se terrer.

hide-and-seek, *Am* **hide-and-go-seek** [haɪdən(gəʊ)'siːk] *n* cache-cache *m*; **to play h.-and-s.,** jouer à cache-cache.

hideaway ['haɪdəweɪ] *n* cachette *f*, *F* planque *f*.

hidebound ['haɪdbaʊnd] *adj* (*person*) aux vues étroites; plein de préjugés; (*idea*) étroit; **the country's h. legal profession,** les hommes de loi conservateurs de ce pays.

hideous ['hɪdɪəs] *adj* hideux, affreux, effroyable; (*crime*) horrible, odieux; **what a h. picture!,** quelle peinture abominable!

hideously ['hɪdɪəslɪ] *adv* hideusement, affreusement.

hideousness ['hɪdɪəsnɪs] *n* hideur *f*, laideur *f*.

hide-out ['haɪdaʊt] *n* cachette *f*, *F* planque *f*.

hiding¹ ['haɪdɪŋ] *n* (*of one's feelings etc*) dissimulation *f*; *Jur* recel *m* (*d'un criminel*); **to go into h.,** se cacher; **to be in h.,** se tenir caché; **to come out of h.,** sortir de sa cachette; **h. place,** cachette *f*.

hiding² *n F* (*beating*) raclée *f*, rossée *f*, volée *f*; **to give s.o. a good h.,** donner une raclée à qn; **to be on a h. to nothing,** n'avoir aucune chance (de réussir).

hid(e)y-hole ['haɪdɪhəʊl] *n F* cachette *f*.

hierarchic(al) [haɪə'rɑːkɪk, -ɪk(ə)l] *adj* hiérarchique; **in h. order,** par ordre hiérarchique.

hierarchy ['haɪərɑːkɪ] *n* hiérarchie *f*.

hieroglyph ['haɪərəglɪf] *n* hiéroglyphe *m*.

hieroglyphic [haɪərə'glɪfɪk] *adj* hiéroglyphique.

hieroglyphics [haɪərə'glɪfɪks] *npl* hiéroglyphes *mpl*, signes *mpl* hiéroglyphiques; *Fig* (*bad handwriting*) hiéroglyphes.

hifalutin(g) [haɪfə'luːtɪn, -tɪŋ] = **HIGHFALUTING**.

hi-fi ['haɪ'faɪ] *adj & n F* hi-fi *f inv*.

higgledy-piggledy ['hɪg(ə)ldɪ'pɪg(ə)ldɪ] *adv F* sans ordre, en pagaïe, pêle-mêle.

high [haɪ] **1** *adj* **(a)** haut, élevé; **house built on h. ground,** maison construite sur un terrain élevé; **this house is much higher (up) than the village,** cette maison est située à beaucoup plus haute altitude que le village; **the highest mountain in the country,** la plus haute montagne du pays; **wall two metres h.,** mur haut de deux mètres *ou* d'une hauteur de deux mètres; **at h. water** *or* **tide,** à la marée haute; **h. neck,** (*on garment*) col montant; **h. cheekbones,** pommettes saillantes; **sun h. above the horizon,** soleil haut sur l'horizon; **with one's head h.,** la tête haute; *Sp* **the h. jump,** le saut en hauteur; **h. jumper,** sauteur, -euse en hauteur; *Br F* **to be for the h. jump,** être sur le point de se faire engueuler; **h. wire,** corde *f* (*pour des funambulistes*);

(b) (*in number, degree*) (*price*) élevé; (*percentage*) gros; (*speed*) grand; **to fetch a h. price,** se vendre cher; **to make a higher bid,** faire une offre supérieure; *Cards & Fig* **to play for h. stakes,** jouer gros (jeu); *Cards* **h. cards,** cartes hautes; **ore with a h. mineral content,** minerai *m* à haute teneur; **h. latitudes,** les hautes latitudes; **highest speed,** vitesse *f* maximum, vitesse de pointe; **to have a h. opinion of s.o.,** tenir qn en haute estime; **to a h. degree,** à un haut degré; **to** *or* **in the highest degree,** au dernier degré; **of the highest importance,** de première importance; **h. fidelity,** haute fidélité; **h. quality,** bonne qualité; *Phys etc* **h. frequency,** haute fréquence; **a h. fever,** une forte *ou* grosse fièvre; **h. winds,** vents forts; **h. treason,** haute trahison;

(c) (*superior, advanced*) (*fashion, society etc*) haut; **of h. rank,** de haut rang; **she is h. up in the government,** elle est haut placée dans le gouvernement; **to be in a h. position,** être haut placé; **higher posts,** postes *ou* emplois supérieurs; *Sch* **higher education,** études supérieures; **higher mathematics,** mathématiques supérieures; *Jur* **a higher court,** instance supérieure; *Sch* **h. school,** *US* = établissement d'enseignement supérieur; *Br* = lycée *m*; **h. definition television,** télévision *f* à haute définition; **h. resolution,** haute résolution; **h. resolution screen,** écran *m* à haute résolution; **she's acting all h. and mighty,** elle agit avec beaucoup d'arrogance; **h. tech(nology),** haute technologie;

(d) (*noble*) élevé, noble; **h. ideals,** idéaux élevés; **she has very h. moral standards,** elle est très exigeante en matière de principes;

(e) (*strong*) **h. colour,** couleur vive; (*of complexion*) vivacité *f* du teint; **h. explosive,** explosif puissant;

(f) (*good*) **to be in h. spirits,** être plein d'entrain; **our spirits were h.,** nous avions le moral; **the h. spot of the match,** le point culminant du match; **one of the h. points of the evening,** un des points forts de la soirée;

(g) *Mus etc* **h. voice,** voix élevée *ou* haute; (*thin*) voix grêle; **h. note,** note aiguë; **to set a song half a tone higher,** hausser un chant d'un demi-ton;

(h) (*principal*) **the H. Street,** la Grand-rue, la Grande rue; **the h. table,** la table d'honneur; *Sch & Univ* la table des professeurs (*au réfectoire*); *Rel* **H. Mass,** la grand-messe, la grande messe; **h. altar,** maître-autel *m*; *Rel* **h. priest/priestess,** grand(e) prêtre/prêtresse; *Jewish Rel* grand sacrificateur; *Fig* **the h. priests of fashion,** les pontifes *mpl* de la mode; *Nau* **the h. seas,** la haute mer;

(i) (*of time*) **h. noon,** plein midi; **h. summer,** plein été; **it's h. time he went to school,** il est grand temps qu'il aille à l'école; *Br Com* **the h. season,** la haute saison; *Br* **h. tea,** = dîner pris assez tôt dans la soirée;

(j) (*meat etc*) avancé, gâté; (*game*) faisandé; **to get h.,** (*of game*) se faisander; **to smell h.,** avoir une forte odeur;

(k) *F* (*person*) **to be h.,** (*drunk*) être ivre; (*drugged*) planer; *Fig* (*euphoric*) être dans un état d'euphorie; **h. on cocaine,** défoncé à la cocaïne; *Fig* **they were h. on success,** ils étaient enivrés par le succès;

(l) (*lively*) **h. jinks,** chahut *m*; **to get up to h. jinks,** faire du chahut; *F* **to have a h. old time,** faire la noce;

(m) *Ling* **H. German,** le haut allemand;

(n) **h. and dry,** (*of ship*) échoué au plein; à sec (*sur la plage etc*); *F* **to be left h. and dry,** (*of person*) être laissé en plan.

2 *adv* **(a)** haut, en haut; **higher (up),** plus haut; **higher and higher,** de plus en plus haut; **to aim h.,** viser haut; *Fig* (*in one's ambitions*) avoir de hautes visées; **to rise h. in the public esteem,** monter très haut dans l'estime publique; **to hunt h. and low for sth,** chercher qch partout; **higher up the river,** en amont;

(b) (*in bidding etc*) **to go as h. as £2,000,** aller jusqu'à 2 000 livres; *Cards etc* **to play** *or* **stake h.,** jouer gros jeu;

(c) (*powerfully etc*) fort, fortement; **to run h.,** (*of sea*) être grosse *ou* houleuse; (*of feeling*) s'échauffer; (*of prices*) être élevés; **tempers were running h.,** les esprits s'échauffaient.

3 *n* **(a)** *St Exch* (*high point*) **highs and lows,** hausses *fpl* et baisses *fpl*; **prices have reached a new h.,** les prix ont atteint un nouveau maximum;

(b) *Met* aire *f* anticyclonique;

(c) (*from drugs etc*) **to be on a h.,** planer;

(d) *Rel* **the Most H.,** le Très-Haut, le Tout-Puissant; **on h.,** en haut; dans le ciel; *Rel & Fig* **from on h.,** d'en haut.

highborn ['haɪbɔːn] *adj* de haute naissance.

highboy ['haɪbɔɪ] *n Am* (*furniture*) commode haute.

highbrow ['haɪbraʊ] *n F* **1** intellectuel, -elle; grosse tête. **2** *adj* (*literature etc*) pour les intellectuels.

highchair ['haɪtʃeər] *n* chaise haute (*de bébé*).

high-class ['haɪ'klɑːs] *adj* (*marchandises etc*) de premier ordre, de première qualité; (*hôtel*) de grande classe; **h.-c. cooking,** la haute cuisine; **h.-c. prostitute,** prostituée *f* de haut vol.

high-density ['haɪ'densɪtɪ] *adj* (*housing*) à forte concentration de population; *Comptr* (*disk, graphics, printing*) haute densité.

highfalutin(g) [haɪfə'luːtɪn, -ɪŋ] *adj F* (*style, discours*) ampoulé, prétentieux, pompeux.

high-fidelity [haɪfɪ'delɪtɪ] *adj* de haute fidélité.

high-flier, -flyer ['haɪ'flaɪər] *n* quelqu'un qui ira loin; *Pej* ambitieux, -euse, carriériste *mf*.

high-flown ['haɪfləʊn] *adj* (*style, discours*) ampoulé, pompeux, déclamatoire.

high-flying ['haɪ'flaɪɪŋ] *adj* qui ira loin; *Pej* ambitieux, -euse, carriériste.

high-frequency [haɪ'friːkwənsɪ] *adj El* (*courant, lampe*) à haute fréquence; (*amplificateur*) de haute fréquence.

high-grade ['haɪ'greɪd] *adj* (*minerai etc*) à haute teneur; (*marchandises*) de première qualité, de (premier) choix; **h.-g. petrol,** supercarburant *m*.

high-handed [haɪ'hændɪd] *adj* autoritaire; (*autorité*) tyrannique.

high-hat ['haɪhæt] *adj & n F* arrogant *m*; snob *m*.

highjack, highjacker *etc* = **HIJACK, HIJACKER** *etc*.

highland ['haɪlənd] **1** *n* pays montagneux; **the Highlands,** les Highlands *mpl*. **2** *adj* des montagnes; (*from Scotland*) des Highlands; **H. cattle,** race bovine des Highlands.

highlander ['haɪləndər] *n* montagnard, -arde; **H.,** (*from Scotland*) Highlander *m*; habitant, -ante de la Haute Écosse; *Mil* = soldat *m* d'un régiment écossais.

high-level ['haɪlevəl] *adj* (*discussion*) de haut niveau; *Comptr* **h.-l. language,** langage *m* de haut niveau.

highlight¹ ['haɪlaɪt] *n* **(a)** (*important moment*) grand moment; clou *m* (*de la fête etc*); point culminant (*d'un match etc*); (*of report*) point saillant; *TV* **they didn't show the whole match, just the highlights,** ils n'ont pas retransmis tout le match, seulement les meilleurs moments; **(b)** (*in a painting*) **highlights,** rehauts *mpl*, clairs *mpl*; **(c)** (*in hair*) **highlights,** reflets *mpl*, mèches *mpl*.

highlight² *vt* **(a)** mettre en vedette; mettre (*un problème*) au premier plan; souligner (*un besoin*); **(b)** (*with coloured marker*) surligner.

highlighter ['haɪlaɪtər] *n* **(a)** (*coloured marker*) surligneur *m*; **(b)** (*for hair*) shampooing-reflets *m*.

highly ['haɪlɪ] *adv* **(a)** **h. placed official,** haut fonctionnaire; **his services are h. paid,** on paie très cher ses services; **to think h. of s.o.,** avoir une haute opinion de qn; **(b)** (*extremely*) fort, très, bien, fortement; **h. amusing,** très amusant; **h. displeased,** fort mécontent; **h. seasoned,** fortement assaisonné; **h. coloured,** (*tableau, style*) haut en couleur; (*récit*) coloré; **to be h. sexed,** avoir une forte libido; **h. strung,** (*of person*) nerveux, impressionnable.

high-minded ['haɪ'maɪndɪd] *adj* aux sentiments nobles, généreux; (*action, nature*) magnanime.

high-mindedness ['haɪ'maɪndɪdnɪs] *n* noblesse *f* de sentiments; magnanimité *f*; grandeur *f* d'âme.

highness ['haɪnɪs] *n* (*title*) Altesse *f*; **His** *or* **Her Royal H.,** son Altesse Royale.

high-octane ['haɪ'ɒkteɪn] *adj* **h.-o. petrol,** essence *f* à indice d'octane élevé.

high-pitched ['haɪpɪtʃt] *adj* **(a)** (*sound*) aigu, -uë; (*voice*) aigu, criard; **(b)** *Constr* **h.-p. roof,** comble *m* à forte inclinaison *ou* à forte pente.

high-powered ['haɪ'paʊəd] *adj* gros (*moteur*); (*voiture*) de haute puissance; *Rad etc* (*poste*) de haute puissance, de grande portée; *Opt* (*jumelles*) à fort grossissement; *Fig* (*person*) dynamique et compétent; (*in high position*) très important; **she is something h.-p. in the City,** elle fait quelque chose d'important dans la Cité.

high-pressure ['haɪ'preʃər] *adj* **(a)** *Tech* (*cylindre, machine*) à haute pression, à haute tension; *Met* (*aire*) anticyclonique; **(b)** *Pej* (*salesman*) importun, agressif.

high-principled ['haɪ'prɪnsɪp(ə)ld] *adj* aux principes élevés.

high-profile ['haɪ'prəʊfaɪl] *adj* (*politician etc*) en vue; (*company*) connu.

high-resolution ['haɪ'rezəluːʃən] *adj Phot TV etc* (*screen, graphics*) à haute résolution.

high-rise ['haɪ'raɪz] *Archit* **1** *n* tour *f*. **2** *adj* **h.-r. building,** tour *f*.

high-risk ['haɪrɪsk] *adj* (*occupation, category etc*) à haut(s) risque(s).

highroad ['haɪrəʊd] *n Old-fashioned* grande route, route nationale.

high-sounding ['haɪsaʊndɪŋ] *adj* (*titre, éloge*) pompeux, prétentieux; ronflant.

high-speed ['haɪ'spiːd] *adj* ultra-rapide; (*machine*) à marche rapide; (*moteur*) & *Phot* (*objectif*) grande vitesse.

high-spirited [haɪ'spɪrɪtɪd] *adj* plein d'ardeur *ou* de feu; (*cheval*) fougueux.

high-street ['haɪstriːt] *adj Br* **h.-s. shops,** magasins *mpl* à succursales; **a h.-s. bank,** une banque connue (ayant de nombreuses succursales).

high-strung ['haɪstrʌŋ] *adj* (*tempérament*) nerveux, impressionnable; (*personne*) au tempérament nerveux.

hightail ['haɪteɪl] *vt esp Am F* **to h. it,** se tirer en vitesse.

high-tech ['haɪtek] *adj see* **HI-TECH**.

high-up ['haɪʌp] *n F* personnage important, *F* gros bonnet, grosse légume.

highway ['haɪweɪ] *n* **(a)** *esp Am* grande voie de communication; grande route; artère *f*; *US* **h. patrolman,** motard *m*; **highways and byways,** chemins et sentiers; **that price is h. robbery,** un prix pareil c'est du vol pur et simple; **(b)** *Br Admin* voie publique; **h. engineer** = ingénieur *m* des Ponts et Chaussées; **H. Code,** Code *m* de la Route.

highwayman, *pl* **-men** ['haɪweɪmən] *n Arch* voleur *m* de grand(s) chemin(s); détrousseur *m*.

hijack ['haɪdʒæk] *vt F* détourner (*un avion en vol*); s'emparer de force de (*un véhicule*); *Fig* **the government hijacked the opposition's policy,** le gouvernement s'est emparé de la politique de l'opposition.

hijacker ['haɪdʒækər] *n F* (*of aircraft*) pirate *mf* de l'air; (*of vehicle*) pirate de la route.

hijacking ['haɪdʒækɪŋ] *n* (*of aircraft*) (*general practice*) piraterie aérienne; (*also single incident*) détournement *m* (*d'avion*); (*of vehicle*) vol armé d'un véhicule et de son contenu.

hike¹ [haɪk] *n* **(a)** (*walk*) (longue) promenade *f* à pied, randonnée *f*; **to go on a h.,** faire une (longue) promenade à pied; *Am F* **he can take a h.!,** il peut aller se faire voir; **(b)** *esp Am* augmentation *f*, hausse *f* (*de prix, de salaire*).

hike² **1** *vi* (*walk*) faire une (longue) promenade à pied. **2** *vt* **(a)** (*climb*) **to h. oneself up on to sth,** grimper (avec difficulté) jusqu'à qch; **(b)** *esp Am* augmenter (*les prix, les salaires*).

hiker ['haɪkər] *n* randonneur, -euse (*à pied*).

hiking ['haɪkɪŋ] *n* tourisme *m* à pied; **to go h.,** faire une (longue) promenade à pied; **h. boots,** bottes *fpl* de randonnée.

hilarious [hɪ'leərɪəs] *adj* **(a)** (*very amusing*) gai, hilarant, *F* marrant; **it was h.!,** c'était à se tordre (de rire)!; **(b)** (*merry*) gai, hilare.

hilariously [hɪ'leərɪəslɪ] *adv* avec hilarité; (*rire*) aux éclats; **it was h. funny,** c'était à se tordre (de rire).

hilariousness [hɪ'leərɪəsnɪs] *n* (*of scene, joke*) caractère hilarant; (*merriness*) hilarité *f*.

hilarity [hɪ'lærɪtɪ] *n* hilarité *f*.

hill [hɪl] *n* **(a)** colline *f*; (*sloping ground*) coteau *m*; **up h. and down dale,** par monts et par vaux; *F* **to be over the h.,** commencer à se faire vieux; **to be as old as the hills,** (*of joke*) dater de *ou* remonter à Mathusalem; **h. country,** pays *m* de collines; **h. station,** (*in India*) station *f* de montagne; *Mil* **h. 304,** la cote 304; **(b)** (*on road*) côte *f*; (*uphill*) montée *f*; (*downhill*) descente *f*; **steep h.,** (*uphill*) montée abrupte; (*downhill*) descente abrupte; *Aut* **h. start,** départ *m* en côte.

hillbilly ['hɪlbɪlɪ] *n US F* villageois(e) un peu rustaud(e); **h. songs,** chants *mpl* folkloriques.

hilliness ['hɪlɪnɪs] *n* vallonnement *m*.

hillock ['hɪlək] *n* petite colline; (*smaller*) butte *f*, tertre *m*.

hillside ['hɪlsaɪd] *n* flanc *m* de coteau, coteau *m*.

hilltop ['hɪltɒp] *n* sommet *m* de (la) colline; hauteur *f*, éminence *f*.

hill-walker ['hɪlwɔːkər] *n* randonneur, -euse (en pays de collines).

hill-walking ['hɪlwɔːkɪŋ] *n* randonnée *f* (en pays de collines).

hilly ['hɪlɪ] *adj* (*country*) montagneux; (*terrain*) accidenté; (*road*) montueux, à fortes pentes.

hilt [hɪlt] *n* (*of sword*) poignée *f*, garde *f*; (*of dagger, knife etc*) manche *m*; *Fig* **right up to the h.,** jusqu'à la gauche; **mortgaged up to the h.,** fortement hypothéqué; **his wife supported him to the h.,** sa femme l'a soutenu à fond.

him [hɪm] *pers pron* (*of person, male animal, certain things personified*) **(a)** (*unstressed*) (*direct*) le, (*before a vowel sound*) l'; (*indirect and reflexive, after prepositions*) lui; **I hate h.,** je le déteste; **do you love h.?,** l'aimez-vous?; **I shall tell h. so,** je le lui dirai; **tell h. I have come,** dites-lui que je suis là; **he took his luggage with h.,** il a pris ses bagages avec lui; **I object to h. borrowing the car,** je m'oppose à ce qu'il emprunte la voiture; **(b)** (*stressed*) lui; *Lit* (*with dem force*) celui; **we are thinking of h.,** nous pensons à lui; **the prize goes to h. who comes in first,** le prix est pour celui qui arrivera le premier; **(c)** (*as complement of verb* **to be**) **it's h.!,** c'est lui!

Himalayan [hɪmə'leɪən] *adj* himalayen, -enne.

Himalayas [hɪmə'leɪəz] *npl* (les montagnes *fpl* de) l'Himalaya *m*.

himself [hɪm'self] *pers pron* **(a)** (*emphatic*) lui-même; **he doesn't want to do it h.,** il ne veut pas le faire lui-même; **he's not (quite) h. again yet,** (*after illness*) il n'est pas encore complètement remis; **he's not h. today,** il n'est pas lui-même aujourd'hui; **(b)** (*reflexive*) se; **he hurt h.,** il s'est fait mal; **he lives by h.,** il vit seul; **(c)** (*used impersonally*) soi(-même); **everyone for h.,** chacun pour soi.

hind¹ [haɪnd] *n* (*female deer*) biche *f*; **h. calf,** faon *m* femelle.

hind² *adj* de derrière, postérieur; **hind legs/feet,** jambes *fpl*/pattes *fpl* de derrière; *F* **to get up on one's h. legs,** (*of person*) se lever (*pour prononcer un discours*).

hinder¹ ['haɪndər] *adj* de derrière, postérieur.

hinder² ['hɪndər] *vt* **(a)** (*impede*) gêner, embarrasser (*qn*); (*delay*) retarder (*qch*); faire obstacle à (*un mouvement*); **(b)** (*prevent*) empêcher, retenir, arrêter (*qn*) (**from doing,** de faire).

Hindi ['hɪndɪ] *n Ling* hindi *m*.

hindmost ['haɪndməʊst] *adj* dernier.

hindquarters ['haɪndkwɔːtəz] *npl* arrière-train *m*.

hindrance ['hɪndrəns] *n* empêchement *m*, obstacle *m*, entrave *f*; **he is a h.,** il gêne; **they were more of a h. than a help,** ils gênaient plus qu'ils n'aidaient.

hindsight ['haɪndsaɪt] *n* sagesse *f* d'après coup; **with (the benefit of) h.,** après coup.

Hindu [hɪn'duː] **1** *adj* hindou. **2** *n* Hindou, -oue.

Hinduism ['hɪnduːɪz(ə)m] *n* (h)indouisme *m*.

Hindustan [hɪndʊ'stɑːn] *n* Hindoustan *m*.

Hindustani [hɪndʊ'stɑːnɪ] *adj & n Ling* hindoustani *m*.

hinge¹ [hɪndʒ] *n* gond *m* (*de porte*); **butt h.,** charnière *f*; **the door came off its hinges,** la porte est sortie de ses gonds; *Philat* **(stamp) h.,** charnière; **h. pin,** broche *f* de charnière.

hinge² **1** *vt* (*mount on hinges*) monter (*une porte etc*) sur ses gonds; (*put hinges on*) mettre les charnières à (*une boîte etc*). **2** *vi* tourner, pivoter (**on,** autour de); **to h. forward,** (*of seat etc*) basculer vers l'avant.

►**hinge on, hinge upon** *vipo* (*depend on*) dépendre de; **everything hinges on his answer,** tout dépend de sa réponse.

hinged [hɪndʒd] *adj* (*porte, couvercle etc*) à charnière(s); **h. flap,** (*of counter etc*) battant *m* rabattable; (*of aircraft*) volet articulé.

hint¹ [hɪnt] *n* **(a)** allusion indirecte; **broad h.,** (*allusion*) allusion évidente *ou* claire; **gentle h.,** allusion discrète; **to give** *or* **drop s.o. a h.,** toucher un mot à qn; **to know how to take a h.,** comprendre à demi-mot; **we can take a h.,** nous avons compris; **(b)** (*sign*) signe *m*, indication *f*, suggestion *f*; **not a h. of surprise,** pas une ombre de surprise; **not the slightest h. of ...,** pas le moindre soupçon de ...; **there was just a h. of garlic in the stew,** il y avait juste un soupçon d'ail dans le ragoût; **(c)** (*piece of advice*) indice *m*; **the book is full of useful hints on how to save money,** le livre est plein de tuyaux pour faire des économies; **can you give me some hints?,** (*about how I should proceed*) pouvez-vous me donner quelques conseils?; (*about the right answer*) pouvez- vous me mettre sur la voie?

hint² *vt & vi* insinuer (*qch*); suggérer *ou* dire (*qch*) à mots couverts; **to h. to s.o. that ...,** laisser entendre à qn que ....

►**hint at** *vipo* laisser entendre (*qch*) à mots couverts; faire une allusion voilée à (*qch*).

hinterland ['hɪntəlænd] *n* arrière-pays *m*.

hip¹ [hɪp] *n* **(a)** *Anat* hanche *f*; **to have narrow/wide hips,** avoir les hanches fines/larges; **he stood with his hands on his hips,** il était debout, les mains sur les hanches; *Fig esp Am* **to shoot from the h.,** traiter (*qn*) *ou* faire (*qch*) par-dessus la jambe; **h. flask,** flacon *m* (de poche); **h. bath,** bain *m* de siège; **h. joint,** articulation *f* de la hanche; *Med* **h. replacement operation,** mise en place d'une prothèse de la hanche; **h. pocket,** poche *f* revolver, *F* poche fessière; **h. size** *or* **measurement,** tour *m* de hanches; **(b)** *Constr* **h. (piece, rafter),** arêtier *m*, arête *f* (*d'un comble*).

hip² *n* (*fruit*) cynor(r)hodon *m*, fruit *m* du rosier.

hip³ *adj F* (*fashionable*) à la page, dans le vent.

hip⁴ *int* **h.! h.!, hurray!,** hip! hip! hourra!

hipbone ['hɪpbəʊn] *n* os *m* iliaque.

hip-huggers ['hɪp'hʌgəz] *npl Am* = **HIPSTERS**.

-hipped [hɪpt] *suff* **broad-h.,** à fortes hanches; **narrow-h.,** aux hanches fines.

hippie ['hɪpɪ] *n F* hippie *mf*.

hippo ['hɪpəʊ] *n F* hippopotame *m*.

Hippocrates [hɪ'pɒkrətiːz] *n* Hippocrate *m*.

Hippocratic [hɪpə'krætɪk] *adj Med* hippocratique; **H. oath,** serment *m* d'Hippocrate.

hippodrome ['hɪpədrəʊm] *n* hippodrome *m*; (*not for racing*) arène *f*.

hippopotamus, *pl* **-muses, -mi** [hɪpə'pɒtəməs, -məsɪz,

-maɪ] *n* hippopotame *m*.

hippy ['hɪpɪ] *n F* hippie *mf*.

hipsters ['hɪpstəz] *npl Br* (*trousers*) pantalon *m* taille basse.

hire¹ [haɪər] *n* **(a)** (*of car, room*) location *f*; **for h.**, (*sign on taxi*) libre; **for** *or* **on h.**, à louer; **h. car,** voiture *f* de location; **(b)** *Am* (*of labour*) embauchage *m*; (*of servant*) louage *m*; **(c)** (*wages*) salaire *m*, gages *mpl*.

hire² **1** *vt* **(a)** louer (*une voiture etc*); soudoyer (*un assassin*); **(b)** *esp Am* embaucher, engager (*un ouvrier etc*); prendre à son service (*un domestique*). **2** *vi esp Am* embaucher.

►**hire out** *vtsep* louer (*qch*), donner (*qch*) en location (**to s.o.,** à qn).

hired ['haɪəd] *adj* **(a)** (*car etc*) de location; **(b)** (*person*) (*assassin*) à gages; *Am* **h. man,** (*servant*) domestique *m*; **h. man** *or* **hand,** (*farmworker*) ouvrier agricole.

hireling ['haɪəlɪŋ] *n Pej* stipendié *m*; laquais *m*.

hire-purchase ['haɪə'pɜːtʃɪs] *n Br Com* location-vente *f*; **to buy sth on h.-p.,** acheter qch en location-vente.

hiring ['haɪ(ə)rɪŋ] *n* **(a)** (*of a car etc*) location *f*; **(b)** *Am* (*of staff etc*) embauchage *m*.

hirsute ['hɜːsjuːt] *adj* hirsute, velu, poilu.

his¹ [hɪz] *poss adj* son, *f*, sa, *pl* ses; **one of h. friends,** un de ses amis, un ami à lui; **h. father and mother,** son père et sa mère; *Admin* ses père et mère; **h. own son,** son propre fils; **he has hurt h. hand,** il s'est fait mal à la main; **h. eyes are brown,** il a les yeux bruns; **I object to h. borrowing the car,** je m'oppose à ce qu'il emprunte la voiture; **H. Majesty,** sa Majesté.

his² *poss pron* le sien, la sienne, les siens, les siennes; **he took my pen as well as h.,** il a pris mon stylo avec le sien; **this book is h.,** ce livre est *ou* appartient à lui, c'est son livre à lui; **a friend of h.,** un de ses amis, un ami à lui; **it is no business of h.,** ce n'est pas son affaire.

Hispanic [hɪs'pænɪk] **1** *adj* hispanique. **2** *n US* Américain, -aine de langue espagnole; Hispano-Américain, -aine.

Hispano-American [hɪ'spænəʊə'merɪk(ə)n] **1** *adj* hispano-américain. **2** *n* Hispano-américain, -aine.

hiss¹ [hɪs] *n* **(a)** (*sound*) sifflement *m*; *Th etc* sifflets *mpl*; **(b)** *Ling* fricative sourde; sifflante *f*.

hiss² *vt & vi* (*of person, steam etc*) siffler; (*of steam, gas*) chuinter; **to h. (at) an actor,** siffler un acteur; **to be hissed,** être sifflé.

hissing ['hɪsɪŋ] **1** *adj* (*voice*) sifflant; (*gas*) qui chuinte; **h. noise,** sifflement *m*; chuintement *m*. **2** *n* sifflement *m*; chuintement *m*.

histamine ['hɪstəmɪn, -miːn] *n Physiol* histamine *f*.

historian [hɪs'tɔːrɪən] *n* historien, -ienne.

historic [hɪs'tɒrɪk] *adj* **(a)** historique; **h. building,** monument *m* historique; **(b)** *Gram* **past h.,** passé *m* simple.

historical [hɪs'tɒrɪk(ə)l] *adj* **(a)** (*character, event*) historique; (*source, document*) de l'histoire; **of purely h. interest,** d'intérêt purement historique; **h. record** *or* **account,** historique *m*; **h. research,** recherche *f* en histoire; **(b)** (*novel, painting*) historique; **(c)** *Ling* **h. linguistics,** linguistique *f* diachronique.

historically [hɪs'tɒrɪklɪ] *adv* historiquement.

historiographer [hɪstɔːrɪ'ɒgrəfər] *n* historiographe *m*.

historiography [hɪstɔːrɪ'ɒgrəfɪ] *n* historiographie *f*.

history ['hɪst(ə)rɪ] *n* **(a)** (*of country, ship etc*) l'histoire *f*; **French h.,** l'histoire de France; **ancient/modern h.,** l'histoire ancienne/moderne; **that's (ancient) history,** ça c'est une vieille histoire; **we're making h.,** nous faisons l'histoire; *Med etc* **there is a h. of heart disease in her family,** il y a des antécédents de maladie cardiaque dans sa famille; *Sch* **h. book/teacher/***etc*, livre *m*/professeur *m*/*etc* d'histoire; **(b)** (*book*) histoire *f*; (*chronological account*) historique *m*; **(c)** (*tradition*) tradition *f*; **there is a long h. of cultural links between the cities,** il existe une longue tradition de liens culturels entre ces villes.

histrionic [hɪstrɪ'ɒnɪk] *adj* **(a)** *Pej* histrionique; **(b)** *Th* théâtral, -aux.

histrionics [hɪstrɪ'ɒnɪks] *npl* **(a)** *Pej* parade *f* d'émotion *ou* d'affection *ou* de colère *etc*; **it is mere h. on her part,** c'est une comédie qu'elle nous joue; **(b)** *Th* l'art *m* du théâtre.

hit¹ [hɪt] *n* **(a)** (*blow*) coup *m*; *F* **that's a h. at you,** c'est à vous que s'adresse l'allusion;

(b) *Mil etc* impact *m*; (*on target*) coup *m* au but; *Fencing* touche *f*, coup; *Billiards* touche; (*hockey*) coup de crosse; *Baseball* coup de batte; **to score a h.,** toucher; *Mil* mettre un coup au but; **to score a direct h. on sth,** (*of bomber etc*) frapper qch de plein fouet; (*of bomb*) tomber directement sur qch; **free h.,** (*hockey*) coup franc; **to answer h. or miss,** répondre au hasard *ou* au petit bonheur; **their method is rather h. or miss,** leur méthode est plutôt aléatoire; **it's h. or miss!,** c'est tout ou rien!;

(c) *Th TV etc* spectacle *m etc* à succès; *Mus* **h. (record),** tube *m*; **she had a h. with her song 'Bye, Bye',** sa chanson 'Bye, Bye' a été un tube; **Frank Sinatra's greatest hits,** les plus grands succès de Frank Sinatra; **to make** *or* **score a h. with s.o.,** faire bonne impression à qn; (*romantically*) faire une touche; **h. parade,** hit parade *m*, palmarès *m*;

(d) *esp US Sl* (*murder*) meurtre prémédité; **h. list,** = liste de victimes à assassiner; **h. man,** tueur *m* à gages;

(e) (*of drugs*) injection *f*.

hit² *v* (*pt & pp* **hit**; *prp* **hitting**) **1** *vt* **(a)** (*of person*) frapper; *Comptr* frapper (sur) (*une touche*); (*of bullet*) atteindre (*qn*); (*of car etc*) percuter (*un arbre, un autobus*); **to h. s.o. in the face,** frapper qn au visage; **to h. one's foot against a stone,** se cogner le pied contre une pierre; (*and stumble*) buter contre une pierre; **to h. one's head on the ceiling,** se cogner la tête contre le plafond; *Nau* **to h. a rock,** (*of ship, boat*) heurter un récif; **the bullet hit her in the arm,** la balle l'a touchée au bras; **to h. the target,** (*with gun, missile etc*) toucher la cible; *Fig* **the remark hit home,** la remarque a fait son effet; *Journ F* **to h. the headlines,** défrayer la chronique; *Fig* **to h. the nail on the head,** tomber juste; *Fig* **to h. the roof,** être furieux; *Sl* **to h. the bottle,** picoler; *Sl* **to h. the hay** *or US* **the sack,** se coucher, se pieuter; **it suddenly hit me that ...,** j'ai réalisé tout d'un coup que ...; **he didn't know what had hit him,** il se demandait ce qui lui était arrivé;

(b) (*reach*) atteindre; *Fencing Billiards* toucher; *Mus* **to h. the wrong note,** (*on the piano etc*) faire une fausse note; (*in singing*) attaquer faux; **I can't h. those high notes anymore,** je ne peux plus chanter ces notes aiguës; **to h. an all-time low,** (*of investment, relationship etc*) être au plus bas;

(c) (*affect*) **to be hard hit,** être sérieusement touché (*par ses pertes etc*); **the strike has hit several factories,** la grève a atteint plusieurs usines;

(d) *US F* (*borrow from*) **he hit his friend for $100,** il a tapé son ami de 100 dollars;

(e) (*guess*) **you've hit it!,** vous y êtes!, vous avez mis le doigt dessus!;

(f) (*arrive at*) arriver à (*un endroit*); **the circus hits town tomorrow night,** le cirque arrive en ville demain soir; **to h. the trail** *or* **the road,** se mettre en route; **when it hits the shops,** quand il arrivera sur le marché;

(g) (*encounter*) buter sur (*un problème, une difficulté*); **the tunnellers hit rock,** les ouvriers qui creusalent le tunnel sont tombés sur de la roche; **we hit a terrible snowstorm,** nous nous sommes trouvés dans une tempête de neige terrible;

(h) *esp US Sl* (*murder*) buter (*qn*).

2 *vi* frapper; **to h. hard,** frapper *ou* cogner fort.

►**hit back** **1** *vi* **(a)** (*return blow*) se défendre; rendre coup pour coup (**at s.o.,** à qn); **(b)** *Fig* (*answer accusation, criticism etc*) riposter, répondre. **2** *vtas* (*return blow*) **to h. s.o. back,** rendre son coup à qn.

►**hit off** *vtsep* **(a)** (*imitate*) (*in satirical drawing*) caricaturer; (*impersonate*) imiter; **he hits the president off very well,** il imite très bien le président; **(b) to h. it off,** bien s'entendre (**with,** avec).

►**hit on** *vipo* (*discover*) trouver (*une idée, une méthode etc*).

►**hit out** *vi* **(a)** (*punch etc*) frapper; **she hit out at her attackers,** elle a frappé ses agresseurs; **he hit out in all directions,** il donnait des coups dans tous les sens; **(b)** (*verbally*) attaquer (verbalement); **George Bush hits out at ...,** George Bush attaque ... .

hit-and-run ['hɪt(ə)n'rʌn] *adj* **(a) h.-and-r. accident,** accident *m* dont l'auteur est coupable de délit de fuite; **killed by a h.-and-r. driver,** tué par un chauffard qui a pris la fuite; **(b)** *Mil* **h.-and-r. raid,** raid *m* éclair.

hitch¹ [hɪtʃ] *n* **(a)** (*difficulty*) empêchement *m*, anicroche *f*, contretemps *m*; **there's a h. somewhere,** il y a quelque chose qui cloche; **there's been a h.,** il y a eu un problème; **without a h.,** sans anicroches, sans accroc; *Rad TV etc* **technical h.,** incident *m* technique; **(b)** (*knot*) nœud *m*; **half h.,** demi-clef *f*; **(c)** *Am F* (*length of time*) **a three-year h. in the army,** (une période de) trois ans dans l'armée; **to do a three-year h. in prison,** faire trois ans de prison; **(d)** (*movement*) saccade *f*, secousse *f*; (*of horse*) léger boitement.

hitch² **1** *vt* **(a)** (*attach*) accrocher, attacher, *Nau* amarrer (*qch*) (**to,** à); **she hitched the horse to a post,** elle a attaché son cheval à un poteau; **they hitched the horses**

to the cart, ils ont attelé les chevaux à la charrette; **(b)** *F* (*hitchhike*) **to h. a lift** *or esp Am* **ride,** faire du stop, *Can* faire de la pouce; **we hitched a ride to Paris,** on nous a pris en stop jusqu'à Paris; **(c)** *F* **to get hitched,** (*married*) se marier. **2** *vi* **(a)** = **HITCHHIKE**; **(b)** (*of person*) **to h. on to sth,** s'accrocher à qch.

►**hitch up** *vtsep* **(a)** (*harness*) harnacher (*un cheval*); **(b)** (*lift*) remonter (*son pantalon, sa jupe*).

hitchhike [ˈhɪtʃhaɪk] *vi* faire de l'auto-stop *ou* du stop, *Can* faire de la pouce; **to h. to Paris,** aller à Paris en stop.

hitchhiker [ˈhɪtʃhaɪkər] *n* auto-stoppeur, -euse.

hitchhiking [ˈhɪtʃhaɪkɪŋ] *n* (auto-)stop *m*.

hi-tech [ˈhaɪtek] **1** *adj* de haute technologie, de technologie pointue; **they've adopted a hi-t. approach,** ils ont eu recours à la technologie de pointe; **we're very hi-t. here,** nous faisons un usage intensif de l'automatisation *ou* de l'informatique ici. **2** *n* technologie *f* de pointe, hi-tech *f*.

hither [ˈhɪðər] *adv Arch & Lit* ici (*exprimant la venue*); **h. and thither,** çà et là.

hitherto [ˈhɪðəˈtuː] *adv* jusqu'ici, jusqu'à présent.

hit-or-miss [ˈhɪtɔːˈmɪs] *adj* (*method*) aléatoire.

HIV [eɪtʃaɪˈviː] *n Med* (*abbr* **human immuno-deficiency virus**) VIH *m*; **to be HIV positive,** être séropositif, avoir une sérologie VIH positive.

hive[1] [haɪv] *n* **(a)** (*for bees*) ruche *f*; *Fig* **a h. of industry,** une véritable ruche *ou* fourmilière; **(b)** (*swarm*) essaim *m*.

hive[2] **1** *vt* mettre (*un essaim*) dans une ruche. **2** *vi* (*of swarm*) entrer dans la ruche.

►**hive off** *vtsep* (*separate*) détacher *ou* séparer (*qch*) d'un tout; **to h. off work,** sous-traiter; *Br Com* **part of the industry was hived off to private ownership,** une partie de cette industrie a été privatisée.

hives [haɪvz] *npl Med* urticaire *f*; **to have h.,** avoir de l'urticaire.

hiya [ˈhaɪjə, haɪˈjɑː] *int F esp Am* salut!

HM [eɪtʃˈem] *n Br abbr* **Her** *or* **His Majesty**.

h'm [hm] *int* (*expressing doubt*) heu!, hum!

HMG [eɪtʃemˈdʒiː] *n Br Admin abbr* **Her** *or* **His Majesty's Government**.

HMI [eɪtʃemˈaɪ] (*abbr* **His** *or* **Her Majesty's Inspector**) inspecteur *m* de l'éducation nationale.

HMS [eɪtʃeˈmes] *n Br Nau abbr* **Her** *or* **His Majesty's Ship**.

HMSO [eɪtʃeˈmesəʊ] *n Br* (*abbr* **Her** *or* **His Majesty's Stationery Office**) = Imprimerie Nationale.

ho [həʊ] *int* **(a)** (*to attract attention*) hé!, ohé!; *Nau* **land ho!,** terre!; **(b)** (*expressing surprise, amusement etc*) oh!

HO *n Br* (*abbr* **Home Office**) = Ministère *m* de l'Intérieur.

hoar [hɔːr] *n* gelée blanche.

hoard[1] [hɔːd] *n* amas *m*; approvisionnement secret (*de vivres etc*); **h. of money,** trésor *m*, *F* magot *m*.

hoard[2] *vt* amasser, accaparer (*le blé etc*); mettre *ou* tenir en réserve (*des vivres etc*); thésauriser (*de l'argent*).

►**hoard up** *vtsep* = **HOARD**[2].

hoarder [ˈhɔːdər] *n* amasseur, -euse, accumulateur, -trice; **h. of money,** thésauriseur, -euse.

hoarding[1] [ˈhɔːdɪŋ] *n* mise *f* en réserve (*de provisions*); thésaurisation *f* (*d'argent*).

hoarding[2] *n* **(a)** *Br* (*for advertising*) panneau *m* d'affichage; **(b)** (*fencing*) clôture *f* en planches; palissade *f* (*de chantier etc*).

hoarfrost [ˈhɔːfrɒst] *n* gelée blanche.

hoarse [hɔːs] *adj* (*voice etc*) enroué, rauque; **to be h.,** être enroué; **to shout oneself h.,** s'enrouer à force de crier.

hoarsely [ˈhɔːslɪ] *adv* d'une voix rauque *ou* enrouée.

hoarseness [ˈhɔːsnɪs] *n* enrouement *m*.

hoary [ˈhɔːrɪ] *adj* **(a)** (*hair*) blanchi, chenu; *Bot Ent* (*foliage, insect*) couvert d'un duvet blanc; **(b)** (*venerable*) vénérable, séculaire; (*old*) vieux.

hoax[1] [həʊks] *n* canular *m*, farce *f*, tour *m*; *Journ F* canard *m*; **(bomb) h.,** fausse alerte à la bombe; **it turned out to be a h.,** c'était un canular; **to play a h. on s.o.,** jouer un tour à qn.

hoax[2] *vt* monter un canular à (*qn*).

hoaxer [ˈhəʊksər] *n* farceur, -euse; (*in bomb hoax etc*) mauvais(e) plaisant(e).

hob [hɒb] *n* plaque *f* (*de cuisinière électrique*); plaque de côté (*d'une grille de cheminée*).

hobble[1] [ˈhɒb(ə)l] *n* **(a)** (*limp*) boitillement *m*; *Arch* **h. skirt,** jupe entravée; **(b)** (*for horses etc*) entrave *f*.

hobble[2] **1** *vi* boitiller, clopiner; **to h. along,** marcher en boitillant. **2** *vt* entraver (*un cheval etc*).

hobby [ˈhɒbɪ] *n* passe-temps *m inv*, hobby *m*, violon *m* d'Ingres.

hobbyhorse [ˈhɒbɪhɔːs] *n* (*toy*) cheval *m* de bois; *Fig* dada *m*, cheval *m* de bataille; *Fig* **to get on one's h.,** enfourcher son dada *ou* son cheval de bataille.

hobgoblin [ˈhɒbgɒblɪn] *n* lutin *m*, gobelin *m*.

hobnail[1] [ˈhɒbneɪl] *n* clou *m*, fer *m* (*pour les chaussures*); **hobnailed boot,** chaussure ferrée.

hobnail[2] *vt* ferrer (*une chaussure*).

hobnob [ˈhɒbnɒb] *vi* (**-bb-**) *F* **to h. with s.o.,** frayer avec qn.

hobo [ˈhəʊbəʊ] *n Am* **(a)** (*tramp*) chemineau *m*, trimardeur *m*; **(b)** (*itinerant worker*) ouvrier ambulant.

Hobson [ˈhɒbsən] *n* **H.'s choice,** = choix qui ne laisse pas d'alternative.

hock[1] [hɒk] *n* (*of horse*) jarret *m*.

hock[2] *n* (*wine*) vin *m* du Rhin.

hock[3] *n F* **in h.,** (*of watch etc*) au clou, en gage; (*in debt*) en gage; **to put sth in h.,** (*pawn*) mettre qch en gage.

hock[4] *vt* mettre (*sa montre etc*) au clou.

hockey [ˈhɒkɪ] *n Sp* **(a) h.,** *Am* **field h.,** (jeu *m* de) hockey *m*; **to play h.,** jouer au hockey; **h. stick,** crosse *f* de hockey; **(b)** *Am* (*ice hockey*) hockey *m* sur glace, *Can* hockey.

hockshop [ˈhɒkʃɒp] *n Am F* crédit municipal, mont-de-piété *m*, *pl* monts-de-piété.

hocus-pocus [ˈhəʊkəsˈpəʊkəs] *n* **(a)** (*formula used by conjurers*) passe-passe *m*; (*trick*) tour *m* de passe-passe; **(b)** (*trickery*) tromperie *f*, supercherie *f*.

hod [hɒd] *n* **(a)** oiseau *m*, hotte *f* (*de maçon*); **h. carrier,** aide-maçon *m*; **(b)** seau *m*, caisse *f* (*à charbon*).

hodgepodge [ˈhɒdʒpɒdʒ] *n esp Am* = **HOTCHPOTCH**.

hoe[1] [həʊ] *n* houe *f*, binette *f*; **(weeding) h.,** sarcloir *m*; **(Dutch) h.,** griffe-bineuse *f*, *pl* griffes-bineuses; **miner's h.,** sape *f*.

hoe[2] *vt* (**hoed; hoeing**) biner (*le sol*); sarcler (*les mauvaises herbes*).

hoedown [ˈhəʊdaʊn] *n esp Am* bal populaire.

hoeing [ˈhəʊɪŋ] *n* binage *m* (*du sol*); sarclage *m* (*des mauvaises herbes*).

hog[1] [hɒg] *n* **(a)** (*castrated pig*) porc châtré; *Am* (*pig*) porc, cochon *m*, pourceau *m*; *F* **to go the whole h.,** aller jusqu'au bout; tout risquer; *US Fig* **to live high on the h.,** manger du pain blanc; **(b)** *Fig* goinfre *m*, glouton *m*.

hog[2] *v* (**-gg-**) **1** *vt* **(a)** *F* (*take, use etc for oneself*) prendre plus que sa part de (*qch*); **to h. the television,** monopoliser la télé; **to h. the limelight,** accaparer la vedette; *Aut* **to h. the road,** tenir toute la route; **(b)** *Nau* donner de l'arc à (*un navire*). **2** *vi* (*of ship, keel*) s'arquer; (*of pipes etc*) cintrer.

Hogmanay [hɒgməˈneɪ] *n Scot* la Saint-Sylvestre.

hogshead [ˈhɒgzhed] *n* tonneau *m*, barrique *f*.

hogtie [ˈhɒgtaɪ] *vt US* lier les quatre pattes de (*un animal*); *Fig* entraver (*l'économie etc*).

hogwash [ˈhɒgwɒʃ] *n* eaux grasses (*que l'on donne aux porcs*); *F* (*nonsense*) foutaise *f*.

hogweed [ˈhɒgwiːd] *n* (*plant*) berce commune.

hoi polloi [ˈhɔɪpəˈlɔɪ] *npl* **the h. p.,** la foule, les masses *fpl*.

hoist[1] [hɔɪst] *n* **(a)** (*act*) levage *m*; (*with a winch*) coup *m* de treuil; *F* **to give s.o. a h. (up),** aider qn à monter, faire la courte échelle à qn; **(b)** (*device*) appareil *m ou* engin *m* de levage; (*winch*) treuil *m*, grue *f*, palan *m*; *Min* bourriquet *m*; (*for goods*) monte-charge *m inv*; **(c)** *Nau* guindant *m* (*de pavillon, de voile*).

hoist[2] *vt* lever, hisser (*un fardeau etc*); *Nau* hisser (*une embarcation, un pavillon*); **to h. boats in/out,** embarquer/débarquer les canots; **h. away!,** hissez!; **she hoisted herself on to the wall,** elle s'est hissée sur le mur; *Fig* **to be hoist with one's own petard,** tomber dans son propre piège.

hoisting [ˈhɔɪstɪŋ] *n* **(a)** levage *m*, hissage *m*; (*by windlass*) guindage *m*; **h. gear** *or* **tackle,** appareil *m ou* engin *m* de levage *ou* de hissage; **(b)** *Mil* **h. the colours,** lever *m* des couleurs.

hoity-toity [ˈhɔɪtɪˈtɔɪtɪ] **1** *int* ta, ta, ta!, taratata! **2** *adj* qui se donne des airs; qui fait l'important.

hokum [ˈhəʊkəm] *n Am F* **(a)** (*in film etc*) niaiseries *fpl*, paroles sentimentales; **(b)** (*nonsense*) bêtises *fpl*.

hold[1] [həʊld] *n* **(a)** (*grip*) prise *f*; *Boxing* tenu *m*; (*in wrestling*) prise; **to have h. of s.o./sth,** tenir qn/qch; **to catch** *or* **get** *or* **take h. of s.o./sth,** saisir *ou* empoigner qn/qch; **where did you get h. of that?,** où vous êtes-vous procuré cela?; **to get h. of the wrong idea,** mal comprendre; **it's difficult to get h. of this book,** (*find a copy of it*) ce livre est difficile à trouver; **to relax one's h.,** relâcher son étreinte; **to let go one's h.,** lâcher prise; **to lose one's h. on reality,** perdre le sens des réalités; **to have a h. on** *or* **over s.o.,** avoir prise sur qn; **to gain a firm h. over s.o.,** acquérir un grand pouvoir sur qn; **no**

holds barred, toutes prises autorisées;

(b) (*in rockclimbing etc*) point *m* d'appui;

(c) on h., (*of project*) en suspens; **the road building programme is on h.,** la construction de la route est interrompue; **to put sth on h.,** mettre qch en suspens; *Tel* **to put s.o. on h.,** faire attendre qn; *Tel* **to be on h.,** (*of caller*) attendre.

hold² *v* (*pt & pp* **held** [held]) **1** *vt* **(a)** (*grip*) tenir (*un enfant etc*); **to h. sth in one's hand,** tenir qch à *ou* dans la main; **to h. sth/s.o. tight(ly),** serrer qch/qn; tenir qch/qn serré; **they held (each other's) hands,** ils se tenaient (par) la main; **to h. one's sides with laughter,** se tenir les côtes de rire; **to h. one's nose,** se boucher le nez; **to h. sth in position,** tenir qch en place; **four screws h. the shelf to the wall,** l'étagère est fixée au mur par quatre vis; **the table is held in place by steel bolts,** la table est maintenue par des boulons d'acier;

(b) (*detain etc*) **she was held without trial for six weeks,** elle a été emprisonnée six semaines sans avoir été jugée; **to h. s.o. prisoner,** retenir qn prisonnier; **to h. s.o. (as) hostage,** retenir qn en otage; **to h. stocks as security,** détenir des titres en garantie;

(c) (*command etc*) **to h. one's ground,** tenir bon, ne pas lâcher pied; **to h. one's own,** se maintenir, se défendre; *Mil* **to h. a fort,** défendre une forteresse; **to h. a position,** tenir une position; **to be able to h. one's drink,** bien supporter le vin; **to h. the stage,** (*of actor*) retenir l'attention de l'auditoire; (*of play*) tenir l'affiche (*pendant longtemps*); *Nau etc* **to h. course,** tenir la route; **car that holds the road well,** voiture qui tient bien la route;

(d) (*carry*) porter; **to h. one's head high,** porter la tête haute; **to h. oneself straight,** se tenir droit; **to h. oneself well,** avoir de la tenue;

(e) (*contain*) contenir, renfermer; **barrel that holds twenty litres,** tonneau d'une contenance de vingt litres; **car that holds six people,** voiture à six places; **to h. water,** (*of cask etc*) être étanche; *Fig* (*of theory, story etc*) tenir debout; **what the future holds,** ce que l'avenir nous réserve; **sport held no interest for them,** pour eux, le sport ne présentait aucun intérêt;

(f) (*conduct etc*) tenir (*une séance etc*); avoir (*une consultation*); célébrer (*une fête etc*); **the meeting willl be held at 8 pm,** la réunion aura lieu à 8 heures du soir; **to h. a conversation with s.o.,** s'entretenir avec qn; **the two sides held talks,** des discussions se sont tenues entre les deux parties;

(g) (*restrain, prevent*) retenir, arrêter; empêcher; **to h. one's breath,** retenir sa respiration; **there's no holding him,** (une fois lancé) il n'y a pas moyen de l'arrêter; **h. your tongue!,** taisez-vous!; *F* **h. it!, h. your horses!,** arrêtez!, attendez!, stop!; **h. it!,** (*at photographer's*) ne bougez plus!; *Mil* **to h. the enemy,** contenir l'ennemi;

(h) (*keep*) **to h. s.o.'s interest,** retenir l'attention de qn; **the film doesn't h. the attention for long,** le film ne retient pas l'attention très longtemps; **to h. one's audience,** retenir l'attention de l'auditoire; **to h. s.o. to their promise,** obliger *ou* contraindre qn à tenir sa promesse; **we can h. a room for you until tomorrow night,** nous pouvons retenir une chambre pour vous jusqu'à demain soir; *Am* **h. the onions,** (*in restaurant*) sans oignons;

(i) avoir, posséder (*un titre, un emploi*); avoir (*une opinion*); détenir (*une charge*); occuper (*une position*); être titulaire de (*une médaille*); *Fin* détenir (*des actions*); **she had held (government) office before,** elle avait déjà assumé des fonctions au gouvernement;

(j) (*consider*) **to h. sth lightly,** faire peu de cas de qch; attacher peu d'importance à qch; **to h. sth sacred,** tenir qch pour sacré; **to h. s.o. responsible,** tenir qn responsable; **to be held in respect,** être respecté de tous;

(k) *Mus* **to h. a note,** tenir *ou* prolonger une note;

(l) *Tel* **h. the line!,** ne quittez pas!; **h. all my calls,** ne me passez aucun appel.

2 *vi* **(a)** (*of rope, nail etc*) tenir (bon); **h. tight!,** (*on bus etc*) = attention au départ!;

(b) (*last*) durer, persister; (*of weather*) se maintenir; **if your luck holds,** si votre chance dure;

(c) (*be valid*) **to h. (good, true),** être vrai *ou* valable; **the same holds true in respect of ...,** il en est de même pour ...;

(d) *Tel* attendre.

hold³ *n Nau* cale *f*.

▶**hold against** *vtaspo* (*dislike for*) **to h. sth against s.o.,** reprocher qch à qn; **I won't h. it against you,** je ne t'en voudrai pas.

▶**hold back 1** *vi* **(a)** (*stay in the background*) rester en arrière; **(b)** (*restrain oneself*) se retenir (**from doing sth,** de faire qch); **buyers are holding back,** les acheteurs s'abstiennent. **2** *vtsep* **(a)** (*restrain*) retenir (*qn, sa colère, ses larmes*); contenir (*sa colère, ses larmes, une foule*); **(b)** (*impede*) freiner, entraver; **lack of investment is holding industry back,** l'absence d'investissements freine l'industrie; **(c)** (*withhold*) cacher, dissimuler (*la vérité*); **he's holding something back,** il cache quelque chose.

▶**hold down** *vtsep* **(a)** (*restrain*) maintenir (*une personne*) à terre; **the government is trying to h. down interest rates,** le gouvernement essaye d'empêcher l'augmentation des taux d'intérêt; **(b) to h. down a job,** (*keep*) garder un emploi; (*occupy*) occuper un poste, avoir un emploi.

▶**hold forth** *vi F* (*speak pompously*) disserter, pérorer (**on sth,** sur qch).

▶**hold in** *vtsep* réprimer (*ses désirs*); maîtriser (*une passion*); serrer la bride à, contenir (*un cheval*); **to h. one's stomach** *or* **oneself in,** rentrer son ventre; **to h. oneself in (emotionally),** se maîtriser.

▶**hold off 1** *vtsep* **(a)** (*keep away*) tenir (*l'ennemi*) à distance; **he held off his assailants,** il a tenu ses assaillants en respect; **she held him off with various excuses,** elle a pris divers prétextes pour le repousser; **(b)** (*not do*) **to h. off doing sth,** remettre qch à plus tard; **to h. off deciding,** remettre une décision à plus tard. **2** *vi* (*keep away*) se tenir à distance (**from,** de); *Nau* tenir le large; **the rain is holding off,** jusqu'ici il ne pleut pas.

▶**hold on 1** *vi* **(a)** (*endure*) tenir, résister; **(b)** (*wait*) attendre; **h. on (a minute)!,** pas si vite!; *Tel* **h. on a moment,** ne quittez pas; **(c)** (*keep one's grip*) se tenir; **h. on (tight)!,** (*on bus, motorbike etc*) tiens-toi bien! **2** *vtas* (*keep attached*) fixer (*un morceau de bois*); **the tiles are held on with glue,** les carreaux sont maintenus en place par de la colle.

▶**hold on to** *vipo* **(a)** (*grip*) s'agripper à (*qch*); *Fig* **to h. on to an idea/a hope/***etc*, se raccrocher à une idée/un espoir/*etc*; **(b)** (*keep*) garder; **h. on to that book,** (*it may be valuable*) garde ce livre précieusement; **she held on to her money,** elle se cramponnait à son argent.

▶**hold out 1** *vtsep* **(a)** (*stretch out*) tendre, offrir (*la main etc*); **(b)** (*offer*) offrir, laisser (*des espérances*); **the doctor doesn't h. out much hope,** le docteur pense qu'il n'y a pas beaucoup d'espoir. **2** *vi* **(a)** (*of person*) tenir (le coup); **to h. out against an attack,** soutenir une attaque; **to h. out for a higher price,** exiger un prix plus élevé; **(b)** (*of supplies etc*) durer.

▶**hold out on** *vipo* (*not give information to*) cacher qch à (*qn*); **you've been holding out on me,** (*I didn't know you played the piano etc*) tu m'as caché des choses.

▶**hold over** *vtsep* (*postpone*) remettre (à plus tard); ajourner (*une décision etc*); arriérer (*un paiement*); **bills held over,** effets en souffrance *ou* en suspens.

▶**hold to** *vipo* (*abide by*) s'en tenir à; **to h. to a belief,** rester attaché à une croyance; **to h. to one's decision,** s'en tenir à *ou* maintenir sa décision.

▶**hold together 1** *vtsep* maintenir (*deux choses*) ensemble; **the two pieces of wood are held together by nails,** les deux morceaux de bois sont cloués ensemble. **2** *vi* tenir (ensemble); (*be cohesive*) garder de la cohésion; **the story doesn't h. together,** l'histoire ne tient pas debout.

▶**hold up 1** *vtsep* **(a)** (*support*) soutenir (*qn, qch*); **these ropes h. the tent up,** ces cordes maintiennent la tente dressée;

(b) (*raise*) lever (*qch*) (en l'air); **h. your head up,** lève la tête; **she held the book up,** (*so that everyone could see*) elle brandit le livre; *Fig* **to h. s.o. up as an example,** citer qn comme exemple; **to h. s.o. up to ridicule,** tourner qn en ridicule;

(c) arrêter (*qn, un train etc*); bloquer (*la circulation etc*); immobiliser (*qn, qch*); **the car was held up at the traffic lights,** la voiture a dû s'arrêter au feu rouge; **our departure was held up by bad weather,** notre départ a été retardé par le mauvais temps; **goods held up at the customs,** marchandises en consigne à la douane; **financial difficulties are holding the project up,** le projet est freiné par des difficultés financières;

(d) (*in order to rob*) attaquer (*qn, une banque*); arrêter (*un train*) à main armée.

2 *vi* **(a)** (*stay in place*) tenir (en place); (*of weather*) se maintenir; **the old building is still holding up,** le vieux bâtiment est toujours debout; **I hope the good weather holds up,** j'espère que le beau temps va durer;

(b) (*of theory etc*) tenir debout.

►**hold with** *vi* (*usu neg*) **I don't h. with his opinions,** je ne partage pas ses opinions; **I don't h. with such behaviour,** je n'approuve pas une telle conduite.

holdall ['həʊldɔːl] *n Br* sac *m* de voyage; fourre-tout *m inv*.

holder ['həʊldər] *n* **(a)** détenteur, -trice (*Fin de titres, d'une lettre de change, Sp du record*); tenant *m* (*d'un championnat*); *Fin* porteur, -euse (*de titres, d'un effet*); titulaire *mf* (*d'un droit, d'un poste etc*); propriétaire *mf* (*d'une terre*); détenteur *m* (*d'un terrain etc hypothéqué*); **(b)** (*device*) support *m*, monture *f*; **(drill) h.**, porte-foret *m*, *pl* porte-forets; **(tool) h.**, porte-outil(s) *m*; **(toothbrush) h.**, porte-brosses *m inv* à dents; **(cigarette) h.**, porte-cigarettes *m inv*; **(c)** (*vessel*) récipient *m*.

holding ['həʊldɪŋ] *n* **(a)** tenue *f* (*d'un objet etc à la main*);
(b) tenue *f* (*d'un congrès etc*);
(c) *MecE* fixation *f*; maintien *m* (en position); *Mil* **h. operation,** (*containment*) opération *f* de fixation (*de l'adversaire*);
(d) conservation *f*; prolongation *f* (*d'un mouvement, d'une action*); *Mus* prolongation (*d'une note*); *Av* attente *f* (*imposée à un avion avant d'atterrir*); *Mil* conservation *f* (*du terrain conquis*); *Av* **h. pattern,** circuit *m* d'attente;
(e) *Agr* terre affermée, ferme *f*;
(f) *Fin* effets *mpl* en portefeuille; **he has holdings in several companies,** il est actionnaire de plusieurs sociétés; **h. company,** holding *m*.

hold-up ['həʊldʌp] *n* **(a)** (*delay*) arrêt *m*; embouteillage *m* (*de voitures*); panne *f* (*du métro etc*); **there have been no h.-ups with the project,** le projet n'a eu à souffrir d'aucun retard; **(b)** (*armed robbery*) attaque *f* à main armée, hold-up *m*, braquage *m*; **this is a h.-up,** c'est un hold-up.

hole¹ [həʊl] *n* **(a)** (*in the ground*) trou *m*, creux *m*, cavité *f*; *Golf* trou; (*of rabbit*) terrier *m*; (*of fox*) tanière *f*; (*of mouse etc*) trou; **to dig a h.,** creuser un trou; **what a h.!,** (*of room etc*) quel (sale) trou!; (*of house*) quel taudis!; (*of town*) quel bled!; *Golf* **a h. in one,** trou réussi en un coup;
(b) (*opening*) trou *m*; perforation *f* (*dans une plaque de métal etc*); point *m* (*d'une courroie*); perce *f* (*d'une flûte*); *Tech* **punched h.,** trou poinçonné; **inspection h.,** orifice *ou* trou de visite; *Min* **blast h.,** trou de mine; *Comptr* **(punch) h.,** perforation; *Med F* **h. in the heart,** trou dans le cœur; **h. in the wall,** restaurant *ou* café *ou* endroit exigu; **to bore a h.,** percer un trou; **to stop (up) a h.,** boucher un trou; **to make a h. in,** faire un trou à (*qch*); trouer (*un vêtement*); *Fig* **to make a h. in one's savings,** (*of expenditure*) grever ses économies; **this jersey is full of holes,** ce tricot est tout troué *ou* est plein de trous; **to pick holes in a theory,** relever les points faibles d'une théorie;
(c) *F* (*difficult situation*) situation difficile; **to be** *or* **find oneself in a h.,** être *ou* se trouver dans une situation délicate.

hole² **1** *vt* **(a)** (*put a hole in*) trouer, percer (*qch*), pratiquer *ou* faire un trou dans (*qch*); **the ship was holed above the water line,** le navire était troué au-dessus de la ligne de flottation; **(b)** (*put into a hole*) faire entrer *ou* mettre (*qch*) dans un trou; *Billiards* bloquer, blouser (*la bille*); *Golf* **to h. the ball,** envoyer *ou* mettre la balle dans le trou; *Fig* **holed in one!,** vous avez deviné juste! **2** *vi* (*of stockings etc*) se trouer, se percer.

►**hole out** *vi Golf* mettre la balle dans le trou.

►**hole up** *vi F* (*hide*) se terrer.

hole-and-corner ['həʊl(ə)n'kɔːnər] *adj F* clandestin, secret.

holey ['həʊlɪ] *adj F* (tout) troué, plein de trous.

holiday¹ ['hɒlɪdɪ, -deɪ] *n* **(a)** (*day of festival*) (jour *m* de) fête *f*, jour férié; **public** *or Br* **bank h.,** fête légale; **(b)** *Br* (*day off*) (jour *m* de) congé *m*; *Sch* **half h.,** après-midi *m* de congé; **I'm going to take a h. today,** je vais prendre un congé aujourd'hui; **(c)** *Br* (*vacation*) vacances *fpl*; **a month's h.,** un mois de vacances; **how much h. do you get?,** combien est-ce que tu as de vacances?; **the summer holidays,** les grandes vacances; **to be on h.,** être en vacances; **when are you going on h.?,** quand est-ce que vous allez prendre vos vacances?; **camping h.,** vacances passées à faire du camping; **h. camp,** camp *m* de vacances; (*for children*) colonie *f* de vacances; **the h. season,** la période des vacances.

holiday² ['hɒlɪdeɪ] *vi Br* passer les vacances.

holiday-maker ['hɒlɪdeɪmeɪkər] *n Br* vacancier, -ière; (*in summer*) estivant, -ante.

holier-than-thou ['həʊlɪəðən'ðaʊ] *adj* (*attitude etc*) hypocritement pieux.

holiness ['həʊlɪnɪs] *n* sainteté *f*; **His/Your H.,** (*of the Pope*) Sa/Votre Sainteté.

holism ['həʊlɪz(ə)m] *n Phil Med* holisme *m*.

holistic [həʊ'lɪstɪk] *adj Phil Med* holistique.

holland ['hɒlənd] *n Tex* toile *f* de Hollande; toile bise.

Holland ['hɒlənd] *n* Hollande *f*.

holler¹ ['hɒlər] *n F* braillement *m*.

holler² *vi F* crier à tue-tête, brailler.

hollow ['hɒləʊ] **1** *adj* **(a)** creux; (*cheek*) creux, rentré; (*eye*) cave; *Mil Hist* **h. square,** carré *m*; *Fig* **to feel h.,** avoir le ventre *ou* l'estomac creux; *Fig* **he's got h. legs,** (*can eat a lot*) il a un appétit insatiable; (*can drink a lot*) il boit comme un trou; **(b)** (*sound*) sourd; **in a h. voice,** d'une voix caverneuse; **(c)** (*promise, friendship etc*) faux, *f* fausse, trompeur, -euse; **(d)** (*worthless*) qui sonne creux; **h. victory,** une victoire sans signification. **2** *adv* **(a) to sound h.,** sonner creux; **(b) to beat s.o. h.,** battre qn à plate(s) couture(s). **3** *n* **(a)** creux *m* (*de la main, d'un arbre etc*); cavité *f* (*d'une dent*); excavation *f*; **(b)** *Geog* (*depression*) enfoncement *m*, dépression *f* (*du sol*); (*basin*) cuvette *f*.

►**hollow out** *vtsep* (*carve, scrape out etc*) creuser, évider; canneler (*une rainure*); (*undermine*) caver (*un rocher etc*); **to h. out the ground,** (*of water*) raviner le terrain.

hollow-cheeked [hɒləʊ'tʃiːkd] *adj* aux joues creuses.

hollow-eyed [hɒləʊ'aɪd] *adj* aux yeux caves.

hollowness ['hɒləʊnɪs] *n* **(a)** (*of a tree etc*) creux *m*, cavité *f*; **(b)** (*of a voice*) timbre caverneux; **(c)** (*of promise etc*) manque *m* de sincérité; **(d)** (*worthlessness*) absence *f* de signification, fausseté *f*, vacuité *f*; **the h. of a victory,** l'absence de signification d'une victoire.

holly ['hɒlɪ] *n* **h. (tree),** houx *m*; **h. berry,** cenelle *f*.

hollyhock ['hɒlɪhɒk] *n* (*plant*) rose trémière.

holm¹ [həʊm] *n Eng Dial* petite île, îlot *m* (*de rivière*).

holm² *n* (*tree*) **h. (oak),** yeuse *f*.

holocaust ['hɒləkɔːst] *n* holocauste *m*.

hologram ['hɒləgræm] *n Phot* hologramme *m*.

holograph ['hɒləgræf] *n* (h)olographie *f*; document *m ou* testament *m* (h)olographe.

hols [hɒlz] *npl Br Sch Sl* vacances *fpl*.

holster ['həʊlstər] *n* (*on saddle, belt*) étui *m* de revolver; (*on saddle*) fonte *f*.

holy ['həʊlɪ] **1** *adj* (**holier, holiest**) **(a)** saint, sacré; **the H. Bible,** la Sainte Bible; **the H. Trinity,** la Sainte Trinité; **the H. Ghost,** le Saint-Esprit; **the H. Father,** le Saint-Père, le Pape; **the H. Land,** la Terre Sainte; **the H. Roman Empire,** le Saint Empire Romain; *Fig F* **that child is a h. terror,** cet enfant est une terreur; **my boss is a h. terror,** mon patron sème la terreur; **to swear by all that is h.,** jurer ses grands dieux; *Fig* **to have a h. fear of sth,** avoir une crainte salutaire de qch; *Sl* **h. cow!, h. smoke!, h. mackerel!,** sapristi!; **h. bread,** pain bénit; **h. ground,** terre sacrée; **h. place,** lieu saint; **h. war,** guerre sainte; **h. water,** eau bénite; **(b)** (*person*) saint, pieux; *F* **a H. Joe,** personne *f* qui se prend pour un saint. **2** *n* **the H. of Holies,** le saint des saints.

holystone¹ ['həʊlɪstəʊn] *n Nau* brique *f* à pont.

holystone² *vt Nau* briquer (*le pont*).

homage ['hɒmɪdʒ] *n* hommage *m*; **to pay** *or* **do h. to s.o.,** rendre hommage à qn.

homburg ['hɒmbɜːg] *n* **h. (hat),** chapeau mou, feutre *m* souple.

home¹ [həʊm] **1** *n* **(a)** maison *f*; appartement *m*; **I've come straight from h.,** je viens (directement) de chez moi; **the Ideal H. Exhibition,** *US* **the H. Show,** ≈ le Salon des Arts Ménagers; **to have a h. of one's own,** avoir un chez-soi *ou* un foyer; **television brings the world into your own h.,** la télévision vous apporte le monde à domicile; *Iron* **don't you have a h. to go to?,** vous avez l'intention de passer la nuit ici? **he showed us his h.,** il nous a montré sa maison *ou* son appartement *ou* son logis; **to buy some things for the h.,** acheter des choses pour sa maison *ou* son appartement; **to make one's h. in France,** s'établir en France; **it's a h. from h.,** on y est comme chez soi; **there's no place like h.,** on n'est nulle part si bien que chez soi; **to leave h.,** quitter la maison; (*for good*) partir (définitivement), quitter la famille; **to be away from h.,** être parti *ou* absent *ou* en voyage; **at h.,** à la maison, chez soi; *Sp* (*jouer*) à domicile; **to stay at h.,** rester à la maison; **how are things at h.?,** comment ça va chez vous?; **these children have problems at h.,** ces enfants ont des problèmes chez eux; **to find no one at h.,** trouver la maison vide; **to feel at h. with s.o.,** se sentir à l'aise avec qn; **I don't feel at h. here,** je me sens dépaysé ici, je ne me sens pas chez moi ici; **he is at h. on** *or* **with any topic,** il est à l'aise sur tous les sujets; **make yourself at h.,** fais comme chez toi; **he insulted me in my own h.!,** il m'a insulté sous mon propre toit!; **ideas received in the**

h., les idées reçues à la maison; **to come from a good h.**, venir d'une bonne famille; **good h. wanted for three kittens,** (*in notice*) on recherche de gentils maîtres pour trois chatons;

(b) (*country, region*) patrie *f*, pays *m* (natal); terre natale; **at h. and abroad,** dans notre pays et à l'étranger; **our policy at h. and abroad,** notre politique intérieure et extérieure; **Glasgow is her second h.**, Glasgow est sa deuxième patrie; **to take an example nearer h.**, sans aller chercher si loin; **Greece, the h. of the arts,** la Grèce, patrie des beaux-arts; **Valencia is the h. of paella,** Valence est le pays de la paella;

(c) *Biol* habitat *m* (*d'un animal, d'une plante*);

(d) (*for old people etc*) asile *m*, hospice *m*; **old people's h.**, maison *f* de retraite (*pour les vieillards*); **rest h.**, maison de repos; **she didn't want her father to go into a h.**, elle ne voulait pas que son père aille à l'hospice; **nursing h.**, clinique *f*; **children's h.**, home *m* d'enfants;

(e) (*in games*) le but;

(f) (*in compounds*) **h. address,** adresse personnelle; *Comptr* **h. banking,** opérations bancaires informatisées effectuées à domicile; *Obst* **h. birth,** accouchement *m* à la maison; **a first-time h. buyer,** personne qui achète une maison pour la première fois; **h. computer,** ordinateur individuel; **h. computing,** informatique *f* à domicile; **h. cooking,** cuisine familiale; (*in restaurant*) cuisine bourgeoise; *Br* **the H. Counties,** les comtés *mpl* avoisinant Londres; **h. economics,** arts ménagers; **h. economist,** spécialiste *mf* des arts ménagers; **h. ground,** terrain *m* du club; *Fig* **to be on h. ground,** être en terrain familier; *Br Hist* **the H. Guard,** = la milice; *Br Admin* **h. help,** aide ménagère; **h. improvements,** travaux *mpl* d'amélioration du logement; **h. journey,** voyage *m* de retour; **h. key,** *Comptr* touche *f* origine; **h. life,** vie *f* de famille; **h. loan,** prêt *m* d'accession à la propriété; **h. market,** marché intérieur; **h. match,** match *m* à domicile; **h. news,** nouvelles *fpl* de l'intérieur; *Br* **the H. Office,** = le Ministère de l'Intérieur; **h. owner,** propriétaire *mf* d'une maison *ou* d'un appartement; **h. ownership is increasing,** le nombre des personnes propriétaires de leur logement augmente; **h. products,** produits *mpl* du pays; *Pol Hist* **H. rule,** autonomie *f*; *Baseball* **h. run,** coup *m* de circuit; **to hit a h. run,** faire un coup de circuit; *Br* **the H. Secretary,** = le Ministre de l'Intérieur; *Comptr Tel* **h. shopping,** téléachat *m*; *Sp* **the h. straight** *or* **stretch,** la dernière ligne droite; *Sp* **h. team** *or* **side,** équipe *f* qui reçoit; **h. town,** ville natale; **a h. truth,** vérité bien sentie; **to tell s.o. a few h. truths,** dire son fait *ou* ses quatre vérités à qn; **h. win,** victoire *f* à domicile.

2 *adv* **(a)** à la maison, chez soi; **to go** *or* **come h.**, rentrer (à la maison); (*after period of absence*) revenir dans sa famille; **on her way h.**, en rentrant *ou* en revenant chez elle; **to bring work h.**, emporter du travail à faire à la maison; **to be h.**, être de retour; **he's h. again!**, il est de retour!; **we'll be h. soon,** nous serons bientôt arrivés;

(b) (*in one's country*) au pays; **to go** *or* **come h.**, retourner au pays; **to send s.o. h. (from abroad),** rapatrier qn;

(c) the blow went h., le coup a porté; **his speech went h.**, son discours fit impression; **it will come h. to him some day,** il s'en rendra compte un jour; **to drive sth h. to s.o.**, faire entrer qch dans la tête à qn;

(d) (*all the way*) à fond; **to screw a piece h.**, visser *ou* serrer une pièce à bloc.

home² **1** *vi* retourner à son gîte; (*of pigeon*) revenir au colombier; (*of aircraft*) revenir à *ou* rallier sa base; (*of aircraft, missile etc*) **to h. on** *or* **towards ...**, mettre le cap sur ..., se diriger vers *ou* sur ... . **2** *vt* diriger (*un avion, un missile etc*) sur un point *ou* un objectif (déterminé) par radioguidage *ou* autoguidage.

►**home in** *vi* (*approach or reach target*) arriver au but.

►**home in on** *vipo* (*aim for*) viser (*qch*); **to h. in on a target,** (*of missile*) se diriger en plein vers un objectif; *Fig* **she homed in on this error,** elle a repéré cette erreur.

home-baked ['həʊm'beɪkt] *adj* (*pain, gâteau*) fait *ou* cuit à la maison; (*pain*) de ménage.

homebird ['həʊmbɜːd] *n F* (*person*) casanier, -ière.

homebody ['həʊmbɒdɪ] *n esp Am F* casanier, -ière.

home-brewed ['həʊmbruːd] *adj* (*beer*) brassé à la maison; (*cider*) de ménage.

homecoming ['həʊmkʌmɪŋ] *n* retour *m* au foyer *ou* à la maison; (*to one's country*) retour au pays.

home-grown ['həʊm'grəʊn] *adj* (*fruits, légumes*) du jardin; (*denrée*) du pays; *Fig* **many people prefer Japanese cars to the h.-g. product,** beaucoup de gens préfèrent les voitures japonaises à celles fabriquées chez eux.

homeland ['həʊmlænd] *n* patrie *f*; (*in South Africa*) bantoustan *m*, homeland *m*.

homeless ['həʊmlɪs] **1** *adj* sans foyer, sans abri; **to be h.**, être sur le pavé. **2** *n* **the h.**, (*used as pl*) les sans-logis *mpl*, les sans-abri *mpl*.

homelessness ['həʊmlɪsnɪs] *n* = fait de ne pas avoir de logis; **h. among the young is growing,** de plus en plus de jeunes sont sans abri.

homeloving ['həʊmlʌvɪŋ] *adj* casanier, -ière.

homely ['həʊmlɪ] *adj* **(a)** (*food*) simple, ordinaire; (*tastes*) modeste; (*atmosphere*) accueillant; **(b)** *Am* (*person*) qui n'est pas spécialement beau.

home-made ['həʊm'meɪd] *adj* (*gâteau, vin*) fait à la maison; (*pain*) de ménage; **the bookshelves looked rather h.**, les étagères semblaient plutôt artisanales.

homemaker ['həʊm'meɪkər] *n Am* **(a)** femme *f ou* homme *m* d'intérieur, ménagère *f*; **(b)** (*social worker*) aide ménagère.

homeopath ['həʊmɪəʊpæθ] *n* homéopathe *mf*.

homeopathic [həʊmɪəʊ'pæθɪk] *adj* homéopathique.

homeopathy [həʊmɪ'ɒpəθɪ] *n* homéopathie *f*.

homer ['həʊmər] *n* **(a)** *Am Baseball F* coup *m* de circuit; **(b)** (*homing pigeon*) pigeon voyageur; **(c)** *Br F* = travail exécuté par un ouvrier à l'insu de son patron.

Homer ['həʊmər] *n* Homère *m*.

Homeric [həʊ'merɪk] *adj* (*poème, rire etc*) homérique.

homesick ['həʊmsɪk] *adj* **(a)** (*for one's country*) nostalgique, qui a le mal du pays; **(b)** (*for one's home*) **a h. little boy,** un petit garçon qui s'ennuie de ses parents; **are you h.?**, tu t'ennuies de chez toi?

homesickness ['həʊmsɪknɪs] *n* mal *m* du pays, nostalgie *f*.

homespun ['həʊmspʌn] **1** *adj* **(a)** (*simple*) simple, sans apprêt; **h. philosophy,** philosophie *f* simple; **(b)** *Tex* (*tissu de laine*) de fabrication domestique; (*drap*) fait *ou* filé à la maison; (*toile*) de ménage. **2** *n Tex* tissu fait à la maison.

homestead ['həʊmsted] *n* **(a)** ferme *f* (*avec dépendances*); **(b)** *US Jur* la concession statutaire de 160 acres.

homeward ['həʊmwəd] **1** *adj* qui se dirige vers sa maison; (*from abroad*) qui se dirige vers son pays; (*of ship*) qui se dirige vers son port d'attache; **h. journey** *or Nau* **voyage,** voyage *m* de retour. **2** *adv* = **HOMEWARDS**.

homeward-bound ['həʊmwəd'baʊnd] *adj Nau* (*navire*) à destination de son port d'attache, retournant au port, sur le retour; (*cargaison*) de retour; **to be h.-b.**, (*of person*) rentrer chez soi.

homewards ['həʊmwədz] *adv* (*to one's house*) vers sa maison, vers sa demeure; (*from abroad*) vers son pays; *Nau* **cargo h.**, cargaison *f* de retour.

homework ['həʊmwɜːk] *n* **(a)** *Sch* devoirs *mpl*; *F* **it was plain that the chairman had not done his h.**, il était évident que le président ne maîtrisait pas son sujet; **(b)** (*paid work*) travail *m* à domicile.

homeworker ['həʊmwɜːkər] *n* travailleur, -euse à domicile.

homey ['həʊmɪ] *adj* accueillant.

homicidal [hɒmɪ'saɪd(ə)l] *adj* homicide, meurtrier.

homicide¹ ['hɒmɪsaɪd] *n* (*criminal*) homicide *mf*.

homicide² *n* (*crime*) homicide *m*; *Jur* **wilful** *or* **culpable h.**, homicide volontaire; meurtre *m*; **justifiable h., h. in self defence,** homicide légitime en état de défense; *esp Am* **three homicides,** trois cas d'homicide.

homily ['hɒmɪlɪ] *n* homélie *f*; **to deliver a h.**, dire *ou* faire une homélie.

homing ['həʊmɪŋ] **1** *adj Tech* directionnel, de radioguidage; **h. device,** appareil *ou* dispositif autodirecteur, autodirecteur *m*; **h. pigeon,** (*bird*) pigeon voyageur. **2** *n* retour *m* au gîte; (*of pigeon*) retour au colombier; (*of aircraft*) (radio-)ralliement *m*; **h. to base,** retour à la base.

hominy ['hɒmɪnɪ] *n Am Culin* maïs concassé et bouilli.

homo ['həʊməʊ] *n F* homosexuel *m*, pédé *m*.

homoeopath, homoepathic *etc* = **HOMEOPATH, HOMEOPATHIC** *etc*.

homogeneity [hɒməʊdʒɪ'niːɪtɪ] *n* homogénéité *f*.

homogeneous [hɒməʊ'dʒiːnɪəs] *adj* homogène.

homogenize [hɒ'mɒdʒənaɪz] *vt* homogénéiser (*du lait*).

homograph ['hɒməgræf] *n* homographe *m*.

homologous [hə'mɒləgəs] *adj Biol Math etc* homologue.

homonym ['hɒmənɪm] *n Ling* homonyme *m*.

homosexual [hɒməʊ'seksjʊəl] *adj & n* homosexuel, -uelle.

homosexuality [hɒməʊseksjʊ'ælɪtɪ] *n* homosexualité *f*.

Hon, the *Br Parl abbr* **the Honourable.**

hone¹ [həʊn] *n* pierre *f* à aiguiser.

hone² *vt* aiguiser, affiler; *Fig* aiguiser (*son humour*); *Fig* **finely honed musicianship,** un sens aigu de la musique.

honest [ˈɒnɪst] *adj* **(a)** (*trustworthy*) honnête, probe, droit; loyal, -aux (*en affaires*); **he has an h. face,** il a une figure d'honnête homme;
(b) (*sincere*) vrai, sincère, de bonne foi; **the h. truth,** la pure vérité; **I gave you an h. answer,** je t'ai répondu de façon sincère; **is that your h. opinion?,** est-ce que c'est ce que tu penses vraiment?; **to be h. (with you),** pour être franc; **if you're h. (with yourself),** si tu étais sincère avec toi-même; **an h. piece of work,** un travail consciencieux; *Sl* **I couldn't help it, h.,** c'était plus fort que moi, je t'assure;
(c) (*legitimate*) juste, légitime; (*moyens*) légitime; **to earn an h. living,** gagner honnêtement sa vie; **an h. day's pay for an h. day's work,** toute peine mérite salaire;
(d) *Old-fashioned & Hum* **to make an h. woman of s.o.,** rendre l'honneur à une femme (*en l'épousant*);
(e) *Old-fashioned* (*usu used condescendingly*) brave, honnête; **they are h. folk,** ce sont de braves gens.

honestly [ˈɒnɪstlɪ] **1** *adv* **(a)** honnêtement; **(b)** (*sincerely*) sincèrement; **quite h.,** en toute sincérité; **I can h. say that ...,** je peux dire franchement que ...; **do you h. believe that?,** est-ce que tu le crois vraiment?; **I didn't do it, h.!,** ce n'est pas moi qui l'ai fait, je t'assure! **2** *int* (*expressing indignation*) **h.! some people!,** y'a des gens, je te jure!

honesty [ˈɒnɪstɪ] *n* **(a)** honnêteté *f*, probité *f*, loyauté *f*; *Prov* **h. is the best policy,** l'honnêteté est la meilleure des tactiques; **(b)** (*sincerity*) véracité *f*, sincérité *f*, bonne foi; franchise *f* (*d'un discours*); **in all h.,** en toute sincérité; **(c)** (*plant*) lunaire *f*, *F* monnaie *f* du pape.

honey [ˈhʌnɪ] *n* **(a)** miel *m*; **clear/thick h.,** miel liquide/grenu; **comb h.,** miel en rayon; **h. coloured,** miellé; **he was all h.,** il a été tout sucre et tout miel; **h. bear,** kinkajou *m*; **(b)** *esp Am* (*term of endearment*) chéri, *f* chérie; **(c)** *esp Am* (*nice person*) amour *m*; (*excellent thing*) bijou *m*; **it's a h. of an apartment,** cet appartement est un bijou.

honeybee [ˈhʌnɪbiː] *n* abeille *f*.

honeybun(ch) [ˈhʌnɪbʌn, -tʃ] *n US F* mon chéri, ma chérie, mon amour.

honeycomb¹ [ˈhʌnɪkəʊm] *n* **(a)** rayon *m* de miel; (*for eating*) gâteau *m* de miel; *Tex* nid *m* d'abeilles; *Geol* **h. structure/formation,** structure/formation alvéolée *ou* alvéolaire; **(b)** (*in metal*) chambre *f*, soufflure *f*.

honeycomb² **1** *vt* cribler (*de petits trous*); *Tex* marquer en nid d'abeilles; **the city was honeycombed with narrow streets,** la ville était un dédale de rues étroites. **2** *vi* (*of metal*) se chambrer, s'affouiller.

honeydew [ˈhʌnɪdjuː] *n* miellée *f*, miellure *f* (*exsudée par les plantes*); **h. melon,** melon *m* d'hiver.

honeyed [ˈhʌnɪd] *adj* (*tones, words*) mielleux; **(b)** (*sweetened with honey*) édulcoré au miel.

honeymoon¹ [ˈhʌnɪmuːn] *n* (*of couple*) & *Fig* lune *f* de miel; **h. (trip),** voyage *m* de noces; **they're on their h.,** ils sont en voyage de noces; **h. couple,** couple *m* en voyage de noces; *Fig* **the h. is over,** la lune de miel est finie.

honeymoon² *vi* aller *ou* être en voyage de noces; **they're honeymooning in Ireland,** ils sont en voyage de noces en Irlande.

honeymooners [ˈhʌnɪmuːnəz] *npl F* couple *m* en voyage de noces.

honeypot [ˈhʌnɪpɒt] *n* pot *m* à miel.

honeysuckle [ˈhʌnɪsʌk(ə)l] *n* (*shrub*) chèvrefeuille *m*.

honk¹ [hɒŋk] *n* **(a)** (*of goose*) cri *m* de l'oie sauvage; **(b)** (*of car horn*) coup *m* de klaxon.

honk² **1** *vi* **(a)** (*of goose, seal etc*) pousser un cri; **(b)** (*of car horn etc*) retentir; *Aut* **she honked twice on the horn,** elle a donné deux coups de klaxon. **2** *vt* **to h. the horn,** klaxonner.

honk³ *vi Br Sl* (*vomit*) dégueuler.

honky [ˈhɒŋkɪ] *n esp Am Offensive Sl* blanc, blanche.

honky-tonk [ˈhɒŋkɪˈtɒŋk] *n Am F* **(a)** (*bar*) **h.-t. (joint),** bouge *m*, bastringue *m*, boui-boui *m*; **(b)** *Mus* musique *f* de bastringue.

honor, honorable *etc US* = **HONOUR, HONOURABLE** *etc.*

honorarium, *pl* **-ia, -iums** [ɒnəˈreərɪəm, -ɪə, -ɪəmz] *n* honoraires *mpl* (*d'un docteur, d'un avocat*).

honorary [ˈɒnərərɪ] *adj* **(a)** (*emploi, service*) honoraire, bénévole; (*président*) d'honneur; *Univ* **h. degree,** grade honorifique *ou* honoris causa; **h. member,** membre *m* honoraire; associé, -ée (*d'un cercle etc*); **h. membership,** honorariat *m*; *Mil* **h. rank,** grade *m* honorifique; **(b)** (*depending on honour*) (*engagement, contrat*) d'honneur.

honorific [ɒnəˈrɪfɪk] *adj* (*épithète*) honorifique.

honour¹, *US* **honor** [ˈɒnər] *n* **(a)** honneur *m*; **in the seat of h.,** assis à la place d'honneur; **to put up a statue in h. of s.o.,** ériger une statue à la gloire de qn; **dinner in your h.,** dîner en votre honneur; *Prov* **h. to whom h. is due, h. where h. is due,** à tout seigneur tout honneur; **in h. of the occasion,** pour l'occasion;
(b) (*privilege*) **to consider it an h. to do sth,** considérer comme un honneur de faire qch; **it is a great h. to be selected for the team,** c'est un grand honneur que d'être sélectionné pour l'équipe; **it was an h. to have worked with her,** ça a été un honneur que de travailler avec elle; **whom have I the h. of addressing?,** à qui ai-je l'honneur de parler?; *Fml* **I don't believe I've had the h. ...,** je ne crois pas avoir eu l'honneur d'être présenté à vous; **we had the h. of a visit from the president,** nous avons eu l'honneur de recevoir la visite du président; **to have the h.,** *Golf* avoir l'honneur; (*at bowls*) avoir la boule; *Fml* **may I have the h.?,** (*at dance*) puis-je avoir l'honneur?, me ferez-vous l'honneur de cette danse?;
(c) (*good name*) **to come out of an affair with h.,** se tirer avec honneur d'une affaire; **she acquitted herself with h.,** (*of player*) elle s'en est tirée honorablement; **their courage does them h.,** leur courage leur fait honneur; **to lose one's h.,** perdre son honneur; **to make (it) a point of h. to do sth,** mettre son (point d')honneur à faire qch; **to be in h. bound to ...,** être obligé par l'honneur à ...; **I felt h. bound to stay,** je sentis que l'honneur me commandait de rester; **man of h.,** homme *m* d'honneur; **debt of h.,** dette *f* d'honneur; **to swear on one's h.,** jurer sur *ou* par sa foi; **to give one's word of h.,** engager sa parole (d'honneur); **on my (word of) h.!,** je vous donne ma parole!, sur l'honneur!; **h. is satisfied,** l'honneur est satisfait;
(d) (*of a woman*) honneur *m*, réputation *f*; **to defend one's h.,** défendre sa réputation;
(e) (*award*) distinction *f* honorifique; **Honours list,** *Univ* palmarès *m*; tableau *m* d'honneur; *Br Admin* = la liste des personnes choisies pour recevoir le titre de MBE etc; **honours course,** programme *m* d'études spécialisées au niveau de la licence; **honours degree,** ≈ licence *f*;
(f) (*civilities*) **to receive s.o. with full honours,** recevoir qn avec tous les honneurs qui lui sont dus; **to do the honours,** (*serve food, pour drinks*) servir; (*do introductions*) faire les présentations; *Mil Hist* **the honours of war,** les honneurs de la guerre; **he was buried with full military honours,** il a été enterré avec tous les honneurs militaires;
(g) *Cards* (*bridge etc*) **honours,** honneurs *mpl* (*as, roi, dame et valet d'atout*);
(h) (*of person*) **to be an h. to one's country,** faire honneur à sa patrie;
(i) (*in title*) *US Jur* **Your** *or* **His H.,** Monsieur le juge;
(j) *Com* **acceptance for h.,** acceptation *f* par intervention.

honour², *US* **honor** *vt* **(a)** honorer (*qn, la mémoire de qn*); *Iron* **the manager honoured us with his presence today,** le directeur nous a fait l'honneur de sa présence aujourd'hui; *Iron* **we are honoured!,** quel honneur!; **(b)** *Fin etc* honorer (*sa signature, Com un effet*); payer, accepter (*un effet*); accepter (*une carte de crédit*).

honourable, *US* **honorable** [ˈɒnərəb(ə)l] **1** *adj* honorable; **he is an h. man,** c'est un homme d'honneur; **to receive h. mention,** recevoir une mention honorable; **are his intentions h.?,** ses intentions sont-elles honorables?; **it's the h. thing to do,** c'est la solution la plus honorable. **2** *n* **(a) the H., the Hon.,** = titre donné aux membres du Parlement britannique; **the H. member for Caithness,** l'honorable député du Caithness; **(b)** = titre donné aux benjamins des familles nobles britanniques; **her fiancé is an h.,** son fiancé est un membre de l'aristocratie.

honourably, *US* **honorably** [ˈɒnərəblɪ] *adv* honorablement; (*to behave etc*) d'une manière honorable; (*to treat prisoners*) décemment.

hooch [huːtʃ] *n Am Sl* (*drink*) gnôle *f*.

hood¹ [hʊd] *n* **(a)** (*of anorak, duffle-coat, monk's etc*) capuchon *m*; (*with eye-holes*) (*of thief, Ku-Klux Klan*) cagoule *f*; (*over hawk's head*) chaperon *m*; **the kidnappers put a h. over her head,** les ravisseurs lui ont couvert la tête d'un sac; **(b)** (*soft top of car*) capote *f*; *US* (*bonnet*) capot *m*; **(c)** (*over cooker, fireplace etc*) hotte *f*; (*of hairdryer*) casque *m*; (*lens hood*) pare-soleil *m*; (*any protective cover, acoustic etc*) couvercle *m*.

hood² *n esp US Sl* (*gangster*) truand *m*; (*ruffian, yobbo*) voyou *m*.

hooded ['hʊdɪd] *adj* **(a)** (*monk*) encapuchonné; (*executioner, thief*) au visage masqué; (*eye*) aux paupières tombantes; (*eyelid*) tombant; **h. men,** cagoulards *mpl*; **(b) h. crow,** corneille mantelée.

hoodlum ['huːdləm] *n esp US* = **HOOD²**.

hoodoo ['huːduː] *n* (*bad luck*) poisse *f*, guigne *f*; (*person*) porte-malheur *m*.

hoodwink ['hʊdwɪŋk] *vt F* berner; **I've been hoodwinked,** je me suis fait avoir; **to h. s.o. into believing sth,** faire croire qch à qn; **I was hoodwinked into signing,** on m'a raconté des bobards pour me faire signer.

hooey ['huːɪ] *n F* **that's all h.,** ce sont des sornettes; **don't talk h.,** arrête de dire des bêtises.

hoof¹, *pl* **hooves** [huːf, huːvz] *n* (*of horse etc*) sabot *m*; (*of devil*) pied fourchu; **500 cattle on the h.,** 500 têtes de bétail sur pied; *US* **h. and mouth disease,** fièvre apteuse.

hoof² *vt F* **to h. it,** aller à pinces; (*to dance*) danser; **to h. s.o. out,** chasser qn à coups de pied.

hoofbeat ['huːfbiːt] *n* **hoofbeats,** (*of horses*) cavalcade *f*.

hoofed [huːft] *adj* (*animal*) à sabots.

hoofer ['huːfər] *n F Hum* danseur *m*, danseuse *f*.

hoo-ha ['huːhɑː] *n F* **there was a lot of h.-ha in the press about ...,** la presse a fait tout un plat de ...; **the announcement caused a great h.-ha at the school,** cette nouvelle a fait beaucoup de bruit à l'école; **when all the h.-ha about the Royal Wedding/government scandal has died down,** quand le mariage princier/le scandale au sein du gouvernement ne sera plus à la une de l'actualité; **now that all the h.-ha is over we can get down to serious business,** maintenant que le calme est revenu nous pouvons nous occuper de choses sérieuses.

hook¹ [hʊk] *n* **(a)** crochet *m*; (*for clothes*) patère *f*; (*for meat*) croc *m*; (*on fishing line*) hameçon *m*; **h. and eye,** agrafe *f*; *Av Nau* **arrester h.,** crosse *f* d'appontage;

(b) *Boxing* crochet *m*; *Golf* hook *m*; **a left/right h.,** un crochet du gauche/droit;

(c) *Geog* pointe *f* de terre; (*larger*) cap *m*; **H. of Holland,** Hoek van Holland;

(d) (*phrases*) **he swallowed it h. line and sinker,** il a tout gobé; **did he fall for it? — yes, h. line and sinker,** est-ce qu'il a marché? — oui, il a tout gobé; **he's fallen for her h. line and sinker,** il est tombé éperdument amoureux d'elle; **we must do it by h. or by crook,** nous devons le faire, coûte que coûte, nous devons à tout prix le faire; **to leave the phone off the h.,** décrocher le *ou* son téléphone; **your phone was off the h.,** tu avais décroché ton téléphone; (*accidentally*) tu avais mal raccroché ton téléphone; **to put the phone back on the h.,** reposer le combiné (sur son support); **that lets you off the h.,** te voilà tiré d'affaire; **thanks for getting me off the h.,** merci de m'avoir tiré d'affaire; **he owned up and got me off the h.,** (*vindicated*) son aveu m'a innocenté; *US Sl* **to get the h.,** (*be sacked*) se faire vider *ou* virer; **to sling one's h.,** foutre le camp; **once she's got her hooks into him ...,** une fois qu'elle lui aura mis le grappin dessus ... .

hook² **1** *vt* **(a)** accrocher (**to sth,** à qch); **to h. the shutters open,** accrocher les volets; **to h. the windows back,** ouvrir les fenêtres et les accrocher; **he got his sweater hooked on a nail/***etc*, il a accroché son tricot à un clou/*etc*; **the two bits of wire had become hooked together,** les deux fils de fer s'étaient pris l'un dans l'autre; **he hooked his legs around the trapeze,** il se suspendit par les jambes au trapèze; **she had her feet hooked up under the chair,** elle avait calé ses pieds sous sa chaise; **h. one end of the wire around ...,** fixer une extrémité du fil de fer autour de ...; **the helicopter hooked him up off the burning roof,** l'hélicoptère est allé le (re)cueillir sur le toit en feu; *Fig F* **she's hooked herself a husband,** elle a décroché un mari; *Fig F* **she'll never manage to h. him,** elle n'arrivera jamais à lui mettre le grappin dessus;

(b) *Boxing* envoyer un crochet à; **to h. s.o. to the jaw,** envoyer un crochet dans la mâchoire de qn; *Golf* faire un hook; *Rugby* (*of hooker*) talonner (*le ballon*); (*in kicking*) envoyer (*le ballon*) à gauche.

2 *vi* **(a)** (*dress etc*) s'agrafer;

(b) *Boxing* envoyer des crochets.

►**hook on** **1** *vi* s'accrocher; **to h. on to s.o.,** s'accrocher à qn. **2** *vtsep* (*caravan to car etc*) accrocher (**to,** à).

►**hook up** **1** *vi* **(a)** (*dress*) s'agrafer; (*wires*) se raccorder; **(b)** *TV etc* **we're now going to h. up with ...,** nous vous proposons maintenant une émission en duplex avec ... . **2** *vtsep* **(a)** (*dress, bra*) agrafer; **could you h. me up please?,** tu peux agrafer mon corsage *ou* soutien-gorge *etc*?; **(b)** (*trailer etc*) accrocher (**to,** à); **(c) to h. up two computers,** connecter deux ordinateurs.

hooked [hʊkt] *adj* **(a)** (*nose*) crochu; **(b)** (*having hooks*) à crochets; **(c) to be h. on,** (*drugs etc*) se droguer à; (*Italian cinema, jazz, tennis etc*) être mordu de, être un fana de; (*person*) être fou de; (*novelist etc*) être un fana de; **he's completely h.,** il est complètement accro.

hookah ['hʊkə] *n* narguilé *m*.

hooker [hʊkər] **(a)** *Rugby* talonneur *m*; **(b)** *F* (*prostitute*) putain *f*.

hookey ['hʊkɪ] *n* = **HOOKY**.

hook-nosed ['hʊknəʊzd] *adj* au nez crochu.

hook-up ['hʊkʌp] *n TV* duplex *m*; (*programme*) émission *f* en duplex; **you can have a direct computer h.-up with your Paris office,** votre ordinateur peut être relié directement à celui de Paris.

hookworm ['hʊkwɜːm] *n* ankylostome *m*.

hooky ['hʊkɪ] *n esp US F* **to play h.,** faire l'école buissonnière.

hooligan ['huːlɪgən] *n* voyou *m*, hooligan *m*.

hooliganism ['huːlɪgənɪz(ə)m] *n* hooliganisme *m*; **the problem of h.,** le problème des voyous.

hoop [huːp] *n* **(a)** (*on barrel*) cercle *m*; (*toy, for skirt, in circus etc*) cerceau *m*; (*in croquet*) arceau *m*; **h. earrings,** anneaux *mpl*, boucles *fpl* d'oreille en forme d'anneau; **(b)** (*coloured ring on plumage, fur etc, stripe*) rayure *f*; (*around animal's neck*) collier *m*; **(c)** *Fig F* **to put s.o. through the hoops,** mettre qn à l'épreuve; (*interrogate*) cuisiner qn; (*accuse*) mettre qn sur la sellette; **to go through the hoops,** passer l'épreuve du feu; **I've really been through the hoops for you,** j'ai sué sang et eau pour toi.

hooped [huːpt] *adj* (*skirt*) à cerceaux.

hoop-la ['huːplɑː] *n* **(a)** jeu *m* des anneaux; **h.-la stall,** stand *m* du jeu des anneaux; **(b)** *US see* **HOO-HA**.

hoopoe ['huːpəʊ] *n* (*bird*) huppe *f*.

hooray [hʊ'reɪ] *int see* **HURRAH**; *Br F* **H. Henry,** fils *m* de famille, jeune homme *m* de la haute.

hoosegow ['huːsgaʊ] *n US Sl* (*prison*) taule *f*.

hoot¹ [huːt] *n* **(a)** (*of owl*) hululement *m*; **(b)** (*mocking*) huée *f*; **hoots of laughter,** des hurlements *mpl* de rire; **she gave a great h. of laughter,** elle partit d'un grand éclat de rire; **(c)** *Aut* coup de klaxon *m*; *Rail* sifflet *m*; *Nau* sirène *f*; **when you hear three hoots on the factory hooter,** quand la sirène de l'usine retentit trois fois; **(d)** *F* **it was a h.!,** c'était tordant!; **he's a h.!,** il est d'un drôle; **(e)** *F* **not to give** *or* **care a h.** *or* **two hoots about s.o./sth;** se ficher éperdument de qn/qch; **I don't give a bloody h.,** je m'en fiche comme de l'an quarante.

hoot² **1** *vi* **(a)** (*of owl*) hululer; **(b) to h. with laughter,** hurler de rire; **they all hooted with derision,** ils poussèrent tous des huées; **(c)** *Aut* klaxonner, donner un coup de klaxon; *Rail* siffler; *Nau* donner un coup de sirène. **2** *vt* (*actor, speaker*) huer; (*play*) siffler; **the speaker was hooted down,** l'orateur fut réduit au silence par les huées générales.

hootenanny ['huːtnænɪ] *n US* improvisation collective de musique folklorique.

hooter ['huːtər] *n* **(a)** *Nau Ind* sirène *f*; *Aut* klaxon *m*; **(b)** *F* (*nose*) pif *m*.

hooting ['huːtɪŋ] *n* **(a)** (*of owl*) hululement *m*; **(b)** (*of person*) (*jeering*) huées *fpl*; (*laughter*) hurlements *mpl* de rire; **(c)** (*of cars*) coups *mpl* de klaxon.

hoover®¹ ['huːvər] *n* aspirateur *m*.

hoover®² **1** *vt* passer à l'aspirateur (*tapis etc*); passer l'aspirateur dans (*pièce*). **2** *vi* passer l'aspirateur.

hoovering ['huːvərɪŋ] *n* **to do the h.,** passer l'aspirateur; **when you've finished with the h.,** quand tu auras passé l'aspirateur; **there's still a lot of h. to do,** nous n'avons pas *ou* je n'ai pas encore fini de passer l'aspirateur.

hooves [huːvz] *npl see* **HOOF¹**.

hop¹ [hɒp] *n Bot* houblon *m*; **hops,** (*for brewing*) le houblon; **h. grower,** houblonnier *m*; **h. field,** houblonnière *f*; **h. picker,** cueilleur, -euse de houblon; **h. picking,** cueillette *f* du houblon.

hop² *n* **(a)** saut *m*; (*on one foot*) saut à cloche-pied; **(b)** *Sp* **h. skip and jump,** triple saut *m*; **(c)** *Fig* **to catch s.o. on the h.,** prendre qn au dépourvu; **to keep s.o. on the h.,** prendre qn au dépourvu; **to keep s.o. on the h.,** ne pas laisser chômer qn; **(d)** *Av* **it's just a short h. from London to Paris,** il n'y a qu'un saut de Londres à Paris; **(e)** *F* (*dance*) soirée dansante.

hop³ **1** *vi* **(a)** sautiller; **to h. on one leg,** sauter à cloche-pied; **(b) to h. out of bed,** sauter du lit; **h. in!,** (*to car etc*) montez!; **I didn't know you'd been hopping into bed with her,** je ne savais pas que tu avais couché avec elle; **he hopped off the bus/his bike,** il sauta du bus/descendit de son vélo; **he hopped on the bus/his bike,** il sauta dans le bus/monta sur son vélo; **I hopped across to France for the weekend,** j'ai fait un saut en France pour le week-end; **she's just hopped out for a second,** elle est sortie deux minutes; **you're always hopping up and down to do something or other,** tu n'arrêtes pas de courir à gauche et à droite; **he's hopped off (with the silver),** il a filé (avec l'argenterie); **h. it!,** fiche le camp!. **2** *vt* **to h. a ride (on a train),** resquiller en train.

►**hop off** *vi Br F* (*clear off*) filer; ficher le camp.

hope[1] [həʊp] *n* **(a)** (*no pl*) espérance *f*, espoir *m*; **to be full of h.,** avoir bon espoir; **to lose h.,** perdre (l')espoir; **there is little/no h. of finding it,** il y a peu d'espoir/aucun espoir de le trouver; **to put one's h. in the future,** compter sur l'avenir; **to live in h. that ...,** caresser l'espoir que ...; *F* **we live in h.!,** c'est l'espoir que fait vivre; *Am* **h. chest,** trousseau *m* (*de mariage*); **the Cape of Good H.,** le cap de Bonne Espérance; **in the h. of ...,** dans l'attente de ..., dans l'espoir de ...;

(b) (*individual instance*) **my last h.,** mon dernier espoir; ma dernière planche de salut; **to have hopes of sth,** avoir qch en vue; **I'm not getting my hopes up,** je ne veux pas commencer à trop espérer; **to have hopes of doing sth,** avoir l'espoir de faire qch; **these events have raised hopes of a peaceful solution,** ces événements ont donné lieu à de plus grands espoirs d'une solution pacifique; **the team's hopes were high,** les espoirs de l'équipe étaient grands; **they had high hopes for their daughter,** ils avaient de grandes espérances pour leur fille; **to set one's hopes on s.o./sth,** mettre tout son espoir en qn/qch; *Iron* **what a h.!, some h.!,** si vous comptez là-dessus!; **she hasn't got a h. (in hell) of winning,** elle n'a aucun espoir de gagner.

hope[2] **1** *vi* espérer; **we must h. against h.,** il faut espérer contre toute espérance; **to h. for sth,** espérer qch; **we'll just have to h. for the best,** nous n'avons plus qu'à espérer que tout aille pour le mieux; **hoped-for victory,** victoire espérée *ou* désirée. **2** *vt* **I h. and pray that ...,** j'espère avec confiance que ...; **I h. to see you again,** j'espère vous revoir; **hoping to hear from you,** (*in letter*) dans l'attente de vos nouvelles; **I was hoping to finish the work today,** j'espérais finir le travail aujourd'hui; **I h. your brother is better,** j'espère que votre frère va mieux; **I h. you may be right,** je souhaite que vous ayez raison.

hopeful ['həʊpfʊl] **1** *adj* **(a)** plein d'espoir; **we must remain h.,** il faut continuer d'espérer; **to be h. that ...,** avoir bon espoir que ...; **(b)** (*promising*) **the situation looks more h.,** la situation est plus encourageante. **2** *n F usu Iron* (*person*) **young h.,** l'espoir *m* de la famille.

hopefully ['həʊpfʊlɪ] *adv* **(a)** (*parler, attendre etc*) avec bon espoir, avec optimisme; **(b)** *F* (*with luck*) **h. the sun will shine tomorrow,** espérons qu'il fera du soleil demain; **do you think he'll come? — h.,** est-ce que vous pensez qu'il viendra? – espérons-le.

hopefulness ['həʊpf(ʊ)lnɪs] *n* **(a)** (*of person*) bon espoir; confiance *f*; **(b)** (*of a situation etc*) bons présages.

hopeless ['həʊplɪs] *adj* **(a)** (*without hope*) sans espoir; désespéré; **h. grief,** douleur *f* inconsolable; **(b)** (*allowing of no hope*) qui ne permet aucun espoir; (*passion etc*) incurable; (*situation*) désespéré; (*projet*) qui n'a aucune chance de réussir; **to be in a h. condition,** (*of patient etc*) être dans un état désespéré; **to give sth up as h.,** renoncer à faire qch; **it is h. to try to ...,** on aurait beau essayer de ...; **(c)** *F* (*very bad*) **I'm a h. singer,** je chante très mal; **you're h.!,** (*you'll never be an artist etc*) tu es épouvantable!; **(d)** *F* (*ivrogne*) incorrigible; **you're h.!,** vous êtes impossible!

hopelessly ['həʊplɪslɪ] *adv* **(a)** (*vivre*) sans espoir; **(b)** (*vaincu*) irrémédiablement; (*amoureux*) sans retour; **h. drunk,** soûl perdu.

hopelessness ['həʊplɪsnɪs] *n* **(a)** (*despair*) désespoir *m*; **(b)** (*of situation*) état désespéré.

hophead ['hɒphed] *n US Sl* toxicomane *mf*, drogué, -ée.

hopper ['hɒpər] *n* **(a)** (*person, animal*) sauteur, -euse; *F* (*insect*) sauterelle *f*; **(b)** *Tech* trémie *f*, huche *f*, hotte *f* (*du moulin*); *Agr* semoir *m*; (*for feeding poultry*) trémie; **h. barge,** marie-salope *f*, *pl* maries-salopes; *Rail* **h. car,** wagon-trémie *m*.

hop-picker ['hɒp'pɪkər] *n Agr* cueilleur, -euse de houblon.

hopping[1] ['hɒpɪŋ] **1** *n* sautillement *m*, sauts *mpl*. **2** *adv F* **to be h. mad,** être fou de colère.

hopping[2] *n* **(a)** (*hop-picking*) cueillette *f* du houblon; **(b)** (*of beer*) houblonnage *m*.

hopscotch ['hɒpskɒtʃ] *n* marelle *f*.

Horace ['hɒrɪs] *n* Horace *m*.

Horatian [hə'reɪʃən] *adj Liter* d'Horace.

horde [hɔːd] *n* (*of barbarians*) *& Fig* horde *f*.

horizon [hə'raɪz(ə)n] *n* horizon *m*; **on the h.,** à l'horizon; **this discovery opens up new horizons,** cette découverte ouvre de nouveaux horizons; **reading broadened my horizons,** la lecture a élargi mes horizons; *Astron Av Nau* **celestial h.,** horizon astronomique; *Av* **artificial h.,** horizon artificiel; **h. bar,** barre *f* d'horizon (*du directeur de vol*).

horizontal [hɒrɪ'zɒnt(ə)l] **1** *adj* horizontal, -aux; *Gym* **h. bar,** barre *f* fixe; *US* **h. increase in salaries of 10%,** augmentation uniforme de 10% sur toutes les rétributions; **I was h. for a few days with the flu,** j'ai été couché *ou* au lit pendant quelques jours avec la grippe. **2** *n* horizontale *f*.

horizontally [hɒrɪ'zɒntəlɪ] *adv* horizontalement.

hormonal [hɔː'məʊn(ə)l] *adj Physiol* hormonal, -aux.

hormone ['hɔːməʊn] *n Physiol* hormone *f*; **h. replacement therapy,** hormonothérapie *f*.

horn[1] [hɔːn] *n* **(a)** corne *f* (*de bétail, de bélier, de limaçon etc*); bois *mpl* (*d'un cerf*); antenne *f* (*de cerf-volant*); aigrette *f* (*d'hibou*); **to draw in one's horns,** (*of animal*) rentrer les cornes; *Fig* (*of person*) restreindre son ardeur, rabattre (de) ses prétentions; **to be on the horns of a dilemma,** être en proie à un dilemme; *Liter* **h. of plenty,** corne d'abondance;

(b) corne *f* (*de la lune*); branche *f* (*d'un estuaire*); *Nau* oreille *f* (*de taquet*); **Cape H., the H.,** le cap Horn; **the h. of Africa,** la péninsule des Somalis;

(c) (*horny matter*) corne *f*; **h. comb,** peigne *m* en corne;

(d) *Mus* cor *m*, cornet *m*; *F* (*brass or woodwind instrument*) cor; **English/French h.,** cor anglais/d'harmonie; **hunting h.,** trompe *f* de chasse; **to sound** *or* **blow the h.,** sonner du cor; *Am* **to blow one's own h.,** se vanter; **h. player,** cor, corniste *m*; **h. section,** (*in popular music*) les cors;

(e) (*on car*) klaxon *m*; **to sound one's h.,** klaxonner;

(f) pavillon *m* (*de haut parleur*).

horn[2] *vt* (*gore*) encorner (*qn*), donner un coup de corne à (*qn*).

►**horn in** *vi* (*interrupt, intrude*) intervenir sans façon (**on a conversation,** dans une conversation); **I don't want him horning in on this deal,** je ne veux pas qu'il s'immisce dans cette affaire.

hornbeam ['hɔːnbiːm] *n* (*tree*) charme *m*.

hornbill ['hɔːnbɪl] *n* (*bird*) calao *m*.

horned [hɔːnd, *Lit* 'hɔːnɪd] *adj* (*animal*) à cornes; (*snake etc*) cornu.

hornet ['hɔːnɪt] *n* (*insect*) frelon *m*; *Fig* **to stir up a h.'s nest,** tomber dans un guêpier.

hornpipe ['hɔːnpaɪp] *n Nau Mus* matelote *f*.

horn-rimmed ['hɔːnrɪmd] *adj* (*lunettes*) à monture en corne.

horny ['hɔːnɪ] *adj* **(a)** (*like horn*) corné; (*beak etc*) de corne, en corne; (*hand etc*) calleux; **to grow h.,** se racornir; **(b)** *Sl* (*lustful*) lascif; (*sexually aroused*) (sexuellement) excité; **to feel h.,** être d'humeur lascive; (*of man*) être chaud lapin.

horology [hɒ'rɒlədʒɪ] *n* **(a)** (*clockmaking*) horlogerie *f*; **(b)** (*measuring time*) horométrie *f*.

horoscope ['hɒrəskəʊp] *n* horoscope *m*; **to cast s.o.'s h.,** faire *ou* dresser l'horoscope de qn; **my h. said that ...,** (*in newspaper etc*) d'après mon horoscope ... .

horrendous [hɒ'rendəs] *adj F* terrible, affreux, horrible.

horrendously [hɒ'rendəslɪ] *adv* (*expensive etc*) terriblement, affreusement, horriblement.

horrible ['hɒrəb(ə)l] *adj* **(a)** horrible, affreux, atroce; (*bruit*) épouvantable; (*temps*) abominable; **how h.!,** quelle horreur!; **(b) = HORRID (b).**

horribly ['hɒrɪblɪ] *adv* **(a)** horriblement, affreusement; **(b) = HORRIDLY (b).**

horrid ['hɒrɪd] *adj* **(a)** horrible, affreux; **h. sight,** chose *f* horrible à voir; **(b)** *F* (*nasty*) méchant; **to be h. to s.o.,** être méchant envers qn; **to say h. things about s.o.,** dire des méchancetés de qn; **don't be h.!,** ne sois pas désagréable!

horridly ['hɒrɪdlɪ] *adv* **(a)** affreusement; **(b)** *F* (*se conduire*) méchamment.

horrific [hɒ'rɪfɪk, hə-] *adj* horrible; **h. injuries,** blessures horribles.

horrify ['hɒrɪfaɪ] *vt* horrifier (*qn*).

horrifying ['hɒrɪfaɪɪŋ] *adj* horrifiant.

horror ['hɒrər] *n* **(a)** horreur *f*; **paralysed with h.,** glacé d'horreur; **to my h.,** à ma grande horreur; **to have a h. of s.o./sth/doing sth,** avoir horreur de qn/qch/faire qch; **he had a h. of being seen naked,** il avait horreur qu'on le voie nu; **h. film,** film *m* d'épouvante; *Liter* **h. story,** histoire *f* d'horreur; *F* **h. stories about hotels where nothing**

worked, des histoires terribles sur des hôtels où rien ne marchait; **(b)** (*terrifying thing*) horreur *f*; **Chamber of Horrors,** Chambre *f* des Horreurs (*d'un musée*); **that child's a little h.,** cet enfant est un petit monstre; *F* **to have the horrors,** grelotter de peur; **it gives me the horrors,** cela me donne le frisson.

horror-stricken, -struck ['hɒrəstrɪk(ə)n, -strʌk] *adj* saisi *ou* glacé *ou* frappé d'horreur.

horse [hɔːs] *n* **(a)** cheval *m*, -aux; *Horseracing* **to put some money on the horses,** jouer aux courses; **draught h.,** cheval de trait; **saddle h.,** cheval de selle, monture *f*; **to mount a h.,** monter à cheval, monter un cheval; **to fall off one's h.,** tomber de cheval; *Fig F* **to get on one's high h.,** monter sur ses grands chevaux; *F* **to eat like a h.,** manger comme un ogre; **I could eat a h.!,** j'ai une faim de loup!; *Fig* **to hear sth from the h.'s mouth,** apprendre qch de source sûre; *F* **hold your horses!,** du calme, du calme!; **sea h.,** (*fish*) hippocampe *m*; **white horses,** (*waves*) vagues *fpl* à crêtes d'écume; **wooden h.,** cheval de bois; **rocking h.,** cheval à bascule; **h. blanket** *or* **rug,** couverture *f* de cheval; **h. brass,** médaillon *m* de cuivre (*fixé sur l'harnachement du cheval*); **h. chestnut,** marron *m* d'Inde; (*tree*) marronier *m* d'Inde; **h. collar,** collier *m* de cheval; **h. dealer** *or* **trader,** maquignon *m*; *F* **h. doctor,** vétérinaire *m*; **h. fair,** foire *f* aux chevaux; **h. laugh,** gros rire bruyant; **h. meat,** viande *f* de cheval; *Am Cin TV* **h. opera,** western *m*; **h. sense,** gros bon sens; **h. racing,** courses *fpl* de chevaux; **h. riding,** équitation *f*; **h. show,** concours *m* hippique; **h. trading,** maquignonnage *m*;
(b) (*in breeding*) cheval mâle, cheval entier; **stud h.,** étalon *m*; **to take a mare to h.,** faire couvrir une jument;
(c) *Mil Hist* (*used as pl*) cavalerie *f*; troupes montées; **regiment of h.,** régiment *m* de cavalerie; **h. artillery,** artillerie montée; **the (Royal) H. Guards,** la Garde Royale (à cheval);
(d) *Gym* **(vaulting) h.,** cheval(-sautoir) *m*; **pommel h.,** cheval d'arçons;
(e) (*for sawing*) chevalet *m*, tréteau *m*, chèvre *f*;
(f) *Nau* (*rope*) marchepied *m*;
(g) *MecE F* = **HORSEPOWER**;
(h) *Sl* (*heroin*) héro *f*.

►**horse about, horse around** *vi* (*play roughly*) se livrer à des jeux brutaux.

-horse [hɔːs] *suff* **one/two/***etc***-h.,** à un cheval/deux chevaux/*etc*; *see* **ONE-HORSE**.

horseback ['hɔːsbæk] *n* **on h.,** à (dos de) cheval; **to ride on h.,** aller à cheval.

horsebox ['hɔːsbɒks] *n* (*trailer*) van *m*; *Rail* wagon *m* à chevaux, wagon-écurie *m*, *pl* wagons-écuries.

horsebreaker ['hɔːsbreɪkər] *n* dresseur, -euse de chevaux.

horse-drawn ['hɔːsdrɔːn] *adj* tiré par des chevaux; **h.-d. vehicle,** véhicule attelé.

horseflesh ['hɔːsfleʃ] *n* **(a)** (*horses*) chevaux *mpl*; **(b)** chair *f ou* viande *f* de cheval.

horsefly ['hɔːsflaɪ] *n* taon *m*.

horsehair ['hɔːsheər] *n* crin *m* (de cheval); *Tex* tissu *m* de crin; **h. mattress,** matelas *m* de crin.

horseman, *pl* **-men** ['hɔːsmən] *n* cavalier *m*, écuyer *m*; **to be a good h.,** bien monter à cheval, être bon cavalier; **the four horsemen of the apocalypse,** les quatre cavaliers de l'apocalypse.

horsemanship ['hɔːsmənʃɪp] *n* équitation *f*; l'art *m* de monter à cheval; **we admired her h.,** nous avons admiré l'art avec lequel elle montait à cheval.

horseplay ['hɔːspleɪ] *n* brutalité *f*; **it's just harmless h.,** c'est une bagarre pour rire; **no h.!,** doucement!, pas de brutalité!, jeux de mains, jeux de vilains!

horsepower ['hɔːspaʊər] *n MecE etc* puissance *f* en chevaux; (*measurement*) cheval-vapeur *m*, *pl* chevaux-vapeur; **brake h.,** puissance au frein; **actual h.,** puissance effective en chevaux.

horseradish ['hɔːsrædɪʃ] *n* (*plant*) raifort *m*; *Culin* **h. sauce,** sauce *f* au raifort.

horseshoe ['hɔːsʃuː, 'hɔːʃ-] *n* fer *m* à cheval; **h. brooch/table/***etc*, broche *f*/table *f*/*etc* en (forme de) fer à cheval.

horsewhip¹ ['hɔːswɪp] *n* cravache *f*.

horsewhip² *vt* (**-pp-**) cravacher, cingler (*qn*).

horsewoman, *pl* **-women** ['hɔːswʊmən, -wɪmɪn] *n* cavalière *f*, amazone *f*, écuyère *f*; **she's a good h.,** elle est bonne cavalière.

horsy, horsey ['hɔːsɪ] *adj* **(a)** chevalin; **h. face,** figure chevaline; **(b)** (*person*) fou, *f* folle de chevaux; **she's terribly h.,** elle ne parle que chevaux.

horticultural [hɔːtɪ'kʌltʃər(ə)l] *n* (*outil*) horticole, d'horticulture; **h. show,** exposition *f* d'horticulture.

horticulture ['hɔːtɪkʌltʃər] *n* horticulture *f*.

horticulturist [hɔːtɪ'kʌltʃərɪst] *n* horticulteur *m*.

hose¹ [həʊz] *n* **(a)** (*pl* **hoses**) tuyau *m*; **fire h.,** tuyau de pompe à incendie; **garden h.,** tuyau d'arrosage; **h. reel,** chariot *m* à tuyaux; *MecE* **(flexible) h.,** tuyau flexible, durite *f*; **air h.,** tuyau d'air flexible; **(b)** (*no pl*) *Com* (*for women*) bas *mpl*; *Hist* (*for men*) chausses *fpl*; **half h.,** chaussettes *fpl* (*d'hommes*).

hose² *vt* **(a)** laver (*la voiture*) au jet; **(b)** arroser (*un gazon etc*) (au jet d'eau).

►**hose down** *vtsep* = **HOSE² (a)**.

►**hose out** *vtsep* (*clean out*) laver au jet.

hosepipe ['həʊzpaɪp] *n* tuyau *m*, flexible *m* (*de lavage, d'incendie etc*); **h. ban,** = interdiction d'utiliser les tuyaux d'arrosage pendant les périodes de sécheresse.

hosier ['həʊzɪər] *n Com* bonnetier, -ière.

hosiery ['həʊzɪərɪ] *n Com* **h. (trade),** bonneterie *f*; **h. counter** *or* **department,** rayon *m* des bas et chaussettes.

hospice ['hɒspɪs] *n* (*for terminally ill*) hospice *m*, mouroir *m*.

hospitable [hɒs'pɪtəb(ə)l] *adj* (*climate*) hospitalier; (*climate, person*) accueillant.

hospitably [hɒs'pɪtəblɪ] *adv* avec hospitalité.

hospital ['hɒspɪt(ə)l] *n* **(a)** hôpital *m*, -aux; **to be in h.,** être à l'hôpital; **she had to go (in) to h.** *or US* **the h.,** elle a dû aller à l'hôpital; **to send s.o. to h.** *or US* **the h.,** hospitaliser qn; **teaching h.,** = centre hospitalier universitaire; **h. bed,** lit *m* d'hôpital; **h. train,** train *m* sanitaire; **h. ship,** navire-hôpital *m*, *pl* navires-hôpitaux; **h. treatment/staff,** traitement/personnel hospitalier; **(b) Chelsea H.,** l'hôpital *m* de Chelsea (*pour les vieux soldats*); **Greenwich H.,** l'Hospice *m* de Greenwich (*pour les invalides de la marine*).

hospitality [hɒspɪ'tælɪtɪ] *n* hospitalité *f*; *Old-fashioned Euph* **to enjoy His** *or* **Her Majesty's h.,** faire de la prison.

hospitalization [hɒspɪtəlaɪ'zeɪʃən] *n* hospitalisation *f* (*des malades*).

hospitalize ['hɒspɪtəlaɪz] *vt* hospitaliser (*un malade*).

host¹ [həʊst] *n* **(a)** (*in private house*) hôte *m*; (*in hotel etc*) hôtelier *m*; aubergiste *m*; *TV etc* (*of chat show etc*) présentateur, -trice; **he was the perfect h.,** il a été un hôte parfait; **(b)** *Biol* hôte *m*; **(c)** *Comptr* **h. computer,** ordinateur-serveur *m*.

host² *vt esp US* recevoir (*qn*), donner l'hospitalité à (*qn*); *TV etc* animer, présenter (*un programme etc*).

host³ *n* **(a)** (*great number*) **a (whole) h.,** (toute) une armée (*de domestiques etc*); **a h. of good restaurants,** une quantité de bons restaurants; **(b)** *Arch & Lit* armée *f*, multitude *f*, foule *f*.

host⁴ *n Rel* hostie *f*.

hostage ['hɒstɪdʒ] *n* otage *m*; **as (a) h.,** en otage, pour otage; **to take s.o. h.,** prendre quelqu'un en otage; **she is being held h.,** elle est gardée en otage; **h. taker,** preneur, -euse d'otage; **h. taking,** prise *f* d'otage(s).

hostel ['hɒstəl] *n* **(a)** (*for the homeless, students*) foyer *m*; **(b)** (*for accommodation*) **youth h.,** auberge *f* de jeunesse.

hosteller, *US* **hosteler** ['hɒstələr] *n* **(youth) h.,** ajiste *mf*.

hostelling, *US* **hosteling** ['hɒstəlɪŋ] *n* **(youth) h.,** ajisme *m*.

hostelry ['hɒstəlrɪ] *n Arch & Br Hum* hostellerie *f*.

hostess ['həʊstɪs] *n* **(a)** (*in private house*) hôtesse *f*; (*in hotel etc*) hôtelière *f*; aubergiste *f*; *TV etc* (*of chat show etc*) animatrice *f*, présentatrice *f*; (*in night club*) entraîneuse *f*; **(b)** *Av* **(air) h.,** hôtesse *f* de l'air.

hostile ['hɒstaɪl, *Am* 'hɒst(ə)l] **1** *adj* (*attitude, climate, environment*) hostile; (*acte*) d'hostilité; (*opposed*) hostile, opposé (**to,** à); **to be h. to s.o.,** être hostile à *ou* envers qn; *St Exch* **h. takeover,** prise *f* de contrôle inamicale. **2** *n US* ennemi *m*.

hostility [hɒs'tɪlɪtɪ] *n* **(a)** hostilité *f* (**to,** contre); **to feel no h. towards s.o.,** n'avoir aucune animosité contre qn; **(b) hostilities,** (*war*) hostilités *fpl*.

hot [hɒt] **1** *adj* (**hotter, hottest**) **(a)** chaud; (*soleil*) ardent; (*feu*) vif; **boiling h.,** bouillant; **burning h.,** brûlant; **to be very h.,** (*of person*) avoir très chaud; (*of water etc*) être très chaud; (*of weather*) faire très chaud; **it was a h. day,** il faisait chaud; **to get** *or* **grow h.,** (*of person*) commencer à avoir chaud; (*of water etc*) devenir chaud, chauffer; (*of weather*) commencer à faire chaud; (*of discussion, contest*) s'échauffer; **to keep a dish h.,** tenir un plat au chaud; *Med* **h. flush,** rougeur brûlante, vive rougeur; *Geol* **h. spring,** source *f* d'eau chaude; *Fig* **to be in h. water,** être dans le pétrin; *Fig* **to get into h. water,**

s'attirer *ou* se créer des ennuis; *F* **it's all h. air,** ce ne sont que des balivernes; *F* **he's full of h. air,** il ne raconte que des foutaises; **a h. meal,** un repas chaud; *Am* **h. cake,** petit pain; **to sell like h. cakes,** se vendre comme des petits pains; *Br* **h. cross bun,** = petit pain à la canelle (*qu'on mange le vendredi saint*); **h. dog,** hot-dog *m*; *Fig* **h. potato,** sujet délicat; *Fig* **to drop s.o. like a h. potato,** laisser tomber qn comme une vieille chaussette *ou* savate;

(b) *Culin* (*spicy etc*) (*poivre*) fort; (*moutarde*) piquant; (*assaisonnement*) épicé; **not all Indian food is h.,** la cuisine indienne n'est pas nécessairement épicée;

(c) (*fresh*) **cakes h. from the oven,** gâteaux sortant du four; **news h. from the press,** nouvelles sortant tout droit de la presse, nouvelles de dernière heure;

(d) (*close*) **to be h. on the scent** *or* **trail,** être sur la bonne piste (*d'un animal, d'un criminel*); **to be in h. pursuit of s.o.,** poursuivre qn de près; **you're getting h.,** (*in guessing game*) tu brûles; *Phys* **h. spot,** point chaud;

(e) (*angry, emotional*) violent; **to have a h. temper,** s'emporter facilement; **h. words,** paroles violentes; *F* **to get all h. and bothered,** devenir tout rouge (d'embarras); *Fig* **to get h. under the collar,** (*with embarrassment*) être embarrassé; (*with anger*) se mettre en colère; **h. tears,** larmes cuisantes;

(f) *F* (*good*) super, sensationnel; **I'm not very h. on history,** je ne suis pas très calé en histoire; **they're not very h. on hygiene,** ils ne sont pas très portés sur l'hygiène; **that record wasn't so h.,** ce disque n'était pas super; **he's h. stuff at tennis,** au tennis c'est un as; **to be h. stuff,** (*of woman*) être canon; (*of man*) être super (bien); **how are you? — not so h.,** comment ça va? — ce n'est pas terrible *ou* fameux;

(g) *Horseracing etc* **h. favourite,** grand favori; **h. tip,** tuyau *m* increvable;

(h) (*dangerous, difficult*) délicat; (*stolen property etc*) recherché par la police; **the place was getting too h. for me,** je me trouvais dans un véritable guêpier; **the situation was too h. to handle,** la situation était trop délicate pour qu'on s'en mêle; **to make things** *or* **it too h. for s.o.,** rendre la vie infernale à qn; **the presence of the army made things h. for the smugglers,** la présence de l'armée a rendu les choses très difficiles pour les contrebandiers; *Fig* **h. seat,** (*difficult position*) situation *f* difficile; *US F* (*electric chair*) chaise *f* électrique; **h. spot,** (*dangerous area*) quartier chaud (*d'une ville*); (*night club*) boîte *f* de nuit;

(i) *Tel* **h. line,** ligne directe; (*USA to Kremlin*) téléphone rouge; (*Élysée to Kremlin*) téléphone vert;

(j) (*colour*) trop vif;

(k) *Aut F* **h. rod,** voiture gonflée, bolide *m*;

(l) *Nucl Phys* radioactif.

(m) *Fin* **h. money,** capitaux *mpl* fébriles.

2 *adv* **to blow h. and cold,** pratiquer la douche écossaise, être d'humeur changeante.

▸**hot up** *F* **1** *vtsep* (*heat*) chauffer (*qch*); *Aut* gonfler (*un moteur*); **to h. up the pace,** (*increase*) forcer l'allure. **2** *vi* (*of campaign etc*) s'échauffer; (*of affair etc*) chauffer; (*of competition*) s'intensifier; **things are beginning to h. up,** l'affaire se corse.

hot-air ['hɒteər] *adj Av* **h.-a. balloon,** montgolfière *f*, ballon *m* à air chaud.

hotbed ['hɒtbed] *n* **(a)** (*in gardening*) couche *f* (*de fumier, de terreau*); **(b)** *Fig* (*of rebellion, intrigue etc*) foyer *m*.

hot-blooded ['hɒt'blʌdɪd] *adj* ardent, passionné; (*race*) au sang fougueux; **to be h.-b.,** avoir le sang chaud.

hotchpotch ['hɒtʃpɒtʃ] *n* mélange confus; **this book's a bit of a h.,** ce livre est de qualité inégale.

hot-dog ['hɒtdɒg] *vi Ski* faire du ski acrobatique.

hot-dogging ['hɒtdɒgɪŋ] *n* ski *m* acrobatique.

hotel [həʊ'tel] *n* hôtel *m*; **private** *or* **residential h.,** = pension de famille; **h. bedroom,** chambre *f* d'hôtel; **h. keeper,** hôtelier, -ière; **the h. trade,** l'industrie hôtelière, l'hôtellerie *f*.

hotelier [həʊ'teljeɪ] *n* hôtelier *m*.

hotfoot¹ ['hɒt'fʊt] *adv* (*s'en aller, arriver*) à toute vitesse, en (toute) hâte.

hotfoot² *vt* **to h. it,** galoper à toute vitesse.

hothead ['hɒthed] *n* exalté, -ée, tête brûlée.

hot-headed ['hɒt'hedɪd] *adj* (*rash*) exalté, impétueux, à la tête chaude; (*quick-tempered*) emporté, violent.

hothouse ['hɒthaʊs] *n* serre chaude; **h. plant,** plante *f* de serre chaude; *Fig* (*person*) plante de serre.

hotly ['hɒtlɪ] *adv* **(a)** (*répondre, protester*) vivement; **(b)** (*poursuivre*) avec acharnement; (*close behind*) de près; **h. contested,** chaudement disputé.

hotplate ['hɒtpleɪt] *n* (*on cooker*) plaque chauffante; (*portable*) chauffe-plats *m inv*.

hotpot ['hɒtpɒt] *n esp Br Culin* = ragoût de viande aux pommes de terre, cuit à l'étuvée.

hots [hɒts] *npl Sl* **to have the h. for s.o.,** (*of woman*) mouiller pour qn; (*of man*) bander pour qn.

hot-shoe ['hɒt'ʃuː] *n Phot* sabot-contact *m*.

hotshot ['hɒtʃɒt] *US F* **1** *adj* magnifique, terrible; **a h. chess player,** un joueur d'échecs super-doué. **2** *n* (*person*) as *m*, crack *m*.

hot-tempered ['hɒt'tempəd] *adj* colérique, coléreux; vif.

Hottentot ['hɒt(ə)ntɒt] **1** *adj* hottentot. **2** *n* Hottentot, -ote.

hot-water [hɒt'wɔːtər] *n* **h.-w. bottle,** bouillotte *f*.

hound¹ [haʊnd] *n* **(a)** (*dog*) chien *m*; (*in hunting*) chien de meute; **the pack of hounds, the hounds,** la meute, l'équipage *m*; **master of hounds,** maître *m* d'équipage; grand veneur; **to ride to hounds,** chasser (le renard); chasser à courre; **(b)** *Sp* coureur *m*, poursuivant *m* (*dans un rallye-paper*); **(c)** *F Pej* (*person*) canaille *f*.

hound² *vt* (*hunt*) chasser (*le gibier*) au chien courant; *Fig* **she was hounded by the press,** elle était traquée *ou* pourchassée *ou* poursuivie (par la presse); **hounded from place to place,** pourchassé d'un endroit à l'autre; **he was hounded out of France,** il fut chassé de France.

▸**hound down** *vtsep* poursuivre (*qn*) avec acharnement, traquer (*qn*).

hour ['aʊər] *n* **(a)** heure *f*; **an h. and a half,** une heure et demie; **half an h.,** *esp Am* **a half hour,** une demi-heure; **a quarter of an h.,** un quart d'heure; **h. by h.,** d'heure en heure; **to pay s.o. by the h.,** payer qn à l'heure; **to be paid £5 an h.,** être payé 5 livres de l'heure; *Ind etc* **output per h.,** puissance *f* horaire; **there's a train every h., on the h.,** il y a un train toutes les heures à l'heure juste; **to take hours over sth,** mettre des heures à faire qch; *F* **we've been waiting hours,** ça fait des heures que nous attendons; **office hours,** heures de bureau; **what are your hours?, what hours do you work?,** quels sont vos horaires de travail?; **to work long hours,** faire de longues journées (de travail); **after hours,** *Br* (*of pub, shop*) après l'heure de la fermeture; (*of office*) après les heures de travail; *Rel* **Book of Hours,** livre *m* d'Heures; **h. hand,** petite aiguille (*de montre, de pendule*);

(b) (*time of day*) **the small hours,** les premières heures (après minuit); **well on into the small hours,** très avant dans la nuit; **people come and go at all hours,** les gens vont et viennent à toute heure; **till all hours,** jusqu'à des heures impossibles; **to keep late hours,** rentrer à des heures indues; (*go to bed late*) se coucher très tard;

(c) (*moment*) l'heure *f*, le moment; **in the h. of need/death,** à l'heure du besoin/de la mort; **his h. has come,** son heure est venue; **her last hours,** ses dernières heures; **he was the man of the h.,** c'était l'homme du moment.

-hour [aʊər] *suff* **one/two/***etc***-h.,** d'une/de deux/*etc* heure(s); **an eight-h. day,** une journée (de travail) de huit heures; **a 30-h. week,** une semaine de trente heures; **a three-h. delay,** un retard de trois heures.

hourglass ['aʊəglɑːs] *n* sablier *m*.

hourlong ['aʊəlɒŋ] *adj* (*meeting*) d'une heure.

hourly ['aʊəlɪ] **1** *adj* de toutes les heures; (*service de trains etc*) à chaque heure; (*débit, rendement, salaire*) horaire, à l'heure; **at h. intervals,** toutes les heures. **2** *adv* toutes les heures; d'heure en heure.

-hourly ['aʊəlɪ] *suff* **two/three/***etc***-h.,** toutes les deux/trois/*etc* heures.

house¹, *pl* **houses** [haʊs, 'haʊzɪz] *n* **(a)** maison *f*; **country h.,** manoir *m*; **private h.,** maison particulière; **we invited him to our h.,** nous l'avons invité à venir chez nous; **from h. to h.,** de porte en porte; **to keep h. for s.o.,** tenir *ou* diriger la maison de qn; **to keep open h.,** tenir table ouverte; **to set up h.,** se mettre en ménage; **the government should put its own h. in order before criticizing others,** le gouvernement devrait balayer devant sa porte avant d'aller voir chez les autres; **they got on like a h. on fire,** ils se sont immédiatement entendus comme larrons en foire; *Br F* **the bus goes all round the houses,** le bus suit un itinéraire très long et peu direct; *Fig F* **to go all round the houses,** tourner autour du pot; **the son/daughter of the h.,** le fils/la fille de la maison; **to move h.,** déménager; **h. of cards,** château *m* de cartes; **h. agent,** agent immobilier; **h. arrest,** assignation *f* à domicile; **to be placed under h. arrest,** être placé en résidence surveillée (à son domicile); **h. guest,** invité *m*; **h. martin,** (*bird*) hirondelle *f* des fenêtres; **h. painter,** peintre *m* en bâtiments; peintre décorateur; **h. party,** partie *f* de campagne; (*guests*) les invités *mpl* à une partie de campagne; **h. plant,** plante *f* d'intérieur, plante d'appartement;

(b) (*institution*) **the h. of God,** la maison de Dieu; **h. of prayer** *or* **worship,** église *f*; (*protestant*) temple *m*; *Br Parl* **the H. of Commons/Lords,** la Chambre des Communes/des Lords; *Br Parl* **the Houses of Parliament,** le Parlement; *US & Austr* **the H. of Representatives,** ≈ l'Assemblée Nationale; **bill before the H.,** loi en cours de vote;

(c) *Com etc* (*company*) maison *f*; **publishing h.,** maison d'édition; *Nau* **h. flag,** pavillon *m* d'armateur *ou* de compagnie (de navigation); **h. organ,** journal *m* de société;

(d) (*restaurant etc*) **to have a drink on the h.,** prendre une consommation aux frais du patron; **h. rule,** règle *f* de la maison; **h. speciality,** *F* **h. special,** spécialité *f* (de la) maison; **h. wine,** vin *m* de la maison; **h. phone,** (*in hotel*) téléphone intérieur;

(e) *Br Sch* (*in boarding school*) maison *f* d'élèves; (*in day school*) groupement *m* d'élèves (*qui rivalise avec un autre pour les activités sportives etc*);

(f) *Med* **h. surgeon/physician,** chirurgien *m*/médecin *m* de permanence (*dans un hôpital*);

(g) *Astrol* maison *f*;

(h) *Tech* cabine *f* (*d'une grue*); *Nau* rouf *m* (*sur le pont*); kiosque *m* (*de la barre etc*); **hen h.,** poulailler *m*;

(i) (*household*) maison *f*; (*dynasty*) famille *f*, maison, dynastie *f*; **the whole h. was down with flu,** toute la maison avait la grippe; *Parl etc* **to make a h.,** (*of assembly*) être en nombre;

(j) **the H. of Stuart/Bourbon,** les Stuarts *mpl*/les Bourbons *mpl*;

(j) *Th* salle *f*, auditoire *m*, assistance *f*; **a full h.,** une salle pleine; **'h. full',** 'complet'; **to play to an empty h.,** jouer devant des banquettes vides, jouer dans *ou* devant une salle vide; **there wasn't a dry eye in the h.,** tout le monde pleurait dans la salle; *Cin* **the first h.,** la première séance; **h. lights,** éclairages *mpl* de la salle.

house² [haʊz] *vt* loger, héberger (*qn*); pourvoir au logement de (*la population*); faire rentrer (*les troupeaux*); rentrer, engranger (*le blé*); mettre à l'abri *ou* à couvert (*une locomotive etc*); emmagasiner (*un avion etc*); *Nau* rentrer (*une voile*).

houseboat ['haʊsbəʊt] *n* péniche *f* (aménagée).

housebound ['haʊsbaʊnd] *adj* obligé de rester à la maison; (*invalid*) immobilisé à la maison.

housebreaker ['haʊsbreɪkər] *n* (*burglar*) voleur *m* avec effraction; cambrioleur *m*.

housebreaking ['haʊsbreɪkɪŋ] *n* (*burglary*) vol *m* avec effraction; cambriolage *m*.

housecoat ['haʊskəʊt] *n* robe *f* d'intérieur.

housefly ['haʊsflaɪ] *n* mouche domestique *ou* commune.

houseful ['haʊsfʊl] *n* **to have a h. of guests,** avoir sa maison pleine d'invités.

household ['haʊshəʊld] *n* **(a)** (*people living in a house*) (membres *mpl* de la) maison *f*; famille *f*; ménage *m*; **h. articles,** articles ménagers; **h. expenses,** frais *mpl* de *ou* du ménage; **h. duties,** (affaires *fpl* du) ménage; **h. goods,** meubles *mpl*, mobilier *m*; **'not for h. use',** (*on industrial cleaning product etc*) usage industriel uniquement; **her name is a h. word, she is a h. name,** son nom est connu de tous; **(b)** (*servants*) les domestiques *mfpl*; **to have a large h.,** avoir une nombreuse domesticité; **the H.,** la Maison du souverain; **the H. troops,** la Garde.

householder ['haʊshəʊldər] *n* (*owner*) propriétaire *mf* (d'une maison); (*tenant*) locataire *mf*.

househusband ['haʊs'hʌzbənd] *n* homme *m* au foyer.

housekeeper ['haʊskiːpər] *n* femme *f* de charge; gouvernante *f* (*d'un prêtre etc*); économe *f*, intendante *f* (*d'un château etc*); **to be a good h.,** être bonne maîtresse de maison.

housekeeping ['haʊskiːpɪŋ] *n* économie *f* domestique; (*work*) les soins *mpl* du ménage; **she knows nothing of h.,** ce n'est pas une femme d'intérieur; **h. book,** carnet *m* de dépenses; **h. (allowance** *or* **money),** l'argent *m* pour le ménage.

housemaid ['haʊsmeɪd] *n* bonne *f*, femme *f* de chambre; *F* **h.'s knee,** hygroma *m* du genou.

houseman, *pl* **-men** ['haʊsmən] *n Br Med* interne *m* (*d'un hôpital*).

housemaster, housemistress ['haʊsmɑːstər, -mɪstrɪs] *n Br Sch* (*in boarding school*) = professeur chargé de la surveillance d'un internat; (*in day school*) = professeur chargé d'un groupe d'élèves.

house-proud ['haʊspraʊd] *adj* **she is very h.-p.,** c'est une femme d'intérieur méticuleuse; *Pej* c'est une véritable maniaque du ménage.

houseroom ['haʊsruːm] *n* place *f* (*pour loger qn, qch*); logement *m*; *F* **I wouldn't give it h.,** je n'en voudrais pas quand même on me le donnerait.

house-sit ['haʊs'sɪt] *vi esp Am* **we used to h.-s. for them,** nous nous occupions de leur maison pendant leur absence.

house-to-house ['haʊstə'haʊs] *adj* (*quête, vente etc*) à domicile; **h.-to-h. canvassing,** le porte à porte; **the police made a h.-to-h. search,** la police a fait une fouille maison par maison.

housetop ['haʊstɒp] *n* toit *m*; *F* **to proclaim sth from the housetops,** crier qch sur tous les toits.

house-train ['haʊstreɪn] *vt Br* dresser (*un chien etc*) à la propreté; **h.-trained,** (*chien etc*) propre.

house-warming ['haʊswɔːmɪŋ] *n* **h.-w. (party),** pendaison *f* de crémaillère, soirée *f* pour pendre la crémaillère; **to give** *or* **have a h.-w.,** pendre la crémaillère.

housewife, *pl* **-wives** *n* **(a)** ['haʊswaɪf, -waɪvz] femme *f* au foyer; **(b)** ['hʌzɪf, -vz] *Br Mil* (*sewing kit*) trousse *f* de couture.

housewifely ['haʊswaɪflɪ] *adj* de femme au foyer.

housewifery ['haʊswɪf(ə)rɪ] *n* économie *f* domestique; (*work*) soins *mpl* du ménage.

housework ['haʊswɜːk] *n* travaux *mpl* domestiques *ou* de ménage; **to do the h.,** faire le ménage.

housey-housey ['haʊsɪ'haʊsɪ] *n* (jeu *m* de) loto *m*.

housing ['haʊzɪŋ] *n* **(a)** (*accommodation*) logement *m* (*de personnes*); *Br* **h. association,** association *f* d'aide au logement; *Br* **h. estate,** cité *f*, résidence *f*; **the h. problem** *or* **shortage,** la crise du logement; **h. stock,** parc *m* de logements; **(b)** rentrée *f* (*des troupeaux, du blé etc*); emmagasinage *m* (*du blé*); mise *f* à l'abri *ou* à couvert (*d'une locomotive etc*); *Nau* rentrée (*d'une voile*); **(c)** *Nau* (*of mast*) partie *f* au-dessous du pont; (*of bowsprit*) partie en dedans de l'étrave; **(d)** *Carp* logement *m*, ruinure *f* (*d'une poutre etc*); *MecE etc* bâti *m*, cage *f* (*d'un laminoir*); coquille *f* (*de moteur*); carter *m* (*de l'engrenage*); *Aut* carter (*du différentiel*).

hove *see* **HEAVE².**

hovel ['hɒv(ə)l] *n* taudis *m*, bouge *m*, masure *f*.

hover ['hɒvər] *vi* **(a)** (*of bird, insect*) planer, se balancer; (*of aircraft*) planer, effectuer un vol stationnaire; **danger is hovering over him,** le danger le menace; **(b)** *Fig* (*of person*) tourner en rond; **a waitress was hovering near our table,** une serveuse tournait près de notre table; **to h. between two courses,** hésiter entre deux possibilités; **he seemed to be hovering on the brink of saying something,** il semblait hésiter à dire quelque chose.

▶**hover around 1** *vipo* (*move about, near*) **to h. around s.o.,** errer *ou* rôder autour de qn. **2** *vi* (*move about nearby*) tourner.

hovercraft ['hɒvəkrɑːft] *n inv* aéroglisseur *m*, *F* hovercraft *m*.

hovering ['hɒvərɪŋ] *n Av* vol *m* stationnaire; (*of bird etc*) vol en suspension.

hoverport ['hɒvəpɔːt] *n* hoverport *m*, gare *f* aéroglisseur.

hovertrain ['hɒvətreɪn] *n* aérotrain *m*.

how [haʊ] **1** *adv* **(a)** (*in what manner*) comment; **h. do you spell this word?,** comment écrit-on ce mot?; *F* **h. the devil ...?, h. on earth ...?, h. in the world ...?,** comment diable ...?; **h. did they find out?,** comment est-ce qu'ils l'ont su *ou* appris?; **tell me h. he did it,** dites-moi comment il l'a fait; **h. was she dressed?,** comment est-ce qu'elle était habillée?, qu'est-ce qu'elle portait?; **h. are you?,** comment allez-vous?, *F* comment ça va?; **h. do you** *or* **d'you do?,** (*when being introduced*) enchanté (de faire votre connaissance); (*hello*) bonjour; **h. is it that ...?,** comment se fait-il que ...?; **h. so?,** comment ça?; *F* **h. come?,** (*why*) et comment ça se fait?; **h. come she didn't tell you?,** comment ça se fait qu'elle ne te l'ait pas dit?; **how's that?,** comment ça?; *Cr* = appel à l'arbitre, pour savoir si le guichet est sauf ou si la balle a été bien attrapée; **suppose I offer you another £500, how's that?,** et si je t'offre 500 livres en plus, qu'est-ce que tu en dis?; **how's that for a sandwich?,** qu'est-ce que tu dis de ce sandwich?; **how's that for size?,** (*of jacket etc*) ça va comme taille?; *F* **and h.!,** et comment!; **h. could you?,** vous n'avez pas honte?; **I don't know h. he can say that!,** je ne sais pas comment il peut dire ça!; **to learn h. to do sth,** apprendre à faire qch; **h. do you like this wine?,** comment trouvez-vous ce vin?; **h. do you like your steak?,** comment voulez-vous votre steak?; **here's h.!,** (*toast*) santé!;

(b) (*to what extent*) **h. much, h. many,** combien (de); **h. many times?, h. often?,** combien de fois?; **h. many are there of you?,** vous êtes combien de personnes?; **you**

know h. useful he is to me, vous savez à quel point il m'est utile; **you don't know h. right you are,** vous ne savez pas combien vous dites vrai; **h. wide is this room?,** quelle est la largeur de cette pièce?; **h. old are you?,** quel âge avez-vous?;

(c) *(in exclamations)* comme, que; **h. pretty she is!,** comme elle est jolie!; **h. disgusting!,** quelle horreur!; **h. kind (of you)!,** comme *ou* que c'est aimable!; **h. she has changed!,** ce qu'elle a changé!; **h. I wish I could!,** si seulement je pouvais!; **h. surprised he was when ...!,** quelle ne fut pas sa surprise lorsque ...!;

(d) *(introducing indirect statement)* que; **I told him h. there had been a great storm,** je lui ai dit qu'il y avait eu un grand orage;

(e) *(making suggestion)* **h. about,** et si; **h. about a game of cards/going out for a meal?,** et si on faisait une partie de cartes?/allait au restaurant?

2 *n* **the hows, whys and the wherefores,** les comment et les pourquoi, tous les détails.

howdy ['haʊdɪ] *int Am F* salut!

how-d'ye-do [haʊdjə'duː] *n Old-fashioned F* **here's a h.-d'ye-do!,** en voilà une histoire!, quelle histoire!

however [haʊ'evər] *adv* **(a)** *(on the other hand)* toutefois, cependant, pourtant; **if, h., you don't agree,** si toutefois cela ne vous convient pas; **there are more important matters, h.,** il y a des problèmes plus importants, pourtant; **(b)** *(in whatever degree)* quelque ... que ...+ *sub*, si ... que ...+ *sub*; **h. good his work is,** si excellent que soit son travail; **h. poor,** si pauvre qu'il *ou* elle *etc* soit; **h. hard she tried, she couldn't do it,** elle a eu beau faire (tout ce qu'elle a pu), elle n'y est pas parvenue; **(c)** *(in whatever way)* de quelque manière que ...; **h. that may be,** quoi qu'il en soit; **h. did she find out?,** comme est-ce qu'elle l'a su?

howitzer ['haʊɪtsər] *n Mil* obusier *m*.

howl¹ [haʊl] *n* hurlement *m (de loup etc)*; braillement *m (de bébé)*; huée *f (de la foule)*; mugissement *m (du vent)*; *Electron* hurlement *m* d'amplificateur; **to give a h. of pain/rage,** hurler de douleur/rage; **there were howls of laughter,** on riait à gorge déployée.

howl² **1** *vi* *(of animals, people)* hurler; pousser des hurlements; *(of wind)* mugir, rugir; *Electron (of loudspeaker)* hurler; **to h. with laughter,** rire à gorge déployée; **to h. with pain/rage,** hurler de douleur/rage. **2** *vt* **(a)** *F (sing badly)* beugler *(une chanson etc)*; **(b)** *(shout)* hurler *(qch)*.

►**howl down** *vtsep* *(silence)* faire taire *(qn)* en poussant des huées.

howler ['haʊlər] *n* **(a)** *F (mistake)* grosse gaffe, bourde *f* énorme; **schoolboy h.,** perle *f*; **(b)** *(person, thing that howls)* hurleur, -euse.

howling ['haʊlɪŋ] **1** *adj* **(a)** *(enfant)* qui hurle; *(foule)* hurlant; *(vent)* furieux; **(b)** *F (very great)* énorme; *(succès)* fou. **2** *n* hurlement *m*; braillement *m (de bébé)*; mugissement *m (du vent, de la tempête)*.

hoyden ['hɔɪd(ə)n] *n* garçon manqué.

hoydenish ['hɔɪd(e)nɪʃ] *adj* *(manner etc)* garçonnier, -ière.

HP, hp [eɪtʃ'piː] *n* **(a)** *MecE (abbr* **horsepower***)* = CV *m*; **(b)** *Br Com abbr* **hire-purchase**.

hq, HQ [eɪtʃ'kjuː] *n Mil (abbr* **headquarters***)* Q.G. *m*.

hr *abbr* **hour**.

HRH [eɪtʃɑː'reɪtʃ] *n Br (abbr* **Her** *or* **His Royal Highness***)* son Altesse Royale.

HRT [eɪtʃɑː'tiː] *n Med abbr* **hormone replacement therapy**.

ht *abbr* **height**.

hub [hʌb] *n* **(a)** moyeu *m (de roue, d'hélice)*; **(b)** *Fig* centre *m* d'activité; **the h. of the universe,** le centre de l'univers.

hubbub ['hʌbʌb] *n* remue-ménage *m*, vacarme *m*, tohu-bohu *m*; **h. of voices,** brouhaha *m* de voix.

hubby ['hʌbɪ] *n F* (petit) mari *m*.

hubcap ['hʌbkæp] *n Aut* enjoliveur *m*.

huckleberry ['hʌk(ə)lberɪ] *n Am (fruit)* airelle *f* myrtille.

huckster ['hʌkstər] *n* **(a)** *(hawker)* colporteur *m*; **(b)** *(profiteer)* mercanti *m*, profiteur *m*; **political h.,** trafiquant *m* politique.

HUD [eɪtʃjuː'diː] *n Mil Av abbr* **head-up display**.

huddle¹ ['hʌd(ə)l] *n* tas confus *(de choses)*; (petit) groupe *m (de personnes)*; *Fig* **to go into a h.,** se réunir en petit comité.

huddle² **1** *vi* **(a)** se blottir; **to h. in a corner/round the fire,** se blottir dans un coin/autour du feu; **(b)** *F* se réunir en petit comité. **2** *vt* = **HUDDLE UP 2 (b)**.

►**huddle together** **1** *vi* *(of people, animals)* s'entasser, se serrer les uns contre les autres. **2** *vtsep* *(form into a bunch)* **to h. things together,** entasser des choses pêle-mêle.

►**huddle up** **1** *vi* *(of person)* se pelotonner. **2** *vtsep* **(a)** *(put in a bunch)* **to h. things up,** entasser des choses pêle-mêle; **(b)** *(usu pass)* **huddled up in bed,** couché en chien de fusil; **huddled up in a corner,** blotti dans un coin.

hue¹ [hjuː] *n* *(colour)* teinte *f*, couleur *f*, nuance *f*.

hue² *n* **h. and cry,** clameur *f* de haro; *Jur* clameur publique; **a h. and cry was raised against this reform,** cette réforme provoqua un tollé général.

huff¹ [hʌf] *n* **to be in a h.,** être froissé *ou* fâché; **to get into a h.,** prendre la mouche, s'offusquer; **he went off in a h.,** il prit la mouche et s'en alla.

huff² **1** *vi* *(blow)* **he huffed and puffed,** il soufflait et haletait. **2** *vt* **to be** *or* **feel huffed,** être offensé *ou* fâché.

huffy ['hʌfɪ] *adj* fâché, vexé.

hug¹ [hʌg] *n* **(a)** *(sign of affection)* étreinte *f*; **to give s.o. a h.,** serrer qn dans ses bras, étreindre qn; **give me a h.,** allez, serre-moi dans tes bras; **(b)** *(in wrestling)* prise *f*; *(of bear)* étreinte *f*.

hug² *vt* (-gg-) **(a)** étreindre, embrasser, serrer *(qn)*; **she hugged the child to her,** elle a serré l'enfant sur son cœur; **clothes that h. the figure,** vêtements qui moulent (la silhouette); *Fig* **to h. s.o. to death,** embrasser qn à l'étouffer; *Fig* **to h. the fire,** se blottir au coin du feu; *Fig* **to h. oneself for doing sth,** se féliciter d'avoir fait qch; **(b)** *(of bear)* étouffer, enserrer *(sa victime)*; **(c)** *(cling to)* chérir *(ses défauts)*; **to h. a belief,** ne pas démordre d'une conviction; **(d)** *(keep close to)* longer, serrer *(le mur)*; *Nau* raser *(la côte)*; *Aut* **to h. the kerb,** serrer le trottoir.

huge [hjuːdʒ] *adj* immense, énorme; *(bâtiment)* énorme, vaste; *(succès)* immense, formidable; *(homme)* colossal; *(différence)* énorme, capital; **h. undertaking,** vaste entreprise *f*.

hugely ['hjuːdʒlɪ] *adv* énormément; *(amusing)* extrêmement.

hugeness ['hjuːdʒnɪs] *n* énormité *f*, immensité *f*.

hugger-mugger ['hʌgəmʌgər] **1** *n* *(confusion)* désordre *m*, confusion *f*. **2** *adj* *(collection)* sans ordre; *(arrangement)* confus. **3** *adv* en désordre; confusément, pêle-mêle.

-hugging ['hʌgɪŋ] *suff* *(of clothes)* **hip/figure/*etc*-h.,** qui moule les hanches/la silhouette/*etc*.

Hugh [hjuː], **Hugo** ['hjuːgəʊ] *n* Hugues *m*.

Huguenot ['hjuːgənɒt, -nəʊ] *n Rel Hist* Huguenot, -ote.

hulk [hʌlk] *n* **(a)** *Nau* carcasse *f* de navire; *(prison)* ponton *m*; **(b)** *Fig (person)* mastodonte *m*.

hulking ['hʌlkɪŋ] *adj* gros, lourd; **h. great man,** mastodonte *m*, mastoc *m*.

hull¹ [hʌl] *n* **(a)** *Nau Av Mil (of ship, tank)* coque *f*; *(in marine insurance)* corps *m*; **h. insurance,** assurance *f* sur corps; **(b)** *(of pea, bean)* cosse *f*, gousse *f*; **(c)** *(of strawberry, raspberry)* calice *m*.

hull² *vt* **(a)** écosser *(des pois)*; monder *(de l'orge)*; baller *(de l'avoine)*; décortiquer *(le riz, l'orge)*; **(b)** *Nau* percer la coque de *(un navire)*.

hullabaloo [hʌləbə'luː] *n* tintamarre *m*, vacarme *m*, boucan *m*.

hullo [hʌ'ləʊ] *int* = **HELLO**.

hum¹ [hʌm] *n* **(a)** bourdonnement *m (d'abeille)*; ronflement *m (de machine)*; vrombissement *m (d'un avion, d'une toupie)*; murmure *m (d'approbation)*; bruit sourd *(de voix)*; brouhaha *m (de conversation)*; *Rad etc* bourdonnement, ronflement; **(b)** *Br Sl (bad smell)* puanteur *f*.

hum² *v* (-mm-) **1** *vi* **(a)** *(of person)* fredonner, chantonner; *(of insect etc)* bourdonner; *(of top)* ronfler, vrombir; *(of aircraft)* vrombir; *Rad (of set)* ronronner, ronfler; **town humming with activity,** ville bourdonnante d'activité; *Fig* **to make things h.,** faire marcher rondement les choses; **(b)** *(say 'hum')* dire hum; **to h. and haw,** *(mumble)* bredouiller, bafouiller; *(hesitate)* hésiter *(à prendre un parti)*; **(c)** *Br Sl (smell bad)* chlinguer, puer. **2** *vt* fredonner, chantonner *(un air)*.

hum³ *int* hmm!, hum!

human ['hjuːm(ə)n] **1** *adj* humain; **he's only h.,** il est humain après tout; **it's only h.,** c'est humain; **the h. body,** le corps humain; **h. being,** être humain; **h. error,** erreur humaine; **h. growth hormone,** hormone *f* somatotrope *ou* de croissance, somatotrophine *f*; *esp Journ* **a h. interest story,** = histoire comique *ou* tragique *ou* touchante; **h. nature,** la nature humaine; **the h. race,** la race humaine; **h. resources,** ressources humaines; **h. rights,** droits *mpl* de l'homme. **2** *n* être humain; **humans,** les humains *mpl*.

humane [hjʊ'meɪn] *adj* **(a)** humain, compatissant; *(œuvre)* humanitaire; *(measure)* bienfaisant; **h. society,** = société visant à promouvoir certaines valeurs humaines; **(b)**

clément; *(killing)* qui évite de faire souffrir.

humanely [hjʊ'meɪnlɪ] *adv* humainement, avec humanité.

humanism ['hjuːmənɪz(ə)m] *n Phil* humanisme *m*.

humanist ['hjuːmənɪst] *n Phil* humaniste *m*.

humanistic [hjʊmə'nɪstɪk] *adj Phil* humaniste.

humanitarian [hjʊmænɪ'teərɪən] *adj & n* humanitaire *mf*.

humanity [hjʊ'mænɪtɪ] *n* **(a)** *(human race)* humanité *f*, *F* le genre humain; **the club was packed with sweaty h.,** le club était plein d'une foule transpirante; **(b)** *(human nature)* nature humaine; **(c)** *(kindness)* humanité *f*; **(d)** *Phil* **the humanities,** les humanités *fpl*, les lettres *fpl*, les sciences humaines; *Sch* **humanities lesson,** cours *m* de sciences humaines.

humanize ['hjuːmənaɪz] *vt* humaniser.

humankind [hjʊm(ə)n'kaɪnd] *n* humanité *f*.

humanly ['hjuːm(ə)nlɪ] *adv* humainement; **to do everything h. possible,** faire tout ce qui est humainement possible.

humanoid ['hjuːmənɔɪd] *adj & n* humanoïde *m*.

humble[1] ['hʌmb(ə)l] *adj* **(a)** *(meek)* humble; **h. prayer,** humble prière *f*; **in my h. opinion,** à mon humble avis; *Old-fashioned* **Your h. servant,** *(ending letter)* je reste votre humble serviteur; **(b)** *(unpretentious)* modeste; **to be of h. origin,** être d'origine modeste; **to eat h. pie,** s'humilier (devant qn); *(make amends)* faire amende honorable.

humble[2] *vt* humilier, mortifier *(qn)*; rabattre *(l'orgueil de qn)*; **to h. oneself,** s'humilier.

humblebee ['hʌmb(ə)lbiː] *n (insect)* bourdon *m*.

humbleness ['hʌmb(ə)lnɪs] *n* humilité *f*.

humbling ['hʌmb(ə)lɪŋ] **1** *adj (experience)* humiliant. **2** *n* humiliation *f (de qn)*; abaissement *m (des grands etc)*.

humbly ['hʌmb(ə)lɪ] *adv (see adj)* **(a)** humblement, avec humilité; **if I may h. suggest ...,** si je peux me permettre de suggérer ...; **(b)** modestement.

humbug ['hʌmbʌg] *n* **(a)** *(nonsense)* bêtises *fpl*; *(deception)* charlatanisme *m*; **h.!,** sottises!; **(b)** *(person) (flatterer)* enjôleur, -euse; *(charlatan)* charlatan *m*; **(c)** *Br (sweet)* berlingot *m*; = bêtise *f* de Cambrai.

humdinger ['hʌmdɪŋər] *n F* quelque chose d'extraordinaire *ou* de fantastique; **a h. of a speech,** un discours formidable *ou* sensationnel.

humdrum ['hʌmdrʌm] **1** *adj* monotone, banal, -als; *(existence)* monotone; **h. daily life,** le train-train quotidien. **2** *n* monotonie *f (de l'existence etc)*.

humerus, *pl* **-i** ['hjuːmərəs, -aɪ, -iː] *n Anat* humérus *m*.

humid ['hjuːmɪd] *adj* humide; *(heat, skin)* moite.

humidifier [hjʊ'mɪdɪfaɪər] *n* humidificateur *m*.

humidify [hjʊ'mɪdɪfaɪ] *vt* humidifier *(l'air etc)*.

humidity [hjʊ'mɪdɪtɪ] *n* humidité *f*.

humidor ['hjuːmɪdɔːr] *n* boîte *f* à cigares (pourvue d'un humidificateur).

humiliate [hjʊ'mɪlɪeɪt] *vt* humilier, mortifier *(qn)*.

humiliating [hjʊ'mɪlɪeɪtɪŋ] *adj* humiliant, mortifiant.

humiliation [hjʊmɪlɪ'eɪʃən] *n* humiliation *f*.

humility [hjʊ'mɪlɪtɪ] *n* humilité *f*.

humming ['hʊmɪŋ] **1** *adj* bourdonnant; **h. top,** toupie *f* d'Allemagne. **2** *n* **(a)** = **HUM**[1] **(a)**; **(b)** fredonnement *m (d'un air)*; **h. noise,** bourdonnement *m*; **(c) h. and hawing,** hésitation *f*.

hummingbird ['hʌmɪŋbɜːd] *n* colibri *m*, oiseau mouche *m*, *pl* oiseaux-mouches.

hummock ['hʌmək] *n* **(a)** tertre *m*, mamelon *m (de terre)*, monticule *m*; **(b)** *(in ice field)* hummock *m*.

humor ['hjuːmər] *n & vt US* = **HUMOUR**[1,2].

humorist ['hjuːmərɪst] *n (writer)* écrivain *m* humoristique, humoriste *m*; *(comedian)* humoriste, comique *m*; *(joker)* farceur *m*; **we've got a h. here,** nous avons un plaisantin parmi nous.

humorous ['hjuːm(ə)rəs] *adj* comique, drôle; *(writer etc)* humoriste, humoristique; *(drawing, remark etc)* humoristique; **she found the situation rather h.,** elle a trouvé la situation plutôt comique.

humorously ['hjuːm(ə)rəslɪ] *adv* drôlement, comiquement; humoristiquement.

humour[1], *US* **humor** ['hjuːmər] *n* **(a)** humour *m*; **the h. of the situation,** le côté comique de la situation; **(b) (sense of) h.,** sens *m* de l'humour; **to have no sense of h.,** ne pas avoir le sens de l'humour; **(c)** *(mood, temper)* humeur *f*, disposition *f*; **to be in the h. for doing sth,** être disposé à faire qch; **good h.,** bonne humeur.

humour[2], *US* **humor** *vt* complaire à *(qn)*; se prêter *ou* se plier à tous les caprices de *(qn)*; *(be nice to)* ménager *(qn)*.

humourless, *US* **humorless** ['hjuːməlɪs] *adj* dépourvu d'humour *ou* du sens de l'humour.

hump[1] [hʌmp] *n* **(a)** *(on flat surface, of hunchback, camel)* bosse *f*; *Rail* butte *f* de triage; **to have a h.,** être bossu; **h. in the road,** dos *m* d'âne; **we're over the h. now,** *(past the worst)* le plus difficile est passé maintenant; **(b)** *Br F* **to have the h.,** *(be depressed)* avoir le cafard; *(be sulking)* faire la tête; **what's he got the h. about?,** pourquoi est-ce qu'il fait la tête?

hump[2] **1** *vt* **(a)** courber, arquer, cambrer; *(of person, animal)* arrondir, arquer *(le dos)*; voûter *(les épaules)*; **(b)** *F (carry)* porter *(un fardeau)* sur son dos; **(c)** *Sl (have sexual intercourse with)* sauter, baiser *(qn)*. **2** *vi Sl (have sexual intercourse)* baiser.

humpback ['hʌmpbæk] *n* **(a)** = **HUNCHBACK**; **(b) h. (whale),** baleine *f* à bosse; **(c)** *Br* **h. (bridge),** pont *m* en dos d'âne.

humpbacked ['hʌmpbækt] *adj* bossu; **h. bridge,** pont *m* en dos d'âne.

humph [hʌmf, hm] *int* hum! hmm!

humus ['hjuːməs] *n (soil)* humus *m*; *(with fertilizer)* terreau *m*.

Hun [hʌn] *n* **(a)** *F (in First World War)* boche *m*; **(b)** *Hist* **the Huns,** les Huns *mpl*.

hunch[1] [hʌntʃ] *n* **(a)** *(intuition)* **to have a h.,** avoir une idée *ou* un pressentiment; **(b)** *(hump)* bosse *f*; **(c)** *(large piece)* gros morceau *(de pain, de fromage)*.

hunch[2] *vt* **to h. one's back,** arrondir le dos; **to h. one's shoulders,** voûter les épaules.

►hunch up *vtsep* = **HUNCH**[2]; **to sit hunched up,** se tenir accroupi le menton sur les genoux.

hunchback ['hʌntʃbæk] *n* bossu, -ue; **to have a h.,** être bossu; **the H. of Notre Dame,** le bossu de Notre Dame.

hunchbacked ['hʌntʃbækt] *adj* bossu.

hundred ['hʌndrəd] **(a)** *(numeral)* cent *m*; **one** *or* **a h.,** cent; **a h. and one,** cent un; **about a h. houses,** une centaine de maisons; **two h. apples,** deux cents pommes; **to live to be a h.,** vivre jusqu'à cent ans; **they were dying in (their) hundreds,** ils mouraient par centaines; **the temperature was in the hundreds,** il faisait plus de 40°; *Culin* **hundreds and thousands,** = vermicelles *fpl*, perlages *mpl*; **to drive at a h. kilometres an hour,** faire du cent à l'heure; **one** *or* **a h. per cent,** cent pour cent; **to be a h. per cent certain,** être sûr à cent pour cent; **I'm not feeling a h. per cent,** je ne me sens pas dans mon assiette; **I'm not feeling a h. per cent yet,** je ne suis pas encore complètement remis; **to sell by the h.,** vendre au cent; *Sp* **the h. metre race, the h. metres,** le cent mètres; *Hist* **the H. Years' War,** la guerre de cent ans;
(b) *F (large number)* **not a h. miles away,** pas si loin d'ici; **a h. and one details,** mille et un détails; **I've told you hundreds of times,** je vous l'ai dit je ne sais combien de fois; **a h. to one it will be a failure,** ça fera un four à coup sûr.

hundredfold ['hʌndrədfəʊld] *adj* centuple; **to increase a h.,** centupler.

hundredth ['hʌndrədθ] **1** *adj* centième; **the two h. anniversary of ...,** le bicentenaire de ...; *Th* **h. performance,** centième *f*. **2** *n (fraction)* centième *m*; **three hundredths,** trois centièmes.

hundredweight ['hʌndrədweɪt] *n* **(a)** *Br* poids *m* de 112 livres, = 50 kg 802; *Can approx* = quintal *m*; **two h., two hundredweights,** un quintal; *Can approx* = deux quintaux; **(b)** *US* poids *m* de 100 livres, = 45 kg 359.

hung[1] [hʌŋ] **1** *see* **HANG**. **2** *adj* **(a)** *F* **to be h. over,** avoir la gueule de bois; **(b)** *Sl* **to be h. up on s.o./sth,** être obsédé par qn/qch.

hung[2] *adj Jur* **h. jury,** = jury aux opinions partagées; **it was a h. jury,** le jury ne parvenait pas à se départager; **h. parliament,** parlement *m* sans majorité.

Hungarian [hʌŋ'geərɪən] **1** *adj* hongrois. **2** *n* **(a)** Hongrois, -oise; **(b)** *Ling* hongrois *m*.

Hungary ['hʌŋgərɪ] *n* Hongrie *f*.

hunger[1] ['hʌŋgər] *n* faim *f*; **h. pains** *or* **pangs,** tiraillements *mpl* d'estomac; **h. strike/striker,** grève *f*/gréviste *mf* de la faim; **to go on h. strike,** faire la grève de la faim; **h. for sth,** ardent désir de qch, soif *f* de qch; **h. for affection,** désir d'affection; **emotional h.,** fort besoin affectif.

hunger[2] *vi esp Lit* avoir faim.

►hunger after, hunger for *vipo esp Lit* être affamé de, avoir soif de (qch); **she hungered for fame,** elle avait soif de célébrité.

hungrily ['hʌŋgrɪlɪ] *adv* avidement, voracement; **she eyed the food h.,** elle regardait la nourriture d'un air vorace; *Fig* **they stared h. at the women,** ils fixaient les femmes avec avidité.

hungry ['hʌŋgrɪ] *adj* **(a)** affamé, qui a faim; **to be** *or* **feel**

h., avoir faim; **to be ravenously h.** *or* **as h. as a wolf** *or US* **a bear,** avoir une faim de loup; **I was getting h.,** je commençais à avoir faim; **to look h.,** avoir l'air famélique; **(b)** *Fig* (*regard, œil*) avide; **to be h. for knowledge,** être avide d'apprendre; **to be h. for love,** avoir soif d'amour.

hunk [hʌŋk] *n* **(a)** gros morceau (*de gâteau, de fromage etc*); quignon *m* (*de pain*); **(b)** *F* (*attractive man*) beau mec, mec bien foutu.

hunky ['hʌŋkɪ] *adj F* (*man*) (*with good body*) bien foutu; (*big and strong*) (bien) baraqué.

hunky-dory ['hʌŋkɪ'dɔːrɪ] *adj F* excellent, au poil.

hunt¹ [hʌnt] *n* **(a)** (*activity*) chasse *f* (*esp* à courre); (*people*) équipage *m* de chasse; (*area*) terrain *m* de chasse; **fox/tiger h.,** chasse au renard/au tigre; **(b)** (*search*) recherche *f*; **he continued his h. for work,** il continuait à chercher un emploi; **local people joined in the h. for the child,** des gens de la région se sont joints aux recherches pour retrouver l'enfant; **I've had a good h. for my gloves,** j'ai cherché mes gants partout.

hunt² **1** *vi* chasser; **to h. for sth/s.o.,** chercher (à découvrir) qch/qn; **to h. for treasure,** aller à la recherche d'un trésor. **2** *vt* **(a)** chasser (*le cerf etc*); pêcher (*la baleine*); **to h. a thief,** (*chase*) poursuivre un voleur; (*try to locate*) être à la recherche d'un voleur; **h. the slipper,** (*game*) jeu *m* du furet; **(b)** (*ride, walk over*) parcourir, battre (*un terrain*); **(c)** (*use in hunting*) monter (*un cheval*) à la chasse; diriger, conduire (*la meute*).

▶**hunt about, hunt around** *vi* (*search*) chercher partout.

▶**hunt down** *vtsep* **(a)** (*chase*) traquer, forcer (*une bête*); traquer (*qn*); **(b)** (*find*) dénicher (*qn, qch*).

▶**hunt out** *vtsep* **(a)** (*expel*) chasser, expulser (*qn*); (*find*) débusquer (*qn*); **(b)** (*find*) déterrer, dénicher (*qch*) (à force de recherches).

▶**hunt up** *vtsep* (*find*) dénicher (*qn, qch*).

hunted ['hʌntɪd] *adj* **he had a h. look,** il avait l'air persécuté.

hunter ['hʌntər] *n* **(a)** chasseur *m*; tueur *m* (*de lions etc*); (*searcher*) pourchasseur *m* (**of,** de); **curio h.,** dénicheur *m* d'antiquités; **dowry h.,** coureur *m* de dots; **(b)** (*horse*) cheval *m* de chasse, hunter *m*; **(c)** (*watch*) (montre *f* à) savonnette *f*; **half h.,** montre à guichet.

hunter-killer ['hʌntə'kɪlər] *adj* **h.-k. submarine,** sous-marin *m* nucléaire d'attaque.

hunting ['hʌntɪŋ] **1** *adj* **h. man,** fervent *m* de la chasse à courre, grand chasseur. **2** *n* chasse *f*; poursuite *f* (*du gibier*); (*science*) vénérie *f*; **fox h.,** chasse au renard; **h. lodge,** pavillon *m* de chasse; **h. horn,** cor *m ou* trompe *f* de chasse; **h. ground,** terrain *m* de chasse; **the Happy H. Grounds,** le Paradis des Peaux-Rouges; **house h.,** recherche *f* d'une maison *ou* d'un logement; **bargain h.,** chasse *f* aux soldes; **a happy h. ground for collectors,** un paradis pour les collectionneurs.

huntress ['hʌntrɪs] *n* chasseuse *f*, *Lit* chasseresse *f*.

huntsman, *pl* **-men** ['hʌntsmən] *n* chasseur *m* (à courre); (*in charge of hounds*) veneur *m*, piqueur *m*.

hurdle¹ ['hɜːd(ə)l] *n* **(a)** (*athletics*) *& Horseracing* haie *f*; **h. race,** course *f* de haies; **400-metre hurdles,** 400 mètres haies; **(b)** *Fig* (*obstacle*) obstacle *m*; **to overcome a h.,** franchir un obstacle; **the next h. will be to persuade the managing director,** le prochain obstacle va être de persuader le directeur général; **(c)** *Agr* claie *f*, clôture *f*.

hurdle² **1** *vt* **(a)** (*jump over*) sauter (*un obstacle*); *Sp* franchir (*une haie*); **(b)** *Agr* entourer (*qch*) de claies. **2** *vi Sp* courir une course de haies.

hurdler ['hɜːdlər] *n* (*athlete*) coureur *m* de haies; (*horse*) cheval *m* de courses de haies.

hurdling ['hɜːd(ə)lɪŋ] *n* (*athletics*) *& Horseracing* saut *m* de haies; (*competition*) courses *fpl* de haies.

hurdy-gurdy ['hɜːdɪgɜːdɪ] *n F* orgue *m* de Barbarie.

hurl¹ [hɜːl] *n* **(a)** lancée *f*, lancement *m*; **(b)** *Sp* crosse *f* de hurling.

hurl² **1** *vt* lancer (*qch*) avec force *ou* violence (**at,** contre); lancer (*des reproches*) (**at s.o.,** à qn); **to h. oneself at s.o.,** se ruer sur qn; **he hurled himself off the bridge,** il s'est jeté du pont; **to h. oneself into the fray,** se jeter à corps perdu dans la mêlée; **to h. abuse,** vociférer des injures. **2** *vi Sp* jouer au hurling.

▶**hurl back** *vtsep* **(a)** relancer (*qch*) avec force *ou* violence; **(b)** *Lit* (*repulse*) refouler, repousser (*l'ennemi etc*).

▶**hurl down** *vtsep* jeter.

hurley ['hɜːlɪ] *n* = **HURLING (b)**.

hurling ['hɜːlɪŋ] *n* **(a)** lancement *m* (*d'un projectile etc*); **(b)** *Sp* (*Ireland*) = variété de jeu de hockey.

hurly-burly ['hɜːlɪ'bɜːlɪ] *n* charivari *m*, tohu-bohu *m*.

hurrah [hʊ'rɑː] **, hurray** [hʊ'reɪ] *int & n* hourra *m*; **h. for the holidays!,** vive(nt) les vacances!

hurricane ['hʌrɪkən, -keɪn] *n Met* ouragan *m*; (*in West Indies*) hurricane *m*; **it was blowing a h.,** le vent soufflait en ouragan; **h. lamp,** lampe-tempête *f*, *pl* lampes-tempête; **h. warning,** avertissement *m* prévenant de l'arrivée d'un ouragan.

hurried ['hʌrɪd] *adj* (*step*) pressé, précipité; (*work*) fait à la hâte; **a few h. words,** (*written*) quelques mots écrits à la hâte; (*spoken*) quelques mots dits à la hâte; **a h. meal,** un repas à la hâte; **a h. conversation,** une conversation rapide.

hurriedly ['hʌrɪdlɪ] *adv* à la hâte, en toute hâte; précipitamment.

hurry¹ ['hʌrɪ] *n* hâte *f*, précipitation *f*; **to go out in a h.,** sortir à la hâte *ou* en courant; **to be always in a h.,** être toujours pressé; **in her h. she forgot her keys,** dans sa précipitation elle a oublié ses clefs; **to do sth in a h.,** faire qch à la hâte; **they were in a h. to complete the work,** ils étaient pressés de terminer le travail; **to be in no h.,** ne pas être pressé, avoir le temps; **you won't see her again in a h.,** vous ne la reverrez pas de sitôt; **I won't do that again in a h.,** je ne suis pas près de recommencer, je ne recommencerai pas de sitôt; **he was in no h. to leave,** il n'était pas pressé de partir; **are you in a h. for it?,** c'est urgent?; **there's no h.,** il n'y a rien qui presse, ça ne presse pas; **so what's the h.?,** qu'est-ce qui presse tant?; **what's your h.?,** pourquoi est-ce que vous êtes aussi pressé?

hurry² **1** *vt* hâter, presser (*qn*); hâter, activer, presser (*le travail*); **don't h. him,** ne le presse pas; **she was hurried to hospital,** elle a été transportée à l'hôpital en (toute) hâte; **work that cannot be hurried,** travail qui demande du temps; **don't h. your meal,** ne mangez pas trop vite. **2** *vi* **(a)** se dépêcher, se hâter, se presser; **don't h.,** ne vous pressez pas; **there's no need to h.,** on a tout son temps; **(b)** (*walk, travel etc*) presser le pas; **she hurried home,** elle s'est dépêchée de rentrer; **to h. into/out of a room,** entrer dans une pièce/sortir d'une pièce en toute hâte; **to h. after s.o.,** courir après qn.

▶**hurry along** **1** *vi* (*move quickly*) marcher d'un pas pressé; **h. along please,** (*we're closing*) dépêchez-vous s'il vous plaît. **2** *vtsep* (*cause to move more quickly*) faire se dépêcher; **he hurried them along,** (*walking*) il les a fait marcher plus vite; **h. him along!,** dis-lui de se presser!; **I tried to h. the work along,** j'ai essayé d'accélérer le travail.

▶**hurry away** **1** *vi* (*move away quickly*) partir précipitamment. **2** *vtsep* (*cause to move away quickly*) emmener précipitamment; **he hurried the children away from the scene of the accident,** il a vite éloigné les enfants du lieu de l'accident.

▶**hurry back** *vi* (*return quickly*) revenir *ou* retourner à la hâte.

▶**hurry off** **1** *vi* (*move away quickly*) partir précipitamment. **2** *vtsep* (*cause to move away quickly*) faire partir précipitamment; **they hurried her off to hospital,** ils l'ont emmenée à l'hôpital en (toute) hâte.

▶**hurry on** **1** *vi* (*proceed quickly*) continuer à la hâte; **she hurried on with the housework,** elle a continué le ménage à la hâte. **2** *vtsep* (*cause to proceed more quickly*) faire hâter le pas à (*qn*); pousser (*qn*) en avant; avancer (*un travail*).

▶**hurry up** **1** *vi* (*move more quickly*) se dépêcher, se hâter; **h. up!,** dépêche-toi!; **h. up and get dressed,** dépêche-toi de t'habiller; **h. up with that packing,** dépêche-toi de faire ces bagages; **h. up with the iron,** dépêche-toi avec le fer. **2** *vtsep* (*cause to move more quickly*) faire se dépêcher; **I'll go and h. them up,** je vais leur dire de se dépêcher.

hurt¹ [hɜːt] **1** *n* **(a)** mal *m*; (*injury*) blessure *f*; **(b)** (*harm*) tort *m*, détriment *m*; **what h. can it do you?,** quel tort cela peut-il vous faire? **2** *adj* (*look, feelings*) blessé.

hurt² *v* (*pt & pp* **hurt**) **1** *vt* **(a)** (*cause pain to*) faire (du) mal à, blesser (*qn*); **to h. oneself,** se faire (du) mal; **to h. one's foot,** se blesser au pied; **to get hurt,** être blessé; **my wound hurts me,** ma blessure me fait mal *ou* me fait souffrir; **it wouldn't h. him to have to wait for a change,** ça ne lui ferait pas de mal de devoir attendre pour changer; **the scandal will h. their prospects,** le scandale nuira à leurs chances;

(b) (*emotionally*) faire de la peine à (*qn*); **it hurt me when they did that,** ça m'a fait de la peine quand ils ont fait ça; **to h. s.o.'s feelings,** blesser qn, peiner qn, offenser qn; **he is easily hurt,** il s'offense facilement; **the thing**

that hurts me most, ce qui me fait le plus mal.
2 *vi* **(a)** (*cause pain*) faire mal; **it hurts,** ça fait mal; **where does it h.?,** où est-ce que ça vous fait mal?; **my foot hurts,** mon pied me fait mal; *F* **I h. all over,** j'ai mal partout; **it hurt when I touched the hot metal,** ça a fait mal quand j'ai touché le métal chaud; **just one drink won't h.,** juste un verre ne te fera pas de mal; **it wouldn't h. to make a few more photocopies,** ça ne fera pas de mal de faire quelques photocopies de plus; **(b)** (*emotionally*) faire souffrir; **it hurts when you say that ...,** ça fait mal de t'entendre dire que ... .

hurtful ['hɜːtfʊl] *adj* préjudiciable (**to,** à); (*thing to say*) blessant, offensant; **he was very h.,** il a été très blessant; **there is nothing so h. as ingratitude,** il n'y a rien qui blesse comme l'ingratitude.

hurtle ['hɜːt(ə)l] **1** *vi* se précipiter, s'élancer (*avec bruit, comme un bolide*); **to h. along,** (*of car etc*) dévorer la route; **a roller skater hurtled into me,** une personne en patins à roulettes s'est élancée sur moi; **to h. down,** dévaler avec fracas (*of rocks etc*). **2** *vt* (*throw*) lancer, faire dévaler (*des pierres etc*).

husband[1] ['hʌzbənd] *n* mari *m*, époux *m*; **h. and wife,** les (deux) époux, les conjoints *mpl*; **h. and wife run the hotel together,** les deux époux s'occupent de l'hôtel ensemble; **to live as h. and wife,** vivre maritalement.

husband[2] *vt* ménager, économiser (*ses ressources, ses forces*); bien gérer (*ses ressources*).

husband-and-wife ['hʌzbəndən'waɪf] *adj* **h.-and-w. team,** équipe formée par deux époux; **h.-and-w. business,** entreprise appartenant à deux époux *ou* à un couple marié.

husbandry ['hʌzbəndrɪ] *n* **(a)** *Agr* agronomie *f*, économie rurale, agriculture *f*; **animal h.,** élevage *m*; **(b)** (*management*) **good h.,** bonne gestion; sage administration *f* (*de son bien*).

hush[1] [hʌʃ] *n* (*quiet*) silence *m*, calme *m*; **there was a h. when** *or* **as ...,** il y eu un silence quand ...; **h. money,** argent donné à qn pour acheter son silence; **he wanted h. money,** il exigeait de l'argent pour se taire.

hush[2] **1** *vt* calmer, faire taire (*un enfant*); imposer silence à (*qn*); étouffer (*un bruit*). **2** *vi* se taire, faire silence.

hush[3] *int* chut!, silence!

►**hush up** *vtsep* (*silence*) étouffer (*un scandale etc*).

hushed [hʌʃt] *adj* à voix basse, étouffé; **h. conversation,** conversation étouffée *ou* discrète; **to talk in a h. voice,** chuchoter, parler à voix basse.

hush-hush ['hʌʃhʌʃ] *adj F* top-secret, -ète, ultra-secret, -ète.

husk[1] [hʌsk] *n* cosse *f*, gousse *f* (*de pois etc*); brou *m* (*de noix*); hérisson *m* (*de châtaigne*); coque *f* (*de grain de café*); tégument *m*, pellicule *f* (*de grain*); enveloppe *f* (*de l'épi du maïs*); **husks,** vannure *f*.

husk[2] *vt* décortiquer; écosser (*des pois*); ébrouer (*des noix*); perler, monder (*le riz, l'orge*); éplucher (*le maïs*); vanner (*le grain*).

huskily ['hʌskɪlɪ] *adv* (*parler*) d'une voix rauque; (*because of sore throat*) d'une voix enrouée.

huskiness ['hʌskɪnɪs] *n* enrouement *m* (*de la voix, d'un son*); empâtement *m* (*de la voix*).

husky[1] ['hʌskɪ] *adj* **(a)** **h. voice,** (*because of sore throat*) voix enrouée *ou* voilée; (*naturally*) voix rauque; **(b)** (*strong*) fort, costaud.

husky[2] *n* (*dog*) chien *m* esquimau.

hussar [hʊ'zɑːr] *n Mil* hussard *m*.

hussy ['hʌsɪ] *n F Arch* coquine *f*, friponne *f*; **you little h.!** petite coquine!

hustings ['hʌstɪŋz] *npl* plate-forme électorale; **to mount the h.,** se présenter aux élections (*pour la Chambre des Communes*).

hustle[1] ['hʌs(ə)l] *n* **(a)** (*energetic activity*) hâte *f*, activité *f* énergique; **h. and bustle,** tourbillon *m* d'activité; **(b)** (*shoving*) bousculade *f*.

hustle[2] **1** *vt* **(a)** (*shove, push*) bousculer, pousser, presser (*qn*); **to be hustled away,** être emmené précipitamment; **I was hustled into a small room,** on m'a fait entrer précipitamment dans une petite pièce; **(b)** (*hurry*) **to h. things on,** pousser le travail, *F* faire activer les choses; **to h. s.o. into a decision,** forcer qn à se décider sans lui donner le temps de respirer; **I won't be hustled,** je ne veux pas qu'on me bouscule. **2** *vi* **(a)** (*hurry*) se dépêcher, se presser; **(b)** (*shove*) **to h. through the crowd,** se frayer un passage à travers la foule; **(c)** *Am Sl* (*swindle*) arnaquer; **(d)** *Am Sl* (*of prostitute*) faire le trottoir.

hustler ['hʌslər] *n* **(a)** (*energetic person*) (*problem-solver etc*) débrouillard *m*; (*with lots of business activities*) brasseur *m ou* remueur *m* d'affaires; **(b)** *Am* (*swindler*) arnaqueur *m*; **(c)** *Am Sl* (*prostitute*) prostituée *f*; **(d)** (*someone who shoves*) bousculeur, -euse.

hut [hʌt] *n* hutte *f*, cabane *f*; **mud h.,** hutte de terre; **Alpine h.,** chalet-refuge *m*, *pl* chalets-refuges.

hutch [hʌtʃ] *n* **(a)** (*for rabbit*) clapier *m*, lapinière *f*; **(b)** *Am* (*cupboard*) vaisselier *m*.

hutments ['hʌtmənts] *npl* baraquements *mpl*.

hyacinth ['haɪəsɪnθ] *n* **(a)** (*flower*) jacinthe *f*; **wood** *or* **wild h.,** jacinthe des bois; **(b)** (*colour*) bleu jacinthe *m inv*, bleu violet *m inv*; **a h. dress,** une robe bleu violet; **(c)** *Miner* hyacinthe *f*.

hyaena [haɪ'iːnə] *n* = **HYENA**.

hybrid ['haɪbrɪd] *Biol Ling etc* **1** *n* hybride *m*. **2** *adj* hybride.

hybridism ['haɪbrɪdɪz(ə)m] *n* hybridisme *m*.

hybridization [haɪbrɪdaɪ'zeɪʃən] *n Biol* hybridation *f*.

hybridize ['haɪbrɪdaɪz] **1** *vt* hybrider. **2** *vi* s'hybrider.

hydra ['haɪdrə] *n* **(a)** (*pl* **hydrae** ['haɪdrɪ]) (*animal*) hydre *f*; **(b)** *Myth* **H.,** Hydre *f* (*de Lerne*).

hydrangea [haɪ'dreɪndʒə] *n* (*shrub*) hortensia *m*.

hydrant ['haɪdrənt] *n* prise *f* d'eau; **fire h.,** bouche *f* d'incendie.

hydrate[1] ['haɪdreɪt] *n Ch* hydrate *m*.

hydrate[2] *vt Ch* hydrater.

hydraulic [haɪ'drɔːlɪk] *adj Phys etc* (*force, frein, puissance etc*) hydraulique; **h. engineering,** technique *f* hydraulique, hydraulique *f*.

hydraulics [haɪ'drɔːlɪks] *npl* (*usu with sing verb*) hydraulique *f*.

hydro ['haɪdrəʊ] *n* **(a)** *Br* (*centre for hydrotherapy*) établissement *m* hydrothérapique; **(b)** *Can F* énergie *f* hydraulique; (*power station*) centrale *f* hydraulique; **to pay the h. bill,** payer la note d'électricité.

hydrocarbon [haɪdrəʊ'kɑːbən] *n Ch* hydrocarbure *m*.

hydrochloric [haɪdrəʊ'klɒrɪk] *adj Ch* (*acid*) chlorhydrique.

hydrochloride [haɪdrəʊ'klɔːraɪd] *n Ch* chlorhydrate *m*.

hydrodynamics [haɪdrəʊdaɪ'næmɪks] *npl* (*usu with sing verb*) hydrodynamique *f*.

hydroelectric [haɪdrəʊɪ'lektrɪk] *adj* hydroélectrique; **h. power,** énergie *f* hydraulique.

hydroelectricity [haɪdrəʊɪlek'trɪsɪtɪ] *n* hydroélectricité *f*.

hydrofoil ['haɪdrəfɔɪl] *n* hydrofoil *m*.

hydrogen ['haɪdrədʒən] *n Ch* hydrogène *m*; **h. bomb,** bombe *f* à hydrogène; **h. peroxide,** eau oxygénée.

hydrography [haɪ'drɒgrəfɪ] *n* hydrographie *f*.

hydrolysis [haɪ'drɒlɪsɪs] *n Ch* hydrolyse *f*.

hydrometer [haɪ'drɒmɪtər] *n* hydromètre *m*.

hydrometry [haɪ'drɒmɪtrɪ] *n Phys* hydrométrie *f*.

hydropathy [haɪ'drɒpəθɪ] *n* hydropathie *f*.

hydrophobia [haɪdrə'fəʊbɪə] *n Med* **(a)** (*rabies*) hydrophobie *f*; **(b)** (*fear*) phobie *f* de l'eau.

hydrophobic [haɪdrə'fəʊbɪk] *adj* hydrophobe.

hydroplane ['haɪdrəpleɪn] *n* **(a)** (*boat*) hydroglisseur *m*; **(b)** *esp US* (*seaplane*) hydravion *m*.

hydroponics [haɪdrəʊ'pɒnɪks] *npl* (*usu with sing verb*) culture *f* hydroponique.

hydrostat ['haɪdrəʊstæt] *n* hydrostat *m*.

hydrostatics [haɪdrəʊ'stætɪks] *npl* (*usu with sing verb*) hydrostatique *f*.

hydrotherapy [haɪdrəʊ'θerəpɪ] *n Med* hydrothérapie *f*.

hydroxide [haɪ'drɒksaɪd] *n Ch* hydroxyde *m*, hydrate *m*.

hyena [haɪ'iːnə] *n* (*animal*) hyène *f*; **laughing h.,** hyène rieuse; **to laugh like a h.,** rire comme un bossu.

hygenic [haɪ'dʒiːnɪk] *adj* hygiénique.

hygenically [haɪ'dʒiːnɪklɪ] *adv* hygiéniquement.

hygiene ['haɪdʒiːn] *n* hygiène *f*.

hymen ['haɪmen] *n* **(a)** *Anat* hymen *m*; **(b)** *Myth* **H.,** Hyménée *f*.

hymn [hɪm] *n* **(a)** *Rel* hymne *f*, cantique *m*; **h. book,** livre *m* de cantiques; **h. singing,** chant *m* d'hymnes; **(b)** (*anthem, poem etc*) hymne *m*.

hymnal ['hɪmn(ə)l] *m* livre *m* d'hymnes *ou* de cantiques.

hype[1] [haɪp] *n* **(a)** *F* (*publicity*) grand battage publicitaire; **it's all h.,** ce n'est que du tapage; **(b)** *Sl* (*hypodermic needle*) aiguille *f* hypodermique.

hype[2] *vt F* (*publicize*) pousser la vente de (*qch*) par un grand battage publicitaire; **to h. a new film/rock group,** lancer un nouveau film/groupe de rock par un grand battage publicitaire.

►**hype up** *vtsep* = **HYPE[2]**; **hyped up,** (*heavily publicized*) lancé par un grand battage publicitaire; (*on drugs*) camé.

hyperacidity [haɪpərə'sɪdɪtɪ] *n* hyperacidité *f*.

hyperactive [haɪpə'ræktɪv] *adj* hyperactif.
hyperbola [haɪ'pɜːbələ] *n Math* hyperbole *f*.
hyperbole [haɪ'pɜːbəlɪ] *n* hyperbole *f*.
hyperbolic(al) [haɪpə'bɒlɪk, -ɪk(ə)l] *adj* (*rhetoric*) *& Math* hyperbolique.
hypercritical [haɪpə'krɪtɪkəl] *adj* hypercritique.
hypermarket ['haɪpəmɑːkɪt] *n* hypermarché *m*.
hypersensitive [haɪpə'sensɪtɪv] *adj* hypersensible.
hypertension [haɪpə'tenʃən] *n Med* hypertension *f* (*artérielle etc*).
hypertext ['haɪpətekst] *n Comptr* hypertexte *m*.
hyphen ['haɪf(ə)n] *n* trait *m* d'union.
hyphenate ['haɪfəneɪt] *vt* mettre un trait d'union à (*un mot*); **hyphenated word,** mot *m* à trait d'union; **is that hyphenated?,** est-ce que ça prend un trait d'union?; *US* **hyphenated American,** étranger naturalisé (*Germano-Américain, Hispano-Américain etc*).
hypnosis [hɪp'nəʊsɪs] *n* hypnose *f*; **under h.,** sous hypnose.
hypnotic [hɪp'nɒtɪk] **1** *adj Psy Pharm* hypnotique; **h. state,** état *m* d'hypnose. **2** *n* **(a)** *Psy* (*person*) hypnotique *mf*; **(b)** *Pharm* (*drug*) hypnotique *m*.
hypnotism ['hɪpnətɪz(ə)m] *n* hypnotisme *m*.
hypnotist ['hɪpnətɪst] *n* hypnotiseur, -euse.
hypnotize ['hɪpnətaɪz] *vt* hypnotiser.
hypoallergenic [haɪpəælə'dʒenɪk] *adj* hypoallergénique, anallergique.
hypochondria [haɪpə'kɒndrɪə] *n Med* hypocondrie *f*.
hypochondriac [haɪpə'kɒndrɪæk] **1** *n* malade imaginaire *mf*, hypocondriaque *mf*. **2** *adj* hypocondriaque.
hypocrisy [hɪ'pɒkrɪsɪ] *n* hypocrisie *f*.
hypocrite ['hɪpəkrɪt] *n* hypocrite *mf*, *F* tartufe *m*.
hypocritical [hɪpə'krɪtɪk(ə)l] *adj* hypocrite.
hypocritically [hɪpə'krɪtɪklɪ] *adv* hypocritement.
hypodermic [haɪpə'dɜːmɪk] **1** *adj* **(a)** (*injection etc*) hypodermique; **h. syringe,** seringue *f* hypodermique; **(b)** *Anat* sous-cutané. **2** *n* (*syringe*) seringue *f* hypodermique; (*needle*) aiguille *f* hypodermique; (*injection*) piqûre *f* hypodermique.
hypotenuse [haɪ'pɒtənjuːz] *n Math* hypoténuse *f*.
hypothermia [haɪpəʊ'θɜːmɪə] *n Med* hypothermie *f*.
hypothesis [haɪ'pɒθəsɪs] *n* hypothèse *f*.
hypothesize [haɪ'pɒθəsaɪz] **1** *vi* supposer, faire des hypothèses *ou* des suppositions. **2** *vt* supposer (*une notion*); admettre comme hypothèse (**that,** que).
hypothetic(al) [haɪpə'θetɪk, -ɪk(ə)l] *adj* hypothétique, supposé.
hypothetically [haɪpə'θetɪklɪ] *adv* hypothétiquement, par hypothèse.
hysterectomy [hɪstə'rektəmɪ] *n Surg* hystérectomie *f*; **to have a h.,** subir une hystérectomie.
hysteria [hɪs'tɪərɪə] *n* **(a)** *Med* hystérie *f*; crise *f* de nerfs; **mass h.,** hystérie collective; **(b)** (*great amusement*) fou rire.
hysteric [hɪs'terɪk] *adj & n* hystérique *mf*.
hysterical [hɪs'terɪk(ə)l] *adj* **(a)** *Med* hystérique, atteint d'hystérie; **(b)** (*very emotional*) en proie à une crise de nerfs; (*laughter*) nerveux, énervé; **h. sobbing,** sanglots convulsifs; **she was h.,** elle était dans tous ses états; *Fig* **the h. reaction of the right wing to the reforms,** la réaction incontrôlée de la droite face aux réformes; **(c)** *F* (*very amusing*) écroulant; **(d)** *F* (*very amused*) **h. laughter,** fou rire.
hysterically [hɪs'terɪklɪ] *adv* **(a)** (*very emotionally*) sans pouvoir maîtriser ses émotions; **he was waving his arms h.,** il agitait ses bras de façon incontrôlée; **to weep h.,** avoir une crise de larmes; **to laugh h.,** être pris d'un rire nerveux; **(b)** *F* **h. funny,** écroulant; **(c)** *F* (*with great amusement*) **to laugh h.,** avoir le fou rire.
hysterics [hɪs'terɪks] *npl* **(a)** *Med* hystérie *f*; **(b)** (*emotional reaction*) attaque *f* de nerfs; crise *f* de nerfs; **to go into h.,** avoir une crise de nerfs; **(c)** *F* (*great amusement*) fou rire; **to be in h.,** être écroulé de rire; **she had us in h.,** elle nous a fait tordre de rire.

I

I[1], **i** [aɪ] *n* (la lettre) I, i *m*; *F* **to dot one's i's (and cross one's t's),** mettre les points sur les i.
I[2] **1** *pers pron* **(a)** *(unstressed)* je *mf*, *(joined to vowel)* j'; **I sing,** je chante; **I accuse,** j'accuse; **here I am,** me voici; **what have I said?,** qu'ai-je dit?; **(b)** *(stressed)* moi *mf*; **he and I,** lui et moi; **I too,** moi aussi. **2** *n* **another I,** un autre moi(-même).
Ia *abbr* **Iowa.**
iambic [aɪ'æmbɪk] *Liter* **1** *adj* *(vers)* iambique; **i. foot,** iambe *m*. **2** *n* *(poem)* iambe *m*.
IATA [aɪ'ɑːtə, iː'ɑːtə] *n Av* (*abbr* **International Air Transport Association**) = association internationale des transports aériens.
Iberia [aɪ'biːrɪə] *n* Ibérie *f*.
Iberian [aɪ'biːrɪən] **1** *adj* *(peuple)* ibérien, ibérique; **the I. peninsula,** la Péninsule ibérique. **2** *n* Ibère *mf*.
ibex, *pl* **-exes** ['aɪbeks, -eksɪz] *n* *(animal)* bouquetin *m* (des Alpes).
ibid ['ɪbɪd] *adv* (*abbr* **ibidem**) ibid.
ibis, *pl* **-ises** ['aɪbɪs, -ɪsɪz] *n* *(bird)* ibis *m*.
ICAO [aɪsiːeɪ'əʊ] *n Av* (*abbr* **International Civil Aviation Organization**) O.A.C.I. *f*.
ice[1] [aɪs] *n* **(a)** *(frozen water)* glace *f*; *Met* givre *m*; **my feet are as cold as i.,** j'ai les pieds glacés; **with i.?,** *(in drink)* vous voulez des glaçons *ou* de la glace?; *Fig* **to break the i.,** briser la glace; *Fig* **to be on** *or* **skate on thin i.,** être sur *ou* toucher à un sujet délicat; *Fig* **to cut no i. with s.o.,** ne faire aucune impression sur qn; *Fig* **to put a project on i.,** mettre un projet en veilleuse; **show on i.,** spectacle sur glace; *Geog* **the i. regions/seas,** les régions/mers glaciales; **drift i.,** glace(s) flottante(s); **pack i.,** (glace de) banquise *f*, pack *m*; **black i.,** verglas *m* *(sur les routes)*; *Geol* **i. age,** période *f* glaciaire; **i. barrier,** muraille *f ou* falaise *f* de glace; **i. bucket,** seau *m* à glace *ou* à rafraîchir; **i. cube,** glaçon *m*; *Sp* **i. dancing,** danse *f* sur glace; *Geog* **i. floe,** banquise *f*, banc *m* de glace; *Sp* **i. hockey,** hockey *m* sur glace, *Can* hockey; **i. house,** glacière *f*; **i. pack,** *(for headache)* sachet *m* de glace; *esp US* **i. man,** *(makes ice)* fabricant *m* de glace; *(sells it)* glacier *m*, marchand *m* de glace; **i. pick,** *(in mountaineering)* pioche *f* à glace; *Culin* poinçon *m* à glace; **i. rink,** patinoire *f*; **i. skate,** patin *m* (à glace); **i. skating,** patinage *m* *(sur glace)*; *Am* **i. water,** eau *f* avec glaçons;
(b) *Culin* **i. (cream),** glace *f*; **strawberry i.,** glace à la fraise; **water i.,** sorbet *m*, glace à l'eau; **i.-cream cone** *or* **cornet,** cornet *m*; **i.-cream man,** marchand *m* de glaces; *esp Am* **i.-cream parlour,** salon *m* de dégustation de glaces; *Br* **i. lolly,** esquimau *m*;
(c) *Ch* **dry i.,** neige *f* carbonique;
(d) *Sl* *(diamonds)* diamants *mpl*.
ice[2] *vt* congeler, geler; rafraîchir *(l'eau, un melon etc)* avec de la glace; frapper *(du champagne)*; *Culin* glacer *(un gâteau)*.
►**ice over** *vi* *(of pond etc)* geler.
►**ice up** *vi* *(of windscreen, propeller etc)* se givrer.
iceberg ['aɪsbɜːg] *n* **(a)** iceberg *m*; *Fig* **this is just the tip of the i.,** ce n'est que l'infime partie d'un tout; **i. lettuce,** laitue croquante; **(b)** *Fig* *(person)* glaçon *m*.
icebound ['aɪsbaʊnd] *adj* *(navire)* retenu *ou* bloqué par les glaces; *(port etc)* fermé par les glaces.
icebox ['aɪsbɒks] *n* **(a)** *(for storing food)* glacière *f* (domestique); *(in fridge)* compartiment *m* à glace; **(b)** *Am* réfrigérateur *m*.
icebreaker ['aɪs'breɪkər] *n Nau* brise-glace *m*.
icecap ['aɪskæp] *n* calotte *f* glaciaire.
ice-cold ['aɪs'kəʊld] *adj* froid comme la glace; *(eau)* glacé; *(vent)* glacial.
iced [aɪst] *adj* *(coffee)* glacé; *(melon)* rafraîchi; *(champagne)* frappé; *Culin* *(gâteau)* glacé; **i. water,** eau *f* avec glaçons.
Iceland ['aɪslənd] *n* Islande *f*.
Icelander ['aɪsləndər] *n* Islandais, -aise.
Icelandic [aɪs'lændɪk] **1** *adj* islandais, d'Islande. **2** *n Ling* islandais *m*.
ice-skate ['aɪs'skeɪt] *vi* faire du patin à glace.
ichthyology [ɪkθɪ'ɒlədʒɪ] *n* icht(h)yologie *f*.
ichthyosaur(us) [ɪkθɪə'sɔːr, -sɔːrəs] *n* icht(h)yosaure *m*.
icicle ['aɪsɪk(ə)l] *n* stalactite *f*.
icily ['aɪsɪlɪ] *adv* **(a)** *(to say, look at)* d'un ton *ou* d'un air glacial; **(b)** *(bitterly)* **it's i. cold,** il fait un froid glacial.
icing ['aɪsɪŋ] *n* **(a)** *esp Br Culin* glaçage *m* *(d'un gâteau)*; *(on cake)* glace *f*; *Fig* **the i. on the cake,** *(final touch)* la cerise sur le gâteau; **i. sugar,** sucre *m* glace; **(b)** *(freezing)* congélation *f*; *Av* givrage *m*.
icky ['ɪkɪ] *adj US F* *(in children's language)* collant.
icon ['aɪkɒn] *n Rel Comptr* icône *f*.
iconoclast [aɪ'kɒnəʊklæst] *n* iconoclaste *mf*.
iconoclastic [aɪkɒnəʊ'klæstɪk] *adj* iconoclaste.
ICU [aɪsiː'juː] *n Med abbr* **intensive care unit.**
icy ['aɪsɪ] *adj* **(a)** *(covered in ice)* couvert de glace; *(route)* verglacé; **(b)** *(very cold)* *(froid, Fig accueil)* glacial; *(mains)* glacé.
ID ['aɪ'diː] *n* (*abbr* **identification**) identité *f*; **have you got any ID?,** est-ce que vous avez une pièce d'identité?; **ID card,** carte *f* d'identité.
I'd [aɪd] **(a)** = **I had,** *see* **HAVE**[2]; **(b)** = **I would,** *see* **WILL**[3].
Ida *abbr* **Idaho.**
idea [aɪ'diːə] *n* idée *f*; **general i.,** idée générale; **the general i. is to ...,** l'idée est de ...; **I can't bear the i. (of it),** je ne peux pas en souffrir l'idée; **I have an i. that I've seen him before,** j'ai l'impression de l'avoir déjà vu; **it's not my i. of pleasure,** ce n'est pas là ma conception du plaisir; **her i. of a joke is ...,** le genre de plaisanterie qu'elle aime, c'est ...; **if this is your i. of a joke,** si tu trouves que c'est drôle; **the i. is to get the ball into the net,** *(of game etc)* le but est de mettre le ballon dans le panier; **I had no i. that ...,** je ne soupçonnais pas que ...; je n'avais aucune idée que ...; **you have no i. how anxious I was,** vous ne vous rendez pas compte combien j'étais inquiet; **can you give me an i.?,** *(of how much it will be, how long it will take)* est-ce que vous pouvez me donner une idée?; **he has some i. of chemistry,** il a des notions de chimie; **a bright i.,** une idée lumineuse; **whose i. was it to do that?,** qui a eu l'idée de faire cela?; **what a funny i.!,** quelle drôle d'idée!; **you've got a funny i. of loyalty,** tu as un sens bizarre de la fidélité; **what a good i.!,** quelle bonne idée!; **I've got a good i.,** j'ai une (petite) idée; **to be full of ideas,** avoir de l'idée; **man of ideas,** homme d'idées; **to get an i. that ...,** s'imaginer que ...; **I got the i. from a film,** c'est un film qui m'a donné l'idée; **to get ideas into one's head,** se faire des idées; **what put that i. into your head?,** qu'est-ce qui vous a donné cette idée?; **what an i.!,** en voilà une idée!; **the (very) i.!,** quelle idée!; **get the i.?,** vous comprenez?; **what's the (big) i.?,** qu'est-ce qui te prend?; **I had some i. of going as far as Paris,** j'avais dans l'idée de pousser jusqu'à Paris.
ideal [aɪ'diːəl] **1** *adj* idéal, -aux; **it's i.!,** c'est le rêve!, c'est l'idéal!; **in an i. world,** dans l'idéal. **2** *n* idéal *m*, *pl* -als, -aux; **the i. of beauty,** l'idéal de la beauté; **a man with no ideals,** un homme sans idéaux; **her high ideals,** sa hauteur de vues.
idealism [aɪ'dɪəlɪz(ə)m] *n* idéalisme *m*.
idealist [aɪ'dɪəlɪst] *n* idéaliste *mf*.
idealistic [aɪdɪə'lɪstɪk] *adj* idéaliste.
idealize [aɪ'dɪəlaɪz] *vt* idéaliser.
ideally [aɪ'diːəlɪ] *adv* **(a)** *(in ideal case)* dans l'idéal; **i., everyone should share alike,** l'idéal serait le partage égal pour tout le monde; **(b)** *(extremely well)* *(situated)* idéalement; *(qualified)* parfaitement; **they're i. matched,** ils vont parfaitement bien ensemble.
identical [aɪ'dentɪk(ə)l] *adj* identique (**with, to,** à); **i.**

copy (of a text), copie textuelle; **i. twins,** vrais jumeaux, vraies jumelles.

identically [aɪ'dentɪk(ə)lɪ] *adv* identiquement.

identification [aɪdentɪfɪ'keɪʃən] *n* **(a)** identification *f* (*d'un cadavre, d'un malfaiteur*); **i. parade,** séance *f* d'identification d'un suspect; **i. papers,** pièces *fpl ou* papiers *mpl* d'identité; *Av Nau* **i. marks,** (lettres *fpl* et numéros *mpl* d')immatriculation *f*; **(b)** (*documents etc*) papiers *mpl* d'identité; **have you got any i.?,** est-ce que vous avez une pièce d'identité?; **(c)** (*association*) **i. of sth with sth,** identification *f* de qch avec qch.

identify [aɪ'dentɪfaɪ] **1** *vt* **(a)** identifier (*qn, qch*); reconnaître (*qn, qch, un navire*); *Biol* déterminer (*un spécimen*); **(b)** (*associate*) **to i. oneself with a cause,** s'identifier à *ou* avec une cause, s'assimiler à une cause; **to be identified with sth,** être associé à qch. **2** *vi* s'identifier (**with s.o.,** à qn); **I can't i. (with it),** ça n'a rien à voir avec moi.

identifying [aɪ'dentɪfaɪɪŋ] *adj* **i. marks,** signes particuliers.

Identikit ® [aɪ'dentɪkɪt] *n* **i. (picture),** portrait-robot *m*, *pl* portraits-robots, photo-robot *m*, *pl* photos-robots.

identity [aɪ'dentɪtɪ] *n* **(a)** identité *f*; **to establish the i. of s.o.,** identifier qn; **to prove one's i.,** établir son identité; **mistaken i.,** erreur *f* sur la personne; *Admin* **i. card,** carte *f* d'identité; *Psy* **i. crisis,** crise *f* d'identité; *Mil* **i. disc/bracelet,** plaque *f*/bracelet *m* d'identité; **i. parade,** séance *f* d'identification d'un suspect; **(b)** (*quality of being identical*) identité *f*; **i. between two things,** identité entre deux choses *ou* de deux choses.

ideogram ['ɪdɪəgræm] **, ideograph** ['ɪdɪəgræf] *n* idéogramme *m*.

ideological [aɪdɪə'lɒdʒɪk(ə)l] *adj Phil etc* idéologique; **i. differences,** différences idéologiques *ou* d'idéologie.

ideologist [aɪdɪ'ɒlədʒɪst] *n* idéologue *mf*.

ideology [aɪdɪ'ɒlədʒɪ] *n* idéologie *f*.

ides [aɪdz] *npl Hist* ides *fpl*.

idiocy ['ɪdɪəsɪ] *n* **(a)** (*stupidity*) bêtise *f*, stupidité *f*; **(b)** (*mental backwardness*) **(congenital) i.,** idiotie *f* (congénitale).

idiolect ['ɪdɪəʊlekt] *n Ling* idiolecte *m*.

idiom ['ɪdɪəm] *n* **(a)** (*expression*) locution *f*, expression *f* idiomatique; **(b)** (*language*) dialecte *m*, idiome *m* (*d'une région*); langue *f*, idiome (*d'un pays*); **(c)** *Art Mus etc* style *m*.

idiomatic [ɪdɪə'mætɪk] *adj* **(a)** idiomatique; **i. phrase,** idiotisme *m*, expression *f* idiomatique; **(b)** qui appartient à la langue courante *ou* familière; **his French is not very i.,** son français n'est pas le français tel qu'on le parle.

idiomatically [ɪdɪə'mætɪklɪ] *adv* (*s'exprimer etc*) de façon idiomatique.

idiosyncrasy [ɪdɪəʊ'sɪŋkrəsɪ] *n* **(a)** particularité *f*, manie *f*; **(b)** *Med etc* idiosyncrasie *f*.

idiosyncratic [ɪdɪəʊsɪŋ'krætɪk] *adj* **(a)** particulier, caractéristique; **(b)** *Med* idiosyncrasique.

idiot ['ɪdɪət] *n* **(a)** imbécile *mf*; **what an i. I've been!,** comme j'ai été bête!; **you i.!,** espèce d'imbécile *ou* d'idiot!; **some i. has ...!,** un espèce d'imbécile a ...!; *Sl* **i. box,** (*television*) télé *f*; **(b)** (*mentally retarded person*) idiot, -ote, imbécile *mf*; **congenital i.,** idiot congénital.

idiotic [ɪdɪ'ɒtɪk] *adj* bête, idiot; **that's i.,** c'est stupide, c'est idiot; **don't be i.!,** ne fais pas l'idiot!

idiotically [ɪdɪ'ɒtɪklɪ] *adv* idiotement.

idiotism ['ɪdɪətɪz(ə)m] *n Am* idiotisme *m*, locution *f* (*d'une langue*).

idle[1] ['aɪd(ə)l] *adj* **(a)** (*unoccupied*) (*person*) inoccupé, oisif, désœuvré; (*machinery, employees*) qui chôme, en chômage; (*machine*) au repos; *MecE* (*wheel*) fou, décalé; (*pignon*) fou, intermédiaire; *El* (*courant*) déwatté; **to be** *or* **stand i.,** (*of person*) rester à ne rien faire; (*of machine*) ne pas servir; **in my i. moments,** à mes heures perdues; **to run i.,** (*of machine*) marcher à vide; (*of engine*) tourner au ralenti; **to lie i.,** (*of money*) dormir; **i. period,** période *f* d'inactivité; (*in mechanical cycle*) temps mort; **(b)** (*lazy*) paresseux, fainéant, indolent; **the i. rich,** les riches désœuvrés; **(c)** (*actions, feelings etc*) inutile, vain, futile; (*larmes*) inutile; (*idée, menace*) en l'air; (*gossip, rumour*) sans fondement; (*boast*) mal placé; **it is i. to speculate,** il est vain de spéculer; **out of i. curiosity,** par simple curiosité.

idle[2] *vi* **(a)** *Aut* (*of engine*) tourner au ralenti; **(b)** (*be lazy*) fainéanter, musarder.

▶**idle away** *vtsep* (*waste*) perdre (*son temps*) (à ne rien faire); **we idled away the afternoon chatting,** nous avons perdu l'après-midi à discuter.

idleness ['aɪd(ə)lnɪs] *n* **(a)** (*inaction*) inaction *f*, oisiveté *f*, désœuvrement *m*; chômage *m* (involontaire) (*d'une fabrique etc*); **(b)** (*laziness*) paresse *f*, fainéantise *f*; **(c)** futilité *f* (*d'une menace, d'un projet etc*).

idler ['aɪdlər] *n* **(a)** (*person*) paresseux, -euse; **(b)** *MecE* (*gear*) pignon fou *ou* intermédiaire; (*wheel*) roue folle *ou* décalée; (*pulley*) poulie folle.

idling ['aɪdlɪŋ] **1** *adj* (*moteur*) au ralenti. **2** *n* **(a)** (*wasting time*) fainéantise *f*; **(b)** (*of engine*) (marche *f* au) ralenti *m*.

idly ['aɪd(ə)lɪ] *adv* **(a)** (*not working*) sans rien faire, sans travailler; **to stand i. by,** rester là à ne rien faire; **(b)** (*lazily*) paresseusement; (*casually*) nonchalamment; **to do sth i.,** faire qch pour passer le temps; **(c)** (*futilely*) inutilement; (*to speculate etc*) vainement.

idol ['aɪd(ə)l] *n* idole *f*; **i. worship,** idolâtrie *f*; **to make an i. of wealth,** idolâtrer l'argent.

idolater [aɪ'dɒlətər] **, idolatress** [aɪ'dɒlətrɪs] *n* **(a)** *Rel* idolâtre *mf*; **(b)** *Fig* adorateur, -trice (**of,** de).

idolatrous [aɪ'dɒlətrəs] *adj* (*vénération*) idolâtre; (*culte*) idolâtrique.

idolatry [aɪ'dɒlətrɪ] *n* culte *m* des idoles; *Fig* idolâtrie *f*.

idolize ['aɪdəlaɪz] *vt* idolâtrer, adorer (*qn, qch*); faire une idole de (*qn*).

idolizing ['aɪdəlaɪzɪŋ] **1** *adj* (*regard etc*) plein d'adoration. **2** *n* idolâtrie *f*.

idyll ['ɪdɪl] *n* idylle *f*.

idyllic [ɪ'dɪlɪk, aɪ-] *adj* idyllique.

ie ['aɪ'iː] (*abbr* **id est**) c.-à.-d..

if [ɪf] **1** *conj* **(a)** si; **if I am late, I apologize,** si je suis en retard, je vous fais mes excuses; **if he does it, he will be punished,** s'il le fait, il sera puni; **let him do it if he dare(s)!,** qu'il le fasse s'il ose!; **if a child can do it so can I,** si un enfant peut le faire, je peux le faire aussi; **if you hesitate (at all),** pour peu que vous hésitiez; **if (it is) necessary,** s'il est nécessaire, s'il le faut, au besoin; **if (it is) possible,** si (c'est) possible; **if (it be) so,** s'il en est ainsi; **if so, when?,** si oui, quand?; **modifications, if any, will have to be made later,** les modifications éventuelles devront être apportées plus tard; **if not,** sinon; **go and see her, if only to please me,** allez la voir, ne serait-ce que pour me faire plaisir; **if and when they arrive we will decide what to do,** s'ils arrivent et seulement à ce moment-là, nous déciderons ce que nous ferons; **if I were you,** si j'étais vous, à votre place; **if it were so,** même s'il en était ainsi; **even if he did say so,** même s'il a dit cela, *Fml* quand même il l'aurait dit; **what if I** *or* **she** *etc* **did?,** qu'est-ce que ça change?; **if I had only known!,** (*exclamatory*) si seulement je l'avais su!; **if only he comes in time!,** pourvu qu'il vienne à temps!; **if only (I could)!,** (*do what you suggest*) si (seulement) je pouvais!; **as if,** comme si; **he looks as if he were drunk,** il a l'air d'être ivre; **as if to show it,** comme pour le montrer; **as if by chance,** comme par hasard; **as if I would allow it!,** comme si j'allais le permettre!; **if I know Sophie ...,** comme je connais Sophie ...;

(b) (*concessive*) **pleasant weather, if rather cold,** temps agréable, bien qu'un peu froid; **well-paid, if uninteresting, work,** travail bien rémunéré à défaut d'être intéressant; **if anything,** (*it's better, worse etc*) en fait;

(c) (*introducing a noun clause,* = **whether**) si; **I asked if it was true,** j'ai demandé si c'était vrai;

(d) (*for second occurrence in a clause*) que; **if he agrees and (if) we have time,** s'il est d'accord et que nous avons le temps.

2 *n* si *m inv*; **your ifs and buts make me tired,** je suis fatigué de vos si et de vos mais; **and it's a very big if,** et je dis bien "si".

iffy ['ɪfɪ] *adj F* aléatoire; **it's looking very i.,** ce ne semble pas du tout évident.

igloo ['ɪgluː] *n* igloo *m*.

igneous ['ɪgnɪəs] *adj* (*rock*) éruptif, igné.

ignite [ɪg'naɪt] **1** *vt* mettre feu à (*qch*); allumer (*une charge de mine*); enflammer (*un mélange explosif*). **2** *vi* prendre feu, s'enflammer, s'allumer.

ignition [ɪg'nɪʃən] *n* **(a)** *Aut* allumage *m*; **to cut off** *or* **switch off the i.,** couper l'allumage; **delayed** *or* **retarded i.,** retard *m* à l'allumage, allumage retardé; **the key was still in the i.,** la clé était encore sur le contact; **i. cable** *or* **lead** *or* **wire,** fil *m* d'allumage *ou* de bougie; **i. key,** clé *f* de contact; **i. spark,** étincelle *f* d'allumage; **i. switch,** contact *m*; **(b)** ignition *f* (*d'une charge de mine etc*).

ignoble [ɪg'nəub(ə)l] *adj* (*act etc*) ignoble, bas, *f* basse, infâme, vil.

ignominious [ɪgnə'mɪnɪəs] *adj* ignominieux, honteux.

ignominiously [ɪgnə'mɪnɪəslɪ] *adv* ignominieusement, honteusement.

ignominy ['ɪgnəmɪnɪ] *n* ignominie *f*, honte *f*.

ignoramus [ɪgnə'reɪməs] *n* ignorant, -ante, ignare *mf.*
ignorance ['ɪgnərəns] *n* ignorance *f*; **through i.,** par ignorance; **to keep s.o. in i. of sth,** laisser qn dans l'ignorance de qch; **I am in complete i. of his intentions,** j'ignore tout de ses intentions; **i. is bliss,** aux innocents les mains pleines; *Jur* **i. of the law is no excuse,** nul n'est censé ignorer la loi.
ignorant ['ɪgnərənt] *adj* ignorant; (*question*) qui trahit l'ignorance; **to be i. of a fact,** ignorer un fait; *Jur* être ignorant du fait; **an i. person,** un ignorant; **he is i. of the world,** (*uninformed*) il ne connaît pas le monde.
ignorantly ['ɪgnərəntlɪ] *adv* (*croire*) par ignorance; (*discourir*) avec ignorance.
ignore [ɪg'nɔːr] *vt* **(a)** (*take no notice of*) feindre d'ignorer (*qch*); passer (*qch*) sous silence; ignorer (*qn, des instructions*); feindre de ne pas voir (*qn*); méconnaître (*les faits*); ne pas répondre à (*une lettre, une invitation*); ne pas relever (*une injure*); ne tenir aucun compte de (*un ordre, un conseil*); brûler (*Rail un signal, Aut un feu rouge*); **I shall i. that!,** je ferai comme si je n'avais rien entendu!; **(b)** *Jur* rejeter (*une plainte*).
iguana [ɪ'gwɑːnə] *n* (*lizard*) iguane *m.*
ikon ['aɪkɒn] *n Rel Comptr* icône *f.*
ilex, *pl* **-exes** ['aɪleks, -eksɪz] *n* (*tree*) ilex *m.*
ilk [ɪlk] *n Scot* (*of landowner bearing the name of his property*) **Moray of that i.,** Moray du domaine de Moray; *Pej* **and others of that i.,** et d'autres du même genre.
ill [ɪl] **1** *adj* **(a)** (*unwell*) malade, souffrant; **to be i.,** être malade; **to feel i.,** se sentir souffrant; **it makes me feel i.,** ça me rend malade; **to fall** *or* **get** *or* **be taken i.,** tomber malade; **he was seriously i. last year,** il a fait une grave maladie l'année dernière; **to look i.,** avoir mauvaise mine; **a very i. woman,** une femme très malade; **he is mentally i.,** c'est un malade mental;
(b) (*repute, health etc*) mauvais; (*deed, nature etc*) méchant, mauvais; (*effect*) pernicieux; **i. breeding,** manque *m* de savoir-vivre; **i. luck** *or* **fortune,** mauvaise chance; **house of i. fame,** maison mal famée; *Prov* **it is an i. wind that blows nobody any good,** à quelque chose malheur est bon; **not to suffer any i. effects,** (*from excessive eating, drinking*) ne pas souffrir de retombées; (*from being imprisoned etc*) ne pas souffrir de séquelles; **i. will,** malveillance *f*; **i. feeling,** rancune *f.*
2 *adv* mal; *Lit* **to take sth i.,** prendre qch en mauvaise part; **to be i. provided with sth,** être mal pourvu de qch; **I can i. afford the expense,** je peux difficilement me permettre cette dépense; **it i. becomes you to...,** il vous sied mal de...; **to be** *or* **feel i. at ease,** (*uncomfortable*) être mal à l'aise; (*anxious*) être *ou* se sentir inquiet (**about,** au sujet de).
3 *n* **(a)** (*evil*) mal *m*; **to speak i. of s.o.,** dire du mal de qn; **to think i. of s.o,** penser du mal de qn;
(b) (*wrong*) dommage *m*, tort *m*; **I have suffered no i. at his hands,** il ne m'a fait aucun tort;
(c) (*misfortune*) **ills,** maux *mpl*, malheurs *mpl.*
ill. *abbr* **illustration**.
Ill *abbr* **Illinois**.
I'll [aɪl] **(a)** = **I will,** *see* **WILL**[3]; **(b)** = **I shall,** *see* **SHALL**.
ill-advised ['ɪləd'vaɪzd] *adj* **(a)** (*person*) malavisé (**to do,** de faire); **(b)** (*action*) peu judicieux.
ill-assorted ['ɪlə'sɔːtɪd] *adj* mal assorti, disparate.
ill-behaved ['ɪlbɪ'heɪvd] *adj* qui se conduit *ou* se tient mal.
ill-bred ['ɪl'bred] *adj* mal élevé, malappris.
ill-concealed ['ɪlkən'siːld] *adj* mal dissimulé.
ill-considered ['ɪlkən'sɪdəd] *adj* (*action, view etc*) peu réfléchi; (*measure etc*) hâtif.
ill-defined ['ɪl'dɪfaɪnd] *adj* mal défini.
ill-disposed ['ɪldɪs'pəʊzd] *adj* **(a)** (*unfriendly, unhelpful*) malintentionné, malveillant; **i.-d. towards s.o.,** mal disposé envers qn; **(b)** (*disinclined*) **to be i.-d. to do sth,** être peu disposé à faire qch.
illegal [ɪ'liːg(ə)l] *adj* illégal, -aux; (*immigrant*) clandestin; (*parking*) irrégulier; **it is i. to ...,** il est illégal de ... .
illegality [ɪlɪ'gælɪtɪ] *n* illégalité *f.*
illegally [ɪ'liːg(ə)lɪ] *adv* illégalement.
illegible [ɪ'ledʒɪb(ə)l] *adj* illisible.
illegibly [ɪ'ledʒɪblɪ] *adv* illisiblement.
illegitimacy [ɪlɪ'dʒɪtɪməsɪ] *n* illégitimité *f.*
illegitimate [ɪlɪ'dʒɪtɪmət] *adj* **(a)** *Jur* (*enfant*) illégitime, bâtard; **(b)** (*in logic*) (*conclusion*) illégitime; (*statement*) non autorisé.
illegitimately [ɪlɪ'dʒɪtɪmətlɪ] *adv* illégitimement.
ill-equipped ['ɪl'ɪkwɪpd] *adj* mal équipé; *Fig* **i.-e. to deal with stress,** démuni contre le stress.
ill-fated ['ɪl'feɪtɪd] *adj* (*enfant*) infortuné; (*jour*) fatal; **the i.-f. expedition,** l'expédition frappée par le destin.
ill-fitting ['ɪl'fɪtɪŋ] *adj* (*garment*) qui va mal, qui ne va pas bien.
ill-founded ['ɪl'faʊndɪd] *adj* (*rumour*) mal fondé, sans fondement.
ill-gotten ['ɪl'gɒtn] *adj* mal acquis; **i.-g. gains,** biens mal acquis *ou* acquis malhonnêtement.
ill-humoured, *US* **-humored** ['ɪl'hjuːməd] *adj* de mauvaise humeur.
illiberal [ɪ'lɪbər(ə)l] *adj* peu libéral, -aux; borné, petit (*d'esprit*); (*ungenerous*) peu généreux, mesquin.
illiberality [ɪlɪbə'rælɪtɪ] *n* illibéralité *f*; (*narrowness*) petitesse *f* (*d'esprit*); (*ungenerosity*) manque *m* de générosité.
illicit [ɪ'lɪsɪt] *adj* illicite.
illicitly [ɪ'lɪsɪtlɪ] *adv* illicitement.
illimitable [ɪ'lɪmɪtəb(ə)l] *adj* illimité.
ill-informed [ɪlɪn'fɔːmd] *adj* **(a)** (*misinformed*) mal renseigné; **(b)** (*poorly informed*) peu instruit; (*criticism etc*) ignorant.
ill-intentioned ['ɪlɪn'tenʃənd] *adj* malintentionné (**towards,** envers).
illiteracy [ɪ'lɪt(ə)rəsɪ] *n* analphabétisme *m.*
illiterate [ɪ'lɪt(ə)rət] *adj & n* illettré, -ée, analphabète *mf.*
ill-judged ['ɪl'dʒʌdʒd] *adj* (*action*) malavisé, peu sage.
ill-kempt ['ɪl'kempt] *adj* (*hair etc*) mal peigné; (*person*) peu soigné, négligé.
ill-mannered ['ɪl'mænəd] *adj* grossier, malappris; **to be i.-m.,** être mal élevé.
ill-natured ['ɪl'neɪtʃəd] *adj* d'un mauvais caractère, désagréable.
illness ['ɪlnɪs] *n* maladie *f.*
illogical [ɪ'lɒdʒɪk(ə)l] *adj* illogique.
illogicality [ɪlɒdʒɪ'kælɪtɪ] *n* illogisme *m.*
illogically [ɪ'lɒdʒɪk(ə)lɪ] *adv* illogiquement.
ill-prepared [ɪlprɪ'peəd] *adj* mal préparé.
ill-starred ['ɪl'stɑːd] *adj* né sous une mauvaise étoile; (*jour*) malheureux, néfaste.
ill-suited ['ɪl'suːtɪd] *adj* (*couple*) mal assorti; **they were i.-s.,** (*of couple*) ils étaient mal assortis, ils n'allaient pas très bien ensemble; **such clothes were i.-s. to a hot climate,** de tels vêtements n'étaient pas adaptés à un climat chaud.
ill-tempered ['ɪl'tempəd] *adj* (*in general*) de mauvais caractère, grincheux; (*on specific occasion*) de mauvaise humeur, grincheux.
ill-timed ['ɪl'taɪmd] *adj* mal à propos, hors de propos; (*arrival*) inopportun; (*plaisanterie*) hors de saison.
ill-treat ['ɪl'triːt] *vt* maltraiter, brutaliser (*qn, un chien*).
ill-treatment ['ɪl'triːtmənt] *n* mauvais traitement.
illuminate [ɪ'luːmɪneɪt] *vt* **(a)** éclairer (*une salle etc*); illuminer (*un édifice*); **(b)** éclairer, élucider (*un sujet, une question*); *Rel Phil* illuminer (*l'esprit*); **(c)** *Art* enluminer (*un manuscrit*).
illuminated [ɪ'luːmɪneɪtɪd] *adj* **(a)** (*room*) éclairé; (*sign*) lumineux; **(b)** *Art* (*manuscrit*) enluminé.
illuminating [ɪ'luːmɪneɪtɪŋ] **1** *adj* **(a)** (*discours, entretien*) qui éclaire la situation; **the programme was very i.,** l'émission était très édifiante; **(b)** (*providing light*) éclairant; (*effect*) lumineux. **2** *n* **(a)** éclairage *m* (*d'une salle*); illumination *f* (*d'un édifice*); **(b)** élucidation *f* (*d'un sujet etc*); **(c)** *Art* enluminure *f* (*d'un manuscrit*).
illumination [ɪluːmɪ'neɪʃən] *n* **(a)** éclairage *m* (*d'une salle etc*); illumination *f* (*d'un édifice*); *esp Br* **we went out to see the illuminations,** (*decorative lights*) nous sommes sortis voir les illuminations; **(b)** *Art* enluminure *f* (*d'un manuscrit*); **(c)** *Opt* éclat *m* (*d'une lentille etc*); *Phys* **(degree of) i.,** éclairement *m*; **(d)** *Rel* illumination *f.*
illuminator [ɪ'luːmɪneɪtər] *n* **(a)** illuminateur, -trice; **(b)** *Art* enlumineur, -euse.
ill-use[1] ['ɪl'juːs] *n* mauvais traitement, sévices *mpl.*
ill-use[2] ['ɪl'juːz] *vt* **(a)** (*maltreat*) maltraiter (*un enfant, une femme*); malmener (*un adversaire*); **(b)** (*behave badly towards*) mal agir envers (*qn*).
illusion [ɪ'luːʒən] *n* illusion *f*; **optical i.,** illusion d'optique; *Cin* (*special effect*) truc *m* d'optique; **to be under an i.,** être (la) victime d'une illusion; **he is under the i. that they will win,** il a l'illusion qu'ils vont gagner; **to cherish an i.,** se bercer d'une illusion; **I have no illusions** *or* **am under no i. on this point,** je ne me fais aucune illusion sur ce point.
illusionist [ɪ'luːʒənɪst] *n* prestidigitateur *m*, illusionniste *mf.*
illusory [ɪ'luːs(ə)rɪ] *adj* illusoire, trompeur.
illustrate ['ɪləstreɪt] *vt* **(a)** illustrer (*le texte d'un livre,*

d'un journal); **illustrated by N. Reed,** illustré par *ou* illustrations de N. Reed; **illustrated magazine,** (journal *m*, magazine *m*) illustré *m*; **(b)** (*explain, give example of*) illustrer, démontrer (*qch*) par des exemples; **to i. my point,** pour illustrer ce que je veux dire; **lectures illustrated by slides,** conférences illustrées par des projections.

illustration [ɪlə'streɪʃən] *n* **(a)** illustration *f*, gravure *f*, image *f* (*dans le texte d'un livre etc*); **text i.,** vignette *f*; **(b)** (*art*) illustration *f*; **she works in i.,** elle est illustratrice; **(c)** illustration *f*, explication *f*, exemple *m*, preuve *f* (*d'un principe etc*); **by way of i.,** à titre d'exemple.

illustrative ['ɪləstr(ə)tɪv] *adj* qui sert à expliquer; **i. of sth,** qui explique *ou* illustre qch.

illustrator ['ɪləstreɪtər] *n* illustrateur, -trice.

illustrious [ɪ'lʌstrɪəs] *adj* illustre, fameux, célèbre.

illustriously [ɪ'lʌstrɪəslɪ] *adv* illustrement.

ILO [aɪe'ləʊ] *n Ind* (*abbr* **International Labour Organization**) O.I.T. *f*.

I'm [aɪm] = **I am,** *see* **BE.**

image ['ɪmɪdʒ] *n* **(a)** (*copy*) image *f*, portrait *m*; **God created man in his own i.,** Dieu créa l'homme à son image; **he's the very** *or* **living** *or F* **spitting i. of his father,** c'est le portrait vivant de son père, *F* c'est son père tout craché; **(b)** (*representation*) image *f* (sculptée); représentation *f*, statue *f* (*d'un dieu etc*); (*for worship*) idole *f*; **(c)** (*mental picture*) image *f*; idée *f*, conception *f*; **he dismissed her i. from his mind,** il chassa son image de sa pensée; **(d)** (*of politician, party*) image *f*; *Com* **brand i.,** image de marque; **its i. is that of a dirty industrial city,** cette ville a la réputation d'être industrielle et sale; **he/it needs a bit of i. building,** il a besoin de rehausser un peu son image de marque; **(e)** *Liter* image *f*, métaphore *f*; **(f)** *Opt* image *f*; **ghost i.,** image blanche; *Phot* **latent i.,** image latente; *Electron TV* **i. distortion,** distorsion *f* d'image; **(g)** *Math* image *f*.

imagery ['ɪmɪdʒ(ə)rɪ] *n* **(a)** *Liter* figures *fpl* de rhétorique, images *fpl*; **(b)** (*pictures, carvings etc*) images sculptées.

imaginable [ɪ'mædʒɪnəb(ə)l] *adj* imaginable; **the finest thing i.,** la plus belle chose qu'on puisse imaginer.

imaginary [ɪ'mædʒɪn(ə)rɪ] *adj* imaginaire.

imagination [ɪmædʒɪ'neɪʃən] *n* imagination *f*; **to have no i.,** n'avoir aucune imagination; **that's your i.!,** vous l'avez rêvé!; **use your i.!,** fais preuve d'un peu d'imagination!; **it's all in your i.,** tout ça c'est dans la tête.

imaginative [ɪ'mædʒɪnətɪv] *adj* (*person, story etc*) imaginatif; (*solution etc*) original, -aux.

imaginativeness [ɪ'mædʒɪnətɪvnɪs] *n* **(a)** (*of person*) imagination *f*, esprit inventif; **(b)** nature imaginative (*d'un poème etc*).

imagine [ɪ'mædʒɪn] **1** *vt* **(a)** (*picture in one's mind*) (s')imaginer, concevoir (*qch*); se figurer, se représenter (*qch*); se faire une idée de (*qch*); (s')imaginer, voir (*qn*); **to i. all sorts of things, to be always imagining things,** se faire des idées; **I can't i. living anywhere else,** je n'imagine pas vivre ailleurs; **you're imagining things,** tu rêves; **you must have imagined it,** tu as dû rêver; **as may (well) be imagined,** comme on peut (se) l'imaginer; **i. meeting you here!,** qui aurait jamais pensé vous rencontrer ici!; **just i. my despair,** imaginez(-vous) un peu mon désespoir; **you can't i. it!,** vous n'avez pas idée!; **I can just i. him saying that,** j'imagine *ou* je conçois tout à fait qu'il dise cela; **I just can't i. you in that hat,** je ne t'imagine *ou* te vois pas du tout avec ce chapeau;

(b) (*suppose*) **I i. them to be fairly rich,** je les crois assez riches; **don't i. that I'm satisfied,** n'allez pas croire que je sois satisfait; **I i. that you must be very tired,** je suppose que vous devez être fatigué.

2 *vi* s'imaginer, imaginer, croire; **I can i.,** je veux bien le croire!, j'imagine!; **well, what did you i.?,** qu'est-ce que tu croyais?, qu'est-ce que tu t'imaginais?

imagined [ɪ'mædʒɪnd] *adj* imaginé, imaginaire.

imaginings [ɪ'mædʒɪnɪŋz] *npl* **the i. of a fevered mind,** les chimères d'un esprit enfiévré.

imam [ɪ'mɑːm] *n* imam *m*.

imbalance [ɪm'bæləns] *n* déséquilibre *m*.

imbecile ['ɪmbɪsiːl] *adj & n* imbécile *mf*.

imbecility [ɪmbɪ'sɪlɪtɪ] *n* **(a)** *Psy* imbécillité *f*; **(b)** *F* (*stupidity*) stupidité *f*, imbécillité *f*.

imbibe [ɪm'baɪb] **1** *vt Fml* (*of person*) absorber, assimiler (*des connaissances, des idées*); boire, avaler (*une boisson*); aspirer (*l'air frais*); (*of thing*) imbiber (*qch*); s'imprégner de (*qch*). **2** *vi F* boire (trop), picoler.

imbroglio [ɪm'brəʊlɪəʊ] *n* imbroglio *m*.

imbue [ɪm'bjuː] *vt Lit* pénétrer, imprégner (*qn*) (**with an idea,** d'une idée); **to be imbued with melancholy/hope/etc,** (*of novel etc*) être empreint de mélancolie/d'espoir/*etc*; **imbued with false principles,** pénétré *ou* imprégné de faux principes.

IMF [aɪe'mef] *n Econ* (*abbr* **International Monetary Fund**) F.M.I. *m*.

imitable ['ɪmɪtəb(ə)l] *adj* imitable.

imitate ['ɪmɪteɪt] *vt* **(a)** (*copy*) imiter, copier (*qn*); **to i. s.o.'s style,** imiter le style de qn; *Art Liter Mus* pasticher qn; **(b)** (*mimic*) singer, mimer (*qn*); contrefaire (*le cri d'un oiseau etc*); **to i. its surroundings,** (*of insect etc*) prendre l'aspect de son milieu.

imitation [ɪmɪ'teɪʃən] *n* **(a)** (*of person*) imitation *f*; **in i. of s.o./sth,** à l'imitation de *ou* imitant qn/qch; **(b)** (*copy*) copie *f*, imitation *f*; *Com* contrefaçon *f*; **i. jewellery,** bijoux *mpl* en faux *ou* en toc; **to wear i. jewellery,** porter du faux; **i. leather,** cuir artificiel, similicuir *m*; **i. silver,** similargent *m*; **i. gold,** similor *m*.

imitative ['ɪmɪtətɪv] *adj* (*son etc*) imitatif; **manner/style i. of s.o.,** manière *f*/style *m* qui imite qn.

imitator ['ɪmɪteɪtər] *n* **(a)** (*copier*) imitateur, -trice; *Com* contrefacteur *m*; *Art Liter Mus etc* pasticheur, -euse; **the Beatles had their imitators,** les Beatles ont eu des imitateurs; **(b)** *F* (*mimic*) singeur, -euse.

immaculate [ɪ'mækjʊlət] *adj* **(a)** (*dress*) immaculé, impeccable; (*desk, room*) dans un ordre parfait; *Fig* **her attendance record is i.,** elle n'a jamais manqué, elle n'a jamais été absente; **(b)** (*pure*) immaculé, sans tache; *Rel* **the I. Conception,** l'Immaculée Conception.

immaculately [ɪ'mækjʊlətlɪ] *adv* (*see adj*) **(a)** (*vêtu*) impeccablement; **(b)** sans tache.

immanent ['ɪmənənt] *adj Phil* immanent.

immaterial [ɪmə'tɪərɪəl] *adj* **(a)** (*unimportant*) peu important, sans conséquence; (*irrelevant*) qui n'a aucun rapport; **that fact is (quite) i.,** cela n'a aucune importance; **(b)** (*ghost etc*) immatériel, incorporel.

immature [ɪmə'tjʊər] *adj* (qui n'est) pas mûr; (*adulte*) qui manque de maturité; *Biol* immature; **the project is i.,** le projet n'est pas suffisamment mûri; **i. work,** œuvre *f* de jeunesse *ou* d'apprenti; **stop being so i.!,** arrête de te comporter comme un gamin!

immaturity [ɪmə'tjʊərɪtɪ] *n* (*of person*) *& Biol* immaturité *f*; manque *m* de maturité (*d'un projet*).

immeasurable [ɪ'meʒərəb(ə)l] *adj* (*espace, abîme*) incommensurable; (*temps*) infini.

immeasurably [ɪ'meʒərəblɪ] *adv* infiniment.

immediacy [ɪ'miːdɪəsɪ] *n* **(a)** caractère immédiat (**of,** de); imminence *f* (*d'un danger*); urgence *f* (*d'un besoin*); **(b)** (*relationship*) relation directe *ou* intime (**of sth with sth,** entre qch et qch).

immediate [ɪ'miːdɪət] *adj* **(a)** (*neighbour, surroundings*) immédiat, direct; **my i. object,** mon premier but; **what are your i. plans?,** que proposez-vous de faire d'abord?; **in the i. future,** dans un avenir immédiat, dans l'immédiat; **the i. family,** les proches parents; **(b)** (*instant*) instantané, sans retard; **i. answer/delivery,** réponse/livraison immédiate; **house for sale with i. possession,** maison à vendre avec jouissance immédiate; **(c)** (*besoin*) pressant, urgent; (*danger*) imminent; **work of i. urgency,** travail de première urgence.

immediately [ɪ'miːdɪətlɪ] **1** *adv* **(a)** (*without delay*) tout de suite, sans délai; (*recognizable*) immédiatement; **please send i. ...,** veuillez (bien) envoyer immédiatement *ou* d'urgence ...; **i. after,** aussitôt après; **(b)** (*directly*) immédiatement, directement; **it does not affect me i.,** cela ne me touche pas directement. **2** *conj Br* dès que; **i. I saw her I knew ...,** dès que je l'ai vu j'ai su que ... .

immemorial [ɪmɪ'mɔːrɪəl] *adj* immémorial, -aux; **from time i.,** de toute antiquité, de temps immémorial.

immense [ɪ'mens] *adj* (*étendue*) immense; (*quantité*) énorme; **of i. size,** de taille immense; **it was an i. success,** ça a été un immense succès.

immensely [ɪ'menslɪ] *adv* **(a)** immensément (*vaste*); énormément (*riche*); **she is i. fat,** elle est terriblement grosse; **(b)** (*to enjoy oneself*) énormément.

immensity [ɪ'mensɪtɪ] *n* **(a)** immensité *f* (*de l'univers, d'une fortune etc*); **(b)** énormité *f* (*d'un crime, d'un problème*).

immerse [ɪ'mɜːs] *vt* **(a)** immerger, plonger (*qn, qch*) (*dans un liquide*); *Rel* baptiser (*qn*) par immersion; **(b) to i. oneself in sth,** (*become absorbed by*) se plonger dans qch; **to be immersed in one's work/thoughts,** être plongé *ou* absorbé dans son travail/ses pensées.

immersion [ɪ'mɜːʃən] *n* **(a)** (*in liquid*) immersion *f*; *Rel* baptême *m* par immersion; **i. (water) heater,** chauffe-eau *m inv* à immersion; **(b)** absorption *f* (*d'esprit*) (**in,** dans).

immigrant ['ɪmɪgrənt] *adj & n (in the process of emigrating)* immigrant, -ante; *(who has emigrated)* immigré, -ée; **i. families,** familles immigrées.
immigrate ['ɪmɪgreɪt] *vi* immigrer.
immigration [ɪmɪ'greɪʃən] *n* immigration *f*; **to go through i.,** *(at port, airport etc)* passer à l'immigration; **i. officer,** agent *m* du service de l'immigration.
imminence ['ɪmɪnəns] *n* imminence *f* **(of,** de).
imminent ['ɪmɪnənt] *adj (danger, disaster, arrival etc)* imminent.
immobile [ɪ'məʊbaɪl] *adj* immobile.
immobility [ɪmə'bɪlɪtɪ] *n* immobilité *f*.
immobilize [ɪ'məʊbɪlaɪz] *vt* **(a)** immobiliser *(un membre blessé etc)*; immobiliser, arrêter *(une armée, la circulation etc)*; **(b)** *Fin* rendre *(des capitaux)* indisponible; immobiliser *(des espèces monnayées)*.
immoderate [ɪ'mɒd(ə)rət] *adj (drinking)* immodéré; *(feeling, attitude)* outré; *(thirst)* démesuré; *(gaiety)* exubérant.
immoderately [ɪ'mɒd(ə)rətlɪ] *adv* immodérément.
immodest [ɪ'mɒdɪst] *adj (personne, tenue)* impudique.
immodestly [ɪ'mɒdɪstlɪ] *adv* impudiquement.
immolate ['ɪməʊleɪt] *vt* immoler *(qn, qch)*.
immoral [ɪ'mɒrəl] *adj* immoral, -aux; *(ouvrage)* contraire à la morale; *Jur* **for i. purposes,** aux fins de débauche; **living on i. earnings,** *(of pimp)* proxénétisme *m*.
immorality [ɪmə'rælɪtɪ] *n* immoralité *f*; *(sexual)* débauche *f*; *(act)* acte immoral; **to incite to i.,** inciter à la débauche.
immorally [ɪ'mɒrəlɪ] *adv* immoralement.
immortal [ɪ'mɔːt(ə)l] **1** *adj* immortel; **the i. memory of ...,** le souvenir impérissable de ... . **2** *n* immortel, -elle.
immortality [ɪmɔː'tælɪtɪ] *n* immortalité *f*.
immortalize [ɪ'mɔːtəlaɪz] *vt* immortaliser *(qn, le nom d'un auteur etc)*; éterniser, perpétuer *(la mémoire de qn)*.
immovable [ɪ'muːvəb(ə)l] **1** *adj* fixe; *(opinion, volonté)* immuable, inébranlable; *(visage)* impassible; *Rel* **i. feast,** fête *f* fixe; *Jur* **i. property,** immeubles *mpl*, biens immobiliers. **2** *npl Jur* **immovables,** immeubles *mpl*, biens immobiliers.
immune [ɪ'mjuːn] *adj* **(a)** *Med* immunisé **(to,** contre); **i. system,** système *m* immunitaire; **(b)** *Fig* **i. to criticism,** imperméable à la critique; **i. to taxation,** exempt d'impôts; **i. from prosecution,** à l'abri de poursuites judiciaires.
immunity [ɪ'mjuːnɪtɪ] *n* **(a)** *Med* immunité *f* **(to,** contre); **(b)** exemption *f* **(from,** de); **diplomatic i.,** immunité *f* diplomatique.
immunization [ɪmjʊnaɪ'zeɪʃən] *n Med* immunisation *f* **(against,** contre).
immunize ['ɪmjʊnaɪz] *vt Med* immuniser *(qn)* **(against,** contre).
immunology [ɪmjʊ'nɒlədʒɪ] *n Med* immunologie *f*.
immunotherapy [ɪmjʊnəʊ'θerəpɪ] *n Med* immunothérapie *f*.
immure [ɪ'mjʊər] *vt Arch* **(a)** *(shut away)* enfermer, cloîtrer *(qn)*; **(b)** *(wall up)* emmurer *(une victime)*.
immutability [ɪmjuːtə'bɪlɪtɪ] *n* immu(t)abilité *f*.
immutable [ɪ'mjuːtəb(ə)l] *adj* immuable, inaltérable.
immutably [ɪ'mjuːtəblɪ] *adv* immuablement.
imp [ɪmp] *n* diablotin *m*, lutin *m*; *F (child)* petit espiègle, petite espiègle.
impact¹ ['ɪmpækt] *n* **(a)** *(shock)* choc *m*, impact *m*, collision *f*; *(of bullet)* impact; point *m* de chute *(d'un projectile)*; *Phys* **i. of one body against another,** choc d'un corps contre un autre; **on i.,** *(of projectile)* à l'impact, à l'arrivée; **point of i.,** *(of projectile)* point d'impact; *Comptr* **i. printer,** imprimante *f* à impact; **(b)** *Fig* répercussion(s) *f(pl)*, impact *m*; **the i. of a publicity campaign,** l'impact d'une campagne publicitaire; **his speech made a great i. on the audience,** son discours eut un effet retentissant sur l'auditoire; **the play has lost some of its i.,** la pièce a perdu une partie de son impact.
impact² [ɪm'pækt] *vt* encastrer, loger **(into,** dans).
impacted [ɪm'pæktɪd] *adj* encastré; *Surg (fracture)* avec impaction; **i. tooth,** dent barrée.
impair [ɪm'peər] *vt* affaiblir *(la vue, l'ouïe, l'esprit)*; altérer, abîmer *(la santé)*; faire perdre, diminuer *(les forces)*; compromettre *(l'autorité de qn)*; **seriously impaired health,** santé gravement altérée.
impairment [ɪm'peəmənt] *n* affaiblissement *m (de la vue, de l'ouïe, de la mémoire)*; altération *f*, ébranlement *m (de la santé)*; diminution *f (des forces)*.
impala [ɪm'pɑːlə] *n (antelope)* impala *m*.
impale [ɪm'peɪl] *vt* empaler; **to be impaled,** être empalé, s'empaler *(sur une grille etc)*.
impalpable [ɪm'pælpəb(ə)l] *adj* **(a)** *(intangible)* impalpable, intangible; **(b)** insaisissable *(à l'esprit)*.
impanel [ɪm'pænəl] *vt* = **EMPANEL**.
impart [ɪm'pɑːt] *vt* **(a)** donner *(du courage etc)*; imprimer, communiquer *(un mouvement)* **(to,** à); transmettre *(de la chaleur)*; **(b)** communiquer *(des connaissances)*; faire connaître, annoncer, confier *(une nouvelle)*; transmettre *(la vérité)* **(to,** à).
impartial [ɪm'pɑːʃəl] *adj (person, conduct)* impartial, -aux **(towards,** envers); **to be i.,** être impartial *ou* équitable.
impartiality [ɪmpɑːʃɪ'ælɪtɪ] *n* impartialité *f* **(to,** envers).
impartially [ɪm'pɑːʃəlɪ] *adv* impartialement, avec impartialité; *(juger)* équitablement.
impassable [ɪm'pɑːsəb(ə)l] *adj (rivière)* infranchissable; *(barrière)* impassable; *(route)* impraticable.
impasse ['æmpɑːs] *n* impasse *f*; **to reach an i.,** arriver à une impasse.
impassioned [ɪm'pæʃənd] *adj (orateur, discours, plaidoyer etc)* passionné; *(style)* chaleureux.
impassive [ɪm'pæsɪv] *adj* impassible; *(visage)* composé.
impassively [ɪm'pæsɪvlɪ] *adv* impassiblement.
impatience [ɪm'peɪʃəns] *n* impatience *f*; **i. to leave,** hâte *f* de partir; *Lit* **i. of sth,** intolérance *f* de qch.
impatient [ɪm'peɪʃənt] *adj* impatient; *(réponse)* vif, emporté; *(ton)* d'impatience; **to get** *or* **grow i.,** s'impatienter; **to be i. for sth,** être désireux *ou* avide de qch; **to be i. to do sth,** être impatient *ou* brûler de faire qch; **to get i. with sth/s.o.,** s'impatienter de qch/contre qn; *Lit* **to be i. of advice,** ne pas supporter les conseils.
impatiently [ɪm'peɪʃəntlɪ] *adv (attendre)* avec impatience; *(répondre)* sur un ton *ou* d'un ton d'impatience.
impeach [ɪm'piːtʃ] *vt* **(a)** *Jur (accuse)* accuser *(qn)* **(of, with a crime,** d'un crime); *Br* **to i. s.o. for high treason,** mettre qn en accusation pour haute trahison; *US* **to i. a public official,** = mettre un haut fonctionnaire en accusation devant le Congrès; **(b)** *(call into question)* attaquer, mettre en doute *(la véracité, la probité de qn)*; *Jur* récuser, reprocher *(un témoin)*; révoquer *(un témoignage)* en doute; **(c)** *(blame)* blâmer, censurer *(les motifs, la conduite de qn)*.
impeachment [ɪm'piːtʃmənt] *n* **(a)** *Jur* mise *f* en accusation *(d'un ministre etc)*; *US* impeachment *m*; **(b)** dénigrement *m (de l'honneur de qn)*; *Jur* reproche *m*, récusation *f (d'un témoin)*.
impeccable [ɪm'pekəb(ə)l] *adj* impeccable, irréprochable.
impeccably [ɪm'pekəblɪ] *adv* irréprochablement, impeccablement.
impecunious [ɪmpɪ'kjuːnɪəs] *adj* impécunieux.
impedance [ɪm'piːdəns] *n El* impédance *f*.
impede [ɪm'piːd] *vt* mettre obstacle à, empêcher, entraver *(le progrès, l'activité etc)*; entraver *(la circulation)*; contrarier *(les mouvements de l'ennemi)*.
impediment [ɪm'pedɪmənt] *n* entrave *f*, empêchement *m*, obstacle *m* **(to,** à); **speech i.,** trouble *m* de la parole; **to have an i. in one's speech,** avoir la parole *ou* la prononciation embarrassée.
impedimenta [ɪmpedɪ'mentə] *npl* impedimenta *mpl*; **all the i. of war,** tout l'attirail de la guerre.
impel [ɪm'pel] *vt* **(-ll-) (a)** *(motivate)* pousser, forcer **(s.o. to do sth,** qn à faire qch); **(b)** *(push)* pousser (en avant).
impelling [ɪm'pelɪŋ] *adj (force etc)* impulsif; *(need etc)* urgent.
impending [ɪm'pendɪŋ] *adj (danger etc)* imminent, menaçant; **her impending arrival,** son arrivée prochaine.
impenetrability [ɪmpenɪtrə'bɪlɪtɪ] *n* impénétrabilité *f*.
impenetrable [ɪm'penɪtrəb(ə)l] *adj* impénétrable **(to, by,** à); *(mystère)* insondable; *(mist)* épais.
impenitence [ɪm'penɪtəns] *n* impénitence *f*.
impenitent [ɪm'penɪtənt] *adj & n* impénitent, -ente.
impenitently [ɪm'penɪtəntlɪ] *adv* sans repentir.
imperative [ɪm'perətɪv] **1** *adj* **(a)** *(need etc)* urgent; **it is i. that he should come,** il faut absolument qu'il vienne; **(b)** *(tone)* impératif, impérieux, péremptoire; **(c)** *Gram (mode)* impératif. **2** *n Gram* (mode *m*) impératif *m*; **in the i.,** à l'impératif.
imperceptible [ɪmpə'septɪb(ə)l] *adj* imperceptible; *(bruit, différence)* insaisissable; *(différence)* insensible.
imperceptibly [ɪmpə'septɪblɪ] *adv* imperceptiblement, insensiblement.
imperfect [ɪm'pɜːfɪkt] **1** *adj* **(a)** *(not perfect)* imparfait; *Mus (cadence)* imparfait; **an i. command of the language,** une connaissance imparfaite de la langue; **(b)** *Gram (tense)* imparfait. **2** *n Gram* imparfait *m*; **verb in the i.,** verbe *m* à l'imparfait.
imperfection [ɪmpə'fekʃən] *n* **(a)** *(flaw)* imperfection *f*,

défectuosité *f*; **(b)** (*state of being imperfect*) caractère imparfait.

imperfectly [ɪm'pɜːfɪktlɪ] *adv* imparfaitement.

imperial [ɪm'pɪərɪəl] **1** *adj* **(a)** (*gouvernement etc*) impérial; **the i. crown,** la couronne impériale; **His** *or* **Her I. Majesty,** sa Majesté Impériale; **(b)** *Br* (*weights and measures*) = qui ont cours légal dans le Royaume-Uni; **i. pint,** pinte légale; **(c)** (*commanding*) majestueux, altier. **2** *n* **(a)** (*papier*) grand jésus; **(b)** (*beard*) impériale *f*.

imperialism [ɪm'pɪərɪəlɪzəm] *n* impérialisme *m*.

imperialist [ɪm'pɪərɪəlɪst] *adj & n* impérialiste *mf*.

imperialistic [ɪmpɪərɪə'lɪstɪk] *adj* impérialiste.

imperially [ɪm'pɪərɪəlɪ] *adv* **(a)** impérialement; **(b)** majestueusement.

imperil [ɪm'perɪl] *vt* (**-ll-**, *US* **-l-**) mettre en péril *ou* en danger; exposer (*sa vie etc*) au danger; compromettre (*sa réputation*).

imperious [ɪm'pɪərɪəs] *adj* (*personne, ton, caractère*) impérieux, dictatorial, -aux; (*ordre*) impératif.

imperiously [ɪm'pɪərɪeslɪ] *adv* (*parler, agir*) impérieusement.

imperishable [ɪm'perɪʃəb(ə)l] *adj* impérissable.

impermanent [ɪm'pɜːmənənt] *adj* impermanent.

impermeable [ɪm'pɜːmɪəb(ə)l] *adj* imperméable.

impersonal [ɪm'pɜːsən(ə)l] *adj* **(a)** (*style etc*) impersonnel; **(b)** *Gram* (*verbe*) impersonnel.

impersonally [ɪm'pɜːsən(ə)lɪ] *adv* impersonnellement, de façon impersonnelle.

impersonate [ɪm'pɜːsəneɪt] *vt* **(a)** se faire passer pour (*qn*); *Th TV etc* (*take off*) imiter; **(b)** *Arch* personnifier (*la vertu etc*).

impersonation [ɪmpɜːsə'neɪʃən] *n* **(a)** (*of person*) usurpation *f* d'identité de (*qn*); **to do impersonations,** faire des imitations (*de personnages*); **(b)** *Arch* personnification *f*.

impersonator [ɪm'pɜːsəneɪtər] *n* personne qui se fait passer pour une autre; imitateur, -trice (*de personnages etc*); **male/female i.,** actrice/acteur qui joue un rôle travesti.

impertinence [ɪm'pɜːtɪnəns] *n* **(a)** impertinence *f*, insolence *f*; **an i., a piece of i.,** une impertinence; **(b)** *Jur* impertinence *f*.

impertinent [ɪm'pɜːtɪnənt] *adj* **(a)** impertinent, insolent; (*remarque*) impertinent, déplacé; **to be i. to s.o.,** être insolent *ou* impertinent envers qn; **(b)** *Jur* (*sujet, récit*) non pertinent, hors de propos.

impertinently [ɪm'pɜːtɪnəntlɪ] *adv* (*see adj*) **(a)** impertinemment, insolemment; d'un ton insolent *ou* impertinent; **(b)** *Jur* (*répondre*) en dehors de la question.

imperturbable [ɪmpə'tɜːbəb(ə)l] *adj* imperturbable.

impervious [ɪm'pɜːvɪəs] *adj* **(a)** inaccessible, rebelle (**to reason,** à la raison); **he's i. to criticism,** il est indifférent à la critique; **(b)** (*material etc*) **i.,** (*to water*) imperméable, étanche; (*to light*) résistant (à la lumière); *Geol* **i. stratum,** couche *f* étanche.

impetigo [ɪmpɪ'taɪgəʊ] *n Med* impétigo *m*, *F* gourme *f*; **to have i.,** avoir *ou* faire de l'impétigo.

impetuosity [ɪmpetjʊ'ɒsɪtɪ] *n* = **IMPETUOUSNESS**.

impetuous [ɪm'petjʊəs] *adj* (*caractère*) fougueux, emporté, impétueux; (*action*) impétueux; **don't be so i.,** ne t'emporte pas comme ça.

impetuously [ɪm'petjʊəslɪ] *adv* impétueusement, avec impétuosité.

impetuousness [ɪm'petjʊəsnəs] *n* impétuosité *f*, fougue *f* (*d'une personne*); impétuosité (*d'une action*).

impetus ['ɪmpɪtəs] *n* **(a)** élan *m*; **to give an i. to sth,** donner l'impulsion à qch; **carried away by my own i.,** emporté par mon propre élan; **(b)** *Phys* vitesse acquise.

impiety [ɪm'paɪətɪ] *n* impiété *f*.

►**impinge on** [ɪm'pɪndʒ] *vipo* empiéter sur (*les droits d'autrui etc*); (*of ray of light etc*) frapper (*qch*); (*affect*) affecter; **it impinges in a big way on all our lives,** ça affecte énormément notre vie à tous; **to i. on s.o.'s conscious mind,** venir à la conscience de qn; **it didn't even i. on his consciousness,** il ne s'en est même pas rendu compte; **insofar as it impinges on our department,** dans la mesure où cela affecte *ou* a des répercussions sur notre service.

impingement [ɪm'pɪndʒmənt] *n* empiètement *m* (*sur les droits de qn etc*); *Old-fashioned* (*collision*) heurt *m*.

impious ['ɪmpɪəs] *adj* impie.

impiously ['ɪmpɪəslɪ] *adv* avec impiété.

impish ['ɪmpɪʃ] *adj* de petit diable, d'espiègle; (*rire*) espiègle, malicieux.

impishly ['ɪmpɪʃlɪ] *adv* en espiègle.

impishness ['ɪmpɪʃnɪs] *n* espièglerie *f*.

implacable [ɪm'plækəb(ə)l] *adj* implacable (**towards,** à, pour, à l'égard de).

implacably [ɪm'plækəblɪ] *adv* implacablement.

implant[1] ['ɪmplɑːnt] *n Surg* implant *m*.

implant[2] [ɪm'plɑːnt] *vt* **(a)** (*insert*) implanter (**in,** dans); **(b)** inculquer (*une opinion*) (**in s.o.,** à qn); implanter (*une idée*) (**in s.o.,** dans la tête de qn); insinuer (*un principe*) (**in s.o.,** à qn); **from his youth this ideal had been implanted in his mind,** dès sa jeunesse cet idéal lui avait été inculqué; **(c)** *Med* implanter.

implausible [ɪm'plɔːzɪb(ə)l] *adj* peu plausible, invraisemblable.

implausibly [ɪm'plɔːzɪblɪ] *adv* invraisemblablement; **to end i.,** (*of book, film etc*) se terminer de façon peu vraisemblable.

implement[1] ['ɪmplɪmənt] *n* outil *m*, instrument *m*, ustensile *m*; **gardening implements,** outils de jardinage.

implement[2] ['ɪmplɪment] *vt* rendre effectif (*un traité etc*); exécuter, remplir (*un engagement*); mettre en œuvre (*un accord, un procédé technique*); mettre à exécution (*un projet*); donner suite à (*une décision*).

implementation [ɪmplɪmen'teɪʃən] *n* exécution *f* (*d'un engagement*); mise *f* en œuvre (*d'un accord, d'un procédé technique*).

implicate ['ɪmplɪkeɪt] *vt* **(a)** impliquer, mêler (**s.o. in a crime,** qn dans un crime); **without implicating anyone,** sans compromettre personne; **(b)** *Fml* (*imply*) impliquer, renfermer; **words implicating contradiction,** mots qui renferment une contradiction.

implication [ɪmplɪ'keɪʃən] *n* **(a)** implication *f*; **by i.,** implicitement; **the full i. of these words,** la portée de ces paroles; **(b)** (*insinuation*) insinuation *f*, sous-entendu *m*, *pl* sous-entendus.

implicit [ɪm'plɪsɪt] *adj* **(a)** (*implied*) (*condition etc*) implicite; (*reconnaissance*) tacite; **(b)** (*absolute*) (*obéissance*) absolu; **i. faith,** confiance *f* aveugle (**in,** dans); *Rel* foi *f* implicite.

implicitly [ɪm'plɪsɪtlɪ] *adv* **(a)** implicitement, tacitement; **(b)** (*absolutely*) (*obéir*) aveuglément; **to trust s.o. i.,** avoir une confiance implicite en qn.

implied [ɪm'plaɪd] *adj* (*consentement*) implicite, tacite; **i. meaning,** signification impliquée, sous-entendu *m*, *pl* sous-entendus.

implode [ɪm'pləʊd] *vi* (*of vacuum tube etc*) imploser.

implore [ɪm'plɔːr] *vt* implorer (*le pardon etc*); implorer, conjurer, supplier (*qn*) (**to do sth,** de faire qch).

imploring [ɪm'plɔːrɪŋ] *adj* (*regard, ton etc*) implorant, suppliant.

imploringly [ɪm'plɔːrɪŋlɪ] *adv* (*to say, look at*) d'un ton *ou* d'un air suppliant.

implosion [ɪm'pləʊʒən] *n* implosion *f* (*d'un tube à vide etc*).

imply [ɪm'plaɪ] *vt* **(a)** (*of person*) donner à entendre, sous-entendre; **you seem to i. that ...,** ce que vous dites laisse supposer que ...; **are you implying that I stole the money?,** est-ce que vous laissez entendre que j'ai volé l'argent?; **(b)** (*of circumstance*) impliquer; **conclusion implied from the evidence,** conclusion qui découle (implicitement) des preuves.

impolite [ɪmpə'laɪt] *adj* impoli (**to, towards,** envers).

impolitely [ɪmpə'laɪtlɪ] *adv* impoliment.

impoliteness [ɪmpə'laɪtnɪs] *n* impolitesse *f*.

impolitic [ɪm'pɒlɪtɪk] *adj* imprudent, peu judicieux.

imponderability [ɪmpɒndərə'bɪlɪtɪ] *n* impondérabilité *f*.

imponderable [ɪm'pɒndərəb(ə)l] *adj & n* impondérable *m*.

import[1] ['ɪmpɔːt] *n* **(a)** *Com Econ* (*item*) article *m* d'importation; (*activity*) importation *f*; **imports,** (*individual imports*) articles *mpl* d'importation; (*collective imports*) importations *fpl*; *Fig* **the art of lacemaking was an i. from France,** l'art de la (fabrication de la) dentelle nous est venu de France; **i. ban,** interdiction *f* d'importation; **i. duty,** droit *m* d'entrée; **(b)** *Fml* sens *m*, signification *f* (*d'un mot*); teneur *f* (*d'un document*); **(c)** (*importance*) importance *f* (*d'un événement*); portée *f* (*d'une observation*); valeur *f* (*d'une découverte etc*); **matter of great i.,** affaire *f* de toute importance.

import[2] [ɪm'pɔːt] *vt* **(a)** *Com Econ* importer (*des marchandises*); **imported goods,** marchandises importées *ou* d'importation; **imported from England,** de provenance anglaise; **(b)** *Comptr* importer; **(c)** *Lit* indiquer; (*mean*) signifier, vouloir dire; (*declare*) déclarer, faire savoir (**that,** que); (*augur*) présager, augurer (*des changements etc*).

importance [ɪm'pɔːtəns] *n* importance *f*; **to give i. to a**

word, mettre un mot en valeur, donner de l'importance à un mot; **to be of i.,** avoir de l'importance; **of vital/strategic/** *etc* **i.,** d'une importance capitale/stratégique/*etc*; **it is of the highest i. to remember that ...,** il importe fort de se souvenir que ...; **it is of no great i.,** cela importe peu; **detail of no i.,** détail *m* négligeable *ou* sans importance; **to attach i. to sth,** mettre *ou* attacher de l'importance à qch; *Pej* **to be full of one's own i.,** (*of person*) être pénétré de son importance.

important [ɪm'pɔːtənt] *adj* important; (*difference*) considérable; **what is more i.?,** qu'est-ce qui est le plus important?; **to become more i.,** (*of nation etc*) s'agrandir; **it is i. for you to know that ..., it is i. that you should know that ...,** il est important *ou* il importe que vous sachiez que ...; **it is i. to know that ...,** il est important *ou* il importe de savoir que ...; **his children/hobbies are very i. to him,** ses enfants/passe-temps sont très importants pour lui; *Pej* **to look i.,** (*of person*) prendre *ou* se donner des airs (d'importance); **to feel i.,** (*of person*) se sentir important.

importantly [ɪm'pɔːtəntlɪ] *adv* (*to look at, say*) d'un air *ou* d'un ton d'importance; **but, more i.,** mais, ce qui est plus important; **they're i. different,** il y a une différence considérable entre eux.

importation [ɪmpɔː'teɪʃən] *n* **(a)** importation *f* (*de marchandises*); **(b)** (*imported article*) importation *f*, article *m* d'importation; **(c)** *Comptr* importation *f*.

importer [ɪm'pɔːtər] *n* importateur, -trice.

import-export ['ɪmpɔːt'ekspɔːt] *n* **i.-e. (trade),** import-export *f*.

importing ['impɔːtɪŋ] **1** *adj* (*pays*) importateur. **2** *n* importation *f* (*de marchandises*).

importunate [ɪm'pɔːtjʊnɪt] *adj Fml* (*créancier, visiteur*) importun.

importune [ɪm'pɔːtjuːn] *vt Fml* importuner (*qn*).

importunity [ɪmpɔː'tjuːnɪtɪ] *n Fml* importunité *f*.

impose [ɪm'pəʊz] **1** *vt* **(a)** imposer (*le silence, sa volonté, des contraintes etc*) **(on s.o.,** à qn); **his bearing imposes respect,** son maintien impose le respect *ou* en impose; **to i. a tax on sugar,** imposer *ou* taxer le sucre; **to i. the maximum penalty provided,** appliquer le maximum de la peine; **(b)** *Typ* imposer (*une feuille*); mettre (*la matière*) en pages; **(c)** *Rel* (*of priest*) **to i. hands on s.o.,** imposer les mains à *ou* sur qn. **2** *vi* **(a)** (*take advantage*) abuser; **I hope I'm not imposing,** je ne voudrais pas abuser de votre hospitalité; **to i. on** *or* **upon s.o.,** abuser de l'amabilité de qn; **to i. upon s.o.'s kindness,** abuser de la bonté de qn; **(b)** (*impose respect*) en imposer.

imposing [ɪm'pəʊzɪŋ] *adj* (*air, ton*) imposant; (*spectacle*) impressionnant.

imposition [ɪmpə'zɪʃən] *n* **(a)** imposition *f* (*d'une tâche, d'une taxe*); (*of fine*) fait *m* d'infliger; **(b)** (*abuse*) abus *m* de la bonne volonté de qn; **this is an i. on your kindness,** c'est abuser de votre bonté; **(c)** *Br Sch* punition *f*; **(d)** *Typ* imposition *f* (*d'une feuille*); **(e)** *Rel* imposition *f* (*des mains*); **(f)** (*tax*) imposition *f*, impôt *m*, taxe *f*.

impossibility [ɪmpɒsɪ'bɪlɪtɪ] *n* impossibilité *f* (*de qch*); **it's an i.,** c'est une impossibilité; **physical i.,** chose *f* matériellement impossible.

impossible [ɪm'pɒsɪb(ə)l] **1** *adj* **(a)** impossible; **it is i. for me to do it,** il m'est impossible de le faire; **to make it i. for s.o. to do sth,** mettre qn dans l'impossibilité de faire qch; **it's not i. that,** il n'est pas impossible que + *sub*; **(it's) i. to say** *or* **tell,** c'est impossible à dire; **(b)** (*unbelievable*) (*histoire, récit*) invraisemblable; **(c)** *F* (*life, person*) impossible; **you're i.!,** vous êtes impossible! **2** *n* impossible *m*; **to attempt the i.,** tenter l'impossible.

impossibly [ɪm'pɒsɪblɪ] *adv* **not i.,** peut-être bien; *F* **the exam was i. difficult,** l'examen était incroyablement difficile; **he's being i. difficult,** il est extrêmement difficile; **i. long,** insupportablement long.

impostor [ɪm'pɒstər] *n* imposteur *m*.

imposture [ɪm'pɒstʃər] *n* imposture *f*, tromperie *f*.

impotence ['ɪmpətəns] *n* **(a)** (*powerlessness*) impuissance *f*; (*weakness*) faiblesse *f*, impotence *f*; **(b)** (*sexual*) impuissance *f*.

impotent ['ɪmpətənt] *adj* **(a)** (*powerless*) impuissant; (*weak*) impotent, faible; **(b)** (*sexually*) impuissant.

impound [ɪm'paʊnd] *vt* **(a)** *Jur* (*confiscate*) confisquer, saisir; **(b)** mettre (*une bête, une voiture etc*) en fourrière.

impounding [ɪm'paʊndɪŋ] *n* **(a)** *Jur* arrêt *m*, saisie *f* (*de marchandises*); prise *f* de possession (*de documents*); **(b)** mise *f* en fourrière (*de bêtes etc*).

impoverish [ɪm'pɒvərɪʃ] *vt* appauvrir (*qn, un pays, le sol*).

impoverished [ɪm'pɒvərɪʃd] *adj* appauvri, pauvre.

impracticability [ɪmpræktɪkə'bɪlɪtɪ] *n* impraticabilité *f*.

impracticable [ɪm'præktɪkəb(ə)l] *adj* infaisable, impraticable; (*théorie*) inapplicable, irréalisable.

impractical [ɪm'præktɪk(ə)l] *adj* (*person*) peu pratique; (*project etc*) peu réaliste.

imprecation [ɪmprɪ'keɪʃən] *n* imprécation *f*, malédiction *f*.

imprecise [ɪmprɪ'saɪs] *adj* imprécis, vague.

imprecision [ɪmprɪ'sɪʒən] *n* imprécision *f*, manque *m* de précision.

impregnable [ɪm'pregnəb(ə)l] *adj* **(a)** (*forteresse*) imprenable, inexpugnable; **i. to attack,** imprenable; **(b)** (*vérité etc*) invincible.

impregnate ['ɪmpregneɪt] *vt* **(a)** *Biol* féconder (*une femelle*); **(b)** *Tech* imprégner, imbiber, saturer **(sth with sth,** qch de qch); **to i. wood,** injecter le bois; *Fig* **to become impregnated with false principles,** s'imprégner *ou* se pénétrer de faux principes.

impregnation [ɪmpreg'neɪʃən] *n* **(a)** *Biol* fécondation *f*; **(b)** imprégnation *f* (*d'un tissu etc*); injection *f*, pénétration *f* (*du bois etc*).

impresario [ɪmpre'sɑːrɪəʊ] *n* impresario *m*.

impress[1] ['ɪmpres] *n* **(a)** (*imprint*) impression *f*, empreinte *f*; **(b)** (*distinctive style etc*) marque distinctive; **the work bore the i. of genius,** l'œuvre portait la marque du génie.

impress[2] [ɪm'pres] **1** *vt* **(a)** (*create strong impression*) frapper, impressionner, faire une impression à (*qn*); **I was deeply impressed by it,** cela m'a fait une grande impression, j'en ai été profondément impressionné; *F* **I'm not impressed,** cela me laisse froid; **he impressed me favourably,** il m'a fait une impression favorable; **she impressed me as hard-working,** elle m'a fait l'impression d'être travailleuse;

(b) (*make understood*) faire bien comprendre **(sth upon s.o.,** qch à qn); inculquer (*une idée*) à qn; **you must i. on him that ...,** il faut bien lui faire sentir que ...;

(c) (*imprint*) **to i. sth on** *or* **upon sth,** imprimer *ou* empreindre qch sur qch; **to i. sth on the mind,** graver qch dans la mémoire; **to i. sth with a seal,** faire une impression sur qch avec un cachet; *Fig* **to i. s.o. with the idea that ...,** inculquer à qn l'idée que ... .

2 *vi* (*of person, remark*) faire impression.

impression [ɪm'preʃən] *n* **(a)** impression *f* (*sur qn, sur les sens*); **to make a good/bad i.,** faire (une) bonne/mauvaise impression **(on, sur)**; **my first i. wasn't favourable,** ma première impression n'a pas été favorable; **to make an i.,** faire impression; **tell us your impressions,** faites-nous part de vos impressions;

(b) (*idea*) idée *f*; **I'm under the i. that I've seen him before,** j'ai l'impression de l'avoir déjà vu; **I had the i. that you liked her,** j'avais l'impression que tu l'aimais bien; **to create** *or* **give the i. that ...,** donner *ou* produire l'impression que ...;

(c) impression *f* (*d'un cachet sur la cire, Typ d'un livre etc*);

(d) (*imprint*) empreinte *f*, impression *f* (*d'un cachet*); *Typ* empreinte (*des caractères sur le papier*); **to take an i. of sth,** prendre l'empreinte *ou* l'impression de qch; **i. cylinder,** cylindre *m* de rotative;

(e) (*in publishing*) tirage *m* (*d'un livre etc*);

(f) (*in engraving*) impression *f*; **proof i.,** épreuve *f* avant la lettre;

(g) (*imitation*) imitation *f*; **to do impressions,** faire des imitations; **this is my i. of you eating,** je t'imite en train de manger.

impressionable [ɪm'preʃənəb(ə)l] *adj* impressionnable, susceptible; **to be at an i. age,** être à un âge impressionnable.

impressionism [ɪm'preʃənɪz(ə)m] *n Art* impressionnisme *m*.

impressionist [ɪm'preʃənɪst] *Art* **1** *adj* impressionniste. **2** *n* impressionniste *mf*.

impressionistic [ɪmpreʃə'nɪstɪk] *adj* impressionniste.

impressive [ɪm'presɪv] *adj* (*spectacle, langage*) impressionnant; **his speech was very i.,** son discours a fait impression.

impressively [ɪm'presɪvlɪ] *adv* d'une manière impressionnante.

imprint[1] ['ɪmprɪnt] *n* **(a)** empreinte *f* (*d'un cachet, des pattes d'un animal etc*); **to take an i. of sth,** prendre l'empreinte de qch; **the events left their i. on her mind,** les événements sont restés gravés dans son esprit, les événements ont laissé leur empreinte dans son esprit; **(b)** **publisher's i.,** firme *f ou* rubrique *f* de l'éditeur; **printer's**

i., nom *m* de l'imprimeur.

imprint² [ɪm'prɪnt] *vt* imprimer; **the shape of an animal's foot was imprinted in the earth,** l'empreinte du pied d'un animal était restée dans la terre; **to i. sth on the memory,** graver *ou* fixer qch dans la mémoire; **to i. sth with sth,** marquer *ou* empreindre qch de qch.

imprison [ɪm'prɪzən] *vt* emprisonner (*qn*), mettre (*qn*) en prison; **to keep s.o. imprisoned,** tenir qn en prison.

imprisonment [ɪm'prɪzənmənt] *n* emprisonnement *m*; **ten days' i.,** dix jours d'emprisonnement *ou* de prison.

improbability [ɪmprɒbə'bɪlɪtɪ] *n* improbabilité *f*, invraisemblance *f*.

improbable [ɪm'prɒbəb(ə)l] *adj* improbable; **it's highly i. that he'll come,** il est très improbable *ou* très peu probable qu'il vienne.

improbably [ɪm'prɒbəblɪ] *adv* improbablement, invraisemblablement.

impromptu [ɪm'prɒmptjuː] **1** *adv* (*faire qch*) sans préparation, (à l')impromptu. **2** *adj* (*poème, discours*) impromptu; **to make an i. speech,** improviser un discours. **3** *n Th Mus* impromptu *m*.

improper [ɪm'prɒpər] *adj* **(a)** (*incorrect*) (*partage*) incorrect; (*expression, dérivation*) impropre; (*terme*) inexact; **to use a word in an i. sense,** donner à un mot un sens abusif; **(b)** (*indecent*) malséant, indécent, inconvenant; **(c)** (*not fitting*) déplacé; **it would be i. to refuse,** il serait de mauvaise grâce de refuser.

improperly [ɪm'prɒpəlɪ] *adv* (*see adj*) **(a)** (*se servir d'une expression*) improprement, incorrectement; **word i. used,** mot employé abusivement; **(b)** (*se conduire*) d'une manière inconvenante *ou* malséante; **(c)** (*parler, se conduire*) d'une façon déplacée.

impropriety [ɪmprə'praɪətɪ] *n* **(a)** inconvenance *f*, indécence *f* (*de conduite, d'un geste etc*); **(b)** impropriété *f*, inexactitude *f* (*de langage etc*).

improve [ɪm'pruːv] **1** *vt* améliorer (*son français, la saveur, une traduction etc*); apporter des perfectionnements à (*une invention*); bonifier (*le vin etc*); nourrir, cultiver (*l'esprit*); étendre, élargir (*ses connaissances*); affiner (*son goût*); *Agr* bonifier, amender (*le sol*); **to i. the appearance of s.o./sth,** embellir qn/qch; **to i. the occasion** *or F* **the shining hour,** profiter de l'occasion, mettre l'occasion à profit. **2** *vi* s'améliorer, devenir meilleur; (*of wine etc*) s'améliorer, se bonifier; *Com* (*of prices, markets*) monter; **the situation has improved,** la situation s'est améliorée; **business is improving,** les affaires reprennent; **his health is improving,** sa santé s'améliore.

►**improve on, improve upon** *vipo* (*make better*) améliorer (*qch*); *Com* **to i. on s.o.'s offer,** offrir plus que qn.

improved [ɪm'pruːvd] *adj* (*situation etc*) amélioré; (*invention*) perfectionné; *Com* (*offer*) supérieur.

improvement [ɪm'pruːvmənt] *n* **(a)** amélioration *f* (*de la situation etc*); perfectionnement *m* (*d'une invention*); embellissement *m* (*d'une ville*); culture *f* (*de l'esprit*); **i. in health,** amélioration de la santé; **any change would be an i.,** n'importe quel changement serait une amélioration; **moral i.,** édification *f* (*du peuple*); **today's weather is an i.,** le temps d'aujourd'hui constitue une amélioration; **to be an i. on s.o./sth,** surpasser qn/qch; **my new car is a great i. on the old one,** ma nouvelle voiture est bien supérieure à l'ancienne; **the cakes were an i. on my first attempt,** les gâteaux étaient mieux réussis que la première fois; **her new boyfriend's a bit of an i.,** son nouveau petit ami est un peu mieux que le(s) précédent(s);

(b) (*usu pl*) **improvements,** améliorations *fpl*, embellissements *mpl*; *Br* **i. grant,** aide financière *ou* subvention *f* pour la modernisation (*d'une maison*).

improvidence [ɪm'prɒvɪdəns] *n* **(a)** (*rashness*) imprévoyance *f*; **(b)** (*prodigality*) prodigalité *f*.

improvident [ɪm'prɒvɪdənt] *adj* **(a)** (*rash*) imprévoyant; **(b)** (*prodigal*) prodigue.

improvidently [ɪm'prɒvɪdəntlɪ] *adv* (*see adj*) **(a)** sans prévoyance; **(b)** de façon prodigue.

improvisation [ɪmprəvaɪ'zeɪʃən] *n Liter Mus etc* improvisation *f*.

improvise ['ɪmprəvaɪz] *Liter Mus etc* **1** *vt* improviser; **improvised speech,** discours improvisé *ou* impromptu; **they improvised bandages from bedsheets,** ils ont fait des bandages de fortune à l'aide de draps; **hastily improvised,** sommairement organisé; **improvised raft,** radeau *m* de fortune. **2** *vi* improviser; **to i. on the piano,** improviser au piano; **you will have to i.,** il faudra que vous débrouilliez avec ce qu'il y a.

improviser ['ɪmprəvaɪzər] *n* improvisateur, -trice.

imprudence [ɪm'pruːdəns] *n* imprudence *f*.

imprudent [ɪm'pruːdənt] *adj* imprudent, malavisé; **i. action,** imprudence *f*.

imprudently [ɪm'pruːdəntlɪ] *adv* imprudemment.

impudence ['ɪmpjʊdəns] *n* impudence *f*, effronterie *f*, insolence *f*, audace *f*.

impudent ['ɪmpjʊdənt] *adj* effronté, audacieux, insolent; **he's an i. fellow,** c'est un insolent.

impudently ['ɪmpjudəntlɪ] *adv* effrontément, insolemment.

impugn [ɪm'pjuːn] *vt* attaquer, contester (*une proposition etc*); mettre en doute *ou* en question (*la véracité de qch, l'honneur, les motifs de qn*); *Jur* récuser (*un témoignage*).

impulse ['ɪmpʌls] *n* **(a)** (*desire*) impulsion *f*, élan *m*; *Psy* pulsion *f* (*sexuelle etc*); **to feel an i. to do sth,** se sentir poussé à faire qch; **on the** *or* **a first i.,** tout d'abord; **rash** *or* **sudden i.,** coup *m* de tête; **to act on i.,** agir spontanément *ou* sur le coup d'une impulsion; **i. buying,** achat spontané; **(b)** (*stimulation, force*) impulsion *f*; *Phys* quantité *f* de mouvement; *El* **electrical impulses,** impulsions électriques; *Fig* **to give an i. to trade/***etc*, donner une impulsion *ou* de l'impulsion au commerce/*etc*; **(c)** *Physiol* **nerve i.,** signal nerveux.

impulsion [ɪm'pʌlʃən] *n* impulsion *f*.

impulsive [ɪm'pʌlsɪv] *adj* **(a)** (*gesture*) involontaire, spontané, primesautier; (*person*) impulsif; **i. action,** coup *m* de tête; **(b)** *MecE* impulsif, propulsif; **i. force,** force impulsive *ou* projective.

impulsively [ɪm'pʌlsɪvlɪ] *adj* (*agir*) par impulsion, spontanément.

impulsiveness [ɪm'pʌlsɪvnɪs] *n* impulsivité *f*.

impunity [ɪm'pjuːnɪtɪ] *n* impunité *f*; **to do sth with i.,** faire qch impunément *ou* en toute impunité.

impure [ɪm'pjʊər] *adj* **(a)** (*sang, air, lait*) impur; **(b)** *Rel Liter* (*hands etc*) impur, souillé; **(c)** (*person, thoughts etc*) impur, impudique.

impurity [ɪm'pjuːrɪtɪ] *n* **(a)** impureté *f* (*de l'eau etc*); **moral i.,** souillure morale; **(b)** (*of thoughts*) impureté *f*.

imputation [ɪmpjuː'teɪʃən] *n* imputation *f*.

impute [ɪm'pjuːt] *vt* imputer, attribuer (*une action etc*) (**to s.o.,** à qn).

in [ɪn] **1** *prep* **(a)** (*of place*) en, à, dans; **in France,** en France; **in Japan,** au Japon; **in the United States,** aux États-Unis; **in Paris,** à Paris; **in the provinces,** en province; **to be in town/in the country,** être en ville/à la campagne; **in his country,** dans son pays; **in prison,** en prison; **in church,** à l'église; **in bed,** au lit; **in the house/city,** dans la maison/ville; **in the water,** dans l'eau; **the key is in the door,** la clef est sur la porte; **in this book,** dans ce livre; **in my hand,** dans ma main; **with a cigar in his mouth,** le cigare à la bouche; **in the distance,** au loin; **in your place,** à votre place; **wounded in the shoulder,** blessé à l'épaule; **to put sth in sth,** mettre qch dans qch;

(b) (*among*) **in the crowd,** dans la foule; **in the thirties,** (*of number*) entre trente et quarante; (*of year*) dans les années trente; **he is in his sixties,** il a la soixantaine;

(c) (*in respect of*) **blind in one eye,** aveugle d'un œil; **expert in economics,** expert en économie politique; **the company is big in computers,** la société fait très fort dans le domaine des ordinateurs; **two metres in length,** long de deux mètres;

(d) (*of ratio*) **one in ten,** un sur dix; **once in ten years,** une fois tous les dix ans;

(e) (*of time*) **in 1927,** en 1927; **in the night,** pendant la nuit; **in the afternoon,** dans l'après-midi; **at four o'clock in the afternoon,** à quatre heures de l'après-midi; **in the evening,** le soir; **in spring/summer/autumn/winter,** au printemps/en été/en automne/en hiver; **in (the month of) April,** au mois d'avril, en avril; **in the future,** à l'avenir; **never in my life,** jamais de ma vie; **in my time,** de mon temps; **to do sth in three hours,** faire qch en trois heures; **he'll be here in three hours,** il sera là dans trois heures; **in a little while,** dans un petit moment; **I haven't seen you in years,** je ne t'ai pas vu depuis des années, ça fait des années que je ne t'ai pas vu;

(f) (*introducing a gerund*) en; **in crossing the river,** en traversant la rivière;

(g) (*of condition, state*) **in good health,** en bonne santé; **in tears,** en larmes; **in despair,** au désespoir; **in a good mood,** de bonne humeur; **cow in calf,** vache pleine; **a rhododendron in bloom,** un rhododendron en pleine floraison; **the person in question,** la personne en question;

(h) (*clothed in etc*) **in his shirt,** en chemise; **in slippers,** en pantoufles; **dressed in white,** habillé de blanc; **wrapped in paper,** enveloppé de papier; *Culin* **in a red**

wine sauce, dans une sauce au vin rouge, accompagné d'une sauce au vin rouge;

(i) (*of weather, light*) **to go out in the rain/snow,** sortir par la pluie/la neige; **in this warm weather,** par ce temps chaud; **to work in the rain,** travailler sous la pluie; **in the sun,** au soleil; **in the dark,** dans l'obscurité; **the fence blew down in the storm,** la barrière est tombée pendant la tempête;

(j) (*engaged in*) **in politics,** en politique; **to be in politics,** être dans la politique; **killed in action,** tué à l'ennemi; **in the navy,** dans la marine; **she's been in a lot of films,** elle a joué dans beaucoup de films; **he wasn't in that race,** il n'a pas pris part à cette course;

(k) (*according to*) **in my opinion,** à mon avis;

(l) (*due to*) dans; **in their hurry,** dans leur précipitation;

(m) (*of manner*) **in a gentle voice,** d'une voix douce; **in a businesslike manner,** d'une façon professionnelle; **in the French style,** à la française; **to be in fashion,** être à la mode;

(n) (*of medium*) **to write in French,** écrire en français; **in writing,** par écrit; **to talk in whispers,** parler en chuchotant;

(o) (*of arrangement*) **to walk in groups,** se promener par groupes; **to stand in a circle,** se tenir en cercle; **in alphabetical order,** par ordre alphabétique;

(p) (*of form*) **I've nothing in your size,** je n'ai rien à *ou* dans votre taille; **in the form of a pill,** sous forme de pilule; **she was curled up in a ball,** elle était roulée en boule; **money in gold,** espèces en or;

(q) (*of degree, extent*) **in large quantities,** en grandes quantités; **in part,** en partie; **in places,** par endroits; **there's nothing in it,** (*there is no difference*) ça tient à peu de choses; (*we're just good friends*) il n'y a rien entre nous;

(r) (*of purpose*) **in reply to ...,** en réponse à ...; **in honour of ...,** en l'honneur de ...; **in search of ...,** à la recherche de ...; **in the cause of humanity,** pour la cause de l'humanité;

(s) (*with reflexive pronoun*) **this product is not a poison in itself,** ce produit n'est pas un poison en soi;

(t) (*of character, ability*) **I didn't think she had it in her,** je ne l'en croyais pas capable; **it's not in her nature to be cruel,** ce n'est pas dans sa nature d'être cruelle.

2 *conj* (*because*) **in that, in so far as,** par ce que, puisque, vu que;

3 *adv* **(a)** (*inside building, room, boundary etc*) (*at home*) à la maison, chez soi; (*in one's office etc*) dans son bureau *etc*; **is he in?,** est-ce qu'il est là?; **is your mother in?,** est-ce que votre mère est à la maison?; *F* **what is he in for?,** (*in prison*) pour quel crime est-ce qu'il est en tôle *ou* taule?; *Agr* **the harvest is in,** la moisson est rentrée; **to be in,** (*bus, plane, mail etc*) être arrivé; **the train is in,** le train est en gare *ou* est arrivé; *Nau* **the sails are in,** les voiles sont serrées *ou* ferlées; **in with you!,** (*come in*) allons, rentrez!; (*go in*) allez-y!; *Tennis* **the ball is in,** la balle est bonne;

(b) (*indoors, inside*) à l'intérieur, dedans;

(c) (*in a situation*) (*in power, in office*) élu; **the Liberals were in,** le parti libéral était au pouvoir; **strawberries are in,** (*in season*) c'est la saison des fraises; **stripes are in this year,** (*in fashion*) les rayures sont à la mode cette année; **I've got my hand in,** (*in practice*) je suis bien en train; je suis en main (*pour dessiner etc*); **to be (well) in with s.o.,** (*in favour*) être en bons termes avec qn, être bien avec qn, être dans les petits papiers de qn; **my luck is in,** je suis en veine; *Cr* **to be in,** battre la balle, *F* être à la batte;

(d) (*phrases*) **to be in for a thousand pounds,** (*have invested etc*) y être pour mille livres; **we're in for a storm,** nous aurons sûrement de l'orage; **he's in for a surprise,** il va être surpris, il va avoir une surprise; *F* **he's in for it,** qu'est-ce qu'il va prendre!; **(now) we're in for it!,** ça va commencer!; **to have it in for s.o.,** avoir une dent contre qn; **to be in at the start/finish of sth,** assister au début/à la fin de qch; **to be in on a secret,** être dans le secret; **I wasn't in on it,** je n'étais pas dans le coup; **day in, day out,** tous les jours (sans exception); **year in, year out,** chaque année (sans exception); **all in,** tout compris; **it will cost you £100 all in,** cela vous coûtera cent livres tout compris; *F* **I'm absolutely all in,** (*exhausted*) je suis absolument éreinté *ou* fourbu; *Tennis* **advantage in,** avantage dedans *ou* au service; **(to go) in and out,** entrer et sortir; **he is always in and out of the house,** (*though he doesn't live there*) il entre et sort comme chez lui; **to know s.o. in and out,** connaître qn à fond.

4 *adj* **(a)** (*fashionable*) **it's the in thing these days,** c'est la mode aujourd'hui; **the in people,** les gens à la mode *ou* *F* dans le coup;

(b) (*exclusive*) **an in joke,** une plaisanterie de coterie;

(c) *Cr* **the in side,** l'équipe qui est à la batte.

5 *n* **(a)** *F* **to know the ins and outs of a matter,** connaître tous les coins et recoins d'une affaire, connaître une affaire dans tous ses détails;

(b) *US F* (*influence*) **to have an in,** avoir de l'influence; **he has an in with the senator,** il a ses entrées chez le sénateur.

inability [ɪnə'bɪlɪtɪ] *n* incapacité *f* (**to do sth,** de faire qch); (*powerlessness*) impuissance *f* (**to do sth,** à faire qch).

inaccessibility [ɪnæksesɪ'bɪlɪtɪ] *n* inaccessibilité *f*.

inaccessible [ɪnæk'sesɪb(ə)l] *adj* (*place, poetry*) inaccessible (**to,** à); (*person*) inabordable.

inaccuracy [ɪn'ækjʊrəsɪ] *n* inexactitude *f*, imprécision *f*; infidélité *f* (*d'une traduction*); **full of inaccuracies,** (*ouvrage*) plein d'inexactitudes.

inaccurate [ɪn'ækjʊrət] *adj* (*calcul, esprit*) inexact; (*esprit*) imprécis; (*avis, sens*) incorrect; (*récit*) infidèle.

inaccurately [ɪn'ækjʊrətlɪ] *adv* (*calculer*) inexactement; (*juger, citer*) incorrectement; (*traduire*) infidèlement.

inaction [ɪn'ækʃən] *n* inaction *f*; **policy of i.,** politique de laisser-faire.

inactive [ɪn'æktɪv] *adj* **(a)** inactif; (*esprit*) inerte; **(b)** *Mil* en non-activité.

inactivity [ɪnæk'tɪvɪtɪ] *n* inactivité *f*.

inadequacy [ɪn'ædɪkwəsɪ] *n* insuffisance *f* (*d'un revenu, d'une personne*); imperfection *f* (*d'un système etc*).

inadequate [ɪn'ædɪkwət] *adj* **(a)** inadéquat, insuffisant; **to be i.,** (*of thing*) être insuffisant (**for,** pour); **she makes me feel i.,** elle me donne des complexes; **(b)** (*style*) inapproprié au sujet.

inadequately [ɪn'ædɪkwətlɪ] *adv* insuffisamment.

inadmissible [ɪnəd'mɪsɪb(ə)l] *adj* (*théorie, prétention*) inadmissible; (*offre*) inacceptable; *Jur* (*témoignage*) irrecevable.

inadvertence [ɪnəd'vɜːtəns] *n* inattention *f*; (*absent-mindedness*) étourderie *f*; **through i.,** par inadvertance.

inadvertent [ɪnəd'vɜːtənt] *adj* (*mistake etc*) commis par inadvertance.

inadvertently [ɪnəd'vɜːtəntlɪ] *adv* par inadvertance; (*absent-mindedly*) par étourderie.

inadvisability [ɪnədvaɪzə'bɪlɪtɪ] *n* imprudence *f*, inopportunité *f* (*d'une action*).

inadvisable [ɪnəd'vaɪzəb(ə)l] *adj* peu sage, imprudent; **it is i. to go there after dark,** il est imprudent d'y aller après la tombée de la nuit.

inalienable [ɪn'eɪlɪənəb(ə)l] *adj* (*bien, droit*) inaliénable.

inane [ɪ'neɪn] *adj* (*person, action*) inepte, stupide, bête; (*smile*) bête, niais; (*answer*) inepte, saugrenu; **i. remark,** ineptie *f*.

inanely [ɪ'neɪnlɪ] *adv* bêtement, stupidement.

inanimate [ɪn'ænɪmət] *adj* (*corps, style etc*) inanimé, sans vie; **i. nature,** le monde inanimé.

inanition [ɪnə'nɪʃən] *n* *Med* inanition *f*.

inanity [ɪ'nænɪtɪ] *n* inanité *f*, niaiserie *f*.

inapplicable [ɪn'æplɪkəb(ə)l] *adj* inapplicable (**to,** à).

inappropriate [ɪnə'prəʊprɪət] *adj* peu approprié, qui ne convient pas (**to,** à); (*word*) impropre; (*speech*) déplacé.

inappropriately [ɪnə'prəʊprɪətlɪ] *adv* d'une façon mal à propos; improprement.

inapt [ɪn'æpt] *adj* **(a)** (*inept*) inepte; (*unskilled*) inhabile, inexpert; **(b)** (*inappropriate*) peu approprié (**to,** à).

inaptitude [ɪn'æptɪtjuːd] *n* **(a)** (*ineptitude*) inaptitude *f* (**for,** à); **(b)** (*inability*) incapacité *f*.

inarticulate [ɪnɑː'tɪkjʊlɪt] *adj* **(a)** (*person*) qui manque de facilité à s'exprimer; (*animal etc*) qui n'a pas le don de la parole; (*dumb*) muet, -ette; (*sound*) inarticulé; *esp Lit* (*desire*) inexprimé; **he's so i.,** il a tellement de mal à s'exprimer; **i. with rage,** bégayant de colère; **(b)** *Biol* inarticulé.

inartistic [ɪnɑː'tɪstɪk] *adj* (*production etc*) peu artistique, sans valeur artistique; (*person*) dépourvu de sens artistique.

inasmuch [ɪnəz'mʌtʃ] *conj* **i. as,** attendu que, vu que, en ce sens que.

inattention [ɪnə'tenʃən] *n* inattention *f*, manque *m* d'attention; **i. to detail,** inattention aux *ou* manque d'attention pour les détails.

inattentive [ɪnə'tentɪv] *adj* **(a)** (*not paying attention*) inattentif, distrait; (*élève*) inappliqué; **(b)** (*negligent*) négligent (**to,** de); **(c)** (*husband, waiter etc*) peu attentionné, peu prévenant (**to, towards,** à l'égard de).

inattentively [ɪnə'tentɪvlɪ] *adv* sans attention, distraitement.

inaudible [ɪn'ɔːdɪb(ə)l] *adj* inaudible; (*son*) imperceptible, inaudible; **it** *or* **he is almost i.**, on l'entend à peine.

inaudibly [ɪn'ɔːdɪblɪ] *adv* de manière inaudible.

inaugural [ɪ'nɔːgjʊrəl] **1** *adj* inaugural, -aux; (*discours*) d'inauguration. **2** *n US* discours *m* d'inauguration; *Br Univ* conférence inaugurale d'un professeur nouvellement nommé.

inaugurate [ɪ'nɔːgjʊreɪt] *vt* inaugurer (*un monument*); faire l'inauguration de (*une fête*); inaugurer, commencer (*une ère nouvelle*); mettre en vigueur (*un nouveau système*); installer (*un chef d'état etc*).

inauguration [ɪnɔːgjʊ'reɪʃən] *n* inauguration *f* (*d'un édifice etc*); commencement *m*, mise *f* en vigueur (*d'un nouveau système etc*); *US* **I. Day**, = jour où le président prend ses fonctions.

inauspicious [ɪnɔːs'pɪʃəs] *adj* qui augure mal, malheureux; (*moment*) malencontreux.

inauspiciously [ɪnɔːs'pɪʃəslɪ] *adv* sous de mauvais auspices, peu favorablement.

in-between [ɪnbɪ'twiːn] **1** *adj* intermédiaire, au milieu. **2** *n* entre-deux *m*.

inborn ['ɪn'bɔːn] *adj* (*instinct, mérite*) inné, infus, naturel; *Med* congénital, -aux.

inbred ['ɪn'bred] *adj* **(a)** (*dog, horse etc*) consanguin; **they are so i. that ...**, la consanguinité chez eux est telle que ...; **(b)** (*innate*) inné.

inbreed ['ɪn'briːd] *v* (*pt, pp* **inbred**) **1** *vt* accoupler (*des chevaux etc*) consanguins. **2** *vi* (*of animals*) s'accoupler avec des consanguins; (*of people*) s'accoupler avec des membres de la même famille.

inbreeding ['ɪn'briːdɪŋ] *n* (*of animals*) accouplement *m* d'animaux consanguins; (*of people*) union consanguine.

in-built ['ɪn'bɪlt] *adj* = **BUILT-IN**.

Inc. [ɪŋk] *adj esp US Com* (*abbr* **Incorporated**) = S.A.R.L..

Inca ['ɪŋkə] **1** *n* Inca *mf*. **2** *adj* inca *inv*.

incalculable [ɪn'kælkjʊləb(ə)l] *adj* incalculable; (*perte*) inestimable.

incalculably [ɪn'kælkjʊləblɪ] *adv* incalculablement.

in camera [ɪn'kæmərə] *adv & adj Jur* à huis clos.

incandescence [ɪnkæn'desəns] *n* incandescence *f*; *Metal* chaleur blanche.

incandescent [ɪnkæn'desənt] *adj* incandescent; (*ampoule, lumière, lampe etc*) à incandescence.

incantation [ɪnkæn'teɪʃən] *n* incantation *f*.

incapability [ɪnkeɪpə'bɪlɪtɪ] *n* incapacité *f*.

incapable [ɪn'keɪpəb(ə)l] *adj* (*unable*) incapable (**of**, de); **i. of movement**, (*of person*) incapable de bouger; **he's i. of doing such a spiteful thing**, il n'est pas capable de faire une méchanceté pareille; **I'm not i.**, je ne suis pas impotent; *Jur* **declared i. of managing his own affairs**, en état d'incapacité légale; **i. of improvement**, (*of thing*) peu susceptible d'amélioration; *Jur* **i. of succeeding to an estate**, (*of person*) incapable de prendre la succession d'un domaine; *Jur* **drunk and i.**, en état d'ivresse manifeste.

incapacitate [ɪnkə'pæsɪteɪt] *vt* **(a)** rendre (*qn*) incapable (**for work**, de travailler); mettre (*un véhicule*) hors d'état de marche; **the alcohol had temporarily incapacitated him**, l'alcool l'avait temporairement rendu incapable de faire quoi que ce soit; **(b)** *Jur* priver (*qn*) de capacité légale, frapper (*qn*) d'incapacité.

incapacity [ɪnkə'pæsɪtɪ] *n* **(a)** incapacité *f*, incompétence *f*; **(b)** *Jur* incapacité légale.

in-car ['ɪn'kɑːr] *adj Aut* (*stereo etc*) installé dans la voiture.

incarcerate [ɪn'kɑːsəreɪt] *vt* incarcérer, mettre en prison, emprisonner.

incarceration [ɪnkɑːsə'reɪʃən] *n* incarcération *f*, emprisonnement *m*.

incarnate¹ [ɪn'kɑːneɪt] *adj Rel* **the Word I.**, le Verbe incarné; **the devil i.**, le diable incarné; **perfection/wisdom i.**, la perfection/la sagesse même.

incarnate² ['ɪnkɑːneɪt] *vt* incarner.

incarnation [ɪnkɑː'neɪʃən] *n Rel etc* incarnation *f* (*du Christ, d'une idée*); **to be the i. of wisdom**, (*of person*) être l'incarnation de la sagesse; **in a previous i.**, dans une vie précédente.

incautious [ɪn'kɔːʃəs] *adj* imprudent; (*remark etc*) inconsidéré; **in an i. moment**, dans un moment d'inattention.

incautiously [ɪn'kɔːʃəslɪ] *adv* imprudemment.

incendiary [ɪn'sendɪərɪ] **1** *adj* (*bombe, dispositif*) incendiaire; *Fig* (*discours*) séditieux. **2** *n* **(a)** (*arsonist*) incendiaire *mf*; auteur *m* volontaire (*d'un incendie*); *Fig* incendiaire; **(b)** (*bomb*) bombe *f* incendiaire.

incense¹ ['ɪnsens] *n* encens *m*; *Rel* **i. bearer**, thuriféraire *m*; **i. burner**, *Rel* encensoir *m*.

incense² [ɪn'sens] *vt* exaspérer, irriter (*qn*).

incensed [ɪn'senst] *adj* enflammé de colère; **to become** *or* **get i.**, s'irriter, se mettre en colère (**with**, contre; **about**, au sujet de).

incentive [ɪn'sentɪv] *n* stimulant *m*, aiguillon *m*; **there is no i. for students here to work hard**, il n'y a rien ici qui incite les étudiants à travailler dur; *Com Ind* **production incentives, i. pay**, primes *fpl* de rendement; **i. scheme**, système *m* de primes; **i. travel**, voyages *mpl* de motivation.

inception [ɪn'sepʃən] *n Fml* commencement *m*, début *m* (*d'une entreprise etc*).

incessant [ɪn'sesənt] *adj* (*noise*) incessant, continuel; (*worry*) éternel.

incessantly [ɪn'sesəntlɪ] *adv* sans cesse, sans relâche; continuellement.

incest ['ɪnsest] *n* inceste *m*.

incestuous [ɪn'sestjʊəs] *adj* incestueux; *Fig* **the i. world of writers**, le monde très fermé *ou* en vase clos des écrivains.

inch [ɪntʃ] *n* (*measurement*) pouce *m* (= 2 centimètres 54); **an i. of rain**, un pouce de pluie; **square/cubic i.**, pouce carré/cube; **he couldn't see an i. in front of him** *or* **of his nose**, il n'y voyait pas à deux pas devant lui; **he's every i. a soldier**, il est soldat jusqu'au bout des ongles; **she won't give way an i.**, elle ne reculera pas d'une semelle; **by inches, i. by i.**, peu à peu, petit à petit; **I know every i. of the neighbourhood**, je connais la région comme ma poche; **give her an i. and she'll take a mile** donnez-lui-en grand comme le doigt, et elle en prendra long comme le bras; **to be within an i. of doing**, être à un poil de faire.

►inch along, inch forward **1** *vi* (s')avancer peu à peu *ou* petit à petit. **2** *vtsep* faire avancer (*qch*) petit à petit; **she inched her way along the window ledge**, elle a progressé petit à petit le long du rebord de la fenêtre.

incidence ['ɪnsɪdəns] *n* **(a)** (*frequency*) fréquence *f* (*des vols etc*); **the i. of cancer has increased**, les cas de cancer se sont multipliés; **(b)** *Opt Electron Av etc* **(angle of) i.**, angle *m* d'incidence; **(c)** incidence *f* (*d'un événement, d'un impôt*) (**on**, sur).

incident¹ ['ɪnsɪdənt] *n* incident *m*; **diplomatic i.**, incident diplomatique; **journey full of incidents**, voyage mouvementé.

incident² *adj* **(a)** *Opt Electron* (*rayon etc*) incident; **(b)** qui arrive; (*related*) qui appartient, qui tient (**to**, à).

incidental [ɪnsɪ'dent(ə)l] **1** *adj* **(a)** (*event*) fortuit, accidentel; (*circumstance etc*) incidentel; (*observation etc*) incident; **i. expenses**, faux frais *mpl*, dépenses accidentelles; **i. music for a play**, la musique pour une pièce; **(b)** (*resulting*) auquel on peut s'attendre; **i. to sth**, qui résulte de qch. **2** *n* chose fortuite; **incidentals**, faux frais *mpl*, dépenses accidentelles.

incidentally [ɪnsɪ'dentəlɪ] *adv* **(a)** (*by the way*) soit dit en passant *ou* entre parenthèses; **i., how is he?**, au fait, comment va-t-il?; **(b)** (*accidentally, secondarily*) incidemment.

incinerate [ɪn'sɪnəreɪt] *vt* incinérer.

incineration [ɪnsɪnə'reɪʃən] *n* incinération *f*.

incinerator [ɪn'sɪnəreɪtər] *n Ind etc* incinérateur *m*; (*in crematorium*) four *m* crématoire.

incipience [ɪn'sɪpɪəns] *n Fml* commencement *m*.

incipient [ɪn'sɪpɪənt] *adj* naissant, qui commence; **i. madness**, folie naissante.

incise [ɪn'saɪz] *vt* **(a)** inciser, faire une incision dans (*qch*); *Surg* inciser, débrider (*une plaie, un tissu*); **(b)** *Art etc* graver (*une inscription etc*).

incision [ɪn'sɪʒən] *n* incision *f*, entaille *f*; **to make an i. in sth**, inciser qch; **i. for a graft**, (*in tree etc*) enture *f*; *Surg* **buttonhole i.**, boutonnière *f*.

incisive [ɪn'saɪsɪv] *adj* (*instrument, ton*) incisif, tranchant; (*ton*) mordant; (*esprit*) pénétrant.

incisively [ɪns'saɪsɪvlɪ] *adv* incisivement; d'un ton tranchant *ou* mordant.

incisor [ɪn'saɪzər] *n Anat* (dent *f*) incisive *f*.

incite [ɪn'saɪt] *vt* inciter, instiguer, animer (**to sth**, à qch; **to do sth**, à faire qch); **to i. racial hatred**, inciter à la haine raciale; **to i. s.o. to crime/violence**, inciter *ou* pousser qn au crime/à la violence.

incitement [ɪn'saɪtmənt] *n* **(a)** (*of people, actions*) incitation *f*, instigation *f*, encouragement *m* (**to**, à); **i. to violence/riot**, incitation *ou* encouragement à la violence/à l'émeute; **(b)** (*motive*) stimulant *m*, aiguillon *m*.

incivility [ɪnsɪ'vɪlɪtɪ] *n* incivilité *f*.

incl **(a)** (*abbr* **inclusive**) inclusivement; **(b)** (*abbr* **including**) y compris.

inclemency [ɪn'klemənsɪ] *n* inclémence *f*, rigueur *f*.

inclement [ɪn'klemənt] *adj* (*climat, temps etc*) inclément, rigoureux, rude; (*juge, sort etc*) inclément.

inclination [ɪnklɪ'neɪʃən] *n* **(a)** (*desire*) inclination *f*, penchant *m* (**to,** à; **for,** pour); **my i. would be to ...,** je serais porté à ...; **to have an i. for sth,** avoir un penchant pour qch; **to have lost all i. for sth,** être revenu de qch; **to show little i. to do sth,** ne pas manifester de fort penchant à faire qch; **to do sth from i.,** faire qch par goût; **(b)** (*to put on weight etc*) tendance *f* (*à qch*); **(c)** (*angle*) inclinaison *f* (*d'un talus, d'un plan etc*); pente *f* (*d'un coteau*); déversement *m*, dévers *m* (*d'un mur*); dévoiement *m* (*d'un tuyau*); **(d)** inclination *f* (*de la tête, du corps*).

incline[1] ['ɪnklaɪn] *n* pente *f*.

incline[2] [ɪn'klaɪn] **1** *vt* **(a)** (*motivate, cause*) porter, inciter; **this inclines me to believe them,** cela me porte à les croire; **her remarks don't i. me to be sympathetic,** ses remarques ne m'incitent pas à faire preuve de compréhension; **(b)** incliner, pencher, faire pencher (*la tête, un vase*). **2** *vi* **(a)** (*of person*) avoir un penchant (**to sth,** pour qch; **to do,** à faire); être enclin *ou* porté *ou* disposé (**to do,** à faire); **to i. to the belief that ...,** incliner à croire que ...; **(b)** (*of thing*) s'incliner, pencher (**to,** à; **towards,** vers); **inclined at an angle of 45°,** incliné à un angle de 45°.

inclined [ɪn'klaɪnd] *adj* **(a)** (*momentarily*) disposé, porté (**to,** à); (*permanently*) enclin, incliné; **to feel** *or* **be i. to do sth,** (*tend to*) avoir tendance à faire qch; (*have desire to*) avoir envie de faire qch; **I am i. to think that he's right,** je suis porté à croire qu'il a raison; **to be favourably i. towards sth,** être favorable à qch; **if ever you should feel so i.,** si jamais l'envie vous en prenait; **prices are i. to fall,** les prix tendent à baisser; **he's i. to put on weight,** il a une tendance à grossir; **i. to laziness** *or* **be lazy,** enclin à la paresse; **if you're that way i.,** (*if you want to*) si cela vous dit; *F* **he's the other way i.,** (*in his sexual orientation*) il serait plutôt de l'autre bord; **I'm not musically i.,** (*I don't like music*) je ne suis pas très porté sur la musique; (*I have no talent*) je n'ai pas de talent musical; **to be well i. towards s.o.,** être bien disposé envers qn; **(b)** *Math etc* (*plan etc*) incliné; (*mur etc*) penchant.

include [ɪn'klu:d] *vt* inclure, comprendre, comporter; **the speech included several references to Soviet history,** le discours comportait plusieurs références à l'histoire de l'Union Soviétique; **the committee includes politicians from all parties,** le comité comprend des politiciens de tous les partis; **men above seventy are not included,** les hommes de plus de soixante-dix ans ne sont pas compris; **the price does not i. accommodation,** le prix ne comprend pas l'hébergement; **there are five of us, not including the children,** nous sommes cinq, sans compter les enfants; **including me,** moi y compris; **if you i. Christmas day,** en comptant le jour de Noël; **up to and including ...,** jusqu'à ... inclus; **to i. s.o. among one's friends,** compter qn parmi *ou* au nombre de ses amis.

▶**include out** *vtsep Hum* **i. me out,** ne compte pas sur moi.

included [ɪn'klu:dɪd] *adj* (y) compris; **all his property was sold, his house i.,** tous ses biens furent vendus, y compris sa maison; **i. in the price are two excursions,** deux excursions sont comprises dans le prix; **service i.,** (*at hotel etc*) service compris; **batteries not i.,** les piles ne sont pas comprises.

inclusion [ɪn'klu:ʒən] *n* inclusion *f*.

inclusive [ɪn'klu:sɪv] *adj* qui comprend; **five i. of the driver,** cinq y compris le chauffeur; **i. terms,** (*at hotel etc*) (prix *m*) tout compris; **from the 4th to the 12th February i.,** du 4 au 12 février inclusivement.

inclusively [ɪn'klu:sɪvlɪ] *adv* inclusivement.

incognito [ɪnkɒg'ni:təʊ] **1** *adj & adv* **to be/travel i.,** être/voyager incognito. **2** *n* (*person*) inconnu, -ue; (*name, disguise*) incognito *m*.

incoherence [ɪnkəʊ'hɪərəns] *n* incohérence *f*.

incoherent [ɪnkəʊ'hɪərənt] *adj* (*speech*) incohérent; (*raisonnement*) qui ne tient pas debout; (*style*) décousu; **to be i.,** (*of person*) s'exprimer de façon incohérente.

incoherently [ɪnkəʊ'hɪərəntlɪ] *adv* d'une manière incohérente.

incombustible [ɪnkəm'bʌstɪb(ə)l] *adj* (*gaz etc*) incombustible.

income ['ɪnkəm] *n* **(a)** revenu, revenu(s) *m*(*pl*); **source of i.,** source(s) *f*(*pl*) de revenu; **earned i.,** revenus salariaux; traitements *mpl*; **their combined i.,** leurs revenus additionnés; **i. from investments,** revenu(s) provenant de placements; **unearned i., private i.,** rente(s) *f*(*pl*); **to have a private i. of £15,000 a year,** avoir quinze mille livres de rente; **to be on a low i.,** avoir un faible revenu; *Econ* **gross/net national i.,** revenu national brut/net; **i. group,** tranche *f* de salaire *ou* de revenus; *Pol* **incomes policy,** politique *f* des revenus; **i. tax,** impôt *m* sur le revenu; **i.-tax return,** déclaration *f* de revenu *ou* d'impôts; **(b)** *Com* (*receipts*) recettes *fpl*, revenus, rentrées *fpl*.

incoming ['ɪnkʌmɪŋ] **1** *adj* qui entre, qui arrive; (*locataire, navire*) entrant; **i. tide,** marée montante; **the i. president,** le président élu; **i. mail,** courrier *m* à l'arrivée; *Tel* **i. call,** appel *m* de l'extérieur; **this telephone takes i. calls only,** ce téléphone ne permet que de recevoir des appels; **i. profit,** profits accrus *ou* réalisés. **2** *npl Com Fin* **incomings,** recettes *fpl*, revenus *mpl*, rentrées *fpl*.

incommensurable [ɪnkə'menʃərəb(ə)l] *adj Math* incommensurable (**with,** avec); (*nombre*) irrationnel.

incommensurate [ɪnkə'menʃərɪt] *adj* pas en rapport, pas en proportion (**with,** avec), disproportionné (**with,** à).

incommode [ɪnkə'məʊd] *vt* incommoder, déranger (*qn*).

incommodious [ɪnkə'məʊdɪəs] *adj* incommode; (*appartement etc*) où l'on est à l'étroit.

incommunicado [ɪnkəmju:nɪ'kɑ:dəʊ] *adv* **to be held i.,** être tenu au secret.

incomparable [ɪn'kɒmpərəb(ə)l] *adj* incomparable (**to, with,** à); (*artiste*) incomparable, sans pareil.

incomparably [ɪn'kɒmpərəblɪ] *adv* incomparablement.

incompatibility [ɪnkəmpætɪ'bɪlɪtɪ] *n* (*of people, theories, medication etc*) incompatibilité *f* (**with,** avec; **between,** entre); inconciliabilité *f* (*de deux théories*).

incompatible [ɪnkəm'pætɪb(ə)l] *adj* (*people, theories, systems, medication etc*) incompatible; (*theory*) inconciliable (**with,** avec); (*metals, fluids etc*) non *ou* peu alliable (**with,** avec); **activities i. with his position,** activités incompatibles avec son poste.

incompetence [ɪn'kɒmpɪtəns] *n* **(a)** incompétence *f* (*de qn*); insuffisance *f* (*du personnel etc*); **(b)** *Jur* incompétence *f* (*d'un tribunal*); incompétence, incapacité *f*, inhabilité *f* (*d'une personne*).

incompetent [ɪn'kɒmpɪtənt] **1** *adj* **(a)** (*person*) incompétent, incapable; **(b)** *Jur* (*juge, tribunal*) incompétent (*à connaître d'une cause*); (*personne*) inhabile (*à accomplir un acte*); **I am i. to act,** je n'ai pas qualité pour agir. **2** *npl* **the incompetents,** les incapables *mpl*.

incomplete [ɪnkəm'pli:t] *adj* (*not complete*) incomplet; (*not finished*) inachevé; (*imperfect*) imparfait.

incompletely [ɪnkəm'pli:tlɪ] *adv* incomplètement; imparfaitement.

incompleteness [ɪnkəm'pli:tnɪs] *n* inachèvement *m*; imperfection *f*.

incomprehensible [ɪnkɒmprɪ'hensɪb(ə)l] *adj* (*situation, speech, person*) incompréhensible; (*writing*) indéchiffrable.

incomprehensibly [ɪnkɒmprɪ'hensɪblɪ] *adv* incompréhensiblement.

incomprehension [ɪnkɒmprɪ'henʃən] *n* incompréhension *f*.

inconceivable [ɪnkən'si:vəb(ə)l] *adj* inconcevable.

inconceivably [ɪnkən'si:vəblɪ] *adv* inconcevablement.

inconclusive [ɪnkən'klu:sɪv] *adj* (*raisonnement, témoignage*) peu concluant.

inconclusively [ɪnkən'klu:sɪvlɪ] *adv* d'une manière peu concluante.

incongruity [ɪnkɒŋ'gru:ɪtɪ] *n* (*of answer, remark*) incongruité *f*.

incongruous [ɪn'kɒŋgrʊəs] *adj* (*behaviour, thing to say, new building*) incongru; (*combination*) bizarre; **the bright red is very i. in this room,** le rouge vif détonne fortement dans cette pièce; **they are such an i. couple,** ils sont tellement bizarrement assortis.

incongruously [ɪn'kɒŋgrʊəslɪ] *adv* incongrûment; (*to say etc*) mal à propos.

inconsequence [ɪn'kɒnsɪkwəns] *n* inconséquence *f*.

inconsequent [ɪn'kɒnsɪkwənt] *adj* = **INCONSEQUENTIAL (b)**.

inconsequential [ɪnkɒnsɪ'kwenʃəl] *adj* **(a)** (*raisonnement*) inconséquent; (*idées*) sans suite; **(b)** (*circonstance, affaire*) sans importance.

inconsiderate [ɪnkən'sɪdərɪt] *adj* (*personne*) sans égards pour les autres; **it was most i. of you to do that,** vous avez manqué d'égards en agissant ainsi; **don't be so i.,** pense un peu aux autres.

inconsiderately [ɪnkən'sɪdərətlɪ] *adv* **to behave i. to s.o.,** manquer d'égards envers qn; **he had i. locked the door,** il avait verrouillé la porte sans égard pour personne.

inconsistency [ɪnkən'sɪstənsɪ] *n* **(a)** (*incompatibility*) inconsistance *f*, contradiction *f* (**between two things,** entre deux choses); **(b)** inconséquence *f*, inconsistance *f*,

illogisme *m* (*d'une personne*); incohérence *f* (*d'un argument*).
inconsistent [ɪnkən'sɪstənt] *adj* **(a)** (*thing*) incompatible, en contradiction, en désaccord (**with,** avec); contradictoire (**with,** à); **his words are i. with his conduct,** ses paroles ne cadrent pas avec sa conduite; **(b)** (*person*) inconsistant, inconséquent; **they're i. in what they say,** leurs dires sont contradictoires; **you're being i.,** tu te contredis.
inconsistently [ɪnkən'sɪstəntlɪ] *adv* inconséquemment, illogiquement.
inconsolable [ɪnkən'səʊləb(ə)l] *adj* inconsolable.
inconspicuous [ɪnkən'spɪkjʊəs] *adj* peu frappant, discret, -ète, peu voyant; **to be** *or* **remain i.,** rester dans l'obscurité; **I tried to look i.,** j'ai essayé de me faire discret.
inconspicously [ɪnkən'spɪkjʊəslɪ] *adv* d'une manière discrète *ou* peu frappante.
inconstancy [ɪn'kɒnstənsɪ] *n* **(a)** (*of weather etc*) instabilité *f*, caractère changeant; **(b)** (*of person, character*) inconstance *f*.
inconstant [ɪn'kɒnstənt] *adj* **(a)** (*vent*) mobile, variable; **(b)** (*personne, caractère*) inconstant, volage.
incontestable [ɪnkən'testəb(ə)l] *adj* incontestable, indéniable.
incontestably [ɪnkən'testəblɪ] *adv* incontestablement.
incontinence [ɪn'kɒntɪnəns] *n Med etc* incontinence *f*; **i. pads,** couches *fpl* pour adultes.
incontinent [ɪn'kɒntɪnənt] *adj Med etc* incontinent.
incontrovertible [ɪnkɒntrə'vɜːtɪb(ə)l] *adj* (*vérité*) incontestable; (*preuve*) irrécusable; (*argument*) irréfutable.
inconvenience¹ [ɪnkən'viːnjəns] *n* inconvénient *m*, incommodité *f*, dérangement *m*; (*more serious*) désagrément *m*; **to cause i. to s.o., to be an i. to s.o.,** incommoder qn, déranger qn; **I am putting you to a great deal of i.,** je vous donne beaucoup d'embarras; **without the slightest i.,** sans le moindre inconvénient *ou* dérangement; **we apologize for any i.,** nous vous demandons de nous excuser pour tout désagrément éventuel; **the i. of living so far from town,** les inconvénients qu'il y a à vivre si loin de la ville.
inconvenience² *vt* déranger, incommoder, gêner (*qn*).
inconvenient [ɪnkən'viːnjənt] *adj* (*time*) inopportun; (*house etc*) incommode, malcommode; (*person*) gênant; **if it is not i. to you,** si cela ne vous gêne pas; **it's very i. living so far from town,** c'est très incommode d'habiter aussi loin de la ville; **Friday's a bit i.,** vendredi ne me convient pas tellement.
inconveniently [ɪnkən'viːnjəntlɪ] *adv* (*located*) incommodément; (*to arrive*) à un moment inopportun.
inconvertible [ɪnkən'vɜːtɪb(ə)l] *adj Fin* inconvertible.
incorporate [ɪn'kɔːpəreɪt] **1** *vt* **(a)** (*include, add*) incorporer, mêler, unir (**with,** à, avec; **in,** dans); **to i. a paragraph in a chapter,** incorporer un paragraphe dans un chapitre; **work that incorporates all the latest discoveries,** ouvrage où se trouvent incorporées toutes les découvertes les plus récentes; **(b)** *Com* constituer (*une association*) en société commerciale; réunir (*des banques*) en société; **(c)** (*merge*) regrouper pour former un tout; **these organizations were incorporated into a national fire brigade,** ces organisations ont été regroupées pour constituer une brigade nationale de pompiers. **2** *vi* **(a)** s'incorporer (**in one body,** en un seul corps; **with others,** avec *ou* à d'autres); **(b)** *US Com* se constituer en société commerciale.
incorporated [ɪn'kɔːpəreɪtɪd] *adj* **(a)** *US Com* **i. company,** association constituée en société commerciale; **Smith I.,** Smith S.A.R.L.; **(b)** incorporé (**in one body,** en un seul corps); faisant corps (**with others,** avec d'autres).
incorporation [ɪnkɔːpə'reɪʃən] *n* **(a)** *Com Jur* constitution *f* (*d'une association*) en société commerciale; **(b)** (*act of incorporating*) incorporation *f* (**in, with, into,** à, avec, dans).
incorrect [ɪnkə'rekt] *adj* **(a)** (*statement, account etc*) inexact; **i. expression,** locution incorrecte; *Com* **i. endorsement,** endos défectueux; **(b)** (*style, behaviour etc*) incorrect.
incorrectly [ɪnkə'rektlɪ] *adv* **(a)** (*reported, stated*) inexactement; (*to speak*) incorrectement; **i. addressed,** (*letter*) mal adressé; **(b)** (*to behave etc*) incorrectement.
incorrigible [ɪn'kɒrɪdʒɪb(ə)l] *adj* (*enfant, paresse etc*) incorrigible; **he's i.,** il est incorrigible.
incorruptible [ɪnkə'rʌptɪb(ə)l] *adj* (*matière, juge*) incorruptible.
increase¹ ['ɪnkriːs] *n* augmentation *f* (*de prix, de recettes, de la population etc*); accroissement *m* (*de vitesse, de la douleur etc*); gain *m* (*de vitesse*); renouvellement *m* (*de zèle, d'attention*); redoublement *m* (*d'efforts, de gaieté*); multiplication *f* (*des êtres, de l'espèce*); **i. in the cost of living,** renchérissement *m* (du coût) de la vie; **i. in value,** plus-value *f* (*d'une propriété etc*); **I've had an i. in salary,** j'ai été augmenté; **to be on the i.,** être en augmentation *ou* en hausse.
increase² [ɪn'kriːs] **1** *vi* (*of prices, population etc*) augmenter; (*of noise, dissatisfaction*) grandir, s'agrandir; (*of speed, pain*) croître, s'accroître; (*of unemployment, dissatisfaction*) s'accentuer; (*in bulk*) grossir, augmenter; **his efforts increased,** ses efforts redoublaient; **to i. in size/value,** augmenter de grandeur/valeur; **to i. in price,** renchérir; **to i. in volume,** (*of earth, lime*) foisonner; **the population is increasing,** la population grossit *ou* augmente.
2 *vt* augmenter (*la vitesse, la production*); grossir, augmenter (*le nombre, la dépense*); accroître, augmenter (*sa fortune*); relever, augmenter (*les salaires*); agrandir (*l'importance*); majorer, augmenter (*les prix*); allonger, augmenter (*la distance*); accentuer, augmenter (*le mécontentement*); **to i. s.o.'s salary,** augmenter (le salaire de) qn; **to i. the dose,** augmenter la dose (*d'un médicament*); **to i. one's efforts,** redoubler d'efforts; **increased cost of living,** renchérissement *m* (du coût) de la vie; *Knitting* **i. two in the next row,** augmenter de deux mailles au rang suivant.
increasing [ɪn'kriːsɪŋ] *adj* (*numbers, use*) croissant; **ever-i. influence,** influence sans cesse croissante.
increasingly [ɪn'kriːsɪŋlɪ] *adv* de plus en plus (*difficile, grand etc*); **i., people are saying that ...,** de plus en plus, les gens disent que ... .
incredible [ɪn'kredɪb(ə)l] *adj* **(a)** (*unbelievable*) incroyable; *F* **it's i.!,** c'est incroyable *ou F* renversant!; **(b)** *F* (*excellent*) incroyable, époustouflant.
incredibly [ɪn'kredɪblɪ] *adv* incroyablement; **he's i. stupid,** il est d'une sottise incroyable; **i., she agreed,** elle a consenti, ce qui est incroyable.
incredulity [ɪnkrɪ'djuːlɪtɪ] *n* incrédulité *f*.
incredulous [ɪn'kredjʊləs] *adj* incrédule (**of,** à l'égard de); (*sourire*) d'incrédulité.
incredulously [ɪn'kredjʊləslɪ] *adv* (*to look at, say*) d'un air *ou* d'un ton incrédule.
increment ['ɪnkrɪmənt] *n* (*increase*) augmentation *f*; *Math* différentielle *f*; **unearned i.,** (*of land, shares*) plus-value *f*.
incriminate [ɪn'krɪmɪneɪt] *vt* **(a)** impliquer (*un complice etc*) (dans une accusation); mêler (*qn*) à une affaire; **(b)** accuser (*qn*) d'un crime.
incriminating [ɪn'krɪmɪneɪtɪŋ] *adj* (*circonstance etc*) qui tend à prouver la culpabilité de qn; **i. documents,** pièces *fpl* à conviction.
incrimination [ɪnkrɪmɪ'neɪʃən] *n* **(a)** incrimination *f*; **(b)** accusation *f* (*de qn*).
incriminatory [ɪn'krɪmɪnətərɪ] *adj* incriminatoire.
incrustation [ɪnkrʌs'teɪʃən] *n* entartrage *m* (*d'une chaudière*); tartre *m*, dépôt *m* calcaire.
incubate ['ɪnkjʊbeɪt] **1** *vt* couver, incuber (*des œufs*). **2** *vi* (*of eggs*) être soumis à l'incubation; (*of disease*) couver.
incubation [ɪnkjʊ'beɪʃən] *n* incubation *f*; *Med* **i. period,** période *f* d'incubation (*d'une maladie*).
incubator ['ɪnkjʊbeɪtər] *n* (*for birds' eggs*) incubateur *m*, couveuse artificielle; (*room*) couvoir *m* (*pour les œufs*); poussinière *f* (*pour poussins*); (*for premature babies*) couveuse; (*in bacteriology*) incubateur *m*.
incubus ['ɪnkjʊbəs] *Myth* incube *m*; *Fig* cauchemar *m*.
inculcate ['ɪnkʌlkeɪt] *vt* inculquer (*une leçon etc*); **to i. sth in s.o., to i. s.o. with sth,** inculquer qch à qn.
inculcation [ɪnkʌl'keɪʃən] *n* inculcation *f*.
incumbent¹ [ɪn'kʌmbənt] *n* **(a)** titulaire *mf* (*d'une fonction administrative*); **(b)** *Rel* bénéficier *m*, bénéficiaire *m*, titulaire *m* (*d'une charge*).
incumbent² *adj* **(a)** (*necessary*) **to be i. on s.o. to do sth,** incomber *ou* appartenir à qn de faire qch; **(b)** (*official*) en place.
incunabulum, *pl* **-a** [ɪnkjuː'næbjʊləm, -ə] *n* incunable *m*.
incur [ɪn'kɜːr] *vt* (**-rr-**) courir (*un risque*); encourir (*un blâme, des frais*); subir (*une perte*); s'attirer (*le courroux de qn*); contracter (*des dettes*); s'attirer (*la haine*).
incurable [ɪn'kjʊərəb(ə)l] *adj* (*maladie, malade*) incurable, inguérissable; *Fig* (*ivrogne*) invétéré; **an i. romantic,** un romantique incurable *ou* incorrigible.
incurably [ɪn'kjʊərəblɪ] *adv* incurablement, incorrigiblement; *Fig* **i. lazy,** d'une paresse incorrigible.
incurious [ɪn'kjʊərɪəs] *adj* incurieux, sans curiosité.

incursion [ɪn'kɜːʃən] *n* incursion *f* (**into,** en).

Ind **(a)** (*abbr* **Independent**) indépendant; **(b)** *abbr* **Indiana.**

indebted [ɪn'detɪd] *adj* **(a)** (*owing money*) endetté; **to be heavily i. to s.o.,** devoir une forte somme à qn; **(b)** *Fig* redevable (**to s.o. for sth,** à qn de qch); **I am i. to Mr Martin for this information,** c'est à M. Martin que je dois ce renseignement.

indebtedness [ɪn'detɪdnɪs] *n* **(a)** (*state of owing money*) dette(s) *f(pl)*; **(b)** *Fig* dette *f* (**to,** envers).

indecency [ɪn'diːsənsɪ] *n* indécence *f*; *Jur* **(public act of) i.,** attentat *m* aux mœurs, outrage *m* (public) aux mœurs.

indecent [ɪn'diːsənt] *adj* indécent; **i. exposure,** exhibitionnisme *m*; **i. behaviour,** attentat *m* aux mœurs; **i. assault,** attentat *m* à la pudeur; **to do sth with I. haste,** faire qch avec une rapidité scandaleuse; *Fig* **he's paid an i. salary,** (*far too much*) on lui paie un salaire exhorbitant; (*far too little*) on lui paie un salaire dérisoire.

indecently [ɪn'diːsəntlɪ] *adv* indécemment.

indecipherable [ɪndɪ'saɪfərəb(ə)l,-frəb(ə)l] *adj* indéchiffrable.

indecision [ɪndɪ'sɪʒən] *n* indécision *f*, irrésolution *f*.

indecisive [ɪndɪ'saɪsɪv] *adj* **(a)** (*argument*) peu concluant; (*battle*) indécis; **(b)** (*person*) indécis, irrésolu.

indecisiveness [ɪndɪ'saɪsɪvnɪs] *n* indécision *f*, irrésolution *f*.

indeclinable [ɪndɪ'klaɪnəb(ə)l] *adj Gram* indéclinable.

indecorous [ɪn'dekərəs] *adj* inconvenant, peu convenable.

indecorously [ɪn'dekərəslɪ] *adv* d'une manière peu convenable.

indecorum [ɪndɪ'kɔːrəm] *n* inconvenance *f*, manque *m* de décorum *ou* de maintien.

indeed [ɪn'diːd] *adv* **(a)** (*certainly*) en effet, vraiment; **he was i. a man of genius,** c'était vraiment un homme de génie; **I am very glad i.,** (*intensive*) je suis très très content; **thank you very much i.,** merci infiniment, merci mille fois; **I may i. be wrong,** (*concessive*) il se peut toutefois que j'aie tort; **(b)** (*what is more*) même, à vrai dire; **I think so, i. I am sure of it,** je le pense et même j'en suis sûr; **(c)** (*with affirmation or negation*) **yes i.!,** mais certainement!, pour sûr!; **i., I have!,** (*been there*) si, j'y suis allé; (*done that*) si, je l'ai fait; **it does i.!, i. it does!,** (*surprise me, mean that etc*) certainement!; **(d)** (*interrogatively*) **I have lived in Paris - i.?,** j'ai vécu à Paris – vraiment?; **have you i.?,** (*expressing doubt, lack of interest, mockery*) ah oui?

indefatigable [ɪndɪ'fætɪgəb(ə)l] *adj* infatigable, inlassable.

indefatigably [ɪndɪ'fætɪgəblɪ] *adv* infatigablement.

indefensible [ɪndɪ'fensɪb(ə)l] *adj* (*place, théorie*) indéfendable, indéfensible; (*conduite*) inexcusable; (*argument*) insoutenable.

indefinable [ɪndɪ'faɪnəb(ə)l] *adj* indéfinissable; (*sentiment*) vague.

indefinite [ɪn'defɪnɪt] *adj* **(a)** (*distance, time, number*) indéfini, indéterminé; (*congé*) illimité, indéfini; **(b)** (*ideas, promises etc*) indéfini, vague; **(b)** *Gram* (*article, pronom*) indéfini.

indefinitely [ɪn'defɪnɪtlɪ] *adv* **(a)** (*remettre*) indéfiniment; **I could go on i.,** je pourrais continuer à l'infini; **(b)** (*promettre*) indéfiniment, vaguement.

indelible [ɪn'delɪb(ə)l] *adj* indélébile, ineffaçable; (*crayon*) violet, à encre indélébile.

indelibly [ɪn'delɪblɪ] *adv* de façon indélébile, ineffaçablement; **i. printed on her mind,** marqué de façon indélébile dans son esprit.

indelicacy [ɪn'delɪkəsɪ] *n* indélicatesse *f*, manque *m* de délicatesse; (*impropriety*) inconvenance *f*.

indelicate [ɪn'delɪkət] *adj* indélicat, qui manque de délicatesse, peu délicat; (*improper*) inconvenant.

indemnification [ɪndemnɪfɪ'keɪʃən] *n* **(a)** (*of person*) indemnisation *f*, dédommagement *m* (**of s.o. for sth,** de qn de qch); **(b)** (*compensation*) indemnité *f*, dédommagement *m*.

indemnify [ɪn'demnɪfaɪ] *vt* **(a)** (*protect*) garantir (*qn*) (**from, against,** contre); **(b)** (*compensate*) indemniser, dédommager (*qn*) (**for a loss,** d'une perte).

indemnity [ɪn'demnɪtɪ] *n* **(a)** garantie *f*, assurance *f* (*contre une perte etc*); **(b)** (*compensation*) indemnité *f*, dédommagement *m*, compensation *f*.

indent[1] ['ɪndent] *n* **(a)** (*notch*) dentelure *f*, entaille *f*; *Carp* adent *m*; **(b)** *esp Br Com* commande *f* de marchandises (*reçue de l'étranger*); **(c)** *Typ* alinéa *m*, retrait *m*.

indent[2] [ɪn'dent] **1** *vt* **(a)** denteler, entailler (*le bord de qch*); *Carp* endenter (*une poutre*); **(b)** *Typ* renfoncer, (faire) rentrer (*une ligne*); **indented line,** ligne *f* en alinéa *ou* en retrait; **(c)** *Jur* passer (*un document*) en partie double. **2** *vi Br Com* **to i. on s.o. for sth,** commander qch à qn.

indent[3] ['ɪndent] *n* (*dent*) creux *m*; (*in metal*) bosselure *f*; brouture *f* (*laissée par l'outil*).

indent[4] [ɪn'dent] *vt* (*dent*) empreindre (en creux); bosseler, bossuer (*une surface*).

indentation [ɪnden'teɪʃən] *n* **(a)** découpage *m* (*des bords de qch*); *Carp* endentement *m* (*de deux poutres*); **(b)** impression *f* (*du sable par les roues etc*); **(c)** (*notched, jagged edge*) dentelure *f*; (*notch*) entaille *f*, découpure *f*; **(d)** *Typ* alinéa *m*, retrait *m*; **(e)** = **INDENT[3]**.

indenture[1] [ɪn'dentʃər] *n Jur* contrat *m* synallagmatique; contrat bilatéral; **indentures,** contrat *ou* brevet *m* d'apprentissage.

indenture[2] *vt* **(a)** (*bind by contract*) lier (*qn*) par contrat; **(b)** *Arch* (*of parent, guardian*) mettre (*qn*) en apprentissage (**to s.o.,** chez qn); (*of employer*) engager (*qn*) par un brevet d'apprentissage.

independence [ɪndɪ'pendəns] *n* indépendance *f* (**of,** de, à l'égard de); indépendance, autonomie *f* (*d'un état*); **the American War of I.,** la Guerre de l'Indépendance (des États-Unis); *US* **I. Day,** jour *m* de l'Indépendance.

independent [ɪndɪ'pendənt] **1** *adj* (*person, inquiry etc*) indépendant; (*état, pays*) indépendant, autonome; **to be i. of s.o./sth,** ne pas dépendre de qn/qch; **to be i.,** être indépendant; **a man of i. means,** un rentier; **his children are i. now,** ses enfants peuvent maintenant pourvoir eux-mêmes à leurs besoins; *Br Admin* **i. school,** = école *f* libre; *Aut* **i. suspension,** suspension indépendante. **2** *n Pol etc* indépendant, -ante.

independently [ɪndɪ'pendəntlɪ] *adv* **(a)** (*to behave etc*) avec indépendance; **(b)** (*not connected*) indépendamment; **i. of that,** indépendamment de cela.

in-depth ['ɪn'depθ] *adj* (*study etc*) approfondi.

indescribable [ɪndɪs'kraɪbəb(ə)l] *adj* (*fureur, misère*) indescriptible; (*joie*) indicible.

indescribably [ɪndɪs'kraɪbəblɪ] *adv* (*angry, wretched*) indescriptiblement; (*happy*) indiciblement; **it was i. awful,** c'était absolument affreux.

indestructible [ɪndɪs'trʌktəb(ə)l] *adj* indestructible.

indeterminate [ɪndɪ'tɜːmɪnət] *adj* (*space etc*) indéterminé; (*thought*) vague, imprécis; *Math* (*quantity*) indéterminé.

indeterminately [ɪndɪ'tɜːmɪnətlɪ] *adv* de façon indéterminée; vaguement.

index[1], *pl* **indexes, indices** ['ɪndeks, 'ɪndeksɪz,'ɪndɪsiːz] *n* **(a)** (*pl* **indexes**) (*of book*) index *m*, table *f* alphabétique; **(b)** (*catalogue*) fichier *m*, répertoire *m*; **(c)** (*pl* **indices**) *Math etc* indice *m*; (*exponent*) exposant *m*; *Opt* **i. of refraction,** indice de réfraction; *Com Econ* **i. number,** chiffre indicateur; indice; **cost of living i.,** indice du coût de la vie; **retail/wholesale price i.,** indice des prix de détail/de gros; **(d)** (*pl* **indexes**) **i. (finger),** index *m*; **(e)** (*pl* **indexes**) *Tech* aiguille *f* (*de cadran etc*); style *m* (*de cadran solaire*); *Typ* main *f*; **(f)** (*pl* **indices**) (*sign*) indice *m*, signe *m* (indicateur).

index[2] *vt* **(a)** faire *ou* dresser l'index de (*un livre*); *Comptr* indexer (*une base de données*); **(b)** répertorier, classer (*un article*); **(c)** (*of wages, pension*) **indexed to inflation,** indexé sur l'inflation.

indexation [ɪndek'seɪʃən] *n* indexation *f*.

index-linked ['ɪndeks'lɪŋkt] *adj* (*wages, pension*) indexé.

index-linking ['ɪndeks'lɪŋkɪŋ] *n* (*of wages etc*) indexation *f*.

India ['ɪndɪə] *n* Inde *f*; **I. ink,** encre *m* de Chine; **I. rubber,** (*eraser*) gomme *f* à effacer; (*material*) caoutchouc *m*, gomme élastique.

Indian ['ɪndɪən] **1** *adj* **(a)** (*of, from India*) de l'Inde, indien; **I. elephant,** éléphant *m* d'Inde; **the I. Ocean,** l'océan Indien; **(b)** (*of Native Americans*) indien, amérindien; des Indiens (d'Amérique), amérindien; **I. file,** file indienne; *Am* **to be an I. giver,** = demander le retour de qch qu'on a donné; **I. reserve,** réserve indienne; **I. summer,** été indien; *Fig* période de succès *ou* de bonheur tardif. **2** *n* **(a)** (*inhabitant, native of India*) Indien, -ienne; **(b)** (*Native American*) Indien, -ienne (d'Amérique), Amérindien, -ienne.

indicate ['ɪndɪkeɪt] **1** *vt* **(a)** (*point to, show*) indiquer, montrer; **to i. sth with the hand,** indiquer qch de la main; **at the time indicated,** à l'heure dite *ou* indiquée; *Aut* **to i. a left/right turn,** mettre son clignotant pour indiquer que l'on va tourner à gauche/droite; **(b)** (*denote*) indiquer, dénoter, témoigner (*qch*); **face that indicates energy,** visage qui révèle *ou* qui dénote l'énergie; **(c)** (*state*) faire savoir (*qch*) en termes brefs; **(d)** (*need*) *Med* **a certain treatment is indicated,** un certain traitement est indiqué; **strong**

measures were clearly indicated, il était évident que la situation demandait des mesures rigoureuses. **2** *vi Aut* mettre son clignotant.

indication [ɪndɪ'keɪʃən] *n* **(a)** (*act of pointing out*) indication *f* (**of sth to s.o.,** de qch à qn); **(b)** (*sign*) indice *m*, signe *m*, indication *f*; **there is every i. of his speaking the truth,** tout porte à croire qu'il dit vrai; **there is no i. of a struggle,** il n'y a aucun signe de lutte; **all the indications are that ...,** tout porte à croire que ...; **he gave early indications of his talent,** il laissa de bonne heure entrevoir son talent; **to take sth as an i. that,** interpréter qch comme une indication du fait que; **(c)** (*warning, statement*) **to give clear i. of one's intentions,** faire connaître clairement ses intentions.

indicative [ɪn'dɪkətɪv] **1** *n Gram* indicatif *m*; **in the i.,** à l'indicatif. **2** *adj* **(a)** (*pointing to*) indicatif (**of,** de); **(b)** *Gram* **i. mood,** mode indicatif.

indicator ['ɪndɪkeɪtər] *n* **(a)** index *m*, aiguille *f* (*de baromètre etc*); *Aut* clignotant *m*; *MecE etc* indicateur *m*; *Nau Av* indicateur, compteur *m* (*de vitesse etc*); *Nucl Phys* **radiation i.,** indicateur *ou* signaleur *m* de rayonnement; **(b)** *Com* **retail-price i.,** indice *m* des prix de détail; **(c)** (*indication, guide*) indicateur *m*, indice *m*; **(d)** (*table with written information*) table *f* d'orientation (*au sommet d'une montagne etc*); **i. (panel),** tableau indicateur; *Rail* **train i., i. board,** tableau *ou* indicateur des arrivées et des départs.

indict [ɪn'daɪt] *vt Jur* accuser (*qn*) (**for,** de), inculper (*qn*) (**for,** pour), traduire *ou* poursuivre (*qn*) en justice (**for,** pour); **she was indicted for murder,** elle a été inculpée pour meurtre.

indictable [ɪn'daɪtəb(ə)l] *adj Jur* (*person*) traduisible en justice; **i. offence,** délit *m*.

indictment [ɪn'daɪtmənt] *n Jur* **(a)** (*of person*) accusation *f*, incrimination *f*, inculpation *f*; (*by public prosecutor*) réquisitoire *m*; *Fig* **it is an i. of our education system that the illiteracy rate is so high,** le fait que le taux d'analphabétisme soit aussi élevé remet en cause notre système éducatif; **(b)** (*document*) acte *m* d'accusation (*au criminel*); **to draw up an i.,** rédiger un acte d'accusation.

Indies (the) [ðɪ'ɪndɪz] *npl* les Indes *fpl*; **the East I.,** l'Insulinde *f*; **the West I.,** les Antilles *fpl*, les Indes occidentales.

indifference [ɪn'dɪfrəns, -fərəns] *n* **(a)** (*lack of interest*) indifférence *f*, manque *m* d'intérêt, apathie *f* (**to, towards sth/s.o.,** pour qch/à l'égard de qn); **it's a matter of complete i. to me,** cela m'est parfaitement indifférent; **(b)** médiocrité *f* (*de talent etc*); **(c)** *Econ* **i. curve,** courbe *f* d'indifférence.

indifferent [ɪn'dɪfrənt, -fərənt] *adj* **(a)** (*not interested*) indifférent (**to,** à); **I am** *or* **feel i. about him,** il m'est indifférent; **(b)** (*meal, cooking*) médiocre, passable; (*painter*) médiocre.

indifferently [ɪn'dɪfrəntlɪ] *adv* (*see adj*) **(a)** indifféremment; **(b)** (*poorly*) médiocrement, ni bien ni mal.

indigence ['ɪndɪdʒəns] *n* indigence *f*, pauvreté *f*.

indigenous [ɪn'dɪdʒɪnəs] *adj* (*plant, product etc*) indigène (**to,** à).

indigent ['ɪndɪdʒənt] *adj* indigent, pauvre.

indigestible [ɪndɪ'dʒestɪbəl] *adj* indigeste.

indigestion [ɪndɪ'dʒestʃən] *n* indigestion *f*, dyspepsie *f*; **to have an attack of i.,** avoir une indigestion.

indignant [ɪn'dɪgnənt] *adj* (*personne, air*) indigné; (*cri*) d'indignation; **to be** *or* **feel i. at sth,** être indigné *ou* s'indigner de qch; **to make s.o. i.,** indigner qn.

indignantly [ɪn'dɪgnəntlɪ] *adv* avec indignation, d'un ton *ou* d'un air indigné.

indignation [ɪndɪg'neɪʃən] *n* indignation *f*; **righteous i.,** une juste indignation.

indignity [ɪn'dɪgnɪtɪ] *n* indignité *f*; **to suffer indignities,** souffrir des affronts; **the i. of it!,** quelle honte!

indigo, *pl* **-o(e)s** ['ɪndɪgəʊ, -əʊz] *n* **(a)** (*in dyeing*) indigo *m*, inde *m*; **i. (blue),** (*colour*) (bleu *m*) indigo *m inv*; (*dye*) indigo bleu; **(b)** *Bot* **i. (plant),** indigotier *m*.

indirect [ɪndɪ'rekt] *adj* **(a)** (*influence, result etc*) indirect; *Gram* **i. speech,** discours indirect; **i. object,** complément d'objet indirect; **(b)** (*route*) détourné; (*answer, costs, tax*) indirect; (*means etc*) détourné, oblique.

indirectly [ɪndɪ'rektlɪ] *adv* indirectement.

indiscernible [ɪndɪ'sɜːnɪb(ə)l] *adj* indiscernable; (*imperceptible*) imperceptible.

indiscipline [ɪn'dɪsɪplɪn] *n* indiscipline *f*.

indiscreet [ɪndɪs'kriːt] *adj* **(a)** indiscret, -ète; **would it be i. to ask you what you are going to do?,** peut-on vous demander sans indiscrétion ce que vous comptez faire?; **(b)** (*unwise*) peu judicieux, imprudent; (*démarche*) inconsidéré.

indiscreetly [ɪndɪs'kriːtlɪ] *adv* **(a)** indiscrètement; **(b)** (*unwisely*) imprudemment.

indiscretion [ɪndɪs'kreʃən] *n* **(a)** (*lack of discretion*) manque *m* de discrétion, indiscrétion *f*; **(b)** (*unwise act*) imprudence *f*; (*social blunder*) écart *m* de conduite; **to be guilty of an i.,** (*blunder*) commettre une inconséquence; (*be caught in compromising situation*) se compromettre (*avec qn*).

indiscriminate [ɪndɪs'krɪmɪnɪt] *adj* (*vengeance, admirateur*) aveugle, qui ne fait pas de distinction, sans discernement; **he was i. in his praise,** il a distribué des compliments sans discernement; **i. slaughter,** tuerie générale.

indiscriminately [ɪndɪs'krɪmɪnɪtlɪ] *adv* (*censurer, frapper*) sans faire de distinction; (*admirer, tuer*) aveuglément.

indispensable [ɪndɪs'pensəb(ə)l] *adj* **(a)** (*person, thing*) indispensable; (*thing*) de première nécessité (**to s.o.,** à qn; **for sth,** pour *ou* à qch); **no one is i.,** personne n'est indispensable; **(b)** (*loi, devoir*) obligatoire, qu'on ne peut négliger.

indisposed [ɪndɪs'pəʊzd] *adj* **(a)** (*ill*) indisposé, souffrant; **to be** *or* **feel i.,** être indisposé *ou* souffrant; **(b)** (*not inclined*) peu enclin, peu disposé (**to do sth,** à faire qch).

indisposition [ɪndɪspə'zɪʃən] *n* **(a)** (*illness*) indisposition *f*, malaise *m*; **(b)** (*lack of inclination*) peu *m* d'inclination (**to do sth,** à faire qch).

indisputable [ɪndɪs'pjuːtəb(ə)l] *adj* incontestable, indiscutable, indisputable; **it is the i. truth,** c'est indiscutablement *ou* incontestablement la vérité.

indisputably [ɪndɪs'pjuːtəblɪ] *adv* indiscutablement, incontestablement.

indissoluble [ɪndɪ'sɒljʊb(ə)l] *adj* (*union, amitié*) indissoluble.

indistinct [ɪndɪs'tɪŋkt] *adj* (*objet, bruit etc*) indistinct, peu distinct; (*bruit*) confus; (*souvenir*) vague.

indistinctly [ɪndɪs'tɪŋktlɪ] *adv* (*voir, parler*) indistinctement; (*sentir*) vaguement; **to speak i.,** manger ses mots.

indistinguishable [ɪndɪs'tɪŋgwɪʃəb(ə)l] *adj* indiscernable, que l'on ne peut distinguer (**from,** de); **the two insects are i.,** les deux insectes ne peuvent pas être distingués.

individual [ɪndɪ'vɪdjʊəl] **1** *adj* **(a)** (*for an individual*) individuel, particulier; **his pupils get i. attention,** il s'occupe de ses élèves individuellement; **every room has its own i. shower,** chaque chambre est équipée de sa propre douche; **(b)** (*taken individually*) **i. animals vary in size,** chaque animal a une taille différente; **(c)** (*unique*) qui se distingue des autres; **he's so i. in his views,** il a des idées si originales. **2** *n* individu *m*; **a private i.,** un simple particulier.

individualism [ɪndɪ'vɪdjʊəlɪzəm] *n* individualisme *m*.

individualist [ɪndɪ'vɪdjʊəlɪst] *n* individualiste *mf*.

individualistic [ɪndɪvɪdjʊə'lɪstɪk] *adj* individualiste.

individuality [ɪndɪvɪdjʊ'ælɪtɪ] *n* individualité *f*.

individualize [ɪndɪ'vɪdjʊəlaɪz] *vt* individualiser.

individually [ɪndɪ'vɪdjʊəlɪ] *adv* individuellement, un par un; **i. wrapped,** emballé individuellement; **he spoke to us all i.,** il nous a parlé à chacun, un par un.

indivisible [ɪndɪ'vɪzɪb(ə)l] *adj* indivisible, insécable.

Indochina ['ɪndəʊ'tʃaɪnə] *n* Indochine *f*.

indoctrinate [ɪn'dɒktrɪneɪt] *vt* endoctriner; **to i. s.o. with an idea,** inculquer une idée à qn.

indoctrination [ɪndɒktrɪ'neɪʃən] *n* endoctrinement *m*.

Indo-European ['ɪndəʊjʊərə'piːən] **1** *adj Ling* indo-européen. **2** *n* **(a)** Indo-Européen, -enne; **(b)** *Ling* indo-européen *m*.

indolence ['ɪndələns] *n* indolence *f*, paresse *f*.

indolent ['ɪndələnt] *adj* indolent, paresseux.

indolently ['ɪndələntlɪ] *adv* indolemment.

indomitable [ɪn'dɒmɪtəb(ə)l] *adj* indomptable; (*courage etc*) invincible.

Indonesia [ɪndəʊ'niːzɪə, -ʒə] *n* Indonésie *f*.

Indonesian [ɪndəʊ'niːzɪən, -ʒ(ə)n] **1** *adj* indonésien. **2** *n* **(a)** Indonésien, -ienne; **(b)** *Ling* indonésien *m*.

indoor ['ɪndɔːr] *adj* (*plante*) d'appartement; (*photographie*) en appartement; **i. games,** (*sport*) sports *mpl* en salle; (*party games*) jeux *mpl* de société; **i. swimming pool,** piscine couverte; **i. aerial,** antenne intérieure.

indoors [ɪn'dɔːz] *adv* (*inside house*) à la maison; (*inside building*) à l'intérieur; **to go i.,** (r)entrer (dans la maison); **to stay i.,** rester à la maison *ou* à l'intérieur; **this job's better, at least it's i.,** ce poste est mieux, au moins je *ou* tu *ou* il *etc* travaille(s) à l'intérieur; *Br Sl* **her i.,** la bourgeoise.

indorse [ɪn'dɔːs] *vt* = **ENDORSE**.
indrawn ['ɪndrɔːn] *adj* (*air*) aspiré; **i. breath,** aspiration *f*.
indubitable [ɪn'djuːbɪtəb(ə)l] *adj* indubitable, hors de doute, incontestable.
indubitably [ɪn'djuːbɪtəblɪ] *adv* indubitablement, sans aucun doute.
induce [ɪn'djuːs] *vt* **(a)** (*persuade*) induire, amener, déterminer (*qn*) (**to do,** à faire); **nothing will i. him to change his mind,** rien ne le fera changer d'idée; **(b)** (*bring about*) amener, produire, occasionner, causer; provoquer (*le sommeil*); *El etc* amorcer, induire (*un courant etc*); *Obst* **to i. labour,** provoquer *ou* déclencher le travail; *Obst F* **she's had to be induced,** on a dû lui faire une piqûre pour provoquer *ou* déclencher le travail; **do not attempt to i. vomiting,** ne pas essayer de provoquer *ou* déclencher des vomissements; **a drug-induced state,** un état provoqué par la drogue; **(c)** induire (*une loi etc*).
induced [ɪn'djuːst] *adj* (*hypnose*) provoqué; **i. draught,** tirage *m* par induction; *El* **i. current,** courant induit *ou* d'induction.
inducement [ɪn'djuːsmənt] *n* **(a)** (*something that persuades someone*) encouragement *m* (matériel); *Jur* incitation *f* (**to,** à); **(b)** *Jur* motif *m* (*d'un acte judiciaire*); cause *f* (*d'un contrat*).
induct [ɪn'dʌkt] *vt* **(a)** installer (*un fonctionnaire*) dans sa charge; *Rel* mettre (*un ecclésiastique*) en possession d'un bénéfice; **(b)** (*initiate*) initier (*qn*) (**into,** à); **he was inducted into the Freemasons,** il a été initié à la franc-maçonnerie; **(c)** *US Mil* **to be inducted,** (*into the army*) être appelé sous les drapeaux.
induction [ɪn'dʌkʃən] *n* **(a)** installation *f* (*d'un ecclésiastique, d'un fonctionnaire*); **(b)** *Obst* (*of labour*) mise *f* en route (artificielle), déclenchement *m* (artificiel); **(c) i. of facts,** énumération *f* des faits (*pour prouver qch*); **(d)** apport *m* de preuves; (*in logic*) *& Math* induction *f*; **(e)** *El* induction *f*; **i. coil,** bobine *f* d'induction, bobine de self; **(f)** *MecE* admission *f*, entrée *f* (*de la vapeur, des gaz*); aspiration *f* (*de gaz*); **i. stroke,** course *f ou* temps *m* d'admission.
inductive [ɪn'dʌktɪv] *adj* **(a)** (*in logic*) *& Math* (*raisonnement*) inductif, par induction; **(b)** *El* (*courant etc*) inducteur.
indulge [ɪn'dʌldʒ] **1** *vt* avoir *ou* montrer trop d'indulgence pour (*qn*); (*spoil*) gâter (*qn*); s'adonner à (*une fantaisie*); nourrir (*un espoir*); se livrer à, donner libre cours à (*une passion*); *Cathol* accorder une indulgence à (*qn*); *Com* accorder un délai à (*le payeur d'une lettre de change*); **to i. oneself,** ne rien se refuser; **to i. s.o.'s fancies,** flatter les caprices de qn. **2** *vi* **to i. in a practice,** s'adonner à une habitude; **to i. in a cigar,** se permettre un cigare; **to i. in a glass of port,** s'offrir un verre de porto; **to i. in speculation,** se laisser aller à des spéculations (**on, about,** sur); **I used to drink a lot but nowadays I rarely i.,** je buvais beaucoup mais maintenant c'est rare que je me le permette; *F* **thanks, but I don't i.,** merci, mais je ne bois *ou* fume pas.
indulgence [ɪn'dʌldʒəns] *n* **(a)** (*doting, leniency*) indulgence *f*, complaisance *f* (**to,** envers); **a mother's i. for her children,** faiblesse *f* d'une mère pour ses enfants; **(b)** (*act, activity*) **i. in strong liquor,** fait de prendre plaisir à boire des liqueurs fortes; **I allow myself the occasional i. in a glass of port,** de temps en temps je m'offre un verre de porto; **sexual i.,** plaisirs *mpl* de la chair; **(c)** *Cathol* indulgence *f*.
indulgent [ɪn'dʌldʒənt] *adj* indulgent (**to,** envers, pour); **over-i. father,** père trop indulgent.
indulgently [ɪn'dʌldʒəntlɪ] *adv* avec indulgence.
industrial [ɪn'dʌstrɪəl] *adj* (*area, city, activity, espionage etc*) industriel; (*conflict*) ouvrier, du travail; (*agitation*) ouvrier; **for i. use only,** usage industriel uniquement; *Br* **to take i. action,** se mettre en grève; **i. disease,** maladie professionnelle *ou* du travail; *Br* **i. estate,** zone industrielle; **i. relations,** relations humaines dans l'entreprise.
industrialism [ɪn'dʌstrɪəlɪz(ə)m] *n* industrialisme *m*.
industrialist [ɪn'dʌstrɪəlɪst] *n* industriel *m*.
industrialization [ɪndʌstrɪəlaɪ'zeɪʃən] *n* industrialisation *f*.
industrialize [ɪn'dʌstrɪəlaɪz] **1** *vt* industrialiser. **2** *vi* s'industrialiser.
industrials [ɪn'dʌstrɪəlz] *npl St Exch* valeurs industrielles.
industrious [ɪn'dʌstrɪəs] *adj* industrieux, travailleur.
industriously [ɪn'dʌstrɪəslɪ] *adv* industrieusement.
industriousness [ɪn'dʌstrɪəsnɪs] *n* assiduité *f* (*au travail*).
industry ['ɪndʌstrɪ] *n* **(a)** industrie *f*; **i. has declined in this country,** l'industrie a décliné dans ce pays; **the i. has declined,** l'industrie a décliné; **i. experts say a strike is unlikely,** les experts de l'industrie rejettent la probabilité d'une grève; **growth i.,** industrie en plein essor; **cottage i.,** industrie artisanale, artisanat *m*; **heavy/light i.,** l'industrie lourde/légère; **aircraft/mining i.,** industrie aéronautique/minière; **the shipping i.,** l'armement *m*; **the record i.,** l'industrie du disque; **(b)** (*diligence*) assiduité *f* (au travail), application *f*.
inebriate[1] [ɪn'iːbrɪət] *Fml* **1** *adj* ivre, gris, enivré. **2** *n* ivrogne *mf*, alcoolique *mf*.
inebriate[2] [ɪn'iːbrɪeɪt] *vt* enivrer, griser.
inebriated [ɪn'iːbrɪeɪtɪd] *adj* ivre, en état d'ébriété.
inebriation [ɪniːbrɪ'eɪʃən] *n* **(a)** (*act of making drunk*) enivrement *m*; **(b)** (*drunkenness*) ivresse *f*, ébriété *f*.
inedible [ɪn'edɪb(ə)l] *adj* non comestible; (*too disgusting to eat*) immangeable.
ineducable [ɪn'edjʊkəb(ə)l] *adj* inéducable.
ineffable [ɪn'efəb(ə)l] *adj* **(a)** (*joy etc*) ineffable, indicible; **(b)** (*sacred name etc*) qu'on n'ose pas prononcer.
ineffective [ɪnɪ'fektɪv] *adj* **(a)** (*moyen, remède*) inefficace; **(b)** (*travail, architecture*) qui manque d'effet artistique; (*discours*) sans effet; (*orateur*) terne; (*style*) plat, terne; **(c)** (*personne*) incapable.
ineffectively [ɪnɪ'fektɪvlɪ] *adv* ineffectivement, vainement.
ineffectual [ɪnɪ'fektjʊəl] *adj* (*effort, raisonnement, personne*) inefficace; (*traitement*) sans résultat; **i. person,** velléitaire *mf*.
inefficacious [ɪnefɪ'keɪʃəs] *adj* inefficace.
inefficaciousness [ɪnefɪ'keɪʃəsnɪs], **inefficacy** [ɪn'efɪkəsɪ] *n* inefficacité *f*.
inefficiency [ɪnɪ'fɪʃənsɪ] *n* (*of method, machine, organization, person*) inefficacité *f*.
inefficient [ɪnɪ'fɪʃənt] *adj* (*measure, person etc*) inefficace.
inefficiently [ɪnɪ'fɪʃəntlɪ] *adv* inefficacement.
inelastic [ɪnɪ'læstɪk] *adj* sans élasticité; *Fig* rigide, raide.
inelegant [ɪn'elɪgənt] *adj* (*style*) inélégant; (*personne, style*) sans élégance.
inelegantly [ɪn'elɪgəntlɪ] *adv* (*dressed*) sans élégance; (*phrased*) inélégamment.
ineligible [ɪn'elɪdʒɪb(ə)l] *adj* (*candidat*) inéligible; **i. for military service,** inapte au service militaire.
ineluctable [ɪnɪ'lʌktəb(ə)l] *adj Lit* inéluctable, inévitable.
inept [ɪn'ept] *adj* **(a)** (*incompetent*) inepte; **(b)** (*inappropriate*) (*remark etc*) déplacé, mal à propos.
ineptitude [ɪn'eptɪtjuːd] *n* **(a)** (*incompetence, foolishness*) ineptie *f*, sottise *f*; **(b)** manque *m* de justesse *ou* d'à-propos (*d'une observation*).
ineptly [ɪn'eptlɪ] *adv* ineptement.
inequality [ɪnɪ'kwɒlɪtɪ] *n* (*social, economic*) inégalité *f*; variabilité *f*, inégalité (*du climat*).
inequitable [ɪn'ekwɪtəb(ə)l] *adj* inéquitable.
ineradicable [ɪnɪ'rædɪkəb(ə)l] *adj* indéracinable, inextirpable.
inert [ɪ'nɜːt] *adj* **(a)** (*masse, substance*) inerte; (*esprit*) inerte, apathique; **(b)** *Ch* inactif, inerte; **the i. gases,** les gaz inertes.
inertia [ɪ'nɜːʃɪə] *n Phys* inertie *f*; (*of person*) paresse *f*, veulerie *f*; **mass i.,** inertie de masse; *Phys* **moment of i.,** moment *m* d'inertie; *Phys* **i. force,** force *f* d'inertie; *Aut* **i. starter,** démarreur *m* à inertie; *Br Com* **i. selling,** = vente par obtention abusive ou frauduleuse de commande.
inertia-reel [ɪ'nɜːʃɪəriːl] *adj Aut* **i.-r. seat-belt,** ceinture *f* (de sécurité) à enrouleur.
inescapable [ɪnɪ'skeɪpəb(ə)l] *adj* inéluctable, inévitable.
inessential [ɪnɪ'senʃəl] *adj* qui n'est pas essentiel.
inestimable [ɪn'estɪməb(ə)l] *adj* (*value, benefit etc*) inestimable.
inevitability [ɪnevɪtə'bɪlɪtɪ] *n* inévitabilité *f*.
inevitable [ɪn'evɪtəb(ə)l] *adj* (*unavoidable*) inévitable; (*certain*) fatal, -als; **his promotion is i.,** il va de soi qu'il sera promu; **there will be accidents, it's i.,** il y aura des accidents, c'est inévitable; **the i. latecomer,** l'inévitable retardataire; **the i. conclusion,** (*of a play, novel*) le dénouement fatal.
inevitably [ɪn'evɪtəblɪ] *adv* inévitablement.
inexact [ɪnɪg'zækt] *adj* (*récit etc*) inexact.
inexactitude [ɪnɪg'zæktɪtjuːd] *n* **(a)** inexactitude *f* (*d'un récit etc*); **(b)** (*mistake*) erreur *f*.
inexactly [ɪnɪg'zæktlɪ] *adv* inexactement.
inexactness [ɪnɪg'zæktnɪs] *n* inexactitude *f* (*d'un récit etc*).
inexcusable [ɪnɪks'kjuːzəb(ə)l] *adj* inexcusable, sans excuse, impardonnable; **that was i. of you,** c'est

impardonnable.
inexcusably [ɪnɪks'kjuːzəblɪ] *adv* inexcusablement, impardonnablement.
inexhaustible [ɪneg'zɔːstɪb(ə)l] *adj* **(a)** (*endless*) inépuisable, inexhaustible; (*source*) intarissable; (*patience*) inépuisable, sans limite; **she had an i. supply of jokes,** elle avait un stock de blagues inépuisable; **(b)** (*person*) infatigable.
inexorable [ɪn'eksərəb(ə)l] *adj* (*personne, destin*) inexorable; (*personne*) inflexible, implacable.
inexorably [ɪn'eksərəblɪ] *adv* inexorablement.
inexpedient [ɪnɪks'piːdɪənt] *adj* inopportun, malavisé.
inexpensive [ɪnɪks'pensɪv] *adj* peu coûteux, bon marché, (qui ne coûte) pas cher; **i. to run,** (*house, car*) économique; **an i. alternative to champagne,** une alternative bon marché pour remplacer le champagne.
inexpensively [ɪnɪks'pensɪvlɪ] *adv* (à) bon marché, à bas prix; (*vivre*) économiquement, à peu de frais.
inexperience [ɪnɪks'pɪərɪəns] *n* inexpérience *f*.
inexperienced [ɪnɪks'pɪərɪənst] *adj* **(a)** (*person*) inexpérimenté, sans expérience; **she is still i.,** elle est encore novice; **he's i. in handling staff,** il n'a pas l'habitude de diriger le personnel; **(b)** (*œil*) inexercé.
inexpert [ɪn'ekspɜːt] *adj* inexpert, maladroit, peu habile (**in,** à).
inexpertly [ɪn'ekspɜː'tlɪ] *adv* d'une manière inexperte, maladroitement.
inexplicable [ɪnɪks'plɪkəb(ə)l] *adj* (*mystery*) inexplicable; (*ingratitude*) inconcevable.
inexplicably [ɪnɪks'plɪkəblɪ] *adv* inexplicablement.
inexpressible [ɪnɪks'presɪb(ə)l] *adj* (*plaisir*) inexprimable, indicible.
inexpressive [ɪnɪks'presɪv] *adj* inexpressif, sans expression.
inextinguishable [ɪnɪks'tɪŋgwɪʃəb(ə)l] *adj* (*feu, rire*) inextinguible.
in extremis [ɪnɪk'striːmɪs] *adv* (*dying*) sur le point de mourir, à l'article de la mort.
inextricable [ɪneks'trɪkəb(ə)l] *adj* inextricable.
inextricably [ɪneks'trɪkəblɪ] *adv* inextricablement.
INF [aɪen'ef] *n Mil* (*abbr* **intermediate-range nuclear forces**) FNI *fpl*.
infallibility [ɪnfælɪ'bɪlɪtɪ] *n Rel etc* infaillibilité *f*.
infallible [ɪn'fælɪb(ə)l] *adj* (*jugement, remède etc*) infaillible.
infallibly [ɪn'fælɪblɪ] *adv* infailliblement.
infamous ['ɪnfəməs] *adj* **(a)** (*personne, conduite*) infâme; (*conduite*) abominable; (*endroit*) mal famé; **(b)** *Jur* (*crime*) infamant.
infamy ['ɪnfəmɪ] *n* infamie *f* (*d'un crime etc*).
infancy ['ɪnfənsɪ] *n* **(a)** (*early childhood*) première enfance, petite enfance; *Fig* débuts *mpl*, première période, enfance (*d'un art, d'une industrie*); **from i.,** dès la plus tendre enfance; *Fig* **science was in its i.,** la science en était à ses balbutiements; **(b)** *Jur* minorité *f*.
infant ['ɪnfənt] **1** *n* **(a)** (*baby*) enfant *mf* du premier âge; (*until umbilical cord drops off*) nouveau-né, nouveau-née *f*; (*until the age of two*) nourrisson *m*; **i. mortality,** mortalité *f* infantile; **i. mortality rate,** taux *f* de mortalité infantile; *Br Sch* **i. class,** la classe enfantine; *Br Sch* **i. school,** école *f* pour les enfants de cinq à huit ans; **i. prodigy,** enfant prodige; **(b)** *Jur* mineur, -eure. **2** *adj* (*child*) en bas âge; *Fig* **an i. science,** une science qui en est à ses balbutiements.
infanticide [ɪn'fæntɪsaɪd] *n* **(a)** (*crime*) (crime *m* d')infanticide *m*; **(b)** (*person*) infanticide *mf*.
infantile ['ɪnfəntaɪl] *adj* **(a)** (*esprit, imagination*) d'enfant; *Med* (*maladie*) infantile; *Med* **i. paralysis,** paralysie infantile; **(b)** *Pej* (*raisonnement etc*) enfantin; (*remarque*) puéril.
infantry ['ɪnfəntrɪ] *n Mil* infanterie *f*; (*foot soldiers*) fantassins *mpl*.
infantryman, *pl* **-men** ['ɪnfəntrɪmən] *n* soldat *m* d'infanterie, fantassin *m*.
infarction [ɪn'faːkʃən] *n Med* infarctus *m*.
infatuated [ɪn'fætjʊeɪtɪd] *adj* entiché (**with,** de); **to become i. with s.o./sth,** s'enticher de qn/de qch.
infatuation [ɪnfætjʊ'eɪʃən] *n* obsession *f*, *F* toquade *f*; **to have an i. for s.o.,** s'enticher de qn; **it's just (an) i.,** ce n'est qu'une toquade.
infect [ɪn'fekt] *vt* **(a)** *Med* contaminer (*qn*); infecter (*une plaie, une ville*); **to i. s.o. with a disease,** communiquer une maladie à qn; **(b)** *Fig* communiquer (*sa gaieté à qn*); (*corrupt, taint*) infecter, corrompre, vicier (*l'air, les mœurs etc*).
infected [ɪn'fektɪd] *adj* (*clothing*) porteur de germes; (*wound*) infecté; **to become i.,** (*of wound*) s'infecter.
infection [ɪn'fekʃən] *n Med* infection *f*, contamination *f*, contagion *f*; *Fig* contagion; **viral i.,** infection virale; **an ear i.,** une otite; **source of i.,** foyer *m* d'infection; **to spread/prevent i.,** répandre/empêcher l'infection.
infectious [ɪn'fekʃəs] *adj Med* (*disease*) infectieux; *F* (*disease, person*) contagieux; *Fig* (*laughter, optimism*) communicatif; **i. rhythms,** rythmes qui donnent envie de danser.
infectiousness [ɪn'fekʃəsnɪs] *n Med* nature infectieuse (*d'une maladie*); *Fig* caractère communicatif.
infelicitous [ɪnfɪ'lɪsɪtəs] *adj* malheureux.
infelicity [ɪnfɪ'lɪsɪtɪ] *n Fig* **(a)** *Lit* (*unhappiness*) malheur *m*, infélicité *f*; **(b)** (*remark*) expression malheureuse; (*action, remark*) gaffe *f*.
infer [ɪn'fɜːr] *vt* (**-rr-**) **(a)** inférer, déduire, conclure (**sth from sth,** qch de qch; **that,** que); **(b)** *F* = **IMPLY**.
inference ['ɪnfərəns] *n* **(a)** (*method*) inférence *f*; **by i.,** par déduction; **(b)** (*conclusion*) inférence *f*, déduction *f*, conclusion *f*; **to draw an i. from sth,** tirer une conclusion *ou* une conséquence de qch.
inferior [ɪn'fɪərɪər] **1** *adj* inférieur; (*ouvrage*) de second ordre; *Bot* (*calice, ovaire*) infère; **the expensive screwdriver was i. to the cheap one,** le tournevis cher était moins bon que celui qui était bon marché; **her second novel is a much i. work,** son deuxième roman est bien moins bon; **i. quality,** qualité inférieure; **to be in an i. position,** être dans une position inférieure *ou* subordonnée; *Astron* **the i. planets,** les planètes inférieures; *Typ* **i. letter,** petite lettre inférieure. **2** *n* **(a)** (*in school position*) inférieur, -eure; (*in rank, grade*) inférieur, -eure, subordonné, -ée, subalterne *mf*; **one's inferiors,** les personnes d'un rang inférieur à soi; **(b)** *Typ* petite lettre inférieure.
inferiority [ɪnfɪərɪ'ɒrɪtɪ] *n* infériorité *f* (**to,** par rapport à); *Psy* **i. complex,** complexe *m* d'infériorité.
infernal [ɪn'fɜːn(ə)l] *adj* **(a)** *F* (*diabolical*) infernal, abominable, diabolique; **(b)** *F* (*intensive*) (*chaleur etc*) d'enfer; (*bruit*) infernal; **it's an i. nuisance,** c'est diablement embêtant; **(c) the i. regions,** l'enfer *m*.
infernally [ɪn'fɜːn(ə)lɪ] *adv F* diablement; **it's i. hot,** il fait une chaleur d'enfer *ou* à crever.
inferno, *pl* **-os** [ɪn'fɜːnəʊ, -əʊz] *n* enfer *m*; *Liter* **Dante's I.,** l'Enfer de Dante; **the house was a raging i.,** la maison était un véritable brasier.
infertile [ɪn'fɜːtaɪl] *adj* (*personne*) stérile; (*terrain*) stérile, infertile, inféconde; (*esprit*) stérile; (*œuf*) clair, non fécondé.
infertility [ɪnfɜː'tɪlɪtɪ] *n* infertilité *f*, stérilité *f*; **i. clinic,** = clinique pour traiter les couples stériles.
infest [ɪn'fest] *vt* (*vermin etc*) infester; **to be infested by rats/cockroaches/***etc*, être infesté de rats/cafards/*etc*; **shark-infested seas,** mers infestées de requins.
infestation [ɪnfes'teɪʃən] *n* invasion *f* (*des plantes par les parasites etc*); *Med* infestation *f*.
infidel ['ɪnfɪdəl] *adj & n* **(a)** *Hist* infidèle *mf*, mécréant, -ante; **(b)** *Pej* incroyant, -ante.
infidelity [ɪnfɪ'delɪtɪ] *n* **(a)** (*of spouse, lover*) infidélité *f*; **(b)** (*disloyalty*) infidélité *f*, déloyauté *f* (*d'un serviteur etc*); **(c)** *Rel* incroyance *f*.
infighting ['ɪnfaɪtɪŋ] *n* **(a)** (*within a group*) querelles intestines; **political i.,** querelles politiques intestines; **(b)** *Boxing* corps à corps *m*.
infill ['ɪnfɪl] *n Constr* remplissage *m*.
infiltrate ['ɪnfɪltreɪt] **1** *vt* **(a)** *Pol etc* (*of subversives etc*) noyauter (*un syndicat etc*); s'infiltrer dans (*l'ennemi etc*); **(b)** (*cause to enter*) faire pénétrer (*un liquide etc*) dans (*qch*); **(c)** (*of liquid*) s'infiltrer *ou* pénétrer dans, imprégner (*une substance*). **2** *vi* (*of fluid, spies etc*) s'infiltrer (**into,** dans; **through,** à travers).
infiltration [ɪnfɪl'treɪʃən] *n* **(a)** (*by spies, troops etc*) infiltration *f*; **to advance by i.,** s'infiltrer; *Pol* **the i. of communists into the trade unions, the i. of the trade unions by communists,** le noyautage des syndicats par les communistes; **(b)** infiltration *f* (*d'un liquide etc*) (**through,** à travers).
infiltrator ['ɪnfɪltreɪtər] *n* agent *m* qui s'infiltre (*dans un parti politique etc*).
infinite ['ɪnfɪnɪt] **1** *adj* **(a)** (*space, wealth etc*) *& Math* infini; **truth of i. importance,** vérité d'une très grande importance; **to go to i. pains to do sth,** avoir une peine infinie à faire qch; *Rel & Hum* **in his i. wisdom,** dans son infinie sagesse; **i. ways of doing sth,** une infinité de façons de faire qch; **i. varieties,** variétés sans nombre; **(b)** [ɪn'faɪnaɪt] *Gram* **i. verb, verb i.,** formes substantives du verbe. **2** *n Rel Math* **the i.,** l'infini *m*.

infinitely ['ɪnfɪnɪtlɪ] *adv* infiniment.

infinitesimal [ɪnfɪnɪ'tesɪməl] *adj* (*quantité*) infinitésimal; (*majorité*) infime; *Math* **i. calculus,** calcul infinitésimal.

infinitive [ɪn'fɪnɪtɪv] *Gram* **1** *n* infinitif *m*; **in the i.,** à l'infinitif. **2** *adj* infinitif.

infinity [ɪn'fɪnɪtɪ] *n* **(a)** (*of space etc*) infinité *f*, infinitude *f*; **(b)** *Math etc* infini *m*; **to i.,** à l'infini; *Phot* **to focus on** *or* **for i.,** mettre au point sur l'infini.

infirm [ɪn'fɜːm] *adj* **(a)** (*person*) infirme, débile; **(b)** (*esprit, jugement*) irrésolu, flottant.

infirmary [ɪn'fɜːmərɪ] *n* **(a)** (*hospital*) hôpital *m*, -aux; **(b)** infirmerie *f* (*d'une école, prison etc*).

infirmity [ɪn'fɜːmɪtɪ] *n* **(a)** (*weakness*) infirmité *f*, débilité *f* (*du corps, de l'esprit*); **(b)** (*affliction*) infirmité *f*; **the infirmities of old age,** les infirmités de la vieillesse; **(c)** (*lack of resolve*) **i. of purpose,** irrésolution *f*.

in flagrante delicto [ɪnflə'græntɪdɪ'lɪktəʊ] *adv Jur* en flagrant délit.

inflame [ɪn'fleɪm] **1** *vt* **(a)** (*stir up*) enflammer (*le courage*); allumer (*les désirs*); attiser (*la discorde*); envenimer (*une querelle*); **(b)** *Med* enflammer (*une plaie*); **(c)** *Fml* (*set on fire*) mettre le feu à, enflammer (*une substance*). **2** *vi* **(a)** *Med* (*of wound, tissue*) s'enflammer; **(b)** *Fml* (*catch fire*) s'enflammer, prendre feu.

inflamed [ɪn'fleɪmd] *adj* **(a)** *Med* (*wound, eye etc*) enflammé; **to become i.,** s'enflammer; **(b)** enflammé (**with,** de); **i. with passion,** brûlant d'amour.

inflammable [ɪn'flæməb(ə)l] **1** *adj* (*substance etc*) inflammable; *Fig* (*person, crowd*) prompt à s'échauffer, inflammable. **2** *npl* **inflammables,** substances *fpl* inflammables.

inflammation [ɪnflə'meɪʃən] *n* **(a)** *Med* inflammation *f*; **(b)** inflammation *f* (*d'un combustible*); inflammation, excitation *f* (*des esprits*).

inflammatory [ɪn'flæmətərɪ] *adj* **(a)** (*discours, brochure*) incendiaire, provocateur, -trice; **(b)** *Med* (*fièvre*) inflammatoire.

inflatable [ɪn'fleɪtəb(ə)l] **1** *adj* (*balloon etc*) gonflable; (*radeau*) pneumatique. **2** *n* (*boat*) bateau *m* pneumatique.

inflate [ɪn'fleɪt] *vt* **(a)** (*fill with air*) gonfler (*un ballon, un pneu, une voile*); **to i. the lungs with air,** (*one's own*) remplir les poumons d'air; (*when giving artificial respiration*) souffler dans les poumons; *Fig* **to i. s.o. with pride,** faire gonfler qn d'orgueil; **(b)** *Fin* hausser, faire monter (*les prix*); *Com* grossir, charger (*un compte*); *Econ* **to i. the currency,** accroître artificiellement la circulation fiduciaire.

inflated [ɪn'fleɪtɪd] *adj* **(a)** (*ballon etc*) gonflé, enflé; **to become i.,** se gonfler (*d'air etc*); *Fig* **i. with pride,** bouffi d'orgueil; **to have an i. opinion of oneself,** avoir une opinion trop flatteuse *ou* surfaite de soi-même; **(b)** *Fin* (*prix*) exagéré; *Econ* **i. currency,** circulation fiduciaire accrue; **(c)** *Liter* (*style*) enflé.

inflation [ɪn'fleɪʃən] *n* **(a)** *Econ* inflation *f*; **rate of i.,** taux *m* d'inflation; **i.-proof,** (*pension etc*) protégé contre les effets de l'inflation; **(b)** gonflement *m*, gonflage *m* (*d'un ballon, pneu etc*); *Med* inflation *f* (*de l'estomac*).

inflationary [ɪn'fleɪʃənərɪ] *adj* (*politique etc*) inflationniste, d'inflation; **i. wage demands,** demandes salariales inflationnistes.

inflect [ɪn'flekt] **1** *vt* **(a)** (*bend*) fléchir, courber (en dedans); *Opt* infléchir (*un rayon*); **(b)** *Gram* donner des flexions à (*un mot*); **(c)** moduler (*la voix*); *Mus* altérer (*une note*). **2** *vi Gram* prendre une marque flexionnelle.

inflected [ɪn'flektɪd] *adj* **(a)** (*curved*) (*position*) courbé; *Archit* (*arc*) renversé; *Opt* (*rayon*) infléchi; **(b)** *Ling* (*langue*) à flexions, flexionnel; (*voyelle*) infléchi; **(c)** *Mus* (*note*) altéré.

inflection [ɪn'flekʃən] *n* = **INFLEXION**.

inflexibility [ɪnfleksɪ'bɪlɪtɪ] *n* inflexibilité *f*, rigidité *f*.

inflexible [ɪn'fleksɪb(ə)l] *adj* inflexible; **i. code of morals,** morale *f* rigide *ou* inflexible.

inflexion [ɪn'flekʃən] *n* **(a)** inflexion *f*, fléchissement *m* (*du corps etc*); *Opt Math* inflexion; **(b)** *Gram* flexion *f* (*d'un mot*); **(c)** inflexion *f* (*de la voix*); *Mus* altération *f* (*d'une note*).

inflict [ɪn'flɪkt] *vt* infliger (**sth on s.o.,** qch à qn); faire (*une blessure*) (**on,** à); faire subir, occasionner (*du chagrin*) (**on,** à); *Jur* infliger (*une punition*) (**on,** à); *F* **to i. oneself on s.o.,** s'imposer.

infliction [ɪn'flɪkʃən] *n* **(a)** (*action*) action *f* d'infliger; **the i. of pain on s.o.,** le fait d'infliger une douleur à qn; **(b)** (*result*) (*pain*) peine infligée; (*punishment*) châtiment *m*; **(c)** (*affliction*) affliction *f*.

in-flight ['ɪn'flaɪt] *adj Av* (*service*) en vol; **in-f. entertainment/meal,** film et programmes radiophoniques diffusés/repas servi pendant le vol.

inflorescence [ɪnflə'resəns] *n Bot* **(a)** (*grouping of flowers*) inflorescence *f*; **(b)** (*flowering*) floraison *f*; **(c)** (*flowers*) fleurs *fpl* (*d'un arbre etc*).

inflow ['ɪnfləʊ] *n* **(a)** (*act of flowing in*) entrée *f*, affluence *f* (*d'un cours d'eau*); affluence *f*, afflux *m* (*de gens, de marchandises*); flot *m* (*d'idées nouvelles*); **i. pipe,** arrivée *f* d'eau; **(b)** vitesse *f* d'appel (*d'air*).

influence¹ ['ɪnflʊəns] *n* influence *f* (**upon, on,** sur); **to exert** *or* **exercise an i. on s.o.,** exercer une influence sur qn, influencer qn; **to be a good/bad/great/***etc* **i. on s.o.,** avoir une bonne/mauvaise/grande/*etc* influence sur qn; **to use one's i. with s.o.,** user de son influence auprès de qn; **man of i.,** homme influent; **he owes his position to i.,** il doit sa situation au piston *ou* au pistonnage; **to have i.,** avoir de l'influence; **to have great i. over s.o.,** avoir beaucoup d'influence sur qn; **under the i. of drink,** *F* **under the i.,** sous l'empire de la boisson; *Jur* **undue i.,** intimidation *f*.

influence² *vt* (*of person*) influencer (*qn, qch*); **to i. one's friends,** influencer *ou* exercer une influence sur ses amis.

influential [ɪnflʊ'enʃəl] *adj* influent; **to be i.,** avoir de l'influence, avoir le bras long; (*of factor etc*) avoir du poids, jouer un rôle; **an i. figure in local politics,** une personnalité influente au niveau de la politique locale.

influenza [ɪnflʊ'enzə] *n Med* grippe *f*.

influx ['ɪnflʌks] *n* entrée *f*, affluence *f* (*d'un cours d'eau etc*); affluence, afflux *m* (*de gens, de marchandises*); afflux (*de gaz*); flot *m* (*d'idées nouvelles*); **a sudden i. of tourists,** un soudain afflux de touristes; *Econ* **i. of gold,** entrée *ou* afflux d'or.

info ['ɪnfəʊ] *n F* renseignements *mpl*, tuyaux *mpl*.

inform [ɪn'fɔːm] **1** *vt* **(a)** (*tell*) **to i. s.o. of sth,** informer *ou* avertir *ou* aviser qn de qch; apprendre *ou* faire savoir qch à qn; renseigner qn sur qch; **to keep s.o. informed of what is happening,** tenir qn au courant de ce qui se passe; **why was I not informed (of this)?,** pourquoi est-ce que je n'en ai pas été informé?; **to i. the police,** avertir la police; **we are writing to i. you of the dispatch of ...,** nous vous avisons de l'envoi de ...; **I regret to have to i. you that ...,** j'ai le regret de vous annoncer que ...; **we are informed that ...,** on nous fait savoir que ...; **to i. s.o. about sth,** (*provide with information*) renseigner qn sur qch; **(b)** *Lit* (*pervade*) imprégner (*les œuvres de qn etc*). **2** *vi Jur* **to i. against** *or* **on s.o.,** dénoncer qn.

informal [ɪn'fɔːməl] *adj* **(a)** (*person, manner, attitude*) simple, décontracté; (*speech, language, words*) familier; (*clothes*) décontracté; (*reception, dinner*) sans cérémonie; **he's very i. for a prime minister,** il est très décontracté pour un premier ministre; **British offices tend to be more i. than German ones,** en Grande-Bretagne l'ambiance dans les bureaux tend à être plus décontractée qu'en Allemagne; **dress: i.,** tenue de ville; **(b)** (*unofficial*) (*meeting*) non-officiel; (*arrangement*) officieux; **could we just have an i. chat?,** est-ce qu'on pourrait avoir un petit entretien?; **the two leaders had i. talks,** les deux dirigeants ont eu des entretiens non-officiels; **(c)** *Jur* irrégulier.

informality [ɪnfɔː'mælɪtɪ] *n* (*of person*) simplicité *f*, décontraction *f*; (*of occasion*) absence *f* de formalité *ou* de cérémonie; (*of talks*) caractère non-officiel.

informally [ɪn'fɔːməlɪ] *adv* **(a)** (*to dine*) sans cérémonie, sans formalités; (*to dress*) simplement; **i. known as ...,** familièrement connu sous le nom de ...; **(b)** (*to discuss*) officieusement, à titre non-officiel.

informant [ɪn'fɔːmənt] *n* informateur, -trice; **I have it from a reliable i.,** je le tiens de bonne source.

informatics [ɪnfɔː'mætɪks] *n sing* informatique *f*.

information [ɪnfə'meɪʃən] *n* **(a)** (*news, facts etc*) renseignement(s) *m(pl)*, information(s) *f(pl)*; **a bit** *or* **piece of i.,** un renseignement, une information; **I am sending you this brochure for your i.,** je vous envoie cette brochure à titre d'information; **I'm afraid your i. is wrong,** je crains qu'on vous ait mal renseigné; *Admin* **(strictly) confidential i.,** renseignements (strictement) confidentiels; **tourist i.,** informations *fpl* touristiques; **to ask for i. on** *or* **about s.o./sth,** demander des renseignements sur qn/qch; **for further i. write to ...,** pour de plus amples informations écrire à ...; **why don't you ask at i.?,** pourquoi est-ce que tu ne demandes pas à l'information *ou* aux renseignements?; **i. bureau,** bureau *m* de renseignements, centre *m* d'information; (*for tourists*) syndicat *m* d'initiative; **i. desk,** (*in hotel etc*) bureau *m* des renseignements;

(b) (*acquired knowledge*) instruction *f*, savoir *m*, connaissances *fpl*; **for my own i.,** pour ma propre information;

(c) *Comptr* information *f*; **i. processing industry,** industrie *f* de l'informatique; **i. theory,** théorie *f* de l'information; **i. processing,** traitement *m* de l'information; **i. science,** sciences *fpl* informatiques; **i. scientist,** informaticien, -ienne; **i. storage,** mémorisation *f* des informations; **i. system,** système *m* informatique; **i. retrieval,** recherche *f* documentaire *ou* des informations; **i. technology,** informatique *f*;

(d) *Jur* dénonciation *f* (**against s.o.,** contre qn), délation *f* (**against s.o.,** de qn); **to lay i. against s.o. with the police,** dénoncer qn à la police, informer contre qn.

(e) *Am Tel* renseignements *mpl*.

informative [ɪn'fɔːmətɪv] *adj* instructif; (*livre*) éducatif; **the documentary/he wasn't very i.,** ce documentaire n'était pas très instructif/il n'a pas dit grand-chose.

informed [ɪn'fɔːmd] *adj* bien renseigné; **i. public opinion,** l'opinion publique bien renseignée *ou* bien au courant; **the i. consumer,** le consommateur averti; **i. estimate/decision,** une évaluation faite/une décision prise en connaissance de cause.

informer [ɪn'fɔːmər] *n Pej* dénonciateur, -trice; *Jur* **common i.,** délateur, -trice; **to turn i.,** dénoncer ses complices.

infraction [ɪn'frækʃən] *n Fml* = **INFRINGEMENT**.

infra dig ['ɪnfrə'dɪg] *adj F* rabaissant; **it would be i. d. for us to reply,** ce serait au-dessous de notre dignité *ou* de nous de répondre.

infrared [ɪnfrə'red] *adj Phys* infrarouge; **i. radiation** *or* **rays,** radiation *f* infrarouge, infrarouge *m*; *Med* **i. lamp,** lampe *f* à rayons infrarouges.

infrastructure ['ɪnfrəstrʌktʃər] *n* infrastructure *f*.

infrequency [ɪn'friːkwənsɪ] *n* rareté *f*.

infrequent [ɪn'friːkwənt] *adj* rare, peu fréquent.

infrequently [ɪn'friːkwəntlɪ] *adv* rarement; **not i.,** assez souvent.

infringe [ɪn'frɪndʒ] *vt* enfreindre, violer (*une loi, un serment*); transgresser (*la loi*); **to i. an author's copyright,** violer *ou* empiéter sur les droits d'un auteur.

►**infringe on** *vipo* **to i. on s.o.'s rights,** empiéter sur les droits de qn.

infringement [ɪn'frɪndʒmənt] *n* infraction *f* (*d'un règlement*); violation *f* (*d'une loi, d'un droit*); **i. of s.o.'s rights,** infraction *ou* atteinte *f* aux droits de qn; **minor i. of the law** *or* **regulations,** contravention *f*; **i. of copyright,** non-respect *m* des droits *f* d'auteur.

infuriate [ɪn'fjʊərɪeɪt] *vt* rendre (*qn, un taureau etc*) furieux.

infuriated [ɪn'fjʊərɪeɪtɪd] *adj* furieux; **to become i.,** entrer en fureur.

infuriating [ɪn'fjʊərɪeɪtɪŋ] *adj* qui rend furieux, exaspérant; **at times I find him i.,** quelquefois il me met hors de moi; **it's i. the way she's always right,** ça me met hors de moi qu'elle ait toujours raison.

infuriatingly [ɪn'fjʊərɪeɪtɪŋlɪ] *adv* d'une façon exaspérante, à rendre furieux; **he's i. smug,** il est d'une suffisance exaspérante; **the computer's i. slow,** l'ordinateur est d'une lenteur exaspérante.

infuse [ɪn'fjuːz] *vt* **(a)** (*instil*) infuser (*du courage, une nouvelle vie*) (**into s.o.,** à qn); **to i. s.o. with ardour,** inspirer de l'ardeur à qn; **(b)** (*soak*) infuser, faire infuser (*du thé, des herbes*).

infuser [ɪn'fjuːzər] *n* infusoir *m*.

infusion [ɪn'fjuːʒən] *n* **(a)** tisane *f*, infusion *f* (*de camomille etc*); *Pharm* infusé *m*; **(b)** infusion *f* (*d'une tisane*); **(c)** *Rel* infusion *f* (*de la vérité etc*).

ingenious [ɪn'dʒiːnɪəs] *adj* (*person, device*) ingénieux.

ingeniously [ɪn'dʒiːnɪəslɪ] *adv* ingénieusement.

ingenuity [ɪndʒɪ'njuːɪtɪ] *n* ingéniosité *f* (*de qn, d'une invention*).

ingenuous [ɪn'dʒenjʊəs] *adj* **(a)** (*frank*) franc, *f* franche, sincère; **(b)** (*naive*) ingénu, simple, candide, naïf, *f* naïve.

ingenuously [ɪn'dʒenjʊəslɪ] *adv* (*see adj*) **(a)** franchement, sincèrement; **(b)** ingénument, naïvement, avec candeur.

ingenuousness [ɪn'dʒenjʊəsnɪs] *n* ingénuité *f*, naïveté *f*, candeur *f*.

ingest [ɪn'dʒest] *vt Physiol* ingérer (*un aliment*).

ingestion [ɪn'dʒestʃən] *n Physiol* ingestion *f*.

inglenook ['ɪŋg(ə)lnʊk] *n* coin *m* du feu.

inglorious [ɪn'glɔːrɪəs] *adj* **(a)** (*shameful*) (*defeat etc*) déshonorant, honteux; **(b)** (*obscure*) (*person*) humble, obscur.

ingloriously [ɪn'glɔːrɪəslɪ] *adv* (*see adj*) **(a)** ignominieusement; **(b)** humblement.

ingot ['ɪŋgət] *n* lingot *m* (*d'or, d'argent*).

ingrain [ɪn'greɪn] *vt* fixer; **certain habits are ingrained in one's nature,** certaines habitudes sont enracinées dans la nature de chacun; **prejudices that become ingrained,** préjugés qui s'incrustent.

ingrained [ɪn'greɪnd] *adj* **(a) i. with dirt,** encrassé; **i. dirt,** crasse *f*; **(b)** (*deep-seated*) enraciné, invétéré.

ingratiate [ɪn'greɪʃɪeɪt] *vt* **to i. oneself with s.o.,** s'insinuer dans les bonnes grâces de qn.

ingratiating [ɪn'greɪʃɪeɪtɪŋ] *adj* insinuant, prévenant, doucereux; (*sourire*) doucereux; **to act/speak in an i. manner,** agir/parler d'une manière doucereuse.

ingratiatingly [ɪn'greɪʃɪeɪtɪŋlɪ] *adv* d'une manière insinuante *ou* prévenante *ou* doucereuse.

ingratitude [ɪn'grætɪtjuːd] *n* ingratitude *f*.

ingredient [ɪn'griːdɪənt] *n* ingrédient *m*; *Fig* **what are the ingredients of her success?,** qu'est-ce qui fait son succès?

ingress ['ɪngres] *n Jur* entrée *f*; **free i.,** droit *m* de libre accès.

ingrowing ['ɪngrəʊɪŋ] , **ingrown** ['ɪngrəʊn] *adj Med* **i. (toe)nail,** ongle incarné.

inhabit [ɪn'hæbɪt] *vt* habiter, habiter dans (*une maison, une ville*); **a fictitious world inhabited by strange people,** un monde fictif peuplé de gens étranges.

inhabitable [ɪn'hæbɪtəb(ə)l] *adj* habitable.

inhabitant [ɪn'hæbɪtənt] *n* habitant, -ante.

inhabited [ɪn'hæbɪtɪd] *adj* habité, peuplé.

inhalant [ɪn'heɪlənt] *n Med* inhalation *f*.

inhalation [ɪnhə'leɪʃən] *n* **(a)** inhalation *f* (*de chloroforme etc*); **(b)** aspiration *f* (*d'un parfum*).

inhale [ɪn'heɪl] **1** *vt Med* inhaler (*de l'éther etc*); aspirer, humer (*un parfum*); respirer, avaler (*la fumée d'une cigarette*). **2** *vi* respirer; (*in smoking*) avaler la fumée.

inhaler [ɪn'heɪlər] *n* **(a)** (*device*) *Med* inhalateur *m*; *Ind* respirateur *m*; **(b)** (*person*) = fumeur qui avale la fumée de sa cigarette.

inhaling [ɪn'heɪlɪŋ] *n* inhalation *f*.

inherent [ɪn'hɪərənt] *adj* inhérent, naturel, propre (**in,** à); **i. stability,** stabilité *f* propre (*d'un avion, d'un navire etc*); **i. fault in the design,** anomalie inhérente à la conception; **power i. in an office,** pouvoir inhérent à une fonction.

inherently [ɪn'hɪərəntlɪ] *adv* fondamentalement; **i. lazy,** né paresseux.

inherit [ɪn'herɪt] **1** *vt* hériter (de) (*qch*); succéder à (*une fortune*); **to i. sth from s.o.,** hériter (de) qch de qn; **often inherited,** (*disease etc*) souvent héréditaire; *Fig* **she has inherited her father's quick temper,** elle a hérité du caractère vif de son père. **2** *vi* **to i. equally,** hériter de parts égales; **to i. jointly,** cohériter.

inheritance [ɪn'herɪtəns] *n* **(a)** (*act of inheriting*) succession *f*; **right of i.,** droit *m* de succession; **law of i.,** droit successif; **(b)** (*money, jewels etc*) patrimoine *m*, héritage *m*; **to come into an i.,** faire un héritage; *Am* **i. tax,** droits *mpl* de succession.

inherited [ɪn'herɪtɪd] *adj* (*bien, trait, goût*) hérité.

inhibit [ɪn'hɪbɪt] *vt* **(a)** *Psy* inhiber (*un sentiment*); **inhibited person,** inhibé, -ée; **to feel inhibited,** (*about doing sth*) avoir honte; **she's not inhibited,** elle n'a pas d'inhibitions; **(b)** *Med* paralyser (*une sécrétion etc*); **(c)** *Jur etc* **to i. s.o. from doing sth,** interdire *ou* défendre à qn de faire qch.

inhibiting [ɪn'hɪbɪtɪŋ] *adj* (*influence etc*) inhibiteur, -trice.

inhibition [ɪnɪ'bɪʃən] *n* **(a)** *Med Psy* inhibition *f*; **person with inhibitions,** inhibé, -ée; **to have no inhibitions,** avoir aucune inhibition; **(b)** *Jur etc* défense expresse, prohibition *f*.

inhibitive [ɪn'hɪbɪtɪv] *adj* (*mandat*) prohibitif; (*jugement*) inhibitoire.

inhibitory [ɪn'hɪbɪt(ə)rɪ] *adj* **(a)** (*nerf, réflexe*) inhibiteur; **(b)** (*mandat*) prohibitif.

inhospitable [ɪnhɒ'spɪtəb(ə)l, ɪn'hɒs-] *adj* (*person, climate, region etc*) inhospitalier.

inhospitably [ɪnhɒ'spɪtəblɪ] *adv* d'une manière inhospitalière.

in-house ['ɪn'haʊs] **1** *adj* **to have an in-h. accountant/computer/***etc*, avoir un comptable/un ordinateur/*etc* sur place; **in-h. newspaper,** journal *m* interne. **2** *adv* **to do sth in-h.,** faire qch sur place; **to keep a job in-h.,** faire un travail sur place.

inhuman [ɪn'hjuːmən] *adj* inhumain; (*coutume*) barbare.

inhumane [ɪnhjuː'meɪn] *adj* inhumain, cruel.

inhumanity [ɪnhjuː'mænɪtɪ] *n* inhumanité *f*, cruauté *f*, barbarie *f* (*d'une personne, d'une action*); **man's i. to man,** la cruauté de l'homme envers l'homme.

inhumation [ɪnhjuː'meɪʃən] *n* inhumation *f*, enterrement *m* (*d'un cadavre*).

inimical [ɪ'nɪmɪk(ə)l] *adj* (*people*) ennemi, hostile; (*conditions*) défavorable, contraire, adverse (**to,** à).
inimitable [ɪ'nɪmɪtəb(ə)l] *adj* inimitable.
inimitably [ɪ'nɪmɪtəblɪ] *adv* d'une manière inimitable.
iniquitous [ɪ'nɪkwɪtəs] *adj* inique.
iniquitously [ɪ'nɪkwɪtəslɪ] *adv* iniquement.
iniquity [ɪ'nɪkwɪtɪ] *n* iniquité *f*.
initial¹ [ɪ'nɪʃəl] **1** *adj* initial, -aux, premier; **her i. delight,** son plaisir initial; **the disease is only in the i. stages,** la maladie n'en est qu'à son stade initial; **the i. difficulties,** les difficultés du début, les premières difficultés; *Com* **i. cost,** coût initial; (*of manufactured product*) prix *m* de revient; *El* **i. charge,** charge principale (*d'un accumulateur*); *Typ* **i. letter,** lettre initiale, lettrine *f*; *Ling* **in i. position,** en position initiale. **2** *n* **(a)** (*usu pl*) **initials,** initiales *f*; (*to alteration of cheque etc*) paraphe *m*; (*of supervisor etc*) visa *m*; (*on garment etc*) monogramme *m*; **(b)** *Typ* lettre initiale, lettrine *f*.
initial² *vt* (**-ll-**, *US* **-l-**) parapher (*un traité, une correction*); viser (*un acte etc*); mettre son paraphe au bas de (*un acte*).
initialize [ɪ'nɪʃəlaɪz] *vt Comptr* initialiser.
initially [ɪ'nɪʃəlɪ] *adv* au départ, au début.
initiate¹ [ɪ'nɪʃɪeɪt] *vt* **(a)** *Fml* (*begin*) commencer, ouvrir (*des négociations etc*); lancer, amorcer (*un projet etc*); instaurer (*des mesures etc*); instituer (*une expérience etc*); inaugurer (*une politique nouvelle*); être l'initiateur de (*une réforme*); *Jur* **to i. proceedings against s.o.,** instituer des poursuites contre qn; **(b)** *Comptr* lancer, faire démarrer (*un programme*); **(c)** (*induct*) initier (*qn*); **to i. s.o. into a secret,** initier qn à un secret; **to i. s.o. into a secret society,** initier qn à *ou* admettre qn dans une société secrète.
initiate² [ɪ'nɪʃɪət] *n* initié, -ée.
initiated [ɪ'nɪʃɪeɪtɪd] **1** *adj* initié. **2** *n* **the i.,** (*used as pl*) les initiés *mpl*.
initiation [ɪnɪʃɪ'eɪʃən] *n* **(a)** (*induction*) initiation *f* (*de qn*) (**into,** à); **i. ceremony,** cérémonie *f* d'initiation; **(b)** (*beginning*) commencement(s) *m(pl)*, début(s) *m(pl)* (*d'une entreprise*); instauration *f*, inauguration *f* (*d'un usage*); **(c)** *Comptr* lancement *m*, déclenchement *m* (*d'un programme etc*).
initiative [ɪ'nɪʃɪətɪv] *n* initiative *f*; **to take the i. in doing sth,** prendre l'initiative pour faire qch; **to do sth on one's own i.,** faire qch de sa propre initiative; **to show/lack i.,** faire preuve/manquer d'initiative; **person with plenty of i.,** personne entreprenante.
initiator [ɪ'nɪʃɪeɪtər] *n* initiateur, -trice; lanceur *m* (*d'une mode etc*).
inject [ɪn'dʒekt] *vt* injecter (*une drogue*) (**into,** dans); (*give injection to*) faire une piqûre (**with sth,** de qch) à (*qn*); **to i. a fluid into a cavity,** injecter un liquide dans une cavité; **to i. a cavity with a fluid,** injecter une cavité d'un *ou* avec un liquide; **to i. s.o. with morphine,** faire une piqûre de morphine à qn; **to i. drugs,** (*of addict*) s'injecter de la drogue, se piquer; *Fig* **to i. new life into sth,** donner un nouvel essor à qch; **to i. capital into a business,** injecter du capital dans une entreprise.
injection [ɪn'dʒekʃən] *n Med etc* injection *f*, piqûre *f*; **anti-tetanus i.,** piqûre *f* antitétanique; **intravenous i.,** (injection) intraveineuse *f*; **course of injections,** série *f* de piqûres; **to give s.o. an i.,** faire une injection *ou* une piqûre à qn, piquer qn; *Fig* **i. of capital into a business,** injection *ou* apport *m* de capital dans une entreprise; **the i. of a drug into a vein,** l'injection d'une drogue dans une veine; *Constr* **i. of cement,** injection de ciment; **i. pump,** pompe *f* à injection; **(fuel) i. pump,** pompe d'injection (de carburant); **i. moulding,** (*of plastics*) moulage *m* par injection.
injudicious [ɪndʒʊ'dɪʃəs] *adj* peu judicieux, malavisé.
injudiciously [ɪndʒʊ'dɪʃəslɪ] *adv* d'une façon peu judicieuse.
Injun ['ɪndʒən] *n US F* Indien, -ienne (d'Amérique); **honest I.!,** vrai de vrai!, sans blague!
injunction [ɪn'dʒʌŋkʃən] *n* **(a)** *Jur* arrêt *m* de suspension, arrêt de sursis; **I shall ask for an i.,** je vais demander un sursis; **(b)** (*command*) injonction *f*, ordre *m*, recommandation *f*; **to give s.o. strict injunctions to do sth,** enjoindre formellement à qn de faire qch.
injure ['ɪndʒər] *vt* **(a)** (*physically*) blesser (*qn*); **to i. oneself,** se blesser, se faire du mal; **she injured her head,** elle s'est blessée à la tête; **fatally injured,** blessé mortellement; *Fig* **to i. s.o.'s pride,** blesser qn dans son amour-propre; **(b)** (*harm*) nuire à, faire tort à (*qn, la réputation de qn*); léser (*qn*); *Jur* porter préjudice à (*qn*); compromettre (*les intérêts de qn*); **(c)** (*damage*) endommager, abîmer, gâter (*qch*); *Com* avarier (*des marchandises*); **to i. one's health,** s'abîmer la santé.
injured ['ɪndʒəd] **1** *adj* **(a)** (*physically*) blessé; **badly/slightly i.,** gravement/légèrement blessé; **(b)** *Fig* (*offended*) offensé, outragé; (*deceived*) trompé, trahi; **the i. party,** l'offensé, -ée; *Jur* la partie lésée; **in an i. (tone of) voice,** d'une voix offensée. **2** *n* **the i.,** (*used as pl*) les blessés *mpl*; (*from accident*) les accidentés *mpl*.
injurious [ɪn'dʒʊərɪəs] *adj* **(a)** (*harmful*) nuisible, pernicieux, préjudiciable (**to,** à); **i. to (the) health,** nocif *ou* nuisible à la santé; **(b)** (*language*) injurieux, offensant.
injury ['ɪndʒ(ə)rɪ] *n* **(a)** (*physical*) blessure *f* (*au corps*); *Med* lésion *f*; **to do oneself an i.,** se blesser; *F* **you'll do yourself an i.,** tu vas te faire du mal; **wearing a seat belt can prevent i.,** le port de la ceinture de sécurité peut éviter des blessures; **he escaped without i.,** il n'a eu aucun mal; **internal injuries,** lésions internes; *Sp* **i. time,** arrêts *mpl* de jeu; **he scored nine minutes into i. time,** il a marqué un but neuf minutes après le début des arrêts de jeu; **(b)** (*wrong*) tort *m*, mal *m*, préjudice *m*; *Jur* lésion *f*; **to do s.o. an i.,** faire du tort à qn; **to suffer i.,** subir un préjudice; **(c)** (*damage*) dommage *m*, dégât *m*; *Nau* avarie *f*.
injustice [ɪn'dʒʌstɪs] *n* **(a)** (*of law, system etc*) injustice *f*; **(b)** (*unjust, act, remark*) **you do him an i.,** vous êtes injuste envers lui.
ink¹ [ɪŋk] *n* **(a)** encre *f*; **written in i.,** écrit à l'encre; **indelible** *or* **waterproof i.,** encre indélébile; **Indian i.,** encre de Chine; **marking i.,** encre à marquer le linge; **i. blot,** (*on paper*) pâté *m*; **i. stain,** tache *f* d'encre; **i. bottle,** bouteille *f* d'encre; **i. pad,** tampon *m* (encreur); **i. pot,** encrier *m*; **(b)** noir *m*, encre *f* (*de seiche*); **i. bag** *or* **sac,** glande *f ou* poche *f* du noir.
ink² *vt* **(a)** noircir d'encre, barbouiller d'encre, tacher d'encre; **(b)** *Typ* encrer (*les lettres*); toucher (*la forme*).
►**ink in** *vtsep Art* **(a)** tracer à l'encre (*des lignes faites au crayon*); **(b)** mettre (*un dessin*) à l'encre.
►**ink out** *vtsep* oblitérer *ou* rayer *ou* biffer (*un mot etc*) à l'encre.
inkblot ['ɪŋkblɒt] *adj Psy* (*in Rorschach test*) tache *f* d'encre; **i. test,** test *m* de la tache d'encre.
inking ['ɪŋkɪŋ] *n Typ* encrage *m* (*des rouleaux*).
inking in *n* (*of drawing*) mise *f* à l'encre.
ink-jet ['ɪŋkdʒet] *adj Comptr* **i.-j. printer,** imprimante *f* à jet d'encre.
inkling ['ɪŋklɪŋ] *n* soupçon *m*; **to give s.o. an i. of sth,** faire pressentir qch à qn; **he had an i. of the truth,** il entrevoyait la vérité; **he has no i. of the matter, he doesn't have an i.,** il ne se doute de rien.
inkstand ['ɪŋkstænd] *n* (grand) encrier *m*.
inkwell ['ɪŋkwel] *n* encrier *m* (de pupitre).
inky ['ɪŋkɪ] *adj* **(a)** (*stained with ink*) taché d'encre; (*blotted with ink*) barbouillé d'encre; **(b) i. (black),** noir comme (de) l'encre; **the night was i. black,** il faisait nuit noire.
inlaid [ɪn'leɪd] *adj* (*furniture*) incrusté (**with,** de); (*with wood*) marqueté; (*floor*) parqueté; **i. work,** marqueterie *f*; **i. enamel work,** niellе *f*, niellage *m*.
inland ['ɪnlænd] **1** *adj* **(a)** (*away from sea*) intérieur; **i. waterways,** voies *fpl* navigables; **i. navigation,** navigation intérieure *ou* fluviale; **(b)** *Br* (*domestic*) du pays; (*commerce*) intérieur; (*produits*) indigène, du pays; (*courrier*) intérieur; **i. postage rates,** (tarif *m* d')affranchissement *m* en régime intérieur; **the I. Revenue,** le fisc. **2** *adv* vers l'intérieur, dans les terres; **to go i.,** pénétrer vers l'intérieur *ou* dans les terres; **the town is situated a few miles i.,** la ville est située à quelques kilomètres dans les terres. **3** *n* (l')intérieur *m* (d'un pays).
in-law ['ɪnlɔː] *n* parent *m* par alliance; **in-laws,** belle-famille *f*; (*mother & father of spouse*) beaux-parents.
inlay¹ ['ɪnleɪ] *n* **(a)** incrustation *f* (*de nacre etc*); (*piece of marqueterie*) marqueterie *f*; **(b)** (*in dentistry*) inlay *m*, incrustation *f* (*de métal, en céramique etc*).
inlay² ['ɪnleɪ, ɪn'leɪ] *vt* (*pt & pp* **inlaid**) incruster (**with,** de); (*with wood*) marqueter (*une table etc*); **to i. with enamel,** nieller; **table inlaid with mother-of-pearl,** table incrustée de nacre.
inlet ['ɪnlet] *n* **(a)** *Geog* (*in shore etc*) petit bras de mer; (*small bay*) crique *f*, anse *f*; goulet *m* (*d'entrée dans un port etc*); **(b)** *Tech* (*opening*) (orifice *m* d')entrée *f*, (orifice d')admission *f* (*d'air etc*); ouïe *f* (*de ventilateur etc*); **(c)** (*act of entering, allowing to enter*) entrée *f*, arrivée *f*, admission *f* (*d'air etc*); **i. pipe,** tuyau *m* d'arrivée (*de vapeur etc*).
inmate ['ɪnmeɪt] *n* détenu, -ue (*dans une prison*); pensionnaire *mf* (*d'une maison de santé, d'un hospice*).
in memoriam [ɪnmɪ'mɔːrɪəm] *prep* en mémoire de.

inmost ['ɪnməʊst] *adj* le plus profond; **our i. thoughts,** nos pensées les plus secrètes; **our i. feelings,** nos sentiments les plus intimes; **our i. being,** le plus profond de nous-mêmes.

inn [ɪn] *n* **(a)** auberge *f*; (*fashionable, restaurant*) hôtellerie *f*, hostellerie *f*; **(b)** *Jur* **Inns of Court,** = les quatre Écoles de droit de Londres qui seules confèrent le droit d'être avocat.

innards ['ɪnədz] *npl* (*of person*) entrailles *fpl*, intestins *mpl*; (*of machine*) entrailles.

innate [ɪ'neɪt] *adj* inné, infus; **i. common sense,** bon sens naturel *ou* foncier; *Phil* **i. ideas,** idées innées.

inner ['ɪnər] **1** *adj* intérieur; (*écorce etc*) interne, de dedans; **on the i. side,** à l'intérieur, en dedans; *Anat* **the i. ear,** l'oreille *f* interne; **i. harbour,** arrière-port *m*, *pl* arrière-ports; *Aut Cycling* **i. tube,** chambre *f* à air; **the i. circle,** le cercle intime (d'amis); le groupe dirigeant (*d'un parti politique*); **the i. city,** les vieux quartiers d'une ville; **i.-city crime/children,** crimes se produisant dans les quartiers pauvres/enfants des quartiers pauvres. **2** *n* premier cercle autour de la mouche (*d'une cible*).

innermost ['ɪnəməʊst] *adj* = **INMOST**.

inning ['ɪnɪŋ] *n Baseball* tour *m* de batte.

innings ['ɪnɪŋz] *n inv Cr* tournée *f*, tour *m* de batte (*de chaque équipe ou de chaque membre de l'équipe*); *Fig* **she had a good i.,** (*of s.o. recently dead*) elle a bien profité de la vie; (*of participant in game show etc*) elle ne s'en est pas mal sortie.

innkeeper ['ɪnki:pər] *n* aubergiste *mf*, hôtelier, -ière.

innocence ['ɪnəsəns] *n* **(a)** innocence *f* (*d'un accusé*); **(b)** (*simplicity*) naïveté *f*, simplicité *f*, innocence *f*; **to lose one's i.,** perdre son innocence; **to take advantage of s.o.'s i.,** abuser de l'innocence de qn; **in all i.,** en toute innocence.

innocent ['ɪnəsənt] **1** *adj* **(a)** (*not guilty*) innocent; **i. of a crime,** innocent d'un crime; **an i. person,** un(e) innocent(e); **the bomb killed several i. bystanders,** la bombe a tué plusieurs innocents qui se trouvaient là; **(b)** (*pure*) innocent; **as i. as a newborn babe,** innocent comme l'enfant qui vient de naître; *Rel Cathol* **Holy Innocents' Day,** la fête des saints Innocents; **(c)** (*naive*) naïf, *f* naïve; (*remark etc*) sans malice; innocent; **to put on an i. air,** faire l'innocent(e), prendre un air innocent; **(d)** (*harmless*) (*jeu, remède*) innocent, inoffensif; **(e)** (*devoid*) dépourvu, vierge (**of,** de); **to be quite i. of Latin,** ne pas savoir un mot de latin. **2** *n* innocent, -ente; **don't come the i. with me,** ne fais pas l'innocent avec moi.

innocently ['ɪnəsəntlɪ] *adv* innocemment, en toute innocence.

innocuous [ɪ'nɒkjʊəs] *adj* inoffensif; **an i. remark,** une remarque anodine.

innocuously [ɪ'nɒkjʊəslɪ] *adv* (*to remark etc*) de façon inoffensive *ou* anodine.

innovate ['ɪnəveɪt] *vi* innover (**in,** à, en, dans).

innovation [ɪnə'veɪʃən] *n* innovation *f*, changement *m* (*dans une méthode etc*).

innovative ['ɪnəveɪtɪv] *adj* (in)novateur, -trice.

innovator ['ɪnəveɪtər] *n* (in)novateur, -trice.

innuendo, *pl* **-o(e)s** [ɪnjʊ'endəʊ, -əʊz] *n* **(a)** (*insinuation*) allusion *f* (malveillante); **to discredit s.o. by i.,** discréditer qn par sous-entendus; **(b)** (*in jokes*) insinuation *f*; **the play is full of i.,** la pièce est pleine d'insinuations *ou* de sous-entendus; **sexual i.,** sous-entendu *m* à connotation sexuelle; **(c)** *Jur* insinuation *f*, mot couvert (*destiné à atteindre qn dans son honneur*).

innumerable [ɪ'nju:mərəb(ə)l] *adj* innombrable; **i. books,** des livres innombrables *ou* sans nombre; **the successes have been i.,** les réussites ne se comptent plus.

inoculate [ɪ'nɒkjʊleɪt] *vt Med* inoculer, vacciner (*qn*) (*contre une maladie*); **to i. s.o. with a virus,** inoculer un virus à qn.

inoculation [ɪnɒkjʊ'leɪʃən] *n Med* inoculation *f*.

inoffensive [ɪnə'fensɪv] *adj* **(a)** (*odeur etc*) sans rien de désagréable; (*observation etc*) qui n'a rien d'offensant; **(b)** (*harmless*) (*médicament, animal, personne*) inoffensif.

inoperable [ɪn'ɒpərəb(ə)l] *adj* **(a)** *Med* inopérable; **(b)** (*system*) qui ne peut pas être exploité, inexploitable.

inoperative [ɪn'ɒpərətɪv] *adj Jur* inopérant.

inopportune [ɪn'ɒpətju:n] *adj* inopportun, intempestif; **i. remarks,** propos *mpl* hors de saison.

inopportunely [ɪn'ɒpətju:nlɪ] *adv* inopportunément, mal à propos.

inordinate [ɪn'ɔ:dɪnət] *adj* démesuré, excessif, immodéré.

inordinately [ɪn'ɔ:dɪnətlɪ] *adv* démesurément, excessivement; **to wait an i. long time,** attendre pendant une durée excessivement longue.

inorganic [ɪnɔ:'gænɪk] *adj* inorganique.

inpatient ['ɪnpeɪʃənt] *n Med* patient hospitalisé.

input¹ ['ɪnpʊt] *n* **(a)** consommation *f* (*d'une usine, d'une machine*); énergie *ou* puissance absorbée; *El Electron* (*current etc*) puissance *f* à l'entrée *ou* d'alimentation; (*terminal*) entrée *f*; *Econ* intrant *m*; **i. transformer,** courant *m ou* transformateur *m* d'entrée; **(b)** *Comptr* entrée *f*, introduction *f* (*des données*); **i. (data),** données introduites; **i./output,** entrée/sortie *f*; **i. program,** programme *m* d'introduction; **(c)** (*contribution*) contribution *f*, apport *m*.

input² *vt Comptr* entrer (*des données*).

inquest ['ɪnkwest] *n* enquête *f* (criminelle); *F* (*into reasons for failure of project etc*) analyse *f*; **coroner's i.,** = enquête judiciaire par-devant jury (*en cas de mort violente ou suspecte*).

inquire [ɪn'kwaɪər] **1** *vt* s'informer de (*qch*) (**of s.o.,** auprès de qn); **to i. the price of sth,** s'informer du prix de qch; **to i. of s.o. what is happening,** s'informer auprès de qn de ce qui se passe. **2** *vi* se renseigner (**about,** sur); **I'd like to i. about ...,** je voudrais des renseignements sur ...; **i. within,** s'adresser ici.

►**inquire after** *vipo* (*ask for news of*) demander des nouvelles de (*qn*); **to i. after s.o.'s health,** s'informer de la santé de qn.

►**inquire into** *vipo* (*seek information about*) faire des recherches sur (*qch*); *Jur* enquêter *ou* faire une enquête sur (*une affaire*).

inquiring [ɪn'kwaɪrɪŋ] *adj* investigateur, -trice; (*mind*) curieux; (*look*) interrogateur.

inquiringly [ɪn'kwaɪrɪŋlɪ] *adv* (*to look at, say*) d'un air *ou* d'un ton interrogateur; **to look i. at s.o.,** interroger qn du regard.

inquiry [ɪn'kwaɪərɪ] *n* **(a)** (*official investigation*) recherche *f*, investigation *f*; (*by police*) enquête *f*; **to conduct** *or* **hold an i. into sth,** procéder *ou* se livrer à une enquête sur qch; **(b)** (*request for information*) demande *f* de renseignements; **to make inquiries,** se renseigner; **to make inquiries about s.o.,** prendre des renseignements sur qn; (*less official*) s'informer *ou* se renseigner sur qn; **private i. agent,** détective *m* (privé); **to make inquiries after s.o.,** s'enquérir de qn; **to make inquiries into sth,** faire des recherches sur qch; **as a result of her inquiries,** à la suite de ses recherches; **i. desk** *or* **office, inquiries,** bureau *m* de renseignements.

inquisition [ɪnkwɪ'zɪʃən] *n* (*investigation*) recherche *f*, investigation *f*; *Jur* enquête *f* (judiciaire); *Rel Hist* **the I.,** l'Inquisition *f*; *F* **the interview turned into an i.,** l'entrevue s'est transformée en une inquisition.

inquisitive [ɪn'kwɪzɪtɪv] *adj* investigateur, -trice; (*mind*) curieux; (*look*) inquisiteur; *Pej* curieux, questionneur.

inquisitively [ɪn'kwɪzɪtɪvlɪ] *adv* avec curiosité; (*to look*) d'un œil inquisiteur.

inquisitiveness [ɪn'kwɪzɪtɪvnɪs] *n* curiosité *f*.

inquisitor [ɪn'kwɪzɪtər] *n* **(a)** *Jur* enquêteur, -euse; **(b)** *Rel Hist & F* inquisiteur *m*.

inquisitorial [ɪnkwɪzɪ'tɔ:rɪəl] *adj* inquisitorial.

inroad ['ɪnrəʊd] *n* **(a)** empiétement *m* (*sur la liberté ou les droits de qn*); **to make inroads into** *or* **on one's capital,** entamer *ou* ébrécher son capital; **(b)** *Mil* (*attack*) incursion *f*.

inrush ['ɪnrʌʃ] *n* irruption *f* (*d'eau, de voyageurs etc*); entrée soudaine (*d'air, de gaz*).

ins **(a)** (*abbr* **insurance**) asse.; **(b)** (*abbr* **inches**) pouces, ppo..

insalubrious [ɪnsə'lu:brɪəs] *adj* insalubre, malsain.

insane [ɪn'seɪn] **1** *adj* **(a)** (*person*) fou, folle; (*mind*) dérangé, aliéné; **to become i.,** perdre la raison; **to be i. with grief/jealousy,** être fou de douleur/jalousie; *Am* **i. asylum,** hospice *m ou* asile *m* d'aliénés; **(b)** *F* (*désir etc*) insensé, fou; **an i. idea,** une idée démente. **2** *n* **the i.,** (*used as pl*) les aliénés *mpl*.

insanely [ɪn'seɪnlɪ] *adv* follement.

insanitary [ɪn'sænɪtrɪ] *adj* insalubre, malsain.

insanity [ɪn'sænɪtɪ] *n* **(a)** *Med* folie *f*, démence *f*, insanité *f*; *Fml* aliénation mentale; **(b)** *F* folie *f* (*d'une démarche etc*); **it's sheer i. doing that,** c'est de la folie pure et simple (que) de faire cela.

insatiable [ɪn'seɪʃɪəb(ə)l] *adj* (*faim, désir etc*) insatiable, inassouvissable.

insatiably [ɪn'seɪʃɪəblɪ] *adv* insatiablement.

inscribe [ɪn'skraɪb] *vt* **(a)** (*carve*) inscrire, graver (**sth on stone,** qch sur la pierre); *Fig* graver (**in s.o.'s memory,** dans la mémoire de qn); **to i. a tomb with a name,**

graver un nom sur un tombeau; **(b)** (*dedicate*) dédier (*une œuvre littéraire*) (**to,** à).

inscription [ɪn'skrɪpʃən] *n* **(a)** (*of name etc*) inscription *f*; **(b)** (*message*) inscription *f* (*sur un monument etc*) inscription, légende *f* (*d'une pièce de monnaie*); (*in book etc*) dédicace *f*.

inscrutability [ɪnskruːtə'bɪlɪtɪ] *n* inscrutabilité *f*.

inscrutable [ɪn'skruːtəb(ə)l] *adj* (*dessein, regard*) impénétrable, inscrutable; (*visage*) fermé.

insect ['ɪnsekt] *n* insecte *m*; **i. eater,** insectivore *m*; **i. powder,** poudre *f* insecticide; **i. repellent,** lotion *f ou* crème *f* anti-insectes.

insecticide [ɪn'sektɪsaɪd] *adj & n* insecticide *m*.

insectivorous [ɪnsek'tɪvərəs] *adj Bot Zool* insectivore.

insecure [ɪnsɪ'kjʊər] *adj* **(a)** (*person*) qui manque d'assurance; **she's very i.,** elle manque beaucoup d'assurance; **to feel i.,** (*mentally or physically*) éprouver un manque d'assurance *ou* un sentiment d'insécurité; **(b)** (*place*) exposé au danger; **(c)** (*not solid, tight etc*) (*verrou etc*) peu sûr; (*terrain*) dangereux; (*pont*) mal affermi; (*espoir*) incertain, peu ferme; (*frontière*) peu sûr.

insecurity [ɪnsɪ'kjʊərɪtɪ] *n* insécurité *f*; danger *m* (*d'une position*); **to have a feeling of i.,** éprouver un manque d'assurance *ou* un sentiment d'insécurité.

inseminate [ɪn'semɪneɪt] *vt Biol* inséminer.

insemination [ɪnsemɪ'neɪʃən] *n Biol* insémination *f*; **artificial i.,** insémination artificielle.

insensate [ɪn'senseɪt] *adj Lit* **(a)** (*insensitive*) (*corps*) insensible; **(b)** (*senseless*) (*projet etc*) insensé.

insensibility [ɪnsensɪ'bɪlɪtɪ] *n* **(a)** (*indifference*) insensibilité *f* (**to,** à), indifférence *f* (**to,** pour); **(b)** (*unconsciousness*) inconscience *f*.

insensible [ɪn'sensɪb(ə)l] *adj* **(a)** (*indifferent*) insensible, indifférent (**to pain,** à la douleur); **(b)** (*unaware*) inconscient; **he was quite i. of the danger he was in,** il ne se doutait pas du danger qui le menaçait; **(c)** (*unconscious*) sans connaissance, évanoui; **to become i.,** perdre connaissance.

insensitive [ɪn'sensɪtɪv] *adj* insensible (**to,** à).

insensitiveness [ɪn'sensɪtɪvnɪs], **insensitivity** [ɪnsensɪ'tɪvɪtɪ] *n* insensibilité *f*.

inseparable [ɪn'sepərəb(ə)l] *adj* inséparable (**from,** de); **they are i.,** (*of people etc*) ils sont inséparables.

inseparably [ɪn'sepərəblɪ] *adv* inséparablement.

insert¹ ['ɪnsɜːt] *n* **(a)** (*something inserted*) pièce rapportée; *Cin* scène-raccord *f, pl* scènes-raccords; (*in magazine etc*) encartage *m*; **(b)** *Typ etc* insertion *f* (*dans une épreuve*); **(c)** *Comptr* insertion *f*; **i. mode,** mode *m* d'insertion; **(d)** *Sewing* incrustation *f*.

insert² [ɪn'sɜːt] *vt* **(a)** introduire, enfoncer (*une clef dans un serrure etc*); insérer (*une page dans un livre etc*); insérer, introduire, apposer (*une clause dans un acte*); **(b)** *Typ* intercaler (*une ligne*); **(c)** *Comptr* insérer.

insertion [ɪn'sɜːʃən] *n* **(a)** (*act of inserting*) insertion *f*, introduction *f* (*de qch dans qch*); insertion (*d'une annonce etc dans un journal*); **(b)** (*something inserted*) = **INSERT¹ (a)**; *Typ* insertion *f*; *Sewing* entre-deux *m inv* (*de dentelle etc*); *Sewing* incrustation *f*; *Ind* pièce *f* d'insertion; *MecE* garniture *f* (*de joint*); *Typ* **i. mark,** renvoi *m*.

inset¹ ['ɪnset] *n* **(a)** (*in bookbinding*) encart *m*, carton *m* (*de 4 ou 8 pages*); **(b)** (*leaf, advertisement*) encartage *m*; **(c)** *Typ* (*map etc*) hors-texte *m inv*; médaillon *m* (*en coin de page*); **(d)** *Sewing* incrustation *f*.

inset² [ˈɪn'set] *vt* (*pt & pp* **inset** *or* **insetted**) **(a)** (*in bookbinding*) encarter (*des feuillets, des annonces*); **(b)** *Typ* insérer en cartouche *ou* en médaillon; **(c)** *Sewing* insérer (*une pièce d'étoffe etc*); faire des incrustations de (*dentelle etc*); **(d)** *Typ* (*indent*) renfoncer (*les lignes, un alinéa*).

inshore ['ɪn'ʃɔːr] *Nau* **1** *adv* près de terre; (*dirigé*) vers la côte; **to keep close i.,** naviguer près de terre, serrer la terre. **2** *adj* (*navigation, pêche*) côtier; **i. wind,** vent *m* du large.

inside 1 ['ɪn'saɪd] *n* **(a)** dedans *m*, (*côté m*) intérieur *m* (*d'un habit etc*); intérieur (*d'une maison etc*); **the door opens from (the) i.,** la porte s'ouvre de l'intérieur; **the door had been locked from the i.,** la porte était verrouillée de l'intérieur *ou* du dedans; **a scar on the i. of his leg,** une cicatrice sur la face interne de sa jambe; **on the i.,** en *ou* au dedans; à l'intérieur; **to walk on the i. (of the pavement),** marcher loin de la chaussée; **a motorbike was coming up on the i.,** une moto arrivait sur la gauche *ou* la droite; *F* **to know the i. of an affair,** connaître les dessous d'une affaire;

(b) *F* (*internal organs*) entrailles *fpl*; (*stomach*) ventre *m*; **to have pains in one's inside(s),** avoir mal au ventre;

(c) i. out ['ɪnsaɪd'aʊt], (*sweater etc*) à l'envers; **to turn sth i. out,** mettre qch à l'envers; *Fig* **to turn everything i. out,** mettre tout sens dessus dessous; *F* **to know sth i. out,** savoir qch à fond; *F* **to know Paris i. out,** connaître Paris comme sa poche.

2 ['ɪnsaɪd] *adj* intérieur; d'intérieur; (*mesure, escalier etc*) dans œuvre; (*diamètre*) interne; **i. leg measurement,** entrejambe *m*; **to take s.o.'s i. leg measurement,** mesurer l'entrejambe de qn; **an i. pocket,** une poche intérieure; **to have an i. accomplice,** avoir un complice à l'intérieur; **it's an i. job,** (*of burglary etc*) c'est un coup monté par quelqu'un de la maison; *Horseracing* **to be on the i. track,** tenir la corde; **i. lane,** (*of road*) voie *f* de gauche *ou* de droite; **to be in the i. lane,** (*in athletics race*) être sur le couloir intérieur; *Fb* **i. left,** intérieur *m ou F* inter *m* gauche; *Rugby* **i. centre,** intérieur centre *m*; **i. information,** renseignements privés; **I speak with i. knowledge,** ce que je dis je le sais de bonne source; **to know the i. story,** connaître les dessous d'une histoire; **to have an i. job,** travailler en intérieur.

3 [ɪn'saɪd] *adv* **(a)** (*on the inside*) intérieurement; (*fermé*) en dedans; (*propre*) à l'intérieur; **with the fur i.,** le côté poil en dedans; **there's nothing i.,** il n'y a rien dedans; **to look i.,** regarder dedans *ou* à l'intérieur; **i. she was angry,** intérieurement elle était en colère; **i. and out,** au dedans et au dehors, à l'intérieur et à l'extérieur;

(b) (*within a building, room, box etc*) dans la maison *ou* la chambre *ou* la salle *etc*; **to push s.o. i.,** pousser qn à l'intérieur *ou* dedans; **come i.!,** entrez!; *Sl* **to be i.,** (*in prison*) être en tôle *ou* taule; *Sl* **to put s.o. i.,** (*in prison*) mettre qn en tôle *ou* taule;

(c) i. of, en moins de; **i. of three hours,** (*faire qch*) en moins de trois heures.

4 [ɪn'saɪd] *prep* **(a)** (*of place*) à l'intérieur de, dans l'intérieur de, dans (*la maison etc*); **i. the country/company,** au sein du pays/de la société; **the telephone is just i. the door,** le téléphone est juste derrière la porte; *F* **get this i. you,** avale-ça; *Th F* **to get right i. a part,** entrer dans la peau d'un personnage;

(b) (*of time*) **i. a week/an hour,** en moins d'une semaine/d'une heure.

insider [ɪn'saɪdər] *n* initié, -ée; *Fin* **i. dealing** *or* **trading,** délit *m ou* opération *f* d'initié.

insidious [ɪn'sɪdɪəs] *adj* (*disease etc*) insidieux; (*reasoning*) captieux, spécieux.

insidiously [ɪn'sɪdɪəslɪ] *adv* insidieusement; (*to reason*) spécieusement.

insight ['ɪnsaɪt] *n* **(a)** (*perspicacity*) perspicacité *f*, pénétration *f*; **i. into character,** finesse *f* psychologique; **(b)** (*understanding*) aperçu *m*; **to get an i. into sth,** avoir un aperçu de qch.

insignia [ɪn'sɪgnɪə] *npl* insignes *mpl* (*de la royauté etc*); *Mil* **i. of rank,** signes distinctifs de grade.

insignificance [ɪnsɪg'nɪfɪkəns] *n* insignifiance *f*.

insignificant [ɪnsɪg'nɪfɪkənt] *adj* insignifiant.

insincere [ɪnsɪn'sɪər] *adj* peu sincère, faux, *f* fausse, *Lit* insincère.

insincerity [ɪnsɪn'serɪtɪ] *n* manque *m* de sincérité, fausseté *f*.

insinuate [ɪn'sɪnjʊeɪt] *vt* **(a)** (*suggest indirectly*) insinuer, laisser entendre, sous-entendre (*qch*); **are you insinuating that ...?,** est-ce que vous insinuez que ...?; **(b)** (*manoeuvre*) **to i. sth into a place,** insinuer *ou* glisser qch dans un endroit; **to i. oneself into s.o.'s favour,** s'insinuer dans les bonnes grâces de qn.

insinuation [ɪnsɪnjʊ'eɪʃən] *n* **(a)** (*indirect suggestion*) insinuation *f*, sous-entendu *m*, *pl* sous-entendus; **(b)** (*manoeuvring*) insinuation *f*, introduction *f* (**of sth into sth,** de qch dans qch).

insipid [ɪn'sɪpɪd] *adj* (*mets*) insipide, fade, sans saveur; (*style, conversation*) fade, plat, insipide.

insipidity [ɪnsɪ'pɪdɪtɪ] *n* insipidité *f*, fadeur *f*.

insist [ɪn'sɪst] **1** *vi* insister (**on doing,** pour faire); **to i. on a point,** insister *ou* appuyer sur un point; **to i. upon one's innocence,** affirmer son innocence avec insistance; **I won't i.,** je n'insiste pas; **very well, if you i.,** très bien, si tu insistes; **he insists on your coming,** il insiste pour que vous veniez; **I i. on it,** je l'exige; **to i. on one's rights,** revendiquer ses droits; **i. on the best,** exigez la meilleure qualité. **2** *vt* **(a)** soutenir, maintenir; **people insisted that they had seen him,** on soutenait l'avoir vu; **he insisted that it was so,** il maintenait qu'il en était ainsi; **(b) I i. that you let me pay,** j'insiste, laisse-moi payer.

insistence [ɪn'sɪstəns] *n* insistance *f*; **he did it at her i.,** il l'a fait parce qu'elle a insisté.

insistent [ɪn'sɪstənt] *adj* qui insiste, insistant; (*creditor*) importun; (*réclamations*) instant; **to be very i.,** insister très fort; **don't be too i.,** n'appuyez *ou* n'insistez pas trop.
insistently [ɪn'sɪstəntlɪ] *adv* instamment, avec insistance.
in situ [ɪn'sɪtjuː] *adv* in situ.
insofar [ɪnsəʊ'fɑːr] *adv US* **i. as,** dans la mesure où.
insole ['ɪnsəʊl] *n* (*of shoe*) (*inner sole*) première semelle; (*separate piece*) semelle intérieure (*de liège, feutre etc*).
insolence ['ɪnsələns] *n* insolence *f* (**to,** envers).
insolent ['ɪnsələnt] *adj* insolent (**to,** envers); **an i. boy,** un (jeune) insolent.
insolently ['ɪnsələntlɪ] *adv* insolemment.
insolubility [ɪnsɒljʊ'bɪlɪtɪ] *n* insolubilité *f*.
insoluble [ɪn'sɒljʊb(ə)l] *adj* **(a)** (*sel etc*) insoluble; **(b)** (*problème*) insoluble, qu'on ne peut pas résoudre.
insolvency [ɪn'sɒlvənsɪ] *n* insolvabilité *f*, *Jur* carence *f*; (*bankruptcy*) faillite *f*.
insolvent [ɪn'sɒlvənt] **1** *adj* (*débiteur*) insolvable; *Com* (*débiteur, société*) en (état de) faillite; **to declare oneself i.,** se déclarer insolvable; *Com* déposer son bilan. **2** *n* débiteur *m* insolvable; *Com* failli *m*.
insomnia [ɪn'sɒmnɪə] *n* insomnie *f*.
insomniac [ɪn'sɒmnɪæk] *n* insomniaque *mf*.
insomuch [ɪnsəʊ'mʌtʃ] *adv* **(a)** = **INASMUCH**; **(b) i. that ...,** à tel point que ... .
inspect [ɪn'spekt] *vt* **(a)** (*examine*) examiner (*qch*), regarder (*qch*) de près; **(b)** (*of official*) inspecter (*une école etc*); contrôler, vérifier (*les livres d'un négociant*); vérifier, inspecter (*une machine etc*); **my mother inspected our hands,** ma mère a passé l'inspection de nos mains; *Sp* **to i. the pitch,** visiter le terrain (*avant le match*); **(c)** *Mil* faire la revue de, faire l'inspection de (*un régiment*), passer (*un régiment*) en revue; **to be inspected,** (*of troops*) être passé en revue.
inspecting [ɪn'spektɪŋ] *adj* **i. officer,** inspecteur *m*.
inspection [ɪn'spekʃən] *n* **(a)** examen *m*; vérification *f* (*de documents etc*); **on close** *or* **closer i.,** en y regardant de plus près; **i. copy,** (*in publishing*) spécimen *m*; **(b)** (*by an official*) inspection *f*, visite *f* (*d'un établissement etc*); contrôle *m* (*des billets, du matériel etc*); **tour of i.,** inspection; **general i.,** inspection générale; **sanitary i.,** contrôle sanitaire; **medical i.,** visite médicale; *Tech* **i. hole** *or* **port,** orifice *m ou* trou *m ou* regard *m* de visite; **(c)** *Mil* revue *f*; **kit i.,** revue d'habillement; **to make** *or* **hold an i.,** passer une revue.
inspector [ɪn'spektər] *n* inspecteur *m* (*des écoles, de police, des mines etc*); *Rail* surveillant *m*; *Br* **detective i.,** = inspecteur de la Sûreté; **health i.,** inspecteur du service sanitaire; **i. of taxes,** inspecteur *ou* contrôleur *m* des contributions directes; *Mil etc* **i. general,** inspecteur général.
inspectorate [ɪn'spektərət] *n* **(a)** (*inspectors*) corps *m* d'inspecteurs; *F* l'inspection *f*; **(b)** (*post*) inspectorat *m*.
inspiration [ɪnspɪ'reɪʃən] *n* **(a)** (*stimulus*) inspiration *f*; **divine i.,** inspiration divine; **he is the i. of the movement,** c'est l'âme du mouvement; **she's an i. to us all,** elle est notre modèle à tous; **to lack i.,** (*of poet etc*) manquer d'inspiration; **to provide the i. for sth,** fournir l'inspiration pour qch; **to have a sudden i.,** avoir une inspiration subite; **(b)** aspiration *f*, inspiration *f* (*d'air etc*).
inspire [ɪn'spaɪər] *vt* **(a)** (*stimulus*) inspirer (*qn, qch*); **to be inspired to do sth,** être inspiré de faire qch; **to i. a thought/a feeling in s.o.,** inspirer une pensée/un sentiment à qn; **to i. s.o. with confidence,** inspirer (de la) confiance à qn; **to i. s.o. with hope,** donner de l'espoir à qn; **inspired with hope,** animé d'espoir; **her example inspired us to ...,** son exemple nous a incités à ...; **I don't know what inspired me to turn back,** je ne sais pas ce qui m'a poussé à revenir sur mes pas; *Iron* **what inspired you to do that?,** qu'est-ce qui t'a pris de faire ça?; **(b)** aspirer, inspirer (*l'air etc*).
inspired [ɪn'spaɪəd] *adj* **(a)** (*poet, verse etc*) inspiré, plein d'inspiration; *F* **no one was (feeling) i.,** personne n'était très inspiré; **to make an i. guess,** bien tomber, tomber juste; **it was just an i. guess,** c'était un coup de chance; **(b)** (*air etc*) aspiré, inspiré.
inspiring [ɪn'spaɪərɪŋ] *adj* (*discours, exemple etc*) inspirant; (*influence*) vivifiant; *F* **the menu wasn't very i.,** le menu n'avait rien de bien tentant.
inst [ɪnst] *Old-fashioned* (*in letter*) (*abbr* **instant**) **on the 5th i.,** le 5 courant.
instability [ɪnstə'bɪlɪtɪ] *n* (*of government etc*) instabilité *f*; *MecE* déséquilibrage *m*; *Met* instabilité (atmosphérique); manque *m* de solidité (*d'un pont etc*); mobilité *f*, instabilité (*de caractère*); **mental i.,** instabilité mentale; *Phys* **thermal i.,** instabilité thermique.
install, *US* **instal** [ɪn'stɔːl] *vt* **(a)** (*fit*) installer, monter (*une machine etc*); installer (*l'électricité etc*); **(b)** (*in a post*) installer (*un évêque, qn dans une fonction*); **(c)** (*settle*) **she installed herself in an armchair,** elle s'est installée dans un fauteuil.
installation [ɪnstə'leɪʃən] *n* **(a)** installation *f* (*du chauffage central dans la maison etc*); installation, montage *m* (*d'une machine etc*); mise *f* en place (*d'un téléviseur etc*); **(b)** (*piece of machinery*) installation *f*; **electrical installations,** installations électriques; **(c)** (*establishment*) installation *f*; **(d)** (*in a post*) installation *f* (*d'un évêque etc*).
instalment, *US* **installment** [ɪn'stɔːlmənt] *n* **(a)** *Com etc* (*part payment*) versement *m*; **final i.,** paiement *m* pour solde; **to pay in** *or* **by instalments,** payer par versements, échelonner *ou* fractionner les paiements; **payable in monthly instalments,** payable par mensualités; *Am* **i. plan,** vente *f* à tempérament; **(b)** (*of part work*) fascicule *m*, livraison *f* (*d'un ouvrage à paraître en fascicules*); *Rad TV* épisode *m* (*d'un feuilleton*).
instance[1] ['ɪnstəns] *n* **(a)** (*example*) exemple *m*, cas *m*; **an isolated i.,** un cas isolé; **in many instances,** dans bien des cas; **for i.,** par exemple; **(b) in the first i.,** en (tout) premier lieu; **in the present i., in this i.,** dans le cas actuel, dans les circonstances actuelles; *Jur* dans l'espèce; **(c)** (*urging*) **to do sth at s.o.'s i.** *or* **at the i. of s.o.,** faire qch à *ou* sur la demande de qn.
instance[2] *vt* citer (*qch, qn*) en exemple; **his cruelty is well instanced by ...,** sa cruauté est bien illustrée par ... .
instant[1] ['ɪnstənt] *adj* **(a)** (*action, dislike etc*) immédiat; **this calls for i. remedy,** il faut y remédier tout de suite *ou* sur-le-champ; **(b)** (*quickly prepared*) (*café*) instantané; **i. potatoes,** pommes de terre déshydratées; **(c)** *Phot* **i. camera,** appareil *m* photographique à développement instantané; **(d)** *Lit* (*urgent*) instant, pressant, urgent; **(e)** *Old-fashioned* (*in letter*) (*of the current month*) courant, de ce mois.
instant[2] *n* **(a)** (*moment*) instant *m*, moment *m*; **come this i.!,** venez immédiatement!; **I just arrived this very i.,** j'arrive à l'instant; **not an i. too soon,** juste à temps; **in an i.,** dans un instant; **the i. I saw him,** dès que je l'ai vu; **(b)** *F* (*instant coffee*) instantané *m*.
instantaneous [ɪnstən'teɪnɪəs] *adj* instantané; *Phot* **i. exposure,** pose instantanée, instantané *m*.
instantaneously [ɪnstən'teɪnɪəslɪ] *adv* instantanément.
instantly ['ɪnstəntlɪ] *adv* tout de suite, immédiatement, sur-le-champ; **she would have died i.,** elle serait morte immédiatement.
instantaneously [ɪnstən'teɪnɪəslɪ] *adv* instantanément.
instead [ɪn'sted] *adv* **(a)** (*in the place of sth*) au lieu de (*qn, qch*); (*in s.o.'s place*) à ma *ou* sa *etc* place; **if John can't come, take me i.,** si Jean ne peut pas venir, emmenez-moi à sa place; **use the hammer i.,** utilise le marteau à la place; **he did not go to Rome but went to Venice i.,** au lieu d'aller à Rome il est allé à Venise; **(b)** (*in prep phrase*) **i. of,** (*in the place of*) au lieu de (*qch*); à la place de (*qn*); **to stand i. of sth,** tenir lieu de qch; **i. of doing sth,** au lieu de faire qch; **i. of diminishing, crime has increased,** au lieu de diminuer, la criminalité a augmenté.
instep ['ɪnstep] *n* **(a)** (*of foot*) cou-de-pied *m*, *pl* cous-de-pied; **foot with a high i.,** pied *ou* cou-de-pied très cambré; **(b)** (*of shoe*) cambrure *f*.
instigate ['ɪnstɪgeɪt] *vt* **(a)** (*cause*) inspirer, susciter (*la révolte*); **(b)** (*incite*) inciter, pousser, provoquer (*qn*) (**to do,** à faire).
instigation [ɪnstɪ'geɪʃən] *n* instigation *f*, incitation *f* (**to a crime,** à un crime); **at s.o.'s i.,** à l'instigation de qn.
instigator ['ɪnstɪgeɪtər] *n* **(a)** instigateur, -trice (*d'un crime etc*); **(b)** auteur *m* (*d'une révolte etc*); fauteur, -trice (*d'une émeute*).
instil, *US* **instill** [ɪn'stɪl] *vt* (*Br* **instils,** *US* **instills,** *Br & US* **instilled, instilling**) instiller (*le courage*) (**into s.o.,** à qn); inspirer (*un sentiment*) (**into s.o.,** à qn); faire pénétrer (*une idée*) (**into s.o.,** dans l'esprit de qn).
instinct ['ɪnstɪŋkt] *n* instinct *m*; **by** *or* **from i.,** d'instinct *ou* par instinct; **my i. was to run away,** mon instinct m'a dit de fuir; **to have an i. for business,** avoir le sens des affaires; **she has a strong business i.,** elle a un fort instinct pour les affaires.
instinctive [ɪn'stɪŋktɪv] *adj* instinctif.
instinctively [ɪn'stɪŋktɪvlɪ] *adv* instinctivement, d'instinct.
institute[1] ['ɪnstɪtjuːt] *n* institut *m*; (*club*) cercle *m*, foyer *m*; **i. for the blind,** établissement *m* pour aveugles.
institute[2] *vt* **(a)** (*set up*) instituer, établir (*un ordre, une loi*); fonder, constituer (*une société*); **(b)** *Jur* (*initiate*)

ordonner, instituer (*une enquête*); **to i. (legal) proceedings against s.o.,** entamer *ou* engager des poursuites contre qn; **(c)** (*install in office etc*) *Rel* **to i. s.o. to a benefice,** investir qn d'un bénéfice; *Jur* **to i. s.o. as heir,** instituer qn héritier.

institution [ɪnstɪ'tjuːʃən] *n* **(a)** (*organization*) institution *f* (*d'éducation etc*); établissement *m* (*public, financier etc*); association *f* (*d'ingénieurs etc*); **charitable i.,** établissement *ou* œuvre *f* de bienfaisance; *Admin* établissement d'intérêt public (*qui ne paie pas d'impôts*); **(b)** (*instituting*) commencement *m*, établissement *m* (*d'une enquête etc*); institution *f*, établissement (*d'une loi etc*); constitution *f* (*d'un comité*); création *f* (*d'un État*); **(c)** (*established practice etc*) institution *f*; **to become a national i.,** devenir une institution nationale; **(d)** (*installing in office etc*) *Rel* investiture *f* (*d'un ecclésiastique*); *Jur* institution *f* (*d'un héritier*).

institutional [ɪnstɪ'tjuːʃən(ə)l] *adj* institutionnel; **i. life,** la vie dans un établissement (*de charité etc*); **he needs i. care,** il a besoin de soins hospitaliers; *Fin* **i. buying,** achats institutionnels; *Fin* **i. investors,** investisseurs institutionnels, grands investisseurs.

institutionalize [ɪnstɪ'tjuːʃənəlaɪz] *vt* **(a)** (*put in a home etc*) placer (*qn*) dans un établissement, faire interner qn; **(b)** (*turn into an institution*) institutionnaliser (*qch*).

institutionalized [ɪnstɪ'tjuːʃənəlaɪzd] *adj* **(a)** (*person*) marqué par la vie en collectivité; **it's less i. in this establishment,** cet établissement a un caractère moins institutionnel; **(b)** (*established*) établi, devenu officiel.

instruct [ɪn'strʌkt] *vt* **(a)** (*teach, train*) instruire (*qn*) (**in sth,** en, dans qch); **(b)** *Fml* (*command*) charger (*qn*) (**to do,** de faire); **I am instructed by the Board to inform you that ...,** la Direction me charge de vous faire savoir que ...; **(c)** *Br Jur* **to i. a solicitor,** donner ses instructions à un avoué; **to i. counsel,** constituer avocat; **(d)** *Fml* (*inform*) informer (*qn*) (**that,** que).

instruction [ɪn'strʌkʃən] *n* **(a)** (*no pl*) (*training*) instruction *f*, enseignement *m*; **we received i. in using the machines,** on nous a appris comment utiliser les machines; *Aut* **driving i.,** leçons *fpl* de conduite;

(b) (*usu pl*) **instructions,** (*orders*) instructions *fpl*, indications *fpl*, directives *fpl*; (*to sentry etc*) consigne *f*; (*to representative etc*) mandat *m*; *Comptr* instructions (du programme); **to give s.o. instructions to do sth,** donner l'instruction à qn de faire qch, ordonner à qn de faire qch; **oral/written instructions,** instructions verbales/écrites; **(book of) standing instructions,** règlement *m*; **strict instructions,** des instructions formelles, des ordres formels; **to carry out instructions,** exécuter des ordres; **to act in accordance with/contrary to one's** *or* **s.o.'s instructions,** se conformer/ne pas se conformer aux instructions reçues; **our instructions were to arrest him,** les instructions *ou* ordres que nous avons reçu(e)s étaient de l'arrêter; **to follow s.o.'s instructions,** suivre les instructions de qn; **to obey s.o.'s instructions,** obéir aux ordres de qn; *Com etc* **we await your instructions,** nous attendons vos instructions; *Br Jur* **to give instructions to a solicitor,** donner ses instructions à un avoué; **instructions (for use),** (*for machine, cleaning product etc*) mode *m ou* notice *f* d'emploi; **i. book(let),** livret *m* d'instruction(s); **i. manual,** manuel *m* d'entretien (*d'une machine etc*).

instructive [ɪn'strʌktɪv] *adj* instructif.

instructor [ɪn'strʌktər] *n* maître *m*, enseignant *m*, professeur *m*; *Am Univ* assistant *m*; *Mil* instructeur *m*; *Ski & Aut* moniteur, -trice; **swimming i.,** professeur *m* de natation.

instructress [ɪn'strʌktrɪs] *n* maîtresse *f*, professeur *m*; monitrice *f* (*de ski, de conduite*).

instrument¹ ['ɪnstrʊmənt] *n* **(a)** *Tech Surg Mus etc* instrument *m*; **scientific/precision i.,** instrument scientifique/de précision; **optical/surgical i.,** instrument d'optique/de chirurgie *ou* chirurgical; **aircraft instruments,** instruments de bord; **flying/landing on instruments, i. flying/landing,** vol *m*/atterrissage *m* aux instruments *ou* sans visibilité; **i. board** *or* **panel,** *Av Aut* tableau *m* de bord; (*on machine*) tableau de commande *ou* de contrôle; *Mus* **wind/stringed i.,** instrument à vent/à cordes; **(b)** *Fml* (*means, agent*) instrument *m*; **to serve as the i. of s.o.'s vengeance,** servir d'instrument à la vengeance de qn; **(c)** *Jur* acte *m* juridique (*de cession etc*); instrument *m*, document officiel; *Com* **negotiable i.,** effet *m* de commerce, titre *m* au porteur.

instrument² ['ɪnstrʊmənt, ɪnstrʊ'ment] **1** *vt* **(a)** *Mus* orchestrer, instrumenter (*un opéra etc*); **(b)** *Tech* équiper *ou* munir (*un atelier etc*) d'instruments. **2** *vi Jur* instrumenter.

instrumental [ɪnstrʊ'ment(ə)l] **1** *adj* **(a)** (*contributing*) contributif (**to,** à); **to be i. in doing sth,** contribuer à faire qch, jouer un rôle décisif dans qch; **(b)** *Tech* de l'instrument, d'instruments; (*équipement*) en instruments; **i. error,** erreur (de lecture) due à l'instrument; **(c)** *Mus* instrumental; **i. performer,** instrumentiste *mf*. **2** *n Mus* version *f* instrumentale.

instrumentalist [ɪnstrʊ'mentəlɪst] *n Mus* instrumentiste *mf*.

instrumentation [ɪnstrʊmen'teɪʃən] *n Mus* instrumentation *f*.

insubordinate [ɪnsə'bɔːdɪnət] *adj* insubordonné, insoumis; (*soldat etc*) mutin.

insubordination ['ɪnsəbɔːdɪ'neɪʃən] *n* insubordination *f*, insoumission *f*.

insubstantial [ɪnsəb'stænʃəl] *adj* **(a)** (*argument*) vide, sans substance; **an i. breakfast,** un petit déjeuner frugal; **(b)** (*unreal*) imaginaire.

insufferable [ɪn'sʌfərəb(ə)l] *adj* insupportable, intolérable.

insufferably [ɪn'sʌfərəblɪ] *adv* insupportablement, intolérablement.

insufficiency [ɪnsə'fɪʃənsɪ] *n* insuffisance *f*.

insufficient [ɪnsə'fɪʃənt] *adj* insuffisant; **i. food supplies,** manque *m* de vivres.

insufficiently [ɪnsə'fɪʃəntlɪ] *adv* insuffisamment.

insular ['ɪnsjʊlər] *adj* **(a)** (*narrow*) (*esprit*) étroit, borné; (*vie etc*) d'insulaire; **to be very i. in one's views,** avoir les idées très bornées; **(b)** *Geog* (*climat etc*) insulaire.

insularity [ɪnsjʊ'lærɪtɪ] *n* insularité *f*.

insulate ['ɪnsjʊleɪt] *vt El* isoler (*un fil etc*); calorifuger (*une conduite*); *Rad etc* insonoriser (*un studio*); **to i. against vibration,** protéger contre les vibrations; *Fig* **insulated from the outside world,** protégé contre le monde extérieur.

insulated ['ɪnsjʊleɪtɪd] *adj El* isolé; (*handle*) isolant; **(heat-)i.,** calorifugé; **(sound-)i.,** insonore, insonorisé.

insulating ['ɪnsʊleɪtɪŋ] *adj* isolant; *El* **i. material,** matériau isolant, matière isolante, isolant *m* électrique; **i. properties,** propriétés isolantes; **i. tape,** ruban isolant, chatterton *m*; **(heat-)i.,** calorifuge; **(sound-)i.,** insonore.

insulation [ɪnsjʊ'leɪʃən] *n* **(a)** (*action, state*) isolation *f*, isolement *m* (*électrique, thermique, acoustique*); **poor i.,** mauvais isolement; **heat** *or* **thermal i.,** isolation thermique; **sound i.,** isolation acoustique, insonorisation *f* (*d'une salle etc*); **(b)** (*substance*) isolant *m* (*électrique, thermique, acoustique*).

insulator ['ɪnsjʊleɪtər] *n El Constr* (*substance*) isolant *m*; (*device*) isolateur *m*; **to be a good/poor i.,** être un bon/mauvais isolant; **heat i.,** isolant thermique, matériau *m ou* matière *f* calorifuge; **sound i.,** isolant acoustique, matériau *ou* matière insonore.

insulin ['ɪnsjʊlɪn] *n Med* insuline *f*; **i. treatment,** insulinothérapie *f*.

insult¹ ['ɪnsʌlt] *n* **(a)** insulte *f*, affront *m*; **to add i. to injury,** doubler ses torts d'un affront; **it's an i. to the intelligence,** c'est un outrage à l'intelligence; **(b)** *Med* blessure *f*, lésion *f* (*du corps*).

insult² [ɪn'sʌlt] *vt* **(a)** insulter (*qn*), faire affront *ou* injure à (*qn*); **to i. s.o.'s intelligence,** faire outrage à l'intelligence de qn; **to feel insulted,** se sentir insulté; **(b)** *Am Med* **foods that i. the body,** nourriture *f* qui nuit à la santé.

insulting [ɪn'sʌltɪŋ] *adj* (*geste, mot*) insultant, offensant, injurieux; **it is i. to suggest that ...,** il est insultant de suggérer que ...; **to use i. language,** employer un langage injurieux; **to be guilty of i. behaviour towards s.o.,** s'être conduit insolemment à l'égard de qn; *Jur* être coupable d'outrages (*à un agent, un magistrat*).

insultingly [ɪn'sʌltɪŋlɪ] *adv* d'une façon insultante *ou* offensante.

insuperable [ɪn'suːpərəb(ə)l] *adj* (*difficulté etc*) insurmontable; (*obstacle*) infranchissable.

insupportable [ɪnsə'pɔːtəb(ə)l] *adj* insupportable.

insurance [ɪn'ʃʊərəns] *n* **(a)** *Com* assurance *f*; **to take out i. on sth** *or* **against a risk,** prendre une assurance *ou* s'assurer sur qch *ou* contre un risque; **he's in i.,** il est dans les assurances; **accident i.,** assurance contre les accidents, assurance-accidents *f*, *pl* assurances-accidents; **fire i.,** assurance contre l'incendie, assurance-incendie *f*, *pl* assurances-incendie; **personal liability i.,** assurance responsabilité civile; **third-party i.,** assurance aux tiers; **all risks** *or* **comprehensive i.,** assurance tous risques; **travel i.,** assurance-voyage; **marine i.,** assurance maritime; **cargo i.,** assurance de la cargaison; **i. agent,** agent *m*

d'assurance(s); **i. broker,** courtier *m* d'assurance(s); **i. company,** compagnie *f* d'assurance(s); **i. policy,** police *f* d'assurance;
(b) (*premium*) prime *f* d'assurance; **to pay the i. on a car,** payer l'assurance d'une voiture;
(c) *Fig* garantie *f*, assurance *f*, protection *f*; **to buy gold as i. against inflation,** acheter de l'or pour se prémunir contre l'inflation.

insure [ɪn'ʃʊər, -ʃɔːr] *vt* **(a)** (*of company*) assurer (*une voiture, des bijoux etc*); (*of client*) (faire) assurer (*des marchandises etc*); **to i. one's life,** s'assurer *ou* se faire assurer sur la vie; **(b)** *esp US* = **ENSURE**.

►**insure against** *vipo* s'assurer, se faire assurer contre (*un risque*); se garantir de (*un danger*).

insured [ɪn'ʃʊəd, -ʃɔːd] **1** *adj* assuré; **i. value,** valeur assurée. **2** *n* **the i.,** (*person*) l'assuré, -ée.

insurer [ɪn'ʃʊərər] *n Com* assureur *m*.

insurgent [ɪn'sɜːdʒənt] **1** *adj* insurgé, révolté. **2** *n* insurgé, -ée, révolté, -ée.

insurmountable [ɪnsə'maʊntəb(ə)l] *adj* (*difficulté, obstacle*) insurmontable; (*obstacle*) infranchissable.

insurrection [ɪnsə'rekʃən] *n* insurrection *f*, soulèvement *m*, rébellion *f*.

insurrectional [ɪnsə'rekʃən(ə)l], **insurrectionary** [ɪnsə'rekʃənərɪ] *adj* insurrectionnel.

insurrectionist [ɪnsə'rekʃənɪst] *n* insurgé, -ée, rebelle *mf*.

intact [ɪn'tækt] *adj* intact.

intaglio [ɪn'tɑːlɪəʊ] *n* intaille *f*; **i. engraving,** gravure *f* en creux.

intake ['ɪnteɪk] *n* **(a)** (*opening*) prise *f* (*d'air, d'eau, El de courant*); arrivée *f*, adduction *f*, admission *f* (*de vapeur*); (*in engine*) entrée *f* (*d'air*); *Min* galerie *f* d'appel d'air; *HydE* aire *f* d'alimentation; **(b)** (*of alcohol*) consommation *f*; **(c)** *Mil* (*of recruits*) contingent *m*; *Sch* (*of pupils, students*) admission(s) *f(pl)*.

intangible [ɪn'tændʒɪb(ə)l] **1** *adj* intangible, impalpable; *Com* **i. assets,** valeurs immatérielles, actif incorporel; *Jur* **i. property,** biens incorporels. **2** *npl Com* **intangibles,** valeurs immatérielles, actif incorporel.

integer ['ɪntɪdʒər] *n Math* (nombre *m*) entier *m*.

integral ['ɪntɪgr(ə)l] **1** *adj* **(a)** (*essential*) intégrant; **to be** *or* **form an i. part of sth,** faire partie intégrante de qch; **to become an i. part of sth,** s'intégrer dans qch; **(b)** *Math* **i. number,** nombre entier; **i. calculus,** calcul intégral; **(c)** *Tech* (*of one piece*) d'une seule pièce; en un seul bloc; (*forming a part of*) incorporé (**with,** à); structural, -aux; qui fait partie intégrante (**with,** de). **2** *n Math* intégrale *f*.

integrate ['ɪntɪgreɪt] **1** *vt* **(a)** (*incorporate*) intégrer (*une minorité*); *US* **to i. a school,** imposer la déségrégation raciale dans une école; **(b)** *Math* intégrer (*une fonction etc*), déterminer l'intégrale de (*une fonction*); **(c)** (*make whole*) compléter, rendre entier (*qch d'incomplet*). **2** *vi* s'intégrer (*dans un milieu social, ethnique etc*); *US* pratiquer la déségrégation raciale.

integrated ['ɪntɪgreɪtɪd] *adj* intégré; *Electron* **i. circuit,** circuit intégré.

integration [ɪntɪ'greɪʃən] *n* **(a)** intégration *f*; **the i. of ethnic minorities,** l'intégration des minorités ethniques; **racial i.,** déségrégation raciale; **(b)** *Math* **i. by parts,** intégration *f* par parties.

integrity [ɪn'tegrɪtɪ] *n* **(a)** (*honesty*) intégrité, honnêteté *f*, probité *f* (*de qn, d'un motif etc*); **woman of i.,** femme intègre; **(b)** (*wholeness*) intégrité *f*, totalité *f* (*d'un texte etc*).

integument [ɪn'tegjʊmənt] *n Biol* tégument *m*.

intellect ['ɪntɪlekt] *n* **(a)** intelligence *f*, esprit *m*, entendement *m*, intellect *m*; **man of i.,** homme intelligent; **he was one of the best intellects of his time,** c'était une des plus grandes intelligences de son époque; **(b)** (*no pl*) **the i. of the country,** tous les meilleurs esprits du pays.

intellectual [ɪntɪ'lektjʊəl] **1** *adj* intellectuel. **2** *n* intellectuel, -elle.

intellectually [ɪntɪ'lektjʊəlɪ] *adv* intellectuellement.

intelligence [ɪn'telɪdʒəns] *n* **(a)** (*mental capacity*) intelligence *f*; (*mind*) esprit *m*; (*understanding*) entendement *m*; **person of good i.,** personne intelligente; *Psy* **i. quotient,** quotient intellectuel; **i. test,** test *m* d'intelligence; **(b)** (*information*) renseignement(s) *m(pl)*; *Mil & Pol* **i. (service),** service *m* de renseignements; = le deuxième Bureau; **to give/receive i. of sth,** donner/avoir avis de qch; **our i. was that,** les informations dont nous disposions étaient que ...; **i. officer,** officier *m* de renseignements.

intelligent [ɪn'telɪdʒənt] *adj* intelligent.

intelligently [ɪn'telɪdʒəntlɪ] *adv* intelligemment, avec intelligence.

intelligentsia [ɪntelɪ'dʒentsɪə] *n* intelligentsia *f*.

intelligibility [ɪntelɪdʒɪ'bɪlɪtɪ] *n* intelligibilité *f*.

intelligible [ɪn'telɪdʒɪb(ə)l] *adj* intelligible; **he was hardly i.,** on le comprenait à peine.

intelligibly [ɪn'telɪdʒɪblɪ] *adv* intelligiblement.

intemperance [ɪn'temp(ə)rəns] *n* intempérance *f*.

intemperate [ɪn'temp(ə)rɪt] *adj* (*person*) intempérant; (*climate*) rude; **person of i. habits,** personne intempérante; (*excessive drinker*) personne adonnée à la boisson.

intend [ɪn'tend] *vt* **(a)** (*mean*) avoir l'intention de, se proposer de (**doing, to do,** faire); compter (**doing, to do,** faire); **was that intended?,** était-ce fait avec intention *ou* à dessein?; **I i. to be obeyed,** je veux qu'on m'obéisse; **I didn't i. her to see it yet,** je ne voulais pas qu'elle le voie déjà; **I intended it as a compliment,** mon intention était de vous faire un compliment; **(b)** (*aim, destine*) **book intended for students,** livre destiné aux étudiants; **this remark is intended for you,** cette observation s'adresse à vous.

intended [ɪn'tendɪd] **1** *adj* **(a)** (*prospective*) projeté; *Old-fashioned* **my i. husband/wife,** mon fiancé/ma fiancée, mon futur/ma future; **the i. effect,** l'effet voulu; **(b)** (*intentional*) intentionnel, fait avec intention. **2** *n Old-fashioned F* **his/her i.,** sa fiancée/son fiancé, sa future/son futur.

intense [ɪn'tens] *adj* **(a)** (*feeling, anxiety*) vif, *f* vive; (*heat, colour, book, activity etc*) intense; (*pain*) vif, intense; (*bombardment*) intensif, -ive; (*hatred*) profond; **(b) i. expression,** expression concentrée; **she's too i.,** elle est trop sérieuse.

intensely [ɪn'tenslɪ] *adv* **(a)** (*greatly*) intensément, profondément; **it was i. hot,** il faisait une chaleur intense; **i. blue eyes,** yeux *mpl* d'un bleu intense; **(b)** (*regarder*) avec intensité, intensément.

intensification [ɪntensɪfɪ'keɪʃən] *n* intensification *f* (*d'un son etc*); *Phot* renforcement *m* (*d'un cliché*).

intensifier [ɪn'tensɪfaɪər] *n Gram* mot qui vient en renforcer un autre.

intensify [ɪn'tensɪfaɪ] **1** *vt* intensifier, augmenter, accroître (*un son, un sentiment*); amplifier (*un son*); renforcer (*une couleur*); *Phot* renforcer (*un cliché faible*). **2** *vi* s'intensifier.

intensity [ɪn'tensɪtɪ] *n* **(a)** intensité *f*; force *f* (*d'une passion*); violence *f* (*d'une douleur*); **with i.,** intensément; **(b)** *Phys* intensité *f* (*d'un son, El du courant etc*); *Ch* énergie *f* (*d'une réaction*); *Phot* densité *f* (*d'un cliché*); *Phys* **luminous i.,** intensité lumineuse.

intensive [ɪn'tensɪv] *adj* intensif; **an i. course,** cours accéléré, formation accélérée; *Med* **i. care unit,** service *m* de soins intensifs; *Med* **to be in i. care,** être dans le service de soins intensifs; **i. farming,** exploitation intensive; *Gram* **i. verb/pronoun,** (verbe *m*/pronom *m*) intensif *m*.

intensively [ɪn'tensɪvlɪ] *adv* intensivement, intensément.

intent¹ [ɪn'tent] *n* intention *f*, dessein *m*, but *m*; **with good i.,** dans une bonne intention; *Jur* **with i. to defraud,** dans l'intention de frauder; **declaration of i.,** déclaration *f* d'intention; **to all intents and purposes,** virtuellement, en fait.

intent² *adj* **(a)** (*follows noun*) **to be i. on sth** *or* **doing sth,** (*determined to*) être résolu *ou* déterminé à faire qch; **they left i. on murder,** ils sont partis, déterminés à commettre un meurtre; **a woman i. on success,** une femme déterminée à réussir; **they're i. on reforming the system,** ils sont déterminés à réformer le système; **(b)** (*follows noun*) **to be i. on sth,** (*engrossed in*) être tout entier à *ou* absorbé par qch; **(c)** (*intense*) (*esprit*) ardent, acharné; (*regard*) profond; (*application*) soutenu.

intention [ɪn'tenʃən] *n* **(a)** intention *f*; **I had no i.** *or* **not the slightest i. of accepting,** je n'avais nullement l'intention d'accepter; **was your i. to ...?,** est-ce qu'il était de ton intention de ...?; **he acted with the best and most honourable intentions,** il a agi en tout bien (et) tout honneur; *Prov* **the road to hell is paved with good intentions,** l'enfer est pavé de bonnes intentions; **her intentions were good,** elle avait de bonnes intentions; *Old-fashioned* **his intentions are honourable,** il a l'intention de l'épouser; **(b)** *Rel* **to celebrate Mass for a special i.,** dire une messe à l'intention spéciale (*de qn, qch*).

intentional [ɪn'tenʃən(ə)l] *adj* intentionnel, voulu, fait à dessein, fait exprès; **it wasn't i.,** je ne l'ai pas *ou* il ne l'a pas *etc* fait exprès.

intentionally [ɪn'tenʃən(ə)lɪ] *adv* à dessein, exprès.

intently [ɪn'tentlɪ] *adv* (*écouter, regarder, étudier*) attentivement; (*réfléchir*) profondément.

inter [ɪn'tɜːr] *vt* (**-rr-**) enterrer, ensevelir, inhumer (*un* *mort*).

interact [ɪntər'ækt] *vi* (*of chemicals, substances*) interagir; *esp Psy* **to encourage a child to i. with its environment,** encourager les échanges d'un enfant avec son environnement; **a situation in which therapist and patient i.,** une situation où il y a interaction entre le thérapeute et son patient; **a person who doesn't i. well with others,** une personne qui a du mal dans ses échanges avec les autres; **the way the two characters in the novel i.,** l'interaction entre les deux personnages dans ce roman.

interaction [ɪntər'ækʃən] *n* interaction *f*; **personal i.,** interaction personnelle.

interactive [ɪntər'æktɪv] *adj* interactif.

interbreed [ɪntə'briːd] *v* (*pt & pp* **interbred**) **1** *vt* **(a)** (*breed from same stock*) accoupler (*des animaux consanguins*); **(b)** (*crossbreed*) (entre)croiser (*des races*). **2** *vi* **(a)** (*in same family group*) (*of people*) se reproduire par mariages *ou* accouplements consanguins; (*of animals*) se reproduire par accouplements consanguins; **(b)** (*crossbreed*) se reproduire par croisement, se croiser.

intercalate [ɪn'tɜːkəleɪt] *vt* intercaler.

intercalation [ɪntɜːkə'leɪʃən] *n* intercalation *f*.

intercede [ɪntə'siːd] *vi* intercéder, plaider (**with s.o.,** auprès de qn) (**for s.o., on s.o.'s behalf,** en faveur de qn, pour qn).

intercept [ɪntə'sept] **1** *vt* intercepter (*la lumière, une lettre, un avion ennemi etc*); arrêter (*qn*) au passage; *Rad etc* capter (*un message*); *Fb* **to i. a pass,** intercepter une passe. **2** *vi Fb* intercepter une passe.

interception [ɪntə'sepʃən] *n* (*of letter etc*) *& Fb* interception *f*; *Rad etc* captation *f* (*de messages, de conversations etc*).

interceptor [ɪntə'septər] *n* **(a)** personne *f* qui intercepte (*un message etc*); **(b)** *Av Mil* **i. (aircraft),** avion *m* d'interception, intercepteur *m*.

intercession [ɪntə'seʃən] *n* intercession *f*.

interchange[1] ['ɪntətʃeɪndʒ] *n* **(a)** échange *m* (*de compliments, d'objets, d'idées*); communication *f* (*d'idées*); **(b)** *Constr* (*on motorway*) échangeur *m*.

interchange[2] [ɪntə'tʃeɪndʒ] **1** *vt* échanger (*des compliments etc*) (**with,** avec); échanger (*des parties d'une machine etc*); **all parts of these machines can be interchanged,** toutes les pièces de ces machines sont interchangeables; **to i. the position of two things,** changer deux choses de place. **2** *vi* s'interchanger.

interchangeable [ɪntə'tʃeɪndʒəb(ə)l] *adj* interchangeable; **these two words are i.,** ces deux mots sont interchangeables.

interchangeably [ɪntə'tʃeɪndʒəblɪ] *adv* (*use*) indifféremment.

inter-city [ɪntə'sɪtɪ] **1** *adj* interurbain; *Br Rail etc* (*service etc*) de grandes lignes. **2** *n Br Rail* train *m* de grandes lignes.

intercom ['ɪntəkɒm] *n Tel F* interphone *m*; **to speak over the i.,** parler dans l'interphone.

intercommunicate [ɪntəkə'mjuːnɪkeɪt] *vi* **(a)** (*of rooms etc*) communiquer; **(b)** (*of prisoners etc*) communiquer entre eux.

intercommunion [ɪntəkə'mjuːnjən] *n Rel* intercommunion *f*.

interconnect [ɪntəkə'nekt] *El Comptr* **1** *vt* interconnecter (*des circuits, des ordinateurs*). **2** *vi* être interconnectés.

interconnection [ɪntəkə'nekʃən] *n* interconnexion *f*.

intercontinental [ɪntəkɒntɪ'nent(ə)l] *adj* intercontinental, -aux; **i. ballistic missile,** missile balistique intercontinental.

intercourse ['ɪntəkɔːs] *n* **(a) (sexual) i.,** rapports sexuels; **to have i. with s.o.,** avoir des rapports sexuels avec qn; **(b)** *Old-fashioned* (*dealings*) commerce *m*, relations *fpl*, rapports *mpl*; **social i.,** la fréquentation du monde.

interdenominational ['ɪntədɪnɒmɪ'neɪʃən(ə)l] *adj Rel* interconfessionnel.

interdepartmental ['ɪntədiːpɑːt'ment(ə)l] *adj* interdépartemental, -aux; entre services; entre départements; **i. rivalry,** rivalité entre services.

interdependence [ɪntədɪ'pendəns] *n* interdépendance *f*.

interdependent [ɪntədɪ'pendənt] *adj* interdépendant.

interdict[1] ['ɪntədɪkt] *n* **(a)** *Jur* défense *f*, interdiction *f*; **(b)** *Rel* interdit *m*.

interdict[2] [ɪntə'dɪkt] *vt* **(a)** *Jur* interdire, prohiber; **(b)** *Rel* frapper d'interdit (*un prêtre, une ville*); interdire (*un prêtre*).

interdiction [ɪntə'dɪkʃən] *n* **(a)** (*action*) interdiction *f*; **(b)** *Rel* (*result*) interdit *m*.

interest[1] ['ɪntərɪst] *n* **(a)** (*curiosity*) intérêt *m* (**in,** à); **to take an i. in s.o./sth,** s'intéresser *ou* porter intérêt à qn/qch; **to have an i. in politics,** s'intéresser à la politique; **to show an i. in sth,** montrer un intérêt pour qch; **her i. in Latin America,** son intérêt à l'égard de l'Amérique latine; **to take no (further) i. in sth, to lose i. in sth,** se désintéresser de qch; **two people have shown an i. in (buying) the house,** deux personnes sont intéressées par l'achat de la maison; **there's little i. in these old chairs nowadays,** on ne s'intéresse pas beaucoup à ces vieilles chaises de nos jours;

(b) (*interesting aspect*) intérêt *m*; **this may be of i. to you,** ceci peut vous intéresser; **what he does is of no i. to me,** ce qu'il fait n'a aucun intérêt pour moi; **there was little of i. on television,** il n'y avait pas grand-chose d'intéressant à la télévision; **buildings of historical/architectural i.,** bâtiments *mpl* d'intérêt historique/architectural; **a little garlic will give i. to a stew,** l'ail donnera un peu de piquant au ragoût;

(c) (*activity, subject of interest*) **I have many interests,** beaucoup de choses m'intéressent; **her interests include skiing and photography,** le ski et la photographie font partie de ses centres d'intérêt;

(d) (*participation*) intérêt *m*, participation *f*; **to have a direct i. in sth,** avoir un intérêt personnel dans qch; **I have no financial i. in the business,** je ne suis pas intéressé dans cette entreprise; **to have a controlling i. in a company,** avoir une participation majoritaire dans une société;

(e) (*group*) **the shipping i.,** les armateurs *mpl*, le commerce maritime; **we look after British interests,** nous défendons les intérêts britanniques;

(f) (*benefit*) intérêt *m*; **the public i.,** l'intérêt public; **it would not be in the public i.,** ça ne serait pas dans l'intérêt public; **to act in/against one's (own) interest(s),** agir dans/contre son propre intérêt; **to act in s.o.'s best interest(s),** agir dans l'intérêt de qn; **it's in my i. to do this,** j'ai intérêt à faire ceci; **it's not in their i. to offend her,** ce n'est pas dans leur intérêt de l'offenser, ils n'ont pas intérêt à l'offenser;

(g) *Fin* intérêt(s) *m(pl)*; **simple i.,** intérêts simples; **fixed i.,** intérêt fixe; **back i.,** arriérages *mpl* (*d'une rente etc*); **i. on capital,** intérêt du capital; **i. on a loan,** intérêt sur prêt; **to pay i. on a loan,** payer des intérêts sur un prêt; **to bear** *or* **yield i.,** porter intérêt *ou* des intérêts; **to yield 5% i.,** rapporter du 5% *ou* un intérêt de 5%; *Fig* **to repay an injury with i.,** rendre le mal avec usure.

interest[2] *vt* intéresser (*qn*); **we couldn't i. her in the idea/in playing cards,** nous ne sommes pas parvenus à éveiller son intérêt à l'égard de cette idée/pour ce qui est de jouer aux cartes; **can I i. you in a drink?,** puis-je vous proposer un verre?; *Iron* **it might i. you to learn** *or* **know that,** ça t'intéressera peut-être d'apprendre *ou* de savoir que.

interested ['ɪntərɪstɪd] *adj* **(a)** (*curious*) intéressé; **to be interested in painting/music,** s'intéresser à la peinture/à la musique; **I am not i.,** cela ne m'intéresse pas; **he wasn't i.,** (*in the offer, suggestion*) il n'était pas intéressé, ça ne l'intéressait pas; **anyone i.?,** il y en a que ça intéresse?, est-ce que quelqu'un est intéressé?; **I should be i. to hear the end of the story,** je serais curieux d'apprendre la fin de l'histoire; **(b)** *Com* intéressé; **the i. parties,** les parties intéressées; *Jur* **i. party,** ayant droit *m*, *pl* ayants droit; **(c)** (*motive*) intéressé; **to act from i. motives,** agir par calcul.

interest-free ['ɪntərɪst'friː] *adj Fin* (*credit, loan*) gratuit.

interesting ['ɪntərɪstɪŋ] *adj* (*livre, travail etc*) intéressant.

interestingly ['ɪntərɪstɪŋlɪ] *adv* de façon intéressante; **i. enough ...,** ce qui est intéressant c'est que ...; **i., a number of the Prime Minister's supporters voted against her,** il est intéressant de noter qu'un certain nombre des partisans du premier ministre ont voté contre elle.

interface[1] ['ɪntəfeɪs] *n Comptr & Fig* interface *f*; **the patient/doctor i.,** les relations médecin-patient; **the extent of the i. between these two subjects,** l'étendue des rapports entre ces deux sujets.

interface[2] **1** *vi* avoir une interface (**with,** avec); **this device interfaces with most PC's,** ce dispositif permet une interface avec la plupart des ordinateurs individuels. **2** *vt* mettre (*deux ordinateurs*) en interface.

interfacing ['ɪntəfeɪsɪŋ] *n* **(a)** *Comptr* constitution *f* d'une interface; **(b)** *Sewing* entoilage *m*.

interfere [ɪntə'fɪər] *vi* **(a)** (*of person*) s'ingérer, s'immiscer, intervenir (**in a matter,** dans une affaire);

s'interposer (*dans une querelle*); **to i. in s.o.'s affairs,** se mêler des affaires de qn; **don't i. in what doesn't concern you,** ne vous mêlez pas de ce qui ne vous regarde pas; **he's always interfering,** il fourre son nez partout, il est toujours à se mêler de ce qui ne le regarde pas; **do not i. with the doors,** ne pas gêner la fermeture des portes; **someone has interfered with the clock,** on a touché à la pendule; *Euph* **was she interfered with?,** est-ce qu'on a abusé d'elle?;

(b) (*of thing*) **to i. with,** gêner, contrarier (*les projets de qn*); gêner (*la circulation etc*); entraver (*la marche des affaires*); **pleasure should not be allowed to i. with business,** il ne faut pas que les plaisirs empiètent sur les affaires; **it interferes with my plans,** cela dérange mes projets;

(c) *Phys etc* (*of light waves etc*) interférer; *Ch* perturber; *Electron Rad* **to i. with a signal,** brouiller *ou* parasiter un signal.

interference [ɪntə'fɪərəns] *n* **(a)** (*by person*) intervention *f*; intrusion *f*, ingérence *f* (**in,** dans); *Sp* obstruction *f* (*d'un adversaire*); **(b)** *Phys* interférence *f* (*des ondes lumineuses etc*); *Ch* perturbation *f*; *Electron Rad* interférence(s), parasite(s) *m(pl)*, brouillage *m*; *Opt* **i. figure** *or* **pattern,** figure *f* d'interférence.

interfering [ɪntə'fɪərɪŋ] *adj* **(a)** (*person*) importun, qui se mêle de ce qui ne le regarde pas; **he's so i.,** il fourre son nez partout; **(b)** *Phys etc* (*waves*) interférent; (*chemical, reagent etc*) perturbateur, -trice; *Electron Rad* qui brouille, parasite.

interferon [ɪntə'fɪərɒn] *n Biol* interféron *m*.

interim ['ɪntərɪm] **1** *n* intérim *m*; *Pol* intérimat *m*; **in the i.,** dans l'intérim. **2** *adj* (*gouvernement, rapport etc*) intérimaire; **the i. period,** l'intérim *m*; *Jur* **i. order,** avant faire droit *m inv*.

interior [ɪn'tɪərɪər] **1** *adj* (*côté, commerce*) intérieur; (*terres etc*) de l'intérieur; *Math* (*angle*) interne; **i. decoration,** décoration *f* d'intérieur; **i. decorator,** décorateur *m*. **2** *n* **(a)** intérieur *m* (*du pays, des terres*); **the i. of a building,** l'intérieur d'un édifice; **(b)** *Art* (tableau *m* d') intérieur *m*.

interior-sprung [ɪn'tɪərɪəsprʌŋ] *adj* **i.-s. mattress,** matelas *m* à ressorts.

interject [ɪntə'dʒekt] *vt* lancer (*une remarque*); émettre (*une protestation*).

interjection [ɪntə'dʒekʃən] *n* **(a)** action *f* de lancer (*une remarque etc*); action d'émettre (*une protestation*); **(b)** *Gram* interjection *f*.

interlace [ɪntə'leɪs] **1** *vt* entrelacer (*des branches etc*); entrecroiser (*des fils*); entremêler (**with,** de). **2** *vi* s'entrelacer, s'entrecroiser; s'entremêler.

interlard [ɪntə'lɑːd] *vt* (entre)larder, entremêler (*un discours, ses récits*) (**with,** de).

interleave [ɪntə'liːv] *vt* interfolier (*un livre*); *Typ* intercaler (*des feuilles*).

interlibrary [ɪntə'laɪbrərɪ] *adj* **i. loan,** prêt *m* interbibliothèque.

interline [ɪntə'laɪn] *vt* **(a)** interligner (*un document, un manuscrit*); **(b)** *Sewing* mettre une doublure intermédiaire à (*un vêtement etc*).

interlining ['ɪntəlaɪnɪŋ] *n* doublure *f* intermédiaire.

interlock [ɪntə'lɒk] **1** *vt* enclencher (*un mécanisme*); engrener (*des roues dentées*); emboîter (*les parties d'un mécanisme*). **2** *vi* (*of questions etc*) s'entrecroiser, s'entremêler; (*of mechanism*) s'enclencher; (*of pinions*) s'engrener; (*of parts*) s'emboîter.

interlocking [ɪntə'lɒkɪŋ] *adj* entrecroisé, entrelacé, entremêlé; *MecE* (*roues*) qui s'engrènent *ou* s'enclenchent.

interlocutor [ɪntə'lɒkjuːtər] *n Fml* interlocuteur, -trice.

interloper ['ɪntələʊpər] *n* intrus, -use.

interlude ['ɪntəluːd] *n Th etc* intermède *m*; **musical i.,** interlude *m*, intermède musical.

intermarriage [ɪntə'mærɪdʒ] *n* (*between families etc*) mariage *m* entre les membres de différentes familles *ou* castes *ou* races *etc*; (*within a family*) mariage entre les membres d'une même famille.

intermarry [ɪntə'mærɪ] *vi* se marier entre soi.

intermediary [ɪntə'miːdɪərɪ] **1** *n* intermédiaire *mf*; **to act as i.,** servir d'intermédiaire. **2** *adj* intermédiaire.

intermediate¹ [ɪntə'miːdɪət] *adj* (*taille etc*) intermédiaire; *Sch* (*cours etc*) (de niveau) moyen; **i. stops,** arrêts *mpl* intermédiaires (*au cours d'un voyage*); *El* **i. frequency,** fréquence moyenne; **i.-range nuclear forces,** forces *fpl* nucléaires intermédiaires.

intermediate² [ɪntə'miːdɪeɪt] *vi* s'entremettre, servir de médiateur, -trice (**between,** entre).

interment [ɪn'tɜːmənt] *n* enterrement *m*, inhumation *f*.

interminable [ɪn'tɜːmɪnəb(ə)l] *adj* (*discussion, voyage*) interminable, sans fin; (*histoires*) à n'en plus finir.

interminably [ɪn'tɜːmɪnəblɪ] *adv* interminablement.

intermingle [ɪntə'mɪŋg(ə)l] **1** *vt* entremêler; mélanger (*des couleurs*). **2** *vi* s'entremêler, se mêler, se confondre (**with,** avec).

intermission [ɪntə'mɪʃən] *n* **(a)** *Cin Th Mus etc* entracte *m*; **(b)** (*pause*) interruption *f*, pause *f*; *Med* intermission *f*, rémission *f* (*de la fièvre*); **without i.,** sans arrêt.

intermittent [ɪntə'mɪtənt] *adj* intermittent.

intermittently [ɪntə'mɪtəntlɪ] *adv* par intervalles, par intermittence, de façon intermittente.

intermodal [ɪntə'məʊdəl] *adj Can* (*transport etc*) intermodal.

intern¹ ['ɪntɜːn] *n Am Med* interne *m* (*des hôpitaux*).

intern² [ɪn'tɜːn] *vt* interner (*des étrangers etc*).

internal [ɪn'tɜːn(ə)l] *adj* **(a)** intérieur, interne; *Med* (*hémorragie, organe etc*) interne; (*maladie*) organique; *Tel* **i. cable,** câble *m* d'immeuble; *MecE* **i. combustion engine,** moteur à combustion interne; **i. telephone,** téléphone intérieur; **(b)** (*commerce*) intérieur; (*droit*) interne; (*législation*) national, interne; *US* **i. revenue,** recettes fiscales; (*authority*) fisc *m*; **i. security,** sécurité intérieure; **i. inquiry,** (*within company etc*) enquête *f* interne; **(c)** (*valeur, preuve*) intrinsèque; **the i. workings of the mind,** les opérations secrètes de l'esprit; **(d)** *Sch* **i. student,** étudiant, -ante d'une université.

internalize [ɪn'tɜːnəlaɪz] *vt* (*skills etc*) assimiler; (*problem*) intérioriser.

internally [ɪn'tɜːn(ə)lɪ] *adv* intérieurement; **i. fired boiler,** chaudière *f* à chauffage intérieur; *Med* **not to be taken i.,** pour usage externe.

international [ɪntə'næʃən(ə)l] **1** *adj* international, -aux; **the i. team,** l'équipe nationale; **i. law,** droit international; **I. Labour Organization,** Organisation internationale du travail; **I. Monetary Fund,** Fonds monétaire international. **2** *n Sp* **(a)** (*player*) (joueur, -euse) international, -ale; **(b)** (*match*) match international.

Internationale (the) [ðiːɪntənæʃjə'nɑːl] *n* l'Internationale *f*.

internationalism [ɪntə'næʃənəlɪz(ə)m] *n* internationalisme *m*.

internationalize [ɪntə'næʃənəlaɪz] *vt* internationaliser.

internationally [ɪntə'næʃənəlɪ] *adv* internationalement; **an i. recognized qualification,** un diplôme reconnu sur le plan international.

interne ['ɪntɜːn] *n* = **INTERN¹**.

internecine [ɪntə'niːsaɪn] *adj* (*guerre etc*) de destruction réciproque.

internee [ɪntɜː'niː] *n* interné, -ée.

internist [ɪn'tɜːnɪst] *n esp Am Med* spécialiste *mf* des maladies organiques.

internment [ɪn'tɜːnmənt] *n* internement *m*; **penal i.,** réclusion *f*; **i. camp,** camp *m* d'internement.

internship ['ɪntɜːnʃɪp] *n Am Med* (*position*) internat *m*.

interpersonal [ɪntə'pɜːsən(ə)l] *adj* **i. relationships,** rapports *mpl* de personne à personne.

interplanetary [ɪntə'plænɪt(ə)rɪ] *adj* (*espace etc*) interplanétaire.

interplay ['ɪntəpleɪ] *n* interaction *f*.

Interpol ['ɪntəpɒl] *n* Interpol *m*.

interpolate [ɪn'tɜːpəleɪt] *vt* **(a)** (*insert*) interpoler, intercaler (*un mot, un passage*); **interpolated sheet,** (*in bookbinding*) feuille *f* intercalaire; **(b)** (*change*) altérer (*un texte*) par interpolation.

interpolation [ɪntɜːpə'leɪʃən] *n* interpolation *f*.

interpose [ɪntə'pəʊz] **1** *vt* **(a)** (*place*) interposer (*un objet entre deux autres*); **(b)** (*use*) opposer (*son veto*); **(c) to i. a remark,** faire une observation (*dans une conversation*). **2** *vi* **(a)** (*intervene*) s'interposer, intervenir; **(b)** (*interrupt*) faire une observation.

interpret [ɪn'tɜːprɪt] *vt* **(a)** (*explain*) interpréter (*une loi, un songe etc*); expliquer (*un texte*); interpréter (*un signal etc*); **to i. s.o.'s words as a threat,** interpréter les paroles de qn comme une menace; **(b)** (*translate*) traduire (*un discours etc*); **(c)** *Th Mus* interpréter. **2** *vi* faire l'interprète; **can you i. for me?,** est-ce que vous pouvez me servir d'interprète?

interpretation [ɪntɜːprɪ'teɪʃən] *n* **(a)** interprétation *f* (*d'un texte, d'un songe etc*); **to put a wrong i. on sth,** donner une fausse interprétation à qch; *Can* **i. centre,** (*at historic site etc*) centre *m* d'interprétation; **(b)** (*at conference etc*) traduction orale, interprétation *f*.

interpretative [ɪn'tɜːprɪtətɪv] *adj* interprétatif; *Br* **i. cen-**

tre, (*at historic site etc*) *Can* centre *m* d'interprétation.

interpreter [ɪn'tɜːprɪtər] *n* **(a)** (*person*) interprète *mf*; **to act as i.**, servir d'interprète; **(b)** *Comptr* (*program*) programme interprétatif; (*machine*) traductrice *f*.

interpreting [ɪn'tɜːprɪtɪŋ] *n* (*occupation*) interprétation *f*; **i. assignment,** mission *f* d'interprète.

interracial [ɪntə'reɪʃəl] *adj* (*mariage etc*) entre des races différentes.

interregnum, *pl* **-ums, -a** [ɪntə'regnəm, -əmz, -ə] *n* interrègne *m*.

interrelated [ɪntərɪ'leɪtɪd] *adj* (*faits*) étroitement reliés entre eux, en corrélation.

interrelation [ɪntərɪ'leɪʃən] *n* corrélation *f*.

interrogate [ɪn'terəgeɪt] *vt* interroger, questionner (*qn*); faire subir un interrogatoire à (*un prévenu*); interroger (*une base de données*).

interrogation [ɪnterə'geɪʃən] *n* **(a)** interrogation *f* (*d'un candidat etc*); interrogatoire *m* (*d'un prévenu*); (*of data base*) interrogation *f*; **under i.**, en train de subir un interrogatoire; *Mil* **i. centre,** centre *m* d'interrogation (*des prisonniers de guerre*); **(b)** *Gram* **i. mark,** *Am* **i. point,** point *m* d'interrogation.

interrogative [ɪntə'rɒgətɪv] **1** *adj* **(a)** (*tone, look etc*) interrogateur, -trice; **(b)** *Gram* (*pronoun etc*) interrogatif. **2** *n Gram* (*pronom etc*) interrogatif *m*; (*symbol*) point *m* d'interrogation.

interrogatively [ɪntə'rɒgətɪvlɪ] *adv* interrogativement; d'un air interrogateur.

interrogator [ɪn'terəgeɪtər] *n* (*person*) interrogateur, -trice.

interrogatory [ɪntə'rɒgətrɪ] *adj* (*look etc*) interrogateur, -trice.

interrupt¹ [ɪntə'rʌpt] **1** *vt* **(a)** (*stop*) interrompre (*une action, une conversation etc*); **am I interrupting something?,** est-ce que je vous dérange?; **to i. s.o.,** interrompre qn, couper la parole à qn; **(b)** (*block*) suspendre (*la circulation*); couper (*les communications*); interrompre (*un circuit électrique*); rompre (*la cadence*); interrompre, former obstacle à (*la vue etc*). **2** *vi* couper la parole à qn; **don't interrupt!,** (*when I'm talking*) ne me coupe pas la parole!; (*when s.o. is talking*) ne coupe pas la parole aux gens!; **I'm sorry to i.,** (*intrude*) je suis désolé de vous interrompre.

interrupt² *n Comptr* interruption *f*; **i. function,** fonction *f* d'interruption.

interruption [ɪntə'rʌpʃən] *n* interruption *f*; (*disturbance*) dérangement *m*; **without i.,** (*without being disturbed*) sans interruption; (*without stopping*) sans arrêt; **I want no more interruptions,** (*let me finish speaking*) je ne veux plus qu'on m'interrompe; (*leave me in peace*) je ne veux plus être dérangé.

interscholastic [ɪntəskə'læstɪk] *adj* (*competition etc*) interscolaire, inter-écoles.

intersect [ɪntə'sekt] **1** *vt* entrecouper, intersecter, entrecroiser (**with, by,** de); (*of street*) croiser; **line that intersects another,** ligne qui en coupe une autre; **to i. one another,** (*of lines, surfaces*) se couper, s'intersecter. **2** *vi Math etc* se couper, s'intersecter, se croiser; (*at several points*) s'entrecouper, s'entrecroiser; **streets that i.,** rues qui s'entrecroisent.

intersection [ɪntə'sekʃən] *n* **(a)** *Math* intersection *f* (*de deux plans etc*); (*in surveying*) recoupement *m*, intersection; **(b)** *esp Am* (*of roads*) croisement *m* de chemins; (*junction*) carrefour *m*; **(point of) i.,** point *m* d'intersection *ou* de recoupement.

interspace [ɪntə'speɪs] *vt* espacer (*des caractères etc*).

intersperse [ɪntə'spɜːs] *vt* entremêler (**between, among,** entre; **with,** de); **to i. a speech with quotations,** émailler un discours de citations; **the roses are interspersed with carnations,** les roses sont entremêlées d'œillets.

interstate [ɪntə'steɪt] **1** *adj* (*commerce etc*) entre États (*des Etats-Unis, de l'Australie etc*). **2** *n US* autoroute *f*.

interstellar [ɪntə'stelər] *adj Astron* interstellaire, intersidéral, -aux, interastral, -aux.

interstice [ɪn'tɜːstɪs] *n* interstice *m*.

intertwine [ɪntə'twaɪn] **1** *vt* entrelacer. **2** *vi* s'entrelacer, s'entremêler.

interurban [ɪntər'ɜːbən] *adj* interurbain.

interval ['ɪntəvəl] *n* **(a)** (*time*) intervalle *m*; *Sch* (période *f* de) récréation *f*; *esp Br Th* entracte *m*; *Fb etc* mi-temps *f inv*, pause *f*; **at intervals,** par intervalles; **after an i. of time,** après un laps de temps; **an hour's i. between two lectures,** une heure de battement entre deux conférences; **at five-minute intervals, at intervals of five minutes,** toutes les cinq minutes; **rainy weather with bright intervals,** temps pluvieux avec éclaircies; *Ind etc* **meal i.,** pause *f*; **(b)** (*space*) écart *m*, espace *m*, écartement *m*; **i. between two beams,** écartement de deux poutres; **trees growing at regular intervals along the road,** arbres qui jalonnent la route; **contour i.,** (*on map*) équidistance *f* des courbes; **vertical i.,** distance verticale; **(c)** *Mus* intervalle *m*.

intervene [ɪntə'viːn] *vi* **(a)** (*take action*) intervenir, s'interposer; **to i. in a quarrel,** intervenir dans une querelle; **the government intervened to save the company,** le gouvernement est intervenu pour sauver la société; **(b)** (*of event*) survenir, arriver; **the war intervened,** la guerre est survenue; **(c)** (*in time and space*) **ten years intervened,** dix ans s'écoulèrent.

intervening [ɪntə'viːnɪŋ] *adj* **(a)** (*event*) survenu; **(b)** (*period, distance*) intermédiaire; **during the i. week,** pendant la semaine qui s'écoula.

intervention [ɪntə'venʃən] *n* (*by government, individual etc*) intervention *f*; interposition *f* (*d'un corps*); *Med* **surgical i.,** intervention chirurgicale; *EC* **i. price,** prix *m* d'intervention.

interventionism [ɪntə'venʃənɪz(ə)m] *n* interventionnisme *m*.

interventionist [ɪntə'venʃənɪst] **1** *adj* (*policy etc*) interventionniste. **2** *n* interventionniste *mf*.

interview¹ ['ɪntəvjuː] *n* **(a)** (*for job, place at university etc*) entrevue *f*, entretien *m*; **I've got an i.,** j'ai un entretien, j'ai une entrevue; **a job i., an i. for a job,** un entretien pour un emploi, un entretien pour du travail; **to invite s.o. to an i.,** convoquer qn à un entretien; **(b)** *Journ TV etc* interview *f*; **he rarely gives interviews,** il donne *ou* accorde rarement des interviews.

interview² **1** *vt* **(a)** (*for job, place at university etc*) (*of interviewer*) faire passer un entretien *ou* une entrevue à; **who interviewed you?,** qui t'a fait passer l'entretien?; **to i. candidates for a post,** examiner les candidats à un poste; **she's being interviewed tomorrow,** on la voit demain, elle est convoquée pour un entretien demain; **(b)** *Journ TV etc* interviewer (*qn*). **2** *vi* **(a)** (*of interviewer*) faire passer des entretiens; **he doesn't i. well,** (*of job candidate etc*) il ne donne pas grand-chose quand on l'interviewe; **(b)** *Journ TV* interviewer.

interviewee [ɪntəvjuː'iː] *n Journ TV* interviewé, -ée; (*for job*) candidat *m*, candidate *f*.

interviewer ['ɪntəvjuːər] *n Journ TV etc* interviewer *m*, intervieweur *m*; (*for research, in canvassing*) enquêteur, -euse; **her skills as an i.,** ses qualités pour faire passer les entretiens *ou* pour examiner les candidats.

inter-war ['ɪntə'wɔːr] *adj* **the i.-w. years** *or* **period,** l'entre-deux-guerres *mf*.

interweave [ɪntə'wiːv] *v* (*pt* **interwove** [ɪntə'wəʊv]; *pp* **interwoven** [ɪntə'wəʊvn]) **1** *vt* **(a)** *Tex* tisser ensemble (*des fils d'or et de laine etc*); entrelacer (*des branches*); **material interwoven with gold threads,** tissu broché d'or; **(b)** *Fig* entremêler (*des sentiments etc*); **closely interwoven systems,** systèmes étroitement liés l'un à l'autre. **2** *vi* s'entrelacer, s'entremêler.

intestate [ɪn'testeɪt] **1** *adj* intestat *inv*; **she died i.,** elle est morte intestat; **i. estate** *or* **succession,** succession *f* ab intestat. **2** *n* intestat *mf*.

intestinal [ɪn'testɪn(ə)l] *adj Anat* intestinal, -aux.

intestine [ɪn'testɪn] *n Anat* intestin *m*; **the large i.,** le gros intestin; **the small i.,** l'intestin grêle.

intimacy ['ɪntɪməsɪ] *n* **(a)** intimité *f*; **in the i. of the family,** dans l'intimité de la famille; **(b)** (*intimate remark etc*) familiarité *f*; **(c)** *Fml* (*sexual intercourse*) rapports *mpl* sexuels; **evidence that i. took place,** preuve de relations intimes.

intimate¹ ['ɪntɪmɪt] **1** *adj* (*amitié, ami, restaurant*) intime; **they're very i.,** ils sont très intimes; **a few i. friends,** quelques intimes; **the i. nature of their conversation,** la nature intime de leur conversation; **to be i. with s.o.,** (*know well*) être intime avec qn; *Fml* (*have sexual intercourse*) avoir des relations intimes avec qn; **to have an i. knowledge of sth,** avoir une connaissance approfondie de qch. **2** *n* intime *mf*.

intimate² ['ɪntɪmeɪt] *vt* **(a)** (*suggest, hint at*) donner à entendre, indiquer, suggérer (**sth to s.o.,** qch à qn); **(b)** *Fml* (*make known*) intimer (*un ordre*); signifier (*ses intentions*); **to i. sth to s.o.,** notifier qch à qn.

intimately ['ɪntɪmətlɪ] *adv* intimement; **i. connected,** étroitement lié; **to know s.o. i.,** (*well*) connaître qn intimement.

intimation [ɪntɪ'meɪʃən] *n* **(a)** (*hint*) avis *m* à mots couverts; (*suggestion*) suggestion *f*; **(b)** (*notice*) avis *m* (*de* *décès etc*); **at the first i.,** au premier avis.

intimidate [ɪn'tɪmɪdeɪt] *vt* intimider (*qn*).

intimidating [ɪn'tɪmɪdeɪtɪŋ] *adj* intimidant, intimidateur, -trice.

intimidation [ɪntɪmɪ'deɪʃən] *n* intimidation *f*; *Jur* menaces *fpl*; **guilty of i.,** coupable de menaces.

into ['ɪntʊ, 'ɪntə] *prep* **(a)** (*motion, direction*) dans; **to go i. a house,** entrer dans une maison; **to fall i. the hands of the enemy,** tomber entre les mains de l'ennemi *ou* aux mains de l'ennemi; **the door opens i. the garden,** la porte donne sur le jardin; **to come i. a property,** (*by inheritance*) hériter d'un bien; **to get i. difficulties,** s'attirer des ennuis; **to work far i. the night,** travailler bien tard dans la nuit; **to walk i. a door/s.o.,** rentrer dans une porte/qn; **to cut i. a piece of cheese,** couper dans un morceau de fromage; **to speak i. a microphone,** parler dans un micro; **I'd like to get i. television,** j'aimerais bien rentrer *ou* entrer à la télévision;

(b) (*change, result*) en; **to change sth i. sth,** changer *ou* transformer qch en qch; **to grow i. a man,** devenir un homme; **to divide i. four,** diviser en quatre; **to break sth i. pieces,** briser qch en morceaux; **to burst i. tears,** fondre en larmes; **to go i. a coma,** tomber dans le coma; **they cajoled her i. agreeing,** ils lui ont arraché son accord à force de cajoleries;

(c) *Math* **three i. six goes two,** six divisé par trois fait deux;

(d) *F* **to be i. s.o./sth,** (*like*) bien aimer qn/qch; **he's i. drugs,** (*uses*) il se drogue; **he's really i. her,** il est fou d'elle; **he's really i. jogging,** il est fou de jogging; **I'm not i. wearing ties,** les cravates, ce n'est pas mon truc; **she's i. the green movement,** elle est à fond *ou* elle donne à fond dans le mouvement écolo; **we're i. French cooking,** nous sommes à fond *ou* nous donnons à fond dans la cuisine française; **I'm not i. computers,** l'informatique, ce n'est pas mon truc; **I'm not really i. that sort of thing,** ces choses-là, ce n'est pas mon truc; **I'm not i. computers the way you are,** je ne suis pas aussi amateur d'informatique que toi; **we're not i. cheating people,** (*that's not our style*) ce n'est pas notre truc d'abuser les gens; **if that's what you're i.!,** si c'est ton truc!;

(e) *Am* **he's i. them for $5,000,** il leur doit cinq mille dollars.

intolerable [ɪn'tɒlərəb(ə)l] *adj* intolérable, insupportable.

intolerably [ɪn'tɒlərəblɪ] *adv* insupportablement.

intolerance [ɪn'tɒlərəns] *n* intolérance *f* **(of,** de); *Med* **i. of a drug/foodstuff,** intolérance à un remède/un aliment.

intolerant [ɪn'tɒlərənt] *adj* (*of other people*) intolérant **(of,** de); **to be very i.,** être d'une extrême intolérance; *Med* **to be i. of a drug,** ne pas tolérer *ou* supporter un médicament.

intolerantly [ɪn'tɒlərəntlɪ] *adv* avec intolérance, de façon intolérante.

intonation [ɪntə'neɪʃən] *n* intonation *f*.

intone [ɪn'təʊn] *vt* **(a)** (*speak*) entonner (*qch*); **(b)** *Rel* psalmodier (*des litanies etc*); entonner (*le chant*).

intoxicate [ɪn'tɒksɪkeɪt] *vt* (*make drunk*) enivrer, griser, rendre ivre; *Fig* griser.

intoxicated [ɪn'tɒksɪkeɪtɪd] *adj* (*drunk*) ivre, gris; **to become i.,** s'enivrer **(with,** de); *Fig* **i. with praise,** grisé d'éloges.

intoxicating [ɪn'tɒksɪkeɪtɪŋ] *adj* (*vin, parfum*) enivrant, grisant; **i. liquors,** boissons *fpl* alcooliques; spiritueux *mpl*.

intoxication [ɪntɒksɪ'keɪʃən] *n* **(a)** (*drunkenness*) ivresse *f*; *Fig* griserie *f*; **(b)** *Med* intoxication *f*.

intractability [ɪntræktə'bɪlɪtɪ] *n* indocilité *f* (*d'un enfant, d'un animal*); (*of illness*) opiniâtreté *f*.

intractable [ɪn'træktəb(ə)l] *adj* (*personne*) intraitable; (*enfant, animal*) insoumis, indocile; (*cheval*) rebours; (*maladie*) opiniâtre, intraitable; (*problème*) très difficile.

intramural [ɪntrə'mjʊərəl] *adj esp Am* intra-muros *inv*.

intramuscular [ɪntrə'mʌskjʊlər] *adj* (*injection*) intramusculaire.

intransigence [ɪn'trænsɪdʒəns] *n* intransigeance *f*.

intransigent [ɪn'trænsɪdʒənt] *adj* intransigeant.

intransitive [ɪn'trænsɪtɪv] **1** *adj Gram* (*verbe*) intransitif. **2** *n Gram* intransitif *m*.

intransitively [ɪn'trænsɪtɪvlɪ] *adv* intransitivement.

intrauterine ['ɪntrə'juːtəraɪn] *adj Anat* intra-utérin, *pl* intra-utérins; **i. device,** dispositif intra-utérin.

intravenous [ɪntrə'viːnəs] *adj Med* intraveineux.

intravenously [ɪntrə'viːnəslɪ] *adv Med* par voie intraveineuse.

in-tray ['ɪntreɪ] *n* corbeille *f* du courrier à traiter.

intrepid [ɪn'trepɪd] *adj* intrépide, brave, courageux.

intrepidity [ɪntre'pɪdɪtɪ] *n* intrépidité *f*.

intrepidly [ɪn'trepɪdlɪ] *adv* intrépidement.

intricacy ['ɪntrɪkəsɪ] *n* complexité *f*, nature compliquée (*d'un mécanisme etc*); caractère embrouillé (*d'une affaire*); **the intricacies of the law,** les dédales *mpl* de la loi.

intricate ['ɪntrɪkət] *adj* (*mécanisme*) compliqué; (*question, affaire*) difficile à démêler, compliqué, complexe; (*dessin*) intriqué; (*thoughts, statements*) enchevêtré, embrouillé, confus; **i. details,** détails compliqués.

intricately ['ɪntrɪkətlɪ] *adv* d'une manière compliquée *ou* embrouillée.

intrigue¹ ['ɪntriːg] *n* **(a)** (*plot, plotting*) intrigue *f*, cabale *f*, machination *f*; **(b)** *Th* intrigue *f* (*d'un drame etc*); **comedy of i.,** comédie d'intrigue.

intrigue² [ɪn'triːg] **1** *vt* intriguer (*qn*), éveiller *ou* piquer la curiosité de (*qn*); **I'm greatly intrigued by the idea,** l'idée m'intrigue énormément. **2** *vi* intriguer, mener des intrigues; **to i. against s.o.,** intriguer contre qn.

intriguing [ɪn'triːgɪŋ] *adj* (*paroles*) mystérieux, intrigant; **all this is very i.,** tout cela est très mystérieux; **I find all this very i.,** tout cela m'intrigue beaucoup.

intrinsic [ɪn'trɪnsɪk] *adj* (*vice, valeur*) intrinsèque.

intrinsically [ɪn'trɪnsɪklɪ] *adv* intrinsèquement.

intro ['ɪntrəʊ] *n F* = **INTRODUCTION (b).**

introduce [ɪntrə'djuːs] *vt* **(a)** (*present*) présenter (*qn*) **(to s.o.,** à qn); **to i. oneself,** se présenter; **who is going to i. us?,** qui est-ce qui va faire les présentations?; **I don't think we've been introduced,** je ne crois pas que nous ayons été présentés; **we've introduced ourselves,** nous nous sommes déjà présentés; **to be introduced to society,** (*of débutante*) faire son entrée dans le monde;

(b) (*initiate*) **to i. s.o. to sth,** faire connaître qch à qn; **he introduced me to Greek,** il m'a initié au grec; **they introduced me to drugs/Rabelais,** ils m'ont fait connaître la drogue/Rabelais;

(c) (*bring, put into etc*) introduire, faire entrer (*une clef dans une serrure*); **to i. a subject,** mettre une question sur le tapis; **to i. s.o. into s.o.'s presence,** introduire qn auprès de qn;

(d) (*have adopted*) établir, faire adopter (*une loi, un usage*); **this fashion was introduced in the fifteenth century,** cette mode a été introduite au quinzième siècle; **the management have introduced new machinery,** la direction a introduit de nouvelles machines;

(e) *Parl* **to i. a bill,** déposer un projet de loi;

(f) *Gram* (*of conjunction, adverb*) commencer (*une phrase*);

(g) *Com* lancer (*une marchandise*); *St Exch* introduire (*des actions*).

introduction [ɪntrə'dʌkʃən] *n* **(a)** (*presentation*) présentation *f* **(of s.o. to s.o.,** de qn à qn); **to make the introductions,** faire les présentations; **letter of i.,** (lettre *f* d')introduction *f*, (lettre de) recommandation *f*;

(b) (*of book*) avant-propos *m inv*, introduction *f* (*d'un livre*); *Mus* introduction;

(c) (*book for beginners*) manuel *m* élémentaire **(to,** de); introduction **(to,** à);

(d) (*act of initiation*) introduction *f* (*dans le monde*); premier contact (*avec qch*); **this was my i. to Shakespeare,** ça a été mon premier contact avec Shakespeare; **this record would be a good i. to her work,** ce disque constituerait une bonne introduction à son œuvre;

(e) (*act of bringing, putting in*) introduction *f* **(of sth into sth,** de qch dans qch);

(f) (*of custom etc*) introduction *f*; **the sport is a recent i. from the United States,** le sport est récemment arrivé des États-Unis;

(g) *Parl* (*of bill*) introduction *f*.

introductory [ɪntrə'dʌktərɪ] *adj* (qui sert) d'introduction; (*page, épître*) liminaire; **after a few i. words,** après quelques mots d'introduction; *Com* **i. price,** prix *m* de lancement.

introit ['ɪntrɔɪt] *n Rel* introït *m*.

introspection [ɪntrə'spekʃən] *n* introspection *f*.

introspective [ɪntrə'spektɪv] *adj* introspectif.

introversion [ɪntrə'vɜːʃən] *n Psy* introversion *f*.

introvert ['ɪntrəvɜːt] *n* introverti, -ie.

introverted [ɪntrə'vɜːtɪd] *adj* (*esprit*) recueilli; *Psy* introverti.

intrude [ɪn'truːd] *vi* faire intrusion **(on s.o.,** auprès de qn); **I hope I am not intruding,** j'espère que je ne vous dérange pas *ou* que je ne suis pas importun; **to i. on s.o.'s privacy,** s'ingérer dans la vie privée de qn.

intruder [ɪn'truːdər] *n* **(a)** (*on other people*) intrus, -use, importun, -une; (*burglar*) intrus; **she felt like an i.,** elle se sentait de trop; **(b)** *Mil Av* chasseur *m* de pénétration.

intrusion [ɪn'truːʒən] *n* intrusion *f* ; **to make an i. upon s.o.,** faire (une) intrusion auprès de qn; **I hope I am not guilty of an i.,** j'espère que je ne suis pas indiscret *ou* que je ne dérange pas.

intrusive [ɪn'truːsɪv] *adj* (*person*) importun, indiscret; *Ling etc* intrusif.

intuition [ɪntjʊ'ɪʃən] *n* intuition *f*.

intuitive [ɪn'tjuːɪtɪv] *adj* intuitif.

intuitively [ɪn'tjuːɪtɪvlɪ] *adv* intuitivement, par intuition.

Inuit ['ɪnjuːɪt] **1** *n* Inuit *m inv*. **2** *adj* inuit *inv*.

inundate ['ɪnʌndeɪt] *vt* inonder (**with,** de); *Fig* **to be inundated with letters,** être submergé de lettres; **to be inundated with phone calls,** recevoir une quantité énorme de coups de téléphone.

inundation [ɪnʌn'deɪʃən] *n* inondation *f*.

inure [ɪ'njʊər] *vt* habituer, endurcir, aguerrir (**to,** à).

inured [ɪ'njʊərd] *adj* **i. to hardships,** habitué aux privations.

invade [ɪn'veɪd] **1** *vt* **(a)** envahir, faire une invasion dans (*un pays etc*); **to i. s.o.'s privacy,** violer la retraite de qn; **(b)** (*encroach*) empiéter sur (*les droits de qn*); porter atteinte à (*un privilège*). **2** *vi* faire invasion.

invader [ɪn'veɪdər] *n* envahisseur *m*.

invading [ɪn'veɪdɪŋ] *adj* envahissant; (*armée*) d'invasion.

invalid¹ [ɪn'vælɪd] *adj* (*argument, ticket*) non valable; *Jur* (*marriage*) invalide, non valide; (*clause*) non valable; (*decision*) nul et non avenu; **your position is morally i.,** d'un point de vue moral votre position ne tient pas.

invalid² ['ɪnvəlɪd] **1** *n* **(a)** (*ill person*) malade *mf*; (*disabled person*) invalide *mf*, infirme *mf*; **i. car,** voiture *f* d'infirme; **i. chair,** fauteuil roulant; **(b)** *Mil etc* (*disabled person*) invalide *mf*. **2** *adj* (*ill*) malade; (*disabled*) invalide, infirme; **she has an i. sister,** (*disabled*) elle a une sœur infirme; *Old-fashioned* (*having poor health*) elle a une sœur d'une santé délicate.

►**invalid out** *vtsep esp Br Mil* **to i. a man out of the army,** réformer un homme.

invalidate [ɪn'vælɪdeɪt] *vt* **(a)** invalider (*une théorie, une thèse etc*); **(b)** *Jur* invalider, rendre nul (*un testament*); vicier (*un acte, un contrat*); casser, infirmer (*un jugement*).

invalidation [ɪnvælɪ'deɪʃən] *n* **(a)** (*of theory etc*) invalidation *f*; **(b)** *Jur* invalidation *f* (*d'un document, d'un contrat*); infirmation *f*, cassation *f* (*d'un jugement*).

invalidity [ɪnvə'lɪdɪtɪ] *n* **(a)** (*disability*) invalidité *f*; **i. pension,** pension *f* d'invalidité; **(b)** (*of passport, contract etc*) invalidité *f*; (*of argument*) nullité *f*.

invaluable [ɪn'væljʊəb(ə)l] *adj* inestimable, très précieux, sans prix; (*trésor*) sans prix; **it's i.,** cela n'a pas de prix, c'est inestimable; **her help was i.,** son aide a été très précieuse.

invariable [ɪn'veərɪəb(ə)l] *adj* invariable; *Gram* **i. particle,** particule *f* invariable.

invariably [ɪn'veərɪəblɪ] *adv* invariablement, immanquablement; **he would i. arrive late,** il arrivait immanquablement en retard.

invasion [ɪn'veɪʒən] *n* **(a)** (*by army*) invasion *f*, envahissement *m*; (*intrusion*) invasion *f*; *Fig* **the annual i. by tourists,** l'invasion annuelle des touristes; **these invasions of my privacy,** ces intrusions *fpl* dans mon intimité; **(b) i. of s.o.'s rights,** violation *f* des droits *ou* empiétement *m* sur les droits de qn.

invective [ɪn'vektɪv] *n* invective *f*; **a torrent of invective(s),** un flot d'invectives *ou* d'injures *fpl*.

inveigh [ɪn'veɪ] *vi* invectiver (**against,** contre).

inveigle [ɪn'veɪg(ə)l, -'viː-] *vt* attirer, séduire, leurrer, enjôler (*qn*); **to i. s.o. into doing sth,** entraîner *ou* amener qn à faire qch.

invent [ɪn'vent] *vt* inventer (*une machine, une histoire etc*); *Fig* **he invented a movie-star mother,** il s'est inventé une mère star de cinéma; **recently invented,** récemment inventé, d'invention récente.

invention [ɪn'venʃən] *n* **(a)** (*something invented*) invention *f*; (*lie*) invention, mensonge *m*; **this is pure i.,** c'est une pure invention; **(b)** (*ability to invent*) capacité *f* à inventer, esprit inventif; **(c)** (*act of inventing*) invention *f* (*d'une machine etc*); **a story of his own i.,** une histoire de son cru; **(d)** *Mus* invention *f*.

inventive [ɪn'ventɪv] *adj* (*esprit*) inventif.

inventiveness [ɪn'ventɪvnɪs] *n* esprit inventif *ou* d'invention; don *m* d'invention.

inventor [ɪn'ventər] *n* inventeur, -trice.

inventory¹ ['ɪnvənt(ə)rɪ] *n* **(a)** *Com* inventaire *m*; **to draw up** *or* **take an i.,** dresser *ou* faire un inventaire; **i. management,** gestion *f* de l'inventaire; **(b)** *esp US* (*stock*) stock(s) *m(pl)*; (*list*) (établissement *m ou* levée *f* d')inventaire *m*.

inventory² *vt* inventorier (*les biens de qn*), dresser l'inventaire de (*les biens de qn*).

inverse [ɪn'vɜːs] **1** *adj* inverse; (*corrélation*) négatif; **in i. order,** en sens inverse; *Math* **i. function,** fonction *f* inverse; **in i. ratio/proportion,** en raison/proportion inverse (**to,** de). **2** *n* inverse *m*, contraire *m* (**of,** de).

inversely [ɪn'vɜːslɪ] *adv* inversement.

inversion [ɪn'vɜːʃən] *n* **(a)** renversement *m* (*d'une image, de l'utérus etc*); *Mus* **i. of a chord,** (*action*) renversement d'un accord; (*result*) accord dérivé; **(b)** inversion *f* (*des mots d'une phrase, Math d'une intégrale etc*); **(c)** *Ch* inversion *f* (*du sucre etc*); **(d)** *Psy* **sexual i.,** inversion sexuelle.

invert¹ ['ɪnvɜːt] **1** *adj* (*sucre*) inverti. **2** *n Psy* inverti, -ie.

invert² [ɪn'vɜːt] *vt* **(a)** (*turn upside down*) renverser, retourner (*un objet*) (le haut en bas); *Mus* renverser (*un accord*); **(b)** (*reverse*) invertir, intervertir, renverser (*l'ordre, les positions*); *Gram* inverser (*le sujet etc*); **(c)** *Ch* invertir (*le sucre*); **(d)** (*turn inside out*) retourner, mettre à l'envers.

invertebrate [ɪn'vɜːtɪbrɪt] *adj & n Zool* invertébré *m*.

inverted [ɪn'vɜːtɪd] *adj* **(a)** (*upside down*) inversé; **i. commas,** guillemets *mpl*; **i. snobbery,** snobisme *m* à l'envers; **i. snob,** personne qui fait preuve de snobisme à l'envers; *Mus* (*accord*) renversé; **(b)** (*reversed*) renversé; *Opt* (*image*) renversé; (*ordre, siphon*) inverse; *Sewing* **i. pleat,** pli inverti *ou* creux; **(c)** *Psy* (*instinct*) inverti.

invest [ɪn'vest] **1** *vt* **(a)** *Fin* placer, investir (*son argent, des fonds*); *Fig* investir (*du temps etc*); **to i. one's money in real estate,** faire des placements dans l'immobilier; **capital invested,** mise *f* de fonds, capital engagé *ou* investi; **(b)** (*give*) investir (*qn*) (*de l'autorité etc*); **to i. s.o. with an office,** investir qn d'une fonction; **(c)** *Lit* (*provide*) revêtir (**with,** de); **to i. a subject with interest,** rendre un sujet intéressant; **(d)** *Mil* investir, cerner (*une place forte*). **2** *vi* investir, faire des placements, placer son argent; **to i. in property,** faire des placements dans l'immobilier; **we're going to i. in three new machines,** nous allons investir dans trois nouvelles machines; *F* **to i. in a new refrigerator,** acheter *ou* se payer un nouveau réfrigérateur.

investigate [ɪn'vestɪgeɪt] **1** *vt* examiner, étudier, sonder, remuer (*une question*); faire une enquête sur, enquêter sur (*un crime*). **2** *vi F* **I'll go and i.,** j'irai voir ce qui se passe.

investigating [ɪn'vestɪgeɪtɪŋ] **1** *n* investigation *f*, recherches *fpl*. **2** *adj* **i. committee,** commission *f* d'enquête; **i. officer,** officier *m* responsable de l'enquête.

investigation [ɪnvestɪ'geɪʃən] *n* investigation *f*; (*by police, tax authority etc*) enquête *f* (**of,** sur); *Jur* instruction *f* (*d'un crime etc*); (*scientific, medical*) recherche *f*; **to conduct** *or* **carry out an i.,** conduire *ou* effectuer une enquête; **question under i.,** question à l'étude; **on further i.,** en poursuivant les recherches; **the police made investigations,** la police a procédé à une enquête.

investigator [ɪn'vestɪgeɪtər] *n* investigateur, -trice; enquêteur, -euse; chercheur, -euse; **private i.,** détective privé.

investiture [ɪn'vestɪtʃər] *n* **(a)** (*installation in office*) investiture *f* (*d'un évêque etc*); **(b)** (*award of decoration*) remise *f* de décorations.

investment [ɪn'vestmənt] *n* **(a)** *Fin* placement *m*, investissement *m*; (*money invested*) investissement, mise *f* de fonds; **good** *or* **safe i.,** placement sûr; **long/short-term i.,** placement à long/court terme; **i. analyst,** analyste *mf* en placements; **i. company,** société *f* de portefeuille *ou* d'investissement; **i. income,** revenu *m* provenant d'investissements; **i. management,** gestion *f* de portefeuille; **(b)** *Mil* investissement *m*, cernement *m* (*d'une place forte*).

investor [ɪn'vestər] *n* actionnaire *mf*, investisseur *m*.

inveterate [ɪn'vetərɪt] *adj* (*ivrogne, joueur*) invétéré; (*fumeur*) acharné, enragé; (*ennemi*) implacable; (*mal, défaut*) invétéré, enraciné.

invidious [ɪn'vɪdɪəs] *adj* **(a)** (*unpleasant*) haïssable, odieux; (*tâche*) ingrat, peu agréable; **to be in an i. position,** être dans une position peu enviable; **(b)** (*comparison*) désobligeant.

invigilate [ɪn'vɪdʒɪleɪt] *Sch Univ* **1** *vi* surveiller les candidats (*à un examen*). **2** *vt* surveiller (*un examen*).

invigilator [ɪn'vɪdʒɪleɪtər] *n Sch Univ* surveillant, -ante (*des candidats à un examen*).

invigorate [ɪn'vɪgəreɪt] *vt* (*of food*) fortifier (*qn*), donner de la vigueur à (*qn*); (*of the air etc*) vivifier, tonifier.

invigorating [ɪn'vɪgəreɪtɪŋ] *adj* (*aliment etc*) fortifiant;

(*air etc*) vivifiant, tonifiant.
invincibility [ɪnvɪnsɪ'bɪlɪtɪ] *n* invincibilité *f*.
invincible [ɪn'vɪnsɪb(ə)l] *adj* invincible.
inviolability [ɪnvaɪələ'bɪlɪtɪ] *n* inviolabilité *f*.
inviolable [ɪn'vaɪələb(ə)l] *adj* inviolable.
inviolably [ɪn'vaɪələblɪ] *adv* inviolablement.
inviolate [ɪn'vaɪəlɪt] *adj* inviolé.
invisibility [ɪnvɪzɪ'bɪlɪtɪ] *n* invisibilité *f*.
invisible [ɪn'vɪzɪb(ə)l] *adj* invisible; **i. to the naked eye,** invisible *ou* indiscernable à l'œil nu; *Econ* **i. earnings,** gains invisibles; **i. mending,** stoppage *m*; **i. ink,** encre *f* sympathique.
invisibly [ɪn'vɪzɪblɪ] *adv* invisiblement; **to mend i.,** stopper (*un trou, un vêtement*).
invitation [ɪnvɪ'teɪʃən] *n* invitation *f* (**to do sth,** à faire qch); **at s.o.'s i.,** sur l'invitation de qn; **i. to lunch,** invitation à déjeuner; *Fig* **speech that is an i. to criticism,** discours qui provoque la critique; **i. card,** carte *f* d'invitation.
invite¹ [ɪn'vaɪt] *vt* **(a)** (*ask*) inviter (*qn*) (**to,** à); convier (*des amis à dîner*); **we weren't invited,** nous n'avons pas été invités; **to i. s.o. in,** inviter qn à entrer; **to i. oneself,** s'inviter soi-même; **the invited guests,** les invités *mpl*; (*at table*) les convives *mpl*; **(b)** (*request*) engager, convier, inviter, appeler (**s.o. to do sth,** qn à faire qch); **she invited me to comment,** elle m'a invité à faire des commentaires; **applications are invited for the position,** des candidatures pour le poste sont attendues; **(c)** (*arouse*) provoquer (*le danger, la critique*); **to i. trouble,** se préparer des ennuis.
invite² ['ɪnvaɪt] *n F* invitation *f*.
►**invite back, invite in, invite round** *etc* = **ASK BACK, ASK IN, ASK ROUND** *etc*.
inviting [ɪn'vaɪtɪŋ] *adj* invitant, attrayant; (*mets*) appétissant; **her eyes were dark and i.,** ses yeux étaient sombres et attirants; **not very i.,** peu invitant, peu attrayant; **the water looks i.,** l'eau a l'air bonne.
invitingly [ɪn'vaɪtɪŋlɪ] *adv* d'une manière attrayante *ou* tentante.
in vitro ['ɪn'viːtrəʊ] *adj* **in v. fertilization,** fertilisation *f* in vitro.
invocation [ɪnvə'keɪʃən] *n* invocation *f*.
invoice¹ ['ɪnvɔɪs] *n Com* facture *f* (*de débit*); note *f* (*de frais*); **to make out an i.,** établir une facture; **as per i.,** suivant la facture; **i. clerk,** facturier, -ière.
invoice² *vt* facturer (*des marchandises*); envoyer la facture à (*qn*); **to i. s.o. for sth,** facturer qch à qn.
invoicing ['ɪnvɔɪsɪŋ] *n* facturation *f* (*de marchandises etc*).
invoke [ɪn'vəʊk] *vt* **(a)** invoquer (*Dieu, la mémoire de qn, une loi etc*); **to i. s.o.'s aid,** appeler qn à son secours; **to i. a blessing on an undertaking,** demander à Dieu de bénir une entreprise; **(b)** (*summon up*) évoquer (*un esprit*).
involuntarily [ɪn'vɒlənt(ə)rɪlɪ] *adv* involontairement.
involuntary [ɪn'vɒləntərɪ] *adj* involontaire.
involve [ɪn'vɒlv] *vt* **(a)** (*in crime, scandal etc*) impliquer (*qn*) (**in,** dans); (*in quarrel*) mêler (*qn*) (**in,** dans); **he is involved in the plot,** il est compromis dans le complot; **about 20 people were involved in the affair,** environ 20 personnes ont été impliquées dans l'affaire; **to become involved in charitable work,** participer à des œuvres de bienfaisance; **he's getting involved with the school orchestra,** il commence à prendre part aux activités de l'orchestre de l'école; **I'm getting really involved in this job,** je commence vraiment à rentrer dans ce travail; **the novel doesn't really i. the reader,** le lecteur ne se sent pas impliqué dans ce roman; **they didn't want to get involved in another war,** ils ne voulaient pas rentrer dans une autre guerre; **the police became involved,** la police s'en est mêlée, la police est intervenue; **no one wanted to get involved,** personne n'a voulu s'en mêler; **he doesn't want to get involved,** (*emotionally*) il ne veut pas s'attacher; **I am too emotionally involved,** cela me concerne de trop près *ou* me touche trop; **he got involved with his friend's wife,** il a eu une liaison avec la femme de son ami;
(b) (*include, entail etc*) impliquer, entraîner; **it will i. a lot of extra work,** cela impliquera *ou* entraînera beaucoup de travail supplémentaire; **my job involves a lot of travel,** je dois beaucoup voyager dans mon travail; **if it involves learning new techniques ...,** si ça implique *ou* entraîne l'apprentissage de nouvelles techniques ...; **what exactly is involved in carrying out a project like this?,** qu'est-ce que ça implique exactement la réalisation d'un tel projet?; **it involves getting to London by 5.30 in the morning,** ça veut dire qu'il faut arriver à Londres à 5h 30 le matin; **all it involves is sitting by the phone,** tout ce qu'il y a à faire, c'est d'être assis à côté du téléphone;
(c) (*have to do with*) concerner; **this discussion doesn't i. you,** cette discussion ne vous concerne pas; **there's been a theft — how much money is involved?,** il y a eu un vol — de combien d'argent s'agit-il?; **he's involved in high finance/language teaching/*etc*,** il est dans la haute finance/l'enseignement des langues/etc; **when I first became involved with teaching,** quand j'ai commencé à enseigner;
(d) *Lit* (*wrap*) envelopper, entortiller (**in,** dans);
(e) (*complicate*) compliquer (*un récit*).
involved [ɪn'vɒlvd] *adj* (*complicated*) (*style, discours*) embrouillé, entortillé, compliqué.
involvement [ɪn'vɒlvmənt] *n* **(a)** (*participation*) participation *f* (**in,** à); implication *f*, *Pej* empêtrement *m* (*de qn dans une affaire*); **her i. with this man,** (*romantic*) sa liaison avec cet homme; **our country's i. in this war,** la participation de notre pays à cette guerre; **(b)** (*confusion*) confusion *f*, imbroglio *m*.
invulnerability [ɪnvʌlnərə'bɪlɪtɪ] *n* invulnérabilité *f*.
invulnerable [ɪn'vʌlnərəb(ə)l] *adj* (*person*) invulnérable; (*position etc*) inattaquable, invincible.
inward ['ɪnwəd] **1** *adj* **(a)** (*internal*) intérieur; **(b)** (*directed to the inside*) (orienté *ou* se dirigeant) vers l'intérieur; **i. traffic of a port,** trafic *m* d'entrée (d'un port); **i. payment,** (*in bookkeeping*) paiement reçu; **i. investment,** investissements étrangers. **2** *adv* = **INWARDS**; **i. opening door,** porte qui s'ouvre vers l'intérieur.
inward-looking ['ɪnwədlʊkɪŋ] *adj* introspectif.
inwardly ['ɪnwədlɪ] *adv* en dedans, intérieurement; **I was i. pleased,** dans mon for intérieur j'étais content.
inwards ['ɪnwədz] *adv* vers l'intérieur; *Com Nau* pour l'importation; **the window opens i.,** la fenêtre s'ouvre vers l'intérieur.
I/O ['aɪ'əʊ] *n Comptr abbr* **input/output**.
iodine ['aɪədiːn] *n Ch* iode *m*; *Pharm* **(tincture of) i.,** teinture *f* d'iode.
iodize ['aɪədaɪz] *vt Med Phot* ioder.
iodoform [aɪ'ɒdəfɔːm] *n Ch Pharm* iodoforme *m*.
ion ['aɪən] *n Phys Ch El* ion *m*; **hydrogen i.,** ion d'hydrogène; **i. beam,** faisceau *m* ionique.
Ionic¹ [aɪ'ɒnɪk] *adj* (*in poetry*) *& Arch* (*ordre, vers*) ionique; *Ling Mus* (*dialecte, mode*) ionien.
ionic² *adj Phys Ch El* ionique.
ionization [aɪənaɪ'zeɪʃən] *n* **(a)** *Phys El* ionisation *f*; **(b)** *Med* (traitement *m* par) ionisation *f*.
ionize ['aɪənaɪz] *Phys El* **1** *vt* ioniser (*l'air, un gaz*). **2** *vi* (*of acid etc*) s'ioniser.
ionosphere [aɪ'ɒnəsfɪər] *n* ionosphère *f*.
iota [aɪ'əʊtə] *n* **(a)** (*in Greek alphabet*) iota *m*; **(b)** (*tiny amount*) iota *m*; **she hadn't changed an i.,** elle n'avait pas changé d'un iota; **not one i.,** pas un iota; **not an i. of truth,** pas un brin de vérité.
IOU, *pl* **IOUs** [aɪəʊ'juː, -'juːz] *n* (= **I owe you**) reconnaissance *f* (de dette); **I'll give you an IOU,** je vais vous faire un billet.
IPA [aɪpiː'eɪ] *n abbr* **International Phonetic Alphabet**.
ipso facto ['ɪpsəʊ'fæktəʊ] *adv* ipso facto.
IQ ['aɪ'kjuː] *n* (*abbr* **intelligence quotient**) QI *m*; **to have an I.Q. of ...,** avoir un QI de ... .
IRA [aɪɑː'reɪ] *n* (*abbr* **Irish Republican Army**) IRA *f*.
Iran [ɪ'rɑːn] *n* Iran *m*.
Iranian [ɪ'reɪnɪən] **1** *adj* iranien. **2** *n* **(a)** Iranien, -ienne; **(b)** *Ling* iranien *m*.
Iraq [ɪ'rɑːk] *n* Irak *m*.
Iraqi [ɪ'rɑːkɪ] **1** *adj* irakien, iraquien. **2** *n* **(a)** Irakien, -ienne, Iraquien, -ienne; **(b)** *Ling* irakien *m*, iraquien *m*.
irascibility [ɪræsɪ'bɪlɪtɪ] *n* irascibilité *f*.
irascible [ɪ'ræsɪb(ə)l] *adj* (*personne*) irascible, coléreux; (*tempérament*) colérique.
irascibly [ɪ'ræsɪblɪ] *adv* irasciblement.
irate [aɪ'reɪt] *adj* (*person*) courroucé, en colère, furieux, irrité; **an i. telephone call,** un coup de téléphone d'une personne en colère.
ire ['aɪər] *n Arch & Lit* courroux *m*, colère *f*.
Ireland ['aɪələnd] *n* Irlande *f*; **Northern I.,** l'Irlande du Nord; **the Republic of I.,** la République d'Irlande.
iridescence [ɪrɪ'desəns] *n* irisation *f*, chatoiement *m* (*d'un plumage, d'un tissu etc*).
iridescent [ɪrɪ'desənt] *adj* irisé, iridescent, chatoyant.
iris ['aɪrɪs] *n* **(a)** (*pl* **irides** ['aɪrɪdiːz]) *Anat* iris *m* (de l'œil); **(b)** (*pl* **irises** ['aɪrɪsɪz]) (*flower*) iris *m*; **yellow i.,** iris jaune *ou* des marais; **(c)** *Myth* **Iris,** Iris *f*.
Irish ['aɪərɪʃ] **1** *adj* (*peuple etc*) irlandais; (*beurre etc*)

d'Irlande; **I. American,** Américain, -aine d'origine irlandaise; **I. coffee,** = café noir au whiskey irlandais couronné de crème fraîche; *Geog* **I. Sea,** mer *f* d'Irlande; **I. setter,** setter irlandais; *Culin* **I. stew,** ragoût à l'irlandaise. **2** *n* **(a)** *Ling* irlandais *m*; **(b) the I.,** (*used as pl*) les Irlandais *mpl.*

Irishman, *pl* **-men** ['aɪərɪʃmən] *n* Irlandais *m*.

Irishwoman, *pl* **-women** ['aɪərɪʃwʊmən, -wɪmɪn] *n* Irlandaise *f*.

irk [ɜːk] *vt* ennuyer, contrarier (*qn*).

irksome ['ɜːksəm] *adj* (*travail*) ennuyeux, ingrat.

iron¹ ['aɪən] *n* **(a)** (*metal*) fer *m*; **old i.,** ferraille *f*; **(made of) i.,** de *ou* en fer; **he has an i. constitution,** il a une santé de fer; **man of i.,** homme dur *ou* sans pitié; **will of i., i. will,** volonté *f* de fer; *Metal* **cast i.,** (fer de) fonte *f*; **crude i.,** fer cru *ou* brut; **wrought i.,** fer forgé; **(sheet) i.,** tôle *f*; **corrugated i.,** tôle ondulée; *Hist* **the I. Age,** l'âge de fer; **i. bar,** barre *f* de fer; **i. bridge,** pont *m* en fer; *Hist* **the I. Curtain,** le rideau de fer; *Fig* **i. discipline,** discipline *f* de fer; **i. filings,** limaille *f* de fer; **an i. fist** *or* **hand in a velvet glove,** une main de fer dans un gant de velours; *Metal* **i. foundry,** fonderie *f* de fonte; **i. grey,** gris *m* fer; **the i. horse,** = la locomotive; **the i. and steel industry,** l'industrie *f* sidérurgique, la sidérurgie; **the I. Lady,** la Dame de Fer; *Med* **i. lung,** poumon *m* d'acier; *Miner Ch* **i. ore,** minerai *m* de fer.

(b) *Med* fer *m*; **i. deficiency,** manque *m* de fer;

(c) (*device, implement*) fer *m* à repasser; **electric i.,** fer électrique; *Arch* **curling i.,** (*for hair*) fer à friser; *Fig* **to have several irons in the fire,** avoir plusieurs cordes à son arc; *Fig* **to have too many irons in the fire,** courir trop de lièvres à la fois; *Carp* **plane i.,** fer *ou* couteau *m* de rabot; *Horseriding* **(stirrup) i.,** étrier *m*;

(d) *Golf* (crosse *f* en) fer *m*; **i. shot,** coup *m* de fer;

(e) *Constr* poutre *f* de fer;

(f) (*for prisoner*) **irons,** fers *mpl*, chaînes *fpl*;

(g) *Med* **irons,** attelles *fpl*;

(h) *Sl* (*handgun*) revolver *m*, pistolet *m*.

iron² *vt* **(a)** repasser (*le linge*); donner un coup de fer à (*un col*); **(b)** garnir (*une porte etc*) de fer, ferrer (*une porte etc*).

►iron out *vtsep* faire disparaître (*un faux pli*) au fer (chaud); *Fig* (*resolve*) résoudre (*un problème*); **to i. out the difficulties,** aplanir les difficultés; **have you ironed out your differences?,** est-ce que vous avez résolu vos différends?

ironclad ['aɪənklæd] **1** *adj* **(a)** à enveloppe de fer; (*vaisseau*) cuirassé; (*puits*) blindé; **(b)** *Fig* (*serment, contrat etc*) strict; (*règlement*) rigoureux. **2** *n Nau Hist* cuirassé *m*.

iron-grey ['aɪən'greɪ] *adj* gris (de) fer.

ironic(al) [aɪ'rɒnɪk, -ɪk(ə)l] *adj* ironique.

ironically [aɪ'rɒnɪklɪ] *adv* ironiquement; (*parler*) avec ironie.

ironing ['aɪənɪŋ] *n* repassage *m*; **I've got a lot of i. to do,** j'ai beaucoup de repassage à faire; **i. board,** planche *f ou* table *f* à repasser.

ironmonger ['aɪənmʌŋgər] *n Br* quincaillier *m*; **i.'s (shop),** quincaillerie *f*.

ironmongery ['aɪənmʌŋgərɪ] *n Br* **(a)** (*goods*) quincaillerie *f*; **(b)** (*shop*) quincaillerie *f*.

ironstone ['aɪənstəʊn] *n* **(clay) i.,** minerai *m* de fer (argileux).

ironware ['aɪənweər] *n* ferronnerie *f*.

ironwork ['aɪənwɜːk] *n* **(a)** (*work in wrought iron*) (travail *m* de) ferronnerie *f*; (*parts made of iron*) ferrure(s) *f(pl)*; ferrements *mpl* (*d'un navire, d'un wagon*); dentelle *f* (*d'une balustrade etc*); **heavy i.,** charpente *f* en fer, grosse serrurerie; **(b)** (*often with sing verb*) **ironworks** (*for smelting*) fonderie *f* de fonte; (*for casting*) usine *f* sidérurgique, forges *fpl*.

irony ['aɪrənɪ] *n* ironie *f*; **the i. is that ...,** l'ironie c'est que ...; **i. of fate,** ironie du sort.

irradiate [ɪ'reɪdɪeɪt] **1** *vt* **(a)** (*of light, heat*) irradier (*la terre etc*); (*of light, rays*) illuminer (*une surface*); **(b)** (*subject to radiation*) irradier (*une substance etc*); *Med* traiter (*un malade*) par irradiation; **irradiated food,** aliments irradiés; **(c)** (*emit*) émettre comme des rayons; **presence that irradiates strength and courage,** présence d'où irradient la force et le courage; **(d)** (*of good humour etc*) faire rayonner (*le visage etc*). **2** *vi* irradier.

irradiation [ɪreɪdɪ'eɪʃən] *n* **(a)** *Phys Opt Physiol* irradiation *f*; (*of a surface*) illumination *f*; **(b)** *Nucl Phys* irradiation *f*; *Med* (traitement *m* par) irradiation, radiothérapie *f*; **(c)** rayonnement *m*, éclat *m* (*d'une source de lumière*).

irrational [ɪ'ræʃən(ə)l] *adj* (*animal etc*) dépourvu de raison, irraisonnable; (*fear, conduct etc*) déraisonnable, absurde, irrationnel; *Math* (*nombre*) irrationnel; **don't be so i.!,** soyez un peu plus rationnel!

irrationally [ɪ'ræʃən(ə)lɪ] *adv* (*to behave*) déraisonnablement, irrationnellement.

irreconcilable [ɪrekən'saɪləb(ə)l] *adj* **(a)** (*ennemi*) irréconciliable; (*haine*) implacable; **(b)** (*croyance, idée*) incompatible, inconciliable (**with,** avec).

irrecoverable [ɪrɪ'kʌvərəb(ə)l] *adj* (*créance*) irrécouvrable; (*perte*) irréparable, irrémédiable.

irredeemable [ɪrɪ'diːməb(ə)l] *adj* **(a)** (*faute*) irrachetable; *Fin* (*fonds*) irrachetable, irréalisable, irremboursable; *Fin* (*papier*) non convertible; **(b)** (*désastre etc*) irrémédiable; (*escroc*) incorrigible.

irreducible [ɪrɪ'djuːsɪb(ə)l] *adj* irréductible.

irrefutable [ɪrɪ'fjuːtəb(ə)l] *adj* (*témoignage, déclaration*) irréfutable; (*témoignage*) irrécusable.

irregular [ɪ'regjʊlər] **1** *adj* **(a)** (*not conforming to rule*) irrégulier, contraire aux règles; (*behaviour*) irrégulier; (*life*) déréglé; *Jur* (*document*) informe; *Gram* (*pluriel, verbe*) irrégulier; **(b)** (*uneven*) asymétrique; (*outline etc*) irrégulier; (*surface*) inégal, -aux; (*forme*) irrégulier; **i. features,** traits irréguliers; **(c)** (*pulse*) irrégulier, déréglé, inégal; (*respiration*) saccadé; **(d)** *Mil* **i. troops,** troupes irrégulières, irréguliers *mpl*. **2** *n* (*usu pl*) *Mil* **irregulars,** troupes irrégulières, irréguliers *mpl*.

irregularity [ɪregjʊ'lærɪtɪ] *n* **(a)** irrégularité *f* (*de conduite etc*); *Admin etc* **to commit irregularities,** commettre des irrégularités (*dans les comptes etc*); **(b)** irrégularité *f* (*des traits*); **irregularities,** accidents *mpl* (*du terrain*).

irregularly [ɪ'regjʊləlɪ] *adv* irrégulièrement.

irrelevance [ɪ'reləvəns], **irrelevancy** [ɪ'reləvənsɪ] *n* **(a)** (*state of being inapplicable*) inapplicabilité *f* (**to,** à); **(b)** (*inappropriateness*) manque *m* d'à-propos; **(c)** (*remark, action*) remarque *f ou* action *f etc* sans rapport avec la question; **the defence of the frontier has become an i.,** la défense de la frontière n'a plus de raison d'être; **irrelevancies,** à-côtés *mpl* qui n'ont rien à voir avec la question.

irrelevant [ɪ'reləvənt] *adj* non pertinent; (*remark etc*) hors de propos; **that is i.,** cela n'a aucun rapport *ou* n'a rien à voir avec la question; **the monarchy had become i.,** la monarchie n'avait plus de raison d'être, la monarchie avait perdu sa raison d'être; **it's i. now whether he changes his mind or not,** maintenant ça ne fait plus rien qu'il change d'avis ou non.

irreligious [ɪrɪ'lɪdʒəs] *adj* irréligieux.

irremediable [ɪrɪ'miːdɪəb(ə)l] *adj* (*mal, faute etc*) irrémédiable, sans remède; (*perte etc*) irrécupérable.

irremediably [ɪrɪ'miːdɪəblɪ] *adv* irrémédiablement, sans remède.

irremovable [ɪrɪ'muːvəb(ə)l] *adj* immuable, fixe; (*fonctionnaire*) inamovible.

irreparable [ɪ'repərəb(ə)l] *adj* (*mal, perte*) irréparable; (*perte*) irrémédiable, irrécupérable.

irreparably [ɪ'repərəblɪ] *adv* irréparablement, irrémédiablement.

irreplaceable [ɪrɪ'pleɪsəb(ə)l] *adj* irremplaçable.

irrepressible [ɪrɪ'presɪb(ə)l] *adj* (*bâillement*) irrésistible, irréprimable; (*force*) irrépressible; (*rire*) inextinguible; (*bonne humeur*) que rien n'entame; **he's i.,** rien ne peut l'abattre.

irrepressibly [ɪrɪ'presɪblɪ] *adv* irrésistiblement; **she's i. cheerful,** rien ne peut entamer sa gaieté.

irreproachable [ɪrɪ'prəʊtʃəb(ə)l] *adj* irréprochable.

irreproachably [ɪrɪ'prəʊtʃəblɪ] *adv* irréprochablement.

irresistible [ɪrɪ'zɪstɪb(ə)l] *adj* irrésistible.

irresistibly [ɪrɪ'zɪstɪblɪ] *adv* irrésistiblement.

irresolute [ɪ'rezəluːt] *adj* indécis, irrésolu; (*esprit*) vacillant, hésitant.

irresolutely [ɪ'rezəluːtlɪ] *adv* irrésolument.

irresoluteness [ɪ'rezəluːtnɪs], **irresolution** [ɪ'rezəluːʃən] *n* indécision *f*, irrésolution *f*.

irrespective [ɪrɪ'spektɪv] **1** *adj* indépendant (**of,** de). **2** *adv* **i. of sth,** indépendamment *ou* sans tenir compte de qch.

irresponsibility [ɪrɪspɒnsɪ'bɪlɪtɪ] *n* **(a)** (*having minor consequences*) irréflexion *f*; (*having major consequences*) irresponsabilité *f*; **(b)** *Jur* irresponsabilité (*d'un aliéné etc*).

irresponsible [ɪrɪ'spɒnsɪb(ə)l] *adj* **(a)** (*person*) (*thoughtless*) étourdi, irréfléchi; (*careless*) irresponsable; (*action*) (*thoughtless*) irréfléchi; (*careless*) irresponsable; **(b)** *Jur* irresponsable.

irresponsibly [ɪrɪ'spɒnsɪblɪ] *adv* **(a)** (*thoughtlessly*) étourdiment; (*carelessly*) de façon irresponsable; **(b)** *Jur* irresponsablement.

irretrievable [ɪrɪ'triːvəb(ə)l] *adj* irréparable, irrémédiable.

irretrievably [ɪrɪ'triːvəblɪ] *adv* irréparablement; (*perdu*) à tout jamais; **to break down i.**, (*of marriage*) se briser à tout jamais.

irreverence [ɪ'revərəns] *n* irrévérence *f* (**towards,** envers, pour).

irreverent [ɪ'revərənt] *adj* irrévérencieux; **i. humour,** humour irrevérencieux.

irreverently [ɪ'revərəntlɪ] *adv* irrévérencieusement.

irreversible [ɪrɪ'vɜːsɪb(ə)l] *adj* **(a)** (*decision etc*) irrévocable; **(b)** (*process, gear etc*) irréversible.

irrevocable [ɪ'revəkəb(ə)l] *adj* irrévocable.

irrevocably [ɪ'revəkəblɪ] *adv* irrévocablement.

irrigable ['ɪrɪgəb(ə)l] *adj* (*terre*) irrigable.

irrigate ['ɪrɪgeɪt] *vt* **(a)** *Agr* irriguer (*des champs*); (*of river*) arroser (*un bassin, une région*); **(b)** *Med* irriguer (*une plaie etc*).

irrigation [ɪrɪ'geɪʃən] *n* **(a)** irrigation *f* (*des champs*); **i. canal** *or* **ditch,** canal *m* d'irrigation; **(b)** *Med* irrigation *f* (*d'une plaie*).

irritability [ɪrɪtə'bɪlɪtɪ] *n* irritabilité *f*, *Lit* irascibilité *f*.

irritable ['ɪrɪtəb(ə)l] *adj* (*caused by sth*) irritable; (*natural trait*) irascible.

irritably ['ɪrɪtəblɪ] *adv* (*to say, answer*) d'un ton irrité; (*to act*) avec humeur.

irritant ['ɪrɪtənt] *adj & n Med* irritant *m*.

irritate ['ɪrɪteɪt] *vt* **(a)** irriter, agacer (*qn, un animal*); exciter (*un animal*); **(b)** *Med* irriter (*un organe*).

irritating ['ɪrɪteɪtɪŋ] *adj* **(a)** irritant, agaçant; **i. little habits,** des petites manies agaçantes; **(b)** *Med* irritant.

irritation [ɪrɪ'teɪʃən] *n* **(a)** irritation *f*; **state of nervous i.,** état d'énervement; **(b)** *Med* irritation *f* (*de la gorge etc*).

is *see* **BE.**

I.S.B.N. [aɪesbiː'en] *n abbr* **International Standard Book Number.**

-ish [ɪʃ] *suff* **(a)** (*with adjective*) **blueish,** bleuâtre; **shortish,** plutôt petit; **(b)** (*with noun*) **girlish,** de petite fille; **wolfish,** de loup.

isinglass ['aɪsɪŋglɑːs] *n* ichtyocolle *f*, isinglass *m*; *Culin* gélatine *f*.

Islam ['ɪzlɑːm] *n* (*religion*) islam *m*; (*people*) l'Islam; **to go over to I.,** embrasser l'islamisme.

Islamic [ɪz'læmɪk] *adj* islamique.

Islamism ['ɪzləmɪzəm] *n* islamisme *m*.

island ['aɪlənd] *n* **(a)** *Geog* île *f*; **small i.,** îlot *m*; **the Pacific Islands,** les îles du Pacifique; **(b)** îlot *m* (*de maisons etc*); (*in supermarket*) gondole *f*; *Nau* îlot, superstructure *f* (*d'un porte-avions*); *Fig* **i. of resistance,** îlot de résistance; *Rail* **i. platform,** quai *m* d'entre-voie, quai entre voies; **traffic i.,** refuge *m* (pour piétons).

islander ['aɪləndər] *n* insulaire *mf*, habitant, -ante de l'île; **Channel Islanders,** habitants *mpl* des îles de la Manche.

isle [aɪl] *n* (*poetic, except in certain proper names*) île *f*; **the British Isles,** les Îles britanniques; **the I. of Man,** l'île de Man.

islet ['aɪlɪt] *n* îlot *m*.

isn't ['ɪz(ə)nt] = **is not,** *see* **BE.**

ISO [aɪe'səʊ] *n* (*abbr* **International Standards Organization**) ISO *f*.

isobar ['aɪsəʊbɑːr] *n Met Phys* isobare *f*.

isolate ['aɪsəleɪt] *vt* **(a)** faire le vide autour de (*qn*); isoler (*un malade, un fil électrique etc*) (**from,** de, d'avec); **she isolated herself from other people,** elle s'est isolée des autres gens; **(b)** *Ch* isoler, dégager (*un corps simple*); *Biol* isoler (*une culture*).

isolated ['aɪsəleɪtɪd] *adj* (*house etc*) isolé, écarté; (*alone*) isolé; **i. instance,** cas isolé.

isolation [aɪsə'leɪʃən] *n* **(a)** (*state of being cut off*) isolement *m*, solitude *f*; **splendid i.,** *Hist* splendide isolement; **if you prefer working in splendid i. ...,** si vous préférez travailler dans l'isolement le plus complet ...; **the only remaining 18th century building stands in splendid i. amid the ...,** le dernier bâtiment du 18e siècle se dresse dans un retranchement magnifique entre les ...; **these problems do not exist in i. (from one another),** ces problèmes n'existent pas isolément; **(b)** *Med* isolement *m* (*d'un malade*); **i. hospital,** hôpital *m* d'isolement de contagieux; **i. ward,** salle *f* des contagieux.

isolationism [aɪsə'leɪʃənɪz(ə)m] *n* isolationnisme *m*.

isolationist [aɪsə'leɪʃənɪst] *adj & n* isolationniste *mf*.

Isolde [ɪ'zɒldə] *n* Iseu(l)t *f*.

isosceles [aɪ'sɒsɪliːz] *adj Math* (*triangle*) isocèle.

isotherm ['aɪsəʊθɜːm] *n Met* isotherme *f*.

isotope ['aɪsəʊtəʊp] *n Ch Phys* isotope *m*.

I-spy ['aɪ'spaɪ] *n Br* = jeu (enfantin) de devinettes.

Israel ['ɪzreɪəl] *n* Israël *m*.

Israeli [ɪz'reɪlɪ] **1** *adj* israélien. **2** *n* (*pl* **Israelis**) Israélien, -ienne.

Israelite ['ɪzrɪəlaɪt] **1** *adj* israélite. **2** *n* Israélite *mf*.

issue[1] ['ɪʃuː] *n* **(a)** (*subject*) problème *m*, question *f*; **an important i.,** une question importante; **the issues of the day,** les questions du jour; *Fig* **I don't want to make an i. of it,** je ne veux pas en faire tout une affaire; **to join i. with s.o.,** discuter l'opinion de qn (**about sth,** au sujet de qch); **the point at i.,** la question pendante; **matters at i.,** matières en contestation; **to be at i.** *or* **take i. with s.o.,** être en désaccord avec qn; **this is not the i.,** ce n'est pas (là) le problème; **to evade** *or* **avoid the i.,** prendre la tangente; **to confuse the i.,** compliquer les choses; *Jur* **i. (of fact/of law),** (*matter*) question *ou* point *m* de fait/de droit; (*conclusion*) conclusion *f*;

(b) *Admin Fin* émission *f* (*de mandats, de billets de banque, de timbres-poste etc*); *Admin Mil etc* distribution *f*, *Mil* versement *m* (*de matériel etc*); parution *f*, publication *f* (*d'un livre*); lancement *m* (*d'un prospectus etc*); *Rail etc* délivrance *f* (*de billets etc*); *Th* contrôle *m* (*des billets*); (*in library*) prêt *m* (*de livres*); *Fin* **i. price,** taux *m* d'émission; *Mil etc* **i. boots/shirts,** bottes *fpl*/chemises *fpl* réglementaires; *US* **government i. equipment,** matériel *m* réglementaire de l'armée; *Mil* **i. of orders,** publication *f* des ordres;

(c) (*of magazine*) numéro *m*; **the November i.,** le numéro de novembre;

(d) (*of smoke etc*) sortie *f*, décharge *f*;

(e) *Med* décharge *f* (*de sang, de pus*);

(f) (*way out*) issue *f*, sortie *f*, débouché *m* (**out of,** de); embouchure *f* (*d'un fleuve*);

(g) (*offspring*) progéniture *f*, descendance *f*; **to die without i.,** mourir sans (laisser de) postérité;

(h) (*outcome*) résultat *m*, dénouement *m*.

issue[2] **1** *vi* **(a)** (*of blood, water*) jaillir, s'écouler (**from,** de); (*of smoke*) sortir; (*of smell*) se dégager; **(b)** (*of children*) provenir, dériver (**from,** de); **the children issuing from this marriage,** les enfants issus de ce mariage.

2 *vt* émettre (*des billets de banque etc*); créer (*un effet de commerce*); publier (*une nouvelle édition, un prospectus etc*); *Fin* fournir (*une lettre de crédit*); *Mil* publier, donner (*un ordre*); *Jur* rendre (*un arrêt*); verser, distribuer (*des provisions etc*); délivrer (*des billets de chemin de fer etc*); (*of lending library*) prêter; **each man will be issued with two uniforms,** chaque homme recevra deux uniformes; **to i. s.o. with sth,** délivrer qch à qn; *Jur* **to i. a summons,** décerner *ou* lancer une citation.

issuing ['ɪʃjuːɪŋ] **1** *adj esp Fin* émetteur, -trice; distributeur, -trice; *Br Fin* **i. house,** banque *f* de placement. **2** *n* émission *f* (*d'un emprunt etc*); publication *f* (*d'un livre, d'un journal*); délivrance *f* (*de billets*); distribution *f* (*de vivres*); (*in library*) prêt *m* (*des livres*).

Istanbul [ɪstæn'buːl] *n* Istanb(o)ul *m*.

isthmus, *pl* **-muses** ['ɪsməs, -məsɪz] *n Geog Anat* isthme *m*.

it [ɪt] **1** *pers pron* (*referring to inanimate objects, animals, and children, but in French taking the gender of the noun for which* it *stands*) **(a)** (*subject*) il, elle; **the house is small but it is my own,** c'est une petite maison mais elle est à moi; **where is your hat? — it's in the cupboard,** où est votre chapeau? – il est dans l'armoire;

(b) (*direct object*) le, la; **I don't believe it,** je ne le crois pas;

(c) (*indirect object*) lui *mf*; **fetch the dog and give it something to eat,** allez chercher le chien et donnez-lui à manger;

(d) *F* (*stressed*) **he thinks he's it,** il se croit sorti de la cuisse de Jupiter; **this book is absolutely IT!,** c'est un livre épatant!; **this is IT!,** nous y voilà!, ça y est!, on est fait!;

(e) (*as unspecified object of a verb*) **to face it,** faire front; **blast it!,** zut!;

(f) (*as unspecified object of a preposition*) **now for it!,** et maintenant allons-y!; **there is nothing for it but to run,** il n'y a qu'une chose à faire, c'est de filer; *F* **he's (in) for it!** qu'est-ce qu'il va prendre! **to have a bad time of it,** en voir de dures;

(g) (*as complement*) **who is it?,** qui est-ce?; **that's it,** c'est ça; (*as encouragement*) ça y est!;

(h) (*as subject of impersonal verb*) **it frightens me,** cela me fait peur; **it doesn't matter,** cela ne fait rien; **it's raining,** il pleut; **it's ten o'clock,** il est dix heures; **it's Mon-**

day, c'est lundi;

(i) it's nonsense talking like that, c'est *ou* il est absurde de parler comme ça; **it is impossible to work in this heat,** c'est *ou* il est impossible de travailler par cette chaleur; **it says in ...,** on lit dans ...; **the fog made it difficult to see,** le brouillard rendait la vision difficile; **I find it hard to understand why,** je trouve difficile de comprendre pourquoi; **you may rely upon it that he will do his best,** vous pouvez être sûr qu'il fera de son mieux;

(j) (*with prepositions*) **to consent to it,** y consentir; **above it** *or* **over it,** au-dessus, dessus; **below it, under(neath) it,** au-dessous, dessous; **as we walked away from it,** tandis que nous nous en éloignions; **he's not bad, far from it,** il n'est pas méchant, loin de là; **give me half of it,** donnez-m'en la moitié; **think of it,** pensez-y; **don't tread on it,** ne marchez pas dessus; **with it,** avec cela, avec lui, avec elle; **the Committee has devoted much care to the task before it,** le comité a accordé beaucoup d'attention à la tâche qui lui incombait; **I cracked his head with it,** je lui ai fendu la tête avec.

2 *n* (*in children's games*) **you're it!,** c'est toi qui y es *ou* qui t'y colles!

Italian [ɪ'tæljən] **1** *adj* italien; (*embassy, ambassador, history*) d'Italie; (*teacher, lesson, dictionary*) d'italien; **I. cooking,** cuisine italienne; **I. hand,** écriture anglaise; **I. Switzerland,** Suisse italienne. **2** *n* **(a)** Italien, -ienne; **(b)** *Ling* italien *m*; **(c)** *F* vermouth italien.

italic [ɪ'tælɪk] *Typ* **1** *adj* (*caractère*) italique. **2** *n* **to print in italic(s),** imprimer en italique(s); **the italics are mine,** c'est moi qui souligne.

italicize [ɪ'tælɪsaɪz] *vt Typ* imprimer *ou* mettre en italiques; **italicized words,** mots en italiques.

Italy ['ɪtəlɪ] *n* Italie *f*.

itch¹ [ɪtʃ] *n* démangeaison *f*; *F* **to have an i. for sth/to do sth,** avoir une envie de qch/de faire qch; **the seven year i.,** l'écueil *m* des sept ans de mariage.

itch² *vi* **(a)** démanger; (*of person*) éprouver des démangeaisons; **my hand itches,** la main me démange; **where does it i.?,** où est-ce que cela vous démange?; **bites that i.,** morsures qui font éprouver des démangeaisons; **(b)** *F* **to i. to do sth,** brûler d'envie de faire qch; **I was itching to speak,** la langue me démangeait (de parler); **she is itching to be off,** ça lui démange de partir.

itching ['ɪtʃɪŋ] **1** *adj* (*plaie etc*) qui démange. **2** *n* démangeaison *f*.

itchy ['ɪtʃɪ] *adj* **I've got an i. hand,** la main me démange; *F* **to have i. feet,** brûler de partir; (*be always on the move*) avoir la bougeotte.

it'd ['ɪt(ə)d] = **it would,** *see* **WILL³**.

item ['aɪtəm] **1** *n Com* article *m*; (*in bookkeeping*) écriture *f*, article, poste *m*, détail *m*; *Journ* entrefilet *m*; **please send us the following items,** prière de nous envoyer les articles suivants; **i. of expenditure,** article *ou* chef *m* de dépense; **the second i. of the contract,** l'article deux du contrat; **the items on the agenda,** les questions *fpl* à l'ordre du jour; *Th etc* **the last i. on the programme,** le dernier numéro du programme; **news items,** faits divers, échos *mpl*. **2** *adv Arch Com* item.

itemize ['aɪtəmaɪz] *vt* détailler (*une facture etc*); **itemized account,** compte spécifié.

iterate ['ɪtəreɪt] *vt* réitérer, répéter (constamment); *Comptr Math* itérer.

iteration [ɪtə'reɪʃən] *n* itération *f*.

itinerant [ɪ'tɪnərənt, aɪ-] *adj* (*marchand, comédien, musicien*) ambulant; (*pasteur, travailleur*) itinérant.

itinerary [aɪ'tɪnərərɪ] *n* itinéraire *m*.

it'll ['ɪt(ə)l] = **it will.**

its [ɪts] **1** *poss adj* son, sa, *pl* ses; (*in the f before a vowel sound*) son; **i. nose, mouth, and eyes,** (*of animal*) son nez, sa bouche, et ses yeux; **i. extent,** (*of forest etc*) son étendue *f*; **a charm of i. own,** un charme qui n'appartient qu'à lui *ou* à elle. **2** *poss pron* (*rare*) le sien, la sienne, *pl* les sien(ne)s.

it's [ɪts] **(a)** = **it is,** *see* **BE**; **(b)** = **it has,** *see* **HAVE²**.

itself [ɪt'self] *pers pron* **(a)** (*emphatic*) lui-même, elle-même, soi-même; **it is simplicity i.,** c'est tout ce qu'il y a de plus simple; **she is kindness i.,** elle est la bonté même; **(b)** (*reflexive*) **the dog hurt i.,** le chien s'est fait mal; **(c)** (*after prepositions*) **the child was left by i.,** l'enfant était laissé(e) tout(e) seul(e); **the thing in i.,** la chose en elle-même; **in i. it's not a bad idea,** en soi l'idée n'est pas mal.

ITV [aɪtiː'viː] *n abbr* **Independent Television.**

IUD [aɪjuː'diː] *n Med abbr* **intra-uterine device.**

I've = **I have.**

ivory ['aɪvərɪ] **1** *n* **(a)** (*substance*) ivoire *m*; (*object*) (objet *m* d')ivoire; **i.-white teeth,** dents d'une blancheur d'ivoire; **i. trade,** ivoirerie *f*; **the I. Coast,** la Côte d'Ivoire; **a collection of ivories,** une collection d'ivoires; *F* **ivories,** *Billiards* billes *fpl*; (*dice*) dés *mpl*; (*teeth*) dents *fpl*; touches *fpl* (*du piano*); **(b)** (*colour*) ivoire *m*. **2** *adj* (*made of ivory*) d'ivoire, en ivoire; *Lit* **i. tower,** tour *f* d'ivoire.

ivy ['aɪvɪ] *n* (*plant*) lierre *m*; **poison i.,** sumac vénéneux; *Can* herbe *f* à la puce; **ground i.,** lierre terrestre *ou* rampant; *US* **I. League,** = qui fait partie ou est caractéristique du cercle des vieilles universités prestigieuses des Etats de l'est.

J

J, j [dʒeɪ] *n* (la lettre) J, j *m*.

jab[1] [dʒæb] *n* **(a)** (*with sharp object*) coup *m* (sec); **(b)** *Br F* (*injection*) piqûre *f*; **(c)** *Boxing* coup droit, direct *m*.

jab[2] *v* (**-bb-**) **1** *vt* **(a)** (*poke, prick*) **to j. s.o./sth,** piquer qn/qch (**with sth,** avec qch, du bout de qch); **to j. s.o. with one's elbow/a knife,** donner un coup de coude/couteau à qn; **(b)** (*thrust*) enfoncer, planter (d'un coup sec) (**into,** dans). **2** *vi* **(a)** (*poke, prick*) **to j. at s.o./sth,** piquer qn/qch (**with sth,** avec qch, du bout de qch); **(b)** *Boxing* envoyer *ou* lancer un coup droit *ou* un direct (**at,** à).

jabber[1] ['dʒæbər] *n* **(a)** (*gibberish*) baragouin *m*; **(b)** (*chatter*) jacasserie *f*.

jabber[2] **1** *vi* **(a)** (*talk fast, unclearly*) baragouiner; **what are you jabbering about?,** qu'est-ce que tu baragouines?; **(b)** (*chatter*) jacasser, bavarder. **2** *vt* bafouiller, bredouiller (*une excuse, une explication*); **to j. a few words in French/***etc*, baragouiner quelques mots de français/*etc*.

▶**jabber away, jabber on** *vi* = **JABBER**[2] **1**.

▶**jabber out** *vtsep* bafouiller, bredouiller (*une excuse*).

jabbering ['dʒæbərɪŋ] *n* **(a)** (*gibberish*) baragouinage *m*; **(b)** (*chattering*) jacasserie *f*.

jabot ['ʒæbəʊ] *n* (*of shirt*) jabot *m*.

jacaranda [dʒækə'rændə] *n* (*shrub*) jacaranda *m*.

jack [dʒæk] *n* **(a)** (*person*) **every man j. (of them** *or* **us** *or* **you),** absolument tout le monde; **j. of all trades,** homme *m ou* femme *f* à tout faire; **(b)** (*lifting device*) *Aut* cric *m*; *Tech* vérin *m*; **(c)** *Cards* (*knave*) valet *m*; **the j. of spades,** le valet de pique; **(d) jacks,** (*game*) (jeu *m* d')osselets *mpl*; **(e)** *Tel* prise *f*; *El* **j. (socket),** prise *ou* fiche *f* femelle; **j. plug,** (*connector*) prise *ou* fiche mâle; **microphone/headphone j.,** prise de microphone/de casque; **(f) j. rabbit,** (*North American hare*) gros lièvre américain.

Jack [dʒæk] *n* (*dimin of* **John**) Jeannot *m*; **J. Frost,** le Bonhomme Hiver; **she was off before you could say J. Robinson,** elle est partie sans qu'on ait eu le temps de dire ouf, elle a disparu en un clin d'œil; *Br F* **I'm all right, J.,** ça marche très bien pour moi (et les autres, je m'en fiche).

▶**jack in** *vtsep Br Sl* plaquer, laisser tomber (*un travail, un projet, sa petite amie*).

▶**jack up** *vtsep Aut Tech* soulever (avec un cric *ou* un vérin); *Fig F* (*increase*) relever (*un prix, des salaires*).

jackal ['dʒækɔːl, -k(ə)l] *n* (*animal*) chacal *m*.

jackass ['dʒækæs] *n* **(a)** (*male donkey*) âne *m* (mâle), *F* baudet *m*; **(b)** *F* (*person*) idiot, -ote, imbécile *mf*; **(c) laughing j.,** (*bird*) dacélo *m*.

jackdaw ['dʒækdɔː] *n* (*bird*) choucas *m*.

jacket[1] ['dʒækɪt] *n* **(a)** (*man's coat*) veste *f*, veston *m*; (*woman's coat*) veste, jaquette *f*; (*bulletproof*) gilet *m*; **single/double-breasted j.,** veston droit/croisé; **bed j.,** liseuse *f*; **dinner j.,** smoking *m*; **leather j.,** (*short*) blouson *m* de cuir; *Nau* **life j.,** gilet *m* de sauvetage; **sheepskin j.,** canadienne *f*; **sports j.,** veste *f* de sport; **(b)** (*of baked potato*) pelure *f*; **j. potatoes, potatoes cooked in their jackets,** pommes de terre en robe des champs; **(c)** (*cover of record, computer diskette*) pochette *f*; (*for documents*) chemise *f*; *Tech* (*of boiler, pipe*) chemise, enveloppe *f*; **(dust) j.,** (*of book*) jaquette *f*.

jacket[2] *vt Tech* garnir *ou* envelopper d'une chemise, chemiser (*un cylindre, une chaudière etc*).

jackhammer ['dʒækhæmər] *n* marteau-piqueur *m*.

jack-in-the-box ['dʒækɪnðəbɒks] *n* (*pl* **jack-in-the-boxes**) diable *m* à ressort, boîte *f* à surprise(s); *F* **to jump up and down like a j.-in-the-b.,** (*be pestered*) ne pas avoir un instant de répit; (*be restless*) ne pas tenir en place.

jackknife[1], *pl* **-knives** ['dʒæknaɪf, -naɪvz] *n* **(a)** couteau *m* de poche, canif *m*; **(b)** *Swimming* **j. (dive),** saut *m* de carpe.

jackknife[2] *vi* **(a)** *Aut* (*of long vehicle*) se mettre en travers (de la route); **(b)** *Swimming* faire un saut de carpe.

jackpot ['dʒækpɒt] *n* **(a)** *Cards* (*in poker etc*) pot *m*; **(b)** (*in competition*) gros lot; **to hit** *or* **win the j.,** gagner le gros lot; *F* **to hit the j.,** (*be successful*) (*of person*) gagner le gros lot, décrocher la timbale; (*of book etc*) faire un malheur *ou* un tabac.

Jacobean [dʒækə'bɪən] *adj* (*furniture etc*) de l'époque de Jacques 1er.

Jacobite ['dʒækəbaɪt] *adj & n Hist* jacobite *m*.

jacuzzi ® [dʒə'kuːzɪ] *n* (*bath, pool*) jacuzzi ® *m*.

jade [dʒeɪd] **1** *n* **(a)** *Miner* jade *m*; **(b)** (*colour*) **j. (green),** vert *m* de jade. **2** *adj* (*colour*) **j.(-green),** couleur *inv* de jade, vert *inv* (de) jade.

jaded ['dʒeɪdɪd] *adj* (*bored*) blasé, revenu de tout; (*exhausted*) éreinté; **j. with,** las de; **j. palate,** palais blasé.

jag [dʒæg] *n* **(a)** *Sl* (*drinking bout*) soûlerie *f*; **to go on a j.,** se soûler, prendre une cuite; **(b)** *Sl* (*indulgence in emotion, activity*) **to go on a crying j.,** avoir une crise de larmes; **to go on a buying j.,** faire de folles dépenses; **(c)** *Br F* (*injection*) piqûre *f*.

Jag [dʒæg] *n F* (*Jaguar* ® *car*) Jag *f*.

jagged ['dʒægɪd] *adj* (*coastline, mountain top*) déchiqueté, découpé; (*edge*) déchiqueté, découpé, irrégulier, dentelé; (*line, tear*) irrégulier; (*knife, blade*) entaillé, ébréché; (*rock*) pointu, dentelé; **the j. outline of the coast,** les dentelures *ou* découpures de la côte.

jaguar [*Br* 'dʒægjʊər, *Am* 'dʒægwɑːr] *n* (*animal*) jaguar *m*.

jail[1] [dʒeɪl] *n* (*place, imprisonment*) prison *f*; **to be in j.,** être en prison; **to put in j., to send to j.,** mettre en prison; **to go to j.,** aller en prison, faire de la prison; **he was sent to j.** *or* **he went to j. for ten years,** il a été condamné à dix ans de prison; **she was in j. for ten years, she went to j. for ten years,** elle a fait dix ans de prison; **to break out of j.,** s'évader de prison; **open j.,** prison ouverte.

jail[2] *vt* mettre en prison, emprisonner; **to j. for theft/***etc*, condamner à la prison pour vol/*etc*; **he was jailed for ten years,** il a été condamné à dix ans de prison.

jailbait ['dʒeɪlbeɪt] *n Am Sl* (*girl*) mineure *f* (*avec qui les relations sexuelles sont interdites*).

jailbird ['dʒeɪlbɜːd] *n F* (*actually in prison*) taulard, -arde; (*constantly going to prison*) cheval *m* de retour.

jailbreak ['dʒeɪlbreɪk] *n* évasion *f* de prison.

jailer ['dʒeɪlər] *n* gardien, -ienne de prison, *Lit* geôlier, -ière.

jailhouse, *pl* **-houses** ['dʒeɪlhaʊs, -haʊzɪz] *n Am* prison *f*.

jailor ['dʒeɪlər] *n* = **JAILER**.

jalop(p)y [dʒə'lɒpɪ] *n F* (vieille) bagnole *f* , (vieux) tacot *m*, (vieille) guimbarde *f*.

jam[1] [dʒæm] *n* **(a)** *Aut* (*congestion*) **(traffic) j.,** bouchon *m*, embouteillage *m*, encombrement *m*; **(b)** (*crowd of people*) foule *f*, presse *f*; **(c)** (*in pipe, machine etc*) engorgement *m*; **(d)** *F* (*difficult situation*) pétrin *m*; **to be in/get into a (bit of a) j.,** être/se mettre dans le pétrin; **to get out of/get s.o. out of a j.,** se tirer/tirer qn du pétrin; **(e)** *Mus* **j. (session),** bœuf *m*, séance *f* de jazz improvisé; **to have a j. (session),** faire un bœuf.

jam[2] *v* (**-mm-**) **1** *vt* **(a)** (*pack, cram*) (en)tasser (*qn, qch*) (**into,** dans); (*thrust, put forcefully*) enfoncer, fourrer (*qch*) (**into,** dans); **to j. one's foot on the brake(s),** écraser le frein *ou* la pédale de frein;

(b) (*squeeze, wedge*) coincer, serrer; **she got her hand jammed** *or* **she jammed her hand in the drawer,** elle s'est coincé la main dans le tiroir; **to j. a door open with a book,** maintenir une porte ouverte à l'aide d'un livre;

(c) (*immobilize, stop from working*) coincer, bloquer (*une fenêtre, un volant etc*); enrayer, bloquer (*une arme, un mécanisme*); boucher (*un tuyau*); **the drawer is jammed,** le tiroir est coincé *ou* bloqué; **to be jammed in the ice,** être bloqué par les glaces;

(d) (*of people, vehicles*) encombrer, bloquer (*une rue, un couloir etc*); envahir (*un immeuble*); **the hall was jammed (with people), people jammed the hall,** la salle était pleine à craquer *ou* bondée *ou* bourrée;

(e) *Rad* brouiller (*une émission, une station*);

(f) *Tel* (*of calls etc*) encombrer (*les lignes*); faire sauter (*le standard*); **the switchboard was jammed,** le standard était saturé.

2 *vi* **(a)** (*of drawer, window etc*) se coincer, se bloquer; (*of gun, machine*) s'enrayer, se bloquer; (*of brake, wheel*) se bloquer;

(b) (*crowd*) s'entasser (**into,** dans).

jam³ *n* (*preserve*) confiture *f*; **strawberry/raspberry/***etc* **j.,** confiture de fraises/framboises/*etc*; **j. jar** *or* **pot,** pot *m* à confitures; **jar** *or* **pot of j.,** pot *m* de confiture(s); **j. tart,** tarte *f* à la confiture; *Br F* **it's money for j.,** c'est grassement payé, c'est de l'argent facilement gagné; *Br F* **what do you want, j. on it?,** ça ne te suffit pas?, que veux-tu de plus?

►jam in 1 *vtsep* **(a)** (*wedge in*) coincer, serrer; **(b)** (*pack or press tightly in*) (en)tasser (*des passagers etc*); bourrer (*des objets*). **2** *vi* (*crowd in*) s'entasser; **they all jammed in,** (*into train*) ils s'y entassèrent tous.

►jam on *vtsep* **(a)** *Aut* **to j. on the brakes,** écraser le frein *ou* la pédale de frein; **(b)** (*put on forcefully or solidly*) enfoncer (*un couvercle, un chapeau etc*).

Jamaica [dʒə'meɪkə] *n* Jamaïque *f*.

Jamaican [dʒə'meɪkən] **1** *adj* jamaïquain, jamaïcain, de la Jamaïque. **2** *n* Jamaïquain, -aine, Jamaïcain, -aine.

jamb [dʒæm] *n* (*side post*) chambranle *m*, jambage *m*, montant *m* (*de porte, de fenêtre, de cheminée*).

jamboree [dʒæmbə'riː] *n* **(a)** (*scouts' meeting*) jamboree *m*; **(b)** *F* (*celebration, party*) fête *f*, réunion *f*; (*festivities*) réjouissances (tapageuses); **village j.,** fête *f* de village.

jammies ['dʒæmɪz] *npl* (*in children's language*) pyjama *m*, *F* pyj *m*.

jamming ['dʒæmɪŋ] *n* **(a)** *Rad* brouillage *m* (délibéré); **(b)** *Tel* encombrement *m* (*des lignes*).

jammy ['dʒæmɪ] *adj Br F* **(a)** (*lucky*) veinard, verni; **he's a j. devil,** quel veinard, celui-là!, il est verni, celui-là!; **(b)** (*easy*) facile; **j. job,** filon *m*, bonne planque.

jam-packed ['dʒæm'pækd] *adj* (*suitcase, bag etc*) plein à craquer, bourré; **j.-p. (with people),** (*hall, bus etc*) plein à craquer, bondé, bourré; (*street*) noir de monde.

Jane [dʒeɪn] *n* **(a)** Jeanne *f*; **(b)** *US Sl* (*woman*) nana *f*; **she's rather a plain J.,** elle n'est pas très jolie, ce n'est pas une beauté; **J. Doe,** (*unidentified woman*) (*under arrest*) inconnue *f*; (*corpse*) morte non identifiée.

jangle¹ ['dʒæŋg(ə)l] *n* (*of metal objects, keys etc*) cliquetis *m* (discordant); (*of bell*) bruit discordant.

jangle² **1** *vi* (*of metal objects, keys etc*) cliqueter (d'une façon discordante); (*of bells*) retentir avec un bruit discordant. **2** *vt* **(a)** faire cliqueter (*des clefs etc*) (d'une façon discordante); faire retentir (*des cloches*) avec un bruit discordant; **(b)** (*upset*) **jangled nerves,** nerfs ébranlés *ou* en pelote.

jangling ['dʒæŋg(ə)lɪŋ] *n* = **JANGLE¹**.

janitor ['dʒænɪtər] *n Am Scot* (*caretaker*) concierge *mf*.

January ['dʒænjʊərɪ] *n* janvier *m*; **in J.,** au mois de janvier, en janvier; **(on) the third of J.,** le trois janvier.

Jap [dʒæp] *Offensive Sl* **1** *n* Japonais, -aise. **2** *adj* japonais.

Japan [dʒə'pæn] *n* Japon *m*.

Japanese [dʒæpə'niːz] **1** *adj* japonais; (*embassy, ambassador, history*) du Japon; (*teacher, lesson, dictionary*) de japonais; **J. lantern,** lanterne vénitienne. **2** *n* **(a)** Japonais, -aise; **the J.,** (*used as pl*) les Japonais *mpl*; **(b)** *Ling* japonais *m*.

jar¹ [dʒɑːr] *n* (*jolt, shock*) & *Fig* choc *m*, secousse *f*; **his fall/the news gave him a nasty j.,** sa chute/la nouvelle l'a fortement ébranlé.

jar² *v* (-rr-) **1** *vi* **(a)** (*make an unpleasant sound*) rendre un son discordant; *Mus* (*of note*) détonner; **to j. on the ears,** écorcher les oreilles; **this noise jars on my nerves,** ce bruit me tape sur les nerfs *ou* me crispe; **(b)** (*of colours, furniture*) détonner, jurer, être en désaccord (**with,** avec); (*of ideas, styles, remarks*) être incompatible, ne pas s'accorder (**with,** avec); **to j. (with each other),** (*of colours, ideas*) se heurter; **to j. on s.o.'s feelings,** froisser qn. **2** *vt* (*of fall, news*) ébranler (*qn*).

jar³ *n* **(a)** (*container*) pot *m*; (*for storing oil etc*) jarre *f*; **(glass) j.,** pot *m*; (*large*) bocal *m*; **(b)** *Br F* (*beer*) pot *m*; **to have a j.,** prendre un pot.

►jar on, jar upon *vipo* (*irritate*) (*of noise*) écorcher (*les oreilles*); **his voice jars (up)on my nerves,** sa voix me tape sur les nerfs *ou* me crispe.

jargon ['dʒɑːgən] *n* **(a)** (*specialized language*) jargon *m*; **legal j.,** jargon juridique, langage *m* du Palais; **to talk (in) j.,** parler en jargon, jargonner; **(b)** (*gibberish*) jargon *m*, baragouin *m*, charabia *m*.

jarring ['dʒɑːrɪŋ] *adj* **(a)** (*noise, voice etc*) discordant; *Mus* (*note*) qui détonne; *Fig* (*incident, behaviour*) qui produit une sensation désagréable; **(b)** (*blow*) qui ébranle tout le corps.

jasmine ['dʒæzmɪn, 'dʒæs-] *n* (*shrub*) **(common** *or* **white) j.,** jasmin *m* (commun *ou* blanc); **winter j.,** jasmin d'hiver; **j. perfume,** (essence *f* de) jasmin; **j. tea,** thé *m* au jasmin.

jaundice ['dʒɔːndɪs] *n* **(a)** *Med* jaunisse *f*, ictère *m*; **neonatal/physiological j.,** ictère du nouveau-né/physiologique; **(b)** *Fig* (*bitterness*) amertume *f*.

jaundiced ['dʒɔːndɪst] *adj* **(a)** *Med* ictérique, bilieux; **(b)** *Fig* (*bitter*) aigri, désenchanté; (*jealous*) jaloux; **to look on the world** *or* **on things with a j. eye,** (*bitterly*) voir tout en noir; (*jealously*) tout regarder d'un œil jaloux; **to take a j. view of a situation,** voir une situation d'un mauvais œil.

jaunt [dʒɔːnt] *n* (petite) excursion *f*, balade *f*, sortie *f*; **on a j.,** en excursion, en balade; **to go on** *or* **for a j.,** faire une (petite) excursion *ou* une balade.

jauntily ['dʒɔːntɪlɪ] *adv* **(a)** (*to remark, play*) d'une manière désinvolte, avec désinvolture; **(b)** (*to walk*) d'un pas vif; **(c)** (*to wear one's hat*) d'une façon désinvolte; (*of woman, stylishly*) coquettement.

jauntiness ['dʒɔːntɪnɪs] *n* **(a)** (*carefreeness*) désinvolture *f*, insouciance *f*; **(b)** (*cheerfulness*) enjouement *m*, vivacité *f*; **the j. of his step,** la vivacité de son pas.

jaunty ['dʒɔːntɪ] *adj* (*manner etc*) désinvolte, insouciant, dégagé; (*cheerful, lively*) enjoué, vif; **with a j. air,** d'un air dégagé; **j. step,** démarche *f* alerte, pas vif; **he wore his cap at a j. angle,** sa casquette était négligemment posée sur sa tête.

Java ['dʒɑːvə] *n* (île *f* de) Java *f*.

Javanese [dʒɑːvə'niːz] **1** *adj* javanais. **2** *n* **(a)** Javanais, -aise; **the J.,** (*used as pl*) les Javanais *mpl*; **(b)** *Ling* javanais *m*.

javelin ['dʒævlɪn] *n* (*weapon*) & *Sp* javelot *m*; **j. thrower/throwing,** lanceur, -euse/lancer *m* du javelot; *Sp* **the j.,** (*event*) l'épreuve *f* de javelot.

jaw¹ [dʒɔː] *n* **(a)** *Anat* mâchoire *f*; **upper/lower j.,** mâchoire supérieure/inférieure; **the lion opened its jaws,** le lion a ouvert la gueule; *Fig* **her j. dropped,** (*in surprise*) elle en est restée bouche bée, les bras lui en sont tombés; *Fig* **to set one's j.,** (*show determination*) décider de s'accrocher, ne pas baisser les bras; **(b)** *Fig* **the jaws of,** (*valley, cave*) l'entrée *f* de; (*volcano*) la bouche de; (*hell*) les portes *fpl* de; **to snatch s.o. from the jaws of death/the enemy,** arracher qn des griffes de la mort/de l'ennemi; **(c)** *Tech* (*of pincer, wrench etc*) mâchoire *f*, mors *m*.

jaw² *n F* (*chat*) papotage *m*, bavardage *m*; (*moralizing talk*) sermon *m*; **to have a (good) j.,** tailler une bavette, papoter.

jaw³ *F vi* (*chat*) papoter, bavarder; (*moralize*) prêcher, moraliser.

jawbone ['dʒɔːbəʊn] *n* (os *m*) maxillaire *m*, mâchoire *f*.

jawbreaker ['dʒɔːbreɪkər] *n* **(a)** *F* (*word*) mot *m* imprononçable; (*name*) nom *m* à coucher dehors; **(b)** *Am* (*candy*) bonbon *m* (très dur).

-jawed [dʒɔːd] *suff* **round/long/***etc***-j.,** à la mâchoire ronde/allongée/*etc*; *Boxing etc F* **glass-j.,** à la mâchoire fragile.

jay [dʒeɪ] *n* (*bird*) geai *m* (des chênes); **blue j.,** geai bleu.

jaywalk ['dʒeɪwɔːk] *vi F* traverser la rue d'une manière imprudente *ou* en dehors des clous.

jaywalker ['dʒeɪwɔːkər] *n F* piéton imprudent (*qui traverse en dehors des clous*).

jaywalking ['dʒeɪwɔːkɪŋ] *n* imprudence *f* (*de la part d'un piéton*).

jazz [dʒæz] *n* **(a)** *Mus* jazz *m*; **j. band/music/***etc***,** orchestre *m*/musique *f*/*etc* de jazz; **(b)** *Sl* (*talk*) baratin *m*; **she gave me a lot of j. about it,** elle m'a fait tout un baratin là-dessus; **what's (all) this j. about your leaving?,** qu'est-ce que c'est que cette histoire comme quoi tu t'en vas?; **(c)** *Sl* (*unspecified matters*) **and all that j.,** et tout le tremblement *ou* bazar.

►jazz up *vtsep* **(a)** *Mus* adapter pour le jazz; **(b)** *Fig* (*enliven*) animer, mettre de l'entrain dans (*une réception*); égayer (*des vêtements, une pièce*); relever (*un plat*).

jazzy ['dʒæzɪ] *adj F* (*tune*) qui évoque le jazz, de jazz; *Fig* (*flashy*) tapageur, voyant; (*elegant*) chic *inv*.

JCB ® [dʒeɪsiː'biː] *n Br* = pelle hydraulique automotrice.

jealous ['dʒeləs] *adj* **(a)** (*fearful of rivals*) jaloux, *f* -ouse; **a j. woman,** une femme jalouse, une jalouse; **(b)** (*envious*) jaloux (**of,** de); **j. of s.o./of s.o.'s happiness,** jaloux de qn/du bonheur de qn; **(c)** (*vigilant, possessive*) jaloux (**of,** de); **with a j. eye,** d'un œil jaloux; **j. of one's good name,** jaloux de sa réputation.

jealously ['dʒeləslɪ] *adv* (*enviously*) jalousement, avec jalousie; (*vigilantly*) avec un soin jaloux.

jealousy ['dʒeləsɪ] *n* jalousie *f*.

jeans [dʒiːnz] *npl* **(pair of) j.,** jean *m*; **she was wearing (a pair of) j.,** elle portait un jean *ou* des jeans; **blue j.,**

blue-jean *m*.

jeep [dʒiːp] *n Aut* jeep *f*.

jeepers (creepers) ['dʒiːpəz('kriːpəz)] *int Old-fashioned Am F* ça alors!

jeer[1] [dʒɪər] *n* raillerie *f*, moquerie *f*; **the jeers of the crowd,** (*boos*) les huées *fpl* de la foule.

jeer[2] **1** *vi* (*boo*) huer, conspuer; (*make fun*) railler. **2** *vt* **to j. s.o.,** (*boo*) huer qn, conspuer qn; (*make fun of*) se moquer de qn, railler qn.

►**jeer at** *vipo* = **JEER**[2] **2.**

jeering ['dʒɪərɪŋ] **1** *adj* railleur, moqueur. **2** *n* railleries *fpl*, moqueries *fpl*; (*of crowd*) huées *fpl*.

jeez [dʒiːz] *int F* mon Dieu!

Jekyll and Hyde [dʒekələnd'haɪd] *n* **he's a (real) J. and H.,** c'est un vrai docteur Jekyll, il mène une double vie; **to have a J.-and-H. personality,** faire un dédoublement de la personnalité.

jell [dʒel] *vi* **(a)** (*of liquid*) se gélifier, prendre (en gelée); **(b)** *Fig* (*of ideas*) prendre corps *ou* forme; (*of plans*) prendre tournure *ou* forme *ou* corps.

jellied ['dʒelɪd] *adj Culin* (*eel, egg etc*) en gelée.

jello ® ['dʒeləʊ] *n Am Culin* gelée *f*.

jelly[1] ['dʒelɪ] *n* **(a)** (*preserve*) gelée *f*; **redcurrant j.,** gelée de groseille(s); *Am* **j. roll,** (*cake*) roulé *m* (à la gelée *ou* à la confiture); **(b)** *Br* (*dessert*) gelée *f*; **my knees were like j.,** j'avais les genoux qui jouaient des castagnettes; **(c)** (*gel-like substance*) gelée *f*; *Culin* gelée (de viande); *Br* **j. baby,** (*sweet*) bonbon gélifié (*en forme de petit bonhomme*); **petroleum j.,** vaseline *f*; **royal j.,** (*from bees*) *& Culin* gelée royale; **(d)** *Br Sl* (*gelignite*) dynamite *f*.

jelly[2] *vt Culin* gélifier, mettre en gelée.

jellybean ['dʒelɪbiːn] *n Am* (*candy*) bonbon mou (*couvert de sucre dur et en forme de haricot*).

jellyfish ['dʒelɪfɪʃ] *n* (*pl* **-fish** *or* **-fishes**) méduse *f*.

jemmy[1] ['dʒemɪ] *n Br* **(burglar's) j.,** pince-monseigneur *f*.

jemmy[2] *vt Br* **to j. (open),** forcer (*une fenêtre etc*) à la pince-monseigneur.

jenny ['dʒenɪ] *n* **(a)** (*female of species*) (*donkey*) ânesse *f*; **j. wren/robin,** troglodyte *m ou* roitelet *m*/rouge-gorge *m* femelle; **(b)** *Bot* **creeping j.,** lysamique *f*; **(c)** *Tex* **spinning j.,** métier *m* à filer.

jeopardize ['dʒepədaɪz] *vt* compromettre, mettre en danger *ou* en péril (*sa santé, son avenir, la vie de qn etc*); compromettre (*ses chances*); laisser péricliter (*ses affaires*).

jeopardy ['dʒepədɪ] *n* danger *m*, péril *m*; **to be in j.,** (*of person, one's life*) être en danger *ou* en péril; (*of one's happiness, career, future etc*) être menacé; **his business is in j.,** son affaire périclite; **to put in j.,** = **jeopardize**; **to put s.o. in j.,** mettre qn en danger *ou* en péril.

jerbil ['dʒɜːbɪl] *n* (*rodent*) gerbille *f*.

jerk[1] [dʒɜːk] *n* **(a)** (*sudden pull, push etc*) secousse *f*, saccade *f*, coup sec; **she gave the rope a j.,** elle a donné une secousse à la corde, elle a tiré d'un coup sec sur la corde; **to move by jerks** *or* **in jerks** *or* **in a series of jerks,** (*of vehicle etc*) avancer par saccades *ou* par à-coups *ou* en faisant des bonds; **(b)** (*sudden start, jump*) sursaut *m*; **to wake up with a j.,** se réveiller en sursaut; **(c)** *Anat* **knee-j.,** réflexe patellaire *ou* rotulien; **(d)** *Sp* (*in weightlifting*) jeté *m*; *Br Gym F* **physical jerks,** gymnastique *f*.

jerk[2] **1** *vt* (*pull, push etc suddenly*) donner une secousse *ou* une saccade à, tirer d'un coup sec; (*repeatedly*) donner des secousses *ou* des saccades à, secouer; **to j. sth out of s.o.'s hands,** arracher qch (d'un coup sec) des mains de qn; **to j. forward/back,** (*of collision etc*) rejeter en avant/en arrière (*la tête ou le corps de qn*).

2 *vi* **(a)** (*shake*) secouer; **to j. (along** *or* **forward),** (*of vehicle*) avancer par saccades *ou* par à-coups, cahoter; **to j. forward/back,** (*of head, body*) être rejeté en avant/en arrière; **to j. to a halt,** (*of vehicle, train*) s'arrêter brusquement (avec des secousses);

(b) (*start, jump*) sursauter;

(c) (*of muscle*) se contracter, avoir un spasme *ou* des spasmes; *Anat* avoir un réflexe *ou* des réflexes.

jerk[3] *n F Pej* **(a)** (*fool*) **(stupid) j.,** crétin, -ine, andouille *f*; **(b)** (*obnoxious person*) abruti, -ie, con(n)ard *m*.

►**jerk off** *vi Vulg* (*masturbate*) se branler.

►**jerk out** *vtsep* balbutier, dire d'une façon saccadée (*des paroles, des excuses etc*).

jerkily ['dʒɜːkɪlɪ] *adv* (*to walk, move*) par saccades, par à-coups; (*to write, speak*) d'une manière saccadée.

jerky ['dʒɜːkɪ] *adj* (*movement, voice, style, speech etc*) saccadé, heurté.

jerrican, jerry can ['dʒerɪkæn] *n* jerrycan *m*, bidon *m*.

Jerry ['dʒerɪ] *n* (*dimin of* **German**) *Old-fashioned F Pej* (*soldier*) Boche *m*, Fritz *m*; (*the Germans*) les Boches.

jerry-building ['dʒerɪbɪldɪŋ] *n Pej* construction *f* en carton-pâte *ou* bon marché.

jerry-built ['dʒerɪbɪlt] *adj Pej* (*house*) en carton-pâte, bon marché, construit comme une cabane à lapins.

jersey ['dʒɜːzɪ] *n* **(a)** (*garment*) tricot *m* (de laine); **(football) j.,** maillot *m* (de footballeur); **(b)** (*material*) jersey *m*; **j. wool/silk, wool/silk j.,** jersey de laine/de soie; **cotton j.,** jersey de coton.

Jersey ['dʒɜːzɪ] *n* **(a)** (*island*) Jersey *f*; **(b) J. (cow),** vache *f* de Jersey *ou* jersiaise.

Jerusalem [dʒə'ruːsələm] *n* **(a)** Jérusalem *mf*; **(b) J. artichoke,** topinambour *m*.

jest[1] [dʒest] *n* (*joke*) plaisanterie *f*; (*witty remark*) mot *m* d'esprit; **in j.,** (*to say, speak etc*) en plaisantant, pour rire, par plaisanterie; **to act in j.,** plaisanter; *Prov* **(there is) many a true word spoken in j.,** on dit souvent la vérité sous le couvert d'une plaisanterie.

jest[2] *vi* (*joke*) plaisanter (**about sth,** sur qch), badiner; (*make witty remarks*) faire des mots d'esprit; **he's not a person to j. with,** on ne plaisante pas *ou* on ne badine pas avec lui.

jester ['dʒestər] *n* (*joker*) farceur, -euse; *Hist* **(court) j.,** bouffon *m ou* fou *m* (du roi).

jesting ['dʒestɪŋ] **1** *adj* (*remark etc*) fait pour plaisanter *ou* pour rire. **2** *n* (*jokes*) plaisanteries *fpl*; (*witty remarks*) mots *mpl* d'esprit.

Jesuit ['dʒezjʊɪt] **1** *n Rel & Fig* jésuite *m*. **2** *adj Rel & Fig* (*argument etc*) jésuite; **J. college,** collège *m* de jésuites.

Jesuitic(al) [dʒezjʊ'ɪtɪk, -'ɪtɪk(ə)l] *adj Rel & Fig* jésuitique.

Jesus ['dʒiːzəs] **1** *n* Jésus *m*; **J. Christ,** Jésus-Christ *m*; *F* **J. freak,** fou *ou* folle de Jésus. **2** *int Sl* **J. (Christ)!,** nom de Dieu!

jet[1] [dʒet] *n* **j. (aircraft),** avion *m* à réaction, jet *m*; **to travel by j.,** voyager en jet *ou* en avion à réaction; **j. engine,** réacteur *m*, moteur *m* à réaction; **j. fighter, fighter j.,** chasseur *m* à réaction; **j. fuel,** kérosène *m*, carburéacteur *m*; **j. lag,** fatigue *f* (due au décalage horaire) (*après un voyage en avion*); **I'm suffering from j. lag,** je suis fatigué (à cause du décalage horaire); **j. propulsion,** propulsion *f* par réaction; **the j. set,** le *ou* la jet set, les riches oisifs.

jet[2] *n* **(a)** (*of liquid, steam etc*) jet *m*; **(b)** (*nozzle*) jet *m*, ajutage *m*, buse *f*; (*of stove*) brûleur *m*; *Aut* gicleur *m*; **(water) j.,** (*in whirlpool, bath etc*) gicleur; **(c)** *Met* **j. stream,** courant-jet *m*, jet *m*, jet-stream *m*.

jet[3] *vi* **(-tt-)** (*of liquid*) sortir en jet, gicler.

jet[4] *n Miner* jais *m*; **j. earrings/necklace,** boucles d'oreille (noires)/collier (noir) de jais; **j. black,** (*colour*) noir *m* de jais; (*hair*) noir comme (du) jais, (noir) de jais.

►**jet off** *vi F* s'envoler (**to,** pour).

jetfoil ['dʒetfɔɪl] *n* hydroglisseur *m*.

jet-lagged ['dʒetlægd] *adj* fatigué (à cause du décalage horaire).

jet-powered [dʒet'paʊəd] **, jet-propelled** [dʒetprə'peld] *adj* (*engine, aircraft*) à réaction.

jetsam ['dʒetsəm] *n* (*no pl*) *Nau & Fig* épaves *fpl*.

jetsetter ['dʒetsetər] *n* membre *m* du *ou* de la jet set, riche oisif, -ive.

jettison ['dʒetɪs(ə)n] *vt Nau* jeter à la mer *ou* par-dessus bord, se délester de (*cargaison*); *Av* larguer (*des bombes, du carburant etc*); *Fig* abandonner, renoncer à (*un espoir, un projet, une tradition etc*).

jetty ['dʒetɪ] *n* **(a)** (*breakwater*) jetée *f*, môle *m*; **(b)** (*for landing*) embarcadère *m*, débarcadère *m*, appontement *m*.

Jew [dʒuː] *n* (*male*) Juif *m*; (*female*) Juive *f*; **the Wandering J.,** le Juif errant; *Mus* **J.'s harp,** guimbarde *f*.

Jew-baiting ['dʒuːbeɪtɪŋ] *n* persécution *f* des Juifs.

jewel ['dʒuːəl] *n* **(a)** (*piece of jewellery*) bijou *m*, joyau *m*; (*gem*) pierre précieuse; *Fig* (*person or thing of value*) perle *f*, bijou; **j. case,** coffret *m ou* écrin *m* à bijoux; **the crown jewels,** les joyaux de la couronne; **(b)** (*of watch*) rubis *m*.

jewelled, *US* **jeweled** ['dʒuːəld] *adj* (*watch*) monté sur rubis.

jeweller, *US* **jeweler** ['dʒuːələr] *n* bijoutier, -ière, joaillier, -ière; **j.'s (shop),** bijouterie *f*.

jewellery, *US* **jewelry** ['dʒuːəlrɪ] *n* bijoux *mpl*, joyaux *mpl*, bijouterie *f*, joaillerie *f*; **a piece of j.,** un bijou.

Jewess ['dʒuːes, -ɪs] *n* Juive *f*.

Jewish ['dʒuːɪʃ] *adj* juif, *f* juive.

Jewry ['dʒuːərɪ] *n* la communauté juive, les Juifs *mpl*.

jib[1] [dʒɪb] *n* **(a)** *Nau* (*sail*) foc *m*; **(b)** *Tech* (*of crane, derrick*) flèche *f*, bras *m*; **(c)** *Old-fashioned Fig* **the cut of**

s.o.'s j., (*s.o.'s manner, style etc*) l'allure *f* de qn.

jib² *vi* (**-bb-**) **(a)** (*of person*) se rebiffer, regimber, rechigner (**at sth**, devant qch); **to j. at doing**, rechigner à faire; **(b)** (*of horse*) regimber, se dérober.

jibe¹ [dʒaɪb] *n & vi* = **GIBE**.

jibe² *vi Am* (*agree*) s'accorder (**with**, avec).

jiffy ['dʒɪfɪ] *n F* **in (half) a j.**, en un instant, en moins de rien, en un clin d'œil; **I won't be (half) a j.!**, je reviens tout de suite *ou* dans un instant!, j'arrive!

Jiffy bag ® ['dʒɪfɪbæg] *n* enveloppe matelassée *ou* rembourrée.

jig¹ [dʒɪg] *n* (*dance, music*) gigue *f*.

jig² *vi* (**-gg-**) **(a)** (*dance*) danser la gigue; **(b)** (*shake*) **to j. (up and down), to j. about** *or* **around**, se trémousser (en dansant), sautiller.

jigger ['dʒɪgər] *n* (*measure for whisky*) = 42 ml.

jiggered ['dʒɪgəd] *adj Br Old-fashioned* **(a)** *F* (*surprised*) étonné; **well, I'm j.!, well, I'll be j.!**, zut alors!; **I'm** *or* **I'll be j. if ...**, (*confounded*) que le diable m'emporte si ...; **(b)** *Sl* (*tired*) claqué.

jiggery-pokery ['dʒɪgərɪ'pəʊkərɪ] *n Br F* manigances *fpl*, micmacs *mpl*.

jiggle ['dʒɪg(ə)l] **1** *vt* **to j. (about** *or* **around)**, secouer légèrement. **2** *vi* **to j. (about** *or* **around)**, être secoué légèrement.

jigsaw ['dʒɪgsɔː] *n* **(a)** *Carp* scie *f* à chantourner; **(b)** (*game*) **j. (puzzle)**, puzzle *m*.

jihad [dʒɪ'hæd] *n* (*Muslim holy war*) djihad *m*.

jilt [dʒɪlt] *vt* laisser tomber, *F* plaquer (*un amant, un amoureux*).

jimjams ['dʒɪmdʒæmz] *npl Sl Hum* **to have the j.**, (*fear*) avoir les chocottes, avoir le frisson; (*revulsion*) avoir le frisson *ou* la chair de poule; (*anxiety*) avoir les nerfs en pelote.

jimmy ['dʒɪmɪ] *n & vt Am* = **JEMMY¹·²**.

jingle¹ ['dʒɪŋg(ə)l] *n* **(a)** (*of bells*) tintement *m*; (*of keys etc*) tintement, cliquetis *m*; **(b)** (*catchy tune*) ritournelle *f*; (*for children*) comptine *f*; *Rad TV* (*in advertisement*) sonal *m*, jingle *m*.

jingle² **1** *vi* (*of bells*) tinter, tintinnabuler; (*of keys, metal objects etc*) tinter, cliqueter. **2** *vt* faire tinter *ou* cliqueter (*sa monnaie, des clefs etc*); faire tinter *ou* tintinnabuler (*des grelots*).

jingling ['dʒɪŋglɪŋ] *n* = **JINGLE¹ (a)**.

jingo ['dʒɪŋgəʊ] *n Old-fashioned F* **by j.!**, nom d'une pipe!

jingoism ['dʒɪŋgəʊɪz(ə)m] *n* chauvinisme *m*.

jingoistic ['dʒɪŋgəʊ'ɪstɪk] *adj* chauvin.

jinks [dʒɪŋks] *npl Old-fashioned F* **high j.**, la rigolade; **it was** *or* **we had high j.**, on a eu une séance de rigolade, on s'est bien marrés; **stop the high j.!**, trêve de rigolade!

jinx¹ [dʒɪŋks] *n F* (*person, object*) porte-malheur *m inv*, porte-guigne *m inv*; (*spell, curse*) maléfice *m*, (mauvais) sort *m*; (*bad luck*) guigne *f*; **to have a j.**, avoir la guigne; **to put a j. on, = jinx²**; **to break the j.**, échapper à la guigne.

jinx² *vt F* porter la guigne à, porter malheur à, jeter un sort à *ou* sur (*qn, un projet etc*); **to be jinxed**, avoir la guigne.

jitterbug¹ ['dʒɪtəbʌg] *n* **(a)** (*dance*) jitterbug *m*; **(b)** *F* (*jittery person*) froussard, -arde.

jitterbug² *vi* (**-gg-**) danser le jitterbug.

jitters ['dʒɪtəz] *npl F* **the j.**, (*anxiety*) la frousse; **to have** *or* **get the j.**, avoir la frousse (**about**, de); **she's got the j. about her exam**, son examen lui fiche la frousse; **it gives me the j.**, ça me fiche la frousse.

jittery ['dʒɪtərɪ] *adj F* (*anxious*) (très) nerveux; **to be j.**, avoir la frousse, être (très) nerveux.

jiujitsu [dʒuː'dʒɪtsuː] *n* jiu-jitsu *m*.

jive¹ [dʒaɪv] *n* **(a)** (*music, dance*) = swing *m*, rock *m*; **(b)** *Am Sl* (*deceiving talk*) baratin *m*; (*foolish talk*) foutaises *fpl*.

jive² **1** *vi* **(a)** (*dance*) danser le swing *ou* le rock; **(b)** *Am Sl* (*talk nonsense*) blaguer. **2** *vt Am Sl* (*mislead*) baratiner (*qn*).

Jnr (*abbr* **junior**) Jr.

Joan [dʒəʊn] *n* Jeanne *f*; **J. of Arc**, Jeanne d'Arc.

job¹ [dʒɒb] *n* **(a)** (*piece of work, task*) travail *m*, tâche *f*, besogne *f*; **to do its j.**, (*of medicine, alcohol etc*) faire son effet; **your tailor has done a first-class j.**, votre tailleur a fait un travail excellent *ou* de l'excellent travail; **to make a good** *or* **successful j. of sth**, bien réussir qch; **I've given it up as a bad j.**, j'y ai renoncé parce que je n'arrivais à rien *ou* parce que je n'ai pas eu de succès; **it's quite a (difficult) j.**, c'est tout un travail (**to mow the lawn/***etc*, que de tondre le gazon/*etc*); *Fig* **to lie down** *or* **fall down on the j.**, (*avoid working*) tirer au flanc; **this shelf isn't strong** *or* **good enough for the j.**, cette étagère ne tiendra pas le coup; **to do odd jobs**, faire des petits travaux, bricoler à droite et à gauche; **odd-j. man**, homme *m* à tout faire, homme (à) toutes mains; *Ind* **it's a precision j.**, c'est un travail de précision; *F* **the car has had a paint j.**, la bagnole a été repeinte; *F* **she wants to have** *or* **get a nose j.**, elle veut se faire rectifier le nez; *Com* **j. lot**, lot *m* (de marchandises); **a j. lot of books/***etc*, des livres *mpl/etc* en vrac, un lot de livres/*etc*; **to buy/sell sth as a j. lot**, acheter/vendre qch en lot *ou* en vrac;

(b) (*responsibility, duty*) travail *m*; **they are only doing their j.**, ils ne font que leur travail; **it's my j. to remind her**, c'est à moi de le lui rappeler; **that's not your j.**, ce n'est pas votre travail, ce n'est pas à vous de faire ça; **I make it my j. to ...**, je me charge de ...; **I'll have the j. of clearing it all up later**, c'est moi qui serai obligé de ranger *ou* qui devrai ranger tout ça plus tard; **that's not part of his j.**, ça n'entre pas dans ses fonctions, ça ne fait pas partie de son travail *ou* de ses attributions;

(c) (*employment, post*) emploi *m*, poste *m*, travail *m*, situation *f*, *F* boulot *m*, job *m*; **to create (new) jobs**, créer des emplois, créer de nouveaux emplois; **she knows her j.**, elle connaît son travail *ou* son affaire *ou* son métier *ou F* son boulot; **to give up one's j., to resign from one's j.**, démissionner; **it's my j. to ...**, je suis chargé de ..., c'est mon travail de ...; *Ind etc* **500 jobs were lost** *or* **axed**, il y a eu 500 suppressions d'emplois; *Br F* **to give jobs to the boys**, placer ses copains, donner des planques aux copains; **it's more than my j. is worth**, ça serait risquer de perdre mon emploi, ça ne vaut pas la peine de perdre mon emploi pour ça; **on-the-j. training**, formation *f* sur le tas; **to be out of a j.**, être au *ou* en chômage *ou* sans travail, chômer; **j. creation**, création *f* d'emplois *ou* de nouveaux emplois; **j. creation scheme**, programme *m* de création d'emplois; **j. description**, profil *m* du poste; **that's not in my j. description**, ça ne fait pas partie de mon travail; **j. hunter**, demandeur, -euse d'emploi; **j. hunting**, chasse *f* à l'emploi; **to go j. hunting**, aller à la recherche d'un emploi; **j. losses**, suppressions *fpl* d'emplois; **j. offers**, offres *fpl* d'emplois; **j. opportunities**, perspectives *fpl* d'emploi, débouchés *mpl*; **j. satisfaction**, satisfaction *f* dans le travail; **j. security**, sécurité *f* de l'emploi; **j. seeker**, demandeur, -euse d'emploi; **j. sharing**, partage *m* des emplois *ou* des fonctions; **j. title**, titre *m* (de fonction);

(d) (*difficulty, trouble*) **to have (quite) a j.** *or* **a difficult j. doing** *or* **to do sth**, avoir du mal à faire qch; *F* **she had the devil** *or Sl* **a hell of a j. doing it**, elle a eu tout le mal du monde *ou* un mal de tous les diables *ou* un mal fou à faire cela; *F* **she's got a real j. on her hands with that baby**, elle a fort à faire avec ce bébé;

(e) *Sl* (*crime*) coup *m*; **they did that bank j.**, ils ont monté le coup de la banque; **a put-up j.**, un coup monté; **an inside j.**, un coup monté avec des complicités de l'intérieur;

(f) *Comptr* travail *m*, élément *m* de travail; **j. control**, gestion *f* des travaux;

(g) *F* (*manufactured object*) **that TV is a really nice j.**, cette télé, c'est du beau travail; **a souped-up j.**, (*car or motorcycle*) une bagnole *ou* une moto au moteur gonflé;

(h) *Fig* (*phrases*) *Br* **it's** *or* **what a good j. (that) ...!**, heureusement que ... + *ind*, c'est heureux que ... + *sub*; *Br F* **he got what he deserved — (and) a good j. too!**, il a eu ce qu'il méritait — et c'est tant mieux *ou* c'est bien fait pour lui *ou* j'en suis très heureux!; **that's just the j.**, c'est exactement ce qu'il faut; *Br F* **the baby has done a (big) j.**, le bébé a fait son caca *ou* un gros caca; *F* **to do a j. on a car/***etc*, (*wreck*) bousiller une voiture/*etc*; *F* **to do a j. on s.o.**, (*beat up*) tabasser qn; (*brainwash*) faire (subir) un lavage de cerveau à qn; **the garage/hairdresser did a good j. on her**, le garage/coiffeur a fait un bon travail.

job² *vi* (**-bb-**) **(a)** (*do small jobs*) faire des petits travaux, bricoler; **(b)** (*do piecework*) travailler à la tâche *ou* à la pièce.

Job [dʒəʊb] *n* Job *m*; **to have the patience of J.**, avoir une patience d'ange; **you're a J.'s comforter**, vous êtes un bien piètre consolateur, vous ne m'êtes pas d'un grand réconfort.

jobbing ['dʒɒbɪŋ] *Br* **1** *adj* (*worker*) (qui travaille) à la tâche *ou* à la pièce; **j. gardener**, jardinier, -ière à la journée. **2** *n* **(a)** (*piecework*) travail *m* à la tâche *ou* à la pièce; **(b)** (*odd jobs*) bricolage *m*.

Jobcentre ['dʒɒbsentər] *n Br* = agence nationale pour l'emploi, ANPE *f*.

jobless ['dʒɒblɪs] **1** *adj* sans travail, au *ou* en chômage. **2** *n* **the j.**, (*used as pl*) les chômeurs *mpl*, les demandeurs *mpl* d'emploi, les sans-emploi *mpl*; **the j. figures**, le nombre des chômeurs *ou* des demandeurs d'emploi.

jock [dʒɒk] *n* **(a)** *Am Univ F* (*sportsman*) sportif *m*; **(b)** *abbr* **jockstrap**.

Jock [dʒɒk] *n Sl* (*Scot*) Écossais, -aise.

jockey¹ ['dʒɒkɪ] *n* **(a)** *Horseracing* (*man*) jockey *m*; (*woman*) femme *f* jockey; **amateur j.**, jockey amateur, gentleman(-rider) *m*; **j. cap,** casquette *f* de jockey; **J.** ® **shorts,** caleçon *m*; **(b)** *Rad etc* **disc j.**, présentateur, -trice de disques, animateur, -trice (de variétés *etc*), disc-jockey *m*.

jockey² **1** *vi* (*scheme*) manœuvrer, intriguer (**for a job/** *etc*, pour obtenir *ou* se faire donner un poste/*etc*); **to j. for position,** manœuvrer *ou* intriguer pour se placer avantageusement. **2** *vt* (*persuade forcefully, deceive*) **to j. s.o. into doing,** amener qn par la ruse à faire; **to j. s.o. out of a job,** évincer *ou* chasser qn d'un poste.

jockstrap ['dʒɒkstræp] *n* slip *m* à coquille.

jocular ['dʒɒkjʊlər] *adj* (*humorous*) facétieux, amusant, jovial; (*jolly*) enjoué; **in (a) j. vein,** (*to say, reply etc*) d'un ton facétieux *ou* amusant *ou* rieur.

jocularity [dʒɒkjʊ'lærɪtɪ] *n* (*humour*) humour *m*; (*jollity*) jovialité *f*.

jocularly ['dʒɒkjʊləlɪ] *adv* (*humorously*) facétieusement; (*with jollity*) jovialement.

jocund ['dʒɒkənd] *adj Lit* jovial, enjoué.

jodhpurs ['dʒɒdpəz] *npl* pantalon *m ou* culotte *f* de cheval, jodhpurs *mpl*.

Joe [dʒəʊ] *n Am F* (*man, fellow*) homme *m*, type *m*; **he's an ordinary J.**, c'est un Monsieur Tout-le-monde; **J. Public,** *F* **J. Blow,** *Sl* **J. Schmo,** *Br* **J. Bloggs,** Monsieur Tout-le-monde, ≈ Monsieur Dupont; *US* **GI J.**, (*soldier*) troufion *m* (américain), GI *m*.

joey ['dʒəʊɪ] *n Austr F* petit kangourou.

jog¹ [dʒɒg] *n* **(a)** (*push*) poussée *f*, coup sec; (*shake*) secousse *f*; (*with elbow*) coup de coude; *Fig* **to give s.o.'s memory a j.**, rafraîchir la mémoire de *ou* à qn; **(b)** (*jolt in vehicle*) cahot *m*, secousse *f*; **(c)** (*run*) **j. (trot),** petit trot; **at a j. (trot),** au petit trot; **to break into a j.**, (*of person, horse*) se mettre à trotter; **(d)** *Sp* **to go for a j.**, faire du jogging.

jog² *v* **(-gg-)** **1** *vt* (*push*) pousser (d'un coup sec); (*shake*) secouer; **she jogged my elbow,** elle m'a poussé le coude; *Fig* **to j. s.o.'s memory,** rafraîchir la mémoire de *ou* à qn; *Fig* **to j. s.o. into action/j. s.o. out of it,** inciter qn à l'action/secouer qn. **2** *vi Sp* faire du jogging; **to go jogging,** faire du jogging.

►jog along *vi* (*of vehicle etc*) cahoter; (*of person*) cheminer; *Fig* (*of person, factory, country etc*) aller tant bien que mal; *Fig* **I'm jogging along quite happily,** je vais mon petit bonhomme de chemin.

jogger ['dʒɒgər] *n Sp* **(a)** (*person*) jogger *m*, joggeur, -euse; **(b)** (*shoe*) chaussure *f* de jogging.

jogging ['dʒɒgɪŋ] *n Sp* jogging *m*; **to like j.**, aimer faire du jogging; **j. outfit** *or* **suit,** tenue *f* de jogging, jogging *m*; **j. shoes,** chaussures *fpl* de jogging.

joggle¹ ['dʒɒg(ə)l] *n* légère secousse.

joggle² **1** *vt* secouer légèrement. **2** *vi* (*shake*) être secoué.

jog-trot ['dʒɒgtrɒt] *vi* **(-tt-)** (*of horse, Fig of person*) aller au petit trot.

john [dʒɒn] *n* **(a)** *Am F* **the j.**, (*lavatory*) le petit coin, les cabinets *mpl*; **(b)** *Am Sl* (*prostitute's client*) micheton *m*; **(c)** *F* **long johns,** (*underwear*) caleçon long.

John [dʒɒn] *n* **(a)** Jean *m*; **J. Bull,** John Bull *m*, l'Anglais *m* typique; (*the English*) les Anglais *mpl*; (*England*) l'Angleterre *f*; *Am* **J. Doe,** (*average person*) l'Américain moyen, ≈ Monsieur Dupont; *F* (*unidentified man*) (*under arrest*) inconnu *m*; (*corpse*) mort non-identifié; *Am F* **one's J. Hancock** *or* **J. Henry,** sa signature, son gribouillis; *Am* **J. Q. Public,** Monsieur Tout-le-monde; **(Saint) J. the Baptist,** saint Jean-Baptiste; **(b)** **J. Dory,** (*fish*) dorée *f*, saint-pierre *m inv*.

Johnny ['dʒɒnɪ] *n* (*dimin of* **John**) Jeannot *m*; *F* **J.-come-lately,** (*new arrival*) nouveau venu; *US Hist F* **J. Reb,** soldat confédéré.

join¹ [dʒɔɪn] *n* (*in wallpaper, masonry etc*) (ligne *f* de) raccord *m*; *Tech* (*junction between elements*) joint *m*; (*in fabric*) couture *f*.

join² **1** *vt* **(a)** (*unite*) joindre, unir (*planches, morceaux d'étoffe etc*); (*connect, link*) relier (*villes, mots, points etc*); rapprocher, réunir (*les bords d'une plaie etc*); raccorder (*tuyaux, fils électriques*); **to j. two things end to end,** joindre deux choses bout à bout; **the Siamese twins are joined at the thigh,** les frères siamois sont rattachés (l'un à l'autre) par la cuisse; **to j. in marriage** *or* **in matrimony,** unir par le mariage; *Mil & Fig* **to j. battle,** engager le combat (**with,** avec); *Fig* **we shall j. forces,** nous unirons nos forces; *Fig* **to j. forces** *or* **hands (with s.o.) to do** *or* **in doing,** se joindre *ou* s'unir (à qn) pour faire; **we joined hands,** nous nous sommes pris par la main, nous nous sommes donné la main;

(b) (*catch up with, meet*) rejoindre, retrouver (*qn*) (**at,** à); (*associate oneself with*) se joindre à (*qn*) (**in doing,** pour faire); (*take part in*) prendre part à (*un jeu*); **to j. a discussion,** se joindre à *ou* prendre part à une discussion; **to j. s.o. in** *or* **for a drink,** prendre un verre avec qn, se joindre à qn pour prendre un verre; **will you j. us?**, voulez-vous vous joindre à nous?; **why don't you j. (us at) our table?**, venez donc vous asseoir à notre table!; **we are joined in the studio by Lord Smith,** Lord Smith vient nous rejoindre *ou* vient se joindre à nous dans notre studio;

(c) (*go to, return to*) rejoindre; *Mil Nau* **to j. one's regiment/ship,** rejoindre son régiment/son bâtiment; **we shall soon j. the motorway,** nous rejoindrons bientôt l'autoroute;

(d) (*intersect with, flow into*) rejoindre; **to j. the sea,** (*of river*) rejoindre la mer, se jeter dans la mer;

(e) (*become a member of*) s'inscrire à, entrer dans, adhérer à (*une association, un club, un parti politique*); entrer dans (*une firme, un groupe, un ordre religieux*); s'engager dans, s'enrôler dans, entrer dans (*l'armée, la marine, la police*); **to j. a convent/a newspaper,** entrer au couvent/au journal; **to j. the queue,** prendre la queue, se mettre à la queue; **to j. a class** *or* **a course,** s'inscrire pour *ou* à un cours.

2 *vi* **(a)** (*of pieces of fabric, planks etc*) se toucher, se joindre; (*of pipes, wires*) se raccorder; (*of rooms in a building*) se toucher, se réunir;

(b) **to j. with s.o.**, (*associate oneself with*) se joindre à qn, s'associer à qn (**in doing,** pour faire);

(c) (*of roads, lines, rivers*) se rejoindre;

(d) (*enrol in club, political party etc*) s'inscrire, devenir membre; (*enlist in the army etc*) s'engager.

►join in **1** *vi* (*take part*) se mettre de la partie, participer, prendre part; **I'll sing first and then you (all) j. in,** je chanterai d'abord et ensuite vous vous joindrez à moi *ou* vous joindrez vos voix à la mienne. **2** *vipo* (*take part in*) prendre part à, participer à (*un jeu, une activité*); prendre part à, se joindre à, participer à (*une discussion*); **to j. in the protest(s),** s'associer aux protestations, joindre sa voix aux protestations; **to j. in the singing,** chanter; **you'll all j. in the chorus,** vous chanterez tous le refrain en chœur.

►join on **1** *vtsep* (*fasten*) attacher (**to,** à); (*add*) ajouter (**to,** à). **2** *vi* (*fasten*) s'attacher (**to,** à); **the paragraph joins on here,** le paragraphe vient s'ajouter ici.

►join together **1** *vtsep* = **JOIN² 1 (a)**. **2** *vi* = **JOIN² 2 (a), (b)**.

►join up **1** *vi* **(a)** *Mil* s'engager (dans l'armée *etc*); (*for class etc*) s'inscrire; **(b)** (*of pieces of fabric*) se toucher, se joindre; (*of pipes, wires*) se raccorder; **(c)** **to j. up with s.o.**, (*catch up with, meet*) rejoindre qn, retrouver qn; **to j. up with the motorway,** rejoindre l'autoroute. **2** *vtsep* joindre, unir (*planches, morceaux d'étoffe etc*); raccorder (*tuyaux, fils électriques*); accoupler (*deux machines*).

joiner ['dʒɔɪnər] *n Br* (*carpenter*) menuisier *m*.

joinery ['dʒɔɪnərɪ] *n Br* menuiserie *f*; **piece of j.**, article *m ou* pièce *f* de menuiserie.

joint¹ [dʒɔɪnt] *n* **(a)** *Anat* articulation *f*, jointure *f*; **hip j.**, articulation de la hanche; **knee j.**, jointure *ou* articulation du genou; **rheumatism of the joints,** rhumatisme *m* articulaire; **to be stiff in the joints,** être tout ankylosé; **to put one's arm/shoulder/***etc* **out of j.**, se démettre *ou* se disloquer *ou* se déboîter le bras/l'épaule/*etc*; *Br Fig* **to put s.o.'s nose out of j.**, (*make envious*) faire pâlir qn (de dépit), dépiter qn;

(b) *Tech* joint *m*, jointure *f*; *Carp* assemblage *m*; **(soldered** *or* **welded) j.**, soudure *f*; *Carp* **dovetail j.**, assemblage à queue d'aronde; *Tech* **universal j.**, cardan *m*, joint universel *ou* de cardan;

(c) *Br Culin* rôti *m*; **j. of beef,** rôti de bœuf; **j. of lamb,** (*leg*) gigot *m* d'agneau; (*shoulder*) épaule *f* d'agneau;

(d) *F Pej* (*nightclub*) boîte *f*; (*restaurant*) restau *m*, gargote *f*; (*place*) endroit *m;* **(gambling) j.**, maison *f* de jeu, tripot *m*;

(e) *Sl* (*cannabis cigarette*) joint *m*.

joint² *vt Culin* découper (*un poulet etc*) (aux jointures).

joint³ *adj* **(a)** (*statement, decision etc*) commun; (*contract, agreement etc between two parties*) bilatéral; (*between more than two parties*) collectif; (*legacy*) conjoint; *Banking* **j. account,** compte joint *ou* commun; *US Mil* **J. Chiefs of Staff,** chefs *mpl* d'état-major des armées; **j. commission/**

committee, commission *f*/comité *m* mixte; *Jur* **j. custody,** garde conjointe; **j. efforts,** efforts conjugués *ou* communs *ou* réunis; **j. financing,** financement conjoint; **j. passport,** passeport conjoint; **we have a j. passport,** nous sommes sur le même passeport; *Com* **j. report,** rapport collectif; **j. signature,** (*of husband and wife etc*) signature conjointe; **j.-stock company,** *Br* société *f* (anonyme) par actions; société *f* en commandite; **j. undertaking** *or* **venture,** coentreprise *f*, société en participation;
(b) (*in partnership with others*) co-; **j. author,** coauteur *m*; **j. heir,** cohéritier, -ière; **j. holder,** (*of record, trophy etc*) codétenteur, -trice; **j. owner,** (*of property*) copropriétaire *mf*; **to be j. owners of,** posséder *ou* détenir en commun (*une voiture, des actions etc*); **j. ownership,** copropriété *f*; *Cin* **j. production,** coproduction *f*.

jointed ['dʒɔɪntɪd] *adj* (*puppet, limb etc*) articulé.

-jointed ['dʒɔɪntɪd] *suff* **large-j.,** aux grosses articulations; **heavy- j.,** aux articulations lourdes.

jointly ['dʒɔɪntlɪ] *adv* conjointement, ensemble (**with,** avec); *Jur* **j. liable, j. responsible,** (*debtors etc*) solidaire; *Jur* **to act j.,** (*of several parties*) agir solidairement; **j. and severally,** conjointement et solidairement.

joist [dʒɔɪst] *n Constr* solive *f*.

joke[1] [dʒəʊk] *n* **(a)** (*remark*) plaisanterie *f*, *F* blague *f*; **to say/do sth for a j.,** dire/faire qch par plaisanterie *ou* pour rire; **to make** *or* **tell** *or* **crack a j.,** faire une plaisanterie (**about,** sur); **to make a j. about,** (*laugh at*) se moquer de; **to make a j. of everything,** prendre tout à la blague *ou* à la rigolade; **the j. is that ...,** le comique *ou* l'amusant de l'histoire, c'est que ...; **it's no j. waiting for hours,** ce n'est pas amusant *ou* drôle d'attendre des heures; **what a j.!,** ce que c'est amusant *ou* drôle!; *F* **that's** *or* **it's no j.!,** (*not easy*) ce n'est pas facile!; (*serious*) ce n'est pas de la blague!; **it's getting beyond a j.,** ça commence à ne plus être drôle, ça dépasse le stade de la plaisanterie; **the j. is on me,** c'est à vous *ou* à eux *etc* de rire; **he's always ready with a j.,** il a toujours le mot pour rire; **she can't take a j.,** elle ne comprend pas la plaisanterie;
(b) (*prank, trick*) **(practical) j.,** farce *f*, plaisanterie *f*, tour *m*, *F* blague *f*; **to play a (practical) j. on s.o.,** faire une farce *ou* une plaisanterie *ou* une blague à qn, jouer un tour à qn;
(c) (*person or thing*) risée *f*.

joke[2] *vi* plaisanter, *F* blaguer; **to j. about,** (*laugh at*) se moquer de; **to j. with s.o.,** plaisanter avec qn; **I was only joking,** ce n'était qu'une plaisanterie, je plaisantais; **you're joking!, you must be** *or* **you've got to be joking!,** vous voulez rire!, sans blague!; **I'm not joking!,** je ne plaisante pas!, sans blague!

joker ['dʒəʊkər] *n* **(a)** farceur, -euse, *F* blagueur, -euse, *Pej* plaisantin *m*; **(b)** *F Pej* (*person*) type *m*, individu *m*; **(c)** *Cards* joker *m*; *Fig* **that's the j. in the pack,** c'est la grande inconnue; *Fig* **she's the j. in the pack,** avec elle, c'est la grande inconnue.

jokey ['dʒəʊkɪ] *adj* = **JOKY**.

jokily ['dʒəʊkɪlɪ] *adv* en plaisantant.

joking ['dʒəʊkɪŋ] **1** *adj* (*tone*) moqueur, de plaisanterie. **2** *n* (*no pl*) plaisanteries *fpl*, *F* blagues *fpl*; **j. apart** *or* **aside,** toute plaisanterie mise à part, *F* blague à part.

jokingly ['dʒəʊkɪŋlɪ] *adv* par plaisanterie, en plaisantant, pour rire.

joky ['dʒəʊkɪ] *adj* (*person*) qui aime raconter des plaisanteries; (*mood, conversation etc*) jovial; (*present etc*) farfelu.

jollies ['dʒɒlɪz] *npl Sl* **to get one's j. (from) doing,** (*get pleasure from*) prendre son pied à faire.

jollification [dʒɒlɪfɪ'keɪsən] *n F* (*merrymaking*) réjouissances *fpl*.

jolliness ['dʒɒlɪnɪs] **, jollity** ['dʒɒlɪtɪ] *n* (*cheerfulness*) jovialité *f*, gaieté *f*; (*merrymaking*) réjouissances *fpl*.

jolly[1] ['dʒɒlɪ] **1** *adj* **(a)** (*cheerful*) jovial, gai, joyeux; *Nau* **the J. Roger,** le pavillon noir (des pirates); **(b)** *F* (*pleasant*) agréable. **2** *adv Br F* (*very*) drôlement, rudement; **it serves him j. well right!,** c'est drôlement *ou* rudement bien fait pour lui!; **yes, I j. well DID do it!,** oui, je l'ai bel et bien fait!; **j. good!,** formidable!; **and a j. good job too!,** et c'est tant mieux!

jolly[2] *vt F* amadouer qn, enjôler qn, encourager qn (par des plaisanteries *ou* des flatteries); **I jollied him into accepting,** je l'ai amadoué *ou* enjôlé tant et si bien qu'il a fini par accepter, je l'ai encouragé à accepter.

▶**jolly along** *vtsep* = **JOLLY**[2].

jolt[1] [dʒəʊlt] *n* **(a)** (*shake*) secousse *f*; (*of vehicle*) cahot *m*, secousse, à-coup *m*; (*of engine*) à-coup, secousse; **(b)** (*start*) sursaut *m*; **to wake up with a j.,** se réveiller en sursaut; **(c)** *Fig* (*shock, surprise*) choc *m*; **it gave me a bit of a j.,** ça m'a fait un choc *ou* un coup.

jolt[2] **1** *vi* (*shake*) secouer; **to j. along,** (*of vehicle*) cahoter, tressauter, avancer en cahotant *ou* par à-coups; **to j. forward,** (*of vehicle, train*) s'ébranler avec une secousse; **to j. forward/back,** (*of head, body*) être rejeté en avant/en arrière; **to j. to a stop,** (*of vehicle, train*) faire un arrêt brutal. **2** *vt* (*shake*) secouer; (*of vehicle*) cahoter, secouer (*des passagers*); *Fig* (*shock, surprise*) secouer (*qn*); **to j. forward/back,** (*of collision etc*) rejeter en avant/en arrière (*la tête ou le corps de qn*); *Fig* **to j. s.o. out of it, to j. s.o. into action,** secouer (les puces à) qn; *Fig* **to j. s.o. out of his smugness,** faire perdre sa suffisance à qn.

jolting ['dʒəʊltɪŋ] *n* (*no pl*) (*of vehicle*) cahots *mpl*.

Jonah ['dʒəʊnə] *n Fig* (*jinx*) porte-malheur *m inv*.

jonquil ['dʒɒŋkwɪl] *n* (*flower*) jonquille *f*.

Jordan ['dʒɔːd(ə)n] *n* (*country*) Jordanie *f*; **the J.,** (*river*) le Jourdain.

Jordanian [dʒɔː'deɪnɪən] **1** *adj* jordanien; (*embassy, ambassador*) de Jordanie. **2** *n* Jordanien, -ienne.

josh[1] [dʒɒʃ] *n Am F* (*joke*) blague *f*.

josh[2] *Am F* **1** *vt* (*tease*) chambrer, vanner (*qn*) (**about,** sur), mettre (*qn*) en boîte (**about,** à cause de). **2** *vi* (*joke*) blaguer.

joss [dʒɒs] *n* **j. stick,** bâton *m* d'encens.

jostle[1] ['dʒɒs(ə)l] *n* (*push*) bousculade *f*.

jostle[2] **1** *vi* (*push each other*) se bousculer; (*use one's elbows*) jouer des coudes (**for sth,** pour obtenir qch); **to j. against s.o.,** bousculer qn; *Fig* **to j. for jobs,** se bousculer pour décrocher un emploi. **2** *vt* bousculer; **to be jostled, to get (oneself) jostled,** se faire bousculer (**by,** par); **to j. s.o. out of the way,** écarter qn à coups de coudes *ou* en jouant des coudes; **to j. one's way (through),** se frayer un chemin à coups de coude.

jostling ['dʒɒs(ə)lɪŋ] *n* (*of crowd*) bousculade(s) *f(pl)*.

jot[1] [dʒɒt] *n* (*used in negatives*) **he doesn't care a j.,** il n'en a rien à faire, il ne s'en soucie pas du tout; **there isn't a j. of truth in what you say,** il n'y a pas la moindre parcelle *ou* part de vérité dans ce que vous dites.

jot[2] *vt* (-tt-) = **JOT DOWN**.

▶**jot down** *vtsep* noter, prendre note de, prendre en note; **to j. down (some) notes,** prendre des notes.

jotter ['dʒɒtər] *n* (*notepad*) bloc-notes *m*.

jottings ['dʒɒtɪŋz] *npl* notes *fpl* (prises à la hâte).

journal ['dʒɜːn(ə)l] *n* **(a)** (*periodical*) revue *f*, journal *m*; **(b)** (*record of events*) journal *m*; *Com* livre *m* de comptes; **(c)** *Tech* **j. bearing,** palier *m*.

journalese [dʒɜːnə'liːz] *n Pej F* style *m ou* jargon *m* journalistique.

journalism ['dʒɜːnəlɪz(ə)m] *n* journalisme *m*.

journalist ['dʒɜːnəlɪst] *n* journaliste *mf*.

journalistic [dʒɜːnə'lɪstɪk] *adj* journalistique.

journey[1] ['dʒɜːnɪ] *n* voyage *m*; (*of short distance*) trajet *m*; **to make** *or* **undertake a j., to set off** *or* **out on a j.,** faire *ou* entreprendre un voyage; **to go (away) on a j.,** partir en voyage; **to get to** *or* **reach the end of one's j.,** arriver à destination, arriver à la fin de son voyage *ou* trajet; **have a good j.!,** bon voyage!; **to have an hour's j. to work,** avoir une heure de trajet pour se rendre à son travail; **a bus/car j.,** un trajet en autobus/voiture; **a train j.,** un voyage par le train; **to go on a train j.,** prendre le train, voyager par le train; **the return j., the j. home** *or* **back,** le voyage de retour, le retour; (*from work*) le trajet de retour; **outward j.,** voyage d'aller, l'aller *m*; **j. time,** (*by train etc*) durée *f* du voyage; (*by car, bus*) durée du trajet.

journey[2] *vi Lit* voyager; **to j. on,** continuer son voyage.

journeyman, *pl* **-men** ['dʒɜːnɪmən] *n* (*craftsman*) compagnon *m*, ouvrier *m*; **j. baker,** ouvrier boulanger; **j. carpenter,** compagnon charpentier.

joust[1] [dʒaʊst] *n Hist & Fig* joute *f*.

joust[2] *vi Hist & Fig* jouter (**against,** contre).

jousting ['dʒaʊstɪŋ] *n Hist & Fig* joutes *fpl*.

jovial ['dʒəʊvɪəl] *adj* jovial, enjoué; **she's in a j. mood,** elle est d'humeur joviale.

joviality [dʒəʊvɪ'ælɪtɪ] *n* jovialité *f*, enjouement *m*.

jovially ['dʒəʊvɪəlɪ] *adv* jovialement.

jowl [dʒaʊl] *n* **(a)** (*jaw*) mâchoire *f*; **(b)** (*hanging flesh*) bajoue *f*.

-jowled [dʒaʊld] *suff* **long/square/***etc***-j.,** à la mâchoire allongée/carrée/*etc*.

joy [dʒɔɪ] *n* **(a)** (*happiness, person, thing*) joie *f*; **to jump** *or* **leap/weep** *or* **cry for j.,** sauter *ou* bondir/pleurer de joie; **wild with j., beside oneself with j.,** fou *ou* ivre de joie; **to our great j.,** à notre grande joie; **the joys of marriage/spring/***etc*, les joies *ou* plaisirs du mariage/du printemps/

etc; **the joys of having children/a car,** les joies qu'apportent les enfants/qu'apporte la voiture; *Fig* **full of the joys of spring,** au comble du bonheur; **I wish you (great) j.,** je vous souhaite beaucoup de plaisir; *Iron* **I wish you j. (of it)!,** je vous souhaite bien du plaisir!, vous m'en voyez fort aise!; **(b)** *Br F* (*no pl*) (*success*) succès *m*; **(did you have** *or* **get) any j.?,** ça a marché?, tu as eu du succès *ou* de la chance?; **no j.!,** un coup pour rien!, ça n'a rien donné!, ça n'a pas marché!

joyful ['dʒɔɪfʊl] *adj* (*person, face, news etc*) joyeux.

joyfully ['dʒɔɪfəlɪ] *adv* joyeusement, avec joie.

joyfulness ['dʒɔɪfʊlnɪs] *n* (grande) joie *f*.

joyless ['dʒɔɪlɪs] *adj* triste, sans joie.

joylessly ['dʒɔɪlɪslɪ] *adv* tristement, sans joie.

joyous ['dʒɔɪəs] *adj* (*occasion, news, person etc*) joyeux.

joyously ['dʒɔɪəslɪ] *adv* joyeusement, avec joie.

joyride¹ ['dʒɔɪraɪd] *n F* virée *f*; **to go for a** *or* **on a j.,** faire une virée; *Am Fig* **it's no j. working with him,** travailler avec lui, ce n'est pas une partie de plaisir, ce n'est pas de tout repos.

joyride² *vi* (*pt* **joyrode** [-rəʊd]; *pp* **joyridden** [-rɪd(ə)n]) *F* faire une virée; **to go joyriding,** faire une virée.

joyrider ['dʒɔɪraɪdər] *n* voleur, -euse (qui prend une voiture pour faire une virée).

joystick ['dʒɔɪstɪk] *n Av* manche *m* à balai; *Comptr* manette *f* (de jeu), manche à balai, poignée *f*.

JP [dʒeɪ'piː] *n Br Jur abbr* **justice of the peace**.

jubilant ['dʒuːbɪlənt] *adj* (*shouts etc*) joyeux, de joie; (*expression*) épanoui, radieux; **to be j.,** (*of person*) déborder de joie, jubiler, exulter; **to be j. at** *or* **about** *or* **over the news/***etc*, être transporté de joie par la nouvelle/*etc*.

jubilantly ['dʒuːbɪləntlɪ] *adv* avec joie.

jubilation [dʒuːbɪ'leɪʃən] *n* (*of person*) (grande) joie *f*, exultation *f*, jubilation *f*; **a sense of j.,** un grand sentiment de joie; **a cause for (great) j.,** l'occasion de (grandes) réjouissances.

jubilee ['dʒuːbɪliː] *n* **(golden) j.,** jubilé *m*, (fête *f* du) cinquantième anniversaire *m* (*de mariage etc*); **silver/diamond j.,** (fête du) vingt-cinquième/soixantième anniversaire.

judas ['dʒuːdəs] *n* **j. (hole** *or* **window),** (*in door*) judas *m*.

Judas ['dʒuːdəs] *n Pej & Bible* Judas *m*; *Bible* **J. Iscariot,** Judas Iscariote; **J. kiss,** baiser *m* de Judas.

judder¹ ['dʒʌdər] *n Br* (*of brakes*) trépidation *f*; (*of clutch, tool*) broutage *m*, broutement *m*.

judder² *vi Br* (*of brakes*) trépider; (*of clutch, tool*) brouter; **to j. to a halt,** (*of train, vehicle*) s'arrêter avec de violentes secousses.

judge¹ [dʒʌdʒ] *n* **(a)** *Jur Sp etc* juge *m*; (*of contest*) juge, membre *m* du jury; *Jur* **examining j.,** juge d'instruction; *Jur* **presiding j.,** président, -ente du tribunal; *Jur* **the judges,** (*the bench*) la magistrature assise; *Bible* **the Book of Judges,** le livre des Juges; *Tennis* **line j.,** juge de ligne; *Rugby* **touch j.,** juge de touche;

(b) *Fig* juge *m*, connaisseur *m*; (*of cars, horses, wine*) spécialiste *mf* (**of,** en); **to be a good** *or* **keen j. of character,** être bon *ou* fin psychologue; **I'll let you be the j. of that,** je vous en fais juge, je vous laisse juge; **I will be the j. of that,** c'est moi qui jugerai de cela.

judge² 1 *vt* **(a)** (*try, give decision about*) juger (*un accusé, un pécheur, un concours, un match etc*);

(b) (*assess critically*) juger (*une personne, une situation, un texte etc*); (*estimate, evaluate*) juger, estimer, évaluer (*la distance, la vitesse etc*); **to j. s.o. by** *or* **on sth,** juger qn sur *ou* d'après qch; **to j. people by appearances,** juger d'après les apparences; **to j. sth at its true** *or* **proper value/on its merits,** juger *ou* apprécier qch à sa juste valeur/selon ses mérites;

(c) (*think, consider*) juger (**that,** que; **if, whether,** si); **to j. it necessary to ...,** juger nécessaire de ... .

2 *vi* (*assess, estimate, pass judgment*) *& Jur Rel* juger; **to j. by appearances,** juger d'après les apparences; **as far as I can j.,** autant que je puisse en juger; **to j. for oneself,** (en) juger par soi-même; **judging by** *or* **from his letter/my first impressions/***etc*, à en juger par *ou* d'après sa lettre/mes premières impressions/*etc*; **who will be judging?,** (*in competition*) qui va faire fonction de juge?

judg(e)ment, *Am* **judgment** ['dʒʌdʒmənt] *n* **(a)** *Jur Rel & Fig* jugement *m*; *Jur* **to pass** *or* **give** *or* **deliver j.,** prononcer *ou* rendre un jugement (**on,** sur); *Jur* **to sit in j.,** (*of court*) siéger; *Fig* **to sit in j. on s.o., to pass j. on s.o.,** porter un jugement sur qn, juger qn; **to sit in j., to pass j.,** porter des jugements *ou* juger (les gens); *Rel* **the Last J., J. Day,** le Jugement dernier;

(b) (*no pl*) (*discernment*) jugement *m*; **to have/lack (good** *or* **sound) j.,** avoir du/manquer de jugement; **to have a very sound j.,** avoir une grande sûreté de jugement, avoir un jugement très sûr;

(c) (*opinion*) jugement *m*; **to give one's j. on,** exprimer *ou* formuler son jugement sur, donner *ou* exprimer son avis sur; **to form a j.,** se faire une opinion, se former un jugement; **in my j.,** à mon sens; **against my better j.,** tout en sachant que je me trompe *ou* me trompais sans doute.

judg(e)mental, *Am* **judgmental** [dʒʌdʒ'ment(ə)l] *adj* (*person*) rigoriste, critique, qui porte des jugements d'ordre moral; (*approach, book etc*) rigoriste, critique, dogmatique; **a j. error,** une erreur de jugement.

judicature ['dʒuːdɪkətʃər] *n* (*administration of justice*) justice *f*; (*system*) organisation *f* judiciaire; (*judges*) magistrature *f*.

judicial [dʒuː'dɪʃ(ə)l] *adj* **(a)** *Jur* (*inquiry, power, proceedings*) judiciaire; **j. murder,** assassinat légal *ou* juridique; *US* **j. review,** = examen *m* de la conformité d'une loi à la constitution; **j. separation,** séparation *f* de corps; **(b)** (*mind, person*) enclin à porter des jugements, critique; **the j. faculty,** le sens critique.

judicially [dʒuː'dɪʃəlɪ] *adv* judiciairement.

judiciary [dʒuː'dɪʃɪərɪ] **1** *adj* judiciaire. **2** *n* (*judges*) magistrature *f*; (*branch of government*) pouvoir *m* judiciaire; (*system of courts*) organisation *f* judiciaire.

judicious [dʒuː'dɪʃəs] *adj* (*person, mind, thought etc*) judicieux.

judiciously [dʒuː'dɪʃəslɪ] *adv* judicieusement.

judiciousness [dʒuː'dɪʃəsnɪs] *n* (*of person, mind*) discernement *m*, bon sens; (*of thought, remark*) bon sens.

judo ['dʒuːdəʊ] *n* judo *m*.

judy, Judy ['dʒuːdɪ] *n Br Sl* (*girl, woman*) nana *f*.

jug¹ [dʒʌg] *n* **(a)** *Br* (*for cream, milk, water*) pot *m*; (*for wine*) pichet *m*; **coffee j.,** (*of electric percolator*) verseuse *f*; **j. kettle,** = bouilloire (électrique) haute; *Am* **j. wine,** vin *m* ordinaire; **(b)** *Old-fashioned Sl* (*prison*) taule *f*, tôle *f*; **in (the) j.,** au trou, en taule *ou* tôle.

jug² *vt* (**-gg-**) *Culin* **jugged hare,** = civet *m* de lièvre.

jugful ['dʒʌgfʊl] *n* (*of cream, milk, water*) (plein) pot *m*; (*of wine*) (plein) pichet *m*.

juggernaut ['dʒʌgənɔːt] *n* **(a)** *Br* (*lorry*) (gros) poids lourd, *F* mastodonte *m*; **(b)** *Fig* (*destructive force*) vague *f* de fond, vague déferlante, raz-de-marée *m inv*.

juggins ['dʒʌgɪnz] *n Old-fashioned Br F* (*simpleton*) nigaud, -aude, cruche *f*.

juggle ['dʒʌg(ə)l] **1** *vi* jongler (*avec des boules etc, Fig avec les chiffres, les faits*). **2** *vt* jongler avec (*des boules etc, Fig des chiffres, des faits*).

juggler ['dʒʌglər] *n* jongleur, -euse.

juggling ['dʒʌglɪŋ] *n* jonglerie *f*, art *m* du jongleur; (*sleight of hand*) tours *mpl* de passe-passe; (*trickery*) fourberie *f*.

Jugoslav ['juːgəʊslɑːv] **1** *adj* yougoslave. **2** *n* Yougoslave *mf*.

Jugoslavia [juːgəʊ'slɑːvɪə] *n* Yougoslavie *f*.

Jugoslavian [juːgəʊ'slɑːvɪən] **1** *adj* yougoslave. **2** *n* Yougoslave *mf*.

jugular ['dʒʌgjʊlər] *Anat* **1** *adj* jugulaire. **2** *n* (veine *f*) jugulaire *f*; *Fig* **to go for the j.,** attaquer toutes griffes dehors *ou* tous azimuts.

juice¹ [dʒuːs] *n* **(a)** (*of fruit, vegetables, meat*) jus *m*; (*of plant*) suc *m*; *Br* **j. extractor,** centrifugeuse *f* (électrique); *Physiol* **gastric** *or* **digestive juices,** sucs gastriques *ou* digestifs; **(b)** *F* (*electricity*) jus *m*, courant *m*; (*gas*) gaz *m*; *Aut* essence *f*.

juice² *vt* extraire le jus de (*pomme, orange etc*).

▶juice up *vtsep Am Sl* **(a)** (*liven up*) mettre de l'animation *ou* de l'ambiance dans (*une réception*); (*add power to*) gonfler (*un moteur*); **(b) to get juiced (up),** (*drunk*) se soûler.

juicer ['dʒuːsər] *n Am* centrifugeuse *f* (électrique).

juiciness ['dʒuːsɪnɪs] *n* (*of fruit*) fondant *m*; (*of meat*) juteux *m*; *Fig* (*of story, detail*) piquant *m*, (côté *m*) croustillant *m*.

juicy ['dʒuːsɪ] *adj* (*fruit*) juteux, fondant; (*meat*) plein de jus, qui rend du jus; *Fig* (*story, detail*) croustillant, piquant; **the j. part of the story,** le plus croustillant de l'histoire; *F* **a j. deal/***etc*, (*lucrative*) une affaire/*etc* juteuse; **a nice j. morsel,** (*of meat etc*) un morceau de choix bien succulent; **a nice j. scandal,** un scandale bien juteux; *Br Sl* **she's a j. bit,** (*sexy*) elle est très excitante, c'est une sacrée allumeuse.

jujitsu [dʒuː'dʒɪtsuː] *n* jiu-jitsu *m*.

juju ['dʒuːdʒuː] *n* (*charm, fetish*) gri(s)-gri(s) *m*.

jukebox ['dʒuːkbɒks] *n* juke-box *m*.

julep ['dʒuːlɪp] *n Am* (*drink*) **(mint) j.**, bourbon frappé à la menthe.

Julian ['dʒuːlɪən] *adj* (*calendar etc*) julien.

Julius ['dʒuːljəs] *n* Jules *m*; **J. Caesar**, Jules César.

July [dʒuː'laɪ, dʒʊ'laɪ] *n* juillet *m*; **in J.**, au mois de juillet, en juillet; **(on) the fourth of J.**, le quatre juillet.

jumble[1] ['dʒʌmb(ə)l] *n* **(a)** (*disorder*) fouillis *m*, pagaïe *f*, pêle-mêle *m inv*, méli-mélo *m*; *Fig* (*of ideas, details etc*) méli-mélo, fouillis, fatras *m*; (*of words*) fatras; **in a j.**, (*papers etc*) en pagaïe; *Fig* (*ideas etc*) (em)brouillé; **(b)** *Br* (*unwanted articles*) bric-à-brac *m inv*; **j. sale**, vente *f* de charité; (*for school, church roof etc*) vente au profit de qch.

jumble[2] *vt* mélanger, brouiller, mettre la pagaïe dans (*documents, jouets, livres etc*); mélanger (*vêtements, chaussures etc*); *Fig* (em)brouiller, mélanger (*idées, détails, mots etc*); **the ribbons lay jumbled on the floor**, les rubans gisaient pêle-mêle sur le sol; **everything was jumbled**, tout était mélangé.

►**jumble together, jumble up** *vtsep* = **JUMBLE[2]**.

jumbo ['dʒʌmbəʊ] **1** *adj* **(a)** *F* géant, énorme; *Com* **the j. size**, la plus grande taille, le plus grand modèle; **(b)** *Av* **j. jet**, avion géant, jumbo-jet *m*, (avion) gros porteur. **2** *n F* (*pl* **-os**) **(a)** (*person, animal, thing*) géant *m*; *Av* avion géant, jumbo-jet *m*, (avion) gros porteur; **(b) J.**, (*elephant*) = surnom *m* de l'éléphant.

jump[1] [dʒʌmp] *n* **(a)** (*leap*) saut *m*, bond *m*; (*by parachute*) saut (en parachute); **to take** *or* **make a j.**, faire un saut *ou* un bond, sauter; **in** *or* **at one j.**, d'un (seul) bond; **running j.**, saut avec élan; *F* **go (and) take a running j.!**, va te faire voir (ailleurs)!, va te faire cuire un œuf!; **to be one j.** *or* **a j. ahead of**, (*be better, cleverer than*) avoir une (petite) longueur d'avance sur; (*be more or bigger than*) être légèrement supérieur à; *F* **to have the j. on s.o.**, (*have a head start*) avoir pris une longueur d'avance sur qn (dès le départ); **j. jet**, avion *m* à décollage vertical; *Br Aut* **j. leads**, câbles *mpl* de démarrage; *Am* **j. rope**, corde *f* à sauter; **j. seat**, strapontin *m*; **j. suit**, combinaison-pantalon *f*; (*for baby*) grenouillère *f*; (*for parachutist*) combinaison *f* de saut;

(b) (*on racecourse etc*) obstacle *m*; **to put a horse over a j.**, faire sauter un obstacle à un cheval;

(c) (*in temperature, unemployment etc*) hausse *f* (soudaine); **the j. in prices**, la flambée des prix, la hausse (soudaine) des prix; **to take a (sudden) j.**, faire un bond;

(d) (*sudden movement, start*) sursaut *m*; **that gave me a j.**, cela m'a fait sursauter *ou* tressauter;

(e) *Comptr* saut *m*, branchement *m*.

jump[2] **1** *vi* **(a)** (*leap*) (*of person, animal etc*) sauter; (*from aircraft*) sauter (en parachute); **j.!**, (*to child, dog*) allez, hop!, saute!; **to j. to one's feet**, se (re)lever d'un bond; **to j. to the ground**, sauter à terre; **to j. for joy**, (*feel elated, leap in the air*) sauter de joie; **to j. (down) from a wall/tree/***etc*, sauter (à bas) d'un mur/arbre/*etc*, sauter du haut d'un mur/arbre/*etc*; **to j. from a train/vehicle**, sauter d'un train/d'un véhicule; **to j. across a ditch/***etc*, franchir un fossé/*etc* (d'un bond), sauter un fossé/*etc*;

(b) (*go directly*) sauter; **to j. from one subject to another** *or* **to the next**, sauter d'un sujet à l'autre; **to j. from the bottom to the top of the list**, remonter toute la liste d'un seul coup;

(c) (*of profit, temperature etc*) faire un bond; (*of price*) flamber, faire un bond;

(d) *Fig* (*phrases*) **to j. at an offer/a chance/a suggestion**, sauter sur une offre/une occasion/une proposition; **you should j. at it**, vous devriez sauter dessus; **to j. to conclusions**, tirer des conclusions prématurées *ou* hâtives; **to j. to the conclusion that ...**, conclure prématurément que ...; **and j. to it!**, et que ça saute!; *F* **to j. down s.o.'s throat**, (*reply sharply to*) rabrouer qn, rembarrer qn, envoyer qn paître *ou* promener; (*criticize*) engueuler qn; *Am F* **to j. all over s.o.**, (*scold, criticize*) passer un savon à qn, engueuler qn;

(e) (*make a sudden movement*) (*of person*) sursauter, tressauter; (*of heart*) faire un bond, bondir; (*of record player needle, chisel, drill*) sauter; **we nearly jumped out of our skins**, (*from surprise*) nous avons failli sauter au plafond; (*from fear, shock*) ça nous a fait *ou F* fichu un de ces coups; **the sight of her (nearly) made me j. out of my skin**, ça m'a fichu un de ces coups de la voir;

(f) *Am Old-fashioned F* **to be (really) jumping**, (*of party, nightclub*) être très animé.

2 *vt* **(a)** (*leap over*) franchir, sauter (par-dessus) (*une haie, un fossé etc*); *Fig* (*skip*) sauter (*un paragraphe, un mot, une page etc*); *Sch* **to j. a class**, sauter une classe; **to j. a** *or* **the groove**, (*of record player needle*) sauter;

(b) (*cause to jump*) faire sauter (*un cheval*); *Sp* **to j. a horse over a hurdle**, faire sauter une haie à un cheval;

(c) *Am* **to j. rope**, sauter à la corde;

(d) (*escape from, pass, leave illegally etc*) *Jur* **to j. bail**, se dérober à la justice (*alors qu'on jouit de la liberté provisoire*); *Aut* **to j. the lights**, griller *ou* brûler un *ou* le feu rouge; *Br* **to j. the queue**, passer avant son tour, resquiller; **to j. the rails**, (*of train*) dérailler; **to j. ship**, (*of sailor*) déserter (le navire);

(e) *Rail Av F* (*get on*) **to j. a train**, sauter dans un train (**to**, à destination de); (*without paying*) prendre un train sans billet;

(f) *F* (*attack, ambush, take over*) **to j. s.o.**, sauter *ou* tomber sur (le paletot de) qn; **to j. a train**, (*of bandits etc*) attaquer un train; *Am* **to j. a claim**, s'emparer illégalement d'une concession.

►**jump about, jump around** *vi* sautiller.

►**jump back** *vi* (*of person, vehicle*) faire un bond en arrière, reculer d'un bond.

►**jump down** *vi* (*from wall etc*) sauter (à terre); **to j. down from a wall/tree/***etc*, sauter (à bas) d'un mur/arbre/*etc*, sauter du haut d'un mur/arbre/*etc*.

►**jump forward** *vi* (*of person, vehicle*) faire un bond en avant.

►**jump in** **1** *vi* (*into pool, river etc*) sauter (dedans); (*into vehicle, train*) monter (vite); *Aut* **j. in!**, montez!; *Fig* **to j. in at the deep end**, se jeter tête baissée dans les problèmes. **2** *vipo* = **JUMP INTO**.

►**jump into** *vipo* sauter dans (*une rivière, un fossé etc*); sauter *ou* monter dans (*une voiture etc*).

►**jump off** **1** *vi* **(a)** (*from wall, train etc*) sauter (**from**, de); **(b)** *Horseriding* faire un barrage. **2** *vipo* sauter de (*bicyclette, train etc*); **to j. off a wall/***etc*, sauter (à bas) d'un mur/*etc*, sauter du haut d'un mur/*etc*.

►**jump on** **1** *vi* (*on to vehicle, train*) monter; (*on to bicycle*) sauter dessus. **2** *vipo* **(a)** monter *ou* sauter dans (*un autobus, un train etc*); sauter sur (*une bicyclette*); **(b)** *F* **to j. on s.o.**, (*reprimand*) passer un savon à qn.

►**jump out** *vi* (*from vehicle, train etc*) descendre, sortir, sauter (**of, from**, de); **to j. out of bed**, sauter (à bas) du lit; **to j. out of the window**, sauter par la fenêtre; *Fig* **to j. out at s.o.**, (*of mistake etc*) sauter aux yeux de qn.

►**jump over** **1** *vipo* franchir, sauter (par-dessus) (*une haie, un fossé etc*). **2** *vi* sauter (par-dessus).

►**jump up** *vi* **(a)** (*to one's feet*) se (re)lever d'un bond; **up she jumped**, d'un bond, elle se (re)leva *ou* elle fut debout; **to j. up and down**, sautiller; **(b)** *F* (*increase suddenly*) = **JUMP[2] 1 (c)**.

jumped-up [dʒʌmp'tʌp] *adj Br F Pej* (*arrogant*) récemment promu (et qui a la grosse tête); (*upstart*) parvenu; **a j.-up salesman**, un (petit) péteux de vendeur.

jumper[1] ['dʒʌmpər] *n* **(a)** *Br* pull(-over) *m*, tricot *m*; **(b)** *Am* robe-chasuble *f*.

jumper[2] *n* **(a)** (*horse, athlete*) sauteur, -euse; **to be a good j.**, être bon sauteur, sauter bien; **(b)** *Am Aut* **jumpers, j. cables**, câbles *mpl* de démarrage; **(c)** *Comptr* **j. (wire)**, cavalier *m*.

jumpily ['dʒʌmpɪlɪ] *adv* (*nervously*) nerveusement.

jumpiness ['dʒʌmpɪnɪs] *n* (*of person*) nervosité *f*; *St Exch* (*of markets*) nervosité, fébrilité *f*.

jumping ['dʒʌmpɪŋ] **1** *adj* **(a)** (*insect*) sauteur; **(b) j. jack**, (*toy figure*) pantin *m*; *Br* (*firework*) pétard *m* à répétition. **2** *n* (*leaps*) sauts *mpl*; *Horseriding* jumping *m*, concours *m* hippique.

jumping-off ['dʒʌmpɪŋ'ɒf] *n* **j.-o. place** *or* **point**, (*for journey*) point *m* de départ (**for**, pour); *Fig* (*for talks, in one's career*) tremplin *m*, point de départ.

jumpmaster ['dʒʌmpmæstər] *n Am Mil* moniteur *m* de parachutisme.

jump-off ['dʒʌmpɒf] *n Horseriding* barrage *m*.

jump-start[1] ['dʒʌmpstɑːt] *n* **to give a j.-s. to**, = **JUMP-START[2]**.

jump-start[2] *vt Br* (*push*) faire démarrer (*une voiture*) en la poussant; *Am* (*with jumper cables*) faire démarrer (*une voiture*) au moyen de câbles de démarrage.

jumpy ['dʒʌmpɪ] *adj* **(a)** (*nervous*) (*person, gestures etc*) nerveux; *St Exch* (*market*) nerveux, fébrile; **(b)** (*fitful, jerky*) (*style, gestures etc*) saccadé.

junction ['dʒʌŋkʃən] *n* **(a)** (*no pl*) (*joining*) jonction *f*; **(b)** (*in roads, railway lines*) embranchement *m*, bifurcation *f*, jonction *f*; (*between two roads*) jonction; (*in rivers*) confluent *m*; (*in pipes*) embranchement, jonction, raccordement *m*; (*crossroads*) carrefour *m*; (*station*) gare *f* de jonction *ou* de raccordement; (*weld*) soudure *f*; *El* connexion *f*; *El* (*of wires*) branchement *m*; *El* **j. box**, boîte *f* de dérivation; *Br*

j. 7, (*on motorway*) (*exit*) la sortie 7; (*entrance*) l'entrée *f* 7.

juncture ['dʒʌŋktʃər] *n* (*critical point in time*) **at this j.,** en ce moment même, dans les circonstances actuelles.

June [dʒu:n] *n* juin *m*; **in J.,** au mois de juin, en juin; **(on) the ninth of J.,** le neuf juin; **J. bug** *or* **beetle,** (*insect*) hanneton *m*.

jungle ['dʒʌŋg(ə)l] *n* (*forest, Fig competitive environment*) jungle *f*; *Fig* **a j. of red tape,** une montagne de paperasseries; **the law of the j.,** la loi de la jungle; **a j. animal/plant/***etc*, une bête/plante/*etc* de la jungle; **j. fever,** paludisme *m*; **j. gym,** (*climbing frame*) cage *f* à l'écureuil; *Sl* **j. juice,** (*alcohol*) tord-boyaux *m* (artisanal); **j. warfare,** combat *m* de jungle.

junior ['dʒu:njər] **1** *adj* **(a)** (*in age*) **to be j. to s.o.,** être plus jeune que qn; **she's three years j. to me, she's j. to me by three years,** elle est plus jeune que moi de trois ans; **j. orchestra/club/***etc*, orchestre *m*/club *m*/*etc* de jeunes; **Hudson Jnr** *or* **Jr** *or* **Jun,** (*the son*) Hudson fils *ou* junior *ou* Jr; (*one of two or more brothers*) Hudson junior *ou* Jr; *Br Sch* **the j. classes,** (*between 7 and 11*) les petites classes; *Am* **j. college,** = institut *m* universitaire du premier cycle; *Am* **j. high (school),** (*between 11 and 15*) = collège *m* d'enseignement secondaire; **j. miss,** (*for clothes' size*) fillette *f*; *Br* **j. school,** (*between 7 and 11*) école *f* primaire; *Am Sch Univ* **j. year,** avant-dernière année; *Sp* **j. event/team,** épreuve *f*/équipe *f* de minimes *ou* de cadets *ou* de juniors.

(b) (*in rank*) subalterne; **to be j. to s.o.,** être au-dessous de qn; **j. teacher/executive/***etc*, jeune professeur *m*/cadre *m*/*etc*; **j. clerk,** *Arch* commis *m* ordinaire, jeune employé, -ée, employé, -ée subalterne; *Br Parl* **j. minister,** secrétaire *mf* d'État **(in,** à); *Com* **j. partner,** jeune associé, -ée;

(c) (*small*) petit; **'j. portions available',** (*in restaurant*) 'menu enfant *ou* junior'; *Com* **j. sizes,** petites tailles.

2 *n* **(a)** (*younger person*) cadet, -ette; **to be s.o.'s j.,** être le cadet de qn, être plus jeune que qn; **she's three years my j., she's my j. by three years,** elle est ma cadette de trois ans, elle est plus jeune que moi de trois ans;

(b) (*subordinate*) (employé, -ée) subalterne *mf*, *F Pej* sous-fifre *m*; **he's our office j.,** (*performing general duties*) c'est notre factotum;

(c) *Br Sch* (*between 7 and 11*) petit(e) élève, élève des petites classes; *Am Sch Univ* étudiant, -ante *ou* élève d'avant-dernière année; *Br* **to go to the juniors, attend the juniors,** (*junior school*) aller à l'école primaire;

(d) *Sp* (*between 13 and 15*) minime *mf*; (*between 15 and 17*) cadet, -ette; (*between 17 and 21*) junior *mf*.

juniper ['dʒu:nɪpər] *n* **j. (tree),** genévrier *m*, genièvre *m*; **j. berries,** baies *fpl ou* grains *mpl* de genièvre; *Pharm* **j. oil,** essence *f* de genièvre.

junk[1] [dʒʌŋk] *n* (*no pl*) **(a)** (*unwanted objects*) bric-à-brac *m inv*; (*outdated objects*) vieilleries *fpl*; (*refuse*) détritus *mpl*, saletés *fpl*; (*waste*) déchets *mpl*; (*old iron*) ferraille *f*; (*inferior goods*) camelote *f*, pacotille *f*, cochonnerie(s) *f(pl)*, saleté(s) *f(pl)*; *Fin* **j. bond,** obligation *f* de pacotille, junk bond *m* (*obligation à haut rendement mais à risque élevé*); **j. dealer,** brocanteur, -euse; **j. food,** aliment peu nutritif; **to eat j. food,** manger des cochonneries, manger n'importe quoi; **j. heap,** (*public*) dépotoir *m*; (*in garden etc*) tas *m* de détritus; (*old car*) tas *m* de ferraille; *Fig* **to throw sth/s.o. on the j. heap,** mettre qch/qn au rebut; *Fig* **young people who end up on the j. heap,** les jeunes qui finissent sous les ponts; *Am* **j. jewelry,** bijoux *mpl* (de) fantaisie; *Pej* **j. mail,** courrier *m* publicitaire, prospectus *mpl*, *F* pub *f*; **j. room,** (pièce *f* de) débarras *m*; **j. shop,** boutique *f* de brocanteur; **at the j. shop,** chez le brocanteur;

(b) *F Fig* (*bad-quality book, play etc*) navet *m*, foutaise *f*, connerie *f*; *Sl* (*nonsense*) foutaises *fpl*, conneries *fpl*;

(c) *Sl* (*heroin etc*) came *f*; **to be on j.,** se camer.

junk[2] *vt F* (*get rid of, discard*) balancer, mettre à la poubelle (*vieux meubles, documents etc*); rejeter (*idées, faits etc*); balancer (*qn*).

junk[3] *n* (*Chinese boat*) jonque *f*.

junket[1] ['dʒʌŋkɪt] *n* **(a)** *Culin* lait caillé (*souvent parfumé*); **(b)** (*feast*) festin *m*, banquet *m*; **(c)** *Am* (*pleasure trip*) partie *f* de plaisir, voyage *m* d'agrément; (*by public official*) voyage (d'agrément) aux frais de la princesse *ou* du contribuable.

junket[2] *vi* **(a)** (*feast*) banqueter, festoyer; **(b)** *Am* (*travel*) faire une partie de plaisir *ou* un voyage d'agrément; (*of public official*) voyager aux frais de la princesse *ou* du contribuable.

junkie ['dʒʌŋkɪ] *n Sl* (*drug addict*) drogué, -ée, camé, -ée, toxico *mf*; *Fig* **a chocolate/sugar j.,** un fou *ou* une folle de chocolat/sucre, un(e) accro du chocolat/sucre; *Fig* **a football/chess j.,** un(e) fana(tique) de football/d'échecs.

junkman, *pl* **-men** ['dʒʌŋkmæn, -men] *n Am* chiffonnier *m*, brocanteur *m*.

junky ['dʒʌŋkɪ] **1** *adj F* (*goods*) de camelote; (*novel, film etc*) nul, sans valeur, à la manque. **2** *n Sl* = **JUNKIE.**

junkyard ['dʒʌŋkjɑ:d] *n* (*for metal*) dépôt *m* de ferrailleur; (*for rags, discarded objects*) dépôt de chiffonnier; *Fig* **their garden is a real j.,** leur jardin est un véritable dépotoir.

Juno ['dʒu:nəʊ] *n Myth Astron* Junon *f*; *Fig* déesse *f*.

Junoesque [dʒu:nəʊ'esk] *adj* d'une grâce souveraine.

junta ['dʒʌntə] *n Mil Pol* junte *f*.

Jupiter ['dʒu:pɪtər] *n* Jupiter *m*; *Astron* Jupiter *f*.

juridical [dʒʊ'rɪdɪk(ə)l] *adj* juridique.

jurisdiction [dʒʊərɪs'dɪkʃən] *n* **(a)** (*legal authority*) juridiction *f*; **area within** *or* **under the j. of ...,** territoire soumis à l'autorité judiciaire *ou* à la juridiction de ...; **to come** *or* **fall within** *or* **under the j. of a court,** (*of question etc*) tomber sous *ou* relever de *ou* rentrer dans la juridiction d'une cour; **(b)** (*general authority*) autorité *f*; **to have j. over s.o.,** avoir autorité sur qn; **he has no j. over his brother's activities,** il n'a aucune emprise *ou* aucun pouvoir sur ce que fait son frère, ce que fait son frère échappe à son contrôle; **(c)** *Fig* (*field of activity*) compétence *f*, ressort *m*; **this matter does not come within** *or* **is not in our j.,** cette affaire ne relève pas de notre compétence, cette affaire n'est pas de notre compétence *ou* de notre ressort.

jurisprudence [dʒʊərɪs'pru:dəns] *n* jurisprudence *f*; **medical j.,** médecine légale.

jurist ['dʒʊərɪst] *n* (*expert*) juriste *mf*, légiste *m*; (*writer*) juriste; *US* (*lawyer*) avocat, -ate; (*student*) étudiant, -ante en droit.

juror ['dʒʊərər] *n* **(a)** *Jur* juré *m*; **woman j.,** femme *f* juré, jurée *f*; **(b)** (*in competition etc*) membre *m* du jury.

jury ['dʒʊərɪ] *n* **(a)** *Jur* jury *m*; **to be** *or* **serve** *or* **sit on the j.,** faire partie *ou* être membre du jury, *F* être de jury; **to pack** *or* **rig** *or* **stack a** *or* **the j.,** composer un jury partisan; **j. service** *or* **duty,** la participation au jury; **to do one's j. service** *or* **duty,** s'acquitter de son devoir de participation au jury; **to be called (up) for j. service** *or* **duty,** être convoqué comme juré; **foreman of the j.,** président *m* du jury; **ladies and gentlemen of the j.!, members of the j.!,** mesdames et messieurs les jurés!; **the j. is out,** le jury est en délibération; *Am Fig F* **the j. is still out on that (one),** (*final decision has not been made*) rien de définitif n'a été décidé; *US Jur* **(federal) grand j.,** = tribunal (fédéral) se prononçant sur la mise en accusation; **special j.,** jury spécial; **j. box,** banc *m* des jurés; **j. fixing,** *Br Sl* **j. nobbling,** corruption *f* de jurés; **j. packing** *or* **rigging** *or* **stacking,** = composition *f* d'un jury partisan;

(b) (*for examination, competition*) jury *m*.

juryman, *pl* **-men** ['dʒʊərɪmən] *n* juré *m*.

jurywoman, *pl* **-women** ['dʒʊərɪwʊmən, -wɪmɪn] *n* femme *f* juré, jurée *f*.

just[1] [dʒʌst] **1** *adj* **(a)** (*person, criticism etc*) juste; **to be j. to** *or* **towards,** être juste pour *ou* envers *ou* à l'égard de; **(b)** (*cause, anger, claim*) juste, légitime; (*reward, punishment*) juste; **it's only j. that ...,** ce n'est que justice que ... + *sub*; **it's only j. to ask such questions,** il est bien normal de poser de telles questions; **as (it) is only j.,** comme de juste; **to show j. cause for concern, to have j. cause to be concerned,** avoir de bonnes raisons de s'inquiéter; **(c)** (*observation, account etc*) juste. **2** *n* **the j.,** (*used as pl*) les justes *mpl*; *Lit* **to sleep the sleep of the j.,** dormir du sommeil du juste.

just[2] *adv* **(a)** (*exactly, precisely*) juste, justement, exactement, précisément; **he's j. the man you are looking for,** c'est juste *ou* justement *ou* exactement *ou* tout à fait l'homme qu'il vous faut; **that's j. what happened,** voilà *ou* c'est justement *ou* exactement *ou* bien ce qui est arrivé; **that's j. what I was wondering,** c'est exactement *ou* précisément *ou* juste *ou* bien ce que je me demandais; **it cost me j. ten pounds** *or Br* **j. on ten pounds,** ça m'a coûté dix livres tout juste; **j. how many are there?,** combien y en a-t-il au juste *ou* exactement?; **j. why does she do it?,** pour quelles raisons exactement le fait-elle?, pourquoi exactement le fait-elle?; **that's j. why she did it,** c'est précisément *ou* exactement pour cela qu'elle l'a fait, c'est justement pourquoi elle l'a fait; **j. as you wish,** (c'est) comme tu veux; **I left the books j. as they were** *or* **j. the way they were,** j'ai laissé les livres exactement comme *ou* tels que je les ai trouvés, j'ai laissé les livres tels quels; **that's j. it** *or* **j. the point!,** précisément!, justement!, voilà!; **j. so!,** (*like this*) exactement comme ça!; *Br* (*that's* *right*) exactement!, précisément!, voilà!; **he set the vase down j. so,** il a posé le vase avec soin; *F usu Pej* **her house is always j. so,** sa maison est toujours archi-impeccable; **it's** *or* **that's j. like him!,** (*typical of him*) c'est bien de lui!; **I have j. the same problem,** j'ai (exactement) le même problème; **j. the same,** (*nevertheless*) cela n'empêche, tout de même;

(b) (*with place*) juste; **j. above/inside/nearby/***etc*, juste au-dessus/dedans/à côté/*etc*; **j. here,** juste ici, ici même;

(c) (*with time: exactly*) juste; **j. then, j. at that moment,** juste à ce moment; **it's j. ten o'clock** *or Br* **j. on ten o'clock,** il est dix heures juste(s) *ou* pile, il est tout juste dix heures; **j. when** *or* **as the door was opening,** au moment même où la porte s'ouvrait; **j. as** *or* **when I was leaving,** juste comme *ou* juste quand *ou* au moment même où je partais; **to be j. about to do,** être sur le point de faire; **she's j. in time for a drink,** elle arrive pile pour *ou* elle arrive juste à temps pour prendre un verre;

(d) (*with time: at this very moment, exactly now*) **he's busy j. now,** il est occupé en ce moment *ou* pour l'instant; **I'm not ready j. now** *or* **j. yet,** je ne suis pas encore prêt, je ne suis pas prêt pour le moment; **she's j. leaving, she's leaving j. now,** elle part (tout de suite *ou* à l'instant); **she's not leaving j. now** *or* **j. yet,** elle ne part pas pour l'instant, elle ne part pas tout de suite; **(I'm) j. coming!, I'm coming j. now!,** j'arrive!; **their cousin is j. over** *or* **is over j. now for a few days,** leur cousin vient d'arriver pour une visite de quelques jours; **my hair is j. turning grey** *or* **is j. beginning to turn grey,** mes cheveux commencent à grisonner;

(e) (*with time: a short while ago, recently*) **to have j. arrived/woken up/written a letter/***etc*, venir d'arriver/de se réveiller/d'écrire une lettre/*etc*; **I've only j. seen him, I've j. now seen him,** je viens seulement de le voir; **I saw him j. now,** je l'ai vu tout à l'heure *ou* à l'instant; **I've only j. this minute seen him,** je viens de le voir à l'instant, je l'ai vu à l'instant; **I saw him j. yesterday, I j. saw him yesterday,** je l'ai vu pas plus tard qu'hier; **he has j. (now) left school,** il sort du lycée; **'j. picked/cooked',** (*newly*) 'cueilli/cuit du jour'; **'j. arrived',** 'fraîchement arrivé';

(f) (*only, no more than*) seulement, juste; **I have come j. to see you,** je viens seulement *ou* juste *ou* uniquement pour vous voir; **we have j. a few copies left,** il nous reste quelques exemplaires seulement *ou* juste quelques exemplaires; **I've got j. one left,** il m'en reste un seul; **she's j. a baby,** ce n'est qu'un bébé; **it costs j. ten dollars,** ça ne coûte que dix dollars, ça coûte dix dollars seulement; **it's j. ten o'clock,** il est seulement dix heures, il n'est que dix heures; **(wait) j. a moment!,** (attendez) un petit instant!, un instant!; **give me j. a tiny bit,** donnez-m'en (juste) un petit peu *ou* rien qu'un petit peu;

(g) (*only a little, slightly*) juste, (un) peu; **j. a little more/less/better,** juste un peu plus/moins/mieux; **j. in front/behind/above/below,** juste devant/derrière/au-dessus/au-dessous; **j. over/under fifty pounds,** un peu plus de/moins de cinquante livres; **it's j. before ten (o'clock),** il est un peu moins de dix heures; **we go to bed j. before ten (o'clock),** nous nous couchons juste avant *ou* peu avant dix heures; **j. after my birthday,** juste après *ou* peu après mon anniversaire;

(h) (*merely, simply*) simplement; **tell him j. to wait,** dites-lui qu'il n'a qu'à attendre; *F* **I'll j. pop in,** je ne ferai qu'entrer et sortir; **j. ask if you need money,** vous n'avez qu'à demander si vous avez besoin d'argent; **they won't accept j. to please ME,** ils n'accepteront pas uniquement pour *ou* rien que pour me faire plaisir à moi; **we j. can't understand it,** nous n'arrivons vraiment pas à comprendre; **why not? — because I j. don't,** pourquoi pas? — parce que c'est comme ça;

(i) (*easily*) **I can j. see him as a doctor,** je le vois très bien médecin;

(j) (*by a narrow margin, barely*) **(only) j.,** de justesse; **he (only) j . (about) managed to catch the train,** il a eu le train de justesse, c'est tout juste *ou* c'est à peine s'il a eu le train; **they (only) j. missed the train,** ils ont manqué le train de peu; **I have (only) j. enough** *or* **j. about enough to live on,** j'ai tout juste de quoi vivre; **she caught the train but (only) j.,** elle a eu le train mais c'était juste *ou* c'était de justesse; **you're (only) j. in time,** vous arrivez à temps, mais c'est de justesse;

(k) (*utterly, completely*) absolument; **it was j. splendid!,** c'était absolument merveilleux!, c'était merveilleux, ni plus ni moins!; *Br* **do you remember? — don't I j.!,** vous vous en souvenez? — et comment (que je m'en souviens), vous pensez (si je m'en souviens)!;

(l) (*in comparisons*) **j. as, j. about as,** tout aussi; **that's j. (about) as good,** c'est tout aussi bien, c'est tout comme; **that will do j. as well,** ça fera aussi bien l'affaire;

(m) (*in threats, orders, exhortations*) **j. (you) try!,** essaie donc un peu!; **j. (you) wait!,** tu n'as qu'à attendre!; (*threat*) attends, tu vas voir!, tu ne perds rien pour attendre!; **j. (you) read this!,** lisez donc cela!; **j. think,** réfléchis donc un peu; **j. look!,** regardez-moi ça!; **j. be quiet, will you!,** veux-tu bien te taire!;

(n) j. about, (*approximately*) plus ou moins, à peu près; **it's j. about ten (o'clock),** il est plus ou moins *ou* à peu près dix heures; **j. about!,** plus ou moins!, à peu près!; *F* **that j. about does it,** (*I'm leaving*) ça suffit comme ça *ou* amplement *ou* largement;

(o) (*indicating preference*) **I would j. as soon stay here,** j'aimerais tout autant rester ici; **he would j. as soon that ...,** il aimerait tout autant que ... + *sub*;

(p) it's j. as well (that), (*fortunate*) heureusement que; **and (it was) j. as well,** et c'était une chance, et tant mieux; **I might j. as well have remained silent,** j'aurais (tout) aussi bien fait de garder le silence; **they could j. as well do without it,** ils feraient (tout) aussi bien de s'en passer.

justice ['dʒʌstɪs] *n* **(a)** (*no pl*) (*power of law*) justice *f*; **to administer** *or* **dispense/exercise j.,** rendre/exercer la justice; **to demand/obtain j.,** demander/obtenir justice; **to bring s.o. to j.,** traduire qn en justice; **to temper j. with mercy,** faire preuve de clémence; *US* **the Department of J., the J. Department,** le Ministère de la Justice; **rough j.,** (*overhard punishment*) punition disproportionnée *ou* exagérée; (*summary justice*) justice sommaire;

(b) (*no pl*) (*fairness*) justice *f*; (*of cause, claim, decision etc*) légitimité *f*; **in all j.,** en toute justice; **in (all) j. to her, we should say ...,** pour être juste envers elle *ou* pour lui rendre justice, on devrait dire ...; **to do s.o. j., to do j. to s.o.,** (*of photo, garment, hairstyle etc*) avantager qn, mettre qn en valeur, montrer qn sous son meilleur jour; **to do j. to a meal,** faire honneur à un repas; **to do oneself j.,** se mettre en valeur, se montrer sous son meilleur jour; *Fml* **with j.,** (*with good reason*) avec juste raison, à juste titre;

(c) (*judge in Supreme Court*) juge *m*; **Mr J. Long,** (*title*) Monsieur le juge Long; **Mrs J. Long,** Madame le juge Long; **j. of the peace,** juge de paix; *Br* **Lord Chief J.,** président *m* de la Haute Cour de justice; *US* **Chief J. (of the United States),** président *m* de la Cour suprême.

justifiable ['dʒʌstɪfaɪəb(ə)l] *adj* justifié, légitime.

justifiably ['dʒʌstɪfaɪəblɪ] *adv* légitimement, à juste titre.

justification [dʒʌstɪfɪ'keɪʃən] *n* **(a)** justification *f* **(for,** de, pour); **in j. of,** comme justification de; **(b)** *Typ Comptr* justification *f* (*d'une ligne etc*).

justify ['dʒʌstɪfaɪ] *vt* **(a)** justifier (*qn, une décision, une action, la conduite de qn etc*); **to j. oneself in the eyes of s.o.,** se justifier aux yeux de qn; **that does not j. your voting for my rival,** cela n'est pas une raison suffisante pour que vous votiez pour mon rival; *Prov* **the end justifies the means,** la fin justifie les moyens; **to be justified in doing sth,** (*have a right to*) être en droit de faire qch, avoir le droit de faire qch; (*have a good reason to*) avoir toutes les bonnes raisons de faire qch, être fondé à faire qch; **a fully justified decison/fear,** une décision/une crainte bien fondée *ou* qui se justifie; **(b)** *Typ Comptr* justifier (*une ligne etc*).

justly ['dʒʌstlɪ] *adv* (*fairly, rightly*) avec justice, justement; **j. famous,** (*deservedly*) célèbre à juste titre.

justness ['dʒʌstnɪs] *n* **(a)** légitimité *f* (*d'une cause, d'une demande etc*); **(b)** justesse *f* (*d'une idée, d'une observation etc*).

▶**jut out** [dʒʌt] *vi* (**-tt-**) (*of balcony, rock etc*) faire saillie, être en saillie, dépasser, avancer; **to j. out over sth,** (*overhang*) surplomber qch, avancer sur qch; **the headland juts out into the sea,** le cap avance (en saillie) dans la mer; **something is jutting out of your pocket,** quelque chose dépasse de votre poche.

jute [dʒuːt] *n* (*plant, fibre*) jute *m*.

juvenile ['dʒuːvɪnaɪl, *Am* -ən(ə)l, -ənaɪl] **1** *adj* **(a)** *Pej* (*behaviour, ideas etc*) puéril; **don't be so j.!,** ne sois pas si puéril *ou* gamin!; **(b)** (*books, games etc*) pour enfants, pour la jeunesse; (*hobbies, activities*) d'enfant(s); *Fml* (*youthful*) juvénile; **j. court,** tribunal *m* pour enfants; **j. delinquency,** délinquance *f* juvénile; **j. delinquent,** jeune délinquant, -ante; *F* petit voyou; **j. offender,** accusé, -ée mineur(e). **2** *n* jeune *mf*, adolescent, -ente.

juxtapose [dʒʌkstə'pəʊz] *vt* juxtaposer.

juxtaposition [dʒʌkstəpə'zɪʃən] *n* juxtaposition *f*; **to be in j.,** se juxtaposer.

K

K[1], **k** [keɪ] *n* **(a)** (la lettre) K, k *m*; **(b)** (*abbr* **kilo**) k.
K[2] *abbr* **(a)** (*thousand*) K; **(b)** *Comptr* Ko.
kaffeeklatsch ['kæfeɪ'klætʃ] *n Am* = réunion de femmes qui bavardent en prenant le café.
Kaffir ['kæfər] *Offensive Sl* **1** *adj* caf(f)re. **2** *n* Caf(f)re *mf*.
Kafkaesque [kæfkə'esk] *adj* kafkaïen.
kaftan ['kæftæn] *n* kaftan *m*.
kale, kail [keɪl] *n* (*cabbage*) **curly k.,** chou frisé.
kaleidoscope [kə'laɪdəskəʊp] *n* kaléidoscope *m*.
kaleidoscopic [kəlaɪdə'skɒpɪk] *adj* kaléidoscopique.
kamikaze [kæmɪ'kɑːzɪ] *n Japanese Hist* kamikaze *m*.
kangaroo [kæŋgə'ruː] *n* **(a)** (*animal*) kangourou *m*; **(b) k. court,** tribunal irrégulier.
Kan(s) *abbr* **Kansas.**
kaolin ['keɪəlɪn] *n* kaolin *m*.
kapok ['keɪpɒk] *n* kapok *m*; **k. tree,** kapokier *m*.
kaput [kə'pʊt] *adj F* fichu, foutu.
karakul ['kærəkʊl] *n* karakul *m*, caracul *m*.
karate [kə'rɑːtɪ] *n Sp* karaté *m*.
kart [kɑːt] *n* kart *m*; **k. racing,** karting *m*.
karting ['kɑːtɪŋ] *n* karting *m*.
Kashmir [kæʃ'mɪər] *n Geog* Cachemire *m*.
Katharine, Katherine ['kæθ(ə)rɪn], **Kathleen** ['kæθliːn] *n* Catherine *f*.
kayak ['kaɪæk] *n Nau* kayac *m*, kayak *m*.
KBE [keɪbiː'iː] *n* (*abbr* **Knight Commander (of the Order) of the British Empire**) Chevalier de l'Ordre de l'Empire britannique.
KCB [keɪsiː'biː] *n* (*abbr* **Knight Commander (of the Order) of the Bath**) Chevalier Commandeur de l'Ordre du Bain.
kebab [kə'bæb] *n Culin* kébab *m*.
kedge[1] [kedʒ] *n Nau* **k. (anchor),** ancre *f* à jet.
kedge[2] *Nau* **1** *vt* haler, touer (*un navire*) sur une ancre à jet. **2** *vi* se touer sur une ancre à jet.
kedgeree [kedʒə'riː] *n Culin* = mets de riz accommodé avec du beurre, des œufs et du poisson.
keel[1] [kiːl] *n Nau Av* quille *f*; *Lit* (*boat*) navire *m*; **bilge k.,** quille latérale *ou* de roulis; **drop k.,** dériveur *m ou* aile *f ou* quille de dérive; **on an even k.,** *Nau* sans différence de tirant d'eau *ou* de calaison; *Fig* **to be back on an even k.,** (*of situation etc*) être de nouveau stable; (*of person*) avoir retrouvé son égalité d'âme; **to put a company/the economy (back) on an even k.,** (re)mettre une entreprise/l'économie d'aplomb; **(b)** *Bot* carène *f* (*de feuille, de pétale etc*).
keel[2] *vt* mettre (*un navire*) en carène.
▶keel over 1 *vi* (*of ship*) chavirer; *F* (*of person*) tomber dans les pommes. **2** *vtsep* faire chavirer (*un navire*).
keelhaul ['kiːlhɔːl] *vt* **(a)** *Nau* faire passer (*un matelot*) sous la quille; **(b)** (*rebuke*) réprimander sévèrement, passer un savon à (*qn*).
keen[1] [kiːn] *adj* **(a)** (*person*) ardent, assidu, zélé; **k. sportsman,** ardent sportif; **k. golfer,** enragé *m* de golf; **he's as k. as mustard,** il brûle de zèle; *F* **to be k. on sth,** avoir la passion de qch; *F* **to be k. on s.o.,** être emballé *ou* avoir le béguin pour qn; **she's k. on sport,** le sport la passionne; **he's not k. on it,** il n'y tient pas beaucoup; **do you want to come? — I'm not k.,** vous voulez venir? — je n'y tiens pas; **she's very k. for us to do it,** elle tient beaucoup à ce que nous le fassions; **k. interest,** vif intérêt; **to take a k. interest in sth,** suivre qch avec un intérêt vif; **k. competition,** concurrence acharnée *ou* âpre; **there is a k. demand for these stocks,** ces fonds sont activement recherchés;

(b) (*œil, regard*) perçant, pénétrant, vif; **to have a k. eye for a bargain,** être prompt à reconnaître une bonne affaire; **to have a k. ear,** avoir l'oreille *ou* l'ouïe fine;

(c) (*esprit*) fin, pénétrant, vif, perçant; **to have a k. awareness of a problem,** être profondément conscient d'un problème; **a k. desire for peace,** un ardent désir de paix; *Com* **k. prices,** prix *mpl* au plus bas, prix étudiés;

(d) (*chagrin*) aigu; (*regret*) poignant; (*remords*) cuisant; **k. pleasure,** vif plaisir; **k. appetite,** rude appétit;

(e) (*froid, vent, air*) vif, piquant, aigre; (*son*) aigu; (*froid*) perçant;

(f) (*couteau etc*) affilé, aiguisé; **k. edge,** fil tranchant; **k. edged,** bien affilé, aiguisé, tranchant;

(g) *US Sl* (*very good*) génial.

keen[2] *n Dial* (*Irish*) mélopée funèbre (chantée en veillant le corps).
keen[3] *vi Dial* (*Irish*) chanter une mélopée en veillant un corps.
keenly ['kiːnlɪ] *adv* **(a)** âprement, vivement; **to be k. interested in ...,** s'intéresser vivement à ...; **(b)** (*to look at*) intensément; **(c) it touched me k.,** cela me toucha profondément; **(d) the wind was blowing k.,** il faisait un vent âpre.
keenness ['kiːnnɪs] *n* **(a)** ardeur *f*, vivacité *f*, empressement *m*, zèle *m* (*de qn*); mordant *m* (*des troupes etc*); **k. on doing sth,** grand désir de faire qch; **(b)** acuité *f* (*de la vision*); finesse *f* (*de l'ouïe*); **(c)** pénétration *f*, finesse (*d'esprit*); **(d)** finesse *f*, acuité *f* (*du tranchant d'un outil*); **(e)** âpreté *f*, rigueur *f* (*du froid*).
keep[1] [kiːp] *n* **(a)** nourriture *f*; (*money*) frais *mpl* de subsistance; **to earn one's k.,** (*earn a living*) subvenir à ses besoins; (*pay one's way*) (*of employee*) mériter son salaire; (*of equipment*) être rentable; **to pay for one's k.,** payer sa pension; **(b)** *F* **for keeps,** pour de bon, pour toujours; **(c)** donjon *m* (*d'un château fort*).
keep[2] *v* (*pt & pp* **kept** [kept]) **1** *vt* **(a)** (*retain*) garder (*qch*); conserver (*son emprise sur qch*); retenir (*l'attention de qn*); garder (*la page dans un livre*); **you can k. the book I lent you,** vous pouvez garder le livre que je vous ai prêté; **to k. one's figure,** garder la ligne; **to k. its shape/colour,** (*of thing*) conserver sa forme/couleur;

(b) (*store*) garder (*des provisions etc*); **the cupboard where I k. the crockery,** l'armoire où je mets la vaisselle; **she keeps her letters under lock and key,** elle garde ses lettres sous clef; **to k. fruit until it is ripe,** garder des fruits jusqu'à ce qu'ils mûrissent; **k. medicines out of reach of children,** ranger les médicaments hors de la portée des enfants;

(c) (*stay in, on etc*) **to k. one's course,** continuer *ou* poursuivre son chemin; **to k. the middle of the road,** garder le milieu de la route; **to k. one's bed/room,** garder le lit/la chambre;

(d) (*maintain*) maintenir (*l'ordre*); garder (*le silence, un secret*); **to k. one's composure,** garder son sang-froid; **they k. themselves to themselves,** il font bande à part; **he keeps himself to himself,** il est très réservé; **to k. a good table,** faire bonne chère; **to k. open house,** tenir maison ouverte;

(e) (*maintain in a condition*) **to k. sth clean/secret,** tenir qch propre/secret; *F* **k. it clean!,** pas de grossièretés!; **to k. oneself warm,** (*by staying in the warmth*) se tenir au chaud; (*by dressing warmly*) s'habiller chaudement; **to k. the door open/shut,** garder *ou* laisser la porte ouverte/fermée; **the noise kept me awake,** le bruit m'a empêché de dormir; **to k. s.o. waiting,** faire attendre qn; **troops were kept on the alert,** les soldats ont été maintenus en état d'alerte; **to k. one's hands in one's pockets,** garder les mains dans ses poches; **to k. one's eyes fixed on sth,** fixer qch du regard; **to k. sth in reserve** *or* **in store,** tenir qch en réserve;

(f) (*look after, tend*) garder (*des moutons, des troupeaux*); entretenir (*un jardin etc*); tenir (*un journal, des comptes, Com les livres*); subvenir aux besoins de (*qn*); **well/badly kept road,** route bien/mal entretenue; **to k. note of sth,** noter qch; **he doesn't earn enough to k. himself,** il ne gagne pas de quoi vivre; **he has his parents to k.,** il a ses parents à (sa) charge; **I've got a family to**

k., j'ai une famille à nourrir; **to k. s.o. in clothes/food,** fournir de l'habillement/de la nourriture à qn;

(g) (*possess*) avoir (*une voiture etc*); élever (*des abeilles, de la volaille etc*); entretenir (*une maîtresse*); tenir (*une école, un magasin etc*); *Com* avoir en magasin (*des marchandises*); **we don't k. them any more,** (*in shop*) nous n'en vendons plus;

(h) (*reserve*) garder (**sth for s.o./for oneself,** qch pour qn/pour soi); **to k. sth for later,** garder *ou* conserver *ou* réserver qch pour plus tard;

(i) (*hold, occupy*) **to k. the field against the enemy,** se maintenir contre les attaques de l'ennemi; **to k. the stage,** tenir la scène; **to k. one's seat,** rester assis;

(j) (*detain*) (*at home, in hospital*) garder; **to k. s.o. in prison,** tenir *ou* retenir qn en prison; **the doctor kept him in bed,** le médecin l'a obligé à garder le lit; **there was nothing to k. me in England,** rien ne me retenait en Angleterre; **what's keeping you?,** qu'est-ce qui vous retient?; **don't let me k. you,** (*from your work etc*) je ne veux pas te retenir;

(k) (*restrain, prevent*) **to k. s.o. from falling,** empêcher qn de tomber;

(l) (*observe*) observer, suivre (*la loi, une règle*); tenir, remplir (*une promesse*); rester fidèle à (*un vœu*); tenir, respecter, observer (*un traité*); ne pas manquer à (*un rendez-vous*); observer (*le jeûne*); **to k. late hours,** se coucher tard; **to k. one's word,** tenir (sa) parole; *Rel* **to k. the commandments,** observer les commandements; **please telephone if you cannot k. the appointment,** veuillez téléphoner si vous ne pouvez pas être présent au rendez-vous:

(m) (*protect*) préserver (**s.o. from evil,** qn du mal); *Mil* défendre (*une forteresse etc*); **God k. (you)!,** Dieu vous garde!; **God k. his soul!,** (que) Dieu ait son âme!; *Sp* **to k. goal,** garder le but; *Cr* **to k. wicket,** garder le guichet;

(n) (*celebrate*) célébrer (*une fête*); fêter, célébrer (*son anniversaire*).

2 *vi* **(a)** (*remain, stay*) rester, se tenir; **to k. well,** rester en bonne santé; **how are you keeping?,** comment allez-vous?; **to k. quiet,** se tenir *ou* rester tranquille; **to k. awake/calm,** rester éveillé/calme; **to k. smiling,** garder le sourire; **the weather is keeping cool/fine,** le temps reste frais/se maintient au beau;

(b) (*continue*) continuer; **to k. working,** continuer de travailler; **to k. hard at it,** travailler sans relâche; **to k. straight on,** continuer tout droit; **to k. doing sth,** ne pas cesser de faire qch; **don't k. asking questions,** ne posez pas tout le temps des questions; **I wish you wouldn't k. saying that,** j'aimerais bien que tu arrêtes de répéter cela;

(c) (*of food etc*) se garder, se conserver; **butter that will k.,** beurre qu'on peut conserver; **the story will k.,** (*you can tell it to me later*) l'histoire n'y perdra rien; **will it k. till later?,** est-ce que ça peut attendre?

►**keep at 1** *vipo* **(a)** (*continue to work at*) travailler (*ses maths*); **(b)** (*nag*) presser (*qn*). **2** *vtaspo* **to k. s.o. at it,** (*working*) faire travailler qn.

►**keep away 1** *vi* ne pas approcher; **she told the children to k. away from the river,** elle a dit aux enfants de ne pas s'approcher de la rivière; **k. away (from me)!,** n'approchez pas!; **I can't k. away from chocolates,** je ne peux pas résister quand je vois des chocolats. **2** *vtas* **k. that dog away from me!,** tenez ce chien loin de moi!; **the wind will k. the rain away,** le vent empêchera la pluie; **to k. matches away from the children,** tenir les allumettes hors de la portée des enfants.

►**keep back 1** *vi* ne pas approcher. **2** *vtsep* **(a)** retenir (*une armée*); contenir, retenir (*une foule*); refouler, retenir (*ses larmes*); **(b)** (*withhold*) **to k. sth back from s.o.'s wages,** retenir une somme sur le salaire de qn; **you're keeping something back (from me),** tu (me) caches quelque chose; **(c)** *Sch* garder (*un élève*) en retenue; (*oblige to repeat a year*) faire redoubler (*un élève*); **(d)** (*delay*) retenir (*qn*).

►**keep down 1** *vi* se baisser. **2** *vtas* baisser (*la tête, la voix*); **I can't k. my food down,** chaque fois que je mange je vomis. **3** *vtsep* **(a)** (*repress*) garder le contrôle sur; **(b)** (*contain*) empêcher (*les prix*) d'augmenter.

►**keep from 1** *vtaspo* **(a)** (*conceal*) **to k. sth from s.o.,** cacher qch à qn; **(b)** (*prevent*) empêcher (*qn*) de (*tomber etc*); **(c)** (*distract*) retenir qn de (*son travail*). **2** *vipo* (*refrain*) **to k. from doing sth,** s'empêcher de faire qch.

►**keep in 1** *vtsep* empêcher (*qn*) de sortir; *Sch* mettre (*un élève*) en retenue; entretenir (*un feu*); **to k. one's hand in,** garder la main. **2** *vtaspo* (*keep supplied with*) **to k. s.o. in sth,** approvisionner qn en qch.

►**keep in with** *vipo F* **to k. in with s.o.,** cultiver (*qn*), rester en bons termes avec (*qn*).

►**keep off 1** *vi* (*stay away*) ne pas approcher. **2** *vipo* **k. off the grass!,** défense de marcher sur le gazon!; **would you please k. off those flower beds,** s'il vous plaît, ne marchez pas sur ces parterres de fleurs. **3** *vtaspo* **k. your hands off that!,** n'y touchez pas!; **k. your hands off me,** (à) bas les mains *ou F* les pattes! **4** *vtas* **to k. one's coat off,** rester sans (son) manteau; **the wind will k. the rain off,** le vent empêchera la pluie.

►**keep on 1** *vi* **(a)** continuer; **to k. on doing sth,** continuer à faire qch, ne pas cesser de faire qch; **don't k. on asking questions,** ne posez pas tout le temps des questions; **(b)** (*annoyingly, naggingly*) **don't k. on so!,** arrête!; **I can't stand the way he keeps on about it,** je ne supporte pas qu'il insiste tout le temps là-dessus. **2** *vtsep* **(a)** (*continue to wear*) garder (*son manteau etc*); **(b)** (*not turn off*) **to k. the central heating on,** maintenir le chauffage central; **to k. the lights/TV/radio on,** laisser les lumières allumées/laisser la télé/la radio allumée *ou F* en route.

►**keep on at** *vipo F* être toujours sur le dos de (*qn*); harceler, tracasser (*qn*).

►**keep out 1** *vi* **(a)** (*stay away*) ne pas s'approcher; **to k. out of danger,** rester à l'abri du danger; **k. out,** (*sign*) défense d'entrer; **(b) k. out of this!,** mêlez-vous de ce qui vous regarde! **2** *vtsep* **(a)** (*put at a distance*) empêcher d'entrer; **(b)** (*not involve*) garder en dehors de.

►**keep to 1** *vipo* **(a)** (*honour*) tenir (*une promesse*); **(b)** (*stay in, on*) garder (*le lit, la chambre*); tenir (*la gauche, la droite*); **to k. to main roads,** rester sur les grandes routes. **2** *vtaspo* **(a)** (*hold*) **to k. s.o. to a promise,** faire tenir une promesse à qn; **to k. delays to a minimum,** minimiser les délais; **(b)** (*not reveal*) **to k. sth to oneself,** taire qch; **to k. one's impressions to oneself,** garder ses impressions pour soi; *F* **you can k. your remarks to yourself!,** tes remarques, tu peux te les garder!; **k. your hands to yourself,** (à) bas les mains *ou F* les pattes.

►**keep up 1** *vi* **(a)** (*of rain, snow etc*) continuer; **(b)** (*remain level, go at same speed*) aller à la même allure; **I can't k. up with you,** vous marchez *ou* parlez *etc* trop vite pour moi; **(c)** (*remain in contact*) **to k. up with s.o.,** rester en contact avec qn; **to k. up with the Joneses,** rivaliser de standing avec ses voisins; **to k. up with the times,** être à la page. **2** *vtsep* **(a)** (*maintain*) entretenir (*un bâtiment, une route, un feu etc*); **(b)** (*continue*) conserver (*un usage*); entretenir (*une correspondance, son français etc*); **we must k. it up,** il nous faut continuer nos efforts; **k. it up!,** continuez!; **(c)** (*stop from falling or waning*) soutenir (*un bâtiment, l'intérêt etc*); soutenir, maintenir (*son courage*); **to k. up appearances,** garder *ou* sauver les apparences; **(d)** (*stop from sleeping*) empêcher (*qn*) de se coucher.

keeper ['kiːpər] *n* **(a)** (*person*) garde *m*; (*in zoo, of park, lighthouse*) gardien *m*; surveillant *m*, gardien (*de prison*); conservateur *m* (*de musée etc*); gardeur, -euse (*de troupeaux*); (*gamekeeper*) garde-chasse *m*, *pl* gardes-chasse(s); tenancier, -ière (*d'un établissement*); *Fb F* goal *m*; **I'm not my brother's k.,** je ne suis pas responsable de mon frère; **(b)** *Tech* (*device*) (*pawl, click*) détente *f*, cliquet *m*; gâche *f* (*de serrure*).

keep-fit ['kiːp'fɪt] *adj* **k.-f. class,** cours *m* de gymnastique.

keeping ['kiːpɪŋ] *n* observation *f* (*d'une règle, d'une promesse*); célébration *f* (*d'une fête*); conservation *f* (*de fruits etc*); **to have s.o./sth in one's k.,** avoir qn/qch en garde *ou* sous sa garde; **in God's k.,** à la garde de Dieu; **in k. with ...,** en harmonie *ou* en accord avec ...; **in k. with his principles,** conforme à ses principes; **out of k. with ...,** en désaccord avec ...; **good k. qualities,** (*of food*) bonnes qualités à la conservation.

keepsake ['kiːpseɪk] *n* souvenir *m*.

keg [keg] *n* caque *f* (*de harengs*); barillet *m* (*de bière, d'eau-de-vie etc*); tonnelet *m* (*d'eau*); **powder k.,** baril *m* de poudre.

kelp [kelp] *n* (*seaweed*) varech *m*.

ken [ken] *n* **within s.o.'s k.,** dans les connaissances *ou* la compétence de qn; **beyond s.o.'s k.,** hors de la compétence de qn.

Ken *abbr* **Kentucky**.

kennel ['ken(ə)l] *n* **(a)** loge *f*, niche *f* (*de chien de garde etc*); chenil *m* (*de chiens de chasse*); **kennels,** établissement *m* d'élevage de chiens; **to put a dog into kennels,** mettre un chien en pension; **the k.,** (*in hunting*) la meute; **(b)** terrier *m* (*de renard*).

kennelmaid ['ken(ə)lmeɪd] *n* employée d'éleveur de chiens *ou* de chenil.

Kenya ['kiːnjə, 'ken-] *n* Kenya *m*.

Kenyan ['kenjən] **1** *adj* kenyan. **2** *n* Kenyan, -ane.
kept¹ [kept] *adj Old-fashioned* **k. woman,** femme entretenue.
kept² *see* **KEEP².**
kerb, *US* **curb** [kɜːb] *n* bordure *f ou* bord *m* de trottoir; **to draw up at the k.,** se mettre en stationnement (le long du trottoir); *St Exch F* **business done on the k.,** opérations en coulisse, après clôture de Bourse; *St Exch F* **k. broker,** coulissier *m ou* courtier *m* en valeurs mobilières; **k. crawler,** personne qui accoste les prostitué(e)s en voiture; **k. crawling,** accostage *m* (*de prostitué(e)s*) en voiture; **k. drill,** précautions pour traverser la rue.
kerbstone, *US* **curbstone** ['kɜːbstəʊn] *n* pierre *f* de parement (*d'un trottoir*); *St Exch F* **k. market,** la coulisse.
kerchief ['kɜːtʃɪf] *n Old-fashioned* (*for head*) mouchoir *m* de tête; (*scarf*) fichu *m*.
kerfuffle [kə'fʌf(ə)l] *n esp Br F* remue-ménage *m*, tohu-bohu *m*.
kernel ['kɜːn(ə)l] *n* **(a)** (*of nut*) intérieur *m*; amande *f* (*de noyau*); pignon *m* (*de pomme de pin*); grain *m* (*de céréale*); graine *f* (*de légumineuse*); *Culin* noix *f* (*de veau*); **(b)** *Fig* noyau *m* (*d'une organisation etc*); fond *m*, essentiel *m* (*d'un problème etc*).
kerning ['kɜːnɪŋ] *n Typ* = réduction de l'espace entre les caractères d'un mot.
kerosene ['kerəsiːn] *n* **(a)** *Ch* kérosène *m*; **(b)** *Am* pétrole lampant.
kestrel ['kestrəl] *n* (*bird*) (faucon *m*) crécerelle *f*.
ketch [ketʃ] *n Nau* ketch *m*, dundee *m*, dindet *m*.
ketchup ['ketʃəp] *n* **(tomato) k.,** ketchup *m*.
kettle [ket(ə)l] *n* (*for boiling water*) bouilloire *f*; (*for cooking*) chaudron *m*; **to boil a k. of water,** mettre une bouilloire d'eau à bouillir; **I'll put the k. on,** je mets l'eau à chauffer pour le thé *etc*; **fish k.,** poissonnière *f*; *Mil* **mess k.,** gamelle *f*; *F* **here's a pretty** *or* **a fine k. of fish!,** nous voilà dans de beaux draps!; **that's quite a different k. of fish,** c'est tout à fait autre chose, ça c'est une autre affaire; *Geol* **giant's k.,** marmite *f ou* chaudière de géant(s).
kettledrum ['ket(ə)ldrʌm] *n Mus* timbale *f*.
key¹ [kiː] **1** *n* **(a)** clef *f*, clé *f* (*de serrure, de porte etc*); **to turn the k. (in the lock),** donner un tour de clef (à la porte); *Old-fashioned F* **to have the k. to the door,** avoir atteint sa majorité; **it was the k. to his success,** cela lui a ouvert les portes du succès; **the k. to understanding sth,** la clé permettant de comprendre qch; **the (House of) Keys,** le Parlement de l'Île de Man; **master k.,** passe-partout *m inv*; **k. bar,** (*in store*) stand *m* de clef-minute; **k. case,** étui *m* porte-clefs; *US* **k. club,** club privé dont les membres possèdent chacun une clef; **k. money,** arrhes *fpl*, *F* pas *m* de porte; **k. rack,** (*in hotel etc*) tableau *m* (des clefs); **k. ring,** porte-clefs *m inv*;
(b) clef *f* (*d'une énigme, d'un chiffre etc*); légende *f* (*d'une carte etc*); *Sch* corrigé *m*; livre *m* du maître; solutions *fpl* (*des problèmes*); *Comptr* indicatif *m*, critère *m* (*de tri, d'identification etc*); **k. numbers,** (*on squared map*) numéros *mpl* de repérage;
(c) *Mus* ton *m*; **major/minor k.,** ton majeur/mineur; **the k. of C,** le ton d'ut; **to be out of k.,** chanter *ou* jouer faux; **k. signature,** armature *f* (de la clef);
(d) *Art etc* caractéristique de luminosité (*d'un tableau, d'une image*); **picture painted in a low k.,** tableau peint dans des tons sombres;
(e) touche *f* (*de piano, d'orgue, de machine à écrire etc*); *Tel Telecom* touche *f* (*d'appel etc*); *El* manette *f*; *Mus* clef (*d'un instrument à vent*); *Tel Telecom* **listening/speaking k.,** touche d'écoute/de conversation; **Morse k.,** clef *ou* manipulateur *m* Morse; *Comptr* **k. punch,** perforatrice *f* à clavier;
(f) *Tech* clef *f*, carotte *f* (*de robinet*); remontoir *m* (*de pendule, de jouet mécanique etc*); **box k.,** (*spanner*) clef à douille;
(g) *Carp* clef *f*; *MecE etc* clavette *f*; cale *f*, coin *m* (*d'arbre*); *Rail* coin (*de coussinet de rail*); *El* fiche *f*; **set k.,** coin prisonnier;
(h) *Constr* rappointis *m*; *Carp* adent *m* (*pour empêcher une poutre etc de glisser*).
2 *adj* (*used attributively*) **k. factor/post/industry,** facteur *m*/poste *m*/industrie *f* clef; **k. person,** cheville ouvrière, pilier *m*, pivot *m* (*d'un établissement, d'une organisation*); **k. word,** mot-clé *m*, *pl* mot-clés, mot-clef *m*, *pl* mots-clefs.
key² *vt* **(a)** *Comptr* taper; taper, saisir (*des données*) **(b)** *MecE* clavet(t)er, coincer, caler (*une poulie sur un arbre*); *Carp* adenter (*une planche*); **to k. sth with sth,** lier qch à qch; *Rail* **to k. the rails,** coincer les rails; **(c)** *Telecom* manipuler.
►**key in** *vtsep Comptr etc* = **KEY² (a)**.
►**key up** *vtsep* **(a)** (*usu passive*) (*make tense*) **crowd keyed up for the match,** foule tendue dans l'attente du match; **to be all keyed up,** être crispé *ou* tendu; **(b)** *Comptr* = **KEY² (a)**; **(c)** *Mus* **to k. up the strings of an instrument,** accorder un instrument.
keyboard¹ ['kiːbɔːd] *n* clavier *m* (*de piano, de machine à écrire, d'ordinateur*); *Mus* **k. instrument,** instrument *m* à clavier; *Mus* **k. player,** joueur, -euse de synthétiseur; **k. skills,** connaissances en dactylo.
keyboard² *vt Comptr* (*text, data*) taper, saisir.
keyboarder ['kiːbɔːdər] *n Comptr* claviste *mf*.
keyboarding ['kiːbɔːdɪŋ] *n Comptr* frappe *f*; saisie *f* (*de données*); **speed of k.,** vitesse de la frappe; **k. problems,** problèmes au niveau de la frappe; **k. error,** faute *f* de frappe.
keyboards ['kiːbɔːdz] *npl Mus* claviers *mpl*.
keyhole ['kiːhəʊl] *n* trou *m* de serrure; **to look through the k.,** regarder par le trou de la serrure; **k. surgery,** chirurgie *f* à incision minimale.
keying ['kiːɪŋ] *n* **(a)** *Comptr* = **KEYBOARDING**; **(b)** *MecE* claret(t)age *m*, calage *m*, coinçage *m*; **(c)** *Telecom* manipulation *f*; **(d)** *Mus* accordage *m* (*d'un piano*).
keying in *n Comptr* = **KEYING (a)**.
keynote ['kiːnəʊt] *n Mus* tonique *f*; note dominante, idée dominante (*d'un discours*); mot *m* d'ordre (*d'une politique*); **k. speech,** discours *m* d'ouverture; **k. speaker,** = **KEYNOTER**.
keynoter ['kiːnəʊtər] *n US* orateur qui prononce le discours d'ouverture.
keypad ['kiːpæd] *n Comptr* **numeric k.,** clavier *m ou* pavé *m* numérique.
keystone ['kiːstəʊn] *n Archit* clef *f* de voûte; *Fig* clef de voûte, pivot *m* (*d'une politique*).
keystroke ['kiːstrəʊk] *n Comptr* touche *f*.
kg (*abbr* **kilogram**) kg.
KG [keɪ'dʒiː] *n abbr* **Knight of the Order of the Garter.**
KGB [keɪdʒiː'biː] *n* KGB *m*; **KGB agent/officer,** agent/officier du KGB.
khaki ['kɑːkɪ] **1** *n Tex* kaki *m*. **2** *adj* kaki *inv*.
kHz (*abbr* **kilohertz**) kHz.
kibbutz, *pl* **-zim** [kɪ'bʊts, kɪbʊt'siːm] *n Agr* kibboutz *m*, *pl* kibboutzim.
kibitzer ['kɪbɪtsər] *n Am F* celui *ou* celle qui donne des conseils non sollicités, donneur, -euse d'avis; (*fusspot, doesn't contribute*) mouche *f* du coche.
kibosh ['kaɪbɒʃ] *n Sl* **to put the k. on sth,** mettre le holà à qch.
kick¹ [kɪk] *n* **(a)** coup *m* de pied; ruade *f* (*d'un cheval etc*); **to give s.o./sth a k.,** donner un coup de pied à qn/qch; **to have a powerful k.,** (*of footballer, horse*) avoir un coup de pied puissant; (*of swimmer*) avoir un battement de pied puissant; *Fb etc* **free k.,** coup de pied franc; **goal k.,** coup de pied de but; *Sp* **k. boxing,** boxe française; *Ski* **k. turn,** conversion *f*; *F* **she just needs a k. up the backside** *or* **in the pants,** elle a juste besoin d'un coup de pied au derrière; *F* **it's better than a k. in the pants,** c'est mieux que rien; *Sl* **a k. in the teeth,** un coup en vache; **k. pleat,** (*in skirt*) pli *m* d'aisance;
(b) (*vigour*) vigueur *f*, énergie *f*; *F* **a drink with a k. in it,** une boisson qui donne un coup de fouet; *F* **to get a k. out of (doing) sth,** prendre plaisir à (faire) qch; *Sl* **to do sth for kicks,** faire qch pour s'amuser; *Sl* **to get one's kicks doing sth,** prendre son pied à faire qch;
(c) (*recoil*) recul *m*, réaction *f*, bourrade *f* (*d'un fusil*); cahot *m*, secousse *f* (*d'un mécanisme etc*);
(d) = **KICKBACK (a)**.
kick² **1** *vi* donner un coup de pied *ou* des coups de pied; (*of animal*) ruer, lancer des ruades; *Sp* (*of athlete*) démarrer; (*of gun*) reculer, repousser; *F* **to k. at** *or* **against sth,** (*rebel against*) regimber contre qch.
2 *vt* (*once*) donner un coup de pied à (*qn, qch*); (*several times*) donner des coups de pied à (*qn, qch*); (*push with foot*) pousser (*qn, qch*) du pied; (*of horse etc*) détacher un coup de pied à (*qn*); *Fb* botter (*le ballon*); marquer (*un but*); **to get kicked,** recevoir un coup de pied *ou* des coups de pied; *Sl* **to get kicked in the teeth,** recevoir un coup en vache; *F* **to k. s.o.'s behind,** flanquer à qn un coup de pied au cul; *Sl* **to k. the bucket,** casser sa pipe, crever; **to k. a man when he's down,** donner le coup de pied de l'âne à qn; **I could have kicked myself,** je me serais donné des gifles; **I could k. myself!,** quel imbécile je fais!; **to k. a (bad) habit,** renoncer à une (mauvaise) habitude.

▶**kick about, kick around** *F* **1** *vi* (*hang around*) traîner; (*of person*) rouler sa bosse; **there are plenty of people like that kicking around,** des gens comme ça, ce n'est pas ça qui manque. **2** *vtsep* **(a)** (*play with*) **to k. a ball around,** taper dans un ballon; *F* explorer (*une idée etc*); **(b)** (*mistreat*) traiter (*qn*) sans ménagements; **you shouldn't let yourself be kicked around like that,** tu ne devrais pas te laisser traiter comme ça.

▶**kick aside** *vtsep* écarter (*qch*) à coups de pied *ou* d'un coup de pied.

▶**kick away** *vtsep* repousser (*qch*) du pied.

▶**kick back 1** *vi* (*recoil*) (*of engine*) donner des retours en arrière; (*of gun*) reculer, repousser. **2** *vtsep* (*return by kicking*) relancer (*un ballon*). **3** *vtas* rendre un coup de pied à (*qn*).

▶**kick in 1** *vtsep* (*break open*) enfoncer (*la porte etc*) à coups de pied; *Sl* **to get one's head kicked in,** se faire casser la tête. **2** *vi F* (*contribute*) payer sa part *ou* son écot.

▶**kick off 1** *vtsep* enlever (*qch*) d'un coup de pied; **to k. off one's shoes,** enlever ses chaussures d'un mouvement brusque du pied. **2** *vi Fb* donner le coup d'envoi; *Fig F* (*start*) démarrer, partir.

▶**kick out 1** *vtsep* chasser (*qn*) à coups de pied; *Fb* renvoyer (*le ballon*); *F* **to be kicked out,** (*of job, house, pub etc*) être mis à la porte. **2** *vi* (*of horse etc*) lancer une ruade *ou* des ruades; (*of person*) donner un coup de pied *ou* des coups de pied.

▶**kick over** *vtsep* (*overturn*) renverser (*qch*) d'un coup de pied.

▶**kick up** *vtsep* (*cause*) *F* **to k. up a fuss,** faire des histoires; **to k. up a row** *or* **a racket,** faire du tapage *ou* du boucan.

kickback ['kɪkbæk] *n* **(a)** (*of engine*) retour *m* en arrière; *F* (*reaction*) réaction violente; **(b)** *F Pej* (*payment*) ristourne *f*, dessous-de-table *m inv*, pot-de-vin *m*.

kicker ['kɪkər] *n* **(a)** (*person who kicks*) donneur *m* de coups de pied; *Rugby* botteur *m*; *Th F* **high k.,** danseuse *f* de can-can *ou* de chahut; **(b)** (*horse etc*) cheval *m etc* qui rue.

kickoff ['kɪkɒf] *n Fb* coup *m* d'envoi; *Fig F* démarrage *m*; **k. at two o'clock,** la partie commence à deux heures; *F* **for a k.,** pour commencer.

kickstand ['kɪkstænd] *n* béquille *f* (*de bicyclette*).

kick-start[1] ['kɪkstɑːt] *n* = **KICK-STARTER**.

kick-start[2] *vt* démarrer au kick (*motorbike, engine*).

kick-starter ['kɪkstɑːtər] *n* (*on motorbike*) démarreur *m* au pied, kick *m*.

kid[1] [kɪd] *n* **(a)** *F* (*child*) mioche *mf*, gosse *mf*; *US* **say k.!,** dis-moi, mon petit *ou* ma petite; **my k. brother,** mon petit frère; **it's k.'s stuff,** (*easy*) c'est facile à faire; (*childish*) c'est (bon) pour les gosses; **(b)** (*animal*) chevreau *m*, *f* chevrette; (*skin*) (peau *f* de) chevreau, cabron *m*; **k. gloves,** gants *mpl* (en peau) de chevreau; *Fig* **to handle s.o. with k. gloves,** ménager qn; *Fig* **you have to handle him with k. gloves (on),** il faut prendre des gants pour l'approcher.

kid[2] *F* **1** *vt* en conter à (*qn*), faire marcher (*qn*); **you're kidding us,** tout ça c'est des blagues; **to k. s.o. that ...,** faire croire à qn que ...; **to k. oneself,** se faire des illusions; **I k. you not,** je ne plaisante pas. **2** *vi* **(I was) only kidding,** je plaisantais; **no kidding!,** sans blague!; **are you kidding?,** (*that's a ridiculous suggestion*) tu plaisantes?

▶**kid on** *vtsep & vi* = **KID[2]**.

kiddie, kiddy ['kɪdɪ] *n F* petit(e) gosse.

kiddo ['kɪdəʊ] *n F* **are you ready, k.?,** tu es prêt(e), mon grand *ou* ma grande.

kidglove ['kɪdglʌv] *adj* **to give s.o. the k. treatment,** ménager qn.

kidnap ['kɪdnæp] *vt* (**-pp-**) kidnapper (*qn*).

kidnapper ['kɪdnæpər] *n* kidnappeur, -euse; ravisseur, -euse (*d'enfant*).

kidnapping ['kɪdnæpɪŋ] *n* kidnapping *m*, enlèvement *m*; *Jur* rapt *m* (*d'enfant*).

kidney ['kɪdnɪ] *n* **(a)** *Anat* rein *m*; *Lit* **a man of his k.,** un homme de sa trempe; **k. donor,** donneur, -euse de rein; **k. machine,** rein artificiel; *Med* **k. stone,** calcul rénal; *Med* **k. tray,** cuvette *f* à pansements réniforme, *F* haricot *m*; **(b)** *Culin* rognon *m*; *Geol* rognon (*de silex etc*); *Culin* **devilled kidneys,** rognons à la diable; **k. bean,** (*French bean*) haricot nain; (*scarlet runner*) haricot d'Espagne *ou* à grappes; **k. vetch,** (*plant*) (anthyllide *f*) vulnéraire *f*, trèfle *m* jaune.

kidney-shaped ['kɪdnɪʃeɪpt] *adj* en forme de haricot, réniforme.

kidology [kɪ'dɒlədʒɪ] *n Br F* **it's all k.,** ce ne sont que des histoires.

kill[1] [kɪl] *n* **(a)** (*in hunting*) mise *f* à mort (*du renard, du cerf etc*); (*animals killed*) gibier tué, le tableau de chasse; **to be in at the k.,** assister à la mise à mort; *Fig* assister au dénouement de qch (et en tirer profit); **(b)** *Mil* descente *f* (*of enemy aircraft*); coulée *f* (*of enemy warship*).

kill[2] **1** *vt* **(a)** tuer; faire mourir (*une plante*); tuer (*les microbes*); *Mil* détruire (*l'ennemi*); tuer, abattre (*un animal*); descendre (*une perdrix, un homme*); (*of butcher*) abattre, tuer (*un bœuf etc*); tuer (*le nerf d'une dent*); (*in hunting*) servir (*la bête*); **to k. oneself,** se suicider; *F* (*overexert oneself*) se tuer (**doing,** à faire); *F* (*with laughing*) être mort de rire; *Iron* **don't k. yourself, will you,** ne te fais pas trop mal; **to k. oneself with work,** se tuer à (force de) travailler; **the shock would k. her,** le choc la tuerait; *F* **I'll kill you!,** (*if you do that again etc*) je t'étrangle!; *F* **this one'll k. you,** (*of joke*) ça va te faire mourir de rire; **k. or cure remedy,** remède *m* héroïque; **this superstition will be hard to k.,** cette superstition aura la vie dure; *Prov* **to k. two birds with one stone,** faire d'une pierre deux coups, faire coup double; **to k. s.o. with kindness,** faire du mal à qn par excès de bonté; *F* **to be dressed to k.,** porter une toilette irrésistible; *F* **my feet are killing me,** mes pieds me font atrocement souffrir;

(b) tuer (*le temps*); éteindre (*l'ambition*); détruire, étouffer (*tout sentiment d'humanité*); *Pol* couler (*un projet de loi*); *Journ etc* supprimer (*un passage*);

(c) amortir (*le son*); *Ch* neutraliser (*un acide etc*); (*in plumbing etc*) décomposer (*l'esprit de sel*); éteindre, amortir (*la chaux*); neutraliser (*les odeurs*);

(d) *Sp Fb* bloquer (*le ballon*); *Tennis* tuer, massacrer (*la balle*).

2 *vi* tuer; **k. or be killed,** tuer ou se faire tuer.

▶**kill off** *vtsep* exterminer (*toute une population etc*); **to k. off a character,** (*of author etc*) faire mourir un personnage.

killer ['kɪlər] *n* **(a)** (*person*) tueur, -euse; (*murderer*) meurtrier *m*; **k. disease,** maladie meurtrière; **k. whale,** épaulard *m*; **(b)** (*in slaughtering*) **humane k.,** revolver *m* d'abattage; **(c) insect** *or* **fly k.,** insecticide *m*; **(d)** *F* (*difficult question*) colle *f*; **the exam was a real k.,** cet examen n'était pas piqué des hannetons; **this hill's a real k.,** (*is very difficult*) cette côte est vraiment mortelle; (*people die on it*) cette côte est meurtrière.

killing ['kɪlɪŋ] **1** *adj* **(a)** (*blow*) meurtrier, assassin; **(b)** (*métier*) tuant, assommant, écrasant; **(c)** *F* (*very amusing*) crevant; **it's too k. for words,** c'est à mourir de rire, c'est à se tordre. **2** *n* **(a)** tuerie *f*, abattage *m* (*d'animaux*); (*murder*) meurtre *m*; *Mil* destruction *f* (*de l'ennemi*); *F* **to make a k.,** (*on Stock Exchange etc*) faire un bénéfice énorme *ou* une affaire à tout casser; **(b)** *Tech* amortissement *m* (*des sons*); *Ch* neutralisation *f* (*d'un acide etc*).

-killing ['kɪlɪŋ] *suff* -icide; **germ-k.,** bactéricide.

killingly ['kɪlɪŋlɪ] *adv* **it's k. funny,** c'est à mourir de rire.

killjoy ['kɪldʒɔɪ] *n* rabat-joie *m inv*.

kiln [kɪln] *n* **(a)** four *m* (céramique); (*for drying*) séchoir *m*, sécherie *f*, étuve *f*; **brick k.,** four à briques; **lime k.,** four à chaux, chaufour *m*; **hop k.,** four *ou* séchoir à houblon; **malt k.,** (*in brewing*) touraille *f*; **k. drying** *or* **seasoning,** séchage *m* au four, étuvage *m*; (*in brewing*) touraillage *m* (*du malt*); **(b) charcoal k.,** meule *f* (de charbon de bois).

kilo ['kiːləʊ] *n* kilo *m*.

kilobyte ['kɪləbaɪt] *n Comptr* kilo-octet *m*.

kilocalorie ['kɪləʊkælərɪ] *n Phys* kilocalorie *f*.

kilocycle ['kɪləsaɪk(ə)l] *n Phys El* kilocycle *m*.

kilogram(me) ['kɪləgræm] *n* kilogramme *m*.

kilohertz ['kɪləʊhɜːts] *n* kilohertz *m*.

kilometre, *US* **kilometer** ['kɪləmiːtər, *esp Am* kɪ'lɒmɪtər] *n* kilomètre *m*; **distance in kilometres,** distance *f* kilométrique.

kilometric [kɪlə'metrɪk] *adj* kilométrique.

kilovolt ['kɪləvəʊlt] *n El* kilovolt *m*.

kilowatt ['kɪləwɒt] *n El* kilowatt *m*.

kilowatt-hour ['kɪləwɒtaʊər] *n El* kilowatt-heure *m*, *pl* kilowatt- heures.

kilt [kɪlt] *n* (*garment*) kilt *m* (écossais).

kilter ['kɪltər] *n* **out of k.,** (*of machine part*) détraqué; (*out of balance*) (*of budget, priorities etc*) déséquilibré.

kimono [kɪ'məʊnəʊ] *n* (*garment*) kimono *m*.

kin [kɪn] *n* parents *mpl*; **his k.,** ses parents, sa parenté; **to be k. to s.o.,** être parent de *ou* apparenté avec qn; **next of k.,** la famille, le parent le plus proche; **to inform the next of k.,** prévenir la famille.

kind[1] [kaɪnd] *n* **(a)** (*class, sort*) genre *m*, espèce *f*, sorte *f*; **what k. is it?,** de quelle sorte *ou* de quel genre (est-ce)?; **what k. of tree is this?,** quelle sorte *ou* quel genre d'arbre est-ce?; **what k. of woman is she?,** quel genre *ou* quelle sorte de femme est-ce?; **people of all kinds,** des gens de toutes sortes; **it's a k. of fish,** c'est une espèce de poisson; **something of the k.,** quelque chose de ce genre; **nothing of the k.,** rien de la sorte; **in a k. of a way,** en quelque façon; **this k. of woman,** ce genre de femmes, les femmes de cette sorte; **this k. of car,** *F* **these k. of cars,** ce genre de voitures, ces types de voitures; **he's not the understanding k.,** il n'est pas du genre compréhensif; **I know your k.!,** je connais les gens de ton espèce!; **she's more the stay-at-home k.,** elle est plus du type *ou* genre à rester à la maison; **well, it's beer of a k. I suppose,** oui, on peut appeler ça de la bière, je suppose; **he speaks French — of a k.,** il parle français – plus ou moins; **we're two of a k.,** nous sommes de la même espèce *ou* race; **it's the only one of its k.,** c'est le seul en son genre; **what k. of person do you think I am!,** pour quel genre de personne me prends-tu?; **he's that k. of person,** il est comme ça; **this is my k. of party,** c'est le genre de soirées que j'aime; **you're my k. of girl,** tu es mon type de femme *ou* le type de femme que j'aime; **I'm not that k. of girl,** ce n'est pas mon genre; **is this the k. of thing you're looking for?,** est-ce que c'est quelque chose de ce genre que vous cherchez?; **that's not the k. of thing I meant,** ce n'est pas exactement ce que je voulais; **this is not the k. of thing you can do overnight,** ce n'est pas le genre de chose qu'on fait du jour au lendemain; *F* **it was a k. of saucer-shaped thing,** c'était une espèce de truc en forme de soucoupe; *F* **there's a k. of bump just here,** il y a comme une bosse ici; *F* **I heard a k. of thump,** j'ai entendu une espèce de *ou* comme un cognement;

(b) (*nature, character*) **difference in k.,** différence *f* spécifique; **payment in k.,** paiement *m* en nature; **to repay s.o. in k.,** (*as opposed to cash*) rembourser qn en nature; (*for an injury, disservice*) rendre à qn la monnaie de sa pièce;

(c) *F* **k. of,** (*with adjectives*) un peu, plutôt; **you look k. of tired,** tu as l'air un peu *ou* plutôt fatigué; **it's k. of late,** il est un peu tard; **I'm k. of worried,** je suis un peu inquiet; **I k. of changed my mind,** je crois bien que j'ai changé d'avis; **I k. of expected it,** je m'y attendais un peu; **I k. of like it,** (*like it a little*) j'aime plus ou moins ça; **actually I k. of like it,** (*quite a bit*) en fait j'aime bien ça; **do you like it? — k. of,** tu aimes ça? – plus ou moins, ça va, comme ça; **do you agree? — k. of,** tu es d'accord? – plus ou moins.

kind² *adj* bon, aimable, bienveillant; **to be k. to s.o.,** se montrer bon pour *ou* envers qn; **it's very k. of you to ...,** c'est bien aimable de votre part *ou* à vous de ...; *Fml* **(would you) be k. enough to** *or* **so k. as to ...,** soyez assez bon pour ..., ayez la bonté de ..., veuillez (bien) ...; **you are really too k.,** vous êtes vraiment trop aimable; **k. to the skin,** (*of detergents etc*) qui n'irrite pas la peau; **they are k. people,** ce sont des gens aimables; **by k. permission of ...,** avec l'aimable autorisation de ...; **give him my k. regards,** faites-lui mes amitiés; **k. words,** paroles bienveillantes.

kinda ['kaɪndə] *F* = **kind of,** *see* **KIND¹(c).**

kindergarten ['kɪndəgɑːt(ə)n] *n Sch* jardin *m* d'enfants, école maternelle.

kind-hearted ['kaɪnd'hɑːtɪd] *adj* (*person*) qui a bon cœur.

kindle ['kɪnd(ə)l] **1** *vt* **(a)** allumer (*une flamme, un feu*); enflammer, embraser (*du charbon, une forêt*); **(b)** allumer (*la haine*); faire naître, susciter (*les passions*); enflammer (*le courage, les désirs*); embraser (*le cœur*); aviver (*les soupçons, le chagrin*); exciter (*le zèle*). **2** *vi* (*of fire, wood, passions etc*) s'allumer, s'enflammer.

kindliness ['kaɪndlɪnɪs] *n* bonté *f*, bienveillance *f*.

kindling ['kɪndlɪŋ] *n* **(a)** (*action*) embrasement *m*, enflammement *m*; **(b) k. (wood),** bois *m* d'allumage, petit bois.

kindly ['kaɪndlɪ] **1** *adv* avec bonté; **she spoke very k. of you,** elle a dit des choses très aimables à votre égard; **to be k. disposed towards s.o./sth,** être bien disposé envers qn/qch; **the council k. agreed to let us use the town hall,** le conseil nous a aimablement autorisé à utiliser l'hôtel de ville; *Com* **k. remit by cheque,** prière de nous couvrir par chèque; **not to take k. to s.o./sth,** ne pas aimer qn/qch. **2** *adj* bon, bienveillant; (*ton, conseil*) bienveillant; (*climat*) doux.

kindness ['kaɪndnɪs] *n* **(a)** bonté *f* (**towards s.o.,** pour qn), bienveillance *f*, amabilité *f* (**towards,** envers); **thanks for your k.,** merci de votre complaisance; **to repay s.o.'s k.,** payer qn de sa gentillesse; **to show k. to s.o.,** témoigner de la bonté à qn; *Fml* **will you have the k. to ...?,** voulez-vous avoir la bonté de ...?; **to be full of the milk of human k.,** être la crème de la bonté; **(b) a k.,** un service (rendu); **to do s.o. a k.,** rendre service à qn.

kindred ['kɪndrɪd] **1** *n* **(a)** (*relatives*) parents *mpl*; (*family*) famille *f*; **(b)** (*blood relationship*) parenté *f* (*de qn avec qn*). **2** *adj* de la même nature, du même genre; **k. spirits,** âmes *fpl* sœurs.

kinematic [kɪnə'mætɪk, kaɪn-] *adj Phys* cinématique.

kinetic [kɪ'netɪk, kaɪ-] *adj Phys etc* (*énergie etc*) cinétique.

kinfolk ['kɪnfəʊk] *npl Am* parents *mpl* et alliés *mpl*.

king [kɪŋ] *n* **(a)** roi *m*; *Fig Ind etc* magnat *m*; **the kings and queens of England,** les souverains *mpl* d'Angleterre; *Bible* **K. of Kings,** Roi des rois; **the three Kings,** les Rois Mages; **the Book of Kings,** le livre des Rois; **to crown s.o. k.,** couronner qn roi; **dish fit for a k.,** morceau *m* de roi; *Fig* **one of the oil kings,** un des rois du pétrole; **k. crab,** (*crustacean*) limule *m*, crabe *m* des Moluques; *Constr* **k. post,** poinçon *m*, aiguille *f* (*d'une ferme de comble*); **k. cobra,** (*snake*) cobra royal; **(b)** *Chess Cards* roi *m*; (*in draughts*) dame *f*.

kingbolt ['kɪŋbəʊlt] *n Constr MecE* cheville maîtresse *ou* ouvrière; pivot central.

kingcup ['kɪŋkʌp] *n* (*plant*) **(a)** (*buttercup*) bouton *m* d'or; **(b)** (*marsh marigold*) populage *m*, souci *m* d'eau.

kingdom ['kɪŋdəm] *n* **(a)** royaume *m*; **the United K.,** le Royaume-Uni; **the k. of heaven,** le royaume des cieux; **(b)** règne *m* (*animal, végétal, minéral*); **in the animal k.,** chez les animaux; **(c)** *Rel* règne *m*; **Thy k. come,** que Ton règne vienne; *F* **k. come,** le paradis; *F* **to send s.o. to k. come,** expédier qn dans l'autre monde; *F* **until k. come,** jusqu'à l'éternité.

kingfisher ['kɪŋfɪʃər] *n* (*bird*) martin-pêcheur *m*, *pl* martins-pêcheurs.

kingly ['kɪŋlɪ] *adj* de roi; (*royal*) royal, -aux.

king-of-arms [kɪŋə'vɑːmz] *n Her* roi *m* d'armes.

kingpin ['kɪŋpɪn] *n* **(a)** *Aut* axe *m* de rotule; *Fig* cheville ouvrière (*d'une organisation, d'une entreprise*); **(b)** (*in tenpin bowling*) quille *f* du milieu.

kingship ['kɪŋʃɪp] *n* royauté *f*.

king-size(d) ['kɪŋ'saɪz, -d] *adj Com* géant; (*cigarette*) long; **a k.-s. headache,** un immense mal de crâne.

kink¹ [kɪŋk] *n* **(a)** vrillage *m*; tortillement *m* (*dans un fil, dans une corde*); grigne *f* (*dans le feutre*); crêpelure *f* (*des cheveux*); *Nau* coque *f* (*dans un cordage*); *Tex* vrille *f*, boucle *f*; *MecE etc* pliure *f* (*d'une pièce mécanique*); **the rope's got a k. in it,** il y a un vrillage dans la corde; **(b)** (*in character*) déséquilibre *m*, aberration *f*; *Br F* **he's got a k.,** (*sexual*) il a des goûts sexuels excentriques.

kink² *vi* (*of rope*) se nouer, se tortiller, vrillonner; *Nau* faire des coques; (*of thread*) vriller.

kinky ['kɪŋkɪ] *adj* **(a)** (*rope etc*) noué; (*hair*) crêpelé, crépu; **(b)** *Sl* (*person*) qui a des goûts sexuels excentriques; *F* (*eccentric*) extravagant; *F* (*clothes etc*) bizarre, extravagant.

kinsfolk ['kɪnzfəʊk] *npl* parents *mpl* et alliés *mpl*.

kinship ['kɪnʃɪp] *n* parenté *f*.

kinsman, *pl* **-men** ['kɪnzmən] *n* parent *m*.

kinswoman, *pl* **-women** ['kɪnzwʊmən, -wɪmɪn] *n* parente *f*.

kiosk ['kiːɒsk] *n* kiosque *m*; **newspaper k.,** kiosque à journaux; *Br* **telephone k.,** cabine *f* téléphonique.

kip¹ [kɪp] *n Br Sl* **(a)** (*sleep*) **to have a k.,** piquer un roupillon; **to get some k.,** roupiller; **an hour's k.,** un roupillon d'une heure; **(b)** (*bed*) pieu *m*, plumard *m*; **to be still in one's k.,** être encore au plumard.

kip² *vi* **(-pp-)** *Br Sl* roupiller.

kip³ *n* (*leather*) peau *f* de veau *ou* d'agneau.

►**kip down** *vi Br Sl* (*make one's bed*) se pieuter.

kipper¹ ['kɪpər] *n Culin* hareng légèrement salé et fumé, kipper *m*.

kipper² *vt* saler et fumer (*des harengs*); **kippered herring,** = **KIPPER¹.**

kir [kɪər] *n* (*drink*) kir *m*.

kirk [kɜːk] *n Scot* église *f*; **the K.,** l'Église (presbytérienne) d'Écosse.

kiss¹ [kɪs] *n* baiser *m*; **to give s.o. a k.,** donner un baiser à qn; **give mother a k.!,** (*to child*) fais une bise à maman!; *Med F* **to give s.o. the k. of life,** faire le bouche-à-bouche à qn; *Fig* **to be the k. of death for s.o./sth,** (*of act, decision*) être fatal pour qn/qch; **k. curl,** accroche-cœur *m*, *pl* accroche-cœurs.

kiss² **1** *vt* **(a)** donner un baiser à, embrasser (*qn*); baiser (*le front, la main, de qn, un objet sacré*); (*ceremonially*) donner l'accolade à (*qn*); **to k. s.o. on the cheek/lips,** embrasser qn sur la joue/les lèvres; **they kissed each other,** ils se sont embrassés; **to k. the book,** baiser la Bible (pour prêter serment); *Lit* **to k. the dust,** mordre la poussière; **to k. s.o. goodbye,** dire au revoir à qn en l'embrassant; *F* **you can k. that promotion goodbye,** tu peux dire au revoir à cet avancement; **(b)** *(touch lightly)* frôler; *Billiards (of ball)* frapper *(une autre)* par contrecoup. **2** *vi* **(a)** *(of two people)* s'embrasser; *F* **to k. and make up,** se réconcilier; **(b)** *(of two objects)* se frôler; *Billiards (of balls)* se frapper par contrecoup.

kissagram ['kɪsəgræm] *n* message délivré par une jeune fille (en tenue légère) et accompagné d'un baiser.

kisser ['kɪsər] *n* **(a)** *(person)* embrasseur, -euse; **to be a great k.,** bien embrasser; **(b)** *Sl (mouth)* gueule *f*.

kissing ['kɪsɪŋ] *n* baisers *mpl*, embrassade *f*; **k. of hands,** baisemain *m*; *Am Med F* **k. disease,** mononucléose infectieuse.

kiss-off ['kɪsɒf] *n Am F* **to give s.o. the k.-o.,** *(of girlfriend etc)* plaquer qn; *(of employer)* virer qn.

kit[1] [kɪt] *n (baggage)* effets *mpl*, bagages *mpl*; *Mil etc* petit équipement; *(personal belongings)* effets (personnels); *(equipment)* matériel *m*, équipement *m*; trousseau *m*, trousse *f (d'outils etc)*; **to pack up one's k.,** plier bagage, faire ses paquets; *F* **the whole k. and caboodle,** tout le bataclan; **repair k.,** nécessaire *m ou* trousse de réparations; **first-aid k.,** trousse de première urgence; **riding k.,** tenue *f* de cheval; **troops in full battle k.,** troupes en tenue de campagne; **to make sth from a k.,** faire qch à partir de pièces détachées; **model k.,** modèle *m* en pièces détachées; **to buy sth in k. form,** acheter qch en prêt-à-monter; *Mil etc* **k. inspection,** revue *f* de détail *ou* d'inspection.

kit[2] *vt* (-tt-) équiper, fournir son équipement à *(un soldat etc)*.

►**kit out, kit up** *vtsep esp Br* = **KIT**[2]; **(all) kitted out,** complètement équipé; *Mil* **to be kitted out,** toucher son paquetage.

kitbag ['kɪtbæg] *n* sac *m* de voyage; sac (de) marin; *Mil* sac à paquetage, sac de grande monture.

kitchen ['kɪtʃɪn] *n* cuisine *f*; **in the k.,** à la cuisine; **mobile k.,** cuisine roulante *(de l'armée)*; *F* **thieves' k.,** repaire *m* de voleurs; *esp Am Pol F* **k. cabinet,** conseillers particuliers; **k. garden,** (jardin *m*) potager *m*; **k. sink,** évier *m*; *F* **k.-sink literature,** littérature *f* boîte à ordures; *F* **everything but the k. sink,** tout, y compris la cage aux serins; **k. stove,** cuisinière *f*; **k. table,** table *f* de cuisine; **k. unit,** bloc-cuisine *m, pl* blocs-cuisines; **k. utensils,** batterie *f* de cuisine.

kitchenette [kɪtʃɪ'net] *n* petite cuisine, cuisinette *f*.

kitchenware ['kɪtʃɪnweər] *n* faïence *f ou* vaisselle *f* de cuisine.

kite [kaɪt] *n* **(a)** *(toy)* cerf-volant *m, pl* cerfs-volants; *Fin F* traite *f* en l'air, billet *m* de complaisance; **k. balloon,** ballon observateur, *F* saucisse *f*; **to fly a k.,** lancer *ou* faire voler un cerf-volant; *F* **as high as a k.,** *(drunk)* ivre, soûl; *(drugged)* drogué, camé; *(very excited)* tout fou, *f* toute folle; **(b)** *Br Av F (aeroplane)* avion *m*, taxi *m*; **(c)** *(bird)* milan *m*.

kith [kɪθ] *n Arch (still used in)* **our k. and kin,** nos parents et amis; **to have neither k. nor kin,** être seul sur la terre.

kitsch [kɪtʃ] *n* kitsch *m*.

kitschy ['kɪtʃɪ] *adj* **it's k.,** c'est du kitsch.

kitten[1] ['kɪt(ə)n] *n (young cat)* chaton *m*; petit(e) chat(te); *esp Am (of rabbit)* jeune lapin *m*; *(of hamster)* jeune hamster *m*; *(term of endearment)* ma petite, ma mignonne; **a cat and her kittens,** une chatte et ses petits; *Br F* **he'll have kittens,** *(of person)* il sera dans tous ses états.

kitten[2] **1** *vt (of cat)* mettre bas *(des petits)*. **2** *vi (of cat)* avoir des petits, chatonner.

kittenish ['kɪtənɪʃ] *adj* **(a)** *(girl, disposition) (lively)* enjoué; *(flirtatious)* coquet; **(b)** *(grâce)* félin.

kittiwake ['kɪtɪweɪk] *n (bird)* mouette *f* tridactyle.

kitty[1] ['kɪtɪ] *n F* chaton *m*; **here k., k.,** minou, minou, viens.

kitty[2] *n* **(a)** *Cards etc* cagnotte *f*; cagnotte, caisse commune *(d'un groupe)*; **(b)** *(at bowls)* cochonnet *m*.

kiwi ['kiːwiː] *n* **(a)** *(bird)* aptéryx *m*, kiwi *m*; **(b)** *F (New Zealander)* **K.,** Néo-Zélandais, -aise; **(c) k. fruit,** *F* **k.,** kiwi *m*.

KKK [keɪkeɪ'keɪ] *n US abbr* **Ku Klux Klan.**

kleptomania [kleptə'meɪnɪə] *n* kleptomanie *f*.

kleptomaniac [kleptə'meɪnɪæk] *adj & n* kleptomane *mf*.

klutz [klʌts] *n Am F* brise-tout *m inv*.

km *(abbr* **kilometre)** km.

km.p.h. *(abbr* **kilometres per hour)** km/h.

knack [næk] *n* talent *m*, chic *m*; *(esp physical)* tour *m* de main; **to have the k. of** *or* **a k. for doing sth,** avoir le talent de faire qch; *(esp physically)* avoir le coup *ou* le tour de main pour faire qch; **you have a k. for telephoning me at exactly the wrong moment,** tu as le chic pour me téléphoner précisément au mauvais moment; **to have lost the k. of sth,** n'avoir plus l'habitude de qch; **there's a k. to it,** il y a un truc.

knacker[1] ['nækər] *n* **(a)** *(of horses)* équarrisseur *m*; **k.'s yard,** chantier *m* d'équarrissage, équarrissoir *m*; **(b)** *(of buildings)* entrepreneur *m* de démolitions; *(of ships)* démolisseur *m* de vieux navires.

knacker[2] *vt Br F* éreinter; **I'm knackered,** je suis crevé; **it's knackered,** *(of machine etc)* c'est foutu.

knapsack ['næpsæk] *n Old-fashioned* havresac *m*, sac *m* à dos; sac alpin *ou* tyrolien; *Mil* sac d'ordonnance.

knave [neɪv] *n* **(a)** *Cards* valet *m*; **k. of clubs,** valet de trèfle; **(b)** *Old-fashioned (scoundrel)* fripon *m*, coquin *m*.

knavery ['neɪvərɪ] *n Old-fashioned* friponnerie *f*, coquinerie *f*.

knead [niːd] *vt* **(a)** pétrir, malaxer, travailler *(la pâte, l'argile)*; **(b)** *Med* masser, pétrir *(les muscles)*.

kneading ['niːdɪŋ] *n* **(a)** pétrissage *m (de la pâte)*; malaxage *m (de l'argile etc)*; **k. trough,** pétrin *m*; **(b)** *Med* massage *m*, foulage *m (des muscles)*.

knee[1] [niː] *n* **(a)** genou *m*, -oux; **to sit on s.o.'s k.** *or* **knees,** s'asseoir sur le genou *ou* les genoux de qn; **he learnt the song at his mother's k.,** il a appris la chanson sur les genoux de sa mère; **to bend** *or* **bow the k. to** *or* **before s.o.,** fléchir le genou devant qn; **to ask for sth on one's (bended) knees** *or* **on bended k.,** demander qch à genoux; **to go down on one's knees,** s'agenouiller; **to fall** *or* **drop to one's knees,** tomber à genoux; **on your knees!,** à genoux!; **to bring s.o. to his knees,** forcer qn à s'agenouiller; *Fig (force to surrender)* obliger qn à capituler; *F* **tennis k.,** foulure *f* du genou *(due au tennis)*; *Vet* **broken knees,** *(of horse)* couronnement *m*; *Anat* **k. reflex, k. jerk,** réflexe patellaire *ou* rotulien;

(b) *MecE Constr* raccord coudé, coude *m*; *(in naval architecture)* courbe *f* (de consolidation); **k. bracket,** console-équerre *f, pl* consoles-équerres; **k. (plate),** gousset *m* (de charpente); *Carp etc* **k. timber,** bois courbant *ou* coudé.

knee[2] *vt (push)* pousser *(qch, qn)* du genou; *(hit)* donner un coup de genou à *(qn, qch)*.

kneecap[1] ['niːkæp] *n Anat* rotule *f*.

kneecap[2] *vt* tirer dans les rotules de *(qn)*.

knee-deep ['niː'diːp] *adj (mud, water)* jusqu'aux genoux; **to be k.-d. in mud,** être enfoncé dans la boue jusqu'aux genoux.

knee-high ['niː'haɪ] *adj & adv* à hauteur du genou; *F* **when I was k.-h. to a grasshopper,** quand j'étais haut comme trois pommes.

kneejerk ['niːdʒɜːk] *adj (reaction)* instinctif, machinal.

kneel [niːl] *vi (pt & pp* **knelt** [nelt], *occ* **kneeled)** s'agenouiller, se mettre à genoux; **to k. to s.o.,** se mettre à genoux devant qn.

knee-length ['niːleŋθ] *adj (robe)* qui descend jusqu'aux genoux; *(boot)* qui monte jusqu'aux genoux.

kneeler ['niːlər] *n* **(a)** *(person)* personne agenouillée; **(b)** *(cushion)* coussin *m* pour s'agenouiller; *(in church)* agenouilloir *m*.

kneeling ['niːlɪŋ] **1** *adj* agenouillé, à genoux. **2** *n* agenouillement *m*.

kneepad ['niːpæd] *n* genouillère *f*.

knees-up ['niːzʌp] *n Br Sl* java *f*; **to have a k.-up,** faire la java.

knell [nel] *n* glas *m*; **to toll the k.,** sonner le glas; **this news/refusal rang the death k. of her hopes,** cette nouvelle/ce refus sonnait le glas de ses espérances.

knelt *see* **KNEEL.**

knickerbocker ['nɪkəbɒkər] *n* **k. glory,** coupe glacée géante.

knickerbockers ['nɪkəbɒkəz] *npl* culotte *f* (bouffante), knickerbockers *mpl*.

knickers ['nɪkəz] *npl* **(a)** culotte *f (de femme)*; *Sl* **to get one's k. in a twist,** perdre les pédales; **(b)** *US* = **KNICKERBOCKERS.**

knick-knack ['nɪknæk] *n* colifichet *m*, babiole *f*, bibelot *m*.

knife[1], *pl* **knives** [naɪf, naɪvz] *n* **(a)** couteau *m*; *(dagger)* couteau, poignard *m*; *Surg (scalpel)* scalpel *m*; *(with narrow blade)* bistouri *m*; **kitchen/table k.,** couteau de cuisine/table; **carving k.,** couteau à découper; **fish/dessert k.,** couteau à poisson/dessert; **k. and fork,** couverts *mpl*; **before you could say k.,** en un rien de temps, en moins de rien; **pocket k.,** couteau de poche, canif *m*; **to get** *or* **have**

one's k. into s.o., en vouloir à qn; **it was war to the k. between them,** ils étaient à couteaux tirés; **he was under the k. for two hours,** (*in operation*) il a passé deux heures sur le billard; **to go under the k.,** passer sur le billard; *Tech* **coopers' hollowing k.,** plane creuse de tonnelier; **putty k.,** spatule *f* de vitrier; couteau à palette *ou* à mastiquer; **k. edge,** bord tranchant; *Tech* pièce *f* (*mécanique etc*) en lame de couteau; couteau *m* (*de balance etc*); (*peak*) arête *f* (de montagne) en lame de couteau; **k. grinder,** (*person*) rémouleur *m*, repasseur *m* de couteaux; (*instrument*) meule *f* à aiguiser; **k. sharpener,** affiloir *m* (pour couteaux);

(b) (*blade*) couteau *m*, lame *f* (*d'un hache-paille etc*); couperet *m* (*de la guillotine*); *Tex* rasoir *m* (*de tondeuse*);

(c) *El* **k. switch,** interrupteur *m ou* commutateur *m* à couteau *ou* à lame(s).

knife² *vt* **(a)** (*stab*) donner un coup de couteau à (*qn*), poignarder (*qn*); **he's been knifed,** il a recu un coup de couteau, il a été poignardé; **(b)** (*depose*) descendre (*un homme politique*) (*par des moyens déloyaux, occultes*).

knife-edge ['naɪfedʒ] *adj* **trousers with a k.-e. crease,** pantalon au pli cassant.

knife-point ['naɪfpɔɪnt] *n* pointe *f* de couteau; **to be robbed at k.-p.,** se faire voler sous la menace d'un couteau.

knife-rest ['naɪfrest] *n* porte-couteau *m*, *pl* porte-couteaux.

knight¹ [naɪt] *n* **(a)** chevalier *m*; *Liter* **the Knights of the Round Table,** les Chevaliers de la Table Ronde; **K. of the Garter,** chevalier de l'Ordre de la Jarretière; **k. errant** [erənt] (*pl* **knights errant**), chevalier errant, paladin *m*; *Hist* **k. service,** service *m* de haubert; **(b)** *Chess* cavalier *m*.

knight² *vt* **(a)** faire *ou* créer (*qn*) chevalier; **(b)** *Hist* armer chevalier (*un écuyer etc*).

knighthood ['naɪthʊd] *n* **(a)** (*title*) **he has just been given a k.,** il vient d'être créé chevalier; **(b)** (*knights*) chevalerie *f*.

knightly ['naɪtlɪ] *adj* (*conduite etc*) chevaleresque, de chevalier.

knit [nɪt] *v* (*pt & pp* **knitted** *or* **knit**) **1** *vt* tricoter (*un vêtement*); faire souder (*les os*); lier (*un liquide, un ciment*); joindre, unir, lier (*des personnes*); **k. two, purl two,** deux à l'endroit, deux à l'envers; **to k. one's brows,** froncer le(s) sourcil(s); **knit (together) by close friendship,** lié d'une étroite amitié; **to k. up,** assembler (*un vêtement*) (en le tricotant); rassembler les fils de (*un argument*). **2** *vi* tricoter, faire du tricot; (*as opposed to purl*) tricoter à l'endroit; (*of bones*) se souder, se rejoindre; (*of liquid, cement*) se lier, prendre.

knitted ['nɪtəd] *adj* **(a)** tricoté, de *ou* en tricot; (*dentelle*) au tricot; **k. fabric,** tricot *m*; **k. goods,** tricots *pl*, articles *mpl* en tricot; **(b) k. eyebrows,** sourcils froncés.

knitter ['nɪtər] *n* tricoteur, -euse.

knitting ['nɪtɪŋ] *n* **(a)** (*activity*) tricotage *m*; soudure *f* (*des os*); **k. needle,** aiguille *f* à tricoter; **k. machine,** machine *f* à tricoter, tricoteuse *f*; **k. pattern,** modèle *m* de tricot; **k. wool,** laine *f* à tricoter; **(b)** (*work*) tricot *m*; **I've brought my k.,** j'ai apporté mon tricot.

knob¹ [nɒb] *n* **(a)** pomme *f* (*de canne, de balustrade*); bouton *m*, poignée *f* (*de porte, de tiroir etc*); (*on surface, forehead etc*) bosse *f*, protubérance *f*; *MecE* **(knurled) k.,** bouton (moleté) (*d'appareil etc*); **control k.,** bouton *ou* molette *f* de réglage; *Electron Rad* **tuning k.,** bouton d'accord; *TV* bouton de réglage; *Br F* **with knobs on,** (*with all refinements etc*) surchoix; *Br F* **the same to you with knobs on!,** c'est celui qui le dit qui l'est!; **(b)** *Am* = **KNOLL**; **(c)** (*piece*) petit morceau (*de fromage etc*); noix *f*, noisette *f* (*de beurre*); **(d)** *Br Vulg* (*penis*) bite *f*.

knobbed [nɒbd] *adj* **(a)** (*surface*) plein de bosses; **(b)** (*stick*) à pommeau.

knobbly ['nɒblɪ] *adj* couvert de bosses; **k. knees,** genoux bosselés.

knock¹ [nɒk] *n* **(a)** (*blow*) coup *m*, heurt *m*, choc *m*; **to give s.o. a k. on the head,** porter à qn un coup à la tête; (*and render unconscious*) assommer qn; **to get a nasty k.,** prendre un vilain coup; *F* **to take the k.,** essuyer de grosses pertes; **to be brought up in the school of hard knocks,** être élevé à la dure; *F* **his pride took a bit of a k.,** sa fierté en a pris un coup; *F* **he's had a few knocks,** (*in business, life*) il en a vu de dures; **k. for k. insurance,** assurance entraînant le remboursement séparé des clients par leurs compagnies respectives; **(b) k. at the door,** coup *m* à la porte; **to hear a k.,** entendre frapper; **to give a loud k.,** frapper très fort; **k., k.!,** toc, toc!, pan, pan!; **(c)** *MecE etc* cognement *m*, cliquetis *m*; détonation *f* (*du carburant dans le moteur*).

knock² **1** *vt* **(a)** frapper, heurter, cogner; **to k. s.o. on the head,** frapper qn sur la tête; (*and render unconscious*) assommer qn; **to k. one's head against sth,** se cogner la tête contre qch; **to k. a nail into a wall,** enfoncer un clou dans un mur; *F* **our plans have been knocked on the head,** nos projets sont tombés à l'eau; *Br F* **to k. s.o. into the middle of next week,** faire voir des étoiles en plein midi à qn; **it's like knocking your head against a brick wall,** c'est peine perdue; **to k. a hole in** *or* **through sth,** faire un trou dans qch; **to k. holes in an argument,** démolir un argument; *F* **that'll k. a bit of sense into her!,** ça lui apprendra!; *Fig* **to k. s.o. sideways,** renverser *ou* abasourdir *ou* stupéfier qn;

(b) *F* (*criticize*) débiner (*qn, qch*).

2 *vi* **(a)** frapper (**at,** à); **to k. at the door,** frapper à la porte; **to k. against sth,** se donner un coup *ou* se heurter *ou* se cogner contre qch; **his knees were knocking,** ses genous s'entrechoquaient;

(b) (*of engine*) cogner, cliqueter; (*of bearings*) tambouriner.

▶**knock about, knock around** **1** *vtsep* **(a)** (*mistreat*) bousculer, maltraiter, malmener (*qn*); **the furniture has been badly knocked about,** les meubles ont été fort maltraités; **they were knocking each other about,** ils se cognaient *ou* se battaient; **(b)** *F* (*discuss*) débattre (*idée, suggestion*). **2** *vi F* (*hang around*) traîner; **to k. about with s.o.,** fréquenter qn. **3** *vipo F* **to k. about the world/countryside,** rouler sa bosse.

▶**knock back** *vtsep F* **(a)** (*drink*) **to k. back a drink,** s'enfiler *ou* s'envoyer un verre; **(b)** (*cost*) coûter; **it knocked me back £200,** ça m'a coûté 200 livres.

▶**knock down** *vtsep* **(a)** (*overturn*) renverser (*qch, qn*); étendre (*qn*) par terre (*d'un coup de poing*); abattre (*un mur etc*); **he was knocked down by a car,** il a été renversé par une voiture; **(b)** (*at auction*) adjuger, vendre (*un article*); **to k. sth down to s.o.,** adjuger qch à qn; **(c)** *F* (*reduce*) baisser; (*reduce price of*) solder; **it's been knocked down to £50,** ça a été soldé à 50 livres.

▶**knock off** **1** *vtsep* **(a)** (*cause to fall off*) faire tomber (*qch*); **to k. a book off the table,** faire tomber un livre de la table; **to k. s.o.'s head** *or* **block off,** flanquer une taloche à qn; *Fig* **I managed to get something knocked off the price,** j'ai réussi à faire rabattre quelque chose du prix; **(b)** *Sl* (*steal*) voler, faucher (*qch*); **to k. off a bank,** se faire une banque; **(c)** *Sl* (*kill*) assassiner, zigouiller (*qn*); **(d)** *F* **k. it off!,** arrêtez!, ça suffit!; **(e)** *F* (*produce quickly*) (*letter, report, song etc*) expédier; **(f)** *Sl* (*have sexual intercourse with*) s'envoyer, se faire. **2** *vi Ind etc* s'arrêter de travailler; (*at end of day*) cesser le travail, débrayer; **we k. off at six,** nous finissons à six heures.

▶**knock out** *vtsep* **(a)** (*remove*) chasser, repousser (*un rivet*); **to k. s.o.'s brains/teeth out,** faire sauter la cervelle/les dents à qn; **(b)** (*make unconscious*) assommer (*qn*) raide; *Boxing* mettre (*son adversaire*) knock-out; **(c)** *Sp* (*in tournament etc*) **to be knocked out,** être éliminé; **(d)** *Mil* (*tank etc*) détruire.

▶**knock over** *vtsep* (*cause to fall*) faire tomber; renverser (*qch, qn*).

▶**knock together** *vtsep* (*assemble hastily*) assembler à la hâte (*un abri, un radeau etc*); former à la hâte (*une équipe*).

▶**knock up** **1** *vtsep* **(a)** (*make hastily*) construire (*un hangar etc*) à la hâte; (*prepare hastily*) improviser (*un repas*); **(b)** *F* (*exhaust*) éreinter, épuiser (*qn*); **(c)** *Br* (*wake*) réveiller, faire lever (*qn*); **(d)** *Cr* **to k. up a century,** faire cent points; **(e)** *Sl* (*make pregnant*) mettre (*une femme*) enceinte. **2** *vi Tennis* faire des balles (avant la partie).

knockabout ['nɒkəbaʊt] **(a)** *adj* (*jeu etc*) violent, bruyant; **k. comedian,** bateleur *m*, bouffon *m*; **k. comedy,** (grosse) farce *f*; **(b) k. clothes,** vêtements usagés (*qu'on met pour faire du bricolage etc*); (*leisurewear*) tenue *f* de loisir *ou* de sport. **2** *n* petit voilier.

knockdown ['nɒkdaʊn] *adj* **(a) k. blow,** coup *m* d'assommoir; **(b)** *Br F* **k. price,** (*at auction*) prix *m* minimum; (*very low*) prix très bas; **(c)** (*machine, furniture etc*) démontable.

knocker ['nɒkər] *n* **(a) (door) k.,** marteau *m* (de porte), heurtoir *m*; **(b)** *Sl* **knockers,** (*breasts*) nichons *mpl*; **(c)** *F* (*critic*) détracteur *m*.

knocking ['nɒkɪŋ] *n* **(a)** coups *mpl* (*à la porte etc*); **(b)** (*of engine*) cognement *m*; **(c)** *Com* **k. copy,** publicité comparative.

knocking-shop ['nɒkɪŋʃɒp] *n Br Sl* bordel *m*.

knock-kneed ['nɒk'niːd] *adj* (*person, horse*) cagneux.

knock-on ['nɒkɒn] *adj* **k.-on effect,** répercussions *fpl*.

knockout ['nɒkaʊt] **1** *adj* **(a)** (*coup*) d'assommoir; **k.**

drops, soporifique *m* (*esp* ajouté à une boisson); **(b)** *Sp* (*concours*) avec (épreuves) éliminatoires; **(c)** *Fig F* (*stunning*) magnifique, mirobolant. **2** *n* **(a)** (*blow*) coup *m* de grâce; *Boxing* knock-out *m*, *pl* knock-outs; **(b)** *F* (*impressive person or thing*) merveille *f*; **he's/she's a k.,** ce qu'il/elle est beau/belle; **(c)** (*at auction*) entente *f* (*entre concurrents pour baisser les prix*); **(d)** *Sp* élimination progressive (*des concurrents, des équipes*).

knock-up [ˈnɒkʌp] *n Tennis* **to have a k.-up,** faire quelques balles (*avant la partie, pour se faire la main*).

knoll [nəʊl] *n* mamelon *m*, tertre *m*, monticule *m*, butte *f*.

knot[1] [nɒt] *n* **(a)** nœud *m*; **to tie/untie a k.,** faire/défaire un nœud; **to tie a k. in one's handkerchief,** faire un nœud à son mouchoir; **reef k.,** nœud plat; **slip k.,** nœud coulant; **sailor's k.,** nœud régate (marine); **k. of hair,** chignon *m*; **k. of ribbons,** nœud de rubans; **(b)** *Nau* (*on log line*) nœud *m ou* division *f* de la ligne de loch; **to make 10 knots,** (*of ship*) filer 10 nœuds; *F* **at a rate of knots,** à toute vitesse; **(c)** nœud *m* (*d'une question, d'un problème*); **(d) the marriage k.,** le lien conjugal *ou* du mariage; *F* **to tie the k.,** se marier; **(e)** nœud *m* (*d'une tige, d'un ligament etc*); nodus *m* (*d'un ligament etc*); nodosité *f* (*arthritique etc*); nœud (*du bois*); **(f)** (*group*) groupe *m*, noyau *m* (*de personnes*); groupe (*d'objets*); bouquet *m* (*d'arbres*).

knot[2] *v* **(-tt-) 1** *vt* faire un nœud *ou* des nœuds à (*une ficelle*); (*of gout etc*) nouer (*les membres*); **to k. together two ropes,** attacher deux cordages ensemble; *Br F* **get knotted!,** va te faire voir! **2** *vi* (*of string*) se nouer, faire des nœuds; (*of joints*) se nouer.

knotting [ˈnɒtɪŋ] *n* nouement *m* (*de cordes*).

knotty [ˈnɒtɪ] *adj* **(a)** (*rope etc*) plein de nœuds; **(b)** (*problem etc*) épineux, embrouillé; (*question*) difficile, épineux; **(c)** (*wood etc*) noueux, raboteux; (*hands*) noueux.

know[1] [nəʊ] *n F* **to be in the k.,** être au courant (de l'affaire); *Sp etc* avoir des tuyaux; **those in the k.,** les initiés *mpl*.

know[2] *v* (*pt* **knew** [njuː]; *pp* **known** [nəʊn]) **1** *vt* **(a)** (*be acquainted with*) connaître (*qn, un lieu*); savoir ce que c'est que (*la pauvreté, le bonheur etc*); **to get** *or* **come to k. s.o.,** faire la connaissance de qn; **when I first knew her,** quand j'ai fait sa connaissance; **he is not a man to k.,** ce n'est pas un homme à fréquenter; **to have known happiness/poverty/***etc*, avoir connu le bonheur/la pauvreté/*etc*; **I've never known anything like it,** je n'ai jamais rien vu de semblable;

(b) (*to have cognizance of*) savoir (*qch*); **I k. that,** ça je le sais; **to k. more than one says,** en savoir plus long qu'on n'en dit; **well, what do you k.!,** sans blague!; **she knows all the answers,** elle a réponse à tout; *F* **to k. a thing or two, to k. one's way about** *or* **around,** être malin *ou* roublard; **he knows his own mind,** il sait ce qu'il veut; **I would have you k. that ...,** sachez que ...; **everyone knows that ...,** personne n'ignore que ...; **I knew (that) she had talent,** je lui connaissais du talent; **how do you k. (that) he will come?,** qui vous dit qu'il viendra?; **do you k. when .../why ...?,** savez-vous quand .../pourquoi ...?; **heaven (only) knows** *or* **God knows when I shall get back,** Dieu sait quand je serai de retour; **she didn't quite k. what to say,** elle ne savait trop que dire; **I don't k. that I do,** (*agree etc*) je n'en suis pas sûr; **I k. him to be a liar,** je sais que c'est un menteur; **she is known to be a keen photographer,** on sait qu'elle aime beaucoup la photographie; **it has been known (to happen),** c'est une chose qu'on a vue se produire, ça c'est vu; **I have never known him tell a lie,** à ce que je sache, il n'a jamais menti; **she doesn't k. what fear is,** elle ne sait pas ce que c'est que d'avoir peur; **to k. what it's like to be happy/poor/***etc*, savoir ce que c'est que d'être heureux/pauvre/*etc*; **nobody knows anything about it,** personne n'en sait rien; **to k. all about cars,** être très calé sur les voitures; **we knew nothing of it,** nous l'ignorions;

(c) (*recognize*) reconnaître; (*distinguish*) distinguer (**from,** de, d'avec); **don't you k. me?,** est-ce que vous ne me reconnaissez pas?; **I'd k. him anywhere,** je le reconnaîtrais n'importe où; **I knew her by her walk,** je l'ai reconnue à son allure *ou* à sa démarche; **I knew him for a German,** j'ai deviné qu'il était allemand; **to k. good from evil,** distinguer le bien du mal; **I didn't k. the one from the other,** je ne pouvais pas les distinguer l'un de l'autre;

(d) savoir, connaître (*un sujet, une langue*); **she knows German,** elle sait parler allemand; **do you k. any physics?,** est-ce que tu connais quelque chose en physique?; **to k. sth by heart,** savoir qch par cœur; **to k. what one is talking about,** savoir de quoi on parle; **to k. how to read/swim/do sth,** savoir lire/nager/faire qch; **to k. how to behave,** savoir se conduire;

(e) (*to be aware of*) **to get to k. sth,** apprendre qch; **how did you get to k. that?,** comment avez-vous appris cela?; **please let us k. whether ...,** veuillez nous faire savoir si ...; **I don't want it known,** je ne veux pas que cela se sache;

(f) *F* **don't I k. it!,** à qui le dites-vous!; **not if I k. Jean-Luc!,** tel que je connais Jean-Luc, sûrement pas; **she is pretty and doesn't she k. it!,** elle est jolie et elle le sait bien!;

(g) to k. better than to ..., bien se garder de ...; **I k. better (than that),** je m'y connais mieux que ça; (*I won't be caught out*) on ne m'y prendra pas, *F* pas si bête!; **he is old enough to k. better,** à son âge il devrait être plus raisonnable; **you k. best,** vous en êtes le meilleur juge; **you k. best what should be done,** vous savez mieux que personne ce qu'il faut faire.

2 *vi* savoir; **had I known,** si j'avais su; **as far as I k., for all I k.,** autant que je sache; *F* **I wouldn't k.,** je ne saurais dire; *F* **you k.,** vous voyez; **as everyone knows,** comme tout le monde le sait; **who knows?,** qui sait?; **to k. about sth,** être informé de qch, être au courant de qch; **I don't k. about that,** je n'en suis pas sûr; **to k. of s.o.,** connaître qn de réputation; avoir entendu parler de qn; **to get to k. of sth,** apprendre qch; *F* **not that I k. of, not as far as I k.,** pas que je sache.

know-all [ˈnəʊɔːl] *n F* je-sais-tout *mf*.

know-how [ˈnəʊhaʊ] *n F* savoir-faire *m*; (*technical*) connaissances *fpl* techniques.

knowing [ˈnəʊɪŋ] **1** *adj* (*intelligent, educated*) intelligent, instruit; (*cunning*) fin, malin, rusé; (*smile*) entendu. **2** *n* **there's no k.,** c'est impossible à dire.

knowingly [ˈnəʊɪŋlɪ] *adv* (*with knowledge of the facts*) sciemment, en connaissance de cause; (*cunningly*) finement, d'un air rusé; (*smile*) d'un air entendu; *Com* **never k. undersold,** si vous trouvez moins cher, avertissez-nous.

know-it-all [ˈnəʊɪtɔːl] *n esp Am F* je-sais-tout *mf*.

knowledge [ˈnɒlɪdʒ] *n* **(a)** connaissance *f* (*d'un fait, d'une personne*); **it has come to my k. that ...,** il est venu *ou* parvenu à ma connaissance que ..., j'ai appris que ...; **I had no k. of it,** je ne le savais pas, je l'ignorais; **lack of k.,** ignorance *f* (**of,** de); **it is (a matter of) common k. that ...,** c'est un fait notoire que ...; **to (the best of) my k.,** à ma connaissance, (autant) que je sache; **not to my k.,** pas que je sache; **without my k.,** à mon insu; **to speak with full k. (of the facts),** parler en connaissance de cause *ou* en pleine connaissance des faits;

(b) (*learning*) savoir *m*, connaissance(s) *f(pl)*; **to have a k. of several languages,** connaître plusieurs langues; **he has a little k.** *or* **a working k. of Latin,** il a quelques connaissances en latin; **her k. is immense,** ses connaissances sont très étendues; **k. of the world,** la connaissance du monde; **k. is power,** savoir c'est pouvoir; *Bible* **the tree of k. of good and evil,** l'arbre *m* de la science du bien et du mal; **to show off one's k.,** étaler sa science; **k. engineer,** (*in artificial intelligence*) cogniticien, -ienne;

(c) carnal k., connaissance charnelle.

knowledgeable [ˈnɒlɪdʒəb(ə)l] *adj* bien informé.

known [nəʊn] *adj* connu; (*voleur, ennemi*) avéré; *Math* (*quantity*) connu; **a k. fact,** un fait bien connu; *Petr* **k. reserves,** réserves prouvées.

knuckle [ˈnʌk(ə)l] *n* **(a)** (*joint*) articulation *f ou* jointure *f* du doigt; **to rap s.o. over the knuckles,** donner sur les doigts à qn; *Fig* taper sur les doigts à qn; **to crack one's knuckles,** faire craquer ses jointures; *F* **that was a bit near the k.,** c'était assez limite; **(b)** *Culin* **k. of a leg of lamb,** (*meat*) souris *f* (d'un gigot); (*bone*) manche *m* (d'un gigot); **k. of veal/pork,** jarret *m* de veau/porc; **k. of ham,** jambonneau *m*; **(c)** *MecE etc* **k. (joint),** articulation *f* à genouillère, joint *m* en charnière; charnière universelle.

►**knuckle down** *vi* **(a)** *F* (*begin working hard*) s'y mettre sérieusement; **to k. down to sth,** se mettre à qch; **(b)** (*at marbles*) appuyer la main à terre (*en lançant la bille*).

►**knuckle under** *vi F* (*give in*) mettre les pouces.

knucklebones [ˈnʌk(ə)lbəʊnz] *npl* (*game*) osselets *mpl*.

knuckle-duster [ˈnʌk(ə)ldʌstər] *n* coup-de-poing *m* (américain), *pl* coups-de-poing.

knurl[1] [nɜːl] *n* **(a)** nœud *m* (*du bois*); **(b)** (*in metalworking*) moletage *m*; (*tool*) molette *f*, godronnoir *m*.

knurl[2] *vt* (*in metalworking*) molet(t)er, godronner.

KO[1], *pl* **KO's** [ˈkeɪˈəʊ, ˈkeɪˈəʊz] *n Boxing etc Sl* K.-O. *m*.

KO[2] *vt* (*3rd person pr* **KO's** [ˈkeɪˈəʊz]; *prp* **KO'ing**; *pp & pt* **KO'd**) *Boxing etc Sl* mettre K.-O..

koala [kəʊˈɑːlə] *n* (*marsupial*) **k. (bear),** koala *m*.

kohlrabi [kəʊl'ræbaɪ, -'rɑːbɪ] *n* (*plant*) chou-rave *m*, *pl* choux-raves, turnep(s) *m*.

kola ['kəʊlə] *n* (*plant*) cola *m*, kola *m*; **k. (tree),** kolatier *m*; **k. nut,** noix *f* de cola *ou* de kola.

kolkhoz ['kɒlkɒz] *n* (*in USSR*) kolkhoze *m*, ferme collective.

kook [kʊk] *n Am F* personne *f* bizarre, drôle *m* d'individu.

kookaburra ['kʊkəbʌrə] *n* (*bird*) dacélo *m*.

Koran (the) [ðəkɔː'rɑːn] *n Rel* le Koran, le Coran.

Koranic [kɔː'rænɪk] *adj* coranique.

Korea [kə'rɪə] *n* Corée *f*; **North/South K.**, Corée du Nord/du Sud.

Korean [kə'rɪən] **1** *adj* coréen. **2** *n* **(a)** Coréen, -enne; **(b)** *Ling* coréen *m*.

korma ['kɔːmə] *n Culin* **chicken/prawn/***etc* **k.**, = poulet/crevettes/*etc* à la sauce indienne au yaourt ou à la crème.

kosher ['kəʊʃər] *adj Jewish Rel* cascher *inv*, kascher *inv*; *F* (*legitimate*) légitime, comme il faut, impec.

kowtow[1] [kaʊ'taʊ] *n* prosternation *f*, prosternement *m* (*à la chinoise*).

kowtow[2] *vi* **(a)** *F* (*act obsequiously*) **to k. to s.o.,** faire des courbettes devant qn; **(b)** (*bow*) se prosterner (**to**, devant).

KP ['keɪ'piː] *n US Mil Sl* (*abbr* **kitchen police**) **to do KP (duty),** être de corvée de patates.

kph [keɪpiː'eɪtʃ] (*abbr* **kilometres per hour**) km/h.

kraft [krɑːft] *n* (*paper*) papier *m* d'emballage fort, papier Kraft.

Krakow ['krɑːkɒf] *n* Cracovie *f*.

Kraut [kraʊt] *n Offensive Sl* boche *mf*.

Kremlin (the) [ðə'kremlɪn] *n* le Kremlin; *F* **K. watcher,** spécialiste *mf* du Kremlin, kremlinologiste *mf*.

Kremlinologist [kremlɪ'nɒlədʒɪst] *n* kremlinologiste *mf*.

krill [krɪl] *n* (*crustacean*) krill *m*.

kudos ['kjuːdɒs] *n* (*prestige*) prestige *m*; (*fame*) célébrité *f*; **to get the k. for sth,** recevoir toute la gloire pour qch; **to receive k.,** être acclamé.

Ku Klux Klan ['kuː'klʌks'klæn] *n US* Ku Klux Klan *m*.

kumquat ['kʊmkwɒt] *n* (*fruit*) kumquat *m*.

kung fu ['kʌŋ'fuː] *n* kung-fu *m*; **a k.-fu expert,** un expert en kung-fu.

Kurd [kɜːd] **1** *adj* k(o)urde. **2** *n* K(o)urde *mf*.

Kurdish ['kɜːdɪʃ] **1** *adj* k(o)urde. **2** *n Ling* k(o)urde *m*.

Kurdistan [kɜːdɪ'stɑːn] *n* K(o)urdistan *m*.

Kuwait [kʊ'weɪt, kjuː-] *n* Koweït *m*.

Kuwaiti [kʊ'weɪtɪ, kjuː-] **1** *adj* koweïtien. **2** *n* Koweïtien, -ienne.

kV (*abbr* **kilovolt**) kV.

kW (*abbr* **kilowatt**) kW.

kWh (*abbr* **kilowatt-hour**) kWh.

Ky *abbr* **Kentucky**.

Kyrie ['kɪrɪeɪ] *n Rel* **K. (eleison** [ɪ'leɪsɒn]**)**, kyrie *m*.

L

L, l [el] *n* **(a)** (la lettre) L, l *mf*; *Ling* **liquid l, palatal(ized) l,** l mouillée; **(b) L iron,** fer *m* cornière, fer en équerre; *Br Aut* **L.-plate,** = plaque obligatoire indiquant que le conducteur est en train d'apprendre à conduire; **L-shaped room,** pièce *f* en forme de L.

l [el] **(a)** (*abbr* **litre**) litre, l.; **(b)** (*abbr* **length**) longueur, long.; **(c)** (*abbr* **line**) ligne; **(d)** (*abbr* **left**) gauche, g..

la [lɑː] *n Mus* la *m*; **sing it to 'la',** chante-le en la.

La *abbr* **Louisiana.**

L.A. [el'eɪ] *n US abbr* **Los Angeles.**

laager ['lɑːgər] *n* (*in South Africa*) & *Fig* camp *m*.

lab [læb] *n F* (= **laboratory**) labo *m*.

Lab *Br Pol* (*abbr* **Labour**) *see* **LABOUR¹ (c)**.

label¹ ['leɪb(ə)l] *n* **(a)** étiquette *f*; **always read the l. on the bottle,** lisez toujours l'étiquette sur la bouteille; **sticky l.,** étiquette gommée; **luggage l.,** étiquette à bagages; **(b)** *Com* label *m*, étiquette *f*; **to record on the Jones l.,** (*of singer, musician etc*) enregistrer sous la marque Jones; **designer l.,** (*on clothes*) marque *f*, griffe *f*; **(c)** *Comptr* label *m* (*de bande, de fichier*); **(d)** qualification *f* (*de qn*); **the l. 'reactionary' stayed with him all his life,** l'étiquette de réactionnaire lui est restée toute sa vie; **(e)** *Chem* marque *f*.

label² *vt* (**-ll-**, *US* **-l-**) **(a)** étiqueter; coller une étiquette sur (*un paquet, une bouteille etc*); **a bottle labelled poison,** une bouteille marquée poison; **all luggage must be clearly labelled,** tous les bagages doivent être clairement étiquetés; **(b)** *Com* attribuer un label (*de garantie, de qualité etc*) à (*un produit*); **(c) to l. s.o. a liar,** qualifier qn de menteur; **(d)** *Chem* marquer.

labellum, *pl* **-bella** [lə'beləm, -ə] *n Bot* labelle *m*.

labial ['leɪbɪəl] **1** *adj* labial, -aux; *Mus* **l. pipe,** tuyau *m* à bouche (*d'un orgue*); *Ling* **l. consonant,** consonne labiale. **2** *n Ling* labiale *f*.

labialize ['leɪbɪəlaɪz] *vt Ling* labialiser.

labiate ['leɪbɪeɪt] *Bot* **1** *adj* labié. **2** *n* labiée *f*.

labiodental [leɪbɪəʊ'dent(ə)l] *adj Ling* labiodental.

labium, *pl* **-a** ['leɪbɪəm, ə] *n* **(a)** *Anat* **labia,** labia *mpl*, lèvres *fpl* (*de la vulve*); **(b)** *Ent* labium *m*; **(c)** *Bot* lèvre *f* (*de corolle labiée*).

labor, labored *etc US* = **LABOUR, LABOURED** *etc*.

laboratory [lə'bɒrətrɪ, *esp Am* 'læbrətɔːrɪ] *n* laboratoire *m*; **research l.,** laboratoire de recherches; **l. tested,** essayé *ou* éprouvé en laboratoire; **dental l.,** laboratoire de prothèse dentaire; **l. assistant,** laborantin, -ine; **l. equipment,** matériel *m* de laboratoire; **l. experiment,** expérience *f* en laboratoire.

laborious [lə'bɔːrɪəs] *adj* **(a)** pénible, fatigant; (*task*) laborieux; **(b)** (*style*) laborieux.

laboriously [lə'bɔːrɪəslɪ] *adv* péniblement.

laboriousness [lə'bɔːrɪəsnɪs] *n* **(a)** pénibilité *f* (*d'un travail, d'une ascension etc*); **(b)** (*of literary style*) caractère laborieux.

labour¹, *US* **labor** ['leɪbər] *n* **(a)** (*work*) travail *m*, labeur *m*, peine *f*; **manual l.,** travail manuel; **division of l.,** division *f* du travail; **l. camp,** camp *m* de travaux forcés;

(b) (*workers*) main-d'œuvre *f*, travailleurs *mpl*; **l. force,** effectifs *mpl*; **male/female l.,** main-d'œuvre masculine/féminine; **skilled/semiskilled/unskilled l.,** main-d'œuvre qualifiée/spécialisée/non spécialisée; **cost of l.,** prix *m* de la main-d'œuvre; **l. shortage,** pénurie *f ou* crise *f* de main-d'œuvre; **l. market,** marché *m* du travail; *US* **l. union,** syndicat *m* (ouvrier); **l. laws,** législation *f* du travail; **capital and l.,** le capital et la main-d'œuvre; **l. dispute,** conflit *m* du travail; **l. unrest,** agitation ouvrière; *Br Admin Arch* **l. exchange,** bureau *m* de placement; **Minister of L.,** ministre *m* du travail; **l. relations,** relations *fpl* dans l'entreprise; **l. intensive,** (*industry*) de main-d'œuvre; **l. supply,** main-d'œuvre disponible; **International L. Organization,** Organisation Internationale du Travail; *Am* **L. Day,** fête *f* du travail;

(c) *Br Pol* **L.,** les Travaillistes *m*; **the L. party,** le parti travailliste; **L. member (of Parliament),** député *m* travailliste; **L. leader,** dirigeant, -ante (du parti) travailliste;

(d) (*task*) **the twelve labours of Hercules,** les douze travaux d'Hercule; **l. of love,** travail *m* fait avec plaisir; **it was a l. of love,** (*for me*) je l'ai fait avec plaisir;

(e) *Obst* travail *m*, couches *fpl*; **premature l.,** accouchement *m* avant terme; **woman in l.,** femme en couches; **l. pains,** douleurs *fpl* de l'enfantement; **she went into l. at 3,** le travail a commencé à 3 heures; **to induce l.,** déclencher l'accouchement; **it was a difficult l.,** ça a été un accouchement difficile; **l. ward,** (*in hospital*) salle *f* d'accouchement.

labour², *US* **labor 1** *vi* **(a)** (*of person*) travailler, peiner; **to l. for sth,** se donner de la peine pour obtenir qch; **he laboured all his life for peace,** il a travaillé toute sa vie pour la paix; **to l. at** *or* **over sth,** travailler à qch, peiner sur qch; **to l. up a hill,** gravir péniblement une côte; **to l. under great difficulties,** être aux prises avec de grandes difficultés; **to l. under a sense of injustice,** nourrir un sentiment d'injustice; **to l. under a misapprehension,** être dans l'erreur, être (la) victime d'une erreur; **(b)** (*of engine*) fatiguer, peiner; (*of ship*) bourlinguer, fatiguer; **to l. uphill,** (*of car*) peiner en côte. **2** *vt* **I won't l. the point,** je ne m'étendrai pas là-dessus.

laboured, *US* **labored** ['leɪbəd] *adj* **(a)** (*respiration*) pénible; **(b)** (*style etc*) trop travaillé, trop élaboré; (*joke*) laborieux.

labourer, *US* **laborer** ['leɪbərər] *n* **(a)** travailleur *m*; *Prov* **the l. is worthy of his hire,** toute peine *ou* tout travail mérite salaire; **(b)** *Ind* manœuvre *m*; **unskilled l.,** ouvrier non spécialisé; **agricultural l.,** ouvrier agricole.

labouring, *US* **laboring** ['leɪbərɪŋ] *adj* **the l. class,** la classe ouvrière; **a l. job,** un travail manuel.

Labourite, *US* **Laborite** ['leɪbəraɪt] *n Br Pol* Travailliste *mf*.

labour-saving, *US* **labor-** ['leɪbəseɪvɪŋ] *adj* (*appareil*) allégeant le travail.

Labrador ['læbrədɔːr] *n* **(a)** *Geog* le Labrador; **(b)** (*dog*) labrador *m*.

laburnum [lə'bɜːnəm] *n* (*tree*) cytise *m* (à grappes).

labyrinth ['læbərɪnθ] *n* **(a)** *Archit etc* labyrinthe *m*, dédale *m;* **(b)** *Anat* labyrinthe *m* (*de l'oreille*).

labyrinthine [læbe'rɪnθaɪn] *adj Archit* en labyrinthe; *Fig* (*politics, procedures, structure*) extrêmement compliqué.

lac [læk] *n* gomme *f* laque, laque *f*.

lace¹ [leɪs] *n* **(a)** dentelle *f*, point *m*; **bobbin** *or* **pillow l.,** dentelle aux fuseaux *ou* au coussin; **l. curtain,** rideau *m* en dentelle; **(b)** lacet *m* (*de soulier*); **(c)** (*braid*) **gold/silver l.,** galon *m* d'or/d'argent.

lace² 1 *vt* **(a)** lacer (*des chaussures*); **to l. sth with sth,** entrelacer qch de *ou* avec qch; **(b)** *F* ajouter de l'alcool (*dans une boisson*); **milk laced with rum,** lait au rhum; **(c)** garnir (*un ouvrage*) de dentelles. **2** *vi* (*of boots etc*) se lacer.

►lace into *vipo* démolir (*qn, qch*).

►lace up *vtsep* lacer (*des chaussures*).

lacemaker ['leɪsmeɪkər] *n* fabricant, -ante de dentelles; (*woman only*) dentellière *f*.

lacemaking ['leɪsmeɪkɪŋ] *n* dentellerie *f*.

lacerate ['læsəreɪt] *vt* lacérer, déchirer.

lacerated ['læsəreɪtəd] *adj* (*hand, skin*) lacéré; **l. feelings,** sentiments profondément blessés.

laceration [læsə'reɪʃən] *n* **(a)** lacération *f*, déchirement *m*; **(b)** *Med etc* déchirure *f*.

lace-up ['leɪsʌp] **1** *n* chaussure *f* à lacets. **2** *adj* (*shoe*) à lacets.

lacewing ['leɪswɪŋ] *n Ent* **l. (fly)** hémérobe *m*.

lacework ['leɪswɜːk] *n* (*objects, art*) dentelles *fpl*; (*art*) dentellerie *f*.

lachrymal ['lækrɪm(ə)l] *adj Anat* (*canal, sac*) lacrymal, -aux; **l. gland,** glande lacrymale; **l. duct,** conduit lacrymal.

lachrymatory ['lækrɪmət(ə)rɪ] *adj* lacrymogène.
lachrymose ['lækrɪməʊs] *adj* larmoyant.
lacing ['leɪsɪŋ] *n* **(a)** *Br F* **to give s.o. a l.**, (*verbally*) passer un savon à qn; (*physically*) administrer une volée à qn; **(b)** (*of drink*) ajout *m* d'alcool (*à une boisson*); **milk with a l. of rum,** lait au rhum; **(c)** (*on uniform*) galon *m*.
lack¹ [læk] *n* manque *m* (**of,** de); **l. of judgment/time,** manque de jugement/temps; **l. of money,** pénurie *f* d'argent; **she was tired from l. of sleep,** elle était fatiguée de n'avoir pas assez dormi; **for l. of ...,** faute de ... .
lack² **1** *vt* manquer de (*expérience, compétence*); être dénué de (*bon sens, d'intelligence, d'humour*); **we l. nothing,** nous ne manquons de rien, il ne nous manque rien. **2** *vi* (*of time*) manquer; **he's lacking in purpose,** il lui manque un but; **they l. for nothing,** ils ne manquent de rien; *F* **to be lacking,** (*mentally*) être (un peu) simplet.
lackadaisical [lækə'deɪzɪk(ə)l] *adj* (*person, manner etc*) apathique.
lackey ['lækɪ] *n* laquais *m*.
lacklustre, *US* **lackluster** ['læklʌstər] *adj* (*eyes, gaze*) terne, sans brillant.
laconic [lə'kɒnɪk] *adj* laconique; (*answer etc*) bref, *f* brève.
laconically [lə'kɒnɪklɪ] *adv* laconiquement.
lacquer¹ ['lækər] *n* **(a)** (*for wood*) laque *f*; (*coloured*) peinture lacquée; **a Chinese red l. screen,** un écran chinois recouvert de laque rouge; **(b)** (*for hair*) laque *f*.
lacquer² *vt* laquer.
lacquerwork ['lækəwɜːk] *n* laque(s) *m*(*pl*).
lacrimal ['lækrɪm(ə)l] *adj* = **LACHRYMAL**.
lacrosse [lə'krɒs] *n Sp* crosse *f*.
lacrymal ['lækrɪm(ə)l] *adj* = **LACHRYMAL**.
lactate [læk'teɪt] *vi* produire du lait.
lactation [læk'teɪʃən] *n Physiol* lactation *f*.
lacteal ['læktɪəl] *adj* lactaire.
lactic ['læktɪk] *adj Ch* lactique; **l. acid,** acide *m* lactique.
lactose ['læktəʊz] *n Ch* lactose *f*, sucre *m* de lait.
lacuna, *pl* **-ae, -as** [læ'kjuːnə, -iː, -əz] *n* lacune *f*; hiatus *m* (*dans un ouvrage*).
lacustrine [lə'kʌstraɪn] *adj* (*plante etc*) lacustre.
lacy ['leɪsɪ] *adj* (*made of lace*) de dentelle; (*resembling lace*) fin comme de la dentelle.
lad [læd] *n* **(a)** (*young man*) jeune homme *m*; (*boy*) garçon *m*; **come on, lads!,** allons, les gars!; **he's only a l.,** ce n'est qu'un gosse; **that's the doctor's l.,** c'est le fils du docteur; **he's a bit of a l.** *or* **quite a l.,** c'est un gaillard; **one of the lads,** un des gars; **(b)** *Br Horseracing* **(stable) l.,** lad *m*.
ladder¹ ['lædər] *n* **(a)** échelle *f*; **it's unlucky to walk under a l.,** ça porte malheur de passer sous une échelle; **extending** *or* **telescopic l.,** échelle à coulisse; **folding l.,** échelle pliante; *Nau* **accommodation l.,** échelle de commandement de coupée; **gangway l.,** échelle de coupée *ou* de côté; **the social l.,** l'échelle sociale; **to climb a rung of the social l.,** gravir un échelon social; **he's got his foot on the l.,** il a le pied sur l'échelle; **to reach the top of the l.,** atteindre le sommet de l'échelle; **fish** *or* **salmon l.,** escalier *m* à poissons; **(b)** *esp Br* (*in stocking*) maille filée; **I've got a l.,** j'ai une maille qui file; **to mend a l.,** rem(m)ailler un bas.
ladder² **1** *vt* **I've laddered my stocking,** j'ai filé mon bas. **2** *vi* (*of stocking etc*) se démailler, filer.
ladder-proof ['lædəpruːf] *adj* (*stockings*) qui ne filent pas.
laddie ['lædɪ] *n Scot F* garçon *m*; (*term of endearment*) mon petit gars.
laden ['leɪd(ə)n] *adj* chargé; **I was l. with shopping,** j'avais les bras chargés de commissions; **fully l. ship,** navire en pleine charge; **(b) heavily l. tree,** arbre chargé de fruits.
la(h)-di-da(h), la-de-da ['lɑːdɪ'dɑː] *adj F* (*air, voice*) affecté.
ladies ['leɪdɪz] *n* toilettes *fpl* (des dames); **can you tell me where the l. is?,** pouvez-vous m'indiquer où sont les toilettes?
lading ['leɪdɪŋ] *n* **(a)** chargement *m* (*d'un navire*); **(b)** mise *f* à bord (*de marchandises*).
ladle¹ ['leɪd(ə)l] *n* **(a) soup l.,** louche *f*; **(b)** *Ind* puisoir *m*, casse *f*; **(c)** *Metal* **foundry l.,** poche *f* de fonderie.
ladle² *vt* **(a) to l. (out) the soup,** servir le potage (avec la louche); **to l. out advice,** prodiguer des conseils; **he ladled out money to all his grandchildren,** il a donné plein d'argent à tous ses petits-enfants; **(b)** *Metal* couler (*la fonte*).
ladleful ['leɪd(ə)lfʊl] *n* pleine louche (**of,** de).
lady, *pl* **-ies** ['leɪdɪ, -ɪz] *n* **(a)** dame *f*; **l. doctor,** femme *f* médecin, docteur *m*; **I insist on a l. doctor,** j'insiste pour que ce soit une femme; **l. of the bedchamber,** (*at court*) dame d'atours; **she's a real l.,** c'est une femme très comme il faut; **she's no l.,** ce n'est pas une femme très comme il faut; **a l. and a gentleman,** un monsieur et une dame; **a young l.,** une jeune fille; (*married*) une jeune dame; **an old l.,** une vieille dame; **how are you, young l.?,** (*to child*) comment allez-vous, ma petite demoiselle?; **listen to me young l.,** écoute-moi un peu ma petite demoiselle; **ladies and gentlemen!,** (*at meeting etc*) mesdames, mesdemoiselles, messieurs!; **come in, ladies!,** entrez donc, mesdames!; **he's a ladies' man,** c'est un homme à femmes; **ladies,** (*on public convenience*) dames; **the l. of the house,** la maîtresse de maison; **painted l.,** (*butterfly*) belle-dame *f*, *pl* belles-dames; **l.'s watch,** montre *f* de dame; *F* **ladies' fingers,** (*vegetable*) gombo(s) *m*(*pl*); **ladies' room,** toilettes *fpl* (des dames); **ladies' tailor,** tailleur *m* pour dames; **l.'s maid,** femme de chambre;
(b) *Rel* **Our L.,** Notre-Dame, la sainte Vierge; **L. chapel,** chapelle *f* de la Vierge; **L. Day,** la fête de l'Annonciation (le 25 mars);
(c) (*title*) **L. Browne,** (*no Fr equivalent*) lady Browne (femme de Sir David Browne); **the l. of the manor,** la châtelaine; *Pej* **l. bountiful,** = dame qui s'adonne aux bonnes œuvres;
(d) *Old-fashioned* femme *f*, épouse *f*; **how's your good l.?,** comment va votre femme?; **this is my l. wife,** voici mon épouse; **my young l.,** ma fiancée, ma future.
ladybird, *Am* **ladybug** ['leɪdɪbɜːd, -bʌg] *n* (*beetle*) coccinelle *f*, *F* bête *f* à bon Dieu.
ladyfinger ['leɪdɪfɪŋgər] *n Culin* langue *f* de chat.
lady-in-waiting ['leɪdɪɪn'weɪtɪŋ] *n* (*at court*) dame *f* d'honneur.
lady-killer ['leɪdɪkɪlər] *n F* bourreau *m* des cœurs, casse-cœur *m inv*, don Juan *m*.
ladylike ['leɪdɪlaɪk] *adj* (*air etc*) distingué; (*woman*) comme il faut, bien élevée; **climbing trees isn't very l.,** les demoiselles comme il faut ne grimpent pas aux arbres.
ladyship ['leɪdɪʃɪp] *n* **her l., your l.,** madame (la comtesse *etc*); *Iron* **her l. doesn't feel like it,** madame n'en a pas envie.
lady's-slipper [leɪdɪz'slɪpər] *n* (*orchid*) sabot *m* de Vénus.
lag¹ [læg] *n* (*delay*) *& El* retard *m*; **jet l.,** fatigue *f* due au décalage horaire; *Ind etc* **time l.,** décalage *m* (*entre deux opérations*); **ignition l.,** (*in engine*) retard à l'allumage.
lag² *vi* **(-gg-)** **(a) to l. (behind),** rester en arrière, se laisser distancer (par les autres); **wages are lagging behind the cost of living,** les salaires restent inférieurs au coût de la vie; **(b)** *El* (*of current*) être déphasé en arrière.
lag³ *n esp Br Sl* **an old l.,** un repris de justice, un récidiviste.
lag⁴ *n* latte *f* (*d'enveloppe de chaudière*).
lag⁵ *vt* envelopper, revêtir (*une chaudière*) d'un calorifuge, calorifuger, isoler (*une chaudière*).
lager ['lɑːgər] *n* bière blonde; *Br F* **l. lout,** voyou *m*; (*drunk*) voyou soûlé à la bière.
laggard ['lægəd] *n* (*in race*) traînard, -arde; (*in class etc*) retardataire *mf*.
lagging ['lægɪŋ] *n* **(a)** (*action*) garnissage *m*, calorifugeage *m* (*d'une chaudière etc*); **(b)** (*material*) revêtement *m* calorifuge (*d'une chaudière etc*).
lagoon [lə'guːn] *n Geog* **(a)** lagon *m* (*d'atoll*); **(b)** (*sand, shingle etc*) lagune *f*; **the city is built on a l.,** la ville est construite sur une lagune.
lah [lɑː] *n* = **LA**.
laid *see* **LAY²**.
laid-back [leɪd'bæk] *adj F* (*person, atmosphere*) relax.
lain *see* **LIE ⁴**.
lair [leər] *n* tanière *f*, repaire *m*, antre *m* (*de bête fauve*); **brigands' l.,** repaire de brigands.
laird [leəd] *n Scot* propriétaire *m* (foncier).
laisser-faire, laissez-faire [leseɪ'feər] *n* laisser-faire *m*; **l.-f. policy,** politique *f* de laisser-faire.
laity ['leɪɪtɪ] *n* **the l.,** les laïques *mpl*.
lake¹ [leɪk] *n* lac *m*; **salt l.,** lac salé; **ornamental l.,** bassin *m*, pièce d'eau décorative; **(the) L. (of) Geneva,** le lac Léman, le lac de Genève; **the Great Lakes,** les Grands Lacs (d'Amérique du Nord); **the L. District, the Lakes,** la région des lacs (au nord-ouest de l'Angleterre); **the L. poets,** les (poètes *mpl*) lakistes *mpl*; **the Common Market's wine l.,** = le surplus de vin du Marché Commun; *Sl* **go jump in the l.,** va te faire foutre; **l. dwelling,**

habitation *f* lacustre; **l. front** *or* **shore** *or* **side,** bord *m* du lac; **they live on the l. front** *or* **shore,** ils habitent au bord du lac; **a l.-side picnic,** un pique-nique au bord du lac.
lake² *n* (*pigment*) laque *f*; **crimson l.,** laque carminée.
lakefront ['leɪkfrʌnt] *n* bord *m* de lac.
Lakeland ['leɪklənd] *n* la région des lacs (au nord-ouest de l'Angleterre).
lam¹ [læm] *n Am Sl* (*flight*) fuite *f*; **to be on the l.,** être en cavale; **to take it on the l.,** partir en cavale.
lam² *vt & vi* (-mm-) *F* **to l. (into) s.o.,** rosser qn, étriller qn.
lama ['lɑːmə] *n Rel* lama *m*; **the Dalai** *or* **Grand L.,** le dalaï *ou* grand Lama.
lamasery ['lɑːməsərɪ] *n* lamaserie *f*.
lamb¹ [læm] *n* **(a)** agneau *m*; **ewe l.,** agnelle *f*; **ewe with l.,** brebis pleine; *Rel* **L. (of God),** Agneau (de Dieu); *F* **he went like a l.,** il s'est laissé faire; **she took my decision like a l.,** elle a accepté ma décision sans broncher; *F* **my l.,** mon petit; **poor l.,** pauvre petit(e); **like a l. to the slaughter,** comme un agneau que l'on emmène à l'abattoir; **l.'s lettuce,** mâche *f*; *F* **l.'s tails,** chatons *mpl* (*du noisetier*); **l.'s wool,** laine *f* d'agneau; **a pure l.'s wool sweater,** un pull en pure laine vierge; **(b)** *Culin* agneau *m*; **l. cutlet** *or* **chop,** côtelette *f* d'agneau; **(c)** (*fur*) **Persian l.,** astrakan *m*, caracul *m*.
lamb² *vi* (*of ewe*) agneler, mettre bas.
lambast [læm'bæst] , **lambaste** [læm'beɪst] *vt* fustiger (*qn*).
lambing ['læmɪŋ] *n* agnelage *m*.
lambskin ['læmskɪn] *n* **(a)** peau *f* d'agneau; **(b)** (*fur*) agnelin *m*.
lame¹ [leɪm] *adj* boiteux; (*through accident etc*) estropié; **l. leg,** jambe boiteuse; **l. horse,** cheval boiteux; **to be l. in one leg,** boiter d'une jambe; **to be l.,** boiter; **to be slightly l.,** boiter légèrement; **to go l.,** se mettre à boiter; *Fig* **l. excuse,** mauvaise *ou* faible excuse; **l. argument,** argument boiteux *ou* qui ne tient pas debout; **l. verses,** vers *mpl* boiteux *ou* qui boitent.
lame² *vt* **(a)** rendre (*qn*) boiteux; **(b)** (*make leg useless*) estropier (*qn*).
lamé ['lɑːmeɪ] *n Tex* **gold/silver l.,** lamé *m* d'or/d'argent; **a gold l. dress,** une robe en lamé d'or.
lamebrain ['leɪmbreɪn] *n F* idiot, -e, abruti, -e.
lamella, *pl* **-ae** [lə'melə, -iː] *n* lamelle *f*.
lamely ['leɪmlɪ] *adv* (*s'excuser etc*) faiblement.
lameness ['leɪmnɪs] *n* claudication *f*; boiterie *f* (*d'un cheval*); *Fig* faiblesse *f* (*d'une excuse etc*).
lament¹ [lə'ment] *n* **(a)** lamentation *f*; **(b)** *Mus Arch* complainte *f*.
lament² **1** *vt* se lamenter sur (*qch*); pleurer (*qch, qn*); **I was lamenting my lost youth,** je pleurais ma jeunesse perdue. **2** *vi* se lamenter (**for, over sth,** sur qch); pleurer (**for, over s.o./sth,** qn/qch).
lamentable [lə'məntəb(ə)l] *adj* (*perte, insuccès etc*) lamentable, déplorable; **it's l.!,** c'est lamentable!
lamentably [lə'məntəblɪ] *adj* lamentablement.
lamentation [læmən'teɪʃən] *n* lamentation *f*; *Bible* **the Lamentations of Jeremiah,** les Lamentations de Jérémie.
lamented [lə'mentɪd] *adj* **the late l. Mr Jones,** le regretté M. Jones.
laminate¹ ['læmɪneɪt] *n* stratifié *m*.
laminate² **1** *vt* **(a)** (*bond*) laminer, lamifier; feuilleter (*du verre*); stratifier (*de la matière plastique*); contreplaquer (*du bois*); **(b)** (*split*) diviser en lamelles; **(c)** (*cover*) plastifier (*du papier etc*). **2** *vi* **(a)** (*bond*) se laminer; **(b)** (*split*) se diviser en lamelles.
laminated ['læmɪneɪtəd] *adj* **(a)** (*glass*) feuilleté; (*wood*) contreplaqué; **l. plate glass,** verre (de sécurité) feuilleté; *Ind* **l. plastics,** matières plastiques stratifiées; *MecE* **l. spring,** ressort *m* à lames (superposées); **(b)** (*paper etc*) plastifié; **l. jacket,** (*of book*) jaquette plastifiée.
Lammas ['læməs] *n* **L. (Day),** le premier août.
lammergeier ['læməgaɪər] *n* (*bird*) gypaète barbu.
lamp [læmp] *n* **(a)** lampe *f*; **oil/paraffin l.,** lampe à huile/à pétrole; **miner's l.,** lampe de mineur; **safety l.,** lampe de sûreté; **portable l., inspection l.,** (*in garage etc*) baladeuse *f*; **street l.,** réverbère *m*; **projector** *or* **projection l.,** lampe de projection; *Rail* **signal l.,** lanterne *f* de signalisation; **table l.,** lampe de table; **standard l.,** lampadaire *m*, lampe sur pied; **l. standard,** torchère *f*; **hanging l.,** suspension *f*; **wall l.,** (lampe d')applique *f*; *Med* **head l.,** lampe frontale; **(b)** *El* (*bulb*) lampe *f*, ampoule *f*; **filament l.,** lampe à filament; **neon l.,** lampe au néon; **incandescent l.,** lampe à incandescence; **ultraviolet l.,** lampe à rayons ultra-violets; **infra-red l.,** lampe infra-rouge.
lampblack ['læmpblæk] *n* noir *m* de fumée.
lamper ['læmpər] *n* **l. eel,** lamproie *f*.
lamplight ['læmplaɪt] *n* lumière *f* de la lampe; **to work by l.,** travailler à la lampe.
lampoon¹ [læm'puːn] *n* libelle *m*, brocard *m*.
lampoon² *vt* lancer des satires *ou* des brocards contre (*qn*), brocarder (*qn*).
lampoonist [læm'puːnɪst] *n* satiriste *m*, chansonnier *m*.
lamppost ['læmppəʊst] *n* **(a)** (*in street*) (montant *m ou* poteau *m* de) réverbère *m*; **(b)** *Ind Constr* (*high*) mât *m* d'éclairage; (*low*) poteau *m* d'éclairage.
lamprey, *pl* **-eys** ['læmprɪ, -ɪz] *n* (*fish*) lamproie *f*.
lampshade ['læmpʃeɪd] *n* abat-jour *m inv*.
lampstand ['læmpstænd] *n* pied *m* de lampe.
LAN [læn] *n Comptr abbr* **local area network.**
lance¹ [lɑːns] *n* **(a)** lance *f*; *Arch & Lit* **to break a l. with s.o.,** rompre une lance avec qn; **(b)** *Mil* **l. corporal,** soldat *m* de première classe.
lance² *vt Med* percer, inciser (*un abcès*).
lanceolate(d) ['lɑːnsɪəleɪt, -ɪd] *adj Bot* lancéolé.
lancer ['lɑːnsər] *n* **(a)** *Mil* lancier *m*; **(b)** (*dance*) **lancers,** (quadrille *m* des) lanciers *mpl*.
lancet ['lɑːnsɪt] *n* **(a)** *Med* lancette *f*, bistouri *m*; **(b)** *Archit* **l. (arch),** lancette; **l. window,** fenêtre *f* en ogive.
Lancs *abbr* **Lancashire.**
land¹ [lænd] *n* **(a)** (*as opposed to sea*) terre *f*; **dry l.,** terre ferme; **on l.,** sur terre; **L.'s End,** la pointe de Cornouaille; **to travel by l.,** voyager par voie de terre; **l. route,** voie *f* de terre; **l. breeze,** brise *f* de terre; *Nau* **l. ho!,** terre (en vue)!; *Nau* **to make l.,** reconnaître la terre; *Fig* **to see how the l. lies,** sonder *ou* tâter le terrain; *Mil* **to attack by l., sea and air,** attaquer par terre, par mer et par air; **l. bridge,** isthme *m*; **l. mine,** mine *f* terrestre; **l. warfare,** guerre *f* sur terre; **l. army,** armée *f* de terre; **l. forces,** armée *f* de terre;
(b) (*earth, soil*) terre *f*, sol *m*; **arable l.,** terre arable *ou* labourable; **ploughed l.,** terre labourée; **waste l.,** terre inculte; (*in city*) terrain vague; **man lives off the l.,** c'est la terre qui nourrit les hommes; *Jur* **l. act,** loi *f* agraire; **l. bank,** crédit foncier, crédit agricole;
(c) (*country*) terre *f*, pays *m*; **the whole l. rose up in rebellion,** le pays entier s'est soulevé; **the best in the l.,** le meilleur du pays; **the l. of the midnight sun,** le pays du soleil de minuit; **distant/unknown lands,** pays lointains/inconnus; **to be still in the l. of the living,** être encore de ce monde; **the Holy L.,** la Terre Sainte; *Bible & Fig* **the Promised L.,** la terre promise; **the l. of dreams,** le pays des rêves;
(d) *Jur* terre(s) *f(pl)*; **private l.,** terrain privé; **the farmer wouldn't allow campers on his l.,** le fermier n'acceptait pas de campeurs sur ses terres; **to buy l.,** acheter des terres; **l. tax,** contributions foncières (*sur les propriétés non bâties*); **l. register,** cadastre *m*.
land² **1** *vt* mettre *ou* faire descendre (*qn*) à terre; mettre (*qch*) à terre; (*from ship, plane*) débarquer (*qn, qch*); *Com* décharger (*des marchandises*); faire atterrir (*un avion*); amener (*un poisson*) à terre; *F* amener, planter (**s.o. somewhere,** qn quelque part); *F* **they landed all the prizes,** ils ont raflé tous les prix; *F* **he's just landed a good job,** il vient juste de se trouver un bon boulot; *F* **that will l. you in prison,** cela vous vaudra de la prison; *F* **you've landed us in a nice mess!,** vous nous avez mis dans de beaux draps!; *F* **to be landed with sth,** rester avec qch sur les bras; *F* **to l. s.o. a blow in the face,** allonger *ou* flanquer à qn un coup au visage.
2 *vi* **(a)** (*of person*) descendre à terre; (*from ship, plane*) débarquer; (*of ship*) aborder, accoster; (*of aircraft, pilot*) atterrir; (*on deck of aircraft carrier*) apponter; **to l. on the moon,** alunir; **to l. on the sea,** amerrir; *Av* **when do we l.?,** quand est-ce que nous atterrissons?;
(b) (*fall*) tomber (à terre); **he slipped and landed in a puddle,** il a glissé et est tombé dans une flaque d'eau; **to l. flat on one's back,** se retrouver les quatre fers en l'air; **to l. on one's feet,** retomber sur ses pieds; *Fig F* **he always manages to land on his feet,** il arrive toujours à retomber sur ses pattes;
(c) (*from a vehicle*) mettre pied à terre; (*after jumping*) tomber, retomber;
(d) (*of gymnast, ski-jumper, horse, after jumping*) se recevoir;
(e) *Sp* (*of horse*) **to l. first,** arriver (le) premier.
►**land up** *vi* (*in a ditch, hospital, jail etc*) se retrouver; **I landed up having to dance with him,** je me suis vue obligée de danser avec lui.
landau ['lændɔː] *n* (*carriage*) landau *m*, *pl* landaus.

landed [lændəd] *adj* **(a)** *Br* **the l. gentry,** la petite noblesse; **l. property,** propriété foncière *ou* territoriale; **l. proprietor,** propriétaire terrien; **l. estate,** propriété foncière; **(b)** *Can Admin* **l. immigrant,** immigrant reçu.

landfall ['lændfɔːl] *n Nau* (*arrival*) atterrissage *m*; (*sight of land*) arrivée *f* en vue de terre; **to make a l.,** (*arrive*) atterrir; (*sight land*) arriver en vue de terre.

landfill ['lændfɪl] *n* décharge *f* en fouille; **to use sth as l.,** utiliser qch pour remblayer *ou* comme remblai; **l. site,** décharge publique en fouille.

landing [lændɪŋ] *n* **(a)** *Nau* débarquement *m*, mise *f* à terre (*de qn, de qch*); *Mil Nau* débarquement; *Av* (*of aircraft*) (*on land*) atterrissage *m*; (*on sea*) amerrissage *m*; (*on deck of ship*) appontage *m*; *Com* déchargement *m*; *Nau* **(passenger's) l. card** *or* **ticket,** ticket *m ou* carte *f ou* carton *m* de débarquement; **l. stage,** débarcadère *m*, embarcadère *m*; **l. force/party,** troupes *fpl*/compagnie *f* de débarquement; **l. operation,** opération *f* de débarquement; **l. craft,** chaland *m ou* engin *m* de débarquement; **blind/instrument l.,** atterrissage sans visibilité/aux instruments; **visual l.,** atterrissage à vue; **forced** *or* **emergency l.,** atterrissage forcé; **to make a crash l.,** faire un atterrissage *ou* atterrir en catastrophe; **l. gear,** train *m* (d'atterrissage); **to retract the l. gear,** relever *ou* rentrer le train; **l. field,** terrain *m* d'atterrissage; **l. strip,** bande *f ou* piste *f* d'atterrissage; *Mil Av* **l. zone,** zone *f* d'atterrissage (*des troupes aéroportées*); **l. flap,** volet *m* d'atterrissage; **l. wheels,** train d'atterrissage; **l. lights,** feux *mpl ou* rampe *f* d'atterrissage;
(b) *Constr* palier *m* (*d'un escalier*); (*corridor*) couloir *m*;
(c) prise *f* (*d'un poisson*); **l. net,** épuisette *f*;
(d) (*of gymnast, ski-jumper*) réception *f*.

landlady ['lændleɪdɪ] *nf* **(a)** propriétaire *f* (*d'un immeuble, d'un pub*); **(b)** (*keeping furnished apartments*) logeuse *f* (en garni); **(c)** aubergiste *f*, hôtelière *f*; **seaside l.,** propriétaire *f* d'une auberge au bord de la mer.

landlegs ['lændlegz] *npl F* (*of sailor*) **to get one's l.,** se familiariser de nouveau avec la terre.

landlocked ['lændlɒkt] *adj* enfermé entre les terres; (*port etc*) entouré de terre; **l. sea,** mer intérieure.

landlord ['lændlɔːd] *n* **(a)** propriétaire *m* (*d'un immeuble*); **(b)** (*keeping furnished apartments*) logeur *m* (en garni); **(c)** *Br* (*of pub*) propriétaire *m*; **(d)** (*landowner*) propriétaire *m* (foncier).

landlubber ['lændlʌbər] *n Nau F* marin *m* d'eau douce.

landmark ['lændmɑːk] *n* **(a)** (point *m* de) repère *m*; *Av* repère, point *m* de repérage (au sol); *Nau* amer *m*, indice *m* (à terre), point à terre; **that clump of trees is a natural l.,** ce groupe d'arbres est un repère naturel; **(b)** (*important event*) point décisif, événement marquant; **to be a l.,** (*of event*) faire époque *ou* date; **l. decision,** décision qui fait époque *ou* date; **(c)** (*boundary marker*) borne *f* limite.

landmass ['lændmæs] *n* masse *f* de terre.

landmine ['lændmaɪn] *n* mine *f* terrestre.

landowner ['lændəʊnər] *n* propriétaire foncier.

landowning ['lændəʊnɪŋ] *adj* **the l. classes,** les classes qui possèdent des terres.

landscape¹ ['lændskeɪp] **1** *n* (*land, painting*) paysage *m*; **these factories are a blot on the l.,** ces usines déparent le paysage; **l. design** *or US* **architecture,** architecture *f* de paysage; **l. designer** *or US* **architect,** paysagiste *mf*; **l. gardener,** jardinier *m* paysagiste; **l. gardening,** paysagisme *m*; *Art* **l. painter,** paysagiste *mf*, peintre *m* de paysages. **2** *adv* (*to print*) à l'italienne.

landscape² *vt* aménager (*un terrain*) en parc; **they had their garden landscaped,** ils ont employé un jardinier paysagiste pour aménager leur propriété.

landscaping ['lændskeɪpɪŋ] *n* paysagisme *m*.

landscapist ['lændskeɪpɪst] *n* paysagiste *mf*.

landslide ['lændslaɪd] *n* **(a)** éboulement *m*, affaissement *m*, glissement *m* (de terrain); **(b)** *Pol* raz de marée *m inv* électoral; **l. victory,** victoire écrasante; **l. majority,** majorité écrasante.

landslip ['lændslɪp] *n* = **LANDSLIDE (a)**.

landward ['lændwəd] **1** *adv* **(to) l.,** du côté de la terre; vers la terre. **2** *adj* **on the l. side,** vers l'intérieur, du côté de la terre.

lane [leɪn] *n* **(a)** (*in country*) chemin vicinal *ou* rural; (*in town*) ruelle *f*, passage *m*; (*in icefield*) passage; **(b)** *Nau* route *f* de navigation; *Av* **air l.,** couloir aérien; **(c)** *Aut etc* **(traffic) l.,** voie *f*; **l. markings,** bandes délimitant les voies; **four l. road,** route à quatre voies (de circulation); **don't change lanes,** ne change pas de voie; **traffic is reduced to two lanes,** la circulation ne se fait plus que sur deux files; **fast/slow l.,** = voie de gauche/de droite; **stay in l.,** restez dans votre file; **get into l.,** = serrez à gauche *ou* à droite; **(d)** *Sp* (*for runner, swimmer*) couloir *m*.

langlauf ['læŋlaʊf] *n* ski *m* de fond; **l. skier,** skieur, -euse de fond.

language ['læŋgwɪdʒ] *n* **(a)** langue *f* (*d'un peuple*); **the English l.,** la langue anglaise; **foreign languages,** langues étrangères; **I never learned to speak the l.,** je n'ai jamais appris à parler la langue; *Fig F* **we don't talk the same l.,** nous ne parlons pas le même langage; **modern languages,** langues vivantes; **l. laboratory,** laboratoire *m* de langues; **l. studies,** études *fpl* de langues; **(b)** (*vocabulary*) langage *m*; **the l. of flowers,** le langage des fleurs; **bad l.,** langage grossier, grossièretés *fpl*; **to use bad l.,** parler vertement, lâcher des gros mots; **(mind your) l.!,** surveillez votre langage!; **code l.,** langage convenu, code *m*; **business l.,** langage *ou* langue des affaires; *Comptr* **computer l., machine l.,** langage machine.

languid ['læŋgwɪd] *adj* languissant, langoureux; (*voice*) traînant; (*movement*) lent, traînant.

languidly ['læŋgwɪdlɪ] *adv* languissamment, langoureusement; (*to say*) d'une voix traînante; (*to move*) lentement.

languidness [læŋgwɪdnɪs] *n* langueur *f*.

languish ['læŋgwɪʃ] *vi* languir, dépérir; (*of plant*) s'étioler; **to l. after** *or* **for s.o./sth,** languir après *ou* pour qn/qch; *F* **it languished in my in-tray for a week,** c'est resté dans ma corbeille à courrier pendant une semaine; **to l. in prison,** languir en prison.

languishing ['læŋgwɪʃɪŋ] *adj* languissant, langoureux.

languor ['læŋgər] *n* langueur *f*.

languorous ['læŋgərəs] *adj* langoureux.

languorously ['læŋgərəslɪ] *adv* langoureusement.

lank [læŋk] *adj* **l. hair,** cheveux plats.

lankiness ['læŋkɪnɪs] *n* taille grande et maigre (*de qn*).

lankness ['læŋknɪs] *n* (*of hair*) aspect *m* terne et sans vigueur.

lanky ['læŋkɪ] *adj* (*person*) grand et maigre.

lanolin(e) ['lænəlɪn] *n Ch Pharm* lanoline *f*, graisse *f* de laine; **l. shampoo,** shampooing *m* à la lanoline.

lantern ['læntən] *n* **(a)** lanterne *f*, falot *m*; *Nau* fanal *m*, -aux; **Chinese l.,** lanterne vénitienne; *Arch* **magic l.,** lanterne magique; **l. slides,** plaques *fpl* de lanterne magique; **(b)** *Archit* lanterne *f*, lanternau *m* (*de dôme*); **(c) l. jaw,** menton *m* en galoche; **l. jaws,** joues creuses.

lantern-jawed [læntən'dʒɔːd] *adj* au menton en galoche.

lanyard ['lænjɑːd, -jəd] *n Nau* aiguillette *f*; ride *f* (*de hauban*); (*of knife etc*) amarrage *m*.

Laos [laʊs] *n* Laos *m*.

Laotian ['laʊʃɪən] **1** *adj* laotien. **2** *n* Laotien, -ienne.

lap¹ [læp] *n* genoux *mpl*; *Lit* giron *m*; **to sit on s.o.'s l.,** s'asseoir sur les genoux de qn; **it's in the l. of the gods,** Dieu seul le sait; **he expects everything to fall into his l.,** il pense qu'il n'y a qu'à se baisser et à prendre; **it's not going to fall into your l.,** (*you'll have to work for it*) ça ne va pas te tomber tout cuit; **to live in the l. of luxury,** vivre dans le luxe; **to drop sth in s.o.'s l.,** coller quelque chose à qn et le laisser se débrouiller avec.

lap² *n* **(a)** *Sp* tour *m* (*de piste, de circuit*); **to do three laps,** faire trois tours de circuit; **they're on the third l.,** ils sont dans le troisième tour; *Fig* **to be on the last l.,** en être à la dernière étape; **l. of honour,** tour d'honneur; **(b)** *MecE* recouvrement *m*; *Constr* chevauchement *m*, recouvrement (*des tuiles, des ardoises*); *Metal* **l. joint,** ourlet *m*; **l. weld(ing),** soudure *f* à recouvrement; **(c)** tour *m* (*d'une corde autour d'un cylindre etc*).

lap³ *v* (-pp-) **1** *vt* **(a)** *Sp* **to l. an opponent,** prendre un tour d'avance sur un concurrent; **to l. the course,** boucler le circuit; **(b) to l. sth round sth,** enrouler qch autour de qch; **(c)** *Constr* enchevaucher (*des planches*); poser (*des planches*) à recouvrement; donner du recouvrement à (*des tuiles etc*); **to l. a joint with sheet metal,** chaperonner un assemblage. **2** *vi* **(a)** *Sp* tourner; **(b) to l. over sth,** dépasser *ou* recouvrir qch; (*of tiles etc*) chevaucher qch.

lap⁴ *n* clapotement *m*, clapotis *m* (*des vagues*).

lap⁵ **1** *vt* (*of animal*) laper (*du lait*). **2** *vi* (*of waves*) clapoter.

►**lap up** *vtsep* **(a)** laper (*du lait*); **(b)** *Fig F* **it was sheer flattery but he lapped it all up,** c'était de la flatterie pure et simple mais il a tout gobé *ou* avalé; **she laps up every new book on gardening,** elle dévore tous les livres qui sortent sur le jardinage.

laparoscope ['læpərəskəʊp] *n Med* laparoscope *m*.

laparotomy [læpə'rɒtəmɪ] *n Surg* laparotomie *f*.

lapdog ['læpdɒg] *n* chien *m* d'appartement; *Fig* béni-oui-oui *m inv*.

lapel [lə'pel] *n* revers *m* (*d'un habit*).
lapidary ['læpɪd(ə)rɪ] *adj & n* lapidaire *m*.
lapis lazuli ['læpɪs'læzʊlɪ] *n* (*stone, colour*) lapis(-lazuli) *m inv*.
Lapland ['læplænd] *n* Laponie *f*.
Laplander ['læplændər] *n* Lapon, -one.
Lapp [læp] **1** *adj* lapon. **2** *n* **(a)** Lapon, -one; **(b)** *Ling* lapon *m*.
lapse¹ [læps] *n* **(a)** (*mistake*) erreur *f*, faute *f*; **l. of memory,** défaillance *f ou* absence *f* de mémoire, oubli *m*; **(b)** (*fault*) faute *f*, défaillance *f*; écart *m* de conduite; (*in standards etc*) baisse *f* (**in,** de); **l. from one's duty,** manquement *m* à son devoir; **it was just a temporary l.,** ce n'était qu'une défaillance temporaire; **(c)** cours *m*, marche *f* (*du temps*); laps *m* de temps; **there was a considerable time l. between the two explosions,** il y a eu un laps de temps considérable entre les deux explosions; **after a l. of three months,** après un délai de trois mois; **(d)** (*expiry*) expiration *f*.
lapse² *vi* **(a)** (*make mistake, err*) **he only lapsed once,** il n'a fait qu'une seule erreur; **his concentration lapsed for a split second,** il a relâché sa concentration pendant une fraction de seconde; **I must have lapsed when I bought that!,** je devais être fou quand j'ai acheté ça!; **if the quality is allowed to l.,** si on laisse baisser la qualité;
(b) (*fall, go*) **to l. into silence,** se taire; **to l. into unconsciousness,** sombrer dans l'inconscience; **he's lapsing back into his old ways,** il est retombé dans ses vieilles habitudes; **it's too easy to l. back into English,** c'est trop facile de revenir à l'anglais;
(c) (*morally*) manquer à ses devoirs; être coupable d'un écart de conduite; faire un faux pas;
(d) *Jur* (*of right, passport etc*) périmer, se périmer; (*of estate*) devenir disponible; (*of legacy*) devenir caduc; (*of law*) tomber en désuétude; (*of insurance policy etc*) cesser d'être en vigueur; *Rel* cesser de pratiquer; **to allow a right to l.,** laisser périmer *ou* laisser tomber un droit; **my club membership has lapsed,** ma carte de membre du club a expiré.
lapsed [læpst] *adj* **(a)** déchu; **a l. Christian,** un chrétien déchu; **(b)** (*postal order etc, right*) périmé; (*inheritance*) tombé en dévolu; (*contract, inheritance*) caduc, *f* caduque; (*insurance policy, membership*) expiré.
lapsus ['læpsəs] *n* lapsus *m*.
laptop ['læptɒp] *n Comptr* portable *m*.
lapweld ['læpweld] *vt Metal* souder en écharpe.
lapwing ['læpwɪŋ] *n* (*bird*) vanneau (huppé).
larceny ['lɑːsənɪ] *n* vol *m*; *Jur* **petty l.,** vol simple, vol minime.
larch [lɑːtʃ] *n* mélèze *m*.
lard¹ [lɑːd] *n Culin* saindoux *m*; *esp Am F* **he's a tub of l.,** c'est un sac de graisse.
lard² *vt Culin* larder, barder, piquer (*la viande*); **larded joint,** larde *f*; *F* **to l. one's writings with quotations,** larder ses écrits de citations.
larder ['lɑːdər] *n* garde-manger *m inv*.
large [lɑːdʒ] **1** *adj* **(a)** grand; (*meal, sum, slice*) gros; **l.(-sized),** de grand format; **a l. woman,** une grosse femme; **l. town,** grande ville; **l. whisky,** double whisky *m*; **l. parcel,** gros paquet, paquet volumineux; **the l. intestine,** le gros intestin; **to grow larger,** grossir; **there she is as l. as life,** la voilà, c'est bien elle!; **the l. size,** (*packet etc*) la grande taille; **have you this dress in a l. size?,** avez-vous cette robe en grande taille?; **a l. sum,** une grosse *ou* forte somme; **l. family,** famille nombreuse; **to a l. extent,** en grande partie; **to trade on a l. scale,** faire les affaires en grand;
(b) (*liberal*) **l. views,** idées *fpl* larges; (*comprehensive*) **l. powers,** pouvoirs larges *ou* étendus.
2 *adv* **by and l.,** à tout prendre, généralement.
3 *n* **to set a prisoner at l.,** élargir *ou* relaxer un prisonnier; **to be at l.,** être libre *ou* en liberté; **the murderer is still at l.,** l'assassin court toujours; **people at l.,** (*in general*) le grand public, la grande masse du public; **teachers at l.,** la masse des professeurs; **at l.,** (*in detail*) tout au long; en détail; **to talk at l.,** parler au hasard; **he was just throwing out ideas at l.,** il lançait juste quelques idées au hasard.
large-handed [lɑːdʒ'hændəd] *adj* généreux.
large-hearted [lɑːdʒ'hɑːtəd] *adj* au grand cœur.
largely ['lɑːdʒlɪ] *adv* **(a)** en grande partie, pour une grande part; **his job is l. administrative,** son travail est surtout administratif; **(b) that is l. sufficient,** cela suffit grandement *ou* largement.
large-minded [lɑːdʒ'maɪndəd] *adj* aux idées larges, à l'esprit large.
largeness ['lɑːdʒnɪs] *n* **(a)** grosseur *f* (*du corps*); grandeur *f*, importance *f* (*des profits, d'une majorité etc*); **(b)** étendue *f* (*d'un pouvoir*); largeur *f* (*d'idées*); grandeur (*d'âme*).
large-print ['lɑːdʒprɪnt] *adj* **l.-p. books,** livres en gros caractères.
large-scale ['lɑːdʒ'skeɪl] *adj* gros (*entreprise*); (*carte*) à grande échelle; **l.-s. farmer,** gros agriculteur; **l.-s. disaster,** grande catastrophe; *Comptr* **l.-s. integration,** intégration à grande échelle.
largess(e) [lɑː'ʒes] *n* largesse *f*.
largish ['lɑːdʒɪʃ] *adj* assez grand; assez gros.
largo, *pl* **-s** ['lɑːgəʊ, -z] *adv & n Mus* largo *m inv*.
lariat ['lærɪət] *n* **(a)** *Am* lasso *m*; **(b)** (*for tethering animals*) corde *f* à piquet.
lark¹ [lɑːk] *n* (*bird*) alouette *f*; **to rise** *or* **get up** *or* **be up with the l.,** se lever au chant du coq; **she sings like a l.,** elle chante comme un rossignol.
lark² *n F* farce *f*, rigolade *f*, blague *f*; **to do sth for a l.,** faire qch histoire de rire *ou* de rigoler; **what a l.!** quelle farce!; **I'd like to know what his little l. is,** je me demande ce qu'il tripote; **I don't like this fancy dress l.,** je n'aime pas du tout cette histoire de bal masqué.
lark³ *vi* (*play joke*) faire des farces; (*have good time*) rigoler.
▶**lark about, lark around** *vi* faire des farces; rigoler; **some children were larking around with an old tyre,** des enfants s'amusaient avec un vieux pneu.
larkspur ['lɑːkspɜːr] *n* (*plant*) pied- d'alouette *m*, *pl* pieds-d'alouette.
larva, *pl* **-vae** ['lɑːvə, -viː] *n Ent* larve *f*.
larval ['lɑːv(ə)l] *adj* **(a)** *Ent* larvaire; en forme de larve; **(b)** *Med* (*disease*) latent, larvé.
laryngitis [lærɪn'dʒaɪtɪs] *n Med* laryngite *f*; **to have l.,** avoir une laryngite.
laryngoscope [lə'rɪŋgəskəʊp] *n* laryngoscope *m*.
larynx ['lærɪŋks] *n Anat* larynx *m*.
lasagne [lə'sænjə] *n Culin* lasagnes *fpl*.
lascivious [lə'sɪvɪəs] *adj* lascif; (*sourire*) provocant.
lasciviously [lə'sɪvɪəslɪ] *adv* lascivement.
lasciviousness [lə'sɪvɪəsnɪs] *n* lasciveté *f*.
laser ['leɪzər] *n* laser *m*; **l. beam,** rayon *m* laser; **l. printer,** imprimante *f* (à) laser; **l. printout/quality,** texte *m*/qualité *f* laser.
lash¹ [læʃ] *n* **(a)** (*blow*) coup *m* de fouet; (*end of whip*) lanière *f* (de fouet); **the l.,** le supplice du fouet; **to receive ten lashes,** recevoir dix coups de fouet; **(b)** *Anat* cil *m*.
lash² **1** *vt* **(a)** (*with whip*) fouetter, cingler (*un cheval etc*); fouetter, flageller (*qn*); (*of rain*) fouetter (*les vitres, le visage de qn*); (*of waves*) battre, fouetter (*le rivage*); **(b)** (*verbally*) cingler; **to l. s.o. with one's tongue,** adresser à qn des paroles cinglantes; **(c)** (*move from side to side*) **to l. its tail,** (*of cat, lion etc*) fouetter l'air de la queue. **2** *vi* **to l. against the windows,** (*of rain*) fouetter les vitres; **to l. against the shore,** (*of waves*) battre *ou* fouetter le rivage; **the rain lashed down on the tent,** la pluie fouettait la tente.
lash³ *vt* (*tie*) lier, attacher; *Nau* amarrer; **to l. down a load on a trailer,** lier *ou* brider une charge sur une remorque; **to l. two wires together,** ligaturer *ou* ligoter deux fils.
▶**lash about** *vi* (*in pain*) se débattre (de douleur).
▶**lash out** **1** *vi* **(a)** (*physically*) envoyer un coup à qn; (*verbally*) lancer des paroles blessantes; **he lashed out at me with his fists,** il m'a envoyé un coup de poing; **(b)** *F* (*spend extravagantly*) faire une folie *ou* des folies; **I'm going to l. out on a new coat,** je vais faire des folies et me payer un nouveau manteau. **2** *vipo F* **I lashed out £10 on a bottle of wine,** je me suis permis la folie de dépenser 10 livres pour une bouteille de vin.
lashing¹ ['læʃɪŋ] **1** *adj* (*of rain*) cinglant. **2** *n* **(a)** (*with whip*) coups *mpl* de fouet, le fouet; **(b)** *Old-fashioned* **tongue l.,** verte réprimande; **(c)** *Br F* **lashings of sth,** des tas *mpl* de qch; **apple-pie with lashings of cream,** de la tarte aux pommes avec une tonne de crème.
lashing² *n* **(a)** (*action*) *Nau* amarrage *m*; ligature *f* (*de câbles, de fils*); **(b)** (*rope*) *Nau* amarre *f*; commande *f* (*de pontons*).
lass [læs] *n esp Scot North Eng* jeune fille *f*; **country l.,** jeune campagnarde.
Lassa ['lɑːsə] *n Med* **L. fever,** fièvre *f* de Lhassa.
lassie ['læsɪ] *n esp Scot* fillette *f*; **a wee l.,** une petite fille.
lassitude ['læsɪtjuːd] *n* lassitude *f*.
lasso¹ [læ'suː] *n* lasso *m*.
lasso² *vt* prendre au lasso.

last¹ [lɑːst] **1** *adj* **(a)** (*in series*) dernier; **the l. guest to arrive,** le dernier des invités à arriver; **the l. but one,** l'avant-dernier, *pl* avant-derniers; **the l. syllable but one,** la syllabe pénultième; **the l. but three,** le troisième avant le dernier; **this is your l. chance,** c'est votre dernière chance; **l. but not least,** le dernier (nommé), mais non le moindre; **you are the l. one who should criticize,** vous devriez être le dernier à critiquer; **you're the l. person I expected to see here,** tu es bien le dernier *ou* la dernière que je pensais rencontrer ici; **that's the l. thing that's worrying me,** ça c'est le cadet de mes soucis; **in the l. resort, as a l. resort,** en dernière ressource, en dernier recours; **you are my l. hope,** vous êtes mon dernier espoir; **in the l. place,** en dernier lieu, pour finir; **after 10 miles we were on our l. legs,** après 10 mil(l)es nous n'en pouvions plus; **in the l. analysis,** en dernière analyse; **to have the l. word,** (*come after other speakers*) parler le dernier; (*in argument*) avoir le dernier mot; **hotel that is the l. word in comfort,** hôtel qui est le summum du confort; **to pay one's l. respects to s.o.,** rendre les derniers devoirs à qn; **I'm down to my l. pound,** il ne me reste plus qu'une livre; **every l. scrap of bread had been eaten,** on avait mangé jusqu'à la dernière miette; **at the l. moment** *or* **minute,** au dernier moment; **the l. day of the month,** le dernier jour du mois; **to do sth l. thing at night,** faire qch en dernier le soir; *Rel* **L. Judgment,** Jugement Dernier; **l. name,** (*surname*) nom *m* de famille; *Cathol* **l. rites,** derniers sacrements;
(b) (*of past or recent time*) **l. Tuesday, Tuesday l.,** mardi dernier; **l. January,** au mois de janvier dernier; **the l. time I saw him,** la dernière fois que je l'ai vu; **l. week,** la semaine dernière, la semaine passée; **l. night,** (*during the night*) la nuit dernière; (*in the evening*) hier soir; **I slept badly l. night,** j'ai mal dormi cette nuit; **I haven't been to church for the l. few weeks,** je n'ai pas été à l'église ces dernières semaines; **in the l. fifty years,** pendant les cinquante dernières années; **this day l. week,** il y a aujourd'hui huit jours; **this day l. year,** l'an dernier à la même date.
2 *n* **(a)** le dernier, la dernière; **am I the l.?,** (*to arrive*) suis-je le dernier?; *Ind* **l. in, first out,** dernier entré, premier sorti; *Bible* **the l. shall be first,** les derniers seront les premiers;
(b) we shall never hear the l. of it, on ne nous le laissera pas oublier; **we haven't heard the l. of it,** tout n'est pas dit; **that's the l. I saw of him,** je ne l'ai pas revu depuis; **to** *or* **till the l.,** jusqu'au bout, jusqu'à la fin; **faithful to the l.,** fidèle jusqu'au bout; **at l., at long l.,** enfin; **now at l. I understand,** finalement je comprends; **that's the l. of the wine,** ce sont les dernières gouttes de vin; **to look one's l. on sth,** voir qch pour la dernière fois; **to breathe one's l.,** mourir;
(c) (*death*) fin *f*; **to be near one's l.,** toucher à sa fin; **towards the l.,** vers la fin.
3 *adv* **(a) when I l. saw him, when I saw him l.,** la dernière fois que je l'ai vu; **when did you l. eat?,** de quand date *ou* à quand remonte votre dernier repas?;
(b) he spoke l., il a parlé le dernier; **to come l.,** (*in race*) arriver dernier; (*in exam*) être dernier;
(c) l., (*I would like to say*) et pour finir; **l. but not least,** enfin et surtout.

last² **1** *vi* durer, se maintenir; **it's too good to l.,** c'est trop beau pour durer; **if the good weather lasts,** si le beau temps se maintient; **cream doesn't l. long,** (*deteriorates quickly*) la crème fraîche ne se garde pas longtemps; **cakes don't l. long in this house,** (*they get eaten quickly*) les gâteaux ne font pas long feu dans cette maison; **the supplies will not l. two months,** les vivres ne feront pas deux mois; **their friendship won't l. long,** leur amitié ne fera pas long feu; **he won't l. long in that job,** il ne fera pas long feu dans cette situation. **2** *vt* **it will l. a lifetime,** j'en ai pour la vie; **it has lasted him well,** ça lui a fait pas mal de temps.

last³ *n* (*for shoe*) forme *f* (à chaussure); *Prov* **let the shoemaker stick to his l.,** cordonnier, mêlez-vous de votre pantoufle!

▸last out **1** *vtsep* **to l. s.o. out,** (*of person*) survivre à qn; (*of thing*) durer autant que qn; **to l. the year,** durer *ou* aller jusqu'au bout de l'année; **my overcoat will l. the winter out,** mon pardessus fera encore l'hiver. **2** *vi* (*of person*) tenir le coup.

last-ditch [lɑːst'dɪtʃ] *adj* (*attempt, effort*) ultime.

lasting ['lɑːstɪŋ] *adj* durable, permanent; (*material etc*) résistant, de bon usage; **l. peace,** paix *f* durable.

lastly ['lɑːstlɪ] *adv* pour finir, en dernier lieu.

last-minute [lɑːst'mɪnɪt] *adj* (*decision*) de dernière heure, de dernière minute.

lat (*abbr* **latitude**) latitude, lat..

latch¹ [lætʃ] *n* **(a)** loquet *m*; pêne *m*, gâche *f* (*de portière de véhicule etc*); (*of front door*) serrure *f* de sûreté (avec clef de maison); **small l.,** (*for shutters etc*) loqueteau; **to leave the door on the l.,** fermer la porte (sans la verrouiller); **(b)** *MecE* verrou *m* (*de levier, d'une pièce mécanique mobile*).

latch² *vt* **(a)** fermer (*la porte*) au loquet; (*not lock it*) fermer (*la porte*) sans mettre le verrou; **(b)** *MecE* verrouiller, bloquer (*un levier, une pièce mécanique mobile*).

▸latch on *vi* **(a)** (*attach oneself*) **to l. on to s.o./sth,** s'accrocher à qn/qch; **(b)** *F* (*understand*) saisir; **to l. on to sth,** saisir qch.

latchkey ['lætʃkiː] *n* clef *f* de maison; clef de porte d'entrée; **l. child** *or F* **kid,** = enfant dont les parents travaillent, et qui doit rentrer seul après l'école.

late [leɪt] **1** *adj* **(a)** (*after the appointed time*) en retard; (*delayed*) retardé; **to be l. (for sth),** être en retard (pour qch); **the train is l./is ten minutes l.,** le train a du retard/a dix minutes de retard; **am I too l. to ...?,** est-il trop tard pour ...?; **we apologize for the l. running of the train,** veuillez nous excuser pour le retard pris par le train; **a l. entry,** (*in competition*) une inscription de dernière minute; **her baby was five days l.,** son bébé est né avec cinq jours de retard;
(b) (*far on in the day etc*) tard; **it is l.,** il est tard; **it is getting l.,** il se fait tard; **it is too l.,** il est trop tard; **I was l. going to bed,** je me suis couché tard; **to keep l. hours,** être un couche-tard; **in the l. afternoon,** tard dans l'après-midi; **in l. summer,** vers la fin de l'été; **to be in one's l. thirties/forties/***etc*, avoir la trentaine/quarantaine/*etc* bien tassée; *Prov* **it's never too l. to mend,** il n'est jamais trop tard pour s'amender; **l. stained glass,** vitraux *mpl* de la dernière époque (*du moyen âge etc*); **in the l. (nineteen) eighties,** vers la fin des années 1980; **a l. marriage,** un mariage sur le tard; **l. edition,** (*of a newspaper*) dernière édition;
(c) (*fruit etc*) tardif; **l. frosts,** gelées tardives *ou* printanières;
(d) feu, défunt, décédé; (*former*) ancien, ex; **my l. father,** feu mon père; **the l. queen,** feu la reine, la feue reine; **the l. minister,** l'ancien ministre, l'ex-ministre;
(e) (*of recent date*) récent, dernier; **the l. war,** la guerre récente; **of l. years,** ces dernières années; **of l.,** récemment.
2 *adv* **(a)** (*after the appointed time*) en retard; **to arrive too l.,** arriver trop tard; *Prov* **better l. than never,** mieux vaut tard que jamais;
(b) (*far on in the day etc*) tard; **he came home very l.,** il est rentré fort tard; **to keep s.o. l.,** attarder qn; **to stay l. at the office,** faire des heures supplémentaires; **to work l.,** travailler tard; **to go to bed l.,** (se) coucher tard; **to sleep** *or* **stay in bed l.,** faire la grasse matinée; **l. into the night,** jusqu'à une heure avancée de la nuit; **l. in the year,** vers la fin de l'année; **l. in life,** à un âge avancé; **to marry l. in life,** se marier tard *ou* sur le tard;
(c) (*recently*) **as l. as last week,** pas plus tard que la semaine dernière;
(d) (*formerly*) **l. of London,** dernièrement domicilié à Londres, autrefois établi à Londres;
(e) *Lit* = **LATELY**.

latecomer ['leɪtkʌmər] *n* retardataire *mf*.

lateen [lə'tiːn] *adj Nau* **l. sail,** voile latine.

lately ['leɪtlɪ] *adv* dernièrement, récemment, ces derniers temps; **what have you been doing l.?** qu'avez-vous fait ces derniers temps?; **it is only l. that the matter has become known,** la chose n'a été sue que ces jours-ci.

latency ['leɪtənsɪ] *n* latence *f*, état latent; **l. period,** temps *m* de latence.

lateness ['leɪtnɪs] *n* **(a)** arrivée tardive (*de qn*); tardiveté *f* (*d'un fruit etc*); **(b) the l. of the hour,** l'heure avancée.

latent ['leɪtənt] *adj* latent; **l. period,** temps *m* de latence; *Phys* **l. heat,** chaleur latente; *Phot Med* **l. disease,** maladie latente; *Jur* **l. defect,** vice caché; *Bot* **l. bud,** œil dormant.

later ['leɪtər] (*comp of* **late**) **1** *adj* postérieur, ultérieur; **I caught a l. train,** j'ai pris un autre train plus tard; **l. events proved that ...,** la suite des événements a démontré que ...; **at a l. meeting,** dans une séance ultérieure; **l. will,** testament subséquent; **in l. life,** plus tard dans la vie. **2** *adv* plus tard; **l. (on) we went to the cinema,** plus tard nous sommes allés au cinéma; **sooner or l.,** tôt ou tard; **no l. than yesterday,** pas plus tard qu'hier; **a moment l.,**

l'instant d'après; **this happened l. (on),** cela est arrivé après *ou* plus tard *ou* ultérieurement; **a few days l.,** à quelques jours de là; **as we shall see l.,** comme nous le verrons plus tard *ou* dans la suite; *F* **see you l.!,** à tout à l'heure!

lateral ['læt(ə)rəl] **1** *adj* latéral, -aux; *MecE* **l. motion,** mouvement latéral; **l. play,** jeu latéral; *Bot* **l. bud,** bourgeon latéral; **he's good at l. thinking,** il sait trouver des approches originales. **2** *n Bot* bourgeon latéral.

laterally ['læt(ə)rəlɪ] *adv* latéralement.

latest ['leɪtɪst] **1** *adj* (*superl of* **late**) dernier; **this author's l. work,** le dernier ouvrage de cet auteur; **his l. views on the subject,** ses vues les plus récentes sur ce sujet; *Com* **l. novelties,** dernières nouveautés; **the very l. improvements,** les tout derniers perfectionnements; **the very l. news,** les informations de toute dernière heure; **l. date,** date *f* limite; *Com Jur* terme de rigueur, délai *m* de rigueur. **2** *n* **at the l.,** au plus tard; **have you heard the l.?,** savez-vous la dernière?; **Wednesday at the l.,** mercredi au plus tard; **the l. I can come,** le plus tard que je puisse venir.

latex ['leɪteks] *n Bot* latex *m*.

lath [læθ, lɑːθ] *n* **(a)** *Constr* latte *f*; **l.-and-plaster partition,** cloison lattée et plâtrée; **(b)** (*of Venetian blind*) lame *f*; **(c)** (*strip of wood*) latte *f*.

lathe [leɪð] *n* tour *m*; **precision l.,** tour de précision; **l. bed,** banc *m ou* bâti *m* de tour; **capstan** *or* **turret l.,** tour (à) revolver; **polishing l.,** touret à polir *ou* de polisseur.

lather¹ ['læðər] *n* **(a)** mousse *f* de savon; **to make a l.,** faire lever la mousse; **(b)** (*on horse*) écume *f*; **horse all in a l.,** cheval couvert d'écume; *F* **to work oneself** *or* **get into a l.,** s'énerver.

lather² **1** *vt* **(a)** savonner (**s.o.'s chin,** le menton à qn); **to l. one's face,** se passer le visage au savon; (*to shave*) se mettre du savon à barbe sur le visage; **(b)** *Old-fashioned F* (*thrash*) rosser (*qn*). **2** *vi* **(a)** (*of soap*) mousser; **(b)** (*of horse*) jeter de l'écume.

lathe-turned ['leɪðtɜːnd] *adj* fait au tour, tourné.

Latin ['lætɪn] **1** *adj* latin; **the L. races,** les races latines; **L. America,** Amérique latine; **L. American,** latino-américain, *pl* latino-américains; **the L. Quarter,** (*in Paris*) le Quartier latin. **2** *n* **(a)** Latin, -ine; **(b)** *Ling* latin *m*; **written in L.,** écrit en latin; *F* **dog L.,** latin de cuisine.

latinize ['lætɪnaɪz] *vt* latiniser.

Latino [læ'tiːnəʊ] *n US* latino *mf*.

latish ['leɪtɪʃ] **1** *adj* **(a)** (*after the appointed time*) un peu en retard; **(b)** (*far on in the day etc*) un peu tardif; **at a l. hour,** à une heure assez avancée. **2** *adv* (*see adj*) **(a)** un peu en retard; **(b)** un peu tard.

latitude ['lætɪtjuːd] *n* **(a)** *Geog* latitude *f*; **in northern/southern latitudes,** dans les latitudes boréales/australes; **at a l. of 30° north,** par 30° (de) latitude nord; **in these latitudes,** sous ces latitudes; **(b)** (*freedom*) **to allow s.o. the greatest l.,** laisser à qn la plus grande latitude *ou* la plus grande liberté d'action; **it doesn't give us much l.,** (*of deadline, timetable etc*) cela ne nous donne pas une grande marge de manœuvre; **(c)** *Astron* **celestial l.,** latitude *f* céleste.

latrine [lə'triːn] *n esp Mil* latrines *fpl*.

latter ['lætər] **1** *adj* **(a)** dernier; (*of two*) seconde; **(b)** (*belonging to the end*) dernier; **the l. years of her life,** les dernières années de sa vie; **the l. half** *or* **part of June,** la deuxième moitié de juin. **2** *n* le dernier, la dernière, les derniers, les dernières; (*of two*) le second, la seconde, les second(e)s.

latter-day ['lætə'deɪ] *adj* **(a)** moderne, d'aujourd'hui; **(b)** *Rel Hist* **the L.-d. Saints,** les Mormons *mpl*.

latterly ['lætəlɪ] *adv* **(a)** vers la fin (*d'une époque*); **(b)** (*recently*) récemment.

lattice ['lætɪs] *n* treillis *m*, treillage *m*; **l. window,** fenêtre à losanges *ou* à vitraux sertis de plomb; *Constr etc* **l. beam** *or* **girder,** poutre *f* en treillis *ou* à croisillons; **l. bridge,** pont *m* en treillis; **l. mast,** *Nau* mât *m* en treillis; *Constr* (*supporting electric wires etc*) pylône *m* métallique; **l. of boughs,** lacis *m* de branchages.

latticed ['lætɪst] *adj* treillissé, treillagé; (*rameaux*) entrecroisé.

latticework ['lætɪswɜːk] *n* treillage *m*, treillis *m*.

Latvia ['lætvɪə] *n* Lettonie *f*.

Latvian ['lætvɪən] **1** *adj* lettonien, letton. **2** *n* **(a)** Lettonien, -ienne, Letton, -one; **(b)** *Ling* letton *m*.

laud [lɔːd] *vt Lit* louer, faire le panégyrique de.

laudable ['lɔːdəb(ə)l] *adj* louable, digne de louanges.

laudably ['lɔːdəblɪ] *adv* louablement; **she was l. restrained,** sa retenue était digne de louanges.

laudanum ['lɔːd(ə)nəm] *n Pharm* laudanum *m*.

laudatory ['lɔːdət(ə)rɪ] *adj* (*speech, remarks etc*) élogieux, louangeur, -euse.

laugh¹ [lɑːf] *n* rire *m*; **to burst into a (loud) l.,** éclater de rire, partir d'un éclat de rire; **to give a short l.,** partir d'un rire bref; **with a l.,** en riant; **he loves a l.,** il aime à rire; **to raise a l.,** faire rire; **look outside if you want a l.,** regarde dehors si tu veux rigoler; *F* **to do sth for a l.,** faire qch histoire de rire; **that's a l.!,** quelle blague!, c'est marrant!; **what a l.!,** que c'est *ou* c'était marrant!; **the laugh's on us,** on nous a bien refaits; **they had the last l.,** ce sont eux qui ont bien ri; **these old films are usually good for a l.,** ces vieux films sont généralement drôles.

laugh² **1** *vi* rire; **to l. heartily,** rire de bon cœur; **to l. and cry at the same time,** pleurer d'un œil et rire de l'autre; **to l. till one cries** *or* **till the tears come,** rire (jusqu')aux larmes; **to l. to oneself,** rire tout seul, rire tout bas; *F* **to l. all the way to the bank,** rire à la caisse; **to l. in** *or* **up one's sleeve,** rire dans sa barbe; **to l. in s.o.'s face,** rire au nez *ou* à la barbe de qn; *Fig F* **to be laughing,** (*in favourable situation*) être à l'aise; *F* **you've finished, you're laughing,** tu as fini, toi, tu es soulagé; *F* **I soon made him l. on the other side of his face,** je lui ai bientôt fait passer son envie de rire; *F* **you'll l. on the other side of your face one of these days,** un de ces jours tu vas rire jaune; *F* **don't make me l.,** laissez-moi rire!; *Prov* **he laughs best who laughs last, he who laughs last laughs longest,** rira bien qui rira le dernier; **to l. at** *or* **over sth,** rire de qch; **there's nothing to l. at,** il n'y a pas de quoi rire; **to l. at s.o.,** se moquer *ou* (se) rire de qn; **I'm afraid of being laughed at,** j'ai peur qu'on se moque de moi.

2 *vt* **he laughed a bitter l.,** il eut un rire amer; **to l. oneself silly,** rire comme un bossu *ou* une baleine; **to l. s.o. out of court,** se moquer des prétentions de qn.

►**laugh down** *vtsep* **to l. down a proposal,** tourner une proposition en ridicule.

►**laugh off** *vtsep* **he laughed the matter off,** il tourna la chose en plaisanterie.

laughable ['lɑːfəb(ə)l] *adj* risible, comique, ridicule; (*offre*) dérisoire.

laughably ['lɑːfəblɪ] *adv* risiblement; (*easy*) ridiculement.

laughing ['lɑːfɪŋ] **1** *adj* (*face*) riant; (*person, eyes, expression*) rieur; **in a l. mood,** d'humeur à rire; **I'm in no l. mood,** je n'ai pas le cœur à rire; **it's no l. matter,** il n'y a pas de quoi rire; **l. gas,** gaz hilarant; **l. hyena,** hyène rieuse; **l. jackass,** (*bird*) dacélo *m*; **l. stock,** (objet *m* de) risée *f*; **to make a l. stock of oneself,** se faire moquer de soi; **to be a l. stock,** être la risée de tous; **to make s.o. a l. stock,** couvrir qn de ridicule; **to make s.o. the l. stock of the village,** faire de qn la risée du village. **2** *n* rires *mpl*; **we could hear the sound of l.,** nous entendions des rires.

laughingly ['lɑːfɪŋlɪ] *adv* **(a)** (*to say*) en riant; **(b) that's l. called art,** on appelle ça de l'art.

laughter ['lɑːftər] *n* rire(s) *m(pl)*; **peals of l.,** éclats *mpl* de rire; **to burst into loud l.,** partir en forts éclats de rire; **to cause l.,** provoquer *ou* exciter les rires *ou* l'hilarité; **there was l. at her words,** ses mots produisirent le rire; **he made us cry with l.,** il nous a fait rire aux larmes; *F* **to split one's sides with l.,** crever *ou* mourir de rire; **uncontrollable fit of l.,** fou rire.

launch¹ [lɔːntʃ] *n Nau* chaloupe *f*; **motor l.,** vedette *f*.

launch² *n* (*of ship, missile, new product etc*) lancement *m*; **l. pad,** (*for rocket etc*) plateforme *f* de lancement; **l. party,** réception *f* (pour le lancement d'un produit); **l. vehicle,** (*for rocket*) véhicule *m* de lancement, lanceur *m*.

launch³ **1** *vt Nau* lancer (*un navire, une torpille*); *Nau* mettre (*un navire*) à l'eau *ou* à la mer; lancer (*qn, une affaire, une enquête, un nouveau produit*); *Mil* déclencher (*une offensive*); **once he is launched on the subject,** une fois lancé sur le sujet. **2** *vi* **to l. into abuse of s.o.,** se répandre en invectives contre qn; **to l. into a story,** se lancer dans une histoire.

►**launch out** *vi* **(a)** (*spend money*) se lancer dans la dépense; **let's l. out and do ...,** lançons-nous et faisons ...; **(b) to l. out on an enterprise,** se lancer dans une affaire; **to l. out on one's own,** (*in business*) faire cavalier seul.

launcher ['lɔːntʃər] *n* appareil *m ou* dispositif *m* de lancement; lanceur *m* (*de projectiles*); rampe *f ou* plateforme *f* de lancement (*de missiles*); *Av* catapulte *f* de lancement (*d'avions*); *Mil* **grenade l.,** lance-grenades *m inv* (à fusil); **rocket l.,** lance-fusées *m inv*.

launching ['lɔːntʃɪŋ] *n Nau* lancement *m*, mise *f* à l'eau (*d'un navire*); mise à l'eau (*d'une embarcation*); lancement (*d'une torpille, d'un projectile, d'une fusée*); **l. cradle,** berceau *m* de lancement; *Com Fin* lancement (*d'une affaire,* *d'un emprunt etc*); *Mil* déclenchement *m*, lancement (*d'une attaque, d'une offensive*); **l. pad** *or* **platform,** plateforme *f* de lancement (*de fusées, de missiles*); **l. ramp,** rampe *f* de lancement; **l. site,** aire *f* de lancement; (*centre*) base *f ou* complexe *m ou* station *f* de lancement (*de fusées, de missiles*); *Av* **l. catapult,** catapulte *f* de lancement.

launder ['lɔːndər] *vt* blanchir (*le linge*); *Fig* **to l. money,** blanchir de l'argent.

Launderette ® [lɔːndə'ret] *n Br* laverie *f* automatique.

laundering ['lɔːndərɪŋ] *n* (*of clothes*) blanchissage *m*; *Fig* (*of money*) blanchiment *m*.

laundress ['lɔːndres] *n* blanchisseuse *f*.

laundrette [lɔːn'dret] *n Br* laverie *f* automatique.

Laundromat ® ['lɔːndrəʊmæt] *n Am* laverie *f* automatique.

laundry ['lɔːndrɪ] *n* **(a)** blanchisserie *f*; (*in house*) *& Can* buanderie *f*; **to send sth to the l.,** envoyer qch à la blanchisserie; **(b)** (*clothes*) lessive *f*; (*clean*) linge blanchi; (*dirty*) linge à blanchir; **to do the l.,** faire la lessive; **l. basket,** panier *m* à linge; **l. list,** liste *f* de blanchissage; **l. room,** (*in house, apartment block*) buanderie *f*.

laureate ['lɔːrɪət] **1** *adj* lauréat; *Br* **Poet L.** (*pl* **Poets Laureate**), poète lauréat (*dignité conférée par la Couronne*). **2** *n* lauréat, -ate.

laurel ['lɒrəl] *n* (*tree*) laurier *m*; **l. wreath,** couronne *f* de lauriers; **crowned with laurel(s),** couronné *ou* ceint de lauriers; **to win laurels,** cueillir *ou* moissonner des lauriers; *Fig* **to rest on one's laurels,** se reposer sur ses lauriers; *Fig* **he must look to his laurels,** il est en passe d'être éclipsé.

lav [læv] *n Br F* petit coin, cabinets *mpl*.

lava ['lɑːvə] *n* lave *f*; **l. stream** *or* **flow,** coulée *f* de lave.

lavabo, *pl* **-os** [lə'veɪbəʊ, -əʊz] *n Rel* lavabo *m*.

lavatory ['lævətrɪ] *n* (*room*) cabinets *mpl*; (*installation*) ensemble *m* W.-C.; **public l.,** W.-C. *mpl*, toilette(s) *f(pl)*; *Br* **l. paper,** papier *m* hygiénique; **l. humour,** humour *m* scatologique; **l. pan,** cuvette *f* de W.-C.

lavender ['lævɪndər] **1** *n* (*shrub*) lavande *f*; **oil of l.,** essence *f* de lavande; **l. water,** eau *f* de lavande. **2** *adj* (*colour*) lavande *inv*.

lavish¹ ['lævɪʃ] *adj* **(a)** (*person*) prodigue (**in, of,** de); **to be l. in one's praise,** prodiguer des louanges, se répandre en éloges; **l. in spending,** prodigue de son argent; **(b)** (*thing*) somptueux; (*meal*) plantureux; (*installation*) princier; **to live in a l. style,** mener la vie à grandes guides; **l. spending,** dépenses folles.

lavish² *vt* prodiguer (*son argent*); **to l. sth on s.o.,** prodiguer qch à qn; **to l. praise on s.o.,** se répandre en éloges sur qn; **to l. care on s.o.,** prodiguer des soins à qn.

lavishly ['lævɪʃlɪ] *adv* **(a)** avec prodigalité; **to spend l.,** dépenser de l'argent à profusion; être prodigue de son argent; **(b)** somptueusement.

lavishness ['lævɪʃnɪs] *n* **(a)** (*of praise*) prodigalité *f*; **(b)** somptuosité *f*.

law [lɔː] *n* **(a)** (*rule*) loi *f*; *Phil* principe *m*; *Parl* **to pass/repeal a l.,** voter/abroger une loi; **labour laws,** législation *f* du travail; **there's no l. against it,** aucune loi ne l'interdit; *Phys* **the laws of gravity,** les lois de la pesanteur; *Econ* **l. of diminishing returns,** loi des rendements décroissants; **l. of supply and demand,** loi de l'offre et de la demande; **l. of averages,** loi des probabilités; **by the l. of averages,** par la loi des probabilités;

(b) (*set of rules*) **the l.,** la loi; *Sp* **the off-side l.,** les règles *ou* le règlement du hors-jeu; **it's the l.,** c'est la loi; **to carry out the l.,** appliquer la loi; **to keep/break the l.,** respecter *ou* observer/enfreindre la loi; **l. and order,** ordre public; **custom that has become l.,** usage qui a passé en loi; **to have the force of l.,** avoir force de loi; **his word is l.,** sa parole a force de loi; **to lay down the l.,** faire la loi (*à qn*) (**about,** sur); **he thinks he's above the l.,** il se croit tout permis; **to be a l. unto oneself,** n'en faire qu'à sa tête; **to have one l. for the rich and another for the poor,** avoir deux poids et deux mesures; **Divine l.,** la loi divine; *Rel Hist* **the L., the l. of Moses,** la loi mosaïque;

(c) *Jur* droit *m*; **civil l.,** = droit civil; **common l.,** (*as opposed to statute law*) droit coutumier; (*of general application*) droit civil; **criminal l.,** droit pénal *ou* criminel, législation criminelle; **commercial l.,** droit commercial, code *m* de commerce; **l. of contract,** = droit des obligations; **Roman l.,** droit romain; **case l.,** droit jurisprudentiel; **judgment quashed on a point of l.,** arrêt cassé pour vice de forme; **to read** *or* **study l.,** étudier le droit, faire son droit; **l. student,** étudiant, -ante en droit; **Bachelor/Doctor of Laws,** = licencié(e)/docteur en droit; **to practise l.,** exercer une profession juridique; **l. officer,** conseiller *m* juridique; *Br* **l. lord,** membre *m* juriste de la Chambre des Lords;

(d) (*justice*) **court of l.,** cour *f* de justice; tribunal *m*, -aux; **to go to l.,** avoir recours à *ou* recourir à la justice; *Sl* **I'll have the l. on you!,** je vais vous poursuivre en justice!; **to hand s.o. over to the l.,** remettre qn à la justice; **action at l.,** action *f* en justice; **to be at l.,** être en procès; **to take the l. into one's own hands,** se faire justice soi-même; *Admin Com* **l. department,** bureau *m ou* service *m* du contentieux, le contentieux; **l. costs,** frais *mpl* de procédure; *F* **the l.,** la police; (*police officer*) un policier, un flic; **arm of the l.,** représentant *m* de la loi.

law-abiding ['lɔːəbaɪdɪŋ] *adj* respectueux des lois, qui observe la loi; **l.-a. people,** amis *mpl* de l'ordre; **I'm just a l.-a. citizen,** je ne suis qu'un citoyen obéissant aux lois.

lawbook ['lɔːbʊk] *n* livre *m* de droit.

lawbreaker ['lɔːbreɪkər] *n* transgresseur *m* de la loi.

lawbreaking ['lɔːbreɪkɪŋ] *n* infraction *f* à la loi.

lawcourt ['lɔːkɔːt] *n* cour *f* de justice; tribunal *m*.

lawful ['lɔːfʊl] *adj* **(a)** (*owner, activities*) légal, -aux; **l. trade,** commerce licite; **(b)** (*droit, union, femme, enfant etc*) légitime; (*contrat*) valide; **l. share** (*of inheritance*) portion virile; **to go about one's l. business,** vaquer à ses occupations personnelles; **(c)** (*revendication etc*) juste.

lawfully ['lɔːfʊlɪ] *adv* légalement, légitimement.

lawgiver ['lɔːgɪvər] *n* législateur *m*.

lawless ['lɔːlɪs] *adj* **(a)** sans loi; (*temps*) d'anarchie; **(b)** (*uncontrolled*) sans frein; **l. passions,** passions effrénées.

lawlessness ['lɔːlɪsnɪs] *n* dérèglement *m*, désordre *m*, licence *f*; (*of times*) anarchie *f*.

lawmaker ['lɔːmeɪkər] *n* législateur *m*.

lawn¹ [lɔːn] *n Tex* batiste *f*; (*fine*) linon *m*.

lawn² *n* pelouse *f*, (parterre *m* de) gazon *m*; **do not walk on the l.,** ne pas marcher sur la pelouse; **l. fertilizer** *or* **food,** engrais *m* à gazon; **l. sprinkler,** arrosoir *m* de pelouse; tourniquet arroseur; **to mow** *or* **cut the lawn,** tondre le gazon; **l. tennis,** tennis *m*.

lawnmower ['lɔːnməʊər] *n* tondeuse *f* (à gazon).

Lawrence ['lɒrəns] *n* Laurent *m*.

lawsuit ['lɔːs(j)uːt] *n* procès *m*, action *f* judiciaire; **to bring a l. against s.o.,** intenter un procès à qn.

lawyer ['lɔːjər] *n* (*provides advice, appears in court*) avocat *m*, avoué *m*; (*authenticates documents*) notaire *m*; (*in company*) conseiller *m* juridique; **we'll have to see a l.,** il nous faudra consulter un avocat.

lax [læks] *adj* **(a)** (*conduct, principles*) relâché; (*person*) négligent, inexact; (*discipline*) lâche; **l. morals,** morale *f* facile *ou* peu sévère; **to be l. in (carrying out) one's duties,** ne pas toujours observer ses devoirs; **(b)** (*vague, imprecise*) vague; **l. use of a word,** emploi peu précis d'un mot; emploi abusif d'un mot; **(c)** (*limp*) mou, *f* molle; **(d)** *Med* (*ventre*) lâche, relâché.

laxative ['læksətɪv] *adj & n Med* laxatif *m*.

laxity ['læksɪtɪ] **, laxness** ['læksnɪs] *n* **(a)** relâchement *m* (*des mœurs, de la discipline*); **l. in one's duties,** inexactitude *f* à remplir ses devoirs; **(b)** vague *m*, imprécision *f*, peu *m* d'exactitude (*de langage etc*).

lay¹ [leɪ] *n* **(a) l. of the land,** configuration *f ou* disposition *f* du pays *ou* du terrain; **(b)** *Sl* **she's an easy l.,** c'est une môme facile *ou* une Marie couche-toi-là; **to be a good l.,** bien baiser.

lay² *v* (*pt & pp* **laid** [leɪd]) **1** *vt* **(a)** (*place horizontally*) coucher; (*of wind, rain*) coucher, abattre (*le blé*); *Sewing* remplier (*un ourlet etc*); **to l. s.o./sth flat,** coucher *ou* étendre qn/qch (par terre); **to l. s.o. flat,** (*with punch*) terrasser qn, abattre qn; **laid low by sickness,** terrassé par la maladie;

(b) (*cause to subside*) abattre (*la poussière etc*); exorciser, conjurer (*un fantôme*); **to l. a fear,** écarter un sujet d'inquiétude;

(c) (*deposit*) mettre, placer, poser (**sth on sth,** qch sur qch); **to l. one's hand on s.o.'s shoulder,** mettre la main sur l'épaule de qn; **to l. a book on the table,** poser un livre sur la table; **to have nowhere to l. one's head,** ne pas avoir où reposer la tête; **to l. s.o. to rest,** enterrer qn; **if you l. a finger on her,** si tu touches à un cheveu de sa tête;

(d) (*of hen etc*) pondre (*un œuf*);

(e) *Sp* faire (*un pari*); parier, miser (*une somme*);

(f) (*place*) **to l. a ship alongside the quay,** faire accoster un navire le long du quai;

(g) (*place*) soumettre (*une question, une demande*) (**before s.o.,** devant qn); **he laid before me all the facts,** il me présenta tous les faits; *Jur* **to l. a complaint,** déposer une plainte, porter plainte; **to l. a matter before the court,** saisir le tribunal d'une affaire; **to l. information,**

présenter une information;

(h) (*impose*) imposer (*une peine, une obligation*) (**upon s.o.,** à qn); infliger (*une amende etc*); **to l. a tax on sth,** frapper qch d'un impôt;

(i) (*dispose, arrange*) poser, jeter, asseoir (*des fondements*); ranger (*des briques*); poser (*une voie ferrée*); poser, immerger (*un câble*); verser (*le béton*) en place; poser, tendre (*un tapis*); préparer (*le feu*); *Nau* poser, mouiller (*une mine*); dresser, tendre (*un piège*); disposer, dresser, placer, tendre (*une embuscade*); former, faire (*un projet*); former, ourdir, tramer, concerter (*un complot*); **to l. the table,** mettre la table; **to l. the table for three,** mettre la table pour trois personnes, mettre trois couverts;

(j) *Sl* **to l. a girl,** s'envoyer une fille; **to get laid,** baiser.

2 *vi* **(a)** *Sl* (*incorrectly used for* **lie**) **to l. in bed,** rester couché;

(b) (*of bird*) pondre;

(c) *Sl* **to l. about one,** frapper de tous côtés.

lay³ [leɪ] *adj* **(a)** laïque; *Rel* **l. brother,** frère lai, frère convers; **l. sister,** sœur laie, sœur converse; **l. preacher** *or* **reader,** prédicateur laïque; **to the l. mind it seems complicated,** aux yeux du profane cela est compliqué; **(b)** *Art* **l. figure,** mannequin *m* (*en bois etc*).

lay⁴ *n* **(a)** (*song*) lai *m*, chanson *f*; **(b)** (*poem*) poème *m* (lyrique).

▶**lay aside** *vtsep* se dépouiller de (*ses préjugés, sa réserve*); abandonner, mettre de côté (*un travail*); mettre (*un papier*) de côté; mettre (*de l'argent*) de côté.

▶**lay away** *vtsep Am* mettre (*de l'argent, qch*) de côté.

▶**lay back** *vtsep* retourner, rabattre (*qch*); (*of horse*) rabattre, coucher (*les oreilles*).

▶**lay by** *vtsep* mettre (*qch*) de côté; réserver (*qch*); **to l. money by,** mettre de l'argent en réserve (*pour l'avenir*), mettre de l'argent de côté.

▶**lay down 1** *vtsep* **(a)** (*deposit*) déposer, poser (*qch*); mettre bas, rendre (*les armes*); *Cards* étaler, abattre (*son jeu*); **(b)** (*place horizontally*) coucher, étendre (*qn*); **to l. oneself down,** se coucher; **(c)** (*abandon*) quitter, se démettre de, résigner (*ses fonctions*); abdiquer (*le pouvoir*); **to l. down one's life,** sacrifier sa vie, faire le sacrifice de sa vie (**for,** pour); **(d)** *Nau* mettre (*un navire*) en chantier *ou* sur cale; **(e)** (*establish*) poser, imposer, établir (*un principe, une règle*); fixer (*des conditions*); spécifier (*des fonctions*); indiquer, prescrire (*une ligne de conduite*); **to l. down that ...,** stipuler que ...; **(f)** (*store*) mettre (*du vin*) en cave *ou* sur chantier. **2** *vi Sl* = **LIE DOWN.**

▶**lay in** *vtsep* faire provision de, s'approvisionner de (*qch*); **to l. in provisions,** faire des provisions; **we've laid in plenty of food for the weekend,** nous avons prévu beaucoup de nourriture pour le week-end; *Com* **to l. in goods** *or* **stock,** emmagasiner des marchandises.

▶**lay into** *vipo F* **to l. into s.o.,** (*hit*) rosser qn; (*verbally*) passer un savon à qn.

▶**lay off 1** *vtsep* **(a)** licencier; (*temporarily*) renvoyer temporairement (*des ouvriers*); **(b)** *Nau* **to l. off a bearing,** porter un relèvement (*sur la carte*); **(c)** (*in insurance*) **to l. off a risk,** effectuer une réassurance; *Horseracing etc* **to l. off a bet,** faire la contrepartie d'un pari; **(d)** *Sp* **to l. the ball off for s.o.,** placer le ballon en bonne position pour qn. **2** *vipo* **(a)** *F* (*abstain from*) s'abstenir de; **the doctor advised him to l. off drink/cigarettes,** le médecin lui a conseillé d'arrêter de boire/fumer; **(b)** *F* (*leave alone*) ficher la paix à qn. **3** *vi* **(a)** *Sl* **l. off!,** fiche-moi la paix!; **l. off him!,** fiche-lui la paix!; **(b)** *Nau* rester au large.

▶**lay on** *vtsep* **(a)** *Br* installer (*le gaz, l'électricité*); amener (*l'eau, le gaz*) (*dans la maison*); *F* arranger, préparer, organiser (*qch*); *F* **I'll l. on the drinks,** je me chargerai de la boisson; *F* **I'll l. on a car for you at the station,** je vais vous faire chercher en voiture à la gare; **the hotel also lays on entertainment,** l'hôtel organise également des spectacles; **(b)** étendre, coucher, appliquer (*un enduit etc*); *Art* **to l. on the paint,** peindre dans la pâte *ou* en pleine pâte; *F* **to l. it on (thick)** *or* **with a trowel,** flatter (*qn*) grossièrement; (*exaggerate*) exagérer, y aller un peu fort.

▶**lay out** *vtsep* **(a)** arranger, disposer (*des objets*); étaler, déployer (*des marchandises*); servir (*un repas*); **(b)** faire la toilette de (*un mort*); *F* étendre (*qn*) d'un coup, coucher (*qn*) par terre *ou* sur le carreau; *Boxing* envoyer (*l'adversaire*) au tapis; **(c) to l. out money,** dépenser *ou* débourser de l'argent; **(d)** (*plan, design*) tracer (*un jardin etc*); (*physically*) disposer; *Typ* mettre (*un texte*) en page.

▶**lay over** *vi Am* (*during journey*) faire (une) halte.

▶**lay up** *vtsep* **(a)** (*store*) mettre (*qch*) en réserve; accumuler, amasser (*des provisions etc*); **(b)** (*take out of service*) désarmer, déséquiper (*un navire*); mettre (*un navire*) en rade; mettre (*une voiture*) sur cales; **(c) to be laid up,** être alité, être obligé de garder le lit.

layabout ['leɪəbaʊt] *n F* paresseux *m*, vaurien *m*.

lay-by ['leɪbaɪ] *n* **(a)** *Br* (*on road*) bande *f* de stationnement; (*on motorway*) = aire *f* (*de stationnement*); **(b)** *Rail* voie *f* de garage.

layer¹ ['leɪər] *n* **(a)** couche *f* (*de peinture etc*); lit *m* (*de fumier*); *Constr* assise *f*, lit (*de béton, de briques etc*); *Geol* couche, strate *f* (*de roches etc*); *Culin* **l. cake,** gâteau fourré (*à la crème*); **the upper layers of the atmosphere,** les couches supérieures de l'atmosphère; **Heaviside l.,** couche de Heaviside; *El* **conducting l.,** couche conductrice; **magnetic l.,** feuillet *m* magnétique; *Phot etc* **sensitive l.,** couche sensible; **(b)** (*hen etc*) **good l.,** bonne pondeuse; **(c)** (*person*) poseur *m* (*de tuyaux, de rails etc*); **l. out,** dessinateur *m* (*de jardins*); (*of the dead*) personne qui fait la toilette des morts; **(d)** (*of plant*) marcotte *f*.

layer² *vt* **(a)** poser *ou* disposer en couches; dégrader (*les cheveux*); **I'd like my hair trimmed and layered,** j'aimerais une coupe d'entretien et un dégradé; **(b)** marcotter (*un rosier etc*).

layette [leɪ'et] *n* layette *f*.

laying ['leɪɪŋ] **1** *adj* **l. hen,** poule pondeuse. **2** *n* **(a)** pose *f* (*de rails, de tuyaux, de câbles etc*); assise *f* (*de fondements*); immersion *f* (*d'un câble sous-marin*); mouillage *m* (*d'une mine*); **(b)** ponte *f* (*des œufs*).

laying down *n* **(a)** établissement *m* (*d'un principe etc*); **(b)** pose *f* (*d'une canalisation, d'un câble*); mise *f* en chantier *ou* sur cale (*d'un navire*); **(c)** dépôt *m* (*des armes*).

laying in *n* emmagasinage *m* (*de marchandises*); approvisionnement *m*.

laying off *n* **(a)** licenciement *m* (*de la main-d'œuvre*); **(b)** (*in insurance*) réassurance *f*.

laying on *n* **(a)** *Rel* **l. on of hands,** imposition *f* des mains; **(b)** *Br* installation *f* (*de l'eau etc*).

laying out *n* toilette *f* (*d'un mort*).

laying up *n* désarmement *m* (*d'un navire*); mise sur cales (*d'une voiture*).

layman, *pl* **-men** ['leɪmən] *n* **(a)** *Rel* laïque *m*; **(b)** personne *f* qui n'est pas du métier, profane *m*.

lay-off ['leɪɒf] *n Ind* licenciement *m* (temporaire).

layout ['leɪaʊt] *n* **(a)** (*plan*) tracé *m* (*d'une construction etc*); dessin *m* (*d'un jardin*); **(b)** (*arrangement*) (*of house, building etc*) plan *m*, agencement *m* des pièces; agencement *ou* disposition *f* des pièces (*dans un ensemble mécanique*); schéma *m* de montage; *Typ* mise *f* en page (*d'un texte etc*); **(c)** étude *f* (*pour la construction d'une machine etc*); *Aut* **chassis l.,** étude de châssis.

layover ['leɪəʊvər] *n Am* escale *f*.

layperson ['leɪpɜːsən] = **LAYMAN.**

laywoman, *pl* **-women** ['leɪwʊmən, -wɪmɪn] *n* **(a)** *Rel* laïque *f*; **(b)** femme *f* qui n'est pas du métier, profane *f*.

Lazarus ['læzərəs] *n Bible* Lazare *m*.

laze [leɪz] *vi* **to l. (about, around),** paresser, fainéanter; **you've spent the whole morning just lazing around,** tu as passé la matinée entière à traînasser; **let's just l. on the beach,** allons simplement faire le lézard sur la plage; **to l. in bed,** traînasser au lit; faire la grasse matinée; **to l. away a couple of hours in the sun,** passer quelques heures à paresser au soleil.

lazily ['leɪzɪlɪ] *adv* paresseusement; (*vivre*) en paresseux.

laziness ['leɪzɪnɪs] *n* paresse *f*, fainéantise *f*.

lazy ['leɪzɪ] *adj* **(a)** paresseux, fainéant; **a l. person,** un paresseux, une paresseuse; **a l. smile,** un sourire nonchalant; **I feel too l. to do it,** je n'ai pas l'énergie de le faire; *Am* **l. Susan,** plateau tournant (*placé au milieu de la table*); **(b)** (*moments*) de paresse; **we spent a l. afternoon in the garden,** nous avons passé l'après-midi à paresser dans le jardin.

lazybones ['leɪzɪbəʊnz] *n F* paresseux, -euse, fainéant, -ante.

lb (*abbr* **libra**) livre, lb.

LBO [elbiː'əʊ] *n Com abbr* **leveraged buy-out.**

lbw [elbiː'dʌb(ə)ljuː] *Cr abbr* **leg before wicket.**

LCD [elsiː'diː] *n Comptr abbr* **liquid crystal display.**

lea [liː] *n Lit* prairie *f*, pâturage *m*.

L.E.A. [eliː'eɪ] *n abbr* **Local Education Authority.**

leach [liːtʃ] **1** *vt* filtrer (*un liquide*); lessiver (*du minerai, de l'écorce*); **to l. away** *or* **out salts,** extraire des sels par lessivage. **2** *vi* (*of liquid*) filtrer (**through,** à travers).

lead¹ [liːd] **(a)** (*in race etc*) **to take the l.,** prendre la direction; (*in race*) prendre la tête; **to take the l. over s.o.,** prendre le pas *ou* les devants sur qn; **to go into the l. from s.o.,** (*in race*) prendre le commandement aux dépens de qn; **to move into the l.,** aller prendre la tête, se lancer vers la tête (*de la course*); **to have a l. of 10 metres,** avoir une avance de 10 mètres; **she's hanging on to her l.,** elle s'accroche en tête; **he's opened up a tremendous l.,** il a pris avance considérable; **to be in the l.,** *Sp & Fig* être en tête; **to lose one's l.,** *Sp & Fig* ne plus être en tête;

(b) (*example*) **to follow s.o.'s l.,** suivre l'exemple de qn;

(c) (*clue*) indice *m*; **the police have no leads,** la police n'a aucune piste; **to give s.o. a l.,** mettre qn sur la voie;

(d) (*in cards*) primauté *f*; **to have the l.,** jouer le premier; **your l.!,** à vous de jouer!; **to follow the l. in clubs,** fournir du trèfle;

(e) *Th* premier rôle; **juvenile l.,** jeune premier, jeune première; **male l.,** premier rôle masculin;

(f) (*for dog etc*) laisse *f*; **dogs must be kept on a l.,** les chiens doivent être tenus en laisse; **l. reins,** (*harness*) grandes guides;

(g) *El* câble *m ou* branchement *m* de canalisation; amenée *f* de courant; fil *m* électrique;

(h) *Journ* (*main story*) **it'll be the l. in tomorrow's papers,** ce sera à la une des journaux demain;

(i) **l. time,** (*to production*) délai *m* de réalisation *ou* de production; (*to delivery*) délai de livraison.

lead² [liːd] *v* (*pt & pp* **led** [led]) **1** *vt* **(a)** (*show the way*) mener, conduire, guider (**s.o. to a place,** qn à un endroit); **she led them to safety,** elle les a conduits en lieu sûr; *Rel* **l. us not into temptation,** ne nous soumets pas à la tentation; **to be led astray,** se laisser entraîner; *Jur* **to l. a witness,** poser des questions tendancieuses à un témoin; **to l. the way,** marcher le premier *ou* en tête; **to l. a team to victory,** mener une équipe à la victoire; **to l. the conversation back to a subject,** ramener la conversation sur un sujet;

(b) (*guide*) conduire, guider (*un aveugle etc*) par la main; mener (*un cheval*) par la bride; tenir (*un chien*) en laisse; **he is easily led,** il va comme on le mène;

(c) (*cause*) amener, porter (**s.o. to do sth,** qn à faire qch); **that leads me to believe that ...,** cela me mène à croire que ...; **I was led to the conclusion that ...,** je fus amené à conclure que ...; **what led you to apply for this job?,** qu'est-ce qui vous a conduit *ou* amené à vous présenter pour ce poste?;

(d) mener (*une vie heureuse, malheureuse*); **to l. s.o. a dog's life,** faire une vie de chien à qn;

(e) (*direct*) mener (*une équipe, la danse*); commander (*une armée*); **leading his troops,** à la tête de ses troupes; **to l. a party,** être chef de parti; **to l. an orchestra,** conduire un orchestre;

(f) (*be ahead of*) **to l. the field,** mener; *Fig* **to l. the field in ...,** être au premier rang en matière de ...; **to l. s.o. by eight points,** mener qn par huit points; **she leads the class in maths,** elle est la première de sa classe en maths; **we l. the world in ...,** nous sommes les leaders mondiaux de ...;

(g) *Cards* **to l. a card,** entamer *ou* attaquer d'une carte; **to l. clubs,** jouer *ou* attaquer trèfle;

(h) amener (*de l'eau à un endroit*); faire passer (*un cordage à travers une poulie*).

2 *vi* **(a)** (*of road*) mener, conduire (**to,** à); **road that leads to the town,** route qui mène *ou* va à la ville; **door that leads into the garden,** porte qui communique avec le jardin *ou* qui donne accès au jardin; **to l. to a good result,** aboutir à un bon résultat, produire un heureux effet; **to l. to a discovery,** conduire *ou* aboutir à une découverte; **drinking too much can l. to violence,** l'excès d'alcool peut conduire à la violence; **one thing leads to another,** une chose en amène une autre; **to l. to nothing,** n'aboutir *ou* ne mener à rien; **action which led to criticism,** action qui a motivé des critiques;

(b) *Journ* **to l. with,** (*of newspaper*) titrer en première page, faire ses gros titres *ou* sa première page sur;

(c) (*in competition, race etc*) mener;

(d) (*barrister*) être l'avocat principal (*dans un procès*); **he led for the prosecution,** avocat principal, il dirigea l'accusation;

(e) *Cards* ouvrir le jeu; jouer le premier, entamer.

lead³ [led] *n* **(a)** plomb *m*; **l. ore,** minerai *m* de plomb; **white l.,** (*ore*) plomb blanc; *Ch* blanc *m* de plomb; **l. content,** indice *m* de plomb (*dans un carburant*); **pig l.,** plomb en saumon; **l. wire,** fil *m* de plomb; **l. glass,** verre *m* de *ou* au plomb; **l. pipe,** tuyau *m* de plomb; *Br Constr* **roof leads,** plombs de couverture; **window leads,** plombs de vitrail *ou* de vitraux; **l. shot,** grenaille *f* de plomb, petit plomb; *Med* **l. poisoning,** intoxication saturnine *ou* par le plomb; *F* **they pumped him full of lead,** ils l'ont truffé *ou* farci de plomb; **(b)** mine *f* (*de crayon*); **l. pencil,** crayon *m* à la mine de plomb; **(c)** *Nau* (plomb *m* de) sonde *f*; **l. line,** ligne *f* de sonde; *F* **to swing the l.,** tirer au flanc; **(d)** *Typ* interligne *f*.

lead⁴ *vt* (**leaded** ['ledɪd]; **leading** ['ledɪŋ]) **(a)** plomber (*un toit*); plomber (*une ligne, un filet*); enchâsser (*des vitraux*) dans les plombs; **leaded windows,** vitres plombées; **(b)** *Typ* interligner (*des lignes de composition*).

►**lead away** *vtsep* emmener (*un prisonnier etc*).

►**lead off 1** *vipo* **(a)** commencer, débuter (**with,** par); **(b)** entamer les débats; jouer le premier; *Billiards* donner l'acquit; (*at dance*) ouvrir le bal; **who's going to l. off the discussion?,** qui va amorcer la conversation?; **to l. off an attack,** lancer une attaque. **2** *vtsep* emmener (*un prisonnier etc*).

►**lead on 1** *vipo* **to l. s.o. on to talk,** encourager qn à parler; **try and l. him on to the subject of football,** essaie de l'amener sur le thème du football *ou F* le brancher sur le football; *F* **to l. s.o. on,** tromper qn, duper qn. **2** *vi* **l. on!,** en avant!

►**lead up 1** *vi* **to l. up to a subject,** amener un sujet; **to l. up to the climax,** amener le dénouement; **I couldn't see what he was leading up to,** je ne voyais pas où il voulait en venir; **the period leading up to the war,** la période précédant la guerre; **there's a path leading up to the ski lift,** il y a un chemin menant au téléski. **2** *vtsep* **he led us up a spiral staircase,** il nous a fait monter un escalier en spirale.

lead-bearing ['ledbeərɪŋ] *adj* plombifère.

leaded [ledɪd] *adj* (*window*) plombé; **l. petrol,** essence *f* au plomb.

leaden ['led(ə)n] *adj* de plomb; (*teint*) plombé; **l. sky,** ciel *m* de plomb; **l.-eyed,** aux yeux ternes; **l. footed,** à la démarche pesante; **l. limbs,** membres inertes.

leader ['liːdər] *n* **(a)** (*of expedition etc*) chef *m*; *Mil* commandant *m* (*de compagnie*); meneur *m* (*d'une émeute*); *Br Mus* premier violon; *US Mus* chef d'orchestre; (*of a group, organization*) chef; *Br Jur* avocat principal (*dans une cause*); **to be a born l.,** être fait pour donner des ordres *ou* commander; **L. of the House of Commons,** chef de la majorité à la Chambre des Communes; *Sp* **team l.,** chef d'équipe; **a major group, l. in its field,** groupe important, leader *m* dans sa branche;

(b) (*in race*) **he's still the l.,** il mène toujours; **the three leaders,** les trois premiers;

(c) (*in horse team*) cheval *m* de tête; (*in dog team*) chien *m* de tête; **the leaders,** l'attelage *m* de devant;

(d) *Agr* conduit *m*; amorce *f* (*de bande magnétique, de film*); *Constr* conduite *f* d'eau; (*of plant*) pousse terminale; bourgeon terminal; *Journ* article principal; *Br* éditorial *m*, -aux; **l. writer,** éditorialiste *mf*; *Com* **loss l.,** produit *m* d'appel (vendu à perte).

leadership ['liːdəʃɪp] *n* **(a)** conduite *f*; (*shown by s.o.*) qualités *fpl* de chef; **the organization lacks l.,** l'organisation n'est pas dirigée correctement; **no one showed any l.,** personne n'a fait preuve d'aucun sens du commandement; **to be under s.o.'s l.,** être sous la conduite de qn; **(b)** *Mil* commandement *m*; fonctions *fpl* de chef; direction *f* (*d'un parti etc*).

lead-free [led'friː] **1** *adj* (*petrol, paint*) sans plomb. **2** *n* (*petrol*) essence *f* sans plomb.

lead-in ['liːdɪn] *n* **(a)** (*introduction*) *& Mus* introduction *f*; **(b)** *El Tel etc* entrée *f* (*de câble, Rad de poste*); **(c)** *Rad etc* descente *f* d'antenne; **l.-in groove,** (*on record*) sillon initial (*de disque*); *Av* guidage *m* (*d'un avion vers une piste d'atterrissage etc*).

leading¹ ['liːdɪŋ] **1** *adj* **(a)** (*chief*) premier, principal, -aux; important; **the l. statesmen of Europe,** les hommes d'État dirigeants de l'Europe; **a l. shareholder,** un des principaux actionnaires; **he's one of Britain's l. novelists,** il est l'un des romanciers les plus en vue de Grande Bretagne; *Journ* **l. article,** *see* **LEADER (d)**; *Cin Th* **l. role** *or* **part,** premier rôle; *Cin Th* **l. man** *or* **lady,** premier rôle; vedette *f*; *Cin Th* **who's going to be your l. man?,** qui sera ton partenaire masculin *ou* ta co-vedette masculine?; **she's a l. light in local politics,** c'est une personnalité très influente *ou* elle a un rôle très influent au niveau de la politique locale; **to play a l. role in a matter,** jouer un rôle prépondérant dans une affaire;

(b) (*in front*) (*voiture*) de tête; *Nau* **the l. ship,** le chef de file; *Mil* **l. patrol,** patrouille *f* de tête; **l. axle** *or* **wheels,** (*of vehicle*) essieu porteur d'avant; *Av* **l. edge,** bord *m* d'attaque (*de l'aile*); **to be on the l. edge of technology,** être à la pointe de la technologie; **l. edge technology,** technologie *f* de pointe; *El* **l. current,** courant déphasé en avant; *Cards* **l. card,** première carte; **l. shoot,** (*of plant*) pousse principale *ou* terminale.

(c) l. question, *Jur* question posée au témoin de manière à suggérer la réponse; *Fig* question tendancieuse.

2 *n* **(a)** conduite *f*, menage *m* (*de chevaux etc*); **l. rein,** (*for horse*) longe *f*, plate-longe *f*, *pl* plates-longes; **l. reins** *or Am* **strings,** (*for child*) rênes *fpl*;

(b) *Mil etc* conduite *f*, commandement *m* (*de la troupe, d'une unité*); direction *f* (*d'une entreprise etc*).

leading² ['lediŋ] *n Typ* interligne *f*.

lead-out ['li:daʊt] *n El Tel* sortie *f* (*de fils etc*); **l.-o. groove,** sillon *m* de sortie (*d'un disque*).

leadsman, *pl* **-men** ['ledzmən] *n Nau* sondeur *m*.

leadwork ['ledwɜ:k] *n Archit* plombs *mpl* (*d'un vitrail*).

leaf, *pl* **leaves** [li:f, li:vz] *n* **(a)** feuille *f* (*de plante, d'arbre*); *Bot* **l. bud,** bourgeon *m* à feuille; **l. mould,** terreau *m* de feuilles; **to put out leaves, to come into l.,** (se) feuiller; **to shed its leaves,** s'effeuiller; **in l.,** couvert de feuilles, en feuilles; **to shake like a l.,** trembler comme une feuille; **l. tobacco,** tabac *m* en feuilles; **outer l. of a cigar,** robe *f* d'un cigare; *Ent* **l. insect,** phyllie *f*; **l. cutting bee,** (abeille)-(dé)coupeuse *f* de feuilles; **l. green,** vert pré *m inv*;

(b) feuillet *m* (*de livre*); **single l.,** (*in bookbinding*) carton *m* de deux pages; **to turn over the leaves of a book,** feuilleter un livre; *Fig* **to turn over a new l.,** (*of person*) tourner la page, changer de conduite; *Fig* **to take a l. out of s.o.'s book,** prendre exemple *ou* modèle sur qn; **counterfoil and l.,** talon *m* et volant *m* (*d'un carnet de chèques etc*);

(c) feuille *f* (*d'argent, d'or etc*);

(d) battant *m*, vantail, -aux *m* (*de porte*); battant (*de contrevent*); panneau *m*, -eaux (*de paravent*); *MecE etc* obturateur *m* (*de vanne*); aile *f* (*de pignon*); lame *f*, feuille *f*, feuillet *m* (*de ressort*); **l. of a table,** (*inserted*) rallonge *f* de table; (*hinged, also* **drop l.,** *US* **fall l.**) battant de table.

►leaf through *vipo* feuilleter (*un livre*).

leaflet¹ ['li:flɪt] *n* feuillet *m* (*de papier*); *Com etc* imprimé *m ou* papillon *m* publicitaire, prospectus *m*; *Pol* tract *m*; **instruction l.,** mode *m* d'emploi.

leaflet² *vt* **to l. an area,** distribuer des prospectus dans une zone.

leafstalk ['li:fstɔ:k] *n Bot* pétiole *m*.

leafy ['li:fɪ] *adj* feuillu; couvert de feuilles; *Lit* **l. canopy,** dais *m* de feuillage *ou* de verdure.

league¹ [li:g] *n* **(a)** (*association*) ligue *f*; **everyone is in l. against them,** tout le monde est ligué *ou* s'est conjuré contre eux; **he was in l. with them,** il était de connivence avec eux; *Hist* **the L. of Nations,** la Société des Nations; *Fb* **l. matches,** matchs *mpl* de championnat (professionnels); **l. table,** tableau *m* de classement du championnat; **l. leaders,** équipe *f* en tête du championnats; **l. champions,** vainqueurs *mpl* du championnat; **(b)** (*category*) catégorie *f*; *F* **I'm not in your l., I'm not in the same l. as you,** je ne suis pas de votre espèce; (*when playing tennis, darts etc*) je ne suis pas de votre niveau; **they're not in the same l.,** ils ne sont pas du même niveau.

league² *n* (*measurement*) lieue *f*.

league³ 1 *vt* **to be leagued with s.o.,** être ligué avec qn; **to be leagued together,** être ligué, être de connivence. **2** *vi* **to l. (together),** se liguer, se conjurer (**with,** avec; **against,** contre; **in order to,** pour).

leak¹ [li:k] *n* **(a)** (*escape*) fuite *f*, écoulement *m* (*d'un liquide*); perte *f* d'eau; (*of gas*) fuite de gaz; *F* fuite (*de secrets officiels etc*); **(b)** (*entry*) infiltration *f*, rentrée *f* (*d'eau etc*); *Nau* voie *f* d'eau; **to spring a l.,** (*of ship*) faire eau, avoir une voie d'eau; (*of shoes*) prendre l'eau; **(c)** *Sl* **to have a l.,** pisser un coup.

leak² 1 *vi* (*of tank etc*) avoir une fuite, fuir; (*of ship etc*) faire eau, avoir une voie d'eau; (*of liquid*) fuir, couler; *F* (*of government official etc*) faire des révélations; **to l. (out),** (*of truth, news etc*) s'ébruiter, transpirer; **roof that leaks,** toit qui laisse entrer la pluie; **my shoes l.,** mes chaussures prennent l'eau. **2** *vt F* divulguer, laisser filtrer (*des informations etc*).

leakage ['li:kɪdʒ] *n* **(a)** (*escape*) fuite *f* (*d'eau, de gaz, d'un tonneau, de secrets officiels*); perte *f*, coulage *m* (*d'eau*); perte, fuite (*d'électricité*) (par dispersion); **(b)** (*water etc*) fuites *fpl*, pertes *fpl*, coulage *m*; **(c)** coulage *m* (*dans une maison de commerce*).

leaky ['li:kɪ] *adj* (*tonneau*) qui coule, qui fuit; (*bateau*) qui fait eau; (*chaussures*) qui prennent l'eau; (*toit*) qui fuit; **l. tap,** robinet qui fuit; *F* **this department is very l.,** il y a plein de fuites dans ce service.

lean¹ [li:n] **1** *adj* **(a)** maigre; (*animal*) efflanqué; **(b)** (*viande*) maigre; **(c)** (*année*) maigre, déficitaire; (*année*) de disette; (*argile*) pauvre; (*houille*) maigre; **we had a l. time,** nous avons connu les vaches maigres; **a l. harvest,** une récolte maigre; **l. diet,** maigre régime; régime frugal. **2** *n* maigre *m* (*de la viande*).

lean² *n* inclinaison *f*.

lean³ *v* (*pt & pp* **leaned** [li:nd] *or* **leant** [lent]) **1** *vi* s'appuyer (**against, on sth,** contre, sur, à qch); **to l. on one's elbow(s),** s'accouder; **leaning against a wall,** appuyé à *ou* contre un mur; **to l. back in one's chair,** se renverser dans son fauteuil; **to l. on s.o.,** (*for support*) s'appuyer sur qn; *F* (*to pay money etc*) serrer la vis à qn; **she still leans on her father for advice,** elle a toujours recours aux conseils de son père; **to l. forward/out of the window,** se pencher en avant/par la fenêtre; **to l. over/towards sth,** se pencher sur/vers qch; **that wall is leaning towards the right,** ce mur incline *ou* penche vers la droite; **to l. towards an opinion,** incliner pour une opinion; **to l. towards socialism,** pencher vers le socialisme; *F* **to l. over backwards to do sth,** se mettre en quatre pour faire qch.

2 *vt* appuyer (*une échelle etc*) (**against a wall,** contre, à un mur); **to l. sth against sth,** (*with its back*) adosser qch à *ou* contre qch; (*with its side*) accoter qch à *ou* contre qch.

leaning ['li:nɪŋ] **1** *adj* penché; (*mur*) qui penche; **the l. tower of Pisa,** la tour penchée de Pise. **2** *n* **(a)** inclinaison *f* (*d'une tour etc*); **(b)** (*tendency*) inclination *f* (**towards,** pour), penchant *m* (**towards,** pour, vers), tendance *f* (**towards,** à); **to have leanings towards communism,** pencher vers le communisme; **to have artistic leanings,** avoir des dispositions artistiques.

leanness ['li:nnɪs] *n* maigreur *f*.

leant *see* **LEAN³**.

lean-to ['li:ntu:] **1** *adj* **l.-to roof,** comble *m* en appentis. **2** *n* appentis *m*.

leap¹ [li:p] *n* **(a)** (*jump*) saut *m*, bond *m*; **to take a l. in the dark,** faire un saut dans l'inconnu; **his heart gave a l.,** son cœur bondit; **to advance by leaps and bounds,** avancer à pas de géant; **with one l. she cleared the ditch,** d'un saut elle franchit le fossé; **the company has taken a great l. forward,** la société a fait un grand bond en avant; **(b)** obstacle *m* (à sauter); **salmon l.,** chute *f* d'eau (que les saumons doivent sauter pour remonter); **(c) l. day,** jour *m* intercalaire; le 29 février; **l. year,** année bissextile.

leap² *v* (*pt & pp* **leaped** [li:pt] *or* **leapt** [lept]) **1** *vi* **(a)** sauter, bondir; **to l. to one's feet,** se lever brusquement; **to l. over a ditch,** sauter un fossé; **to l. at the opportunity,** saisir l'occasion au vol; **to l. for joy,** sauter de joie; (*of the heart*) bondir *ou* tressaillir de joie; **she nearly leapt out of her skin,** elle a sauté au plafond; **(b)** (*of flame etc*) jaillir. **2** *vt* **(a)** sauter (*un fossé*), franchir (*un fossé*) d'un saut; **(b)** (*cause to leap*) **to l. a horse over a ditch,** faire sauter *ou* faire franchir un fossé à un cheval.

►leap up *vi* **(a)** (*of person*) bondir (**to do,** pour faire); **their dog leapt up at me,** leur chien m'a sauté dessus; **(b)** (*of flame*) jaillir.

leapfrog¹ ['li:pfrɒg] *n* **to play l.,** jouer à saute-mouton.

leapfrog² *vt & vi* (**-gg-**) sauter (*qch*) comme à saute-mouton; *Fig* **you can l. the next stage in the selection process,** vous pouvez sauter l'étape suivante dans le processus de sélection.

leapt *see* **LEAP²**.

learn [lɜ:n] *v* (*pt & pp* **learnt** [lɜ:nt], *occ* **learned** [lɜ:nd]) **1** *vt* **(a)** apprendre (*le français, les mathématiques etc*); **to l. to read/drive/***etc*, apprendre à lire/conduire/*etc*; **she's learning the violin,** elle étudie le violon; **to l. a new technique,** s'initier à une nouvelle technique; **he has learnt his lesson,** *Sch* il a appris sa leçon; *Fig* (*he won't do it again*) il a eu une bonne leçon;

(b) apprendre (*une nouvelle, les résultats d'un test etc*); **we are sorry to l. that ...,** nous sommes désolés d'apprendre que ...;

(c) *Arch & Sl* (= **teach**) **to l. s.o. sth,** apprendre qch à qn; *Sl* **that'll l. him!,** ça lui apprendra!

2 *vi* **(a)** apprendre; **they're learning about Victorian times,** ils étudient l'époque Victorienne; **to l. from one's mistakes,** mettre à profit les fautes commises; **it is never too late to l.,** on apprend à tout âge;

(b) (*to hear*) **we learned of your success last week,** nous avons appris votre succès la semaine dernière.

learned ['lɜ:nɪd] *adj* savant, instruit, érudit, docte; **l. treatise,** traité savant; **l. journal,** journal savant; **l. profession,** profession intellectuelle; *Jur* **my l. friend,** mon éminent confrère.

learner ['lɜ:nər] *n* **(a)** celui qui apprend; **to be a quick l.,**

apprendre facilement; **(b)** (*beginner*) élève *mf*, débutant, -ante; *Aut* **l. (driver),** apprenti conducteur.

learning ['lɜːnɪŋ] *n* **(a)** (*action*) action *f* d'apprendre, étude *f*; **his l. capacity is limited,** son aptitude à l'étude est limitée; **l. disability,** difficulté *f* à l'étude *ou* à apprendre; *F* **to have a fast l. curve,** avoir des facultés d'assimilation rapide; *F* **we're back on the l. curve,** il nous faut tout réapprendre (à partir de zéro); **(b)** (*knowledge*) science *f*, instruction *f*, érudition *f*, savoir *m*, connaissances *fpl*; **seat** *or* **centre of l.,** centre intellectuel; **man of great l.,** homme de grand savoir.

learnt *see* **LEARN**.

lease¹ [liːs] *n Jur* bail *m*, *pl* baux; concession *f* (*d'une source d'énergie etc*); (*document*) (contrat *m* de) bail; **l. of a house,** bail à loyer; **l. of a farm** *or* **of land,** bail à ferme; **long l.,** bail à long terme, à longue échéance; **to take a new l.** *or* **to renew the l. of a house,** renouveler le bail d'une maison; *Fig* **to take on a new l. of life,** renaître à la vie, *F* repartir pour un nouveau bail; **it's like a new l. of life,** on se sent renaître; **a little oil will give my bike a new l. of life,** un peu d'huile va donner à mon vélo une nouvelle jeunesse.

lease² *vt* **(a)** (*of owner*) **to l. (out),** louer; donner (*une maison*) à bail, affermer (*une terre*); **(b)** (*of tenant*) prendre (*une maison*) à bail, louer (*une maison*); affermer (*une terre*).

leaseback ['liːsbæk] *n* = location d'un parc de voitures *etc* auprès de la société à laquelle on l'a vendu, cession-bail *f*.

leasehold ['liːshəʊld] **1** *n* **(a)** tenure *f* à bail, *esp* tenure en vertu d'un bail emphytéotique; **(b)** (*property*) propriété *f ou* immeuble *m* loué(e) à bail. **2** *adj* tenu à bail.

leaseholder ['liːshəʊldər] *n* locataire *mf*.

leash¹ [liːʃ] *n* laisse *f*, attache *f*; **to put a dog on the l.,** mettre un chien en laisse *ou* à l'attache; *Fig* **to keep s.o. on a tight l.,** tenir qn étroitement en laisse; **to keep one's emotions on a tight l.,** avoir étroitement en mains les rênes de ses émotions; **to strain at the l.,** (*of dog*) tirer sur la laisse; (*of person*) ruer dans les brancards.

leash² *vt* mettre (*un chien*) à l'attache.

leasing ['liːsɪŋ] *n* (*of house*) location *f* à bail; (*of land*) affermage *m*; *Ind Com* (*of equipment etc*) crédit-bail *m*.

least [liːst] **1** *adj* (*smallest*) **(the) l.,** (le, la) moindre, (le, la) plus petit(e); **she flares up at the l. thing,** elle se fâche pour un rien; **I'm not the l. bit musical,** je ne suis pas musicien pour un sou; **I'm not the l. bit tired,** je ne suis pas du tout fatigué; *Math* **the l. common multiple,** le plus petit commun multiple;

2 *n* **(the) l.,** (le) moins; **to say the l. (of it),** pour ne pas dire plus *ou* mieux, pour ne rien dire de plus; **it's the l. I can do,** c'est la moindre des choses; *Prov* **(the) l. said (the) soonest mended,** moins on en parle mieux cela vaut; **at l.,** (tout) au moins; **I can at l. try,** je peux toujours essayer; **at the very l. they should pay your expenses,** ce serait vraiment la moindre des choses qu'ils remboursent tes dépenses; **it cost him at l. £1,000,** cela lui a coûté 1 000 livres au bas mot; **not in the l.,** pas du tout, *Fml* aucunement, *Fml* nullement; **it doesn't matter in the l.,** cela n'a pas la moindre importance; **I'm not in the l. upset,** je ne suis fâché en aucune manière; **that's the l. of my worries,** ça c'est le moindre de mes soucis.

3 *adv* **(the) l.,** (le) moins; **the l. unhappy,** le moins malheureux; **he deserves it l. of all,** il le mérite moins que personne; **when you l. expect it,** (*that type of thing happens*) au moment où l'on s'y attend le moins.

leastways, *Am* **leastwise** ['liːstweɪz, -waɪz] *adv Dial* ou du moins ... .

leather¹ ['leðər] *n* **(a)** cuir *m*; **l. shoes,** chaussures *fpl* en cuir; **fancy l. goods,** maroquinerie *f*; **(b)** *Br F* (*garment*) cuir *m*; **(c)** cuir *m* (*de pompe, de soupape etc*); **upper l.,** (*of shoe*) empeigne *f*; **stirrup l.,** étrivière *f*.

leather² *vt* **(a)** *F* tanner le cuir à (*qn*); **(b)** garnir (*qch*) de cuir.

leather-bound ['leðəbaʊnd] *adj* (*livre*) relié (en) cuir.

leathercloth ['leðəklɒθ] *n* toile *f* cuir.

leatherette [leðə'ret] *n Old-fashioned* similicuir *m*.

leathering ['leðərɪŋ] *n F* **to give s.o. a l.,** tanner le cuir à qn.

leatherjacket ['leðədʒækɪt] *n Ent* larve *f* de la tipule.

leatherneck ['leðənek] *n US F* soldat *m* de l'infanterie de marine.

leatherwork ['leðəwɜːk] *n* **(a)** travail *m* en cuir; **(b)** cuirs *mpl* (*d'une carrosserie etc*); **fancy l.,** maroquinerie *f*.

leathery ['leðərɪ] *adj* qui ressemble au cuir; (*food*) coriace.

leave¹ [liːv] *n* **(a)** (*permission*) permission *f*, autorisation *f*; **l. to go out,** permission (de sortir); **to ask l. to do sth,** demander la permission de faire qch; **to grant s.o. l. to do sth,** donner *ou* accorder à qn la permission de faire qch; *Arch Fml* **by** *or* **with your l.,** avec votre permission; si vous le voulez bien; **without so much as a by your l.,** sans même en demander la permission;

(b) *Admin Mil etc* (*holiday*) congé *m*; **sick l.,** congé de maladie; **compassionate l.,** congé *ou* permission *f* pour affaires de famille; *Nau* **shore l.,** sortie *f* à terre; *Mil etc* **absence without l.,** absence illégale; **to be on l.,** être en congé; **to take two weeks' l.,** prendre deux semaines de congé;

(c) (*farewell*) adieux *mpl*, congé *m*; **to take one's l.,** prendre congé; **to take l. of s.o.,** faire ses adieux à qn; *F* **to take French l.,** filer à l'anglaise; **to take l. of one's senses,** perdre l'esprit.

leave² *v* (*pt & pp* **left** [left]) **1** *vt* **(a)** (*allow to remain, forget*) laisser; **he left his pen (behind),** il a oublié son stylo; **to l. things (lying) about,** laisser traîner des choses; *F* **take it or l. it,** c'est à prendre ou à laisser; **to l. a wife and three children,** laisser une femme et trois enfants; **to l. one's money to s.o.,** laisser *ou* léguer sa fortune à qn; **to l. the door open,** laisser la porte ouverte; **to l. sth unfinished,** laisser qch inachevé; **he left his supper untouched,** il ne toucha pas à son dîner; **to l. a page blank,** laisser une page en blanc; **l. me alone!,** laissez-moi en paix *ou* tranquille!; **she had been left a widow at thirty,** elle était restée veuve à trente ans; **left to oneself,** livré à soi-même; **let's l. it at that, we'll l. it at that,** (*not do any more work*) arrêtons-nous là; (*not argue any more*) n'en parlons plus, demeurons-en là; **to l. much to be desired,** laisser beaucoup à désirer; **it leaves me cold,** ça me laisse froid; **to l. hold** *or* **go of sth,** lâcher qch; **to l. sth with s.o.,** confier qch à qn; **to l. s.o. in charge of sth,** laisser à qn la garde de qch; **to l. a message for s.o.,** laisser un mot *ou* un message *ou* un billet pour qn; **to l. s.o. to do sth,** laisser qn faire qch; laisser à qn le soin de faire qch; **I l. it to you,** je m'en remets à vous, je m'en rapporte à vous; **l. it to me,** remettez-vous-en à moi, je m'en charge; **nothing was left to chance,** on avait paré à toutes les éventualités; **I l. it to you to decide,** je vous laisse le soin de décider; *Billiards* **to l. the balls in a good/bad position,** donner un bon/mauvais acquit; *Math* **three from seven leaves four,** sept moins trois égale quatre;

(b) (*depart from*) quitter (un endroit, qn); quitter, sortir de (*une pièce*); **he has left London,** il est parti de Londres, il a quitté Londres; **he left Oxford without a degree,** il est sorti d'Oxford sans diplôme; **she left school at 16,** elle a quitté l'école à 16 ans; **she never leaves the house,** elle ne sort jamais de la maison; *Sch* **may I l. the room?,** puis-je sortir?; **his eyes never left her,** il ne la quittait pas des yeux; **to l. the table,** se lever de table; **to l. one's job,** quitter son emploi; *Mil etc* **to l. the service,** quitter le service; *Nau* **to l. harbour,** sortir du port; **to l. one's wife,** quitter sa femme; **to be left behind** *or* **standing,** être dépassé *ou* distancé (par ses concurrents); **to l. the rails,** (*of train*) dérailler; **the car left the road,** la voiture a quitté la route;

(c) to be left, rester; **there are no strawberries left,** il ne reste plus de fraises; **how many are there left?,** combien est-ce qu'il en reste?

2 *vi* partir; **we l. tomorrow,** nous partons demain; **we are leaving for Paris,** nous partons pour Paris; **I was just leaving when ...,** j'étais sur le départ lorsque ... .

►**leave behind** *vtas* **(a)** (*forget*) laisser, oublier (*son chapeau etc*); **(b)** (*leave in a place*) laisser; **he left his family behind in Manchester and ...,** il a laissé sa famille (derrière lui) à Manchester et ...; **they left me behind,** ils sont partis sans moi; **(c)** (*in race etc*) **he's left the other runners (well) behind,** il a laissé les autres concurrents derrière lui, *F* il a largué les autres concurrents; (*at school etc*) **she left the other pupils behind,** elle a laissé les autres élèves derrière elle, *F* elle a largué les autres élèves.

►**leave in** *vtsep* inclure, retenir (*un passage dans un article etc*).

►**leave off 1** *vtsep* **(a)** (*stop doing*) quitter, renoncer à (*qch*); **to l. off work,** cesser le travail; *Sl* **l. off pestering me!,** arrête de m'embêter!; **(b)** (*not replace*) (*lid etc*) ne pas (re)mettre; **(c) l. the light off,** n'allume pas. **2** *vi* cesser, s'arrêter; **where did we l. off?,** où en sommes-nous restés (*dans notre lecture etc*)?; *Sl* **l. off!,** ça suffit comme ça!, arrête!

►**leave on** *vtsep* garder (*son manteau, ses gants etc*); **to l. the light/TV on,** laisser la lumière/la télé allumée.

►**leave out** *vtsep* **(a)** (*omit*) (*a line etc*) omettre; **(b)** (*not* *involve*) **l. her out of this!,** laissez-la en dehors de ça!; **they left me out of their plans,** ils m'ont tenu à l'écart de leurs projets; **to feel left out,** se sentir de trop; **(c)** (*leave ready, available*) **I'll l. your dinner out on the table for you,** je te laisse ton dîner sur la table; **l. the disks out where I can see them,** laisse les disquettes en évidence; **(d)** (*not put away*) **we l. the car out on the street,** nous laissons la voiture dehors dans la rue; **who left the milk out overnight?,** qui a oublié de mettre le lait au frigo hier soir?; **(e)** *Sl* **l. it out!,** arrête!

►**leave over** *vtas* **(a) what's left over?,** qu'est-ce qui reste?; **you can keep what is left over,** vous pouvez garder le surplus; **(b)** (*postpone*) remettre (*qch*) à plus tard.

leaved [li:vd] *adj* feuillé, feuillu.

-leaved [li:vd] *suff* **three-l.,** (*volet, paravent etc*) à trois panneaux; **broad-l. tree,** arbre à larges feuilles; **ivy-l.,** à feuilles de lierre.

leaven¹ ['lev(ə)n] *n* levain *m*.

leaven² *vt* **(a)** faire lever (*le pain, la pâte*); **(b)** modifier, transformer (*le caractère d'un peuple etc*) **(with,** par); imprégner **(with,** de).

leaver ['li:vər] *n* **(school) leavers,** élèves sortants.

leave-taking ['li:vteɪkɪŋ] *n* adieux *mpl*.

leaving ['li:vɪŋ] *n* départ *m*.

leavings ['li:vɪŋz] *npl* restes *mpl* (*d'un repas*).

Lebanese [lebə'ni:z] **1** *adj* libanais. **2** *n* Libanais, -aise.

Lebanon ['lebənən] *n* le Liban; *Bot* **cedar of L.,** cèdre *m* du Liban.

►**lech after** [letʃ] *vipo F* désirer (*qn*).

lecher ['letʃər] *n* débauché *m*, *F* coureur *m* de jupons.

lecherous ['letʃərəs] *adj* libertin, lubrique, débauché; (*look, smile*) lascif.

lecherously ['letʃərəslɪ] *adv* lascivement.

lechery ['letʃərɪ] *n* débauche *f*.

lectern ['lektən] *n Rel* lutrin *m*, aigle *m*; (*for heavy book*) pupitre *m*.

lector ['lektɔ:r] *n Univ* (*for foreign languages*) lecteur, -trice.

lecture¹ ['lektʃər] *n* **(a)** conférence *f* **(on,** sur); *Univ* cours *m*; **to give/attend a l.,** faire/assister à une conférence; **l. hall,** salle *f* de conférences; **l. theatre,** amphithéâtre *m*; **history l.,** cours d'histoire; **l. on Napoleon,** cours sur Napoléon; **(b)** *F* sermon *m*, semonce *f*; **to give** *or* **read s.o. a l.,** faire la morale à qn; (*for wrongdoing*) semoncer qn, sermonner qn.

lecture² **1** *vi* faire une conférence *ou* des conférences; *Univ* faire un cours **(on,** sur); **he lectured on Eastern affairs,** il a traité des affaires d'Orient; **she lectures in economics,** elle donne des cours d'économie à l'université, elle est maître-assistant en économie; **he lectures once or twice a year,** il donne des conférences une ou deux fois par an. **2** *vt F* faire la morale à (*qn*); (*for wrongdoing*) sermonner, semoncer.

lecturer ['lektʃərər] *n* **(a)** conférencier, -ière; **(b)** *Univ* **(junior, assistant) l.,** = maître-assistant; **(senior) l.,** = maître de conférences; **to be a maths l.,** être assistant en maths; **is she a good l.?,** est-ce qu'elle est bon professeur?

lectureship ['lektʃəʃɪp] *n Univ* maîtrise *f* de conférences.

led *see* **LEAD²**.

LED [eli:'di:] *n Comptr abbr* **light-emitting diode**.

ledge [ledʒ] *n* **(a)** rebord *m*, saillie *f*; (*on wall, building*) corniche *f*; **(b)** *Geol* filon *m*, veine *f* (*de minerai etc*); **l. of rock,** plateforme rocheuse; (*awash or under water*) banc *m* de rochers.

ledger ['ledʒər] *n* **(a)** (*in bookkeeping*) grand livre (*de frais, de ventes, d'achats etc*); **payroll l.,** grand livre de paie; *Nau* cahier *m* de solde; **(b)** *Mus* **l. line,** ligne *f* supplémentaire (à la portée).

lee [li:] *n* **(a)** *Nau* côté *m* sous le vent; **l. shore,** terre *f* sous le vent; **(b)** abri *m* (contre le vent); **in the l. of a rock,** abrité par un rocher.

leeboard ['li:bɔ:d] *n Nau* aile *f ou* semelle *f* de dérive.

leech [li:tʃ] *n* **(a)** sangsue *f*; **(b)** *Med* **artificial l.,** sangsue artificielle, ventouse scarifiée; **(c)** *F* (*person*) importun, -e; sangsue *f*, crampon *m*; **to cling** *or* **stick to s.o. like a l.,** se coller à qn comme une sangsue.

leek [li:k] *n* (*vegetable*) poireau *m*.

leer¹ ['lɪər] *n* regard paillard *ou* polisson.

leer² *vi* **to l. at s.o.,** regarder *ou F* reluquer qn d'un air paillard.

lees [li:z] *npl* lie *f* (*de vin etc*).

leeward ['li:wəd] *Nau* **1** *adj & adv* sous le vent; *Geog* **the L. Islands,** (*in South Pacific*) les Îles *fpl* sous le Vent de l'Océanie française; (*in West Indies*) les Îles sous le Vent des Antilles. **2** *n* côté *m* sous le vent; **to pass to l. of a ship,** passer sous le vent d'un navire.

leeway ['li:weɪ] *n* **(a)** (*freedom*) liberté *f* d'action; (*safety margin*) marge *f* de sécurité; **(b)** *Nau* dérive *f*; **to make l.,** dériver (à la voile); *F* **he has considerable l. to make up,** il a un fort retard à rattraper.

left [left] **1** *adj* gauche; **on my l. hand,** à ma gauche; *F* **to have two l. feet,** être empoté. **2** *adv* (*to turn etc*) à gauche; *Mil* **l. turn!,** à gauche, gauche!; **eyes l.!,** tête (à) gauche! **3** *n* (*left hand*) gauche *f*; *Boxing* gauche *m*; **on the l., to the l.,** à gauche; *Aut etc* **to keep (to the) l.,** tenir la gauche; *Pol* **the L.,** la gauche; **l. wing,** *Pol* (*of party, group*) l'aile *f* gauche; *Mil* gauche *f*; *Sp* **to play on the l. wing,** être ailier gauche.

left-hand ['left'hænd] *adj* **(a)** (*poche etc*) de gauche; **l.-h. blow,** coup *m* de la main gauche; **on the l.-h. side,** à gauche; **l.-h. turn,** virage *m* à gauche; *Aut* **to have l.-h. drive,** avoir la conduite à gauche; **(b)** *Tech* (*serrure, vis, foret*) à gauche; **l.-h. thread (of a screw),** filet *m* à gauche, renversé (d'une vis).

left-handed [left'hændɪd] **1** *adj* **(a)** (*person*) gaucher, -ère; (*club de golf etc*) pour gaucher; **(b)** *F* (*awkward*) gauche, maladroit; **(c)** *F* (*ambiguous*) suspect, équivoque; (*compliment*) peu flatteur; **(d)** *Old-fashioned* **l.-h. marriage,** mariage *m* de la main gauche; **(e)** *Tech* = **LEFT-HAND (b)**. **2** *adv* **to play tennis l.,** jouer au tennis de la main gauche.

left-hander [left'hændər] *n* **(a)** (*person*) gaucher, -ère; **(b)** *Boxing* coup *m* du gauche; *F* coup déloyal.

leftie ['leftɪ] *n F* gauchiste *mf*; **he's a bit of a l.,** il est un peu à gauche.

leftist ['leftɪst] **1** *n Pol* gauchiste *mf*. **2** *adj* gauchiste; (*homme*) de gauche.

left luggage ['left'lʌgɪdʒ] *n Br* (*luggage*) bagages déposés à la consigne; **l.-l. lockers,** consigne automatique; **l.-l. (office),** consigne.

leftover ['leftəʊvər] **1** *adj* (*provisions etc*) de surplus, en surplus; *Com* **l. stock,** restes *mpl*. **2** *n* **(a)** *Com Culin* **leftovers,** restes *mpl*; **(b)** survivance *f* (*des temps passés*).

left-wing ['leftwɪŋ] *adj* **(a)** (*politique*) de gauche; **they are very l.-w.,** ils sont très à gauche; **he has slightly l.-w. ideas,** il a des idées gauchisantes; **(b)** *Sp* **l.-w. position,** aile *f* gauche.

left-winger ['left'wɪŋər] *n* **(a)** *Pol* homme *ou* femme de gauche; député *m* de la gauche; **the left-wingers,** la gauche; **(b)** *Sp* ailier *m* gauche.

leg¹ [leg] *n* **(a)** jambe *f* (*d'homme, de cheval*); patte *f* (*de chien, d'oiseau, d'insecte, de reptile*); **wooden l.,** jambe de bois; *Fig* **you don't have a l. to stand on,** vos arguments ne tiennent pas debout; *Fig* **to be on one's last legs,** (*to be tired*) ne plus pouvoir mettre un pied devant l'autre; (*to be dying*) avoir un pied dans la tombe; **the business is on its last legs,** la société est au bord de la faillite; **to give s.o. a l. up,** (*over a wall, fence etc*) faire la courte échelle à qn; (*into the saddle*) aider qn à monter en selle; *F* (*in job etc*) donner à qn un coup d'épaule; *F* **to pull s.o.'s l.,** faire marcher qn; **show a l.!,** (*it's time to get up*) montre le bout de ton nez!; *Sl* **to get one's l. over,** (*have sex*) s'envoyer en l'air; *F* **l. show,** spectacle *m* de music-hall (*où les girls montrent leurs jambes*); *Cr* **l. before wicket,** (mis hors jeu) à pied obstructif; **l. lock,** (*in wrestling*) passement *m* de pied; **l. rest,** appui-jambes *m inv*; bout *m* de pied (*d'une chaise longue*); *Med* étrier *m*; *Med* **l. iron,** prothèse *f* orthopédique;

(b) *Culin* cuisse *f* (*de poulet*); cuisseau *m* (*de veau*); **roast l. of pork,** cuissot *m* de porc rôti; **frogs' legs,** cuisses de grenouille; **l. of lamb,** gigot *m*;

(c) jambe *f* (*de pantalon*); tige *f* (*de bas etc*); **these trousers are a bit short in the l.,** ce pantalon est un peu court au niveau des jambes;

(d) pied *m* (*de table, de chaise*); jambe *f* (*de trépied etc*); montant *m* (*de chevalet*); *Nau* béquille *f* (*pour étayer un bateau échoué*); branche *f* (*de compas*);

(e) *Cr* = le terrain à gauche et en arrière du joueur qui est au guichet; **l. drive,** coup *m* arrière à gauche;

(f) *Sp etc* étape *f*; (*in relay race*) relais *m*; **the first l. of our journey,** la première étape de notre voyage.

leg² *vt* **(-gg-)** *F* **to l. it,** (*walk*) faire la route à pied, *F* aller pedibus; (*hurry*) marcher *ou* courir rapidement, *F* jouer des jambes.

legacy ['legəsɪ] *n Jur* legs *m*; **to come into a l.,** faire un héritage; **to leave s.o. a l.,** laisser un héritage *ou* quelque chose en héritage à qn; *Fig* **this desk is a l. from my predecessor,** j'ai hérité ce bureau de mon prédécesseur; **the l. of the war was a divided Europe,** l'héritage de la guerre fut une Europe divisée.

legal ['li:g(ə)l] *adj* **(a)** (*lawful*) légal, -aux; (*commerce*) licite; **to be l. currency** *or* **tender,** avoir cours; **(b)** *(error)* judiciaire; *(mind, affairs)* juridique; **by l. process,** par voies légales, par voies de droit; **l. redress,** recours *m* à la justice; **l. security,** caution *f* judiciaire; **l. claim to sth,** titre *m* juridique à qch; **l. document,** acte *m* authentique; **l. year,** année civile; *US* **l. holiday,** jour férié; **l. charges,** frais *mpl* judiciaires; **l. department,** *(of bank etc)* service *m ou* bureau *m* du contentieux; **to go into the l. profession,** faire une carrière juridique; **l. medicine,** médicine légale; *esp US* **l. separation,** séparation *f* judiciaire; **l. expert,** expert *m* juridique; avocat *m* conseil; **l. adviser,** conseiller, -ère juridique; **to take l. advice,** = consulter un avocat; **l. aid,** assistance *f* juridique; **l. owner,** propriétaire *m* légitime.

legalese [li:gə'li:z] *n* jargon *m* juridique.

legality [lɪ'gælɪtɪ] *n* légalité *f*.

legalization [li:gəlaɪ'zeɪʃən] *n* légalisation *f*.

legalize ['li:gəlaɪz] *vt* rendre *(un acte)* légal; autoriser *(un acte)*; légaliser, certifier, authentiquer *(un document)*; dépénaliser *(une drogue)*.

legally ['li:gəlɪ] *adv* légalement; **l. responsible,** responsable en droit.

legate¹ ['legɪt] *n Rel Antiq* légat *m*.

legate² [lɪ'geɪt] *vt* léguer.

legatee [legə'ti:] *n* légataire *mf*.

legation [lɪ'geɪʃən] *n* légation *f*.

legato [lɪ'gɑ:təʊ] *adv Mus* legato, coulé.

legend ['ledʒənd] *n (story, inscription etc)* légende *f*.

legendary ['ledʒənd(ə)rɪ] *adj* légendaire.

legerdemain [ledʒədə'meɪn] *n* (tours *mpl* de) passe-passe *m*, prestidigitation *f*.

-legged ['legɪd, legd] *suff* **short/bare/***etc***-l.,** aux jambes courtes/nues/*etc*; **two-l.,** à deux jambes; à deux pattes.

leggings ['legɪŋz] *npl* jambières *fpl*, leggin(g)s *mfpl*.

leggy ['legɪ] *adj (person)* aux longues jambes; *(plant)* étiolé; **a l. girl,** une fille tout en jambes.

legibility [ledʒɪ'bɪlɪtɪ] *n* lisibilité *f (d'une écriture)*.

legible ['ledʒɪb(ə)l] *adj (écriture)* lisible, net.

legibly ['ledʒɪblɪ] *adv (écrire)* lisiblement.

legion ['li:dʒ(ə)n] **1** *n* légion *f*; **the Foreign L.,** la Légion étrangère; **the L. of honour,** la Légion d'honneur. **2** *adj Lit (many)* **their name is l.,** ils sont innombrables; **the difficulties were l.,** les difficultés étaient légion.

legionary ['li:dʒənərɪ] **1** *adj* qui se rapporte à une légion, légionnaire. **2** *n* légionnaire *m*.

legionnaire [li:dʒə'neər] *n* légionnaire *m*; **l.'s disease,** maladie *f* du légionnaire.

legislate ['ledʒɪsleɪt] *vi* faire des *ou* les lois, légiférer; **we can't l. for all possible situations,** nous ne pouvons pas prévoir des lois pour tous les cas de figure possibles.

legislation [ledʒɪs'leɪʃən] *n* **(a)** *(laws)* législation *f*; *(action)* élaboration *f* des lois; **piece of l.,** loi *f*; **(b)** *Parl* programme législatif.

legislative ['ledʒɪslətɪv] *adj* législatif; **the L. Assembly,** l'Assemblée législative; **l. power,** le pouvoir législatif.

legislator ['ledʒɪsleɪtər] *n* législateur, -trice.

legislature ['ledʒɪslətjər] *n (body)* corps législatif.

legist ['li:dʒɪst] *n Fml* légiste *m*.

legit [lɪ'dʒɪt] *adj F* légitime.

legitimacy [lɪ'dʒɪtɪməsɪ] *n* légitimité *f (d'un enfant, d'une opinion etc)*.

legitimate¹ [lɪ'dʒɪtɪmət] *adj (enfant, autorité, raison etc)* légitime; **l. expenditure,** dépenses justifiées; **it's l. to assume that ...,** on peut légitimement penser que ...; **l. stage,** le théâtre traditionnel.

legitimate² [lɪ'dʒɪtɪmeɪt] *vt* légitimer *(un enfant)*.

legitimately [lɪ'dʒɪtɪmətlɪ] *adv* légitimement.

legitimatize [lɪ'dʒɪtɪmətaɪz] **, legitimize** [lɪ'dʒɪtɪmaɪz] *vt* légitimer.

legless ['leglɪs] *adj* sans jambes; **l. cripple,** cul-de-jatte *m*, *pl* culs-de-jatte; *Fig F* **to be l.,** être soûl.

legman, *pl* **-men** ['legmæn, -mən] *n Am* **(a)** reporter qui fait la chronique des chiens écrasés; **(b)** *(errand boy etc)* garçon *m* de courses, coursier *m*.

leg-of-mutton [legəv'mʌt(ə)n] *n* **l.-of-m. sleeves,** manches *fpl* gigot.

leg-pull ['legpʊl] *n F* blague *f*.

leg-puller ['legpʊlər] *n F* blagueur, -euse, farceur, -euse.

legroom ['legrʊm] *n* place *f* pour les jambes; **these little cars don't give you any l.,** dans ces petites voitures on n'a aucune place pour les jambes.

legume ['legju:m] *n* **(a)** fruit *m* d'une légumineuse; **(b) legumes,** légumineuses *fpl*.

leguminous [lɪ'gju:mɪnəs] *adj Bot* légumineux; **l. plant,** légumineuse *f*.

legwarmer ['legwɔ:mər] *n* *(usu pl)* **legwarmers,** jambières *fpl*.

legwork ['legwɜ:k] *n F* **there's a lot of l. in this job,** c'est un travail où l'on marche beaucoup; **I'm the one that gets all the l.,** c'est toujours moi qui me déplace ici.

Leics *abbr* **Leicestershire**.

leisure ['leʒər, *US* 'li:ʒər] *n* loisir(s) *m(pl)*; **to have enough l. for reading,** avoir le loisir *ou* le temps de lire; **to do sth at one's l.,** faire qch à loisir *ou* dans ses moments de loisir; **l. hours,** heures *fpl* de loisir; *F* **I'm a lady of l. at the moment,** je ne travaille pas à présent; **l. time,** temps libre; **l. activities,** activités *fpl* de loisir; **l. centre,** centre *m* de loisirs; **l. wear,** vêtements *mpl* de loisirs.

leisured ['leʒəd] *adj* **(a)** *(life etc)* de loisir; **(b)** *(person)* qui a des loisirs; **the l. classes,** les rentiers *mpl*.

leisureliness ['leʒəlɪnɪs] *n* *(of pace)* caractère mesuré; *(of weekend)* caractère détendu; **compared with the l. of the weekend ...,** par comparaison avec la détente du weekend; **the l. of sea travel,** la détente apportée par une croisière.

leisurely ['leʒəlɪ] **1** *adj* *(person)* qui n'est jamais pressé; *(pace)* mesuré, posé; *(voyage)* par petites étapes; **to go for a l. stroll,** aller se promener tranquillement; **to have a l. weekend,** passer un weekend détendu *ou* relaxe; **to do sth in a l. fashion,** faire qch sans se presser. **2** *adv* *(without haste)* sans se presser.

lemming ['lemɪŋ] *n* lemming *m*; **to follow s.o. like lemmings,** suivre qn comme des moutons (de Panurge).

lemon ['lemən] *n* *(fruit)* citron *m*; *F* personne *f ou* chose *f* qui ne vaut rien; *F* **they squeezed him like a l.,** ils l'ont pressé comme un citron; **fresh l.,** *(drink)* citron pressé; *Culin* **l. cheese** *or* **curd,** (sorte de) confiture *f* au citron; **l. tea,** thé *m* au citron; **l. squeezer,** presse-citrons *m inv*; **l. tree,** citronnier *m*; **I felt a real l.,** je me sentais bien bête; **l. balm,** *(plant)* mélisse officinale; citronnelle *f*; **l. meringue pie,** tourte *f* au citron meringuée; **l. grass,** citronnelle; **l. sole,** *(fish)* plie *f* sole; limande-sole *f*; **l. verbena,** verveine *f* citronnelle. **2** *adj* **l. (coloured),** (jaune) citron *inv*.

lemonade [lemə'neɪd] *n* limonade *f*.

lemony ['lemənɪ] *adj (smell, taste)* citronné.

lemur ['li:mər] *n* *(animal)* maki *m*.

lend [lend] *vt* *(pt & pp* **lent** [lent]) **(a)** prêter **(sth to s.o., s.o. sth,** qch à qn); **to l. money at interest,** prêter de l'argent à intérêt; **(b)** *(give)* **to l. s.o. a (helping) hand,** donner un coup de main à qn; **to l. an ear to ...,** prêter l'oreille à ...; **to l. one's name to a project,** donner son nom à un projet; **to l. dignity to an occasion,** rehausser le prestige d'un événement; **to l. weight to an argument,** donner du poids à un argument; **distance lends enchantment to the view,** tout paraît beau (vu) de loin; **to l. oneself** *or* **itself to sth,** se prêter à qch; **the story doesn't l. itself to dramatization,** l'histoire ne se prête pas à une dramatisation.

lender ['lendər] *n* *(person)* prêteur, -euse; *(institution)* organisme *m* de crédit.

lending ['lendɪŋ] *n* prêt *m (d'un objet, de l'argent)*; *Fin* prêt *m (de capitaux)*; **l. library,** bibliothèque *f* de prêt; **l. bank,** banque *f* de crédit; **l. business,** crédit *m*; **l. country,** pays créancier; **l. policy,** *(of bank, country)* politique *f* de prêt.

lend-lease ['lend'li:s] *n (no pl) Econ* prêt-bail *m*.

length [leŋθ] *n* **(a)** longueur *f*; **to win by a l./half a l.,** *(in race)* gagner d'une longueur/d'une demi-longueur; **the l. and breadth of the country,** dans toute l'étendue du pays; **I fell full l. on the ground,** je suis tombé de tout mon long;

(b) *(in time)* durée *f*; longueur *f (d'un livre, d'un voyage etc)*; **about 300 pages in l.,** *(book)* d'une longueur d'environ 300 pages; **l. of service,** ancienneté *f*; **the l. of time required to do sth,** le temps qu'il faut pour faire qch; **at l.,** *(parler)* longuement; *(expliquer qch)* en détail; *(eventually)* enfin, à la fin;

(c) to go to the l. of doing sth, aller jusqu'à faire qch; **to go to great lengths to do sth,** se donner beaucoup de mal à *ou* pour faire qch; **he would go to any lengths,** il ne reculerait devant rien;

(d) longueur *f (d'une voyelle, d'une syllabe)*;

(e) *Tennis Cr* longueur *f* de balle;

(f) morceau *m*, bout *m (de ficelle etc)*; pièce *f*, coupon *m (d'étoffe)*; morceau *(de bois)*; tronçon *m (de tuyau)*; *Sewing* **dress/trouser l.,** coupon de robe/pantalon; **what l. do I need for ...?,** quel métrage faut-il pour ...?

lengthen ['leŋθən] **1** *vt* allonger, rallonger *(une jupe, une chaîne etc)*; prolonger *(un intervalle, une voyelle etc)*; allonger *(un récit)*. **2** *vi* *(of days etc)* allonger, rallonger; *(of intervals etc)* augmenter.

lengthening ['leŋθənɪŋ] *n* allongement *m*, rallongement *m*; agrandissement *m* (en long).

lengthily ['leŋθɪlɪ] *adv* longuement; (*raconter*) tout au long.

lengthways, *Am* **lengthwise** ['leŋθweɪz, -waɪz] *adv* dans le sens de la longueur, longitudinalement.

lengthy ['leŋθɪ] *adj* (*discours, récit*) long, plein de longueurs, prolixe.

leniency ['liːnɪənsɪ] *n* indulgence *f* (**to, towards,** pour).

lenient ['liːnɪənt] *adj* indulgent (**to, towards,** envers, pour); (*punishment*) peu sévère; *Jur* **a l. sentence,** un jugement clément.

leniently ['liːnɪəntlɪ] *adv* (*to judge*) avec clémence; (*to mark*) avec indulgence.

Lenin ['lenɪn] *n* Lénine *m*.

Leningrad ['lenɪngræd] *n* Léningrad *m*.

Leninism ['lenɪnɪz(ə)m] *n Pol* léninisme *m*.

Leninist ['lenɪnɪst] *n Pol* léniniste *mf*.

lenitive ['lenɪtɪv] *adj & n Med* lénitif *m*.

lens [lenz] *n* **(a)** *Opt* lentille *f*; (*magnifying glass*) loupe *f*, verre grossissant; verre (*de lunettes*); **converging/diverging l.,** lentille convergente/divergente; **concave/convex l.,** lentille concave/convexe; **contact l.,** lentille de contact; **(b)** *Phot* objectif *m* (photographique); **l. holder,** étui *m* à objectif; **l. aperture,** ouverture *f* de l'objectif; **l. cleaning fluid,** produit *m* de nettoyage pour lentilles; **l. cap,** capuchon *m* d'objectif; **mirror l.,** objectif à lentille spéculaire; *Electron* **electron l.,** lentille *f* électronique; **(c)** *Anat* **crystalline l.,** cristallin *m* (*de l'œil*); *F* lentille *f*.

Lent [lent] *n Rel* le Carême; **to keep L.,** faire carême; **to give up sth for L.,** renoncer à qch pour le Carême.

lentil ['lentɪl] *n Culin* lentille *f*; **l. soup,** soupe *f* aux lentilles.

Leo ['liːəʊ] *n* **(a)** Léon *m*; **(b)** *Astron* le Lion; **to be a L.,** être Lion.

leonine ['liːənaɪn] *adj* léonin.

leopard ['lepəd] *n* léopard *m*; *F* **can a l. change his spots?,** il mourra dans sa peau; **American l.,** jaguar *m*; **hunting l.,** guépard *m*; **l. skin,** peau *f* de léopard; **l. skin coat,** manteau *m* en léopard.

leotard ['liːətɑːd] *n* maillot *m* (de danseur), justaucorps *m*.

leper ['lepər] *n Med & Fig* lépreux, -euse; **l. hospital** *or* **colony,** léproserie *f*.

lepidopteran [lepɪ'dɒptərən] *adj & n Ent* lépidoptère *m*.

leprechaun ['leprəkɔːn, -hɔːn] *n Myth* farfadet *m*, lutin *m*.

leprosy ['leprəsɪ] *n Med* lèpre *f*; **to have l.,** avoir la lèpre.

leprous ['leprəs] *adj Med* lépreux.

lesbian ['lezbɪən] **1** *adj* lesbien. **2** *n* lesbienne *f*.

lesbianism ['lezbɪənɪz(ə)m] *n* lesb(ian)isme *m*.

lesion ['liːʒən] *n Jur Med* lésion *f*.

less [les] **1** *adj* (*comp* **lesser**) **(a)** (*smaller*) moindre; **the distance is l. than I thought,** la distance est moindre que je ne le pensais; **to a lesser degree,** à un degré inférieur; **(b)** (*not so much, not so many*) **one mouth l. to feed,** une bouche de moins à nourrir; **in l. time than it takes to tell,** en moins de temps qu'il ne faut *ou* n'en faut pour le dire; **l. trouble/difficulty,** moins de peine/difficulté; **(c)** (*younger*) **he is l. than thirty,** il a moins de trente ans.

2 *prep* moins; **a year l. two days,** une année moins deux jours; **I've £20, l. what I spent on books,** j'ai 20 livres moins ce que j'ai dépensé en livres.

3 *pron* moins; **you have l. than you need,** tu as moins que ce dont tu as besoin; **the l. you know the better,** le moins tu en sais, le mieux c'est; **I don't think any l. of you,** mon estime pour vous n'a pas diminué; **I see l. of her nowadays,** je la vois moins ces temps-ci.

4 *n* moins *m*; **in l. than an hour,** en moins d'une heure; **in l. than no time,** en moins de rien; **I can't sell it at l. than cost price,** je ne peux pas le vendre à moins du prix de revient.

5 *adv* **(a) l. (well) known,** moins (bien) connu; **she is l. musical than her sister,** elle est moins musicienne que sa sœur; **I'm l. happy with that,** ça me satisfait *ou* plaît moins; **I want nothing l.,** (*than that price*) je ne veux rien de moins; (*that's the last thing I want*) cela ne m'arrange pas du tout; **one person l.,** une personne de moins; **not a penny l.,** pas un sou de moins; **l. and l.,** de moins en moins; **no more, no l.,** ni plus ni moins; **the l. said about it the better,** moins on en parle mieux cela vaut; **still l., even l.,** encore moins; **he continued none the l.,** il n'en continua pas moins; **(b) nothing l. than,** (*at the very least*) rien (de) moins que; (*anything rather than*) rien moins que; **it's nothing l. than monstrous!,** c'est absolument monstrueux!; **this wall is no l. than a metre thick,** ce mur n'a pas moins d'un mètre d'épaisseur; **no l. a person than the headmistress,** (*came to see me etc*) la directrice en personne; **l. than six,** moins de six; **they have no l. than six cars,** ils ont six voitures, pas moins; **the letter was signed by Vincent, no l.,** la lettre était signée de Vincent, rien de moins; **he dislikes it no l. than I (do),** il ne le déteste pas moins que moi; **I expected no l. from you,** je n'en attendais pas moins de vous; **they don't own a fridge, much l. a freezer,** ils n'ont pas de réfrigérateur, et encore moins de congélateur; **he's no l. of a man for being a ballet dancer,** pour être danseur de ballet, il n'en est pas moins homme.

lessee [le'siː] *n* **(a)** locataire *mf* (à bail) (*d'un immeuble etc*); tenancier, -ière (*d'un casino etc*); fermier *m* (*d'une ferme*); **(b)** concessionnaire *mf*.

lessen ['les(ə)n] **1** *vi* s'amoindrir, diminuer; (*of symptoms etc*) s'atténuer. **2** *vt* amoindrir, diminuer; atténuer (*le bruit, un crime*); ralentir (*son activité, son ardeur*).

lessening ['les(ə)nɪŋ] *n* amoindrissement *m*, diminution *f*; atténuation *f*.

lesser ['lesər] *adj* **(a)** (*in size*) petit; **(b)** (*in importance*) moindre; **to choose the l. of two evils,** de deux maux choisir le moindre; **to a l. extent,** dans une moindre mesure.

lesson ['les(ə)n] *n* **(a)** leçon *f*; *Sch* cours *m*; (*in primary school*) leçon; **French l.,** cours de français; **swimming l.,** leçon de natation; **private lessons,** leçons particulières; **to be an object l. to s.o.,** servir d'exemple à qn; **to learn a l. from sth,** tirer une leçon de qch; **let that be a l. to you!,** que cela vous serve d'exemple *ou* de leçon!; **it'll teach him a l.,** ça lui servira de leçon; **(b)** *Rel* lecture *f* de l'Écriture sainte.

lessor [le'sɔːr] *n* bailleur, -eresse.

lest [lest] *conj* **(a)** *esp Lit* de peur *ou* de crainte que ... (ne) + *sub*; **l. we forget,** de peur que nous n'oublions; **(b)** *Arch* (*after verbs of fearing*) **I feared l. he should fall,** je craignais qu'il (ne) tombât.

let¹ [let] *n Tennis* **l. (ball),** balle *f* à remettre; balle de filet.

let² *n* location *f*; *F* **when I get a l. for the season I spend the time abroad,** quand je loue ma maison *etc* pour la saison je vais à l'étranger.

let³ *v* (*pt & pp* **let**; *prp* **letting**) **1** *vt* **(a)** (*allow*) permettre, laisser; **to l. s.o. do sth,** laisser qn faire qch, permettre à qn de faire qch; **the police would not l. anyone pass,** la police ne laissait passer personne *ou* ne permettait à personne de passer; **to l. oneself be guided,** se laisser guider; **l. me tell you that ...,** permettez-moi de vous dire que ...; **to l. fall,** laisser échapper (*qch*); **he let go the rope,** il a lâché la corde; **someone has let the dog loose,** quelqu'un a lâché le chien; **to l. s.o. know sth,** faire savoir qch à qn, faire part de qch à qn; **l. me know when ...,** faites-moi savoir quand ...; **I will l. him know you are here,** je vais le prévenir que vous êtes ici; **l. me hear the story,** racontez-moi l'histoire; **(b)** louer (*une maison etc*); **house to l.,** maison à louer; **(c)** *Arch Med* **to l. blood,** pratiquer une saignée; saigner qn.

2 *v aux* (*supplying 1st & 3rd person of imperative*) **let's hurry!,** dépêchons-nous!; **l. us pray,** prions; **don't let's start yet,** ne partons pas encore; **now, don't let's have any nonsense!,** allons, pas de bêtises!; **l. him do it at once!,** qu'il le fasse tout de suite!; *Math* **l. AB be equal to CD,** supposons que AB soit égal à CD; **l. me see!,** voyons!, attendez un peu!; **l. them all come!,** qu'ils viennent tous!; **don't l. me see you here again!,** que je ne vous retrouve plus ici!

let⁴ *conj* **l. alone,** sans parler de, moins encore; **we haven't been to England, l. alone Scotland,** nous n'avons pas été en Angleterre, moins encore en Écosse.

►**let by** *vtas* laisser passer (*qn*).

►**let down** *vtsep* **(a)** baisser (*la glace, un store etc*); **to l. down one's hair,** laisser tomber ses cheveux; *F* abandonner toute réserve; se laisser aller; **(b)** rallonger (*une robe etc*); **(c)** *F* **to l. s.o. down gently,** ne pas être trop sévère avec qn; **(d)** *F* (*disappoint*) faire faux bond à (*qn*); **I won't l. you down,** vous pouvez compter sur moi; **he has been badly let down,** il a été gravement déçu; **the car let us down again,** la voiture nous a encore lâchés; **(e)** dégonfler (*un pneu*).

►**let in** *vtsep* **(a)** laisser entrer, faire entrer, admettre (*qn*); laisser entrer (*l'air, la pluie, un courant d'air*); **to l. in the light,** laisser entrer *ou* passer la lumière; **he's got a key, so he can l. himself in,** puisqu'il a une clef, il peut entrer dans la maison *etc*; **my shoes l. in water,** mes chaussures prennent l'eau; **to l. s.o. in on a secret,** initier qn à un secret; **(b)** *Sewing etc* ajouter, introduire (*une pièce*); **(c)** *F* **I didn't know what I was letting myself in for,** je ne savais pas à quoi je m'engageais; **we're letting ourselves in for a lot of work,** nous nous embarquons pour beaucoup de travail.

►let into *vtaspo* **(a)** laisser *ou* faire entrer (*qn*) dans la maison *etc*; **to l. s.o. into a secret,** dévoiler un secret à qn, mettre qn dans le secret; **(b)** *Sewing etc* **to l. a piece into a skirt,** mettre *ou* ajouter une pièce à une jupe.

►let off 1 *vtsep* **(a)** (*explode, fire*) faire partir (*un fusil, un pétard*); tirer, faire partir (*un feu d'artifice*); décocher (*une flèche etc*); **(b)** (*release*) lâcher, laisser échapper (*de la vapeur*); *Fig* **to l. off steam,** se défouler; **(c)** (*excuse*) **to l. s.o. off from (doing) sth,** décharger qn de qch, dispenser qn de faire qch; **to l. s.o. off,** faire grâce à qn; **you l. him off too easily,** vous lui faites la part trop belle; **I'll l. you off this time,** je vous pardonne (pour) cette fois-ci; **to be let off with a fine,** en être quitte pour une amende; **(d)** (*from vehicle*) laisser (descendre). **2** *vi F* (*fart*) péter.

►let on *vi F* **(a)** (*tell*) **don't l. on that I was there,** n'allez pas dire que j'y étais; **he didn't l. on that he saw her,** (*didn't tell anyone*) il n'a pas dit qu'il l'avait vue; (*didn't acknowledge her*) il a fait semblant de ne pas la voir; **don't l. on!,** pas un mot!; **(b)** (*claim*) feindre, faire semblant; **he wasn't as ill as he let on,** il faisait semblant d'être plus malade qu'il ne l'était.

►let out *vtsep* **(a)** (*release*) laisser sortir (*qn*); laisser échapper (*un oiseau*); élargir (*un prisonnier*); laisser échapper, révéler, divulguer (*un secret*); **the porter let me out,** le gardien m'a ouvert la porte; **I'll l. myself out,** je trouverai le chemin tout seul; **can you l. yourself out?,** vous connaissez le chemin?; *Fig* **that lets me out,** me voilà soulagé; **to l. out the air from,** laisser échapper l'air de (*qch*); dégonfler (*un ballon etc*); **to l. out the bath water,** vider la baignoire; **to l. out a yell,** laisser échapper un cri; **(b)** (*expand*) élargir, agrandir (*un vêtement*); *Nau* lâcher (*un cordage*); larguer (*une voile*); **(c)** (*rent*) louer.

►let through *vtas* laisser passer (*qn, l'eau, la lumière*).

►let up 1 *vi* (*of rain, pressure of business etc*) diminuer; (*of frost etc*) s'adoucir; **once he's started he never lets up,** une fois lancé il ne s'arrête plus. **2** *vtsep* **l. him up,** (*from the ground*) laisse-le se relever.

let-down ['letdaʊn] *n F* déception *f*, déboire *m*.

lethal ['liːθ(ə)l] *adj* mortel; **l. dose,** dose mortelle; *Mil etc* **l. weapon,** arme meurtrière; **that vodka's l.!,** cette vodka est meurtrière!

lethargic [lɪ'θɑːdʒɪk] *adj* léthargique.

lethargically [lɪ'θɑːdʒɪklɪ] *adv* d'une manière léthargique.

lethargy ['leθədʒɪ] *n* léthargie *f*.

let-out ['letaʊt] *n F* (*excuse*) excuse *f*; **a l.-o. clause,** échappatoire *f*.

letter¹ [letər] *n* **(a)** lettre *f*; **business l.,** lettre d'affaires; **I've had a l. from him,** j'ai reçu une lettre de lui; **are there any letters for me?,** y a-t-il du courrier pour moi?; **to notify s.o. by l.,** informer qn par lettre; *Banking Com* **l. of credit/exchange,** lettre de crédit/change; **l. of advice,** lettre d'avis; **l. of acknowledgement,** accusé *m* de réception; **registered l.,** lettre recommandée; **express l.,** lettre exprès; **airmail l.,** lettre par avion; **air l.,** aérogramme *m*; *Sl* **French l.,** capote anglaise; **l. bomb,** lettre piégée; **l. box,** boîte *f* à *ou* aux lettres; **l. card,** carte-lettre *f*, *pl* cartes-lettres; **l. rate,** tarif *m* (d'affranchissement des) lettres; **l. opener,** coupe-papier *m inv*; **l. tray,** corbeille *f*, panier *m* (à lettres, à courrier); **letters patent,** lettres de patentes; **letters patent of nobility,** lettres de noblesse;

(b) lettre *f* (*de l'alphabet*); *Typ* lettre, caractère *m*; **to have letters after one's name,** avoir des titres; **according to the l. of the law,** selon la lettre de la loi; **to obey to the l.,** obéir à la lettre; **code l.,** lettre d'un code de chiffrement, lettre-code *f*, *pl* lettres-code(s); *Rad* indicatif littéral; *Rad etc* **call letters,** indicatif *m* d'appel (*d'une station radio etc*);

(c) letters, (belles-)lettres *fpl*, littérature *f*; **man of letters,** homme *m* de lettres.

letter² *vt* marquer (*un objet*) avec des lettres; (*engrave*) graver des lettres sur (*un objet*).

lettered ['letəd] *adj* **(a)** (*person*) lettré; **(b)** marqué avec des lettres.

letterhead ['letəhed] *n* en-tête *m inv* de lettre (imprimé).

lettering ['letərɪŋ] *n* **(a)** (*action*) lettrage *m*; **(b)** (*result*) lettres *fpl*, inscription *f*.

letterpress ['letəpres] *n* **(a)** *Typ* impression *f* typographique; **l. printing,** typographie *f*; **(b)** texte *m* (accompagnant une illustration); **(c)** presse *f* à copier.

letter-quality ['letə'kwɒlɪtɪ] **1** *adj Comptr* **l.-q. printer,** imprimante *f* qualité courrier. **2** *n* qualité courrier.

letting ['letɪŋ] *n* louage *m*; location *f* (*d'une maison*).

lettuce ['letɪs] *n* laitue *f*; **cabbage l.,** laitue pommée; *Br* **cos l.,** (laitue) romaine *f*; **lamb's l.,** mâche *f*.

let-up ['letʌp] *n F* diminution *f* (**in,** de); changement *m* (*in weather*); relâchement *m* (*in efforts, fighting*); **to work fifteen hours without a l.-up,** travailler quinze heures d'affilée.

leucocyte ['luːkəsaɪt] *n Physiol* leucocyte *m*.

leukaemia, *US* **leukemia** [luː'kiːmɪə] *n Med* leucémie *f*; **to have l.,** avoir la leucémie.

leukaemic, *US* **leukemic** [luː'kiːmɪk] *adj Med* leucémique.

Levant [lɪ'vænt] **1** *n* **the L.,** le Levant. **2** *adj* du Levant; levantin.

Levantine [lə'væntaɪn] **1** *adj* levantin. **2** *n* Levantin, -ine.

levee ['levɪ] *n US Constr* levée *f*, digue *f* (*d'une rivière*).

level¹ ['lev(ə)l] **1** *n* **(a)** (*height*) niveau *m* (*des prix, de la mer etc*); (*in surveying*) & *Geog* altitude *f*, niveau; (*quantity*) niveau (*d'alcool etc*); **mean sea l.,** niveau moyen de la mer; **datum** *or* **reference l.,** (*in surveying*) niveau de référence; **at eye l.,** à (la) hauteur des yeux; **on a l. with sth,** au niveau *ou* à la hauteur de qch, de niveau avec qch; **split l. house,** maison à ressaut *ou* à paliers, *Can* maison à mi-étages; **to maintain prices at a high l.,** maintenir les prix à un niveau élevé; *Phys etc* **energy l.,** niveau énergétique; **noise l.,** niveau de bruit (*d'un moteur etc*); **radiation l.,** niveau de radiation; *MecE* **oil l.,** niveau d'huile; **to be on a l. with s.o.,** être au niveau de qn, être sur un pied d'égalité avec qn; **her ambition is on a l. with mine,** son ambition est du même ordre que la mienne; **to come down to s.o.'s l.,** se mettre au niveau *ou* à la portée de qn; **at ministerial l.,** à l'échelon ministériel;

(b) (*flat ground*) terrain *m* de niveau; *Aut Rail Av* palier *m*; **dead l.,** niveau parfait, palier absolu; **on the l.,** (*built etc*) sur un terrain plat; *F* (*person*) honnête; *F* **is he on the l.?,** est-ce qu'on peut lui faire confiance?; *F* **it's completely on the l.,** c'est tout à fait légal;

(c) (*tool*) niveau *m* (*de charpentier etc*); **spirit l.,** niveau à bulle d'air *ou* à alcool; **l. (rule),** latte *f ou* règle *f* de niveau; **water l.,** niveau d'eau.

2 *adj* **(a)** (*not sloping*) horizontal, -aux; (*terrain*) de niveau, à niveau; (*route etc*) en palier; *Av* **l. flight,** vol horizontal; **hold the tray l.,** tiens le plateau droit;

(b) (*flat*) égal, -aux, uni;

(c) l. with ..., au niveau de ..., à (la) hauteur de ...; *Rail* **l. crossing,** passage *m* à niveau; **l. with the ground,** au ras du sol; à ras de terre; **l. spoonful,** cuillerée rase; *Sp* **to draw l. with ...,** arriver à (la) hauteur de ...; (*in rowing*) venir bord à bord avec ...; **they are about l. in ability,** leurs compétences se valent; **it's l. pegging,** (*between the two*) il y a égalité; **l. tone,** ton soutenu *ou* uniforme; **to keep a l. head,** garder sa tête *ou* son sang-froid; **to do one's l. best,** faire tout son possible, faire de son mieux.

3 *adv Av* **to fly l.,** voler en palier.

level² *v* (**-ll-**, *US* **-l-**) **1** *vt* **(a)** niveler, égaliser (*une surface*); mettre (*un billard etc*) de niveau; araser (*un terrain etc*); **to l. a town (to the ground),** raser une ville; **(b)** pointer (*un fusil*); braquer (*un canon*); diriger (*une longue-vue*) (**at,** sur); **to l. one's gun at s.o.,** ajuster *ou* viser qn avec son fusil, mettre qn en joue; **to l. criticism at s.o.,** émettre des critiques sur qn; **to l. accusations at s.o.,** lancer des accusations contre qn; **to l. a blow at s.o.,** porter un coup à qn; **(c)** (*in surveying*) effectuer des opérations de nivellement dans (*une région*); niveler (*une région*). **2** *vi F* **to l. with s.o.,** parler franchement à qn.

►level down *vi esp Pol* niveler au plus bas.

►level off 1 *vtsep* aplanir (*qch*). **2** *vi* **(a)** s'arrêter à un certain niveau; **demand levels off at this time of year,** la demande se stabilise à cette époque de l'année; **(b)** *Av* voler en palier.

►level out 1 *vtsep* égaliser (*une surface etc*). **2** *vi* **(a)** (*of prices*) s'équilibrer; **(b)** (*of aircraft*) attaquer le palier.

►level up *vi esp Pol* accroître le niveau moyen.

level-headed ['lev(ə)l'hedɪd] *adj* pondéré.

leveller, *US* **leveler** ['lev(ə)lər] *n* **(a)** niveleur, -euse; **(b)** *Pol* égalitaire *mf*; *Lit* **death is a great l.,** tous les hommes sont égaux devant la mort.

levelling, *US* **leveling** ['lev(ə)lɪŋ] *n* **(a)** nivellement *m*; mise *f* à niveau *ou* de niveau; aplanissement *m* (*d'une surface*); égalisation *f* (*de la chaussée*); **l. pole,** (*in surveying*) mire *f* (de nivellement); **(b)** arasement *m* (*d'un* *mur*); **(c)** pointage *m*, braquage *m* (*d'une arme à feu*).

lever[1] ['liːvər, *Am* 'levər] *n* levier *m*; *MecE* levier; manette *f*; **control/operating l.,** levier de commande/ manœuvre; *Aut* **gear l.,** levier de changement de vitesse, levier des vitesses; *Rail* **point** *or* **switch l.,** levier d'aiguille; **arming** *or* **cocking l.,** (*on pistol*) levier d'armement.

lever[2] *vt* **to l. a box open,** ouvrir une caisse avec un levier; **he levered the box open with a piece of wood,** il a ouvert la caisse avec un morceau de bois; *Fig* **he has levered himself into a very strong position,** il s'est hissé jusqu'à une situation très importante.

►**lever off** *vtsep* (*lid, top, tyre*) enlever (avec un levier).

►**lever out** *vtsep* (*object*) extraire; *Fig* (*person*) évincer; **he has been levered out of his job,** on l'a évincé de son emploi.

►**lever up** *vtsep* (*lid etc*) soulever (avec un levier); **he levered himself up onto his elbow,** il s'est soulevé en s'aidant de son coude.

leverage ['liːvərɪdʒ] *n* **(a)** force *f* *ou* puissance *f* de levier; **to bring l. to bear on,** exercer des pesées sur (*une porte etc*); **we have no l. we could bring to bear on him,** nous n'avons pas de prise sur lui; **(b)** (*levers*) système *m* de leviers.

leveraged ['liːvərɪdʒd] *n Com* **l. buy-out,** OPA *f* à crédit.

leveret ['levərɪt] *n* (*animal*) levraut *m*.

leviathan [lɪ'vaɪəθ(ə)n] *n* **(a)** *Bible* léviathan *m*; **(b)** *F* (*something huge*) monstre *m*.

Levis ® ['liːvaɪz] *npl* Levis ® *m*; **a pair of L.,** un Levis.

levitate ['levɪteɪt] **1** *vi* se soulever (par lévitation). **2** *vt* soulever (*qn, qch*) (par lévitation).

levitation [levɪ'teɪʃən] *n* lévitation *f*.

levity ['levɪtɪ] *n* **(a)** légèreté *f*, manque *m* de sérieux; **(b)** *Phys etc* légèreté *f*.

levy[1] ['levɪ] *n* **(a)** (*tax*) impôt *m*, contribution *f*; **capital l.,** prélèvement *m* sur le capital; **import l.,** taxe *f* à l'importation; **(b)** levée *f* (*d'un impôt, Mil des troupes*); réquisition *f* (*des chevaux etc*).

levy[2] *vt* **(a)** lever, percevoir (*un impôt*); infliger (*une amende*); **to l. a duty on goods,** imposer des marchandises; **to l. a fine on s.o.,** frapper qn d'une amende; **(b)** *Mil* lever (*des troupes*).

lewd [luːd] *adj* impudique, lascif, lubrique; (*sourire*) lascif, égrillard.

lewdly ['luːdlɪ] *adv* impudiquement, lascivement.

lewdness ['luːdnɪs] *n* **(a)** (*of joke etc*) impudicité *f*, lasciveté *f*, lubricité *f*; **(b)** (*of lifestyle*) luxure *f*, débauche *f*.

lexical ['leksɪk(ə)l] *adj* lexical.

lexicalize ['leksɪkəlaɪz] *vt* lexicaliser.

lexicographer [leksɪ'kɒgrəfər] *n* lexicographe *mf*.

lexicographical [leksɪkə'græfɪk(ə)l] *adj* lexicographique.

lexicography [leksɪ'kɒgrəfɪ] *n* lexicographie *f*.

lexicology [leksɪ'kɒlədʒɪ] *n* lexicologie *f*.

lexicon ['leksɪkən] *n* lexique *m*.

lh [el'eɪtʃ] *Mus etc* (*abbr* **left hand**) main gauche.

liabilities [laɪə'bɪlɪtɪz] *npl Com Fin* ensemble *m* des dettes, obligations *fpl*, valeurs passives, dettes passives, le passif; (*in bankruptcy*) masse passive (*d'une liquidation après faillite*); **assets and l.,** actif *m* et passif; **to meet one's l.,** faire face à ses engagements.

liability [laɪə'bɪlɪtɪ] *n* **(a)** *Jur* responsabilité *f*; **employer's l.,** responsabilité patronale (*pour les accidents du travail*); **civil l.,** responsabilité civile; **limited l. company,** société *f* à responsabilité limitée; **her firm wouldn't accept l. for the accident,** son entreprise refusa d'assumer la responsabilité de l'accident; **(b)** *Com* (*on bills of exchange*) encours *m*; **(c)** *Fig* désavantage *m*, handicap *m*; **your brother is a l.,** (*to us*) ton frère ne nous attire que des problèmes; **(d)** (*likelihood*) disposition *f*, tendance *f* (**to sth,** à qch; **to do sth,** à faire qch); **l. to a fine,** risque *m* d'amende; **l. for military service,** obligations *fpl* militaires; **l. to explode,** (*of product etc*) danger *m* d'explosion.

liable ['laɪəb(ə)l] *adj* **(a)** *Jur* responsable (**for,** de); **you are l. for the damage,** vous êtes responsable du dommage; **(b)** (*subject*) assujetti, tenu, astreint (**to,** à); **l. to a tax,** assujetti à un impôt, redevable d'un impôt; **l. to a fine,** passible d'une amende; **l. to military service,** astreint au service militaire; **(c)** (*likely*) sujet, apte, exposé (**to,** à); **l. to make mistakes,** enclin à faire des fautes; **she's l. to get sea sick,** elle est sujette au mal de mer; **when he gets angry he is l. to do anything,** quand il se met en colère il est capable de tout; **they're l. to have an accident in that old car,** ils risquent un accident avec cette vieille voiture.

liaise [liː'eɪz] *vi* faire *ou* effectuer la liaison; **to l. with s.o. about sth,** être en liaison avec qn à propos de qch.

liaison [lɪ'eɪzɒn] *n* **(a)** *Mil etc* **l. agent/officer,** agent *m*/ officier *m* de liaison; **(b)** liaison *f* (amoureuse); **(c)** *Ling* **to make a l.,** faire la liaison (entre deux mots).

liana [lɪ'ɑːnə] *n Bot* liane *f*.

liar ['laɪər] *n* menteur, -euse; **you l.!,** menteur que tu es!, quel menteur (tu fais)!

lib [lɪb] *n F* = **LIBERATION (a)**; **women's l.,** MLF *m*.

Lib [lɪb] *Pol* (*abbr* **Liberal**) libéral.

libation [laɪ'beɪʃən] *n* libation *f*.

libel[1] ['laɪb(ə)l] *n* diffamation *f*; *Jur* diffamation (par écrit), écrit *m* diffamatoire; **to utter a l. against s.o.,** publier un article *ou* un écrit diffamant qn; **action for l., l. action,** procès *m* en diffamation; **to sue s.o. for l.,** poursuivre qn en justice pour diffamation; **l. laws,** lois *fpl* contre la diffamation; **that's l.!,** c'est une calomnie *ou* de la diffamation!

libel[2] *vt* (**-ll-**, *US* **-l-**) *Jur* diffamer (*qn*) (*par écrit*); publier une calomnie contre (*qn*); calomnier (*qn*).

libellous, *US* **libelous** ['laɪbələs] *adj* (*écrit*) diffamatoire, diffamant.

liberal ['lɪb(ə)rəl] **1** *adj* **(a)** (*idea etc*) & *Pol* libéral, -aux; (*person*) d'esprit large; **l. education,** éducation libérale; **l. minded,** large d'esprit; **(b)** (*generous*) libéral, généreux; **l. with one's money,** prodigue de son argent; **(c)** (*abundant*) ample; **l. supply of food,** nourriture abondante; **a l. helping,** une portion généreuse. **2** *n Pol etc* libéral, -ale.

liberalism ['lɪb(ə)rəlɪz(ə)m] *n* libéralisme *m*.

liberality [lɪbə'rælɪtɪ] *n* **(a)** libéralisme *m* (*de vues*); **(b)** (*with money etc*) libéralité *f*, générosité *f*.

liberalize ['lɪb(ə)rəlaɪz] *vt* libéraliser.

liberally ['lɪb(ə)rəlɪ] *adv* libéralement.

liberate ['lɪbəreɪt] *vt* **(a)** libérer; **(b)** *Ch* libérer, dégager (*un gaz*); **(c)** *Fin* **to l. capital,** libérer des capitaux.

liberated ['lɪbəreɪtɪd] *adj* libéré; **a l. woman,** une femme libérée; **these are l. times,** on vit à une époque libérée; **her ideas aren't l.,** ses idées ne sont pas émancipées.

liberation [lɪbə'reɪʃən] *n* **(a)** libération *f*; *Hist* **after the l.,** après la libération (de la France); **l. movement,** mouvement *m* de libération; **she doesn't believe in women's l.,** elle ne croit pas à la libération de la femme; **(b)** *Ch Phys* dégagement *m* (*d'un gaz, de chaleur*); **(c)** *Fin* **l. of capital,** mobilisation *f* de capitaux.

liberator ['lɪbəreɪtər] *n* libérateur, -trice.

Liberia [laɪ'bɪərɪə] *n* Libéria *m*.

Liberian [laɪ'bɪərɪən] **1** *adj* libérien. **2** *n* Libérien, -ienne.

libertarian [lɪbə'teərɪən] **1** *n* libertaire *mf*. **2** *adj* (*philosophy, idea, tendency etc*) libertaire.

libertine ['lɪbətaɪn, -tiːn] *adj* & *n* libertin, -ine.

liberty ['lɪbətɪ] *n* liberté *f*; **l. of conscience,** liberté de conscience; **at l.,** (*free*) libre; **to be at l. to do sth,** être libre de faire qch; **Statue of L.,** statue *f* de la Liberté; *Nau* **l. ticket,** permission *f* de terre *ou* d'aller à terre; **to take the l. of doing** *or* **to do sth,** prendre la liberté *ou* se permettre de faire qch; *F* **what a l.!,** quel culot!; **civil liberties,** libertés civiques; **to take liberties with s.o.,** prendre *ou* se permettre des libertés avec qn; **to take liberties with a translation,** se permettre des libertés dans une traduction.

libidinous [lɪ'bɪdɪnəs] *adj* libidineux.

libido [lɪ'biːdəʊ, -'baɪ-] *n Psy* libido *f*.

LIBOR ['laɪbɔːr] *n Br Fin* (*abbr* **London Inter-Bank Offer Rate**) ≈ TIOP *m* (taux interbancaire offert à Paris).

Libra ['liːbrə] *n Astron* la Balance; **to be a L.,** être Balance.

librarian [laɪ'breərɪən] *n* bibliothécaire *mf*.

librarianship [laɪ'breərɪənʃɪp] *n* (*subject*) bibliothéconomie *f*.

library ['laɪbrərɪ] *n* (*of books, Comptr of programs*) bibliothèque *f*; **lending l.,** bibliothèque de prêt; **reference l.,** bibliothèque d'ouvrages de référence; salle *f* de lecture; **mobile l.,** bibliobus *m*; **photographic l.,** photothèque *f*; **film l.,** cinémathèque *f*; **music l.,** musicothèque *f*; **record l.,** discothèque *f*, collection *f* de disques; **tape l.,** magnétothèque *f*; *F* **he's a walking l.,** c'est une encyclopédie vivante; **l. book,** livre *m* de bibliothèque; **l. card** *or* **ticket,** carte *f* de bibliothèque; **l. science,** bibliothéconomie *f*.

librettist [lɪ'bretɪst] *n Th* librettiste *mf*.

libretto, *pl* **-i, -os** [lɪ'bretəʊ, -iː, -əʊz] *n* libretto *m*, *pl* librettos; livret *m* (*d'opéra etc*).

Libya ['lɪbɪə] *n* Libye *f*.

Libyan ['lɪbɪən] **1** *adj* libyen; **the L. desert,** le désert de Libye. **2** *n* Libyen, -yenne.

lice *see* **LOUSE**.

licence, *US* **license** ['laɪsəns] *n* **(a)** *Admin* (*document*) permis *m*, autorisation *f*, patente *f*, licence *f*; (*permission*) permission *f*, autorisation; **under l. from the inventor,**

avec l'autorisation de l'inventeur; **l. to sell beer, wine and spirits,** *Am* **liquor l.,** permis *ou* licence de débit de boissons; **trading l.,** carte *f* de commerce; **manufacturing l.,** brevet *m ou* licence de fabrication; **made/manufactured under l.,** construit/fabriqué sous licence; *Br* **television l.,** (*fee*) redevance *f* télé; **import/export l.,** licence d'importation/ d'exportation; **marriage l., special l.,** = dispense *f* de bans; **they were married by special l.,** ils se sont mariés avec dispense de bans; **shooting l.,** permis de chasse; **gun l.,** permis de port d'arme(s); **dog l.,** taxe *f* sur les chiens; **l. number,** numéro *m* d'immatriculation; *Am* **l. plate,** plaque *f* d'immatriculation; **driving l.,** *Am* **driver's l.,** permis de conduire; **heavy goods (vehicle) l.,** permis poids lourds; *Av* **pilot's l.,** brevet de pilote;
(b) *esp Pej* licence *f*; **poetic l.,** licence poétique;
(c) = **LICENTIOUSNESS.**

license[1] ['laɪsəns] *vt* accorder un permis *ou* une patente *ou* un brevet à (qn); **to l. a car,** (*of owner*) acheter une vignette pour une voiture; **to l. s.o. to sell drink,** autoriser qn à tenir un débit de boissons; **licensed to sell beer, wines and spirits,** autorisé *ou Can* licencié à vendre des boissons alcooliques; **to be licensed to carry a gun,** avoir un permis de port d'arme(s).

license[2] *n US* = **LICENCE.**

licensed ['laɪsənst] *adj Admin* autorisé, patenté; *Av* (*pilote*) breveté; **l. house** *or* **premises,** débit *m* de boissons; **l. victualler,** débitant *m* de boissons *ou* de spiritueux.

licensee [laɪs(ə)n'siː] *n* détenteur, -trice d'une patente *ou* d'un permis *ou* (*for manufacturing*) d'une licence; gérant, -ante, propriétaire *mf* (*d'un pub etc*).

licensing ['laɪsənsɪŋ] *n* autorisation *f* (*de qn à faire qch*); octroiement *m* d'un permis *ou* d'une autorisation (*à qn*); **l. agreement,** accord *m* de licence; **l. hours,** (*of pub*) heures *fpl* d'ouverture; **l. laws,** lois relatives aux débits de boissons alcooliques.

licentiate [laɪ'senʃɪət] *n* **(a)** *Sch* diplômé, -ée; **(b)** *Rel* aspirant *m* à un pastorat (*de l'Église réformée*).

licentious [laɪ'senʃəs] *adj* licencieux; (*person*) dévergondé.

licentiousness [laɪ'senʃəsnɪs] *n* licence *f*; (*of person*) dévergondage *m*.

lichen ['laɪkən, 'lɪtʃən] *n* lichen *m*.

lichgate ['lɪtʃgeɪt] *n* porche d'entrée de cimetière surmonté d'un petit toit.

licit ['lɪsɪt] *adj* licite.

licitly ['lɪsɪtlɪ] *adv* licitement.

lick[1] [lɪk] *n* **(a)** coup *m* de langue; **to give sth,/s.o. a l.,** lécher qch/qn; **give me a l. of your ice cream,** laisse-moi lécher un peu ta glace; *F* **a l. and a promise,** un bout *ou* un brin de toilette; **(b)** *F* petite quantité; **a l. of paint,** une petite couche de peinture; **l. (of hair),** mèche *f*; *F* **at (a) great l., at full l.,** à toute allure, à toute vitesse; **(c) salt l.,** (*provided for cattle*) pain salé; (*place*) terrain *m* salifère (*où les bêtes viennent lécher le sol*).

lick[2] *vt* **(a)** lécher; **to l. one's lips** *or F* **one's chops,** s'en lécher les babines, se (pour)lécher les babines; *Fig* **to l. one's wounds,** se remettre de ses blessures; *F* **to l. s.o.'s boots,** lécher les bottes à qn; *Fig* **to l. s.o. into shape,** former *ou* dégrossir *ou* dégourdir qn; **to l. sth up,** (*of animal*) laper qch; *F* **to l. the plate clean,** torcher le plat; **(b)** *F* (*defeat*) battre, vaincre, écraser (*un adversaire*); (*beat*) battre, rosser (*qn*); **to have s.o. licked,** réduire qn en poussière; **I've got the problem licked,** j'ai surmonté le problème; **this one has got me licked,** (*of problem*) ça me dépasse.

lickety-split ['lɪkɪtɪ'splɪt] *adv Am* très vite, à toute vitesse.

licking ['lɪkɪŋ] *n* **(a)** léchage *m*; **(b)** *F* (*of opponent*) raclée *f*; (*beating*) raclée *f*, rossée *f*; **they gave the other team a l.,** ils ont mis une raclée à l'autre équipe.

lickspittle ['lɪkspɪt(ə)l] *n Old-fashioned* lèche-bottes *m inv*.

licorice ['lɪkərɪs] *n Am* = **LIQUORICE.**

lid [lɪd] *n* **(a)** couvercle *m* (*de boîte, de casserole etc*); *F* **that puts the l. on it!,** ça c'est le comble!; **to take the l. off sth,** ôter le couvercle de qch; *Fig* mettre au grand jour; *Br Sl* **to flip one's l.,** perdre la tête; **to put the l. on information,** tirer un voile sur une information; **(b)** *F* chapeau *m*; **(c)** *Anat* paupière *f*; **(d)** *Biol* opercule *m*.

lidded ['lɪdɪd] *adj* **(a)** (*boîte etc*) à couvercle; **(b)** *Biol* (*capsule etc*) à opercule.

lidless ['lɪdlɪs] *adj* (*eyes*) sans paupières.

lie[1] [laɪ] *n* mensonge *m*; **white l.,** pieux mensonge; **it's all lies** *or* **a pack of lies!,** c'est un tissu de mensonges!; **to tell a l.,** dire un mensonge; **l. detector,** détecteur *m* de mensonges; **to take a l. detector test,** passer au détecteur de mensonges; *Fml* **to give the l. to s.o.,** donner tort à qn; **to give the l. to an argument,** démentir un argument; **to give s.o. the l. (direct),** donner un démenti (formel) à qn.

lie[2] *v* (*pt & pp* **lied** [laɪd]; *prp* **lying** ['laɪɪŋ]) **1** *vi* mentir (**to s.o.,** à qn); **to l. about one's age,** tricher sur sa date de naissance; **to l. in one's teeth,** mentir effrontément. **2** *vt* **she lied her way into the building,** elle a pénétré dans l'immeuble grâce à quelques mensonges; **he always lies his way out of difficulties,** il se sort toujours des difficultés en mentant.

lie[3] *n* **(a)** disposition *f* (*du terrain etc*); *Geol* gisement *m*; *Constr* tracé *m* (*d'une route*); **l. of the land,** configuration *f ou* disposition du terrain, topographie *f*; *Fig* **to find out the l. of the land,** tâter le terrain; **(b)** *Golf* position *f*, assiette *f* (*de la balle*).

lie[4] *vi* (*pt* **lay** [leɪ]; *pp* **lain** [leɪn]; *prp* **lying** ['laɪɪŋ]) **(a)** (*of person, animal*) être couché (à plat); **to l. on one's back/ side,** être couché sur le dos/côté; **to be lying ill in bed,** être (malade et) alité; **we found him lying dead,** nous l'avons trouvé mort; **here lies ...,** (*on gravestone*) ci-gît ...; **to l. in bed,** rester au lit; **to l. awake,** rester éveillé; **to l. hidden,** rester *ou* se tenir caché; **to l. low,** se tapir, rester tapi, *F* rester *ou* se tenir coi; **to l. in wait for s.o.,** se tenir à l'affût de qn, attendre qn à l'affût;
(b) (*of thing*) être, se trouver; **the papers lay on the table,** les papiers étaient (étalés) sur la table; **all her clothes were lying on the floor,** tous ses vêtements étaient étalés par terre; **to l. in ruins,** (*of building*) être en ruines; **the obstacles that l. in our way,** les obstacles qui bloquent notre chemin; *Nau* **ship lying at her berth,** navire mouillé *ou* amarré à son poste; **to l. in the bank,** (*of money*) être déposé à la banque; **it's just lying in the bank doing nothing,** (*of money*) l'argent dort à la banque et ne travaille pas; **the snow did not l.,** la neige n'a pas tenu; **to l. dormant,** (*volcano*) être en sommeil *ou* au repos; **to l. (heavy) on one's stomach,** (*of food*) peser sur l'estomac; **sins that l. heavy on the conscience,** péchés qui pèsent sur la conscience; **the onus of proof lies with them,** c'est à eux qu'incombe la charge de la preuve; **the responsibility lies with the author,** la responsabilité incombe à l'auteur; **town lying in a valley,** ville située dans une vallée; **to know where one's interests l.,** savoir où se trouvent ses intérêts; **the difference lies in this/that ...,** la différence consiste en ceci/que ...; **the fault lies with you,** la faute retombe sur vous; **a vast plain lay before us,** une vaste plaine s'étendait devant nous; **a brilliant future lies before her,** un brillant avenir s'ouvre devant elle; **our way lies through the woods,** notre chemin passe par les bois; **my talents do not l. in that direction,** je n'ai pas de dispositions *ou* de talent pour cela;
(c) *Jur* (*of action, appeal*) être recevable.

▶**lie about** *vi* (*of thing*) traîner (ça et là); (*of person*) traîner; **to leave one's papers lying about,** laisser traîner ses papiers.

▶**lie back** *vi* se laisser retomber; se renverser (*dans son fauteuil*); **when you've finished you can l. back and take things easy,** quand tu auras fini tu pourras te reposer.

▶**lie down** *vi* se coucher, s'étendre; **go and l. down,** va t'allonger; **to l. down on one's bed,** s'étendre sur son lit; **to l. down on the ground,** se coucher *ou* s'allonger par terre; **l. down!,** (*to dog*) couché!; **to take an insult lying down,** ne pas relever une insulte; **he won't take it lying down,** il ne se laissera pas faire.

▶**lie in** *vi* faire la grasse matinée.

▶**lie off** *vi* (*of ship*) rester au large.

▶**lie over** *vi* (*of thing*) être remis à plus tard; **to let a bill l. over,** différer l'échéance d'un effet.

▶**lie to** *vi* (*of ship*) être à la cape, tenir la cape.

▶**lie up** *vi* **(a)** (*because of illness*) garder le lit; garder la chambre; (*hide*) se cacher; **(b)** (*of car*) être en panne; (*of ship*) désarmer.

lie-down ['laɪ'daʊn] *n* **to have a l.-d.,** faire une sieste *ou* un petit somme.

lief [liːf] *adj & adv Arch* **I would as l. ...,** j'aimerais autant ... .

lie-in ['laɪ'ɪn] *n* **to have a l.-in,** faire la grasse matinée.

lien [liː(ə)n] *n Jur* privilège *m* (*sur un meuble etc*), droit *m* de rétention; **to have a l. (up)on a cargo,** avoir un recours sur un chargement.

lieu [ljuː, luː] *n* **in l. of ...,** au lieu de ...; **to stand in l. of ...,** tenir lieu de ...; **I'll take something else in l.,** je prendrai quelque chose d'autre à la place; **two weeks salary in l. of notice,** deux semaines de salaire en guise de préavis.

lieutenant [lef'tenənt, *esp US* luː-] *n Mil & Fig* lieutenant *m*; *Nau* lieutenant de vaisseau; *Mil* **l. colonel** (*pl* **lieutenant colonels**), lieutenant-colonel *m*, *pl* lieutenants-colonels; *Mil* **l. general,** (*pl* **lieutenant generals**), général *m* de corps d'armée; *Nau* **l. commander** (*pl* **lieutenant commanders**), capitaine *m* de corvette; *Mil Av* **flight l.,** capitaine (d'aviation); *Can* **L. Governor,** lieutenant-Gouverneur *m*.

Lieut *n Mil* (*abbr* **Lieutenant**) Lieut., Lt..

Lieut-Col *n Mil* (*abbr* **Lieutenant-Colonel**) Lieut.-Col..

life, *pl* **lives** [laɪf, laɪvz] *n* **(a)** (*existence*) vie *f*; **l. force,** élan vital; **to give l. to s.o.,** donner la vie à qn; **to come to l. again,** revenir à la vie; **it is a matter of l. and death,** c'est une question de vie ou de mort; **to be hovering between l. and death,** être entre la vie et la mort; **to take s.o.'s l.,** tuer qn; **to take one's own l.,** se suicider; **to risk one's l., to risk l. and limb,** risquer sa peau; **to escape with one's l.,** s'en tirer la vie sauve; **to beat s.o. to within an inch of his l.,** battre qn jusqu'à le laisser pour mort; **to lose one's l.,** perdre la vie, périr; **no lives were lost,** personne n'a été tué; **100 lives were lost,** on a eu 100 morts; **the catastrophe resulted in great loss of l.,** la catastrophe a fait beaucoup de victimes; **to believe in l. after death,** croire à la vie après la mort; **run for your lives!,** sauve qui peut!; **a cat has nine lives,** un chat a neuf vies; *F* **not on your l.!,** jamais de la vie!; **he was rowing for dear l.,** il ramait de toutes ses forces; **she can't run to save her l.,** pour tout l'or du monde elle ne pourrait pas courir; *F* **I couldn't for the l. of me think what he wanted,** je ne pouvais absolument pas imaginer *ou* penser ce qu'il voulait; *Art* **to draw from l.,** dessiner sur le vif *ou* d'après nature; *Art* **l. class,** classe *f* où on dessine des nus; **characters taken from l.,** caractères pris sur le vif; **that's her to the l.,** (*in that portrait, play etc*) c'est elle toute crachée; **true to l.,** (*roman etc*) vécu, senti; *F* **there she was as large as l.,** elle était là en chair et en os; **animal/vegetable l.,** la vie animale/végétale; **bird l.,** les oiseaux *mpl*; *Art* **still l.,** nature morte; **l. belt/buoy/jacket/raft,** ceinture *f*/bouée *f*/gilet *m*/radeau *m* de sauvetage; *Br Mil* **the L. Guards,** le corps de cavaliers appartenant à la maison du roi; les Gardes du corps; **l. preserver,** *Am* appareil *m* de sauvetage; *Br* (*weapon*) casse-tête *m inv*, canne plombée;

(b) (*period of existence*) vie *f*, vivant *m* (*de qn*); vie, durée *f* (*d'un phénomène, d'une lampe etc*); **(useful) l.,** vie *ou* durée utile (*d'une machine etc*); **to work all one's l.,** travailler durant toute sa vie; **never in (all) my l.,** jamais de la vie; **in his early l.,** quand il était jeune; **married l.,** vie conjugale; **working l.,** période *f ou* années *fpl* d'activité *ou* de travail; **appointed for l.,** nommé à vie; *F* **to be in for l.,** en avoir pris pour la vie; **to be given a l. sentence, to get l.,** être condamné à vie; **to mate for l.,** (*of animal, bird*) s'unir pour la vie; *Nucl Phys* **average** *or* **mean l.,** vie moyenne (*d'un atome, d'un isotope*); **l. member/membership/subscription,** membre *m*/adhésion *f*/abonnement *m* à vie; **l. annuity/pension,** pension/rente viagère; **l. interest,** usufruit *m* (*d'un bien*); viager *m*; **l. imprisonment,** emprisonnement perpétuel; *Br* **l. peer,** pair *m* à vie; **l. span,** (*of person, animal etc*) espérance *f* de vie; (*of machine*) durée de vie; **l. assurance** *or* **insurance,** assurance *f* sur la vie, assurance-vie *f*; **l. expectancy,** espérance *f* de vie; **l. story,** biographie *f*; **to write s.o.'s l. story,** écrire la biographie de qn;

(c) (*mode of existence*) vie *f*; *F* **to live the l. of Riley,** se la couler douce; **to make a new l. for oneself,** refaire sa vie; **to depart this l.,** mourir, quitter ce monde; **the man/woman in one's l.,** l'homme/la femme de sa vie; **way of l.,** manière *f* de vivre; (train *m* de) vie; **the American way of l.,** le style de vie américain; **high l.,** la vie mondaine; **night l.,** la vie nocturne; **to see l.,** se frotter au monde, s'amuser, faire la noce; **he makes her l. a misery,** il lui rend la vie dure; **to make l. worth living,** (*of sth*) donner un sens à l'existence; **life is worth living when I'm with her,** avec elle la vie vaut la peine d'être vécu; *F* **how's l.?,** comment ça va?; **what a l.!,** quelle vie!; **such is** *or* **that's l.!,** c'est la vie!; **this is the l.!,** voilà ce que j'appelle vivre!;

(d) (*liveliness*) **to come to l.,** s'animer; **the play came to l. in the second act,** la pièce s'est animée au deuxième acte; **to bring a party to l.,** (*of person*) animer une fête; **to bring s.o. to l.,** (*of play, book etc*) faire revivre qn; **full of l.,** (*person*) plein de vie *ou* d'entrain; (*street etc*) plein de mouvement *ou* d'animation; **to put new l. into ,** ranimer (*qn, une entreprise etc*); **the l. and soul of the party,** le boute-en-train de la compagnie; *F* **there's no l. in this place,** ça manque d'entrain ici; **there's l. in the old car yet,** elle marche toujours, la vieille bagnole.

life-and-death [lɑɪfən'deθ] *adj* **a l.-and-d. situation,** une affaire de vie ou de mort; **l.-and-d. struggle,** lutte désespérée; *also Fig* guerre *f* à mort.

lifeblood ['laɪfblʌd] *n* âme *f* (*d'une entreprise etc*); *Lit* sang *m* (*de qn*); **the government are draining the l. from small businesses,** le gouvernement est en train de saigner les petites entreprises; **the l. of the economy,** le pivot de l'économie.

lifeboat ['laɪfbəʊt] *n* **(a) (coastal) l.,** canot *m* de sauvetage; **l. station,** station *f ou* poste *m* de sauvetage; **(b) (ship's) l.,** embarcation *f* de sauvetage.

lifeboatman, *pl* **-men** ['laɪfbəʊtmən] *n* sauveteur *m*.

life-giving ['laɪfgɪvɪŋ] *adj* vivifiant; (*soleil*) fécondant; (*chaleur*) fécond.

lifeguard ['laɪfgɑːd] *n* (*at the seaside*) gardien *m* de plage; (*at swimming pool*) maître nageur; **to be on l. duty,** surveiller la baignade.

lifeless ['laɪflɪs] *adj* sans vie; (*style etc*) mou, inanimé, froid.

lifelessly ['laɪflɪslɪ] *adv* sans vie.

lifelessness ['laɪflɪsnɪs] *n* (*death*) absence *f* de vie; (*of party etc*) manque *m* d'animation.

lifelike ['laɪflaɪk] *adj* (*portrait etc*) vivant, qui a de la vie; **it's very l.,** c'est très réaliste.

lifeline ['laɪflaɪn] *n* **(a)** *Nau* ligne *f* de sauvetage; (*aboard ship*) garde-corps *m inv*, attrape *f*; sauvegarde *f*; corde *f* de communication (*de scaphandrier*); *Fig* **to throw s.o. a l.,** venir à l'aide de qn; *Fig* **for us it was a financial l.,** pour nous cet argent a été une vraie bouée de sauvetage (financière); **(b)** (*in palmistry*) la ligne de vie.

lifelong ['laɪflɒŋ] *adj* (*amitié etc*) de toute la vie; **a l. friend,** un ami de toujours; **l. ambition,** ambition *f* de toujours.

lifer ['laɪfər] *n F* condamné, -ée à perpétuité.

life-saver ['laɪfseɪvər] *n* **(a)** (*person*) sauveteur *m*; **(b)** *Fig* planche *f* de salut; **that cup of tea was a l.!,** cette tasse de thé m'a redonné vie; **you're a l.-s.,** tu me sauves la vie!

life-saving ['laɪfseɪvɪŋ] *n* sauvetage *m*; **l.-s. apparatus,** appareils *mpl ou* engins *mpl* de sauvetage.

life-size(d) ['laɪfsaɪz, -d] *adj* (*portrait etc*) de grandeur naturelle, grandeur nature.

life-support ['lɑɪfsəpɔːt] *adj Med* **l.-s. system** *or* **machine,** respirateur artificiel; *Astron* **l.-s. system,** équipement *m* de survie; *Med* **to be on a l.-s. system** *or* **machine,** être sur respirateur artificiel; **to switch off the l.-s. system** *or* **machine,** arrêter le respirateur artificiel *ou* la respiration artificielle.

life-threatening ['laɪfθretnɪŋ] *adj* (*disease*) qui peut être mortel.

lifetime ['laɪftaɪm] *n* (*of person*) vie *f*; *Phys* durée *f*, vie (*d'un phénomène*); *Nucl Phys* durée de vie, longévité *f* (*d'un atome, d'un isotope*); **in** *or* **during one's l.,** de son vivant; **a l. of happiness,** toute une vie de bonheur; **it's the chance of a l.,** cette chance n'arrive qu'une fois dans la vie; **the holiday of a l.,** des vacances exceptionnelles; **a l. supply,** une réserve pour la vie; **he's bought enough envelopes to last him a l.,** il a acheté suffisamment d'enveloppes pour tenir jusqu'à la fin de ses jours.

lift¹ [lɪft] *n* **(a)** (*raising device*) *Br* (*for people*) ascenseur *m*; *Nau* balancine *f* (*de vergue etc*); **(goods) l.,** monte-charge *m inv*, élévateur *m*; **service l.,** monte-plats *m inv*; **l. shaft,** cage *f* d'ascenseur; **ski l.,** (re)monte-pente *m*, *pl* remonte-pentes; **chair l.,** télésiège *m*; *Mil Av* **bomb l.,** treuil *m* de chargement de bombes;

(b) (*act of raising*) haussement *m*; élévation *f* (*du bras etc*); levée *f* (*d'un fardeau etc*); **to give s.o. a l.,** *esp Br* (*in car*) prendre *ou* emmener qn en voiture; *F* (*cheer up*) remonter le moral à qn; *esp Br* **can I give you a l.?,** est-ce que je peux vous conduire *ou* déposer quelque part?; *esp Br* **to thumb a l.,** faire de l'auto-stop *ou* du stop; **fork l. truck,** chariot *m* (élévateur) à fourche;

(c) (*extent of rise*) hauteur *f* de levage (*d'une grue etc*); hauteur d'élévation (*d'une pompe*); *MecE* levée *f* (*d'un clapet, d'une came*); (hauteur de) chute *f* (*d'un bief*); différence *f* de niveau (*entre paliers etc*); *Min* hauteur verticale (*entre deux galeries*);

(d) (*raising power*) force ascensionnelle (*d'un ballon, d'un gaz*); *Av etc* portance *f*, poussée *f* (aérodynamique), sustentation *f*.

lift² **1** *vt* **(a)** lever, soulever (*un poids*); lever, dresser (*la tête*); lever (*les yeux, le bras*); *Nau* soulager (*une voile*); **to l. weights,** (*as exercise*) faire des haltères; **he never lifts a finger to help,** il ne lève *ou* bouge jamais le petit doigt pour aider; **she has only to l. a finger and everyone comes running,** elle n'a qu'à lever le petit doigt et tout le monde accourt; **to l. sth up again,** soulever qch, relever qch; **to l. s.o. up,** (*who has fallen*) aider qn à se relever; **to l. a child up,** (*take in one's arms*) prendre un enfant dans ses bras; *Lit Rel* **to l. up one's voice,** élever la voix; **to l. sth down,** descendre qch (*d'un rayon etc*); **the wind lifted him off his feet,** il a été soulevé par le vent;

(b) *Agr* arracher (*les pommes de terre*); dépiquer (*les plants pour les repiquer*); *Min* remonter (*le minerai*); *Cer* démouler (*la porcelaine*); *Com* enlever (*des marchandises*);
(c) *Cr Golf* donner de l'essor à (*la balle*); *Tennis* lifter (*un coup*);
(d) *F* (*take, steal*) voler (*qch*); **he had his wallet lifted,** il s'est fait piquer son porte-feuille; **to l. a passage from an author/a book,** plagier un auteur/un livre;
(e) (*remove*) lever (*un embargo*).

2 *vi* **(a)** (*of valve etc*) se lever, se soulever; (*of floor*) se soulever (*sous l'action de l'humidité etc*);
(b) (*disperse*) (*of fog*) se lever, se dissiper; *US* (*of rain*) cesser;
(c) *Nau* (*of vessel*) s'élever à la lame.

►**lift off** *vi* (*of aircraft, rocket*) décoller.
►**lift out** *vtsep* (*from box etc*) enlever (**from,** de); (*Mil*) évacuer (*des troupes etc*) (par avion *ou* hélicoptère).
►**lift up** *vtsep see* **LIFT[2] 1 (a).**

liftboy ['lɪftbɔɪ] *n* liftier *m*.
liftgate ['lɪftgeɪt] *n US Aut* hayon *m* arrière.
lifting ['lɪftɪŋ] *n* **(a)** levage *m*, relevage *m*, soulèvement *m* (*d'un poids etc*); *Aut* **l. ramp** *or* **platform,** pont élévateur; **l. capacity,** force *f ou* puissance *f* de levage; *Av* **l. force** *or* **power,** force de sustentation, puissance ascensionnelle; **(b)** *Agr* arrachage *m* (*des pommes de terre*); *Min* remontée *f* (*du minerai*); *Cer* démoulage *m* (*de la porcelaine*); **(c)** levée *f* (*d'un embargo*); **(d)** *F* (*of wallet etc*) vol *m*; (*of literary work*) plagiat *m*.
liftman, *pl* **-men** [lɪftmæn, -men] *n* liftier *m*.
liftoff ['lɪftɒf] *n* (*of rocket*) décollage *m*; **we have l.,** le lancement est une réussite.
ligament ['lɪgəmənt] *n Anat* ligament *m*; **to tear a l.,** se déchirer un ligament.
ligature[1] ['lɪgətjər] *n* **(a)** *Surg* ligature *f*; **(b)** *Typ* ligature *f*; **(c)** *Mus* liaison *f*.
ligature[2] *vt* **(a)** *Surg* ligaturer, barrer (*une veine*); **(b)** *Typ* entrelacer (*a et e*).
light[1] [laɪt] *n* **(a)** lumière *f*; **artificial/electric l.,** lumière artificielle/électrique; **by the l. of the moon,** au clair *ou* à la clarté de la lune; **the l. of day,** la lumière du jour; le jour; **things will look different in the cold l. of day,** demain il fera jour; **at first l.,** à l'aube; **it's getting l.,** le jour se lève; **to bring sth to l.,** (*of investigations*) mettre qch en évidence, révéler qch; **to come to l.,** (*of crime etc*) être découvert; **to see the l.,** (*realise the truth*) être convaincu *ou* converti; **the l. at the end of the tunnel,** le bout du tunnel; **to (first) see the l. of day,** (*of person*) naître, voir le jour; **to be in s.o.'s l.,** faire de l'ombre à qn; *Phys etc* **bright l.,** lumière vive; **infrared/ultraviolet l.,** lumière infrarouge/ultraviolette; **source of l., l. source,** source lumineuse; **l. beam** *or* **ray,** faisceau *ou* rayon lumineux; **l. wave,** onde lumineuse; *Astron* **l. year,** année-lumière *f*, *pl* années-lumière; **good/bad l.,** bon/mauvais éclairage; **picture hung in a good l.,** tableau accroché dans un bon jour; **against the l., with one's back to the l.,** à contre-jour; **to see s.o./sth in a new l./in its true l.,** voir qn/qch sous un jour nouveau/sous son vrai jour; **to see sth in a different l.,** voir qch sous un jour différent *ou* sous un autre angle; **the question should be considered in the l. of these facts,** on devrait considérer la question dans ce contexte; **in l. of,** (*considering*) prenant en considération *ou* en compte; *Fig* **to throw** *or* **shed l. on,** éclairer, éclaircir (*qch*); **to act according to one's lights,** agir conformément à ses idées; *Rel* **the inner l.,** la parole intérieure du Saint-Esprit; *Comptr* **l. pen,** photostyle *m*;

(b) (*in room etc*) lumière *f*; (*on car, train, ship etc*) feu *m*; *Mil* **lights out,** (sonnerie *f* de) l'extinction *f* des feux; **to put** *or* **turn on the l.,** donner de la lumière, allumer; *F* **to go out like a l.,** (*faint*) s'évanouir; (*fall asleep quickly*) s'endormir aussitôt couché; *F* **one of the leading lights of the town,** une des personnalités de la ville; **traffic lights,** feux *mpl* de circulation *ou* de signalisation routière; feux de croisement, *F* feu rouge; **turn right at the (traffic) lights,** tournez à droite au feu rouge; *Fig* **to see the red l.,** se rendre compte du danger, sentir le danger; **to give s.o. the green l.,** donner le feu vert à qn; *Av* **airport lights,** feux d'aéroport; *Av* **approach l.,** feu d'approche; *Av* **landing/runway light(s),** feu(x) d'atterrissage/de piste; *Nau* **harbour lights,** feux (d'entrée) de port; **flashing l.,** feu à éclats; *Aut* **rear lights,** feux rouges; *Aut* **parking lights,** feux de position *ou* de stationnement; *Aut* **reversing l.,** phare *m* de recul; **signal l.,** fanal *m*; **warning l.,** fanal avertisseur; *Aut* **dip your lights,** roulez en code; *Nau Av* **navigation/position lights,** feux de navigation/position; **she was showing no lights,** (*of ship*) il naviguait *ou* faisait route tous feux éteints; *Tech* **control** *or* **warning l.,** voyant lumineux; *Aut* **dashboard** *or* **panel l.,** lampe du tableau de bord; **courtesy l.,** (*in car*) éclairage intérieur automatique; **l. flare,** fusée éclairante; **l. bulb,** ampoule *f*;
(c) (*lighthouse*) phare *m*;
(d) (*fire*) feu *m*, éclat *m* (*du regard*); **to set l. to sth,** mettre le feu à qch; **could I have a l., please?,** (*of smoker*) pouvez-vous me donner du feu, s'il vous plaît?;
(e) *Archit* (*window*) fenêtre *f*; (*small round*) lucarne *f*; jour *m* (*de fenêtre à meneaux*); carreau *m* (*de serre*); *Jur* **ancient lights,** servitude *f* de vue;
(f) *Art Phot* lumière *f*, clair *m*; **l. effects,** effets *mpl* de lumière; **l. and shade,** les clairs et les ombres, le clair-obscur.

light[2] *vt* (*pt & pp* **lit** [lɪt], *occ* **lighted**) **(a)** allumer (*une lampe etc*); **to l. a fire,** allumer un feu; faire du feu; **(b)** éclairer, illuminer (*une pièce, une rue*); **to l. the way for s.o.,** éclairer qn.
light[3] *adj* **(a)** (*room etc*) clair; (bien) éclairé; **it is/will soon be l.,** il fait/fera bientôt jour; **(b)** (*hair, complexion*) blond; (*colour*) clair; **painted in l. tones,** peint en tons clairs *ou* lumineux; **l. blue,** bleu clair *inv*.
light[4] **1** *adj* **(a)** (*fardeau, coup*) léger; (*terre*) meuble; (*deficient*) (*poids*) faible; **with a l. step,** d'un pas léger; **to be l. on one's feet,** avoir le pas léger; **as l. as a feather,** léger comme une plume; **l. wine,** vin léger; **l. beer,** bière légère; **l. breeze,** brise faible *ou* légère; **l. showers,** menues averses;
(b) *Nau* (*bateau*) lège; (*not of full weight, size etc*) (*aircraft, engine*) léger; *Mil* **l. artillery,** artillerie légère *ou* de petit calibre; **l. infantry,** infanterie légère; = les chasseurs (*à pied*); **l. duty,** service réduit; *Metal* **l. castings,** petites pièces (*de fonderie*); **l. crop,** faible récolte *f*; **to have a l. meal,** prendre un repas léger; **to be a l. sleeper,** avoir le sommeil léger;
(c) (*not difficult or severe*) (*tâche*) facile; **l. punishment,** peine légère; **l. taxation,** faible imposition *f*; **l. work,** petits travaux, travail peu fatigant;
(d) (*not serious*) (*comedy, style, music etc*) léger; **l. reading,** lecture(s) récréative(s) *ou* délassante(s); **l. talk,** propos frivoles *ou* légers; **to make l. of,** traiter (*qch*) à la légère; attacher peu d'importance à (*une accusation*).

2 *adv* légèrement; **to travel l.,** voyager avec peu de bagages.

►**light into** *vipo* (*attack verbally or physically*) tomber dessus, rentrer dedans.
►**light on** *vipo* (*find*) rencontrer (*qn, qch*); trouver (*qn, qch*) par hasard; **his eyes lighted on the picture,** ses yeux rencontrèrent le tableau.
►**light out** *vi Am F* décamper.
►**light up** **1** *vi* (*put lights on*) allumer, mettre la lumière; (*of smoker*) *F* allumer sa cigarette *ou* sa pipe; **his eyes lit up,** ses yeux se sont animés; **the whole sky lit up,** le ciel entier s'est illuminé. **2** *vtsep* éclairer (*une pièce*); allumer (*une cigarette, la pipe*); **the house was lit up,** la maison était illuminée; **a smile lit up her face,** un sourire a illuminé son visage.

light-coloured ['laɪtkʌləd] *adj* clair.
light-emitting ['laɪtɪmɪtɪŋ] *adj Comptr* **l.-e. diode,** diode électroluminescente.
lighten[1] ['laɪt(ə)n] **1** *vt* **(a)** (*light up*) éclairer (*les ténèbres, le visage*); rendre plus clair (*une habitation etc*); **(b)** éclaircir (*une couleur, le ciel*). **2** *vi* **(a)** s'éclairer, s'illuminer; **her face lightened,** son visage s'éclaira; **(b)** **it's thundering and lightening,** il y a du tonnerre et des éclairs.
lighten[2] **1** *vt* alléger; réduire le poids de (*qch*); délester (*un navire*); *Fig* **to l. s.o.'s load,** (*make work or life easier*) rendre la vie plus facile à qn. **2** *vi* **my heart lightened,** mon cœur fut soulagé.
►**lighten up** *esp Am vi* se dérider; **come on, l. up!,** ne prends pas ça tellement au sérieux!
lighter[1] ['laɪtər] *n* **(a)** (*device*) allumeur *m*, allumoir *m*; (*for cigarette*) briquet *m*; **gas l.,** (*for cigarette*) briquet à gaz; (*for gas stove*) allume-gaz *m*; **l. flint/fluid,** pierre *f*/essence *f* à briquet; **(b)** (*person*) allumeur, -euse.
lighter[2] *n Nau* allège *f*, gabare *f*.

lighter³ *vt* décharger (*des marchandises*) par allèges.
lighterage ['laɪtərɪdʒ] *n Nau* **(a)** déchargement *m* par allèges *ou* par gabares, gabarage *m*; **(b)** droits *mpl ou* frais *mpl* d'allège *ou* de gabarage.
lighter-than-air [laɪtəðə'neər] *adj* (*aircraft*) plus léger que l'air.
light-fingered [laɪt'fɪŋgəd] *adj F* **he's l.-f.,** c'est un voleur.
light-footed [laɪt'fʊtɪd] *adj* agile, leste, au pied léger.
light-headed [laɪt'hedɪd] *adj* **(a)** (*dizzy*) **to feel l.-h.,** avoir *ou* se sentir le cerveau vide (*par défaut de nourriture etc*); **(b)** (*frivolous*) à la tête légère, étourdi, écervelé.
light-hearted [laɪt'hɑːtɪd] *adj* au cœur léger, allègre.
lighthouse ['laɪthaʊs] *n Nau* phare *m*; **l. keeper,** gardien *m* de phare.
lighting ['laɪtɪŋ] *n* **(a)** (*lights*) éclairage *m*; **fluorescent l.,** éclairage par fluorescence; **direct/indirect l.,** éclairage direct/indirect; **emergency l.,** éclairage de secours; **street l.,** éclairage urbain *ou* des rues; *Br Admin* **l.-up time,** heure *f* d'éclairage; **l. engineer,** (ingénieur *m*) éclairagiste *m*; *Th* **stage l.,** éclairage scénique, éclairages; **l. effects,** jeux *mpl* de lumière; **(b)** allumage *m* (*d'une lampe etc*); **(c)** éclairage *m*, exposition *f* (*d'un tableau*).
lightly ['laɪtlɪ] *adv* **(a)** légèrement, à la légère; (*marcher*) d'un pas léger; **to sleep l.,** (*generally*) avoir le sommeil léger; (*on one occasion*) dormir d'un sommeil léger; **to stroke sth l.,** effleurer qch; **to skip l. from rock to rock,** sauter agilement de rocher en rocher; **her responsibilities sit l. on her,** ses responsabilités ne lui pèsent pas; **to get off l.,** s'en tirer à bon compte *ou* à bon marché; **(b)** (*to say*) d'un ton léger; **to speak l. of sth,** parler de qch à la légère.
lightness¹ ['laɪtnɪs] *n* (*brightness*) clarté *f*.
lightness² *n* (*in weight etc*) légèreté *f*; **l. of foot,** agilité *f*; **l. of heart,** gaieté *f* de cœur; **l. of touch,** légèreté de main (*d'un médecin etc*); (*of artist*) légèreté de pinceau; (*of writer*) légèreté de style.
lightning ['laɪtnɪŋ] *n* éclairs *mpl*, foudre *f*; **a flash of l.,** un éclair; **struck by l.,** frappé par la foudre; **l. conductor** *or Am* **rod,** paratonnerre *m*; **as quick as l., with l. speed,** *F* **like greased l.,** aussi vite que l'éclair, (rapide) comme l'éclair; **l. doesn't strike twice in the same place,** la foudre ne frappe jamais deux fois au même endroit; **l. attack,** attaque *f* éclair; **l. visit,** visite *f* éclair; *Am* **l. bug,** (*firefly*) luciole *f*.
lightproof ['laɪtpruːf] *adj* opaque.
lights [laɪts] *npl Culin* mou *m* (*de bœuf etc*).
light-sensitive ['laɪt'sensɪtɪv] *adj Phys* photosensible.
lightship ['laɪtʃɪp] *n Nau* bateau-feu *m*, *pl* bateaux-feux, bateau-phare *m*, *pl* bateaux-phares.
lightweight ['laɪtweɪt] **1** *n Boxing* poids léger; *Pej* (*person*) menu fretin. **2** *adj* (*garment etc*) léger.
lignite ['lɪgnaɪt] *n Miner* lignite *m*.
likable ['laɪkəb(ə)l] = **LIKEABLE.**
like¹ [laɪk] **1** *adj* semblable, pareil; **they are of l. temperament,** ils ont le même tempérament; *Math* **l. terms/quantities,** termes *mpl*/quantités *fpl* semblables; *El* **l. poles,** pôles *mpl* semblables *ou* de même nom; **they are as l. as two peas,** ils se ressemblent comme deux gouttes d'eau.

2 *prep* **(a)** (*similar to*) **I want to find one l. it,** je veux trouver le pareil *ou* la pareille; **people l. you,** des gens comme vous; **to be l. s.o./sth,** être semblable à qn/à qch, ressembler à qn/à qch; **we're l. sisters,** nous sommes comme des sœurs; **to taste l. sth,** avoir le même goût que qch; **to look l. sth/s.o.,** ressembler à qch/qn; **what's the weather l.?,** quel temps fait-il?; **you know what she's l.,** vous savez comme elle est; **he was l. a father to me,** il fut pour moi un père; **when I hear things l. that,** quand j'entends des choses semblables; **I know plenty of people l. that,** je connais pas mal de gens comme ça; **something very much l. it,** quelque chose qui y ressemble beaucoup; **it costs something l. £10,** cela coûte quelque 10 livres; **it will cost more l. £20,** ça coûtera plutôt dans les 20 livres; **that's more l. it,** voilà qui est mieux; **we don't have anything l. as many people as we need,** on est loin d'avoir autant de monde que nécessaire; **it's just l. (at) home,** c'est tout comme chez nous; *F* **that's something l. it!,** voilà qui est réussi!; **there's nothing l. it,** il n'y a rien de semblable *ou* de pareil; **she is nothing l. as intelligent as you,** elle est bien loin d'être aussi intelligente que vous; **that's not l. him,** (*not his way of behaving etc*) ça ne lui ressemble pas; **that's just l. a woman/a man!,** voilà bien les femmes/les hommes!; **that's just l. him!,** c'est bien de lui!, voilà comme il est!; **l. father l. son,** tel père, tel fils;

(b) (*in the manner of*) comme; **I think l. you,** je pense comme vous; **just l. anybody else,** tout comme un autre; **to speak French l. a native,** parler français comme un natif; *F* **to run l. blazes** *or* **hell** *or* **mad,** courir comme un dératé; *F* **be l. that then!,** fais comme tu veux puisque c'est ça!; **l. this?,** (*am I doing it correctly?*) comme ça?; **don't talk l. that,** ne parlez pas comme ça; **I'm sorry to keep bothering you l. this,** je suis désolé de vous déranger continuellement comme ça.

3 *adv* (*such as*) **take more exercise, l. jogging,** fais plus d'exercice, du jogging par exemple; *F* **l. enough, very l., (as) l. as not,** probablement, vraisemblablement; *Sl* **he looked angry l.,** il était comme en colère; *Sl* **he just came up behind me, l.,** il est venu juste derrière moi, comme ça.

4 *F conj* (= **as**) comme; **do l. I do,** faites comme moi; **l. I said,** comme je l'ai dit; (= **as if**) **he behaved l. he was scared,** il s'est conduit comme s'il avait peur; **he looked l. he'd seen a ghost,** il avait l'air d'avoir vu un fantôme.

5 *n* semblable *mf*, pareil, -eille; **he and his l., he and the likes of him,** lui et ses semblables; **it's too good for the likes of me,** c'est trop bon pour des personnes comme moi; **the likes of you,** des gens comme toi, *Pej* des gens de ton acabit; **music, painting and the l.,** la musique, la peinture, et autres choses du même genre; **musicians, painters and the l.,** musiciens, peintres et compagnie; *F* **I've never seen the l. of it,** je n'ai jamais vu chose pareille.
like² *n* (*usu pl*) **likes,** goût *m*, préférence *f*, inclination *f*; **likes and dislikes,** sympathies *fpl* et antipathies *fpl*; (*as regards food*) goûts particuliers.
like³ *vt* **(a)** aimer bien (*qn*); aimer (bien) (*qch*); avoir de la sympathie pour (*qn*); **I l. him,** je l'aime bien, il me plaît; **how do you l. him?,** comment le trouvez-vous?; **he likes school,** il se plaît à l'école; **I should l. time to consider it,** j'aimerais avoir le temps d'y réfléchir; **I should l. some tea,** je prendrais bien une tasse de thé; **I should l. nothing better,** je ne demande pas mieux; **do you l. tea?,** aimez-vous le thé?; **I don't l. tea,** je n'aime pas le thé; **I don't l. it at all,** (*situation etc*) cela ne me plaît pas du tout; **if he doesn't l. it he can go elsewhere,** si ça ne lui va pas qu'il aille ailleurs; **whether she likes it or not,** qu'elle le veuille ou non; **these plants don't l. the damp,** ces plantes craignent l'humidité; *F* **(well) I l. that!,** en voilà une bonne!, elle est bien bonne, celle-là!;

(b) (*to want, wish*) aimer (**to do,** (à) faire); **I l. to see them now and again,** j'aime (à) les voir de temps à autre; **he doesn't l. people to talk about it,** il n'aime pas qu'on en parle; **would you l. a cigarette?,** voulez-vous une cigarette?; **I should very much l. to go,** j'aimerais beaucoup y aller; **would you l. me to go with you?,** voulez-vous que je vous accompagne?; **I should l. to know whether ...,** je voudrais bien savoir si ...; **as you l.,** comme vous voudrez; **I can do as I l. with him,** je fais de lui ce que je veux; **she is free to do as she likes,** elle est libre d'agir à sa guise *ou* de faire comme il lui plaira; **to do just as one likes,** en faire à sa tête; **if you l.,** si vous voulez; **when you l.,** quand il vous plaira; **he thinks he can do anything he likes,** il se croit tout permis; **as much as you l.,** tant que vous voudrez; **I didn't l. to mention it,** j'ai préféré ne pas le mentionner; **I wanted to ring you but I didn't l. to,** (*I would have disturbed you, upset you etc*) je voulais te téléphoner mais j'ai préféré ne pas le faire.
likeable ['laɪkəb(ə)l] *adj* (*person*) agréable, sympathique.
likeableness ['laɪkəb(ə)lnɪs] *n* (*of person*) amabilité *f*.
likelihood ['laɪklɪhʊd] *n* vraisemblance *f*, probabilité *f*, apparence *f*; **there is little l. of his succeeding,** il y a peu de chances qu'il réussisse; **there's a strong l. that ...,** il y a une forte probabilité pour que ... + *sub*; **in all l.,** selon toute probabilité, selon toute vraisemblance.
likely ['laɪklɪ] **1** *adj* **(a)** (*probable*) vraisemblable, probable; **it's not a very l. scenario,** ce scénario n'est pas très vraisemblable; **the pub is a l. place to find him,** le pub est probablement l'endroit où le trouver; *F* **that's a l. story!,** la belle histoire!, en voilà une bonne!; **it's more than l.,** c'est plus que probable; **it's not very l.,** c'est peu probable; **it's l. to rain,** il y a des chances pour qu'il pleuve; **she is quite l. to do it,** il est probable qu'elle le fasse;

(b) (*liable*) **books l. to interest young people,** ouvrages *mpl* susceptibles d'intéresser les jeunes; **this plan is most l. to succeed,** ce projet offre le plus de chances de succès; **are the neighbours l. to object?,** est-il probable que les voisins s'y opposent?;

(c) (*candidate*) prometteur; *Dial* **a l. lad,** (*fun-loving*) un joyeux gaillard; (*promising*) un gars qui promet; **a l. candidate/horse/*etc*,** un candidat/cheval/*etc* qui a des chances de gagner.

2 *adv* **most l., very l.,** *US F* **l.,** vraisemblablement, très probablement; **as l. as not,** vraisemblablement; *F* **not l.!,** jamais de la vie!

like-minded [laɪk'maɪndɪd] *adj* dans les mêmes dispositions, du même avis; qui ont les mêmes goûts.

liken ['laɪk(ə)n] *vt* comparer (**s.o. to s.o.,** qn à qn); assimiler, faire ressembler (**sth to sth,** qch à qch).

likeness ['laɪknɪs] *n* **(a)** (*similarity*) ressemblance *f* (**between,** entre; **to,** à); similitude *f* (*de deux personnes, de deux objets*); **God created man in his own l.,** Dieu a créé l'homme à son image; **a close l.,** une ressemblance étroite; **family l.,** air *m* de famille; **(b)** (*image*) portrait *m*, image *f*; **the picture is a good l.,** le portrait est très ressemblant.

likewise ['laɪkwaɪz] *adv* **(a)** (*in addition*) de plus, de même, aussi; **(b)** (*similarly*) **to do l.,** faire de même, en faire autant; **pleased to meet you — l.!,** ravi de vous rencontrer – moi de même!

liking ['laɪkɪŋ] *n* goût *m*, penchant *m*; **to one's l.,** à souhait; **is it to your l.?,** cela est-il à votre goût?, est-ce que cela vous plaît?; **to have a l. for sth,** avoir du goût pour qch, aimer qch; **I have taken a l. to her,** elle m'est devenue sympathique.

lilac ['laɪlək] **1** *n* (*flower, tree*) lilas *m*. **2** *adj* **l.(-coloured),** lilas *inv*.

Lilliputian [lɪlɪ'pjuːʃən] *adj Lit* lilliputien.

Lilo ® ['laɪləʊ] *n* = matelas *m* pneumatique.

lilt [lɪlt] *n* **(a)** rythme *m*, cadence *f* (*des vers*); **a song with a l.,** une chanson au rythme entraînant; **to speak with a Welsh l.,** parler à la cadence galloise; **(b)** *Arch & Scot* chant *m*, air *m*.

lilting ['lɪltɪŋ] *adj* (*rythme*) musical; (*air*) cadencé, scandé.

lily ['lɪlɪ] *n* (*flower*) lis *m*; **tiger l.,** lis tigré; **l. of the valley,** muguet *m*; **l. pad,** feuille *f* de nénuphar.

lily-livered ['lɪlɪlɪvəd] *adj* couard.

lily-white ['lɪlɪwaɪt] *adj* blanc, *f* blanche comme le lis, d'une blancheur de lis; *F* (*character*) blanc comme neige.

limb [lɪm] *n* **(a)** (*of body*) membre *m*; **the lower limbs,** les membres inférieurs; **to tear an animal l. from l.,** mettre un animal en pièces; *esp Br* **l. of the devil** *or* **of Satan,** (*child*) petit diable *ou* monstre; **(b)** (grosse) branche *f* (*d'un arbre*); bras *m* (*d'une croix*); *F* **to be out on a l.,** (*be alone*) être en plan; (*be in dangerous position*) être sur la corde raide; **his refusal to compromise left him out on a l.,** son refus à tout compromis l'a mis dans une position délicate; **to go out on a l.,** prendre des risques.

-limbed [lɪmd] *suff* **loose-l.,** souple; **strong-l.,** aux membres solides, solide.

limber¹ ['lɪmbər] *n Mil* avant-train *m*, *pl* avant-trains (*d'affût de canon*).

limber² *vt Mil* **to l. a gun,** attacher une pièce de canon à l'avant-train.

limber³ *adj* souple.

►**limber up 1** *vi* **(a)** *Sp* s'échauffer; **(b)** *Mil* amener *ou* accrocher *ou* mettre l'avant-train. **2** *vtsep Sp* se chauffer (*les muscles*); **to l. up one's fingers,** (*of pianist etc*) s'échauffer les doigts.

limbering-up [lɪmbərɪŋ'ʌp] *adj* **l.-up exercises,** exercices *mpl* d'assouplissement.

limbless ['lɪmlɪs] *adj* (*personne*) à qui il manque un ou plusieurs membres; (*with no arms or legs*) sans membres; **l. ex-servicemen,** grands mutilés *mpl* de guerre.

limbo ['lɪmbəʊ] *n* **(a)** *Rel* les limbes *mpl*; *also Fig* **to be in l.,** être dans les limbes; **(b)** (*dance*) limbo *m*; **l. dancer,** danseur, -euse de limbo.

lime¹ [laɪm] *n* (*fruit*) lime *f*; (*tree*) limettier *m*; **l. juice,** jus *m* de lime douce *ou* de citron doux; **l. green,** (*colour*) vert citron; **a l.-green coat,** un manteau vert citron.

lime² *n* (*linden tree*) tilleul *m*.

lime³ *n* **(a)** chaux *f*; **slaked l.,** chaux éteinte; **l. pit,** carrière *f* de pierre à chaux; **(b)** (*birdlime*) glu *f*; **l. twig,** gluau *m*.

lime⁴ *vt* **(a)** *Agr* chauler (*un terrain*); **(b)** gluer (*des ramilles*), enduire (*des ramilles*) de glu; **to l. birds,** prendre des oiseaux à la glu *ou* au gluau.

limeade ['laɪmeɪd] *n* jus de citron vert additionné de sucre et d'eau.

limekiln ['laɪmkɪln] *n* four *m* à chaux, chaufour *m*.

limelight ['laɪmlaɪt] *n* **in the l.,** sous les feux de la rampe, très en vue, en vedette; **she doesn't like the l.,** elle n'aime pas sentir les projecteurs braqués sur elle; **an actor who's never out of the l.,** un acteur très en vue.

limerick ['lɪmərɪk] *n* = poème en cinq vers, toujours comique et absurde, aux rimes a a b b a.

limestone ['laɪmstəʊn] *n Geol* calcaire *m*; *Ind etc* pierre *f* à chaux.

limey ['laɪmɪ] *Am Austr Sl* **1** *n* **(a)** Anglais *m*; **(b)** *Old-fashioned* matelot anglais. **2** *adj* anglais.

limit¹ ['lɪmɪt] *n* **(a)** (*boundary*) limite *f*, borne *f*; *MecE* limite (*d'élasticité etc*); (*in insurance*) plein *m*; **within a ten kilometre l.,** dans un rayon de dix kilomètres; **the limits of decency,** les frontières *fpl* de la bienséance; **to fix** *or* **set a l.** *or* **limits (to sth),** fixer *ou* mettre une limite *ou* des limites (à qch); **within limits,** dans une certaine mesure; **I like jazz but within limits,** j'aime le jazz mais jusqu'à un certain point; **age l.,** limite d'âge; **time l.,** limite de temps (*imposée à un orateur etc*); délai *m* (*de paiement etc*); durée *f* (*d'un privilège etc*); **speed l.,** vitesse limite *ou* maximum *ou* maximale; *F* **to be over the (legal) l.,** (*of alcohol*) avoir bu plus qu'il n'est permis au volant; *Fin* **credit l.,** limite *ou* plafond *m* du crédit; **to fix a l.,** (*in insurance*) fixer les pleins; **there's a l. to everything!,** il y a limite à tout!; **there's no l. to her ambition,** son ambition est sans limites; **to know no limits,** ne connaître aucune limite; **his arrogance knows no limits,** son arrogance ne connaît pas de limites; *F* **the sky's the l.,** il n'y a pas de limite; **that's the l.!,** ça c'est le comble!; **he's the l.!,** il est impossible!; **off limits,** (*place*) inaccessible; *Mil* consigné à la troupe; **to be off limits to s.o.,** (*of place*) être inaccessible à qn; *Mil* **to put a public house off limits,** consigner un bar;

(b) *MecE* tolérance *f*; **l. gauge,** (*device*) calibre *m* de tolérance; (*external*) bague *f* à tolérance; (*internal*) bouchon *m* à tolérance.

limit² *vt* limiter, borner, restreindre (*qn, qch*); **I have to l. my calorie intake,** je dois limiter ma consommation de calories; **to l. oneself to ...,** (*in speaking*) se borner à ...; **to l. oneself to strict necessities,** se restreindre au strict nécessaire; **to l. oneself to two whiskies,** se contenter de *ou* se limiter à deux whiskies.

limitation [lɪmɪ'teɪʃən] *n* limitation *f*; **to know one's limitations,** connaître ses limites.

limited ['lɪmɪtəd] *adj* (*nombre etc*) limité, restreint; (*intelligence*) borné; *Com* (*marché*) étroit, restreint; **l. edition,** (*of book*) (édition *f* à) tirage limité; **l. circulation,** circulation restreinte; *Com* **l. company,** société *f* à responsabilité limitée; *Jur* **l. liability,** responsabilité limitée; **l. stop train/bus,** train *m*/bus *m* à nombre d'arrêts limité.

limitless ['lɪmɪtlɪs] *adj* sans bornes, illimité.

limousine [lɪmə'ziːn] **,** *F* **limo** ['lɪməʊ] *n Aut* limousine *f*.

limp¹ [lɪmp] *n* boitement *m*, claudication *f*; **to walk with a l., to have a l.,** boiter.

limp² *vi* boiter, *Lit* claudiquer; *Sp Fig* **to l. home,** (*of runner*) rentrer en clopinant; **to l. along,** aller en boitant *ou* *F* clopin-clopant; (*of ship etc*) avancer péniblement.

limp³ *adj* mou, *f* molle, flasque; **l. binding,** (*of book*) cartonnage *m* souple *ou* à l'anglaise; **to go l.,** (*of person*) s'affaisser; **let your arm go l.,** relâche ton bras; **to become l.,** (*of linen*) devenir mou; (*of starched linen*) se désempeser; **to feel l.,** (*of person*) se sentir mou *ou* sans énergie; **l. with the heat,** abattu par la chaleur.

limpet ['lɪmpɪt] *n* patelle *f*, arapède *m*; *F* (*person*) crampon *m*; **to stick to s.o. like a l.,** suivre qn comme un crampon, cramponner qn; *Mil* **l. mine,** mine *f* magnétique.

limpid ['lɪmpɪd] *adj* (*water etc*) limpide, pellucide, clair; (*style*) limpide.

limping ['lɪmpɪŋ] *adj* boiteux.

limply ['lɪmplɪ] *adv* **(a)** (*without firmness*) mollement, flasquement; **(b)** (*without energy*) sans énergie.

limpness ['lɪmpnɪs] *n* mollesse *f*; manque *m* d'énergie.

limp-wristed [lɪmp'rɪstəd] *adj F* de pédale; **to be l.-w.,** être pédale.

linchpin ['lɪntʃpɪn] *n* esse *f*; cheville *f* d'essieu; *Fig* cheville ouvrière (*d'une organisation etc*).

Lincs *abbr* **Lincolnshire**.

linctus ['lɪŋktəs] *n Pharm* sirop *m*.

linden ['lɪndən] *n* **l. (tree),** tilleul *m*.

line¹ [laɪn] *n* **(a)** ligne *f*, trait *m*; filet *m* (*de lumière*); *Phys* raie *f* (*du spectre*); (*contour*) ligne (*de l'horizon*); contours *mpl* (*d'un rivage, d'un visage*); lignes (*d'une voiture etc*); **straight l.,** (ligne) droite *f*; **to draw a l. under sth,** (*underline it*) souligner qch; **to put a l. through sth,** barrer qch; **l. drawing,** dessin *m* au trait; **broken l.,** trait discontinu; **wavy l.,** trait ondulé; **l. engraving,** gravure *f* au trait; *Nau* **water l.,** ligne de flottaison; **load l.,** ligne de charge; **datum l.,** ligne de référence; *Tennis* **service l.,** ligne de service; *Tennis* **on the l.,** sur la ligne; *TV* **definition of 625 lines,** définition *f* de 625 lignes (d'exploration); *Aut* **white l.,** *US* **yellow l.,** ≈ ligne blanche, bande médiane;

Geol Geog **snow l.,** ligne *ou* limite *f* des neiges; **fault l.,** ligne de faille; **flow l.,** (*of glacier*) ligne de flux; **the lines of the hand,** les lignes de la main; **the lines on one's forehead,** les rides *fpl* de son front; *Geog* **the l.,** la Ligne (équatoriale), l'équateur *m*; *Opt* **l. of sight,** ligne de visée; (*on rifle*) ligne de mire; **l. of vision,** ligne de vision; **l. of fire,** (*of gun*) ligne de tir; *F* **to get a l. on sth,** (*information*) obtenir des tuyaux sur qch; **to give s.o. a l. on sth,** tuyauter qn sur qch; **to get a l. on s.o.,** se renseigner sur qn; **the hard lines of his face,** ses traits durs; **to work on the same lines as s.o.,** travailler d'après le modèle tracé par qn; **to be working on the right lines,** être en bonne voie; **demarcation l.,** (*limit*) ligne de démarcation; **you have to draw the l. somewhere,** il y a une limite à tout; **he doesn't know where to draw the l.,** il ne sait pas où s'arrêter; **that's where I draw the l.,** pour moi c'est la limite à ne pas dépasser; (*warning another person etc*) ça va trop loin; **I draw the l. at lying,** je refuse de mentir; (*referring to other people*) je refuse le mensonge; **to overstep the l.,** dépasser la mesure; **to be out of l.,** (*in what one does, says*) dépasser les bornes; **to lay it on the l. to s.o.,** parler franchement à qn; **to be on the l.,** (*of one's job, reputation etc*) être en jeu;

(b) (*row of people or things*) (*side by side*) ligne *f*, rangée *f*; (*one behind the other*) file *f*; *Am* queue *f*; ligne (*de mots écrits, imprimés*); vers *m* (*de poésie*); **to put things in a l.,** aligner des objets; **to fall** *or* **get into l., to form a l.,** (*of person*) se mettre en ligne; former les rangs; **out of l.,** désaligné; **to get out of l.,** se désaligner; (*of individual*) quitter les rangs, sortir des rangs; **to fall into l. with s.o.'s ideas,** se conformer aux idées de qn; **your decision is not in l.** *or* **is out of l. with government policy,** votre décision n'est pas conforme à *ou* n'est pas en accord avec la politique du gouvernement; **in l. with my decision,** conformément à ma décision; **he's in l. for promotion,** il est sur la liste des promotions (futures); **twenty cars in a l.,** vingt voitures à la file; **l. of traffic,** colonne *f* de véhicules; **to get into the l. of traffic,** (*of vehicle*) prendre la file; *Ind* **assembly l.,** chaîne *f* de montage; **production l.,** chaîne *f* de production; **to work on the production l.,** travailler à la chaîne; **to stand in a l.,** (*of person*) se tenir à la file; *Am* **to stand in l.,** faire la queue; *Mil etc* **fighting l., l. of battle,** ligne de combat *ou* de bataille; **l. of attack,** ligne d'attaque; **the front/rear lines,** le front/l'arrière *m*; **to be in the front l.,** *Mil* être au front; *Fig* être en première ligne; **to win all along the l.,** gagner sur toute la ligne; *Mil* **lines,** lignes (de fortification *etc*); **first l. of a paragraph,** alinéa *m*; **opening/closing lines of a play,** premières/dernières répliques d'une pièce; **new l.,** (*in dictating*) à la ligne; *F* **I'll drop you a l.,** je vous enverrai un petit mot; **just a l. to tell you ...,** deux mots pour vous dire ...; *Fig* **to read between the lines,** lire entre les lignes; **l. space,** interligne *m*; **l. spacing,** interlignage *m*; *Typ etc* **l. printing,** impression *f* ligne par ligne; *Comptr* **l. feed/printer,** avancement *m*/imprimante *f* ligne par ligne; **l. width,** largeur *f* de trait; *Th* **not to know one's lines,** ne pas savoir son rôle; *F* **marriage lines,** acte *m* de mariage;

(c) (*cord, wire etc*) *Nau* ligne *f*, corde *f*, cordage *m*; (*for mooring*) amarre *f*; *Fishing* ligne (de pêche); (*in surveying*) & *Constr* cordeau *m*; **lead** *or* **sounding l.,** ligne de sonde; **clothes l.,** corde à linge; **ground l.,** ligne de fond; **l. fishing,** pêche *f* à la ligne; *Tel* **extension l.,** ligne supplémentaire; *Tel* **shared** *or* **party l.,** ligne partagée; *Tel* **hold the l. please,** restez en ligne s'il vous plaît, ne quittez pas; **the line's very bad,** la communication est mauvaise; **I have Bill on the l.,** j'ai Bill au bout du fil; **she's on the other l.,** elle est sur l'autre ligne; **all the lines to London are busy,** toutes les lignes pour Londres sont occupées; *TV Rad* **the lines are open from 8 o'clock,** (*for viewers and listeners to express their views*) les standards sont ouverts à partir de 8 heures; *El* **high-tension l.,** ligne à haute tension; *El Tel* **overhead/underground l.,** ligne aérienne/souterraine; **laid out by the l.** *or* **by rule and l.,** (*in surveying*) tiré au cordeau; *F* **hard lines on you!,** c'est bien malheureux pour vous!; **hard lines!,** pas de chance!;

(d) (*company*) ligne *f*, compagnie *f* (*de paquebots etc*); **shipping l.,** compagnie de navigation;

(e) (*family*) lignée *f*, ligne *f*; **male/female l.,** ligne masculine/féminine; **long l. of ancestors,** longue suite d'ancêtres; **he comes from a long l. of politicians,** il descend d'une longue lignée d'hommes politiques; **in (a) direct line,** en ligne directe; **to be descended in a direct l. from s.o.,** descendre en droite ligne de qn;

(f) ligne *f* (*de marche, d'intercommunication*); voie *f* (*de communication*); *Rail* (*track*) voie; (*route*) ligne; *F* (*job etc*) métier *m*; *Com* série *f* (*d'articles*); article *m*; *Mil etc* **l. of advance,** direction *f* de marche; **main l.,** voie principale; grande ligne; **single/double-track l.,** ligne à voie unique/à double voie; **l. of conduct,** ligne de conduite; **to be killed in the l. of duty,** (*of policeman*) mourir dans l'exercice de ses fonctions; (*of soldier*) mourir au champ d'honneur; **l. of thought,** suite *f* d'idées; **l. of argument,** raisonnement *m*; **what l. are you going to take?,** quel parti allez-vous prendre?; **along the lines of,** dans le genre *ou* style de; **his talk was along the lines of his latest book,** son discours suivait les grandes lignes de son dernier livre; **what's his l.?,** quel est son métier?, qu'est-ce qu'il fait?; **that's not my l.,** ce n'est pas mon rayon; **that's more (in) my l.,** (*what I'm good at*) cela est plus dans mes compétences *ou F* mes cordes; (*what I like*) cela me ressemble davantage; **a new l. in fast foods,** un nouveau produit dans la restauration rapide; *F* **a rice pudding or something in that l.,** un gâteau de riz ou quelque chose dans ce genre (-là); *F* **don't hand me that l.!,** on ne me la fait pas!;

(g) *Nau* collecteur *m*; *Com* **l. manager,** chef *m* hiérarchique.

line² *vt* **(a)** ligner, régler, rayer (*un morceau de papier*); **to become lined,** (*of forehead, face*) se rider; **(b)** border; **to l. the roads with troops,** aligner des troupes sur les routes; **the crowd lined the street,** la foule s'alignait le long du trottoir; **(c)** érafler, rayer; strier de lignes.

line³ *vt* **(a)** *Sewing etc* doubler (*un vêtement*) (**with,** de); **fur-lined gloves,** gants fourrés; *F* **to l. one's own pockets,** se servir, se remplir les poches; **to l. a box with paper,** tapisser une boîte de papier; *Culin* **to l. a tin with pastry,** foncer un moule de pâte; **nest lined with moss,** nid garni de mousse; **(b)** *Tech* garnir, recouvrir (*un palier*); revêtir, incruster (*un mur, un fourneau*) (**with,** de); cuveler (*un puits*); **to l. a shaft with metal,** blinder un puits.

▶**line up 1** *vtsep* **(a)** aligner, mettre en ligne (*des personnes, des objets*); **(b)** *F* (*plan*) prévoir (*qch, qn*), avoir (*qch, qn*) en vue; **have you got anyone lined up for the job?,** avez-vous quelqu'un en vue pour le poste?; **what have you got lined up for us?,** qu'est-ce que vous nous préparez? **2** *vi* (*of people*) s'aligner, se mettre en ligne, se ranger; (*form queue*) faire la queue.

lineage ['lɪnɪɪdʒ] *n* lignée *f*, lignage *m*; **to boast an ancient l.,** se vanter d'une longue généalogie; **to trace one's l.,** retracer sa généalogie.

lineal ['lɪnɪəl] *adj* linéal, -aux; (*descendant, succession*) en ligne directe.

lineaments ['lɪnɪəmənts] *npl* traits *mpl*, linéaments *mpl*.

linear ['lɪnɪər] *adj* linéaire; *Math* **l. equation,** équation *f* linéaire; **l. measure,** mesure *f* linéaire, mesure de longueur; *Phys* **l. expansion,** dilatation *f* linéaire.

lined¹ [laɪnd] *adj* ligné; (*papier*) réglé, rayé; **deeply l. forehead,** front creusé de rides.

lined² *adj* **(a)** (*manteau*) doublé; (*gant*) fourré; *F* **well l. purse,** bourse bien garnie; **(b)** *Aut* (*frein*) garni; *Min* (*galerie*) coffré; **steel-l.,** (*cylindre*) chemisé d'acier.

linen ['lɪnɪn] *n* **(a)** linge *m*; **table l.,** linge de table; **dirty l.,** linge sale; *F* **don't wash your dirty l. in public,** il faut laver son linge sale en famille; **l. cupboard,** armoire *f* à linge; **l. basket,** panier *m* à linge; **l. room,** lingerie; **(b)** *Tex* toile *f* (de lin); **l. sheets,** draps *mpl* fil; **l. dress,** robe *f* en lin; **l. industry,** industrie linière *ou* toilière; **l. paper,** papier toilé.

line-out ['laɪnaʊt] *n Rugby* touche *f*, remise *f* en jeu.

liner¹ ['laɪnər] *n Nau* (paquebot *m*) transatlantique *m*.

liner² *n* fourreau *m* (*de cylindre*); **bin l.,** sac *m* poubelle.

linesman, *pl* **-men** ['laɪnzmən] *n Fb Tennis* arbitre *m* de lignes; *Fb* arbitre, juge *m* de touche.

line-up ['laɪnʌp] *n* **(a)** *Am* queue *f* (de personnes); rangée *f* de personnes (*assemblées par la police pour l'identification d'un suspect*); **(b)** *Sp* formation *f* (*d'une équipe sur le terrain*); *Rad TV etc* **this evening's l.-up,** (*of guests, stars*) nos invités ce soir.

linework ['laɪnwɜːk] *n Art* dessin *m* au trait.

ling¹ [lɪŋ] *n* (*fish*) lingue *f*.

ling² *n Bot* bruyère commune.

linger ['lɪŋgər] *vi* **(a)** tarder, s'attarder, traîner; **to l. over a meal,** s'attarder sur un repas; **a doubt still lingered,** un doute subsistait encore dans mon *ou* son *etc* esprit; **(b)** (*of invalid*) **to l. (on),** languir, traîner.

lingerie ['lænʒəri] *n* lingerie *f* (pour femmes).

lingering ['lɪŋgərɪŋ] *adj* **(a)** (*regard*) prolongé; (*doute*) qui subsiste encore; **there was a l. hope that ...,** on conservait un vague espoir que ...; **(b)** (*maladie*) qui traîne, chronique; (*mort*) lent; **she died a l. death,** la mort l'a emportée lentement.

lingo, *pl* **-oes** ['lɪŋgəʊ, -əʊz] *n F* **(a) the l. of the country,** (*its language*) la langue du pays; (*its jargon*) le jargon *ou* le patois du pays; **(b)** argot *m* (*du théâtre etc*).

lingua franca ['lɪŋgwə'fræŋkə] *n* langue *f* de communication, langue véhiculaire.

linguist ['lɪŋgwɪst] *n* linguiste *mf*; **to be a good/no l.,** être/ne pas être doué pour les langues.

linguistic [lɪŋ'gwɪstɪk] *adj* linguistique.

linguistically [lɪŋ'gwɪstɪklɪ] *adv* linguistiquement.

linguistics [lɪŋ'gwɪstɪks] *npl* (*usu with sing verb*) linguistique *f*; **structural l.,** linguistique structurale.

liniment ['lɪnɪmənt] *n* liniment *m*.

lining ['laɪnɪŋ] **(a)** (*action*) doublage *m*, garnissage *m*; *Tech* revêtement intérieur; **(b)** (*result*) doublure *f* (*de robe*); coiffe *f* (*de chapeau*); *Tech* garniture *f*, fourrure *f* (*de frein, de coussinet*); chemise *f* (*de fourneau, de pompe*); cuvelage *m* (*de puits*); paroi *f* (*d'un tunnel*); **l. paper,** (*for drawer*) papier *m* pour tiroirs; (*for shelves*) papier pour recouvrir les étagères.

link¹ [lɪŋk] *n* **(a)** chaînon *m*, maillon *m*, maille *f*, anneau *m* (*d'une chaîne*); *Nau* paillon *m* (*de câble-chaîne*); maille (*de tricot*); **cuff links,** boutons *mpl* de manchette; **a weak l. in the chain,** un maillon faible dans la chaîne; **(b)** (*connection*) lien *m*, liaison *f* (**between,** entre); **there's a l. between your health and your job,** il y a un rapport entre votre santé et votre travail; **air/radio, l.,** liaison aérienne/radiophonique; **he is a l. between the old world and the new,** il sert de trait d'union entre le vieux monde et le nouveau; **the weak l.,** le maillon faible; **missing l.,** vide *m*, lacune *f* (*dans une théorie*); *Biol* forme intermédiaire disparue; *F* chaînon manquant; **(c)** *MecE etc* pièce *f* de liaison, tige *f* d'assemblage; *Aut* bielle *f* d'accouplement (*des roues avant*); menotte *f* (*de ressort*); coulisse *f* (*de machine à vapeur*); **(fork) l.,** étrier *m*.

link² **1** *vt* relier (*deux machines, deux villes, deux rives etc*); **a tunnel linking Britain and France,** un tunnel reliant la Grande-Bretagne à la France; **the two companies are in no way linked,** il n'y a aucun lien entre les deux sociétés; **closely linked,** (*of companies, theories etc*) étroitement lié; **to l. negotiations to a discussion of Palestine,** lier des négociations à une discussion sur la Palestine; **I always l. him with my stay in ...,** je l'associe toujours dans mon esprit à mon séjour à ...; **his name has been linked with several well-known actresses,** son nom a été associé à plusieurs actrices bien connues; **it's all linked together,** tout cela se tient; **wages linked to the cost of living,** salaires indexés sur le coût de la vie; **to l. hands/arms,** se donner la main/le bras. **2** *vi* **to l. on to sth, to l. in** *or* **up with sth,** s'attacher *ou* se joindre *ou* s'unir à qch; **we'll l. up with you in Paris,** nous vous rejoindrons à Paris.

linkage ['lɪŋkɪdʒ] *n* **(a)** liaison *f*; raccord *m*; **(b)** *Ch* liaison *f*; enchaînement *m* (*de phénomènes*).

linked [lɪŋkt] *adj* lié, joint; *MecE* articulé; **l. traffic lights,** feux synchronisés.

linking ['lɪŋkɪŋ] *n* enchaînement *m*, liaison *f*; *Astronaut* **l. up,** jonction *f* (*de deux engins spatiaux*).

links [lɪŋks] *npl* (*usu with sing verb*) **(golf) l.,** terrain *m ou* parcours *m* de golf.

linkup ['lɪŋkʌp] *n* lien *m*, liaison *f* (**between,** entre).

linnet ['lɪnɪt] *n* (*bird*) linotte *f* (mélodieuse).

linoleum [lɪ'nəʊlɪəm], *F* **lino** ['laɪnəʊ] *n* linoléum *m*.

linseed ['lɪnsiːd] *n* graine *f* de lin; **l. oil,** huile *f* de lin.

lint [lɪnt] *n* **(a)** *Med* pansement ouatiné; **(b)** peluche *f* (*de coton, de chiffon etc*).

lintel ['lɪnt(ə)l] *n* **(a)** linteau *m*, sommier *m* (*de porte, de fenêtre*); *Archit* **l. course,** plate-bande *f*, *pl* plates-bandes; **(b)** travers *m* (*de manteau de cheminée*).

lint-free [lɪnt'friː] *adj* (*cloth, bandage*) sans peluches.

lion ['laɪən] *n* **(a)** (*animal*) lion *m*; **l. cub,** lionceau *m*; **l. house,** fauverie *f*; **l.'s** *or* **lions' den,** antre *m* du lion; *Fig* **the l.'s share,** la part du lion; *Fig* **to put one's head into the l.'s mouth,** se fourrer dans la gueule du loup; **mountain l.,** lion d'Amérique; couguar *m*; **l. hunter,** chasseur *m* de lion; **l. tamer,** dresseur *m* de lion; **(b)** *Old-fashioned* personnage marquant, lion *m*; **the l. of the day,** la célébrité du jour; **(c)** *Astron* **the L.,** le Lion.

lioness ['laɪənes] *n* (*animal*) lionne *f*.

lionheart ['laɪənhɑːt] *n* homme courageux; *Hist* **(Richard) the L.,** Richard Cœur de Lion.

lion-hearted ['laɪənhɑːtɪd] *adj* au cœur de lion.

lionize ['laɪənaɪz] *vt* faire une célébrité de (*qn*).

lip [lɪp] *n* **(a)** lèvre *f* (*de qn*); babine *f* (*d'un animal*); **to keep a stiff upper l.,** ne pas broncher, serrer les dents; **to do/pay l. service to s.o./sth,** rendre à qn/qch des hommages peu sincères; **a cigar between his lips,** un cigare aux lèvres; **to bite one's lip(s),** se mordre les lèvres; *F* **to keep one's l. buttoned (up),** ne pas souffler mot; **to smack** *or* **lick one's lips over sth,** se lécher les babines; **no complaint ever passes his lips,** jamais il ne se plaint; **to read s.o.'s lips,** lire sur les lèvres de qn; *F* **read my lips,** (*believe what I say*) écoutez-moi bien; **l. gloss,** brillant *m* à lèvres; **l. salve,** baume *m* pour les lèvres;

(b) *Sl* (*impudence*) effronterie *f*, insolence *f*; **none of your l.!, don't give me any of your l.!,** ne te fiche pas de moi!;

(c) lèvre *f* (*d'une plaie*); *Bot* lèvre (*de corolle labiée*); labelle *m* (*d'orchidée*);

(d) (*rim*) bord *m*, rebord *m* (*d'une tasse, d'une cavité*); margelle *f* (*de puits*); bord (*de cratère*); (*projection*) rebord, saillie *f*; couronne *f* (*de came*); lèvre, tranchant *m* (*de mèche anglaise*); **pouring l.,** bec *m* (*de cruche*).

lipped [lɪpt] *adj* **(a)** (*tuyau etc*) à rebord; (*cruche*) à bec; **(b)** *Bot* labié.

-lipped [lɪpt] *suff* **thin-l.,** aux lèvres minces; **thick-l.,** lippu; **red-l.,** aux lèvres rouges; **tight-l.,** (*air, sourire*) pincé.

lippy ['lɪpɪ] *adj Am Sl* effronté.

lip-read ['lɪpriːd] **1** *vi* (*of the deaf*) lire sur les lèvres. **2** *vt* **she can l.-r. what you're saying,** elle peut lire sur vos lèvres.

lip-reading *n* lecture *f* sur les lèvres.

lipstick ['lɪpstɪk] *n* rouge *m ou* crayon *m* à lèvres.

lip-synch ['lɪpsɪnk] *vi* faire une interprétation mimée.

liquefaction [lɪkwɪ'fækʃən] *n* liquéfaction *f*.

liquefied ['lɪkwɪfaɪd] *adj* **l. natural/petroleum gas,** gaz naturel/de pétrole liquéfié.

liquefy ['lɪkwɪfaɪ] **1** *vt* liquéfier (*un gaz etc*). **2** *vi* (*of gas etc*) se liquéfier.

liqueur [lɪ'kɜːr, lɪ'kjʊər] *n* **(a)** liqueur *f* (de dessert); **l. glass,** verre *m* à liqueur; **l. brandy,** fine *f*; **l. chocolates,** bonbons *mpl* à la liqueur; **(b)** (*in winemaking*) liqueur *f* d'expédition.

liquid ['lɪkwɪd] **1** *adj* **(a)** liquide; **to reduce sth to a l. state,** liquéfier qch; **l. oxygen,** oxygène *m* liquide; **l. paraffin,** huile *f* de paraffine; *Comptr* **l. crystal,** cristal *m* liquide; **l. crystal display,** affichage *m* à cristaux liquides; **(b)** (*sound*) doux, *f* douce, clair; **(c)** *Fin* liquide, disponible; **l. assets,** actif *m* liquide; **(d)** *Ling* (*consonne*) liquide. **2** *n* **(a)** liquide *m*; **l. measure,** mesure *f* de capacité pour les liquides; **refrigerating l.,** liquide réfrigérant; **washing-up l.,** produit *m* à vaisselle; **(b)** *Ling* (consonne *f*) liquide *f*.

liquidate ['lɪkwɪdeɪt] *vt* **(a)** liquider (*une société, une dette*); amortir (*une dette*); mobiliser (*des capitaux*); **(b)** (*to kill*) liquider (*qn*).

liquidation [lɪkwɪ'deɪʃən] *n* liquidation *f* (*d'une société, d'une dette*); amortissement *m* (*d'une dette*); mobilisation *f* (*de capitaux*); **to go into l.,** (*of company*) entrer en liquidation.

liquidator ['lɪkwɪdeɪtər] *n* liquidateur, -trice (*d'une société en liquidation*).

liquidity [lɪ'kwɪdɪtɪ] *n* **(a)** liquidité *f* (*d'une substance*); **(b)** *Fin* liquidité *f* (*d'une dette*).

liquidize ['lɪkwɪdaɪz] *vt* **(a)** liquéfier; **(b)** *Culin* passer (*qch*) au mixeur.

liquidizer ['lɪkwɪdaɪzər] *n* mixeur *m*.

liquor ['lɪkər] *n* **(a)** boisson *f* alcoolique, spiritueux *m*, alcool *m*; **he can't hold** *or* **take his l.,** il ne supporte pas l'alcool; *Am* **l. store,** marchand *m* de vins et de spiritueux; **to be the worse for l.,** être ivre; **(b)** *Old-fashioned Culin* jus *m* (*d'un rôti*); eau *f* (*des huîtres*).

▶liquor up **1** *vi* se soûler. **2** *vtsep* soûler; **to be all liquored up,** être soûl.

liquorice, *Am* **licorice** ['lɪkərɪs] *n* réglisse *f*.

Lisbon ['lɪzbən] *n* Lisbonne *f*.

lisle [laɪl] *n Tex* **l. (thread),** fil *m* d'Écosse; **l. stockings,** bas *mpl* de fil.

lisp¹ [lɪsp] *n* zézaiement *m*, chuintement *m*; **to have a l., to speak with a l.,** zézayer, chuinter.

lisp² *vi & vt* zézayer, chuinter.

lissom ['lɪsəm] *adj* souple, agile, leste.

list¹ [lɪst] *n* liste *f*; *Admin etc* bordereau *m*; **alphabetical l.,** liste par ordre alphabétique; **l. of names,** liste nominative; **it's at the top of my list,** ça figure en tête de ma liste; (*I'll do it first*) ça figure en tête de mes priorités; **it's bottom of the l.,** c'est en bas de la liste; (*least important*) ce n'est pas à faire en priorité; **shopping l.,** liste des achats; **check l.,** liste de contrôle *ou* de vérification; **wine l.,** (*in restaurant*) carte *f* des vins; *St Exch* **l. of quotations,** bulletin *m* de cours; *Mil etc* **casualty l.,** état *m* des pertes; *Admin* **civil l.,** liste civile; *Fin etc* **l. of investments,** (bordereau *m* de) portefeuille *m*; **to make out** *or* **draw up a l.,** établir *ou* dresser une liste; **to enter (sth) on a l.,** porter (qch) sur une liste; **price l.,** prix-courant *m*, *pl* prix-courants, tarif *m*; **market price l.,** mercuriale *f*.

list² *vt* inscrire *ou* porter (*des noms etc*) sur une liste; enregistrer (*qch*); inventorier (*des marchandises etc*); **to l. names in alphabetical order,** faire une liste des noms par ordre alphabétique; **the striking workers listed their demands,** les ouvriers en grève énumérèrent leurs revendications.

list³ *n Nau* bande *f*, gîte *f*; **to have** *or* **take a l.,** donner de la bande; prendre de la gîte; **l. to starboard,** gîte à tribord.

list⁴ *vi Nau* donner de la bande (**to starboard,** à tribord), prendre de la gîte; **the ship is listing,** le navire penche sur le côté.

list⁵ *n Arch* **lists,** lice *f*; **to enter the lists,** entrer en lice (**against s.o.,** contre qn).

listed ['lɪstɪd] *adj* **(a)** *Fin* **listed securities** *or* **stock,** valeurs admises *ou* inscrites à la cote (officielle); **(b)** *Archit* **l. building,** immeuble répertorié.

listel ['lɪst(ə)l] *n Archit* listel *m*, *pl* -eaux.

listen ['lɪs(ə)n] *vi* **(a)** écouter; **to l. to s.o./sth,** écouter qn/qch; **to l. with half an ear,** n'écouter que d'une oreille; **you're not listening to a word I'm saying!,** tu n'écoutes pas un traître mot de ce que je dis!; **to l. to s.o. singing,** écouter chanter qn; **l.! I've got an idea,** écoutez donc, j'ai une idée; **(b)** (*pay attention*) faire attention, écouter; **he wouldn't l.,** il n'a rien voulu savoir; **don't l. to such bad advice,** ne tiens pas compte de si mauvais conseils; **you've been listening to tales,** vous vous êtes laissé raconter des histoires; **(c) to l. (out) for sth/s.o.,** tendre l'oreille dans l'attente de qch/qn; **will you l. (out) for the phone?,** veux-tu tendre l'oreille au cas où le téléphone sonnerait?

►**listen in** *vi Rad* **to l. in,** écouter la radio; *Tel* **to l. in to other people's conversations,** écouter les conversations d'autrui; **I'd like to l. in on the discussion,** j'aimerais être témoin de cette discussion.

listener ['lɪsnər] *n* **(a)** auditeur, -trice; (*surreptitious*) écouteur, -euse; **to be a good l.,** savoir écouter; **(b)** *Rad* auditeur, -trice; **(c)** *Mil Tel* écouteur *m*.

listening ['lɪsnɪŋ] *n* écoute *f*; **l. apparatus,** appareil *m* d'écoute; écouteur *m*; **l. post/station,** poste *m*/station *f* d'écoute.

listing ['lɪstɪŋ] *n* listage *m*; *Comptr* listing *m*; **l. paper,** listing; *Am Tel* **do you have a l. for J. Smith?,** est-ce que vous avez un J. Smith dans vos fichiers?

listless ['lɪstlɪs] *adj* apathique, sans énergie.

listlessly ['lɪstlɪslɪ] *adv* sans énergie.

listlessness ['lɪstlɪsnɪs] *n* apathie *f*.

litany ['lɪtənɪ] *n Rel* litanies *fpl*; *Fig* (*of complaints etc*) litanie.

litchi ['liːtʃiː, 'laɪ-] *n* (*fruit*) litchi *m*.

liter ['liːtər] *n US* = **LITRE**.

literacy ['lɪtərəsɪ] *n* fait *m* de savoir lire et écrire; degré *m* d'instruction *ou* d'alphabétisation.

literal ['lɪtərəl] **1** *adj* **(a)** littéral, -aux; (*traduction*) mot à mot; (*of person*) terre à terre, prosaïque; **in the l. sense of the word,** au sens propre du mot; **to take sth in a l. sense,** prendre qch au pied de la lettre; **(b)** *Math* (*coefficient*) littéral; *Typ* **l. error,** coquille *f*. **2** *n Typ* coquille *f*.

literally ['lɪtərəlɪ] *adv* **(a)** littéralement; (*traduire*) mot à mot; **l. speaking,** à proprement parler; **to take sth l.,** prendre qch au pied de la lettre; **(b)** *F* (*intensifier*) littéralement.

literary ['lɪtərərɪ] *adj* (*œuvre, agent, critique etc*) littéraire; **l. man,** homme *m* de lettres.

literate ['lɪtərɪt] **1** *adj* **(a)** qui sait lire et écrire; **computer l.,** formé à l'informatique; **(b)** (*educated*) lettré.

literature ['lɪtərɪtʃər] *n* **(a)** littérature *f*; **French l.,** la littérature française; **(b)** (*giving information*) documentation *f*; *Com etc* prospectus *mpl*, brochures *fpl*; **travel l.,** brochures *fpl* touristiques; **the l. of a subject,** la bibliographie d'un sujet.

lithe [laɪð] *adj* souple, agile.

lithium ['lɪθɪəm] *n Ch* lithium *m*.

lithograph ['lɪθəgræf] *n* lithographie *f*.

lithographic [lɪθə'græfɪk] *adj* lithographique.

lithography [lɪ'θɒgrəfɪ] *n* lithographie *f*, procédés *mpl* lithographiques.

Lithuania [lɪθjʊ'eɪnɪə] *n* Lituanie *f*.

Lithuanian [lɪθjʊ'eɪnɪən] **1** *adj* lituanien. **2** *n* **(a)** Lituanien, -ienne; **(b)** *Ling* lituanien *m*.

litigant ['lɪtɪgənt] *Jur* **1** *adj* **l. parties,** parties plaidantes *ou* en litige. **2** *n* plaideur, -euse.

litigate ['lɪtɪgeɪt] **1** *vi* plaider. **2** *vt* contester (*une question*); mettre (*une question, une propriété*) en litige.

litigation [lɪtɪ'geɪʃən] *n Jur* litige *m*; **in l.,** en litige; **to go to l.,** (*of person*) aller en justice; (*of matter*) être porté en justice.

litigious [lɪ'tɪdʒəs] *adj* **(a)** *Jur* litigieux; **(b)** *Pej* (*person*) chicaneur.

litmus ['lɪtməs] *n Ch* tournesol *m*; **l. paper,** papier *m* (de) tournesol; **l. test,** essai *m* de réaction au papier tournesol; *Fig* test décisif.

litre, *US* **liter** ['liːtər] *n* litre *m*.

litter¹ ['lɪtər] *n* **(a)** (*in public place*) détritus *m*, immondices *fpl*; (*from people eating*) papiers gras; (*untidy belongings*) fouillis *m*, désordre *m*; **please come and clear up your l.,** veuillez venir nettoyer vos ordures; **dropping l. is forbidden,** dépôt d'ordures interdit; **l. bin,** (*in street*) boîte *f* à ordures; *Br Sl* **l. lout,** = malpropre qui salit les rues; **(b)** portée *f* (*d'un animal*); **five young at a l.** *or* **in one l.,** cinq petits d'une portée; **(c)** civière *f* (*pour le transport des blessés*); *Arch* litière *f*; **to be carried in a l.,** être porté en litière; **(d)** *Agr* litière *f* (*de paille etc*); fumier *m* (*d'écurie etc*); (*for cat*) litière.

litter² **1** *vt* **(a)** recouvrir (*les rues*) de détritus *ou* d'immondices; mettre en désordre (*une chambre etc*); **he litters his room with dirty socks,** il parsème sa chambre de chaussettes sales; **table littered with papers,** table encombrée de papiers; *Fig* **beaches littered with tourists,** des plages jonchées de touristes; **(b) to l. (down) a horse,** faire la litière à un cheval; **to l. (down) a stable,** étendre de la paille dans une écurie; **2** *vi* (*of animal*) mettre bas, avoir une portée.

litterbug ['lɪtəbʌg] *n F* personne *f* qui jette des ordures n'importe où.

little ['lɪt(ə)l] **1** *adj* (*comp* **less, smaller,** *F* **littler**; *superl* **least**; **smallest,** *F* **littlest**) **(a)** petit; **l. girl,** petite fille, fillette *f*; **l. ones,** enfants *mpl*, *F* mioches *mpl*; petits *mpl* (*d'un animal*); *Br Hum* **the l. woman,** ma *ou* sa bourgeoise; **I'm fed up with the l. woman role,** j'en ai marre de mon statut de femme au foyer; **poor l. girl!,** pauvre petite!; *F* **a tiny l. house,** une toute petite maison; **wait a l. while!,** attendez un petit moment!; **the l. finger,** le petit doigt; **l. toe,** petit doigt; **l. hand,** (*of clock*) petite aiguille; **a l. something,** (*gift*) une babiole; (*to eat*) un petit quelque chose;

(b) (*not much*) peu (de); **l. money,** peu d'argent; **a l. money,** un peu d'argent; **to gain l. advantage from sth,** ne tirer que peu d'avantage de qch; **we're only a l. way into the discussion,** nous venons juste d'entamer la discussion; *F* **be it ever so l.,** si peu que ce soit; **with what l. French I knew,** avec le peu de français que je connaissais;

(c) *Pej* (*mean*) mesquin; **a l. mind,** un esprit étroit.

2 *n* (*comp* **less**; *superl* **least**) **(a)** peu *m*; **to eat l. or nothing,** manger peu ou point; **he knows very l.,** il ne sait pas grand-chose; **he has done l. for us,** il a peu fait pour nous; **I see very l. of her,** je ne la vois guère; **the l. I know,** le peu que je sais; **to think l. of s.o.,** tenir qn en médiocre estime; **to make** *or* **think l. of sth,** faire peu de cas de qch; *Prov* **every l. helps,** les petits ruisseaux font les grandes rivières; **l. by l.,** peu à peu, petit à petit;

(b) a l. more, encore un peu; **a l. more and he would have died,** peu s'en fallut qu'il ne meure; **for/after a l.,** (*time*) pendant/après un certain temps; (*used adverbially*) **he helped him a l.,** il l'a aidé un peu; **I was not a l. afraid,** j'avais très peur; **wait a l.!,** attendez un peu!

3 *adv* (*comp* **less**; *superl* **least**) **(a)** (*hardly*) peu; **l. known,** peu connu; **l. more than an hour ago,** il n'y a guère qu'une heure; **that's l. less than bribery,** c'est de la corruption pure et simple; **he studied too l.,** il n'a pas assez étudié; **I realized how l. I knew him,** je me suis rendu compte à quel point je le connaissais peu, je me suis rendu compte que je le connaissais fort peu; **if you think how little money they actually have,** si vous pensez à quel point ils manquent d'argent;

(b) he l. knows *or* **thinks** *or* **suspects ...,** il ne se doute guère ...; **l. did I think that ...,** je ne pensais pas du tout que ...; **I l. expected him to come,** je ne m'attendais guère à ce qu'il vienne;

(c) l. enough, assez peu; **you eat l. enough as it is,** tu manges déjà assez peu comme ça.

littoral ['lɪtərəl] **1** *adj* littoral, -aux. **2** *n* littoral *m*.

lit up [lɪt'ʌp] *adj Br Sl* (*drunk*) éméché.
liturgic(al) [lɪ'tɜːdʒɪk, -ɪk(ə)l] *adj* liturgique.
liturgy ['lɪtədʒɪ] *n* liturgie *f*.
livable ['lɪvəb(ə)l] *adj* = **LIVEABLE**.
live[1] [laɪv] **1** *adj* **(a)** vivant, en vie; (*person*) plein de vie; (*question*) d'actualité; (*coal*) ardent; **a restaurant where you order your fish l.**, un restaurant où on commande son poisson vivant; **l. weight,** poids vif *ou* vivant (*d'un animal de boucherie*); *F* **a real l. filmstar,** une vedette en chair et en os; **l. bait,** amorce vive; **l. birth,** enfant né vivant;
(b) *TV Rad* (*émission*) en direct; *TV* **recorded before a l. audience,** enregistré en public;
(c) *Mil* (*ammunition*) actif; (*bomb*) actif, amorcé, armé; (*cartridge*) à balle, réel; *El* **l. wire,** câble *m ou* fil *m* sous tension *ou* en charge *ou* chargé; *F* **she's a l. wire,** elle est énergique, elle a de l'allant;
(d) *Tech* (*load*) roulant, mobile; *MecE* (*essieu*) moteur; **l. steam,** vapeur vive; **l. weight,** charge utile.
2 *adv TV Rad* **to be broadcast l.**, être diffusé en direct; **the show comes l. from New York City,** le spectacle nous arrive en direct depuis New York; **an astronaut speaking l. from Skylab,** un astronaute parlant en direct depuis Skylab.
live[2] [lɪv] **1** *vi* **(a)** (*exist, be alive*) vivre; **while my father lived,** du vivant de mon père; **she'll l. to be 100,** elle ira jusqu'à 100 ans; **she has only a few months to l.**, il ne lui reste plus que quelques mois à vivre; **long l. the king!**, vive le roi!; **as long** *or* **so long as I l.**, tant que je vivrai; *F* **you'll l.!**, tu survivras!; *Prov* **you l. and learn,** on apprend à tout âge; (*wait and see*) qui vivra verra; **l. and let l.**, il faut que tout le monde vive; **they lived happily ever after,** ≈ ils furent heureux et eurent beaucoup d'enfants; **this is what I call living!**, c'est ce que j'appelle vivre!; **his name will l.**, son nom vivra *ou* sera immortalisé; **he lives by his writing,** il vit de sa plume; **to l. in style,** mener grand train; **to l. well,** vivre bien; **she lived only for her husband,** elle n'a vécu que pour son mari; **we're living for the day we emigrate,** nous vivons dans l'attente du jour ou nous émigrerons; **you'll always l. with the guilt,** la culpabilité vous poursuivra toute la vie; **you'll just have to l. with the idea!**, il faudra simplement que tu te fasses à cette idée!; **it's not ideal but I can l. with it,** c'est pas l'idéal mais je peux faire avec;
(b) (*reside*) habiter, vivre; **to l. in Paris,** habiter (à) Paris, vivre à Paris; **to l. in the country,** demeurer *ou* habiter *ou* vivre à la campagne; **where do you l.?**, où est-ce que vous habitez *ou* vivez?; **this house isn't fit to l. in,** cette maison est inhabitable; **the house doesn't seem to be lived in,** la maison ne paraît pas habitée; **to l. with s.o.**, vivre *ou* habiter avec qn; **to l. happily with s.o.**, faire bon ménage avec qn; **he lives with his wife and daughter,** il vit avec sa femme et sa fille.
2 *vt* **to l. a happy life,** mener une vie heureuse; **to l. a life of luxury,** mener un grand train de vie; **once more life seemed worth living,** de nouveau la vie semblait valoir la peine d'être vécue; **to l. a lie,** vivre dans un perpétuel mensonge; *Th* **to l. a part,** entrer dans la peau d'un personnage.
▶**live down** *vtsep* **to l. down one's past,** faire oublier son passé; **this is awful, I'll never l. it down!**, c'est terrible, je n'arriverai jamais à faire oublier cet événement.
▶**live in** *vi* (*of student*) **I'll be living in next year,** je serai interne l'année prochaine; (*of servant*) coucher à la maison; **the employees l. in,** les employés sont logés et nourris.
▶**live off** *vipo* **to live off the land,** vivre de la terre; **to l. off s.o.**, vivre aux crochets de qn.
▶**live on 1** *vi* (*continue to live*) vivre encore; **he lived on for another three years,** il vécut encore trois ans; **his memory will l. on,** sa mémoire lui survivra. **2** *vipo* **to l. on vegetables,** se nourrir de légumes; **to l. on one's capital,** vivre sur son capital; **to l. on s.o.**, vivre aux crochets de qn; **it's not enough to l. on,** ce n'est pas suffisant pour vivre; **to earn enough to l. on,** gagner de quoi vivre.
▶**live out 1** *vi* (*of student*) être externe; (*of servant*) coucher à son domicile, venir en journée. **2** *vtsep* passer (*une période, sa vie*); **they lived out their lives in poverty,** ils vécurent toute leur vie dans la pauvreté; **he won't l. out the year,** il ne passera pas l'année.
▶**live through** *vipo* (*a war, hard times etc*) vivre; (*survive*) survivre à (*une guerre etc*); **anyone who has lived through times like these will know ...**, quiconque a vécu cette époque sait que ...; **he's unlikely to l. through the winter,** il est peu vraisemblable qu'il passe l'hiver.
▶**live together** *vi* vivre ensemble, être en ménage.
▶**live up** *vtsep F* **to l. it up,** faire la noce.
▶**live up to** *vipo* **to l. up to expectations,** (*of person, party, film etc*) tenir ses promesses; **his brother has given him a lot to l. up to,** son frère a placé la barre très haut; **it's too much for me to l. up to,** on m'en demande trop; **to l. up to one's principles,** vivre selon ses principes; **to l. up to one's reputation,** faire honneur à sa réputation; **to l. up to one's promise,** tenir sa promesse.
liveable ['lɪvəb(ə)l] *adj* **(a)** (*house, room*) **l. in,** habitable; **(b)** (*life*) supportable; **(c)** (*person*) **l. with,** avec qui on peut vivre.
lived-in ['lɪvdɪn] *adj* (*house, flat*) accueillant; **to have a l.-in feel (to it),** dégager une chaleur de lieu habité, être accueillant.
live-in ['lɪvɪn] *adj* (*chauffeur, nanny etc*) logé et nourri; *Hum* **l.-in lover,** compagnon *m ou* compagne *f* (avec qui l'on vit).
livelihood ['laɪvlɪhʊd] *n* moyens *mpl* d'existence, gagne-pain *m inv*; **to earn** *or* **gain** *or* **get** *or* **make a l.**, gagner sa vie *ou* son pain, gagner de quoi vivre; **tourism is our l.**, le tourisme est notre gagne-pain; **to lose one's l.**, perdre ses moyens de subsistance.
liveliness ['laɪvlɪnɪs] *n* vivacité *f*, animation *f*, entrain *m*; *Fin* animation (*du marché*).
livelong ['lɪvlɒŋ] *adj Lit* **the l. day,** toute la journée, tout le long du jour; **the l. night,** toute la nuit.
lively ['laɪvlɪ] **1** *adj* **(a)** (*person*) vif, animé, plein d'entrain; (*imagination, pleasure, satisfaction*) vif; (*town, description, party*) animé; **l. conversation,** conversation animée; **l. music,** musique égayante *ou* pleine d'entrain; *F* **to make it** *or* **things l. for s.o.**, rendre la vie dure à qn; **things are getting l.**, ça chauffe; **to take a l. interest in sth,** s'intéresser vivement à qch; **(b)** (*colour*) vif; **(c)** *Nau* (*canot*) léger sur l'eau. **2** *adv* **look l.!**, grouille-toi!
▶**liven up** ['laɪv(ə)n] **1** *vtsep* animer, égayer (*qn, une réunion etc*); activer (*une affaire*); *Th* mouvementer (*l'action*); **to l. up the conversation,** ranimer la conversation; **you need to l. up your style,** vous devriez mettre plus de mouvement dans votre style; **some pictures would l. up the text a bit,** quelques photos égaieraient un peu le texte. **2** *vi* s'animer, s'activer, *F* s'échauffer.
liver[1] ['lɪvər] *n Anat* foie *m*; *Culin* **calf's l.**, foie de veau; **l. pâté,** pâté *m* de foie.
liver[2] *n* (*person*) **fast l.**, viveur, -euse, noceur, -euse; **loose l.**, libertin *m*, débauché *m*.
liveried ['lɪvərɪd] *adj* en livrée.
liverish ['lɪvərɪʃ] *adj F* **to feel l.**, avoir une crise de foie.
Liverpudlian [lɪvə'pʌdlɪən] **1** *adj* de Liverpool. **2** *n* Liverpoolien, -ienne.
liverwurst ['lɪvəwɜːst] *n Am* saucisse *f* de foie.
livery ['lɪvərɪ] *n* **(a)** (*uniform*) livrée *f*; **full l.**, grande livrée; **in l.**, en livrée; **l. company,** corporation *f* d'un corps de métier (de la cité de Londres); **(b) l. horse,** cheval *m* de louage; **l. stables,** écuries *fpl* de chevaux de louage.
livestock ['laɪvstɒk] *n* bétail *m*, bestiaux *mpl*; *Jur* cheptel *m*.
livid ['lɪvɪd] *adj* **(a)** (*angry*) furieux; **to be l. with anger,** *F* **to be absolutely l.**, être blême de colère *ou* furieux; **it makes me l.!**, ça me met en rage!; **(b)** (*teint*) livide, blême; (*ciel*) plombé; **l. bruise,** bleu enluminé.
living ['lɪvɪŋ] **1** *adj* **(a)** vivant, vif; en vie; **while she was l.**, de son vivant; **there is not a l. soul to be seen,** on ne rencontre pas âme qui vive *ou F* pas un chat; **he has done more for them than any man l.**, il a fait plus pour eux que n'importe qui; **within l. memory,** dans la mémoire des vivants; **l. language,** langue vivante; **l. pictures,** tableaux vivants; **a l. death,** une vie pire que la mort; *F* **to scare the l. daylights out of s.o.**, faire mourir de peur qn; *F* **to beat the l. daylights out of s.o.**, arranger le portrait à qn; **to make s.o.'s life a l. hell,** faire de la vie de qn un enfer;
(b) l. water, eau vive; **l. force,** force vive.
2 *n* **(a)** vie *f*; **l. in the country,** la vie à la campagne; **style of l.**, style *m* de vie; *Econ* **standard of l.**, niveau *m* de vie; **to be fond of good l.**, aimer la bonne chère; **fast l. will do him no good,** mener une vie de plaisirs lui fera du mal; **l. room,** (salle *f* de) séjour *m*; **l. space,** espace vital;
(b) (*livelihood*) vie *f*; **to earn one's l.**, gagner sa vie; **to work for one's** *or* **a l.**, travailler pour gagner sa vie; **to write for a l.**, vivre de sa plume; **what does he do for a l.?**, qu'est-ce qu'il fait?, quel est son métier?; **to make a l.**, gagner de quoi vivre; **she makes a l. out of it,** elle en vit; **l. wage,** minimum vital;
(c) the l., (*used as pl*) les vivants *mpl*; **still in the land of the l.**, encore vivant *ou* de ce monde;
(d) *Rel* bénéfice *m*, cure *f*.
-living ['lɪvɪŋ] *suff* **clean-l.**, de bonnes mœurs.

Livy ['lɪvɪ] *n* Tite-Live *m*.
lizard ['lɪzəd] *n* lézard *m*; **l. (skin) handbag,** sac à main en lézard.
Lizzie, Lizzy ['lɪzɪ] *n F* **busy L.,** (*plant*) balsamine *f*, impatiente *f*.
llama ['lɑːmə] *n* (*animal*) lama *m*.
LLB [elel'biː] *n* (*abbr* **Legum Baccalaureus**) ≈ Bachelier en Droit.
LLD [elel'diː] *n* (*abbr* **Legum Doctor**) ≈ Docteur en Droit.
LNG [elen'dʒiː] *n* (*abbr* **liquified natural gas**) GNL *m*.
lo [ləʊ] *int Arch & Lit* voici, voilà; *Hum* **lo and behold, there he was,** et voilà qu'il était là.
loach [ləʊtʃ] *n* (*fish*) loche *f*.
load¹ [ləʊd] *n* **(a)** (*burden*) fardeau *m*; charge *f*, chargement *m* (*d'un camion, d'un navire etc*); (*contents of vehicle*) camion *m*, tombereau *m* (*de gravier etc*); charge (*de bois*); **to carry a l. on one's back,** porter un fardeau sur son dos; **that's a l. off my mind!,** quel soulagement!; **to share the l.,** partager la besogne; **useful l.,** charge utile; *Nau* **l. line,** ligne *f* de charge; **to shed its l. on the motorway,** (*of lorry*) répandre son chargement sur l'autoroute; *F* **it's a l. of rubbish** *or* **nonsense,** (*untrue*) c'est du bidon; (*novel, theory etc*) c'est un tas de bêtises; *Sl* **get a l. of that!,** (*listen*) écoute un peu ça!; (*look*) regarde ça!; *F* **he's got loads of them,** il en a des quantités *ou* des tas; *F* **we've done it loads of times,** nous l'avons fait je ne sais combien de fois; *F* **we've got loads of time,** nous avons largement le temps;
(b) *MecE El* charge *f*; **safe l.,** charge de sécurité; **machine working at full l.,** machine qui fonctionne *ou* travaille à pleine charge; **under l.,** en charge; *El* **to shed the l.,** délester; **l. shedding,** délestage *m*.
load² **1** *vt* **(a)** charger (*un camion, un navire, un appareil-photo etc*); *Comptr* charger; **to l. passengers,** (*of bus*) prendre des voyageurs; **to l. oneself up with luggage,** se charger de bagages; **to l. a washing machine/dishwasher,** mettre du linge dans la machine à laver/de la vaisselle dans le lave-vaisselle; **to l. a program into a computer,** entrer un programme dans un ordinateur; **to l. s.o. with favours,** combler qn de faveurs; **loaded with cares,** accablé de soucis; **loaded with shopping,** chargé d'achats; **I'm going to l. some more work onto you,** je vais vous confier encore un peu de travail; **to l. a gun,** charger un fusil (à balle); **my gun wasn't loaded,** mon fusil *ou* mon revolver n'était pas chargé;
(b) *MecE* serrer, bander (*un ressort*);
(c) piper (*des dés*); *Fig* **the dice were loaded in our favour,** la partie était faussée à notre avantage;
(d) (*in insurance*) majorer (*une prime*).
2 *vi Comptr* (*of software etc*) se charger; (*of ship etc*) faire la cargaison; **ship loading,** navire en chargement *ou* en charge; *Aut* **one can stop for a few minutes to l. and unload,** (*in street*) des arrêts brefs sont autorisés pour charger et décharger; **the camera loads automatically,** l'appareil-photo s'arme automatiquement.
►**load up** **1** *vtsep Comptr* charger. **2** *vi* (*of ship*) faire la cargaison.
loadable ['ləʊdəb(ə)l] *adj Comptr* (*software etc*) qui peut se charger, chargeable.
loaded ['ləʊdɪd] *adj* **(a)** (*camion, navire etc*) chargé; **(b)** *MecE* (*ressort*) bandé; **spring-l. valve,** soupape à ressort; **(c)** (*dés*) pipé; **(d)** (*person*) *Sl* (*wealthy*) richissime; *esp Am* (*drunk*) soûl; *esp Am* (*on drugs*) drogué, camé; **(e) a l. question,** une question insidieuse.
loader ['ləʊdər] *n* **(a)** (*person*) manutentionnaire *m*; (*with shooting party*) chargeur *m* des fusils; **(b)** (*device*) chargeuse *f*; *Constr* chargeur *m*; **bucket l.,** chargeuse à godets.
loading ['ləʊdɪŋ] *n* chargement *m* (*d'un camion, d'un wagon, d'un navire, d'un avion, d'un fusil*); *Phot* chargement (*de l'appareil, des châssis*); *Nucl Phys* chargement (*du réacteur en combustible*); *Comptr* chargement (*de programme*); mise *f* en place (*d'une bande magnétique*); **bulk l.,** chargement en vrac; **l. ramp/bay,** rampe *f*/quai *m* de chargement.
loaf¹, *pl* **loaves** [ləʊf, ləʊvz] *n* **(a)** pain *m*; **a l. of bread,** un pain; **French l.,** baguette *f*; **sandwich l.,** pain de mie; **cottage l.,** ≈ double miche *f*; ≈ calotte bretonne; *Prov* **half a l. is better than no bread,** faute de grives on mange des merles; **(b) sugar l.,** pain *m* de sucre; *Culin* **meat l.,** = hachis *m* de viande moulé en forme de pain; **(c)** *F* tête *f*; **use your l.,** fais un peu travailler tes méninges.
loaf² **1** *vi* **to l. (about** *or* **around),** flâner, traîner. **2** *vt* **to l. away the time,** passer son temps à flâner *ou* à fainéanter.
loafer ['ləʊfər] *n* **(a)** (*person*) flâneur, euse; **(b)** *esp Am* (*shoe*) mocassin *m*.
loam [ləʊm] *n Agr Geol* terreau *m*.
loamy ['ləʊmɪ] *adj* (*soil*) gras.
loan¹ [ləʊn] *n* (*money, object*) (*from borrower's point of view*) prêt *m*; (*from lender's point of view*) emprunt *m*; **l. of money,** prêt *ou* avance *f* d'argent; **can I have a l. of ...?,** puis-je emprunter ...?; **on l. from the Louvre,** prêt du Louvre; **to have sth on permanent l.,** disposer de qch en prêt permanent; **she's on l. to the department from Head Office,** elle est détachée du Siège Central au service; **the video you want is out on l.,** la vidéo que vous voulez est sortie; **government l.,** emprunt d'Etat; **issue of a l.,** émission *f* d'un emprunt; **to take out a l.,** faire un emprunt; **long/short-term l.,** prêt *ou* emprunt à long/court terme; **secured l.,** prêt *ou* emprunt gagé *ou* garanti; **unsecured l., l. without security,** prêt *ou* emprunt à découvert; **l. society,** société *f* *ou* établissement *m* de crédit; **l. account,** compte *m* de prêt; **l.-back facility,** (*in insurance*) possibilité *f* d'emprunt sur le montant de son assurance-vie; *F* **l. shark,** usurier *m*; **to raise a l. on an estate,** emprunter de l'argent sur une terre; **it's a l., you can have it as a l.,** je vous le prête, c'est à titre de prêt; *Ling* **l. word,** mot *m* d'emprunt.
loan² *vt & vi* prêter (**sth to s.o.,** qch à qn); **loaned by the Louvre,** prêt *m* du Louvre.
loanword ['ləʊnwɜːd] *n Ling* mot *m* d'emprunt.
loath [ləʊθ] *adj* **to be l. to do sth,** hésiter à faire qch; **nothing l.,** volontiers.
loathe [ləʊð] *vt* détester, exécrer (*qn, qch*); **I l. milk,** j'ai horreur du lait; **to l. doing sth,** détester faire qch.
loathing ['ləʊðɪŋ] *n* dégoût *m*, répugnance *f* (**for,** pour); **to take** *or* **conceive a l. for s.o.,** prendre qn en dégoût; **to fill s.o. with l.,** (*of s.o., sth*) remplir qn de dégoût, dégoûter qn; **to have a l. for milk,** avoir horreur du lait.
loathsome ['ləʊðsəm] *adj* repoussant, dégoûtant, répugnant; (*smell*) nauséabond.
loathesomeness ['ləʊðsəmnɪs] *n* nature repoussante *ou* dégoûtante (*de qch*).
lob¹ [lɒb] *n Sp* lob *m*, chandelle *f*.
lob² *vt Sp* envoyer (*la balle etc*) en chandelle, lober (*la balle etc*); **he lobbed a stone into the water,** il balança un caillou dans l'eau.
lobby¹ ['lɒbɪ] *n* **(a)** (*corridor*) couloir *m*, antichambre *f*, vestibule *m*; promenoir *m* (*d'un tribunal etc*); entrée *f* (*d'un théâtre*); hall *m* (*d'un hôtel*); **the l. of the House,** (*in Parliament*) la salle des pas perdus; les couloirs de la Chambre; **division lobbies,** = vestibules où passent les députés lorsqu'ils se divisent pour voter; **(b)** *Pol etc* (*pressure group*) lobby *m*, groupe *m* de pression; **the anti-abortion l.,** le groupe de pression contre l'avortement.
lobby² **1** *vi* **(a)** fréquenter la salle des pas perdus de la Chambre (*en quête de nouvelles etc*), faire les couloirs; **(b)** (*of pressure group*) faire pression; **they're lobbying for tax reform,** ils font pression en vue d'une réforme fiscale. **2** *vt* exercer une *ou* faire pression sur (*qn*).
lobbyist ['lɒbɪɪst] *n Pol etc* = membre d'un groupe de pression.
lobe [ləʊb] *n* **(a)** *Anat* lobe *m* (*de l'oreille etc*); **(b)** *Archit Bot* lobe *m* (*d'une rosace, d'une feuille*).
lobelia [ləʊ'biːlɪə] *n* lobélie *f*.
lobotomize [ləʊ'bɒtəmaɪz] *vt* lobotomiser.
lobotomy [ləʊ'bɒtəmɪ] *n Surg* lobotomie cérébrale.
lobster ['lɒbstər] *n* homard *m*; **spiny l.,** langouste *f*; **Norway l.,** langoustine *f*; **l. boat,** homardier *m*; (*for spiny lobster*) langoustier *m*; **l. pot,** casier *m* à homards; (*for spiny lobster*) casier à langoustes.
local ['ləʊk(ə)l] **1** *adj* local, -aux; régional, -aux; **l. authorities,** autorités locales *ou* régionales; **l. government,** ≈ (*in county*) l'administration départementale; (*in town*) ≈ l'administration communale; **l. news,** informations de la région; **l. paper,** journal local; **l. wine,** vin *m* du pays; **l. colour,** couleur locale; **l. time,** heure locale; **6am l. time,** 6 heures du matin heure locale; **the l. doctor,** le médecin du quartier; **a matter of l. politics,** une question de politique locale *ou F* de clocher; **they voted for the l. man,** ils ont voté pour le candidat local; **l. train,** (train *m*) omnibus *m*; **l. showers,** averses éparses; *Comptr* **l. area network,** réseau local; *Fin Com* **l. bill,** effet *m* sur place; *Surg* **l. anaesthetic,** anesthésique local; **to give s.o. a l. anaesthetic,** administrer à qn un anesthésique local.
2 *n* **(a) the locals,** les gens *mpl ou* les habitants *mpl* du pays; *Sp* l'équipe locale *ou* du pays;
(b) *F* anesthésique local;
(c) *F* **the l.,** le bistro du village *ou* du coin.
locale [ləʊ'kɑːl] *n* scène *f*, théâtre *m* (*des événements*).

locality [ləʊ'kælɪtɪ] *n* **(a)** (*neighbourhood*) endroit *m*, lieu *m*; **in our l.,** dans notre pays *ou* région; **in the general l. of the incident,** sur les lieux de l'incident; **(b) to have a good sense of l.** *or F* **the bump of l.,** avoir le sens de l'orientation.

localize ['ləʊkəlaɪz] *vt* localiser (*une épidémie etc*); **to become localized,** (*of disease, pain*) se localiser (**in,** dans).

locally ['ləʊkəlɪ] *adv* localement; (*to live, be well-known etc*) dans le quartier; **l. produced wine,** vin *m* du pays; **we get them printed l.,** nous les faisons imprimer sur place; **I prefer to shop l.,** je préfère faire mes courses sur place; **he set up in business l.,** il a monté une affaire sur place.

locate [ləʊ'keɪt] **1** *vt* **(a)** (*to find*) localiser, situer (*qch*); *El* repérer, localiser (*un dérangement etc*); **to l. sth on a map,** situer qch sur une carte; *Nau* **to l. a ship,** déterminer la position d'un navire (en mer); **(b)** (*to situate*) situer; **the new shopping centre is located in the old market square,** le nouveau centre commercial est situé sur la place du vieux marché. **2** *vi* (*of company etc*) s'installer.

location [ləʊ'keɪʃən] *n* **(a)** (*site, place*) situation *f*, emplacement *m*; **(b)** *Cin* **to be on l.,** tourner en extérieur; **l. shot,** extérieur *m*; **filmed on l.,** filmé en extérieur; **(c)** (*finding*) localisation *f*; *El* repérage *m* (*d'un dérangement etc*); **(d)** (*in South Africa*) réserve *f* indigène.

locative ['lɒkətɪv] *adj & n Gram* locatif *m*.

loch [lɒχ] *n Scot* **(a)** lac *m*; **(b) sea l.,** bras *m* de mer, fjord *m*.

lock¹ [lɒk] *n* **(a)** (*on door etc*) serrure *f*; (*padlock*) cadenas *m*; **mortise l.,** serrure encastrée; **safety/combination l.,** serrure de sûreté/à combinaisons; **under l. and key,** sous clef; (*of person*) sous les verrous; **to pick a l.,** crocheter une serrure; *Rugby* **l. forward,** avant *m* de deuxième ligne; **(b)** *MecE* verrou *m*, *pl* -ous; verrouillage *m*, blocage *m*; *Mil* **breech l.,** verrou de culasse; **(c)** platine *f* (*de fusil*); **he swallowed the story l. stock and barrel,** il a tout avalé; **we sold it l. stock and barrel,** nous avons tout vendu sans exception; **we bought the whole estate l. stock and barrel,** nous avons acheté l'ensemble de la propriété; **the motion was rejected l. stock and barrel,** la motion a été rejetée en bloc; **(d)** (*in wrestling*) étreinte *f*, clef *f*; **arm l.,** clef de bras; **(e)** *Aut etc* angle *m* de braquage; **on full l.,** braqué au maximum; **(f)** (*on river*) écluse *f*; **l. chamber,** sas *m* (d'écluse); **l. gate,** porte *f* d'écluse; **air l.,** sas à air, sas pneumatique; poche *f* d'air (*dans un tuyau etc*).

lock² **1** *vt* **(a)** fermer à clef; donner un tour de clef à (*une porte*); **behind locked doors,** à huis clos; **to l. s.o. in a room,** enfermer qn dans une chambre; **to l. sth (away) in a drawer,** enfermer qch dans un tiroir; **to l. valuables (away) in a safe,** mettre des objets de valeur dans un coffre;

(b) enrayer, bloquer, caler (*les roues*); enclencher (*les pièces d'un mécanisme*); *Mil* verrouiller (*la culasse*); **to l. a keyboard,** (*for capital letters*) bloquer un clavier en majuscules; **ship locked in ice,** navire pris dans les glaces; **to be locked (together) in a struggle,** (*of people*) être engagés corps à corps dans une lutte; **to be locked in each other's arms,** se tenir étroitement embrassés; **his jaws were tightly locked,** il avait les dents serrées; *Fig* **to l. horns with the enemy,** livrer bataille avec l'ennemi; *Fig* **they have locked horns,** (*of people*) ils ont une dispute *ou F* un accrochage.

2 *vi* **(a)** (*of wheels etc*) s'enrayer, se bloquer; **the door locks on the inside,** la serrure (de la porte) se ferme de l'intérieur; **the door locks automatically,** la porte se verrouille automatiquement; **the parts l. into each other,** les parties s'enclenchent l'une dans l'autre;

(b) (*of boat*) passer par une écluse;

(c) *Aut* **to l. left/right,** braquer à gauche/à droite.

lock³ *n* mèche *f*, boucle *f* (*de cheveux*); *Arch & Lit* **locks,** cheveux *mpl*, chevelure *f*.

►lock in *vtsep* enfermer (*qn*) à clef; mettre (*qn*) sous clef; **to get locked in,** se faire enfermer; **to l. oneself in,** s'enfermer; **to be locked into a pension scheme,** être prisonnier d'une caisse de retraite; **to be locked into a company,** (*as a source of supply*) être prisonnier d'une société.

►lock off *vtsep Typ* débloquer; **this key locks the caps on and off,** cette touche bloque et débloque les majuscules.

►lock on *vtsep Typ* bloquer; **l. the caps on before you start typing,** bloque les majuscules avant de commencer à taper.

►lock on to *vipo Electron* (*of radar etc*) accrocher (*un objectif*); *Fig* s'accrocher à (*une idée etc*).

►lock out *vtsep* **(a) to l. s.o. out,** enfermer qn dehors; **I found myself locked out,** en rentrant j'ai trouvé la porte fermée (à clef); **I've locked myself out (of my room),** je me suis enfermé dehors; **(b)** *Ind* lockouter (*le personnel*).

►lock up **1** *vtsep* **(a)** mettre *ou* serrer (*qch*) sous clef; enfermer (*qn, qch*); fermer (*une maison*) à clef; (*in jail*) mettre (*qn*) sous les verrous; **to l. a house up for the winter,** barricader une maison pour l'hiver; **he should be locked up!,** il faudrait l'enfermer!; **(b)** *Fin* immobiliser, bloquer, engager (*des capitaux*). **2** *vi* **it's time to l. up,** c'est l'heure de fermer.

locker ['lɒkər] *n* **(a)** (*for luggage, in school*) casier *m*; **l. room,** vestiaire *m* (*d'une usine, d'un pavillon de sports etc*); **l.-room jokes/language,** plaisanteries *fpl*/langage *m* de vestiaire; **(b)** *Nau* caisson *m*, coffre *m*; **signal l.,** coffre *ou* caisson à signaux.

locket ['lɒkɪt] *n* médaillon *m* (porté en parure).

locking ['lɒkɪŋ] *n* **(a)** fermeture *f* à clef; **(b)** *MecE etc* blocage *m*, enclenchement *m*; **l. device/mechanism,** dispositif *m*/mécanisme *m* de blocage.

locking on *n Electron* (*of radar etc*) accrochage *m* (*d'un objectif*).

locking up *n* mise *f* sous clef; fermeture *f* (*d'une maison etc*); *Fin* immobilisation *f* (*de capitaux*).

lockjaw ['lɒkdʒɔː] *n Med* trismus *m*, trisme *m*, tétanos *m*; **to have l.,** avoir le tétanos.

lock-keeper ['lɒkkiːpər] *n* (*on canal*) gardien *m* d'écluse, éclusier *m*.

locknut ['lɒknʌt] *n* contre-écrou *m*, *pl* contre-écrous.

lock-out ['lɒkaʊt] *n* lock-out *m inv*, grève patronale.

locksmith ['lɒksmɪθ] *n* serrurier *m*.

lockup ['lɒkʌp] *n* **(a)** (*for storage*) hangar *m etc* fermant à clef; **l. shop,** (petit) magasin (construit sans habitation attenante); **l. garage,** box *m*; **(b)** *F* (*police cell*) le violon, le bloc.

loco¹ ['ləʊkəʊ] *n F* (*train*) loco *f*.

loco² *adj US F* (*mad*) fou, *f* folle, *F* dingue.

locomotion [ləʊkə'məʊʃən] *n* locomotion *f*.

locomotive [ləʊkə'məʊtɪv] **1** *adj* locomotif, -ive; *Anat* locomoteur, -trice. **2** *n Rail* locomotive *f*; **diesel l.,** locomotive (à moteur) diesel.

locum ['ləʊkəm] *n* **l. (tenens** ['tenenz]**),** remplaçant, -ante (*d'un médecin, d'un ecclésiastique*); **to take a l. job,** prendre un emploi de remplaçant.

locus, *pl* **loci** ['ləʊkəs, 'ləʊsaɪ, 'ləʊsiː] *n* **(a)** *Math* lieu *m* géométrique; **(b)** *Biol* locus *m* (*d'un chromosome*).

locust ['ləʊkəst] *n* **(a)** *Ent* acridien *m*, criquet *m*; grande sauterelle d'Orient; **(b)** *Bot* **l. (bean),** caroube *f*; **l. (tree),** (*carob tree*) caroubier *m*; (*false acacia*) robinier *m*.

locution [ləʊ'kjuːʃən] *n* locution *f*.

lode [ləʊd] *n Geol Min* filon *m*, veine *f*.

lodestar ['ləʊdstɑːr] *n* **(a)** étoile directrice; **the l.,** l'étoile polaire; **(b)** *Fig* point *m* d'attraction, point de mire (de l'attention etc).

lodestone ['ləʊdstəʊn] *n Miner* aimant naturel.

lodge¹ [lɒdʒ] *n* **(a)** loge *f* (*de concierge etc*); **keeper's l.,** maison *f* de garde-chasse; **(gate) l.,** pavillon *m* d'entrée (*d'une propriété*); pavillon du garde; **l. keeper,** portier *m*; **(b)** (*house*) **shooting l.,** pavillon *m* de chasse; **(c)** loge *f*, atelier *m* (*des francs-maçons*); **the Grand L. of France,** le Grand Orient (de France); **l. (meeting),** tenue *f*; **(d)** *Univ* **master's l.,** résidence *f* du directeur du collège; **(e)** terrier *m* (*de loutre*); hutte *f* (*de castor*); **(f)** hutte *f* (*des Indiens d'Amérique*), wigwam *m*.

lodge² **1** *vt* **(a)** (*accommodate*) loger (*qn*), héberger (*qn*); **to l. oneself,** *esp Mil* prendre position;

(b) (*deposit*) déposer, remettre; consigner *ou* déposer de l'argent (**with s.o.,** chez qn); déposer (*des titres*) (**with a bank,** dans une banque); **securities lodged as collateral,** titres déposés *ou* remis en nantissement; *Jur* **to l. an appeal,** interjeter appel, faire appel; **to l. a complaint,** déposer une plainte; **to l. a complaint against s.o.,** porter plainte contre qn.

2 *vi* **(a)** (*of person*) loger (quelque part); **to l. with s.o.,** (*rent room from*) louer une chambre *ou* des chambres chez qn; (*have meals provided*) être en pension chez qn;

(b) (*of thing*) rester, se loger; **a fishbone lodged in his throat,** il a eu une arête coincée dans son gosier; **a bullet lodged close to his spine,** une balle s'est logée près de sa colonne vertébrale.

lodger ['lɒdʒər] *n* locataire *mf* (*en meublé*); (*who has meals provided*) pensionnaire *mf*; **to take (in) lodgers,** louer des chambres; (*provide meals too*) prendre des pensionnaires.

lodging ['lɒdʒɪŋ] *n* **(a)** (*room etc*) logement *m*; **to find a night's l.,** trouver où coucher pour la nuit; **board and l.,** chambre *f* avec pension; **(b)** (*usu pl*) **lodgings,** logement *m*,

Arch logis *m*, appartement meublé; **to live** *or* **be in lodgings,** loger *ou* habiter en garni *ou* en (hôtel) meublé; **(c)** hébergement *m* (*de qn*); **l. house,** hôtel garni; **(d)** dépôt *m*, consignation *f*, remise *f* (*d'argent, de valeurs etc*); *Jur* déposition *f* (*d'une plainte*); interjection *f* (*d'appel*).

loft¹ [lɒft] *n* **(a)** (*attic*) grenier *m*, soupente *f*; **l. conversion,** loft *m*, soupente aménagée; **(b) pigeon l.,** pigeonnier *m*; **(c)** galerie *f*, tribune *f* (*dans une église, une salle etc*); **organ l.,** tribune de l'orgue.

loft² *vt Golf* donner de la hauteur à (*la balle*); **he lofted the ball out of the ground,** il a envoyé la balle hors du terrain.

loftily ['lɒftɪlɪ] *adv* **(a)** (*situé*) en hauteur; **(b)** (*répondre*) avec hauteur *ou* condescendance.

loftiness ['lɒftɪnɪs] *n* **(a)** (*of mountain etc*) hauteur *f*; **(b)** (*of person*) arrogance *f*, hauteur *f*.

lofty ['lɒftɪ] **1** *adj* **(a)** (*mountain, tree, building etc*) haut, élevé; **(b)** (*person, manner*) hautain, orgueilleux, altier; (*air*) condescendant, protecteur; **(c)** (*aim, desire etc*) élevé; (*style etc*) élevé, relevé, sublime, soutenu. **2** *n F* (*tall person*) **hello, l.!,** salut, mon grand!

log¹ [lɒg] *n* **(a)** (*of wood*) bûche *f*; (*esp for building*) rondin *m*; **to sleep like a l.,** dormir comme une souche; **Yuletide** *or* **Christmas l.,** bûche de Noël; **l. cabin** *or* **hut,** hutte *f* de troncs d'arbre, cabane *f* de bois; **l. fire,** feu *m* de bois; **l. jam,** embâcle *m* de bûches; *Fig* (*in talks etc*) impasse *f*; **l. running,** flottage *m* du bois; **l. transporter,** fardier *m*; **(b)** (*record*) carnet *m* de route *ou* de bord; *Nau* journal *m*, *pl* -aux; *Av* carnet de vol; **ship's l.,** journal de bord; (*giving navigation details*) journal de navigation; **to write up the l.,** noter les détails du voyage; **(c)** *Nau* (*for measuring speed*) loch *m*; (*in engine room*) indicateur *m* de vitesse; **l. line,** ligne *f* de loch.

log² *vt* **(a)** *Nau etc* porter (*un fait*) au journal; *Ind* noter (*des résultats etc*) sur le registre; **the ship's arrival at Southampton was logged at 0800 hours,** l'arrivée du bateau à Southampton a été portée au journal à 0800 heures; *Av* **to l. (up) 1,000 hours,** inscrire 1 000 heures de vol; **(b)** tronçonner (*le bois*); débiter (*le bois*) en bûches; **(c)** (*of ship*) filer (*tant de nœuds*); **(d)** *Rad* repérer, étalonner (*une station*).

log³ *n Math F* log *m*; **l. tables,** tables *fpl* de log.

►log in *vi & vtsep Comptr* = **LOG ON.**

►log off *Comptr* **1** *vi* (*of user*) sortir. **2** *vtsep* faire sortir.

►log on *Comptr* **1** *vi* (*of user*) entrer; **to l. on to a data base,** entrer dans une base de données. **2** *vtsep* faire entrer.

►log out *vi & vtsep Comptr* = **LOG OFF.**

loganberry ['ləʊgənberɪ] *n* (*fruit*) ronce-framboise *f*, *pl* ronces-framboises.

logarithm ['lɒgərɪθ(ə)m] *n* logarithme *m*.

logarithmic [lɒgə'rɪθmɪk] *adj* **(a)** (*courbe, papier*) logarithmique; (*papier*) à divisions logarithmiques; **(b) l. table,** table *f* des logarithmes.

logbook ['lɒgbʊk] *n* **(a)** (*record*) registre *m*; *Av* carnet *m* de vol; *Aut* (*personal record*) carnet de route; journal *m* de travail (*d'une machine*); *Rad* carnet d'écoute; *Nau* **ship's l.,** journal de bord; (*giving navigation details*) journal de navigation; **(b)** *Nau* livre *m* de loch; **(c)** *Old-fashioned Aut F* (*official documents*) ≈ carte grise.

logger ['lɒgər] *n* bûcheron *m*.

loggerheads ['lɒgəhedz] *n F* **to be at l. with s.o.,** avoir un différend avec qn (**about,** au sujet de); **they were constantly at l.,** ils se disputaient tout le temps; **his views were at l. with ...,** ses opinions étaient en contradiction avec ... .

loggia, *pl* **-ias, -ie** ['lɒdʒɪə, -ɪəz, -ɪeɪ] *n Archit* loge *f*, loggia *f*.

logging ['lɒgɪŋ] *n* **(a)** inscription *f* (*d'un fait*) dans le journal *ou* le carnet de route; **(b)** exploitation *f* des bois et forêts; **l. camp,** camp forestier; **(c)** *Rad* étalonnage *m* (*d'une station*).

logic ['lɒdʒɪk] *n* logique *f*; *Comptr* **l. circuit,** circuit *m* logique; **l. analyser,** analyseur *m* logique; **I don't see the logic of it,** je n'en saisis pas la logique.

logical ['lɒdʒɪk(ə)l] *adj* (*conclusion, person*) *& Comptr* logique; **do be l.!,** sois quand même logique!

logically ['lɒdʒɪklɪ] *adv* logiquement.

logistic [lɒ'dʒɪstɪk] *adj Phil Mil* logistique.

logistics [lɒ'dʒɪstɪks] *npl* (*usu with sing verb*) *Mil* logistique *f*; *F* **the l. of the situation,** les données logistiques de la situation.

logo ['ləʊgəʊ] *n* logo *m*.

logrolling ['lɒgrəʊlɪŋ] *n* **(a)** transport *m* des billes à la rivière; **(b)** *US Pol* alliance *f* politique dans un but intéressé.

logwood ['lɒgwʊd] *n Bot* (*wood*) (bois *m* de) campêche *m*; (*tree*) campêcher *m*.

loin [lɔɪn] *n* **(a) loins,** reins *mpl*; *Anat* lombes *mpl*; *Lit* **sprung from the loins of ...,** sorti des reins de ...; **(b)** esquine *f* (*d'un cheval*); *Culin* filet *m* (*de mouton, de veau*); longe *f* (*de veau*); carré *m* (*de mouton*); aloyau *m* et faux-filet (*de bœuf*); échine *f*, filet *m* (*de porc*); **l. chop,** côtelette *f* de filet.

loincloth ['lɔɪnklɒθ] *n* pagne *m*.

loiter ['lɔɪtər] *vi* (*suspiciously*) rôder; (*delay*) s'attarder (en route); *Jur* **to l. (with intent),** rôder (d'une manière suspecte dans un endroit fréquenté).

loitering ['lɔɪtərɪŋ] *n Jur* **l. with intent,** délit *m* d'intention.

loll [lɒl] *vi* **(a)** (*of person*) être étendu (paresseusement); **lolling back in an armchair,** étendu paresseusement dans un fauteuil; **(b)** (*of tongue*) **to l. (out),** pendre.

►loll about *vi* flâner, fainéanter.

lollipop ['lɒlɪpɒp] *n* sucette *f*; *Br F* **l. man/lady,** gardien/gardienne de passage clouté (pour les écoliers).

lollop ['lɒləp] *vi esp Br F* **to l. along,** marcher lourdement; **the rabbit lolloped off,** le lapin s'éloigna en bondissant.

lolly ['lɒlɪ] *n F* **(a)** sucette *f*; **ice(d) l.,** sucette glacée; **(b)** *Austr* bonbon *m*; **(c)** (*money*) fric *m*.

London ['lʌndən] *n* **(a)** Londres; **Greater L.,** le grand Londres; **a L. street,** une rue de Londres; **a L. bus,** un bus londonien; **(b)** *Bot* **L. pride,** saxifrage ombreuse.

Londoner ['lʌndənər] *n* Londonien, -ienne, habitant, -ante de Londres; **a L. born and bred,** un vrai Londonien de Londres.

lone [ləʊn] *adj* **(a)** *esp Lit* (*person, thing*) solitaire, seul; (*place*) isolé, désert; **a l. wolf,** un solitaire; **to be a bit of a l. wolf,** être un peu solitaire; **(b)** *Fig* **to play a l. hand,** agir tout seul; être seul contre tous.

loneliness ['ləʊnlɪnɪs] *n* **(a)** (*isolation*) solitude *f*, isolement *m*; **(b)** (*need for company*) sentiment *m* d'abandon.

lonely ['ləʊnlɪ] *adj* solitaire, isolé; (*endroit*) désert; **to feel very l.,** se sentir bien seul; **are you feeling l.?,** vous vous sentez seul?; **life is very l. since the children left home,** la vie est bien vide depuis que les enfants ont quitté la maison; **l. hearts club/column,** club *m*/rubrique *f* des cœurs solitaires.

loner ['ləʊnər] *n* solitaire *mf*.

lonesome ['ləʊnsəm] **1** *adj esp Am* solitaire, seul; **to feel l.,** se sentir seul. **2** *n F* **to be on one's l.,** être seul avec soi-même; **to do sth all on one's l.,** faire quelque chose tout seul.

long¹ [lɒŋ] (**longer** ['lɒŋgər]; **longest** ['lɒŋgɪst]) **1** *adj* **(a)** long, *f* longue; **to go the l. way round,** (*to a place*) prendre le chemin le plus long; **how l. is the table?,** quelle est la longueur de la table?; **to make sth longer,** allonger qch, rallonger qch; **to be six metres l.,** avoir six mètres de long; **a 20 foot l. swimming pool,** une piscine de 6 mètres de long; **the best by a l. way,** de loin le meilleur; **the l. arm of the law,** le long bras de la justice; **a l. face,** une figure allongée; *Fig* une triste figure; *Fig* **to pull a l. face,** faire la grimace; **l. in the leg,** aux longues jambes; *Br Sp* **l. jump,** saut *m* en longueur; **l. drink,** long drink *m*; *F* **to be long on charm/good ideas/***etc*, être plein de charme/bonnes idées/*etc*; *Math* **l. division,** division *f* à rallonge(s); *F* **l. johns,** (*underwear*) caleçons longs; **l. trousers,** (*for boy*) pantalon long; **l. shot,** (*competitor*) outsider *m*; (*event*) quelque chose d'improbable *ou* de douteux; *Cin* plan général; **not by a l. shot,** loin de là; **patience is not my l. suit,** la patience n'est pas mon fort;

(b) (*in time*) long, *f* longue; **the l. vacation,** les grandes vacances; **we're going away for a l. weekend,** nous partons pour un week-end prolongé; **are you doing anything for the l. weekend?,** est-ce que vous faites quelque chose pendant ce grand week-end?; **the days are getting longer,** les jours rallongent; **it's been a l. night,** la nuit a été longue; **it will take a l. time,** cela prendra longtemps, ce sera long; **a l. time ago,** il y a (bien) longtemps; **it's a l. time since I was (last) in Paris,** ça fait longtemps que je ne suis pas allé à Paris; **I've been wanting to go for a l. time,** ça fait longtemps que j'ai envie d'y aller; **to wait for a l. time,** attendre longtemps; **three days at the longest,** trois jours (tout) au plus; **in the l. term** *or* **run,** à long terme, à longue échéance; **it'll all be alright in the l. run,** tout s'arrangera avec le temps; **to have a l. memory,** avoir la mémoire longue; **to have a l. talk with s.o.,** parler longuement avec qn; **he took a l. drink from the flask,** il but une longue gorgée à la bouteille; **to take a l. hard look at sth,** fixer longuement qch; **l. syllable,** syllabe longue; *Mil* **l. servicemen,** engagés *mpl* à long terme; **it**

was a l. haul, (*of journey*) le voyage a été long; (*to complete this project, make a full recovery from illness etc*) c'était un travail de longue haleine; **friends of l. standing,** amis de longue date; **to take the l. view of sth,** voir quelque chose à long terme;

(c) *Com* **l. hundred,** cent vingt; **l. dozen,** treize.

2 *n* **the l. and short of the matter is that ...,** le fin mot de l'affaire c'est que ...; **that's the l. and short of it,** voilà ni plus ni moins l'affaire, et voilà tout!; **longs and shorts,** (*syllables*) longues *fpl* et brèves *fpl*.

3 *adv* **(a)** longtemps; **I didn't wait l.,** je n'ai pas attendu longtemps; **l. live the King/Queen!,** vive le roi/la reine!; **so l. as, as l. as,** (*for the same length of time as*) aussi longtemps que; (*during the time that*) tant que; (*provided that*) pourvu que; (*since, seeing that*) puisque; **you can take my car so l. as you're careful,** tu peux prendre ma voiture pourvu que tu sois prudent; **as l. as I live,** tant que je vivrai; **to look at s.o./sth l. and hard,** fixer quelque chose longuement; **he was not l. in coming,** il n'a pas tardé à venir; **before l.,** avant peu, sous peu; **for l.,** pendant longtemps; **I won't stay for l.,** je ne resterai pas longtemps; **it won't take l.,** cela ne prendra pas longtemps, cela ne sera pas long; **she won't be l.,** (*will be here soon*) elle ne tardera pas; (*will soon have finished*) elle l'aura vite fait; *F* **so l.!,** au revoir!, à bientôt!;

(b) depuis longtemps; **I have l. been convinced of it,** j'en suis convaincu depuis longtemps; **they have l. since left England,** ça fait longtemps qu'ils ont quitté l'Angleterre; **a l.-awaited event,** un événement longtemps attendu;

(c) how l.?, combien de temps?; **how much longer will he be?,** (*until ready etc*) combien de temps encore lui faut-il?; (*until he arrives*) combien de temps encore lui faudra-t-il pour arriver?;

(d) l. before/after, longtemps avant/après; **not l. before/after,** peu de temps avant/après; **l. before I met you,** longtemps avant que je te rencontre; **l. ago,** il y a longtemps; **not (very) l. ago,** il n'y a pas longtemps; **in the days of l. ago,** autrefois, *Lit* jadis;

(e) (*for the duration of*) **all day/night l.,** tout le long du jour/de la nuit, pendant toute la journée/la nuit; **all winter l.,** tout au long de l'hiver;

(f) I could no longer hear him, je ne pouvais plus l'entendre; **she no longer lives here,** elle n'habite plus ici; **I couldn't wait any longer,** je ne pouvais pas attendre plus longtemps; **five minutes longer,** cinq minutes de plus; encore cinq minutes; **but no longer,** (*I'll wait ten minutes etc*) mais pas plus.

long² *vi* **to l. for sth,** désirer qch fortement *ou* ardemment; **I l. for you,** tu me manques beaucoup; **a much longed-for baby,** un bébé très désiré; **to l. for home,** avoir la nostalgie du foyer; **to l. for s.o.'s return,** attendre impatiemment le retour de qn; **we're longing for them to leave,** nous avons hâte qu'ils partent; **to l. to do sth,** avoir bien envie de faire qch, être impatient de faire qch, rêver de faire qch.

long. [lɒndʒ] *Geog* (*abbr* **longitude**) long..

longboat ['lɒŋbəʊt] *n Nau* chaloupe *f*; (*of Vikings*) drakkar *m*.

longbow ['lɒŋbəʊ] *n Mil Hist* arc *m* (d'homme d'armes); *F* **to draw the l.,** exagérer.

long-dated ['lɒŋ'deɪtɪd] *adj Fin* à longue échéance.

long-distance ['lɒŋ'dɪstəns] **1** *adj Tel* grande distance; (*train*) de grande ligne; (*avion*) long-courrier; *Tel F* **is it l.-d.?,** est-ce que c'est un appel grande distance?; *Br* **l.-d. lorry driver,** conducteur *m* de poids lourd, *F* routier *m*; *Sp* **l.-d. runner,** coureur, -euse de fond. **2** *adv* (*téléphoner*) à grande distance.

long-drawn-out ['lɒŋ'drɔːn'aʊt] *adj* (*sigh etc*) prolongé; (*story, explanation etc*) interminable.

long-established ['lɒŋɪs'tæblɪʃt] *adj* établi depuis longtemps.

longevity [lɒn'dʒevɪtɪ] *n* longévité *f*.

long-forgotten [lɒŋfə'gɒt(ə)n] *adj* oublié depuis longtemps.

longhair ['lɒŋheər] *Am* **1** *adj.* **(a)** (*cat, dog*) à poil(s) long(s); **(b)** *F* qui plaît aux intellectuels; **l. music,** musique *f* classique. **2** *n* **(a)** (*intellectual*) intello *mf*; **(b)** (*hippie*) chevelu *m*.

longhaired ['lɒŋheəd] *adj* **(a)** (*person*) à cheveux longs; (*chien, chat etc*) à poil(s) long(s); *Pej* **one of the l. brigade,** un de la bande des chevelus; **(b)** *Am F* = **LONGHAIR 1 (b)**.

longhand ['lɒŋhænd] *n* écriture ordinaire *ou* courante *ou* non abrégée; **in l.,** (*écrire qch*) en clair.

longing ['lɒŋɪŋ] **1** *adj* qui désire *ou* qui attend ardemment; **to cast l. looks at sth,** jeter des regards plein d'envie à qch. **2** *n* désir ardent, grande envie **(for,** de**)**; **to be filled with l. to do,** être plein d'un ardent désir de faire.

longingly ['lɒŋɪŋlɪ] *adv* avec envie; **to look l. at sth,** couver qch des yeux; **she was looking l. out of the window,** elle regardait languissamment par la fenêtre.

longish ['lɒŋɪʃ] *adj* assez long, plutôt long.

longitude ['lɒndʒɪtjuːd] *n Astron Geog* longitude *f*.

longitudinal [lɒndʒɪ'tjuːdɪn(ə)l] *adj* longitudinal, -aux; **l. beam,** longeron *m*.

longitudinally [lɒndʒɪ'tjuːdɪn(ə)lɪ] *adv* longitudinalement.

long-legged ['lɒŋ'legɪd] *adj* (*person*) à longues jambes; (*horse*) haut-perché, *pl* haut-perchés; (*bird*) à longues pattes.

long-life ['lɒŋ'laɪf] *adj* **l.-l. batteries,** piles *fpl* longue durée; **l.-l. milk/juice,** lait *m*/jus *m* de fruit longue conservation.

long-lived ['lɒŋ'lɪvd] *adj* **(a)** (*person*) qui vit longtemps; **we're a very l.-l. family,** dans la famille on est d'une grande longévité; **(b)** (*erreur*) persistant, tenace; (*célébrité*) de longue durée.

long-lost ['lɒŋ'lɒst] *adj* perdu depuis longtemps; (*person*) disparu depuis longtemps.

long-playing ['lɒŋ'pleɪɪŋ] *adj* **l.-p. record,** disque *m* (de) longue durée, (disque) microsillon *m*.

long-range ['lɒŋ'reɪndʒ] *adj* (*avion*) long-courrier; (*canon, radar*) à longue portée; *Met* **l.-r. forecast,** prévision *f* à longue échéance.

longshoreman, *pl* **-men** ['lɒŋʃɔːmən] *n Am Nau* débardeur *m*.

long-sighted [lɒŋ'saɪtɪd] *adj* **(a)** hypermétrope; (*in old age*) presbyte; **(b)** (*policy, decision*) prévoyant.

long-sightedness [lɒŋ'saɪtɪdnɪs] *n* **(a)** hypermétropie *f*; (*in old age*) presbytie *f*; **(b)** (*of policy, decision*) prévoyance *f*.

long-sleeved [lɒŋ'sliːvd] *adj* (*dress, pullover*) à manches longues.

long-standing [lɒŋ'stændɪŋ] *adj* de longue date; **l.-s. arrangement/friendship,** arrangement *m*/amitié *f* de longue date; **l.-s. accounts,** vieux comptes.

long-suffering [lɒŋ'sʌf(ə)rɪŋ] *adj* patient, endurant; (*tolerant*) indulgent.

long-term ['lɒŋtɜːm] *adj* **(a)** (*détenu*) qui subit un emprisonnement de longue durée; **(b)** *Fin* (*crédit, politique etc*) à long terme.

long-ways ['lɒŋweɪz] *adv* = **LENGTHWAYS**.

long-winded [lɒŋ'wɪndɪd] *adj* **(a)** (*histoire*) de longue haleine, interminable; **(b)** (*speaker*) verbeux, prolixe; (*speech*) verbeux; **(c)** *Sp* (*person, horse*) qui a du souffle.

loo [luː] *n Br F* **the l.,** les cabinets *mpl*, les toilettes *fpl*; **to go to the l.,** aller aux cabinets; **in the l.,** aux cabinets, aux toilettes; **l. paper,** papier *m* hygiénique.

loofah ['luːfə] *n* (*for washing*) & *Bot* loofa(h) *m*, luffa *m*.

look¹ [lʊk] *n* **(a)** (*with eyes*) regard *m*; **to have a l. at sth,** regarder qch; (*quickly*) jeter un coup d'œil sur qch; **let's have a l.,** (*show me*) fais voir; **to take a good l. at s.o.,** scruter qn, dévisager qn; **get the doctor to have a l. at him,** demande au médecin de jeter un coup d'œil sur lui; **to have a l. round the town,** faire un tour dans la ville; **to have a l. through some magazines,** jeter un coup d'œil sur quelques magazines; **we were getting some very odd looks,** nous attirions des regards très étonnés; **if looks could kill ...,** si ses yeux étaient des revolvers ...;

(b) (*appearance*) aspect *m*, air *m*, apparence *f* (*de qn, de qch*); mine *f* (*de qn*); **the business has a suspicious l. about it,** l'affaire paraît suspecte *ou* louche; **I like the l. of him,** il me plaît, je le trouve sympathique; **I don't like the l. of him,** (*he seems suspicious*) sa tête ne me revient pas; (*he looks ill*) son air m'inquiète; **I don't like the l. of the weather,** le temps a l'air inquiétant; **by** *or* **from the l. of her I think it probable,** à la voir cela me paraît très probable; **he has a strange l. in his eyes,** il a un drôle de regard dans les yeux; **she has the l. of her grandfather about her,** elle a des airs qui lui viennent de son grand-père; *Com* **new l.,** nouvelle apparence, nouvelle mode;

(c) (*search*) **to have a l. for sth,** chercher qch;

(d) good looks, belle mine; beauté *f*; **to lose one's looks,** perdre ses charmes; **looks don't matter,** l'apparence ne compte pas; **she's got her mother's looks,** elle a la beauté de sa mère.

look² **1** *vi* **(a)** regarder; **to l. through** *or* **out of the window,** regarder par la fenêtre; **to l. down a list,** parcourir une liste; **to l. the other way,** regarder de l'autre côté; (*avert one's gaze*) détourner les yeux; **to l. into s.o.'s eyes,** regarder dans les yeux de qn, regarder qn dans les yeux; **I'm just looking, thank you,** (*to shop assistant*) je regarde seulement, merci; *Prov* **l. before you leap,** il faut réfléchir avant d'agir; **to l. on the bright side,** voir les choses du bon côté; **l. where you're going!,** regardez où vous allez *ou* marchez!; **I l. to you to help me,** je compte sur votre aide; **the house looks south,** la maison est exposée au sud *ou* orientée vers le sud; **the living room looks on to the garden,** le salon donne sur le jardin; **to l. to** *or* **towards the future,** envisager l'avenir;

(b) (*seem, appear*) avoir l'air, paraître, sembler; **she looks tired,** elle a l'air bien fatigué(e); **to l. old,** paraître *ou* faire vieux; **she's not as stupid as she looks,** elle est moins bête qu'elle n'en a l'air; **he doesn't l. his age,** on ne lui donnerait pas son âge; **to l. ill,** avoir l'air malade, avoir mauvaise mine; **to l. well,** (*of person*) avoir bonne mine; **that dress looks well on you,** cette robe vous va bien; **the crops l. promising,** la récolte s'annonce bien; **things are looking bad** *or* **black,** les choses prennent une mauvaise tournure; **you l. as if you've slept badly,** vous avez l'air d'avoir mal dormi; **it looks as if he didn't want to go,** il semble qu'il ne veuille pas y aller; **what does she l. like?,** comment est-elle?; **it looks like an elephant,** on dirait un éléphant; **he looks the part,** il est fait pour ce rôle; **she looks like winning,** *esp Am* **it looks like she'll win,** on dirait qu'elle va gagner;

(c) l. here!, écoutez donc!, dites donc!, voyons!; **(now) l.,** écoute; *F* **l. alive!, l. sharp!,** dépêchez-vous!, *F* grouillez-vous!;

(d) I'm not looking to cause any trouble, je ne veux pas causer de problème; **they're looking to appoint a new headmaster,** ils envisagent d'engager un nouveau directeur.

2 *vt* **to l. s.o. (full** *or* **straight) in the face,** regarder qn (bien) en face *ou* dans les yeux; **I can never l. her in the face again,** je ne pourrai plus jamais la regarder en face *ou* dans les yeux; **to l. s.o. up and down,** regarder qn de haut en bas.

►**look after** *vipo* **(a)** veiller sur, soigner (*sa vieille mère etc*); (*be careful with*) faire attention à (*ses possessions, un objet*); veiller sur, faire attention à (*sa santé, ses dents etc*); ménager (*ses intérêts*); **can you l. after the house for us?,** peux-tu veiller sur *ou* garder *ou* faire attention à la maison?; **could you l. after my things while I go to ...?,** pourriez-vous veiller sur *ou* surveiller mes affaires pendant que je vais à ...?; **granny's looking after the children this weekend,** mamie garde les enfants ce week-end; **he needs a lot of looking after,** il a bien besoin qu'on s'occupe de lui; **l. after yourself!,** prends bien garde à toi!; **you're well looked after,** vous êtes bien soigné; **he can l. after himself,** il sait se débrouiller; **the garden needs a lot of looking after,** le jardin a bien besoin d'être entretenu; **the car has been well looked after,** la voiture a été bien entretenue;

(b) (*follow with eyes*) suivre (*qn*) des yeux.

►**look around 1** *vi* **(a)** (*look behind one*) regarder derrière soi; **(b)** (*have a look*) regarder partout; (*in town*) faire un tour en ville; (*around the shops*) faire un tour dans les boutiques; **can I just l. around?,** puis-je jeter un coup d'œil?; **(c)** (*search*) chercher; **to l. around for sth,** chercher qch; **I'll go upstairs and l. around,** je monte jeter un coup d'œil. **2** *vipo* **to l. around the house,** (*search*) chercher dans la maison; **to l. around town,** (*have a look*) faire un tour en ville.

►**look at** *vipo* **(a)** regarder (*qn, qch*); **what are you looking at?,** qu'est-ce que vous regardez?; **just l. at that!,** regardez-moi ça!; *F* **she won't l. at a man,** elle dédaigne les hommes; **she still won't l. at him,** (*consider him favourably*) elle continue à le mépriser; **they won't l. at our offer,** ils méprisent *ou* ne font aucun cas de notre offre; **what's he like to l. at?,** quel air a-t-il?; **she's not much to l. at,** ce n'est pas une beauté; **he's not much to l. at,** il n'est pas très beau; **if you l. at the result,** si vous considérez le résultat; **I don't like his way of looking at things,** je n'aime pas la manière dont il voit les choses; **I don't l. at it that way at all,** je ne vois pas ça comme ça du tout; **just l. at the mess we're in!,** regarde les ennuis qu'on a!; **just l. at you!,** (*you look awful, a mess etc*) mais regarde- toi donc!;

(b) (*examine*) regarder, jeter un coup d'œil sur (*les freins, une dent etc*).

►**look back** *vi* regarder en arrière; **to l. back on the past,** faire un retour sur le passé; *F* **he has never looked back since that day,** depuis ce jour il a fait des progrès ininterrompus.

►**look down** *vi* (*from a height*) regarder en *ou* vers le bas; **don't l. down!,** ne regarde pas en bas!; **the chalet looks down on the valley,** le chalet donne sur la vallée.

►**look down on** *vipo* mépriser (*qn*).

►**look for** *vipo* chercher (*qn, qch*); **go and l. for him,** allez le chercher; **he's looking for a new start,** il cherche à faire un nouveau début; **he's looking for trouble,** il cherche les ennuis.

►**look forward** *vi* (*to the future*) regarder vers l'avenir.

►**look forward to** *vipo* attendre (*qch*) avec plaisir; **I'm looking forward to seeing her again,** ce sera un grand plaisir *ou* il me tarde de la revoir; **I'm looking forward to the weekend,** vivement le week-end!; **he hasn't got much to l. forward to in life,** il n'a pas beaucoup à attendre de la vie; **they don't exactly l. forward to a visit to the dentist,** ils appréhendent d'aller chez le dentiste; **I'm not exactly looking forward to going,** je n'ai pas vraiment envie d'y aller; **I'm so looking forward to seeing you all again,** j'aimerais tant vous revoir, ça me ferait tellement plaisir de vous revoir; **I'm not looking forward to it at all,** je n'y tiens pas du tout; **I l. forward to hearing from you,** dans l'attente de vous lire.

►**look in** *vi* **(a)** (*at window etc*) regarder (à l'intérieur), jeter un coup d'œil (à l'intérieur); **(b)** entrer en passant; **I'll l. in again tomorrow,** je repasserai demain.

►**look into** *vipo* examiner, étudier (*une question*), prendre (*une question*) en considération.

►**look on 1** *vi* être spectateur; **while a crowd looked on,** sous les regards d'une foule de gens. **2** *vipo* considérer, envisager (*qn, qch*); **I l. on him as a friend,** je le considère comme un ami.

►**look on to** *vipo* donner sur (*un jardin, la rue etc*).

►**look out 1** *vi* **(a)** (*through window etc*) regarder (à l'extérieur), jeter un coup d'œil (à l'extérieur); **(b)** (*be careful*) prendre garde, être sur ses gardes; **l. out!,** attention!, prenez garde! **2** *vtsep* chercher (*qch*); **I'll l. you out some interesting books,** je vais vous choisir des livres intéressants.

►**look out for** *vipo* **(a)** guetter (l'arrivée de) (*qn*); **(b)** (*be on guard for*) faire attention à (*qn, les pickpockets, les fautes etc*); **(c)** *Am* (*take care of*) prendre soin de (*qn*).

►**look out onto** *vipo* donner sur (*un jardin, la rue etc*).

►**look over** *vipo* jeter un coup d'œil sur (*qch*), examiner (*qch*); parcourir (*des papiers etc*); visiter (*une maison à vendre etc*).

►**look round** *vi* **(a)** regarder autour de soi; **(b)** (*turn one's head*) tourner la tête, se retourner (pour voir); **don't l. round!,** ne regardez pas en arrière!

►**look through 1** *vt* **(a)** parcourir, examiner rapidement (*des papiers etc*); **(b)** (*not see*) **she just looked straight through me,** (*deliberately*) elle m'a ignoré; (*not deliberately*) elle m'a regardé sans me voir. **2** *vi* (*at window etc*) regarder par la fenêtre *ou* par la serrure *etc*.

►**look to** *vipo* **(a)** (*rely on*) compter sur; **we're looking to you to help us,** nous comptons sur vous pour nous aider; **you can't always l. to your parents to provide the money,** on ne peut pas toujours s'en remettre à ses parents pour l'argent; **(b) l. to it that you ...,** faites en sorte de ...; **l. to it that he ...,** faites en sorte qu'il + *sub*; **you should l. to your shortcomings,** tu ferais mieux de te regarder; *Old-fashioned* **l. to your daughter,** faites attention à *ou* surveillez votre fille.

►**look up 1** *vi* **(a)** lever les yeux; **(b) to be looking up,** (*of business*) reprendre; (*of shares*) remonter; **things are looking up,** la situation s'améliore; **things are looking up for her,** sa situation s'améliore. **2** *vtsep* **(a)** chercher (*un mot dans un dictionnaire, un train dans l'indicateur etc*); **(b)** aller voir (*qn*); passer chez (*qn*); **(come and) l. me up,** venez me voir.

►**look upon** *vipo* = **LOOK ON.**

►**look up to** *vipo* respecter, estimer (*qn*).

lookalike ['lʊkəlaɪk] *n* sosie *m*; **she's a Princess Diana l.,** c'est un sosie de la Princesse Diana, c'est la Princesse Diana toute crachée.

looker ['lʊkər] *n F* **(good) l.,** bel homme; belle femme.

looker-on [lʊkə'rɒn] *n* (*pl* **lookers-on**) spectateur, -trice **(at,** de).

look-in ['lʊkɪn] *n F* **(a)** (*chance*) **he won't have** *or* **get a l.-in,** il n'a pas la moindre chance; **everyone gets a l.-in,** tout le monde a sa chance; **(b)** (*visit*) courte visite, visite éclair.

looking-glass ['lʊkɪŋglɑːs] *n* miroir *m*, glace *f*.

lookout ['lʊkaʊt] *n* **(a)** (*action*) surveillance *f*, observation *f*; *Nau* veille *f*; **to keep a l.,** être aux aguets; *Nau* veiller, être en *ou* de vigie; **to be on the l. for,** guetter (*qn*); être à la recherche de (*qch*); **(b)** (*place*) poste *m* d'observation *ou* de guet *ou* de vigie; **(c)** (*person*) *Mil* guetteur *m*; *Nau* homme *m* de veille *ou* de vigie; **(d)** *F* **that's a poor l. for him,** c'est de mauvais augure pour lui; **that's your l.!,** ça c'est ton affaire!, débrouille-toi!

lookover ['lʊkəʊvər] *n* **to give sth a (quick) l.,** jeter un coup d'œil sur qch.

look-see ['lʊksiː] *n F* visite *f ou* coup *m* d'œil d'inspection; **I'll go (and) have a l.-s.,** je vais aller voir.

loom[1] [luːm] *n Tex* métier *m* à tisser.

loom[2] *vi* apparaître indistinctement; **dangers looming ahead,** dangers qui menacent; **to l. large,** (*of event etc*) paraître imminent, être tout proche; **it looms large in his view of things,** cela joue un rôle important dans sa manière de voir les choses.

▶**loom up** *vi* (*of ship, person in authority etc*) surgir.

loon [luːn] *n* **(a)** (*bird*) plongeon *m*, *Can* huart *m*; **(b)** *F* (*fool*) imbécile *mf*.

loony ['luːnɪ] *F* **1** *n* fou, *f* folle; **l. bin,** maison *f* de fous. **2** *adj* fou, *f* folle, loufoque, timbré.

loop[1] [luːp] *n* **(a)** boucle *f* (*de ruban etc*); (*of fingerprint*) anse *f*; méandre *m*, boucle (*de rivière*); (*in skating*) croisé *m*; tour *m*, spire *f* (*de spirale, de bobine*); *Cin* boucle (*de film*); (*contraceptive coil*) stérilet *m*; *Av* boucle, looping *m*; *Am* **to knock** *or* **throw s.o. for a l.,** abasourdir qn; **running l.,** boucle à nœud coulant; **curtain l.,** embrasse *f* de rideau; *Sewing* **l. stitch,** picot *m*; *Rail* **l. (line),** voie *f* d'évitement; voie de raccordement; (*at terminus*) boucle d'évitement; **(b)** *El* boucle *f*, bouclage *m*; *Nucl Phys* boucle, circuit *m* (*de réacteur*); *Comptr* boucle d'itération; *Tel* circuit (branché); ligne dérivée; **l. circuit,** circuit bouclé; **l. current,** courant *m* circulant dans un circuit bouclé; *Electron* **l. antenna** *or* **aerial,** cadre *m* d'antenne.

loop[2] **1** *vt* **(a)** faire une boucle *ou* des boucles à (*une ficelle etc*); **(b)** enrouler (**sth with sth,** qch de qch); **(c)** *Av etc* **to l. the loop,** faire un looping, boucler la boucle; **(d)** *El* boucler. **2** *vi* **(a)** faire une boucle; former des boucles; **(b)** *Comptr* tourner sur une boucle.

▶**loop back 1** *vi* (*of river etc*) faire une boucle; *Comptr* (*of program*) faire une boucle pour retourner (**to,** à). **2** *vtsep* retenir (*un rideau*) avec une embrasse.

looped [luːpt] *adj US F* (*drunk*) soûl.

loophole ['luːphəʊl] *n* **(a)** (*in law etc*) échappatoire *f*; **to find a l.,** trouver une échappatoire; **(b)** (*gap*) trou *m*, ouverture *f*; (*in fortified wall*) meurtrière *f*, créneau *m*.

looping ['luːpɪŋ] *n Av* **l. the loop,** looping *m*.

loopy ['luːpɪ] *adj F* toqué, timbré.

loose[1] [luːs] *adj* **(a)** (*not fastened or attached*) (*fixed part*) dégagé, mal assujetti; branlant; (*page*) détaché; (*knot*) défait, délié; (*board*) désajusté; (*tooth*) qui branle, qui remue; *El* (*connection*) déconnecté, desserré; (*animal*) déchaîné, lâché; (*cable*) volant; *Ch* (à l'état) libre, non-combiné; **to come l., to get l.,** se dégager, se détacher; (*of knot*) se défaire, se délier; (*of screw*) se desserrer; (*of iron bar from stonework etc*) se desceller; **to work l.,** (*of machine parts*) se desserrer, prendre du jeu; (*of tooth*) se déchausser; (*of hair in bun etc*) se dénouer; **to let a dog l.,** lâcher *ou* détacher un chien; **they let their dog run l. in the fields,** ils ont laissé leur chien courir en liberté dans les champs; **to let l. a torrent of abuse,** lâcher un torrent d'injures; *Sp* **l. horse,** cheval *m* sauvage; *MecE* **l. pulley,** roue folle *ou* décalée; **l. end,** bout pendant (*d'une corde*); **to be at a l. end,** se trouver désœuvré *ou* sans rien à faire; *Fig* **to tie up the l. ends,** régler les derniers détails; **l. cash** *or* **change,** menue monnaie; **to buy sth l.,** acheter qch en vrac; *Br* **l. cover,** (*on furniture*) housse *f*;

(b) (*slack*) détendu; (*câble*) mou; (*nœud*) lâche; (*peau*) flasque; (*vêtement*) ample; (*manteau*) flottant; *Med* **l. cough,** toux grasse; **this skirt is much too l. at the waist,** cette jupe est bien trop large à la taille; **l. bowels,** ventre *m* lâche;

(c) (*in structure, arrangement*) (*terre*) meuble; (*terrain*) sans consistance; (*tissu*) lâche, à claire-voie; *Mil* (*ordre*) dispersé;

(d) (*imprecise*) vague, peu exact; (*style*) lâche, décousu; (*translation*) approximatif; **l. ball,** *Cr* balle mal lancée; *Tennis* balle qui traîne;

(e) (*immoral*) dissolu, débauché; (*femme*) de mauvaise vie; **l. living,** mauvaise vie, inconduite *f*; **l. morals,** mœurs relâchées;

(f) (*irresponsible*) **loose talk,** propos inconséquents.

loose[2] *n* **to be on the l.,** (*of prisoner*) être en vadrouille *ou* en cavale; (*of escaped tiger etc*) être en liberté; **there's a horde of lager louts on the l. in town,** il y a une horde de voyous lâchés dans la ville; *Hum* **her husband's on the l. tonight,** son mari est en vadrouille *ou* en rupture de ban ce soir.

loose[3] *adv* **to hang l.,** pendre, flotter (*of rope etc*); *Fig esp US F* (*relax*) se relaxer, se détendre; (*not panic*) rester calme.

loose[4] **1** *vt* **(a)** (*set free*) délier, détacher; **to l. one's hold,** lâcher prise; **(b)** (*untie*) délier, dénouer, défaire (*un nœud etc*); dénouer, détacher (*ses cheveux*); *Nau* larguer (*une amarre*); déferler (*une voile*); **(c)** (*fire*) décocher (*une flèche*).

▶**loose off 1** *vi Mil F* tirer (*avec une mitrailleuse*); lâcher *ou* envoyer une giclée; *Fig* **to l. off at s.o.,** (*tell off*) engueuler qn. **2** *vt* tirer, lâcher (*des balles*).

loose-fitting ['luːsfɪtɪŋ] *adj* non ajusté; (*vêtement*) ample, large; (*col*) dégagé.

loose-leaf ['luːsliːf] *adj* (*album, paper etc*) à feuilles mobiles; **l.-l. binder,** classeur *m*.

loose-limbed ['luːs'lɪmd] *adj* souple.

loosely ['luːslɪ] *adv* **(a)** (*tenir qch*) sans serrer; **to be l. fixed,** être mal serré *ou* mal ajusté; avoir du jeu; **her dress hung l. on her body,** elle flottait dans sa robe; **(b)** (*parler*) sans précision; **l. translated,** traduit approximativement; **the word 'literally' is used l.,** le mot 'littéralement' est employé à tort et à travers; **l. connected** *or* **related,** vaguement lié; **(c)** (*vivre*) d'une manière dissolue.

loosen ['luːs(ə)n] **1** *vt* **(a)** défaire, délier, relâcher (*un nœud*); desserrer, dégager, décoller (*un écrou etc*); relâcher, détendre (*une corde*); desserrer (*sa cravate, ses vêtements*); **to l. s.o.'s bonds,** dénouer les liens de qn; **to l. one's grip,** relâcher son étreinte; **to l. s.o.'s tongue,** délier *ou* dénouer la langue à qn; *Med* **to l. the bowels,** relâcher le ventre; **(b)** détacher (**sth from sth,** qch de qch); **(c)** relâcher (*la discipline*). **2** *vi* (*of knot etc*) se délier, se défaire; (*of screw etc*) se desserrer; (*of rope*) se relâcher; (*of machinery*) prendre du jeu.

▶**loosen up 1** *vi* (*of person*) (*relax*) se mettre à l'aise; (*of rules, discipline*) se relâcher; **exercises to help you l. up before a race,** exercices qui aident à s'échauffer avant une course; **he always loosens up after a few drinks,** il est toujours plus décontracté après quelques verres; **she loosens up once you get to know her,** elle perd de sa froideur une fois qu'on la connaît. **2** *vtsep* relâcher (*les muscles*).

looseness ['luːsnɪs] *n* **(a)** état branlant (*d'une dent, d'une pierre*); desserrage *m* (*d'un écrou*); jeu *m* (*d'une cheville etc*); flaccidité *f* (*de la peau*); **(b)** relâchement *m* (*d'une corde*); ampleur *f* (*d'un vêtement*); **(c)** imprécision *f* (*de terminologie*); **(d)** relâchement *m* (*de la discipline, de la morale etc*).

loosestrife ['luːsstraɪf] *n* (*plant*) **(purple) l.,** salicaire commune.

loot[1] [luːt] *n* **(a)** (*goods*) butin *m*; **(b)** (*action*) pillage *m*; **soldiers on the l.,** soldats *mpl* en maraude *f*.

loot[2] **1** *vt* piller, saccager, mettre à sac (*une ville etc*); piller (*des magasins*); (*of soldiers etc*) voler (*du bétail etc*); **thousands of pounds worth of goods have been looted,** des marchandises d'une valeur de plusieurs milliers de livres ont été volées. **2** *vi* se livrer au pillage.

looter ['luːtər] *n* pilleur, -euse, pillard, -arde.

looting ['luːtɪŋ] *n* pillage *m*.

lop [lɒp] *vt* **(-pp-)** élaguer, ébrancher (*un arbre*); **to l. off a branch,** couper *ou* élaguer une branche.

▶**lope along** [ləʊp] *vi* (*of person*) courir à petits bonds; (*of animal*) avancer en bondissant.

lop-eared ['lɒpɪəd] *adj* (*lapin, chien etc*) aux oreilles pendantes.

lopsided [lɒp'saɪdɪd] *adj* qui manque de symétrie, asymétrique; (*not straight*) de guingois, de travers; (*chaise*) bancale; **a l. group with twice as many women as men,** un groupe déséquilibré comptant deux fois plus de femmes que d'hommes.

loquacious [lɒ'kweɪʃəs] *adj* loquace.

loquaciousness [lɒ'kweɪʃəsnɪs] **, loquacity** [lɒ'kwæsɪtɪ] *n* loquacité *f*.

lord[1] [lɔːd] *n* **(a)** seigneur *m*; **l. of the manor,** châtelain *m*; **our sovereign l. the king,** notre seigneur souverain, le roi; (*in Middle Ages etc*) *& Hum* **her l. and master,** son seigneur et maître; **(b)** *Rel* **L. God Almighty,** Seigneur Dieu Tout-puissant; **the L.,** le Seigneur; **in the year of our L. ....,** en l'an de grâce ...; **the L.'s Prayer,** l'oraison dominicale; **L.'s Day Observance Society,** = Société pour l'Observance du Jour du Seigneur; *F* **(good) L.!, O L.!,** mon Dieu!; **L. knows if ...,** Dieu sait si ...; **(c)** (*title*) lord *m*; *Pol* **the House of Lords, the Lords,** la Chambre des Lords; **to live**

like a l., mener une vie de grand seigneur; **the L. Mayor**, le Lord Maire; **(d)** (*flower*) **lords and ladies**, arum maculé; pied-de-veau *m*, *pl* pieds-de-veau.

lord² *vi F* **to l. it**, agir en maître; **to l. it over s.o.**, vouloir en imposer à qn.

lordly ['lɔːdlɪ] *adj* **(a)** de grand seigneur; noble; **(b)** *Pej* hautain, altier; (*air*) de grand seigneur; **in a l. manner**, avec hauteur.

lordship ['lɔːdʃɪp] *n* **(a)** (*authority*) suzeraineté *f*; **(b) your l.**, *also Hum* votre Seigneurie; (*to nobleman*) monsieur le comte *etc*; (*to judge*) votre honneur.

lordy ['lɔːdɪ] *int esp Am F* Seigneur!

lore [lɔːr] *n* science *f*, savoir *m*; **country l.**, connaissance *f* des choses de la campagne.

lorgnette [lɔː'njet] *n* **(a)** (*spectacles*) face-à-main *m*, *pl* faces-à-main; **(b)** (*opera glasses*) jumelles *fpl* (de théâtre) à manche.

lorry ['lɒrɪ] *n Br* camion *m*; **articulated l.**, véhicule articulé; semi-remorque *mf*, *pl* semi-remorques; **l.-driver**, conducteur *m* de camion, conducteur de poids lourd, *F* routier *m*; *F* **it fell off the back of a l.**, (*is stolen*) je l'ai trouvé.

lose [luːz] *v* (*pt & pp* **lost** [lɒst]; *prp* **losing** [luːzɪŋ]) **1** *vt* **(a)** perdre (*son argent, un pari, un droit etc*); perdre, égarer (*son parapluie etc*); (*through death, injury*) perdre (*son père, son bébé, un bras, la voix etc*); **you will l. nothing by waiting**, vous ne perdrez rien à attendre; **the expression loses something in translation**, l'expression perd quelque chose à la traduction; **to l. one's heart to s.o.**, tomber amoureux de qn; **to l. one's reason**, perdre la raison; **to l. one's reputation**, se perdre de réputation; **he had lost interest in his work**, son travail ne l'intéressait plus; **the patient is losing strength**, le malade baisse; **to l. weight**, perdre du poids; **I've lost 10 kilos**, j'ai perdu 10 kilos, j'ai maigri de 10 kilos; **many lives were lost in the disaster**, la catastrophe a coûté la vie à de nombreuses personnes; **to be lost at sea**, périr en mer; **to l. one's way, to get lost**, perdre son chemin, se perdre, s'égarer; **to l. one's balance**, perdre l'équilibre; **to l. oneself/to be lost in the crowd**, se perdre dans/se mêler à la foule; *F* **I'm lost!, you've lost me!**, je n'y suis plus!; **I lost you when you started using technical terms**, j'ai perdu le fil quand tu as commencé à employer des termes techniques; *Sl* **get lost!**, fiche-moi le camp!; **to l. one's pursuers**, (*of s.o. being chased*) larguer ses poursuivants; **to l. oneself in a book**, s'absorber dans la lecture d'un livre; **to l. sight of s.o.**, perdre qn de vue;

(b) (*waste*) gaspiller, perdre (*son temps*); **the joke was lost on him**, il n'a pas saisi la plaisanterie; **American humour is lost on us**, nous sommes insensibles à l'humour américain; **sarcasm is lost on her**, c'est peine perdue que d'employer des sarcasmes avec elle;

(c) clock that loses five minutes a day, pendule qui retarde de cinq minutes par jour;

(d) (*fail to win*) perdre (*une partie, une bataille, un procès*); être battu dans (*une course*); **the motion was lost**, (*in debate*) la motion a été rejetée;

(e) faire perdre (*qch à qn*); **the decision will l. us our jobs**, la décision nous coûtera nos emplois; **that mistake lost him the match**, cette faute lui coûta la partie.

2 *vi* **(a)** perdre; **to l. heavily**, (*at cards etc*) perdre une forte somme; **to l. in value**, perdre de sa valeur; **both armies lost heavily**, les deux armées ont subi de lourdes pertes; **our team was losing at half-time**, notre équipe perdait à la mi-temps; **we've lost on the sale of the house**, nous avons perdu sur la vente de la maison; **it loses in translation**, on perd un peu à la traduction;

(b) (*of clock, watch*) retarder.

►**lose out** *vi* être (le *ou* la) perdant(e).

►**lose out on** *vipo F* perdre sur (*une affaire*).

loser ['luːzər] *n* **(a)** *Sp etc* perdant, -ante; **the winners and the losers**, les gagnants et les perdants, les vainqueurs et les vaincus; **to be a good/bad l.**, être bon/mauvais joueur; **to back a l.**, miser sur un perdant; **(b) YOU'LL be the l.**, c'est toi qui perdras; **he's a born l.**, il ne réussit jamais.

losing ['luːzɪŋ] *adj* perdant; **l. bargain**, mauvais marché; **to fight a l. battle**, mener une bataille de vaincu; **to play a l. game**, jouer un jeu à perdre; **the l. side**, les vaincus *mpl*; *Sp* l'équipe perdante.

loss [lɒs] *n* **(a)** perte *f* (*d'un parapluie etc*); égarement *m* (*d'un document etc*); perte (*de son père etc*); (*in insurance*) sinistre *m*; **l. of sight**, perte *ou* privation *f* de la vue; **l. of voice**, extinction *f* de voix; *Jur* **l. of civil rights**, perte des droits civiques, dégradation *f* civique; *Rel* **l. of grace**, amission *f* de la grâce; *Mil etc* **to sustain** *or* **suffer heavy losses**, éprouver *ou* subir de grosses pertes; *F* **my brother's a dead l. at tennis**, mon frère est nul au tennis; *Com* **to sell at a l.**, vendre à perte; *Com* **to run at a l.**, (*of business*) tourner à perte; **to cut one's losses**, faire la part du feu; **total l.**, perte totale; *Com* **l. leader**, article *m* d'appel; **she has never recovered from the l. of her mother**, elle ne s'est jamais remise d'avoir perdu sa mère; **he is a great l. to the British theatre**, c'est une grande perte pour le théâtre britannique; **it's no great l. that they're leaving**, leur départ n'est pas une grosse perte;

(b) perte *f* (*de poids, de chaleur etc*); freinte *f*, déperdition (*d'un produit en cours de fabrication ou de transport*); **l. in transit**, freinte *ou* déchet *m* de route; *Med* écoulement *m*, perte; **l. of blood**, écoulement *ou* perte de sang;

(c) to be at a l., être désorienté; **he seemed at a l.**, il avait l'air dépaysé; **to be at a l. to ...**, être en peine de ...; **to be at a l. (to know) what to do/say**, ne savoir que faire/dire; **she's never at a l. for an answer**, elle a *ou* trouve réponse à tout; **he's never at a l. for something to say**, il n'est jamais à court (de mots).

loss-making ['lɒsmeɪkɪŋ] *adj Com* tournant à perte.

lost [lɒst] *adj* perdu; **to give s.o./sth up for l.**, abandonner tout espoir de retrouver qn/qch; **30 people were reported l. at sea**, 30 personnes auraient péri en mer; **to seem** *or* **look l.**, avoir l'air dépaysé; **she's l. to the world**, le monde n'existe plus pour elle; **she's completely l. in her book**, elle est complètement absorbée dans son livre; **to be l. in thought**, être perdu dans ses pensées; **when they talk shop I'm quite l.**, quand ils parlent boutique je suis complètement largué; **l. soul**, âme perdue, âme damnée; **to wander (about) like a l. soul**, errer comme une âme en peine; **he looks like a l. sheep without his wife**, il a l'air d'un enfant égaré sans sa femme; **l. cause**, cause perdue; **l. property office**, *US* **l. and found department**, (service *m* des) objets trouvés; *US* **l. river**, rivière souterraine.

lot [lɒt] *n* **(a) a l. (of) ...**, beaucoup (de) ...; **what a l. of people!**, que de monde!; **such a l. of people**, tant de monde; **quite a l.**, une quantité considérable; **I saw quite a l. of her in Paris**, je l'ai vue assez souvent pendant mon séjour à Paris; **not a l.**, pas beaucoup; **I would have given a l. to ...**, j'aurais donné gros pour ...; **I've got a l. to do before bedtime**, j'ai beaucoup à faire avant ce soir; **I've got a whole l. of things to do**, j'ai un tas de choses à faire;

(b) (*selection*) sort *m*, tirage *m* au sort; **drawn by l.**, tiré au sort; **to draw** *or* **cast lots for sth**, tirer au sort pour qch; tirer qch au sort;

(c) (*destiny*) sort *m*, part *f*, partage *m*; destin *m*, destinée *f*; **it fell to my l. to decide**, c'était à moi de décider; **the poor man's l.**, la condition du pauvre; **to throw** *or* **cast in one's l. with s.o.**, partager le sort *ou* la fortune de qn;

(d) (*land*) (lot *m* de) terrain *m*; *Cin* **(studio) l.**, terrain (de studio); *Am* **parking l.**, parking *m*;

(e) (*at auction*) lot *m*; *Com* lot (*de marchandises*); *Fin* paquet *m* (*de titres, d'actions*); **in lots**, par parties; **to buy/sell in one l.**, acheter/vendre en bloc;

(f) (*referring to person/people*) **a bad l.**, un mauvais sujet, un vaurien; **a nice l. of people**, des gens très agréables; *Iron* **you're a nice l., you are!**, vous êtes admirables, vous!; *F* **that l. next door**, les gens *ou Pej* la bande d'à côté; *F* **listen, you l.!**, écoutez tous; *F* **you arrange to get your l. there in time and ...**, arrangez-vous pour que vos élèves *ou* collègues *etc* soient là à l'heure; **the l.**, tous, tout le monde; **the whole l. of you**, vous tous; **the whole l. of them**, toute la bande;

(g) the l., (*everything*) tout; **I bought the l.**, j'ai acheté le tout; *F* **the whole damn l.**, tout le bazar.

2 *adv* **a l.**, beaucoup; **such a l.**, tellement; **times have changed a l.**, les temps ont bien changé; **he thought a l. before deciding**, il a beaucoup réfléchi avant de se décider; **thanks a l.**, merci beaucoup.

loth [ləʊθ] *adj* = **LOATH**.

lotion ['ləʊʃən] *n* lotion *f*; **setting l.**, (*for hair*) lotion pour mise en plis.

lots [lɒts] *F* **1** *npl* **l. (of)**, beaucoup (de); **I've got l. of things to do**, j'ai beaucoup de *ou* un tas de choses à faire; **he has l. and l. of money**, il a énormément d'argent. **2** *adv* beaucoup.

lottery ['lɒtərɪ] *n* loterie *f*.

lotto ['lɒtəʊ] *n* (*game*) loto *m*.

lotus, *pl* **-uses** ['ləʊtəs, -əsɪz] *n* lotus *m*; **l. position**, (*in yoga*) posture *f* de méditation.

lotus-eater ['ləʊtəsiːtər] *n* mangeur *m* de lotus, lotophage *m*.

loud [laʊd] **1** *adj* **(a)** bruyant, retentissant; (*noise, shout*) grand; (*explosion*) violent; (*laugh*) gros; (*voice*) fort, haut; (*person, behaviour*) bruyant, tapageur; **l. sobs,** gros sanglots; **in a l. voice,** à haute voix; **l. applause,** vifs applaudissements; **l. protests,** protestations bruyantes; **(b)** (*colour etc*) criard, voyant; (*clothes*) tapageur, affichant; **he wore a l. checked suit,** il portait un costume voyant à carreaux. **2** *adv* (*crier, parler*) haut, à haute voix; (*to shout*) fort; **to talk out l.,** parler tout haut; **louder!,** parlez plus haut!; **I hear you l. and clear,** *Rad* je te reçois cinq sur cinq; *F* (*I understand*) j'ai compris.

loud-hailer [laʊd'heɪlər] *n* porte-voix *m inv*.

loudly ['laʊdlɪ] *adv* (*crier*) haut, fort, à voix haute; (*rire*) bruyamment; (*frapper à la porte*) rudement; **you're not speaking l. enough,** vous ne parlez pas assez fort; **he has always dressed rather l.,** il a toujours porté des vêtements assez tapageurs.

loudmouth ['laʊdmaʊθ] *n F Pej* **(a)** gueulard, -arde; **(b)** (*gossip*) grande langue; **to be a l.,** être *ou* avoir une grande langue.

loudmouthed ['laʊdmaʊðd] *adj F Pej* gueulard.

loudness ['laʊdnɪs] *n* **(a)** force *f*, sonorité *f* (*d'un bruit etc*); **(b) the l. of his behaviour,** sa conduite tapageuse.

loudspeaker [laʊd'spiːkər] *n* haut-parleur *m*, *pl* haut-parleurs; **l. van,** camionnette sonorisée.

Louisiana [luːiːzɪ'ænə] *n* Louisiane *f*.

lounge¹ [laʊndʒ] *n* **(a)** (*in house*) salon *m*; (*in hotel*) salon *m*; **cocktail l., l. bar,** bar *m* (*où l'on sert des cocktails etc*); **l. suit,** complet veston *m*; **sun l.,** véranda *m*; **(b)** *Am* (*sofa*) canapé *m*; **l. chair,** fauteuil *m*; *Rail* **l. car,** voiture-salon *f*, *pl* voitures-salons.

lounge² *vi* s'étendre paresseusement (*sur un canapé etc*); **I've been lounging in an armchair all afternoon,** j'ai passé l'après-midi affalé dans un fauteuil.

►**lounge about, lounge around** *vi* flâner.

►**lounge away** *vtsep* **to l. away the time,** passer le temps à flâner.

lounger ['laʊndʒər] *n* **(a)** flâneur, -euse, flemmard -arde; **(b) (sun) l.,** fauteuil *m* de relaxation; *Am* (*settee*) canapé *m*.

louse [laʊs] *n* **(a)** (*insect*) (*pl* **lice**) pou *m*, poux; **infested with lice,** pouilleux; **(b)** *Sl* (*person*) (*pl* **louses**) fripouille *f*, salaud *m*.

►**louse up** *vtsep F* bousiller, gâcher (*qch*); **I've loused up your afternoon,** j'ai gâché votre après-midi.

lousewort ['laʊswɜːt] *n* (*plant*) herbe *f* aux poux.

lousiness ['laʊzɪnɪs] *n F* (*of weather etc*) caractère horrible; (*of service in restaurant etc*) mauvaise qualité.

lousy ['laʊzɪ] *adj* **(a)** pouilleux, plein de poux; *F* **this place is l. with ...,** ça grouille de ...; *F* **to be l. with money,** être un gros richard;

(b) *F* (*headache, cold, day, week*) sale; (*weather*) sale, de chien; (*colour etc*) moche; (*hotel, holiday, party, meal, book, essay*) minable, nul, moche; (*quality, workmanship*) mauvais; (*computer, car, raincoat*) qui ne vaut rien; **that's a l. thing to do/say,** c'est dégueulasse *ou* moche; **a l. trick,** un sale tour; **don't buy them, they're l.,** n'achetez pas ça, c'est de la camelote *ou Vulg* de la merde; **they made a l. job of it,** c'est du travail bâclé; **he's in a l. mood,** il est d'une humeur de chien; **we had a l. time on holiday,** les vacances ont été nulles *ou* minables *ou* dégueulasses; **he's l. to his wife,** il est dégueulasse avec sa femme; **all for a l. £5,** tout ça à cause de 5 malheureuses livres; **to feel/look l.,** se sentir horriblement mal/avoir l'air horrible; **I'm l. at science,** je suis nul en sciences.

lout [laʊt] *n* **(a)** lourdaud *m*, rustre *m*; **you clumsy l.!,** espèce de lourdaud!; **(b)** (*hooligan*) voyou *m*.

loutish ['laʊtɪʃ] *adj* rustre, lourdaud.

louvre, *US* **louver** ['luːvər] *n* **(a)** *Archit* **l. (board),** abat-vent *m inv*, abat-son *m*, *pl* abat-sons (de clocher); **(b)** (*in door, window*) persienne *f*; *Nau* louvre *m*; *Aut Av* persienne, volet *m* (*d'aérage, de capot*); *MecE* ouïe *f* (*de prise d'air*).

louv(e)red ['luːvəd] *adj* **(a)** *Archit* (*clocher*) à abat-sons; **(b)** (*door*) à persiennes; *Nau* muni d'un louvre *ou* de louvres; *Aut Av* (*capot*) à persiennes, à volet.

lovable ['lʌvəb(ə)l] *adj* (*caractère, personne*) sympathique.

lovage ['lʌvɪdʒ] *n Bot Culin* ache *f* de(s) montagne(s).

love¹ [lʌv] *n* **(a)** amour *m*; **l. of** *or* **for,** amour de *ou* pour *ou* envers (*qn*); amour de (*qch*); **he has a great l. for Scotland,** il a une grande affection pour l'Écosse; **there's no l. lost between them,** ils ne peuvent pas se sentir; **a teacher with little l. for his pupils,** un professeur qui n'a pas beaucoup de sympathie pour ses élèves; **for the l. of God,** pour l'amour de Dieu; **give my l. to your parents,** faites mes amitiés à vos parents; **with l. from ...,** (*at end of letter*) affectueuses pensées de ...; **Bill sends his l.,** Bill vous fait ses amitiés; **I wouldn't do it for l. or money,** je ne le ferais pour rien au monde; **to do sth for l.,** faire qch pour le plaisir;

(b) (*between lovers*) amour *m* (*the pl is f in Lit use*); **to be/fall in l. with s.o.,** être/tomber amoureux de qn; **head over heels in l.,** amoureux fou, éperdument amoureux; **to make l. to s.o.,** faire l'amour avec qn; *Old-fashioned* (*to court*) faire la cour à qn; **to marry for l.,** faire un mariage d'amour; **she's the l. of my life,** c'est la femme *ou* l'amour de ma vie; **it was l. at first sight,** c'était le coup de foudre; **first l.,** les premières amours; **l. life,** vie amoureuse; **l. affair,** aventure *f*; **l. nest,** nid *m* d'amour; **l. match,** mariage *m* d'amour; **l. letter,** billet doux; **l. story,** histoire *f ou* roman *m* d'amour; **l. song,** chanson *f* d'amour; **l. seat,** canapé *m* deux places, causeuse *f*; **l. child,** enfant naturel *ou* illégitime;

(c) (*person*) **(my) l.,** mon amour; *esp Eng F* **more coffee, l.?,** tu prends encore du café, mon petit *ou* ma petite?; *esp Eng F* **there you are, l.!,** voilà, ma petite dame *ou* mon (petit) gars *ou* mon petit monsieur!;

(d) L., l'Amour *m*, Cupidon *m*;

(e) *Tennis etc* zéro *m*, rien *m*; **l. fifteen/fifteen l.,** rien à quinze/quinze à rien; **l. game,** jeu blanc; **two sets to l.,** deux sets à rien *ou* à zéro.

love² *vt* **(a)** aimer (*qn*); **to l. one another,** s'aimer; **(b)** (*of lover*) aimer (d'amour); **I l. you!,** je t'aime!; **(c)** aimer (passionnément) (*qch*); adorer (*la musique etc*); **they l. animals,** ils aiment les animaux; **to l. to do sth, to l. doing sth,** aimer (à) faire qch; **will you come with me? I should l. to,** voulez-vous m'accompagner? avec le plus grand plaisir; **she'd l. to see you again,** elle serait enchantée *ou* ravie de vous revoir; **I'd l. to come,** j'aimerais beaucoup venir.

lovebird ['lʌvbɜːd] *n* (*bird*) perruche *f* inséparable; *F* **lovebirds,** tourtereaux *mpl*.

lovebite ['lʌvbaɪt] *n* suçon *m*.

love-in-a-mist ['lʌvɪnə'mɪst] *n* (*plant*) nigelle *f* (de Damas); cheveux *mpl* de Vénus.

loveless ['lʌvlɪs] *adj* sans amour.

love-lies-bleeding ['lʌvlaɪz'bliːdɪŋ] *n* (*plant*) amarante *f* à fleurs en queue.

loveliness ['lʌvlɪnɪs] *n* beauté *f*; charme *m* (*d'une femme, d'un paysage etc*).

lovely ['lʌvlɪ] *adj* **(a)** beau, *f* belle; bon, *f* bonne (*nourriture, idée*); beau (*jour, temps etc*); **what a l. woman!,** quelle femme ravissante!; **have a l. time,** amusez-vous bien; **it's been l. seeing you again,** ça a été charmant de vous revoir; *F* **that's l. and simple,** c'est tout simple; *F* **it's l. and warm,** il fait une chaleur agréable; **(b)** *F* (*personne*) très aimable.

lovemaking ['lʌvmeɪkɪŋ] *n* rapports sexuels; *Old-fashioned* (*courting*) cour *f* (amoureuse).

lover ['lʌvər] *n* **(a)** amant *m*; *Old-fashioned* (*suitor*) amoureux *m*, prétendant *m*; **they were lovers,** ils étaient amants; **(b)** amateur *m*, ami, -e (*de la nature etc*); **music l.,** mélomane *mf*; **animal l.,** ami des animaux.

lovesick ['lʌvsɪk] *adj* qui languit d'amour.

lovesickness ['lʌvsɪknɪs] *n* mal *m* d'amour.

lovey-dovey ['lʌvɪdʌvɪ] *adj Sl* (*parler*) sentimental, mignard; **to get l.-d.,** (*of person*) devenir amoureux.

loving ['lʌvɪŋ] *adj* **(a)** affectueux, affectionné; **a l. husband and father,** un mari et un père aimant; **your l. mother,** (*at end of letter*) ta mère qui t'aime; **(b) l. cup,** coupe *f* de l'amitié.

-loving ['lʌvɪŋ] *suff* **home-l.,** qui aime son chez-soi.

lovingly ['lʌvɪŋlɪ] *adv* affectueusement, tendrement.

low¹ [ləʊ] **1** *adj* **(a)** (*not high*) bas, *f* basse; **l. price,** bas prix, faible prix; **the lowest price,** le dernier prix; **l. wages,** salaires peu élevés; **l. income families,** les familles à faible revenu; **l. temperature,** basse température; **to cook sth over a l. heat** *or* **a l. fire,** faire cuire qch à feu doux; *Cards* **the l. cards,** les basses cartes; **l. relief,** bas-relief *m*; **dress with a l. neckline,** robe décolletée; **l. tide,** marée basse; **my stocks are rather l.,** mes stocks sont un peu dégarnis; **our water supply is getting l.,** notre réserve d'eau baisse; **l. technology,** technologie *f* de base; *Mus* **l. note,** note basse;

(b) (*near the ground*) (*plafond*) bas, *f* basse, peu élevé; **to make s.o. a l. bow,** saluer qn profondément; *Geog* **the L. Countries,** les Pays-Bas; **lower part,** bas *m* (*d'une échelle etc*); **the lower Alps,** les basses Alpes; **lower back,** reins *mpl*; **lower back pain,** mal *m* de reins; **lower jaw,** mâchoire inférieure; *Ling* **l. German,** le bas allemand;

(c) (*inferior*) bas, *f* basse, peu élevé; **l. birth,** basse naissance; **all the people, high and l.,** tous, du haut en bas de l'échelle sociale; **the lower classes,** le bas peuple; **lower ranks,** rangs inférieurs (*de l'armée etc*); *Sch* **the lower school, the lower forms,** les petites classes; **the lower animals,** les animaux inférieurs; **to have a l. opinion of s.o.,** avoir une mauvaise opinion de qn; **l. company,** mauvaise compagnie; **the lowest of the l.,** le dernier des derniers; **that's a l. trick!,** ça c'est un sale coup!; **that was rather a l. thing to do,** ce n'était pas une très jolie chose à faire;

(d) (*depressed*) **to be very l.** *or* **in a very l. state,** (*of invalid*) être bien bas, aller très mal; **to feel l., to be in l. spirits,** se sentir déprimé, *F* avoir le cafard; *Med* **l. physical condition,** mauvaise condition physique;

(e) (*not loud*) bas, *f* basse; **l. murmur,** faible murmure *m*; **in a l. voice,** à voix basse, à mi-voix;

(f) *Rel* **l. Mass,** messe basse; **L. Sunday,** Pâques closes, dimanche *m* de Quasimodo.

2 *adv* **(a)** (*pendre, viser*) bas; **to bow l.,** s'incliner profondément, saluer très bas; **dress cut l. in the back,** robe décolletée dans le dos; *Boxing* **to hit l.,** toucher bas; **to fly l.,** (*of bird, aircraft*) voler bas; **to bring s.o. l.,** humilier qn, abaisser qn; **to lie l.,** (*of animal, person*) se tapir; rester tapi; (*of person*) rester coi, se tenir coi;

(b) the lowest paid employees, les employés les moins payés;

(c) (*parler*) à voix basse; **turn the music down l.,** baisse la musique; **put the heating on l.,** règle le chauffage sur le minimum; *Mus* **to set (a song** *etc*) **lower,** baisser d'une *ou* de deux octaves (une chanson *etc*); **the fire is burning l.,** le feu baisse; **light turned l.,** lumière en veilleuse; **I can't sing that l.,** je ne peux pas chanter aussi bas.

3 *n* **(a)** *Met* zone *f* de basse pression; **(b) to reach a new l.,** descendre encore plus bas; **sterling has reached an all-time l.,** la livre a atteint son plus bas niveau.

low² *vi* (*of cattle*) meugler.

low-alcohol [ləʊ'ælkəhɒl] *adj* (*drink*) peu alcoolisé.

lowboy ['ləʊbɔɪ] *n Am* commode *f*.

lowbrow ['ləʊbraʊ] **1** *adj* peu intellectuel. **2** *n* personne *f* peu intellectuelle.

low-budget [ləʊ'bʌdʒɪt] *adj* économique.

low-calorie [ləʊ'kælərɪ] *adj* (*régime etc*) de basses calories; (*régime*) hypocalorique.

low-capacity ['ləʊkə'pæsɪtɪ] *adj* à faible capacité.

low-class [ləʊ'klɑːs] *adj* vulgaire; sans distinction.

low-cost [ləʊ'kɒst] *adj* à bas prix; (*housing, accommodation*) à loyer modéré.

low-cut [ləʊ'kʌt] *adj* (*dress*) décolleté.

low-down ['ləʊdaʊn] *F* **1** *adj* (*mean*) ignoble; **that's a l.-d. trick,** ça c'est un coup rosse. **2** *n* **to give s.o. the l.-d.,** renseigner qn, tuyauter qn (**on,** sur).

lower¹ ['ləʊər] *vt* **(a)** baisser (*la tête, les yeux, la fenêtre, les stores*); abaisser (*les paupières*); abaisser, rabattre (*son voile, son chapeau*); *Th* **to l. the curtain,** baisser le rideau;

(b) (*reduce*) baisser, rabaisser (*un prix*); réduire (*la pression*); baisser (*la lumière*); abaisser (*la température*); baisser (*la voix, le ton*); déprimer (*le moral de l'ennemi*); (r)abaisser, faire baisser, (r)abattre (*l'orgueil de qn*); abaisser, avilir (*qn*); *Med* **to l. s.o.'s resistance,** (*of tiredness etc*) diminuer la résistance de qn; **to l. oneself,** s'abaisser, se ravaler (**to,** à);

(c) (*reduce in height*) abaisser (*un plafond*); diminuer la hauteur de (*qch*);

(d) (*let down*) descendre (*un tonneau etc*); *Nau* amener, caler (*un mât*); mettre (*une embarcation*) à la mer; **l. away!,** laissez aller!; **to l. s.o. on a rope,** (faire) descendre qn au bout d'une corde; *Fig* **to l. one's guard,** baisser sa garde.

lower² ['laʊər] *vi* **(a)** (*of person*) se renfrogner, froncer les sourcils; **to l. at s.o.,** regarder qn d'un mauvais œil, menacer qn du regard; **(b)** (*of sky*) s'amonceler; (*of storm*) menacer.

lowering¹ ['ləʊərɪŋ] *n* **(a)** abaissement *m*; baissement *m* (*de la tête etc*); **(b)** rabais *m*, diminution *f* (*des prix*); réduction *f* (*de la pression*); **(c)** abaissement *m*; diminution *f* de la hauteur (*de qch*); **(d)** descente *f* (*d'une échelle*); *Nau* calage *m* (*d'un mât*); mise *f* à la mer (*d'une embarcation*).

lowering² ['laʊərɪŋ] *adj* **(a)** (*air*) renfrogné, menaçant; **(b)** (*ciel*) menaçant.

low-flying ['ləʊ'flaɪɪŋ] *adj Av* (*avion*) volant à basse altitude.

low-grade ['ləʊ'greɪd] *adj* **(a)** (*coal etc*) de qualité inférieure; **(b)** (*official*) de grade inférieur.

low-heeled [ləʊ'hiːld] *adj* (*shoe*) à talon plat.

lowing ['ləʊɪŋ] *n* meuglement *m*.

low-key [ləʊ'kiː] *adj* (*film*) de style dépouillé; (*approach*) modéré; (*debate, discussion*) modéré; **to keep sth l.-k.,** contenir qch, modérer qch.

lowland ['ləʊlənd] *n* plaine *f* (basse); **the Lowlands,** (*en Écosse*) les Lowlands *fpl*.

low-level ['ləʊ'levəl] *adj* **(a)** (*radioactivity*) faible; *Med* **l.-l. infection,** infection bénigne; **(b)** (*discussion*) à la base; **(c)** *Comptr* **l.-l. language,** langage *m* de bas niveau.

lowlife ['ləʊlaɪf] *n Sl* crapule *f*.

lowliness ['ləʊlɪnɪs] *n* humilité *f*.

low-loader [ləʊ'ləʊdər] *n* camion *m* à plate-forme surbaissée.

lowly ['ləʊlɪ] *adj Arch & Lit* humble, modeste; (*rang*) infime.

low-lying ['ləʊ'laɪɪŋ] *adj* situé en bas; (*terrain*) bas, enfoncé.

low-necked ['ləʊ'nekt] *adj* (*dress*) décolleté.

lowness ['ləʊnɪs] *n* **(a)** faible hauteur *f* (*d'un mur etc*); faible altitude *f* (*d'une île, des collines*); **(b)** gravité *f* (*d'un son*); faiblesse *f* (*d'un bruit*); **(c)** bassesse *f* (*de conduite*); **(d) l. (of spirits),** abattement *m*, découragement *m*, dépression *f*.

low-pitched ['ləʊ'pɪtʃt] *adj* **(a)** (*son, voix*) grave; (*piano*) accordé à un diapason bas; **(b)** (*comble*) à faible pente.

low-pressure ['ləʊ'preʃər] *adj* **(a)** *Met* (*zone*) de basse pression; **(b)** (*cylindre, machine*) à basse pression *ou* tension.

low-profile [ləʊ'prəʊfaɪl] *adj* (*politician, company etc*) discret, qui adopte *ou* garde un profil bas.

low-rise ['ləʊraɪz] **1** *adj* **l.-r. building,** immeuble peu élevé *ou* bas. **2** *n* immeuble bas.

low-speed ['ləʊ'spiːd] *adj* (*machine*) à petite vitesse.

low-spirited ['ləʊ'spɪrɪtɪd] *adj* abattu, triste, déprimé, découragé.

low-tech [ləʊ'tek] *adj* pas à la pointe des progrès technologiques, *F* à la traîne; **as regards text-processing they're very l.-t.,** en matière de traitement de texte ils ne sont pas très à la page.

loyal ['lɔɪəl] *adj* **(a)** (*ami etc*) fidèle, dévoué (**to,** à), loyal, -aux (**to,** envers); **(b)** fidèle au souverain; **to drink the l. toast,** boire le toast au souverain.

loyalist ['lɔɪəlɪst] *n* loyaliste *mf*.

loyally ['lɔɪəlɪ] *adv* fidèlement.

loyalty ['lɔɪəltɪ] *n* loyalisme *m*; (*to friends, employer etc*) loyauté *f* (**to,** envers); **you'll have to decide where your loyalties lie,** il faudra que tu décides de quel côté tu es; **to have divided loyalties,** être partagé.

lozenge ['lɒzɪndʒ] *n* **(a)** *Pharm* pastille *f*, tablette *f*; **(b)** *Math Her* losange *m*.

LP [el'piː] *n* (*abbr* **long player**) 33 tours *m*.

LSD [eles'diː] *n* (*abbr* **lysergic acid diethylamide**) LSD *m*.

LSI [ele'saɪ] *n Comptr abbr* **large-scale integration**.

Lt *Mil* (*abbr* **Lieutenant**) Lieut., Lt..

LTA [eltiː'eɪ] *n abbr* **Lawn Tennis Association**.

Ltd *Com abbr* **limited**.

lubricant ['luːbrɪkənt] **1** *adj* lubrifiant. **2** *n* lubrifiant *m*; graisse *f*, huile *f* (*pour machines*).

lubricate ['luːbrɪkeɪt] *vt* lubrifier, graisser, huiler; **to l. the wheels,** graisser les roues; *Fig* **we were all well lubricated,** nous étions tous bien imbibés.

lubricating ['luːbrɪkeɪtɪŋ] *n* lubrification *f*; **l. oil,** huile *f* de graissage.

lubrication [luːbrɪ'keɪʃən] *n* lubrification *f*, graissage *m*.

lubricator ['luːbrɪkeɪtər] *n* graisseur *m*, appareil *m* de graissage; **gravity-feed l.,** graisseur par gravité.

lubricity [luː'brɪsɪtɪ] *n* lubricité *f*.

lucerne [luː'sɜːn] *n Bot Agr* luzerne *f*.

Lucerne [luː'sɜːn] *n* Lucerne *f*; **(the) Lake (of) L.,** le lac des Quatre-Cantons.

lucid ['luːsɪd] *adj* (*esprit, style*) lucide; (*explication*) clair; *Med* **l. interval,** intervalle *m* lucide *ou* de lucidité.

lucidity [luː'sɪdɪtɪ] *n* lucidité *f*.

lucidly ['luːsɪdlɪ] *adv* lucidement.

Lucifer ['luːsɪfər] *n Astron Bible* Lucifer *m*.

luck [lʌk] *n* **(a)** (*chance*) chance *f*, fortune *f*; **good l.,** bonne chance, bonheur *m*; **good l. (to you)!,** bonne chance!; *Iron* **good l. to him!, and the best of (British) l. to him!,** qu'il le fasse si ça lui chante!; **good l. with the exams/for Friday,** bonne chance pour les examens/pour vendredi; **better l. next time,** ça ira mieux la prochaine fois; **bad l.,** malchance *f*, mauvaise fortune, *F* déveine *f*; **to be down on one's l.,** avoir de la guigne; **to bring s.o. bad/good l.,** porter malheur/bonheur à qn; **to try one's l.,** tenter sa chance; **don't trust to l.,** n'y compte pas trop; (*when you*

can do something about it) ne laisse rien au hasard; **her l. has changed,** sa chance a tourné; **just my l.!,** c'est bien ma chance!, pas de veine!; **with my l. it won't work,** avec ma chance habituelle, ça ne marchera pas; **hard l.!,** pas de chance!; **I've got to work, worst l.,** il faut que je travaille, pas de chance!; **by good l.,** heureusement; par bonheur; **as l. would have it,** par bonheur; **as l. would have it I was there,** le hasard a voulu que je sois là; **it's the l. of the draw,** c'est le hasard;
(b) (*success*) bonheur *m*, bonne fortune, (bonne) chance *f*; **to keep sth for l.,** garder qch comme porte-bonheur; **bit/piece/stroke of l.,** coup *m* de chance, *F* coup de veine, aubaine *f*; **to wish s.o. l.,** souhaiter bonne chance à qn; **wish me l.!,** souhaite-moi bonne chance!; **to be in l.,** avoir de la chance *ou F* de la veine; **to be out of l.,** ne pas avoir de chance; **no such l.!,** je n'ai pas (eu) cette chance!, hélas pas!; **he has all the l.,** *F* c'est un veinard; **to have the l. of the devil,** avoir une chance de tous les diables.

▶luck out *vi Am* avoir de la chance.

luckily ['lʌkɪlɪ] *adv* heureusement, par bonheur; **l. for her,** par chance pour elle.

luckless ['lʌklɪs] *adj Fml* **(a)** (*person*) malheureux, malchanceux; **(b)** (*jour*) malencontreux; (*heure*) fatal.

lucky ['lʌkɪ] *adj* **to be l.,** avoir de la chance; (*jour*) de veine; (*heure, moment*) propice; **you're a very l. person,** vous avez beaucoup de chance; **who's the l. man?,** (*she's going to marry*) qui est l'heureux élu?; *F* **(you) l. devil!, l. beggar!,** veinard!; *Iron* **you'll be l.!,** tu peux toujours courir!; **to be born l.,** être né coiffé; **to have a l. break,** avoir un coup de chance *ou* de pot; **l. in love/at cards,** heureux en amour/au jeu; **it's l. you came when you did,** c'est une chance que tu sois venu à ce moment; **she's l. to be alive,** elle a de la chance d'être en vie; **l. shot,** coup heureux *ou* de veine; **my l. number,** mon nombre de chance; **to make a l. guess,** tomber juste; **it's not my l. day,** je n'ai pas de chance aujourd'hui; **l. charm,** porte-bonheur *m inv*; **it's l.,** (*of thing*) ça porte bonheur; *Br* **l. dip,** = baquet rempli de son où l'on plonge la main pour en retirer une surprise.

lucrative ['luːkrətɪv] *adj* lucratif.

lucre ['luːkər] *n* lucre *m*; **to do sth for (filthy) l.,** agir par amour de gain *ou* de lucre.

ludicrous ['luːdɪkrəs] *adj* risible, comique, ridicule; **it's l. to do,** c'est ridicule de faire; **he looked faintly l.,** il avait l'air quelque peu grotesque.

ludicrously ['luːdɪkrəslɪ] *adv* ridiculement.

ludo ['luːdəʊ] *n Br* (*game*) jeu *m* des petits chevaux.

luff¹ [lʌf] *n Nau* **(a)** lof *m*, ralingue *f* du vent, chute *f* avant (*d'une voile*); **(b)** épaule *f* (*de l'avant*).

luff² *Nau* **1** *vi* lof(f)er, faire une aulof(f)ée. **2** *vt* **to l. the boat (up),** faire loffer la barque.

lug¹ [lʌg] *vt* **(-gg-)** traîner, tirer (*qch de pesant*); **to l. sth along** *or* **away,** entraîner qch; **to l. sth about with one,** promener *ou* trimbaler qch avec soi.

lug² *n Tech* oreille *f*; *Metal* tasseau *m* (*d'une pièce venue de fonderie*).

lug³ *n Nau* voile *f* à bourcet.

lug⁴ *n* (*lugworm*) arénicole *f*.

luge [luːʒ] *n Sp* luge *f*.

luggage ['lʌgɪdʒ] *n* bagage(s) *m(pl)*; **a piece of l.,** un bagage; **hand l.,** bagages à main; **excess l.,** excédent *m* de bagages; **l. label,** étiquette *f* à bagage; *Rail* **l. van,** fourgon *m* (aux bagages); *Nau* **l. room** *or* **hold,** soute *f* aux bagages; *Av* **l. bay** *or* **compartment,** compartiment *m ou* soute à bagages; **l. rack,** *Rail* filet *m*, porte-bagages *m inv*; *Aut* galerie *f*; **l. locker,** consigne *f* automatique.

lugger ['lʌgər] *n Nau* lougre *m*.

lughole ['lʌghəʊl] *n F* oreille *f*.

lugsail ['lʌgseɪl, 'lʌgs(ə)l] *n Nau* voile *f* à bourcet.

lugubrious [luː'guːbrɪəs] *adj* lugubre.

lugubriously [luː'guːbrɪəslɪ] *adv* lugubrement.

lugworm ['lʌgwɜːm] *n* arénicole *f*.

Luke [luːk] *n* Luc *m*; **Saint L.,** saint Luc.

lukewarm ['luːkwɔːm] *adj* (*water, friendship etc*) tiède; **the critics gave the play a l. reception,** les critiques ont accueilli la pièce avec tiédeur; **to become l.,** tiédir.

lull¹ [lʌl] *n* moment *m* de calme; (*before storm*) bonace *f*; (*in fighting*) répit *m*; *Nau* accalmie *f*, embellie *f*; **there was a l. in the conversation,** la conversation tomba.

lull² *vt* **(a)** bercer, endormir (qn); **to l. a child to sleep,** endormir un enfant; **(b)** endormir (*les soupçons de qn*); **to l. s.o. into a false sense of security,** endormir qn dans un sentiment de sécurité trompeur.

lullaby ['lʌləbaɪ] *n Mus* berceuse *f*.

lumbago [lʌm'beɪgəʊ] *n Med* lumbago *m*; **to have l.,** avoir un lumbago.

lumbar ['lʌmbər] *adj Anat* lombaire; *Med* **l. puncture,** ponction *f* lombaire.

lumber¹ ['lʌmbər] *n* **(a)** objets encombrants; *Br* **l. room,** (pièce *f* de) débarras *m*; **(b)** *Am* bois *m* de charpente *ou* de construction.

lumber² *vt* **(a)** encombrer, embarrasser (*un lieu*); **to l. a room with furniture,** encombrer une pièce de meubles; *F* **too late, we're lumbered!,** (*with the washing-up, babysitting etc*) ça y est, nous sommes bons!; **(b)** *Am* abattre (*des arbres*); débiter (*du bois*).

▶lumber about *vi* se trimbaler çà et là.

▶lumber along *vi* (*of person*) avancer à pas pesants *ou* d'un pas lourd.

▶lumber up *vtsep* = **LUMBER² (a).**

▶lumber with *vtaspo F* (*burden*) **I don't want to be lumbered with him for the whole evening,** je ne veux pas l'avoir sur le dos pendant toute la soirée; **they've lumbered me with the cooking,** ils m'ont mis la cuisine sur les bras.

lumbering ['lʌmbərɪŋ] *adj* lourd, pesant.

lumberjack ['lʌmbədʒæk] *n esp Am* bûcheron *m*.

lumberjacket ['lʌmbədʒækɪt] *n* blouson *m*; (*longer*) canadienne *f*.

lumberman ['lʌmbəmæn] *n Am* bûcheron *m*.

lumberyard ['lʌmbəjɑːd] *n Am* chantier *m* de bois.

luminary ['luːmɪnərɪ] *n* **(a)** *Fig* (*person*) lumière *f*; flambeau *m* (*de la science etc*); **(b)** *Lit* corps lumineux, luminaire *m*, astre *m*.

luminescence [luːmɪ'nesəns] *n Phys* luminescence *f*.

luminescent [luːmɪ'nesənt] *adj Phys* luminescent.

luminosity [luːmɪ'nɒsɪtɪ] *n* luminosité *f*.

luminous ['luːmɪnəs] *adj* lumineux; *Phys* **l. density,** densité lumineuse; luminance *f*; **l. paint,** peinture lumineuse; **l. colours,** couleurs lumineuses *ou* éclatantes; **l. socks,** chaussettes éclatantes.

lumme, lummy ['lʌmɪ] *int F* mon Dieu!

lummox ['lʌməks] *n F* lourdaud, -e.

lump¹ [lʌmp] *n* **(a)** gros morceau, bloc *m* (*de pierre*); motte *f* (*de terre, d'argile*); morceau (*de sucre*); masse *f* (*de plomb etc*); (*in porridge etc*) boule *f*, grumeau *m*; pâton *m* (*dans le papier*); (*caused by bruise*) bosse *f* (*au front etc*); *Med etc* excroissance *f*; grosseur *f*; **l. sum,** somme globale; (*fixed price for contract etc*) prix *m* à forfait; paiement *m* forfaitaire; **to have a l. in one's throat,** avoir la gorge serrée; *Am F* **to take one's lumps,** porter sa croix; **to pay in a l.,** payer tout ensemble; **Parisians, taken in the l., are ...,** les Parisiens en général sont ...; **(b)** *F* (*person*) empoté *m*, pataud *m*; **great l. of a girl,** grosse dondon; **(c)** *Br F* **the l.,** ouvriers indépendants (qui évitent le fisc).

lump² *vt* mettre en bloc *ou* en masse *ou* en tas.

lump³ *vt F* **if he doesn't like it, he can l. it, he can like it or l. it,** si cela ne lui plaît pas, qu'il s'arrange; **you'll have to l. it!,** il faudra que tu fasses avec!

▶lump together *vtsep* réunir (*des choses*) ensemble; **to l. people together,** considérer des personnes en bloc.

lumpectomy [lʌm'pektəmɪ] *n Surg* ablation *f* de tumeur mammaire.

lumpfish ['lʌmpfɪʃ] *n* lompe *m*, lump *m*.

lumpish ['lʌmpɪʃ] *adj* **(a)** (*clumsy*) gros, balourd, pataud; **great l. man,** lourdaud *m*; **(b)** (*stupid*) à l'esprit lent.

lumpy ['lʌmpɪ] *adj* (*earth*) rempli de mottes; (*sauce*) grumeleux; (*surface*) couvert de protubérances; (*forehead etc*) couvert de bosses.

lunacy ['luːnəsɪ] *n* **(a)** *F* action *ou* idée folle; **it's sheer l.,** c'est de la folie (pure et simple); **(b)** *Med* aliénation mentale, folie *f*; *Jur* démence *f*.

lunar ['luːnər] *adj* (*cycle, module, orbit etc*) lunaire; **l. eclipse,** éclipse *f* de lune; **l. landing,** alunissage *m*, atterrissage *m* sur la lune.

lunaria [luː'neərɪə] *n Bot* lunaire *f*.

lunatic ['luːnətɪk] **1** *adj* fou, *f* folle; **l. asylum,** maison *f* de fous; **the l. fringe,** les extrémistes *mpl*, les cinglés *mpl*. **2** *n* fou, *f* folle; *Med* aliéné, -ée.

lunch¹ [lʌntʃ] *n* **(a)** déjeuner *m*; *Can Belg* dîner *m*; **they have l. at one o'clock,** ils déjeunent à une heure; **we had a picnic l.,** nous avons pique-niqué à midi; **what time** *or* **when is l.?,** à quelle heure déjeune-t-on?; **what's for l.?,** qu'y a-t-il pour le déjeuner?; **let's go out for l.,** allons déjeuner dehors; **how long do you get for l.?,** combien de temps tu as pour déjeuner?; **what are you doing for l.?,** que fais-tu à midi?; **she's at l.** *or* **has gone to l.,** elle est sortie prendre son déjeuner; **to go shopping during one's l. hour,** aller en courses à l'heure du déjeuner; **we're having people to l.,** nous avons du monde à déjeuner; *Am Sl*

to be out to l., (*be crazy*) débloquer un peu; **l. hour** *or* **break,** (*in course of working day*) heure *f ou* pause *f* du déjeuner; **l. hour** *or* **time,** (*noon, one o'clock etc*) heure *ou* moment *m* du déjeuner; *Am* **l. counter,** (*in store*) bar de restauration rapide;
(b) *US* petit repas, casse-croûte *m inv* (*pris à n'importe quelle heure*).

lunch[2] **1** *vi* déjeuner; *Can Belg* dîner. **2** *vt* donner à déjeuner à (*qn*), faire déjeuner (*qn*).

lunchbox ['lʌntʃbɒks], *Am* **lunchbucket** ['lʌntʃbʌkɪt] *n* panier-repas *m*.

luncheon ['lʌntʃ(ə)n] *n Fml* déjeuner *m*; **l. meat,** pâté *m* de viande; *Br Com etc* **l. voucher,** chèque-repas *m*, *pl* chèques-repas; chèque-restaurant *m*, *pl* chèques-restaurant.

luncheonette ['lʌnʃə'net] *n Am* petit restaurant, café-restaurant *m*.

lunchpail ['lʌntʃpeɪl] *n Am* panier-repas *m*.

lunchroom ['lʌntʃrʊm] *n Am* = pièce où l'on peut manger ses sandwiches etc à l'heure du déjeuner.

lung [lʌŋ] *n* poumon *m*; **to shout at the top of one's lungs,** crier à tue-tête; **l. cancer,** cancer *m* du poumon; *Med* **iron l.,** poumon d'acier; **l. transplant,** greffe *f* du poumon.

lunge[1] [lʌndʒ] *n* **(a)** mouvement *m* (précipité) en avant; **she made a l. for the ball,** elle a accouru sur la balle; **(b)** *Fencing* botte *f*.

lunge[2] *vi Fencing* se fendre; **to l. at the adversary,** porter *ou* pousser une botte à l'adversaire; **to l. out at s.o.,** allonger un coup de poing à qn.

►**lunge forward** *vi* se précipiter *ou* se jeter en avant.

lupin, *US* **lupine** ['lu:pɪn] *n* (*plant*) lupin *m*.

lupine ['lu:paɪn] *adj* de loup.

lurch[1] [lɜ:tʃ] *n* **to leave s.o. in the l.,** laisser qn en panne *ou* dans le pétrin; (*to desert*) planter là qn.

lurch[2] *n* embardée *f*, coup *m* de roulis (*d'un navire*); (*sideways*) embardée (*d'une voiture*); pas titubant (*d'un ivrogne*); **to give a l.,** (*of ship, car etc*) faire une embardée; **with a l. the train was off again,** le train est reparti avec un à-coup.

lurch[3] *vi* (*of ship, car etc*) faire une embardée.

►**lurch along** *vi* (*of person*) marcher en titubant.

lurcher ['lɜ:tʃər] *n* (*dog*) lévrier bâtard.

lure[1] ['lʊər] *n* **(a)** attrait *m*; **the l. of the sea,** l'attrait de la mer; **(b)** *Fishing & Fig* leurre *m*; (*wooden duck*) appât *m* factice; (*in hunting*) leurre (*de fauconnier*).

lure[2] *vt* **(a)** attirer, séduire, allécher; **to be lured into the trap,** être entraîné dans le piège; **he was lured into it by his friends,** il s'y est laissé entraîner par ses amis; **(b)** leurrer (*un poisson, un faucon etc*).

lurid ['lʊərɪd] *adj* **(a)** (*sensational*) (*récit, langage*) corsé, (*film etc*) à effets corsés; **she gave us a l. description of her operation,** elle nous a fait une description atroce de son opération; **l. details,** détails effroyables; **(b)** (*fiery*) cuivré; (*flames*) rougeoyant; *Pej* (*colour*) criard; **(c)** (*pale*) (*ciel*) blafard; (*teint*) livide; *Biol* luride; **l. light,** lueur blafarde *ou* sinistre.

luridly ['lʊərɪdlɪ] *adv* **(a)** (*to describe*) en corsant les effets; **(b)** (*to glow*) en rougeoyant; **(c)** avec une lueur blafarde; sinistrement.

lurk [lɜ:k] *vi* se cacher; **there's a man lurking in the alleyway,** il y a un homme qui se cache dans la ruelle; **I'll just l. in the background,** je me fondrai dans les décors.

lurking ['lɜ:kɪŋ] *adj* vague (*sentiment etc*); **a l. suspicion,** un vague soupçon; **I have one l. doubt,** j'ai encore un léger doute; **if you have any l. doubts,** s'il vous reste des doutes.

luscious ['lʌʃəs] *adj* succulent, savoureux; (*fruit*) fondant; **a l. blonde,** une blonde alléchante.

lusciousness ['lʌʃəsnɪs] *n* succulence *f* (*d'un fruit*).

lush[1] [lʌʃ] *adj* **(a)** (*grass, plant*) plein de sève, luxuriant; **(b)** (*rich*) **l. surroundings,** environnement luxueux; **a l. sound,** un son riche.

lush[2] *n Am Sl* (*alcoholic*) poivrot, -ote.

lushness ['lʌʃnɪs] *n* luxuriance *f* (*de l'herbe etc*).

lust [lʌst] *n* désir *m* (charnel); *Pej* luxure *f*; *Rel* appétit *m* (coupable); **l. for power,** soif *f* du pouvoir.

►**lust after** *vipo* désirer (*qn*); convoiter (*qch*).

►**lust for** *vipo* convoiter (*qch*); **to l. for power/revenge,** avoir soif de pouvoir/de revanche.

luster, lusterless *etc US* = **LUSTRE, LUSTRELESS** *etc.*

lustful ['lʌstfʊl] *adj* lascif, libidineux.

lustfully ['lʌstfʊlɪ] *adv* lascivement.

lustily ['lʌstɪlɪ] *adv* (*chanter, crier*) à pleine gorge; (*travailler*) vigoureusement, de toutes ses forces.

lustre, *US* **luster** ['lʌstər] *n* **(a)** éclat *m*, brillant *m*, lustre *m*; *Tex* cati *m*, lustre (*du drap*); *Lit* **to add fresh l. to a name,** ajouter un nouveau lustre à un nom; **(b)** pendeloque *f* (*de lustre*); lustre *m* (*de plafond*); **(c)** *Tex* **(cotton) l.,** lustrine *f*.

lustreless, *US* **lusterless** ['lʌstəlɪs] *adj* mat, terne; (*yeux*) sans éclat.

lustreware, *US* **lusterware** ['lʌstəweər] *n Cer* poterie *f* à reflets métalliques, poterie lustrée.

lustrous ['lʌstrəs] *adj* brillant, éclatant; (*material*) lustré, satiné.

lusty ['lʌstɪ] *adj* vigoureux, fort, robuste; **l. voices,** voix puissantes.

lute[1] [lu:t] *n Mus* luth *m*; **l. maker,** luthier *m*; **l. player,** joueur, -euse de luth, luthiste *mf*.

lute[2] *n* (*sealant*) lut *m*, mastic *m*.

lute[3] *vt* luter, boucher, mastiquer.

Lutheran ['lu:θərən] *adj & n Rel Hist* luthérien, -ienne.

luxation [lʌk'seɪʃən] *n* luxation *f*.

Luxemb(o)urg ['lʌksəmbɜ:g] *n* **the Grand Duchy of L.,** le Grand-duché de Luxembourg.

luxuriance [lʌg'zjʊərɪəns, lʌk's-] *n* exubérance *f*, luxuriance *f* (*de la végétation, de style etc*).

luxuriant [lʌg'zjʊərɪənt, lʌk's-] *adj* exubérant, luxuriant; **l. (growth) of hair,** chevelure abondante; **l. beard,** barbe drue.

luxuriantly [lʌg'zjʊərɪəntlɪ, lʌk's-] *adv* avec exubérance; en abondance.

luxuriate [lʌg'zjʊərɪeɪt, lʌk's-] *vi* **to l. in a hot bath,** se prélasser dans un bain chaud.

luxurious [lʌg'zjʊərɪəs, lʌk's-] *adj* **(a)** (*appartement*) luxueux, somptueux; (*vie*) de luxe; **she's got very l. tastes,** elle a des goûts de grand luxe; **(b)** (*person*) adonné au luxe; **(c)** *Arch* sensuel, voluptueux.

luxuriously [lʌg'zjʊərɪəslɪ, lʌk's-] *adv* **(a)** (*furnished*) luxueusement, avec luxe; **(b)** (*to stretch*) avec volupté.

luxuriousness [lʌg'zjʊərɪəsnɪs, lʌk's-] *n* luxe *m*.

luxury ['lʌkʃərɪ] *n* **(a)** luxe *m*; **to live in (the lap of) l.,** vivre dans le luxe; **(b)** objet *m* de luxe; **the little luxuries of life,** les petits plaisirs de la vie; **to indulge in the l. of a cigar,** se payer le luxe d'un cigare; **it's a l. not to have to cook,** c'est un luxe de ne pas avoir à faire la cuisine; **l. flat,** appartement *m* de luxe; **l. car,** voiture *f* de (grand) luxe; **l. holiday,** vacances *fpl* de luxe; **l. tax,** taxe *f* de luxe.

LV [el'vi:] *n Br abbr* **luncheon voucher.**

lychee [laɪ'tʃi:] *n* (*fruit*) litchi *m*.

lychgate ['lɪtʃgeɪt] *n* = **LICHGATE.**

lye [laɪ] *n* lessive *f* (*de soude, de potasse*).

lying[1] ['laɪɪŋ] *adj* couché; étendu.

lying[2] **1** *adj* (*person*) menteur, -euse; (*account*) mensonger. **2** *n* mensonge *m*.

lymph [lɪmf] *n Physiol* lymphe *f*; **l. node** *or Old-fashioned* **gland,** glande *f ou* ganglion *m* lymphatique.

lymphatic [lɪm'fætɪk] *Physiol* **1** *adj* lymphatique; **l. node** *or Old-fashioned* **gland,** glande *f ou* ganglion *m* lymphatique. **2** *n* (vaisseau *m*) lymphatique *m*.

lynch [lɪntʃ] *vt* lyncher.

lyncher ['lɪntʃər] *n* **l. party,** commando lyncheur.

lynching ['lɪntʃɪŋ] *n* lynchage *m*.

lynx [lɪŋks] *n* (*animal*) lynx *m*.

lynx-eyed ['lɪŋksaɪd] *adj* aux yeux de lynx.

lyre ['laɪər] *n Mus* lyre *f*.

lyrebird ['laɪəbɜ:d] *n* oiseau-lyre *m*, *pl* oiseaux-lyres, ménure *m*.

lyric ['lɪrɪk] **1** *adj* (*poète, drame*) lyrique. **2** *n* **(a)** poème *m* lyrique; **(b) lyrics,** paroles *fpl* (*d'une chanson*); **l. writer,** parolier *m*.

lyrical ['lɪrɪk(ə)l] *adj* **(a)** (*poetry etc*) lyrique; **(b)** dit *ou* écrit sur un ton lyrique; *F* **she got positively l. about it,** elle y a montré un enthousiasme fou; **to wax l. about sth,** déborder d'enthousiasme pour qch.

lyrically ['lɪrɪklɪ] *adv* **(a)** lyriquement; **(b)** (*to speak*) avec enthousiasme.

lyricism ['lɪrɪsɪz(ə)m] *n* lyrisme *m*.

lyricist ['lɪrɪsɪst] *n* **(a)** (*of musical etc*) parolier *m*; **(b)** (*poet*) poète *m* lyrique.

lysergic [lɪ'sɜ:dʒɪk, laɪ-] *adj* (*acide*) lysergique.

M

M, m [em] *n* (la lettre) M, m *mf*.
m (*abbr* **metre(s)**) m.
ma [mɑː] *n F* maman *f*.
MA [e'meɪ] *n Univ* (*abbr* **Master of Arts**) ≈ maîtrise *f*; **to have an MA in Russian,** avoir une maîtrise de russe; **Susan Long, MA,** Susan Long, maître ès arts.
ma'am [mɑːm] *n* madame *f*.
mac¹ [mæk] *n F* (*raincoat*) imper *m*.
mac² *n US F* **hey, m.!,** hé, mon vieux *ou* mon pote!
macabre [mə'kɑːbər] *adj* macabre; **a taste for the m.,** le goût du macabre.
macadam [mə'kædəm] *n Constr* macadam *m*.
macadamize [mə'kædəmaɪz] *vt Constr* macadamiser (*une route*); **macadamized road,** macadam *m*.
macaroni [mækə'rəʊnɪ] *n Culin* macaroni *m*; **m. cheese,** macaroni au gratin.
macaroon [mækə'ruːn] *n Culin* macaron *m*.
macaw [mə'kɔː] *n* (*bird*) ara *m*.
mace¹ [meɪs] *n* (*weapon, symbol of office*) masse *f*.
mace² *n Bot Culin* macis *m*.
macebearer ['meɪsbeərər] *n* massier *m*.
macerate ['mæsəreɪt] *vt & vi* macérer.
Mach [mæk] *n Phys* **M. (number),** (nombre *m* de) Mach *m*; **at M. 3,** à Mach 3.
machete [mə'tʃeɪtɪ, -'ʃetɪ] *n* machette *f*.
Machiavellian [mækɪə'velɪən] *adj* machiavélique.
machination [mækɪ'neɪʃən] *n* machination *f*, complot *m*.
machine¹ [mə'ʃiːn] *n* machine *f*; (*person*) automate *m*, robot *m*, machine; **sewing/washing m.,** machine à coudre/à laver; **m. made,** fait à la machine; *Med* **kidney/heart-lung m.,** rein/cœur artificiel; *Com etc* **slot m.,** distributeur *m* automatique, *F* machine à sous; *F* **fruit m.,** tire-pognon *m*; *Pol* **the party m.,** les rouages *mpl* du parti; *Comptr* **m. code** *or* **language,** code *m ou* langage *m* machine; **m. gun,** mitrailleuse *f*; **m. gunner,** mitrailleur *m*; **m. gunning,** mitraillage *m*; **m. shop,** atelier *m* d'usinage; **m. tool,** machine-outil *m*, *pl* machines-outils; *Comptr* **m. translation,** traduction *f* automatique.
machine² *vt* **(a)** *Ind* usiner, façonner (*une pièce*); travailler (*qch*) à la machine; **(b)** *Sewing* coudre *ou* piquer à la machine.
▸machine down *vtsep Ind* amincir (*le métal*).
machine-gun [mə'ʃiːngʌn] *vt* mitrailler.
machine-readable [mə'ʃiːnriːdəb(ə)l] *adj Comptr* (*data*) exploitable par une machine.
machinery [mə'ʃiːnərɪ] *n* **(a)** (*parts*) mécanisme *m*; (*machines*) machines *fpl*, machinerie *f*; **(b)** (*of organization*) **the m. of government,** les rouages *mpl* du gouvernement; **administrative m.,** l'appareil administratif.
machining [mə'ʃiːnɪŋ] *n* **(a)** *Ind* (*of part*) usinage *m*; **(b)** *Sewing* couture *f* à la machine.
machining down *n* (*of metal*) amincissement *m*.
machinist [mə'ʃiːnɪst] *n* **(a)** *Ind* (*operator*) machiniste *m*; mécanicien, -ienne; **(b)** *Sewing* mécanicien, -ienne.
machismo [mæ'tʃɪzməʊ] *n F* machisme *m*.
macho [mætʃəʊ] *adj F* macho.
macintosh ['mækɪntɒʃ] *n* imperméable *m*.
mackerel ['mækrəl] *n* (*pl* **-rel** *or occ* **-rels**) (*fish*) maquereau *m*; **m. sky,** ciel pommelé *ou* moutonné.
mackintosh ['mækɪntɒʃ] *n* imperméable *m*.
macramé [mə'krɑːmɪ] *n* macramé *m*.
macro ['mækrəʊ] *n Comptr* macro *m*, macrocommande *f*.
macrobiotics [mækrəʊbaɪ'ɒtɪks] *npl* (*usu with sing verb*) macrobiotique *f*.
macrocomputing ['mækrəʊkəm'pjuːtɪŋ] *n Comptr* macroinformatique *f*.
macrocosm ['mækrəkɒzəm] *n* macrocosme *m*.
macroeconomics [mækrəʊiːkə'nɒmɪks] *npl* (*usu with sing verb*) macroéconomie *f*.
macron ['mækrɒn] *n Typ* macron *m*.
macroscopic [mækrə'skɒpɪk] *adj* macroscopique.
mad [mæd] **1** *adj* (**madder, maddest**) **(a)** (*insane*) fou, *f* folle, dément; *Med* aliéné; *F* **(stark) raving m., as m. as a hatter** *or* **as a March hare,** fou à lier; **it is enough to drive you m.,** il y a de quoi devenir fou, c'est à vous rendre fou; **to go m.,** devenir fou; **nationalism gone m.,** nationalisme forcené; **m. with fear,** affolé (de peur); **a m. plan,** un projet insensé; *F* **to run like m.,** courir comme un dératé;
(b) (*crazy*) **m. for revenge,** assoiffé de revanche; **there was a m. rush for the door,** on s'est précipité à la porte; **to be m. about s.o./sth,** (*like very much*) être fou de qn/qch; **to be m. about** *or* **on sport,** être un sportif passionné; **to be m. on climbing,** avoir la passion de l'escalade;
(c) *F* (*angry*) furieux, furibond; **to be m. with** *or* **at s.o.,** être furieux contre qn; **m. bull,** taureau furieux *ou* enragé; *Vet* **m. dog,** chien enragé.
2 *adv F* **m. keen on sth,** fou *ou* emballé de qch.
Madagascan [mædə'gæskən] **1** *adj* malgache. **2** *n* Malgache *mf*.
Madagascar [mædə'gæskər] *n* Madagascar *m*.
madam ['mædəm] *n* **(a)** (*as form of address*) madame *f*, mademoiselle *f*; **M. Chairman,** Madame la Présidente; **Dear M.,** (*in letter*) Madame, Mademoiselle; **(b)** (*pl* **madams**) (*in brothel*) tenancière *f* de bordel, maquerelle *f*; **(c)** *Br F* (*pl* **madams**) (*precious girl*) **she's a bit of a m.,** c'est une pimbêche.
madcap ['mædkæp] **1** *adj* écervelé; **m. scheme,** projet insensé. **2** *n* écervelé, -ée.
madden ['mæd(ə)n] *vt* (*make angry, insane*) rendre (*qn*) fou; (*make angry*) exaspérer (*qn*).
maddening ['mæd(ə)nɪŋ] *adj* à rendre fou; (*exasperating*) à rendre fou, exaspérant.
maddeningly ['mæd(ə)nɪŋlɪ] *adv* à rendre fou.
madder ['mædər] *n* **(a)** *Bot* garance *f*; **m. root,** alizari *m*; **(b)** (*in dyeing*) teinture *f* de garance.
madding ['mædɪŋ] *adj Lit* fou, *f* folle; **far from the m. crowd,** loin de la foule et du bruit.
made [meɪd] *adj* fait, fabriqué; **m. in France,** fabriqué en France; *F* **he's a m. man,** son avenir est assuré; sa fortune est faite.
Madeira [mə'dɪərə] *n* **(a)** *Geog* Madère *f*; **(b)** (*wine*) vin *m* de Madère, madère *m*; **(c)** *Culin* **M. cake,** gâteau *m* de Savoie.
made-up [meɪ'dʌp] *adj* **(a)** *F* (*not true*) faux, *f* fausse; (*histoire*) inventé; **(b)** *Sewing* (*vêtement*) tout fait; **(c)** (*wearing make-up*) maquillé, fardé.
madhouse ['mædhaʊs] *n* maison *f* de fous; *F* **this place is a m.!,** on se croirait à Charenton!
madly ['mædlɪ] *adv* **(a)** follement; (*to run*) comme un fou *ou* une folle; **(b)** follement, drôlement; (*aimer*) à la folie, éperdument; **m. in love,** follement amoureux; **it's m. expensive,** c'est fou ce que c'est cher.
madman, *pl* **-men** ['mædmən, -men] *n* fou *m*, aliéné *m*; **like a m.,** (*se battre*) en désespéré, comme un forcené; (*crier*) comme un perdu.
madness ['mædnɪs] *n* folie *f*, démence *f*; **in a fit of m.,** dans un accès *ou* dans un moment de folie; *F* **it's sheer m.,** c'est insensé, c'est de la folie; **it would be m. to ...,** ce serait de la folie de ... .
madonna [mə'dɒnə] *n* madone *f*.
madrigal ['mædrɪg(ə)l] *n* madrigal *m*, -aux.
madwoman, *pl* **-women** ['mædwʊmən, -wɪmɪn] *n* folle *f*.
maelstrom ['meɪlstrəʊm] *n* tourbillon *m*, gouffre *m*; *Fig* **the m. of modern life,** le tourbillon de la vie moderne.
maestro, *pl* **-tros, -tri** ['maɪstrəʊ, -trəʊz, -triː] *n Mus* maestro *m*, *pl* maestros.
Mae West [meɪ'west] *n Old-fashioned F* gilet *m* de sauvetage.
mafia ['mæfɪə] *n* mafia *f*.
mafioso [mæfɪ'əʊsəʊ] *n* mafioso *m*.

mag [mæg] *n F* = **MAGAZINE (a)**.

magazine [mægə'ziːn] *n* **(a)** (*publication*) (revue *f*) périodique *m*; **illustrated m.**, revue illustrée, magazine *m*; **sports m.**, magazine sportif; *Rad TV* **m. (programme)**, magazine; **(b)** (*for cartridges*) chargeur *m*, magasin *m*; *Phot* magasin; **m. rifle**, fusil *m* à répétition *ou* à chargeur; **(c)** *Mil* (*store*) magasin *m*; dépôt *m* (*d'armes etc*); **powder m.**, *Mil* poudrière *f*, dépôt d'explosifs; *Nau* soute *f* aux poudres *ou* à poudre.

magenta [mə'dʒentə] *n & adj* (*colour*) magenta *m inv*.

Maggie ['mægɪ] *n* (*dimin of* **Margaret**) Margot *f*.

maggot ['mægət] *n* ver *m*, asticot *m*.

maggoty ['mægətɪ] *adj* véreux, plein de vers.

Magi ['meɪdʒaɪ] *npl Bible* **the Three M.**, les (trois) rois mages *mpl*.

magic ['mædʒɪk] **1** *n* magie *f*, enchantement *m*; **like m., as if by m.**, comme par enchantement; **some of the m. had gone out of his marriage**, son mariage avait perdu un peu de son charme; **black/white m.**, magie noire/blanche. **2** *adj* **(a)** magique, enchanté; **m. carpet**, tapis volant; **m. lantern**, lanterne *f* magique; *Math* **m. square**, carré *m* magique; **m. wand**, baguette *f* magique; **(b)** *Br Sl* (*excellent*) génial, super; **(that'd be) m.!**, génial!

▶**magic away** *vtsep* (*pt & pp* **magicked**) faire disparaître comme par magie.

magical ['mædʒɪkəl] *adj* magique.

magically ['mædʒɪklɪ] *adv* magiquement; (*to disappear*) (comme) par enchantement.

magician [mə'dʒɪʃən] *n* magicien, -ienne.

magisterial [mædʒɪs'tɪərɪəl] *adj* **(a)** (*air, ton*) magistral, -aux; (*air*) de maître; **(b)** *Jur* de magistrat.

magistrate ['mædʒɪstreɪt] *n* magistrat *m*, juge *m*; **police-court m.**, juge d'instance; **magistrates' court**, ≈ tribunal *m* d'instance.

magma ['mægmə] *n* magma *m*.

Magna Carta ['mægnə'kɑːtə] *n Eng Hist* la Grande Charte (de l'année 1215).

magnanimity [mægnə'nɪmɪtɪ] *n* **(a)** (*generosity*) magnanimité *f*, générosité *f*; **(b)** (*nobility*) grandeur *f* d'âme.

magnanimous [mæg'nænɪməs] *adj* **(a)** (*generous*) magnanime; **(b)** (*noble*) **to be m.**, faire preuve de grandeur d'âme.

magnanimously [mæg'nænɪməslɪ] *adv* (*see adj*) **(a)** magnanimement; **(b)** noblement.

magnate ['mægneɪt] *n* magnat *m* (*de l'industrie etc*).

magnesia [mæg'niːʃə] *n* **(a)** *Ch* magnésie *f*; **(b)** *Pharm* magnésie blanche; **milk of m.**, magnésie hydratée.

magnesium [mæg'niːzɪəm] *n Ch* magnésium *m*.

magnet ['mægnɪt] *n* aimant *m*; (*electromagnet*) électro-aimant *m*, *pl* électro-aimants; **horseshoe m.**, aimant en fer à cheval; *Fig* **the caves have become a m. for tourists**, les grottes attirent les touristes (comme un aimant).

magnetic [mæg'netɪk] *adj* **(a)** (*attraction, field, pole etc*) magnétique; **m. needle**, aiguille aimantée; **m. north**, nord *m* magnétique; *Med* **m. resonance imaging**, imagerie *f* par résonance magnétique; *Comptr* **m. strip** *or* **tape**, bande *f* magnétique; *Comptr* **m. card**, carte *f* magnétique; **m. card/character reader**, lecteur *m* de cartes/caractères magnétiques; **m. tape unit** *or* **drive**, dérouleur *m* de bande magnétique; **(b)** (*personality*) magnétique, hypnotique.

magnetically [mæg'netɪklɪ] *adv* magnétiquement.

magnetism ['mægnɪtɪzəm] *n* magnétisme *m*.

magnetization [mægnɪtaɪ'zeɪʃən] *n Phys* aimantation *f*, magnétisation *f*.

magnetize ['mægnɪtaɪz] **1** *vt* **(a)** aimanter (*une aiguille etc*); **(b)** *Fig* magnétiser, attirer (*qn*) (par magnétisme personnel). **2** *vi* (*of iron etc*) s'aimanter.

magnetizing ['mægnɪtaɪzɪŋ] *adj* (*courant, champ etc*) magnétisant.

magneto [mæg'niːtəʊ] *n El* magnéto *f*.

magneto-electric [mægniːtəʊɪ'lektrɪk] *adj Phys* magnéto-électrique.

magnificat [mæg'nɪfɪkæt] *n Rel* magnificat *m*.

magnification [mægnɪfɪ'keɪʃən] *n Opt etc* grossissement *m*, grandissement *m*; **high m.**, fort grossissement.

magnificence [mæg'nɪfɪsəns] *n* magnificence *f*.

magnificent [mæg'nɪfɪsənt] *adj* magnifique; (*repas*) somptueux.

magnificently [mæg'nɪfɪsəntlɪ] *adv* magnifiquement.

magnifier ['mægnɪfaɪər] *n* verre grossissant.

magnify ['mægnɪfaɪ] *vt* **(a)** grossir, agrandir (*une image*); amplifier (*un son*); grossir, exagérer (*un incident*); **(b)** *Rel Arch* magnifier (*le Seigneur*).

magnifying ['mægnɪfaɪɪŋ] *n Opt etc* grossissement *m*, amplification *f*; **m. power**, pouvoir grossissant, grossissement (*d'une lentille, d'un objectif*); **m. glass**, loupe *f*.

magnitude ['mægnɪtjuːd] *n* grandeur *f*, importance *f*; *Astron* magnitude *f*; *Math* grandeur, valeur *f*; *Astron* **star of the first m.**, étoile *f* de première magnitude; *Fig* **of the first m.**, de premier ordre.

magnolia [mæg'nəʊlɪə] *n* **m. (tree)**, magnolia *m*, magnolier *m*.

magnum, *pl* **-ums** ['mægnəm, -əmz] *n* magnum *m* (*de champagne etc*).

magpie ['mægpaɪ] *n* (*bird*) pie *f*; *F Fig* (*chatterbox*) bavard, -e, pie; (*hoarder*) thésauriseur, -euse.

Magyar ['mægjɑːr] **1** *adj* magyar. **2** *n* Magyar, -are.

maharajah [mɑːhə'rɑːdʒə] *n* maharajah *m*.

maharani [mɑːhə'rɑːniː] *n* maharani *f*.

mahogany [mə'hɒgənɪ] *n* **(a)** (*tree*) acajou *m*; **(b)** (*wood*) (bois *m* d')acajou *m*; **m. table**, table *f* en acajou.

Mahometan [mə'hɒmətən] *adj & n Old-fashioned* musulman, -ane, mahométan, -ane.

maid [meɪd] *n* **(a)** (*servant*) bonne *f*, domestique *f*; **lady's m.**, femme *f* de chambre; **m. of all work**, bonne à tout faire; **m. of honour**, demoiselle *f* d'honneur (*de la reine*); *Am* (*at wedding*) première demoiselle d'honneur; **(b)** *Arch Lit* (*girl*) jeune fille *f*; (*virgin*) vierge *f*; **the M. of Orleans**, la Pucelle (d'Orléans); **old m.**, vieille fille; **to remain an old m.**, rester vieille fille.

maiden ['meɪd(ə)n] *n Lit* (*girl*) jeune fille *f*; (*virgin*) vierge *f*; **m. aunt**, tante non mariée; **m. name**, nom *m* de jeune fille; **m. voyage/flight**, premier voyage/vol; **m. speech**, premier discours; discours de début (*d'un député*).

maidenhair ['meɪd(ə)nheər] *n* **m. (fern)**, adiante *m*, cheveu *m* de Vénus.

maidservant ['meɪdsɜːvənt] *n Arch* domestique *f*.

mail¹ [meɪl] *n* **(a)** (*letters, parcels*) courrier *m*; **it came in the m.**, c'est arrivé au courrier; **incoming/outgoing m.**, courrier (à l')arrivée/(au) départ; *Am* **m. drop**, boîte *f* aux lettres; *Comptr* **m. merge**, publipostage *m*; **(b)** (*postal service*) poste *f*; **m. van**, *Rail* wagon-poste *m*, *pl* wagons-poste; *Aut* voiture *f ou* fourgon *m* des postes; **m. train**, train-poste *m*; *Com* **m. order**, commande *f* par correspondance; **m. order catalogue**, catalogue *m* de vente par correspondance; **m. order company**, société *f* de vente par correspondance; **(c)** *Arch* (*vehicle*) malle *f*, malle-poste *f*, *pl* malles-poste(s); **m. coach**, malle-poste.

mail² *vt esp Am* envoyer par la poste, expédier (*des lettres, des paquets*); mettre (*une lettre*) à la poste.

mail³ *n* (*armour*) mailles *fpl*; **coat of m.**, cotte *f* de mailles.

mailbag ['meɪlbæg] *n* sac postal, sac de dépêches.

mailbox ['meɪlbɒks] *n Am* boîte *f* aux lettres; *Comptr* **electronic m.**, boîte aux lettres électronique.

mailing ['meɪlɪŋ] *n* (*of letter etc*) mise *f* à la poste; **m. list**, mailing *m*, liste *f* de diffusion.

mailman, *pl* **-men** ['meɪlmən] *n Am* facteur *m*.

mailshot¹ ['meɪlʃɒt] *n* publipostage *m*.

mailshot² *vt* envoyer un publipostage à.

maim [meɪm] *vt* estropier, mutiler (*qn*).

main¹ [meɪn] *n* **(a)** (*pipe, cable etc*) canalisation maîtresse *ou* principale; *El* câble *m* de distribution; **(b) mains**, (*network*) secteur *m*; **the house hasn't been connected to the mains**, la maison n'a pas été raccordée au secteur; **electric mains**, canalisations *fpl* électriques; **gas mains**, conduites *fpl* de gaz; **water mains**, canalisations *ou* conduites d'eau; **mains electricity**, courant *m* secteur; **mains water**, eau *f* de ville; *Rad* **mains set**, poste *m* secteur; **(c) in the m.**, (*on the whole*) en général, en gros, en somme, généralement (parlant); **(d)** (*strength*) **with might and m.**, de toutes mes *ou* ses *etc* forces; **(e)** *Nau* grand mât.

main² *adj* principal, -aux, premier, -ière, essentiel, -elle; **m. body**, gros *m* (*de l'armée, de la flotte etc*); **our m. concern**, notre préoccupation majeure; *Agr* **m. crop**, culture principale; **m. entrance**, entrée principale; **m. point** *or* **thing**, l'essentiel, le principal; **m. idea**, idée *f* mère (*d'une œuvre etc*); *Gram* **m. clause**, proposition principale; *Culin* **m. course** *or* **dish**, plat *m* de résistance; **m. road**, grande route; **m. street**, *Am F* **m. drag**, rue principale; **m. sewer**, égout collecteur; *Rail etc* **m. line**, voie principale, grande ligne; *Nau* **m. masts**, les mâts majeurs; **m. deck**, pont principal, premier pont.

mainbrace ['meɪnbreɪs] *n Nau* grand bras de vergue; *Old-fashioned F* **to splice the m.**, boire un coup.

mainframe ['meɪnfreɪm] *n Comptr* ordinateur central.

mainland ['meɪnlænd] *n* continent *m*; **the French m., the m. of France**, la France continentale.

mainline ['meɪnlaɪn] *vi F* (*of drug user*) se piquer, se piquouser.

mainliner ['meɪnlaɪnər] *n F* (*drug addict*) = drogué(e) qui se fait des piqûres intraveineuses.

mainly ['meɪnlɪ] *adv* principalement, surtout; **the tourists come m. from Australia,** les touristes viennent pour la plupart d'Australie; **the passengers were m. old men,** la plupart des passagers étaient des vieux messieurs; **a m. Spanish-speaking population,** une population à majorité hispanophone; **their diet consists m. of insects,** ils se nourrissent essentiellement d'insectes.

mainmast ['meɪnmɑːst, -məst] *n Nau* grand mât.

mainsail ['meɪnseɪl, 'meɪns(ə)l] *n Nau* grand-voile *f*, *pl* grand(s)-voiles.

mainsheet ['meɪnʃiːt] *n Nau* grand-écoute *f*, *pl* grand-écoutes.

mainspring ['meɪnsprɪŋ] *n* **(a)** grand ressort; ressort moteur (*d'une pendule etc*); **(b)** (*motive*) mobile essentiel; (*cause*) cause principale.

mainstay ['meɪnsteɪ] *n* **(a)** *Nau* étai *m* de grand mât; **(b)** (*of economy*) soutien principal; (*of family*) soutien; point *m* d'appui (*d'une cause*).

mainstream ['meɪnstriːm] **1** *n* courant principal; **the m. of French tradition,** l'axe de la tradition française; **a writer who has moved away from the m.,** un auteur qui s'est écarté du courant principal. **2** *adj* **m. Hollywood movies,** films dans la grande tradition hollywoodienne; *Mus* **m. jazz,** = style de jazz entre le traditionnel et le moderne; **m. politics,** les courants politiques dominants.

maintain [meɪn'teɪn] *vt* **(a)** (*keep in good condition*) entretenir (*une route, une machine*); **(b)** (*keep in existence*) entretenir (*une armée*); **(c)** (*keep up*) maintenir (*l'ordre, la discipline*); soutenir (*une lutte, la conversation etc*); entretenir (*des relations etc*); conserver (*la santé*); garder, observer (*une attitude, le silence*); **to m. speed,** conserver l'allure; **(d)** (*support*) entretenir, soutenir, nourrir (*une famille etc*); **(e)** (*defend*) soutenir, défendre (*une cause*); **(f)** (*hold on to*) garder (*un avantage*); *Mil etc* se maintenir dans, tenir (*une position*); **(g)** (*express*) soutenir (*une opinion, un fait*); **to m. that ...,** maintenir *ou* soutenir *ou* prétendre que ...; **he maintains that he is innocent,** il affirme qu'il est innocent.

maintenance ['meɪntɪnəns] *n* **(a)** *Tech* (*of car*) entretien *m*; conservation *f*, maintenance *f* (*du matériel, des routes etc*); *Rail Tel etc* surveillance *f* (*des voies, des lignes*); **m. contract,** contrat *m* de maintenance; *Tel* **m. department,** service *m* de surveillance des lignes; **m. engineer,** ingénieur *m* d'entretien; **m. handbook,** manuel *m* d'entretien; **m. kit,** trousse *f* d'entretien; **m. vehicle,** camion-atelier *m*, *pl* camions-ateliers; **(b)** maintien *m* (*de l'ordre, de qn dans un emploi*); *Com* **resale price m.,** prix imposés; **(c)** entretien *m* (*d'une famille, des troupes etc*); *Jur* pension *f* alimentaire; *Admin Fin* alimentation *f*, financement *m* (*d'un fonds, d'une caisse*); *Sch* **m. grant,** bourse *f* d'entretien; *Jur* **m. order,** obligation *f* alimentaire; **(d)** défense *f* (*de ses droits*).

maintop ['meɪntɒp] *n Nau* grand-hune *f*, *pl* grand-hunes.

maison(n)ette [meɪzə'net] *n* (appartement *m*) duplex *m*.

maître d' [metrə'diː] *n esp Am* (*in restaurant*) maître *m* d'hôtel.

maize [meɪz] *n esp Br* maïs *m*.

Maj *Mil abbr* **major**.

majestic [mə'dʒestɪk] *adj* majestueux, auguste; (*bearing*) plein de majesté.

majestically [mə'dʒestɪklɪ] *adv* majestueusement.

majesty ['mædʒəstɪ] *n* majesté *f*; **God in all His m.,** Dieu dans toute sa majesté; **His M. (the King),** Sa Majesté le Roi; **Her M. (the Queen),** Sa Majesté la Reine; **Your M.,** Votre Majesté; **on His** *or* **Her M.'s Service,** (pour le) service de Sa Majesté (≈ service de l'État); (*on envelope*) ≈ en franchise.

Maj Gen *Mil abbr* **major general**.

major¹ ['meɪdʒər] *n Mil* commandant *m*, chef *m* de bataillon (*d'infanterie*); chef d'escadron (*de cavalerie etc*); **m. general,** général *m* de division.

major² **1** *adj* (*big*) grand; (*main*) le plus grand; (*company*) de première importance, de premier ordre; (*distinction, improvement, changes, difficulties*) de taille, grand; (*problem, cause, concern, interest, new novel*) & *Mus* majeur; (*accident, disaster*) grand; **the m. brands,** les marques les plus importantes; **it's a m. brand,** c'est une des marques les plus importantes; **the m. teams,** les plus grandes équipes; **it's of m. importance,** c'est de la plus haute importance; **the significance of this is quite m.,** la signification de ceci est de tout premier ordre; **the party was a m. disaster,** la fête a été une catastrophe absolue; **any problems? — nothing m.,** des problèmes? — rien d'important; **he's our m. programmer,** c'est notre programmeur principal; **we invested in a m. way,** nous avons investi de manière considérable; **he's taken up Spanish in a m. way,** il s'est mis à fond à l'espagnol; **he's fallen for Susie in a m. way,** il est follement *ou* complètement tombé amoureux de Susie; **the m. portion,** la majeure partie, la plus grande partie; **the m. prophets,** les grands prophètes; **m. decision,** décision capitale; **m. illness,** maladie *f* grave; *Mil* **m. offensive,** vaste offensive *f*; *Mus* **m. key,** ton *ou* mode majeur; *Aut* **m. road,** route principale *ou* à priorité; *Am Sp* **m. league,** première division; *Old-fashioned Br Sch* **Martin m.,** Martin aîné, l'aîné des deux Martin.

2 *n* **(a)** *Jur* (*person*) majeur, -eure;

(b) (*in logic*) majeure *f*;

(c) *US Univ* matière principale (*d'un étudiant*); **philology m.,** (*student*) étudiant, -ante en philologie.

major³ *vi Sch US* **to m. in a subject,** se spécialiser dans un sujet; **to m. in English,** ≈ faire sa licence d'anglais.

Majorca [mə'jɔːkə] *n* Majorque *f*.

Majorcan [mə'jɔːkən] **1** *adj* majorquin. **2** *n* Majorquin, -ine.

major-domo, *pl* **-os** [meɪdʒə'dəʊməʊ, -əʊz] *n* major-dome *m*.

majorette [meɪdʒə'ret] *n Am* **(drum) m.,** majorette *f*.

majority [mə'dʒɒrɪtɪ] *n* **(a)** majorité *f* (*des voix*); la plus grande partie, le plus grand nombre (*des hommes etc*); **absolute m.,** majorité absolue; **a two-thirds m.,** une majorité de deux tiers; **to be in a** *or* **the m.,** être en majorité, avoir la majorité; **elected by a m.,** élu à la pluralité des voix; **by an overwhelming m.,** en nombre écrasant; **in the m. of cases,** dans la majorité des cas; *Fin* **m. holding,** participation *f* majoritaire; **m. party,** parti *m* majoritaire; *Jur* **m. verdict,** verdict *m* de la majorité (*du jury*); **(b)** *Jur* majorité *f*; **to attain one's m.,** atteindre sa majorité, devenir majeur; **(c)** *Mil* grade *m* de commandant.

make¹ [meɪk] *n* **(a)** *Com Ind* marque *f* (*d'un produit*); **cars of all makes,** voitures de toutes marques; **what m. is it?,** c'est quelle marque?; **(b)** (*construction*) façon *f*, fabrication *f*, construction *f*; **of French m.,** de fabrication française; **(c)** caractère *m*, aspect *m* (*de qn*); **(d)** *F* **to be on the m.,** (*financially*) chercher à faire fortune par tous les moyens; (*sexually*) draguer; **(e)** *El* fermeture *f* (*du circuit*); **at m.,** en circuit.

make² *v* (*pt & pp* **made** [meɪd]) **1** *vt* **(a)** (*construct, produce, prepare etc*) faire; construire (*une machine, une boîte etc*); fabriquer, faire (*du papier etc*); effectuer, faire (*un versement, une transaction*); opérer (*un changement*); faire (*un discours, des excuses etc*); commettre, faire (*une erreur*); **God made man,** Dieu a créé l'homme; **the water had made a hole in the rock,** l'eau avait percé la roche; **they seem made for each other,** ils semblent faits l'un pour l'autre; *Knitting* **to m. one/two,** faire un jeté simple/double; **bread is made of flour,** le pain est fait de farine; **the chair is made of wood,** la chaise est en bois; **what is it made of?,** en quoi est-ce?, c'est en quoi?; **to show what one is made of,** donner sa mesure; **I'm not made of money,** je ne suis pas millionnaire; **to m. one's will,** faire son testament; **to m. a bed/the tea,** faire un lit/le thé; **to m. trouble,** provoquer le désordre; (*causing problems*) causer des ennuis (**for s.o.,** à qn); **they made room for one more on the sofa,** ils se sont poussés pour (lui) faire une place sur le canapé; **to m. time to do sth,** trouver le temps de faire qch; **to m. a noise,** faire du bruit; **to m. peace,** faire *ou* conclure la paix; **I m. the rules around here,** ici, c'est moi qui dirige; **to m. a distinction,** faire une distinction; **to m. an attempt to do sth,** essayer de faire qch; **to m. love/war,** faire l'amour/la guerre; **to m. one's escape,** s'échapper, se sauver; **to m. believe,** faire semblant;

(b) (*form*) établir, assurer (**a connection between ...,** le raccordement de ...); *El* (*of contact points*) fermer (*le circuit*); **two and two m. four,** deux et deux font quatre; **they m. a handsome couple,** ils font un beau couple;

(c) (*gain*) faire (*de l'argent*); **to m. £400 a week,** gagner *ou* se faire 400 livres par semaine; **to m. one's fortune,** faire fortune; *F* **to m. a bit on the side,** se faire de la gratte; **to m. a name for oneself,** se faire un nom; **to make an enemy of s.o.,** se faire un ennemi de qn; *Cards* **to m. a trick,** faire une levée;

(d) (*cause to be successful*) faire la fortune de (*qn*); **this book made her** *or* **her name,** ce livre l'a rendue célèbre; **this will m. him or break him,** cela sera ou son succès ou sa ruine; **it made my day,** ça m'a fait très plaisir; **it**

makes all the difference, ça change tout;

(e) (*cause to be*) **to m. s.o. happy/rich,** rendre qn heureux/riche; **to m. s.o. hungry/sleepy,** donner faim/sommeil à qn; **to m. s.o. angry,** fâcher qn; **to m. s.o. one's heir,** constituer qn son héritier; **to m. sth known,** faire connaître qch; **to m. oneself heard,** se faire entendre; **to m. oneself ill,** se rendre malade; **to m. oneself tired,** se fatiguer;

(f) (*cause, compel to do*) **to m. s.o. speak/sleep,** faire parler/dormir qn; **I made him stop,** je l'ai forcé à s'arrêter; **her remarks made me feel more cheerful,** ses remarques m'ont remonté le moral; **m. them see how important it is,** montrez-leur combien c'est important; **what made you say that?,** qu'est-ce qui vous a fait dire cela?; **you can't m. me!,** tu ne peux pas me forcer!; **you MADE me!,** (*do it*) tu m'y a obligé *ou* forcé!;

(g) (*estimate, calculate*) estimer; **what time do you m. it?,** quelle heure avez-vous?; **I m. it five kilometres,** je pense que ça fait cinq kilomètres;

(h) (*reach*) arriver à (*un port etc*); **will we m. the airport in time?,** est-ce que nous arriverons à temps à l'aéroport?; **we'll m. Newport before lunch,** nous serons à Newport avant le déjeuner; **he'll be lucky to m. 50,** il aura de la chance s'il atteint 50 ans; **to m. twenty knots,** (*of ship*) faire vingt nœuds;

(i) *F* (*manage to attend on, at*) se débrouiller pour être là; **can you m. Friday?,** tu peux te libérer vendredi?;

(j) *F* (*establish as*) **let's m. it a day everyone can come,** autant s'arranger pour que tout le monde soit libre ce jour-là; **can we m. it your place?,** est-ce qu'on peut faire ça chez toi?; **better m. it** *or* **that TWO lemonades,** disons deux limonades;

(k) (*become, be*) être; **she'd m. a good diver/singer,** elle ferait une bonne plongeuse/chanteuse; **you'll never m. a diver/singer,** tu ne seras jamais plongeur/chanteur;

(l) (*have sexual intercourse with*) se faire;

(m) *F* **to m. it,** (*arrive in time*) arriver à temps; (*finish in time*) finir à temps; (*be successful*) réussir; (*manage to attend*) se libérer; (*have sexual intercourse*) s'envoyer en l'air; **we'll never m. it,** (*by that time*) nous n'y arriverons jamais; **I made it home for lunch,** je suis arrivé à la maison (à temps) pour le déjeuner; **to m. it in politics,** réussir dans la politique; **I can't m. it on Tuesday,** je ne peux pas me libérer mardi;

(n) to make do, (*cope*) se débrouiller; **we'll just have to m. do,** (*with what we have*) il va falloir faire avec; **we could m. do with ten,** (*though we should have more*) nous pourrions nous débrouiller avec dix; **we'll have to m. the milk do,** il faut nous contenter du peu de lait que nous avons; **I'll just have to m. that do,** il va falloir que je fasse avec.

2 *vi* **(a)** (*act*) **to m. as if** *or* **as though to do sth,** s'apprêter à *ou* faire mine de faire qch; (*pretend*) faire semblant de faire qch; **he made as if to speak,** il a eu l'air de vouloir parler; **she made (as if) to get up,** elle a fait mine de se lever;

(b) (*go*) **he made towards the bar,** il s'est dirigé vers le bar;

(c) (*of tide*) se faire; (*of floodtide*) monter; (*of ebb*) baisser;

(d) *El* (*of current*) **to m. and break,** s'interrompre et se rétablir.

►make away *vi* = **MAKE OFF.**

►make away with *vipo F* **(a)** (*take away*) faire disparaître, enlever (*qch*); **(b)** (*steal*) voler (*de l'argent*); **(c)** (*kill*) tuer, supprimer (*qn*); **to m. away with oneself,** se suicider.

►make for *vipo* **(a)** (*head towards*) se diriger vers (*un endroit, la porte*); **where are you making for?,** où allez-vous?; **the crowd made for the square,** la foule s'est portée vers la place; *Nau* **to m. for ...,** faire route sur ..., mettre le cap sur ...; **ship making for Hull,** navire *m* à destination de Hull; **(b)** (*contribute to*) contribuer à (*le bonheur etc*); **these agreements m. for peace,** ces accords favorisent la paix.

►make of *vipo* **(a)** (*understand*) comprendre; **I don't know what to m. of that remark,** je ne sais pas comment interpréter cette remarque; **what do you m. of her?,** qu'est-ce que tu penses d'elle?; **we couldn't m. much of what he said,** nous n'avons pas compris grand-chose à ce qu'il a dit; (*hear*) nous n'avons pas entendu grand-chose à ce qu'il a dit; **(b)** (*attach importance to*) attacher de l'importance à qch; **you're making too much of this,** tu y attaches trop d'importance; **the Press has made a lot of this visit,** la presse a fait beaucoup de bruit autour de cette visite; **the prosecution made much of this fact,** l'accusation a fait grand cas de ce fait; **to m. much** *or* **a lot of,** (*be attentive to*) être toujours après (*qn*), être aux petits soins pour *ou* auprès de (*qn*); câliner, choyer (*un enfant etc*); (*flatter*) flatter (*qn*).

►make off *vi F* (*leave*) décamper, filer; **the thieves made off in a van.,** les bandits se sont enfuis dans une camionnette.

►make off with *vipo F* (*take, steal*) **to m. off with the cash,** filer avec l'argent; **somebody's made off with my overcoat,** on m'a volé *ou* chipé mon pardessus.

►make out 1 *vtsep* **(a)** (*write*) faire, établir, dresser (*une liste etc*); dresser, rédiger (*un mémoire*); établir, dresser, relever (*un compte*); établir (*un chèque*) (*au nom de qn*); **who do I m. it out to?,** (*the cheque*) je le mets à quel ordre?;

(b) *F* (*claim*) faire croire; **she made out she knew them personally,** elle a fait croire qu'elle les connaissait personnellement; **to m. s.o. out to be richer than he is,** faire qn plus riche qu'il ne l'est; **she's not such a fool as people m. out,** elle n'est pas aussi bête qu'on le dit; **he made me out to be a miser,** il a décrété que j'étais avare;

(c) (*usu with neg*) (*understand, decipher*) comprendre (*une énigme, un problème*); démêler (*les raisons de qn, la signification de qch*); déchiffrer (*une écriture*); débrouiller (*une affaire*); **I can't m. the boy out,** ce garçon est une énigme pour moi; **I can't m. it out,** je ne m'y retrouve pas, je n'y comprends rien;

(d) (*discern*) distinguer, discerner (*qch*);

(e) (*conclude*) **how do you m. that out?,** comment arrivez-vous à ce résultat *ou* à cette conclusion?

2 *vi* **(a)** *F* (*succeed*) réussir, faire son chemin, faire des progrès; **he's making out very well,** il fait de bonnes affaires; **how is she making out at her new school?,** comment ça marche dans sa nouvelle école?;

(b) *Am Sl* (*kiss, fondle*) se peloter; (*have sexual intercourse*) faire l'amour.

►make over *vtsep* (*transfer*) céder, transférer, transmettre (**sth to s.o.,** qch à qn); **she has made the estate over to her granddaughter,** elle a cédé la propriété à sa petite-fille.

►make up 1 *vtsep* **(a)** (*invent*) inventer, forger (*une histoire, des excuses*); **he's making the whole thing up,** ce qu'il dit est inventé de toute pièce;

(b) (*compensate for*) combler, suppléer à (*un déficit*); combler (*une perte*); **we made up the time,** nous avons rattrapé notre retard; **to m. up lost ground,** regagner le terrain perdu; **I'll m. it up to you,** (*for forgetting your birthday etc*) je me rattraperai; (*for helping me*) je te rendrai ça;

(c) (*complete*) compléter, parfaire (*une somme*); **we need two more players to m. up the team,** il nous faut deux joueurs de plus pour compléter l'équipe; **another two players would m. it up to 11,** avec deux joueurs de plus, on arriverait à onze; **I was only invited to m. up the numbers,** je n'ai été invité que pour faire nombre; **to m. up the difference,** parfaire la différence; **I'll make your savings up to the price of a new bike,** je mettrai au bout de tes économies pour que tu puisses acheter un nouveau vélo;

(d) (*form*) constituer; **all the elements that go to m. up a happy marriage,** tout ce qui contribue à faire un bon mariage; **the community is made up primarily of old people,** cette communauté est constituée essentiellement de personnes âgées; **to m. up one's mind,** se décider; **I'll m. up your mind for you,** je vais décider pour toi;

(e) (*prepare, put together*) dresser (*une liste*); faire (*un paquet*); *Pharm* préparer, exécuter (*une ordonnance*); *Com Sewing* faire, confectionner, façonner (*des vêtements*); *Com* **to m. up orders,** préparer des commandes; *Com Sewing* **customer's own material made up,** on travaille à la façon; **to m. up a bed,** faire un lit; **to m. up the fire,** préparer le feu; (*add fuel*) alimenter le feu;

(f) (*in bookkeeping*) régler, établir, arrêter (*un compte*); régler, balancer (*les livres*); **to m. up one's accounts,** vider ses comptes;

(g) (*apply make-up to*) maquiller; **to m. one's face** *or* **oneself up,** se maquiller; **the actors are being made up,** les acteurs se font maquiller;

(h) to make it up, (*settle quarrel*) se réconcilier.

2 *vi* **(a)** (*end quarrel*) se réconcilier;

(b) (*catch up*) rattraper; **he's making up on the leaders,** il rattrape ceux qui sont en tête;

(c) *Typ* mettre en pages;

(d) (*of actor etc*) se maquiller.
►**make up for** *vipo* compenser (*ses pertes*); rattraper, réparer (*le temps perdu*); **that makes up for it,** c'est une compensation; **to m. up for the lack of sth,** suppléer au manque de qch; **how can I m. up for forgetting your birthday?,** comment puis-je me faire pardonner d'avoir oublié ton anniversaire?; **what she lacks in skill she makes up for in enthusiasm,** son manque de savoir-faire est compensé par son enthousiasme.
►**make up to** *vipo* (*make advances to*) faire des avances *ou* faire la cour à qn; (*flatter*) flatter qn.
►**make with** *vipo Am Sl* **(a)** (*produce*) faire; **to m. with the music,** faire de la musique; **m. with the French fries,** (*to waiter etc*) dépêche-toi de servir les frites; (*to cook*) dépêche-toi de faire les frites; **(b)** (*use*) se servir de; **he made with the food mixer,** il s'est servi du mixeur.
make-and-break ['meɪkən'breɪk] *n El* conjoncteur-disjoncteur *m*, *pl* conjoncteurs-disjoncteurs; *Aut* dispositif *m ou* levier *m* de rupture.
make-believe ['meɪkbɪliːv] **1** *n* semblant *m*, feinte *f*, trompe-l'œil *m inv*; **that's all m.-b.,** tout cela est (de la) pure fantaisie; **the land of m.-b.,** le pays des chimères. **2** *adj* **a m.-b. world,** un monde imaginaire.
makefast ['meɪkfɑːst] *n Nau* amarre *f*.
maker ['meɪkər] *n* **(a)** faiseur, -euse; *Com Ind* fabricant *m* (*de drap etc*); constructeur *m* (*de machines*); **(b)** *Rel* **our M.,** le Créateur; **he's gone to meet his M.,** il est monté au ciel; **that's between you and your M.,** ça c'est entre toi et le Seigneur.
make-ready ['meɪkredɪ] *n Typ* mise *f* en train.
makeshift ['meɪkʃɪft] **1** *n* (*solution etc*) expédient *m*; (*object*) moyen *m* de fortune. **2** *adj* de fortune; **a m. clotheshorse,** un séchoir artisanal; **m. equipment,** installation *f* de fortune.
make-up ['meɪkʌp] *n* **(a)** (*cosmetics*) maquillage *m*; (*blusher, eyeshadow, foundation*) fard *m*; **to wear m.-up,** se maquiller; **to put m.-up on,** se maquiller; **m.-up bag,** trousse *f* à maquillage; *Th etc* **m.-up box,** boîte *f* à maquillage; **m.-up remover,** démaquillant *m*; *Th etc* **m.-up man,** maquilleur *m*; **m.-up girl,** maquilleuse *f*; **(b)** (*composition*) composition *f*, arrangement *m* (*de qch*); confection *f* (*des vêtements*); (*of person*) caractère *m*; **(c)** *Typ* mise *f* en pages, imposition *f*; **(d)** *US Sch* examen *m* de rattrapage.
makeweight ['meɪkweɪt] *n* bouche-trou *m*; **they only asked me to join the team as a m.,** ils ne m'ont demandé d'entrer dans l'équipe que parce qu'ils avaient besoin d'un bouche-trou.
making ['meɪkɪŋ] *n* fabrication *f* (*de la toile, du papier*); confection *f*, façon *f* (*de vêtements*); construction *f* (*d'un pont, d'une machine*); création *f* (*d'un poste*); **this failure was the m. of him,** cet échec a réformé son caractère; **history in the m.,** l'histoire en train de se faire; *El* **m. and breaking,** fermeture *f* et ouverture *f* (*du circuit*).
makings ['meɪkɪŋz] *npl* **to have the m. of ...,** avoir tout ce qu'il faut pour devenir ...; **he has the m. of a statesman,** il a l'étoffe d'un homme d'État.
malachite ['mæləkaɪt] *n Miner* malachite *f*.
maladjusted [mælə'dʒʌstɪd] *adj Psy* inadapté, -ée.
maladjustment [mælə'dʒʌstmənt] *n* **(a)** *Psy* inadaptation *f*; **emotional m.,** déséquilibre émotif; **(b)** *MecE* défaut *m* d'ajustage, mauvais réglage; *El Electron* déréglage *m* (*d'un appareil*).
maladministration [mælədmɪnɪs'treɪʃən] *n* mauvaise administration; mauvaise gestion (*des affaires publiques etc*).
maladroit [mælə'drɔɪt] *adj* maladroit.
maladroitly [mælə'drɔɪtlɪ] *adv* maladroitement.
malady ['mælədɪ] *n Fml* mal *m*, maladie *f*.
malaise [mæ'leɪz] *n* malaise *m*.
malaria [mə'leərɪə] *n Med* malaria *f*, paludisme *m*; **to have m.,** avoir la malaria.
malarial [mə'leərɪəl] *adj* paludéen; **m. fever,** fièvre paludéenne, paludisme *m*.
Malawi [mə'lɑːwɪ] *n* **(a)** (*country*) Malawi *m*; **(b)** (*person*) Malawi *mf inv*.
Malay [mə'leɪ] **1** *adj* malais; **the M. Peninsula,** la presqu'île malaise. **2** *n* **(a)** Malais, -aise; **(b)** *Ling* malais *m*.
Malaya [mə'leɪə] *n* Malaisie *f*.
Malayan [mə'leɪən] **1** *adj* malais. **2** *n* Malais, -aise.
Malaysia [mə'leɪzɪə] *n* Malaysia *f*.
malcontent ['mælkəntent] *adj & n* mécontent, -ente.
male [meɪl] **1** *adj* (*enfant, hormone, fleur etc*) mâle; (*sexe*) masculin; *Tech* (*vis*) mâle; **m. chauvinism,** machisme *m*; **m. chauvinist,** phallocrate *m*, macho *m*; *F* **m. chauvinist pig,** macho; **a m. friend,** un ami; **m. nurse,** infirmier *m*; **m. line (of descent),** ligne masculine; **m. menopause,** andropause *f*. **2** *n* mâle *m*.
malediction [mælɪ'dɪkʃən] *n Fml* malédiction *f*.
malefactor ['mælɪfæktər] *n* malfaiteur, -trice.
malevolence [mə'levələns] *n* malveillance *f* (**towards,** envers).
malevolent [mə'levələnt] *adj* malveillant.
malevolently [mə'levələntlɪ] *adv* avec malveillance; (*regarder*) d'un œil malveillant.
malformation [mælfɔː'meɪʃən] *n Med etc* malformation *f*, difformité *f*.
malformed [mæl'fɔːmd] *adj* difforme.
malfunction¹ [mæl'fʌŋkʃən] *n* fonctionnement défectueux *ou* irrégulier (*d'un mécanisme, d'un organe*); dérèglement *m* (*d'une balance*).
malfunction² *vi* mal fonctionner.
Mali ['mɑːlɪ] *n* (*country*) Mali *m*.
Malian ['mɑːlɪən] **1** *adj* malien. **2** *n* Malien, -ienne.
malice ['mælɪs] *n* **(a)** malice *f*, méchanceté *f*; **out of m.,** par malice, par méchanceté; **to bear m. to** *or* **towards s.o., to bear s.o. m.,** vouloir du mal à qn, en vouloir à qn; **(b)** *Jur* intention criminelle *ou* délictueuse; **with m. aforethought,** avec intention criminelle, avec préméditation.
malicious [mə'lɪʃəs] *adj* **(a)** méchant, malveillant; **(b)** *Jur* fait avec intention criminelle *ou* délictueuse, criminel; **m. intent,** intention délictueuse.
maliciously [mə'lɪʃəslɪ] *adv* **(a)** (*to say, do*) avec méchanceté *ou* malveillance; **(b)** *Jur* avec intention criminelle, avec préméditation.
malign¹ [mə'laɪn] *adj* (*thing*) pernicieux, nuisible.
malign² *vt* calomnier, diffamer (*qn*); dire du mal de (*qn*); **much maligned man,** homme calomnié.
malignancy [mə'lɪgnənsɪ] *n* **(a)** (*of person*) malignité *f*, méchanceté *f*; **(b)** *Med* malignité *f*, virulence *f* (*d'une maladie*).
malignant [mə'lɪgnənt] *adj* **(a)** (*person*) malveillant, méchant; **(b)** *Med* (*tumour etc*) malin, *f* maligne.
malignantly [mə'lɪgnəntlɪ] *adv* avec malveillance, méchamment.
malinger [mə'lɪŋgər] *vi* faire le malade, simuler une maladie, *F* tirer au flanc.
malingerer [mə'lɪŋgərər] *n* faux malade, simulateur *m*, *F* tireur *m* au flanc.
malingering [mə'lɪŋgərɪŋ] *n* simulation *f* (de maladie).
mall [mɔːl] *n* **(a)** (*avenue*) mail *m*, promenade publique; **(b)** *Com* **(shopping) m.,** centre commercial (*fermé à la circulation automobile*); **(c)** *Arch* (*game*) (jeu *m* de) mail *m*.
mallard ['mælɑːd] *n* (*duck*) colvert *m*.
malleability [mælɪə'bɪlɪtɪ] *n* (*of person, metal*) malléabilité *f*.
malleable ['mælɪəb(ə)l] *adj* (*person, metal*) malléable.
mallet ['mælɪt] *n* **(a)** (*hammer*) (*small*) maillet *m*; (*large*) mailloche *f*; **(b)** *Sp* maillet *m* (*de croquet, de polo*).
mallow ['mæləʊ] *n* (*plant*) mauve *f*.
malnutrition [mælnjuː'trɪʃən] *n* malnutrition *f*; (*lack of food*) sous-alimentation *f*.
malodorous [mæ'ləʊdərəs] *adj* malodorant.
malpractice [mæl'præktɪs] *n* **(a)** *Jur* (*in professional life*) malversation *f*; négligence *f*, incurie *f* (*d'un médecin*); *esp Am Med* **m. suit,** poursuites *fpl* judiciaires pour négligence; *esp Am Med* **m. insurance,** = assurance souscrite pour parer à des poursuites judiciaires pour négligence; **(b)** (*misdeed*) méfait *m*.
malt¹ [mɔːlt] *n* malt *m*; **m. extract,** extrait *m* de malt; **m. liquor,** bière *f*; **m. (whisky),** whisky *m* de malt.
malt² **1** *vt* (*in brewing*) malter (*l'orge*); **malted milk,** lait malté. **2** *vi* (*of grain*) se convertir en malt.
Malta ['mɔːltə] *n* Malte *f*.
Maltese [mɔːl'tiːz] **1** *adj* maltais; **M. cross,** croix *f* de Malte. **2** *n* **(a)** (*person*) Maltais, -aise; **(b)** *Ling* maltais *m*.
malting ['mɔːltɪŋ] *n* **(a)** (*activity*) maltage *m*; **(b)** (*building*) malterie *f*.
maltreat [mæl'triːt] *vt* maltraiter, malmener (*qn*); maltraiter, déshonorer (*un tableau, un arbre etc*).
maltreatment [mæl'triːtmənt] *n* mauvais traitement.
mam(m)a *n* **(a)** ['mæmə, *Old-fashioned* mə'mɑː] (*mother*) maman *f*; **(b)** ['mæmə] *Am Sl* (*young woman*) nana *f*.
mammal ['mæməl] *n* mammifère *m*.
mammalian [mæ'meɪlɪən] *adj & n* mammifère *m*.
mammaries ['mæmərɪz] *npl* **the m.,** les (glandes *fpl*) mammaires *fpl*.
mammary ['mæmərɪ] *adj Anat* mammaire; **m. glands,** glandes *fpl* mammaires.
mammography [mæ'mɒgrəfɪ] *n Med* mammographie *f*.

Mammon ['mæmən] *n Bible* Mammon *m*; *Fig* **the worship of M.,** l'adoration *f* du Veau d'or.

mammoth ['mæməθ] **1** *n* mammouth *m*. **2** *adj* énorme, gigantesque, colossal.

mammy ['mæmɪ] *n* **(a)** *F* (*mother*) maman *f*; **(b)** *Old-fashioned US* (*black maid, nurse*) bonne *f* d'enfants noire.

man¹, *pl* **men** [mæn, men] *n* **(a)** (*adult male*) homme *m*; *esp Lit* **I've known him m. and boy,** je le connais depuis toujours; **a game that sorts the men from the boys,** un jeu qui distingue les hommes des gamins; **he isn't m. enough to tell me,** il n'est pas assez fort pour me le dire; **men and women,** les hommes et les femmes; **men,** (*on public convenience*) hommes; *Com* **men's department,** rayon *m* hommes; **soap for men,** savon homme; **m. for m.,** homme pour homme; **to make a m. of s.o.,** faire un homme de qn; **he took it like a m.,** il a pris ça courageusement; **to talk to s.o. m. to m.,** parler à qn d'homme à homme; **tell me, m. to m.,** dis-moi, entre nous; **he's just the m. for me,** c'est l'homme qu'il me faut; **to be one's own m.,** être son maître, ne dépendre de personne; **a m.'s m.,** un homme plus à l'aise avec les hommes; **a m. about town,** un homme en vue; **what does the m. in the street think?,** que pense l'homme de la rue?; **come here, young m.!,** venez ici jeune homme!; (*to child*) viens ici mon petit!; **good m.!,** bravo mon vieux!; **an old m.,** un vieillard; **an ambitious m.,** un ambitieux; **a dead m.,** un mort; **an Oxford m.,** (*man from Oxford*) un originaire *ou* un habitant d'Oxford; (*student*) un étudiant de l'Université d'Oxford; (*graduate*) un Oxfordien; **I'm a whisky m. myself,** moi, c'est le whisky que je préfère; **he's a three-pints-a-day m.,** il boit ses trois pintes par jour; **odd-job m.,** homme à tout faire; *F* **the weather m.,** Monsieur Météo; **m. and wife,** mari et femme; **to live as m. and wife,** vivre maritalement; *F* **my old m.,** (*husband*) mon mari, mon homme; (*father*) mon père, mon vieux; *F* **the old m.,** (*boss*) le vieux; (*father*) le vieux, le paternel; *Old-fashioned* **my young m.,** (*sweetheart*) mon amoureux; (*fiancé*) mon fiancé; **m. of God,** homme d'église; **m. Friday,** *Liter* Vendredi *m*; *Fig* homme à tout faire;

(b) *esp US Sl* **hey m.!,** (*hello*) salut mon pote!; (*as interjection*) mec!; **m., am I tired,** bon sang, qu'est-ce que je suis crevé; **you should have seen it, m.,** bon sang tu aurais dû voir ça;

(c) (*individual*) homme *m*; **the rights of m.,** les droits de l'homme; **iron age m.,** homme de l'âge de fer; **any m.,** n'importe qui; **few men,** peu de gens; **the inner m.,** *Rel* l'homme intérieur; *Hum* l'estomac *m*; **every m. jack,** tous sans exception; **they replied as one m.,** ils répondirent d'une seule voix; **they were patriots to a m.,** ils étaient tous patriotes;

(d) (*humanity*) l'homme *m*; **m. proposes, God disposes,** l'homme propose et Dieu dispose; **m. does not live by bread alone,** on ne se nourrit pas que de pain;

(e) (*employee etc*) (*manservant*) domestique *m*, valet *m*; *Hist* (*vassal*) homme *m*; *Ind etc* **employers and men,** les patrons *mpl* et les ouvriers; **our m. in Rome,** *Journ* notre correspondant à Rome; *Com* notre représentant à Rome; *Mil* **officers and men,** officiers *mpl* et hommes de troupe;

(f) *Sp* (*player*) joueur *m*; *Cr* **twelfth m.,** le joueur de réserve;

(g) (*in chess*) pièce *f*; (*in draughts*) pion *m*;

(h) (*black American slang*) **the M.,** (*whites*) les Blancs; (*police*) les flics *mpl*; (*drug peddler*) le dealer.

man² *vt* (**-nn-**) fournir du personnel à (*une organisation etc*); être affecté à (*une organisation etc*); assurer le fonctionnement de (*une machine*); assurer la manœuvre de (*un appareil*); être membre de l'équipe de (*un avion etc*); *Mil* occuper, garnir (*un fort etc*); *Nau* armer, équiper (*un canot*); **to m. a gun,** servir *ou* manœuvrer une pièce d'artillerie; **to m. the barricades,** défendre les barricades; **to m. the pumps,** armer les pompes; **the plane was manned by a crew of three men,** l'avion avait une équipe de trois hommes; **was the spaceship manned?,** y avait-il des hommes à bord du vaisseau spatial?; **someone has to be there to m. the phone,** quelqu'un doit être là pour répondre au téléphone; **who's manning reception today?,** qui assure la réception aujourd'hui?; **reception wasn't manned at the time,** personne n'assurait *ou* n'était à la réception à ce moment-là; **the machines had to be manned all the time,** les machines devaient être sans cesse assistées.

Man [mæn] *n* **the Isle of M.,** l'île *f* de Man.

-man [mæn] *suff* **two-m. toboggan,** luge *f* à deux places; **five-m. crew,** équipage *m* de cinq hommes.

manacle¹ ['mænək(ə)l] *n* (*usu pl*) **manacles,** (*for wrists*) menottes *fpl*; (*for ankles*) entraves *fpl*.

manacle² *vt* mettre les menottes à (*qn*); **manacled to the wall,** attaché au mur par des menottes.

manage ['mænɪdʒ] **1** *vt* **(a)** (*run*) diriger (*une société, une usine, un projet etc*); gouverner (*une banque*); régir (*une propriété*); gérer (*l'économie, son argent, des ressources*); **to m. s.o.'s affairs,** gérer les affaires de qn; **managed fund,** (*in insurance*) fonds géré; **to m. a pop-singer/football team,** être manager d'un chanteur de pop/d'une équipe de football;

(b) (*deal with*) **to know how to m. s.o.,** savoir prendre qn;

(c) (*be able to*) **to m. to do sth,** (*contrive*) s'arranger pour faire qch; (*succeed*) arriver *ou* parvenir à faire qch, trouver moyen de faire qch; **we managed to persuade her,** nous avons réussi à la persuader; **I think I can m. it,** je crois que je pourrai le faire; **I shall never m. to learn it,** jamais je n'arriverai à l'apprendre; **how do you m. not to dirty your hands?,** comment faites-vous pour ne pas vous salir les mains?;

(d) (*be able to produce, consume, carry etc*) **£100 is the most that I can m.,** 100 livres c'est tout ce que je peux offrir *ou* payer; **can you m. a few more cherries?,** pouvez-vous manger encore quelques cerises?; **I can't m. Friday,** (*I'm not free*) je ne peux pas me libérer vendredi; **I can't m. three suitcases,** je ne peux pas porter trois valises; **can you m. the stairs?,** (*carrying so much, being elderly etc*) est-ce que tu arrives à monter les escaliers?

2 *vi* **she manages well,** elle sait s'y prendre; **can you m.?,** (*with all those suitcases etc*) tu y arriveras?; **we shall m. better next time,** nous ferons mieux la prochaine fois; **he'll m. all right,** il se débrouillera; **we could just m.,** (*financially*) on avait juste de quoi vivre.

manageable ['mænɪdʒəb(ə)l] *adj* **(a)** (*thing*) maniable; (*canoe*) manœuvrable; (*hair*) facile à coiffer; **the smaller suitcase was a more m. size,** la valise plus petite était plus maniable; **(b)** (*person*) maniable, traitable, docile; **(c)** (*undertaking*) praticable, faisable; **(d)** (*company*) dirigeable.

management ['mænɪdʒmənt] *n* **(a)** (*of company, factory, project etc*) direction *f*; (*of economy, money, resources*) gestion *f*; **business m.,** gestion des affaires; **bad m.,** mauvaise organisation; **under new m.,** (*change of ownership*) changement *m* de propriétaire; (*change of manager*) nouvelle direction; **m. accounts,** comptes *mpl* de gestion; **m. consultant,** conseil *m* en gestion; **m. consultancy,** (*activity*) conseils pour la gestion (d'entreprise); (*firm*) cabinet *m* (de) conseils; **m. fee,** honoraires *mpl* consultant; **m. skills,** qualités *fpl* de gestionnaire; **m. style,** mode *m* de gestion; **(b)** (*with sing or pl verb*) (*managers, employers*) l'administration *f*, la direction; **senior m.,** les cadres supérieurs, la Direction; **representatives of m. and unions,** des représentants du patronat et des syndicats; **m. buy-out,** = rachat d'une société par la direction; **m. information system,** système intégré de gestion.

manager ['mænɪdʒər] *n* **(a)** (*of bank, company, factory, project*) directeur *m*; (*of café, bar, store*) gérant *m*; (*of department in large store*) chef *m*; (*of funds, money*) gestionnaire *m*; administrateur *m* (*de biens*); régisseur *m* (*d'une propriété*); (*of entertainer, rock band etc*) manager *m*; *US Pol* chef (*d'un parti politique*); (*of home*) ménager, -ère; **I want to see the m.!,** je veux voir le responsable!; **general m.,** directeur général; **sales m.,** directeur commercial; **personnel m.,** chef *ou* directeur du personnel; **she's a good m.,** (*of home etc*) elle est bonne ménagère; **he's a poor m. of money,** il gère mal son argent; **(b)** *Jur* **receiver and m.,** administrateur *m* (*d'une faillite etc*); (*of bankrupt*) syndic *m* de faillite.

manageress [mænɪdʒə'res] *n* directrice *f*, gérante *f*.

managerial [mænɪ'dʒɪərɪəl] *adj* directorial, -aux; (*poste*) de commande; **at m. level,** au niveau de la direction; **m. staff,** les cadres *mpl*; **m. skills,** qualités *fpl* de gestionnaire.

managing ['mænɪdʒɪŋ] *adj* directeur, -trice; **m. director,** président-directeur général.

manatee [mænə'tiː] *n Zool* lamantin *m*.

Manchuria [mæn'tʃʊərɪə] *n* Mandchourie *f*.

Manchurian [mæn'tʃʊərɪən] **1** *adj* mandchou. **2** *n* Mandchou, -oue.

Mancunian [mæŋ'kjuːnɪən] **1** *n* habitant, -ante de Manchester; (*by birth*) originaire *mf* de Manchester. **2** *adj* de Manchester.

mandarin¹ ['mændərɪn] *n* **(a)** *Chinese Hist* mandarin *m*; **nodding m.,** (*toy*) branle-tête *m inv*; **m. collar,** (*on dress etc*) col chinois, col officier; **(b)** *F* (*powerful official*) mandarin *m.*

mandarin², mandarine ['mændəri:n] *n* **(a)** (*fruit*) mandarine *f*; (*tree*) mandarinier *m*; **(b)** (*colour*) mandarine *f inv*; **m. wallpaper,** papier peint couleur mandarine.

Mandarin ['mændərın] *Ling* **1** *n* mandarin *m.* **2** *adj* **M. Chinese,** mandarin *m.*

mandate ['mændeıt] *n* **(a)** (*instructions*) *& Pol* mandat *m*; **the government has a m. to ...,** le gouvernement est mandaté pour ...; **(b)** (*territory*) mandat *m.*

mandatory ['mændətərı] *adj* **(a)** (*obligatory*) obligatoire; **(b)** *Jur* mandataire; **m. writ,** mandement *m.*

mandible ['mændıb(ə)l] *n* **(a)** (*of insect*) mandibule *f*; **(b)** (*of vertebrate*) mâchoire inférieure.

mandolin(e) ['mændəlın] *n Mus* mandoline *f.*

mandrake ['mændreık] *n* (*plant*) mandragore *f.*

mandrel, mandril ['mændrəl] *n MecE* mandrin *m*, arbre *m* (de tour).

mandrill ['mændrıl] *n* (*ape*) mandrill *m.*

mane [meın] *n* (*of horse, lion etc*) *& Fig* crinière *f.*

man-eater ['mæni:tər] *n* (*pl* **man-eaters**) **(a)** (*animal*) mangeur *m* d'hommes; **not all sharks are m.-eaters,** tous les requins ne mangent pas les hommes; **(b)** (*cannibal*) anthropophage *m*, cannibale *m*; *Fig* (*woman*) mangeuse *f* d'hommes.

man-eating ['mæni:tıŋ] *adj* **(a)** (*animal etc*) mangeur d'hommes; **m. shark,** requin bleu, mangeur *m* d'hommes; **(b)** (*tribe etc*) anthopophage, cannibale.

maneuver, maneuvrable *etc US* = **MANOEUVRE, MANOEUVRABLE** *etc.*

manful ['mænfʊl] *adj* vaillant, courageux, hardi.

manfully ['mænfʊlı] *adv* vaillamment, courageusement, hardiment; **he was struggling m. with the suitcases/his second steak,** il se démenait vaillamment avec les valises/son deuxième steak.

manganese [mæŋgə'ni:z] *n Miner Ch* manganèse *m*; **m. steel,** acier *m* au manganèse.

mange [meındʒ] *n Vet* gale *f* (*du chien etc*).

mangel-wurzel ['mæŋg(ə)l'wɜ:z(ə)l] *n* betterave *f* fourragère.

manger ['meındʒər] *n* mangeoire *f*, auge *f* d'écurie; *Bible* crèche *f*; *F* **he's a dog in the m.,** il fait l'empêcheur de tourner en rond.

mangle¹ ['mæŋg(ə)l] *n* (*for clothes*) essoreuse *f* (à rouleaux).

mangle² *vt* essorer (*le linge*) (*dans une essoreuse à rouleaux*).

mangle³ *vt* **(a)** (*mutilate*) déchirer, lacérer, mutiler (*qn, les membres de qn*); charcuter, massacrer (*un morceau de viande*); **their bodies were horribly mangled,** leurs corps ont été atrocement mutilés; **(b)** *Fig* mutiler, déformer (*un mot*); estropier (*une citation*); mutiler, dénaturer (*un texte*).

mango, *pl* **-oes** ['mæŋgəʊ, -əʊz] *n* (*fruit*) mangue *f*; (*tree*) manguier *m*; **m. chutney,** condiment *m* à la mangue.

mangrove ['mæŋgrəʊv] *n* **m. (tree),** manglier *m*, palétuvier *m*; **m. swamp,** mangrove *f.*

mangy ['meındʒı] *adj* **(a)** (*dog*) galeux; **(b)** *F* (*furniture etc*) minable, miteux.

manhandle ['mænhænd(ə)l] *vt* **(a)** (*move by hand*) manutentionner (*des marchandises etc*); transporter, déplacer (*qch*) à la force des bras; **(b)** (*treat roughly*) brutaliser, malmener (*qn*).

manhole ['mænhəʊl] *n* trou *m* d'homme (*de chaudière*); trou de visite, regard *m* (*d'égout*); **m. cover** *or* **lid,** plaque *f* d'égout.

manhood ['mænhʊd] *n* **(a)** (*maturity*) âge *m* d'homme, âge viril; **to reach m.,** devenir un homme; **(b)** (*masculinity*) virilité *f*; **he felt he had to prove his m.,** il pensait devoir prouver sa virilité; **(c)** (*men*) les hommes *mpl*; **British m.,** les hommes britanniques; **(d)** *Hum* (*genitals*) les valseuses *fpl.*

man-hour ['mænaʊər] *n Ind etc* heure-homme *f*, *pl* heures-hommes.

manhunt ['mænhʌnt] *n* chasse *f* à l'homme.

mania ['meınıə] *n* **(a)** (*passion*) passion *f* (*de qch*); **to have a m. for sth,** avoir une obsession pour qch; **(b)** *Med* manie *f*; (*violent*) folie furieuse; **persecution m.,** manie *ou* folie de la persécution; **suicidal m.,** folie du suicide.

maniac ['meınıæk] *n Med* fou furieux, folle furieuse; *Psy* maniaque *mf*; *F* fou, folle; **sex m.,** obsédé sexuel; *F* **a m. driver,** un fou du volant; *F* **a soccer maniac,** un fou de football.

maniacal [mə'naıək(ə)l] *adj* (*laughter etc*) dément.

manic ['mænık] *adj Psy* (*désir etc*) qui tient de la folie; *Fig* **she made m. gestures,** elle faisait des gestes irraisonnés; **at a m. speed,** à une vitesse folle; **m. depression,** psychose maniaque dépressive.

manic-depressive ['mænıkdı'presıv] *adj & n Psy* maniaco-dépressif, -ive.

manicure¹ ['mænıkjʊər] *n* manucure *f*, soin *m* des mains; **to have a m.,** se faire soigner les mains; **to give s.o. a m.,** faire une manucure à qn; **how much is a m.?,** combien coûte une manucure?; **m. set,** trousse *f* de manucure.

manicure² *vt* soigner les mains de (*qn*), faire les mains *ou* les ongles à (*qn*), faire une manucure à (*qn*); **to m. one's nails,** se faire les ongles.

manicurist ['mænıkjʊərıst] *n* manucure *mf.*

manifest¹ ['mænıfest] *adj* manifeste, évident; **to make sth m.,** manifester qch.

manifest² *n* (*document*) *Nau* manifeste *m* (*d'entrée, de sortie*); *Av* état *m* de chargement.

manifest³ **1** *vt* **(a)** (*display*) manifester, témoigner; **to m. itself,** (*of symptom etc*) se manifester, se révéler; **(b)** *Nau* faire figurer (*une marchandise*) sur le manifeste. **2** *vi* (*of ghost, spirit*) se manifester.

manifestation [mænıfes'teıʃən] *n* manifestation *f.*

manifestly ['mænıfestlı] *adv* manifestement; **this was m. not true,** manifestement, ce n'était pas vrai.

manifesto [mænı'festəʊ] *n Pol etc* manifeste *m*, proclamation *f*, déclaration publique.

manifold ['mænıfəʊld] **1** *adj* (*diverse*) divers, varié, de diverses sortes; (*numerous*) multiple, nombreux. **2** *n Phil* diversité *f*; *Tech* tubulure *f*, collecteur *m.*

Manil(l)a [mə'nılə] *n* Manille *f*; **m. rope,** (cordage *m* en) manille *f*; **m. envelope/paper,** enveloppe *f*/papier *m* kraft.

manioc ['mænıɒk] *n* **(a)** *Bot* manioc *m*; **(b)** *Culin* cassave *f.*

manipulate [mə'nıpjʊleıt] *vt* **(a)** (*handle, operate etc*) manipuler (*un objet*); manœuvrer, actionner (*un dispositif mécanique*); agir sur (*un levier, une pédale*); *Med* **to m. bones,** manipuler les articulations; **(b)** *Pej* manipuler (*qn, des comptes*); *St Exch* **to m. the market,** agir sur le marché, travailler le marché.

manipulation [mənıpjʊ'leıʃən] *n* **(a)** (*of object*) manipulation *f*; **(b)** *Pej* manipulation *f*; *St Exch* agiotage *m.*

manipulative [mə'nıpjʊlətıv] *adj* rusé; **m. child,** un enfant roublard.

manipulator [mə'nıpjʊleıtər] *n* **(a)** *Pej* tripoteur *m*; *St Exch* agioteur *m*; **(b)** (*of machine etc*) manipulateur *m.*

Man(it) *abbr* **Manitoba.**

mankind [mæn'kaınd] *n* **(a)** le genre humain, l'humanité *f*, l'espèce humaine; **(b)** (*men*) les hommes *mpl.*

manlike ['mænlaık] *adj* d'homme; mâle; (*woman*) hommasse; (*resembling a man*) semblable à un homme.

manliness ['mænlınıs] *n* caractère viril; virilité *f.*

manly ['mænlı] *adj* (*sport, activity*) d'homme; (*behaviour, character*) mâle, viril.

man-made ['mænmeıd] *adj* artificiel, synthétique; **m.-m. laws,** les lois faites par l'homme; **m.-m. fibres,** fibres *fpl* synthétiques.

manna ['mænə] *n* **(a)** *Bible etc* manne *f*; *Fig* **it was m. from heaven,** cela tombait du ciel; **(b)** *Bot Pharm etc* manne *f* du frêne.

manned [mænd] *adj* (*spacecraft, flight*) habité; *see also* **MAN².**

mannequin ['mænıkın] *n* (*person, dummy*) *& Art* mannequin *m.*

manner ['mænər] *n* **(a)** (*way, method, style*) manière *f*, façon *f* (*de faire qch*); **the m. in which ...,** la manière dont ...; **in a m. of speaking,** en quelque sorte, dans un certain sens; *Gram* **adverb of m.,** adverbe *m* de manière; **he does it (as (if)) to the m. born,** il le fait comme s'il était né pour cela;

(b) (*bearing*) maintien *m*, tenue *f*, air *m*, abord *m*; **I do not like his m.,** je n'aime pas son attitude; **she's got a very abrasive m.,** elle est très acerbe;

(c) (*custom*) (*usu pl*) **manners,** mœurs *fpl*, usages *mpl* (*d'un peuple*);

(d) (*etiquette*) **manners,** manières *fpl*; **bad manners,** mauvaises manières, manque *m* de savoir-vivre, manque d'éducation; **it is bad manners to stare,** il est mal élevé de dévisager les gens; **(good) manners,** bonnes manières, savoir-vivre *m*, politesse *f*; **to teach s.o. manners,** donner à qn une leçon de politesse *ou* de bienséance; **where are your manners?,** (*to child*) c'est comme ça qu'on se tient?, en voilà une tenue!; **he's got no manners,** il ne sait pas se tenir;

(e) (*variety*) espèce *f*, sorte *f*; **all m. of people/things,** toutes sortes de gens/choses; *Lit* **what m. of person is she?,** quel genre de femme est-elle?; **by no m. of means, not by any m. of means,** absolument pas; **they're not**

rich by any m. of means, not by any m. of means are they rich, ils ne sont absolument pas riches.

mannered ['mænəd] *adj Art Lit* maniéré; *Pej* (*person*) affecté; (*style*) recherché, précieux.

mannerism ['mænərɪzəm] *n* **(a)** *Pej* (*of person*) maniérisme *m*, affectation *f*; *Art Lit* maniérisme; **(b)** (*of writer etc*) particularité *f*.

mannerly ['mænəlɪ] *adj* poli, courtois.

man(n)ikin ['mænɪkɪn] *n* **(a)** (*small man*) petit homme; (*dwarf*) nabot *m*; **(b)** *Art Med Surg* mannequin *m*.

mannish ['mænɪʃ] *adj* (*woman*) hommasse; **to be m. in one's dress,** s'habiller d'une manière masculine.

manoeuvrable, *US* **maneuvrable** [mə'nuːvrəb(ə)l] *adj* (*avion etc*) manœuvrable, maniable.

manoeuvre¹, *US* **maneuver** [mə'nuːvər] *n* **(a)** *Mil Nau etc* (*action*) manœuvre *f*; **encircling/evasive m.,** manœuvre d'encerclement/de dérobement; **manoeuvres,** (*exercise*) manœuvres; **troops on manoeuvres,** troupes en manœuvre; **(b)** (*action, remark*) manœuvre *f*; **a clever m.,** une manœuvre habile; **the two cars were very close and there wasn't much room for m.,** les deux voitures étaient très proches et il n'y avait pas beaucoup de place pour faire une manœuvre; *Fig* **there is some room for m. in the negotiations,** ces négociations laissent une certaine marge de manœuvre; *Pej* **manoeuvres,** menées *fpl*, intrigues *fpl*.

manoeuvre², *US* **maneuver 1** *vt* manœuvrer, faire manœuvrer (*une armée, une flotte*); **to m. s.o. into a corner,** acculer qn dans un coin; *Fig* prendre qn au piège, *F* coincer qn. **2** *vi* (*of troops, Fig of politician etc*) manœuvrer; *Nau* (*of ship*) évoluer.

manoeuvring, *US* **maneuvering** [mə'nuːvrɪŋ] *n* manœuvres *fpl*.

man-of-war, *pl* **men-of-war** ['mænəv'wɔːr,'men-] *n* **(a)** *Nau Arch* vaisseau *m ou* bâtiment *m* de guerre; **(b)** **(Portuguese) m.-of-w.,** (*jellyfish*) physalie *f*, galère *f*.

manor ['mænər] *n* **(a)** *Hist* seigneurie *f*; **the lord/lady of the m.,** le châtelain/la châtelaine; **m. (house),** manoir *m*; **(b)** *Br Sl* (*police district*) fief *m*.

manorial [mə'nɔːrɪəl] *adj* seigneurial, -aux.

manpower ['mænpaʊər] *n* **(a)** *Ind etc* (*labour*) main-d'œuvre *f*; *Mil* effectifs *mpl*; **shortage of m.,** crise *f* de main-d'œuvre *ou* d'effectifs; **m. planning,** planification *f* de la main-d'œuvre; **(b)** *MecE* la force des bras.

mansard ['mænsɑːd] *n* **m. (roof),** toit *m* en mansarde.

manse [mæns] *n esp Scot Rel* maison *f* du pasteur.

manservant, *pl* **menservants** ['mænsɜːvənt, 'mensɜːvənts] *n* domestique *m*; (*personal*) valet *m* (de chambre).

mansion ['mænʃən] *n* (*in country*) château *m*; (*in town*) hôtel *m* (particulier); **m. (house),** manoir *m*, château *m*.

mansize(d) ['mænsaɪz, -d] *adj* de la grandeur d'un homme; *Fig* (*handkerchief, helping of food etc*) qui convient à un homme.

manslaughter ['mænslɔːtər] *n Jur* (*through negligence*) homicide *m* involontaire *ou* par imprudence; (*not premeditated*) homicide sans préméditation.

mantel ['mænt(ə)l] *n* = **MANTELPIECE**.

mantelpiece ['mænt(ə)lpiːs] *n* **(a)** (*shelf*) dessus *m ou* tablette *f* de cheminée; **(b)** (*frame*) manteau *m ou* linteau *m ou* chambranle *m* de cheminée.

mantilla [mæn'tɪlə] *n* mantille *f*.

mantis ['mæntɪs] *n* (*insect*) mante *f*; **praying m.,** mante religieuse, prie-Dieu *f inv*.

mantle ['mænt(ə)l] *n* (*covering*) manteau *m* (*de lave, de neige*); *Tech* manchon *m* (*de bec de gaz*); *Constr* parement *m* (*d'un mur*); *Arch* (*cloak*) mante *f*, pèlerine *f* (*de femme*); *Fig* **to take on the m. of office,** assumer les responsabilités qui incombent à un poste.

man-to-man [mæntʊ'mæn] *adj* (*talk*) d'homme à homme.

mantrap ['mæntræp] *n* piège *m* à hommes.

manual ['mænjʊəl] **1** *adj* (*travail, ouvrier etc*) manuel; (*travail*) de manœuvre; **m. typewriter,** machine *f* à écrire mécanique; *Aut* **m. transmission,** transmission *f* mécanique. **2** *n* **(a)** (*handbook*) manuel *m*; **(b)** (*typewriter*) machine *f* à écrire mécanique; (*car*) voiture *f* à embrayage manuel; **to be on m.,** être sur commande manuelle; **(c)** *Mus* clavier *m* (*d'un orgue*).

manually ['mænjʊəlɪ] *adv* manuellement, à la main.

manufacture¹ [mænjʊ'fæktʃər] *n* **(a)** fabrication *f*, élaboration *f* (*d'un produit industriel*); (*of cars, computers*) construction *f*; confection *f* (*de vêtements*); **of Italian m.,** de fabrication italienne; **(b)** (*product*) produit fabriqué *ou* manufacturé.

manufacture² *vt* **(a)** fabriquer (*un produit industriel*); confectionner (*des vêtements etc*); **(b)** *Fig* (*invent*) inventer (de toutes pièces); **to m. an opportunity to do sth,** s'arranger pour faire qch.

manufacturer [mænjʊ'fæktʃərər] *n* fabricant *m*; (*of cars, computers*) constructeur *m*; **send it back to the manufacturers,** renvoyez-le au fabricant; **m.'s recommended price,** prix conseillé par le fabricant.

manufacturing [mænjʊ'fæktʃərɪŋ] **1** *adj* industriel; **the country's m. industry,** le secteur industriel du pays. **2** *n* fabrication *f*; (*of cars, computers etc*) construction *f*; confection *f* (*de vêtements*); **the decline of m.,** le déclin de l'industrie.

manure¹ [mə'njʊər] *n Agr* engrais *m*; **farmyard m.,** fumier *m* (d'étable); **chemical m.,** engrais chimique; **liquid m.,** purin *m*; **m. heap,** tas *m* de fumier.

manure² *vt Agr* fumer, engraisser (*la terre*).

manuscript ['mænjʊskrɪpt] **1** *n* manuscrit *m*; **in m.,** (*book*) sous forme de manuscrit. **2** *adj* manuscrit, écrit à la main.

manway ['mænweɪ] *n US Min* galerie *f* de circulation.

Manx [mæŋks] **1** *adj* de l'île de Man; **M. cat,** chat *m* sans queue de l'île de Man. **2** *n* **(a)** *Ling* mannois *m*; **(b)** (*people*) **the M.,** (*used as pl*) les habitants *m* de l'île de Man.

many ['menɪ] **1** *adj* (*comp* **more,** *superl* **most**) un grand nombre (de); beaucoup (de); bien des; **m. times,** beaucoup de fois, bien des fois; **in m. cases,** dans bien des cas; **for m. years,** pendant de longues années; **m. and varied,** nombreux et très variés; **one of his m. acquaintances,** une de ses nombreuses relations; **like so m. others,** comme tant d'autres; **he told me in so m. words that ...,** il m'a dit en propres termes que ...; **too m. people,** trop de monde; **a card too m.,** une carte de trop; **how m. times?,** combien de fois?; **I have as m. books as you,** j'ai autant de livres que vous; **four accidents in as m. days,** quatre accidents en autant de jours; **a good m. things,** pas mal de choses; **m. a night** *or* **m.'s the night I've done,** maintes nuits j'ai fait; *Prov* **m. hands make light work,** à plusieurs mains l'ouvrage avance vite.

2 *pron* beaucoup; **not m.,** pas beaucoup; **m. of us,** beaucoup d'entre nous; **how m.?,** combien?; **as m. as you like,** autant que vous voulez; **as m. again, as m. more, twice as m.,** deux fois autant; **too m.,** trop; **so m.,** tant.

3 *n* **the m.,** (*used as pl*) la foule, la masse; **the sacrifices made by the few for the m.,** les sacrifices faits par la minorité pour la masse.

many-coloured ['menɪ'kʌləd] *adj* multicolore.

many-sided ['menɪ'saɪdɪd] *adj* **(a)** (*figure*) à plusieurs côtés; **(b)** (*problème*) complexe, compliqué; **(c)** (*personne*) aux talents variés.

Maoist ['maʊɪst] *adj & n Pol* maoïste *mf*.

Maori ['maʊrɪ] **1** *adj* maori. **2** *n* **(a)** Maori, -ie; **(b)** *Ling* maori *m*.

map¹ [mæp] *n* carte *f* (géographique); (*of town*) plan *m*; **relief m.,** carte topographique; *Fig* **it's off the m.,** c'est à l'autre bout du monde; **to put a town on the m.,** mettre une ville en vedette; **this will put us on the m.,** ça va nous faire de la pub; **the village was wiped off the m.,** le village a été rasé; **m. maker,** cartographe *m*; **he's a good m. reader,** il sait bien lire les cartes *ou* les plans; **m. reading,** lecture *f* des cartes; **m. reference,** référence *f* topographique, coordonnées *fpl*.

map² *vt* **(-pp-)** dresser une carte *ou* un plan de (*la région etc*).

▶**map out** *vtsep* tracer (*un itinéraire*); dresser, tracer (*un programme*).

maple ['meɪp(ə)l] *n* **(a)** **m. (tree),** érable *m*; **m. leaf,** feuille *f* d'érable; **m. sugar,** sucre *m* d'érable; **m. syrup,** sirop *m* (de sucre) d'érable; **(b)** (*wood*) (bois *m* d')érable *m*.

mapping ['mæpɪŋ] *n* cartographie *f*; (*act*) levé *m* de carte *ou* de plan.

mar [mɑːr] *vt* **(-rr-)** gâter, gâcher (*le plaisir de qn*); troubler (*la joie de qn*); déparer (*la beauté de qn*); **to make or m. s.o.,** faire la fortune ou la ruine de qn.

marabou ['mærəbuː] *n* (*bird*) marabout *m*.

maraschino [mærəs'kiːnəʊ] *n* marasquin *m*; **m. cherries,** cerises *fpl* au marasquin.

marathon ['mærəθən] *n Sp etc* **m. (race),** marathon *m*; **m. runner,** marathonien *m*; **m. speech,** marathon oratoire; **m. meeting,** conférence-marathon.

maraud [mə'rɔːd] *vi* **to go marauding,** marauder, aller à la maraude.

marauder [mə'rɔːdər] *n* maraudeur, -euse.

marauding [mə'rɔːdɪŋ] **1** *adj* maraudeur, -euse. **2** *n* maraude *f*.

marble¹ ['mɑːb(ə)l] *n* **(a)** (*rock*) marbre *m*; **m. statue,** statue *f* de marbre; **m. floor,** sol *m* de *ou* en marbre; **m.**

cutter, (*person*) marbrier *m*; **m. quarry,** marbrière *f*; **(b)** (*glass ball*) bille *f*; **to play marbles,** jouer aux billes; *F* **she's still got all her marbles,** elle a encore toute sa tête; *F* **to lose one's marbles,** perdre la boule; **(c)** *Art* marbre *m*; **(collection of) marbles,** (collection *f* de) marbres.

marble² *vt* marbrer (*une boiserie etc*); (*in bookbinding*) marbrer, raciner (*les plats*); jasper, marbrer (*les tranches*).

marbled ['mɑːb(ə)ld] *adj* marbré.

marbling ['mɑːblɪŋ] *n* marbrure *f*.

march¹ [mɑːtʃ] *n* **(a)** (*by soldiers etc*) marche *f*; **m. in step,** marche au pas; **m. past,** défilé *m*; **on the m.,** en marche; **it is two days' m. from here,** c'est à deux jours de marche d'ici; **(b)** (*pace*) pas *m*, allure *f*; **quick m.,** pas cadencé; **parade m., slow m.,** pas de parade; **(c)** (*demonstration*) marche *f*, manifestation *f*; **to go on a m.,** participer à une marche; **(d)** (*progress*) marche *f*, progrès *m* (*du temps etc*); **(e)** *Mus* marche *f*; **dead m.,** marche funèbre; **wedding m.,** marche nuptiale.

march² **1** *vi Mil etc* marcher; **to m. off,** se mettre en marche; **to m. by** *or* **past (s.o.),** défiler devant (qn); **quick, m.!,** en avant, marche!; **they marched to the town hall to protest,** ils ont fait une marche de protestation jusqu'à la mairie; **time marches on,** (*I ought to go*) l'heure avance; **she marched into his office,** elle est entrée dans son bureau d'un pas décidé. **2** *vt* faire marcher, mettre en marche (*des troupes*); **he was marched off to prison,** il a été emmené en prison.

March [mɑːtʃ] *n* mars *m*; **in M.,** en mars, au mois de mars; **(on) the first/the seventh of M.,** le premier/le sept mars.

marcher ['mɑːtʃər] *n* **(a)** (*demonstrator*) manifestant, -ante; **peace m.,** marcheur *m* de la paix; **(b)** (*person marching*) marcheur, -euse.

marching ['mɑːtʃɪŋ] *n Mil etc* marche *f*; **in m. order,** en tenue de campagne; (*formation*) en formation de marche; **m. orders,** ordre *m* de mise en route; *Fig F* **to give s.o. their m. orders,** donner son congé à qn, mettre qn à la porte.

marchioness ['mɑːʃənes] *n* marquise *f*.

mare [meər] *n* jument *f*.

mare's-nest ['meəznest] *n* illusion *f*.

margarine [mɑːdʒə'riːn] *n* margarine *f*.

marge [mɑːdʒ] *n Br F* margarine *f*.

margin ['mɑːdʒɪn] *n* **(a)** (*on paper, page etc*) marge *f*, blanc *m*; *Phot* liseré *m* (*d'une épreuve*); **to write sth in the m.,** écrire qch en marge; **there were some notes in the m.,** il y avait quelques notes dans la marge; **m. stop,** (*on typewriter*) margeur *m*; **m. release,** déclenche-marge *m inv*;

(b) (*edge*) bord *m*; lisière *f* (*d'un bois*); bord, rive *f* (*d'un lac etc*); *Biol* marge *f* (*d'une feuille etc*); *Anat* bord, rebord *m* (*d'une cavité, d'un orifice*);

(c) (*space*) marge *f*, écart *m*; *Com Fin* marge; *St Exch* acompte *m* (*versé à un courtier*); **to win by a narrow m.,** (*in race etc*) gagner de justesse; **profit m.,** marge bénéficiaire; **to give s.o. some m.,** accorder quelque liberté à qn; **m. of error,** marge d'erreur; **there is little m. for error,** la marge d'erreur est très faible; *MecE etc* **tolerance/safety m.,** marge de tolérance/sécurité; *Com* **the margins are very tight,** les marges sont très réduites.

marginal ['mɑːdʒɪn(ə)l] **1** *adj* **(a)** marginal, -aux; *Geog* **m. moraine,** moraine marginale; **m. case,** cas *m* limite; *Br Pol* **m. seat,** siège chaudement disputé; *Com etc* **m. profit,** bénéfice marginal; **(b)** (*note*) marginal, en marge; **(c)** (*slight*) léger. **2** *n Pol* siège chaudement disputé.

marginalization [mɑːdʒɪnəlaɪ'zeɪʃən] *n* marginalisation *f*.

marginalize ['mɑːdʒɪnəlaɪz] *vt* marginaliser.

marginally ['mɑːdʒɪn(ə)lɪ] *adv* (*slightly*) légèrement; **the shares were m. lower,** les actions avaient légèrement baissé.

marguerite [mɑːgə'riːt] *n* (*plant*) grande marguerite, marguerite des champs.

Maria [mə'riːə] *n* Maria *f*; *Old-fashioned Br F* **black M.,** [mə'raɪə] panier *m* à salade.

marigold ['mærɪgəʊld] *n* (*plant*) souci *m*; **African m.,** rose *f* d'Inde; **French m.,** œillet *m* d'Inde.

marihuana, marijuana [mærɪ'hwɑːnə] *n* marihuana *f*, marijuana *f*.

marina [mə'riːnə] *n* port *m* de plaisance, marina *f*.

marinade¹ [mærɪ'neɪd] *n Culin* marinade *f*.

marinade², marinate ['mærɪneɪd, -eɪt] *vt Culin* (faire) mariner.

marine [mə'riːn] **1** *adj* (*life, biology*) marin; **m. architect,** ingénieur *m* des constructions navales; **m. engineering,** génie *m* maritime; **m. artist,** peintre *m* de marines; **m. forces,** troupes *fpl* de marine; **m. insurance/risk,** assurance *f*/risque *m* maritime. **2** *n* **(a)** *Mil Nau* (*soldier*) soldat *m* de marine; ≈ fusilier marin; **the Royal Marines, the US M. Corps,** ≈ les fusiliers marins; *F* **tell that to the marines!,** allez raconter ça ailleurs *ou* à d'autres!; **(b)** (*shipping*) marine *f*; **merchant** *or* **mercantile m.,** marine marchande.

mariner ['mærɪnər] *n Old-fashioned Lit Nau* marin *m*.

marionette [mærɪə'net] *n* marionnette *f*.

marital ['mærɪt(ə)l] *adj* **(a)** (*relating to marriage*) matrimonial, -aux; *Admin* **m. status,** situation *f* de famille; **m. obligations,** obligations conjugales; **(b)** *Arch* (*relating to husband*) marital, -aux.

maritime ['mærɪtaɪm] *adj* (*nation, law*) maritime; **m. climate,** climat *m* océanique.

marjoram ['mɑːdʒərəm] *n Bot Culin* marjolaine *f*.

mark¹ [mɑːk] *n* **(a)** (*scratch, stain etc*) marque *f*, trace *f*;

(b) (*trace*) marque *f*, tache *f*, signe *m*, empreinte *f* (*de la souffrance etc*); **to make one's m.,** se faire un nom *ou* une réputation; **he made his m.,** (*because he couldn't write*) il a fait une croix; **years of imprisonment had left their m. on him,** il gardait les traces de ses années d'emprisonnement; **distinguishing m.,** marque distinctive; **identification m.,** marque d'identification; **(assay) m.,** (*on gold, silver*) poinçon *m* de garantie; **punctuation marks,** signes *mpl* de ponctuation; **question m.,** point *m* d'interrogation;

(c) (*sign, proof*) marque *f*, preuve *f*, signe *m*, témoignage *m*; **as a m. of respect,** en signe de respect; **m. of mouth,** (*of horse*) marque d'âge (aux dents);

(d) (*reference on instrument etc*) marque *f*, repère *m*; **reference** *or* **guide m.,** point *m* de repère; *F* **he's not up to the m.,** (*good enough*) il n'est pas à la hauteur; *Br F* **I'm not feeling up to the m.,** je ne suis pas dans mon assiette;

(e) (*target*) but *m*, cible *f*; **to hit the m.,** (*of projectile*) atteindre le but, frapper juste; (*of person*) réussir, tomber *ou* deviner juste; **to miss the m.,** manquer le but; **wide of the m.,** (*far from target*) loin du but; (*far from truth*) loin de la réalité *ou* de la vérité; *F* **an easy m.,** un crédule, une dupe;

(f) *Sch* point *m*, note *f*; **good m.,** bon point; **to get good marks,** avoir de bonnes notes; **she got the highest m.** *or* **marks in the class,** c'est elle qui a eu la *ou* les meilleure(s) note(s) de la classe; **full marks,** (*in a specific subject*) note maximale; **full marks for effort!,** bravo d'avoir essayé!; **bad m., black m.,** mauvais point;

(g) *Nau* amer *m*, point *m* de reconnaissance; (*of a buoy*) voyant *m*; **high-water m.,** niveau *m ou* laisse *f* de la marée haute;

(h) *Sp* ligne *f* de départ; **on your marks! get set! go!,** à vos marques! prêts! partez!; **to be quick off the m.,** (*in race*) démarrer vite; (*to start sth*) se lancer dans qch sans perdre de temps; (*to understand*) avoir l'esprit vif; **to be slow off the m.,** (*in race*) démarrer en douceur; (*to start sth*) prendre son temps pour faire qch; (*to understand*) être lent à la détente; *F* **he wasn't exactly quick off the m. when it came to ordering drinks,** il était plutôt lent à la détente quand il s'agissait de commander les boissons;

(i) *Ind Mil* (*of machine etc*) série *f*; **m. II/III,** série II/III.

mark² *vt* **(a)** (*put mark on*) marquer, chiffrer (*du linge, de l'argenterie etc*); estampiller (*des marchandises*); *Tech* signer (*de la bijouterie etc*); biseauter, piper (*les cartes*); **face marked by** *or* **with smallpox,** visage marqué de *ou* par la petite vérole;

(b) *Com* **to m. (the price of) an article,** mettre le prix à un article; *St Exch* **to m. stock,** coter des valeurs;

(c) *Sch* corriger, noter (*un devoir*); **to m. exam papers,** noter des copies (d'examen); **marked out of 10,** noté sur 10;

(d) (*designate*) **to m. s.o./sth as ...,** désigner *ou* choisir qn/qch pour ...;

(e) (*indicate*) marquer, repérer, indiquer; **to m. a place on the map,** indiquer un lieu sur la carte; **stream that marks the boundary of the estate,** ruisseau qui marque la limite de la propriété; **X marks the spot,** X indique l'endroit;

(f) (*show*) témoigner, montrer (*son approbation, son mécontentement*); accentuer (*le rythme*); **to m. time,** *Mil* marquer le pas; *F* piétiner sur place; attendre; **we're marking time,** on n'avance pas; **to m. an era,** faire époque;

(g) *Sp Fb etc* marquer (*un adversaire*);

(h) (*characterize*) caractériser.

mark³ *n* (*coin*) mark *m*; **gold marks,** marks or.
Mark [mɑːk] *n* Marc *m*; **the Gospel according to Saint M.,** l'évangile selon saint Marc.
▶**mark down** *vtsep* **(a)** *Com* baisser le prix de (*qch*); démarquer (*des marchandises*); **everything has been marked down to half price,** tout a été réduit à moitié prix; **(b)** *Sch* baisser la note de (*une copie*).
▶**mark off** *vtsep* **(a)** (*in surveying*) jalonner (*une ligne, une route*); **to m. off a distance on the map,** (*measure*) mesurer une distance sur la carte; **(b)** (*separate with fence etc*) délimiter (*une zone*).
▶**mark out 1** *vtas* (*distinguish*) distinguer (*qn*) (**from,** de). **2** *vtsep* (*mark with lines*) tracer les lignes de (*un terrain de cricket*).
▶**mark up** *vtsep* **(a)** *Com* élever le prix de (*qch*); **(b)** *Sch* hausser la note de (*une copie*).
markdown ['mɑːkdaʊn] *n Com* réduction *f*.
marked [mɑːkt] *adj* **(a)** (*after accident*) **badly m. face,** visage balafré; **m. cards,** cartes marquées *ou* biseautées; **m. man,** homme marqué (*par ses ennemis*); homme repéré; **he's a m. man,** son sort est réglé; (*he's going to be killed*) c'est un homme mort; **(b)** (*difference*) marqué, prononcé; (*amélioration*) sensible; **strongly m. features,** traits fortement accusés; **a very m. German accent,** un accent allemand très prononcé; **the change is becoming more m.,** le changement s'accentue.
markedly ['mɑːkɪdlɪ] *adv* d'une façon marquée; nettement; **m. better,** nettement meilleur; **m. polite,** d'une politesse marquée.
marker ['mɑːkər] *n* **(a)** (*person*) marqueur, -euse (*de linge, de bétail etc*); (*at games*) marqueur, pointeur *m*; *Mil etc* jalonneur *m*; (*at butts*) marqueur; **(b)** *Ind MecE* (*marking device*) marqueur *m*; (*tool*) marquoir *m*; **m. (pen),** (crayon *m*) marqueur; **(c)** (*indicator*) jalon *m*, repère *m*; (*flag*) fanion *m ou* (*stick*) piquet *m* d'alignement *ou* de jalonnement; *Av etc* (radio)phare *m*, (radio)balise *f*; **boundary m.,** borne *f ou* feu *m* de balisage; balise de délimitation (d'aérodrome); **m. beacon,** (radio)phare de balisage; *Nau* **m. buoy,** bouée *f* de balisage; **(book) m.,** signet *m*.
market¹ ['mɑːkɪt] *n* **(a)** (*collection of stalls*) marché *m*; **open-air m.,** marché en plein air; **covered m.,** halle(s) *f(pl)*, marché couvert; **cattle/fish m.,** marché aux bestiaux/poissons; **m. day,** jour *m* de marché; *esp Br* **m. garden,** jardin maraîcher; *esp Br* **m. gardener,** maraîcher, -ère; *esp Br* **m. gardening,** culture maraîchère, maraîchage *m*; **m. square** *or* **place,** place *f* du marché; **m. town,** ville *f* de marché; *Br* **m. trader,** vendeur qui fait les marchés;
(b) *Com Econ* marché *m*; **commodity m.,** marché des matières premières; **cotton m.,** marché du coton; **the home m.,** le marché intérieur; **foreign m.,** marché extérieur; *Fin St Exch* **foreign exchange m.,** marché des changes; *Fin St Exch* **stock m.,** marché des valeurs, la Bourse (des valeurs); **the Common M.,** le Marché Commun; **black m.,** marché noir; **buyers'/sellers' m.,** marché à la baisse/à la hausse; **to put one's flat on the m.,** mettre son appartement en vente; **the most economical car on the m.,** la voiture la plus économique sur le marché; **to come onto the m.,** arriver sur le marché; **to take sth off the m.,** retirer qch du marché; **to be in the m. for sth,** (*of person*) être acheteur de qch; **to find a m. for sth,** trouver un débouché *ou* des acheteurs pour qch; **there's no m. for these products,** ces produits ne se vendent pas; **m. analysis,** analyse *f* de marché; **m. behaviour,** comportement *m* du marché; **(free) m. economy,** économie *f* de marché; **m. forces,** forces *fpl* du marché; **m. leader,** (*company*) leader *m* du marché; (*product*) produit *m* qui domine le marché; **m. price,** prix courant; **m. research,** étude *f* de marché; **m. share,** part *f* du marché; **m. value,** valeur marchande.
market² *vt* (-t-) vendre, commercialiser (*un produit*).
marketability [mɑːkɪtə'bɪlɪtɪ] *n* fait *m* d'être vendable *ou* commercialisable; **we are doubtful about the m. of these machines,** nous doutons que ces machines soient commercialisables.
marketable ['mɑːkɪtəb(ə)l] *adj* (*goods*) vendable, commercialisable.
marketeer [mɑːkɪ'tɪər] *n* **black m.,** trafiquant *m* du marché noir; *Br* **(pro-) M.,** partisan, -ane du Marché Commun.
market-garden ['mɑːkɪtgɑːd(ə)n] *adj esp Br* **m.-g. produce,** produits maraîchers.
marketing ['mɑːkɪtɪŋ] *n* **(a)** (*buying and selling*) achat *m ou* vente *f* (*de qch*) au marché; **(b)** (*of new product*) commercialisation *f*; **(c)** (*study*) étude *f* des marchés, marketing *m*; **m. campaign,** campagne *f* de marketing; **m. department,** service *m* (de) marketing.
marking ['mɑːkɪŋ] *n* **(a)** marquage *m* (*du linge, du bétail etc*); estampillage *m* (*de marchandises*); poinçonnage *m* (*de l'or, de l'argent etc*); *MecE etc* repérage *m* (*du point mort etc*); **m. ink,** encre *f* à marquer; **(b) markings,** (*distinctive marks*) marques *fpl*; (*on animal*) (*spots*) taches *fpl*; (*stripes*) rayures *fpl*; *Av* **fuselage m.,** cocarde *f*; **(c)** (*stamp*) estampille *f*; **(d)** *Sch* correction *f* (*d'un devoir*); (*work to be marked*) copies *fpl* à corriger.
marksman, *pl* **-men** ['mɑːksmən] *n* tireur d'élite.
marksmanship ['mɑːksmənʃɪp] *n* adresse *f ou* habileté *f* au tir.
mark-up ['mɑːkʌp] *n Com* (*increase*) majoration *f*.
marl [mɑːl] *n Agr* marne *f*; **m. pit,** marnière *f*.
marlin ['mɑːlɪn] *n* (*fish*) poisson *m* épieu.
marline ['mɑːlɪn] *n Nau* lusin *m*.
marlinespike ['mɑːlɪnspaɪk] *n Nau* épissoir *m*.
marly ['mɑːlɪ] *adj* (*sol*) marneux.
marmalade ['mɑːməleɪd] *n Culin* confiture *f* d'oranges.
marmoset ['mɑːməzet] *n* (*animal*) ouistiti *m*, marmouset *m*.
marmot ['mɑːmɒt] *n* (*animal*) marmotte *f*.
maroon¹ [mə'ruːn] *n* **(a)** (*colour*) marron pourpré *inv*, rouge foncé *inv*, bordeaux *m inv*; **a m. blouse,** un chemisier bordeaux; **(b)** (*firework*) fusée *f* à pétard.
maroon² *vt* (*on a desert island*) abandonner (*qn*) (*dans une île déserte*); *Fig* **marooned,** isolé.
marquee [mɑː'kiː] *n* grande tente.
marquess, marquis ['mɑːkwɪs] *n* marquis *m*.
marquetry ['mɑːkɪtrɪ] *n* marqueterie *f*.
marram ['mærəm] *n Bot* **m. grass,** oyat *m*.
marriage ['mærɪdʒ] *n* **(a)** mariage *m*; **a happy m.,** un ménage heureux; **proposal of m.,** demande *f* en mariage; **uncle by m.,** oncle *m* par alliance; **civil m.,** mariage civil; **m. bed,** lit conjugal; **m. ceremony,** cérémonie *f* de mariage; **m. certificate,** *F* **m. lines,** acte *m* de mariage; **m. guidance councillor,** conseiller conjugal; **m. vows,** vœux *mpl* du mariage; **m. settlement,** contrat *m* de mariage; **(b)** *Fig* mariage *m*, union *f* (*entre les choses*); **(c)** *Cards* (*bezique*) mariage *m*.
marriageable ['mærɪdʒəb(ə)l] *adj* (*fille, âge*) nubile; (*fille*) mariable, à marier; **of m. age,** d'âge à se marier.
married ['mærɪd] *adj* marié; **a m. couple,** un ménage; **the young/newly m. couple,** les jeunes/nouveaux mariés; **m. life,** la vie conjugale, le mariage; **m. name,** nom *m* de femme mariée *ou* de mariage; **he's m. to his job,** son travail est sa passion.
marrow ['mærəʊ] *n* **(a)** (*in bone*) moelle *f*; **to be frozen to the m.,** être transi de froid, être glacé jusqu'à la moelle; **(b)** (*essence*) moelle *f*, essence *f* (*de qch*); **(c)** *Br* **(vegetable) m.,** courge *f*.
marrowbone ['mærəʊbəʊn] *n* os *m* à moelle.
marrowfat ['mærəʊfæt] *n* **m. (pea),** pois carré.
marry ['mærɪ] *v* (*pt & pp* **married**) **1** *vt* **(a)** (*get married to*) se marier avec (*qn*), épouser (*qn*); **will you m. me?,** veux-tu m'épouser?; **to get married,** se marier; **(b)** (*of priest, parent*) marier, unir (en mariage); **(c)** (*combine*) marier; *Nau* marier (*deux cordages*). **2** *vi* se marier; **she never married,** elle ne s'est jamais mariée; **to m. for money,** faire un mariage d'argent; **she married into the Smith family/the aristocracy,** elle a épousé un membre de la famille Smith/de l'aristocratie; **to m. again** *or* **a second time,** se remarier; **he says he isn't the marrying kind,** il dit qu'il n'est pas du genre à se marier; **it was a case of 'm. in haste, repent at leisure',** c'était un de ces cas où l'on se marie en vitesse et où l'on passe sa vie à le regretter.
▶**marry off** *vtsep* (*dispose of by marriage*) marier (*qn*).
▶**marry up 1** *vtsep* (*bring two parts together*) joindre. **2** *vi* (*line up, fit*) se joindre; (*of colours*) se marier; **check that the two parts m. up,** vérifier que les deux parties s'ajustent.
marsh [mɑːʃ] *n* marais *m*, marécage *m*; **salt m.,** marais salant; **m. gas,** gaz *m* des marais; **m. marigold,** (*plant*) souci *m* d'eau, populage *m*.
marshal¹ ['mɑːʃəl] *n* **(a)** (*officer*) *Mil* **field m.,** ≈ maréchal (de France); *Mil Av* **M. of the R.A.F.,** ≈ Commandant en Chef des Forces aériennes; **Air Chief M.,** = général d'armée aérienne; **M. of the Diplomatic Corps,** ≈ Chef du Protocole; **(b)** (*in charge of ceremonies*) maître *m* des cérémonies; (*in race, demonstration, march*) membre *m* du service d'ordre; **(c)** *US Jur* = fonctionnaire ayant les attributions d'un shérif; (*police officer*) officier *m* de la police fédérale; **fire m.,** chef *m* du service d'incendie (*dans une région, une usine*).

marshal² *vt* (-ll-, *US* -l-) placer (*des personnes*) en ordre *ou* en rang; *Mil* ranger (*des troupes*); *Rail* classer, trier, manœuvrer (*des wagons*); (*of usher, footman etc*) introduire (**s.o. into a room,** qn dans une salle); **to m. facts,** rassembler des faits et les mettre en ordre.

marshalling, *US* **marshaling** ['mɑːʃəlɪŋ] *n* disposition *f* en ordre (*de personnes, de choses*); *Rail* classement *m*, triage *m* (*des wagons*); *Rail* **m. yard,** gare *f* de triage.

marshland ['mɑːʃlænd] *n* terrain marécageux, marécages *mpl*.

marshmallow [mɑːʃ'mæləʊ] *n* **(a)** *Culin* (pâte *f* de) guimauve *f*; **(b)** (*plant*) guimauve *f*, althée *f*.

marshy ['mɑːʃɪ] *adj* (*sol*) marécageux.

marsupial [mɑː'suːpɪəl] *adj & n* marsupial *m*, -aux.

mart [mɑːt] *n* centre *m* de commerce, marché *m*; **(auction) m.,** salle *f* de vente; **car m.,** marché automobile.

marten ['mɑːtɪn] *n* (*animal*) mart(r)e *f*; **beech** *or* **stone m.,** fouine *f*; **pine m.,** martre des pins; martre commune.

martial ['mɑːʃəl] *adj* martial, -aux, guerrier, -ière; **m. arts,** arts martiaux; **m. law,** loi martiale; **to declare m. law,** proclamer l'état de siège.

Martian ['mɑːʃən] *n* Martien, -ienne.

martin ['mɑːtɪn] *n* (*bird*) **(house) m.,** martinet *m*.

martinet ['mɑːtɪnet] *n Mil etc* officier *m* à cheval sur la discipline; **she's a m.,** c'est un vrai gendarme.

martingale ['mɑːtɪŋgeɪl] *n* **(a)** (*part of harness*) martingale *f*; **(b)** *Nau* **m. (guy** *or* **stay),** martingale *f* du beaupré.

Martinican [mɑːtɪ'niːkən] **1** *adj* martiniquais. **2** *n* Martiniquais, -aise.

Martinmas ['mɑːtɪnməs] *n* la Saint-Martin.

martyr¹ ['mɑːtər] *n* martyr *m*, martyre *f*; **to be a m. to rheumatism,** souffrir (beaucoup) des rhumatismes; **to die a m. in** *or* **to a cause,** mourir martyr d'une cause; *F* **my brother's such a m.,** mon frère se prend pour un vrai martyr.

martyr² *vt* martyriser (*qn*); **a martyred people,** un peuple martyr.

martyrdom ['mɑːtədəm] *n Rel & Fig* martyre *m*.

martyrize ['mɑːtəraɪz] *vt* faire subir le martyre à, martyriser.

marvel¹ ['mɑːv(ə)l] *n* merveille *f*; **to work marvels,** faire des merveilles; (*of treatment etc*) faire merveille; *F* **you're a bloody m.!,** tu es un as!; *Iron* espèce d'andouille!

marvel² *vi* (-ll-, *US* -l-) s'émerveiller, s'étonner (**at,** de).

marvellous, *US* **marvelous** ['mɑːv(ə)ləs] *adj* merveilleux; **it would be m. if ...,** ce serait merveilleux si ...; *Br Iron* **isn't it m.!,** ça c'est le bouquet *ou* le comble!

marvellously, *US* **marvelously** ['mɑːv(ə)ləslɪ] *adv* merveilleusement.

Marxism ['mɑːksɪz(ə)m] *n Econ Pol* marxisme *m*.

Marxism-Leninism ['mɑːksɪz(ə)m'lenɪnɪz(ə)m] *n Econ Pol* marxisme-léninisme *m*.

Marxist ['mɑːksɪst] *adj & n Econ* marxiste *mf*.

Marxist-Leninist ['mɑːksɪst'lenɪnɪst] *adj Econ Pol* marxiste-léniniste.

Mary ['meərɪ] *n* Marie *f*; **M. Stuart, M. Queen of Scots,** Marie Stuart; **Bloody M.,** *Hist F* Marie Tudor; *F* (*cocktail*) = cocktail composé de vodka et de jus de tomate; *Bible* **M. Magdalene,** Marie-Madeleine.

marzipan ['mɑːzɪpæn] *n Culin* massepain *m*, pâte *f* d'amandes; **m. fruits,** fruits *mpl* en pâte d'amandes.

mascara [mæs'kɑːrə] **1** *n* mascara *m*. **2** *vt* **heavily mascara'd eyes,** des cils lourdement chargés de mascara.

mascot ['mæskət] *n* mascotte *f*; *Aut* **radiator m.,** enjoliveur *m* de capot.

masculine ['mæskjʊlɪn] **1** *adj* **(a)** masculin, mâle; (*femme*) masculine, hommasse; **(b)** *Gram* masculin. **2** *n Gram* **in the m.,** au masculin.

masculinity [mæskjʊ'lɪnɪtɪ] *n* masculinité *f*.

maser ['meɪzər] *n Nucl Phys* maser *m*.

mash¹ [mæʃ] *n* **(a)** (*pulp*) **to reduce sth to a m.,** réduire (*du papier etc*) en pâte *ou* en bouillie; **(b)** *Br F* (*mashed potato*) purée *f* de pommes de terre; **(c)** *Agr* mash *m* (*pour chevaux*); pâtée *f* (*pour cochons, volaille*); **bran m.,** pâtée de son; **(d)** (*in brewing*) fardeau *m* (*de malt et d'eau chaude*).

mash² *vt* **(a) to m. (sth) (up),** broyer, écraser (qch); *Culin* (en) faire une purée; **(b)** (*in brewing*) brasser, mélanger, démêler (*le moût*).

mashed [mæʃt] *adj* **m. potato(es),** purée *f* de pommes de terre.

masher ['mæʃər] *n Tech* (*device*) broyeur *m*, écraseur *m*, mélangeur *m*; *Culin* **potato m.,** presse-purée *m*.

mashie, mashy ['mæʃɪ] *n Golf* mashie *m*.

mask¹ [mɑːsk] *n* **(a)** masque *m*; (*silk or velvet*) loup *m*; **to put on a m.,** se masquer; *Fig* **to throw off** *or* **drop the m.,** lever le masque, se démasquer; *Fig* **a m. of good-naturedness,** une apparence de bon naturel; *Fig* **the m. had slipped,** le masque était tombé; **with the m. off,** à visage découvert; **protective m.,** masque de protection; **fencing m.,** masque d'escrime; *Med* **oxygen m.,** masque à oxygène; *Ind* **welder's m.,** masque protecteur pour la soudure; **(b)** moulage *m*, masque *m* (*d'un visage*); **death m.,** masque mortuaire.

mask² *vt* **(a)** (*put a mask on*) masquer; **(b)** (*conceal*) cacher, déguiser (*ses sentiments, ses pensées*); voiler (*ses défauts etc*); **an apparent cheerfulness masked her deep pessimism,** une gaieté apparente masquait son profond pessimisme; **(c)** *Tech Mil etc* masquer (*une batterie, un faisceau lumineux*).

masked [mɑːskt] *adj* **(a)** (*homme, bal*) masqué; **(b)** (*sourire*) dissimulé; *Mil* **m. battery,** batterie masquée.

masking ['mɑːskɪŋ] *n* pose *f* d'un masque *ou* d'un cache; **m. tape,** bande *f* de papier-cache.

masochism ['mæsəkɪz(ə)m] *n Psy* masochisme *m*.

masochist ['mæsəkɪst] *n & adj* masochiste *mf*.

masochistic [mæsə'kɪstɪk] *adj* masochiste.

mason ['meɪs(ə)n] *n* **(a)** maçon *m*; **(b)** (*freemason*) **M.,** franc-maçon *m*, *pl* francs-maçons.

masonic [mə'sɒnɪk] *adj* (franc-)maçonnique; des francs-maçons, de la franc-maçonnerie.

masonry ['meɪsənrɪ] *n* **(a)** maçonnerie *f*; **m. drill,** foret *m* de maçon; **(b)** (*freemasonry*) franc-maçonnerie *f*.

masquerade¹ [mæskə'reɪd] *n* mascarade *f*.

masquerade² *vi* se masquer, faire une mascarade; **to m. as ...,** se déguiser en ...; **dictatorship masquerading as democracy,** dictature qui se déguise en démocratie.

mass¹ [mæs] *n* **(a)** (*large number*) foule *f*, multitude *f* (*de gens*); collection *f*, grande quantité (*de choses, de lettres*); *F* **I've masses (of things) to do,** j'ai un tas de choses à faire; **he was a m. of bruises,** il était tout couvert de meurtrissures; **the (great) m. of the people,** la plus grande partie *ou* la majorité de la population; **the masses,** les masses *fpl*, le grand public; **m. grave,** tombe collective; **m. hysteria,** hystérie collective; **m. media,** les (mass) média *mpl*; **m. meeting,** réunion *f ou* assemblée *f* en masse, grand rassemblement; **m. murder,** meurtre *m ou* tuerie *f* en masse, boucherie *f*; **m. murderer,** boucher *m*; *Ind* **m. production,** fabrication *f ou* production *f* en série; **it goes into m. production next week,** la production en série commence la semaine prochaine; **m. protest,** protestation *f* en masse;

(b) (*body*) masse *f*, amas *m*; *Phys* masse; **air m.,** masse d'air; *Ch* **molecular m.,** masse moléculaire; **atomic m.,** masse atomique de l'atome; **m. number,** nombre *m* de masse (*d'un noyau nucléaire*); *MecE* **unit of m.,** unité *f* de masse.

mass² **1** *vt* masser (*des troupes etc*). **2** *vi* (*of troops*) se masser; (*of clouds*) s'amonceler.

Mass¹ [mæs, mɑːs] *n Rel* messe *f*; **High M.,** grand-messe *f*; **Low M.,** messe basse; **Requiem M., M. for the dead,** messe de requiem, messe des morts; **to celebrate/say M.,** célébrer/dire la messe; **to go to M.,** aller à la messe.

Mass² [mæs] *abbr* **Massachusetts.**

massacre¹ ['mæsəkər] *n* massacre *m*, tuerie *f*; *Sp Fig F* **it was a m.,** c'était un massacre.

massacre² *vt* massacrer (*des hommes, une langue*); faire un massacre de (*gibier*); *Sp Fig F* **they were massacred,** ils ont été massacrés.

massage¹ ['mæsɑːʒ] *n* massage *m*; **(scalp) m.,** friction *f*; **m. parlour,** salon *m* de massage; **m. oil,** huile *f* de massage.

massage² *vt* **(a)** masser (*le corps*); **(b)** *F* (*manipulate*) **to m. the figures,** manipuler les chiffres.

masseur [mæ'sɜːr] *n* masseur *m*.

masseuse [mæ'sɜːz] *n* masseuse *f*.

massif ['mæsiːf] *n Geog* massif *m*.

massive ['mæsɪv] *adj* énorme; (*heart attack*) terrassant; **invasion on a m. scale,** invasion massive; **the m. scale of the Mafia's operations,** l'échelle massive sur laquelle la Mafia opère; *Pharm etc* **m. dose,** dose massive.

massively ['mæsɪvlɪ] *adv* énormément; massivement.

mass-produce [mæsprə'djuːs] *vt Ind* fabriquer en série.

mass-produced [mæsprə'djuːst] *adj Ind* produit en masse.

mast¹ [mɑːst] *n* **(a)** *Nau* mât *m*; **the masts,** les mâts, la mâture; **to sail before the m.,** servir comme simple matelot; **Venetian m.,** mât de pavoisement; **(b)** *Rad* pylône *m*.

mast[2] *vt Nau* **(a)** mâter (*un bâtiment*); **(b)** hisser haut (*une vergue*).

mast[3] *n* **(ground) m.**, faînes *fpl* (*de hêtre*); (*gathered*) faînée *f*.

mastectomy [mæs'tektəmɪ] *n Surg* mastectomie *f*.

masted ['mɑːstɪd] *adj Nau* mâté.

-masted *suff Nau* **three/four/***etc***-m.**, à trois/quatre *etc* mâts.

-master ['mɑːstər] *suff Nau* **three/four/***etc***-m.**, trois-mâts *m inv*/quatre-mâts *etc*, navire *m* à trois/quatre mâts.

master[1] ['mɑːstər] *n* **(a)** (*man in charge*) maître *m*; (*employer*) maître, patron *m*, chef *m*; *Nau* patron (*d'un bateau de pêche*); capitaine *m*, commandant *m* (*d'un navire marchand*); (*esp at Oxford and Cambridge*) directeur *m*, principal *m*, -aux (*de certains collèges universitaires*); (*freemasonry*) vénérable *m*; **the m. of the house,** le maître de la maison; **to be m. in one's own house,** être maître chez soi; **to be one's own m.,** ne dépendre que de soi; **to be m. of the situation,** être maître de la situation; **to meet one's m.,** trouver son maître; **like m. like man,** tel maître, tel valet; **M. of foxhounds,** maître d'équipage, grand veneur; **m. of ceremonies,** maître des cérémonies; *Th* **chorus m.,** répétiteur *m*; **m. bedroom,** chambre principale; *Cards* **m. card,** carte maîtresse; **m. copy,** original *m*; *Comptr* **m. file,** fichier permanent *ou* maître; **m. gauge,** *MecE* calibre *m* mère *ou* d'ensemble; *Rail* gabarit *m* passe-partout; **m. key,** passe-partout *m inv*; **m. plan,** plan *m* d'ensemble détaillé; **m. (record),** (disque *m*) original *m*; *US Mil* **m. sergeant,** sergent-chef *m*; *El* **m. switch,** commutateur *ou* disjoncteur principal; **m. tape,** bande *f* mère;

(b) (*owner of pet*) maître *m*;

(c) (*skilled person*) **to be a m. of one's art,** posséder son art en maître; **she was a m. of the epigrammatic phrase,** elle était un génie du style épigrammatique; **it is the work of a m. hand,** c'est fait de main de maître; *Art* **old m.,** (*painter*) maître *m*; (*painting*) tableau *m* de maître; *Univ* **M. of Arts/Science,** ≈ maître ès lettres/ès sciences; **m. carpenter/mason,** maître charpentier/maçon; **m. mariner,** capitaine marchand;

(d) (*instructor*) **fencing/dancing m.,** maître *m* d'escrime/de danse; **m. class,** (*given by opera singer, actor etc*) cours *m* de maître;

(e) *esp Br Sch* (*in primary school*) maître *m*; instituteur *m*; (*in secondary school*) professeur *m*; **form m.,** professeur principal (*d'une classe*); **French m.,** professeur de français;

(f) *Old-fashioned* (*form of address to small boys*) **M. David Thomas,** Monsieur David Thomas; **M. David,** (*said by servant*) Monsieur David;

(g) *Scot* (*title*) = titre de l'héritier d'une pairie audessous du rang de earl.

master[2] *vt* maîtriser, se rendre maître *ou* maîtresse de (*qn, la situation*); vaincre (*un cheval*); maîtriser, dompter (*ses passions*); surmonter (*une difficulté, sa colère*); apprendre (*un sujet*) à fond; **to have mastered a subject,** posséder un sujet à fond; **I never really mastered the language,** je n'ai jamais eu une maîtrise parfaite de la langue.

masterful ['mɑːstəful] *adj* (*person, manner etc*) impérieux, dominateur, -trice, autoritaire; (*skilful, expert etc*) magistral, -aux.

masterfully ['mɑːstəfʊlɪ] *adv* impérieusement, avec autorité; magistralement.

masterly ['mɑːstəlɪ] *adj* de maître; magistral, -aux; **m. stroke,** coup *m* de maître; **m. work,** œuvre magistrale; **in a m. manner,** de main de maître.

mastermind[1] ['mɑːstəmaɪnd] *n* esprit supérieur *ou* magistral; cerveau *m* (*d'une entreprise etc*); **she was the m. behind the robbery,** c'était elle le cerveau du vol.

mastermind[2] *vt* diriger (*un projet etc*); tramer (*un complot etc*).

masterpiece ['mɑːstəpiːs] *n* chef-d'œuvre *m*, *pl* chefs-d'œuvre.

masterstroke ['mɑːstəstrəʊk] *n* coup *m* de maître.

mastery ['mɑːstərɪ] *n* **(a)** (*control*) maîtrise *f* (**of,** de); autorité *f*, domination *f* (**over,** sur); **(b)** (*knowledge*) maîtrise *f* (*d'un sujet*).

masthead ['mɑːsthed] *n Nau* tête *f ou* ton *m* de mât, haut *m* du mât; (*of newspaper*) ours *m*; *Nau* **m. light,** feu *m* de tête de mât.

mastic ['mæstɪk] *n* **(a)** (*resin*) mastic *m*; **(b)** (*cement*) mastic *m*.

masticate ['mæstɪkeɪt] *vt* **(a)** mâcher, mastiquer (*un aliment*); **(b)** *Ind* triturer (*le caoutchouc etc*); malaxer.

mastiff ['mæstɪf] *n* (*dog*) mastiff *m*.

mastitis [mæs'taɪtɪs] *n Med* mastite *f*.

mastodon ['mæstədɒn] *n* mastodonte *m*.

mastoid ['mæstɔɪd] *adj & n Anat* **m. (process),** (apophyse *f*) mastoïde *f*; *Med F* **mastoids,** mastoïdite *f*.

masturbate ['mæstəbeɪt] **1** *vi* se masturber. **2** *vt* masturber.

masturbation [mæstə'beɪʃən] *n* masturbation *f*.

mat[1] [mæt] *n* **(a)** natte *f* (*de paille, de jonc*); (petit) tapis *m*, carpette *f* (*de laine etc*); (*at entrance*) paillasson *m*; essuie-pieds *m inv*; *Sp* (*in wrestling*) tapis; **table** *or* **place m.,** (*for hot dish*) rond *m* de table, dessous *m* de plat; *F* **to be on the m.,** être sur la sellette; **(b)** *Nau* paillet *m*, sangle *f*, baderne *f*; **chafing m.,** paillet de portage.

mat[2] *v* **(-tt-) 1** *vt* emmêler (*les cheveux etc*). **2** *vi* (*of hair fibres etc*) s'emmêler, se coller ensemble.

mat[3] **1** *adj* (*colour, surface*) mat; **m. paint,** peinture mate; *Phot* **m. paper,** papier mat; **m. varnish,** (vernis *m*) mattolin *m*. **2** *n* (*for gilding*) mat *m*, dorure mate.

mat[4] *vt* **(-tt-)** *Tech* matir (*la dorure*); mater (*le cuivre etc*); dépolir (*le verre*).

matador ['mætədɔːr] *n* matador *m*.

match[1] [mætʃ] *n* **(a)** (*of person*) égal, -ale, -aux; **to meet one's m.,** trouver un adversaire à sa mesure; **to meet more than one's m.,** trouver *ou* s'attaquer à plus fort que soi; **to be more than a m. for s.o.,** être trop fort pour qn; **they were no m. for the other team,** ils n'étaient pas à la hauteur de l'autre équipe; **you're no m. for her,** tu n'es pas à sa hauteur; **to be a bad/good m.,** (*of thing*) aller mal/bien ensemble; **to find a m. for a wallpaper,** (*find curtains etc in suitable colour*) assortir un papier peint; (*find the same*) réassortir un papier peint; **perfect m. of colours,** assortiment parfait de couleurs;

(b) *Sp* (*football, rugby, cricket, baseball*) match *m*; (*tennis, golf*) partie *f*; (*swimming*) compétition *f*; **tennis m.,** partie de tennis; **football m.,** match de football; **to win the m.,** gagner la partie; **m. point,** balle *f* de match; **m. play,** *Tennis* jeu *m* de match; *Golf* partie par trous;

(c) (*marriage*) mariage *m*; **good m.,** beau mariage; **he's a good m.,** c'est un bon *ou* un excellent parti.

match[2] **1** *vt* égaler, être l'égal de (*qn*), rivaliser avec (*qn*); assortir (*des gants, des bas*), rappareiller (*un service à thé etc*); assortir, allier (*des couleurs*); *Carp* bouveter, embrever (*des planches*); **we can't m. their prices,** nous ne pouvons pas rivaliser avec leurs prix; **will their deeds m. their words?,** est-ce que leurs actes seront à la hauteur de leurs paroles?; **there's nobody to m. him,** il n'a pas son pareil; **to m. s.o. against s.o.,** opposer qn à qn; *Sp* **to m. opponents,** matcher des adversaires; **evenly matched,** de force égale; **we will try to m. this material for you,** (*find something similar to*) nous essayerons de trouver un tissu assorti; **a well-matched couple,** un couple bien assorti; **I need a new hat to m. my suit,** j'ai besoin d'un nouveau chapeau qui aille avec mon tailleur; **m. the names to the faces,** (*in competition*) trouvez les noms correspondant aux visages.

2 *vi* (*of colours etc*) (*go well together*) aller (bien) ensemble, être bien assorti; (*be exactly the same*) être exactement les mêmes; (*of fingerprints, description etc*) correspondre; **the carpet doesn't m.,** la moquette n'est pas assortie; **I need some shoes to m.,** il me faut des chaussures assorties; **paper and envelopes to m.,** papier et enveloppes assortis.

match[3] *n* (*for lighting*) allumette *f*; **safety m.,** allumette de sûreté; **box of matches,** boîte *f* d'allumettes; **to strike a m.,** frotter une allumette; **to put a m. to sth,** mettre feu à qch.

►**match up 1** *vtsep* (*combine*) faire correspondre; **to m. up the names with the faces,** faire correspondre les noms et les visages; **to m. up two colours,** harmoniser *ou* assortir deux couleurs; **to m. up a colour,** (*find exact match*) trouver exactement la même couleur. **2** *vi* (*of fingerprints etc*) correspondre.

►**match up to** *vipo* **to m. up to s.o.'s expectations,** répondre aux espérances *ou* à l'attente de qn.

matchbox ['mætʃbɒks] *n* boîte *f* à allumettes.

matching ['mætʃɪŋ] **1** *adj* (*hat, colours etc*) assorti; **these pictures are a m. pair,** ces tableaux se font pendant. **2** *n* assortiment *m* (*de couleurs*); appariement *m* (*d'objets*).

matchless ['mætʃlɪs] *adj* incomparable, sans égal, sans pareil.

matchmaker ['mætʃmeɪkər] *n* faiseur, -euse de mariages, marieur, -euse.

matchmaking ['mætʃmeɪkɪŋ] *n* entremise *f*.

matchstick ['mætʃstɪk] *n* allumette *f*; **to have m. legs,** avoir des jambes comme des balais; **m. figure,** (*drawing*) dessin stylisé.

matchwood ['mætʃwʊd] *n* bois *m* d'allumettes; **smashed** *or* **reduced to m.,** réduit en miettes.

mate¹ [meɪt] *n* **(a)** (*sexual partner*) (*animal*) mâle *m*, femelle *f*; (*person*) époux *m*, épouse *f*; **(b)** *Br F* copain, copine, pote *m*; **watch where you're going m.!,** eh mec, regarde où tu vas!; **team m.,** coéquipier *m*; **(c)** (*assistant*) assistant, -ante, aide *mf*; **plumber's m.,** aide plombier; **(d)** *Nau* (*on merchant vessel*) officier *m*; **first** *or* **chief m.,** second *m*; **second m.,** lieutenant *m*; **(e)** *esp US MecE* pièce qui s'accouple (*avec une autre*), pièce qui s'emboîte (*dans une autre*).

mate² **1** *vt* accoupler (*des oiseaux, des animaux*); *Old-fashioned* marier, unir (**s.o. with s.o.,** qn à qn); *Tech MecE* assembler, réunir (*des éléments*). **2** *vi* (*of birds, animals*) s'accoupler; *MecE etc* (*of parts*) correspondre (**to,** à), s'accoupler (**to,** à), s'emboîter (**to,** dans).

mate³ *n Chess* mat *m*.

mate⁴ *vt Chess* mettre (*le roi*) échec et mat, mater.

mater ['meɪtər] *n Old-fashioned Br F* **the m.,** ma mère, maman *f*.

material [mə'tɪərɪəl] **1** *n* **(a)** (*substance*) matière *f*; (*for building*) matériau *m*, -aux; **raw material(s),** matière(s) première(s); *El* **insulating m.,** matière isolante, isolant *m*; **building materials,** matériaux de construction; **glass is a brittle m.,** le verre est un matériau cassant; **she isn't officer m.,** elle ne ferait pas un bon officier; **the m. for a play,** le matériau d'une pièce; **to collect m. for a book on China,** se documenter pour écrire un livre sur la Chine;
(b) (*requirements, equipment*) **war m.,** matériel *m* de guerre; **photographic materials,** fournitures *fpl ou* accessoires *mpl* pour la photographie; **writing materials,** tout ce qu'il faut pour écrire; **artists' materials,** matériel de l'artiste;
(c) *Tex* tissu *m*, étoffe *f*; **dress m.,** tissu pour robes; **customers' own m. made up,** on travaille à façon.
2 *adj* **(a)** (*point of view etc*) matérialiste; (*comfort, interests*) *& Phil Phys Rel* matériel; **to have enough for one's m. comfort** *or* **needs,** avoir de quoi vivre matériellement;
(b) (*important*) important, essentiel (**to,** pour);
(c) *Jur* (*fait, témoignage*) pertinent; **m. witnesses,** témoins *mpl* de fait.

materialism [mə'tɪərɪəlɪz(ə)m] *n Phil* matérialisme *m*.

materialist [mə'tɪərɪəlɪst] *adj & n* matérialiste *mf*.

materialistic [mətɪərɪə'lɪstɪk] *adj* matérialiste; (*pleasures, mind etc*) matériel.

materialize [mə'tɪərɪəlaɪz] **1** *vi* (*of occurrence*) se réaliser, s'actualiser; (*of plans*) aboutir, se réaliser; (*of psychic ectoplasm*) se matérialiser; **the promised computers never materialized,** (*at my home, in the office etc*) les ordinateurs promis ne se sont jamais matérialisés. **2** *vt* matérialiser (*l'âme, qn*); donner une forme matérielle à (*un esprit*).

materially [mə'tɪərɪəlɪ] *adv* **(a)** *Phil Phys Rel* matériellement, essentiellement; **to benefit m. from sth,** bénéficier matériellement de qch; **(b)** (*appreciably*) sensiblement, d'une manière appréciable.

materiel, matériel [mətɪərɪ'el] *n Mil* matériel *m*.

maternal [mə'tɜːn(ə)l] *adj* maternel; *Fml* **m. grandfather/***etc*, grand-père/*etc* maternel.

maternally [mə'tɜːn(ə)lɪ] *adv* maternellement.

maternity [mə'tɜːnɪtɪ] *n* maternité *f*; **m. benefit,** allocation *f* de maternité; **m. dress,** robe *f* de grossesse; **m. hospital,** maternité; **m. leave,** congé *m* de maternité; **m. ward,** salle *f* des accouchées.

matey ['meɪtɪ] *adj Br F* copain-copain; **to be m.,** être à tu et à toi, être copains; **she's very m. all of a sudden,** elle est bien aimable tout d'un coup.

math [mæθ] *n Am F* = **MATHS**.

mathematical [mæθ(ə)'mætɪk(ə)l] *adj* (*science, calcul*) mathématique; (*connaissance*) des mathématiques; (*connaissances*) en mathématiques; **he's a m. genius,** c'est un mathématicien de génie; **I haven't got a m. mind,** je n'ai pas l'esprit mathématique.

mathematically [mæθ(ə)'mætɪklɪ] *adv* mathématiquement.

mathematician [mæθ(ə)mə'tɪʃən] *n* mathématicien, -ienne.

mathematics [mæθ(ə)'mætɪks] *npl* **(a)** (*usu with sing verb*) mathématiques *fpl*; **pure/applied m.,** mathématiques pures/appliquées; **m. lesson/teacher,** cours *m*/professeur *m* de mathématiques; **(b)** (*calculations*) calculs *mpl*.

maths [mæθs] *npl Br F* math(s) *f(pl)*; **m. lesson/teacher,** cours *m*/professeur *m* de maths.

matinée ['mætɪneɪ] *n* **(a)** *Th Cin* **m. (performance),** (représentation *f* en) matinée *f*; *Old-fashioned Cin* **m. idol,** = acteur idolâtré par les femmes dans les années 30 ou 40; **(b) m. coat,** veste *f* (de bébé).

matiness ['meɪtɪnɪs] *n F* camaraderie *f*.

mating ['meɪtɪŋ] *n* **(a)** accouplement *m* (*d'oiseaux*); **the m. season,** la saison des amours; **m. call,** appel *m* du mâle; **(b)** *Tech* accouplement *m*, raccordement *m*; (*of gears*) conjugaison *f*.

matins ['mætɪnz] *npl Cathol* matines *fpl*; *Church of Eng* office *m* du matin.

matriarch ['meɪtrɪɑːk] *n* femme *f* qui exerce une autorité matriarcale.

matriarchal ['meɪtrɪɑːk(ə)l] *adj* matriarcal, -aux.

matriarchy ['meɪtrɪɑːkɪ] *n* matriarcat *m*.

matric [mə'trɪk] *n F Arch* = **MATRICULATION (b)**.

matricide ['meɪtrɪsaɪd, 'mæ-] *n* **(a)** (*person*) matricide *mf*; **(b)** (*crime*) (crime *m* de) matricide *m*.

matriculate [mə'trɪkjʊleɪt] **1** *vt* immatriculer, inscrire (*un étudiant*). **2** *vi* **(a)** (*of student*) s'inscrire; **(b)** *Arch* passer l'examen d'entrée à l'université (*et prendre ses inscriptions*).

matriculation [mətrɪkjʊ'leɪʃən] *n Sch* **(a)** (*enrolment*) immatriculation *f*, inscription *f* (*comme étudiant*); **(b)** *Arch* examen *m* de fin d'études (*qui admet à l'université*).

matrimonial [matrɪ'məʊnɪəl] *adj* matrimonial, -aux.

matrimony ['mætrɪmənɪ] *n* **(a)** mariage *m*; *Rel* **joined in holy m.,** unis par les saints nœuds du mariage; **(b)** *Cards* mariage *m*.

matrix, *pl* **-ixes, -ices** ['meɪtrɪks, -ɪksɪz, -ɪsiːz] *n* **(a)** *Math etc* matrice *f*; **(b)** *Geol Miner* matrice *f*, gangue *f*, gaine *f*; **(c)** *Metal Typ etc* matrice *f*, moule *m*; *Art Cer* mère *f* (*de moulages en plâtre etc*); **(d)** *Arch Anat* (*womb*) matrice *f*, utérus *m*.

matron ['meɪtrən] *n* **(a)** (*woman*) matrone *f*; **m. of honour,** (*at wedding*) dame *f* d'honneur; **(b)** intendante *f* (*d'une institution, d'un pensionnat*); infirmière *f* en chef (*d'un hôpital*).

matronly ['meɪtrənlɪ] *adj* matronal, -aux, de matrone.

matt [mæt] *adj & n* = **MAT³**.

matted ['mætɪd] *adj* (*cloth etc*) feutré; **m. hair,** cheveux emmêlés *ou* entremêlés.

matter¹ ['mætər] *n* **(a)** (*substance*) matière *f*; *Phil etc* **form and m.,** la forme et la matière; **organic/inorganic m.,** matière organique/inorganique; **vegetable m.,** matières végétales; *Anat* **grey m.,** matière grise; *F* **to have plenty of grey m.,** être très intelligent; **(subject) m.,** matière, sujet *m* (*d'un discours, d'un livre etc*); **reading m.,** lecture *f*, choses *fpl* à lire;
(b) (*affair*) affaire *f*; chose *f*; cas *m*; **let's come back to the m. in hand,** revenons à ce qui nous occupe *ou F* à nos moutons; **it's an easy/no easy m.,** c'est/ce n'est pas facile; **it's no great m.,** ce n'est pas grand-chose; **it is a m. for regret,** c'est à regretter; **it's no laughing m.,** il n'y a pas de quoi rire; **that's quite another m.,** cela c'est tout autre chose; **as matters stand,** au point où en sont les choses; **her remarks made matters worse,** ses remarques n'ont fait qu'empirer les choses; **to make matters worse, it had started to rain,** pour tout arranger, il s'était mis à pleuvoir; **money matters,** affaires d'argent; **business matters,** affaires; **matters of the heart,** affaires de cœur; **in matters of religion,** en ce qui concerne la religion; **to do sth as a m. of course,** faire qch systématiquement; **that's a m. of opinion,** c'est une question d'opinion; **that is a m. for the courts to decide,** sur ce point, c'est à la justice de trancher; **it's simply a m. of time,** c'est une simple question de temps; **it's just a m. of knowing which button to press,** il s'agit juste de savoir sur quel bouton appuyer; **it's just a m. of £100,** c'est une affaire de 100 livres; **within a m. of hours,** au bout de *ou* en quelques heures; **for that m.,** quant à cela; **and so am I for that m.,** moi aussi d'ailleurs; **he isn't very well known in London, or anywhere else for that m.,** il n'est pas très connu à Londres, et nulle part ailleurs en fait; **it's a m. of fact,** c'est un fait; **as a m. of fact,** en fait; **what's the m.?,** qu'est-ce qu'il y a?, qu'y a-t-il?; **what's the m. with you?,** qu'est-ce que vous avez?, qu'avez-vous?; **there's something the m.,** il y a quelque chose; **I don't know what's the m. with me,** je ne sais pas ce que j'ai; **there's something the m. with his throat,** il a quelque chose à la gorge; **there's nothing the m. with you/the television,** tu n'as/la télé n'a rien;
(c) no m.!, n'importe!; **no m. what he does/says,** quoi qu'il fasse/dise; **no m. how,** de n'importe quelle manière;

no m. when, à n'importe quel moment;
(d) *Med* (*pus*) pus *m*;
(e) *Typ* matière *f*, copie *f*; *Admin* **printed m.,** imprimé *m*.

matter² *vi* avoir de l'importance; **what really matters is that ...,** ce qui est vraiment important, c'est que ...; **that is what matters most,** c'est le plus important; **it doesn't m.,** ce n'est pas important, cela ne fait rien, peu importe; **it doesn't m. — perhaps not to you, but it matters to ME,** ce n'est pas important – pour toi, peut-être, mais pour moi c'est important; **it doesn't m. a bit,** cela n'a pas la moindre importance; **what does it m. to you?,** qu'est-ce que cela vous fait?; **nothing else matters,** tout le reste n'est rien; **these things m.,** ces choses-là comptent.

Matterhorn (the) [ðə'mætəhɔːn] *n* le (Mont) Cervin.

matter-of-fact ['mætərə'fækt] *adj* (*person, manner, statement etc*) terre-à-terre, prosaïque; **to say sth in a m.-of-f. tone,** dire qch d'une manière prosaïque.

Matthew ['mæθjuː] *n* Mat(t)hieu *m*.

matting ['mætɪŋ] *n* **(a)** (*of threads etc*) enchevêtrement *m*, emmêlement *m*; (*of straw*) tressage *m*; **(b)** (*material*) natte(s) *f(pl)*, paillassons *mpl*.

mattins ['mætɪnz] *npl* = **MATINS.**

mattock ['mætək] *n Agr* (*tool*) hoyau *m*; pioche *f*.

mattress ['mætrɪs] *n* matelas *m*; **inflatable** *or* **air m.,** matelas pneumatique *ou* de camping.

maturation [mætjʊ'reɪʃən] *n* maturation *f* (*d'un fruit, d'un abcès etc*); développement *m* (*de l'intelligence etc*).

mature¹ [mə'tjʊər] *adj* **(a)** (*fruit, intelligence, person etc*) mûr; (*animal*) adulte; **of m. years,** (*personne*) d'âge mûr; *Br* **would suit a m. person,** (*in job advertisement*) conviendrait à une personne d'âge mûr; **after m. consideration,** après mûre réflexion; **m. cheese,** fromage fait; *Br Univ* **m. student,** = étudiant plus âgé que la moyenne, qui reprend ses études sur le tard; **(b)** *Fin* (*papier*) échu.

mature² **1** *vt* mûrir (*une plante*); vieillir, affiner (*le vin, le fromage*). **2** *vi* **(a)** (*of plant, wine etc*) mûrir; **to let a plan m.,** laisser mûrir un projet; **his plans had not yet matured,** ses projets n'étaient pas encore mûris *ou* mûrs; **(b)** *Fin* (*of bill*) échoir, arriver à échéance.

maturely [mə'tjʊəlɪ] *adv* mûrement.

maturity [mə'tjʊərɪtɪ] *n* **(a)** maturité *f* (*d'un fruit, du vin etc*); **to come to** *or* **reach m.,** arriver à maturité; **the years of m.,** l'âge mûr (*de qn*); **(b)** *Fin Com* **(date of) m.,** échéance *f* (*d'une traite, d'un billet*); **payable at m.,** payable à l'échéance.

maudlin ['mɔːdlɪn] *adj* larmoyant, pleurard; (*drunk*) dans un état d'ivresse larmoyante; **m. sentimentality,** sentimentalité larmoyante; **to become m.,** se mettre à larmoyer *ou* à pleurnicher.

maul¹ [mɔːl] *n* **(a)** (*tool*) maillet *m*, mailloche *f*; **(b)** *Rugby* maul *m*.

maul² *vt* **(a)** (*injure*) meurtrir, malmener (*qn*); *F* éreinter (*un auteur, une œuvre*); **to be mauled by a tiger,** être mutilé *ou* lacéré par un tigre; **to m. s.o. about,** tirer qn de ci de là; **(b)** tripatouiller (*une femme*).

▶**maul about** *vtsep* = **MAUL² (b)**.

mauling ['mɔːlɪŋ] *n* (*by lion etc*) déchiquetage *m*; (*by enemy troops*) *F* tripotée *f*; (*by opposing team*) *F* raclée *f*; (*by critics*) éreintement *m*; **to get a m.,** recevoir une tripotée *ou* une raclée; se faire éreinter.

maunder ['mɔːndər] *vi* **(a)** (*dawdle*) **to m. (along),** flâner, baguenauder; **(b)** (*in speech*) **to m. (on),** radoter.

maundy ['mɔːndɪ] *n Rel* **M. Thursday,** le jeudi saint; *Br* **m. money,** = pièces frappées pour les largesses du jeudi saint.

Mauritania [mɒrɪ'teɪnɪə] *n* Mauritanie *f*.

Mauritian [mə'rɪʃən] **1** *adj* mauricien. **2** *n* Mauricien, -ienne.

Mauritius [mə'rɪʃəs] *n* l'île *f* Maurice.

mausoleum [mɔːsə'liːəm] *n* mausolée *m*.

mauve [məʊv] *adj & n* (*colour*) mauve *m*.

maverick ['mævərɪk] *n* **(a)** (*unorthodox person*) non-conformiste *mf*; **m. politician,** politicien réfractaire *ou* indépendant; **(b)** *Am* (*stray steer*) bouvillon *m* errant sans marque de propriétaire.

maw [mɔː] *n* **(a)** (*stomach*) quatrième poche *f* de l'estomac (*d'un ruminant*); jabot *m* (*d'oiseau*); *F* (*of person*) panse *f*; **(b)** (*mouth*) gueule *f* (*du lion, du brochet*).

mawkish ['mɔːkɪʃ] *adj Pej* **(a)** (*person, novel etc*) d'une sensiblerie outrée; **(b)** (*in taste, smell*) fade, insipide.

mawkishness ['mɔːkɪʃnɪs] *n* **(a)** (*of person, novel*) sensiblerie *f*, sentimentalité excessive; **(b)** (*of taste, smell*) fadeur *f*, insipidité *f*.

max. [mæks] *adj & n* (*abbr* **maximum**) max.

maxi ['mæksɪ] *F* **1** *adj* (*jupe, manteau*) maxi (*no feminine ending*). **2** *n* maxi *mf*.

maxim ['mæksɪm] *n* maxime *f*, dicton *m*.

maximal ['mæksɪməl] *adj* maximal.

maximization [mæksɪmaɪ'zeɪʃən] *n* maximalisation *f*.

maximize ['mæksɪmaɪz] *vt* maximiser, maximaliser (*qch*); porter (*qch*) au maximum.

maximum, *pl* **-a** ['mæksɪməm, -ə] **1** *n* maximum *m*, *pl* -ums, -a; **to the m.,** au maximum; **at the m.,** au (grand) maximum; **to reach one's m.,** plafonner. **2** *adj* maximum; *occ* maximal, -aux; **m. efficiency,** maximum de rendement; **m. load,** charge *f* limite; **m. speed,** vitesse maximale; **m. temperatures,** températures maximales.

may¹ [meɪ] *v aux* (*3rd person sing* **may**; *pt & cond* **might** [maɪt]; *no pres or past participle*) **(a)** (*expressing possibility*) **he m.** *or* **might return at any moment,** il peut *ou* pourrait revenir d'un moment à l'autre; **she m.** *or* **might not be hungry,** elle n'a peut-être pas faim; **that m. or m. not be true,** cela est peut-être vrai ou peut-être pas; **he m.** *or* **might have lost it,** peut-être qu'il l'a perdu; **Queen Anne m. have stayed here,** il se peut que la reine Anne ait séjourné ici; **she refused, as well she might,** rien d'étonnant à ce qu'elle ait refusé; **she might be thirty,** elle aurait peut-être trente ans; **and who m.** *ou* **might YOU be?,** qui êtes-vous, sans indiscrétion?; **and what might YOU be doing here?,** peut-on savoir ce que vous faites là?; **I wonder what I m. have done to offend him,** je me demande ce que j'ai bien pu faire pour le fâcher; **you m.** *or* **might be wondering why I'm doing that,** vous vous demandez peut-être pourquoi je fais cela; **it m.** *or* **might not be the fastest car in the world, but ...,** ce n'est peut-être pas la voiture la plus rapide du monde, mais ...; **it m.** *or* **might be that ...,** il se peut *ou* se pourrait bien que + *sub* ...; **be that as it m.,** quoi qu'il en soit; **that's as m. be,** c'est selon; **whatever faults he m.** *or* **might have he is never dull,** quels que soient ses défauts, il n'est jamais ennuyeux; **he might have arrived in time if ...,** il aurait pu arriver à temps si ...; **I might as well talk to myself!,** autant parler au mur!; **you m.** *or* **might see her if you stay another hour,** vous la verrez peut-être si vous y restez encore une heure; **we m.** *or* **might as well stay where we are,** autant vaut rester où nous sommes; **you might shut the door!,** vous pourriez bien fermer la porte!; **all the same, you might have made less noise,** tout de même vous auriez (bien) pu faire moins de bruit;
(b) (*asking or giving permission*) **m. I?,** *Fml* **might I?,** vous permettez?; **m. I come in?,** puis-je entrer?; *Fml* **m. I write to you? — of course you m.,** pourrais-je vous écrire? bien sûr, je vous en prie; **you m. go,** vous pouvez partir; (*at end of interview*) vous pouvez disposer; **if I m.** *or* **might be allowed to express an opinion,** si vous me permettez d'exprimer mon avis; **if I m.** *or* **might say so,** si j'ose dire;
(c) *Fml* (*be allowed to*) **passengers m. take only one item of hand luggage,** les passagers ne peuvent prendre qu'un bagage à main;
(d) (*in clauses expressing purpose, fear etc*) **I only hope it m. last!,** pourvu que cela *ou* ça dure!; **I was afraid he might have done it,** j'avais peur qu'il ne l'eût fait;
(e) (*expressing a wish*) **m. she rest in peace!,** qu'elle repose en paix!; **much good m. it do you!,** grand bien vous fasse!

may² *n* **m. (blossom),** fleurs *fpl* d'aubépine; **m. tree,** aubépine *f*.

May [meɪ] *n* mai *m*; **in (the month of) M.,** en mai, au mois de mai; **(on) the first/the seventh of M.,** le premier/le sept mai; **M. Day,** le premier mai; **M.-Day parade,** défilé *m* du premier mai; **M. queen,** reine *f* du premier mai; *Ent* **M. bug** *or* **beetle,** hanneton *m*; **M. week,** (*at Cambridge University*) la semaine des courses à l'aviron (*fin mai*).

Maya ['maɪə] *n* **(a)** Maya *mf*; **(b)** *Ling* maya *m*.

Mayan ['maɪən] **1** *adj* maya. **2** *n* Maya *mf*.

maybe ['meɪbiː] **1** *adv* peut-être; **m. yes, m. no,** peut-être bien que oui, peut-être bien que non; **m. she won't accept,** peut-être qu'elle n'acceptera pas, elle n'acceptera peut-être pas. **2** *n F* **(a)** (*person*) indécis, -ise; **(b) I don't want any maybes,** pas de peut-être!

Mayday ['meɪdeɪ] **1** *n* (*distress signal*) mayday *m*, SOS *m*. **2** *int* (*distress signal*) mayday!

mayfly ['meɪflaɪ] *n Ent* éphémère *m* vulgaire.

mayhem ['meɪhem] *n* **(a)** *F* (*uncontrolled behaviour*) grabuge *m*; **there was m. on the streets,** il y a eu du grabuge dans les rues; **(b)** *Jur* mutilation *f*; action *f* d'estropier qn; *Am* **to commit m. on s.o.,** se livrer à des voies de fait contre qn.

mayn't ['meɪənt] = **may not,** *see* **MAY**¹.

mayonnaise [meɪə'neɪz, 'meɪəneɪz] *n Culin* mayonnaise *f*.

mayor ['meər] *n* maire *m*.

mayoress ['meəres] *n* **(a)** (*mayor*) maire *m*, *Old-fashioned* mairesse *f*; **(b)** *esp Br* (*mayor's wife*) mairesse *f*.

maypole ['meɪpəʊl] *n* mai *m*.

maze [meɪz] *n* labyrinthe *m*; *Fig* dédale *m* (*de rues, de statistiques etc*).

Mb *Comptr* (*abbr* **megabyte**) Mo.

MBA [embiː'eɪ] *n Univ* (*abbr* **Master's in Business Administration**) MBA *m*.

MBE [embiː'iː] *n Br abbr* **Member of the Order of the British Empire**.

MBO [embiː'əʊ] *n Com abbr* **management buy-out**.

MC [em'siː] *n abbr* **Master of Ceremonies**.

MCP [emsiː'piː] *n F abbr* **male chauvinist pig**.

Md *abbr* **Maryland**.

MD [em'diː] *n* **(a)** *Med* (*abbr* **Doctor of Medicine**) docteur *m* en médecine; **(b)** *Com* (*abbr* **Managing Director**) P.D.-G. *m*.

Mdd *abbr* **Middlesex**.

me [*unstressed* mɪ, *stressed* miː] *person pron* **(a)** (*unstressed*) me, (*before vowel sound*) m'; (*reflexive, with preposition*) moi; **he knows me,** il me connaît; **he told me so,** il me l'a dit; **listen to me,** écoutez-moi; **lend it (to) me,** prêtez-le-moi; **she wrote me a letter,** elle m'a écrit une lettre; **I'll take it with me,** je le prendrai avec moi; **he's younger than me,** il est plus jeune que moi; **(b)** (*stressed*) moi; **you and me,** vous et moi; **he was thinking of me,** il pensait à moi; **that's for me,** ça c'est pour moi; **(c)** (*complement of verb* **to be**) **it's me!,** c'est moi!; **(d)** (*in int*) **dear me!,** mon Dieu!

Me *abbr* **Maine**.

mead [miːd] *n* (*drink*) hydromel *m*.

meadow ['medəʊ] *n* pré *m*, prairie *f*; **m. grass,** pâturin *m*, herbe *f* des prés; **m. saffron,** (*plant*) colchique *m* d'automne, safran *m* des prés; **m. pipit,** (*bird*) pipit *m* des prés, farlouse *f*.

meadowland ['medəʊlænd] *n* prairie(s) *f*(*pl*).

meadowsweet ['medəʊswiːt] *n* (*plant*) (spirée *f*) ulmaire *f*, reine *f* des prés.

meagre, *US* **meager** ['miːgər] *adj* maigre, pauvre.

meagrely, *US* **meagerly** ['miːgəlɪ] *adv* maigrement, pauvrement.

meal¹ [miːl] *n* repas *m*; **light m.,** repas léger; **I've had a huge m.,** j'ai mangé comme quatre; **to eat between meals,** manger entre les repas; **would you like some wine with your m.?,** est-ce que vous prendrez du vin (avec votre repas)?; **in Spain the evening m. is later,** en Espagne, on dîne plus tard; *F* **don't make a m. of it!,** n'en fais pas toute une histoire!; *F* **the job is just a m. ticket,** ce travail n'est qu'un gagne-pain; *F* **he's just a m. ticket to her,** elle n'est avec lui que pour son argent.

meal² *n* **(a)** farine *f* (*d'avoine, de seigle, de maïs etc*); **(b)** poudre *f* (*de diverses substances*).

meals-on-wheels [miːlzɒn'wiːlz] *n Br Admin* **(a)** (*food*) = repas livrés aux handicapés ou aux personnes âgées; **she gets m.-on-w.,** on lui livre ses repas à domicile; **(b)** (*service*) = service du gouvernement ou d'une œuvre qui organise la livraison à domicile de repas aux handicapés et aux personnes âgées.

mealtime ['miːltaɪm] *n* heure *f* du repas; **they only see each other at mealtimes,** ils ne se voient qu'aux heures des repas.

mealworm ['miːlwɜːm] *n Ent* ver *m* de farine.

mealy ['miːlɪ] *adj* **(a)** (*in consistency*) farineux; (*fruit*) cotonneux; **(b)** (*covered in meal*) saupoudré de farine, poudreux.

mealy-mouthed [miːlɪ'maʊðd] *adj F* doucereux, mielleux, patelin.

mean¹ [miːn] *n* **(a)** (*middle*) milieu *m*, moyen terme; **the golden** *or* **happy m.,** le juste milieu; **(b)** *Math* moyenne *f*.

mean² *adj* (*medium, average*) moyen.

mean³ *adj* **(a)** *esp Br* (*with money*) avare, radin; **he's very m. about tipping,** il n'aime pas donner de pourboires; **(b)** (*low, ignoble*) (*of person, character, action*) bas, méprisable, vil, mesquin; **a m. trick,** un vilain tour, *F* un sale coup; **that's m. of her,** ce n'est pas chic de sa part; *F* **I feel very m. about not going,** j'ai honte de ne pas y aller; **(c)** *esp Am F* (*vicious, tough*) méchant, vicieux; **(d)** (*with* **no**) **no m. ...,** un très bon ...; **he's no m. scholar,** c'est un grand érudit; **it was no m. feat,** ce n'était pas une mince affaire; **(e)** *esp Am F* (*excellent*) formidable; **he plays a m. guitar,** c'est un guitariste formidable; **(f)** *Am F* (*poorly*) **to feel m.,** se sentir mal en train; **(g)** (*wretched*) misérable, pauvre.

mean⁴ *vt* (*pt & pp* **meant** [ment]) **(a)** (*have intention*) avoir l'intention (**to do sth,** de faire qch), se proposer (*de faire qch*); **what do you m. to do?,** que comptez-vous faire?; **I never meant to go,** je n'ai jamais eu l'intention d'y aller; **I m. him no harm,** je ne lui veux pas de mal; **she didn't m. (to do) it,** elle ne l'a pas fait exprès; **without meaning it,** sans le vouloir, sans intention; **I meant to!,** (*do what I did*) c'était bien mon intention!; **to m. well by s.o.,** avoir de bonnes intentions à l'égard de qn; **she means well,** elle a de bonnes intentions; **I m. to be obeyed,** j'entends qu'on m'obéisse; **I m. to succeed,** je veux réussir; **I m. to have it,** je suis résolu à l'avoir;

(b) (*intend*) **I meant this book for you,** je vous destinais ce livre; **the remark was meant for you,** la remarque s'adressait à vous; **the remark wasn't meant to be overheard,** cette remarque n'était pas censée être entendue; **you weren't meant to open the presents until tomorrow,** tu n'étais pas censé ouvrir les cadeaux avant demain; **I have a feeling this was meant to be** *or* **happen,** j'ai le sentiment que ça devait arriver; **do you m. him?,** est-ce de lui que vous parlez?, est-ce lui à qui vous faites allusion?; **this portrait is meant to be the duke,** ce portrait est censé représenter le duc; **we're meant for each other,** nous sommes faits l'un pour autre;

(c) (*signify*) (*of word, phrase, person*) vouloir dire; (*of word, phrase, event etc*) signifier; **what does that word m.?** que signifie ce mot?; **the name means nothing to me,** ce nom ne me dit rien; **what is meant by ...?,** que veut dire ...?; **all this means nothing,** tout cela ne rime à rien; **it doesn't m. anything,** (*what you saw, heard*) cela ne prouve rien; **this means war/the end of our relationship,** c'est la guerre/la fin de notre amitié; **what do you m.?,** que voulez-vous dire?; **what do you m. by that?,** qu'entendez-vous par là?; **I know what you m.!,** (*I quite agree*) et comment!; **what me?, I don't know what you m.!,** qui moi?, je ne vois pas ce que vous voulez dire!; **she knew what it meant to be hungry,** elle savait ce que voulait dire avoir faim; **do you think he meant what he said?,** pensez-vous qu'il l'ait dit sérieusement?; **I didn't m. that,** ce n'est pas cela que je voulais dire; **you don't m. it!,** vous voulez rire!, vous plaisantez!; **I m. it,** je parle sérieusement; **you're my best friend — do you m. that?,** tu es mon meilleur ami — tu le penses vraiment?; **when I say NO, I m. NO,** quand je dis non, c'est non; **the price means nothing to him,** le prix n'est rien pour lui; **doesn't your daughter's education m. anything to you?,** est-ce que l'éducation de ta fille ne t'intéresse pas?; **I cannot tell you what he has meant to me,** je ne saurais vous dire tout ce qu'il a été pour moi; **my Sundays m./independence means a lot to me,** le dimanche/mon indépendance est sacré(e) pour moi.

meander¹ [mɪ'ændər] *n Geog* méandre *m* (*d'un cours d'eau*).

meander² *vi* **(a)** (*of person*) errer çà et là, errer à l'aventure; **(b)** (*of river*) serpenter, se replier; **the river meanders through the plain,** la rivière fait des méandres à travers la plaine.

meandering [mɪ'ændərɪŋ] *adj* **(a)** (*speech etc*) sans plan, sans suite; **(b)** (*river*) qui fait des méandres.

meanie ['miːnɪ] *n F* **(a)** *esp Br* (*miserly person*) rapiat, -ate, pingre *mf*; **(b)** *esp US* (*nasty person*) **what a m.!,** quel chameau!, qu'il est vache!

meaning ['miːnɪŋ] **1** *n* signification *f*, sens *m*, acception *f* (*d'un mot etc*); **what is the m. of this word?,** que signifie *ou* que veut dire ce mot?; **figurative m. of a word,** acception figurée d'un mot; *F* **you don't know the m. of the word!,** tu ne sais même pas ce que ça veut dire!; **life had no m. for him,** la vie n'avait plus aucun sens pour lui; **what's the m. of this?,** (*expressing indignation*) qu'est-ce que cela signifie?; **to understand s.o.'s m.,** comprendre ce que qn veut dire; *F* **if you get my m.,** si tu vois ce que je veux dire; **look full of m.,** regard significatif. **2** *adj* (*regard*) significatif; (*sourire*) d'intelligence.

-meaning ['miːnɪŋ] *suff* **well-m.,** bien intentionné.

meaningful ['miːnɪŋfʊl] *adj* (*full of meaning*) plein de sens; (*expressive*) (*look*) significatif; (*smile*) d'intelligence; *esp Pol* **m. talks,** conversations constructives; **a m. relationship,** une relation sérieuse.

meaningless ['miːnɪŋlɪs] *adj* dénué *ou* vide de sens, qui ne signifie rien; **a m. act** *or* **remark,** un non-sens.

meanly ['miːnlɪ] *adv* **(a)** (*in miserly fashion*) en lésinant; **(b)** (*ignobly*) (*agir, se conduire*) peu loyalement, indignement; **(c)** (*wretchedly*) misérablement, pauvrement.

meanness ['mi:nnɪs] *n* **(a)** (*with money*) avarice *f*, mesquinerie *f*; **(b)** (*nastiness*) vilenie *f*; **(c)** (*baseness*) bassesse *f*, petitesse *f* (*d'esprit*); **(d)** (*poor quality, poverty*) médiocrité *f*, pauvreté *f*, petitesse *f* (*de qch*).

means [mi:nz] *npl* (*often with sing verb*) **(a)** (*method*) moyen(s) *m(pl)*, voie(s) *f(pl)*; **to use every possible m. to do sth,** employer tous les moyens pour accomplir qch; **there is no m. of escape,** il n'y a aucun moyen de fuite; **by all m,** (*by every possible method*) par tous les moyens (possibles); (*certainly*) mais certainement!, mais oui!; **may I come in? — by all m.!,** puis-je entrer? — je vous en prie!; **by no m.**, en aucune façon, nullement; **she is not stupid by any (manner of) m.**, elle est loin d'être stupide; **by some m. or other,** d'une manière ou d'une autre; **by m. of sth,** au moyen *ou* par le moyen de qch; **a m. to an end,** un moyen d'arriver au but;
(b) (*income, wealth*) moyens *mpl* (de vivre), ressources *fpl*; **according to our m.**, selon nos moyens; **to live beyond one's m.**, vivre au-delà de ses moyens; **private m.**, ressources personnelles; **a man of m.**, un homme dont les revenus sont élevés; **to be without m,** (*without resources*) être sans ressources; (*without money, wealth*) être sans fortune; *Admin* **m. test,** = enquête *f* sur la situation (de fortune).

means-test ['mi:nztest] *vt Admin* = étudier les ressources de (*qn*) avant d'accorder une aide sociale.

meant *see* **MEAN⁴**.

meantime, meanwhile ['mi:ntaɪm, -waɪl] *n & adv* **in the meantime, (in the) meanwhile,** dans l'intervalle, pendant ce temps-là, en attendant.

measles ['mi:z(ə)lz] *npl* (*usu with sing verb*) *Med* rougeole *f*; **to have (the) m.**, avoir la rougeole; **German m.**, rubéole *f*.

measly ['mi:zlɪ] *adj F* insignifiant, misérable, minable; **a m. present,** une bricole; **keep your m. money!,** garde ton foutu fric!

measurable ['meʒərəb(ə)l] *adj* mesurable; *Ch etc* (*constituent*) dosable.

measure¹ ['meʒər] *n* **(a)** (*measurement*) mesure *f*; **linear m., m. of length,** mesure linéaire *ou* de longueur; **cubic m.**, mesure de volume; **liquid** *or* **dry m.**, mesure de capacité pour les liquides *ou* les matières sèches; *Typ* **narrow m.**, petite justification; **weights and measures,** poids *mpl* et mesures; **made to m.**, (*clothes etc*) fait sur mesure(s); *Fig* **to take s.o.'s m.**, prendre la mesure de qn, jauger qn;
(b) (*instrument*) mesure *f* (*à grains, à lait etc*); **tape m.**, mètre *m* à ruban;
(c) (*quantity*) dose *f*, mesure *f*; **a m. of whisky,** une dose de whisky; **half m.**, demi-mesure *f*, *pl* demi-mesures; *F* **there are no half measures with her,** avec elle il n'y a pas de demi-mesure; **for good m.**, pour faire bonne mesure; *Fig* **then she insulted the other man for good m.**, elle a aussi insulté l'autre pour ne pas faire de jaloux; **to give s.o. short m.**, donner moins que la mesure à qn;
(d) (*degree*) **in some m.**, dans une certaine mesure; **a m. of independence,** une certaine indépendance;
(e) (*limit*) mesure *f*, limite *f*; **he annoys me beyond m.**, il m'irrite outre mesure;
(f) (*action, step*) mesure *f*, démarche *f*; **to take measures,** prendre des mesures; **security** *or* **safety measures,** mesures de sécurité; **to take extreme measures,** employer les grands moyens; **as an economy m.**, par mesure d'économie;
(g) *Pol* projet *m* de loi;
(h) (*in poetry*) mesure *f*;
(i) *esp Am Mus* mesure *f*.

measure² **1** *vt* mesurer (*une distance, le temps etc*); métrer (*un mur etc*); arpenter (*un terrain*); *Sewing* mesurer, prendre la mesure de (*qn*); **to m. one's length (on the ground),** s'étaler par terre, tomber de tout de son long; **to m. s.o. (with one's eye),** mesurer qn, toiser qn (du regard); **to m. one's strength** *or* **oneself with s.o.**, mesurer ses forces avec qn, se mesurer avec *ou* contre qn; **to m. one's words,** mesurer *ou* peser ses paroles. **2** *vi* mesurer; **column measuring 10 metres,** colonne qui mesure 10 mètres.

▶**measure off** *vtsep* mesurer (*du tissu etc*).

▶**measure out** *vtsep* mesurer (*du blé etc*); (*pour*) verser (*qch*) dans une mesure; (*distribute*) répartir (*qch*); **m. out two cups of flour,** préparez deux mesures de farine.

▶**measure up** **1** *vtsep* mesurer (*du bois*); **they measured each other up,** (*before fight etc*) ils se sont jaugés. **2** *vi* (*be equal*) faire le poids; **to m. up to one's job,** se montrer à la hauteur de sa tâche; **to m. up to s.o./sth,** être à la mesure de qn/qch.

measured ['meʒəd] *adj* **(a)** (*time, distance etc*) mesuré, déterminé; *Nau* **m. ton,** tonneau *m* d'encombrement; **(b)** (*deliberate*) (*mouvement, pas*) cadencé; **m. tread,** marche scandée; **with m. steps,** à pas mesurés *ou* comptés; **(c)** (*langage*) modéré; **to speak in m. tones,** parler sur un ton modéré; **(d)** (*in poetry*) (*vers etc*) mesuré.

measurement ['meʒəmənt] *n* **(a)** (*quantity, length etc*) mesure *f*; (*action*) mesurage *m*; **bust/waist/hip measurements,** (*of person*) tour *m* de poitrine/taille/hanches; **to take a customer's measurements,** mesurer un client; *Constr etc* **inside/outside m.**, mesure dans/hors œuvre; **(b)** *Nau* jaugeage *m* (*d'un bâtiment*); cubage *m*, encombrement *m* (*du fret*).

measuring ['meʒərɪŋ] *n* mesurage *m* (*du drap etc*); métrage *m* (*d'un mur etc*); mesure *f* (*du temps*); arpentage *m* (*d'un terrain*); *Ch etc* dosage *m*; *Culin* **m. cup** *or* **jug,** mesure *f*; **m. spoon,** cuillère *f* à doser; **m. glass,** verre gradué; **m. tape,** mètre *m* à ruban; **m. chain,** (*in surveying*) chaîne *f* d'arpenteur *ou* d'arpentage.

meat [mi:t] *n* viande *f*; **fresh m.**, viande fraîche; *Culin* **cold m.**, viande froide; **luncheon m.**, = pâté *m* de viande; **minced** *or Am* **ground m.**, hachis *m* (de viande), viande hachée; **dog's m.**, viande pour chiens; *Rel* **to abstain from m.**, faire maigre; **m. diet,** régime carné *ou* gras; **m. broth,** bouillon gras; **m. hook,** croc *m* de boucherie, esse *f*; *Old-fashioned* **m. and drink,** le manger et le boire; *Fig* **it was m. and drink to them,** c'était leur plus grand plaisir; *Prov* **one man's m. is another man's poison,** ce qui guérit l'un tue l'autre.

meatball ['mi:tbɔ:l] *n Culin* boulette *f* (de viande).

meathead ['mi:thed] *n US F* crétin, -ine, imbécile *mf*.

meatpacking ['mi:tpækɪŋ] *n Am* abattage *m* et boucherie *f*.

meaty ['mi:tɪ] *adj* **(a)** (*bone, sausage etc*) riche en viande; (*odeur etc*) de viande; *Fig* (*livre etc*) plein de substance; **(b)** (*fleshy*) charnu.

Mecca ['mekə] *n* la Mecque; *Fig* **the town is a m. for antique lovers,** cette ville est un paradis pour les passionnés d'objets anciens.

mechanic [mɪ'kænɪk] *n* mécanicien *m*; **I'm not much of a m.**, je ne suis pas très mécanicien; **motor m.**, mécanicien garagiste.

mechanical [mɪ'kænɪk(ə)l] *adj* **(a)** mécanique; **m. efficiency,** rendement *m* mécanique; **m. drawing,** dessin industriel *ou* géométrique; **m. engineer,** ingénieur *m* mécanicien; **m. engineering,** constructions *fpl* mécaniques; **m. failure,** panne *f* mécanique; **he has no m. skill,** il ne peut pas manier un outil; **(b)** *Fig* (*reply, smile etc*) machinal, -aux, automatique; **her playing is very m.**, (*of pianist etc*) elle joue d'une façon très mécanique.

mechanically [mɪ'kænɪklɪ] *adv* **(a)** mécaniquement; **m. driven,** actionné mécaniquement; **(b)** *Fig* (*to reply, smile etc*) machinalement.

mechanics [mɪ'kænɪks] *npl* (*usu with sing verb*) **(a)** la mécanique; **(b)** (*of human body etc*) mécanisme *m*.

mechanism ['mekənɪz(ə)m] *n* **(a)** appareil *m*, dispositif *m*, mécanisme *m*; **a delicate piece of m.**, un mécanisme délicat; **safety m.**, mécanisme de sécurité; *Mil* **firing m.**, mécanisme de détente; **(b)** *Phil Psy etc* mécanisme *m*; **defence m.**, *Psy* mécanisme de défense; *Zool etc* système *m* de défense.

mechanization [mekənaɪ'zeɪʃən] *n* mécanisation *f*.

mechanize ['mekənaɪz] **1** *vt* mécaniser. **2** *vi* automatiser.

mechanized ['mekənaɪzd] *adj* **m. industry,** industrie mécanisée: *Mil* **m. troops,** troupes motorisées.

Med (the) [ðə'med] *n F* la Méditerranée.

MEd [e'med] *n* (*abbr* **Master of Education**) ≈ C.A.P.E.S. *m*.

medal ['med(ə)l] *n* médaille *f*; **to award a m. to s.o.**, décerner une médaille *ou* une décoration à qn; **the reverse of the m.**, le revers de la médaille.

medallion [mɪ'dæljən] *n* médaillon *m*.

medallist, *US* **medalist** ['medəlɪst] *n Sp etc* médaillé, -ée; **gold m.**, titulaire *mf* d'une médaille d'or.

meddle ['med(ə)l] *vi* (*interfere*) se mêler (**in,** de); (*tamper*) toucher (**with,** à); **to m. with** *or* **in sth,** se mêler de qch; **to m. in other people's affairs,** se mêler des affaires d'autrui.

meddler ['medlər] *n* **he's a terrible m.**, il met son nez partout.

meddlesome ['med(ə)lsəm] *adj* qui se mêle de tout.

meddling ['medlɪŋ] **1** *adj* = **MEDDLESOME**. **2** *n* **(a)** (*action*) intervention *f* (**in, with,** dans); **(b)** (*intrigue, schemes*) manigances *fpl*, menées *fpl*.

media ['mi:dɪə] *npl* **the (mass) m.**, les médias *mpl*; **m.**

coverage, couverture *f* par les médias; **m. event,** événement médiatique; **m. studies,** études *fpl* de communication.

mediaeval [medɪ'iːvəl] *adj* du moyen âge, médiéval, -aux; *F* **you're positively m.!,** tu es moyenâgeux!, tu vis dans le passé!

mediaevalist [medɪ'iːvəlɪst] *n* médiéviste *mf*.

medial ['miːdɪəl] **1** *adj* intermédiaire (**to,** entre); (*letter*) médial. **2** *n Ling* médiale *f*.

medially ['miːdɪəlɪ] *adv* médialement.

median ['miːdɪən] **1** *adj* médian; *Am Aut* **m. strip,** terre-plein central, *Can* médiane *f*. **2** *n* **(a)** *Anat* (*nerve*) nerf médian; (*vein*) veine médiane; **(b)** (*in statistics*) *& Math* médiane *f*.

mediant ['miːdɪənt] *n Mus* médiante *f*.

mediate ['miːdɪeɪt] **1** *vi* (*of person*) agir en *ou* servir de médiateur (**between,** entre). **2** *vt* **to m. a peace,** intervenir en qualité de médiateur pour amener la paix.

mediation [miːdɪ'eɪʃən] *n* médiation *f*; **to go to m.,** recourir à une médiation.

mediator ['miːdɪeɪtər] *n* médiateur, -trice.

medic ['medɪk] *n F* (*student*) étudiant, -ante en médecine, carabin *m*; (*doctor*) toubib *m*.

Medicaid ['medɪkeɪd] *n US* = assistance médicale pour les défavorisés.

medical ['medɪk(ə)l] **1** *adj* médical, -aux; (*livre etc*) de médecine; (*étudiant*) en médecine; **the m. profession,** (*people*) le corps médical; (*activity*) la profession de médecin; **m. practitioner,** médecin *m*; **m. certificate,** certificat médical; **you need m. attention,** il faut vous faire soigner par un médecin; *Admin* **m. officer of health,** = médecin départemental; **m. examination,** examen médical; *esp US* **m. examiner,** médecin légiste; **m. history,** antécédents médicaux; **m. record,** dossier médical. **2** *n* examen médical; **to have a m.,** passer une visite médicale, subir un examen médical.

medically ['medɪklɪ] *adv* médicalement; **to be m. examined,** subir un examen médical.

medicament [me'dɪkəmənt] *n* médicament *m*.

Medicare ['medɪkeər] *n US* **(a)** = assistance médicale pour les personnes âgées et les handicapés; **(b)** *Can* assurance-maladie *f*.

medicate ['medɪkeɪt] *vt* **(a)** donner un traitement médical à, traiter (*un malade*); **(b)** (*make medicated*) rendre (*qch*) médicamenteux.

medicated ['medɪkeɪtɪd] *adj* (*shampooing*) médical, traitant; (*savon*) hygiénique.

medication [medɪ'keɪʃən] *n* **(a)** (*action*) médication *f*; emploi *m* de médicaments; **(b)** (*medicine, drugs*) médicament *m*; médicaments *mpl*.

medicinal [me'dɪsɪn(ə)l] *adj* médicinal, -aux, médicamenteux; **m. plants,** plantes médicamenteuses; **a drug with no m. use,** une drogue sans propriétés médicinales; *Hum* **it's just for m. purposes,** (*having a whisky etc*) c'est mon médicament.

medicinally [me'dɪsɪn(ə)lɪ] *adv* médicalement, comme médicament.

medicine ['medsɪn] *n* **(a)** (*practice, science*) la médecine; **to study/practise m.,** étudier/exercer la médecine; **(b)** (*remedy*) médicament *m*; *Fig* **to give s.o. a taste of his** *or* **her own m.,** rendre la pareille à qn; *Fig* **to take one's m.,** avaler la pilule, supporter les conséquences (de son action); **m. chest** *or* **cabinet,** (coffre *m* à) pharmacie *f*; **(c)** (*among American Indians etc*) (*magic*) sorcellerie *f*, magie *f*; (*spell*) charme *m*; **m. man,** (sorcier *m*) guérisseur *m*; **m. woman,** (sorcière *f*) guérisseuse *f*; **(d)** *Sp* **m. ball,** medecine-ball *m*.

medico ['medɪkəʊ] *n F* (*doctor*) toubib *m*; (*student*) étudiant, -ante en médecine, carabin *m*.

medieval, medievalist = **MEDIAEVAL, MEDIAEVALIST.**

mediocre [miːdɪ'əʊkər] *adj* médiocre.

mediocrity [miːdɪ'ɒkrɪtɪ] *n* **(a)** médiocrité *f* (*de qn, de qch*); **(b)** (*person*) **a m.,** une médiocrité.

meditate ['medɪteɪt] **1** *vi* **(a)** (*consider*) méditer (**on, upon,** sur), réfléchir (**on, upon,** sur, à); **(b)** (*be in or enter into a state of meditation*) méditer. **2** *vt* méditer (*un projet, une entreprise*).

meditation [medɪ'teɪʃən] *n* **(a)** (*thinking*) méditation *f* (**upon,** sur); **(b)** (*state*) recueillement *m*; **(c)** *Lit* **Meditations,** méditations *fpl*.

meditative ['medɪtətɪv] *adj* méditatif, recueilli.

meditatively ['medɪtətɪvlɪ] *adv* d'un air méditatif.

Mediterranean [medɪtə'reɪnɪən] **1** *adj* méditerranéen; **the M. Sea,** la mer Méditerranée. **2** *n* **the M.,** la Méditerranée.

medium[1], *pl* **-a, -ums** ['miːdɪəm, -ə, -əmz] *n* **(a)** (*midpoint*) milieu *m*, moyen terme (**between,** entre); **happy m.,** juste milieu; **(b)** (*intermediary*) intermédiaire *m*, entremise *f*; **through the m. of the press,** par l'intermédiaire de la presse, par voie de presse; **(c)** *Art Mus etc* moyen *m* d'expression; **marble is her favourite m.,** elle préfère travailler le marbre; **television is a powerful m.,** la télévision est un média puissant; **advertising m.,** organe *m* de publicité; **(d)** *Phys* milieu *m*, véhicule *m*; *Biol* culture *m*, bouillon *m* de culture; (*environment*) **(social) m.,** milieu, atmosphère *f*, ambiance *f*; **(e)** (*in spiritualism*) médium *m*.

medium[2] **1** *adj* moyen; **of m. height,** de taille moyenne; **m. rare,** (*lamb, steak*) pas trop saignant; **cook in a m. oven,** cuire à four moyen; **m. sized,** de grandeur moyenne, de taille moyenne; **in the m. term,** à moyen terme; **m. dry wine,** vin demi-sec; *Rad* **m. wave,** onde moyenne. **2** *n* (*something of medium size*) **this teeshirt's a m.,** ce tee shirt est une taille moyenne *ou* un deux; **available in small, m. and large,** disponible en petit, moyen et grand.

medium-range ['miːdɪəm'reɪndʒ] *n* **m.-r. ballistic missile,** missile *m* balistique de moyenne portée.

medlar ['medlər] *n* (*fruit*) nèfle *f*; **m.(-tree),** néflier *m*.

medley ['medlɪ] *n* mélange *m*, confusion *f*, méli-mélo *m*, *pl* mélis-mélos, pêle-mêle *m inv* (*de personnes, d'objets*); *Mus* pot pourri; *Swimming* **400 metres m. race,** 4 x 100 mètres quatre nages.

medulla [me'dʌlə] *n* **(a)** *Bot* médulle *f*, moelle *f*; **(b)** *Anat* moelle *f* (*d'un os, d'un poil*).

meek [miːk] *adj* doux, *f* douce, humble, soumis; *F* **m. and mild,** doux comme un agneau.

meekly [miːklɪ] *adv* avec soumission, humblement.

meekness ['miːknɪs] *n* douceur *f* de caractère, soumission *f*, humilité *f*.

meerschaum ['mɪəʃəm] *n* **(a) m. (pipe),** pipe *f* en écume (de mer); **(b)** *Miner* écume *f* (de mer).

meet[1] [miːt] *n* **(a)** (*in hunting*) rendez-vous *m* de chasse, rassemblement *m* de la meute; **(b)** *esp Am* (*meeting*) réunion *f*.

meet[2] *v* (*pt & pp* **met** [met]) **1** *vt* **(a)** (*by accident*) rencontrer (*qn*), se rencontrer avec (*qn*); **to m. s.o. on the stairs,** croiser qn dans l'escalier; **to m. another car,** croiser une autre voiture;

(b) (*by arrangement*) rejoindre, (re)trouver (*qn*), se rencontrer avec (*qn*); **to go to m. s.o.,** aller au-devant de qn, aller à la rencontre de qn; **to m. s.o. at the station,** aller chercher qn à la gare; **the bus meets the train,** il y a une correspondance entre le train et l'autobus; **I arranged to m. him at three o'clock,** j'ai pris rendez-vous avec lui pour trois heures; **I'll m. you at the crossroads,** on se retrouve au croisement;

(c) (*become acquainted with*) faire la connaissance de (*qn*); **I met her at the Martins',** je l'ai rencontrée chez les Martin; **pleased to m. you,** ravi de faire votre connaissance; **have you met my husband?,** vous connaissez mon mari?; **I get to m. a lot of people in my job,** mon travail m'amène à rencontrer beaucoup de gens; **she's the nicest person I've ever met,** c'est la personne la plus gentille que j'ai jamais rencontrée; **m. Mr Thomas,** je vous présente M. Thomas;

(d) (*join*) **here the road meets the railway,** c'est ici que la route rejoint *ou* croise le chemin de fer;

(e) (*come into contact with*) **my head met the corner of a shelf,** je me suis cogné la tête contre l'angle d'une étagère; **his eyes met mine,** nos regards se sont croisés;

(f) (*be perceived by*) **there's more in this than meets the eye,** on ne voit pas le dessous des cartes; **a strange sound met our ears,** un bruit étrange nous a frappé l'oreille;

(g) (*satisfy*) satisfaire à, parer à, répondre à, remplir (*un besoin*); faire face à (*une demande*); satisfaire à, prévoir, prévenir (*une objection*); *Com* faire honneur à, faire bon accueil à, accueillir (*un effet, une lettre de change*); honorer (*un chèque*); **to m. s.o.'s wishes,** remplir les désirs de qn; **to m. one's commitments,** remplir ses engagements; **to m. expenses,** supporter les dépenses, subvenir aux frais; **the cost will be met by the company,** les frais seront assumés par la compagnie;

(h) (*face*) rencontrer (*l'ennemi*); affronter (*la mort, un danger*); parer à (*un danger*); faire face à (*une difficulté*); **she met her death in an air crash,** elle a péri dans un accident d'avion; *Sp* **he will m. the champion in June,** il rencontrera le champion en juin;

2 *vi* **(a)** (*by accident*) se rencontrer (par hasard);

(b) (*by arrangement*) se recontrer; **let's m. for lunch,** donnons-nous rendez-vous pour le déjeuner; **where shall we m.?,** où se retrouve-t-on?; **when shall we m. again?,** quand nous reverrons-nous?;
(c) (*become acquainted*) se rencontrer, se connaître; **they met in 1980,** ils se sont connus en 1980;
(d) (*of society, assembly*) se réunir en session, s'assembler; **the club meets every other Tuesday,** le cercle se réunit un mardi sur deux;
(e) (*join*) se rencontrer, se réunir, se joindre; **two rivers that m.,** deux rivières qui confluent *ou* qui se rejoignent; **the strap wouldn't** *or* **didn't m. around my wrist,** le bracelet n'était pas assez long pour mon poignet; **to make ends m.,** joindre les deux bouts;
(f) (*come into contact*) se rencontrer; **the two cars met head on,** les deux voitures se sont heurtées de plein fouet; **our eyes met,** nos regards se sont croisés.

meet[3] *adj Arch & Lit* convenable, séant; **it is m. that ...,** il convient que ... .

▶**meet up** *vi* (*meet*) se rencontrer; **in Paris we met up with an Australian,** à Paris, nous avons rencontré un Australien.

▶**meet with** *vipo* **(a)** (*encounter*) rencontrer, trouver, découvrir; **to m. with a refusal,** essuyer un refus; **to m. with difficulties,** éprouver des difficultés; **the proposal has met with fierce opposition,** la proposition s'est heurtée à une opposition très vive; **to m. with failure,** échouer; **the expedition met with disaster,** l'expédition a tourné au désastre; **he has met with an accident,** il lui est arrivé un accident; **the plan didn't m. with her approval,** le projet n'a pas reçu son accord; **(b)** *esp Am* (*meet*) (*for discussion*) rencontrer, retrouver; (*for lunch etc*) retrouver.

meeting ['miːtɪŋ] *n* **(a)** (*encounter*) rencontre *f* (*de personnes, de routes etc*); *Fml Lit* **m. of minds,** communion *f* de pensée; **m. place,** lieu *m* de réunion, rendez-vous *m*; **m. point,** point *m* de jonction; *Math* point de rencontre; **(b)** (*of society, assembly etc*) assemblée *f*, réunion *f*, séance *f*; (*in business, discussion*) réunion *f*, conférence *f*; **he's in a m.,** il est en conférence *ou* réunion; **at our last m.,** lors de notre dernière réunion; **during my first m. with him,** (*when I first met him*) lors de mon premier rendez-vous avec lui; **to hold a m.,** tenir une réunion; **to call a m. of the shareholders,** convoquer les actionnaires; **to open the m.,** déclarer la séance ouverte; **to address the m.,** prendre la parole; **(c)** *Sp* réunion *f*, meeting *m*; *Horseracing* (réunion de) courses *fpl*; **(d)** *Rel* (*of Quakers*) **to go to m.,** aller au temple; **m. house,** temple.

megabuck ['megəbʌk] *n Am Sl* un million de dollars; **megabucks,** une fortune; **m. project,** projet qui coûte une fortune.

megabyte ['megəbaɪt] *n Comptr* méga-octet *m*; **20 m. memory,** mémoire *f* de 20 méga-octets.

megacycle ['megəsaɪk(ə)l] *n El* mégacycle *m*.

megadeath ['megədeθ] *n* mort *f* d'un million de personnes.

megahertz ['megəhɜːts] *n El* mégahertz *m*.

megalith ['megəlɪθ] *n* mégalithe *m*.

megalithic [megə'lɪθɪk] *adj* mégalithique.

megalomania [megələʊ'meɪnɪə] *n* mégalomanie *f*.

megalomaniac [megələʊ'meɪnɪæk] *adj & n* mégalomane *mf*.

megaphone ['megəfəʊn] *n* mégaphone *m*.

megaton ['megətʌn] *n* mégatonne *f*.

megavolt ['megəvəʊlt] *n El* mégavolt *m*.

megawatt ['megəwɒt] *n El* mégawatt *m*.

meiosis [maɪ'əʊsɪs] *n* **(a)** (*in rhetoric*) litote *f*; **(b)** *Biol* méiose *f*.

melancholia [melən'kəʊlɪə] *n Med* mélancolie *f*.

melancholic [melən'kɒlɪk] *adj* mélancolique.

melancholy ['melənkəlɪ] **1** *n* mélancolie *f*. **2** *adj* (*person*) mélancolique, triste, déprimé; (*news*) triste, attristant.

melee ['meleɪ] *n* mêlée *f*.

mellifluous [me'lɪfluəs] *adj* (*words etc*) mielleux, doucereux.

mellow[1] ['meləʊ] *adj* **(a)** (*fruit*) fondant, mûr; (*vin*) moelleux, velouté; **(b)** (*voice, light, sound*) moelleux, doux, *f* douce; (*colour*) doux, tendre, voilé; **(c)** (*esprit, caractère*) mûr; **to grow m.,** mûrir, s'adoucir; **(d)** (*person*) jovial, -aux, enjoué; *F* (*slightly drunk*) un peu gris; **(e)** (*terrain*) meuble.

mellow[2] **1** *vi* **(a)** (*of fruit, wine*) mûrir; (*of wine*) prendre du velouté; (*of sound, light*) prendre du moelleux; **(b)** (*of character*) s'adoucir; **to m. with age,** devenir plus doux avec l'âge. **2** *vt* **(a)** (faire) mûrir (*des fruits*); donner du moelleux à (*un vin, une couleur, un son*); **(b)** mûrir, adoucir (*le caractère de qn*); **age has mellowed her,** l'âge a adouci son caractère; **(c)** ameublir (*le sol*).

mellowing ['meləʊɪŋ] *n* maturation *f*; adoucissement *m*.

mellowness ['meləʊnɪs] *n* **(a)** maturité *f* (*des fruits*); moelleux *m* (*du vin, d'un tableau*); velouté *m* (*du vin*); velouté, moelleux (*de la voix*); douceur *f* (*du caractère*); **(b)** maturité *f*, richesse *f* (*du sol*).

melodic [mɪ'lɒdɪk] *adj Mus* mélodique.

melodious [mɪ'ləʊdɪəs] *adj* mélodieux, harmonieux.

melodiously [mɪ'ləʊdɪəslɪ] *adv* mélodieusement.

melodrama ['melədrɑːmə] *n* mélodrame *m*.

melodramatic [melədrə'mætɪk] *adj* mélodramatique.

melodramatically [melədrə'mætɪklɪ] *adv* d'un air *ou* d'une manière mélodramatique.

melody ['melədɪ] *n* **(a)** *Mus* (*tune*) chant *m*, thème *m*; (*as opposed to harmony*) mélodie *f*; **(b)** (*of sounds*) mélodie *f*.

melon ['melən] *n* **(a)** (*fruit*) melon *m*; **water m.,** pastèque *f*; **m. seeds,** pépins *mpl* de melon; **(b)** *Am F* (*profits, money*) gros bénéfices (à distribuer); **to carve** *or* **cut up the m.,** distribuer les bénéfices.

melt [melt] *v* (*pt & pp* **melted**; *pp adj* **molten** ['məʊlt(ə)n]) **1** *vi* fondre; (*of jelly*) se déprendre; (*of solid in liquid*) fondre, se dissoudre; *Fig* (*of person*) s'attendrir, fléchir; **to m. in the mouth,** fondre dans la bouche; **pear that melts in the mouth,** poire fondante; **to m. into ...,** (*of colour etc*) se fondre dans ..., se perdre dans ...; *Fig* **my heart melted,** j'ai été attendri; **to m. into thin air,** disparaître. **2** *vt* (faire) fondre (*la glace, les métaux*); *Fig* attendrir, émouvoir (*qn*); (faire) fondre, (faire) dissoudre (*un sel etc*); **melted snow,** neige fondue.

▶**melt away** *vi* **(a)** (*of snow*) fondre complètement; **(b)** (*of clouds, vapour*) se dissiper; (*of crowd*) se disperser, disparaître; (*of anger*) s'évaporer.

▶**melt down** *vtsep* fondre (*de la ferraille etc*).

meltdown ['meltdaʊn] *n Nucl Phys* fusion *f*.

melting ['meltɪŋ] **1** *adj* (*neige, cire*) qui (se) fond; (*neige*) fondant; (*voice etc*) attendri; (*fruit*) fondant; (*words, scene etc*) attendrissant, émouvant. **2** *n* **(a)** (*act of melting*) fonte *f*, fusion *f* (*de la neige, des métaux*); **m. point/temperature,** point *m*/température *f* de fusion; *Fig* **everything's in the m. pot,** tout est à refaire; *Fig* **the United States is a m. pot,** les États-Unis sont un creuset *ou* un melting pot; **(b)** *Fig* attendrissement *m* (*des cœurs*).

member ['membər] *n* **(a)** membre *m* (*d'une famille, d'un club etc*); adhérent, -ente (*d'un parti*); **to be a m. of the family,** faire partie de la famille; **M. (***Br Can* **of Parliament,** *US* **of Congress),** député *m*; **M. of Parliament for Newcastle,** le représentant *ou* le député de Newcastle; **(b)** (*limb*) membre *m* (*du corps*); (*organ*) organe *m*; **male m.,** membre (viril), **(c)** *Archit* membre *m* (*d'une façade etc*), *Carp* pièce *f*, élément *m* (*d'une charpente*); *MecE* organe *m* (*d'une machine*); *Gram Math* membre.

membership ['membəʃɪp] *n* **(a)** (*state of being a member*) adhésion *f* (à un parti); **m. of any political party is incompatible with this post,** l'occupant de ce poste ne peut adhérer à aucun parti politique; **she resigned her m. of the party,** elle a rendu sa carte de parti; **my m. expires next month,** mon adhésion expire le mois prochain; **m. card,** carte *f* de membre *ou* d'adhérent; **to pay one's m. (fee),** payer sa cotisation; **(b)** (*members*) nombre *m* des membres, effectif *m* (*d'une société etc*); **club with a m. of a thousand,** club de mille membres; **the majority of our m.,** la majorité de nos membres.

membrane ['membreɪn] *n Biol etc* membrane *f*; **mucous m.,** (membrane *f*) muqueuse *f*.

membranous ['membrənəs] *adj* membraneux.

memento, *pl* **-oes, -os** [mɪ'mentəʊ, -əʊz] *n* mémento *m*, souvenir *m*.

memo ['meməʊ] *n* note *f* de service; **m. pad,** bloc-notes *m*, *pl* blocs-notes.

memoir ['memwɑːr] *n* (*essay*) mémoire *m*, dissertation *f* (*scientifique etc*); (*biography*) notice *f* biographique; **memoirs,** mémoires.

memorable ['memərəb(ə)l] *adj* (*speech, occasion*) mémorable; **a film m. largely for its sex and violence,** un film surtout remarqué pour ses scènes de sexe et de violence.

memorably ['memərəblɪ] *adv* mémorablement.

memorandum, *pl* **-da, -dums** [memə'rændəm, -də, -dəmz] *n* **(a)** *Admin* note *f* de service; **(b)** (*reminder*) note *f*; **(c)** (*in diplomacy*) mémorandum *m*; **(d)** mémoire *m* (*d'un contrat, d'une vente etc*); sommaire *m* des articles (*d'un contrat*); *Jur* **m. of association,** charte constitutive d'une société à responsabilité limitée, acte *m* de société; **(e)** *Com* bordereau *m*; **m. book,** carnet *m*, calepin *m*, agenda *m*.

memorial [mɪ'mɔːrɪəl] **1** *adj* (*statue, festival etc*) commémoratif; *Rel* **m. service,** messe *f* du souvenir. **2** *n* **(a)** (*monument*) monument *m* (commémoratif); **war m.,** monument aux morts; **(b)** *Admin* (*petition*) pétition *f*, demande *f*, requête *f*.

memorize ['meməraɪz] *vt* apprendre (*qch*) par cœur.

memory ['memərɪ] *n* **(a)** (*faculty*) mémoire *f*; **to have a good/bad m.,** avoir (une) bonne/mauvaise mémoire; *F* **m. like a sieve,** mémoire de lièvre; **loss of m.,** perte *f* de mémoire; **it slipped my m.,** cela m'est sorti de la mémoire *ou* de l'esprit; **if my m. serves me right,** si j'ai bonne mémoire; **in** *or* **within living m.,** de mémoire d'homme; **from m.,** (*jouer, réciter, peindre qch*) de mémoire; **to commit sth to m.,** apprendre qch par cœur;
(b) (*something remembered*) mémoire *f*, souvenir *m* (*de qn, de qch*); **childhood memories,** souvenirs d'enfance; **I have very pleasant memories of your friend,** je garde un excellent souvenir de votre ami; **her earliest memories are of music,** ses plus anciens souvenirs sont des airs de musique; **to keep s.o.'s m. alive,** garder le souvenir de qn; **in m. of ...,** en mémoire de ..., à la mémoire de ..., en souvenir de ...;
(c) *Comptr* mémoire *f*; **m. bank,** bloc *m* de mémoire; **m. expansion card,** carte *f* d'extension de mémoire.

menace¹ ['menɪs] *n* menace *f*; **there was m. in his voice,** il parlait d'un ton menaçant; *F* **that kid's a m.,** cet enfant est une catastrophe; *Fig* **that carpet's a m.,** ce tapis est dangereux.

menace² *vt* menacer (*qn*).

menacing ['menəsɪŋ] *adj* menaçant; **in a m. voice,** d'une voix menaçante.

menacingly ['menəsɪŋlɪ] *adv* (*to look, say*) d'un air *ou* d'un ton menaçant.

menagerie [mɪ'nædʒərɪ] *n* ménagerie *f*.

mend¹ [mend] *n* **(a)** (*in fabric etc*) reprise *f*, raccommodage *m*; **(b)** (*improvement*) amélioration *f*; **to be on the m.,** (*of person*) être en voie de guérison.

mend² **1** *vt* **(a)** (*repair*) raccommoder (*un vêtement etc*); repriser (*des bas*); rem(m)ailler (*un filet*); réparer (*un outil, une route, des chaussures etc*); **to m. invisibly,** stopper (*un vêtement*); **(b)** (*put right*) rectifier, corriger; réparer (*une faute, un mal*); **to m. one's ways,** changer de conduite, se corriger; **he promised to m. his ways,** il a promis de changer sa conduite; *Prov* **least said soonest mended,** moins on parle, mieux cela vaut; **it does not m. matters to ...,** cela n'arrange pas les choses de .... **2** *vi* (*of broken bones*) se ressouder; (*of invalid, health etc*) se remettre; (*of condition*) s'améliorer.

mendacious [men'deɪʃəs] *adj* menteur, -euse; (*report*) mensonger.

mendacity [men'dæsɪtɪ] *n* **(a)** (*characteristic*) penchant *m* au mensonge, habitude *f* du mensonge; **(b)** (*falsehood*) fausseté *f*.

Mendelian [men'diːlɪən] *adj Biol* mendélien.

mendicant ['mendɪkənt] **1** *adj* **(a)** *Fml* mendiant, de mendiant; **(b)** *Rel* **m. friar,** moine mendiant. **2** *n* **(a)** *Fml* mendiant, -ante; **(b)** *Rel* moine mendiant.

mendicity [men'dɪsɪtɪ] *n Fml* mendicité *f*.

mending ['mendɪŋ] *n* **(a)** raccommodage *m* (*de vêtements etc*); reprisage *m* (*de bas*); réparation *f* (*d'un mur, d'une route etc*); **invisible m.,** stoppage *m*; rem(m)aillage *m* (*de bas*); **(b)** (*clothes*) **pile of m.,** tas *m* de vêtements à raccommoder.

menfolk ['menfəʊk] *npl* les hommes *mpl* (*par opposition aux femmes*); **the women worked alongside their** *or* **the m.,** les femmes travaillaient aux côtés des hommes.

menial ['miːnɪəl] **1** *adj* (*task, job*) servile, bas, *f* basse. **2** *n usu Pej* laquais *m*; (*in household*) domestique *mf*.

meningitis [menɪn'dʒaɪtɪs] *n Med* méningite *f*; **to have m.,** faire une méningite.

meniscus, *pl* **-ci, -scuses** [mɪ'nɪskəs, -saɪ, -skəsəz] *n* ménisque *m*.

menopausal ['menəʊpɔːzəl] *adj* ménopausique; (*femme*) à la ménopause.

menopause ['menəpɔːz] *n Physiol* ménopause *f*; **to be going through the m.,** traverser la ménopause.

menses ['mensiːz] *npl Physiol* menstrues *fpl*.

menstrual ['menstrʊəl] *adj Physiol* (*cycle*) menstruel.

menstruate ['menstrʊeɪt] *vi Physiol* avoir ses menstrues *ou* ses règles.

menstruation [menstrʊ'eɪʃən] *n Physiol* menstruation *f*.

mensuration [menʃə'reɪʃən] *n* **(a)** (*act of measuring*) mesurage *m*, mesure *f*; **(b)** *Math* mensuration *f*.

menswear ['menzweər] *n Com* vêtements *mpl* d'hommes, habillement *m* pour hommes; **m. (department),** rayon *m* homme.

mental ['ment(ə)l] *adj* **(a)** (*état, âge etc*) mental, -aux; **I made a m. note to speak to her about it,** je me suis dit qu'il ne fallait pas oublier de lui en parler; **I've made a m. note of it,** j'y pense; **m. cruelty,** cruauté mentale; **m. reservation,** réservation *f*; **m. arithmetic,** calcul mental *ou* de tête; **m. deficiency,** déficience *ou* débilité mentale; **m. defective,** déficient, -ente, débile intellectuel(le); **m. health,** santé mentale; **m. hospital** *or* **home,** hôpital *m ou* clinique *f* psychiatrique; **m. illness,** malade *f* mentale; **(b)** *Sl* (*mad*) dingue.

mentality [men'tælɪtɪ] *n* mentalité *f*, état mental (*de qn*); **the oriental m.,** la mentalité orientale.

mentally ['ment(ə)lɪ] *adv* mentalement; **m. deficient** *or* **defective,** débile; **m. ill/handicapped,** malade/handicapé mental; **to be m. ill,** être un malade mental; **the m. ill/handicapped,** les malades/handicapés mentaux.

menthol ['menθɒl] *n Ch* menthol *m*; **m. cigarettes,** cigarettes *fpl* au menthol.

mentholated ['menθəleɪtɪd] *adj Pharm* mentholé.

mention¹ ['menʃən] *n* **(a)** (*reference*) mention *f* (*de qn, de qch*); **m. was made of ...,** on a parlé de ...; **to make no m. of sth,** passer qch sous silence; **there had been no m. of this extra charge in the brochure,** la brochure ne mentionnait pas ce supplément; **at the m. of food,** quand on a parlé de manger; **he gets a brief m. in her autobiography,** elle le mentionne brièvement dans son autobiographie; **(b)** *Sch etc* **honourable m.,** mention *f* (honorable), accessit *m*.

mention² *vt* mentionner, citer, faire mention de, parler de (*qn, qch*); relever (*un fait*); **the sum mentioned,** la somme indiquée; **I had forgotten to m. that ...,** j'avais oublié de vous dire que ...; **she mentioned that she had lived in Bristol,** elle mentionna qu'elle avait vécu à Bristol; **I shall m. it to him,** je lui en toucherai un mot; **too numerous to m.,** trop nombreux pour les citer; **I have no money worth mentioning,** je n'ai pour ainsi dire pas d'argent; **as mentioned above,** comme mentionné ci-dessus; **not to m. ...,** sans parler de ...; **I heard my name mentioned,** j'ai entendu prononcer mon nom; **did she m. my name?,** est-ce qu'elle a parlé de moi?; **to m. s.o. in one's will,** coucher qn sur son testament; *F* **don't m. it!,** (*after being thanked*) il n'y a pas de quoi!; (*drop the subject*) ne m'en parlez pas!, n'en parlez pas!

mentor ['mentɔːr] *n* mentor *m*, guide *m*.

menu ['menjuː] *n* **(a)** *Culin* menu *m*; **today's m.,** la carte du jour; **(b)** *Comptr* menu *m*.

menu-driven ['menjuːdrɪv(ə)n] *adj Comptr* contrôlé par menu(s).

MEP [emiː'piː] *n Br* (*abbr* **Member of the European Parliament**) membre *m* du Parlement Européen.

mercantile ['mɜːkəntaɪl] *adj* commercial, -aux, commerçant; *Pej* mercantile, intéressé; **m. nation,** nation commerçante; **m. marine,** marine marchande; **m. law,** droit commercial, code *m* de commerce.

mercantilism ['mɜːkəntɪlɪzəm] *n* mercantilisme *m*.

mercantilist ['mɜːkəntɪlɪst] *adj & n* mercantiliste *m*.

mercenary ['mɜːsɪnərɪ] **1** *adj* (*âme, esprit*) mercenaire, intéressé. **2** *n* (*soldier*) mercenaire *m*.

mercerized ['mɜːsəraɪzd] *adj Ind* (*cotton*) mercerisé.

merchandise¹ ['mɜːtʃəndaɪz] *n* marchandise(s) *f*(*pl*).

merchandise² *vi* faire du commerce *ou* du négoce.

merchandising ['mɜːtʃəndaɪzɪŋ] *n* marchandisage *m*.

merchant ['mɜːtʃənt] **1** *n* **(a)** *Com* négociant, -ante, commerçant, -ante *ou* marchand, -ande en gros; **wine m.,** négociant en vins; **(b)** *F* **speed m.,** chauffard *m*; **gloom m.,** pessimiste *mf*; **(c)** *Am Com* (*shopkeeper*) marchand, -ande, boutiquier, -ière. **2** *adj* marchand; de commerce; **m. bank,** banque *f* d'affaires; **m. navy** *or* **marine,** marine marchande; **m. ship** *ou* **vessel,** navire marchand.

merchantman, *pl* **-men** ['mɜːtʃəntmən] *n* (*ship*) navire marchand, navire de commerce.

merciful ['mɜːsɪful] *adj* (*God*) miséricordieux (**to,** pour); (*judge*) clément (**to,** envers); **m. heavens!,** grands Dieux!

mercifully ['mɜːsɪfʊlɪ] *adv* **(a)** (*showing mercy*) miséricordieusement; **(b)** (*fortunately*) heureusement.

merciless ['mɜːsɪlɪs] *adj* impitoyable, sans pitié, sans merci.

mercilessly ['mɜːsɪlɪslɪ] *adv* impitoyablement, sans pitié; **the rain beat down m.,** la pluie tombait sans répit.

mercurial [mɜː'kjʊərɪəl] *adj* **(a)** (*lively*) vif, éveillé; à l'esprit prompt; **(b)** (*changeable*) inconstant; d'humeur changeante; **(c)** *Med Pharm* (*produit*) mercuriel.

Mercury ['mɜːkjʊrɪ] *n* **(a)** *Myth Astron* Mercure *m*; **(b)** *Ch* m., mercure *m.*

mercy ['mɜːsɪ] *n* pitié *f*; *Rel* miséricorde *f*; *Rel* **Lord have m.!**, Seigneur prends pitié!; **to show m. to s.o.**, faire miséricorde à qn; **to have m. on s.o.**, avoir pitié de qn; **to be without m.**, être impitoyable *ou* sans pitié; **to call** *or* **beg for m.**, demander grâce; **to throw oneself on s.o.'s m.**, s'abandonner à la merci de qn; **m.!**, grâce!; **m. killing**, euthanasie *f*; **at the m. of s.o./sth**, à la discrétion *ou* à la merci de qn/qch; *Iron* **I leave him to your tender mercies**, je le livre *ou* je l'abandonne à vos soins; **to be thankful for small mercies**, être reconnaissant des moindres bienfaits; **what a m.!**, quel bonheur!, quelle chance!; **works of m.**, œuvres *fpl* de charité; **m. flight**, = vol pour transporter un malade à l'hôpital.

mere [mɪər] *adj* simple, pur, seul; rien que ...; **a m. coincidence**, une pure et simple coïncidence; **it was only by the merest chance that ...**, ce n'est que par le plus grand des hasards que...; **I shudder at the m. thought of it**, je frissonne rien que d'y penser; **he's a m. child**, ce n'est qu'un enfant.

merely ['mɪəlɪ] *adv* simplement, seulement, purement (et simplement); **he m. smiled**, il se contenta de sourire; **I mention this m. to draw attention to ...**, je n'ai dit cela que pour attirer l'attention sur ... .

meretricious [merɪ'trɪʃəs] *adj* (*style etc*) factice, d'un éclat criard.

merge [mɜːdʒ] **1** *vt* fondre, fusionner (*deux systèmes, deux classes*); *Comptr* fusionner (*des fichiers*); **to m. sth in** *or* **into sth**, fondre qch dans qch; amalgamer qch avec qch; **the two regiments were merged (into one)**, les deux régiments ont été regroupés. **2** *vi* se fondre, se perdre (**in, into**, dans); se confondre (**in, into**, avec); *Fin* (*of companies, banks etc*) s'amalgamer, fusionner; **the sea and sky merged**, le ciel et la mer se confondaient.

merger ['mɜːdʒər] *n* **(a)** *Fin* fusion *f* (*de plusieurs sociétés en une seule*); **m. talks**, discussions *fpl* en vue d'une fusion; **(b)** *Jur* extinction *f* par consolidation *ou* par fusion.

meridian [mə'rɪdɪən] **1** *n* **(a)** *Geog* méridien *m*; **Greenwich m.**, méridien de Greenwich; **(b)** *Astron* méridien *m*, point culminant (*d'un astre*). **2** *adj Astron* (*altitude, angle etc*) méridien, -enne; **m. line**, (ligne) méridienne *f*.

meridional [mə'rɪdɪən(ə)l] **1** *adj* méridional, -aux; (*southern*) du sud; (*in France*) du midi de la France. **2** *n* Méridional, -ale, -aux.

meringue [mə'ræŋ] *n Culin* meringue *f*.

merino [mə'riːnəʊ] *n* (*sheep, wool*) mérinos *m*.

merit¹ ['merɪt] *n* **(a)** (*deserving aspect*) mérite *m*; **according to one's merits**, (*être récompensé*) selon ses mérites; *Jur* **the merits of a case**, le bien-fondé d'une cause; **to judge a proposal on its merits**, juger une proposition au fond *ou* en considérant ses qualités intrinsèques; *Rel* **to acquire m.**, gagner du mérite; **her remarks at least had the m. of being frank**, au moins, ses remarques avaient le mérite d'être franches; **(b)** (*worth*) valeur *f*, mérite *m*; **in order of m.**, par ordre de mérite; **these paintings have no m. at all**, ces tableaux n'ont aucune valeur; *Am* **m. system**, régime *m* du mérite; *Am* **m. increase**, augmentation *f* au mérite.

merit² *vt* mériter (*une récompense, une punition*).

meritocracy [merɪ'tɒkrəsɪ] *n* aristocratie *f* du mérite.

meritorious [merɪ'tɔːrɪəs] *adj* (*person*) méritant; (*deed*) méritoire; (*conduct*) digne, méritoire.

meritoriously [merɪ'tɔːrɪəslɪ] *adv* méritoirement.

merlin ['mɜːlɪn] *n* (*bird*) (faucon *m*) émerillon *m*.

mermaid ['mɜːmeɪd] *n Myth* sirène *f*.

merman, *pl* **-men** ['mɜːmæn, -men] *n Myth* triton *m*.

Merovingian [merəʊ'vɪndʒɪən] *Hist* **1** *adj* mérovingien. **2** *n* Mérovingien, -ienne.

merrily ['merɪlɪ] *adv* gaiement, joyeusement.

merriment ['merɪmənt] *n* gaieté *f*, réjouissance *f*, divertissement(s) *m(pl)*, amusement(s) *m(pl)*.

merry ['merɪ] *adj* (*comp* **merrier**; *superl* **merriest**) **(a)** (*happy*) joyeux, gai; jovial, -aux; **to make m.**, se divertir, s'amuser, s'égayer, se réjouir; **m. Christmas!**, joyeux Noël!; *F* **the weather is playing m. hell with the rail timetables**, le mauvais temps a complètement chamboulé l'horaire des trains; *F* **this pain is giving me m. hell**, cette douleur me fait souffrir atrocement; *Prov* **the more the merrier**, plus on est de fous, plus on rit; *Arch & Lit* **m. England**, l'aimable Angleterre; **the m. month of May**, le gentil mois de mai; **Robin Hood and his m. men**, Robin des Bois et ses joyeux *ou* gais lurons; **(b)** *F* (*slightly drunk*) éméché, un peu parti, un peu gris.

merry-go-round ['merɪgəʊraʊnd] *n* manège *m*, *Belg* carrousel *m*.

merrymaking ['merɪmeɪkɪŋ] *n* réjouissances *fpl*, divertissement *m*; (*party*) réunion joyeuse, partie *f* de plaisir.

mescalin(e) ['meskəlɪn] *n Pharm* mescaline *f*.

mesh¹ [meʃ] *n* **(a)** (*of net, sieve etc*) maille *f*; **wire m.**, toile *f* métallique; *Biol* **meshes**, réseau *m* (*vasculaire etc*); **m. stockings**, bas *mpl* filet; **(b)** *MecE* prise *f*, engrènement *m*, engrenage *m*; **in m.**, en prise.

mesh² **1** *vi* (*coordinate*) se coordonner; *MecE* (*of teeth, wheel*) engrener, s'engrener; (*be in mesh*) être en prise (**with**, avec); (*engage*) se mettre en prise (**with**, avec). **2** *vt MecE* endenter, engrener (*des roues dentées*); *Fig* coordonner (*qch à qch*).

meshing ['meʃɪŋ] *n* **(a)** *MecE etc* prise *f*, engrènement *m*; (*act of putting in mesh*) mise *f* en prise; **(b)** mailles *fpl* (*d'un filet*); **wire m.**, trellis *m* métallique *ou* en fil de fer.

mesmeric [mez'merɪk] *adj* magnétique, hypnotique.

mesmerize ['mezməraɪz] *vt* hypnotiser; *Fig* fasciner.

meson ['miːzɒn] *n Nucl Phys* méson *m*.

Mesopotamia [mesəpə'teɪmɪə] *n* Mésopotamie *f*.

mess¹ [mes] *n* **(a)** (*disorder*) fouillis *m*, désordre *m*; (*bungled job etc*) gâchis *m*; **everything's in a m.**, tout est en désordre; **the kitchen's a m.**, la cuisine est en désordre; **what a m.!**, quel désordre!; **you're** *or* **you look a m.!**, tu es dans un triste état!; **my hair's a m.**, mes cheveux sont dans un triste état; **to be in a m.**, (*of person*) être dans le pétrin *ou* dans de beaux draps; **to make a m. of sth**, (*of job, translation, repair etc*) gâcher qch, saboter qch, *F* saloper qch; **the dentist made a real m. of it**, le dentiste a vraiment salopé le travail; **to make a m. of things**, tout gâcher; *F* **after the fight his face was a terrible m.**, après la bagarre il avait le visage tout amoché; *F* **he's a m.**, (*has complexes*) il est bourré de complexes; (*because of drugs etc*) il est foutu;

(b) (*dirt*) saleté *f*; **to make a m. of the tablecloth**, salir la nappe; **dog's m.**, crotte *f* de chien;

(c) *Mil F* (*food*) popote *f* (*des officiers*); ordinaire *m* (*des hommes*); *Nau* plat *m*; (*room*) mess *m* (*des officiers*); réfectoire *m* (*des hommes*); *Nau* carré *m* (*des officiers*); *Nau* **m. deck**, poste *m* des matelots *ou* d'équipage; **m. kit**, ustensiles *mpl ou* matériel *m* d'ordinaire *ou* de campement; **m. tin**, gamelle *f* (individuelle); **m. jacket**, spencer *m*;

(d) (*food*) *Bible* **m. of pottage**, = plat *m* de lentilles.

mess² **1** *vt* salir, souiller (qch). **2** *vi* **(a)** *Mil etc* (*of officers*) faire table; (*of men*) faire plat, manger en commun, faire gamelle (**with**, avec); **to m. together**, manger à la même table; **(b)** *Sl* (*exaggerate*) **no messing!**, sans blagues!, sans mentir!; **there were two hundred of them, no messing!**, ils étaient deux cents sans mentir!; **(c)** (*meddle*) **don't m. with me!**, ne me cherche pas!

►**mess about, mess around** **1** *vi* **(a)** (*play the fool*) faire l'imbécile; **(b)** (*tinker*) tripoter; **don't m. around with something that doesn't belong to you**, ne tripote pas ce qui ne t'appartient pas; **(c)** (*waste time*) glandouiller; **(d)** (*sexually*) **to m. around with s.o.**, avoir des relations avec qn; **stop messing around with my sister!**, laisse ma sœur tranquille! **2** *vtsep* **(a)** (*treat badly*) traiter (*qn*) de façon injuste; **I wish you'd stop messing me about and make up your mind**, j'aimerais bien que tu arrêtes de me tourmenter et que tu te décides; **(b)** (*alter*) chambouler.

►**mess up** **1** *vtsep* **(a)** (*put in disorder*) mettre (*qch*) en désordre, semer la pagaïe dans (*qch*); **you've messed up all my clothes!**, tu as semé la pagaïe dans tous mes vêtements!; **(b)** (*ruin*) gâcher, bousiller (*un travail*); **he's messed everything up**, il a tout gâché. **2** *vi* (*at work, university etc*) tout gâcher; **to m. up on an exam**, merdouiller dans *ou* à un examen.

message ['mesɪdʒ] *n* **(a)** message *m*; communication *f* (*téléphonique etc*); **radio m.**, message radio; **telephone m.**, message téléphoné *ou* téléphonique; **to send a m. to s.o.**, envoyer un message à qn; **to leave a m. for s.o.**, laisser un message *ou* un mot pour qn; **the King's/Queen's m.**, = discours télévisé et radiodiffusé du roi ou de la reine le jour de Noël; *F* **have you got the m.?, is the m. getting across?**, as-tu bien compris?, tu as pigé?; *F* **people seem to be getting the m., the m. seems to be getting across**, les gens ont l'air de commencer à comprendre; *Comptr* **m. switching**, commutation *f* des messages; **(b)** (*meaning*) message *m*, leçon *f* (*spirituelle*); enseignement *m* (*d'un livre etc*); **the film's m. is clear**, le message qui ressort du film est clair; **(c)** (*of a prophet*) prédiction *f*, révélation *f*, évangile *m*; **(d)** *Scot* (*errand*) commission *f*, course *f*.

messenger ['mesɪndʒər] *n* messager, -ère; (*in large offices etc*) coursier, -ière; *Mil* coureur *m*; *Admin* (*in di-*

plomacy) courrier *m* (diplomatique); *Com* commissionnaire *m*; **motorcycle m.**, estafette *f* motocycliste; **m. pigeon,** pigeon voyageur; **King's/Queen's m.**, ≈ courrier d'Etat; **by m.**, par porteur; **m. boy,** garçon *m* de courses.

Messiah [mɪ'saɪə] *n* Messie *m*.

messianic [mesɪ'ænɪk] *adj* messianique.

messily ['mesɪlɪ] *adv* (*to eat*) salement.

messmate ['mesmeɪt] *n Mil etc* commensal, -ale, -aux, camarade *mf* de table; *Nau* camarade de plat.

Messrs ['mesəz] *npl* (*abbr* **Messieurs**) MM.

mess-up ['mesʌp] *n F* gâchis *m*, pagaïe *f*.

messy ['mesɪ] *adj F* **(a)** (*dirty*) sale, malpropre; **a m. eater,** personne qui mange salement, cochon *m*; **(b)** (*that make(s) dirty*) qui salit; salissant; **oranges are a m. fruit (to eat),** les oranges sont difficiles à manger proprement; **(c)** (*untidy*) en désordre; **this room's so m.**, cette pièce est dans un tel désordre!; **(d)** (*unpleasantly complex*) confus, embrouillé; **the official story is getting messier and messier,** l'histoire officielle s'embrouille de plus en plus; **he got involved in some m. business with a drug-taking prostitute,** il a été entraîné dans une sale histoire avec une prostituée qui se drogue; **it's a rather m. solution,** c'est une solution assez compliquée; **his m. private life,** sa vie privée troublée.

mestiza [me'stiːzə] *n* métisse *f*.

mestizo, *pl* **-os** [me'stiːzəʊ, -əʊz] *n* métis *m*.

met¹ [met] *see* **MEET².**

met² *adj Br F* météo; **the m. office,** la météo.

metabolic [metə'bɒlɪk] *adj Biol* métabolique; **m. rate,** taux *m* métabolique.

metabolism [mɪ'tæbəlɪz(ə)m] *n Biol* métabolisme *m*.

metabolize [mɪ'tæbəlaɪz] *vt* transformer (*un tissu etc*) par métabolisme.

metacarpal [metə'kɑːp(ə)l] *adj & n Anat* métacarpien *m*.

metal¹ ['met(ə)l] **1** *n* **(a)** métal *m*, -aux; **precious m.**, métal précieux; **ferrous/non-ferrous metals,** métaux ferreux/non ferreux; **molten m.**, métal en fusion; **sheet m.**, métal en feuilles, tôle *f*; **bearing** *or* **white m.**, métal à coussinets; **m. detector,** détecteur *m* de métal; **m. engraver,** graveur *m* sur métaux; **m. polish,** nettoie-métaux *m inv*; **(b)** *Typ* caractères *mpl*, métal *m*, plomb *m*; **old m.**, vieille matière; **(c)** *Min* pierre *f* de mine; *Constr* (matériau *m* d')empierrement *m*; *Rail* ballast *m* (de voie ferrée); **road m.**, cailloutis *m*, pierraille *f*; **(d)** *Rail etc* **the metals,** les rails *mpl*; **(e)** (*in glassmaking*) verre *m* en fusion. **2** *adj* (*made of metal*) métallique, en métal.

metal² *vt* (**-ll-**, *US* **-l-**) **(a)** empierrer, ferrer, caillouter (*une route*); **metalled road,** route empierrée; **(b)** (*coat with metal*) métalliser (*le bois etc*); doubler de métal (*une carène de navire etc*).

metallic [mɪ'tælɪk] *adj* (*son, voix*) & *Ch El* métallique; (*goût*) de métal; *Fin* **m. currency,** monnaie *f* de métal, monnaie métallique; **m. lustre,** éclat *m* métallique; **a m. blue/green,** un bleu/vert métallique.

metalling, *US* **metaling** ['met(ə)lɪŋ] *n* (*action*) empierrement *m* (*d'une route*); (*surface*) couche *f* d'empierrement.

metallurgic(al) [metə'lɜːdʒɪk, -ɪk(ə)l)] *adj* métallurgique.

metallurgy [me'tælədʒɪ] *n* métallurgie *f*.

metalwork ['met(ə)lwɜːk] *n* (*practice, technique*) travail *m* des métaux; **art m.**, ferronnerie *f ou* serrurerie *f* d'art; *Br Sch* **m. teacher/lesson,** professeur *m*/cours *m* de travail des métaux.

metalworker ['met(ə)lwɜːkər] *n* ouvrier *m* en métaux; **art m.**, ferronnier *m ou* serrurier *m* d'art.

metamorphic [metə'mɔːfɪk] *adj* **(a)** *Geol* métamorphique; **(b)** *Biol* métamorphosique.

metamorphose [metə'mɔːfəʊz] **1** *vt* métamorphoser, transformer (**into,** en). **2** *vi* se métamorphoser (**into,** en).

metamorphosis, *pl* **-oses** [metə'mɔːfəsɪs, -əsiːz] *n* métamorphose *f*.

metaphor ['metəfər] *n* métaphore *f*, image *f* (**for,** symbolisant); **mixed m.**, métaphore multiple.

metaphoric(al) [metə'fɒrɪk, -ɪk(ə)l] *adj* métaphorique.

metaphorically [metə'fɒrɪklɪ] *adv* métaphoriquement.

metaphysical [metə'fɪzɪk(ə)l] *adj* métaphysique.

metaphysics [metə'fɪzɪks] *npl* (*usu with sing verb*) métaphysique *f*.

metatarsal [metə'tɑːs(ə)l] *adj & n Anat* métatarsien *m*.

►**mete out** [miːt] *vtsep* assigner (*des punitions*); distribuer, décerner (*des récompenses*).

meteor ['miːtɪər] *n* météore *m*; **m. shower,** chute *f* de météores.

meteoric [miːtɪ'ɒrɪk] *adj Astron* météorique; *Fig* **m. rise,** ascension *f* météorique.

meteorite ['miːtɪəraɪt] *n* météorite *f*, aérolithe *m*.

meteorological [miːtɪərə'lɒdʒɪk(ə)l] *adj* (*bureau, bulletin etc*) météorologique.

meteorologist [miːtɪə'rɒlədʒɪst] *n* météorologiste *mf*, météorologue *mf*.

meteorology [miːtɪə'rɒlədʒɪ] *n* météorologie *f*.

meter¹ ['miːtər] *n* appareil *m* de mesure, compteur *m*; **electric m.**, compteur électrique; **flow m.**, débitmètre *m*; **gas/water m.**, compteur à gaz/à eau; **slot m.**, compteur à paiement préalable; *Aut* **parking m.**, parc(o)mètre *m*, *Can* compteur de stationnement; **pH meter,** pH-mètre; *Br Aut F* **I'm on a m.**, ma voiture est au parc(o)mètre; *Aut F* **m. maid,** contractuelle *f*; **exposure m.**, *Phot* posemètre *m*; *Opt* **light m.**, luxmètre *m*; **m. reading,** relevé *m* (*de(s) compteur(s)*); **m. reader,** (*person*) releveur, -euse de(s) compteur(s).

meter² *n US* = **METRE¹,².**

methadone ['meθədəʊn] *n Med* méthadone *f*; **to be on m.**, (*of drug addict*) prendre de la méthadone.

methane ['miːθeɪn] *n Ch* méthane *m*.

methinks [mɪ'θɪŋks] *v impers* (*pt* **methought** [mɪ'θɔːt]) *Arch Lit* il me semble.

method ['meθəd] *n* (*in research, science*) méthode *f*; (*manner*) méthode, manière *f* (**of doing sth,** de faire qch); *Admin* **m. of payment,** modalités *fpl* de paiement; **to work without m.**, travailler sans méthode; **there's m. in his madness,** il n'est pas si fou qu'il en a l'air; *Ind* **production m.**, procédé(s) de fabrication *ou* de production; *Th Cin* **M. acting,** jeu *m* selon la méthode de Stanislavski; **M. actor/actress,** acteur/actrice adepte de la méthode de Stanislavski; *Ind* **methods engineer,** ingénieur *m* des méthodes; **methods engineering,** étude *f* des méthodes.

methodical [mɪ'θɒdɪk(ə)l] *adj* méthodique; **to be m.**, avoir l'esprit méthodique, avoir de l'ordre.

methodically [mɪ'θɒdɪklɪ] *adv* méthodiquement, avec méthode.

Methodism ['meθədɪz(ə)m] *n Rel* méthodisme *m*.

Methodist ['meθədɪst] *adj & n Rel* méthodiste *mf*.

methodology [meθə'dɒlədʒɪ] *n* méthodologie *f*.

meths [meθs] *n Br F* alcool *m* à brûler; **m. drinker,** buveur *m* d'alcool à brûler.

Methuselah [mə'θjuːzələ] *n Bible* Mathusalem *m*; *Fig* **as old as M.**, vieux comme Hérode.

methyl ['meθɪl] *n Ch* méthyle *m*; **m. alcohol,** alcool *m* méthylique.

methylated ['meθɪleɪtɪd] *adj* **m. spirits,** alcool dénaturé, alcool à brûler.

methylene ['meθɪliːn] *n Ch* méthylène *m*.

meticulous [mɪ'tɪkjʊləs] *adj* méticuleux; **with m. attention to detail,** avec une attention minutieuse pour les détails.

meticulously [mɪ'tɪkjʊləslɪ] *adv* méticuleusement; (*habillé*) avec un soin méticuleux.

meticulousness [mɪ'tɪkjʊləsnɪs] *n* méticulosité *f*, soin méticuleux.

metre¹, *US* **meter** ['miːtər] *n Liter* (*poetry*) mètre *m*, mesure *f*; **in m.**, en vers.

metre², *US* **meter** *n* (*measurement*) mètre *m*; **square/cubic m.**, mètre carré/cube.

metric ['metrɪk] *adj* (*système*) métrique; **m. area** *or* **volume,** métrage *m*; **m. ton,** tonne *f* (métrique); **to go m.**, adopter le système métrique.

metrical ['metrɪk(ə)l] *adj* métrique.

metrication [metrɪ'keɪʃən] *n* adoption *f ou* introduction *f ou* utilisation *f* du système métrique.

metrics ['metrɪks] *npl Liter* (*poetry*) métrique *f*.

metronome ['metrənəʊm] *n Mus* métronome *m*.

metropolis [mɪ'trɒpəlɪs] *n* (*city*) métropole *f*.

metropolitan [metrə'pɒlɪtən] **1** *adj* (*area etc*) métropolitain; *Eng* **M. Police,** police *f* de Londres. **2** *n* habitant, -ante de la métropole *ou* de la capitale.

mettle ['met(ə)l] *n* **(a)** (*courage*) (*of person*) ardeur *f*, courage *m*, feu *m*; (*of horse*) fougue *f*; **full of m.**, (*person*) courageux, plein de courage, plein d'ardeur; (*horse*) fougueux; **to be on one's m.**, se piquer d'honneur; **(b)** (*character*) caractère *m*, disposition *f*, tempérament *m*; **to show one's m.**, donner sa mesure.

mettlesome ['met(ə)lsəm] *adj* (*person*) ardent, vif, plein de courage; (*horse*) fougueux.

mew¹ [mjuː] *n* miaulement *m* (*du chat*).

mew² *vi* (*of cat*) miauler.

mewing ['mjuːɪŋ] *n* miaulement *m*.

mews [mjuːz] *npl* (*with sing or pl verb*) *Br* **(a)** (*street*) impasse *f*, ruelle *f* (*sur laquelle donnaient des écuries*); **m. house,** = maison aménagée dans une ancienne écurie; **(b)**

Arch (*stables*) écuries *fpl*.
Mexican ['meksɪkən] **1** *adj* mexicain. **2** *n* Mexicain, -aine.
Mexico ['meksɪkəʊ] *n* Mexique *m*; **M. City,** Mexico *f*.
mezzanine ['metsəniːn] *n* **(a)** *Archit* **m. (floor),** mezzanine *f*, entresol *m*; **(b)** *Th Am* premier dessous (*de la scène*).
mezzo ['metsəʊ] *Mus* **1** *adv* mezzo; **m. forte,** mezzo forte. **2** *n* = **MEZZO-SOPRANO**.
mezzo-soprano ['metsəʊsə'prɑːnəʊ] *n Mus* mezzo-soprano *m*, *pl* mezzo-sopranos, -ni.
mezzotint ['metzəʊtɪnt] *n* **(a)** (*technique*) mezzo-tinto *m inv*, gravure *f* à la manière noire; **(b)** (*individual engraving*) estampe *f* à la manière noire.
mfd *Com* (*abbr* **manufactured**) fabriqué.
mg [em'dʒiː] *n* (*abbr* **milligram(s)**) mg *m*.
Mgr *Rel* (*abbr* **monsignor**) Mgr *m*.
Mhz *El* (*abbr* **megahertz**) Mhz *m*.
mi [miː] *n Mus* mi *m*.
MI [e'maɪ] *n Comptr* (*abbr* **machine intelligence**) intelligence artificielle.
MIA [emaɪ'eɪ] *adj & n Am Mil* (*abbr* **missing in action**) porté disparu.
MI5 [emaɪ'faɪv] *n Br* (*abbr* **Military Intelligence Section 5**) MI5 *m* (*contre-espionnage*).
MI6 [emaɪ'sɪks] *n Br* (*abbr* **Military Intelligence Section 6**) MI6 *m* (*espionage*) ≈ deuxième bureau *m*.
miaow¹ [mɪ'aʊ] *n* miaulement *m*, miaou *m* (*du chat*).
miaow² *vi* (*of cat*) miauler.
mica ['maɪkə] *n Miner* mica *m*.
mice *see* **MOUSE**.
Mich *abbr* **Michigan**.
Michael ['maɪk(ə)l] *n* Michel *m*; *Br Sl* **to take the M. out of s.o.,** se payer la tête de qn, se moquer de qn.
Michaelmas ['mɪkəlməs] *n* la Saint-Michel; **M. term,** *Sch* premier trimestre (*de l'année scolaire dans certaines universités*); *Jur* session *f* de la Saint-Michel; **m. daisy,** (*flower*) marguerite *f ou* aster *m* d'automne.
Michelangelo [maɪkə'læn(d)ʒələʊ] *n Art* Michel-Ange *m*.
mickey ['mɪkɪ] *n F* **(a) m. (finn),** boisson droguée (secrètement); **(b)** *Br* **to take the m. out of s.o.,** se payer la tête de qn; **are you taking the m.?,** tu te payes ma tête?
Mickey Mouse ['mɪkɪ 'maʊs] **1** *n* Mickey *m*. **2** *adj Sl* (*car, firm*) de rien du tout; (*job, course*) peinard.
micro ['maɪkrəʊ] *n* **(a)** *Comptr* micro *m*; **(b)** (*microwave oven*) micro-ondes *m*.
microbe ['maɪkrəʊb] *n* microbe *m*.
microbiology [maɪkrəʊbaɪ'ɒlədʒɪ] *n* microbiologie *f*.
microcamera [maɪkrəʊ'kæmərə] *n* appareil *m* de microphotographie.
microcard ['maɪkrəʊkɑːd] *n* microfiche *f*.
microchannel [maɪkrəʊ'tʃæn(ə)l] *adj Comptr* **m. architecture,** architecture *f* à micro-canaux.
microchip ['maɪkrəʊtʃɪp] *n Comptr* puce *f*, pastille *f*.
microcircuit ['maɪkrəʊsɜːkɪt] *n Comptr* microcircuit *m*.
microcircuitry ['maɪkrəʊsɜːkɪtrɪ] *n Comptr* microcircuits *mpl*.
microclimate ['maɪkrəʊklaɪmɪt] *n* microclimat *m*.
microcomputer ['maɪkrəʊkəm'pjuːtər] *n Comptr* micro-ordinateur *m*.
microcosm ['maɪkrəʊkɒzəm] *n* microcosme *m*.
microdot ['maɪkrəʊdɒt] *n* micropoint *m*.
microfiche ['maɪkrəʊfiːʃ] *n* microfiche *f*.
microfilm¹ ['maɪkrəʊfɪlm] *n* microfilm *m*.
microfilm² *vt* microfilmer.
microgroove ['maɪkrəʊgruːv] *n* microsillon *m*.
microlight ['maɪkrəʊlaɪt] *n Av* U.L.M. *m*.
micromesh ['maɪkrəʊmeʃ] *adj* (*bas*) à mailles très fines.
micrometer [maɪ'krɒmɪtər] *n* micromètre *m*.
micron ['maɪkrɒn] *n* (*measurement*) micron *m*.
microorganism [maɪkrəʊ'ɔːgənɪz(ə)m] *n* micro-organisme *m*, *pl* micro-organismes.
microphone ['maɪkrəfəʊn] *n* microphone *m*, micro *m*; **speak into the m.,** parlez dans le micro; **a good m. voice,** une voix qui passe bien à la radio *ou* à l'enregistrement.
microprocessor [maɪkrəʊ'prəʊsesər] *n Comptr* microprocesseur *m*.
microreader ['maɪkrəʊriːdər] *n* microliseuse *f*.
microscope ['maɪkrəskəʊp] *n* microscope *m*; **electron m.,** microscope électronique; **to examine an object under the m.,** examiner un objet au microscope.
microscopic [maɪkrə'skɒpɪk] *adj* **(a)** (*animalcule etc*) microscopique; *F* (*very small*) minuscule; **(b)** (*examen etc*) au microscope.
microscopy [maɪ'krɒskəpɪ] *n* microscopie *f*.
microsecond ['maɪkrəʊsekənd] *n* microseconde *f*.
microspacing ['maɪkrəʊspeɪsɪŋ] *n Comptr* micro-espacement *m*.
microsurgery [maɪkrəʊ'sɜːdʒərɪ] *n* microchirurgie *f*.
microwave¹ ['maɪkrəʊweɪv] *n Electron Rad* micro-onde *f*, *pl* micro-ondes; **m. (oven),** (four *m* à) micro-ondes *m*.
microwave² *vt* cuire (*qch*) au (four à) micro-ondes.
mid [mɪd] *adj* mi-, du milieu; **in m. ocean,** en plein océan; **from m. June to m. August,** de la mi-juin à la mi-août; **m. season,** demi-saison *f*, *pl* demi-saisons; **he stopped in m. sentence,** il s'est interrompu au milieu de sa phrase.
midafternoon [mɪdɑːftə'nuːn] *n* milieu *m* de l'après-midi; **in m.,** au milieu de l'après-midi.
midair [mɪd'ęər] *adj & n* (*collision*) en plein ciel; **in m.,** en plein ciel, entre ciel et terre.
Midas ['maɪdəs] *n* Midas *m*; *Fig* **to have the M. touch,** transformer tout ce qu'on touche en or.
mid-Atlantic [mɪdət'læntɪk] *adj* **m.-A. accent/English,** accent/anglais mi-américain mi-britannique.
midday ['mɪd'deɪ] *n* midi *m*; **at m.,** à midi; **m. meal,** repas *m* de midi.
midden ['mɪd(ə)n] *n Br Dial* (tas *m* de) fumier *m*; **this room is like a m.,** cette pièce ressemble à une porcherie.
middle ['mɪd(ə)l] **1** *adj* du milieu; central, -aux; (*in between*) moyen, intermédiaire; **the m. house/sister,** la maison/la sœur du milieu; **to take a m. course,** prendre un parti moyen *ou* un entre-deux; **man of m. age,** homme d'âge mûr; **in m. age,** à l'âge mûr; **in early m. age he ...,** quand il a atteint l'âge mûr, il ...; **to be past m. age,** être sur le retour; *Hist* **the M. Ages,** le moyen âge; *Mus* **m. C,** do *m* du milieu du piano; **the m. class(es),** la classe moyenne, la bourgeoisie; **in the m. distance,** dans le plan intermédiaire, au second plan; **m. name,** second prénom; *F* **procrastination is your m. name!,** tu remets toujours tout au lendemain; *Ling* **M. English,** moyen anglais; **M. America,** (*sector of society*) l'Amérique moyenne; **the M. East,** le Moyen-Orient; *Anat* **m. ear,** l'oreille moyenne; **m. finger,** médius *m*, doigt *m* du milieu, majeur *m*; *Art* **m. ground,** second plan; **to take the m. ground,** (*in debate*) adopter une position intermédiaire; *Ind etc* **m. management,** cadres *mpl* intermédiaires; **the M. West,** le Midwest.
2 *n* **(a)** milieu *m*, centre *m*; **in the m. of ...,** au milieu de ...; **in the m. of the summer,** en plein été; **about the m. of August,** à la mi-août; **in the m. of the night,** en pleine nuit; **I was in the m. of reading,** j'étais bien en train de lire; **he was driving down the m. of the road,** il roulait au milieu de la route; *F* **they split the money down the m.,** ils ont partagé l'argent en deux parties égales;
(b) *F* (*waist*) taille *f*, ceinture *f*; **round one's m.,** autour de sa taille; **the water came up to his m.,** l'eau lui venait à mi-corps.
middle-aged [mɪd(ə)l'eɪdʒd] *adj* (*person*) entre deux âges, d'un certain âge; **m.-a. spread,** bourrelets *mpl* (qui viennent avec l'âge).
middle-class [mɪd(ə)l'klɑːs] *adj* bourgeois; **she's very m.-c.,** elle est très bourgeoise.
middleman, *pl* **-men** ['mɪd(ə)lmæn, -men] *n Com* intermédiaire *m*, revendeur *m*.
middlemost ['mɪd(ə)lməʊst] *adj* le plus au milieu.
middle-of-the-road ['mɪdləvðə'rəʊd] *adj* (*policy*) modéré, du juste milieu; *Mus Pej* insipide.
middle-roader ['mɪd(ə)l'rəʊdər] *n US Pol* modéré, -ée, partisan, -ane du juste milieu.
middle-sized ['mɪd(ə)l'saɪzd] *adj* de taille moyenne.
middleweight ['mɪd(ə)lweɪt] *n* (*boxer*) poids-moyen *m*; **m. champions,** champions *mpl* poids moyen.
middling ['mɪdlɪŋ] **1** *adj* (*mediocre*) médiocre; (*fairly good*) passable, assez bon; *F* **how are you? — m.,** comment allez-vous? — comme ci comme ça. **2** *adv F* assez bien, passablement, ni bien ni mal.
middy ['mɪdɪ] *n Nau F* midship *m*.
Mideast [mɪd'iːst] *n esp US* (= **Middle East**) le Moyen-Orient.
midfield [mɪd'fiːld] *n Sp Fb etc* milieu *m* de terrain; **to play in m.,** jouer au milieu du terrain; **m. player,** (joueur *m* de) milieu de terrain.
midfielder [mɪd'fiːldər] *n Fb* milieu *m* de terrain.
midge [mɪdʒ] *n* (*insect*) moucheron *m*.
midget ['mɪdʒɪt] *n* (*small person*) nain, naine, nabot, -ote; (*small thing*) miniature *f*; **this car's a m.,** cette voiture a été conçue pour des nains.
midi ['mɪdɪ] **1** *adj* **(a)** (*jupe*) de longueur moyenne, midi; **(b) m. system,** (*in audio*) mini-chaîne *f*. **2** *n* (*skirt*) jupe *f ou* manteau *m etc* de longueur moyenne.
midland ['mɪdlənd] *adj* (*plaine etc*) du centre (*d'un pays*).

Midlands (the) [ðə'mɪdləndz] *npl* = les comtés du centre de l'Angleterre; **a M. accent,** un accent du centre de l'Angleterre.

midlife ['mɪdlaɪf] *n* quarantaine *f*; **m. crisis,** (*in professional life*) crise *f* à l'abord de la quarantaine; (*in sex life*) démon *m* de midi; **to be going through a m. crisis,** (*in professional life*) traverser une crise à l'abord de la quarantaine; (*in sex life*) connaître le démon de midi.

midmorning [mɪd'mɔːnɪŋ] *n* milieu *m* de la matinée; **m. coffee break,** pause-café *f* au milieu de la matinée.

midnight ['mɪdnaɪt] *n* minuit *m*; **at m.,** à minuit; **on the stroke of m.,** sur le coup de minuit; **to burn the m. oil,** travailler *ou* veiller fort avant dans la nuit; **m. feast,** festin *m* nocturne; **m. blue,** (*colour*) bleu *m* de nuit; **m. Mass,** messe *f* de minuit; **a m. snack,** un casse-croûte en plein milieu de la nuit; **m. sun,** soleil *m* de minuit.

midriff ['mɪdrɪf] *n Anat* diaphragme *m*; estomac *m*; **bare m.,** ventre nu, taille nue.

midshipman, *pl* **-men** ['mɪdʃɪpmən] *n Nau* aspirant *m* (*de marine*), *F* midship *m*.

midships ['mɪdʃɪps] *adv Nau* au milieu du navire, par le travers.

midst [mɪdst] *n* **in the m. of sth,** au milieu de qch; **in the m. of winter,** en plein hiver; **in the m. of all this,** sur ces entrefaites; **in the m. of the celebration,** en plein milieu de la fête; **in our/your/their m.,** parmi nous/vous/eux.

midstream [mɪd'striːm] *n* **in m.,** au milieu du courant; *Fig* **she started talking but stopped in m.,** elle a commencé à parler, mais s'est arrêtée en plein milieu de son récit.

midsummer ['mɪdsʌmər] *n* (*middle of summer*) milieu *m* de l'été, cœur *m* de l'été; (*solstice*) solstice *m* d'été; **in m.,** au cœur de l'été; **M. Day,** la Saint-Jean; **A M. Night's Dream,** Le Songe d'une Nuit d'Été.

midterm ['mɪd'tɜːm] *n* **(a)** *US Pol* milieu *m* du mandat présidentiel; **m. elections,** élections *fpl* au milieu d'un mandat présidentiel; **(b)** *Sch* milieu *m* du trimestre.

midway ['mɪdweɪ] *adv* à mi-chemin; **m. up the hill,** à mi-chemin en montant la colline; **m. between ... and ...,** à mi-distance *ou* à mi-chemin entre ... et ...; **a style m. between John's and Paul's,** un style intermédiaire entre celui de John et celui de Paul.

midweek [mɪd'wiːk] *n* milieu *m* de la semaine; **I'll see you m.,** je te verrai vers le milieu de la semaine; **m. show,** spectacle de milieu de semaine.

midwife, *pl* **-wives** ['mɪdwaɪf, -waɪvz] *n* sage-femme *f*, *pl* sages-femmes, accoucheuse *f*.

midwifery ['mɪdwɪfərɪ] *n* **(a)** (*profession*) profession *f* de sage-femme; **(b)** (*obstetrics*) obstétrique *f*.

midwinter ['mɪd'wɪntər] *n* (*middle of winter*) milieu *m* de l'hiver, cœur *m* de l'hiver; (*solstice*) solstice *m* d'hiver.

mien [miːn] *n Lit* mine *f*, air *m*, contenance *f* (*de qn*).

miffed [mɪft] *adj F* **to be m.,** être froissé *ou* piqué *ou* fâché; **I felt a bit m.,** je me suis senti un peu froissé.

might¹ [maɪt] *n* puissance *f*, force(s) *f(pl)*; **with all one's m.,** (*travailler, pousser etc*) de toute sa force, de toutes ses forces; *Prov* **m. is right,** force passe droit.

might² *see* **MAY¹**.

might-have-been ['maɪtəvbiːn] *n F* **he's a m.-h.-b.,** c'est un raté.

mightily ['maɪtɪlɪ] *adv* **(a)** (*powerfully*) puissamment, fortement; **(b)** *F* (*extremely*) extrêmement.

mighty ['maɪtɪ] **1** *adj* (*comp* **mightier**; *superl* **mightiest**) **(a)** (*powerful*) puissant, fort; **a m. nation,** une grande nation; **a m. army,** une armée puissante; **(b)** (*large, imposing*) grand, grandiose; **(c)** *esp Am F* (*considerable*) grand, considérable; **you're in a m. hurry,** vous êtes diablement pressé. **2** *adv F* rudement; **you're making a m. big mistake,** vous commettez là une colossale erreur.

mignonette [mɪnjə'net] *n* (*plant*) réséda *m*.

migraine ['miːgreɪn] *n Med* migraine *f*; **to suffer from m.,** souffrir de migraines; **I had a bad m.,** j'ai eu une forte migraine.

migrant ['maɪgrənt] **1** *adj* = **MIGRATORY (a)**; **m. worker,** travailleur itinérant. **2** *n* (*person, bird etc*) migrateur, -trice.

migrate [maɪ'greɪt] *vi* (*of person*) émigrer; (*of bird*) migrer.

migration [maɪ'greɪʃən] *n* (*of people*) émigration *f*; (*of birds etc*) migration *f*.

migratory ['maɪgrətrɪ, maɪ'greɪtərɪ] *adj* **(a)** (*peuple*) migrateur, nomade; (*oiseau*) migrateur; **(b)** (*mouvement*) migratoire.

mike [maɪk] *n F* micro *m*.

Mike [maɪk] *n* (*dimin of* **Michael**) = Michel *m*; *F* **for the love of M.,** pour l'amour du ciel.

milch [mɪltʃ] *adj Agr & Fig* **m. cow,** (vache *f*) laitière *f*.

mild [maɪld] **1** *adj* **(a)** (*person, remark*) doux, *f* douce; (*answer*) conciliateur; (*criticism*) anodin; **(b)** (*regulation etc*) doux, peu sévère, peu rigoureux; (*punishment*) léger; **(c)** (*climate*) doux, tempéré; (*winter*) doux; **the weather is getting milder,** le temps s'adoucit; **(d)** (*dish*) peu relevé; (*medicine*) doux, bénin, *f* bénigne; (*cigar, tobacco*) doux; **m. beer,** bière brune; **a m. curry,** un curry peu épicé; **(e)** *Med* bénin, *f* bénigne; **a m. form of measles,** une forme bénigne de rougeole; **(f)** (*moderate*) (*exercise*) modéré; (*amusement*) innocent, anodin; **the play was a m. success,** la pièce a obtenu un succès modéré; **(g)** (*steel*) doux. **2** *n Br* bière brune.

mildew¹ ['mɪldjuː] *n* **(a)** (*fungus*) *Agr* rouille *f* (*sur le froment etc*); mildiou *m* (*sur les vignes etc*), oïdium *m* (*des vignes*); chancissure *f* (*sur le pain etc*); **(b)** (*stains*) moisissure *f*, taches *fpl* d'humidité, piqûres *fpl* (*sur le papier, le cuir*).

mildew² **1** *vt* rouiller, moisir (*une plante*); frapper (*une plante*) de mildiou; (*of damp etc*) piquer (*le papier etc*); chancir (*le pain etc*). **2** *vi* (*of plant*) se rouiller, moisir; (*of paper etc*) se piquer.

mildewy ['mɪldjuːɪ] *adj* (*bread*) moisi; (*wallpaper*) piqué par l'humidité, moisi; (*towel*) piqué par l'humidité.

mildly ['maɪldlɪ] *adv* **(a)** (*to say*) doucement, avec douceur; **(b)** (*moderately*) modérément; **to be m. successful,** (*of play*) obtenir un succès modéré; **to put it m.,** pour ne pas en dire plus; **he's a bastard, and that's putting it m.!,** c'est un salaud, et c'est peu dire.

mildness ['maɪldnɪs] *n* **(a)** douceur *f*, clémence *f* (*de qn, du temps*); caractère anodin (*d'une critique*); légèreté *f* (*d'une punition*); **(b)** *Med* bénignité *f* (*d'une maladie*).

mile [maɪl] *n* (*distance*) mil(l)e *m*; **five miles,** cinq mil(l)es, = huit kilomètres; **nautical m.,** mil(l)e marin (= 1853 m 25); *Sp* **four minute m.,** mil(l)e couru en quatre minutes; **square m.,** mil(l)e carré; **a 200 m. journey,** un voyage de 200 mil(l)es; **miles per hour,** mil(l)es par heure; **smaller cars generally do more miles to the** *or* **per gallon/litre,** les voitures relativement petites couvrent une plus grande distance au gallon/litre; **you don't see anyone for miles and miles,** on parcourt des kilomètres sans voir personne; **people came from miles around,** les gens sont venus de kilomètres à la ronde; **it's miles from anywhere,** c'est à des kilomètres de tout; **he lives miles away,** il habite loin d'ici; *F* **to be miles away,** (*be day-dreaming*) être dans la lune; **someone not a thousand** *or* **million** *etc* **miles from us,** une certaine personne qui ne se trouve pas très loin de nous; *F* **I feel miles better,** je me sens beaucoup mieux; *F* **he's miles better than all the others,** il est largement meilleur que tous les autres; *F* **it sticks out a m.,** ça vous crève les yeux, ça se voit comme le nez au milieu de la figure; *F* **I can see you coming a m. off!,** (*I know what you want*) je te vois venir (avec tes gros sabots)!; *F* **he'd run a m.,** (*if that were to happen*) il prendrait ses jambes à son cou.

mileage ['maɪlɪdʒ] *n* **(a)** (*distance travelled*) distance *f* en mil(l)es; *Can* millage *m*; = kilométrage *m*; **car with a very low** *or* **small m.,** voiture qui a très peu roulé; *Admin Com etc* **m. (allowance),** indemnité *f* de déplacement; **(b)** (*per gallon, litre etc*) consommation *f* au mil(l)e; **how much m. do you get?,** combien est-ce que la voiture consomme au cent?; *Fig F* **the opposition got a lot of m. out of the scandal,** l'opposition a largement profité de ce scandale, ce scandale a largement profité à l'opposition; *Fig F* **there's no m. in it,** (*in idea etc*) ça ne nous mènera nulle part, on ne peut rien en tirer.

milestone ['maɪlstəʊn] *n* borne routière, = borne kilométrique; *Fig* événement important; **this discovery is a m. in medical research,** cette découverte marque une étape importante dans la recherche médicale.

milieu ['miːljɜː] *n* milieu *m* (*social, géographique*).

militant ['mɪlɪtənt] **1** *adj* militant; **the Church m.,** l'Église militante. **2** *n Pol etc* militant, -ante.

militarily ['mɪlɪtərɪlɪ] *adv* militairement.

militarism ['mɪlɪtərɪzəm] *n* militarisme *m*.

militarist ['mɪlɪtərɪst] *n* militariste *mf*.

militaristic [mɪlɪtə'rɪstɪk] *adj* militariste.

militarize ['mɪlɪtəraɪz] *vt* militariser.

military ['mɪlɪtərɪ] **1** *adj* (*aircraft, base, service etc*) militaire; **m. man,** militaire *m*; **a strong m. presence,** une forte présence militaire; *Jur* **m. court** *or* **tribunal,** tribunal *m* militaire; **m. police,** police *f* militaire. **2** *n* **the m.,** (*used as pl*) les militaires *mpl*, les soldats *mpl*; l'armée *f*; **the m. were called in,** on a fait venir l'armée.

militate ['mɪlɪteɪt] *vi* (*of fact, reason etc*) militer (**against,** contre).

militia [mɪ'lɪʃə] *n* milice *f*; *US* ≈ garde nationale.

militiaman, *pl* **-men** [mɪ'lɪʃəmən] *n* milicien *m*, soldat *m* de la milice; *US* ≈ garde nationale.

milk[1] [mɪlk] *n* **(a)** lait *m*; **m. fresh from the cow,** lait fraîchement trait; **whole m.,** lait entier; **powdered m.,** lait en poudre; **with m.,** au lait; *Lit* **land of m. and honey,** pays *m* de cocagne; *Prov* **it's no use crying over spilt m.,** à chose faite point de remède; **m. bar,** milk-bar *m*, *pl* milk-bars; **m. bottle,** bouteille *f* à lait; **m. cap,** (*fungus*) lactaire *m*; **m. chocolate,** chocolat *m* au lait; **m. diet,** régime lacté; **m. float,** = véhicule assurant la distribution du lait à domicile; **m. jug,** pot *m* à *ou* au lait; *Culin* **m. pudding,** entremets sucré au lait; crème *f* (*à la vanille etc*); **m. round,** tournée *f* de laitier; *Br Univ F* = tournée de recrutement dans les universités à la fin de l'année; *Av F* **m. run,** vol *m* sans problèmes; *Anat* **m. tooth,** dent *f* de lait; **m. train,** = train de nuit qui s'arrête à toutes les gares; **chocolate m. shake,** milk-shake *m* au chocolat; **cleansing m.,** lait démaquillant; **m. of magnesia,** lait de magnésie; **m. glass,** opaline *f*; **(b)** (*in plant*) lait *m*, eau *f* (*de noix de coco*); **m. of almonds,** lait d'amandes.

milk[2] *vt* **(a)** traire (*une vache etc*); **(b)** *F* (*exploit*) dépouiller, écorcher (*qn*), exploiter (*qn*); **the newspaper milked the story for all it was worth,** les journaux ont tiré tout ce qu'ils ont pu de l'histoire; **they just milked all his ideas,** ils se sont approprié toutes ses idées.

milker ['mɪlkər] *n* **(a)** (*person*) trayeur, -euse; **(b)** (*cow etc*) **good/bad m.,** bonne/mauvaise laitière.

milkiness ['mɪlkɪnɪs] *n* couleur laiteuse, aspect laiteux (*d'un liquide etc*).

milking ['mɪlkɪŋ] *n* traite *f* (*d'une vache*); **m. starts early,** la traite commence de bonne heure; **m. machine,** trayeuse *f* mécanique.

milkmaid ['mɪlkmeɪd] *n* trayeuse *f*; fille *f* de laiterie.

milkman, *pl* **-men** ['mɪlkmən] *n* **(a)** (*delivery man*) livreur *m* de lait; **(b)** (*dairyman*) laitier *m*.

milksop ['mɪlksɒp] *n Old-fashioned F* poule mouillée.

milkweed ['mɪlkwiːd] *n Bot* laiteron *m*, lait *m* d'âne.

milky ['mɪlkɪ] *adj* **(a)** (*containing milk*) qui contient du lait; **I like my coffee m.,** (*with lots of milk*) j'aime mon café avec beaucoup de lait; (*made with milk*) j'aime que mon café soit préparé avec du lait; **(b)** (*colour*) laiteux, *Lit* lactescent; (*gem*) laiteux; **m. white,** blanc laiteux; *Astron* **the M. Way,** la Voie lactée.

mill[1] [mɪl] *n* **(a) (flour) m.,** moulin *m* (à farine); (*large*) minoterie *f*; *F* **he's been through the m.,** il est passé par de rudes épreuves; *F* **run of the m.,** ordinaire; **coffee/pepper m.,** moulin à café/à poivre; **(crushing) m.,** broyeur *m*, concasseur *m*; **(b)** (*in metalworking*) **(rolling) m.,** laminoir *m*, train *m* (de laminage); **(c)** (*tool*) fraise *f*, fraiseuse *f*; **end m.,** fraise en bout; **(d)** (*factory*) usine *f*; **spinning m.,** filature *f*; **cotton m.,** filature de coton; **sugar m.,** raffinerie *f* de sucre; **paper m.,** usine *f* de papier; **m. hand,** ouvrier, -ière textile; **m. owner,** industriel *m* de textile.

mill[2] *vt* moudre (*le blé, la farine*); *Tech* broyer; *Tex* fouler (*le drap*); *MecE* fraiser, tailler (*des engrenages etc*); molet(t)er (*une vis*); créneler (*une pièce de monnaie*).

mill[3] *n Am* millième *m* (de dollar).

►**mill about, mill around** *vi* (*of crowd*) fourmiller, tourner en rond; (*of cattle etc*) tourner sur place.

millboard ['mɪlbɔːd] *n* carton-pâte *m inv*.

milled [mɪld] *adj* **(a)** *MecE* (*écrou*) moleté; (*coin*) crénelé; **m. edge,** (*on coin*) crénelage *m*, grènetis *m*; **(b)** *Tex* foulé.

millennium [mɪ'lenɪəm] *n* **(a)** (*thousand years*) millénaire *m*, mille ans *mpl*; **(b)** *Rel Hist* millénium *m*.

millepede ['mɪlɪpiːd] *n* mille-pattes *m inv*.

miller ['mɪlər] *n* meunier *m*; (*on large scale*) minotier *m*.

millet ['mɪlɪt] *n Bot* millet *m*, mil *m*; **African** *or* **Indian m.,** sorgho *m*, millet d'Afrique *ou* d'Inde.

millibar ['mɪlɪbɑːr] *n Met* millibar *m*.

milligram(me) ['mɪlɪgræm] *n* milligramme *m*.

millilitre, *US* **milliliter** ['mɪlɪliːtər] *n* millilitre *m*.

millimetre, *US* **millimeter** ['mɪlɪmiːtər] *n* millimètre *m*; **a 10 m. gap,** une espace de 10 millimètres.

milliner ['mɪlɪnər] *n* modiste *f*, chapelier, -ière.

millinery ['mɪlɪnərɪ] *n* (articles *mpl* de) modes *fpl*; **m. department,** (*in shop*) rayon *m* des chapeaux.

milling ['mɪlɪŋ] *n* **(a)** (*profession of miller*) métier *m* de meunier *ou* de minoterie, meunerie *f*; (*on large scale*) minoterie *f*; **(b)** mouture *f*, moulage *m* (*du grain*); *Tech* broyage *m*; (*of cloth*) foulage *m*; **(c)** (*in metalwork*) fraisage *m*; moletage *m* (*d'une vis etc*); cordonnage *m* (*d'une pièce de monnaie*); **m. machine,** fraiseuse *f*; **m. cutter,** fraise *f*, fraiseuse; **(d)** cordon *m*, grènetis *m*, tranche cannelée (*d'une pièce de monnaie*).

million ['mɪljən] *n* million *m*; **two m. men,** deux millions d'hommes; **half a m.,** un demi-million; **worth millions,** (*of person*) riche à millions; **an actor who gave pleasure to millions,** un acteur qui a diverti des millions de gens; *F* **she's one in a m.,** elle est unique; **thanks a m.!,** merci mille fois!; *Iron* eh bien, c'est sympa, ça!; *Am F* **I feel like a m. dollars,** je me sens en pleine forme.

millionaire [mɪljə'neər] *n* millionnaire *m*; **to be a m. twice/three times over,** être deux/trois fois millionnaire; **I've got a m. uncle,** j'ai un oncle millionnaire.

millionairess [mɪljə'neərɪs] *n* femme *f* millionnaire.

millionth ['mɪljənθ] *adj & n* millionième *mf*.

millipede ['mɪlɪpiːd] *n* mille-pattes *m inv*.

millpond ['mɪlpɒnd] *n* réservoir *m* de moulin; **sea as calm** *or* **smooth as a m.,** mer calme comme un lac, mer d'huile.

millrace ['mɪlreɪs] *n* bief *m* de moulin.

millstone ['mɪlstəʊn] *n* **(a)** meule *f* (de moulin); **he's a m. round my neck,** c'est un boulet que je traîne; **(b)** *Geol* **m. (grit),** meulière *f*, grès meulier; **m. quarry,** meulière.

millstream ['mɪlstriːm] *n* **(a)** courant *m* d'eau qui actionne la roue d'un moulin; **(b)** = **MILLRACE**.

millwheel ['mɪlwiːl] *n* roue *f* de moulin.

millwright ['mɪlraɪt] *n* constructeur *m* de moulins.

milometer [maɪ'lɒmɪtər] *n Aut etc* compteur *m* de mil(l)es; = compteur kilométrique.

milt [mɪlt] *n* laitance *f*, laite *f* (*des poissons*).

mime[1] [maɪm] *n Th* (*performance, actor*) mime *m*; **a version of Hamlet in m.,** une version d'Hamlet en mime; **m. artist,** mime *m*.

mime[2] **1** *vt* mimer (*une scène*). **2** *vi* jouer par gestes.

mimeograph ®[1] ['mɪmɪəgræf] *n* **(a)** (*machine*) machine *f* à ronéotyper; **(b)** (*document*) polycopie *f*.

mimeograph ®[2] *vt* ronéotyper.

mimic[1] ['mɪmɪk] **1** *n* **(a)** imitateur, -trice; **he's a great m.,** c'est un grand imitateur; **(b)** (*mime artist*) mime *m*. **2** *adj* **(a)** (*gesture etc*) imitateur, -trice; **(b)** (*warfare etc*) factice.

mimic[2] *vt* (*pt & pp* **mimicked**) **(a)** (*impersonate, imitate*) imiter, mimer, contrefaire; *F* singer (*qn*); **(b)** imiter, contrefaire (*la nature etc*).

mimicry ['mɪmɪkrɪ] *n* **(a)** mimique *f*, imitation *f*; **(b)** *Biol* mimétisme *m*.

mimosa [mɪ'məʊzə] *n* (*shrub*) mimosa *m*.

min (a) (*abbr* **minute(s)**) min.; **(b)** (*abbr* **minimum**) min.

minaret [mɪnə'ret] *n* minaret *m*.

mince[1] [mɪns] *n Br Culin* hachis *m* (de viande); **m. pie,** = tarte fourrée au mincemeat.

mince[2] **1** *vt* **(a)** (*chop up*) hacher (menu) (*de la viande etc*); **minced meat,** hachis *m*, viande hachée; **(b)** (*always in negative*) (*speak plainly*) **not to m. one's words,** ne pas mâcher ses mots, parler net; **not to m. matters,** pour parler net. **2** *vi* **(a)** (*walk in affected manner*) marcher d'un air affecté; **(b)** (*talk in affected manner*) parler avec une élégance affectée, parler du bout des lèvres; (*of woman*) minauder; (*of man*) mignarder.

mincemeat ['mɪnsmiːt] *n Culin* = compote de raisins secs, de pommes, de graisse de rognon etc; *F* **to make m. of sth,** pulvériser qch; *F* **to make m. of s.o.,** réduire qn en bouillie.

mincer ['mɪnsər] *n Culin* hachoir *m*.

mincing ['mɪnsɪŋ] *adj* (*manner, tone*) affecté, minaudier.

mind[1] [maɪnd] *n* **(a)** (*thoughts*) esprit *m*; **such a thought had never entered his m.,** une telle pensée ne lui était jamais venue à l'esprit; **to have sth on one's m.,** avoir qch qui vous préoccupe; **it's all in your m.!,** tu te fais des idées!; **in the m.'s eye,** dans l'imagination; **in her m.'s eye she could see them staring at her,** elle se les imaginait la fixant; **a walk will take my m. off it,** une promenade me changera les idées; **to put** *or* **set s.o.'s m. at rest,** rassurer qn; **to be easy/uneasy in one's m.,** avoir/ne pas avoir l'esprit tranquille; **that's a weight off my m.,** voilà qui me soulage l'esprit; **I couldn't get it off my m.,** je ne pouvais pas m'empêcher d'y penser; **she couldn't get their faces out of her m.,** elle ne pouvait oublier leurs visages; **put it out of your m.,** n'y pensez plus; **(b)** (*memory*) mémoire *f*; **to bear** *or* **keep sth in m.,** (*think about*) songer à qch; (*not forget*) ne pas oublier qch, garder qch à l'esprit; (*take into account*) tenir compte de qch; **we must bear in m. that she is only a child,** il ne faut pas oublier que ce n'est qu'une enfant; **I'll bear it in m.,** (*what you suggested*) je m'en souviendrai; **to call sth**

to m., se rappeler *ou* se souvenir de qch; **it brings** *or* **calls to m. a summer's day**, cela rappelle un jour d'été; **to put s.o. in m. of s.o./sth**, rappeler qn/qch à qn; **it went (completely** *or* **clean) out of my m.**, cela m'est (complètement) sorti de l'esprit;

(c) (*opinion*) pensée *f*, avis *m*, idée *f*; **to change one's m.**, changer d'avis *ou* d'idée, se raviser; **I've changed my m. about him**, j'ai changé d'idée à son égard; **I've changed my m. about moving to London**, (*don't want to*) j'ai changé d'avis, je ne veux plus déménager à Londres; (*want to*) j'ai changé d'avis, je veux maintenant déménager à Londres; *F* **I gave him a piece of my m.**, je lui ai dit son fait *ou* ses vérités; **to be of one m., to be of the same m.**, être du même avis, être d'accord; **to my m.**, selon moi, à mon avis; **to speak one's m.**, dire ce qu'on pense; **to keep an open m. about sth**, ne pas se faire une opinion sur qch;

(d) (*purpose, desire*) **to know one's own m.**, savoir ce qu'on veut; **you've got a m. of your own**, tu peux décider toi-même; **the car seemed to have a m. of its own**, la voiture semblait faire ce que bon lui semblait; **to make up one's m.**, se décider; **make up your m.!**, décidez-vous!; **to be in two minds about sth**, être indécis sur qch; **I've a good m. to do it**, je suis bien tenté de le faire; **to set one's m. on sth**, vouloir absolument avoir qch; **to set one's m. on doing sth**, se mettre en tête de faire qch; **I'm in two minds about going**, je ne sais pas si je vais y aller; **to have sth in m.**, avoir qch en vue; **what kind of party did you have in m.?**, à quelle sorte de soirée est-ce que tu pensais?; **I had in m. something smaller**, je pensais à quelque chose de plus petit; **the person I have in m.**, la personne à laquelle je pense; **who did you have in m. for the job?**, à qui pensiez-vous pour le poste?;

(e) (*attention*) **to give one's whole m. to sth**, appliquer toute son attention à qch; **to keep one's m. on sth**, se concentrer sur qch; **keep your m. on your work**, concentre-toi sur ton travail; **your m. is not on the job**, tu n'as pas la tête au travail; **I'm sure if you put your m. to it you could do it**, je suis sûr que si tu te concentrais vraiment, tu pourrais le faire;

(f) (*thought, feeling*) esprit *m*, âme *f*; **state of m.**, état *m* d'esprit; **peace of m.**, tranquillité *f* d'esprit;

(g) (*way of thinking*) **turn of m.**, mentalité *f* (*de qn*); **attitude of m.**, manière *f* de penser; **he has no strength of m.**, c'est un homme sans volonté *ou* sans caractère; **you've got a nasty/dirty m.!**, tu as un mauvais esprit/l'esprit mal placé!; **it's probably just my suspicious m. but I don't trust him**, c'est probablement que je suis trop suspicieux, mais je n'ai pas confiance en lui;

(h) *Phil Psy* (*opposed to body*) âme *f*; (*opposed to matter*) esprit *m*; (*opposed to emotions*) intelligence *f*; **to have a good m.**, être intelligent, avoir la tête bien faite; **to have the m. of a three year old**, avoir l'esprit *ou* l'intelligence d'un enfant de trois ans; **I haven't got a scientific m.**, je n'ai pas l'esprit scientifique;

(i) (*reason*) raison *f*; **to be out of one's m.**, avoir perdu la raison *ou* la tête; *F* (*drunk, from drugs*) être parti; **are you out of your m.?, you must be out of your m.!**, vous êtes fou!; *F* **they were out of their minds with boredom** *or* **bored out of their minds**, ils s'ennuyaient à mourir; **to be in one's right m.**, avoir toute sa raison *ou* toutes ses facultés;

(j) (*person*) **one of the most brilliant minds of the century**, l'un des esprits les plus brillants de ce siècle; *Prov* **great minds think alike**, les grands esprits se rencontrent; **how about a drink? — great minds think alike!**, si on prenait une verre? — les grands esprits se rencontrent!

mind[2] **1** *vt* **(a)** (*pay attention to*) faire attention à, prêter (son) attention à (*qn, qch*); (*concern oneself with*) s'occuper de (*qch*); **never m. the money**, ne regardez pas à l'argent; **don't m. him, he's always like that**, ne fais pas attention à lui, il est toujours comme ça; **m. you, I've always thought that ...**, notez bien, j'ai toujours pensé que ...; **m. your own business!**, occupez-vous *ou* mêlez- vous de ce qui vous regarde!; **m. what you're doing!**, faites attention à ce que vous faites!;

(b) (*take care*) **m. you're not late!**, prenez soin de ne pas être en retard!; **m. you write to him!**, ne manquez pas *ou* n'oubliez pas de lui écrire!; **m. you don't fall!**, prenez garde de tomber!; **m. the step!**, attention à la marche!; **m. your backs (please)!**, dégagez (s'il vous plaît)!; *Br F* **m. how you go!**, fais attention à toi!; *F* **don't be late, m.!**, surtout, ne sois pas en retard!;

(c) (*object to*) **I don't m. trying**, je veux bien essayer; **do you m. my asking ...?**, puis-je vous demander sans indiscrétion ...?; **how much do you earn, if you don't m. my** *or* **me asking?**, combien est-ce que vous gagnez, sans indiscrétion?; **I wouldn't m. a cup of tea**, je prendrais volontiers une tasse de thé;

(d) (*trouble oneself about*) **don't m. them**, ne vous inquiétez pas d'eux; **I don't m. the cold**, le froid ne me gêne pas; **he doesn't m. whose feelings he hurts**, il ne se préoccupe pas des gens qu'il froisse;

(e) (*look after*) soigner (*qn*); surveiller (*des enfants*); garder (*des animaux etc*); garder, veiller sur (*la maison*); **to m. the shop**, s'occuper du magasin;

(f) *Arch & Dial* (*remember*) se souvenir de, se rappeler (*qn, qch*).

2 *vi* **(a)** (*object*) **would you m. if ...?**, cela vous gênerait-il que ...?; **do you m.!**, (*how dare you*) dites donc!; **if you don't m.**, si cela ne vous dérange pas; **I don't m.**, (*it doesn't matter to me*) cela m'est égal; (*go ahead*) je veux bien; **if nobody minds**, si personne n'y voit d'inconvénient; **do you m. if I smoke?**, cela ne vous dérange *ou* gêne pas que je fume?; *F* **another drop of wine? — I don't m. if I do**, encore un peu de vin? — ce n'est pas de refus;

(b) (*trouble oneself*) **never m.!**, (*it doesn't matter*) ça ne fait rien!, tant pis!; (*don't worry*) ne vous inquiétez pas!; **he's dying but no one seems to m.**, il est en train de mourir mais personne n'a l'air de s'inquiéter; *F* **never you m.!**, (*what I earn etc*) ça c'est mon affaire!;

(c) **but, m. you, it was late**, mais, voyez-vous, il était tard.

►**mind out** *vi Br* faire attention (**for**, à).

mind-blowing ['maɪndbləʊɪŋ] *adj Sl* (*drug*) hallucinant; (*experience*) ahurissant, époustouflant.

mind-boggling ['maɪndbɒglɪŋ] *adj F* époustouflant.

minded ['maɪndɪd] *adj* disposé, enclin (*à faire qch*); **commercially m.**, commerçant; **to be mechanically m.**, être bon mécanicien; **feeble m.**, faible d'esprit; **she isn't very money-m.**, (*money isn't important to her*) elle n'est pas très préoccupée par les questions d'argent.

minder ['maɪndər] *n* gardeur, -euse (*de bestiaux*); surveillant, -ante (*d'enfants*); *Sl* (*bodyguard*) garde *m*; *esp Am* **baby m.**, garde-bébé *mf*, *pl* garde-bébés; *Ind* **(machine) m.**, surveillant; *Typ* conducteur *m* de machines.

mindful ['maɪndfʊl] *adj* **(a)** (*keeping in mind*) **to be m. of sth**, se souvenir de qch, ne pas oublier qch; **m. of this warning ...**, se souvenant de cet avertissement ...; **(b)** (*attentive*) attentif (*à sa santé etc*); soigneux (*de*); **he is always m. of others**, il pense toujours aux autres.

mindless ['maɪndlɪs] *adj* **(a)** (*senseless*) (*destruction*) irresponsable; (*task, job*) stupide; **(b)** (*careless*) insouciant (**of**, de), indifférent (**of**, à); (*forgetful*) oublieux (**of**, de).

mind-reader ['maɪndri:dər] *n* liseur, -euse de pensées; **I'm not a m.-r.!**, je ne peux pas deviner *ou* lire dans tes pensées!

mine[1] [maɪn] *n* **(a)** mine *f*; **he went down the m. at 16**, il est descendu dans la mine à 16 ans; **coal m.**, mine de houille *ou* de charbon; **gold/salt m.**, mine d'or/de sel; **opencast m.**, mine à ciel ouvert; *Fig* **a m. of information**, une mine d'information; **m. shaft**, puits *m* de mine; **m. workings**, chantiers *mpl* d'exploitation minière; **(b)** *Mil Nau* mine *f*; **land m.**, mine terrestre; **m. detector**, détecteur *m* de mines; **to lay a m.**, (*on land*) poser une mine; (*at sea*) mouiller une mine.

mine[2] **1** *vt* **(a)** *Min* exploiter (*une couche de houille*); **to m. coal/gold**, exploiter le charbon/l'or; **(b)** *Mil* miner, saper (*une muraille*); *Mil Nau* miner (*un port etc*); **mined area**, zone minée. **2** *vi Min* **to m. for coal/gold**, exploiter le charbon/l'or.

mine[3] **1** *poss pron* **(a)** le mien, la mienne, les miens, les miennes; **this letter is m.**, cette lettre est à moi; **this signature is not m.**, cette signature n'est pas de moi; **I took her hands in m.**, je pris ses mains dans les miennes; **a friend of m.**, un(e) de mes ami(e)s, un(e) ami(e) à moi; **it is no business of m.**, ce n'est pas mon affaire; **(b)** (*my family*) les miens; **(c)** (*my property*) *F* **what's yours is m.**, ce qui est à toi est à moi; **so much money and it's (m.,) all m.!**, tant d'argent, et c'est à moi, rien qu'à moi! **2** *poss adj Arch & Lit* mon, ma, *pl* mes; *Hum* **m. host**, l'aubergiste *m*; **mistress m.!**, ma (belle) maîtresse!

minefield ['maɪnfi:ld] *n Mil Nau* champ *m* de mines; *Fig* terrain miné.

minehunter ['maɪnhʌntər] *n Nau* chasseur *m* de mines.

minelayer ['maɪnleɪər] *n Nau* mouilleur *m* de mines.

minelaying ['maɪnleɪɪŋ] *n Mil* pose *f* de mines; *Nau* mouillage *m* de mines.

miner ['maɪnər] *n Min* mineur *m*; **m.'s lamp**, lampe *f* de mineur.

mineral ['mɪn(ə)rəl] **1** *adj* (*oil, water etc*) minéral, -aux; **the m. kingdom,** le règne minéral; **m. spring,** source (d'eau) minérale; **m. water,** eau minérale. **2** *n* minéral *m*; *Min* **m. deposits,** gisements miniers *ou* minéraux; **the m. resources of a country,** les ressources minières d'un pays; *Br* **minerals,** (*drinks*) boissons gazeuses.

mineralogist [mɪnə'rælədʒɪst] *n* minéralogiste *mf*.

mineralogy [mɪnə'rælədʒɪ] *n* minéralogie *f*.

minesweeper ['maɪnswiːpər] *n Nau* dragueur *m* de mines.

minesweeping ['maɪnswiːpɪŋ] *n Nau* dragage *m* des mines.

mingle ['mɪŋg(ə)l] **1** *vt* mêler, mélanger (**sth with sth,** qch avec qch; **two things together,** deux choses ensemble); **tears mingled with laughter,** le rire mêlé aux larmes. **2** *vi* (*of thing*) se mêler, se mélanger, se confondre (**with,** avec); (*of person*) se mêler (**in** *or* **with a company,** à une compagnie); (*at party*) se joindre aux autres; **to m. with the crowd,** se mêler à *ou* dans la foule.

mingy ['mɪndʒɪ] *adj Br F* **(a)** (*person*) mesquin; **don't be so m.!,** ne sois pas si radin!; **(b)** (*thing*) misérable; **a m. helping,** une portion minuscule.

mini ['mɪnɪ] *n* (*dress etc*) *F* mini *m*.

mini- ['mɪnɪ] *pref* mini(-); **minirecording studio,** ministudio *m* d'enregistrement; **minibiography,** mini-biographie *f*.

miniature ['mɪnɪtʃər] **1** *n* miniature *f*; *Art* (portrait *m* en) miniature; (*figurine*) miniature, statuette *f*; *Com* miniature *f* (*de cognac etc*); **m. painter,** miniaturiste *mf*; **to paint in m.,** peindre en miniature; **Paris in m.,** (*model*) Paris en miniature. **2** *adj* en miniature, en raccourci; (*jardin, bouteille etc*) miniature; (*livre etc*) minuscule; *Phot* (*appareil*) de petit format; **m. golf,** mini-golf *m*; **m. poodle,** caniche nain.

miniaturist ['mɪnɪtʃərɪst] *n Art* miniaturiste *mf*.

miniaturize ['mɪnɪtʃəraɪz] *vt* miniaturiser.

minibudget ['mɪnɪbʌdʒɪt] *n* budget *m* auxiliaire *ou* exceptionnel.

minibus ['mɪnɪbʌs] *n* minibus *m*; **m. service,** service *m* de minibus.

minicab ['mɪnɪkæb] *n Br* radio-taxi *m*, *pl* radio-taxis; **m. firm,** société *f* de radio-taxis.

minicomputer [mɪnɪkəm'pjuːtər] *n Comptr* mini-ordinateur *m*.

minim ['mɪnɪm] *n Mus* blanche *f*; **m. rest,** demi-pause *f*.

minimal ['mɪnɪm(ə)l] *adj* **(a)** (*very small*) (*cost, effect etc*) minime; **(b)** (*minimum*) minimal, -aux, minimum; **m. value,** valeur minimale *ou* minimum.

minimization [mɪnɪmaɪ'zeɪʃən] *n* minimisation *f*.

minimize ['mɪnɪmaɪz] *vt* minimiser (*qch, l'importance de qch*); restreindre (*le bruit, le frottement etc*) au minimum.

minimum, *pl* **-a** ['mɪnɪməm, -ə] **1** *n* minimum *m*, *pl* minimums, minima; **a m. of two years' experience,** un minimum de deux ans d'expérience; **as a m.,** au minimum; **to reduce sth to a m.,** réduire qch au minimum, minimiser qch. **2** *adj* minimum *inv*, minimal; **m. speed,** vitesse minimum *ou* minimale; *Br Fin* **m. lending rate,** taux *m* de prêt minimum; **m. wage,** salaire *m* minimum.

mining ['maɪnɪŋ] *n* **(a)** *Min* exploitation minière; **opencast** *or* **surface m.,** abattage *m*, exploitation *ou* extraction *f* au jour; **m. area/town,** région/ville minière; **m. engineer,** ingénieur *m* des mines; **the m. industry,** l'industrie minière; **(b)** *Mil* sape *f*; *Mil Nau* pose *f* de mines, minage *m*.

minion ['mɪnjən] *n Pej* (*lackey*) larbin *m*; *F Iron* subordonné, -ée; **the minions of the law,** les recors *mpl* de la justice.

minipill ['mɪnɪpɪl] *n* mini-pilule *f*.

miniseries ['mɪnɪsɪəriːz] *n TV* minifeuilleton *m*.

miniskirt ['mɪnɪskɜːt] *n* minijupe *f*.

minister¹ ['mɪnɪstər] *n* **(a)** *Pol* ministre *m* (d'État); *Br* **M. of state,** ministre d'État; *Br* **M. of Defence,** ministre de la Défense; **(b)** *Rel* ministre *m*, pasteur *m* (*d'un culte réformé*); *Cathol* ministre (*des Jésuites*); **m. general,** ministre général.

minister² *vi* **to m. to s.o.** *or* **to s.o.'s needs,** (*take care of*) soigner qn; (*administer to needs*) pourvoir *ou* subvenir aux besoins de qn; *Rel* **to m. to a parish,** desservir une paroisse.

ministerial [mɪnɪ'stɪərɪəl] *adj* **(a)** *Pol* ministériel, gouvernemental, -aux; **(b)** *Rel* sacerdotal, -aux; **(c)** *Jur* exécutif; **m. functions,** fonctions exécutives.

ministering ['mɪnɪstərɪŋ] *adj* (*ange etc*) secourable.

ministration [mɪnɪ'streɪʃən] *n* **(a)** (*assistance*) ministère *m*, soins *mpl*; **(b)** *Rel* sacerdoce *m*; **to receive the ministrations of a priest,** être administré par un prêtre.

ministry ['mɪnɪstrɪ] *n* **(a)** *Pol* (*government*) ministère *m*, gouvernement *m*; (*department*) ministère, département *m*; **to form a m.,** former un ministère; *Br* **the M. of Defence,** le Ministère de la Défense; **(b)** *Rel* **the m.,** le sacerdoce; **he was intended for the m.,** il fut destiné à l'Église; **(c)** (*intervention*) entremise *f* (**of,** de).

mink [mɪŋk] *n* **(a)** (*animal*) **(American) m.,** vison *m*; martre *f* du Canada; **m. farm** *or* **ranch,** visonnière *f*; **(b)** (*fur*) vison; **m. oil,** huile *f* de vison; **m. oil shampoo,** shampooing *m* à l'huile de vison; **a m. coat,** *F* **a m.,** un manteau de vison, un vison.

Minn *abbr* **Minnesota.**

minnow ['mɪnəʊ] *n* (*fish*) vairon *m*; (*also loosely*) épinoche *f*.

Minoan [mɪ'nəʊən] *adj* minoen.

minor¹ ['maɪnər] **1** *adj* (*lesser*) petit, mineur; (*unimportant*) petit, peu important; (*detail, repair*) petit; *Rel* **m. orders,** ordres mineurs; **the film is a m. classic,** le film est un classique de moindre importance; **of m. importance,** sans grande importance; **to play a m. part,** jouer un rôle subalterne *ou* accessoire; **m. roads,** routes secondaires; *Med* **m. operation,** opération *f* d'importance secondaire; *Mus* **m. key,** ton mineur; *Fig* **in a m. key,** plutôt triste; *Old-fashioned Br Sch* **Martin m.,** Martin junior. **2** *n* **(a)** *Jur* mineur, -eure; **(b)** *Rel* **the Minors,** les frères mineurs; **(c)** *US Sch* matière *f* secondaire.

minor² *vi US Sch* **to m. in physics,** étudier la physique comme matière secondaire.

Minorca [mɪ'nɔːkə] *n* Minorque *f*.

minority [mɪ'nɒrɪtɪ, maɪ-] *n* **(a)** (*of total number*) minorité *f*; **to be in a** *or* **the m.,** être en minorité; **to be in a m. of one,** être seul de son opinion; *Fin* **m. holding,** participation *f* minoritaire; *Pol* **m. party/government,** parti *m*/gouvernement *m* minoritaire; **(b)** *Jur* minorité *f*.

Minotaur ['maɪnətɔːr] *n Myth* **the M.,** le Minotaure.

minster ['mɪnstər] *n* grande église; (*attached to abbey*) église abbatiale; **York M.,** la cathédrale d'York.

minstrel ['mɪnstrəl] *n* (*in middle ages*) ménestrel *m*; *Lit* poète *m*, musicien *m*, chanteur *m*; (*actor, singer with blackened face*) acteur *ou* musicien blanc maquillé en noir.

mint¹ [mɪnt] *n* (*plant*) menthe *f*; (*sweet*) bonbon *m* à la menthe; **m. chocolate,** chocolat fourré de crème à la menthe; **m. sauce,** vinaigrette *f* à la menthe; **m. tea,** thé *m* à la menthe; (*herbal*) infusion *f* à la menthe; *esp US* **m. julep,** boisson alcoolique parfumée à la menthe.

mint² *n Fin* **the (Royal) M.,** ≈ (l'hôtel *m* de) la Monnaie; **in m. condition,** à l'état (de) neuf; *F* **to be worth a m.,** (*of person*) rouler sur l'or; (*of thing*) valoir une somme fabuleuse *ou* une fortune; **to make a m.,** gagner une fortune.

mint³ *vt* **(a)** monnayer (*de l'or etc*); **to m. money,** frapper de la monnaie; *Fig* **he must be minting it,** il doit rouler sur l'or; **(b)** *Lit* inventer, forger, créer (*un mot, une expression*).

mintmark ['mɪntmɑːk] *n* (*on coin*) marque *f* de l'atelier monétaire.

minuet [mɪnjʊ'et] *n Mus* menuet *m*.

minus ['maɪnəs] **1** *prep* moins; **ten m. eight leaves two,** dix moins huit égale deux; **he managed to escape, but m. his luggage,** il a réussi à s'échapper, mais sans (ses) bagages; **it's m. twelve degrees,** il fait moins douze degrés. **2** *adj Math* **m. sign,** moins *m*; **m. quantity,** quantité négative; *Sch* **B m.,** B moins. **3** *n Math* (*sign*) moins *m*.

minuscule ['mɪnəskjuːl] *adj* miniscule; *F* **a m. salary,** salaire *m* dérisoire.

minute¹ ['mɪnɪt] *n* **(a)** (*measurement of time*) minute *f*; **it's ten minutes to** *or Am* **of three,** il est trois heures moins dix; **ten minutes past** *or Am* **after three,** trois heures dix; **two m. silence,** deux minutes de silence; **at five-m. intervals, at intervals of five minutes,** toutes les cinq minutes; **a m.'s rest,** un moment de repos; **wait a m.!,** attendez un instant!; **go downstairs this m.!,** descend immédiatement!; **just a m.,** attends un peu; **he's come in this (very) m.,** il rentre à l'instant (même); **the m. my back was turned she ...,** j'avais à peine le dos tourné qu'elle ...; **he'll be here any m.,** il va arriver d'une minute à l'autre; **it'll be ready in a m.,** ça sera prêt dans une minute; **in a few minutes,** dans quelques minutes; **I've just popped in for a m.,** je ne fais qu'entrer et sortir; **m. hand,** grande aiguille (*d'une montre etc*); **a m. timer,** une minuterie;

(b) *Math Astron* minute *f*;

(c) (*note*) note *f* (de service); **to take minutes of a conversation,** noter une conversation; **minutes of a meeting,** compte rendu *m ou* procès-verbal *m* d'une séance.

minute² *vt* prendre note de (*qch*); dresser le procès-verbal *ou* le compte rendu de (*une séance*).

minute³ [maɪ'njuːt] *adj* **(a)** (*small*) tout petit, menu, minuscule, minime; **the minutest details,** les moindres détails; **(b)** (*detailed*) minutieux; **m. examination,** inspection minutieuse.

minutely [maɪ'njuːtlɪ] *adv* minutieusement; en détail.

minutiae [maɪ'njuːʃiː] *npl* petits détails infimes; *Old-fashioned* minuties *fpl*.

minx [mɪŋks] *n F* friponne *f*, coquine *f*; **you little m.!,** petite espiègle!, petite polissonne!

MIPS [mɪps] *n Comptr* (*abbr* **million instructions per second**) MIPS *m*.

miracle ['mɪrək(ə)l] *n* **(a)** *Rel & Fig* miracle *m*; *Fig* prodige *m*; **by a m.,** par miracle; **I can't perform miracles,** je ne peux pas faire de miracles; **it sounds like a m.,** cela tient du miracle; **it's a m. that ...,** c'est (un) miracle que + *sub* ...; *F* **thanks, you're a m.,** merci, tu es fantastique; **m. cure,** guérison miracle *ou* miraculeuse; **m. drug,** remède *m* miracle; **m. worker,** faiseur, -euse de miracles; **(b)** *Lit* **m. play,** miracle *m*.

miraculous [mɪ'rækjʊləs] *adj Rel & Fig* miraculeux; *Fig* extraordinaire, merveilleux; **to have a m. escape,** échapper comme par miracle.

miraculously [mɪ'rækjʊləslɪ] *adv* miraculeusement; par miracle.

mirage ['mɪrɑːʒ] *n* mirage *m*.

mire [maɪər] *n* (*bog*) bourbier *m*; (*mud*) boue *f*, bourbe *f*, fange *f*; *Fig* **to drag s.o. into the m.,** traîner qn dans la boue.

mirror¹ ['mɪrər] *n* miroir *m*, glace *f*; *Opt Phys* **concave/convex m.,** miroir concave/convexe; **hand m.,** glace à main; **shaving m.,** miroir à raser; *Aut* **driving m., rear view m.,** rétroviseur *m*; *Aut* **in my/the m.,** dans mon/le rétroviseur; *Fig* **the press is the m. of public opinion,** la presse est le miroir de l'opinion publique; **m. finish/polish,** fini *m*/polissage *m* spéculaire; **m. image,** (*seen in mirror*) reflet *m*; (*inverted*) image renversé; (*exact copy etc*) copie parfaite; **m. writing,** écriture *f* spéculaire *ou* en miroir.

mirror² *vt Lit & Fig* refléter; **the steeple is mirrored in the lake,** le clocher se reflète *ou* se mire dans le lac.

mirth [mɜːθ] *n* gaieté *f*, allégresse *f*.

mirthful ['mɜːθfʊl] *adj* **(a)** (*amused*) gai, joyeux; **(b)** (*amusing*) amusant.

mirthless ['mɜːθlɪs] *adj* sans gaieté; (*rire*) forcé, sans joie.

MIRV [mɜːv] *n Mil* (*abbr* **multiple independently targeted re-entry vehicle**) = missile à ogives multiples qui sont guidées vers des objectifs éloignés les uns des autres.

miry ['maɪərɪ] *adj* fangeux, bourbeux.

misadventure [mɪsəd'ventʃər] *n* mésaventure *f*, contretemps *m*, avatar *m*; *Jur* **a verdict of death by m.,** un verdict de mort accidentelle.

misalliance [mɪsə'laɪəns] *n* mésalliance *f*.

misanthrope ['mɪzənθrəʊp] *n* misanthrope *mf*.

misanthropic [mɪzən'θrɒpɪk] *adj* (*personne*) misanthrope; (*humeur etc*) misanthropique.

misanthropist [mɪ'zænθrəpɪst] *n* misanthrope *mf*.

misanthropy [mɪ'zænθrəpɪ] *n* misanthropie *f*.

misapply [mɪsə'plaɪ] *vt* **(a)** mal appliquer, mal employer (*qch*); faire un mauvais usage de (*un remède*); **(b)** *Fin* = **MISAPPROPRIATE**.

misapprehend [mɪsæprɪ'hend] *vt* mal comprendre (*qn, qch*); se méprendre sur (*les paroles de qn*).

misapprehension [mɪsæprɪ'henʃən] *n* malentendu *m*, méprise *f*; **to be under a m.,** ne pas avoir bien compris.

misappropriate [mɪsə'prəʊprɪeɪt] *vt* détourner (*des fonds*).

misappropriation ['mɪsəprəʊprɪ'eɪʃən] *n* détournement *m* (*de fonds*).

misbegotten [mɪsbɪ'gɒt(ə)n] *adj* **(a)** *Old-fashioned F* (*badly thought out*) mal conçu; **another of his m. plans!,** encore un de ses projets biscornus!; **(b)** *Arch* (*enfant*) illégitime, bâtard.

misbehave [mɪsbɪ'heɪv] *vi* se conduire mal; (*of child*) se tenir mal.

misbehaviour, *US* **misbehavior** [mɪsbɪ'heɪvjər] *n* (*bad behaviour*) mauvaise conduite; (*more serious*) inconduite *f*.

misc (*abbr* **miscellaneous**) divers.

miscalculate [mɪs'kælkjʊleɪt] **1** *vt* mal calculer (*une somme, une distance etc*); **the government miscalculated the public's response,** le gouvernement a mal prévu la réaction du public. **2** *vi* mal calculer.

miscalculation [mɪskælkjʊ'leɪʃən] *n* erreur *f* de calcul.

miscarriage [mɪs'kærɪdʒ] *n* **(a)** *Obst* fausse couche; **to have a m.,** faire une fausse couche; **(b)** (*failure*) insuccès *m*, échec *m* (*d'un projet*); *Jur* **m. of justice,** erreur *f* judiciaire; (*intentional*) déni *m* de justice; **(c)** (*in post*) égarement *m*, perte *f* (*d'une lettre, d'un colis*).

miscarry [mɪs'kærɪ] *vi* **(a)** *Obst* faire une fausse couche; **(b)** (*of scheme, enterprise*) échouer, ne pas réussir; **(c)** (*of letter*) s'égarer, se perdre; (*reach wrong address*) parvenir à une fausse adresse.

miscast [mɪs'kɑːst] *vt Th Cin etc* donner une mauvaise distribution à (*une pièce*); **he was miscast in the part,** il était mal choisi pour ce rôle.

miscellaneous [mɪsə'leɪnɪəs] *adj* varié, divers; **m. news,** faits *mpl* divers; *Journ* **m. column,** avis *mpl* divers; **m. items,** articles *mpl* divers; *Journ* faits divers.

miscellany [mɪ'selənɪ] *n* **(a)** (*of objects etc*) mélange *m*; collection *f* d'objets variés; **(b)** *Lit* recueil *m*, anthologie *f*; **prose m.,** mélanges *mpl* en prose; **miscellanies,** mélanges.

mischance [mɪs'tʃɑːns] *n* malheur *m*, mésaventure *f*; **by m.,** par malchance.

mischief ['mɪstʃɪf] *n* **(a)** (*trouble*) mal *m*, tort *m*; **to make m.,** apporter le trouble (*dans un ménage etc*); semer la discorde; **(b)** (*of child*) espièglerie *f*; (*malice*) méchanceté *f*; **out of pure m.,** (*naughtiness*) par pure espièglerie; (*malice*) par pure méchanceté; **he's full of m.,** il est très espiègle; **to keep s.o. out of m.,** empêcher qn de faire des sottises *ou* des bêtises; **that'll keep her out of m.,** ça l'occupera, pendant ce temps-là elle ne fera pas de bêtises; **I wonder what m. he's up to,** je me demande ce qu'il fricote; **(c)** *F* (*person*) fripon, -onne, malin, -igne; **little m.,** petit(e) espiègle, petit(e) coquin(e); **(d)** *F* (*injury*) **to do oneself a m.,** se faire du mal.

mischiefmaker ['mɪstʃɪfmeɪkər] *n* brandon *m* de discorde; (*gossip*) mauvaise langue.

mischievous ['mɪstʃɪvəs] *adj* **(a)** (*child*) espiègle, malicieux, coquin; **m. trick** *or* **prank,** espièglerie *f*; **as m. as a monkey,** malin comme un singe; **a m. grin/wink,** un sourire/clin d'œil malicieux; **(b)** (*Pej*) (*person*) méchant, malfaisant; (*thing*) mauvais, malfaisant, nuisible.

mischievously ['mɪstʃɪvəslɪ] *adv* (*see adj*) **(a)** (*to grin, wink*) malicieusement; par espièglerie; **(b)** méchamment; nuisiblement.

mischievousness ['mɪstʃɪvəsnɪs] *n* **(a)** malice *f*, espièglerie *f* (*d'un enfant*); **(b)** *Pej* méchanceté *f*.

misconceive [mɪskən'siːv] *vt* **to have a misconceived idea of sth,** avoir une fausse idée de qch.

misconception [mɪskən'sepʃən] *n* **(a)** (*false idea*) conception erronée, idée fausse; **(b)** (*misunderstanding*) malentendu *m*.

misconduct¹ [mɪs'kɒndʌkt] *n* **(a)** (*of person*) inconduite *f*; *Jur* (*sexual*) adultère *m*; **professional m.,** faute professionnelle; **to be charged with professional m.,** être inculpé pour faute professionnelle; **(b)** mauvaise administration, mauvaise gestion (*d'une affaire*).

misconduct² [mɪskən'dʌkt] *vt* **(a)** mal diriger, mal gérer (*une affaire*); **(b)** *Old-fashioned* **to m. oneself,** se mal conduire.

misconstruction [mɪskən'strʌkʃən] *n* fausse interprétation.

misconstrue [mɪskən'struː] *vt* mal interpréter (*qch*); interpréter (*qch*) à contresens.

miscount¹ ['mɪskaʊnt] *n* (*miscalculation*) faux calcul; (*mistake in addition*) erreur *f* d'addition; *Pol* (*of votes*) erreur dans le dépouillement du scrutin.

miscount² [mɪs'kaʊnt] *vt & vi* mal compter.

miscreant ['mɪskrɪənt] *adj & n* scélérat *m*, misérable *m*.

misdeal¹ [mɪs'diːl] *n Cards* maldonne *f*.

misdeal² *vt & vi* (*pt & pp* **misdealt** [mɪs'delt]) *Cards* **to m. (the cards),** faire maldonne.

misdeed [mɪs'diːd] *n* méfait *m*, mauvaise action; (*crime*) crime *m*, délit *m*.

misdemeanour, *US* **misdemeanor** [mɪsdɪ'miːnər] *n* **(a)** *Jur* acte délictueux; **(b)** (*minor act of misbehaviour*) écart *m* de conduite; (*more serious*) méfait *m*.

misdirect [mɪsdɪ'rekt] *vt* **(a)** mal renseigner, mal diriger (*qn*); **(b)** mal adresser (*une lettre*); **(c)** mal diriger (*un coup*); **(d)** *Jur* **to m. the jury,** (*of judge*) mal instruire le jury.

misdirected [mɪsdɪ'rektɪd] *adj* **(a)** (*letter, parcel etc*) mal adressé; **(b)** (*coup*) frappé à faux; **(c)** (*zèle*) mal employé.

misdirection [mɪsdɪ'rekʃən] *n* **(a)** (*on letter*) erreur *f* d'adresse; **(b)** (*wrong directions*) indication erronée, renseignement erroné.

miser ['maɪzər] *n* avare *mf*.

miserable ['mɪzər(ə)b(ə)l] *adj* **(a)** (*unhappy*) malheureux, triste; **I feel m.,** j'ai le cafard; **don't look so m.,** n'aie pas l'air aussi déprimé; **to make s.o.'s life m.,** rendre la vie dure à qn; **(b)** (*event, condition*) misérable, déplorable; (*journey*) pénible, désagréable; **if only I didn't have this m. cold!,** si je n'avais pas cet affreux rhume!; **what a m. day,** quelle journée épouvantable; **(c)** (*poor, wretched*) misérable, pauvre, pitoyable; (*amount*) insignifiant; (*wage*) dérisoire; **I only need a m. £70 to get straight,** il ne me faudrait que 70 misérables livres pour me remettre d'aplomb.

miserably ['mɪz(ə)rəblɪ] *adv* **(a)** (*unhappily*) d'un air *ou* d'un ton malheureux; **(b)** (*poorly*) pauvrement; **to be m. paid,** avoir un salaire dérisoire; **to fail m.,** échouer lamentablement.

Miserere [mɪzə'rɪərɪ] *n Rel* **(a)** miséréré *m*, miserere *m*; **(b) m. (seat)** = **MISERICORD (b).**

misericord [mɪ'zerɪkɔːd] *n Rel* **(a)** miséricorde *f* (*de monastère*); **(b)** (*seat*) miséricorde *f*, patience *f* (de stalle).

miserliness ['maɪzəlɪnɪs] *n* avarice *f*, ladrerie *f*.

miserly ['maɪzəlɪ] *adj* (*person*) avare, pingre, ladre.

misery ['mɪzərɪ] *n* **(a)** (*suffering*) souffrance(s) *f(pl)*, supplice *m*; **to put s.o. out of their m.,** mettre fin aux souffrances de qn; **to put an animal out of its m.,** donner le coup de grâce à un animal; **(b)** (*unhappiness*) détresse *f*; **to make s.o.'s life a m.,** rendre la vie malheureuse à qn; **(c)** (*person*) *F* geignard, -arde, grincheux, -euse.

misery-guts ['mɪzərɪgʌts] *n F* rabat-joie *m*, empêcheur, -euse de tourner en rond.

misfire¹ [mɪs'faɪər] *n* (*of rifle*) raté *m* (de percussion); **(b)** (*of missile*) *& Aut* raté *m* d'allumage.

misfire² *vi* (*of firearm*) rater, faire long feu; (*of rocket*) avoir un raté d'allumage; (*of engine*) avoir un raté *ou* des ratés; *Fig* (*of joke etc*) manquer son effet, *F* foirer.

misfit ['mɪsfɪt] *n* **(a)** (*person*) inadapté, -ée; **(b)** (*badly fitting garment*) vêtement *etc* manqué *ou* mal réussi; *Com* laissé-pour-compte *m*, *pl* laissés-pour-compte.

misfortune [mɪs'fɔːtʃən] *n* infortune *f*, malheur *m*; **I had the m. to be born on Christmas Day,** j'ai eu le malheur de naître le jour de Noël.

misgiving [mɪs'gɪvɪŋ] *n* doute *m*, crainte *f*, pressentiment *m*, inquiétude *f* (**about sth,** sur qch); **not without misgivings,** non sans hésitation; **to have misgivings,** avoir des doutes (**about s.o.,** à l'égard de qn; **about sth,** au sujet de qch).

misgovern [mɪs'gʌvən] *vt* mal gouverner.

misgovernment [mɪs'gʌvənmənt] *n* mauvais gouvernement, mauvaise administration.

misguided [mɪs'gaɪdɪd] *adj* **(a)** (*person*) malavisé, qui manque de discernement; **these m. people,** ces malheureux; **(b)** (*conduct*) peu judicieux; (*energy*) hors de propos; (*attempt*) malencontreux.

misguidedly [mɪs'gaɪdɪdlɪ] *adv* de façon peu judicieuse, malencontreusement.

mishandle [mɪs'hænd(ə)l] *vt* **(a)** (*handle badly*) mal manier, mal manœuvrer (*une machine, un appareil*); mal gérer, mal mener (*une affaire etc*); **(b)** (*treat badly*) malmener, maltraiter (*qn*).

mishandling [mɪs'hændlɪŋ] *n* **(a)** maniement défectueux (*d'un outil etc*); mauvaise gestion (*d'une affaire etc*); **(b)** mauvais traitements (*à l'égard de qn*).

mishap ['mɪshæp] *n* mésaventure *f*, contretemps *m*; accident *m*; **after many mishaps,** après bien des péripéties.

mishear [mɪs'hɪər] *vt & vi* (*pt & pp* **misheard** [mɪs'hɜːd]) mal entendre; **he misheard them/what they said,** il les a mal entendus/il a mal entendu ce qu'ils ont dit; **I must have misheard her,** j'ai dû mal entendre ce qu'elle a dit.

mishmash ['mɪʃmæʃ] *n F* méli-mélo *m*.

misinformation [mɪsɪnfə'meɪʃən] *n* mauvaise information; **a campaign of m.,** une campagne de mauvaise information.

misinformed [mɪsɪn'fɔːmd] *adj* mal informé, mal renseigné.

misinterpret [mɪsɪn'tɜːprɪt] *vt* mal interpréter (*qn, les paroles de qn*); mal traduire la pensée de (*qn*).

misinterpretation [mɪsɪntɜːprɪ'teɪʃən] *n* **(a)** fausse interprétation; **(b)** (*in translation*) (*opposite meaning to that intended*) contresens *m*; (*wrong meaning*) faux-sens *m*.

misjudge [mɪs'dʒʌdʒ] *vt* mal juger (*qn, qch*); se tromper sur le compte de (*qn*); mal juger de (*qch*); se tromper dans l'estimation de (*la distance*); **it appears I misjudged you,** il semblerait que je vous aie mal jugé.

misjudg(e)ment [mɪs'dʒʌdʒmənt] *n* jugement erroné; fausse estimation (*d'une distance*).

mislay [mɪs'leɪ] *vt* (*pt & pp* **mislaid** [mɪs'leɪd]) égarer, perdre (*son parapluie etc*); **I've just mislaid it somewhere,** je l'ai juste mis quelque part, mais je ne me souviens plus où.

mislead [mɪs'liːd] *vt* (*pt & pp* **misled** [mɪs'led]) **(a)** (*deceive*) induire (*qn*) en erreur, tromper (*qn*) (**as to,** quant à); **her behaviour misled him into thinking her feelings were stronger,** sa conduite lui a laissé croire que ses sentiments étaient plus profonds, mais il n'en était rien; **(b)** *Fml* (*lead in wrong direction, to wrong destination*) égarer, fourvoyer (*qn*); **(c)** *Fml* (*corrupt*) corrompre, dévoyer (*qn*).

misleading [mɪs'liːdɪŋ] *adj* (*advertisement etc*) trompeur, -euse; **it is m. to ...,** il est trompeur de ... .

mismanage [mɪs'mænɪdʒ] *vt* mal conduire, mal diriger, mal gérer (*une affaire, une entreprise*).

mismanagement [mɪs'mænɪdʒmənt] *n* mauvaise administration, mauvaise gestion; **there has been some m.,** l'affaire a été mal menée.

misnomer [mɪs'nəʊmər] *n* **(a)** nom mal approprié; **changes which, by a great m., are called progress,** changements auxquels on donne fort mal à propos le nom de progrès; **(b)** *Jur* erreur *f* de nom.

misogynist [mɪ'sɒdʒɪnɪst, maɪ-] *n* misogyne *f*.

misogyny [mɪ'sɒdʒɪnɪ, maɪ-] *n* misogynie *f*.

misplace [mɪs'pleɪs] *vt* **(a)** mal placer (*ses affections etc*); **misplaced remark,** remarque *f* hors de propos; **misplaced trust,** confiance mal placée; **(b)** (*lose temporarily*) égarer (*un livre etc*); **(c)** *Ling* placer à faux (*l'accent tonique etc*).

misprint¹ ['mɪsprɪnt] *n Typ* erreur *f* typographique, faute *f* d'impression, *F* coquille *f*.

misprint² [mɪs'prɪnt] *vt* imprimer (*un mot*) incorrectement.

mispronounce [mɪsprə'naʊns] *vt* mal prononcer (*un mot*).

mispronunciation [mɪsprənʌnsɪ'eɪʃən] *n* prononciation incorrecte; faute *f* de prononciation.

misquotation [mɪskwəʊ'teɪʃən] *n* citation inexacte.

misquote [mɪs'kwəʊt] *vt* citer (*qch*) à faux *ou* inexactement; citer (*un auteur*) incorrectement; **I've been misquoted,** (*by the press etc*) on m'a cité erronément.

misread [mɪs'riːd] *vt* (*pt & pp* **misread** [mɪs'red]) mal lire, mal interpréter (*un texte etc*); *Fig* **to m. the situation,** mal interpréter la situation; **I misread her remarks,** j'ai mal interprété ses remarques.

misrepresent [mɪsreprɪ'zent] *vt* mal représenter; dénaturer, travestir (*les faits*), présenter (*les faits*) sous un faux jour; **I have been misrepresented in the press as ...,** j'ai été représenté à tort dans la presse comme ... .

misrepresentation [mɪsreprɪzen'teɪʃən] *n* faux rapport; présentation erronée (*des faits etc*); *Jur* fausse déclaration.

misrule [mɪs'ruːl] *n* **(a)** (*inefficient rule*) mauvaise administration, mauvais gouvernement; **(b)** (*disorder*) désordre *m*, confusion *f*.

miss¹ [mɪs] *n* coup manqué; *Billiards* manque *m* de touche; **it was a near m.,** il s'en est fallu de peu, c'était moins une; **we had a near m. with that car,** cette voiture a failli nous percuter; *F* **to give sth a m.,** s'abstenir de faire quelque chose *ou* d'aller quelque part; **I'll give the soup a m.,** je ne prendrai pas de soupe; **to give s.o. a m.,** passer le tour de qn; *Prov* **a m. is as good as a mile,** manquer de près ou de loin, c'est toujours manquer.

miss² 1 *vt* **(a)** (*fail to hit, find, attend etc*) manquer; *F* rater (*le but*); ne pas trouver, ne pas rencontrer (*qn*); manquer, *F* rater (*un train etc*); manquer, laisser échapper, *F* rater (*une occasion*); manquer (*un rendez-vous, un repas*); *F* sécher (*un cours*); **to m. one's mark,** manquer son coup; **to m. the point (in one's answer),** répondre à côté; **you've missed the point,** vous n'avez pas compris; *Th* **to m. one's entrance,** (*of actor*) louper son entrée; **to m. one's cue,** manquer sa réplique; **to m. one's way,** s'égarer; *F* **to m. the boat** *or* **the bus,** rater *ou* laisser échapper l'occasion; **I missed him (by two minutes),** je l'ai manqué *ou F* raté (de deux minutes); **an opportunity not to be missed,** une occasion à ne pas laisser passer; **a life of missed opportunities,** une vie d'occasions manquées; **I've missed my turn,** j'ai perdu mon tour; **I missed the first five minutes of the programme,** j'ai raté les cinq premières minutes de l'émission; *F* **you haven't missed much!,** vous n'avez pas raté grand-chose!; *F* **you don't know what you're missing,** tu ne sais pas ce que tu manques; **I missed my holiday this year,** je n'ai pas eu de vacances cette année; **I never m. going there,** je ne manque jamais d'y aller; **he narrowly** *or* **just missed being killed,** il a failli se faire tuer; **the boss doesn't m. anything,** rien n'échappe au patron; **you can't m. the house,** vous ne pouvez pas manquer de reconnaître la maison;

(b) (*not understand, hear etc*) ne pas saisir (*une plaisanterie*); **I missed that,** (*didn't understand*) je n'ai pas compris; (*didn't hear*) je n'ai pas entendu;

(c) (*omit*) **to m. a word/a line,** omettre *ou* sauter un mot/une ligne; **to m. a stop,** (*of bus etc*) brûler un arrêt;

(d) (*notice absence of*) remarquer l'absence de (*qn, qch*), remarquer qu'il manque (*qn, qch*); **we are sure to be missed,** on va sûrement remarquer notre absence;

(e) (*feel lack of*) **I m. you,** tu me manques; **don't you m. your family?,** est-ce que ta famille ne te manque pas?; **I m. the countryside/my piano,** la campagne/mon piano me manque; *Prov* **you can't m. what you've never had,** ce que l'on n'a jamais eu ne nous manque pas; **I am not allowed cigarettes, but I don't m. them,** on me défend de fumer, mais ça ne me manque pas.

2 *vi* (*miss target*) manquer *ou* rater son coup; **he never misses,** il ne manque jamais son coup; **missed!,** manqué!, *F* raté!

miss[3] *n* **(a) M. Martin,** mademoiselle *ou* Mlle Martin; (*as address*) Mademoiselle Martin; **the M. Martins, the Misses Martin,** les demoiselles Martin; (*as address*) Mesdemoiselles Martin; **thank you, M. Martin,** merci mademoiselle Martin; **M. World,** Miss Monde; **(b)** *Br Sch F* **Yes/good morning M.,** (*to woman teacher*) oui/bonjour madame.

►miss out 1 *vi* (*not benefit*) ne pas bénéficier; **you missed out there,** vous avez raté quelque chose. **2** *vtsep* (*omit*) oublier.

►miss out on *vipo* rater (*un bon film, une soirée super etc*); **a lot of people are missing out on state benefits they are entitled to,** de nombreuses personnes ne profitent pas des allocations auxquelles elles ont droit.

Miss *abbr* **Mississippi.**

missal ['mɪs(ə)l] *n Rel* missel *m*.

misshape [mɪs'ʃeɪp] *n Br Com* (*chocolate, biscuit*) rejet *m*.

misshapen [mɪs'ʃeɪpən] *adj* (*person, limb etc*) difforme, contrefait; (*hat, figure etc*) déformé.

missile ['mɪsaɪl, *Am* 'mɪs(ə)l] *n* **(a)** (*projectile*) projectile *m*; **(b)** *Mil* missile *m*, engin *m*; **guided m.,** missile *ou* engin guidé; **anti-missile m.,** engin antimissile(s); **m. base,** base *f* de lancement de missiles; **m. launcher,** lance-missiles *m inv*.

missing ['mɪsɪŋ] **1** *adj* (*ami etc*) absent; (*objet*) égaré, disparu; (*argent*) qui manque; **m. person,** personne disparue, disparu *m*; **one man is m.,** un homme manque; *Mil etc* **to report s.o. m.,** porter qn disparu; **the m. link,** (*in anthropology, piece of information*) le maillon manquant; **to go m.,** disparaître. **2** *n* **the m.,** (*used as pl*) les disparus.

mission ['mɪʃən] *n* **(a)** (*task*) mission *f*; **to charge** *or* **entrust s.o. with a m.,** charger qn d'une mission, confier une mission à qn; **m. accomplished,** mission accomplie; **minister on a special m.,** ministre *m* en mission spéciale; **she thinks her m. is to ...,** elle croit avoir mission de ...; **space m.,** mission spatiale; **(b)** (*body of persons*) mission *f*; *US* ambassade *f*; représentation *f* diplomatique; **military/trade m.,** mission militaire/commerciale; *Rel* **foreign/home missions,** missions étrangères/métropolitaines; **(c)** (*place*) *Rel* **m. (station),** mission *f*.

missionary ['mɪʃənərɪ] **1** *n* missionnaire *mf*. **2** *adj* (*prêtre, œuvre, esprit*) missionnaire; (*vocation*) de missionnaire; (*tronc*) des missions; *F* **m. position,** position *f* du missionnaire.

missis ['mɪsɪz] *n Sl* = **MISSUS.**

missive ['mɪsɪv] *n Fml* lettre *f*, missive *f*.

misspell ['mɪs'spel] *vt* (*pt & pp* **misspelt** ['mɪs'spelt]) mal épeler, mal orthographier.

misspelling ['mɪs'spelɪŋ] *n* faute *f ou* fautes *fpl* d'orthographe.

misspend ['mɪs'spend] *vt* (*pt & pp* **misspent** ['mɪs'spent]) mal employer (*son argent, son temps*); gâcher (*son argent*); **a misspent youth,** une jeunesse mal employée; (*debauched*) une jeunesse passée dans la dissipation.

missus ['mɪsɪs, 'mɪsɪz] *n Sl* (*wife*) bourgeoise *f*; **the m., my m.,** ma bourgeoise; **your m.,** votre dame.

mist [mɪst] *n* **(a)** *Met* brume *f*, *Nau* brumaille *f*; **Scotch m.,** bruine *f*, crachin *m*; *Fig Hum* **what's this then? Scotch m.?,** (*are you blind?*) tu es aveugle ou quoi?; *Fig* **lost in the mists of time,** perdu dans la nuit des temps; **(b)** buée *f* (*sur une glace etc*); **to see things through a m.,** voir trouble.

►mist over 1 *vi* **(a)** (*of landscape*) disparaître sous la brume; **(b)** (*of mirror*) se couvrir de buée; (*of eyes*) se voiler. **2** *vtsep* couvrir (*une glace etc*) de buée.

►mist up *vi* = **MIST OVER 1 (b); misted-up windscreen,** pare-brise embué.

mistakable [mɪs'teɪkəb(ə)l] *adj* **easily m.,** facile à confondre (**for,** avec).

mistake[1] [mɪs'teɪk] *n* erreur *f*, faute *f*; **m. in calculation/in the date,** erreur de calcul/de date; **exercise full of mistakes,** exercice plein de fautes; **grammatical mistakes,** fautes de grammaire; **it would be a m. to imagine that ...,** ce serait une erreur d'imaginer que ...; **to make a m.,** faire *ou* commettre une faute *ou* une erreur, se tromper (**about, over,** sur, au sujet de, quant à); **you're making a big m.,** tu es en train de commettre une grosse erreur; **to make the m. of doing sth,** avoir le tort de faire qch; **it's an easy m. to make,** c'est une erreur qu'il est facile de faire; **by m.,** (*faire qch*) par erreur, par méprise; **there is** *or* **can be no m. about that,** il n'y a pas à s'y tromper; **there must be some m.,** il doit y avoir une erreur; **make no m.,** que l'on ne s'y trompe pas; *F* **it's warm and no m.!,** il fait chaud, pas d'erreur!; **I'm sorry, my m.,** je suis désolé, je me suis trompé *ou* j'ai fait erreur.

mistake[2] *vt* (*pt* **mistook** [mɪs'tʊk]; *pp* **mistaken** [mɪs'teɪkən]) **(a)** (*misinterpret*) se méprendre sur (*les paroles, les intentions, de qn*); **I have mistaken the house,** je me suis trompé de maison; **if I'm not mistaken,** si je ne me trompe pas; **there's no mistaking it,** il n'y a pas à s'y méprendre; **(b)** (*confuse*) confondre (*qn,qch*) (**for s.o./sth,** avec qn/qch); **I mistook him for someone else,** je l'ai pris pour quelqu'un d'autre.

mistaken [mɪs'teɪkən] *adj* (*opinion*) erroné; (*idea*) faux; **I must be m.,** je dois faire erreur; **in the m. belief that ...,** croyant, à tort, que ...; **under the m. impression that ...,** ayant l'impression erronée que ...; **m. identity,** erreur *f* sur la personne.

mistakenly [mɪs'teɪkənlɪ] *adv* par erreur, par méprise.

mister ['mɪstər] *n Sl* m'sieur *m*; **what's the time, m.?,** quelle heure est-il, m'sieur?

mistime [mɪs'taɪm] *vt* faire (*qch*) mal à propos *ou* à contretemps; mal calculer (*un coup*).

mistimed [mɪs'taɪmd] *adj* inopportun, mal à propos; (*coup*) mal calculé.

mistiness ['mɪstɪnɪs] *n* **(a)** (*obscurity*) état brumeux, obscurité *f*; **(b)** (*mist*) brouillard *m*, brume *f*; (*steam*) vapeurs *fpl*.

mistlethrush ['mɪs(ə)lθrʌʃ] *n* (*bird*) (grive *f*) draine *f*.

mistletoe ['mɪs(ə)ltəʊ] *n Bot* gui *m*.

mistook *see* **MISTAKE[2].**

mistranslate [mɪstræns'leɪt] *vt* mal traduire; interpréter (*une phrase*) à contresens.

mistranslation [mɪstræns'leɪʃən] *n* mauvaise traduction; (*mistake in translation*) erreur *f* de traduction.

mistreat [mɪs'triːt] *vt* maltraiter (*qn, qch*).

mistress ['mɪstrɪs] *n* **(a)** (*woman in charge*) maîtresse *f* (*qui exerce l'autorité*); **to be one's own m.,** être indépendante, être sa propre maîtresse; **to be m. of oneself** *or* **of one's emotions,** être maîtresse de soi(-même); **she was the m. of the situation,** elle était maîtresse de la situation; *Old-fashioned* **the m. of the house,** la maîtresse de maison; **(b)** (*owner of pet*) maîtresse *f*; **(c)** *esp Br Sch* (*woman teacher*) maîtresse *f* (d'école), institutrice *f*; professeur *m* (*de lycée*); **the French m.,** le professeur de français; **(d)** (*lover*) maîtresse *f*; **(e)** *Arch* (*in titles*) Madame *f*.

mistrial [mɪs'traɪəl] *n Jur* jugement entaché d'un vice de procédure; *US* procès ajourné, l'unamité n'ayant pas été atteinte parmi le jury.

mistrust[1] [mɪs'trʌst] *n* méfiance *f*, défiance *f* (**of,** de), manque *m* de confiance (**of,** en).

mistrust[2] *vt* se méfier de, se défier de (*qn, qch*), ne pas avoir confiance en (*qn*).

mistrustful [mɪs'trʌstfʊl] *adj* méfiant, défiant.

mistrustfully [mɪs'trʌstfʊlɪ] *adv* avec méfiance, avec défiance.

misty ['mɪstɪ] *adj* (*weather, place etc*) brumeux, embrumé; (*memory*) vague, confus; (*form*) estompé; **m. eyes,** yeux embués *ou* troublés; **it's m.,** le temps est brumeux; **the windscreen is all m.,** le pare-brise est tout couvert de buée.

misunderstand [mɪsʌndə'stænd] *v* (*pt & pp* **misunderstood** [mɪsʌndə'stʊd]) **1** *vt* **(a)** (*misinterpret*) mal comprendre (*qch, qn*); mal entendre, se méprendre sur (*qch*); mal interpréter (*une action*); **we misunderstood each other,** il y a eu un malentendu entre nous; **(b)** (*misjudge*) méconnaître (*qn*), se méprendre sur le compte de (*qn*). **2** *vi* mal comprendre; **if I have not misunderstood,** si j'ai bien compris.

misunderstanding [mɪsʌndə'stændɪŋ] *n* **(a)**

(*misconception*) conception erronée; (*mistake*) malentendu *m*; (*confusion of two objects or people*) quiproquo *m*; **I think there's been a m.**, je crois qu'il y a eu un malentendu; **(b)** (*disagreement*) mésintelligence *f*, mal-entente *f*.

misuse[1] [mɪs'juːs] *n* abus *m*, mauvais usage, emploi abusif (*de qch*); abus (*d'autorité*); emploi abusif (*des mots*); *Jur* **fraudulent m. of funds,** détournement *m* de fonds.

misuse[2] [mɪs'juːz] *vt* faire (un) mauvais usage *ou* (un) mauvais emploi de (*qch*); abuser de (*son autorité*); employer (*un mot*) à tort *ou* abusivement.

mite [maɪt] *n* **(a)** *Arch & Lit* (*sum of money*) **the widow's m.**, le denier de la veuve; **(b)** (*small amount*) **m. of consolation,** brin *m* de consolation; **it's a m. expensive,** c'est un peu cher; **(c)** (*child*) petit gosse, petite gosse, mioche *mf*; (*animal*) petite bête; **poor little m.!**, pauvre petit!; **(d)** *Zool* mite *f*; **cheese m.**, mite du fromage.

miter ['maɪtər] *n & v US* = **MITRE[1,2,3]**.

mitigate ['mɪtɪgeɪt] *vt* adoucir (*la colère de qn*); adoucir, atténuer (*la souffrance, le chagrin etc*); apaiser (*la douleur*); mitiger, atténuer (*une peine*); tempérer (*la chaleur*); adoucir (*le froid*); *Jur* atténuer (*un crime, une faute*).

mitigating ['mɪtɪgeɪtɪŋ] *adj esp Jur* **m. circumstances,** circonstances atténuantes.

mitigation [mɪtɪ'geɪʃən] *n* adoucissement *m* (*d'une douleur*); mitigation *f*, réduction *f*, atténuation *f*, modération *f* (*d'une peine*); atténuation (*d'une faute*); **if you have anything to say in m. of this offence,** si vous avez quelque chose à ajouter qui pourrait atténuer votre crime.

mitral ['maɪtrəl] *adj Anat* **m. valve,** valvule mitrale.

mitre[1], *US* **miter** ['maɪtər] *n* (*headdress*) mitre *f*.

mitre[2], *US* **miter** *n Carp* **m. (joint),** (assemblage *m* à) onglet *m*; **m. box,** boîte *f* à onglet(s); **m. (square),** équerre *f* (à) onglet.

mitre[3], *US* **miter** *vt Carp etc* **(a)** (*shape*) tailler (*une pièce*) à onglet; **(b)** (*join*) assembler (*deux pièces*) à onglet.

mitt [mɪt] *n* **(a)** = **MITTEN**; *Baseball* gant *m*; **(b)** *F* (*hand*) patte *f*.

mitten ['mɪt(ə)n] *n* **(a)** moufle *f*, *Can* mitaine *f*; **(b)** (*fingerless glove*) mitaine *f*; **(c)** *Boxing F* **mittens,** gants *mpl*, mitaines *fpl*.

mix[1] [mɪks] *n* **(a)** mélange *m* (*de mortier, de plâtre*); **cake m.**, (*in packet*) préparation *f* pour gâteaux; **there was a good/an unusual m. of people at the party,** la soirée regroupait un amalgame intéressant/inhabituel de personnes; *Com* **product m.**, assortiment *m* de produits; **(b)** *Cin* fondu enchaîné; enchaînement *m* (*des images*); **(c)** (*in recording*) mixage *m*; **the 12 inch m.**, (*record*) le trente centimètres.

mix[2] **1** *vt* mêler, mélanger (**several things together,** plusieurs choses ensemble; **sth with sth,** qch à *ou* avec qch); allier (*des métaux*); préparer (*un gâteau, une boisson*); gâcher (*du mortier, du plâtre*); *Culin* retourner, fatiguer (*la salade*); *US Cards* battre, mélanger (*les cartes*); *Pharm* mélanger, mixtionner (*des drogues*); **you should never m. your drinks,** il ne faut jamais mélanger les alcools; **to m. one's metaphors,** confondre deux expressions. **2** *vi* se mêler, se mélanger (**with,** avec, à); (*of fluids*) s'allier; **sport and drug-taking don't m.**, le sport et l'utilisation de drogue ne font pas bon ménage; **to m. with people,** (*of person*) s'associer à *ou* avec des gens, fréquenter des gens; **I don't m. much,** je ne fréquente pas beaucoup de gens; **to m. with the crowd,** se mêler à la foule.

▶**mix up** *vtsep* **(a)** (*prepare*) préparer (*une boisson, un médicament*); **(b)** (*put in disorder*) embrouiller (*ses papiers etc*); **everything had got mixed up,** tout était en pagaille; **(c)** (*confuse*) confondre (**with,** avec); **I was mixing you up with your brother,** je vous confondais avec votre frère; **I was getting all mixed up,** je ne savais plus où j'en étais; **(d)** (*involve*) **to be mixed up in an affair,** être mêlé à une affaire, être compromis *ou* impliqué dans une affaire; **mixed up in something dishonest,** impliqué dans quelque chose de malhonnête; **(e)** *esp US Sl* **to m. it (up),** en venir aux coups.

mixed [mɪkst] *adj* mêlé, mélangé; mixte; **person of m. blood,** sang-mêlé *mf inv*; **m. marriage,** mariage *m* mixte; *Culin etc* **m. grill,** mixed-grill *m*, *pl* mixed-grills; **m. sweets,** bonbons assortis; **m. vegetables,** jardinière *f ou* macédoine *f* de légumes; **m. feelings,** sentiments mêlés; **a m. blessing,** quelque chose qui a du bon et du mauvais; **her resignation was a m. blessing,** sa démission avait du bon et du mauvais; *Econ* **m. economy,** économie *f* mixte; *Nau* **m. cargo,** cargaison *f* mixte, chargement *m* divers; *F* **they were a m. bag,** (*of people or things*) il y en avait de toutes sortes; *Math* **m. number,** nombre *m* fractionnaire; **m. school,** école *f* mixte; *Tennis* **m. doubles,** double *m* mixte; *Old-fashioned* **in m. company,** en présence de personnes des deux sexes.

mixed-up [mɪks'tʌp] *adj F* (*person*) déboussolé, qui ne sait plus où il en est; (*papers etc*) en pagaille; **a crazy m.-up kid,** un adolescent un peu paumé.

mixer ['mɪksər] *n* **(a)** (*machine*) *Ind etc* mélangeuse *f*; agitateur *m*; *Ch* barboteur *m*; *Cin* mélangeur *m* de sons; (*in engine*) diffuseur *m*; **concrete m.**, bétonnière *f*; **(food) m.**, mixeur *m*; **m. (tap),** robinet mélangeur; (*with single control*) mitigeur *m*; **(b)** (*person*) *Metal Ind* brasseur *m*; *Cin* opérateur *m* des sons; **(c) to be a good m.**, (*socially*) être très sociable; **(d)** (*drink*) = boisson non-alcoolisée que l'on utilise pour rallonger certains alcools; **(e)** *esp US Univ F* = soirée pour permettre aux étudiants de faire connaissance.

mixing ['mɪksɪŋ] *n* **(a)** mélange *m* (*de qch avec qch*); gâchage *m* (*du mortier, du plâtre*); *Pharm* mixtion *f* (*d'une préparation etc*); **m. bowl,** terrine *f ou* bol *m* à mélanger; **m. chamber,** (*in engine*) chambre *f* de mélange *ou* de carburation; **m. drum,** mélangeur *m* (à tambour); **(b)** (*in recording*) *& Cin etc* mixage *m*.

mixture ['mɪkstʃər] *n* **(a)** mélange *m* (*de choses, de personnes*); (*combination*) amalgame *m*; **the music is a m. of traditional and modern,** la musique est un amalgame de moderne et de traditionnel; **cake m.**, (*in packet*) préparation *f* pour gâteau; *Ch* **homogeneous/heterogeneous m.**, mélange homogène/hétérogène; **fuel-air m.**, (*in engine*) mélange air-carburant; **lean** *or* **weak m.**, mélange pauvre; **(b)** *Pharm* mixtion *f*, mixture *f*; **cough m.**, sirop *m* pour *ou* contre la toux.

mix-up ['mɪksʌp] *n* (*confusion*) confusion *f*, embrouillement *m*; (*misunderstanding*) malentendu *m*; *F* (*mess*) pagaïe *f*, pagaille *f*; **there's been a m.-up with the reservations,** il y a eu une confusion dans les réservations.

mizzen ['mɪz(ə)n] *n Nau* **m. (sail),** artimon *m*.

mizzenmast ['mɪz(ə)nmɑːst] *n Nau* mât *m* d'artimon.

ml (*abbr* **millilitre(s)**) ml *m*.

MLR [eme'lɑːr] *n Fin* (*abbr* **minimum lending rate**) taux *m* de crédit minimum.

mm (*abbr* **millimetre(s)**) mm *m*.

MNA [eme'neɪ] *n Can* (*in Quebec*) (*abbr* **Member of the National Assembly**) MAN *m* (*abbr* Membre de l'Assemblée Nationale).

mnemonic [nɪ'mɒnɪk] **1** *adj* mnémonique. **2** *n* aide-mémoire *m inv*; moyen *m* mnémotechnique.

mnemonics [nɪ'mɒnɪks] *npl* (*usu with sing verb*) mnémonique *f*, mnémotechnie *f*.

mo [məʊ] *n Br F* instant *m*, minute *f*; **half a mo!**, une petite seconde!

MO [e'məʊ] *n* **(a)** *Mil etc abbr* **medical officer**; **(b)** (*abbr* **modus operandi**) (*of criminal*) façon *f* d'agir; **(c)** (*abbr* **money order**) mandat-poste *m*.

moan[1] [məʊn] *n* **(a)** (*sound*) gémissement *m*, plainte *f*; **(b)** *F* (*complaint*) ronchonnement *m*; **to have a (good) m.**, grogner, ronchonner.

moan[2] **1** *vi* **(a)** (*make sound*) gémir, pousser des gémissements; (*of wind*) gémir; **(b)** *F* (*complain*) ronchonner; **stop moaning!**, arrête de ronchonner!; **to m. about sth,** se plaindre de qch; **he's always moaning (and groaning),** il est toujours à ronchonner. **2** *vt* dire (*qch*) en gémissant.

moaner ['məʊnər] *n F* ronchonneur, -euse, râleur, -euse.

moaning ['məʊnɪŋ] *n* **(a)** (*sounds*) gémissement(s) *m(pl)*; **(b)** *F* (*complaining*) **his constant m.**, ses plaintes continuelles.

moat [məʊt] *n* fossé(s) *m(pl)*, douves *f(pl)*.

mob[1] [mɒb] *n* **(a)** *Pej* **the m.**, (*the masses*) la populace, *F* le populo; **to join the m.**, descendre dans la rue; **m. rule,** voyoucratie *f*; **(b)** (*crowd*) foule *f* (agitée), cohue *f*, rassemblement *m*; attroupement *m*, ameutement *m*; (*people in pursuit*) meute *f*; **(c)** *F* (*gang*) bande *f*, clique *f*; **the M.**, la mafia.

mob[2] *vt* (**-bb-**) (*of angry crowd*) houspiller, attaquer, malmener (*qn*); (*of fans, reporters etc*) assiéger (*qn*).

mobile[1] ['məʊbaɪl] *adj* **(a)** itinérant, mobile; *F* **are you m.?**, vous êtes motorisé?; *Br* **m. library,** bibliothèque itinérante, bibliobus *m*; **m. home,** grande caravane; **(b)** *Mil* (*défense, unité etc*) mobile; **m. warfare,** guerre *f* de mouvement; **(c)** (*in society*) mobile; **upwardly m.**, qui monte; **(d)** (*limb, component etc*) mobile; **m. features,** physionomie changeante.

mobile[2] *n Art* mobile *m*.

mobility [məʊ'bɪlɪtɪ] *n* mobilité *f*; *Br Admin* **m.**

allowance, indemnité *f* pour les déplacements (versée aux personnes handicapées).

mobilization [məʊbɪlaɪ'zeɪʃən] *n* mobilisation *f* (*des troupes, de capitaux etc*); **m. order,** (*general*) appel *m* de mobilisation; (*to individual recruit*) ordre *m* de mobilisation.

mobilize ['məʊbɪlaɪz] **1** *vt* mobiliser (*des troupes, des capitaux*). **2** *vi* (*of army*) entrer en mobilisation.

mobster ['mɒbstər] *n esp Am* gangster *m*.

moccasin ['mɒkəsɪn] *n* (*footwear*) mocassin *m*.

mocha ['mɒkə] *n* **m. (coffee),** (café *m*) moka *m*.

mock¹ [mɒk] *n* **(a) to make a m. of s.o./sth,** se moquer de qn/qch; **(b)** *Sch* examen blanc.

mock² *adj* d'imitation; faux, *f* fausse; **m. tortoiseshell,** écaille *f* imitation; *Culin* **m. turtle soup,** consommé *m* à la tête de veau; **to indulge in m. heroics,** jouer au *ou* se prendre pour un héros; **m. trial,** simulacre *m* de procès; **m. fight,** simulacre de combat; *Sch* **m. examination,** examen blanc; **m. orange,** (*shrub*) seringa(t) *m*.

mock³ **1** *vt* (*ridicule*) narguer (*qn*); (*deceive*) se jouer de, tromper (*qn*); (*imitate*) imiter, singer (*qn*). **2** *vi* **to m. at,** se moquer de (*qn, qch*), railler (*qn, qch*).

mocker ['mɒkər] *n* **(a)** (*person*) moqueur, -euse, railleur, -euse; **(b)** *Br F* **to put the mockers on sth,** (*spoil*) foutre qch en l'air.

mockery ['mɒkərɪ] *n* **(a)** (*action*) moquerie *f*, raillerie *f*; **(b)** (*person, thing*) sujet *m* de moquerie *ou* de raillerie; **this makes a m. of the whole thing,** cela réduit tout à néant; **(c)** (*pretence*) semblant *m*, simulacre *m* (**of,** de); **the trial was a mere m.,** le procès n'a été qu'un simulacre.

mocking ['mɒkɪŋ] **1** *adj* moqueur, -euse, railleur, -euse. **2** *n* moquerie *f*, raillerie *f*.

mockingbird ['mɒkɪŋbɜːd] *n* (*bird*) moqueur *m*.

mockingly ['mɒkɪŋlɪ] *adv* d'un ton moqueur *ou* railleur; par moquerie.

mock-up ['mɒkʌp] *n* maquette *f*.

mod [mɒd] *F* **1** *adj* **m. cons,** confort *m* moderne. **2** *n* **mods and rockers,** ≈ blousons noirs.

MOD [eməʊ'diː] *n Br* (*abbr* **Ministry of Defence**) Ministère *m* de la Défense; **MOD property,** propriété *f* du Ministère de la Défense.

modal ['məʊd(ə)l] *adj* modal, -aux; *Gram* (*auxiliaire etc*) de mode.

modality [məʊ'dælɪtɪ] *n* modalité *f*.

mode [məʊd] *n* **(a)** (*manner*) mode *m*, méthode *f*, manière *f* (**of,** de); **m. of life,** train *m ou* mode de vie; **(b)** (*fashion*) mode *f*; **(c)** *Mus Phil Comptr* mode *m*.

model¹ ['mɒd(ə)l] *n* **(a)** modèle *m*, maquette *f*; (*in naval architecture etc*) gabarit *m*; (*in surveying*) plan *m* en relief; **working m.,** modèle pouvant fonctionner; **m. aircraft,** modèle (réduit) *ou* maquette d'avion; **m. maker,** maquettiste *mf*, modéliste *m*; **(b)** (*example*) *& Art Sewing etc* modèle *m*; **to draw from/without a m.,** dessiner d'après le modèle/de chic; **anatomical m.,** écorché *m*; **to take s.o. as one's m.,** prendre modèle sur qn, prendre qn pour modèle; **to be a m. of virtue,** être un modèle *ou* un exemple de vertu; *Com Ind* **there are several different models,** il y a plusieurs modèles différents; **Paris models,** modèles de la haute couture parisienne; *Econ etc* **feasibility m.,** modèle probatoire; **m. pupil,** écolier, -ière modèle; **(c)** (*person*) *Art* modèle *m*; **(fashion) m.,** mannequin *m*; *Euph* (*prostitute*) hôtesse *f*.

model² (**-ll-**, *US* **-l-**) **1** *vt* **(a)** *Art* modeler (*une figure, un groupe*); **to m. sth after** *or* **on** *or* **upon sth,** modeler qch sur qch; **to m. oneself on s.o.,** prendre exemple sur qn; **(b)** (*of mannequin*) présenter (*une robe etc*). **2** *vi* (*of artist's model*) poser comme modèle; (*of fashion model*) travailler comme mannequin.

modeller, *US* **modeler** ['mɒdələr] *n* modeleur, -euse (**of,** de).

modelling, *US* **modeling** ['mɒdəlɪŋ] *n* **(a)** *Art etc* modelage *m*; **m. clay,** pâte *f* à modeler; **(b)** présentation *f* (*d'une robe etc*); (*occupation*) métier *m* de mannequin.

modem ['məʊdem] *n Comptr* modem *m*.

moderate¹ ['mɒdərɪt] **1** *adj* modéré; (*buveur*) tempéré; (*langage*) mesuré; (*prix*) modéré, modique, moyen; **m. income,** revenu *m* modique; **of m. size,** de grandeur moyenne; **m. wind,** vent modéré; **m. opinions,** opinions modérées. **2** *n Pol* (*person*) modéré, -ée.

moderate² ['mɒdəreɪt] **1** *vt* **(a)** modérer (*ses exigences, ses désirs*); ralentir (*son zèle*); **a moderating influence,** une influence modérante *ou* modératrice; **(b)** présider (*une assemblée, une discussion*). **2** *vi* **(a)** (*of storm*) s'apaiser, se calmer; **(b)** présider (*à une assemblée*).

moderately ['mɒdərɪtlɪ] *adv* (*to eat, drink, like*) modérément; (*fast, well-off*) moyennement; **m. priced,** de prix moyen.

moderation [mɒdə'reɪʃən] *n* **(a)** modération *f*, mesure *f*; sobriété *f* (*de langage*); **in m.,** avec modération, modérément; **taken in m. alcohol is not harmful,** consommé avec modération, l'alcool n'est pas nocif; **(b)** (*at Oxford University*) **Moderations,** = premier examen pour le grade de Bachelor of Arts.

moderator ['mɒdəreɪtər] *n* **(a)** président *m* (*d'une assemblée*); *Rel Scot* **M. of the General Assembly,** modérateur *m ou* président de l'Assemblée générale (de l'Église d'Écosse); **(b)** *Phys* modérateur *m*, ralentisseur *m* (*de réacteur etc*).

modern ['mɒdən] **1** *adj* moderne; **m. times,** les temps modernes; **m. languages,** langues vivantes; **m. Greek,** grec moderne. **2** *n* moderne *m*.

modernism ['mɒdənɪzəm] *n* **(a)** modernisme *m*; **(b)** (*practice*) usage nouveau; *Ling* néologisme *m*.

modernity [mɒ'dɜːnɪtɪ] *n* modernité *f*.

modernization [mɒdənaɪ'zeɪʃən] *n* modernisation *f*.

modernize ['mɒdənaɪz] *vt* moderniser.

modest ['mɒdɪst] *adj* **(a)** (*not boastful*) modeste; **to be m. about one's achievements,** ne pas se vanter de son succès; **(b)** (*moderate*) (*request*) modéré; (*fortune*) modeste; **to be m. in one's requirements,** être peu exigeant; **(c)** (*unpretentious*) (*style etc*) sans prétentions; **(d)** *Old-fashioned* (*chaste*) pudique.

modestly ['mɒdɪstlɪ] *adv* (*see adj*) **(a)** modestement, avec modestie; **(b)** modérément; **(c)** sans prétentions; **(d)** pudiquement; **he m. wrapped a towel around his waist,** il a pudiquement enroulé une serviette autour de sa taille.

modesty ['mɒdɪstɪ] *n* **(a)** (*of person*) modestie *f*; **let it be said with all due m.,** soit dit sans vanité; **(b)** modération *f* (*d'une demande*); modicité *f* (*d'une dépense*); **(c)** (*of style etc*) absence *f* de prétention; **(d)** *Old-fashioned* pudeur *f*.

modicum ['mɒdɪkəm] *n* **a m. of ...,** un minimum de ...; **a m. of truth,** une petite part de vérité.

modification [mɒdɪfɪ'keɪʃən] *n* modification *f*; **to make modifications to sth,** apporter des modifications à qch.

modify ['mɒdɪfaɪ] *vt* **(a)** (*alter*) modifier, apporter des modifications à (*qch*); mitiger, atténuer (*une peine*); rabattre de (*ses prétentions*); **(b)** *Gram Ling* modifier (*le verbe, une voyelle etc*).

modifying ['mɒdɪfaɪɪŋ] *adj* modifiant.

modish ['məʊdɪʃ] *adj* (*chapeau etc*) à la mode.

modishly ['məʊdɪʃlɪ] *adv* (*habillé*) à la mode.

modiste [məʊ'diːst] *n* modiste *f*.

Mods [mɒdz] *npl F* (*at Oxford University*) = premier examen pour le grade de Bachelor of Arts.

modular ['mɒdjʊlər] *adj Archit Math etc* modulaire; (*meuble*) à éléments (composables).

modulate ['mɒdjʊleɪt] **1** *vt* moduler (*sa voix, des sons*); *Phys* moduler (*l'amplitude etc*); **modulating frequency,** fréquence *f* de modulation. **2** *vi Mus* moduler.

modulation [mɒdjʊ'leɪʃən] *n* modulation *f*, inflexion *f* (*de la voix*); *Mus El Electron* modulation.

modulator ['mɒdjʊleɪtər] *n El Electron* modulateur *m*.

module ['mɒdjuːl] *n Archit Astronaut Constr etc* module *m*; *Sch* (*of course*) module; **lunar m.,** module lunaire; **command m.,** module de commande.

modulus, *pl* **-i** ['mɒdjʊləs, -aɪ] *n Math Phys* module *m*, coefficient *m*.

modus operandi ['məʊdəsɒpə'rændaɪ, -diː] *n* modus *m* operandi, façon *f ou* manière *f* d'opérer.

modus vivendi ['məʊdəsvɪ'vendaɪ, -diː] *n* modus *m* vivendi.

moggy ['mɒgɪ] *n Br F* chat *m*.

mogul¹ ['məʊgəl] *n F* (*powerful person*) gros bonnet; **movie m.,** magnat *m* du cinéma.

mogul² *n Ski* bosse *f*.

Mogul ['məʊgəl] *n Hist* mogol *m*.

mohair ['məʊheər] *n* mohair *m*; **m. sweater,** pull *m* en mohair.

Mohammed [məʊ'hæmɪd] *n Rel Hist* Mahomet *m*, Mohammed *m*.

Mohammedan [məʊ'hæmɪd(ə)n] **1** *adj* musulman, -ane, mahométan, -ane. **2** *n* Musulman, -ane, Mahométan, -ane.

mohawk ['məʊhɔːk] *n Am* (*hairstyle*) mohican *m*.

Mohawk ['məʊhɔːk] *n* (*native North American*) Mohawk *m*.

mohican [məʊ'hiːkən] *n Br* (*hairstyle*) mohican *m*.

Mohican [məʊ'hiːkən] *n* (*native North American*) Mohican *m*.

moiré ['mwɑːreɪ] *adj & n Tex* moiré *m*.

moist [mɔɪst] *adj* (*climat, région, chaleur etc*) humide;

(*peau, main, chaleur*) moite; **eyes m. with tears,** yeux mouillés de larmes; **to grow m.,** se mouiller, s'humecter; **a light, m. cake,** un gâteau léger et moelleux.

moisten ['mɔɪs(ə)n] **1** *vt* mouiller, humecter; moitir (*la peau*); arroser (*la pâte etc*); *Tech* humidifier, madéfier; **to m. a cloth with ...,** imbiber un chiffon de ... . **2** *vi* se mouiller, s'humecter.

moistness ['mɔɪstnɪs] *n* humidité *f*; moiteur *f*.

moisture ['mɔɪstʃər] *n* humidité *f*; buée *f* (*sur une glace etc*).

moisturize ['mɔɪstʃəraɪz] *vt* humidifier (*qch*); hydrater (*la peau*).

moisturizer ['mɔɪstʃəraɪzər] *n* crème hydratante, hydratant *m*.

molar ['məʊlər] **1** *n* (dent *f*) molaire *f*. **2** *adj* molaire.

molasses [mə'læsɪz] *npl* (*with sing verb*) mélasse *f*; *Am F* **to be as slow as m. (in winter),** être d'une lenteur de limace *ou* d'escargot *ou* de tortue.

mold, molder *etc US* = **MOULD, MOULDER** *etc*.

mole[1] [məʊl] *n* (*birthmark*) grain *m* de beauté.

mole[2] *n* **(a)** (*animal*) taupe *f*; **m. catcher,** taupier *m*; **m. trap,** taupière *f*; **(b)** (*spy*) taupe *f*.

mole[3] *n* (*breakwater*) môle *m*, brise-lames *m inv*, digue *f*, jetée *f*.

molecular [mə'lekjʊlər] *adj Phys* moléculaire; **m. weight/mass,** masse *f*/poids *m* moléculaire.

molecule ['mɒlɪkju:l] *n Ch Phys* molécule *f*.

molehill ['məʊlhɪl] *n* taupinière *f*.

moleskin ['məʊlskɪn] *n* **(a)** (peau *f* de) taupe *f*; **m. coat,** manteau *m* en taupe; **(b)** *Tex* (*material*) velours *m* de coton.

molest [mə'lest] *vt* **(a)** molester, importuner (*qn*); **(b)** (*sexually*) attenter à la pudeur de (*qn*).

molestation [məʊle'steɪʃən] *n* **(a)** molestation *f*; **(b)** (*sexual*) attentat *m* à la pudeur.

molester [mə'lestər] *n* **(child) m.,** coupable *mf* d'attentat à la pudeur sur un *ou* des enfant(s).

moll [mɒl] *n Sl* **(gangster's) m.,** poule *f ou* môme *f* d'un gangster.

mollify ['mɒlɪfaɪ] *vt* adoucir, apaiser (*qn, la colère de qn*).

mollusc, *US* **mollusk** ['mɒləsk] *n* mollusque *m*.

mollycoddle ['mɒlɪkɒd(ə)l] *vt F* dorloter, câliner (*un enfant*); élever (*un enfant*) dans du coton.

Molotov ['mɒlətɒf] *n* **M. cocktail,** cocktail *m* Molotov.

molt, molting *US* = **MOULT, MOULTING**.

molten ['məʊltən] *adj Metal* fondu, en fusion; **m. lead,** plomb fondu.

molybdenum [mɒ'lɪbdɪnəm] *n* molybdène *m*.

mom [mɒm] *n Am F* maman *f*.

moment ['məʊmənt] *n* **(a)** moment *m*, instant *m*; **the film had its moments,** il y avait quelques bons moments dans le film; **she has her moments of being quite pleasant,** il y a des moments où elle est assez agréable; **I haven't a m. to spare,** je n'ai pas un instant de libre; **wait a m.!, just a m.!, one m.!,** une seconde!, un moment!, un instant!; **he may return at any m.,** il peut revenir d'un instant à l'autre; **I have just** *or* **only this m. heard about it,** je viens de l'apprendre, je l'apprends à l'instant; **just at that m.,** à ce moment précis; **I saw her a m. ago,** je l'ai vue il y a un instant; **the m. he arrives,** dès son arrivée; **at this m.,** en ce moment; **at the (present) m.,** actuellement; **at the last m.,** à la dernière minute; **I'll be with you in a m.,** je suis à vous dans une minute; **nothing else for the m.,** rien de plus pour l'instant; **I don't for one m. believe that this will happen,** je ne crois pas un instant que ça va se produire; **not a m.'s hesitation,** pas un moment d'hésitation; **the man of the m.,** l'homme du jour *ou* du moment; **to live for the m.,** vivre dans l'instant; **the m. of truth,** la minute de vérité; **on the spur of the m.,** sur le moment;

(b) *Phys Math etc* moment *m* (*d'une force*); **m. of inertia,** moment d'inertie;

(c) (*importance*) **of great/little/no m.,** de grande/de petite/d'aucune importance.

momentarily ['məʊməntərɪlɪ] *adv* **(a)** (*very briefly*) momentanément; **(b)** *esp Am* (*very soon*) d'un moment à l'autre.

momentary ['məʊməntərɪ] *adj* momentané, passager.

momentous [məʊ'mentəs] *adj* important; (*decision*) capital; **on this m. occasion,** en cette occasion mémorable.

momentousness [məʊ'mentəsnɪs] *n* importance capitale; (*of an occasion*) importance.

momentum, *pl* **-ta** [məʊ'mentəm, -tə] *n* **(a)** *Phys* force vive, force d'impulsion; *Nucl Phys* impulsion *f* (*d'une particule*); **(b)** (*impetus*) vitesse acquise, élan *m*; *Fig* force vive (*d'une attaque etc*); **carried away by my own m.,** emporté par mon (propre) élan; **to gather m.,** (*of moving object*) acquérir de la force (vive) *ou* de la vitesse; (*of political movement etc*) prendre de l'ampleur, s'amplifier; **we'll never get that m. back again,** on ne retrouvera jamais ce rythme.

Mon (*abbr* **Monday**) lun.

Monaco [mə'nɑ:kəʊ] *n* **(principality of) M.,** (principauté *f* de) Monaco *m*.

monad ['mɒnæd] *n Phil Biol Ch* monade *f*.

Mona Lisa ['məʊnə'li:zə] *n Art* **the M. L.,** la Joconde.

monarch ['mɒnək] *n* monarque *m*.

monarchic(al) [mɒ'nɑ:kɪk, -ɪk(ə)l] *adj* monarchique.

monarchist ['mɒnəkɪst] *n Pol* monarchiste *mf*.

monarchy ['mɒnəkɪ] *n* monarchie *f*.

monastery ['mɒnəstrɪ] *n* monastère *m*.

monastic [mə'næstɪk] *adj Rel & Fig* monastique, monacal, -aux, claustral, -aux; (*attitude*) monastique; **he's a m. sort of person,** il mène une vie de moine.

monasticism [mə'næstɪsɪzəm] *n* **(a)** (*way of life*) vie *f* monastique; **(b)** (*system*) système *m* monastique, monachisme *m*.

monaural [mɒ'nɔ:rəl] *adj* monaural, -aux.

Monday ['mʌndɪ] *n* lundi *m*; **every M.,** tous les lundis; *F* **that M. morning feeling,** le cafard du lundi matin *ou* de l'après-weekend.

monetarism ['mʌnɪtərɪzm] *n Econ* monétarisme *m*.

monetarist ['mʌnɪtərɪst] *Econ* **1** *n* monétariste *mf*. **2** *adj* (*policy etc*) monétariste.

monetary ['mʌnɪt(ə)rɪ] *adj* monétaire; **m. unit,** unité *f* monétaire.

money ['mʌnɪ] *n* **(a)** (*no pl*) argent *m*; **to coin** *or* **mint m.,** frapper de la monnaie; *Econ* **bank m.,** monnaie de banque; **paper m.,** billets *mpl* (de banque), papier-monnaie *m*; *Fin Banking* **cheap** *or* **easy m.,** argent à bon marché; *Com* **ready m.,** argent comptant *ou* liquide; **to pay in ready m.,** payer (au) comptant; **to throw good m. after bad,** s'enfoncer davantage dans une mauvaise affaire; **my own m.,** mon argent personnel; **to put** *or* **invest m. in sth,** investir *ou* placer de l'argent dans qch; **spending m.,** argent pour dépenses courantes; **to be worth a lot of m.,** (*of thing*) avoir de la valeur; (*of person*) être riche; **to have m. to burn,** avoir de l'argent à jeter par les fenêtres; *F* **I'm not made of m.,** je ne suis pas cousu d'or; *F* **to be in the m.,** être en fonds; **to be short of m.,** être à court d'argent; **your m. or your life!,** la bourse ou la vie!; **to earn m.,** gagner de l'argent; **to earn good m.,** bien gagner sa vie; **to make m.,** gagner de l'argent; **the job's boring but the money's good,** le travail est ennuyeux mais ça paye bien; **to do sth for m.,** faire qch pour l'argent; **there's m. to be made in this business,** il y a de l'argent à gagner dans ce métier; **there's no m. in it,** ça ne paye pas; **it was m. for old rope,** c'était de l'argent facile; **m. makes m.,** l'argent va à l'argent; **you've had your m.'s worth,** vous en avez eu pour votre argent; *F* **for my m. Jackson is the better player,** à mon avis, Jackson est le meilleur joueur; **to put m. on a horse/***etc*, mettre de l'argent sur un cheval/*etc*; **to put one's m. where one's mouth is,** passer aux actes; **it's throwing m. away, it's m. down the drain,** c'est de l'argent gaspillé *ou* jeté par la fenêtre; **m. market,** marché monétaire *ou* financier; **m. matters,** affaires *fpl* d'argent, questions financières; **m. order,** mandat-poste *m*, *pl* mandats-poste; **international m. order,** mandat international; **m. belt,** ceinture *f* porte-monnaie; **m. spider,** petite araignée rouge; **m. supply,** masse *f* monétaire;

(b) (*pl* **moneys,** *occ* **monies**) (*coin*) pièce *f* de monnaie; (*currency*) monnaie *f* (particulière); *Arch & Jur* **moneys, monies,** (*sums*) argent *m*, fonds *mpl*, sommes *fpl* (d'argent); **public moneys,** deniers publics.

moneybag ['mʌnɪbæg] *n* **(a)** sac *m* à argent; sacoche *f* (*d'une receveur d'autobus etc*); **(b)** *F Old-fashioned* (*person*) **moneybags,** richard, -arde, rupin, -ine.

moneybox ['mʌnɪbɒks] *n* (*child's bank*) tirelire *f*.

moneychanger ['mʌnɪtʃeɪndʒər] *n* **(a)** (*person*) courtier *m* de change; **(b)** *esp US* (*machine*) = machine qui fait de la monnaie.

moneyed ['mʌnɪd] *adj* riche, qui a de l'argent; **the m. classes,** les gens de fortune; **the m. interest,** les capitalistes *mpl*.

money-grubber ['mʌnɪgrʌbər] *n F* grippe-sou *m*, *pl* grippe-sous, pingre *m*.

money-grubbing ['mʌnɪgrʌbɪŋ] *adj F* grippe-sou.

moneylender ['mʌnɪlendər] *n* (*person*) prêteur *m* d'argent; (*establishment*) maison *f* de prêt.

moneymaker ['mʌnɪmeɪkər] *n* = société *ou* magasin *etc* qui rapporte.

moneymaking ['mʌnɪmeɪkɪŋ] **1** *adj* (*commerce etc*) qui rapporte. **2** *n* acquisition *f* d'argent.

mongol ['mɒŋgəl] *adj* & *n Med* mongolien, -ienne.

Mongol ['mɒŋgəl] **1** *adj Geog* mongol. **2** *n* **(a)** Mongol, -ole; **(b)** *Ling* mongol *m*.

Mongolia [mɒŋ'gəʊlɪə] *n* Mongolie *f*.

Mongolian [mɒŋ'gəʊlɪən] **1** *adj* mongol. **2** *n* **(a)** Mongol, -ole; **(b)** *Ling* mongol *m*.

mongolism ['mɒŋgəlɪz(ə)m] *n Med* mongolisme *m*.

mongoloid ['mɒŋgəlɔɪd] *adj* (*features etc*) de mongolien.

mongoose, *pl* **-ses** [mɒŋ'guːs, -sɪz] *n* mangouste *f*.

mongrel ['mʌŋgrəl] **1** *n* (*dog, animal*) métis, -isse; (*dog*) bâtard, -arde. **2** *adj* (*animal, F peuple*) métis.

moni(c)ker ['mɒnɪkər] *n Sl* (*name*) nom *m*; (*nickname*) surnom *m*.

monitor¹ ['mɒnɪtər] *n* **(a)** (*person*) moniteur, -trice; *Tel* opérateur *m* d'interception; *esp Br Sch* = (*with supervisory role*) élève choisi pour maintenir la discipline; = (*helper*) élève choisi pour aider le professeur dans les travaux pratiques *etc*; *Cin TV* **m. (man),** ingénieur *m* du son; **(b)** (*device*) *Rad* appareil *m* de contrôle *ou* de surveillance, moniteur *m*; *TV* **m. (screen),** écran *m* de contrôle; **m. (speaker),** (*on stage*) = enceinte qui permet aux musiciens de s'entendre jouer; **(c)** *Comptr* moniteur *m*.

monitor² *vt Rad Med etc* surveiller (*des émissions, l'état de qn*); *Tel* entrer en écoute (*sur une conversation*); surveiller (*un circuit de transmissions*); *Cin* contrôler (*l'enregistrement sonore*); **environmental groups monitored the level of pollution,** les groupes de protection de l'environnement ont contrôlé le niveau de pollution.

monitoring ['mɒnɪtərɪŋ] *n Rad* monitoring *m*, interception *f* (*des émissions*); *Tel* écoute *f* (*d'une conversation*); surveillance *f* (*d'un circuit de transmissions*); *Cin* contrôle *m* (*de l'enregistrement sonore*); *Med* surveillance continue (*de malades*); *Rad* **m. station,** station *f ou* centre *m* d'écoute.

monk [mʌŋk] *n* moine *m*; **to live like a m.,** vivre comme un moine.

monkey ['mʌŋkɪ] *n* **(a)** (*animal*) singe *m*; **female m., she-m.,** guenon *f*; **m. house,** pavillon *m* des singes; *F* **you little m.!,** (*child*) petit polisson!, petit(e) espiègle!; **little m. face,** petite frimousse espiègle; *Sl* **to make a m. (out) of s.o.,** se payer la tête de qn; *Sl* **I don't give a m.'s (fart),** je m'en fous comme de l'an quarante; *Am Sl* **to have a m. on one's back,** être toxicomane; *Am* **m. bars,** cage *f* à écureuil; **m. business,** (*scheme*) fricotage *m*, combine *f*; (*underhand dealing*) conduite *f* malhonnête; **m. jacket,** veste courte (*de garçon de café etc*); **m. nut,** cacah(o)uète *f*; **m. puzzle (tree),** araucaria *m*; *US Sl* **m. suit,** smoking *m*; **m. tricks,** espiègleries *fpl*; **(b)** *Constr etc* mouton *m* (*de sonnette*); *Am* **m. wrench,** clef anglaise, clef à molette; **(c)** *Am Sl* (billet *m ou* fafiot *m* de) cinq cents dollars.

▶**monkey about, monkey around** *vi* faire des sottises, faire l'imbécile.

monkfish ['mʌŋkfɪʃ] *n* lotte *f* (de mer), baudroie *f*.

monkish ['mʌŋkɪʃ] *adj* de moine, monacal, -aux.

monkshood ['mʌŋkshʊd] *n* (*plant*) (aconit *m*) napel *m*.

mono ['mɒnəʊ] **1** *adj F* monaural, mono. **2** *n* **recorded in m.,** enregistré en mono.

monochrome ['mɒnəkrəʊm] **1** *adj Art Phot* monochrome; *Art* en camaïeu; *Comptr* **m. screen,** écran monochrome. **2** *n* camaïeu *m*, (peinture *f*) monochrome *m*.

monocle ['mɒnək(ə)l] *n* monocle *m*.

monoclonal ['mɒnəʊkləʊnəl] *adj Biol* **m. antibody,** anticorps monoclonal.

monoculture ['mɒnəʊkʌltʃər] *n Agr* monoculture *f*.

monogamous [mɒ'nɒgəməs] *adj* monogame.

monogamy [mɒ'nɒgəmɪ] *n* monogamie *f*.

monogram ['mɒnəgræm] *n* monogramme *m*.

monogrammed ['mɒnəgræmd] *adj* (*mouchoir*) brodé d'initiales.

monograph ['mɒnəgræf] *n* monographie *f*.

monolingual [mɒnəʊ'lɪŋgwəl] *adj* monolingue.

monolith ['mɒnəlɪθ] *n* monolithe *m*.

monolithic [mɒnə'lɪθɪk] *adj* **(a)** (*monument*) monolithe; **(b)** *Pol etc* monolithique.

monologue ['mɒnəlɒg] *n* monologue *m*.

monomania [mɒnəʊ'meɪnɪə] *n* monomanie *f*.

mononucleosis [mɒnəʊnjuːklɪ'əʊsɪs] *n Med* mononucléose *f*.

monophonic [mɒnəʊ'fɒnɪk] *adj* (*in audio*) monophonique.

monoplane ['mɒnəʊpleɪn] *n Av* monoplan *m*.

monopolist [mə'nɒpəlɪst] *n* **(a)** monopolisateur, -trice, accapareur, -euse; **(b)** *Pol* partisan, -ane du monopole.

monopolization [mənɒpəlaɪ'zeɪʃən] *n* monopolisation *f*.

monopolize [mə'nɒpəlaɪz] *vt* **(a)** *Com* monopoliser, accaparer (*une denrée etc*); **(b)** *Fig* accaparer (*qn, qch*); monopoliser (*qn, qch, la conversation*).

monopoly [mə'nɒpəlɪ] *n Jur etc* monopole *m*; **to have a m. of sth** *or* **on sth,** avoir *ou* faire le monopole de qch, monopoliser qch; **no political party has a m. of morality,** aucun parti politique ne détient le monopole de la moralité.

monorail ['mɒnəʊreɪl] *n Rail etc* monorail *m*.

monosodium [mɒnəʊ'səʊdɪəm] *n* **m. glutamate,** glutamate *m* de sodium.

monosyllabic [mɒnəʊsɪ'læbɪk] *adj* monosyllabe, monosyllabique; **he's rather m.,** il ne s'exprime que par monosyllabes.

monosyllable [mɒnəʊ'sɪləb(ə)l] *n* monosyllabe *m*; **he replied in monosyllables,** il a répondu par monosyllabes.

monotheism ['mɒnəʊθiːɪz(ə)m] *n* monothéisme *m*.

monotheistic [mɒnəʊθiː'ɪstɪk] *adj* monothéiste.

monotone ['mɒnətəʊn] **1** *adj* monotone. **2** *n* débit *m* monotone *ou* uniforme *ou* sans modulation; **to speak in a m.,** parler d'une voix uniforme *ou* monotone.

monotonous [mə'nɒtənəs] *adj* **(a)** (*job*) monotone, sans variété; **(b)** (*sound*) monotone, dont le ton ne varie pas.

monotonously [mə'nɒtənəslɪ] *adv* monotonement.

monotony [mə'nɒtənɪ] *n* monotonie *f*; **to relieve the m.,** rompre la monotonie.

Monotype ® ['mɒnətaɪp] *n Typ* (*machine*) Monotype ® *f*.

monoxide [mɒ'nɒksaɪd] *n Ch* **carbon m.,** oxyde *m* de carbone.

Monsignor [mɒn'siːnjər] *n Rel* monseigneur *m*.

monsoon [mɒn'suːn] *n Met* mousson *f*; **the m. season,** la mousson.

monster ['mɒnstər] **1** *n* **(a)** monstre *m*; monstruosité *f*; *Fig* **a m. of cruelty,** un monstre de cruauté; **(b)** (*large person*) colosse *m*, géant, -ante. **2** *adj F* (*enormous*) monstre, monstrueux, colossal, -aux, énorme, immense.

monstrance ['mɒnstrəns] *n Rel* ostensoir *m*.

monstrosity [mɒn'strɒsɪtɪ] *n* monstruosité *f*; (*building, statue etc*) horreur *f*.

monstrous ['mɒnstrəs] *adj* **(a)** (*creature*) monstrueux; **(b)** (*repugnant*) odieux, monstrueux; **it is perfectly m. that such a thing should be allowed,** c'est monstrueux qu'une telle chose soit permise; **(c)** (*enormous*) monstrueux, énorme, colossal, -aux, immense.

monstrously ['mɒnstrəslɪ] *adv* monstrueusement.

Mont *abbr* **Montana.**

montage ['mɒntɑːʒ] *n Cin* montage *m*.

Monte Carlo [mɒntɪ'kɑːləʊ], *F* **Monte** ['mɒntɪ] *n* Monte-Carlo.

month [mʌnθ] *n* mois *m*; **lunar m.,** mois lunaire; **calendar m.,** mois civil; **in the m. of August,** au mois d'août; **a m. ago today,** il y a aujourd'hui un mois; **a thirteen-m.-old baby, a thirteen months' old baby,** un bébé de treize mois; **from m. to m.,** de mois en mois; **once a m.,** une fois par mois; *F* **never in a m. of Sundays,** jamais de la vie; *F* **to see s.o. once in a m. of Sundays,** voir qn une fois tous les trente-six du mois; **it's that time of the m.,** j'ai mes *ou* elle a ses règles.

monthly ['mʌnθlɪ] **1** *adj* mensuel; *Physiol* **m. periods,** règles *fpl*; *Com* **m. payment** *or* **instalment,** mensualité *f*; *Rail etc* **m. season ticket,** (billet *m* d')abonnement mensuel. **2** *adv* mensuellement; tous les mois. **3** *n* **(a)** revue *ou* publication mensuelle; **(b)** *F* **monthlies,** règles *fpl*.

Montreal [mɒntrɪ'ɔːl] *n* Montréal.

monument ['mɒnjʊmənt] *n* **(a)** monument *m*; **ancient monuments,** monuments historiques; **(b)** (*gravestone*) monument *m* funéraire, pierre tombale.

monumental [mɒnjʊ'ment(ə)l] *adj* **(a)** (*statue etc*) monumental, -aux; (*literary work etc*) monumental; (*ignorance*) prodigieux; (*error, stupidity*) monumental; **(b)** **m. mason,** marbrier *m*.

moo¹ [muː] **1** *n* meuglement *m*, beuglement *m* (*d'une vache etc*). **2** *int* **m.!,** meuh!

moo² *vi* **(mooed)** (*of cow etc*) meugler, beugler.

mooch [muːtʃ] *vt F* emprunter (*qch à qn*), *F* taper (*qch à qn*).

▶**mooch about, mooch around** *vi* flâner, traîner, se balader.

moocow ['muːkaʊ] *n F* (*in children's language*) vache *f*, meu-meu *f*.

mood¹ [muːd] *n* **(a)** (*logic*) & *Gram* mode *m*; **the indicative m.,** l'indicatif *m*; **(b)** *esp US Mus* mode *m*.

mood² *n* humeur *f*, disposition *f*; **to be in a (bad) m.,** être de mauvaise humeur; **to be in a good m.,** être de bonne humeur; **to be in a generous m.,** être en veine de générosité; **to be in the m. for reading,** avoir envie de lire; **he's in no m. for laughing,** il n'est pas d'humeur à rire; **I'm not in the m.,** ça ne me dit rien; **I wasn't in the m. (for it),** je n'étais pas d'humeur à ça; **m. music,** musique *f* d'ambiance.

moodily ['muːdɪlɪ] *adv* d'un air morose, maussadement.

moodiness ['muːdɪnɪs] *n* **(a)** (*sulkiness*) morosité *f*, maussaderie *f*; **(b)** (*changeableness*) humeur changeante.

moody ['muːdɪ] *adj* **(a)** (*sulky*) chagrin, morose, maussade; **(b)** (*changeable*) d'humeur changeante, lunatique.

moon[1] [muːn] *n* **(a)** lune *f*; **new m.,** nouvelle lune; **full m.,** pleine lune; **to land on the m.,** atterrir *ou* se poser sur la lune, *F* alunir; *Fig* **to cry for the m.,** demander la lune; **to promise s.o. the m.,** promettre la lune à qn; *F* **once in a blue m.,** tous les trente-six du mois; *F* **that was many moons ago,** c'était il y a bien longtemps; *F* **to be over the m.,** être enchanté *ou* ravi (**about,** de); **m. buggy,** jeep *f* lunaire; **(b)** *Astron* (*month*) lunaison *f*; *Lit* lune *f*, mois *m*; **(c)** (*on fingernail*) lunule *f*.

moon[2] *Sl* **1** *vi* (*bare one's buttocks*) montrer son cul. **2** *vt* montrer son cul à (*qn*).

►**moon about, moon around** *vi* musarder, flâner.

►**moon over** *vipo* languir pour (*qn, qch*).

moonbeam ['muːnbiːm] *n* rayon *m* de lune.

moonfaced ['muːnfeɪst] *adj* avec des grosses joues.

moonless ['muːnlɪs] *adj* (*nuit etc*) sans lune.

moonlight[1] ['muːnlaɪt] *n* clair *m* de lune; **in the m., by m.,** au clair de lune, à la clarté *ou* la lumière de la lune; *Br F* **m. flit,** déménagement *m* à la cloche de bois; *Br F* **to do a m. flit,** déménager à la cloche de bois.

moonlight[2] *vi F* (*illegally*) faire du travail au noir, travailler au noir.

moonlighter ['muːnlaɪtər] *n F* (*illegal*) travailleur *m* au noir.

moonlighting ['muːnlaɪtɪŋ] *n F* (*illegal*) travail (au) noir.

moonlit ['muːnlɪt] *adj* éclairé par la lune.

moonrise ['muːnraɪz] *n* lever *m* de la lune.

moonshine ['muːnʃaɪn] *n* **(a)** *Am F* alcool illicitement distillé; (*smuggled*) alcool de contrebande; **(b)** (*nonsense*) *F* balivernes *fpl*, fariboles *fpl*, fadaises *fpl*; **that's all m.,** tout ça c'est de la blague; **(c)** (*moonlight*) clair *m* de lune.

moonshot ['muːnʃɒt] *n Astronaut* tir *m* lunaire.

moonstone ['muːnstəʊn] *n* (*gem*) adulaire *f*, feldspath nacré, pierre *f* de lune.

moonstruck ['muːnstrʌk] *adj* à l'esprit dérangé, *F* toqué.

moony ['muːnɪ] *adj* dans la lune, rêveur, -euse.

moor[1] [mʊər] *n* lande *f*, bruyère *f*.

moor[2] *Nau* **1** *vt* amarrer (*un navire*); mouiller (*une bouée, une mine*). **2** *vi* s'amarrer.

Moor [mʊər] *n* Maure, Mauresque, More, Moresque.

moorcock ['mʊəkɒk] *n* (*bird*) lagopède *m* rouge d'Écosse.

moorhen ['mʊəhen] *n* **(a)** (*water bird*) poule *f* d'eau; **(b)** (*red grouse*) lagopède *m* rouge d'Écosse (femelle).

mooring ['mʊərɪŋ] *n* **(a)** (*action*) amarrage *m*; **m. buoy,** (bouée *f* de) corps-mort *m*, *pl* corps-morts, coffre *m* d'amarrage; **m. pile** *or* **post,** pieu *m* *ou* borne *f* d'amarrage; **m. line,** câble *m* d'amarrage; **(b)** (*place*) poste *m* d'amarrage; **ship at her moorings,** navire sur ses amarres.

Moorish ['mʊərɪʃ] *adj* maure, *f* mauresque, more, *f* moresque.

moorland ['mʊələnd] *n* lande *f*, bruyère *f*.

moose [muːs] *n* (*pl* **moose**) **(American) m.,** orignal *m*, élan *m* du Canada; élan.

moot[1] [muːt] *adj* (*question etc*) sujet à controverse, discutable; **it is a m. point,** c'est discutable.

moot[2] *vt* soulever (*une question*).

mop[1] [mɒp] *n* (*for floor*) balai *m* à laver, balai-éponge *m*, *pl* balais-éponges, balai à franges; *Nau* faubert *m*, vadrouille *f*, guipon *m*; (*for dishes*) lavette *f* (à vaisselle); *Fig* **m. of hair,** tignasse *f*.

mop[2] *vt* (**-pp-**) éponger, essuyer (*le parquet*) avec un balai; *Nau* fauberder, fauberter (*le pont*); **to m. one's brow,** s'éponger le front.

►**mop up 1** *vtsep* **(a)** (*clean*) éponger (*de l'eau*); **to take a piece of bread to m. up the sauce,** prendre un morceau de pain pour finir la sauce; **(b)** *Mil etc* liquider (*les derniers résistants*); nettoyer (*une position etc*). **2** *vi* **(a)** (*clean floor etc*) passer la serpillière; **(b)** *Mil etc* nettoyer, faire une opération de nettoyage.

mope [məʊp] *vi* être triste *ou* mélancolique, broyer du noir.

►**mope about, mope around** *vi* = **MOPE**.

moped ['məʊped] *n Br* mobylette ® *f*, *F* mob *f*.

moppet ['mɒpɪt] *n F* gamin, -ine, gosse *mf*.

mopping ['mɒpɪŋ] *n* épongeage *m*, essuyage *m* (*du parquet etc*).

mopping up *n* **(a)** = **MOPPING**; **(b)** *Mil* nettoyage *m* (*d'une position etc*); **m. up operations,** opérations *fpl* de nettoyage.

moquette [mɒ'ket] *n Tex* moquette *f*.

MOR [eməʊ'ɑːr] *adj esp Mus abbr* **middle of the road**.

moraine [mɒ'reɪn] *n Geol* moraine *f*.

moral ['mɒrəl] **1** *adj* (*person, certainty, victory etc*) moral, -aux; **m. standard,** sens moral; **m. life,** vie exemplaire; **I went with him to give him m. support,** je l'ai accompagné pour le soutenir moralement. **2** *n* **(a)** (*lesson*) morale *f*, moralité *f* (*d'un conte*); **there's a m. to that story,** cette histoire a une morale; **story with a m.,** conte moral; **(b)** (*usu pl*) **morals,** moralité *f*, mœurs *fpl*; **man of loose morals,** homme de mœurs dissolues.

morale [mɒ'rɑːl] *n* (*no pl*) moral *m*; **m. in the company is very low/high,** le moral dans la société est très bas/haut; **good for m.,** bon pour le moral; **to undermine the m. (of the army),** démoraliser (les troupes); **to undermine m.,** saper le moral.

moralist ['mɒrəlɪst] *n* moraliste *mf*.

moralistic [mɒrə'lɪstɪk] *adj* moraliste.

morality [mə'rælɪtɪ] *n* **(a)** (*of person, decision, principles*) moralité *f*; **moralities,** principes moraux; **(b)** *Th* **m. (play),** moralité *f*.

moralize ['mɒrəlaɪz] *vi* moraliser, faire de la morale (**(up)on sth,** sur qch).

moralizing ['mɒrəlaɪzɪŋ] *adj* moralisant, moralisateur, -trice.

morally ['mɒrəlɪ] *adv* moralement; **m. bound to do sth,** moralement obligé de faire qch; **m. certain,** moralement certain.

morass [mə'ræs] *n* marais *m*; *Fig* (*of figures etc*) confusion *f*.

moratorium [mɒrə'tɔːrɪəm] *n* moratoire *m*, moratorium *m*, *pl* moratoria (**on,** sur); **to hold a m. on sth,** procéder un moratoire sur qch.

morbid ['mɔːbɪd] *adj* **(a)** (*symptôme, idée*) morbide; **m. curiosity,** curiosité morbide *ou* malsaine; **(b)** *Med* (*anatomie*) pathologique.

morbidity [mɔː'bɪdɪtɪ] *n* **m. (rate),** morbidité *f*.

morbidly ['mɔːbɪdlɪ] *adv* morbidement.

morbidness ['mɔːbɪdnɪs] *n* morbidité *f*; tristesse maladive (*des pensées*).

mordant ['mɔːd(ə)nt] *adj* (*acide, Fig sarcasme*) mordant, caustique.

more [mɔːr] **1** *adj* plus (de); **he has m. patience than I (have),** il a plus de patience que moi; **one m.,** un de plus, encore un; **one or m.,** un ou plusieurs; **one m. hour,** une heure de plus, encore une heure; **there's only one m. problem to solve,** il n'y a plus qu'un problème à résoudre; **(some) m. bread, please!,** encore du pain, s'il vous plaît!; **is there any m. bread?,** est-ce qu'il reste du pain?; **to have some m. wine,** reprendre du vin; **have you (got) any m. books?,** avez-vous d'autres livres?; **that's m. than enough,** c'est plus qu'il n'en faut; **he's m. than 30,** il a plus de 30 ans; **she's m. of an artist than her sister,** elle est plus artiste que sa sœur; **I have no m. money,** je n'ai plus d'argent; **no m. soup, thank you,** plus de potage, merci; **(the) more's the pity,** c'est d'autant plus malheureux *ou* plus regrettable.

2 *n & indef pron* **do you want (any, some) m.?,** en voulez-vous encore?; **what m. can I say?,** que puis-je dire de plus?; **there is nothing m. to be said,** il n'y a plus rien à dire, il n'y a rien à ajouter; **I need still m.,** il m'en faut encore davantage; **I needn't say m.,** pas besoin d'en dire davantage; **he knows m. about it than you (do),** il en sait plus (long) que vous; **she doesn't know any m. about it,** elle n'en sait pas davantage; **we should see m. of each other,** nous devrions nous voir plus; **what is m.,** (et) qui plus est, de plus; **neither m. nor less,** ni plus ni moins; **I have no m.,** je n'en ai plus; **I can do no m.,** je ne peux pas faire plus; **let us say no m. about it,** n'en parlons plus; **say no m.!,** cela suffit!, n'en dites pas plus!; **he's just a good friend, nothing m.,** c'est un bon ami, rien de plus; **the m. you have the m. you want,** plus on a, plus on en veut; **the m. I read, the m. I learn,** plus je lis, plus j'apprends.

3 *adv* **(a)** (*to form comp*) plus; **m. interesting,** plus intéressant; **he became m. and m. drunk,** il est devenu de plus en plus ivre; **m. easily,** plus facilement; **this is far m. serious,** c'est bien *ou* beaucoup plus sérieux;

(b) (*with verbs*) (*to eat, exercise etc*) plus, davantage; **this word is used m.,** ce mot s'emploie plus *ou* davantage; **it's used m. than that one,** il s'emploie plus que celui-là;
(c) (*with adjectives etc*) plus; **he was m. surprised than annoyed,** il était plutôt surpris que fâché; **m. than satisfied,** plus que satisfait; **that's m. like it!,** ça, c'est mieux!; **m. or less,** plus ou moins; **I would think m. of her if ...,** j'aurais une plus haute opinion d'elle si ...; **I am all the m. surprised as ...,** j'en suis d'autant plus étonné que ...; **it makes me all the m. proud,** je n'en suis que plus fier; **he is no m. a lord than I am,** il n'est pas plus lord que moi; **no m. can I,** (ni) moi non plus;
(d) (*in time*) **once m.,** encore une fois, une fois de plus; **I can't see her any m.,** je ne peux plus la voir; **he doesn't drink any m.,** il ne boit plus; *Lit* **he is no m.,** il n'est plus, il est mort.

mor(e)ish ['mɔːrɪʃ] *adj F* fameux; **this cake is very m.,** ce gâteau est fameux.

morel [mɒ'rel] *n* (*fungus*) morille *f*.

morello [mə'reləʊ] *n* **m. (cherry),** griotte *f*; **m. (cherry) tree,** griottier *m*, cerisier *m* aigre.

moreover [mɔː'rəʊvər] *adv* d'ailleurs, du reste, et qui plus est; **and m.,** bien plus.

mores ['mɔːreɪz] *npl* mœurs *mpl*.

Moresque [mɔː'resk] *adj & n Art etc* mauresque *f*.

morganatic [mɔːgə'nætɪk] *adj* morganatique.

morganatically [mɔːgə'nætɪklɪ] *adv* morganatiquement.

morgue [mɔːg] *n* **(a)** morgue *f*, dépôt *m* mortuaire; **(b)** *Journ F* archives *fpl*.

MORI ['mɔːrɪ] *n* (*abbr* **Market and Opinion Research Institute**) ≈ IPSOS *m*.

moribund ['mɒrɪbʌnd] *adj & n* moribond, -onde.

Mormon ['mɔːmən] *adj & n Rel* mormon, -one.

morn [mɔːn] *n Lit* matin *m*.

morning ['mɔːnɪŋ] *n* matin *m*; (*whole period*) matinée *f*; **to work from m. till night** *or* **m., noon and night,** travailler du matin au soir; **this m.,** ce matin; **tomorrow m.,** demain matin; **the next m., the m. after,** le lendemain matin; **the m. before,** la veille au matin; *F* **the m. after (the night before),** le lendemain de la cuite; **four o'clock in the m.,** quatre heures du matin; **early in the m.,** de grand matin; **on Wednesday m.,** mercredi matin; **on the m. of Sunday 1st April,** le dimanche 1er avril au matin; **good m.,** bonjour; **in the course of the m.,** dans la matinée; **m. off,** matinée de congé; **a m.'s work,** une matinée de travail; **early m. tea,** = tasse de thé prise au lit avant de se lever; **m. dress,** habit *m*.

morning-after ['mɔːnɪŋ'ɑːftər] *n F* **m.-a. pill,** pilule *f* du lendemain.

morning-glory ['mɔːnɪŋ'glɔːrɪ] *n* (*plant*) belle-de-jour *f*, liseron *m*.

Moroccan [mə'rɒkən] **1** *adj* marocain. **2** *n* Marocain, -aine.

morocco [mə'rɒkəʊ] *n* (*leather*) maroquin *m*.

Morocco [mə'rɒkəʊ] *n* Maroc *m*.

moron ['mɔːrɒn] *n* **(a)** *F* (*idiot*) idiot, -ote, crétin *m*; **(b)** (homme *m*, femme *f*) faible *mf* d'esprit.

moronic [mə'rɒnɪk] *adj* **(a)** *F* (*stupid*) idiot, crétin; **(b)** faible d'esprit.

morose [mə'rəʊs] *adj* (*person, disposition*) chagrin, morose.

morosely [mə'rəʊslɪ] *adv* d'un air chagrin *ou* morose.

moroseness [mə'rəʊsnɪs] *n* morosité *f*, humeur chagrine *ou* morose.

morpheme ['mɔːfiːm] *n Ling* morphème *m*.

Morpheus ['mɔːfɪəs] *n Myth* Morphée *m*; *Hum* **in the arms of M.,** dans les bras de Morphée.

morphia ['mɔːfɪə] **, morphine** ['mɔːfiːn] *n* morphine *f*; **m. addict,** morphinomane *mf*.

morphological [mɔːfə'lɒdʒɪk(ə)l] *adj* morphologique.

morphology [mɔː'fɒlədʒɪ] *n* morphologie *f*.

morris dance ['mɒrɪs'dɑːns] *n* = sorte de danse folklorique anglaise.

morrow ['mɒrəʊ] *n Arch & Lit* lendemain *m*; **on the m.,** le lendemain.

Morse [mɔːs] *n Telecom* **M. (alphabet/code),** (alphabet *m*/code *m*) Morse *m*.

morsel ['mɔːs(ə)l] *n* (petit) morceau *m*; **choice** *or* **dainty m.,** morceau friand *ou* de choix.

mortadella [mɔːtə'delə] *n* **m. (sausage),** mortadelle *f*.

mortal ['mɔːt(ə)l] **1** *adj* **(a)** mortel; **all men are m.,** tous les hommes sont mortels; **m. remains,** dépouille mortelle; **(b)** (*fatal*) mortel, fatal, -als **(to,** à); **m. blow,** coup mortel; **m. sin,** péché mortel; **(c)** (*until death*) **m. enemy,** ennemi mortel; **m. combat,** combat *m* à mort; **(d)** (*very great*) **to be in m. fear of ...,** avoir une peur mortelle de ...; **(e)** *F* (*conceivable*) **it's no m. use,** ça ne sert absolument à rien. **2** *n* mortel, -elle; **a m.,** un humain; **ordinary mortals like you and me,** des gens comme vous et moi.

mortality [mɔː'tælɪtɪ] *n* **(a)** mortalité *f* (*de l'homme etc*); **(b)** (*human beings*) les mortels *mpl*, les humains *mpl*; **(c)** (*death rate*) mortalité *f*; **infant m.,** mortalité infantile.

mortally ['mɔːt(ə)lɪ] *adv* mortellement; **m. wounded,** blessé à mort; **to be m. afraid,** avoir une peur mortelle.

mortar[1] ['mɔːtər] *n* **(a)** *Constr* mortier *m*; **cement m.,** mortier *ou* enduit *m* de ciment; *F* **to put one's money in bricks and m.,** placer son argent dans la pierre *ou* l'immobilier; **(b)** (*bowl*) *Pharm etc* mortier *m* (*pour piler*); *Culin* égrugeoir *m*; **m. and pestle,** pilon *m* et mortier; **(c)** *Mil* mortier *m*; **m. attack,** attaque *f* au mortier.

mortar[2] *vt Constr* lier (*les pierres*) avec du mortier.

mortarboard ['mɔːtəbɔːd] *n Sch* toque universitaire anglaise.

mortgage[1] ['mɔːgɪdʒ] *n* hypothèque *f*; **first** *or* **prior m.,** hypothèque de premier rang; **second m.,** seconde hypothèque; **to raise a m.,** contracter une hypothèque; **to buy a house on a m.,** prendre une hypothèque pour acheter une maison; **m. bond** *or* **debenture,** obligation *f* hypothécaire; **m. loan,** emprunt *m* hypothécaire; **m. rate,** taux *m* d'emprunt hypothécaire.

mortgage[2] *vt* hypothéquer, grever (*une terre, un immeuble etc*); engager, mettre en gage (*des marchandises, des titres*); *F* **we're mortgaged up to the eyeballs,** on a des crédits jusqu'au cou.

mortgagee [mɔːgɪ'dʒiː] *n* créancier *m* hypothécaire.

mortgager, mortgagor ['mɔːgɪdʒər] *n* débiteur *m* hypothécaire.

mortice ['mɔːtɪs] *n & vt* = **MORTISE**[1,2].

mortician [mɔː'tɪʃən] *n US* entrepreneur *m* de pompes funèbres.

mortification [mɔːtɪfɪ'keɪʃən] *n* **(a)** (*humiliation*) humiliation *f*, *Lit* mortification *f*; **to my m.,** à ma (grande) honte; **(b)** *Rel* mortification *f* (*du corps, des passions*); **(c)** *Med* mortification *f*.

mortify ['mɔːtɪfaɪ] **1** *vt* **(a)** (*humiliate*) humilier, *Lit* mortifier (*qn*); *F* **I was mortified,** j'étais mort de honte; **(b)** *Rel* mortifier, châtier (*son corps, ses passions*); **(c)** *Med* mortifier, gangrener. **2** *vi Med* se gangrener, se mortifier.

mortifying ['mɔːtɪfaɪɪŋ] *adj* (*experience etc*) humiliant, *Lit* mortifiant.

mortise[1] ['mɔːtɪs] *n Carp* mortaise *f*; **m. lock,** serrure encastrée.

mortise[2] *vt Carp* mortaiser; **to m. two beams together,** emmortaiser *ou* emboîter deux poutres.

mortuary ['mɔːtjʊərɪ] **1** *n* morgue *f*. **2** *adj* mortuaire.

mosaic [məʊ'zeɪɪk] *n* **(a)** *Art etc* mosaïque *f*; **m. floor,** dallage *m* en mosaïque; **(b)** *TV* mosaïque *f* (photoélectrique).

Mosaic [məʊ'zeɪɪk] *adj Bible* (*loi etc*) mosaïque, de Moïse.

Moscow ['mɒskəʊ] *n* Moscou.

Moses ['məʊzɪz] **1** *n Bible* Moïse *m*; **M. basket,** moïse *m*. **2** *int F Old-fashioned* **Holy M.!,** grand Dieu!

▶**mosey along** ['məʊzɪ] *vi F* aller son petit bonhomme de chemin; **I'll just m. along to the bar,** je vais faire un tour au bar; **I'll be moseying along now,** (*leaving*) je vais y aller.

Moslem ['mɒzlem] **1** *adj* musulman. **2** *n* Musulman, -ane.

mosque [mɒsk] *n* mosquée *f*.

mosquito, *pl* **-oes** [məs'kiːtəʊ, -əʊz] *n* moustique *m*; **m. bite,** piqûre *f* de moustique; **m. net,** moustiquaire *f*.

moss [mɒs] *n* **(a)** *Bot* mousse *f*; **tree m.,** usnée *f*; **Irish m., pearl m.,** carragheen *m*, mousse perlée (d'Irlande); **m. rose,** rose moussue, *F* rose mousseuse; **(b)** *Miner* **m. agate,** agate mousseuse; **(c)** *Knitting* **m. stitch,** point *m* de riz; **(d)** *Dial* (*bog*) **(peat) m.,** tourbière *f*.

mossy ['mɒsɪ] *adj* moussu.

most [məʊst] (*superl of* **many, much**) **1** *adj* le plus (de); **you have made (the) m. mistakes,** c'est vous qui avez fait le plus de fautes; **m. women,** la plupart des femmes; **in m. cases,** dans la majorité *ou* la plupart des cas; **for the m. part,** (*in greatest number of cases*) pour la plupart; (*most often*) le plus souvent *ou* la plupart du temps.
2 *n & indef pron* **(a)** (*greatest amount*) le plus; **do the m. you can,** faites le plus que vous pourrez; **at the (very) m.,** au maximum, (tout) au plus; **to make the m. of,** tirer le meilleur parti possible de (*qch*); faire valoir (*son argent*); bien employer (*son temps*); exploiter (*son talent*); ménager le plus possible (*ses provisions etc*); **she made the m. of her time in Mexico,** elle a profité au maximum du temps

qu'elle a passé au Mexique; **the opposition made the m. of the scandal,** l'opposition a tiré tout ce qu'elle pouvait du scandale; **make the m. of it,** profitez-en au maximum;

(b) *(majority)* **m. of the work,** la plus grande partie du travail; **m. of the time,** la plupart du temps; **he is more reliable than m.,** on peut compter sur lui plus que sur la plupart des gens.

3 *adv* **(a)** *(to form superl)* le plus; **the m. beautiful woman,** la plus belle femme; **they bought the m. expensive (ones),** ils ont acheté les plus chères; **those who have answered m. accurately,** ceux qui ont répondu le plus exactement;

(b) *(intensive)* très, fort, bien; **m. unhappy,** bien malheureux; **m. likely** *or* **probably,** très probablement; **he has been m. rude,** il a été on ne peut plus impoli;

(c) *(to drink, talk etc)* le plus; **what I want m.,** ce que je désire par-dessus tout; **that's what worries me (the) m.,** c'est ce qui m'inquiète le plus.

mostly ['məʊstlı] *adv* **(a)** *(in the main)* pour la plupart, principalement; **they come m. from Scotland,** ils viennent surtout de l'Écosse; **a m. young audience,** un public composé pour une large part de jeunes, un public composé en majorité de jeunes; **(b)** *(most often)* le plus souvent, (pour) la plupart du temps.

MOT [eməʊ'tiː] *n* **(a)** *Br Admin abbr* **Ministry of Transport**; **(b)** *(test)* = test annuel du Ministère des transports, obligatoire pour toutes les voitures de plus de trois ans; **(b)** *(certificate)* = certificat indiquant qu'une voiture a satisfait aux exigences du Ministère des transports; **6 months' MOT,** *(in advertisement etc)* = la voiture n'aura pas besoin de repasser l'examen avant six mois.

mote [məʊt] *n Lit* atome *m* de poussière; *Bible* **the m. in thy brother's eye,** la paille dans l'œil du voisin.

motel [məʊ'tel] *n* motel *m*; **m. bedroom,** chambre de motel.

motet [məʊ'tet] *n Mus* motet *m*.

moth [mɒθ] *n* *(insect)* papillon *m* nocturne *ou* de nuit; **gipsy m.,** zigzag *m*; **tiger m.,** arctie *f*; **(clothes) m.,** mite *f*; *F* **the moths have been at my fur coat,** mon manteau de fourrure est tout mangé par les mites.

mothball¹ ['mɒθbɔːl] *n* boule *f* de naphtaline; *Fig* **in mothballs,** en conserve; *(of plan)* en réserve; *Fig* **to put a ship in mothballs,** retirer un navire de service actif.

mothball² *vt Fig* retirer *(un navire)* de service actif; mettre *(un plan)* en réserve.

moth-eaten ['mɒθiːt(ə)n] *adj* **(a)** rongé *ou* mangé des mites, mangé aux mites, mité; **(b)** *F* *(in poor condition)* misérable; *(hôtel)* miteux; **(c)** *Old-fashioned F (idea etc)* suranné.

mother¹ ['mʌðər] *n* **(a)** mère *f*; **yes, m.!,** oui, maman!; **m.-to-be,** future maman; **m. of six,** mère de six enfants; *Br F* **shall I be m.?,** *(pour out tea)* est-ce que je fais le service?; **M.'s Day,** fête *f* des Mères; **m. hen,** mère poule; **m. country,** mère-patrie *f*, *pl* mères-patries; métropole *f* *(d'une colonie)*; **M. Nature,** la Nature; **m. tongue,** langue maternelle; **m. wit,** le bon sens inné; **m. church,** église *f* mère; **m. ship,** ravitailleur *m*; *Rel* **reverend m.,** (sœur *f*) supérieure *f*; *(form of address)* ma mère; **the M. Superior,** la Mère supérieure; *Geol etc* **m. rock,** roche *f* mère; *Ch* **m. of vinegar,** mère de vinaigre; **(b)** *US Vulg* = **MOTHERFUCKER.**

mother² *vt* materner *(qn)*.

motherboard ['mʌðəbɔːd] *n Comptr* carte *f* mère.

motherfucker ['mʌðəfʌkər] *n US Vulg* fils *m* de pute.

motherfucking ['mʌðəfʌkıŋ] *adj US Vulg* de merde.

motherhood ['mʌðəhʊd] *n* maternité *f*.

mothering ['mʌðərıŋ] *n* soins maternels; *Br* **M. Sunday,** la fête des Mères.

mother-in-law, *pl* **mothers-in-law** ['mʌðərınlɔː, 'mʌðəz-] *n* belle-mère *f*, *pl* belles-mères; *F* **m.-in-l.'s tongue,** *(plant)* sansevière *f*.

motherland ['mʌðəlænd] *n* patrie *f*, pays natal.

motherless ['mʌðəlıs] *adj* sans mère, orphelin (de mère).

motherly ['mʌðəlı] *adj* maternel, de mère.

mother-of-pearl [mʌðərəv'pɜːl] *n* nacre *f*; **m.-of-p. decoration,** décoration *f* en nacre.

moth-hole ['mɒθhəʊl] *n* piqûre *f ou* trou *m* de mite.

mothproof¹ ['mɒθpruːf] *adj* traité à l'antimite, antimite(s).

mothproof² *vt* traiter à l'antimite.

motif [məʊ'tiːf] *n* motif *m*.

motion¹ ['məʊʃən] *n* **(a)** *Phys etc* mouvement *m*, déplacement *m*; *(of vehicle, apparatus)* marche *f*, mouvement; *Phys* **body in m.,** corps *m* en mouvement; **perpetual m.,** mouvement perpétuel; **car in m.,** voiture en marche; **to put** *or* **set in m.,** mettre *(qch)* en mouvement *ou* en marche *ou* en jeu; embrayer *(une machine)*; faire agir *(la loi)*; **I'll set things** *or* **the wheels in m.,** je vais mettre les choses en route; *esp Am Cin* **m. picture,** film *m*; *MecE* **m. study,** analyse *f* du mouvement, chronophotographie *f*;

(b) *(of arm etc)* mouvement *m*; *(sign)* signe *m*, geste *m*; **he's just going through the motions,** il fait juste semblant; **you could at least go through the motions,** tu devrais au moins le faire pour la forme; *Ind etc* **time and m.,** cadences *fpl*; **time and m. consultant,** organisateur-conseil *m*, *pl* organisateurs-conseil; **time and m. study,** étude *f* des cadences;

(c) *(in meeting, debate)* motion *f*, proposition *f*; **to propose a m.,** faire une proposition; **to put the m.,** mettre la proposition aux voix; **the m. was carried,** la motion fut adoptée;

(d) *Jur* demande *f*, requête *f*.

motion² **1** *vt* **to m. s.o. to do sth,** faire signe à qn de faire qch; **to m. s.o. away/in,** faire signe à qn de s'éloigner/d'entrer. **2** *vi* **to m. to s.o. to do sth,** faire signe à qn de faire qch.

motionless ['məʊʃənlıs] *adj* immobile, sans mouvement; **to remain m.,** ne pas bouger, rester immobile.

motivate ['məʊtıveıt] *vt* motiver *(une action, ses employés)*; **they were motivated by a desire to help others,** ils étaient poussés par un désir d'aider les autres; **I don't understand what motivates him,** je ne comprends pas ses motivations.

motivated ['məʊtıveıtıd] *adj* motivé.

motivation [məʊtı'veıʃən] *n* motifs *mpl*; *esp Psy* motivation *f*; **he lacked the m. to succeed,** la motivation de réussir lui faisait défaut.

motivator ['məʊtıveıtər] *n* **he's a good m.,** il sait motiver les gens.

motive ['məʊtıv] **1** *n* **(a)** *(reason)* motif *m* **(for doing sth,** à *ou* pour faire qch); mobile *m* *(d'une action)*; **interest is a powerful m.,** l'intérêt est un puissant ressort; **I wonder what his m. is,** je me demande pourquoi *ou* pour quelle raison il fait cela; **(b)** *Art* motif *m* *(d'un tableau etc)*. **2** *adj* moteur, -trice; **m. power,** force motrice.

motley ['mɒtlı] **1** *adj* **(a)** *(diverse)* divers, mêlé; **m. crowd,** foule hétéroclite; **(b)** *(of different colours)* bariolé, bigarré. **2** *n* **(a)** *(mixture)* mélange *m* hétéroclite; **(b)** *Arch* *(of jester)* livrée *f* de bouffon de cour.

motocross ['məʊtəʊkrɒs] *n Sp* moto-cross *m*.

motor¹ ['məʊtər] **1** *n* **(a)** moteur *m*; **starting m.,** moteur de démarrage; *El* **electric m.,** moteur électrique; **m. barge,** chaland *m* à moteur; *Rail* **(electric) m. carriage,** (voiture *f*) motrice *f*; **m. vehicle,** voiture automobile; *Sp* **m. racing,** course *f* automobile; **m. scooter,** scooter *m*; **m. show,** salon *m* de l'automobile; *Nau* **m. vessel,** bateau *m* à moteur; **(b)** *Br* *(car)* voiture *f*. **2** *adj* moteur, -trice; *Anat* *(muscle, nerf, centre)* moteur; *Med* **m. paralysis,** paralysie *f* des centres moteurs; *MecE* **m. torque,** couple moteur.

motor² **1** *vi* voyager *ou* circuler en voiture. **2** *vt Old-fashioned* conduire *ou* transporter *(qn)* en voiture.

motorail ['məʊtəreıl] *n Rail* **m. (service),** train(s) *m(pl)* (à) auto-couchettes.

motor-assisted ['məʊtərə'sıstıd] *adj* *(bicyclette)* à moteur.

motorbike ['məʊtəbaık] *n F* = **MOTORCYCLE.**

motorboat ['məʊtəbəʊt] *n* *(fast)* vedette *f* automobile; canot *m* automobile *ou* à moteur.

motorcade ['məʊtəkeıd] *n* défilé *m* de voitures.

motorcar ['məʊtəkɑːr] *n* automobile *f*, voiture *f*.

motorcycle ['məʊtəsaık(ə)l] *n* motocyclette *f*, *F* moto *f*; **m. accident,** accident *m* de moto; **m. gang,** bande *f* de motards; **m. rider,** motocycliste *m*, motard *m*; **m. wheel,** roue *f* de moto.

motorcycling ['məʊtəsaıklıŋ] *n* motocyclisme *m*.

motorcyclist ['məʊtəsaıklıst] *n* motocycliste *mf*.

motor-driven ['məʊtədrıvən] *adj* actionné *ou* commandé par moteur; à (électro)moteur.

motoring ['məʊtərıŋ] *n* automobilisme *m*; **school of m.,** auto-école *f*, *pl* auto-écoles; **m. correspondent,** chroniqueur automobile; **m. offence,** infraction *f* au code de la route.

motorist ['məʊtərıst] *n* automobiliste *mf*.

motorization [məʊtəraı'zeıʃən] *n* motorisation *f*.

motorize ['məʊtəraız] *vt* motoriser; **motorized,** motorisé; *(bicyclette)* à moteur.

motorman, *pl* **-men** ['məʊtəmæn, -men] *n US* wattman *m* *(de tramway)*; conducteur *m* *(de tramway, de train de métro)*.

motorway ['məʊtəweı] *n Br* autoroute *f*; **m. accident,**

accident survenu sur l'autoroute; **m. driving,** conduite *f* sur autoroute; **m. police,** police *f* de l'autoroute.

mottled ['mɒt(ə)ld] *adj* tacheté, moucheté, diapré; (*peau*) marbré; (*tissu*) chiné; (*bois*) madré.

mottling ['mɒtlɪŋ] *n* marbrure *f*, diaprure *f*; *Tex* chinage *m*, chiné *m*.

motto, *pl* **-oes** ['mɒtəʊ, -əʊz] *n* **(a)** devise *f*; **that's my m.,** voilà ma devise; **(b)** *Her* mot *m* (*d'une devise*); **(c)** *Typ* épigraphe *f* (*en tête de chapitre*); **(d)** *Mus* motif *m*; **(e)** (*in Christmas cracker*) (*riddle*) devinette *f*; (*funny saying*) phrase amusante.

mould¹, *US* **mold** [məʊld] *n* moisi *m*, moisissure *f*.

mould², *US* **mold** *n* **(a)** *Art Cer etc* moule *m*; *Typ* matrice *f* (*de caractère*); (*of record*) matrrice (de disque); *Culin* **jelly m.,** moule à gelée; *Lit* **to be cast in a heroic m.,** être de la trempe des héros; **characters cast in the same m.,** caractères sortis du même moule; **a movie star in the John Wayne m.,** une star du cinéma de la trempe de John Wayne; *Fig* **to break the m.,** rompre avec la tradition; *Metal* **casting m.,** moule à fonte; **box m.,** châssis *m* (de moule); **(b)** *Constr etc* (*template*) calibre *m*, profil *m*; *Nau Av* gabarit *m*; **(c)** *Culin* **rice m.,** gâteau *m* de riz; **(d)** *Archit* moulure *f*.

mould³, *US* **mold** *vt* **(a)** (*make from a mould*) mouler; **the bucket is moulded in tough plastic,** le seau est moulé dans du plastique résistant; **(b)** (*shape*) façonner; former, façonner (*le caractère de qn*); **to m. clay/***etc* **into sth,** façonner l'argile/*etc* pour en faire qch; *Fig* **she moulded them into a team,** elle a fait d'eux une équipe; **(c)** (*in baking*) mettre (*le pain*) en forme; **(d)** (*adhere closely to*) **the dress moulded her figure,** la robe moulait sa silhouette.

mould⁴, *US* **mold** *n* (*earth*) terre végétale *ou* meuble; **vegetable m.,** terreau *m*, humus *m*.

moulded, *US* **molded** ['məʊldɪd] *adj* (*plastic*) moulé.

moulder, *US* **molder** ['məʊldər] *vi* tomber en poussière, s'effriter; (*of person*) moisir.

moulding, *US* **molding** ['məʊldɪŋ] *n* **(a)** *Metal etc* moulage *m*; **compression m.,** moulage sous pression; **m. box** *or* **flask,** châssis *m* (à mouler); **(b)** formation *f* (*du caractère etc*); manipulation *f*, mise *f* en condition (*de l'opinion publique*); **(c)** (*in baking*) mise *f* en forme (*du pain*); **(d)** *Archit* (*ornament*) moulure *f*; (*edging strip*) baguette *f*; **drip** *or* **weather m.,** jet *m* d'eau (*de fenêtre, de porte*); larmier *m* (*de mur*); **plain m.,** listeau *m*, listel *m*; **grooved m.,** moulure à gorge.

mouldy, *US* **moldy** ['məʊldɪ] *adj* moisi; **to smell m.,** sentir le moisi.

moult¹, *US* **molt** [məʊlt] *n* mue *f*.

moult², *US* **molt 1** *vi* (*of cat, bird, reptile etc*) muer. **2** *vt* perdre (*ses plumes, sa peau*).

moulting, *US* **molting** ['məʊltɪŋ] **1** *adj* en mue. **2** *n* mue *f*.

mound [maʊnd] *n* (*artificial*) tertre *m*, monticule *m*, butte *f*; *Constr etc* remblai *m*; (*of stones etc*) monceau *m*, tas *m*; (*natural*) monticule; **burial m.,** tumulus *m*.

mount¹ [maʊnt] *n* **(a)** (*mountain*) mont *m*, montagne *f*; **M. Sinai,** le mont Sinaï; **(b)** (*in palmistry*) mont *m*.

mount² *n* **(a)** *Tech* (*support*) montage *m*, support *m*; *Mil etc* affût *m*, trépied *m*; monture *f* (*d'une lentille, d'un prisme*); **lens m.,** porte-objectif *m inv* (*d'un microscope*); **(b)** *Art etc* carton *m* de montage (*d'un tableau etc*); **(c)** (*horse*) cheval *m*, monture *f* (*d'un cavalier*); *Horseracing* (*action*) monte *f*.

mount³ 1 *vt* **(a)** (*climb onto*) monter sur (*un cheval, une bicyclette*); enfourcher (*une bicyclette*); **to m. the scaffold,** monter sur l'échafaud; **to m. the pavement,** (*of car etc*) monter sur le trottoir;

(b) (*mate with*) couvrir, monter (*une femelle*);

(c) (*climb*) monter, gravir (*l'escalier, une colline*); monter à (*une échelle*); monter sur (*un escabeau*);

(d) (*set on*) **to m. s.o. (on a horse),** hisser qn sur un cheval; **to m. a squadron of cavalry,** monter un escadron de cavalerie; **they were mounted on grey horses,** ils chevauchaient des chevaux gris;

(e) *Tech* fixer (*qch*) sur une monture; mettre (*qch*) sur (son) pied *ou* sur (son) socle; *Mil etc* mettre (*un canon, une pièce*) sur (son) affût; monter, installer (*une machine, un moteur etc*); monter, sertir (*une pierre précieuse*); *Art Phot* entoiler, monter (*un tableau, une photographie*);

(f) (*prepare*) monter (*Th une pièce, Mil une offensive etc*); **to m. guard,** monter la garde.

2 *vi* **(a)** *Horseriding* se mettre en selle;

(b) (*rise, climb*) monter; **the blood mounted to his head,** le sang lui est monté à la tête; **the cost was mounting,** le coût s'élevait *ou* augmentait.

►**mount up** *vi* croître, monter, augmenter; **the bill was mounting up,** la facture augmentait; **it all mounts up,** ça finit par chiffrer.

mountain ['maʊntɪn] *n* montagne *f*; **range of mountains, m. range,** chaîne *f* de montagnes; **the Rocky Mountains,** les (montagnes) Rocheuses; **to spend one's holidays in the mountains,** passer ses vacances à la montagne; *Fig* **a m. of work,** un travail monstre; **to make a m. out of a molehill,** se faire une montagne de quelque chose; **m. ash,** (*tree*) sorbier commun *ou* sauvage; **m. bike,** vélo *m* tout-terrain, VTT *m*; **m. climbing,** alpinisme *m*; **m. lion,** puma *m*, couguar *m*; **m. pine,** pin *m* de montagne; **m. rescue,** secours *m* en montagne; **m. rescue service,** service *m* de secourisme en montagne; **m. scenery/stream,** paysage *m*/ruisseau *m* de montagne; **m. sickness,** mal *m* de montagne; **m. side/top,** flanc *m ou* versant *m*/sommet *m* de montagne; **m. tribe,** tribu montagnarde; *Mil* **m. troops,** troupes alpines *ou* de montagne.

mountaineer¹ [maʊntɪ'nɪər] *n* alpiniste *mf*.

mountaineer² *vi* faire de l'alpinisme.

mountaineering [maʊntɪ'nɪərɪŋ] *n* alpinisme *m*.

mountainous ['maʊntɪnəs] *adj* (*pays etc*) montagneux; *Fig* **m. seas,** vagues gigantesques.

mountebank ['maʊntɪbæŋk] *n* charlatan *m*.

mounted ['maʊntɪd] *adj* monté; **the m. police,** la police montée.

Mountie ['maʊntɪ] *n F* = membre de la Gendarmerie Royale du Canada.

mounting ['maʊntɪŋ] **1** *n* **(a)** *Tech* mise *f* (*de qch*) sur (son) pied *ou* sur (son) socle; fixation *f ou* installation *f* (*d'un télescope etc*) sur sa monture; *Mil etc* mise (*d'un canon*) sur (son) affût; *MecE* montage *m*, assemblage *m*, installation (*d'une machine, d'un moteur etc*); *Art Phot* entoilage *m*, montage (*d'une photographie, d'un tableau etc*); **(b)** *Th* montage *m* (*d'une pièce*); **(c)** *Tech* (*support*) support *m*; bâti *m*, socle *m* (*d'une machine, d'un moteur*); monture *f*, garniture *f* (*de fusil etc*); monture (*d'une pierre précieuse*); *Mil* affût *m*; (*of machine gun*) affût, trépied *m*; **engine mountings,** pièces *fpl* d'assemblage d'un moteur. **2** *adj* **m. costs/death toll/***etc*, coût *m*/nombre *m* des morts/*etc* en augmentation.

mounting-block ['maʊntɪŋblɒk] *n* montoir *m*.

mourn [mɔːn] **1** *vt* pleurer (*qn, qch, la mort de qn*). **2** *vi* être en deuil.

►**mourn for** *vipo* **to m. for sth,** pleurer qch, déplorer qch; **to m. for s.o.,** pleurer (la mort de) qn.

►**mourn over** *vipo* = **MOURN FOR.**

mourner ['mɔːnər] *n* **(a)** (*at funeral*) personne qui suit le cortège funèbre; **the mourners,** le convoi, le cortège funèbre; **(b)** (*person grieving*) personne endeuillée, personne qui porte le deuil.

mournful ['mɔːnfʊl] *adj* triste, lugubre, mélancolique.

mournfully ['mɔːnfʊlɪ] *adv* tristement, lugubrement.

mourning ['mɔːnɪŋ] *n* **(a)** (*sadness*) affliction *f*, deuil *m*; **(b)** (*customary behaviour*) deuil *m*; (*clothing*) (habits *mpl* de) deuil; **house of m.,** maison endeuillée; **to go into m.,** se mettre en deuil, prendre le deuil; **to be in m.,** être en deuil.

mouse¹, *pl* **mice** [maʊs, maɪs] *n* **(a)** (*animal*) souris *f*; **we've got mice,** nous avons des souris; **young m.,** souriceau *m*; **field m.,** mulot *m*; **are you a man or a m.?,** t'es un homme ou quoi?; **m. grey, m. colour(ed),** gris *m* (de) souris; **m. hole,** trou *m* de souris; **(b)** *F* (*timid person*) personne *f* timide; **(c)** *Comptr* souris *f*; **m. driver,** programme de commande de la souris.

mouse² *vi* (*of cat etc*) chasser les souris.

mouser ['maʊsər] *n* (*cat etc*) souricier *m*.

mousetrap ['maʊstræp] *n* souricière *f*, tapette *f*; *F* **m. (cheese),** fromage ordinaire, *Can* fromage à souris.

mousse [muːs] *n Culin* mousse *f* (*au chocolat etc*); (*for hair*) mousse.

moustache [məs'tɑːʃ] , *US* **mustache** ['mʌstæʃ] *n* moustache(s) *f(pl)*; **short m., clipped m.,** moustache courte *ou* en brosse.

mousy ['maʊsɪ] *adj* **(a)** (*colour*) gris sale, *F* gris pisseux; **(b)** (*person*) (*timid*) timide; (*hair*) châtain terne; **(c)** (*odeur etc*) de souris.

mouth¹ [maʊθ] *n* (*pl* **mouths** [maʊðz]) **(a)** bouche *f* (*de qn, de cheval, de bœuf etc*); gueule *f* (*de chien, d'animaux carnassiers etc*); **to have one's m. full,** avoir la bouche pleine; **don't speak with your m. full,** ne parle pas (avec) la bouche pleine; *F* **big m.,** gueulard *m*, grande gueule; **he's all m.,** parler, c'est tout ce qu'il sait faire; *Sl* **to shoot one's m. off,** vendre la mèche; **shut your m.!,** ta gueule!;

keep your m. shut about this, garde ça pour toi; **the whole business left a nasty taste in my m.,** cette affaire m'a laissé un arrière-goût désagréable; **to put words into s.o.'s m.,** (*tell them what to say, misquote them*) faire dire à qn ce qu'il ne dit pas; *F* **to be down in the m.,** avoir le cafard; **to have seven mouths to feed,** avoir sept bouches à nourrir; *Horseriding* **horse with a hard m.,** cheval fort en bouche *ou* sans bouche; *Mus* **m. organ,** harmonica *m*;

(b) (*opening etc*) bouche *f* (*de puits, de volcan*); pavillon *m* (*d'entonnoir*); gueule *f* (*de sac, de canon, de four*); ouverture *f*, entrée *f* (*de tunnel, de caverne*); entrée (*de port etc*); embouchure *f* (*de rivière*).

mouth² [maʊð] **1** *vt* **(a)** (*say without sincerity*) dire du bout des lèvres; **they were mouthing a lot of fine sentiments,** ils énonçaient des tas de beaux sentiments du bout des lèvres; **(b)** (*say silently*) former (*des mots*) avec les lèvres (sans faire entendre de son). **2** *vi esp Am* grimacer, faire des grimaces.

mouthful ['maʊθfʊl] *n* **(a)** bouchée *f*; gorgée *f* (*de potage, de vin*); **to swallow sth in** *or* **at one m., to make one m. of sth,** ne faire qu'une bouchée *ou* qu'un morceau de qch; **I swallowed** *or* **got a m. (of water),** j'ai bu une tasse *ou* un bouillon; *esp Am F* **you said a m.,** (*were right*) tu as bien parlé; *Br F* **to give s.o. a m.,** lancer une bordée d'injures à qn; **(b)** *F* (*long word, phrase*) mot *etc* difficile à prononcer; (*name*) nom *m* à coucher dehors; **'cerebral thrombosis' is quite a m.,** thrombose cérébrale est difficile à prononcer.

mouthpiece ['maʊθpiːs] *n* **(a)** embout *m* (*de porte-voix*); tuyau *m*, bout *m* (*de pipe à tabac*); *Mus* bec *m* (*de clarinette etc*); *Mus* (embouchure en) bocal *m* (*de cornet etc*); *Tel* cornet *m*, microphone *m*; **(b)** (*person, magazine*) porte-parole *m inv* (*d'un parti etc*); *US Sl* avocat *m* (au criminel).

mouth-to-mouth ['maʊθtə'maʊθ] *adj Med* **m.-to-m. resuscitation,** bouche-à-bouche *m*; **to give s.o. m.-to-m. resuscitation,** faire du bouche-à-bouche à qn.

mouthwash ['maʊθwɒʃ] *n Pharm* bain *m* de bouche; (*for teeth*) eau *f* dentifrice.

mouthwatering ['maʊθwɔːtərɪŋ] *adj* alléchant, qui fait venir l'eau à la bouche.

mouthy ['maʊðɪ] *adj F* gueulard, grande gueule.

movable ['muːvəb(ə)l] **1** *adj* **(a)** mobile; *Rel* **m. feast,** fête *f* mobile; **(b)** *Jur* mobilier, meuble; **m. property,** biens *mpl* meubles. **2** *npl* **(a) movables,** mobilier *m*; **(b)** *Jur* **movables,** biens *mpl* meubles.

move¹ [muːv] *n* **(a)** (*motion*) mouvement *m*; **to make a m. towards sth,** faire un mouvement vers qch; **there was a general m. towards** *or* **for the door,** tout le monde s'est dirigé vers la porte; **we must make a m.,** il faut partir; **don't make a m.!,** (*or I'll shoot, they'll see us etc*) ne bouge pas!; **don't make a m. without contacting me,** (*don't do anything*) ne fais rien sans me contacter; **to be always on the m.,** ne jamais rester en place; **on the m.,** en marche; *F* **to get a m. on,** se dépêcher, se grouiller, se manier (le train); **get a m. on!,** grouille-toi!, maniez-vous (le train);

(b) (*action, step*) coup *m*, démarche *f*; **smart m.,** coup habile; **at one time there was a m. to ...,** à un moment, il y a eu des démarches pour ...; **what's the next m.?,** qu'est-ce qu'il faut faire maintenant?; **to make the first m.,** faire le premier pas; **when would the enemy make his m.?,** quand l'ennemi allait-il se décider à agir?; **to make a m. on s.o.,** faire des avances à qn;

(c) (*from home, office etc*) déménagement *m*;

(d) *Chess etc* coup *m*; **mate in four moves,** (échec et) mat en quatre coups; **to have first m.,** avoir le trait; **to make a m.,** jouer; **your m.,** à vous de jouer, c'est votre tour.

move² **1** *vt* **(a)** (*shift*) déplacer (*un meuble, des troupes etc*); *Chess etc* jouer (*une pièce*); **to m. sth from its place,** changer qch de place; **to m. one's position,** changer de place; **to m. one's chair near the fire,** approcher son fauteuil du feu; **he was moved to London,** on l'a envoyé (travailler) à Londres; **to m. house,** déménager; **to m. heaven and earth,** déplacer des montagnes;

(b) (*stir*) remuer, bouger (*la tête etc*); (*of wind etc*) agiter, remuer (*les branches etc*); (*set in motion*) mouvoir, animer (*qch*); mettre (*qch*) en mouvement; **not to m. a muscle,** ne pas sourciller; *Med* **to m. one's bowels,** aller à la selle;

(c) (*sway*) ébranler la résolution de (*qn*); **nothing will m. him,** il est inflexible; **to m. s.o. to do sth,** pousser *ou* inciter qn à faire qch;

(d) (*affect emotionally*) émouvoir, toucher, affecter (*qn*); **easily moved,** émotionnable; **to m. s.o. to anger,** provoquer la colère de qn; **to m. s.o. to tears,** émouvoir qn (jusqu')aux larmes; **to m. s.o. to pity,** exciter la pitié de qn;

(e) (*in debate etc*) **to m. a resolution,** proposer une motion, déposer une résolution; **to m. that ...,** faire la proposition que ...; proposer que ... + *sub*.

2 *vi* **(a)** bouger; (*change one's position*) se mouvoir, se déplacer; **to m. to another seat,** changer de place; **to m. in high society,** fréquenter la haute société; **don't m.!,** ne bougez pas!; **I'm stuck, I can't m.,** je suis coincé, je ne peux pas bouger; **could you m. so that we can get in?,** pourriez-vous vous pousser que nous puissions entrer?; **the way the dancers m.,** la façon de se mouvoir *ou* de bouger des danseurs; **she moves like a model,** elle a l'allure d'un mannequin; **I saw the curtains m.,** j'ai vu les rideaux bouger; **something moved in the bushes,** quelque chose a bougé dans les buissons; *F* **come on, m.!,** (*hurry*) allez, magne-toi le train *ou* remue-toi!; **wait till the car stops moving,** attends que la voiture soit arrêtée; *Com* **this product's not moving,** (*not selling*) ce produit ne s'écoule pas;

(b) (*of machine parts etc*) **this part is meant to m.,** cette partie est censée bouger; **what makes it m.?,** qu'est-ce qui le fait tourner *ou* avancer *ou* descendre *etc*?; **it moves upwards and downwards in the ...,** ça monte et ça descend dans le ...; **to m. freely,** jouer librement;

(c) (*progress, advance*) marcher, aller, s'avancer; **the earth moves round the sun,** la terre tourne autour du soleil; **to m. towards a place,** se diriger *ou* s'avancer vers un endroit; **the traffic had slowed down but was still moving,** la circulation avait ralenti mais continuait à avancer; **things are moving slowly,** les choses avancent lentement; **that's really moving!,** (*that's fast*) ça fonce!; (*referring to work*) ça avance!; **it's time we were moving, we must be moving,** il est temps de partir;

(d) (*act*) agir; **it is for him to m. first in the matter,** c'est à lui d'agir le premier dans cette affaire;

(e) (*to new home, office etc*) déménager; **we have moved to new premises,** nous avons déménagé dans de nouveaux locaux; **to m. to the country,** aller s'installer à la campagne.

▶**move about, move around** **1** *vi* bouger, remuer; **I heard someone moving about next door,** j'ai entendu quelqu'un bouger à côté; **he moves around, never staying in one place,** il se déplace sans arrêt. **2** *vtsep* changer (*les meubles*) de place; **they keep moving her around from one department to another,** ils n'arrêtent pas de la faire passer d'un service à l'autre.

▶**move along** **1** *vtsep* (*of police officer*) faire circuler (*les badauds, les gens qui font la quête etc*). **2** *vi* **(a)** (*to make room*) se déplacer, se pousser; **m. along and let the old lady sit down,** poussez-vous un peu pour laisser la vieille dame s'asseoir; **(b)** (*leave*) partir, s'en aller; **I ought to be moving along,** je ferais bien de m'en aller; **the policeman told us to m. along,** le policier nous a dit de circuler; **m. along (please)!,** circulez, s'il vous plaît!; **(c)** (*continue*) **moving along to my next question,** pour passer à ma question suivante.

▶**move away** **1** *vtsep* écarter, éloigner (*qch*). **2** *vi* **(a)** (*go away*) s'éloigner, s'écarter, s'en aller; **(b)** (*go to new home etc*) déménager; **they've moved away from here,** ils ont déménagé.

▶**move back** **1** *vtsep* (faire) reculer. **2** *vi* **(a)** (*of person*) (se) reculer; **(b)** (*to former home etc*) **they have moved back to London,** ils sont revenus *ou* (*gone*) repartis habiter à Londres.

▶**move down** **1** *vtsep* **(a)** (*change position of*) déplacer (*qch*) vers le bas; *Typ etc* **m. this section down,** mettre cette section plus bas; **(b)** (*demote*) dégrader; *Sch* **to be moved down (a class),** descendre de classe. **2** *vi* (*be demoted*) descendre; **the team moved down to the fourth division,** l'équipe est descendue en quatrième division.

▶**move forward** **1** *vtsep* avancer (*la main etc*); faire avancer (*des troupes*). **2** *vi* (s')avancer.

▶**move in** **1** *vtsep* **(a)** (*send*) envoyer (*des troupes*); **(b)** (*install*) emménager (*son mobilier*); faire emménager (*qn*). **2** *vi* **(a)** (*take up residence*) emménager; **he has moved in with his girlfriend,** il est allé habiter chez sa petite amie; **(b)** (*enter situation*) entrer en scène, faire son apparition; **the market changed when the multinationals moved in,** le marché a changé quand les multinationales ont fait leur apparition; **(c)** (*advance*) s'avancer; **troops moved in to quell the riots,** les troupes se sont avancées pour réprimer les émeutes.

▶**move off** *vi* **(a)** *(go away)* s'éloigner, s'en aller; **(b)** *(start journey) (of army, train etc)* se mettre en marche *ou* en branle; *(of car etc)* démarrer.

▶**move on 1** *vtsep* faire circuler *(la foule etc)*. **2** *vi* **(a)** *(go further on journey etc)* avancer, continuer son chemin; **can we m. on to the next item on the agenda?**, pouvons-nous passer à la question suivante à l'ordre du jour?; **(b)** *(make progress) (of science)* faire des progrès, évoluer; **women have moved on,** les femmes ont évolué.

▶**move out 1** *vtsep (remove)* sortir *(qch)*; faire sortir *(qn)*; **the troops will be moved out,** les troupes se retireront; **people were moved out of their homes to make way for the new road,** les gens ont dû quitter leurs maisons pour permettre la construction de la nouvelle route. **2** *vi* **(a)** *(leave home etc)* déménager; **(b)** *(withdraw)* se retirer.

▶**move over** *vi* se déplacer (vers le côté), se ranger; **m. over!,** pousse-toi!

▶**move up 1** *vtsep* **(a)** *(change position of)* déplacer *(qch)* vers le haut; *Typ etc* **move this section up,** mettre cette section plus haut; **the regiment was moved up to the front,** on a fait passer le régiment au front; **(b)** *(promote)* promouvoir; **they've moved her up to be assistant manager,** ils l'ont promue directrice-adjointe; *Sch* **to be moved up (a class),** passer dans la classe supérieure. **2** *vi* **(a)** *(advance)* avancer; **(b)** *(be promoted)* être promu; *Sch* passer dans une classe supérieure; *St Exch (of shares)* se relever; **(c)** *(to make room)* se pousser; **m. up so I can sit down,** pousse-toi *ou* déplace-toi (un peu) que je m'asseoie.

moveable ['mu:vəbəl] *adj* = **MOVABLE**.

movement ['mu:vmənt] *n* **(a)** *(change of place)* mouvement *m*; mouvement, circulation *f (des véhicules)*; mouvement, transport *m (des marchandises)*; *Mil etc* mouvement, manœuvre *f*; *Fin* circulation *(des capitaux etc)*; mouvement (de baisse/de hausse) *(des prix etc)*; **there was a general m. towards the door,** tout le monde s'est dirigé vers la porte; **to watch s.o.'s movements,** surveiller les faits et gestes *ou* les allées et venues de qn; **free m. of labour,** libre circulation de la main-d'œuvre; **(b)** *(motion)* mouvement *m*, geste *m (du bras etc)*; *(in painting, inside building etc)* mouvement; *Physiol* **(bowel) m.,** selle *f*; **(c)** *(group, tendency)* mouvement *m (politique, littéraire etc)*; **(d)** *(mechanism)* mouvement *m*, mécanisme *m (d'horlogerie)*; **(e)** *Mus* mouvement *m (d'une symphonie etc)*.

mover ['mu:vər] *n* **(a)** *(in debate)* auteur *m (d'une motion)*, motionnaire *m*; **(b)** *Am (firm, person)* déménageur *m*; **(c)** **he's a beautiful m.,** ce qu'il bouge bien.

movie ['mu:vɪ] *n esp Am* film *m*; **the movies,** le cinéma; **m. actor/actress,** acteur/actrice de cinéma; **m. camera,** caméra *f*; *Am* **m. house,** cinéma *m*; **m. industry,** industrie *f* cinématographique; **m. star,** vedette *f*; *Am* **m. theater,** cinéma *m*.

moviegoer ['mu:vɪgəʊər] *n* amateur *mf* de cinéma.

moving ['mu:vɪŋ] **1** *adj* **(a)** *(in motion or able to move)* en mouvement, mouvant; *(train, vehicle)* en marche; *(pièce etc)* mobile *m*; *Phys* **m. body,** corps *m* en mouvement; **m. pavement,** *US* **m. sidewalk,** trottoir roulant; **m. staircase,** escalier *m* mécanique; *Mil* **m. target,** but *m ou* cible *f* mobile; *Am Cin* **m. picture,** film *m*; **(b)** *(force etc)* moteur, -trice; **the m. spirit,** l'âme *f (d'une entreprise)*; **(c)** *(scene, story etc)* émouvant, touchant, attendrissant. **2** *n* mouvement *m*, déplacement *m (de qch)*; **m. (out),** déménagement *m*; **m. in,** emménagement *m*; *US* **m. van,** camion *m* de déménagement.

movingly ['mu:vɪŋlɪ] *adv* d'une manière émouvante *ou* touchante.

mow [məʊ] *vt (pt* **mowed** [məʊd]; *pp* **mown** [məʊn]) **(a)** tondre *(le gazon)*; **(b)** *Agr* faucher, moissonner *(le blé, un champ)*.

▶**mow down** *vtsep (slaughter)* faucher.

mower ['məʊər] *n Agr* **(a)** *(machine)* faucheuse *f*; **(lawn) m.,** tondeuse *f (à gazon)*; **(b)** *(person)* faucheur, -euse.

mowing ['məʊɪŋ] *n* **(a)** tonte *f (du gazon)*; **(b)** *Agr* fauchage *m*, moissonnage *m (du foin etc)*.

mown *see* **MOW**.

MP [em'pi:] *n* **(a)** *Parl (abbr* **Member of Parliament**) député *m*; **(b)** *Mil (abbr* **Military Police**) police *f* militaire; **(c)** *Mil (abbr* **Military Policeman**) membre de la police militaire.

m.p.g. [empi:'dʒi:] *n (abbr* **miles per gallon**) mil(l)es au gallon.

m.p.h. [empi:'eɪtʃ] *n (abbr* **miles per hour**) mil(l)es à l'heure.

Mr ['mɪstər] *n (form of address; not used without name)* **Mr Thomas,** Monsieur Thomas; **Mr President,** Monsieur le Président; *F* **Mr Right,** l'homme idéal.

MRBM [emɑ:bi:'em] *n Mil abbr* **medium-range ballistic missile**.

MRI [emɑ:'raɪ] *n Med (abbr* **magnetic resonance imaging**) IRM *f*.

Mrs ['mɪsɪz] *n (form of address; not used without name)* **Mrs Long,** Madame Long.

Ms [mɪz] *n (form of address; not used without name)* **Ms Martin,** *(unmarried)* Mademoiselle Martin; *(married)* Madame Martin.

MS, ms, *pl* **MSS, mss** *abbr* **manuscript**.

MSc [emes'si:] *n abbr* **Master of Science**.

MSG [emes'dʒi:] *n abbr* **monosodium glutamate**.

Mt *(abbr* **Mount**) mont, montagne.

much [mʌtʃ] **1** *adj* beaucoup (de); **m. care,** beaucoup de soin; **I had m. difficulty in convincing her,** j'ai eu beaucoup de mal à la convaincre; *Iron* **m. good may it do you!,** grand bien vous fasse!; **how m. money?,** combien d'argent?; **too m. money,** trop d'argent; **so m. money,** tant d'argent; **as m. money as,** autant d'argent que.

2 *adv* beaucoup, bien; **I don't like them m., I don't m. like them,** je ne les aime pas beaucoup; **m. as I'd like to,** *(I can't accept, be there etc)* pour autant que je le veuille; **(very) m. better,** beaucoup mieux; **m. worse,** bien pire; **it doesn't matter m.,** cela ne fait pas grand-chose; **m. more/less pleasant,** beaucoup plus/moins agréable; **m. the largest,** de beaucoup le plus grand, le plus grand de beaucoup; **m. too small,** beaucoup trop petit; **thank you very m. (for...),** merci beaucoup (de...); **it's (pretty** *or* **very) m. the same thing,** c'est à peu près la même chose; **he's m. the same,** *(of s.o. ill)* son état n'a pas changé; **m. to my astonishment,** à mon grand étonnement; *Sl* **not m. (he doesn't** *etc***)!,** et comment!

3 *pron* **(a)** beaucoup; **m. remains to be done,** il reste beaucoup à faire; **m. has happened while you have been away,** il s'est passé bien des choses pendant votre absence; **there is not m. of it,** il n'y en a pas beaucoup; **it's not worth m.** *or F* **not up to m.,** cela ne vaut pas grand-chose; **this** *or* **that m.,** autant que ceci *ou* cela; **I'll say this m. for him,** je dirai ceci en sa faveur; **there's not (all) that m.,** il n'y en a pas tellement; **I don't think m. of it,** j'en fais peu de cas; **it wasn't m. of a surprise,** ce n'était pas une bien grande surprise; **she isn't m. of a singer,** comme chanteuse, elle n'est pas terrible; **it wasn't m. of a joke,** ce n'était pas terrible comme plaisanterie;

(b) *(phrases)* **m. as,** pour autant; **m. as I like him,** quelle que soit mon affection pour lui; **as m.,** autant (de); **as m. again,** encore autant; **twice as m.,** deux fois autant; **I expected as m.,** je m'y attendais; **I suspected** *or* **guessed** *or* **thought as m.,** je m'en doutais bien; **as m. as,** autant que; **as m. as possible,** autant que possible; **quite as m. as ...,** tout autant que ...; **it is as m. your fault as (it is) mine,** c'est autant votre faute que la mienne; **it is as m. as he can do to read,** c'est tout juste s'il sait lire; **it was as m. as we could do to stand upright,** nous avions le plus grand mal à nous tenir debout; **he looked at me as m. as to say ...,** il me regarda avec l'air de (vouloir) dire ...; **as m. (as), so m. (as),** tant (que), autant (que); **as m. as that?,** (au)tant que cela?; **do you love her as m. as that?,** vous l'aimez donc tant *ou* à ce point-là?; **he went away without so m. as saying goodbye,** il est parti sans même dire au revoir; **I would not so m. as raise a finger to help him,** je ne lèverais pas même le petit doigt pour l'aider; **so m.,** tant, autant; **he has drunk so m. that ...,** il a tellement bu que ...; **so m. the better,** tant mieux; **so m. so that ...,** au point que ...; à tel point que ...; **so m. for his friendship!,** et voilà ce qu'il appelle l'amitié!; **so m. per cent,** tant pour cent; **so m. a kilo,** tant le kilo; **too m.,** trop; **m. too m.,** beaucoup trop (de); **£10 too m.,** 10 livres de trop; **to cost too m.,** coûter trop cher; **this is (really) too m.!,** *F* **that's a bit m.!,** c'est vraiment trop fort!; **you can't have too m. of a good thing,** abondance de biens ne nuit pas.

muchness ['mʌtʃnɪs] *n F* **they're much of a m.,** *(of pictures, books etc)* ils se ressemblent beaucoup; ils sont tous les mêmes; **it's all much of a m.,** c'est toujours la même chose.

mucilage ['mju:sɪlɪdʒ] *n* **(a)** mucilage *m (végétal, animal)*; **(b)** *esp Am* colle *f (de bureau)*.

muck [mʌk] *n* **(a)** *(dung)* fumier *m*; *Agr* **m. spreader,** épandeur *m*; **(b)** *(dirt)* saleté *f*; *(from the streets)* crotte *f*, ordures *fpl*; **(c)** *Br F (rubbish)* saletés *fpl*, choses dégoûtantes; *(worthless objects)* camelote *f*; **I must clear up all this m.,** il me faut me débarrasser de toutes ces saletés; **(d)** *F* (*mess*) **to make a m. of sth,** faire un véritable gâchis de qch.

►**muck about, muck around** *Br F* = **MESS ABOUT, MESS AROUND.**

►**muck in** *vi Br Sl* **to m. in with s.o.,** (*share room with*) crécher avec qn; (*join in with*) participer avec qn (*à un travail etc*); **everyone mucked in,** tout le monde s'y est mis.

►**muck out 1** *vtsep* nettoyer (*une écurie etc*). **2** *vi* nettoyer une écurie *etc*.

►**muck up** *vtsep Br F* **(a)** (*make dirty*) salir, souiller (*qch*); **(b)** (*make a mess of*) gâcher, bousiller (*un travail, une soirée*); déranger (*les projets de qn*).

muckheap ['mʌkhiːp] *n* tas *m* de fumier *ou* d'ordures.

muckraker ['mʌkreɪkər] *n Br F* déterreur *m* de scandales, *Sl* fouille-merde *m inv*.

muckraking ['mʌkreɪkɪŋ] *n Br F* déterrement *m* de scandales.

mucksweat ['mʌkswet] *n Br F* (*perspiration*) **to be in a m.,** être en nage; *Fig* (*nervous, anxious*) se ronger les sangs.

mucky ['mʌkɪ] *adj Br F* sale, souillé; **you're a m. pup!,** que tu es sale!

mucous ['mjuːkəs] *adj* muqueux; **m. membrane,** muqueuse *f*.

mucus ['mjuːkəs] *n* **(a)** *Physiol* mucus *m*, mucosité *f*, glaire *f*; **(b)** *Bot* mucosité.

mud [mʌd] *n* boue *f*; (*in swamp*) bourbe *f*; **(river) m.,** vase *f*; **to get stuck** *or* **to sink in the m.,** s'embourber; (*of ship*) s'envaser; *Fig* **to drag s.o.'s name in the m.,** traîner qn dans la boue; *Fig* **to fling** *or* **sling** *or* **throw m. at s.o.,** lancer des calomnies contre qn; *F* **his name is m.,** sa réputation ne vaut pas cher; *Sl* **here's m. in your eye!,** à votre santé!, à la vôtre!; *F* **as clear as m.,** clair comme du jus de chaussettes; *Med* **m. bath,** bain *m* de boue; **m. hut,** hutte *f* de terre; *Geog etc* **m. flat,** banc *m* de boue; *F* **m. pie,** pâté *m* de sable *ou* de boue (*fait par un enfant*); *Am Culin* = sorte de flan au chocolat.

mudbank ['mʌdbæŋk] *n* (*in river*) banc vaseux.

muddle¹ ['mʌd(ə)l] *n* confusion *f*, emmêlement *m*, embrouillement *m*; **to be in a m.,** (*of things*) être en confusion *ou* en désordre *ou* en pagaille; (*of person*) avoir les idées brouillées; **to get into a m. (about sth),** s'embrouiller (au sujet de qch).

muddle² *vt* **(a)** (*put in disorder*) embrouiller, brouiller (*qch*); emmêler (*une histoire*); brouiller, gâcher (*une affaire*); **to m. things (up),** embrouiller les choses, *F* brouiller les fils; **(b)** (*confuse*) brouiller l'esprit à (*qn*), embrouiller (*qn*).

►**muddle along** *vi* (*cope haphazardly*) vivre au jour le jour; faire son chemin *ou* se débrouiller tant bien que mal.

►**muddle through 1** *vi* (*get through haphazardly*) se débrouiller *ou* s'en tirer tant bien que mal. **2** *vipo* **to m. through a crisis,** traverser une crise tant bien que mal; **to m. through an exam,** passer un examen tant bien que mal.

►**muddle up** *vtsep* (*confuse*) mélanger; **I've muddled the dates up,** j'ai mélangé les dates; **you're muddling me up,** tu m'embrouilles.

muddled ['mʌd(ə)ld] *adj* **(a)** (*things*) brouillé, en désordre; **(b)** (*person, ideas*) confus, embrouillé.

muddleheaded [mʌd(ə)l'hedɪd] *adj* (*person*) à l'esprit confus, brouillon; **m. ideas,** idées confuses *ou* embrouillées.

muddler ['mʌdlər] *n* brouillon, -onne; esprit brouillon.

muddling ['mʌdlɪŋ] *adj* qui embrouille l'esprit.

muddy¹ ['mʌdɪ] *adj* **(a)** (*chemin*) boueux, fangeux, bourbeux; (*cours d'eau*) bourbeux, vaseux; (*vêtement etc*) crotté, couvert de boue; **to taste m.,** avoir un goût de vase; **(b)** (*liquide, vin etc*) trouble; (*couleur*) sale, enfumé; (*teint*) brouillé, terreux.

muddy² *vt* **(a)** encrotter, crotter (*ses habits etc*); **(b)** troubler (*l'eau*); brouiller (*le teint*); *Fig* **to m. the waters,** semer la confusion.

mudflap ['mʌdflæp] *n* pare-boue *m inv*.

mudguard ['mʌdgɑːd] *n* garde-boue *m inv*.

mudlark ['mʌdlɑːk] *n Old-fashioned Sl* gamin *m* des rues.

mudpack ['mʌdpæk] *n* masque *m* à l'argile.

mudskipper ['mʌdskɪpər] *n* (*fish*) gobie *m* des marais.

mudslinger ['mʌdslɪŋər] *n F* calomniateur, -trice.

mudslinging ['mʌdslɪŋɪŋ] *n F* calomnies *fpl*.

mud-stained ['mʌdsteɪnd] *adj* souillé de boue.

muesli ['mjuːzlɪ] *n* müesli *m*.

muezzin [muː'ezɪn] *n* muezzin *m*.

muff¹ [mʌf] *n Old-fashioned Br F* (*bungled attempt*) coup raté.

muff² *vt Br F Old-fashioned* (*bungle*) rater, louper (*qch*); *Golf etc* manquer, rater (*un coup*).

muff³ *n* **(a)** (*for hands*) manchon *m*; **(b)** *MecE* manchon *m* d'accouplement (*de tuyaux*).

muffin ['mʌfɪn] *n Culin* muffin *m*.

muffle¹ ['mʌf(ə)l] *n Metal Cer* moufle *m*.

muffle² *vt* **(a)** (*to deaden sound*) assourdir (*les avirons, une cloche*); *Mus* voiler, assourdir (*un tambour*); **the carpet muffles every footstep,** le tapis éteint *ou* étouffe tout bruit de pas; **(b)** (*wrap*) emmitoufler; **to m. oneself up,** s'emmitoufler.

muffled ['mʌf(ə)ld] *adj* **(a)** (*son*) sourd; (*aviron*) assourdi; (*voice, footstep*) étouffé; **m. drums,** tambours voilés; **(b)** (*wrapped*) **m. (up),** emmitouflé.

muffler ['mʌflər] *n* **(a)** (*scarf*) cache-nez *m inv*, cache-col *m*, *pl* cache-col(s); **(b)** *Am Aut* silencieux *m*; *MecE* **(exhaust) m.,** gueule-de-loup *f*, *pl* gueules-de-loup; **(c)** *Mus* étouffoir *m* (*de piano*).

muffling ['mʌflɪŋ] *n* assourdissement *m* (*d'un tambour, d'une cloche*).

mufti ['mʌftɪ] *n Mil etc* tenue civile; **in m.,** en civil.

Mufti ['mʌftɪ] *n Moslem Rel* mufti *m*, muphti *m*.

mug¹ [mʌg] *n* **(a)** (*for beer*) chope *f*, pot *m*; (*for tea etc*) (grosse) tasse *f*; (*made of metal*) timbale *f*; **(b)** *F* (*face*) visage *m*; **ugly m.,** vilain museau, gueule *f* d'empeigne; *esp Am* **m. (shot),** photo *f* (d'un criminel); **shut your (ugly) m.!,** ta gueule!; **(c)** *F* (*gullible person*) dupe *f*, poire *f*; **it's a m.'s game,** c'est bon pour les poires.

mug² *vt F* (*attack*) attaquer (*qn*), agresser (*qn*).

►**mug up** *Br Sch Sl* **1** *vi* (*study, revise*) plancher, bûcher, potasser; **to m. up on sth,** plancher sur qch. **2** *vtsep* bûcher, potasser (*un sujet*).

mugful ['mʌgful] *n* chope *f*, pot *m* (*de bière*); timbale *f* (*d'eau etc*); grande tasse (*de café*).

mugger ['mʌgər] *n F* agresseur *m*.

mugging ['mʌgɪŋ] *n F* (vol *m* avec) agression *f*.

muggins ['mʌgɪnz] *n Br F* idiot, -ote, nouille *f*; (*oneself*) ma poire; **I suppose m. will have to do it!,** je suppose que ce sera à moi de le faire!

muggy ['mʌgɪ] *adj* (*temps*) chaud et humide.

mugwump ['mʌgwʌmp] *n Pol F* (*independent*) dissident, -ente; (*neutral*) neutre *m*.

mulatto [mjuː'lætəʊ] **1** *adj* mulâtre. **2** *n* mulâtre *mf*, mulâtresse *f*.

mulberry ['mʌlbərɪ] *n* (*fruit*) mûre *f*; **m. (bush, tree),** mûrier *m*.

mulch¹ [mʌltʃ] *n* paillis *m*.

mulch² *vt* pailler.

mulct [mʌlkt] *vt* **(a)** *Jur* frapper (*qn*) d'une amende; **(b)** (*cheat*) **to m. s.o. of sth,** extorquer qch à qch.

mule¹ [mjuːl] *n* **(a) (he) m.,** mulet *m*; **(she) m., m. mare,** mule *f*; **as stubborn as a m.,** têtu comme une mule; **m. driver,** *Am F* **m. skinner,** muletier *m*; **m. path,** sentier muletier; **(b)** *F* (*stubborn person*) tête *f* de mule; **(c)** *Tex* **m. (jenny),** renvideur *m*.

mule² *n* (*slipper*) mule *f*.

muleteer [mjuːlɪ'tɪər] *n* muletier *m*.

mulish ['mjuːlɪʃ] *adj* entêté, têtu (comme une mule).

mulishness ['mjuːlɪʃnɪs] *n* entêtement *m*.

mull [mʌl] *vt* chauffer (*du vin, de la bière*) avec des épices.

►**mull over** *vtsep* (*consider*) ruminer (*une idée*); **I've been mulling it over and ...,** j'y ai réfléchi et ... .

mulled [mʌld] *adj* **m. wine,** vin chaud épicé.

mullet ['mʌlɪt] *n* (*fish*) **grey m.,** muge *m* (capiton), mulet *m*; **red m.,** rouget(-barbet) *m*.

mulligatawny [mʌlɪgə'tɔːnɪ] *n* **m. (soup),** potage *m* au curry.

mullion ['mʌlɪən] *n Archit* meneau *m* (vertical).

mullioned ['mʌlɪənd] *adj Archit* (*fenêtre*) à meneau(x).

multi-access ['mʌltɪ'ækses] *adj Comptr* à accès multiple.

multicoloured ['mʌltɪkʌləd] *adj* multicolore.

multicultural [mʌltɪ'kʌltʃərəl] *adj* (*society, festival etc*) multiculturel.

multifarious [mʌltɪ'feərɪəs] *adj* varié, divers.

multiform ['mʌltɪfɔːm] *adj* multiforme.

multi-functional [mʌltɪ'fʌŋkʃən(ə)l] *adj Comptr* multifonction; **m.-f. keyboard,** clavier *m* multi-fonction.

multilateral [mʌltɪ'lætərəl] *adj* multilatéral, -aux.

multilingual [mʌltɪ'lɪŋgwəl] *adj* (*person*) polyglotte; (*country*) plurilingue.

multimedia [mʌltɪ'miːdɪə] *adj* multimédia.

multimillionaire [mʌltɪmɪlɪə'neər] *adj & n* multimillionnaire *mf*.

multinational [mʌltɪ'næʃən(ə)l] **1** *adj Fin* multinational; **m. company,** multinationale *f*. **2** *n* multinationale *f*.

multiparty [mʌltɪ'pɑːtɪ] *adj* (*state*) pluripartite.

multiple [ˈmʌltɪp(ə)l] **1** *adj* multiple; **m. injuries,** blessures multiples; **m. store,** magasin *m* à succursales (multiples); **m. ownership,** multipropriété *f* (*d'un immeuble etc*); *Psy* **m. personality,** personnalité multiple *ou* alternante; *El* **batteries in m.,** accus *mpl* en parallèle; *Electron Rad etc* **m. reception,** réception *f* multiple; *Tel* **m. circuit,** circuit *m* multiple; **m. switchboard,** multiple *m* (téléphonique); *Med* **m. sclerosis,** sclérose *f* en plaques. **2** *n* **(a)** *Math* multiple *m*; **lowest** *or* **least common m.,** plus petit commun multiple; **(b)** *Tel* multiplage *m*.

multiple-choice [ˈmʌltɪplˈtʃɔɪs] *adj Sch* (*question*) à choix multiples.

multiplication [mʌltɪplɪˈkeɪʃən] *n Math etc* multiplication *f*; **m. table,** table *f* de multiplication.

multiplicity [mʌltɪˈplɪsɪtɪ] *n* multiplicité *f*.

multiplier [ˈmʌltɪplaɪər] *n Math Comptr El* multiplicateur *m*.

multiply [ˈmʌltɪplaɪ] **1** *vt Math etc* multiplier (*des difficultés, des erreurs etc*); **to m. two numbers,** multiplier deux nombres; **to m. 2 by 6,** multiplier 2 par 6. **2** *vi* **(a)** (*of difficulties, species etc*) se multiplier; **(b)** *Math* multiplier, faire une multiplication.

multipurpose [mʌltɪˈpɜːpəs] *adj* (*outil*) à usages multiples; (*véhicule*) (à) tous usages *ou* toutes fins; (*avion*) polyvalent.

multiracial [mʌltɪˈreɪʃəl] *adj* multiracial, -aux.

multistage [ˈmʌltɪsteɪdʒ] *adj Electron MecE* (*amplificateur, compresseur*) à plusieurs étages; *Astronaut* **m. rocket,** fusée composite à étages multiples.

multistorey, *US* **multistory** [mʌltɪˈstɔːrɪ] *adj* (*immeuble, garage*) à plusieurs étages.

multisyllabic [mʌltɪsɪˈlæbɪk] *adj* polysyllabique.

multitasking [mʌltɪˈtɑːskɪŋ] *n Comptr* multitâche *m*.

multitrack [mʌltɪˈtræk] *adj* (*recording*) multipiste, à plusieurs pistes.

multitracking [mʌltɪˈtrækɪŋ] *n* (*in recording*) enregistrement *m* multipiste.

multitude [ˈmʌltɪtjuːd] *n* **(a)** (*large number*) multitude *f*, multiplicité *f* (*de raisons etc*); **(b)** *Fml Lit* (*crowd*) multitude *f*, foule *f*.

multitudinous [mʌltɪˈtjuːdɪnəs] *adj* **(a)** (*numerous*) nombreux, innombrable; **(b)** *Lit* (*varied*) de toutes sortes; **(c)** *Lit* (*immense*) immense, vaste.

multi-user [mʌltɪˈjuːzər] *adj Comptr* pour utilisateurs multiples.

mum[1] [mʌm] *n Br F* maman *f*.

mum[2] **1** *n* **mum's the word!,** motus (et bouche cousue)! **2** *adj* **to keep m. (about sth),** ne pas souffler mot (de qch).

mumble[1] [ˈmʌmb(ə)l] *n* marmonnement *m*, marmottement *m*; **she answered in a m.,** elle a répondu par un marmonnement; **to say in a m.,** dire en marmonnant.

mumble[2] **1** *vt* marmotter, marmonner (*qch*); **he mumbled a few words,** il a prononcé quelques mots entre ses dents. **2** *vi* marmotter, marmonner, parler dans sa barbe, manger ses mots.

mumbo jumbo [ˈmʌmbəʊˈdʒʌmbəʊ] *n* **(a)** (*rites*) culte superstitieux; **(b)** (*language*) baragouin *m*, charabia *m*; **(c)** (*object of worship*) objet auquel on voue un culte ridicule.

mummer [ˈmʌmər] *n* mime *m*.

mummery [ˈmʌmərɪ] *n* momerie *f*.

mummification [mʌmɪfɪˈkeɪʃən] *n* momification *f*.

mummify [ˈmʌmɪfaɪ] **1** *vt* momifier. **2** *vi* se momifier.

mummy[1] [ˈmʌmɪ] *n* (*embalmed body*) momie *f*.

mummy[2] *n Br* maman *f*.

mumps [mʌmps] *npl* (*usu with sing verb*) *Med* oreillons *mpl*; **to have m.,** avoir les oreillons.

munch [mʌntʃ] *vt* mâcher, mâchonner.

►**munch away** *vi* mastiquer; **he was munching away at an apple,** il mastiquait (bruyamment) une pomme.

munchies [ˈmʌntʃɪz] *npl F* petites choses à grignoter.

mundane [mʌnˈdeɪn] *adj* **(a)** (*banal*) banal; **(b)** (*wordly*) mondain.

municipal [mjuːˈnɪsɪp(ə)l] *adj* municipal, -aux; **m. loans,** emprunts *mpl* de ville; **m. buildings,** = mairie *f*; (*in large town*) hôtel *m* de ville; *Can Austr* **m. district,** = municipalité *f*.

municipality [mjuːnɪsɪˈpælɪtɪ] *n* municipalité *f*.

munificence [mjuːˈnɪfɪsəns] *n* munificence *f*.

munificent [mjuːˈnɪfɪsənt] *adj* munificent, généreux.

munitions [mjuːˈnɪʃənz] *n* **m. of war,** munitions *fpl* de guerre; **m. factory,** fabrique *f ou* usine *f* de munitions.

mural [ˈmjʊərəl] *Art* **1** *adj* mural, -aux; **m. paintings,** peintures murales. **2** *n* peinture murale.

murder[1] [ˈmɜːdər] *n* meurtre *m*; *Jur* homicide *m* volontaire; **premeditated m.,** *US* **m. in the first degree,** assassinat *m*; **to commit (a) m.,** commettre un meurtre *ou* un assassinat; **the m. weapon,** l'arme *f* du crime; *F* **it's (sheer, downright) m. in the rush hours,** c'est (absolument) épouvantable *ou* impossible aux heures de pointe; *F* **it's m. trying to park in the town centre,** c'est un vrai cirque pour se garer dans le centre-ville; *F* **to scream blue m.,** crier *ou* gueuler à tue-tête *ou* comme un perdu; *F* **he gets away with m.,** il s'en tire toujours à bon compte; *F* **their kids get away with m.,** leurs gosses font absolument tout ce qu'ils veulent; **m. case,** affaire *f* de meurtre; **m. trial,** procès *m* pour meurtre.

murder[2] **1** *vt* **(a)** (*kill*) assassiner; *F* **I'll m. you (for that)!,** je vais te casser la gueule!; **(b)** *F* (*destroy*) massacrer, saboter, assassiner (*une valse, une chanson*); **(c)** *F* (*defeat heavily*) mettre la pâtée à; **(d)** *Br F* (*drink, eat*) se taper (*une bière, un pizza*); **I could m. a beer/pizza,** je me taperais bien une bière/un pizza. **2** *vi* commettre un meurtre.

murderer [ˈmɜːdərər] *n* meurtrier *m*, assassin *m*.

murderess [ˈmɜːdəres] *n* meurtrière *f*.

murderous [ˈmɜːdərəs] *adj* meurtrier, assassin; **with m. intent,** dans une intention homicide; **a m.-looking knife,** un couteau à l'apparence particulièrement menaçante; **to give s.o. a m. look,** lancer un regard meurtrier à qn.

murk [mɜːk] *n* obscurité *f*, ténèbres *fpl*.

murky [ˈmɜːkɪ] *adj* obscur, ténébreux; (*ciel*) brouillé; **m. past,** passé obscur *ou* ténébreux.

murmur[1] [ˈmɜːmər] *n* **(a)** murmure *m* (*des vagues, d'un ruisseau, de la foule*); bruissement *m* (*de ruisseau*); *Med* **heart m.,** souffle *m* (au cœur); **(b)** murmure *m* (*d'approbation etc*); **without a m.,** (*faire qch*) sans murmurer, sans broncher; **in murmurs,** à voix basse.

murmur[2] **1** *vi* murmurer, susurrer; (*of brook*) bruire. **2** *vt* murmurer (*qch*), dire (*qch*) à voix basse.

murmuring [ˈmɜːmərɪŋ] *n* murmure *m*; **murmurings,** murmures (**against,** contre).

Murphy [ˈmɜːfɪ] *n Am* **M. bed,** lit *m* escamotable; *F* **that's M.'s Law!,** tout s'en mêle pour vous emmerder!

muscatel [mʌskəˈtel] *n* muscat *m*.

muscle [ˈmʌs(ə)l] *n* **(a)** muscle *m*; **she didn't move a m.,** elle était parfaitement immobile; **he has plenty of m.,** il est bien musclé; **man of m.,** homme musculeux *ou* musclé; **m. fibre,** fibres *fpl* musculaires; **(b)** *F* (*political, financial*) pouvoir *m*; **it would give our campaign more m.,** cela donnerait plus de force à notre campagne.

►**muscle in** *vi F* (*force one's way in*) s'immiscer (**on sth,** dans une affaire); s'injecter (*dans une conversation*); **a lot of big companies are muscling in,** de nombreuses grosses sociétés arrivent en force; **to m. in on s.o.'s territory,** s'imposer sur le territoire de qn; **we don't want them muscling in,** nous ne voulons pas qu'ils rappliquent.

muscleman [ˈmʌs(ə)lmæn] *n* monsieur *m* muscle.

Muscovite [ˈmʌskəvaɪt] **1** *adj* moscovite. **2** *n* Moscovite *mf*.

muscular [ˈmʌskjʊlər] *adj* **(a)** *Anat* (*system, tissue, action*) musculaire; *Med* **m. dystrophy,** dystrophie *f* musculaire; **(b)** (*homme*) musculeux, musclé.

musculature [ˈmʌskjʊlətʃər] *n Anat* musculature *f*.

Muse[1] [mjuːz] *n* **(a)** *Myth* Muse *f*; **the (nine) Muses,** les Muses; **(b) the m.,** la muse (*d'un poète*).

muse[2] *vi* méditer, rêver, rêvasser; **'that's queer', he mused,** 'voilà qui est bien étrange', murmura-t-il d'un ton rêveur.

►**muse on** *vipo* méditer sur (*qch*), réfléchir à (*qch*).

museum [mjuːˈzɪəm] *n* musée *m* (*d'antiquités etc*); **m. piece,** pièce *f* de musée.

mush [mʌʃ] *n* **(a)** *Culin esp US* bouillie *f* de farine de maïs; **(b)** *F* (*pulp*) bouillie *f*; **(c)** *F* (*sentimentality*) sentimentalité *f* (à l'eau de rose).

mushroom[1] [ˈmʌʃrʊm] *n* **(a)** (*fungus*) champignon *m* (blanc); **cultivated** *or* **button mushrooms,** champignons de couche *ou* de Paris; **m. cloud,** champignon (atomique); **m. farm,** champignonnière *f*; **m. grower,** champignonnier *m*, champignonniste *m*; *Culin* **m. soup,** potage *m* aux champignons; **m. town,** ville *f* champignon; **(b)** *Sewing* boule *f* à repriser.

mushroom[2] *vi* **(a)** (*gather mushrooms*) ramasser *ou* faire la cueillette des champignons; **(b)** (*grow rapidly*) pousser comme un champignon; (*proliferate*) se multiplier, proliférer.

mushrooming [ˈmʌʃrʊmɪŋ] *n* **(a)** (*gathering of mushrooms*) cueillette *f* des champignons; **to go m.,** aller aux champignons; **(b)** (*rapid growth*) croissance *f* rapide; (*proliferation*) multiplication *f* rapide, prolifération *f*.

mushy [ˈmʌʃɪ] *adj* **(a)** (*food etc*) en bouillie; (*ground etc*) détrempé, bourbeux; (*pear etc*) blet, *f* blette; **(b)** *F* **m. sentimentality,** sensiblerie *f*, sentimentalité *f* (à l'eau de rose).

music ['mju:zɪk] *n* musique *f*; **to set words to m.,** mettre des paroles en musique; **(sheet) m.,** partition *f*; **I can't play without m.,** je ne peux pas jouer sans partition; **chamber m.,** musique de chambre; **background m.,** musique d'ambiance *ou* de fond; **those words were m. to his ears,** il était ravi d'entendre ces mots, ces mots le remplirent d'aise; **m. box,** boîte *f* à musique; **m. case,** porte-musique *m inv*; **m. centre,** combiné *m* stéréophonique; *esp Br* **m. hall,** music-hall *m*, *pl* music-halls; **m. lover,** mélomane *mf*; **m. paper,** papier *m* à musique; **m. stand,** pupitre *m* à musique.

musical ['mju:zɪk(ə)l] **1** *adj* **(a)** musical, -aux; (*instrument*) de musique; **m. evening,** soirée musicale; **m. box,** boîte *f* à musique; **m. chairs,** chaises musicales; *Cin Th* **m. comedy,** comédie musicale; **to be m.,** (*of person*) (*like music*) aimer la musique; (*have talent*) être (bon) musicien *ou* (bonne) musicienne; **(b)** (*sound, voice*) harmonieux, mélodieux. **2** *n* comédie musicale.

musician [mju:'zɪʃən] *n* musicien, -ienne.

musicianship [mju:'zɪʃənʃɪp] *n* sens *m* de la musique.

musicologist [mju:zɪ'kɒlədʒɪst] *n* musicologue *mf*.

musicology [mju:zɪ'kɒlədʒɪ] *n* musicologie *f*.

musing ['mju:zɪŋ] **1** *adj* pensif, rêveur, -euse. **2** *n* rêverie *f* (**on,** à).

musk [mʌsk] *n* (*substance*) musc *m*; (*smell*) odeur *f* fauve (*du corps*); **m. deer,** (*animal*) porte-musc *m inv*, musc; **m. cat,** civette *f*; **m. ox,** (*animal*) bœuf musqué; **m. (plant),** musc; **m. rose,** (*flower*) rose musquée; (*bush*) rosier musqué.

musket ['mʌskɪt] *n Arch* mousquet *m*.

musketeer [mʌskɪ'tɪər] *n Arch* mousquetaire *m*.

musketry ['mʌskɪtrɪ] *n Mil* tir *m* au fusil.

muskrat ['mʌskræt] *n* **(a)** (*North American*) rat musqué, ondatra *m*; **(b)** (*European*) desman musqué.

musky ['mʌskɪ] *adj* musqué, qui sent le musc; **m. smell,** (*of musk*) odeur *f* de musc; (*similar to musk*) odeur fauve.

Muslim ['mʌzlɪm] *adj & n* = **MOSLEM**.

muslin ['mʌzlɪn] *n Tex* mousseline *f*; *Am* calicot *m*.

musquash ['mʌskwɒʃ] *n* **(a)** (*animal*) rat musqué, ondatra *m*; **(b)** (*fur*) rat musqué.

muss [mʌs] *vt Am F* déranger (*la coiffure de qn*); froisser, chiffonner (*une robe*).

▶**muss up** *vtsep Am F* = **MUSS**.

mussel ['mʌs(ə)l] *n* moule *f*; **m. bank** *or* **bed,** banc *m* de moules; (*man-made*) moulière *f*.

must¹ [mʌst] *n F* (*thing not to be missed*) chose *f* à ne pas manquer *ou* à faire à tout prix, must *m*; (*necessity*) nécessité *f*; **this film's a m.,** ça, c'est un film à ne pas manquer; **the ability to speak Russian is a m.,** pouvoir parler le russe est une nécessité absolue; **sunglasses are a m.,** les lunettes de soleil sont indispensables.

must² *modal aux v inv* (**must not** *is often contracted into* **mustn't**) **(a)** (*expressing obligation*) **you m. be ready at four o'clock,** vous devrez être prêt à quatre heures, il faut *ou* faudra que vous soyez prêt à quatre heures; **you m. hurry up,** il faut vous dépêcher; **you mustn't tell anyone,** il ne faut le dire à personne; **they mustn't find out,** il ne faut pas qu'ils le sachent; **plant that m. have continual attention,** plante qui demande des soins continuels; **I simply m. see him,** il faut absolument que je le voie; **if you m.!,** si c'est vraiment nécessaire; **m. you be so silly!,** qu'est-ce que tu peux être bête!; **he is stupid, I m. say,** il est stupide, je dois l'avouer;

(b) (*expressing probability*) **you m. be hungry after your walk,** vous devez avoir faim après votre promenade; **it m. be interesting working there,** ça doit être intéressant de travailler là; **you m. be joking,** tu plaisantes!; *Eng Dial* **she mustn't be very happy,** elle ne doit pas être très heureuse; **I m. have made a mistake,** j'ai dû me tromper; **if he says so it m. be true,** s'il le dit c'est que c'est vrai;

(c) (*past tense*) **if he had looked he m. have seen it,** s'il avait regardé, il l'aurait sûrement vu; **I saw that he m. have suspected something,** j'ai bien vu qu'il avait dû se douter de quelque chose; **just as I was at my busiest he m. come worrying me,** au moment où j'étais le plus occupé il a fallu qu'il vienne me tracasser.

must³ *n* (*in winemaking*) moût *m*, vin doux.

must⁴ *n* (*mould*) moisi *m*, moisissure *f*.

mustache ['mʌstæʃ] *n US* = **MOUSTACHE**.

mustang ['mʌstæŋ] *n* (*horse*) mustang *m*.

mustard ['mʌstəd] *n* **(a)** *Culin* moutarde *f*; **French m.,** ≈ moutarde de Dijon; *Am Sl* **to cut the m.,** se montrer à la hauteur; *Mil* **m. gas,** gaz *m* moutarde; *Med* **m. plaster,** cataplasme *m* à la moutarde; **m. pot,** moutardier *m*, pot *m* à moutarde; **(b)** (*plant*) moutarde *f*; **black m.,** moutarde noire; **white m.,** moutarde blanche; **wild m.,** moutarde sauvage *ou* des champs; **m. and cress,** moutarde blanche et cresson alénois; **m. seed,** graine *f* de moutarde.

muster¹ ['mʌstər] *n* **(a)** (*action*) rassemblement *m* (*de membres etc, esp Austr des troupeaux*); (*roll call*) *Nau etc* appel *m*; *Mil* contrôles *mpl*; **to pass m.,** passer, être passable, être à la hauteur; (*of work*) être acceptable; **m. roll,** feuille *f* d'appel; *Nau* rôle *m* de l'équipage; **to be on the m. roll,** figurer sur les cadres; **(b)** (*result*) assemblée *f*, réunion *f*.

muster² **1** *vt* rassembler (*ses partisans, ses troupeaux etc*); *Nau* faire l'appel de (*les hommes*); *Nau* assembler (*l'équipage*); **society that musters a hundred members,** association qui compte cent membres; **she mustered all her strength,** elle a fait appel à toutes ses forces; **to m. (up) one's courage,** prendre son courage à deux mains. **2** *vi* s'assembler, se réunir, se rassembler.

musty ['mʌstɪ] *adj* (*goût, odeur*) de moisi; (*pain etc*) moisi; **to smell m.,** sentir le moisi; (*of room etc*) sentir le renfermé; (*of food*) sentir l'évent.

mutability [mju:tə'bɪlɪtɪ] *n* mutabilité *f*.

mutable ['mju:təb(ə)l] *adj* **(a)** muable, changeant, variable; **(b)** *Ling* sujet à mutation.

mutant ['mju:tənt] *adj & n* mutant *m*.

mutate [mju:'teɪt] **1** *vi* subir une mutation. **2** *vt* faire subir une mutation à (*qn*).

mutation [mju:'teɪʃən] *n* **(a)** altération *f*, changement *m*; *Biol* mutation *f*; **m. of type,** métatypie *f*; **(b)** *Ling* mutation *f* (*d'une consonne initiale etc*).

mute¹ [mju:t] **1** *adj* **(a)** (*person, appeal etc*) muet; *F* **she stood m. with wonder,** elle restait muette d'étonnement; **(b)** *Ling* muet; (*consonant*) sourd; **h m.,** h muet; **to become m.,** (*of sound*) s'amuïr. **2** *n* **(a)** (*dumb person*) muet, -ette; *Th* personnage muet; *Arch* (*mourner*) pleureur *m*; **(b)** *Ling* consonne sourde; **(c)** *Mus* sourdine *f*.

mute² *vt* **(a)** (*muffle*) amortir, étouffer, assourdir (*un son*); **(b)** *Mus* mettre une sourdine à, assourdir (*un violon etc*).

muted ['mju:tɪd] *adj* (*sound, voice etc*) assourdi, sourd; (*colour*) sourd; (*protest etc*) voilé; (*violin etc*) en sourdine.

mutely ['mju:tlɪ] *adv* silencieusement; en silence.

mutilate ['mju:tɪleɪt] *vt* mutiler, estropier (*qn*); mutiler (*une statue, une pièce de théâtre*); tronquer (*un passage, une citation*).

mutilation [mju:tɪ'leɪʃən] *n* mutilation *f*.

mutineer [mju:tɪ'nɪər] *n* mutiné *m*, mutin *m*.

mutinous ['mju:tɪnəs] *adj* rebelle, mutiné, mutin; (*équipage*) en révolte.

mutiny¹ ['mju:tɪnɪ] *n* révolte *f*, mutinerie *f*.

mutiny² *vi* se révolter, se mutiner (**against,** contre).

mutism ['mju:tɪz(ə)m] *n* mutisme *m*.

mutt [mʌt] *n F* **(a)** *Am* chien *m* (sans race); **(b)** (*idiot*) idiot, -ote, andouille *f*; **poor m.!,** pauvre mec!

mutter¹ ['mʌtər] *n* murmure *m* (*entre les dents*).

mutter² **1** *vt* marmonner, marmotter, grommeler (*qch*), dire (*qch*) dans sa barbe; **a muttered protest,** un marmottement de protestation. **2** *vi* marmonner, marmotter, grommeler, parler dans sa barbe; **he is always muttering,** il est toujours en train de marmonner.

muttering ['mʌtərɪŋ] *n* marmottement *m*, grommellement *m*.

mutton ['mʌt(ə)n] *n Culin* mouton *m*; **leg of m.,** gigot *m*; **m. chop** *or* **cutlet,** côtelette *f* de mouton; *F* **m.-chop whiskers,** favoris *mpl* en côtelette; *F* **m. dressed (up) as lamb,** vieux tableau.

muttonchops ['mʌt(ə)ntʃɒps] *npl* favoris *mpl* en côtelette.

muttonhead ['mʌt(ə)nhed] *n F* idiot, -ote, andouille *f*, cornichon *m*.

mutual ['mju:tʃʊəl] *adj* **(a)** (*feelings etc*) mutuel, réciproque; **the feeling is m.,** c'est réciproque; **m. benefit society,** société *f* de secours mutuels; *Am* **m. fund,** fonds communs de placement; *Fin* **m. insurance,** assurance mutuelle; **(b)** *El Electron* (*attraction, répulsion*) mutuel; **(c)** (*common*) commun; **our m. friends,** nos amis communs.

mutually ['mju:tʃʊəlɪ] *adv* mutuellement, réciproquement.

muzzle¹ ['mʌz(ə)l] *n* **(a)** (*of animal*) museau *m*; **(b)** (*device*) muselière *f* (*pour chiens etc*); bâillon *m* (*pour chevaux*); **(c)** (*of gun*) bouche *f*, gueule *f*; **m. velocity,** vitesse initiale.

muzzle² *vt* museler (*un chien, F la presse etc*); *F* bâillonner (*la presse etc*).

muzzle-loader ['mʌz(ə)l'ləʊdər] *n Mil* pièce *f* se chargeant par la bouche.
muzzy ['mʌzɪ] *adj* (*person*) brouillé (*dans ses idées*); (*idea*) confus, vague; (*outline*) flou, estompé; **I feel m.,** je me sens un peu abruti.
MV [em'viː] *n* **(a)** *El* (*abbr* **megavolt(s)**) MV; **(b)** *Nau* (*abbr* **motor vessel**) bateau *m* à moteur.
MW [em'dʌb(ə)ljuː] *n El* (*abbr* **megawatt(s)**) MW.
my [maɪ] **1** *poss adj* mon, ma, *pl* mes; (*in the f before a vowel sound*) mon; **my hat and gloves,** mon chapeau et mes gants; **in my opinion,** à mon avis; **one of my friends,** un de mes amis, un ami à moi; **my own son,** mon propre fils; **my hair is grey,** j'ai les cheveux gris; **if you don't mind my asking,** si je peux me permettre de vous le demander; **my idea would be to ...,** mon idée à moi serait de ...; **my turn!,** à moi! **2** *int F Old-fashioned* **my! how you've changed!,** mon Dieu, comme vous avez changé!; **my! my! aren't we touchy!,** oh là là! que vous êtes susceptible!; **(oh) my! my! my!,** ça par exemple!
mycology [maɪ'kɒlədʒɪ] *n Bot* mycologie *f*.
myelitis [maɪə'laɪtɪs] *n Med* myélite *f*.
myeloma [maɪə'ləʊmə] *n Med* myélome *m*.
myna(h) ['maɪnə] *n* (*bird*) **m. (bird),** mainate *m*.
myocardial [maɪəʊ'kɑːdɪəl] *n Med* **m. infarction,** infarctus *m* du myocarde.
myopia [maɪ'əʊpɪə] *n* myopie *f*.
myopic [maɪ'ɒpɪk] *adj* **(a)** (*person, eyes, look*) myope; **(b)** (*relating to myopia*) myopique.
myriad ['mɪrɪəd] **1** *n* myriade *f*. **2** *adj Lit* innombrable.
myriapod ['mɪrɪəpɒd] *adj & n Biol* myriapode *m*.
myrmidon ['mɜːmɪd(ə)n] *n F* subordonné *m*.
myrrh [mɜːr] *n* myrrhe *f*.
myrtle ['mɜːt(ə)l] *n* (*shrub*) myrte *m*; *Am* pervenche grimpante; **bog m., Dutch m.,** myrte bâtard *ou* des marais.
myself [maɪ'self] *pers pron* **(a)** (*emphatic*) moi(-même); **I did it m.,** je l'ai fait moi-même; *F* **I'm not quite m.,** je ne suis pas dans mon assiette; **I m. believe that ...,** (quant à) moi *ou* pour ma part, je crois que ...; **(b)** (*reflexive*) me; **I've hurt m.,** je me suis fait mal; **I was enjoying m. very much,** je m'amusais beaucoup; **(c)** (*after preposition*) **I live by m.,** je vis tout seul; **I was laughing to m.,** je riais tout seul; **I'll keep it for m.,** je le garderai pour moi.
mysterious [mɪs'tɪərɪəs] **1** *adj* mystérieux. **2** *n* (*no pl*) **the m.,** le mystère.
mysteriously [mɪs'tɪərɪəslɪ] *adv* mystérieusement.
mysteriousness [mɪs'tɪərɪəsnɪs] *n* caractère mystérieux, mystère *m* (**of,** de).
mystery ['mɪstərɪ] *n* **(a)** mystère *m*; **to make a m. of sth,** faire mystère de qch; **it's a m. to me,** pour moi c'est un mystère; **the key to the m.,** la clef du mystère; **why make such a m. out of it?,** pourquoi (faire) tant de mystères?; **who was the m. benefactor?,** qui était le mystérieux bienfaiteur?; **m. tour,** voyage *m* dont la destination est inconnue; **(b)** *Th* **m. (play),** mystère *m*.
mystic ['mɪstɪk] **1** *adj* **(a)** (*rites, arts*) ésotérique, cabalistique, mystique; (*power*) occulte; (*formula*) magique; **(b)** *Rel* mystique. **2** *n* mystique *mf*.
mystical ['mɪstɪk(ə)l] *adj* mystique.
mysticism ['mɪstɪsɪzəm] *n* mysticisme *m*.
mystification [mɪstɪfɪ'keɪʃən] *n* (*action, result*) mystification *f*; **to our (great) m.,** à notre grande perplexité.
mystify ['mɪstɪfaɪ] *vt* **(a)** (*bewilder*) mystifier (*qn*); **mystified by ...,** intrigué par ...; **I was mystified,** j'étais perplexe; **(b)** (*make mysterious*) mystifier.
mystique [mɪs'tiːk] *n* mystique *f*.
myth [mɪθ] *n* mythe *m*.
mythical ['mɪθɪk(ə)l] *adj* mythique.
mythological [mɪθə'lɒdʒɪk(ə)l] *adj* mythologique.
mythology [mɪ'θɒlədʒɪ] *n* mythologie *f*.
myxomatosis [mɪksəmə'təʊsɪs] *n* myxomatose *f*.

N

N, n [en] *n* **(a)** (la lettre) N, n *m*; **(b) N.,** (*abbr* **North**) N.; **(c)** *Phys* **N.,** (*abbr* **Newton**) N.

n/a, N/A *Admin* n'ayant *ou* sans objet.

NAACP [eneɪeɪsiː'piː] *n US* (*abbr* **National Association for the Advancement of Colored People**) = association nationale pour la promotion des gens de couleur.

NAAFI ['næfɪ] *n Br Mil* (*abbr* **Navy, Army and Air Force Institutes**) = coopérative *f* militaire.

nab [næb] *vt* **(-bb-)** *Sl* **(a)** (*steal*) faucher, chiper (*qch*); **he's nabbed my watch,** il m'a chipé *ou* fauché ma montre; **(b)** (*catch doing sth*) prendre (*qn*) sur le fait; (*arrest*) pincer, choper (*qn*); **to get nabbed,** se faire pincer.

nabob ['neɪbɒb] *n* nabab *m*.

nacelle [næ'sel] *n* **(a)** *Av* carlingue *f*, habitacle *m*; **(engine) n.,** fuseau-moteur *m*, *pl* fuseaux-moteur; **(b)** nacelle *f* (*de dirigeable*).

nacre ['neɪkər] *n* nacre *f*.

nadir ['neɪdɪər] *n Astron* nadir *m*.

naevus, *US* **nevus,** *pl* **-i** ['niːvəs, -aɪ] *n Med* nævus *m*, *pl* nævi.

naff [næf] *adj Br Sl* nul.

►naff off *vi Br Sl* (*go away*) se casser, se tirer.

nag¹ [næg] *n F* (*horse*) bidet *m*, bourrin *m*.

nag² *n* = **NAGGER**.

nag³ *v* **(-gg-) 1** *vi* **he's always nagging,** c'est un enquiquineur, il n'arrête pas de me *ou* te *etc* casser les pieds *ou* harceler; **don't n.!,** arrête de me casser les pieds! **2** *vt* casser les pieds à (*qn*), harceler (*qn*); (*of doubt*) harceler (*qn*); (*of conscience*) ne pas laisser (*qn*) en paix, tourmenter (*qn*); **she's always nagging (at) him to get it fixed,** elle n'arrête pas de lui casser les pieds *ou* de l'enquiquiner pour qu'il le fasse réparer; **he nags her to death,** il la harcèle sans pitié.

►nag at *vipo* = **NAG³ 2.**

nagger ['nægər] *n* enquiquineur, -euse; (*woman also*) chipie *f*; **she's a terrible n.,** elle n'arrête pas de nous *ou* le *etc* harceler.

nagging ['nægɪŋ] **1** *adj* (*pain*) agaçant; **I've got a n. doubt that ...,** je n'arrête pas de me demander si ...; **I've still got this n. doubt about him,** je n'arrête pas de me poser des questions à son sujet; **he has a n. wife,** sa femme est une enquiquineuse. **2** *n* **enough of this n.,** arrête de nous *ou* me *etc* harceler *ou* enquiquiner.

naiad, *pl* **-ads, -ades** ['naɪæd, -ædz, -ədiːz] *n Myth* naïade *f*.

nail¹ [neɪl] *n* **(a)** clou *m*, *pl* clous; *Fig* **another n. in s.o.'s coffin/the coffin of sth,** un autre coup funeste à qn/qch; **to drive in a n.,** enfoncer un clou; *F* **to hit the n. (right) on the head,** tomber juste, mettre le doigt dessus; **bed of nails,** planche *f* à clous; *Fig* situation délicate, affaire épineuse; **n. set** *or* **punch,** chasse-clou *m*, chasse-pointe *m*, *pl* chasse-clous, -pointes; **(b)** (*person, occ of animal, bird*) ongle *m* (*de doigt, d'orteil*); lamelle *f* (*du bec du canard etc*); **to bite one's nails,** se ronger les ongles; **n. scissors,** ciseaux *mpl* à ongles; **n. varnish** *or* **polish** *or esp US* **enamel,** vernis *m* à ongles; **(c)** *F* **to pay on the n.,** payer rubis sur l'ongle.

nail² *vt* **(a)** clouer (**on, to,** à); *Fig* **he stood nailed to the spot,** il est resté cloué au sol; **(b)** clouter (*des chaussures, une porte etc*); **nailed boots,** souliers cloutés; **(c)** *F* (*catch*) attraper, coincer, mettre la main sur (*qn*); *F* **to n. a lie,** exposer un mensonge.

►nail down *vtsep* **(a)** (*fasten*) clouer (*le couvercle d'une boîte*); **(b)** *F* **we couldn't n. him down to anything definite,** nous n'avons pu obtenir aucun engagement précis de sa part; **to n. s.o. down on a date,** obtenir de qn qu'il fixe une date.

►nail up *vtsep* (*close*) clouter (*une caisse*); condamner (*une porte*).

nail-biting ['neɪlbaɪtɪŋ] **1** *adj F* (*finish etc*) anxieux. **2** *n* habitude *f* de se ronger les ongles.

nailbrush ['neɪlbrʌʃ] *n* brosse *f* à ongles.

nailfile ['neɪlfaɪl] *n* lime *f* à ongles.

nailhead ['neɪlhed] *n* **(a)** tête *f* de clou; **(b)** *Archit* pointe *f* de diamant.

nailing up *n* condamnation *f* (*d'une porte*).

naïve, naive [naɪ'iːv] *adj* (*person, manner etc*) naïf, *f* naïve; (*ingenuous*) ingénu; *Art* **n. art,** l'art naïf.

naïvely, naively [naɪ'iːvlɪ] *adv* naïvement.

naïveté, naivety [naɪ'iːvtɪ] *n* naïveté *f*.

naked ['neɪkɪd] *adj* **(a)** (*person*) nu, *F* à poil; (*bras, dos etc*) découvert, nu; (*mur etc*) nu, dégarni; (*pays, arbre*) dénudé; *Biol* (*stalk, tail etc*) nu; **stark n.,** tout nu; **to strip (oneself) n.,** se mettre nu *ou F* à poil; **(b)** (*sword*) nu; **visible to the n. eye,** visible à l'œil nu; **n. facts,** faits bruts; **n. light,** flamme nue; *Min* lampe *f* à feu libre; **(c) the n. truth,** la pure vérité; **n. aggression,** de l'agression pure et simple.

nakedness ['neɪkɪdnɪs] *n* nudité *f*.

NALGO ['nælgəʊ] *n Br* (*abbr* **National and Local Government Officers' Association**) = association des fonctionnaires nationaux et régionaux.

namby-pamby ['næmbɪ'pæmbɪ] **1** *adj* (*style etc*) fade; (*person*) (*ineffectual*) gnangnan *inv*; (*sentimental*) sentimental, -aux. **2** *n* (*ineffectual person*) gnangnan *mf*, mollasson, -onne; (*sentimental person*) sentimental *m*.

name¹ [neɪm] *n* **(a)** nom *m* (*de qn, d'une plante, d'un objet etc*); devise *f*, nom (*d'un navire*); *Com* raison sociale (*d'une maison de commerce, d'une société*); intitulé *m* (*d'un compte*); titre *m* (*d'une pièce de théâtre, d'un roman etc*); **full n.,** nom et prénoms *mpl*; **Christian n., first n.,** *esp Am* **given n.,** prénom; **family n., second n., last n.,** nom de famille; **maiden n.,** nom de jeune fille; **married n.,** nom de femme mariée; **what's your n.?,** quel est votre nom?, comment vous appelez-vous?; **my n. is ...,** je m'appelle ...; *Com* **registered n., trade n.,** nom déposé; **brand n.,** marque *f* de fabrique; **a man by the n. of Smith,** un homme du nom de Smith; **to go by or under the n. of ...,** être connu sous le nom de ...; **he answers to his n.,** (*of dog etc*) il répond quand on l'appelle; **to know s.o. (only) by n.,** (ne) connaître qn (que) de nom; **to mention s.o./sth by n.,** nommer qn/qch; **to put a n. to sth,** donner un nom à qch, mettre un nom sur qch; **I'm sorry, I didn't catch** *or* **get your n.,** désolé, je n'ai pas bien entendu votre nom; **what n. shall I say?,** (*to caller*) qui dois-je annoncer?; **famous n.,** (*person*) célébrité *f*; **a big n. in the theatre,** un nom bien connu dans le monde du théâtre; **to send in one's n.,** se faire inscrire (*dans un concours etc*); (*have oneself announced*) se faire annoncer; **to put one's n. down,** (*in election*) poser sa candidature; (*on list*) s'inscrire (**for sth,** pour qch); **to lend one's n. to an undertaking,** prêter son nom à une entreprise; **list of names,** liste nominative; **in the n. of ...,** au nom de ...; **in the n. of the law/the king,** au nom de la loi/du roi; *F* **what in the n. of goodness are you doing?,** que diable faites-vous là?; **to be master in n. only,** n'être maître que de nom; **insulting n.,** appellation injurieuse; *F* **to call s.o. names,** insulter qn; **she called me a rude n.,** elle m'a insulté; **that's the n. of the game,** c'est ce qui compte; **not to have a penny/a decent pair of shoes/***etc* **to one's n.,** ne pas avoir un centime/une paire de chaussures convenable/*etc* à soi; *Gram* **proper n.,** nom propre; *esp Am* **n. brand** *or* **product,** marque *f*; **n. day,** fête *f* (de qn); **n. part,** rôle *m* qui donne le titre à une pièce *ou* à un film/*etc*;

(b) (*reputation*) réputation *f*, renommée *f*; **she has a good/bad n.,** elle a (une) bonne/(une) mauvaise réputation; **to get a bad n.,** se faire un mauvais renom; **to have several books to one's n.,** être l'auteur de plusieurs livres; **she has a n. for honesty,** elle est connue *ou* réputée pour son honnêteté; **to make a n. for oneself, to make one's n.,** se faire une réputation (**as,** de).

name² *vt* **(a)** nommer, donner un nom à (*qn, qch*);

dénommer (*une nouvelle plante etc*); **he was named Peter,** on lui a donné le nom de Pierre; **someone named Thompson,** un nommé Thompson; **to n. s.o. after s.o** *or US* **for s.o.,** donner à qn le nom de qn;

(b) to n. s.o. to an office, nommer qn à un poste; **she was named best supporting actress,** elle a été élue pour le meilleur second rôle féminin;

(c) désigner (*qn, qch*) par son nom; citer (*un exemple, un fait*); **n. the kings of England,** donnez les noms des rois d'Angleterre; *Parl* **to n. a member,** (*of the Speaker, in House of Commons*) signaler à la Chambre l'indiscipline d'un membre; **to n. names,** donner des noms; **naming no names,** sans nommer personne; *F* **you n. it, she's done it/got it/***etc*, tout ce qu'on peut imaginer, elle l'a fait/le possède/*etc*;

(d) (*set*) fixer (*le jour, une somme*); **n. your price,** donnez-moi un prix.

name-calling ['neɪmkɔːlɪŋ] *n* insultes *fpl*.

named [neɪmd] **1** *adj* nommé; **on the n. day,** à jour nommé. **2** *n Jur* **afore n.,** précité, -ée.

name-dropper ['neɪmdrɒpər] *n F* **she's a terrible n.-d.,** elle ne manque jamais de glisser des noms de personnalités (supposées connues d'elle) dans la conversation.

name-dropping ['neɪmdrɒpɪŋ] *n F* **there was a lot of n.-d. in his speech,** il n'a pas arrêté de glisser des noms de personnalités (supposées connues de lui) dans son discours.

nameless ['neɪmlɪs] *adj* **(a)** (*person etc*) sans nom, inconnu, obscur; **(b)** (*écrivain, tombe etc*) anonyme; **someone who shall be** *or* **remain n.,** quelqu'un dont je tairai le nom; **(c)** (*dread, grief etc*) indéfinissable, indicible, inexprimable; (*vice etc*) abominable.

namely ['neɪmlɪ] *adv* c'est-à-dire, *Fml* (à) savoir.

nameplate ['neɪmpleɪt] *n* plaque *f* (*de porte etc*); écusson *m*, médaillon *m* (*avec le nom*); **manufacturer's n.,** (*on machine etc*) plaque du constructeur.

namesake ['neɪmseɪk] *n* **she's my n.,** (*she's named after me*) on lui a donné mon nom; (*she has the same name as me*) elle porte le même nom que moi, elle s'appelle comme moi.

nametape ['neɪmteɪp] *n* marque *f* à linge.

naming ['neɪmɪŋ] *n* **(a)** attribution *f* d'un nom; baptême *m* (*d'un navire*); **(b)** nomination *f* (*d'un fonctionnaire*); **(c)** fixation *f* (*d'un jour, d'une somme*).

nan[1], nana [næn, -ə] *n F* grand-maman *f*, mémé *f*.

nan[2] *n Culin* **n. (bread),** pain *m* nan.

nancy ['nænsɪ] *Sl* **1** *n* **n. (boy),** (*homosexual*) tapette *f*; (*effeminate man*) homme efféminé. **2** *adj* (*behaviour, ways etc*) efféminé, de tapette.

nanny ['nænɪ] *n* **(a)** bonne *f* d'enfant, nurse *f*; (*in children's language*) nounou *f*; **(b) n. (goat),** chèvre *f*, *F* biquette *f*.

nanosecond ['nænəʊsekənd] *n* nanoseconde *f*.

nap[1] [næp] *n* petit somme; **afternoon n.,** sieste *f*; **to take** *or* **have a n.,** faire un petit somme; (*after lunch*) faire la sieste.

nap[2] *vi* **(-pp-)** faire un petit somme; (*doze*) sommeiller; *Fig* **to be caught napping,** (*off guard*) être pris au dépourvu.

nap[3] *n Tex* (*of velvet, cloth, felt*) poil *m*; (*of cloth*) duvet *m*; **cloth with raised n.,** étoffe molletonnée *ou* tirée à poil *ou* garnie; **against the n.,** à rebrousse-poil, à rebours.

nap[4] *vt Tex* garnir, gratter, lainer (*le drap etc*); molletonner (*la laine, le coton*); faire la peluche de (*un tissu*).

nap[5] *n* **(a)** *Cards* **to go n.,** demander les cinq levées; *F* **to go n. on sth,** être sûr et certain de qch; **to hold a n. hand,** avoir en main toutes les cartes pour réussir; **(b)** *Horseracing* tuyau sûr.

nap[6] *vt Horseracing F* **to n. a winner,** donner un tuyau sûr.

napalm ['neɪpɑːm] **1** *n* napalm *m*; **n. bomb,** bombe *f* au napalm. **2** *vt* bombarder (*qch*) au napalm.

nape [neɪp] *n* **n. (of the neck),** nuque *f*.

naphtha ['næfθə] *n Ind* naphte *m*.

naphthalene ['næfθəliːn] *n Ch Com* naphtaline *f*, naphtalène *m*.

napkin ['næpkɪn] *n* **(a) (table) n.,** serviette *f* (de table); **n. ring,** rond *m* de serviette; **(b)** *Fml* **(baby's) n.,** couche *f* (de bébé); **(c)** *US* **(sanitary) n.,** serviette *f* hygiénique.

Napoleon [nə'pəʊlɪən] *n Hist* Napoléon *m*.

Napoleonic [nəpəʊlɪ'ɒnɪk] *adj* napoléonien.

nappy ['næpɪ] *n Br* couche *f* (de bébé); **cotton n.,** lange *m*; **disposable n.,** couche à jeter; **n. rash,** rougeurs *fpl* aux fesses.

narc [nɑːk] *n US Sl* = agent *m* de la brigade des stup.

narcissism ['nɑːsɪsɪz(ə)m] *n Psy* narcissisme *m*.

narcissistic [nɑːsɪ'sɪstɪk] *adj Psy* narcissique.

narcissus [nɑː'sɪsəs] *n* (*pl* **narcissi, narcissuses** [nɑː'sɪsaɪ, -'sɪsəsɪz]) (*plant*) narcisse *m*.

narcosis [nɑː'kəʊsɪs] *n Med* narcose *f*.

narcotic [nɑː'kɒtɪk] **1** *adj* narcotique, stupéfiant. **2** *n* narcotique *m*, stupéfiant *m*; *US* **narcotics agent,** agent *m* de la brigade des stupéfiants; *US* **narcotics (branch),** (*of police force*) brigade *f* des stupéfiants.

nark[1] [nɑːk] *n Br Sl* **(copper's) n.,** espion *m* de la police, mouchard *m*.

nark[2] *vt Br Sl* (*annoy*) prendre (*qn*) à rebrousse-poil, taper sur les nerfs de (*qn*); **to get narked,** s'énerver, s'exciter.

narrate [nə'reɪt] *vt* narrer, raconter, relater (*qch*).

narration [nə'reɪʃən] *n* **(a)** narration *f* (*d'une histoire etc*); **(b)** (*account*) récit *m*, narration *f*.

narrative ['nærətɪv] **1** *n* **(a)** (*story*) récit *m*, narration *f*; *Liter* **the n.,** le récit; **(b)** (*art*) l'art *m* de la narration. **2** *adj* (*style, poème*) narratif; **n. writer,** narrateur, -trice.

narrator [nə'reɪtər] *n* narrateur, -trice; *Mus* récitant, -ante.

narrow[1] ['nærəʊ] **1** *adj* (*chemin etc*) étroit; (*vallon etc*) resserré; (*passage, chenal*) étranglé; *Ling* (*voyelle*) tendu; (*esprit*) étroit, borné; (*existence*) limité, circonscrit; **to grow** *or* **become n.,** se rétrécir; **within n. bounds,** dans des limites étroites; **to have a n. escape** *or F* **squeak,** l'échapper belle; *Rail* **n. gauge (railway),** (chemin *m* de fer à) voie étroite; **a n. majority,** une faible majorité; **by a n. margin,** (*to win, lose*) de peu; **in the narrowest sense,** dans le sens le plus exact; *Sp* **n. victory,** victoire *f* de justesse; **to take a n. view of sth,** adopter un point de vue étroite sur qch; **the straight and n. way,** la voie étroite. **2** *npl* **narrows,** passe étroite (*entre deux terres*); goulet *m* (*d'un port*); étranglement *m* (*de rivière, de vallée*); pertuis *m* (*de fleuve*).

narrow[2] *vt* resserrer, rétrécir (*une rue etc*); restreindre, limiter, rétrécir (*un espace, les idées etc*); **narrowed eyelids,** paupières mi-closes. **2** *vi* (*of road, path*) devenir plus étroit, se rétrécir; **the gap between rich and poor has narrowed,** l'écart entre les riches et les pauvres s'est resserré.

▶**narrow down** *vtsep* (*limit*) limiter (*qch*); **that narrows it down to two suspects,** cela nous laisse avec *ou* nous ramène à deux suspects.

narrowcasting ['nærəʊkɑːstɪŋ] *n Rad TV* programmation spécialisée.

narrowly ['nærəʊlɪ] *adv* **(a)** (*interpret*) étroitement, strictement; **(b)** (*only just*) de peu; **he n. missed being run over,** il a failli se faire écraser; **they n. escaped being caught,** ils ont failli se faire prendre; **the missile just n. missed them,** le missile les a ratés de peu.

narrow-minded [nærəʊ'maɪndɪd] *adj* (*person*) (d'un esprit) borné, à l'esprit étroit; (*approach*) étroit, limité.

narrow-mindedness [nærəʊ'maɪndɪdnɪs] *n* étroitesse *f* *ou* petitesse *f* d'esprit, mesquinerie *f*.

narrowness ['nærəʊnɪs] *n* étroitesse *f* (*d'un sentier, des épaules etc*); rétrécissement *m* (*d'un passage etc*); petitesse *f*, exiguïté *f* (*d'un espace etc*); limitation *f* (*de la vie, de l'intelligence etc*); **n. of mind,** étroitesse d'esprit.

narw(h)al, narwhale ['nɑːwəl] *n* (*whale*) narval *m*, *pl* narvals.

NASA ['næsə] *n US Astronaut* (*abbr* **National Aeronautics and Space Administration**) NASA *f*.

nasal ['neɪz(ə)l] **1** *adj Anat Ling etc* nasal, -aux; **the n. cavities,** les fosses nasales; **to have a n. voice,** parler du nez. **2** *n Ling* nasale *f*.

nasalize ['neɪzəlaɪz] *vt* nasaliser (*une syllabe etc*).

nasally ['neɪzəlɪ] *adv* nasalement; **to speak n.,** parler du nez, nasiller.

nascent ['neɪsənt, 'næs-] *adj* (*plant, society etc*) naissant; *Ch* (*corps, élément*) à l'état naissant.

nastily ['nɑːstɪlɪ] *adv* (*see adj*) **(a)** désagréablement; **(b)** méchamment; **(c)** indécemment.

nastiness ['nɑːstɪnɪs] *n* **(a)** (*of smell, taste*) caractère *m* désagréable; **the n. of the weather,** le mauvais temps; **(b)** (*of person*) méchanceté *f*; (*of remark, behaviour*) méchanceté, malveillance *f*; **(c)** (*of book, language etc*) indécence *f*, obscénité *f*.

nasturtium [nə'stɜːʃ(ə)m] *n* (*plant*) capucine *f*.

nasty ['nɑːstɪ] *adj* **(a)** désagréable, dégoûtant; **his behaviour left (me with) a n. taste in the mouth,** sa conduite m'a laissé un mauvais souvenir; **n. weather,** sale *ou* mauvais *ou* vilain temps; **n. accident,** accident grave; **n. cold,** méchant rhume; **n. corner,** tournant dangereux; **n. wound,** vilaine blessure; **she's had a n. attack of bronchitis,** elle a fait une mauvaise bronchite; **to give s.o. a n. fright,** faire une sale peur à qn; **(b)** (*person*) méchant, déplaisant, *F* rosse; **to turn n.,** devenir méchant; **to be n. to s.o.,** être méchant envers qn; **don't be n.!,** ne fais donc pas le méchant!; **n. trick,** vilain tour, *F* sale tour; **what a n. little mind you've got!,** qu'est-ce que tu as l'esprit mal tourné!; *F* **he's a n. piece of work,** c'est un sale individu *ou* un sale type; **(c)** (*indecent*) (*language, book etc*) indécent, obscène; **n. word,** vilain mot.

natal ['neɪt(ə)l] *adj* natal, -als, de naissance.

natality [nə'tælɪtɪ] *n esp US* (*birth rate*) natalité *f*.

nation ['neɪʃən] *n* **(a)** (*state*) nation *f*; *Pol* **United Nations (Organization),** (Organisation *f* des) Nations Unies; **(b)** (*people*) **the whole n. rose in arms,** tout le pays se souleva; **to serve the n.,** servir l'Etat.

national ['næʃən(ə)l] **1** *adj* national, -aux; (*costume*) national; (*coutume*) du pays; *Journ* **the n. dailies,** les quotidiens nationaux; *Nau* **n. flag,** pavillon national; *Br* **N. Health Service,** ≈ Sécurité Sociale; *Br* **to get treatment on the N. Health,** se faire soigner sous le régime de la Sécurité Sociale; *Horseracing* **n. hunt (racing),** courses *fpl* d'obstacles; **n. park,** parc national; *esp Br* **n. service,** service *m* militaire. **2** *n* **(a)** ressortissant *m (d'un pays)*; **a French n.,** un(e) Français(e); **(b)** *Journ* national *m*.

nationalism ['næʃənəlɪz(ə)m] *n* nationalisme *m*.

nationalist ['næʃənəlɪst] **1** *n* nationaliste *mf*. **2** *adj* nationaliste; **N. China,** la Chine nationaliste.

nationalistic [næʃənə'lɪstɪk] *adj* nationaliste.

nationality [næʃə'nælɪtɪ] *n* nationalité *f*; **what n. are you?,** de quelle nationalité êtes-vous?; **to take British n.,** prendre la nationalité britannique; **dual n.,** double nationalité.

nationalization [næʃənəlaɪ'zeɪʃən] *n* **(a)** nationalisation *f* (*d'une industrie etc*); **(b)** naturalisation *f* (*d'un étranger*).

nationalize ['næʃənəlaɪz] *vt* **(a)** nationaliser (*un peuple, une industrie etc*); **(b)** naturaliser (*un étranger etc*).

nationally ['næʃənəlɪ] *adv* nationalement.

nation-state [neɪʃən'steɪt] *n Pol* état-nation *m*.

nationwide ['neɪʃənwaɪd] **1** *adj* (*opinion*) répandu dans tout le pays; (*campaign, survey*) au niveau national. **2** *adv* (*to advertise etc*) au niveau national; (*to be known*) dans tout le pays.

native ['neɪtɪv] **1** *n* **(a)** originaire *mf* (*d'un pays, d'une ville*); (*of foreign country, colony*) indigène *mf*; **n. of Australia,** (*person*) Australien, -ienne de naissance; **the koala is a n. of Australia,** le koala est originaire d'Australie; **she speaks English like a n.,** elle parle anglais comme un Anglais; **to go n.,** adopter la manière de vivre des habitants; *Hum* adopter les mœurs des indigènes;

(b) (*plant, animal*) indigène *mf*; **natives,** (*oysters*) = huîtres anglaises (de Colchester).

2 *adj* **(a)** (*country etc*) natal, -als, de naissance; (*costume, huîtres*) du pays; **n. country** *or* **land,** terre natale, patrie *f*, pays natal; **n. language,** langue maternelle; **he returned to his n. London,** il est revenu à Londres, sa ville natale;

(b) (*plant, inhabitant etc*) indigène (**to,** de, à); **n. American,** Americain, -aine de naissance; **n. labour,** main d'œuvre *f* indigène; **a French n. speaker,** personne de langue maternelle française, personne dont la langue maternelle est le français; **I'm not a n. speaker,** ce n'est pas ma langue maternelle;

(c) (*qualities etc*) naturel, inné; **n. wit,** esprit naturel;

(d) (*metals, minerals*) (à l'état) natif.

native-born ['neɪtɪvbɔːn] *adj* indigène, natif; **a. n.-b. German,** un(e) Allemand(e) de naissance.

nativity [nə'tɪvɪtɪ] *n* **(a)** *Rel* **N.,** nativité *f*, naissance *f* (*du Christ, de la Vierge, de saint Jean-Baptiste*); *Rel* **the (festival of the) N.,** la Nativité; *Th* **N. play,** mystère *m* de la Nativité; **N. scene,** crèche *f*; **(b)** *Astrol* horoscope *m*.

Nato, NATO ['neɪtəʊ] *n* (*abbr* **North Atlantic Treaty Organisation**) l'Otan *m*; **N. forces,** les forces *fpl* de l'Otan.

natter[1] ['nætər] *n esp Br F* causerie *f*; **to have a n.,** bavarder, jacter.

natter[2] *vi esp Br F* bavarder, jacter.

natty ['nætɪ] *adj F* **(a)** (*person, dress etc*) chic *inv*; **(b)** (*gadget etc*) habilement exécuté; bien imaginé.

natural ['nætʃərəl] **1** *adj* **(a)** (*droit etc*) naturel; **be n.!,** soyez naturel!; **that'll look more n.,** ça fera plus naturel; **death from n. causes,** mort naturelle; **the n. colour of sth,** la couleur naturelle de qch; **a. n. blonde,** une vraie blonde; **n. childbirth,** accouchement naturel; *Tex* **cloth in n. colour,** tissu *m* beige; **in the n. state,** à l'état naturel *ou* primitif; *Phys Ch* **n. gas,** gaz naturel; **n. law,** loi naturelle *ou* de la nature; **for the rest of one's n. life,** pour le reste de sa vie; **n. mother,** mère naturelle; *Mus* **n. note,** (note) naturelle *f*; **n. resources,** ressources naturelles (*d'un pays*); **n. selection,** sélection naturelle; **n. size,** grandeur *f* nature; *Econ Ind* **n. wastage,** départs *mpl* volontaires;

(b) (*innate*) naturel, natif, inné; **it is n. for a man to ...,** il est dans *ou* de la nature de l'homme de ...; **it's n. (that) ...,** il est (bien) naturel que + *sub*; (*it is not surprising that*) rien de surprenant à ce que + *sub*; **it's only n. that ...,** il est *ou* c'est tout à fait normal que + *sub*; **as is n.,** comme de raison; *Phys* **n. frequency,** fréquence *f* propre; **n. gift,** don naturel; **n. inclination,** penchant naturel; **one's** *or* **the n. reaction is to do ...,** la réaction instinctive est de faire; **to be a n. skier,** être un skieur-né, être né avec des skis; **n. wavelength,** longueur *f* d'onde propre;

(c) **the n. world,** le monde physique; **n. history,** histoire naturelle;

(d) *Arch* (*enfant*) naturel, illégitime.

2 *n* **(a)** **as an actor, he's a n.,** c'est un acteur-né;

(b) (*note*) *Mus* (note *f*) naturelle *f*; (*sign*) bécarre *m*.

natural-born [nætʃərəl'bɔːn] *adj* (*singer, leader etc*) né; **n.-b. Frenchwoman,** française de naissance.

naturalism ['nætʃərəlɪz(ə)m] *n* naturalisme *m*.

naturalist ['nætʃərəlɪst] *adj & n* naturaliste *mf*.

naturalistic [nætʃərə'lɪstɪk] *adj Liter etc* naturaliste.

naturalization [nætʃərəlaɪ'zeɪʃən] *n* **(a)** naturalisation *f* (*d'un étranger, d'un mot étranger*); **to take out (French) n. papers,** se faire naturaliser (français); **(b)** acclimatation *f* (*d'une plante, d'un animal*).

naturalize ['nætʃərəlaɪz] **1** *vt* **(a)** naturaliser (*un étranger, un mot*); **to become naturalized,** (*of person*) se faire naturaliser; **(b)** acclimater (*une plante, un animal*); **(c)** rendre (*l'art etc*) conforme à la nature; donner du naturel à (*son style etc*). **2** *vi* (*of plant etc*) s'acclimater.

naturally ['nætʃərəlɪ] *adv* **(a)** naturellement; (*parler*) naturellement, sans affectation; (*se conduire*) avec naturel; (*mourir*) de mort naturelle; **n. curly hair,** cheveux qui frisent naturellement; **he's n. shy,** il est timide de nature; **it comes n. to him,** c'est un don chez lui; **it comes n. to him to ...,** il a une facilité innée pour ...; **(b)** (*of course*) naturellement.

naturalness ['nætʃərəlnɪs] *n* **(a)** caractère naturel (*d'une action etc*); **(b)** (*of person*) naturel *m*.

nature ['neɪtʃər] *n* **(a)** (*character*) (*of thing*) nature *f*, essence *f*, caractère *m*; (*of person*) nature, naturel *m*, tempérament *m*; **it is in the n. of things that ...,** il est dans l'ordre des choses que ...; **in** *or* **by** *or* **from the n. of things we cannot hope for more,** vu la nature de l'affaire nous ne pouvons espérer mieux; **the n. versus nurture debate,** le débat nature/culture; *Phil* **the true n. of things,** la nature véritable des choses; **a jealous n.,** un caractère jaloux; **to have** *or* **to be of a happy n.,** être d'un heureux naturel; **it's not in her n.,** ce n'est pas dans sa nature (**to do,** de faire); **by n.,** par tempérament, de (sa) nature, naturellement; **shy by n.,** timide de nature, d'un naturel timide; **it has become second n. to her,** elle le fait presque par instinct; **human n.,** nature humaine; **divine n.,** nature divine;

(b) (*sort*) espèce *f*, sorte *f*, genre *m*; **things of this n.,** les choses de ce genre; **something in the n. of a ...,** une espèce *ou* une sorte de ...; *Admin* **n. of contents,** désignation *f* du contenu; *Fml* **what is the n. of your complaint?,** quelle est la nature de votre plainte?;

(c) (*the natural world*) nature *f*; **Mother N.,** la Nature; **the laws of n.,** les lois *fpl* de la nature; *Hum F* **to answer a call of n.,** satisfaire un besoin naturel; **to draw/paint from n.,** dessiner/peindre d'après nature; **crime against n.,** crime *m* contre nature; **return to n.,** retour *m* à l'état de nature; **n. lover,** ami(e) de la nature; **n. reserve,** réserve naturelle; **n. study,** histoire naturelle.

naturism ['neɪtʃərɪz(ə)m] *n* naturisme *m*.

naturist ['neɪtʃərɪst] *n* naturiste *mf*.

naught [nɔːt] *n* **(a)** *Arch & Lit* (*nothing*) rien *m*; **to come to n.,** (*of plans etc*) échouer, n'aboutir à rien; **to bring to n.,** confondre (*les projets de qn*); **(b)** = **NOUGHT**.

naughtily ['nɔːtɪlɪ] *adv* **to behave n.,** se mal conduire, ne pas être sage, être vilain.

naughtiness ['nɔːtɪnɪs] *n* (*of child etc*) mauvaise conduite.

naughty ['nɔːtɪ] *adj* **(a)** (*child*) vilain, méchant, pas sage; **it was very n. of you,** c'était très méchant de ta part; **you n. child!,** petit vilain!; **he's been a n. boy** *or* **n.,** il n'a pas été sage; **(b)** *F* osé; (*story*) grivois; (*chanson*) gaillard.

nausea ['nɔːsɪə] *n* **(a)** *Med* nausée *f*, envie *f* de vomir; **to be overcome with n.,** avoir mal au cœur, avoir des nausées; **(b)** (*disgust*) dégoût *m*, nausée, écœurement *m*.

nauseate ['nɔːsɪeɪt] *vt* **(a)** *Med* donner des nausées *ou* donner mal au cœur à (*qn*); **(b)** (*disgust*) écœurer, dégoûter (*qn*).

nauseating ['nɔːsɪeɪtɪŋ] *adj* **(a)** *Med* nauséeux; **(b)** (*disgusting*) nauséabond, écœurant; *F* **I find him n.,** il m'écœure.
nauseatingly ['nɔːsɪeɪtɪŋlɪ] *adv* d'une façon dégoûtante *ou* écœurante; **he made it look so n. easy,** il l'a fait avec une facilité déconcertante.
nauseous ['nɔːsɪəs] *adj* **(a)** *Med* nauséeux; *Am F* **to feel n.** ['nɔːʃəs], avoir mal au cœur *ou* des nausées; **(b)** (*disgusting*) nauséabond, écœurant.
nautical ['nɔːtɪk(ə)l] *adj* nautique, marin; (*terme*) de navigation, de marine; **n. almanac,** éphémérides *fpl* nautiques; **n. club,** club *m* nautique; **n. mile,** mil(l)e marin.
nautilus, *pl* **-uses, -i** ['nɔːtɪləs, -əsɪz, -aɪ] *n* (*mollusc*) nautile *m*; **paper n.,** argonaute *m*, voilier *m*.
naval ['neɪv(ə)l] *adj* naval, -als; (*puissance*) maritime; **n. architecture,** architecture navale; **n. attaché,** attaché naval; **n. base,** base navale; **the N. College,** l'École navale; **n. dockyard,** arsenal *m* maritime; **n. officer,** officier *m* de marine; **n. stores,** approvisionnements *mpl*, matériel *m*; fournitures *fpl* de navires; **n. war(fare),** guerre navale.
nave[1] [neɪv] *n* moyeu *m* (*de roue*).
nave[2] *n Archit* nef *f* (*d'église*); vaisseau *m* de la nef.
navel ['neɪv(ə)l] *n Anat* nombril *m*, ombilic *m*; *Fig* milieu *m*, centre *m* (*d'un pays etc*); **n. orange,** orange *f* navel *inv*.
navigability [nævɪgə'bɪlɪtɪ] *n* navigabilité *f* (*d'un fleuve, d'un vaisseau*); dirigeabilité *f* (*d'un aérostat*).
navigable ['nævɪgəb(ə)l] *adj* (*fleuve, vaisseau*) navigable; (*aérostat*) dirigeable; **ship in n. condition,** vaisseau en état de prendre la mer.
navigate ['nævɪgeɪt] **1** *vi* naviguer; *Aut* **I'll drive if you n.,** je conduis si vous me dirigez. **2** *vt* naviguer dans *ou* sur (*les mers etc*); diriger (*une voiture*); gouverner (*un navire*); **to n. a ship,** naviguer; *F* **to n. one's way to the door,** se frayer un chemin jusqu'à la porte; **navigating officer,** officier navigateur.
navigation [nævɪ'geɪʃən] *n* navigation *f*; conduite *f* (*d'un navire, d'un aérostat*); **radio n.,** radionavigation *f*; **n. aids,** aides *fpl* à la navigation; **n. lights,** feux *mpl* de navigation; **n. officer,** officier *m* de navigation, officier navigateur.
navigational [nævɪ'geɪʃənəl] *adj* (*instrument etc*) de navigation; (*aides*) à la navigation.
navigator ['nævɪgeɪtər] *n Nau Av* (officier *m*) navigateur *m*; *Aut* navigateur.
navvy[1] ['nævɪ] *n* **(a)** (*worker*) terrassier *m*; **(b)** *Constr etc* **mechanical n.,** excavateur, -trice.
navvy[2] *vi* travailler comme terrassier.
navy ['neɪvɪ] **1** *n* **(a)** marine *f*; marine de guerre, marine militaire; **to serve in the n.,** servir sur mer; **the Royal N.,** la Marine nationale britannique; **the merchant n.,** la marine marchande; **minister** *or US* **secretary for the N.,** ≈ ministre *m* de la Marine; *Com* **n. cut,** carotte de tabac hachée; **(b) n. (blue),** bleu *m* marine *inv*. **2** *adj* (*colour*) bleu marine *inv* ; **n. (blue) socks,** chaussettes bleu marine.
nay [neɪ] **1** *adv Arch Lit & Dial* non; *Lit* (*introducing a more emphatic statement*) (et) même, qui plus est, voire; **I am astounded, n., disgusted,** j'en suis ahuri, voire révolté. **2** *n Arch & Lit* non *m*; **ayes and nays,** (*in voting*) voix *fpl* pour et contre.
Nazarene ['næzəriːn] *adj & n Bible* nazaréen, -éenne.
Nazi ['nɑːtsɪ] *adj & n Hist Pol* nazi, -ie.
Nazism ['nɑːtsɪz(ə)m] *n Hist Pol* nazisme *m*.
NB [en'biː] **(a)** (*abbr* **nota bene**) N.B.; **(b)** *abbr* **New Brunswick**.
NBG, nbg [enbiː'dʒiː] *adj F* (*abbr* **no bloody good**) (*person*) bon à rien; (*book etc*) nul.
NC *abbr* **North Carolina**.
NCO [ensiː'əʊ] *n Mil abbr* **non-commissioned officer**.
Neandert(h)al [nɪ'ændətɑːl] **1** *adj F* (*attitude etc*) qui tient de la préhistoire. **2** *n F* = personne descendue tout droit de l'âge des cavernes; **N. man,** (*in anthropology*) l'homme *m* de Néanderthal.
neap [niːp] **1** *adj* **n. (tide),** marée *f* de morte-eau; **n. tides,** (marées de) mortes-eaux *fpl*. **2** *n* marée *f* de morte-eau.
Neapolitan [nɪə'pɒlɪt(ə)n] **1** *adj* napolitain; **N. ice cream,** tranche napolitaine. **2** *n* Napolitain, -aine.
near[1] [nɪər] **1** *adv* **(a)** (*denoting proximity in space and time*) près, proche; (*closely connected by kinship or intimacy*) proche; **she lives quite n.,** elle habite tout près; **to come** *or* **draw n.,** (s')approcher (**to s.o./sth,** de qn/qch); **come nearer,** venez plus près, approchez-vous; **the time is drawing n.,** l'heure approche; **to bring sth nearer,** rapprocher qch (**to,** de); **nearer and nearer,** de plus en plus proche; **n. at hand,** (*of thing*) tout près, à proximité; (*of event*) tout proche; **keep n. to me,** restez près de moi; **he was standing n. to the table,** il se tenait auprès de la table; **those n. and dear to him,** ceux qui lui touchent de près; **no, it took nearer to three days,** non, ça a pris plutôt trois jours;
(b) (*in extent*) **as n. as I can remember,** autant que je puisse m'en souvenir; **as n. as makes no difference,** à peu de choses près; **I came n. to crying,** j'ai été sur le point de pleurer; **he's nowhere n. so** *or* **as strong as you,** il n'est pas à beaucoup près aussi fort que vous; **she's nowhere n. finished,** elle est loin d'avoir fini; **50 or n. enough** *or* **as n. as makes no difference,** 50 ou peu s'en faut, à peu de choses près 50;
(c) *Arch & Lit* (= **nearly**) presque, à peu près.
2 *prep* **(a)** près de, auprès de (*qn, qch*); **n. the village,** près *ou* auprès du village; **situated n. the church,** situé près (de) l'église; **bring your chair near(er) the fire,** (r)approchez votre chaise du feu; **to come** *or* **draw n. (to) s.o./sth,** (s')approcher de qn/qch;
(b) (*in extent*) près de, sur le point de; **n. death,** sur le point de mourir; **he came n. (to) being run over,** il a failli être écrasé;
(c) (*in resemblance*) **to be** *or* **to come n. s.o./sth,** ressembler à qn/qch; **language that is nearer Latin than Italian,** langue qui est plus près du latin que de l'italien; **nobody can come anywhere n. her,** il n'y a personne à son niveau; **he's nowhere n. it!,** il n'y est pas du tout!
3 *adj* **(a)** (*relative*) proche; (*friend*) intime, cher; **our n. relations,** nos proches (parents);
(b) n. foreleg, (*of horse etc*) pied *m* du montoir; **n. rein,** rêne *f* du dedans;
(c) (*place, time, event*) proche; **go to the nearest chemist's,** allez à la pharmacie la plus proche; **in the n. future,** dans un proche avenir; **the nearest hotel,** l'hôtel le plus proche; **give the measurements to the nearest metre,** donnez les mesures à un mètre près;
(d) (*in extent*) **n. miss,** *Aut Av* collision évitée de justesse; *Av* quasi-collision *f*; **it was a n. miss,** c'était raté de peu *ou* de justesse; **n. race,** course très disputée; **it was a n. thing,** nous l'avons échappé belle, il s'en est fallu de peu, il était moins cinq; **this is the nearest thing we have to a conference room,** c'est ce que nous avons qui ressemble le plus à une salle de conférence.
4 *n* **one's nearest and dearest,** (*used as pl*) ses plus proches parents.
near[2] *vt* (s')approcher de (*qn, qch*); **as we were nearing Oxford,** comme nous approchions d'Oxford; **the road is nearing completion,** la route est près d'être achevée; **we are nearing our goal,** nous touchons au but; *Lit* **he's nearing his end,** il approche de la fin.
near- [nɪər] *pref* **n.-perfect,** presque parfait; **a n.-disaster,** un désastre évité de peu.
nearby **1** [nɪə'baɪ] *adv* tout près, tout proche; **to live n.,** habiter tout près; **in a house n.,** dans une maison voisine. **2** ['nɪəbaɪ] *adj* **she came out of a n. house,** elle est sortie d'une maison avoisinante.
nearly ['nɪəlɪ] *adv* **(a)** presque, à peu près, près de; **it's n. midnight,** il est bientôt minuit; **we're n. there,** (*on journey*) nous sommes presque arrivés; (*in task etc*) nous y sommes presque; **I've got n. all of them,** je les ai presque tous; **very n.,** peu s'en faut; **I n. fell,** j'ai failli tomber; **he very n. died,** il a frôlé la mort; **she's not n. so** *or* **as old as me,** elle est loin d'être aussi âgée que moi; **(b)** (*closely*) (de) près; **we are n. related,** nous sommes proches parents; *Biol* **n. allied species,** espèces voisines.
nearness ['nɪənɪs] *n* (*of time, place*) proximité *f*; (*of place*) voisinage *m*; (*of friends*) intimité *f*.
nearside ['nɪəsaɪd] **1** *n* côté *m* gauche (*d'un cheval*); côté (du) montoir; *Aut* (*in Britain*) gauche *f* (*de la route*); côté gauche (*d'une voiture*); (*in France, US*) côté droit. **2** *adj* du côté gauche *ou* droit; **keep to the n. lane,** serrez à gauche *ou* droit.
near-sighted [nɪə'saɪtɪd] *adj* myope.
near-sightedness [nɪə'saɪtɪdnɪs] *n* myopie *f*.
neat [niːt] *adj* **(a)** (*person*) ordonné, qui a de l'ordre; (*room, drawer etc*) bien rangé, en ordre; (*exercise book etc*) bien tenu, propre; (*garden etc*) bien tenu, *F* propret; (*attire, handwriting*) soigné; **she has a n. figure,** elle est bien faite; **as n. as a new pin,** tiré à quatre épingles; **(b)** (*clothes etc*) simple et de bon goût; (*style*) élégant, choisi; (*phrase, answer etc*) bien tourné, adroit; *esp Am* **a n. plan,** un plan bien pensé; **a n. little gadget,** un petit gadget bien conçu; **a n. manoeuvre,** une manœuvre adroite; **n. piece of work,** ouvrage bien exécuté; **(c)** (*undiluted*) pur, sans eau; **to take** *or* **drink one's whisky n.,** boire son whisky

sec; **(d)** *Am Sl* (*good*) super.

neaten ['niːt(ə)n] *vt* ajuster (*qch*); donner meilleure tournure à (*qch*).

neatly ['niːtlɪ] *adv* **(a)** (*ranger etc*) d'une manière soignée *ou* ordonnée, avec ordre; **n. written,** écrit soigneusement; **everything is n. in its place,** tout est soigneusement rangé à sa place; **(b)** (*cleverly etc*) adroitement; **n. phrased,** bien tourné; **that is n. put,** c'est joliment dit.

neatness ['niːtnɪs] *n* **(a)** ordre *m*, propreté *f* (*d'une personne*); apparence soignée (*d'un jardin*); netteté *f* (*d'écriture, de style*); bon ordre (*d'une chambre etc*); propreté *f* (*d'un cahier etc*); **personal n. is essential,** il est essentiel d'avoir une apparence soignée; **(b)** (*skill, cleverness*) adresse *f*, habileté *f*; tournure adroite (*d'une phrase*).

nebula, *pl* **-æ** *or* **-s** ['nebjʊlə, -iː] *n Astron* nébuleuse *f*.

nebulous ['nebjʊləs] *adj* (*vague*) & *Astron* nébuleux.

necessaries ['nesɪsərɪz] *npl* **(a)** (*food, money etc*) ce qu'il faut pour vivre; **(b)** *Jur* (*means to live*) le nécessaire.

necessarily [nesɪ'serəlɪ] *adv* **(a)** nécessairement; **it's not n. the case,** ce n'est pas nécessairement vrai; **(b)** (*inevitably*) inévitablement, forcément.

necessary ['nesɪsərɪ] **1** *adj* **(a)** nécessaire, indispensable (**to, for s.o./sth,** à qn/qch); **it is n. to do something,** il est nécessaire de faire quelque chose, il faut faire quelque chose; **it is n. for him to return,** il faut qu'il revienne; **I find it n. to ...,** je juge nécessaire de ...; **it is n. that ...,** il est nécessaire *ou* il faut que + *sub*; **it's not n. to be rude,** c'est pas la peine d'être impoli; **to make all n. arrangements,** prendre toutes les dispositions utiles *ou* nécessaires; **to make it n. for s.o. to do sth,** mettre qn dans l'obligation de faire qch; **if n.,** si cela est nécessaire, s'il le faut, le cas échéant, au besoin; **to do what is n.,** faire le nécessaire; **not to do more than is absolutely n.,** ne faire que le strict nécessaire *ou* l'essentiel;

(b) (*résultat, conclusion, loi etc*) nécessaire, inévitable, inéluctable.

2 *n F* **the n.,** (*things, action required*) le nécessaire; (*money*) de l'argent; **his father will provide the n.,** son père fournira les frais de l'entreprise; **to do the n.,** (*take required action*) faire le nécessaire; (*pay*) payer, *F* casquer.

necessitate [nɪ'sesɪteɪt] *vt* nécessiter (*qch*), rendre (*qch*) nécessaire.

necessitous [nɪ'sesɪtəs] *adj* nécessiteux, besogneux.

necessity [nɪ'sesɪtɪ] *n* **(a)** nécessité *f*; **by** *or* **from** *or* **out of n.,** par nécessité, par la force des choses; **of n.,** de (toute) nécessité; **case of absolute n.,** cas *m* de force majeure; *Prov* **n. is the mother of invention,** en cas de besoin on trouve toujours une solution; **(b)** nécessité *f*, besoin *m* (**of doing sth,** de faire qch); **the n. for sth,** le besoin de qch; **if the n. arose** *or* **should arise,** si le besoin s'en faisait sentir; **in case of n.,** au besoin, en cas de besoin; **(c)** (*usu pl*) **necessities,** le nécessaire; **the bare necessities,** le strict nécessaire; **the necessities of life,** les nécessités *fpl* de la vie; **a car is not one of life's necessities,** une voiture n'est pas indispensable; **(d)** (*poverty*) dénuement *m*; **the family live in dire n.,** la famille vit dans le dénuement le plus complet.

neck[1] [nek] *n* **(a)** cou *m* (*d'une personne, d'un animal*); **to have a stiff n.,** avoir un *ou* le torticolis; *F* **to be up to one's n. in work,** avoir du travail par-dessus la tête, être débordé de travail; **he's in it up to his n.,** il y est (mouillé) jusqu'au cou; **to stick one's n. out,** prendre des risques; (*and say s.o. will win etc*) s'engager; **to throw** *or* **fling one's arms round s.o.'s n.,** sauter *ou* se jeter au cou de qn; **to break one's n.,** se casser le cou; *F* **don't break your n. to get there by three o'clock,** ne prends pas de risques pour y être avant trois heures; *Fig F* **to save one's n.,** sauver sa peau; *F* **to get it in the n.,** avoir des ennuis; *Horseracing* **to win by a n.,** gagner d'une encolure; **to finish n. and n.,** arriver à égalité; **it's n. or nothing,** il faut risquer *ou* jouer le tout pour le tout; *F* **what are you doing in this n. of the woods?,** qu'est-ce que tu fais dans le coin?;

(b) *Br Sl* (*cheek*) culot *m*; **to have a n.,** avoir du culot; **to have the n. to do sth,** avoir le culot de faire qch;

(c) encolure *f* (*de robe, de chemise*); **square/round n.,** encolure carrée/ronde; **V-n.,** encolure en pointe *ou* en V; **high n.,** col montant; **low n.,** décolleté *m*;

(d) *Culin* collet *m* (*d'agneau etc*); collier *m* (*de bœuf*);

(e) orifice *m*, tubulure *f*; goulot *m*, col *m* (*de bouteille*); col (*d'un vase*); rétrécissement *m*, étranglement *m* (*de tuyau*); appendice *m*, manchon *m* (*de ballon*); *Anat* col (*de l'utérus*);

(f) langue *f* (*de terre*); collet *m* (*de ciseau, de vis etc*); manche *m*, collet (*d'un instrument à cordes*); coude *m* (*de baïonnette*); gorge *f* (*d'arme à feu*); *Bot* collet (*de champignon etc*);

(g) *Sl* **to have a n., = NECK[2].**

neck[2] *vi Sl* (*of couple*) se bécoter, se faire des papouilles *ou* des mamours.

neckband ['nekbænd] *n* tour-du-cou *m*, *pl* tours-du-cou (*de chemise*); (*of shirt*) col *m*.

neckerchief ['nekətʃɪf] *n Arch* foulard *m*, tour *m* de cou.

necking ['nekɪŋ] *n Sl* papouilles *fpl*, pelotage *m*.

necklace ['neklɪs] *n* collier *m* (*de diamants etc*).

necklet ['neklɪt] *n* collier *m* (*de fourrure etc*).

neckline ['neklaɪn] *n* encolure *f*, échancrure *f* (*d'une robe de jour*); décolletage *m*, décolleté *m* (*d'une robe du soir*); **dress with a plunging n.,** robe *f* au décolleté plongeant.

necktie ['nektaɪ] *n US* cravate *f*.

neckwear ['nekweər] *n Com* cols *mpl*, cravates *fpl*, foulards *mpl*.

necrological [nekrə'lɒdʒɪk(ə)l] *adj* nécrologique.

necrology [ne'krɒlədʒɪ] *n* **(a)** nécrologe *m* (*d'une église, d'une année etc*); **(b)** (*obituary*) nécrologie *f*.

necromancer ['nekrəʊmænsər] *n* nécromancien, -ienne.

necromancy ['nekrəʊmænsɪ] *n* nécromancie *f*.

necrophilia [nekrəʊ'fɪlɪə] *n Med* nécrophilie *f*.

necrophobia [necrəʊ'fəʊbɪə] *n* nécrophobie *f*.

necropolis [ne'krɒpəlɪs] *n* nécropole *f*.

necrosis [ne'krəʊsɪs] *n Med* nécrose *f*.

nectar ['nektər] *n* **(a)** *Myth & Bot* nectar *m*; **(b)** *esp US* (*fruit juice*) nectar *m*.

nectarine ['nektərɪːn] *n* brugnon *m*; **n. tree,** brugnonier *m*.

nectary ['nektərɪ] *n Bot* nectaire *m*.

Ned [ned] *n* (*dimin of* **Edward**) = Édouard *m*.

NEDC [eniːdiː'siː] *n Br Admin* = Agence nationale pour le développement économique.

Neddy ['nedɪ] *n* **(a)** *Br Admin F* = **NEDC**; **(b)** *F* bourricot *m*, âne *m*.

née [neɪ] *adj* née; **Mrs Thomas, n. Long,** Mme Thomas, née Long.

need[1] [niːd] *n* **(a)** (*requirement*) besoin *m*; **to feel/satisfy a n.,** éprouver/satisfaire un besoin; **if need(s) be, in case of n.,** en cas de besoin, au besoin, s'il (en) est besoin, si besoin (en) est; **n. for sth/s.o.,** besoin de qch/qn; **there is no n. to ...,** il n'est pas nécessaire de ..., il n'est pas besoin de ...; **(there's) no n. to wait,** inutile d'attendre; **on a n. to know basis,** lorsqu'une information doit être connue; **the boss works on a n. to know basis,** le patron ne dit que ce qu'on a besoin de savoir; **to be in n.** *or* **have n. of sth,** avoir besoin de qch; (*be lacking*) manquer de qch; **premises badly in n. of repair,** local qui a grand besoin de réparations; **she is in n. of a rest,** elle a besoin de se reposer *ou* de repos; **present needs,** besoins actuels; **to attend to s.o.'s needs,** pourvoir aux besoins de qn; **that will meet my needs,** cela fera mon affaire;

(b) (*difficulty*) adversité *f*, difficulté *f*; (*financial difficulty*) besoin *m*, indigence *f*; **in times** *or* **in the hour of n.,** aux moments difficiles; *Prov* **a friend in n. is a friend indeed,** c'est dans le besoin que l'on reconnaît ses vrais amis; **to be in n.,** être dans la nécessité *ou* dans le besoin; **their n. is greater than mine,** ils en ont plus besoin que moi.

need[2] **1** *vt* (*3rd person sing pr ind* **needs**; *pt & pp* **needed**) **(a)** (*of person*) avoir besoin de (*qn, qch*); (*of thing*) réclamer, exiger, demander (*qch*); **to n. rest,** avoir besoin de repos; **I work because I n. the money,** je travaille par besoin d'argent; **work that needs much care,** travail qui exige *ou* réclame beaucoup de soin; **these facts n. no comment,** ces faits se passent de commentaire; **a much needed lesson,** une leçon dont on avait grand besoin; **what he needs is a thrashing,** ce qu'il lui faudrait c'est une bonne raclée; **to n. to do sth,** être obligé *ou* avoir besoin de faire qch; **he needs to do more work on it,** il faut qu'il y travaille davantage; **they n. to be told everything,** il faut qu'on leur dise tout; **I didn't n. to be reminded of it,** je n'avais pas besoin qu'on me le rappelât; **he didn't n. to be told twice,** il ne se l'est pas fait dire deux fois; **you only needed to ask,** vous n'aviez qu'à demander; *Iron* **that's all I n.!,** j'avais bien besoin de ça!;

(b) *impers* **it needs a great deal of skill for this work,** il faut beaucoup d'habileté pour ce travail.

2 *modal aux v* (*3rd person sing pr ind* **need**; *pt* **need**; *no prp*; *no pp*) **adults only n. apply,** les adultes seuls peuvent postuler; **you needn't trouble yourself,** (vous n'avez) pas besoin de vous déranger; **n. you go yet?,** est-ce qu'il faut que tu partes déjà?; **you needn't wait,** inutile (pour vous) d'attendre; **I n. hardly tell you how grateful I am,** il n'est pas besoin de vous dire combien je vous suis reconnaissant; **it n. not necessarily be true,** ce n'est pas nécessairement vrai.

needful ['ni:dfʊl] **1** *adj* nécessaire (**to,** à; **for,** pour). **2** *n F* = **NECESSARY 2.**

neediness ['ni:dɪnɪs] *n* indigence *f*, nécessité *f*.

needle[1] ['ni:d(ə)l] *n* **(a)** aiguille *f* (*à coudre, à tricoter etc*); *Bot* **(pine) n.,** aiguille *f* (*de pin*); **it's like looking for a n. in a haystack,** c'est comme chercher une aiguille dans une botte de foin; *Br F* **to get** *or* **have the n.,** se mettre en rogne; *Br F* **to give s.o. the n.,** taper sur les nerfs à qn, agacer qn; (*anger*) mettre qn en rogne; *Sp F* **n. match,** match acharné; **hypodermic n.,** aiguille pour injections hypodermiques; **n. lace,** dentelle *f* à l'aiguille; **n.(-)shaped,** en forme d'aiguille; (*stylet etc*) aiguillé; *Bot* **n. gorse,** genêt épineux; **n. threader,** filifère *m*; enfile-aiguilles *m inv*;

(b) *Tech* aiguille *f* (*de tourne-disque, de boussole, d'indicateur de vitesse etc*); aiguille, langue *f*, languette *f* (*de balance*); **compass n.,** aiguille aimantée; *Art* **engraving n.,** pointe *f* pour taille douce; pointe sèche; **n. noise** *or* **scratch,** (*on record player*) bruit *m* d'aiguille; *MecE* **n. valve,** soupape *f* à pointeau *ou* à aiguille;

(c) *Archit* obélisque *m*; *Geol Geog* aiguille *f* (rocheuse); *Ch Miner* **crystalline needles,** aiguilles cristallines;

(d) *Constr* cale *f* d'étayage.

needle[2] *vt F* (*annoy*) irriter, exciter, agacer (*qn*).

needlecord ['ni:d(ə)lkɔ:d] *n Tex* velours *m* mille-raies.

needlecraft ['ni:d(ə)lkrɑ:ft] *n* travaux *mpl* à l'aiguille.

needlepoint ['ni:d(ə)lpɔɪnt] *n* **(a) n. (lace),** dentelle *f* à l'aiguille; **(b)** pointe *f* d'aiguille; **(c)** pointe sèche (*de compas*).

needless ['ni:dlɪs] *adj* inutile, peu nécessaire, superflu; (*remarque*) déplacé; **n. to say we shall refund the money,** il va de soi que nous rembourserons l'argent.

needlessly ['ni:dlɪslɪ] *adv* **(a)** (*superfluously*) inutilement; **(b)** (*unnecessarily*) pour rien; **they travelled all that way n.,** ils ont fait tout ce chemin pour rien.

needlewoman, *pl* **-women** ['ni:d(ə)lwʊmən, -wɪmɪn] *n* (*seamstress*) couturière *f*; **she's a good n.,** elle travaille adroitement à l'aiguille, elle est bonne couturière; **I'm no n.,** je ne sais pas coudre.

needlework ['ni:d(ə)lwɜ:k] *n* travail *m* d'aiguille; travaux d'aiguille; (*school subject*) couture *f*; **she's good at n.,** elle est bonne couturière.

needs [ni:dz] *adv Old-fashioned* (*used only with* **must**) nécessairement, de toute nécessité; **if n. must ...,** s'il le faut ...; **ah well! n. must!,** ah! il le faut bien; **he had no money, but she must n. go and marry him,** il était sans le sou, mais la voilà qui commet la sottise de l'épouser.

needy ['ni:dɪ] **1** *adj* (*person*) nécessiteux, besogneux, indigent. **2** *n* **the n.,** (*used as pl*) les nécessiteux *mpl*.

ne'er [neər] *adv Lit* (= **never**) (ne ...) jamais; **n. the less,** néanmoins.

ne'er-do-well ['neədu:wel] **1** *n* propre-à-rien *mf*. **2** *adj* propre à rien.

nefarious [nɪ'feərɪəs] *adj* (*person, purpose etc*) infâme, scélérat, vilain.

nefariously [nɪ'feərɪəslɪ] *adv* d'une manière infâme.

negate [nɪ'geɪt] *vt* **(a)** *Gram* mettre au négatif; **(b)** annuler (*la loi etc*); **(c)** *Lit* nier.

negation [nɪ'geɪʃən] *n* négation *f* (*d'un fait, d'une proposition etc*).

negative[1] ['negətɪv] **1** *adj* (*reply, result, virtue etc*) & *Math El Phot* négatif; **to maintain a n. attitude,** rester négatif; **he's a very n. sort of person,** il est très négatif; *Math* **n. sign,** (signe *m*) moins *m*; **n. (income) tax,** impôt négatif. **2** *n* **(a)** négative *f*; *Gram* négation *f*; *Math* valeur *ou* quantité négative; **to answer in the n.,** répondre négativement *ou* par la négative; *Gram* **double n.,** double négation; *Gram* **to put a statement into the n.,** mettre une affirmation à la forme négative; **(b)** *Phot* (cliché *m*) négatif *m*; *El* plaque négative (*de pile*); **n. (record),** (*in recording*) poinçon *m*. **3** *adv* (*in answer to a question*) non.

negative[2] *vt* **(a)** s'opposer à, rejeter (*un projet etc*); **(b)** réfuter (*une hypothèse*); contredire, nier (*un rapport*); *Nau etc* annuler (*un signal*); **(c)** neutraliser (*un effet etc*).

negatively ['negətɪvlɪ] *adv* négativement.

negativism ['negətɪvɪz(ə)m] *n* négativisme *m*.

negativity [negə'tɪvɪtɪ] *n* négativité *f*; **because of the n. of his attitude,** à cause de son attitude négative.

neglect[1] [nɪ'glekt] *n* **(a)** (*disregard*) manque *m* d'égards (**of,** envers, pour); (*lack of care*) manque *m* de soin(s); mauvais entretien (*d'une machine etc*); **his n. of his children led to a court case,** le fait qu'il néglige ses enfants a donné lieu à un procès; **to die in total n.,** mourir complètement abandonné; **the equipment was allowed to fall into n.,** le matériel n'a pas été entretenu; **(b)** (*lack of attention*) négligence *f*, inattention *f*; **out of** *or* **from** *or* **through n.,** par négligence; **n. of one's duties,** oubli *m* des devoirs.

neglect[2] *vt* **(a)** négliger (*ses enfants, sa santé etc*); **to n. oneself,** négliger sa personne, se négliger; **the garden looks neglected,** le jardin est mal tenu *ou* à l'abandon; **are you feeling neglected?,** est-ce que vous avez l'impression qu'on vous néglige?; **(b)** (*ignore*) négliger, oublier (*ses devoirs, un avis etc*); laisser échapper (*une occasion*); **he chooses to n. my advice,** il choisit de ne pas tenir compte de mon conseil; **to n. to do sth,** omettre de faire qch.

neglectful [nɪ'glektfʊl] *adj* négligent; **to be n. of sth/s.o.,** négliger qch/qn; être négligent de qch/qn; **n. of one's duty,** oublieux de son devoir.

negligé(e) ['neglɪʒeɪ] *n* négligé *m*, déshabillé *m*.

negligence ['neglɪdʒəns] *n* (*lack of care*) négligence *f*, manque *m* de soins; *Jur* négligence; **through n.,** par négligence; **criminal n.,** négligence coupable *ou* criminelle.

negligent ['neglɪdʒənt] *adj* **(a)** (*neglectful*) négligent; **to be n. of,** négliger (*qch*); être oublieux de (*ses devoirs etc*); **(b)** (*air, ton*) nonchalant, insouciant.

negligently ['neglɪdʒəntlɪ] *adv* (*see adj*) **(a)** négligemment; **(b)** nonchalamment.

negligible ['neglɪdʒɪb(ə)l] *adj* (*amount*) négligeable.

negotiable [nɪ'gəʊʃəb(ə)l] *adj* **(a)** *Fin etc* (*effet, titre etc*) négociable; (*demands, agreement*) à négocier; **not n.,** non-négociable; (*military pension etc*) incessible; **(b)** (*barrière etc*) franchissable; (*chemin etc*) praticable.

negotiate [nɪ'gəʊʃɪeɪt] **1** *vt* **(a)** négocier, traiter (*une affaire, un mariage*); négocier (*un emprunt*); *Fin* négocier, trafiquer (*un effet*); **price to be negotiated,** prix *m* à débattre; **(b)** franchir (*une haie etc*); surmonter (*une difficulté*); *Aut* **to n. a bend,** négocier *ou* prendre un virage. **2** *vi* négocier; **they refuse to n.,** ils refusent de négocier; **to be negotiating with s.o. for ...,** être en traité *ou* en marché avec qn pour ...; **to n. for peace,** entreprendre des pourparlers de paix.

negotiation [nɪgəʊʃɪ'eɪʃən] *n* **(a)** négociation *f* (*d'un traité, d'un emprunt etc*); **under n.,** en négociation; **to be in n. with s.o.,** être en pourparler(s) avec qn; **to break off/resume negotiations,** rompre/reprendre les négociations; **(b)** franchissement *m* (*d'un obstacle*); prise *f* (*d'un virage*).

negotiator [nɪ'gəʊʃɪeɪtər] *n* négociateur, -trice.

Negress ['ni:grɪs] *n* Noire *f*; (*in anthropology*) & *Pej* négresse *f*.

Negro, *pl* **-oes** ['ni:grəʊ, -z] **1** *adj* noir, nègre; **the N. race,** la race noire *ou* nègre; **N. Spiritual,** Négro Spiritual. **2** *n* Noir *m*; (*in anthropology*) & *Pej* nègre *m*.

Negroid ['ni:grɔɪd] *adj* & *n* (*in anthropology*) négroïde *mf*.

neigh[1] [neɪ] *n* hennissement *m*.

neigh[2] *vi* hennir.

neighbour, *US* **neighbor** ['neɪbər] *n* **(a)** (*living nearby*) voisin, -ine; **(b)** *Bible etc* (*fellow human being*) prochain *m*; **love thy n. as thyself,** aime ton prochain comme toi-même.

►**neighbour on,** *US* **neighbor on** *vipo* (*adjoin*) être voisin de.

neighbourhood, *US* **neighborhood** ['neɪbəhʊd] *n* **(a)** (*vicinity*) voisinage *m*, proximité *f* (**of,** de); **to live in the (immediate) n. of ...,** demeurer à proximité de ...; **anyone in the n. of the crime should contact the police,** quiconque se trouvait à proximité du lieu du crime doit contacter la police; *F* **in the n. of 10,** environ 10, dans les 10; **(b)** (*district*) alentours *mpl*, environs *mpl* (*d'un lieu*); voisinage *m*, quartier *m*; **I was in the n.,** j'étais dans le coin *ou* dans le quartier *ou* dans le voisinage; **the whole n. is talking about it,** tout le voisinage en parle; **a very friendly n.,** un quartier très sympa; **she's the n. gossip,** elle est la commère du voisinage; *Br* **n. watch,** = système de surveillance mis en œuvre par les habitants d'un quartier; **(c)** = **NEIGHBOURLINESS.**

neighbouring, *US* **neighboring** ['neɪbərɪŋ] *adj* avoisinant, voisin.

neighbourliness, *US* **neighborliness** ['neɪbəlɪnɪs] *n* (*of person*) (relations *fpl* de) bon voisinage; bons rapports entre voisins.

neighbourly, *US* **neighborly** ['neɪbəlɪ] *adj* (*person*) obligeant, bon voisin; (*action etc*) de bon voisin; (*visite*) de bon voisinage; **to be n. with s.o.,** voisiner avec qn; *esp US* **that was right n. of you,** c'était très obligeant de votre part.

neighing ['neɪɪŋ] *n* hennissement(s) *m(pl)*.

neither ['naɪðər, *esp Am* 'niːðər] **1** *adv* **n. .... nor ...**, ni ... ni ...; **he will n. eat nor drink,** il ne veut ni manger ni boire; **n. (the) one nor the other,** ni l'un ni l'autre; **that's n. here nor there,** (*irrelevant*) ça n'a rien à voir. **2** *conj* non plus; **n. do I,** ni moi non plus; **if you don't go n. shall I,** si vous n'y allez pas, je n'irai pas non plus; **I haven't read it, n. do I intend to,** je ne l'ai pas lu et d'ailleurs je n'en ai pas l'intention. **3** *adj* ni l'un(e) ni l'autre, aucun(e); **n. driver was injured,** ni l'un ni l'autre des conducteurs n'a été blessé; **on n. side,** ni d'un côté ni de l'autre. **4** *pron* **which do you want? — n.,** lequel voulez-vous? — ni l'un ni l'autre; **n. of my two brothers can come,** aucun de mes deux frères ne peut venir; **n. of us is satisfied,** nous ne sommes satisfaits ni l'un ni l'autre.

nelly ['nelɪ] *n Br Sl* **not on your n.!,** jamais de la vie!

nelson ['nels(ə)n] *n* (*in wrestling*) nelson *m*; **double** *or* **full n.,** double nelson.

nematode ['nemətəʊd] *n* (*worm*) nématode *m*.

nemesis ['nemɪsɪs] *n* châtiment mérité.

Nemesis ['nemɪsɪs] *n Myth* Némésis.

neo- [niːəʊ] *pref* néo-.

neoclassic(al) [niːəʊ'klæsɪk, -ɪk(ə)l] *adj* néo-classique.

neoclassicism [niːəʊ'klæsɪsɪz(ə)m] *n* néo-classicisme *m*.

neocolonialism [niːəʊkə'ləʊnɪəlɪz(ə)m] *n Pol* néo-colonialisme *m*.

neofascism [niːəʊ'fæʃɪz(ə)m] *n Pol* néo-fascisme *m*.

neofascist [nɪəʊ'fæʃɪst] *adj & n* néo-fasciste *mf*.

neo-gothic [niːəʊ'gɒθɪk] *adj & n Archit* néo-gothique *m*.

neolithic [niːəʊ'lɪθɪk] *adj* néolithique; **the N. age,** l'âge *m* de la pierre polie, le néolithique.

neologism [nɪ'ɒlədʒɪz(ə)m] *n* néologisme *m*.

neon ['niːɒn] *n Ch* néon *m*; *El* **n. light,** lumière *f* au néon; **n. tube,** tube fluorescent *ou F* au néon; **n. sign,** enseigne *f* au néon.

neonatal [niːəʊ'neɪt(ə)l] *adj Med* néo-natal.

neonazi [niːəʊ'nɑːtsɪ] *adj & n* néo-nazi, -ie.

neophyte ['nɪəʊfaɪt] *n Rel etc* néophyte *mf*.

neoplasm ['niːəʊplæz(ə)m] *n Med* néoplasme *m*.

Nepal [nɪ'pɔːl] *n* Népal *m*.

Nepalese [nepə'liːz] **, Nepali** [ne'pɔːlɪ] **1** *adj* népalais. **2** *n* **(a)** Népalais, -aise; **(b)** *Ling* népalais *m*.

nephew ['nefjuː] *n* neveu *m*.

nephrite ['nefraɪt] *n Miner* néphrite *f*.

nephritic [ne'frɪtɪk] *adj Med* néphrétique.

nephritis [ne'fraɪtɪs] *n Med* néphrite *f*; **to have n.,** avoir une néphrite.

nepotism ['nepətɪz(ə)m, 'niː-] *n* népotisme *m*.

Neptune ['neptjuːn] *n Astron Myth* Neptune *m*.

nerd [nɜːd] *n Pej Sl* nul *m*.

Nereid ['nɪərɪɪd] *n Myth* Néréide *f*.

Nero ['nɪərəʊ] *n Antiq* Néron *m*.

nerve[1] [nɜːv] *n* **(a)** *Anat* nerf *m*; **to take the n. out of a tooth,** (*of dentist*) dévitaliser une dent; **optic/auditory n.,** nerf optique/auditif; **to be in a state of nerves,** être énervé *ou* sur les nerfs; **we're living on our nerves,** nous vivons sur les nerfs; **my nerves won't stand it,** mes nerfs vont lâcher; **he's a bundle of nerves,** c'est un paquet de nerfs; **to get on s.o.'s nerves,** taper sur les nerfs à qn, énerver qn, agacer qn; **she's got nerves of steel,** elle a des nerfs à toute épreuve; **to strain every n. to do sth,** mettre toute sa force à faire qch; **war of nerves,** guerre *f* des nerfs; **n. cell,** neurone *f*; **n. centre,** centre nerveux; *Fig* centre névralgique; **n. ending,** extrémité *f* du nerf; **n. fibre,** fibre nerveuse; *Mil etc* **n. gas,** gaz *m* neurotoxique; *Med* **n. specialist,** neurologue *mf*;

(b) (*courage*) courage *m*; sang-froid *m*; **to lose one's n.,** perdre son sang-froid; **his n. failed him, he lost his n.,** le courage lui a manqué, *Fig* il s'est dégonflé; **a pilot who has lost his n.,** un pilote qui n'est plus mentalement en état de voler; **he never regained his n.,** il n'a jamais retrouvé son courage;

(c) *F* (*cheek*) culot *m*; **to have the n. to do sth,** avoir le toupet *ou* le culot de faire qch; **what a n.!,** quel culot!; **you've got a n.!,** tu es gonflé!;

(d) *Bot Ent Archit* nervure *f*.

nerve[2] *vt* fortifier, donner du courage à (*qn*); donner du nerf *ou* de la force à (*son bras etc*); **to n. oneself to do sth,** s'armer de courage *ou* de sang-froid pour faire qch.

nerveless ['nɜːvlɪs] *adj* **(a)** (*calm*) calme, plein de sang-froid; **(b)** (*person, limb etc*) inerte; (*style etc*) sans vigueur, languissant; **the cup fell from her n. fingers,** la tasse a échappé à ses doigts engourdis.

nerve-(w)racking ['nɜːvrækɪŋ] *adj* éprouvant.

nerviness ['nɜːvɪnɪs] *n* **(a)** (*tension*) nervosité *f*, énervement *m*; **(b)** *Am* (*cheek*) culot *m*.

nervous ['nɜːvəs] *adj* **(a)** (*timid*) (*person, mouse, gazelle etc*) craintif; (*tense, highly strung*) nerveux; (*laugh, smile, gesture*) nerveux; **airports make me n.,** les aéroports me rendent nerveux; **are you n. about the exams?,** est-ce que tu appréhendes les examens?; **he gets terribly n. every time he has to make a speech,** chaque fois qu'il doit faire un discours il devient terriblement nerveux *ou* anxieux; **he's n. about flying,** il appréhende *ou* craint *ou* a peur de voyager en avion; **to be n.** (*before a performance etc*) avoir le trac; **I feel** *ou* **am n. in his presence,** sa présence me rend nerveux; **he makes me n.,** (*is intimidating for me*) il m'intimide; **don't hold your glass like that, you're making me n.,** ne tiens pas ton verre comme ça, tu me rends nerveux *ou* tu me fais peur; **to be n. about doing sth,** avoir peur de faire qch; **I was a bit n. about lending him the car,** j'avais un peu d'appréhension à l'idée de lui prêter ma voiture; **the bank was n. about making the loan,** la banque hésitait à accorder le prêt; **I'm still a little n. about taking on this contract,** j'hésite encore un peu à accepter ce contrat; **if you're n. about offering him the job,** (*are worried*) si vous craignez de lui proposer l'emploi; (*are uncertain*) si vous hésitez à lui proposer l'emploi;

(b) *Anat* (*energy, exhaustion etc*) nerveux; **n. system,** système nerveux; *Med* **n. breakdown,** dépression nerveuse; **to have a n. breakdown,** faire une dépression nerveuse; **n. complaint,** maladie *f* de nerfs; **n. energy,** énergie nerveuse.

nervously [nɜːvəslɪ] *adv* **(a)** (*fearfully*) craintivement; **(b)** (*tensely*) nerveusement; **she laughed n.,** elle a ri nerveusement.

nervousness ['nɜːvəsnɪs] *n* **(a)** timidité *f*; *F* (*before performance*) trac *m*; **(b)** nervosité *f*; état nerveux *ou* d'agitation.

nervy ['nɜːvɪ] *adj* **(a)** *Br F* (*tense*) énervé, irritable; **to feel n.,** être dans un état d'énervement, avoir les nerfs en pelote; **(b)** *Am* (*cheeky*) qui a du culot.

nest[1] [nest] *n* **(a)** nid *m* (*d'oiseaux, de guêpes etc*); *Fig* **the children have all left** *or* **flown the n.,** les enfants ont tous quitté le nid; **n. box,** pondoir *m*, nichoir *m*; *Fig* **n. egg,** argent mis de côté, pécule *m*; **(b)** repaire *m*, nid *m* (*de brigands, mitrailleuses etc*); **(c)** (*nestful*) nichée *f* (*d'oiseaux etc*); **(d)** série *f*, jeu *m* (*d'objets*); **n. of tables,** table *f* gigogne.

nest[2] **1** *vi* **(a)** (*of birds etc*) (se) nicher, faire son nid; **(b)** (*of tables*) s'emboîter. **2** *vt* emboîter (*des tubes etc*).

nestful ['nestfʊl] *n* (*of eggs, fledgelings*) nichée *f*.

nesting ['nestɪŋ] **1** *adj* (*oiseau*) nicheur. **2** *n* **to go (bird) n.,** aller dénicher les œufs *ou* les oisillons; **n. time,** saison *f* de la ponte; **n. box,** pondoir *m*, nichoir *m*.

nestle ['nes(ə)l] **1** *vi* se nicher, se pelotonner; **to n. close to s.o.,** se serrer contre qn; **village nestling in a valley,** village blotti *ou* tapi dans une vallée; **to n. against s.o.'s shoulder,** se blottir contre l'épaule de qn. **2** *vt* **to n. one's face against s.o.'s shoulder,** se blottir contre l'épaule de qn.

▶**nestle up** *vi* = **NESTLE 1**.

nestling ['neslɪŋ] *n* oisillon *m*.

net[1] [net] *n* **(a)** filet *m*; **fishing n.,** filet de pêche; **butterfly n.,** filet à papillons; **to haul in a n.,** relever un filet; *Ind* **guard n.,** filet de protection; *Mil* **camouflage n.,** filet de camouflage; **safety n.,** (*at circus etc*) filet; **hair n.,** filet, résille *f* (à cheveux); **mosquito n.,** moustiquaire *f; Fig* **to be caught in the n.,** être pris au piège; *Fig* **to slip through the n.,** passer à travers les mailles du filet; *Tennis* **n. play,** jeu *m* au filet; **(b)** *Tex* tulle *m*; **Brussels n.,** tulle de Bruxelles; **foundation n.,** mousseline forte; **n. curtain,** rideau *m* de tulle; **(c)** = **NETWORK[1] (a)**.

net[2] (-tt-) *vt* **(a)** (*capture*) prendre (*des poissons, des lièvres, Fig des criminels etc*) au filet; **(b)** tendre des filets dans (*une rivière*); **(c)** *Sp* envoyer (*le ballon, la balle*) dans le filet; *Fb* **he netted the ball twice,** (*scored two goals*) il a marqué deux buts; **(d)** *Mil* camoufler (*un emplacement etc*) avec un filet; **(e)** (*in gardening*) protéger (*des petits pois etc*) avec un filet; **(f)** faire (*un hamac etc*) au filet.

net[3] **1** *adj* (*weight, price etc*) net, *f* nette; **n. proceeds of a sale,** (produit *m*) net *m* d'une vente; **terms strictly n.,** sans déduction; **n. profit,** bénéfice net; **n. of tax,** net d'impôt; **n. earnings,** (*of company*) bénéfices nets; (*of worker*) salaire net; **n. result,** résultat final. **2** *n* prix *m ou* poids *m ou* bénéfice *m etc* net.

net[4] *vt* (-tt-) **(a)** (*of person*) toucher net, gagner net (*tant de bénéfices etc*); **(b)** (*of enterprise etc*) rapporter net, produire net (*une certaine somme*).

netball ['netbɔːl] *n Sp* netball *m*.
nether ['neðər] *adj* inférieur, bas; *Lit* **the n. regions** *or* **world,** l'enfer *m*, les régions infernales; *Hum* **the n. regions of the rue St. Denis,** le bas de la rue St. Denis.
Netherlands (the) [ðə'neðələndz] *npl* les Pays-Bas *mpl*; **in the N.,** dans les *ou* aux Pays-Bas.
nett [net] *adj* = **NET**[3].
netting ['netɪŋ] *n* **(a)** (*nets*) filet(s) *m(pl)* (*de protection, de camouflage*); (*around tennis court etc*) grillage *m*; **wire n.,** treillis *m* métallique, grillage en fil de fer; **(b)** (*action*) fabrication *f* du filet; **n. needle,** navette *f*; **(c)** *Tex* tulle *m*; **(d)** (*in fishing*) pêche *f* au(x) filet(s); (*in hunting*) capture *f* du gibier au(x) filet(s).
nettle[1] ['net(ə)l] *n* (*weed*) ortie *f*; **stinging n.,** ortie brûlante; **dead n.,** ortie blanche; *Med* **n. rash,** urticaire *f*; *Fig* **to grasp the n.,** y aller carrément.
nettle[2] *vt* irriter (*qn*), faire monter la moutarde au nez de (*qn*).
network[1] ['netwɜːk] *n* **(a)** réseau *m*, lacis *m* (*de canaux, de rues etc*); enchevêtrement *m* (*de ronces etc*); *TV Rad* réseau (*de télévision, de radiodiffusion*); *Comptr* réseau; **electricity n.,** réseau électrique; **(b)** réseau *m* (*d'alliances etc*); **spy n.,** réseau d'espionnage; *F* **the old-boy n.,** = la franc-maçonnerie des grandes écoles; **(c)** = **NETTING (a)**.
network[2] **1** *vt* **(a)** (*to cover*) parcourir; **the country was networked with canals,** le pays était parcouru de canaux; **(b)** *TV Rad* **networked programmes,** programmes diffusés en réseau; **(c)** *Comptr* mettre en réseau; **networked systems,** systèmes *mpl* en réseau. **2** *vi* (*exchange information*) établir un réseau de contacts.
networking ['netwɜːkɪŋ] *n* **(a)** *Comptr* travail *m* en réseau; **to have n. capabilities,** (*of terminal*) être conçu pour fonctionner dans un réseau, offrir la possibilité d'intégration à un réseau; **(b)** *esp Am* (*exchanging information*) établissement *m* d'un réseau de contacts.
neural ['njʊərəl] *adj Anat* neural, -aux; *Comptr* **n. network,** réseau neuronal.
neuralgia [njʊ'rældʒə] *n Med* névralgie *f*; **to have n.,** faire *ou* avoir de la névralgie.
neuralgic [njʊ'rældʒɪk] *adj Med* névralgique.
neurasthenia [njʊərəs'θiːnɪə] *n Med* neurasthénie *f*.
neurasthenic [njʊərəs'θiːnɪk] *adj & n Med* neurasthénique *mf*.
neuritis [njʊ'raɪtɪs] *n Med* névrite *f*.
neurological [njʊərə'lɒdʒɪk(ə)l] *adj* neurologique.
neurologist [njʊə'rɒlədʒɪst] *n* neurologue *mf*.
neurology [njʊə'rɒlədʒɪ] *n* neurologie *f*.
neuromuscular [njʊərəʊ'mʌskjʊːlər] *adj* neuromusculaire.
neuron ['njʊərɒn] *n Physiol* neurone *m*.
neuropathology [njʊərəʊpə'θɒlədʒɪ] *n* névropathologie *f*, neuropathologie *f*.
neurosis, *pl* **neuroses** [njʊ'rəʊsɪs, -siːz] *n Med* névrose *f*.
neurosurgeon [njʊərəʊ'sɜːdʒən] *n* neurochirurgien, -ienne.
neurosurgery [njʊərəʊ'sɜːdʒərɪ] *n* neurochirurgie *f*.
neurosurgical [njʊərəʊ'sɜːdʒɪk(ə)l] *adj* neurochirurgical.
neurotic [njʊ'rɒtɪk] **1** *adj* **(a)** (*person*) névrosé; *F* **he's positively n. about it,** c'est une obsession chez lui; **(b)** (*relating to a neurosis*) névrotique. **2** *n* névrosé, -ée.
neurotically [njʊ'rɒtɪklɪ] *adv* de façon névrotique; **to be n. obsessed with sth,** avoir une obsession névrotique de qch.
neuroticism [njʊ'rɒtɪsɪz(ə)m] *n* névrose *f*.
neurotransmitter [njʊərəʊtrænz'mɪtər] *n Biol* neurotransmetteur *m*.
neuter[1] ['njuːtər] **1** *adj* **(a)** *Gram* neutre; **(b)** *Biol* neutre, asexué. **2** *n* **(a)** *Gram* (genre *m*) neutre *m*; **in the n.,** au neutre; **(b)** animal châtré; (*bee*) abeille asexuée *ou* ouvrière.
neuter[2] *vt Vet* châtrer (*un chat etc*).
neutral ['njuːtr(ə)l] **1** *adj Pol etc* (*colour etc*) neutre; *Phys* (*équilibre*) indifférent; **to remain n.,** rester neutre, garder la neutralité. **2** *n* (État *m*, pays *m*) neutre *m*; (*person*) ressortissant, -ante d'un État neutre; *Aut* point mort; *Aut* **in n.,** au point mort.
neutralism ['njuːtrəlɪsm] *n* neutralisme *m*.
neutralist ['njuːtrəlɪst] *n* neutraliste *mf*.
neutrality [njuː'trælɪtɪ] *n Pol etc* neutralité *f*; *Ch* neutralité, indifférence *f* (*d'un sel*).
neutralization [njuːtrəlaɪ'zeɪʃən] *n* neutralisation *f*.
neutralize ['njuːtrəlaɪz] *vt* (*an opposition, a country*) neutraliser; **to n. one another,** (*of chemical agents*) se neutraliser; (*of forces*) se détruire.
neutrino [njʊ'triːnəʊ] *n Phys* neutrino *m*.
neutron ['njuːtrɒn] *n Nucl Phys El* neutron *m*; **n. bomb,** bombe *f* à neutrons; **n. star,** étoile *f* à neutrons.
Nev *abbr* **Nevada**.
never ['nevər] **1** *adv* **(a)** (ne ...) jamais; **I n. go there,** je n'y vais jamais; **n. again,** jamais plus, plus jamais (... ne); **he n. came back,** il n'est jamais revenu; **n. in (all) my life, n. in all my born days,** jamais de la vie; **that n. to be forgotten day,** ce jour inoubliable; **n. say die!,** accroche-toi!; **(b)** (*emphatic neg*) **I n. expected him to come,** je ne m'attendais pas du tout à ce qu'il vînt; **she n. said a word,** elle n'a pas dit un mot; **you (surely) n. left him all alone!,** ne me dites pas que vous l'avez laissé tout seul!; **(c)** *Arch Lit* **be he n. so brave,** quelque courageux qu'il soit, si courageux soit-il. **2** *int* **well I n. (did)!,** ça par exemple!; **n.!,** pas possible!
never-ending [nevə'rendɪŋ] *adj* perpétuel, éternel, sans fin; (*complaints*) incessant; (*tâche*) interminable; **the noise was n.-e.,** le bruit était incessant; **his sermon last Sunday was n.-e.,** son sermon dimanche dernier était interminable; **housework is n.-e.,** le ménage n'est jamais fini.
nevermore [nevə'mɔːr] *adv Lit* (ne ...) plus jamais, (ne ...) jamais plus; **n.!,** jamais plus!, plus jamais!
never-never ['nevə'nevər] **1** *n Br F* **to buy sth on the n.-n.,** acheter qch à crédit *ou* à tempérament. **2** *adj* **n.-n. land,** pays *m* de légende.
nevertheless [nevəðə'les] *adv* néanmoins, quand même, tout de même, pourtant, malgré tout.
nevus ['niːvəs] *n US* = **NAEVUS**.
new [njuː] **1** *adj* **(a)** nouveau, -elle; (*before masculine noun beginning with vowel or silent h*) nouvel; (*esp brand new, not used*) neuf, *f* neuve; **I need a n. set of teeth,** j'ai besoin d'un nouveau dentier; **I would prefer a NEW set of teeth** *or* **a set of teeth that's n.,** je préférerais un dentier qui soit neuf; **we've moved to a n. house,** (*new to us*) nous avons emménagé dans une nouvelle maison; (*newly built*) nous avons emménagé dans une maison nouvelle *ou* neuve; **we visited a n. country,** (*new to us*) nous avons visité un nouveau pays; **America was a n. country,** l'Amérique était un pays neuf; **n. town,** (*newly built*) ville nouvelle; (*new part of town*) ville neuve; **I felt a n. man,** je me sentais un homme nouveau *ou* neuf; **she's got a n. man,** elle a un nouveau mec; **it's made a n. man of him,** cela a fait de lui un autre homme *ou* un homme nouveau *ou* un homme neuf *ou* un nouvel homme; **he's got a n. style,** (*has changed his style*) il a un nouveau style; (*has a new or original type of style*) il a un style nouveau *ou* neuf; **n. page layout,** nouvelle mise en page; **what's n.?,** quoi de neuf *ou* de nouveau?; **that's nothing n.!,** rien de nouveau à cela!; **it's quite n. to me,** c'est tout nouveau *ou* neuf pour moi; **she's n. to this work,** elle débute dans ce travail; **I'm n. to this town,** je suis nouveau venu dans cette ville; **to be dressed in n. clothes,** être habillé de neuf; *Com* **in n. condition, as n.,** à l'état (de) neuf; **to do sth up like n.,** remettre qch à neuf; **n. ideas,** (*modern ideas*) idées neuves; **a completely n. idea,** une idée tout à fait nouvelle *ou* neuve; **the subject is quite n.,** le sujet n'a pas encore été traité; *Sch* **the n. boys,** les nouveaux; *Mil* **the n. guard,** la garde montante; *Am* **n. math,** *Br* **n. maths,** maths *fpl* modernes; **n. moon,** nouvelle lune; **the n. novel,** le nouveau roman; **n. students,** nouveaux étudiants; **n. wave,** nouvelle vague;
(b) (*recently made etc*) (*pain*) frais, *f* fraîche; (*herbe*) tendre; (*pommes de terre*) nouveau, nouvelle; (*vin*) nouveau, jeune; **n. leaves,** jeunes feuilles;
(c) (*in geographical names*) **N. Brunswick,** Nouveau-Brunswick; **N. Caledonia,** Nouvelle-Calédonie; **N. England,** Nouvelle-Angleterre; **N. Guinea,** Nouvelle-Guinée; **N. Mexico,** Nouveau-Mexique; **N. Orleans,** la Nouvelle-Orléans; **N. York,** New York; **N. Yorker,** New-yorkais, -aise; **N. Zealand,** Nouvelle-Zélande; **N. Zealander,** Néo-Zélandais, -aise.
2 *adv* (*used to form compound adj*) nouvellement; **n. blown,** (*fleur*) frais épanoui; **n. mown hay,** foin fraîchement coupé.
newborn ['njuːbɔːn] *adj* **(a)** nouveau-né; **n. baby,** nouveau-né *m*; **(b)** *Rel* régénéré.
newcomer ['njuːkʌmər] *n* nouveau venu.
newel ['njuːəl] *n Constr etc* **(a)** noyau *m* (*d'escalier tournant*); **(b) n. (post),** pilastre *m* (*de rampe d'escalier*).
newfangled ['njuːfæŋg(ə)ld] *adj* nouveau genre; *Pej* (*word, idea etc*) d'une modernité outrée; **n. gadgets,** gadgets à la dernière mode.
Newfie ['njuːfɪ] *n Can F* Terre-neuvien, -ienne; **N. joke,** = plaisanterie sur les Terre-neuviens.

Newfoundland ['nju:fəndlænd, -lənd, -'faʊndlənd] **1** *n* **(a)** Terre-Neuve; **(b) N. (dog),** chien *m* de Terre-Neuve. **2** *adj* terre-neuve *inv.*

Newfoundlander ['nju:fəndlændər, nju:'faʊndləndər] *n* (*native*) Terre-neuvien, -ienne; (*inhabitant*) habitant, -ante de Terre-Neuve.

newish ['nju:ɪʃ] *adj F* (*car, dress etc*) assez neuf, *f* assez neuve.

newly ['nju:lɪ] *adv* (*usu hyphenated in conjunction with adj before n*) récemment, nouvellement; fraîchement; **to be n. arrived,** être fraîchement arrivé; **the n.-elected members,** les députés nouvellement élus; **to be n. shaven,** être rasé de frais; **n.-painted wall,** mur fraîchement peint; **n.-industrializing country,** pays en voie d'industrialisation.

newlyweds ['nju:lɪwedz] *npl* nouveaux mariés, jeunes mariés.

newness ['nju:nɪs] *n* **(a)** nouveauté *f* (*d'une idée etc*); **(b)** état neuf (*d'un vêtement etc*); **(c)** fraîcheur *f* (*du pain etc*); jeunesse *f* (*du vin*).

news [nju:z] *npl* (*usu with sing verb*) **(a)** nouvelle *f*; nouvelles; **what's the n.?,** quelles nouvelles?, quoi de nouveau *ou* de neuf?; **I've some n. for you,** j'ai une nouvelle à vous annoncer; **have you heard the n.?,** est-ce que vous avez appris la nouvelle?; **that's n. to me,** ça, c'est du nouveau; **a sad piece of n., sad n.,** une triste nouvelle; **no n. is good n.,** pas de nouvelles, bonnes nouvelles; **have I got n. for you!,** j'ai une mauvaise *ou* une bonne nouvelle pour vous!; **n. vendor,** marchand, -ande de journaux;

(b) *Rad TV* **the n.,** les informations *fpl*, les actualités *fpl*; *TV* le téléjournal; **to be in the n.,** être en vedette; *esp Pej* défrayer la chronique; **a city that is in the n. a lot these days,** une ville dont on parle beaucoup ces jours-ci; **he's always in the n.,** on parle toujours de lui; **financial n.,** chronique financière; **sports n.,** chronique des sports; **n. in brief,** faits divers; **the n. headlines,** les principaux titres de l'actualité; **official n.,** communiqué officiel; **n. agency,** agence *f* d'information; **n. bulletin,** bulletin *m* d'informations; **n. desk,** service *m* des informations; *Rad TV & (published)* **n. magazine,** magazine *m* d'information;

(c) (*person, event etc*) sujet *m* propre au reportage; **to make n.,** faire sensation; **she's no longer n.,** on ne parle plus d'elle; **the fact that he's leaving is bad n. for the company,** son départ est mauvais pour la société; **dog bites man is not n.,** un chien qui mord un homme, ça n'a plus d'intérêt; *F* **it's bad n.,** (*poor quality, problematic etc*) c'est de la camelote; *F* **he's bad n.,** (*is a problem, unpopular etc*) c'est un enquiquineur.

newsagent ['nju:zeɪdʒənt] *n* marchand, -ande de journaux, dépositaire *m* de journaux.

newscast ['nju:zkɑ:st] *n Rad TV* informations *fpl.*

newscaster ['nju:zkɑ:stər] *n Rad TV* présentateur, -trice.

newsdealer ['nju:zdi:lər] *n US* = **NEWSAGENT**.

newsflash ['nju:zflæʃ] *n Rad TV* flash *m* d'information.

newshawk, newshound ['nju:zhɔ:k, -haʊnd] *n F* reporter *m*, chasseur *m* de copie.

newsletter ['nju:zletər] *n* bulletin *m* (d'informations), circulaire *f*.

newspaper ['nju:zpeɪpər] *n* journal *m*, -aux; **daily n.,** (journal) quotidien *m*; **weekly n.,** (journal) hebdomadaire *m*; **to work for** *or* **on a n.,** travailler dans *ou* pour un journal; **n. report,** reportage *m*; **n. clippings** *or* **cuttings,** coupures *fpl* de journaux; **n. rack,** porte-journaux *m inv*; **n. office,** bureau *m* de la presse; **n. photographer,** photographe *mf* de presse.

newspaperman ['nju:zpeɪpəmæn], **newspaperwoman** ['nju:zpeɪpəwʊmən] *n* **(a)** *Journ* (*reporter*) journaliste *mf*; (*proprietor*) propriétaire *mf* de journal; **I've been a n. all my life,** j'ai été dans le journalisme toute ma vie; **(b)** *Br* (*vendor*) marchand, -ande de journaux.

newsprint ['nju:zprɪnt] *n* papier *m* (de) journal.

newsreader ['nju:zri:dər] *n Rad TV* présentateur, -trice.

newsreel ['nju:zri:l] *n Cin* actualités *fpl.*

newsroom ['nju:zru:m] *n Journ* salle *f* de rédaction des informations.

newsstand ['nju:zstænd] *n* kiosque *m* à journaux.

newsworthy ['nju:zwɜ:ðɪ] *adj Journ* propre au reportage; qui fera parler, qui fera sensation.

newsy ['nju:zɪ] *adj F* (*letter etc*) plein de nouvelles.

newt [nju:t] *n* (*amphibian*) triton *m*; *Br Sl* **pissed as a n.,** soûl comme un âne.

next [nekst] **1** *adj* **(a)** (*in location*) prochain; **the n. bus stop is ...,** le prochain arrêt de bus est à ...; **the n. room,** la pièce voisine *ou* d'à côté; **it's the n. house,** c'est la maison voisine *ou* d'à côté; **the girl (from) next door,** la jeune fille d'à côté; **he lives n. door (to us),** il habite à côté (de chez nous); **n. door neighbours,** voisins d'à côté *ou* immédiats; **we are n. door neighbours,** nous sommes voisins; **it's n. door to madness,** cela confine à la folie;

(b) (*in time*) (*in future*) prochain; (*in past or in listing or enumerating events*) suivant; **see you n. week,** à la semaine prochaine; **the n. week it rained,** la semaine d'après *ou* suivante il a plu; **I leave next month,** je pars le mois prochain; **the n. month was awful,** le mois suivant fut terrible; **in the n. few weeks we will discover ...,** dans les semaines qui vont suivre nous allons découvrir ...; **in the n. four weeks we were to discover that ...,** dans les quatre semaines suivantes nous devions découvrir que ...; **this time n. year,** dans un an d'ici; **n. Friday, (on) Friday n.,** vendredi prochain; **the n. day,** le lendemain, le jour après; **the n. day but one,** le surlendemain; **(the) n. morning,** le lendemain matin; **the week/year after n.,** dans deux semaines/ans; **n. Easter/summer,** à Pâques prochain/l'été prochain; **from one moment to the n.,** d'un instant à l'autre;

(c) (*in order*) prochain; **the next chapter,** le chapitre suivant; **(the) n. time I see him,** la prochaine fois que je le verrai; **ask the n. person you meet,** demandez à la première personne que vous rencontrerez; **the n. thing is to ...,** maintenant il s'agit de ...; **it's the n. station,** c'est la prochaine gare; **take the n. turning on the right,** prenez le prochain tournant à droite; **your name is n. on the list,** votre nom est le prochain sur la liste; **n. (person) please,** au suivant, s'il vous plaît; **n. to speak is ...,** la parole est maintenant à ...; **who's n.?, whose turn (is it) n.?,** à qui le tour?, c'est à qui?; **your train is the n. but one,** ton train n'est pas le prochain, mais celui d'après; **the n. size larger** *or* **up,** la taille au-dessus; **the n. size smaller** *or* **down,** la taille en-dessus.

2 *adv* **(a)** (*afterwards*) ensuite, après; **what shall we do n.?,** qu'est-ce que nous allons faire maintenant; **what did you do n.?,** qu'avez-vous fait après *ou* ensuite?; *F* **whatever n.!,** par exemple!, et quoi encore!; *F* **what will he do n.!,** que ne fera-t-il pas la prochaine fois!;

(b) (*again*) la prochaine fois; **when I n. saw him, when n. I saw him,** quand je l'ai revu; **when shall we meet n.?,** quand nous reverrons-nous?;

(c) n. to, à côté de; **her room is n. to mine,** sa chambre est à côté de la mienne; **seated n. to me,** assis à côté de moi; **I can't bear wool n. to my skin,** je ne peux pas supporter la laine à même la peau; **I got the n. to last loaf,** j'ai eu l'avant-dernière baguette; **n. to my dog I like my sister best,** après mon chien, c'est ma sœur que je préfère; **I got it for n. to nothing,** je l'ai eu pour presque rien *ou* pour une bouchée de pain; **there's n. to nothing left,** il ne reste presque rien; **there is n. to no evidence,** il n'y a pour ainsi dire pas de preuves; **in n. to no time,** en un rien de temps; *US F* **to get n. to s.o.,** se mettre bien avec qn;

(d) the n. best thing would be to ..., à défaut, le mieux serait de ...; **the n. fastest after the Ferrari was ...,** la voiture la plus rapide après la Ferrari était ...; **he's the n. oldest,** (*of all of them*) c'est le second par ordre d'âge; (*in listing*) c'est lui qui vient avant par ordre d'âge; **who's the n. youngest?,** qui est le suivant par ordre d'âge; **the n. highest building in the world is ...,** le deuxième immeuble dans le monde pour la hauteur, c'est ... .

next-of-kin [nekstəv'kɪn] *n* (*relative*) parent le plus proche; (*used as pl*) la famille; **to inform the n.-of-k.,** prévenir la famille.

NH *abbr* **New Hampshire**.

NHI [eneɪtʃ'aɪ] *n Br* (*abbr* **National Health Insurance**) ≈ S.S. *f*.

NHS [eneɪtʃ'es] *n Br* (*abbr* **National Health Service**) ≈ S.S. *f*.

NI [e'naɪ] *n Br* (*abbr* **National Insurance**) ≈ S.S. *f*.

Niagara [naɪ'æg(ə)rə] *n Geog* Niagara *m*; **the N. Falls,** les chutes *fpl* du Niagara.

nib [nɪb] *n* **(a)** (*of pen*) (bec *m* de) plume *f*; **broad n.,** grosse plume, plume à gros bec; **fine n.,** plume fine, plume à bec fin; **(b)** pointe *f* (*d'outil etc*).

nibble¹ ['nɪb(ə)l] *n* **(a)** (*action*) grignotement *m*; **to have a n. at the cake,** grignoter le gâteau; **(b)** *Fishing* touche *f*; **I didn't get** *or* **have a n. all day,** le poisson n'a pas mordu de toute la journée; **(c)** (*food*) juste de quoi grignoter; petit morceau (*de biscuit*); *F* **nibbles,** amuse-gueules *mpl.*

nibble² **1** *vt* grignoter, mordiller (*qch*); **to n. a biscuit,** grignoter un biscuit. **2** *vi* (*of fish, F of person*) mordre à l'hameçon.

▶**nibble at** *vipo* (*eat*) grignoter (*un biscuit*); **to n. at the**

bait, (*of fish, F of person*) mordre à l'hameçon.
▶**nibble on** *vi po* grignoter (*un biscuit*).
nibbler ['nɪblər] *n* grignoteur, -euse.
nibs [nɪbz] *n F Iron* **his n.,** sa majesté.
NIC [enaɪ'siː] *n abbr* **newly-industrializing country.**
Nicaragua [nɪkə'rægjʊə] *n* Nicaragua *m*.
Nicaraguan [nɪkə'rægjʊən] **1** *adj* nicaraguayen. **2** *n* Nicaraguayen, -enne.
nice [naɪs] *adj* **(a)** (*person*) gentil, *f* gentille, agréable, aimable; (*thing*) joli, bon, *f* bonne; (*soirée*) agréable; **to be n. to s.o.,** se montrer gentil *ou* aimable pour *ou* envers qn; **it is n. of you to ...,** vous êtes bien aimable de ...; **sending flowers was a n. gesture,** c'était gentil d'envoyer des fleurs; **it's not n. of you to make fun of him,** ce n'est pas bien de vous moquer de lui; **he's a n. chap,** c'est un gentil garçon; *Iron* **you're a n. one to talk like that!,** c'est du joli de parler comme ça!; **have a n. day!,** bonne journée!; **it's turned out n. again,** il fait encore beau; **the garden is beginning to look n.,** le jardin s'embellit; **to have a n. long chat,** faire une bonne petite causette; **a n. little sum,** une somme rondelette;
(b) (*intensive*) *F* **n. and handy,** bien commode; **it's n. and cool,** le temps est agréablement frais *ou* d'une fraîcheur agréable; **it's n. and easy,** c'est très facile; **a n. cold drink,** une boisson bien fraîche;
(c) (*respectable*) **n. people,** des gens bien; **not n.,** pas tout à fait convenable; **it's not a n. story,** c'est une histoire peu édifiante;
(d) *Iron* **we ARE in a n. mess!,** nous voilà dans de beaux draps!; **that's a n. way to behave!,** en voilà des manières!;
(e) (*experiment, question etc*) délicat; (*taste etc*) subtil, fin, recherché; (*distinction*) subtil;
(f) *Arch Lit* (*person*) difficile, exigeant; *Old-fashioned* scrupuleux; **he is not too n. about the means,** il n'est pas trop scrupuleux quant aux moyens.
nice-looking ['naɪslʊkɪŋ] *adj* beau, *f* belle, joli.
nicely ['naɪslɪ] *adv* **(a)** (*pleasantly, kindly*) gentiment; (*well*) bien; **everything was n. done,** tout était bien fait; **those will do (very) n.,** ceux-là feront très bien l'affaire; **he spoke very n. about you,** il m'a parlé de vous en très bons termes; **(b)** (*judged*) exactement, avec justesse; **(c)** *Arch Lit* minutieusement, scrupuleusement.
niceness ['naɪsnɪs] *n* **(a)** gentillesse *f*, amabilité *f* (*de qn*); agrément *m*, caractère *m* agréable (*de qch*); **(b)** (*delicacy*) délicatesse *f*; (*of taste, distinction*) subtilité *f*; **(c)** (*person*) *Arch Lit* délicatesse exagérée; *Old-fashioned* scrupulosité *f*.
nicety ['naɪsɪtɪ] *n* **(a)** exactitude *f*, précision *f* (*d'un calcul etc*); subtilité *f*, délicatesse *f* (*d'une question etc*); **to a n.,** exactement, à la perfection; **(b) niceties,** minuties *fpl*, finesses *fpl*; **(c)** = **NICENESS**.
niche [nɪtʃ, niːʃ] *n* niche *f* (*pour une statue etc*); (*on market*) créneau *m*; **to make a n. for oneself,** (trouver à) se caser; **n. market,** créneau spécialisé.
Nicholas ['nɪkələs] *n* Nicolas *m*.
nick¹ [nɪk] *n* **(a)** (*in plank etc*) entaille *f*, encoche *f*; (*in tally stick etc*) encoche; brèche *f* (*au tranchant d'une lame*); **(b) in the n. of time,** fort à propos, juste à temps; **you've come just in the n. of time,** vous tombez bien; **(c)** *F* (*condition*) état *m*; **in good n.,** en bon état; **(d)** *Br Sl* (*prison*) taule *f*; **to take s.o. to the (local) n.,** (*police station*) emmener qn au poste; **(e)** (*in dice games*) coup gagnant.
nick² *vt* **(a)** entailler, encocher (*un bâton etc*); ébrécher (*une lame etc*); biseauter (*les cartes*); anglaiser, niqueter (*la queue d'un cheval, un cheval*); **to n. oneself,** se couper; **(b)** *esp Br Sl* (*of police*) pincer, choper (*qn*); **to get nicked,** se faire pincer *ou* épingler; **(c)** *esp Br Sl* (*steal*) chiper, faucher (*qch*); **(d)** *Am Sl* (*overcharge*) **they've nicked me for 50,** je me suis fait avoir de 50.
Nick [nɪk] *n* (*dimin of* **Nicholas**) = Nicolas *m*; *F* **Old N.,** le diable.
nickel¹ ['nɪk(ə)l] *n* **(a)** *Metal* nickel *m*; **n. plating,** nickelage *m*; **(b)** *Am* pièce *f* de cinq cents.
nickel² *vt* (**-ll-**, *US* **-l-**) (*also* **nickel-plate**) nickeler (*des objets en métal oxydable*).
nickel-and-dime [nɪkelen'daɪm] *adj esp US* (*business operation*) de quatre sous.
nickelling, *US* **nickeling** ['nɪk(ə)lɪŋ] *n* nickelage *m*.
nicker ['nɪkər] *n* (*no pl*) *Br Sl* livre *f* sterling.
nickname¹ ['nɪkneɪm] *n* surnom *m*; (*in derision*) sobriquet *m*; (*shortened name*) diminutif *m*.
nickname² *vt* surnommer (*qn*); (*in derision*) donner un sobriquet à (qn); (*use shortened name*) appeler (*qn*) par *ou* de son diminutif.
nicotine ['nɪkətiːn] *n* nicotine *f*; **n. poisoning,** nicotinisme *m*, tabagisme *m*; **n.-stained,** (*fingers, teeth*) jaune de nicotine.
niece [niːs] *n* nièce *f*.
Nielsen ['niːlsən] *n Am TV* **N. rating,** ≈ Audimat *m*.
niff¹ [nɪf] *n Br Sl* puanteur *f*.
niff² *vi Br Sl* puer.
niffy ['nɪfɪ] *adj Br Sl* puant.
nifty ['nɪftɪ] *adj F* **(a)** (*person*) adroit, débrouillard; (*thing*) commode; **that was a n. piece of driving,** c'était un coup de volant adroit; **a n. idea,** une idée géniale; **it's a very n. little car,** c'est une petite voiture très commode *ou* pratique; **(b)** *Am F* (*dress*) coquet, pimpant.
Niger ['naɪdʒər] *n Geog* **(a)** (*river*) Niger *m*; **(b)** (*country*) (République *f* du) Niger *m*.
Nigeria [naɪ'dʒɪərɪə] *n Geog* Nigeria *m*.
Nigerian [naɪ'dʒɪərɪən] *Geog* **1** *adj* nigérian. **2** *n* Nigérian, -ane.
niggard ['nɪgəd] *n* grippe-sou *m*, *pl* grippe-sou(s), pingre *m*, avare *mf*.
niggardliness ['nɪgədlɪnɪs] *n* (*of person*) avarice *f*; (*of sum*) maigreur *f*.
niggardly ['nɪgədlɪ] **1** *adj* (*person*) ladre, pingre, parcimonieux, mesquin; (*sum, portion*) maigre. **2** *adv* chichement, mesquinement.
nigger ['nɪgər] *n Offensive Sl* nègre *m*, *f* négresse; *F* **there's a n. in the woodpile,** il y a anguille sous roche; **he's the n. in the woodpile,** c'est un empêcheur de tourner en rond.
niggle ['nɪg(ə)l] **1** *vi* (*be overfussy*) couper les cheveux en quatre; **he always has something to n. about,** (*complain*) il a toujours quelque chose à redire. **2** *vt* (*doubt etc*) triturer l'esprit à (*qn*); (*annoy*) embêter; **one thing still niggles me,** il y a quelque chose qui me triture l'esprit; **he keeps niggling me to get it done,** il me casse les pieds sans cesse pour que je le fasse.
niggler ['nɪglər] *n* enquiquineur, -euse.
niggling ['nɪg(ə)lɪŋ] *adj* (*details etc*) insignifiant; (*person*) tatillon, -onne; (*pain*) persistant; (*doubt*) insinuant.
nigh [naɪ] *Arch Lit & Dial* **1** *adv* près, proche; **n. unto death,** près de mourir. **2** *prep* près de, auprès de (*qn, qch*).
night [naɪt] *n* (*hours of darkness*) nuit *f*; (*evening*) soir *m*; **last n.,** la nuit dernière; (*in the evening*) hier (au) soir; **the n. before,** la veille (au soir); **tomorrow n.,** demain soir; **I saw him on Thursday n.,** je l'ai vu jeudi soir; **ten o'clock at n.,** dix heures du soir; **it was a warm n.,** la nuit était douce; **all n. long,** toute la nuit; **good n.!,** bonsoir!, bonne nuit!; **to work day and n.** *or* **n. and day,** travailler nuit et jour; **at n.,** (à) la nuit; (*in the evening*) le soir; **in the n.,** (pendant) la nuit; **to travel by n.** *or* **at n.,** voyager de nuit *ou* la nuit; **we stayed the n. (there),** nous y avons passé la nuit; **the n. sky, the sky at n.,** le ciel nocturne; **to make a n. of it,** sortir faire la fête toute la nuit; **n. is falling,** la nuit tombe, il commence à faire nuit, il se fait nuit; **n. clothes,** vêtements *mpl* de nuit; **n. boat/train,** bateau *m*/train *m* de nuit; **n. work,** travail *m* de nuit; **n. shift,** équipe *f* de nuit; **to be on (the) n. shift,** être de nuit; **n. watch,** garde *f*, veille *f* (de nuit); *Nau* quart *m* de nuit; **n. watchman,** veilleur *m* de nuit, garde *m ou* gardien *m* de nuit; *Av* **n. flight,** vol *m* de nuit; **n. blindness,** héméralopie *f*; *Nau* **n. lights,** feux *mpl* de position; **n. bird,** oiseau *m* de nuit *ou* nocturne; *Fig* **n. owl,** oiseau *m* de nuit; **n. nurse,** infirmier, -ière de garde; **n. safe,** (*outside bank*) coffre *m* de nuit; **n. school,** cours *mpl* du soir; *Am* **n. stick,** (*of policeman*) matraque *f*; *Am* **n. table,** table *f* de chevet; *Th etc* **first n.,** première *f*; **Wagner n.,** soirée (consacrée à) Wagner.
nightcap ['naɪtkæp] *n* **(a)** *F* = boisson (alcoolisée) prise avant de se coucher; **would you like a n.?,** prendrez-vous un verre avant de vous coucher?; **(b)** *Arch* bonnet *m* de nuit.
nightclub ['naɪtklʌb] *n* boîte *f* de nuit.
nightdress ['naɪtdres] *n* chemise *f* de nuit (*de femme, d'enfant*); *Can* jaquette *f*.
nightfall ['naɪtfɔːl] *n* tombée *f* du jour *ou* de la nuit; **at n.,** à la nuit tombante.
nightgown ['naɪtgaʊn] *n* = **NIGHTDRESS**.
nighthawk ['naɪthɔːk] *n F* oiseau *m* de nuit.
nightie ['naɪtɪ] *n F* = **NIGHTDRESS**.
nightingale ['naɪtɪŋgeɪl] *n* (*bird*) rossignol *m*.
nightjar ['naɪtdʒɑːr] *n* (*bird*) engoulevent *m* (d'Europe).
nightlife ['naɪtlaɪf] *n* vie *f ou* activité *f* nocturne; **what's the n. like?,** qu'est-ce qu'on peut faire le soir?; **there's not much n.,** il n'y a pas grand-chose à faire le soir.
night-light ['naɪtlaɪt] *n* veilleuse *f*.
nightlong ['naɪtlɒŋ] *adj* (*veille, fête etc*) qui dure toute la nuit.

nightly ['naɪtlɪ] **1** *adj* de toutes les nuits; de tous les soirs; **n. performance,** représentation *f* tous les soirs, soirée quotidienne; **it's a n. occurrence,** c'est comme ça tous les soirs; **there are n. flights,** il y a des vols toutes les nuits; **it's a n. event,** ça arrive tous les soirs; **he would take his n. stroll,** il faisait sa promenade nocturne. **2** *adv* toutes les nuits; tous les soirs; **performances n.,** représentations tous les soirs.

nightmare ['naɪtmeər] *n* cauchemar *m*; **to give s.o. nightmares,** donner des cauchemars à qn; **getting to work was an absolute n.,** se rendre au travail était un véritable cauchemar; **the prospect was a n. to me,** cette perspective me donnait des cauchemars; **a n. journey,** un voyage cauchemardesque.

nightmarish ['naɪtmeərɪʃ] *adj* qui donne des cauchemars, cauchemardesque.

night-night ['naɪt'naɪt] *int F* bonne nuit.

nights [naɪts] *adv* (*to work*) de nuit.

nightshade ['naɪtʃeɪd] *n* (*plant*) **(black) n.,** morelle noire; **woody n.,** douce-amère *f*, *pl* douces-amères; **deadly n.,** belladone *f*.

nightshirt ['naɪtʃɜːt] *n* chemise *f* de nuit.

night-time ['naɪttaɪm] *n* la nuit; **at n.,** la nuit.

nightwear ['naɪtweər] *n* vêtements *mpl* de nuit.

nihilism ['naɪ(h)ɪlɪz(ə)m] *n Phil Pol* nihilisme *m*.

nihilist ['naɪ(h)ɪlɪst] *n* nihiliste *mf*.

nihilistic [naɪ(h)ɪ'lɪstɪk] *adj* nihiliste.

nil [nɪl] *n* rien *m*; (*on report sheet etc*) néant *m*; *Sp* zéro *m*; **they won three n.,** ils ont gagné par trois (buts) à zéro.

Nile [naɪl] *n* Nil *m*.

nimble ['nɪmb(ə)l] *adj* (*person etc*) agile; (*mind etc*) délié, subtil; **n.(-)fingered,** aux doigts agiles *ou* souples *ou* de fée; **n.(-)footed,** aux pieds agiles *ou* légers.

nimbleness ['nɪmb(ə)lnɪs] *n* agilité *f*, souplesse *f* (*de membres etc*); subtilité *f*, vivacité *f* (*d'esprit etc*).

nimbly ['nɪmb(ə)lɪ] *adv* agilement; légèrement.

nimbus, *pl* **-i, -uses** ['nɪmbəs, -aɪ, -əsɪz] *n* **(a)** *Met* nimbus *m*; **(b)** (*of saint*) nuage lumineux; halo *m*; **(c)** *Art* nimbe *m*, auréole *f*; *Met* auréole *f* (autour de la lune).

NIMBY ['nɪmbɪ] *n F* (*abbr* **not in my back yard**) = personne qui s'oppose à la construction d'une centrale nucléaire etc dans sa commune.

nincompoop ['nɪŋkəmpuːp] *n F* nigaud, -aude, niais, -aise.

nine [naɪn] *n* neuf *m*; **n. times out of ten,** neuf fois sur dix; **to have n. lives,** (*person*) avoir l'âme chevillée au corps; *Cards* **the n. of diamonds,** le neuf de carreau; **to dial** *Br* **999** *or Am* **911,** appeler les urgences; *F* **dressed up to the nines,** sur son trente et un; **to work n. to five,** travailler de 9 à 5; **I couldn't stand a n. to five job,** je ne supporterais pas de travailler de 9 à 5.

ninefold ['naɪnfəʊld] **1** *adj* **there's been a n. increase in ...,** ... a été multiplié par neuf. **2** *adv* neuf fois autant; **to increase n.,** (se) multiplier par neuf.

ninepin ['naɪnpɪn] *n* **(a)** (*game*) **ninepins,** (jeu *m* de) quilles *fpl*; **(b)** (*pin*) quille *f*; *F* **to go down like ninepins,** tomber comme des mouches.

nineteen [naɪn'tiːn] *n* dix-neuf *m*; **she is n.,** elle a dix-neuf ans; *F* **to talk n. to the dozen,** bavarder comme une pie.

nineteenth [naɪn'tiːnθ] **1** *adj* dix-neuvième; *Hum* **the n. hole,** (*of golf course*) le bar du golf. **2** *n* (*fraction*) dix-neuvième *m*.

ninetieth ['naɪntɪɪθ] *adj* quatre-vingt-dixième.

ninety ['naɪntɪ] *n* quatre-vingt-dix *m*; *Belg Swiss* nonante; **n.-one/n.-nine,** quatre-vingt-onze/quatre-vingt-dix-neuf; **in the nineties,** dans les années quatre-vingt-dix; **she's in her nineties,** elle est nonagénaire; *Jur* **n.-nine years' lease,** bail *m* emphytéotique de quatre-vingt-dix-neuf ans.

ninny ['nɪnɪ] *n Old-fashioned F* niais, -aise, nigaud, -aude.

ninth [naɪnθ] **1** *adj* neuvième. **2** *n* **(a)** (*fraction*) neuvième *m*; **(b)** *Mus* neuvième *f*.

nip[1] [nɪp] *n* **(a)** pincement *m*, pinçade *f*; **to give s.o. a n.,** pincer qn; **(b)** morsure *f* (*de la gelée, du froid*); (*frost*) coup *m* de gelée; **the n. of the morning air,** le froid *ou* le piquant du petit jour; *F* **there's a n. in the air,** ça pince, l'air est piquant.

nip[2] *v* (**-pp-**) **1** *vt* **(a)** pincer; **to n. one's finger,** se pincer le doigt; **(b)** pincer, éborgner (*des bourgeons etc*); *F* **to n. in the bud,** écraser *ou* détruire *ou* étouffer (*qch*) dans l'œuf; **(c)** (*of cold, frost*) pincer, piquer (*la figure, les doigts etc*); brûler (*les bourgeons etc*); **nipped by the frost,** brûlé par la gelée; **(d)** *Sl* (*snatch, steal*) carotter, faucher. **2** *vi F* (*go quickly*) **just n. across** *or* **along** *or* **down to the baker's,** cours vite chez le boulanger, fais donc un saut chez le boulanger; **to n. in and out of the traffic,** se faufiler adroitement parmi les voitures.

nip[3] *n F* goutte *f*, petit verre, doigt *m* (*de cognac etc*); **to have** *or* **take a n.,** boire *ou* prendre une goutte.

nip[4] *vi* (**-pp-**) *F* boire la goutte, siroter.

Nip [nɪp] *n Br Offensive Sl* jap *mf*.

►**nip in** *vi F* **I just nipped in to see him,** je suis entré juste un instant pour le voir; **if you're passing, do n. in and see us,** si vous passez par ici, rendez-nous donc une petite visite; **as I was passing Harrods I just nipped in and bought ...,** alors que je passais devant Harrods, je suis entré en coup de vent et j'ai acheté ...; **he nipped into the pub,** il s'engouffra dans le pub; **she saw a parking place and quickly nipped in,** elle a vu une place libre et elle s'est empressée de la prendre; **could I just n. in in front of you?,** (*in queue etc*) puis-je vous passer devant?

►**nip off 1** *vi F* filer, s'esquiver. **2** *vtsep* enlever, couper (*qch*) en le pinçant.

►**nip out** *vi F* sortir; **he's just nipped out for a second,** (*from house, office etc*) il est sorti un instant; **I'll n. out and buy a paper,** je sors acheter un journal.

nipper ['nɪpər] *n* **(a)** *Br F* gamin, -ine, gosse *mf*; **(b)** pince *f* (*d'un homard etc*); **(c)** (*usu pl*) **(pair of) nippers,** pince(s) *f(pl)* (de serrage), pincette(s) *f(pl)*, tenaille(s) *f(pl)*.

nipple ['nɪp(ə)l] *n* **(a)** *Anat* mamelon *m*, bout *m* de sein; tétine *f* (*de biberon*); **(b)** *Geog* mamelon *m*; **(c)** *Tech* raccord *m*, jonction *f* (*d'une conduite de vapeur etc*); *MecE* graisseur *m*.

nippy ['nɪpɪ] *adj F* **(a)** *Br* vif, *f* vive; rapide; **look n.!,** grouille-toi!; **a n. little car,** une petite voiture nerveuse; **(b)** (*vent etc*) froid, piquant; **it's a bit n. today,** il fait un froid *ou* un vent vif *ou* mordant aujourd'hui; **(c)** (*dog*) qui a la dent leste; **(d)** (*flavour*) fort.

nirvana [nɪə'vɑːnə, nɜː-] *n Rel* nirvâna *m*.

nisi ['naɪsaɪ] *adj Jur* (*decree, order etc*) provisoire; (*decision*) rendu sous condition.

Nissen ['nɪs(ə)n] *n* **N. hut,** hutte préfabriquée (en tôle).

nit [nɪt] *n* **(a)** lente *f*; **to have nits,** avoir des poux; **(b)** *F* (*person*) nigaud, -aude, andouille *f*; **you silly n.!,** crétin!

niter ['naɪtər] *n US* = **NITRE.**

nitery ['naɪtərɪ] *n US F* boîte *f* de nuit.

nit-pick ['nɪtpɪk] *vi F* chercher la petite bête, chipoter, chinoiser.

nit-picker ['nɪtpɪkər] *n F* chipoteur, -euse, Chinois, -oise.

nit-picking ['nɪtpɪkɪŋ] *F* **1** *n* chipotage *m*, chinoiserie *f*. **2** *adj* (*attitude etc*) chipoteur.

nitrate ['naɪtreɪt] *n Ch* nitrate *m* (*d'argent etc*); **potassium n.,** nitrate de potassium, salpêtre *m*; *Agr* **n. fertilizers,** *F* **nitrates,** engrais azotés.

nitre, *US* **niter** ['naɪtər] *n* salpêtre *m*.

nitric ['naɪtrɪk] *adj Ch* (*oxyde etc*) nitrique; **n. acid,** acide *m* (trioxo)nitrique; *Com* eau-forte *f*.

nitro ['naɪtrəʊ] *n Sl* = **NITROGLYCERIN(E).**

nitrogen ['naɪtrədʒən] *n Ch* azote *m*; **to fix n.,** (*of plant*) fixer l'azote; **n. dioxide,** dioxyde *m* d'azote.

nitroglycerin(e) [naɪtrəʊ'glɪsəriːn] *n* (*explosive*) nitroglycérine *f*.

nitrous ['naɪtrəs] *adj* (*oxyde etc*) nitreux, d'azote.

nitty-gritty ['nɪtɪ'grɪtɪ] *n F* (fin) fond *m*, tréfonds *m* (*d'une affaire*); **when you get down to the n.-g.,** quand on va au fond des choses.

nitwit ['nɪtwɪt] *n F* idiot, -ote, imbécile *mf*.

nix[1] [nɪks] *Am F* **1** *n* rien *m* (du tout), *Sl* que dalle. **2** *int* rien à faire!

nix[2] *vt Am F* refuser, rejeter (*un projet, une proposition*).

NJ *abbr* **New Jersey.**

NM *abbr* **New Mexico.**

NMR [ene'mɑːr] *n Med* (*abbr* **nuclear magnetic resonance**) RMN *f*.

no [nəʊ] **1** *adj* **(a)** (*not any*) pas de, aucun (*with* **ne** *expressed or understood*); **he has no bread,** il n'a pas de pain; **this fact is of no importance whatever,** ce fait n'a aucune importance; **I have no intention of doing it,** je n'ai aucune intention de le faire; **no father was ever more indulgent,** jamais père ne fut plus indulgent; **it's no distance,** ce n'est pas loin; **I am in no way surprised,** je n'en suis aucunement étonné; **no nonsense!,** pas de bêtises!; **no smoking,** défense de fumer; **no man's land,** terrains *mpl* vagues; *Mil* no man's land *m*, zone *f* neutre;

(b) (*not at all*) ne ... pas (du tout); **it's no easy job,** ce n'est pas une tâche facile; **he's no artist,** il n'est pas artiste; **he's no friend of mine,** il n'est pas de mes amis, tant s'en faut; *Cr etc* **no ball,** balle nulle; *F* **no way!,** pas question!; *F* **no way am I/was I going to work on a Saturday,** il n'est pas/n'était pas question que je travaille samedi;

(c) (*with gerund*) ne ... pas; **there's no pleasing him,** il n'y a pas moyen de le satisfaire; **there's no getting out of it,** impossible de s'en tirer.

2 *adv* **(a)** (*with comparatives*) ne ... plus, ne ... pas; **I'm no taller than he (is),** je ne suis pas plus grand que lui; **how is she? — no better,** comment va-t-elle? — pas mieux; **no less that £100,** pas moins de 100 livres; **he's no longer here,** il n'est plus ici;

(b) (*answer*) non; **no, no you're wrong!,** mais non, mais non, vous vous trompez!; **to say no,** dire non; (*deny*) dire que non;

(c) *Arch Lit & Scot* **pleasant or no, it's true,** agréable ou non, c'est vrai; **whether or no,** que cela soit ou non.

3 *n* (*pl* **noes**) non *m inv*; **she won't take no for an answer,** elle n'acceptera pas de refus; **ayes and noes,** (*in voting*) votes *mpl ou* voix *fpl* pour et contre; **the noes have it,** c'est le non qui l'emporte.

No., no. (*abbr* **number**) No, N°, n°.

NO (*abbr* **New Orleans**) Nouvelle-Orléans.

Noah ['nəʊə] *n Bible* Noé *m*; **N.'s ark,** l'arche *f* de Noé.

nob¹ [nɒb] *n Sl* (*head*) caboche *f*.

nob² *n esp Br Sl* aristo *m*; **the nobs,** les rupins *mpl*.

nobble ['nɒb(ə)l] *vt Sl* **(a)** *Horseracing* doper (*un cheval*) (avant la course); *Fig* **to n. s.o.'s chances of doing sth,** bousiller *ou* saboter les chances que qn a de faire qch; **(b)** (*suborn*) soudoyer, acheter (*qn, un journal etc*); **(c)** (*steal*) faucher, filouter, voler (*qch*); **(d)** (*grab*) pincer, choper (*un voleur*); attraper (*qn*) (au passage).

nobility [nəʊ'bɪlɪtɪ] *n* **(a)** noblesse *f* (*de rang, de cœur etc*); *Hist* **patent of n.,** lettres *fpl* d'anoblissement; **(b) the n.,** la noblesse.

noble ['nəʊb(ə)l] **1** *adj* **(a)** (*naissance, personne etc*) noble; **to be of n. descent** *or* **birth,** être de naissance noble; **(b)** (*sentiment etc*) noble, sublime; *F Hum* **I'll be n. and do the washing up,** je vais me montrer grand seigneur et faire la vaisselle; *F Hum* **that's very n. of you,** c'est très généreux *ou* charitable de ta part; **the n. art,** le noble art; **n. soul,** grande âme; **(c)** (*monument, proportions etc*) empreint de grandeur; (*montagne*) altier, imposant; (*édifice*) aux dimensions impressionnantes; **n. wine,** grand vin; **(d)** (*of metals, stones*) noble, précieux; *Ch* **n. gas,** gaz *m* rare. **2** *n* noble *m*, aristocrate *mf*.

nobleman, *pl* **-men** ['nəʊb(ə)lmən] *n* noble *m*, aristocrate *m*.

nobleminded [nəʊb(ə)l'maɪndɪd] *adj* (*person*) magnanime, aux nobles sentiments.

nobleness ['nəʊb(ə)lnɪs] *n* **(a)** noblesse *f* (*de naissance etc*); **(b)** noblesse *f*, magnanimité *f* (*d'esprit, d'une action etc*); grandeur *f* (*d'âme*); **(c)** proportions *fpl* superbes *ou* magnifiques (*d'une statue, d'un cheval etc*); dimensions impressionnantes (*d'un édifice etc*).

noblewoman, *pl* **-women** ['nəʊb(ə)lwʊmən, -wɪmɪn] *n* (femme *f*) noble *f*, aristocrate *f*.

nobly ['nəʊb(ə)lɪ] *adv* **(a)** noblement; **n. born,** noble de naissance; *F Hum* **he n. gave up his weekends,** il a généreusement renoncé à ses week-ends; **(b)** magnifiquement, superbement (*proportionné etc*).

nobody ['nəʊbədɪ] **1** *pron* personne, nul, aucun (*with* **ne** *expressed or understood*); **n. spoke to me,** personne ne m'a parlé; **who's there? — n.,** qui est là? — personne; **n. knows it,** personne ne le sait; **n. is perfect,** nul n'est parfait; **n. was more surprised than me** *or* **than I (was),** personne n'a été plus étonné que moi; **n. who was there heard anything,** aucun de ceux *ou* personne parmi tous ceux qui étaient là n'a rien entendu; **there was n. there** *or* **about,** il n'y avait personne (là); **n. else,** personne d'autre; *F* **like n.'s business,** comme personne *ou* pas un; **the dogs were barking like n.'s business,** les chiens aboyaient à vous rompre les tympans; **she's n.'s fool,** on ne la lui fait pas; **when he was n.,** alors qu'il était encore inconnu. **2** *n* (*person*) nullité *f*, zéro *m*; **they're (mere) nobodies,** ce sont des gens de rien.

no-claim [nəʊ'kleɪm] *n* (*in car insurance*) **no-c. bonus,** bonification *f* pour non-sinistre.

noctambulism [nɒk'tæmbjʊlɪz(ə)m] *n* somnambulisme *m*.

nocturnal [nɒk'tɜːn(ə)l] *adj* nocturne.

nocturnally [nɒk'tɜːn(ə)lɪ] *adv* **a n. active animal,** un animal nocturne *ou* de nuit *ou* qui vit la nuit.

nocturne ['nɒktɜːn] *n* **(a)** *Mus* nocturne *m*; **(b)** *Art* effet *m* de nuit.

nod¹ [nɒd] *n* **(a)** inclination *f* de la tête; (*of consent*) signe *m* d'assentiment, signe de tête affirmatif; (*of command*) signe de tête (impératif); **to answer with a n.,** répondre d'une inclination de tête; *Parl etc F* **on the n.,** sans débats; **a n. is as good as a wink,** pas besoin d'en dire davantage *ou* plus(, on a compris); **(b)** (*greeting*) signe *m* de la tête; **she gave me a n.,** elle m'a fait un petit signe de la tête; **(c) the land of N.,** le pays des songes; *Hum* **to be in the land of N.,** être endormi.

nod² *v* (**-dd-**) **1** *vt* **to n. one's head,** faire un signe de tête (de haut en bas), incliner la tête; **to n. assent,** faire signe que oui, consentir d'un signe de tête. **2** *vi* **(a)** (*in assent*) faire signe que oui, consentir d'un signe de tête; **(b)** (*in sleep*) dodeliner (de) la tête, somnoler, sommeiller; **(c)** (*of plumes etc*) ballotter, danser.

▶**nod off** *vi F* s'endormir.

nodal ['nəʊd(ə)l] *adj Opt Phys* nodal, -aux.

nodding ['nɒdɪŋ] *n* inclination *f* de tête; **to be on n. terms** *or* **have a n. acquaintance with s.o.,** connaître qn de vue.

noddle ['nɒd(ə)l] *n esp Br F* (*head, intelligence*) caboche *f*; **use the n.!,** fais marcher ta caboche *ou* ton ciboulot!

node [nəʊd] *n Astron Math Phys* nœud *m*, point nodal (*d'une orbite d'astre, d'une courbe etc*); *Bot* nœud *m* (*d'un tronc d'arbre etc*); *Med* nœud, nodosité *f*; **lymph n.,** ganglion *m* lymphatique.

nodular ['nɒdjʊlər] *adj Geol Med etc* nodulaire.

nodule ['nɒdjuːl] *n Geol Med Bot* nodule *m*.

Noël [nəʊ'el] *n* **(a)** (*Christmas*) Noël *m*; **(b)** *Arch* (*carol*) Noël *m*.

no-frills [nəʊ'frɪls] *adj* (*airline, travel*) sans prestation de services; (*insurance policy etc*) de base.

nog [nɒg] *n* (*drink*) **egg n.,** lait *m* de poule.

noggin ['nɒgɪn] *n* **(a)** (*container*) (petit) pot *m*; **to have a n.,** prendre un verre; **(b)** *F* (*head*) caboche *f*.

no-go ['nəʊ'gəʊ] *adj* **no-go areas,** = régions où l'autorité du gouvernement est impuissante ou n'est pas reconnue; **this is a no-go area,** c'est un endroit défendu (**for,** à).

no-good ['nəʊgʊd] *F* **1** *adj* bon à rien. **2** *n* vaurien, -ienne.

no-hoper [nəʊ'həʊpər] *n* tocard, -arde; **to be a no-h.,** n'avoir aucune chance (de gagner).

nohow ['nəʊhaʊ] *adv Sl* aucunement, en aucune façon.

noise [nɔɪz] *n* **(a)** (*very loud*) bruit *m*, tapage *m*, vacarme *m*; **n. abatement campaign,** campagne *f ou* lutte *f* contre le bruit; **to make a n.,** faire du bruit *ou* du vacarme *ou* du tapage; *F* (*complain*) faire parler de soi; *F* **the big n.,** le grand manitou (*de l'entreprise*); *F* **shut** *or* **hold your n.!,** ferme-la!; **(b)** (*sound*) bruit *m*, son *m*; *Rad Electron etc* bruit, parasite(s)*m*(*pl*); **she's making noises about retiring,** elle donne à entendre qu'elle va prendre sa retraite; **clicking n.,** cliquetis *m*; **tinkling n.,** tintement *m*; **background n.,** bruit de fond; **n. level,** niveau *m* de bruit.

noiseless ['nɔɪzlɪs] *adj* sans bruit; (*appareil*) silencieux; **with n. tread,** à pas feutrés.

noiselessly ['nɔɪzlɪslɪ] *adv* sans bruit, silencieusement.

noiselessness ['nɔɪzlɪsnɪs] *n* silence *f*, absence *f* de bruit.

noisily ['nɔɪzɪlɪ] *adv* bruyamment, avec grand bruit.

noisiness ['nɔɪzɪnɪs] *n* caractère bruyant, caractère tapageur (*de qn, qch*); turbulence *f* (*des enfants etc*); tintamarre *m* (*des rues*).

noisome ['nɔɪsəm] *adj* **(a)** (*smell*) puant, fétide; **(b)** (*plant, germ*) nocif, nuisible.

noisy ['nɔɪzɪ] *adj* bruyant, tapageur; (*child*) turbulent; (*crowd, street*) tumultueux; **to be n.,** (*of person*) faire du bruit *ou* du tapage *ou* du vacarme.

nomad ['nəʊmæd] *adj & n* nomade *mf*.

nomadic [nəʊ'mædɪk] *adj* nomade.

nom de plume ['nɒmdə'pluːm] *n* (*pl* **noms de plume**) nom *m* de plume, pseudonyme *m* (d'un auteur).

nomenclature [nəʊ'menklətʃər] *n* nomenclature *f*.

nominal ['nɒmɪn(ə)l] *adj* (*in name only*) nominal, -aux; **to be the n. head,** n'être chef que de nom; **n. rent,** loyer insignifiant; **n. price,** prix fictif; **n. value,** valeur nominale.

nominally ['nɒmɪn(ə)lɪ] *adv* (*in name*) de nom.

nominate ['nɒmɪneɪt] *vt* nommer, choisir, désigner (*qn*); proposer, présenter la candidature de (*qn*); **to n. s.o. to** *or* **for a post,** nommer qn à un emploi.

nomination [nɒmɪ'neɪʃən] *n* **(a)** nomination *f* (*de qn à un emploi etc*); **(b)** *Pol* investiture *f* (*d'un candidat*).

nominative ['nɒmɪnətɪv] *Gram* **1** *n* nominatif *m*; **in the n.,** au nominatif. **2** *adj* nominatif.

nominator ['nɒmɪneɪtər] *n* présentateur, -trice.

nominee [nɒmɪ'niː] *n* candidat, -ate, désigné, -ée.

non- [nɒn] *pref* non-; in-; sans; peu.

nonabsorbent [nɒnəb'zɔːbənt] *adj* imperméable.

nonacceptance [nɒnək'septəns] *n Com etc* refus *m* d'acceptation (*d'un effet, d'un traité*).

nonagenarian [nəʊnədʒɪ'neərɪən] *adj & n* nonagénaire *mf*.

nonaggression [nɒnəˈgreʃən] *n* non-agression *f*; **n. pact,** pacte *m* de non-agression.
nonalcoholic [nɒnælkəˈhɒlɪk] *adj* (*drink*) non alcoolisé.
nonaligned [nɒnəˈlaɪnd] *adj Pol* (*pays*) non aligné.
nonalignment [nɒnəˈlaɪnmənt] *n Pol* non-alignement *m*.
nonappearance [nɒnəˈpɪərəns] *n* (*of person*) défaut *m* à comparaître.
nonarrival [nɒnəˈraɪv(ə)l] *n* non-arrivée *f*.
nonattendance [nɒnəˈtendəns] *n* absence *f*.
nonce [nɒns] *n* **(a) for the n.,** pour la circonstance, pour l'occasion; **n. word,** mot créé pour l'occasion, mot de circonstance; **(b)** *Br Sl* (*rapist*) violeur *m*.
nonchalance [ˈnɒnʃələns] *n* nonchalance *f*.
nonchalant [ˈnɒnʃələnt] *adj* nonchalant.
nonchalantly [nɒnʃəˈləntlɪ] *adv* nonchalamment.
noncombatant [nɒnˈkɒmbətənt] *adj & n Mil* noncombattant *m*.
noncommissioned [ˈnɒnkəˈmɪʃənd] *adj Mil* sans brevet; **n. officer,** sous-officier *m*.
noncommittal [nɒnkəˈmɪt(ə)l] *adj* (*of answer etc*) qui n'engage à rien, diplomatique; **to be n.,** (*when answering*) observer une prudente réserve, être très réservé.
noncompletion [nɒnkəmˈpliːʃən] *n* non-achèvement *m* (*d'un travail*); non-exécution *f* (*d'un contrat*).
noncompliance [nɒnkəmˈplaɪəns] *n* refus *m* (de consentement); **n. with an order,** refus d'obéissance à un ordre.
nonconductor [nɒnkənˈdʌktər] *n Phys* non-conducteur *m*, mauvais conducteur; *El* isolant *m*.
nonconformism [nɒnkənˈfɔːmɪz(ə)m] *n* non-conformisme *m*.
nonconformist [nɒnkənˈfɔːmɪst] *adj & n* nonconformiste *mf*.
nonconformity [nɒnkənˈfɔːmɪtɪ] *n* non-conformité *f*.
noncontributory [nɒnkənˈtrɪbjʊt(ə)rɪ] *adj* (*caisse de retraite etc*) sans versements de la part des bénéficiaires.
nondescript [ˈnɒndɪskrɪpt] *adj* (*personne, chose*) quelconque; (*costume*) hétéroclite.
nondestructive [nɒndɪˈstrʌktɪv] *adj* (*test*) non destructif.
nondetachable [nɒndɪˈtætʃəb(ə)l] *adj* inamovible.
nondirectional [nɒndəˈrekʃən(ə)l, -dɪ-] *adj Electron Rad* non directionnel.
non-drip [nɒnˈdrɪp] *adj* (*paint*) qui ne coule pas.
none [nʌn] **1** *pron* **(a)** (*not any*) aucun; **n. of you can tell me,** personne *ou* aucun d'entre vous ne peut me dire; **n. of this concerns me,** rien de ceci ne me regarde; **no news today? — n.,** pas de nouvelles aujourd'hui? — aucune(s); **n. at all,** pas un(e) seul(e); **n. of these vegetables are** *or esp Fml* **is worth keeping,** tous ces légumes sont bons à jeter; **n. of the milk was still fresh,** tout le lait avait tourné; **how much of the wood did you use? — n. of it,** quelle quantité du bois avez-vous employée? — pas un seul morceau; **n. of your impudence!,** pas d'insolences de votre part!; *F* **n. of that!,** pas de ça!; *Arch* **answer came there n.,** de réponse il n'en arriva point;
(b) (*no-one*) personne, nul; **she is aware, n. better, that ...,** elle sait mieux que personne que ...; **the visitor was n. other than the king,** le visiteur n'était autre que le roi;
(c) *Admin* (*in schedules etc*) **n.,** néant.
2 *adv* **(a) I like him n. the better/worse for that,** je ne l'en aime pas plus/moins;
(b) he was n. too soon, il est arrivé juste à temps; **she was n. too happy about it,** elle n'en était pas trop contente; **his position is n. too secure,** sa position n'est rien moins qu'assurée.
nonentity [nɒˈnentɪtɪ] *n* (*person*) personne insignifiante *ou* de peu d'importance.
nonessential [nɒnɪˈsenʃəl] **1** *adj* non essentiel. **2** *n* (*usu pl*) **nonessentials,** superflu *m*; accessoire(s) *m(pl)*; **if you're travelling light forget the nonessentials,** si tu voyages avec peu de bagages, n'emporte rien de superflu.
nonetheless [nʌnðəˈles] *adv* = **NEVERTHELESS**.
nonevent [nɒnɪˈvent] *n F* événement manqué.
nonexecutive [nɒnɪgˈzekjʊtɪv] *n* **n. director,** = administrateur à temps partiel à titre consultatif.
nonexistence [nɒnɪgˈzɪstəns] *n* non-existence *f*, non-être *m*, néant *m*.
nonexistent [nɒnɪgˈzɪstənt] *adj* non-existant, inexistant.
nonferrous [nɒnˈferəs] *adj* non-ferreux.
non-fiction [nɒnˈfɪkʃən] *n* **n.-f. (books),** ouvrages généraux.
non(in)flammable [nɒn(ɪn)ˈflæməb(ə)l] *adj* ininflammable.
nonintervention [nɒnɪntəˈvenʃən] *n Pol* nonintervention *f*.
noninterventionist [nɒnɪntəˈvenʃənɪst] *adj Pol* (*policy*) non interventionniste, de non-intervention.
noniron [nɒnˈaɪən] *adj Tex* lavé-repassé *inv*.
nonmalignant [nɒnməˈlɪgnənt] *adj Med* bénin.
nonmember [nɒnˈmembər] *n* (*at club etc*) invité, -ée; **open to n.-members,** ouvert au public.
non-negotiable [nɒnnɪˈgəʊʃɪəb(ə)l] *adj* (*billet etc*) nonnégociable.
non-nuclear [nɒnˈnjuːklɪər] *adj* (*country*) non-nucléarisé; (*war*) non-nucléaire.
no-no [ˈnəʊnəʊ] *n F* **that's a no-no,** c'est défendu; **ice-cream is a no-no,** (*if you want to lose weight*) la glace est à bannir; **criticizing his cooking is a no-no,** (*if you want to remain friends*) critiquer sa cuisine est fortement déconseillé.
nonobservance [nɒnəbˈzɜːvəns] *n* inobservance *f* (*des lois, du carême etc*).
no-nonsense [nəʊˈnɒnsəns] *adj* (*approach*) direct; **she's a very no-n. kind of person,** c'est quelqu'un de très direct *ou* qui ne plaisante pas.
nonpareil [ˈnɒnpəreɪl] *Lit* **1** *n* personne *ou* chose, sans pareille. **2** *adj* incomparable, sans égal.
nonparticipating [nɒnpɑːˈtɪsɪpeɪtɪŋ] *adj St Exch* (*share*) sans droit de participation.
nonpartisan [nɒnˈpɑːtɪzæn] *adj* neutre.
nonpayment [nɒnˈpeɪmənt] *n* non-paiement *m*.
nonperformance [nɒnpəˈfɔːməns] *n* non-exécution *f*, inexécution *f* (*d'un contrat etc*).
nonplus [nɒnˈplʌs] *vt* (**-ss-**) confondre, interdire, interloquer (*qn*); **to be nonplussed,** être désemparé.
nonpoisonous [nɒnˈpɔɪz(ə)nəs] *adj* non toxique; (*snake*) non venimeux; (*mushroom*) non vénéneux.
non-profit-making [nɒnˈprɒfɪtmeɪkɪŋ], *Am* **nonprofit** [nɒnˈprɒfɪt] *adj* (*association*) sans but lucratif.
nonproliferation [nɒnprəlɪfəˈreɪʃən] *n* (*of nuclear weapons*) non-prolifération *f*; **n. treaty,** traité *m* de nonprolifération.
nonrecurring [nɒnrɪˈkɜːrɪŋ] *adj* exceptionnel, extraordinaire; **n.-r. expenditure,** frais *mpl ou* dépenses *fpl* extraordinaires.
nonresident [nɒnˈrezɪdənt] **1** *n* non-résident *m*; *Sch etc* externe *mf*; (*in hotel*) client, -ente de passage; **open to nonresidents,** (*hotel*) ouvert aux hôtes de passage. **2** *adj* non-résident.
nonreturnable [nɒnrɪˈtɜːnəb(ə)l] *adj* (*bottle*) non consigné; (*deposit for holiday etc*) non remboursable.
nonscheduled [nɒnˈʃedjuːld] *adj* (*flight*) spécial.
nonsectarian [nɒnsekˈteərɪən] *adj* pas sectaire, libéral.
nonsense [ˈnɒns(ə)ns] **1** *n* bêtises *fpl*; **a piece of n.,** une bêtise, une absurdité; **to talk (a lot of) n.,** dire des betises *ou* des sottises; **it's n. to think that ...,** il est absurde de penser que ...; **the Government's action makes a n. of their promises,** l'action du Gouvernement rend absurdes ses promesses; **I won't stand any n.,** je ne supporterai aucune imbécillité; **there's no n. about her,** elle ne plaisante pas; **n. verse,** vers *mpl* amphigouriques; **n. rhyme,** petit poème comique et absurde. **2** *int* **n.!,** quelle(s) blague(s)!
nonsensical [nɒnˈsensɪk(ə)l] *adj* (*speech, reason etc*) absurde, qui n'a pas de sens.
non sequitur [nɒnˈsekwɪtər] *n* (*conclusion*) *& Phil* **his conversation was full of non sequiturs,** il n'y avait pas de suite dans sa conversation; **that's a non s.,** ça manque de suite.
nonshrink [nɒnˈʃrɪŋk] *adj* irrétrécissable.
nonskid [nɒnˈskɪd] *adj* antidérapant; **n. tyre,** (pneu *m*) antidérapant *m*.
nonsmoker [nɒnˈsməʊkər] *n* **(a)** non-fumeur *m*; **she's been a n. all her life,** elle n'a jamais fumé de sa vie; **(b)** *Rail* compartiment *m* non-fumeurs.
nonsmoking [nɒnˈsməʊkɪŋ], **no-smoking** [ˈnəʊsməʊkɪŋ] *adj Rail Av* (*compartiment, zone*) non-fumeurs.
nonstandard [nɒnˈstændəd] *adj* (*size etc*) spécial, -aux.
nonstarter [nɒnˈstɑːtər] *n Sp etc* non-partant *m*; *F* **the project's a n.,** le projet n'a aucune chance *ou F* est fichu d'avance.
nonstick [ˈnɒnˈstɪk] *adj* (*casserole*) avec revêtement antiadhésif, qui n'attache pas.
nonstop [ˈnɒnˈstɒp] **1** *adj* (*train*) direct; (*trajet*) sans arrêt; *Av* (*vol*) sans escale; *Cin* (*spectacle*) permanent. **2** *adv* (*to talk*) sans arrêt; **we flew to Sydney n.,** nous avons fait un vol sans escale jusqu'à Sydney.
nontaxable [nɒnˈtæksəb(ə)l] *adj Admin* (*revenu etc*) non imposable.

nontransferable [nɒn'trænsfərəb(ə)l] *adj* non transmissible, incessible; *(share)* nominatif.
non-U [nɒn'juː] *adj Br F* = pas classe.
nonunion [nɒn'juːnjən] *adj (ouvrier)* non syndiqué.
nonverbal [nɒn'vɜːb(ə)l] *adj* **n. communication,** communication non verbale.
nonvintage [nɒn'vɪntɪdʒ] *adj (wine)* non millésimé.
nonviolence [nɒn'vaɪələns] *n* non-violence *f*.
nonviolent [nɒn'vaɪələnt] *adj (mouvement etc)* non-violent.
nonvoting [nɒn'vəʊtɪŋ] *adj Fin (share)* sans droit de vote.
non-White [nɒn'waɪt] *adj & n (in S. Africa)* (personne *f*) de couleur.
noodle ['nuːd(ə)l] *n* **(a)** *Culin (usu pl)* **noodles,** nouilles *fpl*; **(b)** *F (simpleton)* niais, -aise, nigaud, -aude, nouille *f*.
nook [nʊk] *n* **(a)** *(corner)* coin *m*, recoin *m*; renfoncement *m (dans une pièce)*; **nooks and crannies,** coins et recoins; **(b)** *(retreat)* refuge *m*.
nooky ['nʊkɪ] *n Sl Hum (sex)* crac-crac *m*; **he wants his n.,** il veut s'envoyer en l'air.
noon [nuːn] *n* midi *m*; **it is twelve n.,** il est midi; **to arrive about n.,** arriver vers midi; **at high n.,** au milieu du jour.
noonday ['nuːndeɪ], *Old-fashioned* **noontide** ['nuːntaɪd] *n* midi *m*; **the n. sun,** le soleil de midi.
no-one ['nəʊwʌn] *pron* = **NOBODY 1**.
noose¹ [nuːs] *n* nœud coulant; *(for trapping animals)* lacet *m*, lacs *m*, collet *m*; *(lasso)* lasso *m*; *Fig* **to put one's head in a n.,** signer son arrêt de mort; **hangman's n.,** corde *f* (de potence).
noose² *vt* **(a)** prendre *(un lièvre etc)* au lacet *ou* dans un lacs; attraper *(une bête)* au lasso; **(b)** faire un nœud coulant à *(une corde)*; **to n. a rope round s.o.'s neck,** mettre la corde au cou de qn.
nope [nəʊp] *adv F* non.
nor [nɔːr] *conj* **(a)** *(continuing the force of a neg)* (ne, ni ...) ni; **he has neither father n. mother,** il n'a ni père ni mère, il n'a pas de père ni de mère; **(b)** *(and not)* **I do not know, n. can I guess,** je n'en sais rien et je ne peux pas le deviner; **n. was this all,** et ce n'était pas tout; **he hasn't any, n. have I,** il n'en a pas, ni moi non plus.
nordic ['nɔːdɪk] *adj Sp (event)* nordique.
Nordic ['nɔːdɪk] **1** *adj* nordique, scandinave. **2** *n* Nordique *mf*, Scandinave *mf*.
norm [nɔːm] *n* norme *f*; **according to the n.,** selon la norme; **to deviate from the n.,** sortir de la norme; **it's the n.,** c'est la règle.
normal ['nɔːm(ə)l] **1** *adj* normal, régulier, ordinaire; *Math (line etc)* normal, -aux **(to,** à); *Ch (solution etc)* normal, titré; **he's not quite n.,** il n'est pas complètement normal; **it's n. to do,** c'est normal de faire; **n. person,** personne normale; **n. working** *or* **running,** *(of engine etc)* régime normal; **n. temperature,** température moyenne *ou* normale; **n. salt,** sel *m* neutre. **2** *n* condition normale; *Math* normale *f*, perpendiculaire *f*; **temperature above n.,** température au-dessus de la normale; **things quickly got back to n. after the strike,** les choses rentrèrent rapidement dans l'ordre après la grève.
normality [nɔː'mælɪtɪ] , *US* **normalcy** ['nɔːməlsɪ] *n* normalité *f*.
normalization [nɔːməlaɪ'zeɪʃən] *n* normalisation *f*.
normalize ['nɔːməlaɪz] **1** *vt* normaliser, régulariser. **2** *vi* se normaliser, redevenir normal.
normally ['nɔːməlɪ] *adv* normalement.
Norman ['nɔːmən] **1** *adj* normand; **N. architecture,** l'architecture normande; *(in Britain)* l'architecture romane (anglaise); *Hist* **the N. Conquest,** la conquête normande; *Ling Hist* **N. French,** normand *m*. **2** *n* Normand, -ande *(de la Normandie)*.
Normandy ['nɔːməndɪ] *n* Normandie *f*.
Norse [nɔːs] **1** *adj* norvégien, nordique; **N. mythology,** mythologie *f* scandinave. **2** *n* **(a)** *(used as pl)* Scandinaves *mfpl*; *esp* Norvégiens, -iennes; **(b)** *Ling* nordique *m*, norrois *m*; **Old N.,** vieux norrois; *(in Orkneys, Shetlands etc)* norse *m*.
Norseman, *pl* **-men** ['nɔːsmən] *n Hist* Scandinave *m*.
north [nɔːθ] **1** *n* nord *m*; **true n.,** nord vrai *ou* géographique; **magnetic n.,** nord magnétique; **house facing the n.,** maison exposée au nord; **to the n. of,** au nord de; **in the n.,** au nord, dans le nord; **to live in the n. of England,** habiter dans le nord de l'Angleterre; *US Hist* **the N.,** les États *mpl* du nord *(des États-Unis)*; les États anti-esclavagistes; **the (Canadian) Far N.,** le Grand Nord Canadien.
2 *adv* au nord; *(voyager)* vers le nord; **it's n. of here,** c'est au nord d'ici; **I'm going up n.,** je vais dans le nord (de l'Angleterre); **n. by east/by west,** nord-quart-nord-est/nord-quart-nord-ouest.
3 *adj* nord *inv*; *(pays, vent)* du nord; *(mur etc)* exposé au nord; **on the n. side,** du côté nord; **the N. Country,** le Nord (de l'Angleterre); **he has a strong n.-country accent,** il a un accent du nord prononcé; **N. Africa,** Afrique *f* du Nord; **N. African,** nord-africain; *(person)* Nord-Africain, -aine; **the N. Sea,** la mer du Nord; **N.-Sea gas,** gaz de la mer du Nord; **the N. Pole,** le Pôle Nord; **N. Star,** *(pole star)* étoile *f* polaire; *Archit (in church)* **n. transept,** transept septentrional.
northbound ['nɔːθbaʊnd] *adj (train etc)* allant vers le nord; *(on underground)* en direction de la banlieue nord; *Aut* **the n. carriageway,** la voie nord (de l'autoroute).
northeast [nɔːθ'iːst] , *Nau* **nor'east** [nɔː'riːst] **1** *n* nord-est *m*; *Nau* nordé *m*. **2** *adj* (du) nord-est *inv*; **n. wind,** nord-est. **3** *adv* au nord-est; *(voyager)* vers le nord-est; **n. by east,** nord-est-quart-est; **n. by north,** nord-est-quart-nord.
northeaster [nɔːθ'iːstər] *n (wind)* nord-est *m*.
northeasterly [nɔːθ'iːstəlɪ], *Nau* **nor'easterly** [nɔː'riːstəlɪ] **1** *adj (wind etc)* (du) nord-est *inv*; *(district etc)* (au, du) nord-est; *(direction)* vers le nord-est. **2** *adv* vers le nord-est. **3** *n* = **NORTHEASTER**.
northeastern [nɔːθ'iːstən], *Nau* **nor'eastern** [nɔː'riːstən] *adj* (du) nord-est *inv*.
northerly ['nɔːðəlɪ] **1** *adj (wind etc)* du nord; *(district etc)* (du, au) nord *inv*; *(direction)* vers le nord; **n. aspect,** *(of house)* exposition *f* au nord; **n. lights,** aurore boréale. **2** *adv* vers le nord.
northern ['nɔːðən] *adj* (du) nord *inv*, septentrional, -aux; **N. Ireland,** l'Irlande *f* du Nord; **n. hemisphere,** hémisphère nord; **n. lights,** aurore boréale.
northerner ['nɔːðənər] *n* **(a)** habitant, -ante du Nord *(de l'Angleterre etc)*; **the Northerners,** les gens du Nord; **(b)** *US Hist* nordiste *m*.
Northants *abbr* **Northamptonshire**.
north-northeast [nɔːθnɔːθ'iːst], *Nau* **nor'nor'east** [nɒːnɒː'riːst] **1** *adj & n* nord-nord-est *m inv*. **2** *adv* au nord-nord-est; *(voyager)* vers le nord-nord-est.
north-northwest [nɔːθnɔːθ'west], *Nau* **nor'-nor'west** [nɔːnɔː'west] **1** *adj & n* nord-nord-ouest *m inv*. **2** *adv* au nord-nord-ouest; *(voyager)* vers le nord-nord-ouest.
Northumb. *abbr* **Northumberland**.
northward ['nɔːθwəd] **1** *adj* au *ou* du nord; du côté du nord. **2** *n* nord *m*. **3** *adv* = **NORTHWARDS**.
northwards ['nɔːθwədz] *adv* vers le nord.
northwest [nɔːθ'west], *Nau* **nor'west** [nɔː'west] **1** *n* nord-ouest *m*. **2** *adj* (du) nord-ouest *inv*; **n. wind,** (vent *m* du) nord-ouest. **3** *adv* au nord-ouest; *(voyager)* vers le nord-ouest; **n. by west/n. by north,** nord-ouest-quart-ouest/nord-ouest-quart-nord.
northwester [nɔːθ'westər] *n (wind)* nord-ouest *m*.
northwesterly [nɔːθ'westəlɪ], *Nau* **nor'westerly** [nɔː'westəlɪ] **1** *adj (wind etc)* du nord-ouest; *(district etc)* (au *ou* du) nord-ouest *inv*; *(direction)* vers le nord-ouest. **2** *adv* vers le nord-ouest. **3** *n* = **NORTHWESTER**.
northwestern [nɔːθ'westən], *Nau* **nor'western** [nɔː'westən] *adj* (du) nord-ouest *inv*.
Norway ['nɔːweɪ] *n* Norvège *f*.
Norwegian [nɔː'wiːdʒən] **1** *adj* norvégien. **2** *n* **(a)** Norvégien, -ienne; **(b)** *Ling* norvégien *m*.
nose¹ [nəʊz] *n* **(a)** *(of person, animal)* nez *m*; **n. ring,** anneau nasal, nasière *f (de taureau etc)*; *(of person)* anneau porté au nez; **her n. is bleeding,** elle saigne du nez; **to blow one's n.,** se moucher; **to hold one's n.,** se boucher le nez; **to speak through one's n.,** parler du nez, nasiller; **the parson's** *or* **pope's n.,** *(of fowl)* le croupion; **he can't see any further than the end of his n.,** il ne voit pas plus loin que le bout de son nez; *F* **it's under your n.,** vous l'avez sous le nez; **I did it under his very n.** *or* **right under his n.,** je l'ai fait sous son nez; **to poke one's n. into other people's business,** fourrer *ou* mettre son nez dans les affaires des autres; **to turn up one's n. at sth,** dédaigner qch, tourner le dos à qch; **to look down one's n. at s.o.,** regarder qn de haut en bas; **she walked by with her n. in the air,** elle passa avec un air méprisant *ou* supérieur; *Prov* **that's cutting off your n. to spite your face,** c'est toi le perdant; **to lead s.o. by the n.,** mener qn par le bout du nez; *F* **to pay through the n. for sth,** payer qch une fortune *ou* les yeux de la tête; *F* **to rub s.o.'s n. in it,** retourner le couteau dans la plaie; *F* **to have a n. round,** faire le tour de la maison *etc* en furetant dans tous les recoins; **to get up s.o.'s nose,** *(of person)* taper sur les

nerfs de qn; **it really gets up my n. that ...,** ça me met en boule que ...; **to keep one's n. clean,** se tenir à carreau;

(b) (*sense of smell*) odorat *m*; bouquet *m* (*d'un vin etc*); **to have a good n.,** (*of person*) avoir bon nez *ou* le nez fin *ou* l'odorat fin; *F* **to have a n. for sth,** (*of person*) avoir un flair *ou* du flair pour qch;

(c) *Tech* nez *m*, avant *m* (*d'un véhicule, d'un avion etc*); nez (*du moteur etc*); bec *m*, nez (*d'un outil*); nez (*d'un mandrin etc*); *MecE* ajutage *m* (*d'un tuyau*); bec (*d'un loquet*); mentonnet *m* (*d'une clavette*); pointe *f*, ogive *f* (*d'une balle, d'un missile*); *Nau* cône *m* de choc (*d'une torpille*); *Aut etc* **n. to tail,** (*traffic*) pare-choc(s) contre pare-choc(s); **n. cone,** *Av* cône de nez (*d'un avion*); ogive (*d'une fusée*); *Av* **n. dive,** (vol *m*) piqué *m*; *F* **to take a n. dive,** (*of prices*) descendre en flèche.

nose² **1** *vt* **(a)** (*of dog etc*) pousser du nez; **the ship nosed her way through the fog,** le navire avançait à l'aveuglette à travers le brouillard; **(b)** *Old-fashioned* flairer, sentir (*qch*). **2** *vi* **the ship nosed through the fog,** le navire avançait à l'aveuglette à travers le brouillard.

▶nose about, nose around *vi* fouiller, fureter, fouiner.

▶nose out **1** *vtsep* **(a)** (*of dog*) flairer (*le gibier*); **(b)** *F* découvrir, éventer (*un secret*); dépister, dénicher (*qn*). **2** *vi* (*of car, driver*) sortir prudemment.

nosebag ['nəʊzbæg] *n* musette *f* (mangeoire).

noseband ['nəʊzbænd] *n* (*on harness*) muserolle *f*.

nosebleed ['nəʊzbliːd] *n* saignement *m* de nez; **to have a n.,** saigner du nez.

nose-dive ['nəʊzdaɪv] *vi Av* piquer du nez, descendre en piqué; *Fig* (*of prices*) descendre en flèche.

nosegay ['nəʊzgeɪ] *n* petit bouquet (de fleurs).

nosey ['nəʊzɪ] *adj* = **NOSY**.

nosh¹ [nɒʃ] *n F* (*food*) bouffe *f*.

nosh² *vi F* (*eat*) bouffer.

no-show [nəʊ'ʃəʊ] *n F* = passager ou client etc qui ne se présente pas.

nosh-up ['nɒʃʌp] *n Br Sl* **a good n.-up,** une bonne boustifaille.

nosily ['nəʊzɪlɪ] *adv* indiscrètement.

nosiness ['nəʊzɪnəs] *n* indiscrétion *f*, curiosité *f*.

nostalgia [nɒs'tældʒɪə] *n* nostalgie *f*.

nostalgic [nɒs'tældʒɪk] *adj* nostalgique.

nostalgically [nɒs'tældʒɪklɪ] *adv* nostalgiquement.

nostril ['nɒstrɪl] *n* (*of person*) narine *f*; (*of horse, ox etc*) naseau *m*.

nostrum ['nɒstrəm] *n* panacée *f*, orviétan *m*; (*quack medicine*) remède *m* de charlatan.

nosy ['nəʊzɪ] *adj F* fouinard, fouineur, fureteur; **don't be so n.!,** ne soyez pas si curieux!; **I don't mean to be n. but ...,** je ne veux pas me montrer curieux mais ...; *Br F* **n. parker,** fouinard *m*, fureteur, -euse.

not [nɒt] **1** *adv* **(a)** (*following the aux verb informally affixed as* **n't**) (ne)... pas, (ne)... point; **I don't** *or* **do n. know,** je ne sais pas; **he won't** *or* **will n. come,** il ne viendra pas; **is she coming? — no, she isn't** *or* **she's n.,** vient-elle? — non; **don't move,** ne bougez pas; **I'm n. in the least surprised,** je ne suis nullement étonné; **you understand, don't you?,** vous comprenez, n'est-ce pas?; **she would n. wear a hat!,** (*stressed*) un chapeau, elle n'en porterait pas!;

(b) (*elliptically in answers etc*) **n. at all, n. a bit (of it),** pas du tout; **thank you so much! — n. at all!,** merci beaucoup! — je vous en prie; **n. likely!,** jamais de la vie!; **why n.?,** pourquoi pas?; **whether he likes it or n.,** que cela lui plaise ou non; **little or n. at all,** peu ou pas, peu ou point; **as likely as n. we'll be on holiday,** nous serons probablement en vacances; **I think/hope n.,** je crois/ j'espère que non; **n. always,** pas toujours; **n. yet,** pas encore; **n. even in France,** (non) pas même en France; **n. negotiable,** non négociable; **n. guilty,** non coupable;

(c) (*with a non-finite verb*) **n. wishing to be seen, I drew the curtain,** comme je ne désirais pas être vu, j'ai tiré le rideau; **n. including ..., n. to mention ...,** sans compter ...; *F* **n. to worry!,** ne vous en faites pas!; **she asked me n. to do it,** elle m'a demandé de ne pas le faire;

(d) (*in contrasts*) **she's n. my mother but my aunt,** ce n'est pas ma mère, c'est ma tante; **he is respected but n. loved,** il est respecté mais non pas aimé; **n. only ... but also ...,** non seulement ... mais encore ...;

(e) (*with pronoun or noun*) **n. I,** pas moi; **n. one replied,** pas un(e) n'a répondu; **he'll never pay, n. he!** il ne paiera jamais, c'est sûr!;

(f) (*understatement*) **I wasn't sorry to go,** j'étais bien content de partir; **n. a beautiful town,** une ville pas belle; **n. far from the town,** non loin de la ville; **n. without reason,** non sans raison; *F* **n. half!,** et comment!, tu parles!;

(g) **n. a word was spoken,** on n'a pas dit un mot; **who will believe it? — n. a soul,** qui le croira? — personne.

(h) *Arch & Lit* (*following the verb*) **I know n.,** je ne sais pas; **fear n.,** n'ayez pas peur.

2 *conj* **n. that ...,** ce n'est pas que ..., non (pas) que ...; **n. that I can remember,** pas autant qu'il m'en souvienne.

notability [nəʊtə'bɪlɪtɪ] *n* **(a)** (*person*) notabilité *f*, notable *mf*; **(b)** (*state*) prééminence *f*.

notable ['nəʊtəb(ə)l] **1** *adj* (*person, thing*) notable, insigne, remarquable; (*person*) éminent. **2** *n* notable *mf*.

notably ['nəʊtəblɪ] *adv* notamment, particulièrement.

notarize ['nəʊtəraɪz] *vt* authentifier.

notary ['nəʊtərɪ] *n Jur Scot* **n. (public),** notaire *m*.

notation [nəʊ'teɪʃən] *n Mus etc* notation *f*; *Math* numération *f*.

notch¹ [nɒtʃ] *n* **(a)** (*in wood*) entaille *f*, encoche *f*; cran *m* (*d'une ceinture, d'une crémaillère*); hoche *f* (faite sur une taille); enfourchement *m* (*de tenon*); trait *m* (*de scie*); cran, dent *f* (*d'une roue*); barbe *f* (*de pêne*); *Sewing* cran; brèche *f* (*dans une lame etc*); **to take one's belt in a n.,** resserrer sa ceinture d'un cran; **(b)** *Am* défilé *m*, gorge *f* (*de montagne*).

notch² *vt* entailler, encocher, hocher (*un bâton etc*); denteler, créneler (*une roue etc*); ébrécher (*une lame etc*).

▶notch up *vtsep* marquer (*un point, une victoire etc*).

note¹ [nəʊt] *n* **(a)** (*in writing*) note *f*, mémento *m*; note, commentaire *m*, annotation *f*, remarque *f* (*sur un texte*); (*letter*) billet *m*; *Sch* **lecture notes,** notes de cours; **to make** *or* **take (down) notes,** prendre des notes; **to take** *or* **make a n. of sth,** prendre note de qch; **I must make a n. of it,** il faut que je m'en souvienne; **to lecture without notes,** faire cours sans notes; **to speak from notes,** parler d'après des notes; **to write** *or* **make notes on a text,** annoter un texte; **I wrote a n. to her at once,** je lui ai tout de suite écrit un mot; **diplomatic n.,** note *f* diplomatique, mémorandum *m*;

(b) *Mus* note *f*; touche *f* (*d'un piano etc*); chant *m*, ramage *m* (*d'oiseau*); **to sing** *or* **play a false n.,** faire une fausse note; **there was a n. of impatience in her voice,** son ton indiquait une certaine impatience; **speech that strikes the right n.,** discours dans la note voulue;

(c) *Fin Com* billet *m*; (*money*) billet (de banque); **n. of hand,** reconnaissance *f* (de dette); billet simple; **credit/ debit n.,** note *ou* bordereau *m* de crédit/de débit; **advice n.,** note *ou* lettre *f* d'avis; **hundred-franc notes,** billets *ou* coupures *fpl* de cent francs;

(d) (*distinction*) distinction *f*, marque *f*, renom *m*; **a man of n.,** un homme de marque; **nothing of n.,** rien d'extraordinaire *ou* de spécial;

(e) **to take n. of sth,** noter qch.

note² *vt* noter, remarquer (*qch*); relever (*une erreur*); constater (*un fait*); **which fact is hereby duly noted,** dont acte; **it should be noted that ...,** il est à noter que ...; **we duly n. that ...,** nous prenons bonne note (de ce) que ... .

▶note down *vtsep* écrire, inscrire, prendre note de (*qch*).

notebook ['nəʊtbʊk] *n* carnet *m*, calepin *m*, mémento *m*; (*for shorthand etc*) bloc-notes *m*, *pl* blocs-notes; (*larger*) cahier *m*; **pocket n.,** carnet de poche.

notecase ['nəʊtkeɪs] *n* portefeuille *m*, porte-billets *m inv*.

noted ['nəʊtəd] *adj* (*person*) distingué, éminent; (*thing*) fameux, remarquable (**for sth,** par qch); **the area is n. for its cheese,** la région est fameuse pour son fromage.

notelet ['nəʊtlət] *n* carte-lettre *f*, *pl* cartes-lettres.

notepad ['nəʊtpæd] *n* bloc-notes *m*, *pl* blocs-notes.

notepaper ['nəʊtpeɪpər] *n* papier *m* à lettres.

noteworthy ['nəʊtwɜːðɪ] *adj* (*of fact etc*) remarquable, mémorable; **it is n. that ...,** il convient de noter que ... .

not-for-profit [nɒtfə'prɒfɪt] *adj Am* = **NONPROFIT**.

nothing ['nʌθɪŋ] **1** *pron* rien; **he does n.,** il ne fait rien; **I saw n.,** je n'ai rien vu; **what are you doing? — n.,** que faites-vous? — rien; **it's better than n.,** c'est mieux que rien; **n. could be simpler,** rien de plus simple, c'est tout ce qu'il y a de plus simple; **you can't live on n.,** on ne peut pas vivre de rien; **he let me have it for almost** *or* **next to n.,** il me l'a cédé pour presque rien *ou* pour une bouchée de pain; **it looks like n. (else) on earth,** cela ne ressemble à rien; **as if n. had happened,** comme si de rien n'était; **say n. about it,** n'en dites rien; **to say n. of ...,** sans parler de ...; **she gets angry about n.,** elle se fâche pour un rien; **n. at all,** rien du tout; **there's n. in these rumours,** ces bruits sont sans fondement; *F* **there's n. to it** *or* **in it,** (*it's* *easy*) c'est simple comme bonjour; **he was n. if not discreet,** il était surtout discret, il était discret avant tout; *Prov* **n. ventured, n. gained,** qui ne risque rien n'a rien; **n. new,** rien de nouveau, rien de neuf; **that's n. unusual,** cela n'a rien d'anormal; **n. much,** pas grand-chose; **there is n. more to be said,** il n'y a plus rien à dire; **I have n. to do,** je n'ai rien à faire; **to have n. to do with s.o./sth,** n'avoir rien à voir avec qn/qch; **that's n. to do with you,** ce n'est pas votre affaire, cela ne vous regarde pas; **these people will stop at n.,** ces gens ne reculent devant rien; **there is n. to cry about,** il n'y a pas de quoi pleurer; **to have n. on,** (*no engagement*) être libre; (*no clothes*) être tout nu; **his piano playing has n. on his brother,** la façon dont il joue du piano n'est rien comparée à celle de son frère; **he has n. of his father in him,** il n'a rien de son père; **n. else,** rien d'autre; **n. but ...,** rien que ...; **I have n. (else) to do but ...,** je n'ai rien (d'autre) à faire que de ...; **n. else matters,** tout le reste n'est rien; **n. but the truth,** rien que la vérité; **there's n. else for it,** c'est inévitable; **there's n. like a cold bath in the mornings,** il n'y a rien de tel qu'un bain froid le matin; **to do sth for n.,** (*in vain*) faire qch en vain *ou* inutilement; (*free of charge*) faire qch gratuitement; **it's not for n. that ...,** ce n'est pas sans raison que ...; **all my efforts came to n.,** tous mes efforts se sont révélés inutiles; **to count for n.,** ne compter pour rien; **he is n. to her,** (*she doesn't care for him*) il lui est indifférent; (*she is much better than he is*) elle est bien meilleure que lui ; **£1,000 is n. to her,** 1 000 livres ne sont rien pour elle; **that's n. to what Mum will say,** ce n'est rien par rapport à ce que Maman va dire; **in those days it was n. to see ...,** en ce temps-là on voyait facilement ...; **it's n. to me either way,** cela m'est égal; **to think n. of sth,** (*not think important*) n'attacher aucune importance à qch; (*not hesitate to do*) ne pas se faire scrupule de faire qch; **she thinks n. of walking 10 km,** pour elle 10 km à pied, ce n'est rien; **I can make n. of it,** je n'y comprends rien du tout; **n. doing,** rien à faire, pas question; *F* **to do sth in n. flat,** faire qch en deux temps trois mouvements.

2 *n* **(a)** néant *m*, rien *m*; **to come to n.,** ne pas aboutir; (*of hopes etc*) s'anéantir; (*of scheme etc*) s'effondrer; **(b)** (*trifle*) bagatelle *f*, rien *m*; **a hundred francs? — a mere n.!,** cent francs? — une bêtise!; **to whisper sweet nothings to s.o.,** chuchoter des mots doux à qn; **(c)** *Math* zéro *m*.

3 *adv* **n. like** *or* **near so big** *or* **as big,** loin d'être aussi grand; **she looks n. like her sister,** elle ne ressemble pas du tout *ou* en rien à sa sœur; **it is n. less than** *or* **short of madness,** c'est de la folie ni plus ni moins; **it's n. less than scandalous that ...,** c'est ni plus ni moins un scandale que ... .

nothingness ['nʌθɪŋnɪs] *n* néant *m*.

notice¹ ['nəʊtɪs] *n* **(a)** (*notification*) avis *m*, notification *f*, intimation *f*; (*warning*) préavis *m*, avertissement *m*; (*served by bailiff etc*) exploit *m*; **n. of delivery,** accusé *m* de réception; **to give s.o. n. of sth,** prévenir *ou* avertir qn de qch; **to give official n. that ...,** donner acte que ...; **without (prior) n.,** sans préavis; **n. is hereby given that ...,** le public est avisé que ...; on fait savoir que ...; **public n.,** avis au public; **important n.,** avis important; *Rel* **the weekly notices,** les annonces *fpl* de la semaine; **until further n.,** jusqu'à nouvel ordre *ou* nouvel avis; *Jur* **n. of appeal,** intimation; **n. to pay,** avertissement; **at short n.,** dans un bref délai; **to give s.o. short n.,** prendre qn de court; **that's rather short n.,** c'est un peu court comme délai; **at a moment's** *or* **a minute's n.,** à la minute, à l'instant, sur-le-champ; **without a moment's n.,** sans crier gare; **to require three months' n.,** exiger un préavis de trois mois; **next time give me a bit more n.,** la prochaine fois prévenez-moi un peu plus à l'avance; **n. (to quit),** (avis de) congé *m*; **to be under n. to quit,** avoir reçu son congé; **what n. do you require?,** quel est le terme du congé?; **to give s.o. n.,** (*of landlord, employer*) donner son congé à qn; (*of employer*) licencier qn; **to give n., to give** *or* **hand in one's n.,** (*of tenant, employee*) donner *ou* demander (son) congé; (*of employee*) démissionner; **to give s.o. a week's n.,** donner ses huit jours à qn;

(b) (*giving information*) affiche *f*, placard *m*; (*on a card*) écriteau *m*, pancarte *f*; (*in newspaper etc*) annonce *f*, note *f*; revue *f* (*d'un ouvrage*); **to stick up a n.,** placarder une affiche; **n. board,** panneau *m* d'affichage; (*on house for sale etc*) écriteau; (*in schools, clubs etc*) tableau *m* d'affichage *ou* d'annonces *ou* de publicité; **they put a birth n. in the local paper,** ils ont passé un faire-part de naissance dans le quotidien régional;

(c) (*attention*) attention *f*, connaissance *f*, observation *f*; **to take n. of s.o./sth,** faire attention *ou* prêter (son) attention à qn/qch, tenir compte de qn/qch; **to take no** *or* **not the least n. of sth,** ne pas prêter la moindre attention à qch; **nobody took any n. of me,** personne n'a fait attention à moi; **I should take no n.** *or* **I shouldn't take any n. of it,** je n'y prendrais pas garde; **the fact came to her n. that ...,** son attention a été attirée par le fait que ...; **it has come to my n. that ...,** il est venu à ma connaissance que ...; **to attract n.,** (*of author etc*) commencer à être connu *ou* à percer; **to avoid n.,** se dérober aux regards; **to bring** *or* **call sth/s.o., to s.o.'s n.,** appeler *ou* porter *ou* attirer l'attention de qn sur qch/qn; **the baby is beginning to take n.,** le bébé commence à avoir conscience des choses; *F* **to sit up and take n.,** se réveiller, dresser l'oreille.

notice² **1** *vt* observer, remarquer, s'apercevoir de, prendre garde à (*qn, qch*); relever (*des fautes*); **without his noticing it,** sans qu'il y prenne garde; **to be noticed** *or* **to get oneself noticed by s.o.,** attirer l'attention de qn (sur soi). **2** *vi* remarquer; **nobody will ever n.,** personne ne s'en apercevra jamais.

noticeable ['nəʊtɪsəb(ə)l] *adj* (*evident*) perceptible; **it was very n. that she didn't speak to her husband,** manifestement elle ne parlait pas à son mari; **the difference is very n.,** la différence est très sensible.

noticeably ['nəʊtɪsəblɪ] *adv* perceptiblement, sensiblement.

notifiable [nəʊtɪ'faɪəb(ə)l] *adj* (*maladie*) dont la déclaration aux autorités est obligatoire.

notification [nəʊtɪfɪ'keɪʃən] *n* avis *m*, notification *f*, annonce *f* (*d'un fait etc*); déclaration *f* (*de naissance*); **letter of n.,** lettre notificative.

notify ['nəʊtɪfaɪ] *vt* annoncer, notifier (*qch*); déclarer (*une naissance etc*); **to n. s.o. of sth,** avertir *ou* aviser qn de qch; **to n. the authorities of a fact,** saisir l'administration d'un fait; **to n. the police of sth,** signaler qch à la police; **have you notified the police?,** avez vous prévenu la police?; **to be notified of sth,** recevoir notification de qch, être avisé de qch.

notion ['nəʊʃən] *n* **(a)** (*idea*) notion *f*, idée *f*; **to have no n. of sth,** n'avoir pas la moindre notion de qch; **to have no n. of time,** n'avoir pas le sens de l'heure; **I haven't the first n. about it,** je n'en ai pas la moindre idée; **I have a n. that ...,** j'ai dans l'idée que ...; **(b)** (*whim*) caprice *m*; **as the n. takes him,** selon son caprice; **to have a n. to do sth,** se mettre en tête de faire qch; **(c)** *Phil* notion *f*, concept *m*; **(d)** *Am* **notions,** (*ribbons, needles etc*) mercerie *f*.

notional ['nəʊʃən(ə)l] *adj* **(a)** (*of knowledge etc*) spéculatif; **(b)** (*things, relations etc*) imaginaire.

notoriety [nəʊtə'raɪətɪ] *n* notoriété *f*; **to seek n.,** chercher à se faire remarquer.

notorious [nəʊ'tɔːrɪəs] *adj* d'une triste notoriété; (*menteur etc*) insigne; (*malfaiteur*) reconnu, notoire; (*endroit*) mal famé; (*voleur*) fieffé; **to be n. for being late,** être réputé pour arriver en retard.

notoriously [nəʊ'tɔːrɪəslɪ] *adv* notoirement; **n. cruel,** connu pour sa cruauté; **to be n. difficult/dangerous,** être bien connu pour sa difficulté/ses dangers.

Notts *abbr* **Nottinghamshire**.

notwithstanding [nɒtwɪθ'stændɪŋ] **1** *prep* malgré, en dépit de, *Fml* nonobstant. **2** *adv* quand même, tout de même, néanmoins.

nougat ['nuːgɑː] *n* nougat *m*.

nought [nɔːt] *n* **(a)** *Math* zéro *m*; *Br* **noughts and crosses,** (*game*) ≈ morpion *m*; **(b)** = **NAUGHT (a)**.

noun [naʊn] *n Gram* substantif *m*, nom *m*; **proper n.,** nom propre; **n. clause,** proposition *f*; **n. phrase,** proposition nominale, syntagme nominal.

nourish ['nʌrɪʃ] *vt* **(a)** nourrir (*qn, une plante etc*); alimenter (*qn*); *Ind* nourrir (*le bois*); entretenir (*le cuir*); **to n. s.o. on** *or* **with sth,** nourrir qn de qch; **to be well nourished,** être bien nourri; **(b)** *Old-fashioned* nourrir, entretenir (*un sentiment, un espoir etc*).

nourishing ['nʌrɪʃɪŋ] *adj* nourrissant, nutritif.

nourishment ['nʌrɪʃmənt] *n* **(a)** (*food*) nourriture *f*, aliments *mpl*; **to take (some) n.,** prendre de la nourriture; **(b)** (*action*) alimentation *f*, nourriture *f* (*de qn, qch*); entretien *m* (*du cuir*).

nous [naʊs] *n Br Sl* bon sens; (*know-how*) savoir-faire *m*.

nova, *pl* **-ae** *or* **-s** ['nəʊvə, -iː] *n Astron* nova *f*, *pl* novæ.

Nova Scotia ['nəʊvə'skəʊʃə] *n* Nouvelle-Ecosse *f*.

novel¹ ['nɒv(ə)l] *n* roman *m*; **detective n.,** roman policier.

novel² *adj* nouveau, -elle, original, -aux; **that's a n. idea!,** voilà qui est original!

novelette [nɒvə'let] *n Pej* petit roman à l'eau de rose; *Lit* nouvelle *f*.

novelist ['nɒvəlɪst] *n* romancier, -ière.

novella [nəʊ'velə] *n* nouvelle *f*.

novelty ['nɒvəltɪ] *n* **(a)** (*quality*) nouveauté *f*, étrangeté *f* (*de qch*); **the n. will soon wear off,** l'attrait de la nouveauté ne tardera pas à s'estomper; **(b)** chose nouvelle, innovation *f*; *Com* (article *m* de) nouveauté *f*; **colour television used to be a n.,** la télévision en couleur était une nouveauté; *Com* **novelties** = farces *fpl* et attrapes *fpl*.

November [nəʊ'vembər] *n* novembre *m*; **in N.,** au mois de novembre, en novembre; **(on) the first/the fifth of N.,** le premier/le cinq novembre.

novena [nəʊ'viːnə] *n Rel* neuvaine *f*.

novice ['nɒvɪs] *n* **(a)** novice *mf*, apprenti, -ie, débutant, -ante; **to be a n. in** *or* **at sth,** être novice dans *ou* à qch; **(b)** *Rel* novice *mf*.

noviciate, novitiate [nəʊ'vɪʃɪət] *n Rel* **(a)** (*state, period*) (temps *m* du) noviciat *m*; **(b)** (*living quarters*) noviciat *m*, maison *f* des novices.

now [naʊ] **1** *adv* **(a)** (*at present*) maintenant, à présent, actuellement, à l'heure actuelle; (*in narrative*) alors, à ce moment-là; **what shall we do n.?,** qu'est-ce que nous allons faire maintenant?; *F* **it's (a case of) n. or never,** c'est le moment ou jamais; **n. or never!,** allons-y!; *F* **goodbye for n.!,** à bientôt!; **that'll do for n.,** ça suffit pour le moment; **it's two years n. since his mother died,** ça fait maintenant deux ans que sa mère est morte; **he won't be long n.,** il ne tardera plus guère; **even n., I don't understand,** même maintenant je ne comprends pas; **and n. I must go,** sur ce je vous quitte; **n. is the time to ...,** c'est le bon moment pour ...; **right n.,** tout de suite; **all was n. ready,** dès lors tout était prêt; **he was even n. on his way,** il était déjà en route; **just n.,** (*past*) il y a un instant; (*present*) en ce moment; **I can't do it just n.,** je ne puis pas le faire en ce moment; **(every) n. and then, n. and again,** de temps en temps, de temps à autre; **n. ... n. ..., n. ... then ..., n. ... and again ...,** tantôt ... tantôt ...; **n. here n. there,** tantôt ici tantôt là; **up to n.,** jusqu'ici; **from n. on,** dès maintenant; **in three or four days from n.,** d'ici trois ou quatre jours; **he ought to be here by n., he ought to have been here before n.,** il devrait déjà être arrivé; **until n.,** jusqu'ici, jusqu'à présent; **from n. (on),** dès maintenant;

(b) (*without temporal significance*) (*explanatory, or in development of an argument*) or; **n. to come back to what we were saying,** pour revenir à ce que nous disions; **n. it happened that ...,** (*in story*) or il advint que ...; **n. what's the matter with you!,** qu'avez-vous donc?; **come n.!,** voyons!; **n., n.! stop quarrelling!,** voyons, voyons! assez de querelles!; **well n.!,** eh bien!; **n. then!,** attention!; voyons!, allons!

2 *conj* maintenant que, à présent que; **n. (that) I'm older I think differently,** maintenant que je suis plus âgé je pense autrement.

3 *n* le présent, le temps actuel.

4 *adj esp Am F* (*look, people*) actuel.

nowadays ['naʊədeɪz] *adv* aujourd'hui, de nos jours, actuellement.

nowhere ['nəʊweər] **1** *adv* nulle part; **she was n. to be found,** on ne la trouvait nulle part; **we were getting n. fast,** nous n'avancions pas; **flattery will get you n.,** la flatterie ne vous mènera à rien; **it's n. near the shopping centre,** ce n'est pas du tout dans les parages du centre commercial; **it's n. near enough,** c'est loin d'être suffisant; **he's n. near as intelligent as his sister,** il est loin d'être aussi intelligent que sa sœur; **we're n. near ready,** on est loin d'être prêt; **the rest are n.,** (*in race, sales etc*) les autres ne sont plus dans le coup. **2** *n* le néant; **he seemed to come from n.,** il semblait apparaître tout d'un coup; **a small place in the middle of n.,** un petit trou perdu.

nowt [naʊt] *pron & n Dial* (ne ...) rien *m*; **I don't do owt for n.,** je ne fais rien pour rien.

noxious ['nɒkʃəs] *adj* nocif; (*gas, fumes etc*) délétère, nocif.

nozzle ['nɒz(ə)l] *n* ajutage *m*, jet *m* (*de tuyau*); lance *f* (*de tuyau de pompe à incendie etc*); canule *f* (*de seringue*); bec *m*, tuyau *m*, buse *f* (*de soufflet*); suceur *m* (*d'aspirateur*); tuyère *f*, ajutage (*d'injecteur, de turbine etc*); **petrol pump delivery n.,** pistolet *m* de distributeur d'essence.

NS *abbr* **Nova Scotia**.

NSPCC [enespiːsiː'siː] *n* (*abbr* **National Society for the Prevention of Cruelty to Children**) = comité national pour la prévention des mauvais traitements envers les enfants.

nth [enθ] *adj F* énième; **to the n. degree,** au énième degré; *Math* **to the n. power,** à la puissance n.

nuance ['njuːɒns] *n* nuance *f*.

nub [nʌb] *n* **(a)** bosse *f*, protubérance *f*; **(b)** petit morceau (*de charbon etc*); **(c) the n. of the matter,** l'essentiel *m* de l'affaire.

nubile ['njuːbaɪl] *adj* nubile.

nuclear ['njuːklɪər] *adj* **(a)** (*energy, reactor etc*) nucléaire; **n. physics,** physique *f* nucléaire; **n. fission,** fission *f* nucléaire; **n. fusion,** fusion *f* nucléaire; *Med* **n. magnetic resonance,** résonance *f* magnétique nucléaire; *Med* **n. magnetic resonance scanner,** scanner *m* de résonance magnétique nucléaire; **n. winter,** hiver *m* nucléaire; **n. energy,** énergie *f* nucléaire *ou* atomique; **n. power,** électricité *f* d'origine nucléaire; **n. power station** *or* **plant,** centrale *f* (d'énergie) nucléaire; **n. weapon,** arme *f* nucléaire; **n. war(fare),** guerre *f* nucléaire; *Pol* **the N. Powers,** les puissances *fpl* nucléaires; **(b)** (*family*) nucléaire.

nuclear-free [njuːklɪə'friː] *adj* **n.-f. zone,** zone *f* antinucléaire.

nucleic [njuː'kliːɪk] *adj Ch* (*acide*) nucléique.

nucleus, *pl* **-ei** ['njuːklɪəs, -ɪaɪ] *n* **(a)** *Phys Biol Astron* noyau *m*; *Phys* **atomic n.,** noyau atomique; **(b)** *Fig* noyau *m*, embryon *m* (*d'une organisation etc*); **the n. of a library,** un commencement de bibliothèque; *Mil etc* **n. of resistance,** noyau de résistance.

nuddy ['nʌdɪ] *n Br F Hum* **in the n.,** nu.

nude [njuːd] **1** *adj* (*person, limbs etc*) nu; *Art* **n. figure,** nu *m*, nudité *f*. **2** *n* **(a)** *Art* **(the) n.,** (le) nu, (la) nudité; **to draw/paint from the n.,** dessiner/peindre des nus, dessiner/peindre des académies; **(b) to bathe in the n.,** se baigner tout nu.

nudge¹ [nʌdʒ] *n* coup *m* de coude.

nudge² *vt* pousser (*qn*) du coude, donner un coup de coude à (*qn*).

nudism ['njuːdɪz(ə)m] *n* nudisme *m*, naturisme *m*.

nudist ['njuːdɪst] *n* nudiste *mf*, naturiste *mf* ; **n. camp** *or* **colony,** camp *m* de nudistes.

nudity ['njuːdɪtɪ] *n* nudité *f*.

nugget ['nʌgɪt] *n* pépite *f* (*d'or*); *Fig* (*of useful information etc*) parcelle *f*; **nuggets of chicken,** morceaux *mpl* de poulet.

nuisance ['njuːsəns] *n* **(a)** (*person*) casse-pieds *m inv*, peste *f*, fléau *m*; (*thing*) ennui *m*, incommodité *f*, embêtement *m*; **go away, you('re a) n.!,** va-t'en, tu m'embêtes!; **he's being a n.,** (*of child, drunk*) il m'embête *ou* l'embête *etc*; **to make a n. of oneself,** embêter le monde *ou* les gens; **long skirts are a n.,** les jupes longues sont gênantes; **it's a n. for me to have to ...,** cela me gêne de devoir ...; **that's a n.!,** voilà qui est bien ennuyeux!; **what a n.!,** quel ennui!, que c'est embêtant *ou* agaçant!; **(b)** *Jur* dommage *m*; (*to public at large*) atteinte portée aux droits du public; (*to individual*) atteinte portée aux droits privés des voisins.

NUJ [enjuː'dʒeɪ] *n abbr* **National Union of Journalists**.

nuke¹ [njuːk] *n esp US Sl* bombe *f* nucléaire.

nuke² *vt esp US Sl* atomiser.

null [nʌl] *adj Jur etc* (*decree, act etc*) nul, *f* nulle; (*legacy*) caduc, *f* caduque; **n. and void,** nul et de nul effet; **to declare a contract n. and void,** déclarer un contrat nul et non avenu; **to render n.,** annuler, infirmer, invalider (*un décret, un testament*).

nullification [nʌlɪfɪ'keɪʃən] *n* annulation *f*, invalidation *f*.

nullify ['nʌlɪfaɪ] *vt* annuler; infirmer (*un acte*); invalider (*un décret*); **his marriage was nullified,** son mariage a été déclaré nul.

nullity ['nʌlɪtɪ] *n Jur* nullité *f*, invalidité *f* (*d'un mariage etc*); caducité *f* (*d'un legs etc*); *Jur* **n. suit,** demande *f* en nullité de mariage.

NUM [enjuː'em] *n* (*abbr* **National Union of Mineworkers**) ≈ Syndicat National des Mineurs.

numb¹ [nʌm] *adj* (*limb, mind etc*) engourdi; (*limb*) gourd; **hands n. with cold,** mains engourdies par le froid; **to be n. with shock,** être hébété par le choc; **n. with horror,** glacé d'horreur.

numb² *vt* engourdir (*les membres, l'esprit etc*).

number¹ ['nʌmbər] *n* **(a)** (*quantity*) *&* *Math* nombre *m*; **three-figure n.,** nombre de trois chiffres; **even/odd/prime n.,** nombre pair/impair/premier; **the n. of people present,** le nombre des assistants; **we were in equal numbers,** nous étions en nombre égal; **to swell the number(s),** faire nombre; **they are few in n.,** ils sont peu nombreux; **without n.,** sans nombre; **a n. of ...,** (bon) nombre de ..., un assez grand nombre de ...; (*several*) plusieurs ...; **a large n.**

of men were killed, nombre d'hommes ont été tués; **any n. of ...,** un grand nombre de ..., bon nombre de ...; **to be present in small numbers/in (great) numbers,** être présents en petit nombre/en grand nombre; **they are coming in ever increasing numbers,** ils viennent de plus en plus nombreux; **one of their n.,** (l')un d'entre eux; *Bible* **(the Book of) Numbers,** le Livre des Nombres, les Nombres; *Comptr F* **n. crunching,** calculs *mpl*; *Comptr F* **n. cruncher,** calculateur (puissant);
(b) (*symbol*) chiffre *m*; **to write the n. on a page,** numéroter une page; **the n. eight,** le chiffre huit;
(c) numéro *m* (*d'une maison etc*); (numéro) matricule *m* (*d'un soldat, d'un fusil etc*); **I live at n. 40,** j'habite au (numéro) 40; *Nau* **n. eight uniform,** *F* **n. eights,** = tenue *f* de travail, bleu *m* de chauffe; *F* **to do n. one,** (*in children's language*) faire pipi, faire la petite commission; *F* **to do n. two,** (*in children's language*) faire la grosse commission; *F* **to look after n. one,** tirer la couverture à soi; **my n. one priority,** la première de mes priorités; *F* **to be at n. one,** (*of record*) être (le) numéro un; **he's my n. two,** c'est mon adjoint; *Br F* **N. Ten,** = la résidence officielle du Premier Ministre; **running n.,** numéro de série *ou* d'ordre; *Br Aut* **registration n.,** numéro d'immatriculation; *F* **to have s.o.'s n.,** en savoir long sur qn; *Com* **reference n.,** numéro de commande; *Tel* **telephone n.,** numéro de téléphone; **subscriber's n.,** numéro d'abonné; **to draw a lucky n.,** (*at lottery etc*) tirer un bon numéro; *F* **his number's up,** il a son compte, il est fichu;
(d) *Gram* nombre *m*;
(e) *Th* numéro *m* (*du programme*); *Journ* numéro (*d'un journal etc*); livraison *f*, fascicule *m* (*d'un ouvrage qui paraît par fascicules*); **for my next n. I'd like to sing ...,** j'aimerais vous chanter maintenant ...; **vocal n.,** tour *m* de chant; **current n.,** numéro du jour *ou* de la semaine *ou* du mois, dernier numéro; **back n.,** vieux numéro; *F* **to be a back n.,** (*of person*) être vieux jeu;
(f) *Sl* (*woman*) nana *f*, nénette *f*; **she's a good-looking n.,** c'est une jolie nénette;
(g) *F* **that car/dress is a nice little n.,** elle est pas mal, cette voiture/robe.

number² *vt* **(a)** numéroter (*les maisons d'une rue etc*); *Mil* **to n. (off),** se numéroter; **(b)** compter, dénombrer (*les étoiles etc*); **his days are numbered,** ses jours sont comptés; **to n. s.o. among one's friends,** mettre *ou* compter qn au nombre de *ou* parmi ses amis; **the town/the army numbers thirty thousand,** la ville/l'armée compte trente mille habitants/trente mille hommes.

number-crunch ['nʌmbəkrʌntʃ] *vt F* **the computer then n.-crunches its way through all these statistics,** l'ordinateur fait alors rapidement subir à toutes ces statistiques des calculs longs et complexes.

numbering ['nʌmbərɪŋ] *n* **(a)** comptage *m*, compte *m*, dénombrement *m* (*d'objets, de personnes*); **(b)** numérotage *m* (*de maisons etc*); **n. machine,** numéroteur *m*.

numberless ['nʌmbəlɪs] *adj* innombrable, sans nombre.

numberplate ['nʌmbəpleɪt] *n Br Aut* plaque *f* minéralogique *ou* d'immatriculation.

numbly ['nʌmlɪ] *adv* de manière engourdie, mollement.

numbness ['nʌmnɪs] *n* engourdissement *m* (*des doigts etc*); torpeur *f* (*de l'esprit*).

numbskull ['nʌmskʌl] *n* nigaud, -aude, bêta, -asse.

numeracy ['nju:m(ə)rəsɪ] *n* degré *m* d'aptitude en calcul.

numeral ['nju:m(ə)r(ə)l] **1** *n* chiffre *m*, nombre *m*; **Roman numerals,** chiffres romains; **the cardinal numerals,** les numéraux cardinaux. **2** *adj* (*word, letter etc*) numéral, -aux.

numerate ['nju:mərət] *adj* qui a le sens de l'arithmétique; **applicants should be highly n.,** les candidats doivent avoir des compétences élevées en calcul.

numeration [nju:mə'reɪʃən] *n Math* numération *f*; **binary n.,** numération binaire.

numerator ['nju:məreɪtər] *n Math* numérateur *m*.

numeric [nju:'merɪk] *Comptr* **1** *adj* numérique; **n. coding,** codage *m* numérique. **2** *npl* **numerics,** chiffres *mpl ou* caractères *mpl* numériques.

numerical [nju:'merɪk(ə)l] *adj* (*valeur, supériorité, ordre etc*) numérique; **n. control,** (*of machine, tools*) contrôle *m* numérique.

numerically [nju:'merɪklɪ] *adv* numériquement.

numerous ['nju:m(ə)rəs] *adj* nombreux.

numismatic [nju:mɪz'mætɪk] *adj* numismatique.

numismatics [nju:mɪz'mætɪks] *npl* (*usu with with sing verb*) la numismatique.

numismatist [nju:'mɪz(ə)mətɪst] *n* numismate *mf*.

numskull ['nʌmskʌl] *n* nigaud, -aude, bêta, -asse.

nun [nʌn] *n Rel* religieuse *f*, *F* bonne sœur; **to become a n.,** entrer en religion, se faire religieuse, prendre le voile.

nuncio, *pl* **-s** ['nʌnʃɪəʊ, -z] *n Rel* nonce *m*; **papal n.,** nonce du Pape.

nunnery ['nʌnərɪ] *n* couvent *m* (de religieuses).

nuptial ['nʌpʃəl] *Lit* **1** *adj* nuptial, -iaux. **2** *npl* **nuptials,** noces *fpl*

NUR [enju:'ɑ:r] *n abbr* **National Union of Railwaymen.**

nurse¹ [nɜ:s] *n* **(a)** (*in hospital*) infirmier, -ière; (*privately employed*) garde-malade *mf*, *pl* gardes-malades; **thank you, n.,** merci mademoiselle *ou* madame *etc*; **night n.,** (*in hospital*) infirmière de nuit; (*privately employed*) garde *f* de nuit; **district n.,** infirmière visiteuse; **nursery n.,** puéricultrice *f*; **(b)** nurse *f*, bonne *f* (*d'enfants*); **(wet) n.,** nourrice *f*; **(c)** *Ent* (*of bees, ants*) ouvrière *f*; *Zool* nourrice *f*.

nurse² **1** *vt* **(a)** soigner (*un malade, F un rhume*); **she nursed him back to health,** elle lui a fait recouvrer la santé grâce à ses soins; **(b)** nourrir (de son lait), allaiter (*un enfant*); **(c)** *Fig* soigner, abriter (*des plantes etc*); ménager (*un cheval, une équipe etc*) en vue du dernier effort à donner; nourrir, entretenir (*un sentiment, un espoir etc*); mitonner, mijoter (*un projet*); *Pol* **to n. a** *or* **one's constituency,** chauffer ses électeurs; **to n. an old grievance,** entretenir un grief; **(d)** (*clasp*) bercer, dorloter (*un enfant*); tenir (*qn, qch*) dans ses bras; **to n. one's knee,** tenir son genou dans ses mains. **2** *vi* **(a) she wants to n.,** elle voudrait être infirmière; **(b)** (*of baby*) téter.

nursemaid ['nɜ:smeɪd] *n* bonne *f* d'enfants, nurse *f*; *F* **I'm not your n.!,** je ne suis pas votre bonne!

nursery ['nɜ:s(ə)rɪ] *n* **(a)** (*in house*) chambre *f* des enfants; **(day) n.,** crèche *f*, garderie *f*; **resident n.,** pouponnière *f*; **n. rhyme,** comptine *f*; **n. school,** maternelle *f*; **n. school teacher,** maîtresse *f ou* maître *m* d'école maternelle; **(b) n. (garden),** pépinière *f*; **n. gardener,** pépiniériste *mf*; *Ski* **n. slopes,** pentes *fpl* des débutants.

nurseryman, *pl* **-men** ['nɜ:s(ə)rɪmən] *n* pépiniériste *m*.

nursing ['nɜ:sɪŋ] **1** *adj* **(a) n. mother,** mère qui allaite; **(b)** (*in hospital*) **the n. staff,** les infirmiers, -ières; **n. auxiliary,** aide soignant(e), *pl* aides soignant(e)s; **n. officer,** (*matron*) infirmier *ou* infirmière en chef. **2** *n* **(a)** allaitement *m* (*d'un enfant*); **(b)** culture assidue (*des plantes, d'une terre etc*); ménagement *m*, soin *m* (*d'une affaire*); entretien *m* (*d'un sentiment etc*); **(c)** soins *mpl* (*d'une garde-malade*); **n. home,** (*hospital*) clinique *f*; (*for the mentally ill*) maison *f* de santé; (*residence for elderly people*) maison de retraite; **(d)** (*as profession*) profession *f* d'infirmière; **to go into n.,** devenir infirmière *ou* infirmier; **(e)** bercement *m*, dorlotement *m* (*d'un enfant*) (*dans les bras etc*).

nurture¹ ['nɜ:tʃər] *n* éducation *f*; soins *mpl*.

nurture² *vt* **(a)** (*feed*) nourrir (*les enfants etc*); nourrir, entretenir (*des sentiments etc*); **(b)** (*educate*) élever, faire l'éducation de (*qn*).

NUS [enju:'es] *n* (*abbr* **National Union of Students**) ≈ UNEF *f*.

nut [nʌt] *n* **(a)** noix *f*; **fruit and n. chocolate,** chocolat aux fruits et aux noix; **n. tree,** noyer *m*; *F* **tough** *or* **hard n. to crack,** (*problem*) problème *m* difficile à résoudre; (*person*) personne *f* difficile *ou* peu commode; **(b)** *F* (*head*) caboche *f*; **to be off one's n.,** être timbré *ou* toqué, avoir perdu la boule; *Br Sl* **to do one's n.,** voir rouge; **(c)** *Sl* (*mad person*) dingue *mf*, barjo *mf*; **(d)** *MecE* écrou *m*; **butterfly** *or* **wing n.,** écrou à oreilles, écrou (à) papillon; **n. wrench,** clé *f* à écrous; **a nuts and bolt problem,** un problème pratique; *Fig* **the nuts and bolts of a language,** les éléments de base d'une langue; **(e)** *Mus* sillet *m* (*de violon*); hausse *f* (*d'archet*); **(f)** *Br Com Min* **n. coal, nuts,** gailletin *m*; têtes *fpl* de moineau; **(g)** *esp Am Sl* **nuts,** (*testicles*) couilles *fpl*.

NUT [enju:'ti:] *n* (*abbr* **National Union of Teachers**) ≈ F.E.N.

nut-brown ['nʌtbraʊn] *adj* (couleur) noisette *inv*.

nutcase ['nʌtkeɪs] *n F* dingue *mf*, cinglé, -ée; **he's a complete n.,** il est complètement timbré.

nutcracker ['nʌtkrækər] *n* **(pair of) nutcrackers,** casse-noisette(s) *m inv*, casse-noix *m inv*.

nuthatch ['nʌthætʃ] *n* (*bird*) sittelle *f*.

nuthouse ['nʌthaʊs] *n F* asile *m* d'aliénés, maison *f* de fous.

nutmeg ['nʌtmeg] *n* (noix *f*) muscade *f*; **n. tree,** muscadier *m*; **n. grater,** râpe *f* à muscade.

nutrient ['nju:trɪənt] **1** *adj* nutritif. **2** *n* substance nutritive; aliment *m*.

nutriment ['nju:trɪmənt] *n* nourriture *f*.

nutrition [nju:'trɪʃən] *n* nutrition *f*.

nutritional [nju:'trɪʃənəl] *adj* nutritionnel.

nutritionist [nju:'trɪʃənɪst] *n* nutritionniste *mf*.

nutritious [njuːˈtrɪʃəs] *adj* nutritif, nourrissant.
nutritive [ˈnjuːtrɪtɪv] *adj* nutritif.
nuts [nʌts] *Sl* **1** *adj* **(a)** (*mad*) cinglé; **to go n.,** perdre la boule; **(b)** (*very fond of*) fou, *f* folle (**about,** de); *F* **to be n. about s.o./sth,** raffoler de qn/qch. **2** *int Sl* (*damn*) zut!
nutshell [ˈnʌtʃel] *n* coquille *f* de noix; **that's the whole thing in a n.,** voilà toute l'affaire (résumée) en un mot, en deux mots; **to put it in a n. ...,** pour résumer ...; bref ... .
nutter [ˈnʌtər] *n Br Sl* fou, folle, toqué, -ée.
nutting [ˈnʌtɪŋ] *n* cueillette *f* des noisettes.
nutty [ˈnʌtɪ] *adj* **(a)** (*in taste*) (goût) de noisette, de noix, au goût de noisette *ou* de noix; **(b)** *F* (*mad*) fou, *f* folle, timbré; **to be n. about s.o./sth,** raffoler de qn/qch.
nuzzle [ˈnʌz(ə)l] *vi & vt* **to n. (against) s.o.'s shoulder,** (*of dog, horse*) fourrer son nez sur l'épaule de qn; (*of person*) se blottir sur l'épaule de qn; **the dog nuzzled up to my leg,** le chien me reniflait la jambe.
NY *abbr* **New York.**
NYC *abbr* **New York City.**
nylon [ˈnaɪlɒn] *n Tex* nylon *m*; **n. stockings, nylons,** bas *mpl* nylon.
nymph [nɪmf] *n Myth* nymphe *f*; **tree** *or* **wood n.,** hamadryade *f*; **sea n.,** néréide *f*; **water n.,** naïade *f*.
nymphet [ˈnɪmfɪt] *n* nymphette *f*.
nympho, *pl* **-s** [ˈnɪmfəʊ, -z] *adj & n F* = **NYMPHOMANIAC.**
nymphomania [nɪmfəʊˈmeɪnɪə] *n Med* nymphomanie *f*.
nymphomaniac [nɪmfəʊˈmeɪnɪæk] *adj & n* nymphomane *f*.
NZ *abbr* **New Zealand.**

O

O¹, o [əʊ] *n* **(a)** (la lettre) O, o *m*; *Sch* **O-level (exam),** *Scot* **O-grade (exam),** ≈ BEPC *m* (brevet élémentaire du premier cycle); **(b)** *Tel etc* zéro *m*.

O² *int* **(a)** (*vocative*) O, ô; **(b)** = **OH**.

O³ *abbr* **Ohio**.

oaf, *pl* **-s,** *Arch* **oaves** [əʊf, -s, əʊvz] *n* rustre *m*.

oafish ['əʊfɪʃ] *adj* rustre.

oak [əʊk] *n* **(a) o. (tree),** chêne *m*; **o. apple,** noix *f* de galle; **o. leaf,** feuille *f* de chêne; **o. grove,** chênaie *f*; **o. moth,** (*insect*) tordeuse *f* des chênes; **o. wood,** bois *m* de chênes; **(b) o. (wood),** (bois *m* de) chêne *m*; **o. furniture,** meubles *mpl* de *ou* en chêne; **dark o. (colour),** couleur *f* vieux chêne; **(c)** *Old-fashioned* = porte extérieure (d'un appartement dans les universités d'Oxford et Cambridge); **to sport one's o.,** s'enfermer à double porte.

oaken ['əʊk(ə)n] *adj* de *ou* en chêne.

oakum ['əʊkəm] *n* étoupe *f* (noire), filasse *f*; **to pick o.,** démêler *ou* tirer l'étoupe.

OAP [əʊeɪ'piː] *n Br* (*abbr* **old age pensioner**) retraité, -ée.

oar [ɔːr] *n* aviron *m*, rame *f*; (*as opposed to scull*) aviron de nage; *F* **to put** *or* **stick one's o. in,** mettre son grain de sel; **good o.,** (*rower*) bon rameur.

oarlock ['ɔːlɒk] *n Am* tolet *m* (d'aviron).

oarsman, *pl* **-men** ['ɔːzmən] *n* rameur *m*; *Nau* nageur *m*.

OAS [əʊeɪ'es] *n* (*abbr* **Organization of American States**) OEA *f*.

oasis, *pl* **oases** [əʊ'eɪsɪs, -iːz] *n* oasis *f*; *Fig* **an o. of calm,** une oasis de calme.

oast [əʊst] *n* séchoir *m* (à houblon).

oasthouse ['əʊsthaʊs] *n* sécherie *f* (de houblon).

oat [əʊt] *n* (*cereal*) avoine *f* (commune); **oats,** avoine; **(porridge) oats,** flocons *mpl* d'avoine; *Br Sl* **to get one's oats,** (*have sex*) baiser; *F* **to sow one's wild oats,** faire des fredaines, jeter sa gourme.

oatcake ['əʊtkeɪk] *n Culin* galette *f* d'avoine.

oath, *pl* **oaths** [əʊθ, əʊðz] *n* **(a)** (*pledge*) serment *m*; **o. of allegiance,** serment de fidélité; **to take an o.,** *Jur* **to take the o.,** prêter serment; **witness on o.,** témoin assermenté; **(b)** (*swearword*) juron *m*, gros mot.

oatmeal ['əʊtmiːl] *n* farine *f* d'avoine; (*colour*) beige *m*; *Culin* **o. porridge,** *Am* **o.,** bouillie *f* d'avoine, porridge *m*.

OAU [əʊeɪ'juː] *n* (*abbr* **Organization of African Unity**) OUA *f*.

OB [əʊ'biː] *abbr* **outside broadcast**.

obduracy ['ɒbdjʊrəsɪ] *n* **(a)** (*stubbornness*) entêtement *m*; (*hard-heartedness*) dureté *f*; **(b)** *Rel* impénitence *f*.

obdurate ['ɒbdjʊrɪt] *adj* **(a)** (*stubborn*) obstiné, têtu; (*sinner*) endurci; (*attitude etc*) inflexible; (*stain*) rebelle; **(b)** *Rel* impénitent.

obdurately ['ɒbdjʊrɪtlɪ] *adv* avec entêtement, inflexiblement.

OBE [əʊbiː'iː] *abbr* **Officer of the Order of the British Empire**.

obedience [ə'biːdɪəns] *n* **(a)** obéissance *f* (**to s.o.,** à qn; **to the law,** à la loi); **(b)** *Rel* **the Roman o.,** l'obédience *f* de Rome; *Pol Fml* **countries of the Communist o.,** pays *mpl* d'obédience communiste.

obedient [ə'biːdɪənt] *adj* obéissant; (*animal, child*) obéissant, docile; **to be o. to s.o.,** être obéissant envers qn; *Old-fashioned* **Your o. servant,** (*in letter*) votre serviteur dévoué.

obediently [ə'biːdɪəntlɪ] *adv* docilement.

obeisance [əʊ'beɪsəns] *n Arch & Lit* **(a)** (*greeting*) salut *m*, révérence *f*; **(b)** (*homage*) hommage *m*.

obelisk ['ɒbəlɪsk] *n* **(a)** obélisque *m*; **(b)** *Typ* croix *f*, obèle *m*; **double o.,** diésis *m*.

obese [əʊ'biːs] *adj* obèse.

obesity [əʊ'biːsɪtɪ] **, obeseness** [əʊ'biːsnɪs] *n* obésité *f*.

obey [ə'beɪ] **1** *vt* obéir à (*qn, un ordre*); **to o. the law,** obéir à la loi; **his legs refused to o. him,** ses jambes refusaient d'obéir. **2** *vi* obéir.

obfuscate ['ɒbfʌskeɪt] *vt* obscurcir (*le jugement*).

obituary [ə'bɪtjʊərɪ] *n* nécrologie *f*, notice *f* nécrologique; **o. (list),** registre *m* des morts, nécrologe *m*; *Journ* **the o. column, the obituaries,** la nécrologie; **o. notice,** notice *f* nécrologique.

object¹ ['ɒbdʒɪkt] *n* **(a)** (*thing*) objet *m*, chose *f*; **o. lesson,** bon exemple *m* (**in diplomacy,** de diplomatie; **in how to do,** de comment faire); **o. finder,** (*of microscope*) chercheur *m* d'objet; chariot *m* (*à vernier, de centrage*); *Phil* **formal/material o.,** objet formel/matériel;
(b) (*subject etc*) objet *m*; **o. of** *or* **for pity,** objet de pitié; **to be an o. of ridicule,** être en butte au ridicule;
(c) (*purpose*) but *m*, objectif *m*, fin *f*; **to have sth for** *or* **as an o.,** avoir qch pour objectif *ou* pour but; **with this o. (in view),** dans cette intention, à cette fin; **with the sole o. of doing sth,** à seule fin de faire qch; **what is the o. of all this?,** à quoi vise tout cela?; **to defeat one's o.,** manquer son but; **the o. of the exercise,** le but de l'exercice; **to succeed in** *or* **attain one's o.,** atteindre son but;
(d) (*obstacle*) **expense is no o.,** on ne regarde pas à la dépense; **distance is no o.,** la distance importe peu;
(e) *Gram* **direct/indirect o.,** complément d'objet direct/indirect.

object² [əb'dʒekt] *vi* faire objection (**to sth,** à qch); **to o. to sth,** faire objection *ou* s'opposer à qch; (*of demonstrators etc*) protester *ou* réclamer contre qch; **I don't o. to his** *or* **him coming here but ...,** je ne vois pas d'objection à ce qu'il vienne ici mais ...; **he objects (to it),** il s'y oppose; **I o.!,** je proteste!; **if no one objects,** si personne ne s'y oppose; **to o. to s.o.,** avoir des objections à faire contre qn; *Jur* **to o. to a witness,** récuser un témoin; **to o. to doing sth,** se refuser à faire qch.

objection [əb'dʒekʃən] *n* **(a)** (*protest*) objection *f*; **to raise an o.,** dresser *ou* soulever une objection; *Jur* **o. to a witness,** récusation *f* de témoin; **does anyone have any objection(s)?,** est-ce que quelqu'un a une objection *ou* quelque chose contre?; **does anyone have any objections if I open the window?,** est-ce que quelqu'un a une objection si j'ouvre la fenêtre?; **to make no o. to** *or* **against sth,** ne rien objecter contre qch; **I have no o. to her doing so,** je ne m'oppose pas à ce qu'elle le fasse; **I have no o. to him,** je n'ai rien contre lui; **if you have no o.,** si cela ne vous fait rien, si vous le voulez bien; **(b)** (*disadvantage*) obstacle *m*, inconvénient *m*; **the chief o. to your plan is its cost,** le plus grand inconvénient de votre projet, c'est son coût; **I see no o. (to it),** je n'y vois pas d'inconvénient.

objectionable [əb'dʒekʃənəb(ə)l] *adj* **(a)** (*unpleasant*) désagréable; (*language etc*) choquant; **(b)** (*unacceptable*) répréhensible.

objective [əb'dʒektɪv] **1** *adj* **(a)** objectif; **let's be o.,** voyons les choses objectivement; **to be o.,** être objectif; **(b)** *Gram* (*case*) accusatif. **2** *n* **(a)** (*aim, goal*) but *m*, objectif *m*; **the committee has set out its objectives,** le comité a fixé ses objectifs; **(b)** *Opt* objectif *m*; **(c)** *Gram* cas *m* régime, cas accusatif.

objectively [əb'dʒektɪvlɪ] *adv* objectivement, d'une manière objective.

objectivism [əb'dʒektɪvɪz(ə)m] *n* objectivisme *m*.

objectivity [ɒbdʒek'tɪvɪtɪ] *n* objectivité *f*.

objector [əb'dʒektər] *n* **(a)** (*protestor*) protestataire *mf*; **(b)** (*person who objects*) personne *f* qui soulève des objections, contradicteur *m*.

oblate ['ɒbleɪt] *adj Math etc* aplati (aux pôles), raccourci.

obligate ['ɒblɪgeɪt] *vt* **to o. s.o. to do sth,** imposer à qn l'obligation de faire qch; **to be obligated to do sth,** avoir l'obligation de faire qch; **to feel obligated to s.o.,** se sentir redevable envers qn.

obligation [ɒblɪ'geɪʃən] *n* obligation *f*; **moral o.,** obligation morale; **to be under an o. to do sth,** être dans l'obligation de faire qch; **I am under no o. to go with**

them, rien ne m'oblige à les accompagner; *Com* **without o.,** sans engagement; **to do sth out of (a sense of) o.,** faire qch parce que l'on s'y sent obligé; **to be under an o. to s.o.,** avoir envers qn une dette de reconnaissance; **I am under a great o. to him,** je lui suis redevable de beaucoup; *Com* **to meet one's obligations,** faire face à ses engagements.

obligatory [ɒ'blɪgət(ə)rɪ] *adj* obligatoire; **the wearing of a jacket is o.,** le port d'un veston est de rigueur.

oblige [ə'blaɪdʒ] **1** *vt* **(a)** *(compel) usu Jur* obliger, astreindre (**s.o. to do sth,** qn à faire qch); **to be obliged to do sth,** être obligé *ou* tenu de faire qch; *Admin* être astreint à faire qch; **(b)** *(do a favour for)* obliger *(qn)*, rendre service à *(qn)*; **he did it to o. us,** il l'a fait par pure complaisance; **(c)** *(make indebted) (usu passive)* **to be obliged to s.o.,** *(to be grateful)* être reconnaissant à qn (**for sth,** pour qch); *F* **much obliged,** merci beaucoup; **I would be obliged if you would ...,** je vous serais reconnaissant de bien vouloir ... . **2** *vi* **to be always willing to o.,** être très obligeant *ou* très complaisant; *F* **anything to o.,** tout ce que vous voudrez pour vous faire plaisir; **I'm sorry I can't o.,** je suis désolé, je ne peux pas; **he did it to o.,** il l'a fait par pure complaisance.

obliging [ə'blaɪdʒɪŋ] *adj* obligeant, complaisant.

obligingly [ə'blaɪdʒɪŋlɪ] *adv* obligeamment, complaisamment.

oblique [ə'bliːk] **1** *adj (ligne, angle)* oblique (**to,** à); **o. glance,** regard *m* en biais; *Gram* **o. case,** cas indirect *ou* oblique. **2** *n* (ligne *f*) oblique *f*; *Math* figure *f* oblique; *Anat* (muscle *m*) oblique *m*; *Typ* barre transversale; *Mil etc* (mouvement *m*) oblique *m*.

obliquely [ə'bliːklɪ] *adv* obliquement, de biais; *(indirectly)* d'une façon indirecte, de biais.

obliqueness [ə'bliːknɪs] , **obliquity** [ə'blɪkwɪtɪ] *n* **(a)** *Math Anat* obliquité *f*, biais *m*; **(b)** *(lack of candour)* manque *m* de franchise.

obliterate [ə'blɪtəreɪt] *vt* **(a)** faire disparaître, effacer *(des chiffres etc)*; faire oublier, oblitérer *(le passé)*; oblitérer *(un timbre)*; **(b)** *Anat Med etc* oblitérer *(un conduit etc)*.

obliteration [əblɪtə'reɪʃən] *n* **(a)** effaçage *m*; *(by crossing out)* rature *f*; oblitération *f (d'un timbre)*; **(b)** *Anat Med* oblitération *f (d'un conduit)*.

oblivion [ə'blɪvɪən] *n* (état *m* d')oubli *m*; **to fall** *or* **sink into o.,** tomber dans l'oubli.

oblivious [ə'blɪvɪəs] *adj* oublieux (**of,** de); **I was o. of** *or* **to what was going on,** je n'étais pas conscient *ou* je n'avais pas conscience de ce qui se passait.

oblong ['ɒblɒŋ] **1** *adj* oblong, -ongue; *(visage etc)* allongé. **2** *n* rectangle *m*.

obloquy ['ɒbləkwɪ] *n Fml* opprobre *m*.

obnoxious [əb'nɒkʃəs] *adj (person, action etc)* odieux; *(person)* antipathique (**to s.o.,** à qn); détesté (**to,** par); *(smell etc)* repoussant.

oboe ['əʊbəʊ] *n Mus* hautbois *m*; **o. (player),** hautboïste *mf*.

oboist ['əʊbəʊɪst] *n Mus* hautboïste *mf*.

obscene [əb'siːn] *adj (song, telephone call, word etc)* obscène; *(disgusting)* repoussant, révoltant; *Fig (profits, prices, demands)* scandaleux; **it's o. that they are so rich when people are starving,** il est scandaleux qu'ils soient aussi riches alors qu'il y a des gens qui meurent de faim.

obscenely [əb'siːnlɪ] *adv* d'une manière obscène; **o. rich,** scandaleusement riche.

obscenity [əb'senɪtɪ] *n* obscénité *f*.

obscurantism [ɒbskjʊ'ræntɪz(ə)m] *n* obscurantisme *m*.

obscurantist [ɒbskjʊ'ræntɪst] *adj & n* obscurantiste *mf*.

obscure¹ [əb'skjʊər] *adj* **(a)** *(discours, livre etc)* obscur; **(b)** *(naissance)* obscur; *(auteur, œuvre)* inconnu, peu connu, obscur; *(village etc)* inconnu, ignoré; **(c)** *(sentiment)* vague, obscur; **(d)** *(dark)* obscur, ténébreux; **to grow** *or* **become o.,** s'obscurcir.

obscure² *vt* **(a)** *(hide from view)* cacher; **to o. sth from s.o.'s view,** cacher qch à qn; **(b)** obscurcir *(un argument, les faits)*; **(c)** *(overshadow)* éclipser, surpasser; **(d)** *(darken)* obscurcir, assombrir.

obscurely [əb'skjʊəlɪ] *adv* **(a)** *(parler)* obscurément; **(b)** *(sentir, voir)* vaguement.

obscurity [əb'skjʊərɪtɪ] *n* obscurité *f*.

obsequies ['ɒbsɪkwɪz] *npl* obsèques *fpl*, funérailles *fpl*.

obsequious [əb'siːkwɪəs] *adj* obséquieux.

obsequiously [əb'siːkwɪəslɪ] *adv* obséquieusement.

obsequiousness [əb'siːkwɪəsnɪs] *n* obséquiosité *f*.

observable [əb'zɜːvəb(ə)l] *adj* observable; *(changement)* perceptible; **it was o. that ...,** on a pu observer que ... .

observance [əb'zɜːvəns] *n* **(a)** observation *f*, observance *f* *(d'une loi, d'un usage etc)*; *Rel* règle *f*, observance *(d'un ordre religieux)*; **(b)** *(practice)* **religious observances,** pratiques religieuses.

observant [əb'zɜːvənt] *adj* **(a)** observateur, -trice (**of,** de); **he is very o.,** il est très observateur; **that's very o. of you,** tu es bien observateur; **(b)** *(of law, custom)* respectueux.

observation [ɒbzə'veɪʃən] *n* **(a)** observation *f*; *Mil* surveillance *f (du terrain, de l'ennemi)*; *(in surveying) & Astron* coup *m* de lunette; **to put/keep sth under o.,** mettre/tenir qch en observation; **to put/keep s.o. under o.,** mettre/tenir qn sous surveillance; *Med* **to keep s.o. in hospital for o.,** garder qn en observation à l'hôpital; **to take an o.,** *(in surveying) & Astron* faire une observation; *Nau* faire le point; *Nau* **position by o.,** point observé; *Mil* **aerial o.,** observation aérienne; **o. aircraft,** avion *m* de reconnaissance; *Rail* **o. coach** *or* **car,** voiture *f* panoramique; *Mil* **o. post** *or* **station,** poste *m* d'observation; *Astronaut* **o. satellite,** satellite *m* d'observation; *Med* **o. ward,** salle *f* des malades en observation; **(b)** *(remark)* remarque *f*, observation *f*; **to make an o.,** faire une observation (**about s.o./sth,** sur qn/qch).

observatory [əb'zɜːvət(ə)rɪ] *n* **(a)** *Astron* observatoire *m*; **(b)** *(observation point)* poste *m* d'observation.

observe [əb'zɜːv] **1** *vt* **(a)** observer *(les étoiles etc)*; **to o. the enemy's movements,** surveiller l'ennemi; **(b)** *(notice)* apercevoir, remarquer, noter *(un fait etc)*; **(c)** *(say)* dire, observer; **(d)** *(respect, follow)* observer *(la loi, les convenances, un jeûne)*; se conformer à *(un ordre)*; **to o. silence,** observer le silence; **a two minutes' silence was observed,** deux minutes de silence ont été observées; **to o. the Sabbath,** observer *ou* respecter le sabbat; *(in Christian religion)* observer *ou* respecter le dimanche. **2** *vi* observer; **a man who observes keenly,** un homme qui observe attentivement *ou* à qui rien n'échappe.

observer [əb'zɜːvər] *n* **(a)** *Astron Mil etc* observateur, -trice; **she is a close o. of events there,** elle observe de près les événements là-bas; **to send observers to a conference,** envoyer des observateurs à un congrès; **(b) a strict o. of protocol,** une personne qui respecte *ou* observe le protocole à la lettre.

obsess [əb'ses] *vt* obséder *(qn)*; **to be obsessed with** *or* **by an idea,** être obsédé d'une *ou* par une idée, être hanté par *ou* en proie à une idée; **to be obsessed with s.o.,** être obsédé par qn.

obsession [əb'seʃən] *n* **(a)** *(preoccupation)* obsession *f* (**with,** de); **physical fitness is an o. with her,** la forme physique est une obsession pour elle; **(b)** *Psy* obsession *f*.

obsessional [əb'seʃən(ə)l] *adj Psy* obsessionel.

obsessive [əb'sesɪv] *adj (idea, image)* obsédant; *(person)* à tendances obsessionnelles; *(behaviour)* obsessionnel.

obsessively [əb'sesɪvlɪ] *adv* de manière obsessionnelle; **he's o. concerned with his appearance,** il est obsédé par son apparence.

obsolescence [ɒbsə'les(ə)ns] *n (disuse)* désuétude *f*; *(of word, term)* vieillissement *m*; *Ind etc* obsolescence *f (d'un outillage)*; *Ind* **planned o.,** obsolescence prévue; *Ind Com* **built-in o.,** obsolescence programmée.

obsolescent [ɒbsə'les(ə)nt] *adj (falling into disuse)* qui tombe en désuétude; *(word, term)* qui vieillit, qui a vieilli.

obsolete ['ɒbsəliːt] *adj (word)* désuet, -ète, inusité, tombé en désuétude; *(fashion)* suranné; *(design etc)* démodé, dépassé; *(ship)* déclassé; *(institution)* aboli; *(coin, passport etc)* périmé.

obsoleteness ['ɒbsəliːtnɪs] *n* désuétude *f*.

obstacle ['ɒbstək(ə)l] *n* obstacle *m*; **to be an o. to sth,** faire obstacle à qch; **to put obstacles in s.o.'s way,** faire obstacle à qn; *Mil* **o. course,** parcours *m ou* piste *f* d'obstacles; *Fig* parcours du combattant; *Sp* **o. race,** course *f* d'obstacles.

obstetric(al) [ɒb'stetrɪk, -ɪk(ə)l] *adj* obstétrical, -aux.

obstetrician [ɒbste'trɪʃən] *n* médecin accoucheur, obstétricien, -ienne.

obstetrics [ɒb'stetrɪks] *npl (usu with sing verb)* obstétrique *f*.

obstinacy ['ɒbstɪnəsɪ] *n* **(a)** obstination *f*, entêtement *m*; *(of resistance)* acharnement *m*; **(b)** *Med* persistance *f (d'une maladie)*.

obstinate ['ɒbstɪnɪt] *adj* **(a)** obstiné (**in doing sth,** à faire qch); *(resistance etc)* acharné; **to be o.,** s'entêter; **(b)** *Med (fever)* rebelle; *(cold)* tenace.

obstinately ['ɒbstɪnɪtlɪ] *adv* obstinément; *(to resist)* avec acharnement; **to refuse o.,** s'obstiner à refuser.

obstreperous [əb'strepərəs] *adj (rebellious)* rebelle;

(*noisy*) bruyant, tapageur; **to get o.,** (*complain*) *F* rouspéter; (*get awkward*) faire du scandale.

obstreperously [əb'strepərəslɪ] *adv* (*rebelliously*) *F* en rouspétant; (*noisily*) bruyamment, tapageusement; **to behave o.,** faire du scandale.

obstruct [əb'strʌkt] **1** *vt* obstruer, encombrer (*la rue etc*); boucher (*un tuyau etc*); *Med* oblitérer, obstruer (*l'intestin*); gêner (*la vue*); gêner, entraver, empêcher (*les mouvements de qn*); gêner (*la circulation, la navigation*); **to o. s.o.'s path,** barrer le chemin à qn; *Jur* **to o. the course of justice,** empêcher la justice de suivre son cours; **to o. s.o. in the execution of his duty,** gêner qn dans l'exercice de ses fonctions; *Sp* **to o. another player,** faire obstruction; *Parl* **to o. a bill,** faire obstruction. **2** *vi Sp* faire obstruction.

obstruction [əb'strʌkʃən] *n* **(a)** (*action*) engorgement *m* (*d'un tuyau etc*); *Med* obstruction *f*, oblitération *f* (*de l'intestin*); empêchement *m* (*de qn dans ses affaires, de la circulation etc*); *Sp Pol* obstruction; **(b)** (*blockage*) encombrement *m* (*dans la rue*); entrave *f* (*à la navigation*); engorgement *m* (*dans un tuyau*); **to cause an o.,** (*on road*) gêner la circulation; *Rail* **an o. on the line,** un obstacle sur la voie.

obstructionism [əb'strʌkʃənɪz(ə)m] *n Pol* obstructionnisme *m*.

obstructionist [əb'strʌkʃənɪst] *n Pol* obstructionniste *mf*.

obstructive [əb'strʌktɪv] *adj* (*person*) qui met des bâtons dans les roues; (*tactic*) d'obstruction; *Med* obstructif, obstruant; *Parl etc* **to be o.,** faire obstruction, être obstructionniste.

obtain [əb'teɪn] **1** *vt* obtenir (*qch*); **to o. sugar from beet,** extraire du sucre de la betterave; **I obtained permission to see him,** j'ai obtenu la permission de le voir. **2** *vi Fml* (*of practice etc*) avoir cours.

obtainable [əb'teɪnəb(ə)l] *adj* procurable; **easily o.,** facile à obtenir *ou* à se procurer.

obtrude [əb'tru:d] **1** *vt* mettre (*qch*) en avant; **to o. one's opinions on others,** imposer ses opinions à autrui; **to o. oneself,** s'imposer à l'attention. **2** *vi* (*of person*) s'imposer à l'attention (*de qn*); (*of thing*) être trop en évidence.

obtrusion [əb'tru:ʒən] *n* intrusion *f*.

obtrusive [əb'tru:sɪv] *adj* **(a)** (*person*) importun, intrus; (*behaviour*) indiscret; **(b)** (*smell etc*) pénétrant.

obtrusively [əb'tru:sɪvlɪ] *adv* inopportunément; (*to behave*) indiscrètement.

obtrusiveness [əb'tru:sɪvnɪs] *n* importunité *f*.

obtuse [əb'tju:s] *adj* **(a)** (*esprit*) obtus, peu intelligent; **you're being deliberately o.,** tu fais exprès de ne pas comprendre; **(b)** (*blunt-ended*) obtus, émoussé; *Math* **o. angle,** angle obtus.

obtuseness [əb'tju:snɪs] *n* **(a)** (*of person*) stupidité *f*; **(b)** (*bluntness*) manque *m* de tranchant; (*lack of point*) manque de pointe.

obverse ['ɒbvɜ:s] **1** *adj* **o. side,** avers *m*, obvers *m*, face *f* (*d'une médaille*). **2** *n* avers *m*, obvers *m*, face *f* (*d'une médaille*); opposé *m* (*d'une vérité*).

obviate ['ɒbvɪeɪt] *vt* prévenir, parer à, obvier à (*une difficulté etc*); aller au-devant de (*une objection*); **this obviates the need to ...,** ceci pare à la nécessité de ... .

obvious ['ɒbvɪəs] *adj* évident, clair, manifeste; (*fact, truth*) patent; (*feature*) frappant; **it's quite o. that she is lying,** elle ment, cela saute aux yeux; **you were too o.,** (*unsubtle*) tu n'as pas été très subtil; **it was the o. thing to do,** c'était tout indiqué, cela s'imposait; **an o. comparison would be with the French Revolution,** la première comparaison qui vient à l'esprit est la révolution française; **to state the o.,** enfoncer une porte ouverte; **to miss the o.,** ne pas voir l'essentiel; **his patriotism is a little (too) o.,** son patriotisme sonne faux.

obviously ['ɒbvɪəslɪ] *adv* **(a)** (*in an obvious way*) manifestement; **he's so o. English,** il est si manifestement anglais; **she was very o. shocked,** elle a été manifestement choquée; **he did it so o.,** il l'a fait si ostensiblement; **they are different, but not o.,** ils sont différents, mais ça ne saute pas aux yeux; **he wasn't o. the right choice but ...,** au premier abord il n'était pas évident que c'était le bon choix mais ...; **(b)** (*of course*) évidemment; **do you prefer this? — o.,** préférez-vous cela? — bien sûr *ou* (*in exasperation*) évidemment; **o. not!,** bien sûr que non!, évidemment non!; **I'll o. have to turn the offer down,** il va sans dire que je devrai refuser l'offre; **there'll be ice, so o. be careful,** il va y avoir de la glace, alors fais attention.

obviousness ['ɒbvɪəsnɪs] *n* évidence *f*, clarté *f*.

OC [əʊ'si:] *n Mil* (*abbr* **Officer Commanding**) chef *m* de corps.

ocarina [ɒkə'ri:nə] *n Mus* ocarina *m*.

occasion¹ [ə'keɪʒən] *n* **(a)** (*time*) occasion *f*; **on this o.,** en cette occasion; **on the o. of his daughter's marriage,** à l'occasion du mariage de sa fille; **on one o.,** une fois; **on another o.,** une autre fois; **on several occasions,** à plusieurs reprises; **on rare occasions,** rarement; **on such an o.,** en pareille occasion; **on great occasions,** dans les grandes occasions; **on o.,** (*occasionally*) parfois, de temps en temps; **words appropriate to the o.,** paroles de circonstance; **to dress to suit the o.,** s'habiller pour l'occasion; **we'll make this an o.,** nous allons fêter ça; **(b)** (*opportunity*) occasion *f*; **I'll speak to him on the first o.,** je lui parlerai à la prochaine occasion; **if you have o. to speak to him,** si vous avez l'occasion de lui parler; **(c)** *Fml* (*cause*) sujet *m*, cause *f*; **there's** *or* **you have no o. to be alarmed,** il n'y a pas lieu de vous inquiéter; **should the o. arise,** s'il y a lieu, le cas échéant; **this action was the o. of great suffering,** cette action a donné lieu à de grandes souffrances.

occasion² *vt Fml* occasionner, entraîner (*la mort, un incendie etc*); donner lieu à (*la peur etc*).

occasional [ə'keɪʒ(ə)nəl] *adj* **(a)** (*visit*) espacé, occasionnel; (*incident*) qui se produit de temps en temps, occasionnel; **o. showers,** averses éparses *ou* occasionnelles; **I have the o. cigarette/glass of wine,** il m'arrive de fumer une cigarette/de boire un verre de vin; **(b)** (*pièce, vers*) de circonstance; **o. table,** table volante, guéridon *m*; **o. chair,** chaise volante.

occasionally [ə'keɪʒən(ə)lɪ] *adv* de temps en temps, parfois, occasionnellement.

occident ['ɒksɪdənt] *n* occident *m*, couchant *m*; *Pol etc* **the O.,** l'Occident.

occidental [ɒksɪ'dent(ə)l] *adj* occidental, -aux.

occipital [ɒk'sɪpɪt(ə)l] *Anat* **1** *adj* occipital, -aux. **2** *n* occipital, -aux.

occiput ['ɒksɪpʌt] *n Anat* occiput *m*.

occlude [ə'klu:d] *vt* fermer, boucher (*un orifice etc*); occlure (*les paupières*); *Ch* (*of a metal*) absorber (et retenir) (*un gaz*); occlure (*un gaz*).

occlusion [ə'klu:ʒən] *n* **(a)** occlusion *f*, bouchage *m*, fermeture *f* (*d'un conduit etc*); *Ch* occlusion (*d'un gaz*); **(b)** (*of tooth*) occlusion *f* (molaire *etc*).

occlusive [ə'klu:sɪv] *Ling* **1** *adj* **o. consonant,** consonne occlusive. **2** *n* consonne occlusive.

occult [ɒ'kʌlt] **1** *adj* occulte, secret, -ète; **the o. sciences,** les sciences *fpl* occultes. **2** *n* **the o.,** l'occulte *m*.

occultism ['ɒkʌltɪz(ə)m] *n* occultisme *m*.

occupancy ['ɒkjʊpənsɪ] *n* **(a)** *Jur* possession *f* à titre de premier occupant; **(b)** occupation *f*, habitation *f* (*d'un immeuble*); **multiple o.,** (*of flat, hotel room*) occupation multiple.

occupant ['ɒkjʊpənt] *n* **(a)** occupant, -ante; *Jur* premier occupant; **(b)** voyageur *m*, passager *m* (*d'une voiture etc*); **(c)** titulaire *mf* (*d'un emploi*).

occupation [ɒkjʊ'peɪʃən] *n* **(a)** (*activity*) occupation *f*; (*profession*) métier *m*, profession *f*; **to find s.o. (some) o.,** donner de l'occupation à qn; **(b)** (*of house, land*) occupation *f*; **to be in o. of a house,** occuper une maison; **fit for o.,** (*house*) habitable; *Mil* **army of o.,** armée *f* d'occupation; **troops of o.,** troupes *fpl* d'occupation; *Hist* **the Roman o. of Britain,** l'occupation de la Grande-Bretagne par les Romains; **the O.,** (*of France*) l'Occupation *f*.

occupational [ɒkjʊ'peɪʃən(ə)l] *adj* **o. disease,** maladie professionnelle; **o. hazard,** (*physical danger*) risque *m* du métier; *Hum* déformation professionnelle; **o. therapist,** ergothérapeute *mf*; **o. therapy,** thérapeutique occupationnelle, ergothérapie *f*.

occupied ['ɒkjʊpaɪd] *adj* **(a)** (*house*) habité; *Mil* (*territoire*) occupé; **this seat is o.,** cette place est prise; **in o. France,** dans la France occupée; **(b)** (*busy*) **to be o. in** *or* **with doing sth,** être occupé à faire qch; **to keep s.o. o.,** (*in employment*) occuper qn; **to keep one's mind o.,** s'occuper l'esprit.

occupier ['ɒkjʊpaɪər] *n* occupant, -ante; (*tenant*) locataire *mf*; habitant, -ante (*d'une maison*); **to the o.,** (*on letter*) à l'attention de l'occupant.

occupy ['ɒkjʊpaɪ] *vt* **(a)** occuper, habiter (*une maison etc*); occuper, remplir (*une fonction*); *Mil* occuper (*un pays ennemi*); s'emparer de (*un point stratégique*); **workers have occupied the building,** les ouvriers ont occupé le bâtiment; **(b)** remplir (*un espace*); occuper (*une place, l'attention*); **to o. one's time (in, with) doing sth,** remplir *ou* occuper son temps à faire qch; **her work occupies all her time,** son travail l'absorbe; **to o. one's mind,** s'occuper l'esprit.

occur [ə'kɜ:r] *vi* **(-rr-)** **(a)** (*happen*) (*of event etc*) avoir lieu, survenir, arriver, se produire; (*of opportunity*) se présenter, s'offrir; (*of fire*) se déclarer; **this seldom occurs,** cela arrive rarement; **I hope it will not o. again,** j'espère que cela ne se répétera pas; **(b)** (*be present*) (*of objects, types*) se rencontrer, se trouver, se présenter; **this word occurs twice in the letter,** ce mot se rencontre deux fois dans la lettre; **(c)** (*of idea etc*) venir à l'esprit; **it didn't o. to them that she might be lying,** il ne leur est pas venu à l'esprit qu'elle mentait peut-être.

occurrence [əˈkʌrəns] *n* **(a) two hours before its o.,** deux heures avant que cela eût lieu; **to be of frequent o.,** arriver souvent, se produire fréquemment; **the o. of two murders on the same day,** le fait que deux meurtres aient été commis le même jour; **(b)** (*event*) événement *m*, fait *m*, occurrence *f*; **an everyday o.,** un fait quotidien; **a singular o.,** un fait étrange.

ocean [ˈəʊʃən] *n* océan *m*; **the Atlantic O.,** l'(océan) Atlantique *m*; *Fig* **an o. of sand,** une mer de sable; **o. floor,** fond sous-marin; **o. current,** courant *m* océanique.

ocean-going [ˈəʊʃəngəʊɪŋ] *adj* (*navire*) au long cours, de haute mer.

Oceania [əʊʃɪˈeɪnɪə] *n* l'Océanie *f*.

oceanic [əʊʃɪˈænɪk] *adj* (*voyage, climat*) océanique.

oceanographer [əʊʃəˈnɒgrəfər] *n* océanographe *mf*.

oceanography [əʊʃəˈnɒgrəfɪ] *n* océanographie *f*.

ocelot [ˈɒsəlɒt] *n* (*animal*) ocelot *m*.

ochre, *US* **ocher** [ˈəʊkər] **1** *n Miner* ocre *f*; **red o.,** ocre rouge; **yellow o.,** jaune *m* d'ocre, ocre jaune. **2** *adj* **o.(-coloured),** ocre *inv*.

o'clock [əˈklɒk] *adv* **one o'c.,** une heure; **two/three/***etc* **o'c.,** deux/trois/*etc* heures; **at four o'c.,** à quatre heures; **the seven o'c. train,** le train de sept heures.

OCR [əʊsiːˈɑːr] *n abbr Comptr* **(a) optical character reader; (b) optical character recognition.**

octagon [ˈɒktəgən] *n Math* octogone *m*.

octagonal [ɒkˈtægən(ə)l] *adj Math* octogonal, -aux.

octahedral [ɒktəˈhiːdrəl, -ˈhed-] *adj Math* octaédrique.

octahedron, *pl* **-ons, -a** [ˈɒktəˈhiːdrən, -ˈhed-, -ənz, -ə] *n Math* octaèdre *m*.

octane [ˈɒkteɪn] *n Ch* octane *m*; **o. number** *or* **rating,** indice *m* d'octane.

octave [ˈɒktɪv] *n Rel Mus Fencing* octave *f*; (*in poetry*) huitain *m*; *Mus* **an o. apart,** espacé par un octave.

octavo [ɒkˈteɪvəʊ] *adj & n Typ* in-octavo *m inv*.

octet [ɒkˈtet] *n* **(a)** *Mus* octuor *m*; **(b)** (*in poetry*) huitain *m*; **(c)** *Ch* octet *m*.

October [ɒkˈtəʊbər] *n* octobre *m*; **in O.,** au mois d'octobre, en octobre; **(on) the first/seventh of O.,** le premier/sept octobre; **an O. morning,** un matin d'octobre.

octogenarian [ɒktədʒɪˈneərɪən] **1** *adj* octogénaire. **2** *n* octogénaire *mf*.

octopod [ˈɒktəpɒd] **1** *adj* octopode. **2** *n* octopode *m*.

octopus [ˈɒktəpəs] *n* poulpe *m*, pieuvre *f*.

octosyllabic [ɒktəsɪˈlæbɪk] *adj* (*vers, mot*) octosyllabe, octosyllabique.

octuple [ˈɒktjuːp(ə)l] *adj & n* octuple *m*.

ocular [ˈɒkjʊlər] **1** *adj* (*nerf etc*) oculaire. **2** *n Opt* oculaire *m* (*de microscope etc*).

oculist [ˈɒkjʊlɪst] *n* oculiste *mf*.

OD¹ [əʊˈdiː] *n F* (*abbr* **overdose**) = **OVERDOSE¹**.

OD² (*pt & pp* **OD'd, OD'ed**) *vi F* (*abbr* **overdose**) = **OVERDOSE²**.

odalisk, odalisque [ˈəʊdəlɪsk] *n* odalisque *f*.

odd [ɒd] *adj* **(a)** (*strange*) singulier, drôle; (*person*) excentrique, original; **o. size,** dimension spéciale *ou* non courante; **o.- looking,** bizarre; **the o. thing about it is that ...,** le curieux de l'affaire *ou* ce qui est bizarre c'est que ...; **it's o. your not knowing about it,** il est curieux *ou* singulier que vous n'en sachiez rien; **how o. that he should have forgotten it!,** comme c'est drôle qu'il l'ait oublié!; **(well), that's o.!,** voilà qui est singulier!, c'est curieux!; **an o. way of saying sorry,** une curieuse manière de s'excuser;

(b) *Math etc* (*nombre*) impair; **a hundred o. sheep,** cent et quelques moutons; **twenty pounds o., twenty o. pounds,** un peu plus de vingt livres; **a few o. grammes over,** quelques grammes de plus; **what shall we do with the o. six?,** que ferons-nous avec les six qui restent?; **to be the o. man (out),** être *ou* rester en surnombre; *Fig* ne pas être du métier *ou* de la partie; **to play at o. man out,** jouer à qui sera éliminé; **she was the o. woman out, not being German,** elle se distinguait en n'étant pas allemande; **which of these books is the o. one out?,** lequel de ces livres n'a rien à voir avec les autres?;

(c) (*one of a set*) dépareillé; (*one of a pair*) déparié; **o. glove,** gant déparié *ou* dépareillé; **o. stockings,** bas qui ne vont pas ensemble;

(d) (*random*) quelconque; **any o. piece of cloth,** un bout d'étoffe quelconque; **at o. times,** par-ci par-là; **at o. moments,** dans mes *ou* ses *etc* moments perdus; **we get the o. visitor,** nous avons de la visite de temps en temps; **o. lot,** articles dépareillés; **o. jobs about the house,** petits travaux à faire dans la maison.

oddball [ˈɒdbɔːl] *F* **1** *n* excentrique *mf*. **2** *adj* (*ideas, friends*) excentrique.

oddbod [ˈɒdbɒd] *n F* original, -ale.

oddity [ˈɒdɪtɪ] *n* **(a)** (*strangeness*) singularité *f*, bizarrerie *f*; **he has some little oddities,** il a quelques petits travers; **(b)** (*person*) personne excentrique, original, -ale; (*thing*) chose *f* bizarre, curiosité *f*; **this movie is an o.,** ce film est une œuvre bizarre.

odd-jobman, odd-jobber [ˈɒdˈdʒɒbmæn, -ɒbər] *n* homme *m* à tout faire.

oddly [ˈɒdlɪ] *adv* bizarrement, singulièrement; **o. enough nobody knew anything about it,** chose curieuse, personne n'en savait rien; **an o. lopsided face,** un visage bizarrement irrégulier; **I find her o. attractive,** je la trouve étrangement attirante.

oddment [ˈɒdmənt] *n* (*one of a set*) article dépareillé; (*sale item*) article en solde; (*piece of material*) coupon *m* d'étoffe; **oddments,** fins *fpl* de série; **remnants and oddments,** soldes *mpl* et occasions *fpl*.

oddness [ˈɒdnɪs] *n* singularité *f*, bizarrerie *f*.

odds [ɒdz] *npl* (*occ with sing verb*) **(a)** (*probability*) chances *fpl*; **the o. are against him/in his favour,** les chances sont contre lui/pour lui; **to fight against great** *or* **long o.,** lutter *ou* combattre contre des forces supérieures, avoir affaire à plus fort que soi; **what's the o.?,** (*what does it matter?*) qu'est-ce que ça fait?; **it makes no o.,** ça ne fait rien, cela n'a pas d'importance; *Horseracing* **o. on** *or* **against a horse,** cote *f* d'un cheval; **short/long o.,** faible/forte cote; **the o. are (at) ten to one,** la cote est à dix contre un; **the o. are that he'll succeed,** il y a gros à parier qu'il réussira; **it's against all the o.,** il est fort peu probable; *Sp* **to give s.o. o. of ten to one,** proposer à qn un pari à dix contre un;

(b) (*inequality*) inégalité *f*; **to make o. evens,** égaliser les conditions *ou* les avantages *etc*, répartir les choses également.

(c) to be at o. with s.o., (*be in disagreement*) ne pas être d'accord avec qn; (*be on bad terms*) être brouillé avec qn (**over,** à propos de);

(d) o. and ends *or Br F* **sods,** petits bouts; (*people*) les autres.

odds-on [ɒdˈzɒn] *adj* **o.-on bet,** pari inégal; **o.-on favourite,** grand favori; **it's o.-on that he won't notice,** à coup sûr il ne remarquera pas.

ode [əʊd] *n Liter* ode *f*.

odious [ˈəʊdɪəs] *n* odieux (**to,** à).

odiously [ˈəʊdɪəslɪ] *adv* odieusement.

odium [ˈəʊdɪəm] *n* **(a)** (*hatred*) réprobation *f*, détestation *f*; **to bring** *or* **cast o. upon s.o.,** rendre qn odieux (aux yeux des autres); **(b)** (*hatefulness*) caractère odieux; odieux *m* (*d'une action*).

odometer [əʊˈdɒmɪtər] *n US* compteur *m* (kilométrique).

odontology [ɒdɒnˈtɒlədʒɪ] *n* odontologie *f*.

odor [ˈəʊdər] *n US* = **ODOUR.**

odoriferous [əʊdəˈrɪfərəs] *adj* **(a)** odoriférant, parfumé; **(b)** *F* (*bad-smelling*) malodorant.

odorless [ˈəʊdəlɪs] *adj US* = **ODOURLESS.**

odorous [ˈəʊdərəs] *adj* **(a)** odorant, qui exhale une odeur (*agréable*); **(b)** *F* (*bad-smelling*) malodorant.

odour, *US* **odor** [ˈəʊdər] *n* odeur *f*; (*pleasant smell*) odeur (agréable), parfum *m*; *F* (*bad smell*) mauvaise odeur; **body o.,** odeur corporelle; *Fig* **to be in good/bad o. with s.o.,** être bien/mal vu de qn; **to die in (the) o. of sanctity,** mourir en odeur de sainteté.

odourless, *US* **odorless** [ˈəʊdəlɪs] *adj* inodore, sans odeur.

Odyssey [ˈɒdɪsɪ] *n* **the O.,** l'Odyssée *f*; *Fig* **his journey was a real o.,** son voyage fut une véritable odyssée.

OECD [əʊiːsiːˈdiː] *n Admin* (*abbr* **Organization for Economic Co-operation and Development**) OCDE *f*.

oedema, *US* **edema** [ɪˈdiːmə] *n* œdème *m*.

Oedipal [ˈiːdɪpəl] *adj Psy* œdipien, -ienne.

Oedipus [ˈiːdɪpəs] *n Myth* Œdipe *m*; *Psy* **O. complex,** complexe *m* d'Œdipe.

OEM [əʊiːˈem] *n Comptr* (*abbr* **original equipment manufacturer**) constructeur *m* de systèmes originaux; **OEM sale,** vente *f* OEM.

o'er [ɔːr, 'əʊər] *prep Lit* = **OVER 1**.

oesophagus, *US* **esophagus,** *pl* **-gi, -guses** [iː'sɒfəgəs, -gaɪ, -gəsɪz] *n Anat* œsophage *m*.

oestrogen, *US* **estrogen** ['iːstrədʒen] *n Biol Ch* œstrogène *m*.

oestrous, *US* **estrous** ['iːstrəs] *adj Biol* (*cycle etc*) œstral, -aux.

oestrus, *US* **estrus** ['iːstrəs] *n Biol* œstrus *m*.

of [ɒv, *unstressed* əv] *prep* **(a)** (*indicating separation, origin, cause*) de; **south of,** au sud de; **within a mile of,** à moins d'un mil(l)e de; **free of,** libre de; **cured of,** guéri de; **of noble birth,** de naissance noble; **works of Shakespeare,** œuvres *fpl* de Shakespeare; **to expect sth of s.o.,** s'attendre à qch de qn; **to ask a favour of s.o.,** demander une faveur à qn; **of necessity,** par nécessité; **of one's own accord,** de soi-même; **of my own choice,** de mon propre choix; **she died of grief,** elle mourut de chagrin; **proud of sth,** fier de qch; **I'm sick of it,** j'en ai assez;

(b) (*indicating agency*) **it is very good** *or* **kind of you,** c'est bien aimable de votre part, c'est très gentil à vous; **how clever of her,** comme c'est intelligent de sa part; *Arch* **beloved of all,** aimé de tout le monde;

(c) (*indicating material*) **made of wood,** fait de *ou* en bois; **wall of stone,** mur *m* en *ou* de pierre; **full of water,** plein d'eau;

(d) (*concerning, in respect of*) **to think of s.o.,** penser à qn; **to warn s.o. of sth,** avertir qn de qch; **what do you think of him?,** que pensez-vous de lui?; **of President Taylor it was said that ...,** il a été dit du Président Taylor que ...; **guilty of,** coupable de; **capable of,** capable de; **doctor of medicine,** docteur en médecine; **well, what of it?,** et bien?, et après?; **hard of hearing,** dur d'oreille;

(e) (*in description*) **the city of Rome,** la cité de Rome; **man of genius,** homme de génie; **people of foreign appearance,** gens à l'air étranger; **child of ten,** enfant (âgé) de dix ans; *esp Am* **his wife of twenty years,** la femme qu'il a épousée il y a vingt ans; **to be of no account,** ne pas compter; **to be of interest,** être intéressant, avoir de l'intérêt; **a fine figure of a woman,** une belle femme; **that fool of a sergeant,** cet imbécile de sergent; **all of a tremble,** tout tremblant; **all of a sudden,** tout d'un coup, tout à coup;

(f) (*with grammatical subject*) **the love of a mother,** l'amour d'une mère; (*with grammatical object*) **the fear of God,** la crainte de Dieu; **great drinker of whisky,** grand buveur de whisky;

(g) (*partitive*) **three parts of the whole,** trois quarts du tout; *F* **no more of that!,** plus de cela!; **how much of it do you want?,** combien en voulez-vous?; **many/several of us,** beaucoup/plusieurs d'entre nous; **there were two/several of us,** nous étions deux/plusieurs; **she is one of us,** elle est des nôtres; **one of the best,** un des meilleurs; **to give of one's best,** faire de son mieux; **the best of men,** le meilleur des hommes; **the bravest of the brave,** le brave des braves; **first of all,** avant tout; **he, of all men** *or* **people,** lui entre tous; **this day of all days,** ce jour entre tous;

(h) (*belonging to*) **the husband of the Prime Minister,** le mari du premier ministre; **citizen of London,** citoyen de Londres; **the first of the month,** le premier du mois; **he is a friend of mine,** c'est un de mes amis; **it's no business of yours,** cela ne vous regarde pas, ce n'est pas votre affaire;

(i) (*with expressions of time*) **of late years,** (pendant) ces dernières années; **of late,** dernièrement, récemment; *F* **of an evening,** le soir.

off¹ [ɒf] **1** *adv* **(a)** (*away*) *Nau* au large; **house a mile o.,** maison à un mil(l)e de distance; **some way o.,** à quelque distance; **far o.,** au loin, dans le lointain; **to go** *or F* **be o.,** (*leave*) s'en aller, partir; **I'm o. to London,** je pars pour Londres; **I must be o.,** (il faut que) je me sauve; **be o. with you!,** sauve-toi!, va-t-en!; **they're o.!,** (*of racers, racehorses etc*) ils sont partis!, ils ont pris le départ!; **to go o. (to sleep),** s'endormir; *Th* **to speak o.,** parler à la cantonade;

(b) (*indicating separation*) **to take o. one's coat,** ôter son manteau; **a button has come o.,** un bouton a sauté; **to cut s.o.'s head o.,** décapiter qn; **o. with her head!,** qu'on lui coupe la tête!; **o. with those wet clothes!,** retire-moi ces vêtements humides; **to turn o. the gas,** fermer le gaz; (*at the main*) couper le gaz; **the ignition is o.,** l'allumage est coupé; **the light/radio is o.,** la lumière/radio est éteinte;

(c) *Com* **20%/£5 o.,** 20%/£5 de remise;

(d) (*indicating completion*) **to finish o. a piece of work,** achever un travail;

(e) **have you any time o. during the week?,** avez-vous des heures libres *ou* des loisirs pendant la semaine?; **to take some time o.,** prendre des loisirs; **day o.,** jour *m* de congé; **to give the staff a day o.,** donner congé à son personnel pour la journée; **to arrange to take two days o.,** se libérer pour deux jours;

(f) (*in phrases*) **o. and on, on and o.,** par intervalles, de temps en temps; **right** *or* **straight o.,** immédiatement, sur-le-champ, tout de suite.

2 *prep* **(a)** (*from*) de; **to fall o. sth,** tomber de qch; **to take a ring o. one's finger,** ôter une bague de son doigt; **to cut a slice o. sth,** couper une tranche de qch; **we dined o. a leg of lamb,** nous avons dîné d'une tranche de gigot; *El* **to work o. the mains,** être branché sur le secteur; **a third o. everything,** rabais d'un tiers sur tout; *F* **to borrow money o. s.o.,** emprunter de l'argent à qn; **I caught a cold o. my brother,** mon frère m'a passé un rhume; *Com* **10%/£20 o. a price,** 10%/£20 de remise sur un prix; **o. the top of one's head,** (*to say, answer etc*) sur-le-champ; **o. the cuff,** (*to make a speech*) au pied levé;

(b) (*away from, outside of*) écarté de, éloigné de; **village o. the beaten track,** village éloigné *ou* hors des chemins battus; **street o. the main road,** rue qui donne sur la grande route; **it's just o. Regent Street,** c'est tout près de Regent Street; **to sing/play o. key,** chanter/jouer faux; **o. season,** (*in tourist trade*) pendant la morte-saison; *Comptr* **o. line,** (*processing*) en différé; (*printer etc*) déconnecté; **to put a printer o. line,** déconnecter une imprimante; **to go o. line,** se déconnecter; **he's o. drugs,** il a cessé de prendre de la drogue;

(c) (*on vacation*) **to have time o. work,** avoir du temps de libre; *see also* **1** *adv* **(e)**;

(d) **to be o. one's food,** n'avoir pas d'appétit; **I'm o. coffee at the moment,** en ce moment je n'aime pas le café; *F* **I'm o. her at the moment,** je ne l'aime plus en ce moment;

(e) *Nau* **o. the Cape,** à la hauteur du Cap; au large du Cap; **o. the coast of Spain,** au large de la côte espagnole; **to sail o. the wind,** naviguer vent largue.

3 *adj* **(a)** (*not functioning*) **o. position,** position *f* de repos, position 'zéro' *ou* 'fermé' *ou* 'coupé'; position de desserrage (*des freins*); *El* position de rupture de circuit; position d'extinction (*des lampes*); **o. switch,** commande *f* d'arrêt;

(b) (*not busy*) **o. season,** morte-saison *f*, *pl* mortes-saisons;

(c) (*referring to side*) *Horseriding* **o. leg,** jambe *f* de dehors; *Cr* **o. drive,** coup *m* en avant à droite; **o. side, o. board,** (*in bookbinding*) verso *m*, plat inférieur;

(d) (*unlikely*) **on the o. chance,** au cas peu probable où; **let's go to the office on the o. chance (that) she's there,** allons au bureau au cas peu probable où elle y serait; **I'll take it on the o. chance,** je le prends au cas où;

(e) (*on vacation*) en congé, en vacances: **to be o. sick,** être absent parce qu'on est malade, être en congé maladie; **o. day,** jour où l'on ne travaille pas, jour chômé; **he's o. today,** il n'est pas là aujourd'hui;

(f) (*cancelled, finished*) (*engagement*) rompu; (*marriage*) annulé; **the deal is o.,** le marché est rompu *ou* ne se fera pas; **it's all** *or* **the whole thing is o.,** tout est fini, *F* l'affaire est tombée à l'eau; **this dish is o.,** (*in restaurant*) ce plat est épuisé;

(g) (*not fresh*) **to be o.,** (*of food*) n'être plus frais; (*of meat*) être avarié; (*of milk, orange juice etc*) être tourné; **this beer's o.,** cette bière est éventée;

(h) (*inaccurate*) **his timing was a bit o.,** (*when he asked for a raise etc*) il n'a pas choisi un très bon moment; **an o. day,** un jour où l'on n'est pas en train;

(i) *F* (*improper, unfair*) **that's a bit o.!,** ça c'est pas sympa!;

(j) **to be well/badly o.,** être à l'aise/pauvre; **to be badly o. for sth,** être à court de qch; **he is better o. where he is,** il est bien mieux où il est.

off² *n F* **the o.,** le départ.

offal ['ɒf(ə)l] *n* **(a)** déchets *mpl* d'abattage (de boucherie); (*edible*) abats *mpl*; (*inedible*) issues *fpl*; **(b)** (*waste*) rebut *m*, déchets *mpl*.

offbeat ['ɒfbiːt] **1** *n Mus* temps *m* faible. **2** *adj F* (*person, clothes, music*) original, excentrique.

off-Broadway ['ɒfbrɔːdweɪ] *US Th adj* (*production*) en dehors de Broadway.

off-centre, off-centred, *US* **-center, -centered** [ɒf'sentər, -təd] *adj* décentré, décalé.

off-colour, *US* **off-color** [ɒf'kʌlər] *adj* **(a)** *Br* (*unwell*) pas dans son assiette; **to be** *or* **feel o.-c.,** ne pas se sentir dans son assiette; **to look o.-c.,** ne pas avoir l'air dans son assiette; **(b)** (*joke*) grivois, d'un goût douteux.

off-course ['ɒfkɔːs] *adj* (*pari*) effectué hors des champs de course.

offcut ['ɒfkʌt] *n* découpure *f*; (*from wooden plank, length of cloth*) chute *f*.

offence, *US* **offense** [ə'fens] *n* **(a)** *Jur etc* faute *f*; **minor/serious o.,** faute légère/grave; **to commit an o.,** commettre une infraction; *Jur* **indictable o.,** violation *f* de la loi; *Jur* **petty** *or* **minor o.,** contravention *f* (de simple police); *Jur* **capital o.,** crime capital; *Jur* **second o.,** récidive *f*;

(b) (*no pl*) (*annoyance, displeasure*) blessure faite à la susceptibilité de qn; **to cause o.,** déplaire; **to take o.,** se froisser, se choquer (**at sth,** de qch); **to take o. at the slightest thing,** s'offenser d'un rien; **to cause** *or* **to give o. to s.o.,** offenser *ou* blesser *ou* froisser qn; **I meant no o.,** je ne voulais offenser personne;

(c) (*attack*) attaque *f*, agression *f*.

(d) ['ɒfens] *US Sp* attaque *f*.

offend [ə'fend] **1** *vt* offenser, blesser, choquer (*qn*); **to be offended at** *or* **with** *or* **by sth,** se froisser *ou* s'offenser de qch; **to be easily offended,** être très susceptible, se froisser facilement; **I hope you won't be offended if I ...,** j'espère que vous ne vous froisserez pas si je ...; **to o. the eye,** (*of thing*) choquer les regards *ou* la vue; **harsh sound that offends the ear,** son dur qui offense l'oreille. **2** *vi* **(a)** (*cause offence*) choquer; **I didn't mean to o.,** je ne voulais pas choquer; **(b)** (*infringe rules*) pécher; **to o. against the law,** violer *ou* enfreindre la loi; **to o. against (the laws of) grammar,** pécher contre la grammaire.

offended [ə'fendɪd] *adj* **(a)** (*insulted*) fâché, froissé; **in an o. tone of voice,** d'une voix offensée; **(b)** *Jur* **the o. party,** l'offensé, -ée.

offender [ə'fendər] *n* malfaiteur *m*; *Jur* délinquant, -ante; **a first o.,** un délinquant primaire.

offending [ə'fendɪŋ] *adj* fautif.

offense [ə'fens] *n US* = **OFFENCE**.

offensive [ə'fensɪv] **1** *adj* **(a)** (*word, action*) offensant, blessant, choquant; (*spectacle*) repoussant; (*smell*) nauséabond; **morally o. book,** livre outrageant pour les bonnes mœurs; **the remarks were deeply o. to many people,** ces remarques ont été profondément choquantes pour de nombreuses personnes; **to be o. to s.o.,** (*of person*) insulter qn, injurier qn; **in an o. tone,** d'un ton injurieux; **(b)** *Mil etc* offensif. **2** *n Mil Sp & Fig* offensive *f*; **to take the o.,** prendre l'offensive; **to be on the o.,** être sur l'offensive.

offensively [ə'fensɪvlɪ] *adv* **(a)** (*shockingly*) d'une manière offensante *ou* choquante; (*to say*) d'un ton injurieux; **(b)** *Mil Sp* offensivement.

offensiveness [ə'fensɪvnɪs] *n* **(a)** nature offensante (*d'un spectacle, d'un son*); nature nauséabonde (*d'une odeur*); **(b)** nature injurieuse (*d'une réponse etc*).

offer¹ ['ɒfər] *n* offre *f*, proposition *f*; *Com* **to make an o. for sth,** faire une offre pour qch; **on o.,** en vente; **£500 or nearest o.,** = prix à débattre autour de 500 livres; **special o.,** (*in shop etc*) promotion *f*; *Am* **job offers,** offres d'emploi; **o. of marriage,** demande *f* en mariage; **to make s.o. an o.,** faire une offre *ou* une proposition à qn; *esp Hum* **to make s.o. an o. they can't refuse,** faire à qn une proposition que l'on ne peut refuser.

offer² **1** *vt* offrir (*qch, ses services*); présenter (*des excuses*); tendre (*la main*); faire (*une remarque*); avancer (*une opinion*); proposer (*une définition*); (*of thing*) offrir, présenter (*un beau spectacle*); (*of scheme etc*) présenter (*des difficultés, des avantages*); **to o. s.o. sth,** offrir qch à qn; **he was offered a job,** on lui a offert un emploi; **house offered for sale,** maison mise en vente; **the conditions that we are able to o. you,** les conditions que nous sommes à même de vous faire; **they're offering two weeks' skiing for £200,** ils proposent deux semaines aux sports d'hiver pour 200 livres; **to o. to do sth,** faire l'offre *ou* offrir de faire qch; *Jur* **to o. a plea,** exciper d'une excuse; **to o. resistance,** offrir de la résistance. **2** *vi* (*of occasion etc*) s'offrir, se présenter; **if a good occasion offers,** s'il s'offre une belle occasion.

►**offer up** *vtsep* (*offer*) offrir (*des prières, des remerciements à Dieu*).

offering ['ɒfərɪŋ] *n* **(a)** offre *f*; *Rel* offrande *f*; **this year's offerings from Hollywood,** ce qu'Hollywood nous propose cette année; **burnt o.,** *Rel* holocauste *m*; *Hum* viande brûlée *ou* calcinée, plat brûlé; **(b)** (*action*) offre *f*.

offertory ['ɒfət(ə)rɪ] *n Rel* **(a)** offertoire *m* (*de la messe*); **(b)** quête *f* (*de l'offrande*); (*amount collected*) montant *m* de la quête; **o. box,** tronc *m*.

offhand [ɒf'hænd] **1** *adv* **(a)** (*immediately*) **I don't know o.,** comme ça de but en blanc, je ne le sais pas; **(b)** (*casually*) sans cérémonie, sans façon; (*brusquely*) brusquement. **2** *adj* (*casual*) sans cérémonie, sans façon(s); (*brusque*) brusque, cavalier; **to be o. with s.o.,** se montrer désinvolte à l'égard de qn; **to treat s.o. in an o. manner,** traiter qn cavalièrement *ou* avec désinvolture.

offhanded [ɒf'hændɪd] *adj* = **OFFHAND 2**.

offhandedly [ɒf'hændɪdlɪ] *adv* = **OFFHAND 1(b)**.

offhandedness [ɒf'hændɪdnɪs] *n* (*casualness*) désinvolture *f*; (*brusqueness*) brusquerie *f*.

office ['ɒfɪs] *n* **(a)** bureau *m*; (*of lawyer*) étude *f*; *Am* cabinet *m* de consultation (*d'un médecin, d'un dentiste*); **to work in an o., to have an o. job,** avoir un emploi de bureau; **business o.,** bureau commercial; **head o., registered offices,** (*of company*) siège principal *ou* social; **complaints o.,** bureau *ou* service *m* des réclamations; *Am Tel* **the central o.,** le central; **private o.,** cabinet particulier; **the manager's o.,** le bureau du directeur; **the secretary's o.,** le secrétariat; **government o.,** ministère *m* (d'État); *Br* **the Home O.,** ≈ le ministère de l'Intérieur; *Br* **the Foreign O.,** ≈ le ministère des Affaires étrangères; *Br* **O. of Fair Trading,** = organisme de défense des consommateurs et de régulation des pratiques commerciales; **offices (of a house),** communs *mpl* et dépendances *fpl*; **o. automation,** bureautique *f*; **o. building** *or* **block,** immeuble *m* de bureaux; **o. equipment,** matériel *m* de bureau; **o. hours,** heures *fpl* de bureau; **o. manager,** chef *m* de bureau; **o. party,** soirée entre collègues de bureau; **for o. use only,** (*on form*) (cadre) réservé à l'administration; **o. work,** travail *m* de bureau; **o. worker,** employé, -ée de bureau;

(b) (*position*) charge *f*, fonctions *fpl*; **high o.,** fonctions élevées, haute charge; **the o. of Prime Minister,** la fonction de premier ministre; **he has never held high o.,** il n'a jamais occupé de fonctions élevées; **public o.,** fonctions publiques; **to be in o., to hold o.,** remplir une fonction; (*of government, politician*) être au pouvoir; **to be out of o.,** (*of political party, politician*) ne plus être au pouvoir; **to take o., to come into o.,** entrer en fonctions; (*of government*) prendre le pouvoir; **to seek o.,** chercher à être élu;

(c) (*service*) office *m*, service *m*; **through** *or* **owing to the good offices of a friend,** grâce aux bons offices *ou* par les bons soins d'un ami;

(d) *Rel* **o. of the day,** office *m* du jour; **o. for the dead,** office des morts; *Rel* **last offices,** derniers devoirs (*rendus à un mort*); (*funeral*) obsèques *fpl*.

officeholder ['ɒfɪshəʊldər] *n Am* employé *m* de l'État, fonctionnaire *mf*.

officer ['ɒfɪsər] *n* **(a)** (*official*) fonctionnaire *mf*; **municipal o.,** officier municipal; *Admin* **clerical o.,** secrétaire *mf* d'administration; **administrative o.,** ≈ administrateur civil; **customs o.,** douanier *m*; **police o.,** *US* **o.,** agent *m* *ou* officier de police; *Am* **O. Smith,** officier Smith; **yes, o.,** oui, monsieur l'agent; **(b)** *Mil etc* officier *m*; officier, -ière (*de l'Armée du Salut*); **army/naval o.,** officier de l'armée de terre/de marine; **field o.,** officier supérieur; **first o.,** (*in Merchant Navy*) (commandant *m* en) second *m*; **radio o.,** radionavigant *m*; **(c) high o.,** grand dignitaire (*d'un ordre*).

official [ə'fɪʃəl] **1** *adj* (*statement, visit, strike etc*) officiel; (*language*) administratif; (*style*) bureaucratique; *Pharm* officinal, -aux, autorisé par la pharmacopée; **o. letter,** pli officiel *ou* de service; **o. opening,** (*of new factory etc*) inauguration *f*; **to act in one's o. capacity,** agir dans l'exercice de ses fonctions; *Fin* **o. quotation,** cote officielle; *Sp* **o. record,** record homologué; **the o. organist,** le titulaire de l'orgue. **2** *n* fonctionnaire *mf*; *Pej* bureaucrate *m*; (*at sports meeting etc*) commissaire *mf*; *US Sp* arbitre *m*; **minor officials,** petits fonctionnaires; **the o. at the entrance,** le préposé à l'entrée; **railway/post-office o.,** employé, -ée des chemins de fer/des Postes.

officialdom [ə'fɪʃəldəm] *n* **(a)** (*no pl*) (*officials*) l'administration *f*; **(b)** *Pej* bureaucratie *f*, fonctionnarisme *m*.

officialese [əfɪʃə'liːz] *n F* jargon administratif.

officialism [ə'fɪʃəlɪz(ə)m] *n* bureaucratie *f*, fonctionnarisme *m*, chinoiseries *fpl* (*de l'administration*).

officially [ə'fɪʃəlɪ] *adv* officiellement.

officiate [ə'fɪʃɪeɪt] *vi* **(a)** *Rel* **to o. at a service,** officier à un office; **to o. at a church,** desservir une église; **officiating minister,** (ministre *m*) officiant *m*; **(b)** *Old-fashioned* **to o. as host,** remplir *ou* exercer les fonctions d'hôte.

officious [ə'fɪʃəs] *adj* trop zélé, officieux.

officiously [ə'fɪʃəslɪ] *adv* avec trop de zèle; **to behave o.,** faire l'empressé.

offing ['ɒfɪŋ] *n Nau* **in the o.,** au large; *Fig* **a general election is in the o.,** une élection générale est en vue; **there's a pay rise in the o.,** il y a une augmentation de salaire en perspective; **Christmas is in the o.,** Noël se profile à l'horizon.

off-licence ['ɒflaɪsəns] *n Br Com Jur* **(a)** (*premises*) = magasin ou bar où l'on peut acheter des boissons alcoolisées à emporter; **(b)** (*licence*) = licence permettant la vente de boissons alcoolisées à emporter.

off-line ['ɒflaɪn] *adj Comptr* (*processing*) en différé; (*printer*) déconnecté.

off-load [ɒf'ləʊd] *vt* débarquer (*un excédent de marchandises etc*); *Fig* **he offloads most of his work on his colleagues,** il se décharge de la plus grande partie de son travail sur ses collègues.

off-peak ['ɒf'piːk] *adj* **o.-p. hours,** heures creuses *ou* hors pointe; *El* **o.-p. tariff,** tarif *m* de nuit; *Rail* **o.-p. fare,** = billet à prix réduit avec lequel on peut voyager en dehors des heures de pointe.

off-piste [ɒf'piːst] *adj & adv Sp* (*in skiing*) hors piste.

offprint ['ɒfprɪnt] *n* tirage *m* à part, tiré *m* à part.

off-putting [ɒf'pʊtɪŋ] *adj Br F* **(a)** (*événement*) déconcertant, déroutant; **it can be very o.-p.,** ça peut être très déconcertant; **(b)** (*caractère*) répugnant.

off-road ['ɒfrəʊd] *adj Aut* **o.-r. vehicle,** véhicule *m* tout terrain.

off-sales ['ɒfseɪlz] *npl Br* = ventes des boissons alcoolisées à emporter.

offscreen ['ɒfskriːn] *Cin* **1** *adv* **o. he's a modest man,** dans le privé c'est un type modeste. **2** *adj* (*life*) privé.

off-season ['ɒfsiːz(ə)n] *adj* (*tarif etc*) hors-saison.

offset¹ ['ɒfset] *n* **(a)** (*compensation*) compensation *f*, dédommagement *m*; (*in bookkeeping*) compensation (*d'une écriture*); **as an o. to my losses,** en compensation de mes pertes; **(b)** (*counterbalance*) repoussoir *m*; **(c)** *Archit* ressaut *m*, saillie *f*; retrait *m* (*d'un mur*); *MecE etc* désaxage *m*, décalage *m*, décentrement *m*; rebord *m* (*de piston etc*); bord biseauté (*d'une roue*); double coude *m*, siphon *m* (*d'un tuyau etc*); **(d)** (*in surveying*) perpendiculaire *f*; ordonnée *f*; **(e)** *Typ* offset *m*; **printed in o.,** tiré en offset; **(f)** (*of plant*) rejeton *m*.

offset² *vt* (*pt & pp* **offset**; *prp* **-setting**) **(a)** compenser (*ses pertes*); **to o. one thing against another,** compenser quelque chose par quelque chose d'autre; **(b)** *MecE* désaxer, décentrer (*une roue*); déporter, décaler (*un organe*); faire déborder (*une pièce*); prévoir un dégagement *ou* une courbure à (*un outil*); faire un double coude à (*un tuyau*); **(c)** *Typ* imprimer (*un livre*) en offset.

offshoot ['ɒfʃuːt] *n* rejeton *m* (*d'un arbre, d'une famille*); *Fig* ramification *f*; **an o. of a political party/an artistic movement,** une ramification d'un parti politique/d'un mouvement artistique.

offshore ['ɒfʃɔːr] **1** *adv* vers le large, au large; **to drill o.,** forer au large; **to live o.,** (*of oil workers etc*) vivre au large. **2** *adj* **(a)** **o. wind,** vent *m* de terre *ou* d'aval; **(b)** (*near coast*) côtier, littoral; (*far from coast*) éloigné de la côte; *Petr* (*prospection, forage*) au large, offshore; **o. fishing,** pêche côtière; *Petr* **o. installations,** installations pétrolières marines; *Petr* **o. oilfield,** champ (pétrolifère) au large *ou* offshore; **(c)** (*taking place abroad*) **o. purchases,** achats *mpl* à l'étranger.

offside [ɒf'saɪd] **1** *n Aut* (*in Britain*) côté droit; (*in France, US*) côté gauche; *Horseriding* côté hors montoir; *Horseracing* extérieur *m* de la piste. **2** *adj* **(a)** *Sp* hors jeu; **the o. rule,** la règle du hors jeu; **(b)** *Aut* (*in Britain*) du côté droit; (*in France, US*) du côté gauche. **3** *adv* hors jeu.

offspring ['ɒfsprɪŋ] *n* (*no pl*) **(a)** *Biol* (*young*) progéniture *f*, descendance *f*, descendants *mpl*; (*children*) enfants *mfpl*; **(b)** *Fig* **the o. of much research,** le fruit de beaucoup de recherches.

offstage [ɒf'steɪdʒ] **1** *adv* (*parler, fracas etc*) derrière la toile; **his life o.,** (*of actor*) sa vie privée. **2** *adj* (*life*) privé.

off-street ['ɒfstriːt] *adj* **o.-s. parking,** (stationnement *m* dans un) parking *m*.

off-the-cuff [ɒfðə'kʌf] *adj* (*remark*) impromptu.

off-the-peg [ɒfðə'peg] , *Am* **off-the-rack** [ɒfðə'ræk] *adj* (*clothes*) de prêt-à-porter.

off-the-record [ɒfðə'rekɔːd] *adj* (*comment, briefing*) officieux.

off-the-wall [ɒfðə'wɔːl] *adj F* (*humour*) bizarre, dément.

off-white ['ɒf'waɪt] **1** *adj* blanc cassé. **2** *n* blanc légèrement teinté *ou* cassé.

oft [ɒft] *adv Lit* (*esp in poetry*) souvent; **many a time and o.,** maintes et maintes fois.

oft- [ɒft] *pref* **o.-visited/-quoted/***etc*, souvent visité/cité/*etc*.

often ['ɒf(ə)n, 'ɒft(ə)n] *adv* souvent, fréquemment; **I don't see her very o. now,** je ne la vois plus très souvent maintenant; **how o.?,** (*how many times*) combien de fois?; (*at what intervals*) tous les combien?; **how o. have I told you!,** combien de fois ne vous l'ai-je pas dit!; **as o. as I saw him,** toutes les fois *ou* chaque fois que je l'ai vu; **as o. as not, more o. than not,** assez souvent, le plus souvent; **every so o.,** de temps en temps, de temps à autre; **it cannot be repeated too o.,** on ne saurait trop le répéter; **once too o.,** une fois de trop.

ogee ['əʊdʒiː] *n Archit* **o. (moulding),** cimaise *f*, talon *m*; **o. arch,** arc *m* en accolade.

ogival [əʊ'dʒaɪv(ə)l] *adj Archit* ogival, -aux.

ogive ['əʊdʒaɪv] *n Archit* ogive *f*.

ogle¹ ['əʊg(ə)l] *n* œillade *f* (amoureuse).

ogle² *vt* lorgner, guigner (*qn*), lancer des œillades à (*qn*).

ogre ['əʊgər] *n* ogre *m*.

ogress ['əʊgrɪs] *n* ogresse *f*.

oh [əʊ] *int* (*expressing surprise etc*) oh; **oh how tired I am!,** ah! que je suis fatigué!; **oh no!,** oh non!

ohm [əʊm] *n El* ohm *m*.

OHMS [əʊaɪtʃem'es] *Br* (*abbr* **On Her** *or* **His Majesty's Service**) = au service de sa majesté.

oho [əʊ'həʊ] *int* (*expressing triumph*) ah ah!

oik [ɔɪk] *n Br Offensive Sl* prolo *mf*.

oil¹ [ɔɪl] *n* **(a)** (*edible*) & *Art* huile *f*; **vegetable o.,** huile végétale; **olive/groundnut o.,** huile d'olive/d'arachide; **linseed o.,** huile (de graine) de lin; **cooking o.,** huile de cuisine; **whale o.,** huile *f* de baleine; **sperm o.,** huile de blanc de baleine; **cod-liver o.,** huile de foie de morue; **to cook in** *or* **with o.,** faire la cuisine à l'huile; **fried in o.,** frit à l'huile; **to paint in oils,** peindre à l'huile; *Rel* **holy o.,** les saintes huiles (*pour l'extrême-onction etc*); *Fig* **to add o. to the flames,** jeter de l'huile sur le feu; *Fig* **to pour o. on troubled waters,** calmer la tempête; **o. paint,** peinture *f* à l'huile; **o. painting,** peinture à l'huile; *Fig* **he's** *or* **she's no o. painting,** ce n'est pas une beauté; **o. cake,** tourteau *m* de lin;

(b) *Ind* (*petroleum*) pétrole *m*; **mineral o.,** huile minérale; **crude o.,** pétrole brut; **fuel o.,** mazout *m*; *Aut* **to check the o.,** vérifier le niveau d'huile; *Tech* **lubricating o.,** huile à graisser *ou* de graissage; *MecE* **motor o.,** huile de moteur; **o. company,** compagnie pétrolière; **o. cooling,** refroidissement *m* par huile; **o. drum,** bidon *m* à pétrole; **o. heating,** chauffage *m* au mazout; **o. industry,** industrie pétrolière; **o. lamp,** lampe *f* à pétrole; **o. refinery,** raffinerie *f* de pétrole; **o. rig,** derrick *m*; (*offshore*) plate-forme *f* de forage; **o. slick,** nappe *f* de pétrole; *St Exch* **o. shares, oils,** valeurs *fpl* pétrolières, pétroles; **o. tanker,** pétrolier *m*; **o. well,** puits *m* pétrolifère.

(c) **essential o.,** essence *f*; **o. of cloves/lavender,** essence *f* de girofle/lavande.

oil² **1** *vt* **(a)** huiler, graisser, lubrifier (*une machine*); **to o. the wheels,** graisser les roues; *Fig* mettre de l'huile dans les rouages, faciliter les choses; **(b)** huiler (*la toile etc*); **to o. one's skin,** s'enduire la peau d'huile. **2** *vi Nau* faire le plein de mazout.

►**oil up** **1** *vtsep* encrasser (*d'huile*). **2** *vi* (*of sparking plug etc*) s'encrasser (*d'huile*).

oil-bearing ['ɔɪlbeərɪŋ] *adj Geol* pétrolifère.

oilcan ['ɔɪlkæn] *n* **(a)** (*for applying oil*) burette *f*; **(b)** (*large container*) bidon *m*, estagnon *m* à huile.

oilcloth ['ɔɪlklɒθ] *n* toile cirée.

oil-cooled ['ɔɪlkuːld] *adj MecE* refroidi par huile.

oiled [ɔɪld] *adj* **(a)** huilé; *F* **to be well o.,** (*drunk*) être (un peu) éméché; **(b)** (*papier*) huilé; **o. silk,** taffetas *m* imperméable.

oiler ['ɔɪlər] *n* **(a)** *Nau* (*tanker*) pétrolier *m*; **(b)** (*oilcan*) burette *f* à huile; *MecE* (*lubricating device*) graisseur *m*, godet graisseur *ou* de graissage; **(c)** (*person*) graisseur *m*.

oilfield ['ɔɪlfiːld] *n* gisement *m ou* champ *m* pétrolifère.

oilfired ['ɔɪlfaɪəd] *adj* **o. central heating,** chauffage central au mazout.

oiliness ['ɔɪlɪnɪs] *n* **(a)** état graisseux; (*appearance*) aspect graisseux; **(b)** *Pej* onctuosité *f* (*de qn*).

oiling ['ɔɪlɪŋ] *n* **(a)** graissage *m*, huilage *m* (*d'un mécanisme etc*); **(b)** enduisage *m* (*d'un nageur etc*) de graisse.

oiling up *n* encrassement *m* (*d'une bougie, d'allumage etc*).

oilpaper ['ɔɪlpeɪpər] *n* papier huilé.

oil-producing ['ɔɪlprədjuːsɪŋ] *adj* **(a)** (*shale etc*) pétrolifère; (*pays*) producteur de pétrole; **(b)** (*plant*) oléifère; (*substance etc*) oléifiant.

oilrich ['ɔɪlrɪtʃ] *adj* (*countries*) enrichi par le pétrole.

oilskin ['ɔɪlskɪn] *n* (*fabric*) toile cirée; (*garment*) ciré *m*.

oilstone ['ɔɪlstəʊn] *n* pierre *f* à huile (*pour affûter*).

oily ['ɔɪlɪ] *adj* **(a)** (*hands, rag*) graisseux; (*paper*) imprégné d'huile; **(b)** *Pej* (*manner etc*) onctueux; (*voice*) gras.

ointment ['ɔɪntmənt] *n* onguent *m*, pommade *f*; *Fig* **a fly in the o.**, un cheveu (dans la soupe).

O.K.[1], **okay**[1] [əʊ'keɪ] *F* **1** *adj* **(a)** (*in order, fine*) correct, exact, OK; **everything's O.K.**, tout est en règle *ou* OK; **to be O.K.**, (*unhurt*) aller bien; **but is the car O.K.?**, mais est-ce que la voiture n'a rien?; **that's O.K. by** *or* **with me**, d'accord!; **is that O.K. by** *or* **with your mother**, est-ce que ta mère est d'accord?; **is it O.K. to bring my friend?**, est-ce que ça vous dérange si je viens avec mon ami?; **no, it is NOT O.K.**, pas question; **O.K.!**, OK!, bon!, d'accord!; **O.K.?**, OK?, d'accord?; **O.K.**, (*on document*) vu et approuvé; **clothes like that are O.K. for a party but not for the office**, des vêtements comme ça conviennent pour aller à une soirée mais pas pour aller au bureau; **O.K., O.K. it wasn't a great movie**, (*but that was no reason to boo etc*) bon, d'accord, ce n'était pas un film super;

(b) (*passable*) **to be O.K.**, (*of thing*) aller; (*of person*) être assez sympa; **how are things? — O.K.**, comment ça va? — ça peut aller, c'est OK; **the meal was O.K.**, le repas était pas mal;

(c) (*understanding*) **she was O.K. about it**, elle n'a pas fait d'histoires.

2 *n* **to give one's O.K. to**, approuver (*une commande*); contresigner, parafer (*un ordre*); **to give the O.K.**, donner le feu vert.

O.K.[2] (*pt & pp* **O.K.'d**), **okay**[2] *vt F* passer, approuver (*une commande*); contresigner, parafer (*un ordre*).

okapi [əʊ'kɑːpɪ] *n* (*animal*) okapi *m*.

okey-doke, okey-dokey, okie-doke, okie-dokey [əʊkɪ'dəʊk, -kɪ] *int F* ça va!, d'accord!

Okla *abbr* **Oklahoma**.

okra ['ɒkrə] *n* (*plant*) okra *m*.

old [əʊld] *adj* **(a)** (*aged*) vieux, *f* vieille, *pl* vieux, vieilles, âgé; (*in sing before a qualified noun beginning with a vowel or h mute*) vieil; **my o. friend**, mon vieil ami; **you're as o. as you feel**, on a l'âge de ses artères; **to be growing** *or* **getting o.**, prendre de l'âge, vieillir; **to grow older**, vieillir; **an o. man**, un homme âgé, un vieillard, *F* un vieux; **an o. woman**, une vieille femme, *F* une vieille; **o. people, o. folk(s)**, les vieux; **o. age**, la vieillesse; **to die at a good o. age**, mourir à un âge avancé; **in o. age she was still beautiful**, dans sa vieillesse elle était encore très belle: **he's saving for his o. age**, il économise pour ses vieux jours; **as o. as the hills**, vieux comme le monde; **o. age pension**, retraite *f*; **o. age pensioner**, retraité, -ée; **o. clothes**, vieux habits; **o. clothes shop**, friperie *f*; **o. clothes man/woman**, fripier/fripière; *US F* **O. Glory**, la bannière étoilée; **o. gold**, (*colour*) vieil or; **to be o. hat**, être démodé; *Old-fashioned* **o. maid**, vieille fille; *Fig* **he's a bit of an o. maid**, il a des manies de petite vieille; **o. wine**, vin vieux; *Art* **o. master**, (*painter*) maître *m*; (*painting*) tableau *m* de maître; **o. rose**, (*colour*) vieux rose; **the o. guard**, la vieille garde;

(b) (*with specific age*) **how o. are you?**, quel âge avez-vous?; **the oldest of the tribe**, l'aîné, -ée de la tribu; **to be five years o.**, avoir cinq ans, être âgé de cinq ans; **she is older than I am**, elle est plus âgée que moi; **when you're older**, (*to child*) quand tu seras plus grand; **at six years o.**, à (l'âge de) six ans; **a two-year-o. child, a two-year-o.**, un enfant (âgé) de deux ans; **to be o. enough to do sth**, être d'âge à faire qch;

(c) (*long-established*) vieux, ancien; (*famille*) de vieille souche; (*dette*) d'ancienne date; **he's an o. friend of mine**, c'est un de mes vieux amis; **an o. story**, une vieille histoire; **that's an o. dodge**, c'est un coup classique; **that's an o. one**, (*of joke*) c'est une vieille blague; **to go over o. ground**, revenir sur un terrain déjà parcouru;

(d) (*experienced*) vieux; **o. hand**, ouvrier expérimenté; *Nau* vétéran *m*; **to be an o. hand at sth**, avoir le coup pour faire qch;

(e) (*former*) ancien; **o. boy** *or* **pupil**, ancien élève; **o. girl** *or* **pupil**, ancienne élève; *Br* **the o. boy network, the o. school tie**, = la franc-maçonnerie des écoles privées et des universités; **o. memories**, souvenirs *mpl* du temps passé; (*of youth*) souvenirs de jeunesse; **in the o. days**, autrefois; **a boss of the o. school**, un patron de la vieille école; **the O. World**, l'ancien monde; **O. English/French**, l'ancien anglais/français; **the O. Testament**, l'Ancien Testament;

(f) *F* (*intensifier*) **any o. how**, n'importe comment; **any o. thing**, n'importe quoi; **it's a strange o. world**, c'est un drôle de monde; **we had a fine o. time**, nous avons passé un sacré bon moment; **o. Fred**, Fred; **your o. book**, ton bouquin; **your o. bike**, ton clou;

(g) **o. man** *or* **chap** *or* **fellow** *or* **boy**, mon vieux, mon pote; *F* **the o. man**, (*father*) papa; (*boss*) le patron; *Nau* (*captain*) le capitaine; *Mil* (*colonel*) le colonel; *Sl* **my o. man**, (*father*) mon vieux; (*husband*) mon homme; **the o. woman** *or* **lady**, (*wife*) ma femme, *Sl* la bourgeoise; (*mother*) ma vieille; *F* **to be (a bit of) an o. woman**, être soupe au lait;

(h) *Lit* **in the days of o.**, autrefois, au temps jadis; **I know him of o.**, je le connais depuis longtemps.

2 *n* **the o.**, (*used as pl*) les vieux; **popular with o. and young**, apprécié des jeunes et des moins jeunes.

olden ['əʊld(ə)n] *adj Lit* **in o. times, in the o. days**, au temps jadis.

old-established ['əʊldɪs'tæblɪʃt] *adj* ancien, établi depuis longtemps.

olde-worlde ['əʊldɪ'wɜːldɪ] *adj* (*maison, village etc*) qui a un aspect factice d'antan.

old-fashioned [əʊld'fæʃənd] **1** *adj* (*dress, hat etc*) démodé, passé de mode; (*person*) partisan, -ane des anciens usages; (*manner*) de l'ancien temps; (*ideas*) arriéré, vieillot, vieux jeu; **o.-f. Christmas**, Noël à l'ancienne; **you can call me o.-f. but ...**, tu vas peut-être me trouver vieux jeux, mais ...; *F* **o.-f. look**, regard *m* de travers. **2** *n* = cocktail composé de whisky, d'amers, de sucre et d'eau de seltz.

oldie ['əʊldɪ] *n F* **(a)** (*old thing*) vieillerie *f*, antiquaille *f*; (*song*) ancienne chanson populaire; **that's a real o.**, (*of song, joke etc*) il est vieux celui-là; **(b)** (*old person*) vieillard, -arde.

oldish ['əʊldɪʃ] *adj* vieillot, -otte, assez vieux *ou* vieille.

oldster ['əʊldstər] *n* vieillard *m*, vieille *f*.

old-style ['əʊld'staɪl] *adj* à l'ancienne mode; *Hist* **the o.-s. calendar**, le calendrier ancien style.

old-time ['əʊld'taɪm] *adj* du temps jadis; **o.-t. dancing**, danses *fpl* du bon vieux temps.

old-timer [əʊld'taɪmər] *n* **(a)** (*experienced person*) vieux de la vieille, personne *f* qui s'y connaît; **(b)** *esp Am* (*old man*) vieux *m*.

old-world ['əʊld'wɜːld] *adj* **(a)** (*of former times*) des temps anciens; de l'ancien temps; (*not modern*) = de l'ancien monde opposé au monde moderne; (*European*) = de l'ancien monde opposé à l'Amérique; **(b)** (*village*) qui n'a pas changé au cours des siècles.

oleander [əʊlɪ'ændər] *n* (*shrub*) oleandre *m*, laurier-rose *m*, *pl* lauriers-rose(s).

oleograph ['əʊlɪəʊgræf] *n Typ* oléographie *f*.

olfactory [ɒl'fæktərɪ] *adj* (*bulbe, nerf etc*) olfactif.

oligarchic(al) [ɒlɪ'gɑːkɪk, -ɪk(ə)l] *adj* oligarchique.

oligarchy ['ɒlɪgɑːkɪ] *n* oligarchie *f*.

olive ['ɒlɪv] **1** *n* **(a)** (*fruit*) olive *f*; **o. oil**, huile *f* d'olive; **(b)** **o. (tree)**, olivier *m*; *Bible* **the Mount of Olives**, le Mont *ou* le Jardin des Oliviers; **o. grove** *or* **plantation**, oliv(er)aie *f*; **o. grower**, oléiculteur *m*; **o. branch**, rameau *m* d'olivier; *Fig* **to hold out the o. branch**, présenter l'olivier; **(c)** **o. (wood)**, (bois *m* d')olivier *m*; **(d)** *Culin* **beef o.**, paupiette *f*; **(e)** (*colour*) **o. (green)**, (vert *m*) olive *m inv*. **2** *adj* (*teint etc*) olivâtre.

Oliver ['ɒlɪvər] *n* Olivier *m*.

Olympiad [ə'lɪmpɪæd] *n Sp* olympiade *f*.

Olympian [ə'lɪmpɪən] **1** *adj* (*air, calme etc*) olympien; (*dieu*) de l'Olympe. **2** *n* Olympien, -ienne.

Olympic [ə'lɪmpɪk] **1** *adj Antiq Sp* (*stade etc*) olympique; **the O. Games**, les jeux *mpl* olympiques. **2** *npl* **the Olympics**, les Jeux olympiques.

Olympus [ə'lɪmpəs] *n* l'Olympe *m*.

Oman [əʊ'mæn] *n* Oman *m*.

ombudsman, *pl* **-men** ['ɒmbʊdzmən] *n* ombudsman *m*, médiateur *m*; *Belg* commissaire *m* du Parlement.

omega ['əʊmɪgə] *n* (*in Greek alphabet*) oméga *m*.

omelette, *US* **omelet** ['ɒmlɪt] *n Culin* omelette *f*; **ham o.**, omelette au jambon; *Fig* **you can't make an o. without breaking eggs**, on ne fait pas d'omelette sans casser d'œufs.

omen[1] ['əʊmen] *n* présage *m*, augure *m*, auspice *m*; **to take sth as a good o.**, prendre qch à bon augure; **bird of ill o.**, oiseau *m* de mauvais augure.

omen[2] *vt* augurer, présager.

ominous ['ɒmɪnəs] *adj* de mauvais augure; **o.-looking sky**, ciel menaçant; **an o. silence**, un silence lourd de menaces; **I heard an o. crack,** j'entendis un craquement qui ne présageait rien de bon; **a bus strike? — that sounds o.,** une grève des bus? — ça ne présage rien de bon.

ominously ['ɒmɪnəslɪ] *adv* d'une façon menaçante *ou* inquiétante.

omission [əʊ'mɪʃən] *n* **(a)** omission *f* (*d'un mot etc*); *Com* **errors and omissions excepted,** sauf erreur ou omission; **(b)** (*negligence*) négligence *f*, oubli *m*; *Rel* omission *f*; *Rel* **sin of o.,** péché *m ou* faute *f* d'omission; **(c)** *Typ* bourdon *m*.

omit [əʊ'mɪt] *vt* (**-tt-**) **(a)** omettre (*des détails*); **(b) to o. to do sth,** (*forget*) oublier *ou* omettre de faire qch; (*fail*) manquer à faire qch; **not to o. to do sth,** ne pas manquer de faire qch.

omnibus, *pl* **-uses** ['ɒmnɪbəs, -bəsɪz] **1** *n* **(a)** (*book*) recueil *m*; **detective o.,** recueil de romans policiers; **(b)** *Arch* (*vehicle*) **(horse) o.,** omnibus *m*; **motor o.,** autobus *m*. **2** *adj* (*in publishing*) **o. volume** *or* **edition,** gros recueil (*de contes, de poèmes etc*); publication *f* en un volume de plusieurs ouvrages d'un auteur.

omnidirectional ['ɒmnɪdɪ'rekʃən(ə)l] *adj Rad etc* (*aerial, microphone*) omnidirectionnel.

omnipotence [ɒm'nɪpətəns] *n* omnipotence *f*, toute-puissance *f*.

omnipotent [ɒm'nɪpətənt] **1** *adj* omnipotent, tout-puissant, *pl* tout-puissants. **2** *n* **the O.,** le Tout-Puissant.

omnipresence [ɒmnɪ'prezəns] *n* omniprésence *f*.

omnipresent [ɒmnɪ'prezənt] *adj* omniprésent.

omniscience [ɒm'nɪsɪəns] *n* omniscience *f*.

omniscient [ɒm'nɪsɪənt] *adj* omniscient.

omnivorous [ɒm'nɪvərəs] *adj* omnivore; *F* (*lecteur*) qui lit de tout.

on [ɒn] **1** *prep* **(a)** (*indicating position*) sur; **on the table,** sur la table; **do not tread on it,** ne marchez pas dessus; **on the high seas,** en haute mer; **room on the second floor,** chambre *f* du second (étage); **on the train,** dans le train; **on foot/horseback,** à pied/cheval; **on a bicycle,** à bicyclette; **he had his rucksack on his back,** il portait son sac au dos; **to swear sth on the Bible,** jurer qch sur la Bible; **hanging on the wall,** pendu au mur; **on the ceiling,** au plafond; **he has a ring on his finger,** il a une bague au doigt; **have you any money on you?,** avez-vous de l'argent sur vous?; **dog on the lead,** chien en laisse; **to be on the phone,** (*speaking*) parler *ou* être au téléphone; (*have a telephone*) avoir le téléphone; **to be on the committee,** (*member of*) être membre du comité; **to be on a newspaper,** être attaché à la rédaction d'un journal; **he played it on his violin,** il l'a joué sur son violon; **on page four,** à la quatrième page, à la page quatre; **house on the main road,** maison sur la grande route; *Am* **she lives on Sixth Avenue,** elle habite dans la Sixième Avenue; **on the right/left,** à droite/gauche; **on this side,** de ce côté; *Comptr* **on line,** connecté, en ligne, en direct; **to go on line,** passer au mode connecté *ou* en ligne *ou* en direct; **to put a printer on line,** mettre une imprimante en ligne; **to be on line to s.o./sth,** être en ligne avec qn/qch; **live on stage,** en direct sur scène; **what's on (the) television?,** qu'est-ce qu'il y a à la télévision?;

(b) (*indicating direction*) **on (to),** sur, à; **room that looks on (to) the street,** pièce qui donne sur la rue; **to march on London,** avancer vers *ou* sur Londres; **to turn one's back on s.o.,** tourner le dos à qn; **to hit s.o. on the head,** frapper qn sur la tête; **shame on you!,** vous devriez avoir honte!;

(c) (*according to*) **based on a fact,** fondé sur un fait; **to have sth on good authority,** savoir qch de source certaine *ou* de bonne part; **arrested on a charge of murder,** arrêté sous l'inculpation de meurtre; **on pain** *or* **penalty of death,** sous peine de mort; **on (an) average,** en moyenne; **tax on tobacco,** impôt *m* sur le tabac; **interest on capital,** intérêt du capital; **to retire on a pension of £5,000 a year,** prendre sa retraite avec une pension de 5 000 livres par an; **on condition that ...,** à condition que + *sub* ...;

(d) (*in expressions of time*) **on Sunday,** dimanche; **on Sundays,** le(s) dimanche(s); **on the day of my arrival,** le jour de mon arrivée; **on the following day,** le lendemain; **on April 3rd,** le trois avril; **on a fine day in June,** par une belle journée de juin; **on and after the fifteenth,** à partir du quinze; **on or about the twelfth,** vers le douze; **on that occasion,** à cette occasion; **on the death of his mother,** à la mort de sa mère; **on my arrival,** à mon arrivée; **on application,** sur demande; **on examination,** après examen; **payable on sight,** payable à vue; **on (my) entering the room,** quand j'entrai *ou* en entrant dans la pièce, à mon entrée dans la salle; **on the count of three,** à trois; **on time,** ponctuel, à l'heure; **just on a year ago,** (*approximately*) il y a près d'un an; **just on 5 o'clock,** (*approximately*) tout près de cinq heures;

(e) (*indicating manner*) **on the cheap,** à bon marché; **on the sly,** en cachette, en douce;

(f) (*indicating state*) en; **on sale,** en vente; **on tap,** en perce;

(g) (*about, concerning*) **a book on France,** un livre sur la France; **a lecture on history,** une conférence d'histoire; **to congratulate s.o. on his success,** féliciter qn de son succès; **keen on sth,** porté sur qch, amateur de qch; **mad on s.o.,** fou *ou* entiché de qn;

(h) (*indicating activity*) **I am here on business,** je suis ici pour affaires; **on tour,** en tournée; **on holiday,** en vacances; **to be working on sth,** travailler à qch;

(i) (*indicating person, thing affected*) **to have pity on s.o.,** avoir pitié de qn; **effect of sth on s.o.,** effet de qch sur qn; **attack on s.o.,** attaque contre qn; **decision binding on s.o.,** décision obligatoire pour qn; **this round (of drinks) is on me,** c'est moi qui paie; **the police have nothing on him,** la police n'a rien contre lui; **cheque on a bank,** chèque sur une banque;

(j) (*indicating source of support*) **to live on one's private income,** vivre de ses rentes; **many live on less than that,** beaucoup vivent avec moins que ça; **he's on insulin,** il prend de l'insuline; **to be on drugs,** se droguer; **she's on the pill,** elle prend la pilule; **to travel on a British passport,** voyager avec un passeport britannique;

(k) (*added to*) **disaster on disaster,** désastre sur désastre;

(l) *Horseracing etc* **to put money on a horse,** parier sur un cheval; **to put money on a colour,** miser sur une couleur.

2 *adv* **(a)** (*indicating direction, position*) **to put the cloth on,** mettre la nappe; **to put the kettle on,** mettre la bouilloire à chauffer; **to fall on** *or* **onto sth,** tomber sur qch; **to climb onto a wall,** grimper sur un mur; **to be on,** (*of actor*) être en scène; **to put on one's clothes,** s'habiller; **what had she got on?,** comment était-elle vêtue?; **to have nothing on,** être tout nu; **to be sideways on to sth,** présenter le côté à qch;

(b) (*expressing continuation*) **to go/march/work on,** continuer son chemin/sa marche/son travail; **to burn/drive/sail/talk on,** continuer à brûler/rouler/naviguer/parler; **go on!,** allez-y!; **move on!,** circulez!; **the speech/he went on and on,** le discours/il n'en finissait pas; **and so on,** et ainsi de suite; **on with the show!,** que le spectacle continue!;

(c) (*in time*) **later on,** plus tard; **from that day on,** à dater de ce jour; **well on in years,** d'un âge avancé;

(d) (*in operation*) (*machine, engine*) en marche; (*light, television, radio*) allumé; (*gas*) ouvert; **to turn on the tap,** ouvrir le robinet; **the brakes are on,** les freins sont serrés; **is the electricity on?,** est-ce que l'électricité est mise?;

(e) (*taking place*) **on with the show!,** que le spectacle commence!; **the play was on for weeks,** la pièce a tenu l'affiche pendant des semaines; **what's on tonight?,** (*what's happening*) qu'est-ce qui se passe ce soir?; *Rad* qu'est-ce qu'ils donnent ce soir?; *TV* qu'est-ce qui passe ce soir?; (*what are we doing?*) que fait-on ce soir?; *TV Rad* **there's nothing good on,** il n'y a rien de bien; **what's on at the cinema?,** qu'est-ce qu'on joue au cinema?; **have you anything on this evening?,** avez-vous quelque chose en vue pour ce soir?; **is the party still on?,** est-ce que la soirée se fait toujours?;

(f) *F* (*anxious to take part*) **I'm on!,** je suis de la partie!; **you're on!,** d'accord!, c'est bon!;

(g) *F* (*acceptable*) **that sort of behaviour isn't on,** cette sorte de comportement n'est pas admissible; **it's not on, charging £10 a ticket!,** c'est incroyable, faire payer un billet £10!; **it's not on,** (*I refuse your offer*) rien à faire!;

(h) to be on to sth, comprendre *ou* saisir *ou F* piger qch; **they were on to him at once,** ils ont tout de suite vu clair dans son jeu; **to be on to a good thing,** être sur une bonne affaire; **the police are on to her,** la police est sur sa piste; **I was on to him on the phone,** je lui ai parlé au téléphone; **I'll put you on to her,** je vais vous passer la communication;

(i) he's always on at *or* **to me,** il s'en prend toujours à moi;

(j) *Horseracing* **to have a bet on,** (*make a bet*) faire un pari; (*have made a bet*) avoir fait un pari;

(k) on and off *see* **OFF[1] 1(f).**

3 *adj* **(a) on position,** position *f* de serrage (*des freins*); position de mise en marche (*d'un moteur*); *El* position de fermeture (*du circuit*); **on/off switch,** interrupteur *m* marche/arrêt;

(b) *Cr* **drive to the on side, on drive,** coup *m* avant à gauche;

(c) *F* **it was not one of his on days,** il n'était pas dans un de ses meilleurs jours.

once [wʌns] *adv* **(a)** une fois; **o. only,** une seule fois; **more than o.,** plus d'une fois; **o. a week,** tous les huit jours; **o. or twice,** une ou deux fois, une fois ou deux; **o. in a while,** une fois de temps en temps; **o. more, o. again,** une fois de plus, encore une fois; **o. too often,** une fois de trop; **o. and for all,** une fois pour toutes; **you may do so this o.** *or* **just for (this) o.,** je vous le permets pour une fois *ou* pour cette fois(-ci); **for o. you are right,** pour une fois tu as raison; **o. a thief always a thief,** qui a volé volera; **(if) o. you hesitate you're lost,** dès que vous hésitez, vous êtes fichu; **a o.-in-a-lifetime opportunity,** une occasion qui ne se présente qu'une fois;

(b) (*formerly*) autrefois; **o. upon a time there was a princess,** il était une fois une princesse; **o. (upon a time) children used to respect their elders,** il fut un temps où les enfants respectaient leur aînés; **I knew him o.,** je l'ai connu autrefois *ou* dans le temps;

(c) at o., (*immediately*) tout de suite, immédiatement; (*at the same time*) à la fois, en même temps; **all at o. we were home,** tout à coup nous étions arrivés à la maison; **to do several things at o.,** faire plusieurs choses à la fois; **it all happened at o.,** tout est arrivé en même temps.

once-over ['wʌnsəʊvər] *n F* **to give s.o./sth the o.-o.,** jeter un coup d'œil (scrutateur) sur qn/qch; **to give a room a o.-o.,** donner un coup de torchon à une chambre.

oncology [ɒŋ'kɒlədʒɪ] *n* oncologie *f*.

oncoming ['ɒnkʌmɪŋ] *adj* **(a)** (*approaching*) approchant, qui approche; **the o. traffic,** (*for vehicle*) les véhicules venant en sens inverse; (*for pedestrian*) les véhicules qui approchent; **(b)** *Ind* **o. shift,** poste entrant.

OND [əʊen'diː] *n Br* (*abbr* **Ordinary National Diploma**) ≈ diplôme d'études techniques.

one [wʌn] **1** *adj* **(a)** un; **twenty-o. apples,** vingt et une pommes; **fifty-o.,** cinquante et un; **seventy-o.,** soixante et onze; **eighty-o.,** quatre-vingt-un; **a hundred and o.,** cent un; **a thousand and o.,** mille un; *F* **to have a thousand** *or* **a million and o. things to do,** avoir des tas de choses à faire; **o. or two people saw it,** une ou deux personnes l'ont vu; **o. day out of two,** un jour sur deux; **o. stormy evening in January,** par une soirée orageuse de janvier; **o. man in a hundred,** un homme entre *ou* sur cent; **for o. thing I'm short of cash,** entre autres raisons je suis à court d'argent; **it was o. hell of a journey,** c'était un voyage horrible; **o. way and another,** (*on balance*) à tous les points de vue;

(b) (*single*) seul, unique; **my o. and only suit,** mon seul et unique complet; **my o. and only daughter,** ma fille unique; **her o. care,** son seul *ou* unique souci; **no o. man can do it,** il n'y a pas d'homme qui puisse le faire à lui seul *ou* tout seul; **they cried out with o. voice** *or* **as o. man,** ils s'écrièrent d'une seule voix; **all in o. direction,** tous dans la même direction; **o. and the same thought came into our minds,** une seule et même pensée nous est venue à l'esprit; *F* **it's all o.,** cela revient au même; *F* **it's all o. to me,** ça m'est égal.

2 *n* **(a)** un *m*; **chapter o.,** chapitre un, chapitre premier; **number o.,** numéro un; *Sp* **o., two, three, go!,** un(e), deux, trois, partez!; **o. fifty,** (*a hundred and fifty*) cent cinquante; (*one pound and fifty pence*) une livre cinquante (pence); (*one dollar fifty cents*) un dollar cinquante (cents); (*ten minutes to two*) deux heures moins dix, une heure cinquante; **o. (o'clock),** une heure; *Horseracing* **the odds are (at) ten to o.,** la cote est à dix contre un; *F* **it's ten to o.** *or Am* **o. will get you ten that he's at the office,** je parie (à) dix contre un qu'il est au bureau;

(b) (*individual thing, person*) **there's only o. left,** il n'en reste qu'un; *F* **there's o. born every minute,** comment peut-on être aussi stupide!; **the top** *or* **bottom stair but o.,** l'avant-dernière marche; **to arrive in ones and twos,** arriver un par un ou deux par deux; **two for the price of o.,** deux pour le prix d'un; **two volumes in o.,** deux volumes en un; **chauffeur and gardener in** *or* **rolled into o.,** chauffeur et jardinier en un; **to be at o. with s.o.,** être d'accord avec qn; **I landed him o.,** je lui ai flanqué un marron; **o. for the road,** le coup de l'étrier; **to have o. too many,** boire un verre de trop; *Sp* **to be o. up on an opponent,** être en avance d'un point *ou* d'un jeu *ou* d'un but *etc* sur un concurrent; *F* **to be o. up on s.o.,** avoir l'avantage sur qn; *Knitting* **to make o.,** faire une augmentation;

(c) (*in dominoes*) as *m*; **double o.,** double-un *m*, *pl* double-uns;

(d) *St Exch* unité *f*; unité de mille livres (*au prix nominal des actions*).

3 *dem pron* **this o.,** celui-ci, celle-ci; *F* **these ones,** ceux-ci, celles-ci; **that o.,** celui-là, celle-là; *F* **those ones,** ceux-là, celles-là; **which o. do you prefer?,** lequel *ou* laquelle préférez-vous?; **the o. I spoke of,** celui *ou* celle dont j'ai parlé; **to pick the ripe plums and leave the green ones,** cueillir les prunes mûres et laisser les vertes; **the ones with the long sleeves,** ceux avec les manches longues; **the scheme was a good o. on paper,** le plan était excellent en théorie; **that's a good o.!,** elle est bonne, celle-là!; **have you heard the o. about ...?,** est-ce que tu as déjà entendu la blague du ...?; **that's a hard o.,** (*a difficult question*) vous me posez une colle; **our loved** *or* **dear ones,** ceux qui nous sont chers; (*our dead friends, relatives*) nos chers disparus; **the little ones,** les petits enfants; **he's a strange o., that boy,** il est bizarre ce garçon.

4 *indef pron* **(a)** (*pl* **some, any**) **I haven't a pencil, have you got o.?,** je n'ai pas de crayon, en avez-vous un?; **this question is o. of extreme delicacy,** ce problème est délicat entre tous; **o. of them,** un d'entre eux, l'un d'eux; **o. of these days,** un de ces jours; **she is o. of the family,** elle fait partie de la famille, elle est de la famille; **he is o. of us,** il est des nôtres; **o. of my friends,** un de mes amis, un ami à moi; **any o. of us,** n'importe lequel d'entre nous; **o. and all,** tous sans exception; **Merry Christmas to o. and all,** Joyeux Noël à tous; **o. for all and all for o.,** un pour tous et tous pour un; **(the) o. ... the other,** l'un ... l'autre; **you can't have o. without the other,** l'un ne va pas sans l'autre; **o. after the other,** l'un après l'autre; **o. by o.,** un à un, une à une;

(b) (*particular person*) **I want the opinion of o. better able to judge,** je voudrais avoir l'opinion de quelqu'un qui soit plus capable de juger; **o. Anne Martin,** une certaine Anne Martin; **I, for o., do not believe it,** pour ma part je n'en crois rien; **I'm not o. to complain,** je ne suis pas homme *ou* femme à me plaindre; **I'm not much of a o. for sweets,** je ne suis pas grand amateur de bonbons; *Old-fashioned* **you ARE a o.!,** vous êtes fameux *ou* impayable, vous!;

(c) *esp Fml* (*people in general*) on; **o. cannot always be right,** on ne peut pas toujours avoir raison; **if o. wanted to do it,** si l'on voulait le faire; **it is enough to kill o.,** il y a de quoi vous faire mourir; **o.'s,** son, sa, *pl* ses; votre, *pl* vos; **to give o.'s opinion,** donner son avis; **to cut o.'s finger,** se couper le doigt; **if o. loses o.'s** *or* (*US*) **his ...,** si on perd son ...;

(d) o. another, l'un l'autre; les uns les autres; **to look at o. another,** se regarder.

one-armed ['wʌnɑːmd] *adj* à un seul bras; (*person*) manchot, -ote; *Br F* **o.-a. bandit,** tire-pognon *m*, *pl* tire-pognons.

one-eyed ['wʌnaɪd] *adj* (*person*) borgne; *Zool* unioculé; **o.-e. man** *or* **woman,** borgne *mf*.

one-horse ['wʌnhɔːrs] *adj F* **o.-h. town,** petite ville de rien du tout, trou perdu.

one-legged [wʌn'legɪd] *adj* qui n'a qu'une jambe; *Zool* monopode; **o.-l. man** *or* **woman,** unijambiste *mf*.

one-liner [wʌn'laɪnər] *n* bon mot *m*.

one-man ['wʌnmæn] *adj* (*tâche etc*) pour un seul homme; **o.-m. band,** homme-orchestre *m*; *Fig* entreprise individuelle; **o.-m. show,** *Art* exposition individuelle; *Th* (spectacle *m*) solo *m*; *Fig* entreprise individuelle; *Com* **o.-m. company,** société à une seule personne *ou* à personne unique *ou* unipersonnelle.

oneness ['wʌnnɪs] *n* **(a)** (*unity*) unité *f*; accord *m* (*d'opinions*); **(b)** (*uniqueness*) caractère *m* unique.

one-night ['wʌn'naɪt] *adj F* **o.-n. stand,** *Th Mus etc* représentation *f* unique; (*sexual encounter*) histoire *f ou* rencontre *f* sans lendemain.

one-off ['wʌnɒf] **1** *adj Com* (*article*) spécial, hors série; (*film*) en exclusivité; (*in publishing*) (*livre*) à tirage limité; **a o.-o. design,** un modèle exclusif. **2** *n* (*thing*) objet *m ou* exemplaire *m* unique; (*person*) personnalité *f* unique; **the mistake was a o.-o.,** cette erreur ne se reproduira pas.

one-one, one-on-one ['wʌn'wʌn, wʌnɒn'wʌn] *adj Am* = **ONE-TO-ONE**.

one-parent ['wʌnpeərənt] *adj* **o.-p. family,** famille monoparentale.

one-piece ['wʌn'piːs] *adj* d'une seule pièce; (*casting*) monobloc *inv*; **o.-p. swimsuit,** maillot *m* une pièce.

oner ['wʌnər] *n Br Sl* **to down a drink in a o.,** faire cul sec; **he got it in a o.,** (*understood*) il a tout de suite pigé; (*got answer*) il a tout de suite trouvé la solution.

onerous ['ɒnərəs, 'əʊ-] *adj* (*impôt etc*) onéreux; (*tâche*) lourd.

oneself [wʌn'self] *pron* **(a)** (*reflexive*) se, soi(-même); **to flatter o.,** se flatter; **to look after o.,** se soigner; **to speak of o.,** parler de soi; **to keep o. to o.,** être peu sociable; **to feel o. again,** se sentir rétabli; **(b)** (*emphatic*) soi-même; **one must do it o.,** il faut le faire soi-même; **to do sth all by o.,** faire qch tout seul.

one-sided [wʌn'saɪdɪd] *adj* **(a)** (*unfair*) (*contract*) inégal, -aux, inéquitable; (*judgment*) partial, -aux; (*relationship*) à sens unique; **(b)** (*unilateral*) (*contract*) léonin; **(c)** (*asymmetric*) (*shape*) asymétrique.

one-step ['wʌnstep] *n* (*dance*) one-step *m*.

one-time ['wʌntaɪm] *adj* **Mr Martin, o.-t. mayor,** M. Martin ancien maire.

one-to-one ['wʌntə'wʌn] *adj* univoque; **o.-to-o. relationship,** (*between figures etc*) correspondance *f* univoque; **o.-to-o. tuition,** cours particuliers.

one-track ['wʌntræk] *adj* **o.-t. mind,** esprit obsédé par une seule idée; **you've got a o.-t. mind!,** tu ne penses qu'à une chose.

one-upmanship [wʌn'ʌpmənʃɪp] *n F* l'art de se faire passer pour supérieur aux autres.

one-way ['wʌnweɪ] *adj* **(a)** (*billet*) simple; *Com* (*emballage*) perdu; **(b)** (*rue, circulation*) à *ou* en sens unique; **o.-w. street,** sens *m* unique; **their relationship was all o.-w.,** leurs rapports étaient à sens unique.

ongoing ['ɒngəʊɪŋ] *adj F* continu; **o. discussions,** discussions actuelles *ou* en cours.

onion ['ʌnjən] *n* **(a)** oignon *m*; **spring o.,** ciboule *f*; **string of onions,** chapelet *m ou* corde *f* d'oignons; **o. skin,** pelure *f* d'oignon; *Culin* **o. soup,** soupe *f* à l'oignon; **(b)** *Sl* (*head*) ciboulot *m*; **(c)** *Br Sl* **she knows her onions,** elle connaît son affaire, elle s'y connaît.

oniony ['ʌnjənɪ] *adj* (*in smell*) qui sent l'oignon; (*in taste*) qui a un goût d'oignon.

on-line [ɒn'laɪn] *adj Comptr* connecté, en ligne, en direct.

onlooker ['ɒnlʊkər] *n* spectateur, -trice.

only ['əʊnlɪ] **1** *adj* seul, unique; **o. child,** enfant unique; **only son/daughter,** (*sole child*) fils/fille unique; (*sole son/daughter*) unique fils/fille; **her one and o. hope,** son seul et unique espoir; **his o. answer was to ...,** pour toute réponse il a ...; **we are the o. people who know it,** nous sommes seuls à le savoir; **you are not the o. one,** vous n'êtes pas le seul; **the o. thing is that it's rather expensive,** seulement ça coûte cher; **the one and o. Marilyn Monroe,** la seule et l'unique Marilyn Monroe.

2 *adv* seulement, ne ... que, ne rien que; **she has o. one brother,** elle n'a qu'un seul frère; **it's o. a scratch,** c'est seulement une égratignure, ce n'est qu'une *ou* ce n'est rien qu'une égratignure; **o. half an hour more,** plus qu'une demi-heure; **one man o.,** un seul homme; **(entrance for) season ticket holders o.,** entrée réservée aux abonnés; **o. an expert could advise us,** seul un expert pourrait nous conseiller; **I o. touched it,** je n'ai fait que le toucher; **he has o. to ask for it,** il n'a qu'à le demander; **I will o. say that I disagree,** je me bornerai à dire que je ne suis pas de cet avis; **I shall be o. too pleased to come,** je ne serai que trop heureux de venir; **o. if you agree,** seulement si tu es d'accord; **o. think what pleasure it gave me,** imaginez un peu le plaisir que cela m'a fait; **if o. I knew where he was!,** si seulement je savais où il est!; **if o. they knew, if they o. knew!,** si seulement ils savaient!, s'ils savaient!; **not o. useful but also decorative,** non seulement utile, mais aussi décoratif; **o. yesterday,** hier encore; (*no later than yesterday*) pas plus tard qu'hier; **I saw her o. yesterday,** je l'ai vue pas plus tard qu'hier; **o. last week he was walking normally,** la semaine dernière encore, il marchait normalement; **o. just,** à peine; **it's o. me,** (*wanting to come in, speak to you etc*) ce n'est que moi.

3 *conj* mais; **the book is interesting, o. rather too long,** le livre est intéressant, mais un peu long; **I would do it o. I can't spare the time,** je le ferais si j'avais le temps.

only-begotten [əʊnlɪbɪ'gɒt(ə)n] *adj & n* **the o.-b. (Son) of the Father,** le Fils unique du Père.

ono [əʊen'əʊ] *adv abbr* **or near(est) offer.**

onomatop(o)eia [ɒnəmætə'piːə] *n* onomatopée *f*.

onomatop(o)eic [ɒnəmætə'piːɪk] *adj* onomatopéique.

onrush ['ɒnrʌʃ] *n* ruée *f*, attaque *f*.

onset ['ɒnset] *n* **(a)** (*attack*) assaut *m*, attaque *f*; **(b)** (*beginning*) **at the o.,** d'emblée, de prime abord; **from the o.,** dès l'abord; **the o. of a disease,** la première attaque d'une maladie.

onshore ['ɒnʃɔːr] *adj* **(a)** (*vent etc*) du large; **(b)** (*installation pétrolière etc*) à terre.

on-site ['ɒnsaɪt] *adj* (*supervision, maintenance*) sur place.

onslaught ['ɒnslɔːt] *n* assaut *m*, attaque *f*.

Ont *abbr* **Ontario**.

on-the-job ['ɒnðə'dʒɒb] *adj* **on-the-j. training,** formation *f* sur le tas *ou* par la pratique.

onto ['ɒntʊ, *unstressed* 'ɒntə] *prep* = **ON TO,** *see* **ON.**

ontological [ɒntəʊ'lɒdʒɪk(ə)l] *adj Phil* ontologique.

ontology [ɒn'tɒlədʒɪ] *n Phil* ontologie *f*.

onus ['əʊnəs] *n* responsabilité *f*, charge *f*; **the o. is on the government to compensate the victims,** il incombe au gouvernement d'indemniser les sinistrés; *Jur* **o. of proof,** charge de la preuve.

onward ['ɒnwəd] **1** *adv* = **ONWARDS. 2** *adj* (*motion etc*) en avant.

onwards ['ɒnwədz] *adv* en avant, plus loin; **from tomorrow o.,** à partir de demain; **from this time o.,** désormais, dorénavant.

onyx ['ɒnɪks] *n Miner* onyx *m*.

oodles ['uːd(ə)lz] *npl Sl* **there's o. of it,** il y en a un tas *ou* des tas *ou* une tapée; **to have o. of money,** avoir un paquet *ou* une tonne de fric; **o. of cream,** des tonnes de crème.

ooh [uː] *int* (*expressing surprise, awe, pleasure*) oh!

oolite ['əʊəlaɪt] *n* (*rock*) oolithe *m*.

oomph [ʊmf] *n Sl* **(a)** (*energy*) énergie *f*; **to have plenty of o.,** avoir la pêche; **(b)** (*sex appeal*) sex-appeal *m*.

oops [uːps] *int* **(a)** (*to child who has fallen down*) houp-là!; **(b)** (*after s.o. has made a mistake*) oh là là!

oops-a-daisy ['uːpsə'deɪzɪ] *int* = **OOPS (a)**.

ooze¹ [uːz] *n* **(a)** (*mud*) vase *f*, limon *m*; (*muddy ground*) marais *m*, fond bourbeux; **(b)** suintement *m* (*d'un liquide*).

ooze² **1** *vi* suinter; **water that oozes out from the rock,** eau qui sourd du rocher; **the walls were oozing with water,** les murs suintaient, l'eau suintait des murs. **2** *vt* suer, suinter, laisser dégoutter (*l'eau*); *Fig* **to o. charm,** faire du charme; *Fig* **the place just oozes wealth,** cet endroit respire l'opulence.

op¹ [ɒp] *n Med F etc* opération *f*.

op² *adj Art* **o. art,** op art *m*.

opacity [əʊ'pæsɪtɪ] *n* opacité *f* (*d'un corps etc*).

opal ['əʊp(ə)l] *n* **(a)** (*mineral*) opale *f*; **o. necklace,** collier *m* d'opale; **(b)** (*colour*) opale *m inv*; **(c) o. (glass),** verre opale, opaline *f*.

opalescence [əʊpə'lesəns] *n* opalescence *f*.

opalescent [əʊpə'lesənt] *adj* opalescent; (*hue*) opale *inv*; (*haze etc*) opalisé.

opaline ['əʊpəlaɪn] **1** *adj* opalin. **2** *n* (*glass*) opaline *f*.

opaque [əʊ'peɪk] *adj* opaque; **to become o.,** s'opacifier.

opaqueness [əʊ'peɪknɪs] *n* opacité *f* (*d'un liquide etc*).

OPEC ['əʊpek] *n Petr* (*abbr* **Organization of Petroleum-Exporting Countries**) OPEP *f*; **OPEC countries/prices,** les pays *mpl*/prix *mpl* de l'OPEP.

open¹ ['əʊp(ə)n] **1** *adj* **(a)** (*box, door, window etc*) ouvert; **to fling** *or* **throw the door wide o.,** ouvrir la porte toute grande; **the door flew o.,** la porte s'ouvrit brusquement; **my door is always o.,** ma porte t'est *ou* vous est *etc* toujours ouverte; **half o.,** entrouvert, entrebâillé; **to keep o. house,** tenir table ouverte; **to cut o.,** couper, ouvrir; **to read s.o. like an o. book,** lire à livre ouvert dans la pensée de qn; **o. from ten to five,** (*of shop etc*) ouvert de dix heures à cinq heures; **we're not o. yet,** nous ne sommes pas encore ouverts; **o. to the public,** (*museum etc*) ouvert *ou* accessible au public; **o. all night,** ouvert la nuit; **o. late,** ouvert en nocturne; **in (the) o. court,** en plein tribunal; **career o. to very few,** carrière très fermée; *Sp* **o. competition,** tournoi ouvert; *Golf* **o. championship,** championnat open *ou* ouvert; **o. invitation,** invitation permanente; **o.** *Br* **day** *or Am* **house,** journée *f* porte(s) ouverte(s); **o. market,** marché public; **o. prison,** prison ouverte; *Culin* **o. sandwich,** canapé *m*; *Ind* **o. shop,** atelier qui admet les ouvriers non-syndiqués; *Br Sch* **O. University,** = enseignement universitaire par correspondance doublé d'émissions de télévision ou de radio;

(b) (*unobstructed*) **o. country,** pays découvert; **in the o. air,** au grand air, à ciel ouvert; **to sleep in the o. air,** coucher à la belle étoile; **in the o. country,** en pleine *ou* rase campagne; **the o. sea,** la haute mer, le large;

(c) (*not enclosed*) découvert, non couvert; (*coast, position*) exposé **(to,** à); **o. carriage,** voiture découverte; **o. to all the winds,** ouvert à tous les vents; *Fb* **to leave the goal o.,** dégarnir ses buts; **to lay oneself o. to,** prêter le flanc *ou* donner prise à (*une accusation, la critique*); s'exposer à (*la calomnie*); **o. to doubt,** douteux; **o. to ridicule,** qui prête au ridicule; **to be o. to conviction,** être accessible à la conviction; **o. to any reasonable offer,** disposé à considérer toute offre raisonnable; **to be o. to suggestions,** être ouvert à toute suggestion;

(d) (*publicly known*) manifeste, public, *f* -ique; (*not hidden*) ouvert; (*frank*) franc, *f* franche; **o. scandal,** scandale public; **o. secret,** secret *m* de Polichinelle; **o. letter,** lettre ouverte (*dans la presse*); **o. enemy,** ennemi déclaré; **her o. dislike,** son aversion déclarée; **they are in o. revolt,** ils ne dissimulent pas leur révolte; **o. hostilities,** guerre ouverte; **to be o. with s.o.,** parler franchement à qn, ne rien cacher à qn; **he is o. about his homosexuality,** il ne cache pas son homosexualité;

(e) (*flower, lips, hand*) ouvert; **with eyes o. wide,** les yeux écarquillés; **o. wound,** (*gaping*) plaie béante; (*not healed*) plaie non cicatrisée; **o. at the neck,** (*of dress*) échancré; (*of shirt*) à col ouvert; *Ling* **o. vowel,** voyelle ouverte; **to welcome with o. arms,** accueillir (*qn*) à bras ouverts; accueillir (*qch*) avec enthousiasme;

(f) (*clear, unobstructed*) libre, non obstrué; (*bowels*) libre; **road o. to traffic,** route ouverte à la circulation; **o. view,** vue dégagée; **to keep the bowels o.,** tenir le ventre libre; **to keep a day o. for s.o.,** réserver un jour pour qn; **the job is still o.,** la place est toujours vacante; **membership o. to anyone over 18,** inscription ouverte à toute personne de plus de 18 ans; **two courses are o. to us,** deux moyens s'offrent à nous; *Mus* **o. string,** corde *f* à vide;

(g) (*unresolved*) non résolu; (*question*) pendant; **to keep an o. mind on sth,** rester impartial *ou* réserver son opinion sur qch; **to leave the matter o.,** réserver la question; **I want to leave the return date o.,** (*on ticket*) pour l'instant, je ne veux pas réserver pour le retour; **o. ticket,** billet *m* open; **o. verdict,** verdict *m* de décès sans cause déterminée;

(h) *Fin Com* **o. account,** compte ouvert, compte courant; **o. cheque,** chèque *m* en blanc; **o. credit,** crédit *m* à découvert, crédit en blanc;

(i) *Fb etc* (*play*) (*free-flowing*) ouvert, dégagé.

2 *n* **in the o.,** (*in open air*) au grand air, à ciel ouvert; (*not hidden*) au grand jour; **to sleep in the o.,** dormir à la belle étoile; **to bring sth out into the o.,** mettre qch au grand jour; **their mutual dislike was out in the o.,** ils affichaient ouvertement l'antipathie qu'ils avaient l'un pour l'autre; **to come out into the o. about sth,** révéler qch; **let's get all this out in the o.,** jouons cartes sur table.

3 *adv Culin* **to o. freeze sth,** congeler qch à découvert.

open² **1** *vt* **(a)** ouvrir (*une porte, un livre etc*); ouvrir, déboucher, entamer (*une bouteille*); ouvrir, écailler (*une huître*); ouvrir, décacheter (*une lettre*); ouvrir, défaire (*un paquet*); ouvrir, déplier (*un journal*); ouvrir, lâcher (*une écluse*); ouvrir, dépouiller (*le courrier*); présider à l'inauguration de, inaugurer (*une institution, un établissement*); **to o. the door wide,** ouvrir la porte toute grande; *Med* **to o. the bowels,** relâcher les intestins; **to o. one's shop,** (*in morning etc*) ouvrir son magasin; **to o. a new shop,** ouvrir *ou* monter un nouveau magasin; **to o. a park to the public/a road (to traffic),** ouvrir un parc au public/une route à la circulation; **to o. Parliament,** ouvrir la session du Parlement;

(b) écarter (*les jambes etc*); ouvrir (*la main, les yeux*);

(c) (*lay bare*) découvrir, exposer, révéler; **to o. one's heart,** ouvrir son cœur, s'ouvrir (**to s.o.,** à qn); **that opens new prospects for me,** cela m'ouvre de nouveaux horizons;

(d) (*begin*) commencer; entamer, engager (*des négociations, une conversation, un débat*); ouvrir (*le feu, les hostilités*); **to o. an account in s.o.'s name,** ouvrir un compte à qn *ou* en faveur de qn; *Jur* **to o. the case,** exposer les faits.

2 *vi* **(a)** s'ouvrir; **to half o.,** (*of door etc*) s'entrebâiller, s'entrouvrir; **door that opens into the garden,** porte qui donne sur le jardin; **o. wide!,** (*said by doctor, dentist etc*) ouvrez grand la bouche!;

(b) (*of shop*) ouvrir; (*of bank, museum*) ouvrir ses portes; **as soon as the season opens,** dès l'ouverture de la saison;

(c) (*of view, prospects*) s'étendre; (*of flower*) s'épanouir, s'ouvrir; (*of bay*) s'ouvrir;

(d) (*begin*) commencer; **the play opens with a death scene,** la pièce s'ouvre sur une scène de mort; *St Exch* **coppers opened firm,** les valeurs cuprifères ont ouvert fermes;

(e) *El* (*of cutout*) décoller.

▶**open out 1** *vi* **(a)** (*of flower*) s'ouvrir; (*of wings*) se déployer; (*of view, prospects*) s'ouvrir, s'étendre. **2** *vtsep* **(a)** (*unfold*) ouvrir, déplier (*une feuille de papier*); **(b)** (*develop*) développer (*une entreprise*); **(c)** (*widen*) élargir, aléser, agrandir (*un trou*); évaser, mandriner (*la bouche d'un tuyau*).

▶**open up 1** *vi* **(a)** (*of flower*) s'ouvrir; **(b)** (*of view, prospects*) s'ouvrir, s'étendre; **new markets are opening up,** de nouveaux marchés sont en train de s'ouvrir; **(c)** (*of shopkeeper etc*) ouvrir; **this is the police — o. up!,** police! ouvrez!; **(d)** (*of new shop etc*) ouvrir; **(e)** (*of person*) s'ouvrir (**to s.o.,** à qn); **(f)** *Mil* ouvrir le feu. **2** *vtsep* **(a)** ouvrir (*un journal*) (en grand); **(b)** exposer, révéler (*une perspective etc*); **(c)** (*make accessible*) ouvrir (*un pays au commerce, une mine*); frayer, rendre praticable (*un chemin*); **the rain forest is being opened up for development,** on commence à exploiter la forêt tropicale; **(d)** (*develop*) ouvrir (*une carrière professionnelle*); **to o. up opportunities,** donner des chances; **(e)** (*start*) **to o. up a business,** ouvrir *ou* monter une affaire; **to o. up shop,** (*in the morning etc*) ouvrir la boutique.

open-air [əʊpə'neər] *adj* (*restaurant, marché, vie etc*) en plein air; **she's an o.-a. girl,** elle aime la vie *ou* les occupations en plein air.

open-and-shut [əʊpənən'ʃʌt] *adj* **an o.-and-s. case,** une affaire vite classée.

opencast ['əʊpənkɑːst] *adj* (*chantier, exploitation*) à ciel ouvert.

open-door ['əʊpəndɔːr] *adj* **o.-d. policy,** (*for immigrants*) politique d'ouverture des frontières; (*of university etc*) politique d'ouverture.

open-ended ['əʊpən'endɪd] *adj* sans limites fixes, non déterminé; **o.-e. discussion,** libre discussion; **it's a bit too o.-e.,** c'est un peu trop vague.

opener ['əʊpənər] *n* **(a)** *Th* premier numéro; *Cards* **openers,** cartes avec lesquelles on peut ouvrir (*au poker*); *F* **for openers,** pour commencer; **(b)** (*device*) **bottle o., crown cork o.,** décapsulateur *m*; **can** *or* **tin o.,** ouvre-boîtes *m inv*; **(c)** (*person*) ouvreur, -euse.

open-eyed ['əʊpə'naɪd] *adj* qui a les yeux ouverts; **to look at s.o. in o.-e. astonishment,** regarder qn les yeux écarquillés de surprise.

open-handed [əʊpən'hændɪd] *adj* libéral, -aux; **to be o.-h.,** avoir la main ouverte.

open-heart ['əʊpən'hɑːt] *adj* (*chirurgie*) à cœur ouvert.

open-hearted [əʊpən'hɑːtɪd] *adj* **(a)** (*frank*) ouvert, franc, *f* franche; **(b)** (*kind*) au cœur tendre *ou* compatissant.

open-hearth ['əʊpənhɑːθ] *adj Metal* **o.-h. furnace,** four *m* à sole; four Martin.

opening ['əʊpənɪŋ] *n* **(a)** ouverture *f* (*de la porte, d'un magasin, de son cœur, d'un compte*); ouverture, débouchage *m* (*d'une bouteille*); ouverture, décachetage *m* (*d'une lettre*); ouverture, dépouillement *m* (*de son courrier*); *Com* **late o. Friday,** ≈ nocturne le vendredi; **formal o.,** inauguration *f*; **the o. of Parliament,** l'ouverture du Parlement; **o. ceremony,** cérémonie *f* d'inauguration; **o. hours,** heures *fpl* d'ouverture; *Br* **o. time,** (*of pub, bar*) = heure à laquelle les pubs peuvent commencer à servir des boissons alcoolisées;

(b) (*beginning*) commencement *m*, début *m* (*d'une pièce de théâtre, d'une ère nouvelle*); ouverture *f* (*de négociations*); *Jur* exposition *f* des faits; **o. address** *or* **speech,** discours *m* d'ouverture; *Cards* **o. bid,** annonce *f* d'entrée *ou* d'indication; *Th* **the o. lines,** les premières lignes; *Th* **the o. scene,** la scène d'ouverture; *Th* **o. night,** première *f*; **o. day,** jour *m* d'ouverture;

(c) épanouissement *m*, éclosion *f* (*d'une fleur*); déploiement *m* (*des ailes d'un oiseau*);

(d) (*open space*) trou *m*, percée *f* (*à travers un mur*); percée, éclaircie *f* (*dans une forêt*); embrasure *f*, baie *f* (*dans un mur*); échappée *f* (*entre les arbres*); embouchure *f* (*d'un sac*); *Min* cloche *f* (*d'une carrière*); amorce *f* (*d'une galerie*);

(e) (*opportunity*) occasion *f* favorable; (*job*) poste *m*, place *f*; *Com* débouché *m* (*pour une marchandise*); **I didn't get an o.,** (*to mention it*) je n'ai pas eu l'occasion.

openly ['əʊpənlɪ] *adv* ouvertement; (*publicly*) publiquement; (*in front of everyone*) au vu (et au su) de tous; (*parler*) sans réticence; **to act o.,** agir à découvert *ou* cartes sur table, jouer franc jeu.

open-minded [əʊpən'maɪndɪd] *adj* qui a l'esprit ouvert *ou* large; **to be o.-m. on** *or* **about sth,** ne pas avoir de parti pris *ou* d'idée préconçue sur qch.

open-mouthed [əʊpən'maʊðd] *adj* **to stand o.-m.** *or* **in o.-m. astonishment,** rester bouche bée.

openness ['əʊpənnɪs] *n* **(a)** (*frankness*) franchise *f*, candeur *f*; **(b)** largeur *f*, libéralité *f* (*d'esprit*); **(c)** situation exposée (*d'une côte etc*); aspect découvert (*du terrain*).

open-plan ['əʊpənplæn] *adj (office)* décloisonné; **our office is o.-p., we have an o.-p. office,** nous avons un bureau décloisonné, *Can* nous avons l'aménagement paysager.
openwork ['əʊpənwɜːk] *n (embroidery)* ouvrage ajouré *ou* à jour; *(holes)* ajours *mpl*, jours *mpl*; **o. stockings,** bas ajourés *ou* à jour.
opera ['ɒp(ə)rə] *n* **(a)** opéra *m*; **o. tickets,** billets *mpl* pour l'opéra; **comic o., o. bouffe,** opéra bouffe *ou* comique; *TV F* **soap o.,** feuilleton *m*; **o. glasses,** jumelles *fpl* de théâtre; **o. goer,** amateur *m* d'opéra; **o. singer,** chanteur, -euse d'opéra; **(b) o. (house),** opéra *m*; **(c) o. (company),** (compagnie *f* d')opéra *m*.
operable ['ɒp(ə)rəb(ə)l] *adj* **(a)** *Surg (malade, tumeur)* opérable; **(b)** *(système etc)* utilisable, praticable.
operate ['ɒpəreɪt] **1** *vi* **(a)** *(of machine)* fonctionner; *(of burglar, company etc)* opérer, travailler; **the wage increase will o. from the first of January,** l'augmentation des salaires prendra effet à partir du premier janvier; **(b)** *Surg* opérer; **to o. (on s.o.) for appendicitis,** opérer (qn) de l'appendicite; **to be operated on,** subir une opération *ou* une intervention chirurgicale; **(c)** *St Exch* faire des opérations. **2** *vt* **(a)** *(of person)* manœuvrer *(une machine)*; actionner *(les freins)*; *(of part of machine)* commander, actionner; **operated by electricity,** actionné par l'électricité; **(b)** *Com* exploiter *(un chemin de fer, une ligne d'autobus etc)*.
operatic [ɒpə'rætɪk] **1** *adj* d'opéra; **o. society,** groupe *m* d'opéra d'amateurs. **2** *npl F* **operatics,** opéra *m* d'amateurs.
operating ['ɒpəreɪtɪŋ] **1** *adj* qui opère. **2** *n* **(a)** fonctionnement *m*; manœuvre *f*, commande *f (d'une machine)*; **o. instructions,** instructions *fpl ou* règlements *mpl* de service; **o. lever,** levier *m* de commande; **(b)** *Com* exploitation *f (d'une compagnie de chemins de fer)*; **o. costs,** frais *mpl* d'exploitation; **(c)** *Surg* **o. table,** table *f* d'opération, *F* (le) billard; **o.** *Br* **theatre** *or US* **room,** salle *f* d'opération; **(d)** *Comptr* **o. system,** système *m* d'exploitation.
operation [ɒpə'reɪʃən] *n* **(a)** opération *f*; fonctionnement *m*; marche *f (d'un appareil, d'une machine)*; jeu *m (d'un mécanisme)*; **in o.,** *(machine)* en marche, en fonctionnement; *(law)* en application, en vigueur; **to come into o.,** *(of machine)* commencer à fonctionner; *(of law)* entrer en application *ou* en vigueur;
(b) commande *f (d'une machine etc)*; exploitation *f (d'un réacteur, d'un navire, d'un réseau de transport)*;
(c) *(process)* travail *m*, -aux; unité *f (de fabrication etc)*; **it's a tricky o.,** c'est un travail délicat; **(mathematical) o.,** opération *f* mathématique; *Comptr* **(computer) o.,** opération machine; **operations research,** recherche opérationnelle; **a firm's operations,** les activités *fpl* d'une entreprise; **the company is moving its soft drinks o.,** la société déménage sa branche de boissons non alcoolisées: *St Exch* **credit o.,** opération à terme;
(d) *Mil etc* **airborne o.,** opération aéroportée; **operations room,** salle *f* d'opérations (d'un état-major); **O. Snow,** opération Neige;
(e) *Surg* opération *f*, intervention *f* (chirurgicale); **an o. to have one's appendix out,** une opération de l'appendicite; **to perform an o. on s.o.,** opérer qn **(for,** de); **to undergo** *or* **have an o.,** se faire opérer, subir une opération **(for,** de); **a throat o.,** une opération de la gorge.
operational [ɒpə'reɪʃənəl] *adj* **(a)** *Mil etc* opérationnel; **o. training,** instruction *f* tactique, entraînement *m* de guerre *ou* au combat; **(b)** *(machine)* opérationnel, en état de marche *ou* de fonctionnement *ou* de service; **the new power station should be o. next year,** la nouvelle centrale électrique devrait être opérationnelle l'an prochain.
operative ['ɒpərətɪv] **1** *adj* **(a)** actif; **to become o.,** *(of law)* entrer en vigueur, prendre effet; **to make a decree o.,** rendre un décret opérant; **the o. word,** le mot qui compte; **(b)** *Surg (méthode, champ)* opératoire. **2** *n* **(a)** *(worker)* ouvrier, -ière; opérateur, -trice *(d'une machine etc)*; **(b)** *US (detective)* détective *m*; **(c)** *(secret agent)* agent secret.
operator ['ɒpəreɪtər] *n* **(a)** *(person)* opérateur, -trice *(d'une machine)*; *Tel* téléphoniste *mf*; *Telecom* télégraphiste *mf*; *Com Ind* exploitant *m* (d'une entreprise); *F* brasseur *m* d'affaires; **radio** *or* **wireless o.,** (opérateur de) radio *m*; *Tel* **switchboard o.,** standardiste *mf*; *F* **he's a pretty slick o.,** il se débrouille plutôt bien; **(b)** *Math* opérateur *m (de logarithme)*; *MecE* appareil *m ou* mécanisme *m* de commande; opérateur *(d'une machine-outil)*.
operetta [ɒpə'retə] *n Mus* opérette *f*.
ophthalmic [ɒf'θælmɪk] *adj* **(a)** ophtalmique; **(b)** *(hôpital)* ophtalmologique.
ophthalmologist [ɒfθæl'mɒlədʒɪst] *n Med* ophtalmologiste *mf*, ophtalmologue *mf*.
ophthalmology [ɒfθæl'mɒlədʒɪ] *n Med* ophtalmologie *f*.
opiate ['əʊpɪɪt] *n Pharm* opiacé *m*, opiat *m*.
opine [əʊ'paɪn] *vt Old-fashioned & Am (be of opinion)* être d'avis **(that,** que); *(state opinion)* exprimer l'avis **(that,** que).
opinion [ə'pɪnjən] *n* opinion *f*, avis *m*; **in my o.,** à mon avis; **in the o. of experts,** de l'avis *ou* au dire des experts, suivant *ou* selon l'opinion des experts; **to be of the o. that ...,** être d'avis *ou* estimer que ..., **to be of the same o. as s.o.,** être du même avis que qn; **to express** *or* **put forward an o.,** exprimer une opinion; **to ask s.o.'s o.,** demander l'avis de qn, consulter qn; **I'd like your o.,** j'aimerais avoir ton opinion *ou* savoir ce que tu en penses; **to form an o. on s.o./sth,** se faire une opinion sur *ou* de qn/qch; **what is your o. of him?,** que pensez-vous de lui?; **opinions differ,** les avis sont partagés; **that's a matter of o.,** chacun ses opinions; **to have a high/low o. of s.o.,** avoir une bonne/mauvaise opinion de qn; **public o.,** l'opinion (publique); **o. poll** *or* **survey,** sondage *m* d'opinion publique; **o. pollster,** sondeur, -euse d'opinion; **you ought to have a second o.,** *Med* vous devriez consulter un autre médecin; *(generally)* vous devriez consulter quelqu'un d'autre.
opinionated [ə'pɪnjəneɪtɪd] *adj (esprit, ton)* dogmatique; *(personne)* entêté.
opium ['əʊpɪəm] *n* opium *m*; **o. addict,** opiomane *mf*; **o. den,** fumerie *f* d'opium.
Oporto [ə'pɔːtəʊ] *n* Porto *m*.
opossum [ə'pɒsəm] *n (animal)* opossum *m*.
opp *(abbr* **opposite)** en face.
opponent [ə'pəʊnənt] *n* adversaire *mf*; *Pol etc* opposant, -ante **(of,** à).
opportune ['ɒpətjuːn] *adj (time)* opportun, convenable; *(action)* à propos; **you have come at an o. moment,** vous arrivez à propos, vous tombez bien.
opportunely [ɒpə'tjuːnlɪ] *adv* opportunément, en temps opportun.
opportunism [ɒpə'tjuːnɪz(ə)m] *n* opportunisme *m*.
opportunist [ɒpə'tjuːnɪst] *n* opportuniste *mf*.
opportunistic [ɒpətjuː'nɪstɪk] *adj* **(a)** opportuniste; **(b)** *Med (disease)* opportuniste.
opportunity [ɒpə'tjuːnɪtɪ] *n* occasion *f* **(for doing sth, to do sth,** de faire qch); **golden o.,** affaire *f* en or; **at the first** *or* **earliest o.,** à la première occasion; **if I get an o.,** si l'occasion se présente; **to miss an o.,** laisser passer *ou* perdre une occasion; **a job with opportunities,** un emploi qui offre des perspectives.
oppose [ə'pəʊz] *vt* **(a)** *(resist)* s'opposer à *(qn, qch)*; mettre obstacle *ou* opposition à *(qch)*; résister à *(qn, qch)*; **to be opposed to sth,** être opposé à qch; **as opposed to,** par contraste à *ou* avec; *Jur* **to o. an action/a marriage,** s'opposer à un acte/mariage; **(b)** *(contrast)* opposer; mettre *(deux couleurs etc)* en opposition *ou* en contraste.
opposed [ə'pəʊzd] *adj* opposé; **directly o. evidence,** témoignages en contradiction directe.
opposing [ə'pəʊzɪŋ] *adj (armies, characters)* opposé; *(party)* opposant; *Sp* **o. team,** équipe *f* adverse.
opposite ['ɒpəzɪt] **1** *adj (page, characters)* opposé; *(opinion)* contraire; *(end of room etc)* autre; *(wall)* d'en face, opposé; **the o. sex,** l'autre sexe; **in the o. direction,** en sens inverse, dans le sens opposé; **they went in o. directions,** ils prirent des directions opposées; **see the diagram on the o. page,** voir la figure ci-contre; **o. number,** *(of politician etc)* homologue *m*; *Mil* correspondant *m* en grade.
2 *n* contraire *m*.
3 *adv* en face; **the house o.,** la maison (d')en face.
4 *prep* en face de, vis-à-vis (de); **to stand** *or* **sit o. s.o.,** faire vis-à-vis à qn; **house o. the church,** maison en face de l'église *ou* qui fait face à l'église; **we live o. them,** nous habitons en face de chez eux; *Th Cin* **she played o. many stars,** elle a joué avec beaucoup de vedettes pour partenaires.
opposition [ɒpə'zɪʃən] *n* opposition *f*; résistance *f*; *Com (competition)* concurrence *f*; **to act in o. to public opinion,** agir contrairement à l'opinion publique; **to meet with fierce o.,** recontrer une farouche opposition; **to break down all o.,** vaincre toutes les résistances; *Pol* **to be in o.,** être dans l'opposition; **the o.,** le camp adverse; *Pol* (le parti de) l'opposition; **member of the o.,** membre *m* de l'opposition; *Astron* **in o.,** en opposition.
oppress [ə'pres] *vt* opprimer *(un peuple vaincu)*; accabler *(l'esprit)*.

oppressed [ə'prest] **1** *adj* (*peuple*) opprimé. **2** *n* **the o.,** (*used as pl*) les opprimés *mpl*.
oppression [ə'preʃən] *n* **(a)** oppression *f* (*d'un peuple*); *Jur* abus *m* d'autorité; **(b)** accablement *m* (*de l'esprit*).
oppressive [ə'presɪv] *adj* **(a)** (*law, régime*) oppressif, opprimant; **(b)** (*atmosphere*) lourd, étouffant; (*mental burden*) accablant; (*heat*) accablant, étouffant.
oppressively [ə'presɪvlɪ] *adv* (*see adj*) **(a)** d'une manière oppressive; **(b)** d'une manière étouffante; **it was o. hot,** il faisait une chaleur accablante *ou* étouffante.
oppressiveness [ə'presɪvnɪs] *n* **(a)** caractère oppressif; **(b)** lourdeur *f* (*du temps*).
oppressor [ə'presər] *n* oppresseur *m*; **the oppressors and the oppressed,** les oppresseurs et les opprimés.
opprobrious [ə'prəʊbrɪəs] *adj Fml* injurieux, outrageant.
opprobrium [ə'prəʊbrɪəm] *n Fml* opprobre *m*.
opt [ɒpt] *vi* opter (**for,** pour; **between,** entre); **to o. to do sth,** choisir de faire qch.
▶**opt in** *vi* (*join*) choisir de participer.
▶**opt into** *vipo* (*join*) **to o. into an association/the Common Market** *etc*, entrer dans une association/le Marché Commun/*etc*.
▶**opt out** *vi* choisir de ne pas participer; **to o. out of an association,** quitter une association; **to o. out of a competition,** abandonner un concours; **I'm opting out,** je ne veux pas participer; *Br* **to o. out (of the state education system),** (*of school*) devenir privé.
optative ['ɒptətɪv] *adj & n Gram* optatif *m*.
optic ['ɒptɪk] **1** *adj* **(a)** optique; *Anat* **o. nerve,** nerf *m* optique; **(b) o. measure,** = mesure transparente (*utilisée dans les bars*). **2** *n* **(a)** *Opt* (*lens*) lentille *f*; (*mirror*) miroir *m*; (*prism*) prisme *m*; **(b) o.** ®, = mesure transparente (*utilisée dans les bars*).
optical ['ɒptɪk(ə)l] *adj* optique; (*instrument*) d'optique; **o. axis/centre,** axe *m*/centre *m* optique (*d'une lentille*); *Comptr* **o. character reader,** lecteur *m* optique de caractères; *Comptr* **o. character recognition,** reconnaissance *f* optique des caractères; *Comptr* **o. disk,** disque *m* optique; **o. fibre,** fibre *f* optique; **o. fibre cable,** câble à fibre optique; **o. illusion,** illusion *f* d'optique.
optician [ɒp'tɪʃən] *n* opticien, -ienne; **at the o.'s,** chez l'opticien.
optics ['ɒptɪks] *npl* (*usu with sing verb*) optique *f*.
optimal ['ɒptɪm(ə)l] *adj* optimal, -aux.
optimism ['ɒptɪmɪz(ə)m] *n* optimisme *m*.
optimist ['ɒptɪmɪst] *n* optimiste *mf*.
optimistic [ɒptɪ'mɪstɪk] *adj* optimiste.
optimistically [ɒptɪ'mɪstɪklɪ] *adv* d'une manière optimiste, avec optimisme.
optimum, *pl* **-ima** ['ɒptɪməm, -ɪmə] **1** *n* optimum *m*. **2** *adj* **o. conditions,** conditions les meilleures, conditions optimum; **o. population density,** optimum *m* de population.
option ['ɒpʃən] *n* **(a)** (*choice*) option *f*, choix *m*; **the military o.,** l'option militaire; **to have the o. of doing sth,** avoir la faculté *ou* le choix de faire qch; **we have no o. but to agree,** nous ne pouvons faire autrement que de consentir; **I haven't got any o., I've got no o.,** je n'ai pas le choix; *Jur* **imprisonment without the o. of a fine,** emprisonnement sans substitution d'amende; **which of them is the best o.?,** lequel est le meilleur choix?; **there was no soft o.,** il n'y avait pas de solution facile; **it's best to leave your options open,** il est préférable d'envisager toutes les possibilités; **we have the o. of staying here,** nous avons la possibilité de rester ici;
(b) *St Exch etc* option *f*; (marché *m* à) prime *f*; **to take an o. on all the future works of an author,** prendre une option sur tous les ouvrages à paraître d'un auteur; *St Exch* **buyer's/seller's o.,** prime acheteur/vendeur; *St Exch* **to take up an o.,** lever une prime; *St Exch* **o. deal,** opération *f* à prime.
optional ['ɒpʃən(ə)l] *adj* facultatif; **evening dress is o.,** l'habit n'est pas de rigueur; **o. extras,** accessoires *mpl* en option; **o. retirement at sixty,** retraite à soixante ans sur demande; *Sch* **o. subjects,** (*one must be chosen*) matières *fpl* à option *ou* optionnelles; (*possible to choose none*) matières facultatives.
optometrist [ɒp'tɒmɪtrɪst] *n* optométriste *mf*.
opulence ['ɒpjʊləns] *n* opulence *f*, richesse *f*.
opulent ['ɒpjʊlənt] *adj* **(a)** (*wealthy*) opulent, riche; **(b)** (*plentiful*) abondant.
opulently ['ɒpjʊləntlɪ] *adv* avec opulence.
opus ['əʊpəs, 'ɒp-] *n* opus *m*; **magnum o.,** chef-d'œuvre *m*, *pl* chefs-d'œuvre.
or [ɔːr; *unstressed* ər] *conj* ou; (*with neg*) ni; **do you want beef or ham?,** voulez-vous du bœuf ou du jambon?; **either one or the other,** soit l'un soit l'autre, l'un ou l'autre; **either come in or (else) go out,** entrez ou (bien) sortez; **either you or he has done it,** c'est vous ou (c'est) lui qui l'a fait; **without money or luggage,** sans argent ni bagages; **in a day or two,** dans un ou deux jours; **a mile or so,** environ un mil(l)e; **did she do it or not?,** est-ce qu'elle l'a fait ou pas?; **don't move, or I'll shoot,** ne bougez pas, sinon je tire; **we could go to the beach or we could go to the zoo,** nous pourrions aller soit à la plage soit au zoo; **or else,** sinon; *F* **do it now or else,** fais-le tout de suite ou sinon.
oracle ['ɒrək(ə)l] *n* oracle *m*; (*priest, priestess*) (prêtre, -esse d')oracle; **the Delphic o.,** l'oracle de Delphes; **to pronounce** *or* **utter an o.,** rendre un oracle; **to consult the o.,** consulter les oracles.
oracular [ɒ'rækjʊlər] *adj* (*style etc*) d'oracle, oraculaire; (*réponse etc*) équivoque, obscur.
oral ['ɔːrəl] **1** *adj* (*agreement, tradition, contraceptive, sex*) oral, -aux; (*vaccin*) buccal; (*administration d'une drogue*) par la bouche, par voie orale; *Anat* **o. cavity,** cavité orale *ou* buccale; *Sch* **o. examination,** (examen *m*) oral *m*. **2** *n Sch* (examen *m*) oral *m*.
orally ['ɔːrəlɪ] *adv* oralement, de vive voix; *Med* par la bouche, par voie orale.
orange ['ɒrɪndʒ] *n* **(a)** (*fruit*) orange *f*; **blood o.,** (orange) sanguine *f*; **o. juice,** jus *m* d'orange; **o. marmalade,** confiture *f* d'orange(s); **o. peel,** peau *f ou* écorce *f ou Culin* zeste *m* d'orange; **o. segment,** quartier *m*, tranche *f* (d'une orange); **(b) o. (tree),** oranger *m*; **mock o.,** (*shrub*) seringa odorant; **o. blossom,** fleurs *fpl* d'oranger; **o. flower water,** eau *f* de fleur d'oranger; **o. grove,** orangeraie *f*; **o. stick,** (*for nails*) bâtonnet *m*; **(c)** (*colour*) orangé *m*, orange *m*. **2** *adj* (*colour*) orangé, orange *inv*; **o. red,** rouge orangé.
Orange ['ɒrɪndʒ] *n* **(a)** *Geog* **the O. (River),** l'Orange *m*; **the O. Free State,** l'Etat *m* libre d'Orange; **(b)** *Hist* **the Prince of O.,** le prince d'Orange.
orangeade [ɒrɪn'dʒeɪd] *n* orangeade *f*.
Orangeman, *pl* **-men** ['ɒrɪndʒmən] *n Br* = orangiste (*du parti protestant de l'Irlande du Nord*).
orangery ['ɒrɪndʒərɪ] *n* orangerie *f*.
orang-outang, -utan [ɔːræŋ'uːtæŋ, -tæn] *n* (*ape*) orang-outan(g) *m*, *pl* orangs-outan(g)s.
oration [ɔː'reɪʃən] *n* allocution *f*, discours *m*; **funeral o.,** oraison *f* funèbre.
orator ['ɒrətər] *n* orateur, -trice.
oratorical [ɒrə'tɒrɪk(ə)l] *adj* (*style, talent*) oratoire.
oratorio [ɒrə'tɔːrɪəʊ] *n Mus* oratorio *m*.
oratory¹ ['ɒrət(ə)rɪ] *n* art *m* oratoire; éloquence *f*; **a brilliant piece of o.,** un brillant spécimen d'art oratoire; **flight of o.,** envolée éloquente.
oratory² *n Rel* oratoire *m*.
orb [ɔːb] *n* globe *m*, sphère *f*; (*of regalia*) globe; *Arch Lit* (*planet etc*) orbe *m*; **the o. of the sun,** le globe du soleil; **the o. and the sceptre,** l'orbe et le sceptre.
orbit¹ ['ɔːbɪt] *n* **(a)** orbite *f* (*d'une planète, d'un véhicule spatial*); **in o.,** en orbite; **to enter** *or* **go into o.,** se mettre *ou* se placer en orbite; **to send a satellite into o.,** lancer un satellite en orbite, mettre un satellite sur orbite; **(b)** *Anat* orbite *f* (*de l'œil*).
orbit² **1** *vt* **to o. the sun,** décrire une orbite *ou* orbiter autour du soleil. **2** *vi* (*of satellite etc*) orbiter, décrire une orbite.
orbital ['ɔːbɪt(ə)l] **1** *adj* **(a)** *Astron etc* orbital, -aux; *Br* **o. road,** périphérique *m*; **(b)** *Anat* (*cavité etc*) orbitaire. **2** *n Br* (*road*) périphérique *m*.
Orcadian [ɔː'keɪdɪən] **1** *n* habitant, -ante des îles Orcades. **2** *adj* des îles Orcades.
orchard ['ɔːtʃəd] *n* verger *m*; **apple o.,** pommeraie *f*.
orchestra ['ɔːkɪstrə] *n* **(a)** *Mus* orchestre *m*; **string o.,** orchestre à cordes; *Th* **o. pit,** orchestre; **(b)** *Th* orchestre *m*; **the o. stalls,** *Am* **the o.,** les fauteuils *mpl* d'orchestre.
orchestral [ɔː'kestr(ə)l] *adj* orchestral, -aux.
orchestrate ['ɔːkɪstreɪt] *vt Mus* orchestrer (*une symphonie etc, Fig une campagne de presse etc*).
orchestration [ɔːkɪs'treɪʃən] *n* orchestration *f*.
orchid ['ɔːkɪd] *n* (*plant*) orchidée *f*; (*wild*) orchis *m*; **o. grower,** cultivateur, -trice d'orchidées.
orchis ['ɔːkɪs] *n* (*plant*) orchis *m*.
ordain [ɔː'deɪn] *vt* **(a)** (*decree*) ordonner, fixer; décréter (*une mesure*); **fate ordained** *or* **it was ordained that we should meet,** le sort a voulu que nous nous rencontrions; **(b)** *Rel* ordonner (*un prêtre*); **to be ordained,** recevoir les ordres.
ordeal [ɔː'diːl] *n* **(a)** épreuve *f*; danger *m* (*qui éprouve la*

force et le courage); **to go through a terrible o.,** passer par une rude épreuve; **it is an o. for me to make a speech,** je suis au supplice quand je dois faire un discours; **they spoke of their o.,** ils ont évoqué l'épreuve qu'ils ont vécue; **(b)** *Hist* épreuve *f* judiciaire, ordalie *f*; **o. by fire,** épreuve du feu.

order[1] ['ɔːdər] *n* **(a)** (*instruction*) ordre *m*; *Mil* ordre, consigne *f*; **verbal/written o.,** ordre verbal/écrit; **standing orders,** ordres permanents; règlement(s) *m(pl)* (*d'une assemblée etc*); **I have orders to remain here,** j'ai ordre de rester ici; **to give orders/an o.,** donner des ordres/un ordre; **to obey orders,** obéir aux ordres, suivre la consigne; **our orders are to ...,** nous avons l'ordre de ...; **and that's an o.!,** c'est un ordre!; *F* **I don't take (my) orders from him,** je ne dépends pas de lui; **until further o.,** jusqu'à nouvel avis; **by o. of the King,** de par le roi; *Mil* **arms at the o.,** l'arme au pied; *Fin* **pay to the o. of J. Martin,** payez à l'ordre de J. Martin; **pay J. Martin or o.,** payez à J. Martin ou à son ordre; **cheque to o.,** chèque *m* à ordre; **I can't do it to o.,** ça ne se commande pas;

(b) *Com* commande *f*; **to call for orders,** (*of representative*) passer prendre les commandes; **to place an o. with s.o., to give s.o. an o.,** confier *ou* passer une commande à qn, commander qch à qn; **another firm got the o.,** ils ont passé la commande auprès d'une autre compagnie; **have you given your o.?,** (*in restaurant*) avez-vous commandé?; **cash with o.,** payable à la commande; **it's on o.,** c'est commandé; **made to o.,** fabriqué sur commande; (*suit*) fait sur mesure; *F* **that's a tall o.,** ce que vous demandez là n'est pas facile; **to deliver an o.,** livrer une commande; *Am* **an o. of French fries,** une portion de frites; **o. book,** carnet *m* de commandes; **the o. books are full,** les carnets de commandes sont pleins; **o. form,** bon *m ou* bulletin *m* de commande;

(c) (*document*) ordre *m*; *Com Admin* bon *m*; *Fin* mandat *m*; **o. in council,** = décret *m* du gouvernement; arrêté ministériel; (*statutory order*) décret-loi *m*, *pl* décrets-lois; **o. to pay** *or* **for payment,** ordonnance *f* de paiement; ordonnancement *m*; **o. to view,** permis *m* de visiter (une maison à vendre); *Jur* **o. of the court,** injonction *f* de la cour; **deportation o.,** arrêté *m* d'expulsion; *Mil* **daily orders,** décision journalière; **battle orders,** mémorandum *m* de combat; *Nau* **sailing orders,** ordre d'appareiller, instructions *fpl* pour l'appareillage; **sealed orders,** ordres cachetés; *Com* **delivery o.,** bon *m* de livraison; **purchase o.,** bon d'achat *ou* de commande; *Fin* **banker's o., standing o.,** ordre de transfert permanent;

(d) (*peace, harmony*) ordre *m*; **law and o.,** l'ordre public; **to keep o. in a town,** assurer *ou* maintenir l'ordre dans une ville; *Sch* **to keep o. in class,** maintenir la discipline dans une classe; **to restore o.,** rétablir l'ordre;

(e) (*condition*) **machine in (good) working o.,** machine en (bon) état de fonctionnement *ou* de marche; **out of o.,** (*mécanisme*) détraqué, dérangé; (*compas*) déréglé; (*téléphone*) en dérangement; (*ascenseur, machine*) en panne;

(f) (*in meeting etc*) **o. of the day,** ordre *m* du jour; *Parl* **o. paper,** copie *f* de l'ordre du jour; **to rule a question out of o.,** statuer qu'une interpellation n'est pas dans les règles; *Br F* **you're out of o.!,** tu as dépassé les bornes!; *F* **I think a celebration is in o.,** je pense que ça mérite d'être fêté; **to call s.o. to o.,** rappeler qn à l'ordre; **o.! o.!,** à l'ordre!; *Rel* **o. of service,** office *m*;

(g) in o., (*as it should be*) en ordre; (*document*) en règle, conforme à la règle; **to put things in o.,** mettre des choses en ordre; **to put** *or* **set one's affairs in o.,** mettre ses affaires en ordre; régler ses affaires; *Fig* **to set one's house in o.,** remettre de l'ordre dans ses affaires;

(h) (*system*) ordre *m*; **the established o.,** l'ordre établi; **it's not in the natural o. of events,** ce n'est pas dans l'ordre des choses;

(i) (*sequence*) ordre *m*; **in alphabetical/chronological o.,** en *ou* par ordre alphabétique/chronologique; **in o. of age,** par rang d'âge; *Th Cin* **in o. of appearance,** par ordre d'apparition; **in ascending/descending o.,** en *ou* par ordre croissant/décroissant;

(j) *Mil* (*disposition*) **in close o.,** en ordre serré; **o. of battle,** ordre de bataille;

(k) (*class*) classe *f*, ordre *m*; *Biol* ordre (*d'un règne*); **the higher/lower orders (of society),** les classes supérieures/inférieures; **workmanship of the highest o.,** travail de premier ordre; **population of** *or* **in** *or Am* **on the o. of 100,000,** population de l'ordre de 100 000 habitants; **a disaster/a project/investment of this o.** (**of magnitude**), un désastre/un projet/des investissements de cette envergure; *Archit* **Ionic/Doric o.,** ordre ionique/dorique; *Rel* **holy orders,** ordres sacrés; **major orders,** ordres majeurs; **minor orders,** ordres mineurs; **to be in holy orders,** être prêtre *ou* moine *ou* religieuse; **monastic o.,** ordre religieux; communauté *f*; **o. of knighthood,** ordre de chevalerie; **the O. of the Garter,** l'Ordre de la Jarretière; *Br* **O. of Merit,** ≈ Ordre *m* du Mérite, **to be wearing one's orders,** porter ses décorations;

(l) in o. to do sth, afin de *ou* pour faire qch; **in o. that they understand,** afin qu'ils *ou* pour qu'ils puissent comprendre.

order[2] **1** *vt* **(a)** *Med* prescrire, ordonner (*un traitement à qn*); **to o. s.o. to do sth,** ordonner *ou* commander à qn de faire qch; **he's been ordered to report tomorrow,** il a reçu l'ordre de se présenter demain; *Jur* **to be ordered to pay costs,** être condamné aux dépens; *Fig* **that's just what the doctor ordered,** c'est tout à fait ce qu'il faut pour l'occasion;

(b) *Com* commander (*qch*); **to o. goods from Paris,** commander des articles à Paris; **we can o. it for you,** nous pouvons vous le commander; **to o. a taxi,** (faire) demander un taxi; **what have you ordered for dinner?,** qu'avez-vous commandé pour le dîner?;

(c) (*arrange*) arranger, ranger, ordonner (*des meubles etc*); classer, ranger (*des papiers*); *Mil* **o. arms!,** reposez armes!

2 *vi* (*in restaurant*) commander.

►**order about, order around** *vtsep F* faire marcher, faire aller (*qn*); **he likes ordering people about,** il aime (à) commander les autres; **you can't o. me about!,** je n'ai pas d'ordres à recevoir.

►**order off** *vtsep Sp* **to o. a player off,** expulser un joueur du terrain.

►**order out** *vtsep* **to o. s.o. out,** (*of the room, house*) mettre (*qn*) à la porte.

ordered ['ɔːdəd] *adj* ordonné; (*in good order*) en bon ordre; **an o. life,** une vie régulière *ou* réglée.

orderliness ['ɔːdəlınıs] *n* **(a)** (*methodical nature*) méthode *f*; **(b)** (*habits*) habitudes *fpl* d'ordre; **(c)** (*discipline*) discipline *f*; bonne conduite (*d'une foule etc*).

orderly ['ɔːdəlı] **1** *adj* **(a)** (*arrangement*) ordonné, méthodique; (*life*) réglé, rangé, régulier; **to be very o.,** (*of person*) avoir beaucoup de méthode; **leave the building in an o. fashion,** quittez l'immeuble dans l'ordre et le calme; **(b)** (*crowd*) discipliné. **2** *n* **(a)** *Mil* planton *m*; **to be on o. duty,** être planton; *Mil* **o. room,** salle *f* des rapports; **o. officer,** officier *m* de service; **(b) hospital o., medical o.,** aide-infirmier, -ière; *Mil* infirmier *m*, ambulancier *m*.

ordinal ['ɔːdın(ə)l] **1** *adj* (*nombre*) ordinal, -aux. **2** *n* adjectif ordinal.

ordinance ['ɔːdınəns] *n* **(a)** (*decree*) ordonnance *f*, règlement *m*; **(b)** *Rel* rite *m*, cérémonie *f* (*du culte*).

ordinarily ['ɔːdın(ə)rılı, *Am* ɔːdı'neərılı] *adv* ordinairement, d'ordinaire, d'habitude.

ordinary ['ɔːdın(ə)rı] **1** *adj* (*habitual*) ordinaire; **o. Englishman,** Anglais moyen *ou* typique; **she was just an o. tourist,** c'était une touriste comme une autre; **this is no o. house/car,** ce n'est pas une maison/voiture ordinaire; *Pej* **a very o. kind of man,** un homme tout à fait quelconque; *Br Sch* (*not Scot*) **O. level,** *Scot Sch* **O. grade,** ≈ BEPC *m* (brevet élémentaire du premier cycle); *Br Nau* **o. seaman,** matelot *m*; *Br Fin* **o. share,** action *f* ordinaire. **2** *n* **(a)** ordinaire *m*; **out of the o.,** exceptionnel, peu ordinaire, qui sort de l'ordinaire; **nothing out of the o. happened,** il n'est rien arrivé d'inhabituel; **(b)** (*person*) *Jur Scot* juge *m*; *Rel Jur* ordinaire *m* (archevêque *ou* évêque); **(c)** *Rel* **the O. (of the Mass),** l'Ordinaire *m* (de la messe); **(d)** *Her* pièce *f* honorable.

ordinate ['ɔːdınıt] *n Math* ordonnée *f*.

ordination [ɔːdı'neıʃən] *n Rel* ordination *f*.

ordnance ['ɔːdnəns] *n* **(a)** *Mil* (service *m* du) matériel *m*; **Royal Army O. Corps,** *US* **O. Service,** Service *m* du Matériel; **o. and supplies,** les ravitaillements *mpl*; **(b)** *Mil* (*artillery*) artillerie *f*; **piece of o.,** bouche *f* à feu; pièce *f* d'artillerie; **o. factory,** manufacture *f* d'artillerie; **(c)** *Br* **O. Survey,** ≈ Institut Géographique National; *Br* **o.(-survey) map,** ≈ carte de l'Institut Géographique National.

ordure ['ɔːdjʊər] *n* ordure *f*.

ore [ɔːr] *n* minerai *m*; **iron o.,** minerai de fer; **rich** *or* **high-grade o.,** minerai à *ou* de haute teneur; **crude o.,** minerai brut; **o. deposit,** gisement *m* de minerai.

Ore(g) *abbr* **Oregon.**

oregano [ɒrı'gɑːnəʊ] *n Bot Culin* origan *m*.

organ ['ɔːgən] *n* **(a)** *Mus* orgue *m*; *Rel* orgues *fpl*; **grand o.,** grand orgue, grandes orgues; **choir o.,** orgue du chœur; **to play the o.,** jouer de l'orgue; **American o.,** orgue de salon; **street o.,** orgue de Barbarie; **o. builder,** facteur *m* d'orgues; **o. loft** *or* **gallery,** tribune *f* d'orgues; **o. pipe,** tuyau *m* d'orgue; **o. stop,** jeu *m* d'orgue; **(b)** *Anat* organe *m* (*du corps humain, d'une plante*); *Euph* (*of male*) membre *m*; **o. of hearing,** organe de l'ouïe; **the vocal organs,** l'appareil vocal; **o. transplant,** transplantation *f* d'organe; **(c)** organe *m* (*de gouvernement*); (*medium*) journal *m*, -aux, organe, porte-parole *m inv* (*du gouvernement, d'un parti*); **an efficient o. of propaganda,** un organe de propagande efficace; **the official o.,** l'organe officiel.

organdie ['ɔːgəndɪ] *n Tex* organdi *m*; **o. dress,** robe *f* d'organdi.

organ-grinder ['ɔːgəngraɪndər] *n* joueur, -euse d'orgue de Barbarie; *F* **I want to speak to the o.-g. not his monkey,** je veux parler à Dieu et non pas à ses saints.

organic [ɔː'gænɪk] *adj* **(a)** (*dépôt, engrais*) organique; biologique; (*chimie, acide, composé*) organique; **o. farming,** agriculture *f* biologique; **o. foods,** aliments *mpl* biologiques; **o. gardening,** jardinage *m* biologique; **o. chemist,** organicien, -ienne; **(b)** (*maladie, fonction*) organique; **(c) o. beings,** êtres organisés; **the law of o. growth,** la loi de croissance organisée; **(d)** (*made up of parts*) systématisé; **an o. whole,** un ensemble systématique; **(e)** (*fundamental*) organique, fondamental, -aux; **o. part of the whole,** partie essentielle de la totalité.

organically [ɔː'gænɪklɪ] *adv* **(a)** organiquement; **o. grown foods,** aliments produits à l'aide d'un engrais organique; **(b)** (*basically*) fondamentalement, foncièrement.

organism ['ɔːgənɪz(ə)m] *n* organisme *m*; **living o.,** organisme vivant.

organist ['ɔːgənɪst] *n* organiste *mf*.

organization [ɔːgənaɪ'zeɪʃən] *n* **(a)** (*action*) organisation *f*; *Ind* **o. of labour,** régime *m* du travail; (*trade unionism*) syndicalisme *m*; **o. and methods,** organisation scientifique du travail; **o. chart,** (*of company*) organigramme *m*; **(b)** (*association*) organisation *f*, organisme *m*; **charity o.,** organisation charitable, œuvre *f* de charité; **youth o.,** mouvement *m* de jeunesse.

organizational [ɔːgənaɪ'zeɪʃən(ə)l] *adj* (*défaut etc*) d'organisation, de structure, organisationnel.

organize ['ɔːgənaɪz] **1** *vt* **(a)** organiser; **workmen organized into trade unions,** ouvriers organisés en syndicats; **(b)** (*arrange, bring about*) organiser, arranger (*un concert*); aménager (*ses loisirs*); *F* se faire accorder (*un congé etc*); **she organized it so that we got in free,** elle s'est arrangée pour que nous puissions entrer sans payer; *F* **to o. a bottle of rum,** dénicher une bouteille de rhum. **2** *vi* **(a)** s'organiser; **(b)** (*of workers*) se syndiquer.

organized ['ɔːgənaɪzd] *adj* **(a)** (*society, crime, person*) organisé; **o. labour,** = les organisations ouvrières; *Sch* **o. games,** jeux dirigés; **(b)** *Biol* organisé.

organizer ['ɔːgənaɪzər] *n* (*person*) organisateur, -trice; (*personal organizer*) organisateur *m*; **she's a born o.,** elle a le sens de l'organisation, c'est une organisatrice née.

organizing ['ɔːgənaɪzɪŋ] *n* **(a)** organisation *f*; **o. ability,** qualités *fpl* d'organisation; **(b)** (*arranging*) aménagement *m* (*de ses loisirs*).

orgasm ['ɔːgæz(ə)m] *n Physiol* orgasme *m*; **to have an o.,** avoir un orgasme.

orgasmic [ɔː'gæzmɪk] *adj Physiol* orgastique; *Sl* (*success etc*) fantastique.

orgiastic [ɔːdʒɪ'æstɪk] *adj* orgiastique.

orgy ['ɔːdʒɪ] *n* (*sexual, Fig of colour*) orgie *f*; (*of violence*) déchaînement *m*; (*sexual*) débauche *f*; **orgies,** (*in ancient Greece, Rome*) orgies, bacchanales *fpl*; **drunken o.,** beuverie *f*.

oriel ['ɔːrɪəl] *n Archit* **o. (window),** oriel *m*.

orient¹ ['ɔːrɪənt] *n* orient *m*; **the O.,** l'Orient.

orient² ['ɔːrɪent] *vt & vi* = **ORIENTATE**.

oriental [ɔːrɪ'ent(ə)l] **1** *adj* oriental, -aux; **o. rug,** tapis *m* d'Orient. **2** *n* Oriental, -ale.

orientalist [ɔːrɪ'entəlɪst] *n* orientaliste *mf*.

orientate ['ɔːrɪənteɪt] **1** *vt* orienter (*une carte, une église*); **to o. oneself,** (*physically, psychologically*) s'orienter. **2** *vi* s'orienter.

orientation [ɔːrɪən'teɪʃən] *n* orientation *f*; *esp Am* **o. course,** cours *m* d'introduction.

oriented ['ɔːrɪentɪd] *adj* orienté.

-oriented ['ɔːrɪentɪd] *suff* **profit-o.,** qui cherche le profit; **youth-o.,** qui vise la jeunesse; *Comptr* **computer-o. language,** langage adapté au calculateur; **export-o.,** (*company, industry*) exportateur, -trice.

orienteering [ɒrɪən'tɪərɪŋ] *n Sp* exercice *m* d'orientation (sur le terrain).

orifice ['ɒrɪfɪs] *n* orifice *m*, ouverture *f*.

origami [ɒrɪ'gɑːmɪ] *n* (art *m* du) pliage *m*.

origin ['ɒrɪdʒɪn] *n* **(a)** origine *f*; **the o. of the universe,** la genèse des mondes; **to trace an event back to its o.,** remonter à l'origine d'un événement; **to have its origins in ...,** tirer son origine de ...; **the custom has its o.** *or* **origins in ...,** l'origine de cette coutume est ...; *Archit* **point of o.,** point *m* d'origine (*d'une courbe etc*); **word/woman of Greek o.,** mot *m*/femme *f* d'origine grecque; **a man of humble o.,** un homme d'humble origine *ou* extraction; *Com* **country of o.,** pays *m* de provenance; **certificate of o.,** certificat *m* d'origine; **(b)** *Anat* attache *f* (*d'un muscle*).

original [ə'rɪdʒɪn(ə)l] **1** *adj* (*manuscrit, tableau, écrivain, style*) original, -aux; (*first*) premier; (*innate*) originel, originaire; (*play, script*) inédit; **the o. colour,** la couleur initiale; **the o. four members of the band,** les quatre premiers membres du groupe; **o. idea of a work,** idée mère d'une œuvre; **that's quite on o. idea,** c'est vraiment une idée originale; **o. meaning of a word,** sens premier d'un mot; *Com* **o. packing,** emballage *m* d'origine; **in the o. Chinese,** dans le texte original en chinois; **o. defect,** vice *m* originaire; *Rel* **o. sin,** péché originel; **o. edition,** édition princeps *ou* originale; *Fin Com* **o. invoice,** facture originale.

2 *n* **(a)** original *m* (*d'un tableau, d'une facture*); (*in lithography*) matrice *f*; *Fin* primata *m* (*d'une traite*); **to copy sth from the o.,** copier qch sur l'original; **to read the classics in the o.,** lire les classiques dans le texte; **(b)** (*person*) personne originale, original, -ale.

originality [ərɪdʒɪ'nælɪtɪ] *n* originalité *f*.

originally [ə'rɪdʒɪn(ə)lɪ] *adv* **(a)** à l'origine, au départ; **the building was o. used as a warehouse,** à l'origine *ou* au départ, l'immeuble servait d'entrepôt; **o. we come from Hampshire,** nous sommes originaires de Hampshire; **where do you come from o?.,** d'où êtes-vous originaire?; **that's what I o. thought,** c'est ce que je pensais au départ; **(b)** (*in an unusual way*) originalement, d'une façon originale.

originate [ə'rɪdʒɪneɪt] **1** *vt* donner naissance à, être l'auteur de (*qch*); amorcer (*une réforme etc*). **2** *vi* tirer son origine, dériver, provenir (**from, in,** de); (*of river*) prendre sa source (**from, in,** dans); **the fire originated under the floor,** le feu a pris naissance sous le plancher; **the scheme originated with me,** je suis l'auteur de ce projet; **the custom originated in France,** cette coutume est née en France.

originator [ə'rɪdʒɪneɪtər] *n* créateur, -trice; (*of scheme*) auteur *m*, initiateur, -trice; promoteur *m* (*d'une industrie*).

oriole ['ɔːrɪəʊl] *n* (*bird*) **(a)** loriot *m*; **golden o.,** loriot (jaune d'Europe); **(b)** *Am* troupiale *m*; *Can* oriole *m*.

Orkneys (the) [ðɪ'ɔːknɪz] *npl* les Orcades *fpl*.

ormolu ['ɔːməluː] *n* simili-or *m*.

ornament¹ ['ɔːnəmənt] *n* **(a)** (*no pl*) (*decoration*) ornement *m* (*du style, d'architecture etc*); agrément *m*, garniture *f* (*sur une robe etc*); **by way of o.,** pour ornement; **(b)** (*individual item*) ornement *m*; **vases and other ornaments,** vases et autres ornements; **(c)** *Mus* **ornaments,** ornements *mpl*.

ornament² ['ɔːnəment] *vt* orner, ornementer (*une chambre etc*); agrémenter, embellir (*une robe etc*); orner (*son style*) (**with,** de).

ornamental [ɔːnə'ment(ə)l] **1** *adj* décoratif, ornemental, -aux, d'ornement, d'agrément; *F* (*person*) décoratif; **purely o.,** purement décoratif; **o. tree/plant,** arbre *m*/plante *f* d'ornement. **2** *n* (*plant*) plante *f* d'ornement; (*tree*) arbre *m* d'ornement.

ornamentation [ɔːnəmen'teɪʃən] *n* ornementation *f*, embellissement *m*.

ornate [ɔː'neɪt] *adj* orné; *Pej* surchargé (d'ornements); **o. style,** style imagé *ou* fleuri.

ornately [ɔː'neɪtlɪ] *adv* de façon décorative; *Pej* avec une surabondance d'ornements; (*written*) dans un style très fleuri.

ornery ['ɔːnərɪ] *adj Am F* désagréable; (*bad-tempered*) rouspéteur; (*stubborn*) têtu.

ornithological [ɔːnɪθə'lɒdʒɪk(ə)l] *adj* ornithologique.

ornithologist [ɔːnɪ'θɒlədʒɪst] *n* ornithologue *mf*, ornithologiste *mf*.

ornithology [ɔːnɪ'θɒlədʒɪ] *n* ornithologie *f*.

orphan¹ ['ɔːfən] **1** *n* orphelin, -ine; **to be left an o.,** rester *ou* devenir orphelin; **war o.,** pupille *mf* de la Nation. **2** *adj* **an o. child,** un orphelin, une orpheline.

orphan² *vt* rendre (*qn*) orphelin, -ine; **orphaned of both parents,** orphelin de père et (de) mère.

orphanage ['ɔːf(ə)nɪdʒ] *n* orphelinat *m*.

Orpheus ['ɔːfjuːs] *n Myth* Orphée *m*.

orris [ˈɒrɪs] *n Pharm* **o. root,** racine *f* d'iris.
orthodontics [ɔːθəʊˈdɒntɪks] *npl* (*usu with sing verb*) orthodontie *f*.
orthodontist [ɔːθəʊˈdɒntɪst] *n* orthodontiste *mf*.
orthodox [ˈɔːθədɒks] **1** *adj* **(a)** *Rel* orthodoxe; **the O. Church,** l'Église *f* orthodoxe; **(b)** (*historien etc*) traditionaliste; (*méthode, opinion etc*) orthodoxe. **2** *n* **the o.,** (*used as pl*) les orthodoxes *mpl*.
orthodoxy [ˈɔːθədɒksɪ] *n* **(a)** orthodoxie *f* (*d'une doctrine, des opinions de qn etc*); **(b)** (*in Jewish religion*) judaïsme *m* rabbinique.
orthogonal [ɔːˈθɒgən(ə)l] *adj Math* orthogonal, -aux.
orthographic(al) [ɔːθəˈgræfɪk, -ɪk(ə)l] *adj* orthographique.
orthographically [ɔːθəˈgræfɪklɪ] *adv* orthographiquement.
orthography [ɔːˈθɒgrəfɪ] *n* **(a)** (*spelling*) orthographe *f*; **(b)** *Math* projection orthogonale.
orthop(a)edic [ɔːθəˈpiːdɪk] *adj Med* (*traitement, appareil*) orthopédique; **o. surgeon,** (chirurgien *m*) orthopédiste *mf*.
orthop(a)edics [ɔːθəˈpiːdɪks] *npl* (*usu with sing verb*) *Med* orthopédie *f*.
orthop(a)edist [ɔːθəˈpiːdɪst] *n Med* orthopédiste *mf*.
ortolan [ˈɔːtələn] *n* (*bird*) **o. bunting,** ortolan *m*.
oryx [ˈɒrɪks] *n* (*antelope*) oryx *m*.
Oscar [ˈɒskər] *n Cin* Oscar *m*; **O.-winning picture,** film primé aux Oscars; **in her O.-winning film,** dans le rôle qui lui a valu l'Oscar.
oscillate [ˈɒsɪleɪt] **1** *vi Phys Rad* (*of pendulum etc*) osciller; *Fig* **to o. between two opinions,** osciller *ou* balancer *ou* hésiter entre deux opinions. **2** *vt* balancer, faire osciller.
oscillating [ˈɒsɪleɪtɪŋ] *adj* oscillant, oscillatoire, d'oscillation; (*électron*) oscillateur.
oscillation [ɒsɪˈleɪʃən] *n* oscillation *f* (*d'un pendule etc*).
oscillator [ˈɒsɪleɪtər] *n* oscillateur *m*; **o. valve** *or* **tube,** lampe oscillatrice.
oscillatory [ˈɒsɪleɪt(ə)rɪ] *adj* oscillant, oscillatoire.
oscillogram [ɒˈsɪləgræm] *n* oscillogramme *m*.
oscillograph [ɒˈsɪləgræf] *n* oscillographe *m*.
oscilloscope [ɒˈsɪləskəʊp] *n El* oscilloscope *m*.
osculate [ˈɒskjʊleɪt] *vi* **(a)** *Hum* (*kiss*) embrasser; **(b)** *Math* **curve that osculates with a line,** courbe osculatrice à une ligne (**at a point,** en un point); **(c)** *Biol* avoir des traits en commun (**with,** avec).
osculation [ɒskjʊˈleɪʃən] *n Math* osculation *f*; **point of o.,** point *m* d'attouchement.
osier [ˈəʊzɪər, ˈəʊʒər] *n* osier *m*; **o. bed,** oseraie *f*; **o. basket,** panier *m* d'osier.
osmosis [ɒzˈməʊsɪs] *n Ch Physiol* osmose *f*.
osmotic [ɒzˈmɒtɪk] *adj Ch Physiol* osmotique.
osprey [ˈɒsprɪ, -preɪ] *n* **(a)** (*bird*) balbuzard pêcheur *ou* fluviatile; *Can* aigle pêcheur; **(b)** (*feather*) aigrette *f*.
ossicle [ˈɒsɪk(ə)l] *n Anat* osselet *m* (*de l'oreille*).
ossification [ɒsɪfɪˈkeɪʃən] *n* ossification *f*.
ossified [ˈɒsɪfaɪd] *adj* (*cartilage*) ossifié; *Fig* (*esprit*) sclérosé.
ossify [ˈɒsɪfaɪ] **1** *vi* (*of cartilage*) s'ossifier; *Fig* (*of person*) se fossiliser; (*of government*) se scléroser. **2** *vt* ossifier (*un cartilage*); *Fig* amener *ou* entraîner la sclérose dans (*le gouvernement*).
ossuary [ˈɒsjʊərɪ] *n* ossuaire *m*.
Ostend [ɒsˈtend] *n* Ostende.
ostensible [ɒsˈtensɪb(ə)l] *adj* prétendu.
ostensibly [ɒˈstensɪblɪ] *adv* en apparence; **he went out o. to buy some tobacco,** il sortit sous prétexte d'acheter du tabac *ou* soi-disant pour acheter du tabac.
ostentation [ɒstenˈteɪʃən] *n* ostentation *f*.
ostentatious [ɒstenˈteɪʃəs] *adj* plein d'ostentation; (*personne, attitude*) prétentieux, ostentatoire.
ostentatiously [ɒstenˈteɪʃəslɪ] *adv* avec ostentation, d'une manière ostentatoire; **to display sth o.,** faire ostentation de qch.
ostentatiousness [ɒstenˈteɪʃəsnɪs] *n* ostentation *f*.
osteoarthritis [ɒstɪəʊɑːˈθraɪtɪs] *n Med* arthrose *f*; **to have o.,** souffrir d'arthrose.
osteomyelitis [ɒstɪəʊmaɪˈlaɪtɪs] *n Med* ostéomyélite *f*.
osteopath [ˈɒstɪəpæθ], *US also* **osteopathist** [ɒstɪˈɒpəθɪst] *n Med* (médecin *m*) ostéopathe *m*.
osteopathy [ɒstɪˈɒpəθɪ] *n Med* ostéopathie *f*.
osteoporosis [ɒstɪəʊpɔˈrəʊsɪs] *n Med* ostéoporose *f*.
ostler [ˈɒslər] *n* valet *m* d'écurie, garçon *m* d'écurie.
ostracism [ˈɒstrəsɪz(ə)m] *n* ostracisme *m*.
ostracize [ˈɒstrəsaɪz] *vt* frapper (*qn*) d'ostracisme, mettre (*qn*) au ban de la société; **she's been ostracized at work,** on l'a mise en quarantaine au travail.
ostrich [ˈɒstrɪtʃ] *n* autruche *f*; *Fig* **o. policy,** politique *f* de l'autruche.
OTC [əʊtiːˈsiː] *n Br Sch abbr* **Officers' Training Corps.**
other [ˈʌðər] **1** *adj* autre; **the o. one,** l'autre; **every o. day/week,** un jour/une semaine sur deux, tous les deux jours/toutes les deux semaines; **the o. day,** l'autre jour; **the o. four,** les quatre autres; **potatoes and (some) o. vegetables,** les pommes de terre et d'autres légumes; **o. people have seen it,** d'autres l'ont vu; **o. people's property,** le bien d'autrui; **any o. book,** tout autre livre; **no one o. than he knows it,** nul autre que lui *ou* personne d'autre ne le sait, il n'y a que lui qui le sache; **somebody o. than me** *or* **you** *or* **her** *etc*, quelqu'un d'autre; **all verbs o. than those in -er,** tous les verbes autres que ceux en -er; *Br Mil* **o. ranks,** = ensemble des militaires non gradés; **the o. woman/man,** (*in relationship*) l'autre.

2 *pron* autre *mf*; **one after the o.,** l'un après l'autre; **the others,** les autres, le reste; **all the others are there,** tous les autres sont là; **some ... others ...,** les uns ... les autres ...; **have you got any others?,** (*have you got any more?*) en avez-vous encore?; (*have you got any different ones?*) en avez-vous d'autres?; **I have no o.,** je n'en ai pas d'autre; **for this reason, if for no o.,** pour cette raison, à défaut d'une autre; **no** *or* **none o. than the great actress Greta Garbo,** nulle autre que la grande Greta Garbo; **one or o. of us will see to it,** l'un de nous y veillera; **some woman** *or* **o.,** une femme; **this day of all others,** ce jour entre tous; **others,** d'autres; (*not as subject also*) autrui *m*; **to be somewhere or o.,** être dans les parages; **to see oneself as others see one,** se voir comme les autres vous voient; **they prefer you to all others,** ils vous préfèrent à tout autre.

3 *adv* autrement; **to see things o. than as they are,** voir les choses autrement qu'elles ne le sont; **o. than that everything is fine,** à part ça, tout va bien; **she never speaks of them o. than admiringly,** c'est toujours avec admiration qu'elle parle d'eux.

4 *n Am Hum* **significant o.,** (*husband*) mon *ou* ton *etc* mari; (*wife*) ma *ou* ta *etc* moitié; *F Hum* (*sex*) **to have a bit of the o.,** prendre un peu son pied.
otherwise [ˈʌðəwaɪz] **1** *adv* **(a)** (*differently*) autrement (**than,** que); **he could not do o.,** il n'a pas pu faire autrement; **to think o.,** penser autrement; **if she's not o. engaged,** si elle n'est pas occupée à autre chose; (*socially*) si elle n'a pas d'autres obligations; **except where o. stated,** sauf indication contraire; **all people rich or o.,** tout le monde, riches et pauvres;

(b) (*apart from that*) sous d'autres rapports; **o. he is quite sane,** à part cela il est complètement sain d'esprit.

2 *adj* **the facts were o.,** les faits étaient différents; **should it be o.,** dans le cas contraire, *Fml* s'il en était autrement.

3 *conj* autrement, sans quoi, sans cela; **do what I tell you, o. everything will go wrong,** faites ce que je vous dis, autrement *ou* sans cela tout ira de travers; **o. we will take legal proceedings against you,** faute de quoi nous vous poursuivrons en justice.
otherworldly [ʌðəˈwɜːldlɪ] *adj* détaché de ce monde.
otic [ˈəʊtɪk] *adj Anat* (*nerf, ganglion*) otique.
otitis [əʊˈtaɪtɪs] *n Med* otite *f*.
OTT [əʊˈtiːtiː] *esp Br Sl abbr* **over the top.**
otter [ˈɒtər] *n* (*animal*) loutre *f*; **sea o.,** loutre de mer *ou* marine; **o. hound,** chien *m* pour la chasse aux loutres.
ottoman¹ [ˈɒtəmən] *n* (*furniture*) ottomane *f*.
Ottoman² *n Hist* **1** *adj* ottoman. **2** *n* Ottoman, -ane.
ouch [aʊtʃ] *int* (*expressing pain*) aïe!
ought¹ [ɔːt] *v aux* (*with present and past meaning; inv;* **o. not** *is frequently abbreviated to* **oughtn't**) **(a)** (*obligation*) **this o. to have been done before,** on aurait dû *ou* il aurait fallu le faire auparavant; **to behave as one o.,** se conduire comme il convient; **to drink more than one o.,** boire plus que de raison; **I thought I o. to let you know about it,** j'ai cru devoir vous en faire part; **one o. never to be unkind,** il ne faut *ou* on ne doit jamais être malveillant;

(b) (*vague desirability or advantage*) **you o. to go and see it,** vous devriez aller le voir; **you o. not to have waited,** vous n'auriez pas dû attendre; **I o. to be going,** il est temps que je parte; **you o. to have seen it!,** il fallait voir ça!;

(c) (*probability*) **they o. to be in Paris by now,** ils doivent être à Paris maintenant; **you o. to be able to get £50 for it,** tu devrais pouvoir en tirer 50 livres sterling;

your horse o. to win, votre cheval a de grandes chances de gagner; **you o. to know,** vous êtes bien placé pour le savoir.

ought² *n Arch & Lit* (= **aught**) quelque chose *m*.

Ouija ® ['wiːdʒə] *n* **O. (board),** oui-ja *m*.

ounce¹ [aʊns] *n* (*measurement*) once *f*; **(avoirdupois) o.,** = 28,35g.; **Troy o.,** = 31,1035 g.; **fluid o.,** = 28,4 cm^3; *Fig* **if you had an o. of sense,** si tu avais un gramme de bon sens; *Fig* **he hasn't an o. of courage,** il n'a pas pour deux sous de courage.

ounce² *n* (*animal*) once *f*, panthère *f* des neiges.

our ['aʊər] *poss adj* notre, *pl* nos; **o. friends,** nos ami(e)s; **o. father and mother,** notre père et notre mère, nos père et mère; **o. two,** les deux nôtres; *Com* **o. Mr Martin,** M. Martin de notre maison.

ours ['aʊəz] *poss pron* le nôtre, la nôtre, les nôtres; **your house is larger than o.,** votre maison est plus grande que la nôtre; **this is o.,** ceci est à nous, ceci nous appartient; **o. is a nation of travellers,** nous sommes une nation de voyageurs; **a friend of o.,** un(e) de nos ami(e)s, un(e) ami(e) à nous; **it's no business of o.,** cela ne nous regarde pas.

ourself [aʊə'self] *pers pron* (*said by monarch, editor etc*) nous-même.

ourselves [aʊə'selvz] *pers pron pl* **(a)** (*emphatic*) nous-mêmes; **we o. do not believe it,** nous, pour notre part, ne le croyons pas; **(b)** (*reflexive*) nous; **we are enjoying o. very much,** nous nous amusons bien; **(c)** (*after preposition*) nous, nous-mêmes; **we say to o.,** nous nous disons; **we shouldn't talk about o.,** on ne doit pas parler de soi; **instead of fighting among o.,** au lieu de nous battre entre nous.

ousel ['uːz(ə)l] *n* = **OUZEL.**

oust [aʊst] *vt* **(a)** évincer, supplanter, déplacer (*qn*); **the ousted ruler,** le dirigeant évincé; **to o. s.o. from his post,** déloger qn de son poste; **(b)** *Jur* déposséder, évincer (*qn*) **(of,** de).

out [aʊt] **1** *adv* **(a)** (*outside*) dehors; **to go** *or* **walk o.,** sortir; **to run o.,** sortir en courant; **it's colder inside than o.,** il fait plus froid à l'intérieur qu'à l'extérieur; **where are you going? — o.,** où allez-vous? — dehors; **o. you go!,** hors d'ici!, allez, hop!; **voyage o.,** voyage *m* d'aller;

(b) (*not in, not at home*) **I was only o. for a minute,** je n'ai été absent qu'une minute; **my father is o.,** mon père est sorti; **he's o. in September,** (*of prisoner*) il sort en septembre; **I am dining o. this evening,** je dîne en ville *ou* au restaurant *ou* chez des amis ce soir; **he is o. and about again,** il est de nouveau sur pied; **she's o. picking mushrooms,** elle est sortie (pour aller) cueillir des champignons; **we had a night o. on Saturday,** nous sommes sortis samedi soir; **the mob was o.,** la populace était descendue dans la rue; **the men are o.,** (*on strike*) les ouvriers sont en grève; **the jury was o. for two hours,** le jury s'est retiré pendant deux heures pour délibérer; **the tide is o.,** la marée est basse;

(c) (*distant*) **a long way o.,** loin, éloigné; **o. at sea,** en mer, au large; **four days o. from Rio,** à quatre jours de Rio; **o. there,** là-bas; **she does not live far o. (of the town),** elle n'habite pas loin de la ville; **o. in the country,** dans la campagne; *F* **way o.,** très avant-garde; *F* **far o.!,** fantastique!, terrible!;

(d) (*outwards*) **to turn one's toes o.,** tourner les pieds en dehors; **to lean o. (of the window),** se pencher au dehors; **to be o. at the elbow(s),** (*of garment*) être troué *ou* percé aux coudes;

(e) (*uncovered, in the open*) découvert, exposé; (*secret*) échappé, éventé; (*sail*) déployé; (*flower*) épanoui; **the sun is o.,** il fait du soleil; *F* **the best game o.,** le meilleur jeu qui soit; **the book is o./just o.,** le livre est paru/vient de paraître; **the secret is o.,** le secret est connu; **to whip o. a revolver,** tirer *ou* sortir vivement un revolver; **o. loud,** tout haut, à haute voix; **to say sth straight** *or* **right o.,** dire qch carrément *ou* sans détours; *F* **o. with it!,** allons, dites-le!, expliquez-vous!; *Prov* **murder will o.,** tôt ou tard la vérité se fait jour; **the cherry tree is o.,** le cerisier est en fleur;

(f) (*indicating aim*) **he's simply o. for money,** tout ce qui l'intéresse c'est l'argent; **I am not o. to reform the world,** je n'ai pas entrepris de réformer le monde; **to go all o. for sth,** mettre toute son énergie pour faire aboutir qch, se démener pour obtenir qch; **I'm o. for big results,** je vise aux grands résultats;

(g) (*indicating exertion*) **all** *or* **flat o.,** à toute vitesse, à toute allure; *Aut* **she does 80 (when she's going) flat o.,** elle fait du 130 quand on la laisse filer;

(h) (*not in place*) **shoulder o. (of joint),** épaule luxée; **I'm o. of practice,** je n'ai plus la main, j'ai perdu le tour de main; *Pol* **the party that's o.,** le parti qui n'est pas au pouvoir; **long skirts are o. this year,** les jupes longues ne sont plus à la mode cette année; **the players who are o. (of the game),** les joueurs qui sont hors jeu *ou* éliminés; *Cr* **not o.,** = encore au guichet (*à la fin de l'innings, de la journée*); **to be fifty pounds o. (of pocket),** en être pour cinquante livres (de sa poche);

(i) (*inaccurate*) dans l'erreur; **to be o. in one's calculations,** s'être trompé dans son calcul; **I was not far o.,** je ne me trompais pas de beaucoup; **the shot was only a centimetre o.,** le coup n'a manqué le but que d'un centimètre; **he was miles o.,** il était totalement à côté;

(j) (*not functioning*) **the fire/gas is o.,** le feu/gaz est éteint; **the light was o.,** la lumière était éteinte; *Mil* **lights o.,** extinction *f* des feux; *Nau* **to steam with all lights o.,** naviguer tous feux éteints;

(k) (*indicating completion*) à bout, achevé; **my pipe is smoked o.,** j'ai fini ma pipe; **before the week is o.,** avant la fin de la semaine; *Rad* **o.!,** terminé!; **hear me o.,** écoutez-moi jusqu'à la fin;

(l) (*unconscious*) *F* **to be o. cold,** être K.O.; **to be o. for seven seconds,** (*of boxer*) rester au plancher pendant sept secondes; *F* **to be o. on one's feet,** tomber de fatigue; **I went o. like a light,** (*asleep*) je me suis endormi tout de suite;

(m) from o. (of) the open window came bursts of laughter, par la fenêtre ouverte arrivaient des éclats de rire;

(n) out of, hors de, en dehors de; **o. of danger,** hors de danger; **o. of sight,** hors de vue; **to be o. of the country,** être à l'étranger; **o. of doors,** = **OUTDOORS 1**; **hardly were the words o. of my mouth,** à peine avais-je prononcé ces mots; **I'm glad I'm o. of the whole business,** je suis content d'en être quitte; **to feel o. of it,** se sentir de trop; **o. of season,** hors de saison; **o. of date,** suranné, vieilli; (*no longer fashionable*) passé de mode, démodé; (*theory*) désuet; (*passport*) périmé; **o. of fashion,** démodé, passé de mode; **to be o. of one's mind,** avoir perdu la raison; **to go o. of the house,** sortir de la maison; **is there a way o. of it?,** y a-t-il (un) moyen d'en sortir?; **to throw sth/to jump o. of the window,** jeter qch/sauter par la fenêtre; **to turn s.o. o. of the house,** mettre *ou* flanquer qn à la porte; **to get money o. of s.o.,** obtenir de l'argent de qn; **I got ten pounds o. of it,** j'y ai gagné dix livres; **Gladiator by Monarch o. of Gladia,** (*in breeding*) Gladiateur par *ou* issu de Monarch et Gladia; **to drink o. of a glass,** boire dans un verre; **to drink o. of the bottle,** boire à (même) la bouteille; **to copy sth o. of a book,** copier qch dans un livre; **the firemen are paid o. of the rates,** on paie les pompiers sur le budget de la ville; **choose one o. of these ten,** choisissez-en un parmi les dix; **three days o. of four,** trois jours sur quatre; **one o. of every three,** un sur trois; **hut made o. of a few old planks,** cabane faite de quelques vieilles planches; **o. of respect for you,** par respect pour vous; **o. of friendship/curiosity,** par amitié/curiosité; **to act o. of fear,** agir sous le coup de la peur; **to be o. of tea,** ne plus avoir de thé, être à court de thé; **o. of cash,** démuni d'argent; *Com* **I am o. of this article,** je n'ai plus cet article pour le moment; **the shop was o. of sugar,** le magasin était à court de sucre.

2 *int* **(a) o. (with you)!,** sortez!, hors d'ici!;

(b) *Tennis* out!

3 *adj* (*outward*) vers l'extérieur; **the o. door,** la (porte de) sortie; *Com* **o. (tray),** corbeille *f* de documents à envoyer; *Archit* **o. thrust,** poussée *f* en dehors.

4 *n* **(a)** *esp US* (*from difficult situation*) échappatoire *f*; **always leave yourself an o.,** garde toujours une échappatoire; *Pol etc F* **the outs,** ceux qui ne sont pas au pouvoir;

(b) *Tennis* balle *f* (qui tombe) en dehors des limites.

5 *prep* **to go o. the door,** sortir par la porte; **to look o. the window,** regarder par la fenêtre.

outage ['aʊtɪdʒ] *n* **(a)** (*shortage*) **stock o.,** rupture *f* de stock; **(b)** coupure *f*; (*of machine*) panne *f*.

out-and-out [aʊtə'naʊt] **1** *adj* (*républicain etc*) convaincu, intransigeant; (*menteur*) fieffé, achevé. **2** *adv* (*wrong etc*) complètement.

outasight [aʊtə'saɪt] *adj & int Sl* fantastique, terrible.

outback *Austr* **1** ['aʊtbæk] *n* **the o.,** l'intérieur *m*. **2** [aʊt'bæk] *adv* à l'intérieur.

outbid [aʊt'bɪd] *vt* (*pt* **outbid**; *pp* **outbid, -bidden** ['bɪdən]) (*at auction*) (r)enchérir *ou* surenchérir sur (*qn*).

outboard ['aʊtbɔːd] **1** *adj Nau* (*rigging etc*) extérieur, hors bord; *Av* extérieur (au fuselage); **o. motor,** moteur *m* hors bord. **2** *adv Nau* (*attaché etc*) au dehors, hors bord; (*jeter qch*) par-dessus bord; *Av* à l'extérieur (du fuselage). **3** *n Nau* (*motor*) moteur *m* hors bord; (*boat*) hors-bord *m inv*.

outbound ['aʊtbaʊnd] *adj* en partance.

outbox ['aʊtbɒks] *vt* boxer mieux que; **he was completely outboxed,** il a été complètement dominé.

outbreak ['aʊtbreɪk] *n* **(a)** éruption *f* (*volcanique*); début *m*, commencement *m* (*des hostilités*); première manifestation (*d'une épidémie*); déclenchement *m* (*de violence*); **there's been an o. of flu,** il y a eu de nombreux cas de grippe; **precautions against an o. of typhus,** précautions contre le typhus; **o. of fire,** incendie *m*; **at the o. of war,** quand la guerre a éclaté; **(b)** (*revolt*) révolte *f*; (*disturbance*) émeute *f*.

outbuilding ['aʊtbɪldɪŋ] *n* bâtiment extérieur; **outbuildings,** dépendances *fpl*.

outburst ['aʊtbɜːst] *n* éruption *f*, explosion *f*; élan *m* (*de générosité*); déchaînement *m* (*de la haine etc*); **o. of temper,** accès *m ou* éclat *m* de colère.

outcast ['aʊtkɑːst] **1** *n* expulsé, -ée, proscrit, -ite; **an o. of society, a social o.,** un paria. **2** *adj* expulsé, proscrit.

outclass [aʊt'klɑːs] *vt* surclasser (*un concurrent*).

outcome ['aʊtkʌm] *n* issue *f*, résultat *m*; **the o. of our labours,** le fruit de nos travaux; **I don't know what the o. will be,** je ne sais pas ce qui en résultera.

outcrop ['aʊtkrɒp] *n* **(a)** *Min* affleurement *m*, pointement *m*; **(b)** (*projecting part*) saillie *f*.

outcry ['aʊtkraɪ] *n* (*protest*) protestations *fpl*, tollé *m*; **there was a public o. when the hospital was closed,** un tollé général s'est élevé contre la fermeture de l'hôpital; **to raise an o. against s.o.,** crier haro sur qn.

outdated [aʊt'deɪtɪd] *adj* démodé, désuet, périmé.

outdistance [aʊt'dɪstəns] *vt* distancer, dépasser.

outdo [aʊt'duː] *vt* (*pt* **outdid** [aʊt'dɪd]; *pp* **outdone** [aʊt'dʌn]) surpasser (**s.o. in sth,** qn en qch), l'emporter *ou* renchérir sur (*qn*); **they are all anxious to o. each other,** c'est à qui fera le mieux; **not to be outdone,** pour ne pas être en reste (**in,** de).

outdoor ['aʊtdɔːr] *adj* (*vie, jeux*) au grand air, en plein air, de plein air; (*piscine*) de plein air, découvert; **she's an o. person,** c'est une personne qui aime le grand air *ou* qui aime être dehors; *Rad* **o. aerial,** antenne extérieure; **o. clothes,** vêtements *mpl* de ville *ou* de sortie; *Cin* **o. scenes** *or* **shots,** extérieurs *mpl*; **o. work,** travail (à l')extérieur *ou* en plein air.

outdoors [aʊt'dɔːz] **1** *adv* dehors, au dehors; (*in open air*) en plein air; **to sleep o.,** coucher à la belle étoile; **to sow o.,** (*in gardening*) semer en pleine terre; **the machine had been left o.,** la machine avait été laissée dehors. **2** *n* **the o.,** la vie en plein air; **the great o.,** la nature sauvage; **she's an o. person,** c'est une personne qui aime le grand air *ou* qui aime être dehors.

outer ['aʊtər] **1** *adj* extérieur, externe; *Archit* **o. door,** avant-portail *m*, *pl* avant-portails; **o. garments,** vêtements *mpl* de dessus; **O. Mongolia,** Mongolie-Extérieure *f*; **o. space,** l'espace intersidéral; **the o. world,** le monde extérieur. **2** *n* (*in range shooting*) cercle extérieur (*de la cible*); (*shot*) balle *f* dans le cercle extérieur.

outermost ['aʊtəməʊst] *adj* **(a)** (*closest to outside*) le plus à l'extérieur; **(b)** (*most remote*) le plus écarté; **to the o. parts of the earth,** jusqu'aux extrémités de la terre.

outfall ['aʊtfɔːl] *n* (*of pipe*) embouchure *f*.

outfit[1] ['aʊtfɪt] *n* **(a)** (*clothes*) ensemble *m*; *Mil* équipement *m*; **(b)** (*equipment*) appareil *m*, appareillage *m*, équipement *m*; *Nau* armement *m* (*d'un navire*); **repair(ing) o.,** nécessaire *m ou* trousse *f* de réparation; **(c)** (*organization*) établissement *m*, organisation *f*; *F* (*of workers*) équipe *f* d'ouvriers; *F Mil* (*unit*) unité *f*; *F* (*company etc*) boîte *f*; *F* (*rock band etc*) groupe *m*.

outfit[2] *vt* équiper (*qn, qch*).

outfitter ['aʊtfɪtər] *n* **(a)** *esp Br* (*for clothes*) spécialiste *m* de la confection; **(b)** *Am* (*for hunting etc equipment*) fournisseur *m*.

outflank [aʊt'flæŋk] *vt* **(a)** *Mil* déborder, tourner (*une position adverse*); **outflanking movement,** mouvement débordant *ou* tournant; **(b)** *Fig* circonvenir (*qn*).

outflow ['aʊtfləʊ] *n* écoulement *m* (*d'un liquide*); coulée *f* (*de lave*); décharge *f* (*d'un égout*); *Fin* sortie *f* (*d'or, de devises*); **o. per hour,** débit *m* par heure.

outfox [aʊt'fɒks] *vt* se montrer plus rusé que (*qn*).

outgoing ['aʊtgəʊɪŋ] **1** *adj* **(a)** (*departing*) (*locataire, fonctionnaire*) sortant; (*ministère*) démissionnaire; (*avion, navire, train*) en partance; *Tel* (*communication*) de sortie; **o. mail,** courrier *m* à expédier; *Ind* **o. shift,** équipe sortante *ou* relevée; **o. tide,** marée descendante; **(b)** (*sociable*) sociable, qui se lie facilement; (*extrovert*) extraverti. **2** *npl Fin* **outgoings,** dépenses *fpl*, débours *mpl*.

outgrow [aʊt'grəʊ] *vt* (*pt* **outgrew** [aʊt'gruː]; *pp* **outgrown** [aʊt'grəʊn]) **(a)** devenir trop grand pour (*ses vêtements etc*); **to o. one's strength,** grandir trop vite; **(b)** perdre (*une habitude*) avec le temps *ou* en vieillissant; **to o. one's friends,** ne plus avoir grand-chose en commun avec ses amis; **(c)** croître plus vite que (*qn, qch*), devenir plus grand que (*qn, qch*).

outgrowth ['aʊtgrəʊθ] *n* excroissance *f*; *Geol* apophyse *f* (éruptive).

outguess [aʊt'ges] *vt* déjouer les intentions de (*qn*).

out-Herod [aʊt'herəd] *vt* **to o.-H. Herod,** se montrer plus cruel qu'Hérode.

outhouse ['aʊthaʊs] *n* bâtiment extérieur, dépendance *f*; *Am* lieux *mpl* d'aisance.

outing ['aʊtɪŋ] *n* (*excursion*) excursion *f*, sortie *f*, partie *f* de plaisir; (*drive, walk etc*) promenade *f*; *Sp* match *m*, concours *m*; **day's o.,** (*in a car etc*) randonnée *f*; **school o.,** sortie scolaire.

outlandish [aʊt'lændɪʃ] *adj* (*manner, dress*) incongru, bizarre; (*language*) barbare.

outlast [aʊt'lɑːst] *vt* durer plus longtemps que (*qch*); survivre à (*qn*).

outlaw[1] ['aʊtlɔː] *n* hors-la-loi *m inv*.

outlaw[2] *vt* **(a)** mettre (*qn*) hors la loi, proscrire (*qn*); **(b)** proscrire, bannir (*un usage etc*).

outlay ['aʊtleɪ] *n* débours *mpl*, frais *mpl*, dépenses *fpl*; **to get back** *or* **recover one's o.,** rentrer dans ses fonds *ou* dans ses débours; **without any great o.,** (*by company*) sans grande mise de fonds; (*by individual*) à peu de frais.

outlet ['aʊtlet] *n* **(a)** orifice *m* d'émission; issue *f* (*de tunnel*); sortie *f*, départ *m* (*d'air, de gaz*); échappement *m* (*de vapeur*); débouché *m* (*de tuyau*); *HydE* **o. pipe** *or* **drain,** tuyau *m* d'écoulement; **to find an o. for one's energy,** trouver un exutoire pour son trop-plein d'énergie; **(b)** *Com* débouché *m* (*pour marchandises*); **retail o.,** magasin *m*; **(c)** *El* prise *f* de courant.

outlier ['aʊtlaɪər] *n Geol* butte *f* témoin.

outline[1] ['aʊtlaɪn] *n* **(a)** (*form*) **outline(s),** contour(s) *m(pl)*, profil *m* (*d'une colline*); configuration *f* (*de la terre*); silhouette *f* (*de qn, d'un édifice*); ligne *f* (*d'une voiture*); **(b)** (*drawing*) dessin *m* au trait, tracé *m*; argument *m*, canevas *m* (*d'une pièce, d'un roman*); **drawn in o.,** dessiné au trait; **rough o.,** premier jet; **o. plan,** plan *m* schématique *ou* d'ensemble; **main** *or* **general** *or* **broad outlines,** grandes lignes, données générales, aperçu *m* (*d'un projet*); **to give a general o. of sth,** décrire qch à grands traits; **an o. of French history,** un résumé de l'histoire de France; **outlines of astronomy,** éléments *mpl* d'astronomie.

outline[2] *vt* **(a)** silhouetter (*le profil de qch*); **(b)** esquisser (*un dessin, un roman, un projet*); tracer les grandes lignes de (*un projet*); ébaucher, indiquer (*un plan d'action*).

outlive [aʊt'lɪv] *vt* survivre à (*qn, une défaite*); **he will o. us all,** il nous enterrera tous; **to have outlived its usefulness,** (*of machine*) ne plus servir (à rien).

outlook ['aʊtlʊk] *n* **(a)** (*view*) vue *f*, perspective *f*; **the political o.,** l'horizon *m* politique; **the o. is gloomy,** (*for industry, economy, weather etc*) les perspectives ne sont pas réjouissantes; **(b)** (*attitude*) façon *f* de voir les choses; **o. on life,** conception *f* de la vie; **(c)** *Old-fashioned* (*act of looking out*) guet *m*; **to be on the o. for sth,** guetter qch.

outlying ['aʊtlaɪɪŋ] *adj* éloigné, écarté; (*rock, island, village*) isolé; **o. areas,** régions *fpl* périphériques.

outmanoeuvre, *US* **outmaneuver** [aʊtmə'nuːvər] *vt Mil* l'emporter sur (*l'ennemi*) en tactique; *Fig* déjouer (*qn*).

outmatch [aʊt'mætʃ] *vt* se montrer supérieur à (*qn*).

outmoded [aʊt'məʊdɪd] *adj* démodé, passé de mode.

outnumber [aʊt'nʌmbər] *vt* l'emporter en nombre sur (*l'ennemi etc*); **we were heavily outnumbered,** nous étions très minoritaires; **they outnumbered us three to one,** ils étaient en majorité de trois à un par rapport à nous.

out-of-doors [aʊtəv'dɔːz] *adv* = **OUTDOORS 1**.

out-of-pocket [aʊtəv'pɒkɪt] *adj* **o.-of-p. expenses,** menues dépenses, débours *mpl*.

out-of-the-way [aʊtəvðə'weɪ] *adj* **(a)** (*place etc*) écarté, loin de tout et de tous; **(b)** (*unusual*) peu ordinaire, peu commun, insolite.

out-of-town [aʊtəv'taʊn] *adj* (*store*) situé en dehors du centre-ville.

out-of-towner [aʊtəv'taʊnər] *n F* **he's an o.-of-t.,** il n'est pas d'ici.

outpace [aʊt'peɪs] *vt* dépasser, distancer (*un concurrent etc*); **demand has outpaced production,** la demande a dépassé la production.
outpatient ['aʊtpeɪʃənt] *n* malade *mf* qui vient consulter à l'hôpital; **outpatients' department,** service *m* des consultations externes.
outplacement ['aʊtpleɪsmənt] *n esp US* = licenciement accompagné d'aide et de conseils fournis par l'employeur pour trouver un autre emploi.
outplay [aʊt'pleɪ] *vt* jouer mieux que (*qn*); **she was outplayed,** son adversaire a joué mieux qu'elle; **to o. the other side,** dominer la partie.
outpost ['aʊtpəʊst] *n Mil* poste avancé; **o. of the Empire,** poste colonial éloigné.
outpouring ['aʊtpɔːrɪŋ] *n* épanchement *m* (*de sentiments*); **outpourings of the heart,** effusions *fpl* du cœur.
output¹ ['aʊtpʊt] *n* **(a)** production *f*, rendement *m* (*d'une exploitation, d'un travailleur*); débit *m*, rendement (*d'une machine*); débit, refoulement *m* (*d'une pompe*); *El* débit (*d'une génératrice*); **literary o. of an author,** production littéraire d'un auteur; **(b)** *MecE etc* puissance *f*, rendement *m* (*d'un moteur*); *El* **power o.,** puissance débitée *ou* de sortie; **o. voltage,** tension *f* de sortie; **(c)** *Comptr* sortie *f* (*de données, de renseignements*); résultat(s) *m(pl)* (*d'un traitement de données*); **o. card,** carte sortie, carte résultat; **o. device,** dispositif *m* de sortie.
output² *vt* (*pt & pp* **output**) **(a)** (*of factory etc*) produire; **(b)** *Comptr* sortir (**to,** sur).
outrage¹ ['aʊtreɪdʒ] *n* **(a)** (*vicious act*) outrage *m*; (*violation of decency*) scandale *m*; **to commit an o. on** *or* **against s.o./sth,** faire outrage à qn/à qch; **$200 a ticket?! — it's an o.!,** 200 dollars un billet?! — c'est un scandale!; **o. against humanity,** crime *m* de lèse-humanité; **plastic bomb o.,** (*in headline*) attentat au plastic; **(b)** (*indignation*) indignation *f* (**at,** de, contre).
outrage² *vt* **(a)** outrager, faire outrage à (*la religion etc*); **(b)** (*make indignant*) faire éclater l'indignation de (*qn*); **I am outraged,** je suis scandalisé *ou* outré.
outrageous [aʊt'reɪdʒəs] *adj* (*cruelty*) immodéré; (*price*) excessif, exorbitant; (*statement, accusation*) outrageant; (*conduct*) scandaleux; **it's o.!,** cela dépasse toutes les bornes!; *F* **an o. get-up,** une tenue impossible.
outrageously [aʊt'reɪdʒəslɪ] *adv* immodérément, outre mesure; (*expensive*) scandaleusement; (*to behave*) d'une façon scandaleuse; (*to dress*) de façon impossible, outrageusement.
outrank [aʊt'ræŋk] *vt* **(a)** (*be of higher rank than*) être supérieur en grade à (*qn*); **(b)** (*take precedence over*) avoir *ou* prendre le pas sur (*qch*).
outreach [aʊt'riːtʃ] *n Admin* = activité visant à encourager les gens à profiter des avantages sociaux.
outrider ['aʊtraɪdər] *n* (*on horseback*) cavalier *m* d'escorte; **motor-cycle o.,** motard *m* d'escorte.
outrigger ['aʊtrɪgər] *n* **(a)** (*in rowing*) porte-nage *m inv* en dehors; (*boat*) outrigger *m*; **(b)** (*on canoe*) balancier *m*; **(c)** *Nau* (*spar*) espar *m* en saillie.
outright [aʊt'raɪt] **1** *adv* **(a)** (*completely*) complètement; (*immediately*) du premier coup, sur le coup; **to buy sth o.,** acheter qch comptant *ou* à forfait *ou* à un prix forfaitaire; **he was killed o.,** il fut tué net; **(b)** (*bluntly*) sans ménagement; (*frankly*) franchement, carrément; **to refuse o.,** refuser tout net. **2** *adj* (*before noun* ['aʊtraɪt]) **(a) o. sale,** vente *f* à forfait; **o. gift,** don pur et simple; **it's o. wickedness,** c'est de la pure méchanceté; **(b)** (*manner*) carré.
outrival [aʊt'raɪv(ə)l] *vt* (**-ll-**, *US* **-l-**) surpasser, devancer, l'emporter sur (*qn*).
outrun [aʊt'rʌn] *vt* (*pt* **outran** [aʊt'ræn]; *pp* **outrun;** *prp* **outrunning**) **(a)** (*go faster than*) dépasser, gagner (*qn*) de vitesse; **(b)** (*exceed*) **his zeal outruns his discretion,** son ardeur l'emporte sur son jugement.
outrunner ['aʊtrʌnər] *n Hist* piqueur *m*.
outs [aʊts] *npl esp Am F* **to be on the o. with s.o.,** être brouillé avec qn; **they're on the o.,** ils sont brouillés.
outsell [aʊt'sel] *vt* (*pt & pp* **outsold** [aʊt'səʊld]) se vendre mieux que (*qch*).
outset ['aʊtset] *n* commencement *m*; **at the o.,** au départ, au début; **from the o.,** dès le début.
outshine [aʊt'ʃaɪn] *vt* (*pt & pp* **outshone** [aʊt'ʃɒn]) **(a)** (*shine brighter than*) briller plus que; **(b)** *Fig* (*surpass*) surpasser, éclipser, dépasser (*qn, qch*).
outside 1 ['aʊtsaɪd] *n* extérieur *m* (*d'une maison, d'un livre*); **on the o. of sth,** à l'extérieur de qch; **the fruit is yellow on the o.,** le fruit est jaune à l'extérieur; **friends on the o.,** (*of prisoner*) des amis dehors; **to open a door from the o.,** ouvrir une porte du dehors; **to turn a sweater o. in,** retourner un pull; **you've got it on o. in,** (*your sweater etc*) tu l'as mis à l'envers; **at the o.,** tout au plus, au maximum; **to come up on the o.,** (*in race*) arriver sur l'extérieur.
2 ['aʊtsaɪd] *adj* **(a) it was an o. job,** (*of theft*) les voleurs étaient étrangers à la maison; **o. aerial,** antenne extérieure; **o. broadcast,** production extérieure; **o. broker,** coulissier *m*; **o. diameter,** diamètre extérieur; **o. interests,** intérêts en dehors de son travail *ou* de sa famille; **o. lane,** *Aut* (*in Britain*) voie *f* de droite; (*in France, Germany etc*) voie de gauche; (*on athletic track*) couloir extérieur; *Tel* **o. line,** ligne extérieure; *St Exch* **o. market,** coulisse *f*; *Constr* **o. measurements,** dimensions *fpl* hors d'œuvre; **o. work,** travail extérieur *ou* à l'extérieur *ou* (*in open air*) au grand air *ou* en plein air; **o. worker,** ouvrier, -ière à domicile; **the o. world,** le monde extérieur;
(b) it's an o. chance, il y a tout juste une chance (de réussir); **I think we have an o. possibility,** je pense que nous avons une toute petite chance;
(c) *Sp* **o. left/right,** ailier gauche/droit; *Rugby* **o. half,** demi *m* d'ouverture; *Rugby* **o. centre,** extérieur centre *m*.
3 [aʊt'saɪd] *adv* dehors, à l'extérieur, au dehors; **to go o.,** aller dehors; **the taxi is o.,** le taxi vous attend dehors; **seen from o.,** vu de dehors; **vase that is black o. and in,** vase qui est noir à l'extérieur et à l'intérieur; *F* **o. of,** à l'extérieur de, en dehors de; **to get o. of a good dinner,** s'envoyer un bon dîner; **get o. of that,** (*drink, meal etc*) avale ça; **o. of a few friends nobody knows anything about it,** sauf quelques amis, personne n'en sait rien.
4 [aʊt'saɪd] *prep* **(a)** en dehors de, hors de, à l'extérieur de; **o. my bedroom,** (*at the door*) à la porte de ma chambre; (*below the windows*) sous les fenêtres de ma chambre; **I'll meet you o. the cinema,** je vous rencontrerai devant le cinéma; **o. the town,** en dehors de la ville;
(b) he's o. the family, il n'appartient pas à la famille; **that's o. our agreement,** ça ne fait pas partie de notre accord;
(c) (*apart from*) en dehors de; **o. a few friends,** en dehors de quelques amis.
outsider [aʊt'saɪdər] *n* **(a)** (*socially*) étranger, -ère, profane *mf*; **a rank o.,** un intrus; **(b)** (*in election*) & *Horse-racing Sp etc* outsider *m*; **(c)** *St Exch* coulissier *m*.
outsize ['aʊtsaɪz] **1** *n* **(a)** (*large size*) dimension *f ou* pointure *f* hors série, taille exceptionnelle; (*in men's clothes*) très grand patron; **(b)** (*large person*) personne de taille exceptionnelle; **for outsizes,** pour les grandes tailles. **2** *adj* **(a) o. dress,** robe *f* en taille exceptionnelle; **o. shoes,** pointure *f* hors série; **(b)** (*paquet etc*) géant, énorme.
outskirts ['aʊtskɜːts] *npl* **(a)** (*outer parts*) limites *fpl*, (a)bords *mpl*; lisière *f* (*d'une forêt*); faubourgs *mpl* (*d'une ville*); banlieue *f*, périphérie *f* (*d'une grande ville*); **(b)** (*approaches*) approches *fpl* (*d'une ville etc*).
outsmart [aʊt'smɑːt] *vt* surpasser (*qn*) en finesse.
outsourcing ['aʊtsɔːsɪŋ] *n Ind* (*of supplies, parts etc*) achat *m* à l'étranger.
outspoken [aʊt'spəʊkən] *adj* (*person*) franc, *f* franche, carré; **to be o.,** parler franc, ne pas mâcher ses mots; **o. criticism,** critique franche.
outspokenly [aʊt'spəʊkənlɪ] *adv* franchement, carrément, rondement.
outspokenness [aʊt'spəʊkənnɪs] *n* franchise *f*, franc-parler *m*.
outspread [aʊt'spred] *adj* étendu, étalé, déployé; **with wings o., with o.** ['aʊtspred] **wings,** les ailes déployées.
outstanding [aʊt'stændɪŋ] *adj* **(a)** (*detail, feature, person, incident*) marquant; (*artist*) hors ligne, éminent, exceptionnel; (*novel, film etc*) marquant, hors du commun, exceptionnel; **man of o. personality/merit,** homme à la personnalité/valeur exceptionnelle; **matter of o. importance,** affaire de la première importance; **she plays o. tennis,** elle joue un tennis excellent; **(b)** (*unresolved*) (*affaire*) en suspens, en cours de règlement; (*problème*) pas encore résolu; *Fin* (*compte*) impayé, à recouvrer, à percevoir; *Fin* (*paiement*) arriéré, en retard; *Fin* (*intérêt*) échu, arriéré; **o. debts (due to us),** créances *fpl* à recouvrer, recouvrements *mpl*.
outstandingly [aʊt'stændɪŋlɪ] *adv* éminemment, exceptionnellement.
outstay [aʊt'steɪ] *vt* rester plus longtemps que (*qn*); **to o. one's welcome,** lasser l'amabilité de ses hôtes; **I hope I haven't outstayed my welcome,** j'espère ne pas avoir abusé de votre hospitalité.
outstretched ['aʊtstretʃt] *adj* déployé, étendu; (*bras*) tendu; **with arms o., with o. arms,** les bras étendus.
outstrip [aʊt'strɪp] *vt* (**-pp-**) devancer, dépasser (*qn à la*

course); *Sp* distancer (*un concurrent*); (*surpass*) surpasser (**s.o. in sth,** qn en qch).

outtake ['aʊtteɪk] *n Cin TV* coupure *f*.

outvote [aʊt'vəʊt] *vt* (*usu in pass*) **we were outvoted,** la majorité des voix a été contre nous.

outward ['aʊtwəd] **1** *adj* **(a)** (*direction etc*) en dehors; *Nau* pour l'étranger; **o. voyage,** voyage *m* d'aller; **o. half (of ticket),** billet *m* aller; **(b)** (*appearance*) extérieur, de dehors; **o. form,** extérieur *m*, dehors *m*. **2** *adv* = **OUTWARDS**; *Nau* **o.-bound,** (*navire*) en partance; (*for foreign destination*) en route pour l'étranger; *Sch* **o.-bound course,** école *f* d'endurcissement (en plein air). **3** *n* extérieur *m*, dehors *m*.

outwardly ['aʊtwədlɪ] *adv* (*see adj*) **(a)** à l'extérieur, extérieurement; **(b)** en apparence.

outwards ['aʊtwədz] *adv* vers l'extérieur; **to turn one's feet o.,** tourner les pieds en dehors.

outwear [aʊt'weər] *vt* (*pt* **outwore** [aʊt'wɔːr]; *pp* **outworn** [aʊt'wɔːn]) user complètement; **outworn doctrine,** doctrine désuète *ou* périmée.

outweigh [aʊt'weɪ] *vt* **(a)** (*be more important than*) l'emporter sur (*qch*); **(b)** (*weigh more than*) peser plus que (*qch*).

outwit [aʊt'wɪt] *vt* (**-tt-**) **(a)** se montrer plus malin que (*qn*); (*thwart plans of*) déjouer les intentions *ou* les menées de (*qn*); **(b)** (*of hunted animal or person*) dépister (*les chiens, la police*).

outwith [aʊt'wɪθ] *prep Scot* = **OUTSIDE 4(b),(c)**.

ouzel ['uːz(ə)l] *n* (*bird*) **ring o.,** merle *m* à plastron *ou* à collier; **water o.,** cincle plongeur, merle d'eau.

oval ['əʊv(ə)l] **1** *adj* ovale, en ovale; (*bouton*) à olive; *US* **the O. Office,** = le bureau du Président des États-Unis. **2** *n* ovale *m*.

ovarian [əʊ'veərɪən] *adj Anat Bot* ovarien.

ovary ['əʊvərɪ] *n Anat Bot* ovaire *m*.

ovate ['əʊveɪt] *adj Biol* ové, ovale.

ovation [əʊ'veɪʃən] *n* ovation *f*; **to give s.o. an o./a standing o.,** faire une ovation *ou* un triomphe à qn/se lever pour applaudir qn.

oven ['ʌv(ə)n] *n* **(a)** four *m*; **electric o.,** four électrique; **gas o.,** four à gaz; **to put sth in the o.,** mettre qch au four; **to cook sth in a slow/quick o.,** cuire qch à four doux/vif; *F* **it's like an o. in here,** il fait extrêmement chaud ici; **o. gloves** *or* **mitts,** gants *mpl* de cuisine; **(b)** *Ind* **drying o.,** étuve *f ou* four *m* de séchage.

oven-proof ['ʌv(ə)npruːf] *adj* (*plat*) allant au four.

oven-ready ['ʌv(ə)nredɪ] *adj* prêt à mettre au four; (*chicken, meat*) prêt à rôtir.

ovenware ['ʌv(ə)nweər] *n* vaisselle *f* allant au four.

over ['əʊvər] **1** *prep* **(a)** (*on surface of*) sur, dessus, par-dessus; **to spill ink o. the table,** répandre de l'encre sur la table; **to spread a cloth o. sth,** étendre une toile sur *ou* par-dessus qch; **all o. the north of England,** sur tout le nord de l'Angleterre; **to search all o. Paris,** chercher dans tout Paris; **famous all o. the world,** célèbre dans le monde entier; **to glance o. sth,** parcourir qch des yeux *ou* du regard; **length o. all,** longueur totale; *F* **to be all o. s.o.,** (*be excessively polite*) faire l'empressé auprès de qn; (*be excessively physical*) ne pas quitter qn d'une semelle; **o. (the top of) sth,** par-dessus (qch); *F* **o. the top,** (*behaviour etc*) exagéré; **to throw sth o. the wall,** jeter qch par-dessus le mur; **to read o. s.o.'s shoulder,** lire par-dessus l'épaule de qn; **with his coat o. his shoulder,** le manteau sur l'épaule; **he wore an old coat o. his uniform,** il portait un vieux manteau par-dessus son uniforme; **to stumble** *or* **trip o. sth,** buter contre qch;

(b) (*above*) **directly o. our heads,** juste au-dessus de nos têtes; **bending o. his work,** courbé sur son travail; **to have a chat o. a glass of wine,** bavarder tout en prenant un verre de vin; **to discuss sth o. lunch,** discuter de qch pendant le déjeuner; **to go to sleep o. one's work,** s'endormir sur son travail; **I couldn't hear her o. the noise of the machine,** je ne pouvais pas l'entendre à cause du bruit de la machine; **with his hat o. his eyes,** le chapeau enfoncé jusqu'aux yeux; *Math* **a o. b,** a divisé par b; **to have an advantage o. s.o.,** avoir un avantage sur qn; **to reign o. a country,** régner sur un pays;

(c) (*about*) **to laugh o. sth,** rire de qch; **we had trouble o. the tickets,** nous avons eu des ennuis au sujet des billets; **to fight o. sth,** se battre au sujet de qch; (*in order to obtain it*) se battre pour (obtenir) qch;

(d) (*across*) **to cross o. the road,** traverser la rue; **the house o. the way,** la maison d'en face; **o. the border,** au-delà de la frontière; **to live o. the river,** demeurer de l'autre côté de la rivière; **from o. the seas,** de par delà les mers; **the bridge o. the river,** le pont qui traverse *ou* sur la rivière;

(e) (*in excess of*) **numbers o. a hundred,** numéros au-dessus de cent; **o. ten pounds,** plus de dix livres; **not o. 250 grams,** (*in post office*) jusqu'à 250 gr.; **to be o. the limit,** dépasser la limite; (*of drunk driver*) avoir dépassé la limite d'alcool; **children o. five (years of age), the o. fives,** les enfants au-dessus de cinq ans; **he's o. fifty,** il a (dé)passé la cinquantaine; **he spoke for o. an hour,** il a parlé pendant plus d'une heure; **he receives tips o. and above his wages,** il reçoit des pourboires en sus de son salaire;

(f) (*in the course of*) **o. the last three years,** au cours des trois dernières années; **o. Christmas,** à Noël; **I'll do it o. the weekend,** je le ferai pendant le week-end; **o. a period of several weeks,** pendant plusieurs semaines; (*scheduling etc*) sur une période de plusieurs semaines;

(g) (*recovered from the effects of*) **I'm** *or* **you're** *or* **she's** *etc* **o. the worst,** le plus mauvais moment est passé; **to be o. a cold,** être guéri d'un rhume.

2 *adv* **(a) famous the world o.,** célèbre dans le monde entier; **to ache all o.,** avoir mal partout; **he's French all o.,** il est français jusqu'au bout des ongles; **that's you all o.,** je vous reconnais bien là;

(b) (*indicating repetition*) **I've had to do it all o. again,** j'ai dû le faire de *ou* à nouveau *ou* encore une fois; **ten times o.,** dix fois de suite; **twice o.,** à deux reprises; **o. and o. (again),** maintes et maintes fois, à n'en plus finir;

(c) (*over edge*) **the milk boiled o.,** le lait s'est sauvé;

(d) (*down*) **to knock sth o.,** renverser qch; **and o. I went,** et me voilà par terre;

(e) (*to other side*) **please turn o.!,** voir au dos!, tournez s'il vous plaît!; **to turn sth o. and o.,** tourner et retourner qch; **to bend sth o.,** replier qch; *Nau* **hard o.!,** la barre toute!; *Aut* **to put the wheel hard o.,** braquer à fond;

(f) (*across*) **he led me o. to the window,** il m'a conduit à la fenêtre; **to cross o.,** traverser (*la rue etc*); faire la traversée (*de la Manche etc*); **o. there,** là-bas; **o. here,** ici, de ce côté; **ask him o.,** demandez-lui de venir (chez nous); **our friends are coming o. tomorrow,** nos amis vont venir nous voir demain; **to deliver sth o. to s.o.,** remettre qch à qn; **to hand sth o. to s.o.,** remettre qch entre les mains de qn; **o.,** *Rad* à vous!; **o. to you,** (*it's your turn*) c'est votre tour, c'est à vous;

(g) (*in excess*) en plus, en excès; **cook for an hour, but allow five minutes o.,** faire cuire pendant une heure, mais ajoutez-y cinq minutes; **children of fourteen and o.,** les enfants qui ont quatorze ans et plus; **three into seven goes twice and one o.,** sept divisé par trois donne deux, et il reste un; **you will keep what is (left) o.,** vous garderez l'excédent *ou* le surplus; **I have one card left o.,** il me reste encore une carte; **he didn't look o. cheerful,** il n'était pas d'une gaieté folle; **we're not o. busy,** nous n'avons pas trop à faire;

(h) (*until later*) **to hold o.,** remettre (à plus tard) (*une décision*); **bills held o.,** effets en souffrance *ou* en suspens.

3 *adj* (*finished*) fini, achevé; **the danger is o.,** le danger est passé; **the rain is o.,** la pluie a cessé; **the game is o.,** la partie est finie; **the holidays are o.,** les vacances sont terminées; **the war was just o.,** la guerre venait de finir; **when the strike is o.,** quand la grève sera finie; **it is (all) o.,** c'est fini; **it is all o. with me,** c'en est fait de moi; **it's all o. between us,** c'est fini entre nous; **that's o. and done with,** voilà qui est fini et bien fini.

4 *n* **(a)** *Com* **shorts and overs,** déficits *mpl* et excédents *mpl*; **overs,** (*in publishing*) exemplaires *mpl* de passe;

(b) *Cr* série *f* de six balles.

overabundance [əʊvərə'bʌndəns] *n* surabondance *f*.

overabundant [əʊvərə'bʌndənt] *adj* surabondant.

overachieve [əʊvərə'tʃiːv] *vi* essayer de trop bien faire.

overachiever [əʊvərə'tʃiːvər] *n* = quelqu'un qui essaie de trop bien faire.

overact [əʊvə'rækt] **1** *vt* outrer, charger, exagérer (*un rôle etc*). **2** *vi* (*of actor*) forcer son jeu.

overactive [əʊvər'æktɪv] *adj* trop actif.

overall ['əʊvərɔːl] **1** *adj* **(a)** (*from one end to the other*) hors tout; **o. length,** longueur totale *ou* hors tout; **(b)** (*taken as a whole*) général, -aux; **o. efficiency,** (*total efficiency*) efficacité totale; (*efficiency in general*) rendement global; **o. plan,** plan *m* d'ensemble. **2** *adv* dans l'ensemble, globalement; **England came third o.,** au classement général l'Angleterre a fini troisième; **yacht measuring ... o.,** yacht dont le longueur hors tout est de ... . **3** *n* blouse *f*; (*child's*) tablier *m*, blouse; **overalls,** combinaison *f* (de travail); salopette *f*; *F* bleus *mpl* (de travail).

overanxious [əʊvər'æŋkʃəs] *adj* **(a)** (*excessively worried*)

extrêmement *ou* trop inquiet; **(b)** (*excessively zealous*) qui fait des excès de zèle.
overarm ['əʊvərɑːm] **1** *adj Tennis* **o. service,** *Cr* **o. bowling,** service *m* au-dessus de la tête; *Swimming* **o. stroke,** brasse indienne, nage (à l')indienne. **2** *adv Tennis* **to serve o.,** *Cr* **to bowl o.,** servir par en dessus.
overawe [əʊvə'rɔː] *vt* intimider (*qn*); **don't be overawed by him,** ne te laisse pas intimider par lui, ne sois pas intimidé par lui.
overbalance [əʊvə'bæləns] **1** *vi* (*of person*) perdre l'équilibre; (*of thing*) se renverser. **2** *vt* (*knock over*) renverser (*qch*).
overbearing [əʊvə'beərɪŋ] *adj* autoritaire; **in an o. manner,** autoritairement.
overboard ['əʊvəbɔːd] *adv Nau* par-dessus bord; **to be washed o.,** être enlevé par une lame; **to throw o.,** jeter (*qch*) par-dessus (le) bord *ou* à la mer; *F* abandonner (*un projet*); **to throw s.o. o.,** jeter qn par-dessus bord; *Fig F* abandonner *ou* trahir qn; **to fall o.,** tomber à la mer; **man o.!,** un homme à la mer!; *F* **to go o.,** (*be enthusiastic*) s'emballer (**for sth/s.o.,** pour qch/qn).
overbook [əʊvə'bʊk] *vt & vi* (*a flight etc*) surréserver, surbooker; **the flight was overbooked,** il y a eu surréservation sur ce vol.
overbooking [əʊvə'bʊkɪŋ] *n* surréservation *f*, surbooking *m*.
overboot ['əʊvəbuːt] *n* couvre-chaussure *m*, *pl* couvre-chaussures.
overburden [əʊvə'bɜːd(ə)n] *vt* surcharger, accabler (**with,** de); *Fig* **not overburdened with principles,** qui ne s'encombre pas de principes.
overcapitalization [əʊvəkæpɪtəlaɪ'zeɪʃən] *n Fin* surcapitalisation *f*.
overcapitalize [əʊvə'kæpɪtəlaɪz] *vt Fin* surcapitaliser (*une société*).
overcast ['əʊvəkɑːst] *adj* (*ciel*) couvert, sombre, nuageux; (*temps*) bouché; (*visage*) assombri.
overcharge [əʊvə'tʃɑːdʒ] **1** *vt* **(a)** faire payer trop cher un article à (*qn*); majorer (*une facture*); **you've overcharged me,** vous m'avez fait payer trop (cher); **(b)** (*overload*) surcharger (*une batterie d'accus*); surcharger (*un livre, un portrait etc*) (**with details** *etc*, de détails *etc*). **2** *vi* (*of shopkeeper etc*) faire payer trop cher.
overcoat ['əʊvəkəʊt] *n* pardessus *m*.
overcome [əʊvə'kʌm] *vt* (*pt* **overcame** [əʊvə'keɪm]; *pp* **overcome**) **(a)** triompher de, vaincre (*ses adversaires etc*); venir à bout de, avoir raison de (*qn, qch*); dominer, maîtriser (*son émotion*); surmonter, vaincre (*un obstacle*); **to o. a disability,** surmonter un handicap; **(b) to be o. with** *or* **by,** être accablé de (*douleur*); être paralysé par (*la peur*); être gagné par (*le sommeil, les larmes*); succomber à (*l'émotion, la chaleur*); être asphyxié par (*des gaz*); **I was quite overcome,** j'ai été bouleversé.
overcompensate [əʊvə'kɒmpenseɪt] **1** *vt* surcompenser (*une inégalité etc*). **2** *vi Psy* manifester une surcompensation.
overconfidence [əʊvə'kɒnfɪdəns] *n* **(a)** (*excessive confidence*) confiance exagérée (**in,** en); **(b)** (*self-importance*) suffisance *f*, présomption *f*.
overconfident [əʊvə'kɒnfɪdənt] *adj* **(a)** (*self-important*) trop confiant; **(b)** (*about winning, finding a job etc*) présomptueux.
overcook [əʊvə'kʊk] *vt* trop cuire.
overcritical [əʊvə'krɪtɪk(ə)l] *adj* **to be o.,** être trop critique, *F* chercher la petite bête.
overcrowd [əʊvə'kraʊd] *vt* trop remplir (*un autobus etc*); surpeupler (*une ville etc*).
overcrowded [əʊvə'kraʊdəd] *adj* trop rempli (**with,** de); surchargé, bondé (*de gens*); (*town etc*) surpeuplé.
overcrowding [əʊvə'kraʊdɪŋ] *n* remplissage excessif (*d'un autobus*); encombrement *m* (*d'une pièce etc*); surpeuplement *m* (*d'une ville, d'une forêt*); **o. is a problem in our schools,** les sureffectifs sont un problème dans nos écoles.
overdeveloped [əʊvədɪ'veləpt] *adj Phot etc* trop développé.
overdo [əʊvə'duː] *vt* (*pt* **overdid** [əʊvə'dɪd]; *pp* **overdone** [əʊvə'dʌn]) **(a)** outrer (*les choses*); charger (*un rôle etc*); **they overdid the welcome,** ils ont exagéré l'accueil; *F* **to o. it** *or* **things,** (*exaggerate*) forcer la note, exagérer; (*work too hard*) se surmener; **you've been overdoing it** *or* **things,** (*you need a rest*) tu en as trop fait; **(b)** *Culin* trop cuire.
overdose¹ ['əʊvədəʊs] *n* dose excessive, surdose *f*, overdose *f*.
overdose² [əʊvə'dəʊs] **1** *vt* administrer à (*qn*) des remèdes à trop forte(s) dose(s); **to o. oneself,** prendre des médicaments *ou* des drogues à trop fortes doses. **2** *vi* prendre une overdose; **he overdosed on heroin,** (*took an overdose*) il a pris une overdose d'héroïne; (*died*) il est mort d'une overdose d'héroïne.
overdraft ['əʊvədrɑːft] *n Banking* découvert *m*, solde débiteur; **to have an o.,** avoir un découvert; **to pay off an/one's o.,** rembourser un/son découvert; **o. facility,** découvert autorisé.
overdraw [əʊvə'drɔː] *vt* (*pt* **overdrew** [əʊvə'druː]; *pp* **overdrawn** [əʊvə'drɔːn]) **(a)** *Banking* **to o. one's account,** mettre son compte à découvert; **overdrawn account,** compte à découvert, compte désapprovisionné; **to be overdrawn,** être à découvert; **to be £100 overdrawn,** avoir un découvert de 100 livres; **(b)** charger (*le portrait de qn*); trop colorer (*un récit*).
overdress [əʊvə'dres] *vi* faire trop de toilette; **to be overdressed,** (*wearing too many clothes*) être trop couvert; (*for the occasion*) être habillé de façon trop élégante.
overdrive ['əʊvədraɪv] *n Aut* vitesse surmultipliée; **in o.,** en surmultipliée; *Fig* **to be in o.,** avoir passé (à) la vitesse supérieure.
overdue [əʊvə'djuː] *adj* (*account*) arriéré, échu; (*interest*) qui n'a pas été payé à l'échéance; (*person, train etc*) en retard; (*baby*) tardif; (*reform etc*) qui tarde à être réalisé; **he's long o.,** il devrait être là depuis longtemps; **this law was long o.,** cette loi faisait défaut depuis longtemps; **the baby was two weeks o.,** le bébé aurait dû naître deux semaines plus tôt; **she's o.,** (*of pregnant woman*) elle a dépassé le terme.
overeat [əʊvə'riːt] *vi* (*pt* **overate** [əʊvə'ret]; *pp* **overeaten** [əʊvə'riːt(ə)n]) manger avec excès, trop manger.
overeating [əʊvə'riːtɪŋ] *n* excès *mpl* de table.
overemphasis [əʊvə'remfəsɪs] *n* accentuation excessive.
overemployment [əʊvərɪm'plɔɪmənt] *n* suremploi *m*.
overenthusiastic [əʊvərɪnθjuːzɪ'æstɪk] *adj* (par) trop enthousiaste.
overestimate [əʊvə'restɪmeɪt] *vt* surestimer, surévaluer (*le coût, les talents de qn*); exagérer (*le danger*); trop présumer de (*ses forces*); *Com* majorer (*son actif*); **to o. one's own importance,** surestimer sa propre importance.
overexcite [əʊvərek'saɪt] *vt* surexciter.
overexcitement [əʊvərek'saɪtmənt] *n* surexcitation *f*.
overexert [əʊvəreg'zɜːt] *vt* surmener, fatiguer outre mesure; **to o. oneself,** trop se fatiguer, se surmener.
overexertion [əʊvəreg'zɜːʃən] *n* surmenage *m*.
overexpose [əʊvəreks'pəʊz] *vt Phot* surexposer.
overexposure [əʊvəreks'pəʊʒər] *n Phot* surexposition *f*.
overfamiliar [əʊvəfə'mɪlɪər] *adj* **to be o. with s.o.,** se montrer trop familier *ou* prendre des libertés excessives avec qn; **I'm not o. with the rules,** les règlements ne me sont pas tellement familiers.
overfeed [əʊvə'fiːd] **1** *vt* suralimenter. **2** *vi* se suralimenter, trop manger.
overflow¹ ['əʊvəfləʊ] *n* **(a)** (*action*) débordement *m* (*d'un liquide*); (*water*) eau débordée; (*flood*) inondation *f*; *Fig* surplus *m* (*de population*); **o. meeting,** réunion *f* supplémentaire (*pour ceux qui ont trouvé salle comble*); **(b)** (*outlet*) trop-plein *m inv*; **o. pipe,** (tuyau *m* de) trop-plein; déversoir *m* (*d'une citerne*).
overflow² [əʊvə'fləʊ] **1** *vt* (*of liquid*) déborder de (*la coupe*); (*of river*) inonder (*un champ*); **to o. its banks,** (*of river*) sortir de son lit. **2** *vi* (*of liquid*) déborder, s'épancher; (*of gutter, stream*) dégorger; (*of cup, heart*) déborder; **room overflowing with people,** salle qui regorge de monde; **the guests overflowed into the other rooms,** les invités se répandaient dans les autres pièces.
overflowing [əʊvə'fləʊɪŋ] **1** *adj* débordant, plein à déborder; (*kindness*) surabondant. **2** *n* débordement *m*; **full to o.,** plein à déborder.
overfly [əʊvə'flaɪ] *vt* (*pt* **overflew** [əʊvə'fluː]; *pp* **overflown** [əʊvə'fləʊn]) survoler.
overfond ['əʊvəfɒnd] *adj* trop attaché (**of,** à); **I'm not o. of oranges,** je n'aime pas trop les oranges.
overfull [əʊvə'fʊl] *adj* trop plein (**of, with,** de).
overgrown [əʊvə'grəʊn] *adj* **(a)** couvert (**with sth,** de qch); **o. with weeds,** (*jardin*) envahi par les mauvaises herbes; **o. with ivy,** tapissé de lierre; **(b) he's like an o. schoolboy,** il est resté très écolier.
overhang¹ ['əʊvəhæŋ] *n* surplomb *m*; *Constr* **to have an o.,** porter à faux; **a balcony with an o. of three feet,** un balcon avec une saillie d'un mètre.
overhang² [əʊvə'hæŋ] *v* (*pt & pp* **overhung** [əʊvə'hʌŋ]) **1** *vt* surplomber, faire saillie au-dessus de (*qch*). **2** *vi* sur-

plomber, faire saillie, être en porte-à-faux.
overhanging [əʊvə'hæŋɪŋ] *adj* surplombant, en surplomb, en porte-à-faux; (*mur*) déversé; **the o. threat,** la menace suspendue sur nos *ou* leurs têtes.
overhaul¹ ['əʊvəhɔːl] *n* **(a)** (*examination*) révision *f* (*d'une machine etc*); **complete o.,** révision complète; **(b)** (*repairs*) remise *f* en état (*d'un véhicule, d'une machine*).
overhaul² [əʊvə'hɔːl] *vt* **(a)** (*examine*) examiner en détail, réviser; vérifier (*les machines, les contacts*); *Nau* repasser (*le gréement*); **(b)** (*repair*) remettre en état *ou* au point, réviser (*une machine*); **(c)** *Nau etc* (*overtake*) rattraper, dépasser (*un autre navire*).
overhead [əʊvə'hed] **1** *adv* en haut, en l'air; au-dessus (*de la tête*). **2** *adj* (*câble etc*) aérien; *Constr Rail* **o. crossing,** croisement supérieur; *Com* **o. expenses** *or* **charges,** frais généraux; *Art Phot MecE* **o. lighting,** éclairage vertical; **o. railway,** chemin de fer aérien; **o. projector,** rétroprojecteur *m*; **o. valves,** soupapes *fpl* en dessus *ou* en tête; *Tennis* **o. volley,** volée rattrapée au-dessus de la tête. **3** ['əʊvəhed] *n Com Am* **o.,** *Br* **overheads,** frais généraux.
overhear [əʊvə'hɪər] *v* (*pt & pp* **overheard** [əʊvə'hɜːd]) **1** *vt* surprendre (*une conversation etc*); **they were overheard discussing it,** ils ont été surpris en train d'en parler. **2** *vi* surprendre une conversation; **I couldn't help overhearing,** je n'ai pas pu m'empêcher de surprendre la *ou* leur *ou* votre *etc* conversation.
overheat [əʊvə'hiːt] **1** *vt* surchauffer, trop chauffer (*un four etc*); **to get overheated,** (*of person*) trop s'échauffer; (*of engine, brakes etc*) chauffer. **2** *vi* (*of engine etc*) chauffer.
overheating [əʊvə'hiːtɪŋ] *n* **(a)** surchauffe *f*, surchauffage *m*; **(b)** *MecE* échauffement *m* (anormal).
overindulge [əʊvərɪn'dʌldʒ] **1** *vt* montrer trop d'indulgence envers (*qn*); (*spoil*) gâter (*qn*). **2** *vi* trop manger; trop boire; **to o. (in sth),** abuser (*de qch*).
overindulgence [əʊvərɪn'dʌldʒəns] *n* **(a)** indulgence excessive (**of s.o.,** envers qn); **(b)** (*in food, drink etc*) abus *m*.
overjoyed [əʊvə'dʒɔɪd] *adj* transporté *ou* rempli de joie.
overkill ['əʊvəkɪl] *n* surcapacité *f* de tuer; *Fig* **putting on three coats of paint was an o.,** faire trois couches de peinture était exagéré.
overland **1** *adv* [əʊvə'lænd] par voie de terre. **2** *adj* ['əʊvəlænd] **o. route,** voie *f* de terre; *Av* trajet survolant la terre; **o. journey,** voyage *m* par voie de terre.
overlap¹ ['əʊvəlæp] *n* **(a)** (*act, state of overlapping*) recouvrement *m*; *Constr* chevauchement *m*, imbrication *f* (*des tuiles etc*); empiètement *m*, chevauchement (*d'une opération sur une autre*); **an o. of two inches,** un chevauchement de 5 cm; **there is some o. between philosophy and religion,** il y a un domaine commun entre la philosophie et la religion; **(b)** (*overlapping part*) partie chevauchante *ou* débordante.
overlap² [əʊvə'læp] *vt & vi* (**-pp-**) **(a)** recouvrir (partiellement); (*of categories etc*) avoir un domaine commun; (*in time*) se chevaucher; **to o. (one another),** (*of tiles, slates*) chevaucher; **(b)** (*go beyond*) dépasser, outrepasser (*l'extrémité de qch*); (*in time*) déborder.
overlay¹ ['əʊvəleɪ] *n* (*of paint, varnish*) couche *f*.
overlay² [əʊvə'leɪ] *vt* (*pt & pp* **overlaid** [əʊvə'leɪd]) recouvrir, couvrir (**with,** de).
overleaf [əʊvə'liːf] *adv* au dos (de la page); **see o.,** voir au verso *ou* au dos.
overlie [əʊvə'laɪ] *vt* (*pt* **overlay** [əʊvə'leɪ]; *pp* **overlain** [əʊvə'leɪn]) recouvrir, couvrir.
overload¹ ['əʊvələʊd] *n* **(a)** *El* surcharge *f*, surélévation *f* d'intensité; (*of engine*) excès *m* d'injection; *MecE etc* **o. running,** marche *f* en surcharge; **(b)** (*of vehicle*) (poids *m* en) surcharge *f*.
overload² [əʊvə'ləʊd] *vt* **(a)** surcharger, surmener (*une machine*); **(b)** surcharger (*un véhicule etc*).
overlong [əʊvə'lɒŋ] **1** *adv* trop longtemps. **2** *adj* trop long, trop longue.
overlook [əʊvə'lʊk] *vt* **(a)** (*look out over*) avoir vue sur (*qch*); (*of building*) dominer, commander (*un vallon*); (*of window*) donner sur (*la rue*); **we are overlooked by our neighbours,** nos voisins ont vue sur nous; **(b)** (*fail to notice, disregard*) oublier, laisser passer (*l'heure*); négliger, laisser échapper (*une occasion*); fermer les yeux sur (*qch*); laisser passer (*une erreur*); **I overlooked the fact,** ce fait m'a échappé; **I cannot o. this insolence,** je ne peux pas laisser passer cette insolence.
overlord ['əʊvəlɔːd] *n* suzerain *m*.
overly ['əʊvəlɪ] *adv* trop, à l'excès, excessivement; **not o.,** pas trop.
overlying [əʊvə'laɪɪŋ] *adj* superposé; (*stratum*) surjacent.
overman [əʊvə'mæn] *vt* **to be overmanned,** avoir un personnel trop nombreux; *Ind* avoir du surplus de main-d'œuvre.
overmanning [əʊvə'mænɪŋ] *n Ind* surplus *m* de main-d'œuvre.
overmuch [əʊvə'mʌtʃ] *adv* (par) trop, à l'excès, outre mesure.
overnight **1** *adv* [əʊvə'naɪt] (pendant) la nuit; (*changer etc*) du jour au lendemain; **to stay o.,** rester jusqu'au lendemain, passer la nuit; **leave to soak o.,** laisser tremper toute la nuit; **he became famous o.,** il est devenu célèbre du jour au lendemain. **2** *adj* ['əʊvənaɪt] d'une nuit (de durée); **to be an o. success,** devenir célèbre du jour au lendemain; **o. bag,** sac *m* de voyage; **o. case,** mallette *f*; **o. guest,** ami, -e qui passe la nuit (*chez qn*); client, -e qui passe la nuit (*dans un hôtel*); **o. stay,** séjour *m* d'une nuit; (*in hotel*) nuitée *f*; **o. stop,** arrêt *m* pour la nuit.
overoptimism [əʊvə'rɒptɪmɪz(ə)m] *n* excès *m* d'optimisme, optimisme exagéré.
overoptimistic [əʊvərɒptɪ'mɪstɪk] *adj* excessivement *ou* par trop optimiste.
overparticular [əʊvəpə'tɪkjʊlər] *adj* (par) trop exigeant, trop méticuleux.
overpass ['əʊvəpɑːs] *n Constr* (*for pedestrians*) passerelle surélevée.
overpay [əʊvə'peɪ] *vt* (*pt & pp* **overpaid** [əʊvə'peɪd]) surpayer, trop payer (*qn*); **he's overpaid for what he does,** il est trop payé pour ce qu'il fait.
overpayment [əʊvə'peɪmənt] *n* **(a)** (*in purchasing*) surpaiement *m*, paiement *m* en trop; (*of taxes*) trop-perçu *m*, *pl* trop-perçus; **(b)** rémunération excessive (*d'un employé*).
overplay [əʊvə'pleɪ] *vt* **to o. one's hand,** *Cards* annoncer au-dessus de ses moyens; *Fig* surestimer ses chances de réussir.
overpolite [əʊvəpə'laɪt] *adj* trop poli.
overpopulated [əʊvə'pɒpjʊleɪtɪd] *adj* surpeuplé.
overpopulation [əʊvəpɒpjʊ'leɪʃən] *n* surpeuplement *m*, surpopulation *f*.
overpower [əʊvə'paʊər] *vt* maîtriser (*un bandit, ses passions*); **to be overpowered by superior numbers,** succomber *ou* être écrasé sous le nombre.
overpowering [əʊvə'paʊərɪŋ] *adj* (*emotion, heat etc*) accablant; (*desire etc*) tout-puissant, irrésistible; **I find him/her o.,** je le/la trouve par trop imposant/imposante.
overprice [əʊvə'praɪs] *vt* fixer une prix excessif à (*qch*).
overpriced [əʊvə'praɪst] *adj* d'un prix excessif.
overprint¹ ['əʊvəprɪnt] *n* **(a)** *Typ* impression *f* en surcharge; surcharge *f* (*sur un timbre-poste etc*); *Phot* surimpression *f*; **(b)** (*postage stamp*) timbre-poste surchargé.
overprint² [əʊvə'prɪnt] *vt Typ* imprimer (*une rectification*) en surcharge; surcharger (*un timbre-poste*); *Phot* tirer en surimpression.
overprinting [əʊvə'prɪntɪŋ] *n Typ* impression *f* en surcharge; *Phot* (tirage *m* en) surimpression *f*.
overproduce [əʊvəprə'djuːs] *vt & vi* surproduire.
overproduction [əʊvəprə'dʌkʃən] *n* surproduction *f*.
overrate [əʊvə'reɪt] *vt* surévaluer, surestimer (*qn, qch*), faire trop de cas de (*qn, qch*); exagérer (*les qualités de qn*); **overrated restaurant,** restaurant surfait.
overreach [əʊvə'riːtʃ] **1** *vt* **to o. oneself,** trop présumer de ses forces. **2** *vi* (*of horse*) (s')attraper.
overreact [əʊvərɪ'ækt] *vi* réagir de façon excessive (**to,** à; **against,** contre).
overreaction [əʊvərɪ'ækʃən] *n* réaction trop forte *ou* excessive.
override¹ [əʊvə'raɪd] *n* dispositif *m* de prise de priorité; **manual o.,** (*on automatic camera, lift etc*) commande *f* de passage en mode manuel.
override² *v* (*pt* **overrode** [əʊvə'rəʊd]; *pp* **overridden** [əʊvə'rɪd(ə)n]) **1** *vt* **(a)** outrepasser (*ses ordres*); passer outre à (*la loi*); fouler aux pieds (*les droits de qn*); avoir plus d'importance que, avoir la priorité sur (*qch*); **decision that overrides a former decision,** décision qui annule une décision antérieure; **(b)** surmener (*un cheval*); **(c)** (*of mounted troops*) ravager (*une région ennemie*). **2** *vi* (*of ends of fractured bone*) chevaucher.
overriding [əʊvə'raɪdɪŋ] *adj* principal, -aux; (*principe*) premier.
overripe [əʊvə'raɪp] *adj* trop mûr; (*cheese*) trop fait.
overrule [əʊvə'ruːl] *vt* décider contre (*qn, l'avis de qn*); *Jur* annuler, casser (*un arrêt*); rejeter (*une réclamation*); passer à l'ordre du jour sur (*une objection*); *US Jur* **objection overruled,** objection rejetée.

overrun¹ ['əʊvərʌn] *n* **(a)** *Typ* (*at end of line*) chasse *f*; (*at end of page*) report *m*, ligne(s) *f*(*pl*) à reporter; **(b)** **(cost) overruns,** dépassement *m* du coût estimé.
overrun² [əʊvə'rʌn] *v* (*pt* **overran** [əʊvə'ræn]; *pp* **overrun**; *prp* **overrunning**) **1** *vt* **(a)** (*of invaders*) se répandre sur, envahir (*un pays*); **garden o. with weeds,** jardin envahi par les mauvaises herbes; **house o. with mice,** maison infestée de souris; **(b)** dépasser (*la limite, le temps prévu*); *Rail* brûler (*un signal*); **to o. a budget,** dépasser un budget; **(c)** *Typ* reporter (*un mot*) à la ligne *ou* à la page suivante; **words that o. the line,** mots qui chassent. **2** *vi* **words that o. (into the margin),** mots qui chassent; **the TV programme overran,** le programme télévisé a duré plus longtemps que prévu.
overseas 1 *adj* ['əʊvəsiːz] (*colonie, commerce*) d'outre-mer. **2** *adv* [əʊvə'siːz] à l'étranger; *Lit* par delà les mers; **most of our products go o.,** la plupart de nos produits vont à l'étranger; **from o.,** d'outre-mer.
oversee [əʊvə'siː] *vt* (*pt* **oversaw** [əʊvə'sɔː]; *pp* **overseen** [əʊvə'siːn]) surveiller (*un atelier, un chantier etc*).
overseer ['əʊvəsɪər] *n* surveillant, -ante; *Ind* contremaître, -tresse; *Constr* chef *m* de chantier; *Typ* prote *m*.
oversell ['əʊvəsel] *vt* (*pt & pp* **oversold** [əʊvə'səʊld]) **(a)** vendre trop de (*qch*); **(b)** exagérer les mérites de, surfaire (*qch*).
oversensitive [əʊvə'sensɪtɪv] *adj* hypersensible.
oversew ['əʊvəsəʊ] *vt* (*pt & pp* **oversewn** ['əʊvəsəʊn]) *Sewing* surjeter; surfiler (*un bord*).
oversexed [əʊvə'sekst] *adj* à tendances sexuelles exagérées; **you're o.,** vous êtes un obsédé sexuel.
overshadow [əʊvə'ʃædəʊ] *vt* **(a)** (*spread shadow over*) ombrager, couvrir de son ombre; *Fig* **the negotiations were overshadowed by gloom,** une atmosphère morose planait sur les négociations; **(b)** (*eclipse*) éclipser (*qn*); surpasser (*qch, qn*) en éclat.
overshoe ['əʊvəʃuː] *n* couvre-chaussure *m*, *pl* couvre-chaussures, galoche *f*; **rubber overshoes,** caoutchoucs *mpl*.
overshoot [əʊvə'ʃuːt] *v* (*pt & pp* **overshot** [əʊvə'ʃɒt]) **1** *vt* dépasser, outrepasser (*le point d'arrêt*); (*with gun etc*) dépasser (*la cible*); (*of shot, gun*) porter au delà de (*qch*); **to o. the mark,** dépasser le but; *Fig* dépasser les bornes; *Av* **to o. the runway,** atterrir *ou* se présenter trop long (sur la piste); (*deliberately*) survoler la piste; **to o. a production target,** dépasser *ou* excéder un objectif de production. **2** *vi* (*fail to stop in time*) dépasser *ou* outrepasser le point d'arrêt; (*of bullet, person firing etc*) dépasser la cible; (*of plane, pilot*) atterrir *ou* se présenter trop long sur la piste.
overshot ['əʊvəʃɒt] *adj HydE* (*roue*) en dessus.
oversight ['əʊvəsaɪt] *n* **(a)** (*omission*) oubli *m*, omission *f*, inadvertance *f*; **through** *or* **by an o.,** par mégarde, par inadvertance, par oubli; **(b)** (*supervision*) surveillance *f*.
oversimplification [əʊvəsɪmplɪfɪ'keɪʃən] *n* simplification excessive.
oversimplify [əʊvə'sɪmplɪfaɪ] *vt & vi* trop simplifier.
oversized ['əʊvəsaɪzd] *adj* surdimensionné; *F* (*very big*) énorme.
oversleep [əʊvə'sliːp] *vi* (*pt & pp* **overslept** [əʊvə'slept]) s'éveiller après l'heure, *F* avoir une panne d'oreiller.
oversleeve ['əʊvəsliːv] *n* manchette *f*.
overspend [əʊvə'spend] *v* (*pt & pp* **overspent** [əʊvə'spent]) **1** *vi* dépenser trop; **to o. by ...,** dépenser ... de trop. **2** *vt* dépenser au delà de (*ses moyens etc*).
overspending [əʊvə'spendɪŋ] *n* dépense excessive.
overspill ['əʊvəspɪl] *n* **o. population,** surplus *m ou* déversement *m* de population; **o. town,** = ville servant à décongestionner une agglomération surpeuplée.
overstaffed [əʊvə'stɑːft] *adj* qui a un personnel trop nombreux.
overstaffing [əʊvə'stɑːfɪŋ] *n* **problems of o.,** des problèmes d'excédent de personnel.
overstate [əʊvə'steɪt] *vt* exagérer (*les faits etc*); **I am neither overstating nor understating the case,** je n'exagère ni dans un sens ni dans l'autre.
overstay [əʊvə'steɪ] *vt* dépasser (*son congé etc*); **to o. one's welcome,** lasser l'amabilité de ses hôtes.
oversteer [əʊvə'stɪər] *vi Aut* survirer.
overstep [əʊvə'step] *vt* (**-pp-**) outrepasser; *Fig* **to o. the mark,** dépasser les bornes.
overstock [əʊvə'stɒk] *vt* encombrer (*le marché etc*) (**with,** de); trop meubler (*une ferme*) de bétail; surcharger (*un étang*) de poissons; **to be overstocked,** (*of shop*) avoir des stocks excessifs.
oversubscribe [əʊvəsəb'skraɪb] *vt Fin* sursouscrire (*une émission*).
overt [əʊ'vɜːt] *adj* patent, évident, manifeste; *Jur* **o. act,** acte *m* manifeste.
overtake [əʊvə'teɪk] *vt* (*pt* **overtook** [əʊvə'tʊk]; *pp* **overtaken** [əʊvə'teɪk(ə)n]) **(a)** rattraper (*qn*); *esp Br* doubler, dépasser, devancer (*un concurrent, une voiture*); **demand has overtaken supply,** la demande a dépassé l'offre; **overtaken by events,** devancé par les événements; **(b)** (*of accident*) arriver à (*qn*); (*of fate etc*) s'abattre sur (*qn*); **darkness overtook us,** la nuit nous surprit.
overtaking [əʊvə'teɪkɪŋ] *n esp Br* dépassement *m*; *Aut* **o. lane,** voie *f* de dépassement; **no o.,** défense de doubler.
overtax [əʊvə'tæks] *vt* **(a)** accabler (*la nation*) sous les impôts; surtaxer, surimposer (*qn*); **(b)** (*overburden*) surmener (*qn*); **to o. one's strength,** se surmener, abuser de ses forces.
over-the-counter [əʊvəðə'kaʊntər] *adj* (*ventes*) au comptant; (*médicament*) vendu sans ordonnance; *Fin* **o.-the-c. market,** marché *m* hors cote.
overthrow¹ ['əʊvəθrəʊ] *n* subversion *f*, renversement *m* (*d'un empire*); défaite *f* (*de qn, d'un projet*).
overthrow² [əʊvə'θrəʊ] *vt* (*pt* **overthrew** [əʊvə'θruː]; *pp* **overthrown** [əʊvə'θrəʊn]) **(a)** défaire, vaincre (*qn*); abattre, mettre à bas (*un empire*); renverser (*un ministère etc*); réduire à néant (*les projets de qn*); **(b)** (*knock down*) abattre (*un adversaire*).
overtime ['əʊvətaɪm] **1** *n* **(a)** *Ind* heures *fpl* supplémentaires; **to do o.,** faire des heures supplémentaires; **wages, including o.,** le salaire, y compris le paiement d'heures supplémentaires; **(b)** *US Sp* temps *m* supplémentaire. **2** *adv* **to work o.,** faire des heures supplémentaires; *Fig* **your imagination is working o.,** tu te laisses emporter par ton imagination; **my imagination was working o.,** mon imagination battait la campagne.
overtire [əʊvə'taɪər] *vt* surmener (*qn*); **to o. oneself,** se fatiguer outre mesure, se surmener; **to be overtired,** (*of child*) être trop fatigué.
overtly [əʊ'vɜːtlɪ] *adv* ouvertement.
overtness [əʊ'vɜːtnɪs] *n* franchise *f*.
overtone ['əʊvətəʊn] *n* **(a)** (*suggestion*) nuance *f*, soupçon *m* (*de tristesse, d'amertume*); **there are overtones of violence in her books,** ses livres sont empreints d'une certaine violence; **the phrase has an o. of disparagement,** l'expression comporte un soupçon *ou* un rien de dénigrement; **(b)** *Mus* harmonique *m*.
overtop [əʊvə'tɒp] *vt* (**-pp-**) **(a)** (*be taller than*) dépasser (*qn, qch*) en hauteur; dominer (*qch*); **(b)** (*surpass*) l'emporter sur (*qn*).
overture ['əʊvətjʊər] *n Mus* ouverture *f*; *Fig* **to make overtures to s.o.,** faire des avances à qn.
overturn [əʊvə'tɜːn] **1** *vt* renverser (*une table*); faire verser (*une voiture*); faire chavirer (*un canot*); abattre, mettre à bas (*un empire*); ruiner, réduire à néant (*les projets de qn*); **the bill was overturned in the Senate,** le projet de loi a été rejeté par le Sénat. **2** *vi* se renverser; (*of vehicle*) verser; (*of boat*) chavirer; (*turn turtle*) *Aut Av* capoter.
overuse¹ [əʊvə'juːs] *n* emploi excessif (**of,** de); **the phrase has been made meaningless by o.,** l'expression a perdu tout son sens à force d'être trop employée.
overuse² [əʊvə'juːz] *vt* trop employer.
overvalue [əʊvə'væljuː] *vt* **(a)** *Com* surestimer, majorer (*l'actif*); estimer (*un objet*) au-dessus de sa valeur; **(b)** faire trop de cas de (*la capacité de qn*).
overview ['əʊvəvjuː] *n* (*of a situation etc*) vue *f* d'ensemble.
overwater [əʊvə'wɔːtər] *vt* arroser à l'excès, trop arroser.
overwatering [əʊvə'wɔːtərɪŋ] *n* arrosage excessif.
overweening [əʊvə'wiːnɪŋ] *adj* (*person*) outrecuidant, présomptueux; (*ambition*) sans bornes.
overweight 1 ['əʊvəweɪt] *n* (*excess weight*) surpoids *m*, poids *m* en excès; excédent *m* (*de bagages*); (*of person*) embonpoint *m*. **2** [əʊvə'weɪt] *adj* (*luggage*) au-dessus du poids réglementaire; (*person, animal*) au-dessus du poids normal; **he's o.,** il est trop lourd.
overwhelm [əʊvə'welm] *vt* écraser, accabler (*l'ennemi*); combler (*qn de bontés*); confondre (*qn de honte*); **to be overwhelmed with work,** être accablé *ou* débordé de travail; **I am overwhelmed by your kindness,** je suis confus de vos bontés; **overwhelmed with joy,** au comble de la joie.
overwhelming [əʊvə'welmɪŋ] *adj* irrésistible, accablant; (*defeat, majority*) écrasant.
overwhelmingly [əʊvə'welmɪŋlɪ] *adv* irrésistiblement.
overwind [əʊvə'waɪnd] *vt* (*pt & pp* **overwound** [əʊvə'waʊnd]) trop remonter (*une montre etc*).

overwork¹ [əʊvə'wɜːk] *n* surmenage *m*, travail *m* outre mesure; **suffering from o.,** surmené.
overwork² **1** *vt* surmener (*qn*), surcharger (*qn*) de travail; abuser de (*un truc, une idée etc*). **2** *vi* se surmener, travailler outre mesure.
overworking [əʊvə'wɜːkɪŋ] *n* surmenage *m*.
overwrite¹ ['əʊvəraɪt] *n Comptr* **o. mode,** mode *m* de superposition.
overwrite² [əʊvə'raɪt] *vt Comptr* superposer (*des données*).
overwrought [əʊvə'rɔːt] *adj* (*with emotion*) accablé; (*exhausted*) épuisé; **the child was o.,** l'enfant était à bout.
overzealous [əʊvə'zeləs] *adj* trop zélé, qui fait trop de zèle.
Ovid ['ɒvɪd] *n* Ovide *m*.
oviduct ['əʊvɪdʌkt] *n Biol* oviducte *m*.
ovine ['əʊvaɪn] *adj* (*animal etc*) ovin.
oviparous [əʊ'vɪpərəs] *adj Biol* ovipare.
ovoid ['əʊvɔɪd] **1** *adj* ovoïde. **2** *n* figure *f* ovoïde.
ovulate ['ɒvjʊleɪt] *vi Biol* ovuler.
ovulation [ɒvjʊ'leɪʃən] *n Biol* ovulation *f*.
ovule ['ɒvjuːl] *n Biol* ovule *m*.
ovum, *pl* **ova** ['əʊvəm, 'əʊvə] *n Biol* ovule *m*.
ow [aʊ] *int* aïe!
owe [əʊ] *v* (*pp & pt* **owed** [əʊd]) **1** *vt* devoir (*de l'argent, du respect, de l'obéissance etc*) (**to s.o.,** à qn); **to o. s.o. sth, to o. sth to s.o.,** devoir qch à qn; **the sum owed (to) her by her brother,** la somme qui lui est due par son frère; **I still o. you for the petrol,** je vous dois encore l'essence; **what** *or* **how much do I o. you?,** qu'est-ce que je te dois?, combien est-ce que je te dois?; **I o. you an apology/an explanation,** je vous dois des excuses/une explication; **you o. it to yourself to do your best,** vous vous devez à vous-même de faire de votre mieux; **I o. my life to you,** je vous dois la vie; **to whom** *or* **to what do I o. this honour?,** qu'est-ce qui me vaut cet honneur?; **he owes his success to his parents' influence,** il doit son succès à l'influence de ses parents.
2 *vi* **he owes for three months' rent,** il doit trois mois de loyer.
owing ['əʊɪŋ] *adj* **(a) there is £5 o.,** 5 livres restent dues; **all the money owing to me,** tout l'argent qui m'est dû; **(b) o. to,** à cause de, en raison de; **o. to a recent bereavement,** en raison d'un deuil récent.
owl [aʊl] *n* (*bird*) hibou *m*, -oux; **tawny o.,** chouette *f* hulotte; **barn o.,** (chouette) effraie *f*; **eagle o.,** grand-duc *m* (d'Europe); *Fig* **a wise old o.,** un vieux sage; **Brown O.,** (*in Brownies*) cheftaine *f*; *F* **o. glasses,** lunettes (parfaitement) rondes.
owlet ['aʊlɪt] *n* (*bird*) jeune hibou *m*.
owlish ['aʊlɪʃ] *adj* de hibou; **o. look,** air *m* de faux sage.
own¹ [əʊn] **1** *vt* **(a)** posséder, être propriétaire de (*une terre, une maison etc*); **I've never owned a suit,** je n'ai jamais possédé de costume; **who owns this land?,** qui est le propriétaire de cette terre?; **he behaves as if he owned the place,** il se conduit comme en pays conquis; **you don't o. me!,** je ne t'appartiens pas!; **company owned by the state,** compagnie qui appartient à l'État; **(b)** (*recognize*) reconnaître; avouer (*un enfant*); (*admit*) avouer (*qch*); **dog nobody will o.,** chien que personne ne réclame; **I o. I was wrong,** j'ai eu tort, je l'avoue *ou* je le reconnais; **to o. oneself beaten,** se reconnaître vaincu. **2** *vi* **to o. to a mistake,** reconnaître *ou* avouer une erreur; **he owns to being forty,** (*admits he is*) il admet qu'il a quarante ans; (*claims he is*) il avoue quarante ans.
own² **1** *adj* propre; **her o. money,** son propre argent; **I saw it with my o. eyes,** je l'ai vu de mes propres yeux; **o. brother/sister,** frère germain/sœur germaine; **my o. brother! — and you won't even lend me £10!,** mon propre frère! — et tu ne veux même pas me prêter 10 livres!; **I had my o. table,** j'avais ma table à moi; **I do my o. cooking,** je fais la cuisine moi-même, je fais ma propre cuisine; **the supermarket does its own baking,** le supermarché produit son propre pain; **to roll one's o. cigarettes,** rouler ses cigarettes; **to score an o. goal,** *Fb* marquer un but pour l'équipe adverse; *Fig* apporter de l'eau au moulin de l'adversaire.
2 *pron* **my/his/one's/***etc* **o.,** le mien/le sien/*etc*; **to look after one's o.,** (*property*) soigner son bien; (*friends, relatives*) s'occuper des siens; **I have money of my o.,** j'ai de l'argent à moi; **a child of his o.,** un enfant à lui; **the house is my o.,** la maison est à moi *ou* m'appartient; **to make sth one's o.,** s'approprier qch; **she took the song and made it her o.,** elle s'est approprié la chanson; **he has a copy of his o.,** il a un exemplaire à lui *ou* en propre; **for reasons of his o.,** pour des raisons qui le regardent; **a style of one's o.** *or* **all one's o.,** un style original *ou* propre *ou* spécifique; *F* **to roll one's o.,** rouler ses cigarettes; **the landscape has a wild beauty of its o.,** le paysage a une beauté sauvage qui lui est propre; **may I have it for my (very) o.?,** est-ce que je peux l'avoir pour moi seul?; **there's not a thing here that I can call my o.,** il n'y a pas ici un objet qui m'appartienne en propre; **his ideas are his o.,** ses idées lui sont propres; **my time is my o.,** mon temps est à moi *ou* m'appartient, je suis libre de mon temps; **to come into one's o.,** (*blossom*) s'épanouir; (*inherit*) entrer en possession de son bien; (*receive one's reward*) recevoir sa récompense; **to get one's o. back,** se venger; **to hold one's o.,** (*of patient*) se maintenir; **my o. (sweetheart)!,** ma chérie!; **to do sth on one's o.,** (*without company*) faire qch tout seul; (*on one's own initiative*) faire qch de sa propre initiative *ou* de son chef; **to be** *or* **work on one's o.,** travailler tout seul; (*be in business alone*) être établi à son propre compte; **I am (all) on my o.,** je suis seul.
►**own up** *vi* (*confess*) avouer; **to o. up to a crime/to having done sth,** avouer un crime/avoir fait qch.
own-brand [əʊn'brænd], **own-label** [əʊn'leɪbəl] *adj* **our o.-b. butter,** du beurre sous notre propre marque.
owner ['əʊnər] *n* propriétaire *mf*; patron, -onne (*d'une maison de commerce*); **rightful o.,** possesseur *m* légitime; *Jur* ayant *m* droit; **cars parked here at the owners' risk,** stationnement *m* des voitures à la responsabilité de leurs propriétaires; **a dog o.,** le propriétaire d'un chien; *Aut* **o. driver,** conducteur *m* propriétaire; *Nau* **the owners (of a ship),** les armateurs *mpl*, l'armement *m*.
ownerless ['əʊnələs] *adj* sans propriétaire; (*chien*) sans maître.
owner-occupancy ['əʊnər'ɒkjʊpənsɪ] *n* fait d'être propriétaire du logement qu'on occupe; **o.-o. has increased,** de plus en plus de gens sont propriétaires de leurs logements.
owner-occupier ['əʊnər'ɒkjʊpaɪər] *n* propriétaire-occupant *m*, *pl* propriétaires-occupants.
ownership ['əʊnəʃɪp] *n* propriété; (*right*) (droit *m* de) propriété *f*; **change of o.,** *Com* changement *m* de propriétaire; *Jur* mutation *f*; **under new o.,** (*notice in shop, restaurant etc*) nouveau propriétaire; **during her o. of the property,** pendant qu'elle possédait la propriété; **the bus company is now in private o.,** la compagnie de bus est maintenant aux mains du secteur privé.
owt [aʊt] *n Eng Dial* n'importe quoi; quelque chose.
ox, *pl* **oxen** [ɒks, 'ɒks(ə)n] *n* bœuf *m*; **humped ox,** zébu *m*; **ox cart,** char *m* à bœufs; *Culin* **ox heart/tongue,** cœur *m*/langue *f* de bœuf.
oxalic [ɒk'sælɪk] *adj Ch* oxalique.
oxblood ['ɒksblʌd] *adj & n* rouge sang *m inv*.
oxbow ['ɒksbəʊ] *n Geog* **o. (lake),** bras mort (d'un cours d'eau).
Oxbridge ['ɒksbrɪdʒ] *n* les universités d'Oxford et de Cambridge. **2** *adj* (*graduate etc*) de l'université d'Oxford ou de Cambridge.
oxen *see* **OX**.
oxeye ['ɒksaɪ] *n* (*flower*) **o. daisy, white o.,** marguerite *f* des champs.
Oxfam ['ɒksfæm] *n Br* = œuvre de bienfaisance travaillant pour le Tiers Monde; **O. shop,** magasin où l'on vend des articles d'occasion et d'artisanat au profit du Tiers Monde.
Oxford ['ɒksfəd] *n* **O. bags,** (*trousers*) pantalon *m* très large; **O. blue,** bleu foncé *m inv*; **O. shoes, oxfords,** souliers *mpl* richelieu.
oxherd ['ɒkshɜːd] *n* bouvier, -ière.
oxhide ['ɒkshaɪd] *n* cuir *m* de bœuf.
oxidation [ɒksɪ'deɪʃən] *n Ch* oxydation *f*.
oxide ['ɒksaɪd] *n Ch* oxyde *m*.
oxidization [ɒksɪdaɪ'zeɪʃən] *n Ch* oxydation *f*.
oxidize ['ɒksɪdaɪz] **1** *vt Ch* oxyder. **2** *vi Ch* s'oxyder.
Oxonian [ɒk'səʊnɪən] **1** *adj* oxfordien, -ienne, oxonien, -ienne. **2** *n* membre *m* de l'Université d'Oxford.
oxtail ['ɒksteɪl] *n Culin* queue *f* de bœuf; **o. soup,** soupe *f* de queue de bœuf.
oxyacetylene [ɒksɪə'setɪliːn] *n* **o. cutting,** découpage *m* au chalumeau; **o. burner** *or* **torch,** chalumeau *m* oxyacétylénique de découpage.
oxygen ['ɒksɪdʒən] *n Ch* oxygène *m*; **o. bottle** *or* **cylinder,** bouteille *f* d'oxygène; **o. mask/tent,** masque *m*/tente *f* à oxygène.
oxygenate ['ɒksɪdʒɪneɪt, ɒk'sɪ-] *vt* oxygéner.
oxygenation [ɒksɪdʒɪ'neɪʃən] *n* oxygénation *f*.
oxygenize ['ɒksɪdʒɪnaɪz] *vt* oxygéner.

oyez [əʊ'jeɪ, əʊ'jes] *int* **o.! o.!,** oyez! (= *interjection par laquelle le crieur public réclame le silence*).

oyster ['ɔɪstər] *n* huître *f*; **pearl o.,** (huître) perlière *f*; *Fig* **the world is your o.,** le monde t'appartient; *F* **he shut up like an o.,** il est resté muet comme une carpe; **o. bed** *or* **bank,** huîtrière *f*, banc *m* d'huîtres, parc *m* à huîtres; **o. breeder** *or* **farmer,** ostréiculteur, -trice; **o. farm** *or* **park,** parc à huîtres; **o. knife,** couteau *m* à huîtres; **o. shell,** écaille *f* d'huître; **o. mushroom,** pleurote *f*.

oystercatcher ['ɔɪstəkætʃər] *n* (*bird*) huîtrier *m*.

oz *abbr* **ounce(s)**.

Oz [ɒz] *n Sl* Australie *f*.

ozone ['əʊzəʊn] *n Ch* ozone *m*; **o. depletion,** appauvrissement *m* en ozone; **o. layer,** couche *f* d'ozone; *Met* ozonosphère *f*.

ozone-friendly ['əʊzəʊn'frendlɪ] *adj* (*product, spraycan*) qui ne détruit pas la couche d'ozone, qui préserve la couche d'ozone.

P

P, p [piː] *n* **(a)** (la lettre) P, p *m*; *F* **to mind one's P's and Q's,** (*be careful in one's behaviour*) se surveiller; (*take care over details*) faire bien attention aux détails; **(b)** *Br F* (*penny*) penny *m*, *pl* pence; **a 20p stamp,** un timbre à 20 pence; *Arch* **a half p.,** un demi-penny.
p. *n* (*abbr* **page**) p..
pa [pɑː] *n F* papa *m*.
p.a. ['piː'eɪ] *adv* (*abbr* **per annum**) par an; **£16,000 p.a.,** 16 000 livres par an.
Pa. *n abbr* **Pennsylvania.**
PA ['piː'eɪ] *n* **(a)** (*abbr* **public address**) **PA (system),** (système *m* de) sonorisation *f*, *F* sono *f*; **an announcement over the PA,** une annonce par haut-parleurs; **(b)** *abbr* **personal assistant.**
pace¹ [peɪs] *n* **(a)** (*step*) pas *m*; **ten paces off,** à dix pas de distance; *Mil etc* **one p. forward!,** un pas en avant!;
(b) (*gait*) allure *f*; amble *m* (*d'un cheval etc*); **to put a horse through its paces,** faire passer un cheval à la montre; **to put a car/machine through its paces,** mettre une voiture/une machine à l'épreuve; **to put s.o. through his** *or* **her paces,** mettre qn à l'épreuve;
(c) (*speed*) vitesse *f*, train *m*, allure *f*; **at a smart p.,** à vive allure; **at a slow p.,** à petite allure; **at a walking p.,** au pas; **to keep p. with s.o.,** marcher du même pas que qn; **supply is keeping p. with demand,** l'offre suit la demande; **the company did not keep p. with developments in the industry,** la société n'a pas suivi le rythme des développements dans l'industrie; **to force/slacken the p.,** forcer/ralentir le pas *ou* l'allure; **to set the p.,** donner le pas (*à qn*); *Sp* donner *ou* régler l'allure; (*of company etc*) mener le train; **to stand the p.,** tenir le rythme; **he can't stand the p.,** il ne tient pas le rythme.
pace² **1** *vi* marcher à pas mesurés; (*of horse etc*) aller l'amble; **to p. about** *or* **up and down,** faire les cent pas. **2** *vt* arpenter (*une rue, une pièce etc*); *Sp* tirer (*qn*).
▶**pace off, pace out** *vtsep* mesurer (*une distance*) au pas.
pacemaker ['peɪsmeɪkər] *n* **(a)** *Sp* meneur, -euse de train (*d'un coureur*); **(b)** *Med* (*device*) stimulateur *m* (cardiaque), pacemaker *m*; **(c)** *Anat* nœud sinusal cardiaque.
pachyderm ['pækɪdɜːm] *n* (*animal*) pachyderme *m*.
pacific [pə'sɪfɪk] *adj* **(a)** *Geog* **the P. (Ocean),** l'océan *m* Pacifique, le Pacifique; **(b)** (*not aggressive*) pacifique; **(c)** (*peaceful*) paisible.
pacifically [pə'sɪfɪklɪ] *adv* pacifiquement.
pacification [pæsɪfɪ'keɪʃən] *n* pacification *f* (*d'un pays etc*); apaisement *m* (*de qn*).
pacifier ['pæsɪfaɪər] *n* **(a)** (*person*) pacificateur, -trice; **(b)** *esp Am* (*for babies*) sucette *f*, tétine *f*.
pacifism ['pæsɪfɪz(ə)m] *n Pol* pacifisme *m*.
pacifist ['pæsɪfɪst] *n & adj* pacifiste *mf*.
pacify ['pæsɪfaɪ] *vt* pacifier (*une foule, un pays etc*); apaiser, adoucir, calmer (*qn, la colère de qn*).
pack¹ [pæk] *n* **(a)** (*bundle etc*) paquet *m*, ballot *m* (*de linge, de marchandises etc*); ballot (*de colporteur*); (*backpack*) sac *m* (porté sur le dos); bât *m* (*de bête de somme*); *Mil* **p. drill,** exercice *m* en tenue de campagne (à titre de punition), *Sl* le bal; **p. animal,** animal *m* de bât *ou* de charge, bête *f* de somme; **p. train,** convoi *m* de bêtes de somme; *Av* **parachute p.,** (*parachute*) parachute *m* (plié et prêt à servir); (*container*) enveloppe *f ou* sac de parachute; **a p. of lies,** un tissu de mensonges;
(b) (*group*) (*of robbers*) bande *f*; (*of game*) volée *f*; (*of people*) presse *f*; (*of wolves, foxhounds*) meute *f*; (*of staghounds*) équipage *m*; (*of cub scouts, Brownies*) meute; (*of Brownies*) ronde *f*; **wolves hunt in packs,** les loups chassent en meutes; **to lay on the p.,** laisser courre; **p. of fools,** tas *m* d'imbéciles; *Rugby Fb* **the p.,** le pack;
(c) (*set, collection*) jeu *m* (*de cartes, de dominos*); paquet *m* (*de cartes*);
(d) *esp Am* paquet *m* (*de cigarettes*); **an economy p. of washing powder,** un paquet de lessive de taille économique; **a four-** *or* **six-p. of beer,** un pack de bière;
(e) (*in oceanography*) **(ice) p.,** banquise *f*; **p. ice,** pack *m*;
(f) *Med* **wet/cold p.,** enveloppement humide/froid.
pack² **1** *vt* **(a)** (*wrap*) emballer, empaqueter (*des objets*); (*put in luggage*) mettre (*ses effets*) dans sa valise *ou* sa malle; *Com* conserver (*de la viande*) en boîtes; embariller (*des harengs etc*); baguer (*des marchandises périssables*); *Med* faire un enveloppement froid à (*un malade*); **to p. one's bags,** faire ses bagages; **did you p. any towels?,** est-ce que tu as mis des serviettes dans les bagages?; **we're not packed,** nous n'avons pas fait nos bagages; **to p. a pistol,** porter un revolver; *F* **to p. a punch,** (*of person*) cogner dur; (*of drink*) donner un coup de fouet;
(b) (*cram*) entasser, serrer (*des voyageurs dans une voiture etc*); tasser (*de la terre dans un trou etc*); **we were packed like sardines,** nous étions serrés *ou* pressés comme des harengs (en caque) *ou* comme des sardines; *Nau* **to p. on all sail,** mettre toutes voiles dehors;
(c) (*fill*) remplir, bourrer (**sth with sth,** qch de qch); *Constr Min etc* remblayer (*un fossé etc*); bâter (*un mulet etc*); **to p. one's case,** faire sa valise; **the train was packed,** le train était bondé; **the hall was packed,** la salle était comble; **book packed with information,** livre bourré de faits; **to p. the house,** faire la salle;
(d) *MecE* garnir, étouper (*un gland etc*); fourrer (*un assemblage*); garnir (*un piston*);
(e) *esp Am* transporter (*qch*) dans un sac à dos; **if you p. it in, p. it out,** = remmenez vos ordures;
(f) **to p. a jury,** se composer un jury favorable; **to p. a meeting,** s'assurer un nombre prépondérant de partisans à une réunion; *Cards* **to p. the cards,** apprêter les cartes.
2 *vi* **(a)** (*prepare luggage*) faire sa valise *ou* ses valises; **we haven't finished packing,** nous n'avons pas fini de faire nos bagages; **tent that packs easily,** tente facile à emballer; *F* **to send s.o. packing,** envoyer promener qn;
(b) (*of earth etc*) se tasser;
(c) *Rugby Fb* former le pack.
▶**pack away** *vtsep* **(a)** (*store*) ranger (*ses vêtements d'hiver*); **(b)** *F* (*eat a lot*) avaler, engouffrer (*de la nourriture*); **I've never seen anyone p. it away like him,** je n'ai jamais vu personne engouffrer de la nourriture comme lui.
▶**pack down** **1** *vi* (*be compacted*) **to p. down hard,** (*of snow etc*) se tasser dur. **2** *vtsep* tasser (*la terre*).
▶**pack in** **1** *vtsep* **(a)** (*cram in*) faire rentrer; **I couldn't p. anything more in,** je ne pouvais pas en faire rentrer plus; **this movie is packing them in,** ce film attire les foules; **we were packed in like sardines,** nous étions serrés *ou* pressés comme des harengs (en caque) *ou* comme des sardines; **(b)** *Br F* (*stop, give up*) arrêter; **p. it in!,** assez!; **tell them to p. the noise in,** dis-leur d'arrêter ce bruit; **she packed it (all) in,** elle a tout laissé tomber; **he's packed her in,** il l'a larguée *ou* jetée. **2** *vi* **(a)** (*crowd in*) s'entasser; **(b)** *F* (*stop working*) tomber en panne; **the photocopier's just packed in on me,** la photocopieuse vient de me lâcher.
▶**pack off** *vtsep F* (*send, dispatch*) expédier; **to p. the kids off to school/bed,** envoyer les enfants à l'école/au lit; **his father packed him off to America/to boarding school,** son père l'a embarqué pour l'Amérique/l'a expédié en pension.
▶**pack out** *vtsep F* (*fill completely*) remplir (*une salle*) à craquer; **the hall/pub was packed out,** la salle/le bar était comble.
▶**pack up** **1** *vtsep* **(a)** faire (*ses valises*); emballer (*ses effets*); (*at end of class, work etc*) ranger (*ses livres, outils etc*); **(b)** *F* (*stop*) **p. it up!,** assez! **2** *vi* **(a)** (*prepare luggage*) faire ses valises *ou* bagages; **(b)** (*store things away*

at end of class, work etc) ranger ses affaires; *F* (*finish work*) remballer; **(c)** *F* (*of machine etc*) tomber en panne; **my car's packed up,** ma voiture ne marche plus.

package¹ ['pækɪdʒ] *n* **(a)** (*parcel*) paquet *m*, colis *m*; **(b)** *Comptr* **software p.,** logiciel *m*; **(c)** (*offer*) proposition *f*, offre *f*; **the p. includes a company car,** l'offre comprend une voiture de société; **you get all these services in a complete p.,** vous obtenez tous ses services selon un marché global; **I didn't know this would be extra, I thought we were buying a p.,** je ne savais pas que ce serait en supplément, je pensais que tout était compris; **we offer copywriting and typesetting as a p.,** nous offrons un service global *ou* forfaitaire de rédaction d'annonces et composition; **all new arrivals are given a p. of financial and legal aid,** tous les nouveaux arrivants se voient attribuer un ensemble d'avantages financiers et juridiques; **the employment p. includes ...,** les avantages accompagnant ce poste sont ...; *Com etc* **p. deal,** contrat global; **p. tour/holiday,** voyage *m*/vacances *fpl* à prix forfaitaire; **(d)** *US* **p. store,** = magasin qui vend des boissons alcoolisées (à emporter).

package² *vt Com etc* emballer, conditionner; *F* **to p. s.o.,** (*pop star, candidate etc*) créer l'image de marque de qn.

packager ['pækɪdʒər] *n* (*in publishing*) packager *m*.

packaging ['pækɪdʒɪŋ] *n Com* emballage *m*, conditionnement *m*; *F* (*of pop star, candidate etc*) image *f* de marque.

packed [pækt] *adj* **(a)** (*bus, train etc*) bondé; **(b) p. lunch,** panier-repas *m*, *pl* paniers-repas, pique-nique *m*, *pl* pique-niques.

packer ['pækər] *n* **(a)** (*person*) *Com etc* emballeur, -euse, empaqueteur, -euse; **fruit p.,** emballeur de fruits; **(b)** (*device*) machine *f* à emballer *ou* à empaqueter; (*for tamping down*) bourroir *m*.

packet ['pækɪt] *n* **(a)** paquet *m* (*de thé, de cigarettes etc*); sachet *m* (*d'aiguilles*); *Comptr* paquet (*de données*); **I made the sauce from a p.,** j'ai fait la sauce à partir d'un sachet; **pay p.,** paie *f*; **wage p.,** salaire *m*; **(postal) p.,** colis *m* (postal), paquet poste; *Sl* **to make a p.,** gagner un argent fou; *Sl* **that'll cost a p.,** ça va coûter les yeux de la tête; **p. soup,** bouillon *m ou* potage *m* en sachet; *Comptr* **p. switching,** commutation *f* par paquets; **(b)** *Old-fashioned* **p. (boat),** paquebot *m*.

packhorse ['pækhɔːs] *n* cheval *m* de somme; *F* **I'm not your p.!,** je ne suis pas ton porteur.

packing ['pækɪŋ] *n* **(a)** *Com etc* (*act of wrapping etc*) emballage *m*, empaquetage *m*; *Nau* arrimage *m* (*de la cargaison*); embarillage *m* (*des harengs etc*); mise *f* en conserve (*de la viande etc*); *Med* enveloppement *m* (*dans un drap mouillé*); *Com* **postage and p.,** frais *mpl* d'emballage et d'envoi; **to do one's p.,** faire sa valise *ou* ses valises; **there isn't much p. (to do),** il n'y a pas beaucoup de bagages à faire; **p. case,** caisse *f ou* boîte *f* d'emballage; **p. list,** *Com* liste *f* de colisage; (*of holidaymaker*) liste du contenu des bagages;

(b) (*material used*) matériel *m* d'emballage; *Med* pansement *m*; **non-returnable p.,** emballage perdu;

(c) (*action of insertion, of pressing down*) *Constr etc* remblayage *m* (*d'un fossé etc*); tassement *m* (*de la terre etc*); *Nucl Phys* tassement (*des particules*); *MecE etc* bourrage *m*, étoupage *m*, garnissage *m* (*d'un joint etc*); *Med* tamponnement *m*; **p. box,** presse-étoupe *m inv*; **p. ring,** *MecE* rondelle *f ou* bague *f* de garniture; bague de fond (*d'un cylindre*); segment *m*, bague, garniture *f* (*de piston*);

(d) (*material, object, added or inserted*) *Constr etc* remblai *m* (*pour combler un fossé etc*); *Nucl Phys* masse *f* (*spécifique, apparente*); *MecE etc* garniture *f* (*d'un joint, d'un piston etc*); joint *m* (*d'un gland etc*); *Med* tampon *m*;

(e) manipulation *f* (*du choix des membres d'un jury etc*).

packsaddle ['pæksæd(ə)l] *n* bât *m*.

pact [pækt] *n* pacte *m*, convention *f*, contrat *m*; **suicide p.,** accord de suicide collectif passé entre deux personnes ou plus; **to make a p. with s.o.,** faire un pacte avec qn, pactiser avec qn.

pad¹ [pæd] *n* **(a)** (*for protection, to prevent chafing etc*) bourrelet *m*, coussinet *m*; sellette *f* (*de cheval de trait*); coussinet (*de selle, de collier*); *Fencing* plastron *m*; tampon *m* (*d'ouate etc*); *Med* tampon, compresse *f*; (*for feminine hygiene*) serviette *f* hygiénique; *Sp* **shin pads,** *Cr* **pads,** jambières *fpl*; **shoulder p.,** (*in dress, jacket*) épaulette *f*;

(b) (*on body*) pulpe *f* (*du doigt, de l'orteil*); patte *f* (*de renard, de lièvre etc*); pelote digitale (*de certains animaux*);

(c) (*block*) bloc *m* (*de papier à écrire etc*); (*on desktop*) sous-main *m inv*; **memo** *or* **scribbling p.,** bloc-notes *m*, *pl* blocs-notes; **inking p.,** tampon encreur; **stamp p.,** tampon à timbrer;

(d) (*drill chuck*) mandrin *m* (*de vilebrequin*); (*handle*) manche *m* porte-outils;

(e) *MecE* (*base*) semelle *f*, support *m* (*de moteur etc*); patin *m* (*d'appui*); patin (*de butée*); (*strap*) bride *f*, patte *f*; **mounting p.,** bride de fixation *ou* de montage;

(f) *Av etc* aire *f* de décollage et d'atterrissage (*pour hélicoptères*); **launching p.,** aire *ou* plate-forme *f* de lancement (*d'une fusée*);

(g) *Rad* atténuateur *m* (*d'amplitude*) non réglable;

(h) *Sl* (*home*) logement *m*, piaule *f*.

pad² *vt* (**-dd-**) **(a)** bourrer, rembourrer (*un coussin etc*); matelasser (*une porte etc*); capitonner (*un fauteuil*); ouater (*un vêtement*); garnir (*les épaules d'un manteau*); **(b)** *F* (*fill out*) délayer, étoffer (*un discours, une dissertation etc*); cheviller (*un vers*); **to p. a book,** ajouter des pages de remplissage dans un livre.

pad³ *n* (*sound*) (*of animal*) pas sourds; (*of person*) pas feutrés.

pad⁴ *vt & vi* (**-dd-**) **to p. (along),** (*of dog etc*) trotter à pas sourds; **to p. about the room,** (*of person*) aller et venir à pas feutrés.

▶pad out *vtsep* (*fill out*) délayer, étoffer (*un discours, une dissertation etc*); **they included two old songs to p. the album out,** ils ont inclu deux vieilles chansons pour étoffer l'album.

padded ['pædɪd] *adj* (*door, wall etc*) matelassé; **p. cell,** cabanon *m*; **p. shoulders,** (*fashion*) épaulettes *fpl*; *Sp* épaules rembourrées.

padding ['pædɪŋ] *n* **(a)** (*action*) remplissage *m*, rembourrage *m*; garnissage *m* (*avec de la bourre etc*); (*lining with cotton wool*) ouatage *m*, ouatinage *m*; **(b)** (*material*) bourre *f*, ouate *f*, rembourrage *m* (*d'un coussin etc*); matelassure *f* (*d'un siège etc*); **(c)** *F* délayage *m* (*d'un discours, d'une dissertation etc*).

paddle¹ ['pæd(ə)l] *n* **(a)** (*for canoe*) pagaie *f*; **double p.,** pagaie à double pale; **(b)** (*blade*) aube *f*, pale *f*, palette *f* (*de roue hydraulique, de bateau à roues*); vannelle *f* (*de porte d'écluse*); **p. boat/steamer,** bateau *m*/vapeur *m* à aubes *ou* à roues; **p. wheel,** roue *f* à aubes *ou* à palettes; **(c)** (*of animal*) nageoire *f* (*de cétacé, de manchot, de tortue*); patte *f* (*de canard*); **(d)** (*table tennis bat*) raquette *f* de ping-pong.

paddle² **1** *vt* pagayer; *Fig* **to p. one's own canoe,** (*get by on one's own*) se débrouiller (tout seul), arriver par soi-même; (*mind one's own business*) s'occuper de ses affaires. **2** *vi* (*in canoe*) pagayer; (*in rowing boat*) tirer en douce.

paddle³ *n* (*walk in water*) barbotage *m*; **to go for a p.,** (*of child*) aller barboter dans l'eau.

paddle⁴ *vi* barboter (*dans l'eau etc*); patauger, patouiller (*dans la boue etc*); **paddling pool,** bassin *m* à patauger.

paddock ['pædək] *n* paddock *m*; *Austr* champ *m*; **to put a horse in the p.,** parquer un cheval.

paddy¹ ['pædɪ] *n* **(a)** *Br F* **to be/get in a p.,** être/se mettre en colère; **(b)** *US F* **p. wagon,** panier *m* à salade.

paddy² *n* **(a) p. field,** rizière *f*; **(b)** *Com* (*rice*) paddy *m*.

Paddy ['pædɪ] *n* **(a)** (*dimin of* **Patrick**) = Patrice *m*, Patrick *m*; **(b)** *Sl* (*Irish person*) Irlandais *m*.

padlock¹ ['pædlɒk] *n* cadenas *m*.

padlock² *vt* cadenasser; fermer (*une porte etc*) au cadenas; **he padlocked his bike to the fence,** il a cadenassé son vélo à la grille.

padre ['pɑːdreɪ] *n* prêtre *m*; *Mil* aumônier *m* (militaire).

paean ['piːən] *n* péan *m*, pæan *m*.

paediatric, *US* **pediatric** [piːdɪ'ætrɪk] *adj* (*hôpital etc*) de pédiatrie; (*spécialiste*) en pédiatrie.

paediatrician, *US* **pediatrician** [piːdɪə'trɪʃən] *n* pédiatre *mf*.

paediatrics, *US* **pediatrics** [piːdɪ'ætrɪks] *n* pédiatrie *f*.

paedology, *US* **pedology** [piː'dɒlədʒɪ] *n* pédologie *f*.

paedophile, *US* **pedophile** ['piːdəufaɪl] *n* pédophile *mf*.

paedophilia, *US* **pedophilia** [piːdəu'fɪlɪə] *n* pédophilie *f*.

pagan ['peɪgən] *adj & n* païen, -ïenne.

paganism ['peɪgənɪz(ə)m] *n* paganisme *m*.

page¹ [peɪdʒ] *n* page *f*; **three pages later,** trois pages plus loin; **front p.,** la une (*d'un journal*); **on p. 6,** à la page 6; *Journ etc* **continued on p. 6/on back p.,** suite *f* (en) page 6/en dernière page; **p. number,** numéro *m* de page; **p. numbering,** numérotage *m* des pages; *Comptr* **p. preview,** visualisation *f* de la page complète sur l'écran; *Comptr* **p. printer,** imprimante *f* page par page; **p. proofs,** épreuves *fpl* en pages; *Typ* **p. make-up,** mise *f* en pages.

page² *vt* paginer (*un livre*).

page³ *n* (*boy*) jeune chasseur *m* (*d'hôtel*); (*at wedding*) page *m* (d'honneur); (*attending person of rank*) page.

page⁴ *vt* (*call*) **to p. s.o., to have s.o. paged,** (*by loudspeaker*) appeler qn par haut-parleur; (*by messenger*) envoyer chercher qn par un chasseur; (*by radio*) appeler qn par radio portative.

pageant ['pædʒənt] *n* (*display*) spectacle pompeux; (*of historical events*) cortège *m ou* cavalcade *f* historique.

pageantry ['pædʒəntrɪ] *n* apparat *m*, pompe *f*.

pageboy ['peɪdʒbɔɪ] *n* **(a) p. (style)**, (*hairstyle*) coiffure *f* à la page; **(b)** = **PAGE³**.

pager ['peɪdʒər] *n Telecom* récepteur d'appel *ou* de poche.

page-turner ['peɪdʒtɜːnər] *n* (*book*) = livre passionnant.

paginate ['pædʒɪneɪt] *vt* paginer (*un livre*).

pagination [pædʒɪ'neɪʃən] *n* pagination *f*.

pagoda [pə'gəʊdə] *n Archit* pagode *f*.

pah [pɑː] *int* pouah!

paid [peɪd] **1** *see* **PAY²**. **2** *adj* **(a)** (*person, work*) rétribué, rémunéré; **p. holidays,** congés payés; **p. worker,** travailleur salarié; **(b)** *Com* (*goods, bill*) payé.

paid-up ['peɪdʌp] *adj* **(a) (fully) p.-up member,** membre *m* (*d'un parti etc*) qui a payé sa cotisation; **(b)** *Fin* (*capital*) versé; (*shares*) libéré; **to make a life assurance policy p.-up,** cesser de cotiser à une assurance-vie (sans l'annuler).

pail [peɪl] *n* (*bucket*) seau *m*; **milking p.,** seille *f* à traire; **a p. of water,** un seau d'eau.

pain¹ [peɪn] *n* **(a)** douleur *f*, souffrance *f*; (*mental*) peine *f*; **I have a p. in my leg,** j'ai une douleur à la jambe; **to give s.o. p.,** (*of tooth*) faire mal à qn, faire souffrir qn; (*of incident etc*) faire de la peine à qn; **to be in (great) p.,** souffrir beaucoup; **is he in p.?,** souffre-t-il?; **the p. was unbearable,** la douleur était insupportable; **to put a wounded animal out of its p.,** achever un animal blessé; **shooting pains,** élancements *mpl*, douleurs lancinantes; **labour pains,** douleurs de l'accouchement; *F* **he's a p. (in the neck** *or Vulg* **arse),** il est casse-pieds *ou Sl* emmerdant; *F* **working can be a p. sometimes,** travailler peut être casse-pieds quelquefois;
(b) (*trouble*) (*usu pl*) **pains,** peine *f*; **to take pains** *or* **be at great pains to do sth,** se donner de la peine *ou* du mal pour faire qch; **as she was at pains to explain,** ce qu'elle se donnait du mal à expliquer; **to take pains over sth,** s'appliquer à qch; **to have nothing for one's pains,** en être pour sa peine;
(c) *Arch still used in* **on** *or* **under p. of (death** *etc*), sous peine de (mort *etc*).

pain² *vt* faire souffrir (*qn*), faire mal à (*qn*); (*mentally*) faire de la peine à (*qn*), peiner, affliger (*qn*); **it pained her to see them quarrel,** cela lui faisait de la peine de les voir se disputer.

pained [peɪnd] *adj* attristé, peiné (**at,** de); **p. expression,** air affligé *ou* peiné.

painful ['peɪnfʊl] *adj* **(a)** (*wound, part of the body*) douloureux; **I find walking p.,** marcher me fait souffrir; **to become p.,** (*of limb etc*) s'endolorir; **(b)** (*spectacle, effort*) pénible; **p. subject,** sujet *m* pénible; **it was p. to see,** il était pénible de voir; **the expensive shops were a p. reminder of their poverty,** les boutiques chères leur rappelaient péniblement leur pauvreté; **(c)** *Arch* (*travail*) laborieux, pénible.

painfully ['peɪnfʊlɪ] *adv* (*see adj*) **(a)** douloureusement; **(b)** péniblement; **(c)** laborieusement.

painkiller ['peɪnkɪlər] *n* calmant *m*, analgésique *m*.

painkilling ['peɪnkɪlɪŋ] *adj* calmant, analgésique.

painless ['peɪnlɪs] *adj* indolore; (*extraction etc*) sans douleur; *F Fig* **replacing the fan belt was fairly p.,** remplacer la courroie de ventilateur n'a pas posé beaucoup de problèmes.

painlessly ['peɪnlɪslɪ] *adv* sans douleur; *F Fig* (*effortlessly*) sans effort, sans problème.

painstaking ['peɪnzteɪkɪŋ] *adj* soigneux, assidu; (*travail*) soigné.

painstakingly ['peɪnzteɪkɪŋlɪ] *adv* avec (grand) soin.

paint¹ [peɪnt] *n* peinture *f*; *Art* couleur *f*; *Med* badigeon *m*; *F* (*face make-up*) fard *m*; **coat of p.,** couche *f* de peinture; **gloss p.,** peinture brillante *ou* laquée; **oil p.,** peinture *ou* couleur à l'huile; **pot of p.,** pot *m* de peinture; **wet p.!, mind the p.!,** (*on sign*) attention, peinture fraîche!; **box of paints,** boîte *f* de couleurs; **tube of p.,** tube *m* de peinture *ou* de couleurs; **p. gun/roller,** pistolet *m*/rouleau *m* à peinture; **p. pot,** pot à peinture; **p. shop,** magasin *m* de couleurs, marchand *m* de couleurs; *Ind* (*in factory etc*) atelier *m* de peinture.

paint² **1** *vt* **(a)** *Art* peindre; **to p. a portrait in oils,** peindre un portrait à l'huile; **(b)** (*coat with paint*) peindre (*une pièce, une porte etc*) (**green,** en vert); *Med* badigeonner (*la gorge etc*); **the kitchen needs painting,** il faut faire repeindre la cuisine; *Th* **to p. the scenery for a play,** brosser les décors d'une pièce; *F* **to p. the town red,** faire la noce *ou* la bringue; *F* **to p. one's face,** se farder; **(c)** (*depict*) dépeindre; **what words can p. the scene?,** comment dépeindre cette scène?; **to p. everything in rosy colours,** peindre tout en rose. **2** *vi* faire de la peinture; **I've always wanted to p.,** j'ai toujours voulu faire de la peinture; **I wish I could p. like that!,** si seulement je pouvais peindre comme cela!; **to p. in water-colours,** faire de l'aquarelle.

paintbox ['peɪntbɒks] *n* boîte *f* de couleurs.

paintbrush ['peɪntbrʌʃ] *n* pinceau *m*.

painter¹ ['peɪntər] *n Art* peintre *m*; coloriste *mf* (*de jouets etc*); **she was a famous p.,** elle fut un peintre célèbre; **landscape/portrait p.,** paysagiste *mf*/portraitiste *mf*; **(house) p.,** peintre en bâtiments; **J. Smith, painters and decorators,** J. Smith, peintre et décorateur.

painter² *n Nau* bosse *f* (*d'embarcation, de lof*); **to cut the p.,** couper l'amarre.

painting ['peɪntɪŋ] *n* **(a)** (*of house etc*) *& Art* peinture *f*; **to study p.,** étudier la peinture; **landscape/portrait p.,** peinture de paysages/portraits; **(house) p.,** peinture (*de bâtiments etc*); **(b)** (*picture*) tableau *m*.

paintwork ['peɪntwɜːk] *n* les peintures *fpl*; (*on car etc*) peinture *f*.

pair¹ [peər] *n* **(a)** paire *f* (*de chaussures, de vases, de ciseaux, de jambes etc*); attelage *m* (*de deux chevaux*); (*man and woman, male and female animal*) couple *m*; (*in rowing*) deux *m*; **in pairs,** deux par deux, par paires, par couples; **the p. of you,** vous deux; **they can go to bed without their supper, the p. of them!,** qu'ils aillent au lit sans manger tous les deux!; **what a p.!,** (*of two people*) quelle paire!; **a p. of trousers,** un pantalon; *Old-fashioned* **a p. of scales,** une balance; **carriage and p.,** voiture *f* à deux chevaux; **these two pictures are a pair,** (*match*) ces deux tableaux se font pendant; **stockings that are not a p.,** bas dépareillés *ou* qui ne vont pas ensemble; **where is the p. of this glove?,** où se trouve l'autre gant de cette paire?; **p. royal,** *Cards* brelan *m*; (*dice*) rafle *f*; *Nucl Phys* **electron/ion p.,** paire d'électrons/d'ions; **p. of steps,** marchepied *m* (volant), escabeau *m*;
(b) *Br Parl* (= *two MPs from opposing parties*) paire de membres de partis adverses qui se sont associés (pour un vote); (= *MP from opposing party*) membre du parti adverse avec qui on peut s'associer.

pair² **1** *vi* faire la paire (**with s.o./sth,** avec qn/qch); (*of birds etc*) s'accoupler, s'apparier (**with,** avec); *Br Parl* s'associer (**with s.o.,** avec qn). **2** *vt* appareiller, apparier, assortir (*des gants etc*); accoupler, apparier (*des oiseaux etc*).

▶**pair off** **1** *vi* former un couple *ou* des couples. **2** *vtsep* arranger (*des personnes, des objets*) deux par deux; **he's trying to get them paired off,** il essaie de les mettre ensemble.

paired [peəd] *adj* deux par deux, par paires, par couples; *Med* (*organs etc*) pairs; (*guns*) jumelés, conjugués; (*cylinders*) accouplés; *Tel* (*cables*) à paires.

paisley ['peɪzlɪ] *n Tex* **p. pattern,** (dessin *m*) cachemire *m*.

pajamas [pə'dʒɑːməz] *npl US* pyjama *m*.

Paki ['pækɪ] *n & adj Br Offensive Sl* = **PAKISTANI**; (*restaurant*) restaurant pakistanais; (*corner shop*) épicerie tenue par un Pakistanais.

Paki-bashing ['pækɪbæʃɪŋ] *n Br Offensive Sl* persécution *f* des Pakistanais.

Pakistan [pɑːkɪ'stɑːn] *n* Pakistan *m*.

Pakistani [pɑːkɪ'stɑːnɪ] **1** *adj* pakistanais. **2** *n* Pakistanais, -aise.

pakora [pə'kɔːrə] *npl Culin* = beignets *mpl* de légumes.

pal [pæl] *n F* copain, *f* copine; **watch where you're going p.!,** regarde où tu vas mon vieux *ou* (*more aggressively*) mon coco!

▶**pal up** *vi F* (*become friends*) (*of two people*) devenir copains; **to p. up with s.o.,** devenir copain avec qn.

palace ['pælɪs] *n* **(a)** palais *m*; **Bishop's/Archbishop's p.,** palais épiscopal/archiépiscopal; *Pol* **p. revolution,** révolution *f* de palais; **(b)** *Br* **(Buckingham) P.,** Buckingham; **the P. raised no objections to the visit,** Buckingham n'a élevé aucune objection concernant la visite; **a P. spokesperson,** un porte-parole de Buckingham; **(c)** (*hotel etc*) palace *m*; *Old-fashioned* **picture p.,** cinéma *m*.

paladin ['pælədɪn] *n* paladin *m*.

palaeographer [pælɪ'ɒgrəfər] *n* paléographe *mf*.

palaeography [pælɪ'ɒgrəfɪ] *n* paléographie *f*.

Palaeolithic [pælɪəʊ'lɪθɪk] *adj* paléolithique; **the P. age,** le paléolithique, l'âge *m* de la pierre taillée.

palaeontologist [pælɪɒn'tɒlədʒɪst] *n* paléontologiste *mf*, paléontologue *mf*.

palaeontology [pælɪɒn'tɒlədʒɪ] *n* paléontologie *f*.

palatable ['pælətəb(ə)l] *adj* d'un goût agréable, agréable au palais; (*vin*) qui se laisse boire; (*doctrine etc*) agréable (**to**, à).

palatal ['pælət(ə)l] **1** *adj Anat Ling* palatal, -aux. **2** *n Ling* palatale *f*.

palatalize ['pælətəlaɪz] *vt Ling* palataliser, mouiller (*un l, la combinaison gn*).

palate ['pælɪt] *n Anat* palais *m*; **hard p.**, palais (dur), voûte *f* du palais, voûte palatine; **soft p.**, voile *m* du palais; **cleft p.**, palais fendu; **to have a delicate p.**, avoir le palais fin.

palatial [pə'leɪʃəl] *adj* (*édifice*) magnifique, grandiose.

palatinate [pə'lætɪnɪt] *n* palatinat *m*.

palaver¹ [pə'lɑːvər] *n* **(a)** *F* (*fuss*) embarras *mpl*; **what's all the p. about?**, qu'est-ce qu'il y a qui cloche?; **(b)** (*discussion*) palabre *f*; **after a long p.**, après de longues palabres.

palaver² *vi* palabrer.

pale¹ [peɪl] *adj* pâle; (*because ill, angry, afraid etc*) blême, pâle; (*colour*) pâle, clair; **p. as death, deadly p.**, pâle comme un mort; d'une pâleur mortelle; **to grow** *or* **become p.**, pâlir; **to turn p. with fright**, pâlir de terreur; **p. blue dress**, robe *f* bleu pâle; **by the p. light of the moon**, à la lumière blafarde de la lune.

pale² *vi* pâlir, blêmir; **my adventures p. beside yours**, mes aventures semblent bien pâles auprès des vôtres; **to p. into insignificance**, devenir insignifiant.

pale³ *n* **(a)** pieu *m* (*de clôture*); **(b)** *Arch* (*limits*) bornes *fpl*; *still used in* **beyond the p.**, au ban de la société; (*of person*) pas fréquentable.

paleface ['peɪlfeɪs] *n* visage *m* pâle.

pale-faced ['peɪlfeɪst] *adj* au visage *ou* au teint pâle.

paleness ['peɪlnɪs] *n* pâleur *f*.

Palestine ['pælɪstaɪn] *n* Palestine *f*; **the P. Liberation Organisation**, l'Organisation *f* de Libération de la Palestine.

Palestinian [pælɪ'stɪnɪən] **1** *adj* palestinien. **2** *n* Palestinien, -ienne.

palette ['pælɪt] *n Art* palette *f*; **p. knife**, couteau *m* à palette.

palfrey ['pɔːlfrɪ] *n Arch & Lit* palefroi *m*.

palimony ['pælɪmənɪ] *n F* pension alimentaire versée au concubin.

palimpsest ['pælɪmpsest] *adj & n* palimpseste *m*.

palindrome ['pælɪndrəʊm] *n* palindrome *m*.

paling ['peɪlɪŋ] *n* palissade *f*, palis *m*.

palisade [pælɪ'seɪd] *n* palissade *f*.

pall¹ [pɔːl] *n* **(a)** *Rel* poêle *m*; **(b)** *Fig* voile *m* (*de fumée etc*); manteau *m* (*de neige etc*).

pall² *vt Rel* couvrir d'un poêle; *Fig* voiler.

pall³ **1** *vi* (*become uninteresting*) s'affadir, devenir fade *ou* insipide (**on s.o.**, pour qn); **it never palls**, on ne s'en dégoûte jamais. **2** *vt* blaser, émousser (*les sens*).

pallbearer ['pɔːlbeərər] *n* porteur *m* (*d'un cordon du cerceuil*).

pallet¹ ['pælɪt] *n* (*straw mattress*) paillasse *f*; (*poor bed*) grabat *m*.

pallet² *n* **(a)** *Com* palette *f* (*de manutention*); **p. truck**, transpalette *f*; **(b)** *Art* palette *f*.

palletizable [pælɪ'taɪzɪb(ə)l] *adj Com* palettisable.

palletize ['pælɪtaɪz] *vt* palettiser.

palletizing ['pælɪtaɪzɪŋ] *n Com* palettisation *f*.

palliasse ['pælɪæs] *n* paillasse *f*.

palliate ['pælɪeɪt] *vt* pallier (*la misère, une faute, une maladie etc*); lénifier (*une maladie*); pallier, atténuer (*un vice etc*).

palliative ['pælɪətɪv] *adj & n* palliatif *m*.

pallid ['pælɪd] *adj* pâle, décoloré; (*light, moon etc*) blafard; (*face*) blême.

pallidness ['pælɪdnɪs] , **pallor** ['pælər] *n* pâleur *f*.

pally ['pælɪ] *adj F* **to be p. with s.o.**, être copain avec qn.

palm¹ [pɑːm] *n* **(a)** **p. (tree)**, palmier *m*; **date p.**, dattier *m*; **p. cabbage**, (chou *m*) palmiste *m*; **p. grove** *or* **plantation**, palmeraie *f*; **p. leaf**, feuille *f* de palmier; *Archit* **p. leaf (moulding)**, palmette *f*; **p. oil**, huile *f* de palme *ou* de palmier; **(b)** (*branch*) palme *f*; *Rel* rameau *m*, buis *m* (béni); **P. Sunday**, le Dimanche des Rameaux, *F* les Rameaux; *Fig* **to bear** *or* **win the p.**, remporter la palme.

palm² *n* paume *f* (*de la main*); empaumure *f* (*d'un gant*); *F* **to grease s.o.'s p.**, graisser la patte à qn; *F* **to hold s.o. in the p. of one's hand**, avoir qn sous sa coupe.

palm³ *vt* (*conceal*) **to p. a card**, empalmer *ou* escamoter une carte; (*in conjuring*) filer la carte.

▶**palm off** *vtsep* **(a)** (*dispose of something unwanted*) faire passer, *F* refiler (**sth on s.o.**, qch à qn); **to p. off a bad coin on s.o.**, refiler une fausse pièce à qn; **they're palming the children off on us for the weekend**, ils vont nous refiler les enfants pour le week-end; **(b)** (*give something worthless to*) **when I complained, they palmed me off with a form letter**, quand je me suis plaint, ils m'ont refilé une lettre toute faite.

palmist ['pɑːmɪst] *n* chiromancien, -ienne.

palmistry ['pɑːmɪstrɪ] *n* chiromancie *f*.

palmy ['pɑːmɪ] *adj* (*prosperous, flourishing*) **p. days**, époque florissante (*d'une nation etc*); **in his p. days**, dans ses beaux jours.

palpable ['pælpəb(ə)l] *adj* **(a)** (*tangible*) palpable, que l'on peut toucher; **(b)** (*obvious*) palpable, manifeste; (*mensonge*) évident; (*différence*) sensible.

palpably ['pælpəblɪ] *adv* manifestement.

palpate ['pælpeɪt] *vt Méd* palper.

palpation [pæl'peɪʃən] *n Med* palpation *f*, palper *m*.

palpitate ['pælpɪteɪt] *vt & vi* palpiter.

palpitating ['pælpɪteɪtɪŋ] *adj* palpitant.

palpitation [pælpɪ'teɪʃən] *n* palpitation *f*; **to get** *or* **have palpitations**, avoir des palpitations.

palsy ['pɔːlzɪ] *n Med* paralysie *f*; **cerebral p.**, paralysie cérébrale.

paltry ['pɔːltrɪ] *adj* (*amount, sum*) misérable, malheureux; **p. excuses**, piètres excuses.

pampa ['pæmpə] *n Geog* pampa *f*; **the Pampa(s)**, la Pampa; **pampas grass**, herbe *f* des pampas.

pamper ['pæmpər] *vt* choyer, dorloter (*un enfant*); **a hotel where you will be pampered**, un hôtel où l'on sera à vos petits soins; **pampered tastes**, goûts difficiles.

pamphlet ['pæmflɪt] *n* brochure *f*; (*literary, scientific*) opuscule *m*; (*libellous, scurrilous*) pamphlet *m*.

pamphleteer [pæmflɪ'tɪər] *n* auteur *m* de brochures; (*scurrilous*) pamphlétaire *m*.

pan¹ [pæn] *n* **(a)** *Culin* (*for cooking*) casserole *f*; **frying p.**, poêle *f*; **roasting p.**, plat *m* à rôtir; **pots and pans**, batterie *f* de cuisine; **p. scourer**, éponge *f* à récurer les casseroles; **(b)** (*dish, vessel*) plateau *m*, plat *m*, bassin *m* (*d'une balance*); *Min* (*for gold*) batée *f*; **(lavatory) p.**, cuvette *f* de W.C.; **(c)** *Geol etc* cuvette *f*, bassin *m* de déposition *ou* de sédimentation; **salt p.**, marais salant, saline *f*, salin *m*; **(d)** *Hist* **(priming) p.**, bassinet *m* (*d'un fusil*).

pan² *v* (-nn-) **1** *vt Min* laver (*le gravier etc*) à la batée. **2** *vi* laver le gravier à la batée; **to p. for gold**, laver le gravier à la batée pour en extraire l'or.

pan³ *vt* (-nn-) *F* (*of critic etc*) décrier, éreinter (*qn, qch*).

pan⁴ *v* (-nn-) *Cin F* **1** *vt* prendre (*une vue*) en panoramique. **2** *vi* **the camera pans around the bay**, la caméra prend la baie en panoramique *ou* fait un panoramique de la baie.

Pan [pæn] *n Myth* (le dieu) Pan.

▶**pan out** **1** *vtsep Min* (*wash*) laver (*le gravier etc*) à la batée. **2** *vi F* (*turn out*) **it didn't p. out (well)**, cela n'a pas réussi.

panacea [pænə'sɪə] *n* panacée *f*.

panache [pə'næʃ] *n* **(a)** (*style*) panache *m*; **(b)** (*plume*) panache *m* (*de casque*).

Pan-African [pæn'æfrɪkən] *adj* panafricain.

Pan-Africanism [pæn'æfrɪkənɪz(ə)m] *n* panafricanisme *m*.

Panama [pænə'mɑː] *n* **(a)** (*country*) Panama *m*; **the P. Canal**, le canal de Panama; **(b)** **p. (hat)**, panama *m*.

Panamanian [pænə'meɪnɪən] **1** *adj* panaméen. **2** *n* Panaméen, -éenne.

Pan-American [pænə'merɪkən] *adj* panaméricain.

Pan-Americanism [pænə'merɪkənɪz(ə)m] *n* panaméricanisme *m*.

pancake¹ ['pænkeɪk] *n* **(a)** *Culin* crêpe *f*; *Scot Culin* **P. Day**, mardi gras; **(b)** *Nau* **p. ice**, gâteaux *mpl* de glace, glace *f* en fragments; **(c)** *Av* **p. (landing)**, atterrissage brutal.

pancake² *vi Av* faire un atterrissage brutal.

panchromatic [pænkrəʊ'mætɪk] *adj Phot* (*plaque*) panchromatique.

pancreas ['pæŋkrɪəs] *n Anat* pancréas *m*.

pancreatic [pæŋkrɪ'ætɪk] *adj* pancréatique.

panda ['pændə] *n* (*animal*) panda *m*; **giant p.**, panda géant; *Br* **p. car**, voiture *f* pie (de la police).

pandemic [pæn'demɪk] *Med* **1** *adj* pandémique. **2** *n* pandémie *f*.

pandemonium [pændɪ'məʊnɪəm] *n* pandémonium *m*; **it's p.**, c'est un désordre indescriptible.

pander ['pændər] *vi* **these films p. to our worst instincts,** ces films font appel à nos pires instincts; **to p. to s.o.,** encourager bassement qn; **to p. to a vice,** encourager un vice; **to p. to s.o.'s whims,** se prêter aux exigences de qn.

P & L [piːə'nel] *n Com Fin abbr* **profit and loss.**

Pandora [pæn'dɔːrə] *n Myth* Pandore *f*; **P.'s box,** la boîte de Pandore.

pandowdy [pæn'daʊdɪ] *n US Culin* = genre de tourte, surtout aux pommes.

p & p [piːən'piː] *n Br Com* (*abbr* **postage and packing**) frais *mpl* d'envoi.

pane¹ [peɪn] *n* vitre *f*, carreau *m* (*de fenêtre*); (*in glassmaking*) plat *m* (*de verre*).

pane² *n* panne *f* (*d'un marteau*).

panegyric [pænɪ'dʒɪrɪk] *adj & n* panégyrique *m*.

panel¹ ['pæn(ə)l] *n* **(a)** panneau *m* (*de lambris etc*); placard *m* (*de porte*); caisson *m* (*de plafond*); *Sewing* panneau; (*shaped*) volant *m*; *Archit Constr* entre-deux *m inv*; **sunk p.,** panneau en retrait; **sliding p.,** panneau mobile *ou* coulissant; *MecE etc* **access/inspection p.,** panneau d'accès/de visite; *Aut Av* **instrument p.,** tableau *m* de bord; *Tel* **distribution p.,** tableau de distribution; *Comptr* **control p.,** pupitre *m ou* tableau de commande; *Com* **advertisement p.,** panneau d'affichage *ou* de publicité, panneau-réclame *m*, *pl* panneaux-réclame; *Aut etc* **p. beater,** tôlier *m*; **p. light,** lampe *f ou* éclairage *m* de tableau de bord;

(b) *Jur* (*of jury members*) tableau *m ou* liste *f* du jury; (*of committee members*) liste des membres d'un comité *ou* d'une commission; comité, commission (*d'enquête etc*); (*working party*) groupe *m* de travail; (*round table*) table ronde; **the p.,** *Jur Rad TV* le jury; *Scot* (*the accused*) l'accusé; les accusés; **p. of experts,** comité *ou* commission d'experts; **p. game,** jeu télévisé *ou* radiophonique par équipes.

panel² *vt* (**-ll-**, *US* **-l-**) recouvrir de panneaux; lambrisser (*une paroi*); plaquer (*une surface*).

pannelled, *US* **panneled** ['pæn(ə)ld] *adj* (*room*) boisé, lambrissé; (*wall*) revêtu de boiseries.

panelling, *US* **paneling** ['pæn(ə)lɪŋ] *n* **(a)** (*action*) lambrissage *m* (*d'une pièce*); **(b)** (*finished result*) lambris *m*, boiserie *f*, placage *m*; **oak p.,** lambris *mpl* de chêne; **(c)** (*material*) aubage *m*.

panellist, *US* **panelist** ['pæn(ə)lɪst] *n Jur Rad TV* membre *m* du jury; (*of committee*) membre de comité; (*of working party*) membre du groupe de travail.

pang [pæŋ] *n* angoisse *f*, douleur *f*; **pangs of jealousy,** tourments *mpl* de la jalousie; **to feel a p.,** sentir une petite pointe au cœur; **a p. of conscience,** un soubresaut de conscience; **pangs of hunger,** tiraillements *mpl* d'estomac.

panhandle ['pænhænd(ə)l] *vi Am F* mendier.

panhandler ['pænhændlər] *n Am F* mendiant, -ante.

panic¹ ['pænɪk] *n* panique *f*; **to create a p.,** causer une panique; **to throw the crowd into a p.,** affoler la foule; **in a p.,** pris de panique; *F* **it was p. stations,** c'était la panique totale *ou* l'affolement général; **p. attack,** crise *f* de panique; **p. button,** bouton *m* déclencheur du signal d'alarme; *Fig* **to hit the p. button,** paniquer; *Fin* **p. buying/selling,** achat *m*/vente *f* sous le coup de la panique; **p. measures,** mesures dictées par la panique; **p. reaction,** réaction *f* de panique.

panic² *v* (**panicked**) **1** *vt* remplir de panique, affoler (*la foule etc*); *F* paniquer (*qn*). **2** *vi* être pris de panique, s'affoler, paniquer; **don't p.!,** ne t'affole pas!; **he panicked,** il a paniqué.

panic³ *n Bot* **p. (grass),** panic *m* (d'Italie).

panicky ['pænɪkɪ] *adj F* (*feelings*) panique; (*person*) sujet à la panique; (*market etc*) enclin à la panique; **don't get p.,** ne vous affolez pas.

panic-stricken ['pænɪkstrɪk(ə)n] *adj* pris de panique, affolé.

panjandrum [pən'dʒændrəm] *n Old-fashioned F* gros bonnet.

pannier ['pænɪər] *n* (*basket*) panier *m*; panier de bât (*d'une bête de somme*).

panning¹ ['pænɪŋ] *n Min* lavage *m*.

panning² *n Cin* panoramique *m*; **p. shot,** prise *f* panoramique.

panoply ['pænəplɪ] *n* panoplie *f*.

panorama [pænə'rɑːmə] *n* panorama *m*.

panoramic [pænə'ræmɪk] *adj* (*vue etc*) panoramique; *Aut* **p. mirror,** rétroviseur *m* panoramique.

panpipes ['pænpaɪps] *npl Mus* flûte *f* de Pan.

pansy ['pænzɪ] *n* **(a)** (*flower*) pensée *f*; **(b)** *F* (*male homosexual*) pédéraste *m*, pédale *f*, tante *f*; (*effeminate man*) homme efféminé.

pant¹ [pænt] *n* souffle pantelant *ou* haletant.

pant² **1** *vi* **(a)** (*gasp*) panteler, haleter; (*of animal*) battre du flanc; **to p. for breath,** chercher à reprendre haleine; **(b)** *F* (*be eager*) **he's panting to do it,** il a tellement envie de le faire. **2** *vt* **'listen to me', she panted,** 'écoute-moi' a-t-elle haleté.

▶**pant out** *vtsep* (*say*) dire (*qch*) en haletant.

pantechnicon [pæn'teknɪkən] *n Old-fashioned Br* camion *m* de déménagement.

pantheism ['pænθɪɪz(ə)m] *n* panthéisme *m*.

pantheist ['pænθɪɪst] *adj & n* panthéiste *mf*.

pantheistic [pænθɪ'ɪstɪk] *adj* panthéiste.

pantheon ['pænθɪən] *n* panthéon *m*.

panther ['pænθər] *n* (*animal*) **(a)** panthère *f*; **Black P.,** Panthère noire; **(b)** *Am* couguar *m*, puma *m*.

panties ['pæntɪz] *npl* culotte *f*, slip *m* (*de femme*).

pantihose ['pæntɪhəʊz] *n Am* collant *m*.

panting ['pæntɪŋ] *n* essoufflement *m*, halètement *m*.

panto ['pæntəʊ] *n Br Th F* = **PANTOMIME (a)**.

pantograph ['pæntəgræf] *n* **(a)** *Art* pantographe *m*, singe *m*; **(b)** *El* pantographe *m* (*de locomotive électrique etc*).

pantomime ['pæntəmaɪm] *n Th* **(a)** *Br* (*traditional winter show*) = revue-féerie à grand spectacle (présentée aux environs de Noël); **(b)** (*dumb show*) pantomime *f*; **(c)** *Br F* (*confused situation*) cirque *m*, sérénade *f*.

pantry ['pæntrɪ] *n* (*cupboard*) (grand) placard *m* à provisions, *Old-fashioned* dépense *f*; *Av* bar *m*; **(butler's) p.,** office *mf*.

pants [pænts] *npl* (*underwear*) slip *m*; (*boxer shorts*) caleçon *m* (*d'homme*); slip (*de femme*); *esp Am* (*trousers*) pantalon *m*; *F* **to give s.o. a kick in the p.,** donner un coup de pied au derrière à qn; *F* **to beat the p. off s.o.,** mettre une sacrée volée à qn; *F* **to scare the p. off s.o.,** faire une peur bleue à qn; *F* **to bore the p. off s.o.,** barber qn comme ce n'est pas permis; *F* **to be caught with one's p. down,** être pris dans une situation fort embarrassante; *F* **it's clear who wears the p. around here,** il n'y a pas de doute sur qui porte le pantalon ici.

panty ['pæntɪ] *n* **p. girdle,** gaine-culotte *f*, *pl* gaines-culottes.

pantyhose ['pæntɪhəʊz] *n Am* collant *m*.

pap [pæp] *n* bouillie *f*; *Pej* idioties *fpl*, stupidités *fpl*.

Pap [pæp] *n Med* **P. test** *or* **smear,** frottis vaginal.

papa [pə'pɑː] *n Old-fashioned* papa *m*.

papacy ['peɪpəsɪ] *n* papauté *f*.

papadum ['pæpɪdəm] *n* = **POPPADOM.**

papal ['peɪp(ə)l] *adj* papal, -aux.

paparazzi [pæpə'rætsɪ] *npl Journ Phot Pej* paparazzi *mpl*.

papaw [pə'pɔː] **, papaya** [pə'paɪə] *n Bot* **(a)** (*asimina triloba*) (*fruit*) asimine *f*; (*tree*) asiminier *m*; **(b)** = **PAPAYA.**

papaya [pə'paɪə] *n* (*carica papaya*) papaye *f*; **p.(-tree),** papayer *m*.

paper¹ ['peɪpər] *n* **(a)** papier *m*; (*for wall*) papier peint; **rice p.,** papier de Chine *ou* de riz; **India p.,** papier bible, papier pelure; **blotting p.,** (papier) buvard *m*; **carbon p.,** papier carbone; **emery p.,** papier émeri; **glass p.,** papier de verre; **brown p., wrapping p.,** papier kraft; **cigarette p.,** papier à cigarettes; *Phot* **sensitized p.,** papier sensible; **tracing p.,** papier-calque *m*; **writing p.,** papier à écrire; **drawing p.,** papier à dessin; **rough p.,** papier brouillon; **toilet** *or Br F* **loo p.,** papier hygiénique *ou* toilette; **a sheet/a piece of p.,** une feuille/un morceau de papier; **a pile of p.,** une pile de papier; **to put sth down on p.,** mettre qch sur papier; **on p. it is an army of 300,000,** sur le papier *ou* en théorie, c'est une armée de 300 000 hommes; **it's a good plan on p.,** ce projet est excellent en théorie; **p. bag,** sac *m* en papier; *Comptr* **p. feed,** entraînement *m ou* alimentation *f* du papier; **p. handling equipment,** matériel *m* de façonnage; **the p. industry,** l'industrie papetière, la papeterie; **p. mill,** usine *f* à papier; (*on small scale*) fabrique *f* de papier; *Comptr* **p. tray,** bac *m* à feuilles; **p. profits,** profits fictifs; **p. cup,** (*for drinking*) gobelet *m* en carton; (*for small cake*) caissette *f*;

(b) (*document*) écrit *m*, document *m*, pièce *f*; *Fin etc* papier *m* valeur; (*banknotes*) billets *mpl* (*de banque*); **private** *or* **personal papers,** papiers personnels; **identity papers,** papiers d'identité; *Mil etc* **call-up papers,** ordre *m* d'appel (*sous les drapeaux*); **to send** *or* **hand in one's papers,** donner sa démission; *Fin* **long/short p.,** papier à long/court terme; **negotiable p.,** papier négociable; **p. securities,** papiers valeurs, titres *mpl* fiduciaires; **p. money** *or* **currency,** papier-monnaie *m*, *pl* papiers-monnaie; **voting p.,** bulletin *m* de vote;

(c) *Sch* **(examination) p.,** (*questions*) questions *fpl* d'examen, épreuve écrite; (*answer(s)*) copie *f*; **to correct** *or* **mark papers,** corriger l'écrit;

(d) (*study, report*) étude *f*, mémoire *m* (*sur un sujet scientifique etc*); **to read a p.,** faire une communication (*à une société savante etc*); (*give a talk*) faire une conférence *ou* un exposé, *F* lire un papier; *Parl* **white p.,** livre blanc;

(e) (*newspaper*) journal *m*, -aux; **daily p.,** quotidien *m*; **weekly p.,** hebdomadaire *m*; **p. round,** tournée *f* de distribution des journaux; *Br F* **p. shop,** marchand *m* de journaux.

paper² *vt* doubler (*une boîte*) de papier; tapisser (*une chambre*).

►paper over *vtsep* masquer (*qch*) en le tapissant; *F* **to p. over the cracks,** (*disguise faults*) déguiser les défauts (*de qch*); (*disguise disagreements*) déguiser les mésententes (*entre deux personnes*).

paperback ['peɪpəbæk] **1** *n* livre *m* de poche; **available in p.,** disponible en livre de poche; **p. sales,** ventes de livres de poche. **2** *adj* **p. book/edition,** livre *m*/édition *f* de poche.

paperboard ['peɪpəbɔːd] *n* carton *m*.

paperboy ['peɪpəbɔɪ] *n* (*deliverer*) livreur *m* de journaux; (*seller*) vendeur *m* de journaux.

paperclip ['peɪpəklɪp] *n* trombone *m*.

papergirl ['peɪpəgɜːl] *n* (*deliverer*) livreuse *f* de journaux; (*seller*) vendeuse *f* de journaux.

paperhanger ['peɪpəhæŋər] *n* **(a)** (*decorator*) peintre-décorateur *m*; **(b)** *US Sl* faux-monnayeur *m*.

paperknife ['peɪpənaɪf] *n* coupe-papier *m inv*.

paperless ['peɪpəlɪs] *adj* **the p. office,** = le bureau dans lequel on n'utilise pas de papier, tout étant informatisé.

paperweight ['peɪpəweɪt] *n* presse-papiers *m inv*.

paperwork ['peɪpəwɜːk] *n* paperasseries *fpl*.

papery ['peɪpərɪ] *adj* semblable au papier; (*thin*) mince comme du papier.

papier-mâché ['pæpjeɪ'mæʃeɪ] *n* carton-pâte *m*.

papist ['peɪpɪst] *n & adj Pej* papiste *mf*.

papistry ['peɪpɪstrɪ] *n Pej* papisme *m*.

paprika ['pæprɪkə, pə'priːkə] *n* paprika *m*.

Papua ['pæpjʊə] *n Hist* Papouasie *f*; **P. New Guinea,** Papouasie-Nouvelle-Guinée *f*.

Papuan ['pæpjʊən] **1** *adj* papou. **2** *n* Papou, -oue.

papyrus, *pl* **-ri** [pə'paɪrəs, -raɪ] *n* papyrus *m*.

par [pɑːr] *n* **(a)** (*equality*) pair *m*, égalité *f*; **to be on a p. with s.o./sth,** être au niveau de *ou* aller de pair avec qn/qch; **(b)** *Fin* **p. of exchange,** pair *m* du change; **above/below p.,** au-dessus/au-dessous du pair; **at p.,** au pair; **(c)** (*average*) moyenne *f*; **above/below p.,** au-dessus/au-dessous de la moyenne; *F* **to feel below p., not to feel up to p.,** ne pas être dans son assiette; **(d)** *Golf* par *m*; *Fig F* **that's about p. for the course,** c'est ce à quoi il faut s'attendre.

para ['pɑːrə] *n* **(a)** (*abbr* **paragraph**) par.; **(b)** *Mil F* (*abbr* **paratrooper**) para *m*.

parable ['pærəb(ə)l] *n* parabole *f*; **teaching in parables,** enseignement parabolique *ou* en paraboles.

parabola [pə'ræbələ] *n Math* parabole *f*.

parabolic [pærə'bɒlɪk] *adj Math etc* (*courbe, miroir etc*) parabolique.

paracetamol ® [pærə'siːtəmɒl] *n* paracétamol *m*; **take two p.** *or* **paracetamols,** prenez deux cachets de paracétamol.

parachute¹ ['pærəʃuːt] *n* parachute *m*; **to drop s.o./sth by p.,** larguer qn/qch par parachute, parachuter qn/qch; **brake** *or* **tail p.,** parachute de freinage (à l'atterrissage); **p. flare,** fusée *f* (éclairante) à parachute; **p. harness,** ceinture *f ou* harnais *m* de parachute; **p. jump/descent,** saut *m*/descente *f* en parachute; **to make a p. jump,** sauter en parachute.

parachute² **1** *vi* descendre en parachute. **2** *vt* parachuter (*qn, qch*), larguer (*qn, qch*) par parachute.

►parachute in 1 *vtsep* (*send*) envoyer par parachute. **2** *vi* se faire parachuter.

parachuting ['pærəʃuːtɪŋ] *n* **(a)** parachutisme *m*; **(b)** parachutage *m* (*de qn, de qch*).

parachutist ['pærəʃuːtɪst] *n* parachutiste *mf*.

parade¹ [pə'reɪd] *n* **(a)** *Mil* (*exercise*) exercice *m*; **church p.,** rassemblement *m* (*du bataillon etc*) pour assister à l'office du dimanche; **on p.,** à l'exercice; **to go on p.,** parader; **p. ground,** place *f* d'armes; **(b)** (*procession*) défilé *m*; *Rel* procession *f*; **fashion p.,** défilé de mannequins; **(c)** (*display*) parade *f*; **to make a p. of one's knowledge/feelings,** étaler sa culture/ses sentiments; **(d)** (*esplanade*) esplanade *f*; boulevard *m* (*le long d'une plage*); **(e)** *Fencing* parade *f*.

parade² **1** *vt* **(a)** *Mil* faire parader, faire défiler (*les troupes*); (*assemble*) rassembler (*un bataillon*); **(b)** faire parade *ou* ostentation *ou* étalage de (*ses richesses, ses connaissances etc*). **2** *vi* **(a)** *Mil* parader (*pour l'exercice, pour l'inspection*); **to p. through the streets,** défiler dans les rues; **(b)** (*show off*) **young people parading up and down the beach with next to nothing on!,** des jeunes gens qui se pavanent sur la plage avec presque rien sur le dos!

paradigm ['pærədaɪm] *n* paradigme *m*.

paradise ['pærədaɪs] *n Rel & Fig* paradis *m*; **an earthly p.,** un paradis sur terre; **to go to p.,** aller au paradis; **bird of p.,** (*bird*) paradisier *m*, oiseau *m* de paradis; **p. crane,** grue *f* de paradis.

paradisiac [pærə'dɪzɪæk], **paradisiacal** [pærədɪ'zaɪək(ə)l] *adj* paradisiaque.

paradox ['pærədɒks] *n* paradoxe *m*.

paradoxical [pærə'dɒksɪk(ə)l] *adj* paradoxal, -aux.

paradoxically [pærə'dɒksɪklɪ] *adv* paradoxalement.

paraffin ['pærəfɪn] *n* paraffine *f*; **p. (oil),** pétrole *m* (lampant), kérosène *m*; *Pharm* **liquid p.,** huile *f* de vaseline, vaseline *f* liquide; **to coat with p.,** paraffiner; **p. lamp,** lampe *f* à pétrole; **p. wax,** paraffine solide.

paragliding ['pærəglaɪdɪŋ] *n Sp* parapente *m*.

paragon ['pærəgən] *n* modèle *m* (*de beauté, de vertu etc*).

paragraph¹ ['pærəgræf] *n* **(a)** paragraphe *m*, alinéa *m*; **new p.,** (*when dictating*) à la ligne; *Typ* **p. (mark),** pied *m* de mouche; **(b)** *Journ* (*short article*) entrefilet *m*.

paragraph² *vt* **(a)** diviser (*un document*) en paragraphes; **(b)** *Journ* écrire un entrefilet sur (*qn, qch*).

Paraguay ['pærəgwaɪ] *n* Paraguay *m*.

Paraguayan [pærə'gwaɪən] **1** *adj* paraguayen. **2** *n* Paraguayen, -enne.

parakeet ['pærəkiːt] *n* (*bird*) perruche *f*.

parallel¹ ['pærəlel] **1** *adj* **(a)** *adj* parallèle (**to, with sth,** à qch); **to be** *or* **run p. to sth,** être parallèle à qch; *Gym* **p. bars,** barres *fpl* parallèles; *El* **p. circuits,** circuits *mpl* parallèles; **p. connection,** couplage *m ou* montage *m* en parallèle *ou* en dérivation; *Comptr* **p. interface,** interface *f* parallèle; *Math etc* **p. lines,** lignes *fpl* parallèles; *Ski* **p. turn,** virage *m* en parallèle; *Aut* **p. parking,** stationnement *m* en créneau; *Comptr* **p. port,** port *m* parallèle; *Comptr* **p. printer,** imprimante en parallèle; *Comptr* **p. processing,** traitement *m* en simultanéité; **p. rule(r),** règle *f* à (tracer des) parallèles, parallèle *m*;

(b) (*analogous*) pareil, semblable; (*cas*) analogue (**to, with sth,** à qch); **the two cases are exactly p.,** les deux cas sont analogues.

2 *n* **(a)** (ligne *f*) parallèle *f*; *Geog Astron* parallèle *m* (*de latitude, de déclinaison*); *Mil* (*trench*) (tranchée *f*) parallèle; *Typ* **parallels,** barres *fpl*;

(b) *El* (*connected*) **in parallel,** en parallèle, en dérivation; **out of p.,** (*of dynamo*) déphasé, hors de phase, hors de synchronisme;

(c) (*analogy*) parallèle *m*, comparaison *f*; **to draw a p. between two things,** établir un parallèle *ou* une comparaison entre deux choses; **without p.,** sans pareil.

parallel² *vt* **(-l-)** **(a)** (*make parallel*) placer parallèlement (*des objets*); *El* mettre (*deux circuits, deux piles etc*) en parallèle; (*be parallel to*) être parallèle à (*qch*); **(b)** (*compare*) mettre (*deux choses*) en parallèle, comparer (*deux choses*); **(c)** (*find a parallel to*) trouver un parallèle à (*qch*); (*be equivalent, similar to*) être égal *ou* pareil à (*qch*).

parallelism ['pærəlelɪz(ə)m] *n* parallélisme *m*.

parallelogram [pærə'leləgræm] *n* parallélogramme *m*.

paralyse, *US* **paralyze** ['pærəlaɪz] *vt Med* paralyser; **paralysed in one leg,** paralysé d'une jambe; *Fig* **laws that p. industry,** lois qui paralysent l'industrie; **paralysed with fear,** paralysé par l'effroi, glacé d'effroi.

paralysing, *US* **paralyzing** ['pærəlaɪzɪŋ] *adj* (*poison, fear etc*) paralysant.

paralysis [pə'ræləsɪs] *n Med* paralysie *f*; *Fig* paralysie, impuissance *f*.

paralytic [pærə'lɪtɪk] **1** *adj* **(a)** *Med* paralytique; **p. stroke,** attaque *f* de paralysie; **(b)** *Br F* (*very drunk*) **he's p.,** il est ivre mort. **2** *n* paralytique *mf*.

paralyze, paralyzing *US* = **PARALYSE, PARALYSING.**

paramedic [pærə'medɪk] **1** *n* auxiliaire médical. **2** *adj* (*skills, qualification*) paramédical.

parameter [pə'ræmɪtər] *n Math etc* paramètre *m*; *Fig* **within the parameters of an enquiry,** dans les limites fixées par les paramètres de l'enquête.

paramilitary [pærə'mɪlɪtrɪ] *adj & n* paramilitaire.

paramount ['pærəmaʊnt] *adj* (*chief, leader*) suprême; (*nécessité*) de toute première urgence; **it is of p. importance,** c'est d'une importance primordiale; **the interests of the nation are p.,** les intérêts de la nation sont primordiaux.

paramour ['pærəmʊər] *n Arch* amant *m*, amante *f*.

paranoia [pærə'nɔɪə] *n Med* paranoïa *f*; *F* **you're suffering from p.,** tu es parano.

paranoiac [pærə'nɔɪɪk] *adj & n* paranoïaque *mf*.

paranoid ['pærənɔɪd] *adj* paranoïaque; paranoïde (*délire, folie*); *F* **he's p. about being cheated,** il est convaincu qu'on cherche à l'avoir; *F* **you're being p.,** tu es parano.

paranormal [pærə'nɔːməl] **1** *adj* (*experience, phenomenon etc*) paranormal. **2** *n* **the p.,** le paranormal.

parapet ['pærəpet] *n* **(a)** *Mil* (*in fortress*) parapet *m*; berge *f* (*de tranchée*); **(b)** (*wall*) parapet *m*; (*railing*) garde-fou *m, pl* garde-fous; garde-corps *m inv* (*d'un pont etc*).

paraphernalia [pærəfə'neɪlɪə] *npl* (*things*) affaires *fpl*; (*equipment*) attirail *m*, accessoires *mpl*; *F* **all the p.,** tout le bazar.

paraphrase¹ ['pærəfreɪz] *n* paraphrase *f*.

paraphrase² *vt* paraphraser.

paraplegia [pærə'pliːdʒɪə] *n Med* paraplégie *f*.

paraplegic [pærə'pliːdʒɪk] *adj & n Med* paraplégique *mf*.

parapsychology [pærəsaɪ'kɒlədʒɪ] *n* parapsychologie *f*, métapsychique *f*.

parasite ['pærəsaɪt] *n* (*animal, plant*) & *Fig* parasite *m*; **to be a p. on society,** (*of person*) parasiter la société.

parasitic [pærə'sɪtɪk] *adj* (*insecte, plante, personne*) parasite (**on,** de); *Electron etc* **p. noise,** (bruit *m*) parasite *m*.

parasitism ['pærəsaɪtɪz(ə)m] *n* parasitisme *m*.

parasitize ['pærəsɪtaɪz] *vt* parasiter.

parasitology [pærəsaɪ'tɒlədʒɪ] *n* parasitologie *f*.

parasol ['pærəsɒl] *n* ombrelle *f*; **p. pine,** pin *m* parasol; **p. mushroom,** coulemelle *f*.

paratrooper ['pærətruːpər] *n Mil* parachutiste *m*.

paratroops ['pærətruːps] *npl Mil* (soldats *mpl*) parachutistes *mpl*.

paratyphoid [pærə'taɪfɔɪd] *n* paratyphoïde *f*.

parboil ['pɑːbɔɪl] *vt Culin* faire cuire à demi (dans l'eau).

parcel¹ ['pɑːs(ə)l] *n* **(a)** (*bundle, packet*) paquet *m*, colis *m*; **to do up goods into parcels,** empaqueter des marchandises; **parcel(s) office,** bureau *m* des messageries, messageries *fpl*; **to send sth by p. post,** envoyer qch par colis postal; **(b)** pièce *f*, parcelle *f* (*de terrain*); *St Exch* paquet *m* (*de titres*); (*batch*) lot *m* (*de marchandises*); (*shipment*) envoi *m* (*de marchandises*).

parcel² *vt* (**-ll-**, *US* **-l-**) empaqueter (*du thé etc*).

▶**parcel out** *vtsep* (*distribute*) parceller, partager (*un héritage*); lotir (*des terres etc*); répartir (*des vivres etc*).

▶**parcel up** *vtsep* (*wrap*) mettre en paquets, emballer (*des livres etc*).

parch [pɑːtʃ] *vt* (*of sun*) dessécher (*l'herbe etc*); rôtir, griller, sécher (*des céréales*); (*of fever*) brûler (*qn*); **to be parched with thirst,** avoir une soif dévorante; *F* **I'm parched,** je meurs de soif.

parchment ['pɑːtʃmənt] *n* parchemin *m*; **p. paper,** papier parchemin *ou* parcheminé.

pardon¹ ['pɑːd(ə)n] *n* **(a)** pardon *m*; **I beg your p.!,** je vous demande pardon!; **(I beg your) p.?,** (*what did you say?*) pardon?, comment?; (*shocked, taken aback*) *F* hein?; **(b)** *Rel* indulgence *f*; **(c)** *Jur* (*document*) lettre *f* de grâce; **free p.,** grâce *f*; **to grant s.o. a free p.,** (*of monarch*) faire grâce à qn; **to receive the King's** *or* **Queen's p.,** être gracié; **general p.,** amnistie *f*.

pardon² *vt* **(a)** pardonner, excuser, passer (*une faute etc*); **p. my contradicting you, p. me for contradicting you,** pardonnez(-moi) si je vous contredis; **(b) to p. s.o.,** pardonner à qn; **you could be pardoned for thinking so,** il est facile de croire cela; *Am* **p. me!,** (*I apologize*) je vous demande pardon!; (*I'm sorry, I didn't hear what you said*) pardon?; *Iron* **p. me!,** hou là là, excusez-moi; *Rel* **to p. s.o. sth,** absoudre qn de qch; **(c)** *Jur* gracier, amnistier (*qn*).

pardonable ['pɑːdənəb(ə)l] *adj* **(a)** pardonnable, excusable; **(b)** *Jur* graciable.

pardonably ['pɑːdənəblɪ] *adv* excusablement.

pare [peər] *vt* éplucher (*un légume etc*); rogner (*ses ongles etc*); parer (*le sabot d'un cheval*); **expenses have been pared to the bone,** les dépenses ont été réduites au maximum.

▶**pare down** *vtsep* réduire (*ses dépenses etc*).

parent ['peərənt] *n* père *m*, mère *f*, *pl* parents *mpl*; **when you first become a p.,** quand on devient père *ou* mère; **the p./child relationship,** la relation parents-enfant; **each p. should ...,** le père et la mère devraient ...; **if neither p. can ...,** si ni le père ni la mère ne peuvent ...; *Sch* **p. teacher association,** association *f* de parents d'élèves; *Com* **p. company,** société *f* mère, maison *f* mère.

parentage ['peərəntɪdʒ] *n* origine *f*; **of unknown p.,** parents inconnus.

parental [pə'rent(ə)l] *adj* (*autorité etc*) des parents, des père et mère; (*pouvoir*) paternel.

parenthesis, *pl* **-theses** [pə'renθəsɪs, -iːz] *n* **(a)** (*bracket*) parenthèse *f*; **in parentheses,** entre parenthèses; **(b)** (*interval*) intermède *m*.

parenthesize [pə'renθəsaɪz] *vt* mettre (*des mots*) entre parenthèses.

parenthetic(al) [pæren'θetɪk, -ɪk(ə)l] *adj* **(a)** entre parenthèses; **(b)** *Gram* **p. clause,** incidente *f*.

parenthetically [pæren'θetɪklɪ] *adv* par parenthèse; **could I just say p. ...,** je voudrais faire une parenthèse et dire que ... .

parenthood ['peərənthʊd] *n* paternité *f*; maternité *f*.

parenting ['peərəntɪŋ] *n* l'art *m* d'être parent.

pariah [pə'raɪə] *n* paria *m*; **p. dog,** chien paria, chien métis des Indes.

paring ['peərɪŋ] *n* **(a)** (*action*) épluchage *m* (*de légumes etc*); rognage *m* (*des ongles etc*); *Culin* **p. knife,** couteau *m* à légumes; **(b)** (*result*) (*usu pl*) **parings,** épluchures *fpl* (*de légumes etc*); (*of nails*) rognures *fpl*; (*of metal*) cisaille *f*.

pari passu [pærɪ'pæsʊ] *adv* **to go p. p. with ...,** marcher de pair avec ... .

Paris ['pærɪs] *n* Paris *m*; **the P. basin,** le bassin parisien.

parish ['pærɪʃ] *n Rel* paroisse *f*; **civil p.,** commune *f*; **p. boundary,** limites *fpl* de la paroisse; **p. church,** église paroissiale; **p. council,** = conseil municipal (*d'une petite commune*); **p. hall,** salle *f* d'œuvres (*de la paroisse*); **p. priest,** prêtre *m* de la paroisse; **p. pump issue,** histoire *f* de clocher; **p. register,** registre paroissial; **p. school,** école communale.

parishioner [pə'rɪʃənər] *n* paroissien, -ienne; *Admin* habitant, -ante de la commune.

Parisian [pə'rɪzɪən] **1** *adj* parisien. **2** *n* Parisien, -ienne.

parity ['pærɪtɪ] *n* **(a)** (*equality*) égalité *f* (*de rang etc*); parité *f*; **ambulance staff want p. with firemen,** les ambulanciers veulent être considérés sur un pied d'égalité avec les pompiers; **(b)** *Fin* **exchange at p.,** change *m* à (la) parité *ou* au pair; **exchange parities,** parités de change; **p. value,** valeur *f* au pair; **(c)** *Comptr* **even p.,** parité *f*; **no p.,** non-parité *f*; **odd p.,** imparité *f*; **(d)** (*analogy*) analogie *f*, comparaison *f*; **p. of reasoning,** raisonnement *m* analogue.

park¹ [pɑːk] *n* **(a)** parc *m*; (*in hunting*) réserve *f*; **deer p.,** parc (clôturé) réservé aux cerfs; **national p.,** parc national; **(public) p.,** jardin public, parc; **p. keeper** *or* **officer,** gardien *m* de parc; **(b)** *Br* **car p.,** parc *m* de stationnement pour voitures, parking *m*; **(c)** *Ind Com* **business** *or* **industrial p.,** zone commerciale *ou* industrielle; **(d)** *Old-fashioned Mil* **ammunition p.,** parc *m* à munitions.

park² *vt* **(a)** parquer, garer (*une voiture*); **to be double parked,** (*of car, driver*) être garé en double file; *F* **to p. oneself,** s'installer, se planquer (*chez qn, dans un fauteuil etc*); **(b)** *Comptr* **to p. a hard disk,** parquer la tête de lecture; **(c)** parquer (*des moutons*); **(d)** mettre (*de l'artillerie etc*) en parc. **2** *vi* (*of car, aircraft etc*) stationner, se garer; (*of person*) se garer; **it's impossible to p. in the city centre,** il est impossible de se garer dans le centre-ville.

parka ['pɑːkə] *n* (*coat*) parka *f*.

park-and-ride ['pɑːkənraɪd] *n* = système consistant à garer sa voiture près d'une gare et à continuer son trajet en train, en métro *etc*.

parked [pɑːkd] *adj* (*avion, voiture etc*) en stationnement.

parking ['pɑːkɪŋ] *n* **(a)** (mise *f* en) stationnement *m* (*de véhicules, d'avions etc*); **p. is a problem in town,** il est difficile de se garer en ville; **no p.,** défense de stationner; **p. prohibited,** stationnement interdit; **double p.,** stationnement en double file; **p. area,** aire *f* de stationnement, parking *m*; **p. attendant,** gardien *m* de parking *ou* de voitures; **p. bay,** emplacement *m* pour le stationnement; *Am Aut* **p. brake,** frein *m* à main; **p. fees,** tarif *m* de stationnement; *Aut* **p. lights,** feux *mpl* de position; *Am* **p. lot,** parcage *m*, parking; **p. meter,** parc(o)mètre *m*; **p. place** *or* **space,** (*for one vehicle*) (*in street, car park*) place *f* de parking; **there's more p. (space) behind the restaurant,** il y a encore des places de parking derrière le restaurant; **to get a p. ticket,** avoir une amende pour stationnement illégal; **(b)** parcage *m* (*d'animaux etc*); **(c)** *Astronaut* **p. orbit,** orbite *f* d'attente.

Parkinson ['pɑːkɪnsən] *n* **(a)** *Med* **P.'s disease,** maladie *f* de Parkinson; **(b)** *Hum* **P.'s law,** = plus on a de temps pour accomplir une tâche plus on prend de temps pour l'accomplir.

parkland ['pɑːklænd] *n* espace vert.

parkway ['pɑːkweɪ] *n Am* = grande voie de communication.

parky ['pɑːkɪ] *adj Br F* (*weather*) frisquet.

parlance ['pɑːləns] *n* langage *m*, parler *m*; **in common p.,** dans la langue familière, en langage courant; **in legal p.,** en termes de pratique.

parley¹ ['pɑːlɪ] *n* conférence *f*; *Mil* pourparlers *mpl* (*avec l'ennemi*); **to hold a p.,** parlementer (**with,** avec).

parley² *vi* être *ou* entrer en pourparlers; parlementer (**with the enemy,** avec l'ennemi).

Parliament ['pɑːləmənt] *n* le Parlement; **the Houses of P.,** le palais *ou* les chambres du Parlement; **in P.,** au Parlement.

parliamentarian [pɑːləmen'teərɪən] *n Parl* (*member of parliament*) parlementaire *m*, membre *m* du Parlement; (*expert in parliamentary procedures*) député rompu aux débats de la Chambre.

parliamentary [pɑːlə'ment(ə)rɪ] *adj Parl* (*régime, gouvernement*) parlementaire; **p. election,** élection législative; **p. candidate,** candidat *m* à la Chambre des communes; (*in France*) candidat à la députation; **p. privilege,** immunité *f* parlementaire; *Br* **p. private secretary,** = député détaché auprès d'un ministre pour l'aider dans ses devoirs parlementaires; *Br* **p. secretary,** ≈ ministre d'État.

parlour, *US* **parlor** ['pɑːlər] *n* parloir *m* (*d'un couvent*); *Old-fashioned & Am* (*living room*) salon *m*; **p. games,** petits jeux de salon *ou* de société; **beauty p.,** salon de beauté; *Am* **beer p.,** bar *m* (où on sert de la bière); *US* **funeral p.,** entreprise *f* de pompes funèbres; *Am* **ice-cream p.,** glacier *m*.

parlourmaid ['pɑːləmeɪd] *n* bonne *f* (*affectée au service de table*).

parlous ['pɑːləs] *adj Lit* périlleux, précaire.

Parma ['pɑːmə] *n* Parme; **P. ham,** jambon *m* de Parme.

Parmesan [pɑːmɪ'zæn] *n* **P. (cheese),** parmesan *m*.

Parnassus [pɑː'næsəs] *n* Parnasse *m*.

parochial [pə'rəʊkɪəl] *adj* communal, -aux; *Rel* paroissial, -aux; *Pej* provincial, -aux; **p. outlook,** esprit *m* de clocher; *Am* **p. school,** école religieuse.

parochialism [pə'rəʊkɪəlɪz(ə)m] *n Pej* esprit *m* de clocher; patriotisme *m* de clocher.

parodist ['pærədɪst] *n* parodiste *m*.

parody¹ ['pærədɪ] *n* parodie *f*, pastiche *m*; travestissement *m* (*de la justice*).

parody² *vt* parodier, pasticher; travestir (*la justice etc*).

parole¹ [pə'rəʊl] *n* (*from jail*) libération conditionnelle; **prisoner on p.,** prisonnier (*de droit commun*) libéré conditionnellement; *Can* libéré conditionnel; *Mil* prisonnier *m* sur parole *ou* sur sa foi; **to be put on p.,** être libéré sur parole; **to break one's p.,** manquer à sa parole; **day p.,** libération conditionnelle de jour; **p. supervisor,** surveillant de liberté conditionnelle.

parole² *vt Mil* libérer (*un prisonnier*) sur parole; *Jur* libérer (*un prisonnier*) conditionnellement; **paroled inmate,** libéré conditionnel.

paroxysm ['pærəksɪz(ə)m] *n Med* paroxysme *m* (*d'une fièvre etc*); crise *f* (*de fou rire etc*).

parquet ['pɑːkeɪ] *n* **(a) p. (floor),** parquet *m*; **p. flooring,** parquetage *m*; **(b)** *US Th* premiers rangs du parterre.

parricide ['pærɪsaɪd] *n* **(a)** (*person*) parricide *mf*; **(b)** (*crime*) (crime *m* de) parricide *m*.

parrot¹ ['pærət] *n* (*bird, Fig person*) perroquet *m*; *Br F* **to be as sick as a p.,** être dégoûté.

parrot² *vt* répéter (*qch*) comme un perroquet.

parrot-fashion ['pærətfæʃən] *adv F* **to repeat sth p.-f.,** répéter qch comme un perroquet.

parrotfish ['pærətfɪʃ] *n* perroquet *m* de mer.

parry¹ ['pærɪ] *n Fencing Boxing* parade *f*.

parry² **1** *vt Fencing Boxing etc* parer (*un coup*); *Fig* détourner, éviter (*un danger*); *Fig* parer (*une question*). **2** *vi* **to p. and thrust,** *Fencing* parer et tirer; *Fig* riposter, répondre du tac au tac.

parse [pɑːz] *vt* **(a)** *Gram* faire l'analyse (grammaticale) de, analyser (grammaticalement) (*une phrase, un mot*); **(b)** *Comptr* analyser.

Parsee ['pɑːsiː, pɑː'siː] *adj & n* Parsi, -ie.

parsimonious [pɑːsɪ'məʊnɪəs] *adj Pej* pingre, mesquin.

parsimoniously [pɑːsɪ'məʊnɪəslɪ] *adv* mesquinement.

parsimony ['pɑːsɪmənɪ] *n* pingrerie *f*, mesquinerie *f*.

parsing ['pɑːzɪŋ] *n* **(a)** *Gram* analyse grammaticale; **(b)** *Comptr* analyse *f* syntaxique (*du programme source*).

parsley ['pɑːslɪ] *n Bot Culin* persil *m*; *Culin* **p. sauce,** sauce *f* au persil, sauce persillée.

parsnip ['pɑːsnɪp] *n* panais *m*.

parson ['pɑːs(ə)n] *n Rel* **(a)** (*priest holding benefice*) titulaire *m* d'un bénéfice; **the p.'s nose,** (*of chicken etc*) le croupion; **(b)** (*clergyman*) ecclésiastique *m*; (*Catholic priest*) prêtre *m*; (*Protestant priest*) pasteur *m*.

parsonage ['pɑːsənɪdʒ] *n* ≈ presbytère *m*, cure *f*.

part¹ [pɑːt] **1** *n* **(a)** (*portion, component*) partie *f*; *Ind etc* pièce *f*, organe *m*, élément *m*; (*in publishing*) fascicule *m*, livraison *f* (*d'un ouvrage*); **p. of the house is to let,** une partie de la maison est à louer; **good in parts,** bon en partie; **it's not bad in parts,** il y a des parties qui ne sont pas mal; **the funny/odd p. about it is that ...,** ce qu'il y a de comique/d'étrange c'est que ...; **the best/worst p. was when he started laughing,** le mieux/le pire ça a été quand il s'est mis à rire; **the hard p. is remembering,** le plus dur c'est de se souvenir; **in the early p. of the week,** dans les premiers jours de la semaine; **for the best** *or* **greater p. of five years,** (*to wait, last etc*) presque cinq ans; **the greater p. of the population,** la plus grande partie de la population; **p. of her wanted to agree with them,** une partie d'elle-même voulait être d'accord avec eux; **to be** *or* **form p. of sth,** faire partie de qch; **it's all p. of growing up,** c'est ce qui se passe quand on grandit; **it is p. and parcel of ...,** c'est une partie intégrante *ou* essentielle de ...; **to contribute in p. to the expenses,** contribuer pour partie aux frais; **this is due in p. to inflation,** c'est en partie dû à l'inflation; **for the most p.,** pour la plupart; **will you take it in p. exchange?,** voulez-vous le reprendre?; **ten parts of water to one of milk,** dix parties d'eau pour une partie de lait; **the parts of the body,** les parties du corps; **moving parts,** (*of machine*) organes *ou* parties en mouvement; **spare parts, parts,** pièces détachées *ou* de rechange; *Gram* **parts of speech,** parties du discours; *Gram* **principal parts,** temps principaux (*d'un verbe*); **to buy a work in parts,** (*in publishing*) acheter un ouvrage par fascicules; **p. two,** (*of book, TV programme*) deuxième partie; **in that p. of the world,** dans cette partie du monde; **in those parts,** dans cette région; **they are not from our p. of the world,** ils ne sont pas de chez nous; **in these parts,** par ici; **what are you doing in these parts?,** qu'est-ce que vous faites ici *ou* dans ces parages?; **p. owner,** copropriétaire *mf*; *Nau* coarmateur *m*; **p. work,** (*in publishing*) ouvrage *m* à fascicules;

(b) (*active role*) part *f*; *Th etc* rôle *m*; *Th* (*character*) personnage *m*; **to take (a) p. in sth,** prendre part à qch, participer à qch; **to take p. in the conversation,** prendre part à *ou* se mêler à la conversation; **she takes an active p. in decision-making,** elle participe activement dans le processus de prise de décision; *TV etc* **those taking p. were ...,** avec le concours de ...; **to take no p. in sth,** se désintéresser de qch; **I had no p. in it,** je n'y suis pour rien; **I want no p. of it,** (*I don't want to be involved*) je ne veux pas y participer; **to play a p.,** (*act, pretend*) faire semblant; **to play a p. in sth,** (*be involved in, contribute to*) jouer un rôle dans qch; *Th etc* **supporting p.,** second rôle; *Th etc* **small p., bit p.,** petit rôle; **bit parts,** utilités *fpl*; **she took** *or* **played the p. of Esmerelda,** elle a joué le rôle d'Esmerelda; **to play one's p.,** jouer *ou* remplir son rôle; **imagination plays a large p. in all this,** dans tout ceci l'imagination entre pour beaucoup; *Mus* **orchestral parts,** parties *fpl* d'orchestre; **p. music,** musique *f* d'ensemble; **p. singing,** chant *m* à plusieurs voix; **p. song,** chanson *f* à plusieurs voix;

(c) (*side*) parti *m*; **to take s.o.'s p.,** prendre parti pour qn, prendre fait et cause pour qn; **an indiscretion on the p. of ...,** une indiscrétion de la part de ...; **for my p.,** pour ma part;

(d) to take sth in good/bad p., prendre qch en bonne/mauvaise part, prendre qch du bon/mauvais côté;

(e) *Fml* (*abilities*) (*usu pl*) **parts,** moyens *mpl*, facultés *fpl*; **man of many parts,** homme à facettes;

(f) *Am* (*parting*) raie *f* (dans les cheveux).

2 *adv* partiellement, en partie; **p. silk p. cotton,** mi-soie mi-coton; **a mythical creature, p. woman, p. fish,** une créature mythique mi-femme, mi-poisson; **p. one and p. the other,** moitié l'un moitié l'autre.

part² **1** *vt* séparer en deux; (*of island*) diviser (*un cours d'eau*); (*of person*) fendre (*la foule*); séparer (**sth from sth,** qch de qch); rompre (*une amarre etc*); **to p. one's hair,** se faire une raie (dans les cheveux); **to p. one's hair in the middle/at the side,** se faire *ou* porter la raie au milieu/sur le côté; **his hair was parted on the left/in the middle,** il avait la raie à gauche/au milieu; **they can't bear to be parted,** ils ne supportent pas d'être séparés; **to p. company,** (*of associates, friends*) se séparer; *Hum* **to p. company with one's horse/bike,** tomber de son cheval/vélo; **this is where I p. company with you,** (*I'm going in the opposite direction*) je te quitte ici; (*where I begin to disagree with you*) c'est là que je ne suis plus d'accord.

2 *vi* (*of crowd etc*) se diviser; (*of two people*) se quitter, se séparer; (*of two things*) se séparer; (*of roads*) diverger; (*of cable etc*) rompre, se rompre, partir, céder; **her lips parted in a smile,** un sourire se dessina sur ses lèvres; **to p. good friends,** se quitter bons amis; **to p. from s.o.,** quitter qn; (*separate*) se séparer de *ou* d'avec qn; **to p. with,** (*get rid of*) se défaire de (*qch*); (*give up*) céder (*qch*); *Jur* aliéner (*un droit, un bien*); **he hates to p. with (his) money,** il n'aime pas débourser.

partake [pɑːˈteɪk] *vi* (**partook** [pɑːˈtʊk]; **partaken** [pɑːˈteɪkən]) **to p. in *or* of sth,** participer à qch (**with s.o.,** avec qn); *Old-fashioned* **to p. of a meal,** prendre un repas; *Rel* **to p. of the Sacrament,** s'approcher des sacrements.

parthenogenesis [pɑːθənəʊˈdʒenɪsɪs] *n Biol* parthénogénèse *f*.

partial [ˈpɑːʃəl] *adj* **(a)** (*biassed*) partial, -aux (*envers qn*); (*unjust*) injuste; *F* **to be p. to,** avoir un faible *ou* une prédilection pour (*qn, qch*); avoir un penchant pour (*qn*); **I am p. to a pipe after dinner,** je fume volontiers une pipe après dîner; **(b)** (*in part*) partiel, -ielle; **p. eclipse,** éclipse partielle; **p. loss,** perte partielle; **p. disability,** (*of person*) incapacité partielle.

partiality [pɑːʃɪˈælɪtɪ] *n* (*bias*) partialité *f* (**for,** pour; **to,** envers); (*injustice*) injustice *f*; (*favouritism*) favoritisme *m*; (*liking*) prédilection *f*, préférence marquée, faible *m* (**for,** pour); (*inclination*) penchant *m* (**for,** pour).

partially [ˈpɑːʃəlɪ] *adv* (*see adj*) **(a)** avec partialité; **(b)** partiellement, en partie; **p. sighted,** malvoyant; **the p. sighted,** les malvoyants *mpl*.

participant [pɑːˈtɪsɪpənt] *adj & n* participant, -ante (**in,** à).

participate [pɑːˈtɪsɪpeɪt] *vi* (*of person*) prendre part, participer (**in sth,** à qch); (*of thing*) participer, tenir (**of sth,** de qch); **to p. in s.o.'s joy/work,** s'associer à la joie/aux travaux de qn.

participating [pɑːˈtɪsɪpeɪtɪŋ] *adj* qui participe, participant; **hand this coupon in at any p. store,** remettez ce coupon dans n'importe quel magasin participant; **the p. nations,** (*in sports' contest etc*) les nations participantes.

participation [pɑːtɪsɪˈpeɪʃən] *n* participation *f* (**in sth,** à qch); **thank you for your p.,** merci d'avoir participé.

participial [pɑːtɪˈsɪpɪəl] *adj Gram* participial, -aux.

participle [ˈpɑːtɪsɪp(ə)l] *n Gram* participe *m*; **present/past p.,** participe présent/passé.

particle [ˈpɑːtɪk(ə)l] *n* **(a)** particule *f*, parcelle *f* (*de matière*); paillette *f* (*de métal*); grain *m* (*de sable*); *Nucl Phys* particule, corpuscule *m*; **there's not a p. of truth in the story,** il n'y a pas l'ombre de vérité dans ce récit; **p. accelerator,** accélérateur *m* de particules; *Constr* **p. board,** panneau *m* d'aggloméré; **(b)** *Gram* particule *f*.

parti-coloured, *US* **-colored** [ˈpɑːtɪkʌləd] *adj* bigarré, bariolé.

particular [pəˈtɪkjʊlər] **1** *adj* **(a)** (*specific*) particulier; (*special*) spécial, -aux; (*object*) déterminé; **that p. book,** ce livre-là, ce livre en particulier; **p. branch,** (*of a service*) spécialité *f*; **my own p. feelings,** mes sentiments particuliers *ou* personnels; **to take p. care over (doing) sth,** faire qch avec un soin particulier; **to take p. care to do sth,** mettre un soin particulier à faire qch; **I left for no p. reason,** je suis parti sans raison précise; **I didn't notice anything p.,** je n'ai rien remarqué de particulier; **in p.,** en particulier;

(b) (*account etc*) détaillé, circonstancié;

(c) (*person*) méticuleux, minutieux, soigneux; (*fussy*) pointilleux; **to be p. about one's food,** (*demanding*) être exigeant sur la nourriture; (*difficult*) être difficile sur la nourriture; **to be p. about one's dress,** soigner sa mise *ou* sa tenue; **he is p. in his choice of friends,** il est difficile dans le choix de ses relations; **don't be too p.,** ne vous montrez pas trop exigeant; *F* **I'm not p. (about it),** je n'y tiens pas plus que ça.

2 *n Fml* détail *m*, particularité *f*; **alike in every p.,** semblables en tout point; **to give particulars of sth,** donner les détails de qch; **to ask for fuller particulars about sth,** demander des précisions *ou* des indications supplémentaires sur qch; **for further particulars apply to ...,** pour plus amples détails *ou* renseignements s'adresser à ... .

particularity [pətɪkjʊˈlærɪtɪ] *n* **(a)** (*special quality*) particularité *f*; **(b)** méticulosité *f*; minutie *f* (*d'une description etc*).

particularization [pətɪkjʊləraɪˈzeɪʃən] *n* particularisation *f*.

particularize [pəˈtɪkjʊləraɪz] **1** *vt* particulariser, spécifier. **2** *vi* entrer dans les détails, préciser.

particularly [pəˈtɪkjʊləlɪ] *adv* particulièrement, spécialement, en particulier; **it's cold here, p. at night,** il fait froid ici, particulièrement la nuit; **note p. that ...,** notez en particulier que ...; **I asked him to be p. careful,** je lui ai demandé de prendre particulièrement soin; **not p.,** pas particulièrement *ou* spécialement; **she's not p. rich,** elle n'est pas tellement riche.

parting [ˈpɑːtɪŋ] *n* **(a)** (*division*) séparation *f*; (*of waters*) partage *m*; **to be at the p. of the ways,** (*of two roads*) se trouver là où deux routes se séparent; *Fig* être au carrefour *ou* à la croisée des chemins; **(b)** (*leave-taking*) départ *m*; séparation *f*; **it was a painful p.,** la séparation a été douloureuse; **p. kiss,** baiser *m* d'adieu; **p. shot,** riposte *f* (*lancée en partant*); **(c)** (*breaking*) rupture *f* (*d'un câble etc*); **(d)** *Br* (*of hair*) raie *f*; **centre p.,** raie médiane.

partisan [pɑːtɪˈzæn] **1** *n* **(a)** (*supporter*) partisan, -ane; **(b)** (*resistance fighter*) partisan -ane. **2** *adj* **(a)** partisan; **to act in a p. spirit,** (*of politician etc*) faire preuve d'esprit de parti; (*be prejudiced*) faire preuve de parti pris; **(b)** *Mil* partisan.

partisanship [pɑːtɪˈzænʃɪp] *n* partialité *f*; (*of politician etc*) esprit *m* de parti.

partition¹ [pɑːˈtɪʃən] *n* **(a)** partage *m* (*d'un pays vaincu, d'un héritage etc*); division *f*, découpage *m* (*en plusieurs parties*); **(b)** (*screen*) cloison *f*, cloisonnage *m*; (*wall*) paroi *f*; compartiment *m* (*de cale etc*); *Constr* **internal p., p. wall,** mur *m* de refend *ou* de séparation; **wooden p.,** pan *m* de bois; **glass p.,** vitrage *m*; (*in vehicle*) glace *f* de séparation.

partition² *vt* **(a)** diviser (*qch en plusieurs parties*); partager (*un héritage etc*); démembrer, partager (*un pays vaincu*); **(b)** = **PARTITION OFF.**

▶**partition off** *vtsep* (*separate*) cloisonner (*une pièce*); séparer (*une partie d'une pièce*) par une cloison.

partitive [ˈpɑːtɪtɪv] *adj & n Gram* partitif *m*.

partly [ˈpɑːtlɪ] *adv* partiellement, en partie; **wholly or p.,** en tout ou en partie; **p. by force, p. by persuasion,** moitié de force, moitié par persuasion; **a p. eaten sandwich,** un sandwich à moitié mangé.

partner¹ [ˈpɑːtnər] *n* associé, -ée (**with s.o. in sth,** de qn dans qch); partenaire *mf* (*au tennis etc*); (*in dancing*) cavalier, -ière; (*boyfriend, girlfriend etc*) ami, amie; **they became partners,** ils se sont associés; **to be s.o.'s p. in a crime,** être associé à qn dans un crime; *Com* **senior p.,** associé principal; **full p.,** associé à part entière; **sleeping p., silent p.,** (associé) commanditaire *m*, bailleur *m* de fonds; *Cards* **to cut *or* draw for partners,** = faire les rois.

partner² *vt* être associé *ou* s'associer à *ou* avec (*qn*); (*in games*) être le partenaire de (*qn*).

partnership [ˈpɑːtnəʃɪp] *n* **(a)** association *f* (**in sth with s.o.,** avec qn dans qch); **p. in crime,** association dans le crime; *Com etc* **to enter *or* go into p. with s.o.,** entrer en association avec qn, s'associer avec qn; **to take s.o. into p.,** prendre qn comme associé; **(b)** *Com etc* (*company*) société *f*; **general p.,** société commerciale en nom collectif; **sleeping p.,** (société en) commandite *f* (simple).

partridge [ˈpɑːtrɪdʒ] *n* (*pl* **partridges, partridge**) perdrix *f*; *Culin* perdreau *m*; **a brace of p.,** un couple de perdrix.

part-time [pɑːtˈtaɪm] **1** *adj* (*job, work*) à temps partiel, à mi-temps; **p.-t. worker/employee,** ouvrier, -ière/employé, -ée qui travaille à temps partiel *ou* à mi-temps. **2** *adv* (*to work*) à temps partiel.

part-timer [pɑːtˈtaɪmər] *n F* = **PART-TIME WORKER/EMPLOYEE.**

partway [ˈpɑːtweɪ] *adv* **they were p. through the rehearsal,** ils avaient commencé à répéter depuis déjà un moment; **I'm only p. through it,** (*the book, the task*) je ne l'ai pas encore fini.

party¹ [ˈpɑːtɪ] *n* **(a)** *Pol* parti *m*; **the Labour P.,** le Parti Travailliste; **p. leader/man,** chef *m*/homme *m* de parti; **a p. member, a member of the p.,** un membre du parti; **p. quarrels,** querelles partisanes; *TV Rad* **p. political broadcast,** émission *f* des partis politiques; **p. politics/spirit,** politique *f*/esprit *m* de parti; **he's just making a p. political point,** il se perd dans une querelle politicienne; **to follow *or* toe the p. line,** obéir aux directives du parti;

(b) (*gathering*) réunion *f* (*privée, intime*); (*reception*) réception *f*; (*evening party*) soirée *f*; **dinner p.**, dîner *m*; **birthday p.**, fête *f* d'anniversaire; **children's tea p.**, goûter *m* d'enfants; **I love parties!**, j'adore les soirées; **may I wear my p. dress?**, (*of child*) puis-je mettre ma belle robe?; **p. games**, jeux auxquels on joue dans les soirées *ou* les fêtes; *F* **he's caught the p. spirit**, il s'est abandonné aux joies de la fête; *Am F* **p. pooper**, trouble-fête *mf inv*;

(c) (*group*) groupe *m*, bande *f* (*de touristes etc*); brigade *f*, équipe *f*, groupe (*de mineurs etc*); atelier *m* (*d'ouvriers etc*); *Mil etc* détachement *m*; *Mil* parti *m* (*détaché pour battre la campagne*); **the official p.**, le groupe des officiels, les officiels *mpl*; **rescue p.**, équipe de secours; *Admin etc* **working p.**, comité *m* d'étude; *Mil* **the advance p.**, les éléments *mpl* d'avant-garde; *Mil* **firing p.**, peloton *m* d'exécution; *Mil* **landing p.**, compagnie *f* de débarquement; **shooting p.**, partie *f* de chasse; **will you join our p.?**, voulez-vous être des nôtres?; **we're a small p.**, nous sommes peu nombreux; **I was one of the p.**, j'étais de la partie; *Tel* **p. line**, ligne partagée;

(d) (*participant*) *Jur* (*to a suit, to a dispute*) partie *f*; **the parties to the case**, les parties en cause; **to be p. to a suit**, être en cause; *Com etc* **parties to a bill of exchange**, intéressé(e)s à une lettre de change; **a third p.**, un tiers, une tierce personne; **third p. insurance**, *F* **third p.**, assurance *f* au tiers; **to be/become (a) p. to a crime**, être/se rendre complice d'un crime; **I would never be (a) p. to such a thing**, je ne donnerais jamais mon consentement *ou* je ne m'associerais jamais à une chose pareille;

(e) *F* (*person*) individu *m*, type *m*.

party² *vi Sl* faire la bringue, faire la fête; **let's p.!**, faisons la bringue.

partygoer ['pɑːtigəʊər] *n* habitué *m* des soirées.

PASCAL ['pæskæl] *n Comptr* PASCAL *m*.

paschal ['pæsk(ə)l] *adj* pascal, -aux.

pass¹ [pɑːs] *n* (*in mountains, hills*) col *m*, défilé *m*.

pass² *n* **(a)** (*permit*) permis *m*, passe *f*, permission *f*, laissez-passer *m inv*; **(free) p.**, *Rail etc* titre *m ou* carte *f* de circulation; *Th etc* (*free ticket*) billet gratuit *ou* de faveur; **p. book**, carnet *m ou* livret *m* de banque; **p. key**, (clef *f*) passe-partout *m inv*;

(b) *esp Br Sch* (*in examination*) **to obtain** *or* **get a p.**, être reçu; **p. mark**, moyenne *f*;

(c) (*movement*) (*of footballer, magician etc*) passe *f*; *Fencing* passe, passade *f*, botte *f*; **good p.**, belle passe; *Fb etc* **back p.**, passe en arrière; **the aircraft made two low passes over the village**, l'avion a effectué deux passages à basse altitude au-dessus du village; **to make a p. at s.o.**, faire des propositions à qn;

(d) *Metal* passe *f*, passage *m* (*du métal dans le laminoir*);

(e) *F* (*situation*) **things have come to a pretty p.!**, voilà donc où en sont les choses!; **things came to such a p. that ...**, les choses en vinrent à ce point *ou* à tel point que ... .

pass³ **1** *vi* **(a)** (*go past*) passer; *Aut* doubler; *Cards* passer, renoncer, passer parole; (*at dominoes*) bouder; **as we were passing**, comme nous passions; **the tourists passed into the dining hall**, les touristes ont défilé dans le réfectoire; **words passed between them**, ils ont eu une altercation; **to p. along a street**, passer par une rue; **the procession passed slowly by**, le cortège passa *ou* défila lentement; **everyone smiles as he passes**, tout le monde sourit à son passage; **the motorway passes close to the village**, l'autoroute passe tout près du village; **to let s.o. p.** *or* **allow s.o. to p.**, laisser passer qn; **they shall not p.!**, ils ne passeront pas!; *Rail etc* **p. along** *or* **down the car!**, avancez!, dégagez la portière!; **to p. unobserved**, passer inaperçu; **let it p.!**, passe pour cela!; **I'd like to say in passing**, soit dit en passant; *Aut* **no passing**, défense de doubler; *Cards & Fig* **p.!**, je passe!;

(b) (*of time*) (se) passer, s'écouler; **when five minutes had passed**, au bout de cinq minutes; **how time passes!**, comme le temps passe (vite)!; **to let the opportunity p.**, laisser passer l'occasion;

(c) (*be transferred*) **water passes from a liquid to a solid state when it freezes**, l'eau passe de l'état de liquide à celui de solide quand il gèle; **the expression has passed into the language**, l'expression est passée dans la langue;

(d) (*disappear*) disparaître; (*of clouds etc*) s'en aller;

(e) *Old-fashioned* (*take place*) avoir lieu, se passer; **I don't know what passed between them**, je ne sais pas ce qui s'est passé entre eux; *Arch & Lit* **to come to p.**, arriver, avoir lieu; **it came to p. that ...**, or il arriva *ou* advint que ...;

(f) (*be accepted*) **it would p. in certain circles**, cela passerait dans certains milieux; *F* **you'd p. in a crowd!**, tu n'es pas si mal que ça!; **she could p. for an Italian**, elle pourrait passer pour une Italienne;

(g) *Sch etc* (*succeed in examination etc*) réussir, être reçu.

2 *vt* **(a)** (*go past*) passer près de *ou* à côté de (*qn, la fenêtre etc*); (*without stopping*) passer (sans s'arrêter); dépasser (*le but*); outrepasser (*les bornes de qch*); passer, franchir (*une frontière etc*); *Nau* dépasser, doubler (*un cap*); (*surpass*) surpasser (*qn*); (*go faster than*) gagner (*qn*) de vitesse; (*overtake*) dépasser, rattraper (*qn, un autre navire etc*); doubler (*une autre voiture*); *Sp etc* devancer (*un concurrent*); **to p. s.o. on the stairs/in the street**, croiser qn dans l'escalier/la rue;

(b) *Sch etc* (*succeed in*) être reçu *ou* admis à (*un examen*); **to p. a test**, subir une épreuve avec succès;

(c) (*be accepted by*) **bill that has passed the House of Commons**, projet de loi qui a été voté par la Chambre des Communes; **to p. the censor/the customs**, être accepté par la censure/la douane;

(d) (*approve*) approuver, admettre, apurer (*une facture*); allouer (*une dépense*); *Parl etc* passer, voter, adopter (*un projet de loi, une résolution*); **to p. a dividend of 5%**, (*of company*) approuver un dividende de 5%; **the censor has passed the play/the film**, le censeur a accordé le visa; *Sch* **to p. a candidate**, recevoir un candidat, admettre un candidat; *Mil etc* **to be passed fit**, être reconnu apte;

(e) (*give, transfer*) (faire) passer; (faire) passer, écouler, *F* refiler (*un faux billet de banque etc*); **to p. sth from hand to hand**, passer qch de main en main; **p. me the salt, please**, passez-moi le sel, s'il vous plaît; **p. the cakes round**, faites passer les gâteaux; *Fb etc* **to p. the ball**, passer le ballon; **to p. an item to current account**, (*in book-keeping*) passer *ou* porter un article en compte courant;

(f) (*put*) passer; **to p. one's hand between the bars**, passer *ou* glisser sa main à travers les barreaux; **to p. a rope round sth**, passer une corde autour de qch; **to p. vegetables through a sieve**, passer des légumes; **to p. a sponge over sth**, passer l'éponge sur qch;

(g) *Mil* **to p. troops in review**, passer des troupes en revue;

(h) **to p. the time**, passer le temps; **it passes the time**, cela fait passer le temps;

(i) (*utter*) **to p. criticism on sth**, faire la critique de qch; **to p. remarks**, faire des commentaires *ou* des observations (**on sth**, sur qch); *Jur* **to p. sentence**, prononcer le jugement; **to p. judgement on s.o.**, porter un jugement sur qn, juger qn;

(j) *Physiol* **to p. water**, uriner; *Med* **to p. blood**, être affecté d'hématurie, *F* pisser du sang;

(k) **to p. understanding**, dépasser l'entendement.

►**pass away** *vi* **(a)** *Euph* (*die*) mourir; **(b)** (*disappear*) disparaître.

►**pass by** **1** *vi* **(a)** (*go past*) passer; **luckily a taxi was passing by**, heureusement un taxi passait par là; **(b)** (*of time*) passer. **2** *vipo* (*go past*) passer devant (*une maison etc*). **3** *vtas* (*ignore*) **do you ever feel that life has passed you by?**, est-ce que tu as quelquefois l'impression que les années ont passé sans que tu aies eu le temps de vivre?

►**pass down** *vtsep* **(a)** (*hand down*) passer; **p. me down that cup**, passez-moi cette tasse; **(b)** (*knowledge, story etc*) transmettre; (*clothing etc*) passer (**from ... to**, de ... en).

►**pass off** **1** *vi* **(a)** (*take place*) **everything passed off well**, tout s'est bien passé; **(b)** (*end*) (*of pain*) se passer, disparaître; **is the nausea passing off?**, est-ce que la nausée se passe? **2** *vtsep* **(a)** (*pretend to be*) **to p. off one's goods as those of another make**, faire passer ses propres produits pour ceux d'une autre marque; **to p. oneself off as an artist**, se faire passer pour artiste; **she passed him off as a duke**, elle l'a fait passer pour un duc; **(b)** (*dismiss*) **to p. sth off as a joke**, (*accept as a joke*) prendre qch en riant; (*claim to be a joke*) dire qu'on a fait qch pour rire.

►**pass on** **1** *vi* **(a)** *Euph* (*die*) mourir, passer à la vie éternelle; **(b)** (*proceed*) (*on journey*) continuer son chemin *ou* sa route; **to p. on to another subject**, passer à un nouveau sujet. **2** *vtsep* (*tell or give to other people*) faire circuler (*qch*); (*give to other people*) (faire) passer (*qch à qn*); **read this and p. it on**, lisez ceci et faites circuler; **these cost reductions have been passed on to the consumer**, ces baisses des coûts ont été répercutées sur le consommateur.

►**pass out** **1** *vi* **(a)** (*faint*) s'évanouir; **(b)** (*leave*) sortir (*d'une salle etc*); **don't let this document p. out of your hands**, gardez soigneusement ce document; **(c)** *Sch etc* (*after final examination*) sortir; **cadets passing out**, élèves sortants; **passing-out list,** classement *m* de sortie. **2** *vtsep* (*distribute*) distribuer, faire passer; **to p. out leaflets,** faire passer des dépliants.

▶**pass over 1** *vtsep* (*ignore*) **to p. s.o. over,** (*for promotion*) passer par-dessus le dos à qn, faire un passe-droit; **they passed over the subject in silence,** ils ont passé la question sous silence. **2** *vipo* (*cross*) traverser, franchir (*une rivière etc*); franchir, passer sur (*un obstacle*); passer (*qch*) sous silence; passer sur, glisser sur (*une difficulté etc*). **3** *vi* **(a)** *Euph* (*die*) mourir, passer à la vie éternelle; **(b)** (*end*) (*of storm*) se dissiper, finir; **(c) to p. over to the enemy,** passer à l'ennemi.

▶**pass through 1** *vi* (*travel through*) traverser; **I was just passing through,** je ne faisais que passer. **2** *vipo* **(a)** (*travel through*) traverser (*un pays etc*); **he was (only) passing through Paris,** il était de passage à Paris; **(b)** (*experience*) traverser (*une crise*).

▶**pass up** *vtsep* **(a)** *F* (*not take*) refuser; **she passed up the offer of a job,** elle a refusé une offre d'emploi; **(b)** (*hand up*) passer; **p. (me) up that hammer,** passe-moi ce marteau.

passable ['pɑːsəb(ə)l] *adj* **(a)** (*of acceptable quality*) passable, assez bon; **it's p.,** ce n'est pas si mauvais *ou* trop mal; **(b)** (*rivière, bois etc*) traversable, franchissable; (*route*) praticable.

passably ['pɑːsəblɪ] *adv* passablement, assez.

passage ['pæsɪdʒ] *n* **(a)** (*act of passing*) (*journey*) passage *m*; *esp Nau* traversée *f*; *Pol* adoption *f* (*d'un projet de loi*); **bird of p.,** oiseau *m* de passage; *Nau* **to have a bad** *or* **rough p.,** avoir *ou* faire une mauvaise traversée; *Nau* **to work one's p.,** gagner son passage (en travaillant à bord); **to force a p.,** se forcer un passage; *Jur* **right of p.,** droit *m* de passage;

(b) (*corridor*) couloir *m*, corridor *m*; (*alley*) passage *m*, ruelle *f*; (*at end of street*) échappée *f*; **underground p.,** passage souterrain; *Geog* **the North-West/North-East p.,** le passage Nord-Ouest/Nord-Est;

(c) *MecE* canalisation *f*, conduit *m*, conduite *f*; **air p.,** conduit d'aérage, conduit(e) à air; *Anat* **air passages,** voies aérifères; *F* **the back p.,** le rectum;

(d) p. of arms, passe *f* d'armes; (*argument*) échange *m* de mots vifs;

(e) (*from book etc*) passage *m*; **selected passages,** morceaux choisis.

passageway ['pæsɪdʒweɪ] *n* **(a)** (*space*) passage *m*; **to leave a p.,** laisser le passage libre; **(b)** (*alley*) passage *m*, ruelle *f*; (*corridor*) couloir *m*, corridor *m*.

passé ['pɑːseɪ] *adj* (*outdated*) qui n'est plus à la mode, dépassé.

passel ['pæs(ə)l] *n US F* tas *m* (*de personnes etc*).

passenger ['pæsəndʒər] *n* **(a)** voyageur, -euse (*on train*); (*on ship, aircraft, in car*) passager, -ère; *Av* **p. aircraft,** avion *m* pour le transport de passagers; *Rail* **p. coach** *or* **carriage** *or Am* **car,** voiture *f ou* wagon *m* à voyageurs; *Aut* **p. seat,** siège du passager; **p. ship,** paquebot *m*; *Rail* **p. train,** train *m* de voyageurs; **(b)** *esp Br F* (*non-contributing member*) non-valeur *f*, *pl* non-valeurs, poids mort; **we can't take passengers,** on ne peut pas embarquer des poids morts; **(c)** *Arch* (*bird*) **p. pigeon,** pigeon migrateur.

passe-partout [pɑːspɑː'tuː] *n* **(a)** (*key*) (clef *f*) passe-partout *m inv;* **(b)** *Art Phot* ruban *m* de bordure (*de photographie sous verre etc*); **p.-p. framing,** encadrement *m* sous verre.

passer-by ['pɑːsə'baɪ] *n* (*pl* **passers-by**) passant, -ante.

passing ['pɑːsɪŋ] **1** *adj* passant, qui passe; (*remarque*) en passant; (*fleeting, temporary*) passager, éphémère; (*désir etc*) fugitif; *Lit* **the p. hour,** l'heure fugitive; *Tennis* **p. shot,** passing-shot *m*.

2 *n* **(a)** (*going past*) passage *m* (*d'un train, d'oiseaux etc*); (*overtaking*) dépassement *m*, doublement *m* (*d'une autre voiture*); *Com* passation *f* (*d'un dividende*); **in p.,** à propos; entre parenthèses; **p. place,** (*on road*) = emplacement ménagé pour laisser passer un véhicule venant en sens inverse; *Rail* voie *f* d'évitement *ou* de dédoublement;

(b) écoulement *m* (*du temps*); *Old-fashioned* disparition *f* (*de la beauté de qn*); (*death*) mort *f*; **p. bell,** glas *m*;

(c) (*approval*) *Sch etc* admission *f* (*d'un candidat*); *Pol etc* adoption *f* (*d'une résolution etc*); vote *m* (*d'une loi*); *Fin Com* approbation *f* (*des comptes*);

(d) (*giving*) transmission *f* (*d'un message etc*); *Fb etc* passes *fpl* (*du ballon*);

(e) *Jur* prononcé *m* (*du jugement*).

3 *adv Arch & Lit* **p. fair,** de toute beauté.

passion ['pæʃən] *n* **(a)** (*strong interest*) passion *f*; **to have a p. for music/painting,** avoir la passion de la musique/peinture; **(b)** (*anger*) colère *f*, emportement *m*; (*outburst*) accès *m* de colère; **to fly into a p.,** s'emporter; **(c)** (*love*) passion *f*; **to have a p. for s.o.,** aimer qn passionnément *ou* à la folie; *Jur* **crime of p.,** crime passionnel; **(d)** *Rel* **the P. (of Christ),** la Passion (de Jésus-Christ); **P. Sunday/week,** le dimanche/la semaine de la Passion; *Mus* **the Saint Matthew P.,** la Passion selon saint Matthieu; *Lit* **p. play,** mystère *m* de la Passion; **p. fruit,** fruit *m* de la passion.

passionate ['pæʃənɪt] *adj* **(a)** (*discours*) véhément; **a p. plea for justice,** un véhément appel à la justice; **(b)** (*quick-tempered*) emporté, irascible; **(c)** (*love, lover*) passionné, ardent; (*embrace*) passionné; (*relationship*) passionnel; **to make p. love,** faire l'amour avec passion; **a p. weekend,** un week-end de passion.

passionately ['pæʃənɪtlɪ] *adv* passionnément, ardemment, avec passion; (*to speak*) avec passion, avec véhémence; **to be p. in love with s.o.,** aimer qn passionnément *ou* à la folie; **to be p. fond of (doing) sth,** être passionné de qch, avoir la passion de (faire) qch.

passionflower ['pæʃənflaʊər] *n* (*plant*) passiflore *f*.

passionless ['pæʃənlɪs] *adj* sans passion; (*calm*) impassible.

passive ['pæsɪv] **1** *adj* **(a)** passif; *Com* (*dettes*) ne portant pas d'intérêt; *Metal El* (*iron, electrode etc*) passif; **p. resistance,** résistance passive *ou* inerte; **p. smoking,** fait de respirer la fumée des autres; **(b)** *Gram* passif; **the p. voice,** la voix passive. **2** *n Gram* **the p.,** la voix passive, le passif; **verb in the p.,** verbe *m* au passif.

passively ['pæsɪvlɪ] *adv* passivement.

passiveness ['pæsɪvnɪs], **passivity** [pæ'sɪvɪtɪ] *n* passivité *f* (*de l'esprit, d'un métal etc*).

passkey ['pɑːskiː] *n* (clef *f*) passe-partout *m inv*.

Passover ['pɑːsəʊvər] *n* la Pâque.

passport ['pɑːspɔːt] *n* passeport *m*; **ship's p.,** permis *m* de navigation; *Fig* **this job was her p. to fame,** ce travail a été son passeport pour la célébrité; **money is a p. to anything,** l'argent est un passe-partout.

password ['pɑːswɜːd] *n Mil Comptr etc* mot *m* de passe; **to give the p.,** donner le mot de passe.

past¹ [pɑːst] **1** *adj* passé; **those days are p.,** ces jours sont passés; **in p. times., in times p.,** autrefois, *Lit* au temps jadis; **p. chairman,** (*retiring chairman*) président sortant; (*former chairman*) ancien président; **she's a p. master at (doing) it,** elle est experte en la matière, elle est passée maître dans l'art de le faire; *Gram* **p. participle,** participe passé; **in the p. tense,** au passé; **the p. week,** la semaine dernière *ou* passée; **the p. two months,** les deux derniers mois, les deux mois passés; **for some time p.,** depuis quelque temps.

2 *n* **(a) the p.,** le passé; **in the p.,** autrefois; **it is a thing of the p.,** (*no longer exists*) ça n'existe plus; (*is old-fashioned*) c'est périmé; **to live in the p.,** vivre dans le passé;

(b) (*background*) (*of person*) antécédents *mpl*; **woman with a p.,** femme qui a eu des aventures *ou* qui a un passé; **town with a p.,** ville *f* historique; **our country's glorious p.,** le glorieux passé de notre pays;

(c) *Gram* **in the p.,** au passé; **p. perfect,** passé composé; **p. historic,** passé simple.

past² 1 *prep* (*beyond*) au delà de; **a little p. the bridge,** un peu plus loin que le pont; **to walk p. the house,** passer (devant) la maison; **it is p. four (o'clock),** il est quatre heures passées; **half/a quarter p. four,** quatre heures et demie/et quart; *Br* **ten (minutes) p. four,** quatre heures dix; **it is half p.,** il est la demie; **this bread is p. its sell-by date,** ce pain a dépassé sa date limite de vente; **p. all understanding,** qui dépasse toute compréhension; **p. endurance,** insupportable; **that's p. all belief,** cela est incroyable; **I'm p. work,** je ne suis plus d'âge à travailler; **to be p. caring for sth,** être revenu de qch; **I'm p. caring,** (*what happens, what you or they have done etc*) je n'en ai plus rien à faire; *F* **he's p. it,** il est trop vieux (*pour travailler, pour jouer au tennis etc*); *F* **I wouldn't put it p. her,** elle en est bien capable.

2 *adv* **to walk** *or* **go p.,** passer; **to run p.,** passer en courant; **to march p.,** défiler.

pasta ['pæstə] *n Culin* pâtes *fpl* (alimentaires).

paste¹ [peɪst] *n* **(a)** (*malleable substance*) pâte *f*; *Cer* **hard/soft p.,** pâte dure/tendre; *Culin* **anchovy p.,** pâte d'anchois; **fish p.,** = mousse *f* de poisson; **(b)** (*glue*) colle *f* (*de pâte*); **p. pot,** pot *m* de colle; **(c)** *Culin* (*for pastry*) pâte *f* (à pâtisserie); **(d)** (*jewellery*) stras(s) *m*; **it's only p.,** ce n'est que du toc.

paste² ** *vt* **(a) (*glue*) coller (*une affiche*); afficher (*un avis*); **to p. pictures on a screen,** coller des images sur un

écran; **(b)** *F* (*beat up*) battre, rosser (*qn*); (*defeat heavily*) mettre la pâtée à (*qn*).
pasteboard ['peɪstbɔːd] *n* carton *m*.
pastel ['pæst(ə)l] *n Art* (*crayon*) (crayon *m*) pastel *m*; (*drawing*) pastel; **p. drawing, drawing in p.,** (dessin *m* au) pastel; **p. blue,** bleu pastel; **p. shades,** tons pastels.
paste-up ['peɪstʌp] *n* (*in publishing*) maquette *f*.
pasteurization [pæstəraɪ'zeɪʃən] *n* pasteurisation *f*.
pasteurize ['pæstəraɪz] *vt* pasteuriser; **pasteurized milk,** lait pasteurisé.
pastiche [pæ'stiːʃ] *n* pastiche *m*.
pastille ['pæstɪl] *n* **(a)** pastille *f*; **fruit pastilles,** = pâtes *fpl* de fruits; **(b)** (*for fumigating the air*) pastille *f* à brûler.
pastime ['pɑːstaɪm] *n* passe-temps *m inv*, distraction *f*, divertissement *m*.
pastiness ['peɪstɪnɪs] *n* **(a)** (*of face*) teint terreux; **(b)** consistance pâteuse (*du pain etc*).
pasting ['peɪstɪŋ] *n* **(a)** (*gluing*) collage *m* (*d'affiches etc*); **(b)** *F* (*beating*) rossée *f*, raclée *f*; *Sp* **to get a p.,** être battu à plate(s) couture(s); *Sp* **to give s.o. a p.,** mettre la pâtée à qn.
pastor ['pɑːstər] *n Rel* pasteur *m*.
pastoral ['pɑːstərəl] **1** *adj* **(a)** (*rural*) pastoral, -aux; **p. land,** (terre *f* en) pâturages *mpl*; **(b)** *Rel* pastoral, -aux; **p. letter,** (lettre *f*) pastorale *f*, mandement *m* (*de l'évêque*); **(c)** *Sch* (*care*) qui concerne la santé physique et spirituelle des élèves. **2** *n* **(a)** *Liter Mus Art Th* pastorale *f*; **(b)** *Rel* (lettre *f*) pastorale *f*, mandement *m* (*de l'évêque*).
pastrami [pə'strɑːmɪ] *n Culin* = genre de viande fumée épicée.
pastry ['peɪstrɪ] *n* (*substance*) pâte *f*; (*cake*) pâtisserie *f*; **short p.,** pâte brisée; **flaky** *or* **puff p.,** pâte feuilletée; **choux p.,** pâte à choux; **p. board,** planche *f* à pâtisserie; **p. brush,** pinceau *m* à pâtisserie; **p. case,** fond *m* de tarte; **p. cutter,** emporte-pièce *m inv*; **p. cream,** crème pâtissière.
pastrycook ['peɪstrɪkʊk] *n* pâtissier, -ière.
pasturage ['pɑːstʃərɪdʒ] *n* **(a)** (*right*) (droit *m* de) pâturage *m ou* pacage *m*; **(b)** (*land*) = **PASTURE¹**.
pasture¹ ['pɑːstʃər] *n* **p. (ground** *or* **land),** (lieu *m* de) pâture *f*, pâturage *m*, herbage *m*; *F* **to be put out to p.,** être mis à la retraite *ou* au vert.
pasture² **1** *vi* paître, pâturer, pacager. **2** *vt* (*of shepherd*) (faire) paître (*les bêtes*); (*of animals*) pâturer (*un pré*).
pasty¹ ['peɪstɪ] *adj* **(a)** (*face*) terreux, brouillé; **(b)** (*texture*) pâteux.
pasty² ['pæstɪ] *n Culin* = (petit) pâté en croûte (*cuit sans moule*); **Cornish p.,** = pâté (en croûte) qui contient du bœuf, des pommes de terre et autres légumes.
pat¹ [pæt] *n* **(a)** (*tap*) petite tape; (*affectionate tap*) caresse *f*; **to give s.o. a p. on the back,** donner une tape dans le dos à qn; *Fig* (*congratulate*) féliciter qn; **(b)** (*sound*) bruit sourd (*de pas etc*); **(c)** (*lump*) rondelle *f*, médaillon *m* (*de beurre*); **cow p.,** bouse *f* de vache.
pat² *vt* (-tt-) taper, tapoter; caresser (*un animal etc*); flatter (*qn, un animal etc*) de la main; **to p. one's hair,** se tapoter les cheveux; **she patted the little boy's head,** elle a caressé la tête du petit garçon; **to p. s.o. on the back,** donner une tape dans le dos à qn; *Fig* (*congratulate*) féliciter qn; *Fig* **to p. oneself on the back,** se féliciter.
pat³ *adv* **his answer came p.,** il a répondu du tac au tac; **to know** *or* **have sth off p.,** savoir qch par cœur; **to stand p.,** *Cards* jouer d'autorité; *esp Am* (*not give in*) refuser de bouger.
pat⁴ **(a)** (*abbr* **patent**) brev.; **p. no.,** brev. no.; **(b)** (*abbr* **patented**) breveté.
pat down *vtsep* (*soil, cement etc*) tasser (doucement).
patch¹ [pætʃ] *n* **(a)** pièce *f* (*pour raccommoder un vêtement*); (*on garment*) pièce rapportée; *Comptr* (*correction*) correction *f*; *Nau* placard *m*; **to put a p. on a garment,** rapiécer un vêtement; *F* **his last novel isn't a p. on the others,** son dernier roman est loin de valoir les autres; **p. pocket,** poche rapportée *ou* appliquée; *El Tel* **p. board,** tableau *m* de commutation (à cordon); **p. cord,** cordon *m* de commutation; *Aut etc* **(rubber) p.,** (*for inner tube*) pastille *f*; (*for outer cover*) emplâtre *m*, guêtre *f*; **eye p.,** couvre-œil *m*, *pl* couvre-œils;

(b) (*mark*) tache *f* (*de couleur, de lumière etc*); nappe *f* (*de brume*); flaque *f* (*d'huile*); plaque *f* (*de verglas*); **p. of blue sky,** pan *m ou* coin *m ou* échappée *f* de ciel bleu; **rough patches,** (*on wood, metal etc*) aspérités *fpl*; **book that is good in patches,** livre qui contient de bons passages; *F* **to be going through** *or* **to strike a bad p.,** traverser une mauvaise période;

(c) (*area*) morceau *m*, coin *m*; lopin *m*, parcelle *f* (*de terre*); carré *m*, plant *m* (*de légumes*); *F* (*of police*) secteur *m*; **keep off my p.!,** (*territory*) ça c'est mon territoire (à moi)!
patch² *vt* mettre une pièce à, rapiécer (*un vêtement etc*); poser une pastille à (*une chambre à air*); placarder (*une voile*).
►**patch together** *vtsep F* (*temporarily join*) réunir (*les fragments de qch*); **they patched together a documentary,** ils ont monté un documentaire; *Pej* **the whole thing is a bit patched together,** tout est un peu mal fichu.
►**patch up** *vtsep F* **(a)** (*repair temporarily*) rafistoler (*qch, Fig son mariage*); *Med F* retaper (*qn*); **I managed to p. the car up,** j'ai réussi à retaper la voiture; **(b)** arranger (*une querelle*); **we've patched things up,** (*after quarrel, argument*) nous avons réussi à arranger les choses.
patching ['pætʃɪŋ] *n* rapiéçage *m*, rapiècement *m* (*d'un vêtement*); **we can use that old jacket for p.,** nous pouvons utiliser cette vieille veste pour faire du rapiècement *ou* rapiéçage.
patching up *n* rafistolage *m*.
patchwork ['pætʃwɜːk] *n* **(a)** *Sewing* patchwork *m*; *Fig* ouvrage fait de pièces et de morceaux *ou* de pièces disparates; **p. quilt,** couverture *f* en patchwork; **(b)** *Fig* **p. of fields,** campagne bigarrée.
patchy ['pætʃɪ] *adj* (*paintwork etc, Fig novel etc*) inégal, -aux.
pate [peɪt] *n Arch & F* (*head*) caboche *f*; **bald p.,** crâne *m* chauve.
pâté ['pæteɪ] *n Culin* pâté *m*; **liver p.,** pâté de foie; **p. sandwich,** sandwich *m* au pâté.
patella, *pl* **-ae, -as** [pə'telə, -iː, -əz] *n Anat* rotule *f*.
paten ['pæt(ə)n] *n Rel* patène *f*.
patent¹ ['peɪtənt, 'pæt-] **1** *adj* **(a)** (*protected by patent*) breveté; **p. medicine,** spécialité pharmaceutique *ou* médicale; **p. food,** spécialité alimentaire; **p. leather,** cuir verni; **p.-leather shoes,** chaussures vernies;

(b) *Jur* **letters p.,** lettres patentes *ou* de noblesse; (*of inventor*) lettres patentes, brevet *m* d'invention *ou* d'inventeur;

(c) (*evident*) manifeste, clair, évident; **how can we deny p. facts?,** comment nier l'évidence même?

2 *n* **(a)** (*right*) brevet *m* d'invention; (*invention*) invention *ou* fabrication brevetée; **to take out a p. for an invention,** faire breveter une invention; **p. applied for, p. pending,** (une) demande de brevet (a été) déposée; **infringement of a p.,** contrefaçon *f*; **p. agent,** agent *m* en brevets (d'invention); **p. application,** demande *f* de brevet; *US* **p. attorney,** conseil *m* en matière de brevets; **P. Office,** bureau *m* des brevets; office national de la propriété industrielle; **p. rights,** propriété industrielle;

(b) (*grant of nobility*) lettres patentes; **p. of nobility,** lettres d'anoblissement *ou* de noblesse.
patent² *vt* (*of authorities*) protéger par un brevet, breveter (*une invention*); (*of inventor*) faire breveter, prendre un brevet pour (*une invention*); **patented,** (*of invention etc*) breveté.
patentable ['peɪtəntəb(ə)l] *adj* brevetable.
patentee [peɪtən'tiː] *n* détenteur *m* d'un brevet.
patently ['peɪtəntlɪ] *adv* manifestement, clairement; **he was p. lying,** il était manifeste qu'il mentait; **it was p. obvious that ...,** il était absolument évident que ... .
patentor ['peɪtəntər] *n* organisme *m* délivrant un brevet.
pater ['peɪtər] *n Old-fashioned F* papa *m*, le paternel.
paterfamilias [peɪtəfə'mɪlɪæs] *n* chef *m* de famille.
paternal [pə'tɜːnəl] *adj* paternel; **the p. roof,** la maison paternelle; **the p. side,** le côté paternel.
paternalism [pə'tɜːnəlɪz(ə)m] *n* paternalisme *m*.
paternally [pə'tɜːnəlɪ] *adv* paternellement.
paternity [pə'tɜːnɪtɪ] *n* paternité *f*; **there are doubts about his p.,** on n'est pas sûr de l'identité de son père; *Jur* **p. suit,** procès *m* en paternité.
path, *pl* **paths** [pɑːθ, pɑːðz] *n* **(a)** chemin *m*, sentier *m*; (*in garden*) allée *f*; *Fig* (*in research etc*) voie *f*; **mule p.,** sentier muletier; *Fig* **the p. of glory,** le chemin de la gloire; **he killed everyone in his p.,** il a tué tout le monde sur son chemin; **in the p. of a vehicle,** sur le chemin d'un véhicule; **their paths had crossed before,** leurs chemins s'étaient déjà croisés; **(b)** (*course*) cours *m*, trajet *m*, course *f* (*d'un corps en mouvement*); trajectoire *f* (*d'un projectile, d'une particule, d'une planète etc*); passage *m*, trajet *m* (*d'un rayon de lumière*); route *f* (*du soleil*); **p. of a bullet,** (*through the air*) trajectoire d'une balle; (*through the body*) trajet *m ou* sillon *m* d'une balle; *Av* **flight p.,** ligne *f* de vol; **glide p.,** axe *m* de descente, trajectoire d'atterrissage.
pathetic [pə'θetɪk] *adj* **(a)** (*sight etc*) pathétique, touchant,

attendrissant; *F* (*excuse, game etc*) lamentable, pitoyable; **she's a p. creature,** c'est une créature pitoyable; *Br F* **you're p.!,** tu me fais pitié!, tu es lamentable!; *F* **how p.!, it's p.!, isn't it p.?,** c'est malheureux *ou* pitoyable!; **(b)** *Lit* **the p. fallacy,** l'attribution des caractéristiques humaines à la nature.

pathetically [pə'θetɪklɪ] *adv* **(a)** pitoyablement; **they wept p.,** ils pleuraient d'une façon pitoyable; **she looked at him p.,** elle lui jeta un regard pitoyable; **(b)** *F* (*ridiculously*) lamentablement; **some p. easy questions,** des questions d'une facilité invraisemblable; **that's a p. weak excuse,** c'est une excuse lamentable; **he's so p. arrogant,** il est d'une arrogance ridicule, il est arrogant à en être ridicule.

pathfinder ['pɑːθfaɪndər] *n* **(a)** (*pioneer*) pionnier *m*; **(b)** *Av* avion éclaireur.

pathological [pæθə'lɒdʒɪk(ə)l] *adj* (*hatred, liar etc*) pathologique.

pathologically [pæθə'lɒdʒɪklɪ] *adv* pathologiquement.

pathologist [pə'θɒlədʒɪst] *n* pathologiste *mf*; **(forensic) p.,** médecin *m* légiste.

pathology [pə'θɒlədʒɪ] *n* pathologie *f*.

pathos ['peɪθɒs] *n* pathétique *m*; *Phil* pathos *m*.

pathway ['pɑːθweɪ] *n* sentier *m*.

patience ['peɪʃəns] *n* **(a)** patience *f*; **to try** *or* **tax s.o.'s p.,** éprouver la patience de qn; **my p. is exhausted** *or* **is at an end,** ma patience est à bout, je suis à bout de patience; **(have) p.!,** (prenez) patience!; **to lose p.,** perdre patience; **I've no p. with him,** il m'impatiente; **p. is a virtue,** la patience est une vertu; **to suffer in p.,** souffrir avec patience; **(b)** *Br Cards* réussite *f*; **to play p.,** faire des réussites.

patient ['peɪʃənt] **1** *adj* patient, endurant; **to be p.,** patienter, prendre patience; **you will have to be p.,** il vous faudra être patient. **2** *n* malade *mf*, patient, -ente; (*in operation*) opéré, -ée; **a doctor and his patients,** un médecin et ses clients *ou* patients; **p. care,** soins administrés aux patients.

patiently ['peɪʃəntlɪ] *adv* patiemment; **to wait p.,** attendre patiemment *ou* avec patience.

patina ['pætɪnə] *n* patine *f*; **to take on a p.,** (*of bronze*) se patiner.

patio ['pætɪəʊ] *n Archit* patio *m*.

patriarch ['peɪtrɪɑːk] *n Rel etc* patriarche *m*; *Br* fondateur *m* (*d'une organisation etc*).

patriarchal [peɪtrɪ'ɑːk(ə)l] *adj* patriarcal, -aux.

patriarchy ['peɪtrɪɑːkɪ] *n* patriarcat *m*, système patriarcal.

patrician [pə'trɪʃən] *adj & n Antiq etc* patricien, -ienne.

patricide ['pætrɪsaɪd] *n* **(a)** (*person*) parricide *mf*; **(b)** (*offence*) (crime *m* de) parricide *m*.

patrimony ['pætrɪmənɪ] **(a)** (*inheritance*) patrimoine *m*; **(b)** (*of church*) biens-fonds *mpl ou* revenu *m* d'une église.

patriot ['peɪtrɪət, 'pæ-] *n* patriote *mf*.

patriotic [peɪtrɪ'ɒtɪk, pæ-] *adj* (*person*) patriote; (*speech etc*) patriotique.

patriotically [peɪtrɪ'ɒtɪklɪ, pæ-] *adv* patriotiquement, en patriote, avec patriotisme.

patriotism ['peɪtrɪətɪz(ə)m, 'pæ-] *n* patriotisme *m*.

patrol¹ [pə'trəʊl] *n* patrouille *f*; (*of police*) patrouille (*de surveillance*); (*of nightwatchman, police officer on foot*) ronde *f*; **security p.,** patrouille de sûreté *ou* de protection; **to be on p.,** être en patrouille, patrouiller; *Av* **fighter p.,** patrouille de chasse; **traffic p.,** patrouille de la circulation (routière); **A.A. p.,** (*person*) patrouilleur *m* de l'Automobile Association; (*car*) voiture *f* de patrouille de l'Automobile Association; **p. bomber,** patrouilleur de bombardement, bombardier patrouilleur; **p. car,** voiture *f* de reconnaissance *ou* de liaison policière; *Nau* **p. craft** *or* **vessel,** patrouilleur, vedette *f* de surveillance; **p. leader,** (*in scouts*) chef *m* de patrouille.

patrol² *v* **(-ll-) 1** *vi* patrouiller, aller en patrouille. **2** *vt* faire la patrouille dans (*un quartier*); patrouiller à (*la frontière*).

patrolman, *pl* **-men** [pə'trəʊlmən] *n* **(a)** *Br* (*employee of AA, RAC etc*) patrouilleur *m*; **(b)** *US* agent *m* de police (en service de ronde).

patrolwoman, *pl* **-women** [pə'trəʊlwʊmən, -wɪmɪn] *n US* femme *f* agent de police (en service de ronde).

patron ['peɪtrən] *n* **(a)** protecteur *m*, mécène *m* (*des artistes, des arts etc*); patron *m* (*d'une œuvre de charité etc*); *Rel* patron, collateur *m* (*d'un bénéfice*); *Rel* **p. saint,** (saint) patron, (sainte) patronne; **(b)** *Com* client, -ente (*d'un magasin*); (*regular*) habitué, -ée.

patronage ['pætrənɪdʒ] *n* **(a)** protection *f*; (*of art*) mécénat *m*; (*of charity*) patronage *m*; *Pej* air protecteur (*envers qn*); **concert under the p. of ...,** concert patronné par ...; **(b)** clientèle *f* (*d'un hôtel etc*); **(c)** *Church of Eng* droit *m* de présentation (*à un bénéfice*).

patroness ['peɪtrənɪs] *n Old-fashioned* protectrice *f* (*des arts etc*); (dame *f*) patronnesse *f* (*d'une œuvre de charité*).

patronize ['pætrənaɪz] *vt* **(a)** patronner, protéger (*un artiste etc*); encourager (*un art*); subventionner (*un hôpital etc*); souscrire pour *ou* à (*une œuvre de bienfaisance*); **(b)** *Pej* traiter (*qn*) d'un air protecteur *ou* avec condescendance; **(c)** *Com* accorder sa clientèle à (*une maison*); être un habitué de (*un cinéma, un restaurant etc*); **a restaurant patronized by the famous,** un restaurant fréquenté par des gens célèbres.

patronizing ['pætrənaɪzɪŋ] *adj* (*ton, air*) condescendant, paternaliste.

patronizingly ['pætrənaɪzɪŋlɪ] *adv* (*to look*) d'un air de condescendance; (*to say*) d'un ton de condescendance *ou* paternaliste.

patronymic [pætrə'nɪmɪk] **1** *adj* patronymique. **2** *n* patronyme *m*, nom *m* patronymique.

patsy ['pætsɪ] *n Am Sl* (*dupe*) gobeur *m*, jobard *m*.

patten ['pæt(ə)n] *n* socque *m* (*pour protéger les chaussures contre la boue*).

patter¹ ['pætər] *n* petit bruit (*de pas précipités etc*); trottinement *m* (*de souris*); fouettement *m* (*de la pluie*); **soon we'll be hearing the p. of tiny feet,** la famille s'élargira bientôt.

patter² *vi* trottiner *ou* marcher à petits pas rapides; (*of rain*) fouetter.

patter³ *n* (*of sales person*) baratin *m*, boniment *m*; (*of comedian*) bagout *m*; (*chatter*) bavardage *m*.

patter⁴ 1 *vt* marmotter, expédier (*ses prières etc*). **2** *vi* (*chatter*) bavarder sans arrêt, jaser, caqueter.

►**patter about** *vi* (*walk, run with rapid small steps*) trottiner çà et là.

pattern¹ ['pæt(ə)n] *n* **(a)** (*design*) dessin *m*, motif *m* (*de papier peint etc*); *Tex* broché *m* (*d'un tissu*); grille *f* (*de mots croisés*); groupement *m* (*des points d'impact de projectiles sur une cible, sur le sol etc*); gerbe *f* (*d'un fusil tirant des cartouches à plombs*); *Comptr* combinaison *f* (*de perforations*); **streets arranged in an orderly p.,** rues établies suivant un plan ordonné; **the normal p. of trade,** la tendance normale du marché; **some clear patterns emerge from the statistics,** des tendances nettes ressortent des statistiques; *Mil Av* **p. bombing,** bombardement *m* systématique;

(b) (*model*) modèle *m*, dessin *m*, maquette *f*; *Sewing etc* patron *m* (*en papier etc*); *Knitting* modèle; *Metal* modèle, gabarit *m*, calibre *m* (*de fonderie*); **machines all built to one p.,** machines construites *ou* fabriquées toutes sur le même modèle; *Sewing* **to cut out a shirt to** *or* **from a p.,** tailler une chemise sur un patron; *Ind* **p. designer,** dessinateur, -trice de modèles;

(c) (*example*) modèle *m*, exemple *m*; **to be a p. of virtue,** être un exemple *ou* un modèle de vertu;

(d) *Com* échantillon *m*; **p. book/card,** livre *m*/carte *f* d'échantillons.

pattern² *vt* **(a)** (*draw patterns on*) tracer des dessins *ou* des motifs sur (*qch*); (*decorate with patterns*) orner (*qch*) de motifs; **(b)** (*model*) **to p. sth after** *or* **(up)on sth,** modeler qch sur qch.

patterned ['pætənd] *adj* à dessins.

patty ['pætɪ] *n Culin* pâté *m* (en croûte).

paucity ['pɔːsɪtɪ] *n* (*of information, proof etc*) manque *m*; (*rarity*) rareté *f*.

paunch [pɔːntʃ] *n* panse *f*, ventre *m*, *F* bedaine *f* (*de qn*); panse, rumen *m* (*des ruminants*); **to develop a p.,** prendre du ventre.

paunchy ['pɔːntʃɪ] *adj* ventru.

pauper ['pɔːpər] *n* indigent, -ente; **to die a p.,** mourir dans l'indigence; *Arch* **p.'s grave,** fosse commune.

pause¹ [pɔːz] *n* **(a)** pause *f*, arrêt *m*; (*in recording*) blanc *m* sonore; (*in conversation etc*) silence *m*; **to make a p.,** faire une pause; **(b)** (*in poetry*) repos *m*; (*caesura*) césure *f*; **(c)** *Mus* point *m* d'orgue; (*over a rest*) point d'arrêt; **(d)** *esp Lit* **to give s.o. p.,** faire hésiter qn.

pause² *vi* **(a)** (*stop*) (*when working*) faire une pause; (*when speaking, leaving etc*) marquer un temps; **he paused at the door to say to me ...,** il s'est arrêté à la porte pour me dire ...; **to p. for breath/thought,** faire une pause pour reprendre son souffle/réfléchir; **(b)** (*hesitate*) hésiter; **to make s.o. p.,** faire hésiter qn; (*make someone think*) donner à réfléchir à qn; **(c) to p. on a word,** s'arrêter sur un mot; *Mus* **to p. on a note,** tenir une note.

pave [peɪv] *vt* paver (*une rue etc*); carreler (*une cour etc*); **to p. the way,** préparer le terrain (**for sth,** pour qch); **the streets here aren't paved with gold,** on ne roule pas sur l'or ici.

pavement ['peɪvmənt] *n* **(a)** *esp Br* (*path beside road, street*) trottoir *m*; **p. artist,** artiste *mf* de trottoir; **p. café,** café *m* en terrasse; **(b)** *Am* (*roadway*) chaussée *f*; **(c)** (*material*) pavé *m*; **wood(-block) p.,** pavé en bois; **cobblestone** *or* **cobbled p.,** empierrement *m* en cailloux.

pavilion [pə'vɪlɪən] *n* **(a)** *Br Sp etc* pavillon *m*; *Mus* **Chinese p.,** chapeau chinois; **(b)** *Archit* pavillon *m*.

paving ['peɪvɪŋ] *n* **(a)** (*action*) pavage *m*; carrelage *m*; **p. stone,** pierre *f* à paver, pavé *m*; **p. tile,** carreau *m* (de pavage); **(b)** (*surface*) pavé *m*, dalles *fpl*.

Pavlova [pæv'ləʊvə] *n Culin* vacherin *m*; **raspberry P.,** vacherin à la framboise.

Pavlovian [pæv'ləʊvɪən] *adj Biol* (*treatment, reaction, response*) pavlovien.

paw¹ [pɔː] *n* patte *f* (*d'animal onguiculé, F de qn*); *F* **paws off!,** bas les pattes!; *F* **you're not getting your dirty** *or* **sweaty paws on my new bike!,** il n'est pas question que tu touches à mon nouveau vélo.

paw² **1** *vt* **(a)** (*of animal*) donner des coups de patte *ou* de griffe à (*qn, qch*); **to p. the ground,** (*of horse*) gratter (la terre) du pied; **(b)** *F* (*of person*) tripoter, peloter (*qn*). **2** *vi* (*of horse*) gratter la terre du pied.

pawky ['pɔːkɪ] *adj Scot* rusé.

pawl [pɔːl] *n MecE etc* linguet *m*, ginguet *m* (*de cabestan etc*); cliquet *m* (*d'arrêt*); **p. and ratchet wheel,** roue *f ou* encliquetage *m* à rochet.

pawn¹ [pɔːn] *n* **(a)** (*object pawned*) gage *m*, nantissement *m*; **(b)** **in p.,** en gage; **to put one's watch in p.,** mettre sa montre en gage *ou* au mont-de-piété *ou F* au clou; **p. ticket,** reconnaissance *f* (de dépôt de gage).

pawn² *vt* mettre (*qch*) en gage, engager (*qch*); engager (*sa vie, son honneur*).

pawn³ *n Chess* pion *m*; *Fig* **to be s.o.'s p.,** être le jouet de qn.

pawnbroker ['pɔːnbrəʊkər] *n* prêteur, -euse sur gage(s).

pawnbroking ['pɔːnbrəʊkɪŋ] *n* prêt *m* sur gage(s).

pawnshop ['pɔːnʃɒp] *n* bureau *m* de prêt sur gage(s).

pawpaw ['pɔːpɔː] *n* = **PAPAW**.

pax [pæks] **1** *n Rel* paix *f*. **2** *int Old-fashioned* pouce!

pay¹ [peɪ] *n* **(a)** paie *f*; salaire *m* (*d'un ouvrier etc*); gages *mpl* (*d'un domestique*); traitement *m* (*d'un fonctionnaire*); indemnité *f* (*d'un parlementaire*); *Mil* solde *f*; **basic p.,** salaire *ou* traitement de base; **take-home p.,** salaire net; **back p.,** arrérages *mpl ou* rappel *m* de traitement *ou* de salaire; **to get an extra £10 a week in one's p.,** toucher 10 livres de salaire en plus par semaine; **the p.'s good/terrible,** ça paie bien/mal; *Pej* **to be in s.o.'s p.,** être à la solde *ou* aux gages de qn; **p. award** *or* **increase,** augmentation *f* de salaire; *Mil* **p. book,** livret *m* de solde; **p. cheque,** chèque *m* de règlement de traitement *ou* de salaire; **p. packet,** paie; salaire; **p. rise,** augmentation de salaire; **p. slip,** bulletin *m ou* feuille *f* de paie;

(b) (*payment*) **p. bed,** lit *m* pour malade payant (*dans un hôpital*); **p. desk,** caisse *f*; **p. phone,** téléphone public; (*enclosed*) cabine téléphonique; **p. TV,** télévision *f* à péage.

pay² *v* (*pt & pp* **paid** [peɪd]) **1** *vt* **(a)** payer, régler, acquitter (*un compte, une facture*); payer (*une amende*); payer, liquider, régler, acquitter (*une dette*); rembourser (*un créancier*); **to p. s.o. £100,** payer 100 livres à qn; **how much do you p. for tea?,** combien coûte le thé?; **I expect to p. my way,** je m'attends à payer mon écot; **to be paid in four instalments,** payable en quatre versements; **to p. cash (down)** *or* **ready money,** payer (argent) comptant, payer au comptant; **p. self, p. cash,** (*on cheque*) payez (à l'ordre de) moi-même; **to p. money into s.o.'s account,** verser de l'argent au compte de qn; **paid,** (*on receipted bill*) pour acquit; *F* **to put paid to,** anéantir (*un espoir, un projet*); **carriage paid,** port payé;

(b) payer (*ses employés etc*); **to be paid by the hour/the week,** être payé à l'heure/la semaine; **badly paid job,** situation mal payée; **to p. s.o. to do sth,** payer qn pour faire qch; **I wouldn't do it if you paid me,** je ne le ferais pas même si on me payait;

(c) (*give*) **to p. tribute** *or* **homage to s.o.,** rendre hommage à qn; **to p. one's respects to s.o.,** présenter ses respects à qn; **to p. a visit to s.o.,** rendre visite à qn; **p. attention to what you are doing,** faites attention à ce que vous faites;

(d) (*profit*) **it will p. you to do it,** c'est dans votre intérêt de le faire.

2 *vi* **(a)** payer; *F* **to make s.o. p. through the nose,** écorcher qn; **who's paying?,** qui paie?; **p. at the gate** *or* **door,** entrée payante; **p. as you earn** *or Am* **as you go,** retenue *f* (de l'impôt sur le revenu) à la base *ou* à la source; **how would you like to p.?,** comment souhaitez-vous régler?; **to p. by cheque,** payer par chèque; **to p. on account,** verser une somme à titre de provision;

(b) *Com Fin etc* **to p. on demand,** payer à vue *ou* à présentation; **p. to the order of ...,** payez à l'ordre de ...;

(c) (*be profitable*) **business that doesn't p.,** affaire qui ne rapporte pas *ou* qui ne paie pas *ou* qui n'est pas rentable; **it wouldn't p.,** cela ne rapporterait pas; **it pays to advertise,** la publicité rapporte; **it pays to be honest,** l'honnêteté est toujours récompensée.

▶**pay back** *vtsep* **(a)** rembourser, restituer (*un emprunt*); **I'll p. you back tomorrow,** je te rembourserai demain; *Fig* **to p. s.o. back in his own coin,** rendre la pareille à qn; **(b)** (*have revenge on*) **I'll p. you back for this!,** je te le revaudrai!, tu me le paieras!

▶**pay for** *vipo* payer (*qch*); **his uncle paid for his schooling,** son oncle a subvenu aux frais de ses études; *F* **he'll p. for this!, I'll make him p. for this!,** il me le payera!

▶**pay in** *vtsep* encaisser (*un chèque*).

▶**pay off** **1** *vtsep* **(a)** (*finish paying*) liquider, régler (*une dette etc*); rembourser (*un créancier*); purger (*une hypothèque*); **(b)** (*dismiss*) congédier (*des ouvriers etc*); licencier (*des troupes*); débarquer (*des marins*); **(c)** *F* (*bribe*) soudoyer (*qn*), donner des pots de vin à (*qn*). **2** *vi* (*of deal etc*) être payant *ou* rentable *ou* fructueux; (*of efforts etc*) porter des fruits; **all these years of work have paid off at last,** nous sommes enfin récompensés après toutes ces années de travail.

▶**pay out** **1** *vtsep* **(a)** (*spend*) payer, verser, débourser; **I've had to p. out a lot on car repairs this year,** j'ai eu beaucoup à débourser pour les réparations de voiture cette année; **(b)** (*issue*) payer (*les salaires*); **(c)** (*pt* **payed**) *Nau* (laisser) filer (*un câble*). **2** *vi* (*spend money*) débourser.

▶**pay up** **1** *vi* (*pay debt*) payer, *F* s'exécuter; **I finally made him p. up,** j'ai finalement réussi à le faire payer *ou* débourser. **2** *vtsep* (*pay*) payer; **she finally paid up what she owed me,** elle a fini par me payer ce qu'elle me devait.

payable ['peɪəb(ə)l] **1** *adj* **(a)** payable; **rates p. by the tenant,** = impôts à la charge du locataire; *Com* **p. at sight/to order/to bearer,** payable à vue/à ordre/au porteur; **to make a bill p. to s.o.,** faire un billet à l'ordre de qn; **cheque p. to bearer,** chèque *m* au porteur; **bonds made p. in francs,** bons libellés en francs; **bills p.,** factures *fpl* à payer; **(b)** *Min* (*seam etc*) exploitable. **2** *US npl* **payables,** factures *fpl* à payer.

paycheck ['peɪtʃek] *n Am* chèque *m* de règlement de traitement *ou* de salaire.

payday ['peɪdeɪ] *n* jour *m* de paie.

PAYE [piːeɪwaɪ'iː] *n Br abbr* **pay as you earn**.

payee [peɪ'iː] *n* bénéficiaire *mf* (*d'un bon de poste etc*); *Com* porteur *m* (*d'un effet*).

payer ['peɪər] *n* payeur, -euse; **he's a good/bad p.,** c'est un bon/mauvais payeur.

paying ['peɪɪŋ] **1** *adj* **(a)** (*élève etc*) payant; **p. guest,** pensionnaire *mf*; **(b)** (*business etc*) rémunérateur, -trice, profitable, qui rapporte. **2** *n* paiement *m*, versement *m* (*d'argent*).

paying back *n* remboursement *m*, restitution *f* (*d'un emprunt*).

paying in *n* versement *m* (*d'argent à la banque etc*); **p.-in book,** carnet *m* de versements.

paying off *n* **(a)** liquidation *f*, règlement *m* (*d'une dette*); purge *f* (*d'une hypothèque*); **(b)** congédiement *m* (*des ouvriers etc*); licencement *m* (*de troupes*); débarquement *m* (*de marins*).

paying out *n* **(a)** (*of money*) déboursement *m*; **(b)** *Nau* filage *m* (*d'un câble etc*).

paying up *n* = **PAYING OUT (a)**.

payload ['peɪləʊd] *n* charge payante *ou* utile (*d'un véhicule*); charge utile (*d'un missile*); *Av* poids *m* utile.

paymaster ['peɪmɑːstər] *n* intendant *m*, caissier *m*, payeur *m*; *Mil etc* trésorier *m*; *Nau* commissaire *m*; **the terrorists' p.,** le commanditaire des terroristes.

payment ['peɪmənt] *n* **(a)** (*act or fact of paying*) paiement *m*, versement *m* (*d'argent*); paiement, règlement *m*, acquittement *m* (*d'une dette etc*); remboursement *m* (*d'un créancier*); **terms of p.,** conditions *fpl* de paiement; **cash p.,** paiement (au) comptant; **p. by cheque,** paiement par chèque; **to stop p. on a cheque,** faire opposition sur un chèque; **p. by instalments,** paiement par acomptes *ou* échelonné; **(hire purchase) p.,** traite *f*; **I'm behind on the**

payments, j'ai du retard dans les paiements; **on p. of £100,** contre paiement de 100 livres; **non p.,** défaut *m* de paiement; **to present a bill for p.,** présenter un effet au paiement *ou* à l'encaissement;

(b) (*remuneration*) paiement *m*, rémunération *f*; **as (a) p. for your services,** en rémunération de vos services; **she would not accept p.,** elle n'a pas voulu accepter de paiement.

payoff ['peɪɒf] *n* **(a)** (*final payment*) paiement *m*, règlement *m*; **(b)** *F* (*bribe*) pot-de-vin *m*, *pl* pots-de vin; **(c)** *F* (*ending*) dénouement *m* (*de l'histoire*); **(d)** (*outcome*) (*retribution*) rétribution *f*; (*reward*) récompense *f*.

payroll ['peɪrəʊl] *n* **(a)** (*list of employees*) feuille *f* des appointements *ou* des salaires; *Mil etc* feuille *ou* état *m* de solde; **to be on the p.,** étre salarié; **how many do you have on the p.?,** combien d'employés avez-vous?; *Pej* **he's on our p.,** (*we're bribing him*) on l'a acheté; **(b)** (*money paid*) masse salariale.

pc ['piː'siː] *n* **(a)** *Comptr* (*abbr* **personal computer**) O.I. *m*; **(b)** *abbr* **postcard.**

PC ['piː'siː] *n Br* (*abbr* **Police Constable**) = agent *m* de police.

PCB [piːsiː'biː] *n* **(a)** *Ch* (*abbr* **polychlorinated biphenyl**) polychlorobiphényle *m*; **(b)** *Comptr abbr* **printed circuit board.**

PD ['piː'diː] *n US* (*abbr* **Police Department**) service *m* de police.

pdq [piːdiː'kjuː] *adv Sl* (*abbr* **pretty damn(ed) quick**) illico presto, rapido.

PDSA [piːdiːe'seɪ] *n Br* (*abbr* **People's Dispensary for Sick Animals**) ≈ SPA.

PE ['piː'iː] *n Sch* (*abbr* **physical education**) EPS *f*; **PE lesson/teacher,** cours *m* /professeur *m* d'EPS.

pea [piː] *n* pois *m*; *Culin* **(green) peas,** petits pois; **split peas,** pois cassés; **sweet p.,** (*flower*) pois de senteur; **p. green,** vert feuille *m inv*; *Nau* **p. jacket,** caban *m*; **p. pod,** cosse *f* de pois; **like two peas in a pod,** comme deux gouttes d'eau; **p. soup,** soupe *f* aux pois (cassés); (*thick*) purée *f* de pois.

peace [piːs] *n* **(a)** paix *f*; (*treaty*) traité *m* de paix; **at p.,** en paix (**with,** avec); **to live in p. with one's neighbours,** (*of person, tribe, country*) vivre en harmonie avec ses voisins; **in time of p.,** en temps de paix; **to make (one's) p. with s.o.,** faire la paix *ou* se réconcilier avec qn; **p. treaty,** traité *m* de paix; **p. campaigner,** militant *m* pour la paix, pacifiste *mf*; *US* **P. Corps,** = organisme américain de coopération; **p. movement,** mouvement *m* pacifiste; **p. negotiations,** négociations pour la paix; **p. pipe, pipe of p.,** calumet *m* de la paix; **p. studies,** études *fpl* sur la paix; **p. offering,** cadeau *m* de réconciliation; **the P. of Amiens,** la Paix d'Amiens;

(b) (*public order*) **p. and order,** la paix et l'ordre public, le repos public; **to keep the p.,** (*of citizen*) ne pas troubler l'ordre public; (*of police, troops*) veiller à l'ordre public; **to break** *or* **disturb the p.,** troubler *ou* violer l'ordre public; (*at night*) faire du tapage nocturne; **justice of the p.,** = juge *m* de paix;

(c) (*tranquillity*) tranquillité *f* (*de l'âme, du soir etc*); **for the sake of p. and quiet,** pour avoir la paix; **to leave s.o. in p.,** laisser qn tranquille; **he gave me no p. until ...,** il ne m'a pas laissé en paix tant que ...; *esp Rel* **go in p.!,** allez en paix!; **p. of mind,** tranquillité d'esprit; **it will give you p. of mind,** ça te tranquillisera; **to be at p.,** (*of dead person*) reposer en paix; **to hold one's p.,** se taire.

peaceable ['piːsəb(ə)l] *adj* **(a)** pacifique, qui aime la paix; **p. man,** homme *m* de paix; **(b)** = **PEACEFUL (b)** .

peaceably ['piːsəblɪ] *adv* pacifiquement.

peaceful ['piːsfʊl] *adj* **(a)** (*calm*) paisible, calme, tranquille; (*death*) tranquille; **(b)** (*not warlike, aggressive*) pacifique, qui ne trouble pas la paix; **p. settlement of a dispute,** règlement *m* pacifique d'un litige.

peacefully ['piːsfʊlɪ] *adv* (*see adj*) **(a)** paisiblement, tranquillement; **p., at home,** (*in death notice*) mort dans son lit; **(b)** pacifiquement.

peacefulness ['piːsfʊlnɪs] *n* tranquillité *f*, paix *f*.

peacekeeping ['piːskiːpɪŋ] *n* maintien *m* de la paix; *Mil* **p. force,** force *f* de maintien de la paix.

peace-loving ['piːslʌvɪŋ] *adj* (*nation*) pacifique, qui aime la paix.

peacetime ['piːstaɪm] *n* temps *m* de paix; **in p.,** en temps de paix.

peach¹ [piːtʃ] *n* pêche *f*; **p. (tree),** pêcher *m*; **p. (colour),** (couleur *f*) fleur de pêcher *inv*; *F* **she's a p.,** c'est une jolie pépée; *F* **it's a p.,** c'est magnifique.

peach² *vi Sl Old-fashioned* **to p. on s.o.,** moucharder qn.

peacock ['piːkɒk] *n* (*bird*) paon *m*; **as proud as a p.,** fier comme un paon; **p. (blue),** bleu paon *m inv*; **p. butterfly,** paon (du jour).

peahen ['piːhen] *n* paonne *f*.

peak¹ [piːk] *n* **(a)** pic *m*, cime *f*, sommet *m* (*de montagne*); **the highest peaks,** les plus hauts sommets; *Culin* **whisk the egg white until it forms stiff peaks,** battre le blanc en neige bien ferme; **(b)** (*maximum point*) pointe *f*, apogée *m* (*d'une courbe, d'une charge*); *Med* pointe, poussée *f* (*d'une fièvre*); *Phys* crête *f* (*d'une onde*); **p. load,** charge *f* maximum; débit *m* maximum (*d'un générateur*); **prosperity was at its p.,** la prospérité était à son apogée *ou* à son maximum; *El TV etc* **p. hours** *or* **period,** (*for traffic*) heures *fpl* de pointe; (*in shop etc*) heures d'affluence; *TV* **p. viewing hours,** heures d'écoute maximale; **(c)** visière *f* (*de casquette etc*); bec *m* (*d'une selle de bicyclette, d'une ancre etc*); pointe *f* (*de barbe, de toit etc*); **widow's p.,** pointe de cheveux sur le front; **(d)** *Nau* coqueron *m* (*de la cale*); pic *m*, corne *f*, empointure *f* (*de voile*).

peak² **1** *vi* **(a)** (*of curve etc*) passer par son apogée; **inflation peaked at 10%,** l'inflation a fait une pointe à 10%, l'inflation a atteint un niveau record de 10%; **(b)** (*of whale*) plonger (à pic). **2** *vt Nau* apiquer (*une vergue*).

▶**peak out** *vi* (*reach top limit*) atteindre un niveau record.

peaked [piːkt] *adj* (*casquette*) à visière.

peaky ['piːkɪ] *adj F* pâlot, malingre, souffreteux; **to look p.,** avoir les traits tirés.

peal¹ [piːl] *n* (*bells*) carillon *m*; (*noise*) carillonnement *m*; grondement *m* (*du tonnerre, de l'orgue*); coup *m* (*de tonnerre*); **to ring a p.,** sonner un carillon, carillonner; **peals of laughter,** éclats *mpl* de rire.

peal² **1** *vi* (*of bells*) (*chime*) carillonner; (*ring out loudly*) sonner à toute volée; (*of thunder, of the organ*) retentir, gronder; (*of laughter*) résonner. **2** *vt* sonner (*les cloches*) à toute volée; carillonner (*un air*).

peanut ['piːnʌt] *n* cacah(o)uète *f*, cacahouette *f*; **p. oil,** huile *m* d'arachide; **p. butter,** beurre *m* de cacah(o)uète; *F* **peanuts,** deux fois rien.

pear [peər] *n* poire *f*; **butter p.,** beurré *m*; **p. (tree),** poirier *m*; *El* **p. switch,** (interrupteur *m* à) poire.

peardrop ['peədrɒp] *n* bonbon parfumé à la poire.

pearl¹ [pɜːl] *n* perle *f*; **cultured p.,** perle cultivée *ou* de culture; *Prov* **to cast pearls before swine,** jeter des perles aux pourceaux; *F* **she's a p.,** c'est une perle *ou* un trésor; **he comes out with some real pearls,** (*amusing comments etc*) il sort de vraies perles; **mother of p.,** nacre *f* (de perle); **p. button,** bouton *m* de nacre; **p. diver,** pêcheur *m* de perles; **p. grey,** gris de perle *inv*, gris perle *inv*; **p. oyster,** huître perlière; **p. necklace,** collier *m* de perles; *El* **p. lamp,** ampoule opale; **p. barley/tapioca,** orge/tapioca perlé; **pearls of dew,** perles de rosée; **p. moss,** mousse perlée *ou* d'Irlande.

pearl² **1** *vi* **(a)** (*of moisture etc*) perler, former des gouttelettes; **(b)** (*dive for pearls*) pêcher des perles. **2** *vt* perler (*de l'orge*); *Culin* cuire (*le sucre*) au perlé.

pearl³ *n* = **PURL¹.**

pearl⁴ *vt* = **PURL².**

pearly ['pɜːlɪ] **1** *adj* perlé; **p. (white) teeth,** dents perlées *ou* de perle; *F* **the P. Gates,** les portes du Paradis; **p. king/queen,** = marchand/marchande des quatre saisons de Londres (*qui porte les jours de fête un costume couvert de boutons de nacre*); **p. nautilus,** (*mollusc*) nautile *m*, nautilus *m*. **2** *n* **(a)** (*button*) bouton *m* de nacre; **(b)** (*person*) = membre d'une famille de pearly kings.

peasant ['pezənt] *n* paysan, -anne; *Pej* rustre *mf*.

peasantry ['pezəntrɪ] *n* (*people*) les paysans.

pease [piːz] *n* **p. pudding,** purée *f* de pois (cassés).

peashooter ['piːʃuːtər] *n* petite sarbacane.

peasouper ['piːsuːpər] *n esp Br F* (*fog*) purée *f* de pois, brouillard *m* (jaune) à couper au couteau.

peat [piːt] *n* tourbe *f*; **turf** *or* **sod** *or* **block of p.,** motte *f* de tourbe; **p. bog,** tourbière *f*; **p. cutting** *or* **digging,** tourbage *m*; **p. cutter,** tourbier *m*; **p. moss,** (*for garden*) tourbe horticole.

peaty ['piːtɪ] *adj* (*sol*) tourbeux; (*goût*) de fumée de tourbe.

pebble ['peb(ə)l] *n* **(a)** caillou *m*, -oux; *F* **you're not the only p. on the beach,** il n'y a pas que toi au monde; **p. beach,** plage *f* de galets; *Constr* **p. dash,** crépi *m* (moucheté); **p.-dash finish,** crépi *m*; **(b)** *Opt* (*crystal*) cristal *m* de roche; (*lens*) lentille *f* en cristal de roche.

pebble-dash ['peb(ə)ldæʃ] *vt Constr* crépir (*un mur*).

pebbly ['peblɪ] *adj* caillouteux; (*plage*) à galets.

pecan ['piːkən, pɪ'kæn] *n* **p. (nut),** noix *f* de pecan, *Can* pacane *f*; **p. (tree),** pacanier *m*; *Am Culin* **p. pie,** tourte *f*

aux noix de pecans *ou* aux pacanes.
peccadillo [pekə'dɪləʊ] *n* peccadille *f*.
peccary ['pekərɪ] *n* (*animal*) pécari *m*.
peck[1] [pek] *n* coup *m* de bec; *F* (*kiss*) bécot *m*; **to give s.o. a p.,** (*kiss*) bécoter qn.
peck[2] **1** *vt* (*of bird*) picoter, becqueter (*qch*); donner un coup de bec à (*qn*); *F* (*kiss*) bécoter, baisoter (*qn*). **2** *vi* **to p. (at sth),** picoter (qch), donner des coups de bec (à qch); **to p. at one's food,** pignocher, mangeotter son repas.
peck[3] *n* picotin *m* (*d'avoine etc*); *Fig* **she's had a p. of trouble,** elle a eu bien des malheurs.
pecker ['pekər] *n* **(a)** (*bird*) *F* pic vert; **(b)** *Br Sl* (*spirits*) courage *m*, cran *m*; **keep your p. up!.** (du) courage!; **(c)** *esp Am Vulg* (*penis*) bite *f*.
pecking ['pekɪŋ] *n* becquetage *m*; **p. order,** (*among birds*) hiérarchie *f* du becquetage; *Fig* hiérarchie sociale.
peckish ['pekɪʃ] *adj F* **to be** *or* **feel p.,** avoir un creux.
pectin ['pektɪn] *n Ch* pectine *f*.
pectoral ['pektər(ə)l] **1** *adj Anat Med etc* pectoral, -aux; **p. cross,** croix pectorale (*d'évêque*); **p. fin,** (*of fish*) nageoire pectorale. **2** *n* **(a)** *Jewish Rel Hist* pectoral *m*; **(b)** *Anat* (muscle *m*) pectoral *m*.
peculate ['pekjʊleɪt] **1** *vi* détourner des fonds. **2** *vt* détourner (*des fonds*).
peculation [pekjʊ'leɪʃən] *n* malversation *f*, détournement *m* de fonds.
peculiar [pɪ'kjuːlɪər] *adj* **(a)** (*strange*) singulier, bizarre; (*eccentric*) original, -aux; (*taste*) insolite; **well, that's p.,** voilà qui est singulier, tiens, c'est bizarre!; **he** *or* **she is a little p.,** c'est un(e) excentrique; **(b)** (*characteristic*) particulier; **this gait is p. to him,** cette façon de marcher lui est particulière *ou* lui est propre; **smell p. to an animal,** odeur spécifique à un animal; **(c)** (*special*) spécial, -aux, particulier; **of p. interest,** d'un intérêt tout particulier.
peculiarity [pɪkjuːlɪ'ærɪtɪ] *n* **(a)** (*strangeness*) bizarrerie *f*, singularité *f*; (*eccentricity*) originalité *f*, excentricité *f*; **(b)** (*distinctive feature*) trait distinctif, particularité *f*.
peculiarly [pɪ'kjuːlɪəlɪ] *adv* **(a)** (*strangely*) singulièrement, bizarrement; **(b)** (*specially*) particulièrement.
pecuniary [pɪ'kjuːnɪərɪ] *adj* pécuniaire; **p. difficulties,** embarras financiers, ennuis *mpl* d'argent.
pedagogic(al) [pedə'gɒdʒɪk, -ɪk(ə)l] *adj* pédagogique.
pedagogue ['pedəgɒg] *n* pédagogue *m*; *Pej* pédant, -ante.
pedagogy ['pedəgɒdʒɪ] *n* pédagogie *f*.
pedal[1] ['ped(ə)l] *n* **(a)** pédale *f* (*de machine, de véhicule, de bicyclette, d'instrument de musique etc*); **soft/loud p.,** (*of piano*) petite/grande pédale; **p. keyboard,** (*of organ*) pédalier *m*; *Aut etc* **accelerator p.,** pédale d'accélérateur; **clutch p.,** pédale de débrayage *ou* d'embrayage; **gear(-change) p.,** pédale de changement de vitesse; **brake p.,** pédale de frein; **p. bin,** poubelle *f* à pédale; **p. boat,** pédalo *m*; **p. car,** voiture *f* à pédales; **p. pushers,** (*trousers*) (pantalon *m*) corsaire *m*; **(b)** *Mus* **p. (note),** (note *f* de) pédale *f*.
pedal[2] *vi* (**-ll-**, *US* **-l-**) **(a)** *Cycling etc* pédaler; **(b)** *Mus* (*in playing organ*) jouer sur le pédalier; (*in playing piano*) mettre la pédale.
pedal-operated ['ped(ə)lɒpəreɪtɪd] *adj MecE etc* commandé par pédale(s).
pedant ['pedənt] *n Pej* pédant, -ante.
pedantic [pɪ'dæntɪk] *adj* pédant.
pedantically [pɪ'dæntɪklɪ] *adv* en pédant; (*to say*) d'un ton pédant.
pedantry ['pedəntrɪ] *n* pédantisme *m*, pédanterie *f*.
peddle ['ped(ə)l] **1** *vi* faire le colportage. **2** *vt* colporter (*des marchandises*); **to p. drugs,** trafiquer des drogues, faire le trafic de drogues.
peddler ['pedlər] *n* **(a)** **(drug) p.,** trafiquant *m* de drogues; **(b)** *US* = **PEDLAR.**
pederast ['pedəræst, 'piː-] *n* pédéraste *m*.
pederasty ['pedəræstɪ, 'piː-] *n* pédérastie *f*.
pedestal ['pedɪst(ə)l] *n* **(a)** *Archit Art etc* piédestal *m*, -aux, socle *m*; *Fig* **to put s.o. on a p.,** mettre qn sur un piédestal; **(b)** socle *m* (*de pompe etc*); support *m*, colonne *f* (*de projecteur etc*); **p. table,** guéridon *m*; **p. washbasin,** lavabo *m* à pied.
pedestrian [pɪ'destrɪən] **1** *adj* pédestre; (*style etc*) prosaïque, terre à terre. **2** *n* piéton *m*; *Br* **p. crossing,** passage *m* pour piétons, passage clouté; **p. precinct,** zone piétonnière.
pedestrianize [pɪ'destrɪənaɪz] *vt* aménager (*une rue*) en zone piétonnière.
pediatric, pediatrician *etc US* = **PAEDIATRIC, PAEDIATRICIAN** *etc*.
pedicure[1] ['pedɪkjʊər] *n* **(a)** (*activity*) pédicure *f*; **to have a p.,** se faire faire une pédicure; **(b)** (*person*) pédicure *mf*.
pedicure[2] *vt* pédicurer.
pedigree ['pedɪgriː] *n* **(a)** certificat *m* d'origine, pedigree *m* (*d'un chien etc*); **to have a p.,** (*of a dog*) être un chien de race, avoir un pedigree; **p. dog/bull,** chien *m*/taureau *m* de (pure) race *ou* de bonne lignée; **(b)** (*background*) histoire *f*, antécédents *mpl*; **she had an impeccable political p.,** ses antécédents politiques sont irréprochables; **(c)** (*ancestry*) ascendance *f*, généalogie *f* (*de qn*); **(d)** (*genealogical table*) arbre *m* généalogique.
pediment ['pedɪmənt] *n Archit* fronton *m*; (*small*) fronteau *m*.
pedlar ['pedlər] *n* colporteur *m*, marchand ambulant, (marchand) forain *m*.
pedological, pedology *US* = **PAEDOLOGICAL, PAEDOLOGY.**
pedometer [pe'dɒmɪtər] *n* podomètre *m*.
pedophile, pedophilia *US* = **PAEDOPHILE, PAEDOPHILIA.**
pee[1] [piː] *n F* pipi *m*, *Sl* pisse *f*; **to go and have a p.,** aller faire pipi, *Sl* aller pisser; **cat's p.,** pisse *f* de chat.
pee[2] *vi F* faire pipi, *Sl* pisser.
peek[1] [piːk] *n* regard furtif, coup *m* d'œil (furtif); **to take** *or* **have a p. (at sth/s.o.),** jeter un coup d'œil (furtif) (à *ou* sur qch/qn).
peek[2] *vi* jeter un regard *ou* un coup d'œil furtif (**at s.o./sth,** sur *ou* à qn/qch); risquer un coup d'œil; **no peeking!,** on ne regarde pas!
peekaboo ['piːkəbuː] **1** *int* coucou! **2** *adj* (*corsage etc*) (*see-through*) d'un tissu transparent; (*with holes*) avec *ou* en broderie(s) ajourée(s).
peel[1] [piːl] *n* pelure *f* (*de pomme etc*); écorce *f*, peau *f*, *Culin* zeste *m* (*de citron, d'orange*); **candied p.,** zeste confit; (*of orange*) orangeat *m*; (*of lemon*) citronnat *m*.
peel[2] **1** *vt* peler (*un fruit*); éplucher (*des pommes de terre etc*); décortiquer (*un chêne, des amandes*); écorcer (*un bâton etc*); **to p. the bark/skin,** enlever l'écorce/la peau; **to keep one's eyes peeled,** ouvrir l'œil. **2** *vi* (*of paint etc*) s'écailler; (*of skin*) peler; *Med* se desquamer; (*of nose etc*) peler; (*of tree*) se décortiquer; (*of wall*) se décrépir; **you're peeling,** tu pèles.
►**peel off** **1** *vtsep* (*remove*) enlever (*l'écorce, la peau*); **to p. off one's clothes,** se déshabiller. **2** *vi* **(a)** (*become detached*) (*of paint, nail varnish etc*) s'écailler; (*of skin*) peler; *Av* se détacher (*de la formation*); **(b)** (*undress*) se déshabiller.
peeler ['piːlər] *n* **(a)** éplucheur *m*; **potato p.,** économe *m*; **(b)** *Arch Br* (*policeman*) agent *m* de police.
peeling ['piːlɪŋ] *n* **1 (a)** (*of potato*) épluchage *m*; (*of stick*) écorçage *m*; **(b)** (*of paint*) écaillement *m*; *Med* desquamation *f* (*de l'épiderme*); **(c) peelings,** épluchures *fpl* (*de pommes de terre etc*).
peeling off *n* = **PEELING (b).**
peep[1] [piːp] *n* **(a)** (*furtive glance*) coup d'œil furtif; **to have** *or* **take a p. at sth,** jeter un regard furtif sur qch; **to get a p. at sth,** entrevoir qch; **(b)** filtrée *f* (*de lumière*).
peep[2] *vi* **(a)** (*glance furtively*) **to p. at s.o./sth,** regarder qn/qch à la dérobée, jeter un coup d'œil furtif sur qn/qch; **to p. through the door,** glisser un œil par la porte; **I saw you peeping through the keyhole,** je vous ai vu regarder par le trou de la serrure; **no peeping!,** on ne regarde pas!; **a Peeping Tom,** un voyeur; **(b)** (*be visible*) se laisser entrevoir, se montrer; (*of flower*) percer, pointer; **violets peeping (up) from the grass,** violettes qui pointent au milieu de l'herbe.
peep[3] *n* (*sound*) piaulement *m*, pépiement *m* (*d'oiseau*); cri *m* (*de souris*); *F* **if I hear so much as a p. out of you,** si tu fais le moindre bruit; *F* **we haven't heard a p. from him for months,** ça fait des mois qu'il n'a pas fait le moindre signe de vie.
peep[4] *vi* (*of bird*) piauler, pépier; (*of mouse*) crier.
►**peep out** *vi* (*be visible*) se laisser entrevoir, se montrer; (*of flower*) percer, pointer.
peep-bo ['piːpbəʊ] **1** *int* coucou! **2** *n* **to play at p.-bo,** jouer à cache-cache (*avec un enfant*).
peephole ['piːphəʊl] *n* **(a)** (*in door*) judas *m*; **(b)** *MecE etc* (trou *m* de) regard *m*; regard *ou* orifice *m* de visite.
peepshow ['piːpʃəʊ] *n* vues *fpl* stéréoscopiques; (*modern*) peepshow *m*.
peer[1] [pɪər] *n* **(a)** (*equal*) pair *m*; **a jury of one's peers,** un jury de ses pairs; **you will not find his p.,** vous ne trouveriez pas son pareil; **p. group,** pairs; **p. pressure,** influence *f* de ses pairs; **(b) p. of the realm,** pair *m* du Royaume-Uni; **life p.,** pair à vie.

peer² *vi* **to p. at s.o./sth,** scruter qn/qch du regard; **he peered (out) into the night,** il cherchait à percer l'obscurité; **to p. round the corner,** risquer un coup d'œil au coin de la rue.
peerage ['pɪərɪdʒ] *n* **(a)** (*noble title, rank*) pairie *f*; **life p.,** pairie à vie; **to confer a p. on s.o., to raise s.o. to the p.,** élever qn à la pairie; **(b)** (*no pl*) **the p.,** les pairs *mpl*; **(c) p. (book),** (almanach *m*) nobiliaire *m*.
peeress ['pɪəres] *n* pairesse *f*.
peerless ['pɪəlɪs] *adj Lit* sans pareil, sans égal, hors pair, incomparable.
peeve [piːv] *vt F* fâcher, irriter (*qn*); **to be peeved,** être fâché *ou* irrité.
peevish ['piːvɪʃ] *adj* maussade, irritable; (*enfant*) *F* grognon.
peevishly ['piːvɪʃlɪ] *adv* avec (mauvaise) humeur.
peevishness ['piːvɪʃnɪs] *n* maussaderie *f*, mauvaise humeur.
peewit ['piːwɪt] *n* (*bird*) vanneau *m* (huppé); **p. (gull),** mouette rieuse.
peg¹ [peg] *n* **(a)** cheville *f* (*en bois*), fiche *f*; fausset *m*, fosset *m* (*d'un tonneau*); *MecE* cheville, clavette *f*, goupille *f*, goujon *m*, ergot *m*; ranche *f*, enture *f* (*d'échelier*); piquet *m* (*de tente etc*); *Mus* cheville (*de violon etc*); bouton *m* (*de corde de harpe*); *Cards* **cribbage p.,** fiche *f*; **hat** *or* **coat p.,** patère *f*; *esp Br* **clothes off the p.,** vêtements *mpl* de confection; *Br* **clothes p.,** pince *f* à linge; *F* **to be a square p. in a round hole,** ne pas être à sa place; **to take s.o. down a p. (or two),** remettre qn à sa place; **that's a p. to hang a grievance on,** voilà un prétexte de plainte; **p. leg,** (*wooden leg*) jambe *f* de bois, pilon *m*; (*person*) = personne qui a une jambe de bois; **(b)** pointe *f*, fer *m* (*de toupie*); pied *m*, pique *f* (*de violoncelle*); **p. top,** toupie *f*; **(c)** doigt *m* (*de whisky etc*).
peg² *vt* **(-gg-) (a)** cheviller (*un assemblage etc*); **to p. clothes on the line,** accrocher du linge sur la corde (*avec des pinces*); **(b)** (*in games*) marquer (*des points*); **(c)** *St Exch Fin* stabiliser (*les prix*); **to p. the market,** stabiliser le marché; maintenir le marché ferme.
►peg away *vi F* (*work hard*) travailler assidûment, bosser (*à qch*); **to p. away at one's algebra,** piocher *ou* bûcher son algèbre.
►peg down *vtsep* (*fix*) fixer, assujettir (*un filet etc*) avec des piquets; **pegged down by regulations,** entravé par des règlements.
►peg out 1 *vtsep* **(a)** (*mark with pegs*) piqueter, jalonner, borner (*une concession*); jalonner (*une ligne*); *Constr* **to p. out the ground plan,** implanter le tracé des fondations; **(b)** (*hang*) **to p. out clothes on the line,** accrocher du linge sur la corde (*avec des pinces*). **2** *vi* **(a)** *Sl* (*die*) casser sa pipe; **(b)** (*in croquet*) toucher le piquet final (et se retirer de la partie).
pegboard ['pegbɔːd] *n* **(a)** (*for hanging things*) panneau alvéolé; **(b)** (*for game*) table *f* à trous.
pegging ['pegɪŋ] *n* **(a)** (*assembling with pegs*) chevillage *m*; **(b)** *Sp etc* **it's still level p.,** ils sont encore à égalité; **(c)** *St Exch Fin* stabilisation *f* (*du marché etc*).
PEI [piːiː'aɪ] *n Geog* (*abbr* **Prince Edward Island**) IPE *f*.
pejorative [pɪ'dʒɒrətɪv, 'piːdʒ-] **1** *adj* péjoratif. **2** *n* (mot *m*) péjoratif *m*.
pejoratively [pɪ'dʒɒrətɪvlɪ, 'piːdʒ-] *adv* péjorativement.
peke [piːk] *n F* (chien *m*) pékinois *m*.
Pekinese [piːkɪ'niːz] **1** *adj* pékinois. **2** *n* **(a)** (*person*) Pékinois, -oise; **(b)** (*dog*) (chien *m*) pékinois *m*.
Peking [piː'kɪŋ] *n* Pékin.
Pekingese [piːkɪŋ'iːz] *adj & n* = **PEKINESE**.
pelagic [pɪ'lædʒɪk] *adj* pélagien, pélagique.
pelargonium [pelə'gəʊnɪəm] *n* (*plant*) pélargonium *m*, *F* géranium *m*; **trailing p.,** géranium lierre.
pelican ['pelɪkən] *n* **(a)** (*bird*) pélican *m*; **(b)** *Br* **p. crossing,** passage clouté avec feux opérés par les piétons.
pellagra [pe'lægrə, -'leɪ-] *n Med* pellagre *f*.
pellet ['pelɪt] *n* boulette *f* (*de papier etc*); pelote *f* (*d'argile etc*); pastille *f* (*de matière plastique*); (*in shotgun cartridge*) grain *m* de plomb; *Pharm* pilule *f*, grain *m*, bol *m*; *Med* pellet *m*; boulette d'aliments regurgités (*par les hiboux etc*); *Agr* granulé *m*; *Metal Ch* boulette.
pell-mell ['pel'mel] **1** *adv* pêle-mêle; (*courir etc*) à la débandade. **2** *adj* (*dash*) confus. **3** *n* pêle-mêle *m*, confusion *f*.
pellucid [pe'luːsɪd] *adj Lit* pellucide, transparent; (*style, esprit etc*) lucide.
pelmet ['pelmɪt] *n* lambrequin *m*.
Peloponnese (the) [peləpə'niːs] *n* le Péloponnèse.
Peloponnesian [peləpə'niːsɪən] *adj* péloponnésien, du Péloponnèse.
pelota [pə'lɒtə] *n* (*game*) pelote *f* basque.
pelt¹ [pelt] *n* **(a)** (*skin*) peau *f*, fourrure *f* (*de mouton ou de chèvre*); **(b)** (*hide*) (*with hair on*) peau verte; (*without hair*) peau en tripe.
pelt² *n* **(at) full p.,** (*courir, s'enfuir*) à toute vitesse, ventre à terre.
pelt³ 1 *vt* **to p. s.o. with stones/snowballs,** bombarder qn des pierres/boules de neige; **he pelted abuse at them,** il les a criblés d'injures. **2** *vi* **(a)** (*of rain etc*) tomber à verse; **it was pelting with rain,** la pluie tombait à verse; **pelting rain,** pluie battante; **(b)** (*go fast*) aller à toute vitesse *ou* à toute allure, *F* foncer; **he came pelting round the corner,** il a débouché du coin à toute allure; **the kids pelted off down the street,** les gosses ont descendu la rue à toute allure *ou* ventre à terre; **he pelted upstairs,** il est monté comme une flèche *ou* ventre à terre; **she's really pelting through her work,** elle abat son travail à toute allure.
pelvic ['pelvɪk] *adj Anat* pelvien; **p. bone,** os *m* du bassin; **p. fins,** pelviennes *fpl*; **p. girdle,** ceinture pelvienne.
pelvis ['pelvɪs] *n Anat* **(a)** bassin *m*, pelvis *m*; **(b)** bassinet *m* (*du rein*).
pen¹ [pen] *n* stylo *m*; **fountain p.,** stylo à plume; **ball(point) p.,** stylo à bille, stylo-bille *m*; **felt p.,** crayon *m* feutre; **quill p.,** plume *f* (d'oie); **drawing** *or* **mapping p.,** plume à dessin; **p. (-and-ink) drawing,** dessin *m* à la plume *ou* à l'encre; **stroke of the p.,** trait *m* de plume; **to put p. to paper,** prendre la plume (en main), écrire; **to earn one's living by one's p.,** vivre de sa plume; **p. compass,** compas *m* à tire-ligne; *Prov* **the p. is mightier than the sword,** la plume blesse souvent plus que l'épée; **p. friend** *or* **pal,** correspondant, -ante; **p. name,** nom *m* de plume; (*of journalist*) nom de guerre; **p. (nib),** plume.
pen² *vt* **(-nn-)** écrire, rédiger (*une lettre, un article etc*).
pen³ *n* **(a)** parc *m*, enclos *m* (*à moutons etc*); *Nau* cage *f*; **bull p.,** toril *m*; **pig p.,** *US* **hog p.,** porcherie *f*; **play p.,** parc; **(b)** *Nau* abri *m* (*de sous-marins*); **(c)** *Am Sl* (*penitentiary*) tôle *f*, taule *f*, trou *m*.
pen⁴ *vt* **(-nn-,** *Lit* **pent)** parquer (*des moutons etc*).
pen⁵ *n* (*female swan*) cygne *m* femelle.
►pen in, pen up *vtsep* (*enclosure*) parquer (*des moutons etc*); **to feel penned up,** se sentir à l'étroit; **we were penned up in the room for weeks,** nous sommes restés parqués dans la pièce pendant des semaines.
penal ['piːn(ə)l] *adj* (*laws, code*) pénal, -aux; (*offence*) qui comporte *ou* entraîne une pénalité; *Arch* **p. colony** *or* **settlement,** colonie *f* pénitentiaire; **p. servitude,** travaux forcés (*d'une durée minimum de trois ans*).
penalization [piːnəlaɪ'zeɪʃən] *n* infliction *f* d'une peine (**of s.o.,** à qn); *Sp* pénalisation *f*.
penalize ['piːnəlaɪz] *vt* **(a)** (*impose a penalty on*) infliger une peine à (*qn*); *Sp* pénaliser (*un concurrent, un joueur*); déclasser (*un coureur*); *Sp* (*handicap*) handicaper; **(b)** sanctionner (*un délit*) d'une peine *ou* d'une pénalité; (*attach a penalty to*) attacher une peine à (*un délit*).
penalty ['penəltɪ] *n* **(a)** peine *f*, pénalité *f*; (*disadvantage*) désavantage *m*; *Com* amende *f* (*pour retard de livraison etc*); *Admin* sanction *f* (pénale); **to impose penalties,** prendre des sanctions; **p. clause,** (*in contract*) clause pénale (*de dommages-intérêts*); **the death p.,** la peine de mort; **on** *or* **upon** *or* **under p. of death,** sous peine de mort; **the p. for this is death/excommunication/***etc*, la peine encourue pour ce crime est la mort/l'excommunication/*etc*; **to pay the p. of one's foolishness,** subir les conséquences *ou* être puni de sa sottise; **to pay the p. of fame,** payer la rançon de la gloire;
(b) *Sp* pénalisation *f*, pénalité *f*; (*handicap*) handicap *m*; **p. box,** (*in ice hockey*) banc *m* de pénalité; *Golf* **p. stroke,** coup *m* d'amende; *Fb* **p. (kick),** penalty *m*; *Fb* **p. area/spot,** surface *f*/point *m* de réparation; *Fb* **p. shootout,** épreuve *f* des penalties.
penance ['penəns] *n Rel* **the sacrament of p.,** le sacrement de la pénitence; **to do p.,** faire pénitence (**for,** de, pour); **to do sth as a p.,** faire qch par pénitence.
pence [pens] *see* **PENNY**.
penceworth ['penswɜːθ] *n* **to buy ten p. of sweets,** acheter pour dix pence de bonbons.
pencil ['pens(ə)l] *n* **(a)** crayon *m*; **lead p.,** crayon à mine de plomb; **coloured p.,** crayon de couleur; **indelible p.,** crayon (à encre) indélébile; **to mark/write sth in p.** *or* **with a p.,** marquer/écrire qch au crayon; **p. sketch,** croquis *m*; **drawing in p., p. drawing,** (dessin *m* au) crayon, crayonnage *m*; **slate p.,** crayon d'ardoise; **eyebrow p.,** (*make-up*) crayon à sourcils; **p. case,** plumier *m*;

p. lead, mine *f* de crayon; **p. mark,** trait *m ou* marque *f* au crayon; **p. sharpener,** taille-crayon(s) *m inv*; *Math* faisceau (*de courbes etc*); **(b)** *Opt* **p. of light rays,** faisceau *m* de lumière.

pencil² *vt* (-ll-, *US* -l-) **(a)** (*mark with a pencil*) marquer (*qch*) au crayon; (*draw, sketch in pencil*) dessiner *ou* esquisser (*une figure*) au crayon; crayonner (*un billet*); **a pencilled note,** un billet écrit au crayon; **to p. one's eyebrows,** se faire les sourcils (au crayon); **pencilled eyebrows,** sourcils tracés au crayon.

▶**pencil in** *vtsep* (*write*) écrire (*qch*) au crayon; **the date had been pencilled in,** on a fixé provisoirement la date; **p. me in for Friday,** inscrivez-moi provisoirement pour vendredi; *Fig* en principe, vous pouvez compter sur moi vendredi.

pendant ['pendənt] *n* **(a)** pendentif *m* (*de collier*); breloque *f* (*de bracelet*); pendeloque *f* (*de lustre*); *Archit* clef pendante; cul-de-lampe *m*, *pl* culs-de-lampe; **ear p.,** pendant *m* d'oreille; **electric light p.,** (lampe *f* à) suspension *f;* **(b)** *Nau* (*rope*) pantoire *f*; **(c)** ['penənt] (*flag*) flamme *f*, guidon *m*.

pending ['pendɪŋ] **1** *adj* (*procès*) pendant, en instance; (*négociations*) en cours; *Admin Com* (*documents*) en attendant, en attente; **p. tray,** corbeille *f* pour les documents en attente. **2** *prep* en attendant (*le retour de qn etc*); **p. further news,** en attendant de plus amples nouvelles.

pendulous ['pendjʊləs] *adj* (*branch, lip, ear etc*) pendant.

pendulum ['pendjʊləm] *n* (*clockmaking*) *& Phys* pendule *m*, balancier *m*; **p. ball** *or* **bob,** lentille *f* de pendule *ou* de balancier; **p. clock,** horloge *f* à pendule *ou* à balancier.

penetrable ['penɪtrəb(ə)l] *adj* pénétrable.

penetrate ['penɪtreɪt] **1** *vt* pénétrer, percer; pénétrer (*le marché*); **darkness that the eye could not p.,** ténèbres que l'œil ne pouvait percer; **to p. s.o.'s mind,** voir clair dans l'esprit de qn; **to p. s.o. with a feeling,** pénétrer qn d'un sentiment. **2** *vi* pénétrer; **the water is penetrating everywhere,** l'eau s'introduit partout; **to p. through sth,** passer à travers qch; **to p. into a forest,** pénétrer dans une forêt; **the custom has not penetrated to this part of the country,** cette coutume n'est pas parvenue jusqu'à cette partie du pays; **it hasn't penetrated,** (*hasn't been understood*) ça n'a pas fait le tour.

penetrating ['penɪtreɪtɪŋ] *adj* (*wind, cold*) pénétrant; (*sound, voice*) mordant; (*bullet, shell*) perforant; (*esprit*) pénétrant; **to have a p. eye,** avoir des yeux perçants.

penetration [penɪ'treɪʃən] *n* pénétration *f*.

penguin ['peŋgwɪn] *n* pingouin *m*; (*at South Pole*) manchot *m*, gorfou *m*.

penholder ['penhəʊldər] *n* porte-plume *m inv*.

penicillin [penɪ'sɪlɪn] *n* pénicilline *f*.

peninsula [pɪ'nɪnsjʊlə] *n* péninsule *f*, presqu'île *f*; **the Iberian P.,** la péninsule Ibérique.

peninsular [pɪ'nɪnsjʊlər] *adj* péninsulaire.

penis, *pl* **-nes** ['piːnɪs, -niːz] *n Anat* pénis *m*, verge *f*.

penitence ['penɪtəns] *n* pénitence *f*, repentir *m*, contrition *f*.

penitent ['penɪtənt] **1** *adj* pénitent, repentant, contrit. **2** *n* pénitent, -ente.

penitential [penɪ'tenʃəl] **1** *adj* pénitentiel; (*psaumes*) de la pénitence. **2** *n* (*book*) pénitentiel *m*.

penitentiary [penɪ'tenʃərɪ] **1** *n* **(a)** *Am* (*prison*) pénitencier *m*; **(b)** *Cathol* (*person*) pénitencier *m*; (*tribunal*) pénitencerie *f*. **2** *adj Am* (*délit*) puni de réclusion dans une maison pénitentiaire.

penitently ['penɪtəntlɪ] *adv* d'un air contrit.

penknife ['pennaɪf] *n* canif *m*.

penman, *pl* **-men** ['penmən] *n* **(a) good** *or* **expert p.,** calligraphe *m*; **to be a poor p.,** écrire mal; **(b)** (*author*) homme *m* de plume.

penmanship ['penmənʃɪp] *n* (*calligraphy*) calligraphie *f*.

Penn(a). *n abbr* **Pennsylvania**.

pennant ['penənt] *n* **(a)** *Nau* flamme *f*, guidon *m*; **(b)** = **PENNON**.

penniless ['penɪlɪs] **1** *adj* sans le sou; **to be p.,** n'avoir pas le sou *ou* pas un sou vaillant; **to leave s.o. p.,** laisser qn sans le sou. **2** *n* **the p.,** (*used as pl*) les sans-le-sou *mpl*.

Pennine ['penaɪn] *adj* **the P. Chain,** la chaîne Pennine.

Pennines (the) [θə'penaɪnz] *npl* la chaîne Pennine.

pennon ['penən] *n* flamme *f*, banderole *f*.

Pennsylvania [pensɪl'veɪnɪə] *n* Pennsylvanie *f*.

penny ['penɪ] *n* **(a)** *Br* (*coin*) (*pl usu* **pennies**) penny *m*; **they haven't a p. (to their name,** *Old-fashioned* **to bless themselves with),** ils sont sans le sou *ou* sans un sou vaillant; **pennies from heaven,** une aubaine; *Prov* **take care of the pennies and the pounds will take care of themselves,** les petits ruisseaux font les grandes rivières; **to count every p.,** compter ses sous; **it was worth every p.,** c'était un bon investissement; **you'd better start saving (up) your pennies,** tu ferais mieux de commencer à mettre de l'argent de côté; *F* **the penny's dropped,** j'y suis, ça y est; *Br F* **to spend a p.,** aller téléphoner, aller faire pipi;

(b) *Br* (*pl* **pence** [pens]) (*value*) **I paid 60 pence for it,** je l'ai payé 60 pence; **a ten/fifty pence piece,** une pièce de dix/cinquante pence; **a (new) p.,** = un nouveau penny; **an (old) p.,** (*before 1971*) = un ancien penny; **they're two a p. nowadays,** c'est monnaie courante à l'heure actuelle; **a p. for your thoughts** *or F* **for them,** à quoi rêvez-vous *ou* pensez-vous?; *Prov* **in for a p. in for a pound,** quand le vin est tiré il faut le boire; *esp Br F* **a bad p.,** (*rogue, worthless person*) bon à rien *m*; **it didn't cost them a p.,** ça ne leur a pas coûté un centime; **that'll cost a pretty p.,** cela coûtera cher; **to make a pretty p. out of sth,** tirer une petite fortune de qch; **to earn** *or* **turn an honest p.,** gagner honnêtement sa vie; *Mus* **p. whistle,** flûteau *m*;

(c) *US & Can* (*cent*) cent *m*.

penny-dreadful [penɪ'dredfʊl] *n Old-fashioned F* roman *m* à deux sous *ou* à sensation.

penny-in-the-slot [penɪɪnðə'slɒt] *adj Old-fashioned* (*machine*) à sous.

penny-pincher ['penɪpɪntʃər] *n* pingre *mf*, radin *m*.

penny-pinching ['penɪpɪntʃɪŋ] **1** *adj* (*person*) radin, pingre, qui fait des économies de bouts de chandelle; (*action, step*) mesquin. **2** *n* pingrerie *f*.

penny-wise ['penɪwaɪz] *adj* **to be p.-w. and pound foolish,** économiser les sous et prodiguer les louis.

pennyworth ['penɪwɜːθ] *n* **a p. of sweets,** un pence de bonbons; **not a p.,** rien du tout.

penology [piː'nɒlədʒɪ] *n* pénologie *f*.

penpusher ['penpʊʃər] *n F Pej* gratte-papier *m inv*, scribouillard, -arde.

penpushing ['penpʊʃɪŋ] *F Pej* **1** *adj* (*clerk etc*) sans responsabilités. **2** *n* paperasse *f*, paperasserie *f*.

pension¹ *n* **(a)** ['penʃən] pension *f*; **government** *or Br* **state p.,** pension sur l'État; **to be on a p.,** (*of elderly person*) vivre d'une pension; **p. plan,** régime *m* de pension; **retirement** *or* **old age p.,** pension de retraite; **p. fund,** (*money*) capital *m* retraite; (*company*) caisse *f* de retraite; **p. scheme,** caisse *f* de retraite; **to retire on a p.,** prendre sa retraite; **(b)** ['pɔːnsɪɔːn] pension *f* de famille; **en p.,** (*at hotel*) en pension.

pension² ['penʃən] *vt* pensionner (*qn*).

▶**pension off** *vtsep* (*retire*) mettre (*qn*) à la retraite; *F* mettre (*qch*) au rebut.

pensionable ['penʃənəb(ə)l] *adj* **(a)** (*person*) qui a droit à une pension *ou* à sa retraite; **(b)** (*injury etc*) qui donne droit à une pension; **p. age,** âge *m* de la mise à la retraite; **(c)** (*job*) donnant droit à une pension.

pensioner ['penʃənər] *n* pensionné -ée; **old-age p.,** retraité, -ée.

pensive ['pensɪv] *adj* pensif, méditatif, rêveur.

pensively ['pensɪvlɪ] *adv* pensivement; d'un air pensif.

pent [pent] *see* **PEN⁴**.

pentagon ['pentəgən] *n Math* pentagone *m*; *US Mil* **the P.,** le Pentagone.

pentagonal [pen'tægən(ə)l] *adj* pentagonal.

pentameter [pen'tæmɪtər] *n* (*in poetry*) pentamètre *m*.

Pentateuch (the) [ðə'pentətjuːk] *n Bible* le Pentateuque.

pentathlete [pen'tæθliːt] *n* pentathlonien, -ienne.

pentathlon [pen'tæθlən] *n Sp* pentathlon *m*.

Pentecost ['pentɪkɒst] *n Rel* la Pentecôte.

pentecostal [pentɪ'kɒst(ə)l] *adj Rel* de la Pentecôte.

penthouse ['penthaʊs] *n Constr* **(a)** (*apartment*) = appartement construit sur le toit d'un immeuble; **(b)** (*shed*) appentis *m*.

pent-up [pen'tʌp] *adj* (*emotion*) refoulé, contenu.

penultimate [pe'nʌltɪmɪt] **1** *adj* pénultième, avant-dernier. **2** *n* pénultième *f*; *Ling* avant-dernière syllabe.

penumbra [pe'nʌmbrə] *n* pénombre *f*.

penurious [pe'njʊərɪəs] *adj* pauvre.

penury ['penjʊrɪ] *n* **(a)** (*poverty*) pénurie *f*, indigence *f*; **(b)** (*dearth*) manque *m*, disette *f* **(of,** de).

peony ['piːənɪ] *n* (*plant*) pivoine *f*.

people¹ ['piːp(ə)l] *n* (*with pl verb except for* **(b)** *where pl is usu* **peoples) (a)** gens *mpl*; **young p.,** jeunes gens; **old p.,** les vieux; **old p.'s home,** maison *f* de retraite pour personnes âgées; **thousands of p.,** des milliers de gens; **there were not many p.,** il n'y avait pas beaucoup de monde; **most p.,** la plupart des gens; **he's one of those p.**

who il est de ceux qui ...; c'est un homme qui ...; **there were five p. in the room,** il y avait cinq personnes dans la pièce; **it's a question of knowing the right p.,** il faut avoir des relations; **we're having p. to dinner tonight,** nous aurons des invités *ou* du monde à dîner ce soir; **blind/ deaf p.,** les aveugles/les sourds; **stop annoying p.,** arrête d'embêter le monde; **p. don't like being told they're wrong,** les gens n'aiment pas qu'on leur dise qu'ils ont tort; **p. are less patient nowadays,** de nos jours, les gens sont moins patients; **p. say that ...,** on dit que ...; *Myth* **the little p., the good p.,** les fées *fpl*; **she's a p. person,** elle est très sociable; **p. power,** pouvoir *m* populaire;

(b) *(nation)* peuple *m*, nation *f*; **the French p.,** les Français; **the Sikhs/Russians are a proud p.,** les Sikhs/ les Russes sont un peuple fier; **English-speaking peoples,** peuples *ou* nations de langue anglaise;

(c) *(citizens)* citoyens *mpl (d'un Etat)*; **p.'s republic,** république *f* populaire; **the will of the p.,** la volonté du peuple; **the (common) p.,** le peuple; *Pej* la populace; **a man of the p.,** un homme sorti du peuple; **a king and his p.,** un roi et ses sujets;

(d) *(population)* peuple *m*, habitants *mpl*; **the p. of Paris,** les habitants de Paris;

(e) *(employees)* employés, -ées; ouvriers, -ières; **I'll get one of my p. to do it,** un de mes employés *ou* ouvriers le fera; **the police sent their p.,** la police a envoyé ses hommes; **our p. in Moscow,** *(representatives)* nos représentants à Moscou; *(compatriots)* nos compatriotes installés à Moscou; **the p. in accounts,** les gens de la comptabilité;

(f) *(parents)* parents *mpl*; *(family)* famille *f*; **how are your p.?,** comment va votre famille?

people² *vt* peupler **(by, with,** de); **a country peopled by many different races,** un pays multiracial; *Lit* **a room peopled with antique chairs,** une pièce meublée de chaises d'époque.

pep [pep] *n F* entrain *m*, fougue *f*; **full of p.,** plein de sève *ou* d'allant; **p. pill,** excitant *m*, stimulant *m*; **p. talk,** petit discours d'encouragement.

►pep up *vtsep* **(-pp-)** *F (enliven)* ragaillardir *(qn)*; revigorer *(qn, qch)*; **to p. up a business,** remonter une affaire.

peplum ['pepləm] *n (on jacket)* basque *f*.

pepper¹ ['pepər] *n* **(a)** *(spice)* poivre *m*; **p. (plant),** poivrier *m*; *Culin* **black/white p.,** poivre noir/gris; **Cayenne p.,** poivre de Cayenne; **Jamaica p.,** poivre de la Jamaïque, piment *m*; **p. mill,** moulin *m* à poivre; **p. pot,** poivrière *f*; *Culin* **p. steak,** steak *m* au poivre; **(b)** *(vegetable)* **sweet p.,** piment doux, poivron *m*; **green/red/yellow p.,** poivron vert/rouge/jaune.

pepper² *vt* **(a)** poivrer *(de la viande etc)*; **(b)** *Fig* cribler *(l'ennemi etc)* de balles; **her conversation was liberally peppered with swearwords,** sa conversation était largement pimentée de jurons.

pepper-and-salt ['pepərən'sɔːlt] *adj (hair)* poivre et sel.

peppercorn ['pepəkɔːn] *n* **(a)** grain *m* de poivre; **(b)** *Jur* **p. rent,** loyer nominal *ou* insignifiant.

peppermint ['pepəmɪnt] *n* **(a)** *(plant, flavour)* menthe poivrée; *(flavour)* peppermint *m*; **(b)** *(sweet)* bonbon *m* à la menthe, pastille *f* de menthe.

peppery ['pepərɪ] *adj* **(a)** *(dish etc)* poivré; **(b)** *F (person)* irascible, coléreux, colérique.

peppy ['pepɪ] *adj F (person)* plein de sève *ou* d'allant.

pepsin ['pepsɪn] *n Ch Physiol* pepsine *f*.

peptic ['peptɪk] *adj Physiol* peptique; **p. ulcer,** ulcère *m* de l'estomac *ou* gastro-duodénal.

peptone ['peptəʊn] *n Bio Ch* peptone *f*.

Péquiste [peɪ'kiːst] *n Can (member, supporter of Parti québécois)* péquiste *mf*.

per [pɜːr] *prep Com etc* par; **p. annum,** par an; **p. capita,** par personne; **the highest p. capita income in Europe,** le revenu par habitant le plus élevé en Europe; **sent p. carrier,** envoyé par messagerie; **p. cent,** pour cent; **a five p. cent increase, an increase of five p. cent,** une augmentation de cinq pour cent; **p. day,** par jour; **100 km p. hour,** cent kilomètres à l'heure; **as p. invoice,** suivant facture; **as p. your instructions,** conformément à vos instructions; **ten francs p. kilo,** dix francs le kilo; **as p. sample,** conformément à l'échantillon; **p. se,** en soi; **it is not a bad idea p. se,** en soi, ce n'est pas une mauvaise idée; **as p. usual,** comme d'habitude.

peradventure [pɜːrəd'ventjər] *adv Arch* **(a)** *(by chance)* par aventure, par hasard; **(b)** *(perhaps)* peut-être.

perambulate [pə'ræmbjʊleɪt] *vt Fml* parcourir, se promener dans *(son jardin etc)*.

perambulator [pə'ræmbjʊleɪtər] *n Arch & Lit* landau *m*.

perceive [pə'siːv] *vt* **(a)** *(notice)* percevoir *(un son, une odeur)*; s'apercevoir de *(qch)*; apercevoir *(qn)*; **he perceived that he was being watched,** il s'aperçut qu'on l'observait; **(b)** *(understand)* percevoir *(la vérité etc)*.

percentage [pə'sentɪdʒ] *n* **(a)** *(proportion)* **p. of acid/ alcohol/***etc*, teneur *f* en acide/en alcool/*etc*; **(b)** *Com* pourcentage *m*; **to allow a p. on all transactions,** allouer un pourcentage *ou* un tantième sur toutes les opérations; *F* **what's my p.?,** quel pourcentage je touche?

perceptibility [pəseptɪ'bɪlɪtɪ] *n* perceptibilité *f*.

perceptible [pə'septɪb(ə)l] *adj* perceptible (à l'esprit); *Phil* cognoscible; *(différence)* sensible; **p. to the eye,** visible; **p. to the ear,** perceptible à l'oreille, audible.

perceptibly [pə'septɪblɪ] *adv* perceptiblement, sensiblement.

perception [pə'sepʃən] *n* **(a)** *(act of perceiving)* perception *f*; **organs of p.,** organes percepteurs; **(b)** *(ability to perceive)* faculté perceptive; sensibilité *f (aux impressions extérieures)*; **(c)** *(understanding)* façon *f* dont on perçoit *ou* ressent qch; **the public's p. of the government's role,** la façon dont l'opinion publique perçoit le rôle de l'Etat.

perceptive [pə'septɪv] *adj* **(a)** *(perspicacious)* perspicace; sensible; **(b)** *(able to perceive)* perceptif; **p. faculties,** facultés perceptives.

perceptiveness [pə'septɪvnɪs] *n* **(a)** *(perspicacity)* perspicacité *f*; **(b)** *(ability to perceive)* (faculté *f* de) perception *f*.

perch¹ [pɜːtʃ] *n* **(a)** perchoir *m*; *(in cage)* bâton *m*; *F* **to knock s.o. off his** *or* **her p.,** *(depose)* détrôner qn; *(force to abandon pretensions)* rabattre le caquet à qn; **(b)** *Arch (measurement)* perche *f* (de 512 yards, *approx* = 5 m.).

perch² **1** *vi (of bird, F of person)* percher, se percher **(on,** sur); *(of poultry)* jucher; **perching bird,** oiseau percheur. **2** *vt* **castle perched on a hill,** château perché sur (le sommet d')une colline; **to p. oneself,** se percher, se jucher **(on,** sur).

perch³ *n (fish)* perche *f*.

perchance [pə'tʃɑːns] *adv Arch* peut-être.

percipient [pə'sɪpɪənt] *adj* percepteur, -trice *(de sensations etc)*.

percolate ['pɜːkəleɪt] **1** *vi* s'infiltrer; *(of coffee etc)* filtrer, passer. **2** *vt (of liquid)* filtrer à travers, s'infiltrer dans *(le sable)*; *(of person, filter etc)* filtrer *(un liquide)*; passer *(le café)*.

percolator ['pɜːkəleɪtər] *n* cafetière *f* à pression; *(for large quantities)* percolateur *m*.

percussion [pə'kʌʃən] *n* **(a)** *Mus* **p. instruments,** instruments *mpl* de *ou* à percussion; **p. player,** percussionniste *mf*; **p. (section),** la batterie; **(b)** *(in firearm)* percussion *f*; **p. gun,** fusil *m* à percussion; *Mil* **p. pin,** rugueux *m* (de fusée).

percussive [pə'kʌsɪv] *adj* percutant.

perdition [pə'dɪʃən] *n* perte *f*, ruine *f*, *Rel* perdition *f*.

peregrination [perɪgrɪ'neɪʃən] *n* pérégrination *f*.

peregrine ['perɪgrɪn] *n* **p. falcon,** (faucon *m*) pèlerin *m*.

peremptorily [pə'remptərɪlɪ] *adv* péremptoirement; *(to order)* dictatorialement.

peremptory [pə'remptərɪ] *adj* péremptoire; *(refusal)* absolu, décisif; *(tone)* dogmatique, impératif; *(person)* impérieux, autoritaire; *Jur* **p. writ,** mandat *m* de comparaître en personne.

perennial [pə'renɪəl] **1** *adj* éternel, perpétuel; *(plant)* vivace, persistant. **2** *n* plante *f* vivace.

perennially [pə'renɪəlɪ] *adv* à perpétuité, éternellement.

perestroika [perə'strɔɪkə] *n* perestroïka *f*.

perfect¹ ['pɜːfɪkt] **1** *adj* **(a)** parfait; **God alone is p.,** Dieu seul est parfait; **no one's p.,** personne n'est parfait; **p. example,** exemple parfait; **a p. piece of work,** un travail achevé; **her English is p.,** son anglais est impeccable; **to be p.,** être parfait; **to be p., to be in p. condition,** être intact *ou* sans défaut; **p.!,** parfait!; **the p. gift,** le cadeau idéal; **a wine that is the p. accompaniment for fish,** un vin qui accompagne parfaitement le poisson; **in p. sincerity,** en toute sincérité; **he's a p. stranger to me,** il m'est tout à fait inconnu; *F* **he's a p. idiot,** c'est un parfait imbécile;

(b) *Math (nombre, carré)* parfait; *Mus (intervalle)* juste; *(accord)* parfait; *(flower, insect)* parfait; *(in bookbinding) (reliure)* arraphique, sans couture; **p. cadence,** cadence parfaite; *Gram* **the p. tense,** le parfait, le passé composé; *Gram* **future p.,** futur antérieur.

2 *n Gram* **the p.,** le parfait, le passé composé; **verb in the p.,** verbe au parfait.

perfect² [pə'fekt] *vt* **(a)** (*make perfect*) rendre parfait, perfectionner, parfaire (*une méthode etc*); mettre (*une invention, un dessin*) au point; **(b)** *Typ* imprimer *ou* mettre (*une feuille*) en retiration.

perfecting [pə'fektɪŋ] *n* **(a)** perfectionnement *m* (*d'une méthode, d'un travail*); mise *f* au point (*d'un dessin, d'un projet etc*); **(b)** *Typ* (impression *f* en) retiration *f*; **p. machine,** presse *f* à retiration.

perfection [pə'fekʃən] *n* **(a)** (*state*) perfection *f*; **p. itself,** la perfection même; **to attain p.,** toucher *ou* arriver à la perfection; **to do sth to p.,** faire qch à la perfection; **(b)** (*action*) perfectionnement *m* (*d'un travail etc*); **(c)** développement complet (*d'une plante, d'un insecte*).

perfectionism [pə'fekʃənɪz(ə)m] *n* perfectionnisme *m*.

perfectionist [pə'fekʃənɪst] **1** *n* perfectionniste *mf*; **she's such a p.,** elle est tellement perfectionniste. **2** *adj* perfectionniste.

perfective [pə'fektɪv] *Gram* **1** *adj* perfectif. **2** *n* aspect perfectif.

perfectly ['pɜːfɪktlɪ] *adv* parfaitement; (*savoir qch*) à fond; (*faire qch*) à la perfection; **she's p. right,** elle a parfaitement raison; **I'm p. capable of doing,** je suis tout à fait capable de faire; **you know p. well,** (*what I mean*) tu le sais très bien.

perfidious [pə'fɪdɪəs] *adj* perfide; *Lit* **p. Albion,** la perfide Albion.

perfidiously [pə'fɪdɪəslɪ] *adv* perfidement.

perfidiousness [pə'fɪdɪəsnɪs], **perfidy** ['pɜːfɪdɪ] *n* perfidie *f*.

perforate ['pɜːfəreɪt] **1** *vt* **(a)** perforer, percer, transpercer; poinçonner (*une tôle, un billet etc*); grillager (*une plaque etc*); *Tech* perforer (*un papier etc*) en pointillé. **2** *vi Med* (*of ulcer*) déterminer une perforation.

perforated ['pɜːfəreɪtɪd] *adj* perforé; (*stamps*) dentelé.

perforation [pɜːfə'reɪʃən] *n* **(a)** (*action*) perforage *m*, perçage *m*; **(b)** (*hole*) (petit) trou *m*; *Anat* orifice *m*; *Med* perforation *f*; (*for counterfoils etc*) (perforation(s) en) pointillé *m*; (*of postage stamp*) dentelure *f*; **tear along the perforations,** déchirer selon les pointillés.

perforce [pə'fɔːs] *adv Lit* forcément.

perform [pə'fɔːm] **1** *vt* **(a)** célébrer (*un rite*); remplir (*son devoir*); *Surg* **to p. an operation on s.o.,** opérer qn; **(b)** *Th etc* jouer, représenter (*une pièce*); exécuter (*une danse*); exécuter, jouer (*un morceau de musique*); tenir, remplir (*un rôle*). **2** *vi* **(a)** (*of machine*) marcher; **to p. well/badly/***etc*, (*of vehicle, machine etc*) avoir de bons/mauvais/*etc* résultats *ou* de bonnes/mauvaises/*etc* performances; (*of student etc*) avoir de bons/mauvais/*etc* résultats; **how are your shares performing?,** comment vos actions marchent-elles *ou* se tiennent-elle?; **how does he p. in bed?,** comment est-il au lit?; **(b)** *Th* **to p. in a play,** tenir un rôle *ou* jouer dans une pièce; **to p. on the flute,** jouer de la flûte.

performance [pə'fɔːməns] *n* **(a)** exécution *f* (*d'un contrat, d'un opéra*); accomplissement *m* (*d'une tâche*); célébration *f* (*d'un rite*);

(b) *Sp etc* performance *f*; *Ind* cadence *f* (*de travail d'un ouvrier*); *MecE* fonctionnement *m*, marche *f* (*d'une machine*); rendement *m*, performance (*d'un avion, d'un appareil, d'un moteur etc*); comportement *m*, tenue *f* (*d'un matériel*); **to put up a good p.,** (*of team, army etc*) accomplir une bonne performance; **a good/poor p. in exams,** de bons/mauvais résultats à des examens; *Th Mus* **she gave a superb p.,** son interprétation était fantastique; **p. appraisal,** (*of employee*) appréciation *f ou* évaluation *f* du rendement; *Aut* **p. car,** voiture puissante;

(c) *Th etc* représentation *f* (*d'une pièce*); séance *f* (*de cinéma*); **first p.,** première *f*; *Cin* **continuous p.,** cinéma permanent; **there is no p. tonight,** il y a relâche ce soir; **he made such a p. about having to wash his hair,** il a fait toute une histoire parce qu'il devait se laver les cheveux; **what a p.!,** quel spectacle!; **it's such a p. cooking Christmas dinner!,** qu'est-ce que c'est compliqué de préparer un dîner de Noël!

performative [pə'fɔːmətɪv] *Ling* **1** *adj* performatif. **2** *n* performatif *m*.

performer [pə'fɔːmər] *n* **(a)** *Mus* exécutant, -ante, artiste *mf*, interprète *mf*; **(b)** *Th* acteur, -trice; artiste *mf*; **a good/bad/***etc* **p.,** (*student*) un bon/mauvais/*etc* élève; (*vehicle*) une voiture performante/peu performante/*etc*.

performing [pə'fɔːmɪŋ] **1** *adj* (*chien*) savant; **p. arts,** arts *mpl* du spectacle. **2** *n* **(a)** (*execution*) accomplissement *m*, exécution *f* (**of,** de); **(b)** *Th Mus etc* représentation *f* (*d'une pièce*); **p. rights,** *Th* droits *mpl* de représentation; *Mus* droits d'exécution.

perfume¹ ['pɜːfjuːm, *Am* pə'fjuːm] *n* parfum *m*; (*pleasant smell*) odeur *f* agréable; **bottle of p.,** flacon *m* de parfum; **p. counter,** (*in shop*) rayon *m* parfumerie.

perfume² [pə'fjuːm] *vt* parfumer.

perfumed ['pɜːfjuːmd] *adj* (*soap etc*) parfumé.

perfumery [pə'fjuːmərɪ] *n* parfumerie *f*.

perfunctorily [pə'fʌŋktrɪlɪ] *adv* superficiellement; (*negligently*) par manière d'acquit.

perfunctory [pə'fʌŋkt(ə)rɪ] *adj* **(a)** (*inquiry etc*) fait pour la forme, superficiel; **to give sth a p. glance,** donner un bref coup d'œil à qch; **the examination was p.,** l'examen a été une pure formalité; **p. inquiry,** enquête peu poussée *ou* superficielle; (*careless*) renseignements pris par manière d'acquit; **(b)** (*person*) (*negligent*) négligent; (*lacking zeal*) peu zélé.

pergola ['pɜːgələ] *n* pergola *f*.

perhaps [pə'hæps, præps] *adv* peut-être; **p. (so)/not,** peut-être (bien) que oui/que non; **p. we shall come back tomorrow,** peut-être reviendrons-nous demain; **p. you would like to try it on,** voulez-vous l'essayer?

perigee ['perɪdʒiː] *n Astron* périgée *m*.

perihelion [perɪ'hiːlɪən] *n Astron* périhélie *m*.

peril ['perɪl] *n* péril *m*, danger *m*; **in p.,** en danger, en péril; **in p. of one's life,** en danger de mort; **to do sth at one's (own) p.,** faire qch à ses risques et périls; **peril(s) of the sea,** (*in marine insurance*) fortune(s) *f(pl)* de mer.

perilous ['perɪləs] *adj* périlleux, dangereux.

perilously ['perɪləslɪ] *adv* dangereusement; **p. close to the edge of the cliff,** dangereusement proche du bord de la falaise.

perimeter [pə'rɪmɪtər] *n* périmètre *m*; **p. fence,** clôture *f*.

perinatal [perɪ'neɪt(ə)l] *adj Med* (*treatment, care, death*) périnatal.

perineum [perɪ'niːəm] *n Anat* périnée *m*.

period ['pɪərɪəd] *n* **(a)** période *f*; *Sch* heure *f* de cours; *Astron* cycle *m*, période (*de la révolution d'une planète*); *Phys* période (*d'une onde, d'un courant alternatif*); *Nucl Phys* période (*d'un corps radioactif etc*); **for a p. of three months,** pendant une période de trois mois; **within the agreed p.,** dans les délais convenus; *Com etc* **accounting p.,** exercice *m*; *Banking* **deposit for a fixed p.,** dépôt *m* à terme fixe; *Met* **clear periods,** éclaircies *fpl*; *Med* **incubation p.,** période d'incubation; *Physiol* **(monthly) period(s),** règles *fpl*;

(b) (*age*) époque *f*, âge *m*; (*era*) ère *f*; **p. costume,** toilette *f* d'époque; **p. dress,** robe *f* de style; **p. furniture,** meubles *mpl* de style *ou* d'époque; **p. play/novel,** comédie *f*/roman *m* historique;

(c) *esp Am Gram Typ* point *m*; *Am F* **he's no good at maths! — he's no good, p.!,** il est nul en math! — il est nul, un point c'est tout!; *Am* **you're not going to the party, p.!,** tu n'iras pas à cette soirée, un point c'est tout!;

(d) *Liter* phrase *f*; *Mus* phrase complète.

periodic [pɪərɪ'ɒdɪk] *adj* **(a)** périodique; *Ch* **p. table,** tableau *m* de Mendéleiev; **(b)** (*style*) périodique, riche en périodes.

periodical [pɪərɪ'ɒdɪk(ə)l] **1** *adj* périodique. **2** *n* (publication *f*) périodique *m*.

periodically [pɪərɪ'ɒdɪklɪ] *adv* périodiquement.

peripatetic [perɪpə'tetɪk] *adj* ambulant, itinérant.

peripheral [pə'rɪfərəl] **1** *adj* **(a)** (*région, Opt vision etc*) périphérique; **this issue is p. to the central debate,** ce problème est accessoire au débat principal; **(b)** *Comptr* périphérique; **p. device** *or* **unit,** unité *f* périphérique; **p. equipment,** matériel *m* périphérique, périphériques *mpl*. **2** *n* périphérique *f*.

periphery [pə'rɪfərɪ] *n* périphérie *f*, circonférence *f*, pourtour *m*; **on the p. of ...,** en bordure de ... .

periphrasis, *pl* **-es** [pə'rɪfrəsɪs, -iːz] *n* périphrase *f*, circonlocution *f*.

periscope ['perɪskəʊp] *n* périscope *m*.

perish ['perɪʃ] **1** *vi* **(a)** (*of person*) périr, mourir; **p. the thought!,** loin de nous cette pensée!; **(b)** (*of rubber*) se détériorer, se gâter, s'altérer; (*of leather*) s'avachir. **2** *vt* détériorer, altérer; (*of frost*) brûler, griller (*la végétation*).

perishable ['perɪʃəb(ə)l] **1** *adj* périssable; *Nau* **p. cargo,** chargement *m* périssable. **2** *npl* **perishables,** marchandises *fpl* périssables.

perished ['perɪʃt] *adj F* (*very cold*) **I'm p.,** je meurs de froid; **my hands are p.,** j'ai les mains gelées.

perisher ['perɪʃər] *n Br Sl* saligaud *m*; *F* **little p.,** petit coquin.

perishing ['perɪʃɪŋ] *adj* **(a)** *F* (*very cold*) très froid; **it's p.,** il fait un froid de canard; **I'm p.,** je meurs de froid; **(b)** *Br Sl* (*intensifier*) sacré; **p. idiot,** sacré idiot.

peristyle ['perɪstaɪl] *n Archit* péristyle *m*.

peritoneum [perɪtə'niːəm] *n Anat* péritoine *m*.
peritonitis [perɪtə'naɪtɪs] *n Med* péritonite *f*.
periwig ['perɪwɪg] *n Arch* perruque *f*.
periwinkle[1] ['perɪwɪŋk(ə)l] *n* (*plant*) (petite) pervenche *f*; **p. (blue),** bleu pervenche *m inv*.
periwinkle[2] *n* (*mollusc*) bigorneau *m*.
perjure ['pɜːdʒər] *vt* **to p. oneself,** se parjurer.
perjurer ['pɜːdʒərər] *n* parjure *mf*.
perjury ['pɜːdʒərɪ] *n* (*moral offence*) parjure *m*; *Jur* faux serment; **to commit p.,** se parjurer.
perk[1] [pɜːk] *n Br F* à-côté *m*; **perks,** petits bénéfices; **perks include ...,** les avantages acquis comprennent ...; **free tickets are one of the perks of the job,** un des avantages de ce travail est que l'on peut obtenir des billets gratuits; **clean air is a p. of working in the country,** l'air pur est un des avantages du travail à la campagne.
perk[2] *F* **1** *vi* (*of coffee*) passer. **2** *vt* faire (*le café*).
►**perk up 1** *vi* (*become more cheerful*) se ragaillardir; (*after illness*) se ravigoter; (*of party*) s'animer; (*of appetite*) revenir. **2** *vtsep* **(a)** *F* (*revive*) requinquer, ravigoter (*qn*); **to p. up an old dress,** donner un nouvel éclat à une vieille robe; **to p. up s.o.'s appetite,** stimuler l'appétit de qn; **(b)** (*raise*) **to p. up its ears,** (*of dog*) dresser les oreilles.
perkily ['pɜːkɪlɪ] *adv* d'un air éveillé; (*to answer, say*) d'un ton dégagé.
perky ['pɜːkɪ] *adj* (*lively*) éveillé; (*cheerful*) guilleret; (*tone*) dégagé, désinvolte.
perm[1] [pɜːm] *n F* (*hairdressing*) permanente *f*; **to have a p.,** se faire faire une permanente.
perm[2] *vt F* (*hairdressing*) **to have one's hair permed,** se faire faire une permanente.
perm[3] *n Br* (*in football pool*) permutation *f*.
permafrost ['pɜːməfrɒst] *n Geol* permafrost *m*.
permanence ['pɜːmənəns] *n* permanence *f*.
permanency ['pɜːmənənsɪ] *n* **(a)** permanence *f*; **(b)** (*post*) emploi permanent.
permanent ['pɜːmənənt] **1** *adj* permanent; (*employee*) à vie, permanent; (*établissement*) à demeure; (*assemblée*) en permanence; (*résidence, adresse*) fixe; (*ink, stain*) indélébile; **p. hearing loss,** perte définitive de l'ouïe; **p. press,** plissé permanent; **p. job,** situation permanente; **she was in a p. state of depression,** elle était dans un état de dépression permanent; **p. wave,** (*hairdressing*) permanente *f*; *Br Rail* **p. way,** voie *f* (ferrée). **2** *n* (*in hair*) permanente *f*.
permanganate [pə'mæŋgəneɪt] *n Ch* permanganate *m*.
permeability [pɜːmɪə'bɪlɪtɪ] *n* perméabilité *f*, pénétrabilité *f*.
permeable ['pɜːmɪəb(ə)l] *adj* perméable, pénétrable.
permeate ['pɜːmɪeɪt] **1** *vt* **(a)** (*penetrate*) filtrer *ou* passer à travers (*qch*); **water permeates everywhere,** l'eau s'infiltre partout; **the soil was permeated with water,** le sol était saturé d'eau; **a smell of flowers permeated the room,** des fleurs embaumaient la pièce; **(b)** *Fig* (*of feeling, idea etc*) imprégner; **this attitude permeated 18th-century thought,** la pensée du 18e siècle a été imprégnée par cette attitude. **2** *vi* passer; **to p. through sth,** filtrer *ou* passer à travers qch.
permissible [pə'mɪsɪb(ə)l] *adj* admissible, acceptable.
permission [pə'mɪʃən] *n* permission *f*; autorisation *f*; **to ask/give/refuse s.o. p. to do sth,** demander/donner/refuser à qn la permission *ou* l'autorisation de faire qch; **with your p.,** avec votre permission; **you have my p.,** je te donne la permission.
permissive [pə'mɪsɪv] *adj* **(a)** (*tolerant*) permissif; **p. morals,** morale *f* commode; **p. society,** société permissive; **(b)** (*législation*) facultatif.
permissively [pə'mɪsɪvlɪ] *adv* peu strictement.
permissiveness [pə'mɪsɪvnɪs] *n* **(a)** (*tolerance*) tolérance *f*; (*excessive*) laxisme *m*; **(b)** légalité *f* (*d'une action*).
permit[1] ['pɜːmɪt] *n* permis *m*; (*allowing entry*) laissez-passer *m inv*; (*at Customs*) acquit-à-caution *m*, *pl* acquits-à-caution; passavant *m*; **export p.,** autorisation *f* d'exporter; **work p.,** permis de travail; **p. holders only,** (*on sign*) réservé aux personnes autorisées.
permit[2] [pə'mɪt] *v* **(-tt-) 1** *vt* permettre; **to p. s.o. to do sth,** permettre à qn de faire qch, autoriser qn à faire qch; **larger telescopes p. us to ...,** des télescopes plus performants nous permettent de ...; **if I may be permitted,** si vous me le permettez; **p. me to tell you ...!,** (*angrily*) laissez-moi vous dire que ...!; *Br Admin* **permitted hours,** = heures légales de la vente des boissons alcooliques. **2** *vi* **if time permits,** si j'ai *ou* nous avons *etc* le temps; **weather permitting,** si le temps le permet.
►**permit of** *vipo* (*admit possibility of*) admettre (*qch*); **this permits of only one explanation,** ceci n'admet qu'une explication.
permutation [pɜːmjʊ'teɪʃən] *n* permutation *f*.
permute [pə'mjuːt] *vt Ling Math* permuter.
pernicious [pə'nɪʃəs] *adj* pernicieux; (*doctrine etc*) malsain, délétère; *Med* **p. anaemia,** anémie pernicieuse.
perniciously [pə'nɪʃəslɪ] *adv* pernicieusement.
pernickety [pə'nɪkɪtɪ] *adj F* (*person*) tatillon, vétilleux, pointilleux; (*job*) délicat, minutieux; **to be p. about one's food,** être difficile sur la nourriture.
perorate ['perəreɪt] *vi* **(a)** (*conclude speech*) faire la péroraison; **(b)** (*speak at length*) discourir longuement.
peroration [perə'reɪʃən] *n* **(a)** (*conclusion*) péroraison *f*; **(b)** (*long speech*) discours prolongé *ou* de longue haleine.
peroxide[1] [pə'rɒksaɪd] *n Ch* peroxyde *m*; *F* **p. blonde,** fausse blonde.
peroxide[2] *vt* faire blondir (*ses cheveux*) à l'eau oxygénée.
perpendicular [pɜːpən'dɪkjʊlər] **1** *adj* perpendiculaire (**to,** à); (*wall, cliff etc*) vertical, -aux; (*upright, straight*) à plomb; (*cliff*) à pic; **line p. to another,** ligne perpendiculaire à une autre; *Eng Arch* **p. style,** style *m* (gothique) perpendiculaire. **2** *n* **(a)** fil *m* à plomb; **out of (the) p.,** hors d'aplomb, hors d'équerre; **(b)** *Math* perpendiculaire *f*.
perpendicularly [pɜːpən'dɪkjʊləlɪ] *adv* perpendiculairement; verticalement; d'aplomb; **the cliff rose p.,** la falaise s'élevait tout droit.
perpetrate ['pɜːpɪtreɪt] *vt* commettre, perpétrer (*un crime*); être l'auteur de (*une gaffe, une farce*).
perpetration [pɜːpɪ'treɪʃən] *n* perpétration *f* (*d'un crime etc*).
perpetrator ['pɜːpɪtreɪtər] *n* auteur *m* (*d'un crime etc*).
perpetual [pə'petjʊəl] *adj* (*eternal*) perpétuel, éternel; (*incessant*) sans fin, continuel, incessant; **p. motion,** mouvement perpétuel.
perpetually [pə'petjʊəlɪ] *adv* (*eternally*) perpétuellement, éternellement; (*ceaselessly*) sans cesse; (*continually*) continuellement.
perpetuate [pə'petjʊeɪt] *vt* perpétuer, éterniser; **to p. s.o.'s memory,** préserver le nom de qn de l'oubli; **to p. the species,** perpétuer l'espèce.
perpetuation [pəpetjʊ'eɪʃən] *n* perpétuation *f*, éternisation *f*; (*of s.o.'s memory*) préservation *f* de l'oubli.
perpetuity [pɜːpɪ'tjuːɪtɪ] *n* **(a)** perpétuité *f*; **in** *or* **to** *or* **for p.,** à perpétuité; **(b)** *Jur* jouissance *f* (*d'un bien*) à perpétuité; **(rent in) p.,** rente constituée en perpétuel, rente perpétuelle.
perplex [pə'pleks] *vt* confondre, troubler (*qn*); **to be perplexed,** être perplexe.
perplexing [pə'pleksɪŋ] *adj* (*problem etc*) troublant; (*book, person etc*) difficile (à comprendre); **it's very p.,** on n'y comprend rien.
perplexity [pə'pleksɪtɪ] *n* perplexité *f*, confusion *f*.
perquisite ['pɜːkwɪzɪt] *n Br Fml* = **PERK**.
perry ['perɪ] *n* poiré *m*.
persecute ['pɜːsɪkjuːt] *vt* persécuter (*des hérétiques etc*); tourmenter, harceler (*qn*); brimer (*des recrues, des nouveaux élèves etc*).
persecution [pɜːsɪ'kjuːʃən] *n* persécution *f*; **p. mania,** délire *m ou* manie *f* de la persécution; *Psy* **p. complex,** complexe *m* de persécution.
persecutor ['pɜːsɪkjuːtər] *n* persécuteur, -trice.
perseverance [pɜːsɪ'vɪərəns] *n* persévérance *f* (*dans le travail etc*).
persevere [pɜːsɪ'vɪər] *vi* persévérer (*dans son travail, à faire qch*) (**with sth,** dans qch); **to p. in one's belief that ...,** persister à croire que ... .
persevering [pɜːsɪ'vɪərɪŋ] *adj* persévérant.
Persia ['pɜːʃə] *n* Perse *f*.
Persian ['pɜːʃən] **1** *adj* persan; *Antiq* perse; (*chat, cheval*) persan; (*tapis*) de Perse; **the P. Gulf,** le Golfe persique. **2** *n* **(a)** (*person*) Persan, -ane; *Antiq* Perse *mf*; **(b)** (*cat*) chat persan; **(c)** *Ling* perse *m*.
persimmon [pɜː'sɪmən] *n* **(a)** (*fruit*) plaquemine *f*; (*from Japan*) kaki *m*; **(b) p. (tree),** plaqueminier *m*.
persist [pə'sɪst] *vi* **(a)** persister, s'obstiner (**in doing sth,** à faire qch); **to p. in one's opinion,** persister *ou* s'obstiner dans son opinion; **(b)** (*of fog, fever etc*) persister, continuer.
persistence [pə'sɪstəns] *n* **(a)** persistance *f*, ténacité *f*, obstination *f* (**in doing sth,** à faire qch); **(b)** (*of fog, fever etc*) persistance *f*, continuité *f*.
persistent [pə'sɪstənt] *adj* **(a)** (*person*) persistant, opiniâtre, tenace; (*pluie*) qui s'obstine; **(b)** (*incessant*) persistant; *Com* **p. demand for ...,** demande suivie pour ...; **(c)** *Bot*

(*feuillage*) persistant.
persistently [pə'sɪstəntlɪ] *adv* avec persistance.
persnickety [pə'snɪkɪtɪ] *adj US* = **PERNICKETY**.
person ['pɜːs(ə)n] *n* **(a)** personne *f*, individu *m*; *Pej* individu, type *m*; **he/she is a kind/strange p.**, c'est une personne charmante/étrange; **he's/she's not an outdoor p.**, il est casanier *ou F* pantouflard/elle est casanière *ou F* pantouflarde; **private p.**, (simple) particulier *m*; **to act through a third p.**, passer par une tierce personne; **there is no p. of that name here,** il n'y a personne de ce nom ici; *Jur* **some p. or persons unknown,** un certain quidam; **what's he/she like as a p.?**, il/elle est comment sur le plan moral?; **I like her as a p.**, je l'aime en tant que personne; **who is this p.?**, qui est cette personne?; **in (one's own) p.**, en (propre) personne; **help came, in the p. of Amanda,** on a trouvé de l'aide, en la personne d'Amanda; **he came in p.**, il est venu en personne; **to be delivered in p.**, à remettre en main(s) propre(s); **to carry weapons on one's p.**, porter des armes sur soi; *Jur* **natural p.**, personne physique *ou* naturelle; *Jur* **artificial p.**, personne *ou* personnalité morale *ou* civile *ou* juridique;
(b) *Gram* **verb in the first p.**, verbe à la première personne; **the second p. plural,** la deuxième personne du pluriel; **the story is told in the first p.**, l'histoire est racontée à la première personne;
(c) (one) God in three Persons, la Trinité.
-person ['pɜːs(ə)n] *suff* **chairp.**, directeur, -trice; **spokesp.**, porte-parole *m inv*; **salesp.**, vendeur, -euse.
personable ['pɜːsənəb(ə)l] *adj* bien (fait) de sa personne; **he's very p.**, il présente bien.
personage ['pɜːsənɪdʒ] *n* personnage *m*.
personal ['pɜːsən(ə)l] *adj* **(a)** personnel; **p.**, (*on letter*) personnelle; **to be careless about one's p. appearance,** négliger sa tenue; **to make a p. appearance,** venir *ou* paraître en personne; *Sp etc* **3 mins 22 secs is my p. best,** mon record est 3 min 22; **p. assistant,** (*of executive etc*) assistant, -ante; (*with secretarial duties*) secrétaire *mf* de direction; *Journ* **p. column,** petites annonces; *Comptr* **p. computer,** ordinateur individuel; **to do sth as a p. favour,** rendre un service à titre personnel; **p. friend,** ami(e) personnel(le); **p. hygiene,** hygiène *f*; *Br Banking* **p. identification number,** code confidentiel; *Admin* **p. income,** revenu *m* des personnes physiques; **p. liberty,** liberté individuelle; *Banking* **p. loan,** prêt personnel; **it's a p. matter,** c'est une affaire privée *ou* personnelle; **my p. opinion** *or* **view is that ...**, à mon avis ...; **for p. reasons,** pour des raisons personnelles; **don't be p., don't make p. remarks,** ne faites pas des allusions personnelles; **it's nothing p. but ...**, ça n'a rien de personnel mais ..., **p. stereo,** baladeur *m*; **to give a p. touch to sth,** donner une touche personnelle à qch; **I want it for my p. use,** j'en ai besoin pour mon usage personnel; **articles for p. use,** (*at customs*) effets à usage personnel;
(b) *Jur* **p. action,** action mobilière; **p. estate** *or* **property,** biens personnels *ou* meubles *ou* mobiliers; **p. effects,** effets personnels;
(c) *Gram* (*pronoun*) personnel.
personality [pɜːsə'nælɪtɪ] *n* **(a)** (*character*) personnalité *f*; **he's got no p.**, il n'a aucune personnalité; *Psy* **p. disorder,** trouble *m* de la personnalité; **(b)** (*well-known person*) personnalité *f*; **(c)** *Old-fashioned* (*personal remark*) (*often pl*) **to indulge in personalities,** faire des remarques personnelles.
personalize ['pɜːsənəlaɪz] *vt* personnaliser; **a personalized shirt/***etc*, une chemise/*etc* personnalisée; **personalized letter,** lettre personnelle.
personally ['pɜːsən(ə)lɪ] *adv* personnellement; (*intervenir*) en personne; **to attend to sth p.**, s'occuper de qch en personne *ou* personnellement; **p. I think ...**, pour ma part je pense ...; **that belongs to me p.**, cela m'appartient en propre; **to deliver sth to s.o. p.**, remettre qch à qn en main(s) propre(s); **don't take it p.**, (*what was said, done*) n'en faites pas une affaire personnelle.
personalty ['pɜːsənəltɪ] *n Jur* biens meubles, biens mobiliers.
personification [pɜːsɒnɪfɪ'keɪʃən] *n* personnification *f*; **to be the p. of meanness,** être l'avarice même *ou* l'avarice en personne.
personify [pɜː'sɒnɪfaɪ] *vt* personnifier; **he's meanness personified,** il est *ou* c'est l'avarice même *ou* l'avarice en personne.
personnel [pɜːsə'nel] *n* personnel *m*; **I work in p.**, (*that department*) je travaille au service du personnel; (*that field*) je suis dans la branche du personnel; *Mil* **armoured p. carrier,** véhicule blindé de transport de personnel; **anti-p. mine,** mine *f* anti-personnel; **p. department/manager,** service *m*/directeur *m* du personnel.
perspective [pə'spektɪv] **1** *n* **(a)** *Math Art* perspective *f*; **drawing in p.**, dessin *m* en perspective; **picture out of p.**, tableau dont la perspective est fausse; **to see a matter in its true p.**, voir une affaire sous son vrai jour; **to put sth in(to) p.**, remettre qch à sa (vraie) place; voir les choses comme elles sont; **let's keep things in p.**, n'exagérons rien; **(b)** (*view*) vue *f*; **a fine p. opened out before his eyes,** une belle perspective s'ouvrit devant ses yeux; **with a long p. of happy days before us,** avec devant nous une longue perspective de jours heureux. **2** *adj* (*dessin etc*) perspectif, en perspective; **p. lines of a picture,** fuyants *mpl* d'un tableau.
perspicacious [pɜːspɪ'keɪʃəs] *adj* (*person*) perspicace; (*comment*) fin.
perspicaciously [pɜːspɪ'keɪʃəslɪ] *adv* avec perspicacité.
perspicacity [pɜːspɪ'kæsɪtɪ] *n* perspicacité *f*; clairvoyance *f*, discernement *m*.
perspicuity [pɜːspɪ'kjuːɪtɪ] *n* (*of person*) perspicacité *f*; clarté *f*, netteté *f*, lucidité *f* (*du style etc*).
perspicuous [pə'spɪkjʊəs] *adj* clair, net, *f* nette, lucide.
perspicuously [pə'spɪkjʊəslɪ] *adv* clairement, nettement.
perspiration [pɜːspə'reɪʃən] *n* (*act of perspiring*) transpiration *f*; (*sweat*) sueur *f*; **beads of p.**, gouttes *fpl* de sueur; **bathed in** *or* **dripping with p.**, trempé de sueur, en nage.
perspire [pə'spaɪər] *vi* transpirer, suer.
persuade [pə'sweɪd] **1** *vt* persuader, convaincre (*qn*) (**to do,** de faire); **to p. s.o. not to do sth,** déconseiller à qn *ou* dissuader qn de faire qch; **nothing could p. her,** aucun argument n'a pu la convaincre. **2** *vi Fml* **the argument fails to p.**, cet argument n'est pas très convaincant.
persuasion [pə'sweɪʒən] *n* **(a)** (*act of persuading, ability to persuade*) persuasion *f*; **power of p.**, force *f* de persuasion; **the art of p.**, l'art de persuader; **(b)** (*beliefs*) **(religious) p.**, (*religion*) religion *f*, foi *f*, confession *f*; (*sect*) secte *f*, communion *f*; **(political) p.**, opinions *fpl* en matière de politique, idéologie *f*; **to be of the Catholic p.**, être de religion catholique; *Hum* **a person of the male/female p.**, un homme/une femme; *Fml* **she is of a different p.**, elle est d'une autre obédience; *Old-fashioned* **it's my p. that ...**, je suis persuadé *ou* convaincu que ... .
persuasive [pə'sweɪzɪv, -sɪv] *adj* (*person*) persuasif; (*argument*) convaincant; **she can be very p.**, elle a un grand pouvoir de persuasion.
persuasively [pə'sweɪzɪvlɪ, -sɪvlɪ] *adv* (*to say*) d'un ton persuasif.
persuasiveness [pə'sweɪzɪvnɪs, -sɪv-] *n* force persuasive, persuasion *f*.
pert [pɜːt] *adj* **(a)** (*impertinent*) effronté, hardi; **(b)** (*lively*) guilleret, plein d'entrain.
pertain [pə'teɪn] *vi Fml* **(a)** (*belong*) appartenir (*à qch*); **the house and the land pertaining to it,** la maison et le terrain qui fait partie de la propriété; **(b) to p. to,** (*have reference*) regarder (*qch*).
pertinacious [pɜːtɪ'neɪʃəs] *n* obstiné, opiniâtre.
pertinaciously [pɜːtɪ'neɪʃəslɪ] *adv* obstinément, opiniâtrement.
pertinence ['pɜːtɪnəns] *n* pertinence *f* (*d'une raison, d'une remarque*); à-propos *m*, justesse *f* (*d'une remarque*).
pertinent ['pɜːtɪnənt] *adj* (*reason, remark*) pertinent; (*remark*) à propos, juste; **to be p. to,** avoir rapport à (*une question*); relever de (*une affaire etc*).
pertinently ['pɜːtɪnəntlɪ] *adv* d'une manière pertinente.
pertly [pɜːtlɪ] *adv* (*see adj*) **(a)** (*to say*) d'un ton effronté; **(b)** (*to look*) d'un air guilleret.
pertness ['pɜːtnɪs] *n* **(a)** (*impertinence*) effronterie *f*; **(b)** air guilleret.
perturb [pə'tɜːb] *vt* **(a)** (*worry*) troubler, inquiéter, agiter; **to be perturbed,** être agité *ou* troublé *ou* inquiet; **(b)** (*put into confusion*) jeter le désordre *ou* la perturbation dans (*un royaume etc*); **(c)** *Astron* dévier (*un astre*); *Phys* affoler (*l'aiguille d'une boussole*).
perturbation [pɜːtə'beɪʃən] *n* **(a)** agitation *f*, inquiétude *f*, trouble *m* (*de l'esprit*); **(b)** affolement *m* (*de l'aiguille aimantée*); **(c)** (*putting into disorder*) perturbation *f*, désordre *m*.
Peru [pə'ruː] *n* Pérou *m*.
perusal [pə'ruːz(ə)l] *n* lecture *f*; **for p.**, (*of document*) en communication.
peruse [pə'ruːz] *vt* lire attentivement, prendre connaissance de (*qch*).
Peruvian [pə'ruːvɪən] **1** *adj* péruvien. **2** *n* Péruvien, -ienne.
perv [pɜːv] *n Sl* = **PERVERT[1]**.

pervade [pɜː'veɪd] *vt* s'infiltrer dans, se répandre dans (*qch*); **the scent of pine trees pervaded the air,** l'air était embaumé de l'odeur des pins.
pervading [pɜː'veɪdɪŋ] *adj* (*smell*) pénétrant; **(all-)p.,** qui se répand partout; (*influence etc*) régnant, dominant.
pervasive [pɜː'veɪsɪv] *adj* qui se répand partout; (*gloom*) envahissant; (*perfume etc*) subtil.
perverse [pə'vɜːs] *adj* pervers, perverti; (*stubborn*) entêté; (*contrary*) contrariant, désobligeant; (*cantankerous*) revêche, acariâtre; **to take a p. pleasure in doing,** prendre un malin plaisir à faire.
perversely [pə'vɜːslɪ] *adv* perversement, avec perversité; (*contrarily*) d'une manière contrariante.
perverseness [pə'vɜːsnɪs], **perversity** [pə'vɜːsɪtɪ] *n* perversité *f*; (*contrariness*) esprit contraire *ou* contrariant; (*cantankerousness*) caractère *m* revêche *ou* acariâtre.
perversion [pə'vɜːʃən] *n* **(a)** (*act of perverting*) action *f* de pervertir; (*state*) pervertissement *m*; **(b)** (*perverted action, form*) perversion *f*; **a p. of the truth,** un travestissement de la vérité; **sexual perversions,** perversions sexuelles.
pervert¹ ['pɜːvɜːt] *n Psy* **(sexual) p.,** pervers(e) (sexuel(le)).
pervert² [pə'vɜːt] *vt* **(a)** (*divert*) détourner (*qch de son but*); **to p. the course of justice,** égarer la justice; **(b)** (*corrupt*) pervertir (*qn*); dépraver (*le goût*); **(c)** (*distort*) altérer, dénaturer (*les faits, les mots de qn*).
pervious ['pɜːvɪəs] *adj* perméable (*à l'eau etc*).
pesky ['peskɪ] *adj Am F* maudit, sacré.
pessary ['pesərɪ] *n Med* pessaire *m*.
pessimism ['pesɪmɪz(ə)m] *n* pessimisme *m*.
pessimist ['pesɪmɪst] *n* pessimiste *mf*.
pessimistic [pesɪ'mɪstɪk] *adj* pessimiste.
pessimistically [pesɪ'mɪstɪklɪ] *adv* avec pessimisme.
pest [pest] *n* **(a)** (*insect, plant etc*) animal *m ou* insecte *m ou* plante *f* nuisible; **rabbits are a p. here,** ici les lapins sont un fléau; **p. control,** (service *m* de) dératisation *f ou* désinsectisation *f etc*; **(b)** *F* (*nuisance*) **he's a perfect p.!,** c'est un vrai casse-pieds!; **stop being a p.!,** arrête d'embêter le monde!
pester ['pestər] *vt F* tourmenter, importuner (*qn*); **to p. s.o. with questions,** importuner *ou* assommer *ou* harceler qn de (ses) questions; **to p. s.o. for money,** harceler qn pour obtenir de l'argent.
pesticide ['pestɪsaɪd] *n* pesticide *m*.
pestiferous [pes'tɪfərəs] *adj* (*air*) pestilentiel; (*insects*) nuisible; (*doctrine*) pernicieux.
pestilence ['pestɪləns] *n* peste *f*.
pestilential [pestɪ'lenʃəl] *adj* (*disease*) pestilentiel, pestiféré; (*smell*) pestilentiel, infect; *F* (*irritating*) assommant, empoisonnant.
pestle ['pes(ə)l] *n* pilon *m* (*pour mortier*).
pet¹ [pet] *n* **(a)** (*animal*) animal familier *ou* de compagnie; **do you have a p.?,** est-ce que tu as un animal?; **she's got a p. monkey/budgerigar/*etc*,** elle a un singe/une perruche/*etc* apprivoisé(e); **p. shop,** animalerie *f*; **p. food,** nourriture *f* pour chiens *ou* chats *etc*; **sorry no pets!,** (nos amis) les animaux ne sont pas admis; **(b)** (*favourite child*) enfant gâté; **mother's/teacher's p.,** le chouchou de sa maman/du professeur; **my p.!,** mon chéri!, mon petit chou!; **my p. hate,** ma bête noire; **p. name,** (*diminutive*) diminutif *m*; (*used by friends, relatives*) surnom *m*; **p. subject,** sujet *m* de prédilection.
pet² *vt* **(-tt-) (a)** (*make a pet of*) choyer, chouchouter (*qn*); **(b)** (*stroke, pat*) caresser, câliner (*qn, un chien etc*); **(c)** (*kiss, touch*) peloter (*qn*).
pet³ *n Old-fashioned F* **to be in a p.,** (*to sulk*) bouder; être de mauvaise humeur.
petal ['pet(ə)l] *n* (*of flower*) pétale *m*; *F* **thanks, p.,** merci mon chou.
petard [pe'tɑːd] *n* **to be hoist with one's own p.,** être pris à son propre piège.
Pete [piːt] *n* (*dimin of* **Peter**) Pierrot *m*; *F* **for P.'s sake!,** pour l'amour du ciel!
peter ['piːtər] *n Sl* (*safe*) coffre-fort *m*.
Peter ['piːtər] *n* (*name*) Pierre *m*; *Nau* **Blue P.,** (*flag*) pavillon *m* de partance *ou* de départ; **P. Pan collar,** col *m* Claudine.
▸**peter out** *vi F* (*of conversation, interest, enthusiasm*) tarir; (*of scheme*) aboutir à rien; (*of stream, path*) disparaître; (*of flame etc*) mourir.
peterman ['piːtəmæn] *n Sl* (*safe-breaker*) casseur *m* de coffre-fort.
petersham ['piːtəʃəm] *n Tex* gros-grain *m*.
petite [pə'tiːt] *adj* (*woman*) menue.
petition¹ [pɪ'tɪʃən] *n* pétition *f*, supplique *f*, requête *f*; prière *f* (*à Dieu*); **to grant a p.,** faire droit à une pétition; **to hand in/sign a p.,** déposer *ou* remettre/signer une pétition; *Jur* **p. for mercy,** recours *m* en grâce; **p. for a divorce,** demande *f* en divorce; **p. in bankruptcy,** (*made by creditors*) requête des créanciers; (*made by bankrupt*) requête du négociant insolvable.
petition² **1** *vt* adresser *ou* présenter une pétition *ou* une requête à (*la cour, un souverain etc*); supplier (*le souverain*) (**to do sth,** de faire qch). **2** *vi* pétitionner; **to p. for sth,** demander *ou* requérir *ou* solliciter qch; **to p. for mercy,** se pourvoir *ou* recourir en grâce.
petitioner [pɪ'tɪʃənər] *n* pétitionnaire *mf*; *Jur* requérant, -ante.
petrel ['petrəl] *n* (*bird*) pétrel *m*; **storm(y) p.,** pétrel tempête.
petrifaction [petrɪ'fækʃən] *n* pétrification *f*.
petrified ['petrɪfaɪd] *adj* (*bois etc*) pétrifié; *F* **p. with fear,** pétrifié *ou* paralysé de terreur; *F* **I was p. he would shoot me,** j'étais mort de peur à l'idée qu'il me tire dessus.
petrify ['petrɪfaɪ] **1** *vt* pétrifier (*le bois etc*); *F* (*with fear*) pétrifier, méduser, paralyser (*qn*). **2** *vi* se pétrifier.
petrifying ['petrɪfaɪɪŋ] *adj* pétrifiant; *F* paralysant.
petrochemical [petrəʊ'kemɪk(ə)l] **1** *adj* (*industrie etc*) pétrochimique. **2** *npl* **petrochemicals,** produits *mpl* pétrochimiques.
petrodollar ['petrəʊdɒlər] *n* pétrodollar *m*.
petrol ['petrəl] *n Ch* essence *f* (minérale); *Br Aut* essence, *Swiss* benzine *f*; **anti-knock p.,** essence antidétonante; **high-grade** *or* **four-star p.,** = supercarburant *m*, *F* super *m*; **p. bomb,** cocktail *m* Molotov; **p. can,** bidon *m* à essence; **p. cap,** bouchon *m* de réservoir; **p. pump,** (*at petrol station, in car*) pompe *f* à essence; **p. tank,** réservoir *m* à essence; **p. station,** station-service *f*.
petroleum [pə'trəʊlɪəm] *n* pétrole *m*; **crude p.,** pétrole brut; **p. jelly,** vaseline *f*.
petrology [pe'trɒlədʒɪ] *n* pétrologie *f*.
petticoat ['petɪkəʊt] *n* jupon *m*, combinaison *f*; *F* **p. government,** régime *m* de cotillons.
pettifogging ['petɪfɒgɪŋ] *adj* (*detail*) insignifiant; (*objection*) de pure chicane; (*person*) chicanier; **p. lawyer,** avocassier *m*.
pettiness ['petɪnɪs] *n* (*insignificance*) insignifiance *f*; (*small-mindedness*) mesquinerie *f*.
petting ['petɪŋ] *n* pelotage *m*; **heavy p.,** attouchements *mpl*.
pettish ['petɪʃ] *adj* de mauvaise humeur, maussade, irritable.
pettishly ['petɪʃlɪ] *adv* avec mauvaise humeur.
petty ['petɪ] *adj* **(a)** (*insignificant, minor*) petit, insignifiant; **p. annoyances,** tracasseries *fpl*, petits ennuis (*de la vie quotidienne*); *Com* **p. cash,** petite caisse; **these are only p. differences,** ce ne sont que des différences insignifiantes *ou* sans importance; *Jur* **p. larceny,** vol *m* simple; **p. offences,** contraventions *fpl*; *Nau* **p. officer,** second maître *m*; **chief p. officer,** maître *m*; **(b) p.(-minded),** mesquin.
petty-mindedness [petɪ'maɪndɪdnɪs] *n* mesquinerie *f*.
petulance ['petjʊləns] *n* irascibilité *f*; **an outburst of p.,** un accès de mauvaise humeur.
petulant ['petjʊlənt] *adj* irritable, susceptible.
petulantly ['petjʊləntlɪ] *adv* (*to look at, say*) d'un air *ou* ton irrité.
petunia [pɪ'tjuːnɪə] *n* (*plant*) pétunia *m*.
pew [pjuː] *n* banc *m* d'église; *F* **take a p.!,** assieds-toi!
pewter ['pjuːtər] *n* étain *m*; **p. (ware),** étains *mpl*, vaisselle *f* d'étain; **I like p. (ware),** j'aime les étains.
PG [piː'dʒiː] *n Cin* (*abbr* **parental guidance**) = film etc qui exige une autorisation parentale.
pH [piː'eɪtʃ] *n Ch* pH *m*; **to have a pH of 9,** avoir un pH de 9.
phalanx ['fælæŋks] *n* **(a)** (*pl usu* **phalanxes** ['fælæŋksɪz]) (*in ancient armies*) *& Fig* phalange *f*; **(b)** *Anat Bot* (*pl usu* **phalanges** [fæ'lændʒiːz]) phalange *f*.
phallic ['fælɪk] *adj* phallique; **p. symbol,** symbole *m* phallique.
phallus ['fæləs] *n* phallus *m*.
phantasm ['fæntæz(ə)m] *n* (*illusion*) illusion *f*; (*ghost*) apparition *f*.
phantasmagoria [fæntæzmæ'gɒrɪə] *n* fantasmagorie *f*.
phantasy ['fæntəsɪ] *n* = **FANTASY**.
phantom ['fæntəm] *n* fantôme *m*, spectre *m*; *Tel* **p. circuit,** circuit *m* fantôme; *Med* **p. limb,** membre *m* fantôme; **p. ship,** vaisseau *m* fantôme.
Pharaoh ['feərəʊ] *n Antiq* pharaon *m*.
pharisee ['færɪsiː] *n* pharisien *m*.
pharmaceutical [fɑːmə'sjuːtɪk(ə)l] **1** *adj* pharma-

ceutique. **2** *npl* **pharmaceuticals,** industrie *f* pharmaceutique; **I'm in pharmaceuticals,** je suis dans la pharmaceutique; **pharmaceuticals company,** société *f* pharmaceutique.

pharmacist ['fɑːməsɪst] *n* pharmacien, -ienne.

pharmacological [fɑːməkə'lɒdʒɪk(ə)l] *adj* pharmacologique.

pharmacologist [fɑːmə'kɒlədʒɪst] *n* pharmacologiste *mf*, pharmacologue *mf*.

pharmacology [fɑːmə'kɒlədʒɪ] *n* pharmacologie *f*.

pharmacopoeia [fɑːməkəʊ'piːə] *n* (*book*) pharmacopée *f*; (*collection of drugs*) pharmacie *f*.

pharmacy ['fɑːməsɪ] *n* pharmacie *f*.

pharyngitis [færɪn'dʒaɪtɪs] *n Med* pharyngite *f*.

pharynx ['færɪŋks] *n Anat* pharynx *m*.

phase¹ [feɪz] *n* phase *f* (*d'un phénomène, d'un processus etc*); **initial/final p.,** phase initiale/finale; **to enter upon a new p.,** entrer dans une nouvelle phase; **it's just a p. (he's/she's going through),** ça lui passera; *Phys MecE* **in p.,** en phase; **out of p.,** hors de phase, déphasé; *Fig* déphasé; *El* **single/two/three-p. current,** courant monophasé/diphasé/triphasé.

phase² *vt* **(a)** faire (*qch*) progressivement; développer (*un projet*) en phases successives; échelonner (*un programme de fabrication etc*); **(b)** *El etc* mettre en phases, caler en phase.

►phase in *vtsep* introduire *ou* adopter progressivement (*de nouvelles méthodes etc*); mettre en place progressivement (*de nouvelles installations etc*).

►phase out *vtsep* éliminer progressivement (*de vieilles méthodes, de vieux équipements etc*).

phased [feɪzd] *adj* **(a)** par phases, par stades, progressif, échelonné; (*évacuation*) par échelons, par étapes; **(b)** *El* phasé; (*lumière*) cohérent.

phasing ['feɪzɪŋ] *n* **(a)** exécution par phases *ou* par stades *ou* progressive (*de qch*); échelonnement *m* (*d'un programme de fabrication etc*); **(b)** *El etc* mise *f* en phase, calage *m* en phase.

phasing in *n* adoption *ou* introduction progressive (*de nouvelles méthodes etc*); mise en place progressive (*de nouvelles installations etc*).

phasing out *n* élimination progressive (*de vieilles méthodes, de vieux équipements etc*).

PhD [piːeɪtʃ'diː] *n Univ* (*abbr* **Doctor of Philosophy**) (*diploma*) = doctorat *m*; *F* (*person*) docteur *m*, titulaire *mf* d'un doctorat; **to have a PhD in Maths,** avoir un doctorat en maths.

pheasant ['fez(ə)nt] *n* faisan *m*; **cock p.,** (coq *m*) faisan; **hen p.,** (poule *f*) faisane *f*; **young p., p. poult,** faisandeau *m*; **golden p.,** faisan doré; **p. shoot,** faisanderie *f*; **p. shooting,** chasse *f* au faisan.

phenix ['fiːnɪks] *n US Myth* phénix *m*.

phenobarbitone [fiːnəʊ'bɑːbɪtəʊn] *n Pharm* phénobarbital *m*.

phenol ['fiːnɒl] *n Ch* phénol *m*.

phenomenal [fɪ'nɒmɪn(ə)l] *adj* (*very great*) phénoménal, prodigieux; *Phil* phénoménal, -aux.

phenomenally [fɪ'nɒmɪn(ə)lɪ] *adv* phénoménalement, prodigieusement.

phenomenological [fənɒmənə'lɒdʒɪk(ə)l] *adj* phénoménologique.

phenomenologist [fənɒmə'nɒlədʒɪst] *n* phénoménologue *mf*.

phenomenology [fənɒmə'nɒlədʒɪ] *n* phénoménologie *f*.

phenomenon, *pl* **-mena** [fɪ'nɒmɪnən, -mɪnə] *n* phénomène *m*.

phew [fjuː] *int* pfff!; (*disgust*) pouah!

phial ['faɪəl] *n* fiole *f*, flacon *m*, ampoule *f*.

Phil *abbr* **Philadelphia.**

philander [fɪ'lændər] *vi Old-fashioned* courir le jupon.

philanderer [fɪ'lændərər] *n* coureur *m* de jupons.

philanthropic [fɪlən'θrɒpɪk] *adj* philanthropique; (*person*) philanthrope.

philanthropist [fɪ'lænθrəpɪst] *n* philanthrope *mf*.

philanthropy [fɪ'lænθrəpɪ] *n* philanthropie *f*.

philatelic [fɪlə'telɪk] *adj* philatélique.

philatelist [fɪ'lætəlɪst] *n* philatéliste *mf*.

philately [fɪ'lætəlɪ] *n* philatélie *f*.

-phile [faɪl] *suff* -phile; **Anglop./Francop./***etc*, anglophile *mf*/francophile *mf*/*etc*.

philharmonic [fɪlə'mɒnɪk] **1** *adj* philharmonique. **2** *n* philharmonique *f*.

-philia [fɪlɪə] *suff* -philie; **necrop./Anglop./***etc*, nécrophilie *f*/anglophilie *f*/*etc*.

Philippine ['fɪlɪpiːn] **1** *adj* philippin. **2** *n* **the Philippines,** les (îles *fpl*) Philippines *fpl*.

Philistine ['fɪlɪstaɪn] **1** *n Bible* Philistin *m*; *Art Lit* philistin *m*. **2** *adj Art Lit* philistin.

Phillips ® ['fɪlɪps] *adj* **P. screw/screwdriver,** vis *f*/tournevis *m* à empreinte cruciforme.

philodendron [fɪlə'dendrən] *n* (*house plant*) philodendron *m*.

philological [fɪlə'lɒdʒɪk(ə)l] *adj* philologique.

philologist [fɪ'lɒlədʒɪst] *n* philologue *mf*.

philology [fɪ'lɒlədʒɪ] *n* philologie *f*.

philosopher [fɪ'lɒsəfər] *n* philosophe *mf*; **the p.'s stone,** la pierre philosophale.

philosophic(al) [fɪlə'sɒfɪk, -ɪk(ə)l] *adj* philosophique; (*person*) philosophe; **she was p. about her defeat,** elle a pris sa défaite en philosophe *ou* avec philosophie.

philosophically [fɪlə'sɒfɪklɪ] *adv* philosophiquement; (*to react etc*) en philosophe, avec philosophie.

philosophize [fɪ'lɒsəfaɪz] *vi* philosopher.

philosophy [fɪ'lɒsəfɪ] *n* philosophie *f*; **moral p.,** philosophie morale; **natural p.,** sciences *fpl* de la nature; **a personal p.,** une philosophie personnelle; **one's own p. about sth,** sa conception personnelle d'une chose; *F* **my p. is, ...,** ma philosophie c'est ...; **with p.,** (*supporter des malheurs*) avec philosophie, en philosophe.

philtre, *US* **philter** ['fɪltər] *n* philtre *m*.

phiz [fɪz] **, phizog** ['fɪzɒg] *n esp Br F* visage *m*, binette *f*.

phlebitis [flɪ'baɪtɪs] *n Med* phlébite *f*.

phlegm [flem] *n* **(a)** (*mucus*) flegme *m*, pituite *f* (bronchiale); **to cough up p.,** tousser gras; **(b)** (*composure*) flegme *m*, calme *m*.

phlegmatic [fleg'mætɪk] *adj* flegmatique.

phlegmatically [fleg'mætɪklɪ] *adv* flegmatiquement.

phlox [flɒks] *n* (*plant*) phlox *m*.

-phobe [fəʊb] *suff* -phobe; **Anglop./xenop./***etc*, anglophobe *mf*/xénophobe *mf*/*etc*.

phobia ['fəʊbɪə] *n* phobie *f*; **to have a p. about sth,** avoir une phobie pour qch.

-phobia ['fəʊbɪə] *suff* -phobie; **Anglop./agorap./***etc*, anglophobie *f*/agoraphobie *f*/*etc*.

phobic ['fəʊbɪk] *adj & n Med* phobique *mf*.

-phobic ['fəʊbɪk] *suff* -phobe; **Anglop./agorap./***etc*, anglophobe/agoraphobe/*etc*.

Phoenician [fɪ'niːʃən] *Antiq* **1** *adj* phénicien. **2** *n* **(a)** Phénicien, -ienne; **(b)** *Ling* phénicien *m*.

phoenix, *US* **phenix** ['fiːnɪks] *n Myth* phénix *m*.

phone¹ [fəʊn] *n* téléphone *m*; **to be on the p.,** (*talking*) être au téléphone; (*have a telephone*) avoir le téléphone; **he was on the p. for an hour,** il a passé une heure au téléphone; **to get on the p. to s.o.,** téléphoner à qn; **get off the p.!,** raccroche!; **to speak to s.o. on the p.,** parler à qn au téléphone; **p. bill,** facture *f* de téléphone; **p. book,** annuaire *m* (du téléphone); **p. box,** cabine *f* téléphonique; **p. call,** coup *m* de téléphone; **p. number,** numéro *m* de téléphone.

phone² **1** *vt* **to p. s.o.,** téléphoner à (*qn*), appeler (*qn*) au téléphone, donner un coup de téléphone à (*qn*); **to p. the office/police,** téléphoner au bureau/à la police; **to p. a piece of news,** téléphoner une nouvelle. **2** *vi* téléphoner; **to p. home,** téléphoner à la maison.

phone³ *n Ling* phonème *m*.

►phone up *vtsep* = **PHONE² 1.**

-phone [fəʊn] *suff* -phone; **Anglo/Franco/***etc***-p.,** anglophone/francophone/*etc*.

phonecard ['fəʊnkɑːd] *n Br Tel* télécarte *f*.

phone-in ['fəʊnɪn] *Rad TV* **1** *n* programme *m* à ligne ouverte. **2** *adj* **p.-in programme,** programme *m* à ligne ouverte.

phoneme ['fəʊniːm] *n Ling* phonème *m*.

phonemic [fə'niːmɪk] *adj* phonémique.

phonetic [fə'netɪk] *adj* phonétique; **p. alphabet,** alphabet *m* phonétique.

phonetically [fə'netɪklɪ] *adv* phonétiquement.

phonetician [fəʊnə'tɪʃən] *n* phonéticien, -ienne.

phonetics [fə'netɪks] *npl* phonétique *f*.

phoney, *esp US* **phony** ['fəʊnɪ] *F* **1** *adj* (*comp* **phonier**; *superl* **phoniest**) faux, *f* fausse; (*story etc*) bidon; **he's p. (*US* as a two-dollar bill),** il est faux comme un jeton, il est faux-jeton. **2** *n* (*imposter*) imposteur *m*; (*insincere person*) comédien, -ienne; (*fake object*) faux *m*.

phonic ['fɒnɪk, 'fəʊnɪk] *adj* phonique.

phonograph ['fəʊnəgræf] *n Am* phonographe *m*.

phonology [fə'nɒlədʒɪ] *n* phonologie *f*.

phony ['fəʊnɪ] *adj & n* = **PHONEY**; *Hist* **p. war,** drôle de guerre.

phooey ['fuːɪ] *int* peuh!

phosgene ['fɒzdʒi:n] *n Ch* phosgène *m*.
phosphate¹ ['fɒsfeɪt] *n Ch* phosphate *m*; **p. of lime, calcium p.**, phosphate de chaux; **p. mine** *or* **works**, phosphaterie *f*.
phosphate² *vt Agr* phosphater.
phosphide ['fɒsfaɪd] *n Ch* phosphure *m*.
phosphite ['fɒsfaɪt] *n Ch* phosphite *m*.
phosphoresce [fɒsfə'res] *vi* être phosphorescent, luire par phosphorescence.
phosphorescence [fɒsfə'resəns] *n* phosphorescence *f*.
phosphorescent [fɒsfə'resənt] *adj* phosphorescent.
phosphoric [fɒs'fɒrɪk] *adj Ch* phosphorique.
phosphorous ['fɒsfərəs] *adj* phosphoreux.
phosphorus ['fɒsfərəs] *n Ch* phosphore *m*.
photo ['fəʊtəʊ] *n* photo *f*; **to take good photos,** prendre de bonnes photos; **to take a good p.,** (*be photogenic*) être photogénique; **p. album,** album *m* (de) photos; *Sp* **p. finish,** photo-finish *f inv*; **p. opportunity,** *Cin TV* **p. call,** séance *f* de photos.
photocell ['fəʊtəʊsel] *n* photocellule *f*.
photocopier ['fəʊtəʊkɒpɪər] *n* photocopieur *m*, photocopieuse *f*.
photocopy¹ ['fəʊtəʊkɒpɪ] *n* photocopie *f*.
photocopy² *vt* photocopier.
photoelectric [fəʊtəʊɪ'lektrɪk] *adj* photoélectrique; **p. cell,** photocellule *f*.
photoelectron [fəʊtəʊɪ'lektrɒn] *n Phys* photoélectron *m*.
photoengraving [fəʊtəʊɪn'greɪvɪŋ] *n* photogravure *f*.
Photofit® ['fəʊtəʊfɪt] *n* **P. (picture),** portrait-robot *m*.
photogenic [fəʊtə'dzenɪk] *adj* photogénique.
photograph¹ ['fəʊtəgræf] *n* photographie *f*; **to have a p. of sth,** avoir qch en photo; **to take s.o.'s p.,** prendre une photographie de qn; **he had his p. taken,** il s'est fait photographier; **she takes a good p.,** elle est photogénique; **p. album,** album *m* de photos.
photograph² **1** *vt* photographier, prendre en photographie (*qn, qch*). **2** *vi* **to p. well,** (*of person*) être photogénique.
photographer [fə'tɒgrəfər] *n* photographe *mf*; **she's a good/bad p.,** elle prend de bonnes/mauvaises photos; *Journ* **press p.,** reporter *m* photographe, photographe de presse.
photographic [fəʊtə'græfɪk] *adj* (*procédé, papier, description etc*) photographique; **to have a p. memory,** avoir une mémoire photographique.
photographically [fəʊtə'græfɪklɪ] *adv* photographiquement.
photography [fə'tɒgrəfɪ] *n* photographie *f*; **aerial p.,** photographie aérienne; **colour p.,** photographie en couleurs.
photogravure [fəʊtəʊgrə'vjʊər] *n* photogravure *f*.
photojournalism [fəʊtəʊ'dʒɜ:nəlɪz(ə)m] *n* photoreportage *m*.
photojournalist [fəʊtəʊ'dʒɜ:nəlɪst] *n* reporter *mf* photographe.
photolithography [fəʊtəʊlɪ'θɒgrəfɪ] *n* photolithographie *f*.
photoluminescence [fəʊtəʊlu:mɪ'nesəns] *n* photoluminescence *f*.
photometer [fəʊ'tɒmɪtər] *n Phys* photomètre *m*.
photometry [fəʊ'tɒmɪtrɪ] *n Phys* photométrie *f*.
photomontage ['fəʊtəʊmɒn'tɑ:ʒ] *n* photomontage *m*.
photon ['fəʊtɒn] *n Opt* photon *m*.
photosensitive [fəʊtəʊ'sensɪtɪv] *adj* photosensible.
Photostat ¹® ['fəʊtəʊstæt] *n* photostat *m*.
Photostat ²® **1** *vt* faire un photostat de (*qch*). **2** *vi* faire des photostats.
photosynthesis [fəʊtəʊ'sɪnθɪsɪs] *n* photosynthèse *f*.
photosynthesize [fəʊtəʊ'sɪnθɪsaɪz] *vt* photosynthétiser.
phototropism [fəʊtəʊ'trəʊpɪz(ə)m] *n Biol* phototropisme *m*.
photovoltaic [fəʊtəʊvɒl'teɪɪk] *adj* photovoltaïque; **p. cell,** cellule *f* photovoltaïque, photopile *f*; **p. effect,** effet *m* photovoltaïque.
photovoltaics [fəʊtəʊvɒl'teɪɪks] *npl* énergie *f* photovoltaïque; **p. industry,** l'industrie *f* de l'énergie photovoltaïque; **to work in p.,** travailler dans l'énergie photovoltaïque.
phrasal ['freɪzəl] *adj Eng Gram* **p. verb,** verbe à particule, verbe composé.
phrase¹ [freɪz] *n* **(a)** locution *f*, expression *f*; *Mus* phrase *f*; *Gram* locution *f* (adverbiale *etc*), membre *m* de phrase; **noun p.,** syntagme nominal; **p. book,** manuel *m ou* guide *m* de conversation; **in Voltaire's p.,** comme disait Voltaire.
phrase² *vt* **(a)** exprimer (*sa pensée etc*); donner un tour à (*sa pensée*); **that is how he phrased it,** voilà comment il s'est exprimé, voilà comment il a tourné cela; **(b)** *Mus* phraser.
phraseology [freɪzɪ'ɒlədʒɪ] *n* phraséologie *f*.
phrasing ['freɪzɪŋ] *n* **(a)** (*of text*) phraséologie *f*; (*of thought*) expression *f*; **(b)** *Mus* phrasé *m*.
phrenology [frɪ'nɒlədʒɪ] *n* phrénologie *f*.
phthisis ['θaɪsɪs] *n Med* phtisie *f*.
phut [fʌt] *F* **1** *n* bruit sourd (*de deux objets qui se heurtent etc*). **2** *adv F* **to go p.,** (*of business, engine etc*) claquer; (*of rope etc*) se casser; **the light went p.,** nous avons eu une panne d'électricité.
phylactery [fɪ'læktərɪ] *n Jew Rel* phylactère *m*.
phylloxera [fɪlɒk'sɪərə] *n* (*insect*) phylloxéra *m*.
phylum, *pl* **-la** ['faɪləm, -lə] *n Biol* phylum *m*.
physic ['fɪzɪk] *n Old-fashioned* médecine *f*, médicament *m*.
physical ['fɪzɪk(ə)l] **1** *adj* **(a)** (*relating to the body*) physique; *Med* (*symptoms*) somatique; **rugby is a very p. sport,** le rugby est un sport dans lequel il y a beaucoup de contacts physiques; **the game got very p.,** le jeu est devenu très physique; **p. contact,** contact *m* physique; **p. education,** culture *f ou* éducation *f* physique; *Med* **p. examination,** visite médicale; **p. exercises** *or* **training** *or* *F* **jerks,** exercices *mpl* physiques *ou* d'assouplissement; **p. fitness,** bonne forme physique; **p. strength,** force *f* physique;
(b) (*concrete, material*) physique; **p. body,** corps matériel; **p. features,** topographie *f*; **p. geography,** géographie *f* physique; **p. impossibility,** impossibilité *f* physique;
(c) p. chemistry, chimie *f* physique; **p. property,** propriété *f* physique; **p. sciences,** sciences *fpl* physiques.
2 *n Med* visite médicale; **to have a p.,** passer une visite médicale.
physically ['fɪzɪklɪ] *adv* **(a)** physiquement; **p. fit,** en forme; **to be p. handicapped,** être handicapé physique; **(b)** (*materially*) physiquement, matériellement; **seeing it on TV isn't the same as being p. there,** le voir à la télévision ce n'est pas la même chose que d'y assister en personne.
physician [fɪ'zɪʃən] *n* médecin *m*.
physicist ['fɪzɪsɪst] *n* physicien, -ienne.
physics ['fɪzɪks] *npl* (*usu with sing verb*) physique *f*; **nuclear/quantum p.,** physique nucléaire/quantique.
physio ['fɪzɪəʊ] *n Med F* **(a)** = **PHYSIOTHERAPIST**; **(b)** = **PHYSIOTHERAPY**.
physiognomy [fɪzɪ'ɒnəmɪ] *n* **(a)** (*of person*) physionomie *f*; **(b)** (*art*) physiognomonie *f*.
physiological [fɪzɪə'lɒdʒɪk(ə)l] *adj* physiologique.
physiologically [fɪzɪə'lɒdʒɪklɪ] *adv* physiologiquement.
physiologist [fɪzɪ'ɒlədʒɪst] *n* physiologiste *mf*, physiologue *mf*.
physiology [fɪzɪ'ɒlədʒɪ] *n* physiologie *f*; **plant p.,** physiologie végétale.
physiotherapist [fɪzɪəʊ'θerəpɪst] *n* kinésithérapeute *mf*.
physiotherapy [fɪzɪəʊ'θerəpɪ] *n* kinésithérapie *f*.
physique [fɪ'zi:k] *n* physique *m* (*de qn*); **fine p.,** beau physique; **he hasn't the p. for it,** il n'a pas le physique de l'emploi.
pi [paɪ] *n* (*in Greek alphabet*) pi *m*.
piaffe [pɪ'æf] *n Horseriding* piaffé *m*.
pianissimo [pɪə'nɪsɪməʊ] *adv & n* pianissimo *m*.
pianist ['pɪənɪst] *n* pianiste *mf*.
piano¹ [pɪ'ænəʊ], **pianoforte** [pɪænəʊ'fɔ:rtɪ] *n* piano *m*; **grand p.,** piano à queue; **upright p.,** piano droit; **to play the p.,** jouer du piano; **sonata for p. and violin,** sonate pour piano et violon; **p. concerto,** concerto *m* pour piano; **p. key,** touche *f* de piano; **p. player,** joueur, -euse de piano, pianiste *mf*; **p. stool,** tabouret *m* de piano.
piano² [pɪ'ɑ:nəʊ] *Mus* **1** *adv* piano, doucement. **2** *n* piano *m*.
piastre [pɪ'æstər] *n* (*currency*) piastre *f*.
piazza [pɪ'ætsə] *n* (*esp in Italy*) place *f* (publique); *Br* galerie *f*.
pic [pɪk] *n F* **(a)** (*picture*) image *f*; (*photograph*) photo *f*; **(b) the pics,** le ciné, le cinéma.
pica ['paɪkə] *n Typ* pica *m*, cicéro *m*, corps *m* 12.
picador ['pɪkədɒr] *n* picador *m*.
Picardy ['pɪkədɪ] *n* Picardie *f*.
picaresque [pɪkə'resk] *adj* (*roman*) picaresque.
piccalilli [pɪkə'lɪlɪ] *n Culin* pickles *mpl* à la moutarde.
piccaninny [pɪkə'nɪnɪ] *n Offensive Sl* négrillon, -onne.
piccolo ['pɪkələʊ] *n Mus* piccolo *m*.
pick¹ [pɪk] *n* choix *m*, élite *f*; **the p. of the bunch,** le dessus du panier, *F* le gratin (du gratin); **we had first p.,** nous avons été les premiers à choisir; **take your p.,** choisissez.
pick² *vt* **(a)** (*choose*) choisir, sélectionner; trier (*du minerai*

etc); **(hand-)picked men,** hommes *mpl* d'élite; **to p. one's words,** choisir ses mots; **to p. the winners,** repérer les gagnants; **to p. and choose,** se montrer difficile, faire le *ou* la difficile; **to p. one's way through a field,** traverser un champ en regardant où on met les pieds; **you picked a fine time to tell me,** tu as bien choisi ton moment pour me le dire;

(b) (*gather*) cueillir (*des fleurs, des fruits etc*);

(c) crocheter (*une serrure*); **to p. s.o.'s pocket,** prendre *ou* voler qch dans la poche de qn; **to p. s.o.'s brains,** exploiter l'intelligence *ou* les connaissances de qn; **can I p. your brains a minute?,** est-ce que je peux faire appel à tes connaissances une minute?;

(d) (*pull apart*) mettre (*qch*) en pièces; détisser, effilocher (*des chiffons etc*);

(e) (*make holes in*) piocher (*la terre etc*); **to p. a hole in sth,** faire un trou dans *ou* à qch (*avec une pioche, ses ongles etc*); *F* **to p. holes in sth,** trouver à redire à qch; **she's constantly picking holes,** elle n'arrête pas de chercher la petite bête;

(f) (*remove material from*) épailler, échardonner (*de la laine*); époutier (*un tissu*); démêler (*l'étoupe*); **to have a bone to p. with s.o.,** avoir un compte à régler avec qn; **to p. one's nose/teeth,** se curer le nez/les dents; **to p. a spot,** gratter un bouton (*du bout de l'ongle*);

(g) *Mus* **to p. a guitar,** pincer la guitare;

(h) (*of birds*) picoter, becqueter (*le blé etc*);

(i) **to p. a fight,** chercher la bagarre (**with s.o.,** à qn).

2 *vi* (*choose*) choisir; **you p. first,** choisis d'abord; **to p. and choose,** faire le *ou* la difficile.

pick³ *n* **(a)** (*tool*) pic *m*, pioche *f*; **miner's p.,** pic à main; **p. and shovel man,** terrassier *m*; **(b)** **lobster p.,** fourchette *f* à homard; **(c)** *Mus* (*plectrum*) plectre *m*, médiator *m*.

►**pick at** *vipo* picorer (*ses légumes etc*); **to p. at one's food,** picorer; **to p. at a scab,** gratter une croûte.

►**pick off** *vtsep* **(a)** (*remove*) enlever, ôter (*les fleurs fanées d'une plante etc*); **p. those papers off the ground,** ramassez ces papiers de sur le sol; **(b)** (*of gunman, sniper*) descendre, abattre un à un (*des soldats, ennemis etc*).

►**pick on** *vipo* **(a)** (*victimize*) s'en prendre à qn; **stop picking on her,** arrête de t'en prendre à elle; **why p. on me?,** pourquoi s'en prendre à moi?; **p. on s.o. your own size!,** ne t'attaque pas à qn de plus faible que toi!; **(b)** (*choose*) choisir; **who have you picked on for your bridesmaid?,** qui as-tu choisi comme demoiselle d'honneur?

►**pick out** *vtsep* **(a)** (*remove*) extirper, enlever (*qch*); ôter (*qch*) (*avec les doigts etc*); **(b)** (*select*) désigner, choisir (*qch*); **he picked out the best peaches,** il a choisi les meilleures pêches; **to p. out a criminal,** (*in identification parade*) identifier un criminel; **(c)** (*recognize*) repérer; **she was easy to p. out in her orange coat,** elle était bien reconnaissable avec son manteau orange; **(d)** (*highlight*) **picked out in gold,** à filets d'or.

►**pick over** *vtsep* trier (*des fruits etc*).

►**pick up 1** *vtsep* **(a)** (*lift up*) prendre; ramasser, relever (*qch par terre*); décrocher (*le téléphone*); *Knitting* relever (*une maille*); *Nau* recueillir (*des naufragés*); **to p. up the odd pound or two,** gagner un peu d'argent; **to p. up a child,** (*in one's arms*) prendre un enfant dans les bras; (*after falling*) relever un enfant (*qui est tombé*); **to p. oneself up,** (*after falling*) se relever; *Fig* (*recover from crisis*) se remettre; (*after breaking sth*) & *Fig* **to p. up the pieces,** ramasser les morceaux; **we were left to p. up the bill,** c'est nous qui avons dû casquer; **let me p. up the bill,** laisse-moi payer;

(b) (*collect*) **I'll p. you up at the station,** je viendrai vous chercher à la gare; **the train stops to p. up passengers,** le train s'arrête pour prendre des voyageurs;

(c) (*catch*) **to p. up a cold/***etc*, ramasser *ou* attraper un rhume/*etc*;

(d) (*acquire*) **to p. sth up cheap,** acheter qch bon marché; **she's good at picking up bargains,** elle a du flair pour les bonnes affaires;

(e) *F* (*make casual acquaintance*) **to p. up a man/woman,** lever un homme/une femme; **he tried to p. me up,** il m'a draguée; **I'm going to (try and) p. up a woman/man,** je vais draguer; **to p. up a customer,** (*of prostitute*) raccrocher un client;

(f) (*arrest*) arrêter; **the police picked him up in a bar,** la police l'a arrêté dans un bar;

(g) (*locate*) trouver; *El* prendre, capter (*le courant*); capter, recevoir (*un message*); (*of searchlight*) repérer (*un avion*); **the police have picked up a trail,** la police a trouvé une piste; **you can p. up a lot of foreign stations on short wave,** on peut capter beaucoup de stations étrangères sur les ondes courtes;

(h) (*learn*) apprendre (*un tour, un fait, une langue etc*); recueillir (*des nouvelles, des informations*); **to p. up a habit,** prendre une habitude;

(i) (*notice*) trouver, retrouver, relever (*une erreur*);

(j) (*continue*) **to p. up again,** reprendre (*le fil de la conversation etc*); **we soon picked up the road again,** nous avons vite retrouvé notre chemin;

(k) (*reprimand*) **to p. s.o. up sharply,** reprendre qn vertement; **I'd like to p. Chris Jones up on that (point),** (*in debate*) j'aimerais reprendre Chris Jones sur ce thème;

(l) (*gather*) *Aut etc* **to p. up speed,** reprendre de la vitesse; **to p. up strength,** (*of person*) reprendre des forces.

2 *vtas* (*make better*) **that will p. you up,** voilà qui vous remontera.

3 *vi* **(a)** (*improve*) s'améliorer; (*after illness*) retrouver la santé *ou* ses forces, se rétablir; **business is picking up,** les affaires reprennent; **the weather looks like picking up,** le temps a l'air de se remettre;

(b) (*continue*) reprendre;

(c) *Sp etc* **to p. up on s.o.,** rattraper qn; **this engine picks up well,** ce moteur a de bonnes reprises.

pick-a-back ['pɪkəbæk] *adv, adj & n* = **PIGGYBACK**.

pickaninny [pɪkə'nɪnɪ] *n Offensive Sl* = **PICCANINNY**.

pickaxe¹, *US* **pickax** ['pɪkæks] *n* (*tool*) pioche *f*, pic *m*.

pickaxe², *US* **pickax** *vt & vi* piocher.

picker ['pɪkər] *n* **(a)** cueilleur, -euse (*de fleurs, de fruits etc*); **(b)** éplucheur, -euse (*de laine etc*); démêleur, -euse (*de coton etc*).

pickerel ['pɪkərəl] *n Am* (*fish*) doré *m*, brochet *m*.

picket¹ ['pɪkɪt] *n* **(a)** *Ind etc* piquet *m* (*de grévistes*); (*one person*) gréviste *m* en faction; **p. line,** piquet de grève; **(b)** *Mil etc* (*detachment*) piquet *m* (*d'hommes*); (*one soldier*) factionnaire *m*; **to be on p.,** être de piquet; **(c)** (*stake*) piquet *m*, pieu *m* (*d'une clôture etc*); piquet d'attache (*pour chevaux etc*); **p. fence,** palis *m*, palissade *f*.

picket² *vt* **(-t-)** **(a)** *Ind etc* **to p. a factory,** mettre un piquet de grève aux portes d'une usine (*pour en interdire l'accès*); **(b)** *Mil* détacher (*des soldats*) en grand'garde; **(c)** (*fence*) entourer (*un terrain*) de piquets *ou* de pieux; palissader (*un terrain*); **(d)** (*fasten*) mettre (*des chevaux*) au(x) piquet(s); attacher (*une chèvre*).

picking ['pɪkɪŋ] *n* **(a)** (*money etc*) (*usu pl*) **pickings,** bénéfices *mpl*; **(b)** (*choosing*) triage *m* (*du minerai etc*); **hand p.,** triage à la main; **(c)** cueillette *f*, cueillage *m* (*de fruits, de fleurs etc*); **p. season,** cueillette; **(d)** crochetage *m* (*d'une serrure*); **(e)** démêlage *m*, démêlement *m* (*de l'étoupe*); **(f)** échardonnage *m*, épaillage *m* (*de la laine etc*); époutiage *m* (*des étoffes*).

pickle¹ ['pɪk(ə)l] *n* **(a)** **pickles,** pickles *mpl*, conserves *fpl* au vinaigre; **mixed pickles,** mélange *m* de pickles; **(b)** (*marinade*) marinade *f*, saumure *f*; **(c)** *F* (*predicament*) **to be in a fine p.,** être dans de beaux draps *ou* dans le pétrin.

pickle² *vt* mariner, saumurer, conserver (au vinaigre, à la saumure).

pickled ['pɪk(ə)ld] *adj* **(a)** mariné, saumuré; **p. cabbage/onions,** chou rouge/oignons au vinaigre; **(b)** *F* (*drunk*) gris.

pickling ['pɪk(ə)lɪŋ] *n* marinage *m*, saumurage *m*, conservation *f* au vinaigre; **p. onions,** petits oignons.

picklock ['pɪklɒk] *n* **(a)** (*person*) crocheteur *m* (*de serrures*); **(b)** (*key*) crochet *m*, rossignol *m*.

pick-me-up ['pɪkmɪʌp] *n F* remontant *m*; **that's a good p.-me-up!,** voilà qui vous remonte!

pickpocket ['pɪkpɒkɪt] *n* voleur, -euse à la tire, pickpocket *m*.

pick-up ['pɪkʌp] *n* **(a)** (*collection*) ramassage *m* (*de qch*); *Electron Rad* captage *m* (*des ondes, d'un signal*); **a p.-up point,** (*for passengers on coach journey etc*) point *m* de ramassage, arrêt *m*; (*for goods*) point *m* de ramassage; **(b)** (*on record player*) lecteur *m* (phonographique), pick-up *m inv*; *Electron etc* capteur *m*, détecteur *m* (*d'ondes, de vibrations*); **p.-up arm,** bras *m* de pick-up; **(c)** (*vehicle*) pick-up *m inv*, camionnette *f* à ridelles basses *ou* à plateau; **(d)** *F* (*man, woman*) partenaire *mf* de rencontre; **(e)** *F* (*improvement*) amélioration *f*; (*of business etc*) reprise *f*.

picky ['pɪkɪ] *adj F* difficile, délicat.

picnic¹ ['pɪknɪk] *n* pique-nique *m*, *pl* pique-niques; **to go on a p.,** aller en pique-nique, aller pique-niquer; **we'll take a p. (meal) with us,** nous emporterons un pique-nique; *F* **it was no p.,** cela n'a guère été une partie de plaisir; **p. basket** *or* **hamper,** panier garni (pour pique-niques).

picnic² *vi* (*pt & pp* **picnicked**) pique-niquer, faire un pique-nique.

picnicker [ˈpɪknɪkər] *n* pique-niqueur, -euse.
Pict [pɪkt] *n Hist* Picte *mf*.
Pictish [ˈpɪktɪʃ] *adj* picte, pictique.
pictogram [ˈpɪktəgræm] *n* pictogramme *m*.
pictograph [ˈpɪktəgræf] *n* pictographe *m*.
pictorial [pɪkˈtɔːrɪəl] **1** *adj* (*périodique etc*) illustré; (*représentation*) par une image, par images; (*talent etc*) pictural, -aux; (*écriture*) en images; **p. dictionary,** dictionnaire *m* par images. **2** *n* périodique illustré, journal illustré.
pictorially [pɪkˈtɔːrɪəlɪ] *adv* par images.
picture¹ [ˈpɪktʃər] *n* tableau *m*, peinture *f*; (*in picture book etc*) image *f*; (*illustrating text*) illustration *f*; *Br Cin F* film *m*; (*photograph*) photo *f*; **the political/economic p.,** la situation politique/économique; **to paint a p.,** faire *ou* peindre un tableau; **to paint a bleak p. of the future,** présenter une triste image de l'avenir; **to get one's p. in the paper,** avoir sa photo dans le journal; *F* **she's a p.,** elle est à peindre; *F* **to be in the p.,** être au courant *ou* au fait *ou* à la page; *F* **put me in the p.,** mets-moi au courant; *F* **I get the p.,** je vois (ce dont il s'agit); **to be out of the p.,** être dépassé, être en dehors du coup; **it doesn't come into the p.,** cela n'entre pas en ligne de compte; *Jur* **identikit p.,** portrait *m* robot; **he's the p. of health,** il respire la santé; **this book gives a more accurate p. of the general,** ce livre offre un portrait plus fidèle du Général; **a clearer p. is emerging of what is taking place in the city,** une idée plus claire se fait jour sur ce qui se produit dans la ville; **to get a mental p. of sth,** se représenter qch; *Med* **clinical p.,** facies *m ou* tableau *m* clinique; *TV* **the picture's terrible,** l'image est très mauvaise; *Br* **to go to the pictures,** aller au cinéma; **p. book,** livre *m* d'images; (*travel book etc*) livre illustré; *Cards* **p. card,** figure *f*; **p. dealer,** marchand *m* de tableaux; **p. dictionary,** dictionnaire *m* par images; **p. gallery,** musée *m* de peinture; **p. hat,** chapeau *m* gainsborough; **p. library,** banque *f* d'images; **p. postcard,** carte postale illustrée; **p. puzzle,** rébus *m*; **p. research,** documentation *f* iconographique; **p. researcher,** documentaliste *mf* iconographique; **p. window,** baie vitrée; **p. writing,** pictographie *f*.
picture² *vt* **(a)** peindre, dépeindre, représenter (*qn, qch*); **(b) to p. (to oneself),** s'imaginer, se figurer, se représenter (*qch*).
picturesque [pɪktʃəˈresk] *adj* pittoresque; (*expressions*) qui font image.
picturesquely [pɪktʃəˈresklɪ] *adv* pittoresquement.
picturesqueness [pɪktʃəˈresknɪs] *n* pittoresque *m*.
piddle [ˈpɪd(ə)l] *vi F* faire pipi.
piddling [ˈpɪdlɪŋ] *adj F* insignifiant, ridicule.
pidgin [ˈpɪdʒɪn] *n* **(a)** pidgin *m*; **p. (English** *etc*), = petit nègre.
pie¹ [paɪ] *n* **(veal and ham** *etc*) **p.,** = pâté *m* en croûte; **chicken p.,** = croustade *f* de volaille; **cottage p.** *or* **shepherd's p.,** hachis parmentier; **fish p.,** = timbale *f* de poissons; **(apple** *etc*) **p.,** = tourte *f* (aux pommes *etc*); *esp Am* tarte *f* (aux pommes *etc*); **custard p.,** = tarte à la crème; *F* **p. in the sky,** le miel de l'autre monde; *F* **as easy as p.,** simple comme bonjour; *Math etc* **p. chart,** camembert *m*; **p. dish,** tourtière *f*, terrine *f* (pour pâtés en croûte).
pie² *n Typ* (composition tombée en) pâte *f*, pâté *m*.
piebald [ˈpaɪbɔːld] **1** *adj* (*cheval etc*) pie. **2** *n* (cheval *m*) pie *m*.
piece¹ [piːs] *n* **(a)** morceau *m* (*de papier, de pain etc*); bout *m* (*de ruban, de ficelle etc*); parcelle *f* (*de terrain*); morceau *m*, tranche *f* (*de gâteau*); morceau *m*, coupon *m* (*de drap*); morceau *m*, fragment *m*, éclat *m* (*de verre etc*); **p. by p.,** morceau à morceau; **to break sth in** *or* **to pieces,** briser qch, mettre qch en morceaux; **to fall to pieces,** tomber en morceaux; (*of house etc*) se délabrer, crouler; **my coat is falling to pieces,** mon manteau part en morceaux; *F* **to go (all) to pieces,** (*of person*) perdre tout empire sur soi-même; *Sp* (*of team etc*) s'effondrer; **to tear to pieces,** déchirer (*du papier, une lettre*); mettre (*de l'étoffe*) en lambeaux; déchirer (*une proie*) à belles dents; démolir (*un argument*); **the dog tore the armchair to pieces,** le chien a mis le fauteuil en morceaux *ou* en pièces; *F* **they'll tear you to pieces,** vous allez vous faire écharper; *F* **to pull s.o./a play to pieces,** critiquer qn/une pièce sévèrement;
(b) (*of machine etc*) partie *f*, pièce *f*; (*of jigsaw puzzle*) pièce; **to take a machine to pieces,** démonter une machine;
(c) *Com* pièce *f* (*de drap etc*); **to sell sth by the p.,** vendre qch à la pièce; **p. dyeing,** teinture *f* en pièces; *Tex* **p. goods,** marchandises *fpl ou* tissus *mpl* à la pièce; *Ind* **p. rate,** salaire *m* à la tâche *ou* à la pièce;
(d) all in one p., tout d'une pièce, d'une seule pièce, d'un seul tenant; *F* **they are all of a p.,** (*of people*) ils sont tous du même acabit; *Metal* **to cast cylinders in one p.,** couler des cylindres d'un seul jet *ou* en bloc; **cast** *or* **pressed** *or* **made in one p.,** monobloc *inv*; **to be still in one p.,** (*of person, car etc after accident*) être encore en un seul morceau, être encore entier;
(e) (*sample, instance*) **a p. of work,** un travail; (*manual*) un ouvrage; **a p. of my work,** un échantillon de mon travail; **p. out of a book,** passage *m* d'un livre; **p. of bravery/folly,** acte *m* de bravoure/folie; **p. of good luck,** coup *m* de chance; **what a p. of luck!,** quelle chance!; **a p. of advice,** un conseil; **a p. of carelessness,** une étourderie; **a p. of cruelty,** une cruauté; **a p. of (bad) news,** une (mauvaise) nouvelle; **a p. of luggage,** une valise; **to give s.o. a p. of one's mind,** dire ses quatre vérités à qn; **a p. of furniture,** un meuble; **a p. of clothing,** un vêtement;
(f) morceau *m* (*de musique, de poésie*); *Journ* article *m*, papier *m*; **to say one's p.,** prononcer son discours;
(g) *Mus* (*instrument*) instrument *m* de musique;
(h) (*in backgammon*) dame *f*; (*in dominoes*) domino *m*, dé *m*; *Draughts* pion *m*; *Chess* **pieces and pawns,** pièces et pions;
(i) *esp Br* (*coin*) **five-/fifty-pence/***etc* **p.,** pièce *f* de cinq/cinquante/*etc* pence;
(j) *Metal* **punched/shaped p.,** pièce estampée/profilée;
(k) *Mil* pièce *f* (*d'artillerie*); (*firearm*) pistolet *m*; **to be carrying a p.,** porter une arme, être armé; **fowling p.,** fusil *m* de chasse;
(l) *Sl* (*girl*) nana *f*.
piece² *vt* **(a)** (*patch*) rapiécer, raccommoder; mettre une pièce à (*un habit etc*); **(b)** (*join*) joindre, unir (**one thing to another,** une chose à une autre).
▶**piece together** *vtsep* (*assemble*) joindre, assembler (*des cordages etc*); coordonner (*des faits etc*); **detectives are piecing together a picture of the events,** les enquêteurs sont en train de se faire petit à petit une idée des événements.
-piece [piːs] *suff* **one/two/three/***etc***-p.,** une/deux/trois/*etc* pièce/pièces; **one-p. overalls,** combinaison *f*; **two/three-p. suit,** costume deux/trois pièces; *Mus* **three-p. ensemble,** trio *m*; **a nine-p. jazz band,** groupe de jazz de neuf musiciens *ou* éléments.
piecemeal [ˈpiːsmiːl] **1** *adv* par morceaux, pièce à pièce; (*gradually*) peu à peu; **the collection was sold p.,** les pièces de la collection ont été vendues séparément. **2** *adj* fragmentaire; (*travail etc*) fait pièce à pièce.
piecework [ˈpiːswɜːk] *n Ind* travail *m* à la tâche *ou* à la pièce.
piecrust [ˈpaɪkrʌst] *n* croûte *f* de pâté (en croûte).
pied [paɪd] *adj* bigarré, panaché; *Lit* **the P. Piper of Hamelin,** le Joueur de flûte d'Hamelin.
pied-à-terre [pjedaˈteər] *n* pied-à-terre *m inv*.
Piedmont [ˈpiːdmɒnt] *n* Piémont *m*.
pie-eyed [ˈpaɪaɪd] *adj Sl* (*drunk*) rond, bourré.
pier [pɪər] *n* **(a)** (*at seaside resort*) jetée *f*; (*of stone*) jetée, môle *m*, digue *f*; (*on piles*) estacade *f*; **landing p.,** embarcadère *m*, débarcadère *m*; **floating p.,** ponton *m*; **(b)** *Constr* pilier *m* (*de maçonnerie*).
pierce [pɪəs] **1** *vt* percer, transpercer (*qch*); percer (*un trou*); *Metal* épingler (*un moule, l'âme*); **to have one's ears pierced,** se faire percer les oreilles; **to p. the darkness,** (*of light*) percer les ténèbres; **to p. the air with one's cries,** percer l'air de ses cris. **2** *vi* **to p. through the enemy's lines,** pénétrer les lignes de l'ennemi.
piercing [ˈpɪəsɪŋ] *adj* (*outil, regard, cri etc*) aigu, perçant, pénétrant; (*froid, vent*) pénétrant.
pierhead [ˈpɪəhed] *n* musoir *m*.
pierrot [ˈpɪərəʊ] *n Th* pierrot *m*.
piety [ˈpaɪətɪ] *n* piété *f*.
piffle [ˈpɪf(ə)l] *n F* futilités *fpl*, bêtises *fpl*, niaiseries *fpl*; **to talk p.,** dire des futilités.
piffling [ˈpɪflɪŋ] *adj F* (*occupation, activity*) futile; (*discours etc*) creux.
pig¹ [pɪg] *n* **(a)** (*animal*) porc *m*, cochon *m*, pourceau *m*; *Am* (*young pig*) cochonnet *m*, porcelet *m*; (*person*) *F* (*glutton*) goinfre *m*, glouton *m*; *F* (*unpleasant person*) sale type *m*; *Sl Pej* (*police officer*) flic *m*; **suck(l)ing p.,** cochon de lait; **roast p.,** rôti *m* de porc; **p.'s wash,** = **PIGSWILL**; *F* **to buy a p. in a poke,** acheter chat en poche; **when pigs fly,** à *ou* dans la semaine des quatre jeudis, quand les poules auront des dents; *Br F* **to make a p.'s ear of sth,**

saloper qch; **to eat like a p., to make a p. of oneself,** manger comme un goinfre; **wild p.,** sanglier *m*; *Am* marcassin *m*, jeune sanglier; **you dirty little p.!,** petit cochon!; **he's a greedy p.,** c'est un goinfre; **what a selfish p.!,** quel sale égoïste!; *Sl* **the filing cabinet was a p. to move,** ça a été vachement difficile de déplacer le classeur; **p. farm,** porcherie *f*;
(b) *Metal* gueuse *f* (*de fonte*); saumon *m* (*de plomb, d'étain etc*); **p. iron,** fer *m* de première coulée; fonte brute *ou* en gueuses.

pig² *v* (**-gg-**) **1** *vi* (*of sow*) mettre bas, cochonner. **2** *vt* **(a)** *F* **to p. oneself,** (*eat excessively*) se goinfrer; **(b) to p. it,** (*be untidy, dirty*) vivre comme un cochon.

►pig out *vi Am F* (*eat excessively*) se goinfrer (**on sth,** de qch).

pigeon ['pɪdʒɪn] *n* **(a)** (*bird*) pigeon *m*; **fantail p.,** pigeon paon; **homing** *or* **racing** *or* **carrier p.,** pigeon voyageur; **wood p.,** (pigeon) ramier *m*; *Sp* **clay p.,** pigeon (d'argile); **clay p. shooting,** ball-trap *m*; **p. fancier,** colombophile *mf*; **p. loft,** colombier *m*, pigeonnier *m*; **p. post,** transport *m* de dépêches par pigeons voyageurs; **(b)** *F* **that's my p.,** ça c'est mon affaire.

pigeon-chested [pɪdʒɪn'tʃestɪd] *adj* qui a la poitrine en saillie.

pigeonhole¹ ['pɪdʒɪnhəʊl] *n* **(a)** case *f*, casier *m* (*de bureau etc*); **(b)** boulin *m* (*de colombier*).

pigeonhole² *vt* **(a)** (*classify*) caser, classer (*des papiers etc*); classer (*une réclamation etc*); reléguer (*qch*) dans sa mémoire; étiqueter, cataloguer, mettre une étiquette à (*qn*); **I don't like being pigeonholed,** je n'aime pas qu'on me catalogue; **(b)** (*defer*) remettre.

pigeon-toed [pɪdʒɪn'təʊd] *adj* qui marche les pieds tournés en dedans.

piggery ['pɪgərɪ] *n* porcherie *f*.

piggish ['pɪgɪʃ] *adj F* (*person*) (*dirty*) sale, malpropre; (*gluttonous*) goinfre; (*selfish*) égoïste; (*unpleasant*) désagréable.

piggy ['pɪgɪ] *F* **1** *n* (*in children's language*) cochonnet *m*, petit cochon; **p. bank,** (cochon *m*) tirelire *f*. **2** *adj* (*person*) goinfre.

piggyback ['pɪgɪbæk] **1** *adv* **(a)** (*on one's back*) sur le dos; sur les épaules; **to ride p. on s.o.,** monter à dos sur qn; **(b)** *Comptr* superposition *f*; **to mount sth p. on sth,** superposer qch sur qch. **2** *adj Comptr* **p. board,** carte fille *f*. **3** *n* **to give s.o. a p.,** porter qn sur le dos.

pig-headed [pɪg'hedɪd] *adj* obstiné, entêté.

pigheadedly [pɪg'hedɪdlɪ] *adv* obstinément.

pigheadedness [pɪg'hedɪdnɪs] *n* obstination *f*, entêtement *m*.

piglet [pɪglɪt], **pigling** ['pɪglɪŋ] *n* cochonnet *m*.

pigment¹ ['pɪgmənt] *n* **(a)** *Art etc* couleur *f*, colorant *m*, pigment *m*; **(b)** *Physiol* pigment *m*; **p. cell,** cellule *f* pigmentaire.

pigment² *vt & vi* (se) pigmenter; **pigmented,** pigmenté.

pigmentation [pɪgmən'teɪʃən] *n* pigmentation *f*.

pigmy ['pɪgmɪ] *n* = **PYGMY**.

pigpen ['pɪgpen] *n Am* = **PIGSTY**.

pigskin ['pɪgskɪn] *n* (*leather*) peau *f* de porc *ou* de truie; **p. purse,** bourse *f* en peau de porc.

pigsty ['pɪgstaɪ] *n* **(a)** porcherie *f*; **(b)** *F Fig* (*house, room*) (sale) taudis *m*, porcherie *f*; **your room is a p.,** ta chambre est une vraie porcherie.

pigswill ['pɪgswɪl] *n* pâtée *f* pour les porcs; eaux grasses (*de cuisine*); *F* (*food*) pâtée pour chiens.

pigtail ['pɪgteɪl] *n* natte *f* (*de cheveux*).

pike¹ [paɪk] *n* **(a)** (*weapon*) pique *f*; **p. bearer,** piquier *m*; **(b)** *Br Dial* (*in the Lake District*) pic *m* (*de montagne*).

pike² *n* (*fish*) brochet *m*.

pike³ *n esp Am* = **TURNPIKE**.

pikestaff ['paɪkstɑːf] *n* **(a)** (*of weapon*) bois *m ou* hampe *f* de pique; **(b)** (*for walking*) bâton *m* à pointe de fer.

pilaf(f) ['piːlæf] *n Culin* pilaf *m*, pilau *m*.

pilaster [pɪ'læstər] *n Archit* pilastre *m*.

Pilate ['paɪlət] *n* **Pontius P.,** Ponce Pilate.

pilau, pilaw ['piːlaʊ, -ləʊ, -lɔː] *n* = **PILAF(F)**.

pilchard ['pɪltʃəd] *n* (*fish*) pilchard *m*.

pile¹ [paɪl] *n* **1 (a)** (*heap*) tas *m* (*de bois, de pierres etc*); monceau *m* (*d'or, de détritus etc*); amas *m*, amoncellement *m* (*d'objets, de marchandises etc*); pile *f* (*d'assiettes, de linge etc*); *Mil* faisceau *m* (*d'armes*); *F* (*fortune*) fortune *f*, magot *m*; **funeral p.,** bûcher *m* (funéraire); **to put in(to) a p., to make a p.,** mettre en tas, empiler; *F* **to make a** *or* **one's p.,** (*make a, one's fortune*) faire fortune; *F* **to have a p. of ironing/work/***etc* **to do,** avoir un tas de repassage/travail/*etc* à faire; **(b)** *El* **(electric) p.,** pile *f* (électrique); *Nucl Phys* **(atomic) p.,** pile, réacteur *m* (atomique); **(c)** (*building*) édifice *m*; masse *f* (*d'un édifice*).

pile² **1** *vt* entasser, amonceler (*de la terre etc*); mettre (*des objets*) en tas; empiler (*du bois, des livres etc*), mettre (*des objets*) en pile; **they piled food onto my plate,** ils ont amoncelé de la nourriture dans mon assiette; *Mil* **to p. arms,** former les faisceaux; **to p. a table with dishes,** charger une table de plats; **the table was piled high with dishes,** les plats s'empilaient haut sur la table. **2** *vi* s'entasser, s'amonceler; **seven of them piled into the car,** sept d'entre eux se sont entassés dans la voiture.

pile³ *n* **(a)** *Tex* poil *m* (*d'un tapis etc*); **p. fabrics,** tissus *mpl* à poil; **(b)** poil *m* (*de chameau etc*); laine *f* (*de mouton*).

pile⁴ *n Constr* pieu *m*, pilot *m*; **to drive piles,** enfoncer des pieux, piloter; **built on piles,** bâti sur pilots; **p. dwelling,** (*in prehistoric times*) habitation *f* lacustre.

pile⁵ *vt Constr* soutenir (*un édifice*) au moyen de pilots; piloter (*un terrain*).

►pile in 1 *vi* (*enter in large numbers, quantity*) (*of people*) s'entasser. **2** *vtsep* (*cause to enter in large numbers, quantity*) entasser.

►pile on *vtsep* (*give in large numbers, quantity*) amonceler; **my plate was full, but they piled on more,** mon assiette était pleine mais ils m'ont resservi une platée; **to p. on the agony,** dramatiser; *F* **to p. it on,** exagérer, charrier.

►pile out *vi* (*leave in large numbers, quantity*) partir en masse; **fifteen piled out of the compartment,** quinze personnes ont quitté le compartiment en masse.

►pile up 1 *vi* (*form into pile(s)*) s'amonceler, s'entasser, s'empiler; (*of cars*) caramboler; **dirty dishes were piling up,** la vaisselle sale s'empilait; **work was piling up on her desk,** le travail s'amoncelait sur son bureau; **the clouds are piling up,** les nuages s'amoncellent. **2** *vtsep* **(a)** (*form into pile(s)*) entasser, empiler; **p. the leaves up here,** entasse les feuilles ici; **to p. up money,** amasser de l'argent; **(b)** *F* (*crash, wreck*) **to p. up one's plane/a car,** bousiller son appareil/une voiture; **ship piled up on the rocks,** navire échoué sur les rochers.

piled [paɪld] *adj* **p. (up),** entassé, en tas, en pile.

pile-driver ['paɪldraɪvər] *n Constr* sonnette *f*; *F* (*blow*) coup *m* d'assommoir; *Fb* shoot vigoureux.

piles [paɪlz] *npl Med F* hémorroïdes *fpl*; **to have p.,** avoir des hémorroïdes.

pile-up ['paɪlʌp] *n Aut F* carambolage *m*, emboutissage *m ou* téléscopage *m* en série.

pilfer ['pɪlfər] *vt & vi* chaparder, marauder (**sth from s.o.,** qch à qn).

pilferage ['pɪlfərɪdʒ] *n* petits vols, larcins *mpl*; **the percentage lost through p.,** le pourcentage perdu imputable aux petits vols.

pilferer ['pɪlfərər] *n* chapardeur, -euse.

pilfering ['pɪlfərɪŋ] *n* = **PILFERAGE**.

pilgrim ['pɪlgrɪm] *n* **(a)** pèlerin, -ine; **(b)** *Hist* **the P. Fathers,** les (pères *mpl*) Pèlerins *mpl*.

pilgrimage ['pɪlgrɪmɪdʒ] *n* pèlerinage *m*; **to go on (a) p., to make a p.,** aller en pèlerinage, faire un pèlerinage.

pill [pɪl] *n Pharm* pilule *f*; *F* **the p.,** la pilule; **she's on the p.,** elle prend la pilule; **(sugar coated) p.,** dragée *f*; **sleeping p.,** cachet *m* pour dormir, somnifère *m*; **to sugar the p.,** dorer la pilule; *F* **to be a p. popper,** se bourrer de médicaments.

pillage¹ ['pɪlɪdʒ] *n* pillage *m*.

pillage² **1** *vt* piller, saccager, mettre (*une ville*) au pillage *ou* à sac. **2** *vi* se livrer au pillage, piller.

pillager ['pɪlɪdʒər] *n* pilleur, -euse, pillard, -arde.

pillar ['pɪlər] *n* **(a)** *Archit etc* pilier *m*, colonne *f*; *Min* pilier, stappe *m*; pied central (*d'une table, d'un guéridon*); (*in surveying etc*) borne *f*, colonne (*de démarcation, de signalisation etc*); *Fig* **a p. of the Church,** un pilier *ou* une colonne de l'Église; **I've been rushing around from p. to post,** je n'ai pas arrêté de courir d'un endroit à l'autre; **to drive s.o. from p. to post,** envoyer qn de droite à gauche *ou* d'un endroit à l'autre; *Min* **p. and stall system,** méthode *f* de piliers et galeries; **p. of fire/smoke,** colonne de feu/fumée; *Br* **p. box,** boîte *f* aux lettres; **p. box red,** ≈ rouge-drapeau; **(b)** *MecE* colonne *f*, montant *m* (*d'une machine-outil*); (*small and round*) chandelle *f*; *Aut* **door p.,** montant de porte.

pillared ['pɪləd] *adj* à piliers, à colonnes.

pillbox ['pɪlbɒks] *n* **(a)** boîte *f* à pilules, pilulier *m*; **(b) p. (hat),** petit chapeau rond sans bord; **(c)** *Mil* blockhaus *m*.

pillion ['pɪljən] *n* (*on motor cycle*) **p. (seat),** siège *m* arrière, selle *f* tandem, tan-sad *m*, *pl* tan-sads; **to ride p.,** monter derrière; **p. rider** *or* **passenger,** passager, -ère (de derrière).

pillory¹ ['pɪlərɪ] *n* pilori *m.*

pillory² *vt Hist & Fig* mettre (*qn*) au pilori; dénoncer (*un abus*).

pillow¹ ['pɪləʊ] *n* oreiller *m*; **(lace) p.,** carreau *m*, coussin *m* (*pour dentelle*); oreiller (*pour dentelle aux fuseaux*); **p. fight,** bataille *f* d'oreillers *ou* de polochon(s); **p. talk,** conversation *f* sur l'oreiller.

pillow² *vt* **to p. one's head on one's arms,** reposer sa tête sur ses bras.

pillowcase, pillowslip [pɪləʊkeɪs, -slɪp] *n* taie *f* d'oreiller.

pilot¹ ['paɪlət] *n* **(a)** *Av* pilote *m*; **airline p.,** pilote de ligne; **automatic p.,** pilote automatique; **test p.,** pilote d'essais; *Mil Av* **fighter p.,** pilote de chasse; **p. officer,** sous-lieutenant *m* (aviateur);

(b) *Nau* pilote *m*; **p. waters,** zone *f* de pilotage; **p. boat** *or* **cutter,** bateau-pilote *m*, *pl* bateaux-pilotes; **p. flag,** pavillon *m* de *ou* du pilote; **p. house,** (kiosque *m* de) timonerie *f*;

(c) *TV* émission *f* pilote;

(d) (*person acting as guide*) guide *m*, mentor *m*; **p. fish,** poisson *m* pilote;

(e) *MecE* guide *m*; axe-guide *m*, *pl* axes-guides; **p. light** *or* **flame** *or* **jet** *or* **burner,** veilleuse *f* (*de bec de gaz etc*); *El etc* **p. light** *or* **lamp,** lampe *f* témoin, lampe pilote; témoin *m* de contrôle; *Av etc* **p. parachute,** parachute extracteur; *Met* **p. balloon,** ballon-sonde *m*, *pl* ballons-sondes; **p. factory** *or* **plant,** usine *f* pilote; *Ind Com* **p. run** *or* **series,** présérie *f*; **p. scheme,** projet *m* d'essai; **p. study,** enquête *f* pilote;

(f) *Rail* **p. (engine),** locomotive *f* estafette; locomotive pilote.

pilot² *vt* **(a)** piloter (*un navire, un avion, une auto de course etc*); mener, conduire (*qn à travers des obstacles etc*); *MecE etc* guider (*la mèche*).

pimento [pɪ'mentəʊ] *n* (*plant*) *& Culin* piment *m.*

pimp¹ [pɪmp] *n* souteneur *m*, proxénète *m*; *Sl* maquereau *m.*

pimp² *vi* exercer le métier de proxénète; **to p. for s.o.,** maquer qn.

pimpernel ['pɪmpənel] *n* (*flower*) **scarlet p.,** mouron *m* rouge.

pimple ['pɪmp(ə)l] *n* bouton *m* (*sur la peau*); **to come out in pimples,** boutonner, bourgeonner.

pimply ['pɪmplɪ] *adj* boutonneux, couvert de boutons.

pin¹ [pɪn] *n* **(a)** épingle *f*; (*for hair*) épingle (à cheveux); (*brooch*) broche *f*; **(safety) p.,** épingle à nourrice; **you could have heard a p. drop,** on aurait entendu voler une mouche; **as bright** *or* **clean as a new p.,** propre comme un sou neuf; **for two pins I'd punch his face,** pour un rien je lui casserais la figure; **pins and needles,** fourmillements *mpl*; *Br* **drawing p.,** punaise *f*; **p. money,** (*money for small purchases*) argent *m* de poche; *Arch* (*money given to wife*) argent pour le ménage; *Sewing* **p. tuck,** nervure *f*;

(b) *MecE* axe *m* (*de fixation etc*); goupille *f*, clavette *f*; pivot *m* (*d'une grue etc*); axe, verge *f* (*de girouette*); broche *f* (*de clef, de serrure*); gond *m* (*de penture, de paumelle*); tourillon *m* (*de porte*); *El* broche (*de fiche mâle*); *Comptr* (*on connector*) broche; (*of printhead*) aiguille *f*; *Surg* broche, clou *m* (*pour fracture*); **firing p.,** percuteur *m* (*d'une arme à feu*); *MecE* **split p.,** goupille fendue; **(safety) p.,** (*of grenade*) goupille;

(c) *Culin* **rolling p.,** rouleau *m* à pâtisserie;

(d) *Golf* drapeau *m* de trou;

(e) (*at ninepins*) quille *f*; **p. table,** billard chinois *ou* japonais;

(f) *F* (*legs*) **pins,** quilles *fpl*, cannes *fpl*; **to feel a bit shaky on one's pins,** (*after illness etc*) ne pas se sentir très sûr sur ses cannes.

pin² *vt* **(-nn-) (a)** épingler, attacher *ou* assujettir *ou* fixer avec une épingle *ou* des épingles; **to p. a map to** *or* **on the wall,** fixer une carte au mur (avec des punaises), punaiser une carte au mur; **(b)** *MecE etc* cheviller, goupiller, mettre une goupille à (*qch*); (*with a cotter*) claveter; **(c)** (*hold still*) fixer, clouer; **to p. s.o. against a wall,** clouer *ou* plaquer qn contre un mur; **to p. s.o.'s arms to his sides,** coller *ou* plaquer les bras de qn au corps; **to be pinned under a fallen tree,** se trouver pris *ou* coincé sous un arbre déraciné; *Fig F* **to p. sth on s.o.,** rendre qn responsable de qch; **you can't p. this on me,** tu ne peux pas me la mettre sur le dos, celle-là; **to p. one's hopes on s.o./sth,** mettre tous ses espoirs en qn/dans qch; **(d)** étayer, étançonner (*un mur etc*).

►**pin down** *vtsep* **(a)** (*trap*) coincer; **he pinned me down,** (*in fight etc*) il m'a coincé; **they were pinned down by the wreckage,** ils ont été coincés dans les décombres; *Mil* **to p. down the enemy,** coincer l'ennemi; **pinned down by enemy fire,** coincé par le feu de l'ennemi;

(b) (*force to be definite*) obliger (*qn*) à s'engager; **I tried to p. her down to a time,** j'ai essayé de lui faire donner une heure précise; **to p. s.o. down to do sth,** obliger *ou* contraindre qn à faire qch; **without pinning himself down to anything,** sans s'engager à rien;

(c) (*identify*) identifier, isoler; **we couldn't p. down the source of the noise,** nous ne pouvions pas identifier la source du bruit; **a feeling that's difficult to p. down,** un sentiment qu'il est difficile d'isoler *ou* d'identifier; **it's difficult to p. it down,** c'est difficile de mettre le doigt dessus.

►**pin up** *vtsep* **(a)** (*fasten to wall etc*) fixer au mur, punaiser; **to p. up a photograph/poster/map/***etc*, punaiser une photo/un poster/une carte/*etc*; **(b)** (*fasten*) **to p. up one's hair,** épingler ses cheveux; **to p. up a hem,** rabattre un ourlet avec des épingles.

PIN [pɪn] *n Br Banking* (*abbr* **personal identification number**) code confidentiel.

pinafore ['pɪnəfɔːr] *n* **(a)** *esp Br* tablier *m* (*d'enfant etc*); **(b)** *Br* **p. (dress),** robe *f* à bretelles, robe chasuble.

pinball ['pɪnbɔːl] *n* (*machine, game*) flipper *m*; **p. machine** *or* **game** *or* **table,** flipper *m.*

pincer ['pɪnsər] *n* (*of crab, insect etc*) pince *f*; *Mil* **p. movement,** mouvement *m ou* manœuvre *f* en tenailles.

pincers ['pɪnsəz] *npl* (*tool*) **(pair of) p.,** pince *f*, tenaille(s) *f(pl)*.

pinch¹ [pɪntʃ] *n* **(a)** action *f* de pincer; pincement *m*; **to give s.o. a p.,** pincer qn; **the p. of hunger,** la morsure de la faim; *F* **to feel the p.,** tirer le diable par la queue; **at a p.,** à la rigueur; **(b)** pincée *f* (*de sel etc*); prise *f* (*de tabac*).

pinch² *vt* **(a)** (*nip*) pincer (*qn, la joue de qn etc*); **(b)** (*restrict*) serrer, gêner (*qn*); **(c)** *F* chiper, faucher (*qch*) **(from s.o.,** à qn); arrêter, pincer, choper (*un voleur etc*); **I've had my purse pinched,** on m'a piqué mon porte-monnaie; **to get pinched,** (*of thief etc*) se faire pincer *ou* épingler. **2** *vi* **(a)** (*nip*) blesser; **shoe that pinches,** chaussure qui blesse *ou* qui serre; *Fig* **that's where the shoe pinches,** c'est là que le bât (le) blesse; **(b) to p. and scrape,** faire des économies de bouts de chandelle.

►**pinch off** *vtsep* (*remove*) enlever (*qch*) en pinçant (*avec les ongles etc*); **to p. off a bud,** épincer un bourgeon.

►**pinch out** *vtsep* enlever en pinçant.

pinchbeck ['pɪntʃbek] **1** *n* toc *m.* **2** *adj* simili, en toc.

pinched ['pɪntʃt] *adj* **(a)** (*face etc*) tiré, hâve; **to be p. with hunger,** être tenaillé par la faim; **(b)** étroit; **to be (a bit) p. for money/time/***etc*, être à court d'argent/de temps/*etc.*

pinch-hit ['pɪntʃhɪt] *vi* **to p.-h. for s.o.,** *Baseball* frapper à la place de (*qn*); *Fig* remplacer qn.

pinch-hitter ['pɪntʃhɪtər] *n Baseball* frappeur *m* d'urgence *ou* suppléant.

pinch-runner ['pɪntʃrʌnər] *n Baseball* coureur *m* d'urgence *ou* suppléant.

pincushion ['pɪnkʊʃən] *n* pelote *f* à épingles.

pine¹ [paɪn] *n* **(a) p. (tree),** pin *m*; **Norway p.,** pin sylvestre *ou* suisse; **Scotch p.,** sapin *m* du Nord *ou* de l'Écosse; **pitch p.,** pitchpin *m*; **p. cone,** pomme *f ou* cône *m* de pin, pigne *f*; **p. forest,** forêt *f* de pins, pinède *f*; **p. needle,** aiguille *f* de pin; **p. nut,** pignon *m*; **(b)** (*wood*) (bois *m* de) pin *m*; **p. furniture,** meubles *mpl* en pin.

pine² *vi* languir, se consumer; **to p. with grief,** languir de tristesse.

►**pine away** *vi* = **PINE².**

►**pine for** *vipo* languir pour *ou* après (*qn, qch*); **to p. for home,** avoir la nostalgie du foyer.

pineapple ['paɪnæp(ə)l] *n* ananas *m*; **p. juice,** jus *m* d'ananas.

ping¹ [pɪŋ] *n* cinglement *m*, fouettement *m* (*d'une balle de fusil etc*); (*of sth hitting wine glass, small bell etc*) petit bruit clair.

ping² *vi* (*of bullet etc*) cingler, fouetter; (*of sth hitting wine glass, small bell etc*) faire un petit bruit clair.

pinger ['pɪŋər] *n* (*timer*) compte-minutes *m inv.*

ping-pong ['pɪŋpɒŋ] *n* ping-pong *m*; **p.-p. table/ball,** table *f*/balle *f* de ping-pong.

pinhead ['pɪnhed] *n* **(a)** tête *f* d'épingle; **smaller than a p.,** plus petit qu'une tête d'épingle; **(b)** *F* (*stupid person*) idiot, -iote, abruti, -ie.

pinhole ['pɪnhəʊl] *n* **(a)** trou *m* d'épingle; *Opt* très petite ouverture (*dans un écran etc*); *Phot* sténopé *m*; **p. source**

of light, source de lumière punctiforme *ou* ponctuelle; **(b)** *Tech* trou *m* de cheville *ou* de goujon.

pining ['paɪnɪŋ] *n* **(a)** langueur *f*, languissement *m*; **(b)** (*strong desire*) désir ardent (**for sth,** de qch); (*for home*) nostalgie *f*.

pinion¹ ['pɪnɪən] *n Orn* (*flight feathers*) penne *f*, rémige *f*.

pinion² *vt* **(a)** (*tie*) lier les bras à, ligoter (*qn*); lier (**s.o. to a tree,** qn à un arbre); **to p. s.o.'s arms,** lier les bras de qn; **(b)** rogner les ailes à (*un oiseau*).

pinion³ *n Mec E* pignon *m*; (*on shaft*) tympan *m*; **rack and p.,** crémaillère *f* et pignon; **p. wheel,** roue *f* à pignon.

pink¹ [pɪŋk] **1** *n* **(a)** (*colour*) (couleur *f* de) rose *m*; **to turn** *or* **go p.,** (*with embarrassment etc*) rosir; **p. champagne,** champagne rosé; *Am F* **p. collar job,** = emploi typiquement féminin; *Am F* **p. collar workers,** employées de bureau; **salmon p.,** rose saumon *inv*; **shocking p.,** rose vif; **(hunting) p.,** rouge *m*, écarlate *m*; *US F* **p. slip,** avis *m* de licenciement; **to get one's p. slip,** être licencié; **(b)** (*flower*) œillet *m*; **garden p.,** (œillet) mignardise *f*; **(c) in the p. of condition** *or* **health,** en excellente *ou* parfaite santé; (*of racehorse etc*) entraîné à fond; **to be in the p.,** (*of person*) se porter à merveille. **2** *adj* **(a)** (couleur *f* de) rose; **to see p. elephants,** voir double; **p. eyes,** (*of albino*) yeux rouges; **(b)** *F* = **PINKO**.

pink² *vt* **(a)** (*pierce slightly*) percer, toucher (*son adversaire*); **(b)** *Sewing etc* (*with pinking shears*) denteler *ou* hocher *ou* découper les bords (*de qch*); travailler à jour, évider (*le cuir etc*).

pink³ *vi* (*of engine*) cliqueter.

pinkeye ['pɪŋkaɪ] *n Med* conjonctivite aiguë contagieuse.

pinkie ['pɪŋkɪ] *n Am & Scot* petit doigt, auriculaire *m*.

pinking¹ ['pɪŋkɪŋ] *n Sewing etc* découpage *m*, découpure *f*; **p. shears** *or* **scissors,** ciseaux *mpl* à cranter *ou* à denteler; **p. iron,** emporte-pièce *m inv*.

pinking² *n* (*of engine*) cliquetis *m* (*produit par les auto-allumages*).

pinkish ['pɪŋkɪʃ] *adj* rosâtre, rosé.

pinko ['pɪŋkəʊ] *F* **1** *n* personne *f* à tendances gauchistes. **2** *adj* gauchisant.

pinky¹ ['pɪŋkɪ] *n* = **PINKIE**.

pinky² *adj F* rosâtre; **p. grey,** gris rosâtre *inv*.

pinnace ['pɪnɪs] *n Nau* chaloupe *f*, grand canot.

pinnacle ['pɪnək(ə)l] *n* **(a)** cime *f* (*d'une montagne etc*); *Fig* **on the highest p. of fame,** à l'apogée *ou* au sommet de la gloire; **(b)** *Archit* pinacle *m*, clocheton *m*; couronnement *m* (*de faîte etc*).

pinny ['pɪnɪ] *n esp Br F* tablier *m*.

pinpoint¹ ['pɪnpɔɪnt] *n* (*tip of a pin*) pointe *f* d'épingle; (*very small point*) point infime *ou* infinitésimal; **p. accuracy,** haute précision; *Mil* **p. bombing/firing,** bombardement *m*/tir *m* de précision; **p. target,** objectif ponctuel.

pinpoint² *vt* (*point out*) indiquer exactement, mettre le doigt sur (*qch*); (*locate*) localiser *ou* repérer (*qch*) avec exactitude *ou* avec précision; souligner (*un fait*); *Mil* (*aim at*) viser (*un objectif*) avec précision; (*fire on, bomb*) effectuer un tir *ou* un bombardement de précision sur (*un objectif*); **to p. a problem,** isoler un problème, mettre le doigt sur un problème.

pinprick ['pɪnprɪk] *n* piqûre *f* d'épingle; *F* **pinpricks,** tracasseries *fpl*.

pinstripe ['pɪnstraɪp] *n Tex* rayure fine (*de couleur*); **p. suit,** costume rayé.

pint [paɪnt] *n* (*measurement*) pinte *f* (= 0,568 litre; *US* = 0,473 litre); *Br F* **a p.,** (*drink*) une pinte de bière; **I'm going for a p.,** je vais prendre une bière.

pinta ['paɪntə] *n Br F* une pinte de lait.

pintail ['pɪnteɪl] *n* **(a)** (*wild duck*) pilet *m*; **(b)** (*grouse*) tétras *m* à longue queue, *Can* gelinotte *f* à queue fine.

pinto ['pɪntəʊ] *adj & n Am* (cheval *m*) pie *m*.

pint-size(d) ['paɪntsaɪz, -d] *adj F* minuscule.

pin-up ['pɪnʌp] *n F* (*woman, picture of woman*) pin-up *f inv*; **he's a real p.-up,** c'est un vrai canon.

Pinyin ['pɪn'jɪn] *n* pinyin *m*.

pioneer¹ [paɪə'nɪər] *n* pionnier *m*.

pioneer² **1** *vt* frayer (*un chemin*) en pionnier; **to p. a new method,** être le premier *ou* l'un des premiers à développer une nouvelle méthode. **2** *vi* faire œuvre de pionnier.

pioneering [paɪə'nɪərɪŋ] *adj* (*work*) de pionnier; (*scientist etc*) qui fait œuvre de pionnier; **to do p. work in a science,** défricher le terrain d'une science, faire œuvre de pionnier dans une science, ouvrir la voie dans une science; **in p. days,** au temps des pionniers.

pious ['paɪəs] *adj* pieux; **p. fraud,** pieux mensonge; *F* (*person*) hypocrite.

piously ['paɪəslɪ] *adv* pieusement, avec piété.

piousness ['paɪəsnɪs] *n* piété *f*.

pip¹ [pɪp] *n* pépin *m* (*de fruit*).

pip² *n* **(a)** (*on card, die etc*) point *m*; **(b)** *Br Mil F* **to get one's third p.,** ≈ recevoir sa troisième ficelle; **(c)** *Rad* (*sound*) top *m*; (*on radar*) top d'écho; *Rad* **the pips,** = les bips sonores.

pip³ *vt* (-pp-) *Old-fashioned* (*defeat*) vaincre, battre (*qn*); *F* **to be pipped at the post,** se faire coiffer *ou* battre sur le poteau.

pip⁴ *n* **(a)** (*poultry disease*) pépie *f* (*de la volaille*); **(b)** *Br F* **to give s.o. the p.,** embêter qn.

pipe¹ [paɪp] *n* **(a)** (*tube*) tuyau *m*, tube *m*, conduit *m*, conduite *f*; **water/gas p.,** tuyau *ou* conduite d'eau/de gaz; **pipes and fittings,** tuyauterie *f* et accessoires *mpl* de tuyauterie; **connecting p.,** tuyau de communication, raccord *m*; **elbow p.,** coude *m*, raccord coudé; **(b)** *Mus* chalumeau *m*; *Nau* sifflet *m* (*du maître d'équipage*); chant *m* (*d'oiseau*); **the pipes,** la cornemuse; **organ p.,** tuyau *m* d'orgue; **reed p.,** tuyau à anche; *Mil* **p. major,** cornemuse-chef *m*; **(c)** (*for smoking*) pipe *f*; **to smoke a p.,** fumer une pipe; **p. of peace, peace p.,** calumet *m* de (la) paix; *F* **put that in your p. and smoke it!,** mettez ça dans votre poche et votre mouchoir par-dessus!; **p. cleaner,** cure-pipe *m*, *pl* cure-pipes; **p. dream,** rêve *m* (chimérique), projet *m* illusoire; **p. rack,** porte-pipes *m inv*.

pipe² **1** *vi Mus* jouer du chalumeau; (*play the bagpipes*) jouer de la cornemuse; (*of bird etc*) siffler; (*of person*) parler d'une voix flûtée; *Nau* donner un coup de sifflet. **2** *vt* **(a)** installer *ou* poser des canalisations dans (*une maison etc*); canaliser (*l'eau, le pétrole etc*); **piped water,** eau courante; **to p. oil to a refinery,** amener le pétrole à une raffinerie par oléduc *ou* par pipeline; *F* **piped music,** musique *f* de fond; **(b)** *Mus Arch* jouer (*un air*) au chalumeau; (*on bagpipes*) jouer à la cornemuse; (*sing*) chanter (*un air*) d'une voix flûtée; *Nau* siffler (*un commandement*); *Nau* **to p. s.o. aboard,** rendre les honneurs du sifflet à qn; **(c)** *Sewing etc* passepoiler (*une robe etc*); **(d)** *Culin* décorer (*un gâteau*) avec une douille.

▶**pipe down** *vi F* **(a)** (*make less noise*) faire moins de bruit; **p. down!,** moins de bruit!; **(b)** (*not talk*) se taire; **p. down!,** boucle-la!; **he piped down when he realised she knew a lot more about it,** il s'est tu quand il a réalisé qu'elle en savait bien plus que lui.

▶**pipe in** *vtsep* **to p. in the guests,** (*in Scotland*) jouer de la cornemuse en tête de la procession (lors de l'entrée solennelle des invités).

▶**pipe up** *vi* (*start to speak*) commencer à parler; **a little voice piped up,** une petite voix s'est fait entendre.

pipeclay ['paɪpkleɪ] *n* terre *f* de pipe; blanc *m* de terre à pipe (*pour astiquage*).

pipeline ['paɪplaɪn] *n* **(a)** (*large pipe*) canalisation *f*, conduite *f*; (*for gas*) conduite de gaz naturel, gazoduc *m*; (*for petrol*) oléoduc *m*, pipeline *m*; **(b)** canal *m ou* voie *f* d'acheminement (*des nouvelles, du matériel etc*); *F* **it's in the p.,** c'est en route; *F* **there's a pay rise in the p.,** une augmentation de salaire se dessine à l'horizon.

piper ['paɪpər] *n Mus* joueur *m* de chalumeau; (*of bagpipes*) joueur de cornemuse, cornemuseur *m*, cornemuseux *m*; *Prov* **he who pays the p. calls the tune,** qui paye a bien le droit de choisir.

pipette [pɪ'pet] *n Ch etc* pipette *f*, compte-gouttes *m inv*.

piping ['paɪpɪŋ] **1** *adj* (*son*) aigu, *f* aiguë, sifflant; (*voix*) flûté. **2** *adv* **p. hot,** tout chaud, tout bouillant. **3** *n* **(a)** (*installation of pipes*) installation *f ou* pose *f* de tuyaux *ou* de canalisations (*dans un immeuble etc*); (*system*) canalisation *f* (*de l'eau, du gaz etc*); (*pipes collectively*) conduites *fpl*, tuyaux *mpl*, tuyauterie *f*; **(b)** *Mus etc* (*sound of pipe*) son *m* du chalumeau; (*sound of bagpipes*) son de la cornemuse; gazouillement *m*, gazouillis *m* (*d'oiseaux*); *Nau* commandement *m* au sifflet; **(c)** *Sewing etc* passepoil *m*; **(d)** *Culin* décoration (*d'un gâteau etc*) faite avec une douille; **p. bag,** poche *f* à douilles.

pipistrelle [pɪpɪ'strel] *n* **p. (bat),** pipistrelle *f*.

pipit ['pɪpɪt] *n* (*bird*) pipit *m*.

pippin ['pɪpɪn] *n* (*apple*) (pomme *f*) reinette *f*.

pipsqueak ['pɪpskwiːk] *n F* (*person*) petit bonhomme de rien du tout, gringalet *m*.

piquancy ['piːkənsɪ] *n* **(a)** goût piquant (*d'un mets*); **(b)** sel *m*, piquant *m* (*d'un conte, d'une affaire etc*).

piquant ['piːkənt] *adj* (*flavour, story etc*) piquant.

piquantly ['piːkəntlɪ] *adv* d'une manière piquante, avec du piquant.

pique¹ [piːk] *n* pique *f*, ressentiment *m*; **in a fit of p.,**

dans un accès de dépit.

pique² *vt* **(a)** (*offend*) piquer, dépiter (*qn*); **to p. s.o.'s pride,** piquer *ou* blesser qn dans son orgueil; **(b)** (*arouse*) piquer, exciter (*la curiosité de qn*).

piquet [pɪ'ket] *n Cards* piquet *m*.

piracy ['paɪrəsɪ] *n* **(a)** *Nau etc* piraterie *f*, flibusterie *f*; **an act of p.,** un acte de piraterie; **air p.,** piraterie de l'air; **(b)** (*of copyright*) atteinte *f* au droit d'auteur; pillage *m*, vol *m* (*des idées etc*); **film p.,** piratage *m* de films.

piranha [pɪ'rɑːnə] *n* (*fish*) piranha *m*, piraya *m*.

pirate¹ ['paɪrɪt] *n* **(a)** *Nau* (*person*) pirate *m*, flibustier *m*; (*ship*) navire *m* pirate; **p. captain,** capitaine *m* des pirates; **(b)** *Rad* (*person*) pirate *m*; **p. radio,** radio *f* pirate; **p. station,** poste *m ou* émetteur *m* pirate; **(c)** contrefacteur *m* (*d'un ouvrage littéraire etc*); voleur, -euse (*d'idées etc*); **p. cassettes/videos,** cassettes/vidéos pirates.

pirate² *vt* **(a)** *Nau* saisir (*un navire*) en pirate *ou* en flibustier; **(b)** s'approprier, voler (*une invention etc*); contrefaire (*une marque de fabrique*); pirater (*une cassette*); **to p. a book,** (*republish without permission*) republier un livre sans autorisation; (*copy*) contrefaire *ou* démarquer un livre.

piratical [paɪ'rætɪk(ə)l] *adj* **(a)** *Nau* de pirate, de flibustier; **(b)** (*reproduction etc*) de contrefacteur, de contrefaçon.

pirouette¹ [pɪrʊ'et] *n* (*in dancing*) pirouette *f*.

pirouette² *vi* pirouetter.

Pisa ['piːzə] *n* Pise *f*.

Pisces ['paɪsiːz] *n Astron* les Poissons *mpl*; **I'm a P.,** je suis poisson.

piss¹ [pɪs] *n Sl* pisse *f*; **to have a p.,** pisser; **to take the p. out of,** se foutre de la gueule de (*qn*); se foutre de (*qn, qch*); **you're taking the p.!,** tu te fous de moi!; **p. artist,** (*bungler*) maladroit *m*; (*braggart*) vantard *m*; (*drunk*) soûlard *m*; (*fool, idiot*) espèce *f* de con.

piss² *Sl* **1** *vi* pisser. **2** *vt* pisser (*du sang etc*).

►**piss about, piss around** *vi Sl* **(a)** (*behave foolishly*) faire le con, déconner; **(b)** (*waste time*) glandouiller.

►**piss down** *vi Sl* (*rain*) **it's pissing down,** il pleut des cordes *ou Sl* à vache qui pisse.

►**piss off** *Sl* **1** *vi* **(a)** (*go away*) foutre le camp; **p. off!,** fous le camp! **2** *vtsep* (*annoy*) faire chier; **that really pisses me off,** ça me fait vraiment chier; **to be pissed off,** en avoir marre.

pissed [pɪst] *adj* **(a)** *Br Sl* (*drunk*) soûl; **as p. as a newt,** rond comme une queue de pelle; **(b)** *US Sl* (*angry*) en rogne, en boule.

piss-taker ['pɪsteɪkər] *n Br Sl* personne qui se fout du monde.

piss-up ['pɪsʌp] *n Br Sl* biture *f*, soûlerie *f*; **they couldn't organise a p.-up in a brewery,** ils ne sont pas foutus d'organiser quoi que ce soit correctement.

pistachio [pɪ'stɑːʃɪəʊ] *n* **p. (nut),** pistache *f*; **p. (tree),** pistachier *m*.

piste [piːst] *n Ski* piste *f*.

pistil ['pɪstɪl] *n Bot* pistil *m*.

pistol ['pɪst(ə)l] *n* (*gun*) pistolet *m*; **cap p.,** pistolet à amorces; **to hold a p. to s.o.'s head,** tenir un pistolet braqué contre la tempe de qn; *Fig* mettre le couteau sous la gorge à qn; **p. shot,** coup *m* de pistolet; **(b)** *Tech* pistolet *m* (*d'un outil pneumatique etc*); **p. grip,** poignée *f* pistolet (*d'un outil*).

pistol-whip ['pɪstəlwɪp] *vt* **(-pp-)** *US* frapper (*qn*) avec un pistolet.

piston ['pɪstən] *n MecE etc* piston *m*; *Mus* piston (*d'instrument à vent en cuivre*); **p. engine,** moteur *m* à pistons; **p. head,** tête *f ou* fond *m* du piston.

pit¹ [pɪt] *n* **(a)** (*hole in ground*) fosse *f*; (*roughly dug*) fouille *f*; piège *m*, fosse (*à attraper les animaux*); *Min* puits *m* (*de mine*); (*coal mine*) mine *f* (*de houille*); **to dig a p.,** creuser une fosse; *Metal* **casting p.,** fosse de coulée (*de fonderie*); **tan p.,** cuve *f ou* fosse à tanner; *Aut etc* **inspection p.,** fosse de visite; *Lit* **the (bottomless) p.,** (*hell*) l'enfer *m*, les enfers; *Min* **to work in the pits,** être mineur (de fond); **he went down the pits when he was 16,** il est descendu à la mine à 16 ans; **chalk p.,** carrière *f* à chaux; *Min* **p. prop,** poteau *m ou* étai *m* de mine; étançon *m*; *Min* **p. pony,** cheval *m* de mine; *Sl* **this town is the pits,** cette ville est minable; *Sl* **it's the pits,** c'est nul;

(b) *Th* parterre *m*; *Am* marché *m* (*à la Bourse*); arène *f* (*de combat de coqs*); fosse *f* (*à ours*); **orchestra p.,** fosse d'orchestre; **wheat p.,** Bourse *f* des blés; *Sp* **the pits,** les stands *mpl* de ravitaillement;

(c) (*mark*) piqûre *f*, alvéole *mf* (*dans un métal etc*);

(d) *Med* cicatrice *f*, marque *f* (*de la petite vérole*); *Anat* **the p. of the stomach,** le creux de l'estomac;

(e) *Br F* (*bed*) pieu *m*; **he's still in his p.,** il est encore au pieu.

pit² *n* noyau *m* (*de cerise etc*).

pit³ *vt* **(-tt-)** dénoyauter (*des cerises etc*).

pit⁴ *vt* **(-tt-)** **(a) to p. s.o. against s.o.,** mettre qn aux prises avec qn, opposer qn à qn; **to p. oneself against s.o.,** se mesurer à qn; **(b)** (*of acids etc*) piquer, trouer (*le métal etc*); *Med* (*of smallpox*) grêler, marquer (*le visage*).

pita ['pɪtə] *n* **p. bread,** pain grec non levé et de forme ovale.

pit-a-pat ['pɪtə'pæt] **1** *adv* **to go p.-a-p.,** (*of rain etc*) crépiter; (*of feet*) trottiner; (*of the heart*) faire toc-toc. **2** *n* crépitement *m* (*de la pluie*); battement *m* (*du cœur*).

pitch¹ [pɪtʃ] *n* **(a)** (*act of throwing*) lancement *m* (*d'une pierre, d'une balle etc*);

(b) (*place*) place *f*, emplacement *m* (*dans un marché etc*); place habituelle (*d'un marchand forain, d'un mendiant etc*); terrain *m* (*de football etc*); *Cr* terrain entre les guichets;

(c) *Archit* hauteur *f* (*du plafond*);

(d) *Mus* hauteur *f* (*d'un son*); **to have perfect p.,** avoir l'oreille absolue; **to give the orchestra the p.,** donner l'accord à un orchestre; **to rise in p.,** monter de ton; **p. pipe,** diapason *m* à bouche;

(e) (*degree*) degré *m* (*d'insolence etc*); **to such a p. that ...,** à tel point que ..., au point que ...; **to the highest p.,** au plus haut degré, au plus haut point; **expectation had reached fever p.,** l'attente était fébrile;

(f) (sales) p., baratin *m*, boniment *m* publicitaire; *Am Sl* **to make a p. for,** (*express support for*) vanter les mérites de (*qn, qch*);

(g) (*slope*) pente *f*, rampant *m* (*d'un toit, d'un comble, d'un escalier*); chute *f*, inclinaison *f* (*d'un toit, d'un comble*); *Min* plongement *m* (*d'un filon*); *Tech* inclinaison, basile *f* (*d'un fer de rabot*);

(h) *Nau Av* (*of ship, aircraft*) (*type of movement*) tangage *m*; (*instance*) coup *m* de tangage; **angle of p., p. angle,** angle *m* de tangage;

(i) (*spacing*) espacement *m*, écartement *m* (*des rivets, des trous*); pas *m* (*d'une roue dentée, d'une vis, d'une hélice etc*); **p. circle,** cercle primitif; ligne *f* d'engrènement (*d'une roue*).

pitch² **1** *vt* **(a)** (*throw*) jeter, lancer (*une balle*); (*baseball*) lancer; **to p. the hay onto the cart,** jeter le foin sur la charrette; **(b)** (*set up*) dresser (*une tente*); établir (*un camp*); *Cr* planter, dresser (*les guichets*); **(c)** *Mus* jouer (*un morceau*) dans une clef donnée; **to p. one's voice higher/lower,** hausser/baisser le ton de sa voix; **(d)** (*aim*) **to p. an estimate too low,** arrêter un devis trop bas; **to p. one's aspirations too high,** viser trop haut; **stories pitched at older children,** histoires écrites pour des enfants plus âgés; **(e)** *F* **to p. a yarn,** raconter des histoires. **2** *vi* **(a)** (*in baseball*) lancer; **(b)** (*fall*) tomber; **to p. forward,** (*be thrown*) être projeté en avant; (*fall*) piquer du nez; **the ball pitched on a stone,** le ballon a rebondi sur une pierre; **(c)** *Nau Av* (*of ship, aircraft*) tanguer.

pitch³ *n* (*substance*) poix *f*; (*from coal tar*) brai *m*; **black** *or* **dark as p.,** (*hair, eyes*) noir comme le jais; (*room, night*) noir comme dans un four.

pitch⁴ *vt* (*coat with pitch*) brayer (*qch*), enduire (*qch*) de poix *ou* de brai.

►**pitch in** *vi* **(a)** (*start working*) se mettre à la besogne; **(b)** (*contribute to a task*) s'y mettre; (*contribute money etc*) payer son écot; **she pitched in with an offer of help,** elle s'y est mise en proposant d'aider.

►**pitch into** *vipo F* **(a)** (*physically*) s'attaquer à (*qn*); (*verbally*) dire son fait à (*qn*); **to p. into a task,** se mettre à une tâche; **(b)** (*fall*) tomber la tête la première dans (*une mare etc*).

►**pitch on** *vipo* (*choose*) décider pour, choisir (*qch, qn*).

pitch-black [pɪtʃ'blæk] *adj* noir comme poix; **it's p.-b.,** (*I can't see*) il fait noir comme dans un four.

pitch-dark [pɪtʃ'dɑːk] *adj* **it's p.-d.,** (*outside*) il fait nuit noire; (*in cellar etc*) il fait noir comme dans un four.

pitched [pɪtʃt] *adj* **p. battle,** bataille rangée.

pitcher¹ ['pɪtʃər] *n* (*large jug*) cruche *f*, broc *m*, pichet *m*; *esp Am* (*small jug*) pot *m* (*à lait etc*); *F* **little pitchers have big ears,** = pas devant les enfants.

pitcher² *n Baseball* lanceur *m*.

pitchfork¹ ['pɪtʃfɔːk] *n Agr* fourche *f*, fouine *f* (*à foin*); (*two-pronged*) bident *m*.

pitchfork² *vt* lancer (*une gerbe etc*) avec la fourche; *Fig F* (*force*) propulser (*qn à un poste*).

pitching ['pɪtʃɪŋ] *n* **(a)** lancement *m*, jet *m* (*d'une pierre etc*); **(b)** dressage *m* (*d'une tente*); établissement *m* (*d'un*

camp); **(c)** *Nau Av* tangage *m* (*d'un navire, d'un avion*).
piteous ['pɪtɪəs] *adj* pitoyable, piteux.
piteously ['pɪtɪəslɪ] *adv* pitoyablement, piteusement.
pitfall ['pɪtfɔːl] *n* (*pit*) trappe *f*, fosse *f*; (*trap*) piège *m*; **the pitfalls of the English language,** les pièges de l'anglais.
pith [pɪθ] *n* **(a)** peau blanche (*d'une orange etc*); *Bot* (*medulla*) mœlle *f*; **p. helmet,** casque *m* (colonial) en sola; **(b)** *Fig* moelle *f*, essence *f* (*d'un livre etc*); piquant *m* (*d'une histoire*).
pithead ['pɪthed] *n* bouche *f* de puits; **p. ballot,** vote *m* des mineurs; **p. baths,** bains *mpl ou* douches *fpl* de la mine.
pithiness ['pɪθɪnɪs] *n* concision *f*.
pithy ['pɪθɪ] *adj* **(a)** (*orange etc*) couvert de peau blanche; (*stem etc*) moelleux; **(b)** (*style etc*) concis; **p. phrase,** phrase *f* lapidaire.
pitiable ['pɪtɪəb(ə)l] *adj* pitoyable, piteux; (*appearance, object*) minable, lamentable; **she was in a p. state,** elle était dans un état à faire pitié.
pitiful ['pɪtɪfʊl] *adj* pitoyable, apitoyant; *Pej* lamentable; **it's p. to see him,** il fait pitié.
pitifully ['pɪtɪfʊlɪ] *adv* pitoyablement; **she was p. thin,** elle était d'une maigreur pitoyable.
pitiless ['pɪtɪlɪs] *adj* impitoyable; (*vent, froid*) cruel.
pitilessly ['pɪtɪlɪslɪ] *adv* impitoyablement, sans pitié.
piton ['piːtɒn] *n* (*in mountaineering*) piton *m*.
pitta ['pɪtə] *n* **p. bread,** pain grec non-levé et de forme ovale.
pittance ['pɪtəns] *n* maigre salaire *m*; **to work for a p.,** travailler pour un salaire dérisoire.
pitted ['pɪtɪd] *adj* (*metal etc*) piqué, alvéolé (*par un acide etc*); (*skin*) grêlé (*par la petite vérole*).
pitter-patter ['pɪtə'pætər] *n & vi* = **PATTER**[1,2].
pituitary [pɪ'tjuːɪt(ə)rɪ] *Anat* **1** *n* **p. (gland),** hypophyse *f*, glande *f* pituitaire. **2** *adj* pituitaire.
pity[1] ['pɪtɪ] *n* pitié *f*; **to have** *or* **take p. on s.o.,** prendre qn en pitié; **to show no p.,** ne manifester aucune pitié; **out of p. for s.o.,** (*faire qch*) par pitié pour qn; **for p.'s sake,** par pitié; **what a p.!,** quel dommage!; **it's a great p. that ...,** il est bien malheureux *ou* dommage que ...; **more's the p.,** c'est bien dommage.
pity[2] *vt* plaindre (*qn*), avoir pitié de, s'apitoyer sur (*qn*); **he is to be pitied,** il est à plaindre, il fait pitié.
pitying ['pɪtɪɪŋ] *adj* compatissant; (*regard*) de pitié.
pityingly ['pɪtɪɪŋlɪ] *adv* avec pitié.
Pius ['paɪəs] *n* Pie *m*.
pivot[1] ['pɪvət] *n* **(a)** *MecE etc* pivot *m*, axe *m* (*de rotation*); pivot (*d'une grue etc*); (*of axle etc*) tourillon *m*; **(b)** *Fig* (*person*) pivot *m*, cheville ouvrière (*d'une entreprise etc*); *Mil* **p. (man),** pivot, guide *m*, homme *m* de base (*d'un mouvement d'ordre serré*).
pivot[2] *v* **(-t-) 1** *vt* monter (*une pièce*) sur pivot. **2** *vi* pivoter, tourner (**on sth,** sur qch).
pivotal ['pɪvət(ə)l] *adj* pivotal, -aux; (*point*) cardinal; (*position*) clef *inv*.
pix [pɪks] *npl F* (= **pics**) *see* **PIC**.
pixel ['pɪksəl] *n Comptr* pixel *m*.
pixie, pixy ['pɪksɪ] *n* (*elf*) lutin *m*; (*fairy*) fée *f*.
pixil(l)ated ['pɪksɪleɪtəd] *adj esp US Sl* (*drunk*) bourré.
pizza ['piːtsə] *n Culin* pizza *f*; **p. parlour,** pizzeria *f*.
pizzazz [pə'zæz] *n* = **PZAZZ**.
pizzeria [piːtsə'riːə] *n* pizzeria *f*.
pkg *n abbr* **package**.
pkt *n abbr* **packet**.
pl *n Gram* (*abbr* **plural**) pl.
Pl. *n* (*abbr* **Place**) = rue.
placard[1] ['plækɑːd] *n* (*written notice*) écriteau *m*; (*poster*) affiche *f*.
placard[2] *vt* placarder (*un mur*).
placate [plə'keɪt] *vt* apaiser, calmer, concilier.
place[1] [pleɪs] *n* **(a)** (*location*) lieu *m*, endroit *m*; (*in street names*) cour *f*, passage *m*, rue *f*, ruelle *f*; **this would be an ideal p. for a picnic,** voilà un endroit idéal pour piqueniquer; **a good p. to meet people,** un bon endroit pour rencontrer des gens; **this is the p.!,** nous voilà arrivés!; **to move from one p. to another,** se déplacer d'un lieu *ou* d'un endroit à un autre; **in places,** par endroits; **all over the p.,** (*in many different places*) partout; (*in disorder*) dans tous les sens; *F* **the team were all over the p.,** l'équipe a joué n'importe comment; *F* **these figures are all over the p.,** (*are a mess*) ces chiffres ont été calculés n'importe comment; *F* **to go places,** réussir (dans la vie); *Br Univ F* **the other p.,** (*at Oxford*) Cambridge; (*at Cambridge*) Oxford; **p. of refuge,** lieu de refuge; **p. of amusement,** lieu de divertissement; **p. of worship,** édifice consacré au culte; **my p. of work,** l'endroit où je travaille, mon bureau *etc*; **meeting p.,** (lieu de) rendez-vous *m inv*; **the village/museum/*etc* was an interesting p.,** le village/musée/*etc* était intéressant; **I'm looking for a p. to stay,** je cherche un logement; **can you recommend a p. to eat?,** pouvez-vous me recommander un restaurant?; **p. of residence,** résidence *f*, demeure *f*, domicile *m* (réel); **a little p. in the country,** une petite maison à la campagne; *F* **nice p. you've got here,** c'est bien chez vous!; *F* **come round to my p.,** venez chez moi; *F* **your p. or mine?,** on va chez toi ou chez moi?; **this is no p. for you,** vous n'avez que faire ici; *Mil* **fortified p.,** place forte, place de guerre; **p. of payment,** lieu de paiement; *Br* **p. of safety order,** (*for child*) = décision de mise en sûreté; **p. name,** nom *m* de lieu;
(b) (*assigned to s.o., sth*) place *f*; **everything in its p.,** chaque chose à sa place; **in its proper time and p.,** en temps et lieu; **to find a p. for sth,** trouver une place pour qch; (*to get out of the way*) caser qch; **this town has a special p. in my affections,** j'ai une tendresse particulière pour cette ville; **to hold sth in p.,** tenir qch en place; **this remark is out of p.,** cette observation est déplacée *ou* hors de propos *ou* mal à propos; **to look out of p.,** (*of person*) (sembler) ne pas être à sa place *ou* dans son élément; (*of thing*) ne pas être à sa place, *F* venir comme un cheveu sur la soupe; **to book a p.,** réserver une place; **if I get there first I'll keep a p. for you,** si j'y arrive le premier je te garderai une place; **to lose/find one's p.,** (*in a book*) perdre/retrouver la page; **to change places with s.o.,** changer de place avec qn; **to keep s.o.'s p. in a queue,** garder la place de qn dans une file d'attente; **his anger gave p. to pity,** sa colère a fait place à un sentiment de pitié; **to take s.o.'s p.,** remplacer qn; (*oust*) prendre la place de qn; **a woman's p. is in the home,** la place d'une femme est à la maison; **to get a p. at university,** être admis à l'université; **p. card,** carte *f* portant le nom du convive; **p. mat,** napperon *m*, set *m* de table; **p. (setting),** (*at table*) couvert *m*; **the dishwasher takes 12 p. settings,** le lave-vaiselle contient jusqu'à 12 couverts;
(c) (*situation*) **put yourself in my p.,** mettez-vous à ma place; **if I were in your p. I'd go,** à votre place, j'irais;
(d) to take p., (*happen*) avoir lieu; **the marriage will not take p.,** le mariage n'aura pas lieu *ou* ne se fera pas; **many changes have taken p.,** il y a eu beaucoup de changements; **while this was taking p.,** tandis que cela se passait;
(e) (*in society, competition etc*) place *f*, rang *m*; **to keep s.o. in his p.,** garder les distances avec qn; **to know one's p.,** observer les distances; *Iron* **I know my p.,** je sais tenir mon rang; *F* **to put s.o. in his p.,** remettre qn à sa place; **in the first/second p.,** en premier/second lieu; **he came in second p.,** il est arrivé à la deuxième place *ou* en deuxième position; *Horseracing* **to back a horse for a p.,** jouer un cheval placé; *Math* **to three places of decimals,** à trois décimales;
(f) (*prerogative*) **it's not my p. to do it,** ce n'est pas à moi de le faire;
(g) *Rugby Fb* **p. kick,** coup de pied placé.
place[2] **1** *vt* **(a)** placer, mettre; *Com Fin* placer, vendre (*des marchandises, des actions*); passer (*une commande*); placer, négocier (*un emprunt*); adjuger, concéder (*un contrat*); faire (*un pari*); **to p. a book back on a shelf,** remettre un livre (en place) sur un rayon; **strategically placed airfields,** des terrains d'aviation stratégiquement situés; **to be awkwardly placed,** (*of person*) être dans une situation délicate; **how are you placed?,** (*for time, money*) quelles sont vos possibilités?; **you're better placed than I am to answer that,** tu es mieux placé que moi pour répondre à cela; **to p. a book with a publisher,** confier un livre à un éditeur; **to p. a matter in s.o.'s hands,** mettre une affaire dans les mains de qn; **I p. myself at your disposal,** je me mets à votre disposition; **to p. a child in s.o.'s care,** confier un enfant à la garde de qn;
(b) (*find a job for*) placer, donner un emploi à (*qn*);
(c) (*class*) **I would p. him among the outstanding biographers of the century,** je le classerais parmi les meilleurs biographes du siècle; *Sch Sp etc* **to be placed third,** se classer troisième;
(d) *Archeol etc* assigner une date à, dater (*un tombeau etc*); localiser (*un son*); **I know his face but I can't p. him,** je le reconnais mais je n'arrive pas à le remettre.
2 *vi esp Horseracing* bien se classer.
placebo [plæ'siːbəʊ] *n Med* placebo *m*.
placement ['pleɪsmənt] *n* (*arrangement*) placement *m*, mise *f* en place; (*finding job*) placement *m*; **the p. of**

children in care/with foster parents, le placement d'enfants à l'Assistance publique/dans des familles d'accueil; **to get a p.,** (*of trainee*) avoir un stage; **if you get a p.,** si tu trouves un stage.

placenta [plə'sentə] *n Anat Bot* placenta *m.*

placid ['plæsɪd] *adj* placide, calme, tranquille.

placidity [plæ'sɪdɪtɪ], **placidness** ['plæsɪdnɪs] *n* placidité *f*, calme *m*, tranquillité *f*.

placidly ['plæsɪdlɪ] *adv* placidement, tranquillement.

placing ['pleɪsɪŋ] *n* placement *m* (*de qch*); *Com Fin* placement, vente *f* (*de marchandises, d'actions*); *Sp etc* classement *m.*

placket ['plækɪt] *n Sewing* patte *f*.

plagiarism ['pleɪdʒərɪz(ə)m] *n* **(a)** (*activity*) (habitude *f* du) plagiat *m*; **(b)** (*copy*) plagiat *m.*

plagiarist ['pleɪdʒərɪst] *n* plagiaire *mf.*

plagiarize ['pleɪdʒəraɪz] **1** *vt* plagier (*une œuvre, un auteur*); faire un plagiat de, contrefaire (*une œuvre*). **2** *vi* se livrer à des plagiats.

plague¹ [pleɪg] *n* **(a)** *Med* peste *f*; *Vet* **cattle p.,** peste bovine; *F* **to avoid s.o. like the p.,** fuir qn comme la peste; **(b)** (*scourge*) fléau *m*, plaie *f*.

plague² *vt F* tourmenter, harceler, embêter (*qn*); **to p. s.o.'s life,** empoisonner l'existence de qn; **to p. s.o. with questions,** harceler qn de questions; **our journey was plagued by minor problems,** notre voyage a été gâché par de petits ennuis.

plaice [pleɪs] *n* (*fish*) carrelet *m*, plie *f* (franche).

plaid [plæd, *Scot* pleɪd] *n* **(a)** *Tex* (*material*) tartan *m*, écossais *m*; **(b)** (*part of Highland costume*) plaid *m*; (*travelling rug*) plaid *m.*

plain¹ [pleɪn] **1** *adj* **(a)** (*clear*) clair, évident; **to make sth p. to s.o.,** faire comprendre qch à qn; **they made their contempt for him p.,** ils n'ont pas caché leur mépris pour lui; **it's as p. as (p.) can be** *or* **as p. as a pikestaff** *or F* **as the nose on your face,** c'est on ne peut plus clair, c'est clair comme le jour; **it's p. to see that you don't like me,** il est évident que vous ne m'aimez pas; **in p. English,** clairement; *Com* **marked in p. figures,** marqué en chiffres connus; **p. text,** (*not in code*) texte *m* en clair;

(b) (*simple*) (*style*) simple, uni; (*mobilier, robe, couture*) simple; (*cigarettes*) sans filtre; (*papier*) non réglé; **p. (post)card,** carte *f* de correspondance; **under p. cover,** sous pli discret; **in p. clothes,** en civil; **p.-clothes policeman,** agent *m* en civil; *Knitting* **one p. one purl,** une maille à l'endroit, une maille à l'envers; **p. knitting,** tricot *m* à l'endroit; *Tex* **p. material,** tissu uni; **p. cooking,** cuisine simple *ou* bourgeoise; **p. chocolate,** chocolat *m* à croquer; **p. flour,** farine *f*; **p. living,** vie *f* simple; **the p. truth,** la franche *ou* pure *ou* simple vérité; **I'll be quite p. with you,** je vais vous parler franchement; **p. answer,** réponse carrée; **that's just p. foolishness/ignorance/***etc*, c'est de la pure bêtise/ignorance/*etc*; **p. speech, p. speaking,** le franc parler; **p. country people,** de simples campagnards;

(c) (*not beautiful*) sans beauté; **to be p.,** manquer de beauté; **a p. Jane,** une jeune fille plutôt laide.

2 *adv F* **(a)** (*simply*) simplement; **he's just p. ignorant,** il est tout simplement ignorant;

(b) (*frankly*) franchement; **to speak p.,** parler franc *ou* sans détours.

3 *n* **in p.,** (*not in code*) en clair.

plain² *n Geog* plaine *f*; **alluvial p.,** plaine alluviale; **the Great Plains,** la Prairie (américaine).

plainchant ['pleɪntʃɑːnt] *n* = **PLAINSONG.**

plainly ['pleɪnlɪ] *adv* **(a)** (*voir*) distinctement, nettement; (*parler*) distinctement, clairement; **I can see p. that ...,** il est évident que ...; **p. I was not wanted,** il était clair que j'étais de trop; **they were p. exhausted,** ils étaient de toute évidence épuisés; **(b)** (*vivre*) simplement; (*s'habiller*) simplement, sans recherche; **to speak p.,** (*be frank*) parler carrément *ou* franchement.

plainness ['pleɪnnɪs] *n* **(a)** (*clarity*) clarté *f* (*de langage*); netteté *f* (*des objets lointains*); **(b)** (*simplicity*) simplicité *f* (*de vie etc*); franchise *f*, rondeur *f* (*de langage*); **(c)** (*lack of beauty*) manque *m* de beauté.

plainsong ['pleɪnsɒŋ] *n Mus* plain-chant *m.*

plain-spoken [pleɪn'spəʊkən] *adj* (*person*) franc, *f* franche.

plaint [pleɪnt] *n Jur* plainte *f*.

plaintiff ['pleɪntɪf] *n Jur* demandeur, -eresse; plaignant, -ante.

plaintive ['pleɪntɪv] *adj* plaintif.

plaintively ['pleintɪvlɪ] *adv* plaintivement.

plaintiveness ['pleɪntɪvnɪs] *n* ton plaintif.

plait¹ [plæt] *n* natte *f*, tresse *f* (*de cheveux etc*).

plait² *vt* natter, tresser (*les cheveux etc*).

plan¹ [plæn] *n* **(a)** (*proposal, intention*) projet *m*, plan *m*; **p. of battle,** plan de bataille; *Fin* **investment p.,** plan d'investissement; *Econ* **five year p.,** plan quinquennal; *Av* **flight p.,** plan de vol; **to change one's plans,** changer de projets; **to have no fixed plan(s),** ne pas avoir de projet bien déterminé; **everything went according to p.,** tout a marché comme prévu; **the best p. would be to ...,** la meilleure solution serait de ...; **it would be a good p. to ...,** ce serait une bonne idée *ou* on ferait bien de ...; **what are your plans for the summer?,** quels sont vos projets pour cet été?; **I've thought of a p.,** j'ai imaginé un plan; **to have other plans,** avoir d'autres projets; **(b)** (*drawing etc*) plan *m* (*d'un bâtiment, d'une ville etc*); (*in surveying*) plan, levé *m* (*d'un terrain*); cadre *m*, plan (*d'un roman etc*); **ground p.,** plan géométral; **sketch p.,** plan sommaire, croquis *m*; **to draw a p.,** tracer *ou* dessiner un plan.

plan² *v* (-nn-) **1** *vt* **(a)** (*arrange*) projeter (*un voyage etc*); combiner (*une attaque etc*); comploter, tramer (*un crime*); **to p. to do sth,** projeter de faire qch; **this had been planned,** cela avait été prévu; **they were planning to rob a bank,** ils projetaient de voler une banque; **(b)** faire *ou* dessiner le plan de (*qch*); *Econ* planifier (*la production etc*); faire *ou* établir *ou* élaborer le plan de (*son nouveau roman etc*); **the school was planned for 500 pupils,** l'école a été prévue pour 500 élèves. **2** *vi* faire des projets; **to p. for the future,** faire des projets d'avenir.

▶**plan on** *vipo* (*have intention of*) prévoir; **to p. on sth/doing sth,** prévoir qch/de faire qch, projeter de faire qch; **we're planning on going to Brazil/on a trip to Brazil,** nous avons l'intention de partir au Brésil, nous projetons un voyage au Brésil.

▶**plan out** *vtsep* (*make detailed plans for*) prévoir (en détail); **he had planned it all out,** il en avait établi tous les détails.

plane¹ [pleɪn] **1** *adj* plan, uni; *Math etc* (*angle, geometry etc*) plan; **p. surface,** surface plane; *Math* **p. trigonometry,** trigonométrie *f* rectiligne. **2** *n* **(a)** *Math etc* plan *m*; **horizontal/vertical p.,** plan horizontal/vertical; *Opt* **focal p.,** plan focal; *Geol* **bedding p., p. of stratification,** plan de stratification; **fault p.,** plan de faille; **on the economic p.,** sur le plan économique; **a higher p. of intelligence,** un niveau intellectuel supérieur; **(b)** *MecE* **inclined p.,** plan incliné; **(c)** *Av* (*surface*) plan *m*; **tail p.,** plan fixe horizontal.

plane² *n* (*aeroplane*) avion *m*; *F* **I came by p.,** je suis venu en avion.

plane³ *vi* (*of bird, aircraft*) planer; **to p. down,** descendre en vol plané *ou* en planant; **to p. along the water,** (*of hydroplane*) glisser à la surface de l'eau.

plane⁴ *n* (*tool*) rabot *m.*

plane⁵ *vt Carp etc* raboter (*le bois*); aplanir, planer (*le bois, le métal*); dégauchir (*le bois*).

plane⁶ *n* **p. (tree),** platane *m.*

planer ['pleɪnər] *n Carp etc* **(a)** (*person*) raboteur *m*; **(b)** (*machine*) raboteuse *f*, planeuse *f*.

planet ['plænɪt] *n Astron* planète *f*; **the biggest country on the p.,** le plus grand pays de la planète.

planetarium [plænɪ'teərɪəm] *n* planétarium *m.*

planetary ['plænɪt(ə)rɪ] *adj Astron* (*système, heure, mouvement*) planétaire.

planing ['pleɪnɪŋ] *n Carp etc* (*of wood*) rabotage *m*; (*of wood, metal*) planage *m*, aplanissage *m*; **p. machine,** raboteuse *f*.

planisphere ['plænɪsfɪər] *n* planisphère *m* céleste.

plank¹ [plæŋk] *n* **(a)** *Carp Constr etc* planche *f* (épaisse), madrier *m*; **to walk the p.,** passer à la planche; **(b)** *Pol* **p. in the party platform,** article *m* du programme du parti.

plank² *vt Constr* planchéier (*un plancher etc*).

▶**plank down** *vtsep* (*put down heavily*) déposer brusquement.

planking ['plæŋkɪŋ] *n* **(a)** (*action*) planchéiage *m*; **(b)** (*planks*) planches *fpl*, madriers *mpl.*

plankton ['plæŋktən] *n* plancton *m.*

planned ['plænd] *adj* **(a) the p. meeting never took place,** la réunion qui avait été prévue n'a jamais eu lieu; **well/badly p.,** bien/mal conçu; (*complot, crime*) bien/mal concerté *ou* organisé; **(b)** *Econ etc* planifié; **p. economy,** économie dirigée.

planner ['plænər] *n* planificateur, -trice; **town p.,** urbaniste *mf.*

planning ['plænɪŋ] *n* **(a)** conception *f*, organisation *f* (*d'un projet, d'un complot etc*); **the expedition will require careful p.,** il faudra une organisation minutieuse pour mener à bien cette expédition; **it's still at the p. stage,** c'est encore à l'état de projet; **(b)** *Econ etc* dirigisme *m*, planification *f*, *F* planning *m*; **economic p.,** planification économique; *Admin* **to get p. permission to build sth** *or* **for sth,** obtenir un permis de construire qch; **(c)** tracé *m* (*d'une autoroute*); **town p.,** urbanisme *m*; **(d) family p.,** planning familial.

plant¹ [plɑːnt] *n* **(a)** plante *f*; **flowering p.,** plante à fleurs; **(indoor) pot p., house p.,** plante d'appartement; **bedding p.,** plant *m* à repiquer; **ice p.,** ficoïde cristalline *ou* glaciaire; **tobacco p.,** (*species*) tabac *m*; (*single plant*) pied *m* de tabac; **p. biology,** phytobiologie *f*; *Agr* **p. breeder,** phytogénéticien, -ienne; **p. life,** (*life of plants*) vie végétale; (*plants*) flore *f* (*d'une région*); **p. physiology,** physiologie végétale; **(b)** *Ind* (*equipment*) appareil(s) *m(pl)*, appareillage *m*; équipement *m*, matériel *m* (industriel); (*facility*) installation *f* (industrielle); (*factory*) usine *f*; **cooling p.,** appareil de refroidissement; **(electric) power p., generating p.,** centrale *f* électrique; **(c)** *Sl* (*spy*) taupe *f*; (*from police*) mouchard *m*; (*something planted*) coup monté.

plant² *vt* **(a)** planter (*un arbre etc*); **to p. a field with wheat,** mettre une terre en blé; **(b)** (*insert, place*) planter (*un piquet dans la terre etc*); *Nau* mouiller (*une mine*); *Mil* poser, déposer (*une bombe*); *F* planter (*un espion chez qn*); **to p. an idea in s.o.'s mind,** implanter une idée dans l'esprit de qn; *F* **a well planted blow,** un coup bien asséné *ou* bien appliqué; *F* **he planted a big kiss on her cheek,** il lui planta un gros baiser sur la joue; *F* **to p. oneself in front of s.o.,** se planter devant qn; **to p. incriminating evidence on s.o.,** fabriquer de fausses preuves contre qn.

►plant out *vtsep* repiquer (*des semis*).

plantain¹ ['plæntɪn] *n* (*plant*) plantain *m*.

plantain² *n* **(a)** (*fruit*) banane *f* des Antilles; **(b) p. (tree),** bananier *m* du paradis.

plantation [plæn'teɪʃən] *n* plantation *f*, pépinière *f* (*d'arbres*); plantation (*de coton etc*).

planter ['plɑːntər] *n* **(a)** (*worker*) planteur *m* (*de choux etc*); (*plantation owner*) planteur, propriétaire *m* d'une plantation; **coffee p.,** planteur de café; **(b)** (*tool*) planteuse *f*.

plaque [plɑːk] *n* **(a)** plaque *f* (commémorative) (*de bronze, de marbre etc*); **(b)** (*on teeth*) plaque *f* dentaire.

plash¹ [plæʃ] *n* clapotement *m*, clapotis *m* (*des vagues, d'un ruisseau etc*); flac *m* (*d'un corps qui tombe dans l'eau*).

plash² **1** *vt* plonger (*qch dans l'eau*) avec un flac. **2** *vi* (*of liquids*) clapoter, faire un clapotis; (*of falling object etc*) faire flac (*sur l'eau etc*).

plasm [plæz(ə)m] *n* protoplasme *m*.

plasma ['plæzmə] *n* plasma *m*; **(blood) p.,** plasma (sanguin); *Comptr* **p. display,** affichage *m* à plasma.

plasmapheresis [plæzmə'ferəsɪs] *n Med* plasmaphérèse *f*, échange *m* plasmatique.

plaster¹ ['plɑːstər] *n* **(a)** *Constr etc* plâtre *m*; **p. was falling from the ceiling,** du plâtre tombait du plafond; **p. of Paris,** plâtre de Paris, plâtre de moulage; **to put a leg in p.,** plâtrer une jambe, mettre une jambe dans le plâtre; **p. cast,** *Surg* plâtre; *Art* (moulage *m* en) plâtre; empreinte *f* en plâtre; **(b)** *Med* (*Br* **sticking) p.,** pansement adhésif, sparadrap *m*; **corn p.,** emplâtre *ou* pansement coricide.

plaster² *vt* **(a)** *Constr etc* plâtrer, ravaler (*un mur*), enduire (*un mur*) de plâtre; **wall plastered with advertisements,** mur tapissé d'affiches; **plastered with mud,** (*person*) plâtré *ou* tout couvert de boue; *F* **to p. the enemy,** bombarder l'ennemi; *Sl* **to get plastered,** se soûler; *Sl* **he's plastered,** il est soûl; **(b)** *Med* mettre un emplâtre sur (*une plaie etc*).

plasterboard ['plɑːstəbɔːd] *n Constr* Placoplâtre ® *m*.

plasterer ['plɑːstərər] *n* plâtrier *m*.

plasterwork ['plɑːstəwɜːk] *n* plâtrage *m*; (*esp on walls and ceilings*) plâtres *mpl*.

plastic ['plæstɪk] **1** *n* plastique *m*; **laminated p.,** (plastique) stratifié *m*, lamifié *m*; **moulded p.,** plastique moulé; **wrapped in transparent p.,** emballé dans un plastique transparent; **p. bag,** sac *m* en plastique; **p. bullet,** balle *f* de plastique; **a p. cup,** une tasse en (matière) plastique; **the plastics industry,** l'industrie *f* des plastiques; **p. (money),** monnaie *f* électronique. **2** *adj Art etc* plastique; *Phys etc* (*déformation, stabilité*) plastique; **the p. arts,** les arts *mpl* plastiques; **p. surgery,** chirurgie *f* plastique; (*cosmetic*) chirurgie esthétique; **p. surgeon,** plasticien; chirurgien esthétique; *Fig* **p. nature,** caractère *m* malléable; **p. bomb,** (bombe *f* au) plastic *m*; **to attack a house with a p. bomb,** plastiquer une maison; **p. explosive,** plastic *m*.

Plasticine ® ['plæstɪsiːn] *n* pâte *f* à modeler.

plasticity [plæs'tɪsɪtɪ] *n* plasticité *f*; *Art Cin* effet *m* plastique.

plate¹ [pleɪt] *n* **(a)** (*for food*) assiette *f*; **dinner/soup p.,** assiette plate/creuse; *Fig F* **to have a lot on one's p.,** avoir du pain sur la planche; *Fig F* **I've already got far too much on my p.,** j'ai déjà beaucoup trop à faire; *Fig F* **I've got enough on my p. without him causing problems,** j'ai déjà suffisamment de pain sur la planche sans qu'il ne crée des problèmes; *Fig F* **to hand s.o. sth on a p.,** apporter qch à qn sur un plateau; *Fig F* **he got it handed to him on a p.,** ça lui est venu sur un plateau; *Rel etc* **(collection) p.,** plateau de quête; **to pass round the p.,** faire la quête; **p. rack,** égouttoir *m*; **p. warmer,** chauffe-assiettes *m inv*;

(b) (*small piece*) (petite) plaque *f*, lamelle *f* (*de métal, de verre, de matière plastique etc*); *Geol* plaque *f*; **(dental) p.,** (*for straightening teeth*) appareil *m* (dentaire); (*dentures*) dentier *m*; **p. glass,** vitre *f*; **p. glass window,** baie vitrée; *Geol* **p. tectonics,** plaque *f* tectonique;

(c) *Metal* plaque *f*; (grande) feuille *f* (*de métal*); plaque, plate *f* (*d'armure*); *MecE etc* plaque (*de montage etc*); plateau *m* (*de balance etc*); platine *f*, palastre *m* (*de serrure*); paumelle *f* (*de gond de porte*); *Mil Nau* **p. armour,** blindage *m*; *Nau* **bilge p.,** tôle *f* de bouchain; **bulkhead p.,** tôle de cloison; *Aut* **p. clutch,** embrayage *m* à disque *ou* à plateau; **hot p.,** plaque chauffante (*de cuisinière*); (*single plate*) réchaud *m* (*électrique, à gaz*); (*plate warmer*) chauffe-assiettes *m inv*; **name p.,** (*on door*) plaque de porte; (*of street*) plaque de rue; plaque d'identification *ou* de série (*d'une machine*); *Br Aut etc* **number p.,** plaque d'immatriculation;

(d) *El* plaque *f*, lame *f* (*de batterie etc*); *Electron* plaque, anode *f* (*de tube électronique*); **accumulator p.,** plaque d'accumulateur;

(e) (*engraving*) *& Typ* plaque *f*; (*engraving*) *& Phot etc* cliché *m* (*photographique, imprimant*); cliché (*de photogravure*); (*engraving*) planche *f*, gravure *f*, estampe *f*; *Phot* **(photographic) p.,** plaque (photographique); **dry p.,** plaque sèche; **p. cylinder,** cylindre *m* de plaque; **half-tone p.,** cliché de similigravure; **full-page p.,** hors-texte *m inv*, planche; **p. 12 (a),** (*in book*) planche 12 (a);

(f) *Constr* (poutre *f*) sablière *f*; panne *f*; **wall p.,** plaque *f* d'assise (*de poutre*); lambourde *f* (*pour les solives du plancher*);

(g) (*plated metal*) (*gold*) orfèvrerie *f*; **silver p.,** argenterie *f*; **it's (only) p.,** c'est du plaqué;

(h) *Sp* coupe *f* (*d'or, d'argent*) (*donnée en prix*).

plate² *vt* **(a)** (*protect with plates of metal*) blinder, recouvrir *ou* garnir (*qch*) de plaques; **(b)** (*add layer of metal to*) métalliser; (*with gold*) plaquer en or; (*with silver*) plaquer en argent; étamer (*une glace*); **(c)** *Typ* clicher (*les pages*).

plateau, *pl* **-eaux, -eaus** ['plætəʊ, -əʊz] *n Geog & Fig* plateau *m*.

plated ['pleɪtɪd] *adj* **(a)** (*protected with metal plates*) recouvert *ou* garni de plaques; **armour p.,** blindé; **(b)** (*coated with metal*) plaqué; **gold p.,** doublé d'or; **silver p.,** argenté; **chromium p.,** chromé.

plateful ['pleɪtfʊl] *n* assiettée *f*, assiette *f*.

platelayer ['pleɪtleɪər] *n Br Rail* poseur *m* de rails.

platelet ['pleɪtlɪt] *n* (*in blood*) plaquette *f*.

platform ['plætfɔːm] *n* **(a)** (*raised flat surface*) plate-forme *f*; *Rail* (*where passengers stand*) quai *m*; (*where train stops*) voie *f*; tablier *m* (*de bascule, de pont etc*); passerelle *f* (*de grue*); *Nau* parquet *m*, plancher *m*; plate-forme (*de cale, de soute*); *Petr* **drilling p.,** plate-forme de forage; **launching/firing p.,** plate-forme de lancement/de tir (*de missiles*); *Rail* **the train waiting at p. one,** le train au départ voie no 1; **to wait on the p.,** (*of person*) attendre sur le quai; *Rail* **what p. is it for London?,** quel quai est-ce pour Londres?; *Rail Am* **p. car,** (wagon *m*) plate-forme; *Rail* **p. ticket,** ticket *m* de quai; **arrival/departure p.,** quai d'arrivée/de départ;

(b) (*at public meeting*) estrade *f*, tribune *f*; *Fig Pol* plate-forme *f*, programme *m* (*d'un parti*);

(c) (*raised ground*) terrasse *f*;

(d) (*on shoe*) semelle compensée; **p. shoes,** chaussures *f* à semelles compensées.

plating ['pleɪtɪŋ] *n* **(a)** (*layer of metal plates*) revêtement *m* en tôle; armature *f* (*de four etc*); (*plates*) tôles *fpl*; **steel** *or* **armour p.,** blindage *m*; *Nau* **deck p.,** bordé *m* de pont; **(b)** (*coating with metal*) placage *m*; **copper p.,** cuivrage *m*; **silver p.,** argentage *m*, argenture *f*; **gold p.,** dorage *m*, dorure *f*; **(c)** *Typ* clichage *m*.

platinum ['plætɪnəm] **1** *n* platine *m*; **p. blond hair,** cheveux platinés; **she's a p. blonde,** c'est une blonde platinée; **p. record,** disque *m* de platine. **2** *adv* **to go p.,** (*of record*) devenir disque de platine.

platitude ['plætɪtjuːd] *n* (*remark*) platitude *f*, lieu commun.

platitudinize [plætɪ'tjuːdɪnaɪz] *vi* débiter des platitudes *ou* des banalités.

platitudinous [plætɪ'tjuːdɪnəs] *adj* (*style*) plat, banal.

Plato ['pleɪtəʊ] *n* Platon *m*.

Platonic [plə'tɒnɪk] *adj* (*philosophie etc*) platonicien; (*amour*) platonique.

platoon [plə'tuːn] *n Mil* section *f* (*dans l'infanterie*); peloton *m* (*dans les blindés, le train*); **p. commander,** chef *m* de section *ou* de peloton.

platter ['plætər] *n* **(a)** *esp Hist* (*plate*) écuelle *f*; (*wooden plate*) plat *m* de bois, planche *f*; **(b)** *Am F* (*record*) disque *m*.

platypus ['plætɪpəs] *n* (*animal*) ornithor(h)ynque *m*.

plaudits ['plɔːdɪts] *npl esp Lit* (salve *f* d') applaudissements *mpl*; **the new menus on trains have won the p. of passengers,** les passagers ont applaudi aux nouveaux menus servis dans les trains.

plausibility [plɔːzə'bɪlɪtɪ] *n* plausibilité *f*.

plausible ['plɔːzəb(ə)l] *adj* **(a)** (*argument, excuse etc*) plausible, vraisemblable; (*prétexte etc*) spécieux; **(b)** (*person*) convaincant; (*con-man etc*) captieux, aux belles paroles.

plausibly ['plɔːzəblɪ] *adv* plausiblement; (*argue etc*) de façon convaincante.

play¹ [pleɪ] *n* **(a)** *Th* pièce *f* (*de théâtre*); **Shakespeare's plays,** le théâtre de Shakespeare;

(b) (*movement*) jeu *m*, mouvement *m*, activité *f*; jeu (*d'un escrimeur*); maniement *m*, manipulation *f* (*d'une arme*); *MecE* course *f*, jeu (*du piston d'un moteur etc*); *MecE etc* jeu (*d'un boulon etc dans son logement*); jeu, reflets *mpl* (*de lumière*); chatoiement *m*, reflets (*de couleurs*); **there's still too much p. in the brakes,** il y a encore trop de jeu dans les freins; **to come into p.,** entrer en jeu, intervenir; **to bring** *or* **call** *or* **put into p.,** mettre (*qch*) en jeu *ou* en œuvre; exercer (*ses facultés*); *F* **to make a p. for sth,** jouer le grand jeu pour obtenir qch; **to make a p. for s.o.,** (*try to seduce*) faire des avances à qn; **to give** *or* **allow full p. to one's imagination,** donner libre cours à son imagination;

(c) (*of children etc*) jeu *m*, amusement *m*; **to be at p.,** être en train de jouer; **to say sth in p.,** dire qch en plaisantant *ou* pour rire; **p. on words,** calembour *m*, jeu de mots;

(d) *Sp* **p. began at one o'clock,** la partie a commencé à une heure; **after some very boring p. in the first half ...,** après une première mi-temps très ennuyeuse ...; **there was some incredibly fast p. in the final set,** il y a eu des échanges très rapides au dernier set; **what a good piece of p.!,** quel beau coup!, que c'était bien joué!; *Cr* **rain stopped p.,** la partie a été interrompue par la pluie; **ball in p.,** ballon *m* en jeu; **ball out of p.,** ballon hors jeu;

(e) (*gambling*) jeu *m* (de hasard); **to lose at p.,** perdre au jeu; **high/low p.,** gros/petit jeu.

play² **1** *vi* **(a)** (*have fun*) jouer, s'amuser; (*of animals*) folâtrer, gambader; **to p. at soldiers,** jouer aux soldats; **to p. at keeping shop,** jouer à la marchande; **to p. at doing sth,** (*not be serious*) faire qch en amateur; *F* **what d'you think you're playing at?,** à quoi tu joues?; **to p. with a doll,** jouer *ou* s'amuser avec une poupée; **to p. with one's glasses,** jouer (distraitement) avec ses lunettes; **to p. with fire,** jouer avec le feu; **to p. with s.o.'s affections,** jouer avec l'affection de qn; **to p. on** *or* **with words,** jouer sur les mots;

(b) (*participate in game*) jouer; **to p. against s.o./a team,** jouer contre qn/une équipe; **who plays first?,** à qui de commencer?; (*at bowling*) à qui la boule?; *Golf* à qui l'honneur?; **to p. fair,** jouer franc jeu; **to p. for money,** (*in gambling*) jouer pour de l'argent; **to p. high** *or* **for high stakes,** (*in gambling*) jouer gros (jeu); *Cards* **to p. high/low,** jouer une forte/basse carte; **do you p.?,** est-ce que tu sais jouer?;

(c) (*move*) (*of light, colour*) se jouer, chatoyer; (*of fountain*) jouer; (*of part of mechanism etc*) jouer, se mouvoir (librement); (*of bolt etc*) avoir du jeu; **the sun is playing on the water,** le soleil se joue sur l'eau;

(d) *Th* (*act*) **to p. on the stage,** (*of actor*) jouer *ou* se produire sur la scène; **production/film now playing at ...,** pièce/film qui passe actuellement à ...;

(e) *Mus* (*of instrument, musician, band*) jouer;

(f) **to p. into s.o.'s hands,** faire le jeu de qn.

2 *vt* **(a)** *Sp etc* jouer (*une partie de tennis*); disputer (*un match*); (*include on one's team*) inclure (*qn*) dans son équipe; **to p. s.o. at chess,** faire une partie d'échecs avec qn; **Real Madrid played Dynamo Kiev,** le Real de Madrid a affronté le Dynamo de Kiev; *Fb etc* **to p. left back,** jouer arrière gauche; **the team was playing two reserves,** l'équipe jouait avec deux réserves; *Sp* **to p. a shot/ball/ etc,** jouer un coup/une balle/*etc*; *Cards* **to p. a card,** jouer une carte; **to p. clubs/spades,** jouer trèfle/pique; *Horse-racing* **to p. the favourite,** jouer le favori; *F* **to p. a hunch,** jouer *ou* agir par intuition; **I'll p. you for the drinks,** je vous joue les consommations;

(b) *Th Cin* jouer (*un rôle*); jouer, représenter (*une tragédie*); **to p. Macbeth,** jouer *ou* tenir le rôle de Macbeth; **to p. an important part,** jouer un rôle important; *F* **to p. the fool,** faire l'idiot *ou* l'imbécile;

(c) *Mus* **to p. the piano/the flute,** jouer du piano/de la flûte; **to p. a piece,** jouer un morceau; **to p. a record-player,** faire marcher un tourne-disques; **to p. a record/a tape,** passer un disque/une bande; **the neighbours were playing loud music,** les voisins faisaient beaucoup de bruit avec leur musique;

(d) **to p. a joke** *or* **a trick on s.o.,** jouer un tour à qn;

(e) *esp Lit* **to p. s.o. false,** trahir qn;

(f) (*direct*) diriger (**upon, over,** sur); **to p. a hose on the fire,** diriger la lance sur le feu.

▸play about, play around *vi* **(a)** (*play*) jouer, s'amuser (*avec qch*); **stop playing around with that gun!,** arrête de jouer avec ce revolver!; **(b)** (*not be serious*) s'amuser; **it's time he stopped playing about and settled down,** il est temps qu'il arrête de s'amuser et qu'il se fixe; **(c)** (*consider possibilities*) **to p. around with an idea,** retourner une idée dans sa tête; **they played around with the words to find a good slogan,** ils jonglaient avec les mots pour trouver un bon slogan; **(d)** (*sexually*) avoir des aventures; **to p. around with s.o.,** avoir une aventure avec qn.

▸play along **1** *vi* (*cooperate*) coopérer. **2** *vtas* (*manipulate*) manipuler (*qn*).

▸play back *vtsep* (faire) repasser (*une bande*).

▸play down *vtsep* minimiser (*l'importance de qch*); dédramatiser (*un problème*); **the government is trying to p. down its role,** le gouvernement tente de minimiser l'importance de son rôle.

▸play in *vtsep* **(a)** *Sp* **to p. oneself in,** (*become accustomed*) s'accoutumer *ou* se faire au jeu; **(b)** (*with music*) accueillir en musique.

▸play off **1** *vtas* (*oppose*) **to p. s.o. off against s.o.,** opposer qn à qn; **they played their enemies off against each other,** ils ont dressé leurs ennemis les uns contre les autres. **2** *vi Sp* (*attempt to break tie*) faire *ou* jouer la belle.

▸play on **1** *vi* (*continue to play*) continuer à jouer. **2** *vipo* (*exploit*) **to p. on s.o.'s feelings,** jouer sur les sentiments de qn.

▸play out *vtsep* **(a)** (*act*) **the events being played out on the world's stage,** les événements qui se déroulent dans le monde; **(b)** *F* (*usu passive*) (*exhaust*) **to be played out,** (*of person, horse etc*) être très fatigué *ou* vanné *ou* éreinté; (*of idea etc*) être vieux jeu *ou* démodé; **(c)** (*with music*) **they were played out to the strains of ...,** leur départ a été accompagné par l'air de ... .

▸play up **1** *vi* **(a)** (*of car, child, horse etc*) faire des siennes; **(b)** *F* (*flatter*) **to p. up to s.o.,** flatter qn. **2** *vtas* (*cause difficulties to*) énerver, *F* taper sur le système de (*qn*); **my rheumatism is playing me up,** mon rhumatisme me fait mal. **3** *vtsep* (*emphasize*) faire ressortir (*qch*); exploiter (*un incident, un scandale*).

playable ['pleɪəb(ə)l] *adj* (*pitch etc*) praticable.

play-act ['pleɪækt] *vi* jouer la comédie.

play-acting ['pleɪæktɪŋ] *n* **it's just p.-a.,** c'est de la comédie.

playback ['pleɪbæk] *n* réécoute *f*.

playbill ['pleɪbɪl] *n Th* (*poster*) affiche *f* (de théâtre); *Am* (*programme*) programme *m*.

playboy ['pleɪbɔɪ] *n* playboy *m*.

player ['pleɪər] *n* **(a)** *Sp* joueur, -euse; (*team member*) équipier, -ière; **card/billiards p.,** joueur de cartes/billard; **(b)** *Mus* musicien, -ienne; joueur, -euse (*d'un instrument*); **a good guitar p.,** un bon guitariste; **the band's piano p.,** le pianiste du groupe; **p. piano,** piano *m* mécanique; **(c)** (*machine*) **record p.,** tourne-disques *m*; **cassette p.,** magnétophone *m* à cassettes; **(d)** *Th* acteur, -trice; interprète *mf* (*d'un rôle*).

playfellow ['pleɪfeləʊ] *n Old-fashioned* = **PLAYMATE**.

playful ['pleɪfʊl] *adj* enjoué, espiègle, taquin.
playfully ['pleɪfʊlɪ] *adv* gaiement; en badinant.
playfulness ['pleɪfʊlnɪs] *n* enjouement *m*, badinage *m*, espièglerie *f*.
playgoer ['pleɪgəʊər] *n* habitué, -ée du théâtre.
playground ['pleɪgraʊnd] *n* **(a)** *Sch* cour *f* (de récréation); (*en dehors de l'école*) parc *m* à jeux; **covered p.,** préau *m*; **(b)** (*popular place*) lieu *m* de villégiature.
playgroup ['pleɪgru:p] *n* ≈ (école *f*) maternelle *f*.
playhouse ['pleɪhaʊs] *n* théâtre *m*.
playing ['pleɪɪŋ] *n* jeu *m*; **p. card,** carte *f* à jouer; **p. field,** terrain *m* de jeux *ou* de sports.
playmate ['pleɪmeɪt] *n* camarade *mf* (de jeu); (*friend*) copain, *f* copine.
play-off ['pleɪɒf] *n Sp* belle *f*.
playpen ['pleɪpen] *n* parc *m* à bébé *ou* pour enfants.
playroom ['pleɪru:m] *n* salle *f* de jeux.
playschool ['pleɪsku:l] *n* ≈ (école *f*) maternelle *f*.
plaything ['pleɪθɪŋ] *n* jouet *m*, joujou *m*; **the children treat the dog like a p.,** les enfants se servent du chien comme d'un jouet.
playtime ['pleɪtaɪm] *n Sch* récréation *f*.
playwright ['pleɪraɪt] *n* auteur *m* dramatique, dramaturge *m*.
plaza ['plɑ:zə] *n US* **(a)** (*square*) place *f*; **(b)** (*shopping centre*) centre commercial; **(c)** (*motorway service area*) aire *f* de service.
plc, PLC [pi:el'si:] *n Br Com* (*abbr* **public limited company**) ≈ SARL *f*; **Smith plc,** Smith SARL.
plea [pli:] *n* **(a)** (*appeal*) **p. for mercy,** appel *m* à la clémence; **(b)** (*excuse*) excuse *f*, prétexte *m*, justification *f* (**for doing sth,** pour faire qch); **(c)** *Jur* défense *f*; **incidental p.,** exception *f*; **special p.,** exception péremptoire; **to make a p. of guilty/not guilty,** plaider coupable/non coupable; **to put forward a p. of insanity,** (*of counsel*) plaider la folie; *Am* **p. bargaining,** = accord entre le juge et l'accusé qui permet à l'accusé de voir ses charges réduites en échange de sa coopération.
plead [pli:d] *v* (*pt & pp* **pleaded**, *occ Am* **pled** [pled]) **1** *vi* **(a)** (*entreat*) **to p. with s.o. for s.o./sth,** intervenir *ou* intercéder *ou* plaider auprès de qn pour qn/qch; **they were pleading with him to stop,** ils le suppliaient de s'arrêter; **(b)** *Jur* plaider (**for,** pour; **against,** contre); **to p. guilty/not guilty,** plaider coupable/non coupable. **2** *vt* **(a)** *Jur* plaider (*une cause*); **to p. s.o.'s cause with s.o.,** intercéder pour qn auprès de qn, plaider la cause de qn auprès de qn; **to p. insanity,** (*of counsel*) plaider la folie; **(b)** (*claim*) prétexter (*l'ignorance etc*); invoquer, alléguer (*une excuse*).
pleading ['pli:dɪŋ] **1** *adj* suppliant, implorant. **2** *n* **(a)** prières *fpl*, intercession *f* (**for,** en faveur de); **(b)** *Jur* plaidoyer *m*; (*action*) plaidoirie *f*; (*art*) l'art *m* de plaider.
pleadingly ['pli:dɪŋlɪ] *adv* (*to say*) d'un ton suppliant; (*to look*) d'un regard suppliant.
pleasant ['plezənt] *adj* agréable; (*person*) agréable, charmant, aimable; **story that makes p. reading,** histoire agréable à lire; **p. breeze,** brise douce *ou* agréable; **to keep a p. memory of s.o.,** garder un doux *ou* agréable souvenir de qn; **it's a p. day,** il fait bon aujourd'hui; **to have a p. day,** passer agréablement la journée; **goodnight, p. dreams,** bonne nuit, faites de beaux rêves; **a man p. to deal with,** un homme d'humeur facile; **to make oneself p., to be p. (to s.o.),** se rendre agréable (auprès de qn); **he was very p.,** il s'est montré très affable *ou* très gentil.
pleasantly ['plezəntlɪ] *adv* agréablement; d'une manière agréable; **to be p. surprised,** être agréablement surpris.
pleasantness ['plezəntnɪs] *n* agrément *m*, charme *m* (*d'un endroit etc*); (*of person, manner etc*) affabilité *f*.
pleasantry ['plezəntrɪ] *n* **(a)** (*joke*) plaisanterie *f*; **(b) pleasantries,** (*polite remarks*) civilités *fpl*.
please [pli:z] **1** *int* s'il vous plaît; s'il te plaît; **come in, p.,** entrez, s'il vous plaît, entrez, je vous prie; **p. don't cry,** ne pleurez pas, je vous en supplie; **p., daddy, p.,** s'il te plaît, papa; **p. tell me ...,** voudriez-vous bien me dire ...; **may I? — p. do,** vous permettez? — je vous en prie!; **p. sit down** *or* **take a seat,** veuillez vous asseoir; **p. don't interrupt!,** veuillez bien ne pas nous interrompre; **p. do not walk on the grass,** (*on sign*) prière de ne pas marcher sur le gazon; **would you like some cake?/to come with me?, — yes, p.,** est-ce que vous voulez un peu de gâteau/venir avec moi? — oh, oui, avec plaisir; *Sch* **p., sir!,** pardon, monsieur!
2 *vt* plaire à (*qn*); (*give pleasure to*) faire plaisir à (*qn*); (*make content*) contenter (*qn*); **you can't p. everybody,** on ne peut plaire à tout le monde; **he's hard to p.,** il est difficile (à contenter); **music that pleases the ear,** musique qui flatte l'oreille; **p. yourself!,** faites comme il vous plaira *ou* comme vous voudrez; **to set out to p. s.o.,** chercher à plaire à qn; *Fml* **His Majesty has been graciously pleased to ...,** il a plu à sa gracieuse Majesté de ....
3 *vi* **(a)** (*like*) **to do as one pleases,** agir à sa guise *ou* à son gré; **do as you p.,** faites comme vous voudrez; **he will only do as he pleases,** il n'en fera qu'à sa tête; *F* **just as you p.,** c'est *ou* ce sera comme vous voudrez; *F* **if you p.,** s'il vous plaît; s'il te plaît; *Iron* **and then if you p. he blamed me for it!,** et puis il a dit que c'était de ma faute!; **(b)** (*give pleasure*) faire plaisir; **he tries hard to p.,** il fait tout pour me *ou* te *etc* faire plaisir; **anything to p.,** à tes ordres.
4 *v impers Arch & Lit* **may it p. your Majesty,** plaise *ou* n'en déplaise à votre Majesté; **p. God!,** plaise à Dieu!, Dieu le veuille!
pleased [pli:zd] *adj* (*satisfied*) satisfait, content; (*happy*) heureux; (*sourire*) de satisfaction; **to be p. with sth,** être satisfait de qch; **he's very** *or* **highly p. with himself,** il est très content *ou* fort satisfait de lui-même *ou Pej* de sa petite personne; **I'm very p. she's coming,** cela me fait grand plaisir *ou* je suis très content *ou* je suis ravi qu'elle vienne; *F* **he's as p. as Punch,** il est heureux comme un roi; (*proud*) il en est fier comme Artaban; **to be p. to do sth,** faire qch avec plaisir; **I'll be p. to come,** je viendrai avec plaisir; **I'm very p. to see you,** je suis très content *ou* cela me fait grand plaisir de vous voir; **I'm p. to say that ...,** je suis heureux de pouvoir vous dire que ...; *Com* **I am p. to inform you that ...,** j'ai le plaisir de vous aviser que ...; **to be p. for s.o.,** être content pour qn.
pleasurable ['pleʒərəb(ə)l] *adj* agréable.
pleasurably ['pleʒərəblɪ] *adv* agréablement.
pleasure¹ ['pleʒər] *n* **(a)** plaisir *m*; **to take** *or* **find (a) p. in doing sth,** éprouver du plaisir à faire qch, prendre *ou* avoir (du) plaisir à faire qch; **I have p. in informing you that ...,** je suis heureux de vous apprendre que ...; **her books gave p. to many people,** beaucoup de gens ont pris du plaisir à lire ses livres; **it gave me great p.,** cela m'a fait grand plaisir; **it's a real p. to see you looking so cheerful,** cela me fait (infiniment de) plaisir de vous voir si gai; **it is a p. to listen to him,** on a plaisir à l'écouter; **thank you very much — (it was) a p.,** merci beaucoup — de rien; **the p. was all mine,** tout le plaisir était pour moi; **I haven't the p. of knowing her** *or* **of her acquaintance,** je n'ai pas le plaisir de la connaître; **Mr Stevens requests the p. of the company of Miss Miller at ...,** (*invitation*) M. Stevens prie Mlle Miller de lui faire le plaisir d'assister à ...; **with p.,** avec plaisir, volontiers; **with the greatest (of) p.,** avec le plus grand plaisir;
(b) (*enjoyment*) plaisir(s) *m(pl)*, jouissances *fpl*; **life given up to p., life of p.,** vie adonnée au plaisir; **to take one's p.,** s'amuser, se divertir; **to travel for p.,** voyager pour son plaisir; **p. boat,** bateau *m* de plaisance; *Psy* **p. principle,** recherche *f* du plaisir; **p. seeker,** jouisseur, -euse; **p. seeking,** recherche *f* des plaisirs; **p. trip,** partie *f* de plaisir;
(c) (*will*) volonté *f*, bon plaisir; **at s.o.'s p.,** au gré de qn, au bon plaisir de qn; **during the King's p.,** pendant le bon plaisir du roi.
pleasure² *Arch* **1** *vt* faire plaisir à (*qn*). **2** *vi* se plaire, prendre plaisir (**in sth,** à qch; **in doing sth,** à faire qch).
pleat¹ [pli:t] *n Sewing etc* pli *m*; **box p.,** double pli; **inverted p.,** pli creux *ou* rentré *ou* inverti.
pleat² *vt* plisser, faire des plis à (*une jupe etc*).
pleated ['pli:tɪd] *adj* (*skirt etc*) plissé.
pleating ['pli:tɪŋ] *n* **(a)** plissage *m*; **(b)** (*no pl*) (*pleats*) plissé(s) *m(pl)*.
pleb [pleb] *n F* plébéien, -ienne; *F* **the plebs,** le prolétariat.
plebeian [plə'bi:ən] **1** *n* plébéien, -ienne. **2** *adj* plébéien, vulgaire.
plebiscite ['plebɪsɪt] *n* plébiscite *m*; **to hold a p.,** organiser un plébiscite; **to vote for (s.o., sth) by p.,** plébisciter (qn, qch).
plectrum ['plektrəm] *n Mus* (*for guitar etc*) médiator *m*.
pledge¹ [pledʒ] *n* **(a)** (*oath*) promesse *f*, vœu *m*; **I am under a p. of secrecy,** j'ai fait vœu de garder le secret; **to take** *or* **sign the p.,** promettre de s'abstenir d'alcool; **(b)** (*object of value*) gage *m*, nantissement *m*; **p. holder,** détenteur, -trice de gage(s), (créancier *m*) gagiste *m*; **unredeemed p.,** gage non retiré; **to hold in p.,** (dé)tenir en gage *ou* en nantissement; **to redeem a p.,** retirer un gage; **to take sth out of p.,** dégager qch; **(c)** (*sign*) **p. of good faith,** garantie *f* de bonne foi.
pledge² *vt* **(a)** (*promise*) engager (*sa parole etc*); **to p.**

oneself *or* **one's word to do sth,** s'engager à faire qch; **to be pledged to do sth,** avoir pris l'engagement de faire qch; **to p. one's honour,** donner sa parole d'honneur; s'engager sur l'honneur (**to do sth,** à faire qch); **to p. money,** (*in radio, television appeal*) promettre un don; **to p. one's allegiance to the king,** vouer obéissance au roi; **(b)** donner, mettre (*qch*) en gage, déposer (*qch*) en gage *ou* en nantissement, engager, gager (*qch*).

pleiad, *pl* **-ads, -ades** ['plaɪəd, -ædz, -ədiːz] *n* **(a)** *Liter* pléiade *f*; **(b)** *Myth Astron* **the Pleiads, the Pleiades,** les Pléiades *fpl*.

plenary ['pliːnərɪ] *adj* complet, -ète, entier; **p. power,** (*of dictator*) pouvoir absolu; (*of president*) pleins pouvoirs; **p. assembly,** assemblée plénière.

plenipotentiary [plenɪpə'tenʃ(ə)rɪ] *adj & n* plénipotentiaire *m*.

plenitude ['plenɪtjuːd] *n* plénitude *f*.

plentiful ['plentɪfʊl] *adj* abondant, copieux, ample; **to be p.,** abonder, affluer.

plentifully ['plentɪfʊlɪ] *adv* abondamment, copieusement.

plenty ['plentɪ] **1** *n* abondance *f*; **p. of ...,** beaucoup de ...; **money in p.,** de l'argent en abondance; **to have p. of courage,** avoir beaucoup de courage, ne pas manquer de courage; **you've got p. of time,** vous avez largement le temps; **to arrive in p. of time,** arriver de bonne heure; **to have p. to live on,** avoir grandement de quoi vivre; **that's p.,** (*when being served food, drink*) ça suffit; **land of p.,** pays *m* de cocagne; **year of p.,** année *f* d'abondance. **2** *adv F* **it's p. big enough,** c'est bien assez gros. **3** *adj Arch & US* abondant, ample; **money is p.,** l'argent abonde.

pleonasm ['pliːənæz(ə)m] *n* pléonasme *m*.

pleonastic [pliːə'næstɪk] *adj* pléonastique, redondant; **to be p.,** (*of word*) être un pléonasme.

plethora ['pleθərə] *n* **(a)** pléthore *f*, surabondance *f* (*de biens etc*); **(b)** *Med* pléthore *f*.

pleurisy ['plʊərɪsɪ] *n Med* pleurésie *f*; **to have p.,** faire une pleurésie.

plexus ['pleksəs] *n* **(a)** *Anat* plexus *m*; **solar p.,** plexus solaire; **(b)** enchevêtrement *m* (*de rues etc*).

pliability [plaɪə'bɪlɪtɪ] *n* flexibilité *f*, souplesse *f* (*d'une tige*); docilité *f*, souplesse (*de caractère*).

pliable ['plaɪəb(ə)l] *adj* pliable, pliant, flexible; (*cuir*) souple; (*caractère etc*) docile, malléable, souple.

pliers ['plaɪəz] *npl* (*tool*) pince(s) *f(pl)*, tenaille(s) *f(pl)*; **a pair of p.,** des tenailles; **universal p.,** pinces universelles; **surgical p.,** pince(s) chirurgicale(s).

plight¹ [plaɪt] *n* condition *f ou* état *m* critique; **to be in a sorry** *or* **sad p.,** (*of person, country, economy*) être dans une mauvaise passe; **she saw my p. and helped me get up,** elle a vu que ça n'allait pas et m'a aidé à me relever; **what a p. you're in!,** comme vous voilà fait!

plight² *vt Lit* engager, promettre (*sa foi etc*); **to p. one's troth to s.o.,** donner sa foi à qn; *Arch* (*promise to marry*) se fiancer à qn.

Plimsoll ['plɪmsəl] *n Nau* **P. line** *or* **mark,** ligne *f* de Plimsoll.

plimsolls ['plɪmsəlz] *npl Br* (chaussures *fpl* de) tennis *mpl*.

plinth [plɪnθ] *n Archit* plinthe *f*; socle *m* (*d'une statue, d'une colonne*).

Pliny ['plɪnɪ] *n* **P. the Elder/the Younger,** Pline l'Ancien/le Jeune.

PLO [piːe'ləʊ] *n* (*abbr* **the Palestine Liberation Organization**) OLP *f*; **PLO representatives,** les représentants de l'OLP.

plod¹ [plɒd] *n* **(a)** démarche lourde *ou* lente; **(b)** (*heavy work*) travail *m* pénible.

plod² *vi* (**-dd-**) **(a)** marcher lourdement *ou* péniblement; **to p. one's way,** avancer *ou* marcher d'un pas lent; **to p. on,** continuer sa marche pénible; **(b)** = **PLOD AWAY**.

►**plod along** *vi* **(a)** (*walk slowly*) avancer *ou* marcher d'un pas lent; **(b)** (*work slowly*) travailler laborieusement.

►**plod away** *vi* (*work slowly*) travailler laborieusement; peiner, trimer (**at,** à).

plodder ['plɒdər] *n* travailleur, -euse, persévérant, -ante; **he's a p.,** il est dur à la besogne.

plodding ['plɒdɪŋ] **1** *adj* (*démarche*) pesant, lourd; (*personne*) qui travaille laborieusement. **2** *n* (*walk*) démarche lourde; (*work*) travail assidu.

plonk¹ [plɒŋk] *n* (*sound*) bruit sourd.

plonk² *vt* = **PLONK DOWN**.

plonk³ *n F* (*wine*) pinard *m*; gros rouge.

►**plonk away** *vi* (*on guitar*) tapoter; **to p. away on a piano,** pianoter.

►**plonk down** *vtsep* poser (*qch*) lourdement et sans façons; **just p. it down there,** mets-le juste par là; **to p. oneself down in an armchair,** se laisser tomber dans un fauteuil.

►**plonk out** *vtsep* (*play clumsily*) **to p. a tune out on a guitar/piano/*etc*,** jouer maladroitement un air à la guitare/au piano/*etc*.

plonker ['plɒŋkər] *n Br Sl* **(a)** (*penis*) bite *f*, *Hum* zizi *m*; **(b)** (*fool*) branleur *m*.

plook [plʊk] *n Scot F* bouton *m*.

plop¹ [plɒp] **1** *n* **(a)** (*splash*) flac *m*, plouf *m* (*de qch tombant dans l'eau*); **(b)** (*soft sound*) pouf *m*. **2** *adv* **to go p.,** (*of sth falling into water etc*) faire plouf; (*of sth landing softly*) faire pouf.

plop² *vi* (**-pp-**) **(a)** (*splash*) faire flac, tomber (dans l'eau) en faisant flac *ou* plouf; **(b)** (*land softly*) tomber en faisant pouf.

plosive ['pləʊsɪv] *Ling* **1** *adj* (*consonne*) explosif. **2** *n* explosive *f*.

plot¹ [plɒt] *n* **(a)** (*conspiracy*) complot *m*, conspiration *f*; **a p. on s.o.'s life,** un complot pour tuer qn; **to hatch a p.,** tramer *ou* ourdir un complot; **(b)** *Liter Th Cin* intrigue *f*, action *f* (*d'une pièce de théâtre, d'un roman etc*); **the p. thickens,** l'affaire se corse; **(c)** *Math etc* tracé *m*; (*graph*) graphe *m*, graphique *m*; courbe *f* (*d'un point mobile etc*); (*in surveying*) relèvement *m*; *Av Nau* tracé, graphe (*de la route d'un avion, d'un navire etc*); (*on radar*) pointé *m*; **(d)** (*land*) (parcelle *f ou* lot *m* de) terrain *m*; coin *m*, lopin *m*, quartier *m* (*de terre*); **building p.,** terrain à bâtir, lotissement *m*; **vegetable p.,** (*in garden*) potager *m*.

plot² *v* (**-tt-**) **1** *vt* **(a)** (*plan*) comploter, combiner (*la ruine de qn*); **(b)** *Math Phys* tracer *ou* faire le graphe *ou* le graphique de (*une courbe etc*); tracer, relever (*un diagramme, un graphe*); (*in surveying etc*) dresser *ou* lever le plan de, faire le levé de, lever (*un terrain etc*); tracer, rapporter (*une figure géométrique, un levé topographique*); marquer, tracer, repérer (*un point*) (*sur une carte*); (*on radar*) marquer, relever (*un pointé de radar*); *Comptr* tracer; **to p. a course,** relever *ou* tracer une route (*d'avion, de navire etc*); *Av Nau* **to p. the position,** faire le point. **2** *vi* (*conspire*) comploter, conspirer (**against s.o.,** contre qn).

plotter ['plɒtər] *n* **(a)** (*conspirator etc*) conspirateur, -trice, comploteur *m*; **(b)** *Math etc* (*person*) traceur, -euse; marqueur, -euse, plotteur *m* (*de pointés de radar*); *Comptr* traceur.

plotting ['plɒtɪŋ] *n* **(a)** (*conspiring*) complots *mpl*; **(b)** (*in surveying etc*) (*act*) report *m* (*d'un point repéré sur le terrain*); levé *m* (*d'un terrain*); pointage *m* (*d'une carte*); report (*des cotes relevées sur un appareil enregistreur etc*); report, marquage *m* (*des pointés de radar*); *Comptr* traçage *m*; **p. of details,** levé *m* des détails; *Comptr* **p. board** *or* **table,** table traçante, traceur *m* de courbes; **(c)** (*diagram etc*) représentation *f* graphique; tracé *m* (*d'une courbe*); *Av Nau* tracé (*de la route*).

plough¹, *US* **plow** [plaʊ] *n* **(a)** charrue *f*; (*ploughed land*) terres *fpl* de labour, labours *mpl*; *Fig* **to put one's hand to the p.,** mettre la main à la pâte; **to follow the p.,** être laboureur; **(b)** *Astron* **the P.,** la Grande Ourse; **(c)** *Br Sch F Old-fashioned* échec *m* (*à un examen*).

plough², *US* **plow 1** *vt* **(a)** labourer (*un champ etc*); tracer, creuser (*un sillon*); (*of ship*) fendre, sillonner (*les flots*); **to p. the soil,** retourner la terre (à la charrue); **ploughed land,** terres *fpl* de labour, labours *mpl*; **(b)** *Br Sch F Old-fashioned* **to p. an exam,** échouer à un examen; **to be** *or* **get ploughed in an exam,** être recalé *ou* collé à un examen. **2** *vi* labourer la terre.

►**plough back,** *US* **plow back** *vtsep Com Fin* **profits ploughed back into the business,** bénéfices réinvestis dans l'affaire.

►**plough in,** *US* **plow in** *vtsep* enterrer *ou* enfouir (*le fumier etc*) dans le sol en labourant.

►**plough into,** *US* **plow into** *vipo* (*of vehicle*) rentrer dans, foncer dans.

►**plough on,** *US* **plow on** *vi* (*continue laboriously*) **as negotiations p. on,** pendant que les négociations continuent avec difficulté.

►**plough through,** *US* **plow through 1** *vipo* (*move laboriously*) **to p. through the snow,** avancer péniblement dans la neige; **to p. through a book,** lire laborieusement un livre jusqu'au bout. **2** *vtsep* **to p. one's way through the snow,** avancer péniblement dans la neige.

►**plough up,** *US* **plow up** *vtsep* **(a)** (*turn over*) faire passer la charrue dans *ou* sur (*un champ*); *Fig* (*of bombs etc*) effondrer, défoncer (*le terrain*); **(b)** (*remove*) déraciner *ou* arracher (*des mauvaises herbes etc*) avec la charrue.

ploughing, *US* **plowing** ['plaʊɪŋ] *n* labourage *m*, labour *m*.

ploughing back, *US* **plowing back** *n* **p. back of profits,** réinvestissement *m* des bénéfices.
ploughland, *US* **plowland** ['plaʊlænd] *n* (*cultivated land*) terre labourée *ou* cultivée; (*ploughed land*) terres *fpl* de labour, labours *mpl*; (*arable land*) terre arable *ou* labourable.
ploughman, *US* **plowman,** *pl* **-men** ['plaʊmən] *n* laboureur *m*; *Br* **p.'s lunch,** = du pain, du fromage et des pickles.
ploughshare, *US* **plowshare** ['plaʊʃeər] *n* soc *m* de charrue.
plover ['plʌvər] *n* (*bird*) pluvier *m*; **golden p.,** pluvier doré; *Culin* **p.'s eggs,** œufs *mpl* de vanneau.
plow, plowland *etc US* = **PLOUGH, PLOUGHLAND** *etc*.
ploy [plɔɪ] *n* stratagème *m*, *F* truc *m*.
pluck[1] [plʌk] *n* (*courage*) courage *m*, cran *m*; **she's got plenty of p.,** elle a du cran, elle a du cœur au ventre.
pluck[2] *n* (*pull*) pincement *m* (*de corde de guitare etc*).
pluck[3] **1** *vt* **(a)** (*pull out*) arracher (*des cheveux, des plumes etc*); cueillir (*une fleur*); *Fig* **they were plucked from danger by a helicopter,** un hélicoptère les a arrachés au danger; **(b)** (*pull*) **to p. s.o.'s sleeve,** tirer qn par la manche; *Mus* **to p. a guitar/***etc*, pincer la guitare/*etc*; **(c)** (*remove feathers from*) plumer (*une volaille*); **to p. one's eyebrows,** s'épiler les sourcils. **2** *vi* **to p. at s.o.'s sleeve,** tirer qn par la manche.
▶**pluck up** *vtsep* (*summon*) **to p. up (one's) courage to do sth,** rassembler son courage pour faire qch.
pluckily ['plʌkɪlɪ] *adv* courageusement, avec courage.
pluckiness ['plʌkɪnɪs] *n Old-fashioned* courage *m*.
plucky ['plʌkɪ] *adj* courageux; **to be p.,** avoir du courage *ou* du cran.
plug[1] [plʌg] *n* **(a)** (*stopper*) bouchon *m*, tampon *m*; bonde *f*, crapaudine *f* (*de bassin, de réservoir etc*); bouchon (*d'évier*); (*dentistry*) *& Surg* tampon (*d'ouate, de coton*); *Geol* culot *m* volcanique; **waste p.,** tampon, soupape *f* (*de baignoire, de lavabo*);
(b) *Tech* fiche *f*; *El* fiche (mâle), prise *f* de courant, prise mâle; broche *f* (*de lampe etc*); (*for nail, screw in wall*) fiche; tampon *m* (*de scellement*); scellement *m*; *Rail* cale *f*, coin *m* (*pour coussinet de rail*); *El* **two-/three-pin p.,** fiche à deux/trois broches; *El* **wall p.,** prise de courant (murale); **spark(ing) p.,** (*in engine*) bougie *f*; **to pull the p. out,** (*disconnect electrical appliance*) débrancher; *Fig* **to pull the p. on a project,** enrayer un projet; *Comptr* **p. compatible,** compatible; **p. socket,** prise de courant (femelle);
(c) fire hydrant p., bouche *f* d'incendie;
(d) chasse *f* d'eau (*de w.c.*); **to pull the p.,** tirer la chaîne;
(e) *Old-fashioned* **p. of tobacco,** chique *f* de tabac;
(f) *F Com* (*publicity*) pub *f*; **the DJ gave the album a p.,** l'animateur a fait la pub de l'album;
(g) *F* (*blow*) coup *m* de poing.
plug[2] *v* **(-gg-) 1** *vt* **(a)** (*block*) boucher, obturer (*une ouverture, un tuyau*); tamponner (*une ouverture, une plaie*); *Nau* taper (*un écubier etc*); (*dentistry*) obstruer (*une cavité dentaire*); **to get plugged (up),** (*of pipe etc*) se boucher, s'obstruer; **(b)** *Tech* enfoncer des chevilles dans (*un mur etc*); **(c)** *F* (*promote*) faire de la réclame *ou* du battage *ou* de la pub pour (*un produit etc*); **(d)** *Sl* (*shoot*) fusiller, flinguer (*qn*); (*hit*) flanquer un coup à (*qn*). **2** *vi* (*block*) se boucher, s'obstruer.
▶**plug away** *vi F* (*persevere*) persévérer (**at,** dans), s'acharner (**at sth,** à qch).
▶**plug in** *El* **1** *vtsep* brancher (*une lampe etc*); connecter (*une imprimante etc*). **2** *vi* (*insert plug*) brancher.
▶**plug into** *El* **1** *vtaspo* (*connect*) **to p. sth into sth,** brancher qch sur qch. **2** *vipo* (*connect*) **the TV plugs into that socket,** le télé se branche sur cette prise.
plughole ['plʌghəʊl] *n* bonde *f*, trou *m* d'écoulement (*d'évier, de baignoire*).
plug-ugly ['plʌgʌglɪ] *adj F* (*man*) affreux.
plum [plʌm] **1** *n* **(a)** (*fruit*) prune *f*; **p. (tree),** prunier *m*; **p. brandy,** eau *f* de vie de prunes; *Culin* **p. cake,** cake *m*, gâteau *m* aux raisins; **p. jam,** confiture *f* de prunes; **p. pudding,** pudding *m* de Noël; **(b)** *F* (*job*) travail bien rétribué; (*part in play etc*) rôle *m* en or; **to have a p. job,** avoir une place en or. **2** *adj* (*colour*) prune *inv*; **p. jacket,** une veste (couleur) prune.
plumage ['plu:mɪdʒ] *n* plumage *m*.
plumb[1] [plʌm] *n* **(a)** (*perpendicular*) aplomb *m*; **out of p.,** hors d'aplomb; (*mur*) qui porte à faux; **p. (bob),** plomb *m* (*d'un fil à plomb*); **p. line,** (*weighted string*) fil *m* à plomb; (*vertical line*) verticale *f*; **(b)** *Nau* **p. (line)** (ligne *f* de) sonde *f*.
plumb[2] *vt* **(a)** (*in surveying*) vérifier l'aplomb de (*qch*), plomber (*un mur etc*); **(b)** *Nau* sonder (*la mer etc*); *Lit* **to p. the depths,** toucher le fond du désespoir.
plumb[3] **1** *adj* droit, vertical, -aux, d'aplomb; *Am F* **p. nonsense,** pure sottise. **2** *adv* perpendiculairement (**with sth,** à qch); à la verticale, à l'aplomb (**with sth,** de qch); *F* **p. in the centre,** en plein milieu, au beau milieu; (*of target*) en plein dans le mille; *F* **p. crazy,** complètement fou.
▶**plumb in** *vtsep* (*install*) raccorder (*une machine à laver*).
plumbago [plʌm'beɪgəʊ] *n Miner* plombagine *f*.
plumber ['plʌmər] *n* plombier *m*.
plumbing ['plʌmɪŋ] *n* **(a)** (*action*) plomberie *f*, plombage *m*; **(b)** (*pipes*) tuyauterie *f*, tuyaux *mpl*; (*toilets, washbasins etc*) installations *fpl* sanitaires; *F* **to inspect the p.,** (*urinate*) aller faire pipi.
plume[1] [plu:m] *n* **(a)** *Arch & Lit* (*feather*) plume *f*; *Fig* **in borrowed plumes,** paré des plumes du paon; **(b)** (*ornament*) panache *m*, aigrette *f*; plumet *m* (*de casque*).
plume[2] *vt* **(a)** (*ornament*) orner *ou* garnir de plumes; **black-plumed,** aux plumes noires; **plumed helmet,** casque empanaché; **(b)** (*preen*) **to p. itself,** (*of bird*) se lisser les plumes; *Old-fashioned* **to p. oneself on sth,** (*of person*) se glorifier de qch.
plummet[1] ['plʌmɪt] *n* (*weight*) plomb *m* (*de fil à plomb, de sonde, de ligne de pêche*).
plummet[2] *vi* plonger *ou* tomber verticalement; (*of prices etc*) s'effondrer; (*of blood pressure etc*) tomber soudainement; **the aircraft plummeted to the ground,** l'avion s'est écrasé au sol.
plummy ['plʌmɪ] *adj Br F* **(a)** (*voice*) de la haute, snob; **(b)** (*job*) agréable, bien payé.
plump[1] [plʌmp] *adj* (*person*) grassouillet, dodu, boulot, bien en chair; (*baby, fowl*) dodu; (*hands*) potelé.
plump[2] **1** *n* (*sound*) bruit sourd (*de chute*); (*esp in water*) floc *m*, plouf *m*. **2** *adv* **to fall p. into the mud,** tomber dans la boue en faisant floc. **3** *adj* (*denial*) catégorique.
plump[3] **1** *vt* **to p. oneself into an armchair,** s'affaler dans un fauteuil. **2** *vi* (*fall heavily*) tomber lourdement; (*make sound*) faire pouf.
▶**plump down** *vtsep* déposer brusquement (*une valise etc*).
▶**plump for** *vipo* (*choose*) choisir.
▶**plump out** *vi* = **PLUMP UP 2.**
▶**plump up 1** *vtsep* (*shake*) secouer, brasser (*un oreiller*). **2** *vi* (*become fat*) devenir dodu.
plumpness ['plʌmpnɪs] *n* embonpoint *m*, rondeur *f*.
plunder[1] ['plʌndər] *n* (*act*) pillage *m*; (*result*) butin *m*.
plunder[2] **1** *vt* piller, mettre à sac, dépouiller (*un pays etc*); dépouiller (*qn*). **2** *vi F* brigander.
plundering ['plʌndərɪŋ] **1** *adj* pillard. **2** *n* pillage *m*.
plunge[1] [plʌndʒ] *n* plongeon *m*; **to take a p.,** faire un plongeon, plonger (**into,** dans); *Fig* (*of profits etc*) s'effondrer; *F* **to take the p.,** (*resolve to do sth*) prendre le taureau par les cornes; (*get married*) se marier.
plunge[2] **1** *vt* plonger, immerger (*le linge dans la lessive etc*); **to p. a dagger into s.o.'s back,** plonger un poignard dans le dos de qn; **plunged in darkness,** plongé dans l'obscurité; **to p. s.o. into despair,** plonger qn dans le désespoir. **2** *vi* plonger, se jeter (la tête la première) (*dans l'eau etc*); s'enfoncer, s'engouffrer (*dans un bois etc*); se jeter (à corps perdu) (*dans une affaire etc*); (*of ship*) tanguer, piquer du nez; (*in gambling*) jouer sans compter *ou* gros jeu; (*of profits*) s'effondrer; **the lorry plunged over the cliff,** le camion plongea par-dessus la falaise; **she plunged to her death,** elle fit une chute mortelle; **necklines have plunged this year,** cette année les décolletés sont plus profonds; **to p. forward,** s'élancer en avant.
plunger ['plʌndʒər] *n* **(a)** (*device*) piston *m* (*de pompe, de cafetière, de seringue etc*); manette *f* (*de détonateur*); **(rubber) p.,** (*for clearing sink etc*) ventouse *f*; **(b)** *F* (*gambler*) flambeur, -euse.
plunging ['plʌndʒɪŋ] **1** *adj* **p. neckline,** décolleté plongeant. **2** *n* (*diving, immersing*) plongement *m*; (*immersing*) immersion *f*; tangage *m* (*d'un bateau*).
plunk [plʌŋk] *vt* **(a)** pincer les cordes de (*un banjo etc*); **(b)** (*drop heavily*) laisser tomber lourdement (*qch*).
▶**plunk down** *vtsep F* déposer (*qch*) lourdement.
pluperfect ['plu:pɜ:fɪkt] *Gram* **1** *adj* plus-que-parfait; **p. subjunctive,** plus-que-parfait du subjonctif. **2** *n* plus-que-parfait *m*; **in the p.,** au plus-que-parfait.
plural ['plʊər(ə)l] **1** *adj* **(a)** *Gram* pluriel; **(b)** *Pol* **p. vote,** vote plural. **2** *n Gram* **in the p.,** au pluriel.

pluralism ['plʊərəlɪz(ə)m] *n* **(a)** *Phil etc* pluralisme *m*; **(b)** (*holding of several posts*) cumul *m* de fonctions *ou Rel* de bénéfices.

plurality [plʊə'rælɪtɪ] *n* **(a)** pluralité *f*; **(b)** cumul *m* (*de fonctions, Rel de bénéfices*); *Rel* (*individual benefice*) bénéfice détenu par cumul; **(c)** *Pol* majorité *f* (*des voix*).

plus [plʌs] **1** *prep* plus; **seven p. nine,** sept plus neuf; **two floors p. an attic,** deux étages plus un grenier. **2** *adj* (*quantity, number, electric charge*) positif; **on the p. side of the account,** à l'actif du compte; *F* **on the p. side the bicycle is very light,** la légèreté est l'un des avantages de cette bicyclette; **p. fours,** culotte (bouffante) de golf; *F* **fifteen p.,** au-dessus de quinze ans. **3** *n* (*pl* **plusses** ['plʌsɪz]) *Math* (*symbol*) plus *m*; (*positive quantity*) quantité positive; (*advantage*) avantage *m*, atout *m*; *Math* **p. sign,** (*symbol*) signe *m* d'addition; (*in formula*) signe positif.

plush[1] [plʌʃ] *n Tex* peluche *f*, panne *f*.

plush[2] *adj* **(a)** *Tex* en peluche; **(b)** *F* (*appartement etc*) somptueux, luxueux.

Plutarch ['pluːtɑːk] *n* Plutarque *m*.

Pluto ['pluːtəʊ] *n Myth Astron* Pluton *m*.

plutocracy [pluː'tɒkrəsɪ] *n* ploutocratie *f*.

plutocrat ['pluːtəkræt] *n* ploutocrate *m*.

plutocratic [pluːtə'krætɪk] *adj* ploutocratique.

plutonium [pluː'təʊnɪəm] *n Ch* plutonium *m*.

pluviometer [pluːvɪ'ɒmɪtər] *n* pluviomètre *m*.

ply[1] [plaɪ] *n* **(a)** (*layer*) pli *m* (*de tissu appliqué en plusieurs plis*); placage *m*, épaisseur *f* (*de contre-plaqué*); pli (*d'un pneu*); **two-p. paper handkerchief,** mouchoir *m* en papier double épaisseur; **(b)** (*strand*) brin *m*, fil *m* (*de corde, de laine*); toron *m* (*de corde*); **three-p. wool,** laine *f* trois fils; **(c)** *F* = **PLYWOOD**; **three-p.,** contre-plaqué *m* à trois plis.

ply[2] **1** *vt* **(a)** (*use*) manier vigoureusement (*un outil etc*); faire courir (*l'aiguille*); exercer (*un métier*); **(b)** (*supply*) **to p. s.o. with questions,** presser qn de questions; **to p. s.o. with drink,** verser force rasades à qn; **to p. s.o. with food,** donner abondamment à manger à qn; **(c) to p. an ocean,** (*of ship*) faire la traversée; **to p. a route,** (*of ship, bus etc*) assurer une liaison (avec). **2** *vi* (*of ship, bus etc*) faire le service *ou* la navette (**between ... and ...,** entre ... et ...); **to p. for hire,** (*of taxi etc*) prendre des voyageurs.

plywood ['plaɪwʊd] *n* (bois *m*) contre-plaqué *m*.

pm ['piːem] *adv abbr* **post meridiem**; **6 pm,** 18h.

PM [piː'em] *n Br & Can Pol abbr* **Prime Minister**.

PMS [piːe'mes] *n Med abbr* **premenstrual syndrome**.

PMT [piːem'tiː] *n Med* (*abbr* **premenstrual tension**) = tension prémenstruelle.

pneumatic [njuː'mætɪk] *adj* (*machine, outil*) pneumatique; **p. drill,** marteau *m* pneumatique; **p. tyre,** pneumatique *m*, pneu *m*.

pneumatically [njuː'mætɪklɪ] *adv* **p. operated,** (*appareil*) à marche pneumatique, à air comprimé.

pneumatics [njuː'mætɪks] *npl Phys* (*usu with sing verb*) pneumatique *f*.

pneumonia [njuː'məʊnɪə] *n Med* pneumonie *f*; **to have p.,** avoir une pneumonie.

po [pəʊ] *n Br F* pot *m* de chambre, Jules *m*.

PO [piː'əʊ] *n* **(a)** (*abbr* **Post Office**) **P.O. Box,** B.P.; **(b)** *abbr* **postal order**; **(c)** *Nau abbr* **petty officer**.

poach[1] [pəʊtʃ] *vt Culin* pocher (*des œufs*); **poached egg,** œuf poché.

poach[2] **1** *vt* (*steal*) braconner (*le gibier etc*); (*steal from*) braconner dans (*un bois etc*). **2** *vi* braconner; **to p. on s.o.'s preserves,** braconner sur la chasse réservée de qn; *Fig* empiéter sur les prérogatives de qn.

poacher[1] ['pəʊtʃər] *n* **(egg) p.,** pocheuse *f* (à œufs).

poacher[2] *n* (*thief*) braconnier *m*.

poaching ['pəʊtʃɪŋ] *n* braconnage *m*.

pock [pɒk] *n Med* pustule *f* (*de la petite vérole*).

pocket[1] ['pɒkɪt] *n* **(a)** poche *f* (*de vêtement*); **waistcoat p.,** gousset *m*; *F* **to line one's pockets,** faire sa pelote; **to put one's hands in one's pockets,** mettre les mains dans ses poches; **to go through s.o.'s pockets,** faire les poches à qn; *F* **to have s.o. in one's p.,** avoir qn dans sa poche; *F* **to live in each other's** *or* **one another's pockets,** ne pas se lâcher d'une semelle; **prices to suit every p.,** des prix à la portée de tout le monde; **he's always got his hand in his p.,** il a toujours la main sur le portefeuille, il est toujours à débourser; **to be in p.,** être en bénéfice *ou* en gain; **to be out of p. (over a transaction),** être en perte, ne pas rentrer dans ses fonds; **how much are you out of p.?,** combien est-ce que vous avez dépensé?; *Nau* **p. battleship,** cuirassé *m* de poche; **p. comb/handkerchief,** peigne *m*/mouchoir *m* de poche; **p. calculator,** calculatrice *f* de poche; **p. dictionary,** dictionnaire *m* de poche; **p. money,** argent *m* de poche; **p. park,** parc *m* miniature; **p. size,** (*in bookbinding*) format *m* de poche;

(b) (*bag*) sac *m* (*de houblon, de laine*); *Billiards* blouse *f*; *Aut* **car p.,** (*in door etc*) poche intérieure;

(c) *MecE* (*in engine*) chambre *f* (*de soupape*);

(d) *Min* poche *f*, nid *m*, sac *m* (*de minerai*); poche (*d'eau, de gaz*); nid (*de grisou*); **air p.,** *Av* trou *m* d'air; *HydE etc* poche d'air (*dans une canalisation*);

(e) *Fig* (*small area*) poche *f* (*de résistance, de rébellion etc*).

pocket[2] *vt* (**-t-**) **(a)** (*put in pocket*) empocher (*qch*), mettre (*qch*) dans sa poche; *Pej* empocher, *F* chiper (*qch*); **(b)** avaler, empocher, encaisser (*un affront, une insulte etc*); **(c)** faire taire (*ses sentiments*); **to p. one's pride,** faire taire son amour-propre; **(d)** *Billiards* blouser (*la bille*).

pocketbook ['pɒkɪtbʊk] *n Am* **(a)** (*handbag*) sac *m* à main; **(b)** (*small book*) livre *m* de poche.

pocketful ['pɒkɪtfʊl] *n* pleine poche; **pocketfuls of sweets,** des poches pleines de bonbons.

pocketknife ['pɒkɪtnaɪf] *n* couteau *m* de poche, canif *m*.

pockmark ['pɒkmɑːk] *n* marque *f* de la petite vérole.

pockmarked ['pɒkmɑːkt] *adj* (*face*) grêlé; (*surface of the moon etc*) plein de trous.

pod[1] [pɒd] *n* **(a)** cosse *f*, gousse *f* (*de fèves, de pois etc*); **senna pods,** follicules *mpl* de séné; **(b)** cocon *m* (*de ver à soie*); **(c)** *Fishing* nasse *f* (*pour anguilles*); **(d)** *Fishing Av* nacelle *f*, fuseau *m* (*de réacteur etc*); **engine p.,** nacelle-moteur *f*, *pl* nacelles-moteur.

pod[2] *v* (**-dd-**) **1** *vi* (*of plant*) former des cosses *ou* des gousses. **2** *vt* écosser, écaler (*des pois etc*).

podgy ['pɒdʒɪ] *adj* (*person*) boulot, -otte; (*finger*) boudiné, rondelet.

podium, *pl* **-ia** ['pəʊdɪəm, -ɪə] *n* podium *m*.

poem ['pəʊɪm] *n* poème *m*, poésie *f*.

poet ['pəʊɪt] *n* poète *m*; **p. laureate,** poète lauréat.

poetaster [pəʊɪ'tæstər] *n Pej* mauvais poète, rimailleur *m*.

poetess ['pəʊɪtɪs] *n Old-fashioned* femme *f* poète, poétesse *f*.

poetic(al) [pəʊ'etɪk, -ɪk(ə)l] *adj* poétique; **poetic justice,** justice divine; **poetic licence,** licence *f* poétique.

poetically [pəʊ'etɪklɪ] *adv* poétiquement.

poetry ['pəʊɪtrɪ] *n* poésie *f*; **to write p.,** écrire des vers; **the art of p.,** l'art *m* poétique.

po-faced ['pəʊfeɪst] *adj Sl* avec une figure d'enterrement; **why are you looking so po-f.?,** pourquoi fais-tu une telle figure d'enterrement?; **the po-f. old cow!,** sale gueule de vache!

pogo ['pəʊgəʊ] *n* **p. stick,** = échasse *f* à ressort.

pogrom ['pɒgrəm] *n* pogrom(e) *m*.

poignancy ['pɔɪnjənsɪ] *n* caractère poignant (*d'une émotion etc*).

poignant ['pɔɪnjənt] *adj* (*feeling*) poignant, vif; (*regret etc*) amer, -ère.

poignantly ['pɔɪnjəntlɪ] *adv* d'une façon poignante.

poinsettia [pɔɪn'setɪə] *n* (*plant*) poinsettia *f*.

point[1] [pɔɪnt] *n* **1 (a)** (*in space*) point *m*; **p. of arrival/departure,** point d'arrivée/de départ; **assembly p.,** lieu *m* de rassemblement; **observation p.,** point d'observation; *Mil* **key points,** points stratégiques; *Com* **p. of sale,** point de vente; **p. of view,** point de vue; **to consider sth from all points of view,** considérer qch sous tous ses aspects; **p. source,** (*of pollution*) source ponctuelle;

(b) *Gram* **full p.,** point *m* (*de ponctuation*); *Math* **decimal p.,** virgule *f* (décimale); **three p. five (3.5),** = trois virgule cinq (3,5);

(c) point *m*, détail *m* (*d'un raisonnement etc*); **the chief p. of an argument,** l'important *ou* l'essentiel d'un raisonnement; **figures that give p. to his argument,** chiffres qui ajoutent du poids à sa thèse; **on that p. we disagree,** là-dessus nous ne sommes pas d'accord; **I take your p.,** je vois ce que vous voulez dire; **p. taken!,** très juste!; **she has a p.,** elle a raison; **to make a p.,** faire ressortir un argument; **my p.** *or* **the p. I'm making is that ...,** là où je veux en venir c'est que ...; **the teacher went through the essay p. by p.,** le professeur a repris la dissertation point par point; **to make a p. of doing sth,** se faire un devoir de faire qch; (*regularly*) ne pas manquer de faire qch; **p. of grammar/of law,** question *f* de grammaire/de droit; **in p. of fact,** en fait, à vrai dire; **a case in p.,** un exemple; **p. of honour,** point d'honneur; **the p.,** le sujet, la question; **the p. is (that) ...,** c'est que ...; **that's the p.,** c'est bien de cela qu'il s'agit; **that's not the p.,** il ne s'agit pas de cela; **beside the p.,** à côté de la question, hors sujet; **on this p.,** à cet égard, à ce propos; **this is very much to the p.,** c'est bien parlé *ou* bien dit; **to stick to the p.,** ne pas s'écarter du sujet; **to come to the p.,** en venir au fait; **what would be the p. (of doing sth)?,** à quoi bon (faire qch)?; **there is no p. in (doing) it,** cela ne servirait à rien; **I can't see the p.,** (*of doing it*) je ne vois pas l'intérêt; **I don't see the p. of the story,** je ne vois pas où cette histoire veut en venir; **p. of interest,** détail intéressant; **to have its good points,** avoir ses bons côtés; **its price is a p. in its favour,** son prix est un de ses atouts;

(d) (*precise moment*) **at this p. in time,** en ce moment même; **at one p. I thought we would all be killed,** à un certain moment, j'ai cru que nous allions tous être tués; **to be on the p. of doing sth,** être sur le point de faire qch; **on** *or* **at the p. of death,** sur le point de mourir, à l'article de la mort; **to be on the p. of departure,** être sur le point de partir; **p. of no return,** point de non-retour; **critical p.,** point critique; **a high/low p. in s.o.'s life,** un moment fort/difficile de la vie de qn; **when it came to the p.,** quand le moment critique est arrivé; **there comes a p. in everyone's life when ...,** dans la vie de chacun il arrive un moment où ...; **up to a (certain) p.,** jusqu'à un certain point; **she had reached the p. where she was no longer interested,** elle en était arrivée à ne plus être intéressée; **severe to the p. of cruelty,** sévère jusqu'à la cruauté;

(e) (*in game, exam etc*) point *m*; **to score so many points,** marquer *ou* obtenir tant de points; **you get three points for a correct answer,** une bonne réponse vaut trois points; *Cards etc* **to play ten pence a p.,** jouer à dix pence le point; *Boxing* **to win on points,** gagner aux points; **beaten on points,** battu aux points; *Tennis* **match/set p.,** balle *f* de match/de set; **p. system,** (*at school etc*) barème *m*, système *m* de notation *f*; (*in game etc*) système d'attribution des points; *Cycling* **points competition,** classement *m* par points;

(f) (*measure*) *Typ etc* point *m*; **the thermometer went up/down two points,** le thermomètre a monté/a baissé de deux degrés *ou* divisions; **freezing/melting/boiling p.,** point de congélation/de fusion/d'ébullition; *St Exch* **rise/fall of one p.,** (*of price*) hausse *f*/baisse *f* d'un point;

(g) (*sharp end*) pointe *f* (*d'une aiguille, d'un clou, d'une épée, d'un outil etc*); mouche *f* (*d'un foret*); bec *m* (*d'une plume à écrire*); *Geog* pointe, promontoire *m*; **to dance on points,** faire des pointes; **on (full) p.,** sur la pointe; **on demi-p.,** sur la demi-pointe; **p. work,** pointes; **to end in a p.,** aller *ou* se terminer en pointe; **to give a p. to a pencil,** tailler un crayon; **p. of a joke,** piquant *m ou* sel *m* d'une plaisanterie; **points,** extrémités *fpl* (*d'un cheval etc*); (*in hunting*) cors *mpl* (*du cerf*); **not to put too fine a p. on it ...,** pour dire les choses clairement;

(h) (*tool*) pointe *f*, poinçon *m*;

(i) *El* (point *m* de) prise *f* de courant (*sur le secteur*); **power p.,** prise de courant (force); **eight-p. distributor,** (*in engine*) distributeur *m* (d'allumage) à huit plots;

(j) *Rail* points *mpl*, aiguillage *m*; **p. duty,** (*of police officer*) service *m* de la circulation; **policeman on p. duty,** agent *m* de circulation; **to be on p. duty,** être à la circulation;

(k) the points of the compass, les aires *fpl* du vent; **p. of the compass,** quart *m* (de vent); **to alter course 16 points,** venir de 16 quarts;

(l) (*in backgammon*) flèche *f*, pointe *f*, case *f*;

(m) (*in lacemaking*) **p. (lace),** dentelle *f* à l'aiguille; point *m*; guipure *f*; *Tex* **p. paper,** carte *f*.

point² **1** *vt* **(a)** (*aim*) pointer, braquer (*un canon*); diriger, orienter, braquer (*une longue-vue*) **(at,** sur); **to p. a gun at s.o.,** pointer une arme sur qn; **to p. a camera at sth/s.o.,** braquer un appareil photo sur qch/qn; *F* **just p. me in the right direction,** dites-moi simplement quelle direction je dois prendre;

(b) to p. the way, indiquer *ou* montrer le chemin (**to s.o.,** à qn; **to a place,** vers un endroit);

(c) (*make sharp*) tailler en pointe (*un bâton etc*); appointer (*un outil, un clou etc*); donner du piquant à (*des remarques etc*); **to p. the toe** *or* **the foot,** (*in dancing*) pointer le pied;

(d) *Constr* jointoyer (*un mur*);

(e) (*in hunting*) (*of hound*) arrêter (*le gibier*).

2 *vi* **(a)** (*indicate*) **the magnetic needle always points north,** l'aiguille aimantée est toujours tournée vers le nord; **this points to the fact that ...,** cette circonstance laisse supposer *ou* fait ressortir que ...; **everything seems to p. to success,** tout semble indiquer le succès;

(b) (*with finger etc*) **to p. at s.o.,** montrer *ou* désigner qn du doigt *etc*; **don't p., it's rude,** ne montre pas du doigt, ce n'est pas poli;

(c) (*in hunting*) (*of hound*) tomber en arrêt.

▶**point off** *vtsep Math* séparer (*les décimales*) par une virgule.

▶**point out** *vtsep* **(a) to p. out sth to s.o. (with one's finger),** désigner *ou* montrer qch du doigt à qn; **she pointed out some of the famous sights,** elle a désigné (du doigt) certaines des vues les plus célèbres; **(b)** (*indicate, show*) signaler, relever (*une erreur etc*); faire ressortir, faire valoir (*un fait etc*); **to p. out sth to s.o.,** attirer l'attention de qn sur qch, signaler *ou* faire remarquer qch à qn; **to p. out to s.o. that he is wrong,** démontrer à qn qu'il a tort; **to p. out to s.o. the advantages of sth,** (dé)montrer à qn les avantages de qch; **might I p. out that ...?,** permettez-moi de vous faire observer que ...; **he has been pointed out to me as a capable man,** on me l'a signalé comme un homme capable.

▶**point up** *vtsep* (*highlight*) mettre en évidence.

point-blank ['pɔɪnt'blæŋk] **1** *adj Mil etc* (*tir*) direct, à bout portant; *F* (*question*) posé de but en blanc; (*refus*) net, catégorique; **to fire at p.-b. range,** tirer à bout portant; **he was shot at p.-b. range,** on lui a tiré dessus à bout portant. **2** *adv* **to fire p.-b. at s.o.,** tirer sur qn à bout portant; **he asked me p.-b. whether ...,** il m'a demandé de but en blanc si ...; **to refuse p.-b.,** refuser catégoriquement *ou* carrément *ou* (tout) net.

point-by-point ['pɔɪntbaɪ'pɔɪnt] *adj* **p.-by-p. analysis,** analyse *f* point par point.

pointed ['pɔɪntɪd] *adj* **(a)** (*having a sharp point*) pointu, à pointe; (*barbe*) en pointe; *Tech* aléné; **(b)** (*réflexion*) sarcastique, mordant; (*allusion*) peu équivoque, peu voilé.

pointedly ['pɔɪntɪdlɪ] *adv* (*to say*) d'un ton mordant; (*to refer*) explicitement, nettement; (*markedly*) d'une manière marquée; **not too p.,** sans appuyer.

pointedness ['pɔɪntɪdnɪs] *n* mordant *m* (*d'une remarque*); caractère *m* explicite (*d'une allusion*).

pointer ['pɔɪntər] *n* **(a)** aiguille *f* (*d'horloge*); aiguille, languette *f* (*d'une balance*); *Sch* baguette *f* (*du tableau noir*); **optical** *or* **illuminated p.,** (*for slides*) flèche lumineuse; **(b)** *F* (*advice*) tuyau *m*; **to give s.o. a few pointers on sth,** donner à qn quelques indications *ou* tuyaux à propos de qch; **(c)** (*dog*) pointer *m*; **(d)** (*tool*) pointe *f* (*de maçon etc*).

pointillism ['pwæntɪlɪz(ə)m] *n Art* pointillisme *m*.

pointing ['pɔɪntɪŋ] *n* **(a)** pointage *m*, braquage *m* (*d'un canon etc*); **(b)** (*making sharp*) taillage *m* en pointe; (*of knife*) affûtage *m*; **(c)** *Constr* jointoiement *m* (*d'un mur*); (*cement*) gobletis *m*.

pointless ['pɔɪntlɪs] *adj* (*story etc*) qui ne rime à rien; (*joke*) fade, sans sel; (*remark etc*) qui n'a rien à voir avec la question; (*action*) inutile; **it would be p.,** ce serait inutile, cela ne servirait à rien (**to do,** de faire).

pointlessly ['pɔɪntlɪslɪ] *adv* inutilement, vainement.

pointlessness ['pɔɪntlɪsnɪs] *n* (*of joke etc*) fadeur *f*; (*of remark etc*) manque *m* d'à-propos; (*of action*) inutilité *f*.

pointsman ['pɔɪntsmən] *n Br Rail* aiguilleur *m*.

point-to-point ['pɔɪnttə'pɔɪnt] *adj Sp* **p.-to-p. (race),** cross *m* à cheval, hippocross *m*.

pointy-headed [pɔɪntɪ'hedɪd] *adj US Pej* intello.

poise¹ [pɔɪz] *n* **(a)** (*balance*) **(equal, even, just) p.,** équilibre *m*, aplomb *m*; **to have p.,** (*of person*) avoir de la prestance; **a man of p.,** un homme pondéré; **(b)** port *m* (*de la tête, du corps*).

poise² *vt* équilibrer; (*in hand*) tenir (*qch*) en équilibre; **to be poised,** être en équilibre; (*of person*) être équilibré; **the cat was poised ready to spring,** le chat se tenait prêt à bondir; **Rome was poised to conquer the known world,** Rome se tenait prête à conquérir le monde connu.

poison¹ ['pɔɪzən] *n* poison *m*, toxique *m*; **to take p.,** s'empoisonner; *F* **what's your p.?,** qu'est-ce que tu veux boire?; **p. gas,** gaz *m* toxique; **p. gland,** (*of animal*) glande *f* à venin; **p. ivy,** (*plant*) sumac vénéneux; **p. pen letter,** lettre anonyme venimeuse.

poison² *vt* empoisonner (*qn, qch*); intoxiquer (*qn*); corrompre, pervertir (*l'esprit*); empoisonner (*la vie de qn*); **to p. s.o.'s mind against s.o.,** monter qn contre qn; **poisoned food,** nourriture empoisonnée.

poisoner ['pɔɪzənər] *n* empoisonneur, -euse.

poisoning ['pɔɪzənɪŋ] *n* (*of person, food*) empoisonnement *m*; (*of person*) intoxication *f*; corruption *f* (*de l'esprit*); **food p.,** intoxication alimentaire.

poisonous ['pɔɪzənəs] *adj* toxique, intoxicant; (*gas*) asphyxiant, toxique; (*animal*) venimeux; (*plant*) vénéneux; (*doctrine*) pernicieux.

poke¹ [pəʊk] *n* **(a)** (*push*) poussée *f*; (*nudge*) coup *m* de coude; (*with the finger*) coup du bout du doigt; **to give s.o.**

a p. in the ribs, donner une bourrade (amicale) à qn; **(b)** *Sl* (*act of sexual intercourse*) baise *f*.

poke² **1** *vt* **(a)** pousser (*qn, qch*) du bras *ou* du coude; piquer (*qch*) du bout d'un bâton; **to p. s.o. in the ribs,** donner une bourrade (amicale) à qn; **to p. a hole in sth,** faire un trou dans qch; crever qch (*avec le doigt etc*); **(b)** (*insert*) mettre, fourrer (*qch*) (**into,** dans); **to p. one's head through the window,** passer la tête par la fenêtre; *F* **to p. one's nose into other people's business,** fourrer son nez dans les affaires des autres; **(c)** tisonner, attiser (*le feu*); **(d) to p. fun at s.o./sth,** se moquer de qn/qch; **(e)** *Sl* (*have sexual intercourse with*) baiser (*qn*). **2** *vi* **to p. at sth,** tâter qch du bout du doigt *ou* d'un bâton *etc*; **to p. in every corner,** fouiller *ou* fureter dans tous les coins; *F* **to p. into other people's business,** fourrer son nez dans les affaires des autres.

poke³ *n Dial* (*pocket*) sac *m*, poche *f*; *F* **to buy a pig in a p.,** acheter chat en poche.

►**poke about, poke around** **1** *vi* **(a)** (*search*) fouiller; **a dog was poking about in the bushes,** un chien fouinait dans les buissons; **(b)** (*make unwanted enquiries*) fourrer son nez partout, fouiner; **that social worker is always poking about,** cette assistante sociale est toujours en train de fourrer son nez dans les affaires des autres. **2** *vi po* (*search in*) fouiller dans (*un magasin d'antiquités*).

►**poke out** **1** *vi* (*protrude*) sortir de, dépasser; **her umbrella was poking out (of her bag),** son parapluie dépassait de son sac. **2** *vtsep* **(a)** (*push out*) **to p. one's head out (of the window),** passer *ou* sortir la tête par la fenêtre; **(b) to p. s.o.'s eye out,** éborgner qn.

poker¹ ['pəʊkər] *n* **(a)** (*for fire*) tisonnier *m*; *Ind* fourgon *m*; (*for furnace*) ringard *m*; **(b)** pointe *f* métallique (*pour pyrogravure*); **p. work,** pyrogravure *f*.

poker² *n Cards* poker *m*; **p. dice,** dés *mpl* pour jouer au poker; *F* **p. face,** visage *m* impassible; **p.-faced,** au visage impassible; **p. game,** partie *f* de poker.

poky ['pəʊkɪ] *adj* (*room*) exigu, -uë; **to live in a p. little place,** être logé à l'étroit *ou* étroitement.

Polack ['pəʊlæk] *n Am Offensive Sl* polaque *mf*.

Poland ['pəʊlənd] *n* Pologne *f*.

polar ['pəʊlər] *adj Geog Math Phys* polaire; **p. bear,** ours polaire *ou* blanc.

polarimeter [pəʊlə'rɪmɪtər] *n Opt* polarimètre *m*.

polarity [pəʊ'lærɪtɪ] *n Phys* polarité *f*.

polarization [pəʊlərаɪ'zeɪʃən] *n Phys* polarisation *f*; *Fig* radicalisation *f*.

polarize ['pəʊləraɪz] **1** *vt* **(a)** *Phys* polariser (*la lumière, une barre de fer etc*); **(b)** (*make extreme*) radicaliser (*les opinions*). **2** *vi* se polariser.

Polaroid ® ['pəʊlərɔɪd] *n* **(a)** *Phot* (*camera*) Polaroid ® *m*; (*photograph*) photographie *f* instantanée; **(b)** *Opt* Polaroid ® *m*.

pole¹ [pəʊl] *n* **(a)** perche *f* (*à houblon etc*); (*for plants*) échalas *m*, rame *f*; mât *m* (*d'échafaudage*); hampe *f* (*d'un drapeau*); bras *m* (*de civière*); barre *f* (*d'écurie*); *Nau* flèche *f* (*de mât*); **tent p.,** mât de tente; **telegraph p.,** poteau *m* télégraphique; *Sp* **p. vault(ing),** saut *m* à la perche; *Br F* **to be up the p.,** être timbré *ou* toqué; **(b)** *Arch* (*measurement*) perche *f*.

pole² *n El etc* pôle *m*; *Geog* **North p.,** pôle nord *ou* arctique *ou* boréal; **South p.,** pôle sud *ou* antarctique *ou* austral; **magnetic/true p.,** pôle magnétique/géographique; **to be poles apart,** être aux antipodes l'un de l'autre; (*of views etc*) être diamétralement opposé; **opposite poles,** (*of magnet*) pôles contraires; **p. star,** étoile *f* polaire.

Pole [pəʊl] *n* Polonais, -aise.

poleax(e)¹ ['pəʊlæks] *n* merlin *m*.

poleax(e)² *vt* assommer (*qn*); abattre (*un animal*) avec un merlin; **to be poleaxed,** (*shocked*) être assommé (*par une nouvelle etc*).

polecat ['pəʊlkæt] *n* (*animal*) putois *m*.

polemic [pə'lemɪk] **1** *adj* polémique. **2** *n* polémique *f*; (*person*) polémiste *mf*.

polemicist [pə'lemɪsɪst] *n* polémiste *mf*.

polemics [pə'lemɪks] *npl* polémique *f*.

pole-vault ['pəʊlvɔːlt] *vi Sp* sauter à la perche.

pole-vaulter ['pəʊlvɔːltər] *n Sp* sauteur, -euse à la perche, perchiste *m*.

police¹ [pə'liːs] *n inv* (*with pl verb*) **the p. (force),** la police; **twenty p. were on duty,** vingt agents étaient de service; **military p.,** police militaire; **traffic p.,** police de la circulation *ou* de la route; **to be a member of the p. force, to be in the p.,** être de *ou* dans la police; *US* **p. captain,** ≈ commissaire *m* de police; **p. car,** voiture *f* de police; *Br* **p. constable,** agent *m* de police; *US* **p. department,** Police *f*; **p. dog,** chien policier; *Br* **the P. Federation,** = syndicat de la police britannique; **p. informer,** indicateur, -trice; *Br* **p. inspector,** inspecteur *m* de police; (*in the CID*) commissaire *m* de police; **p. officer,** officier *m* de police; **p. state,** état policier; **p. station,** poste *m* de police; (*bigger*) commissariat *m*; **p. van,** (*for transporting prisoners*) voiture *f* cellulaire, *F* panier *m* à salade; (*for transporting police*) car *m* de police; **hours of careful p. work,** des heures d'un travail poussé de la part de la police.

police² *vt* assurer la police de (*l'Etat etc*); maintenir l'ordre dans (*le pays etc*); **to p. a football match/demonstration,** assurer l'ordre à un match de football/une manifestation.

policeman, *pl* **-men** [pə'liːsmən] *n* agent *m* (de police); **traffic p.,** agent de la circulation; **motor-cycle p.,** agent motocycliste, motard *m*.

policewoman, *pl* **-women** [pə'liːswʊmən,-wɪmɪn] *n* femme-agent (de police), *pl* femmes-agents (de police).

policing [pə'liːsɪŋ] *n* maintien *m* de l'ordre; **the p. of the match/demonstration was inadequate,** le service d'ordre du match/de la manifestation était inadéquat; **p. policy,** politique *f* de maintien de l'ordre.

policy¹ ['pɒlɪsɪ] *n* (*plan etc*) politique *f*; **foreign p.,** politique étrangère *ou* extérieure; **economic/agricultural p.,** politique économique/agricole; **prices and incomes p.,** politique des prix et des salaires; **my p. is not to tell him anything,** ma politique, c'est de ne rien lui dire; **sales p.,** méthodes *fpl* de vente; **p. changes, changes of p.,** changements *mpl* de politique.

policy² *n* (*in insurance*) police *f* (d'assurance); **(fully) comprehensive** *or* **all-risks p.,** police tous risques; **life insurance** *or* **assurance p.,** police d'assurance (sur la) vie; **fire insurance p.,** police d'assurance (contre l')incendie.

policyholder ['pɒlɪsɪhəʊldər] *n* assuré, -ée.

polio ['pəʊlɪəʊ] *n Med* polio *f*; **to have p.,** avoir la polio.

poliomyelitis [pəʊlɪəʊmaɪə'laɪtɪs] *n Med* poliomyélite *f*.

polish¹ ['pɒlɪʃ] *n* **(a)** (*finish*) poli *m*, brillant *m*, lustre *m* (*d'une surface etc*); brunissure *f* (*des métaux*); **high p.,** poli brillant; **to lose its p.,** se dépolir; **to take the p. off sth,** dépolir qch, ternir qch; **to give the table a p.,** cirer la table; **(b)** (*substance*) crème *f ou* pâte *f* à polir; **boot** *or* **shoe p.,** cirage *m ou* crème pour chaussures; **floor p.,** encaustique *f ou* cire *f* à parquet; **metal p.,** produit *m* pour faire briller les métaux *m inv*; **nail p.,** vernis *m* à ongles; **(c)** (*refinement*) belles manières, savoir-vivre *m inv*; **to have a certain p.,** avoir un certain savoir-vivre; **to lack p.,** manquer d'éducation *ou* de savoir-vivre.

polish² *vt* **(a)** polir (*le bois, le fer, etc*); brunir (*l'or, l'argent*); cirer (*des chaussures*); astiquer (*le cuivre etc*); lisser (*une pierre etc*); encaustiquer (*les meubles, les dalles*); cirer (*le parquet*); glacer, polir (*le riz*); **(b)** (*make more refined*) polir, dégrossir (*qn, les mœurs*).

Polish ['pəʊlɪʃ] **1** *adj* polonais. **2** *n Ling* polonais *m*.

►**polish off** *vtsep F* expédier, dépêcher (*un travail*); vider (*un verre*); achever (*un plat*); expédier (*un repas*); régler le compte de, en finir avec (*qn*); (*put finishing touch to*) mettre la dernière main à (*un travail*).

►**polish up** *vtsep* **(a)** faire reluire (*qch*); astiquer, brunir, lustrer (*des objets en cuivre*); **(b)** (*improve*) dérouiller (*son français*); polir (*son style*).

polished ['pɒlɪʃt] *adj* **(a)** poli; (*bois*) ciré; **(b)** (*manners etc*) poli, distingué; **(c)** (*style etc*) châtié, raffiné.

polisher ['pɒlɪʃər] *n* **(a)** (*person*) polisseur, -euse, brunisseur, -euse (*de métaux etc*); astiqueur, -euse (*de cuivre etc*); **(b)** (*tool*) instrument *m* à polir, polissoir *m*; brunissoir *m* (*pour métaux*); **electric floor p.,** cireuse *f* électrique à parquet.

polishing ['pɒlɪʃɪŋ] *n* polissage *m*, brunissage *m*; cirage *m* (*des chaussures etc*); encaustiquage *m* (*des meubles, des parquets*); astiquage *m* (*des cuirs etc*).

politburo ['pɒlɪtbjʊərəʊ] *n Pol* politburo *m*.

polite [pə'laɪt] *adj* **(a)** (*courteous*) poli, courtois (**to s.o.,** envers, avec qn); **p. refusal,** refus poli; **to be p.,** être poli; **(b)** (*cultivated, refined*) **p. society,** (*well-mannered people*) les gens bien élevés; **this word is not used in p. society,** ce mot ne s'utilise pas chez les gens bien élevés.

politeness [pə'laɪtnɪs] *n* politesse *f*, courtoisie *f*.

politic ['pɒlɪtɪk] *adj* **(a)** (*person, conduct*) politique, avisé; *Pej* rusé, astucieux; **it would not be p. to ...,** ce ne serait pas prudent de ...; **(b) the body p.,** le corps politique; (*the state*) l'État *m*.

political [pə'lɪtɪk(ə)l] *adj* **(a)** (*parti etc*) politique; **he isn't very p.,** il n'a pas une très forte conscience politique; **she's a very p. animal,** elle ne pense qu'en termes de politique; **p. beliefs,** opinions *fpl* politiques; **p. prisoner,** prisonnier *m* politique; **p. science,** sciences *fpl* politiques; **(b)** *Fig* **things are getting far too p. in the office,** ça devient vraiment intenable au bureau avec toutes ces manigances *ou F* magouilles; **it's normally the more p. sort of executive who will succeed,** d'habitude, le cadre qui réussit le mieux, c'est celui qui s'y connaît le plus en manigances *ou F* magouilles *ou* qui est le plus doué pour les manigances *ou F* magouilles.

politically [pə'lɪtɪklɪ] *adv* **(a)** politiquement; **(b)** *Fig* **p., that wouldn't be a wise thing to say,** du point de vue tactique, ce ne serait pas une chose à dire.

politician [pɒlɪ'tɪʃən] *n* **(a)** homme *ou* femme politique; *esp Pej* politicien, -ienne; **(b)** *esp Am Pej* politicard *m*.

politicize [pə'lɪtɪsaɪz] **1** *vt* politiser (*un débat, un problème etc*). **2** *vi* (*talk politics*) parler politique.

politicking ['pɒlɪtɪkɪŋ] *n* activité électorale en vue d'obtenir des suffrages.

politico-economical [pə'lɪtɪkəʊiːkə'nɒmɪk(ə)l] *adj* politico-économique.

politics ['pɒlɪtɪks] *npl* (*usu with sing verb*) la politique; **to be interested in p.,** être intéressé par la politique; **to talk p.,** parler politique; **foreign p.,** politique étrangère; **office p.,** intrigues *fpl* de bureau; **his p. are right of centre,** (politiquement parlant,) il se situe à droite; **what are her p.?,** de quel bord est-elle?

polity ['pɒlɪtɪ] *n Pol* **(a)** (*state*) constitution *f* politique; régime *m*; État *m*; **(b)** (*management*) administration *f* politique.

polka ['pɒlkə] *n Mus* polka *f*; *Tex* **blue p. dot tie,** cravate bleue à pois (blancs).

poll¹ [pəʊl] *n* vote *m* par tête; vote *m* (par bulletins), scrutin *m*; **(public) opinion p.,** sondage *m* d'opinion; **to go to the polls,** aller aux urnes; **to head the p.,** arriver en tête de scrutin; **heavy/light p.,** forte/faible participation électorale; *Br* **p. tax,** = impôt local.

poll² **1** *vt* **(a)** (*of polling clerk*) recueillir le bulletin de vote de (*qn*); (*of candidate*) réunir (*tant de voix*); **to p. a vote for s.o.,** donner sa voix à *ou* voter pour qn; **(b)** étêter, écimer (*un arbre*); décorner (*un taureau etc*). **2** *vi* voter (*à une élection*); aller aux urnes.

poll³ *n* (*animal*) (vache *f etc*) sans cornes.

pollard¹ ['pɒləd] *n* (*tree*) arbre étêté; (*animal*) animal *m* sans cornes.

pollard² *vt* étêter, écimer (*un arbre*).

pollen ['pɒlən] *n Bot* pollen *m*; **p. sac,** sac *m* pollinique; **p. count,** taux *m* de pollen.

pollinate ['pɒlɪneɪt] *vt Bot* polliniser.

pollination [pɒlɪ'neɪʃən] *n Bot* pollinisation *f*, fécondation *f*; **self p.,** pollinisation directe; **cross p.,** pollinisation croisée.

polling ['pəʊlɪŋ] *n* scrutin *m*, élections *fpl*; **p. day,** jour *m* des élections *ou* du scrutin; **p. booth,** isoloir *m*; **p. station,** bureau *m* de vote.

polliwog ['pɒlɪwɒg] *n Am* (*tadpole*) têtard *m*.

pollster ['pəʊlstər] *n Am* = enquêteur, -euse ou organisateur, -trice d'un sondage.

pollutant [pə'luːtənt] *n* polluant *m*.

pollute [pə'luːt] *vt* **(a)** polluer (*une rivière etc*); **(b)** profaner, violer (*un lieu saint etc*).

polluter [pə'luːtər] *n* pollueur, -euse.

pollution [pə'luːʃən] *n* **(a)** (*contamination*) pollution *f*, souillure *f*; **atmospheric p., p. of the atmosphere,** pollution atmosphérique *ou* de l'air; **the river is full of p.,** la rivière est très polluée; **(b)** (*of holy ground*) profanation *f*.

Polly ['pɒlɪ] *n F* **(a)** (*dimin of* **Mary**) Marie *f*, Mariette *f*; **(b)** (*parrot*) **(pretty) P.,** = Jacquot *m*.

Pollyanna [pɒlɪ'ænə] *n esp Am* optimiste *mf*.

pollywog ['pɒlɪwɒg] *n Am* (*tadpole*) têtard *m*.

polo ['pəʊləʊ] *n Sp* polo *m*; **to play p.,** jouer au polo; **p. pony,** poney *m* de polo; **p. stick,** maillet *m*; **p. neck,** col roulé; **p. neck sweater,** pullover *m* à col roulé.

polonaise [pɒlə'neɪz] *n Mus* polonaise *f*.

poltergeist ['pɒltəgaɪst] *n* esprit frappeur.

poly ['pɒlɪ] *n Br F* = **POLYTECHNIC 2**.

polyandrous [pɒlɪ'ændrəs] *adj Bot etc* polyandre.

polyandry [pɒlɪ'ændrɪ] *n* polyandrie *f*.

polyanthus [pɒlɪ'ænθəs] *n* (*plant*) primevère *f* des jardins.

polychrom(at)ic [pɒlɪkrəʊ'mætɪk, -'krəʊmɪk] *adj* polychrome.

polychrome ['pɒlɪkrəʊm] **1** *adj* polychrome. **2** *n* polychromie *f*.

polyclinic [pɒlɪ'klɪnɪk] *n Med* polyclinique *f*.

polyester [pɒlɪ'estər] *n Ch* polyester *m*.

polyethylene [pɒlɪ'eθɪliːn] *n esp Am Ch* polyéthylène *m*, polythène *m*.

polygamist [pə'lɪgəmɪst] *n* polygame *mf*.

polygamous [pə'lɪgəməs] *adj* polygame.

polygamy [pə'lɪgəmɪ] *n* polygamie *f*.

polyglot ['pɒlɪglɒt] *adj & n* polyglotte *mf*.

polygon ['pɒlɪgən] *n Math* polygone *m*.

polygonal [pə'lɪgən(ə)l] *adj Math etc* polygonal, -aux.

polygraph ['pɒlɪgræf] *n* détecteur *m* de mensonges; **to take a p. test,** subir un test au détecteur de mensonges.

polyhedron [pɒlɪ'hiːdrən] *n Math* polyèdre *m*.

polymer ['pɒlɪmər] *n Ch* polymère *m*.

polymerization [pɒlɪməraɪ'zeɪʃən] *n Ch* polymérisation *f*.

polymorphic [pɒlɪ'mɔːfɪk], **polymorphous** [pɒlɪ'mɔːfəs] *adj Biol Ch* polymorphe, polymorphique.

polymorphism [pɒlɪ'mɔːfɪz(ə)m] *n Biol Ch* polymorphisme *m*, polymorphie *f*.

Polynesia [pɒlɪ'niːzɪə] *n* Polynésie *f*.

Polynesian [pɒlɪ'niːzɪən] **1** *adj* polynésien. **2** *n* Polynésien, -ienne.

polyneuritis [pɒlɪnjʊ'raɪtɪs] *n Med* polynévrite *f*.

polynomial [pɒlɪ'nəʊmɪəl] *n Math* polynôme *m*.

polyp ['pɒlɪp] *n Zool & Med* polype *m*.

polyphase ['pɒlɪfeɪz] *adj El* polyphasé.

polyphonic [pɒlɪ'fɒnɪk] *adj Mus Ling* polyphonique.

polyphony [pə'lɪfənɪ] *n Mus Ling* polyphonie *f*.

polypropylene [pɒlɪ'prəʊpɪliːn] *n Ch* polypropène *m*, polypropylène *m*.

polypus ['pɒlɪpəs] *n Med* polype *m*.

polysaccharide [pɒlɪ'sækəraɪd] *n Ch* polysaccharide *m*, polyoside *m*.

polystyrene [pɒlɪ'staɪriːn] *n Ch* polystyrène *m*; **p. packaging,** un emballage en polystyrène.

polysyllabic [pɒlɪsɪ'læbɪk] *adj* polysyllabe, polysyllabique.

polysyllable ['pɒlɪsɪləb(ə)l] *n* polysyllabe *m*.

polytechnic [pɒlɪ'teknɪk] **1** *adj* polytechnique. **2** *n Br Sch* ≈ Institut *m* universitaire de technologie.

polytheism ['pɒlɪθiːɪz(ə)m] *n* polythéisme *m*.

polytheistic [pɒlɪθiː'ɪstɪk] *adj* polythéiste.

polythene ['pɒlɪθiːn] *n* polyéthylène *m*, polythène *m*; **p. bag,** sac *m* en plastique.

polyunsaturated [pɒlɪʌn'sætjʊreɪtɪd] *adj Ch* polyinsaturé; **p. fats,** graisses polyinsaturées.

polyurethane [pɒlɪ'jʊərɪθeɪn] *n Ch etc* polyuréthane *m*.

polyvalent [pɒlɪ'veɪlənt] *adj Ch* polyvalent.

polyvinyl [pɒlɪ'vaɪnɪl] *n Ch* polyvinyle *m*; **p. chloride,** chlorure *m* de polyvinyle.

pom [pɒm] *n Austr F* Anglais, -aise.

pomegranate ['pɒmɪgrænɪt] *n* **(a)** (*fruit*) grenade *f*; **(b) p. (tree),** grenadier *m*.

Pomerania [pɒmə'reɪnɪə] *n* Poméranie *f*.

Pomeranian [pɒmə'reɪnɪən] **1** *n* (*dog*) loulou *m* (de Poméranie). **2** *adj* de Poméranie; **P. dog,** loulou *m* (de Poméranie).

pommel¹ ['pɒm(ə)l] *n* **(a)** pommeau *m* (*d'épée*); **(b)** pommeau *m* (*de selle*); **(c)** *Gym* **p. horse,** cheval *m* d'arçons.

pommel² *vt* (**-ll-**, *US* **-l-**) battre, rosser (*qn*), bourrer (*qn*) de coups.

pommie, pommy ['pɒmɪ] *n Austr F* Anglais, -aise; **p. bastard,** salaud *m* d'Anglais, sale Anglaise.

pomp [pɒmp] *n* pompe *f*, éclat *m*, faste *m*; **p. and circumstance,** (grand) apparat *m*.

Pompeii [pɒm'peiː] *n* Pompéi.

pom-pom ['pɒmpɒm] *n Mil* canon-mitrailleuse *m*, *pl* canons-mitrailleuses (*système Maxim*).

pompom, pompon ['pɒmpɒm, -pɒn] *n* (*tuft*) pompon *m*.

pomposity [pɒm'pɒsɪtɪ] *n Pej* emphase *f*, suffisance *f*.

pompous ['pɒmpəs] *adj Pej* (*person*) suffisant, qui fait l'important; (*style*) emphatique, pompeux.

pompously ['pɒmpəslɪ] *adv Pej* (*see adj*) avec suffisance; avec emphase.

pompousness ['pɒmpəsnɪs] *n Pej* (*of person*) suffisance *f*; (*of style*) emphase *f*.

ponce¹ [pɒns] *n esp Br Sl* **(a)** (*effeminate man*) homme efféminé; **(b)** (*pimp*) maquereau *m*.

ponce² *vi esp Br Sl* (*of pimp*) maquer.

▸**ponce about, ponce around** *vi Br Sl* **(a)** (*waste time*) glandouiller; **(b)** (*of effeminate man*) se pavaner.

poncey ['pɒnsɪ] *adj esp Br Sl* (*manner etc*) efféminé.

poncho, *pl* **-os** ['pɒntʃəʊ, -əʊz] *n* poncho *m*.

poncy ['pɒnsɪ] *adj esp Br Sl* (*manner etc*) efféminé.

pond [pɒnd] *n* étang *m*; bassin *m*, pièce *f* d'eau (*de parc*);

mare *f* (*de village*); vivier *m*, réservoir *m* (*pour le poisson*); réservoir (*de moulin*); **p. life,** = vie animale des eaux stagnantes.

ponder ['pɒndər] **1** *vt* réfléchir sur (*une question*); considérer, peser (*un avis*); méditer (sur) (*la situation*); ruminer (*une idée*). **2** *vi* méditer; **to p. on** *or* **over sth,** réfléchir à *ou* méditer sur qch.

ponderable ['pɒndərəb(ə)l] *adj* pondérable.

ponderous ['pɒndərəs] *adj* **(a)** (*large*) massif, lourd, pesant; **(b)** (*travail*) laborieux; **(c)** (*style*) lourd, pesant.

ponderously ['pɒndərəslı] *adv* lourdement.

pondweed ['pɒndwiːd] *n* (*plant*) épi *m* d'eau.

pone [pəʊn] *n US* **(corn) p., p. bread,** pain *m* de maïs.

pong[1] [pɒŋ] *n Br F* puanteur *f*; **what a p.!,** comme ça pue!

pong[2] *vi Br F* puer, schlinguer.

pontiff ['pɒntıf] *n Rel* pontife *m*; **the sovereign p.,** le souverain pontife.

pontifical [pɒn'tıfık(ə)l] **1** *adj* **(a)** *Rel* pontifical, -aux; **(b)** *Pej* pontifiant. **2** *n* (*book*) pontifical *m*.

pontificate[1] [pɒn'tıfıkeıt] *n Rel* pontificat *m*.

pontificate[2] *vi Rel & Pej* pontifier.

Pontius Pilate ['pɒnʃəs'paılət] *n Bible* Ponce Pilate.

pontoon[1] [pɒn'tuːn] *n* **(a)** (*float*) ponton *m*; **(b)** *Mil* bateau *m* (*d'un pont de bateaux*); **p. bridge,** pont *m* de bateaux, pont flottant; **(c)** *Av* (*on aeroplane*) flotteur *m*.

pontoon[2] *n Cards* vingt-et-un *m*.

pony ['pəʊnı] *n* **(a)** (*animal*) poney *m*; *US* (*small horse*) petit cheval, *esp* mustang *m*; *US* **cow p.,** cheval de ranch; **p. trekking,** randonnées *fpl* à dos de poney; **(b)** *Br Sl* vingt-cinq livres sterling; **(c)** *US Sch F* (*in exam*) traduction *f* (juxtalinéaire); **(d)** (*drinking glass*) petit verre (sans pied); **(e) p. engine,** *Rail Old-fashioned* locomotive *f* de manœuvre.

ponytail ['pəʊnıteıl] *n* (*hairstyle*) queue *f* de cheval.

pooch [puːtʃ] *n Sl* (*dog*) cabot *m*, clebs *m*.

poodle ['puːd(ə)l] *n* caniche *mf*.

poof [pʊf], **poofter** ['pʊftər] *n Br Offensive Sl* pédé *m*, tante *f*.

poofy ['pʊfı] *adj Br Sl* de pédé; **to look p.,** avoir l'air d'un pédé.

pooh [puː] **1** *int* bah! peuh! **2** *n* (*in children's language*) (*faeces*) caca *m*.

pooh-pooh ['puː'puː] *vt* traiter légèrement, ridiculiser (*une idée, une théorie etc*); se moquer de, faire peu de cas de (*une idée, un avertissement*); repousser (*un conseil*) avec mépris.

pool[1] [puːl] *n* mare *f*; (*puddle*) flaque *f* (*d'eau etc*); (*ornamental*) pièce *f* d'eau; (*left on beach by tide*) bâche *f*; clame *m* (*dans une rivière*); **(swimming) p.,** piscine *f*; **paddling p.,** pataugeoire *f*; **lying in a p. of blood,** étendu dans une mare de sang.

pool[2] *n* **(a)** (*group etc*) groupe *m* (*de travail*); *Com* groupement *m* (*pour opérations en commun*), pool *m*; syndicat *m* de placement (*de marchandises etc*); *Econ* fonds commun, *F* pool; **typing p.,** central *m* dactylographique, pool de dactylos; **(b)** (*in games*) (*kitty*) poule *f*, cagnotte *f*; *Billiards Fencing* poule; **(c)** *Br* **football pools,** *F* **the pools,** = concours de pronostics de matchs de football.

pool[3] *vt* mettre en commun (*ses capitaux, ses bénéfices etc*); grouper (*ses moyens*); *Com etc* grouper (*les commandes*); **we pooled our resources,** nous avons fait bourse commune.

pool[4] *n* (*game*) billard américain; **p. hall,** salle *f* de billard; **p. table,** (table *f* de) billard.

poolroom ['puːlrʊm] *n Am* salle *f* de billard.

poop [puːp] *n Nau* **(a) p. (deck),** (pont *m* de) dunette *f*; gaillard *m* d'arrière; **(b)** (*raised part*) poupe *f*.

pooped [puːpt] *adj Sl* (*exhausted*) claqué, vanné.

poor [pʊər] **1** *adj* **(a)** (*having little wealth*) pauvre; **a p. man/woman,** un pauvre/une pauvre; **as p. as a church mouse** *or US* **as Job's cat,** pauvre comme Job; **I'm poorer by a thousand francs,** j'en suis pour mille francs; *Rel* **p. box,** tronc *m* pour les pauvres;

(b) (*inferior*) de mauvaise qualité, mauvais, médiocre; (*qualité*) inférieur; (*santé*) débile; (*sol*) maigre, peu fertile; (*temps*) mauvais; **p. harvest,** mauvaise récolte; **p. excuse,** piètre excuse; **I've a p. memory,** je n'ai pas de mémoire; **to be p. at maths,** être faible en math(s); **his French is very p.,** son français est très faible; **to cut a p. figure,** faire piètre figure; **the patient had a p. night,** le malade a passé une mauvaise nuit; **p. reception,** (*unwelcoming*) mauvais accueil; *Rad etc* mauvaise transmission;

(c) (*to be pitied*) **p. creature!, p. thing!,** pauvre petit!, pauvre petite!; **p. Philippe!,** le pauvre Philippe!; **I'm so sorry for the p. man,** je le plains bien, le pauvre homme; **when p. Alice was alive,** (*of person who has died*) du vivant de la pauvre Alice.

2 *n* **the p.,** (*used as pl*) les pauvres *mpl*.

poorhouse ['pʊəhaʊs] *n Arch* asile *m* des pauvres.

poorly ['pʊəlı] **1** *adv* pauvrement; **p. dressed,** pauvrement vêtu; **p. lit,** mal éclairé; **he did p. in his exams,** il a eu de mauvais résultats aux examens. **2** *adj F* (*person*) souffrant, indisposé; **she's looking p.,** elle a mauvaise mine; **I'm feeling p.,** je ne suis pas dans mon assiette.

poorness ['pʊənıs] *n* **(a)** (*of person, soil*) pauvreté *f* (*du sol*); **(b)** (*inferiority*) médiocrité *f*.

pop[1] [pɒp] **1** *int* crac!, pan!; **to go p.,** éclater, crever; **p. goes the cork!,** paf! le bouchon saute. **2** *n* **(a)** (*sound*) bruit sec (*de bouchon qui saute etc*); **(b)** *Br F* (*fizzy drink*) boisson gazeuse.

pop[2] *v* (-pp-) **1** *vi* **(a)** éclater, péter; (*of cork*) sauter, péter; (*of balloon*) crever; **(b)** *F* (*go quickly*) **to p. over** *or* **across** *or* **down to the grocers,** faire un saut (jusque) chez l'épicier; **I'm going to p. into town,** je vais faire un saut en ville; **to p. into bed,** se glisser dans le lit. **2** *vt* **(a)** crever (*un ballon*); faire sauter (*un bouchon*); **(b)** (*put quickly*) **to p. sth into a drawer,** mettre *ou* fourrer qch dans un tiroir; **to p. one's head out of the window,** sortir (tout à coup) la tête à la fenêtre; **(c)** *F* **then he popped the question,** alors il lui a *ou* m'a demandé de l'épouser; **(d)** *F* **to p. pills,** se bourrer de comprimés; **(e)** *Old fashioned Br Sl* (*pawn*) mettre (*sa montre etc*) en gage *ou* au clou.

pop[3] *n F* papa *m*.

pop[4] *F* **1** *adj* pop; **p. art,** pop'art *m*, pop *m*; **p. music,** musique *f* pop; **p. singer,** chanteur, -euse de pop; **p. song,** chanson *f* pop. **2** *n* pop *f*.

►**pop in** *vi F* entrer en passant *ou* pour un instant (*chez qn*); **I've just popped in,** je ne fais que passer.

►**pop off** *vi* **(a)** *F* (*leave abruptly*) filer, partir; **(b)** *Sl* (*die*) claquer (subitement).

►**pop out** *vi F* (*go out*) sortir; **I only popped out for five minutes,** je ne suis sorti que cinq minutes; **his eyes were popping out of his head,** les yeux lui sortaient de la tête.

►**pop up** *vi F* **(a)** (*rise suddenly*) surgir; **a head popped up through the trap door,** une tête a surgi de la trappe; **(b) this question has popped up again,** cette question est revenue sur le tapis; **he popped up again years later in Miami,** il a fait sa réapparition quelques années après à Miami.

pop. *n abbr* **population.**

popcorn ['pɒpkɔːn] *n* pop-corn *m*.

pope [pəʊp] *n Rel* (*in Roman Catholic Church*) pape *m*; (*in Eastern Orthodox Church*) pope *m*; *Culin* **the p.'s nose,** le croupion.

popemobile ['pəʊpməbiːl] *n* papamobile *f*.

popery ['pəʊpərı] *n Pej* papisme *m*, romanisme *m*.

popeyed ['pɒpaıd] *adj F* (*having protuberant eyes*) aux yeux exorbités; (*with surprise*) aux yeux écarquillés.

popgun ['pɒpgʌn] *n* (*toy*) fusil *m* à bouchon.

popinjay ['pɒpındʒeı] *n Arch* fat *m*, freluquet *m*.

popish ['pəʊpıʃ] *adj Pej* papiste.

poplar ['pɒplər] *n* (*tree*) peuplier *m*.

poplin ['pɒplın] *n Tex* popeline *f*.

popover ['pɒpəʊvər] *n* **(a)** *Culin* (genre *m* de) beignet soufflé; **(b)** (*garment*) robe *f* jumper (pour enfant).

poppadom, poppadum ['pɒpədəm] *n Culin* poppadum *m*.

popper ['pɒpər] *n Br F* (*on clothing, bags etc*) bouton-pression *m*, *pl* boutons-pression.

poppet ['pɒpıt] *n F* **she's a p.,** elle est charmante; **my p.,** (*to boy, man*) mon chéri; (*to girl, woman*) ma chérie; (*to boy or girl*) mon (petit) chou.

poppy ['pɒpı] *n* (*plant*) pavot *m*; **corn p., field p.,** coquelicot *m*, pavot rouge; **opium p.,** pavot somnifère; **p. (coloured), p. red,** rouge coquelicot *m inv*; *F* **P. Day,** anniversaire *m* (du jour) de l'Armistice; **p. seed,** graine(s) *f(pl)* de pavot.

poppycock ['pɒpıkɒk] *n F* bêtises *fpl*, inepties *fpl*.

poppyhead ['pɒpıhed] *n* tête *f* de pavot.

Popsicle ® ['pɒpsık(ə)l] *n Am Culin* ≈ Esquimau ® *m*.

popsy ['pɒpsı] *n Old-Fashioned Br F* pépée *f*, nana *f*.

populace ['pɒpjʊləs] *n* **the p.,** le peuple; *Pej* la populace.

popular ['pɒpjʊlər] *adj* (*person, action etc*) populaire; (*in vogue*) à la mode, en vogue; (*music, song*) populaire; (*of the people*) populaire, du peuple; **to make oneself p.,** se rendre populaire; **his views have not made him p. with the authorities,** à cause de ses opinions, il est mal vu par les autorités; **she is p. with her colleagues,** elle est très populaire auprès de *ou* appréciée par ses collègues; **with p. appeal,** qui plaît au grand public; **this was not a p. decision,** cette décision n'était pas populaire; **p. error,** erreur courante; **p. prices,** prix *mpl* à la portée de tous; **p. work** *or* **treatise,** ouvrage *m* de vulgarisation; **contrary to p. belief,** contrairement à ce que les gens croient.

popularity [pɒpjʊ'lærɪtɪ] *n* popularité *f*; succès *m* (*d'un produit etc*) auprès du (grand) public; **the president's p. has fallen** *or* **diminished,** la popularité du président a baissé; **the sport has gained in p.,** le sport est de plus en plus populaire; **p. rating,** taux *m* de popularité.

popularization [pɒpjʊlərai'zeɪʃən] *n* popularisation *f*; vulgarisation *f* (*d'une science etc*).

popularize ['pɒpjʊləraɪz] *vt* populariser (*une idée, une science*); vulgariser (*des connaissances etc*); propager (*une méthode etc*); rendre (*qn*) populaire; mettre (*une mode etc*) en vogue.

popularly ['pɒpjʊləlɪ] *adv* populairement; **p. known as ...,** (*of plant etc*) dont le nom vulgaire est ...; (*of person*) familièrement appelé ...; **it is p. believed that ...,** les gens croient que ..., il est communément admis que ... .

populate ['pɒpjʊleɪt] *vt* peupler; **densely** *or* **thickly populated country,** pays très peuplé; **sparsely populated,** (*région*) à faible peuplement *ou* population.

population [pɒpjʊ'leɪʃən] *n* population *f*; **p. control,** contrôle *m* démographique; **p. explosion,** explosion *f* démographique; **p. statistics,** statistique(s) *f(pl)* démographique(s).

populism ['pɒpjʊlɪz(ə)m] *n Pol* populisme *m*.

populist ['pɒpjʊlɪst] *Pol* **1** *n* populiste *mf*. **2** *adj* populiste.

populous ['pɒpjʊləs] *adj* populeux, très peuplé.

pop-up ['pɒpʌp] *adj* (*grille-pain*) automatique; *Comptr* **p.-up menu,** menu déroulant de bas en haut.

porcelain ['pɔːslɪn] *n* porcelaine *f*; **p. manufacturer,** porcelainier *m*; **p. plate,** assiette *f* en porcelaine.

porch [pɔːtʃ] *n* **(a)** (*over door*) porche *m*; **(glass) p.,** marquise *f* (*d'hôtel etc*); **p. roof,** auvent *m*; **(b)** *Am* (*veranda*) véranda *f*.

porcine ['pɔːsaɪn] *adj* porcin, de porc.

porcupine ['pɔːkjʊpaɪn] **(a)** (*animal*) porc-épic *m*, *pl* porcs-épics; **(b) p. fish,** poisson-globe *m*.

pore [pɔːr] *n Anat Bot etc* pore *m*.

▶**pore over** *vipo* (*examine closely*) se plonger dans la lecture *ou* dans l'étude de (*un livre*); être plongé dans (*un livre*); **to p. over a map,** étudier soigneusement une carte; **to p. over a problem,** méditer longuement un problème.

pork [pɔːk] *n* **(a)** (viande *f* de) porc *m*; **salt p.,** porc salé; **roast p.,** rôti *m* de porc; **p. chop,** côtelette *f* de porc; **p. pie,** pâté *m* de porc en croûte; **p.-pie hat,** chapeau de feutre rond à forme aplatie; **(b)** *US F Pol* **the p. barrel,** ≈ l'assiette au beurre.

porker ['pɔːkər] *n* **(a)** (*young pig*) jeune porc engraissé, destiné à la boucherie; **(b)** *F* (*fat person*) cochon *m*.

porn [pɔːn] *F* **1** *n* pornographie *f*; **soft/hard p.,** pornographie soft/hard. **2** *adj* porno.

pornographic [pɔːnə'græfɪk] *adj* pornographique.

pornography [pɔː'nɒgrəfɪ] *n* pornographie *f*.

porosity [pɔː'rɒsɪtɪ] *n* porosité *f*.

porous ['pɔːrəs] *adj* poreux, perméable.

porousness ['pɔːrəsnɪs] *n* porosité *f*.

porphyry ['pɔːfɪrɪ] *n Miner* porphyre *m*.

porpoise ['pɔːpəs] *n* (*animal*) marsouin *m*.

porridge ['pɒrɪdʒ] *n* **(a)** *Culin* bouillie *f* d'avoine, porridge *m*; **p. oats,** flocons *mpl* d'avoine; **(b)** *Br Sl* **to do p.,** purger sa peine en prison.

porringer ['pɒrɪndʒər] *n Arch* écuelle *f*.

port¹ [pɔːt] *n* (*harbour, town*) port *m*; **the p. of London,** le port de Londres; **river p.,** port fluvial; **in p.,** au port; **to put into p.,** relâcher; **to call at a p.,** faire escale à un port; *Fig* **any p. in a storm,** (*any place will do*) à la guerre comme à la guerre; **p. of call,** port d'escale *ou* de relâche; **p. of refuge,** port de refuge; **fishing p.,** port de pêche; *Com* **free p.,** port franc; **naval p.,** port de guerre, port militaire; **p. charges** *or* **dues,** droits *mpl* de port.

port² *n* **(a)** *Nau* (*opening*) sabord *m*; **p.(-lid),** mantelet *m ou* panneau *m ou* volet *m* de sabord; contre-sabord *m*, *pl* contre-sabords; **air** *or* **ventilation p.,** sabord d'aération; **gangway p.,** sabord de coupée; **(b)** *Tech* orifice *m*, lumière *f* (*d'un cylindre etc*); **admission** *or* **inlet p.,** orifice *m ou* pipe *f* d'admission; **(c)** *Comptr* port *m*; **input/output p.,** port entrée/sortie; **printer p.,** sortie *f* imprimante.

port³ *n Nau* **p. (side),** bâbord *m*; **land to p.!,** la terre par bâbord!; **on the p. bow,** par bâbord devant.

port⁴ *n* (*wine*) vin *m* de Porto, porto *m*.

portability [pɔːtə'bɪlɪtɪ] *n* transportabilité *f*.

portable ['pɔːtəb(ə)l] **1** *adj* portatif, transportable, mobile, portable. **2** *n* téléviseur *m ou* ordinateur *m etc* portable *ou* portatif; *Comptr* portable *m*, portatif *m*.

portage ['pɔːtɪdʒ] *n* **(a)** (*transport*) transport *m*, port *m* (*de marchandises*); (*of canoe etc between waterways*) portage *m*; **(b)** (*costs*) frais *mpl* de port *ou* de transport.

portal ['pɔːt(ə)l] *n Archit* portail *m* (*de cathédrale*).

portcullis [pɔːt'kʌlɪs] *n* (*of castle*) herse *f*, sarrasine *f*.

portend [pɔː'tend] *vt* présager, augurer, faire pressentir (*qch*).

portent ['pɔːtent] *n* **(a)** (*sign*) présage *m*; **(b)** (*event*) prodige *m*; **(c)** (*importance*) portée *f*.

portentous [pɔː'tentəs] *adj* **(a)** (*ominous*) de mauvais présage *ou* augure; **(b)** (*amazing*) prodigieux; **(c)** (*solemn*) solennel; **(d)** (*over-serious*) pompeux, pontifiant.

porter¹ ['pɔːtər] *n* **(a)** *Rail* porteur *m* (*de bagages etc*); chasseur *m*, garçon *m* (*d'hôtel*); *Am Rail* garçon *m* (*de wagon-lit etc*); **(b)** *esp Br* (*doorkeeper*) portier *m*, concierge *m* (*de musée etc*); concierge (*d'un immeuble*); **p.'s lodge,** loge *f* de concierge; maisonnette *f* du portier (*à l'entrée d'une grande propriété*).

porter² *n Br* (*beer*) bière brune (anglaise), porter *m*.

porterage ['pɔːtərɪdʒ] *n* **(a)** (*carrying*) transport *m*, factage *m* (*de marchandises, de colis*); **(b)** (*cost*) prix *m* de transport, factage *m*.

porterhouse ['pɔːtəhaʊs] *n Culin* **p. steak,** = châteaubriand *m*.

portfolio [pɔːt'fəʊlɪəʊ] *n* **(a)** serviette *f* (*pour documents etc*); carton *m* (*à dessins, à estampes*); **candidates are asked to bring a p. of their recent work,** on a demandé aux candidats d'apporter un dossier contenant leurs travaux récents; **minister's p.,** portefeuille *m* de ministre; **minister without p.,** ministre *m* sans portefeuille; **(b)** *Fin* (*of shares*) portefeuille *m*; **securities in p.,** valeurs *fpl* en portefeuille.

porthole ['pɔːthəʊl] *n Nau* sabord *m*, hublot *m*.

portico, *pl* **-o(e)s** ['pɔːtɪkəʊ, -əʊz] *n Archit* portique *m*.

portion¹ ['pɔːʃən] *n* **(a)** (*part*) partie *f*; part *f* (*dans un partage*); portion *f*, ration *f* (*de viande etc*); **the portions there are small/big,** les portions y sont petites/grosses; **this p. to be given up,** (*on ticket*) côté *m* à détacher; *Jur* **p. (of inheritance),** part d'héritage; **(marriage) p.,** dot *f*; **(b)** *Arch & Lit* (*destiny*) destinée *f*, sort *m*.

portion² *vt* = **PORTION OUT**.

▶**portion out** *vtsep* partager (*un bien etc*); répartir (*une somme*); distribuer (*les parts*).

portliness ['pɔːtlɪnɪs] *n* corpulence *f*, embonpoint *m*.

portly ['pɔːtlɪ] *adj* corpulent, ventru.

portmanteau, *pl* **-eaus, -eaux** [pɔːt'mæntəʊ, -əʊz] *n* valise *f*; **p. word,** mot-valise *m*, *pl* mots-valises.

portrait ['pɔːtreɪt] *n Art & Fig* portrait *m*; **to have one's p. painted, to sit for one's p.,** se faire peindre; **p. painter,** portraitiste *mf*; **p. bust,** (portrait en) buste *m*; **p. gallery,** galerie *f* de portraits.

portraitist ['pɔːtrətɪst] *n* portraitiste *mf*.

portraiture ['pɔːtrətjər] *n* **(a)** (*picture*) portrait *m*; **(b)** (*art*) art *m* du portrait.

portray [pɔː'treɪ] *vt* **(a)** (*depict*) dépeindre, décrire (*une scène etc*); **in the film the soldiers are portrayed as monsters,** dans le film les soldats sont dépeints comme des monstres; **(b)** *Arch & Lit* (*paint portrait of*) faire le portrait de (*qn*).

portrayal [pɔː'treɪəl] *n* **(a)** (*depiction*) peinture *f*, description *f* (*d'une scène, des mœurs d'une époque*); *Th Cin* (*by actor, actress*) interprétation *f*; **(b)** *Arch & Lit* (*portrait*) portrait *m*.

Portugal ['pɔːtjʊg(ə)l] *n* Portugal *m*.

Portuguese [pɔːtjʊ'giːz] **1** *adj* portugais; **P. man of war,** (*jellyfish*) physalie *f*, galère *f*. **2** *n* **(a)** Portugais, -aise; **(b)** *Ling* portugais *m*.

pose¹ [pəʊz] *n* **(a)** pose *f*, attitude *f* (*du corps*); pose (*d'un modèle*); **to strike a p.,** (*of model*) prendre une pose; **(b)** (*affectation*) pose *f*, affectation *f*; **it's just a p.,** c'est juste un air qu'il *ou* elle *etc* se donne.

pose² **1** *vt* **(a)** *Art* faire prendre une pose à (*qn*) (*pour son portrait*); faire poser (*un modèle*); **(b)** poser (*un problème*); émettre, énoncer (*une opinion*). **2** *vi* poser (*pour son portrait*); poser (*comme modèle*); *F* (*affect behaviour*) poser, se donner des airs (affectés); **to p. for s.o.,** (*as a model*) poser pour qn; **young men posing in motorbike jackets,** des jeunes gens se donnant des airs avec leurs blousons de moto; **to p. as a Frenchman,** se faire passer pour un Français; **to p. as a socialist,** se faire passer pour un socialiste.

poser ['pəʊzər] *n F* **(a)** (*difficult question*) colle *f*; **to give**

s.o. a p., poser une colle à qn; **(b)** *Pej* (*person*) poseur, -euse.

poseur [pəʊ'zɜːr] *n* = **POSER (b)**.

posh [pɒʃ] *adj Br F* **(a)** *occ Pej* (*upper-class*) bien, comme il faut, distingué; **p. accent**, accent distingué; **a p. area**, un quartier chic *ou* bourgeois; **(b)** (*nice-looking, sounding etc*) chic; **it looks p.**, ça fait bien.

posit ['pɒzɪt] *vt Phil etc* avancer (*une proposition*); poser en principe (**that**, que).

position¹ [pə'zɪʃən] *n* **(a)** (*posture etc*) position *f*, posture *f*, attitude *f* (*du corps*); **horizontal/vertical p.**, position horizontale/verticale; **prone p.**, position couchée;

(b) (*mental, attitude*) position *f*, point *m* de vue; **to take up an uncompromising p.**, adopter une attitude intransigeante (**about sth**, à l'égard de qch); **what is the American p. on this issue?**, quelle est la position des Américains sur ce problème?; **her p. is that ...**, ce qu'elle pense c'est que ..., son point de vue est que ...;

(c) (*place*) position *f*; place *f* (*d'un objet*); situation *f* (*d'une ville etc*); *Banking etc* guichet *m*; *Av Nau* position (*d'un avion, d'un navire*); *Mil* emplacement *m*, position; **in p.**, en place; **out of p.**, déplacé; **to put** *or* **get sth into p.**, mettre qch en place; *Fb* **what p. do you play?**, en quelle position jouez-vous?, quelle est votre position sur le terrain?; *Nau* **to take up p. ahead/astern**, prendre poste en tête/derrière; **p. closed**, (*in bank etc*) guichet fermé; **estimated p.**, point estimé; **to fix** *or* **work out one's p.**, faire le point; **p. finding**, orientation *f*; *Mil* goniométrie *f*; *Mil* **to move into p.**, se mettre en place *ou* en position; **to bring guns into p.**, mettre des pièces en batterie *ou* en position; **defensive p.**, position défensive *ou* de défense; **p. warfare**, guerre *f* de position;

(d) (*situation*) état *m*, situation *f*; (*social status*) condition *f*, état, rang social; **to be in an awkward p.**, se trouver dans une situation difficile *ou* délicate; **to be in a strong p.**, être bien placé; **put yourself in my p.**, mettez-vous à ma place; **to be in a p. to do sth**, être à même *ou* en mesure *ou* en état de faire qch; **financial p.**, situation financière; **what is the p. of the firm?**, quelle est la situation (financière) de cette maison?; **to keep up one's p.**, (*in society*) tenir son rang; **to be in seventh p.**, (*in race etc*) être en septième position;

(e) *Old-fashioned* (*job*) emploi *m*, situation *f*; **to work one's way up to a good p.**, se faire une belle situation; **key p.**, position *f* clef; **p. of trust**, poste *m* de confiance.

position² *vt* **(a)** (*place*) mettre (*qch, des troupes*) en place *ou* en position; **(b)** (*locate*) déterminer la position de (*qch*); **(c)** (*in marketing*) positionner.

positioning [pə'zɪʃənɪŋ] *n* mise *f* en place *ou* en position.

positive ['pɒzɪtɪv] **1** *adj* **(a)** (*affirmative*) positif; (*absolute*) (*fait etc*) authentique, indiscutable; **p. answer**, (*yes*) réponse affirmative; (*indicating willingness to do*) réponse positive *ou* favorable; **p. proof**, preuve positive *ou* manifeste; *Med etc* **p. reaction**, réaction positive; *Med* **the test was p.**, le test était positif; *F* **a p. miracle**, un véritable miracle; *F* **it's a p. shame**, c'est une véritable honte;

(b) (*certain*) convaincu, certain, sûr (**of**, de); **I'm p. on that point**, je n'ai aucun doute à ce sujet; **I'm p. (that) I saw him**, je suis certain de l'avoir vu;

(c) (*constructive*) (*person, philosophy*) positif; (*proposition, aide*) constructif; **he described the talks as 'p.'**, il a décrit les discussions comme 'positives'; **p. discrimination** *or* **action**, *Can* action positive;

(d) *Math El* positif; *Phot* **p. print**, positif *m*, épreuve positive;

(e) *Gram* **p. degree**, degré positif (*d'un adjectif, d'un adverbe*).

2 *n* **(a)** *Phil* le positif, la réalité;

(b) *Phot* positif *m*, épreuve positive;

(c) *Gram* degré positif.

positively ['pɒzɪtɪvlɪ] *adv* **(a)** (*affirmatively*) positivement; **the body has not been p. identified**, le corps n'a pas été identifié de façon certaine; *F* **p. not**, absolument pas; **smiling? — she was p. beaming!**, souriante? — elle était littéralement radieuse!; **(b)** (*certainly*) assurément, certainement, sûrement; **(c)** *El* **p. charged**, à charge positive; *MecE* **p. driven**, à commande directe.

positivism ['pɒzɪtɪvɪz(ə)m] *n Phil* positivisme *m*.

positivist ['pɒzɪtɪvɪst] *adj & n Phil* positiviste *mf*.

poss. *adj abbr* **possible**.

posse ['pɒsɪ] *n* détachement *m* (*d'agents de police*); troupe *f*, bande *f* (*de personnes*).

possess [pə'zes] *vt* **(a)** posséder (*un bien*); être en possession de (*qch*); avoir, posséder (*une qualité, une faculté*); **all I p.**, tout mon avoir; *Lit* **to be possessed of a property**, posséder un bien; **(b)** (*of evil spirit*) posséder (*qn*); **possessed by fear**, pris de terreur; *F* **what possessed you to do that?**, qu'est-ce qui vous a pris de faire cela?; **to be possessed with an idea**, être obsédé d'une idée; **to scream like one possessed**, crier comme un possédé; **(c)** *Lit* **to p. oneself in patience**, se munir de patience.

possession [pə'zeʃən] *n* **(a)** (*ownership*) possession *f*, jouissance *f* (**of**, de); **to have sth in one's p.**, avoir qch en sa possession; **to be in p. of sth**, être en possession de qch; **how did the car come into your p.?**, comment la voiture est-elle entrée en votre possession?; **to take p. of an estate, to come** *or* **enter into p. of an estate**, entrer en possession *ou* en jouissance d'un bien; **to take** *or* **get p. of sth**, s'emparer de qch; **the information in my p.**, les renseignements dont je dispose; **in full p. of one's faculties**, en pleine possession de ses facultés; **vacant p.**, libre possession (*d'un immeuble*); **(b)** (*object possessed*); possession *f*; **possessions**, possessions, biens *mpl*, avoir *m*; (*colonies*) possessions, colonies *fpl*; **overseas possessions**, possessions d'outre-mer; **(c)** possession *f* (*par le démon*).

possessive [pə'zesɪv] **1** *adj* **(a)** (*parent etc*) possessif; **(b)** *Gram* **p. adjective/pronoun**, adjectif/pronom possessif; **the p. case**, le cas possessif. **2** *n* adjectif *ou* pronom possessif; **the p.**, le cas possessif.

possessiveness [pə'zesɪvnɪs] *n* possessivité *f*.

possessor [pə'zesər] *n* possesseur *m*.

possibility [pɒsɪ'bɪlɪtɪ] *n* **(a)** possibilité *f*, éventualité *f* (*d'un événement*); **have you considered the p. of his being dead?**, avez-vous envisagé la possibilité qu'il soit mort?; **within the range** *or* **the bounds of p.**, dans la limite du possible; **there's a p. that it will rain**, il est possible qu'il pleuve; **(b)** (*possible event, outcome*) événement *m* possible, éventualité *f*; **that is a distinct p.**, c'est bien possible; **to allow for all possibilities**, parer à toute éventualité; **(c)** (*potential*) (*often pl*) **possibilities**, possibilités *fpl* de succès; **the plan has possibilities**, ce projet offre des chances de succès; **the flat has possibilities**, l'appartement a un bon potentiel.

possible ['pɒsɪb(ə)l] **1** *adj* possible; **it's p.**, c'est possible; **that's quite p.**, c'est très *ou* fort possible; **anything's p.**, tout est possible; **it is p. that he will come**, il se peut qu'il vienne; **is it p. to see her?**; y a-t-il moyen de la voir?; **as cheap/soon/***etc* **as p.**, aussi bon marché/tôt/*etc* que possible; **the best p.**, le meilleur possible; **the shortest p. route**, l'itinéraire le plus court possible; **to give as many details as p.**, donner le plus de détails possible *ou* tous les détails possibles; **what p. interest can you have in it?**, mais quel intérêt cela peut-il donc avoir pour vous?; **there's no p. reason why he should have done it**, il n'avait absolument aucune raison de le faire; **if p.**, (*I will do it*) si possible; **if it's p. to ...**, si c'est possible de ...; **as far as p.**, dans la mesure du possible; **the p. nomination of ...**, la nomination éventuelle de ...; **to insure against p. accidents**, s'assurer contre les accidents éventuels.

2 *n* **(a) it's in the realms of the p.**, c'est dans le domaine du possible;

(b) *F* (*person*) candidat *m* possible *ou* acceptable; (*thing*) chose *f* possible.

possibly ['pɒsɪblɪ] *adv* **(a) I can't p. do it**, il ne m'est pas possible de le faire; **I'll do all I p. can**, je ferai tout mon possible; **you can't p. mean that!**, vous ne pouvez pas dire ça sérieusement!; **I can't p. allow you to do that!**, je ne peux vraiment pas vous permettre de faire cela!; **they can't p. have left yet!**, il est tout à fait impossible qu'ils soient déjà partis; **it can't p. cost that much!**, c'est absolument impossible que ça coûte autant que ça!; **(b)** (*perhaps*) peut-être (bien); **he has p. heard of you**, il se peut qu'il ait entendu parler de vous; **p.!** c'est possible, cela se peut.

possum ['pɒsəm] *n F* (*animal*) opossum *m*; **to play p.**, faire le mort; (*keep low profile*) se tenir coi.

post¹ [pəʊst] *n* **(a)** (*of fence*) pieu *m*; (*of frame*) montant *m*; *Constr etc* poteau *m*, pilier *m*; (*of door, window*) montant, jambage *m*; arbre *m*, fût *m* (*de grue*); **bed p.**, colonne *f* de lit; **telegraph p.**, poteau télégraphique; **(b)** *Min* pilier *m* (*de houille*); **(c)** *Nau* **(stern) p.**, étambot *m*; **(d)** *Horseracing etc* **starting p.**, (poteau *m* de) départ *m*; **winning p.**, (poteau d')arrivée *f*; **(e) to be left at the p.**, rater le départ; **to be beaten** *or F* **pipped at the p.**, se faire coiffer *ou* battre sur le poteau.

post² *vt* **(a)** (*on wall etc*) placarder, coller (*des affiches etc*); afficher (*un avis etc*); placarder (*un mur*); **p. no bills**, (*on sign*) défense d'afficher; **(b)** (*on list*) inscrire *ou* porter (*qn*) sur une liste; (*in marine insurance*) porter (*un navire*) disparu; **to be posted for night duty,** être sur la liste (du personnel) de service de nuit; **to be posted missing,** être porté disparu, être porté manquant.

post[3] *n Br* **(a)** (*mail*) courrier *m*; (*service*) la poste; **by return of p.,** par retour du courrier; **when does the next p. go?,** à quelle heure est la prochaine levée?; **to miss the p.,** manquer la levée; **the first p.,** la première distribution; **there's no p. today,** pas de courrier *ou* pas de lettres aujourd'hui; **the P. Office,** (*government department*) ≈ les Postes et Télécommunications; **p. office,** bureau *m* de poste; **to send sth by p.,** envoyer qch par la poste; **to take a letter to the p.,** porter une lettre à la poste; **p.-office box,** boîte postale; **p. office van,** ≈ camionnette *f* des PTT; **(b)** *Arch* **p. (coach),** (malle-)poste *f*, *pl* malles-poste(s); **p. chaise,** chaise *f* de poste.

post[4] *vt* **(a)** *Br* (*send*) mettre (*une lettre*) à la poste *ou* à la boîte, poster (*une lettre*); **I'll p. it to you,** je vous l'enverrai par la poste; **(b)** (*in bookkeeping*) passer écriture de (*un article*); *F* **I'll keep you posted,** je vous tiendrai au courant.

post[5] *n* **(a)** *Mil etc* poste *m* (*de combat etc*); *US* (*permanent station*) camp *m*, fort *m* (*servant de lieu de garnison*); (*garrison*) garnison *f*; **to be/die at one's p.,** être/mourir à son poste; **advanced** *or* **outlying p.,** (*place, group of men*) poste avancé; **lookout p.,** poste de guet *ou* d'observation; **frontier p.,** poste frontière; **(b)** *Hist* **trading p.,** comptoir *m*, établissement *m* (*aux Indes, au Canada etc*); *Av* **staging p.,** escale aérienne; **(c)** *Fml* (*job*) poste *m*, emploi *m*; **to take up a p.,** entrer en fonction.

post[6] *vt* **(a)** (*assign*) *Mil etc* désigner (*qn*) à un commandement; **to be posted to a different branch,** (*of store, bank*) être muté dans une autre succursale; **to be posted to a unit/a ship,** être affecté à une unité/un navire; **(b)** *Mil etc* (*position*) poster, placer (*qn à un endroit*); poster, placer, mettre en faction (*une sentinelle*); aposter (*un espion*); **she posted herself at the window,** elle s'est postée à la fenêtre.

post[7] *n Br Mil* **first p.,** première partie de la sonnerie de la retraite; **last p.,** dernière partie (de la sonnerie); (*for the dead*) (la) sonnerie aux morts; **to sound the last p. (over the grave),** jouer la sonnerie aux morts.

postage ['pəʊstɪdʒ] *n* affranchissement *m*, port *m* (*d'une lettre etc*); **add 10% (for) p. and packing,** ajouter 10% pour les frais d'emballage et d'expédition; **additional p.,** (*on insufficiently stamped letter*) surtaxe *f* (postale); **p. paid,** port payé; **p. rates,** tarifs postaux; **p. stamp,** timbre(-poste) *m*.

postal ['pəʊst(ə)l] *adj* postal, -aux; **p. charges,** frais *mpl* d'envoi, port *m* (*d'une lettre etc*); **p. order,** mandat postal; **p. services,** les services postaux; *US* **p. card,** carte postale.

postbag ['pəʊstbæg] *n esp Br* sac postal *ou* de dépêches; *Rad TV* **our p. has been heavy this week,** vous avez été nombreux à nous écrire cette semaine.

postbox ['pəʊstbɒks] *n esp Br* boîte *f* aux lettres.

postcard ['pəʊstkɑːd] *n* carte postale.

postcode ['pəʊstkəʊd] *n Br* code postal.

postdate[1] ['pəʊstdeɪt] *n* postdate *f*.

postdate[2] [pəʊst'deɪt] *vt* postdater.

poster ['pəʊstər] *n* affiche murale; placard *m* (*de publicité*); *Art* **p. paint,** gouache *f*.

poste restante ['pəʊstres'tɒnt] *n & adv Br* poste restante.

posterior [pɒs'tɪərɪər] **1** *adj* postérieur (**to,** à). **2** *n F* le postérieur, le derrière (*de qn*).

posterity [pɒs'terɪtɪ] *n* postérité *f*; **to preserve sth for p.,** garder qch pour la postérité.

postern ['pəʊstɜːn] *n* poterne *f*.

postgraduate [pəʊst'grædjʊɪt] **1** *adj* **p. student,** = licencié(e) qui continue ses études; **p. studies,** = études supérieures (après la licence). **2** *n* (*student*) étudiant titulaire de la licence.

posthaste ['pəʊst'heɪst] *adv* en toute hâte.

posthumous ['pɒstjʊməs] *adj* (*œuvre*) posthume.

posthumously ['pɒstjʊməslɪ] *adv* à titre posthume.

postil(l)ion [pɒs'tɪlɪən] *n* postillon *m*, cocher *m*.

postimpressionism [pəʊstɪm'preʃənɪz(ə)m] *n Art* postimpressionnisme *m*.

postimpressionist [pəʊstɪm'preʃənɪst] *adj & n Art* postimpressionniste *mf*.

postindustrial [pəʊstɪn'dʌstrɪəl] *adj* post-industriel.

posting[1] ['pəʊstɪŋ] *n* **(a)** (*sending*) envoi *m* (*d'une lettre*) par la poste; **(b)** (*in bookkeeping*) passation *f* (*d'écritures*).

posting[2] *n Mil etc* **(a)** (*of person*) affectation *f* (*à un poste etc*); **she's got a p. to Switzerland,** elle a été affectée en Suisse; **(b)** mise *f* en faction (*de sentinelles etc*).

postman, *pl* **-men** ['pəʊstmən] *n* facteur *m*; **p.'s knock,** ≈ mariage chinois.

postmark[1] ['pəʊstmɑːk] *n* cachet *m* de la poste, (cachet d')oblitération *f*; **date as p.,** cachet *m* de la poste faisant foi.

postmark[2] *vt* oblitérer (*une lettre*); **the letter was postmarked London,** la lettre était timbrée (au départ) de Londres.

postmaster ['pəʊstmɑːstər] *n* receveur *m* (des postes); **P. General,** = *Arch* ministre des Postes et Télécommunications; *Can* Ministre des Postes.

post meridiem [pəʊstmə'rɪdɪəm] *adv* de l'après-midi, du soir.

postmistress ['pəʊstmɪstrɪs] *n* receveuse *f* des postes.

postmodernism [pəʊst'mɒd(ə)nɪz(ə)m] *n Archit Art etc* post-modernisme *m*.

postmodernist [pəʊst'mɒd(ə)nɪst] *adj n Archit Art* postmoderniste *mf*.

postmortem [pəʊst'mɔːtəm] **1** *adj* **p. examination,** autopsie *f* (*d'un cadavre*); **to hold a p. examination,** faire une autopsie. **2** *n* autopsie *f* (*d'un cadavre*); *Fig* analyse rétrospective *ou* après coup; **please, no postmortems,** inutile de revenir sur ce qui est terminé.

postnatal [pəʊst'neɪt(ə)l] *adj* postérieur à la naissance; (*medical case etc*) post-natal, -als; **p. depression,** dépression post-natale.

postoperative [pəʊst'ɒpərətɪv] *adj Med* (*choc etc*) postopératoire.

post-paid [pəʊst'peɪd] *adj* port payé.

postpone [pəʊst'pəʊn] *vt* remettre, ajourner, renvoyer à plus tard, reculer (*un départ, un projet, une décision etc*); différer, arriérer (*un paiement*); **to p. a matter for a week,** remettre *ou* renvoyer une affaire à huitaine; **postponed action** *or* **trial,** cause remise.

postponement [pəʊst'pəʊnmənt] *n* remise *f* à plus tard; ajournement *m* (*d'une réunion, d'une cause*); renvoi *m* (*d'une cause*).

postposition [pəʊstpə'zɪʃən] *n Gram* postposition *f*.

postprandial [pəʊst'prændɪəl] *adj usu Hum* après le repas; **to go for a p. stroll,** faire une promenade digestive.

postscript ['pəʊsskrɪpt] *n* post-scriptum *m inv*; **by way of p.,** en post-scriptum.

postulant ['pɒstjʊlənt] *n Rel* postulant, -ante.

postulate[1] ['pɒstjʊlɪt] *n* (*logic*) *& Math* postulat *m*.

postulate[2] ['pɒstjʊleɪt] *vt* **(a)** (*logic &*) *Math* postuler (*qch*); poser (*qch*) en postulat; **(b)** postuler, demander, réclamer (*qch*).

posture[1] ['pɒstʃər] *n* posture *f*, pose *f*, attitude *f* (*du corps*); **to have good p.,** avoir une bonne posture, bien se tenir.

posture[2] *vi* (*physically*) prendre une pose; (*in behaviour, attitude*) se donner des airs.

posturing ['pɒstʃərɪŋ] *n* (*physical*) pose *f*; (*in behaviour, attitude*) affectation *f*.

postwar ['pəʊst'wɔːr] *adj* d'après-guerre; **the p. period,** l'après-guerre *m inv*.

posy ['pəʊzɪ] *n* petit bouquet (*de fleurs*).

pot[1] [pɒt] *n* **(a)** (*receptacle*) pot *m*; (*for cooking*) marmite *f*; *Sp Sl* (*trophy*) coupe remportée en prix; **flower p.,** pot à fleurs; **coffee p.,** cafetière *f*; **a p. of tea,** un thé; un thé servi dans une petite théière; **chamber p.,** pot de chambre; **pots and pans,** batterie *f* de cuisine; **it's (a case of) the p. calling the kettle black,** c'est la paille et la poutre; *F* **to go to p.,** (*country, economy*) aller à la ruine; **his health/marriage has gone to p.,** il/son mariage est mal en point, sa santé/son mariage s'est délabré(e); **p. plant,** plante *f* en pot; *F* **to take a p. shot at sth,** (*fire at*) tirer à l'aveuglette sur qch; (*make attempt at*) faire qch au petit bonheur (la chance), faire qch au pif; **(b)** *F* **pots of money,** des tas d'argent; **to have pots of money,** rouler sur l'or; **we have pots of time,** nous avons tout le temps; **(c)** *Sl* (*cannabis*) herbe *f*; (*marijuana*) marijuana *f*; (*hashish*) hachisch *m*.

pot[2] *v*(-tt-) **1** *vt* **(a)** mettre en pot (*le beurre, la viande salée etc*); mettre en pot, empoter (*une plante*); mettre (*un bébé*) sur son pot (*de chambre*); *Billiards* blouser (*une bille*); **(b)** *F* (*shoot*) abattre (*du gibier etc*). **2** *vi* (*shoot*) **to p. at,** lâcher un coup de fusil à (*une pièce de gibier*).

▶**pot on** *vtsep* rempoter (*une plante*).

▶**pot up** *vtsep* mettre en pot, empoter (*une plante*).

potable ['pəʊtəb(ə)l] *adj Fml* potable, buvable.

potash ['pɒtæʃ] *n* potasse *f*.

potassium [pə'tæsɪəm] *n Ch* potassium *m*; **p. chloride,** chlorure *m* de potassium.

potato, *pl* **-oes** [pəˈteɪtəʊ, -əʊz] *n* pomme *f* de terre; **to dig up** *or* **lift potatoes,** arracher des pommes de terre; *Culin* **roast potatoes,** pommes de terre rôties au four; **boiled potatoes,** pommes de terre à l'eau *ou* à l'anglaise; **French fried potatoes,** pommes (de terre) frites, *F* frites *fpl*; **p. crisps,** *Am* **p. chips,** (pommes) chips *mpl*; **mashed potatoes,** purée *f* (de pommes de terre); **baked** *or* **jacket potatoes,** pommes de terre en robe de chambre *ou* en robe des champs; *F* **hot p.,** affaire épineuse; *F* **to drop s.o. like a hot p.,** laisser tomber qn (avant d'avoir des ennuis avec lui); **p. masher,** presse-purée *m inv*; **p. peeler,** économe *m*, éplucheur (de pommes de terre), *F* épluche-patate(s) *m*; **p. salad,** salade *f* de pommes de terre; **sweet p.,** patate *f* (douce).

potbellied [pɒtˈbelɪd] *adj F* ventru, bedonnant.

potbelly [ˈpɒtbelɪ] *n F* gros ventre, bedon *m*.

potboiler [ˈpɒtbɔɪlər] *n F* œuvre *f* alimentaire.

poteen [pɒˈtiːn] *n* = whisky irlandais distillé en fraude.

potency [ˈpəʊtənsɪ] *n* force *f*, puissance (*d'un argument*); efficacité *f*, activité *f* (*d'un médicament*); force, degré *m* (*d'une boisson alcoolique*); **sexual p.,** puissance sexuelle.

potent [ˈpəʊtənt] *adj* (*drug etc*) efficace, puissant, actif; (*motive etc*) convaincant, décisif; (*drink*) très fort; (*poison*) violent; (*man*) viril; (*dictator etc*) puissant.

potentate [ˈpəʊtənteɪt] *n* potentat *m*.

potential [pəˈtenʃəl] **1** *adj Math etc* potentiel; (*danger*) possible, latent; (*ennemi, criminel*) en puissance; (*client*) éventuel; **p. value of mineral deposit,** valeur virtuelle d'un gîte métallifère; *Phys* **p. energy,** énergie potentielle; *Gram* **the p. mood,** le potentiel. **2** *n Phys* potentiel *m* (électrique); *El* tension *f*, potentiel; *Gram* **the p.,** le potentiel; **human p.,** potentiel humain; **to reach one's p.,** atteindre son maximum; **to have p.,** avoir du potentiel; **the building has a lot of** *or* **considerable p.,** le bâtiment offre de grandes possibilités d'aménagement; **this idea has great p.,** cette idée ouvre de grandes possibilités; **there is the p. for a major accident,** tous les risques d'un grave accident sont réunis; *El* **operating p.,** tension *f* de fonctionnement.

potentiality [pətenʃɪˈælɪtɪ] *n* potentialité *f*.

potentially [pəˈtenʃəlɪ] *adv* potentiellement.

pother [ˈpɒðər] *n Dial* (*confusion*) agitation *f*, confusion *f*; (*din*) tapage *m*, vacarme *m*.

pothole [ˈpɒthəʊl] *n Geol* marmite torrentielle *ou* de géants; (*in road*) trou *m*.

potholer [ˈpɒthəʊlər] *n* spéléologue *mf*.

potholing [ˈpɒthəʊlɪŋ] *n* spéléologie *f*; **to go p.,** faire de la spéléologie.

pothook [ˈpɒthʊk] *n* crémaillère *f* (*de foyer*).

pothunter [ˈpɒthʌntər] *n Sl Sp* coureur, -euse de prix.

potion [ˈpəʊʃən] *n* potion *f*; **love p.,** philtre *m* d'amour.

potluck [pɒtˈlʌk] *n F* **to take p.,** choisir au hasard, **it was just p.,** c'était un pur hasard; **come round for a meal, but you'll have to take p.,** venez manger à la maison, mais ça sera à la fortune du pot.

potpourri [pəʊˈpʊərɪ] *n* (*dried flowers*) fleurs séchées; *Mus Liter* pot-pourri *m*, *pl* pots-pourris.

pot-roast [ˈpɒtrəʊst] **1** *n* morceau de viande cuit à l'étouffée. **2** *vt* cuire à l'étouffée.

pottage [ˈpɒtɪdʒ] *n Arch* potage *m* (épais); potée *f* (*de viande et de légumes*); *Bible* **mess of p.,** = plat de lentilles.

potted [ˈpɒtɪd] *adj* (conservé) en pot, en terrine; *F* (*biography etc*) abrégé, condensé; **p. meat,** terrine *f* de porc *etc*; **p. shrimps,** crevettes en conserve cuites dans du beurre.

potter¹ [ˈpɒtər] *n Art* potier *m*; **p.'s clay,** terre *f* de potier *ou* à potier; **p.'s wheel,** tour *m* de potier.

potter² *vi* **(a)** (*do odd jobs*) s'occuper de bagatelles; **(b)** (*walk about slowly*) traîner, traînasser.

▶**potter about, potter around** *vi* **(a)** (*do odd jobs*) s'occuper de bagatelles; **to p. about at odd jobs,** bricoler; **to p. about the house,** faire des petits travaux dans la maison; **(b)** (*move about slowly*) (*of person*) traîner, traînasser; **pottering about in country lanes in her old car,** en se baladant dans les chemins de campagne au volant de sa vieille voiture.

▶**potter along** *vi* (*move slowly in work*) (*of person*) traîner, traînasser; *Aut etc* aller doucement.

pottery [ˈpɒtərɪ] *n* (*art, works*) poterie *f*; **a piece of p.,** une poterie; **some p.,** des poteries.

potting [ˈpɒtɪŋ] *n* mise *f* en pot (*des plantes etc*); *Billiards* mise en blouse; **p. shed,** serre *f* de bouturages.

potty¹ [ˈpɒtɪ] *adj Br F* **(a)** (*crazy*) toqué, timbré; **to go p.,** devenir fou *ou* maboul; **to be p. about s.o./sth,** être toqué de qn/qch; **(b)** (*insignificant*) insignifiant; **a p. little state,** un petit État de rien du tout.

potty² *n* (*in children's language*) pot *m* (de chambre) (*d'enfant*); **p. training,** apprentissage *m* de la propreté; **is he/she p. trained?,** est-ce qu'il/elle est propre?

pouch [paʊtʃ] *n* **(a)** (*small bag*) (petit) sac *m*; (*for money*) bourse *f*; (*of dispatch rider, courier*) sacoche *f*; (*for ammunition*) étui *m*; **tobacco p.,** blague *f* à tabac; **(b)** (*of marsupial*) poche ventrale.

pouf(fe) [puːf] *n* (*item of furniture*) pouf *m*.

poult [pəʊlt] *n* (*young chicken*) (jeune) poulet *m*; (*young turkey*) dindonneau *m*; (*young pheasant, partridge*) pouillard *m*.

poulterer [ˈpəʊltərər] *n* marchand, -ande de volaille.

poultice [ˈpəʊltɪs] *n Med* cataplasme *m*.

poultry [ˈpəʊltrɪ] *n* (*no pl*) volaille *f*; **p. farming,** aviculture *f*, élevage *m* de volaille.

pounce¹ [paʊns] *n* **to make a p. on,** (*of bird, beast*) fondre *ou* s'abattre *ou* bondir sur (*sa proie*); *F* (*of person*) se précipiter *ou* se jeter sur (*qch*).

pounce² *vi* **(a)** (*of bird, beast*) bondir; **to p. on the prey,** fondre *ou* s'abattre *ou* bondir sur la proie; **(b)** *F* (*of person*) se précipiter, se jeter (**on,** sur).

pound¹ [paʊnd] *n* **(a)** (*measurement of weight*) livre *f* (de 453, 6 grammes); **to sell sth by the p.,** vendre qch à la livre; **40 pence a p.,** quarante pence la livre; *Fig* **to demand one's p. of flesh,** exiger son dû de qn; *Culin* **p. cake,** quatre-quarts *m inv*; **(b)** (*currency unit*) **p. (sterling),** livre *f* (sterling); **p. coin,** pièce *f* d'une livre; **p. note,** billet *m* d'une livre; **p. sign,** signe *m* de la livre (sterling).

pound² *n* (*enclosure*) fourrière *f* (*pour animaux errants, pour voitures saisies par la police*).

pound³ *vt* (*enclose*) mettre (*des animaux*) en fourrière.

pound⁴ **1** *vt* (*crush etc*) broyer, piler, concasser (*des pierres etc*); égruger (*du sel, du sucre*); casser, briser (*des mottes de terre*); pilonner (*la terre, une drogue*); battre, rosser (*qn*); *Mil* pilonner, marteler (*une position*); **to p. sth to pieces,** réduire qch en miettes *ou* en morceaux; **to p. the beat,** (*policeman*) patrouiller; **you'll be back to pounding the beat,** (*demoted*) on vous remettra à la circulation; **to p. the streets,** battre le trottoir. **2** *vi* frapper *ou* taper dur; (*of heart*) battre à grands coups; **to p. at** *or* **on sth,** cogner dur sur qch; **to p. on the door,** donner de grands coups à la porte; **feet were heard pounding on the stairs,** on entendait résonner lourdement des pas sur l'escalier.

▶**pound away** *vi* (*guns*) tirer; (*waves*) se briser (**at, against,** sur); **he sat pounding away at the piano,** il martelait le piano, il jouait du piano comme un forcené; **he was pounding away at the typewriter,** il tapait comme un fou sur la machine à écrire.

▶**pound along** *vi* (*on foot*) marcher d'un pas lourd; (*on horse*) chevaucher.

poundage [ˈpaʊndɪdʒ] *n* **(a)** (*weight*) poids *m* en livres; **(b)** (*tax etc*) taxe *ou* commission proportionnelle au poids *ou* à la valeur.

-pounder [ˈpaʊndər] *suff* **two/three/***etc***-p.,** poisson de deux/de trois/*etc* livres (de poids); *Mil* **thirty-p.,** canon *m ou* pièce *f* de trente.

pounding [ˈpaʊndɪŋ] *n* **(a)** (*crushing*) broyage *m*, broiement *m*; pilage *m*; concassage *m* (*de pierres etc*); martellement *m* (*de qch*); **the p. of the waves,** le martellement des vagues; **to take a p.,** (*of boat*) être fortement secoué; (*of troops, city etc*) être durement attaqué, subir une attaque violente; (*of team etc*) être battu à plate(s) couture(s); **(b)** (*of heart*) battement *m* frénétique; grands coups (*à la porte*); (*of drums*) battement.

pour [pɔːr] **1** *vt* verser (*qch dans qch*); *Metal* couler (*le métal*); **to p. s.o. a drink,** verser un verre à qn; **she poured some tea into the cup,** elle a versé du thé dans la tasse; *Fig* **the government poured money into the industry,** le gouvernement a investi des sommes énormes dans l'industrie. **2** *vi* **(a) it's pouring (with rain), the rain's pouring down,** il pleut à verse, la pluie tombe à torrents; **water was pouring into the cellar,** l'eau entrait à flots dans la cave; **sweat was pouring off him,** il ruisselait de sueur; **tourists were pouring into the palace,** des touristes entraient dans le château en foule; **(b)** (*of jug etc*) **this jug doesn't pour well,** le broc ne verse pas bien; **shall I p.?,** puis-je faire le service?

▶**pour in** **1** *vi* (*of water*) se déverser, entrer à flots; **the crowd came pouring in,** on entrait à flots *ou* en foule; **invitations came pouring in,** ça a été une avalanche d'invitations. **2** *vtsep* verser (*un liquide*); **the government poured money in,** le gouvernement a investi des sommes énormes.

►**pour off** *vtsep* vider.
►**pour out 1** *vi* (*of water*) se déverser, sortir à flots; (*of people*) sortir en foule; **smoke was pouring out of the window,** la fumée sortait en grande quantité par la fenêtre; **the words just poured out,** les mots sont venus en flots continus. **2** *vtsep* verser (*le thé, le café etc*); répandre (*sa colère*); donner libre cours à (*ses sentiments*); (*of chimney*) cracher, vomir (*de la fumée*); **the factories were pouring out cars,** les usines produisaient des voitures à un rythme incroyable; **Japanese products are being poured out onto the market,** les produits japonais arrivent sur le marché à flots continus; **to p. out a torrent of abuse at s.o.,** déverser un torrent d'injures sur qn.
pouring ['pɔːrɪŋ] **1** *adj* (*pluie*) torrentiel. **2** *n Metal* coulée *f*; **p. ladle,** cuillère *f* de fondeur.
pout[1] [paʊt] *n* moue *f*.
pout[2] *vi* faire la moue; (*sulk*) bouder; **her pouting lips,** ses lèvres boudeuses.
pouter ['paʊtər] *n* **p. (pigeon),** pigeon *m* boulant.
poverty ['pɒvətɪ] *n* **(a)** pauvreté *f*; **extreme** *or* **abject p.,** misère *f*; **to live in p.,** vivre dans la gêne *ou* la misère; **to live below the p. line,** vivre en-dessous du seuil de pauvreté; **to be caught in the p. trap,** = perdre des avantages sociaux à cause d'une augmentation de revenus; **(b)** (*lack*) disette *f*, manque *m*, pénurie *f* (*de denrées etc*); (*poor quality*) pauvreté *f* (*du sol*); **p. of ideas,** pauvreté d'idées; **p. of the mixture,** (*in engine*) pauvreté du mélange.
poverty-stricken ['pɒvətɪstrɪk(ə)n] *adj* (*person*) indigent, réduit à la misère; (*dwelling, area etc*) misérable; **a. p.-s. country,** un pays souffrant de la misère.
P.O.W. [piːəʊ'dʌb(ə)ljuː] *n* (*abbr* **prisoner of war**) P.G..
powder[1] ['paʊdər] *n* poudre *f*; (*gunpowder*) poudre, explosif *m*; **to reduce sth to p.,** réduire qch en poudre, pulvériser qch; *Fig* réduire qch en poussière *ou* en miettes; **milk p.,** lait *m* en poudre; **soap p.,** savon *m* en poudre; **washing p.,** lessive *f*, détergent *m*; **(face) p.,** poudre (de riz); **talcum p.,** (poudre de) talc *m*; **tooth** *or* **dental p.,** poudre dentifrice; *Fig* **to smell p. for the first time,** recevoir le baptême du feu; *Am Sl* **to take a p.,** ficher le camp; **p. blue,** (*colour*) bleu clair *inv*; **p. compact,** poudrier *m*; *Lit* **p. keg,** baril *m* de poudre; **p. puff,** houppe *f*, houppette *f*; *Euph* **p. room,** (*in hotel etc*) toilettes *fpl* pour dames.
powder[2] *vt* **(a)** saupoudrer (*un gâteau de sucre etc*); **landscape powdered with snow,** paysage saupoudré de neige; **to p. one's face,** se poudrer (le visage); *F* **to go and p. one's nose,** aller aux cabinets *ou* aux toilettes; **(b)** (*convert to powder*) réduire (*qch*) en poudre; (*pulverize*) pulvériser (*qch*).
powdered ['paʊdəd] *adj* **(a)** (*milk etc*) en poudre; (*charbon etc*) pulvérisé; **(b)** (*face*) poudré.
powdery ['paʊd(ə)rɪ] *adj* poudreux; (*crumbly*) friable.
power[1] ['paʊər] *n* **(a)** (*capacity*) pouvoir *m*; **I'll do everything in my p.,** je ferai tout ce qui est en mon pouvoir *ou* tout mon possible; **the p. of reason,** la puissance de la raison; **mental powers,** facultés intellectuelles; **man of great intellectual powers,** homme de hautes facultés; **to be at the height of one's powers,** être à l'apogée de sa puissance; **p. of speech,** la parole; **p. of observation,** dons *mpl* d'observation; *Phys Ch* **p. of absorption,** capacité *f* d'absorption; **heating p.,** pouvoir calorifique; *Tech* **braking p.,** puissance de freinage; *Econ* **purchasing p.,** pouvoir d'achat;
(b) (*physical strength*) vigueur *f*, force *f*, énergie *f* (physique); *F* **more p. to your elbow!,** allez-y!;
(c) *Tech* puissance *f* (*d'une machine etc*); force *f* (*d'un aimant etc*); énergie *f* (*électrique, hydraulique etc*); (*electricity*) courant *m*; **magnifying p.,** grossissement *m* (*d'une lentille*); *MecE etc* **full p.,** puissance maximale; **nuclear p.,** énergie nucléaire; *MecE* **motive p.,** force motrice; **to shut off/turn on the p.,** couper/mettre le courant; *Tech* mettre hors/sous tension; *MecE* **p. driven,** à propulsion mécanique; **p. cut** *or* **failure,** panne *f* de courant; **p. line,** ligne *f* électrique; *El* **p. pack,** bloc *m* d'alimentation; **p. plant,** (*engine in car, lorry*) groupe moteur; *El* centrale *f* électrique; **p. point,** prise *f* de courant; *Ind* **p. press,** presse *f* mécanique; **p. station,** centrale électrique; *Aut* **p. steering,** direction assistée; **p. tool,** outil *m* à moteur; **p. strike,** grève *f* des employés de l'électricité;
(d) (*authority, control*) pouvoir *m*, autorité *f*; *Jur* procuration *f*, mandat *m*, pouvoir; **absolute p.,** pouvoir absolu; **executive/legislative p.,** pouvoir exécutif/législatif; **to come into p.,** arriver au pouvoir; **to be in p.,** être au pouvoir; *Pol* **the party in p.,** le parti au pouvoir; **p. of life and death,** droit *m* de vie et de mort; **to have s.o. in one's p.,** avoir qn à sa merci; **to be in s.o.'s p.,** être à la merci de qn; **to act with full powers,** agir de pleine autorité; **this lies beyond his powers,** cela ne rentre pas dans ses attributions; *Jur* **p. of attorney,** procuration *f*; **to give s.o. p. of attorney,** donner une procuration à qn; *Jur* **delegation of powers,** délégation *f* de pouvoirs; *Jur* **to furnish s.o. with full powers,** donner pleins pouvoirs à qn; **the police have been given greater powers,** la police a reçu des pouvoirs plus importants; **they constitute Le Pen's p. base,** ils constituent le groupe d'où Le Pen tire son pouvoir; **p. structure,** structure *f* du pouvoir; **p. struggle,** lutte *f* de pouvoir;
(e) (*person in power etc*) puissance *f*; **the powers that be,** les autorités *fpl*; *Rel* **the powers of darkness,** les puissances des ténèbres; **world p.,** (*country*) puissance mondiale; **the great powers,** les grandes puissances;
(f) *F* **that'll do you a p. of good,** ça vous fera énormément de bien;
(g) *Math* puissance *f* (*d'un nombre*); **three to the p. of ten (3^{10}),** trois (à la) puissance dix *ou* à la dixième puissance.
power[2] **1** *vt* (*provide with power*) fournir de l'énergie *ou* de l'électricité à (*une machine*); (*propel*) propulser; **powered by two engines,** actionné par deux moteurs. **2** *vi* (*move fast*) **he powered round the final bend,** il avalait la dernière courbe à toute allure; **the rocket powered up into the sky,** la fusée filait de toute sa puissance vers les étoiles.
►**power down** *vi* (*of engine etc*) être arrêté.
►**power up** *vi* (*of computer, machine*) être mis en marche.
power-assisted ['paʊərəsɪstɪd] *adj Aut* (*steering*) assisté.
powered ['paʊəd] *adj* actionné mécaniquement; **nuclear p.,** à propulsion atomique *ou* nucléaire.
powerful ['paʊəful] **1** *adj* **(a)** puissant; (*physically strong*) fort, vigoureux; (*blow*) vigoureux, énergique; (*argument, incentive*) efficace, de poids; (*story*) fort; (*language, prose style*) vigoureux, qui a de l'impact; (*music, passage*) plein de vigueur; (*speaker, actor*) qui a de la présence, qui en impose; **to become more p.,** augmenter en puissance; (*of state*) s'agrandir; **p. dose,** forte dose (*d'un médicament*); **a p. new novel/film,** un nouveau roman/film très fort; **a p. image,** une image chargée de force, une image-choc; **(b)** *F Old-fashioned* **a p. lot of people,** un tas de gens. **2** *adv esp US* **I was p. tired,** j'étais rudement fatigué.
powerfully ['paʊəfʊlɪ] *adv* puissamment; **p. built,** (*man*) à forte carrure.
powerhouse ['paʊəhaʊs] *n El* centrale *f* électrique; *F* (*person*) personne vigoureuse et dynamique.
powerless ['paʊəlɪs] *adj* impuissant; **p. to act,** impuissant à agir; **I am p. to help you,** je ne puis rien faire pour vous aider.
power-up [paʊə'rʌp] *n Tech* (*of computer, machine*) mise *f* sous tension.
pow-wow[1] ['paʊwaʊ] *n* (*of American Indians*) assemblée *f*; *F* (*talk, discussion*) palabre *f*, discussion *f*.
pow-wow[2] *vi* (*of American Indians*) tenir une assemblée; *F* palabrer; **to p.-w. about sth,** discuter qch.
pox [pɒks] *n F* **the p.,** la syphilis, la vérole; *Arch* **a p. on ...!,** maudit soit ...!; maudits soient ...!
poxy ['pɒksɪ] *adj Sl* (*worthless*) merdique; (*unpleasant*) sale.
pp [piː'piː] *adv* (*abbr* **per procurationem**) **pp Jane Smith,** p.p. Jane Smith.
pp. [piː'piː] *npl* (*abbr* **pages**) p., pp.; **see pp. 44 - 47,** voir pp. 44 à 47.
P.P.E. [piːpiː'iː] *n Sch abbr* **philosophy, politics and economics**.
pps [piːpiː'es] *abbr* **post postscriptum**.
PQ [piː'kjuː] *n Can abbr* **(a) Province of Quebec**; **(b) Parti québécois**.
PR [piː'ɑr] *n* **(a)** (*abbr* **public relations**) **we need better PR,** il nous faut améliorer nos relations publiques; **a skilful PR man,** un homme qui excelle dans les relations publiques; **(b)** *Pol* (*abbr* **proportional representation**) R. P. *f*.
practicability [præktɪkə'bɪlɪtɪ] *n* réalisabilité *f*, faisabilité *f*; (*of road etc*) praticabilité *f*.
practicable ['præktɪkəb(ə)l] *adj* **(a)** (*feasible*) faisable; **(b)** (*road, ford*) praticable.
practical ['præktɪk(ə)l] **1** *adj* **(a)** pratique; (*proposition*) réalisable; **he's very p.,** il a l'esprit pratique; **we must be p.,** il faut que nous soyons raisonnables; **p. application,** mise *f* en pratique (*d'une théorie etc*); réalisation *f*

(pratique) (*d'une invention etc*); **it appeals to p. minds,** cela plaît aux esprits positifs; **for all p. purposes,** en fin de compte; **of no p. use** *or* **value,** inutilisable dans la pratique; **p. joke,** farce *f*; **p. joker,** farceur, -euse; *Sch* **p. work,** travaux *mpl* pratiques; **(b)** (*virtual*) **with p. unanimity,** d'un consentement presque unanime. **2** *n Sch* (*lesson*) travaux dirigés *ou* pratiques; (*examination*) épreuve *f* pratique.

practicality [præktɪ'kælɪtɪ] *n* **(a)** (*feasibility*) aspect *m* pratique, caractère *m* pratique; **(b)** (*of person, mind*) sens *m ou* esprit *m* pratique.

practically ['præktɪklɪ] *adv* **(a)** pratiquement, en pratique; **(b)** (*almost*) pour ainsi dire; **there has been p. no snow,** il n'y a presque pas eu de neige; **p. the whole of the audience,** la quasi-totalité de l'auditoire.

practice¹ ['præktɪs] *n* **(a)** pratique *f*; **to put one's ideas into p.,** mettre ses idées en pratique, donner suite à ses idées; **in p.,** en *ou* dans la pratique;

(b) (*of profession etc*) exercice *m*; (*of doctor etc*) clientèle *f*; (*of solicitor*) étude *f*; **to be in p.,** (*of doctor etc*) exercer; **private p.,** clientèle privée, cabinet (*médical etc*) privé; **group p.,** cabinets de groupe; groupement médical *ou* dentaire;

(c) (*custom*) habitude *f*, coutume *f*, usage *m*; *Ind etc* technique *f*; méthodes *fpl*; **to make a p. of doing sth,** se faire une habitude *ou* une règle de faire qch; **it's the usual p.,** c'est l'usage; **in hospitals it's standard p. to throw needles away,** dans les hôpitaux, la règle est de jeter les seringues usagées;

(d) (*exercise, training*) exercice(s) *m(pl)*; *Sp etc* entraînement *m*; **it takes years of p.,** cela demande des années de pratique; **I don't get much p.,** (*at driving, playing sport, music etc*) je ne m'entraîne pas souvent; **I need more p.,** j'ai besoin de m'entraîner davantage; **to do 2 hours' p. a day,** s'entraîner deux heures par jour; **to keep in p.,** se maintenir en forme; **to get out of p.,** perdre l'habitude *ou* la main, se rouiller; **Alain Prost did 3.25 in p.,** Alain Prost a fait 3 mn. 25 aux essais; *Mus* **choir p.,** répétition *f* (chorale); **piano p.,** travail *m* au piano; *Prov* **p. makes perfect,** c'est en forgeant qu'on devient forgeron; **target p.,** tir à la cible *ou* au but; *Sp* **p. match,** match *m* d'entraînement;

(e) (*dealings*) (*usu pl*) **practices,** agissements *mpl*; pratiques *fpl*.

practice² *v US* = **PRACTISE.**

practiced, practicing *adj US* = **PRACTISED, PRACTISING.**

practise, *US* **practice** ['præktɪs] **1** *vt* **(a)** (*carry out*) pratiquer (*une vertu etc*); suivre (*une méthode*); mettre en pratique *ou* en action (*un principe etc*); **to p. what one preaches,** montrer l'exemple; **to p. a custom,** suivre une coutume; **(b)** pratiquer, exercer (*une profession*); exercer (*la médecine*); **(c)** (*do exercises etc in*) étudier (*le piano etc*); s'exercer à (*la flûte*); *Tennis Billiards etc* s'exercer à (*un coup*); **to p. one's French,** essayer son français (**on s.o.,** sur qn). **2** *vi* **(a)** (*of doctor*) exercer; **(b)** (*do exercises etc*) s'exercer; *Sp* s'entraîner.

practised, *US* **practiced** ['præktɪst] *adj* exercé, expérimenté; (*orateur etc*) habile.

practising, *US* **practicing** ['præktɪsɪŋ] *adj* qui pratique; (*doctor, solicitor etc*) en exercice; (*chrétien, catholique*) pratiquant; **a p. homosexual,** un(e) homosexuel(le) déclaré(e).

practitioner [præk'tɪʃənər] *n Fml* praticien, -ienne; **medical p.,** médecin *m*; **general p.,** (médecin) généraliste *mf*, omnipraticien, -ienne.

pragmatic [præg'mætɪk] *adj* pragmatique.

pragmatism ['prægmətɪz(ə)m] *n* pragmatisme *m*.

pragmatist ['prægmətɪst] *n* pragmatiste *mf*.

prairie ['preərɪ] *n* prairie *f* (*de l'Amérique du Nord*); **the Prairies,** les Prairies; **p. dog,** chien *m* de prairie; **p. oyster,** œuf cru assaisonné; **p. wolf,** coyote *m*.

praise¹ [preɪz] *n* (*deserved*) éloge(s) *m(pl)*; (*adulatory or in worship*) louange(s) *f(pl)*; **in p. of s.o./sth,** à la louange de qn/qch; **to sing the praises of sth/s.o.,** chanter *ou* célébrer les louanges de qch/qn; **to sing one's own praises,** faire son propre éloge; **I have nothing but p. for him,** je n'ai rien pour lui que des louanges; **she deserves special p.,** elle mérite toutes les louanges; **his conduct is beyond all p.,** sa conduite est au-dessus de tout éloge; **p. be (to God)!,** Dieu soit loué!

praise² *vt* louer, faire l'éloge de (*qn, qch*); **to p. God,** glorifier Dieu.

praiseworthy ['preɪzwɜːðɪ] *adj* digne d'éloges, louable; (*travail*) méritoire.

praline ['preɪliːn] *n Culin* praline *f*; (*almond*) amande pralinée; (*pecan*) pacane pralinée.

pram [præːm] *n Br* voiture *f* d'enfant, landau *m*.

prance [prɑːns] *vi* **(a)** (*of horse*) caracoler; **prancing horse,** un cheval fringant; **(b)** (*of person*) se pavaner; **to p. in/out,** entrer/sortir d'un pas dégagé.

►prance about *vi* (*of horse*) caracoler; (*of person*) se pavaner.

prang¹ [præŋ] *n Old-fashioned Br F* **to have a p.,** (*in car*) avoir un accrochage.

prang² *vt Old-fashioned Br F* amocher (*son avion, sa voiture*); (*write off*) bousiller.

prank [præŋk] *n* **(a)** (*escapade*) folie *f*, frasque *f*, fredaine *f*; **to play all sorts of pranks,** faire les cent coups; **(b)** (*practical joke*) tour *m*, farce *f*, espièglerie *f*; **to play pranks on s.o.,** jouer des tours à qn.

prat [præt] *n Br Sl* crétin, -ine.

prate [preɪt] *vi* dire *ou* débiter des niaiseries *ou* des absurdités (*d'un air important*); (*chatter*) jaser, bavarder.

pratfall ['prætfɔːl] *n Am* **to do a p.,** tomber sur les fesses.

prattle¹ ['præt(ə)l] *n* babil *m*, babillage *m* (*d'enfants*); bavardage *m*, caquet *m* (*de commères*).

prattle² *vi* (*of children*) babiller; (*of adults*) jaser, bavarder.

prawn [prɔːn] *n* crevette *f* rose; (*bigger*) bouquet *m*; **Dublin Bay p.,** langoustine *f*; *Culin* **p. cocktail,** cocktail *m* de crevettes.

pray [preɪ] **1** *vi* **(a)** prier; **to p. to God,** prier Dieu; **to p. for s.o.,** prier pour qn; **to p. for sth,** prier pour avoir qch; **to p. for s.o.'s soul,** prier pour (le repos de) l'âme de qn; *F* **he's past praying for,** il est perdu; **(b)** *Arch* **p. be seated,** veuillez (bien) vous asseoir. **2** *vt* prier, implorer, supplier (**s.o. to do sth,** qn de faire qch).

prayer [preər] *n* prière *f*; **the Lord's P.,** le Notre Père; **p. for the dead,** prière pour les morts; **to say one's prayers,** dire *ou* réciter ses prières; *Sch* **prayers,** la prière du matin en commun; *Church of Eng* **Morning/Evening P.,** office *m* du matin/du soir; **his p. was granted,** sa prière a été exaucée; *F* **he doesn't have a p.,** il n'a aucune chance; **p. beads,** chapelet *m*; **p. book,** livre *m* de messe, missel *m*; **p. mat/wheel,** tapis *m*/moulin *m* à prières; **p. meeting,** réunion *f* pour prières en commun.

praying ['preɪɪŋ] **1** *adj* en prières; **p. mantis,** mante religieuse. **2** *n* prière(s) *f(pl)*.

preach [priːtʃ] **1** *vi* prêcher; **to p. to the converted,** prêcher à un converti; **to p. against s.o.,** prêcher contre qn; *F* **he's always preaching at me,** il est toujours à me sermonner; **stop preaching!,** arrête ton sermon! **2** *vt* prononcer (*un sermon*); **to p. the gospel,** annoncer l'Evangile; **to p. a new doctrine,** se faire l'évangéliste d'une doctrine nouvelle; **she preaches austerity and lives in luxury,** elle prêche l'austérité mais elle vit dans le luxe.

preacher ['priːtʃər] *n* prédicateur *m*; *US* pasteur *m*; *Pej* prêcheur, -euse; **he's a poor p.,** il prêche mal.

preachify ['priːtʃɪfaɪ] *vi F* faire la morale.

preaching ['priːtʃɪŋ] **1** *adj* prêcheur. **2** *n* prédication *f*; *Pej* sermons *mpl*.

preachy ['priːtʃɪ] *adj F* prêcheur, sermonneur.

preamble ['priːæmb(ə)l] *n* **(a)** (*to legal text*) préambule *m*; (*of book*) introduction *f*, préface *f*; préliminaires *mpl* (*d'un traité etc*); **(b)** *Jur* exposé *m* (*d'un projet de loi*).

preamplifier [priː'æmplɪfaɪər] *n Electron* préamplificateur *m*.

prearrange [priːə'reɪndʒ] *vt* arranger au préalable *ou* d'avance; **at a prearranged signal,** sur un signal convenu.

prebend ['prebənd] *n Rel* **(a)** (*stipend*) prébende *f*; **(b)** (*person*) = **PREBENDARY.**

prebendary ['prebənd(ə)rɪ] *n Rel* prébendier *m*, chanoine *m*.

precarious [prɪ'keərɪəs] *adj* précaire, incertain; **to make a p. living,** gagner sa vie précairement; **p. life,** vie précaire.

precariously [prɪ'keərɪəslɪ] *adv* précairement.

precariousness [prɪ'keərɪəsnɪs] *n* état *m* précaire.

precast ['priːkɑːst] *adj* (*concrete*) prémoulé.

precaution [prɪ'kɔːʃən] *n* (*act*) précaution *f*; (*attitude*) prévoyance *f*; **to take precautions,** prendre ses précautions (**against sth,** contre qch); **air-raid precautions,** défense passive; **as a p.,** par mesure de précaution.

precautionary [prɪ'kɔːʃən(ə)rɪ] *adj* (*measure*) de précaution, préventif (**against,** contre).

precede [prɪ'siːd] *vt* **(a)** (*occur before*) précéder; **the calm that precedes the storm,** le calme qui précède la tempête; **the conference was preceded by a reception,** une réception a eu lieu avant la conférence; **(b)** (*take precedence over*) avoir le pas *ou* la préséance sur (*qn*).

precedence ['presɪdəns] *n (of rank)* préséance *f*; (*of urgency etc*) priorité *f*; **to have** *or* **take p. over s.o.,** avoir le pas *ou* la préséance sur qn, prendre le pas sur qn; **duty that takes p. over all others,** devoir qui prime tout; **this translation takes p.,** cette traduction est à faire en priorité.

precedent ['presɪdənt] *n* **(a)** précédent *m*; **to create a p.,** créer un précédent; **there's no p. for it,** il n'y en a point d'exemple; **according to p.,** conformément à la tradition; **(b)** *Jur* décision *f* judiciaire faisant jurisprudence; **to set p.,** faire jurisprudence.

preceding [prɪ'siːdɪŋ] *adj* précédent; **the p. day,** la veille; **in the p. article,** dans l'article ci-dessus.

precentor [prɪ'sentər] *n Rel* maître *m* de chapelle.

precept ['priːsept] *n* **(a)** précepte *m*; commandement *m* (*de Dieu*); **(b)** *Jur* mandat *m* d'amener *ou* d'arrêt.

preceptor [prɪ'septər] *n* précepteur, -trice.

precinct ['priːsɪŋkt] *n* **(a)** (*enclosed area*) enceinte *f*, enclos *m*; **precincts,** enceinte *f*, enclos *m* (*d'une cathédrale etc*); environs *mpl* (*d'un endroit*); **pedestrian p.,** zone piétonnière; **shopping p.,** centre commercial (fermé à la circulation automobile); **(b)** (*boundary*) limite *f* (*du pourtour*); **(c)** *US* (*electoral district*) circonscription électorale; (*police district*) circonscription administrative.

precious ['preʃəs] **1** *adj* précieux; de grande valeur; *Lit* (*style*) précieux; **p. metals,** métaux précieux; **p. stones,** pierres précieuses; **we wasted a lot of p. time,** nous avons perdu beaucoup d'heures précieuses; **a few p. drops of water,** quelques précieuses gouttes d'eau; **that photo is very p. to me,** je tiens beaucoup à cette photo; **you and your p. dictionary!,** toi et ton sacré dictionnaire! **2** *n* (*term of endearment*) **my p.!,** mon trésor!, mon amour! **3** *adv F* **there are p. few of them,** il n'y en a guère; **there's p. little hope,** il n'y a guère d'espoir; **you'd better take p. good care of it!,** tu ferais mieux d'y faire très attention!

precipice ['presɪpɪs] *n* précipice *m*, escarpement abrupt, paroi *f* à pic; **to fall over a p.,** tomber dans un précipice; *Fig* **to be on the p. of war/bankruptcy,** être au bord de la guerre/de la faillite.

precipitance [prɪ'sɪpɪtəns], **precipitancy** [prɪ'sɪpɪtənsɪ] *n* précipitation *f*; (*haste*) empressement *m*; (*rashness*) manque *m* de réflexion.

precipitant [prɪ'sɪpɪtənt] **1** *adj* = **PRECIPITATE[2]**. **2** *n Ch Phys* précipitant *m*.

precipitate[1] [prɪ'sɪpɪtɪt] *n* **(a)** *Ch* précipité *m*; **to form a p.,** (se) précipiter; **(b)** *Met* eau *f* de condensation.

precipitate[2] *adj* **(a)** (*sudden, abrupt*) précipité, fait *ou* pris à la hâte; **(b)** (*hasty*) précipité, trop empressé; (*rash*) irréfléchi.

precipitate[3] [prɪ'sɪpɪteɪt] **1** *vt* précipiter (*qn, qch*) (*dans qch*); hâter (*un événement*); *Ch* précipiter (*une substance solide*); *Met* condenser (*la rosée*); **to p. a war/an argument,** faire éclater une guerre/une dispute; **to p. matters,** brusquer les choses. **2** *vi Ch Phys* (se) précipiter; *Met* se condenser.

precipitately [prɪ'sɪpɪtətlɪ] *adv* (*see adj*) **(a)** précipitamment; **(b)** avec précipitation, sans réfléchir.

precipitation [prɪsɪpɪ'teɪʃən] *n* **(a)** *Ch Phys* précipitation *f*; *Met* précipitations; **annual p.,** précipitations annuelles; **(b)** (*haste*) **to act with p.,** agir avec précipitation *ou* précipitamment.

precipitous [prɪ'sɪpɪtəs] *adj* **(a)** (*steep*) escarpé, abrupt; (*sheer*) à pic; **(b)** (*départ etc*) précipité.

precipitously [prɪ'sɪpɪtəslɪ] *adv* **(a)** de façon abrupte; (*monter, descendre*) à pic; **(b)** précipitamment.

précis[1], *pl* **précis** ['preɪsiː, 'preɪsiːz] *n* résumé *m*; *Sch* **p. writing,** compte-rendu *m* de lecture.

précis[2] *vt* faire un résumé de (*qch*).

precise [prɪ'saɪs] *adj* **(a)** (*exact*) précis, exact; **to give p. orders,** donner des ordres précis; **p. movements,** mouvements précis; *Horseriding* mouvements écoutés; **there were a few people — five to be p.,** il y avait quelques personnes — cinq pour être précis; **at the p. moment when ...,** au moment précis où ..., juste au moment où ...; **(b)** (*person*) (*meticulous*) méticuleux; (*punctilious*) formaliste; (*scrupulous*) scrupuleux.

precisely [prɪ'saɪslɪ] *adv* avec précision; **at six (o'clock) p.,** à six heures précises; **p.!,** précisément!, exactement!

preciseness [prɪ'saɪsnɪs] *n* **(a)** (*of figure, calculation etc*) précision *f*; **(b)** (*of person*) (*meticulousness*) méticulosité *f*; (*punctiliousness*) formalisme *m*.

precision [prɪ'sɪʒ(ə)n] *n* précision *f*, exactitude *f*; **lack of p.,** manque *m* de précision, imprécision *f*; **with mathematical p.,** avec une précision (toute) mathématique; **p.-engineered,** de haute technologie; **p. instruments,** instruments *mpl* de précision; **p.-made,** de (haute) précision; **p. work/engineering,** travail *m*/mécanique *f* de précision.

preclude [prɪ'kluːd] *vt* prévenir, exclure (d'avance) (*une objection, un malentendu etc*); **to p. s.o. from doing sth,** empêcher qn de faire qch.

precocious [prɪ'kəʊʃəs] *adj* (*plant*) précoce, hâtif; **p. child,** enfant précoce.

precociously [prɪ'kəʊʃəslɪ] *adv* précocement, avec précocité.

precociousness [prɪ'kəʊʃəsnɪs] *n* précocité *f*.

precognition [priːkɒg'nɪʃən] *n Phil etc* connaissance anticipée *ou* antérieure.

precombustion [priːkəm'bʌstʃən] *n* précombustion *f*.

preconceive [priːkən'siːv] *vt* préconcevoir; **preconceived idea,** idée préconçue.

preconception [priːkən'sepʃən] *n* idée *ou* opinion préconçue; (*prejudice*) préjugé *m*; **to free oneself from all preconceptions,** se libérer de toute opinion préconçue.

preconcerted [priːkən'sɜːtɪd] *adj* convenu *ou* arrangé *ou* concerté d'avance.

precondition[1] [priːkɒn'dɪʃən] *n* condition *f* préalable *ou* requise *ou* indispensable (**of sth,** à qch; **for doing,** pour faire).

precondition[2] *vt* conditionner (*qn*) (**to do sth,** à faire qch).

precooked [priː'kʊkt] *adj (food)* précuit.

precursor [prɪ'kɜːsər] *n* (*person*) précurseur *m*; (*sign, event*) avant-coureur *m*, *pl* avant-coureurs.

precursory [prɪ'kɜːsərɪ] *adj* précurseur; (*symptôme*) avant-coureur, *pl* avant-coureurs; (*observation*) préliminaire.

predate [priː'deɪt] *vt* **(a)** (*precede*) précéder (*un fait historique etc*); **(b)** antidater (*un document*).

predator ['predətər] *n* prédateur *m*; (*bird*) rapace *m*.

predatory ['predət(ə)rɪ] *adj* prédateur, -trice; (*animal, person*) rapace; **p. instincts,** instincts de bête de proie *ou* prédateurs.

predecease [priːdɪ'siːs] *vt* prédécéder.

predecessor ['priːdɪsesər] *n* **(a)** prédécesseur *m*; devancier, -ière (*d'un dignitaire etc*); **my (immediate) p. (in the job),** mon prédécesseur (à ce poste); **my new desk is much better than its p.,** mon nouveau bureau est bien mieux que le précédent; **(b)** (*ancestor*) ancêtre *m*.

predestination [priːdestɪ'neɪʃən] *n* prédestination *f*.

predestine [priː'destɪn] *vt* destiner d'avance (**to,** à); *Rel* prédestiner (à); **to be predestined to do,** être prédestiné à faire.

predetermination [priːdɪtɜːmɪ'neɪʃən] *n* prédétermination *f*.

predetermine [priːdɪ'tɜːmɪn] *vt* **(a)** déterminer *ou* arrêter d'avance; **(b)** *Rel Phil* prédéterminer; **motives that p. man's actions,** mobiles qui (pré)déterminent les actions de l'homme.

predicament [prɪ'dɪkəmənt] *n* **(a)** (*difficult situation*) situation difficile *ou* fâcheuse, conjoncture malheureuse; **to be in an awkward p.,** être dans une mauvaise passe; **(b)** (*logic*) & *Phil* prédicament *m*, catégorie *f*.

predicate[1] ['predɪkət] *n Ling* prédicat *m*; *Gram* attribut *m*.

predicate[2] ['predɪkeɪt] *vt* **(a)** affirmer; **(b)** *Am* **to p. sth on sth,** (*base*) baser qch sur qch; *Am* **this view is predicated on ...,** (*is based on*) ce point de vue se base *ou* se fonde sur ...; **(c)** *Phil* **to p. sth of sth,** (*ascribe to as a quality*) affirmer de qch qu'il *ou* elle est qch; **to p. a quality of sth,** attribuer une qualité à qch.

predicative [prɪ'dɪkətɪv] *adj* affirmatif; (*logic*) & *Gram* prédicatif.

predict [prɪ'dɪkt] *vt* (*forecast*) prédire (*un événement*).

predictable [prɪ'dɪktəb(ə)l] *adj* qui peut être prédit; *F* **the film was too p.,** ce film était sans surprise; **there was the p. standing ovation,** comme c'était à prévoir, le public s'est levé pour l' *ou* les *etc* ovationner.

predictably [prɪ'dɪktəblɪ] *adv* comme on s'y attendait.

prediction [prɪ'dɪkʃən] *n* prédiction *f*.

predilection [priːdɪ'lekʃən] *n* prédilection *f* (**for,** pour).

predispose [priːdɪs'pəʊz] *vt* prédisposer; **to p. s.o. in s.o.'s favour,** prédisposer qn en faveur de qn; **this life had predisposed him to gout,** cette vie l'avait prédisposé à la goutte.

predisposition [priːdɪspə'zɪʃən] *n* prédisposition *f* (**to,** à).

predominance [prɪ'dɒmɪnəns] *n* prédominance *f*; **there is a p. of women in the profession,** il y a une

prédominance de femmes dans ce métier.
predominant [prɪ'dɒmɪnənt] *adj* prédominant, prévalent.
predominantly [prɪ'dɒmɪnəntlɪ] *adv* d'une manière prédominante; **cars sold here are p. Russian,** la plupart des voitures vendues ici sont soviétiques.
predominate [prɪ'dɒmɪneɪt] *vi* **(a)** (*prevail*) prédominer, l'emporter (**over,** sur); **(b)** (*be in the majority*) être plus nombreux *ou* supérieur, prédominer.
predominating [prɪ'dɒmɪneɪtɪŋ] *adj* prédominant.
pre-election [priːɪ'lekʃən] *adj* préélectoral, -aux.
preemie ['priːmɪ] *n Am Sl* (*premature baby*) avorton *m*.
pre-eminence [prɪ'emɪnəns] *n* prééminence *f*; **this country's sporting p.,** la prééminence de ce pays sur le plan sportif.
pre-eminent [prɪ'emɪnənt] *adj* (*remarkable*) prééminent.
pre-eminently [prɪ'emɪnəntlɪ] *adv* (*supremely*) d'une manière prééminente, souverainement, par excellence.
pre-empt [prɪ'empt] *vt* **(a)** (*prevent, frustrate*) devancer (*qn*); **(b)** *Jur* préempter (*une terre, un bien*); *US* occuper (*un terrain*) afin d'obtenir un droit d'achat préférentiel.
pre-emption [prɪ'empʃən] *n Jur* (droit *m* de) préemption *f*.
pre-emptive [prɪ'emptɪv] *adj* **(a)** *Jur* (*droit*) de préemption; **(b)** *Cards* (*at bridge*) **p.-e. bid,** ouverture préventive; appel élevé (*pour s'assurer l'enchère*); **(c)** *Mil* (*strike, attack*) préventif.
preen [priːn] *vt* (*of bird*) lisser *ou* nettoyer (*ses plumes*) avec le bec; **to p. itself,** (*of bird*) se lisser les plumes; **to p. oneself,** (*of person*) (*make oneself attractive*) se faire beau *ou* belle; (*look smug*) prendre un petit air satisfait.
pre-establish [priːɪs'tæblɪʃ] *vt* préétablir.
pre-established [priːɪs'tæblɪʃt] *adj* préétabli.
pre-exist [priːɪg'zɪst] *vi* préexister.
pre-existence [priːɪg'zɪstəns] *n* préexistence *f*.
pre-existent [priːɪg'zɪstənt] *adj* préexistant.
prefab ['priːfæb] *n F* maison préfabriquée.
prefabricate [priː'fæbrɪkeɪt] *vt* préfabriquer; **prefabricated house,** maison préfabriquée.
preface[1] ['prefɪs] *n* **(a)** préface *f*, avant-propos *m inv* (*d'un livre*); **(b)** préambule *m* (*d'un discours*).
preface[2] *vt* **(a)** (*introduce*) préluder à (*un discours*); **to p. one's remarks with an anecdote,** faire précéder ses remarques d'une anecdote; **the events that prefaced the crisis,** les événements qui ont précédé la crise; **(b)** (*write preface to*) préfacer (*un ouvrage*).
pre-faded ['priːfeɪdɪd] *adj* (*denims*) délavé.
prefatory ['prefətərɪ] *adj* (*remarque*) préliminaire, d'introduction.
prefect ['priːfekt] *n* **(a)** *Br Sch* = élève des grandes classes chargé de la discipline; **(b)** *Admin* (*French etc official*) préfet *m*.
prefecture ['priːfektjʊər] *n* (*in France*) préfecture *f*.
prefer [prɪ'fɜːr] *vt* (**-rr-**) **(a)** (*like better*) préférer; **to p. sth to sth,** préférer qch à qch, aimer mieux qch que qch; **I p. her to her sister,** je la préfère à sa sœur; **which would you p., wine or beer?,** tu préfères du vin ou de la bière?; **I p. meat well done,** je préfère la viande bien cuite; **I would p. to stay at home,** j'aimerais mieux rester à la maison; **I would p. that you did not repeat this,** je préférerais que tu ne répètes pas ça; **(b)** (*of police*) émettre (*des accusations*); intenter (*une action en justice*); **to p. charges,** déposer *ou* porter plainte (**against,** contre); **(c)** (*appoint*) nommer, élever (*qn à un emploi, à une dignité*); **to be preferred to an office,** être promu à un emploi.
preferable ['prefərəb(ə)l] *adj* préférable; **anything was p. to this uncertainty,** tout était préférable à cette incertitude.
preferably ['prefərəblɪ] *adv* de préférence; **would you like to make the presentations? — p. not,** voudriez-vous faire les présentations – je n'y tiens pas.
preference ['prefərəns] *n* **(a)** préférence *f*; **to give sth p.,** donner *ou* accorder la préférence à qch (**over sth,** sur qch); **in p. to ...,** de préférence à ...; **in order of p.,** par ordre de préférence; **(b)** (*thing preferred*) **this is my p.,** voilà celui que je préfère; **I have no p.,** je n'ai pas de préférence; **(c)** *Econ* tarif *m ou* régime *m* de faveur; (*preferential treatment*) traitement préférentiel; **imports entitled to p.,** importations ayant droit à un régime de faveur; **(d)** droit *m* de priorité; *Br Fin* **p. shares,** actions privilégiées *ou* de priorité.
preferential [prefə'renʃəl] *adj* **(a)** (*traitement etc*) préférentiel; *Econ* (*tarif*) préférentiel, de faveur; **to get p. treatment,** (*of people*) bénéficier d'un traitement de faveur *ou* privilégié; *Com* **p. price,** prix *m* de faveur; **p. voting,** vote préférentiel; **(b)** *Jur* **p. claim** *or* **right,** privilège *m*; **p. creditor,** créancier privilégié; **p. dividend,** dividende privilégié *ou* de priorité.
preferment [prɪ'fɜːmənt] *n* (*promotion*) avancement *m*, promotion *f* (**to an office,** à une fonction).
preferred [prɪ'fɜːd] *adj US Fin* **p. stock,** actions privilégiées *ou* de priorité.
prefiguration [priːfɪgə'reɪʃən] *n* préfiguration *f*.
prefigure [priː'fɪgər] *vt* préfigurer.
prefix[1] ['priːfɪks] *n* **(a)** *Gram etc* préfixe *m*; **(b)** particule *f ou* (*title*) titre *m* (*précédant un nom propre*).
prefix[2] *vt* préfixer, mettre un préfixe à (*un mot*).
preflight ['priː'flaɪt] *adj* (*inspection etc*) avant vol.
prefrontal [priː'frʌnt(ə)l] *adj Anat* préfrontal, -aux.
preggers ['pregəz] *adj Br F* enceinte.
pregnancy ['pregnənsɪ] *n* grossesse *f*; **p. test,** test *m* de grossesse.
pregnant ['pregnənt] *adj* **(a)** (*woman*) enceinte; (*animal*) pleine; **she's three months p.,** elle est enceinte de trois mois; **to become or get p.,** devenir enceinte; **to get s.o. p.,** mettre qn enceinte; **(b)** *Fig* (*fertile*) fécond (**with,** en); **p. with meaning,** chargé de sens.
preheat [priː'hiːt] *vt* préchauffer.
prehensile [prɪ'hensaɪl] *adj* préhensile.
prehistoric [priːhɪs'tɒrɪk] *adj* préhistorique.
prehistory [priː'hɪst(ə)rɪ] *n* préhistoire *f*.
pre-ignition [priːɪg'nɪʃən] *n* (*in engine*) préallumage *m*.
prejudge [priː'dʒʌdʒ] *vt* **(a)** préjuger (*une question etc*); **(b)** condamner (*qn*) d'avance.
prejudice[1] ['predʒʊdɪs] *n* **(a)** (*preconception*) préjugé *m* (*contre, en faveur de qn, qch*), parti pris *m*; **racial p.,** préjugés raciaux; **I have a p. against that sort of thing,** j'ai des préjugés contre de telles choses; **(b)** *Fml* (*harm*) préjudice *m*, tort *m*, dommage *m*; *Jur* **without p. (to my rights),** sans préjudice de mes droits; **without p. to the solution of the question,** sans préjuger la solution de la question; **without p.,** sous toutes réserves.
prejudice[2] *vt* **(a)** (*bias*) prévenir, prédisposer (*qn contre qn, en faveur de qn*); **(b)** (*harm*) nuire *ou* faire tort *ou* porter préjudice à (*une réputation etc*); préjuger (*une solution etc*); **without prejudicing my rights,** sans préjudice de mes droits.
prejudiced ['predʒʊdɪst] *adj* **to be p.,** avoir des préjugés (**in favour of,** pour; **against,** contre); **racially p.,** plein de préjugés raciaux.
prejudicial [predʒʊ'dɪʃəl] *adj* préjudiciable, nuisible (**to,** à); **to be p.,** porter *ou* faire préjudice (**to,** à).
prelate ['prelɪt] *n* prélat *m*.
prelim ['priːlɪm] *n F* **(a)** *Sch* examen *m* préliminaire; **(b)** *Typ* **prelims,** pages *fpl* de départ.
preliminary [prɪ'lɪmɪnərɪ] **1** *adj* préliminaire, préalable, préparatoire; **after a few p. remarks,** après quelques avant-propos; *Jur* **p. investigation,** instruction *f* (d'une affaire); *Constr etc* **p. scheme** *or* **plan,** avant-projet *m*, *pl* avant-projets; *Min* **p. work,** travaux *mpl* de premier établissement. **2** *n* **(a)** prélude *m* (*à une conversation etc*); **by way of** *or* **as a p.,** préalablement, en guise d'introduction; **(b) preliminaries,** préliminaires *mpl* (*d'un traité etc*).
prelude[1] ['preljuːd] *n Mus etc* prélude *m* (**to,** à).
prelude[2] *vt* précéder.
premarital [priː'mærɪt(ə)l] *adj* prénuptial, -aux; **p. sex,** rapports avant le mariage *ou* préconjugaux.
premature ['premətjʊər] *adj* prématuré; **p. birth,** accouchement avant terme; **to be two weeks p.,** (*of baby*) être prématuré de deux semaines; *F* **you're being a bit p.!,** tu vas trop vite!
prematurely ['premətjʊəlɪ] *adv* prématurément; (*né*) avant terme.
premed ['priːmed] *n F* préparation *f* pour une opération.
premeditate [priː'medɪteɪt] *vt* préméditer (*un coup etc*).
premeditated [priː'medɪteɪtɪd] *adj* prémédité; (*crime*) réfléchi; (*insolence*) calculé.
premeditation [priːmedɪ'teɪʃən] *n* préméditation *f*.
premenstrual [priː'menstrʊəl] *adj* prémenstruel; **p. tension** *or* **syndrome,** syndrome prémenstruel.
premier ['priːmɪər, 'prem-] **1** *adj* (tout) premier. **2** *n* premier ministre.
première[1] ['prəmɪeər, 'prem-, *Am* prɪ'mɪər] *n Th Cin* première *f*.
première[2] **1** *vt* donner la première de (*une pièce de théâtre, un film*). **2** *vi* **the play premiered in New York,** la première de la pièce a eu lieu à New York.
premiership ['priːmɪəʃɪp, 'prem-] *n* fonctions *fpl* de premier ministre; **during her p.,** pendant qu'elle était premier ministre.
premise[1] ['premɪs] *n* (*in logic*) (*also* **premiss**) prémisse

f; **to argue from different premises,** discuter à partir de prémisses différentes.

premise² [prɪˈmaɪz] *vt* poser en principe (**that,** que); (*in logic*) poser (*un fait*) en prémisse; poser en prémisse (**that,** que).

premises [ˈpremɪsɪz] *npl* **(a)** (*property*) **the p.,** le local, les locaux; les lieux *mpl*; **business p.,** locaux commerciaux; **drinks to be consumed on/off the p.,** boissons à consommer dans/hors de l'établissement; **she's still on the p.,** elle est encore dans le bâtiment; **(b)** *Jur* **premises,** intitulé *m* (*d'un document*).

premium [ˈpriːmɪəm] *n* **(a)** (*for insurance*) prime *f*; **(b)** *Fin etc* **(exchange) p.,** agio *m*; prix *m ou* prime *f* du change; **to issue shares at a p.,** émettre des actions au-dessus du pair *ou* de leur valeur nominale; *Br* **p. bonds,** obligations *fpl* à primes *ou* à lots; **to sell sth at a p.,** vendre qch à prime *ou* à bénéfice; **antiques are at a p.,** (*are sought after*) les antiquités sont très recherchées; (*sell at high prices*) les antiquités se vendent à prix d'or; *Fig* **to put** *or* **place a p. on sth,** (*of people*) accorder beaucoup d'importance à qch; (*of circumstances*) mettre l'accent sur qch; **(c)** (*bonus*) prime *f*, prix *m*, récompense *f*; **(d)** prix convenu, indemnité *f* (*pour l'apprentissage à une profession libérale*); **(e) p. grade petrol,** *Am* **p. fuel** *or* **gasoline,** = supercarburant *m*, *F* super *m*.

premolar [priːˈməʊlər] *adj & n Anat* (dent *f*) prémolaire *f*.

premonition [priːməˈnɪʃən] *n* prémonition *f*, pressentiment *m* (*de malheur etc*); **to have a p.,** avoir un pressentiment.

premonitory [prɪˈmɒnɪtərɪ] *adj* prémonitoire; (*signe*) précurseur.

prenatal [priːˈneɪt(ə)l] *adj* prénatal, -als, -aux.

preoccupation [priːɒkjʊˈpeɪʃən] *n* préoccupation *f* (**with,** de); préoccupation (*de l'esprit*).

preoccupied [priːˈɒkjʊpaɪd] *adj* préoccupé; absorbé (*par un souci*); **to be p.,** être préoccupé; **to be p. with sth,** s'occuper de qch.

preoccupy [priːˈɒkjʊpaɪ] *vt* préoccuper, absorber (*l'esprit*).

preordain [priːɔːˈdeɪn] *vt* **(a)** (*decree*) ordonner *ou* régler d'avance; **(b)** (*destine*) prédéterminer; **it was preordained,** c'était prédestiné.

prep¹ [prep] *Br Sch F* **1** *n* (*esp in private school*) étude *f* (du soir); devoirs *mpl* (du soir); **p. room,** (salle *f* d')étude; **p. period,** (heure *f* de) permanence *f*. **2** *adj* **p. school,** école primaire (privée).

prep² *vt* **(-pp-)** *F* préparer; **to p. s.o. for an operation,** préparer qn pour une opération.

prepack [priːˈpæk] *vt* préconditionner, préemballer.

preparation [prepəˈreɪʃən] *n* **(a)** préparation *f* (*de la nourriture, d'un médicament etc*); mise *f* en état (*de fonctionner, d'être utilisé*); *Constr* appareillage *m* (*des pierres à bâtir*); **in course of p.,** en cours de préparation; **they broke the news to her without any p.,** ils lui ont annoncé la nouvelle sans aucune préparation;

(b) (*measures*) (*usu pl*) **preparations,** préparatifs *mpl*; **preparations for war,** préparatifs de guerre; **to make (one's) preparations for,** prendre ses mesures *ou* ses dispositions *ou* faire des préparatifs en vue de (*qch*); se préparer à *ou* pour (*un voyage*);

(c) *Br Sch* (*esp in private school*) étude *f* (du soir); devoirs *mpl* (du soir);

(d) (*substance*) préparation *f* (*pharmaceutique, microscopique etc*).

preparative [prɪˈpærətɪv] **1** *adj* préparatoire. **2** *n* acte *m ou* signal *m* préparatoire; **preparatives,** préparatifs *mpl*.

preparatory [prɪˈpærətərɪ] *adj* préparatoire, préalable (**to,** à); **p. school,** école primaire (privée).

prepare [prɪˈpeər] **1** *vt* préparer (*un repas etc*); monter, préparer (*une attaque etc*); mettre (*qch*) en état (*de fonctionner, d'être utilisé*); *Constr* appareiller (*des pierres à bâtir*); **to p. a surprise for s.o.,** ménager une surprise à qn; **to p. the way for negotiations,** préparer la voie pour des négociations; **to p. s.o. for an exam,** préparer qn à un examen; **their training had prepared them for most eventualities,** leur entraînement les a préparés à toutes les éventualités; **prepared from the finest ingredients,** préparé avec les meilleurs ingrédients.

2 *vi* se préparer, se disposer, s'apprêter (**for sth,** à qch; **to do sth,** à faire qch); se mettre en devoir (**to do sth,** de faire qch); **to p. for departure,** faire ses préparatifs de départ; **to p. for an examination,** préparer un examen.

prepared [prɪˈpeəd] *adj* **(a)** (*willing*) **I am (quite) p. to ...,** je suis prêt *ou* disposé à ...; **he was/was not p. to lie,** il était/n'était pas disposé à mentir; **(b)** (*ready*) **to be p. for anything,** être prêt à tout; **be p.,** (*Scout's motto*) toujours prêt; **I wasn't p. for this reaction,** je ne m'attendais pas à cette réaction; **a p. speech,** un discours préparé (à l'avance); **(c)** (*made*) préparé; **well p. dish,** mets bien préparé; **(d)** (*finished*) en état; **p. timber,** bois refait.

preparedness [prɪˈpeərɪdnɪs] *n* état *m* de préparation; *Mil* **to be in a state of p.,** être en état d'alerte (préventive).

prepay [priːˈpeɪ] *vt* (*pt & pp* **prepaid**) payer *ou* régler (*qch*) d'avance; affranchir (*une lettre etc*); **to send sth carriage prepaid,** envoyer qch port payé *ou* franc de port *ou* franco; *Telecom* **prepaid answer,** réponse payée.

prepayment [priːˈpeɪmənt] *n* paiement *m* à l'avance.

preponderance [prɪˈpɒndərəns] *n* prépondérance *f* (**over,** sur); **there was a p. of French books on the shelf,** il y avait une majorité de livres français sur l'étagère.

preponderant [prɪˈpɒndərənt] *adj* prépondérant.

preponderantly [prɪˈpɒndərəntlɪ] *adv* à un degré prépondérant; **the guests were p. French,** les invités étaient pour la majeure partie français.

preponderate [prɪˈpɒndəreɪt] *vi* l'emporter sur la balance (**over,** sur).

preposition [prepəˈzɪʃən] *n Gram* préposition *f*.

prepositional [prepəˈzɪʃən(ə)l] *adj* prépositif.

prepositionally [prepəˈzɪʃən(ə)lɪ] *adv* (*employé*) comme préposition.

prepossess [priːpəˈzes] *vt* **(a)** (*engross*) préoccuper (*qn*); **(b)** (*influence*) influencer (*qn*).

prepossessing [priːpəˈzesɪŋ] *adj* (*visage*) agréable, prévenant; **p. appearance,** aspect engageant *ou* attrayant; (*of person*) air *m* sympathique.

preposterous [prɪˈpɒstərəs] *adj* absurde.

preposterously [prɪˈpɒstərəslɪ] *adv* d'une façon absurde.

preposterousness [prɪˈpɒstərəsnɪs] *n* absurdité *f*.

preppy [prepɪ] *F* **1** *adj* (*look, clothes etc*) ≈ b.c.b.g. **2** *n* ≈ (personne *f*) b.c.b.g..

preprogram [priːˈprəʊgræm] *vt Comptr etc* préprogrammer; **the theory that humans are preprogrammed to behave in certain ways,** la théorie selon laquelle les êtres humains sont conditionnés à se comporter d'une certaine façon.

preprogrammed [priːˈprəʊgræmd] *adj Comptr etc* préprogrammé.

prepuce [ˈpriːpjuːs] *n Anat* prépuce *m*.

Pre-Raphaelite [priːˈræfəlaɪt] *adj & n Art* préraphaélite *m*.

prerecord [priːrɪˈkɔːd] *vt* préenregistrer; *TV Rad* **prerecorded broadcast,** émission *f* en différé; **prerecorded cassette,** cassette préenregistrée.

prerecording [priːrɪˈkɔːdɪŋ] *n* préenregistrement *m*; *TV Rad* (émission *f* en) différé *m*.

prerelease [priːrɪˈliːs] *Cin* **1** *n* avant-première *f* (*d'un film*). **2** *adj* **p. publicity,** bande-annonce *f*.

prerequisite [priːˈrekwɪzɪt] **1** *adj* préalablement nécessaire, indispensable. **2** *n* nécessité *f ou* condition *f* préalable.

prerogative [prɪˈrɒgətɪv] *n* prérogative *f*, privilège *m*; **the royal p.,** la prérogative royale; **to exercise the royal p.,** faire acte de souverain.

Pres. *n Pol etc abbr* **President.**

presage¹ [ˈpresɪdʒ] *n Lit* (*sign*) présage *m*; (*foreboding*) pressentiment *m*.

presage² [ˈpresɪdʒ, prɪˈseɪdʒ] *vt Lit* présager, augurer de (*une catastrophe etc*).

Presbyterian [prezbɪˈtɪərɪən] *adj & n Rel* presbytérien, -ienne.

Presbyterianism [prezbɪˈtɪərɪənɪz(ə)m] *n Rel* presbytérianisme *m*.

presbytery [ˈprezbɪt(ə)rɪ] *n Rel* **(a)** (*in church*) sanctuaire *m*; **(b)** *Cathol* presbytère *m*; **(c)** (*in Presbyterian Church*) consistoire *m*.

preschool [priːˈskuːl] *adj* (*âge etc*) préscolaire.

prescience [ˈpresɪəns] *n* prescience *f*.

prescient [ˈpresɪənt] *adj* prescient.

prescribe [prɪˈskraɪb] *vt* **(a)** prescrire, ordonner; indiquer, imposer (*une ligne de conduite*); **prescribed task,** tâche imposée; **in the prescribed time,** dans le délai prescrit; **(b)** *Med* **to p. sth for s.o.,** prescrire *ou* ordonner qch à qn.

prescription [prɪˈskrɪpʃən] *n* **(a)** (*order*) prescription *f*; **(b)** *Med* ordonnance *f*; **available only on (a doctor's) p.,** délivré seulement sur ordonnance; **p. charges,** frais *mpl* pharmaceutiques; **p. drugs,** médicaments délivrés uniquement sur ordonnance.

prescriptive [prɪˈskrɪptɪv] *adj* **(a)** (*prescribing action*) normatif; **(b)** (*established by custom*) consacré par l'usage *ou* par la coutume.

prescriptivism [prɪ'skrɪptɪvɪz(ə)m] *n Phil* normativisme *m*.

presence ['prezəns] *n* **(a)** présence *f*; **in the p. of ...,** en présence de ...; **say nothing about it in his p.,** n'en parlez pas devant lui; *Fml* **to be admitted to the p.,** être admis en présence (*du roi etc*); **the police maintained a discreet p.,** (*at demonstration etc*) la police a assuré une surveillance discrète; **the Soviet (military) p.,** la présence militaire soviétique; **to make one's p. felt,** se faire remarquer, faire sentir sa présence; **(b) p. of mind,** présence *f* d'esprit; **to keep one's p. of mind,** garder son sang-froid; **to have the p. of mind to do,** avoir la présence d'esprit de faire; **(c)** (*bearing*) air *m*, mine *f*, extérieur *m*, maintien *m*; **to have a good p.,** bien présenter; **he has p.,** il a de la prestance, il en impose.

present[1] ['prezənt] **1** *adj* **(a)** (*in attendance*) présent; **to be p. at a ceremony,** être présent *ou* assister à une cérémonie; **he cannot be interviewed without a lawyer being p.,** on ne peut pas l'interroger sans la présence d'un avocat; **all p. heard it,** toute l'assistance l'a entendu; **some of you p. here,** quelques-uns d'entre vous, ici présents; **minerals which are p. in the solution,** minéraux qui se trouvent dans la solution;

(b) (*in time*) actuel; (*under discussion*) en question; **the p. king,** le roi actuel; **at the p. time,** à présent; (*at this moment*) en ce moment; (*in this period of time*) à l'époque actuelle; (*nowadays*) aujourd'hui; **up to the p. time,** jusqu'ici; **the p. writer,** l'auteur du présent article *etc*; **in the p. case,** dans le cas qui nous occupe; *Gram* **p. tense,** temps présent; *Gram* **p. subjunctive,** présent du subjonctif; *Gram* **p. perfect,** passé composé.

2 *n* **(a)** (*time*) présent *m*; **the p.,** le présent; *Gram* le présent; **up to the p.,** jusqu'à présent, jusqu'ici; **at p.,** à présent, maintenant, actuellement; **no more at p.,** rien de plus pour le moment; **as things are at the p.,** (*at the stage things have reached*) au point où en sont les choses; (*nowadays*) par les temps qui courent; **for the p.,** pour le moment;

(b) *Jur* **by these presents,** par la présente.

present[2] *n* (*gift*) cadeau *m*; **to make s.o. a p. of sth, to give sth to s.o. as a p.,** faire cadeau de qch à qn, donner qch en cadeau à qn; **it's for a p.,** (*when buying*) c'est pour offrir.

present[3] [prɪ'zent] **1** *vt* **(a)** (*introduce, put forward*) présenter; **to p. s.o. to s.o.,** présenter qn à qn; **to p. s.o. at court,** présenter qn à la cour; *Th* **to p. a play,** (*of company etc*) présenter *ou* donner une pièce; *TV Rad* **to p. a programme,** (*of presenter*) présenter une émission; **to p. oneself at** *or* **for an examination,** se présenter à *ou* pour un examen; **a good opportunity presents itself,** une bonne occasion se présente (**for doing sth,** de faire qch); **to p. s.o./sth in a good/bad light,** présenter qn/qch sous un jour favorable/défavorable; **his attempts to mount the horse presented a strange spectacle,** ses tentatives pour monter le cheval offraient un curieux spectacle;

(b) (*give*) donner; **to p. sth to s.o., to p. s.o. with sth,** remettre qch à qn; **to p. one's compliments to s.o.,** présenter ses compliments à qn; **they were presented with an empty goalmouth,** ils se trouvèrent devant un but vide; *Mil & Fig* **to p. s.o. with an easy target,** offrir une bonne cible à qn;

(c) *Jur* déposer (*une plainte etc*); *Com* **to p. a bill for acceptance,** présenter une traite à l'acceptation; *Jur* **to p. a plea,** introduire une instance;

(d) *Parl* présenter, introduire (*un projet de loi*); **to p. a plan to a meeting,** soumettre un plan à une assemblée;

(e) *Mil* **to p. arms,** présenter les armes; **p. arms!,** présentez armes!

2 *vi Obst* (*of foetus*) se présenter; *Med* **to p. with sth,** avoir qch.

presentable [prɪ'zentəb(ə)l] *adj* (*person, thing*) présentable; (*garment*) portable, mettable; *F* **he's not p.,** il n'est pas présentable.

presentation [prezən'teɪʃən] *n* **(a)** présentation *f* (*de qn*); présentation, représentation *f* (*d'une pièce de théâtre*); présentation (*d'une théorie etc*); soutenance *f* (*d'une thèse, d'un mémoire*); **to give a p.,** faire un exposé; **(b)** (*giving*) remise *f* (*d'un cadeau, d'une médaille etc à qn*); (*gift*) cadeau *m* (*offert à qn*); **to make a p. to s.o.,** offrir un cadeau à qn; **p. ceremony,** cérémonie *f* de remise des prix *ou* des médailles *etc*; **p. copy,** (*book*) (*sent by publisher*) = exemplaire envoyé à titre gracieux par l'éditeur; (*given by author*) = exemplaire offert à titre d'hommage par l'auteur; **(c)** *Com* **payable on p. of the coupon,** payable contre remise du coupon; **on p. of the invoice,** au vu de la facture; **(d)** *Obst* présentation *f* (*du fœtus*).

present-day [prezənt'deɪ] *adj* actuel, d'aujourd'hui.

presenter [prɪ'zentər] *n Rad TV etc* présentateur, -trice.

presentiment [prɪ'zentɪmənt] *n* pressentiment *m*.

presently ['prezəntlɪ] *adv* **(a)** (*soon*) bientôt; **(b)** *esp Am* (*now*) actuellement, à présent.

presentment [prɪ'zentmənt] *n* **(a)** *Com* présentation *f* (*d'une traite etc*); **(b)** *Jur* déclaration *f* émanant du jury.

preservation [prezə'veɪʃən] *n* **(a)** conservation *f*; maintien *m* (*de la paix*); naturalisation *f* (*d'une fleur, d'un spécimen*); (*of goods etc*) traitement *m* avant stockage; **in a good state of p.,** en bon état de conservation; **(b)** (*protection*) préservation *f* (**from a danger,** d'un danger).

preservative [prɪ'zɜːvətɪv] **1** *adj* préservateur, -trice; (*assurant la conservation*) conservateur, -trice. **2** *n* (*in foods*) conservateur *m*; préservateur *m*.

preserve[1] [prɪ'zɜːv] *n* **(a)** (*often pl*) **(apricot** *etc***) preserve(s),** confiture *f* (d'abricots *etc*); **(b)** (*area*) **game p.,** réserve *f*; *esp US* **wildlife p.,** réserve zoologique; *Fig* **engineering is no longer a male p.,** le métier d'ingénieur n'est plus réservé aux hommes.

preserve[2] *vt* **(a)** préserver, garantir (*qn*) (**from sth,** de qch); **(b)** conserver (*un bâtiment, une coutume etc*); maintenir (*la paix etc*); garder, observer (*le silence etc*); conserver, mettre en conserve (*des fruits etc*); naturaliser (*une plante*); **(c)** élever (*du gibier*) dans une réserve; élever (*des poissons*) dans un vivier.

preserved [prɪ'zɜːvd] *adj* **(a)** conservé; (*fruit*) confit; **p. food,** conserves *fpl*; **p. meat,** conserve *f* de viande; **(b) well/badly p.,** (*bâtiment etc*) en bon/mauvais état de conservation; *Hum* **well p.,** (*person*) bien conservé.

preserver [prɪ'zɜːvər] *n* **(a)** (*person*) conservateur, -trice (*de choses*); **(b)** (*thing*) **dress p.,** dessous *m* de bras; **life p.,** (*life belt*) ceinture *f ou* gilet *m* de sauvetage; *F* (*club*) matraque *f*.

preserving [prɪ'zɜːvɪŋ] *n* **(a)** (*protection*) préservation *f* (**from,** de); **(b)** conservation *f* (*des aliments*); **p. pan,** bassine *f* à confitures; **(c)** = **PRESERVATION**.

preset [priː'set] *vt* (*pt & pp* **preset**; *prp* **presetting**) *Tech Electron* prérégler (*le fonctionnement d'un mécanisme etc*).

presetting [priː'setɪŋ] *n* préréglage *m*.

preshrink [priː'ʃrɪŋk] *vt* (*pt* **preshrank**; *pp* **preshrunk**) rendre (*un tissu*) irrétrécissable.

preshrunk [priː'ʃrʌŋk] *adj* (*tissu*) rétréci en cours de fabrication.

preside [prɪ'zaɪd] *vi* présider; **p. at** *or* **over a meeting,** présider une réunion.

presidency ['prezɪdənsɪ] *n* présidence *f*; **to assume the p.,** assumer la présidence.

president ['prezɪdənt] *n* président *m*.

president-elect ['prezɪdəntɪ'lekt] *n Pol* président élu.

presidential [prezɪ'denʃəl] *adj* présidentiel; **p. elections,** (élections *fpl*) présidentielles *fpl*; **p. hopeful,** présidentiable *mf*.

presidium [prɪ'sɪdɪəm, -'zɪd-] *n Pol* présidium *m*.

press[1] [pres] *n* **(a)** (*act of pushing*) pression *f* (*sur qch*); (*crowd*) foule *f*; mêlée *f* (*de la bataille*); **give it a slight p.!,** appuyez légèrement là-dessus!; **give your trousers a p.,** donne un coup de fer à ton pantalon; **to force one's way through the p.,** fendre la foule, se frayer un chemin à travers la foule; **p. stud,** (*on clothing*) bouton *m* (à) pression;

(b) (*device*) **wine p.,** pressoir *m*; **cider/oil p.,** pressoir à cidre/à huile; **tennis racquet p.,** presse *f* à raquette; **trouser p.,** presse pour pantalons, presse-pantalon *m*, *pl* presse-pantalons; *Ind etc* **hydraulic p.,** presse hydraulique; **coining p.,** presse monétaire; *Typ* **(printing) p.,** presse d'imprimerie; **rotary/offset p.,** presse rotative/offset; **to go to p.,** être mis sous presse, aller à l'impression; **at the time of going to p.,** au moment d'être mis sous presse; **ready for p.,** prêt à mettre sous presse; **to pass a proof for p.,** donner le bon à tirer; **the Jones P.,** (*in name of firm*) (*printing firm*) l'Imprimerie Jones; (*publishing firm*) les Editions Jones;

(c) *Journ* **the p.,** la presse, les journaux; **the liberty** *or* **freedom of the p.,** la liberté de la presse; **to write for the p.,** écrire pour les journaux; **to have a good/bad p.,** avoir bonne/mauvaise presse; **the story appeared in the p.,** on a parlé de cette affaire dans la presse; **p. attaché** *or* **officer,** attaché *m* de presse; **p. conference/campaign,** conférence *f*/campagne *f* de presse; **p. copy,** (*of book*) exemplaire *m* de publicité; **p. cutting** *or* **clipping,** coupure *f* de journal *ou* de presse; **p. photographer,** photographe *mf* de presse; **p. release,** communiqué *m* de presse; *Typ* **p. run,** tirage *m* (*en une seule fois*); **p. run of 5,000,** tirage à *ou* de *ou* en

5 000 exemplaires; **p. agent,** (*for film star, organization etc*) agent *m* de publicité;
(d) *Hist* **p. gang,** presse *f*, enrôleurs *mpl*;
(e) (*in weightlifting*) développé *m*;
(f) *Scot* **linen** *or* **clothes p.,** armoire *f* à linge.

press² **1** *vt* **(a)** (*push*) appuyer sur (*qch*); (*squeeze*) serrer; **he pressed my hand in his,** il a serré ma main dans la sienne; **to p. (the juice out of) a lemon,** presser un citron;
(b) *Tech* mettre (*qch*) sous presse; matricer, estamper (*le métal*); matricer, presser (*un disque*); calandrer (*le papier, un tissu*); mouler (*le verre, le plastique*); pressurer, fouler (*le raisin*); presser, pressurer (*le fromage*); repasser, donner un coup de fer à (*un vêtement*); **to p. a seam,** rabattre une couture;
(c) (*put pressure on*) **to p. the enemy hard** *or* **closely,** serrer l'ennemi de près, talonner l'ennemi; **to p. s.o. hard,** mettre qn à la dernière extrémité; **pressed by one's creditors,** harcelé par ses créanciers; **to be pressed for time/money,** être à court de temps/d'argent; **to p. s.o. to do sth,** presser qn de faire qch; **if you p. her she'll tell you,** si tu insistes, elle te le dira; **to p. a point,** insister sur un point; **to p. a claim,** insister sur une demande; **to p. a gift on s.o.,** forcer qn à accepter un cadeau; *Jur* **to p. charges,** porter plainte.
2 *vi* **(a)** (*push*) appuyer, exercer une pression; **don't p. too hard,** n'appuyez pas trop fort; **the crowd was pressing forward towards the exit,** la foule se pressait pour gagner la sortie; **to p. close against s.o.,** se serrer contre qn; **stop pressing!,** ne poussez pas!;
(b) **time is pressing,** le temps presse; **nothing presses,** rien ne presse; **to p. for an answer,** insister pour avoir une réponse immédiate.
►**press down** **1** *vtsep* appuyer sur; (*with force*) enfoncer. **2** *vi* **to p. down on s.o.,** (*of heavy object*) appuyer sur qn, peser sur qn; (*of worries etc*) peser sur qn.
►**press on** *vi* (*walk, travel faster*) presser *ou* forcer le pas; (*continue one's journey*) continuer son chemin; (*persevere with activity*) persévérer, ne pas abandonner; (*continue activity*) continuer; **to p. on with one's work,** poursuivre son travail; **p. on regardless!,** allons-y et tant pis!
►**press out** *vtsep* exprimer (*le jus etc*).

press-button ['presbʌt(ə)n] *adj Tel* **p.-b. dialling,** numérotation *f* à touches.

pressed [prest] *adj* pressé, serré, comprimé; (*coton, foin*) en balles; (*metal*) matricé, estampé; *Culin* **p. beef,** bœuf salé, bouilli et moulé en forme.

press-gang ['presgæŋ] *vt Hist* **to p.-g. s.o. into the navy/army,** enrôler qn de force dans la marine/l'armée; *F* **to p.-g. s.o. into doing sth,** forcer la main à qn pour qu'il fasse qch.

pressie ['prezɪ] *n Br F* cadeau *m*.

pressing ['presɪŋ] **1** *adj* (*danger*) pressant; (*travail*) urgent; (*dette*) criard; **the matter is p.,** il y a urgence; **there is a p. need for action,** il faut agir vite. **2** *n* **(a)** (*act of pressing*) pression *f* (*sur qch*); mise *f* en balle (*du coton etc*); foulage *m*, pressurage *m* (*du raisin*); pressurage (*des fromages*); estampage *m*, matriçage *m* (*de disques, de métal*); moulage *m* (*du verre, du plastique etc*); calandrage *m* (*des tissus, du papier*); repassage *m* (*des vêtements*); *Com* pressing *m*; **(b)** (*pressed metal*) pièce matricée; **(c)** (*usu pl*) **pressing(s),** pressée *f*, pressis *m* (*de pommes etc*).

pressman, *pl* **-men** ['presmən] *n* journaliste *m*, reporter *m*.

pressmark ['presmɑːk] *n* cote *f* (*d'un livre dans une bibliothèque*).

press-up ['presʌp] *n Gym* **to do p.-ups,** faire des tractions *ou F* des pompes.

pressure¹ ['preʃər] *n* **(a)** pression *f* (*exercée sur qch*); **I felt the slight p. of his hand on my arm,** j'ai senti la légère pression de sa main sur mon bras; *Fig* **to bring p. to bear** *or* **to put p. on s.o.,** exercer une pression sur qn; **to act under p.,** agir sous la pression des circonstances; **I can't take p.,** je ne supporte pas le stress; **he's been under a lot of p. lately,** il est très stressé depuis peu; **financial p.,** embarras financiers; **p. of business/work,** le poids des affaires/du travail; **to work at high p.,** travailler au plus fort; *F* **there's no p. — don't come if you don't want to,** rien ne t'oblige, si tu ne veux pas venir, ne viens pas; *Pol etc* **p. group,** groupe *m* de pression;
(b) *Phys MecE etc* pression *f*; poussée *f* (*d'un fluide, d'un corps pesant*); *El* pression (électrique), tension *f*, voltage *m*; *Met* **high/low-p. area,** zone *f* anticyclonique/cyclonique, zone de hautes/basses pressions; *Aut* **tyre p.,** pression des pneus; *Physiol* **blood p.,** tension artérielle; *Med* **high/low blood p.,** hypertension *f*/hypotension *f*; *El* **drop in p.,** chute *f* de tension; *MecE* **p. chamber,** réservoir *m* d'air comprimé; *Culin* **p. cooker,** cocotte-minute *f*, autocuiseur *m*; **p. gauge,** jauge *f* de pression; *Astronaut* **p. suit,** combinaison pressurisée.

pressure² *vt* **(a)** exercer une pression sur (*qn*); **stop pressuring me!,** arrête de me presser comme ça!; **(b)** pressuriser (*la cabine d'un avion etc*).

pressure-cook ['preʃəkʊk] *vt Culin* (faire) cuire sous pression *ou* à la cocotte-minute.

pressurization [preʃəraɪ'zeɪʃən] *n* pressurisation *f*, mise *f ou* maintien *m* sous pression.

pressurize ['preʃəraɪz] *vt* **(a)** *Tech* pressuriser; mettre *ou* maintenir en *ou* sous pression; *Av Astronaut* **pressurized cabin/suit,** cabine/combinaison pressurisée; *Nucl Phys* **pressurized water reactor** réacteur *m* à eau sous pression; **(b)** (*put moral pressure on*) exercer une pression sur (*qn*); **to p. s.o. into doing sth,** contraindre *ou* obliger qn à faire qch; **he was pressurized into it,** il a été contraint de le faire, il l'a fait sous la contrainte.

Prestel ® ['prestel] *n Br TV* ≈ Minitel *m*.

prestidigitation [prestɪdɪdʒɪ'teɪʃən] *n* prestidigitation *f*.

prestidigitator [prestɪ'dɪdʒɪteɪtər] *n* prestidigitateur *m*.

prestige [pres'tiːʒ] *n* prestige *m*; **it would mean a loss of p.,** ce serait déchoir *ou* déroger; **p. flats,** appartements *mpl* de grand standing; **a p. job,** un poste prestigieux.

prestigious [pres'tɪdʒəs] *adj* prestigieux.

presto¹ ['prestəʊ] *adj, adv & n Mus* presto *m*.

presto² *int* **hey p.!,** le tour est joué!

prestressed [priː'strest] *adj* (*béton*) précontraint.

presumably [prɪ'zjuːməblɪ] *adv* **p. she will come,** il est à croire qu'elle viendra; **he is p. dead,** il est vraisemblablement mort; **p. you told him that ...,** je suppose que vous lui avez dit que ...; **have they left? — p.,** ils sont partis? — je pense.

presume [prɪ'zjuːm] **1** *vt* présumer; **to p. s.o. innocent,** présumer qn innocent *ou* que qn est innocent; **he was presumed dead,** (*by family etc*) on le croyait mort; (*by authorities*) on l'a considéré comme décédé; **missing, presumed dead,** porté disparu; **I p. you've written to him,** je suppose que vous lui avez écrit; **I wouldn't p. to question her decision,** je n'oserais pas mettre en question sa décision. **2** *vi* se montrer présomptueux; prendre des libertés (*avec qn*); **to p. too much,** y aller un peu fort; **to p. on one's friendship with s.o.,** abuser de l'amitié de qn.

presuming [prɪ'zjuːmɪŋ] *adj* présomptueux.

presumption [prɪ'zʌmpʃən] *n* **(a)** présomption *f*; **the p. is that she is dead,** on présume qu'elle est morte; *Jur* **p. of law,** présomption légale; **p. of fact,** présomption de fait; **(b)** (*arrogance*) présomption *f*, arrogance *f*.

presumptive [prɪ'zʌmptɪv] *adj Jur etc* **p. evidence,** (preuve *f* par) présomption *f*; **heir p.,** héritier présomptif.

presumptuous [prɪ'zʌmptjʊəs] *adj* présomptueux.

presumptuously [prɪ'zʌmptjʊəslɪ] *adv* présomptueusement.

presumptuousness [prɪ'zʌmptjʊəsnɪs] *n* présomption *f*.

presuppose [priːsə'pəʊz] *vt* présupposer.

presupposition [priːsʌpə'zɪʃən] *n* présupposition *f*.

pretence, *US* **pretense** [prɪ'tens] *n* **(a)** (faux-)semblant *m*, simulation *f*, affectation *f*; **to make a p. of doing sth,** faire semblant de faire qch; **under the p. of friendship,** sous prétexte d'amitié; **under the p. that ...,** sous prétexte que ...; **under** *or* **on the p. of consulting me,** sous prétexte de me consulter; *Jur* **false pretences,** faux-semblant; présentation mensongère (*en vue d'escroquer*); **to obtain sth by** *or* **under false pretences,** obtenir qch par fraude *ou* par des moyens frauduleux; **she makes no p. to photographic skills,** elle ne prétend pas avoir des dons de photographe; **(b)** (*pretension*) prétention *f*, vanité *f*; **devoid of all p.,** sans aucune prétention.

pretend¹ [prɪ'tend] **1** *vt* **(a)** feindre, simuler (*qch*); **to p. ignorance,** simuler l'ignorance, faire l'ignorant; **to p. to be ill,** faire le malade; **to p. to do sth,** faire semblant de faire qch; **she pretended to be angry,** elle a fait mine d'être fâchée; **they pretended that nothing had happened,** ils ont fait comme si rien ne s'était passé; **let's p. that we're astronauts,** on dirait qu'on était astronautes; **it's no use pretending (that) I'm still young,** ce n'est pas la peine de prétendre que je suis encore jeune; **he pretended he was a doctor,** il s'est fait passer pour médecin; **pretending that he had a lot of work to do, he left early,** sous prétexte d'avoir beaucoup de travail à faire, il est parti de bonne heure;
(b) (*claim*) prétendre; **she does not p. to be artistic,**

elle ne prétend pas être artiste.
2 *vi* **(a)** (*put on act*) faire semblant, jouer la comédie; **he appeared interested, but he was just pretending,** il s'est montré intéressé mais il jouait la comédie;
(b) *Arch* (*lay claim*) **to p. to sth,** prétendre à qch, revendiquer son droit à qch; **to p. to the throne,** prétendre au trône.

pretend² *n F* **it was only p.!,** c'était pour rire!

pretended [prɪˈtendɪd] *adj* (*emotion*) feint, simulé, faux; (*doctor, duke etc*) soi-disant, supposé, prétendu.

pretender [prɪˈtendər] *n* **(a)** (*person who puts on act*) simulateur, -trice; **(b)** (*claimant*) prétendant *m* (**to,** à); *Hist* **the Old P.,** le Prétendant; **the Young P.,** le Jeune Prétendant.

pretense [prɪˈtens] *n US* = **PRETENCE.**

pretension [prɪˈtenʃən] *n* **(a)** (*false claim*) prétention *f* (**to,** à); **man of no pretension(s),** homme sans prétentions; **to have pretensions to literary taste,** se piquer de littérature; **to have social pretensions,** vouloir arriver; **(b)** (*right*) droit *m*, titre *m*; prétention justifiée; **(c)** = **PRETENTIOUSNESS.**

pretentious [prɪˈtenʃəs] *adj* prétentieux.

pretentiously [prɪˈtenʃəslɪ] *adv* prétentieusement.

pretentiousness [prɪˈtenʃəsnɪs] *n* prétention *f*.

preterite [ˈpretərɪt] *n Gram* prétérit *m*, passé simple.

preternatural [priːtəˈnætʃrəl] *adj* surnaturel.

pretext [ˈpriːtekst] *n* prétexte *m*; **to give sth as a p.,** alléguer qch comme prétexte; **he came under** *or* **on the p. of consulting his sister,** il est venu sous prétexte de consulter sa sœur.

prettify [ˈprɪtɪfaɪ] *vt* enjoliver.

prettily [ˈprɪtɪlɪ] *adv* joliment; gentiment.

prettiness [ˈprɪtɪnɪs] *n* (*of woman*) charmes *mpl*; *Pej* mignardise *f* (*de style etc*).

pretty [ˈprɪtɪ] **1** *adj* (*woman, child*) joli, mignon; (*thing*) joli; **as p. as a picture,** joli *ou* mignon comme tout; **a p. thatched cottage,** une jolie chaumière; **p. picture/song,** (*with Pej nuance*) joli petit tableau/jolie petite chanson; *Pej* **to make p. speeches,** dire des gentillesses; *Sp* **that was p. play,** c'était bien joué; *Iron* **a p. state of affairs!, a p. mess!,** c'est du joli *ou* du propre!; (*that we're in*) nous voilà dans de beaux draps!; *F* **that'll cost me a p. penny!,** ça va me coûter cher! **2** *adv* **(a)** (*fairly*) assez, passablement; **I'm p. well,** ça ne va pas trop mal; **p. good,** (*not bad*) pas mal *ou* mauvais; (*very good*) vraiment bon; **it's p. difficult,** c'est plutôt difficile; **p. nearly** *or* **much** *or* **well the same,** à peu près la même chose; **(b)** *F* **to be sitting p.,** ne pas avoir à s'en faire.

pretty-pretty [ˈprɪtɪprɪtɪ] *adj Pej* affecté, minaudier.

pretzel [ˈpretz(ə)l] *n Culin* bretzel *m*.

prevail [prɪˈveɪl] *vi* **(a)** (*come out strongest*) prévaloir, avoir l'avantage; **let us hope that justice/reason prevails,** espérons que la justice/la raison l'emportera; **to p. over** *or* **against s.o.,** prévaloir sur *ou* contre qn, avoir l'avantage *ou* l'emporter sur qn; **(b) to p. on s.o. to do sth,** (*persuade*) amener *ou* décider qn à faire qch; **he was prevailed (up)on by his friends to ...,** il se laissa persuader par ses amis de ...; **(c)** (*predominate*) prédominer, régner; (*of theory etc*) dominer, avoir cours; **the conditions prevailing in France,** les conditions qui règnent en France.

prevailing [prɪˈveɪlɪŋ] *adj* (pré)dominant; **p. winds,** vents dominants; **the p. opinion,** l'opinion la plus répandue; **the p. cold,** le froid qui règne en ce moment; **p. fashions,** la mode actuelle.

prevalence [ˈprevələns] *n* prédominance *f* (*d'une opinion etc*); **p. of bribery,** caractère généralisé de la corruption; **p. of typhus,** fréquence *f* des cas de typhus.

prevalent [ˈprevələnt] *adj* (pré)dominant; (*wind*) dominant; **the disease is p. here,** la maladie est très répandue ici.

prevaricate [prɪˈværɪkeɪt] *vi* user d'équivoques, tergiverser.

prevarication [prɪværɪˈkeɪʃən] *n* équivoques *fpl*, tergiversation *f*.

prevaricator [prɪˈværɪkeɪtər] *n* tergiversateur, -trice.

prevent [prɪˈvent] *vt* (*stop*) empêcher, mettre obstacle à (*un mariage*); prévenir, détourner (*un malheur*); parer à (*un accident etc*); **to p. s.o. (from) doing sth, to p. s.o.'s doing sth,** empêcher qn de faire qch, empêcher que qn ne fasse qch; **to p. a disease from spreading,** empêcher une maladie de s'étendre; **there is nothing to p. our doing so,** il n'y a rien qui nous en empêche; **to be unavoidably prevented from doing sth,** être dans l'impossibilité matérielle de faire qch; **I cannot p. him,** je ne peux pas l'en empêcher; **to p. any scandal,** pour éviter tout scandale; **the police prevented the murderer from being lynched,** la police a empêché que l'assassin ne soit lynché.

preventable [prɪˈventəb(ə)l] *adj* évitable.

preventative [prɪˈventətɪv] *adj & n* = **PREVENTIVE.**

prevention [prɪˈvenʃən] *n* prévention *f*; **p. of accidents,** prévention *f* des accidents; **p. of disease,** prévention de la maladie; **rust p.,** protection *f* contre la rouille; **society for the p. of cruelty to children/to animals,** société protectrice des enfants/des animaux; *Prov* **p. is better than cure,** mieux vaut prévenir que guérir.

preventive [prɪˈventɪv] **1** *adj* (*médicament etc*) préventif; **p. medicine,** médecine préventive, prophylaxie *f*; **p. measures,** mesures préventives *ou* de précaution; *Jur* **p. detention,** détention préventive. **2** *n* (*measure*) mesure préventive; (*medication*) médicament préventif; **rust p.,** antirouille *m*.

preventively [prɪˈventɪvlɪ] *adv* préventivement.

preview¹ [ˈpriːvjuː] *n Cin etc* avant-première *f*, *pl* avant-premières; *esp US Cin* (*advertising film*) bande-annonce *f*, *pl* bandes-annonces (*d'un film*); **we've got a p. of the latest computers,** on a eu un aperçu des derniers ordinateurs.

preview² *vt Cin etc* voir en avant-première.

previous [ˈpriːvɪəs] **1** *adj* précédent; (*in time*) précédent, antérieur (**to,** à); **the p. day,** le jour précédent, la veille; **her p. job,** son travail précédent; **p. engagement,** engagement antérieur; *F* **you're a bit (too) p.!,** vous êtes trop pressé!, vous allez trop vite! **2** *adv* **p. to my departure,** avant mon départ.

previously [ˈpriːvɪəslɪ] *adv* précédemment, antérieurement; **he had p. denied this,** il avait précédemment nié cela; **three days p.,** trois jours auparavant.

prewar [priːˈwɔːr] *adj* (*prix etc*) d'avant-guerre; **the p. period,** l'avant-guerre *m*.

prey [preɪ] *n* proie *f*; **birds of p.,** oiseaux *mpl* de proie, rapaces *mpl*; **beasts of p.,** bêtes *fpl* de proie; **to pursue its p.,** (*of beast*) poursuivre sa proie; **to be a p. to,** être la proie de (*qch*); être en proie à (*la peur etc*); **to fall p. to temptation,** tomber en proie à la tentation.

▶**prey on, prey upon** *vipo* (*be predator of*) faire sa proie de (*qch, qn*); *Fig* **something is preying on his mind,** il y a quelque chose qui le travaille *ou* le tourmente; **to p. on old people,** (*of confidence man etc*) abuser des personnes âgées.

prezzie [ˈprezɪ] *n Br F* cadeau *m*.

price¹ [praɪs] *n* prix *m*; *Horseracing* cote *f*; **cost p.,** prix coûtant, prix de revient; **to sell under cost p.,** vendre à perte; **full p.,** prix fort; **manufacturer's p.,** prix de fabrique *ou* d'usine; **wholesale p.,** prix de *ou* en gros; **published p.,** (*of book*) prix de catalogue; *Rail Th etc* **half p.,** demi-tarif *m*; **to sell sth (at) half p.,** vendre qch à moitié prix; **at a reduced p.,** à prix réduit, au rabais, en solde; **to rise** *or* **increase in p.,** (*of goods*) augmenter; **what p. is that article?,** quel est le prix de cet article?; **car prices have fallen,** le prix des voitures a chuté; **he charges reasonable prices,** il pratique des prix raisonnables; **to quote** *or* **name a p.,** faire le prix; **his pictures fetch huge prices,** ses tableaux se vendent à prix d'or; **to be beyond** *or* **without p.,** être (d'un prix) inestimable *ou* hors de prix *ou* sans prix, ne pas avoir de prix; **you can buy it at a p.,** vous pouvez l'acheter en y mettant le prix; **this must be done at any p.,** il faut que cela se fasse à tout prix *ou* coûte que coûte; **not at any p.,** à aucun prix; *Fig* **to pay the p. (for sth)** payer le prix (pour qch); *Fig* **the p. paid for progress,** la rançon du progrès; **to set a high p. on sth,** faire grand cas de qch; **it's too high a p. (to pay),** c'est trop cher; *Fig* c'est trop cher payé; **to put** *or* **set a p. on s.o.'s head,** mettre à prix la tête de qn; **every man has his p.,** il n'y a pas d'homme qu'on ne puisse acheter; *Horseracing* **long/short p.,** forte/faible cote; *F* **what p. my chances of being appointed?,** quelles sont mes chances d'être nommé?; **what p. glory!,** pour ce qu'elle rapporte, la gloire!; *Fin* **issue p.,** taux *m* d'émission (*de titres*); **slump in prices,** effondrement *m* des prix *ou* des cours; *St Exch* **closing p.,** cours *m* de fermeture; **market p.,** cours du marché; **prices and incomes policy,** politique *f* des prix et des salaires; **p. control,** contrôle *m ou* régulation *f* des prix; **p. cut,** réduction *f* des prix; **p. freeze,** blocage *m* des prix; **p. increase,** hausse *f* des prix; **p. list,** liste *f ou* barème *m* des prix, tarif *m*; **p. range,** écart *m* des prix; **what is your p. range?,** combien voulez-vous mettre?; **it's not in my p. range,** ce n'est pas dans mes prix; **p. rigging,** alignement *m* des prix; **p. ring,** monopole *m* des prix; **p. tag,** étiquette *f*; **p. war,** guerre *f* des prix.

price² *vt* **(a)** *(indicate cost of)* mettre un prix à *(qch)*; *(decide cost of)* fixer un prix pour *(qch)*; **the book is priced at £10,** le livre se vend (au prix de) dix livres; **(b)** *(of customer)* s'informer du prix de *(qch)*; **(c)** *Com* **to p. competitors out of the market,** éliminer la concurrence en pratiquant des prix déloyaux; **to p. oneself out of the market,** perdre sa clientèle en demandant des prix inabordables; **(d)** *(attach value, regard to)* estimer, évaluer; **to p. sth high/low,** faire grand/peu de cas de qch.

►**price down** *vtsep Com (reduce price of)* baisser le prix de *(qch)*.

►**price up** *vtsep Com (increase price of)* augmenter le prix de *(qch)*.

priced [praɪst] *adj* **(a) high/low-p.,** de haut/bas prix; **(b)** *(marked with price)* marqué d'un prix, chiffré; **everything in the window is p.,** à la vitrine tous les prix sont marqués.

price-fixing ['praɪsfɪksɪŋ] *n* alignement *m* des prix.

priceless ['praɪslɪs] *n (invaluable)* inestimable, qui n'a pas de prix; *F (joke, person etc)* très amusant, impayable.

pricey ['praɪsɪ] *adj F* cher, coûteux.

pricing ['praɪsɪŋ] *n* **(a)** *(setting price(s))* fixation *f* du prix **(of sth,** de qch); **p. policy,** politique *f* des prix; **(b)** *(value, regard)* évaluation *f*.

prick¹ [prɪk] *n* **(a)** piqûre *f (d'une aiguille etc)*; **pricks of conscience,** aiguillons *mpl* de la conscience; **to have a p. of conscience,** être titillé par sa conscience; **p. ears,** oreilles pointues *(d'un chien)*; **(b)** *Vulg (penis)* bite *f*, queue *f*; *(man)* connard *m*; **p. teaser,** allumeuse *f*.

prick² **1** *vt (pierce)* piquer *(qch, qn)*; faire une piqûre à *(qch)*; crever, percer *(un ballon)*; ponctionner *(une ampoule)*; **to p. one's finger,** se piquer au *ou* le doigt; **his conscience is pricking him,** sa conscience l'aiguillonne *ou* le tourmente; **to p. a hole in sth,** faire un trou d'épingle dans qch; **to p. a design on sth,** piquer un dessin sur qch. **2** *vi (of the skin)* avoir des picotements, picoter, fourmiller.

►**prick out** *vtsep* **(a)** *(plant)* repiquer *(des plants)*; **(b)** *(mark)* piquer *(un dessin)* **(on,** sur).

►**prick up** **1** *vtsep (raise)* **to p. up one's ears,** *(of animal)* dresser les oreilles; *(of person)* tendre *ou* dresser l'oreille. **2** *vi (rise)* **his ears pricked up,** *(of dog)* ses oreilles se sont dressées; *(of person)* il a dressé l'oreille.

pricking ['prɪkɪŋ] **1** *adj* piquant; **p. sensation,** picotement *m*, fourmillement *m*. **2** *n* piquage *m*; *Med* ponction *f*; picotement *m*, fourmillement *m (de la peau)*; **prickings of conscience,** remords *mpl* (de conscience).

pricking out *n* repiquage *m (de plantes)*.

prickle¹ ['prɪk(ə)l] *n* piquant *m (de plante, d'animal)*; épine *f (de plante)*; *(of skin)* picotement *m*.

prickle² **1** *vt* piquer, picoter, aiguillonner. **2** *vi (of parts of body)* fourmiller, avoir des picotements.

prickling ['prɪklɪŋ] **1** *adj (sensation)* de picotement, de fourmillement. **2** *n* picotement *m*, fourmillement *m*.

prickly ['prɪklɪ] *adj* **(a)** *(plant, animal)* hérissé; *(plant)* épineux; *(question etc)* épineux; *Bot* **p. pear,** *(tree)* figuier *m* de Barbarie; *(fruit)* figue *f* de Barbarie; *F* **he's very p. today,** il est très irritable aujourd'hui; **(b)** *(sensation)* de picotement, de fourmillement; *Med* **p. heat,** miliaire *f*, sudamina *mpl*.

pride¹ [praɪd] *n* **(a)** *(satisfaction)* fierté *f*, orgueil *m*; *(self-esteem)* amour-propre *m*, orgueil; *Pej* orgueil, vanité *f*; **the sin of p.,** le péché d'orgueil; **puffed up** *or* **blown up** *or* **swollen with p.,** bouffi d'orgueil; **false p.,** vanité *f*; **proper p.,** orgueil légitime; **I have my p.!,** j'ai ma fierté!; **to have too much p. to do sth,** être trop fier pour faire qch; **to hurt** *or* **wound s.o.'s p.,** blesser l'amour-propre *ou* l'orgueil de qn; **to take (a) p. in sth,** être fier de qch; **to take p. in one's work,** mettre son amour-propre dans son travail; **he takes great p. in his daughter's achievements,** il est très fier des succès de sa fille; *Prov* **p. comes** *or* **goes before a fall,** de grande montée grande chute;

(b) *(person, thing)* **he is the p. of the family,** il fait l'orgueil de la famille; **the p. of the fleet,** l'orgueil de la flotte; **she's his p. and joy,** elle fait toute sa fierté; **that antique table is her p. and joy,** elle tient à cette table ancienne comme à la prunelle de ses yeux;

(c) to have p. of place, avoir *ou* tenir la place d'honneur;

(d) troupe *f (de lions)*.

pride² *vt* **to p. oneself (up)on (doing) sth,** être fier de (faire) qch; *Pej* s'enorgueillir *ou* se piquer *ou* se faire gloire de (faire) qch; **to p. oneself on one's knowledge of literature,** se piquer de littérature.

priest [priːst] *n* prêtre *m*; **the priests,** le clergé; *Cathol* **parish p.** = curé *m*; **assistant p.,** vicaire *m*; **to become a p.,** devenir prêtre.

priestess ['priːstɪs] *n* prêtresse *f*.

priesthood ['priːsthʊd] *n* **(a)** *(state)* prêtrise *f*, sacerdoce *m*; **to enter the p.,** se faire prêtre; **(b)** *(priests)* **the p.,** le clergé.

priestly ['priːstlɪ] *adj* sacerdotal, -aux, de prêtre.

prig [prɪg] *n* poseur à la vertu; **he's a real little p.,** il fait toujours le petit saint.

priggish ['prɪgɪʃ] *adj* collet monté *inv*, suffisant; *(woman)* bégueule.

priggishness ['prɪgɪʃnɪs] *n* suffisance *f*.

prim¹ [prɪm] *adj* **(a)** *(person)* collet monté *inv*; *(manner)* guindé, compassé; **she's so p. and proper,** *(morally)* elle est tellement prude; *(in appearance, tidiness etc)* elle est tellement maniaque; **(b)** *(garden)* méticuleusement entretenu.

prim² *vt* **(-mm-) to p. (up) one's mouth** *or* **one's lips,** prendre un air pincé, pincer les lèvres.

prima ['priːmə] *adj* **p. donna,** prima donna *f*; **p. ballerina,** première danseuse étoile; *Fig* **he has a real p. donna mentality,** il a *ou* fait des caprices de star.

primacy ['praɪməsɪ] *n* **(a)** primauté *f*, prééminence *f*; **(b)** *Rel* primatie *f*.

primaeval [praɪ'miːv(ə)l] *adj* = **PRIMEVAL**.

prima facie ['praɪmə'feɪʃɪ] *adv & adj* de prime abord; *Jur* **p. f. case,** = affaire qui d'après les premiers témoignages paraît bien fondée; *Fig* **this is a p. f. case of ...,** à première vue c'est une affaire de ...; **p. f. evidence,** commencement *m* de preuve.

primal ['praɪm(ə)l] *adj* **(a)** primitif, originel; *Psy* **p. scream,** cri primal; **(b)** *(duty etc)* principal, -aux, fondamental, -aux.

primarily [praɪ'mərɪlɪ] *adv (see adj)* **(a)** principalement, essentiellement; **(b)** originairement.

primary ['praɪmərɪ] **1** *adj (original, first)* premier, primitif, originel; *(fundamental, main)* premier, principal, -aux; *El Phys etc (bobine, courant, électron etc)* primaire; **p. cause,** cause première; *El* **p. cell,** élément *m* de pile; **p. colours,** couleurs fondamentales; *Sch* **p. education/school,** enseignement *m*/ école *f* primaire; *US Pol* **p. election,** (élection *f*) primaire *f*; *Econ* **p. industries,** secteur *m* primaire; *Med* **p. infection,** primo-infection *f*, *pl* primo-infections; *Med* **p. lesion,** lésion *f ou* accident *m* primaire; **p. meaning of a word,** sens premier d'un mot; *Astron* **p. planet,** planète principale *ou* primaire; **p. product,** produit *m* de base, matière première, produit brut; *Geol* **p. rocks,** roches *fpl* primaires; *Gram* **p. tenses,** temps primitifs.

2 *n* **(a)** *Astron* planète principale, grande planète;

(b) *El* bobine *f* primaire;

(c) *(colour)* couleur fondamentale;

(d) *Orn (feather)* rémige *f*;

(e) *US Pol (election)* (élection *f*) primaire *f*; *(assembly)* assemblée *f* primaire.

primate ['praɪmeɪt] *n* **(a)** *Rel* primat *m*; **the P. of All England,** l'archevêque *m* de Cantorbéry; **(b)** *(animal)* primate *m*.

prime¹ [praɪm] *adj* **(a)** *(most important)* premier, principal, -aux; **p. minister,** premier ministre; **p. ministerial,** de *ou* du premier ministre; **p. ministership,** poste *m* de premier ministre; **during her p. ministership,** pendant qu'elle était premier ministre; **of p. importance,** d'importance capitale, de (toute) première importance; **p. motive,** principal mobile **(of,** de); **p. mover,** *MecE* force motrice; âme *f (d'un complot etc)*; *Phil* premier moteur; *TV* **p. time,** heures *fpl* de grande écoute; **(b)** *(excellent)* excellent, de qualité supérieure, de première qualité; **p. quality meat,** viande *f* de premier choix; *Tex* **p. wool,** prime *f*; **(c)** *(original)* premier, primitif; *(fundamental)* de base; *Math* **p. number,** nombre premier; **p. meridian of Greenwich,** méridien *m* (d')origine de Greenwich.

prime² *n* **(a)** *(best time)* **p. of youth,** fleur *f* de la jeunesse; **in the p. of life, in one's p.,** à *ou* dans la fleur de l'âge; **to be past one's** *or* **its p.,** ne plus être de première jeunesse; **(b)** *Rel* prime *f*; **to say/sing the p.,** dire/chanter prime; **(c)** *(beginning)* commencement *m*; **(d)** *Fencing* prime *f*; **(e)** *Math* nombre premier; **n p.,** n prime.

prime³ *vt* **(a)** amorcer *(un obus, une pompe etc)*; *(in engine)* enrichir *(le mélange au départ)*; **(b)** *(provide with information)* **to p. s.o. for a speech,** préparer qn à faire son discours; **to be well primed (with alcohol),** être bien parti; **(c)** *(in painting)* apprêter, donner l'apprêt à *(la surface à peindre)*.

primer¹ ['praɪmər] *n* **(a)** *(in engine)* enrichisseur *m (du mélange au départ)*; injecteur *m (de départ)*; *(of explosive)* amorce *f*; **p. detonator,** amorce-détonateur *f, pl* amorces-détonateurs; **(b)** (*paint*) (couche *f* d')apprêt *m*.

primer² *n* (*book*) premier livre de lecture; introduction *f* (*à l'étude des mathématiques etc*); **geography p.,** premier cours de géographie.

primeval [praɪ'miːv(ə)l] *adj* primitif; **p. forest,** forêt primitive.

priming ['praɪmɪŋ] *n* **(a)** amorçage *m* (*d'une pompe, d'un carburateur*); enrichissement *m* (*du mélange au départ*); injection *f* (*de carburant au départ*); **p. (powder),** (*explosive*) amorce *f*; **p. charge,** charge *f* d'amorçage; **(b)** (*in painting*) apprêtage *m* (*de boiserie etc*); (*paint*) couche *f*, apprêt *m*.

primitive ['prɪmɪtɪv] **1** *adj* primitif, primaire; (*method etc*) primitif, rude, grossier; **p. language,** langue primitive; **the plumbing is very p.,** les installations sanitaires sont rudimentaires. **2** *n Art* (peintre *m*, tableau *m*) primitif *m*; (*in anthropology*) primitif, -ive; *Math* primitive *f*; *Art* **the primitives,** les (peintres) primitifs.

primitively ['prɪmɪtɪvlɪ] *adv* primitivement.

primitiveness ['prɪmɪtɪvnɪs] *n* caractère primitif; (*of manners*) grossièreté *f*, rudesse *f*; (*of a people*) rudesse *f*.

primitivism ['prɪmɪtɪvɪz(ə)m] *n* primitivisme *m*.

primly ['prɪmlɪ] *adv* d'un air collet monté, d'un air guindé.

primness ['prɪmnɪs] *n* (*of person*) pruderie *f*.

primogeniture [praɪməʊ'dʒenɪtʃər] *n* primogéniture *f*; **(right of) p.,** droit *m* d'aînesse.

primordial [praɪ'mɔːdɪəl] *adj* primordial, -aux.

primordially [praɪ'mɔːdɪəlɪ] *adv* primordialement.

primp [prɪmp] **1** *vi* (*dress up*) se mettre sur son trente et un, *Pej* s'attifer. **2** *vt* **to p. oneself up,** se mettre sur son trente et un, *Pej* s'attifer.

primrose ['prɪmrəʊz] *n* (*plant*) primevère *f*; *Fig* **the p. path,** le chemin de velours.

primula ['prɪmjʊlə] *n* (*plant*) primula *f*, primevère *f*.

primus ® ['praɪməs] *n* **p. (stove),** réchaud portatif (à pétrole vaporisé sous pression).

prince [prɪns] *n* prince *m*; **p. of the blood,** prince du sang; **p. charming,** prince charmant; *Eng Hist* **the Black P.,** le Prince Noir; *Fig* **the P. of darkness,** le prince des ténèbres; **p. consort,** prince consort; **the P. of Wales,** le Prince de Galles; *Can Geog* **P. Edward Island,** Île-du-Prince-Édouard *f*.

princeling ['prɪnslɪŋ] *n* principicule *m*.

princely ['prɪnslɪ] *adj* princier; (*cadeau*) magnifique; **to get a p. salary,** être payé princièrement.

princess [prɪn'ses] *n* princesse; **p. line dress,** robe *f* princesse; *Br* **p. royal,** = titre conféré de temps en temps à la fille aînée de la reine ou du roi.

principal¹ ['prɪnsɪp(ə)l] *adj* principal, -aux; **p. events in one's life,** événements capitaux de la vie; *Th* **p. part,** rôle principal; **p. boy,** (*in pantomine*) = rôle du héros (*joué par une femme*); *Gram* **p. clause,** proposition principale.

principal² *n* **(a)** (*person*) principal *m*, -aux, directeur, -trice (*d'école, de collège*); *Com Jur* (*in transaction*) mandant *m*, commettant *m*; *St Exch* donneur *m* d'ordre; *Jur* auteur *m* (*d'un crime*); *Mus* soliste *mf*; *Th* (acteur, -trice qui joue le) rôle principal; *Jur* **p. and agent,** commettant et préposé; **principals in a duel,** adversaires *mpl* dans un duel; **(b)** *Com* capital *m*, principal *m* (*d'une dette*).

principality [prɪnsɪ'pælɪtɪ] *n* principauté *f*.

principally ['prɪnsɪplɪ] *adv* principalement, surtout.

principle ['prɪnsɪp(ə)l] *n* **(a)** (*idea*) principe *m*; **fundamental p.,** principe premier *ou* fondamental; **the Archimedean p.,** le principe d'Archimède; **in p.,** en principe; **to reach an agreement in p.,** aboutir à un accord de principe; **machines that work on the same p.,** machines qui fonctionnent sur *ou* d'après le même principe; **(b)** (*moral rule*) principe *m*, règle *f*; **guiding p.,** principe directeur; **to have high principles,** avoir des principes; **man of no principles,** homme sans principes; **on p.,** par principe; **to do sth on p.,** avoir pour principe de faire qch; **to stick to one's principles,** rester fidèle à ses principes; **it's the p. of the thing,** c'est une question de principe; **(c)** *Phil* loi *f*; **p. of causality,** loi de causalité.

principled ['prɪnsɪp(ə)ld] *adj* (*behaviour*) dicté par des principes; (*person*) qui a des principes; **to be p.,** (*of person*) avoir des principes.

prink [prɪŋk] *vt* = **PRIMP.**

print¹ [prɪnt] *n* **(a)** (*imprint*) empreinte *f*, impression *f*; marque *f*, trace *f* (*du pied*); **thumb p.,** empreinte du pouce; **(b)** *Typ* (*printed matter*) matière imprimée; (*characters*) caractères *mpl*; **to appear in p.,** (*of writings*) paraître; (*of author*) se faire imprimer; **edition in p.,** édition en vente (courante); **out of p.,** épuisé; **large/small p.,** gros/petits caractères; **p. shop,** imprimerie *f*; **the p. unions,** les syndicats des typographes; **always read the small p.,** (*of contract, guarantee etc*) il faut toujours lire les petits caractères; **(c)** (*engraving*) estampe *f*, gravure *f*, image *f*; **p. room,** (*in museum*) cabinet *m* d'estampes; **(d)** *Phot* épreuve *f*; **to take a p. from a negative,** tirer une épreuve d'un cliché; **contact p.,** épreuve par contact; **(e)** *Tex* (*material*) indienne *f*; **(cotton) p.,** imprimé *m*; **(f)** *Comptr* **p. drum,** tambour *m* d'impression; **p. head,** tête *f* d'impression; **p. menu,** menu *m* d'impression; **p. speed,** vitesse *f* d'impression.

print² **1** *vt* **(a)** *Typ* imprimer (*un livre etc*); tirer (*des exemplaires*); imprimer, tirer (*un journal*); **(b)** (*imprint*) imprimer (**sth on sth,** qch sur qch); **incidents that p. themselves on the memory,** incidents qui se gravent dans la mémoire; **(c)** (*write*) mouler (*des lettres*); écrire (*une adresse, son nom*) en lettres moulées; **please p.,** (*on form etc*) veuillez écrire en lettres d'imprimerie; **(d)** *Phot* **to p. a negative,** tirer une épreuve d'un cliché; **(e)** *Tex* imprimer (*du coton etc*). **2** *vi* (*of printer*) imprimer; **the book is now printing,** le livre est à l'impression *ou* est actuellement sous presse.

▶**print off** *vtsep* imprimer.

▶**print out** *vtsep Comptr* imprimer.

printable ['prɪntəb(ə)l] *adj Lit Fig* imprimable.

printed ['prɪntɪd] *adj* imprimé; *El* **p. circuit board,** carte *f* de circuits imprimés; *Tex* **p. cotton,** indienne imprimée; **p. matter,** (*sent by post*) imprimés *mpl*; **p. paper rate,** (*at post office*) tarif *m* imprimés; **such is the power of the p. word,** tel est le pouvoir de l'écrit.

printer ['prɪntər] *n* **(a)** *Typ etc* (*person*) imprimeur *m* (typographique), typographe *m*; (*worker*) ouvrier *m* typographe; (*machine*) *Comptr* imprimante *f*; *Telecom* téléscripteur *m*; **p.'s devil,** apprenti imprimeur; *Comptr* **p. driver,** programme *f* de commande d'impression; **p.'s error,** faute *f* d'impression, coquille *f*; **p.'s reader,** correcteur, -trice d'épreuves; **(b)** *Phot* (*person*) tireur, -euse d'épreuves; (*machine*) tireuse *f*.

printing ['prɪntɪŋ] *n* **(a)** impression *f*, tirage *m* (*d'un livre*); (*craft*) imprimerie *f*, typographie *f*; (*writing*) écriture *f* en caractères moulés; **p. ink,** encre *f* d'imprimerie; **p. press,** presse *f* d'imprimerie; **p. paper,** papier *m* d'impression; **(b)** *Phot* tirage *m*; **(c)** *Tex* **cotton p.,** impression *f* sur coton.

printout ['prɪntaʊt] *n Comptr* listing *m*.

printrun ['prɪntrʌn] *n Typ* tirage *m*.

print-through ['prɪntθruː] *n Comptr* **p.-t. paper,** papier *m* à effet d'empreinte.

prior¹ ['praɪər] **1** *adj* préalable, précédent, antérieur (**to sth,** à qch); **to have a p. claim,** avoir des prétentions antérieures; **to have p. knowledge of sth,** être déjà au courant de qch. **2** *adv* **p. to my departure,** avant mon départ.

prior² *n Rel* prieur *m*.

prioress ['praɪərɪs] *n Rel* prieure *f*.

prioritization [praɪɒrɪtaɪ'zeɪʃən] *n* **the p. of all these jobs,** la définition d'un ordre de priorité pour toutes ces tâches; **they decided on the p. of expansion,** ils ont décidé de donner la priorité à l'expansion.

prioritize [praɪ'ɒrɪtaɪz] *vt* (*several tasks etc*) donner un ordre de priorité à; (*one task etc*) donner la priorité à.

priority [praɪ'ɒrɪtɪ] *n* priorité *f*; **to give p. to s.o./sth,** donner la priorité à qn/qch; **to have p.,** (*of job etc*) être prioritaire; (*of person, in driving*) avoir la priorité; **to have** *or* **take p. over s.o.,** avoir la préséance *ou* la priorité sur qn; **hygiene has a high p.,** l'hygiène est tout à fait prioritaire; **our first p. is to buy the tickets,** en priorité il faut que nous achetions les billets; **p.,** (*on message*) urgent; **to have one's priorities right/wrong,** faire/ne pas faire la part des choses, ne pas se tromper/se tromper de priorité(s); **p. of claim,** priorité; **p. holder,** prioritaire *mf*; *Jur* **p. rights,** droits *mpl* de priorité *ou* de préférence; droits prioritaires; *St Exch* **p. share,** action privilégiée; **to get p. treatment,** (*of task*) être exécuté *ou* fait en priorité.

priory ['praɪərɪ] *n Rel* prieuré *m* (de couvent).

prise [praɪz] *vt* = **PRIZE⁴.**

prism ['prɪz(ə)m] *n* prisme *m*; **p. binoculars,** jumelle(s) *f(pl)* à prismes *ou* prismatiques.

prismatic [prɪz'mætɪk] *adj* (*forme, couleur etc*) prismatique; **p. binoculars,** jumelle(s) *f(pl)* à prismes *ou* prismatiques.

prison ['prɪz(ə)n] *n* prison *f*; **to send s.o. to p., to put s.o. in p., to throw s.o. into p.,** emprisonner qn; mettre *ou* jeter qn en prison; **to be sent to p.,** être incarcéré; **he's**

been in p., il a fait de la prison; **open p.**, établissement ouvert; **p. camp,** camp *m* de prisonniers; **p. officer,** gardien, -ienne de prison; **p. visitor,** visiteur, -euse de prison; **p. yard,** cour *f* de prison.

prisoner ['prɪz(ə)nər] *n* **(a)** prisonnier, -ière; *Mil* **p. of war,** prisonnier de guerre; **p. of war camp,** camp *m* de prisonniers de guerre; **to take s.o. p.,** faire qn prisonnier; **to take prisoners,** faire des prisonniers; **to hold s.o. p.,** retenir qn prisonnier; **p.'s base** (*game*) (jeu *m* de) barres *fpl*; **(b)** *Jur* détenu, -ue; (*after sentence*) détenu, prisonnier; **p. at the bar,** prévenu, -ue; (*for serious crimes*) accusé, -ée.

prissy ['prɪsɪ] *adj* (*fussy*) maniaque; (*prudish*) prude; (*effeminate*) efféminé.

pristine ['prɪstaɪn, -iːn] *adj* (*spotless*) sans tache, à l'état (de) neuf; **in p. condition,** comme neuf.

prithee ['prɪðɪ] *int Arch* je te prie.

privacy ['praɪvəsɪ, 'prɪ-] *n* **the p. of one's home,** l'intimité *f* du chez-soi; **desire for p.,** désir de se cacher aux regards indiscrets; **I like my p.,** j'aime avoir un peu d'intimité; **to disturb s.o.'s p.,** faire intrusion chez qn; **there is no p. here,** on n'est jamais seul ici; **to be married in strict p.,** se marier dans la plus stricte intimité; *Can* **P. Commissioner,** Commissaire *m* à la protection de la vie privée.

private ['praɪvɪt] **1** *adj* **(a)** (*individual, personal*) privé, particulier; **p. citizen,** simple particulier; **the p. life of an actor,** la vie privée d'un acteur; **p. income** *or* **means,** rentes *fpl*; **this is his own p. room,** c'est sa pièce à lui; **in p. life,** dans la vie privée, dans le privé; **can I talk to you about something p.?,** puis-je discuter avec vous de quelque chose de personnel?; **can we go somewhere p.?,** est-ce que nous pourrions discuter en privé?; **p. motives,** motifs personnels; **p. parts,** parties génitales; **p. persons,** particuliers *mpl*; *Parl* **p. member,** = simple député *m*; *Parl* **p. member's bill,** = proposition de loi faite par un simple député; *Mil* **p. soldier,** simple soldat *m*; **for my p. use,** pour mon usage personnel; *Jur* **p. wrong,** atteinte *f* aux droits d'un individu; **p. secretary,** secrétaire personnel;

(b) (*secret*) secret, -ète; **to keep a matter p.,** tenir une affaire secrète; **he is very p. about his affairs,** il est très réservé au sujet de ses affaires;

(c) (*confidential*) intime; **p. and confidential,** secret et confidentiel; **to mark a letter p.,** marquer sur une lettre 'confidentiel' *ou* 'personnel'; **you stay out of this! — it's p. between John and me,** reste en dehors de tout ça! — ça ne regarde que John et moi; **to be received in p. audience,** être reçu en audience particulière; **p. conversation,** conversation *f* intime;

(d) (*not business*) **p. house,** maison particulière; **p. car,** voiture particulière *ou* privée;

(e) (*for personal use*) **p. bus,** bus réservé; **p. office,** cabinet particulier; **p. room,** (*in hotel etc*) salon réservé;

(f) (*to which public not admitted*) **the funeral will be p.,** les obsèques auront lieu dans la plus stricte intimité; **P.,** (*on sign*) entrée interdite au public; **p. dance,** bal *m* sur invitation; **p. fishing,** pêche réservée; *Tel* **p. line,** ligne intérieure; *Th* **p. performance,** représentation *f* à bureaux fermés; **p. party,** (*gathering*) réunion privée *ou* intime; (*group*) groupe *m* de particuliers; **p. property,** propriété privée; **p. road,** chemin privé;

(g) p. education, (*not state*) enseignement privé; (*by a tutor*) enseignement par un précepteur; **p. detective** *or* **investigator** *or F* **eye,** détective privé; **p. enterprise,** entreprise privée; (*principle*) la libre entreprise; **p. patient,** malade *mf* privé(e); **p. patients,** clientèle privée; **p. industry,** le privé; **p. nursing home,** clinique privée; **p. practice,** clientèle privée, cabinet (médical *etc*) privé; **to work in the p. sector,** travailler dans le privé; **p. sector salaries,** les salaires du secteur privé; **p. room,** (*in hospital*) chambre particulière;

2 *n* **(a)** (*in private life*) dans la vie privée; (*with close family*) dans l'intimité; (*with friends etc, not in public*) dans le privé; (*confidentially*) en privé; **married in p.,** marié dans l'intimité; **to sit in p.,** (*of assembly*) se réunir en séance privée; *Jur* **to hear a case in p.,** juger une affaire à huis clos; **to speak to s.o. in p.,** parler à qn en particulier; **in p. she admitted she was worried,** en privé elle a admis qu'elle était inquiète; (*to herself*) dans son for intérieur elle a admis qu'elle était inquiète;

(b) *Mil* (*ordinary soldier*) soldat *m* de 2e classe, simple soldat, homme du rang; **the privates and the N.C.O.'s,** la troupe et les gradés;

(c) privates, (*genitals*) parties génitales.

privateer [praɪvə'tɪər] *n Hist* (*ship*) (bâtiment armé en) corsaire *m*; (*person*) corsaire.

privateering [praɪvə'tɪərɪŋ] *n Hist* course *f*.

privately ['praɪvɪtlɪ] *adv* (*see also* **in private**) **(a)** (*by an individual*) en simple particulier; **p. owned,** qui appartient à un particulier; (*not public*) qui appartient au (secteur) privé; **(b)** (*in private*) en particulier; **to speak to s.o. p.,** parler à qn en particulier; **p. he admitted he was worried,** en privé, il a admis qu'il s'inquiétait; **sold p.,** vendu à l'amiable *ou* de gré à gré; **(c)** (*personally*) en personne; **to benefit p. from sth,** bénéficier personnellement de qch; **(d) I had it done p.,** (*of treatment at doctor's, dentist's etc*) je l'ai fait faire à mes frais.

privation [praɪ'veɪʃən] *n* privation *f* (**of,** de); **to live in p.,** vivre dans la privation, vivre de privations.

privatization [praɪvɪtaɪ'zeɪʃən] *n* privatisation *f*.

privatize ['praɪvɪtaɪz] *vt* privatiser.

privet ['prɪvɪt] *n* (*plant*) troène *m*; **p. hedge,** haie *f* de troènes.

privilege¹ ['prɪvɪlɪdʒ] *n* **(a)** privilège *m*, prérogative *f*; **to grant s.o. certain privileges,** octroyer certains avantages à qn; **to enjoy the p. of doing sth,** jouir du privilège *ou* avoir le privilège de faire qch; **it is my p. to introduce ...,** j'ai le grand honneur de vous présenter ...; **it was a p. to work with her,** c'était un privilège de travailler avec elle; **I had the p. of knowing** *or* **to know him personally,** j'ai eu le privilège de le connaître personnellement; **(b)** *Jur* immunité *f* contre les poursuites en diffamation (*accordée aux juges, avocats et témoins*); **parliamentary p.,** immunité *f* parlementaire.

privilege² *vt* privilégier (*qn*).

privileged ['prɪvɪlɪdʒd] **1** *adj* privilégié; **the p. classes,** les classes privilégiées; **a p. few,** quelques privilégiés; **to be p. to do sth,** jouir du privilège *ou* avoir le privilège de faire qch. **2** *n* **the p.,** (*used as pl*) les privilégiés.

privily ['prɪvɪlɪ] *adv Arch* en secret.

privy ['prɪvɪ] **1** *adj* **(a) to be p. to sth,** (*have knowledge of*) avoir connaissance de qch; **(b)** (*private*) **the P. Council,** le Conseil privé (*du souverain*); **the P. Purse,** = la cassette du souverain. **2** *n* (*toilet*) cabinets *mpl* (*souvent en dehors de la maison*).

prix [priː] *n inv Sp* **Grand P.,** grand prix (automobile).

prize¹ [praɪz] *n* **(a)** (*award*) prix *m* (remporté); (*what is at stake, to be won*) enjeu *m*; *F* **no prizes for guessing,** pas difficile de deviner; **consolation p.,** prix de consolation; **the Nobel p.,** le prix Nobel; **to win** *or* **carry off the p.,** remporter le prix; **p. bull,** taureau primé; *Sch* **p. day,** jour *m* de la distribution des prix; **p. list,** palmarès *m*; **p. money,** prix en espèces; *Boxing* **p. ring,** ring *m* des professionnels; **my p. tulips/sheep/***etc*, mes tulipes/moutons/*etc* primé(e)s; **(b)** (*in a lottery*) lot *m*; **to win first p.,** gagner le gros lot.

prize² *vt* (*value*) évaluer, estimer, priser; **to p. sth highly,** faire grand cas de qch; **her most prized possession,** l'objet qu'elle prise au-dessus de tout.

prize³ *n Nau* (*ship*) prise *f*, capture *f*; *Mil* (*spoils*) butin *m* de guerre.

prize⁴ *vt* (*force*) **to p. sth up,** soulever qch à l'aide d'un levier; **to p. a lid open,** forcer un couvercle avec un levier; **she prized the fighting boys apart,** elle a séparé les garçons qui se battaient.

prizefight ['praɪzfaɪt] *n* (*professional boxing match*) match *m* de boxe professionnel.

prizefighter ['praɪzfaɪtər] *n* boxeur professionnel.

prizefighting ['praɪzfaɪtɪŋ] *n* (*professional boxing*) boxe professionnelle.

prizegiving ['praɪzgɪvɪŋ] *n* distribution *f* des prix.

prizewinner ['praɪzwɪnər] *n* gagnant, -ante (du prix); *Sch* lauréat, -ate.

prizewinning ['praɪzwɪnɪŋ] *adj* (*roman etc*) primé.

pro¹ [prəʊ] *n* **(a)** *Sp etc F* (*professional person*) pro *mf inv*; **she was a real p.,** (*actress, singer etc*) c'était une vraie pro; **(b)** *Sl* (*prostitute*) professionnelle *f*.

pro² **1** *adj & prep* pour; **he was very p. (the idea),** il était tout à fait pour (cette idée). **2** *npl* **the pros and cons,** le pour et le contre.

PRO [piːɑːr'əʊ] *n* **(a)** (*abbr* **public relations officer**) responsable *mf* des relations publiques; **(b)** (*abbr* **Public Record Office**) ≈ Archives nationales *fpl*.

proactive [prəʊ'æktɪv] *adj* qui prend les devants; *esp Am Can Admin* **p. staffing,** dotation *f* par anticipation.

pro-am ['prəʊ'æm] *adj Golf* (*abbr* **professional-amateur**) **p.-a. tournament,** = tournoi opposant équipes composées chacune d'un professionel et d'un amateur.

probability [prɒbə'bɪlɪtɪ] *n* probabilité *f*; **in all p.,** selon toute probabilité *ou* vraisemblance; **the p. is that it will**

get hotter, vraisemblablement, il va faire plus chaud; *Math* **calculation of probabilities, calculus of p.,** calcul *m* des probabilités; **p. laws,** lois *fpl* des probabilités.

probable ['prɒbəb(ə)l] **1** *adj* probable; (*histoire, excuse*) vraisemblable; **it's p. that he'll come,** il est probable qu'il viendra; **p. cause of death,** cause de la mort probable; *Math* **p. error,** erreur *f* probable. **2** *n* (*likely candidate, participant*) candidat *m ou* participant *m* probable; (*candidate, participant with greatest chance*) candidat *ou* participant qui a les meilleures chances; *esp Am* (*probable thing, event*) chose *f ou* événement *m* probable, probabilité *f*; **certainties and probables,** certitudes *fpl* et probabilités.

probably ['prɒbəblɪ] *adv* probablement, vraisemblablement; **will they come? — p. not,** viendront-ils? — probablement pas.

probate ['prəʊb(e)ɪt] *n Jur* **(a) (grant of) p.,** validation *f*, homologation *f* (*d'un testament*); **to grant p. (of a will),** homologuer un testament; *Am* **p. court, court of p.,** tribunal *m* des successions et des tutelles; **(b)** (*will*) testament revêtu de la formule exécutoire.

probation [prə'beɪʃən] *n* **(a)** (*trial period*) période *f* d'essai; (*esp in Civil Service*) stage *m*; *Rel* probation *f* (*d'un novice*); **to be on p.,** faire sa période d'essai *ou* son stage; **period of p.,** (période *f* de) stage; **(b)** *Jur* probation *f*; **he'll probably get p.,** on lui accordera probablement la liberté surveillée; **p. system,** régime *m* de la liberté surveillée; **on p.,** en liberté surveillée; **p. officer,** agent *m* de probation.

probationary [prə'beɪʃən(ə)rɪ] *adj* **p. period,** (période *f* de) stage *m*; *Rel* probation *f*.

probationer [prə'beɪʃənər] *n* **(a)** (*person on trial period*) stagiaire *mf*; *Rel* novice *mf*; **(b)** *Jur* jeune délinquant, -ante en liberté surveillée.

probe¹ [prəʊb] *n* **(a)** *Surg* (*instrument*) sonde *f*; (*act*) coup *m* de sonde; **(b)** *Min* lance *f ou* tête *f* de sonde; *Av* perche *f*; (fusée *f*) sonde *f*; *Tech* **sensing p.,** détecteur *m*; **space p.,** (*rocket*) sonde spatiale; **(c)** (*enquiry*) enquête *f*, sondage *m*.

probe² **1** *vt Med* sonder, explorer (*une plaie etc*); sonder (*qn*); fouiller (dans) (*le passé*); approfondir, fouiller (*un mystère etc*). **2** *vi* **to p. into the past,** fouiller dans le passé; **to p. (deeply into) the human heart,** (*of novelist*) pénétrer (profondément) dans le cœur humain; **if you'd probed more deeply,** (*journalist etc*) si vous aviez fait des recherches plus approfondies; **to p. into people's private lives,** fouiller dans la vie des gens.

probing ['prəʊbɪŋ] **1** *adj* (*question*) approfondi. **2** *n Med* sondage *m*, exploration *f* (*d'une plaie*); (*enquiries*) enquête *f*, sondage.

probity ['prəʊbɪtɪ] *n* probité *f*, honnêteté *f*.

problem ['prɒbləm] *n* problème *m* (*de mathématiques etc*); **that's your p.,** c'est ton problème; **their p. is that they don't have enough time,** leur problème c'est qu'ils n'ont pas assez de temps; **money isn't a p.,** l'argent n'est pas un problème; **and I thought I had problems!,** moi qui pensais que j'avais des problèmes!; **I can't pay until next week — that's not a p.,** je ne pourrai pas payer avant la semaine prochaine — ce n'est pas un problème, pas de problème; *F* **I haven't got a car — no p., I'll take you,** je n'ai pas de voiture — pas de problème, je t'emmènerai; **social problems,** problèmes sociaux; **the housing p.,** la crise du logement; **she likes solving problems,** elle aime trouver des solutions aux problèmes (pratiques); **it's a p. to know what to do,** il est bien difficile de savoir quoi faire; **p. area,** source *f* de difficultés; **p. car,** voiture *f* qui pose des problèmes; **p. child,** enfant à problèmes; **p. families,** familles à problèmes; **he's a p.,** c'est un cas *ou* c'est un problème, celui-là; **I don't want to be a p.,** je ne veux pas créer de problème(s); **what seems to be the p.?,** qu'est-ce qu'il y a?, où est le problème?

problematic(al) [prɒblɪ'mætɪk, -ɪk(ə)l] *adj* (*question, opinion, résultat etc*) problématique.

problematically [prɒblɪ'mætɪklɪ] *adv* problématiquement.

problem-oriented ['prɒbləmɔːrɪəntɪd] *adj Comptr* **p.-o. language,** langage orienté vers le problème.

problem-solving ['prɒbləmsɒlvɪŋ] *n* résolution *f* des problèmes.

proboscis, *pl* **proboscises** [prəʊ'bɒsɪs, prəʊ'bɒsɪsɪz] *n* **(a)** trompe *f* (*d'éléphant*); (*of insect*) proboscide *f*; **p. monkey,** nasique *m*; **(b)** *Hum* (*nose*) nez *m*.

procedural [prə'siːdʒər(ə)l] *adj* **(a)** *Jur* procédural, -aux; **(b)** *Tech* de mode opératoire.

procedure [prə'siːdʒər] *n* procédure *f*; **the correct p.,** la marche à suivre; **what's the p. for renewing a passport?,** quelle est la marche à suivre pour faire renouveler un passeport?; **p. in case of fire,** marche à suivre en cas d'incendie; **rules** *or* **order of p.,** réglement intérieur (*d'une assemblée*); règles *fpl* de procédure; **code of criminal p.,** code *m* de procédure pénale.

procedure-orientated [prə'siːdʒərɔːrɪənteɪtɪd] *adj Compta* **p.-o. language,** langage procédural.

proceed [prə'siːd] *vi* **(a) to p. (on one's way),** continuer son chemin, poursuivre sa route; **before we p. any further,** avant d'aller plus loin; **to p. to(wards) a place,** (*go to a place*) aller *ou* se rendre à un endroit; (*go towards a place*) se diriger vers un endroit; **to p. with caution,** agir avec prudence; **how shall we p.?,** quelle est la marche à suivre?; *esp Fml* **how does one p.?,** quelle est la marche à suivre?, comment est-ce qu'on s'y prend?; **to p. to do sth,** (*begin*) se mettre à faire qch; **he then proceeded to unlock the safe,** puis il se mit en devoir d'ouvrir le coffre; **to p. to business,** (*at meeting etc*) passer aux affaires; **I will now p. to another matter,** je passe maintenant à une autre question;

(b) (*continue*) (se) continuer, se poursuivre; **the play proceeded without further interruption,** la pièce se poursuivit sans nouvelle interruption; **the project is proceeding well,** le projet se déroule bien; **negotiations are now proceeding,** des négociations sont en cours; **to pay as the work proceeds,** payer au fur et à mesure de l'ouvrage; **he immediately proceeded to say the opposite,** et le voilà qui se met à dire le contraire; **to p. with sth,** poursuivre qch, continuer qch; **p.!,** continuez!, allez toujours!;

(c) *Jur* **to p. against s.o.,** poursuivre qn (en justice);

(d) (*originate*) **sounds proceeding from a room,** bruits qui sortent *ou* proviennent d'une pièce.

proceeding [prə'siːdɪŋ] *n* **(a)** (*way of acting*) façon *f* d'agir; **the best p.,** la meilleure marche à suivre; **(b)** (*event*) procédé *m*, acte *m*; **proceedings,** faits et gestes; débats *mpl* (*d'une assemblée*); (*of conference*) actes *fpl*; **the whole proceedings were disgraceful,** toute l'affaire a été menée d'une façon indigne; **to conduct the proceedings,** diriger les débats; **the proceedings were orderly,** la réunion s'est déroulée dans le calme; **(c)** *Jur* **(legal) proceedings,** procès *m*, poursuites *fpl* judiciaires *ou* en justice; **to take** *or* **institute proceedings against s.o.,** intenter une action contre *ou* un procès à qn, poursuivre qn en justice; **to order proceedings to be taken against s.o.,** instrumenter contre qn.

proceeds ['prəʊsiːdz] *npl* produit *m*, montant *m* (*d'une vente etc*); bénéfices *mpl* (*d'une œuvre de charité*).

process¹ ['prəʊses] *n* **(a)** processus *m*; **evolutionary p.,** processus de l'évolution; **it's a slow p.,** c'est un long travail; **to be in the p. of doing sth,** être en train de faire qch; **during the p. of dismantling,** au cours du démontage; **the work is in p.,** le travail est en cours; **(b)** *Tech* procédé *m* (*industriel*); réaction *f* (*chimique*); *Typ Phot* procédés photomécaniques; *Comptr* procédé, opération *f*, traitement *m*; **manufacturing p.,** procédé de fabrication; *Metal* **Bessemer p.,** procédé Bessemer; *Ch* **dry/wet p.,** voie sèche/humide; **p. engineering,** ingénierie *f* de procédé; **(c)** *Jur* procès *m*, action *f* en justice; (*summons*) sommation *f* de comparaître; *US* **by due p. of law,** par voies légales; **(d)** *Anat* excroissance *f*; *Bot* proéminence *f*.

process² *vt* **(a)** *Ind* traiter, transformer (*une matière première, un produit*); préparer *ou* confectionner industriellement (*des aliments*); *Tex* apprêter; *Comptr* traiter (*une information*); *Admin* traiter (*documents, candidatures à un poste*); **your request is being processed,** votre demande est en cours de traitement; **processed food,** aliment(s) industriel(s); (*precooked*) plat(s) cuisiné(s) industriellement; **process(ed) cheese,** fromage industriel; **(b)** *Jur* intenter un procès à (*qn*), poursuivre (*qn*); **(c)** *Phot* développer.

process³ [prə'ses] *vi* (*go in a procession*) défiler en cortège.

processing ['prəʊsesɪŋ] *n* traitement *m*, travail *m*, transformation *f* (*d'une matière première, d'un produit*); opérations *fpl* (*d'une fabrication*); confection *ou* préparation industrielle (*d'aliments*); *Phot* développement *m*, traitement (*d'un film*); *Admin* examen préalable (*de documents, de candidat*); acheminement *m* (*de documents*); *Comptr* **computer p.,** traitement sur ordinateur; **data/information p.,** traitement des données informatiques/des informations; **food p. industry,** l'industrie alimentaire; **p. of mail,** acheminement du courrier; *Ind* **p. plant,** (*for sewage, waste*) usine *f* de retraitement; *Comptr* **p. speed,** vitesse *f* de traitement; *Comptr* **p. unit,** unité *f* de traitement; *Comptr* **p. language,** langage *m* de traitement.

procession [prə'seʃən] *n* cortège *m*, défilé *m*; file *f* (*de* *voitures*); (*religious*) procession *f*; **funeral p.,** cortège funèbre; **to go or walk in p.,** aller en cortège *ou* en procession, défiler; *Fig* **he had had a p. of private tutors,** les précepteurs avaient défilé chez lui.

processional [prə'seʃən(ə)l] **1** *adj* processionnel. **2** *n Rel* (*book*) processionnal *m*, -aux; (*hymn*) hymne processionnel.

processor ['prəusesər] *n Comptr* processeur *m*.

process-server ['prəuses'sɜːvər] *n Jur* huissier *m* (qui dresse des exploits).

pro-choice ['prəu'tʃɔɪs] *adj* (*pro-abortion*) en faveur de la liberté de l'avortement.

proclaim [prə'kleɪm] *vt* **to p. s.o. king,** proclamer qn roi; **to have sth proclaimed through the town,** faire annoncer *ou* faire crier qch par la ville; **to p. a state of emergency,** déclarer l'état d'urgence.

proclamation [prɒklə'meɪʃən] *n* proclamation *f*, déclaration *f* (publique); publication *f* (*des bans etc*); **to make** *or* **issue a p.,** faire une proclamation.

proclivity [prəu'klɪvɪtɪ] *n* penchant *m* (**for,** *pour, à qch*).

proconsul [prəu'kɒnsəl] *n Hist* proconsul *m*.

procrastinate [prəu'kræstɪneɪt] *vi* remettre au lendemain; **stop procastinating,** arrêtez de remettre les choses au lendemain.

procrastination [prəukræstɪ'neɪʃən] *n* **there's too much p.,** on a trop tendance à remettre les choses au lendemain; *Prov* **p. is the thief of time,** il ne faut pas remettre au lendemain ce que l'on peut faire le jour même.

procrastinator [prəu'kræstɪneɪtər] *n* **she's a terrible p.,** il faut toujours qu'elle remette les choses au lendemain.

procreate ['prəukrɪeɪt] *vt* procréer.

procreation [prəukrɪ'eɪʃən] *n* procréation *f*.

proctor ['prɒktər] *n* **(a)** *Univ* (*at Oxford, Cambridge*) membre exécutif du conseil de discipline; censeur *m*; **(b)** *Jur* avoué *m* (*devant une cour ecclésiastique*); **Queen's/King's p.,** procureur *m* de la reine/du roi; **(c)** *Rel* procureur *m*.

procurable [prə'kjuərəb(ə)l] *adj* procurable.

procuration [prɒkju'reɪʃən] *n Jur* procuration *f*; **letters of p.,** procuration, mandat *m*.

procurator ['prɒkjureɪtər] *n* **(a)** *Jur* fondé *m* de pouvoir(s); *Scot* **p. fiscal,** procureur général; **(b)** *Hist* procurateur *m*.

procure [prə'kjuər] **1** *vt* **(a)** (*obtain*) obtenir, procurer; **to p. sth for s.o.,** procurer qch à qn; **to p. sth (for oneself),** se procurer qch; **(b)** (*for prostitution*) procurer (*une femme*). **2** *vi* faire du proxénétisme.

procurement [prə'kjuəmənt] *n* acquisition *f* (**of,** de); *Ind* équipement *m*; **p. officer,** agent *m* des achats.

procurer [prə'kjuərər] *n* **(a)** (*of prostitutes*) proxénète *mf*; **(b)** personne *f* qui procure (*qch pour qn*).

procuress [prə'kjuərɪs] *n* entremetteuse *f*.

procuring [prə'kuərɪŋ] *n* (*for prostitution*) proxénétisme *m*.

prod¹ [prɒd] *n* **(a)** (*act*) coup *m* (*donné du bout du doigt etc*); *F* **give him a p.,** aiguillonnez-le un peu; *Fig F* **he needs an occasional p.,** il a besoin qu'on le pousse de temps en temps; **thanks for the p.,** (*reminder*) merci de me l'avoir rappelé; **(b)** (*object*) instrument pointu; aiguillon *m*, poinçon *m*.

prod² *v* (-dd-) **1** *vt* **(a) to p. s.o./sth,** tâter *ou* pousser qn/qch (**with sth,** du bout de qch); **(b)** *F* aiguillonner, pousser (*qn*) (**into doing sth,** à faire qch); **he needs a lot of prodding,** il faut toujours le pousser. **2** *vi* **to prod at,** = **PROD² 1.**

prodigal ['prɒdɪg(ə)l] *adj & n* prodigue *mf*; *Fml* **to be p. of sth,** être prodigue de qch; *Bible* **the P. Son,** l'enfant *m* prodigue.

prodigality [prɒdɪ'gælɪtɪ] *n* prodigalité *f*.

prodigally ['prɒdɪglɪ] *adv* (*to spend etc*) avec prodigalité.

prodigious [prə'dɪdʒəs] *adj* prodigieux; (*amazing*) merveilleux; (*in size*) énorme.

prodigiously [prə'dɪdʒəslɪ] *adv* (*see adj*) prodigieusement; merveilleusement; énormément.

prodigiousness [prə'dɪdʒəsnɪs] *n* merveille *f*; (*of size*) énormité *f*.

prodigy ['prɒdɪdʒɪ] *n* prodige *m*, merveille *f*; **child** *or* **infant p.,** enfant *mf* prodige.

produce¹ ['prɒdjuːs] *n* **(a)** rendement *m* (*d'un champ de blé etc*); (*product*) produit *m*, résultat *m*; **(b)** (*no pl*) produits *mpl*, denrées *fpl*; **home p.,** produits du pays; **p. of Spain,** (*on packaging*) produit d'origine espagnole; **agricultural/dairy p.,** produits agricoles/laitiers.

produce² [prə'djuːs] *vt* **(a)** produire, fabriquer (*des marchandises*); (*yield*) rapporter, rendre (*un profit*); **this writer has produced about thirty novels,** cet auteur a écrit une trentaine de romans; **(b)** (*present*) présenter, exhiber (*son billet, son passeport*); fournir, donner (*des raisons*); *Jur* produire, fournir (*des documents, un alibi*); faire comparaître (*un témoin*); **she produced a ten-pound note/a gun,** elle a sorti un billet de dix livres/un revolver; **(c)** (*create*) créer; *El* faire jaillir (*une étincelle*); provoquer (*un effet*); **to p. a vacuum,** produire *ou* faire le vide; **to p. a sensation,** faire sensation; **(d)** *Th* (*of producer*) mettre (*une pièce*) en scène; (*of company*) produire, représenter (*une pièce*); produire (*un film, une émission de radio*); **badly produced play,** pièce mal montée.

producer [prə'djuːsər] *n* **(a)** (*person*) producteur, -trice; (*of manufactured goods*) fabricant *m* (**of,** de); **the company/country is an important p. of coffee** *or* **coffee p.,** cette entreprise/ce pays est un important producteur de café; **p. goods,** biens *mpl* de production *ou* d'équipement; **(b)** *Th* metteur *m* en scène; *Cin Rad* producteur, -trice; **television p.,** producteur, -trice (d'émissions de télévision); **(c)** *Ind* **gas p.,** gazogène *m*.

producing [prə'djuːsɪŋ] *adj* producteur, -trice; (*centre*) de production.

-producing [prə'djuːsɪŋ] *suff* **coffee/oil/***etc***-p.,** producteur, -trice de café/de pétrole/*etc*; **oil-p. country,** pays producteur de pétrole.

product ['prɒdʌkt] *n* **(a)** produit *m*; *Econ* **gross national p.,** produit national brut; *Ind* **finished p.,** produit fini; **the p. of ten years' work,** le produit de dix années de travail; **the disaster was the p. of bad planning,** ce désastre était le résultat d'une mauvaise organisation; **she was a p. of her age,** c'était un pur produit de son époque; **p. information sheet,** fiche *f* technique; **(b)** *Math* produit *m*.

production [prə'dʌkʃən] *n* **(a)** production *f*, fabrication *f* (*de marchandises*); **to go into p.,** (*of car etc model*) entrer en production; **to go out of p.,** cesser d'être produit; **is it in p. yet?,** est-il encore fabriqué?; *F* **to make a p. (number) (out) of sth,** (*make fuss*) faire des histoires; **mass p.,** production en masse; **drop in p.,** chute *f ou* baisse *f* de la production; **p. costs,** frais *mpl* de production; **p. line,** chaîne *f* de fabrication; **to work on a p. line,** travailler à la chaîne; *Petr* **p. platform,** plate-forme *f* de production; **(b)** (*presentation*) production *f* (*de documents*); présentation *f* (*d'un billet*); **(c)** *Phys* production *f*, génération *f* (*d'énergie, de vapeur*).

productive [prə'dʌktɪv] *adj* **(a)** productif; (*mine etc*) en plein rapport, en plein rendement; (*discussions*) positif; (*worthwhile*) profitable, utile; (*land etc*) fécond; **p. period of an author,** années productives d'un auteur; **the meeting wasn't very p.,** la réunion n'a pas été très productive; *Fml* **to be p. of sth,** être générateur, -trice de qch; **(b)** *Econ* (*travail*) productif; **(c) to be p. of,** (*giving rise to*) engendrer, produire.

productively [prə'dʌktɪvlɪ] *adv* **to use one's time p.,** employer son temps de façon efficace.

productivity [prɒdʌk'tɪvɪtɪ] *n* productivité *f*; productivité financière, rentabilité *f* (*d'une entreprise*); **p. bonus,** prime *f* à la productivité.

prof [prɒf] *n F* prof *m* (*de faculté*).

Prof [prɒf] *n Sch* (*abbr* **Professor**) **P. Jones,** M. Jones.

profanation [prɒfə'neɪʃən] *n* profanation *f*.

profane¹ [prə'feɪn] *adj* **(a)** (*blasphemous*) (*acte*) profane; (*langage*) impie, blasphématoire; (*person*) qui blasphème à tout propos; **(b)** (*secular*) profane; **things sacred and p.,** le sacré et le profane.

profane² *vt* profaner (*une chose sainte, un talent*).

profanity [prə'fænɪtɪ] *n* **(a)** (*word, remark*) blasphème *m*, juron *m*; **to utter profanities,** blasphémer; **(b)** nature *f* profane (*d'un écrit*); impiété *f* (*d'une action*).

profess [prə'fes] *vt* **(a)** professer, faire profession de (*sa foi etc*); déclarer; **to p. oneself a socialist,** se déclarer socialiste, faire profession de socialisme; **I do not p. to be a scholar,** je ne prétends pas être savant; **to p. one's ignorance,** avouer son ignorance; **(b)** *Rel* **to p. oneself (in an order),** faire profession (dans un ordre); **(c)** *Fml* exercer (*un métier etc*); *Sch* professer (*l'histoire etc*).

professed [prə'fest] *adj* **(a)** (*ennemi*) déclaré; (*marxiste*) avéré; (*pretended*) prétendu (*savant*); **(b)** (*monk, nun*) profès, -esse.

professedly [prə'fesɪdlɪ] *adv* (*on one's own admission*) de son propre aveu; (*according to one's claims*) soi-disant.

profession [prə'feʃən] *n* **(a)** (*occupation*) profession *f*, carrière *f*; (*people*) (les membres *mpl* de) la profession; *F* (*the theatre*) le théâtre; **the teaching p.,** le corps professoral, le professorat; **the (learned) professions,** les professions libérales; **writer by p.,** écrivain professionnel; **she is a doctor by p.,** elle est médecin de (sa) profession; *Hum* **the oldest p. (in the world),** le plus vieux métier du monde; **(b)** (*declaration*) profession *f*, déclaration *f*; **p. of faith,** profession de foi.

professional [prə'feʃən(ə)l] **1** *adj* (*danseur, photographe etc*) professionnel; (*soldat, diplomate*) de carrière; **conduct that is not p.,** conduite contraire aux usages de la profession (*de médecin etc*); **she is very p.,** elle est très professionnelle; **to take p. advice on sth,** consulter une personne du métier *ou* un professionnel sur qch; (*on legal, medical matter*) consulter un avocat/un médecin; *Euph* **I think she needs p. help,** je pense qu'elle a besoin d'aller voir un psychiatre; **the p. army,** l'armée de métier; **p. football,** le football professionnel; **they made a very p. job of the repair,** la réparation qu'ils ont faite est digne d'un professionnel; **to take a p. interest in sth,** s'intéresser professionnellement à qch; *Pej* **a p. liar/hypochondriac/***etc*, un menteur/un hypocondriaque/*etc* professionnel; **p. man/woman,** homme/femme qui exerce une profession libérale; *Sp* **p. player,** joueur professionnel.

2 *n* professionnel, -elle; **it's best to leave such work to the professionals,** il vaut mieux laisser ce genre de travail à des professionnels *ou* à des gens du métier; **he was a true** *or* **real p.,** (*of actor, athlete etc*) c'était un vrai professionnel; **a rugby p.,** un professionnel de rugby; **to turn** *or* **go p.,** devenir professionnel.

professionalism [prə'feʃənəlɪz(ə)m] *n* professionnalisme *m*; (*of job done*) caractère professionnel.

professor [prə'fesər] *n Univ* professeur *m* (de faculté); **she's a p.,** elle est professeur; **P. Martin,** Monsieur Martin.

professorial [prɒfɪ'sɔːrɪəl] *adj* professoral, -aux.

professorship [prə'fesəʃɪp] *n* chaire *f* (*de l'enseignement supérieur*); **to get a p.,** obtenir une chaire.

proffer ['prɒfər] *vt* **(-r-)** *Fml* offrir, présenter; **to p. one's hand,** tendre la main (*à qn*); **to p. one's resignation,** démissionner.

proficiency [prə'fɪʃənsɪ] *n* capacité *f*, compétence *f* (**in a subject,** en une matière).

proficient [prə'fɪʃənt] *adj* capable, compétent (**in,** dans).

proficiently [prə'fɪʃəntlɪ] *adv* avec compétence.

profile[1] ['prəʊfaɪl] *n* profil *m* (*de qn, du visage*); *TV Journ* profil (*de qn, d'une société*); *Tech* profil (*du terrain, d'une aile d'avion*); configuration *f* (*des ailes d'un avion*); *Archit* coupe *f* perpendiculaire; (*on graph*) graphique *m*, courbe *f*; *Art* **drawn in p.,** dessiné *ou* esquissé de profil; **to keep a low p.,** (*of person*) se tenir coi; **to have a high p.,** (*of person*) être (très) en vue; (*of issue*) être d'actualité.

profile[2] *vt* **(a)** (*draw in profile*) dessiner *ou* montrer (*qch*) de profil; (*draw outline of*) dessiner *ou* tracer le contour de (*qch*); (*silhouette*) silhouetter (*qch*); *Archit* dessiner (*qch*) en coupe perpendiculaire; *TV Journ* faire le portrait de; **the trees are profiled against the horizon,** les arbres se profilent sur l'horizon; **(b)** *Ind* profiler.

profit[1] ['prɒfɪt] *n* profit *m*, bénéfice *m*; (*advantage*) avantage *m*, gain *m*, fruit *m*; **to turn sth to p.,** tirer profit *ou* bénéfice de qch; **to make a p.,** (*of seller, company*) faire un bénéfice; (*of goods*) être vendu avec bénéfice; **we made a p. on the sale of the house,** nous avons réalisé un profit sur la vente de la maison; *Com* **gross/net p.,** bénéfice brut/net; **£100 clear p.,** 100 livres de bénéfice net; **p. on a transaction,** rendement *m* d'une opération; **profits were down/up this year,** les bénéfices ont diminué/augmenté cette année; **at a p.,** (*vendre qch*) à profit, à bénéfice; (*exploiter une mine*) avec profit; **to derive (a) p. from sth,** retirer un profit de qch; **p. and loss,** profits et pertes; **p. and loss account,** compte *m* de pertes et profits; **p. margin,** marge *f* bénéficiaire; **p.-making association,** association *f* à but lucratif.

profit[2] *v* **(-t-) 1** *vt* bénéficier *ou* profiter à (*qn*), faire du bien à (*qn*), être avantageux pour (*qn*). **2** *vi* **to p. by sth,** profiter *ou* bénéficier de qch, tirer profit de qch; **to p. by** *or* **from s.o.'s advice,** mettre à profit le conseil de qn.

profitability [prɒfɪtə'bɪlɪtɪ] *n* rentabilité *f*.

profitable ['prɒfɪtəb(ə)l] *adj* profitable, avantageux; (*deal, speculation*) lucratif, rémunérateur, -trice, rentable; (*business company*) rentable, lucratif; **it will be more p. for us to sell it,** nous aurons plus d'avantage à le vendre; **it would be a more p. use of your time,** ça serait pour vous une meilleure manière d'utiliser votre temps.

profitably ['prɒfɪtəblɪ] *adv* profitablement, avantageusement; **to use one's time p.,** employer utilement son temps.

profiteer[1] [prɒfɪ'tɪər] *n Pej* affairiste *mf*; **war profiteers,** profiteurs *mpl* de guerre.

profiteer[2] *vi* faire des bénéfices excessifs.

profiteering [prɒfɪ'tɪərɪŋ] *n Pej* mercantilisme *m*, affairisme *m*.

profitless ['prɒfɪtlɪs] *adj* sans profit.

profit-making ['prɒfɪtmeɪkɪŋ] *adj* (*association*) à but lucratif.

profit-sharing ['prɒfɪtʃeərɪŋ] *n* participation *f* aux bénéfices, intéressement *m*; **p.-s. scheme,** plan *m* de participation aux bénéfices, plan d'intéressement.

profligacy ['prɒflɪgəsɪ] *n* **(a)** (*debauchery*) débauche *f*; (*shamelessness*) dévergondage *m*; **(b)** (*extravagance*) prodigalité *f*.

profligate ['prɒflɪgət] **1** *adj* **(a)** (*debauched*) débauché; (*shameless*) dévergondé; **(b)** (*extravagant*) prodigue; dissipateur, -trice. **2** *n* **(a)** (*debauchee*) débauché, -ée; **(b)** (*extravagant person*) prodigue *mf*.

pro forma [prəʊ'fɔːmə] **1** *adv* pour la forme. **2** *adj Com* **p. f. invoice,** facture *f* pro forma. **3** *n Com* (*invoice*) facture *f* pro forma.

profound [prə'faʊnd] *adj* (*thought, study*) profond; **p. bow,** révérence profonde; **there is a p. difference,** il y a une profonde différence.

profoundly [prə'faʊndlɪ] *adv* profondément; **to be p. grateful,** être profondément reconnaissant.

profundity [prə'fʌndɪtɪ] *n* profondeur *f*.

profuse [prə'fjuːs] *adj* prodigue; (*copious*) profus, abondant; **to be p. in one's apologies,** se confondre en excuses; **p. bleeding,** hémorragie abondante.

profusely [prə'fjuːslɪ] *adv* profusément; **to apologize p.,** se confondre en excuses; **to perspire p.,** transpirer abondamment; **to thank s.o. p.,** remercier qn avec profusion.

profuseness [prə'fjuːsnɪs] *n* profusion *f*.

profusion [prə'fjuːʒən] *n* (*abundance*) profusion *f*, abondance *f*; **flowers in p.,** des fleurs à profusion.

prog [prɒg] *n Old-fashioned F TV Rad* émission *f*.

progenitor [prəʊ'dʒenɪtər] *n* (*ancestor*) aïeul *m*, aïeule *f*, *pl* aïeux, ancêtre *m*; *Fig* précurseur *m* (*de qch*).

progeny ['prɒdʒɪnɪ] *n* **(a)** (*offspring*) progéniture *f*; **(b)** (*descendants*) descendants *mpl*.

progesterone [prəʊ'dʒestərəʊn] *n Bio Ch* progestérone *f*.

prognosis, *pl* **-oses** [prɒg'nəʊsɪs, -əʊsiːz] *n* **(a)** *Med* pronostic *m*; (*art*) prognose *f*; **(b)** (*forecast*) prévision(s) *f(pl)*, pronostic *m*; **to make a p.,** faire un pronostic *ou* des prévisions.

prognostic [prɒg'nɒstɪk] **1** *adj* (*essai etc*) de pronostic, pronostique. **2** *n* **(a)** *Med* signe *m* pro(g)nostique; **(b)** (*sign*) pronostic *m*, présage *m*.

prognosticate [prɒg'nɒstɪkeɪt] *vt* (*of person, sign etc*) pronostiquer, présager, prédire (*qch*).

prognostication [prɒgnɒstɪ'keɪʃən] *n* **(a)** (*action*) pronostication *f*, prédiction *f*; (*premonition*) pressentiment *m*; **(b)** = **PROGNOSTIC 2(b).**

program[1] ['prəʊgræm] *n & vt Am* = **PROGRAMME**[1,2].

program[2] *n Comptr* programme *m*; **p. card,** carte *f* programme.

program[3] *vt & vi Comptr* programmer.

programmable [prəʊ'græməb(ə)l] *adj Comptr* (*computer, oven etc*) programmable.

programme[1], *Am* **program** ['prəʊgræm] *n* **(a)** programme *m* (*de spectacle, politique etc*); *F* **what's the p. for today?,** quel est le programme aujourd'hui?; **training p.,** programme d'instruction *ou* de formation; *Cin* **supporting p.,** film(s) d'appoint; *Mus* **p. music,** musique *f* à programme; *Th* **p. seller,** vendeur, -euse de programmes; **(b)** *TV Rad* programme *m*, émission *f*; (*channel*) chaîne *f*; **current affairs p.,** programme *ou* émission d'actualités.

programme[2], *Am* **program** *vt* programmer; **to p. sth to do sth,** programmer qch pour faire qch; **programmed teaching** *or* **learning,** enseignement programmé.

programmer ['prəʊgræmər] *n Comptr* (*person*) programmeur, -euse; *TV Rad & Tech* programmateur, -trice; *Comptr* (*device*) programmateur *m*.

programming ['prəʊgræmɪŋ] *n* **(a)** *Comptr* programmation *f*; **p. language,** langage *m* de programmation; **(b)** *TV Rad* programmation *f*.

progress[1] ['prəʊgres] *n* (*no pl*) **(a)** (*improvement*) progrès *m*; **age of p.,** siècle de progrès; **to make p. in one's studies,** faire des progrès dans ses études; **to make great p.,** avancer à pas de géant; (*of industry*) prendre un grand essor; **negotiations are making good p.,** les négociations sont en bonne voie; **I am satisfied with her p.,** je suis satisfait de ses progrès; *Iron* **that's p. for you!,** c'est ça le progrès!;

(b) (*forward movement*) marche *f* (*du temps, d'une maladie etc*); cours *m* (*des événements*); avancement *m* (*d'un travail*); *Chess* **the knight's p.,** la marche du cavalier; **the work is now in p.,** le travail est en voie d'exécution; **the**

negotiations in p., les négociations en cours; **p. report**, compte-rendu *m* (*sur l'évolution de qch*); *Ind* **p. chart**, diagramme *m* de l'avancement des travaux.

progress² [prə'gres] **1** *vi* **(a)** (*improve*) (*of person*) faire des progrès, progresser; (*of project*) progresser, avancer; **to p. with one's studies**, faire des progrès dans ses études; **I never progressed beyond the first lesson**, je ne suis pas allé plus loin que la première leçon; **the patient is progressing satisfactorily**, le malade fait des progrès satisfaisants; **(b)** (*move forwards*) s'avancer; **to p. towards a place**, s'approcher d'un endroit (par étapes successives); **as the inquiry progresses**, à mesure que l'enquête avance; **as the year progresses**, au cours de l'année. **2** *vt esp Com* (*advance*) faire progresser.

progression [prə'greʃən] *n* (*movement*) *& Math Mus* progression *f*; marche *f* (*d'un astre*); *Mil* avance *f*; *Math* **arithmetical/geometrical p.**, progression arithmétique/géométrique; *Mus* **chord p.**, progression harmonique.

progressive [prə'gresɪv] **1** *adj* **(a)** (*mouvement*) progressif, en avant; *Med* **p. disease**, maladie progressive; **p. increase in taxation**, progressivité *f* (de l'impôt); *Fin* **p. rate**, taux progressif; **(b)** (*forward-looking*) (*siècle*) de progrès; (*littérature, musique*) d'avant-garde; **to be p.**, avoir des idées avancées; **p. ideas**, idées avancées *ou* progressistes; **the p. party**, le parti progressiste; **(c)** *Gram* **the p. form**, la forme progressive. **2** *n* **(a)** *Pol* progressiste *mf*; **(b)** *Gram* temps progressif.

progressively [prə'gresɪvlɪ] *adv* progressivement.

progressiveness [prə'gresɪvnɪs] *n* progressivité *f*.

prohibit [prə'hɪbɪt] *vt* (*forbid*) prohiber, défendre, interdire (*qch*); **smoking prohibited**, défense de fumer; **to p. s.o. from doing sth**, défendre *ou* interdire à qn de faire qch.

prohibition [prəʊɪ'bɪʃən] *n* **(a)** prohibition *f*, interdiction *f*, défense *f* (**from doing sth**, de faire qch); **(b)** *US Hist* prohibition; **p. party**, parti prohibitionniste.

prohibitionist [prəʊɪ'bɪʃənɪst] *adj & n Econ etc* prohibitionniste *mf*.

prohibitive [prə'hɪbɪtɪv] *adj* prohibitif; **p. price**, prix prohibitif *ou* inabordable; **the price of flowers is p.**, les fleurs sont hors de prix.

project¹ ['prɒdʒekt] *n* projet *m*; plan *m* (*conçu, envisagé*); *Sch* étude *f* pratique (*individuelle ou collective*); *Constr* ouvrage *m* d'art (*projeté, réalisé*); travaux *mpl* (*d'assèchement, d'irrigation etc*); **(housing) p.**, lotissement *m*; **p. manager**, directeur *m* de projet.

project² [prə'dʒekt] **1** *vt* **(a)** projeter (*un plan, un voyage*); **projected motorway**, autoroute projetée; **(b)** (*propel*) projeter *ou* lancer (*qch*) en avant; **to p. one's voice**, projeter sa voix; **(c)** *Cin etc* projeter (*une image, un film*) (**onto a screen**, sur un écran); *Math* projeter (*un plan, une ligne*); tracer la projection de (*un plan*); **projected angle**, angle projeté; *Art* **projected shadow**, ombre portée; **(d)** (*predict*) extrapoler (*des résultats*); **the projected sales figures**, les chiffres d'affaires escomptés; **(e)** (*imagine*) **to p. oneself into the past/the future**, se transporter dans le passé/l'avenir; *Psy* **to p. one's needs onto other people**, projeter ses besoins sur les autres. **2** *vi* faire saillie; (*protrude*) déborder, dépasser, (s')avancer, sortir; (*of balcony*) porter à faux; **the balcony projects over the pavement**, le balcon surplombe le trottoir.

projectile [prə'dʒektaɪl] **1** *adj* (*force*) impulsif, projectif; **p. weapons**, armes *fpl* de jet. **2** *n* projectile *m*.

projecting [prə'dʒektɪŋ] *adj Archit* saillant, en saillie; (*balcony*) en porte-à-faux; **p. part of a roof**, avancée *f* d'un toit.

projection [prə'dʒekʃən] *n* **(a)** projection *f*; départ *m*, lancement *m* (*d'un projectile*); *Cin* **p. of an image on a screen**, projection d'une image sur un écran; **the p. of one's voice**, la projection de sa voix; *Cin* **p. room** *or* **booth**, cabine *f* de projection; **(b)** (*in mapmaking*) planisphère *m*; **conical p.**, projection conique; **(c)** (*prediction*) **demographic projections**, projections démographiques; **(d)** *Psy* projection *f*; **(e)** (*of roof etc*) avancée *f* (en dehors); (*protruding part*) saillie *f*; *Archit* partie *f* qui fait saillie; (*of balcony*) porte-à-faux *m inv*; avant corps *m inv* (*de façade*).

projectionist [prə'dʒekʃənɪst] *n Cin etc* projectionniste *mf*.

projective [prə'dʒektɪv] *adj* **(a)** *Archit* saillant, en saillie; **(b)** *Math* (*plan*) de projection; (*géométrie*) projectif; **(c)** *Psy* (*imagination*) tendant à s'extérioriser; **p. test**, test projectif.

projector [prə'dʒektər] *n Cin* projecteur *m* (de cinéma, cinématographique); **slide p.**, projecteur de diapositives.

prolapse¹ ['prəʊlæps] *n Med* prolapsus *m* (*de l'utérus etc*).

prolapse² *vi Med* (*of organ*) descendre, tomber; **prolapsed**, prolabé.

proletarian [prəʊlɪ'teərɪən] **1** *adj* prolétarien, -ienne, prolétaire. **2** *n* prolétaire *mf*.

proletarianize [prəʊlɪ'teərɪənaɪz] *vt* prolétariser.

proletariat [prəʊlɪ'teərɪət] *n* prolétariat *m*.

pro-life ['prəʊ'laɪf] *adj* **the p.-l. movement**, le mouvement pour le respect de la vie.

pro-lifer [prəʊ'laɪfər] *n F* = personne en faveur du respect de la vie.

proliferate [prə'lɪfəreɪt] *vi & vt* proliférer; (*of human beings*) se multiplier.

proliferation [prəlɪfə'reɪʃən] *n* prolifération *f*.

prolific [prə'lɪfɪk] *adj* prolifique, fécond, fertile (**in, of,** en); **a p. writer**, un écrivain prolifique *ou* fécond.

prolifically [prə'lɪfɪklɪ] *adv* abondamment, fertilement.

prolix ['prəʊlɪks] *adj* prolixe, diffus; (*style*) délayé.

prolixity [prəʊ'lɪksɪtɪ] *n* prolixité *f*.

prologue ['prəʊlɒg] *n* prologue *m* (**to**, de).

prolong [prə'lɒŋ] *vt* prolonger (*la vie etc*); continuer, prolonger (*une ligne*); *F* **don't p. the agony**, ne me faites pas souffrir plus longtemps.

prolongation [prəʊlɒŋ'geɪʃən] *n* prolongation *f* (*de la durée de qch*); prolongement *m* (*d'une ligne etc*).

prolonged [prəʊ'lɒŋgd] *adj* prolongé; **p. applause**, acclamations nourries.

prom [prɒm] *n F* **(a)** *Br* = **PROMENADE¹**; **(b)** *Br Mus* (*concert*) concert-promenade *m*, *pl* concerts-promenade; **(c)** *Am Sch* (*dance*) = bal *m* d'étudiants.

PROM [prɒm] *n Comptr* (*abbr* **Programmable Read Only Memory**) mémoire morte programmable.

pro(-)marketeer [prəʊmɑːkɪ'tɪər] *n* = personne qui est pour l'appartenance de la Grande-Bretagne au Marché Commun.

promenade¹ ['prɒmənɑːd] *n esp Br* (*place for walking*) (lieu *m* de) promenade *f*; (*at seaside*) front *m* de mer; *Th* promenoir *m* (*du parterre*); *Nau* **p. deck**, pont-promenade *m*, *pl* ponts-promenades; **p. concert**, concert-promenade *m*, *pl* concerts-promenade.

promenade² **1** *vi* se promener (*à pied, en voiture etc*). **2** *vt* exhiber (*qn, qch*).

promenader ['prɒmənɑːdər] *n Br Mus* auditeur, -trice à un concert-promenade.

prominence ['prɒmɪnəns] *n* **(a)** (*of issue, person etc*) éminence *f*; **to bring sth into p., to give sth p.**, faire ressortir qch; **to come into p.**, (*of person*) percer, arriver à un rang éminent; (*of thing*) devenir plus important; (*of idea etc*) se faire jour; **(b)** (*of land, feature etc*) proéminence *f*, relief *m*; (*part sticking up*) saillie *f*, protubérance *f*.

prominent ['prɒmɪnənt] *adj* **(a)** (*projecting*) saillant, en saillie, proéminent; (*pommette*) saillant; (*nez*) prononcé; **(b)** (*obvious*) saillant, remarquable; (*well-known*) éminent; **p. features**, traits prononcés *ou* saillants (*d'un paysage, d'un caractère etc*); **in a p. position**, très en vue; **to hold a p. position**, occuper une position très importante; **p. people**, personnages de marque.

prominently ['prɒmɪnəntlɪ] *adv* éminemment; **to display a sign p.**, mettre une affiche bien en vue.

promiscuity [prɒmɪs'kjuːɪtɪ] *n* **(a)** promiscuité *f* (sexuelle); **(b)** (*mixing*) promiscuité *f*; (*mixture*) confusion *f*.

promiscuous [prə'mɪskjʊəs] *adj* **(a)** (*behaviour*) de débauche sexuelle; **to be p.**, coucher avec tout le monde; **(b)** (*mixed*) confus, mêlé; (*foule*) hétérogène.

promiscuously [prə'mɪskjʊəslɪ] *adv* (*see adj*) **(a)** de manière débauchée; **(b)** confusément; au hasard.

promise¹ ['prɒmɪs] *n* promesse *f*; **to make a p.**, faire une promesse; **to keep one's p.**, tenir sa promesse; **to break one's p.**, manquer à sa parole, ne pas tenir sa promesse; **a p. is a p.**, chose promise, chose due; **promises, promises!**, rien que des promesses!; **empty promises**, promesses vaines; **child who shows p., child full of p.**, enfant qui promet; **young man with every p. of a brilliant future**, jeune homme promis à un brillant avenir; **to hold out a p. of sth to s.o.**, faire espérer qch à qn.

promise² **1** *vt* **to p. s.o. sth**, promettre qch à qn; **to p. (s.o.) to do sth**, promettre (à qn) de faire qch; **he promised me he'd do it**, il m'a promis qu'il le ferait *ou* de le faire; **they were promised help**, on leur promit de l'aide; **to p. oneself sth**, se promettre qch; *F* **you'll be sorry, I p. you**, je vous promets que vous le regretterez. **2** *vi* promettre; **I'll pay you back, I p.**, je te rembourserai, c'est promis; **I'll wait for you — (do you) p.?,** je t'attendrai — tu le promets?; **but you promised!,** mais tu avais promis!; **it promises to be hot,** le temps promet d'être *ou* s'annonce chaud; **the scheme promises well,** le projet s'annonce bien.

promised ['prɒmɪst] *adj* promis; *Bible* **the P. Land,** la Terre promise.

promising ['prɒmɪsɪŋ] *adj* plein de promesses, qui promet, prometteur; (*jeune femme, homme*) d'avenir; **she's made a p. start,** elle a fait des débuts prometteurs; **the future looks p.,** l'avenir promet *ou* s'annonce bien.

promisingly ['prɒmɪsɪŋlɪ] *adv* d'une façon prometteuse *ou* qui promet.

promissory ['prɒmɪsərɪ] *adj* (*oath*) promissoire, de promesse; *Com* **p. note,** billet *m* à ordre.

promo ['prəʊməʊ] *n Com F* **(a)** (*video*) vidéo promotionnelle; (*for record*) clip *m*; **(b)** (*promotion*) promo *f*.

promontory ['prɒmənt(ə)rɪ] *n* promontoire *m*.

promote [prə'məʊt] *vt* **(a)** (*raise in rank*) promouvoir (*qn*), donner de l'avancement à (*qn*); **to be promoted to (the rank of) captain,** être promu (au grade de) capitaine; passer capitaine; **to be promoted,** être promu, monter en grade; *Fb* (*of team*) monter (*en première division etc*); **(b)** (*encourage*) encourager (*les arts, un projet*); favoriser (*le succès*); faciliter (*le progrès*); avancer (*les intérêts de qn*); amener, contribuer à (*un résultat*); servir (*une cause*); lancer, fonder (*une société anonyme*); *Com* (*stimulate sales*) faire la promotion de (*un produit*); *Ch* amorcer, provoquer (*une réaction*); *Pol* **to p. a bill,** prendre l'initiative d'un projet de loi.

promoter [prə'məʊtər] *n* instigateur, -trice, auteur *m* (*d'un projet*); monteur *m*, lanceur *m* (*d'affaires*); *Sp* promoteur, -trice; **sales p.,** promoteur de ventes.

promotion [prə'məʊʃən] *n* **(a)** (*in rank*) promotion *f*, avancement *m*, nomination *f* à un grade supérieur; *Fb* (*of team*) ascension *f*, promotion; **to get p.,** être promu, obtenir de l'avancement; **(b)** *Com* promotion *f* (*d'un produit*); **to have a Chanel p.,** avoir des produits Chanel en promotion; **sales p.,** promotion *f* des ventes.

promotional [prə'məʊʃən(ə)l] *adj Com* promotionnel; **p. literature,** prospectus *mpl* promotionnels; **p. video,** = **PROMO (a)**.

prompt[1] [prɒmpt] **1** *adj* **(a)** (*not delayed*) prompt, vif, rapide; **p. service,** service rapide; **to be p. to act,** être prompt à agir; **to take p. action,** prendre des mesures immédiates; **her p. action saved his life,** la rapidité de sa réaction lui a sauvé la vie; **p. reply,** *Com* (*to letter etc*) prompte réponse, réponse rapide; **(b)** *Com* (*coton, sucre*) livrable sur-le-champ et comptant. **2** *adv* **at three o'clock p.,** à trois heures précises.

prompt[2] *n* **(a)** (*reminder*) *Th* **to give an actor a p.,** souffler à un acteur; **p. box,** trou *m* du souffleur; **p. copy,** exemplaire *m ou* manuscrit *m* du souffleur; **p. side,** côté jardin, *US* côté *m* cour; **opposite p. side,** côté cour, *US* côté jardin; **(b)** *Comptr* invite *f*; (*with wording*) message *m* d'invite; **DOS p.,** invite du DOS.

prompt[3] *vt* **(a)** (*cause*) **to p. s.o. to do sth,** pousser *ou* porter qn à faire qch; (*suggest*) suggérer à qn de faire qch; **what prompted you to come?,** qu'est-ce qui vous a donné l'idée de venir?; **these events prompted her to ...,** ces événements l'ont poussée à ...; **to be prompted by a feeling of pity,** être animé par un sentiment de pitié; **(b)** *Th etc* souffler (*qch à un acteur, un élève*); rappeler (*qch*) à la mémoire de (*qn*); **to p. s.o. with an answer,** suggérer une réponse à qn.

prompter ['prɒmptər] *n Th* souffleur, -euse; **p.'s box,** trou *m* du souffleur.

prompting ['prɒmptɪŋ] **(a)** (*suggestion*) *n* suggestion *f*; incitation *f* (**to do sth,** à faire qch); **to do sth at s.o.'s p.,** faire qch sur les instances de qn; **the promptings of conscience,** l'aiguillon *m* de la conscience; **he needed no p.,** il n'a pas été nécessaire de le pousser; **(b)** *Th etc* action *f* de souffler (*à un acteur, un élève*); *Sch* **no p.!,** ne soufflez pas!

promptitude ['prɒmptɪtjuːd], **promptness** ['prɒmptnɪs] *n* promptitude *f*, empressement *m*.

promptly ['prɒmptlɪ] *adv* promptement; (*rapidly*) avec empressement; (*immediately*) sur-le-champ, immédiatement; **to pay p.,** payer promptement *ou* ponctuellement; *F* **she screamed, and p. dropped the tray,** elle jeta un cri, et du coup laissa tomber le plateau.

promulgate ['prɒməlgeɪt] *vt* **(a)** promulguer (*une loi, un édit*); **(b)** disséminer, répandre (*une idée etc*); proclamer (*une nouvelle*).

promulgation [prɒməl'geɪʃən] *n* **(a)** promulgation *f* (*d'une loi, d'un édit*); **(b)** dissémination *f* (*d'une idée, d'une doctrine*); proclamation *f* (*d'une nouvelle*).

prone [prəʊn] *adj* **(a)** (*person, animal etc*) couché (sur le ventre), étendu face à terre; **(b)** (*inclined*) **to be p. to (do) sth,** être enclin *ou* porté à (faire) qch; **to be p. to a disease,** être prédisposé à une maladie.

proneness ['prəʊnnɪs] *n* disposition *f*, inclination *f*, propension *f* (**to,** à).

prong [prɒŋ] *n* fourchon *m*, dent *f* (*de fourche*); griffe *f* (*de mandrin etc*); pointe *f* (*d'andouiller*).

pronged [prɒŋd] *adj* à fourchons, à pointes; **two-p. fork,** fourchette à deux dents *ou* à deux fourchons; *Mil* **two/three/***etc*- **p. attack,** attaque *f* sur deux/trois/*etc* fronts.

pronominal [prəʊ'nɒmɪn(ə)l] *adj Gram* pronominal, -aux.

pronominally [prəʊ'nɒmɪn(ə)lɪ] *adv* pronominalement.

pronoun ['prəʊnaʊn] *n Gram* pronom *m*.

pronounce [prə'naʊns] **1** *vt* **(a)** prononcer (*un mot etc*); **this letter is not pronounced,** cette lettre ne se prononce pas; **(b)** (*declare*) déclarer; *Jur* prononcer (*un arrêt, un jugement*); rendre (*un arrêt*); **to p. s.o. (to be) a genius,** déclarer que qn est un génie; **I now p. you husband and wife,** (*in marriage service*) je vous déclare mari et femme. **2** *vi* **to p. on a subject,** se prononcer sur un sujet; (*of tribunal*) statuer sur une question; **to p. for** *or* **in favour of s.o./against s.o.,** se prononcer *ou* se déclarer pour/contre qn.

pronounceable [prə'naʊnsəb(ə)l] *adj* prononçable; **a barely p. foreign name,** un nom étranger tout juste prononçable.

pronounced [prə'naʊnst] *adj* prononcé, marqué; (*traits*) accusé; **the change is becoming more p.,** le changement s'accentue.

pronouncement [prə'naʊnsmənt] *n* déclaration *f*.

pronouncing [prə'naʊnsɪŋ] **(a)** prononciation *f* (*d'un mot etc*); **p. dictionary,** dictionnaire *m* de prononciation; **(b)** déclaration *f* (*d'une opinion*); *Jur* prononcé *m* (*d'un jugement, d'une sentence*).

pronto ['prɒntəʊ] *adv F* sur-le-champ, illico.

pronuclear ['prəʊnjuːklɪər] *adj* (*policy, statement etc*) en faveur du nucléaire; **to be p.,** (*of person*) être pour le nucléaire.

pronunciation [prənʌnsɪ'eɪʃən] *n* prononciation *f* (*d'un mot, d'une langue*).

proof[1] [pruːf] *n* **(a)** (*evidence*) preuve *f*; **you have no p.,** tu n'as pas de preuve; **positive p., p. positive,** preuve patente; **clear p. of guilt,** preuve évidente de culpabilité; **to give p. of,** faire preuve de (*qch*); annoncer, indiquer (*l'intelligence*); **this is p. that he is lying,** cela prouve qu'il ment; **in p. of** *or* **as a p. of one's good faith,** comme preuve *ou* en témoignage de sa bonne foi; **to produce p. to the contrary,** fournir la preuve contraire; *Jur* **the onus** *or* **the burden of p. lies with ...,** la charge de la preuve incombe à ...; **p. of one's identity,** preuve d'identité; **p. of purchase,** (*receipt etc*) preuve d'achat;

(b) (*test*) épreuve *f*; **to put sth/s.o. to the p.,** mettre qch/qn à l'épreuve; *Prov* **the p. of the pudding is in the eating,** c'est à l'œuvre que l'on connaît l'artisan;

(c) *Typ* **printer's p.,** épreuve *f* (d'imprimerie); **galley p.,** (épreuve *f* en) placard *m*; **page proofs,** épreuves en page; **to read proofs,** corriger les épreuves; **to pass the proofs,** donner le bon à tirer; **p. engraving,** (*in engraving*) épreuve avant la lettre; **signed p.,** épreuve signée;

(d) (*of alcoholic drink*) teneur *f* en alcool.

proof[2] *adj* **(a)** (*resistant*) **p. against sth,** résistant à qch, à l'épreuve de qch; **p. against damp,** imperméable, étanche; *Tech* hydrofuge; **to be p. against danger/disease,** être à l'abri du danger/immunisé contre la maladie; **p. against temptation,** (*person*) inaccessible *ou* insensible à la tentation; **(b) to be 0.9% p.,** (*of alcohol*) contenir 0,9% d'alcool.

proof[3] *vt* **(a)** *Typ* tirer une épreuve de (*la page, l'estampe etc*); **(b)** imperméabiliser (*un tissu etc*); rendre (*qch*) étanche (*à la poussière etc*); rendre (*qch*) résistant *ou* inattaquable (*aux acides etc*).

-proof [pruːf] *suff* **bulletp./heatp./***etc*, à l'épreuve des balles/de la chaleur/*etc*.

proofing ['pruːfɪŋ] *n* **(a)** (*action*) imperméabilisation *f*; **(b)** (*coating*) enduit *m* imperméable.

proofread ['pruːfriːd] *Typ* **1** *vi* corriger les épreuves. **2** *vt* corriger les épreuves de.

proofreader ['pruːfriːdər] *n Typ* correcteur, -trice (*d'épreuves*).

proofreading ['pruːfriːdɪŋ] *n* correction *f* d'épreuves.

prop[1] [prɒp] *n* **(a)** (*support*) appui *m*, support *m*, étai *m*;

Constr etc étançon *m*; étrésillon *m*; *Rugby Fb* pilier *m* (*de mêlée*); *Min* **pit p.**, étai *ou* étançon de mine; **(b)** (*for plant*) échalas *m* (*de vigne etc*); tuteur *m* (*d'un plant*); rame *f* (*pour les haricots etc*); écuyer *m* (*d'un arbre*); **(c)** *Fig* **he was the p. of his father's old age,** c'était lui qui soutenait son père âgé.

prop² *vt* (-pp-) appuyer, soutenir; *Constr* étayer, étançonner (*un mur etc*); *Constr* étrésillonner (*une tranchée etc*); *Min* boiser, buter (*une mine*); échalasser (*des vignes etc*); (*in gardening*) ramer (*des haricots, des pois*); tuteurer (*un arbuste etc*); **to p. a ladder against a wall,** appuyer une échelle contre un mur.

prop³ *n Av F* = **PROPELLER (a)**.

prop⁴ *n Th etc* accessoire *m*; **props,** (*person*) accessoiriste *mf*; *Fig* **the rock star's guitar was just a p.,** la guitare du chanteur de rock n'était qu'un accessoire.

►**prop up** *vtsep* (*support*) appuyer, soutenir; **to p. up a patient on his/her pillow,** redresser un/une malade sur son oreiller; **to p. a ladder up against a wall,** appuyer une échelle contre un mur; **to p. up a wall,** soutenir *ou* étayer un mur; *Fig* **the régime is being propped up by the military,** le régime est maintenu en place par l'armée; *Br Hum* **he's always propping up the bar,** c'est un vrai pilier de bar; **to p. oneself up against sth,** s'appuyer contre qch.

prop. *n abbr* **proprietor**.

propaganda [prɒpə'gændə] *n* propagande *f*; **p. film,** film *m* de propagande.

propagandist [prɒpə'gændɪst] *n* propagandiste *mf*.

propagate ['prɒpəgeɪt] **1** *vt Bot Phys etc* propager; propager, disséminer (*des idées*). **2** *vi* (*of animal, plant*) se propager.

propagation [prɒpə'geɪʃən] *n* propagation *f* (*d'une espèce etc*); propagation, dissémination *f* (*d'une doctrine, des idées etc*); *Phys* propagation (*de la lumière, du son etc*).

propagator ['prɒpəgeɪtər] *n* (*for seedlings*) = mini-serre *f*.

propane ['prəʊpeɪn] *n Ch* propane *m*.

propel [prə'pel] *vt* (-ll-) propulser, donner une impulsion à (*qch*); **propelled by ambition,** poussé *ou* animé par l'ambition.

propellant, propellent [prə'pelənt] *n* propulseur *m*; (*fuel*) combustible *m*; propergol *m* (*pour fusées*); **liquid/solid (rocket) p.,** propergol liquide/solide.

propellent [prə'pelənt] *adj* propulseur (*no f*); propulsif.

propeller [prə'pelər] *n* **(a)** *Nau Av* hélice *f*; **p. blade,** pale *f* d'hélice; *Nau* **p. shaft,** arbre *m* porte-hélice; **(b)** (*person, thing that propels*) propulseur *m*.

propelling [prə'pelɪŋ] *adj* propulsif; **p. pencil,** porte-mine *m inv*.

propensity [prə'pensɪtɪ] *n* propension *f*, penchant *m*, tendance *f* (**to sth,** à, vers qch; **to do, for doing sth,** à faire qch).

proper ['prɒpər] **1** *adj* **(a)** (*true, real*) vrai, juste; **the p. word,** le mot juste; **p. meaning of a word,** signification *f* propre d'un mot; **what's its p. name?,** comment ça s'appelle au juste?; **it'll be good to sleep in a p. bed,** ça va être agréable de dormir dans un vrai lit; **to get a p. night's sleep,** avoir une bonne nuit de sommeil; **architecture p.,** l'architecture proprement dite; *Math* **p. fraction,** fraction *f* moindre que l'unité;

(b) (*most suitable, suited*) convenable (*comportement, modèle etc*) approprié; (*correct in behaviour*) convenable, comme il faut; **at the p. time,** en temps utile, au moment voulu; **to apply to the p. person,** s'adresser à qui de droit; **to put sth in the p. place,** mettre qch à sa place; **to think p. to do sth,** juger à propos *ou* bon de faire qch; **do as you think p.,** faites comme bon vous semblera; *F* **to do the p. thing by s.o.,** agir honnêtement avec qn; **the p. way to do it,** la meilleure façon de le faire; **the p. use of the subjunctive,** l'emploi correct du subjonctif; **paid at the p. rate,** payé au taux *ou* au prix convenable; **a very p. old lady,** une vieille dame très comme il faut; (*very dignified*) une vieille dame très digne; *Old-fashioned* **it's not the p. thing to do,** cela ne se fait pas; **that's not the p. way to behave!,** en voilà des manières!, tiens-toi convenablement!; **she thanked him, as is p.,** elle l'a remercié comme il se doit;

(c) (*characteristic*) **p. to sth,** propre *ou* particulier à qch; **p. use of a drug,** emploi rationnel d'un remède; **to put sth to its p. use,** utiliser rationnellement qch; *Gram* **p. noun,** nom *m* propre;

(d) *Br F* (*intensifier*) **we're in a p. mess,** nous voilà dans de beaux draps!; **he's a p. fool,** c'est un parfait imbécile *ou* une vraie andouille.

2 *adv Sl* **they got it good and p.,** ils ont reçu ce qu'ils méritaient; **he was p. angry,** il était drôlement en colère.

properly ['prɒpəlɪ] *adv* **(a)** (*correctly*) correctement; (*well*) bien, de la bonne façon; **word used p.,** mot employé correctement; **p. speaking,** proprement dit, à proprement parler; **do it p. or not at all,** faites-le comme il faut ou pas du tout; **(b)** (*suitably*) convenablement; (*correctly in behaviour*) comme il faut; **to behave p.,** se conduire comme il faut; **he very p. refused,** il a refusé, comme il le fallait; **I haven't been sleeping p.,** je dors mal ces temps-ci; **(c)** *F* (*intensive*) **he was p. drunk,** il était complètement soûl; **(d)** *Jur* (*agir*) de bon droit.

propertied ['prɒpətɪd] *adj* possédant.

property ['prɒpətɪ] *n* **(a)** (*possessions*) propriété *f*, biens *mpl*, avoir(s) *m(pl)*; (*buildings*) immeuble(s) *m(pl)*; (*land*) propriété (foncière), terre *f*; matériel *m* (*appartenant à l'État*); **that's my p.,** cela m'appartient; **personal p.,** effets personnels; **damage to p.,** dommages matériels; **a small p. in the country,** une petite propriété à la campagne; **lost p. office,** service *m* des objets trouvés; **to be on s.o.'s p.,** être sur les terres de qn; **get off my p.!,** sortez de ma propriété!; **p. is theft,** la propriété, c'est le vol; **p. developer,** promoteur *m* (immobilier); **the p. market,** le marché immobilier;

(b) *Jur* (droit *m* de) propriété *f*; **literary p.,** propriété littéraire;

(c) (*quality*) (*of person, thing*) qualité *f* (propre); (*of thing*) propriété *f*; **(inherent) p.,** attribut *m*; **plants with healing properties,** plantes qui ont la vertu de guérir;

(d) *Th etc* **properties,** accessoires *mpl*; **p. man,** accessoiriste *m*; **p. mistress,** accessoiriste *f*.

propfan ['prɒpfæn] *n Av* biturbopropulseur *m*.

prophecy ['prɒfɪsɪ] *n* prophétie *f*.

prophesier ['prɒfɪsaɪər] *n* prophète, -étesse.

prophesy ['prɒfɪsaɪ] **1** *vi* parler en prophète, prophétiser. **2** *vt* prophétiser, prédire (*un événement*).

prophet ['prɒfɪt] *n* prophète *m*; *Bible* **the major/minor prophets,** les grands/petits prophètes; **the P.,** (*in Islamic religion*) le Prophète (Mahomet); *Prov* **no man is a p. in his own country,** nul n'est prophète en son pays; *F* **the prophets of doom,** les prophètes de malheur.

prophetess ['prɒfɪtes] *n* prophétesse *f*.

prophetic [prə'fetɪk] *adj* prophétique; **these deeds were p. of his future greatness,** ces actions annonçaient sa grandeur future.

prophetically [prə'fetɪklɪ] *adv* prophétiquement.

prophylactic [prɒfɪ'læktɪk] *adj & n Med* prophylactique *m*.

prophylaxis [prɒfɪ'læksɪs] *n Med* prophylaxie *f*.

propinquity [prɒ'pɪŋkwɪtɪ] *n* **(a)** (*proximity*) proximité *f* (de lieu); **(b)** (*of blood relationship*) (proche) parenté *f*; **(c)** affinité *f* (**of ideas,** entre les idées).

propitiate [prə'pɪʃɪeɪt] *vt* apaiser (*qn que l'on a offensé*).

propitiation [prəpɪʃɪ'eɪʃən] *n* apaisement *m* (*des dieux courroucés etc*).

propitiatory [prə'pɪʃɪət(ə)rɪ] *adj* propitiatoire.

propitious [prə'pɪʃəs] *adj* propice, favorable (*à qn, à une entreprise*).

propitiously [prə'pɪʃəslɪ] *adv* d'une manière propice.

propman ['prɒpmæn] *n Th* accessoiriste *m*.

proportion¹ [prə'pɔːʃən] *n* **(a)** (*relationship*) rapport *m*, proportion *f*; *Math* proportion (*arithmétique, géométrique*); **friction in p. to the load,** frottement proportionnel à la charge; **the same ingredients in different proportions,** les mêmes ingrédients dans des proportions différentes; **in p. to ...,** proportionnellement à ...; en fonction de ...; **out of all p. to ...,** sans commune mesure avec ...; **the payment is out of all p. to the work involved,** la rétribution n'est pas du tout proportionnelle au travail requis; **in perfect p.,** en parfaite harmonie; **out of p.,** mal proportionné, disproportionné; **a Greek temple of classical proportions,** un temple grec d'une harmonie classique; **he has no sense of p.,** il n'a pas le sens de la mesure; **to lose all sense of p.,** ne garder aucune mesure; **let's keep a sense of p.,** remettons les choses à leur place; **you're getting this all out of p.,** tu as une impression complètement déformée de tout cela; **inverse p.,** rapport inversel;

(b) (*part*) partie *f*, proportion *f*, dose *f* (*d'un ingrédient dans un mélange*);

(c) **proportions,** proportions *fpl* (*d'un édifice, du corps humain*); dimensions *fpl* (*d'une machine*).

proportion² *vt* **(a)** proportionner, mesurer (*la punition au crime etc*); **(b)** doser (*des ingrédients, un mélange*); **(c)** *Ind* déterminer les dimensions de (*une pièce*); coter (*un dessin*).

proportional [prə'pɔːʃən(ə)l] **1** *adj* proportionnel; en

proportion (**to,** de); **inversely p. to ...,** inversement proportionnel à ...; *Admin* **p. assessment,** coéquation *f*; *Pol* **p. representation,** représentation proportionnelle; *Typ* **p. spacing,** espacement proportionnel. **2** *n Math* proportionnelle *f*.
proportionally [prə'pɔːʃən(ə)lɪ] *adv* en proportion, proportionnellement (**to,** à).
proportionate [prə'pɔːʃənɪt] *adj* proportionné (**to,** à); **the result was not p. to the effort made,** le résultat n'était pas proportionnel à l'effort fourni.
proportionately [prə'pɔːʃənɪtlɪ] *adv* proportionnellement (**to,** à).
proportioned [prə'pɔːʃənd] *adj* **well/badly p.,** bien/mal proportionné.
proposal [prə'pəʊz(ə)l] *n* **(a)** (*offer*) proposition *f*, offre *f*; **to make a p.,** faire *ou* formuler une proposition; **p. (of marriage),** demande *f* en mariage, offre de mariage; **to receive a p. of marriage,** recevoir une demande en mariage; **p. of peace,** proposition de paix; **(b)** (*plan*) dessein *m*, projet *m*; **the p. to turn the building into a museum,** le projet de transformer ce bâtiment en musée.
propose [prə'pəʊz] **1** *vt* proposer (*qch, un candidat, une motion*); **he proposed that ...,** il a proposé que ... + *sub*; **to p. a toast,** porter un toast; **to p. s.o.'s health,** porter un toast à la santé de qn; **to p. to do sth** *or* **doing sth,** se proposer *ou* avoir l'intention de faire qch; **they p. making the street one-way,** ils suggèrent mettre cette rue en sens unique. **2** *vi* **(a)** (*make offer of marriage*) faire une demande en mariage; **he proposed to her,** il lui a demandé de l'épouser; **when did he p.?,** quand a-t-il fait sa demande en mariage?; **(b) man proposes, God disposes,** l'homme propose et Dieu dispose.
proposed [pre'pəʊzd] *adj* (*planned*) proposé, projeté.
proposer [prə'pəʊzər] *n* auteur *m* d'une offre *ou* d'une proposition; (*at club etc*) parrain *m*, marraine *f* (*d'un candidat*); **p. of a motion,** promoteur *m* d'une motion.
proposition¹ [prɒpə'zɪʃən] *n* **(a)** (*suggestion*) proposition *f*, offre *f*; *F* (*matter*) affaire *f*; **I've got a p. (to put to you),** j'ai une proposition (à te faire); **paying p.,** affaire rentable *ou* qui rapporte; **it's a tough p.,** c'est difficile; **that's a very different p.,** c'est tout à fait autre chose; **he's a tough p.,** il est peu commode; **(b)** (*logic*) *& Gram* proposition *f*.
proposition² *vt* **(a)** (*sexually*) faire des avances à (*qn*); **(b)** *F* (*make an offer to*) proposer un projet à (*qn*).
propound [prə'paʊnd] *vt* proposer (*une théorie etc*); émettre (*une idée*); exposer (*un programme*).
proprietary [prə'praɪɪt(ə)rɪ] *adj* (*droit etc*) de propriété, de propriétaire; *Com* **p. article,** spécialité *f*, article breveté; **p. medicines,** spécialités pharmaceutiques; **p. name,** nom déposé.
proprietor [prə'praɪətər] *n* propriétaire *mf*; patron *m* (*d'un hôtel etc*).
proprietorial [prəpraɪə'tɔːrɪəl] *adj* (*attitude*) de propriétaire; (*rights*) du propriétaire.
proprietorship [prə'praɪətəʃɪp] *n* **to dispute the p. of sth,** disputer la propriété de qch; **under his p.,** alors qu'il est *ou* était propriétaire.
proprietress [prə'praɪətrɪs] *n* propriétaire *f*; patronne *f* (*d'un hôtel etc*).
propriety [prə'praɪətɪ] *n* **(a)** à-propos *m inv* (*d'une expression etc*); correction *f* (*de langage, de manières*); rectitude *f* (*de conduite*); opportunité *f* (*d'une action, d'une démarche*); **(b)** (*decency*) bienséance *f*, décence *f*; **to observe the proprieties,** observer les convenances.
propulsion [prə'pʌlʃən] *n MecE* propulsion *f*; **means of p.,** moyen(s) *m(pl)* *ou* mode *m* de propulsion; **jet p.,** propulsion par réaction.
propulsive [prə'pʌlsɪv] *adj* propulsif; (*mouvement, effort*) de propulsion; (*force*) moteur, -trice.
pro rata ['prəʊ'rɑːtə] *adv & adj* au prorata.
prorogation [prəʊrəʊ'geɪʃən] *n* prorogation *f*.
prorogue [prəʊ'rəʊg] *vt* proroger.
prosaic [prəʊ'zeɪɪk] *adj* (*style, esprit etc*) prosaïque, banal, -als.
prosaically [prəʊ'zeɪɪklɪ] *adv* prosaïquement.
proscenium [prəʊ'siːnɪəm] *n Th* avant-scène *f*, *pl* avant-scènes; **p. arch,** manteau *m* (d'Arlequin).
proscribe [prəʊ'skraɪb] *vt* **(a)** (*outlaw*) proscrire (*qn*), mettre (*qn*) hors la loi; **(b)** (*prohibit*) proscrire, interdire, défendre (*une pratique*).
proscription [prəʊ'skrɪpʃən] *n* **(a)** (*outlawing*) proscription *f* (*de qn*), mise *f* (*de qn*) hors la loi; **(b)** (*prohibiting*) proscription *f*, interdiction *f* (*d'une pratique etc*).
prose¹ [prəʊz] *n* **(a)** prose *f*; **p. poem, poem in p.,** poème *m* en prose; **p. writer,** prosateur *m*; **(b)** *Sch* (*translation*) **Latin/French p.,** thème latin/français.
prose² *vi Old-fashioned* tenir des discours ennuyeux.
prosecute ['prɒsɪkjuːt] **1** *vt* **(a)** *Jur* poursuivre (*qn*) (en justice); **prosecuting counsel** *or US* **attorney,** ≈ le Ministère public; **(b)** *Fml* intenter (*une action*); poursuivre (*une réclamation, ses activités, une guerre etc*). **2** *vi Jur* **to decide to p.,** décider d'engager des poursuites judiciaires.
prosecution [prɒsɪ'kjuːʃən] *n* **(a)** *Jur* poursuites *fpl* judiciaires, accusation *f*; **Director of Public Prosecutions,** ≈ le procureur de la République; **the p.,** les plaignants *mpl*; (*in Crown case*) ≈ le Ministère public; **witness for the p.,** témoin *m* à charge; **(b)** *Fml* (*of action etc*) poursuite *f*.
prosecutor ['prɒsɪkjuːtər] *n Jur* plaignant *m*; **the Public P.,** ≈ le procureur de la République.
proselyte ['prɒsɪlaɪt] *n* prosélyte *mf*.
proselytism ['prɒsɪlɪtɪz(ə)m] *n* prosélytisme *m*.
proselytize ['prɒsɪlɪtaɪz] **1** *vt* convertir (*qn*), faire un prosélyte de (*qn*). **2** *vi* faire du prosélytisme *ou* des prosélytes.
prosodic [prə'sɒdɪk] *adj* prosodique.
prosody ['prɒsədɪ] *n* prosodie *f*.
prospect¹ ['prɒspekt] *n* **(a)** (*expectation*) perspective *f*; **to open up a new p. to s.o.,** ouvrir une nouvelle perspective à qn; **there is very little p. of it,** on ne peut guère y compter; **no p. of agreement,** aucune perspective d'accord; **(b) prospects,** avenir *m*, espérances *fpl*; **future prospects,** perspectives *fpl* d'avenir; **prospects of success,** chances *fpl* de succès; **his prospects are brilliant,** un brillant avenir l'attend; **to have prospects,** (*of person*) avoir un avenir prometteur; **a job with prospects,** un poste comportant des ouvertures; **(c)** *Com* client éventuel; **(d)** (*view*) vue *f*; perspective *f*.
prospect² [prə'spekt] **1** *vi Min etc* prospecter; **to p. for gold,** chercher de l'or. **2** *vt* prospecter (*un terrain, une mine*).
prospecting [prə'spektɪŋ] *n* prospection *f*, recherche(s) *f(pl)*; **oil p.,** prospection pétrolière.
prospective [prə'spektɪv] *adj* **(a)** (*valeur*) d'avenir; **p. obligation,** obligation future; **(b)** (*likely*) en perspective; à venir; **my p. son-in-law,** mon futur gendre; **p. buyer,** acheteur éventuel *ou* potentiel.
prospector [prə'spektər] *n* (*person*) prospecteur, -trice; **oil p.,** chercheur de pétrole, (géologue *m*) pétrolier *m*.
prospectus, *pl* **-tuses** [prə'spektəs, -təsɪz] *n Com* prospectus *m*, réclame *f*; *Fin* appel *m* à la souscription publique; *Sch* brochure *f* d'information.
prosper ['prɒspər] **1** *vi* prospérer, réussir. **2** *vt Arch & Lit* faire prospérer, faire réussir.
prosperity [prɒs'perɪtɪ] *n* prospérité *f*.
prosperous ['prɒspərəs] *adj* **(a)** (*wealthy*) prospère; **(b)** *Lit* (*favourable*) **p. winds,** vents *mpl* favorables.
prosperously ['prɒspərəslɪ] *adv* d'une manière prospère.
prosperousness ['prɒspərəsnɪs] *n* prospérité *f*.
prostaglandin [prɒstə'glændɪn] *n Physiol* prostaglandine *f*.
prostate ['prɒsteɪt] *n Anat* **p. (gland),** prostate *f*.
prosthesis ['prɒsθɪsɪs] *n Gram Surg* prothèse *f*.
prostitute¹ ['prɒstɪtjuːt] *n* prostituée *f*; **male p.,** prostitué *m*.
prostitute² *vt* prostituer (*son corps, son talent etc*); **to p. oneself,** se prostituer.
prostitution [prɒstɪ'tjuːʃən] *n* prostitution *f* .
prostrate¹ ['prɒstreɪt] *adj* **(a)** (*lying*) prosterné; couché (*à terre*); **to lie p.,** être prosterné; **(b)** (*exhausted*) abattu, accablé; *Med* prostré; **p. with grief,** terrassé par le chagrin.
prostrate² *vt* **(a)** (*lie down*) coucher, étendre (*à terre*); **to p. oneself before s.o.,** se prosterner devant qn; **(b)** (*exhaust*) abattre, renverser; *Med* mettre dans un état de prostration; **prostrated by the heat,** accablé par la chaleur.
prostration [prɒs'treɪʃən] *n* **(a)** (*lying down*) prosternation *f*; **(b)** (*exhaustion*) abattement *m*; *Med* prostration *f*.
prosy ['prəʊzɪ] *adj F* (*style*) fastidieux; *Old-fashioned* (*person*) verbeux, ennuyeux.
protagonist [prə'tægənɪst] *n* protagoniste *m*.
protect [prə'tekt] *vt* **(a)** protéger; sauvegarder (*les intérêts de qn etc*); **to p. s.o./sth from** *or* **against,** préserver *ou* défendre *ou* garder qn/qch de (*qch*); abriter qn/qch de (*la pluie etc*); **the law can't p. us,** la loi ne peut pas nous protéger; **well protected against the cold,** bien protégé du froid; **to p. s.o. against s.o.'s anger,** soustraire qn à la colère de qn; **(b)** *Econ* protéger (*une industrie*).

protected [prə'tektɪd] *adj* protégé; **p. area,** zone protégée; **p. species,** espèce protégée.

protection [prə'tekʃən] *n* **(a)** protection *f*, défense *f* (**against,** contre); sauvegarde *f* (*des intérêts de qn etc*); **to be under s.o.'s p.,** être sous la protection de qn; **under police p.,** sous la protection de la police; **to claim the p. of the law,** demander la protection de la loi; **society for the p. of birds,** société protectrice des oiseaux; *F* **p. (money),** = argent versé à qn en échange de sa protection; *F* **p. (racket),** racket *m*; **(b)** *Econ* protectionnisme *m*; (*of industry*) protection *f*; **(c)** (*thing*) abri *m*, protection *f* (**against,** contre); **suntan lotion gives** *or* **provides** *or Fml* **affords some p. against the sun,** le lait solaire protège du *ou* contre le soleil; **p. factor,** (*of suntan lotion*) indice *m* de protection.

protectionism [prə'tekʃənɪz(ə)m] *n Econ* protectionnisme *m*.

protectionist [prə'tekʃənɪst] *adj & n Econ* protectionniste *mf*.

protective [prə'tektɪv] *adj* protecteur, -trice; **he is very p. towards his children,** il se montre très protecteur envers ses enfants; **p. clothing,** vêtements protecteurs *ou* de protection (*contre la radiation etc*); *Aut* **p. cage,** cage *f* de sécurité; *Biol* **p. colouring** *or* **coloration,** mimétisme *m* des couleurs.

protectively [prə'tektivlɪ] *adv* d'une manière protectrice; (*with protective gesture*) d'un geste protecteur.

protector [prə'tektər] *n* **(a)** (*person*) protecteur, -trice; **(b)** (*device*) (dispositif *m*) protecteur *m* (*d'une machine, d'un appareil etc*); **ear p.,** protège-oreilles *m inv*.

protectorate [prə'tektərɪt] *n Pol* protectorat *m*.

protectress [prə'tektrɪs] *n* protectrice *f*.

protégé, -ée ['prɒteʒeɪ] *n* protégé, -ée.

protein ['prəʊtiːn] *n* protéine *f*.

protest[1] ['prəʊtest] *n* **(a)** protestation *f*; **to make a p.,** protester, faire des protestations; **to raise a strong p.,** élever des protestations énergiques; **to give rise to protests,** (*of action*) soulever des protestations; *Jur* **p. in writing,** réserve *f*; **under p.,** (*signer etc*) sous réserve; (*faire qch*) à son corps défendant, en protestant; *Jur* **to act under p.,** protester de violence; **she resigned in p. (at this decision/***etc***),** elle a démissionné en signe de protestation (contre cette décision/*etc*); **p. meeting,** réunion *f* de protestation; **p. song/singer,** chanson/chanteur, -euse engagé(e); *Pol* **p. vote,** vote *m* de protestation; **(b)** *Com* protêt *m*; **p. for non-acceptance,** protêt faute d'acceptation.

protest[2] [prə'test] **1** *vt* **(a)** protester de (*son innocence etc*); **to p. that ...,** protester en disant que ...; *Com* **to p. a bill,** (faire) protester un effet *ou* une lettre de change; **(b)** *Am* (*protest against*) protester contre (*qch*). **2** *vi* protester, réclamer (**against,** contre); **many people protested against the decision,** beaucoup de gens ont protesté contre cette décision; **demonstrators protesting against** *or* **about the new tax,** les manifestants qui protestent contre le nouvel impôt; **really, I p., that's too much!,** non, vraiment, je proteste, c'est trop!

Protestant ['prɒtɪstənt] *adj & n Rel* protestant, -ante; **the P. Church,** = l'église réformée.

Protestantism ['prɒtɪstəntɪz(ə)m] *n Rel* protestantisme *m*.

protestation [prɒtes'teɪʃən] *n* protestation *f*; **in spite of his protestations of innocence,** bien qu'il ait clamé son innocence.

protester [prə'testər] *n* protestataire *mf*; **anti-nuclear/peace p.,** militant, -ante contre le nucléaire/pour la paix.

protocol ['prəʊtəkɒl] *n* **(a)** (*in diplomacy etc*) protocole *m*; **(b)** *Jur etc* protocole *m* (*d'une charte etc*).

proton ['prəʊtɒn] *n Nucl Phys* proton *m*.

protoplasm ['prəʊtəplæz(ə)m] *n Biol* protoplasme *m*, protoplasma *m*.

prototype ['prəʊtətaɪp] *n* prototype *m*; **p. aircraft/car,** avion *m*/voiture *f* prototype.

protract [prə'trækt] *vt* prolonger; faire traîner (*une affaire*) en longueur; **protracted stay,** séjour prolongé.

protraction [prə'trækʃən] *n* **(a)** prolongation *f* (*d'un procès etc*); longueur *f* (*d'une procédure etc*); **(b)** *Anat* protraction *f* (*d'un muscle*).

protractor [prə'træktər] *n* **(a)** *Math* rapporteur *m*; **(b)** *Anat* **p. (muscle),** (muscle *m*) protracteur *m*.

protrude [prə'truːd] **1** *vt* (faire) sortir, pousser en avant, avancer. **2** *vi* s'avancer, faire saillie, déborder; **his teeth p. (too far),** il a les dents proéminentes.

protruding [prə'truːdɪŋ] *adj* en saillie, saillant; (*mâchoire, dents*) proéminent; (*yeux*) exorbité, saillant.

protrusion [prə'truːʒ(ə)n] *n* **(a)** (*state*) sortie *f*, saillie *f*; poussée *f* en avant; **(b)** (*thing*) saillie *f*, protubérance *f*; *Anat* protrusion *f*.

protuberance [prə'tjuːbərəns] *n* protubérance *f*.

protuberant [prə'tjuːbərənt] *adj* protubérant.

proud [praʊd] **1** *adj* **(a)** fier, orgueilleux; **as p. as a peacock** *or* **as Punch,** fier comme Artaban; **too p. to complain,** trop fier pour se plaindre; **I'll sit here, I'm not p.,** je m'assiérai là, je ne suis pas exigeant; **to be p. of sth/of having done sth,** être fier *ou* s'enorgueillir de qch/d'avoir fait qch; **I'm p. to have known her,** je suis fier de l'avoir connue; **it made me feel p. to be Welsh,** cela m'a rendu fier d'être gallois; **we're all p. of you,** nous sommes tous fiers de toi; **he's the p. owner of ...,** il est l'heureux possesseur de ...;

(b) *Lit* (*haughty*) altier, hautain; (*view, city etc*) noble, imposant, magnifique; **a p. beauty,** une beauté orgueilleuse.

2 *adv F* **to do s.o. p.,** faire beaucoup d'honneur à qn; se mettre en frais pour qn; **to do oneself p.,** ne se priver de rien; **you've done me p.,** vous m'avez régalé; **they do you p. at that restaurant,** on se régale dans ce restaurant.

proudly ['praʊdlɪ] *adv* fièrement, orgueilleusement.

prove [pruːv] *v* (*pp* **proved,** *esp Am Scot* **proven** ['pruːv(ə)n, 'prəʊ-]) **1** *vt* **(a)** (*demonstrate*) prouver, démontrer, établir (*la vérité de qch*); constater (*un fait*); justifier de (*son identité*); témoigner de (*sa bonne volonté*); *Jur* homologuer (*un testament*); **I can't p. it,** je ne peux pas le prouver; **the evidence goes to p. that ...,** les témoignages concourent à prouver que ...; **she/this assertion was proved wrong,** on a prouvé qu'elle avait tort/que cette affirmation était fausse; **this letter proves him to be still alive,** cette lettre prouve qu'il est encore en vie; *Jur Scot* **not proven,** (verdict *m* de) culpabilité non prouvée; *Prov* **the exception proves the rule,** l'exception confirme la règle; **to p. oneself,** faire ses preuves; **what are you trying to p.?,** qu'est-ce que tu cherches à prouver?; **to do sth to p. a point,** faire qch pour démontrer un point de vue; **that proves my point,** ceci confirme ce que je disais;

(b) *Arch & Tech* éprouver; essayer (*une arme à feu*); *Typ* tirer une épreuve d'essai; *Culin* faire lever (*la pâte*); **proven remedy,** remède éprouvé; *Math Old-fashioned* **to p. a sum,** faire la preuve d'un calcul.

2 *vi* se montrer, se trouver; **if what you say proves (to be) true,** si ce que vous dites se confirme; **many of his observations have proved correct,** beaucoup de ses observations se sont avérées justes; **the news proved false,** la nouvelle s'est révélée fausse; **to p. unequal to one's task,** se montrer au-dessous de sa tâche.

provenance ['prɒvənəns] *n* provenance *f*, origine *f*.

Provençal [prɒvɒn'sɑːl] **1** *adj Geog* provençal, -aux. **2** *n* **(a)** Provençal, -ale; **(b)** *Ling* provençal *m*.

provender ['prɒvɪndər] *n Agr* fourrage *m*.

proverb ['prɒvɜːb] *n* proverbe *m*; *Bible* **the Book of Proverbs,** le Livre des Proverbes.

proverbial [prə'vɜːbɪəl] *adj* proverbial, -aux.

proverbially [prə'vɜːbɪəlɪ] *adv* proverbialement.

provide [prə'vaɪd] **1** *vt* **(a)** (*supply*) fournir; **to p. s.o. with sth,** fournir qch à qn, pourvoir *ou* munir qn de qch; **they were well provided with food,** ils étaient bien approvisionnés *ou* ravitaillés; **this provided her with an excuse,** ça lui a fourni une excuse; **to p. an explanation,** donner *ou* fournir une explication; **to p. an exit,** (*of passage*) offrir une sortie; (*of architect*) ménager une sortie; **to p. a regular bus service,** assurer un service d'autobus régulier; **the factory will p. 500 new jobs,** cette usine procurera 500 nouveaux emplois; **(b)** (*stipulate*) stipuler (**that,** que); **the law provides that ...,** la loi porte *ou* dispose que ... . **2** *vi* **the Lord will p.,** Dieu y pourvoira.

►**provide against** *vipo* se prémunir *ou* prendre des mesures contre (*une attaque etc*); parer à (*un danger*).

►**provide for** *vipo* **(a)** (*supply needs of*) pourvoir *ou* subvenir aux besoins de (*qn*); **to p. for oneself,** se suffire; **to be well** *or* **amply provided for,** avoir grandement de quoi vivre; **he provided for everything,** il a subvenu à tout; **he left his family well provided for,** il laissa sa famille à l'abri du besoin; **(b)** (*allow for*) **to p. for an eventuality,** pourvoir à *ou* parer à une éventualité; **expenses provided for in the budget,** dépenses prévues au budget; **this has been provided for,** on y a pourvu.

provided [prə'vaɪdɪd] *conj* **p. (that),** pourvu que + *sub*, à condition que + *sub*; **p. there is enough,** pourvu qu'il y en ait assez, si seulement il y en a assez.

providence ['prɒvɪdəns] *n* **(a)** *Rel* providence *f* (divine); **by a special p.,** par une intervention providentielle; **(b)**

(*foresight*) prévoyance *f*, prudence *f*; (*management of finances etc*) économie *f*.

provident ['prɒvɪdənt] *adj* prévoyant; (*good at managing*) économe; *Br* **p. society,** société *f* de prévoyance.

providential [prɒvɪ'denʃəl] *adj (secours etc)* providentiel.

providentially [prɒvɪ'denʃəlɪ] *adv* providentiellement.

providently ['prɒvɪdəntlɪ] *adv* avec prévoyance.

provider [prə'vaɪdər] *n* fournisseur, -euse.

providing [prə'vaɪdɪŋ] *conj* **p. (that),** = **PROVIDED.**

province ['prɒvɪns] *n* **(a)** province *f* (*d'un pays, d'un archevêque*); **in the provinces,** en province; **(b)** *Jur* juridiction *f*, ressort *m*, compétence *f* (*d'un tribunal*); **that is not (within) my p.,** ce n'est pas de mon ressort.

provincial [prə'vɪnʃəl] **1** *adj* provincial, -aux, -ales; (*théâtre*) de province. **2** *n* provincial, -ale, *pl* -aux.

provincialism [prə'vɪnʃəlɪz(ə)m] *n* provincialisme *m*.

proving ['pru:vɪŋ] *n* **(a)** preuve *f*, démonstration *f* (*de la vérité de qch*); constatation *f* (*d'un fait*); *Jur* homologation *f* (*d'un testament*); **(b)** (*testing*) épreuve *f*; essai *m* (*de bon fonctionnement*); **p. ground,** terrain *m* d'essai *ou* d'expériences.

provision¹ [prə'vɪʒən] *n* **(a)** *Com* provision *f*, réserve *f*; **provisions,** provisions (de bouche); **to lay in a store of provisions,** faire provision de vivres; **wholesale p. business,** maison *f* d'alimentation en gros;

(b) (*supplying*) *Com* **p. of capital,** prestation *f* de capitaux; **there was little p. for education in the budget,** la part du budget consacrée à l'éducation était faible;

(c) (*allowance*) **p. for/against sth,** prise *f* des dispositions nécessaires pour assurer qch/pour parer à qch; **to make p. for sth,** pourvoir à qch; **the law makes no p. for a case of this kind,** la loi ne prévoit pas un cas semblable; **to make p. for one's family,** pourvoir aux besoins de sa famille; (*in the long term*) assurer l'avenir de sa famille; **to make p. against sth,** prendre des mesures contre qch;

(d) article *m* (*d'un traité*); clause *f*, stipulation *f* (*d'un contrat*); **provisions of an act,** dispositions *fpl* d'un décret; **to come within the provisions of the law,** être prévu par la loi.

provision² *vt* approvisionner, ravitailler (*une armée, un navire etc*).

provisional [prə'vɪʒən(ə)l] **1** *adj* provisoire; *Jur* provisionnel; (*jugement*) par provision; *Aut* **p. driving licence,** permis *m* de conduire provisoire; **p. government,** gouvernement *m* provisoire. **2** *n* **the Provisionals,** membres *mpl* de l'IRA provisoire.

provisionally [prə'vɪʒən(ə)lɪ] *adv* provisoirement; *Jur* provisionnellement; (*nommer qn*) à titre provisoire.

proviso, *pl* **-os** [prə'vaɪzəʊ, -əʊz] *n* (*in document*) clause conditionnelle; condition *f* (*d'un contrat*); (*stipulation*) stipulation *f*; **with the p. that ...,** à condition que ... .

provisory [prə'vaɪzərɪ] *adj* conditionnel.

Provo ['prəʊvəʊ] *n F* membre *m* de l'IRA provisoire.

provocation [prɒvə'keɪʃən] *n* provocation *f*; **to act under p.,** agir en réponse à une provocation; **without p.,** sans provocation.

provocative [prə'vɒkətɪv] *adj* provocateur, -trice, provocant; (*sourire, robe etc*) provocant, aguichant; **he's just being p.,** il le fait seulement pour provoquer.

provocatively [prə'vɒkətɪvlɪ] *adv* (*to smile, be dressed*) d'une manière provocante.

provoke [prə'vəʊk] *vt* **(a)** provoquer, pousser, inciter (**s.o. to do sth,** qn à faire qch); (*irritate*) irriter, contrarier, agacer, exaspérer (*qn*); exciter (*un chien*); **to p. s.o. to anger,** mettre qn en colère; **I was provoked,** on m'a provoqué *ou F* cherché; **(b)** (*arouse*) exciter, faire naître (*la curiosité etc*); provoquer (*la gaieté*); stimuler (*l'appétit*); soulever (*une passion, l'indignation*).

provoking [prə'vəʊkɪŋ] *adj* irritant, agaçant, exaspérant.

provokingly [prə'vəʊkɪŋlɪ] *adv* d'une manière irritante *ou* exaspérante.

provost *n* **(a)** ['prɒvəst] *Sch & Univ* principal *m*; **(b)** ['prɒvəst] *Scot* maire *m*; **(c)** [prə'vəʊ] *Mil* **p. marshal,** grand prévôt; **p. duty,** service prévôtal; prévôté *f*.

prow [praʊ] *n Nau* proue *f*, avant *m* (*d'un navire*).

prowess ['praʊɪs] *n* **(a)** (*skill*) talent *m*, habileté *f*; **her p. at tennis** *or* **as a t. player,** son talent au tennis *ou* en tant que joueuse de tennis; **(b)** (*courage*) prouesse *f*, vaillance *f*.

prowl¹ [praʊl] *n* action *f* de rôder (*en quête de proie*); **to go on the p.,** (*of lion etc, Fig*) partir en chasse; *US F* **p. car,** voiture *f* de patrouille (*de police*).

prowl² **1** *vi* (*of animal*) rôder en quête de proie; **to p. about the streets,** rôder par toute la ville. **2** *vt* **to p. the streets,** rôder les rues.

prowler ['praʊlər] *n* rôdeur, -euse; **there's a p. in the neighbourhood,** il y a quelqu'un qui rôde dans le voisinage.

prox. *Old-fashioned Com abbr* **proximo.**

proximity [prɒk'sɪmɪtɪ] *n* **(a)** (*closeness*) proximité *f*; **its p. to London,** sa situation à proximité de Londres; **in p. to,** à proximité de, près de; **in close p. to,** juste à proximité *ou* tout près de; **(b)** *Fig* **p. of blood,** proximité *f* du sang, proche parenté; **(c)** *Mil* **p. fuse,** fusée *f* à influence; fusée de proximité.

proximo ['prɒksɪməʊ] *adv Old-fashioned Com* (du mois) prochain.

proxy ['prɒksɪ] *n* **(a)** (*power*) procuration *f*, délégation *f* de pouvoirs, pouvoir *m*, mandat *m*; **to vote by p.,** voter par procuration; **(b)** (*person*) mandataire *mf*, fondé *m* de pouvoir(s), délégué, -ée; **to make s.o. one's p.,** déléguer ses pouvoirs à qn; **p. bomb,** = bombe amenée sur les lieux par une personne agissant sous la contrainte.

prude [pru:d] *n* prude *mf*, bégueule *mf*; **don't be such a p.!,** ne soyez pas si prude!

prudence ['pru:dəns] *n* prudence *f*; (*common sense*) sagesse *f*.

prudent ['pru:dənt] *adj* prudent; (*sensible*) sage.

prudential [pru:'denʃəl] *adj US* **p. committee,** = comité *m* de surveillance (*d'une municipalité, d'une société*).

prudently ['pru:dəntlɪ] *adv* prudemment.

prudery ['pru:dərɪ] *n* pruderie *f*, pudibonderie *f*.

prudish ['pru:dɪʃ] *adj* prude, pudibond.

prudishness ['pru:dɪʃnɪs] *n* = **PRUDERY.**

prune¹ [pru:n] *n* pruneau *m*; *Fig F* **old p.,** (*old woman*) vieille bique ratatinée.

prune² *vt* **(a)** tailler (*un rosier, un arbre fruitier*); rafraîchir (*les racines d'un arbre*); châtrer (*une plante*); émonder (*un arbre*); **to p. a branch,** élaguer une branche; **(b)** *Fig* faire des coupures dans, émonder, élaguer (*un article etc*).

►prune away, prune off *vtsep* élaguer (*une branche, Fig un texte*).

pruner ['pru:nər] *n* (*person*) tailleur *m* d'arbres, élagueur *m*, émondeur *m*.

pruning ['pru:nɪŋ] *n* **(a)** taille *f* (*d'un rosier etc*); émondage *m* (*d'une branche*); élagage *m* (*d'un arbre*); **p. hook,** émondoir *m*; **p. knife,** serpette *f*; **p. shears,** cisailles *fpl*; **(b)** *Fig F* (*of article etc*) élagage *m*.

prurience ['prʊərɪəns], **pruriency** ['prʊərɪənsɪ] *n* lascivité *f*, lubricité *f*.

prurient ['prʊərɪənt] *adj* (à l'esprit) lascif; **to take a p. interest in sth,** porter un intérêt lascif à qch.

Prussia ['prʌʃə] *n* Prusse *f*.

Prussian ['prʌʃən] **1** *adj* prussien; **P. blue,** bleu *m* de Prusse. **2** *n* Prussien, -ienne.

prussic ['prʌsɪk] *adj Ch* (*acide*) prussique, cyanhydrique.

pry¹ [praɪ] *vi* (*pt & pp* **pried**) (*into particular matter*) fouiller, fureter, chercher à voir (*dans qch*); (*generally*) fourrer son nez partout; **I don't mean to p., but why did you do it?,** je sais que ça ne me regarde pas mais pourquoi est-ce que tu as fait ça?; **to p. into a secret,** chercher à pénétrer un secret.

pry² *vt* (*pt & pp* **pried**) (*force*) soulever *ou* mouvoir à l'aide d'un levier.

►pry loose *vtsep* décoller, détacher (*qch*).

►pry open *vtsep* forcer (*une porte, un coffret etc*).

prying ['praɪɪŋ] *adj* curieux, indiscret, -ète, fureteur; **safe from p. eyes,** à l'abri des regards indiscrets.

PS ['pi:es] *n* (*abbr* **postscript**) P.S.; **to add a PS to a letter,** ajouter un P.S. à une lettre; **PS see you next week,** P.S. à la semaine prochaine.

psalm [sɑ:m] *n* psaume *m*; **p. book,** livre *m* de psaumes, psautier *m*; *Bible* **(the Book of) Psalms,** (le Livre des) Psaumes.

psalmist ['sɑ:mɪst] *n* psalmiste *m*.

psalmodize ['sɑ:mədaɪz] *vi* psalmodier.

psalmody ['sɑ:mədɪ] *n* psalmodie *f*.

psalter ['sɔ:ltər] *n* psautier *m*.

PSBR [pi:esbi:'ɑ:r] *n Br* (*abbr* **public sector borrowing requirement**) = besoins d'emprunt du secteur public non couverts par les rentrées fiscales.

psephological [sefə'lɒdʒɪk(ə)l] *adj* relatif à l'étude scientifique des élections, politologique.

psephologist [se'fɒlədʒɪst] *n* spécialiste *mf* de l'étude des élections, politologue *mf*.

psephology [se'fɒlədʒɪ] *n* étude *f* scientifique des élections, politologie *f*.

pseud [sju:d] *n F* comédien, -enne.

pseudo ['sju:dəʊ] *adj F* faux, *f* fausse, pseudo-.

pseudonym ['sju:dənɪm] *n* pseudonyme *m*; **to write sth**

under a p., écrire qch sous un pseudonyme.
pshaw [(p)ʃɔː] *int Old-fashioned (indicating disgust)* peuh!
psi [piːe'saɪ] *Phys (abbr* **pounds per square inch***)* livres par pouce carré.
psittacosis [sɪtə'kəʊsɪs] *n Med Vet* psittacose *f*.
psoriasis [sə'raɪəsɪs] *n Med* psoriasis *m*.
psst [pst] *int (to attract attention)* psitt!, pst!; *(to warn)* chut!
PST [piːes'tiː] *n Am (abbr* **Pacific Standard Time***)* PST.
PSV [piːes'viː] *n Admin (abbr* **public service vehicle***)* véhicule *m* de transport en commun.
►**psych out** [saɪk] *vtsep* = **PSYCHE OUT**.
►**psych up** *vtsep* = **PSYCHE UP**.
psyche ['saɪkɪ] *n* psyché *f*, psychè *f*.
►**psyche out** [saɪk] *vtsep F (unnerve)* démoraliser *(qn)*, déstabiliser *(qn)*.
►**psyche up** *vtsep F (prepare)* **to p. oneself up (for sth),** se préparer (mentalement) (à faire qch); **to p. s.o. up for sth,** préparer qn mentalement pour qch.
psychedelic [saɪkə'delɪk] *adj* psychédélique.
psyched-up [saɪk'tʌp] *adj* préparé, *F* gonflé à bloc.
psychiatric [saɪkɪ'ætrɪk] *adj* psychiatrique; *Br* **p. social worker,** assistant social en psychiatrie.
psychiatrist [saɪ'kaɪətrɪst] *n* psychiatre *mf*.
psychiatry [saɪ'kaɪətrɪ] *n* psychiatrie *f*.
psychic ['saɪkɪk] **1** *adj (also* **psychical** ['saɪkɪk(ə)l]) psychique; *(phénomène etc)* métapsychique; *F* **I'm not p.!,** je ne suis pas devin! **2** *n* médium *m*.
psycho ['saɪkəʊ] *adj & n F* psychopathe *mf*.
psychoanalyse, *US* **-analyze** [saɪkəʊ'ænəlaɪz] *vt* psychanalyser *(qn)*.
psychoanalysis [saɪkəʊə'nælɪsɪs] *n* psychanalyse *f*.
psychoanalyst [saɪkəʊ'ænəlɪst] *n* psychanalyste *mf*.
psychoanalytic(al) [saɪkəʊænə'lɪtɪk,-ɪk(ə)l] *adj* psychanalytique.
psychobabble ['saɪkəʊbæbəl] *n F* jargon *m* des psys.
psychological [saɪkə'lɒdʒɪk(ə)l] *adj* psychologique; **the p. moment,** le moment psychologique; **p. warfare,** guerre *f* psychologique.
psychologically [saɪkə'lɒdʒɪklɪ] *adv* psychologiquement.
psychologist [saɪ'kɒlədʒɪst] *n* psychologue *mf*; **child p.,** psychologue *mf* pour enfants.
psychology [saɪ'kɒlədʒɪ] *n* psychologie *f*; **the p. of the football hooligan,** la psychologie des hooligans du football; *F* **to use p.,** faire preuve de psychologie.
psychomotor ['saɪkəʊməʊtər] *adj* psychomoteur, -trice.
psychoneurosis [saɪkəʊnjʊ'rəʊsɪs] *n Med* psychonévrose *f*.
psychopath ['saɪkəʊpæθ] *n Psy* psychopathe *mf*.
psychopathic [saɪkəʊ'pæθɪk] *adj* psychopathe; *(état, personnalité)* psychopathique.
psychopathology [saɪkəʊpə'θɒlədʒɪ] *n* psychopathologie *f*.
psychophysiology [saɪkəʊfɪzɪ'ɒlədʒɪ] *n* psychophysiologie *f*.
psychosis, *pl* **-oses** [saɪ'kəʊsɪs, -əʊsiːz] *n Med* psychose *f*.
psychosomatic [saɪkəʊsə'mætɪk] *adj Med (illness etc)* psychosomatique.
psychotherapist [saɪkəʊ'θerəpɪst] *n* psychothérapeute *mf*.
psychotherapy [saɪkəʊ'θerəpɪ] *n* psychothérapie *f*.
psychotic [saɪ'kɒtɪk] *adj & n Med* psychotique *mf*.
PT [piː'tiː] *n abbr* **physical training**.
PTA [piːtiː'eɪ] *n Sch abbr* **Parent-Teacher Association**.
ptarmigan ['tɑːmɪgən] *n (bird)* **p.,** *Am* **rock p.,** lagopède muet, *Can* lagopède des rochers.
Pte *n Mil (abbr* **private***)* soldat *m*.
pterodactyl [terəʊ'dæktɪl] *n* ptérodactyle *m*.
PTO [piːtiː'əʊ] *(abbr* **please turn over***)* T.S.V.P.
ptomaine ['təʊmeɪn] *n Ch* ptomaïne *f*; **p. poisoning,** intoxication *f* alimentaire (par les ptomaïnes).
pub [pʌb] *n Br F* = café *m*, bistro(t) *m*, pub *m*; **p. food** *or F* **grub,** = nourriture servie dans un pub; **p. lunch,** déjeuner *m* simple *(servi dans un pub)*.
pub-crawl¹ ['pʌbkrɔːl] *n Br* tournée *f* des bars; **to go on a p.-c.,** faire la tournée des bars, aller de bar en bar; *Can F* partir sur une brosse.
pub-crawl² *vi Br* faire la tournée des bars, aller de bar en bar.
puberty ['pjuːbətɪ] *n Physiol* puberté *f*; **at p.,** à la puberté; **to reach p.,** atteindre l'âge de la puberté.
pubescence [pjuː'besəns] *n* **(a)** *Bot* pubescence *f*; **(b)** *Physiol* puberté *f*.
pubescent [pjuː'besənt] *adj* **(a)** *Bot* pubescent, velu; **(b)** *Physiol* pubère.
pubic ['pjuːbɪk] *adj Anat* pubien; **p. hair,** poils *mpl ou (single)* poil du pubis *ou* pubien(s).
public ['pʌblɪk] **1** *adj* public, *f* publique; *F* **to go p.,** *(of firm)* émettre *ou* placer des actions dans le public; *(reveal information)* tout dire *ou* raconter; **to make p.,** rendre *(qch)* public; publier *(une nouvelle etc)*; **p. address system,** sonorisation *f*; **to make a p. appearance,** paraître en public; *US* **p. assistance,** assistance publique; **p. authorities,** pouvoirs publics; **p. call box,** cabine (téléphonique) publique; *US Jur* **p. defender,** = avocat spécialisé dans l'aide judiciaire; *F* **p. enemy number 1,** ennemi public numéro 1; **at p. expense,** aux frais du contribuable; **to work for the p. good,** travailler pour le bien public; **p. health official,** représentant *m* de la santé publique; **p. holiday,** fête légale; *Br* **p. house,** = café *m*, *Fml* débit *m* de boissons; **p. convenience** *or* **lavatory,** toilettes publiques; *Br* **p. lending right,** = droit d'auteur sur les livres empruntés dans une bibliothèque municipale; **p. life,** vie publique; *Br* **p. limited company,** = société à responsabilité limitée; **p. opinion,** opinion publique; **p. opinion poll,** sondage *m* d'opinion publique; **p. park,** jardin public; **in a p. place,** dans un lieu public; **to make a p. protest,** protester publiquement; **p. relations,** relations publiques; **p. relations officer,** agent *m* de(s) relations publiques; *Sch* **p. school,** *Am* école publique; *Br* école privée; *Br* **a p.-school education,** une scolarité faite dans une école privée; *Econ* **p. sector,** secteur public; **p. sector earnings,** les revenus du secteur public; **p. service,** *(civil service)* fonction publique; *TV Rad* **p. service broadcasting,** (une chaîne/station du) service public; **p. speaking,** art *m* de parler en public; **p. spirit,** civisme *m*; **p. transport,** transports *mpl* en commun; **p. utility (service),** service public; **p. works,** travaux publics.
2 *n* **the (general) p.,** le (grand) public; **book aimed at a wide p.,** livre qui s'adresse à un large public; *Fin* **to issue shares to the p.,** placer des actions dans le public; **my p. like the old songs,** mon public aime les vieilles chansons; **in p.,** en public, publiquement.
publican ['pʌblɪkən] *n Br* patron, -onne d'un pub.
publication [pʌblɪ'keɪʃən] *n* **(a)** publication *f (d'un livre, d'une nouvelle, des bans etc)*; promulgation *f (d'une ordonnance, d'un décret)*; **p. date,** *(of book)* date *f* de parution; **(b)** *(published work)* ouvrage publié, publication *f*; **a recent p.,** une publication récente.
publicist ['pʌblɪsɪst] *n* **(a)** publicitaire *mf*; **(b)** *Old-fashioned* journaliste *mf*.
publicity [pʌb'lɪsɪtɪ] *n* publicité *f (donnée à une affaire etc)*; *Com* publicité, réclame *f*; **the football team has received a lot of free p. as a result of this scandal,** ce scandale a fait beaucoup de publicité (gratuite) à l'équipe de football; **p. campaign,** campagne *f* de publicité; **p. department,** *Com* la publicité; **p. manager,** chef *m* de publicité.
publicize ['pʌblɪsaɪz] *vt* faire connaître *(qch)* au public; *(advertise)* faire de la réclame pour *(un produit)*; **her resignation was widely publicized,** on a fait beaucoup de battage autour de sa démission.
publicly ['pʌblɪklɪ] *adv* publiquement, en public.
public-spirited ['pʌblɪkspɪrɪtɪd] *adj (person)* qui a le sens civique.
publish ['pʌblɪʃ] **1** *vt* **(a)** *(of publisher)* éditer, publier, faire paraître *(un livre)*; **just published,** *(of book)* vient de paraître; **she's had two novels published,** on a publié deux de ses romans; **(b)** publier *(un édit, des bans de mariage)*; publier, révéler, divulguer *(une nouvelle)*. **2** *vi* **they decided not to p.,** ils ont décidé de ne pas faire publier la nouvelle *ou* leur ouvrage *ou* un article *etc*.
publisher ['pʌblɪʃər] *n* **(a)** éditeur, -trice; **(b)** *Am (newspaper owner)* propriétaire *m* d'un journal.
publishing ['pʌblɪʃɪŋ] *n* **(a)** publication *f*, mise *f* en vente *(d'un livre)*; **to work** *or* **be in p.,** travailler dans l'édition; **p. house** *or* **firm,** maison *f* d'édition; **the p. trade,** l'édition *f*; **(b)** publication *f (des bans etc)*.
puce [pjuːs] *adj & n* (couleur *f*) puce *m inv*.
puck¹ [pʌk] *n (elf)* lutin *m*, farfadet *m*.
puck² *n Sp* palet *m* en caoutchouc *(pour le hockey sur glace)*.
pucker¹ ['pʌkər] *n* ride *f*, pli *m (du visage)*; faux pli, godet *m*, *(d'un tissu)*.
pucker² **1** *vt* rider *(le visage)*; plisser, froncer, faire goder *(un tissu)*; froncer *(les sourcils)*; plisser *(les lèvres)*. **2** *vi* = **PUCKER UP**.
►**pucker up** **1** *vi (of garment, material)* faire des faux plis, goder; **his face puckered up,** sa figure s'est crispée. **2** *vtsep* avancer *(les lèvres)*.

puckish ['pʌkɪʃ] *adj* malicieux, espiègle.

pud [pʊd] *n Br F* pudding *m*; (*dessert*) dessert *m*.

pudding ['pʊdɪŋ] *n Culin* **(a)** (*dish*) **(suet) p.,** pudding *m*, pouding *m*; **p. basin,** moule *m* à puddings; **milk p.,** entremets sucré au lait; **rice p.,** (*milky*) riz *m* au lait; (*solid*) gâteau *m* de riz; **black p.,** boudin (noir); *Sl Hum* **to be in the p. club,** (*be pregnant*) avoir un polichinelle dans le tiroir; **(b)** (*dessert*) dessert *m*; **what's for p.?,** qu'est-ce qu'il y a comme *ou* pour le dessert?; **(c)** *F* (*chubby person*) petit gros, petite grosse; (*baby*) gros bébé.

puddingface ['pʊdɪŋfeɪs] *n F* visage empâté.

puddinghead ['pʊdɪŋhed] *n F* idiot, -ote, andouille *f*.

puddingstone ['pʊdɪŋstəʊn] *n* poudingue *m*.

puddle¹ ['pʌd(ə)l] *n* flaque *f* d'eau *ou* d'huile; (*small pool*) petite mare; *F* **the dog's made a p. on the carpet,** le chien a fait pipi sur le tapis.

puddle² *vt* rendre (*l'eau*) boueux; corroyer, malaxer (*l'argile*); *Metal* puddler (*le fer*).

pudenda [pu:'dendə] *npl* vulve *f*.

pudgy ['pʌdʒɪ] *adj F* (*person*) rondelet, dodu.

puerile ['pjʊəraɪl] *adj Pej* puéril, enfantin.

puerility [pjʊə'rɪlɪtɪ] *n* puérilité *f*.

puerperal [pju:'ɜ:pərəl] *adj Med* puerpéral, -aux.

Puerto Rican [pweətəʊ'ri:kən] *Geog* **1** *adj* portoricain. **2** *n* Portoricain, -aine.

Puerto Rico [pweətəʊ'ri:kəʊ] *n* Porto Rico.

puff¹ [pʌf] *n* **(a)** souffle *m* (*de la respiration, d'air*); bouffée *f* (*d'air, de fumée*); échappement soudain (*de vapeur*); **to take a p. at one's pipe,** tirer une bouffée de sa pipe; *F* **out of p.,** essoufflé, à bout de souffle; *F* **let me get my p. back,** laissez-moi récupérer; **p. adder,** (*snake*) vipère heurtante; **(b)** *Sewing* bouillon *m* (*de robe*); bouffant *m* (*d'une manche*); *US* (*quilt*) édredon *m*; **p. sleeves,** manches bouffantes; **(c) powder p.,** houppe *f*, houppette *f*; **(d)** *Culin* **p. pastry,** pâte feuilletée; **cream p.,** feuilleté *m* à la crème; **(e)** *F Old-fashioned* (*advertisement*) réclame *f* (tapageuse); **(f)** *Sl* (*male homosexual*) tante *f*.

puff² **1** *vi* souffler; lancer des bouffées (*de fumée, de vapeur*); émettre des jets de vapeur; **to p. and blow** *or* **pant,** haleter; **to p. at one's pipe,** tirer sur sa pipe, tirer des bouffées de sa pipe; **the steam engine puffed into view,** la fumée indiqua l'arrivée du train. **2** *vt* émettre, lancer (*des bouffées de fumée, d'air*); fumer (*un cigare*) par petites bouffées; gonfler (*le riz*); *F Old-fashioned* pousser, vanter (*ses marchandises*); **to p. smoke into s.o.'s face,** envoyer de la fumée à la figure de qn.

▸**puff out** *vtsep* **(a)** gonfler (*les joues*); faire ballonner (*une manche etc*); **(b)** (*emit*) émettre, lancer (*des bouffées de fumée*); **(c)** *F* (*exhaust*) épuiser, *F* crever; **that walk has puffed me out,** cette marche m'a crevé.

▸**puff up** *vtsep* gonfler (*les joues*).

puffball ['pʌfbɔ:l] *n F* (*fungus*) vesse-de-loup *f*, *pl* vesses-de-loup.

puffed [pʌft] *adj* **(a)** *Sewing* **p. sleeves,** manches bouffantes; *Culin* **p. rice,** riz gonflé; **p. out,** ballonné; **p. up (with pride),** gonflé *ou* bouffi d'orgueil; **(b)** *F* **p. (out),** (*person*) essoufflé, à bout de souffle.

puffin ['pʌfɪn] *n* (*bird*) macareux *m*, moine *m*, puffin *m*.

puffiness ['pʌfɪnɪs] *n* aspect bouffi (*du visage etc*).

puffy ['pʌfɪ] *adj* **(a)** (*swollen*) bouffi, boursouflé; (*face*) bouffi, boursouflé; (*eyes*) gonflé; **to be p. under the eyes,** avoir les yeux bouffis; **(b)** (*person*) (*short-winded*) à l'haleine courte, poussif; (*out of breath*) hors d'haleine.

pug [pʌg] *n* **p. (dog),** carlin *m*; **p. nose,** nez écrasé *ou* camus; **p.-nosed,** au nez camus.

pugilism ['pju:dʒɪlɪz(ə)m] *n* boxe *f*.

pugilist ['pju:dʒɪlɪst] *n* pugiliste *m*; boxeur *m*.

pugnacious [pʌg'neɪʃəs] *adj* querelleur, -euse, batailleur, -euse, *Lit* pugnace.

pugnaciously [pʌg'neɪʃəslɪ] *adv* d'une manière querelleuse *ou* batailleuse *ou Lit* pugnace.

pugnaciousness [pʌg'neɪʃəsnɪs], **pugnacity** [pʌg'næsɪtɪ] *n* caractère querelleur *ou* batailleur, *Lit* pugnacité *f*.

puke¹ [pju:k] *n Sl* (*vomit*) dégueulis *m*; **to have a p.,** dégueuler.

puke² *vt & vi Sl* dégueuler; **it makes me p.,** c'est à gerber; **you make me p.,** vous êtes dégueulasse.

pukey ['pju:kɪ] *adj Sl* merdique.

pukka ['pʌkə] *adj* authentique; **a p. Englishman,** un vrai Anglais d'Angleterre.

pull¹ [pʊl] *n* **(a)** (*act of pulling*) tirage *m*; traction *f*; force *f* d'attraction (*d'un aimant*); tension *f*, tirage (*d'une courroie etc*); (*in rowing*) coup *m* (d'aviron); *Horseracing* manœuvre *f* (*pour retenir un cheval*); **give it a hard p.!,** tirez fort!; **gravitational p.,** gravitation *f*; **bell p.,** cordon *m* de sonnette; **(b)** *F* gorgée *f*, lampée *f* (*de bière etc*); **to take a p. at one's pipe,** tirer une bouffée de sa pipe; **(c)** (*influence*) influence *f*; **to have plenty of p.,** avoir le bras long; **(d)** *Golf Cr* longue crossée à gauche; coup tiré; **(e)** *Typ* première épreuve.

pull² **1** *vt* **(a)** tirer (*une corde, les cheveux de qn etc*); se déchirer (*un muscle*); manier (*un aviron*); *Horseracing etc* retenir, tirer (*un cheval*); **p.,** (*on door*) tirez, tirer; **pulled muscle,** élongation *f*; **to p. the trigger,** presser sur la détente *ou* la gâchette; **p. your chair up to** *or* **nearer the fire,** approchez votre fauteuil du feu; **to p. sth to pieces,** déchirer qch, mettre qch en morceaux; **to p. s.o. to pieces,** (*criticize severely*) critiquer sévèrement qn; **to p. one's hat over one's eyes,** renfoncer *ou* rabattre son chapeau sur les yeux;

(b) traîner, tirer (*une charrette etc*); (*of barge etc*) haler (*un bateau*);

(c) *Com etc* (*attract*) attirer (*la clientèle, une foule*); *Sl* (*attract sexually*) attirer;

(d) (*extract*) **to p. a cork,** déboucher une bouteille; **to p. a plant,** déraciner *ou* arracher une plante; **to p. a tooth,** arracher une dent; **to have a tooth pulled,** se faire arracher une dent; *F* **to p. a gun on s.o.,** mettre un pistolet sous le nez de qn; *F* **to p. a fast one on s.o.,** avoir qn;

(e) to p. a face, faire une grimace;

(f) *Typ* tirer (*une épreuve*);

(g) *Sp* **to p. the ball,** renvoyer la balle vers la gauche; *Golf* faire un coup tiré.

2 *vi* **(a)** tirer; (*in rowing*) ramer, souquer; **to p. on** *or* **at a rope,** tirer sur un cordage; **to p. at one's pipe,** tirer sur sa pipe; *Horseriding* **horse that pulls,** cheval qui résiste au mors;

(b) *Aut etc* **the engine is pulling heavily,** le moteur fatigue *ou* peine; **they're pulling in different directions,** ils ne s'entendent pas, ils ne sont pas d'accord, *F* ils tirent à hue et à dia;

(c) *Sp* renvoyer la balle d'un coup tiré à gauche; *Golf* faire un coup tiré;

(d) *Sl* (*to attract s.o. sexually*) être attirant.

▸**pull about** *vtsep* tirailler (*qch*); (*mistreat*) malmener (*qn*).

▸**pull ahead** *vi Sp* (*in race*) se détacher du peloton *ou* prendre la tête.

▸**pull apart** **1** *vtsep* (*break up*) déchirer qch; mettre qch en petits morceaux; (*separate*) séparer. **2** *vi* **it's designed to p. apart,** c'est conçu pour se détacher quand on tire dessus.

▸**pull away** **1** *vtsep* (*remove forcefully*) **to p. sth away from sth/s.o.,** arracher qch de qch/des mains de qn; **they pulled the distraught father away (from the burning car),** ils ont tiré le père affolé loin de la voiture en feu. **2** *vi* **(a)** (*of train, car*) démarrer; **she's beginning to p. away,** (*in race*) elle commence à prendre de l'avance; **(b)** (*in rowing*) **p. away!,** souquez!

▸**pull back** *vi* (*hesitate*) hésiter; (*not continue with project etc*) refuser de continuer; *Mil* décrocher.

▸**pull down** *vtsep* **(a)** (*lower*) baisser, faire descendre (*un store etc*); descendre (*sa jupe*); **to p. one's hat down over one's eyes,** renfoncer *ou* rabattre son chapeau sur ses yeux; **(b)** (*demolish*) démolir, abattre (*une maison etc*); **(c)** (*of illness*) abattre, affaiblir (*qn*); (*of circumstances*) décourager (*qn*); **(d)** *Comptr* appeler (en mémoire ou sur l'écran); **(e)** *Am F* (*earn*) toucher (*un salaire*); gagner (*de l'argent*); **he doesn't p. down much of a salary,** il ne touche pas des masses.

▸**pull in** **1** *vtsep* **(a)** rentrer (*un filet etc*); **(b)** (*attract*) attirer (*le public*); **(c)** *F* (*of police*) arrêter (*un suspect*); **they pulled him in for questioning,** ils l'ont arrêté pour l'interroger; **to be pulled in (for speeding),** être arrêté (pour excès de vitesse); **(d)** *Aut* **to p. one's car in to the kerb,** se ranger près du trottoir; **(e) to p. oneself in,** rentrer son ventre; **(f)** *Horseriding* (*hold back*) retenir (*son cheval*), tirer les rênes de (*son cheval*). **2** *vi* **(a)** (*stop at side of road*) (*of vehicle, driver*) s'arrêter, se garer; **p. in here,** arrête-toi là; **we'll p. in to the next garage we see,** on s'arrêtera à la prochaine station-service; **(b)** *F* (*arrive*) (*of train, bus, person*) arriver; **the express pulled in two hours late,** l'express est arrivé avec deux heures de retard.

▸**pull into** *vipo* (*arrive at*) (*of train, bus, person etc*) arriver à; **the train was pulling into the station,** le train entrait en gare; *Aut* **to p. into the kerb,** se ranger près du trottoir.

▸**pull off** **1** *vtsep* **(a)** (*remove*) détacher (*qch de qch*); **to p. off one's clothes,** enlever ses vêtements; **I pulled off**

the plastic wrapping, j'ai enlevé l'emballage en plastique; **(b)** *F* (*win*) gagner, remporter, décrocher (*un prix*); **to p. off a deal,** réussir une opération, boucler une affaire; **to p. off a daring bank raid/an ambitious project,** réussir un hold-up audacieux/un projet ambitieux; **he pulled it off,** il a réussi. **2** *vi* **the lid simply pulls off,** il faut tirer pour enlever le couvercle.

►**pull on** *vipo* mettre (*un pull, ses vêtements*).

►**pull out 1** *vtsep* **(a)** (*extract*) arracher (*une dent*); **to p. sth out of sth,** tirer *ou* sortir qch de qch; **p. me out, I'm stuck in this mud!,** sors-moi de là, je suis enlisé dans la boue!; *F* **to p. out all the stops,** donner le maximum; **(b)** (*withdraw*) retirer (*des troupes*). **2** *vi* **(a)** *Aut* (*move out to overtake*) déboîter; **to p. out from behind a vehicle,** déboîter de derrière une voiture; **(b)** *F* (*leave*) (*of train, bus, person etc*) partir; **when do we p. out?,** quand est-ce qu'on part?; **(c)** (*withdraw*) (*of troops, of firm from project*) se retirer; (*of firm from place*) quitter une région *ou* une ville *etc*.

►**pull out of** *vipo* (*leave*) (*of train, bus, person etc*) partir de; **the train was pulling out of the station,** le train sortait de la gare; *Av* **to p. out of a dive,** arrêter de piquer.

►**pull over 1** *vtsep* **(a)** (*cause to fall*) faire tomber; **careful you don't p. that wardrobe over on top of you!,** fais attention de ne pas te prendre l'armoire sur la tête!; **(b) she pulled her sweater over her head,** (*when putting it on*) elle (s')enfila son pull; (*when taking it off*) elle ôta son pull. **2** *vi* **she's pulling over to let the other runners past,** elle se range *ou* se met sur le côté pour laisser passer les autres coureurs.

►**pull round 1** *vtas* (*help regain consciousness*) remonter (*qn*), remettre (*qn*) sur pied; **I was very depressed but my friends pulled me round,** j'étais très déprimé mais mes amis m'ont remonté le moral. **2** *vi* (*regain consciousness, recover from illness*) se remettre.

►**pull through 1** *vtas* **(a)** (*of doctor etc*) remettre (*qn*) sur pied; **(b)** (*help survive difficulty*) tirer (*qn*) d'embarras *ou* d'affaire; **he says his faith pulled him through,** il dit que c'est la foi qui lui a permis de s'en sortir. **2** *vi* **(a)** (*recover from illness*) s'en tirer; **(b)** (*survive difficulty*) se tirer d'affaire, s'en tirer, surmonter ses difficultés.

►**pull to** *vtsep* tirer, fermer (*la porte*).

►**pull together 1** *vtsep* (*become calm, more organized*) **to p. oneself together,** se reprendre, se remettre, reprendre ses esprits; **p. yourself together!,** remettez-vous! **2** *vi F* (*co-operate*) être d'accord, s'entendre; **they're not pulling together,** ils ne s'entendent pas, ils ne sont pas d'accord; **if we all p. together on this,** si nous y mettons tous du nôtre; **p. together!,** (*in rowing*) avant partout!

►**pull up 1** *vtsep* **(a)** (*raise*) hausser, lever (*un store*); retrousser, relever (*sa jupe*); arracher (*les mauvaises herbes*); **to p. one's socks up,** tirer *ou* remonter ses chaussettes; *F Fig* se remuer, s'activer; **to p. up a plant,** déraciner *ou* arracher une plante; **p. up a chair!,** prends une chaise!;

(b) (*stop*) *Horseriding* arrêter (*un cheval*); **to p. oneself up,** s'arrêter (*quand on est sur le point de dire ou faire qch d'indiscret*);

(c) *F* (*reprimand*) réprimander, rembarrer (*qn*); **he pulled me up for being late,** il m'a enguirlandé parce que j'étais en retard; *Aut* **to be pulled up (by the police),** se faire arrêter (par un agent).

2 *vi* **(a)** (*stop*) s'arrêter; **he pulled up at the traffic lights,** il s'est arrêté au feu rouge; **the horse pulled up lame,** le cheval s'est arrêté en boitant;

(b) (*close gap*) **to p. up (on another competitor),** réduire la distance (qui vous sépare d'un autre concurrent).

pull-back ['pʊlbæk] *n* **(a)** (*device*) dispositif *m* de rappel; **(b)** (*withdrawal*) retrait *m* (*de troupes*); **(c)** *Billiards* **p.-b. (stroke),** rétro *m*.

pull-down ['pʊldaʊn] *adj Comptr* **p.-d. menu,** menu déroulant.

pullet ['pʊlɪt] *n* poulette *f*; (*fattened*) poularde *f*.

pulley ['pʊlɪ] *n* poulie *f*; **grooved p.,** poulie à gorge; **p. housing,** carter *m* de poulie; **band** *or* **belt p.,** poulie à courroie; **fixed p.,** poulie fixe; **p. block,** palan *m*, moufle *mf*; **p. wheel,** réa *m*, rouet *m*.

pull-in ['pʊlɪn] *n* (*café*) = restoroute *m*; (*for parking*) parking *m* (*esp près d'un restaurant*).

pulling ['pʊlɪŋ] *n* **(a)** (*act of pulling*) tirage *m*; traction *f*; **(b)** *Typ* tirage *m* d'épreuves.

Pullman ['pʊlmən] *n Rail* **P. (car),** voiture *f* Pullman.

pull-off ['pʊlɒf] *n US Aut* (*rest area*) aire *f* de repos.

pull-out ['pʊlaʊt] **1** *adj* (*section in magazine*) détachable. **2** *n Journ* supplément *m* détachable.

pullover ['pʊləʊvər] *n* (*garment*) pull-over *m*, *pl* pull-overs, *F* pull *m*.

pullulate ['pʌljʊleɪt] *vi* pulluler.

pull-up ['pʊlʌp] *n* **(a)** arrêt *m* (*d'une voiture etc*); **(b)** (*café*) = restoroute *m*.

pulmonary ['pʌlmənərɪ] *adj Anat Med* pulmonaire.

pulp¹ [pʌlp] *n* pulpe *f*, chair *f* (*des fruits*); **dental p.,** pulpe dentaire; **paper p.,** pâte *f ou* pulpe à papier; **to reduce sth to (a) p.,** réduire qch en pulpe; *F* **I reduced him to a p.,** je l'ai mis en bouillie; **p. novels,** romans *mpl* de *ou* à quatre sous.

pulp² *vt* réduire en pulpe *ou* en pâte; mettre (*des livres*) au pilon.

pulping ['pʌlpɪŋ] *n* réduction *f* en pulpe *ou* en pâte; **p. machine,** (*in papermaking*) pilon *m*.

pulpit ['pʊlpɪt] *n* chaire *f* (*du prédicateur*).

pulpwood ['pʌlpwʊd] *n* (*for papermaking*) bois *m* à pâte.

pulpy ['pʌlpɪ] *adj* pulpeux, charnu.

pulsar ['pʌlsər] *n Astron* pulsar *m*.

pulsate [pʌl'seɪt] *vi* palpiter; (*vibrate*) vibrer; (*of heart etc*) battre; *El* **pulsating current,** courant *m* pulsatoire.

pulsation [pʌl'seɪʃən] *n Physiol El Astron* pulsation *f*; battement *m* (*du cœur*).

pulse¹ [pʌls] *n* **(a)** *Physiol* pouls *m*; **quick p.,** pouls fréquent *ou* précipité; **strong/weak p.,** pouls fort/faible; **to feel** *or* **take s.o.'s p.,** prendre le pouls à qn; *Fig* **to have one's finger on the p.,** être à la page; **to keep one's finger on the pulse of ...,** se tenir étroitement au courant de ...; **p. rate,** fréquence *f* du pouls; **(b)** pulsation *f*, battement *m* (*du cœur etc*); *Phys* vibration *f* (*de la lumière, du son etc*); *Electron Rad* impulsion *f*; (*poetry*) *& Mus* cadence *f*, rythme *m*.

pulse² 1 *vi* (*of heart*) palpiter, battre; **to p. through the arteries,** (*of blood*) circuler dans les artères par pulsations rythmées; **the pulsing music,** le rythme saccadé de la musique. **2** *vt El etc* moduler (*un courant*) en impulsions.

pulse³ *n* (*no pl*) plantes légumineuses, légumes *mpl* à gousse.

pulverization [pʌlvəraɪ'zeɪʃən] *n* pulvérisation *f*.

pulverize ['pʌlvəraɪz] *vt* pulvériser, réduire en poudre; broyer (*le charbon*); atomiser (*de la peinture liquide etc*); *F* **to p. s.o.,** (*beat badly*) démolir qn; (*criticize severely*) démolir le discours de qn.

puma ['pju:mə] *n* (*animal*) puma *m*, couguar *m*.

pumice¹ ['pʌmɪs] *n* **p. (stone),** (pierre *f*) ponce *f*.

pumice² *vt* poncer (*une surface*), passer (*une surface*) à la pierre ponce.

pummel¹ ['pʌm(ə)l] *n* = **POMMEL.**

pummel² *vt* (**-ll-**, *US* **-l-**) battre, rosser.

pummelling, *US* **pummeling** ['pʌm(ə)lɪŋ] *n* volée *f* de coups; **to give s.o. a good p.,** donner une bonne raclée à qn.

pump¹ [pʌmp] *n* pompe *f*; *Phys MecE* **force p.,** pompe refoulante; **hand p.,** pompe à bras *ou* à main; **air p.,** pompe à air; **vacuum p.,** pompe à vide; **bicycle p.,** pompe à bicyclette; **the village p.,** la pompe du village; **(petrol) p. attendant,** pompiste *mf*; *Med* **stomach p.,** pompe stomacale; **breast p.,** tire-lait *m*; **p. room,** (*at spa*) pavillon *m* (*où l'on prend les eaux*); **p. water,** eau *f* de pompe; *Min* eau de puits.

pump² 1 *vt* pomper (*de l'eau etc*); puiser (*l'eau*) à la pompe; *F* **to p. s.o.'s hand,** serrer vigoureusement la main à qn; **to p. a well dry,** assécher *ou* épuiser un puits; *F* **to p. s.o.,** (*pour avoir des renseignements*) tirer les vers du nez à qn; **to p. water into a boiler,** refouler de l'eau dans une chaudière; *F* **athletes were pumped full of drugs,** les athlètes étaient complètement dopés; *Sl* **to p. s.o. full of lead,** faire la peau à qn; **to p. air into s.o.'s lungs,** insuffler de l'air dans les poumons de qn; **the government pumped money into the region,** le gouvernement a injecté des capitaux dans cette région. **2** *vi* (*of heart, machine etc*) pomper.

pump³ *n* (*shoe*) escarpin *m*.

►**pump in** *vtsep* refouler (*de l'eau etc*); *Fig* **more money will have to be pumped in,** il faudra injecter plus d'argent.

►**pump out** *vtsep* pomper (*de l'eau etc*); *Nau* **to p. out the holds,** assécher les cales; **to p. out s.o.'s stomach,** faire (subir) un lavage d'estomac à qn.

►**pump up** *vtsep* gonfler (*un pneu*).

pumping ['pʌmpɪŋ] *n* pompage *m*, extraction *f* (*de l'eau etc*); **p. (out),** épuisement *m* (*des eaux dans une mine etc*); asséchage *m* (*d'un puits*); **p. (up),** gonflage *m* (*d'un pneu*); **p. station,** station *f* de pompage.

pumpkin ['pʌmpkɪn] *n* potiron *m*, citrouille *f*.

pun[1] [pʌn] *n* (*play on words*) calembour *m*, jeu *m* de mots (**on sth**, sur qch).

pun[2] *vi* (-nn-) (*play on words*) faire des calembours *ou* des jeux de mots.

punch[1] [pʌntʃ] *n Tech etc* (*tool*) poinçon *m*; perçoir *m*; (*machine*) poinçonneuse *f*; **ticket p.**, poinçon (*de contrôleur de chemin de fer etc*); (*in station*) composteur *m*; **centre p.**, poinçon *m*; **hollow p.**, emporte-pièce *m inv*, découpoir *m*; **paper p.**, perforateur *m* à papier; *Comptr* **card/tape p.**, perforateur de cartes/de bande; **p. card/tape**, carte/bande perforée; *Ind* **p. operator**, mécanographe *mf*.

punch[2] *vt* percer, découper (*à l'emporte-pièce*); faire, percer (*un trou*); poinçonner, composter (*un billet*); perforer (*le cuir etc*); estamper, étamper (*une plaque de fer*); *Comptr* perforer (*une carte, une bande*); **punched card**, carte perforée.

punch[3] *n* **(a)** (*blow*) coup *m* de poing; *Boxing* coup de poing, punch *m*; **to pack a good p.**, (*hit hard*) cogner dur; *F* (*of drink*) être corsé; **to pull a p.**, retenir *ou* adoucir un coup; **he didn't pull his punches**, (*hit hard*) il n'y est pas allé de main morte; (*spoke frankly*) il n'a pas mâché ses mots; **a documentary that pulls no punches**, un documentaire sans complaisance; **(b)** *F* (*energy*) force *f*, énergie *f*; **style that has p.**, style incisif; **style that lacks p.**, style plat; **p. line**, pointe *f* (*d'une plaisanterie*).

punch[4] *vt* (*hit*) donner des coups de poing à (*qn*), cogner sur (*qn*); **to p. s.o. on the nose**, donner un coup de poing sur le nez de qn; **he punched him on the chin**, il lui a donné un coup de poing au menton; *Am* **to p. cattle**, être cowboy.

punch[5] *n* (*drink*) punch *m*; **milk p.**, lait *m* au rhum.

Punch [pʌntʃ] *n* = Polichinelle *m*, Guignol *m*; **P. and Judy show**, = (théâtre *m* de) Guignol.

►**punch in** *vtsep* (*lid etc*) crever (*qch*) d'un coup de poing; *F* **to p. s.o.'s face in**, casser la gueule à qn.

►**punch out** *vtsep Tech* chasser (*une goupille*).

punchball ['pʌntʃbɔːl] *n Boxing* punching(-ball) *m*.

punchbowl ['pʌntʃbəʊl] *n* **(a)** bol *m* à punch; **(b)** *Geog* cuvette *f* (*entre collines*).

punch-drunk ['pʌntʃdrʌŋk] *adj F esp Boxing* abruti (par les coups); *Fig* abruti.

puncher[1] ['pʌntʃər] *n* **(a)** *Tech* (*person*) poinçonneur *m*, perceur *m* (*de tôle etc*); *Comptr* perforeur, -euse (*de cartes, de bandes*); (*in metalworking*) estampeur *m*, frappeur *m*; **(b)** (*device*) poinçonneuse *f* (*de tôles*); perforatrice *f* (*dans les mines*); emporte-pièce *m inv* (*pour le carton, le cuir etc*); *Comptr* perforatrice (*de cartes, de bandes*).

puncher[2] *n Boxing* puncheur *m*; **cow p.**, cowboy *m*.

punching[1] ['pʌntʃɪŋ] *n* **(a)** (*action*) perçage *m*, poinçonnage *m*; **p. (out)**, découpage *m* (à l'emporte-pièce); poinçonnage, compostage *m* (*des billets etc*); *Comptr* perforation *f* (*des cartes, des bandes*); **(b)** (*punched object*) pièce étampée; **punchings**, confetti *mpl* de perforation; *Comptr etc* perforations *fpl*.

punching[2] *n* (*blows*) coups *mpl* de poing; *Am Boxing* **p. bag**, punching-bag *m*.

punch-up ['pʌntʃʌp] *n Br F* bagarre *f*.

punchy ['pʌntʃɪ] *adj F* **(a)** (*slogan etc*) incisif, marquant; **(b)** = **PUNCH-DRUNK**.

punctilious [pʌŋk'tɪlɪəs] *adj* **(a)** (*paying attention to detail*) pointilleux, méticuleux, formaliste; **(b) to be very p.**, (*in social behaviour*) être très pointilleux.

punctiliously [pʌŋk'tɪlɪəslɪ] *adv* scrupuleusement, dans les moindres détails.

punctiliousness [pʌŋk'tɪlɪəsnɪs] *n* **(a)** (*attention to detail*) scrupule *m* des détails; **(b)** (*observance of etiquette*) souci *m* du protocole.

punctual ['pʌŋktjʊəl] *adj* ponctuel; **he's always p.**, il est toujours à l'heure *ou* toujours ponctuel.

punctuality [pʌŋktjʊ'ælɪtɪ] *n* ponctualité *f*.

punctually ['pʌŋktjʊəlɪ] *adv* ponctuellement, à l'heure.

punctuate ['pʌŋktjʊeɪt] *vt* **(a)** (*in writing*) ponctuer (*une phrase etc*); **(b)** ponctuer (*ses mots en parlant*); donner plus de force à (*une remarque etc*); souligner (*une phrase*) (**with sighs**, de soupirs); **speech punctuated with anecdotes**, discours agrémenté d'anecdotes; **speech punctuated with applause**, discours entrecoupé d'applaudissements.

punctuation [pʌŋktjʊ'eɪʃən] *n* ponctuation *f*; **p. mark**, signe *m* de ponctuation.

puncture[1] ['pʌŋktʃər] *n* **(a)** crevaison *f*, perforation *f* (*d'un pneu, d'un abcès*); (*action*) *Surg* ponction *f* (*d'une ampoule, d'un abcès*); **lumbar p.**, ponction lombaire; *Med* **p. wound**, trace *f* de piqûre; **(b)** (*in tyre*) crevaison *f*; (*hole*) piqûre *f*, perforation *f*; *Br Aut* **to have a p.**, crever; **p. patch**, pastille adhésive (*pour réparer un pneu*); *Cycling* **p. repair kit**, sacoche *f* à outils.

puncture[2] **1** *vt* crever, perforer (*un pneu*); ponctionner (*une ampoule, un abcès*); **to p. s.o.'s self-esteem**, rabattre le caquet à qn. **2** *vi* (*of tyre*) crever.

pundit ['pʌndɪt] *n* **(a)** (*expert*) pontife *m* (*de la politique etc*), *F* ponte *m*; **according to the pundits**, si l'on en croit les spécialistes *ou F* les grands pontes; **(b)** (*in India*) pandit *m*.

pungency ['pʌndʒənsɪ] *n* **(a)** goût piquant (*d'une épice etc*); odeur forte *ou* piquante (*d'un parfum*); **(b)** âcreté *f*, aigreur *f* (*de paroles*); piquant *m*, mordant *m* (*d'un sarcasme*); saveur *f* (*d'un récit, du style*); causticité *f* (*du style etc*).

pungent ['pʌndʒənt] *adj* **(a)** (*style, sarcasm etc*) mordant, caustique; **(b)** (*smell etc*) âcre, piquant, irritant; (*taste*) piquant; **p. sauce**, sauce relevée *ou* épicée.

pungently ['pʌndʒəntlɪ] *adv* d'une manière piquante.

Punic ['pjuːnɪk] *adj Hist* punique.

puniness ['pjuːnɪnɪs] *n* faiblesse *f*.

punish ['pʌnɪʃ] *vt* **(a)** punir (*un malfaiteur, une faute, un enfant*); **to p. s.o. with imprisonment**, punir qn de prison; **to p. s.o. for a crime**, punir qn pour un crime; **to p. s.o. for having done sth** *or* **for doing sth**, punir qn pour avoir fait qch; *Jur* **to p. s.o. by** *or* **with a fine**, frapper qn d'une amende; **(b)** *Sp etc F* taper dur sur (*qn*); malmener (*un adversaire*); *Horseracing* fouetter, malmener (*un cheval*); *Aut* fatiguer, forcer (*le moteur*); **he really punishes himself in training**, il se donne à fond à son entraînement.

punishable ['pʌnɪʃəb(ə)l] *adj* punissable; *Jur* délictueux; **p. by a fine**, passible d'amende.

punishing ['pʌnɪʃɪŋ] **1** *adj* dur; (*coup*) violent; (*jeu*) rude; (*travail*) éreintant; **p. race**, course épuisante. **2** *n* punition *f*.

punishment ['pʌnɪʃmənt] *n* **(a)** punition *f*, châtiment *m*; *Jur* peine *f*; **corporal p.**, châtiment corporel, punition corporelle; **capital p.**, peine capitale; **as a p. for sth**, en punition de qch; **to inflict a p. on s.o.**, donner *ou* infliger une punition à qn; **to escape p.**, échapper à la punition; **to make the p. fit the crime**, proportionner la punition au crime; *Mil* **summary p.**, sanction *f* disciplinaire; **(b)** *F* (*blows etc*) **to take a lot of p.**, (*of boxer etc*) encaisser; (*of army, warship, tank, car, boat etc*) se faire malmener; (*of shoes, clothes etc*) ne pas être épargné; **to inflict severe p. on a team**, administrer une cruelle défaite à une équipe.

punitive ['pjuːnɪtɪv], **punitory** ['pjuːnɪt(ə)rɪ] *adj* répressif; (*taxation*) très sévère; *Mil* **p. expedition**, expédition punitive; *Jur* **p. justice**, justice répressive; **p. damages**, dommages-intérêts *mpl*.

Punjab [pʌn'dʒɑːb] *n* le Pendjab.

Punjabi [pʌn'dʒɑːbɪ] **1** *adj* du Pendjab. **2** *n* **(a)** habitant, -ante du Pendjab; (*by birth*) originaire *mf* du Pendjab; **(b)** *Ling* pendjab *m*.

punk[1] [pʌŋk] *n* **(a)** punk *mf*; **p. (rock)**, le punk (rock); **(b)** *F Pej* (*worthless person*) vaurien *m*, crapule *f*.

punk[2] *adj F* (*worthless*) qui ne vaut rien.

punnet ['pʌnɪt] *n esp Br* carton *m*, petit panier (*à fraises etc*).

punster ['pʌnstər] *n* faiseur, -euse de calembours *ou* de jeux de mots.

punt[1] [pʌnt] *n* bateau plat (*de rivière, conduit à la perche*); **p. pole**, perche *f* (*pour la conduite d'un bateau plat*).

punt[2] **1** *vt* conduire (*un bateau*) à la perche; transporter (*qn*) dans un bateau plat. **2** *vi* **to go punting**, faire un tour dans un bateau à fond plat.

punt[3] *n Fb & Rugby* coup *m* de volée.

punt[4] **1** *vt Fb & Rugby* envoyer (*le ballon*) d'un coup de volée. **2** *vi* donner un coup de pied de volée.

punt[5] *n Cards* (*person*) ponte *m*.

punt[6] *vi* **(a)** *Cards* ponter; **to p. high**, ponter gros; **(b)** *Horseracing* parier.

punter[1] ['pʌntər] *n* **(a)** *Horseracing* parieur *m*; **(b)** *Br F* (*person*) mec *m*; **the punters**, (*the public*) le public; **the average p.**, l'homme de la rue; **(c)** *Cards* ponte *m*.

punter[2] *n* (*in boat*) canotier *m* qui conduit à la perche.

puny ['pjuːnɪ] *adj* (*person, hands etc*) chétif; (*effort*) malheureux; **a p. little fellow**, un petit gringalet; **our p. little guns**, nos pauvres *ou* malheureux petits canons; **what a p. excuse!**, quelle piètre excuse!; **a p. argument**, un piètre argument; **a p. 50p**, cinquante malheureux pence.

pup [pʌp] *n* **(a)** (*of dog*) jeune chien, chiot *m*; (*of seal*) jeune phoque *m*; (*of wolf*) louveteau *m*; (*of rat*) raton *m*; **a bitch and her pups**, une chienne et ses petits; **to be in p.**, (*of bitch*) être grosse; *F* **to be sold a p.**, se faire rouler; **(b)**

F (*young man*) (*self-important*) freluquet *m*; (*impertinent*) impertinent *m*.

pupa, *pl* **-ae** ['pju:pə, -i:] *n* (*insect*) nymphe *f*, chrysalide *f*.

pupate ['pju:peɪt] *vi* (*of insect*) se métamorphoser en nymphe *ou* en chrysalide.

pupil¹ ['pju:p(ə)l] *n* **(a)** *Sch* élève *mf*, écolier, -ière; **(b)** *Jur* pupille *mf*.

pupil² *n Anat* pupille *f* (*de l'œil*).

pupil(l)age ['pju:pɪlɪdʒ] *n Jur* **(a)** (*of minor*) minorité *f*; **(b)** pupillarité *f*; **child in p.,** enfant en pupille *ou* en tutelle.

puppet ['pʌpɪt] *n* marionnette *f*; *Fig* (*person*) marionnette, fantoche *m*; **glove** *or* **hand p.,** marionnette à gaine; *Fig* **p. government,** gouvernement *m* fantoche; **p. player,** marionnettiste *mf*; **p. show** *or* **play,** (spectacle *m* de) marionnettes; **p. theatre,** (théâtre *m* de) marionnettes.

puppeteer [pʌpɪ'tɪər] *n* marionnettiste *mf*.

puppetry ['pʌpɪtrɪ] *n* art *m* des marionnettes; (*puppet making*) fabrication *f* de marionnettes.

puppy ['pʌpɪ] *n* **(a) p. (dog),** jeune chien *m*, chiot *m*; **p. love,** premier amour, amour juvénile; **p. fat,** adiposité *f* d'enfance *ou* d'adolescence; **(b)** *F* (*young man*) (*self-important*) freluquet *m*; (*impertinent*) petit impertinent.

purblind ['pɜ:blaɪnd] *adj* **(a)** (*almost blind*) presque aveugle; **(b)** (*obtuse*) obtus; (*politique*) aveugle.

purchase¹ ['pɜ:tʃɪs] *n* **(a)** (*act of buying*) achat *m*, acquisition *f*; (*thing bought*) achat; **to make some purchases,** faire des achats *ou* des emplettes; **p. order,** ordre *m* d'achat, commande *f*; **p. price,** prix *m* d'achat; **(b)** (*grip*) prise *f*; (*thing gripped*) (point *m* d') appui *m*; **to get** *or* **secure a p. on sth,** trouver prise à qch.

purchase² *Fml* **1** *vt* acheter, acquérir, faire l'acquisition de (*qch*). **2** *vi* **now is the time to p.,** c'est maintenant qu'il faut acheter.

purchaser ['pɜ:tʃəsər] *n* acheteur, -euse, acquéreur, -euse.

purchasing ['pɜ:tʃəsɪŋ] *n* achat *m*; *Econ* **p. power,** pouvoir *m* d'achat.

purdah ['pɜ:də] *n Muslim Rel* = système qui astreint les femmes à une vie retirée; *F* **to go into p.,** se retirer, ne voir personne.

pure [pjʊər] *adj* **(a)** pur; (*alcool*) rectifié; **the p. and simple truth,** la vérité pure et simple; **p. Arab (horse),** (cheval *m*) arabe *m* de race pure; **p. chance,** pur hasard; **p. mathematics,** les mathématiques pures; *Phil* **p. reason,** la raison pure; **p. silk/wool,** pure soie/laine; **(b)** (*free from taint*) (*style, taste*) pur; (*person*) innocent, chaste; *Bible* **blessed are the p. in heart,** bienheureux ceux qui ont le cœur pur; **p. English,** l'anglais pur; **p.-minded,** pur d'esprit; **p. thoughts,** des pensées pures.

pure(-)blood ['pjʊəblʌd] **1** *adj* (*person, animal*) pur sang, de pure race; (*cheval*) pur sang. **2** *n* (*horse*) pur sang *m inv*.

pure(-)blooded ['pjʊəblʌdɪd] *adj* = **PURE-BLOOD 1.**

purebred ['pjʊəbred] **1** *adj* (*chien, taureau*) de race (pure), pur sang. **2** *n* animal *m* de race; (*horse*) pur sang *m*.

purée¹ ['pjʊəreɪ] *n Culin* purée *f*; **potato p.,** purée de pommes de terre.

purée² *vt Culin* écraser (*un aliment*) en purée.

purely ['pjʊəlɪ] *adv* **(a)** purement; **(b)** (*simply*) simplement; **p. routine questioning,** interrogatoire *m* de simple routine; **it was p. by chance that we met,** notre rencontre n'était qu'un pur hasard; **it was p. accidental,** c'était un pur hasard.

pureness ['pjʊənɪs] *n* pureté *f*.

purgation [pɜ:'geɪʃən] *n* **(a)** purge *f* (*de l'intestin*); **(b)** *Rel* purgation *f* de l'âme (*au purgatoire*).

purgative ['pɜ:gətɪv] *adj & n Med* purgatif *m*.

purgatory ['pɜ:gət(ə)rɪ] *n Rel* purgatoire *m*; **the souls in p.,** les âmes du purgatoire, les âmes en peine; **to live a life of p.,** souffrir les peines du purgatoire de son vivant; *F* **it was sheer p.,** c'était l'enfer.

purge¹ [pɜ:dʒ] *n* **(a)** *Med Pharm* purgatif *m*, purge *f*; **(b)** purgation *f*; épuration *f*, purge *f*, nettoyage *m* (*d'un parti politique etc*).

purge² *vt* **(a)** *Med* purger (*qn*); **(b)** nettoyer (*un égout*); épurer (*les mœurs, un parti politique etc*); *Rel* **to p. oneself of** *or* **from sin,** se laver de ses péchés; **(c)** *Jur* **to p. oneself of a charge,** se disculper, se justifier; **(d)** *Jur* expier (*une faute*); purger (*sa peine*); *US* **to p. one's contempt,** faire amende honorable (*pour outrage aux magistrats*).

▶purge away *vtsep* **to p. away one's sins,** expier ses fautes.

purging ['pɜ:dʒɪŋ] *n* **(a)** *Med etc* purge *f*, purification *f* (*du corps*); **(b)** nettoyage *m* (*d'un égout*); épuration *f* (*des mœurs, d'un parti politique etc*); assainissement *m* (*des finances publiques*).

purification [pjʊərɪfɪ'keɪʃən] *n* **(a)** purification *f*; épuration *f* (*du gaz, de l'huile etc*); **(b)** *Rel* **Feast of the P. (of the Virgin Mary),** (fête *f* de) la Purification.

purifier ['pjʊərɪfaɪər] *n* épurateur *m* (*de gaz, d'huile etc*); assainisseur *m* (*d'air*).

purify ['pjʊərɪfaɪ] *vt* purifier (*l'air etc*); épurer (*le gaz, l'huile, une langue etc*); dépurer (*le sang*); sublimer (*le cœur, l'esprit etc*); **to p. s.o. of** *or* **from his sins,** purger qn de ses péchés.

purist ['pjʊərɪst] *n* puriste *mf*.

puritan ['pjʊərɪt(ə)n] *adj & n* **(a)** *Hist* puritain, -aine; **(b)** puritain, -aine, rigoriste *mf*.

puritanical [pjʊərɪ'tænɪk(ə)l] *adj* (de) puritain, rigoriste.

puritanism ['pjʊərɪtənɪz(ə)m] *n* puritanisme *m*, rigorisme *m*.

purity ['pjʊərɪtɪ] *n* pureté *f*; **degree of p.,** (degré *m* de) pureté (*de l'eau etc*); titre *m* (*de l'or*).

purl¹ [pɜ:l] *n* **(a)** *Knitting* **p. stitch,** maille *f* à l'envers; **(b)** picot *m*, engrêlure *f* (*de dentelle etc*).

purl² *vt* **(a)** *Knitting* tricoter (*un rang*) en mailles à l'envers; **knit one, p. one,** une maille à l'endroit, une maille à l'envers; **(b)** engrêler (*de la dentelle etc*).

purler ['pɜ:lər] *n Old-fashioned Br Sl* **to come a p.,** se ramasser une gamelle.

purlieu ['pɜ:lju:] *n* **(a)** (*limits*) limites *fpl*, bornes *fpl*; **(b)** (*surrounding area*) **purlieus,** alentours *mpl*, environs *mpl*.

purloin [pɜ:'lɔɪn] *vt Fml* voler, dérober.

purloining [pɜ:'lɔɪnɪŋ] *n Fml* vol *m*.

purple ['pɜ:p(ə)l] **1** *adj* violet; *Arch* pourpre, pourpré; **he turned** *or* **went p. (with rage** *etc*), il est devenu cramoisi (de rage *etc*); **face p. with cold,** visage violacé par le froid; *F* **p. heart,** = comprimé violet de drinamyl en forme de cœur; *US* **P. Heart,** = décoration remise à un blessé de guerre; *Liter* **p. patch,** morceau *m* de bravoure; **p. prose,** prose *f* héroïque. **2** *n* (*colour*) violet *m*; (*dye*) pourpre *f*; **born in the p.,** né dans la pourpre.

purplish ['pɜ:plɪʃ] *adj* violacé, violâtre; (*face*) cramoisi.

purport¹ ['pɜ:pɔ:t] *n Fml* sens *m*, signification *f* (*d'un document*); portée *f*, force *f* (*d'un argument*).

purport² [pɜ:'pɔ:t] *vt* **to p. to be sth,** (*of person*) prétendre être qch; (*of thing*) être présenté comme étant qch.

purpose ['pɜ:pəs] *n* **(a)** (*object, aim*) dessein *m*, objet *m*, but *m*, intention *f*; (*resolve*) résolution *f*; **fixed p.,** dessein bien arrêté; **to gain** *or* **achieve one's p.,** accomplir son dessein; **for** *or* **with the p. of doing sth,** dans le but de *ou* afin de faire qch; **to do sth on p.,** faire qch exprès *ou* à dessein *ou* de propos délibéré; **to give s.o. a sense of p.,** motiver qn; **man of p.,** homme résolu *ou* décidé;

(b) (*use*) **intended p.,** destination *f*, affectation *f* (*d'un bâtiment, d'une somme d'argent*); **to serve no p.,** ne servir à rien; **once she had served her p. they abandoned her,** une fois qu'elle a eu tenu son rôle, ils l'ont abandonnée; **this will suit** *or* **serve your p.,** cela vous arrangera, cela fera votre affaire; **made for that very p.,** fait tout exprès; **for all purposes,** à toutes fins, à tous usages; **general p. vehicle,** véhicule tous usages; **general p. formula,** formule passe-partout; **intended for practical purposes,** destiné à des usages pratiques; **to set up a commission for the p. of investigation,** former un comité à des fins d'enquête; **for the p. of this article...,** (*in lease, contract etc*) au sens du présent article ...; **for our purposes we can assume this is true,** en ce qui nous concerne, nous pouvons admettre que c'est vrai;

(c) to speak to the p., parler à propos; **very much to the p.,** fort à propos; **we're (talking) at cross purposes,** il y a malentendu (entre nous);

(d) to some p., utilement, avantageusement, efficacement; **all that is to no p.,** tout cela ne sert à rien.

purpose-built ['pɜ:pəs'bɪlt] *adj* construit en vue d'un usage précis.

purposeful ['pɜ:pəsfʊl] *adj* (*person*) réfléchi, avisé; (*determined*) tenace; (*intentional*) prémédité, intentionnel.

purposefully ['pɜ:pəsfʊlɪ] *adv* dans un but précis.

purposely ['pɜ:pəslɪ] *adv* à dessein, de propos délibéré; **he p. looked the other way,** il a regardé exprès de l'autre côté; **I came p. to see her,** je suis venu exprès pour la voir.

purr¹ [pɜ:r] *n* ronron *m*, ronronnement *m* (*de chat*); ronflement *m* (*d'une machine*); vrombissement *m* (*d'un moteur etc*); **she's got a very loud p.,** (*of cat*) elle ronronne très fort.

purr² *vi* (*of cat, person, engine*) ronronner; (*of car etc*) ronfler; (*of engine*) vrombir.

purring ['pɜ:rɪŋ] **1** *adj* (*chat*) qui ronronne, qui fait ronron. **2** *n* = **PURR¹.**

purse[1] [pɜːs] *n* **(a)** bourse *f*, porte-monnaie *m inv*; *Am* (*handbag*) sac *m* à main; **the public p.,** les finances *fpl* de l'État; le Trésor; *Boxing* **to put up a p.,** constituer et offrir une somme d'argent pour une rencontre sportive; *Boxing* **how big is the p.?,** à combien se monte le prix?; *Prov* **you cannot make a silk p. out of a sow's ear,** on ne saurait faire d'une buse un épervier; *F* **she holds the p. strings,** c'est elle qui tient les cordons de la bourse; **(b)** *Fishing* **p. crab,** crabe *m* des cocotiers; **p. seine** *or* **net,** senne *f ou* seine *f* à poche.

purse[2] *vt* **to p. (up) one's lips** *or* **mouth,** pincer les lèvres.

purser ['pɜːsər] *n Nau* commissaire *m* (*de la marine marchande*); **p.'s mate,** cambusier *m*.

pursuance [pə'sjuːəns] *n Fml* exécution *f*; **in p. of your instructions,** conformément à vos instructions.

pursuant [pə'sjuːənt] *adv Fml* **p. to your instructions,** conformément à vos instructions.

pursue [pə'sjuː] *vt* **(a)** (*chase*) poursuivre (*qn*); rechercher (*le plaisir*); aspirer à (*un but*); être à la poursuite de (*le bonheur*); **to be pursued by misfortune,** être poursuivi par le malheur; **(b)** (*continue*) continuer, suivre (*son chemin*); donner suite à, poursuivre (*une enquête, une politique*); suivre (*une ligne de conduite*); faire, exercer (*un métier*); **the subject was pursued no further,** on ne s'attacha pas davantage à débattre ce sujet.

pursuer [pə'sjuːər] *n* **(a)** poursuivant, -ante; **(b)** *Scot Jur* plaignant, -ante.

pursuit [pə'sjuːt] *n* **(a)** poursuite *f*; recherche *f* (*du bonheur etc*); **pack in eager** *or* **hot p.,** meute acharnée à la poursuite; **to be in p. of s.o.,** être à la poursuite de qn; **in p. of his aim,** en poursuivant son but; **in p. of happiness,** à la poursuite *ou* en quête du bonheur; *Av* **p. plane,** chasseur *m*, avion *m* de chasse; *Cycling* **p. race,** (course *f*) poursuite *f*; **(b)** (*occupation*) occupation *f*; (*hobby*) passe-temps *m inv*; **ambitious pursuits,** visées ambitieuses; **literary pursuits,** travaux *mpl* littéraires; **hunting is his favourite p.,** la chasse est son occupation favorite.

purulence ['pjʊərʊləns] *n Med* **(a)** purulence *f*; **(b)** (*pus*) pus *m*.

purulent ['pjʊərʊlənt] *adj Med* purulent.

purvey [pə'veɪ] *vt* fournir (*des provisions*).

purveyance [pə'veɪəns] *n* fourniture *f* de provisions, approvisionnement *m*.

purveyor [pə'veɪər] *n* fournisseur, -euse (de provisions), appovisionneur, -euse.

purview ['pɜːvjuː] *n* **(a)** *Jur* corps *m*, articles *mpl* (*d'une loi*); **(b)** (*scope*) limites *fpl*, portée *f* (*d'un projet*).

pus [pʌs] *n Med* pus *m*.

push[1] [pʊʃ] *n* **(a)** poussée *f*, impulsion *f*; *Constr* poussée (*d'une voûte*); **to give sth a p.,** pousser qch; **to give s.o. a p.,** pousser qn; **she's got a good mind, she just needs a little p.,** elle n'est pas bête, elle a juste besoin qu'on l'encourage un petit peu; *F* **to get the p.,** recevoir son congé; *F* **to give s.o. the p.,** (*from job*) flanquer qn à la porte; (*from relationship*) plaquer qn; *El* **p. button,** (bouton-)poussoir *m*, *pl* (boutons-)poussoirs; (*of doorbell*) bouton de sonnette *ou* d'appel; **to give a car a p. start,** faire démarrer une voiture en la poussant; *Billiards* **p. (stroke),** coup queuté;

(b) (*effort*) effort *m*, coup *m* de collier; *Mil* attaque *f* en masse; (*energy*) énergie *f*; (*enterprise*) hardiesse *f*, initiative *f*; **to have plenty of p.,** (*energy*) avoir beaucoup d'initiative *ou* d'énergie; (*be ambitious*) être ambitieux;

(c) (*difficult moment*) moment *m* difficile, circonstance *f* critique; **at a p.,** au besoin; **when it comes to the p.,** au moment critique; *Am* **if p. comes to shove,** si la situation l'exige;

(d) *Sl esp Austr* (*gang*) bande *f*, clique *f* (*de voyous, de pickpockets*).

push[2] **1** *vt* **(a)** pousser; **p.,** (*on door*) poussez, pousser; **to p. a wheelbarrow,** pousser une brouette; **to p. a button,** appuyer sur un bouton;

(b) (*shove, thrust*) pousser; **to p. s.o. into the room,** pousser qn (pour le faire entrer) dans la pièce; **don't p. (me)!,** ne (me) poussez pas!, ne (me) bousculez pas!; **did he fall or was he pushed?,** il est tombé ou on l'a poussé?; **to p. s.o. out of the way,** faire écarter qn; **to p. one's way through the crowd,** se frayer *ou* s'ouvrir un chemin à travers la foule; **to p. one's way in,** (*to party, conversation etc*) s'immiscer; **to p. oneself forward,** se mettre en avant; **to p. an attack home,** pousser à fond une attaque; *Fig* **to p. oneself,** (*make an effort*) se forcer; *Fig* **he needs pushing,** il faut toujours le pousser;

(c) faire la réclame pour (*sa marchandise*); vendre, fournir (*des drogues*); *F* **the government is pushing the idea of people setting up small businesses,** le gouvernement pousse les gens à créer de petites entreprises; **to p. one's demands,** revendiquer ses droits; *St Exch* **to p. shares,** placer des valeurs douteuses;

(d) to p. s.o. into doing sth, (*force*) pousser qn à faire qch; **her parents didn't p. her into the law,** ses parents ne l'ont pas poussée à faire du droit; **to p. s.o. for payment,** harceler qn pour se faire payer; **don't p. him too far,** ne le poussez pas à bout; *F* **to p. one's luck,** aller un peu fort; *F* **that's pushing it a bit,** tu y vas *ou* il y va *etc* un peu fort; **I'm terribly pushed (for time),** je suis très pressé; **to be pushed for money,** être à court d'argent;

(e) *F* **he's pushing sixty,** il frise la soixantaine.

2 *vi* **(a)** pousser; **to p. against sth,** pousser *ou* s'appuyer sur qch; **we'll have to get out and p.,** il va falloir descendre pousser; **stop pushing!,** arrêtez de pousser!; *Fig* **you have to p. to get your way,** pour réussir il faut savoir se mettre en avant; **the unions are pushing for 10%,** les syndicats font pression pour obtenir 10%;

(b) (*move forward*) avancer (avec difficulté); **to p. through the crowd,** se frayer *ou* s'ouvrir un chemin à travers la foule; **he pushed past me,** il m'a poussé pour me dépasser.

►**push ahead** *vi* **(a)** (*continue*) continuer, persévérer; **(b)** (*advance*) avancer, progresser; **research is pushing ahead,** la recherche fait des progrès.

►**push along 1** *vtsep* (*move by pushing*) pousser; **she pushed the pram along,** elle poussait le landau. **2** *vi F* (*leave*) partir, y aller; **I suppose I should be pushing along soon,** il va bientôt falloir que j'y aille.

►**push around** *vtsep F* (*bully*) marcher sur les pieds de (*qn*), mener (*qn*) par le bout du nez; **we're sick and tired of being pushed around,** nous en avons marre d'être menés par le bout du nez.

►**push aside** *vtsep* (*shove out of way*) écarter (*d'une poussée*).

►**push away** *vtsep* (*shove from oneself*) repousser, éloigner (*qn, qch*).

►**push back 1** *vtsep* (*shove away*) repousser, faire reculer; **I pushed him back,** je l'ai repoussé; **the police pushed back the crowd,** la police a fait reculer la foule. **2** *vi* (*retreat*) reculer.

►**push forward 1** *vtsep* (*cause to move*) pousser en avant, (faire) avancer. **2** *vi* (*move forward*) avancer.

►**push in 1** *vtsep* (*insert*) enfoncer, refouler, repousser (*qch*); **the side of the car was pushed in,** le flanc de la voiture était enfoncé; **he was standing by the pool and someone pushed him in,** il était au bord de la piscine et quelqu'un l'a poussé dedans; *F* **to p. s.o.'s face in,** casser la gueule à qn. **2** *vi* (*jump queue*) resquiller.

►**push off 1** *vtas* (*cause to fall*) faire tomber. **2** *vtaspo* (*cause to fall*) **he pushed me off the wall,** il m'a poussé du haut du mur. **3** *vtsep* (*remove by pushing*) pousser; **p. the lid off,** pousse le couvercle. **4** *vi F* (*leave*) partir; *Nau* pousser au large; *F* **time to p. off,** il est temps de partir; *Sl* **p. off!,** fiche le camp!, file!, tire-toi!

►**push on 1** *vi* (*continue with work, journey etc*) continuer; **to p. on to** *or* **as far as a place,** pousser jusqu'à un endroit; **it's time to p. on,** (*with journey*) il est temps de nous remettre en route; **to p. on with the work,** se remettre au travail. **2** *vtsep* **(a)** (*apply pressure to*) forcer; **you just p. the lid on,** il faut juste appuyer un peu pour mettre le couvercle; **(b)** (*encourage*) encourager.

►**push out** *vtsep* **(a)** (*cause to leave*) pousser dehors, faire sortir, mettre (*qn*) à la porte; **(b)** (*launch*) mettre (*une embarcation*) à l'eau; *F* **to p. the boat out,** faire la fête.

►**push over** *vtsep* (*cause to fall*) faire tomber (*qn, qch*).

►**push through 1** *vtsep* **(a)** (*cause to pass through*) faire passer (*qch*) à travers (*qch*); faire accepter (*un projet de loi etc*); **(b)** (*bring to completion*) mener à bien, parvenir à terminer (*un travail*). **2** *vi* (*shove through*) se frayer un chemin. **3** *vipo* (*shove through*) se frayer *ou* se faire un chemin à travers; **to p. through a crowd,** se frayer un chemin dans la foule.

►**push to** *vtas* pousser, fermer (*la porte, les volets*).

►**push up** *vtsep* **(a)** (*lift by pushing*) relever (*qch*) en poussant; **(b)** (*help climb by pushing*) aider (*qn*) à monter (*en le poussant*); **(c)** (*increase*) faire monter (*les prix etc*).

push-bike ['pʊʃbaɪk] *n Br F* vélo *m*, *F* bécane *f*.

push-button ['pʊʃbʌtən] *adj* **p.-b. operation,** fonctionnement *m* automatique; **p.-b. telephone,** téléphone *m* à touches; **p.-b. war,** la guerre presse-bouton.

pushcart ['pʊʃkɑːt] *n* voiture *f* à bras, charrette *f* à bras.

pushchair ['pʊʃtʃeər] *n* poussette *f* (*d'enfant*).

pusher ['pʊʃər] *n* **(a)** (*person pushing*) personne *f* qui pousse (*une voiture etc*); **(b)** (*ambitious person*) ambitieux, -euse; **(c)** *F* **(drug) p.,** dealer *m*; **(c) (baby's) p.,** raclette *f*.

pushing ['pʊʃɪŋ] **1** *adj* (*full of drive*) entreprenant, énergique. **2** *n* **(a)** poussée *f*; **no p.!,** ne poussez pas!; **(b)** vente *f* (*de marchandises*); fourniture *f* (*de drogues etc*).

pushover ['pʊʃəʊvər] *n* **(a)** *F* (*thing*) chose facile à faire; **it's a p.,** c'est un jeu d'enfant; **(b)** *F* (*opponent*) adversaire *m* facile; (*gullible person*) personne crédule, poire *f*; **when it comes to red-heads, I'm a p.,** quand il s'agit des rousses, je ne peux pas me retenir.

pushpin ['pʊʃpɪn] *n US* punaise *f* (*pour planche à dessin*).

push-pull ['pʊʃpʊl] *n Electron* push-pull *m inv*; **p.-p. circuit/amplifier,** circuit *m*/amplificateur *m* push-pull; **p.-p. train,** train *m* réversible.

pushrod ['pʊʃrɒd] *n* (*in engine*) poussoir *m*.

push-start ['pʊʃstɑːt] *vt Aut* faire démarrer (*une voiture etc*) en la poussant.

push-up ['pʊʃʌp] *n Gym* **to do p.-ups,** faire des tractions *ou F* des pompes.

pushy ['pʊʃɪ] *adj F* **(a)** (*self-assertive*) sûr de soi, *Pej* arrogant; **(b)** (*ambitious*) arriviste; **he's a very p. man,** c'est un ambitieux; il sait se pousser dans le monde.

pusillanimity [pjuːsɪlə'nɪmɪtɪ] *n* pusillanimité *f*.

pusillanimous [pjuːsɪ'lænɪməs] *adj* pusillanime.

puss [pʊs] *n* **(a)** *F* (*cat*) minet *m*, minette *f*, minou *m*; **P. in Boots,** le Chat botté; **(b)** *Sl* (*girl, woman*) nana *f*; (*face*) figure *f*.

pussy ['pʊsɪ] *n* **(a)** *F* **p. (cat),** minet *m*, minette *f*, minou *m*; **(b)** *Vulg* (*female genitals*) chatte *f*; **(c)** *F* (*catkin*) chaton *m* (*du saule etc*); **p. willow,** (*tree*) saule *m*.

pussyfoot¹ ['pʊsɪfʊt] *n F* **he's a p.,** il ne veut pas se mouiller.

pussyfoot² *vi F* **(a)** (*walk stealthily*) marcher à pas étouffés *ou* sur la pointe des pieds; **(b)** *Fig* (*avoid committing oneself*) ne pas se mouiller.

pustule ['pʌstjuːl] *n Med Vet* pustule *f*.

put¹ [pʊt] *n* **(a)** *Sp* lancer *m*, lancement *m* (*du poids*); **(b)** *St Exch* **p. (option),** option *f* de vente.

put² *v* (*pt & pp* **put**; *prp* **putting**) **1** *vt* **(a)** (*place in a spot*) mettre; **p. it on the table,** mettez-le *ou* placez-le *ou* posez-le sur la table; **to p. an advertisement in the paper,** mettre une annonce dans le journal; **to p. a man on the moon,** envoyer un homme sur la lune; **to p. sth into s.o.'s hands,** mettre *ou* glisser qch dans la main à qn; *F* **p. it there!,** (*shake hands*) touchez là!, **to p. oneself into s.o.'s hands,** s'en remettre à qn; **to p. a matter into s.o.'s hands,** confier une affaire à qn; **to p. s.o. in his** *or* **her place,** remettre qn à sa place; **to p. the horse to the cart,** atteler la voiture; **to p. one's signature to sth,** apposer sa signature sur *ou* à qch; **to p. honour before riches,** préférer l'honneur à l'argent; **to p. s.o. in the wrong,** prendre qn en faute; **to p. a matter right,** arranger une affaire, remettre les choses au point; **to p. s.o. out of suspense,** tirer qn de doute; **to p. s.o. against s.o.,** monter qn contre qn; **to p. an article on the market,** mettre un article en vente *ou* sur le marché; **to p. a play on the stage,** monter une pièce; **to p. one's thoughts into words,** traduire ses pensées par des mots; **to p. money into an undertaking,** verser des fonds dans une affaire; **to p. money on a horse,** miser *ou* parier sur un cheval; **to p. energy into finishing a job,** mettre de l'énergie à achever une tâche; **to p. a lot of work into sth,** travailler dur pour qch;

(b) (*present*) **to p. a question to s.o.,** poser une question à qn; **to p. a case before s.o.,** soumettre un cas à qn; **to p. a resolution to the meeting,** présenter une résolution à l'assemblée; *Jur* **I p. it to you that ...,** n'est-il pas vrai que ...?; **I put it to him that it would be better to ...,** je lui ai suggéré qu'il vaudrait mieux ...; **to p. the case clearly,** exposer clairement la situation; **to p. it bluntly,** pour parler franc; **if one may p. it in that way,** si l'on peut s'exprimer ainsi; **I don't know how to p. it,** je ne sais comment dire; **'to encourage the others', as Voltaire puts it,** 'pour encourager les autres' comme dirait Voltaire; **what did you p. for question three?,** qu'est-ce que tu as mis à la question trois?;

(c) (*estimate*) **to p. the population at 10,000,** estimer *ou* évaluer la population à 10 000;

(d) to p. an end *or* **a stop to sth,** mettre fin à qch;

(e) to p. s.o. to do sth, (*to make, have s.o. do sth*) faire faire qch à qn; (*to designate s.o. to do sth*) désigner qn pour faire qch; *Mil* **to p. a man on extra fatigue,** désigner un homme de corvée; **to p. a guard on the door,** faire surveiller la porte; **to p. s.o. to bed,** mettre qn au lit; **to p. a child to bed,** coucher un enfant; **to p. sth to a good use,** employer qch à un bon usage; **to p. s.o. through an ordeal,** faire subir une rude épreuve à qn; *F* **to p. s.o. through it,** faire passer un mauvais quart d'heure à qn; **to p. s.o. to the test,** soumettre qn à l'épreuve; **to p. a resolution to the vote,** mettre une résolution aux voix; **to p. the enemy to flight,** mettre l'ennemi en fuite; **to p. s.o. to sleep,** endormir qn; *F* **to have a dog put to sleep,** faire piquer un chien; **I'm putting you to a lot of trouble,** je vous donne beaucoup d'embarras;

(f) to p. a bullet through s.o.'s head, loger une balle dans la tête de qn; **to p. one's fist through the window,** enfoncer la fenêtre d'un coup de poing; *Sp* **to p. the shot,** lancer le poids.

2 *vi Nau* **to p. (out) to sea,** mettre à la mer, prendre la mer; **to p. into port,** relâcher, faire relâche.

►**put about 1** *vtsep* **(a)** (*spread*) faire circuler (*un bruit*); **to p. it about that ...,** faire circuler le bruit *ou* la nouvelle que ...; **(b)** *Nau* **to p. a ship about,** virer de bord. **2** *vi* virer de bord.

►**put across** *vtsep* **(a)** (*communicate*) faire comprendre, faire accepter (*qch à qn*); **to p. a message across,** communiquer un message; **she knows how to p. her ideas across,** elle sait bien faire passer ses idées; **(b)** *F* **to p. one across on s.o.,** (*trick*) abuser qn, *F* (bien) avoir qn.

►**put aside** *vtsep* (*place on one side*) poser (*son livre etc*) à côté de soi; *Fig* (*save*) mettre (*de l'argent etc*) de côté; **p. aside all gloomy thoughts,** laisse tomber toutes ces pensées maussades.

►**put away** *vtsep* **(a)** (*tidy away*) ranger (*qch*); (*return to its place*) remettre (*qch*) à sa place; garer (*une voiture*); **p. your money** *or* **wallet away,** (*I'm paying*) range ton argent *ou* ton porte-feuille; **(b)** (*save*) mettre de côté (*de l'argent*); **to p. something away for one's old age,** mettre quelque chose de côté pour sa retraite; **(c)** *Sl* (*lock up*) (*in prison*) mettre (*qn*) en prison, coffrer (*qn*); (*in asylum*) (faire) enfermer (*qn*) (dans un asile *etc*); **(d)** *F* (*eat*) bouffer, expédier (*de la nourriture*); (*drink*) siffler; **he can really p. it away,** il a une bonne descente.

►**put back 1** *vtsep* **(a)** (*restore to position*) remettre (*qch*) à sa place; **(b)** (*postpone*) reporter (*une réunion etc*); (*delay*) retarder (*une pendule etc*); **this decision has put the clock back,** cette décision nous a ramenés en arrière; *Sch* **his absence has put him back,** son absence l'a retardé dans ses études. **2** *vi Nau* retourner *ou* revenir *ou* rentrer au port.

►**put by** *vtsep* mettre de côté (*de l'argent*); mettre en réserve (*des provisions etc*); **to have sth put by,** (*to have savings*) avoir des économies; (*to have reserves*) avoir des réserves.

►**put down** *vtsep* **(a)** (*set down*) poser, déposer; **to p. sth down on the ground,** déposer qch par terre; *Tel* **to p. down the receiver,** raccrocher; **p. that gun down!,** pose ce revolver!; **to p. down passengers,** (*of bus etc*) débarquer *ou* déposer *ou* laisser descendre des voyageurs; **to p. down roots,** (*of plant, Fig of person*) s'enraciner; **I couldn't p. it down,** (*of book*) je l'ai lu d'un trait;

(b) (*suppress*) réprimer (*une révolte*); vaincre (*l'opposition*); supprimer, faire cesser, mettre fin à (*un abus*);

(c) (*close*) fermer (*un parapluie*);

(d) (*write*) noter (*sur papier*); mettre *ou* coucher par écrit; **to p. down one's name,** s'inscrire, se faire inscrire **(for,** pour); *F* **p. me down for a ticket/to play,** mets-moi sur la liste pour les tickets/des joueurs; **p. it down to me** *or* **to my account,** inscrivez-le *ou* mettez-le à *ou* sur mon compte; *Fig* **to p. sth down to experience,** tirer une leçon de qch; **I should p. her down at thirty,** je lui donne trente ans; **to p. down sth to s.o.,** mettre qch au compte de qn;

(e) (*attribute*) **to p. sth down to s.o./sth,** attribuer *ou* imputer qch à qn/qch; **I p. his success down to luck,** j'attribue son succès à la chance;

(f) (*pay*) **to p. some money down as a deposit,** déposer une caution;

(g) (*kill*) tuer, abattre (*un animal*); **to have a dog put down,** faire piquer un chien;

(h) (*say negative things about*) dire du mal de; **you're always putting me down,** tu n'arrêtes pas de me critiquer; **you shouldn't p. yourself down,** tu ne devrais pas te sous-estimer;

(i) (*wine*) mettre en cave.

2 *vi Av* atterrir.

►**put forward** *vtsep* **(a)** (*suggest*) avancer, proposer, mettre en avant (*une théorie, un projet etc*); émettre (*une prétention*); **to p. s.o.** *or* **s.o.'s name forward (for a**

post), suggérer qn *ou* le nom de qn (pour un poste); **to p. oneself forward,** se mettre en avant; **to p. one's best foot forward,** (*walk faster*) presser le pas; *Fig* se mettre en devoir de faire de son mieux; **(b)** (*advance*) avancer (*la pendule, l'heure d'une réunion etc*).

►put in 1 *vtsep* **(a)** (*place in*) mettre (*qch*) *ou* introduire (*qch*) (dans qch); **to p. one's contact lenses in,** mettre ses lentilles; **to p. one's head in at the window,** passer la tête par la fenêtre; **you only get out what you p. in,** on ne récolte que ce qu'on sème; **to p. a word in,** placer un mot (dans la conversation); **to p. in a good word for s.o.,** dire un mot en faveur de qn;

(b) (*install*) installer; **we're having a new telephone put in,** on nous installe un nouveau téléphone;

(c) (*enter*) **to p. in a claim,** présenter une réclamation; **we're putting him in for the 500 metres,** nous le présentons pour le 500 mètres; *Sch* **to p. pupils in for an examination,** présenter des élèves à un examen;

(d) (*spend time doing*) **to p. in an hour's work,** faire une heure de travail; **she's put in a lot of time on this project,** elle a passé beaucoup de temps sur ce projet.

2 *vi* **(a)** *Nau* **to p. in at a port,** entrer *ou* relâcher dans un port, faire escale dans un port;

(b) (*apply*) **to p. in for an election/for a job,** poser sa candidature à une élection/à un poste; **to p. in for two days' leave,** demander un congé *ou Mil* une permission de 48 heures.

►put off 1 *vtsep* **(a)** (*postpone*) remettre, différer, ajourner, renvoyer; arriérer, différer, reculer (*un paiement*); **to p. off doing sth,** remettre qch à plus tard; **don't keep putting things off,** ne remettez pas toujours à plus tard; **never p. off till tomorrow what you can do today,** il ne faut jamais remettre au lendemain ce que l'on peut faire le jour même; **let's p. lunch off to another time,** nous déjeunerons ensemble une autre fois; **we shall have to p. our guests off,** il va falloir décommander nos invités;

(b) (*make excuses to*) **to p. s.o. off,** donner le change à qn; **to p. s.o. off with an excuse,** se débarrasser de qn *ou* renvoyer qn avec une excuse;

(c) (*allow to get off bus etc*) laisser descendre; (*force to get off*) faire descendre; **could you p. me off at the High Street?,** pourriez-vous me laisser descendre *ou* m'arrêter à High Street?; **the bus driver put the boys off because of their misbehaviour,** le chauffeur de bus a fait descendre les garçons parce qu'ils se tenaient mal;

(d) (*switch off*) éteindre (*le téléviseur etc*).

2 *vtas* **(a)** (*disturb*) déconcerter, dérouter, troubler (*qn*); **these interruptions p. me off,** ces interruptions me dérangent; **the noise was putting her off her tennis,** le bruit l'empêchait de bien jouer au tennis; **the worry was putting me off my food,** l'inquiétude me coupait l'appétit;

(b) (*cause dislike in*) dégoûter (*qn*); **there's something about him that puts me off,** il y a quelque chose en lui qui me dégoûte; **the mere smell of that cheese puts me off,** la seule odeur de ce fromage suffit à m'écœurer.

3 *vi Nau* déborder du quai; pousser au large; **to p. off from the shore,** quitter la côte.

►put on *vtsep* **(a)** (*put on oneself*) mettre (*ses vêtements*); revêtir (*un pardessus*); enfiler (*son pantalon*); chausser (*ses pantoufles, ses lunettes, ses éperons*); **to p. on one's shoes,** se chausser;

(b) (*act*) **to p. on an air of injured innocence,** affecter *ou* prendre *ou* se donner un air innocent; **to p. on an act,** faire la comédie; **to p. on an accent,** prendre un accent; *F* **you're putting it on!,** tout ça c'est de l'affectation *ou* de la pose *ou* du chiqué!;

(c) *F* (*deceive*) **she's putting you on,** elle te mène en bateau;

(d) (*present*) *Th* monter (*une pièce de théâtre*); *TV Rad* diffuser, passer (*une émission*); **why can't they p. something decent on for a change?,** ils ne pourraient pas passer quelque chose d'intéressant pour une fois?;

(e) (*add to weight, price etc*) **to p. on weight,** grossir, prendre du poids; **I've put on five kilos,** j'ai grossi de cinq kilos; **they've put 2p on the price,** on a augmenté le prix de 2 pence; *F* **they know how to p. it on,** ils s'entendent à saler la facture;

(f) (*switch on*) mettre (*la lumière*); allumer (*le gaz*); faire marcher, allumer (*la radio, la télévision*); **to p. the kettle on,** mettre la bouilloire à chauffer; **to p. the potatoes/***etc* **on,** mettre les pommes de terre/*etc* à cuire; **to p. on a record/a tape,** passer un disque/une bande; **to p. on the brake,** freiner;

(g) (*put into service*) mettre (*un train*) en service; **to p. on speed,** prendre de la vitesse;

(h) *Horseracing etc* **to p. on £1,** miser 1 livre;

(i) (*advance*) avancer (*la pendule*).

►put on to *vtaspo* **(a)** (*provide information about*) **to p. s.o. on to sth,** indiquer qch à qn, *F* tuyauter qn; **who put you on to it?,** qui est-ce qui vous a donné le tuyau?; **who put the police on to me?,** qui m'a dénoncé à la police?;

(b) *Tel* **would you p. me on to Mr Lawrence?,** voulez-vous me passer M. Lawrence?

►put out 1 *vtsep* **(a)** (*place outside*) mettre dehors; **to p. the cat out,** mettre le chat dehors; *Nau* **to p. out a boat,** mettre un canot à l'eau; **to p. one's head out of the window,** passer la tête par la fenêtre, sortir la tête à la fenêtre; **to p. out one's tongue,** tirer la langue; **the snail put out its horns,** l'escargot a sorti ses cornes;

(b) (*arrange for use*) préparer; **I've put your clothes out (on the bed),** tes vêtements sont préparés (sur le lit);

(c) (*extend*) avancer, tendre (*la main*); allonger, étendre (*le bras*);

(d) (*issue*) (*new record, edition, model etc*) sortir;

(e) (*extinguish*) éteindre (*une bougie, le feu, la lumière*); fermer (*le gaz*); **to p. s.o.'s eyes out,** crever les yeux à qn;

(f) (*make unconscious*) endormir (*un patient*).

2 *vtas* **(a)** (*make angry*) ennuyer, fâcher, contrarier (*qn*); **to be put out about sth,** être mécontent de qch;

(b) (*inconvenience*) déranger, incommoder, gêner (*qn*); **you mustn't p. yourself out for me,** il ne faut pas vous déranger *ou* vous mettre en frais pour moi; **would one more guest p. you out?,** est-ce qu'un invité de plus te dérangerait?; **I don't want to p. anyone out,** je ne veux déranger personne;

(c) (*dislocate*) **to p. one's back/shoulder out,** se démettre le dos/l'épaule;

(d) (*disturb*) déconcerter, décontenancer, interloquer (*qn*); (*confuse*) brouiller les idées à (*qn*); (*cause to lose train of thought*) faire perdre le fil de ses idées à (*qn*);

(e) to p. a cow out to grass, mettre une vache en pâture; **to p. money out (to interest),** placer de l'argent (à intérêt).

►put over *vtsep F* **(a)** = **PUT ACROSS**; **(b)** *US* (*postpone*) remettre, différer (*qch*); **(c) to p. one over on s.o.,** l'emporter sur qn.

►put through 1 *vtsep* **(a)** (*carry through*) mener à bien, faire aboutir (*un projet*); (*have accepted*) faire accepter (*un marché*); **(b)** *Tel* (*connect*) **to p. s.o. through to s.o.,** donner à qn la communication avec qn; **I'll p. you through to him,** je vous le passe. **2** *vtaspo* (*cause to suffer*) causer; **you've put your mother through a lot of worry,** tu as causé beaucoup d'inquiétude à ta mère; *F* **to p. s.o. through it,** (*at interview etc*) mettre qn à l'épreuve.

►put to *vtas* (*only in passive*) **to be hard put to it to do sth,** avoir beaucoup de mal à faire qch.

►put together *vtsep* **(a)** (*place side by side*) mettre (*deux choses*) côte à côte; rapprocher, comparer (*des faits*); **(b)** (*assemble*) assembler, mettre ensemble (*les parties d'un tout*); monter, assembler (*une machine etc*); **I'm trying to p. together a team,** j'essaie de monter une équipe; *F* **to p. two and two together,** tirer ses conclusions; **I'll just p. a few things together (in my bag),** je vais faire rapidement ma valise; **she's got more brains than the rest of them put together,** elle est plus intelligente qu'eux tous mis ensemble.

►put up 1 *vtsep* **(a)** (*raise*) relever (*ses cheveux, le col de son manteau etc*); ouvrir (*un parapluie*); **p. up your hands!,** haut les mains!; **I'm going to p. my feet up for a few minutes,** je vais me reposer un peu;

(b) (*erect*) dresser (*une échelle, une tente etc*); construire, bâtir (*une maison etc*); ériger (*un monument*); installer, monter (*un échafaudage*);

(c) (*attach to wall*) fixer, accrocher (*un tableau*); poser (*un rideau*); coller (*une affiche*); afficher (*un avis etc*);

(d) (*increase*) augmenter, hausser (*les prix*);

(e) (*provide accommodation for*) loger, héberger; **I can't p. you up,** je ne peux pas vous coucher;

(f) (*offer*) proposer (*un candidat aux élections*); **to p. sth up for sale,** mettre qch en vente; **to p. a picture up for auction,** mettre une peinture aux enchères; **to p. up resistance** *or* **a fight,** (*physically*) opposer une résistance; (*object*) s'y opposer;

(g) (*provide*) fournir (*une somme d'argent*); **to p. up the money for an undertaking,** fournir les fonds d'une entreprise;

(h) *Horseracing* faire courir (*un jockey*), donner une monte à (*un jockey*);

(i) (*in hunting*) (faire) lever, faire partir (*une perdrix etc*).

2 *vi* (a) (*stay*) **to p. up at a hotel/***etc*, descendre *ou* séjourner à un hôtel/*etc*; **I've been putting up at a hotel for three weeks,** j'ai passé trois semaines à l'hôtel;

(b) (*of candidate*) **to p. up for the council,** poser sa candidature comme conseiller;

(c) *F* **p. up or shut up!,** montrez la couleur de votre argent d'abord!

▶**put upon** *vipo F* (*impose on*) **to p. upon s.o.,** en imposer à qn; (*abuse*) abuser de qn; (*exploit*) exploiter qn; **I won't be put upon,** je refuse qu'on abuse de moi *ou* se joue de moi *ou* se fiche de moi.

▶**put up to** *vtaspo F* **to p. s.o. up to sth,** (*incite*) inciter qn à faire qch; **who put you up to it?,** qui vous a fait faire ça?

▶**put up with** *vipo* (*tolerate*) supporter, souffrir; **we'll have to p. up with it,** il faut l'accepter *ou* nous y résigner; **I don't know how you p. up with the noise,** je ne sais pas comment tu peux supporter ce bruit; **I'll have to p. up with him,** il faudra que je le tolère *ou F* que je l'encaisse.

putative ['pju:tətɪv] *adj Jur* (*mariage, père*) putatif.

put-down ['pʊtdaʊn] *n F* affront *m*.

put-in ['pʊtɪn] *n Rugby* introduction *f*.

put-on ['pʊtɒn] *adj* (*air*) affecté; (*joie*) feint.

put-put¹ ['pʌtpʌt] *n* (*sound*) teuf-teuf *m*.

put-put² *vi* (*of small engine etc*) faire teuf-teuf.

putrefaction [pju:trɪ'fækʃən] *n* putréfaction *f*.

putrefy ['pju:trɪfaɪ] 1 *vt* putréfier, pourrir. 2 *vi* (*of carrion etc*) se putréfier, pourrir; (*of living tissue*) (*suppurate*) suppurer, s'envenimer.

putrescence [pju:'tresəns] *n* putrescence *f*.

putrescent [pju:'tresənt] *adj* putrescent, en putréfaction.

putrid ['pju:trɪd] *adj* (a) putride; (b) *F* (*disgusting, horrible*) sale.

putridity [pju:'trɪdɪtɪ] *n* putridité *f*.

putsch [pʊtʃ] *n* putsch *m*.

putt¹ [pʌt] *n Golf* putt *m*; **to hole a long p.,** rentrer un long putt.

putt² *vt & vi Golf* putter.

putter¹ *n* (a) ['pʌtər] *Golf* (*club*) putter *m*; (*person*) **good/bad p.,** joueur *ou* joueuse qui putte bien; (b) ['pʊtər] *Sp* **shot p.,** lanceur *m* de poids.

putter² ['pʌtər] *vi US* = **POTTER.**

putting ['pʌtɪŋ] *n* (*game*) *& Golf* putting *m*; **to practise p.,** s'exercer à putter; **p. green,** (putting-)green *m*; **p. iron,** putter *m*.

putto, *pl* **putti** ['pʊtəʊ, -ti:] *n Art* putto *m*, *pl* putti.

putty¹ ['pʌtɪ] *n* mastic *m*; **to fill a hole with p.,** mastiquer un trou; **p.-faced,** (*person*) au visage de papier mâché; **p. knife,** spatule *f* de vitrier; **to be like p. in s.o.'s hands,** être comme un petit enfant dans les mains de qn.

putty² *vt* mastiquer (*un trou*), boucher (*un trou*) au mastic.

put-up ['pʊtʌp] *adj F* **a p.-up job,** une affaire machinée à l'avance; (*trap*) un coup monté.

put-upon ['pʊtəpɒn] *adj* **she was feeling p.-u.,** elle avait l'impression qu'on abusait de sa gentillesse.

put-you-up ['pʊtju:ʌp] *n* canapé-lit *m*.

puzzle¹ ['pʌzl] *n* (a) (*manual*) casse-tête *m inv*; (*mental*) devinette *f*, problème *m*; **jigsaw p.,** puzzle *m*; **crossword p.,** mots croisés; (b) (*mystery*) question troublante, énigme *f*; (c) (*perplexity*) embarras *m*, perplexité *f*.

puzzle² 1 *vt* embarrasser, déconcerter; **puzzled look,** air perdu; **I was puzzled,** je ne savais que penser; **this remark puzzled me,** cette remarque m'intrigua; **he puzzles me,** il m'intrigue, il est une énigme pour moi. 2 *vi* **to p. about sth,** chercher à comprendre (qch).

▶**puzzle out** *vtsep* résoudre (*un problème*); trouver (*une solution*); **I'm still trying to p. out how he did it,** je cherche toujours à comprendre comment il l'a fait.

▶**puzzle over** *vipo* (*wonder about*) chercher à comprendre (*qch*).

puzzler ['pʌzlər] *n F* énigme *f*; **that's a p.!,** voilà une question difficile!

puzzling ['pʌzlɪŋ] *adj* inexplicable, curieux, bizarre.

PVC [pi:vi:'si:] *n* (*abbr* **polyvinyl chloride**) P.V.C. *m*; **a PVC belt,** ceinture en P.V.C.

PW [pi:'dʌb(ə)lju:] *n* (*abbr* **policewoman**) femme *f* policier.

PWR [pi:dʌb(ə)lju:'a:r] *n Nucl Phys* (*abbr* **pressurized-water reactor**) R.E.P. *m* (réacteur à eau pressurisée).

PX [pi:'eks] *n US Mil* (*abbr* **post exchange**) foyer *m*.

pygmy ['pɪgmɪ] 1 *n* pygmée *m*. 2 *adj* pygmée.

pyjama [pə'dʒɑ:mə] *n esp Br* (*garment*) **(pair of) pyjamas,** pyjama *m*; **he's in pyjamas,** il est en pyjama; **p. bottoms** *or* **trousers,** pantalon *m* de pyjama; **p. top,** veste *f* de pyjama.

pylon ['paɪlən] *n* (a) pylône *m* (*en charpente métallique, en béton armé*); **(electricity) p.,** pylône; (b) *Archit* (*gateway*) pylône *m*.

pyorrhea [paɪə'rɪə] *n Med* pyorrhée *f*.

pyramid ['pɪrəmɪd] *n Archit Math* pyramide *f*; **p. selling,** vente *f* à la boule de neige.

pyramidal [pɪ'ræmɪd(ə)l] *adj* pyramidal, -aux.

pyre ['paɪər] *n* bûcher *m* (funéraire).

Pyrenean [pɪrə'ni:ən] *adj* pyrénéen, des Pyrénées; **P. mountain dog,** saint-bernard *m* des Pyrénées.

Pyrenees (the) [ðəpɪrə'ni:z] *npl* les Pyrénées *fpl*.

pyrethrum [paɪ'ri:θrəm] *n* (*plant*) pyrèthre *m*.

pyretic [paɪ'retɪk] *adj Med* pyrétique.

Pyrex ® ['paɪreks] *n* Pyrex ® *m*; **P. dish,** plat *m* en Pyrex.

pyrites [paɪ'raɪti:z] *n Miner* pyrite *f*; **iron p.,** sulfure *m* de fer, fer sulfuré.

pyritic [paɪ'rɪtɪk] *adj Miner* pyriteux.

pyromaniac [paɪrəʊ'meɪnɪæk] *n* pyromane *mf*.

pyrotechnic [paɪrəʊ'teknɪk] *adj* pyrotechnique; **p. display,** feu *m* d'artifice.

pyrotechnics [paɪrəʊ'teknɪks] *npl* (*usu with sing verb*) pyrotechnie *f*; (*fireworks*) feux *mpl* d'artifice; *Fig* (*of style etc*) fioritures *fpl*.

Pyrrhic ['pɪrɪk] *adj Antiq* de Pyrrhus; **P. victory,** victoire *f* à la Pyrrhus, victoire désastreuse.

Pythagoras [paɪ'θægərəs] *n* Pythagore *m*.

Pythagorean [paɪθægə'ri:ən] *adj* pythagoricien.

python ['paɪθən] *n* python *m*.

pyx [pɪks] *n Rel* ciboire *m*; **p. cloth,** custode *f*.

pzazz [pə'zæz] *n F* (*flair*) punch *m*.

Q

Q, q [kjuː] *n* (la lettre) Q, q *m*.
q [kjuː] *Sch etc* (*abbr* **question**) q.
QC [kjuːˈsiː] *n Br Jur abbr* **Queen's Counsel**.
QED [kjuːiːˈdiː] (*abbr* **quod erat demonstrandum**) C.Q.F.D. (ce qu'il fallait démontrer).
QE2 [kjuːiːˈtuː] *n F* (*abbr* **Queen Elizabeth II**) = le (paquebot) reine Elizabeth II.
QM [kjuːˈem] *n abbr* **Quartermaster**.
QMG [kjuːemˈdʒiː] *n Mil abbr* **Quartermaster General**.
qt, *pl* **qts** *abbr* **quart,** *pl* **quarts**.
q.t. [kjuːˈtiː] *n F* (*abbr* **quiet**) **to do sth on the q.t.,** faire qch en douce; **to tell s.o. sth on the q.t.,** dire qch à qn discrètement *ou* en confidence.
qty *Com abbr* **quantity**.
quack[1] [kwæk] **1** *int* **q.! q.!,** coin-coin! **2** *n* **(a)** (*cry*) coin-coin *m inv*; **(b)** (*in children's language*) **q.-q.,** canard *m*.
quack[2] *vi* **(a)** (*of duck*) cancaner, *F* faire coin-coin; **(b)** *F* (*of person*) cancaner.
quack[3] *n* **(a) q. (doctor),** charlatan *m*; **q. remedy,** remède *m* de charlatan; **(b)** *F* (*doctor*) médecin *m*, toubib *m*.
quackery [ˈkwækərɪ] *n* charlatanisme *m*, charlatanerie *f*.
quad[1] [kwɒd] *n Sch F* = **QUADRANGLE (b)**.
quad[2] *n F* (*child*) = quadruplé, -ée; **they've got quads,** ils ont des quadruplés.
quad[3] *adj Comptr F* **q. density,** densité *f* quadruple.
quadragenarian [kwɒdrədʒəˈneərɪən] *adj & n* quadragénaire *mf*.
Quadragesima [kwɒdrəˈdʒesɪmə] *n Rel* **Q. (Sunday),** (le dimanche de) la Quadragésime.
quadrangle [ˈkwɒdræŋg(ə)l] *n* **(a)** *Math* figure *f* quadrangulaire, quadrilatère *m*; **(b)** (*courtyard*) cour *f* (carrée) (*d'un palais, d'une école etc*).
quadrangular [kwɒˈdræŋgjʊlər] *adj* quadrangulaire.
quadrant [ˈkwɒdrənt] *n* **(a)** *Astron Math* (*of circle*) quart *m* de cercle; (*of surface*) quadrant *m*; *Nau* octant *m*; *Mil* niveau *m* (de pointage); **(b)** *MecE* secteur *m*; **(c)** *Archit Carp* quart-de-rond *m*, *pl* quarts-de-rond.
quadraphonic [kwɒdrəˈfɒnɪk] *adj* **q. sound,** son *m* tétraphonique.
quadraphonics [kwɒdrəˈfɒnɪks] *npl* (*with sing verb*) quadriphonie *f*, tétraphonie *f*.
quadrate [kwɒˈdreɪt] *vt Math* réduire (*une surface etc*) au carré équivalent; faire cadrer (**sth with** *or* **to sth,** qch avec qch).
quadratic [kwɒˈdrætɪk] *adj* **(a)** *Math* (*équation*) quadratique, du second degré; **(b)** *Miner* quadratique.
quadrature [ˈkwɒdrətʃər] *n Math Astron* quadrature *f*; **q. of the circle,** quadrature du cercle.
quadrennial [kwɒˈdrenɪəl] *adj* quadriennal, -aux.
quadri- [ˈkwɒdrɪ] *pref* quadri-.
quadrilateral [kwɒdrɪˈlætər(ə)l] **1** *adj* quadrilatéral, -aux. **2** *n Math etc* quadrilatère *m*, tétragone *m*.
quadrille [kwəˈdrɪl] *n Mus* quadrille *m*.
quadrillion [kwɒdˈrɪlɪən] *n* quadrillion *m* (10^{24}); *Am* mille billions (10^{15}).
quadriplegia [kwɒdrɪˈpliːdʒɪə] *n Med* tétraplégie *f*, quadriplégie *f*.
quadriplegic [kwɒdrɪˈpliːdʒɪk] *adj & n Med* tétraplégique *mf*, quadriplégique *mf*.
quadroon [kwɒˈdruːn] *adj & n* quarteron, -onne.
quadruped [ˈkwɒdrʊped] *adj & n* quadrupède *m*.
quadruple[1] [ˈkwɒdrʊp(ə)l] *adj & n* quadruple *m*.
quadruple[2] *vt & vi* quadrupler.
quadruplet [ˈkwɒdrʊplet] *n* **(a)** (*child*) quadruplé, -ée; **(b)** *Mus* quartolet *m*.
quadruplex [ˈkwɒdrʊpleks] *adj* quadruple.
quadruplicate[1] [kwɒˈdruːplɪkət] *adj* quadruplé, quadruple; **in q.,** en quatre exemplaires.
quadruplicate[2] [kwɒˈdruːplɪkeɪt] *vt* **(a)** (*multiply by four*) quadrupler, multiplier par quatre; **(b)** (*make four copies of*) faire *ou* tirer quatre exemplaires de (*une lettre etc*).
quaff [kwɒf] *vt Lit* boire (*du vin*) à longs traits; vider (*une coupe*) d'un trait.
quagmire [ˈkwægmaɪər, ˈkwɒg-] *n* (*bog*) marécage *m*.
quail[1] [kweɪl] *n inv* (*in hunting*) (*bird*) caille *f* (des blés); *Can* colin *m*; **q.'s eggs,** œufs de caille.
quail[2] *vi Lit* (*of person*) fléchir, faiblir (**before,** devant); **his heart quailed,** son cœur défaillit.
quaint [kweɪnt] *adj* (*unusual*) étrange, bizarre; (*old-fashioned*) suranné; **q. ideas,** (*unusual*) idées baroques *ou* cocasses; (*old-fashioned*) idées un peu surannées; **q. style,** (*unusual*) style singulier *ou* original; (*old-fashioned*) style d'un archaïsme piquant; **a q. little cottage,** une petite chaumière pittoresque.
quaintly [ˈkweɪntlɪ] *adv* (*unusually*) étrangement, bizarrement; (*picturesquely*) pittoresquement.
quaintness [ˈkweɪntnɪs] *n* (*unusualness*) étrangeté *f*, bizarrerie *f*; (*old-fashioned charm*) pittoresque suranné.
quake[1] [kweɪk] *n* **(a)** (*shaking*) tremblement *m*; **(b)** *F* (*earthquake*) tremblement *m* de terre.
quake[2] *vi* **(a)** (*of person*) trembler, frémir (**for, with fear,** de crainte); **to q. in one's shoes,** trembler dans sa peau; **quaking grass,** (*plant*) brize *f*; **(b)** (*of thing*) trembler, branler.
Quaker [ˈkweɪkər] *n Rel* quaker *m*, *f* quakeresse.
Quakerism [ˈkweɪkərɪz(ə)m] *n Rel* quakerisme *m*.
qualification [kwɒlɪfɪˈkeɪʃən] *n* **(a)** (*competence*) aptitude *f*, compétence *f*; (*diploma etc*) diplôme *m*; **to have the necessary qualifications for a job,** (*skills etc*) avoir les qualités requises pour remplir une fonction; (*diplomas*) avoir les diplômes requis pour remplir une fonction; **professional qualifications,** qualification professionnelle; **what are your qualifications?,** quels diplômes avez-vous?; **a q. in translating, a translating q.,** un diplôme en traduction, un diplôme de traduction; **one of the qualifications for this job is a sense of humour,** une des qualités requises à *ou* pour ce poste est le sens de l'humour; **(b)** (*reservation*) réserve *f*, restriction *f*; **to accept without q.,** (*without reservation*) accepter sans réserve; (*without conditions*) accepter sans conditions; **(c)** (*description*) qualification *f* (**of s.o. as sth,** de qn de qch).
qualificative [ˈkwɒlɪfɪkətɪv] *adj & n Gram* qualificatif *m*.
qualified [ˈkwɒlɪfaɪd] *adj* **(a)** qui a les qualités requises (*pour un poste etc*); (*pilote etc*) breveté; *Jur* capable (**to,** de); **she's very highly q.,** elle a d'excellents diplômes; **to be q. to do sth,** être apte à faire qch, avoir les capacités pour faire qch; **I am q. to speak about it,** (*I know about it*) je suis bien placé pour en parler; **to be q. to speak,** (*at meeting etc*) avoir voix au chapitre; **q. persons,** personnes compétentes; **(b)** (*modified*) restreint, modéré; **q. approval,** approbation modérée.
qualifier [ˈkwɒlɪfaɪər] *n* **(a)** *Sp* (*person, team that qualifies*) qualifié, -ée; **(b)** *Gram* qualificatif *m*; **(c)** (*reservation*) restriction *f*, réserve *f*.
qualify [ˈkwɒlɪfaɪ] **1** *vt* **(a) to q. s.o. for (doing) sth/to do sth,** donner à qn les qualités requises pour (faire) qch, rendre qn apte à (faire) qch; *Jur* donner qualité à qn pour (faire) qch; **my knowledge qualifies me to undertake this work,** mes connaissances me qualifient pour entreprendre cet ouvrage; **what do you think qualifies you for this job?,** en quoi vous considérez-vous comme qualifié pour cet emploi?;

(b) (*modify*) apporter des réserves à (*un consentement etc*); restreindre (*une affirmation*); modérer, diminuer (*un plaisir*);

(c) (*describe*) **to q. s.o./sth as sth,** qualifier qn/qch de qch;

(d) *Gram* qualifier.

2 *vi* acquérir les qualités *ou* les connaissances requises, se préparer, se qualifier (**for sth,** pour qch); *Sp* se qualifier (**for,** pour); **to q. as a doctor,** être reçu médecin; **to q. as**

a pilot, obtenir son brevet de pilote; **you don't q. for a grant,** vous ne présentez pas les conditions requises à l'octroi d'une prime; **that doesn't q. as news,** ceci n'a pas qualité de nouvelles.

qualifying ['kwɒlɪfaɪɪŋ] *adj* **(a) q. examination,** examen *m* pour certificat d'aptitude; examen d'entrée (*à une école etc*); *Sp* **q. round,** série *f* éliminatoire; **(b)** (*modifying*) modificateur, -trice; **q. statement,** déclaration corrective; **(c)** *Gram* (*adjectif*) qualificatif; (*adverbe*) modificatif.

qualitative ['kwɒlɪtətɪv] *adj Gram Ch* qualitatif.

qualitatively ['kwɒlɪtətɪvlɪ] *adv Gram Ch* qualitativement.

quality ['kwɒlɪtɪ] *n* **(a)** (*degree of excellence*) qualité *f*; **of good q.,** de bonne qualité; **of high/poor q.,** de qualité supérieure/inférieure; *Com* **q. goods,** marchandises de qualité; **high/poor q. goods,** marchandises *fpl* de bonne/mauvaise qualité; **q. matters more than quantity,** la qualité importe plus que la quantité; **q. control,** contrôle *m* de la qualité; **q. newspaper,** journal sérieux; **the q. of life,** la qualité de la vie;

(b) (*of person*) qualité *f*, trait *m*; (*of thing*) qualité, avantage *m*; **one of the qualities I look for in a friend,** une des qualités que je recherche chez un ami; **moral/intellectual qualities,** qualités morales/intellectuelles; **he has many (good) qualities,** il a beaucoup de qualités;

(c) qualité *f*, timbre *m* (*d'un son, de la voix*);

(d) qualité *f*, logique *f* (*d'une proposition*);

(e) to act in the q. of ..., agir en qualité de ...;

(f) *Arch* **person of q.,** personne *f* de qualité.

qualm [kwɑːm] *n* **(a)** (*pang of conscience*) scrupule *m*, remords *m*; **to have no qualms about doing sth,** ne pas se faire le moindre scrupule à faire qch; **don't you feel any qualms about getting married?,** n'éprouves-tu aucune inquiétude à l'idée de te marier?; **I sometimes have qualms about what I did,** j'ai parfois des remords pour ce que j'ai fait; **(b)** (*premonition*) pressentiment *m* de malheur; (*anxiety*) inquiétude *f*; **(c)** (*nausea*) soulèvement *m* de cœur, nausée *f*.

quandary ['kwɒnd(ə)rɪ] *n* situation embarrassante, difficulté *f*; **to be in a q.,** (*unable to decide what to do*) ne pas trop savoir que faire.

quango ['kwæŋgəʊ] *n* (*abbr* **quasi-autonomous non-governmental organization**) = organisation non gouvernementale quasi-autonome.

quantifier ['kwɒntɪfaɪər] *n* (*logic*) *& Math* quantificateur *m*.

quantify ['kwɒntɪfaɪ] *vt* **(a)** (*determine quantity of*) déterminer la quantité de (*qch*); (*measure*) mesurer, évaluer; **success is hard to q.,** la réussite est difficile à évaluer; **(b)** (*in logic*) quantifier (*le prédicat*).

quantitative ['kwɒntɪtətɪv] *adj Ch etc* quantitatif.

quantitatively ['kwɒntɪtətɪvlɪ] *adv Ch etc* quantitativement.

quantity ['kwɒntɪtɪ] *n* **(a)** quantité *f*; **a small q. of,** une petite quantité de; **to buy sth in large quantities,** acheter qch en quantité considérable *ou* en grande quantité; **to produce sth in q.,** produire qch en quantité; *Constr* **bill of quantities,** devis *m*; **q. surveyor,** métreur *m* (vérificateur); **q. surveying,** métrage *m*, métré *m*, toisé *m*; **(b)** *Math* quantité *f*; **unknown q.,** inconnue *f*; **she's an unknown q.,** (*nothing is known of her*) on ne sait rien d'elle; (*it's hard to tell what she'll do, how she'll react etc*) on ne peut pas prévoir ce qu'elle va faire *ou* comment elle va réagir *etc*; **negligible q.,** quantité négligeable; **(c)** (*in prosody*) quantité *f*; **q. mark,** signe *m* de quantité; **(d)** (*in logic*) quantité *f* (*d'une proposition*); **(e)** *Econ* **q. theory,** théorie quantitative.

quantum, *pl* **-a** ['kwɒntəm, -ə] *n* quantum *m*; **q. leap,** saut *m* quantique; *Phys* **q. mechanics/optics/physics,** mécanique *f*/optique *f*/physique *f* quantique; *Phys* **q. theory,** théorie *f* des quanta, théorie quantique.

quarantine¹ ['kwɒrəntiːn] *n* quarantaine *f*; **to be in q.,** (*of person, animal*) être en quarantaine.

quarantine² *vt* mettre (*qn, un navire*) en quarantaine.

quark [kwɑːk] *n* **(a)** *Nucl Phys* quark *m*; **(b)** (*cheese*) ≈ fromage blanc.

quarrel¹ ['kwɒr(ə)l] *n* (*dispute*) querelle *f*, dispute *f*, brouille *f*; (*cause for complaint*) motif *m* de plainte; **to pick a q. with s.o.,** faire une scène à qn, se quereller avec qn; **to try to pick a q. with s.o.,** chercher querelle *ou* noise à qn; **they've had a q.,** ils sont brouillés; **the q. between them,** la brouille qui les divise; **to make up a q.,** raccommoder un différend; **I have no q. with** *or* **against him,** je n'ai rien à lui reprocher; **my q. with you is that ...,** ce que je te reproche c'est que ...; **she has no q. with that,** elle n'a rien à redire là-dessus.

quarrel² *vi* (**-ll-**, *US* **-l-**) **(a)** se quereller, se disputer (**with s.o. over, about sth,** avec qn à propos de qch); se brouiller (**with s.o.,** avec qn); **they've been quarrelling,** ils se sont disputés; **I don't want to q.,** je ne veux pas me bagarrer; **they're always quarrelling,** ils *ou* elles sont toujours à se quereller; **(b) to q. with s.o. for doing sth,** (*to find fault with*) reprocher à qn de faire qch; **to q. with sth,** (*to take exception to*) trouver à redire à qch; (*to complain about*) se plaindre de qch; **while I wouldn't q. with your figures ...,** quoique je ne contesterais pas vos chiffres ... .

quarrelling, *US* **quarreling** ['kwɒr(ə)lɪŋ] **1** *adj* querelleur, -euse. **2** *n* querelle(s) *f(pl)*, dispute(s) *f(pl)*.

quarrelsome ['kwɒr(ə)lsəm] *adj* querelleur, batailleur; **in a q. mood,** d'humeur batailleuse *ou* querelleuse.

quarrier ['kwɒrɪər] *n* = **QUARRYMAN**.

quarry¹ ['kwɒrɪ] *n* (*in hunting, Fig person*) proie *f*; gibier *m* (*poursuivi à courre*).

quarry² *n* carrière *f* (*de pierres, d'ardoises etc*); **open q.,** carrière à ciel ouvert; **q. stone,** moellon *m*; **q. tile,** carreau *m* (de céramique).

quarry³ **1** *vt* extraire *ou* tirer (*des minerais etc*) de la carrière. **2** *vi* exploiter une carrière.

►**quarry out** *vtsep* (*extract from ground*) extraire (*des minerais etc*).

quarrying ['kwɒrɪɪŋ] *n* exploitation *f* de carrières.

quarryman, *pl* **-men** ['kwɒrɪmən] *n* (ouvrier *m*) carrier *m*; **slate q.,** perrayeur *m*, perrier *m*.

quart¹ [kwɔːt] *n* (*liquid measurement*) = (*in UK*) 1,136 litres; (*in US*) 0,946 litre.

quart² [kɑːt] *n* **(a)** *Fencing* quarte *f*; **(b)** *Cards* quatrième *f*.

quartation [kwɔː'teɪʃən] *n Metal* quartation *f*, inquartation *f*, inquart *m*.

quarte [kɑːt] *n Fencing* quarte *f*.

quarter¹ ['kwɔːtər] *n* **(a)** (*portion*) quart *m* (*de pomme, de cercle, de siècle etc*); quartier *m* (*d'orange, de la lune*); *Am* (*coin*) pièce *f* de vingt-cinq cents; *Am* (*sum*) quart de dollar; *Culin* quartier (*de bœuf, d'agneau*); *Her* quartier, franc-quartier *m*, *pl* francs-quartiers; *Her* écart *m*, partition *f* (*de l'écu*); *Nau* (*in naval architecture*) hanche *f*; quartier (*de chaussure*); (*in farriery*) quartier (*de sabot*); **to divide sth in(to) quarters,** diviser qch en quatre; **three quarters,** trois quarts; **three and a q.,** trois et quart; **a q. (of a pound) of coffee,** un quart (de livre) de café; *Sp* **q. (mile),** (course *f* d'un) quart de mille; **bottle one q.** *or* **a q. full,** bouteille au quart pleine; *Culin* **fore/hind q.,** quartier de devant/de derrière; **(hind) quarters,** arrière-train *m*, train *m* de derrière (*d'une bête*); arrière-main *mf* (*du cheval*); **moon at the first q.,** lune au premier quartier; **moon in its last q.,** lune dans son dernier quartier *ou* sur son décroît; **I can get it for you for a q. of the price,** je peux vous l'avoir pour le quart du prix; *Nau* **wind on the q., q. wind,** vent grand largue, vent de la hanche; **q. binding,** (*in bookbinding*) demi-reliure *f*; *Sp* **q. final,** quart de finale; *esp Am Mus* **q. note,** noire *f*;

(b) (*of time*) (*three-month period*) trimestre *m*; terme *m* (*de loyer*); **to be paid by the q.,** être payé par trimestre; **in the first q. of 1990,** pendant le premier trimestre de l'année 1990; **in the first q. of the century,** pendant le premier quart du siècle; **q. day,** (jour *m* de) terme; *Jur* **q. sessions,** assises trimestrielles, cour trimestrielle de comté; **a q. to six,** *Am* **a q. of six,** six heures moins le quart; **it's a q. to,** il est moins le quart; **a q. past** *or Am* **after six,** six heures et quart; **it's a q. past,** il est le quart; **there's a train at a q. to and a q. past every hour,** il y a un train à moins le quart et au quart de chaque heure;

(c) *Nau* quart *m* d'aire de vent (= 2º 48' 45''); (*direction*) aire *f* de vent, quart, côté *m*; **the wind is in the right q.,** le vent vient du bon côté;

(d) (*region*) région *f*, partie *f*; quartier *m* (*d'une ville*); **the four quarters of the globe,** les quatre parties du globe; **news from all quarters,** nouvelles de partout; **what is he doing in these quarters?,** que fait-il dans ces parages?; **an order from high quarters,** un ordre d'en haut; **in some quarters there is talk of rebellion,** on parle de rébellion dans certains milieux; **to apply to the proper q.,** s'adresser à qui de droit; **you'll get no help from THAT q.,** vous n'obtiendrez aucune aide de ce côté; **the slum q.,** le quartier des taudis; **the residential q.,** le quartier d'habitation *ou* résidentiel;

(e) quarters, *Mil* quartier *m*, cantonnement *m*, logement *m*; *Nau* poste *m* de combat; **living quarters,** (*for servants*) appartements *mpl* (domestiques); **married quarters,** appartements pour familles; *Av* **crew's quarters,** locaux affectés au personnel du bord; *Nau* **to beat** *or* **pipe to**

quarters, battre *ou* sonner le branle-bas; *Nau* **general quarters,** branle-bas de combat;

(f) (*mercy*) quartier *m*, merci *f*; **to give q.,** faire quartier, accorder merci; **to give no q.,** ne pas faire de quartier.

quarter² *vt* **(a)** diviser (*une pomme etc*) en quatre; diviser (*un bœuf etc*) par quartiers, équarrir (*un bœuf*); *Min* quarter; *Hist* écarteler (*un condamné*); *Her* écarteler (*l'écu*); *MecE etc* caler à 90°; **to q. (the ground),** (*of hunting dogs*) bricoler, quêter; **(b)** *Mil* cantonner, caserner, loger (*des troupes*); *Nau* désigner leurs postes à (*les hommes*); **to be quartered with s.o.,** loger chez qn.

quarterback ['kwɔːtəbæk] *n Am Fb* arrière *m*; *F* **to be a Monday morning q.,** être sage après l'heure.

quarterdeck ['kwɔːtədek] *n* **(a)** *Nau* plage *f* arrière; **(b)** *Nau* (*no pl*) **the q.,** (*officers*) les officiers *mpl*.

quarterfinal [kwɔːtə'faɪnəl] *n* (*of competition*) quart *m* de finale.

quartering ['kwɔːtərɪŋ] *n* **(a)** (*division*) division *f* en quatre; équarrissage *m* (*d'un bœuf, d'un tronc d'arbre*); *Her* écartelure *f* (*d'un écusson*); *MecE etc* calage *m* à 90°; *Hist* écartèlement *m* (*d'un condamné*); **(b)** *Mil* logement *m*, cantonnement *m*, stationnement *m* (*de troupes*); *Nau* désignation *f* des postes (*de combat etc*); **(c)** (*of hunting dogs*) quête *f*; **(d)** *Petr Min* échantillonnage *m* du minerai.

quarterly ['kwɔːtəlɪ] **1** *adj* trimestriel; (*abonnement*) au trimestre. **2** *n* publication trimestrielle. **3** *adv* trimestriellement, tous les trimestres, tous les trois mois.

quartermaster ['kwɔːtəmɑːstər] *n Nau* maître *m* de timonerie; *Mil* officier chargé des vivres et des fournitures; **Q. General,** = Directeur *m* de l'Intendance (militaire); **q. sergeant,** fourrier *m*.

quarterstaff ['kwɔːtəstɑːf] *n Arch* **(a)** (*staff*) bâton *m* (à deux bouts); **to fence with quarterstaffs,** jouer du bâton; **(b)** (*fighting*) escrime *f* au bâton.

quartet(te) [kwɔː'tet] *n* **(a)** *Mus* quatuor *m*; **string q.,** quatuor à cordes; **(b)** *Biol* quartette *f*.

quartile ['kwɔːtaɪl] *n* quartile *m*.

quarto ['kwɔːtəʊ] *adj & n* in-quarto *m inv*.

quartz [kwɔːts] *n Miner* quartz *m*; **smoky q.,** quartz enfumé; **rose q.,** pseudo-rubis *m*, rubis *m* de Bohême; **q. crystal,** cristal *m* de quartz; **q. watch,** montre *f* à quartz; **q. lamp,** lampe *f* (à vapeur de mercure) à tube de quartz.

quartzite ['kwɔːtsaɪt] *n Miner* quartzite *f*.

quasar ['kweɪzɑːr] *n Astron* quasar *m*.

quash [kwɒʃ] *vt* **(a)** étouffer (*un sentiment, un projet*); écraser (*une révolte*); *F* **to q. s.o.,** rabattre le caquet à qn; **(b)** *Jur* casser, infirmer, annuler (*un jugement, une décision*); invalider (*une élection*); **to q. proceedings** *or* **an action,** arrêter les poursuites.

quasi ['kweɪsaɪ, 'kwɑːzɪ] *pref* quasi, presque; **q. contract,** quasi-contrat *m, pl* quasi-contrats.

quatercentenary [kwɒtəsen'tiːnərɪ] *n* quatrième centenaire *m*.

quaternary [kwə'tɜːnərɪ] **1** *adj Ch Geol Math* quaternaire; *Geol* **the Q. era,** ère *f* quaternaire. **2** *n Geol* **the Q.,** le quaternaire.

quatrain ['kwɒtreɪn] *n* (*in prosody*) quatrain *m*.

quaver¹ ['kweɪvər] *n* **(a)** *Mus* (*note*) croche *f*; **(b)** (*trembling*) tremblement *m*, chevrotement *m* (*de la voix*); *Mus* trille *m*, tremolo *m*; **to have a q. in one's voice,** parler d'une voix tremblante.

quaver² **1** *vi* (*of voice*) chevroter, trembloter; *Mus* (*of singer*) faire des trilles; (*on instrument*) faire un tremolo; **quavering voice,** voix tremblotante *ou* chevrotante, voix mal assurée. **2** *vt* **to q. (out),** trembloter, chevroter (*un air*); *Mus* triller (*une note etc*).

quay [kiː] *n* quai *m*; (*on piles*) appontement *m*; **alongside the q.,** à quai; *Com* **ex-q.,** (*goods*) à prendre *ou* livrable à quai.

quayside ['kiːsaɪd] *n* (terrain *m* au bord du) quai *m*; **q. worker/crane,** ouvrier *m*/grue *f* de quai.

queasiness ['kwiːzɪnɪs] *n* nausées *fpl*; (*about what one has done*) malaise *m*.

queasy ['kwiːzɪ] *adj* (*person*) sujet à des nausées; (*estomac*) délicat; **I feel q.,** j'ai mal au cœur.

Quebec [kwɪ'bek] *n* Québec *m*; **I'm from Q.,** je suis Québecois, -oise.

queen¹ [kwiːn] *n* **(a)** reine *f*; **Q. Anne,** la reine Anne; **a Q. Anne house,** une maison de l'époque de la reine Anne; **the kings and queens of England,** les souverains *mpl* d'Angleterre; *Jur* **Q.'s counsel,** conseiller *m* de la reine; **beauty q.,** reine de beauté; **Q. of heaven,** reine du ciel; **Q. of hearts,** reine des cœurs; **she is the q. of my heart,** elle règne sur mon cœur; **the rose is the q. of flowers,** la rose est la reine des fleurs; *Bot* **q. of the meadows,** reine des prés; **q. of the night,** (cactus *m*) reine de la nuit; **q. mother,** reine mère; **(b)** *Cards* dame *f*; *Chess* reine *f*; **to go to q.,** (*of pawn*) aller à dame; **(c)** (*insect*) reine *f* (*des fourmis etc*); **q. bee,** (*insect*) abeille *f* mère, reine des abeilles; *Fig* maîtresse *f* femme; **she's the q. bee around here,** c'est elle qui règne sur ces lieux; **(d)** *Offensive Sl* (*male homosexual*) pédale *f*, tante *f*.

queen² **1** *vt* **(a)** *F* **to q. it,** faire la reine (**over s.o.,** avec qn); **(b)** *Chess* damer (*un pion*). **2** *vi Chess* (*of pawn*) aller à dame.

queer¹ ['kwɪər] *n* **(a)** *Offensive Sl* (*male homosexual*) pédé *m*, pédale *f*; **(b)** *US Sl* (*counterfeit money*) fausse monnaie.

queer² *adj* **(a)** (*strange*) bizarre, étrange, singulier; **that's q.,** c'est bizarre; **a q.-looking person,** une drôle de tête; **q. ideas,** idées bizarres *ou F* biscornues; *F* **q. in the head,** toqué, timbré; *F* **to be in Q. Street,** être dans une situation (financière) délicate; **(b)** (*suspicious*) suspect, louche; *US* **q. money,** fausse monnaie; **(c)** *Offensive Sl* (*homosexual*) de tante, de pédale; **his q. friends,** ses copains pédales *ou* tantes; **(d)** *F* (*unwell*) pas bien; **I feel very q.,** je me sens tout chose *ou* tout drôle; *Sl* **to come over** *or* **to be taken q.,** avoir un malaise.

queer³ *vt F* **to q. the pitch for s.o., to q. s.o.'s pitch,** bouleverser *ou* faire échouer les plans de qn.

queer-bashing ['kwɪəbæʃɪŋ] *n Br Offensive Sl* chasse *f* aux pédés.

queerly ['kwɪəlɪ] *adv* bizarrement, étrangement.

queerness ['kwɪənɪs] *n* étrangeté *f*, bizarrerie *f*.

quell [kwel] *vt Lit* réprimer, étouffer (*une révolte, une émotion*); dompter (*qn, une passion*).

quench¹ [kwentʃ] *n* (*in metalwork*) trempe *f*.

quench² *vt* **(a) to q. one's thirst,** étancher *ou* assouvir sa soif, se désaltérer; **(b)** (*extinguish*) éteindre (*un feu, une flamme*); **(c)** (*cool*) (*in metalwork*) tremper, éteindre (*le métal*); refroidir (*l'enthousiasme de qn*); **(d)** (*suppress*) réprimer, étouffer (*un désir*); *El* étouffer (*une étincelle*); amortir (*des oscillations*).

quenching ['kwentʃɪŋ] *n* **(a)** assouvissement *m* (*de la soif*); **(b)** extinction *f* (*du feu*); (*in metalwork*) trempe *f* (*à l'eau, à l'huile*).

querulous ['kwerʊləs] *adj* qui se plaint toujours, grognon; (*ton*) plaintif, dolent.

querulously ['kwerʊləslɪ] *adv* d'un ton plaintif.

query¹ ['kwiːərɪ] *n* **(a)** question *f*; *Comptr* interrogation *f*; **I have a q.,** j'ai une question; **to settle a q.,** résoudre une question (*de méthode, de routine etc*); **there was a note of q. in her voice,** il y avait une note d'interrogation dans sa voix; **q. is this accurate?,** (*in margin of document etc*) s'assurer de l'exactitude de cette déclaration; *Comptr* **q. language,** langage *m* d'interrogation; **(b)** *Gram Typ* point *m* d'interrogation.

query² *vt* **(a) to q. if** *or* **whether ...,** s'informer si ...; **(b)** (*question*) mettre (*une affirmation*) en question *ou* en doute; (*mark with question mark*) marquer (*qch*) d'un point d'interrogation; *US* poser des questions à (*qn*); **how much is that?, he queried,** combien est-ce?, s'enquit-il; **she queried the bill,** elle a posé des questions sur la facture; **I would q. it if I were you,** à votre place je le vérifierais; *Comptr* **to q. a data base,** interroger une banque de données.

quest [kwest] *n Lit* quête *f*, recherche *f*; **to go in q. of s.o.,** se mettre *ou* aller *ou* partir à la recherche de qn *ou* en quête de qn; **her q. for justice,** sa bataille pour que justice soit faite; **the quest for the Holy Grail,** la quête du Graal.

question¹ ['kwestʃən] *n* **(a)** (*interrogation*) question *f*; **to ask s.o. a q.,** *esp Fml* **to ask a q. of s.o., to put a q. to s.o.,** poser *ou* adresser une question à qn; *Parl* adresser une interpellation à qn; **does anyone have any questions?,** quelqu'un a-t-il une question?; **I have a q.,** j'ai une question; **the q. is, did she know?,** la question est de savoir si elle était au courant; *F* **to pop the q.,** faire sa demande; *Gram* **direct/indirect q.,** interrogation directe/indirecte; *Sch etc* **list** *or* **set of questions,** questionnaire *m*; **multiple choice questions,** questions à choix multiples; *Typ* **q. mark,** point *m* d'interrogation; *Fig* **a q. mark hangs over the project,** il y a un point d'interrogation quant au projet; *Rad TV* **q. master,** animateur, -trice, meneur *m* de jeu (d'un jeu-concours); *Parl* **q. time,** heure consacrée aux questions;

(b) (*doubt*) doute *m*; **without q.,** sans aucun doute, sans contredit; **to obey without q.,** obéir aveuglément; **courage beyond q.,** courage *m* indiscutable; **that is beyond q.,** c'est incontestable; **his honesty has never been in q.,** sa probité n'a jamais été mise en doute; **to call s.o.'s**

honesty into q., mettre en question l'honnêteté de qn; **there is no q. about it,** il n'y a pas de doute là-dessus; **there is no q. of going back,** il n'est pas question de revenir en arrière; **it's open to q. whether ...,** on peut se demander si ...;

(c) (*subject of discussion*) question *f*; **that's the q.,** c'est là la question; **that is not the q., that is beside the q.,** ce n'est pas là la question, il ne s'agit pas de cela; **the q. is whether ...,** il s'agit de savoir si ...; **it is out of the q.,** c'est impossible, c'est hors de question; **it is quite out of the q. for us to ...,** il ne saurait être question pour nous de ...; **a merger is out of the q.,** fusionner est hors de question; **there's no q. of you going back to work at the moment,** il n'est pas question que vous retourniez au travail pour le moment; **it's not a q. of who's right,** la question n'est pas de savoir qui a raison; **the Middle East q.,** la question du Moyen Orient; **a q. of life or death,** une question de vie ou de mort; **a q. of money/time,** une question d'argent/de temps; **the matter/person in q.,** l'affaire/la personne en question; **the case in q.,** le cas en litige; **there was some q. of ...,** il a été question de ...;

(d) (*questioning*) interrogation *f*; *Arch* **to put s.o. to the q.,** (*torture*) mettre qn à la question, appliquer la question à qn.

question² *vt* **(a)** questionner, interroger (*qn*) (**about,** sur, à propos de); **to be questioned,** subir un interrogatoire; **the people questioned in the survey,** les personnes interrogées dans le cadre du sondage; **she was questioned on her views,** (*in interview etc*) on l'a interrogée sur ses opinions; **(b)** (*cast doubt on*) mettre (*qch*) en question *ou* en doute *ou* en cause; contester (*qch*); **I q. whether he will come,** je doute qu'il vienne; **I q. whether it would not be better...,** je me demande s'il ne vaudrait pas mieux ... .

questionable ['kwestʃənəb(ə)l] *adj* **(a)** contestable, discutable, douteux; **of q. authenticity,** (*document etc*) d'une authenticité (fort) douteuse; **this is the most democratic country — that's very q.,** c'est le pays le plus démocratique — c'est très discutable; **(b)** *Pej* (*conduct etc*) suspect, équivoque; **in q. taste,** d'un goût douteux.

questioner ['kwestʃənər] *n* interrogateur, -trice; (*likes asking questions*) questionneur, -euse.

questioning ['kwestʃənɪŋ] **1** *adj* (*regard etc*) interrogateur; **to have a q. mind,** avoir un esprit curieux. **2** *n* questions *fpl*, interrogation *f*; *Mil etc* interrogatoire *m* (*d'un prisonnier*); **to be held for q.,** (*by police*) être détenu pour un interrogatoire.

questioningly ['kwestʃənɪŋlɪ] *adv* (*to look at s.o.*) d'un air interrogateur.

questionnaire [kwestʃə'neər] *n* questionnaire *m*.

quetzal ['ketsəl] *n* **(a)** (*bird*) quetzal *m*, *pl* quetzals; **(b)** (*pl* **quetzales** [ket'sɑːleɪs]) (*coin*) quetzal *m*, *pl* quetzales.

queue¹ [kjuː] *n* **(a)** *esp Br* (*line*) queue *f* (*de personnes, de voitures*); **is this the q?.,** (*for tickets etc*) est-ce que c'est la queue?; **to form a q., to stand in a q.,** faire la queue; **to join the q.,** prendre la file, se mettre à la queue; *F* **to jump the q.,** resquiller, carotter; **(b)** *Arch* queue *f* (*de cheveux, de perruque*).

queue² *vi* faire la queue; **why don't you q. like everyone else?,** pourquoi ne faites-vous pas la queue comme tout le monde!; **I spent ages queuing for a bus,** j'ai passé des heures à faire la queue pour un bus.

▶**queue up** *vi* = **QUEUE²**; **people queued up to shake his hand,** les gens faisaient la queue pour lui serrer la main.

queue-jump ['kjuːdʒʌmp] *vi* resquiller, carotter.

queue-jumper ['kjuːdʒʌmpər] *n F* resquilleur *m*.

quibble¹ ['kwɪb(ə)l] *n* argutie *f*, chicane *f* sur les mots.

quibble² *vi* (*equivocate*) ergoter, chicaner sur les mots; (*split hairs*) chipoter, vétiller, couper les cheveux en quatre.

quibbler ['kwɪblər] *n* ergoteur, -euse, chicaneur, -euse.

quibbling ['kwɪb(ə)lɪŋ] *n* arguties *fpl*, chicanerie *f*, ergoterie *f*.

quiche [kiːʃ] *n Culin* quiche *f*.

quick [kwɪk] **1** *adj* (*movement, growth etc*) rapide; *Mus* animé, vif; **that was q.!,** ça a été rapide!; **as q. as lightning** *or* **as a flash,** aussi vite que l'éclair, en un clin d'œil; **to be q. about** *or* **over sth,** (*of person*) faire qch vite; **be q. (about it)!,** faites vite!, dépêchez-vous!; **he's q.,** il a des facilités; **q. to act/to anger,** prompt à agir/à se fâcher; **don't be so q. to criticize,** ne critique donc pas si vite; **she was q. to realize what had happened,** elle a été prompte à réaliser ce qui s'était passé; **q. ear** *or* **hearing,** oreille fine; **q. mind,** esprit prompt *ou* vif; *F* **let's have a q. one,** (*drink*) viens prendre un petit verre; **I'll just have a q. bath,** je vais juste prendre un petit bain; **q. recovery (from illness),** prompt rétablissement (d'une maladie); **q. temper,** tempérament emporté, irascibilité *f*; **she has a q. temper,** elle s'emporte facilement; *Cards* **q. trick,** levée assurée; **the quickest way there,** le chemin le plus court (pour y arriver).

2 *n* **(a)** (*flesh*) vif *m*; **to bite one's nails to the q.,** ronger ses ongles jusqu'au vif; *Fig* **to sting** *or* **cut s.o. to the q.,** blesser *ou* piquer qn au vif;

(b) *Rel* **the q. and the dead,** (*used as pl*) les vivants et les morts.

3 *adv F* vite, rapidement; **as q. as possible,** aussi vite que possible; **to run quicker,** courir plus vite; **he just wants to get rich q.,** il ne pense qu'à s'enrichir à tout prix; **q.-acting, q.-action,** (*mécanisme*) à action rapide *ou* immédiate; (*drogue, médicament*) à action rapide; **q.-firing rifle,** fusil *m* à tir rapide; **q.-growing,** (*plante etc*) à croissance rapide; *Constr Culin etc* **q.-setting,** (*mortier, gelée*) à prise rapide.

quick-change [kwɪk'tʃeɪndʒ] *adj Th* (*artiste*) à transformations rapides.

quicken ['kwɪk(ə)n] **1** *vt* hâter, presser, accélérer (**one's pace,** le pas); *Med* accélérer (*le pouls*); *Tech* activer, accélérer (*la combustion, le tirage*); (*stimulate*) animer, stimuler (*qn*); exciter, aiguiser (*le désir, l'appétit*); *Lit* donner la vie à, (r)animer (*les hommes, les plantes*); *Sp* **to q. the pace,** accélérer le pas *ou* le rythme. **2** *vi* (*of pace, pulse etc*) devenir plus rapide, s'accélérer; (*of nature, hope etc*) s'animer, se ranimer; (*of foetus*) donner des signes de vie.

quickening ['kwɪkənɪŋ] *adj* **(a)** (*pas*) qui s'accélère; **his q. interest,** son intérêt qui s'aiguise; **(b)** (*stimulating*) animateur, -trice; **a q. force,** une force vive. **2** *n* accélération *f* (*du pas, du pouls*); retour *m* à la vie (*de la nature etc*); *Obst* premiers mouvements du foetus.

quick-freeze [kwɪk'friːz] *vt Culin* congéler (*qch*) rapidement.

quickie ['kwɪkɪ] **1** *n F* (*quick drink*) consommation prise sur le pouce; (*something done quickly*) chose faite à la hâte; **let's have a q.,** (*drink*) viens prendre un petit verre; (*sex*) faisons l'amour en vitesse. **2** *adj Am F* **a q. divorce,** divorce *m* à la hâte.

quicklime ['kwɪklaɪm] *n* chaux vive.

quickly ['kwɪklɪ] *adv* vite, rapidement, vivement.

quickness ['kwɪknɪs] *n* **(a)** (*rapidity*) vitesse *f*, rapidité *f*, vivacité *f*; fréquence *f* rapide (*du pouls*); **(b)** (*sharpness*) acuité *f* (*de vision*); finesse *f* (*d'oreille*); promptitude *f*, vivacité *f* (*d'esprit*); **q. of temper,** caractère emporté *ou* irascible.

quicksand ['kwɪksænd] *n* lise *f*, sable(s) mouvant(s) (*du bord de la mer*); **to get caught in a q.** *or* **in the quicksands,** s'enliser.

quickset ['kwɪkset] **1** *adj* vif. **2** *n* **q. (hedge),** haie vive.

quicksilver ['kwɪksɪlvər] *n* vif-argent *m*, mercure *m*; **he's** *or* **she's just like q.,** c'est du vif-argent.

quickstep ['kwɪkstep] *n* (*dance*) fox-trot *m* rapide.

quick-tempered [kwɪk'tempəd] *adj* emporté, colérique, coléreux, irascible; **to be q.-t.,** s'emporter facilement.

quick-witted [kwɪk'wɪtɪd] *adj* vif, éveillé, à l'esprit vif.

quid¹ [kwɪd] *n Br Sl* (*inv in pl*) livre *f* (sterling).

quid² *n* chique *f* (*de tabac*).

quid pro quo [kwɪdprəʊ'kwəʊ] *n* équivalent *m*, compensation *f*; *Econ* contrepartie *f*.

quiescence [kwaɪ'esəns] *n* repos *m*, tranquillité *f*.

quiescent [kwaɪ'esənt] *adj* en repos, tranquille.

quiet¹ ['kwaɪət] *n* (*calm*) tranquillité *f*, repos *m*, calme *m*, quiétude *f*; (*silence*) silence *m*; **to enjoy perfect peace and q.,** jouir d'une parfaite tranquillité; **the q. of the night,** le calme de la nuit; *Br F Pej* **to do sth on the q.,** faire qch en cachette *ou* à la dérobée *ou* clandestinement.

quiet² *adj* **(a)** (*with little sound or motion*) tranquille, calme, silencieux; (*mer*) calme; (*moteur*) silencieux; **can we go somewhere q.?,** est-ce que nous pouvons aller dans un endroit tranquille?; **q. neighbourhood,** quartier *m* tranquille; **the wind grew q.,** le vent s'est apaisé; **to keep q.,** se tenir *ou* rester tranquille, se tenir coi *ou* en repos; **we must keep q. about it,** il ne faut pas en parler; **keep it q.,** pas un mot; **she was very q. about her background,** elle n'a pas dit grand-chose de ses antécédents; **to keep a child q.,** faire taire un enfant; **be q.!,** tais-toi!, taisez-vous!; **q. please!,** silence, s'il vous plaît!; **could I have a q. word (with you)?,** est-ce que je peux vous prendre à part pour vous dire deux mots?; **I'll have a q. word with her,** je la prendrai à part pout lui dire deux mots;

(b) (*gentle*) doux, *f* douce; **he's a very q. kind of chap,** c'est un type très tranquille; **q. disposition,** caractère doux *ou* calme; **q. horse,** cheval doux *ou* tranquille *ou* sage; **(c)** (*subdued*) (*dress, colours etc*) simple, discret, -ète, sobre; **we had a q. laugh over it,** nous en avons ri entre nous; **you're very q., is anything wrong?,** tu est drôlement silencieux, est-ce que quelque chose ne va pas?; **q. irony,** ironie voilée; **it's very pretty countryside, in a q. sort of way,** c'est un très joli paysage, dans le genre paisible; **q. wedding,** mariage célébré dans l'intimité; **(d)** (*undisturbed*) calme, tranquille, paisible; **to lead a q. life,** mener une vie calme; *F* **anything for a q. life!,** n'importe quoi du moment qu'on me fiche la paix!; **to spend a q. evening,** passer une soirée tranquille; **all q. on the western front,** à l'ouest rien de nouveau; *Com* **business is very q.,** les affaires sont très calmes; **it's very q. in here tonight,** (*in the pub, shop etc*) c'est très calme ce soir.

quiet³ *vt* = **QUIETEN.**

►quiet down = **QUIETEN DOWN 1 (a).**

quieten ['kwaɪət(ə)n] *vt* apaiser, calmer; tranquilliser (*qn, sa conscience*); faire taire (*un enfant*); apaiser, calmer (*un tumulte*); dissiper (*les craintes, les soupçons*); assoupir (*une douleur, les sens*).

►quieten down 1 *vi* **(a)** (*become quiet*) se taire; **(b)** (*become calm*) (*of person*) se calmer; (*of business*) ralentir. **2** *vtsep* **(a)** (*make quiet*) faire taire; **(b)** (*make calm*) calmer, apaiser (*qn*).

quietly ['kwaɪətlɪ] *adv* (*see adj*) **(a)** silencieusement, sans bruit; **(b)** tranquillement, doucement; **to be q. determined to do sth,** être froidement décidé à faire qch; **(c)** (*vêtu etc*) simplement, discrètement, sobrement; **to get married q.,** se marier sans cérémonie *ou* dans l'intimité; **(d) we live very q.,** nous menons une vie très simple.

quietness ['kwaɪətnɪs] *n* **(a)** (*lack of sound*) silence *m*; **(b)** (*of person*) calme *m*; (*of horse*) tranquillité *f*, sagesse *f*; **(c)** (*of dress, colour etc*) sobriété *f* (*de tenue etc*); **(d)** (*of life*) tranquillité *f*; (*of business*) manque *m* d'activité.

quietude ['kwaɪətjuːd] *n Lit* quiétude *f*.

quiff [kwɪf] *n* **q. (of hair),** toupet *m*.

quill [kwɪl] *n* **(a)** tuyau *m* (*de plume*); **q. (feather),** penne *f*; **q. (pen),** plume *f* d'oie (*pour écrire*); **(b)** piquant *m* (*de porc-épic etc*).

quilt¹ [kwɪlt] *n* couverture piquée *ou* matelassée; (*eiderdown*) édredon piqué; **continental q.,** couette *f*, *Swiss* duvet *m*.

quilt² 1 *vt* **(a)** piquer, ouater, ouatiner, matelasser (*un vêtement etc*); **quilted jacket,** veste matelassée; **(b)** piquer (*deux morceaux d'étoffe*). **2** *vi* faire du piquage.

quilting ['kwɪltɪŋ] *n* **(a)** (*technique, act*) piquage *m*, ouatinage *m*, matelassage *m*; **(b)** (*result*) piqué *m*, étoffe ouatée, ouatine *f*, matelassé *m*.

quin [kwɪn] *n F* (*child*) quintuplé, -ée.

quince [kwɪns] *n* **(a)** (*fruit*) coing *m*; **q. jelly,** gelée *f* de coings; **(b) q. (tree),** cognassier *m*.

quincentenary [kwɪnsen'tiːnərɪ] **1** *adj* de cinq cents ans. **2** *n* cinquième centenaire *m*.

quinine [kwɪ'niːn] *n Ch* quinine *f*.

quinquagenarian [kwɪŋkwədʒə'neərɪən] *adj & n* quinquagénaire *mf*.

Quinquagesima [kwɪŋkwə'dʒesɪmə] *n Rel* **Q. (Sunday),** (le dimanche de) la Quinquagésime.

quinsy ['kwɪnzɪ] *n Med* angine phlegmoneuse.

quint [kwɪnt] *n* **(a)** *Mus* quinte *f*; **(b)** [*also* kɪnt] *Cards* (*at piquet*) quinte *f*; **(c)** *Fencing* = **QUINTE.**

quintal ['kwɪnt(ə)l] *n* (*measurement*) quintal *m* métrique (de 100 kg).

quinte [kænt] *n Fencing* quinte *f*.

quintessence [kwɪn'tesəns] *n* quintessence *f*.

quintessential [kwɪntɪ'senʃəl] *adj* quintessenciel, quintessencié.

quintet(te) [kwɪn'tet] *n Mus* quintette *m*.

quintillion [kwɪn'tɪljən] *n* quintillion *m* (10^{30}); *Am* trillion *m* (10^{18}).

quintuple¹ ['kwɪntjʊp(ə)l] *adj & n* quintuple *m*.

quintuple² 1 *vt* quintupler. **2** *vi* (se) quintupler.

quintuplet [kwɪn'tjuːplɪt, 'kwɪntjʊplɪt] *n* **(a)** (*child*) quintuplé, -ée; **(b)** (*group of five*) groupe *m* de cinq; *Mus* quintolet *m*.

quip¹ [kwɪp] *n* (*sarcastic remark*) sarcasme *m*, raillerie *f*; (*witty remark*) trait *m ou* mot *m* d'esprit; (*riposte*) repartie *f*.

quip² (-pp-) **1** *vi* (*make sarcastic remark*) railler; (*be witty*) dire des mots d'esprit. **2** *vt* (*say sarcastically*) dire (*qch*) de façon sarcastique; (*say wittily*) dire (*qch*) avec esprit.

quire ['kwaɪər] *n* **(a) q. of paper (24 sheets),** *approx* = main *f* de papier (25 feuilles); **(b)** *Typ* **in quires,** en feuilles.

quirk [kwɜːk] *n* (*of character*) bizarrerie *f* de caractère; **he's got a lot of little quirks,** il y a plein de choses bizarres chez lui; **a q. of fate,** un caprice du sort; **by a q. they both went to Rome,** par un effet du hasard, ils sont tous les deux allés à Rome.

quirky ['kwɜːkɪ] *adj* (*sense of humour etc*) bizarre.

quisling ['kwɪzlɪŋ] *n Pej* collaborateur, -trice.

quit¹ [kwɪt] *adj Fml* quitte, libéré; **to be q. of s.o./sth,** être débarrassé de qn/qch.

quit² *v* (*pt & pp* **quitted,** *Dial & US* **quit**; *prp* **quitting**) **1** *vi* (*resign*) démissionner; (*in fight*) céder, baisser pavillon; *Comptr* sortir; **you can't fire me, I q.,** vous ne pouvez pas me mettre à la porte, je démissionne; **to receive notice to q.,** (*of tenant*) recevoir son congé. **2** *vt* **(a)** *Lit* quitter (*qn, un endroit*); **(b)** *Comptr* sortir de (*une base de données, un programme*); **(c) to q. office,** se démettre de ses fonctions; **to q. one's job,** quitter son emploi, démissionner; **to q. doing sth,** cesser de faire qch; **q. annoying me, will you!,** tu veux bien arrêter de m'ennuyer!; **to q. (work),** cesser le travail.

quite [kwaɪt] *adv* **(a)** (*entirely*) tout à fait, entièrement, complètement; **she's q. happy,** elle est tout à fait heureuse; **he's q. happy to let others do the work,** ça ne le dérange absolument pas de laisser les autres faire le travail; **q. finished,** tout à fait fini; **q. recovered,** complètement rétabli; **he was q. obviously drunk,** il était manifestement ivre; **q. the best story of its kind,** sans exception la meilleure histoire de ce genre; **q. as much,** tout autant; **q. enough,** bien assez; **q. apart from the fact that ...,** tout à fait en dehors du fait que ...; **q. right,** tout à fait; (*of sum*) parfaitement juste; (*of clock*) bien à l'heure; **you are q. right,** vous avez bien *ou* tout à fait raison; **q. so!,** parfaitement!, d'accord!; **I'm afraid I'll be a bit late — that's q. all right,** je crains d'être un peu en retard — ce n'est pas grave; **not q.,** pas tout à fait; **not q. 300,** pas tout à fait 300; **it's not q. 2 o'clock,** il n'est pas tout à fait 2 heures; **q. the opposite,** bien au contraire; **I don't q. know what he will do,** je ne sais pas trop ce qu'il fera; **you know q. well what I mean,** vous savez très bien ce que je veux dire; **I q. understand,** je comprends bien, je me rends parfaitement compte; **I don't q. understand,** je ne comprends pas bien; **I can't q. remember when it happened,** je ne me souviens pas tout à fait quand ça s'est passé; **in q. another tone,** sur un tout autre ton; **(b)** (*fairly, rather*) assez; **q. big/small,** assez gros/petit; **q. frequently/recently,** assez fréquemment/récemment; **this furniture is q. sought after,** ces meubles sont assez recherchés; **I q. like him,** je l'aime bien; **she is q. happy,** elle est plus ou moins heureuse; **q. a lot of people/money,** un assez grand nombre de gens/une assez grosse somme d'argent; **q. a few people,** pas mal de gens; **(c)** (*really*) **q. a beauty,** une vraie beauté; **it was q. a surprise,** c'était une véritable surprise; *F* **it's been q. a day,** quelle journée! **she's q. a girl,** elle est formidable; **that film was q. something,** ce film c'était vraiment quelque chose; **it's q. something when ...,** c'est vraiment quelque chose quand ... .

quits [kwɪts] *adj* quitte(s); **to be q.,** être quitte(s); **double or q.,** quitte ou double; **I'll be q. with him yet,** je lui rendrai la pareille, il me le paiera; **let's call it q.,** (*agree to end game, dispute*) restons-en là.

quittance ['kwɪt(ə)ns] *n* quittance *f*, décharge *f*, acquit *m*.

quitter ['kwɪtər] *n F* lâcheur, -euse; **she's not a q.,** ce n'est pas une lâcheuse.

quiver¹ ['kwɪvər] *n* (*arrow holder*) carquois *m*; *esp Lit Fig* **to have an arrow** *or* **a shaft left in one's q.,** n'être pas à bout de ressources.

quiver² *n* (*of person*) tremblement *m*, frisson *m*, frémissement *m*; (*of leaves, lips*) tremblement *m*; (*of flesh*) palpitation *f*; **with a q. in one's voice,** d'une voix frémissante *ou* mal assurée.

quiver³ 1 *vi* (*of person*) trembler, frémir, frissonner; (*of leaves, lips*) trembler; (*of voice, light*) trembloter; (*of flesh*) palpiter, frémir; **to q. with fear,** frémir de crainte; **voice quivering with emotion,** voix vibrante d'émotion. **2** *vt* (*of bird*) **to q. its wings,** agiter ses ailes.

quivering ['kwɪvərɪŋ] **1** *adj* (*person, leaves, lips*) tremblant; (*person*) frissonnant, frémissant; (*flesh*) palpitant; **the experience had reduced him to a q. mass** *or* **jelly,** l'expérience l'avait réduit à l'état de masse tremblante. **2** *n* (*of person*) tremblement *m*, frémissement *m*, frissonnement *m*; (*of flesh*) palpitation *f*; battement *m* (*de paupières*).

qui vive [kiː'viːv] *n* **to be on the q. v.,** être sur le qui-vive.

Quixote (Don) [dɒn'kwɪksəʊt, -kiː'həʊtɪ] *n Liter* Don Quichotte *m*.
quixotic [kwɪk'sɒtɪk] *adj* (*visionary*) exalté, visionnaire; donquichottesque.
quixotically [kwɪk'sɒtɪklɪ] *adv* en Don Quichotte.
quiz[1] [kwɪz] *n Rad TV etc* jeu-concours *m*; (*questioning*) interrogatoire *m*; *Sch* examen oral; *Rad TV* **q. show** *or* **programme,** jeu télévisé *ou* radiophonique.
quiz[2] *vt* (**-zz-**) questionner; *Am Sch* faire passer l'oral à (*un candidat*); **they quizzed me on my political views,** ils m'ont interrogé sur mes opinions politiques.
quizmaster ['kwɪzmɑːstər] *n Rad TV etc* animateur *m*, meneur *m* de jeu.
quizzical ['kwɪzɪk(ə)l] *adj* (*regard, air*) interrogateur; (*mocking*) railleur, -euse.
quizzically ['kwɪzɪk(ə)lɪ] *adv* d'un air interrogateur; (*mockingly*) d'un air railleur.
quod [kwɒd] *n Arch Br Sl* (*prison*) taule *f*; **in q.,** en taule.
quoin[1] [kɔɪn] *n* **(a)** *Constr* pierre *f* d'angle; coin *m* (*de mur*); (*internal*) encoignure *f*; **(b)** (*wedge*) *MecE* coin *m* (*pour caler*); *Typ* coin, cale *f*.
quoin[2] *vt* caler, coincer.
quoit [kɔɪt] *n* (*game*) palet *m*; **to play (at) quoits,** jouer au palet.
quorate ['kwɔːreɪt] *adj Fml* **to be q.,** être en nombre.
quorum ['kwɔːrəm] *n* quorum *m*; **to have a q.,** être en nombre; **to form a q.,** constituer un quorum.
quota ['kwəʊtə] *n* (*share*) quote-part *f*, *pl* quotes-parts, quotité *f*; (*stipulated quantity, number*) contingent *m*, quota *m*; **import/export quotas,** contingents d'importation/d'exportation; **to apportion** *or* **fix quotas for import,** contingenter une importation, déterminer les contingents d'importation; **I've had my q. of bad luck,** j'ai eu ma dose de malchance; **we've had more than our q. of rain recently,** nous avons eu plus que notre quota *ou* dose de pluie dernièrement.
quotable ['kwəʊtəb(ə)l] *adj* **(a)** (*able to be quoted*) rapportable; **a very q. phrase,** une expression qui se prête bien à citation; **(b)** *St Exch* cotable.
quotation [kwəʊ'teɪʃən] *n* **(a)** citation *f* (*empruntée à un auteur etc*); *Typ* **q. marks,** guillemets *mpl*; **to put a word in q. marks,** mettre un mot entre guillemets; **(b)** *Com* prix *m*; (*for repair work etc*) devis *m*; *St Exch* cotation *f*, cote *f*, cours *m*, prix *m*; *Ind* **q. for plant,** prix pour matériel; *St Exch* **stock admitted to q.,** valeurs admises à la cote officielle; **to ask for a q.,** (*for proposed work*) demander un prix *ou* un devis; **they gave me a q. of £500,** ils m'ont donné un prix *ou* fait un devis de 500 livres.
quote[1] [kwəʊt] *n F* **(a)** citation *f*; **a q. from Shakespeare,** une citation de Shakespeare; **(b) quotes,** guillemets *mpl*; **in quotes,** entre guillemets; **(c)** *Com* = **QUOTATION (b)**.
quote[2] **1** *vt* **(a)** citer (*un auteur, un passage*); alléguer, citer (*une autorité, une preuve*); **to q. from an author/a book,** tirer une citation *ou* des citations d'un auteur/d'un livre; **she said q. ...,** et voici exactement ce qu'elle a dit ...; **his 'friends' q. unquote,** ses amis entre guillemets; **can I q. you on that?,** est-ce que je puis vous citer?; **don't q. me but ...,** ce n'est pas encore officiel *ou* définitif mais ...; **to q. s.o. as an example,** citer qn pour *ou* en exemple; *Admin Com* **in reply please q. this number,** prière de rappeler ce numéro dans toute correspondance ultérieure; **(b)** *Com* établir, faire (*un prix*); *St Exch* coter (*une valeur*); **they quoted me £500 for the work,** ils m'ont fait un devis de 500 livres pour ce travail; *St Exch* **stock officially quoted,** valeur admise à la cote officielle.
2 *vi Com* donner un prix, donner un devis.
quoth [kwəʊθ] *vt Arch* **no, q. I,** non, dis-je.
quotient ['kwəʊʃənt] *n Math* quotient *m*; *Phy* **intelligence q.,** quotient intellectuel.
qv [kjuː'viː] (*abbr* **quod vide**) cf.
qwerty ['kwɜːtɪ] *n* **q. keyboard,** clavier *m* qwerty.

R

R, r [ɑːr] **1** *n* (la lettre) R, r *m*; *Fig* **the three R's** (*Reading, (w)Riting and (a)Rithmetic*), l'enseignement *m* primaire. **2** *adj Am Cin abbr* **Restricted (to persons over 17)**.

rabbet ['ræbɪt] *n Carp* feuillure *f*, rainure *f*.

rabbi ['ræbaɪ] *n Rel* rabbin *m*; **chief r.**, grand rabbin.

rabbinic(al) [ræ'bɪnɪk, -ɪk(ə)l] *adj* rabbinique.

rabbit ['ræbɪt] *n* **(a)** (*also fur*) lapin *m*; *Fig* **they breed like rabbits,** ils se reproduisent comme des lapins; **to produce a r. out of a hat,** (*of conjuror*) faire sortir un lapin d'un chapeau; *Fig* trouver une solution miracle; **to run like a scared r.,** courir comme un lapin; **buck r.,** lapin mâle; **doe r.,** lapine *f*; **young r.,** lapereau *m*; **wild r.,** lapin de garenne; *Am Fig F* **r. ears,** (*TV aerial*) antenne *f* portative; *Pej F Hum* **r. food,** crudités *fpl*; **I'm fed up with all this r. food,** avec toutes ces salades j'ai l'impression d'être un lapin; **r.'s foot** *or* **paw,** (*lucky charm*) patte *f* de lapin; **r. hole,** terrier *m* de lapin; **r. hutch,** (*also Fig*) clapier *m ou* cage *f* à lapin; *Boxing etc* **r. punch,** coup *m* du lapin; **r. warren,** terrier *m*; *Fig* labyrinthe *m*;
(b) *Culin* **stewed r.,** ragoût *m* de lapin;
(c) *Sp* (*pacemaker*) lièvre *m*;
(d) *Old-fashioned Fig Sp* nullard *m*.

►**rabbit on** *vi Br F* parler pour ne rien dire; **she rabbited on to us about her son-in-law all evening,** elle nous a débité toute la soirée des histoires sur son beau-fils; **do stop rabbiting on,** arrête ton char; **what is he rabbiting on about?,** qu'est-ce qu'il raconte?

rabbiting ['ræbɪtɪŋ] *n* **to go r.,** faire la chasse au lapin, chasser le lapin.

rabble ['ræb(ə)l] *n* **(a)** (*disorderly mob*) foule *f*; **(b)** *Pej* (*lower classes*) **the r.,** la populace, la masse, *Old-fashioned* la canaille; **r. rouser,** agitateur, -trice; **r. rousing,** incitation *f* à la révolte; **r.-rousing speech,** discours *m* qui incite à la révolte.

Rabelaisian [ræbə'leɪzɪən] *adj* (*humour etc*) rabelaisien.

rabid ['ræbɪd] *adj* **(a)** *Vet* (*dog etc*) enragé; **(b)** *Fig* (*socialist etc*) enragé, fanatique; (*hatred*) farouche.

rabies ['reɪbiːz] *n Vet* rage *f*; **the dog is a r. carrier,** le chien est porteur de la rage; **r. vaccine,** vaccin *m* contre la rage.

RAC [ɑːreɪ'siː] *n Br Aut abbr* **Royal Automobile Club**.

raccoon [rə'kuːn] *n* (*animal*) raton laveur; **r. skin hat,** toque *f* en raton laveur.

race[1] [reɪs] *n* **(a)** *Sp* course *f*; **it's anybody's r.,** les chances sont égales; **there is a r. meeting at Newmarket tomorrow,** on court demain à Newmarket, il y a des courses demain à Newmarket; **a r. against time,** une course contre la montre; *Pol* **the arms r.,** la course aux armements; **bicycle r.,** course de vélos; **boat r.,** régates *fpl*; **dog r.,** course de lévriers; **horse r.,** course de chevaux; **relay r.,** (course de) relais *m*; **hundred metres r.,** course sur cent mètres, un cent mètres; *Horseracing* **r. card,** programme *m* des courses;
(b) (*channel for water*) canal *m*; **mill r.,** bief *m* d'un moulin;
(c) (*tide*) raz *m*, ras *m*;
(d) *Tech* (*for ball bearings etc*) **ball r.,** chemin *m* de roulement à billes;
(e) *Horseracing* **the races,** les courses *fpl*; **to go to the races,** aller aux courses; **he loves the races,** c'est un passionné des courses.

race[2] **1** *vi* **(a)** (*move quickly*) (*of person, animal*) courir à toute vitesse, galoper; **to r. for a bus/train,** galoper pour attraper un bus/train; **to r. down the street,** dévaler la rue à toute vitesse; **she raced to answer the door,** elle se précipita pour ouvrir la porte; **the ambulance raced to the scene of the accident,** l'ambulance fonça sur les lieux de l'accident; **to r. up the stairs,** monter les escaliers quatre à quatre; **easy, don't r. so!,** doucement, c'est pas la course!; **he raced through his meal,** il a avalé son repas à toute vitesse; **the horse raced towards the winning post,** le cheval galopait vers la ligne d'arrivée; **the weekend just raced by,** le weekend a passé très vite; **the work is racing ahead,** le travail avance très vite; **the clouds are racing across the sky,** les nuages filent dans le ciel;
(b) *Sp* (*of cyclist, driver*) participer à une épreuve de vitesse; (*of jockey*) monter; (*of athlete, horse*) courir; *Horseracing* (*of owner*) faire courir des chevaux;
(c) (*of engine*) s'emballer;
(d) (*of pulse*) être rapide; **my heart is racing,** mon cœur bat la chamade.
2 *vt* **(a)** (*against person, thing*) faire la course avec (*qn etc*); **I'll r. you home!,** le premier arrivé à la maison a gagné!; **he raced me round the block,** il a fait la course avec moi autour du pâté de maisons; **the car is racing the bus to the traffic lights,** la voiture fait la course avec le bus pour arriver la première aux feux de signalisation;
(b) (*enter for races*) faire courir (*un cheval*);
(c) (*transport quickly*) **he raced me to the airport** il m'emmena à l'aéroport à toute vitesse;
(d) *Aut* emballer (*le moteur*).

race[3] *n* (*species*) race *f*; **the human r.,** la race humaine; **r. relations,** relations interraciales; **r. riot,** émeute raciale.

racecourse ['reɪskɔːs] *n* champ *m* de courses, hippodrome *m*, turf *m*.

racegoer ['reɪsgəʊər] *n* turfiste *mf*.

racehorse ['reɪshɔːs] *n* cheval *m* de course.

raceme [ræ'siːm] *n Bot* grappe *f*.

racer ['reɪsər] *n* **(a)** (*person*) coureur, -euse; **(b)** cheval *m ou* vélo *m ou* voiture *f ou* moto *f* de course; *Nau* yacht *m* de course, racer *m*.

racetrack ['reɪstræk] *n* **(a)** (*for cars*) circuit *m*; **(b)** (*for bikes*) piste *f*; **(c)** *Horseracing* champ *m* de courses, hippodrome *m*.

raceway ['reɪsweɪ] *n* **(a)** (*channel for water*) canal *m*; **(b)** *esp Am El* conduite *f* pour câbles; **(c)** (*in car racing*) circuit *m*; **(d)** *esp Am Horseracing* champ *m* de courses, hippodrome *m*; **(e)** *esp Am Tech* chemin *m* de roulement à billes.

racial ['reɪʃəl] *adj* (*discrimination, prejudice*) racial; **r. slur,** propos *mpl* racistes.

racialism ['reɪʃəlɪz(ə)m] *n* racisme *m*.

racialist ['reɪʃəlɪst] *adj & n* raciste *mf*.

racially ['reɪʃəlɪ] *adv* **r. biased policy,** politique *f* de discrimination raciale; **they were r. discriminated against,** ils ont souffert de discrimination raciale; **a r. slanted article,** un article à tendance raciste.

raciness ['reɪsɪnɪs] *n* **(a)** (*of writing, style*) piquant *m*, verve *f*; **(b)** (*of story, joke*) grivoiserie *f*.

racing ['reɪsɪŋ] **1** *n* **(a)** course *f*; **motor r.,** la course automobile; **(b)** *Horseracing* les courses *fpl* (de chevaux), hippisme *m*, turf *m*; **(c)** *Aut* emballement *m* (du moteur); **(d)** (*of heart*) palpitations *fpl*. **2** *adj* **(a)** **r. bicycle/car,** vélo *m*/voiture *f* de course; **r. colours,** couleurs *fpl* de l'écurie; **r. driver,** coureur *m* automobile, pilote *m* de courses; **r. man,** turfiste *m*; **r. pigeon,** pigeon voyageur de compétition; **r. stable,** écurie *f* de courses; **(b)** **r. engine,** moteur emballé *ou* qui s'emballe; **(c)** **r. pulse,** pouls élevé; **a r. heart may be a warning sign of a heart attack,** avoir des palpitations peut être un signal avant-coureur d'une crise cardiaque.

racism ['reɪsɪz(ə)m] *n* racisme *m*.

racist ['reɪsɪst] *adj & n* raciste *mf*.

rack[1] [ræk] *n* (*only in the phrase*) **to go to r. and ruin,** aller à la ruine; (*of house etc*) se délabrer; (*of health, economy, business*) se détériorer.

rack[2] *n* **(a)** *Agr* (*for hay etc*) râtelier *m*; (*sectioned*) casier *m*; (*set of shelves*) étagère *f*; **bicycle r.,** (*for luggage*) porte-bagages *m inv*; (*for storage*) râtelier pour deux roues; *Mil Av* **bomb r.,** râtelier à bombes; **bottle r.,** (*vertical*) casier à bouteilles; (*horizontal*) porte-bouteilles *m inv*; **coat r.,** portemanteau *m*; **display r.,** présentoir *m*; **letter r.,**

porte-lettres *m inv*; **luggage r.,** porte-bagages; **newspaper r.,** porte-journaux *m inv*; **pipe r.,** râtelier à pipes; **plate r.,** égouttoir *m*; *Aut* **roof r.,** galerie *f*; **toast r.,** porte-toasts *m inv*; **vegetable r.,** casier à légumes; **(b)** *Comptr* châssis *m*; *Tech* crémaillère *f*; **r. and pinion,** crémaillère (et pignon *m*); *Aut* **r. and pinion steering,** direction *f* à crémaillère; *Rail* **r. (and pinion) railway,** chemin *m* de fer à crémaillère; **(c)** *Culin* **r. of lamb,** carré *m* d'agneau.

rack³ *n* **(a)** *Hist* chevalet *m* (de torture); **(b)** *Fig* **to be on the r.,** être à la torture, être au supplice; **to keep s.o. on the r.,** faire mourir qn à petit feu.

rack⁴ *vt* **(a)** (*of disease, pain etc*) tourmenter, torturer (*qn*), faire souffrir le martyre à (*qn*); **to be racked with pain,** être tourmenté de douleur; **racking pain,** douleur atroce *ou* déchirante; **(b) to r. one's brains,** se creuser la tête.

►**rack up** *vtsep* accumuler (*des points*).

racket¹ ['rækɪt] *n* **(a)** raquette *f* (*de tennis etc*); **r. cover,** housse *f* de raquette; **r. press,** presse-raquette *m*, presse *f*; **(b)** (*game*) **rackets,** jeu *m* de paume.

racket² *n F* **(a)** (*falling plates etc*) fracas *m*; (*uproar*) tapage *m*, vacarme *m*; (*discordant sounds*) tintamarre *m*; **to make a r.,** faire du boucan; **(b)** (*criminal activity*) escroquerie *f*, racket *m*, supercherie *f*; **it's a r.,** c'est une escroquerie *ou* du vol; **(c)** *Hum* (*occupation*) métier *m*.

racketeer [rækɪ'tɪər] *n* criminel *m*, racketter *m*, racketteur *m*.

racketeering [rækɪ'tɪərɪŋ] *n* racket *m*.

rack-rent ['rækrent] *n* loyer excessif *ou* exorbitant.

racoon [rə'kuːn] *n* (*animal*) raton laveur.

racquet ['rækɪt] *n* = **RACKET¹**.

racy ['reɪsɪ] *adj* **(a)** (*description, writing*) piquant; **r. story,** anecdote corsée *ou* croustillante *ou* osée; **(b)** (*person etc*) vif, plein de verve; (*style*) plein de verve.

rad *n abbr* **(a)** (*radiation*) rd *f*; **(b)** *esp Am* (*heating system*) radiateur *m*.

RADA ['rɑːdə] *n Br Art abbr* **Royal Academy of Dramatic Art**.

radar ['reɪdɑːr] *n* radar *m*; **ground r.,** radar au sol; **r. operator,** radariste *mf*, opérateur, -trice radar; **r. screen,** écran *m* (de) radar; **r. station,** station *f* radar; *Aut* **r. trap,** contrôle *m* radar.

raddled ['ræd(ə)ld] *adj* (*face*) (*worn-out*) ravagé; *Old-fashioned* (*over made-up*) peinturluré.

radial ['reɪdɪəl] **1** *adj* **(a)** *Tech Math etc* radial; *Aut* **r. engine,** moteur *m* en étoile; **r. (ply) tyre,** pneu radial; **r. road,** radiale *f*; **(b)** *Anat* (*artery etc*) radial. **2** *n* (*tyre*) pneu radial.

radially ['reɪdɪəlɪ] *adv* radialement.

radiance ['reɪdɪəns] *n* **(a)** (*of light, sun*) rayonnement *m*; **(b)** (*of beauty, smile*) éclat m.

radiant ['reɪdɪənt] **1** *adj* **(a)** (*light, sun*) radiant, rayonnant; **r. energy,** énergie *f* de rayonnement; *Phys* **r. heat,** chaleur radiante *ou* rayonnante; **r. heating,** chauffage *m* à rayonnement; **r. point,** point radiant; **(b)** (*beauty, smile etc*) radieux, rayonnant; **a woman of r. beauty,** une femme d'une beauté éblouissante; **the bride was r.,** la mariée était radieuse; **to be r. with joy,** rayonner de joie. **2** *n* **(a)** *Phys* point radiant; **(b)** (*of heater*) foyer *m* de rayonnement; **(c)** *Astron* radiant *m*.

radiantly ['reɪdɪəntlɪ] *adv* radieusement; **r. happy,** rayonnant de bonheur.

radiate ['reɪdɪeɪt] **1** *vi* (*from centre*) rayonner; (*of heat*) irradier. **2** *vt* (*heat, light*) émettre; **to r. happiness,** rayonner de bonheur.

radiation [reɪdɪ'eɪʃən] *n* **(a)** (*radioactivity*) radiation *f*; **to be exposed to r.,** être exposé à des radiations; *Med* **r. sickness,** mal *m* des rayons; **r. therapy,** radiothérapie *f*; **(b)** (*heat*) rayonnement *m*; **(c)** (*light*) irradiation *f*; **ultraviolet r.,** rayons ultraviolets.

radiator ['reɪdɪeɪtər] *n* **(a)** (*for heating*) radiateur *m*; *Can* calorifère *m*; **(b)** *Aut* radiateur *m*; **r. cap,** bouchon *m* du radiateur; **r. grille,** calandre *f*.

radical ['rædɪk(ə)l] **1** *adj* **(a)** (*opinion, policy etc*) radical, -aux; **to make a r. alteration in sth,** changer qch radicalement; **(b)** *Ling* (*word*) radical, primitif; *Math* (*axis, centre*) radical; *Bot* (*leaf*) radical. **2** *n* **(a)** *Pol* radical, -ale; **(b)** *Ch Ling Math* radical *m*.

radicalism ['rædɪkəlɪz(ə)m] *n Pol* radicalisme *m*.

radically ['rædɪklɪ] *adv* radicalement, fondamentalement.

radicle ['rædɪk(ə)l] *n* **(a)** *Bot* (*embryo*) radicule *f*; (*root*) radicelle *f*; **(b)** *Ch* radical *m*.

radio¹ ['reɪdɪəʊ] *n* **(a)** poste *m* (de radio), radio *f*; **to put** *or* **switch** *or* **turn the r. on/off,** allumer/éteindre la radio; **she was on the r. last night,** elle est passée à la radio hier soir; **portable r.,** poste portatif, radio portative; **r. alarm,** radio-réveil *m*, *pl* radio-réveils; **r. announcer,** présentateur, -trice de radio; **r. broadcast,** émission *f* de radio; **r. cassette,** radio-cassette *f*; **R. Moscow,** Radio Moscou; **r. producer,** producteur, -trice d'émissions de radio; **r. set,** poste *m* (de radio), radio *f*; **r. station,** station *f* de radio;

(b) (*service, system*) **the French r.,** la radiodiffusion française;

(c) *Telecom* radio(télégraphie) *f*; (*in taxi, ship etc*) radio *f*; **to communicate by r.,** communiquer par radio; **to send a message by r.,** envoyer un message radio; **ship-to-shore r.,** liaison *f* radio navire-sol; **r. beacon,** radiobalise *f*, radiophare *m*; **r. communication,** contact *m* radio, radiocommunications *fpl*; **r. engineer,** ingénieur *m* radio; **r. frequency,** radiofréquence *f*; **r. link,** liaison *f* radio; **r. mast,** antenne *f* (radio); **r. operator,** (*on plane*) radio *m*; (*on ship*) radionavigant *m*; **r. receiver,** radiorécepteur *m*; *Nau* **r. room,** poste *m* radio de bord; **r. station,** poste *m* radiotélégraphique; **r. taxi,** radio-taxi *m*, *pl* radio-taxis; **r. transmitter,** (poste) émetteur *m*; *Phys* **r. astronomy,** radioastronomie *f*; **r. spectrum,** spectre *m* radio *ou* radioélectrique *ou* des fréquences radioélectriques; **r. telescope,** radiotélescope *m*; **r. waves,** ondes hertziennes.

radio² **1** *vt* envoyer par (la) radio; **to r. information,** envoyer des renseignements par radio; **to r. a person/ship,** contacter une personne/un bateau par radio; **to r. one's position,** signaler sa position par radio. **2** *vi* **to r. for assistance** *or* **help,** demander de l'aide par radio.

radioactive [reɪdɪəʊ'æktɪv] *adj* radioactif; **r. dust,** poussières radioactives; **r. fallout,** retombées radioactives; **r. material,** matière radioactive; **r. substance,** substance radioactive; **r. waste,** déchets radioactifs.

radioactivity [reɪdɪəʊæk'tɪvɪtɪ] *n* radioactivité *f*.

radiocarbon [reɪdɪəʊ'kɑːbən] *n* radiocarbone *m*, carbone *m* 14; **r. dating,** datation *f* au radiocarbone *ou* au carbone 14.

radio-controlled [reɪdɪəʊkən'trəʊld] *adj* télécommandé.

radiogram ['reɪdɪəʊgræm] *n* **1** *Rad* radiophono *f*, *F* radio *m*. **2** *Med* = **RADIOGRAPH**.

radiograph ['reɪdɪəʊgrɑːf] *n Med etc* radiographie *f*.

radiographer [reɪdɪ'ɒgrəfər] *n Med etc* radiographe *mf*.

radiography [reɪdɪ'ɒgrəfɪ] *n Med* radiographie *f*.

radioisotope [reɪdɪəʊ'aɪsətəʊp] *n* radio-isotope *m*.

radiological [reɪdɪəʊ'lɒdʒɪk(ə)l] *adj* radiologique.

radiologist [reɪdɪ'ɒlədʒɪst] *n Med* radiologue *mf*.

radiology [reɪdɪ'ɒlədʒɪ] *n Med* radiologie *f*.

radio-pager [reɪdɪəʊ'peɪdʒər] *n* récepteur *m* d'appel *ou* de poche.

radioscopic [reɪdɪəʊ'skɒpɪk] *adj Med etc* radioscopique.

radioscopy [reɪdɪ'ɒskəpɪ] *n Med etc* radioscopie *f*.

radiotelegram [reɪdɪəʊ'telɪgræm] *n* radiotélégramme *m*, radiogramme *m*, *F* radio *m*.

radiotelephone [reɪdɪəʊ'telɪfəʊn] *n* radiotéléphone *m*.

radiotelephony [reɪdɪəʊtɪ'lefənɪ] *n* radiotéléphonie *f*, *Old-fashioned* téléphonie *f* sans fil, T.S.F. *f*.

radiotherapist [reɪdɪəʊ'θerəpɪst] *n* radiothérapeute *mf*.

radiotherapy [reɪdɪəʊ'θerəpɪ] *n* radiothérapie *f*.

radish ['rædɪʃ] *n* radis *m*.

radium ['reɪdɪəm] *n Ch* radium *m*; **r. treatment,** radiumthérapie *f*.

radius, *pl* **-ii** ['reɪdɪəs, -ɪaɪ] *n* **(a)** (*of circle*) rayon *m*; *Av* rayon (d'action), autonomie *f*; **within a r. of ten miles,** dans un rayon de dix milles; **(b)** (*of crane*) portée *f*; **(c)** *Anat* radius *m*.

radix, *pl* **-ices** ['reɪdɪks, -ɪsiːz] *n* **(a)** *Math* (*logarithms etc*) base *f*; **(b)** *Ling* radical *m*.

RAF [ɑːreɪ'ef] *n Br Mil* (*abbr* **Royal Air Force**) ≈ armée *f* de l'air.

raffia ['ræfɪə] *n Bot* raphia *m*; **r. mat,** tapis *m* en raphia.

raffish ['ræfɪʃ] *adj* (*look*) canaille; **to have r. friends,** avoir des amis qui mènent une vie dissolue *ou* de patachon.

raffle¹ ['ræf(ə)l] *n* tombola *f*; **I won it in a r.,** je l'ai gagné dans une tombola; **r. ticket,** billet *m* de tombola.

raffle² *vt* (*often with* **off**) mettre (*qch*) en tombola; **they're raffling off a car,** le lot de la tombola est une voiture.

raft¹ [rɑːft] *n* **(a)** radeau *m*; **(inflatable) life r.,** canot *m* (pneumatique) de sauvetage; **(b) timber r.,** *Am* **lumber r.,** train *m* de bois *ou* de flottage; **(c)** *Am Fig* (*great quantity*) **I have a r. of papers on my desk,** j'ai une montagne de papiers sur mon bureau.

raft² **1** *vt* (*wood*) flotter en trains; **they rafted the logs to the paper mill,** ils ont flotté les troncs jusqu'à la papeterie. **2** *vi* **to r. across the river,** traverser le fleuve sur un radeau.

rafter¹ ['rɑːftər] *n Constr* chevron *m*; **main r.,** arbalétrier *m*; **the rafters,** le chevronnage.

rafter² *vt* **a room with a raftered ceiling,** une pièce à poutres apparentes.

rag¹ [ræg] *n* **(a)** (*piece of cloth*) chiffon *m*; **any mention of his ex-wife is like a red r. to a bull,** dès qu'on parle de son ex-femme, il voit rouge; **to chew the r.,** (*discuss complainingly*) râler (**about,** contre); *Fig* **to feel like a wet r.,** être lessivé *ou* ramollo *ou* vidé; **r. book,** livre *m* en tissu; **r. content,** (*of paper*) pourcentage *m* de peille; **r. doll,** poupée *f* de chiffon; **r. paper,** papier *m* à base de peille; **r. picker,** chiffonnier *m*; **r. rug,** catalogne *f*;
(b) (*clothing*) guenille *f*, lambeau *m*; *Hum* **I've had this r. for years,** ça fait des années que j'ai cette guenille; **r. trade,** la confection; **rags (and tatters),** haillons *mpl*, guenilles, loques *fpl*; **to be in rags,** être en guenilles *ou* en haillons; **to go from rags to riches,** passer de la pauvreté à la richesse; **a rags to riches story,** (*through own achievement*) l'histoire d'une réussite; (*through fate, luck*) un conte de fées; **to put one's glad rags on,** se mettre sur son trente et un;
(c) *F Pej* (*newspaper*) torchon *m; **you don't read that r., do you?,*** tu ne lis pas ce torchon!; **the local r.,** le journal du coin.

rag² *n* **(a)** (*joking etc*) blague *f*, canular *m*, farce *f*; **I did it for** *or* **as a r.,** c'était une blague; **(b) students' r.,** carnaval *m* d'étudiants; **the students collected a lot of money for the hospital on r. day,** les étudiants ont ramassé beaucoup d'argent pour l'hôpital lors du carnaval.

rag³ *vt* (-gg-) **(a)** (*tease*) taquiner (*qn*) (**about,** sur); **(b)** (*teacher etc*) chahuter, *F* asticoter, *F* mettre en boîte.

raga ['rægə] *n Mus* raga *m*.

ragamuffin ['rægəmʌfɪn] *n* **(a)** (*child*) gamin *m* des rues; **you little r.!,** petit polisson!; **(b)** (*person in rags*) gueux, -euse.

rag-and-bone [rægən'bəʊn] *adj* **r.-and-b. man,** chiffonnier *m*.

ragbag ['rægbæg] *n* **(a)** *Fig* (*of things, ideas etc*) collection *f* hétéroclite; **(b)** (*bag*) sac *m* à chiffons.

rage¹ [reɪdʒ] *n* **(a)** (*of person*) colère *f*, fureur *f*, rage *f*; **to be in a r.,** être furieux *ou* fou de rage; **to get** *or* **fly into a r.,** se mettre en colère, piquer une colère; **to have a fit of r.,** avoir un accès de fureur; **to weep with r.,** pleurer de rage; **(b)** *F* **to be all the r.,** (*of dance, music etc*) faire fureur; **it's all the r.,** c'est la grande mode, ça fait fureur.

rage² *vi* **(a)** (*of person*) être furieux, rager; **to r. against** *or* **at s.o.,** être furieux *ou* tempêter contre qn; **(b)** (*of river, ocean*) être déchaîné *ou* démonté *ou* en furie; **(c)** (*of epidemic, war*) régner, sévir; (*of battle, fire, storm*) faire rage; (*of wind*) souffler avec rage *ou* en tempête.

ragged ['rægɪd] *adj* (*garment etc*) en lambeaux, en loques; (*person*) en haillons, en guenilles, déguenillé; **a shirt with r. cuffs,** une chemise à manchettes élimées; *Mus* **the execution is r.,** l'exécution manque d'ensemble; *F* **to run oneself r.,** s'éreinter; *Typ* **r. right/left,** non-justifié à droite/à gauche; *Typ* **to print sth r.,** imprimer qch sans justification; *Bot* **r. robin,** nielle *f* des prés; **r. vegetation,** broussailles *fpl*.

raggle-taggle [ræg(ə)l'tæg(ə)l] *adj* dépareillé; **a r.-t. army,** une armée hétéroclite.

raging ['reɪdʒɪŋ] **1** *adj* (*person*) furieux, en colère; **to be in a r. temper,** être furieux; **r. fever/thirst,** fièvre/soif ardente; **r. sea,** mer déchaînée *ou* démontée *ou* en furie; **r. toothache,** rage *f* de dents. **2** *n* (*of person*) colère *f*, fureur *f*, rage *f*; (*of sea, wind*) fureur *f*.

raglan ['ræglən] **1** *n* **r. (coat),** raglan *m*. **2** *adj* raglan *inv*; **r. sleeves,** manches *fpl* raglan; **r. sweater,** pull *m* raglan.

ragman, *pl* **-men** ['rægmən, -men] *n* chiffonnier *m*.

ragout ['ræguː] *n Culin* ragoût *m*.

ragtag ['rægtæg] *n* **the r. and bobtail,** la racaille.

ragtime ['rægtaɪm] *n Mus* ragtime *m*.

ragweed ['rægwiːd] *n Bot* herbe *f* à poux.

ragwort ['rægwɜːt] *n Bot* séneçon *m*, *F* herbe *f* de saint-Jacques.

rah-rah ['rɑːrɑː] *adj Sp esp Am* enthousiaste; *Fig* **he's very r.-r. about the President,** c'est un fervent admirateur du Président.

raid¹ [reɪd] *n* (*on bank etc*) hold-up *m*, braquage *m*; (*by police*) descente *f*, rafle *f*; *Mil Av Nau* raid *m* (**on,** sur, contre); *Mil Av* **bombing r.,** bombardement aérien; **daylight/night r.,** attaque *f* (aérienne) de jour/de nuit; *St Exch* **dawn r.,** tentative *f* surprise de rachat.

raid² *vt* (*attack*) braquer (*une banque*); (*by police*) faire une descente *ou* une rafle dans (*un bar*); *Mil* faire un raid *ou* des raids; **the terrorists raided the presidential palace,** les terroristes ont fait un raid sur le palais présidentiel; **the soldiers raided the ammunitions store,** les soldats ont fait un raid sur les munitions dans le magasin; *Fig* **the children raided the fridge,** les enfants ont fait une razzia dans le frigo.

raider ['reɪdər] *n* (*of banks*) braqueur *m* de banques; *Mil* (*boat*) raider *m*; (*plane*) bombardier *m*; *Fin* raider *m*; *Mil* raider, commando *m*.

rail¹ [reɪl] *n* **(a)** (*metal or wooden fence or gate*) barre *f*;
(b) (*for protection, support*) (*escalator, stairway*) main courante; (*balcony*) balustrade *f*; (*banister*) rampe *f*; *Nau* lisse *f*; **guard-r.,** garde-fou *m*; **hand-r.,** barre *f* d'appui;
(c) (*for hanging things*) **curtain r.,** tringle *f* à rideaux; **picture r.,** cimaise *f*; **towel r.,** porte-serviettes *m inv*;
(d) *Rail* (*track*) rail *m*; **conductor** *or* **live r.,** rail conducteur *ou* sous tension; **to travel by r.,** voyager en train; **free on r.,** prix *m* franco-wagon; **r. transport,** transport *m* par chemin de fer *ou* train; **r. traffic,** trafic *m* ferroviaire; **r. workers,** (*general*) employés *mpl* de chemin de fer; (*for track, rolling stock*) cheminots *mpl*;
(e) the rails, *Horseracing* corde *f*; *Nau* bastingage *m*, garde-corps *m inv*, rambarde *f*; **he was pushed to the rails by the other jockeys,** il a été forcé de tenir la corde par les autres jockeys; *Rail* **to jump** *or* **leave the rails,** dérailler, sortir des rails; *Fig* **to go off the rails,** dérailler, s'écarter du bon sens; (*morally*) s'écarter du droit chemin; **to get the economy back on the rails,** remettre l'économie sur les rails; **I did my best to get him back on the rails after his breakdown,** j'ai fait de mon mieux pour le remettre sur pieds après sa dépression nerveuse.

rail² *n* (*bird*) râle *m*; **water r.,** râle d'eau.

►**rail at, rail against** *vipo* s'en prendre à (*qn*); **to r. at fate,** s'en prendre au sort.

►**rail in** *vtsep* clôturer, entourer d'une clôture.

►**rail off** *vtsep* fermer avec une clôture *ou* une barrière; **the path down to the beach was railed off after the accident,** le chemin qui mène à la plage a été fermé après l'accident.

railcar ['reɪlkɑːr] *n Rail* autorail *m*.

railcard ['reɪlkɑːd] *n Br* carte *f* d'abonnement (ferroviaire).

railhead ['reɪlhed] *n Rail etc* tête *f* de ligne.

railing¹ ['reɪlɪŋ] *n* (*also* **railings**) **(a)** (*barrier*) (*placed horizontally*) clôture *f* à claire-voie; (*of metal*) grille *f*; (*of wood*) palissade *f*; **iron railings,** grille; **(b)** (*in dangerous place*) garde-fou *m*, garde-corps *m inv*; **(c)** (*for support*) (*staircase*) rampe *f*; (*balcony*) balustrade *f*.

railing² *n* (*complaints*) invectives *fpl* (**at, against,** contre).

raillery ['reɪlərɪ] *n* (*teasing*) raillerie *f*.

railman, *pl* **-men** ['reɪlmən] *n* = **RAILWAYMAN**.

railroad¹ ['reɪlrəʊd] *n US* chemin *m* de fer; **to travel by r.,** voyager en chemin de fer; **underground r.,** métro *m*; *Am Hist* réseau clandestin de libération des esclaves; **r. car,** wagon *m*.

railroad² *vt* **(a)** *F* (*force acceptance of*) **to r. a bill through Parliament,** imposer un projet de loi au Parlement; **(b)** *F* (*force into action*) **to r. s.o. into doing sth,** faire pression sur qn pour qu'il fasse qch; **to be railroaded into doing sth,** être forcé à faire qch; **I don't want to r. you, but ...,** je ne voudrais pas te forcer mais ...; **stop railroading me!,** arrête de faire pression sur moi!; **she was railroaded into this job,** on a fait pression sur elle pour qu'elle prenne ce poste; **(c)** *esp Am F Jur* (*convict*) (*by false charges*) condamner (*qn*) à l'aide de fausses inculpations; (*hastily*) juger sommairement (*qn*); **(d)** *Am* (*transport*) transporter (*qch*) par chemin de fer.

railway ['reɪlweɪ] *n Br & Can* (*system*) chemin *m* de fer; (*track*) voie ferrée; **to travel by r.,** voyager en chemin de fer; **to work on the railway(s),** être employé des chemins de fer; **Canadian National Railways,** Chemins de fer nationaux du Canada; **underground r.,** métro *m*; *US Hist* réseau clandestin de libération des esclaves; **r. engineer/guide/strike/worker/yard,** ingénieur *m*/indicateur *m*/grève *f*/employé *m*/dépôt *m* des chemins de fer; **r. bridge,** pont *m* ferroviaire; **r. carriage,** voiture *f* de train; **r. crossing,** (*over road*) passage *m* à niveau; **r. cutting,** traversée *f* en déblai; **r. embankment,** remblai *m*; **r. engine,** (*Am* = **locomotive**) locomotive *f*; **r. line,** (*system*) ligne *f* de chemin de fer; (*track*) voie (ferrée); **to cross the r. line,** traverser la voie (ferrée); **r. network** *or* **system,** réseau *m* ferroviaire *ou* de chemin de fer; **r. signal,** signal *m* ferroviaire; **r. station,** gare *f*; **r. ticket,** billet *m* de train; **r. timetable,** fiche *f* horaire, horaire *m* des chemins de fer; **r. track(s),** voie ferrée.

railwayman, *pl* **-men** ['reɪlweɪmən] *n* (*administrative employee*) employé *m* des chemins de fer; (*technical em-*

ployee) cheminot *m*; *Br* **National Union of Railwaymen,** = syndicat des employés de chemins de fer de Grande-Bretagne.

raiment ['reɪmənt] *n Arch* vêtements *mpl*.

rain[1] [reɪn] *n* **(a)** pluie *f*; **in the r.,** sous la pluie; **it looks like r.,** on dirait qu'il va pleuvoir, le temps est à la pluie; *Br* **it's pouring with r.,** il pleut des cordes *ou* à flots *ou* à seaux *ou* à torrents; **they had some r. during their holiday,** ils ont eu de la pluie pendant leurs vacances; **a river swollen with r., a r.-swollen river,** une rivière gonflée par les pluies; **the rains,** la saison des pluies; **(come) r. or shine,** (*whatever the weather*) qu'il pleuve ou qu'il vente; (*whatever the circumstances*) quoiqu'il arrive; *F* **two days in bed and you'll be as right as r.,** deux jours au lit et tu seras remis; *Fig* **he doesn't have the sense to come in out of the r.,** il n'a pas inventé le fil à couper le beurre; **acid r.,** pluies acides; **driving/fine r.,** pluie battante/fine; **freezing r.,** pluie verglaçante; **heavy r.,** forte *ou* grosse pluie; **light r.,** pluie fine; **r. belt,** zone *f* des pluies; **r. cape,** pèlerine *f*; *Am* **r. check,** (*for sports event*) = billet *m* valable pour une réunion remise à cause du mauvais temps; (*for sales*) = bon *m* qui garantit le prix d'un produit soldé et qui est donné à la suite de l'épuisement des stocks avant la fin de la période des soldes; *Am* **or would you rather take a r. check?,** (*issuing invitation*) ou est-ce que tu préfères remettre ça à plus tard?; **I'll take a r. check on that,** (*replying to invitation*) ça sera pour une autre fois; **r. cloud,** nuage *m* de pluie; **r. dance,** danse *f* de la pluie; **r. gauge,** pluviomètre *m*; **r. hat,** capuche *f*; **r. hood,** capuche *f*; (*attached to anorak, jacket etc*) capuchon *m*; **r. shower,** averse *f*;
(b) *Fig (large quantity)* (*of abuse, blows etc*) pluie *f*.

rain[2] **1** *v impers* pleuvoir; **it rains, it is raining,** il pleut; **it is raining hard,** il pleut à verse; *Br F* **it's raining cats and dogs** il tombe des cordes, il pleut comme vache qui pisse; *Prov* **it never rains but it pours,** (*of misfortune*) un malheur ne vient jamais seul; (*of good fortune*) jamais deux sans trois. **2** *vi* (*of abuse, blows etc*) pleuvoir (**on,** sur). **3** *vt* **to r. gifts/flowers on s.o.,** couvrir qn de cadeaux/fleurs; **to r. blows on s.o.,** rouer qn de coups.

▶**rain down 1** *vi* = **RAIN**[2] **2**. **2** *vtsep* = **RAIN**[2] **3**.

▶**rain off** *vtsep Sp etc* **to be rained off** *or Am* **out,** (*of match etc*) être annulé à cause du mauvais temps.

rainbird ['reɪnbɜːd] *n* pivert *m*, pic-vert *m*, pic vert.

rainbow ['reɪnbəʊ] *n* arc-en-ciel *m*; **all the colours of the r.,** toutes les couleurs de l'arc-en-ciel; **a dress in all the colours of the r.,** une robe arc-en-ciel; *Fig* **to chase rainbows,** se nourrir d'illusions; **r. trout,** truite *f* arc-en-ciel.

raincoat ['reɪnkəʊt] *n* imperméable *m*, *F* imper *m*.

raindrop ['reɪndrɒp] *n* goutte *f* de pluie.

rainfall ['reɪnfɔːl] *n* (*shower*) chute *f* de pluie; (*amount*) précipitations *fpl*; **average r.,** précipitations moyennes, taux *m* de pluviosité; **low/high r.,** précipitations faibles/importantes.

rainforest ['reɪnfɒrɪst] *n* **(tropical) r.,** forêt tropicale humide.

rainless ['reɪnlɪs] *adj* (*day etc*) sans pluie.

rainmaker ['reɪnmeɪkər] *n* (*magician*) faiseur *m* de pluie.

rainmaking ['reɪnmeɪkɪŋ] *adj* (*ritual etc*) pour faire pleuvoir.

rainout ['reɪnaʊt] *n* **(a)** (*pollution, radioactive fallout*) retombées entraînées par la pluie; **(b)** *Am Sp* match annulé à cause du mauvais temps.

rainproof[1] ['reɪnpruːf] *adj* (*coat, fabric etc*) imperméable.

rainproof[2] *vt* imperméabiliser (*un tissu*).

rainstorm ['reɪnstɔːm] *n* pluie torrentielle.

rainwater ['reɪnwɔːtər] *n* eau *f* de pluie.

rainwear ['reɪnweər] *n* (*clothing*) vêtements *mpl* de pluie.

rainy ['reɪnɪ] *adj* (*climate, weather*) pluvieux; **a r. day,** un jour de pluie; **the r. season,** la saison des pluies; **it has been very r. recently,** il a beaucoup plu récemment; *Fig* **to put something by** *or* **keep something for a r. day,** garder une poire pour la soif; *Fig* **she puts ten pounds a week by for a r. day,** elle met dix livres de côté par semaine en cas de besoin.

raise[1] [reɪz] *n* **(a)** *Am* (*pay increase*) augmentation *f* (de salaire); **to get a r.,** être augmenté; **(b)** *Cards* (*poker*) relance *f*; (*bridge*) enchère *f*.

raise[2] *vt* **(a)** (*lift, cause to rise*) lever (*l'ancre, la main, les yeux*); relever (*un voile*); lever, soulever (*un poids*); monter (*un store*); hisser (*un drapeau*); renflouer (*un navire coulé*); **to r. a cloud of dust,** soulever un nuage de poussière; *Th* **to r. the curtain,** lever le rideau; **to r. dough,** faire lever la pâte; **to r. an eyebrow** *or* **one's eyebrows,** (*in disapproval*) froncer les sourcils, sourciller; (*in surprise*) avoir l'air étonné; **he raised an eyebrow at the news,** la nouvelle l'a fait sourciller; **to r. an eyebrow** *or* **eyebrows,** (*in others*) (*in disapproval*) faire sourciller; (*in surprise*) étonner, surprendre; **that will r. a few eyebrows** *or* **an eyebrow or two,** cela va en surprendre plus d'un; **eyebrows were raised yesterday when ...,** il y a eu un mouvement de surprise hier quand ...; **to r. one's fist to s.o.,** menacer qn du poing; **to r. one's glass,** lever son verre (**to s.o.,** à la santé de qn); **to r. one's glass to one's lips,** porter son verre à ses lèvres; **to r. s.o.'s hackles,** hérisser qn; **to r. one's hand to s.o.,** lever la main sur qn; **to r. one's hat to s.o.,** donner un coup de chapeau à qn; *Fig* tirer son chapeau à qn; **to r. one's head,** (*from lowered position*) lever la tête; (*hold erect*) dresser la tête; **to r. oneself to one's knees,** se hisser sur les genoux; **to r. a patient to a sitting position,** soulever un malade pour l'asseoir; *Mil & Fig* **to r. one's sights,** viser plus haut; **to r. standards,** (*of education, morality*) élever le niveau; (*of cleanliness, safety*) améliorer les conditions; **to r. the standard of living,** améliorer le niveau de vie; **to r. s.o.'s hopes,** donner l'espoir à qn; **to r. s.o.'s spirits,** remonter le moral à qn; **to r. the tone** *or* **level of the conversation,** élever le niveau de la conversation; **to r. the tone** *or* **level of the neighbourhood,** rehausser le prestige du quartier; **to r. the rafters,** (*make noise*) faire un foin d'enfer *ou* un boucan de tous les diables; **to r. the roof,** (*make noise*) faire un foin d'enfer *ou* un boucan de tous les diables; (*complain*) faire une scène terrible *ou* de tous les diables;
(b) (*increase in amount*) augmenter (*la production, un salaire*); augmenter, monter (*un prix*); faire monter (*la température*); monter (*la mise*); **to r. production to a maximum,** porter la production au maximum; **to r. the school-leaving age,** prolonger la scolarité; **they've raised the age limit to ...,** l'âge limite est passé à ...; *Fig* **she raised the temperature of the room by her condemnation of party policy,** les esprits se sont échauffés lorsqu'elle a condamné la politique du parti; *Am* **to r. a cheque,** falsifier le montant d'un chèque; *Cards* **I'll r. you ten,** (*at poker*) plus dix; *Math* **to r. a number to the ninth power,** élever un nombre à la puissance neuf;
(c) (*increase in height*) rehausser, surélever (*un parterre*); **to r. (the level of) a wall,** rehausser *ou* surélever un mur; **to r. the level of the ground,** rehausser le niveau du sol; **to r. the ceiling on wage increases,** augmenter le plafond des salaires; **she raised herself to her fullest height,** elle se fit aussi grande que possible;
(d) (*increase in intensity*) **to r. s.o.'s consciousness (of sth),** (*inform*) sensibiliser qn (à qch); (*emphasize*) faire prendre conscience à qn (de qch); **to r. one's voice,** (*speak more loudly*) élever la voix; (*speak in anger*) hausser le ton; **no one raised his voice (to answer** *or* **speak),** personne ne souffla mot;
(e) (*create, produce*) soulever (*un problème, un sujet de discussion*); susciter (*des craintes, des doutes, de la méfiance*); **to r. an objection,** élever *ou* soulever une objection; *F* **to r. hell** *or* **a stink,** (*complain*) faire une scène terrible *ou* de tous les diables; **to r. a blush/laugh,** faire rougir/rire; **to r. a cheer,** (*of people*) crier hourra; (*of announcement, speech etc*) soulever des hourras; **to r. a shout,** (*of people*) pousser un cri; (*of announcement, speech etc*) faire pousser des cris; **to r. a question,** (*make query*) poser une question; **his attitude raises certain questions,** son attitude pose *ou* soulève *ou* suscite certaines questions; **his attitude raises questions about his loyalty,** son attitude remet en question sa loyauté; **to r. a smile,** (*in oneself*) esquisser un sourire; (*in others*) provoquer *ou* faire naître un sourire; **to r. a storm of laughter/protest,** déchaîner *ou* déclencher *ou* soulever une tempête de rires/protestations; **to r. the alarm,** donner *ou* sonner l'alarme; **to r. a loan,** (*of government*) émettre *ou* lancer un emprunt; (*of individual*) faire un emprunt (**on,** sur); **to r. steam,** (*in boiler*) chauffer la chaudière; (*in train*) chauffer la locomotive;
(f) (*collect together*) réunir (*de l'argent*); **to r. an army,** réunir une armée, mettre une armée sur pied; **to r. funds,** (*for charity*) (*of volunteers*) faire une collecte (**for,** pour, au profit de); (*for business, government programme*) se procurer des fonds; **how much (money) did you r. on the car when you sold it?,** combien t'es-tu fait sur la vente de la voiture?; **he wanted a new motorbike but couldn't r. the money,** il voulait une moto neuve mais il n'a pas pu trouver l'argent nécessaire; **to r. taxes,** lever des impôts;
(g) (*erect*) construire (*un édifice, une grange etc*); ériger

(*une statue*);

(h) (*rear, grow*) élever (*des enfants*); élever, faire l'élevage de (*bétail, poulets etc*); cultiver (*du blé, des légumes*);

(i) (*promote*) *Mil & Fig* **to r. s.o. from the ranks,** promouvoir qn; *Mil* **to r. s.o. to the rank of lieutenant,** promouvoir qn lieutenant; **to r. s.o. from the gutter,** tirer qn du caniveau; **to r. s.o. to the peerage,** (*give hereditary title to*) anoblir qn; (*give life title to*) conférer à qn un titre de pair;

(j) (*contact*) (*by telephone*) joindre, contacter (*qn*); (*by radio*) entrer en contact (radio) avec (*un navire*); *Nau* **to r. land,** apercevoir la terre;

(k) (*awaken, rouse*) **to r. Cain,** (*make noise*) faire un foin d'enfer *ou* un boucan de tous les diables; (*complain*) faire une scène terrible *ou* de tous les diables; **to r. the devil,** (*complain*) faire une scène terrible *ou* de tous les diables; **to r. s.o. from (his** *or* **her) bed,** faire lever qn, sortir qn du lit; **to r. s.o. from the dead,** ressusciter qn des morts; **to r. a ghost,** faire apparaître un fantôme; **to r. a spirit,** évoquer un esprit;

(l) (*stir up*) exciter, soulever (*un peuple*); soulever (*une rébellion*);

(m) (*end*) lever (*un blocus, un embargo, un siège*).

►**raise up** *vtsep* lever, soulever; **she raised herself up out of her chair,** elle se leva de son fauteuil.

raised [reɪzd] *adj* **(a)** (*lifted*) (*arm*) levé; (*head*) dressé; **r. voices,** des éclats de voix; **to say in a r. voice,** dire d'une voix forte; **(b)** (*elevated*) (*deck, flowerbed, wall*) surélevé; **(c)** (*embossed*) (*design, letter, motif*) en relief; **(d)** *Am Culin* au levain.

raiser ['reɪzər] *n* (*breeder*) (*of cattle etc*) éleveur *m*.

raisin ['reɪz(ə)n] *n* (*fruit*) raisin sec; **r. bread,** pain *m* aux raisins.

raising ['reɪzɪŋ] *n* **(a)** (*of curtain*) lever *m*; (*of sunken ship*) renflouage *m*; (*of standards*) élévation *f*; **(b)** (*of prices, rents, salaries*) augmentation *f*; **(c)** (*of army*) levée *f*; (*of funds for charity*) collecte *f*; (*of taxes*) imposition *f*; **(d)** (*of barn, building*) construction *f*; (*of monument, statue*) érection *f*; **(e)** (*of animals*) élevage *m*; (*of children*) éducation *f*; (*of crops*) culture *f*; **(f)** (*of blockade, embargo, siege*) levée *f*; **r. of the dead,** résurrection *f* des morts; **r. of the school-leaving age,** prolongation *f* de la scolarité; **consciousness r.,** (*of general public*) sensibilisation *f*; (*in psychoanalysis*) prise *f* de conscience; *Culin* **r. agent,** levure *f*.

raj [rɑːdʒ] *n* (*government, rule*) souveraineté *f*, autorité *f*; *Br Hist* **the R.,** l'empire *m* britannique.

raja(h) ['rɑːdʒə] *n* ra(d)ja(h) *m*.

rake¹ [reɪk] *n* **(a)** (*for croupier, gardener*) râteau *m*; **(b)** (*for grate*) râble *m*, ringard *m*; **as thin as a r.,** maigre comme un clou.

rake² *vt* **(a)** (*collect or level with rake*) ratisser (*une allée, des feuilles, le sol*); **(b)** *Mil* (*fire on*) (*with machine gun*) mitrailler (*l'ennemi, les tranchées*); **(c)** (*search*) (*with eyes*) détailler minutieusement (*le groupe*); (*with searchlights*) balayer (*le ciel, la mer*); **to r. one's memory,** fouiller dans ses souvenirs.

rake³ *n* (*dissolute man*) coureur *m*, débauché *m*, libertin *m*, *Old-fashioned* roué *m*; **The R.'s Progress,** La Carrière du roué.

rake⁴ *n* (*slope*) (*of aircraft wings, funnel, mast, seat back, steering wheel*) (angle *m* d')inclinaison *f*; (*of floor, stage*) pente *f*; **a stage with a steep r.,** une scène fortement inclinée.

rake⁵ 1 *vi* (*of aircraft wings, funnel, mast, seat back, steering wheel*) être incliné; (*of floor, stage*) être en pente. **2** *vt* incliner (*une cheminée, un mât*); construire (*un plancher, une scène*) en pente; **a steeply raked stage,** une scène fortement inclinée.

►**rake about, rake around** *vi* (*search*) fouiller (**among, in,** dans).

►**rake in** *vtsep* **(a)** (*in garden*) enfouir (*de l'engrais*) au râteau; (*in casino*) ratisser (*les mises*); **(b)** *F* (*acquire*) amasser (*de l'argent*); **you must be raking it in!,** tu dois t'en mettre plein les poches!; **that shop is raking in a fortune,** ce magasin ramasse une fortune.

►**rake off** *vtsep* **(a)** (*remove*) enlever (*des cailloux, des feuilles*) au râteau; **(b)** (*take*) empocher (*50 livres*), se mettre (*50 livres*) dans la poche.

►**rake out** *vtsep* **(a)** (*remove ashes from*) retirer *ou* enlever les cendres de; **(b)** *F* (*find*) dégoter (*une écharpe, des gants*) (**from,** dans).

►**rake over** *vtsep* ratisser (*le sol*); *Fig* **to r. s.o. over the coals,** (*scold*) réprimander vertement qn; *Fig* **to r. over the past,** (*revive*) remuer le passé.

►**rake through** *vipo* (*search*) fouiller dans (*ses poches, un tiroir*); **the down-and-out was raking through the dustbins,** le clochard faisait les poubelles.

►**rake up** *vtsep* **(a)** (*collect with rake*) ratisser (*des feuilles*); **(b)** (*revive*) attiser (*le feu*); *Fig* **to r. up an old quarrel,** attiser *ou* exhumer *ou* faire revivre une ancienne querelle; *Fig* **to r. up the past,** remuer le passé; *Fig* **to r. up s.o.'s past,** fouiller dans le passé de qn; **(c)** *F* (*find with difficulty*) dégoter, dénicher (*de l'argent, une histoire*).

rake-off ['reɪkɒf] *n* **(a)** *F* (*share of profits*) (*legal*) commission *f*; (*illegal*) ristourne *f*; **what's her r.-o.?,** (*legal*) quelle est sa part?; (*illegal*) combien se met-elle dans la poche?; **(b)** *Am* (*deduction*) rabais *m*, réduction *f* (**on,** sur).

raki [rɑː'kiː] *n* (*drink*) raki *m*.

rakish ['reɪkɪʃ] *adj* **(a)** (*dissolute*) (*behaviour, life*) libertin, débauché; **(b)** (*jaunty*) (*air*) cavalier, désinvolte; **to wear one's hat at a r. angle,** porter son chapeau avec désinvolture; *Nau* **a ship built on r. lines,** un navire élancé *ou* effilé.

rally¹ ['rælɪ] *n* **(a)** (*meeting*) grand rassemblement; (*protest*) manifestation *f*; *Hist* **the Nuremberg Rallies,** les congrès *mpl* du Parti national-socialiste de Nuremberg; **(b)** (*improvement*) (*in health*) amélioration passagère, mieux momentané; (*on Stock Exchange*) redressement *m*; **(c)** *Sp* (*in tennis etc*) long échange; (*car race*) rallye *m*; **r. driver,** pilote *m* de rallye.

rally² 1 *vt* **(a)** (*unite, win over*) rallier (*des troupes, des partisans*); **(b)** (*recover*) reprendre (*courage, ses forces*). **2** *vi* **(a)** (*unite, support*) se rallier (**to, round,** à); **to r. for the attack,** se regrouper pour attaquer; **to r. round s.o.,** (*help*) venir en aide à qn; **all the neighbours rallied round to help,** tous les voisins sont venus apporter leur soutien; **to r. to s.o.'s defence,** accourir à la défense de qn; **(b)** (*recover*) (*of shares*) se redresser; (*of patient*) se remettre momentanément; (*of athlete*) se reprendre, se ressaisir; **(c)** *Sp* (*enter car rally*) courir *ou* participer à un rallye; *Tennis* **they've been rallying for five minutes,** l'échange dure depuis cinq minutes.

rallycross ['rælɪkrɒs] *n Aut* rallycross *m*.

rallyer ['rælɪər] *n* concurrent, -ente d'un rallye.

rallying ['rælɪɪŋ] *n* **(a)** (*of supporters, troops*) ralliement *m*; **r. cry/point/***etc*, cri *m*/point *m*/*etc* de ralliement; **(b)** *Aut* **to go r.,** courir *ou* participer à un rallye.

ram¹ [ræm] *n* **(a)** (*animal*) bélier *m*; (*astrological sign*) Bélier; **(b)** (*machine*) (*part of pile driver*) marteau *m*; (*part of hydraulic press*) (piston *m*) plongeur *m*; **battering r.,** bélier *m*; **hydraulic r.,** bélier hydraulique; **(c)** *Fig F* (*sexually active man*) étalon *m*; **(d)** *Nau Hist* éperon *m*.

ram² ** *vt* **(-mm-) (a) (*crash into*) (*of ship*) entrer en collision avec, aborder (*un autre navire, un sous-marin*); *Hist* éperonner (*un galion*); (*of car*) heurter, percuter (*un arbre, un camion*); **(b)** (*force into place*) enfoncer (*un clou, un pieu*) (**into,** dans).

►**ram down** *vtsep* (*compact*) tasser (*le sol*); *Fig* **to r. one's hat down on one's head,** enfoncer son chapeau (sur la tête); **she's always ramming religion down my throat,** elle me rebat toujours les oreilles avec sa religion.

►**ram home** *vtsep* (*emphasize*) insister sur (*l'importance de*); **he kept ramming it home that we should ...,** il insistait indéfiniment sur le fait que nous devions ...; *Mil* **to r. home a charge,** bourrer un canon *ou* un fusil.

►**ram into 1** *vtaspo* (*pack*) **to r. clothes into a suitcase,** bourrer une valise de vêtements; **to r. a charge into a gun,** bourrer un fusil; *Fig* **the teacher rammed the dates into them,** le professeur leur enfonçait *ou* leur faisait entrer les dates dans la tête; **to r. food into one's mouth,** se gaver. **2** *vipo* (*collide with*) emboutir; **a Jag rammed into the back of me,** une Jag a embouti l'arrière de ma voiture.

►**ram through** *vtsep* (*force acceptance of*) imposer (*une nomination*).

RAM [ræm] *n* **(a)** *Comptr* (*abbr* **random access memory**) mémoire vive; **R. chip,** puce *f* de mémoire vive; **(b)** [ɑːreɪ'em] *Br Mus abbr* **Royal Academy of Music.**

Ramadan [ræmə'dɑːn] *n Rel* ramadan *m*; **during R.,** pendant la période du ramadan.

ramble¹ ['ræmb(ə)l] *n* (*walk*) (*spontaneous*) balade *f*, grande promenade; (*planned*) excursion *f*; **to go on** *or* **for a r.,** (*spontaneously*) faire une balade *ou* une grande promenade; (*planned*) partir en excursion.

ramble² *vi* **(a)** (*walk*) (*spontaneously*) se balader, faire une grande promenade (**over, through,** dans); (*in organized fashion*) partir en excursion; **(b)** (*talk in disconnected fashion*) parler sans suite (**about,** de); **(c)** (*be delirious*) divaguer, *F* battre la campagne; **(d)** (*meander*) (*of stream*) courir (**through,** dans); **there was ivy rambling all over the ruins,** le lierre rampait sur les ruines; **the path that rambles through the fields,** le chemin sinueux qui traverse les champs.

▶**ramble on** *vi* tenir des discours sans fin, discourir; **to r. on about nothing in particular,** parler pour ne rien dire; **what are you rambling on about now?,** qu'est-ce que tu racontes maintenant?

rambler ['ræmblər] *n* **(a)** (*walker*) promeneur, -euse; (*hiker*) excursionniste *mf*; **(b)** (*flower*) rosier grimpant; **(c)** *Am* (*house*) ranch *m*.

rambling ['ræmblıŋ] **1** *adj* **(a)** (*conversation, letter, speech etc*) décousu; **(b)** (*path, stream etc*) sinueux; **a r. house,** une maison pleine de coins et de recoins; **a r. town,** une ville construite au hasard; **(c) r. rose,** rosier grimpant. **2** *n* **(a)** (*walking*) balades *fpl*; (*hiking*) excursions *fpl*; **(b) ramblings,** (*delirium*) divagations *fpl*; **the ramblings of old age,** les radotages *mpl* de la vieillesse.

rambunctious [ræm'bʌŋ(k)ʃəs] *adj US F* **(a)** (*boisterous*) (*behaviour, child*) chahuteur, tapageur; **(b)** (*noisy*) (*meeting*) mouvementé; (*party*) bruyant.

RAMC [ɑːreıem'siː] *n Br Mil abbr* **Royal Army Medical Corps.**

ramee ['ræmı] *n Tex* = **RAMIE.**

ramekin, ramequin ['ræmıkın] *n* ramequin *m*.

ramie ['ræmı] *n Tex* ramie *f*; **r. fabric/sweater/***etc*, tissu/pull/*etc* en ramie.

ramification [ræmıfı'keıʃən] *n* ramification *f*.

ramify ['ræmıfaı] **1** *vt* ramifier. **2** *vi* se ramifier.

ramjet ['ræmdʒet] *n* **r. (engine),** statoréacteur *m*.

rammer ['ræmər] *n* (*for road-making*) dame *f*; (*for metal-working*) fouloir *m*, batte *f*; (*for civil engineering*) engin *m* de compactage du sol.

ramp¹ [ræmp] *n* **(a)** (*slope*) rampe *f*; **(b)** *Aut* (*in garage*) pont élévateur; *Am Aut* (*connecting road*) bretelle *f*; **(beware) r.!,** dénivellation *f*, dénivellement *m*; *Av* **boarding r.,** passerelle *f*; *Am Av* **parking r.,** (*for aircraft*) parc *m* de stationnement.

ramp² *n Br Sl* (*deception*) supercherie *f*, coup monté.

rampage¹ ['ræmpeıdʒ] *n F* **to be** *or* **go on the r.,** (*lose control*) se déchaîner; (*cause damage*) saccager; *Hum* **the boss is on the r.,** le patron est complètement déchaîné; **the hooligans went on a r.,** les hooligans ont tout saccagé sur leur passage.

rampage² [ræm'peıdʒ] *vi* **to r. (about** *or* **around),** se déchaîner; **they were rampaging through the streets,** ils saccageaient tout dans les rues.

rampancy ['ræmpənsı] *n* (*of behaviour, person*) déchaînement *m*; (*of plant*) exubérance *f*.

rampant ['ræmpənt] *adj* **(a)** (*corruption, poverty, vice*) qui sévit; (*plant*) exubérant, luxuriant; **to be r.,** régner, sévir; *F* **he's a bit r. tonight,** il est émoustillé ce soir; **r. inflation,** inflation galopante; **(b)** *Her* rampant; **the Lion R.,** (*flag*) le Lion rampant.

rampart ['ræmpɑːt] *n* (*fortification*) rempart *m*; **to walk round the ramparts,** se promener sur les remparts.

ramrod ['ræmrɒd] *n Mil* (*for cleaning rifle*) écouvillon *m*; (*for loading cannon*) refouloir *m*; **to be as stiff as a r.,** être raide comme un piquet; **to sit as straight as a r.** *or* **r.-straight,** être raide comme un piquet sur sa chaise.

ramshackle ['ræmʃæk(ə)l] *adj* (*building, farm*) délabré, qui tombe en ruines; (*furniture*) bancal; *Fig* (*economy, government*) qui s'effrite *ou* s'effondre; **r. old car,** vieille guimbarde.

ranch¹ [rɑːntʃ] *n* ranch *m*, ferme *f* d'élevage; **cattle/mink r.,** ferme d'élevage de bétail/du vison; **r. hand,** employé *m* de ranch; **r. house,** ranch *m*; *Am* **r. mink,** vison *m* d'élevage.

ranch² **1** *vi Am* avoir *ou* exploiter *ou* tenir un ranch. **2** *vt* élever, faire l'élevage de (*bétail, visons*).

rancher ['rɑːntʃər] *n* propriétaire *m* d'un ranch; **cattle/mink r.,** éleveur *m* de bétail/visons.

ranching ['rɑːntʃıŋ] *n* (*of cattle, mink*) élevage *m*.

rancid ['rænsıd] *adj* rance; **to go r.,** rancir; **to smell r.,** sentir le rance.

rancidity [ræn'sıdıtı], **rancidness** ['rænsıdnıs] *n* (*of butter, oil*) rancidité *f*, rancissure *f*.

rancorous ['ræŋkərəs] *adj* (*attitude, remark*) rancunier, -ière.

rancour, *US* **rancor** ['ræŋkər] *n* (*malice*) rancune *f*, rancœur *f*; **full of r.,** (*remark etc*) amer; **he is full of r.,** (*permanent condition*) il est aigri; **to be full of r. against s.o.,** avoir beaucoup de rancœur pour qn.

rand [rænd] *n* (*money*) rand *m*; *Geog* **the R.,** le Rand.

R & B [ɑːrən'biː] *n Mus abbr* **rhythm and blues.**

R & D [ɑːrən'diː] *n* (*abbr* **research and development**) **R & D expenditure,** dépenses *fpl* pour recherche et développement.

random ['rændəm] **1** *adj* (*choice*) fait au hasard; (*sample*) prélevé au hasard; (*pattern*) irrégulier; *Math* (*error, number*) aléatoire; **to fire at r.,** tirer à l'aveuglette; **I just made a r. guess,** j'ai deviné tout à fait par hasard; **a r. selection of people were asked if ...,** on a demandé à des gens choisis au hasard si ...; *Comptr* **r. access,** accès aléatoire *ou* sélectif; *Comptr* **r. access memory,** mémoire vive; **r. check/sampling,** contrôle *m*/échantillonnage *m* au hasard; **r. killings,** tuerie *f* aveugle *ou* au hasard; **r. shot,** coup tiré au hasard; *Math* **r. variable,** (variable *f*) aléatoire *f*; **r. violence,** violence gratuite. **2** *n* **at r.,** au hasard.

R & R [ɑːrən'dɑːr] *n US Mil abbr* **rest and recreation.**

randy ['rændı] *adj Br F* émoustillé, allumé; **to get** *or* **become r.,** s'échauffer; **to make s.o. r.,** allumer qn; **to be feeling r.,** être excité; **he's a r. devil,** c'est un chaud lapin.

ranee [rɑː'niː] *n* rani *f*.

range¹ [reındʒ] *n* **(a)** (*of missile, telescope, weapon*) portée *f*; (*of car, plane*) autonomie *f*; *Mil* **out of r.,** hors de portée (de tir); *Mil* **within r.,** à portée de tir; **at point blank r.,** à bout portant; **at a r. of 1,000 metres,** à une distance de 1 000 mètres; **to fire at short/long r.,** tirer à petite/grande distance *ou* à courte/longue portée; **long-r. ballistic missile,** engin *m* balistique à longue *ou* à grande portée; **short/medium/long-r. aircraft,** court/moyen/long-courrier *m*; *Met* **short/long-r. forecast,** prévisions *fpl* météorologiques à court/long terme; **to be within hearing r.,** être à portée de voix; **r. of vision,** champ visuel; *Av* **cruising r.,** autonomie à vitesse de croisière; **firing r.,** distance de tir; **operating r.,** rayon *m* d'action; **r. finding,** télémétrie *f*;

(b) (*target practice area*) **rifle/shooting r.,** *Mil* champ *m* de tir; (*at funfair*) stand *m* de tir; **rocket/torpedo r.,** zone *f* d'essai de fusées/torpilles;

(c) (*scale*) (*of prices, salaries*) échelle *f*, éventail *m*; (*of instrument, voice*) étendue *f*, registre *m*, tessiture *f*; **beyond one's r.,** (*of price*) au-dessus de ses moyens; (*of note*) hors de son registre; **within one's r.,** (*of price*) dans ses prix; (*of note*) dans son registre; **what is your price r.?,** quel prix voulez-vous mettre?; **a house/property at the lower end of the r.,** une maison/propriété bas de gamme; **r. of expression,** variété *f* de moyens d'expression; **temperature r.,** écart *m* *ou* variation *f* de température;

(d) (*scope*) (*of knowledge, research*) étendue *f*; (*of inquiry, investigation*) domaine *m*; **she has a wide r. of interests,** elle s'intéresse à beaucoup de choses;

(e) (*collection, series*) (*of colours, feelings, products*) gamme *f*; (*of patterns, sizes*) choix *m*; (*of hills, mountains*) chaîne *f*; **the shop carries a wide/limited r. of ...,** le magasin offre un grand choix/choix limité de ...; **the coat comes in a wide r. of colours/sizes,** le manteau existe dans une gamme variée de couleurs/un grand choix de tailles;

(f) (*territory*) (*of animal, plant*) habitat *m*; *Am* (*grazing area*) prairie *f*, pâturages *mpl*; **r. cattle,** bétail élevé dans la prairie;

(g) (*in surveying*) alignement *m*, direction *f*; **r. pole** *or* **rod,** jalon *m*;

(h) *Culin* **kitchen r.,** fourneau *m* de cuisine.

range² **1** *vt* **(a)** (*arrange in row*) faire aligner (*des troupes, des élèves*); ranger (*des assiettes, des livres*) (**along,** le long de);

(b) (*travel*) parcourir, sillonner (*la forêt, la mer*) (**in search of, looking for,** à la recherche de);

(c) (*aim*) braquer (*une arme, un télescope*) (**on,** sur);

(d) *Am* **to r. cattle,** élever du bétail dans la prairie;

(e) (*classify*) classer (**among,** parmi); *Fig* **to r. oneself with s.o.,** se ranger du côté de qn; (*in political, scientific etc matters*) s'aligner sur la position de qn; **to r. oneself against s.o.,** s'opposer à qn.

2 *vi* **(a)** (*extend*) (*of ages, colours, marks*) aller (**from ... to,** de ... à); (*of prices, temperatures*) varier (**from ... to,** entre ... et); **incomes ranging from £12,000 to £15,000** *or* **between £12,000 and £15,000,** revenus de l'ordre de 12 000 à 15 000 livres; **their discussions will r. over a great many topics,** leurs discussions couvriront un grand nombre de sujets; **the plant ranges over a very small area,** la plante pousse dans une zone très restreinte;

(b) (*travel*) (*of animals, people*) parcourir; (*of projectiles*) porter (**over a given distance,** à une distance donnée); **these guns r. over six miles,** ces canons ont une portée de six mil(l)es; *Fig* **his eyes ranged over the audience,** il parcourut des yeux l'auditoire;

(c) (*adjust aim*) (*of gunner*) régler le tir.
rangefinder ['reɪndʒfaɪndər] *n* télémètre *m*.
rangeland ['reɪndʒlænd] *n Am* prairie *f*.
ranger ['reɪndʒər] *n* **(a)** (*in forest, park*) garde forestier; **(b)** *US* (*State police officer*) policier *m*; (*soldier*) commando *m*; **(c)** *Br* **R. (Guide),** (guide *f*) aînée *f*.
ranging ['reɪndʒɪŋ] *n* **(a)** (*of objects*) rangement *m*; (*of troops etc*) alignement *m*; **(b)** *Mil* (*adjustment of weapon*) réglage *m* du tir; **r. fire,** tir *m* de réglage; **r. pole** *or* **rod,** (*surveying instrument*) jalon *m*.
rangy ['reɪndʒɪ] *adj* (*thin*) élancé.
rani [rɑː'niː] *n* rani *f*.
rank¹ [ræŋk] *n* **(a)** (*position*) (*in army, navy*) grade *m*; (*in society*) rang *m* (social), classe *f*; *Br* **badge of r.,** (*Am* = **rating badge**) insigne *m* de grade; **officer of high r.,** officier *m* de grade élevé *ou* de haut grade; **to hold the r. of colonel,** avoir le grade de colonel; **to reduce in r.,** rétrograder; *Mil* **the ranks,** les hommes *mpl* (du rang); *Fig* **the ranks of the homeless/unemployed,** les rangs des sans-abri/chômeurs; *Mil* **to have risen from the ranks,** être sorti des rangs; *Fig* être parti de rien; **to reduce an NCO to the ranks,** casser un gradé; **to have served in the ranks,** avoir servi comme simple soldat; **all ranks,** les militaires de tous grades; *Br Mil* **officers and other ranks,** gradés et simples soldats; **the higher ranks of the civil service,** les hauts fonctionnaires; **person of (high) r.,** personne *f* de haut rang; **actor/dancer of the first r.,** comédien *m*/danseur *m* de premier ordre; *Br* **a Minister of Cabinet r.,** un ministre du Cabinet;
(b) (*row*) (*of chessmen, trees etc*) rangée *f*; (*of people*) rang *m*; **r. upon r.,** (*of objects*) rangée après rangée; (*of people*) rang après rang; **to arrange in ranks,** (*objects*) mettre en rangées; (*people*) disposer en rangs; *Mil* **close ranks!,** serrez!; *Mil* **to break/close ranks,** rompre/serrer les rangs; *Fig* **to break ranks,** désolidariser (**with,** de, d'avec); **to close ranks,** solidariser (**on,** sur); *Mil* **front r.,** premier rang; *Br* **(taxi) r.,** (*Am* = **cabstand**) station *f* de taxis, stationnement *m* pour taxis; **at the head of the (taxi) r.,** en tête de file *ou* de station.
rank² **1** *vt* **(a)** (*classify*) classer, compter, placer (*un athlète, un écrivain*) (**among,** parmi, au nombre de);
(b) *esp Am* (*outrank*) (*in army*) occuper un rang supérieur à (*qn*); (*in office, organization etc*) être le supérieur de (*qn*);
(c) (*arrange in rows*) mettre (*les pièces d'un jeu*) en rangées; disposer (*des soldats*) en rangs.
2 *vi* **(a)** (*occupy position*) être classé *ou* compté *ou* placé (**among,** parmi, au nombre de); **to r. above s.o.,** être le supérieur de *ou* occuper un rang supérieur à qn; **to r. below s.o.,** occuper un rang inférieur à qn; **to r. equally,** être du même rang (**with,** que); **to r. with s.o.,** avoir le même rang que qn; **this must** *or* **has to r. as the best/biggest/worst ...,** ceci doit être le meilleur/plus grand/pire ...; **a sports car does not r. high in my order of priorities,** une voiture de sport ne vient pas en tête de mes priorités;
(b) *esp Am Mil* (*be most senior*) être le plus haut en grade.
rank³ *adj* **(a)** (*excessive*) (*vegetation, weeds*) envahissant, luxuriant; **to grow r.,** pousser (très) rapidement; **(b)** (*foul-smelling*) fétide, qui sent fort; **to be r. with sweat,** sentir fort la sueur; **to smell r.,** sentir fort; **(c)** (*thorough*) complet, absolu; **he's a r. outsider,** (*in competition*) c'est un outsider; (*in society*) il n'est pas des nôtres; **r. beginner,** novice parfait; **r. imposter,** imposteur fieffé; **r. injustice,** injustice flagrante; **r. stupidity,** stupidité grossière.
rank-and-file [ræŋkən'faɪl] *n* **(a)** *Mil* (*soldiers*) simples soldats *mpl*; **ten officers and two hundred r.-and-f.,** dix officiers et deux cents hommes; **r.-and-f. feelings/opinions/***etc*, les sentiments *mpl*/opinions *fpl*/*etc* des simples soldats; **(b)** (*majority*) (*in political party*) membres *mpl*; (*in union*) base *f*; **r.-and-f. feelings/opinions/***etc*, les sentiments/opinions/*etc* des membres *ou* de la base.
rank-and-filer [ræŋkən'faɪlər] *n* (*individual*) (*in army*) simple soldat *m*; (*in political party*) membre *m*; (*in union*) syndiqué, -e.
ranker ['ræŋkər] *n Mil* (*soldier*) simple soldat *m*; (*officer*) officier sorti du rang.
ranking ['ræŋkɪŋ] **1** *n* (*classification*) classement *m*; **his r. is number four,** il est classé quatrième. **2** *adj* (*authority, economist*) éminent; **high/low r.,** (*officer*) de haut grade/grade inférieur; (*diplomat, official*) de premier rang/rang inférieur; *Am Mil* **the r. officer,** l'officier le plus haut en grade.
rankle ['ræŋk(ə)l] *vi* rester sur le cœur; **it rankled with me,** je l'avais sur le cœur; **their attitude still rankles with her,** leur attitude lui est restée sur le cœur.
rankness ['ræŋknɪs] *n* **(a)** (*of vegetation*) exubérance *f*, luxuriance *f*; **(b)** (*of rotting food etc*) odeur forte *ou* fétide; **(c)** (*of stupidity etc*) grossièreté *f*.
ransack ['rænsæk] *vt* **(a)** (*search*) fouiller, mettre (*une pièce, un tiroir*) sens dessus dessous; **(b)** (*pillage*) dévaliser, piller, mettre à sac (*un magasin, une ville*).
ransom¹ ['rænsəm] *n* **(a)** (*money*) rançon *f*; **to pay r.,** payer une rançon; **to hold s.o. to r.,** mettre qn à rançon, rançonner qn; *Fig* **he said that the strikers were holding the country to r.,** il a dit que les grévistes exerçaient un chantage sur le pays; *F* **it will cost a king's r.,** ça coûtera les yeux de la tête; **(b)** *Rel* (*redemption*) rachat *m*.
ransom² *vt* racheter (*un prisonnier*).
rant [rænt] *vi* déclamer avec véhémence, *F* déblatérer (**about, at,** contre); **to r. and rave,** fulminer *ou* tempêter (**about, at,** contre).
►**rant on** *vi* = **RANT**.
ranting ['ræntɪŋ] **1** *adj* (*style*) déclamatoire; (*speaker*) tonitruant. **2** *n* déclamation *f*; **sectarian rantings,** déclamations *fpl ou* fulminations *fpl* sectaires; **r. and raving,** discours délirant.
ranunculus, *pl* **-uses, -i** [ræ'nʌŋkjʊləs, -əsɪz, -aɪ] *n Bot* renoncule *f*.
rap¹ [ræp] *n* **(a)** (*slight blow*) petit coup sec; **I heard a r. at the door,** j'ai entendu frapper à la porte; **to give s.o. a r. on** *or* **over the knuckles,** taper sur les doigts de qn; *Fig* **the saleswoman was given a r. over the knuckles for being rude to a customer,** la vendeuse s'est fait taper sur les doigts pour avoir été malpolie avec un client; **(b)** *US Sl* (*accusation, charge*) **to beat the r.,** échapper à la condamnation; **to take the r. for sth,** trinquer pour qch; **you let me take the r. for you,** tu m'as laissé trinquer à ta place; **a bum r.,** une peine injuste; *Jur* **r. sheet,** casier *m* judiciaire; **(c)** *US Sl* (*conversation*) **we had a r. session last night,** hier soir, on s'est taillé une bavette; **(d)** *Fig* (*small amount*) **he doesn't care** *or* **give a r.,** il s'en moque *ou* s'en fiche éperdument.
rap² *v* **(-pp-)** **1** *vt* (*strike*) frapper à (*la fenêtre, la porte*); taper sur (*les doigts*); *Fig Br* **to r. s.o.'s knuckles** *or* **s.o. on** *or* **over the knuckles,** *Am* **to r. s.o.,** taper sur les doigts de qn. **2** *vi* **(a)** frapper (**at,** à; **on,** sur); **(b)** *US Sl* (*talk*) tailler une bavette, papoter.
rap³ *n Mus* rap *m*.
►**rap out** *vtsep* **(a)** lancer (*un ordre, une réponse*); lâcher (*un juron*); **(b)** (*in spiritualism*) communiquer (*un message*) au moyen de coups frappés par le guéridon.
rapacious [rə'peɪʃəs] *adj* rapace; **to be r.,** (*of person*) être avide *ou* rapace.
rapaciously [rə'peɪʃəslɪ] *adv* avec rapacité.
rapacity [rə'pæsɪtɪ] *n* rapacité *f*.
rape¹ [reɪp] *n* **(a)** viol *m*; **to commit r.,** violer; **attempted r.,** tentative *f* de viol; *Jur* **statutory r.,** détournement *m* de mineur; **r. crisis centre,** centre *m* S.O.S. viol; **r. victim,** personne violée; **(b)** *Old-fashioned* (*abduction*) enlèvement *m*; **the R. of the Sabine Women,** l'enlèvement des Sabines; **(c)** *Fig* **the r. of tropical forests,** la destruction des forêts tropicales.
rape² **1** *vt* **(a)** violer; **she was gang raped,** elle a été la victime d'un viol collectif; **(b)** *Old-fashioned* (*abduct*) enlever; **(c)** *Fig* mettre à sang et à feu (*un pays, une région*); détruire (*la forêt, la mer*). **2** *vi* violer.
rape³ *n Bot* **(summer) r.,** colza *m*, navette *f*; **r. (seed) oil,** huile *f* de colza *ou* de navette.
raphia ['ræfɪə] **1** *n Bot* raphia *m*. **2** *adj* en raphia.
rapid ['ræpɪd] *adj* (*developments, improvement, progress*) rapide; *Fig* **we are making r. strides towards a cure for cancer,** on a fait des progrès rapides *ou* un grand pas en avant pour guérir le cancer; **they have had six children in r. succession,** ils ont eu six enfants très rapprochés; *Fig* **a comedian with r.-fire delivery,** un comédien au débit rapide; **r. eye movement,** sommeil paradoxal, phase *f* de mouvements oculaires; **r. fire,** feu accéléré *ou* continu; **r.-fire** *or* **r.-firing gun,** canon *m* à tir rapide; **r. pulse,** pouls *m* rapide; **r. strides,** de longues enjambées.
rapidity [rə'pɪdɪtɪ] *n* rapidité *f*.
rapidly ['ræpɪdlɪ] *adv* rapidement.
rapids ['ræpɪdz] *npl Geog* rapides *mpl*; **to shoot the r.,** descendre les rapides.
rapier ['reɪpɪər] *n* rapière *f*; *Fig* **she has a r.-like wit,** elle a un esprit mordant; **r. thrust,** coup *m* d'estoc *ou* de pointe; *Fig* (*of wit*) trait *m* d'esprit.
rapist ['reɪpɪst] *n* violeur *m*, auteur *m* d'un viol.
►**rappel down** [ræ'pel] *vi* (*in mountaineering*) descendre

en rappel.

rapport [ræ'pɔːr] *n* sympathie *f*, affinité *f*; **there was an instant r. between them,** ils ressentirent une sympathie immédiate; **he had a r. with his music teacher,** il avait des affinités avec son professeur de musique.

rapporteur [ræpɔː'tɜːr] *n* (*report writer*) rapporteur *m*.

rapprochement [ræ'prɒʃmɒn] *n* rapprochement *m*; **to effect a r.,** se rapprocher (**with s.o.,** de qn).

rapt [ræpt] *adj* (*attention, interest*) profond; (*look, smile*) ravi; **there was a r. look on her face as she listened,** il y avait une expression d'extase sur son visage pendant qu'elle écoutait; **to be r. in a book,** être absorbé dans un livre; **to be r. in contemplation,** être plongé dans la contemplation.

raptor ['ræptər] *n Orn* rapace *m*.

rapture ['ræptʃər] *n* ravissement *m*, extase *f*; **to be filled with r.,** être ravi (**at, over,** à); **to be in raptures,** être ravi *ou* enchanté (**with, over,** de); **in raptures of delight,** transporté de joie; **to go into raptures,** s'extasier (**at, over,** devant); **he goes into raptures over his new grandchild,** il est en extase devant son dernier petit-enfant.

rapturous ['ræptʃərəs] *adj* (*cries*) de ravissement; (*applause*) frénétique; (*reception, welcome*) enthousiaste; **they were r. about their daughter's success,** ils étaient en extase devant *ou* émerveillés par le succès de leur fille.

rare [reər] *adj* **(a)** (*uncommon*) rare; **very** *or* **extremely r.,** très *ou* extrêmement rare, rarissime; **it is r.** *or* **a r. thing for him to do that,** c'est rare qu'il fasse quelque chose comme ça; *F* **you're a r. bird in these parts since you got that promotion,** vous vous faites rare depuis que vous avez été promu; *Ch* **r. earths,** terres *fpl* rares; **r. gas,** gaz *m* rare; **(b)** *Culin* (*on purpose*) bleu; (*by accident*) pas assez cuit; **medium r.,** saignant; **(c)** (*lacking oxygen*) (*air, atmosphere*) raréfié; **(d)** *Old-fashioned* **we had r. fun** *or* **a r. old time,** on s'est fameusement amusé; **he's a r. one for a fight,** il est toujours prêt à se battre.

rarebit ['ræbɪt, 'reəbɪt] *n Culin* **Welsh r.,** = tranche de pain grillée recouverte de fromage fondu souvent mélangé à de la moutarde et de la bière.

rarefied ['reərɪfaɪd] *adj* (*thin*) (*air, gas*) raréfié; *Fig* **to live in a r. atmosphere,** vivre dans un monde à part.

rarefy ['reərɪfaɪ] **1** *vt* raréfier (*l'air, un gaz*). **2** *vi* (*of air, gas*) se raréfier.

rarely ['reəlɪ] *adv* rarement; **I have I** *or* **I have r. encountered anyone like him,** j'ai rarement rencontré quelqu'un comme lui; **she is r. ill,** elle est rarement malade, il est rare qu'elle soit malade.

rareness ['rɛənɪs] *n* (*uncommonness*) rareté *f*.

raring ['reərɪŋ] *adj F* (*eager*) **r. to start/***etc*, impatient de commencer/*etc*; **to be r. to go,** (*of person, animal*) trépigner d'impatience.

rarity ['reərɪtɪ] *n* **(a)** (*uncommonness*) rareté *f*; **a fine day is a r. here,** une belle journée est un événement rare ici; **wild flowers are becoming (something of) a r.,** les fleurs sauvages se font de plus en plus rares; **(b)** (*lack of oxygen*) rareté *f*.

rascal ['rɑːsk(ə)l] *n* **(a)** coquin *m*, fripon *m*; *F* **you little r.!,** petit coquin!, petite canaille!; *F* **she's a right little r.,** elle est bien coquine; **(b)** *Old-fashioned* (*scoundrel*) coquin *m*, vaurien *m*.

rascally ['rɑːskəlɪ] *adj Old-fashioned* (*behaviour, habit*) de coquin; (*lawyer*) retors; **r. fellow,** coquin *m*, vaurien *m*; **r. trick,** méchant tour, tour de coquin.

rase [reɪz] *vt* = **RAZE**.

rash¹ [ræʃ] *n* **(a)** *Med* éruption *f*; (*caused by allergy*) urticaire *f*; (*caused by chickenpox, measles, scarlet fever*) exanthème *m*, *F* boutons *mpl*; **to come out** *or* **break out in a r.,** avoir une éruption; (*because of allergy*) avoir une crise d'urticaire; **heat r.,** éruption miliaire; **nettle r.,** urticaire causée par les orties; **(b)** *Fig* (*of anonymous letters, resignations*) épidémie *f*.

rash² *adj* (*person*) imprudent, téméraire; (*action, word*) imprudent, inconsidéré, irréfléchi; **don't make any r. promises!,** ne faites pas de promesses en l'air!; **we decided in a r. moment to ...,** nous avons décidé dans un moment d'enthousiasme de ...; **that was a bit r. of you,** c'était un peu risqué de ta part; *Hum* **don't do anything r., will you?,** ne prends pas de risques, hein?

rasher ['ræʃər] *n Br* tranche *f* de lard maigre.

rashly ['ræʃlɪ] *adv* (*to behave, act, speak*) à la légère, sans réfléchir, imprudemment; (*to agree, decide*) dans un moment d'enthousiasme.

rashness ['ræʃnɪs] *n* (*of person*) imprudence *f*, témérité *f*; (*of action*) imprudence, irréflexion *f*; **once again I paid for my r.,** encore une fois j'ai payé pour mes imprudences; **the r. of the chairman's statement,** la déclaration inconsidérée du président.

rasp¹ [rɑːsp] *n* **(a)** (*file*) râpe *f*; **(b)** (*sound*) grincement *m*; **the r. in his voice,** le ton rauque *ou* âpre de sa voix; **(c)** *Scot* (*abbr* **raspberry**) framboise *f*.

rasp² **1** *vt* **(a)** (*use file*) râper; *Fig* **the cat rasped its tongue over my face,** le chat me râpa le visage de sa langue; *Fig* **he rasped his hand over his unshaven chin,** il frotta sa main sur son menton râpeux; **(b)** dire (*qch*) d'une voix rauque. **2** *vi* **(a)** (*make hoarse sound*) **her breath rasped in her lungs,** elle avait une respiration sifflante; **to rasp out an answer/a plea,** répondre/demander d'une voix rauque; **(b)** (*irritate*) **to r. on the ears,** écorcher les oreilles; **the constant creaking of the door was rasping on their nerves,** le grincement constant de la porte leur portait sur les nerfs.

raspberry ['rɑːzb(ə)rɪ] *n* **(a)** (*fruit*) framboise *f*; **r. bush, r. cane,** framboisier *m*; **r. jam,** confiture *f* de framboise; **r. pink,** (*colour*) rose *m* framboise; **r. tart,** tarte *f* à la framboise; **(b)** *F* (*jeer*) (*Am* = **Bronx cheer**) **to blow** *or* **give s.o. a r.,** siffler qn; **to get a r.,** se faire siffler.

rasping ['rɑːspɪŋ] **1** *n* **(a)** (*noise*) grincement *m*; **(b)** (*shaving*) (*of metal, wood*) copeau *m*. **2** *adj* (*sound*) grinçant; **r. cough,** toux rauque *ou* sèche; **r. voice,** voix *f* rauque *ou* âpre.

raspings ['rɑːspɪŋz] *npl Culin* chapelure *f*.

Rasta ['ræstə] *n & adj Rel* (*abbr* **Rastafarian**) rasta *mf inv*.

Rastafarian [ræstə'feərɪən] *n & adj Rel* rastafari *mf inv*.

Rastafarianism [ræstə'feərɪənɪz(ə)m] *n Rel* rastafarisme *m*.

rat¹ [ræt] *n* **(a)** (*animal*) rat *m*; **to be caught like a r. in a trap,** être fait comme un rat; **to look like a drowned r.,** être trempé jusqu'aux os; **with her hair all in rats' tails,** avec ses cheveux en queues de vache; *Fig* **to smell a r.,** se douter de qch; *Am Fig* **to be a pack r.,** ne jamais rien jeter; *Fig* **that child is a real water r.,** cet enfant passerait sa vie dans l'eau; *Br Old-fashioned* **rats!,** (*exclamation of irritation*) zut!; (*exclamation of disbelief*) mon œil!; **black r.,** rat noir; **desert r.,** (*animal*) gerboise *f*; *Mil* = soldat britannique qui s'est battu en Afrique du Nord pendant la deuxième guerre mondiale; **pet r.,** rat apprivoisé; **sewer** *or* **grey r.,** rat d'égout, rat gris, surmulot *m*; **water r.,** rat d'eau, mulot *m*, campagnol *m*; **r. catcher,** chasseur *m* de rats; *Am F* **r. cheese,** (*Br* = **mousetrap**) cheddar *m*; **r. extermination,** dératisation *f*; **r. poison,** *Old-fashioned* **r.'s bane,** mort-aux-rats *f*; *Fig* **r. race,** (*daily routine*) course *f* au bifteck; (*jungle*) foire *f* d'empoigne, jungle *f*; **to get out of the r. race,** sortir du système *ou* de l'engrenage;
(b) *F Pej* (*unreliable person*) lâcheur, -euse; **you r.!,** salaud!, ordure!;
(c) *US F Pej* (*informer*) mouchard, -arde, indic *m*;
(d) *F Pej* (*scab*) jaune *m*, briseur *m* de grève.

rat² *vi* **(-tt-)** (*reveal information*) cafarder, moucharder.

►**rat on** *vipo* (*to friends, parents etc*) cafarder, dénoncer (*qn*); (*to police*) balancer (*qn*); (*desert*) lâcher (*qn*); **you should not r. on a promise,** tu ne devrais pas revenir sur une promesse; **they ratted on our deal,** ils nous ont laissés tomber dans cette affaire.

ratable ['reɪtəb(ə)l] *adj Br Fin* (*house, property*) imposable; **r. value,** valeur locative nette; *Admin* loyer matriciel.

ratafia [rætə'fɪə] *n* (*drink*) ratafia *m*; *Br* **r. (biscuit),** macaron *m*.

ratan [ræ'tæn] *n Bot* rotin *m*; **r. furniture/seat/***etc*, meubles *mpl*/siège *m*/*etc* en rotin.

rat-arsed ['rætɑːst] *adj Br Sl* (*drunk*) rond comme une queue de pelle.

ratatat-tat¹ ['rætətættæt] *n* (*also* **ratatat**) (*on door*) toc toc *m*; (*on drum*) rantanplan *m*; (*of machine gun*) pétarade *f*; (*of typewriter*) tac-tac-tac *m*.

ratatat-tat² *vi* **(-tt-)** (*on door*) frapper; (*of machine gun*) pétarader; **I could hear the typewriter ratatat-tatting angrily,** je pouvais entendre le tac-tac-tac furieux de la machine à écrire.

ratatouille [rætə'tuːiː] *n Culin* ratatouille *f*.

ratbag ['rætbæg] *n Sl* con, conne; *Hum* **you r.!,** mon salaud!

rat-catcher ['rætkætʃər] *n* chasseur *m* de rats.

ratchet ['rætʃɪt] *n Tech* rochet *m*; **r. mechanism,** (dispositif *m* d')encliquetage *m*; **r. wheel/screwdriver,** roue *f*/tournevis *m* à cliquet.

rate¹ [reɪt] *n* **(a)** (*of inflation, tax etc*) taux *m*; **birth/crime/death r.,** taux de la natalité/la criminalité/la mortalité; **divorce r.,** nombre *m* de divorces; **pass/failure r.,** (*in exam etc*) pourcentage *m* de réussite/d'échecs; **success r.,** (*of operation, treatment etc*) chances *fpl* de succès; **at**

the r. of, (*amount*) à raison de; **to be paid at the r. of five pounds an hour,** être payé (à raison de) cinq livres de l'heure; **to strike for higher rates of pay,** faire la grève pour une augmentation de salaire;

(b) (*speed*) vitesse *f*; (*of pulse*) fréquence *f*; **the fearful r. of technological advance,** le rythme effrayant du progrès technologique; **at the r. of ...,** à une vitesse de ...; *F* **she headed for the station at a r. of knots,** elle s'est dirigée vers la gare à toute allure; **at this rate,** à ce rythme-là; (*slow speed*) à ce train-là; **at the r. things are going,** du train où vont les choses; **at any r.,** en tout cas; *Av* **r. of climb,** vitesse ascensionnelle; **r. of flow,** (*of rivers, turbines*) débit *m*; **r. of production,** (*in factory*) cadence *f* de production; **heart r.,** rythme cardiaque;

(c) *Com Fin* taux *m*; **economic growth r.,** taux de croissance économique; **r. of return,** (*on investment*) taux de rendement; **bank** *or Am* **discount r.,** taux bancaire; **buying/selling r.,** (*of currency*) taux acheteur/vendeur; **discount/interest r.,** taux d'escompte/d'intérêt; **minimum lending r.,** taux de crédit minimum; **mortgage r.,** taux d'intérêt sur un emprunt immobilier; **prime r.,** *Br* taux préférentiel, *US* taux de base.

(d) (*price, charge*) tarif *m*; **what's the going r. for a computer/translator these days?,** quel est le prix/salaire d'un ordinateur/traducteur ces jours-ci?; **what are your rates?,** (*for hotel room etc*) quel est le tarif *ou* le prix?; (*for service*) quels sont vos tarifs?; **to pay the full r.,** payer plein tarif; **insurance rates,** primes *fpl* d'assurance; **letter r.,** tarif lettres; **postage** *or* **postal r.,** tarif d'affranchissement; **off-peak r.,** (*for electricity, gas*) tarif de nuit; (*for phone call*) tarif réduit; **peak r.,** (*for electricity, gas, phone*) plein tarif;

(e) *Br* (*tax*) (*usu pl*) **rates,** impôts locaux; **rates and taxes,** impôts et contributions; **the r. is 60p in the pound,** le taux est de soixante pence par livre; **r. collector,** receveur, -euse municipal, -ale; **r. rebate,** dégrèvement *m* d'impôts locaux; **rates office,** recette *f* municipale.

rate² **1** *vt* **(a)** (*classify*) classer (*un athlète, un pianiste*) (**among,** parmi); considérer (*qn, qch*) (**as,** comme); **I r. him among my friends,** je le compte au nombre de *ou* le considère comme un de mes amis;

(b) (*evaluate*) apprécier, évaluer (*un élève, un concert, un film*); **to r. highly,** apprécier beaucoup; **to be highly rated,** être très apprécié; **how do you r. their chances of a contract?,** à votre avis, quelles sont leurs chances de décrocher un contrat?; **I r. this restaurant very highly,** je trouve ce restaurant excellent; *Br Sl* **I don't r. him,** je n'ai pas grande estime pour lui;

(c) (*deserve*) mériter (*une augmentation de salaire*); **that win should r. him a place on the team,** après sa victoire il mérite une place dans l'équipe; **a battle that didn't r. a mention in the history books,** une bataille qui n'a pas mérité d'apparaître dans les livres d'histoire;

(d) *Br* (*set amount of taxes on*) établir *ou* calculer le montant des impôts locaux sur (*une propriété*); **their house has been rated higher this year,** les impôts locaux sur leur maison ont été augmentés cette année.

2 *vi* (*be classified*) se classer, être classé (**as,** comme); **in terms of efficiency, she rates higher than anyone else,** en ce qui concerne l'efficacité, elle bat tout le monde; **to r. with,** (*please*) être beaucoup apprécié par, gagner l'estime de.

-rate [reɪt] *suff* **first/second/***etc* **-r.,** de premier/second/*etc* ordre.

rateable ['reɪtəb(ə)l] *adj Br Fin* (*house, property*) imposable; **r. value,** valeur locative nette; *Admin* loyer matriciel.

rate-cap ['reɪtkæp] *vt Br Fin* fixer un taux plafond pour les impôts locaux de (*une municipalité*).

rate-capping ['reɪtkæpɪŋ] *n Br Fin* plafonnement *m* des impôts locaux.

rated ['reɪtɪd] *adj Tech* (*load, speed, voltage*) nominal.

rateen [ræ'tiːn] *n Tex* = **RATINE.**

ratepayer ['reɪtpeɪər] *n Br* (*local taxpayer*) contribuable *mf* assujetti(e) aux impôts locaux.

ratfink ['rætfɪŋk] *n US Pej Sl* salaud *m*, ordure *f*.

rather ['rɑːðər] *adv* **(a)** (*preferably*) plutôt (**than,** que); **I'd r. stay,** j'aimerais mieux *ou* préférerais rester (**than,** que); **I would** *or* **had r. that you came,** je préférerais que vous veniez; **I'd r. not,** je n'y tiens pas; **r. than leave/***etc*, plutôt que de partir/*etc*; **anything r. than that,** tout sauf ça; **r. you than me!,** plutôt toi que moi!; **accept? — I'd r. die first!,** accepter? — plutôt mourir!;

(b) (*more precisely*) **or r.,** ou plus précisément, ou pour être plus précis;

(c) (*fairly*) plutôt; (*quite*) assez; (*to a degree*) un peu; **she's a r.** *or* **r. a beautiful woman,** c'est une femme plutôt belle; **she is r. plain,** elle n'est pas très jolie; **r. a lot of people,** pas mal de monde; **I r. think you know him,** je crois bien *ou* il me semble que vous le connaissez; **it tastes r. like a pear,** ça rappelle le goût de la poire; **I am r. inclined to agree with you,** je suis plutôt de votre avis; **I r. liked it,** ça m'a assez plu; **it's r. nice,** c'est bien; **r. more tired/***etc*, un peu plus fatigué/*etc* (**than,** que);

(d) ['rɑː'ðɜː] (*certainly*) (*when accepting offer*) oui alors, et comment; (*when answering question*) et comment.

ratification [rætɪfɪ'keɪʃən] *n* (*by government*) ratification *f*; (*by sports authorities*) homologation *f*.

ratify ['rætɪfaɪ] *vt* ratifier (*un traité*); homologuer (*un record*); **to r. a contract,** approuver un contrat.

ratine [ræ'tiːn] *n Tex* ratine *f*; **r. coat/***etc*, manteau *m*/*etc* de ratine.

rating ['reɪtɪŋ] *n* **(a)** (*classification*) classement *m*; (*of machine, sailor, ship*) classe *f*; (*of candidates, politicians*) cote *f* de popularité; (*of wage etc*) indice *m*; *TV* **the ratings,** l'indice d'écoute; **to boost the ratings,** améliorer l'indice d'écoute; **to stand high in the ratings,** avoir un indice d'écoute élevé; *Fin* **credit r.,** solvabilité *f*; *Aut* **octane r.,** indice d'octane; *Am Mil* **r. badge,** *Br* **badge of r.,** insigne *m* de grade; **(b)** (*evaluation*) (*of employee, student etc*) appréciation *f*, évaluation *f*; **(c)** *Br* (*of property*) montant *m* des impôts locaux; **(d)** *Br* (*sailor*) matelot *m*; **the ratings,** les matelots et gradés.

ratio, *pl* **-os** ['reɪʃɪəʊ, -əʊz] *n* (*proportion, relationship*) proportion *f*, rapport *m*; **in a r. of 25 to 1,** dans une proportion *ou* un rapport de 25 pour 1; **in direct r.,** directement proportionnel, en rapport direct (**to,** avec), en raison directe (**to,** de); **the school has a teacher-pupil r. of 1 to 10,** l'école a un rapport professeur-élève de 1 pour 10; *Math* **arithmetical r.,** raison *ou* proportion arithmétique; *Aut* **compression r.,** taux *m* de compression.

ration¹ ['ræʃən, *Am* 'reɪʃən] *n* (*of bread, sugar etc*) ration *f*; **to come off the r.,** cesser d'être rationné; **to be on r.,** être rationné; **rations,** (*food supplies*) provisions *fpl*; **to be on short rations,** avoir des rations réduites; **to put s.o. on short rations,** réduire les rations de qn; **full rations,** rations complètes; *Mil* **to draw rations,** toucher sa ration; *Am Mil* **C rations,** vivres *mpl*; *Br Mil* **iron rations,** vivres de réserve; **r. book** *or* **card,** carte *f* de rationnement.

ration² *vt* rationner (*le pain, le sucre etc*); **I was rationed to ...,** ma ration était de ...; **she rations herself to one film a week,** elle se limite à un film par semaine; **I will r. you to half an hour's television a day,** je ne t'autoriserai à regarder la télévision que pendant une demi-heure par jour.

rational ['ræʃən(ə)l] *adj* **(a)** (*sensible*) (*behaviour, person*) raisonnable, sensé; **it seemed like the r. thing to do,** il me semblait que c'était ce qu'il y avait de plus logique à faire; **(b)** (*sane*) rationnel; (*lucid*) lucide; **to be quite r.,** avoir toute sa tête; **she is not quite r. when the subject of divorce comes up,** elle n'a pas un comportement raisonnable lorsqu'on parle de divorce; **(c)** (*based on or using reason*) (*decision, thought etc*) rationnel; (*animal, creature*) doué de raison; **(d)** *Math* (*number*) rationnel.

rationale [ræʃə'nɑːl] *n* (*reasoning*) raisonnement *m* (**for,** de); (*written or spoken*) exposé raisonné.

rationalism ['ræʃənəlɪz(ə)m] *n* rationalisme *m*.

rationalist ['ræʃənəlɪst] *adj & n* rationaliste *mf*.

rationalistic [ræʃənə'lɪstɪk] *adj* rationaliste.

rationality [ræʃə'nælɪtɪ] *n* (*of decision, thought*) rationalité f.

rationalization [ræʃənəlaɪ'zeɪʃən] *n* **(a)** (*of action, behaviour etc*) justification *f*, rationalisation *f* (**of,** de); **(b)** *Br Ind* (*of company etc*) rationalisation *f*.

rationalize ['ræʃənəlaɪz] **1** *vt* **(a)** justifier, rationaliser (*un acte, un comportement etc*); **to r. one's dislike/fears,** trouver une explication logique *ou* rationnelle à son antipathie/ses peurs; **(b)** *Br Ind* rationaliser (*une société etc*). **2** *vi* **he rationalized by telling himself that his wife took a job because they needed the money,** il s'est raisonné en se disant que sa femme avait pris un emploi parce qu'ils avaient besoin d'argent; **(do) stop rationalizing!,** arrête de chercher des excuses!

rationally ['ræʃənəlɪ] *adv* **(a)** (*sensibly*) raisonnablement; **(b)** (*sanely*) rationnellement; **(c)** (*to decide, think*) rationnellement.

rationing [ræʃənɪŋ, *Am* 'reɪʃənɪŋ] *n* (*of bread, sugar etc*) rationnement *m* (**of,** de); **food r.,** rationnement alimentaire.

ratlin(e) ['rætlɪn] *n Nau* enfléchure *f*.

ratrack ['rætræk] *n Ski* ratrack *m*.

rat-tail ['rætteɪl] *n (file)* (lime *f*) queue-de-rat *f*.
rattan [ræ'tæn] *n Bot* rotin *m*; **r. furniture/seat/***etc*, meubles *mpl*/siège *m*/*etc* en rotin.
rat-tat ['rættæt] *n & vi* = **RATATAT-TAT**.
ratteen [ræ'tiːn] *n Tex* = **RATINE**.
ratter ['rætər] *n (animal)* ratier *m*.
rattiness ['rætɪnɪs] *n Br F (irritability)* irritabilité *f*.
ratting ['rætɪŋ] *n* **to go r.**, faire la chasse aux rats.
rattle¹ ['ræt(ə)l] *n* **(a)** *(for baby)* hochet *m*; *(on pram)* boulier *m*; *(for sports fan)* crécelle *f*; *(of snake)* sonnette *f*; **(b)** *(noise)* *(of bottles, chains, coins, keys)* cliquetis *m*; *(of engine)* bruit *m* de ferraille; *(of gunfire, hailstones)* crépitement *m*; *(of door, window)* vibration *f*.
rattle² **1** *vi (make noise)* faire du bruit; *(of bottles)* cliqueter, s'entrechoquer; *(of chains, coins, keys)* cliqueter; *(of door, window)* vibrer; *(of engine)* faire un bruit de ferraille; *(of gunfire, hailstones)* crépiter; **the door rattled in the wind,** le vent faisait vibrer la porte. **2** *vt* **(a)** *(make noise with)* secouer *(une boîte)*; entrechoquer *(des bouteilles)*; ébranler, faire vibrer *(une porte, des vitres)*; **(b)** *F (make nervous)* démonter, décontenancer, ébranler *(qn)*, faire perdre son sang froid à *(qn)*; **to get rattled,** perdre son sang froid; **don't get rattled!,** pas de panique!; **we got them rattled,** on a semé la panique parmi eux; **she was badly rattled by the news,** la nouvelle l'a complètement démontée; **to be easily rattled,** être facilement démonté.
▶**rattle along** *vi* **(a)** *(move noisily)* *(of car, train)* rouler dans un bruit de ferraille; **(b)** *(move quickly)* *(in car, train)* rouler à toute allure.
▶**rattle around** *vi (be somewhere too large)* **he's been rattling around in that enormous house since his wife died,** il est perdu dans cette grande maison depuis la mort de sa femme.
▶**rattle away** *vi (talk rapidly)* jacasser, baratiner.
▶**rattle down** *vi (of stones etc)* tomber avec fracas.
▶**rattle off** *vtsep (lines, recitation etc)* débiter.
▶**rattle on** *vi (speak at length)* ne pas arrêter de parler (**about,** de).
▶**rattle through** *vipo (homework, task etc)* expédier.
rattlebrain ['ræt(ə)lbreɪn], **rattlehead** ['ræt(ə)lhed], **rattlepate** ['ræt(ə)lpeɪt] *n Old-fashioned F (foolish person)* cervelle *f* d'oiseau, tête *f* de linotte.
rattlesnake ['ræt(ə)lsneɪk], *Am* **rattler** ['rætlər] *n* serpent *m* à sonnette, crotale *m*.
rattletrap ['ræt(ə)ltræp] *n Old-fashioned F (car)* vieille guimbarde *ou* bagnole.
rattling ['ræt(ə)lɪŋ] **1** *n* = **RATTLE¹**. **2** *adj* **(a)** *(noisy)* bruyant; **r. noise,** cliquetis *m*; **(b)** *(fast)* rapide; **to set a r. pace,** aller *ou* marcher très vite *ou* à une cadence rapide; *(in race)* mener à une cadence rapide. **3** *adv Old-fashioned (extremely)* **r. good,** *(lunch, story)* excellent, fameux.
rat-trap ['rættræp] *n* **(a)** *(for animals)* piège *m* à rats, ratière *f*; **(b)** *Am (rundown building)* taudis *m*.
ratty ['rætɪ] *adj* **(a)** *Br (irritable)* irritable; *(annoyed)* irrité; **to get r.,** *(of adult)* prendre la mouche; *(of child)* devenir grognon; **(b)** *Am (shabby)* *(building, clothes)* miteux.
raucous ['rɔːkəs] *adj* **(a)** *(hoarse)* rauque; **r. voice,** voix rauque *ou* éraillée; **(b)** *(loud, rowdy)* **r. laughter,** rires *mpl* gras; **a r. party,** une soirée tapageuse *ou* bruyante; **things got a bit r. as the evening wore on,** la soirée a pris une tournure tapageuse.
raucously ['rɔːkəslɪ] *adv (see adj)* **(a)** d'une voix rauque; **(b)** tapageusement.
raucousness ['rɔːkəsnɪs] *n* **(a)** *(hoarseness)* raucité *f*; **(b)** *(rowdiness)* **the r. of the party was not to his liking,** il n'aimait pas le côté tapageur de la soirée.
raunch [rɔːntʃ] *n Am F (crudeness)* obscénité *f*.
raunchiness ['rɔːntʃɪnɪs] *n* **(a)** *(of joke, song)* grivoiserie *f*; **(b)** *(of dance, voice)* sensualité *f*.
raunchy ['rɔːntʃɪ] *adj F* **(a)** *(joke, song)* *(dirty)* cochon; *(in more light-hearted way)* grivois; **that's much too r. for our viewers,** c'est beaucoup trop grivois pour nos téléspectateurs; **(b)** *(sexy)* *(dance, voice)* sexy *inv*; **there is something a little r. about her,** elle a un petit quelque chose de sexy.
ravage¹ [rævɪdʒ] *n (damage)* *(of alcohol, disease, grief, time etc)* *(usu pl)* **ravages,** ravages *mpl*.
ravage² *vt (destroy)* ravager, dévaster *(les récoltes, une région)*; ravager *(qn)*; **the invading army ravaged the land,** l'armée d'invasion a mis la terre à feu et à sang; **ravaged face,** visage ravagé.
rave¹ [reɪv] *n F (praise)* éloge *m* enthousiaste; *Br Sl* **to have a r.,** délirer (**about,** sur); **it's the latest r.,** c'est la dernière mode *ou* le dernier cri *ou* en vogue; **r. notice** *or* **review,** critique *f ou* revue *f* dithyrambique.
rave² *vi* **(a)** *(be delirious)* délirer; **(b)** *(talk nonsense)* divaguer, délirer; *F* **you're raving!,** vous divaguez!, tu délires!; **to r. (on),** *(rage)* tempêter (**about, at,** contre); **he's been raving on for an hour,** ça fait une heure qu'il tempête; **to r. at** *or* **against s.o.,** s'emporter contre qn, être *ou* se mettre en colère contre qn; **(c) to r. about s.o.,** *(praise)* délirer sur qn; **to r. about sth,** ne pas tarir d'éloges sur qch, faire l'éloge de qch.
raven ['reɪv(ə)n] **1** *n (bird)* corbeau *m*. **2** *adj (colour)* (noir comme du) jais, de jais; **a r.-haired beauty,** une beauté aux cheveux noir corbeau *ou* de jais.
ravening ['ræv(ə)nɪŋ] *adj (hungry)* vorace; *Hum* **the r. hordes,** les rapaces *mpl*.
ravenous ['ræv(ə)nəs] *adj (animal)* vorace; *(person)* affamé; *(appetite)* vorace, féroce; **to be r.,** avoir une faim dévorante *ou* de loup; *Fig* **to be r. for,** *(fame, power)* avoir faim de, être affamé *ou* assoiffé *ou* avide de.
ravenously ['ræv(ə)nəslɪ] *adv (to eat)* voracement; **to be r. hungry,** avoir une faim dévorante *ou* de loup.
raver ['reɪvər] *n Br Sl (socially active person)* fêtard, -arde, noceur, -euse; **he's a bit of a r.,** il est noceur.
rave-up ['reɪvʌp] *n Br Sl (party)* fiesta *f*, nouba *f*; **to have a r.-up,** faire la fiesta *ou* nouba; **the neighbours had a right old r.-up last night,** les voisins ont fait une de ces fiestas *ou* noubas hier soir.
ravine [rə'viːn] *n* ravin *m*, ravine *f*.
raving ['reɪvɪŋ] **1** *adj* **(a)** *(delirious)* délirant; **(b)** *(crazy, angry)* furieux; **a r. lunatic,** un fou furieux; *Br F* **you are stark r. mad** *or* **bonkers,** tu es complètement givré *ou* fêlé; **to be r. mad,** *(crazy)* être complètement fou; *F (angry)* être furax (**about,** au sujet de; **with,** contre); *Fig* **she is a r. beauty,** elle est d'une beauté ravageuse; *Fig* **she is no r. beauty,** ce n'est pas une beauté; *Fig* **to be a r. success,** avoir un succès fou. **2** *n* **(a)** *(delirium)* délire *m*; **(b)** *(wild talk)* divagation *f*; **the ravings of a madman,** les divagations d'un fou.
ravioli [rævɪ'əʊlɪ] *n (pasta)* ravioli *mpl*.
ravish ['rævɪʃ] *vt* **(a)** *(delight)* enchanter, ravir *(qn)*; **(b)** *Old-fashioned (abduct)* enlever, ravir *(une femme)*; *(rape)* violenter, violer *(une femme)*.
ravisher ['rævɪʃər] *n Old-fashioned (abductor)* ravisseur *m*; *(rapist)* violeur *m*.
ravishing ['rævɪʃɪŋ] *adj (sight, view)* magnifique, ravissant; **a r. woman, a woman of r. beauty,** une femme ravissante *ou* d'une grande beauté.
ravishingly ['rævɪʃɪŋlɪ] *adv (to play, sing)* à ravir; **r. beautiful,** d'une beauté ravissante.
ravishment ['rævɪʃmənt] *n* **(a)** *(delight)* enchantement *m*, ravissement *m*; **(b)** *Old-fashioned (abduction)* enlèvement *m*; *(rape)* viol *m*.
raw¹ [rɔː] *adj* **(a)** *(uncooked)* *(meat, shellfish, vegetables)* cru;
(b) *(unprocessed)* *(data, statistics, water)* brut; **r. edge,** *(of material)* bord coupé; **r. materials,** matières premières; *Fig* **he uses his former colleagues as r. material for his plays,** il s'inspire de ses anciens collègues pour ses pièces; **r. milk,** lait cru; **r. sewage,** eaux d'égout non traitées; **r. silk,** soie brute *ou* crue *ou* écrue *ou* grège; **r. spirits,** alcool pur; **r. sugar,** sucre brut *ou* non raffiné;
(c) *F (immature)* inexpérimenté; **r. hand,** novice *mf*, personne *f* sans expérience; **a r. recruit,** un bleu; *Mil* **r. troops,** troupes inaguerries *ou* non aguerries;
(d) *(sore)* *(wound)* à vif; *(skin)* écorché; **her hands were r. with the cold,** ses mains étaient bleues à cause du froid; *Fig* **the memory was still r.,** le souvenir était encore douloureux; *Fig* **my nerves are r.,** j'ai les nerfs à vif *ou* à fleur de peau; *Fig* **a r. deal,** *(unfair treatment)* un coup dur; *Fig* **he's had a r. deal out of life,** il n'a pas été gâté par la vie; *Fig* **working mothers get a r. deal from the government,** les mères qui travaillent sont très défavorisées par le gouvernement;
(e) *(unpleasant)* *(climate, weather)* froid et humide; **a r. wind,** un vent âpre *ou* pénétrant; **it's a r. day,** il fait froid et humide;
(f) *Am (frank)* réaliste; **the film paints a r. picture of penitentiary life,** le film peint la vie carcérale de façon réaliste.
raw² *n* **in the r.,** nu, tout nu, *F* à poil; **life in the r.,** la vie telle qu'elle est; **to get** *or* **touch s.o. on the r.,** piquer *ou* toucher qn au vif.
rawboned ['rɔːbəʊnd] *adj (animal, person)* maigre, efflanqué.
rawhide ['rɔːhaɪd] *n* **(a)** *(untreated leather)* cuir brut *ou*

vert; **r. bag/belt/***etc*, sac *m*/ceinture *f*/*etc* en cuir vert; **(b)** (*whip*) fouet *m* à lanières.

Rawlplug ® ['rɔːlplʌg] *n* cheville *f*, tampon *m*.

rawness ['rɔːnɪs] *n* **(a) the r. of the data/statistics makes it impossible to ...**, le fait que les données/statistiques sont à l'état brut rend impossible de ...; **(b)** (*immaturity*) (*of recruit etc*) inexpérience *f*; **(c)** (*soreness*) (*of skin*) écorchure *f*, éraflure *f*; **(d)** (*unpleasantness*) (*of climate, weather*) froid *m* humide; (*of wind*) âpreté *f*; **(e)** *Am* (*frankness*) réalisme *m*, crudité *f*.

ray [reɪ] *n* **(a)** (*of light, sun etc*) *& Phys* rayon *m*; *Fig* **that child has brought a r. of sunshine into my life**, cet enfant, c'est mon rayon de soleil; *Iron* **you're a real little r. of sunshine, aren't you!**, tu as vraiment le mot pour rire, toi!; **(b)** *Fig* (*of hope, intelligence*) lueur *f*; **(c)** (*fish*) raie *f*; **electric r.**, torpille *f*; **(d)** *Mus* ré *m*.

rayon ['reɪɒn] *n Tex* rayonne *f*; **r. dress/shirt/***etc*, robe *f*/chemise *f*/*etc* en rayonne.

raze [reɪz] *vt* **to r. (to the ground)**, (*destroy*) raser (*un édifice*).

razor ['reɪzər] *n* rasoir *m*; *Fig* **on a r.** *or* **the r.'s edge**, (*in difficulty*) au bord du précipice *ou* du gouffre; **her life was on the r.'s edge for days**, sa vie n'a tenu qu'à un fil pendant plusieurs jours; **electric r.**, rasoir électrique; **lady's r.**, rasoir pour femme; **r. blade**, lame *f* de rasoir; **r. cut**, (*hairstyle*) coupe *f* au rasoir; **to have a r. cut**, se faire couper les cheveux au rasoir; **r. edge**, fil tranchant; (*mountain ridge*) arête effilée *ou* aiguë; **r. slash**, taillade *f* au rasoir; **r. wire** *or Am* **ribbon**, barbelés tranchants.

razorback ['reɪzəbæk] *n* **(a)** (*whale*) rorqual *m*; **(b)** *US* (*wild pig*) cochon *m* sauvage.

razorbacked ['reɪzəbækt] *adj* (*animal*) au dos tranchant.

razorbill ['reɪzəbɪl] *n* (*bird*) petit pingouin.

razor-cut ['reɪzəkʌt] *vt* couper (*les cheveux*) au rasoir.

razor-sharp ['reɪzəʃɑːp] *adj* (*knife*) coupant comme un rasoir; *Fig* (*intelligence, mind*) vif; (*wit*) acéré.

razor-shell ['reɪzəʃel] *n Br* (*Am* = **razor clam, jack-knife clam**) (*shellfish*) couteau *m*, solen *m*.

razz [ræz] *vt esp Am F* **(a)** (*tease*) taquiner (*qn*); **(b)** (*deride*) brimer (*qn*); **(c)** (*heckle*) chahuter (*qn*).

razzle-dazzle ['ræz(ə)ldæz(ə)l] *n F* (*flashy display*) tape-à-l'œil *m*, clinquant *m*; *Br* **to be** *or* **go on the r.-d.**, faire la bringue *ou* la fête *ou* la nouba.

razzmatazz ['ræzmətæz] *n F* (*flashy display*) tape-à-l'œil *m*, clinquant *m*; **the r. side of politics**, le côté tape-à-l'œil de la politique.

RC [ɑː'siː] *n & adj Rel abbr* **Roman Catholic**.

RCMP [ɑːsiːem'piː] *n Can* (*abbr* **Royal Canadian Mounted Police**) GRC *f*.

Rd *n* (*abbr* **Road**) Rte.

re¹ [reɪ] *n Mus* ré *m*.

re² [riː] **1** *prep* (*with reference to*) *Com* (*at top of letter*) objet *m*; (*in body of letter etc*) en référence *ou* suite à. **2** *n Jur* **(in) r. Martin v Thomas**, dans l'affaire Martin contre Thomas.

re- [riː-] *pref* (*before consonant*) re-, ré-; **rebaptize**, rebaptiser; **rehabituate**, réhabituer; (*before vowel*) r-, ré- ; **reassure**, rassurer; **readjust**, rajuster, réajuster.

reach¹ [riːtʃ] *n* **(a)** (*accessibility*) atteinte *f*, portée *f*; **beyond the r. of the authorities**, à l'abri des *ou* hors de la portée des autorités; **he was beyond the r. of human help**, on ne pouvait plus rien faire pour lui; **a subject beyond my r.**, une matière qui dépasse mon entendement; **out of r.**, (*object*) hors de portée; **I'll be out of r. for a week**, on ne pourra pas me contacter pendant une semaine; **keep out of the r. of children**, (*instruction on medicine bottles, plastic bags etc*) ne pas laisser à la portée d'enfants; **within r. of**, à portée de; (*near*) à proximité *ou* proche de; **within arm's r.**, à portée de *ou* sous la main; **within easy r.**, (*object*) à portée de *ou* sous la main; (*banks, shops etc*) facilement accessible; **within everyone's r.**, (*affordable*) à la portée de tous *ou* de toutes les bourses;

(b) (*length of arm*) extension *f*; *Boxing* allonge *f*; **he has a longer r. than any of the other contenders**, il a la meilleure allonge de tous les concurrents; **she made a r. for the gun**, elle étendit la main pour prendre le revolver; *Fig* **your r. should always exceed your grasp**, dans la vie, il faut toujours viser plus haut;

(c) (*area, region*) (*of forest*) étendue *f*; (*of river*) partie *f*; (*of canal*) bief *m*; **in the further reaches of the empire**, au fin fond de l'empire.

reach² **1** *vt* **(a)** (*arrive at*) arriver à (*une conclusion, une destination*); atteindre (*un but, un objectif, une hauteur*); (*of letter, news, parcel*) parvenir à (*qn*); **to r. (an) agreement**, aboutir à un accord (**on**, sur); **to r. a ceiling**, (*of imports, wages*) plafonner; **to r. a decision**, prendre une décision; **to r. the end of one's journey**, arriver au bout du voyage; **which page have you reached?**, à quelle page en es-tu?; **it has reached my ears that ...**, j'ai entendu dire *ou* appris que ...; **production has reached rock bottom** *or* **an all time low**, la production est descendue à son plus bas; **unemployment is reaching the two million mark**, le nombre de chômeurs atteint le seuil des deux millions;

(b) (*gain access to*) accéder à (*une plage, une maison*); (*contact*) (*by telephone etc*) joindre, contacter (*qn*); **easy/difficult to r.**, (*house etc*) facile/difficile d'accès; *Fig* **he's so bitter about his wife's death that no-one can r. him**, la mort de sa femme l'a rendu tellement amer qu'on ne peut pas communiquer avec lui; **the adverts are intended to r. the over-40s**, les pubs sont faites pour toucher les *ou* sont destinées aux *ou* sont à l'intention des plus de 40 ans;

(c) (*stretch as far as*) arriver (jusqu')à (*l'épaule, la taille*); **can you r. the ceiling?**, pouvez-vous toucher le plafond?; **are the curtains long enough to r. the floor?**, est-ce que les rideaux sont suffisamment longs pour descendre jusqu'au sol?;

(d) (*hand*) passer (*le journal, le sel*); **to r. s.o. (over, up) sth**, passer qch à qn; **to r. sth down**, (*from coat-rack*) décrocher qch; (*from cupboard, shelf*) descendre qch;

(e) *Am F* (*corrupt*) corrompre, suborner (*un témoin*).

2 *vi* (*extend*) (*of forest, property etc*) s'étendre (**to**, jusqu'à); (*of noise, voice*) porter (**to**, jusqu'à); **as far as the eye can r.**, à perte de vue; **can you r.?**, est-ce que tu peux y arriver?; **to r. for sth**, attraper qch, étendre le bras pour prendre qch; **she reached to get** *or* **for it**, elle étendit le bras pour le prendre; **the policeman reached for his gun**, l'agent de police s'apprêta à dégainer son revolver; *Am* **r. (for the sky)!**, haut les mains!; **to r. into**, (*drawer, pocket*) mettre la main dans (**for**, pour prendre).

►**reach across**, *vi* (é)tendre le bras (**for**, pour prendre); **to r. across the table for sth**, (é)tendre le bras pour prendre qch sur la table.

►**reach back** *vi Fig* (*of records, files etc*) remonter (**to**, à).

►**reach down** **1** *vi* (*of coat, curtains, hair etc*) descendre (**to**, jusqu'à); (*of person*) (é)tendre le bras (**for**, pour prendre). **2** *vtsep* = **REACH² 1 (d)**.

►**reach out** **1** *vi* (é)tendre le bras (**for**, pour prendre); **I reached out and grabbed her**, je l'ai attrapée au vol. **2** *vtsep* **he reached out his hand for the glass**, il tendit la main vers le verre.

►**reach over** *vi* = **REACH ACROSS**.

►**reach up** **1** *vi* (*of person*) lever le bras (**for**, pour prendre); (*of snow, water*) monter (**to**, jusqu'à); **boots reaching halfway up his legs**, bottes lui montant à mi-jambe. **2** *vtsep* = **REACH² 1 (d)**.

reachable ['riːtʃəb(ə)l] *adj* (*place*) accessible; (*object*) accessible, à portée.

reach-me-down ['riːtʃmɪdaʊn] *n Old-fashioned Br* vieux vêtement.

react [rɪ'ækt] **1** *vi* réagir (**against**, contre; **on**, sur; **to**, à); **to be slow to r.**, (*of person*) être lent à réagir; (*of chemical*) avoir une réaction lente; **an acid can r. with a base to form a salt**, un acide et une base peuvent réagir ensemble et former un sel. **2** *vt Ch* faire réagir (**sth with sth**, qch avec qch).

reactance [rɪ'æktəns] *n El* réactance *f*.

reactant [rɪ'æktənt] *n Ch* réactif *m*.

reaction [rɪ'ækʃən] *n* **(a)** (*response*) (*of chemical, person*) réaction *f*; **to show no r.**, rester sans réaction; **what was her r.?**, quelle fut sa réaction?, comment a-t-elle réagi?; **in r. to**, en *ou* par réaction contre; *Med* **adverse r.**, mauvaise réaction; *Av* **r. engine** *or* **motor**, moteur *m* à réaction, réacteur *m*; **r. time**, temps *m* de réaction; **r. turbine**, turbine *f* à réaction; **(b)** *Pol Pej* **the forces of r.**, les réactionnaires *mpl*, *F* les réacs *mpl*.

reactionary [rɪ'ækʃən(ə)rɪ] *adj & n Pol* réactionnaire *mf*; **the reactionaries**, les réactionnaires *mpl*, *F* les réacs *mpl*.

reactivate [rɪ'æktɪveɪt] *vt* **(a)** (*start again*) reconstituer (*un club*); reformer (*un groupe*); **(b)** *esp Am Mil* (*return to active status*) remettre (*un navire*) en service.

reactive [rɪ'æktɪv] *adj Ch Phys* réactif; *El* (*load, power*) réactif, déwatté; **r. current**, courant réactif.

reactivity [rɪæk'tɪvɪtɪ] *n Ch Phys* réactivité *f*.

reactor [rɪ'æktər] *n Ch* réacteur *m*; *Nucl* réacteur atomique.

read¹ [riːd] *n F* **to have a (bit of a) r.**, faire un peu de lecture; *F* **just have a r. of this!**, (*expression of astonishment, disgust*) lis-moi ça!; *Br F* **can I have a r. of your**

magazine?, est-ce que je peux jeter un coup d'œil sur votre magazine *ou* emprunter votre magazine?; *F* **this book's a good r.,** ce livre est agréable à lire; **I've always enjoyed a good r.,** j'ai toujours aimé avoir un bon livre à lire; **he was having a quiet r.,** il lisait tranquillement; *Th* **to have a r. through,** (*of play*) lire la pièce.

read² *v* (*pt & pp* **read** [red]) **1** *vt* **(a)** (*of person*) *& Comptr* lire (*un journal, un livre, le braille*); lire, déchiffrer (*l'écriture, une partition*); **I r. Italian,** je lis *ou* je peux lire l'italien; **to r. Proust in the original,** lire Proust dans le texte; **have you something to r.?,** avez-vous de quoi lire *ou* quelque chose à lire?; **have you enough to r.?,** avez-vous assez de lecture?; **do you r. me?,** *Rad* est-ce que vous me recevez?; *Fig* est-ce que tu me comprends?; **I r. you loud and clear,** *Rad* je vous reçois cinq sur cinq; *Fig* oui, oui j'ai compris; *Admin* **read** [red] **and approved,** (*stamp on document*) lu et approuvé; *Fig* **to take sth as read,** (*evident*) considérer qch comme allant de soi; (*agreed upon*) considérer qch comme entendu; *Admin* **to take the minutes as read,** passer sur la lecture du procès-verbal; *Comptr* **r. head,** tête *f* de lecture;

(b) (*interpret*) lire (l'avenir dans) (*les lignes de la main*); **to r. s.o.'s mind** *or* **thoughts,** lire dans la pensée de qn; **to r. the future,** lire *ou* prédire l'avenir; **she can r. him like a(n open) book,** elle sait toujours ce qu'il pense; **I read** [red] **it as 24, but it was actually 224,** j'ai vu 24 mais en fait c'était 224; **to r. an electricity meter,** relever un compteur d'électricité; **don't r. too much into what she says,** ne donne pas à ce qu'elle dit plus de signification que ça n'en a;

(c) (*say aloud*) lire (*une lettre, un texte*) (à haute voix); **to r. s.o. sth** *or* **sth to s.o.,** lire qch à qn; **r. me that last bit again,** relis-moi le dernier passage; **to r. a child a bedtime story,** lire une histoire à un enfant pour qu'il s'endorme; **the colonel always reads the lesson,** c'est toujours le colonel qui lit un passage de l'Évangile; *Fig* **to r. s.o. a lesson** *or* **a lecture,** faire la leçon à qn; **to r. a paper at a conference,** présenter un exposé à une conférence; *Fig* **to r. s.o. the riot act,** (*reprimand*) chapitrer qn; *Jur* **to r. a will,** exécuter la lecture d'un testament;

(d) (*spend time reading*) **to r. oneself to sleep,** lire jusqu'à ce qu'on s'endorme; **he read** [red] **me to sleep,** il m'a fait la lecture jusqu'à ce que je m'endorme; **to r. sth over and over,** lire et relire qch; **to be widely read,** (*of magazine, author etc*) être très lu (**by,** parmi); (*of person*) avoir beaucoup lu; **she is widely read in history,** elle a lu beaucoup de livres d'histoire;

(e) *Br Univ* (*study*) étudier (*le français, l'histoire*); **to r. law/medicine,** faire son droit/sa médecine;

(f) (*show*) (*of measuring instrument*) indiquer (*une température, une pression*); **the inscription on the monument reads ...,** on peut lire sur le monument ...; **the calendar invariably reads January before I ...,** janvier arrive toujours avant que je ... + *sub*.

2 *vi* **(a)** (*understand printed word*) lire; **she taught her daughter (how) to r.,** elle a appris à lire à sa fille; **the child reads very well for his age,** c'est un enfant qui lit très bien pour son âge; **for 'least', r. 'lease',** remplacer 'least' par 'lease'; **we read** [red] **of his death in the newspaper,** nous avons appris sa mort dans le journal;

(b) (*interpret*) **to r. between the lines,** lire entre les lignes; **she read** [red] **in the cards that I would be famous,** elle a lu dans les cartes que je serais célèbre;

(c) (*spend time reading*) lire; **I'm very fond of reading,** j'aime beaucoup lire *ou F* bouquiner; **to r. aloud,** lire à haute voix; **r. quietly to yourselves,** lisez en silence; **to r. to s.o.,** faire la lecture à qn; **to r. about s.o./sth,** lire qch sur qch/qn; **what are you reading about?,** qu'est-ce que tu lis?;

(d) *Br Univ* **to r. for a degree,** préparer un diplôme; **to r. for the Bar,** faire des études de droit;

(e) (*be worded*) **to r. well,** (*of text*) se lire bien; **his text reads like a translation,** son texte sent la traduction; **the telegram reads as follows,** le télégramme est libellé comme suit.

►**read in** *vtsep Comptr* (*enter*) emmagasiner (*des données*).

►**read off** *vtsep* (*names etc*) énumérer (**from,** sur).

►**read on** *vi* (*continue to read*) **now r. on,** lisez la suite; **to r. on from ...,** lire à partir de ... .

►**read out** *vtsep* **she read out the names of the dead,** elle donna les noms des personnes décédées.

►**read over** *vtsep* (*skim*) parcourir; *esp Am* (*read again*) relire.

►**read through** *vtsep* (*skim*) parcourir; (*examine closely*) lire en détail, examiner; *Th* **to r. through a play,** faire la lecture d'une pièce.

►**read up** *vtsep* étudier (*un sujet*).

►**read up on** *vipo* = **READ UP**.

readability [riːdə'bɪlɪtɪ] *n* (*of book, handwriting*) lisibilité *f*.

readable ['riːdəb(ə)l] *adj* **(a)** (*enjoyable*) (*book etc*) lisible, qui se laisse lire *ou* qui est intéressant à lire; **(b)** (*legible*) (*handwriting*) lisible; **not r.,** illisible.

readdress [riːə'dres] *vt* **(a)** (*alter address*) réadresser (*un colis, une lettre*); **(b)** (*forward*) faire suivre (*une lettre*); **(c)** (*speak to again*) reprendre la parole devant (*les Communes*).

reader ['riːdər] *n* **(a)** (*of books, newspapers etc*) lecteur, -trice; *Am* (*company librarian*) documentaliste *mf*; **she is a great** *or* **an avid r.,** c'est une grande liseuse, elle lit beaucoup; *F* **he's not much of a r.,** il n'aime guère la lecture, il n'est pas liseur; **(proof) r.,** correcteur, -trice d'épreuves; **publisher's r.,** lecteur, -trice dans une maison d'édition; **(b)** (*university teacher*) *Br* maître *m* de conférences; *US* (*Can* = **teaching assistant**) assistant, *Can* chargé de cours; **(c)** (*book*) (*for teaching reading*) livre *m* de lecture; (*for pupils*) livre, manuel *m*; (*anthology*) recueil *m*; **French/geography r.,** livre de français/géographie; **a Melville r.,** un recueil d'extraits de Melville; **(d)** (*machine*) lecteur *m*.

readership ['riːdəʃɪp] *n* **(a)** (*of magazine, author etc*) lecteurs *mpl*, public *m*; (*esp of paper*) lectorat *m*; **what is the paper's r.?,** combien de personnes lisent le journal?; **(b)** *Br Univ* **she holds a r. in mathematics,** elle est maître de conférences de mathématiques.

readies ['redɪz] *npl Br Sl* (*cash*) liquide *m*; **£500 in r.,** 500 livres en liquide; **I want the r. first,** je veux le fric d'abord.

readily ['redɪlɪ] *adv* (*willingly*) de bonne grâce, volontiers; (*easily*) facilement.

readiness ['redɪnɪs] *n* **(a)** (*willingness*) empressement *m* (**to do,** à faire); **(b)** (*agility*) (*of speech, tongue*) facilité *f* d'expression; (*of mind, wit*) vivacité *f* d'esprit; **(c)** (*preparedness*) **to be in r.,** être prêt (**for,** pour); **to have everything in r.,** avoir tout prêt.

reading ['riːdɪŋ] **1** *n* **(a)** (*action, pastime*) lecture *f*; **r. is not his favourite activity,** lire *ou* la lecture n'est pas son passe-temps favori; **I have a lot of r. to catch up on,** j'ai beaucoup de retard à rattraper dans mes lectures; **we've brought you some r.,** nous vous avons apporté de la lecture *ou* de quoi lire; **I like a bit of light r.,** j'aime avoir un livre facile à lire; **his thesis makes (for) boring r.,** sa thèse est ennuyeuse à lire; **a young woman of wide r.,** une jeune femme très cultivée *ou* érudite *ou* lettrée;

(b) (*saying aloud*) (*of play, poetry, will*) lecture *f*; *Parl* **first/second/third r.,** première/seconde/troisième lecture;

(c) (*measurement*) (*of meter*) relevé *m*; (*by instrument*) indication *f*; **the fuel gauge is giving the wrong r.,** l'indicateur d'essence est faussé; **to take a barometric/temperature r.,** lire le baromètre/le thermomètre;

(d) (*interpretation*) (*of facts, situation*) interprétation *f*; *Th* (*by actor*) interprétation; (*by director*) version *f*;

(e) (*variant*) variante *f*.

2 *adj* (*book*) de lecture; **she has a r. age well in advance of her years,** elle a un niveau de lecture très avancé pour son âge; **to have a r. age of ten,** lire comme un enfant de dix ans; **children of r. age,** des enfants en âge de lire; **I have a r. knowledge of Arabic,** je peux lire l'arabe; **r. glasses,** lunettes *fpl* pour lire; *Comptr* **r. head,** tête *f* de lecture; **r. lamp,** (*on desk*) lampe *f* de bureau *ou* de travail; (*by bed*) lampe de chevet; **r. light,** (*on plane, train*) liseuse *f*; **r. list,** liste *f* de livres *ou* d'ouvrages recommandés; **r. material,** de la lecture, de quoi lire; **the r. public,** les lecteurs *mpl*; **r. room,** (*in library*) salle *f* de lecture; (*in university*) salle d'étude; **r. speed,** (*of child, computer*) vitesse *f* de lecture.

readjust [riːə'dʒʌst] **1** *vt* (*correct*) rajuster, réajuster (*les prix, les salaires*); remettre au point (*un microscope*); **to r. one's clothing,** se rajuster. **2** *vi* (*of person*) se réadapter (**to,** à).

readjustment [riːə'dʒʌstmənt] *n* **(a)** (*of prices, wages*) rajustement *m*, réajustement *m*; **some r. of the telescope is necessary,** il faut régler de nouveau le télescope; **(b)** (*of person*) réadaptation *f*.

readmission [riːəd'mɪʃən] *n* (*to club, political party*) réintégration *f* (**to,** dans); **his r. to hospital was seen as a bad sign,** le fait qu'il soit réadmis à l'hôpital fut interprété comme un mauvais signe.

readmit [riːəd'mɪt] *vt* (*take in again*) réintégrer (*qn*) (**to,** dans); **they readmitted him** *or* **he was readmitted (to hospital) last night,** il a été réadmis à l'hôpital la nuit dernière.

read-only [riːd'əʊnlɪ] *adj Comptr* **r.-o. memory,** mémoire morte.

read-out ['riːdaʊt] *n Comptr* affichage *m*; **r.-o. device,** unité *m* d'affichage.

readvertise [riː'ædvətaɪz] **1** *vt* repasser une annonce de (*offre d'emploi*). **2** *vi* repasser une annonce (**for,** pour trouver); **they're readvertising,** ils ont repassé l'annonce.

readvertisement [riːəd'vɜːtɪsmənt] *n* deuxième annonce *f*; **this is a r.,** (*notice on jobs page*) deuxième annonce d'offre d'emploi.

read-write ['riːdraɪt] *adj Comptr* **r.-w. head,** tête *f* de lecture et d'écriture; **r.-w. memory,** mémoire *f* lecture-écriture.

ready[1] ['redɪ] **1** *adj* **(a)** (*prepared*) prêt (**to do,** à faire; **for sth,** à, pour qch); *Sp* **(get) r.! (get) set! go!,** à vos marques! prêts! partez!; **to make** *or* **get sth r.,** préparer qch; (*food*) apprêter qch; **dinner is r.,** le dîner est servi, *F* à table; **r. for use,** prêt à l'usage; **to get r.,** se préparer, s'apprêter (**to do,** à faire; **for sth,** à qch); **to get r. for school,** se préparer pour aller à l'école; **to get a patient r. for an operation,** apprêter un malade pour une opération; **to get a room r. for a guest,** préparer *ou* faire une chambre pour un invité; **she's r. for anything,** elle est prête à tout; **are you r. to order?,** (*in restaurant*) avez-vous choisi *ou* fait votre choix?; **I'm r. if you are,** quand tu veux; **to make r.,** faire des préparations, se préparer (**for,** pour); **r. to serve,** (*food*) prêt à servir, tout prêt; **I'm r. to drop,** (*exhausted*) je tombe de fatigue; **r. to hand,** sous la main, à portée de main; **r. cash** *or* **money,** argent *m* liquide; **to pay in r. money,** payer en espèces *fpl ou* argent liquide; *Com* **r. reckoner,** barème *m*;
(b) (*willing*) prêt, disposé (**to do,** à faire); **don't be too r. to believe him,** ne le croyez pas trop facilement;
(c) (*quick*) prompt, facile; **to have a r. wit,** avoir l'esprit prompt *ou* d'à-propos *ou* de repartie; **r. understanding,** intelligence ouverte; **to be always r. with an answer,** avoir la réplique prompte; **he's very r. with his fists,** il est prompt à se battre; **goods that meet with a r. sale,** marchandises de vente facile *ou* courante; **the story found r. acceptance,** l'histoire a été acceptée sans difficulté; **a r. source of income,** une source de revenu facile; **you're always a bit too r. with advice,** tu es toujours un peu trop pressé pour donner conseil.
2 *n* **(a)** *F* (*money*) argent *m* liquide; **have you enough of the r. on you?,** as-tu assez de liquide?;
(b) *Mil* **to come to the r.,** apprêter l'arme; **at the r.,** (*guns*) prêt à tirer; **the reporter had her notebook at the r.,** la journaliste avait son carnet tout prêt; **with notebook at the r., she ...,** son carnet tout prêt, elle ... .

ready[2] **1** *vt* préparer (*la maison*); **to r. oneself for action,** se préparer à l'action. **2** *vi* se préparer (**for,** pour).

ready- [redɪ-] *pref* **r.-cut/***etc*, pré-coupé/*etc*.

ready-made [redɪ'meɪd] **1** *adj* (*shoes, suit*) de confection, prêt-à-porter; (*curtains, excuses, phrases*) tout fait; **r.-m. clothes,** vêtements *mpl* de confection, le prêt-à-porter; **to wear r.-m. clothes,** s'habiller en confection *ou* prêt-à-porter; *Fig* **to have a r.-m. family,** avoir une famille toute faite. **2** *n* (*garment*) (vêtement *m* de) confection *f*.

ready-mix ['redɪmɪks] *adj* (*buns, cake etc*) fait à partir d'une préparation; (*concrete*) prémalaxé.

ready-to-wear [redɪtə'weər] **1** *adj* (*clothes*) de confection, prêt-à-porter. **2** *n* (*garment*) (vêtement *m* de) confection *f*, prêt-à-porter *m*.

reaffirm [riːə'fɜːm] *vt* affirmer de nouveau, réaffirmer (*sa loyauté*).

reafforest [riːə'fɒrɪst] *vt* = **REFOREST**.

reafforestation [riːəfɒrɪ'steɪʃən] *n* = **REFORESTATION**.

Reaganite ['reɪgənaɪt] *n* partisan *m* de Reagan; **R. budget/programme/***etc*, budget *m*/programme *m*/*etc* reaganien.

Reaganomics [reɪgə'nɒmɪks] *npl* (*usu with sing verb*) reaganisme *m*.

reagent [rɪ'eɪdʒənt] *n Ch* réactif *m*.

real [rɪəl] **1** *adj* **(a)** (*authentic*) (*diamond, pearl*) vrai; (*gold, leather*) véritable; (*silk, flowers, mother etc*) naturel; **a r. friend/idiot,** un véritable ami/idiot; **a r. disaster/shock,** un vrai désastre/choc; **that's what I call a r. man,** ça, c'est ce que j'appelle un (vrai) homme; **the r. reason,** la vraie raison (**for,** pour); **she has no r. feeling for poetry,** elle n'a pas le vrai sentiment de la poésie; **what is his r. name?,** quel est son nom véritable?; *Br* **r. ale,** ale *f* véritable; *Br* **Campaign for R. Ale,** Campagne *f* pour l'ale véritable; *Br* **he's a r. gentleman,** c'est un véritable *ou* vrai gentleman; *F* **it's the r. McCoy** *or* **thing,** c'est du vrai de vrai; *F* **she swears it's the r. thing this time,** elle jure que cette fois-ci c'est le grand amour; *F* **this is not a fire drill, it's the r. thing** *or* **for r.,** ce n'est pas un exercice, c'est pour de vrai; *esp Am* **is that man for r.?,** est-ce que cet homme est sérieux?; *esp Am* **is that for r.?,** c'est vrai?;
(b) (*actual*) (*cost, salary, world etc*) *& Math Phys* réel; **what does that mean in r. terms?,** qu'est-ce que ça signifie en termes réels?; **in r. life,** dans la réalité *ou* la vie; *Fin* **r. value,** valeur effective *ou* réelle; *Rel* **r. presence,** présence réelle; *Comptr* **r. time,** temps réel;
(c) (*immovable*) **r. estate,** immobilier *m*; **she's in r. estate,** elle travaille dans l'immobilier; **r. estate agent,** agent immobilier; **r. estate agency,** agence immobilière; **r. estate developer,** promoteur *m*;
(d) *Sp* **r. tennis,** (jeu *m* de) paume *f*; **to play r. tennis,** jouer à la paume.
2 *adv F* (*very*) vraiment, très; *Am* **a r. fine day,** vraiment une belle journée, une très belle journée; *Am* **that's r. nice of you,** c'est très gentil de votre part; *Am* **I'll see you r. soon,** à très bientôt.

realism ['rɪəlɪz(ə)m] *n Art Phil etc* réalisme *m*.

realist ['rɪəlɪst] *adj & n Art Phil* réaliste *mf*.

realistic [rɪə'lɪstɪk] *adj* (*person, proposal*) réaliste; (*style*) plein de réalisme.

realistically [rɪə'lɪstɪklɪ] *adv* (*to act, behave*) avec réalisme.

reality [rɪ'ælɪtɪ] *n* réalité *f*; **in r.,** en réalité; **to bring s.o. back to r.,** ramener qn à la réalité; **described with extraordinary r.,** décrit avec un réalisme extraordinaire; **to become a r.,** (*of dream, hope etc*) se réaliser, devenir réalité; **to make a dream/project a r.,** réaliser un rêve/projet; **the realities of everyday life,** les réalités de tous les jours.

realizable ['rɪəlaɪzəb(ə)l] *adj* (*plan, project etc*) *& Fin* réalisable.

realization [rɪəlaɪ'zeɪʃən] *n* **(a)** (*of plan, project etc*) *& Fin* réalisation *f*; **(b)** (*awareness*) (prise *f* de) conscience *f*; **there is a growing r. that ...,** on commence à se rendre compte que ...; **the sudden r. that ... made her weep,** elle a pleuré quand tout d'un coup elle s'est rendu compte que ... .

realize ['rɪəlaɪz] **1** *vt* **(a)** réaliser (*un projet*); *Fin* réaliser (*un actif, des bénéfices*); **to r. a high price,** (*of goods*) atteindre un haut prix; (*of seller*) obtenir un haut prix; **our worst fears have been realized,** nos pires craintes se sont réalisées; **our hopes were realized,** nos espoirs se sont réalisés *ou* concrétisés; **(b)** (*know, be aware of*) se rendre compte de, réaliser (*qch*); **I r. that, but ...,** je sais bien, mais ...; **(c)** (*become aware of*) s'apercevoir de, se rendre compte de (*qch*); **we realized that he was blind,** nous nous sommes aperçus qu'il était aveugle; **I realized it at the first glance,** je m'en suis rendu compte au premier coup d'œil. **2** *vi* **I'm sorry, I didn't r.,** je suis désolé, je ne m'en étais pas rendu compte *ou* je n'avais pas réalisé.

really ['rɪəlɪ] **1** *adv* vraiment; **things that r. exist,** choses qui existent réellement; **that is r. a matter for the manager,** c'est là proprement l'affaire du gérant; **you r. MUST go to it,** il faut absolument que vous y alliez; **is it r. true?** est-ce bien vrai? **2** *int* **r.?** vraiment?; **not r.!** pas possible!; **(well) r.!,** ça alors!, c'est le comble!

realm [relm] *n* (*kingdom*) royaume *m*; *Fig* (*of dreams, fancy etc*) monde *m*; (*of politics, science etc*) domaine *m*; **peer of the R.,** pair *m* du royaume; **within the r. of possibility,** dans le domaine du possible; **health is no longer the exclusive r. of doctors,** la santé n'est plus l'apanage du médecin.

real-time [rɪəl'taɪm] *adj Comptr* **r.-t. clock,** horloge *f* temps réel; **r.-t. computer,** ordinateur exploité en temps réel; **r.-t. system,** système *m* utilisable *ou* d'exploitation en temps réel.

realtor ['rɪəltər] *n Am* (*Br* = **estate agent**) agent immobilier.

realty ['rɪəltɪ] *n Jur* biens immobiliers, (biens *mpl*) immeubles *mpl*.

ream[1] [riːm] *n* (*of paper*) rame *f*; *F* **to write reams,** écrire des pages et des pages; *F* **reams of information,** des quantités *fpl* d'informations.

ream[2] *vt* **(a)** (*clean out*) curer (*une pipe*); **(b)** (*bore*) aléser (*une pièce*); **(c)** (*squeeze*) presser (*un citron*).

reamer ['riːmər] *n* **(a)** (*for pipe*) cure-pipe(s) *m*; **(b)** (*for part*) alésoir *m*; **(c)** (*for lemon*) presse-citron *m inv*.

reaming ['riːmɪŋ] *n* (*of part*) alésage *m*.

reanimate [riː'ænɪmeɪt] *vt Med* r(é)animer (*un asphyxié*).

reap [riːp] **1** *vt* moissonner (*le blé, un champ*); *Prov* **he who sows the wind shall r. the whirlwind,** qui sème le vent récolte la tempête; *Fig* **to r. the rewards of one's labours,** recueillir le fruit de ses travaux; *Fig* **I r. no benefit from it,** je n'en retire aucun avantage. **2** *vi* moissonner, faire la moisson.

reaper ['riːpər] *n* (*machine*) moissonneuse *f*; (*person*) moissonneur, -euse; **r. binder,** moissonneuse-lieuse *f*; *Fig* **the (Grim) R.,** la Mort.

reaping ['riːpɪŋ] *n* (*of wheat etc*) moisson *f*; **r. machine,** moissonneuse *f*.

reappear [riːə'pɪər] *vi* (*of person, sun etc*) reparaître; (*of ghost, mirage, sun*) réapparaître.

reappearance [riːə'pɪərəns] *n* (*of person, sun etc*) réapparition *f*.

reapply [riːə'plaɪ] **1** *vt* réappliquer (*crème, lotion etc*). **2** *vi* (*for grant, job, loan etc*) renouveler sa demande (**for,** de); **r. as necessary,** (*of cream, lotion etc*) réappliquer au besoin.

reappoint [riːə'pɔɪnt] *vt* renommer (*qn*).

reappointment [riːə'pɔɪntmənt] *n* (*of chairman etc*) nomination *f* pour la deuxième fois de suite.

reappraisal [riːə'preɪz(ə)l] *n* **(a)** *Fin* (*of property*) réévaluation *f*; **(b)** (*of policy*) réexamen *m*.

reappraise [riːə'preɪz] *vt* **(a)** *Fin* réévaluer (*une propriété*); **(b)** réexaminer (*une politique*).

rear¹ [rɪər] *n* **(a)** (*back part*) (*of building, car, train*) arrière *m*; (*of military column*) queue *f*; **in the r.,** en arrière, à l'arrière; **to attack the enemy in the r.,** attaquer l'ennemi par l'arrière; **in the r. of the train,** en queue du train; **at** *or Am* **in the r. of,** (*behind*) derrière; **from the r.,** par derrière; **to bring up the r.,** (*come at end*) (*of military column*) fermer la marche; (*of procession*) venir en queue; (*be in last place*) être à la queue; *Pej* être la lanterne rouge; **to protect one's r.,** *Mil* protéger ses arrières; *Fig* assurer ses arrières; *Aut* **r. axle/door/wheel/window,** essieu *m*/portière *f*/roue *f*/lunette *f* arrière *inv*; *Br Aut* **r. lights** *or* **lamps,** feux *mpl* arrière; **r.-engined** (*car etc*) avec le moteur à l'arrière, à moteur arrière; **r. legs,** (*of animal*) pattes de derrière; *Nau* **r. admiral,** contre-amiral *m*, *pl* contre-amiraux; **r. entrance,** (*of building*) entrée *f* de derrière; **r.-mounted,** (*engine, gun*) monté à l'arrière; **r. portion,** (*of train*) rame *f ou* groupe *m* de queue; *Aut* **r.-view** *or Am* **vision mirror,** rétroviseur *m*; *Aut* **r.-wheel drive,** (*vehicle*) traction *f* arrière; **car/***etc* **with r.-wheel drive,** voiture *f*/*etc* à traction arrière.

(b) *F* (*buttocks*) **r. (end),** cul *m*, derrière *m*, fesses *fpl*; **he needs a kick in the r.,** il lui faut un coup de pied au cul.

rear² **1** *vt* **(a)** (*nurture*) élever (*un enfant, des moutons*); cultiver (*des plantes*); **(b)** (*lift*) relever (*la tête*); *Fig* **to r. its ugly head** (*of racism, violence etc*) faire son apparition. **2** *vi* **to r. (up),** (*of horse*) se cabrer; **high cliffs r. above the shore,** de hautes falaises se dressent au-dessus du rivage.

rear-end [rɪər'end] *vt esp Am Aut* **to r.-e. s.o.,** (*collide with*) emboutir l'arrière de la voiture de qn.

rearguard ['rɪəgɑːd] *n Mil* arrière-garde *f*, *pl* arrière-gardes; **r. action,** combat *m* d'arrière-garde; **to fight** *or* **mount a r. action,** mener un combat d'arrière-garde.

rearing ['rɪərɪŋ] *n* **(a)** (*of children*) éducation *f*; (*of animals*) élevage *m*; (*of plants*) culture *f*; **(b)** (*of horse*) cabrage *m*.

rearm [riː'ɑːm] *vt & vi* réarmer.

rearmament [riː'ɑːməmənt] *n* (*of country, soldiers etc*) réarmement *m*.

rearmost ['rɪəməʊst] *adj* (*carriage, compartment*) dernier, de queue.

rearrange [riːə'reɪndʒ] *vt* réarranger (*des livres, des fleurs etc*); réajuster (*ses vêtements*); changer, décaler (*un rendez-vous*); **to r. a room,** déménager une pièce.

rearrangement [riːə'reɪndʒmənt] *n* (*of books, flowers etc*) réarrangement *m*; (*of clothing*) réajustement *m*; (*of appointment*) changement *m*, décalage *m*.

rearward ['rɪəwəd] **1** *n* (*position in rear*) arrière-garde *f*, derrières *mpl*; **in** *or* **to r.,** à l'arrière (**of,** de). **2** *adj* **(a)** (*at back*) (*compartment etc*) (situé à l')arrière; **(b)** (*backward*) (*glance, movement*) en arrière. **3** *adv esp Am* = **REARWARDS.**

rearwards ['rɪəwədz] *adv esp Br* (*be situated*) à l'arrière; (*to glance, move*) vers l'arrière.

reason¹ ['riːz(ə)n] *n* **(a)** (*cause*) raison *f* (**for,** de); **the r. why,** la raison; **I don't know the r. why,** je ne sais pas pourquoi; **the r. (why) he left,** la raison pour laquelle il est parti; **there is a r. for his doing so,** il y a une raison pour qu'il le fasse; **to state one's reasons for a decision,** motiver une décision; **for reasons of health,** pour raisons de santé; **reasons of state,** la raison d'État; **for reasons best known to themselves,** pour des raisons qu'eux seuls connaissent *ou* qu'ils sont les seuls à connaître; **for some** *or* **one r. or other,** pour une raison ou pour une autre; **for no other r. than that I forgot,** pour la simple raison que j'ai oublié; **for no particular r.,** sans aucune raison spéciale; **for no r. at all,** sans raison; **for that very r.,** pour cette raison même; **for the very r. that he had been asked not to do it,** précisément parce qu'on l'avait prié de ne pas le faire; **the r. (for which** *or* **why) he came, his r. for coming,** la raison pour laquelle il est venu; **what's the r. for it?,** à quoi cela tient-il?, quelle en est la raison?; **what r. did you give for your absence?,** comment as-tu expliqué ton absence?; **to have every r. to believe/***etc*, avoir tout lieu de croire/*etc*; **I have (good) r. to believe that he's lying,** j'ai de bonnes raisons de croire qu'il ment; **she complains and with (good) r.,** elle se plaint et pour cause; **it's not without (good) r. that I detest him,** ce n'est pas pour rien que je le déteste; **to give s.o. good r. for doing sth,** donner de bonnes raisons à qn de faire qch; **give me one good r. why I should!,** donne-moi une seule bonne raison pour le faire *ou* pour que je le fasse!; **all the more r. for going there** *or* **why I should go there,** raison de plus pour y aller *ou* pour que j'y aille; **by r. of his infirmity,** en raison de son infirmité; **to be found not guilty by r. of insanity,** être déclaré non-coupable pour cause de démence;

(b) (*sanity, common sense*) raison *f*; **he lost his r.,** il a perdu la raison; **to listen to** *or* **hear** *or* **see r.,** entendre raison; **to bring s.o. to r.,** faire entendre raison à qn; **it stands to r.,** il va de soi *ou* sans dire (**that,** que); **that stands to r.,** cela va sans dire, cela coule de source, c'est logique; **to do everything within r. to ...,** faire tout ce qu'il est raisonnable de faire pour ... .

reason² **1** *vi* raisonner (**on, about,** sur); **to r. with s.o.,** raisonner (avec) qn; *Hum* **ours is not to r. why,** il ne faut pas chercher à comprendre; **to r. from past experience,** fonder ses raisons sur l'expérience du passé. **2** *vt* **to r. that,** calculer que.

▶**reason out** *vtsep* déduire la solution de (*un problème*).

reasonable ['riːz(ə)nəb(ə)l] *adj* (*person, price, demand*) raisonnable; (*price*) équitable; (*offer*) acceptable, raisonnable; (*effort*) acceptable; **(do) be r.,** tâchez d'être raisonnable; **to believe sth beyond all r. doubt,** croire qch en son âme et conscience; **r. suspicions,** soupçons bien fondés; **r. excuse,** excuse *f* valable (**for,** de); **with a r. amount of luck,** avec un peu de chance; **the weather was r.,** le temps était passable.

reasonableness ['riːz(ə)nəb(ə)lnɪs] *n* (*of person, offer, effort etc*) caractère *m* raisonnable; (*of suspicion*) bien fondé *m*.

reasonably ['riːz(ə)nəblɪ] *adv* **(a)** (*to behave, act*) raisonnablement; **r. priced,** (*house etc*) d'un prix équitable *ou* raisonnable; **(b)** (*fairly, rather*) assez; **r. fit,** en assez bonne forme; **if we are r. lucky,** avec un peu de chance.

reasoned ['riːzənd] *adj* (*analysis, decision etc*) raisonné.

reasoning ['riːzənɪŋ] **1** *n* raisonnement *m*; **power of r.,** (*ability*) capacité *f* de raisonnement; **there's no r. with him,** il n'y a pas moyen de lui faire entendre raison, on ne peut pas raisonner avec lui; **the r. behind the decision,** les raisons de cette décision. **2** *adj* (*creature etc*) doué de raison; (*ability, process etc*) de raisonnement.

reassemble [riːə'semb(ə)l] **1** *vt* **(a)** (*gather*) rassembler (*des troupes*); **(b)** (*put together*) remonter (*une machine*); rassembler (*une charpente*). **2** *vi* (*of troops*) s'assembler de nouveau; **Parliament will r. on ...,** le Parlement rouvrira le ... .

reassert [riːə'sɜːt] *vt* réaffirmer (*une conviction*); **her self-confidence reasserted itself,** sa confiance est revenue.

reassess [riːə'ses] *vt* **(a)** reconsidérer, réexaminer (*une politique, une situation*); **(b)** *Fin* réévaluer (*des dommages*); **you have been reassessed,** votre situation fiscale a été réexaminée.

reassessment [riːə'sesmənt] *n* **(a)** (*of policy, situation*) réexamen *m*; **(b)** *Fin* (*of damages*) réévaluation *f*.

reassign [riːə'saɪn] *vt* (*transfer*) muter (*un employé, un policier etc*) (**to,** à).

reassignment [riːə'saɪnmənt] *n* **(a)** (*transfer*) (*of employee, policeman etc*) mutation *f*; **(b)** (*duties*) nouveau poste, nouvelles fonctions.

reassume [riːə'sjuːm] *vt* assumer (*ses fonctions*) de nouveau.

reassurance [riːə'ʃʊərəns] *n* **(a)** (*comfort*) réconfort *m*; (*guarantee*) assurance *f*; **to give reassurances,** rassurer (**about,** quant à); assurer (**that,** que); **(b)** *Br Fin* réassurance *f*.

reassure [riːəˈʃʊər] *vt* **(a)** rassurer (*qn*) (**on, about,** sur); **to r. s.o. of one's esteem,** assurer qn de son estime; **to feel reassured,** se sentir rassuré (**about,** sur); **(b)** *Br Fin* réassurer.

reassuring [riːəˈʃʊərɪŋ] *adj* (*person, news etc*) rassurant.

reassuringly [riːəˈʃʊərɪŋlɪ] *adv* (*to behave, act*) d'une manière rassurante.

reawaken [riːəˈweɪk(ə)n] **1** *vt* réveiller (*un dormeur*); ranimer (*l'intérêt, un sentiment*); faire renaître (*l'espoir, l'intérêt, un sentiment*). **2** *vi* (*of person*) se réveiller de nouveau; (*of affection, feelings, interest*) se ranimer.

reawakening [riːəˈweɪk(ə)nɪŋ] *n* (*of person, feeling etc*) réveil *m*; (*of idea*) renaissance *f*.

rebate [ˈriːbeɪt] *n Com etc* **(a)** (*refund*) remboursement *m* (partiel); (*of rates, tax*) dégrèvement *m*; **(b)** (*discount on purchase*) rabais *m*, ristourne *f*.

rebec [ˈriːbek] *n Mus* rebec *m*.

rebel[1] [ˈreb(ə)l] *n* (*opponent*) (*of government*) rebelle *mf*; (*armed*) insurgé, -ée; (*of society*) révolté, -ée; *US Hist* **the Rebels,** les confédérés; **r. army/camp/***etc*, armée *f*/camp *m*/*etc* rebelle; **r. forces/MPs/***etc*, forces *fpl*/parlementaires *mpl*/*etc* rebelles; **r. leader,** chef *m* des rebelles.

rebel[2] [rɪˈbel] *vi* (**-ll-**) (*against government*) se rebeller, se soulever (**against,** contre); (*against society*) se révolter (**against,** contre); **to r. against one's fate,** se révolter *ou* s'insurger contre son destin.

rebellion [rɪˈbeljən] *n* (*against government*) rébellion *f*, soulèvement *m* (**against,** contre); (*against society*) révolte *f* (**against,** contre); **to be in r. against,** être en rébellion contre; **to rise up in r.,** se soulever (**against,** contre).

rebellious [rɪˈbeljəs] *adj* (*soldier, troops etc*) insubordonné; (*student*) révolté, en révolte; (*behaviour, child, hair etc*) rebelle; **r. act,** acte *f* de rébellion.

rebelliously [rɪˈbeljəslɪ] *adv* (*to behave, act*) d'une façon rebelle.

rebelliousness [rɪˈbeljəsnɪs] *n* (*of troops*) insubordination *f*; (*of students etc*) esprit *m* de rébellion.

rebirth [riːˈbɜːθ] *n Fig* (*of country etc*) renaissance *f*.

reboot [riːˈbuːt] *Comptr* **1** *vt* réamorcer. **2** *vi* se réamorcer.

rebore[1] [ˈriːbɔːr] *n Aut* réalésage *m*; **my car needs a r.,** le cylindre de ma voiture a besoin d'être réalésé *ou* d'un réalésage.

rebore[2] *vt Aut* réaléser (*un cylindre*).

reborn [riːˈbɔːn] *adj* né à nouveau; **to be r.,** renaître; *Fig* **hope was r.,** l'espoir est revenu; *Fig* **to feel r.,** (*physically*) se sentir comme neuf; (*spiritually*) se sentir renaître.

rebound[1] [ˈriːbaʊnd] *n* **(a)** (*of bullet*) ricochet *m*; (*of spring*) détente *f*; *Fig* **she married him on the r.,** elle l'a épousé à cause d'une déception amoureuse; *Fig* **he caught her on the r.,** il a commencé à la fréquenter au moment où elle sortait d'une déception amoureuse; **(b)** *Sp* (*ball, puck*) rebond *m*, rebondissement *m*; *Basketball* (prise *f* du) ballon *m* qui fait rebond; **to hit a ball on the r.,** frapper une balle au rebond.

rebound[2] [rɪˈbaʊnd] *vi* **(a)** (*of ball etc*) rebondir; (*of stone*) ricocher; (*of cry, noise*) faire écho (**from,** contre); *Fig* (*of joke, lie etc*) se retourner (**on,** contre); **the trick he played rebounded on him,** son mauvais tour a fait boomerang; **(b)** (*recover*) (*of person*) se ressaisir (**from,** après); (*of share prices, business*) reprendre, se redresser (**from,** après).

rebuff[1] [rɪˈbʌf] *n* (*of person*) rebuffade *f*; (*of suggestion etc*) refus *m*; **to meet with** *or* **suffer a r.,** (*of person*) essuyer une rebuffade; (*of suggestion etc*) être repoussé.

rebuff[2] *vt* (*reject*) repousser (*qn, des avances*); rejeter (*une offre, une suggestion*); **to feel rebuffed,** se sentir repoussé.

rebuild [riːˈbɪld] *v* (*pt & pp* **rebuilt** [riːˈbɪlt]) **1** *vt* reconstruire (*un immeuble, une société*); reconstruire, refaire (*sa vie*); remettre à neuf, refaire (*un appareil, un moteur*). **2** *vi* reconstruire.

rebuilding [riːˈbɪldɪŋ] *n* (*of house, company*) reconstruction *f*; (*of life*) reconstruction *f*, réfection *f*; (*of machine, engine*) réfection *f*, remise *f* à neuf.

rebuke[1] [rɪˈbjuːk] *n* (*scolding*) réprimande *f*; **to administer a r. to s.o.,** réprimander qn, faire une réprimande à qn.

rebuke[2] *vt* (*scold*) réprimander (*qn*) (**for doing,** pour avoir fait qch).

rebus [ˈriːbəs] *n* rébus *m*.

rebut [rɪˈbʌt] *vt* (**-tt-**) (*disprove*) réfuter (*une accusation, une hypothèse etc*).

rebutment [rɪˈbʌtmənt], **rebuttal** [rɪˈbʌt(ə)l] *n* (*of accusation, hypothesis etc*) réfutation *f*.

rec [rek] *n F* **(a)** *Br* **r. (ground),** terrain *m* de jeux; **(b)** *Am* récréation *f*, récré *f*; **r. room,** (*in home*) salle *f* de jeux.

recalcitrance [rɪˈkælsɪtrəns] *n* (*of animal, person, disease*) récalcitrance *f*.

recalcitrant [rɪˈkælsɪtrənt] **1** *adj* (*horse, person*) récalcitrant; (*disease*) récalcitrant, réfractaire. **2** *n* récalcitrant, -ante.

recall[1] [rɪˈkɔːl] *n* **(a)** (*remembering*) **she has remarkable powers of r.,** elle a une mémoire remarquable; **to have instant r.,** avoir une mémoire vive; **to have total r.,** être capable de se souvenir de tous les détails de quelque chose; **(b)** (*calling back*) (*of troops, library book, defective goods etc*) rappel *m*; (*of Parliament*) reconvocation *f*; *Mil* **to sound the r.,** battre le rappel; **it's past r.,** c'est irrémédiable; **beyond r.,** irrévocable; **lost beyond r.,** perdu irrévocablement; **r. slip,** (*for library book*) fiche *f* de rappel.

recall[2] **1** *vt* **(a)** (*remember*) se souvenir de, se rappeler (*qch*); **to r. doing sth,** se rappeler avoir fait qch; **to r. sth to s.o.,** rappeler qch à qn; **legends that r. the past,** légendes évocatrices du passé *ou* qui évoquent le passé; **how vividly I r. the scene!,** avec quelle netteté je revois ce spectacle!; **(b)** (*call back*) rappeler (*des troupes, des articles défectueux etc*); demander le retour de (*un livre*); **the sound of the telephone recalled her to the present,** la sonnerie du téléphone la ramena à la réalité. **2** *vi* **as I r.,** si je me rappelle bien; **as you may r.,** comme vous vous en souvenez *ou* le rappelez peut-être; **as you will r.,** comme vous vous en souvenez sans doute.

recant [rɪˈkænt] **1** *vt* (*disavow*) rétracter, revenir sur (*une opinion*); abjurer (*une erreur de doctrine*); désavouer (*une doctrine*). **2** *vi* se rétracter.

recantation [riːkænˈteɪʃən] *n* (*of faith, statement*) rétractation *f*, abjuration *f* (**of,** de).

recap[1] [ˈriːkæp] *n* **(a)** *F* (*summary*) récapitulation *f*; **let's do a r.,** faisons le point; **(b)** *Am Aut* pneu rechapé.

recap[2] *v* (**-pp-**) **1** *vt* **(a)** *F* = **RECAPITULATE 1 (a)**; **(b)** *Am Aut* rechaper (*un pneu*); **2** *vi* = **RECAPITULATE 2**.

recapitulate [riːkəˈpɪtjʊleɪt] **1** *vt* **(a)** (*summarize*) récapituler, faire un résumé de (*une discussion etc*); **let us r. the facts,** faisons le point; **(b)** *Mus* reprendre (*un thème*). **2** *vi* récapituler.

recapitulation [riːkəpɪtjʊˈleɪʃən] *n* **(a)** (*of discussion etc*) récapitulation *f*, résumé *m*; **(b)** *Mus* reprise *f*.

recapture[1] [riːˈkæptʃər] *n* (*of prisoner, town*) reprise *f*.

recapture[2] *vt* **(a)** (*take again*) reprendre (*un prisonnier, une ville*); **(b)** (*recreate*) faire revivre, recréer (*une époque*); faire revivre (*une ambiance, de bons moments*); **(c)** (*rediscover*) retrouver (*sa jeunesse*).

recast [riːˈkɑːst] *vt* (*pt & pp* **recast**) **(a)** (*reshape*) remanier (*une phrase, une œuvre littéraire*); **(b)** *Th* (*find new cast for*) trouver de nouveaux acteurs pour (*une pièce*); (*find new part for*) donner un nouveau rôle à (*un acteur*); **the part has been recast,** le rôle a été donné à quelqu'un d'autre;

recce [ˈrekɪ] *n F* (*exploration*) reconnaissance *f*; **to make a quick r.,** faire une reconnaissance rapide (**of,** de).

recede [rɪˈsiːd] *vi* **(a)** (*of tide, sea*) se retirer, descendre; (*of coastline, person, thing*) s'éloigner, reculer; *Art* (*of background*) s'éloigner; **the colour receded from his face,** il devint livide; **as memories of the past r.,** à mesure que les souvenirs du passé s'effacent; **(b)** (*slope backwards*) (*of chin, forehead*) fuir; **to have a receding chin/forehead,** avoir le menton/front fuyant; **his hair(line)** *or* **he is receding,** ses tempes se dégarnissent; **(c)** (*lose value*) décliner en valeur; **the company's shares have receded five points,** les actions de la société ont reculé de *ou* perdu cinq points.

receipt[1] [rɪˈsiːt] *n* **(a)** (*of letter, parcel etc*) réception *f*; **on r. of this letter,** dès réception de cette lettre; **on r. of the news,** à la nouvelle (**about,** de); **within one week of r.,** dans un délai d'une semaine après réception; **to pay on r.,** payer à (la) réception; **to acknowledge r.,** accuser réception (**of,** de); **(b)** *Com* (*for payment*) reçu *m* (**for,** de); (*for letter, parcel*) récépissé *m*, accusé *m* de réception; **to give a r.** (*for meal, taxi fare etc*) donner un reçu; (*for rent*) donner acquit *ou* quittance; **(c) receipts,** (*takings*) recettes *fpl*, rentrées *fpl*; **receipts and expenditure,** recettes et dépenses *fpl*;

receipt[2] *vt* **to r. a bill,** (*in writing*) acquitter une facture; (*with stamp*) apposer le tampon 'pour acquit' sur une facture.

receivable [rɪˈsiːvəb(ə)l] *Com* **1** *adj* (*account, bill etc*) à recevoir. **2** *n* compte *m ou* effet *m* à recevoir.

receive [rɪˈsiːv] **1** *vt* **(a)** (*take delivery of*) recevoir (*un don, une nouvelle, une lettre*); toucher (*de l'argent, son traitement etc*); **I have received your letter,** votre lettre m'est parvenue; **received with thanks,** (*on bill*) pour acquit; *Rad TV* **to r. a broadcast,** recevoir une émission; **to r. a station,** capter un poste; **are you receiving me?,** (*on radio*) est-ce que vous me recevez?; **to r. (the) service,** (*of tennis or badminton player*) recevoir le service; *Jur* **to r. stolen goods,** receler des objets volés;

(b) (*be given*) recevoir (*une salutation, un coup, la communion etc*); essuyer (*un refus*); faire l'objet de (*critique*); **to r. thirty days,** être condamné à un mois de prison; **I received from her the impression that ...,** elle m'a donné l'impression que ...; *Prov* **it is better to give than to r.,** il y a plus de joie à donner qu'à recevoir;

(c) (*welcome*) recevoir (*des invités*); **to be cordially received,** (*of visitor etc*) trouver un accueil chaleureux, être bien reçu; **the proposal was well/badly received,** la proposition reçut un accueil favorable/défavorable *ou* a été bien/mal reçue; **to r. s.o. into the Church,** admettre qn dans l'Église; **to r. s.o. into one's family,** admettre *ou* recevoir qn dans sa famille.

2 *vi* (*of tennis or badminton player*) recevoir le service.

received [rɪ'siːvd] *adj* (*idea*) reçu; (*opinion*) admis; **the r. view is that ...,** il est communément admis *ou* accepté que ..., on admet communément que ...; **r. pronunciation,** = la prononciation des gens cultivés; **r. wisdom,** sagesse *f* populaire.

receiver [rɪ'siːvər] *n* **(a)** (*of stolen goods*) receleur, -euse; **(b)** *Tel* récepteur *m*; **r. rest,** berceau *m* du récepteur; **to lift** *or* **pick up the r.,** décrocher; **to replace the r.,** raccrocher; **(c)** *Rad* récepteur *m*; **(d)** *Jur* **r. in bankruptcy, official r.,** mandataire liquidateur, syndic *m* de faillite; **to be in the hands of the r.,** être en règlement judiciaire.

receivership [rɪ'siːvəʃɪp] *n* **to go into r.,** se mettre en règlement judiciaire.

receiving [rɪ'siːvɪŋ] *n* **(a)** (*of goods etc*) réception *f*; (*of money*) recette *f*; **r. body of water,** cours *m* d'eau récepteur; *F* **to be at** *or* **on the r. end,** écoper; *F* **I've been on the r. end of customers' complaints all day,** les clients sont venus se plaindre à moi toute la journée; *F* **it's different when you're on the r. end,** c'est tout autre chose quand c'est à toi que ça arrive; *Am* **r. blanket,** petite couverture légère pour bébé; **(b)** (*of stolen goods*) recel *m*; **he is doing two years for r.,** il fait deux ans de prison pour recel; **(c)** *Telecom Rad* **r. station,** station réceptrice, poste récepteur.

recent ['riːsənt] *adj* (*development, event, past*) récent; (*acquaintance*) nouveau, *f* nouvelle; **event of r. date,** événement récent; **r. news,** nouvelles récentes *ou* fraîches; **all that is quite r.,** tout cela n'est que *ou* ne date que d'hier; **in r. months,** au cours des derniers mois; **in r. times,** ces derniers temps; **the most r. edition,** (*of book etc*) la dernière édition; **her most r. novel,** son dernier roman.

recently ['riːsəntlɪ] *adv* récemment; **as r. as yesterday,** pas plus tard qu'hier; **until quite r.,** jusqu'à ces derniers temps; **I saw her quite r.,** je l'ai vue tout dernièrement.

receptacle [rɪ'septək(ə)l] *n* **(a)** (*for litter, paper, water etc*) récipient *m*; **(b)** *Am El* prise *f* de courant (femelle).

reception [rɪ'sepʃən] *n* **(a)** (*of guests, new members*) réception *f*; (*of announcement, book etc*) accueil *m*; **the r. (desk),** (*in hotel*) la réception; **at** *or* **to r.,** à la réception; **to give s.o. a chilly/warm r.,** réserver à qn un accueil glacial/chaleureux; **what kind of r. did you get?,** quel accueil t'ont-ils réservé?, comment est-ce qu'ils t'ont reçu?; **the play has had a favourable r.,** la pièce a été accueillie favorablement *ou* bien reçue; **r. centre,** (*for refugees etc*) centre *m* d'accueil; *Br Sch* **r. class,** première année de maternelle; *Am* **r. clerk,** réceptionniste *mf*; **r. committee,** comité *m* d'accueil;

(b) (*party*) réception *f*; **wedding r.,** réception de mariage; **we are going to a r.,** nous allons à une soirée; **r. room,** (*in hotel*) salle *f* de réception; (*in private house*) salon *m*;

(c) *Rad & TV* réception *f*; **the r. is bad,** on ne reçoit pas bien.

receptionist [rɪ'sepʃənɪst] *n* réceptionniste *mf*.

receptive [rɪ'septɪv] *adj* (*audience, listener*) réceptif (**to an idea/etc,** à une idée/*etc*); **r. to s.o.,** compréhensif envers qn.

receptiveness [rɪ'septɪvnɪs], **receptivity** [riːsep'tɪvɪtɪ] *n* (*of audience, listener*) réceptivité *f* (**to,** à).

receptor [rɪ'septər] *n* **(a)** (*for antibody, drug*) récepteur *m*; **r. site,** (site *m*) récepteur; **(b)** (*for radio signals*) récepteur *m*.

recess[1] [rɪ'ses, *Am* 'rɪses] *n* **(a)** *Br* (*of law courts, Parliament*) vacances *fpl*; **while Parliament is in r.,** pendant les vacances parlementaires; **(b)** *esp Am Sch* récréation *f*; **(c)** *Am Jur* suspension *f* d'audience; **the court is now in r.,** l'audience est maintenant suspendue; **we will take a ten minute r.,** nous allons suspendre l'audience pendant dix minutes; **(d)** (*nook*) *& Fig* recoin *m*; (*for bed etc*) renfoncement *m*; (*for statue*) niche *f*; **dining r.,** coin *m* repas, coin salle à manger; **in the innermost recesses of the soul,** dans les replis les plus secrets de l'âme.

recess[2] **1** *vt* **(a)** mettre (*qch*) dans un renfoncement; encastrer (*éclairage, interrupteur etc*); **(b)** pratiquer un renfoncement dans (*une muraille*). **2** *vi* **(a)** *Br* **Parliament will r. next week,** les vacances parlementaires commenceront la semaine prochaine; **(b)** *Am* (*of assembly*) suspendre la séance; (*of court*) suspendre l'audience.

recession [rɪ'seʃən] *n Econ* récession *f*; **in (a) r.,** en récession.

recessionary [rɪ'seʃənərɪ] *adj* (*conditions, policy etc*) de récession; **to have a r. effect,** (*of policy etc*) entraîner une récession.

recessive [rɪ'sesɪv] *adj Biol* (*gene, character*) récessif.

recharge [riː'tʃɑːdʒ] **1** *vt* recharger (*un accumulateur*); *F* **to r. one's batteries,** recharger ses batteries, reprendre du poil de la bête. **2** *vi* (*of battery*) se recharger.

rechargeable [riː'tʃɑːdʒəb(ə)l] *adj* (*battery*) rechargeable.

recherché [rə'ʃeəʃeɪ] *adj* (*film, topic*) recherché.

recidivism [rɪ'sɪdɪvɪz(ə)m] *n Jur* récidivisme *m*.

recidivist [rɪ'sɪdɪvɪst] *n Jur* récidiviste *mf*.

recidivistic [rɪsɪdɪ'vɪstɪk] *adj Jur* (*tendency etc*) à récidiver.

recipe ['resɪpɪ] *n Culin & Fig* recette *f*; *Pharm* formule *f*, recette; **r. for a happy life,** recette pour vivre heureux; **r. for failure,** le meilleur moyen pour échouer; **those two working together would be a r. for disaster,** si ces deux-là travaillaient ensemble ce serait l'échec assuré; **r. book,** livre *m* de recettes; **r. card,** fiche-recette *f*.

recipient [rɪ'sɪpɪənt] *n* (*of gift, letter etc*) destinataire *mf*; (*of cheque, money*) bénéficiaire *mf*; (*of award, honour*) récipiendaire *mf*; *Med* (*of organ transplant*) receveur, -euse.

reciprocal [rɪ'sɪprək(ə)l] **1** *adj* **(a)** (*agreement, friendship*) réciproque; (*concessions, trade*) mutuel, réciproque; **he dislikes me and it's r.,** il ne m'aime pas et c'est réciproque *ou* je le lui rends bien; **(b)** *Gram* réciproque; **(c)** *Math* réciproque, inverse. **2** *n Math* (*of quantity*) réciproque *f*, inverse *f*.

reciprocally [rɪ'sɪprəklɪ] *adv* (*to trade*) réciproquement, mutuellement.

reciprocate [rɪ'sɪprəkeɪt] **1** *vt* retourner (*un sentiment, un compliment, des vœux*); **to r. s.o.'s kindness,** repayer qn de leur amabilité. **2** *vi* **(a)** (*do the same*) en faire autant; (*counter-attack*) riposter; **(b)** *MecE* (*of piston etc*) avoir un mouvement alternatif *ou* de va-et-vient.

reciprocating [rɪ'sɪprəkeɪtɪŋ] *adj MecE* (*movement*) alternatif; (*machine*) à mouvement alternatif *ou* de va-et-vient; **r. engine,** moteur alternatif.

reciprocation [rɪsɪprə'keɪʃən] *n* **(a)** (*of feeling*) action *f* de donner en retour; (*of compliment*) retour *m*; **these feelings met with no r.,** ces sentiments n'ont pas été payés de retour; **in r. for ...,** en retour de ...; **(b)** *MecE* (*of movement*) mouvement alternatif, va-et-vient *m inv*.

reciprocity [resɪ'prɒsɪtɪ] *n* réciprocité *f*.

recital [rɪ'saɪt(ə)l] *n* **(a)** (*of event etc*) récit *m*, narration *f*, relation *f*; **(b)** (*of complaints, details etc*) énumération *f*; **(c)** (*of poetry*) récitation *f*; **(d)** *Mus* récital *m*; **to give a r.,** donner un récital; **Bach/***etc* **r.,** récital des œuvres de Bach/*etc*.

recitation [resɪ'teɪʃən] *n* (*of poem etc*) récitation *f*; **to give a r.,** réciter; **to give a r. from Burns,** réciter du Burns.

recitative [resɪtə'tiːv] *n Mus* récitatif *m*.

recite [rɪ'saɪt] **1** *vt* **(a)** réciter (*un événement, un poème etc*); **(b)** énumérer (*des plaintes, des détails etc*). **2** *vi* réciter; **will you r. to us?,** voulez-vous nous réciter quelque chose?

reckless ['reklɪs] *adj* (*rash*) (*attempt, person*) téméraire; (*driving, gambler*) imprudent; **to be a r. spender,** dépenser sans compter; *Aut* **r. driver,** conducteur imprudent, *F* chauffard *m*.

recklessly ['reklɪslɪ] *adv* (*to attempt*) témérairement; (*to drive, gamble*) imprudemment; (*to spend*) sans compter.

recklessness ['reklɪsnɪs] *n* (*of attempt, person*) témérité *f*; (*of driving, gambling*) imprudence *f*.

reckon ['rekən] **1** *vt* **(a)** (*consider*) considérer (*qn*) (**as,** comme); **to r. s.o. among the greatest writers,** mettre qn au rang *ou* au nombre des plus grands écrivains;

(b) (*calculate, count*) calculer, compter (*une somme etc*); **if we r. £50 that should be enough,** si nous comptons 50 livres ça devrait suffire;
(c) *F* (*think*) penser; **I r. he is forty,** je lui donne quarante ans; **I r. he will consent,** à mon avis, il consentira; **maybe we should go, what do you r.?,** nous devrions peut-être y aller, qu'est-ce que tu en penses?;
(d) *F* (*regard favourably*) **I don't r. her chances,** je ne donne pas cher de sa réussite.
2 *vi* **(a)** (*calculate*) compter, calculer; **reckoning from today,** à partir *ou* à compter d'aujourd'hui; **he had reckoned without his rivals,** il n'avait pas tenu compte de ses rivaux;
(b) (*expect, plan*) compter (**to go**/*etc*, partir/*etc*); **you must r. without me tomorrow,** ne compte pas sur moi demain.

▶**reckon in** *vtsep* compter; **did you r. in what you left in tips?,** est-ce que tu as compté ce que tu as laissé en pourboires?

▶**reckon on** *vipo* **to r. on sth,** compter sur qch; **they had not reckoned on finding me here,** ils ne comptaient pas me trouver ici.

▶**reckon up 1** *vtsep* additionner; **to r. up a bill,** faire une facture. **2** *vi* faire la note.

▶**reckon with** *vipo* compter avec; **to have s.o. to r. with,** avoir affaire à qn; **she's a force to be reckoned with,** c'est une femme qu'il ne faut pas sous-estimer.

reckoner ['rek(ə)nər] *n* (*person*) calculateur, -trice; **ready r.,** barème *m*.

reckoning ['rekənɪŋ] *n* **(a)** (*of bill, interest etc*) compte *m*, calcul *m*; **by my r.,** d'après mon calcul *ou* mes comptes; **to be out in one's r.,** s'être trompé dans son calcul *ou* ses comptes; **you're a long way out in your r.,** vous êtes loin du compte; *Rel* **day of r.,** jour *m* du Jugement dernier; **(b)** (*of chances*) estimation *f*; **to the best of his r.,** autant qu'il en puisse juger; **(c)** (*of ship's position*) estime *f*; **(d)** *Arch* (*bill*) note *f*.

reclaim [rɪ'kleɪm] *vt* **(a)** mettre (*une terre*) en valeur; (*from undergrowth*) défricher (*un terrain*); assécher (*un marais*); **to r. land from the sea/the desert,** conquérir du terrain sur la mer/le désert; **(b)** récupérer (*une valise, un objet perdu*); réclamer (*un objet perdu*); **luggage** *or* **baggage r.,** (*in airport*) retrait *m* des bagages; **(c)** *Ind* régénérer (*le caoutchouc etc*); récupérer (*un sous-produit*).

reclamation [reklə'meɪʃən] *n* **(a)** (*of land*) mise *f* en valeur; (*from undergrowth*) défrichement *m*; (*of marsh*) assèchement *m*; **(b)** (*of suitcase, lost property etc*) récupération *f*; (*of lost property*) réclamation *f*; **(c)** (*of rubber etc*) régénération *f*; (*of by-product*) récupération *f*.

reclassify [riː'klæsɪfaɪ] *vt* reclasser (*une plante etc*); reclassifier (*un document etc*).

recline [rɪ'klaɪn] **1** *vt* appuyer (*sa tête*) (**against,** contre; **on,** sur); incliner le dossier de (*un siège*). **2** *vi* (*of person*) être allongé (**on,** sur); (*of head*) être appuyé (**on,** sur); (*of seat*) avoir un dossier inclinable *ou* réglable; **to r. on a couch,** être *ou* rester étendu sur un canapé.

recliner [rɪ'klaɪnər] *n* (*for sunbathing*) chaise longue; (*armchair*) fauteuil *m* de relaxation.

reclining [rɪ'klaɪnɪŋ] *n* (*on couch etc*) action de se reposer; **to be in a r. position,** (*of person*) être en position allongée; (*of seat*) être incliné; **r. seat,** (*in aircraft etc*) siège *m* à dossier inclinable *ou* réglable.

recluse [rɪ'kluːs] *n* (*hermit*) reclus, -use; **to live** *or* **lead the life of a r.,** vivre en reclus *ou* ermite; **she has become a bit of a r.,** elle est devenue assez solitaire.

recognition [rekəg'nɪʃən] *n* **(a)** (*identification*) (*of person, style etc*) reconnaissance *f*; **sign of r.,** signe *m* de reconnaissance; **to change beyond** *or* **out of all r.,** devenir méconnaissable; **brand r.,** (*in advertising*) identification *f* de la marque; **(b)** (*acknowledgement*) (*of fact, government, speaker etc*) reconnaissance *f*; **to win r.,** (*of artist etc*) s'imposer (**from,** aux yeux de); **to withhold r. from,** refuser de reconnaître (*un gouvernement*); **in r. of his courage,** en reconnaissance de son courage; **she received no r.,** on ne lui accordait aucune considération.

recognizable [rekəg'naɪzəb(ə)l] *adj* (*person, style etc*) reconnaissable; **he's so changed as to be no longer r.,** il est devenu méconnaissable; **to be barely** *or* **scarcely r.,** être à peine reconnaissable.

recognizably [rekəg'naɪzəblɪ] *adv* **she is r. your daughter,** on voit bien que c'est votre fille.

recognizance [rɪ'kɒ(g)nɪzəns] *n Jur* (*promise*) engagement *m*; (*money paid*) caution personnelle; **to enter into recognizances,** donner caution; **to enter into recognizances for s.o.,** se porter garant *ou* caution pour qn, cautionner qn; **to be released on one's own recognizances,** être remis en liberté sur engagement personnel.

recognize ['rekəgnaɪz] *vt* **(a)** (*know again*) reconnaître (*une ville, une personne*) (**by,** à); **to r. the truth when one sees it,** être capable de savoir si quelque chose est vrai ou non, savoir discerner le vrai du faux;
(b) (*acknowledge*) reconnaître (*un gouvernement etc*); *Sp* homologuer (*un record*); **to r. s.o. as king,** reconnaître qn comme *ou* en tant que roi; **to r. defeat,** accepter *ou* admettre sa défaite; **to be the first to r. a fact,** être le premier à se rendre compte d'un fait; **to r. a member,** (*of chairman of a meeting etc*) donner la parole à un membre; **to be recognized,** (*of speaker*) avoir la parole; **to be a recognized authority,** être une autorité (**on,** en);
(c) (*greet*) saluer (*un admirateur*) (**with,** avec, de); **he recognized me,** il m'a fait un signe de (re)connaissance.

recognized ['rekəgnaɪzd] *adj* (*government etc*) reconnu; (*truth*) admis, accepté; (*method etc*) classique; **it is a r. fact that ...,** c'est un fait avéré *ou* reconnu que ...; **the r. term,** le terme consacré (**for,** pour); *Com* **r. agent,** agent accrédité (**for,** pour).

recoil¹ ['riːkɔɪl] *n* (*of gun, rifle*) recul *m*; (*of spring*) détente *f*; (*of person*) mouvement *m* de recul.

recoil² [rɪ'kɔɪl] *vi* (*of gun, rifle*) reculer, repousser; (*of spring*) se détendre; (*of person*) reculer (**from doing,** à l'idée de faire); (*in disgust*) se révolter (**from,** contre); *Fig* (*of joke etc*) se retourner (**on,** contre).

recoilless [rɪ'kɔɪllɪs] *adj* (*rifle, weapon*) sans recul.

recollect [rekə'lekt] **1** *vt* se rappeler (*qch*), se souvenir de (*qch*); **r. where/who you are!,** n'oublie pas où/qui tu es!; **to r. oneself,** se recueillir. **2** *vi* **as far as I r.,** autant que je m'en souvienne.

recollection [rekə'lekʃən] *n* souvenir *m*; **my earliest recollections,** mes premiers souvenirs; **her r. differs from mine,** ses souvenirs et les miens *ou* nos souvenirs ne concordent pas; **I have some r. of it,** j'en ai un vague souvenir; **I have no r. of it,** je n'en ai *ou* je n'en garde aucun souvenir; **I have no r. of doing it,** je ne me souviens pas l'avoir fait; **to the best of my r.,** pour autant que je me souvienne; **such a thing has never occurred within my r.,** cela ne s'est jamais produit de mon temps.

recombinant [riː'kɒmbɪnənt] *adj Biol* **r. DNA,** ADN recombinant.

recommend [rekə'mend] *vt* **(a)** (*praise*) recommander (*un livre, un restaurant, un médecin*) (**to,** à; **for,** pour); **the hotel is to be recommended for its cooking,** l'hôtel se recommande par sa cuisine; **the hotel has little to r. it,** on ne peut pas dire grand-chose en faveur de cet hôtel (**apart from, except,** en dehors de); **the hotel comes recommended,** on dit beaucoup de bien de l'hôtel; **I would r. him as a driver,** je vous le recommande comme chauffeur;
(b) (*advise*) conseiller (*prudence*); **to r. s.o. to do sth,** recommander *ou* conseiller à qn de faire qch; **I have been recommended (to come) to you,** on m'a adressé à vous; **the jury recommended the murderer to mercy,** les jurés ont signé le recours en grâce du meutrier; **recommended price,** prix conseillé;
(c) *Old-fashioned* (*entrust*) **to r. sth to the care of s.o.** *or* **to s.o.'s care,** recommander qch aux soins de qn; **to r. one's soul to God,** recommander son âme à Dieu.

recommendable [rekə'mendəb(ə)l] *adj* (*book, person etc*) recommandable; (*action*) à conseiller.

recommendation [rekəmen'deɪʃən] *n* **(a)** (*advice*) recommandation *f*; **I have come on the r. of one of your customers,** je viens sur la recommandation d'un de vos clients; **through personal r.,** par recommandation personnelle; **the jury made a r. for mercy,** les jurés ont signé le recours en grâce; **my r. is that ...,** ce que je recommande *ou* conseille c'est que ...; **(b)** (*commendation*) recommandation *f*; **the hotel's sole r. is its location,** l'hôtel ne peut se recommander que par son emplacement.

recompense¹ ['rekəmpens] *n* **(a)** (*compensation*) récompense *f* (**for,** de); **in r. for ...,** en récompense de ...; **(b)** (*for damage, loss*) dédommagement *m*, compensation *f* (**for,** de, pour); **as r.,** en dédommagement.

recompense² *vt* **(a)** récompenser (*qn*) (**for,** de); **(b)** *Jur* dédommager (*qn*) (**for sth,** de qch).

reconcilable [rekən'saɪləb(ə)l] *adj* (*people, ideas, opinions*) conciliable.

reconcile ['rekənsaɪl] *vt* **(a)** réconcilier (*qn*) (**with,** avec); **to become reconciled,** se réconcilier; **to r. s.o. to sth,** faire accepter qch à *ou* par qn; **to r. oneself** *or* **become reconciled to sth,** se résigner à quelque chose; **(b)** (*settle*) ajuster, arranger, mettre fin à (*une querelle*); **let**

us r. our differences, essayons de nous entendre; **(c)** (*make agree*) concilier, faire accorder (*des opinions, des faits*); mettre d'accord (*deux points de vue*); *Fin* **to r. accounts,** faire accorder les comptes; **evidence which cannot be reconciled with the known facts,** témoignage qui ne saurait être concilié avec les faits connus.

reconciliation [rekənsɪlɪ'eɪʃən] *n* **(a)** (*of people*) réconciliation *f* (**between,** entre; **with,** avec); **(b)** (*of differences*) conciliation *f*, arrangement *m*; **(c)** (*of opinions*) conciliation.

recondite [re'kɒndaɪt] *adj* (*subject, knowledge*) profond, mystérieux.

recondition [riːkən'dɪʃən] *vt* remettre (*un moteur etc*) à neuf.

reconditioning [riːkən'dɪʃənɪŋ] *n* (*of engine etc*) remise *f* à neuf.

reconfiguration [riːkənfɪgə'reɪʃən] *n Comptr* (*of keyboard, system etc*) reconfiguration *f*.

reconfigure [riːkən'fɪgər] *vt Comptr* reconfigurer (*un clavier, un système*).

reconnaissance [rɪ'kɒnɪsəns] *n Mil & Fig* reconnaissance *f*; **to make a r.,** faire une reconnaissance; **to be on r.,** être en reconnaissance; **r. flight/mission/satellite/***etc*, vol *m*/mission *f*/satellite *m*/*etc* de reconnaissance.

reconnect [riːkə'nekt] *vt El* rebrancher (*un téléphone, un câble etc*); raccorder (*un tuyau*); **to r. the water supply,** rétablir l'alimentation en eau; *Tel* **to r. s.o.,** (*of operator*) rétablir la communication; (*of telephone company*) rebrancher le téléphone.

reconnection [riːkə'nekʃən] *n El* (*of cable, telephone etc*) rebranchement *m*; (*of pipe*) raccordement *m*; (*of water supply, telephone call*) rétablissement *m*; *Tel* **r. charge,** (*for disconnected telephone*) frais *mpl* de rebranchement.

reconnoitre, *US* **reconnoiter** [rekə'nɔɪtər] **1** *vt Mil & Fig* reconnaître (*le terrain*); faire une reconnaissance de (*l'ennemi*). **2** *vi* faire une reconnaissance.

reconquer [riː'kɒŋkər] *vt* reconquérir (*un pays etc*).

reconquest [riː'kɒŋkwest] *n* (*of country etc*) reconquête *f*.

reconsider [riːkən'sɪdər] **1** *vt* considérer de nouveau, repenser (*une question*); réexaminer (*une décision*); (*alter*) revenir sur (*une décision*). **2** *vi* y repenser; **won't you please r.?,** est-ce que vous ne pourriez pas y repenser *ou* reconsidérer la question?

reconsideration [riːkənsɪdə'reɪʃən] *n* (*of matter, question*) reconsidération *f*; (*of decision*) réexamen *m*; (*altered decision*) révision *f*.

reconstitute [riː'kɒnstɪtjuːt] *vt* reconstituer (*un comité etc, du lait en poudre etc*).

reconstitution [riːkɒnstɪ'tjuːʃən] *n* reconstitution *f*.

reconstruct [riːkən'strʌkt] *vt* reconstruire, rebâtir (*une maison etc*); reconstituer (*un fichier détruit, une société etc*); *Fig* reconstituer (*des faits, un crime*); reconstruire (*sa vie, un pays*).

reconstruction [riːkən'strʌkʃən] *n* (*of house, country, life etc*) reconstruction *f*; (*of file, company etc*) *& Fig* reconstitution *f*; **economic and financial r.,** restauration économique et financière.

record[1] ['rekɔːd] *n* **(a)** (*of attendance*) registre *m*; (*of proceedings*) procès-verbal *m*, *pl* procès-verbaux; (*of verdict, fact*) enregistrement *m*; **I can find no r. of it,** je n'en trouve aucune mention; **to be on r.,** (*of verdict, fact*) être enregistré *ou* authentique; **to be on r. as saying sth,** avoir déclaré qch; **to go on r. as a pacifist,** se déclarer pacifiste; **to say sth off the r.,** dire qch en confidence; **this is strictly off the r.,** ceci est strictement confidentiel, ceci doit rester entre nous; **for the r.,** *F* **to keep the r. straight,** pour mémoire; **to put sth on r.,** noter qch, consigner qch; **it is on r.** *or* **a matter of r.,** c'est un fait établi (**that,** que); **this is the coldest winter on r.,** c'est l'hiver le plus froid dont on se souvienne; *Jur* **to strike sth from the r.,** rayer qch du procès-verbal; **is this for the r.?,** est-ce que cela est officiel?; **just for the r., let me say that ...,** pour que les choses soient claires, permettez moi de dire que ...; **to put** *or* **set the r. straight,** mettre les choses au clair, dissiper tout malentendu; **to leave few records,** (*of ancient civilization*) laisser peu de témoignages;

(b) (*file*) dossier *m*; *Comptr* (*in database*) article *m*; *Hist & Jur* archive *f*; *Admin* registre *m*; **our records do not go back that far,** nos archives ne remontent pas aussi loin; **r. office,** bureau *m* des archives; *Jur* greffe *m*; **r. card,** fiche *f*; *Admin* **records management,** gestion *f* des dossiers;

(c) (*personal history*) antécédents *mpl*; (*of criminal*) casier *m* judiciaire; (*achievements*) résultats *mpl*; **to have a good/bad safety r.,** (*of company etc*) avoir une bonne/mauvaise réputation en ce qui concerne la sécurité; *Mil & Fig* **he has a good r.,** ses états de service sont bons; **his past r.,** sa conduite passée *ou* dans le passé; **given your r. as a late payer,** vu vos antécédents de mauvais payeur; **to have a clean r.,** avoir un casier judiciaire vierge; **he has a r.,** il a des condamnations antérieures; **he has a r. of breaking and entering,** il s'est déjà rendu coupable de plusieurs effractions; *Med* **case r.,** fiche *f* de patient *ou* d'observation;

(d) (*recording*) *Mus* disque *m*; **to make** *or F* **cut a r.,** faire *ou* enregistrer un disque; **to play** *or* **put on a r.,** mettre *ou* passer un disque; **to change a r.,** changer un disque; *Hum* **change the r., will you?,** change un peu de disque!; **r. company/producer/***etc*, maison *f*/producteur *m*/*etc* de disques; **r. buff** *or* **collector** *or* **enthusiast,** discophile *mf*; **r. library,** discothèque *f*, phonothèque *f*; **r. player,** tourne-disques *m inv*; **r. deck,** platine *f* (tourne-disque); **r. shop,** disquaire *mf*; **r. token,** bon-cadeau pour acheter des disques;

(e) (*best performance*) record *m;* **to set a r.,** établir un record; **to break** *or* **beat the r.,** battre le record (**for, by,** de); **to break all records,** battre tous les records; **to hold the r.,** détenir le record (**for,** de); **in r. time,** en un temps record; **unemployment is at a r. high/low,** le chômage a atteint son chiffre le plus haut/bas.

record[2] [rɪ'kɔːd] **1** *vt* **(a)** (*write down*) enregistrer (*un fait*); mettre (*ses pensées, ses idées etc*) sur papier; (*of policeman*) consigner (*qch*); *Jur* minuter (*un jugement*); relever (*la température*); rapporter, relater (*des événements*); *Parl* **to r. a vote,** voter; **throughout recorded history,** aussi loin que les archives remontent; **to send a letter (by) recorded delivery,** envoyer une lettre en recommandé; **to r. one's opposition,** indiquer par écrit son opposition; (*in speech*) faire part de son opposition;

(b) (*tape*) enregistrer (*une chanson, un programme*); **this is a recorded message,** (*on telephone*) ceci est un message enregistré; **r. button,** (*on machine*) touche *f* pour l'enregistrement;

(c) (*register*) enregistrer (*un tremblement de terre*); **the thermometer records ten degrees,** le thermomètre marque dix degrés;

(d) (*be evidence of*) rappeler, commémorer (*une bataille*).

2 *vi* (*of machine, performer*) enregistrer; (*of sound*) s'enregistrer.

record-breaking ['rekɔːdbreɪkɪŋ] *adj* (*jump, performance, success*) qui bat tous les records, jamais égalé.

recorder [rɪ'kɔːdər] *n* **(a)** (*machine*) (appareil *m*) enregistreur *m*; **radio cassette r.,** magnétophone *m* avec radio; **(tape) r.,** magnétophone *m*; **(b)** *Mus* flûte *f* à bec.

record-holder ['rekɔːdhəʊldər] *n* détenteur, -trice du record.

recording [rɪ'kɔːdɪŋ] *n* **(a)** (*on tape*) enregistrement *m*; **to play a r.,** passer un enregistrement; **r. barometer,** baromètre enregistreur; **r. instrument** *or* **machine,** appareil enregistreur; **r. room,** central *m* d'enregistrement; **r. tape,** ruban *m ou* bande *f* d'enregistrement; **(b)** (*in writing*) relation *f* par écrit, consignation *f*.

recount [rɪ'kaʊnt] *vt* (*relate*) raconter (*qch*) (**to,** à).

re-count[1] ['riːkaʊnt] *n* (*of people, money etc*) recomptage *m*; *Pol* (*of votes*) nouveau dépouillement du scrutin; **to do a r.,** (*of money, people etc*) recompter; *Pol* **to demand a r.,** exiger un nouveau dépouillement.

re-count[2] *vt* recompter (*son argent etc*); compter de nouveau (*les votes*).

recoup [rɪ'kuːp] **1** *vt* récupérer (*son argent, une perte*); *Jur* défalquer, faire le décompte de (*qch*); **to r. s.o. for his** *or* **her losses,** dédommager *ou* indemniser qn de ses pertes. **2** *vi* se rattraper de ses pertes.

recourse [rɪ'kɔːs] *n* recours *m*; **to have r. to sth/s.o.,** avoir recours *ou* recourir à qch/qn; **my only r. is,** mon seul recours est (**to do,** de faire); **she cannot remember without r. to her notes,** elle ne peut pas se souvenir sans avoir recours à ses notes; **right of r.,** droit *m* de recours.

recover [rɪ'kʌvər] **1** *vt* **(a)** (*get back, find again*) recouvrer, retrouver (*un objet perdu*); retrouver (*son appétit, sa voix*); regagner (*l'affection de qn*); *Comptr* récupérer (*un dossier, des donnees*); **to r. one's looks,** (*after illness etc*) retrouver son apparence normale; **to r. one's breath/courage,** reprendre haleine/courage; **to r. consciousness,** reprendre connaissance, revenir à soi; **I am recovering my strength,** mes forces me reviennent; **to r. one's money,** récupérer son argent, rentrer dans ses fonds; **to r. sth from s.o.,** reprendre qch à qn; **to r. one's health,** guérir, se rétablir; **to r. oneself,** (*gain self-control*) se ressaisir; **to r. one's balance,** recouvrer *ou* retrouver son équilibre;

(b) (*obtain, collect*) récupérer (*des corps*); (*from sea*) repêcher (*un noyé, un vaisseau spatial*); récupérer (*un sous-produit*).

2 *vi* (*from shock etc*) se remettre (**from,** de); (*get better*) guérir, se remettre (**from,** de); (*of export market, business*) reprendre; (*of stock market, economy, country*) se redresser; (*of currency*) remonter; (*in competition, race etc*) se ressaisir; **to be quite recovered,** être tout à fait remis *ou* guéri *ou* rétabli.

re-cover ['riːkʌvər] *vt* recouvrir (*une chaise etc*).

recoverable [rɪ'kʌvərəb(ə)l] *adj* **(a)** (*something lost*) recouvrable; (*money*) récupérable; **(b)** (*by-product, computer file etc*) récupérable; *Petr* **r. resources,** ressources *fpl* exploitables.

recovery [rɪ'kʌvərɪ] *n* **(a)** (*of something lost*) recouvrement *m*; (*of money*) récupération *f*; **beyond** *or* **past r.,** irrécupérable; *Jur* **action for r. of property,** (action *f* en) revendication *f*; **r. of damages,** obtention *f* de dommages-intérêts;

(b) (*of by-product, computer file etc*) récupération *f*; *Br Aut* **r. service,** service *m* de dépannage; **r. ship** *or* **vessel,** navire *m* de récupération; *Br Aut* **r. vehicle,** dépanneuse *f*;

(c) (*from illness*) guérison *f*; **to be on the way** *or* **road to r.,** être sur la voie de la guérison; **the patient is making a good r.,** le malade est en bonne voie de guérison; **she made a quick r.,** elle s'est vite rétablie; **he is past** *or* **beyond r.,** il est dans un état désespéré; **I wish you a speedy r.,** je vous souhaite une prompte guérison; **r. room,** salle *f* post-opératoire;

(d) (*of economy*) redressement *m*; (*of export market, business*) reprise *f*; (*of currency*) remontée *f*; **to make a r.,** (*in competition, race etc*) se ressaisir.

re-create [riːkrɪ'eɪt] *vt* (*in film, play etc*) recréer, reconstituer (*une époque etc*).

recreation [rekrɪ'eɪʃən] *n* récréation *f*, loisirs *mpl*; *Sch* **during (the) r.,** pendant la récréation; **r. centre/facilities/***etc*, centre *m*/équipements *mpl*/*etc* de loisirs; **r. ground,** terrain *m* de jeux; **r. room,** (*in hotel, hospital*) salle *f* de récréation; (*in home*) salle de jeux.

re-creation [riːkrɪ'eɪʃən] *n* (*of era etc, in film, play etc*) recréation *f*.

recreational [rekrɪ'eɪʃən(ə)l] *adj* (*centre, facility etc*) de loisirs; **r. area,** (*country park etc*) aire réservée aux loisirs; (*playground*) terrain *m* de jeux; *Am* **r. vehicle,** camping-car *m*.

recrimination [rɪkrɪmɪ'neɪʃən] *n* récrimination *f* (**against,** contre).

recriminatory [rɪ'krɪmɪnət(ə)rɪ] *adj* (*remark etc*) de récrimination.

recrudescence [riːkruː'desəns] *n* (*of disease, disorder etc*) recrudescence *f*.

recrudescent [riːkruː'desənt] *adj* (*disease, disorder etc*) recrudescent.

recruit¹ [rɪ'kruːt] *n Mil* recrue *f*, conscrit *m*; (*in organization, company etc*) recrue.

recruit² **1** *vt* recruter (*une armée, des employés etc*); embaucher (*qn*) (**as,** pour le poste de); *Fig* **to r. s.o. to do sth,** embaucher qn pour faire qch. **2** *vi Mil* recruter; (*of company*) recruter, embaucher (**for,** pour); *Fig* embaucher.

recruiting [rɪ'kruːtɪŋ] *n* (*of soldier, employee etc*) recrutement *m*; **r. agent/office,** agent *m*/bureau *m* de recrutement; **r. officer,** (*for army*) officier recruteur; (*for company*) (agent) recruteur *m*.

recruitment [rɪ'kruːtmənt] *n* (*of soldier, new employee etc*) recrutement *m*; **r. campaign/company/scheme/***etc*, campagne *f*/société *f*/programme *m*/*etc* de recrutement; **r. consultant,** conseil *m* en recrutement.

rectal ['rekt(ə)l] *adj Med Anat* rectal; **r. cancer,** cancer *m* du rectum; **r. examination,** examen rectal *ou* du rectum.

rectangle ['rektæŋg(ə)l] *n* rectangle *m*.

rectangular [rek'tæŋgjʊlər] *adj* (*room etc*) rectangulaire; **to be r. in shape,** être rectangulaire.

rectification [rektɪfɪ'keɪʃən] *n* (*of calculation, situation etc*) rectification *f*; (*of oversight*) réparation *f*; *Ch Math* rectification; *El* redressement *m*.

rectifier ['rektɪfaɪər] *n Ch* rectificateur *m*; *El* redresseur *m*.

rectify ['rektɪfaɪ] *vt* rectifier, corriger (*un calcul*); rectifier (*une erreur, une situation*); réparer (*un oubli*); *Fin* rectifier (*une écriture*); *Ch Math* rectifier; *El* redresser.

rectilineal [rektɪ'lɪnɪəl], **rectilinear** [rektɪ'lɪnɪər] *adj* (*geometrical figure, street etc*) rectiligne; *TV* **r. scanning,** analyse *f* par lignes.

rectitude ['rektɪtjuːd] *n* rectitude *f*.

recto ['rektəʊ] *n Typ* recto *m*.

rector ['rektər] *n* **(a)** *Rel Church of Eng* = ecclésiastique préposé à l'administration d'une paroisse et titulaire du bénéfice et de la dîme; (*of seminary*) supérieur *m*; **(b)** *Univ* recteur *m*; *Scot Sch* directeur *m* (d'une école secondaire).

rectorial [rek'tɔːrɪəl] *adj* (*decision, duties*) rectoral; **r. election,** élection d'un recteur.

rectory ['rekt(ə)rɪ] *n Rel* (*residence*) presbytère *m*.

rectoscope ['rektəskəʊp] *n* rectoscope *m*.

rectoscopy [rek'tɒskəpɪ] *n* rectoscopie *f*.

rectum, *pl* **-ums, -a** ['rektəm, -əmz, -ə] *n Anat* rectum *m*.

recumbent [rɪ'kʌmbənt] *adj* couché, étendu; **to be r.,** être couché (**on,** sur); **r. figure,** (*on tomb*) gisant *m*.

recuperate [rɪ'kuːpəreɪt, -'kjuː-] **1** *vt* récupérer (*ses forces, de l'argent, de la chaleur*). **2** *vi* (*of person*) se remettre, se rétablir (**from,** de); *F* récupérer; **he had gone to the South of France to r.,** il était allé dans le Midi pour achever de se rétablir; **she is still recuperating,** elle est encore en convalescence.

recuperation [rɪkuːpə'reɪʃən, -'kjuː-] *n* **(a)** (*of strength, money, heat*) récupération *f*; **(b)** (*from illness*) rétablissement *m*; **powers of r.,** capacités *fpl* de rétablissement.

recuperative [rɪ'kuːpərətɪv, -'kjuː-] *adj* (*powers*) de rétablissement.

recur [rɪ'kɜːr] *vi* **(-rr-)** (*of theme*) revenir; (*of event*) se reproduire; (*of illness*) réapparaître; *Math* (*of figures*) se reproduire; **to r. to the mind,** revenir à la mémoire; **festival that recurs every ten years,** fête qui revient tous les dix ans.

recurrence [rɪ'kʌrəns] *n* (*of illness*) réapparition *f*; (*of infectious disease*) récurrence *f*, récidive *f*; **has there been any r. of the symptoms?,** les symptômes se sont-ils manifestés à nouveau?

recurrent [rɪ'kʌrənt] *adj* (*event*) périodique, qui revient périodiquement; (*fever, symptom*) récurrent; (*dream, nightmare*) qui revient souvent; *Med* **r. bronchial catarrh,** bronchite *f* chronique; **r. expenses,** dépenses *fpl* qui reviennent périodiquement; *Math* **r. series,** série récurrente.

recurring [rɪ'kɜːrɪŋ] *adj* périodique; (*dream, nightmare*) qui revient souvent; *Math* **r. decimal,** fraction décimale périodique.

recyclable [riː'saɪkləbəl] *adj* (*container etc*) recyclable.

recycle [riː'saɪk(ə)l] *vt* recycler (*des eaux usées, du papier etc*); *Fin* **to r. funds,** remettre des fonds en circulation.

recycling [riː'saɪklɪŋ] *n* (*of paper etc*) recyclage *m*; (*of funds*) remise *f* en circulation; **r. facility/plant/***etc*, installation *f*/usine *f*/*etc* de recyclage.

red [red] **1** *adj* (*comp* **redder**, *superl* **reddest**) **(a)** (*dress, wine etc*) rouge; (*beard, hair*) roux, *f* rousse; (*lips*) vermeil; **r.(-rimmed) eyes,** yeux *mpl* rouges; **to turn** *or* **go r.,** (*of person*) rougir, devenir rouge; (*of thing*) rougir; (*of hair, leaves etc*) roussir; (*of sky*) rougeoyer; **to be r. in the face** *or* **have a r. face,** (*permanent state*) être rougeaud; **to be r. (in the face) with anger/embarrassment/***etc*, être rouge de colère/gêne/*etc*; **was my face r.!,** ce que j'étais gêné!; **there will be some r. faces on the Opposition benches,** cela va causer de l'embarras dans les rangs de l'Opposition; **to be as r. as a beetroot,** (*with embarrassment*) être rouge comme une tomate; **to be as r. as a lobster,** (*with sunburn*) être rouge comme une écrevisse; **to put** *or* **roll out the r. carpet for s.o.,** recevoir quelqu'un en grande pompe, dérouler le tapis rouge pour recevoir quelqu'un; **I got the r.-carpet treatment wherever I went,** on m'a reçu en grande pompe partout où je suis allé; *Am F* **it isn't worth a r. cent,** ça ne vaut pas un centime; *Mil & Fig* **to be on r. alert,** être en état d'alerte maximale; *Mil & Fig* **to go to r. alert,** se mettre en état d'alerte maximale; **Little R. Riding Hood,** Le Petit Chaperon rouge;

(b) *Pol* rouge; **the r. flag,** le drapeau rouge; **the R. Flag,** (*song*) l'Internationale *f*; **R. China,** la Chine communiste; *F* **r. shirt,** anarchiste *mf*; *Italian Hist* **the R. Shirts,** les Chemises rouges;

(c) (*compounds*) **r. card,** (*in soccer*) carton *m* rouge; **to be shown the r. card,** (*of soccer player*) recevoir un carton rouge; **R. Crescent,** Croissant-Rouge *m*; **R. Cross,** Croix Rouge *f*; *Astron* **r. dwarf/giant,** étoile naine/géante; **r. herring,** (*food*) hareng *m* saur; *Fig* **it was just a r. herring,** (*false trail*) ce n'était qu'une diversion; *Fig* **she's always introducing r. herrings into the conversation,** (*avoiding the issue*) elle détourne toujours la conversation; (*getting sidetracked*) elle fait toujours des digressions; *Am Fin* **r. herring (prospectus),** prospectus *m* préliminaire; **R.**

Indian, *Old-fashioned* **r. man,** peau *f* rouge; *Am F* **r. ink,** déficit *m*; *Am* **to go into r. ink,** (*of person*) se mettre à découvert; (*of company*) être en déficit; *Aut* **r. light,** feu *m* rouge; *Aut* **to go through a r. light,** brûler le rouge; *Fig* **to see the r. light,** sentir le danger; *F* **r.-light district,** quartier des prostituées, quartier chaud; *Culin* **r. meat,** viande *f* rouge; **r. pepper,** (*vegetable*) poivron *m* rouge; *Geog* **the R. Sea,** la mer Rouge; **r. setter,** (*dog*) setter irlandais; **r. snapper,** (*fish*) vivaneau *m*; **r. squirrel,** écureuil *m*; **r. tape,** (*on documents*) ruban *m* rouge, bolduc *m* (rouge); *Fig* bureaucratie *f*, *F* paperasse *f*.

2 *n* **(a)** (*colour*) rouge *m*; **r. is my favourite colour,** le rouge est ma couleur préférée; **dressed in r.,** habillé de *ou* en rouge; *F* **to see r.,** (*be angry*) voir rouge;

(b) *Fin F* **to be in the r.,** (*of company, person*) être dans le rouge, avoir un découvert; (*of account*) avoir un solde déficitaire; **at last I'm out of the r.,** j'ai enfin un compte en crédit;

(c) *Pol* rouge *mf*; **to see reds under the bed,** avoir la phobie des communistes; **the reds under the bed syndrome,** la phobie anti-communiste;

(d) (*in billiards*) bille *f* rouge; (*on roulette table*) rouge *f*.

red-blooded [red'blʌdɪd] *adj* (*person*) vigoureux, robuste; (*policy, response etc*) musclé; **the average r.-b. male,** n'importe quel homme digne de ce nom.

redbreast ['redbrest] *n* (*bird*) **(robin) r.,** rouge-gorge *m*, *pl* rouges-gorges.

redbrick ['redbrɪk] *adj* (*house, building*) en brique rouge; *Fig* **r. universities,** = universités de province modernes (par opposition à Oxford et Cambridge).

redcap ['redkæp] *n* **(a)** *Br Mil* soldat *m* de la police militaire; **(b)** *Am* porteur *m*.

redcoat ['redkəʊt] *n Br Hist* soldat anglais (du dix-huitième siècle).

redcurrant ['redkʌrənt] *n* groseille *f* (rouge); **r. bush,** groseillier *m*; **r. jelly,** gelée *f* de groseille(s).

redden ['red(ə)n] **1** *vt* rendre (*qch*) rouge, rougir (*qch*). **2** *vi* (*of sky*) rougeoyer; (*of leaves*) roussir; (*of person*) rougir.

reddish ['redɪʃ] *adj* (*light, colour*) rougeâtre; **r. hair,** cheveux *mpl* qui tirent sur le roux.

redecorate [riː'dekəreɪt] **1** *vt* refaire (*un appartement etc*). **2** *vi* refaire la peinture et les papiers.

redecoration [riːdekə'reɪʃən] *n* (*of flat etc*) remise *f* à neuf de la peinture et des papiers.

redeem [rɪ'diːm] *vt* **(a)** (*recover*) dégager (*un objet mis en gage*); **to r. one's good name,** dégager son honneur (**by,** en); **(b)** (*pay off*) racheter, dégager (*une propriété hypothéquée*); **to r. a mortgage,** (*of mortgagor*) éteindre une hypothèque; (*of purchaser of mortgaged property*) purger une hypothèque; **(c)** (*convert*) obtenir le remboursement de (*une obligation remboursable*); encaisser (*un coupon*); (*for cash*) rembourser (*un coupon*); **(d)** (*compensate for*) racheter, compenser (*des défauts*); **to r. oneself,** se racheter; **it's his** *or* **her** *or* **its sole redeeming feature,** c'est sa seule qualité; **(e)** (*free*) libérer, racheter (*un esclave, un prisonnier*); *Rel* (*of Christ*) racheter (*le genre humain*).

redeemable [rɪ'diːməb(ə)l] *adj Fin* (*share etc*) remboursable; **coupons are r. for cash,** les coupons sont remboursables en espèces.

redeemer [rɪ'diːmər] *n Rel* **the R.,** le Rédempteur.

redemption [rɪ'dem(p)ʃən] *n* **(a)** (*of item pawned*) dégagement *m*; **(b)** (*of property*) rachat *m*; (*of mortgage*) (*by mortgagor*) extinction *f*; (*by purchaser*) purge *f*; **(c)** (*of coupon, gift token*) encaissement *m*; **r. date,** date *f* de remboursement; **(d)** (*of fault*) rachat *m*; **(e)** (*of slave, prisoner*) rachat *m*; *Rel* rédemption *f*; *Fig* **this setback proved his r.,** ce revers de fortune fut son salut.

redeploy [riːdɪ'plɔɪ] *vt Mil* redéployer (*des troupes etc*); *Admin* réorganiser (*des employés etc*).

redeployment [riːdɪ'plɔɪmənt] *n* (*of troops etc*) redéploiement *m*; (*of staff etc*) réorganisation *f*.

redevelop [riːdɪ'veləp] *vt* réaménager, revaloriser (*un quartier pauvre*); **the Cardiff docks are being redeveloped,** les docks de Cardiff sont en cours de réaménagement.

redevelopment [riːdɪ'veləpmənt] *n* (*of town, street etc*) réaménagement *m*, remise *f* en valeur; **scheduled for r.,** dont le réaménagement est prévu; **r. area,** zone *f* de réaménagement; **r. costs/plans/***etc*, frais *mpl*/projets *mpl*/*etc* de réaménagement.

red-eye ['redaɪ] *n* **(a)** *Am Av F* **r.-e. (flight),** = vol tard dans la nuit *ou* tôt le matin; **(b)** *Phot* **to avoid the r.-e. effect ...,** pour éviter que le sujet apparaisse avec des yeux rouges ... .

red-eyed ['redaɪd] *adj* aux yeux rouges; **to be r.-e.,** avoir les yeux rouges (**from doing,** de faire; **with,** de).

red-faced ['red'feɪst] *adj* (*naturally*) rougeaud, rubicond; (*with anger, embarrassment*) rougissant (**with,** de); **a r.-f. admission,** un aveu confus.

red-haired ['red'heəd] *adj* aux cheveux roux; **r.-h. man/woman,** roux *m*/rousse *f*.

red-handed ['red'hændɪd] *adj Fig* **to be caught r.-h.,** être pris en flagrant délit *ou F* la main dans le sac.

redhead ['redhed] *n* roux *m*, rousse *f*.

red-headed [red'hedɪd] *adj* **(a)** (*person*) = **RED-HAIRED**; **(b)** (*bird, animal*) à tête rouge.

red-hot [red'hɒt] *adj* (*dish, plate etc*) brûlant; (*metal*) chauffé au rouge; *Fig* (*supporter, revolutionary etc*) ardent; *Fig* (*enthusiasm*) chauffé à blanc; *Fig F* (*very good*) sensass *inv*; **to make sth r.-h.,** porter qch au rouge; *Fig* **r.-h. news,** nouvelle de dernière heure *ou* toute chaude; **r.-h. poker,** (*flower*) tritoma *m*.

redial[1] [riː'daɪəl] *v* (**-ll-,** *US* **-l-**) *Tel* **1** *vt* **to r. a number,** refaire un numéro. **2** *vi* refaire le numéro.

redial[2] ['riːdaɪəl] *n Tel* **r. (feature),** rappel *m* du dernier numéro; **the latest model has automatic r.,** le dernier modèle est muni du système de rappel du dernier numéro.

redirect [riːdɪ'rekt, -daɪ-] *vt* **(a)** faire suivre (*une lettre etc*); **(b)** donner un nouvel itinéraire à (*un avion etc*).

redirection [riːdɪ'rekʃən, -daɪ-] *n* **(a)** (*of letter etc*) réacheminement *m*, réexpédition *f*; **(b)** (*of plane*) détournement *m* sur un nouvel itinéraire.

rediscover [riːdɪs'kʌvər] *vt* redécouvrir, retrouver.

redistribute [riːdɪs'trɪbjuːt] *vt* redistribuer (*les richesses, les tâches*); *Pol* **to r. seats,** redécouper les circonscriptions électorales.

redistribution [riːdɪstrɪ'bjuːʃən] *n* (*of wealth, labour*) redistribution *f*; *Pol* (*of seats*) nouvelle répartition.

red-letter ['red'letər] *adj* **r.-l. day,** *Rel* jour férié *ou* de fête; *Fig* jour à marquer d'une pierre blanche; **this has been a r.-l. day for everyone,** ceci a été un jour mémorable pour tout le monde.

redneck ['rednek] *n Am Pej* rustre *m*, péquenaud *m*; *Fig* réactionnaire *mf*; *Fig* **r. attitude/behaviour/***etc*, attitude *f*/comportement *m*/*etc* réactionnaire.

redness ['rednɪs] *n* (*of face, sky, wine etc*) rougeur *f*, couleur *f* rouge; (*of hair*) rousseur *f*.

redo [riː'duː] *vt* refaire (*une tâche, un appartement*).

redolent ['redələnt] *adj* (*sweet smelling*) odoriférant, parfumé; (*strong-smelling*) qui a une odeur forte (**of,** de); *Fig* (*reminiscent*) évocateur, suggestif; **r. of spring,** qui exhale une odeur de printemps; *Fig* **a house r. of the past,** une maison qui évoque *ou* suggère le passé.

redouble [riː'dʌb(ə)l] **1** *vt* redoubler (*ses cris, ses instances*); **to r. one's efforts,** redoubler ses efforts, redoubler d'efforts *ou* de zèle; *Cards* **to r. spades,** surcontrer pique. **2** *vi* (*of noise, rain etc*) redoubler; *Cards* surcontrer.

redoubt [rɪ'daʊt] *n Mil* redoute *f*.

redoubtable [rɪ'daʊtəb(ə)l] *adj* (*fearsome*) formidable; (*opponent*) redoutable.

redound [rɪ'daʊnd] *vi Fml* contribuer (**to,** à); **to r. to s.o.'s advantage,** contribuer *ou* tourner à l'avantage de qn.

red-pencil ['red'pens(ə)l] *vt* (**-ll-,** *US* **-l-**) corriger, réviser (*un texte*).

redraft[1] ['riːdrɑːft] *n* (*of proposal, submission*) refonte *f*.

redraft[2] [riː'drɑːft] *vt* refondre (*une proposition, soumission*).

redress[1] [rɪ'dres] *n* (*of grievance*) réparation *f*; **to seek r.,** demander réparation (**for,** de); **there is no r.,** il n'y a pas de recours.

redress[2] *vt* (*rectify*) réparer (*un tort*); **to r. the balance,** rétablir l'équilibre.

re-dress [riː'dres] *vt* **to r. a wound,** refaire un pansement.

redshank ['redʃæŋk] *n* (*bird*) chevalier *m* gambette.

redskin ['redskɪn] *n Pej* Peau-Rouge *m*.

redstart ['redstɑːt] *n* (*bird*) rouge-queue *m* à front blanc.

reduce [rɪ'djuːs] *vt* **(a)** (*lessen*) baisser, diminuer, réduire (*un prix*); réduire (*un dessin, une photographie*); alléger (*un impôt*); diminuer, réduire (*les dépenses*); faire baisser (*la température*); *Culin* faire réduire (*une sauce*); **oranges have been reduced,** les oranges ont diminué; **reduced to 10 from 15,** réduction: 10 au lieu de 15, en vente à 10 au lieu de 15; **to r. speed,** diminuer *ou* réduire la vitesse, ralentir; *Ind* **to r. output,** ralentir la production; **to r. a prison sentence,** accorder *ou* consentir une remise de peine; **are these shoes reduced?,** est-ce que ces chaussures sont soldées *ou* en solde?;

(b) (*bring to a certain state*) **to r. sth to ashes/dust/**

etc, réduire qch en cendres/poussière/*etc;* **to r. s.o. to despair/silence,** réduire qn au désespoir/silence; **his words reduced her to tears,** ses paroles l'ont fait fondre en larmes; **to r. s.o. to helpless laughter,** faire mourir qn de rire; **to be reduced to doing sth,** en être réduit à faire qch; **is this what I've been reduced to?,** j'en suis donc réduit à cela?;

(c) (*simplify*) convertir (*kilos*) (**to,** en); ramener (*un problème, une question*) (**to,** à); **to r. a fraction to its lowest terms,** simplifier une fraction, ramener une fraction à sa plus simple expression; **to r. two fractions to the same denominator,** réduire deux fractions au même dénominateur.

2 *vi* (*slim*) maigrir.

reduced [rɪ'djuːst] *adj* (*smaller*) réduit; **on a r. scale,** à une échelle réduite; **at (greatly) r. prices,** au rabais, en solde; **at (a) r. rate,** (*billet*) à tarif réduit; **'everything r. by ten per cent',** remise de dix pour cent sur tous nos articles; **reduced to clear,** (*sale notice*) (soldes) coup de balai; **to be/live in r. circumstances,** être/vivre dans la gêne.

reducer [rɪ'djuːsər] *n El* réducteur *m*; *Phot* affaiblisseur *m*.

reducible [rɪ'djuːsɪb(ə)l] *adj* réductible (**to,** à).

reduction [rɪ'dʌkʃən] *n* **(a)** (*of prices*) baisse *f*, diminution *f*, réduction *f*; (*of taxes*) allègement *m*; (*of costs, speed, spending*) diminution *f*, réduction; (*of drawing, photograph, scale*) réduction; (*of temperature, voltage*) baisse *f*; **I'll give you a r.,** (*on purchase*) je vous fais un prix; **big reductions,** (*sale notice*) rabais, soldes intéressantes; *Jur* **r. of sentence,** remise *f* de peine; *Tech* **r. gear,** (engrenage *m*) démultiplicateur *m*; **(b)** (*of equation*) réduction *f*.

redundancy [rɪ'dʌndənsɪ] *n* **(a)** *Ind* (*dismissal*) licenciement *m*; (*unemployment*) chômage *m*; **redundancies have been heavy,** il y a eu beaucoup de licenciements; **the strike caused over three hundred redundancies,** la grève a causé le licenciement de plus de trois cents ouvriers; **r. notice,** avis *m* de licenciement; **r. payment** *or* *F* **money,** indemnité *f* de licenciement; **(b)** (*of details, factory etc*) inutilité *f*; *Comptr* redondance *f*; **(c)** *Liter* redondance *f*.

redundant [rɪ'dʌndənt] *adj* **(a)** (*worker*) licencié; **to make s.o. r.,** (*of technology etc*) entraîner le licenciement de qn; **to be made r.,** être licencié; **she has been r. for six months,** elle est au chômage depuis six mois; **(b)** (*details, factory etc*) superflu; *Comptr* (*file, information*) redondant; **(c)** *Liter* redondant.

redwood ['redwʊd] *n* (*tree*) séquoia *m*.

re-echo [riː'ekəʊ] **1** *vt* (*repeat*) répercuter, renvoyer (*un son*); *Fig* répéter. **2** *vi* (*of noise, voice etc*) retentir, résonner; **the hall echoed and re-echoed to the sound of applause,** la salle retentissait d'acclamations.

reed [riːd] *n* **(a)** (*plant*) roseau *m*; **bed of reeds, r. bed,** roselière *f*; *F* **broken r.,** personne sur laquelle on ne peut (pas) compter; **r. warbler,** (*bird*) rousserolle *f* des roseaux; **r. bunting,** (*bird*) bruant *m* des roseaux; **(b)** *Mus* anche *f*; **the reeds,** les instruments *mpl* à anche; **r. stop,** (*on organ*) jeu *m* d'anches.

re-edit [riː'edɪt] *vt* rédiger (*un texte*) à nouveau; *Comptr* rééditer.

re-educate [riː'edjʊkeɪt] *vt* rééduquer (*un délinquant, un membre*).

re-education [riːedjʊ'keɪʃən] *n* (*of criminal, limb*) rééducation *f*.

reedy ['riːdɪ] *adj* **(a)** (*covered in reeds*) abondant en roseaux, plein *ou* couvert de roseaux; **(b)** (*shrill*) (*instrument*) aigu; (*voice*) flûté, grêle.

reef¹ [riːf] *n* (*rocks*) écueil *m*, récif *m*; *Fig* écueil; **to hit a r.,** (*of ship*) faire naufrage sur un récif.

reef² *n Nau* ris *m*; **r. knot,** nœud plat.

reef³ *vt Nau* prendre un *ou* des ris à (*une voile*); **to r. the sails,** prendre les ris.

reefer ['riːfər] *n* **(a)** (*jacket*) caban *m*, vareuse *f*; **(b)** *Old-fashioned F* cigarette *f* de marihuana, joint *m*; **(c)** *Am* (*for transporting goods*) camion *m ou* navire *m ou* wagon *m* frigorifique; (*refrigerator*) chambre *f* frigorifique.

reefing ['riːfɪŋ] *n* (*of sail*) prise *f* de ris; **r. jacket,** caban *m*, vareuse *f*.

reek¹ [riːk] *n* (*bad smell*) puanteur *f*.

reek² *vi* puer; **to r. of sth,** (*smell*) *& Fig* puer qch; **this room reeks,** ça pue ici.

reel¹ [riːl] *n* **(a)** *Br* (*for film, paper, thread*) bobine *f*; (*film itself*) bande *f*; (*for fishing line*) moulinet *m*; (*for cable, hose etc*) dévidoir *m*; *Am F* **(right) off the r.,** (*continuously*) d'une seule traite, d'affilée; (*immediately*) sans hésiter, sur-le-champ; **(b)** (*dance, music*) reel *m*, quadrille écossais.

reel² *vi* (*sway*) chanceler; (*not walk straight*) tituber; **to go reeling down the street,** descendre la rue en titubant; *Fig* **to make s.o.'s senses r.,** donner le vertige à qn; *Fig* **my head is reeling,** la tête me tourne; *Fig* **I'm still reeling,** (*after news*) je n'en suis toujours pas revenu; **to send s.o. reeling,** (*of punch*) faire valser qn; *Fig* (*of news, scene etc*) abasourdir qn; *Fig* **his mind** *or* **brain reeled at the thought,** cette pensée lui donnait le vertige; *Fig* **the whole room was reeling,** toute la salle tournoyait autour de moi *ou* de lui *etc*.

►**reel in** *vtsep* **to r. a fish in,** remonter un poisson.

►**reel off** *vtsep* débiter (*un discours etc*).

re-elect [riːɪ'lekt] *vt* réélire (*un député*); **she is sure to be re-elected,** sa réélection est assurée; **he was re-elected (as) president,** on l'a réélu président.

re-election [riːɪ'lekʃən] *n* (*of MP etc*) réélection *f*; **to stand** *or Am* **run for r.,** se représenter.

reeling ['riːlɪŋ] *adj* (*head*) qui tourne; (*person*) qui chancelle; (*not walking straight*) qui titube; (*gait*) titubant.

re-embark [riːɪm'bɑːk] **1** *vt* rembarquer (*des passagers*). **2** *vi* (se) rembarquer; *Fig* **to r.-e. on sth,** recommencer qch.

re-embarcation [riːɪmbɑː'keɪʃən] *n* (*of passengers*) rembarquement *m*.

re-emerge [riːɪ'mɜːdʒ] *vi* (*of person*) ressortir; (*of sun*) reparaître.

re-employ [riːɪm'plɔɪ] *vt* réemployer (*un ancien employé*).

re-employment [riːɪm'plɔɪmənt] *n* (*of former employee*) r(é)emploi *m*.

re-enact [riːɪ'nækt] *vt* **(a)** (*enforce*) remettre en vigueur (*une loi*); **(b)** (*depict*) reconstituer (*un accident, un crime*); reproduire (*une scène*).

re-enactment [riːɪ'næktmənt] *n* **(a)** (*of law*) remise *f* en vigueur; **(b)** (*of crime, accident*) reconstitution *f*; (*of scene*) reproduction *f*.

re-engage [riːɪn'geɪdʒ] **1** *vt* **(a)** réemployer (*un ancien employé*); **(b)** *Tech* rengrener (*une roue dentée*); *Aut* **to r. the clutch,** rembrayer.

re-engagement [riːɪn'geɪdʒmənt] *n* **(a)** (*of former employee*) r(é)emploi *m*; **(b)** *Tech* (*of cogwheel*) rengrènement *m*; *Aut* (*of clutch*) rembrayage *m*.

re-enlist [riːɪn'lɪst] *vi Mil* se rengager.

re-enter [riː'entər] **1** *vi* (*of person, spacecraft*) rentrer; (*of musical instrument*) faire une *ou* sa rentrée; *Th* **r. Macbeth,** Macbeth rentre; **to r. for an examination,** se présenter de nouveau à un examen. **2** *vt* **(a)** rentrer dans (*un endroit, l'atmosphère*); **he never re-entered that house,** il n'a jamais remis les pieds dans cette maison; **to r. the job market,** se remettre à chercher du travail; **(b)** réinscrire, inscrire de nouveau (*la date, son nom*).

re-entrant [riː'entrənt] **1** *adj* (*angle etc*) rentrant. **2** *n* angle rentrant.

re-entry [riː'entrɪ] *n* **(a)** (*of person, spacecraft*) rentrée *f*; **to make its r.,** (*of spacecraft*) rentrer dans l'atmosphère; **(b)** (*of date, name*) réinscription *f*.

re-establish [riːɪ'stæblɪʃ] *vt* rétablir (*communications, relations diplomatiques etc*).

re-establishment [riːɪ'stæblɪʃmənt] *n* (*of communications, relations etc*) rétablissement *m*.

reeve [riːv] *vt* (*pt* **rove** [rəʊv], **reeved;** *pp* **reeved, rove**) *Nau* passer (*un cordage*) (**through a block,** dans une poulie).

re-examination [riːɪgzæmɪ'neɪʃən] *n* **(a)** (*of file, question etc*) réexamen *m*; **(b)** *Jur* (*of witness*) nouvel interrogatoire.

re-examine [riːɪg'zæmɪn] *vt* **(a)** (*review*) réexaminer (*un dossier, une question etc*); **(b)** *Jur* interroger (*un témoin*) de nouveau.

re-export¹ [riː'ekspɔːt] *n* (*of goods*) réexportation *f*.

re-export² [riːeks'pɔːt] *vt* réexporter (*des marchandises*).

ref [ref] **(a)** *Br F abbr* **referee; (b)** *Com abbr* **with reference to.**

refectory [rɪ'fekt(ə)rɪ] *n* réfectoire *m*; **r. table,** = table longue et étroite, souvent en chêne massif, comme on en trouve dans les châteaux.

refer [rɪ'fɜːr] *v* (**-rr-**) **1** *vt* (*direct*) soumettre (*une affaire, une proposition etc*) (**to,** à); **to r. a cheque to drawer,** (*of bank*) refuser d'honorer un chèque; **r. to drawer,** (*notice on cheque*) voir le tireur; **to r. a matter to s.o.,** en référer à qn *ou* à l'avis de qn; **to r. a question to s.o. for (a) decision,** s'en rapporter *ou* s'en remettre à la décision de qn; **to r. a matter to a tribunal,** soumettre une affaire à un tribunal; **the reader is referred to ...,** (*in book*) se reporter à ...; **readers are referred to our previous article,** nous renvoyons les lecteurs à notre article précédent; **to r. a patient to a specialist,** envoyer un malade à un spécialiste; **she's going to r. me,** elle va m'envoyer à un spécialiste; **to r. a customer to another department,** renvoyer un client à un autre service; **he just referred me back to you,** il m'a renvoyé à vous; *Med* **referred pain,** douleur irradiée.

2 *vi* **(a) to r. to,** (*consult*) se référer *ou* se reporter à; **to r. (back) to an authority,** s'en rapporter à *ou* se référer à une autorité; **to r. to a work,** consulter un ouvrage;

(b) to r. to, (*allude to*) faire allusion à; (*speak of*) parler de; (*apply to*) s'appliquer à; **this remark refers to you,** cette remarque fait allusion à vous; (*is aimed at*) cette remarque s'adresse à vous; **who are you referring to?,** de qui parlez-vous?; **it's you I'm referring to,** c'est de toi que je parle; **referred to as ...,** désigné sous le nom de ...; **he never refers to it,** il n'en parle jamais; **we won't r. to it again,** n'en reparlons plus; *Com* **referring to ...,** nous référant à ...; **referring to your letter,** suite à votre lettre.

referee[1] [refə'riː] *n* **(a)** *Sp* arbitre *m*; **(b)** (*for job etc*) répondant, -ante; **please give at least two referees,** (*in job advert*) veuillez fournir aux moins deux références; **will you act as my r.?,** voulez-vous me fournir des références?

referee[2] *vi & vt* (**refereed**) *Sp* arbitrer.

reference ['ref(ə)rəns] *n* **(a)** (*to higher authority*) renvoi *m*, référence *f*; **terms of r.** (*of person, investigating body*) compétence *f*; (*of law*) étendue *f*; **it is outside the committee's terms of r.,** c'est hors de la compétence du comité;

(b) (*consultation*) consultation *f*; (*source*) référence *f*; **without r. to the Board,** sans consulter le conseil d'administration; **page r.,** (numéro *m* de) la page; **can we have some page references?,** voulez-vous nous donner les numéros des pages auxquelles on devrait se référer?; **to keep sth for future r.,** garder qch à titre d'information; **for future r., please note ...,** pour votre information à l'avenir, veuillez noter ...; **for r. only,** (*on book*) consultation sur place; (*on document etc in circulation*) pour information seulement; **r. book/work,** livre *m*/ouvrage *m* de référence; **r. library,** bibliothèque *f* d'ouvrages à consulter; **r. point, point of r.,** point *m* de repère; **r. room,** (*in public library*) salle *f* de lecture; (*in university*) salle de consultation;

(c) (*allusion*) allusion *f* (**to,** à); (*mention*) mention *f* (**to,** de); (*connection*) rapport *m* (**to,** avec); (*in book*) (*allusion*) référence *f*; (*cross-reference*) renvoi *m*; (*on map*) coordonnées *fpl*; **to make r. to a fact,** faire mention d'un fait; **if any r. is made to me,** si on parle de moi; **with r. to what was said ...,** en référence à ce qui a été dit ...; **a talk on the environment with particular r. to ...,** un colloque sur l'environnement s'intéressant particulièrement à *ou* et plus particulièrement sur ...; **with r. to my letter of the 20th March,** me référant *ou* suite à ma lettre du 20 mars; **in r.** *or* **with r. to your letter,** en ce qui concerne votre lettre; **r. AB,** (*at head of letter*) référence AB; **our/your r.,** (*on letter*) notre/votre référence;

(d) (*from bank, employer etc*) référence *f*; **to give s.o. a r.,** faire *ou* donner une référence à qn; **to have good references,** avoir de bonnes références; **to take up references,** prendre contact avec *ou* contacter des références; **to give s.o. as a r.,** se recommander de qn; **you may use my name as (a) r.,** vous pouvez donner mon nom comme référence, vous pouvez vous recommander de moi.

referendum [refə'rendəm] *n* *Pol* référendum *m*, referendum *m*; **to hold a r.,** faire un référendum; **the matter has been decided in a** *or* **by r.,** la question a été décidée par référendum.

referral [rɪ'fɜːrəl] *n* (*of case*) envoi *m*; **he/the case is a r. from Dr. Smith,** c'est un patient/un cas envoyé par le Docteur Smith.

refill[1] ['riːfɪl] *n* (*for lighter, pen*) recharge *f*, cartouche *f*; (*for propelling pencil*) mine *f* de rechange; (*for notebook*) feuilles *fpl* de rechange; *F* (*of drink*) autre verre *m*; **I'll have a r.,** (*to barman*) un autre verre; (*to friend*) la même chose; **she handed me her glass for a r.,** elle m'a tendu son verre pour que je la serve à nouveau.

refill[2] [riː'fɪl] **1** *vt* remplir (*un verre etc*) (à nouveau) (**with,** de); recharger (*un briquet, un stylo etc*); regarnir (*un rayon*) (**with,** de). **2** *vi* (*of container*) se remplir à nouveau.

refillable [riː'fɪləb(ə)l] *adj* (*lighter, pen*) rechargeable.

refinance [riː'faɪnæns] *Fin* **1** *vt* refinancer (*un emprunt*). **2** *vi* (*of company*) se refinancer (**on the money market,** auprès du marché monétaire).

refinancing [riː'faɪnænsɪŋ] *n* *Fin* refinancement *m*; **to get r. from a bank,** se refinancer auprès d'une banque.

refine [rɪ'faɪn] *vt* **(a)** affiner (*un métal*); purger (*l'or*); raffiner (*le sucre, le pétrole*); *Fig* raffiner (*les plaisirs, les mœurs*); **(b)** perfectionner (*une technique, une machine*).

►**refine on, refine upon** *vipo* (*improve*) raffiner sur.

refined [rɪ'faɪnd] *adj* (*metal*) affiné; (*gold*) fin; (*petroleum, sugar*) raffiné; (*person, taste*) raffiné; (*person*) distingué, cultivé; *Pej* maniéré.

refinement [rɪ'faɪnmənt] *n* **(a)** *Fig* (*of manners, taste, person*) raffinement *m*, distinction *f*, délicatesse *f*; (*of thought*) raffinement, subtilité *f*; **of great r.,** (*person*) très distingué; **lack of r.,** vulgarité *f*; **without going into refinements,** sans entrer dans des subtilités; **(b)** (*of technique*) perfectionnement *m*; **machine with all the latest refinements,** machine avec les perfectionnements les plus récents; **to make refinements to sth,** perfectionner qch; **(c)** (*of metal etc*) = **REFINING**.

refiner [rɪ'faɪnər] *n* (*of sugar, oil*) raffineur *m*; (*of metal*) affineur *m*.

refinery [rɪ'faɪnərɪ] *n* (*for petroleum, sugar*) raffinerie *f*; (*for metal*) affinerie *f*.

refining [rɪ'faɪnɪŋ] *n* (*of petroleum, sugar*) raffinage *m*; (*of metal*) affinage *m*.

refit[1] ['riːfɪt] *n* (*of ship*) réparation *f*, remise *f* en état; (*of factory*) réaménagement *m*; **the yacht is under r.,** le yacht est en cours de réparation.

refit[2] [riː'fɪt] *v* (**-tt-**) **1** *vt* (*alter*) réparer; remettre (*un navire*) en état; réaménager (*une usine*). **2** *vi* (*of ship*) être en cours de réparation; (*of factory*) être en cours de réaménagement; **while we're refitting,** pendant les réparations *ou* le réaménagement.

reflate [riː'fleɪt] *vi* relancer l'économie.

reflation [riː'fleɪʃən] *n* *Econ* relance *f*.

reflationary [riː'fleɪʃənərɪ] *adj* **r. measures/policy/***etc*, mesures *fpl*/politique *f*/*etc* de relance.

reflect [rɪ'flekt] **1** *vt* **(a)** (*mirror*) réfléchir, refléter (*une image*); *Fig* refléter (*qch*); **to be reflected,** se réfléchir (**in,** sur); (*send back*) réfléchir (*la lumière*); renvoyer (*la chaleur, une image, la lumière*); **to be reflected on s.o. (else),** (*of behaviour*) rejaillir sur qn; **(b)** (*think*) **to r. that ...,** penser *ou* se dire que ... . **2** *vi* **(a)** (*of person*) réfléchir (**on,** à, sur); **(b) to r. on s.o.'s honesty,** (*of action etc*) porter atteinte à *ou* émettre des doutes sur l'honnêteté de qn; **to r. (badly) on s.o.,** (*of action etc*) faire du tort à qn, nuire à (la réputation de) qn; **how is that going to r. on the company?,** quelles en seront les conséquences *ou* répercussions pour la société?

reflecting [rɪ'flektɪŋ] *adj* (*mirror, surface, water*) réfléchissant.

reflection [rɪ'flekʃən] *n* **(a)** (*in mirror, glass*) reflet *m*, image *f* (réfléchie); *Fig* reflet; **to see one's r. in a mirror,** voir son image dans un miroir; **(b)** (*of light, sound, image*) reflexion *f*; **(c)** (*on honesty, character etc*) blâme *m*, critique *f* (**on,** de); **to cast reflections on s.o.,** critiquer qn, blâmer qn, faire des réflexions à qn; **this is a r. on your character,** c'est une atteinte à votre intégrité; **it's no r. on your performance,** il ne s'agit pas d'une remise en cause de votre performance, cela ne remet pas votre performance en cause; **(d)** (*thought*) réflexion *f* (**on,** sur); **on r.,** à la réflexion, en y réfléchissant, tout bien réfléchi; **to do sth without due r.,** faire qch étourdiment *ou* sans avoir suffisamment réfléchi; **reflections,** réflexions, pensées *fpl*; **reflections on history,** considérations *fpl* sur l'histoire.

reflective [rɪ'flektɪv] *adj* **(a)** (*person*) réfléchi; **(b)** (*surface*) réfléchissant; **r. power,** pouvoir réfléchissant.

reflectively [rɪ'flektɪvlɪ] *adv* d'un air *ou* d'un ton réfléchi *ou* pensif.

reflector [rɪ'flektər] *n* (*on bicycle, vehicle*) réflecteur *m*, cataphote ® *m*, catadioptre *m*; (*of heat*) réflecteur.

reflex[1] ['riːfleks] *n* (*reaction*) réflexe *m*; **to have good reflexes,** avoir de bons réflexes; **to test s.o.'s reflexes,** tester les réflexes de qn; **your reflexes aren't what they should be,** vos réflexes sont défaillants.

reflex[2] *adj* **(a)** réflexe; **r. action,** réflexe *m*; **(b)** *Math* (*angle*) rentrant; *Phot* **r. camera,** (appareil *m*) reflex *m*.

reflexion [rɪ'flekʃən] *n* = **REFLECTION**.

reflexive [rɪ'fleksɪv] *Gram* **1** *adj* (*pronoun, verb*) réfléchi. **2** *n* (*verb*) verbe réfléchi; (*pronoun*) pronom (personnel) réfléchi.

reflexively [rɪ'fleksɪvlɪ] *adv* *Gram* au sens réfléchi.

reflexology [riːflek'sɒlədʒɪ] *n* (*massage*) réflexologie *f*.

refloat [riː'fləʊt] *vt* **(a)** renflouer, (re)mettre à flot (*un navire échoué*); **(b)** *Fin* émettre de nouveau (*un emprunt*); renflouer (*une entreprise*).

reflux ['riːflʌks] *n* reflux *m*.

reforest [riː'fɒrɪst] *vt* reboiser (*une région, un terrain*).

reforestation [riːfɒrɪ'steɪʃən] *n* reboisement *m*; **r. costs/programme/***etc*, coûts *mpl*/programme *m*/*etc* de reboisement.

reform¹ [rɪ'fɔːm] *n* **(a)** (*of abuse, institution etc*) réforme *f*; **to introduce reforms,** introduire *ou* apporter des réformes; **to make reforms,** faire des réformes; **(b)** (*of person*) retour *m* à la vertu; *Old-fashioned Br* **r. school,** maison *f* de correction *ou* de redressement.

reform² **1** *vt* (*correct*) réformer (*une institution, un abus etc*); améliorer (*un système*); corriger (*qn*), ramener (*qn*) à la vertu; **he's a reformed character,** il s'est assagi, il a changé en bien; **Reformed Church,** Église réformée. **2** *vi* (*of person*) se corriger, s'amender.

re-form [riː'fɔːm] **1** *vt* reformer (*un bataillon, un groupe etc*). **2** *vi* (*of group, troops etc*) se reformer.

reformat [riː'fɔːmæt] *vt & vi* (**-tt-**) reformater.

reformation [refə'meɪʃən] *n* **(a)** (*of abuse, calendar, society etc*) réforme *f*; *Rel Hist* **the R.,** la Réforme; **(b)** (*of person*) retour *m* à la vertu *ou* à une conduite meilleure.

reformatory [rɪ'fɔːmət(ə)rɪ] **1** *adj* (*measures etc*) réformateur. **2** *n Am* centre *m* d'éducation surveillée; *Hist* maison *f* de correction *ou* de redressement.

reformatting [riː'fɔːmætɪŋ] *n* (*of text etc*) reformatage *m*.

reformer [rɪ'fɔːmər] *n* (*of religion, society*) réformateur, -trice.

reformist [rɪ'fɔːmɪst] *adj & n* réformiste *mf*.

refract [rɪ'frækt] *vt Phys* réfracter (*la lumière*); **to be refracted,** se réfracter; **refracting angle,** angle *m* de réfraction; **refracting medium,** milieu réfringent.

refraction [rɪ'frækʃən] *n Phys Opt* réfraction *f*; **double r.,** biréfringence *f*.

refractive [rɪ'fræktɪv] *adj Phys* réfringent; **r. index,** indice *m* de réfraction.

refractivity [riːfræk'tɪvɪtɪ] *n Phys* réfringence *f*.

refractor [rɪ'fræktər] *n* **(a)** *Phys* (*material*) milieu réfringent; (*object*) dispositif réfringent; **(b)** *Opt* réfracteur *m*, lunette *f* astronomique, longue-vue *f*.

refractory¹ [rɪ'frækt(ə)rɪ] *adj* (*person*) réfractaire, récalcitrant, insoumis; (*animal*) récalcitrant; (*illness*) rebelle.

refractory² *n Ch* réfractaire *m*.

refrain¹ [rɪ'freɪn] *n Mus Fig* refrain *m*.

refrain² *vi* se retenir, s'abstenir (**from doing,** de faire); **to r. from comment,** s'abstenir de tout commentaire; **he couldn't r. from smiling,** il n'a pu s'empêcher de sourire; **kindly r. from smoking/talking/***etc*, (*on notice*) prière de ne pas fumer/parler/*etc*.

refrangible [rɪ'frændʒɪb(ə)l] *adj Phys Opt* réfrangible.

re-freeze [riː'friːz] *vt* remettre (*des aliments*) au congélateur.

refresh [rɪ'freʃ] *vt* (*of bath, drink*) rafraîchir, remonter, *F* requinquer (*qn*); (*of rest, amusement*) reposer, délasser (*qn*); (*of rain*) rafraîchir (*l'air*); **to r. oneself,** (*with food*) se restaurer; (*with drink, bath*) se rafraîchir; **to awake refreshed,** s'éveiller bien reposé; *Hum* **to r. the inner man,** se refaire, se restaurer; **to r. one's memory,** se rafraîchir la mémoire; **can I r. your drink for you?,** voulez-vous que je vous remplisse votre verre?

refresher [rɪ'freʃər] *n* **r. course,** cours *m* de recyclage *m*.

refreshing [rɪ'freʃɪŋ] *adj* (*breeze, drink*) rafraîchissant; (*sleep*) réparateur, reposant; **r. cup of tea,** tasse de thé revigorante *ou* ravigotante; **it is r. to encounter such honesty,** cela change agréablement de *ou* il est réconfortant de rencontrer une telle honnêteté.

refreshingly [rɪ'freʃɪŋlɪ] *adv* d'une manière qui repose *ou* fait du bien; **r. honest,** d'une honnêteté réconfortante.

refreshment [rɪ'freʃmənt] *n* (*drink*) rafraîchissement *m*; (*snack*) collation *f*; **to have some r.,** manger *ou* boire qch; **to order some r.,** commander à manger *ou* à boire; **refreshments,** rafraîchissements; sandwichs, boissons *etc* (*servis à un buffet etc*); **refreshments will be served,** on servira une collation; *Rail* **r. room,** buffet *m* (de gare).

refrigerant [rɪ'frɪdʒərənt] *n* (mélange *m*) réfrigérant *m*.

refrigerate [rɪ'frɪdʒəreɪt] **1** *vt* réfrigérer, frigorifier (*un aliment etc*); **r. after opening,** (*notice on packet, tin*) conserver au réfrigérateur après ouverture; **keep refrigerated,** (*notice on packet*) conserver au réfrigérateur; **refrigerated meat,** viande frigorifiée, *F* congelé *m*; **refrigerated lorry,** camion *m* frigorifique. **2** *vi* se refroidir, se réfrigérer.

refrigeration [rɪfrɪdʒə'reɪʃən] *n* (*of food etc*) réfrigération *f*; **r. industry,** industrie *f* du froid.

refrigerator [rɪ'frɪdʒəreɪtər] *n* (*domestic*) réfrigérateur *m*, frigidaire ® *m*, *F* frigo *m*; (*industrial*) réfrigérateur, chambre *f ou* appareil *m* frigorifique; *Rail* **r. van** *or Am* **car,** wagon *m* frigorifique.

refuel [riː'fjuəl] *v* (**-ll-**, *US* **-l-**) **1** *vt* ravitailler (*un navire, un avion, une voiture de course*); *Fig* **to r. speculation,** alimenter *ou* encourager la spéculation. **2** *vi* (*of ship, aircraft, racing car*) se ravitailler; **to r. in flight,** se ravitailler en vol.

refuelling, *US* **refueling** [riː'fjuəlɪŋ] *n* (*of ship, plane*) ravitaillement *m* (en combustible); **to stop for r.** *or* **make a r. stop,** (*of aircraft*) faire escale pour le ravitaillement; (*of racing car*) s'arrêter pour se ravitailler; **during a r. stop,** (*of aircraft*) au cours d'une escale de ravitaillement *ou* d'une escale technique; (*of racing car*) pendant le ravitaillement.

refuge ['refjuːdʒ] *n* **(a)** (*from danger*) refuge *m*, asile *m*; (*from weather*) abri *m* (**from,** contre); *Br* (*in road*) refuge; (*for battered women*) asile; **place of r.,** lieu *m* de refuge *ou* d'asile; **to seek r.,** chercher refuge *ou* asile; **to take r.,** (*from danger*) se réfugier (**with,** chez); **to take r. from the storm,** s'abriter de l'orage; **to take r. in lying,** se réfugier dans le mensonge; **(b)** (*source of help*) refuge *m*; **God is my r.,** Dieu est mon refuge.

refugee [refjʊ'dʒiː] *n* réfugié, -ée; **economic r.,** migrant économique; **r. camp,** camp *m* de réfugiés; **r. status,** statut *m* de réfugié.

refund¹ ['riːfʌnd] *n* (*for ticket, tax etc*) remboursement *m*; **to obtain a r. for sth,** se faire rembourser qch; **I'm due a r.,** on me doit *ou* je dois recevoir un remboursement.

refund² [riː'fʌnd, rɪ-] *vt* rembourser (*de l'argent, un paiement etc*); **to r. s.o.,** rembourser qn (**sth,** de qch).

refurbish [riː'fɜːbɪʃ] *vt* remettre à neuf (*un appartement, un restaurant etc*).

refurbishment [riː'fɜːbɪʃmənt] *n* (*of flat, restaurant etc*) remise *f* à neuf.

refusal [rɪ'fjuːz(ə)l] *n* (*of offer, invitation etc*) refus *m* (**to do,** de faire); **to give a flat r.,** refuser (tout) net; **to meet with (a) r.,** se heurter à *ou* essuyer un refus; **she shook her head in r.,** elle a fait non de la tête; **that's his third r.,** (*of show-jumper*) c'est son troisième refus; **to have (the) first r. on sth,** avoir la première offre de qch; **to give s.o. first r.,** donner à qn la première offre (**on sth,** de qch); **you promised me first r. on the car,** tu m'as promis que je serais le premier à qui tu proposerais (d'acheter) la voiture.

refuse¹ ['refjuːs] *n Br* (*rubbish*) ordures *fpl*, détritus *m*; (*waste materials*) déchets *mpl*; **household r.,** ordures ménagères; **r. bag,** sac *m* à ordures; **r. bin,** (*in street*) boîte *f* à ordures; (*in home*) poubelle *f*; **r. chute,** vide-ordures *m inv*; **r. collection,** service *m* de voirie, ramassage *m* des ordures; **r. collector,** éboueur *m*; **r. disposal,** traitement *m* des ordures; **r.-disposal unit,** broyeur *m* d'ordures; **r. dump,** dépôt *m* d'ordures, *F* dépotoir *m*; **r. material,** détritus *m*.

refuse² [rɪ'fjuːz] **1** *vt* refuser (*une invitation, une offre, un obstacle etc*); rejeter, repousser (*une requête*); **to r. to do sth,** refuser de *ou* se refuser à faire qch; **I r. to believe that,** (*it is a lie*) je refuse de croire ça; (*it is impossible*) je ne peux pas croire ça; **to r. to comment,** se refuser à tout commentaire; **to r. to fight,** refuser le combat; **the car refuses to start,** la voiture ne veut pas démarrer; **to r. s.o. sth,** refuser qch à qn; **to r. s.o. admittance,** refuser (de laisser entrer) qn; **they were refused admittance,** on ne les a pas laissés entrer; **to be refused sth,** essuyer un refus; **I don't see how we can r. them,** je ne vois pas comment on peut le leur refuser; **she made me an offer I couldn't r.,** elle m'a fait une proposition impossible à refuser; **she refused him,** (*would not marry him*) elle l'a rejeté. **2** *vi* (*of person*) refuser, se refuser; (*of horse*) refuser l'obstacle.

refus(e)nik [rɪ'fjuːznɪk] *n Pol* refuznik *m*.

refutation [refjʊ'teɪʃən] *n* (*of argument, theory*) réfutation *f*.

refute [rɪ'fjuːt] *vt* réfuter (*un argument, une théorie etc*); **to r. a statement,** démontrer la fausseté d'une déclaration; (*incorrect use*) (*to deny*) **to r. an allegation,** nier une allégation.

regain [rɪ'geɪn] *vt* **(a)** (*get back*) regagner (*de l'argent perdu, la confiance de qn*); récupérer (*ses forces, de l'argent*); retrouver (*ses forces, la santé, la vue*); reprendre (*ses forces, son équilibre, sa liberté*); recouvrer (*la liberté, la santé*); **to r. possession of sth,** rentrer en *ou* reprendre possession de qch; **to r. consciousness,** reprendre connaissance, revenir à soi; **to r. lost ground,** regagner du terrain; **(b)** (*reach*) regagner (*un endroit, sa place*).

regal ['riːg(ə)l] *adj* (*offer, salary, splendour etc*) royal; (*air, person*) majestueux.

regale [rɪ'geɪl] *vt* régaler (*qn*) (**with,** de).

regalia [rɪ'geɪlɪə] *npl* (*of monarch*) insignes royaux; (*of*

Freemason etc) insignes; **the mayor came first in all his r.**, le maire est venu en premier avec tous les insignes de ses fonctions; *Hum* **here comes Mrs Smith in full r.**, voilà Mme Smith dans ses plus beaux atours.

regally [ˈriːg(ə)lɪ] *adv* (*to entertain*) royalement; (*to behave, act*) majestueusement.

regard¹ [rɪˈgɑːd] *n* **(a)** (*admiration, respect*) (*for person*) respect *m*, estime *f*; (*for skill, talent etc*) respect *m*; **to have great r. for s.o.**, avoir beaucoup d'estime pour qn; **to hold s.o. in great** *or* **high r.**, tenir qn en grande *ou* haute estime; **out of r. for s.o.**, par respect pour qn; **to give** *or* **send one's regards**, faire ses hommages; **(please give) my kindest** *or* **best regards to the family**, (présentez) mon meilleur souvenir *ou* mes sincères amitiés à toute la famille; **kind** *or* **best regards**, (*at end of letter*) meilleur souvenir, sincères amitiés, bien amicalement;
(b) (*consideration*) égard *m* (**to**, à; **for**, pour), considération *f* (**to, for**, pour); **out of r. for**, par égard pour; **without** *or* **with no r. to**, sans égard pour; **without r. to race** *or* **colour**, sans distinction de race ni de couleur; **to pay r. to**, avoir égard à; **to pay no r. to**, ne faire aucune attention à; **to have no r. for human life**, faire peu de cas de la vie humaine;
(c) (*connection*) égard *m*, point *m* (de vue); **in this** *or* **that r.**, à cet égard; **in my r.**, quant à moi, à mon égard; **in all regards**, à tous (les) égards; **with r. to**, en ce qui concerne, quant à; **with r. to your letter of ...**, relativement à votre lettre du ....; **having r. to**, si l'on tient compte de, eu égard à.

regard² *vt* **(a)** (*admire, respect*) avoir de l'estime pour (*qn*); **to r. s.o. highly**, avoir beaucoup d'estime pour qn; **(b)** (*consider*) considérer (*qch, qn*) (**as**, comme), tenir (*qch, qn*) (**as**, pour); **(c)** (*concern*) concerner (*qn*); **as regards ...**, en ce qui concerne ..., quant à ...; **she is very strict as regards discipline**, elle est très sévère sur le chapitre de la discipline.

regarding [rɪˈgɑːdɪŋ] *prep* (*about*) en ce qui concerne, concernant; *F* **what's it r.?**, de quoi s'agit-il?

regardless [rɪˈgɑːdlɪs] *adv* **(a) r. of**, (*consequences, danger, noise etc*) sans se soucier de; **r. of expense**, sans regarder à la dépense; **(b)** *F* quand même; *F* **press on r.!**, allez-y quand même!

regatta [rɪˈgætə] *n* régates *fpl*.

regency [ˈriːdʒənsɪ] *n* régence *f*; *Br & Fr Hist* **the R.**, la Régence; **R. armchair/furniture/***etc*, fauteuil *m*/meubles *mpl*/*etc* Régence.

regenerate [rɪˈdʒenəreɪt] **1** *vt Rel* régénérer, faire renaître (*qn*); *Physiol* reconstituer, reproduire (*un organe*); *Ch* régénérer (*une substance*); *Fig* **to feel regenerated**, se sentir comme neuf. **2** *vi* (*of tail etc*) repousser; (*of substance*) se régénérer.

regenerating [rɪˈdʒenəreɪtɪŋ] *adj* régénérateur.

regeneration [rɪdʒenəˈreɪʃən] *n* (*of missing organ*) & *Rel Ch* régénération *f*; *Physiol* reconstitution *f*.

regenerative [rɪˈdʒenərətɪv] *adj* régénérateur.

regent [ˈriːdʒənt] **1** *adj Hist* régent; **prince r.**, prince régent. **2** *n Hist & Am Sch* régent, -ente.

reggae [ˈregeɪ] *n Mus* reggae *m*; **r. group/musicians/***etc*, groupe *m*/musiciens *mpl*/*etc* reggae.

regicide [ˈredʒɪsaɪd] *n* (*crime*) régicide *m*; (*person*) régicide *mf*.

regime, régime [reɪˈʒiːm] *n Pol* régime *m*; **the old r.**, l'ancien régime.

regimen [ˈredʒɪmen] *n* **(a)** *Med* régime *m*; **(b)** *Old-fashioned* (*government*) régime *m*.

regiment¹ [ˈredʒɪmənt] *n Mil & Fig* régiment *m*; **there's enough to feed a r.**, il y en a pour un régiment.

regiment² *vt* réglementer, organiser (*des gens*); **life at boarding school is very regimented**, la vie en pensionnat est très stricte; **it's a very regimented organization**, c'est une organisation très rigide.

regimental [redʒɪˈment(ə)l] **1** *adj* (*badge, flag etc*) régimentaire, du régiment; **r. number**, numéro *m* matricule; **r. band**, musique *f* du régiment; **r. sergeant major**, adjudant-chef *m*. **2** *npl* **regimentals**, (*uniform*) uniforme *m* (militaire), tenue *f* militaire; **in full regimentals**, en grande tenue d'apparat.

regimentation [redʒɪmenˈteɪʃən] *n Pej* discipline excessive.

region [ˈriːdʒ(ə)n] *n* (*of country, body etc*) région *f*; *Fig* **in the r. of**, environ; **somewhere in the r. of £500**, dans les 500 livres.

regional [ˈriːdʒən(ə)l] *adj* (*accent, development, office etc*) régional; **r. writer**, (écrivain *m*) régionaliste *mf*.

regionalization [riːdʒən(ə)laɪˈzeɪʃən] *n* régionalisation *f*.

regionalism [ˈriːdʒənəlɪz(ə)m] *n* **(a)** (*special treatment*) régionalisme *m*; **(b)** *Ling* régionalisme *m*, mot régional.

register¹ [ˈredʒɪstər] *n* **(a)** (*record*) registre *m*; *Sch* cahier *m* d'appel; *Admin etc* sommier *m*; **to enter sth in a r.**, inscrire qch sur *ou* dans un registre; **to keep a r.**, tenir un registre; *Sch* **to take the r.**, faire l'appel; **r. of births, marriages and deaths**, ≈ le registre de l'état civil; *Br* **r. office**, bureau *m* de l'état civil; **electoral** *or* **parliamentary r., r. of voters**, liste électorale; **(b)** (*range*) (*of instrument*) registre *m*; (*of voice*) étendue *f*; **(c)** (*style*) (*of speaking, writing*) registre *m*; **(d)** *Comptr* registre *m*; **(e)** (*machine*) **(cash) r.**, caisse enregistreuse; **(f)** (*plate*) (*on furnace*) registre *m*; (*in fireplace*) tablier *m*, rideau *m*.

register² **1** *vt* **(a)** (*enter in records*) enregistrer (*une plainte, un acte notarié*); inscrire (*un membre, un étudiant*); immatriculer (*un véhicule, un navire*); faire enregistrer (*une société*); déclarer (*un décès, un mariage, une naissance*); déposer (*une marque de fabrique*); **to r. a letter**, recommander une lettre; **I want to send it registered**, je voudrais l'envoyer en recommandé; **is the car registered in your name?**, est-ce que la voiture est à votre nom?; **she is not registered at this hotel**, nous n'avons personne de ce nom;
(b) (*indicate, make known*) (*of thermometer etc*) indiquer (*une température*); (*of person*) manifester, exprimer (*son étonnement, mécontentement*); **his face registered disappointment/disapproval**, son visage reflétait la déception/désapprobation;
(c) (*realize*) réaliser (*un fait*);
(d) (*achieve*) réaliser (*un progrès, une victoire*).
2 *vi* **(a)** (*for course etc*) s'inscrire (**for**, à); (*at hotel*) signer le registre; (*of voter*) se faire inscrire sur la liste électorale; **to r. with the police**, se faire inscrire à la police;
(b) (*of gauge, machine*) détecter; (*of amount, measurement*) être enregistré *ou* indiqué, apparaître;
(c) *F* (*of fact, joke etc*) être compris; **he explained it to me yesterday but it didn't r.**, il me l'a expliqué hier, mais je n'ai pas compris; **it didn't r. (with him/her)**, il/elle n'a rien pigé; **I did give them the address but I don't think it registered**, je leur ai bien donné l'adresse mais je ne crois pas qu'ils aient réalisé.

registered [ˈredʒɪstɜːd] *adj* (*complaint, deed*) enregistré; (*member, voter*) inscrit; (*vehicle*) immatriculé; **to send sth by r. mail**, envoyer qch en recommandé; **r. letter**, lettre recommandée, envoi *m* en recommandé; *Fin* **r. capital**, capital social déclaré; *Am* **r. nurse**, *Br* **r. general nurse**, infirmière diplômée (d'État); *Can Fin* **r. retirement savings plan**, régime enregistré d'épargne-retraite; *Fin* **r. stock**, effets nominatifs; **R. Trademark**, marque déposée; **r. unemployed**, inscrit au chômage; **the r. unemployed**, les personnes inscrites au chômage.

registrar [ˈredʒɪstrɑːr, redʒɪsˈtrɑːr] *n* **(a)** (*in registry office*) officier *m* de l'état civil; (*in college, university*) secrétaire général; **r.'s office**, ≈ le bureau de l'état civil; **the R. General**, le Conservateur des actes de l'état civil; **r. of companies**, directeur *m* du registre des sociétés; **(b)** *Br Med* interne *mf*.

registration [redʒɪsˈtreɪʃən] *n* (*of complaint, deed*) enregistrement *m*; (*of student*) inscription *f*; (*of voter*) inscription sur la liste électorale; (*of vehicle*) immatriculation *f*; (*of birth, death, marriage*) déclaration *f*; (*of trademark*) dépôt *m*; (*of letter*) recommandation *f*; **when does r. start?**, (*for university, evening classes*) quand les inscriptions commencent-elles?; **r. fee**, (*for course, exam etc*) droit *m* d'inscription; (*for letter*) taxe *f* de recommandation; *Aut* **r. document**, ≈ carte grise; **r. (number)**, (*of car*) numéro *m* minéralogique *ou* d'immatriculation; (*of student*) (numéro) matricule *m*.

registry [ˈredʒɪstrɪ] *n* **(a)** *Br* **r. (office)**, bureau *m* de l'état civil; **to be married at a r. office**, se marier civilement, ≈ se marier à la mairie; **r. office wedding**, mariage civil; **(b)** *Nau* **a ship of Canadian r.**, un navire immatriculé au Canada; **certificate of r.**, lettre *f* de mer, certificat *m* d'inscription; (*of French ship*) acte *f* de francisation; **port of r.**, port *m* d'attache.

regrade [riːˈgreɪd] *vt* **(a)** reclasser (*une infirmière, un employé etc*); **(b)** *Am Sch* renoter (*des devoirs*).

regrading [riːˈgreɪdɪŋ] *n* (*of nurse, employee etc*) reclassement *m*; **r. dispute/strike/guidelines/***etc*, conflit *m*/grève *f*/directives *fpl*/*etc* concernant le reclassement.

regress [rɪˈgres] *vi* (*lose ground*) régresser, rétrograder.

regression [rɪˈgreʃən] *n* régression *f*.

regressive [rɪˈgresɪv] *adj* (*gene etc*) régressif.

regret¹ [rɪˈgret] *n* (*sorrow*) regret *m* (**for**, de); **to feel r.**, éprouver *ou* avoir du regret (**at, about,** à; **about doing,** de faire); **to express one's r.,** exprimer ses regrets; **to have** *or* **feel a pang of r.,** éprouver une pointe de regret; **to have no regrets,** n'avoir aucun regret, ne rien regretter (**about,** au sujet de); **I have no regrets,** je ne regrette rien; **my only r. is that ...,** je n'ai qu'un regret, c'est de + *inf*; **(much) to my r.,** à (mon) (grand) regret; **it is with deep r. that we inform you,** c'est à grand regret que nous vous informons; **she sends (you/us) her regrets,** (*is unable to come*) elle vous/nous prie de l'excuser.

regret[2] *vt* (-**tt**-) (*be sorry for*) regretter (*qch*); **we r. any inconvenience to passengers,** nous regrettons les éventuels désagréments subis par les voyageurs; **to r. doing** *or* **having done sth,** regretter d'avoir fait qch; **you'll r. this,** tu le regretteras; **I r. to have to say it,** je regrette d'avoir à le dire; **I r. to (have to) inform you that ...,** je regrette de (devoir) vous annoncer que ...; **then, I r. to say, she ...,** alors, je regrette de devoir dire qu'elle ...; **he bitterly regretted having spoken,** il s'est mordu la langue d'avoir parlé; **I r. to hear that ...,** je suis désolé d'apprendre que ...; **it is to be regretted that ...,** il est regrettable *ou* à regretter que + *sub*.

regretful [rɪ'gretfʊl] *adj* (*glance, expression*) plein de regrets; (*feeling*) de regret; **to be r.,** avoir des regrets (**about,** au sujet de, quant à).

regretfully [rɪ'gretfəlɪ] *adv* (*to say*) avec regret; **r., I cannot,** je regrette, je ne peux pas.

regrettable [rɪ'gretəb(ə)l] *adj* (*sad*) regrettable, à regretter; (*inconvenient*) fâcheux; **it is r. that ...,** il est regrettable *ou* à regretter *ou* fâcheux que + *sub*.

regrettably [rɪ'gretəblɪ] *adv* malheureusement; **r. few people were present,** il est regrettable que si peu de personnes soient venues.

regroup [riː'gruːp] **1** *vt* regrouper (*des soldats etc*). **2** *vi* (*of soldiers etc*) se regrouper.

regrouping [riː'gruːpɪŋ] *n* (*of soldiers etc*) regroupement *m*.

regular ['regjʊlər] **1** *adj* **(a)** (*steady, even*) (*features, pulse, service etc*) régulier; (*surface*) uni; **bran will keep you r.,** le son vous fera aller régulièrement à la selle; **to be as r. as clockwork,** être d'une régularité infaillible *ou* d'horloge; **to do sth as r. as clockwork,** faire qch avec une régularité infaillible *ou* d'horloge; **he's there every Tuesday, (as) r. as clockwork,** il est là tous les mardis, ça ne manque jamais *ou* c'est réglé comme du papier à musique; **to keep r. hours,** (*have strict timetable*) avoir un emploi de temps précis; (*go to bed and rise at reasonable time*) se lever et se coucher à heures régulières; **you should keep more r. hours,** vous devriez vous coucher plus tôt; **man of r. habits,** homme rangé (dans ses habitudes);

(b) (*usual*) (*doctor etc*) habituel; (*customer, verb*) régulier; (*price, size*) normal, *Can* régulier; (*reader, listener*) fidèle; (*staff*) permanent; *Am Aut* (*gas*) ordinaire; **my r. time for going to bed,** l'heure habituelle à laquelle je me couche; **you can stay up past your r. bedtime,** tu peux te coucher plus tard que d'habitude; **a r. visitor to the house,** un des habitués de la maison; **r. customer,** habitué, -ée; *Ind* **r. model,** modèle courant;

(c) (*professional*) (*army, soldier*) régulier;

(d) *F* (*real, thorough*) (*fool, slave etc*) vrai, véritable; **a r. hero,** un vrai héros; *esp Am* **a r. guy,** un gars réglo *ou* sympa.

2 *n* **(a)** (*in bar, restaurant etc*) habitué, -ée; (*in shop*) client régulier;

(b) *Am Aut* (*gas*) ordinaire *m*;

(c) (*professional*) *Mil* régulier *m*; *Rel* régulier *m*, religieux *m*.

regularity [regjʊ'lærɪtɪ] *n* (*of features, pulse etc*) régularité *f*; **to do sth with unfailing r.,** faire qch avec une régularité infaillible.

regularly ['regjʊləlɪ] *adv* (*to attend, visit etc*) régulièrement; *Am* **the coat is r. priced at ...,** le manteau coûte normalement ... .

regularize ['regjʊləraɪz] *vt* régulariser (*une situation*).

regulate ['regjʊleɪt] *vt* **(a)** (*adjust*) régler, régulariser (*la marche d'une machine etc*); régler (*une montre*); **(b)** (*control*) réglementer (*des gens*); **he leads a well-regulated life,** il mène une vie très réglée; **rules regulating the use of additives,** les réglementations qui régissent l'emploi des additifs.

regulating ['regjʊleɪtɪŋ] *adj* (*knob, switch, valve*) de réglage; (*hormone, mechanism*) régulateur; **self-r.,** à réglage automatique.

regulation [regjʊ'leɪʃən] *n* **(a)** (*of machine, watch etc*) réglage *m*; (*of voltage*) régulation *f*; **(b)** (*of people, use of additives etc*) réglementation *f*; **(c)** (*rule*) règlement *m*; (*instruction*) prescription *f*; **r. dress/speed/uniform/***etc*, tenue *f*/vitesse *f*/uniforme *m*/*etc* réglementaire; **black shoes are r. wear,** le port de chaussures noires est réglementaire; **regulations,** règlement(s); **contrary to** *or* **against (the) regulations,** contraire au règlement; **in accordance with the regulations,** selon le règlement; **it's not in accordance with the regulations,** ce n'est pas réglementaire; **under the regulations,** en vertu du règlement; **safety regulations,** prescriptions relatives à la sécurité.

regulator ['regjʊleɪtər] *n* (*of temperature, speed etc*) régulateur *m*.

regulatory ['regjʊlətərɪ, regjʊ'leɪtərɪ] *adj* (*framework, provisions etc*) réglementaire.

regulo ['regjʊləʊ] *n Br* thermostat *m*.

regurgitate [rɪ'gɜːdʒɪteɪt] **1** *vt* régurgiter (*sa nourriture, Fig un cours*). **2** *vi* (*of liquids etc*) refluer, regorger.

regurgitation [rɪgɜːdʒɪ'teɪʃən] *n* (*of food, Fig lecture notes*) régurgitation *f*.

rehabilitate [riːə'bɪlɪteɪt, riːh-] *vt* **(a)** (*return to society*) réhabiliter, réintégrer (*un délinquant*); *Med* rééduquer (*un handicapé etc*); désintoxiquer (*un alcoolique, un drogué*); réadapter (*un soldat blessé*); **(b)** (*restore reputation of*) réhabiliter (*un politicien*); **(c)** (*restore*) réhabiliter, remettre en état, rénover (*un immeuble, un quartier*).

rehabilitation [riːəbɪlɪ'teɪʃən, riːh-] *n* (*of criminal, politician, building*) réhabilitation *f*; (*of disabled*) réadaptation *f*, rééducation *f*; (*of alcoholic, drug addict*) désintoxication *f*; (*of young offender*) rééducation; *Med* **r. centre,** centre *m* de réinsertion.

rehash[1] ['riːhæʃ] *n F* (*of book, script etc*) réchauffé *m*; **it's just a r.,** c'est du réchauffé; **it was a r. of her first novel,** c'était son premier roman réchauffé.

rehash[2] [riː'hæʃ] *vt F* (*rework*) remanier (*un vieux conte etc*); ressasser, rabâcher (*de vieux arguments etc*).

rehearsal [rɪ'hɜːs(ə)l] *n* (*of play, speech etc*) répétition *f*; **to have** *or* **hold a r.,** faire une répétition; **to put a play into r.,** mettre une pièce en répétition; **we go into r. next week,** nous commençons les répétitions la semaine prochaine; *Fig* **the naval exercises were just a r. for the real thing,** les exercices navals n'étaient qu'un entraînement; *Th* **dress r.,** (répétition) générale *f*.

rehearse [rɪ'hɜːs] **1** *vt* (*practise*) répéter (*une pièce, son rôle, un morceau, un ballet*); faire répéter (*qn*); **I rehearsed what I was going to say,** j'ai préparé mon petit discours; **the demonstration looked a bit rehearsed,** la manifestation n'avait pas l'air très spontané. **2** *vi* (*of actor, musician etc*) répéter.

rehouse [riː'haʊz] *vt* reloger (*qn*).

rehousing [riː'haʊzɪŋ] *n* relogement *m*.

Reich [raɪk] *n* (*empire*) Reich *m*; *Hist* **the Third R.,** le IIIe Reich.

reign[1] [reɪn] *n* (*of monarch, champion etc*) règne *m*; **in** *or* **during the r. of ...,** sous le règne de ...; **their r. of terror/violence is at an end,** la terreur/violence qu'ils faisaient régner a pris fin.

reign[2] *vi* (*of monarch, silence, champion etc*) régner (**over,** sur); **to r. supreme,** régner en maître; **to r. for ten years,** régner (pendant) dix ans.

reigning ['reɪnɪŋ] *adj* (*monarch*) régnant; (*champion*) en titre.

reimburse [riːɪm'bɜːs] *vt* rembourser (*de l'argent*); **to r. s.o. (for) sth,** rembourser qn de qch.

reimbursement [riːɪm'bɜːsmənt] *n* (*of money, person*) remboursement *m*.

reimport [riːɪm'pɔːt] *vt* réimporter (*des marchandises*).

reimportation [riːɪmpɔː'teɪʃən] *n* (*of goods*) réimportation *f*.

reimpose [riːɪm'pəʊz] *vt* réimposer (*une taxe*).

Reims [riːmz] *n* Reims.

rein [reɪn] *n* (*for rider*) rêne *f*; (*for coachman*) guide *f*; (*for child*) sangle *f*; **to pull at** *or* **on the reins,** (*of horse, rider*) tirer sur les rênes; **to give a horse the reins** *or* **free r.,** lâcher les rênes *ou* la bride à un cheval; *Fig* **to give s.o. a free r.,** lâcher la bride à qn; *Fig* **to give free r. to one's imagination,** donner libre cours à son imagination; *Fig* **to keep a tight r. on** *or* **over s.o.,** tenir la bride serrée *ou* haute à qn; *Fig* **to keep a tight r. on one's spending,** surveiller étroitement ses dépenses; **to keep a tight r. on one's emotions,** ne pas se laisser aller à ses émotions; **to keep a tight r. on one's imagination,** ne pas se laisser emporter par son imagination; *Fig* **to assume** *or* **take over/hold the reins of government,** prendre/tenir les rênes du gouvernement; *Fig* **to hand over the reins,** (*of *politician, businessman etc*) passer les rênes du pouvoir (**to,** à).

►**rein back 1** *vtsep* faire arrêter (*un cheval*). **2** *vi* (*of rider*) faire arrêter son cheval.

►**rein in 1** *vtsep* serrer la bride *ou* les rênes à (*un cheval*); *Fig* **to r. s.o. in,** retenir qn, ramener qn à la discipline; **to r. in one's enthusiasm,** modérer son enthousiasme; **to r. in one's spending,** limiter ses dépenses. **2** *vi* (*of rider*) ramener son cheval au pas.

reincarnate¹ [riːɪn'kɑːnɪt, -eɪt] *adj* réincarné.

reincarnate² [riːɪn'kɑːneɪt] *vt* **to be reincarnated,** se réincarner (**as,** sous les traits de, sous la forme de).

reincarnation [riːɪnkɑː'neɪʃən] *n* réincarnation *f*.

reindeer ['reɪndɪər] *n* (*animal*) renne *m*; **r. moss** *or* **lichen,** cladonie *f*.

reinforce [riːɪn'fɔːs] *vt* renforcer (*une armée, un mur, un tissu*); consolider (*des fondations*); armer (*le béton, le verre*); *Fig* étayer (*un argument*) (**with,** par); appuyer (*une demande*) (**with,** avec); **that just reinforces what I've been saying all along,** ça ne fait que confirmer ce que j'ai toujours dit.

reinforcement [riːɪn'fɔːsmənt] *n* **(a)** (*of troops, wall, material*) renforcement *m*; (*of foundations*) consolidation *f*; (*of concrete, glass*) armature *f*; **(b)** (*for army, police*) renfort *m*; **to await reinforcements,** attendre un renfort *ou* des renforts; **to call up reinforcements,** demander des renforts.

reinsert [riːɪn'sɜːt] *vt* réinsérer (*une annonce, une pièce de monnaie, une clause*).

reinstate [riːɪn'steɪt] *vt* réintégrer, rétablir (*qn*) (dans ses fonctions); réintroduire (*une clause etc*).

reinstatement [riːɪn'steɪtmənt] *n* (*of person*) réintégration *f*, rétablissement *m* (**as,** en tant que, au poste de); (*of clause etc*) réintroduction *f*.

reinsurance [riːɪn'ʃʊərəns, -'ʃɔːr-] *n* (*of insurer*) réassurance *f*.

reinsure [riːɪn'ʃʊər, -'ʃɔːr-] *vt* réassurer (*un assureur*).

reintroduce [riːɪntrə'djuːs] *vt* réintroduire.

reintroduction [riːɪntrə'dʌkʃən] *n* réintroduction *f*.

reinvest [riːɪn'vest] *vt Fin* réinvestir (*des fonds*).

reinvestment [riːɪn'vestmənt] *n Fin* nouveau placement, réinvestissement *m*.

reissue¹ [riː'ɪʃuː] *n* (*of book*) réédition *f*; (*of bank note etc*) nouvelle émission.

reissue² *vt* rééditer (*un livre*); émettre de nouveau (*un billet de banque etc*).

reiterate [riː'ɪtəreɪt] *vt* réitérer (*une demande, une promesse etc*).

reiteration [riːɪtə'reɪʃən] *n* (*of request, promise etc*) réitération *f*.

reiterative [riː'ɪtərətɪv] *adj* réitératif.

reject¹ ['riːdʒekt] *n* (*object*) article *m* de rebut; *Fig* (*for job*) candidat refusé *ou* qui a échoué; *Fig* **I'm not going out with one of your rejects!,** (*former boyfriend or girlfriend*) je ne sors pas avec un de tes ex!; **export rejects,** marchandises *fpl* impropres à l'exportation; **r. china**/*etc*, articles *mpl* en porcelaine/*etc* présentant de légers défauts; **r. shop,** magasin *m* de soldes, solderie *f*.

reject² [rɪ'dʒekt] *vt* (*refuse*) rejeter, repousser (*un conseil, une offre, une proposition*); (*of animal, parent*) rejeter (*ses petits, un enfant*); réprouver (*une doctrine*); refuser (*des marchandises, un manuscrit, un candidat*); éconduire (*un soupirant*); **to feel rejected,** se sentir rejeté; **to r. food,** (*not want*) refuser la nourriture; (*vomit*) rendre la nourriture; *Ind* **to r. a part,** mettre une pièce au rebut; *Med* **to r. a transplant,** rejeter un greffon; **the machine keeps rejecting this coin,** la machine n'arrête pas de refuser cette pièce.

rejection [rɪ'dʒekʃən] *n* (*of bill, offer, suggestion, transplant*) rejet *m*; (*of applicant, goods, manuscript*) refus *m*; (*of food*) (*by stomach*) régurgitation *f*; **to meet with r.,** essuyer un refus; **r. slip,** note *f* refusant un manuscrit.

rejig [riː'dʒɪg] *vt* (**-gg-**) *F* réaménager (*une usine, une pièce etc*); **famous scenes from films are being rejigged as commercials,** on adapte des scènes de films célèbres pour en faire des publicités.

rejoice [rɪ'dʒɔɪs] *vi* se réjouir (**at, over,** de; **in doing,** de faire); **to r. in one's freedom/independence/***etc*, jouir de sa liberté/son indépendance/*etc*; **we r. to hear that you are safe,** nous sommes ravis d'apprendre que vous êtes en sécurité; *Hum* **he rejoiced in the name of Winterbottom,** il avait la chance de s'appeler Winterbottom.

rejoicing [rɪ'dʒɔɪsɪŋ] *n* réjouissance *f*, allégresse *f* (**at, over,** à); **there was much r. at the announcement,** la nouvelle a donné lieu à une grande allégresse; **it was an occasion for general r.,** ce fut la grande liesse *ou* la liesse générale; **there were great rejoicings on the day of the Coronation,** il y a eu de grandes réjouissances le jour du couronnement.

rejoin¹ [rɪ'dʒɔɪn] *vt & vi* (*retort*) répliquer.

rejoin² [riː'dʒɔɪn] **1** *vt* **(a)** (*attach*) rejoindre, réunir (*qch*) (**to,** à); **(b)** (*return to*) rejoindre, retrouver (*qn*); *Mil* rallier, rejoindre (*son unité, son régiment*); **to r. one's ship,** rallier le bord; **to r. a political party,** rallier un parti politique de nouveau. **2** *vi* (*of roads, lines etc*) se réunir, se rejoindre.

rejoinder [rɪ'dʒɔɪndər] *n* (*retort*) réplique *f*; **sharp r.,** riposte *f*.

rejuvenate [rɪ'dʒuːvɪneɪt] **1** *vt* rajeunir (*qn*); **I feel quite rejuvenated after a week off,** je me sens requinqué après une semaine de vacances; *Fig* **to r. the economy,** donner un coup de fouet à l'économie. **2** *vi* (*of person*) rajeunir.

rejuvenating [rɪ'dʒuːvɪneɪtɪŋ] *adj* (*effect etc*) rajeunissant.

rejuvenation [rɪdʒuːvɪ'neɪʃən] *n* rajeunissement *m*.

rekindle [riː'kɪnd(ə)l] **1** *vt* rallumer (*un feu*); *Fig* ranimer, raviver (*l'enthousiasme, l'espoir, la haine*); rallumer (*la haine*); *Fig* **a romantic dinner to r. the flame** *or* **spark,** un dîner en amoureux pour ranimer la flamme. **2** *vi* se rallumer.

relapse¹ [rɪ'læps] *n Med* rechute *f*; **to have** *or* **suffer a r.,** avoir *ou* faire une rechute, rechuter; **his relapses into alcoholism,** ses rechutes dans l'alcoolisme.

relapse² *vi Med* avoir *ou* faire une rechute, rechuter; **to r. into unconsciousness,** reperdre connaissance; *Fig* **to r. into alcoholism,** retomber dans l'alcoolisme.

relate [rɪ'leɪt] **1** *vt* **(a)** (*narrate*) raconter, *Fml* conter (*une histoire etc*); faire le récit de (*ses aventures*); **strange to r.,** (chose) étonnante à dire;

(b) (*connect*) établir un rapport entre (*deux faits*); *Biol etc* apparenter (*deux espèces*); **to r. sth to sth,** (*link*) rattacher qch à qch.

2 *vi* **(a)** (*of question etc*) se rapporter, avoir rapport, avoir trait (**to,** à); **agreement relating to ...,** convention ayant trait à ...;

(b) (*of person*) communiquer *ou* s'entendre avec; **he finds it difficult to r., he can't r. (to others),** il lui est difficile de communiquer avec les autres; **he doesn't r. very well to his mother,** il ne s'entend pas très bien avec sa mère; **I can't r. to modern music,** je ne peux pas apprécier la musique moderne; **I don't r. to my home town any more,** je ne me sens plus d'attaches à ma ville natale.

related [rɪ'leɪtɪd] *adj* **(a)** (*things*) lié, ayant rapport (**to,** à); (*languages, styles*) apparenté; **the cost of the project is directly r. to the amount of work involved,** le coût du projet est directement lié à la quantité de travail nécessaire; **questions r. to a subject,** questions relatives à un sujet; **r. ideas,** idées connexes; **the two events are r.,** les deux événements sont liés; **closely r. species,** espèces voisines;

(b) (*people*) apparenté (**to,** à); (*by blood*) parent (**to,** de); (*by marriage*) parent par alliance (**to,** à); **are you two r.?,** êtes-vous apparentés *ou* parents *ou* de la même famille, vous deux?; **we are not really r., I just call her 'auntie',** nous ne sommes pas parents *ou* de la même famille, je l'appelle juste 'ma tante' comme ça; **she is r. to me by marriage,** elle et moi sommes parents par alliance; **we're r. by marriage,** nous sommes parents par alliance; **he is closely/distantly r. to me,** nous sommes proches parents/parents éloignés.

-related [rɪ'leɪtɪd] *suff* **space/industry/***etc***-r.,** lié à l'espace/l'industrie/*etc*.

relating [rɪ'leɪtɪŋ] *adj* **r. to,** (*about*) relatif à, qui se rapporte à; *Admin Jur* afférent à.

relation [rɪ'leɪʃən] *n* **(a)** (*relative*) parent, -ente; **r. by marriage,** parent par alliance; **what r. is he to you?,** quelle est son lien de parenté avec vous?; **are you any r. to ...?,** avez-vous un lien de parenté avec ...?; **he's no r. to me** *or* **of mine,** il ne fait pas partie de ma famille; **she is my closest living r.,** elle est la plus proche parente qui me reste; **I have relations in Montreal,** j'ai de la famille à Montréal; **we've invited all the relations,** nous avons invité toute la famille;

(b) (*connection, relationship*) relation *f*, rapport *m* (**between,** entre; **with,** avec); **in** *or* **with r. to,** relativement à, par rapport à; **to bear no r.,** n'avoir aucun rapport (**to,** avec); **to bear little r.,** avoir peu de rapport (**to,** avec); **relations between us are rather strained,** nos relations sont plutôt tendues; **to have** *or* **enjoy friendly relations,** entretenir des relations amicales *ou* des rapports amicaux (**with,** avec); **how are relations between you?,**

comment est-ce que vous vous entendez?; **to enter into relations with s.o.,** entrer *ou* se mettre en rapport *ou* en relations avec qn; **to break off all relations with s.o.,** rompre toute relation *ou* cesser tout rapport avec qn; **to have (sexual) relations,** avoir des rapports sexuels (**with,** avec);

(c) (*telling*) (*of adventures, story etc*) relation *f*, récit *m*.

relational [rɪ'leɪʃən(ə)l] *adj Comptr* **r. database,** base de données relationnelle.

relationship [rɪ'leɪʃənʃɪp] *n* **(a)** (*relations*) (*between people*) rapport *m*, relation *f*; (*sexual*) liaison *f*; **to have a love-hate r. with s.o./sth,** avoir avec qn/qch une relation dans laquelle se mêlent l'amour et la haine; **she has a good r. with her mother-in-law,** elle s'entend bien avec sa belle-mère; **our r. is going nowhere,** notre relation ne mène nulle part; **patient-doctor r.,** rapports patient-médecin *ou* entre le patient et le médecin; **to have a r.,** (*affair*) avoir une liaison (**with,** avec); **I'm already in a r.,** j'ai déjà quelqu'un; **he finds it difficult to have relationships with people,** ça lui est difficile d'avoir des relations avec les autres; **our r. is purely professional,** nos rapports *ou* relations sont purement professionnel(le)s; **what exactly is your r. with her?,** quelle est la nature de *ou* quels sont vos rapports avec elle?;

(b) (*kinship*) (*between people of same family*) lien(s) *m(pl)* de parenté; (*by marriage*) parenté *f* par alliance; (*between languages, styles etc*) parenté; **family r.,** lien *m* de parenté; **blood r.,** parenté, (degré *m* de) consanguinité *f*; **what was your r. to the deceased?,** quel était votre lien de parenté avec la personne décédée?;

(c) (*connection*) (*between things*) rapport *m* (**between ... and,** entre ... et); **in r. to,** relativement à;

relative ['relətɪv] **1** *adj* relatif; **r. to,** (*compared to*) relativement à; (*in terms of*) en fonction de, par rapport à; *Gram* **r. clause,** (proposition *f*) relative *f*; **r. pronoun,** (pronom *m*) relatif *m*. **2** *n* **(a)** = **RELATION (a)**; **(b)** *Phil* **the r.,** le relatif.

relatively ['relətɪvlɪ] *adv* relativement, assez; **r. few people were there,** il y avait assez *ou* relativement peu de gens; **r. speaking,** relativement parlant.

relativism ['relətɪvɪz(ə)m] *n Phil* relativisme *m*.

relativistic [relətɪ'vɪstɪk] *adj* relativiste.

relativity [relə'tɪvɪtɪ] *n* relativité *f*; **r. theory, theory of r.,** théorie *f* de la relativité.

relax [rɪ'læks] **1** *vt* **(a)** (*of bath, meditation etc*) (*physically*) délasser (*qn*); (*mentally*) détendre, relaxer (*qn*); **(b)** (*loosen*) relâcher, décontracter, relaxer (*ses muscles*); relâcher (*la discipline, son attention*); assouplir (*une politique, une loi*); **to r. one's hold** *or* **grip,** desserrer son étreinte; **to r. one's efforts,** relâcher ses efforts. **2** *vi* **(a)** (*of person*) (*mentally*) se détendre, se relaxer; (*physically*) se délasser; **to r. for an hour,** se détendre pendant une heure; **r.!,** (*calm down*) relaxe!, du calme!; **r.!, I'm not going to hurt you,** détends-toi, je ne vais pas te faire mal; **(b)** (*of muscles*) se relâcher, se détendre; **to r. in one's efforts,** se relâcher dans ses efforts.

relaxant [rɪ'læks(ə)nt] *n* (*activity*) détente *f*; (*drug, drink etc*) sédatif *m*; *Med* **muscle r.,** myorelaxant *m*, décontracturant *m*.

relaxation [riːlæk'seɪʃən] *n* **(a)** (*of person*) (*physical*) délassement *m*; (*mental*) détente *f*, relaxation *f*; **r. after the day's work,** détente après le travail de la journée; **fishing is his only r.,** la pêche est sa seule détente; **she finds r. in reading,** elle se détend à lire; **reading is one of my favourite forms of r.,** lire est une de mes façons préférées de me détendre; **(b)** (*of muscles*) décontraction *f*, relaxation *f*; (*of discipline*) relâchement *m*; (*of policy, law*) assouplissement *m*.

relaxed [rɪ'lækst] *adj* (*atmosphere, person*) décontracté, détendu; **she takes a very r. approach** *or* **is very r. in her approach to bringing up children,** elle a une attitude très décontractée quant à l'éducation des enfants.

relaxing [rɪ'læksɪŋ] *adj* (*climate, medication*) relaxant; **I've had a very r. day,** j'ai eu une vraie journée de détente; **a r. place for a holiday,** un endroit tranquille pour passer des vacances.

relay¹ ['riːleɪ] *n* **(a)** (*of people, horses*) relais *m*; (*of workers*) relève *f*; **to work in relays,** se relayer; **to do sth in relays,** faire qch en se relayant; **(b)** *Sp* **r. (race),** course *f* de relais; **she's in the r.,** elle participe à la course de relais; **(c)** *El Electron Tel* relais *m*; *Rad TV* (*broadcast*) retransmission *f*, radiodiffusion relayée; **r. (station),** (station *f ou* émetteur *m*) relais.

relay² [rɪ'leɪ, riː-] *vt* (*pt & pp* **relayed**) *El Tel Rad etc* relayer (*un message téléphonique, une émission etc*).

re-lay [riː'leɪ] *vt* reposer (*un tapis, des carreaux etc*).

release¹ [rɪ'liːs] *n* **(a)** (*of hostage, prisoner*) délivrance *f*, libération *f*; (*from care, worry*) délivrance, libération (**from,** de); (*from obligation, responsibility*) décharge *f*, libération (**from,** de); *Fig* **it was a merciful r.,** (*when he or she died*) ça a été une véritable délivrance; *Jur* **order of r.,** (ordre *m* de) levée *f* d'écrou; *Jur* **r. on bail,** mise *f* en liberté sous caution; *Br* **day r.,** = jour de congé accordé aux employés d'une maison pour se perfectionner;

(b) (*of bomb*) largage *m*; (*of balloon, pigeon*) lâcher *m*; (*of funds*) déblocage *m*; (*of gas etc*) libération *f*, dégagement *m*; (*of steam*) échappement *m*; (*of pressure*) relâchement *m*; *Phys* (*of energy*) libération; (*of spring*) détente *f*; (*of mechanism*) déclenchement *m*; (*of blocked part*) dégagement *m*; (*of clutch*) débrayage *m*; *Phot* **(shutter) r.,** (*action*) déclenchement; (*mechanism*) déclencheur *m*; **r. button** *or* **knob,** bouton *m* de déclenchement, démarreur *m*; **r. (lever),** (*on typewriter*) levier *m ou* touche *f* de dégagement du chariot; **r. of goods (from warehouse),** libération de marchandises;

(c) (*of book, record etc*) sortie *f*, mise *f* en vente; (*of film*) sortie; (*of document*) diffusion *f*; (*of computer software*) version *f*; **(press) r.,** communiqué *m* de presse; **is the film on general r.?,** est-ce que le film passe dans les salles?; **her latest r.,** (*record*) son dernier disque; (*film*) son dernier film.

release² *vt* **(a)** (*liberate*) délivrer, libérer (*un otage, un prisonnier*); (*from hospital*) autoriser (*qn*) à sortir (**from,** de); (*from work*) libérer; **to r. s.o. from his** *or* **her promise,** délier *ou* relever qn de sa promesse; **to r. s.o. from a duty,** dispenser qn d'une corvée; *Jur* **released on bail,** remis en liberté sous caution;

(b) (*let go*) lâcher (*un ballon, un pigeon voyager*); lâcher, larguer (*une bombe*); **to r. s.o.'s hand,** lâcher la main à qn; **to r. one's hold,** desserrer son étreinte, lâcher prise;

(c) (*emit*) dégager, laisser échapper (*un gaz*); émettre (*de la fumée etc*); **to be released,** (*of energy etc*) se libérer;

(d) (*unblock*) dégager (*une pièce coincée etc*); lâcher, détendre (*un ressort*); desserrer (*le frein*); débloquer (*des fonds*); *Phot* déclencher (*l'obturateur*); **to r. the safety catch,** (*on gun*) libérer le cran de sûreté; *Aut* **to r. the clutch,** débrayer;

(e) (*make available*) sortir, mettre en vente (*un livre, un disque etc*); sortir (*un film*); rendre public (*une nouvelle*); diffuser (*un document*).

relegate ['relɪgeɪt] *vt* (*downgrade*) reléguer (**to,** à); *Fb* **to r. a team (to the next division),** reléguer une équipe à la division inférieure (de la Ligue).

relegation [relɪ'geɪʃən] *n* (*of furniture, person etc*) relégation *f* (**to,** à); (*of soccer club*) renvoi *m* à la division inférieure (de la Ligue).

relent [rɪ'lent] *vi* (*of person*) s'adoucir, se radoucir; (*as result of argument, persuasion*) se laisser fléchir; (*of storm, wind, rain*) diminuer de violence.

relentless [rɪ'lentlɪs] *adj* (*person*) implacable, inflexible, intransigeant; (*hatred*) implacable; (*persecution, pain*) sans rémission; **to be r. in doing sth,** mettre de l'acharnement à faire qch.

relentlessly [rɪ'lentlɪslɪ] *adv* (*to beat etc*) implacablement; (*to continue, persecute etc*) sans rémission, avec acharnement; (*to blow, rain*) sans interruption.

relet [riː'let] *vt* relouer (*une maison etc*).

relevance ['reləvəns], **relevancy** ['reləvənsɪ] *n* **(a)** (*aptness*) (*of facts, remarks etc*) pertinence *f* (**to,** à); **(b)** (*significance*) intérêt *m*; **Latin no longer has any r. in the school curriculum,** le latin n'a plus aucune utilité *ou* aucun intérêt dans les programmes scolaires; **(c)** (*connection*) rapport *m* (**to,** avec); **to have** *or* **bear some r.,** avoir un rapport (**to,** avec).

relevant ['reləvənt] *adj* **(a)** (*apt*) pertinent (**to,** à); **r. facts,** faits pertinents; **the r. documents,** les documents qui se rapportent à l'affaire; *Jur* les pièces justificatives; **to be r.,** être pertinent, avoir quelque chose à voir; **that's not r.,** ça n'a rien à voir (**to,** avec); **that's hardly r.,** ça n'a pas grand-chose à voir, ça n'a pas grand intérêt; **(b)** (*appropriate, proper*) approprié; **(c)** (*significant*) important; (*useful*) utile; **all r. information,** tous renseignements utiles; **to be highly r.,** (*of experience, situation*) être très utile (**for,** pour); **to be/remain r.,** (*of book, play, institution etc*) être/rester d'actualité.

reliability [rɪlaɪə'bɪlɪtɪ] *n* (*of person, firm, information etc*) sérieux *m*; (*of information, source, testimony*) sûreté *f*; (*of device, machine*) fiabilité *f*.

reliable [rɪ'laɪəb(ə)l] *adj* (*firm, information, person*) sérieux; (*person*) sur qui on peut compter; (*information, source, testimony*) sûr; (*car, machine etc*) fiable; **to have sth from a r. source** *or* **on r. evidence,** tenir qch de bonne source; **my memory isn't r.,** je n'ai pas bonne mémoire; **the weather is not very r.,** on ne peut pas se fier au temps.

reliably [rɪ'laɪəblɪ] *adv* (*to operate, perform etc*) de façon fiable; **to be r. informed that ...,** savoir de bonne source que ... .

reliance [rɪ'laɪəns] *n* (*trust*) confiance *f*; (*dependence*) dépendance *f* (**on,** de); **to place r. in** *or* **on s.o.,** mettre sa confiance en qn, se fier à qn.

reliant [rɪ'laɪənt] *adj* **to be r. on,** (*trusting*) avoir confiance en; (*dependent on*) dépendre de (**for,** pour).

relic ['relɪk] *n* **(a)** (*reminder of past, remnant*) vestige *m*; **the last surviving r. of,** les derniers vestiges de; **relics of the past,** vestiges du passé; *Hum* **their old r. of a car,** leur vieille bagnole toute pourrie; **relics,** (*corpse*) dépouille mortelle; **(b)** *Rel* relique *f*.

relief [rɪ'li:f] *n* **(a)** (*of pain, anxiety, poverty etc*) soulagement *m* (**from,** de); **to bring r. to s.o.,** apporter du soulagement à qn; **to heave a sigh of r.,** pousser un soupir de soulagement; **that's** *or* **what a r.!,** ouf! on respire!, quel soulagement!; **for the r. of pain,** (*of pills etc*) pour soulager la douleur; **to my great** *or* **much to my r.,** à mon grand *ou* vif soulagement; **to feel r.,** se sentir soulagé, ressentir du soulagement (**about, at, over,** à propos de, à); **his feelings of r. were short-lived,** son soulagement a été de courte durée; **you can imagine my r.** *or* **the r. that I felt,** tu peux imaginer mon soulagement; **to provide light** *or* **comic r.,** détendre l'atmosphère, introduire une note comique; **by way of light r.,** pour passer à des choses plus gaies; *Br Aut* **r. road,** route *f* de délestage; **r. valve,** soupape *f* de sûreté, clapet *m* de décharge;
(b) (*help*) secours *m*, assistance *f*, aide *f*; *Am* **to be on r.,** recevoir l'aide sociale; **disaster/famine/***etc* **r.,** secours *ou* assistance *ou* aide aux victimes d'un désastre/d'une famine/*etc*; **r. agency,** organisme *m* d'assistance; **r. fund,** caisse *f* de secours; **r. official,** responsable *mf* d'assistance; **r. work,** assistance; **r. worker,** employé(e) d'un organisme d'assistance; (*after disaster*) secouriste *mf*;
(c) (*replacement*) *Mil Nau* relève *f*; *F* **my r. didn't show up,** ma relève ne s'est pas pointée; **r. driver,** chauffeur qui assure la relève; **r. train,** (train *m*) supplémentaire *m*; **r. worker,** suppléant, -ante;
(d) (*liberation*) (*of city etc*) délivrance *f*; **r. troops,** (troupes *fpl* de) secours *m*;
(e) *Art* relief *m*, modelé *m*; **printed in r.,** imprimé en relief; **blank wall without r.,** mur d'une nudité monotone; **to stand out in r.,** ressortir, se détacher (**against,** sur); **to stand out in bold** *or* **sharp r.,** ressortir ou se détacher nettement; **to bring** *or* **throw sth into r.,** relever *ou* faire ressortir qch; **high/low r.,** haut/bas-relief; **r. printing,** typographie *f*;
(f) *Geog* relief *m* (terrestre); **an area of low r.,** une zone au relief peu élevé; **r. map,** carte *f ou* plan *m* en relief.

relieve [rɪ'li:v] *vt* **(a)** (*alleviate*) soulager (*la douleur, l'inquiétude, la misère etc*); dissiper (*l'ennui*); remédier à (*la situation*); réduire (*la pression*); **I'm very relieved to hear it,** c'est un grand soulagement pour moi de l'apprendre; **to feel relieved,** se sentir soulagé; **to be relieved at the news,** être soulagé en entendant la nouvelle; **to r. one's feelings,** se décharger le cœur, se soulager (**by doing,** en faisant); *F* **to r. oneself,** (*go to lavatory*) faire ses besoins, se soulager; **black dress relieved by** *or* **with white lace,** robe noire agrémentée de dentelle blanche; **to r. the monotony we went for a walk,** pour nous changer les idées nous sommes allés nous promener; *Aut & Med* **to r. congestion in,** décongestionner;
(b) (*help*) secourir, soulager (*qn*);
(c) (*replace*) relever, relayer (*qn*); *Mil & Nau* relever (*la garde, le quart*);
(d) (*liberate*) (*from doubt*) délivrer, tirer (**from,** de); (*from obligation*) dégager, affranchir (**from,** de); *Mil* délivrer, dégager (*une ville*); **to r. s.o. of a burden,** soulager qn d'un fardeau; **to r. s.o. of their coat,** débarrasser qn de son manteau; **to r. s.o. of their duties,** relever *ou* destituer qn de ses fonctions; **relieved of all anxiety,** débarrassé de toute inquiétude; *F* **to r. s.o. of their wallet,** délester *ou* soulager qn de son portefeuille.

religion [rɪ'lɪdʒən] *n* religion *f*; (*Catholic, Protestant*) culte *m*; *Admin* confession *f*; **freedom of r.,** liberté *f* du culte; *F Pej* **to get r.,** attraper le virus de la religion; *Fig* **to make a r. of (doing) sth,** se faire une obligation de (faire) qch; *Fig* **football is a r. with some people,** le football est une religion pour certains.

religious [rɪ'lɪdʒəs] **1** *adj* (*person*) religieux, dévot; (*fanatic, order, service*) religieux; (*war, book*) de religion; *Fig* (*care*) scrupuleux; *Fig* (*silence*) religieux; **he is very r.,** il est très croyant *ou* pieux; *Fig* **his r. attendance at every football match,** sa fréquentation scrupuleuse de tous les matches de football; *Fig* **to be r. about doing sth,** mettre un soin religieux à faire qch, **r. beliefs,** croyances religieuses; **r. life,** vie religieuse *ou* de religion; **r. persuasion,** confession *f*. **2** *n inv Rel* religieux, -ieuse.

religiously [rɪ'lɪdʒəslɪ] *adv* (*to behave, act*) religieusement, pieusement; *Fig* (*to attend, obey*) scrupuleusement.

religiousness [rɪ'lɪdʒəsnɪs] *n* (*of person*) piété *f*, dévotion *f*; (*of music, art*) caractère religieux; *Fig* (*of attendance, obedience*) caractère scrupuleux.

reline [ri:'laɪn] *vt* remettre une doublure à (*un manteau*); *Aut* **to r. the brakes,** changer les garnitures de freins; **brakes relined,** (*notice in garage etc*) changement de garnitures de freins.

relinquish [rɪ'lɪŋkwɪʃ] *vt* **(a)** (*give up*) abandonner (*une habitude, tout espoir*); renoncer à (*un projet, un droit, une succession*); **to r. all thoughts of doing sth,** abandonner toute pensée de faire qch; **to r. (one's hold on) sth,** (*let go*) lâcher qch.

relinquishment [rɪ'lɪŋkwɪʃmənt] *n* (*of hope etc*) abandon *m* (**of,** de); (*of right etc*) renonciation *f* (**of,** à).

reliquary ['relɪkwərɪ] *n Rel* reliquaire *m*.

relish¹ ['relɪʃ] *n* **(a)** (*liking, taste*) goût *m* (**for,** pour); **to eat sth with r.,** manger qch de bon appétit, savourer qch; **(b)** (*pleasure*) plaisir *m*; **danger gives r. to an adventure,** le danger donne du piquant à une aventure; **he used to tell the story with great r.,** il se délectait à raconter cette histoire; **... she said with great r., ...** dit-elle avec délectation; **(c)** *Culin* (*pickle*) achar(d) *m*.

relish² *vt* (*enjoy*) goûter, savourer (*un mets*); trouver goût à (*qch*); trouver bon (*qch*); **to r. doing sth,** trouver du plaisir à *ou* aimer faire qch; **I didn't r. the prospect,** cette perspective ne me disait rien; **I didn't r. the prospect of telling her,** j'appréhendais de le lui dire; **we didn't r. the idea,** l'idée ne nous souriait pas.

relive [ri:'lɪv] *vt* revivre (*sa vie, le passé*).

reload [ri:'ləʊd] **1** *vt* recharger (*un navire, appareil photo, un fusil etc*). **2** *vi* (*of ship, photographer etc*) recharger.

relocate [ri:ləʊ'keɪt] **1** *vt* (*move*) réimplanter (*une usine, une société*). **2** *vi* (*of person, shop*) déménager; (*of company*) se réimplanter; **the firm is relocating out of Glasgow,** la société se réimplante hors de Glasgow.

relocation [ri:ləʊ'keɪʃən] *n* (*of person, shop*) déménagement *m*; (*of company*) réimplantation *f*; **r. assistance,** (*from employer*) contribution *f* aux frais de déménagement; **r. expenses,** frais *mpl* de déménagement.

reluctance [rɪ'lʌktəns] *n* (*unwillingness*) répugnance *f*; **to show (some) r. to do sth,** montrer quelque répugnance à faire qch, se montrer peu disposé *ou* empressé à faire qch; **to do sth with r.,** faire qch à regret *ou* à contrecœur.

reluctant [rɪ'lʌktənt] *adj* (*consent, greeting, promise etc*) accordé à contrecœur; **to be r. to do sth,** hésiter *ou* être peu disposé à faire qch; **to feel r.,** hésiter, éprouver de la répugnance (**to do,** à faire); **a r. teacher/***etc*, un professeur/*etc* malgré lui.

reluctantly [rɪ'lʌktəntlɪ] *adv* (*to consent, greet, promise etc*) avec répugnance, à contrecœur; **I say it r.,** il m'en coûte de le dire.

►rely on, rely upon [rɪ'laɪ] *vipo* **(a)** (*count on*) compter sur, avoir confiance en; **I'm relying on it,** j'y compte (bien); **it's a car you can r. on,** c'est une voiture fiable; **he's a lawyer you can r. on,** c'est un avocat sur lequel on peut compter; **we can't r. on the weather,** le temps n'est pas sûr; **(b)** (*be dependent on*) dépendre de (*qn*) (**for sth,** pour qch).

REM [rem] **(a)** *abbr* **rapid eye movement**; **(b)** (*abbr Biol* **roentgen equivalent man**) rem *m*.

remain [rɪ'meɪn] *vi* **(a)** (*stay behind*) rester;
(b) (*continue to be*) (*of doubts*) rester, demeurer; **to r. faithful to s.o./sth,** rester fidèle à qn/qch; **please r. in your seats,** veuillez rester assis; **let it r. as it is,** laissez-le comme cela; **one thing remains certain,** une chose reste certaine; **the fact remains that ...,** il n'en est pas moins vrai que ..., toujours est-il que ...; *Old-fashioned Br* **I r., Sir, yours truly,** (*at end of letter*) veuillez agréer, Monsieur, l'expression de mes sentiments distingués;
(c) (*be left*) rester; **all that remains of ...,** tout ce qui reste de ...; **much yet remains to be done,** il reste encore beaucoup à faire; **it (only) remains for me to ...,** il ne me reste qu'à ..., je n'ai plus qu'à ...; **it remains to be seen**

whether, reste à savoir si; **that remains to be seen,** c'est ce que nous verrons, c'est ce qu'on va voir.

remainder¹ [rɪ'meɪndər] *n* **(a)** (*of time, wine etc*) reste *m*; (*of salary, specific quantity*) restant *m*; (*of amount due*) reliquat *m*; **the r. of his life,** le reste *ou* le restant de sa vie; **the r.,** (*remaining people*) les autres *mfpl*; **(b)** *Math* reste *m*; **division with no r.,** division *f* sans reste; **the r. is one,** il reste un; **(c)** (*book*) invendu soldé.

remainder² *vt* solder (*un livre*).

remaining [rɪ'meɪnɪŋ] *adj* (*food, money, wine etc*) qui reste, restant; **the r. travellers,** le reste des *ou* les autres voyageurs; **our only r. hope,** le seul espoir qui nous reste.

remains [rɪ'meɪnz] *npl* (*of fortune, meal*) restes *mpl*; (*of damaged building*) ruines *fpl*, vestiges *mpl*; **human r.,** restes d'un cadavre, ossements *mpl*; **(literary) remains,** œuvres *fpl* posthumes.

remake¹ ['riːmeɪk] *n* (*of film, TV series, record*) remake *m*; **to do a r. of,** faire un remake de.

remake² [riː'meɪk] *vt* (*pt & pp* **remade** [riː'meɪd]) refaire (*un film, un lit etc*); faire un remake de (*un film*).

remand¹ [rɪ'mɑːnd] *n Jur* **to be on r.,** (*in custody*) être en détention préventive; (*on bail*) être en liberté provisoire; **r. centre** *or* **home,** maison *f* de détention préventive.

remand² *vt Jur* **to r. (in custody)** placer en détention préventive; **to r. a prisoner on bail,** mettre un inculpé en liberté sous caution.

remark¹ [rɪ'mɑːk] *n* **(a)** (*comment*) remarque *f*, observation *f*, commentaire *m*; **to make** *or* **pass a r.,** faire une remarque *ou* une observation *ou* un commentaire (**about,** sur); **to let sth pass without r.,** laisser passer qch sans remarque *ou* observation *ou* commentaire; **to venture** *or* **hazard a r.,** se permettre un mot, hasarder une remarque *ou* une observation *ou* un commentaire; **no remarks, please!,** pas de commentaires, s'il vous plaît!; **(b)** (*notice*) attention *f*; **worthy of r.,** digne d'attention; **it could not escape r. that ...,** on ne pouvait pas ne pas remarquer que ..., le fait que ... ne pouvait pas passer inaperçu; **her reaction could not escape r.,** sa réaction n'a pu passer inaperçue.

remark² **1** *vt* **(a)** (*comment*) faire la remarque, faire remarquer (que); **(b)** (*note*) remarquer, observer (*qn, qch*); noter (*qch*); **it may be remarked that ...,** constatons que .... **2** *vi* faire une remarque, faire des remarques (**on,** sur); **I remarked on it to my mother,** j'en ai fait la remarque à ma mère.

remarkable [rɪ'mɑːkəb(ə)l] *adj* (*change, coincidence, progress etc*) remarquable (**for,** par).

remarkably [rɪ'mɑːkəblɪ] *adv* (*to change, progress etc*) remarquablement, notablement; (*good, intelligent*) remarquablement; (*bad, stupid*) incroyablement.

remarriage [riː'mærɪdʒ] *n* remariage *m*.

remarry [riː'mærɪ] **1** *vt* **(a)** se remarier avec (*qn*); épouser de nouveau (*son premier mari*); **(b)** (*of registrar etc*) remarier (*des divorcés*). **2** *vi* se remarier.

remediable [rɪ'miːdɪəb(ə)l] *adj* (*situation*) remédiable; (*illness*) curable.

remedial [rɪ'miːdɪəl] *adj* (*treatment etc*) curatif; *Med* **r. exercises,** gymnastique corrective; *Sch* **r. class,** classe *f* de rattrapage; **r. education,** éducation spécialisée; **r. teacher,** enseignant chargé d'une classe de rattrapage.

remedy¹ ['remɪdɪ] *n* (*for illness*) & *Fig* remède *m* (**for,** pour, contre); **a r. for flu,** un remède pour *ou* contre la grippe; *Fig* **work is the best r. for boredom,** le travail est le meilleur remède contre l'ennui; **it's past** *or* **beyond r.,** c'est irrémédiable *ou* sans remède.

remedy² *vt* remédier, (ap)porter remède à (*une situation*).

remember [rɪ'membər] **1** *vt* **(a)** (*recall*) se souvenir de (*qn, qch*); se rappeler (*qch*); **I r. him as being very generous,** je me souviens de lui comme de quelqu'un de très généreux; **they r. me as a child,** ils se souviennent de moi lorsque j'étais enfant; **do you r. turning off the lights?,** est-ce que tu te souviens (d')avoir éteint les lumières?; **the chairman, you will r., cannot vote,** vous vous souvenez certainement que le président ne peut pas voter; **I can't r. his name for the moment,** son nom m'échappe pour l'instant; **don't you r. me?,** (est-ce que) vous ne vous souvenez pas de moi?; **it will be something to r. you by,** ce sera un souvenir de vous;

(b) (*not forget*) retenir, ne pas oublier (*une leçon*); **I'll r. to do it,** je n'oublierai pas de le faire; **that's worth remembering,** cela est à noter; **r.** *or* **you must r. (that) he's only ten years old,** n'oubliez pas qu'il n'a que dix ans; **did you r. to turn off the lights?,** est-ce que tu as pensé à éteindre les lumières?; **r. that we're going to the theatre next week,** n'oublie pas que nous allons au théâtre la semaine prochaine; **she will long be remembered for her achievements,** on se souviendra longtemps d'elle pour ses exploits; **he will be remembered as the man who ...,** on se souviendra de lui comme de l'homme qui ...; **r. where we are!,** ressaisis-toi!;

(c) (*give gift to*) ne pas oublier; **she always remembers the children at Christmas,** elle n'oublie jamais les enfants à Noël; **he remembered me in his will,** il ne m'a pas oublié dans son testament;

(d) (*speak of*) **let us r. them in our prayers,** prions pour eux; **r. me (kindly) to them,** rappelez-moi à leur bon souvenir, dites-leur bien des choses de ma part; **he asks to be remembered to you,** il me prie de le rappeler à votre bon souvenir;

(e) (*of service, monument etc*) commémorer (*les morts*).

2 *vi* se souvenir, se rappeler; **as I r.,** d'après ce que je me souviens; **as far as I r.,** pour autant que je me souvienne; **if I r. rightly,** si je m'en souviens bien, si j'ai bonne mémoire; **for as long as I can r.,** aussi loin que remontent mes souvenirs.

remembrance [rɪ'membrəns] *n* **(a)** (*memory*) souvenir *m*, mémoire *f*; **in r. of s.o./sth,** en souvenir *ou* mémoire de qn/qch; **garden of r.,** jardin commémoratif; *Br & Can* **R. Day** *or* **Sunday,** (*in France*) l'Armistice *m*; (*in Canada*) le Jour du Souvenir; **(b)** *Old-fashioned* (*keepsake*) souvenir *m*; **(c)** *Old-fashioned* (*greeting*) **give my kind remembrances to him,** rappelez-moi à son bon souvenir.

remind [rɪ'maɪnd] *vt* (*make remember*) rappeler à (*qn*) (**that,** que); **to r. s.o. of sth,** rappeler qch à qn; **he reminds me of my brother,** il me fait penser à *ou* me rappelle mon frère; **that reminds me of my childhood,** cela me rappelle mon enfance; **to r. s.o. to do sth,** faire penser à qn à faire qch; **r. me about it tomorrow,** rappelle-le-moi demain; **that** *or* **which reminds me!,** à propos!; **I would r. you that ...,** permettez-moi de vous rappeler que ... .

reminder [rɪ'maɪndər] *n* (*of event & letter*) rappel *m*; (*to jog memory*) pense-bête *m*; **to send s.o. a r. about sth,** envoyer un rappel à qn à propos de qch; **the exhibition is a stark r. of the horrors of war,** l'exposition constitue un brutal rappel des horreurs de la guerre; **such events are a r. that ...,** de tels événements nous rappellent que ...; **it's a r. to myself to ...,** c'est pour me rappeler de ....

reminisce [remɪ'nɪs] *vi* (*of person*) raconter ses souvenirs (**about,** de); (*in thoughts*) repenser au passé; **to r. about the old days,** évoquer le bon vieux temps.

reminiscence [remɪ'nɪsəns] *n* (*of past*) souvenir *m* (**about, of,** de); **to write one's reminiscences,** écrire ses souvenirs.

reminiscent [remɪ'nɪsənt] *adj* **(a) to be in a r. mood,** être enclin à *ou* d'humeur à évoquer des souvenirs; **she gave a r. smile,** elle a eu le sourire de quelqu'un qui évoque un souvenir; **(b) r. of** (*film, music, scene etc*) qui fait penser à *ou* rappelle *ou* évoque.

reminiscently [remɪ'nɪsəntlɪ] *adv* **to smile r.,** sourire à un souvenir; **to talk r. of sth,** évoquer des souvenirs de qch.

remiss [rɪ'mɪs] *adj* (*negligent*) négligent; **that was very r. of her,** c'était très négligent de sa part; **he has been very r.,** il a été très négligent (**in doing,** de faire).

remission [rɪ'mɪʃən] *n* **(a)** (*of prison sentence*) remise *f*; **(b)** *Med* rémission *f*; **to go into r.,** (*of disease, patient*) entrer en phase de rémission; **(c)** *Rel* pardon *m*, rémission *f*; **to pray for the r. of sins,** prier pour la rémission des péchés; **(d)** (*of debt*) remise *f*; (*of duty, fee, payment*) dispense *f*; (*of tax*) dispense, exemption *f*.

remit¹ [rɪ'mɪt] *v* **(-tt-)** **1** *vt* **(a)** (*send back*) remettre, soumettre (*une question*) (**to,** à); *Jur* renvoyer (*un procès*) à un autre tribunal; **to r. a sum to s.o.,** envoyer *ou* remettre une somme à qn, faire envoi d'une somme à qn; **(b)** (*lessen*) remettre (*une peine*); relâcher (*ses efforts*); **(c)** (*forgive*) pardonner, absoudre (*un péché*); **(d)** (*cancel*) remettre, faire remise de (*une dette*); **to r. s.o.'s fees,** dispenser qn de ses frais; **to r. s.o.'s income tax,** dispenser *ou* exempter qn d'impôt; **(e)** (*postpone*) remettre, différer (*une affaire*). **2** *vi* **(a)** (*of debtor*) régler, payer; **please r. by cheque,** veuillez régler par chèque; **(b)** (*abate*) (*of efforts, zeal etc*) se relâcher; (*of pain, storm*) se calmer.

remit² ['riːmɪt] *n* (*area of authority*) attributions *fpl*, compétence *f*; **to exceed one's r.,** outrepasser ses compétences; **it is outside** *or* **not part of our r.,** ceci ne relève pas de nos attributions *ou* de notre compétence.

remittance [rɪ'mɪtəns] *n Com* (*of money*) remise *f*, envoi *m* de fonds; (*money sent*) paiement *m*, règlement *m*; **return the form with your r.,** renvoyez le formulaire avec votre paiement.

remix ['ri:mɪks] *n Mus* (*record*) remix *m*.

remnant ['remnənt] *n* **(a)** (*of food*) reste *m*, restant *m*; *Fig* (*of imperialism, former glory*) vestige *m*; *Fig* **remnants of one's dignity/an army,** ce qui subsiste de sa dignité/d'une armée; **(b)** (*of fabric*) coupon *m*; (*of carpet*) chute *f*; **r. sale,** (*of fabric*) soldes *mpl* de fins de série; **remnants,** (*of fabric*) soldes *mpl*, fins *fpl* de série.

remodel [ri:'mɒd(ə)l] *vt* (**-ll-**, *US* **-l-**) remanier, refondre (*un ouvrage*); transformer (*une maison*); **he's having his nose/chin remodelled,** il va se faire refaire le nez/le menton.

remonstrance [rɪ'mɒnstrəns] *n* **(a)** (*scolding*) remontrance *f*; **(b)** (*protest*) protestation *f*.

remonstrate ['remənstreɪt] **1** *vi* **to r. with s.o.,** faire des remontrances à qn (**about,** au sujet de); **to r. against sth,** protester contre qch. **2** *vt* protester (**that,** disant que).

remorse [rɪ'mɔ:s] *n* (*regret*) remords *m* (**for, about,** de); **without r.,** (*not sorry*) sans remords; (*in doing*) sans scrupules *ou* pitié; **to feel r.,** éprouver *ou* avoir du *ou* des remords (**for having done,** d'avoir fait); **a feeling/twinge of r.,** un sentiment/une pointe de remords; **in a fit of r.,** dans un accès de remords; **to be full of** *or* **filled with r.,** être plein de remords; **to show r.,** manifester des remords.

remorseful [rɪ'mɔ:sful] *adj* (*confession, mood*) plein de remords.

remorsefully [rɪ'mɔ:sfəlɪ] *adv* (*to say*) d'un ton plein de remords.

remorseless [rɪ'mɔ:slɪs] *adj* (*person, wind*) impitoyable; (*cruelty*) sans pitié; *Fig* (*ambition, logic, self-interest etc*) implacable; **he was r. in his pursuit of the criminal,** il était impitoyable dans sa poursuite du criminel.

remorselessly [rɪ'mɔ:slɪslɪ] *adv* (*to hit, pursue etc*) impitoyablement; (*ambitious, logical etc*) implacablement.

remorselessness [rɪ'mɔ:slɪsnɪs] *n* (*of person*) absence *f* de pitié.

remote [rɪ'məʊt] *adj* **(a)** (*far-off*) (*house, village etc*) éloigné, lointain; (*isolated, hard to reach*) reculé; (*cousin, ancestor*) lointain; (*future*) lointain; (*past*) reculé; **r. from,** loin de; **in the remotest part of Asia,** au fin fond de l'Asie; **r. antiquity,** la haute antiquité;

(b) (*removed, not connected*) éloigné (**from,** de); **his plays are r. from everyday life,** ses pièces sont éloignées de la vie quotidienne; **r. control,** (*for model aircraft, door, television etc*) télécommande *f*; (*for bomb*) commande *f* à distance; **it's all done by r. control,** tout est effectué par télécommande *ou* par commande à distance; **r. sensing,** télédétection *f*; *Comptr* **r. batch processing,** télétraitement *m* par lots; **r. job entry,** soumission *f* de travaux à distance; **r. loading,** téléchargement *m*; **r. maintenance,** télémaintenance *f*; **r. management,** télégestion *f*; **r. processing,** télétraitement *m*;

(c) (*aloof*) distant, réservé; (*with mind elsewhere*) absent; **she had a rather r. look on her face,** (*looked aloof*) elle avait une expression plutôt distante; (*was thinking of other things*) elle avait une expression plutôt absente;

(d) (*slight*) (*chance, connection, resemblance*) vague; (*possibility, resemblance*) vague, faible; (*prospect*) peu probable; **I haven't the remotest idea of what he meant,** je n'ai pas la moindre idée de ce qu'il voulait dire; **there is a r. possibility that ...,** il y a une vague possibilité que + *sub*; **in the r. event of a water shortage,** dans l'hypothèse improbable d'une pénurie d'eau.

remote-controlled [rɪ'məʊtkən'trəʊld] *adj* (*model aircraft, door, television*) télécommandé; (*bomb*) commandé à distance.

remotely [rɪ'məʊtlɪ] *adv* **(a)** (*situated*) loin, au loin; (*related*) de loin; **(b)** (*to answer etc*) (*aloofly*) d'un ton distant; (*absent-mindedly*) d'un ton absent; **(c)** (*possible*) vaguement, faiblement; **it's only r. connected with the subject,** cela n'a qu'un faible rapport avec le sujet; **it isn't even r. connected with the subject,** cela n'a même pas le moindre rapport avec le sujet; **I'm not r. interested in science fiction,** la science fiction ne m'intéresse pas le moins du monde; **not r. aware/***etc*, nullement conscient/*etc*.

remoteness [rɪ'məʊtnɪs] *n* **(a)** (*of house, past etc*) éloignement *m*; (*isolation*) isolement *m*; **(b)** (*aloofness*) distance *f*; (*absent-mindedness*) absence *f*; **the r. of his expression,** (*aloofness*) son expression distante *ou* réservée; (*absent-mindedness*) son expression absente; **(c)** (*of resemblance*) faible degré *m*; **the r. of her chances of success,** l'improbabilité *f* de sa réussite.

remould¹ ['ri:məʊld] *n Br Aut* pneu rechapé.

remould² [ri:'məʊld] *vt Br* **(a)** *Aut* rechaper (*un pneu*); **(b)** (*shape again*) remouler (*une figurine*).

remount [ri:'maʊnt] **1** *vt* **(a)** (*get on again*) remonter à (*une bicyclette, un cheval*); **(b)** (*place on new support*) rentoiler (*un tableau*); remonter (*un bijou*). **2** *vi* remonter à bicyclette *ou* à cheval.

removable [rɪ'mu:vəb(ə)l] *adj* **(a)** (*component, lid, lining etc*) amovible; **(b)** (*mark, spot, stain etc*) qui s'enlève.

removal [rɪ'mu:v(ə)l] *n* **(a)** (*of rubbish, plate*) enlèvement *m*; (*of stain etc*) nettoyage *m*; (*of appendix, kidney, tumour etc*) ablation *f*; (*of doubt, fear*) dissipation *f*; (*of burden, worry*) soulagement *m*; (*of obstacle, threat, word*) suppression *f*; **the r. of stains from a jacket,** le détachage d'une veste; **for the r. of stains,** pour enlever les taches, pour détacher; **(b)** (*of coat, glove etc*) enlèvement *m*; (*of tyre*) démontage *m*; (*of seal*) levée *f*; **(c)** (*dismissal*) révocation *f*; (*of civil servant, judge etc*) destitution *f*; **(d)** (*moving house*) déménagement *m*; **r. company/van/***etc*, entreprise *f*/camion *m*/*etc* de déménagement; **r. expenses,** frais *mpl* de déménagement; **r. man,** déménageur *m*.

remove¹ [rɪ'mu:v] *n* (*degree of difference*) distance *f*; **at a certain r.,** à une certaine distance; **it is but** *or* **only one r. from ...,** cela est tout près de ...; **her account is several removes from the truth,** son récit est assez loin de la vérité.

remove² **1** *vt* **(a)** (*take away*) enlever (*des ordures, une assiette*); enlever, faire partir (*une tache*) (**from,** de); procéder à l'ablation de, enlever (*un appendice, un rein, une tumeur*); emmener (*qn*) (**to,** à); **to have a mole/wart removed,** se faire enlever un grain de beauté/une verrue; **to r. one's make-up,** se démaquiller; **to r. s.o.'s name from a list,** rayer qn d'une liste; **she's having the plaster removed tomorrow,** on lui enlève son plâtre demain; **to r. a burden from s.o.,** soulager qn d'un fardeau; **now that the threat has been removed,** maintenant que la menace a été supprimée; **to r. oneself and all one's belongings,** faire place nette; **to r. a child from school,** retirer un enfant de l'école; **police removed the demonstrators,** la police a fait partir les manifestants; **the judge ordered her to be removed from the court room,** le juge a ordonné qu'on la fasse sortir de la salle de tribunal; **he has been removed to hospital,** il a été transporté à l'hôpital; **death has removed him from our midst,** la mort nous l'a enlevé;

(b) (*take off*) enlever (*son manteau, ses gants, son chapeau*) (**from s.o.,** à qn); retirer (*son chapeau*); démonter (*un pneu*); lever (*un scellé*);

(c) (*dismiss*) révoquer (*un cadre, un directeur*); destituer (*un fonctionnaire, un magistrat*); **to r. s.o. from his** *or* **her position,** révoquer *ou* destituer qn de son poste (**as,** de);

(d) (*of furniture movers*) déménager (*meubles etc*).

(e) *F* (*kill*) supprimer (*qn*).

2 *vi Old-fashioned* (*of people, company*) déménager (**to,** à).

removed [rɪ'mu:vd] *adj* (*distant*) **his feeling was not far r. from love,** son sentiment n'était pas très éloigné de l'amour; **her explanation is far r. from the truth,** son explication est très loin de la vérité; **first cousin once r.,** cousin(e) issu(e) de germain, cousin(e) au deuxième degré.

remover [rɪ'mu:vər] *n* **(a)** (*company, person*) déménageur *m*; **(b)** (*substance*) (*for paint*) décapant *m*; (*for stains*) détachant *m*; (*for hair*) (d)épilatoire *m*; (*for nail varnish*) dissolvant *m*; (*for make-up*) démaquillant *m*.

removing [rɪ'mu:vɪŋ] *adj* **r. cream,** (*for hair*) crème *f* (d)épilatoire; (*for make-up*) crème démaquillante; (*for wrinkles*) crème antirides.

remunerate [rɪ'mju:nəreɪt] *vt* rémunérer (*qn*) (**for,** de); rémunérer, rétribuer (*un service*).

remuneration [rɪmju:nə'reɪʃən] *n* (*for service etc*) rémunération *f* (**for,** de).

remunerative [rɪ'mju:nərətɪv] *adj* (*position, business*) rémunérateur; **medicine is a highly r. field,** la médecine est une profession très rémunératrice.

renaissance [rɪ'neɪsəns] *n* (*of industry etc*) renaissance *f*.

Renaissance [rɪ'neɪsəns] *n Art etc* Renaissance *f*; **R. art/literature/***etc*, art *m*/littérature *f*/*etc* de la Renaissance; *Fig* **he's a R. man,** c'est un humaniste.

renal ['ri:n(ə)l] *adj Anat* (*artery, failure etc*) rénal.

rename [ri:'neɪm] *vt* débaptiser (*qn, une rue*); *Comptr* changer le nom de, renommer (*un fichier*); **the street has been renamed,** la rue a changé de nom *ou* a été débaptisée; **the street has been renamed 'Brown Avenue',** la rue s'appelle maintenant 'avenue Brown'.

renascence [rɪ'næsəns, -'neɪ-] *n* (*of interest, nationalism etc*) renaissance *f*.

renascent [rɪ'næsənt, -'neɪ-] *adj* (*interest, nationalism etc*) renaissant.

rend [rend] *vt* (*pt & pp* **rent** [rent]) **(a)** (*pierce*) déchirer (*le silence*); **the air was rent with her screams,** l'air était déchiré par ses hurlements; **(b)** *Lit* (*tear*) déchirer (*qch*); **to r. sth asunder** *or* **apart,** déchirer *ou* fendre qch en deux; **he was rent from my arms,** il a été arraché à mes bras; **a country rent by war,** un pays déchiré par la guerre.

render ['rendər] *vt* **(a)** *Fml* (*give*) rendre (*hommage, service*); **to r. good for evil,** rendre le bien pour le mal; **to r. thanks to God,** rendre grâce à Dieu; *Bible* **r. unto Caesar the things which are Caesar's,** rendez à César ce qui appartient à César; **to r. an account of sth,** (*describe*) rendre compte de qch; *Fin* **to r. an account to s.o.,** remettre un compte à qn; *Fin* **as per** *or* **to account rendered,** suivant notre compte *ou* compte remis; **to r. assistance to s.o.,** prêter secours à qn; **to r. (up) a fortress,** rendre une forteresse; **to r. up one's soul,** (*die*) rendre l'âme;

(b) (*make, cause to be*) rendre; **the blow/news rendered her unconscious,** le coup/la nouvelle l'a rendue inconsciente;

(c) (*depict*) rendre (*la luminosité*); (*perform*) interpréter (*un morceau de musique*);

(d) (*translate*) rendre, traduire (*une expression française*) (**in, into,** en);

(e) (*plaster*) enduire (*un mur etc*) de ciment;

(f) *Culin* **to r. (down) fat,** faire fondre de la graisse.

rendering ['rendərɪŋ] *n* **(a)** (*of account*) reddition *f*; **(b)** (*of expression, features in painting*) rendu *m*; (*of music*) interprétation *f*; **(c)** (*of phrase*) traduction *f*; **(d)** (*of wall*) enduit *m* (de ciment); **(e)** (*of fat*) fonte *f*.

rendezvous[1] ['rɒndɪvuː, *pl* -vuːz] *n* (*meeting, meeting-place*) rendez-vous *m* (**for,** de); **to make a r. with s.o.,** prendre rendez-vous avec qn; **to keep a r.,** se rendre à un rendez-vous.

rendezvous[2] *vi* (*pt & pp* **rendezvoused** [-vuːd]; *prp* **rendezvousing** [-vuːɪŋ]) (*meet by arrangement*) se rencontrer, se réunir, se retrouver; **to r. with s.o.,** retrouver qn.

rendition [ren'dɪʃən] *n* (*of role etc*) interprétation *f*; (*of phrase*) traduction *f*; **to give a r. of,** (*role etc*) interpréter; (*of phrase*) traduire; **they finished with a r. of the Marseillaise,** ils ont terminé en chantant *ou* jouant la Marseillaise.

renegade ['renɪgeɪd] *n* **(a)** (*traitor*) renégat, -ate; **r. priest,** prêtre *m* parjure; **(b)** (*outlaw*) hors-la-loi *m inv*.

renege, renegue [rɪ'neɪg] *vi* **(a)** manquer à *ou* revenir sur sa promesse (**on doing sth,** de faire qch); **she has reneged,** (*on promise*) elle a manqué à sa promesse; (*on deal*) elle est revenue sur notre *ou* leur *etc* marché; **(b)** *Cards* faire une fausse renonce.

renew [rɪ'njuː] *vt* **(a)** (*resume*) renouer (*une conversation*); **to r. one's acquaintance with s.o.,** renouer *ou* renouveler connaissance avec qn; **to r. pressure on s.o.,** recommencer à faire pression sur qn (**to do,** pour que + *sub*); *Mil* **to r. an attack,** réitérer une attaque; *Fig* **to r. one's attack,** revenir à la charge (**on,** concernant); **renewed activity,** activité redoublée; **renewed outbreak of a fire,** recrudescence *f* d'un incendie; **renewed bombing/outbreaks of violence,** recrudescence des bombardements/de la violence;

(b) (*restate*) renouveler (*une demande, une promesse*);

(c) (*extend*) renouveler (*un bail, un passeport*); **to r. one's subscription,** se réabonner, renouveler son abonnement (**to,** à); **to r. a library book,** faire renouveler *ou* prolonger le prêt d'un livre de bibliothèque; **this book may only be renewed once,** le prêt de ce livre ne peut être renouvelé qu'une fois;

(d) (*replace*) remplacer (*un pneu*); **to r. one's wardrobe,** renouveler sa garde-robe.

renewable [rɪ'njuːəb(ə)l] *adj* (*lease, passport etc*) renouvelable; **this book is r. only once,** le prêt de ce livre n'est renouvelable qu'une fois; **your subscription is r. at the end of the year,** (*must be renewed*) votre abonnement doit être renouvelé à la fin de l'année; (*may be renewed*) votre abonnement peut être renouvelé à la fin de l'année; **r. resources,** ressources *fpl* renouvelables.

renewal [rɪ'njuːəl] *n* **(a)** (*of acquaintance*) renouvellement *m*, renouement *m*; (*of hostilities, violence*) reprise *f*; (*of bombing, violence*) recrudescence *f*; **r. of activity,** reprise *ou* regain *m* d'activité; **(b)** (*of promise, request*) renouvellement *m*; **(c)** (*of lease, passport etc*) renouvellement *m*; (*of library book*) renouvellement de prêt; **r. date,** (*of library book*) date *f* de renouvellement de prêt; **r. of subscription,** réabonnement *m*, renouvellement d'abonnement (**to,** à); **(d)** (*of enthusiasm, hopes*) regain *m*; **(e)** (*of tyre*) remplacement *m*; (*of wardrobe*) renouvellement *m*.

renewed [rɪ'njuːd] *adj* (*effort*) renouvelé; (*attempt, hope*) nouveau; (*enthusiasm*) neuf; **with r. vigour/***etc*, avec un regain de vigueur/*etc*.

rennet ['renɪt] *n* présure *f*.

renounce [rɪ'naʊns] *vt* **(a)** (*abandon, give up*) renoncer à (*un droit, un titre, l'alcool, la violence etc*); répudier (*une succession*); **to r. the world,** renoncer au monde; **to r. one's bad habits,** renoncer à *ou* abandonner ses mauvaises habitudes; **to r. all thought of doing sth,** renoncer à toute idée de faire qch; **(b)** (*disown*) répudier, dénoncer (*un traité*); renier, désavouer (*un ami*); renier (*ses principes*); **to r. one's faith,** renoncer à sa foi, apostasier; **to r. Satan and all his works,** renoncer à Satan, à ses pompes et à ses œuvres.

renouncement [rɪ'naʊnsmənt] *n* = **RENUNCIATION**.

renovate ['renəveɪt] *vt* rénover (*une maison*).

renovation [renə'veɪʃən] *n* (*of house etc*) rénovation *f*; **closed for r.,** (*notice in shop window*) fermé pour cause de travaux de rénovation; **to be under r.,** être en cours de rénovation; **to undergo renovations,** subir des rénovations, être en rénovation; **r. project/work/***etc*, projet *m*/travaux *mpl*/*etc* de rénovation.

renovator ['renəveɪtər] *n* rénovateur, -trice.

renown [rɪ'naʊn] *n* (*fame*) renommée *f*, renom *m*; **woman of great** *or* **high r.,** femme de grand renom; **to win r.,** acquérir une renommée, se faire une renommée (**as,** en tant que; **for,** pour).

renowned [rɪ'naʊnd] *adj* (*town, person*) renommé, célèbre (**for,** pour); (*wine*) fameux; (*artist, writer*) illustre; **he is r. for being late,** il est réputé pour être toujours en retard; **Dr Hector Smith, the r. psychiatrist,** le Dr Hector Smith, célèbre psychiatre; **to be r. as,** être renommé *ou* célèbre comme.

rent[1] [rent] *n* (*on flat, house etc*) loyer *m*; *esp Am* **for r.,** (*property*) à louer; **to pay the r.,** payer le loyer; **how much do you pay in r.?, how much r. do you pay?,** combien est-ce que tu paies de loyer?; **how much is the r.?,** à combien le loyer s'élève-t-il?; **to live somewhere free of r.,** habiter quelque part sans payer de loyer; **to be behind with the r.,** être en retard pour (payer) le loyer; **Friday is r. day, it's r. day on Friday,** on doit payer le loyer vendredi; *Br* **r. book,** livre *m* de location; *Br F* **r. boy,** = jeune garçon qui se prostitue; **r. collector,** receveur *m ou* encaisseur *m* de loyers; **r. strike,** grève *f* des loyers.

rent[2] **1** *vt* louer (*un appartement, une vidéo, une voiture*) (**from, to,** à); **to r. (out) rooms,** louer des chambres; (**from, to,** à); **she lives in a rented house,** elle habite dans une maison qu'elle loue. **2** *vi* **it rents at** *or Am* **for ...,** cela se loue à ... .

rent[3] *n* (*in clothing*) déchirure *f*, accroc *m*; (*in clouds*) déchirure; (*in relations*) rupture *f*.

rental ['rent(ə)l] *n* **(a)** (*hire*) (*of car, flat, house etc*) location *f*; **r. car/charges/company,** voiture *f*/frais *mpl*/société *f* de location; **r. office,** (*for car*) bureau *m* de location; **r. property,** propriété *f* à louer; **(b)** (*money received*) **r. income,** revenus *mpl* locatifs; **(c)** (*money paid*) (*for flat, house*) loyer *m*; (*for car, equipment, holiday flat*) (prix *m* de) location *f*; (*for telephone*) abonnement *m*; **to pay a telephone/television r. of ...,** payer ... d'abonnement pour le téléphone/de location pour la télévision; *Tel* **fixed r.,** redevance *f* d'abonnement.

rent-free [rent'friː] *adj* (*accommodation, flat etc*) exempt de loyer; **to live somewhere r.-f.,** habiter quelque part sans payer de loyer; **a house is available r.-f.,** il y a une maison où l'on peut habiter gratuitement *ou* sans payer de loyer.

rentier ['rɒntɪeɪ] *n Pej* rentier *m*.

renunciation [rɪnʌnsɪ'eɪʃən] *n* **(a)** (*of right, title, alcohol, violence etc*) renonciation *f*; (*of bad habits*) abandon *m*; **(b)** (*of treaty*) répudiation *f*, dénonciation *f*; (*of friend, principles*) reniement *m*; (*of friend*) désaveu *m*; (*of world*) renoncement *m*.

reoccupy [riː'ɒkjʊpaɪ] *vt* réoccuper (*un territoire*).

reopen [riː'əʊp(ə)n] **1** *vt* **(a)** rouvrir (*un livre, une frontière, une enquête etc*); *Fig* **to r. an old wound,** raviver une plaie; **(b)** (*resume*) recommencer, reprendre (*les hostilités*); reprendre (*les pourparlers*). **2** *vi* (*of wound*) se rouvrir; (*of shop, theatre etc*) rouvrir; (*of school, law court*) rentrer; (*of hostilities*) reprendre, recommencer; (*of talks*) reprendre; **the border has reopened,** la frontière a été réouverte.

reopening [riː'əʊp(ə)nɪŋ] *n* (*of border, investigation etc*) réouverture *f*; (*of hostilities, talks*) reprise *f*.

reorder[1] [riː'ɔːdər] *n* (*to obtain more supplies*) nouvelle commande; (*reminder to supplier*) commande renouvelée;

to send *or* **put a r. in,** envoyer *ou* passer une nouvelle commande (**for,** de); **r. form/procedure/***etc,* formulaire *m*/procédure *f*/*etc* de renouvellement de commande.

reorder² *vt* (*order more*) faire une nouvelle commande de (*qch*); (*order again*) renouveler la commande de (*qch*).

reorganization [riːɔːgənaɪ'zeɪʃən] *n* (*of company, education, files etc*) réorganisation *f*.

reorganize [riː'ɔːgənaɪz] **1** *vt* réorganiser (*une société, un système de classement etc*). **2** *vi* (*of company etc*) se réorganiser.

rep¹ [rep] *n F* (= **representative**) (*door to door*) représentant, -ante; (*for large company*) représentant, V.R.P. *m* (**for,** chez); **sales r.,** représentant, V.R.P.

rep² *vi F* travailler comme représentant, -ante (**for,** chez).

rep³ *n Br F* = **REPERTORY.**

Rep [rep] *n US Pol abbr* **(a) Representative; (b) Republican.**

repaint [riː'peɪnt] *vt* repeindre (*un mur*).

repair¹ [rɪ'peər] *n* **(a)** (*of shoes, watch etc*) réparation *f*; (*of building, road*) réparation, réfection *f*; (*of machine*) remise *f* en état; (*of clothing*) raccommodage *m*; **to be in need of r.,** nécessiter des réparations, avoir besoin d'être réparé; **to be (damaged) beyond r.,** être irréparable; **road under r.,** (*road sign*) travaux; **(shoe) repairs while you wait,** (*notice in shop*) cordonnerie minute; **to make repairs to sth,** faire des réparations sur qch; **to carry out repairs,** (faire) effectuer des réparations; **to undergo repairs** *or* **be under r.,** être en réparation; **r. kit,** trousse *f* de réparation; **r. shop,** atelier *m* de réparations; **(b)** (*condition*) état *m*; **to be in good/bad r.,** être en bon/mauvais état, être bien/mal entretenu; **to keep a road/car/property/***etc* **in (good) r.,** entretenir une route/voiture/propriété/*etc*.

repair² *vt* (*mend*) réparer (*des souliers, une montre, un bâtiment, une route*); remettre en état (*une machine*); dépanner (*une voiture*); raccommoder (*un vêtement*).

repairer [rɪ'peərər] *n* (*of shoes*) cordonnier, -ière; (*of watch*) réparateur, -trice; (*of heavy machines*) dépanneur, -euse.

repairman [rɪ'peəmæn] *n* (*of shoes*) cordonnier *m*; (*of watch*) réparateur *m*; (*of heavy machines*) dépanneur *m*.

repairwoman [rɪ'peəwʊmən] *n* (*of shoes*) cordonnière *f*; (*of watch*) réparatrice *f*; (*of heavy machines*) dépanneuse *f*.

repaper [riː'peɪpər] *vt* retapisser (*une pièce*).

reparation [repə'reɪʃən] *n* (*of wrong, omission*) réparation *f*; **in r. of ...,** en réparation de ...; **to make r. for sth,** réparer qch; **he has made r.,** il a réparé; **(war) reparations, r. payments,** réparations.

repartee [repɑː'tiː] *n* (*banter*) repartie *f*; **to be good** *or* **quick at r.,** avoir la repartie facile, avoir de la repartie; **to engage in r.,** faire de l'esprit.

repast [rɪ'pɑːst] *n Lit* repas *m*.

repatriate¹ [riː'pætrɪeɪt] *vt* rapatrier (*un prisonnier de guerre, des capitaux*) (**to,** vers).

repatriate² [riː'pætrɪət] *n* rapatrié, -ée.

repatriation [riːpætrɪ'eɪʃən] *n* (*of prisoner of war, capital*) rapatriement *m*.

repay [riː'peɪ, rɪ-] *vt* (*pt & pp* **repaid** [riː'peɪd, rɪ-]) (*pay back*) rendre (*de l'argent*); rembourser (*un prêt, qn*); (*award*) récompenser (*qn*) (**for,** de); (*give in return for*) rendre (*un service*); **to r. good for evil,** rendre le bien pour le mal; **to r. s.o. with ingratitude,** payer qn d'ingratitude; **to r. a kindness,** payer une gentillesse de retour; **is this how you r. us?,** et c'est comme ça que tu nous remercies?; **I can never r. you for all you've done,** je ne pourrai jamais vous remercier assez pour tout ce que vous avez fait; **how can I ever r. you?,** comment pourrais-je vous remercier assez?

repayable [riː'peɪəb(ə)l] *adj* (*loan, mortgage etc*) remboursable.

repayment [riː'peɪmənt] *n* **(a)** (*of loan, mortgage etc*) remboursement *m*; **the repayments are spread over five years,** les remboursements sont échelonnés sur cinq ans; *Br* **r. mortgage,** = prêt hypothécaire qu'on rembourse et qui ne produit pas de rente; **(b)** (*of kindness*) récompense *f*.

repeal¹ [rɪ'piːl] *n* (*of law*) abrogation *f*; (*of decree*) révocation *f*.

repeal² *vt* abroger (*une loi*); révoquer (*un décret*).

repeat¹ [rɪ'piːt] *n* (*of event, motif, attempt*) répétition *f*; (*of item in programme*) bis *m*; *Mus* (*passage*) reprise *f*; *Mus* (*mark*) barre *f* de reprise, renvoi *m*; *Rad TV* rediffusion *f*, reprise; **there's nothing on (television) but repeats,** il n'y a que des rediffusions; **we get a lot of r. business,** beaucoup de nos clients reviennent; **it will be a r. of last year's final,** ça sera comme la finale de l'année dernière; *Comptr* **r. function,** fonction *f* de répétition; *Jur* **r. offender,** récidiviste *mf*; **r. order,** commande renouvelée; **r. performance,** deuxième représentation *f*; *Med* **r. prescription,** ordonnance renouvelée.

repeat² [rɪ'piːt] **1** *vt* **(a)** (*do again*) répéter (*une action, un motif, une tentative*); renouveler (*ses efforts, une ordonnance*); (*as encore*) bisser (*une chanson, un mouvement*); *Sch* redoubler (*une classe*); *Rad TV* rediffuser (*une émission*); **history repeats itself,** l'histoire se répète; **cannot be repeated,** (*notice in shop*) sans suite;

(b) (*say again*) répéter (*une question*); réitérer (*une menace, un ordre, une promesse*); **it can't be repeated too often,** on ne saurait trop le répéter; **r.,** (*after a line of a song etc*) bis; **to r. oneself,** se répéter; **am I repeating myself?,** est-ce que je me répète?; *Hum* est-ce que je radote?; **I don't want to have to r. myself,** je ne veux pas avoir à le répéter; **r. after me, ...,** répétez après moi ...;

(c) (*say to others*) répéter (*un secret*); **don't r. this, but ...,** ne le répète pas, mais ... .

2 *vi* **(a)** (*of decimal figure*) se répéter;

(b) (*of food*) donner des renvois, remonter; **it's repeating on me,** j'ai des renvois;

(c) (*of watch, alarm clock, rifle*) être à répétition.

repeated [rɪ'piːtɪd] *adj* (*action etc*) répété; (*question etc*) réitéré; (*effort*) renouvelé; **after r. failures/warnings/***etc,* après des échecs/des avertissements/*etc* répétés.

repeatedly [rɪ'piːtɪdlɪ] *adv* (*to fail, tell, warn etc*) à maintes reprises.

repeater [rɪ'piːtər] *n* (*alarm clock*) réveil *m* à répétition; (*rifle*) fusil *m* à répétition; (*watch*) montre *f* à répétition.

repeating [rɪ'piːtɪŋ] **1** *adj* **(a)** (*alarm clock, rifle, watch*) à répétition; **(b)** (*decimal*) périodique. **2** *n* (*of word, action*) répétition *f*; **his language doesn't bear r.,** les mots qu'il emploie ne sont pas à répéter.

repel [rɪ'pel] *vt* (**-ll-**) **(a)** (*repulse*) repousser (*un assaillant*); **to r. moisture,** empêcher l'infiltration de l'humidité; **like poles r. (each other),** les pôles semblables se repoussent; **a spray that repels greenfly,** un aérosol qui éloigne les pucerons; **(b)** (*disgust*) répugner à, dégoûter (*qn*); **she was repelled by the sight,** elle a été dégoûtée par ce qu'elle a vu.

repellent [rɪ'pelənt] **1** *adj* (*person*) repoussant, répugnant; (*sight etc*) repoussant; **he finds her/the idea quite r., she/the idea is quite r. to him,** elle/l'idée lui répugne; **r. (to water)** imperméable. **2** *n* (*for insects*) insectifuge *m*.

-repellent [rɪ'pelənt] *suff* **moth/rust/***etc***-r.,** antimites/antirouille/*etc*; **cat/dog/***etc***-r.,** qui éloigne les chats/les chiens/*etc*.

repent [rɪ'pent] **1** *vi* (*feel remorse*) se repentir (**of,** de). **2** *vt* se repentir de (*qch*); **he has bitterly repented it,** il s'en est repenti amèrement.

repentance [rɪ'pentəns] *n* (*remorse*) repentir *m* (**for,** pour); **to show r.,** manifester du repentir; *Rel* venir à résipiscence; **to show no sign of r.,** ne manifester aucun signe de repentir.

repentant [rɪ'pentənt] *adj* (*sinner etc*) repentant (**of,** de).

repentantly [rɪ'pentəntlɪ] *adv* (*to say, look at*) d'un ton *ou* d'un air repentant.

repercussion [riːpə'kʌʃən] *n* **(a)** *Fig* (*reverberation*) répercussion *f*; (*of scandal*) retentissement *m*; (*consequence*) contrecoup *m*; **to have repercussions,** avoir des répercussions (**for, on,** sur); **the repercussions are still being felt,** on ressent encore les répercussions; **(b)** (*from impact, of sound*) répercussion *f*.

repertoire ['repətwɑːr] *n* (*of jokes, songs etc*) répertoire *m*; **to have a wide/limited r.,** avoir un vaste répertoire/un répertoire restreint; *Th* **the two plays will be performed in r.,** les deux pièces seront jouées en alternance.

repertory ['repət(ə)rɪ] *n Th* répertoire *m*; **they have both worked in r.,** ils ont tous les deux fait du théâtre de répertoire; **what's on at the local r.?,** qu'est-ce qu'on joue au théâtre municipal?; *Br* **r. company,** troupe *f* à demeure; *Br* **r. theatre,** théâtre *m* de répertoire.

répétiteur [repetɪ'tɜːr] *n Th* (*of opera singer etc*) maître *m* de musique.

repetition [repɪ'tɪʃən] *n* (*of word etc*) répétition *f*; (*of action*) répétition, réitération *f*; (*of effort*) renouvellement *m*; *Mus* reprise *f*; **it was an exact r. of last year's final,** c'était exactement comme la finale de l'année dernière; **I don't want any r. of your behaviour,** que cela ne se reproduise pas!

repetitious [repɪ'tɪʃəs] *adj* (*book, speech etc*) plein de répétitions.

repetitive [rɪ'petɪtɪv] *adj* (*person*) rabâcheur; (*work*) répétitif.

rephrase [riː'freɪz] *vt* formuler à nouveau, reformuler (*une* *question*); **could you r. that?,** est-ce que tu pourrais me redire ça autrement *ou* d'une autre façon?

repine [rɪ'paɪn] *vi Lit* être mécontent, se plaindre (**against, at,** de).

replace [rɪ'pleɪs] *vt* **(a)** (*put back*) replacer (*qch*), remettre (*qch*) en place; **I replaced the book on the shelf,** j'ai replacé le livre sur l'étagère; **r. the book when you've finished with it,** remets le livre à sa place quand tu n'en auras plus besoin; *Tel* **to r. the receiver,** raccrocher (le récepteur); **(b)** (*substitute for*) remplacer (*qn, qch*) (**as,** en tant que; **with,** par); **to be replaced by** *or* **with,** être remplacé par; **it can be replaced,** (*of broken cup etc*) c'est facile à retrouver.

replaceable [rɪ'pleɪsɪb(ə)l] *adj* (*broken cup etc*) facile à retrouver.

replacement [rɪ'pleɪsmənt] *n* **(a)** (*putting back*) (*of object*) remise *f* en place; **(b)** (*substitution*) (*of person, thing*) remplacement *m*, substitution *f* (**of ... by,** de ... par); **(c)** (*substitute*) (*for person*) remplaçant, -ante; (*for component*) pièce *f* de rechange; **we are looking for a r. for our secretary,** nous cherchons une remplaçante à notre secrétaire; **r. hip/knee joint/***etc*, prothèse *m* de hanche/de rotule/*etc*; **r. staff,** personnel *m* de remplacement.

replant [riː'plɑːnt] *vt* replanter (*un arbuste, un jardin*).

replay¹ ['riːpleɪ] *n Sp* second match; *TV* **(action** *or* **instant) r.,** répétition immédiate (au ralenti); *TV* **to give** *or* **show a(n action** *or* **instant) replay,** repasser une séquence (au ralenti).

replay² [riː'pleɪ] *vt* **(a)** *Sp* rejouer (*un match*); *Tennis* **to r. a point,** rejouer un point; **(b)** repasser (*un enregistrement*).

replenish [riː'plenɪʃ] *vt* remplir (*une tasse etc*) de nouveau (**with,** de); **to r. one's supplies,** se réapprovisionner (**with,** de); **she kept his glass replenished,** elle veillait à ce que son verre fût toujours plein; *F* **do you need replenishing?,** est-ce que je remplis ton verre?

replenishment [rɪ'plenɪʃmənt] *n* (*of cup etc*) remplissage *m*; **r. of supplies,** réapprovisionnement *m*.

replete [rɪ'pliːt] *adj* **(a)** (*well-fed*) rassasié, gorgé (**with,** de); **(b)** (*well-supplied*) rempli, plein (**with,** de).

repletion [rɪ'pliːʃən] *n* satiété *f*; **to eat to r.,** manger à satiété *ou* jusqu'à être rassasié.

replica ['replɪkə] *n* (*of statue, painting*) reproduction *f*, réplique *f*; (*of document*) reproduction, copie *f*; *Fig* (*of person*) portrait *m*; **she is a r. of her grandmother,** elle est (tout) le portrait de sa grand-mère.

replicate ['replɪkeɪt] *vt* copier (*un document*); **the gene can r. itself,** le gène peut se reproduire.

reply¹ [rɪ'plaɪ] *n* (*to letter, query etc*) réponse *f*; **I made no r.,** je n'ai rien répondu; **his r. to that was ...,** (*in speech*) il a répondu à cela que ...; **his r. to that was to do ...,** il a réagi à cela en faisant ...; **what did you say in r.?,** qu'est-ce que tu as répondu?; **what did you do in r.?,** comment est-ce que tu as réagi?; **there was no r.,** (*to telephone call*) on n'a pas répondu, *F* ça ne répondait pas; (*to knock on door*) on n'a pas ouvert; **in r. to your letter,** en réponse à votre lettre; *Com* **r. card,** carte-réponse *f*, *pl* cartes-réponses; **(international) r. coupon,** coupon-réponse *m* (international), *pl* coupons-réponses (internationaux); **r. paid,** réponse payée.

reply² *vt & vi* répondre (**to,** à); (*retort*) répliquer (**to,** à); **yes, madam, he replied,** oui, madame, a-t-il répondu; **she replied to the criticism with a counterattack,** elle a répondu à la critique en contre-attaquant.

repo ['riːpəʊ] *n US Sl* (*abbr* **repossession**) **r. man,** = personne chargée par une société de saisir des meubles *etc* non payés.

report¹ [rɪ'pɔːt] *n* **(a)** (*account*) rapport *m* (**on,** sur); (*of meetings*) compte rendu; (*in writing*) procès-verbal, *pl* procès-verbaux; *m*; (*in newspaper*) (*short*) exposé *m*, récit *m*; (*long*) reportage *m*; (*on radio, television*) reportage; (*by eyewitness*) témoignage *m*; *Comptr* état *m*; **to draw up** *or* **make a r. on sth,** faire *ou* rédiger un rapport sur qch; (*of police officer*) dresser procès-verbal de qch; *Parl* **the bill has reached the r. stage,** le rapport a été présenté; *Am Sch* **book r.,** compte rendu de lecture; *Sch* **end-of-term r.,** bulletin *m* (trimestriel); **progress r.,** rapport périodique *ou* d'avancement (des travaux); *Mil* **sick r.,** rôle *m* des malades; *Sch* **r. (card),** carnet *m* (de notes), bulletin scolaire; *Sch* **to get a good r. card,** avoir un bon carnet; *Comptr* **r. form,** rapport *m* (d'édition);

(b) (*rumour*) bruit *m* (qui court), rumeur *f*;

(c) (*sound*) (*of shot*) détonation *f*, coup *m* de fusil *ou* canon; (*of explosion*) bruit *m* d'explosion, détonation;

(d) *Arch* (*reputation*) renom *m*; **man of good r.,** homme de bonne réputation.

report² **1** *vt* **(a)** (*give account of*) rapporter (*un fait*); rendre compte de (*qch*); faire le compte rendu de (*un discours etc*); *Journ* faire le reportage de, faire un reportage sur (*qch*); **to r. progress to s.o.,** tenir qn au courant de la marche d'une affaire; *Gram* **reported speech,** discours indirect; **the president was reported by the newspapers to have ...,** les journaux ont rapporté *ou* raconté que le président a ...; **she is reported to be dead,** on dit qu'elle est morte, on la dit morte; **it is reported that,** on dit que; **they are reported to be in France,** ils seraient en France;

(b) (*make known*) signaler (*un accident, un vol*) (**to,** à); (*announce*) annoncer (**that,** que); **I'm going to r. you,** (*complain about*) je vais me plaindre contre vous; **to r. s.o. to the police,** dénoncer qn à la police; **to r. a pupil to the headmaster,** (*of teacher*) signaler la mauvaise conduite d'un élève au directeur; **to r. a pupil for smoking,** signaler le nom d'un élève surpris en train de fumer; **I'm going to r. you for smoking,** je dirai au directeur que je t'ai surpris en train de fumer; *Mil* **to r. s.o. sick/missing,** porter qn malade/absent; **to r. s.o. missing,** (*to police*) signaler la disparition de qn; **she has been reported missing,** on a signalé sa disparition; **she was reported missing five years ago,** elle a été portée disparue il y a cinq ans.

2 *vi* **(a)** (*present oneself*) se présenter (**to,** à, devant); **please r. to reception,** veuillez vous présenter à la réception; **you've to r. to the headmaster,** tu dois aller chez le directeur; *Mil* **to r. sick,** se faire porter malade; *Mil* **to r. fit,** reprendre son service après la maladie; *Mil* **to r. to one's unit,** rallier son unité; **to r. for duty,** prendre son service; **you will r. for duty on Monday,** vous serez à votre poste lundi; **to r. back from leave,** reprendre son service après un congé;

(b) (*give account*) faire un rapport (**on,** sur); (*of journalist*) faire un reportage (**on,** sur); **to r. to s.o.,** rendre compte à qn (**on,** de), faire son rapport à qn (**on,** sur); *Parl* **to r. on a bill,** rapporter un projet de loi; *Parl* **to r. back to a committee,** faire son rapport à un comité; **to r. (for a newspaper),** faire des reportages (pour un journal); *TV Rad* **reporting from Geneva is our foreign affairs correspondent ...,** de Genève, notre correspondant pour les affaires étrangères; **this is Mary Smith reporting for ITN news,** Mary Smith pour le journal d'informations d'I.T.N.; **nothing to r.,** rien à signaler; (*on form*) néant, R.A.S..

▶report to *vipo* (*be accountable*) relever de; **who do you r. to?,** de qui relevez-vous?

reportage [repɔː'tɑːʒ] *n Journ etc* reportage *m*.

reportedly [rɪ'pɔːtɪdlɪ] *adv* à ce qu'on dit; **the President r. said that ...,** le Président aurait dit que ...; **she is r. unharmed,** elle serait indemne; **he is r. resident in Paris,** il résiderait à Paris.

reporter [rɪ'pɔːtər] *n* (*for newspaper, TV*) journaliste *mf*; (*for magazine*) reporter *m*; (*in the field*) envoyé, -ée.

reporting [rɪ'pɔːtɪŋ] *n* **(a)** (*of news*) reportage *m*; **his r. of the facts is always accurate,** sa version *ou* son récit des faits est toujours fidèle; **r. restrictions have been imposed,** on a imposé des restrictions quant aux reportages; **(b)** (*accountability*) **r. structure,** structure *f* hiérarchique.

repose¹ [rɪ'pəʊz] *n* **(a)** (*calm*) repos *m*, tranquillité *f*; **her face is beautiful in r.,** son visage au repos est très beau; **(b)** *Lit* (*rest*) repos *m*; (*sleep*) sommeil *m*.

repose² **1** *vt* **(a)** *Fml* **to r. trust in s.o.,** placer *ou* mettre sa confiance en qn; **(b)** *Old-fashioned* reposer (*sa tête*); **to r. oneself,** se reposer. **2** *vi* **(a)** (*of argument, plan*) reposer (**on,** sur); **(b)** *Old-fashioned* se reposer.

reposition [riːpə'zɪʃən] *vt Com* (*change market image of*) repositionner (*un produit*).

repositioning [riːpə'zɪʃənɪŋ] *n Com* (*of product*) repositionnement *m*.

repository [rɪ'pɒzɪt(ə)rɪ] *n Am* (*for books, furniture etc*) dépôt *m*, entrepôt *m*.

repossess [riːpə'zes] *vt* (*for non-payment*) saisir (*des meubles, une voiture etc*).

repossession [riːpə'zeʃən] *n* (*of furniture etc*) saisie *f* (**of,** de).

repot [riː'pɒt] *vt* rempoter (*une plante*).

reprehensible [reprɪ'hensɪb(ə)l] *adj* (*behaviour, act*) répréhensible; **that was most r. of you,** c'était très répréhensible de votre part.

reprehensibly [reprɪ'hensɪblɪ] *adv* (*to behave, act*) de façon répréhensible.

represent [reprɪ'zent] *vt* **(a)** (*depict, portray*) représenter (*qch, qn*);

(b) (*act as agent for*) *& Jur Pol* représenter (*une société, qn etc*); **the Queen will be represented by ...,** la Reine sera représentée par ...; **(c)** (*constitute*) représenter, constituer; **this represents a great improvement,** cela constitue un grand progrès; **(d)** (*symbolize, embody*) symboliser (*la nation*); **(e)** (*typify*) représenter; **the government's policy does not r. my opinions,** la politique du gouvernement n'est pas représentative de mes opinions; **(f)** (*describe*) présenter (*qn, qch*) (**to be, as,** comme); **he represents himself as a model of virtue,** il se donne pour un modèle de vertu; **(g)** *Fml* (*state, express*) faire remarquer, signaler (*qch*) (**to,** à); **I will r. your grievances to management,** je ferai part de vos griefs à la direction.

re-present [riːprɪ'zent] *vt* présenter (*un chèque, une facture etc*) à *ou* de nouveau.

representation [reprɪzen'teɪʃən] *n* **(a)** *Pol* représentation *f*; **they have increased their r. to six,** le nombre de leurs délégués est passé à six; **(b)** (*in painting*) représentation *f*; *Th* (*of role*) interprétation *f*; **(c)** (*of views, facts etc*) exposé *m* des faits; **this is a fair r. of their point of view,** cela représente bien leur point de vue; **representations,** (*complaints*) remontrances *fpl*; **to make representations,** faire des démarches (**about,** concernant; **to,** auprès de).

representational [reprɪzen'teɪʃən(ə)l] *adj* (*art*) figuratif.

representative [reprɪ'zentətɪv] **1** *n* **(a)** (*of group, company, organization etc*) représentant, -ante; (*for mail-order firm*) délégué, -ée; **(sales) r.,** représentant, V.R.P. *m*; **to send a r. to a conference,** se faire représenter à une conférence; **sole representatives of a firm,** représentants *ou* agents exclusifs d'une maison; **last r. of an illustrious race,** dernier descendant d'une race illustre; **(b)** *Pol* député *m*; *US* **the House of Representatives,** la Chambre des Représentants. **2** *adj* **(a)** (*symbolic*) symbolique; **to be r. of sth,** représenter qch, symboliser qch; **(b)** (*typical*) typique; **a r. cross-section of the French population,** un échantillon représentatif de la population française; *Com* **r. sample,** échantillon type; **(c)** *Pol* (*government*) représentatif.

repress [rɪ'pres] *vt* **(a)** réprimer (*ses désirs, ses passions*); retenir (*ses larmes*); réprimer (*une sédition*); **(b)** *Psy* (*unconsciously*) refouler; (*consciously*) réprimer; **he is very repressed,** il est très renfermé; **she had a very repressed adolescence,** elle a eu une adolescence très réprimée.

repression [rɪ'preʃən] *n* **(a)** (*of desire, riot etc*) répression *f*; **(b)** *Psy* (*unconscious*) refoulement *m*; (*conscious*) répression *f*.

repressive [rɪ'presɪv] *adj* (*government, law*) répressif; (*measures*) de répression.

reprieve¹ [rɪ'priːv] *n* *Jur* (*for condemned prisoner*) (*definitive*) commutation *f* de la peine capitale; (*temporary*) *& Fig* sursis *m*; **to grant a r.,** accorder une commutation de peine *ou* un sursis; **this is a r. for the government,** cela constitue un sursis pour le gouvernement; *F* **we've got a r.,** (*for project etc*) on nous a donné un peu plus de temps.

reprieve² *vt* *Jur* accorder (*à un condamné*) une commutation de la peine capitale *ou* un sursis; *Fig* **the shipyard has been reprieved by the government's decision,** le chantier naval bénéficie d'un sursis grâce à la décision du gouvernement.

reprimand¹ ['reprɪmɑːnd] *n* (*of child*) réprimande *f*; (*of employee, accused person*) blâme *m*; **to be given a r.,** (*of child*) recevoir une réprimande; (*of employee etc*) recevoir un blâme; **she was let off with a r.,** elle s'en est tirée avec une réprimande *ou* un blâme.

reprimand² *vt* (*admonish*) réprimander (*un enfant*) (**for,** pour); blâmer (*un employé, un accusé*) (**for,** pour).

reprint¹ ['riːprɪnt] *n* (*of book*) réimpression *f*; (*of article*) nouvelle parution, nouvelle publication; **the book is going into its fourth r.,** le livre va être réimprimé pour la quatrième fois; **separate r.,** (*of article from journal*) tirage *m* à part.

reprint² [riː'prɪnt] **1** *vt* réimprimer (*un livre*); faire paraître *ou* publier (*un article*) à nouveau; **article reprinted from The Times,** article reproduit du Times. **2** *vi* (*of book*) être en réimpression.

reprisal [rɪ'praɪz(ə)l] *n* représailles *fpl*; **to carry out** *or* **take reprisal(s),** exercer des représailles, user de représailles (**against,** contre); **to threaten reprisals,** menacer de représailles; **there have been threats of r.,** il y a eu des menaces de représailles; **as a** *or* **in r. for ...,** en *ou* par représailles pour ...; **r. attack/raid/etc,** attaque *f*/raid *m*/*etc* de représailles.

reprise [rɪ'priːz] *n* *Mus* reprise *f*.

reproach¹ [rɪ'prəʊtʃ] *n* **(a)** (*blame*) reproche *m*; **she heaped reproaches on him,** elle l'a accablé de reproches; **look of r.,** regard *m* de reproche; **there was a note of r. in his voice,** il y avait une pointe *ou* une nuance de reproche dans sa voix; **a letter of r.,** une lettre de reproches; **beyond** *or* **above r.,** (*conduct*) irréprochable; (*person*) à qui on n'a rien à reprocher, sans reproche; **(b)** (*shame*) honte *f*; **to be a r. to ...,** être la honte de...; **it is a r. to the government that ...,** c'est une honte pour le gouvernement que ...; **things that have brought r. upon him,** choses qui ont jeté le discrédit sur lui.

reproach² *vt* reprocher (**s.o. for, with sth,** qch à qn); **to r. oneself,** se faire des reproches; **I have nothing to r. myself with** *or* **for,** je n'ai rien à me reprocher; **she reproached him for not keeping his promise,** elle lui a reproché de n'avoir pas tenu sa promesse, elle lui a fait des reproches pour ne pas avoir tenu sa promesse.

reproachful [rɪ'prəʊtʃfʊl] *adj* (*look, tone*) de reproche, plein de reproche(s).

reproachfully [rɪ'prəʊtʃfəlɪ] *adv* (*to say, look at*) d'un ton *ou* d'un air de reproche *ou* plein de reproche(s).

reprobate ['reprəbeɪt] *n* réprouvé *m*; *Old-fashioned Hum* vaurien *m*.

reprocess [riː'prəʊses] *vt* *Ind etc* retraiter (*déchets etc*).

reprocessing [riː'prəʊsesɪŋ] *n* (*of waste*) retraitement *m*; **r. plant,** usine *f* de retraitement.

reproduce [riːprə'djuːs] **1** *vt* (*copy*) reproduire (*un tableau*); copier (*un texte*). **2** *vi* *Biol Bot* se reproduire; (*of photocopier*) reproduire; **this print will r. well,** cette estampe se prêtera bien à la reproduction.

reproduction [riːprə'dʌkʃən] *n* (*of document, picture etc*) *& Biol Bot* reproduction *f*; **thousands of reproductions have been made of this picture,** ce tableau a été reproduit à des milliers d'exemplaires.

reproductive [riːprə'dʌktɪv] *adj* *Biol* reproducteur; **r. organs,** organes *mpl* de la reproduction *ou* reproducteurs; **r. system,** (*of animal etc*) appareil *m* reproducteur.

reprography [re'prɒgrəfɪ] *n* reprographie *f*.

reproof¹ [rɪ'pruːf] *n* réprobation *f*; (*in speech, writing*) blâme *m*; **he looked at her with r.,** il l'a regardée avec réprobation; **word/look of r.,** mot *m*/regard *m* de réprobation.

reproof² [riː'pruːf] *vt* réimperméabiliser (*un manteau*).

reprove [rɪ'pruːv] *vt* reprendre (*un enfant*); réprimander (*qn*) (**for,** pour); condamner (*une action*).

reproving [rɪ'pruːvɪŋ] *adj* (*look, tone*) réprobateur.

reprovingly [rɪ'pruːvɪŋlɪ] *adv* (*to say, look at*) d'un ton *ou* d'un air réprobateur.

reptile ['reptaɪl] *n* reptile *m*; **r. house,** (*in zoo*) vivarium *m* pour les reptiles.

reptilian [rep'tɪlɪən] **1** *adj* (*animal*) reptilien; *Pej* (*features*) de reptile. **2** *n* reptile *m*.

republic [rɪ'pʌblɪk] *n* république *f*.

republican [rɪ'pʌblɪkən] *adj & n* républicain, -aine.

Republican [rɪ'pʌblɪkən] *adj & n* *US Pol* républicain, -aine.

republicanism [rɪ'pʌblɪkənɪz(ə)m] *n* républicanisme *m*.

repudiate [rɪ'pjuːdɪeɪt] *vt* *esp Fml* répudier (*une épouse, une idée etc*); désavouer (*un ami, une opinion*); repousser (*une offre*); nier (*une dette, une accusation*); **to r. the authorship of a book,** désavouer la paternité d'un livre.

repudiation [rɪpjuːdɪ'eɪʃən] *n* *esp Fml* (*of spouse, idea etc*) répudiation *f*; (*of friend, opinion*) désaveu *m*; (*of offer*) refus *m*; (*of debt, accusation*) reniement *m*.

repugnance [rɪ'pʌgnəns] *n* (*abhorrence*) répugnance *f* (**for,** pour); **to have a r. for sth/for doing,** avoir de la répugnance pour qch/à faire.

repugnant [rɪ'pʌgnənt] *adj* (*deed, person etc*) répugnant (**to,** à); **to be r. to s.o.,** répugner à qn.

repulse¹ [rɪ'pʌls] *n* (*of person*) rebuffade *f*; (*of assistance, offer etc*) refus *m*; *Mil* échec *m*; **to meet with a r.,** (*of person, offer*) essuyer un refus.

repulse² *vt* repousser (*qn, une demande*); repousser, refouler (*un assaut, un ennemi*).

repulsion [rɪ'pʌlʃən] *n* **(a)** (*of person*) répulsion *f*, aversion *f* (**for,** à l'égard de); **to feel r. for sth/s.o.,** éprouver de la répulsion *ou* de l'aversion à l'égard de qch/qn; **(b)** *Phys* répulsion *f*.

repulsive [rɪ'pʌlsɪv] *adj* **(a)** (*person, sight, smell*) repoussant; (*person, habit, idea etc*) répugnant; **(b)** *Phys* répulsif.

repulsively [rɪ'pʌlsɪvlɪ] *adv* **r. ugly,** d'une laideur repoussante.

repulsiveness [rɪ'pʌlsɪvnɪs] *n* **(a)** (*of person, sight etc*) caractère repoussant; (*of person, habit etc*) caractère répu-

gnant; *Phys* force répulsive.
reputable ['repjʊtəb(ə)l] *adj* (*person*) honorable, réputé; (*job*) honorable; (*shop, company*) réputé, qui a bonne réputation.
reputation [repjuː'teɪʃən, repjʊ-] *n* (*of person, shop etc*) réputation *f*; **to make a r. (for oneself),** se faire une réputation; **to have a good/bad r.,** avoir (une) bonne/mauvaise réputation (**as,** en tant que); **to have a r. for frankness/***etc*, avoir la réputation d'être franc/*etc*; *Pej* **he has a bit of a r.,** il n'a pas très bonne réputation; **to live up to one's reputation,** (*of person*) se montrer à la hauteur de sa réputation; (*of book, restaurant etc*) être à la hauteur de sa réputation.
repute¹ [rɪ'pjuːt] *n esp Fml* réputation *f*, renom *m*; **to know s.o. by r.,** connaître qn de réputation; **to be held in high r.,** avoir une haute réputation; **of r.,** (*doctor etc*) réputé, de grand renom; **house of ill r.,** maison *f* de passe.
repute² *vt* (*usu passive*) **to be reputed wealthy,** avoir la réputation d'être riche; **he is reputed to be a good doctor,** il a la réputation d'être (un) bon médecin, il est réputé pour être bon médecin; **his reputed father,** son père putatif.
reputedly [rɪ'pjuːtɪdlɪ] *adv* (*supposedly*) censément, à ce qu'on dit; **she is r. the best heart specialist,** elle a la réputation d'être le meilleur cardiologue.
request¹ [rɪ'kwest] *n* demande *f*, requête *f*; (*urgent*) prière *f*; **r. for money,** demande d'argent; **at the r. of s.o., at s.o.'s r.,** à la demande de qn; **samples sent on r.,** échantillons sur demande; **to make a r.,** faire *ou* formuler une demande (**for,** de); **by (popular) r.,** à la demande générale; *Rad* **to play a r.,** passer un disque demandé par un auditeur; *Rad* **to send in a r.,** envoyer une demande; *Rad* **r. programme** *or* **show,** programme *m* des auditeurs; *Br* **r. stop,** (*for bus*) arrêt facultatif.
request² *vt* **to r. sth of s.o.,** demander qch à qn, solliciter qch de qn; **to r. s.o. to do sth,** demander à qn de faire qch; (*as a matter of urgency*) prier qn de faire qch; **passengers are requested not to smoke,** les passagers sont priés de ne pas fumer; **as requested,** (*on compliments slip etc*) conformément à votre demande.
requiem ['rekwɪəm] *n Rel* **r. (mass),** (messe *f* de) requiem *m*, messe des morts; *Mus* requiem; **to have a r. mass for s.o.,** faire dire une messe de requiem pour qn.
require [rɪ'kwaɪər] *vt* (*necessitate*) demander; (*demand*) exiger; (*of person*) avoir besoin de; **to r. sth of s.o.,** (*order*) exiger qch de qn; **to r. s.o. to do sth,** exiger de qn qu'il fasse qch; **he had done all that was required by law,** il s'était conformé à toutes les exigences de la loi; **my services are no longer required,** on n'a plus besoin de mes services; *Euph* (*I've been dismissed*) j'ai été remercié; **this plant requires plenty of water,** cette plante demande beaucoup d'eau; **have you everything you r.?,** avez-vous tout ce qu'il vous faut?; **I shall do whatever is required,** je ferai tout ce qu'il faudra; **the qualifications required for this job,** les qualités requises pour ce poste; **if required,** s'il le faut, si besoin est; **when required,** au besoin; **in the required time,** en temps voulu, dans le délai prescrit; **required reading,** ouvrage *m* à lire absolument; (*for student*) ouvrages au programme, lectures *fpl* obligatoires; **staff required,** (*notice in shop*) on recherche du personnel.
requirement [rɪ'kwaɪəmənt] *n* (*need*) exigence *f*; (*condition*) condition *f* (requise); *Univ* **requirements for the course,** conditions préalables d'admission; **a qualification in Greek is no longer a r.,** un diplôme en grec n'est plus nécessaire; **to meet s.o.'s requirements,** (*wishes*) répondre aux désirs de qn; (*demands*) satisfaire les *ou* aux exigences de qn.
requisite ['rekwɪzɪt] **1** *adj* (*money, papers etc*) requis (**to,** pour), nécessaire (**to,** à). **2** *n* **(a)** (*for travel etc*) article *m*; **toilet requisites,** articles *ou* nécessaire *m* de toilette; **(b)** = **REQUIREMENT**.
requisition¹ [rekwɪ'zɪʃən] *n* demande *f*; *Mil* réquisition *f*; *Com etc* **r. for supplies,** commande *f* pour fournitures; **r. number,** numéro *m* de référence.
requisition² **1** *vt Mil* réquisitionner (*des vivres etc*) (**from,** de); *Com* commander, faire la demande de (*fournitures*); *Fig* réquisitionner (*qn*) (**to do,** pour faire); recourir à, avoir recours à (*services de qn*). **2** *vi* faire des réquisitions.
requisitioning [rekwɪ'zɪʃənɪŋ] *n Mil* **r. officer,** officier chargé des réquisitions.
requital [rɪ'kwaɪt(ə)l] *n* (*for service*) récompense *f*; (*of love*) retour *m*; **in r. of** *or* **for her services,** en récompense de ses services.
requite [rɪ'kwaɪt] *vt* récompenser (*un service*); se venger de, venger (*une injure*); **to r. s.o. for sth,** récompenser qn de qch; **to r. s.o.'s love,** répondre à l'amour de qn.
reread [riː'riːd] *vt* relire.
reredos ['rɪədɒs] *n* (*in church*) retable *m*.
reroute [riː'ruːt] *vt* dérouter (*un avion, un train etc*) (**through,** via).
rerun¹ ['riːrʌn] *n* (*of film, tape*) reprise *f*; *Rad TV* rediffusion *f*; *Fig* (*of disaster etc*) répétition *f*.
rerun² [riː'rʌn] *vt* repasser (*un film, une cassette*); *Rad TV* rediffuser (*un programme*).
resale [riː'seɪl] *n* revente *f*; **r. price maintenance,** prix imposé(s) (par le fabricant).
reschedule [riː'ʃedjuːl] *vt* modifier l'heure *ou* la date de (*un rendez-vous, un vol, un départ*); rééchelonner (*une dette*).
rescheduling [riː'ʃedjuːlɪŋ] *n* (*of appointment, flight, departure*) modification *f* d'horaire *ou* de date; (*of debt*) rééchelonnement *m*.
rescind [rɪ'sɪnd] *vt* rescinder, abroger (*une loi*); annuler, résilier (*un contrat*).
rescue¹ ['reskjuː] *n* (*action*) sauvetage *m* (**of,** de); (*help, troops etc*) secours *mpl*; (*setting free*) délivrance *f*; **to the r.,** à la rescousse; **to come/go to s.o.'s r.,** venir/aller au secours de qn; **r. archaeology,** fouilles *fpl* de sauvetage; **r. party,** équipe *f* de sauvetage *ou* de sauveteurs; **r. operation,** opération *f* de sauvetage; **r. worker,** secouriste *mf*.
rescue² *vt* (*from death, difficult or embarrassing situation*) sauver, secourir; (*set free*) délivrer (**from,** de); **to r. s.o. from danger,** arracher qn à un danger, sauver qn d'un danger; **to r. s.o. from drowning,** sauver qn qui se noie; **to r. a company from bankruptcy,** sauver une société de la faillite; **the rescued,** (*used as pl*) les rescapés.
rescuer ['reskjuːər] *n* (*from shipwreck, fire etc*) secouriste *mf*, sauveteur *m*; (*from embarrassing situation*) sauveur *m*; (*from captivity*) libérateur, -trice.
research¹ [rɪ'sɜːtʃ] *n* recherche *f* (**into,** sur); **some r.,** de la recherche; **a piece of r. (work),** un travail de recherche; **r. and development,** recherche et développement; **to do** *or* **be engaged in r.,** faire des recherches (**on, into,** sur); **r. establishment/laboratory/team/***etc*, centre *m*/laboratoire *f*/équipe *f*/*etc* de recherche; **r. finding,** découverte effectuée à l'occasion de recherches; **r. work,** recherches, travaux *mpl* de recherche; **r. worker** *or* **assistant,** (*scientific*) chercheur, -euse; *Am* (*literary*) documentaliste *mf*; **r. scientist,** maître *m* de recherche.
research² **1** *vt* faire des recherches sur (*qch*); **he spent two years researching his book/thesis,** il a passé deux ans à faire des recherches pour son livre/sa thèse; **a well researched book,** un livre bien documenté. **2** *vi* faire des recherches (**on, into,** sur).
researcher [rɪ'sɜːtʃər] *n* chercheur, -euse.
reseat [riː'siːt] *vt* **(a) to r. oneself,** se rasseoir; **(b)** remettre un fond à (*un pantalon, une chaise*); **(c)** roder (*une soupape*).
resection [riː'sekʃən] *n Surg* résection *f*.
resell [riː'sel] *vt* (*pt & pp* **resold** [riː'səʊld]) revendre (*une maison*).
resemblance [rɪ'zembləns] *n* (*of person, thing*) ressemblance *f* (**to,** à, avec; **between,** entre); **to bear a r. to s.o./sth,** ressembler à qn/qch; **his testimony bears no r. to the facts,** il n'y a aucune ressemblance entre son témoignage et les faits.
resemble [rɪ'zemb(ə)l] *vt* ressembler à (*qn, qch*); **to r. one another,** se ressembler.
resent [rɪ'zent] *vt* **(a)** (*be angry about*) être indigné de, ne pas aimer (*qch*); **I r. your remarks,** je n'aime pas du tout vos remarques; **I r. that,** je n'aime pas ça du tout; **(b)** (*be bitter about*) éprouver de l'amertume à l'égard de (*qch*); **you r. my being here,** ma présence vous déplaît; **your children r. me,** tes enfants m'en veulent.
resentful [rɪ'zentfʊl] *adj* (*remark, look*) plein de ressentiment, amer; **to be** *or* **feel r.,** éprouver de l'amertume *ou* du ressentiment (**about,** à propos de, concernant).
resentfully [rɪ'zentfəlɪ] *adv* (*to behave, act*) avec ressentiment *ou* amertume; (*to speak*) d'un ton plein de ressentiment *ou* d'amertume, d'un ton rancunier; (*to look*) d'un air rancunier.
resentment [rɪ'zentmənt] *n* amertume *f*, ressentiment *m* (**at,** à; **over,** concernant; **of,** à l'égard de); **to feel r. against s.o.,** avoir de la rancune contre qn; **there is a lot of r. about her appointment,** sa nomination suscite beaucoup d'amertume.
reservation [rezə'veɪʃən] *n* **(a)** (*booking*) (*in restaurant*

etc) réservation *f*; **to make a r.**, réserver; **to make a r. for nine o'clock,** (*in restaurant*) réserver une table pour neuf heures; **do you have a r.?**, (*in restaurant*) est-ce que vous avez réservé?; (*in hotel, train*) est-ce que vous avez une réservation?; **for reservations, call ...**, pour réserver appeler ...; *Am* **r. clerk,** préposé aux réservations; **r. desk,** bureau des réservations; **(b)** (*doubt*) (*about idea, plan etc*) réserve *f*; **without r.**, sans réserve, sans arrière-pensée; **not without** *or* **with some r.**, non sans réserves; **with this r.**, à cette restriction près; **to have reservations about sth,** avoir des doutes à propos de qch; **to have no reservations in doing sth,** n'avoir aucune hésitation à faire qch; **(c)** *Am* (*land*) terrain réservé; **Indian r.**, réserve indienne; *Br Aut* **central r.**, terre-plein *m*, *pl* terres-pleins.

reserve[1] [rɪ'zɜːv] *n* **(a)** (*stock*) (*of money etc*) réserve *f*; **to have great reserves of energy,** avoir beaucoup d'énergie en réserve; **he still has a r. of support in the country,** il bénéficie encore d'un certain soutien parmi les électeurs; **to draw on one's reserves,** (*of courage, money, skill*) puiser dans ses réserves; *Min* **known reserves,** réserves prouvées; **to keep sth in r.**, tenir qch en réserve (**for,** pour); **to have nothing in r.**, ne rien avoir en réserve; **r. power/energy,** réserve de puissance/énergie; *Aut Av* **r. tank,** réservoir *m* de secours;
(b) *Mil etc* **the reserves,** les réserves *fpl*, les réservistes *mpl*; **r. officer,** officier *m* de réserve;
(c) *Sp* remplaçant, -ante;
(d) (*for birds, game*) réserve *f*; **nature r.**, réserve naturelle; *Can* **Indian r.**, réserve indienne;
(e) (*limitation*) réserve *f*, restriction *f*; **without r.**, sans réserve, sans restriction;
(f) *Br* (*at sale*) **r. (price),** prix *m* minimum, mise *f* à prix; **to put a r. on sth,** fixer un prix minimum à qch; **the item did not reach its r.**, l'article n'a pas atteint sa mise à prix;
(g) (*reticence*) réserve *f*; **when he breaks through his r.**, quand il sort de sa réserve.

reserve[2] *vt* **(a)** (*book*) réserver (*une table*); **(b)** (*keep*) mettre (*qch*) en réserve; **to r. a seat for s.o.**, réserver *ou* retenir une place à qn; **reserved seat,** (*on train*) place réservée; (*at theatre, concert etc*) place louée; **to r. the right to do sth,** se réserver le droit de faire qch; **to r. one's strength,** ménager ses forces; **all rights reserved,** tous droits de reproduction réservés; **(c)** (*withhold*) **to r. judgement on sth/s.o.**, réserver son jugement sur qch/qn.

reserved [rɪ'zɜːvd] *adj* (*shy*) réservé, peu communicatif; (*introverted*) renfermé; **to be r. with s.o.**, être réservé *ou* se tenir sur la réserve avec qn.

reservedly [rɪ'zɜːvɪdlɪ] *adv* avec réserve, de manière réservée.

reservist [rɪ'zɜːvɪst] *n Mil etc* réserviste *m*.

reservoir ['rezəvwɑːr] *n* (*for water*) réservoir *m*, bassin *m* de retenue; (*for oil*) réservoir.

reset [riː'set] *v* (*pt & pp* **reset**; *prp* **resetting**) **1** *vt* **(a)** remettre (*une montre*) à l'heure; **to r. a timer,** remettre un minuteur à zéro; **to r. an alarm clock,** régler la sonnerie du réveil; *Comptr* **r. button** *or* **switch,** bouton *m* de remise à zéro; **(b)** remonter (*une pierre précieuse etc*); *Surg* (*fracture*) réduire; (*dislocation*) remettre, remboîter; **(c)** *Typ* recomposer (*un texte*). **2** *vi* (*of alarm*) se réenclencher.

resettle [riː'set(ə)l] **1** *vt* implanter (*des réfugiés*); repeupler (*une région*). **2** *vi* se réinstaller (**in,** dans).

resettlement [riː'set(ə)lmənt] *n* (*of refugees*) implantation *f*; (*of area*) repeuplement *m*.

reshape [riː'ʃeɪp] *vt* réorganiser (*une industrie etc*).

reshuffle[1] [riː'ʃʌf(ə)l] *n* (*of Cabinet, jobs, responsibilities etc*) remaniement *m*.

reshuffle[2] *vt* **(a)** remanier (*un personnel etc*); **(b)** battre de nouveau (*les cartes*).

reside [rɪ'zaɪd] *vi* (*of person*) résider (**at, in,** à, dans); *Fig* (*of power, quality*) résider (**in,** dans).

residence ['rezɪdəns] *n* **(a)** (*stay*) séjour *m*; **to take up r. in a country,** se fixer *ou* s'établir dans un pays; **to be in r.**, être en résidence; **in r.**, (*doctor, poet*) sur place; (*students*) sur le campus; *Br Sch* **hall of r.**, résidence *f* universitaire; **place of r.**, lieu *m* de résidence; **six months r.**, séjour de six mois; **r. permit,** permis *m* de séjour; **(b)** (*home*) demeure *f*, maison *f*; (*of students*) foyer *m*; **desirable r. for sale,** belle propriété à vendre.

residency ['rezɪdənsɪ] *n* **(a)** *Am Med* internat *m*; **to do one's r.**, faire son internat; **(b)** (*of governor etc*) résidence officielle.

resident ['rezɪdənt] **1** *adj* résidant, qui réside; (*population*) fixe; (*correspondent*) permanent; **to be r. in London,** résider à Londres; **r. teacher,** professeur à demeure, professeur résident. **2** *n* **(a)** (*of country, street*) habitant, -ante; (*of hotel*) pensionnaire *mf*; (*foreigner*) résident, -ente; **to be a permanent r.**, être résident permanent (**of,** de); **residents' association,** association *f* de riverains; **residents' parking bay** *or* **place,** emplacement réservé aux riverains; **(b)** *Am Med* interne *mf*.

residential [rezɪ'denʃəl] *adj* **(a)** (*area, neighbourhood etc*) résidentiel; **the building is reverting to r. use,** l'édifice va être à nouveau utilisé pour l'habitation; **(b)** (*course*) à temps complet; **(c)** (*staff*) à demeure.

residual [rɪ'zɪdjʊəl] **1** *adj* **(a)** (*unrest, resentment etc*) qui reste, restant; **r. income,** revenu net; **(b)** *Ch* résiduel. **2** *n* **(a)** *Cin TV* **residuals,** droits *mpl*; **(b)** *Ch* résidu *m*.

residuary [rɪ'zɪdjʊərɪ] *adj Jur* **r. legatee,** légataire *m* (à titre) universel.

residue ['rezɪdjuː] *n* **(a)** (*of army, fortune etc*) reste(s) *m(pl)*; *Jur* (*of estate*) reliquat *m*; **(b)** *Ch Ind etc* résidu *m*, reliquat *m*.

residuum, *pl* **-a** [rɪ'zɪdjʊəm, -ə] *n Ch* résidu *m*.

resign [rɪ'zaɪn] **1** *vi* démissionner, donner sa démission (**from,** de); **he has resigned as Prime Minister,** il a démissionné de son poste de Premier ministre; *Parl* **r.!, r.!,** démission! démission! **2** *vt Admin* résigner (*une fonction*); abandonner (*un droit*); **to r. one's job,** démissionner de son poste; **to r. sth to s.o.**, abandonner *ou* céder qch à qn; **to r. oneself to sth/to doing sth,** se résigner à qch/à faire qch; **to r. oneself/be resigned to one's fate,** se résigner à/être résigné à son sort.

resignation [rezɪg'neɪʃən] *n* **(a)** (*from job*) démission *f*; **to give (in)** *or* **send in** *or Fml* **tender one's r.**, donner sa démission; **(b)** (*of claim, right*) abandon *m* (**of,** de); **(c)** (*attitude*) résignation *f*; **to accept one's fate with r.**, se résigner à son sort.

resignedly [rɪ'zaɪnɪdlɪ] *adv* avec résignation, d'un ton *ou* d'un air résigné.

resilience [rɪ'zɪlɪəns] *n* (*of material, metal etc*) élasticité *f*; *Fig* (*of person*) (*physical*) résistance *f*; (*mental*) ressort *m*; (*of economy*) faculté *f* de reprise; **to have r.**, (*of person*) avoir du ressort.

resilient [rɪ'zɪlɪənt] *adj* (*material, metal*) élastique; *Fig* (*person*) **to be r.**, (*physically*) être résistant; (*mentally*) avoir du ressort; **children are more r. than adults,** les enfants se remettent plus vite que les adultes; **the economy is proving remarkably r.**, l'économie fait preuve d'une capacité remarquable de reprise.

resin ['rezɪn] *n* résine *f*; **to tap trees for r.**, gemmer des arbres.

resinated ['rezɪneɪtɪd] *adj* (*wine*) résiné.

resinous ['rezɪnəs] *adj* résineux.

resist [rɪ'zɪst] **1** *vt* résister à (*une attaque, la corrosion, la tentation etc*); s'opposer à, résister à (*une influence, une tentative*); s'opposer à, ne pas aimer (*des changements*); repousser (*une suggestion*); **I couldn't r. telling him,** je n'ai pas pu m'empêcher *ou* me retenir de le lui dire; **I can't r. chocolates,** je ne peux pas résister devant des chocolats; **he can't r. her,** il ne peut pas lui résister. **2** *vi* résister; **it's best not to r.**, mieux vaut ne pas offrir de résistance *ou* ne pas résister.

resistance [rɪ'zɪstəns] *n* **(a)** (*to attack, corrosion, temptation etc*) résistance *f* (**to,** à); (*to influence, change etc*) opposition *f*; **to put up (a)** *or* **offer r.**, résister, offrir de la résistance (**to,** à); **to offer no r.**, n'offrir *ou* n'opposer aucune résistance; **she made no r.**, elle s'est laissé faire; **to meet with no r.**, ne rencontrer aucune résistance; **to have no r. left,** (*to illness etc*) ne plus avoir de résistance; *Fig* **to take the line of least r.**, aller au plus facile, suivre la loi du moindre effort; *Pol etc* **r. (movement),** résistance; **r. fighter,** résistant, -ante; **(b)** *El Phys etc* résistance *f*; **r. coupling,** couplage par résistance; **r. thermometer,** thermomètre *m* à résistance; **r. welding,** soudure *f* électrique par résistance.

resistant [rɪ'zɪstənt] *adj* résistant (**to,** à); **to be r. to change,** (*of person*) s'opposer à *ou* ne pas aimer les changements; *Med* **r. to,** rebelle à.

-resistant [rɪ'zɪstənt] *suff* **corrosion/heat/***etc***-r.**, résistant à la corrosion/la chaleur/*etc*.

resistor [rɪ'zɪstər] *n El* résistance *f*.

resit[1] ['riːsɪt] *n Univ F* (*exam*) **the resits are scheduled for August,** la session de rattrapage est prévue pour le mois d'août; **how many resits do you have?**, combien d'u.v. *ou* d'unités de valeur est-ce que tu as à repasser?

resit[2] [riː'sɪt] *vt* (*pt & pp* **resat** [riː'sæt]; *prp* **resitting**) repasser (*un examen*); **to r. one's driving test,** repasser le permis de conduire.

resolute ['rezəluːt] *adj* (*person*) résolu, déterminé;

(*answer, voice*) résolu, ferme; (*refusal, opposition*) ferme.

resolutely ['rezəlu:tlɪ] *adv* (*to refuse, say etc*) résolument.

resoluteness ['rezəlu:tnɪs] *n* (*of person*) résolution *f*, fermeté *f*.

resolution [rezə'lu:ʃən] *n* **(a)** (*of individual*) résolution *f*; **to make a r. to do sth,** prendre la résolution de *ou* se résoudre à faire qch; **have you made any New Year resolutions?,** est-ce que tu as pris de bonnes résolutions pour le nouvel an?; **to keep/break a New Year r.,** tenir/ne pas tenir une résolution prise à l'occasion du nouvel an;
(b) (*of committee, meeting etc*) résolution *f*; **to put a r. to the meeting,** soumettre *ou* proposer une résolution à l'assemblée; **to pass** *or* **carry** *or* **adopt a r.,** adopter une résolution; **the committee passed a r. that he should be expelled** *or* **to expel him,** le comité a adopté la résolution de l'expulser; **all those in favour of the r.,** tous ceux qui sont en faveur de la résolution; **the r. was rejected,** la résolution a été refusée;
(c) (*firmness*) résolution *f*, fermeté *f*; **her r. was strengthened by their refusal,** sa résolution s'est trouvée renforcée par leur refus; **there was a note of r. in his voice,** il y avait une pointe de détermination dans sa voix;
(d) (*solving*) (*of difficulty, problem etc*) résolution *f*;
(e) *Med* (*of tumour*) résolution *f*;
(f) *TV* définition *f*; **high r. screen,** écran *m* à haute définition.

resolve[1] [rɪ'zɒlv] *n* **(a)** = **RESOLUTION (a)**; **(b)** = **RESOLUTION (c)**.

resolve[2] **1** *vt* **(a)** (*of individual*) se résoudre à, prendre la résolution de (*partir*); **to be resolved to do sth,** être résolu *ou* décidé à faire qch; **(b)** (*of committee etc*) résoudre de, adopter la résolution de, décider de (*poursuivre une enquête*); **the committee has resolved that ...,** le comité a décidé que ...; **(c)** résoudre (*un problème, une difficulté*); trouver la solution à (*une crise, une situation*); **(d)** *Ch* résoudre (*qch*) en ses éléments; **to r. itself,** (*of substance*) se résoudre; **the House resolved itself into a committee,** la Chambre s'est constituée en commission. **2** *vi* **(a)** (*of person*) **to r. (up)on/against doing,** décider de *ou* se résoudre à faire/ne pas faire; **(b)** (*of chemical etc*) se résoudre (**into,** en); **(c)** (*of tumour*) se résoudre, se résorber.

resolving [rɪ'zɒlvɪŋ] *n* **r. power,** (*of lens*) pouvoir *m* de résolution.

resonance ['rez(ə)nəns] *n* (*of instrument*) *& Electron* résonance *f*; (*of voice*) sonorité *f*; *Electron* **r. curve,** courbe *f* de résonance.

resonant ['rezənənt] *adj* (*sound, room etc*) *& Electron* résonnant; (*voice, room*) sonore; **to be r. with,** résonner de; *Electron* **r. frequency,** fréquence *f* de résonance.

resonate ['rezəneɪt] *vi* résonner, retentir (**with,** de); **his voice resonated with emotion,** sa voix vibrait d'émotion.

resonator ['rezəneɪtər] *n Electron etc* résonateur *m*.

resort[1] [rɪ'zɔ:t] *n* **(a)** (*recourse*) recours *m* (**to,** à); (*person resorted to*) recours *m*, ressource *f*; **in the** *or* **as a last r.,** en dernier recours *ou* ressort, en désespoir de cause; **she would be my last r.,** elle serait ma dernière ressource *ou* mon dernier recours; **without r. to,** sans avoir recours à, sans recourir à; **(b) (holiday) r.,** lieu *m* de vacances; **health r.,** station *f* climatique *ou* thermale; **ski r.,** station de ski; **(c)** (*haunt*) lieu *m* de rendez-vous (**of,** pour), *Pej* repaire *m* (**of,** de).

resort[2] *vi* **to r. to,** avoir recours à, recourir à; **to r. to doing sth,** en venir à faire qch; **to r. to drink,** se rabattre sur la boisson; **to r. to violence,** avoir recours à *ou* user de la violence; **to r. to s.o. (for help),** avoir recours *ou* faire appel *ou* recourir à qn.

resound [rɪ'zaʊnd] *vi* (*of place*) résonner, retentir (**with,** de); (*of voice*) résonner; *Fig* (*of event*) avoir du retentissement.

resounding [rɪ'zaʊndɪŋ] *adj* (*applause, defeat, failure*) retentissant; (*laugh*) sonore; (*success, victory*) éclatant, retentissant; **her first novel was a r. success/failure,** son premier roman a connu un succès/échec retentissant.

resoundingly [rɪ'zaʊndɪŋlɪ] *adv* d'une manière retentissante; **to be r. successful,** (*of author, play etc*) connaître un succès retentissant.

resource[1] [rɪ'sɔ:s, -'zɔ:s] *n* **(a)** (*wealth*) **resources,** ressources *fpl*; **human resources,** ressources humaines; **(b)** (*expedient, recourse*) ressource *f*; **to be at the end of one's resources,** être au bout de ses *ou* à bout de ressources; **he was left to his own resources,** il a dû se débrouiller tout seul; *Am* **r. person,** (*contact*) contact *m*; **(c)** (*ingenuity*) ressource *f*; **person of r.,** personne *f* (pleine) de ressource(s).

resource[2] *vt* financer (*un projet*).

resourceful [rɪ'sɔ:sfʊl, -'zɔ:s-] *adj* (*person, scheme*) habile, ingénieux; (*person*) (plein) de ressources; **to be r.,** être plein de ressources, *F* être débrouillard.

resourcefully [rɪ'sɔ:sfəlɪ, -'zɔ:s-] *adv* habilement, ingénieusement.

resourcefulness [rɪ'sɔ:sfʊlnɪs, -'zɔ:s-] *n* (*of person, scheme*) ingéniosité *f*, habileté *f*.

resourcing [rɪ'sɔ:sɪŋ] *n Br* (*for project etc*) financement *m*; **r. officer,** agent *m* de financement.

respect[1] [rɪ'spekt] *n* **(a)** (*admiration*) respect *m* (**for,** pour); **to earn** *or* **gain** *or* **win s.o.'s r.,** gagner le respect de qn; **to have great r. for s.o., to hold s.o. in great r.,** avoir beaucoup de respect pour qn; **he knows how to command r.,** il sait se faire respecter; **her achievements command r.,** ses succès suscitent le respect;
(b) (*consideration*) respect *m* (**for,** pour); **to have r. for s.o.,** avoir *ou* témoigner du respect à *ou* envers *ou* pour qn; **she has little r. for the truth/other people's property,** elle fait peu de cas de la vérité/du bien d'autrui, elle a peu de respect pour la vérité/le bien d'autrui; **he took his hat off as a mark of r.,** il a ôté son chapeau en signe de respect; **in a tone of r.,** d'un ton respectueux; **he shows little r. for his parents,** il ne se montre guère respectueux envers ses parents; **show your father a little more r.!,** sois un peu plus respectueux *ou* montre un peu plus de respect à l'égard de *ou* envers ton père; **out of r. for ...,** par respect *ou* égard *ou* considération pour ...; **respects,** respects, hommages *mpl*; **(give** *or* **send) my respects to your mother,** (présentez *ou* envoyez) mes hommages à votre mère; **to pay one's respects to s.o.,** présenter ses respects *ou* ses hommages à qn; **to pay one's last respects,** (*at funeral etc*) faire ses adieux (**to,** à); **treat those plates with r.,** (*they are fragile*) fais attention à ces assiettes; **treat matches with r.,** (*they are dangerous*) utilisez les allumettes avec prudence; **treat mountains with r.,** soyez prudent en montagne; **with all due r. (to you),** sauf votre respect, sauf le respect que je vous dois, sans vouloir vous vexer *ou* offenser; **with the greatest r. to my colleague, I feel that her approach is wrong,** sans vouloir critiquer ma collègue, je pense que sa démarche n'est pas la bonne; **with the greatest r., sir, I cannot agree,** sans vouloir vous offenser, Monsieur, je ne suis pas d'accord;
(c) *esp Com* (*reference*) rapport *m*, égard *m*; **with r. to, in r. of,** en ce qui concerne, concernant;
(d) (*aspect*) rapport *m*, égard *m*; **in some** *or* **certain respects,** à certains égards; **in at least two respects,** à au moins deux égards; **in all respects** *or* **every r.,** sous tous les rapports, à tous (les) égards; **in this r.,** à cet égard, sous ce rapport; **in other respects,** sous d'autres rapports, à d'autres égards.

respect[2] *vt* **(a)** (*admire*) respecter, avoir du respect pour (*qn*) (**for,** pour); **he was greatly respected,** il était très respecté; **to be universally respected,** être respecté de tous; **(b)** (*show consideration for*) respecter (*qch*); **he respected my wish to be alone,** il a respecté mon désir d'être seul; **to r. s.o.'s opinion,** respecter l'opinion de qn; **I r. myself too much to do that,** je me respecte trop pour faire cela; **(c)** (*comply with*) respecter (*la loi*); **to r. the speed limit,** respecter la limite de vitesse.

respectability [rɪspektə'bɪlɪtɪ] *n* (*of person*) respectabilité *f*.

respectable [rɪ'spektəb(ə)l] *adj* **(a)** (*honourable, decent*) (*family, person etc*) respectable, digne de respect; (*upbringing, pub etc*) comme il faut; (*behaviour, clothes*) convenable, comme il faut; **he always looked so r.!,** il avait toujours l'air tellement comme il faut; **I'm not r., YOU answer the door,** va ouvrir, je ne suis pas dans une tenue convenable; **(b)** (*fairly good or large etc*) respectable; (*salary, mark, result*) honnête; **a r. number of people,** un bon nombre de gens; **a r. sum,** une somme respectable *ou* rondelette.

respectably [rɪ'spektəblɪ] *adv* de manière respectable; (*to behave, dress*) convenablement; (*brought up*) comme il faut; (*rather well*) plutôt bien.

respecter [rɪ'spektər] *n* **to be no r. of the law,** ne pas respecter la loi; **to be no r. of persons,** (*of death, taxes etc*) ne faire acception de personne; (*of person*) ne s'en laisser imposer par personne.

respectful [rɪ'spektfʊl] *adj* respectueux (**to, towards,** envers; **of,** de); **to stand at a r. distance,** se tenir à distance respectueuse.

respectfully [rɪ'spektfəlɪ] *adv* (*to listen, say etc*) respectueusement, avec respect; *Old-fashioned* **(I remain) yours r.,** veuillez agréer l'expression de mes sentiments respectueux.

respectfulness [rɪ'spektfəlnɪs] *n* (*of person*) respect *m*; (*of answer*) caractère respectueux.

respecting [rɪ'spektɪŋ] *prep* concernant, relatif à.

respective [rɪ'spektɪv] *adj* respectif.

respectively [rɪ'spektɪvlɪ] *adv* respectivement.

respiration [respɪ'reɪʃən] *n* respiration *f*.

respirator ['respɪreɪtər] *n Med* respirateur *m*; (*gas mask*) masque *m* à gaz; **the baby's on a r.,** le bébé est sous respirateur.

respiratory [rɪ'spaɪərət(ə)rɪ, rɪ'spɪrɪt(ə)rɪ] *adj* (*disease, organ, system*) respiratoire; **r. failure,** insuffisance *f* respiratoire.

respire [rɪ'spaɪər] *vt & vi* respirer.

respite ['respaɪt] *n* **(a)** (*from worry etc*) répit *m*; (*rest*) relâche *mf*; **to work without r.,** travailler sans relâche; **the weekend was a welcome r.,** le weekend a constitué un répit bienvenu; **(b)** (*from obligation*) sursis *m*, délai *m*; **to get/grant a r.,** obtenir/accorder un délai.

resplendence [rɪ'splendəns] *n Fml* splendeur *f*, resplendissement *m*.

resplendent [rɪ'splendənt] *adj Fml* resplendissant, éblouissant.

resplendently [rɪ'splendəntlɪ] *adv* de manière resplendissante *ou* éblouissante.

respond [rɪ'spɒnd] *vi* **(a)** (*answer*) répondre, faire une réponse (**to,** à); *Rel* réciter *ou* chanter les répons; **(b)** (*react*) (*to affection, kindness etc*) répondre, être sensible (**to,** à); (*to order*) répondre, réagir (**to,** à); **he responded with a smile,** il a répondu par un sourire; **to fail to r. to s.o.'s advances,** ne pas répondre aux avances de qn; **to r. generously to an appeal,** répondre généreusement à un appel; *Fig* **to r. to pressure,** réagir à la pression; *Med* **to r. to treatment,** (*of patient*) réagir positivement au traitement; *Med* **she is not responding,** elle ne réagit pas; *Av Aut* **to r. well,** répondre bien; *Aut Av* **to r. to the controls,** obéir aux commandes.

respondent [rɪ'spɒndənt] *n* **(a)** *Jur* (*esp in divorce case*) défendeur, -eresse; (*in appeal case*) intimé, -ée; **(b)** (*in opinion poll*) personne interrogée *ou* sondée; **the respondents,** les sondés.

response [rɪ'spɒns] *n* **(a)** (*answer*) réponse *f*, réplique *f*; *Rel* répons *m*; **he made no r.,** il n'a fait aucune réponse; *Rel* **to make the responses at Mass,** répondre la messe; **what was her r.?,** (*answer*) quelle a été sa réponse?; (*reaction*) quelle a été sa réaction?; **he smiled in r.,** il a souri en guise de réponse; **in r. to your question,** en réponse à votre question, pour répondre à votre question; **(b)** (*reaction*) *Med* réaction *f*; *Physiol* réponse *f*, réaction; **the appeal met with a generous r.,** on a répondu généreusement à l'appel; **the decision was taken in r. to ...,** la décision a été prise en *ou* par réaction à ...; *Mil* **flexible r.,** réponse graduée; **r. time,** temps *m* de réponse.

responsibility [rɪspɒnsɪ'bɪlɪtɪ] *n* **(a)** (*authority*) responsabilité *f*; **sense of r.,** sens *m* des responsabilités; **to assume** *or* **accept a r.,** accepter une responsabilité; **to do sth on one's own r.,** faire qch sous sa (propre) responsabilité *ou* de son (propre) chef;

(b) (*blame*) responsabilité *f*; **to take** *or* **accept full r. for sth,** prendre *ou* accepter la responsabilité de qch; **we accept no r. for lost or stolen items,** (*notice in restaurant etc*) nous déclinons toute responsabilité pour les objets perdus ou volés; **to refuse to accept any** *or Fml* **to disclaim all r. for the accident,** décliner toute responsabilité au sujet de l'accident; **no-one has yet claimed r. for the attack,** personne n'a encore revendiqué l'attaque; **the r. is mine,** c'est moi qui suis responsable;

(c) (*obligation*) responsabilité *f*; **you have a r. to your family,** vous avez une responsabilité envers votre famille;

(d) (*task*) responsabilité *f*; **his new responsibilities give him no time for leisure,** ses nouvelles fonctions *ou* responsabilités ne lui laissent pas de loisirs; **answering the phone is your r., not mine,** c'est ta responsabilité de répondre au téléphone, pas la mienne; **it's my r.,** c'est ma responsabilité (**to do,** de faire); **bringing up children is quite a r.,** élever des enfants est une grande responsabilité.

responsible [rɪ'spɒnsɪb(ə)l] *adj* **(a)** (*trustworthy*) sérieux; (*sensible*) responsable; **r. job,** poste *m* à responsabilités; **no r. parent would have left the children alone,** un parent responsable n'aurait pas laissé les enfants tout seuls; **try to be a bit more r. in future,** essaye d'être un peu plus responsable à l'avenir;

(b) (*for accident, mistake etc*) responsable (**for,** de); **to hold s.o. r.,** tenir qn (pour) responsable (**for,** de); *Jur* **to be r. for s.o.'s actions,** être solidaire des actes de qn; **he is not r. for his actions,** il n'est pas responsable de ses actes;

(c) (*accountable*) chargé (**for,** de; **to s.o.,** devant qn); **you and she will be jointly r. for the project,** vous et elle partagerez la responsabilité du projet; **to make s.o. r. for sth,** donner à qn la responsabilité de qch; **to be r. for s.o./sth,** avoir la responsabilité de qn/qch; **to be r. to s.o.,** (*be junior to in rank*) relever de qn; **I will be r. for his safety,** je me porte garant de sa sécurité.

responsibly [rɪ'spɒnsɪblɪ] *adv* (*to behave, act*) de façon responsable, avec sérieux.

responsive [rɪ'spɒnsɪv] *adj* (*reacting*) qui réagit bien; (*alert*) éveillé; (*attentive*) qui fait attention; *Med* (*illness, virus etc*) qui réagit bien (**to,** à); *Aut* (*brakes, steering etc*) qui répond bien; **r. to,** (*kindness*) sensible à; (*idea, suggestion*) réceptif à; **he is very r. to my needs,** il est très attentif à mes besoins; **to be r. to sth,** (*of person*) être sensible à qch; **they're not very r. tonight,** (*of audience*) il n'y a pas grand-chose à en tirer ce soir.

responsiveness [rɪ'spɒnsɪvnɪs] *n* (*of person*) (*to kindness*) sensibilité *f* (**to,** à); (*to idea etc*) réceptivité *f*; (*of illness etc*) (bonne) réaction *f*.

respray[1] ['riːspreɪ] *n* **the car's had a r.,** la voiture a été repeinte.

respray[2] [riː'spreɪ] *vt* repeindre (*qch*) au pistolet.

rest[1] [rest] *n* **(a)** (*repose*) repos *m*; **to have** *or* **take a r.,** prendre du repos, se reposer (**from,** de); **to have a good night's r.,** passer une bonne nuit; **I need a r.,** j'ai besoin de me reposer, j'ai besoin de repos; **my arms need a r.,** j'ai besoin de me reposer les bras; **we've earned a r.,** nous avons mérité un peu de repos; **to stop for a r.,** faire une pause; **at r.,** au repos, en repos; **to put** *or* **set s.o.'s mind at r.,** calmer *ou* tranquilliser l'esprit de qn, dissiper les craintes *ou* inquiétudes de qn; **to give s.o. a r. from sth,** permettre à qn de se reposer de qch; *F* **give it a r., will you!,** (*stop doing, talking etc*) laisse tomber *ou* arrête cinq minutes, tu veux bien!; *F* **give that music a r.!,** arrête un peu cette musique!; **give studying a r. for a day or two,** arrête d'étudier pendant un ou deux jours; **she's giving tennis a r. this year,** elle a arrêté le tennis cette année; **those children give her no r.,** ces enfants ne lui laissent aucun repos; **his conscience gave him no r.,** sa conscience ne lui laissait pas de répit; **you must get some more r.,** vous devez vous reposer davantage; **a day of r., a day's r.,** un jour de repos; **the day of r.,** le jour du Seigneur, le repos dominical; **to come to r.,** (*of ball etc*) s'arrêter, s'immobiliser; (*of bird, eyes*) se poser (**on,** sur); *Am Mil* **r. and recreation,** permission *f*; **two days r. and recreation,** deux jours de permission; *Euph* **to be laid to r.,** être enterré; *Euph* **to be** *or* **lie at r.,** reposer en paix; *Euph* **to lay s.o. to r.,** porter qn en terre, enterrer qn; *Fig* **to lay** *or* **put a plan/suggestion/project/***etc* **to r.,** (*terminate*) renoncer à *ou* abandonner un projet/une suggestion/*etc*; *Fig* **to lay** *or* **put allegations/doubts/suspicions to r.,** dissiper des allégations/des doutes/des suspicions; *Am* **r. room,** toilettes *fpl*; *Am* **r. stop,** *Austr* **r. area,** aire *f* de repos; *Am* **to make a r. stop,** faire une pause pour se détendre;

(b) (*support*) support *m*; (*for arm*) accoudoir *m*; (*for head*) appui(e)-tête *m*, *pl* appuis-tête, appuie-tête, reposetête *m inv*; (*for feet*) repose-pieds *m inv*; (*for billiard cue*) chevalet *m*; (*for telephone receiver*) étrier *m*; (*for knife*) porte-couteau *m*, *pl* porte-couteau(x); (*for telescope*) trépied *m*;

(c) *Mus* (*silence*) pause *f*, silence *m*.

rest[2] **1** *vi* **(a)** (*relax*) se reposer, prendre du repos; **you need to r. (up),** il vous faut le repos complet; **to r. from one's work,** se reposer de son travail; **to feel rested,** se sentir (bien) reposé *ou* frais et dispos; **to be resting,** (*of actor*) = se trouver sans engagement; (*of field*) être en jachère; **she is resting comfortably,** (*after operation etc*) son état est satisfaisant; **I won't r. until ...,** je n'aurai de repos que ... + *sub*; **to r. on,** (*of argument, fame, roof etc*) reposer sur; **he was resting on his shovel,** il s'appuyait sur sa pelle; *Fig* **to r. on one's oars,** se reposer, *F* souffler;

(b) (*be buried*) être enterré, reposer; **may they r. in peace!,** qu'ils reposent en paix!; **r. in peace,** (*inscription on gravestone*) repose en paix;

(c) (*remain*) **there the matter rests,** l'affaire en reste *ou* en est là; **I won't let it r. at that,** cela ne se passera pas ainsi; **let it r.!,** n'en parlons plus!; **can't we let it r.?,** (*stop talking about it*) est-ce que nous pouvons laisser tomber la question?; **r. assured,** soyez assuré (**that,** que); **a heavy responsibility rests (up)on them,** une lourde responsabilité pèse sur eux; **to r. with,** (*of decision, responsibility etc*) incomber à; **it rests with you to ...,** il vous incombe de ...;

(d) *Jur* **the defence/prosecution rests,** = plaise au tribunal d'adopter mes conclusions.

2 *vt* **(a)** (*repose*) reposer, faire reposer (*qn*); **to r. one's men/horses/***etc*, faire *ou* laisser reposer ses hommes/chevaux/*etc*; **to r. one's eyes/legs/***etc*, se reposer les yeux/les jambes/*etc*; *Agr* **to r. a field,** mettre un champ en jachère; **(God) r. his soul!,** Dieu donne le repos à son âme!;

(b) (*lean*) appuyer (*ses coudes*) (**on,** sur); reposer (*la tête*) (**on,** sur);

(c) (*base*) fonder (*un argument, une théorie*) (**on,** sur);

(d) *esp Am Jur* **to r. one's case,** conclure son plaidoyer; *Fig* **I r. my case,** j'ai dit ce que j'avais à dire.

rest³ *n* (*remainder*) reste *m*, restant *m* (**of,** de); **where's the r. of it?,** (*of money, food*) où est le reste *ou* le restant?; **I'm keeping the r. of it for tomorrow,** je garde le reste *ou* le restant pour demain; **do you want to watch the r. of the news?,** est-ce que tu veux regarder le reste des actualités?; **(as) for the r.,** quant au reste, pour le reste; **and (all) the r. of it,** et tout le reste; **the r.,** (*others*) les autres *mfpl*; **the r. of us,** nous autres; les autres (d'entre nous); **the r. of the men/***etc*, les autres hommes/*etc*; **it's just another day like all the r.,** c'est un jour comme tous les autres.

restart [riːˈstɑːt] **1** *vt* recommencer, reprendre (*un travail etc*); (re)mettre (*une machine*) en marche; relancer (*un moteur*). **2** *vi* (*of job etc*) recommencer, reprendre; (*of machine*) se remettre en marche.

restate [riːˈsteɪt] *vt* **(a)** (*repeat*) exposer de nouveau (*une théorie, un point de vue*); *Mus* reprendre (*un thème*); **(b)** (*rephrase*) formuler de nouveau (*une question*).

restatement [riːˈsteɪtmənt] *n* (*of theory, viewpoint*) nouvel exposé; (*of question*) nouvelle formulation.

restaurant [ˈrestrɒnt] *n* restaurant *m*; **r. manager/***etc*, gérant *m/etc* de restaurant; *Br Rail* **r. car,** wagon-restaurant *m*, *pl* wagons-restaurants; **r. supply shop** *or* **store,** magasin *m* de fournitures pour restaurants.

restaurateur [restərəˈtɜːr] *n* restaurateur, -trice.

rest-cure [ˈrestkjʊər] *n* cure *f* de repos; *Fig* **this job is no r.-c.,** ce travail n'est pas une sinécure.

rest-day [ˈrestdeɪ] *n* (*of cricketer, tennis player etc*) jour *m* de repos; (*of shift worker*) jour de congé.

restful [ˈrestfʊl] *adj* (*holiday, weekend, place etc*) reposant, tranquille; **Paris is not the most r. of places,** Paris n'est pas l'endroit le plus reposant qu'on puisse imaginer; **r. to the eyes,** (*colour, lighting*) qui repose les yeux, reposant pour la vue.

restfully [ˈrestfəlɪ] *adv* (*to spend time*) paisiblement, tranquillement.

rest-home [ˈresthəʊm] *n* (*for convalescents*) maison *f* de repos; (*for elderly*) hospice *m*; **to go into a r.-h.,** aller à l'hospice; **to put s.o. in a r.-h.,** mettre qn à l'hospice.

resting [ˈrestɪŋ] *n* **r. place,** (lieu *m* de) repos *m*; **last r. place,** dernière demeure.

restitution [restɪˈtjuːʃən] *n* (*of stolen property*) restitution *f*; (*compensation*) réparation *f*; **to make r. of sth,** (*give back*) restituer qch; **to make r. for sth,** (*compensate for*) verser une compensation pour qch; **he should make full r.,** il devrait verser une compensation intégrale.

restive [ˈrestɪv] *adj* (*nervous*) agité; (*apt to rebel*) rétif.

restiveness [ˈrestɪvnɪs] *n* (*of horse*) nature rétive; (*of person, child*) indocilité *f*, nature récalcitrante; (*of crowd*) agitation *f*.

restless [ˈrestlɪs] *adj* (*person*) nerveux, agité; (*child*) agité, remuant; (*sea*) agité; (*wind*) incessant; **to be r. in one's sleep** *or* **a r. sleeper,** avoir le sommeil agité *ou* troublé; **I've had** *or* **spent a r. night,** j'ai passé une nuit agitée; **r. mind,** esprit agité; **she's feeling a bit r.,** (*in present job, situation etc*) elle a envie de voir *ou* de faire autre chose; **the audience was getting r.,** l'auditoire s'impatientait.

restlessly [ˈrestlɪslɪ] *adv* (*to move*) (*of person, sea*) avec agitation; (*of wind*) incessamment.

restlessness [ˈrestlɪsnɪs] *n* (*of person*) inquiétude *f*, agitation *f*; (*of mind*) nervosité *f*, état fiévreux; (*of sea*) agitation *f*; (*of wind*) mouvement incessant; (*of audience*) impatience *f*.

restock [riːˈstɒk] **1** *vt* réapprovisionner (*un rayon, un magasin*) (**with,** en); refaire le plein de (*un congélateur*). **2** *vi* (*of shop*) se réapprovisionner.

restoration [restəˈreɪʃən] *n* **(a)** (*of monument, building, furniture etc*) restauration *f*; **r. fund/project/work/***etc*, caisse *f*/projet *m*/travail *m/etc* de restauration; **(b)** (*of communications, law and order, health*) rétablissement *m*; **(c)** (*of lost property*) remise *f*; (*of fortune*) relèvement *m*; (*of dynasty*) restauration *f*, rétablissement *m* sur le trône; *Br Hist* **the R.,** la Restauration; **R. comedy/literature/poetry/***etc*, comédie *f*/littérature *f*/poésie *f/etc* de (l'époque de) la Restauration.

restorative [rɪˈstɔːrətɪv, -ˈstɒr-] **1** *n* (*food*) fortifiant *m*, reconstituant *m*; (*medicine*) cordial *m*. **2** *adj* **the r. powers of sleep,** les pouvoirs reconstituants du sommeil.

restore [rɪˈstɔːr] *vt* **(a)** restaurer (*un monument, un bâtiment, un meuble etc*); **to r. sth to its former glory,** rendre son ancienne gloire à qch; *Fig* **to r. one's reputation,** se refaire une réputation; **(b)** (*bring back*) rétablir (*l'ordre, la paix etc*); faire renaître (*le calme, la confiance*); restaurer (*la paix, la discipline, une dynastie*); **order is being restored,** l'ordre est en cours de rétablissement; **to r. s.o. to health,** rétablir la santé de qn; **I feel quite restored,** je me sens remis sur pied; **to r. s.o. to life,** ramener qn à la vie; **to r. s.o.'s strength,** redonner des forces à qn; **to r. the circulation,** réactiver la circulation; **(c)** (*give back*) restituer, rendre (*qch*); **to r. sth to s.o.,** rendre qch à qn; **to r. sth to its place/former condition,** remettre qch en place/en état; **to r. s.o.'s sight/hearing,** rendre la vue/l'ouïe à qn.

restorer [rɪˈstɔːrər] *n* **(a)** (*of building, picture etc*) restaurateur, -trice; **(b)** (*for hair*) régénérateur *m* capillaire.

restrain [rɪˈstreɪn] *vt* retenir, empêcher (*qn*) (**from,** de); refréner (*ses passions*); retenir, contenir (*une foule*); retenir (*un chien*); contenir, refouler (*sa colère, ses larmes*); retenir (*ses larmes, sa curiosité*); **to r. oneself,** se maîtriser, se contenir; **he had to be forcibly restrained,** il a fallu le retenir de force; **to r. s.o.'s activities,** mettre un frein aux activités de qn.

restrained [rɪˈstreɪnd] *adj* (*feelings*) contenu; (*tone, terms*) mesuré; (*style*) sobre; (*silence*) prudent; (*response*) mitigé; **her manner was very r.,** son attitude était très réservée.

restraining [rɪˈstreɪnɪŋ] *adj* (*influence*) modérateur; *Jur* qui retient, restrictif.

restraint [rɪˈstreɪnt] *n* **(a)** (*moderation*) (*of person*) mesure *f*; (*of style*) sobriété *f*; **lack of r.,** manque *m* de mesure; **to throw aside all r.,** ne garder aucune mesure; **to show** *or* **exercise great r.,** faire preuve d'une grande mesure; **to urge r.,** demander instamment qu'on fasse preuve de mesure (**in doing,** dans); **(b)** (*restriction*) contrainte *f*, restriction *f*; (*of mental patient*) contention *f*; (*of powers, wages*) limitation *f*; **to put a r. on s.o.,** contraindre qn; **to break free of all r.,** se donner libre cours; **to be under no r.,** avoir ses coudées franches; **without r.,** (*to laugh etc*) sans contrainte; **to impose restraints,** imposer des restrictions (**on,** sur); **r. of trade,** restrictions du commerce.

restrict [rɪˈstrɪkt] *vt* restreindre, limiter (*la vitesse etc*) (**to,** à); **to r. oneself to ...,** se limiter à ...; **he is restricted to one glass of wine a day,** on ne lui permet qu'un verre de vin par jour; **fog is restricting visibility,** le brouillard limite la visibilité; **membership is restricted to the over-20s,** la qualité de membre est réservée aux personnes âgées de plus de 20 ans.

restricted [rɪˈstrɪktɪd] *adj* (*sense, space, use*) restreint; (*sale*) contrôlé; **r. access,** (*notice on factory gate etc*) accès réservé; **restricted area,** *Aut* zone à vitesse limitée; *Admin Mil* zone interdite; *Admin* **r. document,** document secret; **to be on a r. diet,** suivre un régime sévère *ou* strict; **she feels less r. wearing trousers,** elle se sent plus libre (de ses mouvements) lorsqu'elle porte un pantalon.

restriction [rɪˈstrɪkʃən] *n* restriction *f*; (*of speed etc*) limitation *f*; **to place** *or* **set restrictions on sth,** apporter des restrictions à qch.

restrictive [rɪˈstrɪktɪv] *adj* (*clause, measure etc*) restrictif; *Br Ind* **r. practices,** pratiques restrictives.

restring [riːˈstrɪŋ] *vt* (*pt & pp* **restrung** [riːˈstrʌŋ]) enfiler de nouveau (*des perles*); remonter (*un violon*); recorder (*une raquette*).

restructure [riːˈstrʌktʃər] *vt* restructurer (*une société, l'industrie, l'économie*).

restructuring [riːˈstrʌktʃərɪŋ] *n* (*of company etc*) restructuration *f*.

result¹ [rɪˈzʌlt] *n* **(a)** (*of action, behaviour etc*) & *Math* résultat *m* (**of,** de); **the r. is that ...,** il en résulte que ...; **to yield** *or* **show results,** donner des résultats; **as a r. of,** par suite de; **without r.,** sans résultat; **results,** (*of exam etc*) résultats; **I made some jam, with disastrous results,** j'ai fait des confitures et j'ai obtenu des résultats désastreux; **this paint gives excellent results,** cette peinture donne d'excellents résultats; **to be a** *or* **the r. of sth,** résulter *ou* être le résultat de qch; **with the r. that, as a r.,** en conséquence; **to have little or no r.,** avoir peu ou pas de résultat; **she knows how to get results,** elle sait comment s'y prendre pour obtenir ce qu'elle veut; **what was the r.?,** (*of soccer match*) quel était le résultat?; **end r.,** résultat final; **(b)** *Br F* (*win, in soccer etc*) victoire *f*; **we need a r.,** il faut qu'on fasse quelque chose.

result² *vi* résulter, découler (**from,** de); **it results from this that ...,** il s'ensuit que ...; **consequences resulting from,** conséquences découlant de; **to r. in,** entraîner, avoir pour résultat *ou* conséquence de; **this will r. in unpleasantness,** cela entraînera des désagréments.

resultant [rɪ'zʌltənt] **1** *adj* résultant; **the r. economic benefits,** les avantages économiques qui en résultent. **2** *n* résultante *f*.

resume [rɪ'zjuːm] **1** *vt* reprendre, renouer (*des relations*); (*after short break*) continuer, poursuivre (*un discours, des négociations, des discussions, un voyage*); **to r. one's seat,** reprendre sa place, se rasseoir; **to r. doing sth,** se remettre à faire qch; **to r. work,** se remettre au travail; **to r. one's duties,** reprendre son service *ou* ses fonctions; **she resumed her maiden name,** elle a repris son nom de jeune fille. **2** *vi* (*of music, speaker etc*) continuer, reprendre; **we** *or* **the meeting will r. after lunch,** nous reprendrons *ou* la réunion reprendra après le déjeuner; *Cr* **play resumed at four,** le match a repris à quatre heures.

résumé [reɪ'zjuːmeɪ, -uːmeɪ] *n* **(a)** *Br* (*summary*) résumé *m*, abrégé *m*; **for a r. of the situation, here is our foreign affairs correspondent,** voici notre correspondant dans le domaine des affaires étrangères, qui nous donne un résumé de la situation; **to give a r. of sth,** faire un résumé de qch; **(b)** *Am* (*curriculum vitae*) curriculum (vitae) *m inv*.

resumption [rɪ'zʌmpʃən] *n* (*of relationship, negotiations etc*) reprise *f*.

resurface [riː'sɜːfɪs] **1** *vt* refaire le revêtement de (*une route*). **2** *vi* (*of submarine*) revenir à la surface; *Hum* **when did he eventually r.?,** quand est-ce qu'il a fini par refaire surface?

resurgence [rɪ'sɜːdʒəns] *n* (*of nationalism, trend*) réapparition *f*, renouveau *m*; (*of disease*) réapparition; (*of idea, ideology etc*) résurrection *f*; (*of company etc*) reprise *f*.

resurgent [rɪ'sɜːdʒənt] *adj* (*idea, nationalism etc*) renaissant; (*company etc*) qui connaît une reprise.

resurrect [rezə'rekt] *vt* ressusciter (*les morts, une mode*); faire revivre (*une époque*); réveiller (*une querelle, une dispute*).

resurrection [rezə'rekʃən] *n* (*of the dead*) *& Fig* résurrection *f*; (*of argument*) réveil *m*; **the R.,** la résurrection du Christ.

resuscitate [rɪ'sʌsɪteɪt] *vt* ranimer, ressusciter (*qn*).

resuscitation [rɪsʌsɪ'teɪʃən] *n* réanimation *f*, ranimation *f*; **all attempts at r. failed,** toutes les tentatives de réanimation ont échoué.

resuscitator [rɪ'sʌsɪteɪtər] *n* (*machine*) appareil *m* de réanimation.

retail¹ ['riːteɪl] *n Com* (vente *f* au) détail *m*; **to buy/sell goods r.** *or Am* **at r.,** acheter/vendre des marchandises au détail; **wholesale and r. business,** commerce *m* en gros et au détail; **r. price/trade/***etc*, prix *m*/commerce/*etc* de détail; **r. dealer,** détaillant *m*; **r. outlet,** magasin *m* de détail; **r. chain,** chaîne *f* de vente au détail; **r. customer,** client, -ente qui achète au détail; **r. price index,** indice *m* des prix de détail; **r. sales,** vente *f* au détail.

retail² **1** *vt* **(a)** détailler, vendre au détail (*des marchandises*); **(b)** (*spread*) colporter (*un potin*). **2** *vi* (*of goods*) se vendre au détail, se détailler (**at, for,** à).

retailer ['riːteɪlər] *n* marchand, -ande au détail, détaillant, -ante.

retain [rɪ'teɪn] *vt* **(a)** (*keep*) conserver, garder (*un bien, le contrôle etc*); conserver (*une coutume, la chaleur etc*); **to r. the power to do,** se réserver le droit de faire; **(b)** *Old-fashioned* (*employ*) prendre (*qn*) à son service; **to r. s.o.'s services,** s'assurer les services de qn; *Br Jur* **to r. a barrister** *or* **counsel,** retenir un avocat (à l'avance); *Jur* **retaining fee,** avance *f*, provision *f*; **(c)** (*hold in place*) retenir, maintenir (*qch*); *Constr* **retaining wall,** mur *m* de soutènement *ou* de retenue; **(d)** (*remember*) garder (*qch*) en mémoire.

retainer [rɪ'teɪnər] *n* **(a)** (*fee*) avance *f*, provision *f*; **to pay s.o. a r.,** verser une provision à qn; **(b)** *Old-fashioned* (*servant*) serviteur *m*.

retake¹ ['riːteɪk] *n* **(a)** *Cin TV* reprise *f*; **(b)** *esp Univ* (*exam*) nouveau passage; (*candidate*) candidat *m* qui repasse un examen.

retake² [riː'teɪk] *vt* (*pt* **retook** [riː'tʊk]; *pp* **retaken** [riː'teɪk(ə)n]) **(a)** *Cin TV* refaire, filmer à nouveau (*un plan*); **(b)** *esp Univ* repasser (*un examen*); **(c)** reprendre (*une place forte etc*); rattraper (*un prisonnier etc*).

retaliate [rɪ'tælɪeɪt] *vi* riposter, rendre la pareille; (*in speech*) riposter; *esp Mil* user de représailles (**with,** par); **to r. for an attack,** riposter à une attaque (**by doing,** en faisant).

retaliation [rɪtælɪ'eɪʃən] *n* riposte *f*, revanche *f*, représailles *fpl* (**against,** contre); **r. for the attack,** les représailles contre l'attaque; **in r.,** par mesure de représailles; **in r. for,** en représailles de.

retaliatory [rɪ'tælɪət(ə)rɪ] *adj* **r. measures,** représailles *fpl*; *Econ* mesures *fpl* de rétorsion; **r. weapons,** armes *fpl* de représailles.

retard¹ ['riːtɑːd] *n F Pej* demeuré *m*.

retard² [rɪ'tɑːd] *vt* retarder la croissance *ou* le développement de; **to be severely (mentally) retarded,** être très attardé; **mentally retarded person,** (personne) attardé(e), arriéré(e); **the retarded,** (*used as pl*) les attardés *mpl*, les arriérés *mpl*.

-retardant [rɪ'tɑːdənt] *suff* **heat/flame/***etc***-r.,** qui ralentit la propagation de la chaleur/des flammes/*etc*.

retardation [riːtɑː'deɪʃən] *n* (*of growth*) retard *m*; (*of mechanism*) retardement *m*; **(mental) r.,** arriération *f*.

retch [retʃ] *vi* avoir des haut-le-cœur *ou* la nausée; *Fig* **to make s.o. r.,** donner des haut-le-cœur *ou* la nausée à qn.

retching [retʃɪŋ] *n* haut-le-cœur *mpl*; **r. noises were coming from the bathroom,** on entendait quelqu'un qui avait des haut-le-cœur dans la salle de bain.

retd *abbr* **retired.**

retell [riː'tel] *vt* (*pt & pp* **retold** [riː'təʊld]) raconter (*une histoire, un conte*) de nouveau.

retention [rɪ'tenʃən] *n Med* (*of urine etc*) rétention *f*; (*of custom, weapon etc*) conservation *f*; (*of authority*) maintien *m*; (*of fact, impression etc*) mémoire *f*; **to have limited powers of r.,** avoir peu de mémoire; **to have great powers of r.,** avoir une excellente mémoire.

retentive [rɪ'tentɪv] *adj* (*memory*) tenace, fidèle.

retentiveness [rɪ'tentɪvnɪs] *n* (*of memory*) fidélité *f*, ténacité *f*.

rethink¹ ['riːθɪŋk] *n* **to have a r. (on sth),** repenser *ou* reconsidérer (qch); **the plan needs a complete r.,** le projet doit être complètement repensé.

rethink² [riː'θɪŋk] *vt* (*pt & pp* **rethought** [-'θɔːt]) repenser, reconsidérer (*une question, un projet*).

reticence ['retɪsəns] *n* réticence *f*; **without any r.,** sans réticence(s).

reticent ['retɪsənt] *adj* peu communicatif, taciturne; **to be r. about sth,** ne pas vouloir parler de qch, faire mystère de qch.

reticently ['retɪsəntlɪ] *adv* avec réticence *ou* réserve.

reticle ['retɪk(ə)l] *n Opt* réticule *m*.

reticular [rɪ'tɪkjʊlər], **reticulate(d)** [rɪ'tɪkjʊlət, -leɪtɪd] *adj esp Biol* réticulé.

reticulation [rɪtɪkjʊ'leɪʃən] *n esp Biol* réticulation *f*.

reticule ['retɪkjuːl] *n* **(a)** *Opt* réticule *m*; **(b)** *Old-fashioned* (*bag*) réticule *m*.

retina, *pl* **-as, -ae** ['retɪnə, -əz, -iː] *n* (*of eye*) rétine *f*.

retinal ['retɪnəl] *adj* (*image etc*) rétinien.

retinue ['retɪnjuː] *n* (*of prince etc*) *& Hum* suite *f*.

retire [rɪ'taɪər] **1** *vi* **(a)** (*of employee*) prendre la retraite; **to r. from a company,** prendre sa retraite d'une société; **to r. from teaching,** prendre sa retraite de l'enseignement; **when I r.,** quand je prendrai ma retraite; **to r. early,** prendre une retraite anticipée; **to have retired,** être à la retraite; **(b)** (*withdraw*) se retirer (**to,** dans, à; **from,** de); (*of troops*) reculer, se replier (**to,** vers); (*from match, competition etc*) se retirer, abandonner; **to r. into oneself,** rentrer en soi-même; *Fml* **to r. from the room,** quitter la pièce; *Fml* **to r. (to bed, for the night),** (aller) se coucher; **to r. from boxing/the race,** abandonner la boxe/la course. **2** *vt* **(a)** mettre (*qn*) à la retraite; **(b)** *Mil* replier (*les troupes*); *Sp* (*from race etc*) retirer (*un athlète*).

retired [rɪ'taɪəd] *adj* **(a)** (*police officer, doctor etc*) retraité, à la retraite; **to be r.,** être à la retraite; **to put** *or* **place s.o. on the r. list,** mettre qn à la retraite; **Admiral John Smith, r.,** Amiral John Smith, retraité; **(b)** (*life*) retiré; (*place etc*) retiré, écarté.

retiree [rɪtaɪ'riː] *n US* retraité, -ée.

retirement [rɪ'taɪəmənt] *n* **(a)** (*from work, army etc*) retraite *f*; **on my retirement,** (*when I retire*) quand je serai à la retraite; (*when I retired*) quand j'ai pris ma retraite; **to take early r.,** prendre une retraite anticipée; **she's been offered early r.,** on lui a proposé de prendre *ou* de faire valoir ses droits à la *ou* une retraite anticipée; **to come out**

of r., reprendre sa carrière; **to live in r.**, (*no longer employed*) être à la retraite; (*quietly*) vivre retiré du monde; **compulsory r.**, retraite d'office; **r. age**, âge *m* de la retraite; **r. flat**, appartement *m* pour retraités; **r. lifestyle**, vie *f* de retraité; **r. pension**, (pension *f* de) retraite; **r. present**, cadeau *m* de départ en retraite; **(b)** (*withdrawal*) (*of troops*) retraite *f*, repli *m*; (*from match, competition etc*) abandon *m*.

retiring [rɪ'taɪərɪŋ] *adj* **(a)** (*reserved*) réservé; **to have** *or* **be of a r. nature**, avoir une *ou* être d'une nature réservée; **(b)** (*employee*) qui prend la retraite; (*elected official*) sortant; **r. age**, âge *m* de la retraite.

retool [riː'tuːl] **1** *vt* rééquiper (*une usine*); *Am F* réorganiser (*une société*). **2** *vi* (*of factory*) se rééquiper; *Am F* (*of company*) se réorganiser.

retort¹ [rɪ'tɔːt] *n* réplique *f* (**to**, à), riposte *f*; **to make a r.**, lancer une réplique.

retort² *vt & vi* répliquer, riposter.

retort³ *n Ch Ind* cornue *f*.

retouch [riː'tʌtʃ] *vt* retoucher (*une photographie etc*).

retouching [riː'tʌtʃɪŋ] *n* (*of photograph etc*) retouche *f*.

retrace [rɪ'treɪs] *vt* remonter à l'origine de (*qch*); reconstituer, retracer (*le passé*); **to r. one's steps**, revenir sur ses pas, rebrousser chemin; **to r. s.o.'s movements**, (*of police etc*) reconstituer les faits et gestes de qn.

retract [rɪ'trækt] **1** *vt* **(a)** rétracter (*ce qu'on a dit*); reprendre, revenir sur (*sa parole, une déclaration, une offre etc*); désavouer, rétracter (*une opinion etc*); **(b)** (*of animal*) rentrer (*ses griffes*); *Av* **to r. the undercarriage**, escamoter *ou* rentrer le train d'atterrissage. **2** *vi* **(a)** (*of person*) se rétracter; **(b)** (*of cat's claws*) rentrer; (*of undercarriage*) s'escamoter, rentrer; (*of handle*) s'escamoter.

retractable [rɪ'træktəb(ə)l] *adj Av* (*undercarriage*) rentrant, escamotable; (*handle etc*) escamotable; (*ballpoint pen*) à pointe rétractable.

retraction [rɪ'trækʃən] *n* **(a)** (*of word*) rétractation *f*; (*of opinion*) désaveu *m*, reniement *m*; **to publish a r.**, (*of newspaper*) publier un désaveu; **(b)** (*of claws etc*) rétraction *f*.

retrain [riː'treɪn] **1** *vt* recycler (*un employé*); *Med* rééduquer (*un muscle*). **2** *vi* (*of employee*) se recycler.

retraining [riː'treɪnɪŋ] *n* (*of person*) recyclage *m*; *Med* (*of muscle*) rééducation *f*.

retread¹ ['riːtred] *n Aut* (pneu *m*) rechapé *m*.

retread² [riː'tred] *vt Aut* rechaper (*un pneu*).

retreat¹ [rɪ'triːt] *n* **(a)** *Mil* retraite *f*; *Mil* **to sound/beat the r.**, sonner/battre la retraite; *Fig* **to beat a r.**, battre en retraite; **(b)** (*of flood waters*) retrait *m*, recul *m*; (*of glacier*) recul; **(c)** *Rel* retraite *f*; **to go into** *or* **on r.**, faire une retraite; **(d)** (*place*) abri *m*, retraite *f*, refuge *m*; (*of pirates etc*) repaire *m*; **a holiday/weekend r.**, une maison paisible pour les vacances/le week-end; **country r.**, une maison paisible à la campagne.

retreat² *vi* **(a)** *Mil* battre en retraite; (*of crowd, spectators etc*) reculer, se retirer, s'éloigner (**from**, de); *Fig* **to r. into a world of one's own**, s'isoler dans son petit monde (à soi); **to r. from the public eye**, se retirer du monde; **to r. a few hundred yards**, reculer de quelques centaines de mètres; **(b)** (*of flood waters, glacier*) reculer.

retrench [rɪ'trentʃ] **1** *vt* restreindre (*ses dépenses*); faire des coupures dans (*une œuvre littéraire*). **2** *vi* restreindre ses dépenses, faire des économies.

retrenchment [rɪ'trentʃmənt] *n* (*of expenditure*) réduction *f*; **policy of r.**, politique *f* d'économies.

retrial [riː'traɪ(ə)l] *n Jur* nouveau procès.

retribution [retrɪ'bjuːʃən] *n* châtiment *m*; **in r. for sth**, comme châtiment pour qch; **the Day of R.**, le jour du jugement; **just r. of** *or* **for a crime**, juste récompense *f* d'un crime.

retributive [rɪ'trɪbjʊtɪv] *adj* (*measure etc*) de châtiment, punitif.

retrievable [rɪ'triːvəb(ə)l] *adj* (*loss, error*) réparable; *Comptr* accessible; *Fin* (*amount*) recouvrable.

retrieval [rɪ'triːv(ə)l] *n Fin* recouvrement *m*; *Comptr* (*of data*) recherche *f*; (*of error, loss*) réparation *f*; (*of fortunes*) rétablissement *m*; **information r. system**, système *m* de recherche documentaire; (*computer system*) système de recherche d'information; **beyond** *or* **past r.**, irréparable.

retrieve [rɪ'triːv] **1** *vt Fin* recouvrer (*des biens*); retrouver (*un objet perdu, sa liberté*); *Comptr* retrouver, extraire (*une instruction*); réparer (*une perte, une erreur etc*); rétablir (*son honneur, sa fortune*); (*of dog*) rapporter (*un ballon, du gibier etc*); **to r. one's losses**, se refaire; **to r. the situation**, sauver la situation. **2** *vi* (*of dog*) rapporter.

retriever [rɪ'triːvər] *n* (*dog*) chien *m* d'arrêt, retriever *m*.

retro ['retrəʊ] *adj* (*fashion etc*) rétro *inv*.

retro- ['retrəʊ-] *pref* rétro-.

retroactive [retrəʊ'æktɪv] *adj* (*increase, measure etc*) rétroactif; **the increase is r. to last January**, l'augmentation a un effet rétroactif à compter de janvier dernier; **laws are not r.**, les lois ne sont pas rétroactives.

retroactively [retrəʊ'æktɪvlɪ] *adv* (*to increase, come into effect etc*) rétroactivement.

retrofit ['retrəʊfɪt] *vt* moderniser (*un avion, une machine*) (**with**, en y intégrant).

retrograde ['retrəgreɪd] *adj* (*movement, step etc*) rétrograde.

retrogress [retrə'gres] *vi* rétrograder.

retrogression [retrə'greʃən] *n* rétrogradation *f*, rétrogression *f*; *Biol* régression *f*.

retrogressive [retrə'gresɪv] *adj* rétrograde; *Biol* régressif.

retrorocket ['retrəʊrɒkɪt] *n Astronaut* rétrofusée *f*.

retrospect ['retrəspekt] *n* **in r.**, rétrospectivement, après coup; **when I consider these events in r.**, quand je pense à ces événements rétrospectivement.

retrospective [retrə'spektɪv] **1** *adj* (*review*) rétrospectif; (*measure*) à effet rétrospectif. **2** *n* (*of film director's, artist's etc work*) rétrospective *f*.

retrospectively [retrə'spektɪvlɪ] *adv* (*to consider etc*) rétrospectivement, après coup; (*to take effect*) rétroactivement.

retroussé [rə'truːseɪ] *adj* (*nose*) retroussé.

retrovirus ['retrəʊvaɪrəs] *n Biol* rétrovirus *m*.

retry [riː'traɪ] *vt Jur* juger (*qn*) à *ou* de nouveau.

retsina [ret'siːnə] *n* (vin) résiné *m*.

retune¹ ['riːtjuːn] *n Aut* (*of engine*) réglage *m*; **the engine needs a r.**, il faut faire régler le moteur.

retune² [riː'tjuːn] *vt Aut* régler (*un moteur*).

return¹ [rɪ'tɜːn] *n* **(a)** (*of person, peace, spring etc*) retour *m*; (*to house*) rentrée *f*; **on my r.**, dès *ou* à mon retour; **the r. to school**, la rentrée (des classes); **on his r. to France**, à son retour en France; **by r. (of post)**, par retour (du courrier); **many happy returns (of the day)!**, bon anniversaire!; **r. journey**, (voyage *m* de) retour; *Br Rail etc* **r. (ticket)**, billet *m* de retour, aller *m* (et) retour; **day r.**, billet d'aller (et) retour valable pour la journée seulement; **cheap day r.**, billet d'aller (et) retour à tarif réduit valable pour la journée seulement; **I've lost the r. half of my ticket**, j'ai perdu mon billet *ou* coupon de retour; **how much is the r. fare?**, combien coûte l'aller (et) retour?; **r. flight/voyage/***etc*, vol *m*/voyage/*etc* de retour; **point of no r.**, point *m* de non-retour;

(b) (*of object to original place*) remise *f*; (*of goods to supplier*) renvoi *m*; (*of stolen property*) restitution *f*; (*of overpayment*) ristourne *f*; *Tennis* renvoi *m* (de la balle); (*of library book*) rentrée *f*; (*of politician*) élection *f*; **r. (key)**, (*on keyboard*) touche *f* de retour; **carriage r.**, (*on typewriter, keyboard*) retour *m ou* rappel *m* de chariot; *Tennis* **to make a good r. of service**, bien renvoyer le service; **r. to office**, (*of politician*) reprise *f* de fonctions; **on sale or r.**, (marchandises) vendues avec faculté de retour *ou* à condition; **no deposit, no r.**, (*notice on bottle*) ni retour, ni consigne; *Th* **returns may be available on the day of the performance**, des places peuvent se libérer le jour de la représentation; **r. address**, adresse *f* de l'expéditeur; *Com* **returns**, rendus *mpl*; (*of books, newspapers*) invendus *mpl*, *F* bouillons *mpl*; *Pol* **to announce the returns of the election**, annoncer les résultats du scrutin; **early returns indicate a win for the incumbent**, les premiers résultats laissent prévoir une victoire du candidat sortant;

(c) *Fin* (*yield*) rapport *m* (**on**, de); **how much r. do you get on your investment?**, combien est-ce que ton investissement te rapporte?; **returns**, (*profit*) bénéfices *mpl*; **quick returns**, un prompt débit, une vente rapide; **small profits and quick returns**, faibles bénéfices et rentes rapides; **to bring (in) a fair r.**, rapporter un bénéfice raisonnable;

(d) (*form*) rapport officiel; (*for tax*) déclaration *f*; *Admin* (*of population etc*) recensement *m*;

(e) (*for something given*) échange *m*; (*for something done*) récompense *f*, remerciement *m*; **to give sth in r.**, donner qch en échange; (*for favour, service*) donner qch en guise de récompense *ou* de remerciement; **in r. for which ...**, moyennant quoi ...; **if you will do sth in r.**, si vous voulez bien faire qch en retour; **in r. for this service ...**, en récompense *ou* retour de ce service ...; **you must expect the same treatment in r.**, il faut vous attendre à la pareille; **it's a small r. for all your kindness**, c'est une modeste récompense pour votre bonté; *Sp* **r. match** *or* game, match *m* retour, revanche *f*; **I'll give you a r. match** *or* **game next week,** on disputera le match retour *ou* la revanche la semaine prochaine.

return[2] **1** *vi* (*come back*) revenir; (*go back*) retourner; (*of anxiety, fear*) revenir, reprendre; **I was returning from a journey,** je rentrais de voyage; **to r. home,** rentrer (chez soi); **he/spring has returned,** il/le printemps est revenu *ou* de retour; **to r. from the dead,** ressusciter d'entre les morts; **her colour returned,** elle a repris des couleurs; *Nau* **to r. to port,** rentrer au port; **to r. to a task,** reprendre une tâche; **to r. to a subject,** revenir à un sujet; **to r. to one's old habits,** reprendre ses vieilles habitudes; **r. to sender,** (*on undelivered letter*) renvoyer à l'expéditeur, retour à l'envoyeur.

2 *vt* **(a)** (*give back*) rendre (*un livre, un compliment, un verdict etc*); restituer (*un objet volé etc*); renvoyer (*un cadeau, une balle etc*); rembourser (*un emprunt*); élire (*un député*); **returned letter,** lettre renvoyée à l'expéditeur; **to r. a book to its place,** remettre un livre à sa place; *Tennis* **to r. (the) service,** renvoyer la balle; **the jury returned a verdict of guilty/not guilty,** le jury a déclaré l'accusé coupable/non coupable; **to r. an animal to the wild,** faire retourner un animal à l'état sauvage; *Mil* **to r. fire,** riposter (au feu adverse); **to r. s.o.'s greeting,** rendre un salut à qn; **to r. good for evil,** rendre le bien pour le mal; **to r. s.o.'s love,** aimer qn en retour;

(b) *Com Fin* (*produce*) rapporter (*un bénéfice*);

(c) *Pol* **to r. the result of the poll,** annoncer les résultats du scrutin;

(d) *Old-fashioned* (*answer*) répondre, répliquer.

returnable [rɪ'tɜːnəb(ə)l] *adj* (*purchase, ticket etc*) qui peut être rendu *ou* renvoyé; (*bottle*) consigné; **sale items are not r.,** (*notice in shop*) les articles en solde ne sont ni échangés ni repris; **empties are not r.,** on ne reprend pas les bouteilles, les bouteilles ne sont pas consignées.

returning [rɪ'tɜːnɪŋ] *n Pol* **r. officer,** directeur, -trice du scrutin.

reunification [riːjuːnɪfɪ'keɪʃən] *n* (*of country*) réunification *f*.

reunify [riː'juːnɪfaɪ] *vt* réunifier (*un pays*).

reunion [riː'juːnɪən] *n* réunion *f*, assemblée *f*, retrouvailles *fpl*; *Am* **class r.,** réunion d'anciens élèves de la même classe *ou* promotion; **to have** *or* **hold a r.,** organiser une réunion *ou* des retrouvailles; **r. celebration/dinner/***etc*, célébration *f*/dîner *m*/*etc* de retrouvailles.

reunite [riːjʊ'naɪt] **1** *vt* (*after quarrel*) réconcilier (*une famille etc*); **the freed hostage was reunited with his wife,** l'otage libéré a retrouvé sa femme; **the dog was reunited with its owner,** le chien a retrouvé son maître. **2** *vi* se réunir.

reupholster [riːʌp'həʊlstər] *vt* regarnir (*un fauteuil etc*).

reusable [reɪ'juːzəb(ə)l] *adj* (*paper, bottle etc*) réutilisable; (*battery*) rechargeable.

reuse[1] [riː'juːs] *n* (*of paper, bottle etc*) réutilisation *f*, remploi *m*.

reuse[2] [riː'juːz] *vt* réutiliser (*du papier, une bouteille*).

rev[1] [rev] *n Aut F* (*abbr* **revolution**) tour *m* (à la minute *ou* minute); **to do three thousand revs,** faire trois mille tours à la minute *ou* minute; **r. counter,** compte-tours *m inv*.

rev[2] *v* **(-vv-)** *Aut* **1** *vt* (faire) emballer (*le moteur*); **he revs the engine too hard,** il fait tourner le moteur trop vite. **2** *vi* (*of engine*) s'emballer; (*of driver*) emballer le moteur.

Rev *n Rel abbr* **Reverend.**

►rev up *vtsep & vi* = **REV**[2].

revaluation [riːvæljʊ'eɪʃən] *n* **(a)** (*of currency*) revalorisation *f*, réévaluation *f*; **(b)** (*of property etc*) réévaluation *f*, réestimation *f*.

revalue [riː'væljuː] *vt* **(a)** revaloriser, réévaluer (*une monnaie*); **(b)** réévaluer, réestimer (*une propriété etc*).

revamp[1] ['riːvæmp] *n F* (*of method, play etc*) remaniement *m*; (*of policy*) modification *f*, remaniement; (*of company*) réorganisation *f*, restructuration *f*; (*of house etc*) remise *f* en état.

revamp[2] [riː'væmp] *vt F* remanier (*une méthode, une pièce etc*); modifier, remanier (*une politique*); réorganiser, restructurer (*une entreprise*); retaper (*une maison etc*).

revanchisme [rɪ'væntʃɪz(ə)m] *n* revanchisme *m*.

revanchiste [rɪ'væntʃɪst] *n & adj* revanchiste *mf*.

Revd *Rel abbr* **Reverend.**

reveal [rɪ'viːl] *vt* révéler (*un objet caché, un secret, un nom*); faire connaître (*un fait*); laisser voir (*une qualité etc*); **to r. one's identity,** se faire connaître; **the police do not want to r. the identity of the victim,** la police ne veut pas révéler l'identité de la victime; **the reporter refused to r. his sources,** le reporter a refusé de révéler ses sources; **a medical examination revealed two cracked ribs,** un examen médical a permis de découvrir deux côtes fêlées; **it was revealed yesterday that ...,** on a révélé hier que ... .

revealing [rɪ'viːlɪŋ] *adj* (*sign, comment etc*) révélateur; (*dress*) décolleté; (*skirt*) qui ne cache pas grand-chose.

revealingly [rɪ'viːlɪŋlɪ] *adv* (*to say, look at*) d'un ton *ou* d'un air révélateur; **a r. low dress,** une robe tellement décolletée qu'elle ne cache pas grand-chose.

reveille [rɪ'vælɪ] *n Mil* le réveil, la diane; **to sound r.,** sonner *ou* battre le réveil.

revel[1] ['rev(ə)l] *n Old-fashioned* (*often pl*) divertissement(s) *m(pl)*, réjouissances *fpl*.

revel[2] *vi* **(-ll-,** *US* **-l-)** se réjouir, se divertir, *F* faire la noce; **to r. in sth/in doing sth,** se délecter à qch/à faire qch; **to r. in one's freedom,** se réjouir de sa liberté.

revelation [revə'leɪʃən] *n* (*of secret etc*) révélation *f*; **it was a r. to me,** cela a été une révélation pour moi; *Bible* **(the Book of) Revelations,** l'Apocalypse *f*.

reveller, *US* **reveler** ['rev(ə)lər] *n* joyeux convive, *F* noceur, -euse; **late-night r.,** oiseau *m* de nuit.

revelling ['rev(ə)lɪŋ], **revelry** ['revəlrɪ] *n* festivités *fpl*.

revenge[1] [rɪ'vendʒ] *n* **(a)** vengeance *f*; **r. is sweet,** la vengeance est douce; **to take** *or* **get** *or* **have (one's) r.,** se venger (**for,** de; **on,** sur); **to want one's r.,** vouloir prendre sa revanche; **in r.,** pour se venger (**for,** de); **to do sth out of r.,** faire qch par revanche; **(b)** *Fig* (*esp in games*) revanche *f*, contre-partie *f*; **to give s.o. his** *or* **her r.,** laisser qn prendre sa revanche.

revenge[2] *vt* venger (*une injure*) (**(up)on s.o.,** sur qn); **to r. oneself** *or* **be revenged,** se venger (**on,** sur; **for,** de); **Liverpool revenged last week's defeat with a resounding win over Everton,** Liverpool a pris la revanche de sa défaite de la semaine dernière avec une victoire éclatante sur Everton.

revengeful [rɪ'vendʒfʊl] *adj* (*attitude, person etc*) vindicatif; (*act*) vengeur, de vengeance.

revengefully [rɪ'vendʒfʊlɪ] *adv* (*to do*) par esprit de vengeance; (*to say*) d'un air vengeur.

revenger [rɪ'vendʒər] *n* vengeur, -eresse (**of,** de).

revenue ['revənjuː] *n* revenu *m*; (*from land, property*) rentes *fpl*; (*from sales*) recettes *fpl*; **advertising r.,** recettes de publicité; **oil r.,** revenu pétrolier; **the Inland** *or Am* **Internal R.,** le fisc; **tax r.,** recettes fiscales.

reverberate [rɪ'vɜːbəreɪt] **1** *vi* (*of sound*) retentir, résonner (**off,** contre); (*of light, heat*) se réverbérer (**off,** contre); **the warehouse was reverberating with the noise,** l'entrepôt retentissait du bruit; *Fig* **the news reverberated round the world,** la nouvelle a fait du bruit partout dans le monde; (*had an effect*) la nouvelle a eu des répercussions partout dans le monde. **2** *vt* renvoyer, répercuter (*le son*); réverbérer, réfléchir (*la lumière, la chaleur*).

reverberation [rɪvɜːbə'reɪʃən] *n* (*of sound*) répercussion *f*; (*of light, heat*) réverbération *f*; *Fig* **the announcement is still causing reverberations,** la nouvelle continue à avoir des répercussions.

revere [rɪ'vɪər] *vt* (*treat with respect*) révérer; (*regard with respect*) vénérer (*qn*) (**for,** pour)

reverence[1] ['rev(ə)rəns] *n* révérance *f*; (*for artist, doctor etc*) vénération *f*; *Rel* respect religieux; **to hold s.o. in r.,** révérer qn; *Rel* **Your** *or* **His R.,** monsieur l'abbé.

reverence[2] *vt* révérer (*qn*).

reverend ['rev(ə)rənd] **1** *adj* **(a)** vénérable; **(b)** *Rel* le révérend; **the R. Father Martin,** *Anglican* le révérend père Martin; *Cathol* l'abbé *ou* le père Martin; **the R. Mother Superior,** la révérende mère supérieure; **Right R.,** (*bishop*) très révérend; **Very R.,** (*dean*) très révérend; **Most R.,** (*archbishop*) révérendissime. **2** *n* révérend *m*; (*Anglican clergyman*) pasteur *m*; *Cathol* abbé *m*; *Cathol* **Your R.,** mon père.

reverent ['rev(ə)rənt] *adj* (*gesture, tone*) respectueux, plein de vénération; **to be very r. towards s.o.,** être très respectueux à l'égard de *ou* envers qn.

reverential [revə'renʃəl] *adj* (*act*) révérenciel; (*tone, gesture etc*) révérencieux.

reverently ['rev(ə)rəntlɪ] *adv* (*to treat*) avec révérence; (*to act, speak etc*) avec grand respect *ou* vénération, très respectueusement.

reverie ['revərɪ] *n* rêverie *f*; **in a r.,** rêveur; **to be lost in r.,** être perdu dans ses rêves; **to fall into a r.,** se mettre à rêver (**about,** à, de).

revers [rɪ'vɪəz] *npl* (*on jacket*) revers *mpl*.

reversal [rɪ'vɜːs(ə)l] *n* **(a)** (*of opinion, policy, situation*) revirement *m*; (*of roles*) renversement *m*; (*of fortune*) revers *m*; **to suffer a r.,** (*of person*) essuyer un revers de fortune; **(b)** *Jur* (*of decision*) réforme *f*, annulation *f*.

reverse[1] [rɪ'vɜːs] *adj* **(a)** (*opposite*) contraire (**to,** à); **(b)** (*order, image*) inverse; **r. side,** (*of coin etc*) revers *m*, envers *m*; (*of fabric*) envers; (*of paper*) verso *m*; (*of painting*) dos *m*; **in r. order,** à l'envers; *Br Tel* **r.-charge call,** communication *f* en P.C.V.; *Am* **r. discrimination,** discrimination *f* à l'envers; *Aut* **r. gear,** marche *f* arrière; **r. turn,** marche *f* arrière; **to do** *or* **make a r. turn,** faire (une) marche arrière.

reverse[2] *n* **(a)** (*opposite*) contraire *m*; **to be (quite) the r.**

of sth, être (tout) le contraire *ou* l'opposé de qch; **she was the r. of calm,** elle était tout sauf calme; **quite the r.!,** bien au contraire!; **printed in r.,** écrit à l'envers; **(b)** (*back*) (*of coin, fabric*) revers *m*; (*of paper*) verso *m*; **(c)** (*defeat*) échec *m*; (*misfortune*) revers *m*; **to suffer a r.,** essuyer un revers de fortune; (*be defeated*) essuyer un échec; **(d)** *Aut* (*gear*) marche *f* arrière; (*turn*) virage *m* en marche arrière; **in r.,** en marche arrière; **to put a car into r.,** mettre une voiture en marche arrière; **to do a r.,** faire une marche arrière.

reverse³ 1 *vt* **(a)** (*turn in opposite direction*) retourner (*un habit, un tableau*); **to r. the cuffs on a shirt,** retourner les poignets d'une chemise; *Br Tel* **to r. the charge(s),** demander une communication en P.C.V.; *Can* faire un appel à frais virés; **I want to r. the charges please,** je voudrais appeler en P.C.V. s'il vous plaît; *Mil* **to r. arms,** renverser les fusils; *Tech* **to r. steam,** renverser la vapeur;
(b) (*alter*) inverser (*un ordre, une politique*); renverser (*une situation*); annuler (*une décision*); **to r. a trend,** renverser une tendance; **the roles are reversed,** les rôles sont intervertis;
(c) *Aut* **to r. one's car,** faire marche arrière; **to r. the car out of the garage,** sortir du garage en marche arrière.
2 *vi Aut* faire marche arrière; **to r. into a lamppost,** rentrer dans un réverbère en faisant une marche arrière; **to r. out (of the garage),** sortir (du garage) en marche arrière.

reversed [rɪ'vɜːst] *adj* (*situation*) renversé; (*order, policy*) inverse; *Br Tel* **r. charge call,** communication *f* en P.C.V., *Can* appel *m* à frais virés; **will you accept a r. charge call?,** acceptez-vous un appel en P.C.V.? **(from,** de).

reversible [rɪ'vɜːsəb(ə)l] *adj* (*fabric, jacket etc*) réversible, à double face; (*film*) inversible; (*decree, judgment, sentence*) révocable, réformable.

reversing [rɪ'vɜːsɪŋ] *n Aut* marche *f* arrière; **r. light,** phare *m* de recul.

reversion [rɪ'vɜːʃən] *n* **(a)** (*to previous condition*) retour *m* **(to,** à); *Biol* retour à l'état antérieur, régression *f*; **r. to type,** retour au type primitif; **(b)** *Jur* (*of property*) retour *m*, réversion *f*; **right of r.,** réversion; **estate in r.,** bien grevé d'une réversion.

reversionary [rɪ'vɜːʃən(ə)rɪ] *adj* **(a)** *Biol* (*characteristic, organ*) atavique; **(b)** *Jur* (*right*) de réversion, réversible.

revert [rɪ'vɜːt] *vi* **(a)** (*of conversation, thoughts*) revenir **(to,** à); *Biol* retourner à l'état sauvage; **to r. to type,** *Biol* revenir *ou* retourner au type primitif; *Fig* laisser le naturel reprendre le dessus; **we shall r. to this matter,** nous reviendrons sur cette question; **reverting to your question,** pour (en) revenir à votre question; **the garden has reverted to a wilderness,** le jardin s'est retourné à l'état sauvage; **to r. to one's maiden name,** (*of divorced woman*) reprendre son nom de jeune fille; **(b)** *Jur* (*of property*) revenir, retourner **(to,** à).

revetment [rɪ'vetmənt] *n Constr* revêtement *m*; **r. wall,** mur *m* de revêtement, épaulement *m*.

review¹ [rɪ'vjuː] *n* **(a)** (*of past etc*) examen *m*, passage *m* en revue, révision *f; (of policy, salary etc)* révision, examen; (*of situation*) bilan *m*; **prices are subject to r.,** les prix peuvent faire l'objet d'une révision; **to come up for r.,** (*of salary, contract etc*) devoir être révisé; **to be under r.,** (*of policy, salary etc*) faire l'objet d'une révision, être en cours de révision; **they are keeping the question of salaries/student grants under r.,** la question des salaires/des allocations d'études fait l'objet de réexamens perpétuels; **to keep a question under r.,** suivre une question de très près; **to give a r. of sth,** passer qch en revue; **a r. of the year,** une rétrospective des événements de l'année;
(b) (*of book, play, film etc*) critique *f*, compte rendu; **her last novel got very bad reviews,** son dernier roman a eu de très mauvaises critiques; **he gave it a good r.,** il en a fait une bonne critique; **r. copy,** (*of book*) exemplaire fourni au critique;
(c) (*publication*) revue *f*;
(d) *Th* revue *f*;
(e) *Mil* revue *f*; **to hold a r.,** passer une revue; **to pass troops in r.,** passer en revue des troupes;
(f) *Jur* (*of trial*) révision *f*.

review² 1 *vt* **(a)** revoir, examiner (*des événements passés*); réviser, examiner (*une politique, un salaire*); passer (*des faits etc*) en revue; faire le bilan *ou* le point de (*une situation*); **your progress will be reviewed every six weeks,** on fera le point sur *ou* le bilan de vos progrès toutes les six semaines; **(b)** faire la critique *ou* le compte rendu de (*un livre, un film*); **(c)** *Mil* passer (*les troupes*) en revue; **to be reviewed,** (*of troops*) passer en revue; **(d)** *esp Am* (*revise*) revoir (*des leçons*); **(e)** *Jur* revoir, réviser (*un procès*). **2** *vi* **(a) he reviews for the Sunday Times,** il rédige des critiques pour le Sunday Times; **(b)** *esp Am* faire de la révision.

reviewer [rɪ'vjuːər] *n* (*of book, play etc*) critique *m*.

revile [rɪ'vaɪl] *vt* injurier (*qn*) **(for,** pour).

revise¹ [rɪ'vaɪz] *n Typ* épreuve *f* de révision, seconde *f*; **second** *or* **final r.,** troisième épreuve, tierce *f*.

revise² 1 *vt* **(a)** (*amend*) revoir, réviser (*un texte*); corriger, réviser (*des épreuves*); réviser (*une loi, la constitution*); revenir sur (*une décision*); **to r. one's opinion of s.o.,** (*change one's mind about*) changer son opinion à l'égard de qn; **to r. figures upwards/downwards,** corriger des chiffres à la hausse/à la baisse, corriger des calculs à la hausse/à la baisse; **(b)** (*study*) repasser, revoir, réviser (*une leçon*). **2** *vi* (*for exam*) réviser, faire des révisions **(for,** pour).

revised [rɪ'vaɪzd] *adj* (*text, lesson*) revu; (*proof, law*) révisé; **r. edition,** (*of book etc*) édition revue et corrigée; **the R. Version,** la traduction de la Bible de 1884.

reviser [rɪ'vaɪzər] *n* réviseur *m*; (*of proof*) correcteur, -trice.

revision [rɪ'vɪʒən] *n* (*of text, lesson etc*) révision *f*; **for r.,** à revoir; **to do some r.,** faire des révisions.

revisionism [rɪ'vɪʒənɪz(ə)m] *n Pol* révisionnisme *m*.

revisionist [rɪ'vɪʒənɪst] *adj & n* révisionniste *mf*.

revisit [riː'vɪzɪt] *vt* visiter de nouveau, revisiter (*un endroit*); **Brideshead Revisited,** Retour à Brideshead; *Fig* **nuclear power revisited,** un nouveau regard *ou* une nouvelle perspective sur la question de l'énergie nucléaire.

revitalize [riː'vaɪtəlaɪz] *vt* ranimer, revigorer (*qn*); relancer (*l'économie*); donner un nouvel essor à (*l'industrie, les arts, le mouvement syndical etc*); **to feel revitalized,** se sentir revigoré.

revival [rɪ'vaɪv(ə)l] *n* **(a)** (*of person*) retour *m* à la vie; (*to health*) retour des forces; (*to consciousness*) reprise *f* des sens; **all attempts at r. failed,** toutes les tentatives de réanimation ont échoué; **(b)** (*of arts, industry, hope*) renaissance *f*; (*of custom, fashion*) réapparition *f*; (*of interest*) réveil *m*; (*of law*) remise *f* en vigueur; (*of economy*) reprise *f*; **the r. of trade,** la reprise des affaires; **(c)** (*of play etc*) reprise *f*; **to put on a r. of Blithe Spirit,** monter une reprise de Blithe Spirit; **(d)** *Rel* réveil *m*, renouveau *m*; **religious r.,** renouveau religieux; **r. meeting,** = réunion dans le but de ranimer la foi (dans une ville).

revivalism [rɪ'vaɪv(ə)lɪz(ə)m] *n Rel* = mouvement visant à ranimer la foi.

revivalist [rɪ'vaɪvəlɪst] *n Rel* = personne qui vise à ranimer la foi; **r. meeting,** réunion *f* dans le but de ranimer la foi (dans une ville).

revive [rɪ'vaɪv] **1** *vt* **(a)** ranimer (*une personne évanouie*); réanimer (*un moribond*); **that will r. you,** voilà qui vous remontera; **(b)** ranimer (*un souvenir, une conversation*); ressusciter (*un usage, une mode*); faire renaître (*l'espoir, l'intérêt*); remettre (*une loi*) en vigueur; **to r. s.o.'s spirits,** remonter le moral à qn; **(c)** *Th* remonter (*une pièce*). **2** *vi* **(a)** (*of unconscious person*) reprendre connaissance; (*of dying person*) ressusciter; **(b)** (*of feelings*) se ranimer, renaître; (*of hope*) renaître; (*of custom*) se renouveler, reprendre; (*of fashion*) rentrer en vogue; (*of arts*) renaître; (*of business, commerce*) reprendre; **his spirits revived,** il a repris courage; **to feel one's hopes reviving,** sentir renaître l'espoir; **hopes have revived of finding the miners alive,** l'espoir renaît de trouver les mineurs vivants.

revivify [rɪ'vɪvɪfaɪ, riː-] *vt Lit* revivifier (*qch, qn*).

revocable [rɪ'vəʊkəb(ə)l] *adj* (*contract, law, will etc*) révocable; (*decision*) sur laquelle on peut revenir; (*order*) que l'on peut annuler.

revocation [revə'keɪʃən] *n* (*of will*) révocation *f*; (*of decision, order, contract, law*) annulation *f*.

revoke¹ [rɪ'vəʊk] *n Cards* fausse renonce.

revoke² 1 *vt* révoquer (*un testament*); annuler (*un ordre, un contrat, une loi*); revenir sur (*une décision*); rétracter, revenir sur (*une promesse*); retirer (*un permis de conduire*). **2** *vi Cards* faire une fausse renonce.

revolt¹ [rɪ'vəʊlt] *n* révolte *f*; **to rise in r.,** se soulever, se révolter **(against,** contre); **to be in r.,** être en révolte **(against,** contre).

revolt² 1 *vi* (*of troops*) se révolter, s'insurger, se soulever **(against, at,** contre). **2** *vt* (*disgust*) révolter, dégoûter; **to be revolted by sth,** être révolté par qch.

revolting [rɪ'vəʊltɪŋ] *adj* **(a)** (*troops etc*) insurgé, en révolte; **(b)** (*action*) révoltant, dégoûtant; **it smells r.,** ça a une odeur révoltante; **it tastes r.,** ça a un goût infâme; **that sounds r.,** (*what has just been described*) ça semble répugnant.

revoltingly [rɪ'vəʊltɪŋlɪ] *adv* d'une façon révoltante *ou* dégoûtante; **a r. bad smell,** une odeur infecte.

revolution [revə'luːʃən] *n* **(a)** *Pol & Fig* révolution *f*; *Hist* **the French R.,** la Révolution française; **the Industrial R.,** la Révolution industrielle; **this process has brought about a complete r. in the industry,** ce procédé a révolutionné *ou* complètement transformé l'industrie; **(b)** (*of wheel*) tour *m*, révolution *f*; (*of record, turntable, propeller*) tour; (*of planet*) révolution; **r. counter,** compte-tours *m* *inv*; **to make** *or Fml* **describe a r.,** faire *ou* décrire une révolution *ou* un tour; **revolutions per minute,** tours à la minute.

revolutionary [revə'luːʃən(ə)rı] *adj & n Pol & Fig* révolutionnaire *mf*.

revolutionize [revə'luːʃənaız] *vt Fig* révolutionner, transformer complètement (*une industrie*).

revolve [rı'vɒlv] **1** *vt* faire tourner (*une roue etc*); *Fig* **to r. a problem in one's mind,** retourner un problème dans son esprit. **2** *vi* (*of wheel etc*) tourner; **to r. around sth/s.o.,** (*of thoughts*) tourner autour de qch/qn; **all my thoughts r. around you,** je ne pense qu'à toi; **the play revolves around ...,** la pièce est centrée sur ... .

revolver [rı'vɒlvər] *n* (*firearm*) revolver *m*.

revolving [rı'vɒlvıŋ] *adj* **(a)** (*planet etc*) en rotation, qui accomplit sa révolution; **(b)** (*chair etc*) tournant, pivotant; (*stage*) tournant; *Banking* **r. credit,** crédit permanent, revolving *m*; **r. door,** (porte *f* à) tambour *m*; *Am Fig* = le va-et-vient de fonctionnaires haut-placés entre les services publics et le secteur privé; **r. fund,** fonds *m* de roulement.

revue [rı'vjuː] *n Th* revue *f*.

revulsion [rı'vʌlʃən] *n* (*disgust*) répugnance *f*, révulsion *f*; (*of feeling*) revirement *m*; **r. from s.o.,** réaction *f* contre qn; **to draw back in r.,** reculer dans un mouvement de dégoût *ou* de révulsion; **to be filled with r.,** être rempli de dégoût; **to fill s.o. with r.,** (*of scene, cruelty etc*) remplir qn de dégoût.

reward¹ [rı'wɔːd] *n* (*for information, service etc*) récompense *f*; **to offer a r.,** offrir une récompense (**for,** pour); **as a** *or* **in r. for ...,** en récompense de *ou* pour ...; **to get a fair r. for** *or* **from one's labour,** tirer de son travail une récompense légitime.

reward² *vt* récompenser, rémunérer (*qn*) (**for,** de; **with,** par); **that's how he rewards me for my loyalty,** voilà comment il me récompense de mon dévouement.

rewarding [rı'wɔːdıŋ] *adj* qui (en) vaut la peine; (*satisfying*) satisfaisant; (*financially*) rémunérateur, -trice.

rewind [riː'waınd] *vt* (*pt & pp* **rewound** [riː'waʊnd]) **(a)** rembobiner (*un film*); **r. (button),** (*on tape deck*) touche *f* 'rewind', touche pour rembobiner la bande; **(b)** remonter (*une montre, un réveil*).

rewire [riː'waıər] *vt* refaire l'installation électrique de (*une maison, un appartement etc*); réinstaller (*une prise*).

reword [riː'wɜːd] *vt* recomposer, rédiger à nouveau (*un paragraphe etc*).

rework [riː'wɜːk] *vt* retravailler sur (*une idée, un thème*); retravailler (*un texte*); **your thesis needs reworking,** votre thèse a besoin d'être retravaillée.

rewrite¹ ['riːraıt] *n* (*of article etc*) **here's the r. you asked for,** voici la nouvelle version que vous m'avez demandée.

rewrite² [riː'raıt] *vt* (*pt* **rewrote** [riː'rəʊt]; *pp* **rewritten** [riː'rıt(ə)n]) récrire, réécrire, rédiger à nouveau (*une lettre, un article*).

Rgt (*abbr* **regiment**) rég.

rh [ɑːr'eıtʃ] *Mus etc* (*abbr* **right hand**) main droite.

Rh *Physiol abbr* **Rhesus**.

rhapsodic(al) [ræp'sɒdık, -ık(ə)l] *adj Fig* (*description, welcome etc*) excessivement élogieux, dithyrambique; *Mus* r(h)apsodique.

rhapsodize ['ræpsədaız] *vi Fig* (*of person*) s'extasier (**over,** sur).

rhapsody ['ræpsədı] *n Fig* transports *mpl*, dithyrambe *m*; *Mus* r(h)apsodie *f*; *Fig* **to be in** *or* **go into rhapsodies,** s'extasier (**over,** sur); **to send s.o. into rhapsodies,** provoquer l'extase chez qn.

rhea ['riːə] *n* (*bird*) nandou *m*.

Rheims [riːmz] *n* Reims.

Rhenish ['renıʃ] *adj Geog* rhénan, du Rhin; **R. (wine),** vin *m* du Rhin.

rheo ['riːəʊ] **, rheostat** ['riːəʊstæt] *n El* rhéostat *m*.

rhesus ['riːsəs] *n* **(a)** *Zool* **r. (monkey),** (macaque) rhésus *m*; **(b)** *Physiol* **r. factor,** (facteur) rhésus *m*; **r. positive/negative,** (*blood*) rhésus positif/négatif; **I'm r. negative,** je suis rhésus négatif; **r. negative mother,** mère *f* rhésus négatif; **r. baby,** enfant *m* rhésus positif souffrant d'incompatibilité avec le rhésus négatif de la mère.

rhetoric ['retərık] *n* **(a)** *Pej* rhétorique *f*, emphase *f*; **his speech contained nothing but r.,** son discours ne consistait qu'en de belles phrases vides de sens; **(b)** rhétorique *f*.

rhetorical [rı'tɒrık(ə)l] *adj* **(a)** *Pej* (*style*) emphatique, ampoulé; **(b)** (*term etc*) de rhétorique; **r. question,** question *f* de pure forme.

rhetorically [rı'tɒrıklı] *adv* **(a)** *Pej* (*to speak*) avec emphase; **(b)** (*to ask*) pour la forme.

rhetorician [retə'rıʃən] *n* **(a)** *Pej* rhéteur *m*; **(b)** rhétoricien, -ienne.

rheumatic [ruː'mætık, rʊ-] **1** *adj Med* (*pain etc*) rhumatismal; (*person*) rhumatisant; (*finger, joint*) affligé de rhumatisme; **r. fever,** rhumatisme articulaire aigu. **2** *n* rhumatisant, -ante.

rheumaticky [ruː'mætıkı, rʊ-] *adj F* = **RHEUMATIC 1**.

rheumatics [ruː'mætıks, rʊ-], **rheumatism** ['ruːmətız(ə)m, 'rʊ-] *n* rhumatisme *m*; **to have** *or* **suffer from r.,** avoir des rhumatismes.

rheumatoid ['ruːmətɔıd, 'rʊ-] *adj* rhumatoïde; **r. arthritis,** polyarthrite *f* rhumatoïde.

rheumatologist [ruːmə'tɒlədʒıst, rʊ-] *n Med* rhumatologue *mf*.

rheumatology [ruːmə'tɒlədʒı, rʊ-] *n Med* rhumatologie *f*.

rheumy ['ruːmı] *adj* **r. eyes,** yeux chassieux.

Rhine (the) [ðə'raın] *n* le Rhin; **R. wines,** vins *mpl* du Rhin.

Rhineland (the) [ðə'raınlənd] *n* les pays rhénans, la Rhénanie.

rhinestone ['raınstəʊn] *n* strass *m*; **r. earring/***etc*, boucle d'oreille/*etc* en strass.

rhino ['raınəʊ] *n* **(a)** (*animal*) rhino(céros) *m*; **(b)** *Br Sl* (*money*) pèze *m*, blé *m*, fric *m*.

rhinoceros [raı'nɒsərəs] *n* (*animal*) rhinocéros *m*; *Fig* **to have a hide** *or* **skin like a r.,** ne pas être très sensible.

rhizome ['raızəʊm] *n Bot* rhizome *m*.

Rhode Island [rəʊd'aılənd] *n* Rhode Island *f*; **R. I. red,** (*chicken*) Rhode-Island *f*.

Rhodes¹ [rəʊdz] *n* (l'île *f* de) Rhodes *f*.

Rhodes² *n Sch* **R. scholarship,** bourse *f* de Rhodes; **R. scholar,** titulaire *mf* de la bourse de Rhodes.

Rhodesia [rəʊ'diːʒə, -zıə] *n Hist* Rhodésie *f*.

Rhodesian [rəʊ'diːʒən, -zıən] *Hist* **1** *adj* rhodésien, de Rhodésie. **2** *n* Rhodésien, -ienne.

rhododendron, *pl* **-ons, -a** [rəʊdə'dendrən, -ənz, -ə] *n* rhododendron *m*; **r. bush,** rhododendron, buisson *m* de rhododendron.

rhomb [rɒm] *n Math* losange *m*, rhombe *m*.

rhombic ['rɒmbık] *adj* rhombique.

rhomboid ['rɒmbɔıd] *adj & n Math* rhomboïde *m*.

rhombus, *pl* **-uses, -i** ['rɒmbəs, -əsız, -aı] *n Math* = **RHOMB**.

Rhone (the) [ðə'rəʊn] *n* le Rhône; **the R. valley,** la vallée du Rhône; **R. wines,** vins *mpl* du Rhône.

rhubarb ['ruːbɑːb] *n Bot Pharm* rhubarbe *f*; **r. jam,** confiture *f* de rhubarbe; **r. tart/desert/***etc*, tarte *f*/dessert *m*/*etc* à la rhubarbe.

rhumb [rʌm] *n Nau* **r. (line),** r(h)umb *m*.

rhumba ['rʌmbə, rʊm-] *n* = **RUMBA**.

rhyme¹ [raım] *n* **(a)** (*sound*) *& Fig* rime *f*; **can you think of a r. for ...?,** est-ce que tu peux trouver une rime pour ...?; **without r. or reason,** sans rime ni raison; **there's neither r. nor reason about it,** cela ne rime à rien *ou* n'a ni rime ni raison; **there's no r. or reason to such behaviour,** un tel comportement ne rime à rien *ou* n'a ni rime ni raison; **(b)** (*poem*) vers *mpl*; **to make up a r.,** faire *ou* composer un vers (**about,** sur).

rhyme² **1** *vi* **(a)** (*of words*) rimer (**with,** avec); **(b)** (*of person*) rimer, faire des vers; **rhyming slang,** = système de rimes cockney dans lequel on remplace un mot par un autre mot ou locution rimant avec celui-ci; **rhyming dictionary,** dictionnaire *m* des rimes. **2** *vt* mettre (*un récit*) en vers; **to r. a word with another,** faire rimer un mot avec un autre.

rhymed [raımd] *adj* rimé, en vers (rimés).

rhymester ['raımstər] *n Pej* rimailleur *m*.

rhythm ['rıð(ə)m] *n Mus etc* rythme *m*; (*pace*) rythme, cadence *f*; **to have a sense of r.,** avoir du rythme; **to keep up a steady r.,** maintenir un rythme régulier; (*of worker*) travailler à un rythme régulier; **r. of work,** rythme *ou* cadence de travail; **r. section,** (*in jazz band etc*) section *f* rythmique; **r. and blues,** rhythm and blues *m*; **r. method,** (*of birth control*) méthode *f* d'abstention périodique.

rhythmic(al) ['rıðmık, -ık(ə)l] *adj* rythmique, cadencé; **to be r.,** (*of person*) avoir le sens du rythme; **r. tread,** marche scandée; **r. dancing,** dance *f* rythmique; **r. breathing,** respiration cadencée.

rhythmically ['rıðmıklı] *adv* (*to breathe, dance etc*) avec rythme, de façon cadencée.

rial ['raıəl] *n* (*coin*) rial *m*.

rib¹ [rıb] *n* **(a)** (*of person, animal*) côte *f*; *F* **his ribs stick out,** on lui voit les côtes; *Culin* **r. roast,** côte de bœuf; **spare ribs,** côtes découvertes; **r.-tickling joke/story/***etc*, une plaisanterie/histoire/*etc* (qui fait rire) à s'en tenir les côtes; **(b)** (*on aeroplane, book, ceiling, leaf*) nervure *f*; (*of umbrella*) baleine *f*; (*of ship*) membre *m*, membrure *f*; (*in knitting*) côte *f*; **knit two inches in r.,** tricoter environ cinq centimètres (au point) de côtes; **the ribs left on the sand,** les rides laissées sur le sable.

rib² *v* (**-bb-**) **1** *vt* **(a)** *F* taquiner (*qn*) (**about,** à propos de, au sujet de); **(b)** garnir (*qch*) de côtes *ou* nervures. **2** *vi Knitting* **r. for two inches,** tricoter environ cinq centimètres (au point) de côtes.

ribald ['rıbəld, 'raı-] *adj* (*joke, person, song*) grivois, paillard; (*laughter*) gras; **r. joke,** grivoiserie *f*, paillardise *f*.

ribaldry ['rɪbəldrɪ, 'raɪ-] *n* grivoiserie *f*, paillardises *fpl*.

rib(b)and ['rɪbənd] *n Old-fashioned* = **RIBBON**.

ribbed [rɪbd] *adj* (*ceiling*) à nervures, nervuré; (*glass*) à côtes, cannelé; (*sand*) ridé; (*fabric*) côtelé; *Knitting* au point de côtes; *Archit* **r. vault,** voûte *f* d'ogives.

ribbing ['rɪbɪŋ] *n* **(a)** taquinerie *f*; **their constant r. was getting me down,** leurs taquineries incessantes me donnaient le cafard; **to take a r.,** se faire mettre en boîte; **(b)** (*on ceiling*) nervurage *m*, nervures *fpl*; (*of fabric, knitting*) côtes *fpl*; (*of boat*) membrure *f*.

ribbon ['rɪbən] *n* **(a)** (*for hair, package, typewriter*) ruban *m*; **a piece of r.,** un morceau de ruban; **tied with r.,** attaché avec du ruban; **to hang in ribbons,** (*of clothes, curtains etc*) pendre en lambeaux; *Horseriding* **ribbons,** (*reins*) guides *fpl*; **to tear to ribbons,** (*clothes etc*) mettre en lambeaux, déchiqueter, lacérer; *F* (*film, performance etc*) éreinter; **(b)** (*on medal*) ruban *m*; (*of order*) cordon *m*; **(c)** *Fig* (*of land, road etc*) bande *f*, ruban *m*; (*of smoke*) filet *m*; **r. development,** extension urbaine en bordure de route.

ribcage ['rɪbkeɪdʒ] *n Anat* cage *f* thoracique.

riboflavin(e) [raɪbəʊ'fleɪvɪn] *n Ch* riboflavine *f*.

ribonucleic [raɪbəʊnjuː'kliːɪk] *adj Ch* **r. acid,** acide *m* ribonucléique.

rice[1] [raɪs] *n* riz *m*; **long/short grain r.,** riz à grains longs/courts; **brown r.,** riz complet; **to grow r.,** cultiver le riz; **r. bowl,** bol *m* de riz; **r. field** *or* **paddy,** rizière *f*; **r. grower,** riziculteur *m*; **r. growing,** riziculture *f*; **r.-growing,** (*country, region*) producteur de riz; *Culin* **r. pudding,** riz au lait; **r. paper/straw/water/***etc*, papier *m*/paille *f*/eau *f*/*etc* de riz; **r. wine,** alcool *m* de riz, saké *m*.

rice[2] *vt Am* passer (*des légumes*) au presse-purée.

ricer ['raɪsər] *n Am* presse-purée *m inv*.

rich [rɪtʃ] **1** *adj* (*person, country*) riche; (*profit*) gros; (*food*) riche; (*banquet*) somptueux; (*soil*) riche, fertile; (*vegetation*) luxuriant; (*harvest, supply*) abondant; (*costume, dress*) riche, somptueux; (*furniture*) luxueux; (*colour*) chaud; (*voice*) étoffé, ample, plein; (*incident, situation*) très divertissant, impayable; **r. people,** les riches *mpl*; **extremely r.,** richissime; **to get** *or* **grow r.,** s'enrichir; **a get-r.-quick scheme,** un système pour s'enrichir rapidement; **I'm richer by a hundred pounds** *or* **a hundred pounds richer,** j'ai une centaine de livres de plus; **r. in ...,** riche *ou* abondant en ...; **r. dish,** plat riche *ou* composé d'ingrédients de choix; **I can't eat r. food,** je ne digère pas les aliments riches; *Aut* **r. mixture,** mélange *m* riche; **r. green,** vert *m* intense; *Iron* **that's r. coming from you,** venant de toi, c'est un peu fort. **2** *n* **(a) riches,** (*of country, seabed etc*) richesse(s) *f(pl)*; **(b) the r.,** (*used as pl*) les riches *mpl*.

-rich [rɪtʃ] *suff* **cotton/protein/***etc***-r.,** riche *ou* à haute teneur en coton/protéines/*etc*.

Richard ['rɪtʃəd] *n* **R. the Lion-Heart,** Richard *m* Cœur de Lion.

richly ['rɪtʃlɪ] *adv* (*to dress*) richement, somptueusement; (*to decorate*) richement; **r. deserved,** bien mérité.

richness ['rɪtʃnɪs] *n* (*of person, country, food, fuel mix, style*) richesse *f*; (*of harvest, supply*) abondance *f*; (*of banquet*) somptuosité *f*; (*of soil*) richesse, fertilité *f*; (*of voice*) ampleur *f*; (*of colour*) chaleur *f*.

Richter ['rɪktər] *n* **R. scale,** échelle *f* de Richter; **to measure five on the R. scale,** (*of earthquake*) atteindre cinq sur l'échelle (de) Richter.

rick[1] [rɪk] *n* (*of hay, straw etc*) meule *f*.

rick[2] *vt* mettre (*le foin etc*) en meule(s).

rick[3] *n* (*in back, ankle etc*) torsion *f*; (*in neck*) torticolis *m*; **I have a r. in my lower back,** je me suis donné un tour de reins; **I have a r. in my neck,** j'ai attrapé un torticolis.

rick[4] *vt* se tordre (*la cheville*); **to r. one's back,** se donner un tour de reins; **to r. one's neck,** attraper un torticolis.

rickets ['rɪkɪts] *npl Med* rachitisme *m*; **to have r.,** être rachitique.

rickety ['rɪkɪtɪ] *adj* **(a)** *F* (*furniture*) bancal; (*staircase*) branlant, délabré; (*bridge*) branlant; (*table*) boiteux, branlant; **(b)** *Med* rachitique.

rickrack ['rɪkræk] *n* **r. (braid),** soutache *f*, galon *m* en forme de zigzag.

rickshaw ['rɪkʃɔː] *n* pousse(-pousse) *m inv*; **r. driver,** conducteur *m* de pousse(-pousse); **r. passenger,** personne se déplaçant en pousse(-pousse).

ricochet[1] ['rɪkəʃeɪ, *occ* -ʃet] *n* (*of ball, bullet etc*) ricochet *m*.

ricochet[2] *vi* (**ricochetted** ['rɪkəʃeɪd]; **ricochetting** ['rɪkəʃeɪɪŋ]) (*of ball, bullet etc*) ricocher (**off,** contre).

ricrac ['rɪkræk] *n* = **RICKRACK**.

rictus *pl* **-tus, -tusses** ['rɪktəs, -əsɪz] *n* rictus *m*.

rid [rɪd] *vt* (*pt* **ridded, rid**; *pp* **rid**; *prp* **ridding**) débarrasser, délivrer (*qn*) (**of,** de); débarrasser (*un endroit*) (**of,** de); **to r. a country of bandits,** purger un pays de bandits; **to r. the world of poverty,** délivrer le monde de la pauvreté; **to r. oneself of one's illusions,** se défaire de ses illusions; **to r. s.o. of his enemies,** délivrer qn de ses ennemis; **the kidneys r. the body of waste,** les reins débarrassent le corps des déchets; **to get rid** *or* **to r. oneself of sth,** se débarrasser *ou* se défaire de qch; **I'll get rid of it for you,** je vais t'en débarrasser; **I've got rid of my car,** je me suis débarrassé de ma voiture; **we can't get rid of the house,** nous n'arrivons pas à vendre la maison; *Cards* **to get rid of a card,** se défausser d'une carte; **to get rid of s.o.,** (*dismiss*) (*servant*) renvoyer; (*government, politician etc*) *F* balayer qn, débarquer qn; (*murder*) supprimer qn; **I thought we were never going to get rid of them,** j'ai cru que nous n'allions jamais arriver à nous en débarrasser; **to get rid of a cold,** se débarrasser d'un rhume.

riddance ['rɪd(ə)ns] *n* débarras *m*; **good r.!,** bon débarras!

ridden ['rɪd(ə)n] *adj* **to be r. with** *or* **by guilt,** être bourrelé de remords *ou* accablé par le remords; **to be r. with fear,** être dévoré par la peur.

-ridden ['rɪd(ə)n] *suff* **debt-r.,** criblé *ou* accablé de dettes; **disease-r.,** rongé par la maladie; **guilt-r.,** bourrelé de remords, accablé par le remords.

riddle[1] ['rɪd(ə)l] *n* (*puzzle*) devinette *f*; *Fig* (*person, event*) énigme *f*; **to speak** *or* **talk in riddles,** parler par énigmes; **to ask s.o. a r.,** poser une devinette à qn.

riddle[2] *n* (*for earth, gravel etc*) crible *m*.

riddle[3] *vt* cribler (*le gravier*); **to r. the grate,** secouer la grille; *Fig* **to r. s.o. with bullets,** cribler qn de balles; *Fig* **riddled with,** (*holes*) criblé de; (*spelling mistakes*) cousu de; (*corruption*) en proie à; (*cancer*) rongé par.

ride[1] [raɪd] *n* **(a)** (*journey*) (*on bicycle, horse*) promenade *f*; (*in car*) promenade, voyage *m*; (*in taxi*) course *f*; (*in train*) voyage, trajet *m*; (*on merry-go-round*) tour *m*; (*in boat, helicopter, plane*) voyage; **to go for a r. in a car** *or* **a car r.,** aller se promener *ou* aller faire un tour en voiture; **we went for a r. in my car,** nous sommes allés faire un tour dans ma voiture; **to go for** *or* **take a r.,** (*on bicycle*) aller se promener *ou* aller faire un tour à bicyclette; (*on horse*) faire une promenade à cheval; **she goes for a r. every morning,** elle fait une promenade à cheval chaque matin; **to have a r. on,** (*bicycle*) monter sur; (*horse*) monter à; **to give a child a r. on one's back,** porter un enfant sur son dos; **the car gives a very smooth r.,** la voiture est bien suspendue *ou* a une bonne suspension; *Fig* **he did not have an easy r.,** (*at interview, press conference etc*) on ne l'a pas épargné; *Fig* **to give s.o. a rough r.,** en faire baver *ou* voir à qn; **we're in for a bumpy r.,** (*in plane*) ça va secouer; *Fig* nous sommes bien partis pour en baver; **to be along for the r.,** venir juste pour voir; *Can* **Musical R.,** (*of RCMP*) Carrousel *m*; **he has three rides today,** (*of jockey*) il a trois montes aujourd'hui; **to take s.o. for a r.,** emmener qn faire une promenade (**on horse,** à cheval; **in car,** en voiture); *F* (*cheat*) faire marcher qn, duper qn; *Am* (*in order to kill*) emmener qn en voiture pour le tuer; *F* **he's been taken for a r.,** (*cheated*) il s'est fait avoir;

(b) (*distance*) trajet *m*; **it's a 70p r. on the bus,** il y en a pour 70p en autobus; **it's only a short r. away by car,** il n'y en a pas pour longtemps en voiture; **it's a quarter of an hour's r. on a bicycle,** il y en a pour un quart d'heure à bicyclette;

(c) *Am Aut* (*lift*) **can I give you a r.?,** est-ce que je peux vous emmener *ou* conduire quelque part?; **could you give me a r. into town?,** est-ce que tu peux m'emmener *ou* me conduire en ville?; **does everyone have a r. to the church?,** est-ce que tout le monde a un véhicule pour aller à l'église?; **do you have a r. to the airport?,** est-ce que quelqu'un vous emmène *ou* conduit à l'aéroport?;

(d) (*in forest*) allée cavalière;

(e) *Am* (*at funfair*) manège *m*.

ride[2] *v* (*pt* **rode** [rəʊd]; *pp* **ridden** ['rɪd(ə)n], *Nau* **rode**) **1** *vi* **(a)** (*on horse*) chevaucher, aller *ou* se promener *ou* monter *ou* être monté à cheval, être à cheval; (*in car*) aller *ou* se promener en voiture; (*in bus*) aller *ou* venir *ou* être en autobus; **can you r.?,** savez-vous monter à cheval?; **she doesn't r. much,** elle ne monte pas souvent à cheval; **I'm going riding this morning,** je vais aller faire une promenade à cheval ce matin; **he rides well,** il monte bien (à cheval), il est bon cavalier; **to r. to hounds,** faire de la chasse à courre; **to r. on an elephant,** aller à dos d'éléphant; **it's the first time I've ridden in a Porsche,** c'est la première fois que je roule en Porsche; **to r. on s.o.'s shoulders,** être monté sur les épaules de qn; **to r. on s.o.'s knee,** (*of child*) être à califourchon sur le genou de qn; *Fig* **there's a lot riding on this election,** l'enjeu de cette élection est important; **to r. to a place,** se rendre à un endroit (**on horseback,** à cheval; **on bicycle,** à bicyclette); **to r. to work on the bus,** se rendre en bus à son travail; **to be riding for a fall,** courir à sa perte; **you are riding for a fall investing in a company you know nothing about,** tu cours à ta perte en investissant dans une société dont tu ne sais rien; **to be riding high,** connaître une période de succès; **to r. up/down,** (*in lift*) monter/descendre; **to r. 50 kilometres,** aller *ou* faire 50 kilomètres (à cheval, en voiture, *etc*); **he rides at 56 kilos,** (*of jockey*) il pèse 56 kilos en selle; **she's riding in the 3.30,** (*taking part in horserace*) elle dispute la course de 3h30; **the moon was riding high in the heavens,** la lune voguait haut dans le ciel; *Fig* **to let sth r.,** laisser courir qch; *Am* **I don't mind riding in** (*Br* **the**) **back,** je veux bien m'asseoir à l'arrière;

(b) *Aut* **how does she r.?,** comment est-ce qu'elle tient la route?; **this car rides very smoothly,** cette voiture est bien suspendue;

(c) (*of ship*) **to r. at anchor,** être au mouillage; **the ship was riding over the waves,** le navire voguait sur les eaux.

2 *vt* **(a)** monter, être monté sur (*un cheval*); aller à *ou* en (*bicyclette*); **she rode her horse across the fields,** elle a fait traverser le champ à son cheval; **she rode her horse at the fence,** elle a dirigé son cheval sur la barrière; **he's a very easy horse to r.,** c'est un cheval très facile à monter; *Horseracing* **Comet ridden by Martin,** Comet monté par Martin; **to r. an ass/elephant,** être monté à dos d'âne/d'éléphant; *esp Am F* **to r. s.o.,** être (toujours) sur le dos de qn; **stop riding me!,** fiche-moi la paix!; **witches r. broomsticks,** les sorcières chevauchent des balais *ou* des manches à balai; **to know how to r. a bike,** savoir faire de la bicyclette; **can I r. your bike?,** puis-je monter sur ta bicyclette?; *Fig* **to r. an idea to death,** être féru d'une idée; *Fig* **he rides this theory to death,** cette théorie est son cheval de bataille; **to r. the waves,** (*of ship*) voguer sur les flots; (*of surfer*) chevaucher les vagues; *Nau* **to r. the storm,** soutenir le choc de la tempête; **to r. a punch,** (*of boxer*) encaisser un coup; *Am* **to r. s.o. up/down,** (*in elevator*) faire monter/descendre qn; **to r. s.o. down,** (*on horse*) (*trample*) piétiner qn; (*overtake*) dépasser qn;

(b) *Am* (*travel in*) prendre (*l'autobus, le train*) **(to,** jusqu'à);

(c) (*take part in*) **to r. a race,** disputer une course.

►ride out 1 *vtsep* **to r. out the storm,** *Nau* étaler la tempête; *Fig* surmonter la crise; *Am* **to r. s.o. out of town,** faire quitter la ville à qn. **2** *vi* **we rode out to meet them,** nous sommes partis à leur rencontre en vélo *ou* à cheval.

►ride up *vi* (*of skirt etc*) remonter.

rider ['raɪdər] *n* **(a)** (*on horse*) cavalier, -ière; (*on racehorse*) jockey *m*; (*in circus*) écuyer, -ère; (*on bicycle*) cycliste *mf*; (*on motorcycle*) motocycliste *mf*; **to be a good r.,** monter bien à cheval, être bon cavalier; **(b)** (*to bill*) clause additionnelle; (*to document*) ajouté *m*, annexe *f*; (*to contract*) avenant *m*; **to add a r. (recommending) that ...,** ajouter une clause recommandant que ... .

riderless ['raɪdəlɪs] *adj* (*horse*) sans cavalier; (*motorcycle*) sans conducteur.

ridership ['raɪdəʃɪp] *n Am* nombre total d'utilisateurs des transports en commun.

ridesharing ['raɪdʃeərɪŋ] *n Am* = le fait pour plusieurs personnes de partager un véhicule pour se rendre sur leur lieu de travail.

ridge¹ [rɪdʒ] *n* **(a)** (*of roof, mountain*) arête *f*, crête *f*; **r. roof,** toit *m* en dos d'âne; **r. tile,** (tuile) faîtière *f*; **(b)** (*of hills, mountains*) chaîne *f*; *Met* **r. of high pressure,** dorsale *f* barométrique; **(c)** (*on surface*) strie *f*; (*on sand*) ride *f*; (*in field*) crête *f* de labour.

ridge² *vt* **(a)** enfaîter (*un toit*); **(b)** sillonner, canneler, strier (*une surface*); rider (*le sable*).

ridgepole ['rɪdʒpəʊl] *n* (*of roof*) panne faîtière; (*of tent*) mât *m* de faîte.

ridgetree ['rɪdʒtriː] *n* (*of roof*) panne faîtière.

ridgeway ['rɪdʒweɪ] *n Br* route *f* des crêtes.

ridicule¹ ['rɪdɪkjuːl] *n* ridicule *m*, dérision *f*; **to hold s.o./sth up to r.,** tourner qn/qch en ridicule *ou* en dérision; **to lay oneself open to r.,** s'exposer au ridicule; **object of r.,** objet *m* de risée; **to be an object of r.,** *F* être en butte au ridicule.

ridicule² *vt* ridiculiser (*qn, qch*), tourner (*qn, qch*) en ridicule *ou* en dérision **(for,** à cause de).

ridiculous [rɪ'dɪkjʊləs] **1** *adj* (*behaviour, person etc*) ridicule; **to make s.o./sth r.,** rendre qn/qch ridicule, ridiculiser qn/qch; **to make oneself r.,** se rendre ridicule, prêter à rire; **it's r. that ...,** il est ridicule que ...; **to pay a r. price for sth,** (*pay little*) payer un prix ridicule *ou* dérisoire pour qch; (*pay a lot*) payer un prix exagéré pour qch; *F* **don't be r.,** ne sois pas ridicule. **2** *n* ridicule *m*; **from the sublime to the r.,** du sublime au ridicule.

ridiculously [rɪ'dɪkjʊləslɪ] *adv* (*to act, dress etc*) ridiculement, d'une façon ridicule; (*easy, expensive, low etc*) ridiculement.

ridiculousness [rɪ'dɪkjʊləsnɪs] *n* (*of appearance, behaviour, situation etc*) ridicule *m*.

riding ['raɪdɪŋ] *n* **(a)** (*of horse*) équitation *f*; (*skill*) monte *f*; **r. is her favourite hobby,** l'équitation est son passe-temps favori; **r. cap,** bombe *f*; **r. boots,** bottes *fpl* de cheval; **r. breeches,** culotte *f* de cheval; **r. costume,** tenue *f* de cheval; **r. habit,** amazone *f*; **r. lesson,** leçon *f* d'équitation; **r. techniques,** techniques *fpl* de l'équitation; **r. crop** *or* **whip,** cravache *f*; **r. school,** école *f* d'équitation, manège *m*; **r. instructor,** professeur *m* d'équitation, maître *m* de manège; **(b)** *Aut* **smooth r.,** suspension douce; **(c)** *Can* circonscription électorale; *Br* **the East/West/North R.,** la division est/ouest/nord du comté d'Yorkshire.

rife [raɪf] *adj* (*widespread*) répandu; **to be r.,** (*of corruption, crime, disease etc*) régner, sévir; (*of rumour*) courir; **the city was r. with disease/rumours,** la ville était en proie à la maladie/aux rumeurs, la maladie/les rumeurs ré-gnai(en)t dans la ville; **the police force is r. with corruption,** la corruption règne dans la police.

riffle¹ ['rɪf(ə)l] *n Am* (*ripple*) rides *fpl* sur l'eau, ondulations *fpl* de l'eau; (*shoal*) banc *m*.

riffle² 1 *vt* **(a)** battre (*les cartes*); feuilleter (*des pages*); **(b)** troubler (*la surface de l'eau*). **2** *vi* **to r. through,** feuilleter.

riffraff ['rɪfræf] *n* canaille *f*, racaille *f*; **all the r.,** tout le rebut de la société.

rifle¹ ['raɪf(ə)l] *vt* piller (*un endroit*); vider (*les poches de qn, un classeur, un tiroir*); violer (*un tombeau*).

rifle² *n* fusil *m*; (*for hunting*) carabine *f* (de chasse); **r. club,** société *f* de tir; **r. practice,** (exercice *m* de) tir *m* au fusil; **r. shot,** coup *m* de fusil; **within r. shot,** à portée de fusil; *Mil* **R. Corps,** corps *m* des fusiliers *ou* des chasseurs à pied.

rifleman, *pl* **-men** ['raɪf(ə)lmən] *n Mil* fantassin *m*, fusilier *m*.

rifling ['raɪflɪŋ] *n* (*on gun barrel*) (*grooves*) rayures *fpl*; (*action of cutting grooves*) rayage *m*.

rift [rɪft] *n* (*in earth, rock etc*) fissure *f*, crevasse *f*; (*in clouds etc*) éclaircie *f*; *Fig* (*in relationship*) rupture *f*; *Pol* (*in party*) scission *f*; *Geol* **r. valley,** rift *m*, fossé *m* (tectonique).

rig¹ [rɪg] *n* **(a)** (*of ship*) gréement *m*; **(b)** (*equipment*) équipement *m*, installation *f*, accessoires *mpl*; **(oil) r.,** derrick *m*; (*at sea*) plate-forme pétrolière; **(c)** *Am Aut* semi-remorque *m*; **(d)** = **RIG-OUT.**

rig² *vt* **(-gg-) (a)** *Nau* gréer, équiper (*un navire*); **(b)** *F* (*fix dishonestly*) truquer (*une élection*); **a rigged election,** une élection bidon *ou* truquée; *Fin* **to r. the market,** provoquer une hausse *ou* une baisse factice; **to r. prices,** fixer illégalement les prix; **to r. a game,** truquer un jeu.

►rig out *vtsep* (*dress*) attifer, accoutrer (*qn*) **(as,** en); **to r. oneself out,** s'accoutrer **(in, dans,** avec).

►rig up *vtsep* (*aerial, shelter*) monter, installer; *F* **to r. something up,** faire une installation de fortune.

rigamarole ['rɪgəmərəʊl] *n F* = **RIGMAROLE.**

rigger ['rɪgər] *n* **(a)** (*of ship*) gréeur *m*, mâteur *m*; **square r.,** (*ship*) navire gréé en carré; **(b)** (*of plane*) monteur-régleur *m*.

rigging¹ ['rɪgɪŋ] *n* **(a)** (*of machine*) montage *m*; **(b)** (*on ship*) gréement *m*; (*of ship*) gréage *m*.

rigging² *n* (*of election*) truquage *m*; (*of market*) hausse *f ou* baisse *f* factice; (*of prices*) fixation illégale.

right¹ [raɪt] **1** *adj* **(a)** (*correct, accurate*) (*answer etc*) bon, *f* bonne, exact, juste; (*word*) juste; **that can't be r.,** ça ne peut pas être ça, ça ne peut pas être juste; **have you the r. amount?,** avez-vous le compte *ou* la monnaie exacte?; **is this the r. house?,** est-ce (bien) la bonne maison?; **what's the r. time?,** quelle heure est-il (exactement)?, quelle est l'heure juste *ou* exacte?; **my watch is r.,** ma montre est à l'heure; **to be r.,** (*of person*) avoir raison **(to do,** de faire); **you're quite r.!,** vous avez bien raison!; **you were r. about him being a crook,** vous aviez raison de dire que c'est une canaille; **the r. thing to do,** la meilleure chose à faire; **it doesn't look r.,** (*of answer, dress etc*) ça ne va pas; **the r. side of the material,** l'endroit *m* du tissu; **r. side** *or* **way up,** à l'endroit; **we're on the r. road,** nous sommes sur le bon chemin *ou* la bonne route; **that's r.!,** parfaitement!, c'est ça!; **r. (you are)!,** entendu!, d'accord!; *F* **r.?,** d'acc.?; *Am* **r. on!,** *Austr* **too r.!,** exactement!, bien parlé!; **he's on the r. side of forty,** il n'a pas encore quarante ans; **to get on the r. side of s.o.,** s'insinuer dans les bonnes grâces de qn; **to keep on the r. side of the law,** respecter la loi;

(b) (*morally good*) bon, juste; (*fair*) juste; **it's not r. to steal,** ce n'est pas bien de voler; **it doesn't look r.,** ça ne fait pas bien; **it's only r.,** ce n'est que justice; **I thought it r. to attend,** j'ai jugé bon *ou* à propos d'y aller; **to do the r. thing,** se conduire honnêtement *ou* honorablement; *Old-fashioned Br* **I hope he's going to do the r. thing by you,** (*marry you*) j'espère qu'il va agir honorablement à ton égard;

(c) *Math* (*angle*) droit; *Am* **r. triangle,** triangle *m* rectangle; **at r. angles to ...,** à angle droit avec ..., perpendiculaire à ...;

(d) (*most appropriate*) **in the r. place,** bien placé, à sa place; **to be in the r. place at the r. time,** être là où il faut quand il le faut; **the r. man/woman in the r. place,** l'homme/la femme qu'il faut pour la tâche; **you came at the r. time,** vous êtes venu au bon moment; **to wait for the r. moment,** attendre le bon moment *ou* le moment opportun; **to know the r. people,** avoir des relations, avoir des relations utiles; **r. whale,** baleine franche;

(e) (*mentally, physically well*) **to be in one's r. mind,** avoir toute sa raison, être en possession de toutes ses facultés; *F* **he's not quite r. in the head,** il n'a pas toute sa tête; **no one in their r. mind would do such a thing,** aucune personne sensée ne ferait une chose pareille; **I'm not feeling quite r.,** je ne me sens pas très bien, *F* je ne me sens pas dans mon assiette; **as r. as rain** *or Am* **a trivet,** en parfaite santé; **all r.,** *see* **ALL RIGHT**;

(f) *F* (*idiot, swindle etc*) vrai; **I felt a r. fool,** je me suis senti vraiment stupide; **he's all r.,** c'est un brave type; *Sl* **she's a bit of all r.!,** voilà une jolie pépée!;

(g) (*righthand*) droit; **on the r. side,** à *ou* sur la droite; **r. hand,** main droite; **on my r. hand,** sur ma droite; **he's my r. hand,** il est mon bras droit; **r. bank,** (*of river*) rive droite; **r. wing,** *Mil Sp* aile droite; *Pol* la droite.

2 *n* **(a)** (*morality*) droit *m*, bien *m*; **r. and wrong,** le bien et le mal; **to know r. from wrong,** faire la différence entre le bien et le mal; **to be in the r.,** avoir raison; **by rights,** en toute justice;

(b) (*entitlement*) droit *m* (**to,** à; **to do,** de faire); **to exercise a r.,** exercer un droit; **r. to vote,** droit de vote; **r. of abode,** (*of refugee etc*) droit de séjour; **r. of way,** *Jur* servitude *f ou* droit de passage; *Aut* priorité *f*; **there is no r. of way across this land,** il n'y a pas de droit de passage sur cette terre; **to have r. of way,** (*on road*) avoir (la) priorité; **it belongs to him by r.,** cela lui appartient de droit; **to possess sth in one's own r.,** avoir qch en propre; **she is famous in her own r.,** elle est elle-même célèbre; **animal/human rights,** les droits de l'animal/ l'homme; **women's rights,** les droits de la femme; **to be within one's rights,** être dans son droit (**in doing,** en faisant); **to know one's rights,** connaître ses droits; *St Exch* **rights issue,** émission de nouvelles actions à taux préférentiel;

(c) (*authority, claim*) droit *m*; **to hold the film/ translation rights to a book,** détenir les droits d'adaptation cinématographique/de traduction d'un livre; **all rights reserved,** tous droits réservés; **by what r.?,** de quel droit?, à quel titre?; **what r. have you to do that?,** de quel droit faites-vous cela?;

(d) (*order*) **to put** *or* **set sth to rights,** arranger qch, mettre qch en ordre *ou* en règle;

(e) (*right-hand side*) droite *f*, côté droit; **on the r.,** à droite; **on your r.,** à votre droite; **to drive on the r.,** rouler *ou* conduire à droite; **to keep to the r.,** tenir la droite;

(f) (*blow*) coup *m* du droit;

(g) *Pol* **the r.,** la droite, les conservateurs *mpl*; **to be to the r.,** être à droite.

3 *adv* **(a)** (*straight*) (tout) droit; **to put a mistake r.,** corriger *ou* rectifier une erreur; **to put things r.,** arranger les choses *ou* une affaire; **to put one's watch r.,** mettre sa montre à l'heure; **to put s.o. r.,** (*give directions*) mettre qn sur la (bonne) voie; (*open eyes*) détromper qn, désabuser qn (**about,** au sujet de); **he went r. at him,** il est allé droit vers lui; **to do sth r. away** *or* **off,** (*immediately*) faire qch sur-le-champ *ou* immédiatement; (*easily*) faire qch du premier coup; **I'll be r. back,** je reviens tout de suite; **r. now,** (*immediately*) tout de suite; *Am* (*at the moment*) en ce moment;

(b) (*completely*) tout à fait; **a wall r. round the house,** un mur tout autour de la maison; **he turned r. round,** il a fait un tour complet; *Br Dial F* **I was r. glad to hear it,** j'étais fort heureux de l'apprendre; **r. reverend/ honourable,** très révérend/honorable;

(c) (*exactly*) **r. at the top,** tout en haut; **r. in the middle,** au beau *ou* en plein milieu; **r. in the middle of the harvest,** en pleine moisson; **r. behind,** juste derrière; **the wind was r. behind us,** nous avions le vent en plein dans le dos; **it was r. here on the table,** il était là sur la table; **he parked r. in front of the gate,** il s'est garé en plein devant le portail; *F* **I'll be waiting r. here,** j'attends ici, je ne bouge pas;

(d) (*correctly*) juste; (*to answer*) correctement; (*to guess*) juste; **if I remember r.,** si je me souviens bien; **you did r. to wait,** vous avez bien fait d'attendre; **to act r.,** agir bien; **did I hear r.?,** est-ce que j'ai bien entendu?;

(e) (*well*) bien; **nothing goes r. with me,** rien ne me réussit; **I got your letter all r.,** j'ai bien reçu votre lettre; **he's to blame r. enough,** c'est bien de sa faute (à lui); **to see s.o. r.,** (*financially*) veiller à ce que qn ne soit pas à court d'argent; **that'll put you r.,** voilà qui vous remontera;

(f) (*to look, turn*) à droite; *F* **r., left and centre,** (*everywhere*) de tous les côtés; *F* **he owes money r., left, and centre,** il doit de l'argent à droite et à gauche; *F* **he cheated us r., left and centre,** il nous a eus sur tous les tableaux.

right² *vt* **(a)** redresser (*un canot, une voiture etc*); **to r. itself,** (*of boat*) se redresser; **(b)** redresser, réparer (*un tort*); corriger, rectifier (*une erreur*); **to r. itself,** (*of faulty machine*) s'arranger.

right-angled ['raɪtæŋg(ə)ld] *adj* à angle droit; (*triangle etc*) rectangle, rectangulaire.

righteous ['raɪtʃəs] **1** *adj* (*person*) droit, vertueux; *Bible* juste; (*anger, indignation*) juste, justifié; *Pej* **r. tone of voice,** ton satisfait. **2** *n* **the r.,** (*used as pl*) les bons *mpl*, les justes *mpl*.

righteously ['raɪtʃəslɪ] *adv* vertueusement; (*angry, indignant*) de manière offensée; *Pej* (*to say*) d'un ton satisfait.

righteousness ['raɪtʃəsnɪs] *n* (*of person*) droiture *f*, vertu *f*; *Bible* **those who hunger and thirst after r.,** ceux qui ont faim et soif de justice.

rightful ['raɪtfʊl] *adj* (*heir, king*) légitime; (*claim, owner*) légitime, juste, justifié; (*inheritance*) auquel on a droit; **to have one's r. share,** avoir sa juste part.

rightfully ['raɪtfəlɪ] *adv* légitimement; (*inherited*) à juste titre; **it is r. mine,** cela m'appartient légitimement.

right-hand ['raɪthænd] *adj* (*glove etc*) de la main droite; (*bend, drawer etc*) de droite; **to have r.-h. drive,** (*of car*) avoir la conduite à droite, avoir le volant à droite; **on the r.-h. side,** au côté droit; *Fig* **r.-h. man** *or* **woman,** bras droit.

right-handed [raɪt'hændɪd] **1** *adj* (*person*) droitier; (*tool, scissors etc*) pour la main droite; (*screw*) vis *f* dont le pas est à droite; **r.-h. blow,** coup *m* du droit. **2** *adv* (*to play, hit etc*) de la main droite.

right-hander [raɪt'hændər] *n* **(a)** (*person*) droitier, -ière; **(b)** (*blow*) coup *m* du droit.

righting ['raɪtɪŋ] *n* (*of boat, wrong*) redressement *m*.

rightist ['raɪtɪst] *adj* (*ideas, politics etc*) de droite.

rightly ['raɪtlɪ] *adv* **(a)** (*to act, judge*) bien; **(b)** (*believe, answer*) correctement, à juste titre; (*annoyed, concerned etc*) à raison; **r. or wrongly,** à tort ou à raison; **I can't r. say,** je ne saurais dire au juste; **I don't r. know,** je ne sais pas exactement *ou* au juste; **and r. so,** et à juste titre.

right-minded [raɪt'maɪndɪd] *adj* (*person*) sensé.

rightness ['raɪtnɪs] *n* (*of decision*) justesse *f*; (*of answer*) justesse, exactitude *f*; (*of cause*) justesse.

righto [raɪ'təʊ], **rightyho** [raɪtɪ'əʊ] *int Br F* entendu!, d'accord!

right-thinking [raɪt'θɪŋkɪŋ] *adj* sensé.

right-to-lifer [raɪttə'laɪfər] *n Am* partisan *m* du droit à la vie, personne *f* qui est contre l'avortement.

right-wing [raɪt'wɪŋ] *adj Pol* (*attitude, government, thinking etc*) de droite; **r.-w. policy,** politique *f* de droite; **he is very r.-w.,** il est très à droite.

right-winger [raɪt'wɪŋər] *n Pol* personne *f* de droite.

rigid ['rɪdʒɪd] *adj* (*metal, plastic etc*) rigide, raide; *Fig* (*discipline, principles, rules etc*) sévère, strict, inflexible; (*etiquette*) rigide; **she's very r. in her ideas,** elle a des idées inflexibles; *Br F* **to be bored r.,** s'ennuyer ferme; *Br F* **it shook me r.,** (*shocked me*) ça m'en a fichu un sacré coup.

rigidity [rɪ'dʒɪdɪtɪ] *n* (*of metal, plastic*) rigidité *f*, raideur *f*; *Fig* (*of discipline, principles, rules etc*) sévérité *f*, intransigeance *f*; (*of etiquette*) rigidité.

rigidly ['rɪdʒɪdlɪ] *adv* rigidement; (*censored, controlled*) sévèrement, strictement; **r. opposed to ...,** rigoureusement opposé à ... .

rigmarole ['rɪgmərəʊl] *n F* (*speech*) galimatias *m*; (*process*) procédure compliquée; **to go through a whole r.,** en passer par tout un cirque (**of doing,** consistant à faire).

rigor ['rɪgər] *n* **(a)** *US* = **RIGOUR**; **(b)** *Med* **r. mortis** ['mɔːtɪs], rigidité *f* cadavérique.

rigorous ['rɪgərəs] *adj* (*discipline, training, climate, analysis etc*) rigoureux.

rigorously ['rɪgərəslɪ] *adv* (*to discipline, train*) rigoureusement.

rigorousness ['rɪgərəsnɪs] *n* (*of discipline, training, climate, analysis etc*) rigueur *f*.

rigour, *US* **rigor** ['rɪgər] *n* rigueur *f*; **the r. of the law,** la rigueur de la loi; **the rigours of prison life,** les rigueurs de la vie en prison; **the rigours of the Scottish climate,** les rigueurs du climat écossais.

rigout ['rɪgaʊt] *n F* (*outfit*) tenue *f*; *Pej* accoutrement *m*; **to be in full r.,** être en grande tenue.

rile [raɪl] *vt F* agacer, exaspérer (*qn*); **to r. s.o. (up) about sth,** faire (en)rager qn à propos de qch; **don't get riled!,** ne t'énerve pas!

rill [rɪl] *n* ruisselet *m*, petit ruisseau.

rim¹ [rɪm] *n* (*of wheel*) jante *f*; (*of cup, glass etc*) bord *m*; (*of crater*) bord *m*; (*of dirt, soap etc*) trace *f*; **spectacle rims,** monture *f* de lunettes; **countries on the Pacific R.,**

pays de la ceinture pacifique; **Pacific R. economy,** économie des pays de la ceinture pacifique.
rim² *vt* (-mm-) janter (*une roue*); (*of hills etc*) border, encercler (*une vallée*); **nails rimmed with dirt,** des ongles ourlés de crasse.
rime¹ [raɪm] *n* givre *m*, gelée blanche.
rime² *n & v* = **RHYME¹,²**.
rimless ['rɪmlɪs] *adj* (*spectacles*) sans monture.
-rimmed ['rɪmd] *suff* **horn/steel/***etc* **-r.,** avec une monture en corne/en acier/*etc*.
rind [raɪnd] *n* (*of fruit, vegetable*) peau *f*, pelure *f*; (*of melon, lemon*) écorce *f*; (*of cheese*) croûte *f*; (*of bacon*) couenne *f*; **a piece of orange/lemon r.,** un zeste de citron/d'orange.
ring¹ [rɪŋ] *n* **(a)** (*band*) (*for finger*) anneau *m*; (*with stone*) bague *f*; (*for marking birds*) bague; (*for keys*) porte-clés *m inv*; (*for curtain*) anneau; (*for napkin*) rond *m*; (*on ski pole*) rondelle *f*; **r. binder,** classeur *m* à anneaux; **r. finger,** annulaire *m*; *Gym* **the rings,** les anneaux; *Mus* **The R. (Cycle** *or* **of the Nibelung),** La Tétralogie;
(b) (*circle*) (*of people, chairs etc*) cercle *m*; (*in water*) rond *m*; (*burner on stove*) brûleur *m*; (*round planet*) anneau *m*; (*round sun, moon*) halo *m*; (*of smoke*) rond; (*of tree*) anneau *ou* cercle annuel; (*stain*) tache *f*, marque *f*; **the cup will leave a r.,** la tasse va faire une marque; **sitting in a r.,** assis en cercle *ou* en rond; *Geol* **R. of Fire,** ceinture *f* de feu; **to have rings round one's eyes,** avoir les yeux cernés; *F* **make** *or* **run rings round s.o.,** surpasser qn, l'emporter sur qn; **they formed a r. round her,** ils ont formé un cercle autour d'elle; **to draw** *or* **put a r. round sth,** entourer qch d'un cercle; *Br* **r. road,** route *f* de ceinture; (*motorway*) périphérique *m*; **swimming r.,** bouée *f*;
(c) (*enclosure*) (*at circus*) arène *f*, piste *f*; (*for boxing, wrestling*) enceinte *f*, ring *m*; (*for bullfight*) arène; (*for showjumping*) enceinte *f*; *Fig* **to throw** *or* **toss one's hat in the r.,** faire connaître son intention de descendre dans l'arène;
(d) (*organization*) (*of people*) groupe *m*, petit cercle; (*gang*) bande *f*; *Com* syndicat *m*, cartel *m*; (*of spies, drug traffickers*) réseau *m*; **the r.,** (*boxing as sport*) la boxe *f*; **to retire from the r.,** se retirer du ring; *St Exch* **the R.,** le Parquet.
ring² *vt* **(a)** baguer (*un oiseau*); **(b)** (*of police, troops etc*) encercler (*un édifice etc*); (*item on list etc*) entourer d'un cercle; **to r. s.o./sth round** *or* **about** *or* **in,** (*surround*) encercler *ou* entourer *ou* cerner qn/qch (**with,** de).
ring³ *n* **(a)** (*sound*) (*of bells, telephone*) sonnerie *f*; (*of small bell, coins*) tintement *m*; (*of voice*) timbre *m*, intonation *f*; **there was a r. at the door,** on sonnait; **to answer a r.,** (*at door*) aller ouvrir; **r. of bells,** (*in church etc*) carillon *m*; *Fig* **it has a hollow r.,** cela sonne creux; *Fig* **the r. of truth,** l'accent *m* de la vérité; *Tel* **I hung up on the sixth r.,** j'ai raccroché à la sixième sonnerie; **(b)** *Br Tel* (*communication*) appel *m* téléphonique, coup *m* de téléphone; **to give s.o. a r.,** passer un coup de fil à qn.
ring⁴ *v* (*pt* **rang** [ræŋ]; *pp* **rung** [rʌŋ]) **1** *vi* **(a)** (*of bell, telephone*) sonner; (*of small bell*) tinter; (*of person*) sonner; (*of alarm*) retentir; (*of street etc*) résonner, retentir (**with,** de); **this will cause the alarm to r.,** cela déclenchera l'alarme; **to r. at the door,** sonner à la porte; **the bell is ringing for dinner,** on sonne pour le dîner; **to r. for s.o.,** sonner qn; **to r. for some coffee,** sonner pour demander du café; **to r. true/false,** (*of coin*) sonner vrai/faux; *Fig* **his answer did not r. true,** sa réponse a sonné faux; **her words still r. in my ears,** ses paroles résonnent encore à mes oreilles; **my ears are ringing,** mes oreilles bourdonnent;
(b) *esp Br Tel* téléphoner; **to r. round,** passer une série de coups de fil; **to r. for room service,** (*in hotel*) sonner pour appeler le garçon d'étage.
2 *vt* **(a)** (faire) sonner (*une cloche*); déclencher (*une alarme*); **to r. the doorbell,** sonner à la porte; *F* **does that r. a bell?** est-ce que cela vous rappelle *ou* vous dit quelque chose?; *Fig* **to r. the changes,** introduire des changements;
(b) *esp Br Tel* téléphoner à, appeler (*qn*).
►**ring back** *esp Br* **1** *vi* rappeler. **2** *vtsep* rappeler (*qn*).
►**ring down** *vtsep Th* **to r. down the curtain,** sonner pour la chute du rideau; *Fig* **to r. down the curtain on sth,** marquer la fin de qch.
►**ring in 1** *vi esp Br* **to r. in sick,** appeler pour dire qu'on est malade; **the boss wants her to r. in every hour when she's not in the office,** le patron veut qu'elle appelle toutes les heures quand elle n'est pas au bureau. **2** *vtsep* **to r. in the New Year,** marquer la nouvelle année par une volée de cloches.
►**ring off** *vi esp Br* raccrocher (l'appareil).
►**ring out 1** *vi* (*of bell*) sonner; (*of voice, shot*) retentir. **2** *vtsep* **to r. out the Old Year,** sonner *ou* carillonner la fin de l'année.
►**ring up** *esp Br* **1** *vi* téléphoner. **2** *vtsep* **(a)** téléphoner à (*qn*), appeler (*qn*); **(b)** *Th* **to r. up the curtain,** sonner pour faire lever le rideau; (*in France*) frapper les trois coups; *Fig* **to r. up the curtain on sth,** marquer le début de qch; **to r. an amount up,** (*on cash register*) enregistrer une somme.
ringed [rɪŋd] *adj* **(a)** (*bird*) bagué; **(b)** (*plover etc*) à collier.
ringer ['rɪŋər] *n* **(a)** (*of bell*) sonneur *m*, carillonneur *m*; **(b)** (*on telephone*) sonnerie *f*; **(c)** *Am Horseracing* cheval substitué à un autre; **(d)** *F* **to be a dead r. for s.o.,** être le sosie de qn.
ringing¹ ['rɪŋɪŋ] *n* (*of bird*) baguage *m*.
ringing² 1 *adj* (*bell*) qui tinte *ou* sonne; (*voice etc*) sonore, retentissant; **in r. tones,** d'une voix vibrante. **2** *n* **(a)** son *m*; (*of large bell, telephone*) sonnerie *f*; (*of small bell*) tintement *m*; **(b)** (*of telephone*) appel *m*, sonnerie *f*; *Br* **r. tone,** tonalité *f*; **(c)** (*in ears*) bourdonnement *m*.
ringleader ['rɪŋliːdər] *n Pej* (*of gang*) chef *m* de bande; (*of rebellion, in mischief etc*) meneur, -euse.
ringlet ['rɪŋlɪt] *n* (*curl*) anglaise *f*, boucle *f* (de cheveux); **to wear one's hair in ringlets,** porter les cheveux en boucles, porter des anglaises.
ringmaster ['rɪŋmɑːstər] *n* (*of circus*) maître *m* de manège.
ring-necked ['rɪŋnekt] *adj* (*bird, snake*) à collier; **r.-n. dove,** pigeon ramier, palombe *f*.
ring-pull ['rɪŋpʊl] *n* **r.-p. can,** boîte *f* à anneau que l'on tire.
ringside ['rɪŋsaɪd] *n* premier rang; **to have a r. seat,** (*at circus, boxing match*) avoir une place au premier rang; *Fig* être aux premières loges; **to have a r. view of sth,** être bien placé pour voir qch.
ring-tailed ['rɪŋteɪld] *adj* à queue zébrée.
ringworm ['rɪŋwɜːm] *n Med* teigne *f*.
rink [rɪŋk] *n* (*for ice-skating*) patinoire *f*; (*for roller-skating*) piste *f*.
rinkydink [rɪŋkɪ'dɪŋk] *adj US F* de mauvaise qualité.
rinse¹ [rɪns] *n* **(a)** (*of bottle, hands etc*) rinçage *m*; **to give sth a r.,** rincer qch; **r. cycle,** (*in washing machine*) cycle *m* de rinçage; **(b)** (*hair colouring*) shampooing colorant, rinçage *m* (colorant); **to have a r.,** se faire faire un shampooing colorant *ou* un rinçage (colorant).
rinse² *vt* **(a)** rincer (*le linge*); **to r. sth out,** rincer qch; **to r. sth out of sth,** rincer qch pour en éliminer qch; **to r. one's hands,** se passer les mains à l'eau; (*remove soap*) se rincer les mains; **(b)** (*with hair colouring*) faire un shampooing colorant *ou* un rinçage colorant à.
►**rinse down** *vtsep* faire passer (*un repas, un cachet*) en buvant qch.
►**rinse out** *vtsep* = **RINSE²**.
riot¹ ['raɪət] *n* (*uprising*) émeute *f*; (*demonstration*) manifestation violente; *Fig* **there will be a r.,** (*when people find out*) ça va faire scandale; *Fig* **a r. of colour,** une orgie de couleurs; **to run r.,** (*of person, inflation etc*) se déchaîner; (*of plants*) pulluler; *F* **he's/it's a r.,** c'est un/c'est rigolo; **the r. police,** la police anti-émeute, ≈ les CRS *mpl*; **r. gear,** matériel anti-émeute.
riot² *vi* (-t-) **(a)** (*rise up*) faire une émeute, s'ameuter; **(b)** (*fight*) se bagarrer.
rioter ['raɪətər] *n* émeutier, -ière; (*demonstrator*) manifestant, -ante violent(e).
rioting ['raɪətɪŋ] **1** *adj* qui fait émeute; **r. mob,** bande *f* d'émeutiers. **2** *n* émeutes *fpl*, manifestations violentes; (*fighting*) bagarres *fpl*; **r. broke out when ...,** les bagarres ont commencé quand ... .
riotous ['raɪətəs] *adj* (*crowd etc*) tapageur; *Jur* **to charge s.o. with r. behaviour,** accuser qn d'avoir eu un comportement séditieux; **r. living,** vie déréglée.
riotously ['raɪətəslɪ] *adv* tapageusement, de façon tapageuse; (*funny*) à se tordre.
rip¹ [rɪp] *n* (*in fabric*) déchirure *f*; **there's a r. in your jacket,** il y a une déchirure à ta veste.
rip² *v* (-pp-) **1** *vt* déchirer (*un tissu etc*); **to r. to pieces** *or* **shreds,** déchirer (*qch*) en lambeaux; *Fig* éreinter (*une pièce etc*); **it's ripped to pieces** *or* **shreds,** c'est en lambeaux. **2** *vi* (*of fabric etc*) se déchirer; **to r. (along),** aller *ou* avancer à toute vitesse *ou* à fond de train; **let her r.!,** (*of car*) mettez les gaz!, fonce!; *F Old-fashioned* **to let r.,** (*be angry*) laisser éclater sa colère (**about,** au sujet de); **to let r. at s.o.,** s'en prendre à qn (**about,** au sujet de); **to let r. against the government,** laisser éclater sa colère à l'égard du gouvernement (**for,** au sujet de).
►**rip away** *vtsep* arracher, déchirer (*qch*).
►**rip into** *vipo F* attaquer (*qn*).
►**rip off** *vtsep* **to r. sth off,** arracher qch, déchirer qch; *F* **to r. s.o. off,** (*cheat*) rouler qn; **you were ripped off,** tu t'es fait rouler; *F* **to r. sth off,** (*steal*) voler qch.
►**rip open** *vtsep* éventrer (*qn*); découdre (*un vêtement*); **to r. open a letter,** décacheter une lettre en la déchirant; **to r. open a package,** ouvrir un paquet en le déchirant.
►**rip out** *vtsep* **to r. out a fireplace,** enlever une

cheminée.

▶**rip up** *vtsep* déchirer.

RIP [ɑːraɪ'piː] (*abbr* **Rest In Peace**) Repose en paix.

riparian [raɪ'peərɪən] *adj & n* riverain, -aine.

ripcord ['rɪpkɔːd] *n* (*on parachute*) corde *f* d'ouverture, cordelette *f* de déclenchement; (*on hot-air balloon*) corde de déchirure.

ripe [raɪp] *adj* (*fruit, grain*) mûr; (*cheese*) bien fait, bien à point; **to grow r.,** mûrir; **to live to a r. old age,** vivre vieux, vivre jusqu'à un âge avancé; *Hum* **the r. old age of sixteen,** l'âge considérable de seize ans; *Fig* **the time is r. for speaking the truth,** le temps est venu de dire la vérité; **the time is not yet r.,** le temps n'est pas encore venu; **r. for mischief,** prêt à faire le mal; **a site r. for development,** un site bon pour le développement; **to smell r.,** (*of fruit*) avoir un parfum de fruit mûr; *Pej* (*of person*) sentir mauvais.

ripen ['raɪp(ə)n] **1** *vt* (faire) mûrir (*un fruit, une céréale*); affiner (*le fromage*). **2** *vi* **(a)** (*of fruit, plan etc*) mûrir; (*of cheese*) se faire; *Fig* **to r. into manhood,** atteindre l'âge d'homme.

ripeness ['raɪpnɪs] *n* (*of fruit, grain etc*) maturité *f*.

ripening ['raɪp(ə)nɪŋ] **1** *adj* **(a)** (*sun*) qui fait mûrir; **(b)** (*fruit, grain*) mûrissant, qui mûrit; (*cheese*) qui se fait. **2** *n* (*of fruit, grain*) maturation *f*, mûrissage *m*, mûrissement *m*; (*of cheese*) affinage *m*.

rip-off ['rɪpɒf] *n F* **it's a r.-o.!,** c'est du vol!; **this book/package holiday is a r.-o.,** ce livre/voyage organisé n'est qu'un attrape-nigaud.

riposte[1] [rɪ'pɒst] *n* (*of fencer, speaker etc*) riposte *f*; **to make a r.,** riposter.

riposte[2] *vi* (*of fencer, speaker etc*) riposter.

ripper ['rɪpər] *n* (*killer*) éventreur *m*.

ripping ['rɪpɪŋ] **1** *adj Old-fashioned Br F* épatant, formidable. **2** *n* (*of fabric, clouds*) déchirement *m*.

ripple[1] ['rɪp(ə)l] *n* **(a)** (*wave*) (*on water*) ride *f*; (*in corn, hair*) ondulation *f*; (*of muscles*) saillie *f*; *Fig* **a r. of excitement ran through the crowd,** un frémissement d'excitation a parcouru la foule; *Fig* **r. effect** (*of action, investment etc*) effet multiplicateur; **(b)** (*noise*) (*of stream*) gazouillement *m*; (*of conversation, voices*) murmure(s) *m(pl)*; (*of laughter, applause*) cascade *f*; **(c)** (*ice-cream*) **raspberry/strawberry/***etc* **r.,** = glace panachée à la framboise/fraise/*etc*.

ripple[2] **1** *vi* (*of water*) se rider; (*of corn, hair*) onduler, ondoyer; (*of muscles*) saillir; (*of stream*) murmurer; **laughter/applause rippled through the audience,** des vagues de rires/d'applaudissements ont traversé le public. **2** *vt* (*of wind*) rider (*l'eau, le sable*); **he rippled his muscles,** il a fait saillir ses muscles.

rip-roaring ['rɪprɔːrɪŋ] *adj F* (*party*) tumultueux; **a r.-r. success,** un succès retentissant.

ripsaw ['rɪpsɔː] *n* scie *f* à refendre.

riptide ['rɪptaɪd] *n* courant *m* de retour.

rise[1] [raɪz] *n* **(a)** (*appearance*) (*of sun*) lever *m*; (*of moon*) apparition *f*; **to give r. to sth,** donner lieu à qch; **it would give r. to misunderstandings,** cela donnerait lieu à des malentendus;

(b) (*ascent*) (*of theatre curtain*) lever *m*; (*of leader, party*) ascension *f*; (*to power*) accession *f*; (*in rank*) avancement *m*, élévation *f*; (*of industry, technology*) essor *m*; (*in ground*) éminence *f*; **her r. to fame came overnight,** son ascension vers la célébrité s'est faite du jour au lendemain; *F* **to take** *or* **get a r. out of s.o.,** (*anger*) mettre qn en colère;

(c) (*increase*) (*in pressure, price etc*) hausse *f* (**in,** de); (*in river*) crue *f*; (*of temperature*) élévation *f*, relèvement *m*; (*of tide*) montée *f*; (*of price*) augmentation *f*; *Br* **(pay) r.,** augmentation (de salaire); **r. and fall,** (*of chest*) mouvement *m* de montée et de descente; (*of sea*) flot et jusant *m*, flux et reflux *m*; (*of politician etc*) grandeur *f* et décadence; **food prices are on the r.,** le prix des denrées est en hausse; **a big r. in house prices is on the way,** une augmentation importante des prix de l'immobilier se prépare; **to get a r.,** (*in salary*) être augmenté.

rise[2] *vi* (*pt* **rose** [rəʊz]; *pp* **risen** ['rɪz(ə)n]) **(a)** (*get up*) (*from bed, chair*) se lever; (*from knees, after fall*) se relever; *Rel* ressusciter; (*of Parliament, court*) (*at end of day*) lever la séance; (*at end of session*) entrer en vacances; *Am* **all r.!,** (*in courtroom*) levez-vous s'il vous plaît!; **to r. from table,** se lever de table; **to r. on its hind legs,** (*of horse*) se cabrer; **to r. early/late,** se lever tôt/tard; *F* **r. and shine!,** debout les morts!; **Christ is risen,** le Christ est ressuscité;

(b) (*appear, emerge*) (*of sun, star*) se lever; (*of moon*) faire son apparition; (*of fish*) monter à la surface; **I saw the sun r.,** j'ai vu le soleil se lever; **a picture rose in my mind,** une image s'est présentée à mon esprit; **a feeling of panic rose in me,** un sentiment de panique s'est élevé en moi; **new buildings are rising all the time,** de nouveaux bâtiments se construisent constamment;

(c) (*ascend*) (*of theatre curtain*) se lever; (*of ground, road etc*) monter, s'élever; (*of ground*) se relever; (*of sap*) monter; (*in society*) s'élever; (*of smoke, balloon*) monter, s'élever (**from,** de); **to r. off the ground,** (*of plane*) quitter le sol; **to r. in the saddle,** faire du trot enlevé; **to r. to the surface,** (*of fish, anger*) faire surface; **a murmur rose from the crowd,** une rumeur s'est élevée parmi la foule; **the boat rose and fell on the water,** le bateau se balançait sur l'eau; **it makes my stomach r.,** cela me soulève le cœur; **trees rising a hundred feet above the plain,** arbres qui s'élèvent à trente mètres au-dessus de la plaine; **his voice rose above the noise of the crowd,** sa voix s'élevait au-dessus du bruit de la foule; **the book never rises above the level of potboiler,** ce livre n'est que de la littérature alimentaire; *Fig* **to r. above events/one's difficulties,** dépasser les événements/vaincre ses difficultés; *Fig* **to r. to the occasion/challenge/task,** se montrer à la hauteur de la situation/du défi/de la tâche; **to r. to fame,** connaître une ascension vers la célébrité; **to r. to power,** accéder au pouvoir; **to r. in the world,** faire son chemin, parvenir; **he rose from nothing,** il est parti de rien; **to r. to the rank of colonel,** monter au grade de colonel; **to r. in s.o.'s esteem,** monter dans l'estime de qn;

(d) (*increase in amount, intensity*) (*of temperature*) monter, s'élever; (*of wind*) se lever; (*of voice, water level*) s'élever; (*of hope*) grandir; (*of tide, pressure*) monter; (*of dough*) lever; (*of river*) être en crue; (*of prices*) monter, augmenter; **prices are rising,** les prix sont à la *ou* en hausse; **everything has risen in price,** tout a augmenté de prix *ou* a renchéri; **the river has risen by two metres,** la rivière est montée de deux mètres; **the wind has risen to gale force,** le vent a pris la force d'une tempête; **my spirits rose at the sight of the mountains,** j'ai repris courage à la vue des montagnes; **her colour rose,** ses joues s'empourpraient;

(e) (*become erect*) (*of hair*) se hérisser; **the dog's hackles rose,** le chien s'est hérissé de colère; **the hair on the back of her neck rose,** ses poils se sont hérissés; **it makes my hackles r.,** ça me hérisse;

(f) (*revolt*) se soulever, se révolter (**against,** contre); **to r. (up) in arms,** prendre les armes; **to r. in protest against sth,** se soulever *ou* se révolter contre qch;

(g) (*originate*) (*of river*) prendre sa source (**at,** à; **in,** dans); (*of difficulty, quarrel*) provenir, naître (**from,** de).

▶**rise up** *vi* = **RISE[2] (f).**

riser ['raɪzər] *n* **(a) early r.,** lève-tôt *mf inv*; **late r.,** lève-tard *mf inv*; **(b)** (*on staircase*) contremarche *f*; **(c)** (*pipe*) tuyau *m* de montée.

risibility [rɪzɪ'bɪlɪtɪ] *n Lit Pej* (*of situation etc*) caractère *m* risible *ou* ridicule.

risible ['rɪzɪb(ə)l] *adj Lit Pej* (*idea, plan etc*) risible, ridicule; (*offer*) dérisoire.

rising ['raɪzɪŋ] **1** *adj* **(a)** (*sun*) levant; **(b)** (*road*) qui monte; (*artist, politician etc*) d'avenir; **r. trot,** trot enlevé; **r. ground,** élévation *f* du terrain, éminence *f*; *Constr* **r. damp,** humidité *f* qui monte du sol; **the r. generation,** la nouvelle *ou* la jeune génération; **(c)** (*pressure, temperature*) en hausse; (*tide*) montant; **r. prices,** la hausse des prix. **2** *n* **(a)** (*of Parliament*) levée *f*, clôture *f*; **I don't like early r.,** je n'aime pas me lever tôt; **(b)** (*of sun*) lever *m*; (*of star*) lever, ascension *f*; (*of moon*) apparition *f*; **(c)** (*of theatre curtain*) lever *m*; (*of sap*) montée *f*; **(d)** (*of water*) crue *f*; **(e)** (*revolt*) ameutement *m*, insurrection *f*, révolte *f*, soulèvement *m*. **3** *prep* **he's r. sixty,** il va sur (ses) soixante ans.

risk[1] [rɪsk] *n* (*danger*) risque *m* (**of doing,** de faire); (*in insurance*) risque; **at r.,** (*life, person, child*) en danger; (*job*) menacé; **is there any r. of that happening?,** est-ce qu'il y a un risque que cela se produise?; **to be full of risks,** comporter beaucoup de risques; **to run risks,** courir des risques; **to run the r. of losing everything,** courir le risque *ou* risquer de tout perdre; **to take risks,** prendre des risques; **she takes too many risks,** elle prend trop de risques; **I'm not taking any risks,** je ne veux rien risquer; **I'll take that r.,** j'en prends le risque; **with no r. of infection,** sans risque d'infection; **at the r. of his life,** au risque *ou* péril de sa vie; **at the r. of sounding conceited,** au risque de paraître prétentieux; **at considerable r. to herself,** en courant (elle-même) un risque considérable; **at one's own r.,** à ses risques et périls; **it's too much of a r.,** c'est un trop grand risque; *esp Br Fin* **r. capital,** capital *m* à risque; **r. management,** gestion *f* du risque; **risks and perils at sea,** fortune *f* de mer; **a good/bad r.,** (*person, thing*) un bon/mauvais risque; **to be a fire/health/security/***etc* **r.,** constituer un risque d'incendie/pour la santé/pour la sécurité/*etc*.

risk[2] *vt* **(a)** (*endanger*) risquer (*sa vie, réputation etc*); **to r. one's neck** *or* **skin,** risquer sa peau; **(b)** (*take the chance of*) aventurer, hasarder (*qch*); **I'll r. it,** je vais risquer le coup; **we'll just have to r. it,** il va simplement falloir que nous en prenions le risque; **to r. defeat/failure,** courir le risque d'une défaite/d'un échec; **to r. s.o.'s anger,**

s'exposer à la colère de qn; **she won't r. leaving,** (*take the risk*) elle ne se risquera pas à partir; **to r. breaking one's leg,** risquer de *ou* courir le risque de se casser une jambe.
riskiness ['rɪskɪnɪs] *n* (*of venture etc*) risques *mpl*.
risky ['rɪskɪ] *adj* (*job, venture etc*) risqué.
risotto [rɪ'zɒtəʊ] *n Culin* risotto *m*.
risqué ['rɪskeɪ, 'riː-] *adj* (*story etc*) osé.
rissole ['rɪsəʊl] *n Culin* croquette *f*.
rite [raɪt] *n Rel* rite *m*; (*tradition*) cérémonie *f*; *Rel* **the last rites,** les derniers sacrements; **r. of passage,** rite de passage; *Mus* **The R. of Spring,** le Sacre du printemps.
ritual ['rɪtjʊəl] **1** *adj* (*dance, killing*) rituel. **2** *n Rel & Fig* rituel *m*; *Fig* **to make a r. of sth,** (se) faire un rituel de qch; *Fig* **he went through his nightly r. of locking the doors,** il a verrouillé les portes selon son rituel de tous les soirs.
ritualism ['rɪtjʊəlɪz(ə)m] *n Pej* ritualisme *m*.
ritualist ['rɪtjʊəlɪst] *adj & n Pej* ritualiste *mf*.
ritualistic [rɪtjʊə'lɪstɪk] *adj Pej* ritualiste.
ritually ['rɪtjʊəlɪ] *adv* (*killed*) rituellement, selon les rites.
ritz ['rɪts] *n Am F* tape-à-l'œil *m*; **to put on the r.,** se mettre sur son trente et un; *Pej* faire du tape-à-l'œil.
ritzy ['rɪtsɪ] *adj F* (*party, occasion etc*) luxueux, classe.
rival[1] ['raɪv(ə)l] **1** *adj* (*company, faction etc*) rival; (*forces, claim etc*) opposé. **2** *n* rival, -ale, concurrent, -ente; **to be rivals for sth,** être en compétition pour qch; **to be rivals in business/love/***etc*, être rivaux en affaires/amour/*etc*; **to be without** *or* **have no r.,** ne pas avoir d'égal.
rival[2] *v* (**-ll-**, *US* **-l-**) *vt* **(a)** (*compete with*) rivaliser avec (*qn, qch*) (**in,** de); **(b)** (*equal*) égaler (**for, in,** en); **it rivals anything to be seen in Paris,** ça vaut largement tout ce que l'on peut voir à Paris; **New York cannot r. London for historic interest,** New York ne vaut pas Londres du point de vue de l'intérêt historique.
rivalry ['raɪvəlrɪ] *n* rivalité *f* (**between,** entre); **the party is torn by personal rivalries,** le parti est divisé par des rivalités d'ordre personnel; **in r. with s.o.,** en concurrence *ou* rivalité avec qn (**for,** pour).
rive [raɪv] *v* (*pt* **rived** [raɪvd]; *pp* **riven** ['rɪv(ə)n]) *vt Lit* fendre (*le bois, la roche etc*); **a country riven by war,** un pays déchiré par la guerre.
river ['rɪvər] *n* (*small*) rivière *f*; (*major, flowing into sea*) fleuve *m*; *Fig* (*of lava*) coulée *f*; (*of blood*) flot *m*; *F* **to sell s.o. down the r.,** trahir qn, vendre qn; *US F* **he's up (the) r.,** (*in prison*) il est en taule; **the R. Thames,** la Tamise; **r. bank,** rive *f*; **r. port/traffic/***etc*, port/trafic/*etc* fluvial; **r. basin,** bassin *m* du fleuve; **r. mouth,** embouchure *f* de la rivière; **r. safety,** sécurité *f* de la navigation fluviale; **r. users,** utilisateurs *mpl* des rivières.
riverbed ['rɪvəbed] *n* lit *m* de la rivière.
riverside ['rɪvəsaɪd] *n* bord *m* de l'eau, rive *f*; **to walk along the r.,** marcher le long de la rive; **r. house/pub/***etc*, maison *f*/pub *m*/*etc* au bord de l'eau; **r. properties,** propriétés riveraines.
rivet[1] ['rɪvɪt] *n* (*pin*) rivet *m*; **r. head/hole/***etc*, tête *f*/trou *m*/*etc* de rivet; **r. gun,** pistolet *m* à river.
rivet[2] *vt* river, riveter (*qch*); *Fig* fixer (*les yeux*) (**on,** sur); *Fig* **to be riveted to the spot,** être rivé *ou* cloué sur place; **I was riveted to the television,** j'étais cloué devant la télévision; **to be absolutely riveted,** être absolument fasciné (**by,** par); **riveted together,** rivés ensemble; **riveted joint,** rivure *f*.
riveter ['rɪvɪtər] *n* (*person*) riveur, -euse; (*machine*) riveteuse *f*, riveuse *f*.
riveting ['rɪvɪtɪŋ] **1** *n* rivetage *m*; **r. machine,** riv(et)euse *f*. **2** *adj Fig* (*story etc*) fascinant.
Riviera (the) [ðərɪvɪ'eərə] *n* **the (French) R.,** la Côte d'Azur.
rivulet ['rɪvjʊlɪt] *n* ruisselet *m*; *Fig* (*of sweat etc*) filet *m*.
Riyadh [rɪ'jæd] *n* R(i)yad, Riad.
riyal [rɪ'jæl] *n* (*coin*) rial *m*.
RN [ɑː'ren] *abbr* **(a)** *Br Mil* **Royal Navy**; **(b)** *Am Med* **registered nurse**.
RNA [ɑːren'eɪ] *n* (*abbr* **ribonucleic acid**) ARN *m*.
RNLI [ɑːrenel'aɪ] *n abbr* **Royal National Lifeboat Institution**.
roach [rəʊtʃ] *n* **(a)** (*fish*) gardon *m*; **(b)** *Am* (*cockroach*) blatte *f*, cafard *m*, cancrelat *m*; **(c)** *Sl* (*of marijuana cigarette*) mégot *m* de joint; **r. clip,** pince *f* pour joint.
road [rəʊd] *n* **(a)** route *f* (**to,** de); (*small*) chemin *m*; (*in town*) rue *f*; (*roadway*) chaussée *f*; *Fig* (*path*) voie *f*, chemin *m* (**to,** de); **the London/Paris/***etc* **r.,** la route de Londres/Paris/*etc*; **the r. into town,** le chemin de la ville; **across** *or* **over the r.,** (*building etc*) en face; **by r.,** par la route; **get out of the r.!,** ne bloque pas le passage!; **to be off the r.,** (*of car*) ne pas être en état de marche; (*of driver*) ne pas pouvoir conduire; (*banned*) s'être fait retirer son permis de conduire; **to step into the r.,** quitter le trottoir; **to hold the r. well,** (*of car*) bien tenir la route, avoir une bonne tenue de route; **the r. is up,** la route est en travaux; *esp Am* **to burn up the r.,** (*of driver*) brûler de la gomme; **down the r.,** un peu plus loin dans cette rue; *Fig* à l'avenir; *F* **one for the r.,** un petit coup avant de partir; **r. works** *or* **repairs,** travaux *mpl* de voirie; *Prov* **all roads lead to Rome,** tous les chemins mènent à Rome; **approach r.,** route d'accès; **r. conditions,** état *m* des routes; **r. system/transport/***etc*, réseau *m*/transports *mpl*/*etc* routier(s); **r. accidents/user,** accidents *mpl*/usager *m* de la route; **r. map,** carte routière; *Aut* **r. tax,** taxe différentielle sur les véhicules à moteur; **have you paid your r. tax?,** est-ce que tu as acheté ta vignette?; **r. tax disc,** ≈ vignette *f*; *Aut* **r. test,** essai(s) *m(pl)* sur route; **after three hours on the r.,** après trois heures de route; **to be on the r.,** (*travelling*) être en route *ou* chemin *ou* voyage; (*work as salesman*) être représentant; (*of salesman, theatre company, pop group etc*) être en tournée; *Fig* **to be on the r. to recovery/success/***etc*, être sur le chemin de la guérison/du succès/*etc*; **to be on the right r.,** être sur la bonne voie; *Fig* **we'd like to go a little further down this r.,** nous aimerions aller un peu plus loin dans ce sens *ou* cette direction; *Fig* **to come to the end of the r.,** (*of relationship etc*) toucher à sa fin; *F* **let's get this show on the r.,** allez, c'est parti, on y va!; *F* **let's hit the r.!,** en route!; *Am Sl* **r. apple,** crottin *m*; *Am Th* **r. company,** troupe itinérante; *F* **r. hog,** chauffard *m*; **r. junction,** carrefour *m*; **r. manager,** (*of pop group etc*) organisateur *m* de tournées; *Br* **r. metal,** empierrement *m*; **r. sense,** sens *m* de la route; **r. race,** course *f* cycliste; **r. racer,** (*bicycle*) bicyclette *f* de compétition; (*competitor*) participant à une course cycliste; **r. show,** tournée *f*, spectacle itinérant; **r. sign,** panneau *m* (routier *ou* de signalisation); **r. train,** convoi routier;
(b) *Nau* **road(s),** rade *f*;
(c) *US* chemin *m* de fer.
roadbed ['rəʊdbed] *n* (*for road*) encaissement *m*; *Rail* terre-plein *m*.
roadblock ['rəʊdblɒk] *n* barrage routier; *Fig* obstacle *m*.
road-fund ['rəʊdfʌnd] *adj* **r.-f. licence,** ≈ vignette *f*.
roadholding ['rəʊdhəʊldɪŋ] *n* (*of car*) **r. (ability),** tenue *f* de route.
roadhouse ['rəʊdhaʊs] *n* hôtellerie *f* en bord de route.
roadie ['rəʊdɪ] *n F* = membre du personnel technique qui accompagne une vedette ou un groupe en tournée.
roadroller ['rəʊdrəʊlər] *n* rouleau *m* compresseur.
roadside ['rəʊdsaɪd] *n* bord *m* de la route; **r. inn,** auberge *ou* café situé(e) au bord de la route; *Aut* **r. repairs,** (*by driver*) réparations *fpl* de fortune; (*by mechanic*) dépannage *m*.
roadstead ['rəʊdsted] *n Nau* rade *f*.
roadster ['rəʊdstər] *n* **(a)** (*bicycle*) bicyclette routière; **(b)** *Old-fashioned Aut* torpédo *m*.
road-test ['rəʊdtest] *vt* essayer (*une voiture*) sur route.
roadway ['rəʊdweɪ] *n* chaussée *f*.
roadwork ['rəʊdwɜːk] *n* (*by boxer, athlete etc*) entraînement *m* consistant à courir le long de la route; **to do r.,** courir le long de la route.
roadworthiness ['rəʊdwɜːðɪnɪs] *n* (*of vehicle*) bon état de marche.
roadworthy ['rəʊdwɜːðɪ] *adj* (*vehicle*) en état de marche *ou* de rouler.
roam [rəʊm] **1** *vi* errer; **to r. about the streets,** (*of child etc*) traîner dans les rues; **to r. about the world,** courir le monde. **2** *vt* parcourir (*les rues*); sillonner (*les mers*).
roamer ['rəʊmər] *n* vagabond, -onde; **to be (something** *or* **a bit of) a r.,** aimer rouler *ou* traîner sa bosse.
roaming ['rəʊmɪŋ] **1** *adj* errant, vagabond. **2** *n* course *f* à l'aventure.
roan [rəʊn] **1** *adj* (*horse, cow*) rouan. **2** *n* (*horse*) (cheval *m*) rouan *m*; (*cow*) vache rouanne.
roar[1] [rɔːr] *n* (*of person*) hurlement *m*, rugissement *m*; (*of anger*) vocifération *f*; (*of lion, wind, engine*) rugissement; (*of thunder*) grondement *m*; (*of sea*) mugissement *m*; (*of crowd, spectators etc*) clameurs *fpl*; (*of furnace*) ronflement *m*; (*of applause*) tonnerre *m*; (*of traffic*) vrombissement *m*; **to give a r.,** (*of person*) hurler; (*of lion*) rugir; **the crowd gave a r. of approval,** la foule a poussé un hurlement d'approbation; **roars of laughter,** grands éclats de rire.
roar[2] **1** *vi* (*of person*) hurler, rugir; (*with anger*) vociférer (**with,** de); (*of crowd*) hurler; (*of lion, wind, engine*) rugir; (*of thunder*) gronder; (*of sea*) mugir; (*of furnace*) ronfler; **to r. with laughter,** éclater de rire. **2** *vt* hurler, vociférer (*un ordre*); **to r. one's approval,** manifester son approbation par des hurlements.
▶**roar by** *vi* (*of car etc*) passer dans un bruit de tonnerre.
▶**roar out** *vtsep* = **ROAR**[2] **2**.
▶**roar past** *vi* = **ROAR BY**.
roaring ['rɔːrɪŋ] **1** *adj* (*person*) hurlant; (*lion, wind, engine*) rugissant; (*thunder*) grondant; *F* **to be r. drunk,** être complètement bourré *ou* rond; **a r. fire,** une belle flambée; **the R. Forties,** les quarantièmes *mpl* rugissants; *F* **to do a r. trade,** faire un gros commerce, vendre

beaucoup (**in**, de); **r. success,** succès fou. **2** *n* = **ROAR[1]**.

roast[1] [rəʊst] **1** *n* **(a)** *Culin* rôti *m*; **a pork r., a r. of pork,** un rôti de porc; **pot r.,** rôti à la cocotte; **(b)** *Am F* (*of celebrity etc*) = soirée ou émission en l'honneur d'une vedette, et au cours de laquelle cette dernière fait l'objet de taquineries et de flatteries. **2** *adj Culin* (*pork, chestnuts etc*) rôti; **r. beef,** rosbif *m*.

roast[2] **1** *vt* **(a)** (faire) rôtir (*la viande*); rôtir (*des marrons*); griller (*du café, des amandes*); **to r. oneself in front of the fire,** se rôtir *ou* se griller devant le feu; **(b)** *Am* railler, *F* mettre (*qn*) en boîte. **2** *vi* (*of meat etc*) rôtir; (*of coffee*) se torréfier; *F* **I was roasting in the sun,** je grillais au soleil; *F* **it's roasting in here,** il fait une chaleur à crever ici; *F* **we're roasting here,** on cuit ici.

roaster ['rəʊstər] *n* **(a)** *Br Culin* volaille *f* à rôtir; **(b)** (*for coffee*) brûloir *m*, torréfacteur *m*.

roasting ['rəʊstɪŋ] **1** *adj F* **r.(-hot),** brûlant. **2** *n* **(a)** (*of meat*) rôtissage *m*; (*of coffee*) torréfaction *f*; **r. jack,** tournebroche *m*; **r. pan,** plat *m* à rôtir; **(b)** *Old-fashioned F* semonce *f*; **to give s.o. a r.,** (*scold*) passer un savon à qn.

rob [rɒb] *vt* (**-bb-**) voler (*qn*); dévaliser (*une banque, une maison*); piller (*un verger*); **to r. s.o. of sth,** voler qch à qn; (*deprive*) priver qn de qch; **to r. the till,** voler la caisse; **to r. Peter to pay Paul,** faire un trou pour en boucher un autre, déshabiller Pierre pour habiller Paul; *Sp* **he was robbed of victory,** on lui arracha la victoire; *esp Fb* **we were robbed!,** nous aurions dû gagner!

robber ['rɒbər] *n* voleur, -euse.

robbery ['rɒbərɪ] *n* vol *m*; **armed r.,** vol à main armée; **highway r.,** vol de grand chemin, brigandage *m*; *Fig* **it's highway** *or* **daylight r.!,** c'est du vol organisé!

robe[1] [rəʊb] *n* **(a)** (*of priest, judge etc*) robe *f*; **(baby's) christening r.,** robe de bâptème; **magistrate in his robes,** magistrat en robe; **(b)** (*dressing gown*) (*heavy*) robe *f* de chambre; (*light, for women*) peignoir *m*; (*bathrobe*) sortie *f* de bain, peignoir; **(c)** *Am* couverture *f*.

robe[2] **1** *vt* revêtir (*qn*) d'une robe. **2** *vi* (*of judge etc*) revêtir sa robe.

robin ['rɒbɪn] *n* **r.(-redbreast)** (*bird*) rouge-gorge *m*; **r.'s-egg blue,** (*colour*) bleu vert.

Robin ['rɒbɪn] *n* (*dimin of* **Robert**) Robert *m*, Bob *m*; **R. Hood,** Robin des Bois.

robing ['rəʊbɪŋ] *n* revêtissement *m* des robes de cérémonie; **r. room,** (*for judge etc*) vestiaire *m*.

robot ['rəʊbɒt] *n* robot *m*; *Fig* robot, automate *m*.

robotics [rəʊ'bɒtɪks] *n* robotique *f*; **r. research/expert/** *etc*, recherche *f*/expert *m*/*etc* dans le domaine de la robotique.

robotize, robotise ['rəʊbətaɪz] *vt esp Am* robotiser (*une chaîne de montage*).

robust [rəʊ'bʌst] *adj* (*person, faith, appetite*) robuste, solide; (*machine, suitcase etc*) solide; (*coffee, wine*) corsé; (*defence, speech, statement*) vigoureux, musclé.

robustness [rəʊ'bʌstnɪs] *n* (*of person, faith*) nature *f* robuste; (*of person*) bonne santé; (*of machine, suitcase, appetite*) solidité *f*; (*of coffee, wine*) goût corsé; (*of defence, speech etc*) vigueur *f*.

roc [rɒk] *n Myth* rock *m*.

rock[1] [rɒk] *n* **(a)** (*substance*) roche *f*; (*at seaside, boulder, rockface*) rocher *m*; *Am* (*stone*) pierre *f*; *Fig* roc *m*; **fall of rocks,** éboulis rocheux; **cut in(to) the r.,** creusé dans le roc; **r. face,** paroi rocheuse; **r. climbing,** varappe *f*; **r. climber,** varappeur, -euse; **to go r. climbing,** faire de la varappe *ou* du rocher; **to reach** *or* **hit r. bottom,** (*of prices*) être au plus bas; (*of person, morale*) toucher le fond; *Fig* **r. solid,** (*support, morale etc*) solide comme le roc; **to be as solid as a r.,** être solide comme le roc; *Am* **to be between a r. and a hard place,** tomber de Charybde en Scylla; *Am F* **r. hound,** (*professional*) géologue *mf*; (*amateur*) collectionneur, -euse de pierres; *Miner* **r. crystal,** cristal *m* de roche, quartz hyalin; **r. salt,** sel *m* gemme; *Br* **r. salmon,** roussette *f*; *Rel* **the R. of Ages,** Jésus-Christ; *Geog* **the R. of Gibraltar,** *F* **the R.,** le Rocher de Gibraltar; *Nau* **to run onto** *or* **strike the rocks,** se jeter sur des rochers, donner sur les écueils; *F* **on the rocks,** (*person*) sans le sou, fauché, à sec; (*marriage, relationship*) en pleine débâcle; (*company*) en faillite; (*whisky*) avec des glaçons, *Can* sur glace; *Culin* **r. bun** *or* **cake,** rocher; **r. garden,** rocaille *f*; *Am* **r. melon,** cantaloup *m*; **r. painting,** peinture *f* rupestre; **r. plant,** plante *f* rupestre; **r. pool,** (*at seaside*) mare *f* dans les rochers;
(b) *Am Sl* (*jewel*) diamant *m*;
(c) *Br* sucre *m* d'orge.

rock[2] *n* **(a)** (*of child*) bercement *m*; (*of cradle*) balancement *m*; **to give the cradle a r.,** balancer un peu le berceau; **(b)** *Mus* rock *m*; **r. 'n' roll,** rock-and-roll *m*; **r. concert/group/singer/***etc*, concert *m*/groupe *m*/chanteur *m*/*etc* de rock.

rock[3] **1** *vt* bercer, balancer (*un enfant, une barque*); balancer (*un berceau*); (*violently*) & *Fig* secouer, ébranler (*un édifice, qn*); *Fig* **to r. the boat,** faire des vagues. **2** *vi* **(a)** (*sway*) se balancer; (*of building, ground*) trembler; **to r. (backwards and forwards) in one's chair,** se balancer sur sa chaise; **to r. with laughter,** être secoué par le fou-rire; **(b)** danser le rock.

rock-bottom ['rɒkbɒtəm] *adj* (*prices*) les plus bas, très bas.

rock-bound ['rɒkbaʊnd] *adj* (*bay etc*) encerclé de rochers.

rock-climb ['rɒkklaɪm] *vi* faire de la varappe *ou* du rocher.

rocker ['rɒkər] *n* **(a)** (*on cradle, rocking chair etc*) bascule *f*; *F* **to be off one's r.,** être timbré *ou* un peu fou; **(b)** *Am F* rocking-chair *m*, fauteuil *m* à bascule, *Can* berceuse *f*; **(c)** *Br* (*person*) rocker *m*.

rockery ['rɒkərɪ] *n* (*in garden*) rocaille *f*.

rocket[1] ['rɒkɪt] *n* (*firework, missile*) fusée *f*; **to fire** *or* **launch a r.,** lancer une fusée; *F* **to give s.o. a r.,** engueuler qn (**about**, au sujet de); *F* **he's just had a r. from the boss,** il vient de se faire engueuler par le patron; **r. attack,** attaque *f* par fusées; **r. base,** base *f* de lancement de fusées; **r. launcher,** lance-fusée(s) *m*, lance-roquettes *m*.

rocket[2] *vi* (*of prices*) monter en flèche; **to r. to fame,** faire une ascension météorique vers la célébrité; **to r. away/past,** (*of car etc*) filer/passer à toute allure.

rocket[3] *n* (*plant*) roquette *f*.

rocketry ['rɒkɪtrɪ] *n* (*science*) l'étude *f ou* la technologie *ou* la technique des fusées; (*weaponry*) l'arsenal *m* des fusées.

rockfall ['rɒkfɔːl] *n* éboulement *m*.

rock-hard [rɒk'hɑːd] *adj* (*soil etc*) dur comme la pierre *ou* le roc.

Rockies (the) [ðə'rɒkɪz] *npl* les (Montagnes) Rocheuses *fpl*.

rocking ['rɒkɪŋ] **1** *adj* (*movement*) oscillant; (*building*) branlant; **r. chair,** rocking-chair *m*, fauteuil *m* à bascule, *Can* berceuse *f*; **r. horse,** cheval *m* à bascule. **2** *n* (*of baby, boat, cradle*) balancement *m*; (*of baby, boat*) bercement *m*; (*of chair*) oscillation *f*.

rockslide ['rɒkslaɪd] *n* (*action*) avalanche *f* de rochers; (*result*) traînée *f* d'éboulis.

rocky ['rɒkɪ] *adj* **(a)** (*path*) rocailleux; (*soil*) pierreux; (*shoreline*) rocheux, plein de rochers; (*terrain, bottom*) de roche; **r. outcrop,** affleurement rocheux; **the R. Mountains,** les Montagnes Rocheuses; **(b)** *Fig* difficile; (*marriage etc*) instable, branlant; **his business is in a r. condition,** ses affaires vont mal; **I feel a bit r.,** (*unwell*) je ne suis pas dans mon assiette; **it's been a r. year for the oil industry,** ça a été une année difficile pour l'industrie pétrolière; **to have a r. road ahead,** avoir des problèmes en perspective; **to go through a r. patch,** traverser une période difficile.

rococo [rə'kəʊkəʊ] *adj & n Art etc* rococo *m*.

rod [rɒd] *n* **(a)** (*stick*) (*wooden*) baguette *f*; (*metal*) tige *f*; (*of curtain*) tringle *f*; (*for fishing*) canne *f* à pêche; (*for administering punishment*) verge *f*; **r. and line,** ligne *f* de pêche; **to fish with r. and line,** pêcher à la ligne; **r. fishing,** pêche *f* à la ligne; **fuel r.,** barreau *m* de combustible; **(b) to make a r. for one's own back,** se préparer des ennuis; *Old-fashioned* **to have a r. in pickle for s.o.,** garder à qn un chien de sa chienne; *Prov* **spare the r. and spoil the child,** qui aime bien châtie bien; **a r. to beat oneself with,** des verges pour se faire battre; **that would be giving them a r. to beat us with,** ce serait leur donner des verges pour nous faire battre; **to rule s.o. with a r. of iron,** gouverner qn avec une main de fer; **(c)** (*symbol of office*) verge *f*; **(d)** *Old-fashioned* perche *f* (= approx 5m); **(e)** *Am Sl* (*gun*) revolver *m*; **(f)** *Sl* (*penis*) bite *f*.

rodent ['rəʊdənt] *n* rongeur *m*; **r. characteristics/habitat/***etc*, caractéristiques/habitat/*etc* des rongeurs; *Br* **r. operative,** employé chargé de la dératisation.

rodeo ['rəʊdɪəʊ, rəʊ'deɪəʊ] *n* rodéo *m*; **r. rider,** cavalier *m* pratiquant le rodéo.

Roderick ['rɒd(ə)rɪk] *n* Rodrigue *m*, Roderic *m*.

rodomontade [rɒdəmɒn'teɪd, -'tɑːd] *n* rodomontade *f*.

roe[1] [rəʊ] *n Zool* **r. (deer),** chevreuil *m*.

roe[2] *n* (*of fish*) œufs *mpl* (de poisson); **soft r.,** laite *f*, laitance *f*.

roebuck ['rəʊbʌk] *n* chevreuil *m* (mâle).

roentgen ['rɜːntgən] *n* Röntgen, Roentgen; **r. equivalent man,** = unité employée pour évaluer l'effet biologique d'un rayonnement radioactif; **measurements are given in r. equivalent man,** les mesures sont données en Röntgen Equivalent Man.

rogation [rəʊ'geɪʃən] *n Rel* Rogations *fpl*; **R. Week,** la semaine des Rogations; **R. Sunday,** le dimanche avant l'Ascension.

roger ['rɒdʒər] *vt Br Vulg* baiser (*une femme*).

Roger ['rɒdʒər] **1** *int* **R.!,** (*in radio message*) = reçu et compris!, d'accord! **2** *n* Roger *m*.

rogue [rəʊg] *n* (*dishonest*) filou *m*, crapule *f*; (*mischievous*) espiègle *mf*, coquin, -ine; **rogues' gallery,** collection *f* de portraits de criminels; *Hum* ensemble *m* de personnes ayant des mines de criminels; **r. (elephant/buffalo),** (éléphant *m*/buffle *m*) solitaire *m*; **r. gene,** gène aberrant; **r. policeman/politician/*etc*,** policier/politicien *etc* corrompu.

roguery ['rəʊgərɪ] *n* (*mischievousness*) coquinerie *f*, friponnerie *f*; (*of child*) espièglerie *f*.

roguish ['rəʊgɪʃ] *adj* (*smile, look etc*) espiègle, coquin.

roguishly ['rəʊgɪʃlɪ] *adv* (*to smile, wink*) avec espièglerie, d'un air coquin.

roguishness ['rəʊgɪʃnɪs] *n* = **ROGUERY**.

roisterer ['rɔɪstərər] *n* tapageur, -euse, fêtard, -arde.

role, rôle [rəʊl] *n Th & Fig* rôle *m*; *Psy* **r. model,** modèle *m*, exemple *m*; **children need a r. model,** les enfants ont besoin de quelqu'un à qui s'identifier.

role-playing, rôle-playing, ['rəʊlpleɪɪŋ] *n* (*for training purposes, at school*) jeu *m* de rôle; (*in psychotherapy*) psychodrame *m*.

rolf [rɒlf] *vi Am Sl* vomir.

roll¹ [rəʊl] *n* **(a)** (*of paper, film, cloth*) rouleau *m*; (*of fat, flesh*) bourrelet *m*; *esp Am* (*of paper money*) liasse *f*;
(b) (*bread*) petit pain; *Br* **jam r.,** (gâteau *m*) roulé *m* à la confiture; **spring r.,** rouleau *m* de printemps; **ham/cheese/*etc* r.,** ≈ sandwich *m* au jambon/fromage/*etc*;
(c) (*noise*) (*of drum, thunder*) roulement *m*;
(d) (*movement*) (*of ball, vehicle, dice etc*) roulement *m*; (*of ship*) roulis *m*; (*of sea*) houle *f*; (*of aircraft*) (vol *m* en) tonneau *m*; (*of hills, prairie*) ondulation *f*; (*in canoe*) esquimautage *m*; **to walk with a r.,** se balancer *ou* dandiner en marchant; **to have a r. on the ground,** (*of horse etc*) se rouler par terre; **to do a r.,** (*in high jump*) sauter en rouleau; *F* **to have a r. in the hay** *or* **sack,** se rouler dans le foin; **to be on a r.,** (*of gambler*) *& Fig* avoir la chance de son côté; **western r.,** (*high jump*) rouleau costal;
(e) (*list*) liste *f*; **r. call,** appel (nominal); **to call the r.** *or* **have a r. call,** faire l'appel; *Br* **r. of honour,** *US* **honor r.,** liste *f* de ceux qui sont morts pour la patrie; *Jur* **to strike s.o. off** *or* **from the rolls,** rayer qn du tableau *ou* barreau.

roll² **1** *vt* **(a)** rouler (*une bille, une cigarette etc*); rouler, enrouler (*du papier, un tapis*); **to r. sth along the ground,** faire rouler qch sur le sol; **to r. string into a ball,** rouler de la ficelle en pelote; **to r. one's own,** (*cigarettes*) se rouler ses cigarettes; **to r. a snowball,** faire une boule de neige; *Cin* **r. 'em!,** tournez!; **to r. one's eyes,** rouler les yeux; **to r. one's r's,** rouler les r, grasseyer; *Culin* **loin of mutton boned and rolled,** carré de mouton roulé; **to r. an umbrella,** plier un parapluie; **to r. oneself into a ball,** (*of animal*) se rouler en boule; **he is a chauffeur and gardener rolled into one,** il est à la fois chauffeur et jardinier; **this book/play/programme is ... rolled into one,** ce livre/cette pièce/ce programme est à la fois ...; **to r. about,** rouler (*qch*) çà et là;
(b) rouler, passer au rouleau (*le gazon*); cylindrer (*une route*); laminer (*un métal*); planer (*l'or*); **to r. out,** (*dough*) étendre au rouleau; *Am Sl* **to r. a drunk,** (*rob*) dévaliser un ivrogne.
2 *vi* **(a)** (*of ball, ship etc*) rouler; (*of person, animal*) se rouler; (*of aircraft*) faire des tonneaux; **the car rolled to a stop,** la voiture s'est progressivement arrêtée; *Fig* **heads will r.,** des têtes vont tomber; **someone's head will r. for this,** quelqu'un va payer pour cela; *F* **to be rolling (in money** *or* **it),** rouler sur l'or; **to r. with laughter** *or* **in the aisles,** se tordre *ou* se tenir les côtes de rire; *F* **to get sth rolling,** (*started*) mettre qch en route; **to r. with the punches,** (*of boxer*) encaisser les coups de l'adversaire;
(b) (*of thunder*) gronder, rouler; **to hear the drums rolling,** entendre le roulement des tambours;
(c) (*of hills, prairie*) onduler;
(d) (*of camera, machine etc*) tourner.

►**roll about** *vi* (*of marble, ball etc*) rouler çà et là; (*of person, animal*) se rouler; (*of ship*) rouler; **to r. about on the floor/ground,** (*of person*) se rouler sur le sol; (*of object*) rouler sur le sol; **to r. about in pain/laughing,** se tordre de douleur/de rire.

►**roll along** *vi F* (*of person*) arriver, se pointer; **to r. along in one's car,** rouler dans sa voiture.

►**roll around** *vi* = **ROLL ROUND**.

►**roll away** **1** *vi* (*of marble, ball etc*) s'éloigner (en roulant); (*of clouds, mist*) se retirer. **2** *vtsep* **to r. sth away,** rouler qch.

►**roll back** **1** *vi* (*of car*) rouler en arrière; (*of eyes*) chavirer. **2** *vtsep Mil* **to r. back the enemy,** faire reculer l'ennemi; **to r. back a carpet,** enrouler un tapis (pour faire de la place); **to r. back prices,** baisser les prix.

►**roll by** *vi* (*of car*) passer (en roulant); (*of time*) s'écouler.

►**roll down** **1** *vi* (*of tears*) couler; **to r. down a hill,** (*of car, children*) débouler une pente; **the tears rolled down his cheeks,** les larmes coulaient sur ses joues; **perspiration rolled down her face,** la transpiration coulait sur son visage; **rain rolled down the windowpane,** la pluie coulait le long de la vitre. **2** *vtsep* **to r. sth down,** descendre qch (en roulant); **to r. down a blind,** baisser un store; **she rolled down the car window,** elle a baissé la vitre.

►**roll in** **1** *vi* **(a)** (*of waves*) déferler; *F* (*of orders, spectators etc*) affluer; *F* (*of person*) rappliquer, s'amener; **she rolled in to work three hours late,** elle s'est amenée au travail avec trois heures de retard; **(b)** (*at hockey*) remettre la balle en jeu. **2** *vtsep* **to r. sth in,** faire entrer qch en roulant; **to r. the ball in,** (*in hockey*) remettre la balle en jeu.

►**roll off** *vi* **(a)** tomber (en roulant); **to r. off the shelf/the table,** tomber de l'étagère/de la table en roulant; **(b) cars are rolling off the production line,** les voitures sortent de la chaîne de production.

►**roll on** **1** *vi* (*of time*) s'écouler; *F* **r. on tonight/the holidays/*etc*!,** vivement ce soir/les vacances/*etc*! **2** *vtsep* **to r. paint on,** étendre de la peinture au rouleau.

►**roll out** **1** *vi* (*of person*) sortir en titubant; (*of ball etc*) rouler (dehors); **to r. out of bed,** (*of person*) rouler hors du lit; *F* **we rolled out of the pub at midnight,** nous sommes sortis du pub à minuit. **2** *vtsep* **to r. sth out,** faire sortir qch en le roulant; **to r. a carpet out,** dérouler un tapis; **to r. out any bumps,** (*in grass*) faire disparaître des inégalités au rouleau.

►**roll over** **1** *vi* (*of person*) (*once*) se retourner; (*many times*) se rouler; (*of car etc*) capoter; **to r. over on the ground,** rouler sur le sol. **2** *vtsep* **to r. a stone over,** retourner une pierre; **to r. s.o. over,** retourner qn.

►**roll round** *vi* (*of season etc*) arriver.

►**roll up** **1** *vi* (*of blind*) s'enrouler; *F* (*arrive*) (*of guests*) arriver, se pointer, s'amener; (*of customers, spectators*) arriver en foule; **to r. up into a ball,** (*of animal*) se mettre *ou* se rouler en boule; **r. up!, r. up!,** venez nombreux! **2** *vtsep* (*map etc*) rouler, enrouler; (*trousers*) relever, retrousser; **to r. sth up in sth,** (*for protection*) envelopper qch (**in,** de qch); **to r. up one's sleeves,** retrousser les manches; *Fig* se mettre au travail; **to r. oneself up in a blanket,** s'enrouler dans une couverture; **to r. up a blind,** monter un store; **to r. up the car window,** remonter la vitre.

rollaway ['rəʊləweɪ] **1** *n esp Am* (*bed*) lit pliant sur roulettes. **2** *adj* **r. bed/table/*etc*,** lit *m*/table *f*/*etc* pliant(e) sur roulettes.

rollback ['rəʊlbæk] *n Am* (*of prices, inflation*) baisse *f*, réduction *f*.

rollbar ['rəʊlbɑːr] *n* (*on vehicle*) arceau *m* de sécurité.

rolled [rəʊld] *adj* **(a)** (*paper etc*) en rouleau, roulé; **r. in a blanket/*etc*,** enveloppé d'une couverture/*etc*; **(b)** (*lawn*) passé au rouleau, roulé; (*metal etc*) laminé; (*umbrella*) plié; **r. gold,** plaqué or; **r.-gold watch,** montre en plaqué or; **r. oats,** flocons *mpl* d'avoine.

rolled-up [rəʊl'dʌp] *adj* (*sleeves, trousers*) retroussé; (*paper, carpet etc*) enroulé.

roller ['rəʊlər] *n* **(a)** (*for hair, paint, garden etc*) rouleau *m*; (*for metal*) laminoir *m*; **to put rollers in (one's hair), to put one's hair in rollers,** se mettre des rouleaux *ou* des bigoudis; **my hair's in rollers,** j'ai des bigoudis sur la tête; **road r.,** rouleau compresseur; **r. bandage,** bandage enroulé; **r. blind/map/*etc*,** store *m*/carte *f*/*etc* sur rouleau; **r. coaster,** (*at funfair*) montagnes *fpl* russes; **(b)** (*on chair etc*) roulette *f*; (*for moving heavy objects*) rouleau transporteur; **r. bearing,** roulement *m* à rouleaux; **r. conveyor,** transporteur *m* à rouleaux; **r. skate,** patin *m* à roulettes; **(c)** (*in sea*) lame *f* de houle; **(d)** *Am F* **high r.,** (*gambler*) gros parieur.

roller-coaster ['rəʊlə'kəʊstər] *vi esp Am* (*of road*) être très accidenté, faire des montagnes russes; (*of economy*) connaître des hauts et des bas prononcés.

roller-skate ['rəʊləskeɪt] *vi* faire du patin à roulettes.

roller-skating ['rəʊləskeɪtɪŋ] *n* patin *m* à roulettes; **r.-s. rink/clothes/*etc*,** piste *f*/vêtements *mpl*/*etc* de patin à roulettes; **to go r.-s.,** aller faire du patin à roulettes.

rollick ['rɒlɪk] *vi* faire la fête *ou* la noce *ou* la bombe.

rollicking ['rɒlɪkɪŋ] **1** *adj* (*person*) joyeux, d'une gaieté exubérante; **r. laughter,** rires bruyants; **to have a r. good time,** bien se marrer. **2** *n Br F* **to give s.o. a r.,** (*tell off*) engueuler qn.

rolling ['rəʊlɪŋ] **1** *adj* **(a)** roulant, qui roule; (*mist*) qui avance; (*boat*) qui roule, qui a du roulis; *Prov* **a r. stone gathers no moss,** pierre qui roule n'amasse pas mousse; *Fig* **he's a r. stone,** il a roulé sa bosse; *F* **to be r. drunk,** être ivre-mort, être rond comme une queue de pelle; *Fig* **r. strikes,** grèves tournantes; **(b)** (*thunder*) qui gronde; **(c)** (*hills, prairie*) ondulant; (*ground, gait*) onduleux; **to have a r. gait,** se balancer *ou* se dandiner en marchant; **r. countryside,** paysage ondulant *ou* ondulé; **(d)** (*sea*) gros, houleux. **2** *n* **(a)** (*of ship, aircraft, vehicle*) roulis *m*; *Rail* **r. stock,** matériel roulant; **(b)** *Ind* (*of road, lawn*) cylindrage *m*; (*of metal*) laminage *m*; **r. mill,** laminoir *m*; *Culin* **r. pin,** rouleau *m* (à pâtisserie).

rollmop ['rəʊlmɒp] *n Culin* rollmops *m*.

rollneck ['rəʊlnek] **1** *adj* (*sweater*) à col roulé. **2** *n* (*sweater*) col roulé.
roll-on ['rəʊlɒn] *n* **(a)** (*deodorant*) déodorant *m* à bille; **r.-on deodorant,** déodorant *m* en flacon à bille; **(b)** *Old-fashioned* (*corset*) gaine *f* (élastique).
roll-on/roll-off [rəʊl'ɒnrəʊl'ɒf] *adj* (*ferry, traffic etc*) de type roll on-roll off, roulier; (*port*) à roulage direct; (*cargo*) à manutention horizontale *ou* de type roll on-roll off.
roll-top ['rəʊltɒp] *n* **r.-t. (desk),** bureau *m* à cylindre.
roll-up ['rəʊlʌp], **roll-your-own** [rəʊljɔː'rəʊn, -jə-] *n Br F* (*cigarette*) cigarette roulée.
roly-poly ['rəʊlɪ'pəʊlɪ] **1** *n* **(a)** *F* (*plump person*) boudin *m*; **(b)** *Culin* **r.-p. (pudding),** gâteau roulé à la confiture. **2** *adj* (*person*) boulot, grassouillet.
ROM [rɒm] *n Comptr* (*abbr* **read only memory**) mémoire morte.
romaine [rəʊ'meɪn] *n Am* **r. (lettuce),** (laitue) romaine *f*.
roman ['rəʊmən] *n & adj Typ* romain *m*; **in r.,** (*word, abbreviation*) en romain.
Roman ['rəʊmən] **1** *adj* (*law, numeral etc*) romain; **R. nose,** nez busqué *ou* aquilin; **R. candle,** (*firework*) chandelle romaine; **the Holy R. Empire,** le Saint Empire romain (germanique); *Rel* **R. Catholic,** catholique; **R. Catholicism,** catholicisme *m*. **2** *n* Romain, -aine; *Rel Pej* catho *mf*; *Bible* **Epistle to the Romans,** Épître *f* aux Romains.
romance¹ [rə'mæns, 'rəʊ-] *n* **(a)** (*book, film*) histoire *f ou* roman *m* d'amour; *Hist* roman de chevalerie *ou* d'aventures *etc*; **the age of r.,** les temps chevaleresques; **(b)** (*love*) amour *m*; (*affair*) aventure amoureuse, idylle *f*; **a holiday r.,** un amour *ou* une idylle de vacances; **r. is in the air,** il y a de l'amour dans l'air; **(c)** (*charm*) poésie *f*; **(d)** *Mus* romance *f*.
romance² **1** *vi Old-fashioned* exagérer, inventer à plaisir. **2** *vt esp Am* faire la cour à (*qn*).
Romance [rə'mæns, 'rəʊ-] *n Ling* roman *m*, la langue romane; **R. languages/words/***etc*, langues *fpl*/mots *mpl*/*etc* roman(e)s; **student of R. languages,** romaniste *mf*.
romancing [rə'mænsɪŋ, 'rəʊ-] *n* exagération *f*, invention *f*.
Romanesque [rəʊmə'nesk] *adj Archit* roman.
Romania [rə'meɪnɪə] *n* Roumanie *f*.
Romanian [rə'meɪnɪən] **1** *adj* roumain. **2** *n* **(a)** Roumain, -aine; **(b)** *Ling* roumain *m*.
romanize ['rəʊmənaɪz] *vt Typ* transcrire (*un texte*) en caractères romains.
Romans(c)h [rəʊ'mænʃ] *adj & n Ling* romanche *m*.
romantic [rə'mæntɪk, rəʊ-] **1** *adj* **(a)** (*love, tenderness etc*) romantique; (*idea, notion*) romanesque; **to play the r. lead,** (*in film, play*) être le jeune premier; **r. play/comedy/***etc*, pièce *f*/comédie *f*/*etc* romantique; **r. adventure,** aventure *f* romanesque; **r. novelist,** auteur *m* de romans d'amour; **r. young woman,** jeune fille sentimentale *ou* romantique; **r. landscape,** paysage *m* romantique; **r. spot,** coin *m* romantique; **a r. dinner for two,** un dîner romantique *ou* en tête à tête; **he's very r.,** il est très romantique; **(b)** *Art Liter Mus* romantique. **2** *n* (*person*) romantique *mf*.
romantically [rə'mæntɪklɪ, rəʊ-] *adv* (*to behave*) de façon romantique; **to be r. involved with s.o.,** avoir des relations amoureuses avec qn.
romanticism [rəʊ'mæntɪsɪz(ə)m] *n* **(a)** *Art Liter Mus* romantisme *m*; **(b)** (*of person*) idées *fpl* romanesques.
romanticist [rə'mæntɪsɪst, rəʊ-] *n* romantique *mf*.
romanticize [rə'mæntɪsaɪz, rəʊ-] **1** *vt* romancer (*une idée, un incident etc*); faire tout un roman de (*qch*); **to r. war,** glorifier la guerre. **2** *vi* donner dans le romanesque.
Romany ['rəʊmənɪ] **1** *adj* (*custom, life etc*) tzigane. **2** *n* **(a)** tzigane *mf*; **(b)** *Ling* langue *f* tzigane.
Rome [rəʊm] *n* **(a)** Rome *f*; *Prov* **R. was not built in a day,** = Paris ne s'est pas fait en un jour; *Prov* **when in R., (do as the Romans do),** à Rome faites comme les Romains; **(b)** *Rel* **(the Church of) R.,** l'Église romaine, le catholicisme; **to go over to R.,** passer au catholicisme.
Romeo ['rəʊmɪəʊ] *n* Roméo *m*; *Hum* **he's a bit of a R.,** c'est un Roméo.
romp¹ [rɒmp] *n* ébats *mpl*.
romp² *vi* (*of child, animal etc*) s'ébattre (bruyamment), gambader; **to r. away with a race,** gagner une course haut la main; **to r. home,** (*of candidate, horse, runner*) arriver dans un fauteuil; **to r. through an examination,** passer un examen sans effort, *F* passer un examen les doigts dans le nez; **to r. through one's work,** faire son travail sans effort.
romper ['rɒmpər] *n* (*for baby*) **r. suit, rompers,** barboteuse *f*.
rondo ['rɒndəʊ] *n Mus* rondeau *m*.
roneo®¹ ['rəʊnɪəʊ] *n* document *etc* ronéotypé *ou F* ronéoté.
roneo®² *vt* ronéotyper, *F* ronéoter (*un document*).
roo [ruː] *n Austr F* kangourou *m*; **r. bar,** = arceau *m* de sécurité.
rood [ruːd] *n* **(a)** *Rel* crucifix *m*; **r. arch,** arche *f* du jubé; **r. loft,** (galerie *f* du) jubé *m*; **r. screen,** jubé; **(b)** *Arch* (*measurement*) rood *m*, quart *m* d'arpent.
roof¹ [ruːf] *n* (*of building, vehicle*) toit *m*; (*of tunnel, cave, mine*) plafond *m*; *Br F* **to go through** *or* **hit the r.,** sortir de ses gonds; *F* **to go through the r.,** (*of inflation, prices*) connaître une flambée; **to be without** *or* **not have a r. over one's head,** se trouver sans logement; **at least you have a r. over your head,** au moins tu as quelque part où vivre; **to live under one** *or* **the same r.,** habiter sous le même toit *ou* dans le même bâtiment; **shops and sports facilities under one** *or* **the same r.,** des boutiques et des aménagements sportifs dans un même endroit; **not under MY r.,** pas chez moi; **the r. of heaven,** la voûte des cieux; **r. of the mouth,** voûte du palais; *Fig* **the r. of the world,** le toit du monde; **r. garden,** jardin aménagé sur un toit; **r. light,** lucarne *f*; (*in vehicle*) plafonnier *m*; **r. rack,** (*on car*) galerie *f*; **r. timbering** *or* **timbers,** les combles *mpl*.
roof² *vt Constr* couvrir (*une maison etc*) (**with,** de); **to r. sth in** *or* **over,** recouvrir qch d'un toit; **a house roofed with slate/thatch/***etc*, une maison à toit d'ardoises/de chaume/*etc*.
-roofed [ruːft] *suff* **slate/***etc***-r.,** à toit d'ardoises/*etc*.
roofer ['ruːfər] *n Constr* (*of building etc*) couvreur *m*.
roofing ['ruːfɪŋ] *n* (*operation*) pose *f* de la toiture; (*material*) toiture *f*; **r. material/tiles/felt/***etc*, matériaux *mpl*/tuiles *fpl*/feutre *m*/*etc* de couverture; **r. strip,** (latte) volige *f*.
roofless ['ruːflɪs] *adj* (*building*) sans toit, à ciel ouvert.
rooftop ['ruːftɒp] *n* toit *m*; **to shout sth from the rooftops,** crier *ou* publier qch sur les toits.
rooftree ['ruːftriː] *n* poutre *f* de faîte, faîtage *m*.
rook¹ [rʊk] *n* **(a)** (*bird*) freux *m*; **(b)** (*in chess*) tour *f*.
rook² *vt F* (*cheat*) rouler (*qn*) (**out of,** de).
rookery ['rʊkərɪ] *n* (*of rooks, seals, penguins*) colonie *f*, rookerie *f*.
rookie ['rʊkɪ] *n F* (*in army*) recrue *f*, bleu *m*; (*in sport*) novice *mf*; (*addition to a team*) nouveau membre; *Am* **r. cop,** flic débutant, bleu.
room¹ [ruːm] *n* **(a)** (*in house etc*) pièce *f*; (*in hotel*) chambre *f*; (*bedroom*) chambre; (*large, public*) salle *f*; **one's rooms,** son appartement; **to live in rooms,** vivre en meublé; **(furnished) rooms to let,** chambres garnies à louer; **r. and board,** chambre et pension; **double/single r.,** chambre à deux personnes/une personne; **r. with twin beds,** chambre à deux lits; **r. 22 wants some coffee,** (*in hotel*) du café pour la chambre 22; *F* **the smallest r. in the house,** les cabinets *mpl*, le petit coin; *Am* **men's r., ladies r.,** toilettes *fpl*; **the r. fell silent,** le silence s'est fait dans la pièce; **the whole r. burst out laughing,** toute la salle a éclaté de rire; **serve at r. temperature,** (*of wine*) servir chambré; **to keep sth at r. temperature,** garder qch à la température ambiante *ou* de la pièce; **r. divider,** cloison *f*, écran *m*; **r. service,** (*in hotel*) service *m* (des repas *etc*) dans les chambres, room-service *m*; **to provide r. service,** servir dans les chambres; **to call r. service,** appeler le garçon d'étage;
(b) (*space*) place *f* (**for,** pour); **(some) r.,** de la place; **there's no r. to breathe in here,** on étouffe ici; **to give s.o. r. to move,** donner à qn plus d'espace *ou* de place pour bouger; **there's no r. to move in his flat,** on n'a pas la place de bouger dans son appartement; **to have r. for manoeuvre,** avoir une marge de manœuvre; **to make r. for s.o.,** faire place à qn; *Fig* laisser le champ libre à qn; **to make r. for sth,** faire de la place pour qch; **is there r. for one more?,** est-ce qu'il y a assez de place pour une personne en plus?; **r. for one more inside!,** (*on bus*) il y a assez de place pour une personne en plus; *Fig* **there's r. for doubt,** le doute est permis; **no r. for doubt,** aucun doute possible; **there is r. for improvement,** cela laisse à désirer, on peut faire mieux; **there's no r. for slackers in this company,** les fainéants n'ont pas leur place dans cette société.
room² *vi Old-fashioned* vivre en meublé; *Am* **to r. with s.o.,** partager un logement avec qn; **to r. together,** vivre ensemble dans le même logement.
-roomed [ruːmd] *suff* **two/three/***etc***-r.,** (*house etc*) de deux/trois/*etc* pièces.
roomer ['ruːmər] *n Am* locataire *mf* en meublé.
roomette [ruː'met] *n Am Rail* compartiment *m* avec couchette.
roomful ['ruːmfʊl] *n* (*of people, objects etc*) salle pleine; (*of soldiers*) chambrée *f*.
roominess ['ruːmɪnɪs] *n* (*of house etc*) dimensions spacieuses *ou* généreuses; (*of clothing*) coupe *f* confortable *ou* ample; (*of car*) dimensions spacieuses.
rooming ['ruːmɪŋ] *n Am* **r. house,** maison *f* de rapport.
roommate ['ruːmmeɪt] *n Br* compagnon, -agne *ou* camarade *mf* de chambre; *Am* (*flatmate*) = personne avec qui on partage un appartement.
roomy ['ruːmɪ] *adj* (*house*) spacieux, où l'on a de la place;

(*clothes*) ample; (*car*) spacieux.

roost¹ [ruːst] *n* (*for domestic fowl*) juchoir *m*; (*for wild birds*) perchoir *m*, *Fig* logement *m*, gîte *m*; **to go to r.**, (*of domestic fowl*) se jucher; (*of wild birds*) se percher; *Fig* **to come home to r.**, (*of crime, mistake etc*) se retourner contre son auteur; *Fig* **your chickens have come home to r.**, ça s'est retourné contre toi, ça a fait boomerang.

roost² *vi* (*of domestic fowl*) se jucher; (*of wild birds*) se percher.

rooster ['ruːstər] *n* coq *m*.

root¹ [ruːt] *n* (*of plant*) & *Math Fig* racine *f*; (*of problem etc*) cause *f*, origine *f*; **to pull up a plant by the roots**, déraciner une plante; **to pull s.o.'s hair out by the roots**, arracher les cheveux de qn; **to touch up one's roots**, (*of person with dyed hair*) se retoucher les racines; **to take r.**, (*of plant*) & *Fig* prendre racine *ou* pied; *Fig* **my roots are in Canada**, mes racines sont au Canada; **I don't have any roots**, je n'ai pas de racines; *Fig* **to put down roots**, s'enraciner; **to get back to one's roots**, retrouver ses racines; **to have its roots in**, (*of crisis etc*) avoir ses origines dans; **money is the r. of all evil**, l'argent est la source de tous les maux; **to get to the r. of things**, aller au fond des choses; **to strike at the r. of sth**, aller à la source de qch; **to destroy sth r. and branch**, extirper qch; **a r. and branch reform**, une réforme complète; *Am* **r. beer**, boisson gazeuse (faite avec les racines de certaines plantes); **r. cause**, cause première; **r. canal**, (*of tooth*) canal *m* de la racine; **to have r. treatment**, subir un traitement endodontique; *Am* **r. cellar**, = cave où l'on stocke les légumes à racine comestible; *Agr* **r. crops**, (cultures *fpl* de) racines alimentaires; **r. vegetable**, légume *m* à racine comestible.

root² **1** *vt* enraciner (*des boutures, plantes*) (**in**, dans); **to remain rooted to the spot** *or* **ground**, rester cloué *ou* figé sur place; *Fig* **her behaviour is rooted in her political convictions**, son comportement trouve ses origines dans ses convictions politiques. **2** *vi* (*of plants*) s'enraciner, prendre racine.

root³ **1** *vi* (*of pig*) fouiller avec le groin. **2** *vt* (*of pig*) fouiller (*la terre*).

►**root about, root around** *vi* fouiller; **to r. about** *or* **around for**, fouiller pour trouver.

►**root for** *vipo esp Am F* (*cheer, support*) encourager; **to r. for a candidate**, appuyer un candidat; **we'll be rooting for you**, nous sommes de votre côté.

►**root out** *vtsep* **(a)** déraciner (*une plante*); **to r. out abuses**, déraciner *ou* extirper des abus; **(b)** *F* (*find*) trouver, dénicher (*qch*); *F* **see if you can r. him out of the pub**, essayez de le dénicher du pub.

►**root up** *vtsep* déraciner (*une plante*); (*dig up*) ramasser (*les pommes de terre*); arracher (*les carottes*).

rooted ['ruːtɪd] *adj* (*plant*) enraciné; (*cutting*) qui a des racines; *Fig* (*prejudice*) enraciné, invétéré; **deeply r.**, bien enraciné (**in**, dans).

rooting ['ruːtɪŋ] *n* enracinement *m*; **r. compost**, compost *m* favorisant l'enracinement.

rooting out *n* (*of abuse etc*) déracinement *m*, extirpation *f*, éradication *f*.

rootless ['ruːtlɪs] *adj* (*plant, person*) sans racines.

rootstock ['ruːtstɒk] *n* (*of plant*) rhizome *m*, souche *f*.

rope¹ [rəʊp] *n* corde *f*; *Nau* cordage *m*; (*of pearls*) sautoir *m*; (*of onions*) glane *f*, chapelet *m*; **to be on the ropes**, (*of boxer*) se retrouver dans les cordes; *Fig* (*of company, economy etc*) battre de l'aile; *Boxing etc* **the ropes**, les cordes, *F* les ficelles *fpl*; *Br F* **he's getting money for old r.**, il est payé à faire un travail qui ne vaut rien; **wire r.**, câble *m* métallique; **piece of r.**, corde; **bell r.**, (*in house*) cordon *m* de sonnette; (*in belltower*) corde d'une cloche; **to put on the r.**, s'encorder; **(climbers on the) r.**, (alpinistes en) cordée *f*; *F* **to know the ropes**, connaître son affaire, être au courant; *F* **to learn the ropes**, apprendre les ficelles; *F* **to show s.o. the ropes**, mettre qn au courant, former qn; **the r.**, (*death by hanging*) la pendaison; **to bring back the r.**, remettre la pendaison en vigueur; *Fig* **to give s.o. enough r. (to hang himself** *or* **herself)**, donner à qn la corde pour se pendre; *Fig* **to give s.o. lots** *or* **plenty of r.**, donner du mou à qn; **r. dancer**, danseur, -euse de corde; **r. ladder**, échelle *f* de corde; **r. maker**, cordier *m*; **r. yard**, corderie *f*.

rope² *vt* corder (*une malle*); lier (*qn*) (**to**, à); *Am* prendre (*un animal*) au lasso; **to r. climbers (together)**, encorder des alpinistes; **climbers roped together**, (alpinistes en) cordée *f*.

►**rope in** *vtsep F* **to r. s.o. in**, (*to help*) embrigader (*qn*) (**to do**, pour faire).

►**rope off** *vtsep* séparer (*qch*) (par une corde); **part of the field has been roped off**, une partie du champ a été fermée par des cordes.

►**rope up** *vi* (*of climbers*) s'encorder.

rope-soled ['rəʊpsəʊld] *adj* (*sandal etc*) à semelles de corde.

rop(e)y ['rəʊpɪ] *adj Br F* (*furniture, hotel, translation*) minable; (*person*) patraque; **to feel a bit r.**, ne pas être dans son assiette.

ropiness ['rəʊpɪnɪs] *n Br F* (*of furniture, hotel etc*) mauvaise qualité.

ro-ro ['rəʊrəʊ] *adj* = **ROLL-ON/ROLL-OFF**.

Rorschach ['rɔːʃɑːk] *n Psy* **R. test**, test *m* de Rorschach *ou* des taches d'encre.

rosary ['rəʊzərɪ] *n Rel* rosaire *m*, chapelet *m*; **to say a r.**, réciter son chapelet.

rose [rəʊz] *n* **(a)** (*flower*) rose *f*; (*on hat etc*) rosette *f*; (*on watering can*) pomme *f*; (*on ceiling*) rosace *f*; *Fig* **life is not a bed of** *or* **all roses**, tout n'est pas rose dans la vie; **her life wasn't a bed of roses**, elle n'avait pas la vie bien rose; *Prov* **there is no r. without a thorn**, il n'y a pas de rose sans épine; *Fig* **to come up smelling of roses**, s'en sortir toujours très bien; *Fig* **to come up roses**, marcher parfaitement; *Fig* **to put the roses back in s.o.'s cheeks**, (*of holiday, sea air etc*) faire reprendre des couleurs à qn; *Fig* **to be a real English r.**, (*of woman*) avoir le teint clair (typique des Anglaises); *Hist* **the Wars of the Roses**, la guerre des Deux-Roses; **r. bed**, parterre *m* de rosiers; **r. (bush)**, rosier *m*; **r. diamond**, diamant (taillé) en rose; **r. garden**, roseraie *f*; **r. grower**, rosiériste *mf*; **r. petal**, pétale *m* de rose; *Archit* **r. window**, rosace, rose; **(b)** (*colour*) (couleur *f* de) rose *m*; **r. brick/paint/***etc*, brique *f*/peinture *f*/*etc* rose; **r. pink**, rose *m*; **r. red**, vermillon *m*.

rosé ['rəʊzeɪ] *n* (vin) rosé *m*.

roseate ['rəʊzɪeɪt] *adj Fml* rose.

rosebay ['rəʊzbeɪ] *n Bot* laurier-rose *m*.

rosebud ['rəʊzbʌd] *n* bouton *m* de rose; **r. mouth**, bouche *f* en cerise.

rose-coloured ['rəʊzkʌləd] *adj* couleur de rose, rose *inv*, rosé; **to see things** *or* **the world through r.-c. glasses** *or* **spectacles**, voir tout en rose, voir la vie en rose.

rose-cut ['rəʊzkʌt] *adj* (*diamond etc*) (taillé) en rose.

rosehip ['rəʊzhɪp] *n* églantine *f*; **r. jelly**, gelée *f* d'églantine; **r. syrup**, sirop *m* d'églantine.

rosemary ['rəʊzmərɪ] *n Bot Culin* romarin; **r. bush**, buisson *m* de romarin.

rose-pink [rəʊz'pɪŋk] *adj* (*dress etc*) (couleur *m* de) rose, rosé, incarnat.

rose-red [rəʊz'red] *adj* (*complexion etc*) vermeil.

rosetree ['rəʊztriː] *n* rosier *m* sur tige.

rosette [rəʊ'zet] *n* **(a)** (*decoration*) (*on parcel*) chou *m*; *Sp* (*prize*) cocarde *f*; (*badge*) rosette *f*; **(b)** *Archit* rosette *f*.

rose-water ['rəʊzwɔːtər] *n* eau *f* de rose; **r.-w. perfume**, parfum *m* à l'eau de rose.

rosewood ['rəʊzwʊd] *n* bois *m* de rose; **r. desk/table/***etc*, bureau *m*/table *f*/*etc* en bois de rose.

rosie ['rəʊzɪ] *n Br Sl* **r. (lee)**, (*tea*) thé *m*.

rosin¹ ['rɒzɪn] *n* colophane *f*.

rosin² *vt* traiter (*un archet*) à la colophane.

rosiness ['rəʊzɪnɪs] *n* couleur *f* rose; **the r. of her cheeks**, le rose de ses joues.

ROSPA ['rɒspə] *n Br* (*abbr* **Royal Society for the Prevention of Accidents**) ≈ société *f* pour la prévention des accidents.

roster¹ ['rɒstər] *n Mil etc* **(duty) r.**, liste *f* (de service).

roster² *vt esp Am* mettre (*qn*) sur une liste (de service).

rostrum, *pl* **-a, -ums** ['rɒstrəm, -ə, -əmz] *n* (*for speaker*) estrade *f*, tribune *f*; (*for prizewinner*) podium *m*; (*for conductor*) estrade.

rosy ['rəʊzɪ] *adj* (*pink*) rose, rosé; *Fig* (*future*) tout en rose; **r. cheeks**, joues vermeilles; **her r. complexion**, son teint de rose; *Fig* **to paint everything in r. colours**, peindre tout en rose; *Fig* **to paint a r. picture of sth**, dépeindre qch sous un jour optimiste; *Fig* **a r. prospect**, une perspective attrayante; *Fig* **to take a r. view of things**, voir les choses sous un jour optimiste.

rot¹ [rɒt] *n* **(a)** (*in plant, wood etc*) pourriture *f*; (*of food*) putréfaction *f*; **(b)** *F* (*nonsense*) bêtises *fpl*, inepties *fpl*; **to talk (utter** *or* **absolute) r.**, dire des imbécillités; **r.!**, n'importe quoi!; **what r.!**, quelle idiotie!; **(c)** *Fig* (*in sport, war etc*) démoralisation *f*; **the r. has set in**, la démoralisation s'est installée; **to stop the r.**, parer à la démoralisation.

rot² *v* (**-tt-**) **1** *vi* (*of leaves, wood, material etc*) pourrir; (*of food*) se décomposer, se putréfier; (*of manure*) se décomposer. **2** *vt* (faire) pourrir, décomposer, putréfier; *Agr* **rotted manure**, fumier décomposé; **oil rots rubber**, l'huile désagrège le caoutchouc; **soft drinks r. your teeth**, les boissons sucrées gâtent les dents *ou* donnent des caries; *Fig* **they let him r. in prison**, ils l'ont laissé pourrir dans un cachot.

►**rot away** *vi & vtsep* = **ROT²**.

rota ['rəʊtə] *n esp Br* liste *f* de service; **we have a r. for the housework**, nous faisons le ménage à tour de rôle; **according to a r.**, à tour de rôle.

Rotarian [rəʊ'teərɪən] *n* rotarien *m*.

rotary ['rəutərɪ] **1** *adj* (*movement*) rotatif, de rotation; (*switch*) tournant; *Typ* **r. printing press,** (machine) rotative *f*, *F* roto *f*; **r. clothesline** *or* **clothes dryer,** séchoir *m* parapluie; **r. engine,** moteur rotatif; **r. pump,** pompe rotative; *Am* **r. tiller,** herse rotative. **2** *n Am Aut* (*roundabout*) sens *m* giratoire.

Rotary ['rəutərɪ] *n* **R. Club,** Rotary Club *m*.

rotate [rəʊ'teɪt] **1** *vi* **(a)** (*of earth etc*) tourner; (*on pivot*) pivoter; **(b)** (*in job*) remplir des fonctions à tour de rôle; **the presidency rotates every two years among members,** les membres assument la présidence à tour de rôle tous les deux ans. **2** *vt* **(a)** (faire) tourner (*un bouton*); **(b)** remplir (*des fonctions*) à tour de rôle; faire (*le ménage*) à tour de rôle; *Agr* alterner (*les cultures*).

rotating [rəʊ'teɪtɪŋ] **1** *adj* (*can move*) tournant, rotatif; (*is moving*) en rotation. **2** *n* rotation *f*; (*of crops*) alternance *f*.

rotation [rəʊ'teɪʃən] *n* **(a)** (*of planet*) rotation *f*; (*of machine*) rotation, tour *m*; **rotations per minute,** tours-minute *mpl*; **(b)** (*in job*) succession *f* tour à tour, rotation *f*, roulement *m*; **by** *or* **in r.,** par roulement, à tour de rôle; *Agr* **r. of crops,** alternance *f* des cultures, assolement *m*.

rotative ['rəutətɪv, rəʊ'teɪtɪv] *adj* rotatif.

rotator [rəʊ'teɪtər] *n* **(a)** appareil rotateur; **(b)** *Anat* (muscle) rotateur *m*.

rotatory [rəʊ'teɪtərɪ] *adj* rotatoire, de rotation.

rote [rəut] *n* **r. learning,** apprentissage *m* par cœur; **to learn by r.,** apprendre par cœur.

rotgut ['rɒtgʌt] *n Br F* (*wine, spirits*) tord-boyau *m*.

rotisserie [rəʊ'tiːsərɪ, -'tɪs-] *n* (*spit*) rôtissoire *f*.

rotogravure ['rəutəugrə'vjuər] *n* rotogravure *f*.

rotor ['rəutər] *n* (*of turbine, helicopter*) rotor *m*.

rotovator ® ['rəutəveɪtər] *n Br* motoculteur *m*.

rotten ['rɒt(ə)n] *adj* **(a)** (*leaves, wood, egg, fruit etc*) pourri; **to smell r.,** sentir le pourri;

(b) *F* (*book, film etc*) nul, pourri; (*actor, golfer etc*) nul; (*job, trick etc*) sale; **you r. bastard!,** espèce de pourriture!; **what a r. bastard he is,** quelle pourriture; **to feel r.,** (*ill*) être mal fichu; (*sorry*) être malade (**about,** de); **I felt r. about it,** j'en étais malade; **to look r.,** avoir l'air mal fichu; **don't be r.!,** ne sois pas salaud!; **that was a r. thing to do,** c'était un sale tour; **she's r. to the core,** elle est corrompue jusqu'à la moelle des os; **he played a r. game,** il a joué abominablement; **r. luck!,** quelle guigne; **to have r. luck,** avoir la guigne; **r. weather,** temps *m* de chien; **the weather was r.,** il a fait un temps de chien; **it's been a r. summer,** (*the weather has been bad*) ça a été un été pourri; **she's been having a r. time of it lately,** elle vient de traverser une sale période.

rottenly ['rɒt(ə)nlɪ] *adv* (*to behave, play*) de façon abominable *ou* épouvantable.

rottenness ['rɒt(ə)nnɪs] *n* **(a)** (*of leaves etc*) pourriture *f*, décomposition *f*; **(b)** *F* (*of performance etc*) caractère *m* lamentable *ou* abominable, nullité *f*.

rotter ['rɒtər] *n Old-fashioned Br F* sale type *m*, propre *m* à rien.

rotting ['rɒtɪŋ] **1** *adj* qui pourrit, en pourriture. **2** *n* pourriture *f*, putréfaction *f*.

rotund [rəʊ'tʌnd] *adj* (*round*) rond; (*plump*) arrondi, rondelet; (*speech, style*) grandiloquent; **his r. figure,** ses formes arrondies.

rotunda [rəʊ'tʌndə] *n Archit* rotonde *f*.

rotundity [rəʊ'tʌndɪtɪ] *n* (*of person*) rotondité *f*, embonpoint *m*; (*of speech, style*) grandiloquence *f*.

rouble, *US* **ruble** ['ruːb(ə)l] *n* (*currency*) rouble *m*.

roué ['ruːeɪ] *n Old-fashioned* vieux roué, vieux débauché.

rouge¹ [ruːʒ] *n* **(a)** (*make-up*) rouge *m* (à joues); **(b)** *Cards* **r. et noir** ['ruːʒeɪ'nwɑːr], trente et quarante *m*.

rouge² *vt & vi* **to r. (one's cheeks),** se mettre du rouge aux joues, se farder.

rough¹ [rʌf] **1** *adj* **(a)** (*uneven, not smooth*) (*material*) rude, rugueux, raboteux; (*surface, skin*) rèche, rugueux; (*road*) raboteux; (*terrain etc*) accidenté; (*ground*) inégal, raboteux; *F* **to give s.o. the r. edge of one's tongue,** parler brutalement à qn;

(b) (*unrefined, unpolished*) (*manners*) brut, grossier, fruste; (*speech*) bourru, rude; (*style*) fruste; **in the r. state,** à l'état brut; **r. sketch,** ébauche *f*, esquisse *f*; **r. draft,** premier jet, brouillon *m*; **r. paper,** papier brouillon; *Sch* **r. work,** brouillon *m*;

(c) *F* (*ill, not working properly*) **to feel r.,** se sentir patraque; **you look a bit r.,** tu as l'air un peu patraque; **the engine sounds a bit r.,** le moteur ne semble pas tourner très rond;

(d) (*violent*) grossier, brutal, rude, dur; (*wind*) violent; **r. sea,** mer grosse *ou* houleuse; *F* **r. customer,** mauvais coucheur; **to have a r. crossing,** faire une mauvaise traversée; **r. handling,** *F* **r. stuff,** brutalités *fpl*; *Sl* **r. trade,** (*in homosexual relationship*) partenaire violent ramassé au hasard; *Sl* **he's into r. trade,** il recherche les partenaires violents; **to be r. with s.o.,** brutaliser qn, rudoyer qn; **you were too r.,** tu as été trop rude; **don't be so r. with her,** sois moins rude avec elle; **this is a r. neighbourhood,** ce quartier est mal fréquenté;

(e) (*harsh, hard*) (*voice*) rude, rauque, âpre; (*wine*) gros, grossier, âpre, rude; *F* **to give s.o. a r. time,** traiter qn avec sévérité, être vache avec qn; *F* **he's had a r. deal** *or* **ride** *or* **time of it,** il en a bavé, il a bouffé de la vache enragée; *F* **it was r. on her,** c'était dur pour elle; **r. work,** le gros ouvrage, *F* le plus gros; **r. justice,** justice *f* sommaire; **divorce is r. on children,** le divorce est dur pour les enfants; **you were too r. on them,** tu as été trop sévère avec eux; **it's r. having to work on Saturdays,** c'est dur de devoir travailler le samedi; **r. luck!,** dommage!, pas de chance!; **they've had a lot of r. luck recently,** ils n'ont pas eu beaucoup de chance récemment;

(f) (*approximate*) (*calculation, estimate etc*) approximatif; **r. guess,** approximation *f*; **at a r. guess** *or* **estimate,** approximativement; **as a r. guide one metre equals three feet,** un mètre équivaut approximativement à trois pieds; **could you give me a r. idea of how long it will take?,** pourriez-vous me donner une idée approximative du temps que ça va prendre?; **I have a r. idea of what it's about,** j'ai une petite idée de ce dont il s'agit;

(g) (*uncultured*) (*land, pasture*) en friche.

2 *adv* rudement, grossièrement; **to play r.,** jouer brutalement; *F* **to sleep r.,** coucher à la dure; *F* **to live r.,** vivre dans des conditions rudimentaires.

3 *n* **(a)** terrain accidenté; *Fig* le côté désagréable des choses; *Golf* **to be in the r.,** être dans l'herbe longue; *Fig* **to take the r. with the smooth,** prendre le bon avec le mauvais;

(b) (*hooligan*) voyou *m*;

(c) (*of drawing etc*) ébauche *f*; **to do sth in r.,** faire qch au brouillon.

rough² *vt* ébouriffer (*les cheveux*); faire hérisser (*le poil*); **to r. it,** vivre à la dure, en voir de dures; **we've** *or* **you've** *etc* **got to r. it,** à la guerre comme à la guerre.

▶**rough out** *vtsep* (*drawing etc*) ébaucher; (*plan, project, play, novel*) concevoir dans ses grandes lignes.

▶**rough up** *vtsep* **(a)** ébouriffer (*les cheveux*); **(b) to r. s.o. up,** rudoyer *ou* malmener *ou* maltraiter qn.

roughage ['rʌfɪdʒ] *n* (*in food*) fibres *fpl* (alimentaires).

rough-and-ready [rʌfən'redɪ] *adj* (*meal*) vite préparé; (*accommodation, construction*) sommaire; (*person*) rustre; (*conditions, solution*) grossier.

rough-and-tumble [rʌfən'tʌmb(ə)l] *n* bousculade *f*, mêlée *f*; *Fig* **the r.-and-t. of politics/***etc*, la jungle de la politique/*etc*; **the r.-and-t. world of publishing,** la jungle de l'édition.

roughcast¹ ['rʌfkɑːst] *n Constr* crépi *m*; **r. surface/wall/***etc*, mur *m*/surface *f*/*etc* crépi(e).

roughcast² *vt* (*pt & pp* **roughcast**) *Constr* crépir (*un mur etc*).

rough-coated ['rʌfkəutɪd] *adj* (*horse*) à poil long; (*dog*) à poil dur.

roughen ['rʌf(ə)n] **1** *vt* rendre (*une surface*) rude *ou* rugueux *ou* âpre. **2** *vi* **(a)** devenir rude *ou* rugueux *ou* âpre; **(b)** (*of sea*) grossir, devenir houleux.

rough-hew [rʌf'hjuː] *vt* (*pt* **rough-hewed**; *pp* **rough-hewn**) dégrossir (*du bois d'œuvre, une statue etc*)

roughhouse¹ ['rʌfhaus] *n F* (*disorderly behaviour*) chahut *m*; (*noise*) boucan *m*; **there was a bit of a r. in the pub last night,** il y a eu de la bagarre au pub hier soir.

roughhouse² **1** *vi* chahuter. **2** *vt* malmener (*qn*).

roughing ['rʌfɪŋ] *n* (*of wall*) crépissage *m*, ravalement *m*; **r. (down** *or* **out),** dégrossissage *m*, dégrossissement *m*, ébauchage *m*; **r. tool,** ciseau *m* à dégrossir, ébauchoir *m*.

roughly ['rʌflɪ] *adv* **(a)** (*to build*) grossièrement; **r. made table,** table grossière; **to sketch sth r.,** faire un croquis sommaire de qch; **(b)** (*to handle, behave, answer*) rudement, brutalement; **to treat s.o. r.,** maltraiter *ou* malmener *ou* rudoyer qn; **(c)** (*approximately*) approximativement, en gros; **r. speaking,** en général, généralement parlant; **to estimate sth r.,** estimer qch approximativement; **they live in r. the same area,** ils habitent approximativement dans le même quartier.

roughneck ['rʌfnek] *n Am* **(a)** *F* voyou *m*; **(b)** (*on oil rig*) = personne travaillant sur une plate-forme pétrolière.

roughness ['rʌfnɪs] *n* **(a)** (*of surface, skin*) caractère rèche *ou* rugueux; (*of road, ground*) rugosité *f*, inégalité *f*; **(b)** (*of diamond etc*) état brut; **(c)** (*of sea*) agitation *f*; (*of wind*) violence *f*; **(d)** (*of voice*) âpreté *f*, rudesse *f*.

roughrider ['rʌfraɪdər] *n* dresseur *m* de chevaux.

roughshod ['rʌfʃɒd] *adj Fig* **to ride r. over,** fouler (*qn*) aux pieds, traiter (*qn*) cavalièrement; fouler (*des principes*) aux pieds.

rough-spoken [rʌf'spəuk(ə)n] *adj* au langage grossier.

roulette [ruː'let] *n* roulette *f*; **to play r.,** jouer à la roulette; **game of r.,** partie *f* de roulette; **Russian r.,** roulette russe; **r. table,** table *f* de roulette; **r. wheel,** roulette *f*.

Roumania [ruː'meɪnɪə, rʊ-] *n* Roumanie *f*.

Roumanian [ruː'meɪnɪən, rʊ-] **1** *adj* roumain. **2** *n* **(a)**

Roumain, -aine; **(b)** *Ling* roumain *m.*

round¹ [raʊnd] **1** *adj* **(a)** (*in shape*) rond, circulaire; **r. brackets,** parenthèses *fpl*; **the R. Table,** la Table ronde; *Pol Ind etc* **r. table (conference),** table ronde; **to become r.,** s'arrondir; **r. shoulders,** épaules voûtées; **r. cheeks,** joues rebondies; **r. hand,** (écriture) ronde *f*; **r. dance,** ronde *f*; *Am* **r. trip,** voyage *m* aller et retour; **r. robin,** pétition revêtue de signatures en cercle; *Sp* poule *f*;

(b) (*number*) rond; **in r. figures,** en chiffres ronds; **r. sum,** compte rond; **a r. dozen,** une bonne douzaine; **a good r. sum, a r. sum of money,** une somme rondelette;

(c) (*declaration etc*) franc, *f* franche.

2 *n* **(a)** (*shape*) (*of butter, pastry etc*) cercle *m*, rond *m*; (*of bread*) tranche *f*, tartine *f*; (*sandwich*) sandwich *m*; *Art* **sculpture in the r.,** ronde(-)bosse *f*; **theatre in the r.,** théâtre en rond; *Culin* **r. of beef,** gîte *m* à la noix;

(b) (*stage*) *Sp Pol* manche *f*; (*of golf*) partie *f*; *Boxing* round *m*; *Tennis* tour *m*, série *f*; **to play a r. of golf,** faire une partie de golf; **he only went three rounds,** (*of boxer*) il n'a fait que trois rounds; **in the first r.** *or* **R. One,** (*of boxing match*) au cours du premier round; **to have a r. of cards,** faire une partie de cartes; *Horseriding* **clear r.,** sans-faute *m inv*; **to have** *or* **get a clear r.,** faire un sans-faute; **to be** *or* **get through to the next r.,** se qualifier pour la manche suivante;

(c) (*series*) (*of talks*) série *f*; (*of drinks, visits*) tournée *f*; **to stand a r. of drinks,** payer une tournée (générale); **whose r. is it?,** qui paye cette tournée?; **it's my r.,** c'est moi qui paye cette tournée, c'est ma tournée;

(d) (*route*) **rounds,** (*of milkman etc*) tournée *f*; (*of doctor*) visites *fpl*; (*of policeman*) ronde *f*; **delivery r.,** livraisons *fpl*, tournée *f*; **the daily r.,** la routine de tous les jours; **the daily r. of cooking and cleaning,** les travaux quotidiens de cuisine et de ménage; **one continual r. of pleasure,** une succession perpétuelle de plaisirs; **the story went the rounds (of the village/***etc***),** l'histoire a fait le tour (du village/*etc*); **there's a virus going the rounds,** il a un virus qui se promène; **to be on** *or* **make** *or* **do one's rounds,** faire sa tournée; **to do a hospital r.,** faire sa visite à l'hôpital; **to do a paper r.,** distribuer le journal; **to do** *or* **go the rounds of travel agencies/***etc*, faire les agences de voyage/*etc*;

(e) *Mil* (*shot*) balle *f*; (*ammunition*) cartouche *f*; *Mil* **r. of ten shots,** salve *f* de dix coups; **to fire a r.,** tirer un coup; *Fig* **r. of applause,** applaudissements *mpl*; **let's have a big r. of applause for her,** on l'applaudit bien fort!;

(f) *Mus* canon *m*, fugue *f*; (*dance*) ronde *f*.

round² **1** *adv* autour; **garden with a wall right** *or* **all r.,** jardin avec un mur tout autour; **taking it** *or* **taken all r.,** dans l'ensemble, en général; **the villages r. about,** les villages des alentours; **the people r. about,** les gens des alentours; **r. here,** par ici; **the long way r.,** le chemin le plus long; **to have one's hat/jumper/***etc* **on the wrong way r.,** avoir son chapeau/son pull/*etc* à l'envers; **all (the) year r.,** (pendant) toute l'année; **it's the other way r.,** c'est (tout) le contraire; **to go r. (to s.o.'s),** passer (chez qn); **to order the car r.,** demander qu'on amène la voiture; **to ask s.o. r.,** inviter qn chez soi; **he brought his friend r. (with him),** il a amené son ami (avec lui); **he'll be r.,** il passera; **if you are r. this way next week,** si vous passez par ici la semaine prochaine.

2 *prep* **(a)** (*position*) autour de; **sitting r. the table,** assis autour de la table; **he's 95 cm round the chest,** il fait 95 cm de tour de poitrine; **shells were exploding r. (about) him,** des obus éclataient autour de lui; **r. about,** environ; **r. about midday,** vers midi; **she's r. about forty,** elle a la quarantaine; *Br* **he's r. the pub,** il est au pub; *Br* **he's r. his brother's,** il est chez son frère;

(b) (*motion*) autour de; **to look r. the room,** jeter un coup d'œil autour de la pièce; **to go r. (and r.) sth,** tourner autour de qch; **to go r. an obstacle,** contourner un obstacle; **to go r. the corner,** (*of person*) tourner le coin; (*of vehicle*) prendre le virage; **the grocer r. the corner,** l'épicier du coin.

round³ *vt* **(a)** (*shape*) arrondir (*qch*); *Ling* arrondir (*une voyelle*); **(b)** (*move past*) contourner (*un obstacle*); *Nau* doubler, franchir (*un cap*); contourner (*une île*); **to r. a corner,** (*of car*) prendre un virage; (*of person*) tourner un coin.

►**round down** *vtsep* arrondir **(to,** à).

►**round off** *vtsep* (*angle, sentence etc*) arrondir; (*negotiations etc*) achever; **to r. off one's speech,** achever son discours; **to r. things off ...,** pour finir ...; **we rounded the meal off with a bottle of brandy,** nous avons fini le repas avec une bouteille de cognac.

►**round up** *vtsep* rassembler (*le bétail*); faire une rafle de (*filous*); **to r. everyone up for a meeting,** rassembler tout le monde pour une réunion; **to r. an amount up,** arrondir une somme **(to,** à).

roundabout ['raʊndəbaʊt] **1** *n Br* **(a)** (*at fairground*) manège *m*; (*in playground*) carrousel *m*; *F* **what you gain on the swings you lose on the roundabouts,** à tout prendre on ne gagne ni ne perd; **(b)** *Aut* rond-point *m*, *pl* ronds-points; *Admin* carrefour *m* à sens giratoire. **2** *adj* (*method, statement etc*) détourné, indirect; **to take a r. way,** faire un détour; **to hear of sth in a r. way,** apprendre qch indirectement; **to lead up to a question in a r. way,** aborder une question de biais.

rounded ['raʊndɪd] *adj* arrondi; **r. cheeks,** joues rebondies.

roundel ['raʊnd(ə)l] *n* (*on wood, stone*) œil-de-bœuf *m*; (*on aircraft*) cocarde *f*.

rounders ['raʊndəz] *npl Br Sp* = jeu similaire au baseball.

round-eyed ['raʊn'daɪd] *adj* aux yeux ronds; **to listen in r.-e. amazement,** écouter les yeux ronds.

Roundhead ['raʊndhed] *n Br Hist* têtes rondes; **R. army/victory/***etc*, armée *f*/victoire *f*/*etc* des têtes rondes.

roundhouse ['raʊndhaʊs] *n Rail* rotonde *f*.

roundly ['raʊndlɪ] *adv* (*parler etc*) rondement, franchement, carrément.

roundness ['raʊndnɪs] *n* rondeur *f*.

round-shouldered [raʊnd'ʃəʊldəd] *adj* (*person*) au dos voûté; **to be r.-s.** avoir le dos voûté.

roundsman, *pl* **-men** ['raʊndzmən] *n Com* livreur *m*.

round-the-clock [raʊndðə'klɒk] *adj* (*activity etc*) de jour et de nuit, vingt-quatre heures sur vingt-quatre; **open r.-the-c.,** ouvert vingt-quatre heures sur vingt-quatre.

round-trip ['raʊnd'trɪp] *adj Am* (*ticket etc*) aller-retour; **r.-t. memo,** note *f* de service circulaire.

roundup ['raʊndʌp] *n* (*of cattle*) rassemblement *m*; (*of criminals*) rafle *f*; **here is a r. of the news,** voici un résumé des nouvelles.

rouse [raʊz] *vt* **(a)** (*from sleep*) (r)éveiller (*qn*); (*from day-dreaming*) tirer (*qn*) de sa torpeur; (*make more active*) remuer, activer (*qn*); soulever (*l'indignation etc*); susciter (*l'admiration etc*); **to r. the camp,** donner l'alerte au camp; **to r. oneself,** se secouer; **to r. s.o. to action,** inciter qn à agir; **(b)** (*anger*) mettre (*qn*) en colère; **he is terrible when roused,** il est terrible quand il est en colère; *Lit* **to r. the passions,** éveiller les passions.

rousing ['raʊzɪŋ] *adj* qui (r)éveille, qui excite; (*speech*) stimulant; (*welcome*) enthousiaste; (*music*) allegro; **r. cheers,** applaudissements chaleureux.

roustabout ['raʊstəbaʊt] *n F Am* débardeur *m*; *Austr* homme *m* à tout faire, manœuvre *m*.

rout¹ [raʊt] *n Mil* déroute *f*; **to put troops to r.,** mettre des troupes en déroute; *Fig* **to put s.o. to r.,** mettre qn en fuite; *Fig* **the election was a r. for the government,** l'élection a été une débâcle pour le gouvernement.

rout² *vt Mil* mettre (*une armée*) en déroute; mettre (*l'ennemi*) en fuite.

►**rout out** *vtsep* dénicher (*qn*), faire sortir (*qn*) **(from, of,** de).

route¹ [ruːt, *Am also* raʊt] *n* **(a)** (*of traveller*) itinéraire *m*; (*of plane, ship*) route *f*, voie *f*; (*of parade*) parcours *m*; (*on mountain*) course *f*; *Am* (*of mailman etc*) tournée *f*; *Fig* (*to failure, success etc*) voie; **to map out a r.,** tracer un itinéraire; **sea r.,** route maritime; **bus r.,** (*service*) ligne *f* d'autobus; (*direction taken*) itinéraire *ou* parcours d'autobus; **are you on a bus r.?,** est-ce qu'un autobus passe près de chez vous?; **all routes,** (*road sign*) toutes directions; **r. map,** levé *m* d'itinéraire; *Mil* **r. march,** marche *f* d'entraînement (au pas de route); **(b)** *Am* (*highway*) route nationale.

route² *vt* router, acheminer (*un colis etc*) **(through, via,** par).

routine [ruː'tiːn] *n* **(a)** (*habit*) routine *f*; **to do sth as a matter of r.,** faire qch d'office *ou* de façon systématique; **the daily r.,** le train-train quotidien; **it's just r.,** c'est une simple formalité; **it was a r. flight,** c'était un vol sans rien de particulier; **r. examination,** examen *m* de routine; *Pej* **r. job/performance/rendering/***etc*, travail *m*/représentation *f*/rendu *m*/*etc* qui n'a rien de particulier; **r. work,** travail de routine, travail routinier; **r. enquiries,** (*of police*) constatations *fpl* d'usage; **it's just a r. enquiry,** (*that we're making*) nous venons simplement faire les constatations d'usage; **(b)** *Th* (*of dancer*) enchaînement *m* (de pas de danse); (*of comic*) numéro *m*; **to go through one's r.,** faire son numéro; **to practise one's r.,** répéter son numéro; **don't give me that r.,** ne me fais pas ton numéro; **(c)** *Comptr* sous-programme *m*.

routinely [ruː'tiːnlɪ] *adv* (*to check, proceed etc*) (*systematically*) d'office; (*as usual*) comme d'habitude.

rove [rəʊv] **1** *vi* (*of person*) rôder, vagabonder; **his eyes roved from one to the other,** ses yeux erraient de l'un à l'autre. **2** *vt* parcourir (*la campagne, un pays*); (*of pirate*) écumer (*les mers*).

rover ['rəʊvər] *n* **(a)** rôdeur, -euse, vagabond, -onde; **(b)** (*scout*) routier *m*.

roving ['rəʊvɪŋ] **1** *adj* vagabond; (*ambassador, reporter*) itinérant; **r. commission,** grande liberté de manœuvre; *F*

to have a r. eye, avoir l'œil égrillard. **2** *n* vagabondage *m*; **r. life,** vie nomade.

row[1] [rəʊ] *n* (*of chairs, knitting*) rang *m*; (*of trees*) rangée *f*; (*of houses*) ligne *f*, rangée; (*in street names*) rue *f*; (*of cars*) file *f*; **r. of figures,** (*horizontal*) ligne *f* de chiffres; (*vertical*) colonne *f* de chiffres; **r. of lights,** rampe *f* (de lumières); **r. of medals,** brochette *f* de décorations; **in a r.,** en rang *ou* ligne; **to put things in a r.,** mettre des objets en rang, aligner des objets; **in rows,** par rangs; **in two rows,** sur deux rangs; **two Sundays in a r.,** deux dimanches de suite *ou* d'affilée; **in the front/third r.,** (*seat etc*) au premier/troisième rang; *Am* **r. house,** maison *f* en rangée.

row[2] *n* promenade *f* en canot; **to go for a r.,** canoter.

row[3] **1** *vi* (*in boat*) ramer; **to r. hard,** faire force de rames. **2** *vt* faire aller (*un canot*) à la rame; transporter (*qn*) en canot.

row[4] [raʊ] *n* **(a)** (*noise*) chahut *m*, tapage *m*, vacarme *m*; **I can't concentrate with all this r. going on,** je ne peux pas me concentrer avec tout ce chahut; **make less r.!,** faites moins de vacarme!; **to make** *or* **kick up a r.,** (*be noisy*) faire du chahut *ou* tapage; (*protest*) faire toute une histoire (**about,** au sujet de);

(b) (*quarrel*) querelle *f*, dispute *f*, *F* scène *f*; **family r.,** querelle de famille; **to have a r.,** se quereller, se disputer (**with,** avec); *F* **to get into a r.,** (*from parents, teacher etc*) se faire attraper, se faire laver la tête; **I got into a r. with the bus driver,** je me suis disputé avec le chauffeur d'autobus; *Scot* **the boss gave me a r. for being late,** le patron m'a enguirlandé parce que j'étais en retard; **the r. in Parliament over defence policy,** la controverse au Parlement au sujet de la politique de défense.

row[5] *vi* se quereller, se disputer (**with,** avec; **about,** à propos de).

rowan ['raʊən, 'rəʊ-] *n* (*tree*) sorbier *m* (domestique), cormier *m*; (*berry*) sorbe *f*, corme *f*.

rowboat ['rəʊbəʊt] *n Am* bateau *m* à rames.

rowdiness ['raʊdɪnɪs] *n* tapage *m*, chahut *m*.

rowdy ['raʊdɪ] **1** *adj* tapageur, chahuteur; **to be r.,** chahuter. **2** *n* (*person*) voyou *m*.

rowdyism ['raʊdɪɪz(ə)m] *n* tapage *m*, chahut *m*.

rowel ['raʊəl] *n* (*on spur*) molette *f*.

rower ['rəʊər] *n* (*of boat*) rameur, -euse.

rowing[1] ['rəʊɪŋ] *n* canotage *m*; *Sp* aviron *m*; *Br* **r. boat,** bateau *m* à rames; *Gym* **r. machine,** machine *f* à ramer.

rowing[2] ['raʊɪŋ] *n* querelles *fpl*, disputes *fpl*.

rowlock ['rɒlək] *n Br* tolet *m*.

royal ['rɔɪəl] **1** *adj* (*visit etc*) royal; *Fig* (*splendid*) royal, princier, magnifique; **His** *or* **Her R. Highness,** son Altesse Royale; **Their R. Highnesses,** leurs Altesses Royales; **Your R. Highness,** votre Altesse Royale; **the Princess R.,** la princesse Royale; *Hum* **the r. we,** le 'nous' de majesté; *Br Mil* **R. Canadian Air Force,** armée *f* de l'air canadienne; **R. Canadian Mounted Police,** Gendarmerie royale du Canada; *Br* **R. Commission,** = commission de recherche nommée par le monarque sur recommandation du premier ministre; *Br Mil* **R. Engineers,** = section du génie civil de l'armée britannique; **r. blue,** bleu *inv* (de) roi *ou* (de) France; **r. charter,** acte *m* du souverain; *Cards* **r. flush,** quinte royale; **r. jelly,** gelée royale; **r. warrant,** brevet *m* de fournisseur du souverain.

2 *n F* membre *m* de la famille royale; **the royals,** la famille royale.

royalism ['rɔɪəlɪz(ə)m] *n* royalisme *m*.

royalist ['rɔɪəlɪst] *adj & n* royaliste *mf*.

royally ['rɔɪəlɪ] *adv* (*to entertain, welcome etc*) royalement.

royalty ['rɔɪəltɪ] *n* **(a)** royauté *f*; **hotel patronized by r.,** hôtel fréquenté par les personnages royaux; **(b)** (*for invention etc*) redevance *f*; **royalties** (*in publishing etc*) droits *mpl* d'auteur; *Petr* royalties *fpl*.

rozzer ['rɒzər] *n Br Sl* (*policeman*) flic *m*.

RP [ɑː'piː] *n abbr* **received pronunciation.**

rpm [ɑːpiː'em] *n Aut* (*abbr* **revolutions per minute**) tours/minute *mpl*.

RRP [ɑːrɑː'piː] *n Br* (*abbr* **recommended retail price**) prix conseillé.

RSC [ɑːres'siː] *n Br Th abbr* **Royal Shakespeare Company.**

RSM [ɑːre'sem] *n* **(a)** *Br Mil* (*abbr* **regimental sergeant-major**) adjudant-chef *m*; **(b)** *Br abbr* **Royal School of Music.**

RSPB [ɑːrespiː'biː] *n Br* (*abbr* **Royal Society for the Protection of Birds**) ≈ ligue *f* pour la protection des oiseaux.

RSPCA [ɑːrespiːsiː'eɪ] *n Br* (*abbr* **Royal Society for the Prevention of Cruelty to Animals**) ≈ SPA *f*.

RSVP [ɑːresviː'piː] *abbr* (*on invitation*) RSVP.

Rt Hon *Br Pol abbr* **Right Honourable.**

rub[1] [rʌb] *n* frottement *m*, friction *f*; **to give sth a r.,** (*to dry it*) donner un coup de torchon à qch; (*to polish it*) frotter qch, astiquer qch; *Fig* **there's the r.!,** c'est là la difficulté!

rub[2] *v* (**-bb-**) **1** *vt* (*massage*) frotter; (*polish*) astiquer; **to r. one's eyes/chin/***etc*, se frotter les yeux/le menton/*etc*; **to r. one's leg with liniment,** se frotter *ou* se frictionner la jambe avec du liniment; **to r. one's hand's (together) (in** *or* **with satisfaction),** se frotter les mains (de satisfaction); **to r. s.o.'s hands,** frotter les mains à qn; *Fig* **to r. shoulders with,** côtoyer, coudoyer; *F* **to r. s.o. up the wrong way,** prendre qn à rebrousse-poil; **to r. sth dry,** sécher qch en le frottant; **to r. sth through a sieve,** passer qch au tamis; *Fig* **I don't have two pennies to r. together,** je n'ai pas un rond. **2** *vi* frotter (**up against,** contre); **these shoes r.,** ces chaussures me font mal.

►**rub along** *vi F* se débrouiller; **we r. along (together) very well,** nous nous accordons très bien.

►**rub away** *vtsep* = **RUB OFF.**

►**rub down** *vtsep* (*wall*) regratter; (*paintwork*) poncer; **to r. a horse down,** bouchonner un cheval; **to r. s.o. down,** frictionner qn.

►**rub in** *vtsep* **to r. a hole in sth,** trouer qch à force de le frotter; **to r. sth in,** faire pénétrer qch en frottant; *F* **there's no need to r. it in!,** ce n'est pas la peine d'insister; *Fig* **to r. s.o.'s nose in it,** mettre le nez de qn dans son caca; *Fig* **to r. salt in a wound,** remuer le couteau dans la plaie.

►**rub into** *vtaspo Culin* **to r. the butter into the flour,** mélanger (avec les doigts) le beurre et la farine.

►**rub off 1** *vtsep* enlever (*qch*) par le frottement. **2** *vi* **this paint rubs off easily,** cette peinture s'enlève facilement; *F* **it rubs off on them,** cela déteint sur eux.

►**rub out** *vtsep* (*word etc*) effacer, gommer; *Sl* **to r. s.o. out,** (*murder*) éliminer qn.

rubber[1] ['rʌbər] *n* **(a)** *Br* (*eraser*) gomme *f*; (*for blackboards*) effaceur *m*;

(b) (*substance*) caoutchouc *m*, gomme *f* élastique; *Fig* **my legs feel like r.,** j'ai les jambes en coton; *Am F* **the r. chicken circuit,** = série de visites dans des petites villes au cours d'une campagne; **r. ball/gloves/***etc*, balle *f*/gants *mpl*/*etc* en caoutchouc; *Br* **r. band,** élastique *m*; *Am* **r. boots,** bottes *fpl* en caoutchouc; *F* **r. cheque,** chèque *m* en bois; **r. dinghy,** bateau *m* pneumatique; **r. stamp,** tampon *m*; *F* (*person*) béni-oui-oui *m inv*; *F* **r. stamp parliament,** parlement ratificateur; **r. tree,** arbre *m* à gomme; **r. plant,** caoutchouc, caoutchoutier *m*; **r. overshoes,** *Am* **rubbers,** caoutchoucs; **r. plantation,** plantation *f* d'hévéas; **r. planter,** planteur *m* de caoutchouc;

(c) *Am Sl* préservatif *m*, capote anglaise; **r. goods,** préservatifs.

rubber[2] *n Cards* rob(re) *m*; **to play a r.,** faire un robre.

rubberize ['rʌbəraɪz] *vt* caoutchouter (*un tissu*).

rubberneck[1] ['rʌbənek] *n Am F* **(a)** (*at scene of accident etc*) badaud, -aude, curieux, -ieuse; **(b)** (*tourist*) touriste *mf*.

rubberneck[2] *vi Am F* **(a)** (*at scene of accident etc*) faire le badaud; **(b)** (*of tourist*) excursionner, visiter.

rubber-stamp [rʌbə'stæmp] *vt* apposer un cachet sur (*qch*), estampiller (*qch*); *Fig F* approuver (*une décision*) sans discussion.

rubbery ['rʌbərɪ] *adj* caoutchouteux.

rubbing ['rʌbɪŋ] *n* frottage *m*; *Med etc* friction *f*; (*of brass*) frottis *m*; *Am* **r. alcohol,** alcool à 90 (degrés); **to take a r. of an inscription,** prendre un frottis d'une inscription; **r. down,** = **RUBDOWN.**

rubbish[1] ['rʌbɪʃ] *n Br* (*refuse*) ordures *fpl*, détritus *mpl*; (*waste*) déchets *mpl*; (*junk*) saleté(s) *f(pl)*; *Fig* (*nonsense*) bêtises *fpl*, sottises *fpl*; **r. bin,** boîte *f* à ordures, poubelle *f*; **r. chute,** vide-ordures *m inv*; **r. collection,** ramassage *m* d'ordures; **r. dump** *or* **heap,** dépotoir *m*, décharge publique; **to throw sth on the r. heap,** se débarrasser de qch; *Fig* **to throw s.o. on the r. heap,** se débarrasser de qn; *F* **good riddance to bad r.,** bon débarras; **to talk r.,** dire des bêtises; **(what) r.!, what a load of (old) r.!,** quelle foutaise!; **the play is absolute r.,** la pièce est nulle.

rubbish[2] *vt F* éreinter (*un livre, un projet*).

rubbishy ['rʌbɪʃɪ] *adj Br* (*worthless*) sans valeur; (*poor quality*) de mauvaise qualité; (*book, play*) nul.

rubble ['rʌb(ə)l] *n* décombres *mpl*; **to reduce a town to r.,** réduire une ville à des décombres; **streets strewn with r.,** des rues jonchées de décombres.

rubdown ['rʌbdaʊn] *n* (*of person*) frictionnement *m*; (*of horse*) brossage *m*; (*of wood, paintwork*) frottement *m*; **to give s.o. a good r.,** bien frictionner qn.

rube [ruːb] *n Am F* paysan *m*, rustaud *m*.

Rube Goldberg ['ruːb'gəʊldbɜːg] *adj Am* (*device, plan etc*) trop compliqué.

rubella [ruː'belə] *n Med* rubéole *f*; **r. injection/vaccine/***etc*, injection *f*/vaccin *m*/*etc* contre la rubéole.

Rubicon ['ruːbɪkən] *n* Rubicon *m*; *Fig* **to cross the R.,** franchir le Rubicon, sauter le pas.

rubicund ['ruːbɪkənd] *adj* rubicond, rougeaud.

ruble ['ruːb(ə)l] *n US* rouble *m*.

rubric ['ruːbrɪk] *n Typ etc* rubrique *f*.

ruby ['ruːbɪ] **1** *n* (*gem*) rubis *m*; **r. earrings/necklace/***etc*, boucles *fpl* d'oreille/collier *m/etc* en rubis; **2** *adj* **r. (red),** rouge, rubis *inv*; **r. port,** porto *m* rouge; **r. lips,** lèvres vermeilles; **r. wedding,** noces *fpl* de vermeil.

RUC [ɑːjuːˈsiː] *n Br* (*abbr* **Royal Ulster Constabulary**) = police de l'Irlande du Nord.

ruche¹ [ruːʃ] *n* (*on sleeves etc*) ruché *m*.

ruche² *vt* garnir (*une manche etc*) d'un ruché.

ruck¹ [rʌk] *n Sp* (*of runners etc*) peloton *m*; (*in rugby*) mêlée ouverte; *Fig* **the (common) r.,** le commun (du peuple); *Fig* **to get out of the r.,** sortir du rang.

ruck² *n* (*in cloth*) faux pli; **to smooth out the rucks,** lisser les faux plis.

ruck³ **1** *vt* froisser (*un drap*). **2** *vi* (*of sheet*) se froisser.

rucksack [ˈrʌksæk] *n Br* sac *m* à dos.

ruckus [ˈrʌkəs] *n F* (*noise*) chahut *m*, vacarme *m*; (*argument, controversy*) dispute *f*, bagarre *f*; **what's all this r. about?,** qu'est-ce que c'est que ce chahut?; **to make a r.,** faire du chahut; **to cause a r.,** (*of announcement etc*) faire du foin.

ruction [ˈrʌkʃən] *n F* dispute *f*; **there'll be ructions,** il va y avoir du grabuge *ou* de la casse.

rudder [ˈrʌdər] *n* (*on boat*) gouvernail *m*; (*on plane*) gouverne *f*; *Av* **rudders,** empennage *m*.

rudderless [ˈrʌdəlɪs] *adj* (*ship*) sans gouvernail; *Fig* (*country etc*) qui va à la dérive.

ruddiness [ˈrʌdɪnɪs] *n* (*of complexion*) teint coloré; (*of sky etc*) teinte *f* rougeâtre.

ruddy [ˈrʌdɪ] **1** *adj* (*complexion*) coloré, haut en couleur; (*cheeks*) coloré; (*sky*) rougeâtre; **r. glow,** (*of fire*) lueur rouge; *Br Sl* **you r. fool!,** espèce d'imbécile!; *Br Sl* **r. hell!,** nom de dieu! **2** *adv Br Sl* **it's r. cold,** il fait bigrement froid; **r. fast/slow/***etc*, bigrement rapide/lent/*etc*.

rude [ruːd] *adj* **(a)** (*impolite*) impoli (**to,** envers); **(b)** (*indecent*) indécent, obscène; **he made a r. gesture,** il a fait un geste obscène; **(c)** *Lit* (*primitive*) (*tool*) grossier, rudimentaire; (*drawing*) primitif; **r. beginnings,** commencements *mpl* informes; **(d)** (*violent*) violent; *Fig* **to receive a r. awakening,** recevoir un choc; *Fig* **it was a bit of a r. awakening,** le réveil a été brutal; **(e)** *Fig* **to be in r. health,** jouir d'une santé robuste.

rudely [ˈruːdlɪ] *adv* **(a)** (*to speak, interrupt*) impoliment, grossièrement; **(b)** (*to gesture*) de façon obscène; **(c)** (*made, drawn*) primitivement, grossièrement; **(d)** violemment; **r. awakened,** brusquement éveillé; *Fig* qui a reçu un choc.

rudeness [ˈruːdnɪs] *n* **(a)** (*of person*) impolitesse *f*, grossièreté *f*; **(b)** (*of joke, story*) obscénité *f*; **(c)** (*of tool*) caractère primitif; (*of drawing*) manque *m* d'art.

rudiment [ˈruːdɪmənt] *n Anat* rudiment *m*; *Fig* **rudiments,** (*of grammar etc*) rudiments, notions *fpl* élémentaires.

rudimentary [ruːdɪˈment(ə)rɪ] *adj* (*tail, knowledge etc*) rudimentaire; (*equipment, tool etc*) rudimentaire, de base; **to have a r. grasp of sth,** comprendre les rudiments de qch; **I speak Russian and r. Chinese,** je parle russe et j'ai des rudiments de chinois.

rue¹ [ruː] *vt Fml* regretter amèrement (*une action*); **to r. the day when ...,** regretter le jour où ...; **you'll r. the day,** (*that you did this*) tu vas le regretter.

rue² *n Bot Culin* rue *f*.

rueful [ˈruːfʊl] *adj* (*glance, smile*) désabusé.

ruefully [ˈruːfʊlɪ] *adv* (*to laugh, say*) d'un air désabusé.

ruefulness [ˈruːfʊlnɪs] *n* (*of glance, smile*) caractère désabusé.

ruff¹ [rʌf] *n* (*on costume*) fraise *f*, collerette *f*; (*on bird, animal*) collier *m*, cravate *f*.

ruff² *vt Cards* couper (*qn*) (avec un atout).

ruffian [ˈrʌfɪən] *n* brute *f*, bandit *m*; *F* **young ruffians,** petits polissons.

ruffle¹ [ˈrʌf(ə)l] *n* **(a)** (*at wrist*) manchette *f* (en dentelle); (*at throat*) jabot plissé; (*of bird*) collier *m*, cravate *f*; **(b)** (*on water*) rides *fpl*.

ruffle² **1** *vt* troubler, rider (*la surface de l'eau*); agiter (*l'herbe*); ébouriffer (*les cheveux de qn*); **hair ruffled by the breeze,** cheveux agités par la brise; **to r. its feathers,** (*of bird*) hérisser ses plumes; **to r. s.o.** *or* **s.o.'s feelings** *or F* **s.o.'s feathers,** froisser *ou* irriter *ou* contrarier *ou* troubler qn; **to smooth s.o.'s ruffled feathers,** apaiser qn qui a été contrarié; **to be ruffled,** (*annoyed, irritated*) être froissé *ou* énervé; **to get ruffled,** (*of person*) se froisser; **to r. s.o.'s composure,** faire perdre contenance à qn; **to r. the pages of a book,** feuilleter rapidement les pages d'un livre. **2** *vi* (*of hair*) s'ébouriffer; (*of feathers*) se hérisser; (*of sea*) s'agiter, se rider.

rug [rʌg] *n* **(a)** (*blanket*) couverture *f*; **travelling r.,** couverture de voyage, plaid *m*; **(b)** (*carpet*) (petit) tapis *m*, *Can* carpette *f*; **to pull the r. out from under s.o.'s feet,** couper l'herbe sous le pied de qn; **(c)** *Am Sl* (*toupee*) toupet *m*.

rugby [ˈrʌgbɪ] *n* **r. (football),** rugby *m*; **r. ball/ground/***etc*, ballon *m*/terrain *m*/*etc* de rugby; **r. league,** rugby *ou* jeu *m* à treize; **r. player,** rugbyman *m*, joueur *m* de rugby; **r. union,** rugby à quinze.

rugged [ˈrʌgɪd] *adj* **(a)** (*ground, country*) accidenté; (*rock, hill*) déchiqueté; **r. features,** traits rudes *ou* irréguliers; **a man with r. good looks,** un bel homme aux traits rudes; **(b)** (*equipment, vehicle etc*) vigoureux, robuste; **(c)** (*manners*) bourru, rude; **r. independence,** indépendance *f* farouche; **r. individualist,** individualiste farouche *ou* forcené; **r. life,** vie rude *ou* dure.

ruggedness [ˈrʌgɪdnɪs] *n* **(a)** (*of ground, country*) aspect accidenté; (*of rock*) aspect déchiqueté; **(b)** (*of vehicle etc*) robustesse *f*.

rugger [ˈrʌgər] *n Br F* rugby *m*.

ruin¹ [ˈruːɪn] *n* (*of building etc*) *& Fig* ruine *f*; **the castle is a r.,** le château est en ruine(s); **to fall/lie in ruin(s),** tomber/être en ruine(s); **to be in ruins,** (*of building*) être en ruine(s); *Fig* (*of career*) être fini; (*of hopes*) s'être écroulé; **the ruins of my career/hopes/***etc*, la fin de ma carrière/mes espoirs/*etc*; **to go to r.,** tomber en ruine(s); **he's on the road to r.,** il va *ou* court à la ruine *ou* à sa perte; **to be the r. of s.o.,** ruiner qn, perdre qn; **it will be the r. of him,** ça le perdra; **gambling has led to his r.,** le jeu l'a perdu; **r. is staring us in the face,** la ruine nous pend au nez; *Br Sl* **mother's r.,** gin *m*.

ruin² *vt* abîmer (*la récolte, une robe*); gâcher (*sa vie, son avenir*); ruiner (*qn*); **to r. one's eyes,** s'user la vue *ou* les yeux; **to r. one's health,** se ruiner la santé; **ruined castle,** château *m* en ruine(s); **to r. oneself gambling,** se ruiner au jeu; **the meal's ruined,** le repas est gâché; **to r. s.o.'s plans/chances/***etc*, faire échouer les projets/les chances/*etc* de qn; **we're ruined,** (*financially*) nous sommes ruinés; **tourists are ruining the country,** les touristes gâchent le pays; **they're ruining that child,** ils gâtent cet enfant.

ruination [ruːɪˈneɪʃən] *n* ruine *f*, perte *f*; **to be the r. of s.o.,** faire la ruine de qn.

ruinous [ˈruːɪnəs] *adj Fig* (*expense etc*) ruineux.

ruinously [ˈruːɪnəslɪ] *adv* **r. expensive,** ruineux.

rule¹ [ruːl] *n* **(a)** (*principle*) règle *f*; (*regulation*) règlement *m*; (*custom*) coutume *f*; **it's the** *or* **a r. that ...,** il est de règle que ... + *sub*; **I'm sorry, but that's the r.,** je suis désolé mais c'est le règlement; **to lay** *or* **set sth down as a r.,** établir qch en règle générale; **as a (general) r.,** en règle générale; **the exception proves the r.,** l'exception confirme la règle; **snow is the r. rather than the exception in winter,** en hiver, le plus souvent, il neige; **to make it a r. to do sth,** se faire une règle de faire qch; **we must make it a r. that everyone contributes equally,** nous devons nous faire une règle que chacun contribue à part égale; **rules and regulations,** statuts *mpl* et règlements; **there are too many rules and regulations,** il y a trop de règlements; *Ind* **work(ing) to r.,** grève *f* du zèle; **to work to r.,** faire la grève de zèle; **to play according to** *or* **to observe the rules (of the game),** jouer selon les règles (du jeu); **it's against the rules,** c'est contre les règles; **rules of conduct,** règles de conduite; **the r. of the road,** (*for cars*) le code de la route; (*for ships*) les règles de route; **r. of three,** règle de trois; **r. of thumb,** méthode *f ou* procédé *m* empirique; **as a r. of thumb, allow one pound of meat for four people,** en règle générale, compter une livre de viande pour quatre personnes; **ground r.,** règle de base; **Queensberry rules,** (*in boxing*) règles du marquis de Queensberry;

(b) (*authority*) autorité *f*; *Pol* gouvernement *m*; **under British r.,** sous l'autorité britannique; **the r. of law,** l'autorité de la loi; **majority r.,** règle majoritaire;

(c) (*for measuring*) règle *f*; **pocket r.,** règle *ou* mètre *m* de poche; **folding r.,** mètre pliant.

rule² **1** *vt* **(a)** gouverner (*un état, un peuple*); maîtriser, commander à (*ses passions*); **to r. a nation,** régner sur une nation; **to r. s.o.,** (*dominate*) mener qn; **don't let him r. your life,** ne le laisse pas mener ta vie; **don't let your heart r. your head,** ne laisse pas tes émotions l'emporter sur la raison; **to r. the waves,** tenir la mer, être maître *ou* maîtresse des mers; *Fig* **to r. the roost,** régner, faire la loi; **(b)** décider (**that,** que); **(c)** régler, rayer (*du papier*); **ruled paper,** papier réglé *ou* ligné. **2** *vi* (*of monarch*) régner (**over,** sur); (*of judge*) statuer (**against,** contre; **on,** sur); **to r. in favour of/against s.o.,** (*of judge, umpire etc*) décider en faveur de/contre qn.

▶**rule out** *vtsep* **to r. sth out,** (*exclude*) exclure qch; (*make impossible*) rendre qch impossible; **a possibility that can't be ruled out,** une possibilité que l'on ne saurait écarter *ou* éliminer.

ruler [ˈruːlər] *n* **(a)** (*of country*) dirigeant, -ante; (*sovereign*) souverain, -aine (**of, over,** de); **(b)** (*for measuring*) règle *f*.

ruling [ˈruːlɪŋ] **1** *adj* (*passion*) dominant; (*class*) dirigeant; *Pol* (*party*) au pouvoir. **2** *n* (*of judge, umpire etc*) décision *f*; **to give a r. in favour of s.o.,** décider en faveur de qn.

rum¹ [rʌm] *n* rhum *m*.

rum² *adj* (*comp* **rummer**, *superl* **rummest**) *Br F* (*story etc*) drôle, bizarre; **a r. character,** un drôle de type *ou* de numéro.

Rumania [ruːˈmeɪnɪə, rʊ-] *n* Roumanie *f*.

Rumanian [ruːˈmeɪnɪən, rʊ-] **1** *adj* roumain. **2** *n* **(a)** Roumain, -aine; **(b)** *Ling* roumain *m*.

rumba [ˈrʌmbə] *n* (*dance, music*) rumba *f*; **to do the r.,** faire la rumba; **to play a r.,** jouer une rumba; **r. tune/step**/*etc*, air *m*/pas *m*/*etc* de rumba.

rumble[1] [ˈrʌmb(ə)l] *n* **(a)** (*of thunder*) grondement *m*; (*of voices*) bruit confus; (*of cart*) roulement *m*; (*of stomach*) borborygmes *mpl*; **my stomach gave a r.,** mon estomac a fait entendre des borborygmes *ou* a gargouillé; **(b)** *Am Sl* (*gang-fight*) échauffourée *f*.

rumble[2] **1** *vi* **(a)** (*of thunder etc*) gronder (sourdement); (*of stomach*) gargouiller; **a cart rumbled along the street,** une charrette est passée bruyamment dans la rue; **(b)** *Am Sl* (*of street gang*) prendre part à une échauffourée. **2** *vt F* flairer, se douter de, subodorer (*qch*); voir venir (*qn, qch*); **I soon rumbled him,** j'ai bien vite deviné son jeu; **we've been rumbled,** on a deviné notre jeu.

rumbling [ˈrʌmblɪŋ] *n* **(a)** (*of thunder*) grondement *m*; (*of cart*) roulement *m*; (*of stomach*) borborygmes *mpl*; **(b)** *Fig* (*of discontent etc*) grognement *m*; **there have been rumblings about the proposal,** la proposition a suscité des grognements.

rumbustious [rʌmˈbʌstjəs] *adj F* turbulent, tapageur, chahuteur.

ruminant [ˈruːmɪnənt] *adj & n Zool* ruminant *m*.

ruminate [ˈruːmɪneɪt] *vi* **(a)** (*of person*) ruminer, méditer; **to r. on sth,** ruminer qch, méditer qch; **(b)** (*of animal*) ruminer.

rumination [ruːmɪˈneɪʃən] *n* **(a)** *Fig* rumination *f*, méditation *f*; **(b)** (*of animal*) rumination *f*.

ruminative [ˈruːmɪnətɪv] *adj* (*look, voice*) méditatif.

ruminatively [ˈruːmɪnətɪvlɪ] *adv* (*to say etc*) d'un ton méditatif.

rummage [ˈrʌmɪdʒ] *n* fouille *f*; **to have a r. (around),** fouiller (**in,** dans); *Am* **r. sale,** vente *f* de charité *ou* de bienfaisance.

▶**rummage about, rummage around** *vi* fouiller, fourrager; **to r. about** *or* **around among old papers,** fouiller *ou* fourrager dans de vieux papiers.

▶**rummage in, rummage through** *vipo* fouiller dans; fourrager dans (*ses poches, un tiroir etc*).

rummy [ˈrʌmɪ] *n Cards* rami *m*; **to play r.,** jouer au rami; **a game of r.,** une partie de rami.

rumour[1], *US* **rumor** [ˈruːmər] *n* rumeur *f*, bruit *m* (qui court); **r. has it** *or* **there's a r. going round that ...,** le bruit court que ..., on raconte que ..., il y a une rumeur selon laquelle ...; **rumours have been circulating,** des rumeurs ont circulé (**that,** selon lesquelles; **about,** au sujet de); **so r. has it,** c'est ce qu'on dit; **to hear a r. that ...,** entendre dire que ...; **there are rumours of a takeover,** on parle de prise de contrôle; **have you heard any rumours about what's going to happen?,** est-ce que vous avez entendu des rumeurs sur ce qui va se passer?; **it's only a r.,** ce n'est qu'un on-dit; **r. monger,** personne qui fait courir des bruits.

rumour[2], *US* **rumor** *vt* (*always passive*) **it is rumoured that ...,** le bruit court que ...; **he is rumoured to be ...,** le bruit court *ou* on dit qu'il est...; **he was rumoured to be in hiding,** le bruit courait qu'il se cachait; **so it was rumoured,** c'est ce qu'on a dit.

rumoured [ˈruːməd] *adj* (*engagement, takeover etc*) au sujet duquel *ou* dont le bruit court.

rump [rʌmp] *n* **(a)** (*of animal*) croupe *f*; (*of bird*) croupion *m*; *F* (*of person*) postérieur *m*; **r. steak,** romsteck *m*; **(b)** *F* (*of army, political party etc*) restant *m*; **r. Parliament,** Parlement *m* croupion.

rumple [ˈrʌmp(ə)l] *vt* chiffonner, friper, froisser (*une robe, etc*); froisser (*des draps*); ébouriffer (*les cheveux*); **to look rumpled,** (*of person*) avoir l'air ébouriffé.

rumpus [ˈrʌmpəs] *n F* (*noise*) chahut *m*, vacarme *m*; (*argument, protest*) bagarre *f*; **to kick up** *or* **make a r.,** (*be noisy*) faire un chahut à tout casser; (*protest*) faire toute une histoire (**about,** au sujet de); **there's been a bit of a r. about her appointment,** il y a eu toute une histoire au sujet de sa nomination; *Am* **r. room,** salle *f* de jeu.

run[1] [rʌn] *n* **(a)** (*on foot*) course *f*; **he took a short r. and cleared the gate,** après un court élan il a franchi la barrière; **at a r.,** en courant; **to break into a r.,** se mettre à courir; **to go for a r.,** (*jog*) aller courir; **to take the dog for a r.,** emmener le chien se dégourdir les jambes; **we've got them on the r.,** nous les avons mis en déroute; **criminal on the r.,** malfaiteur en fuite; **to be on the r.,** (*from police*) être en fuite *ou* recherché par la police; (*of soldiers, rebels etc*) être en fuite; (*losing competition etc*) être en déroute; (*be busy*) courir; *F* **to make a r. for it,** (*escape*) s'enfuir, se sauver; (*to get out of rain, catch train etc*) se dépêcher; *F* **to have a (good) r. for one's money,** en avoir pour son argent; *F* **to give s.o. a (good) r. for their money,** en donner pour son argent à qn; **to make ten runs,** (*in cricket match*) marquer dix points; *F* **to have the runs,** (*diarrhoea*) avoir la courante;
(b) (*for pleasure, in car etc*) promenade *f*; **to go for a r.,** faire une promenade (en voiture).
(c) (*journey*) trajet *m*; **our town is two hours' r. (by train/by car) from London,** notre ville est à deux heures (de train/de voiture) de Londres; **he used to do the Glasgow r.,** (*of pilot, steward*) il faisait le vol à destination de Glasgow; (*of bus or train driver*) il faisait le trajet à destination de Glasgow;
(d) (*of book*) tirage *m*; (*of product*) série *f*;
(e) (*sequence, series*) cours *m*, marche *f*; **the recent r. of events,** la récente succession d'événements; **a r. of bad luck,** une suite de malheurs; **we had a r. of good luck last week,** la semaine dernière la chance nous a souri; *Cards* **r. of three,** séquence *f* de trois; **the r. of the cards was against me,** la suite de cartes n'était pas en ma faveur; **in the long r.,** à la longue, en fin de compte; **in the short r.,** à court terme; **to have a long r.,** (*of fashion*) rester longtemps en vogue; (*of play*) tenir longtemps l'affiche; **after its record r. in London the play is moving to New York,** après avoir tenu l'affiche pendant un temps record à Londres la pièce va se jouer à New York; *Th* **during its six-month r.,** pendant les six mois où elle a tenu l'affiche; **it will soon finish its r.,** cela ne sera bientôt plus à l'affiche;
(f) (*rush*) (*on bank*) descente *f*; (*on stock exchange*) ruée *f*; **a r. on the banks,** un retrait massif de dépôts bancaires; **r. on the red,** (*in roulette etc*) série *f* à la rouge; **a r. on the dollar,** une ruée sur le dollar; **there's been a big r. on tickets,** il y a eu une ruée énorme sur les tickets;
(g) généralité *f*, commun *m* (des hommes); **the ordinary r. of mankind,** le commun des mortels; **the ordinary r. of things,** la routine de tous les jours; **out of the common r.,** hors du commun; **it's just r. of the mill,** c'est ce qu'il y a de plus ordinaire;
(h) (*freedom*) libre accès *m*; **to give s.o. the r. of one's house,** mettre sa maison à la disposition de qn; **to have the r. of the house,** être libre d'aller partout dans la maison;
(i) (*in stocking*) maille *f* qui file, échelle *f*;
(j) (*for skier*) piste *f*;
(k) (*of salmon*) remontée *f*;
(l) (*competition*) **she's making a r. for the Premiership,** elle ambitionne les fonctions de premier ministre;
(m) *Mus* roulade *f*.

run[2] *v* (*pt* **ran** [ræn]; *pp* **run;** *prp* **running) 1** *vi* **(a)** courir (**towards,** à, vers); **to come running towards s.o.,** accourir vers qn; **to r. up/down the street,** monter/descendre la rue en courant; **r. up to your grandmother's,** cours chez ta grand-mère; **I'll just r. across** *or* **round** *or* **over to the grocer's,** je vais faire un saut chez l'épicier; **to r. after s.o.,** (*chase*) courir après qn; (*coddle*) dorloter qn; *Fig* **to r. after men/women,** courir les garçons/filles; **r. along!,** allez-vous-en!; **he's running scared,** il a la frousse; **don't come running to me for help,** n'accours pas vers moi quand tu auras besoin d'aide; **to r. for Parliament,** se présenter à la députation; **to r. for office,** se porter candidat;
(b) (*flee*) fuir, s'enfuir, se sauver; **r. for it!,** sauve qui peut!;
(c) (*of salmon*) remonter les rivières, faire la montaison;
(d) (*of ship*) courir, filer, faire route; **to r. before the wind,** courir vent arrière; **to r. aground,** échouer;
(e) (*go*) aller, marcher; **this train is not running today,** ce train est supprimé aujourd'hui; **the buses stop running at midnight,** après minuit il n'y a plus d'autobus; **to be running late,** (*of bus, train etc*) avoir du retard; (*of person*) être en retard; **TV programmes are running ten minutes later than advertised,** les émissions télévisées commencent avec dix minutes de retard; **the table runs on wheels,** la table peut se rouler; **trains running to Paris,** trains à destination de Paris; **trains running between London and the coast,** trains qui font le trajet entre Londres et la côte; **a murmur ran through the crowd,** un murmure a parcouru la foule; **that song keeps running through my head,** cette chanson me trotte dans la tête; **it runs in the family,** cela tient de la famille; **the conversation ran something like this,** la conversation suivait à peu près ces lignes; **the lease has only a year to r.,** le bail n'a plus qu'un an à courir; *Th* **the play has been running for a year,** la pièce tient l'affiche depuis un an; **to r. to,** (*of amount, number*) monter à, s'élever à; **this paper runs to 32 pages,** ce journal est publié sur 32 pages; **I can't** *or* **my money won't r. to a car,** je n'ai pas assez d'argent pour acheter *ou* avoir *ou* entretenir une voiture;
(f) (*operate*) (*of machine*) fonctionner, marcher; *Comptr* **the software runs on this machine,** le logiciel peut être utilisé sur cette machine; **the house is too expensive to r.,** la maison coûte trop cher à entretenir; **the engine's running,** le moteur marche *ou* tourne *ou* est en marche; **the engine is running smoothly,** le moteur tourne rond; **the**

car runs on unleaded petrol, la voiture roule à l'essence sans plomb; *El* **this machine runs off the mains,** cet appareil se branche *ou* marche sur le secteur; **few buses are running because of the strike,** peu d'autobus circulent à cause de la grève; **the hotel runs like clockwork,** l'hôtel marche sans problème;

(g) (*of colour in fabric*) déteindre; (*of ink*) s'étendre; (*of dye*) couler (au lavage); **colour that runs in the wash,** couleur qui déteint au lavage;

(h) (*of stocking*) filer, se démailler;

(i) (*flow*) couler; **the river runs into a lake,** la rivière débouche *ou* se jette dans un lac; **there was a heavy sea running,** la mer était grosse; **the floor was running with water,** le parquet ruisselait; **the streets were running with blood,** le sang coulait dans les rues; **my nose is running,** j'ai le nez qui coule; **the ice cream is beginning to r.,** la glace commence à fondre; **money runs through his fingers like water,** l'argent lui brûle les doigts, c'est un panier percé;

(j) (*go in certain direction*) s'étendre; **the road runs alongside the river,** la route suit *ou* longe la rivière; **to r. north and south,** être orienté du nord au sud; **the line runs from ... to ...,** la ligne s'étend depuis ... jusqu'à ...; **the road runs quite close to the village,** la route passe tout près du village; **to r. to extremes,** pousser les choses à l'extrême; **to r. to seed,** (*of plant*) monter en graine; **to r. to fat,** (*of person*) prendre de l'embonpoint; **feelings are running high,** les esprits sont échauffés; **his funds are running low,** ses fonds baissent; **our stores are running low,** nos provisions s'épuisent *ou* tirent à leur fin.

2 *vt* **(a) to r. a race,** courir *ou* disputer une course; **to r. a kilometre,** courir un kilomètre; **to r. an errand,** faire une course; **to r. the blockade,** forcer le blocus; **things must r. their course,** il faut que les choses suivent leur cours; **to r. a fox to earth,** chasser un renard jusqu'à son terrier; **to r. s.o. hard** *or* **close,** presser qn, serrer qn de près; *F* **I'm run off my feet,** je suis éreinté;

(b) (*drive*) **to r. the car into the garage,** rentrer la voiture dans le garage; **to r. s.o. (in)to town/back home,** conduire qn en ville/reconduire qn chez lui; **to r. one's car into a wall/tree/***etc*, rentrer dans un mur/un arbre/*etc* avec sa voiture;

(c) (*smuggle*) faire la contrebande de (*drogues, armes*);

(d) (*operate*) faire fonctionner, faire travailler (*une machine*); *Comptr* **this computer runs most software,** sur cet ordinateur on peut utiliser la plupart des logiciels; *Comptr* **to r. a programme,** exécuter *ou* faire tourner un programme; **I can't afford to r. a car,** je n'ai pas les moyens d'entretenir une voiture; **to r. trains between Glasgow and Inverness,** établir un service de trains entre Glasgow et Inverness; **they are running an extra train,** il y aura un train supplémentaire; *Av* **to r. the engines,** (*for checking*) faire le point fixe; **to r. tests,** effectuer des essais;

(e) (*manage*) diriger (*une affaire*); tenir (*un magasin, un hôtel*); exploiter (*une ferme*); diriger (*un théâtre*); éditer, gérer (*un journal, une revue*);

(f) (*enter in competition*) faire courir (*un cheval*); *Pol* **to r. a candidate,** mettre un candidat en avant;

(g) (*pass*) (faire) passer; **to r. the vacuum cleaner over the carpet,** passer l'aspirateur sur la moquette; **to r. pipes through a wall,** faire passer des tuyaux à travers un mur; **to r. one's fingers over sth,** promener ses doigts sur qch; **to r. a comb/brush through one's hair,** se donner un coup de peigne/de brosse; **he ran his hand through his hair,** il a passé sa main dans ses cheveux;

(h) (faire) couler (*de l'eau etc*) (**into sth,** dans qch); **to r. a bath,** faire couler un bain;

(i) (*have, carry*) **to r. a (high) temperature,** faire de la température, avoir (de) la fièvre; **to r. a deficit,** avoir un déficit; **to r. a story,** (*of newspaper etc*) publier un récit.

►**run about 1** *vi* courir çà et là (**in,** dans); *F* (*be busy*) courir; **I've been running about all day,** j'ai couru toute la journée. **2** *vipo* courir (*les magasins*); **to r. about the streets,** (*of children etc*) courir dans les rues.

►**run across** *vipo* rencontrer (*qn, qch*) par hasard.

►**run around** *vi & vipo* = **RUN ABOUT**.

►**run around with** *vipo* (*be friendly with*) fréquenter (*qn*); (*have affair with*) sortir avec (*qn*).

►**run away** *vi* (*of person*) s'enfuir, se sauver; (*of child, teenager etc*) faire une fugue; (*of horse*) s'emballer, s'emporter; **they have run away to get married,** ils se sont enfuis pour se marier; **to r. away from the facts,** se refuser à l'évidence; **to r. away with s.o.,** s'enfuir avec qn; **to r. away with sth,** emporter qch, enlever qch; **to r. away with the idea that ...,** se mettre dans la tête que ...; **don't r. away with the idea that I'm rich,** ne t'imagine pas que je suis *ou* sois riche; **his imagination runs away with him,** son imagination galope; **she lets her enthusiasm r. away with her,** son enthousiasme lui joue des tours; **last year's holiday ran away with most of my savings,** les vacances de l'année dernière ont englouti la plus grande partie de mes économies; **the favourite ran away with the race,** le favori a gagné la course haut la main.

►**run back** *vi* (*of person*) revenir en courant; *F* **to come running back,** (*of errant husband etc*) revenir bien vite.

►**run down 1** *vi* **(a)** (*of person*) descendre en courant; **(b)** (*of clockwork, clock*) s'arrêter (faute d'être remonté); (*of battery*) se décharger. **2** *vtsep* **(a)** (*in car etc*) écraser (*qn*); **(b)** (*find*) découvrir, dénicher (*qn, qch*); **(c)** (*criticize*) rabaisser, dénigrer (*qn, qch*); **(d)** (*reduce*) diminuer (*les effectifs*); laisser épuiser (*les stocks*); restreindre la production de (*une industrie, une usine*); **you've run the battery down,** vous avez déchargé la pile; (*of car*) vous avez vidé la batterie; **to be run down,** (*of person*) être épuisé.

►**run in 1** *vi* entrer en courant. **2** *vtsep* **(a)** *Br F* arrêter (*qn*); **to be** *or* **get run in,** se faire ramasser (**for,** pour); **(b)** roder (*un moteur*); *Br Aut* **running in,** (*notice on car*) en rodage.

►**run into** *vipo* (*of vehicle*) entrer en collision avec (*une voiture, un arbre*); heurter, entrer dans (*un autre véhicule etc*); (*of person*) heurter, se heurter contre (*qn*); *Fig* (*meet*) rencontrer (*qn*) par hasard; **to r. into debt,** faire des dettes, s'endetter; **to r. into difficulties,** rencontrer des difficultés; **the project will r. into massive losses,** le projet va occasionner des pertes énormes; **takings r. into five figures,** la recette atteint les cinq chiffres; **the cost will r. into millions,** le coût va s'élever à des millions.

►**run off 1** *vi* **(a)** fuir, s'enfuir, se sauver; **to r. off with the cash,** filer avec l'argent; **to r. off with s.o.,** (*elope with*) s'enfuir avec qn; **(b)** (*of liquid*) s'écouler; *Am Sl* **to r. off at the mouth,** parler sans arrêt. **2** *vtsep* **(a)** copier, reproduire; *Typ* **machine that runs off ten copies a minute,** machine qui imprime dix feuilles par minute; **(b)** écrire *ou* rédiger (*un article*) rapidement; **(c)** (*remove*) faire écouler (*un liquide*); **you'll soon r. off those few extra pounds,** vous perdrez vite ces quelques kilos en trop en courant.

►**run on 1** *vi* **(a)** (*of person*) continuer à courir; **(b)** (*of verse*) enjamber; *Typ* (*of words*) se rejoindre, être lié; (*of text*) suivre sans alinéa; **r. on,** (*instruction*) alinéa à supprimer; *F* **he DOES r. on, doesn't he!,** (*talks a lot*) il n'en finit pas, hein? **2** *vtsep Typ* **to r. on the text,** faire suivre sans alinéa.

►**run out 1** *vi* **(a)** sortir en courant; *F* **to r. out on s.o.,** abandonner qn; **the tide is running out,** la mer se retire; **(b)** (*of lease*) expirer; **we're/you're/***etc* **running out of time, time is running out,** il nous/vous/*etc* reste peu de temps; **to r. out of provisions,** épuiser ses provisions; **we are running out of sugar,** nous allons nous trouver à court de sucre; **I've run out of cigarettes,** je n'ai plus de cigarettes; **I'm running out of patience,** je perds patience (**with,** avec). **2** *vtsep Cr* mettre (*un batteur*) hors jeu pendant sa course; **to r. s.o. out of town,** faire quitter la ville à qn.

►**run over 1** *vtsep* **(a)** parcourir (*un document*); **to r. over one's lines,** revoir son texte; *Mus* **to r. one's fingers over the keys,** passer les doigts sur les touches (du piano); **(b)** *Aut* écraser (*qn*); **he's been run over,** il s'est fait écraser; **the car ran over his legs,** la voiture lui est passé sur les jambes; **(c)** (*exceed*) **to r. over the allotted time,** excéder le temps imparti. **2** *vi* (*of vessel or contents*) déborder; **to r. over with energy/enthusiasm/***etc*, déborder d'énergie/d'enthousiasme/*etc*.

►**run past 1** *vi* passer en courant. **2** *vtaspo Am F* **can I r. something past you?,** puis-je vous demander votre avis?; **r. that one past me again,** dis-moi ça encore une fois.

►**run through 1** *vi* traverser *ou* passer en courant. **2** *vipo* **(a)** parcourir (*un document*); feuilleter (*un livre*); *Th* **to r. through one's part,** répéter son rôle; **I'll r. through your speech with you,** je vous ferai répéter votre discours; **(b)** gaspiller, dissiper (*une fortune*); **he runs through a dozen shirts a week,** il salit une douzaine de chemises par semaine. **3** *vtsep* transpercer (*qn*) (**with a sword,** d'une épée).

►**run up 1** *vi* (*to the flat etc above*) monter en courant; **people came running up,** (*to me etc*) des gens sont arrivés en courant; **to r. up to s.o.,** courir vers qn. **2** *vtsep* **(a)** laisser grossir (*un compte*); laisser accumuler (*des dettes*); **I'm running up your phone bill,** je t'augmente ta facture de téléphone; **(b)** hisser (*un drapeau*); **(c)** confectionner (*une robe etc*) à la hâte.

►**run up against** *vipo* buter contre, se heurter à (*des difficultés*).

runabout ['rʌnəbaʊt] *n Aut* petite voiture.

run-around ['rʌnəraʊnd] *n F* **to give s.o. the r.-a.,** éviter de donner une réponse directe à qn; **to get the r.-a.,** recevoir des réponses très vagues; **he's giving her the r.-a.,** il la fait marcher.

runaway ['rʌnəweɪ] **1** *n* (*person*) fuyard, -arde, fugitif,

-ive; (*child, teenager*) fugueur, -euse; (*horse*) cheval emballé *ou* échappé. **2** *adj* **(a)** (*marriage*) à la suite d'une fugue; **r. lorry/train/***etc*, camion/train/*etc* fou; **(b)** (*victory*) remporté haut la main; **the play has been a r. success,** la pièce a connu un immense succès; **(c)** (*inflation*) galopant.

run-down [rʌn'daʊn] *adj* **(a)** (*battery*) à plat, épuisé; **(b)** (*building*) délabré; (*person*) épuisé.

rundown ['rʌndaʊn] *n* **(a)** (*summary*) résumé détaillé; **give me a r. on what's been happening,** racontez-moi en détail ce qui s'est passé; **(b)** (*of staff*) diminution *f*; (*of production*) restriction *f*.

rune [ru:n] *n* rune *f*.

rung [rʌŋ] *n* (*on ladder*) échelon *m*, barreau *m*; (*on chair*) bâton *m*.

runic ['ru:nɪk] *adj* (*letters, verse*) runique.

run-in ['rʌnɪn] *n F* prise *f* de bec; **to have a r.-in with s.o.,** avoir une prise de bec avec qn (**about,** au sujet de).

runnel ['rʌn(ə)l] *n* ruisseau *m*; (*in street*) caniveau *m*.

runner ['rʌnər] *n* **(a)** (*in race*) coureur, -euse; **she's a very fast r.,** elle court très vite; *Horseracing* **five runners,** cinq partants; **(b)** (*messenger*) messager *m*, courrier *m*; *esp US* **bank r.,** garçon *m* de recette; **(c)** (*of guns, drugs etc*) contrebandier *m*; **(d)** (*on plant*) coulant *m*, stolon *m*; (*on strawberry*) marcotte *f*; **r. bean,** haricot *m* d'Espagne, haricot à rames; **(e)** (*on sleigh*) patin *m*; (*on skate*) lame *f* de patin; (*on drawer*) coulisseau *m*; **(f)** (*for stairs, table*) chemin *m*.

runner-up [rʌnə'rʌp] *n* (*in race, competition etc*) second, -onde (**to,** après); **fifteen runners-up will also receive prizes,** les quinze suivants recevront également des prix.

running ['rʌnɪŋ] **1** *adj* (*person, water*) courant; (*pattern etc*) continu; *Sp* **r. jump,** saut *m* avec élan; *Sl* **go (and) take a r. jump!,** va te faire foutre!; **to keep up a r. battle,** se battre sans discontinuer; *Fig* lutter continuellement (**with,** avec); **they have a r. battle about housework,** ils se bagarrent continuellement au sujet des travaux ménagers; **to give a r. commentary,** donner un commentaire simultané (**on, about,** de); **three years r.,** trois ans de suite; **we talked for two hours r.,** nous avons parlé pendant deux heures de suite; **room with r. water,** (*in hotel*) chambre *f* avec eau courante; **to keep a r. total of sth,** totaliser qch au fur et à mesure; *Aut* **r. board,** marchepied *m*; **r. expenses,** dépenses courantes; *Mil* **r. fire,** feu roulant; **r. hand,** écriture cursive; **r. repairs,** réparations courantes; **r. sore,** plaie *f* qui suppure; *Sewing* **r. stitch,** point devant, point droit; **r. stream,** ruisseau coulant; *Typ* **r. head** *or* **title,** titre courant.

2 *n* **(a)** course(s) *f(pl)*; **r. is her hobby,** la course est son passe-temps; (*in race*) *& Fig* **to make the r.,** mener la course; *Fig* **to make all the r.,** (*in relationship*) toujours prendre les devants; **to be in the r.,** avoir des chances d'arriver (**for,** à); **he's out of the r.,** il n'a aucune chance (*d'être nommé, d'arriver*); *US Pol* **r. mate,** colistier *m*; **r. shoe,** chaussure *f* de course; **r. track,** piste *f*;

(b) (*of machine*) marche *f*, fonctionnement *m*; (*of car*) roulement *m*; (*of train*) marche, circulation *f*; **r. in,** (*of engine*) rodage *m*; **we apologise for the late r. of this train,** nous vous prions d'excuser le retard de ce train; **in r. order,** en bon état (de marche); **r. costs,** frais *mpl* d'entretien; *Nau* **r. lights,** feux *mpl* de position;

(c) (*of hotel, restaurant etc*) direction *f*; (*of railway*) exploitation *f*;

(d) (*of arms, drugs*) introduction *f* en contrebande;

(e) (*of water*) écoulement *m*, ruissellement *m*;

(f) *Comptr* (*of program*) exécution *f*.

running down *n* **(a)** (*of person, play etc*) ravalement *m*, dénigrement *m*; **(b)** (*of staff*) diminution *f*; (*of industry, factory*) restriction *f* de la production.

runny ['rʌnɪ] *adj* (*mixture*) liquide; *Pej* trop liquide; (*nose*) qui coule.

run-off ['rʌnɒf] *n* **(a)** *Sp* (course) finale *f*; *Pol* élection *f* pour départager deux candidats; **a r.-o. will decide the winner,** une course finale décidera du vainqueur; **r.-o. race,** (course) finale; **r.-o. election,** élection pour départager deux candidats; **(b)** (*from field etc*) eaux *fpl* de ruissellement; **(c)** *Am* (*desk*) rallonge *f*.

run-of-the-mill [rʌnəvðə'mɪl] *adj* (*film, play etc*) ordinaire, sans rien de particulier.

run-on ['rʌnɒn] *n Typ* texte continu sans alinéa.

run-out ['rʌnaʊt] *n Ski* zone *f* d'arrivée.

run-proof ['rʌnpru:f], **run-resist** [rʌnrɪ'zɪst] *adj* (*stocking etc*) indémaillable.

runt [rʌnt] *n* (*of litter*) petit dernier; *Fig Pej* avorton *m*.

run-through ['rʌnθru:] *n* (*of text etc*) lecture *f* rapide; *Th* répétition *f* rapide; **to have a r.-t.,** répéter rapidement.

run-up ['rʌnʌp] *n* **(a)** (*of high-jumper, pole-vaulter, bowler*) élan *m*; *Av* **the pilot was making his r.-up to the target,** le pilote fonçait sur l'objectif; **(b)** période *f* préparatoire; **in the r.-up to the exams/election/***etc*, au cours de la période qui précède les examens/les élections/*etc*, dans l'attente des examens/des élections/*etc*.

runway ['rʌnweɪ] *n Av* piste *f*; **r. lights,** feux *mpl* de piste d'atterrissage.

rupee [ru:'pi:] *n* (*currency*) roupie *f*.

rupture¹ ['rʌptʃər] *n* (*in negotiations etc*) rupture *f*; (*in marriage, friendship*) brouille *f*; (*of container, pipeline etc*) rupture; *Med* (*of artery*) éclatement *m*, rupture; (*hernia*) hernie *f*.

rupture² **1** *vt* rompre (*des relations*); *Med* se rompre (*un vaisseau sanguin, l'appendice etc*); se faire éclater (*la rate*); **to r. oneself,** se donner une hernie. **2** *vi* (*of blood vessel, appendix*) se rompre; (*of spleen*) éclater.

ruptured ['rʌptʃəd] *adj* (*relations etc*) rompu; *Med* hernié; (*blood vessel, appendix*) rompu; (*spleen*) éclaté; **to be r.,** (*of person*) avoir une hernie.

rural ['rʊər(ə)l] *adj* (*life, custom etc*) rural; *Rel* **r. dean,** doyen rural.

ruse [ru:z] *n* ruse *f*, stratagème *m*, subterfuge *m*; **the r. worked,** la ruse a marché.

rush¹ [rʌʃ] *n* **(a)** (*plant*) jonc *m*; **r. bed,** jonchaie *f*; **(b)** (*material*) paille *f*; **made from rushes,** fait de joncs; **r.-bottomed chair,** chaise à fond de paille; **r. mat,** natte *f* de jonc; **r. matting,** tapis *m* en jonc.

rush² *n* **(a)** course précipitée, ruée *f*; **the gold r.,** la ruée vers l'or; **to make a r. at s.o.,** s'élancer *ou* se jeter *ou* se précipiter sur qn; **to make a r. for the exit/the phones/***etc*, se précipiter vers la sortie/les téléphones/*etc*; **general r.,** ruée générale, bousculade *f*; **there was a r. for the papers,** on s'arrachait les journaux; **we had a r. (of customers) in the afternoon,** les clients sont arrivés en masse l'après-midi; **the r. hour,** les heures d'affluence *ou* de pointe; **r. hour traffic,** circulation *f* aux heures de pointe; **let's leave before the r. starts,** partons avant l'heure de pointe; partons avant la bousculade;

(b) hâte *f*, empressement *m*; **there's no r. (for it),** ce n'est pas pressé; **life is too much of a r. in London,** la vie à Londres est trop enfiévrée; **to be in a (bit of a) r.,** être (un peu) pressé; *F* **to be in a tearing r.,** être très pressé; **we left in such a r. that ...,** nous sommes partis avec une telle précipitation que ...; **what's all the r. for?,** qu'est-ce qui presse tant?; **there's a bit of a r. on,** il y a quelque chose d'assez pressé; **a r. job,** un travail d'urgence; **to have a r. job on,** avoir un travail urgent à faire; **r. order,** commande urgente; **r. work,** travail *m* de première urgence;

(c) (*surge*) **a r. of cold air,** une bouffée d'air glacé; **a r. of water,** une arrivée soudaine d'eau; **a r. of blood to the head,** un coup de sang;

(d) (*demand*) ruée *f* (**on,** sur);

(e) *Cin* **rushes,** épreuves *fpl*; **to see the rushes,** voir les épreuves.

rush³ **1** *vi* (*move fast*) se précipiter, se ruer (**at,** sur; **towards,** vers); (*hurry*) se dépêcher (**to do,** de faire); (*of blood*) affluer (**to,** à); (*of vehicle*) foncer; **I must r.,** il faut que je mette les bouts; **there's no point in rushing,** ça ne sert à rien de se précipiter; **he came rushing down the stairs,** il a dégringolé l'escalier; **a stream that rushes down the mountain side,** un ruisseau qui dévale de la montagne; *Prov* **fools r. in (where angels fear to tread),** = agir sans réfléchir peut avoir des conséquences fâcheuses; **to r. to conclusions,** conclure trop hâtivement *ou* à la légère; **the blood rushed to his cheeks/head,** le sang lui est monté au visage/à la tête; **to r. upstairs,** monter l'escalier à la hâte.

2 *vt* **(a)** faire (*un travail*) trop vite; *Pej* **a rushed job,** un travail fait à la hâte; **he was rushed to hospital,** on l'a transporté d'urgence à l'hôpital; **to r. s.o. into an undertaking,** entraîner qn dans une entreprise sans lui donner le temps de réfléchir; **I don't want to r. you,** je ne voudrais pas vous bousculer; **don't r. me,** laissez-moi le temps de souffler, ne me bousculez pas; **I won't be rushed,** je ne veux pas qu'on me bouscule; **to be rushed off one's feet,** courir à droite et à gauche; **I've been rushed off my feet all day,** j'ai passé ma journée à courir à droite et à gauche; **to be rushed into doing sth,** être forcé à faire qch; **to be rushed into a decision/answer/***etc*, être forcé à prendre une décision/donner une réponse/*etc* à la hâte; **don't let yourself be rushed into anything,** ne te sens pas obligé de faire quoi que ce soit à la hâte; **please r. me your latest catalogue,** (*notice on advertising material*) envoyez-moi votre dernier catalogue d'urgence; **let's not r. things,** ne nous précipitons pas; **a horse that rushes his fences,** un cheval qui se précipite sur l'obstacle avec trop d'impétuosité; *F* **don't r. your fences!,** réfléchissez donc!;

(b) *Mil* prendre d'assaut (*une position*); **to rush s.o.,** (*attack*) attaquer qn; **the audience rushed the platform,** le public a envahi l'estrade;

(c) *Br F* (*charge a lot*) **how much did they r. you for that?,** combien est-ce qu'ils t'ont fait casquer pour ça?

►**rush about** *vi* courir çà et là.

►**rush away** **1** *vi* partir précipitamment; **do you have to r. away?,** est-ce qu'il faut vraiment que vous partiez

aussi vite? 2 *vtsep* emmener (*qn*) d'urgence.
▶**rush back** *vi* revenir en toute hâte *ou* en vitesse.
▶**rush into** *vipo* **to r. into a room,** entrer précipitamment *ou* faire irruption dans une pièce; **to r. into things,** agir sans réfléchir *ou* à la hâte *ou* étourdiment; **to r. into marriage/divorce/***etc*, se marier/divorcer/*etc* à la hâte.
▶**rush off** *vi* = **RUSH AWAY**.
▶**rush out 1** *vi* sortir précipitamment (**of,** de). **2** *vtsep* sortir (*un produit*) à la hâte; envoyer (*des troupes*) d'urgence.
▶**rush through 1** *vipo* **the wind was rushing through the tunnel,** le vent s'engouffrait dans le tunnel; **to r. through one's work,** faire son travail à la hâte.
2 *vtsep* **to r. a bill through (the House),** faire passer un projet de loi à la hâte; **to r. an order/application/***etc* **through,** traiter une commande/une demande/*etc* en urgence.
▶**rush up 1** *vi* (*upstairs etc*) monter à toute vitesse; **to r. up to s.o.,** (*to say hello etc*) de précipiter sur qn. **2** *vtsep Mil* **to r. up reinforcements,** amener *ou* envoyer des renforts en toute hâte.
rushing ['rʌʃɪŋ] *adj* (*wind, river*) impétueux.
rusk [rʌsk] *n* biscotte *f*; (*for baby*) gros biscuit.
russet ['rʌsɪt] **1** *n* (*apple*) reinette grise. **2** *adj* roussâtre, roux, *f* rousse, couleur feuille-morte *inv*.
Russia ['rʌʃə] *n* Russie *f*.
Russian ['rʌʃən] **1** *adj* russe; (*history*) de Russie; (*teacher, lesson, dictionary*) de russe; **R. language student,** russisant, -ante; **R. roulette,** roulette *f* russe; **R. salad,** salade *f* russe. **2** *n* **(a)** Russe *mf*; **(b)** *Ling* russe *m*.
Russianization [rʌʃənaɪ'zeɪʃən] *n* (*of population, republic etc*) russification *f*.
Russianize ['rʌʃənaɪz] *vt* russifier.
Russophile ['rʌsəʊfaɪl] *adj & n* russophile *mf*.
rust¹ [rʌst] *n* (*on metal, wheat etc*) rouille *f*; **to be covered with** *or* **in r.,** être couvert de rouille; *Br F* **r. bucket,** (*car*) bagnole toute rouillée; **r. inhibitor, r. preventer** antirouille *m inv*; **r. (coloured), r. red,** roux, roussâtre.
rust² 1 *vi* (*of metal, wheat etc*) se rouiller; (*of metal*) s'oxyder. **2** *vt* rouiller (*le fer etc*); **to be badly rusted,** être très rouillé.
▶**rust away, rust through** *vi* (*of metal etc*) être rongé *ou* mangé par la rouille.
rustic ['rʌstɪk] **1** *adj* (*bench, charm etc*) rustique; *Pej* (*manners etc*) rustre. **2** *n* paysan, -anne, campagnard, -arde; *Pej* rustaud, -aude.
rusticate ['rʌstɪkeɪt] **1** *vt Br Univ* renvoyer temporairement (*un étudiant*). **2** *vi Fml Lit* habiter la campagne.
rustication [rʌstɪ'keɪʃən] *n* **(a)** *Br Univ* (*of student*) renvoi *m* temporaire; **(b)** *Fml Lit* vie *f* à la campagne.
rusticity [rʌs'tɪsɪtɪ] *n* rusticité *f*.
rustiness ['rʌstɪnɪs] *n* (*of metal, wheat*) rouillure *f*, rouille *f*; *Fig* **because of the r. of my French,** parce que mon français est un peu rouillé.
rusting ['rʌstɪŋ] *n* rouillure *f*.
rustle¹ ['rʌs(ə)l] *n* (*of leaves*) bruissement *m*, frémissement *m*; (*of silk, dress*) frou-frou *m*; (*of paper*) froissement *m*.
rustle² 1 *vi* (*of leaves*) bruire, frémir; (*of silk, dress*) faire frou-frou, froufrouter; **to hear papers rustling,** entendre des froissements de papier. **2** *vt* faire bruire, faire frémir (*les feuilles*); faire froufrouter (*la soie*); froisser (*le papier*).
rustle³ *vt* voler (*du bétail etc*).
▶**rustle up** *vtsep F* **to r. up support,** rassembler des partisans; **she can always r. up a good meal,** elle peut toujours confectionner un bon repas; **to r. up some coffee,** (*order*) faire venir du café; (*make*) faire du café.
rustler ['rʌslər] *n* (*of cattle*) voleur, -euse.
rustling ['rʌslɪŋ] *n* **(a)** = **RUSTLE¹**; **(b)** (*of cattle*) vol *m*.
rustproof¹ ['rʌstpruːf] *adj* antirouille *inv*.
rustproof² *vt* protéger (*le métal*) contre la rouille.
rustproofing ['rʌstpruːfɪŋ] *n* (*substance*) produit *m* antirouille; (*process*) application *f* d'un produit antirouille (**of,** sur).
rust-resistant ['rʌstrɪzɪstənt] *adj* (*metal*) résistant à la rouille.
rusty ['rʌstɪ] *adj* **(a)** (*iron etc*) rouillé; **to get r.,** se rouiller; *Fig* **my French is getting r.,** mon français se rouille; **my playing is very/a bit r.,** mon jeu est très/un peu rouillé; **the pianist/batsman sounded/looked a bit r.,** le pianiste/batteur semblait n'avoir pas joué depuis longtemps; **(b)** (*colour*) couleur de rouille; **a r. red,** un marron rouille.
rut¹ [rʌt] *n* ornière *f*; *Fig* **to get into a r.,** s'encroûter, s'enliser dans la routine; *Fig* **to be in a r.,** être prisonnier d'une routine; *Fig* **to get out of a r.,** sortir de la routine.
rut² *vt* (**-tt-**) sillonner (*un chemin*) d'ornières; **deeply rutted,** (*path etc*) coupé d'ornières.
rut³ *n* (*of stag etc*) rut *m*.
rut⁴ *vi* (**-tt-**) (*of stag etc*) être en rut.
rutabaga [ruːtə'beɪgə] *n Am* rutabaga *m*.
ruthless ['ruːθlɪs] *adj* (*person*) impitoyable, sans pitié; (*act*) brutal; (*determination*) inflexible; (*schedule, pace*) impitoyable; **to be r. in enforcing the law,** être impitoyable dans l'application de la loi; **we have to be r.,** nous devons être impitoyables.
ruthlessly ['ruːθlɪslɪ] *adv* (*to act, say*) impitoyablement.
ruthlessness ['ruːθlɪsnɪs] *n* (*of person, act*) nature *f* impitoyable.
rutting ['rʌtɪŋ] *n* rut *m*; **r. season,** saison *f* du rut.
RV [ɑː'viː] *n* **(a)** *Am Aut* (*abbr* **recreational vehicle**) = véhicule *m* de loisirs; **(b)** *abbr* **Revised Version** (*de la Bible*).
rye [raɪ] *n* **(a)** (*plant*) seigle *m*; **r. bread,** pain *m* de seigle; **(b)** *Am* **r. (whisky),** whisky *m* de seigle.
rye-grass ['raɪgrɑːs] *n* ivraie *f* vivace.

S

S, s [es] *n* **(a)** (la lettre) S, s *m*; **(b) S(-shaped) hook,** crochet *m* en S; *Aut* **S bend,** virage *m* en S; **(c) S** (*abbr* **south**) S; (*on clothes label*) (*abbr* **small**) S; **(d)** *Arch* (*abbr* **solidus**) shilling *m*.

's [s, z] **(a)** (*shortened form of* **is; us; has**) **it's raining,** il pleut; **he's found a knife,** il a trouvé un couteau; **let's go!,** partons!; **(b)** (*genitive case*) **the pupil's books,** les livres de l'élève; **the pupils' books,** les livres des élèves; **in an hour's time,** dans une heure; **(c)** (*forming pl*) **the Thomas's,** les Thomas, la famille Thomas; **a series of o's,** une série d'o.

SA [es'eɪ] **(a)** *abbr* **Salvation Army**; **(b)** *abbr* **South Africa.**

Saar [sɑːr] *n* **the S.,** la Sarre.

Sabbath ['sæbəθ] *n* **(a)** *Rel* **S. (day),** (jour *m* du) sabbat *m* (*des Juifs*); dimanche *m* (*des chrétiens*); **S. day observance,** observation *f* du dimanche; **to keep/break the S.,** (*in Jewish religion*) observer/violer le sabbat; (*in Christian religion*) observer/violer le dimanche; **(b) witches' S.,** sabbat *m* (de sorcières).

sabbatical [sə'bætɪk(ə)l] **1** *n Sch etc* année *f ou* trimestre *m* sabbatique (*accordé(e) à un professeur etc pour faire des recherches etc*); **to be on s.,** (*of teacher etc*) être en cours d'année *ou* de trimestre sabbatique. **2** *adj Sch etc* **s. year/term,** année *f*/trimestre *m* de congé (*accordé(e) à un professeur etc pour faire des recherches etc*).

sable¹ ['seɪb(ə)l] *n* **(a)** (*animal*) zibeline *f*; **(b) s. (fur),** zibeline *f*; **s. coat,** manteau *m* de zibeline; **(c)** *Art* **s. (brush),** pinceau *m* en poil de martre.

sable² **1** *n* (*colour*) *Arch & Lit* sable *m*; *Her* sable *m*. **2** *adj Arch & Lit* noir; *Her* (*écusson etc*) sable; *Zool* **s. antelope,** antilope noire.

sabot ['sæbəʊ] *n* (*clog*) sabot *m*.

sabotage¹ ['sæbətɑːʒ] *n* sabotage *m*.

sabotage² *vt* saboter (*un pont, un fusil*); *Fig* saboter, faire échouer (*un projet*).

saboteur [sæbə'tɜːr] *n* saboteur, -euse.

sabre, *US* **saber** ['seɪbər] *n Mil* sabre *m*; **s. cut,** (*blow*) coup *m* de sabre; (*scar*) balafre *f*; *Fig* **s. rattling,** propos *mpl* belliqueux.

sac [sæk] *n Biol* sac *m*; **yolk s.,** membrane vitelline; **ink s.,** (*of squid, sepia etc*) poche *f* d'encre.

saccharin ['sækərɪn] *n Ch etc* saccharine *f*.

saccharine ['sækəriːn] *adj Ch* saccharin; *Fig* (*of smile*) mielleux.

sacerdotal [sæsə'dəʊt(ə)l] *adj* sacerdotal, -aux.

sachet ['sæʃeɪ] *n* sachet *m*.

sack¹ [sæk] *n* **(a)** (*bag*) (grand) sac *m*; **s. of coal/flour,** sac de charbon/farine; *Sp* **s. race,** course *f* en sac; *F* **to hit the s.,** se coucher, se pieuter; **(b)** *F* **to give s.o. the s.,** virer qn, sa(c)quer qn, mettre *ou* flanquer qn à la porte; **to get the s.,** être viré *ou* sa(c)qué.

sack² *vt* **(a)** *F* (*dismiss from job*) virer, sa(c)quer (*qn*), mettre *ou* flanquer (*qn*) à la porte; **(b)** (*put in sack*) ensacher, mettre en sac (*du charbon etc*).

sack³ *n Mil etc* (*plundering*) sac *m*, pillage *m* (*d'une ville etc*).

sack⁴ *vt Mil etc* (*plunder*) saccager, piller, mettre à sac (*une ville etc*).

sackcloth ['sækklɒθ] *n* **(a)** *Tex* toile *f* à sacs, grosse toile, toile d'emballage; **(b)** *Bible etc* sac *m*; **s. and ashes,** le sac et la cendre; *Fig* **he wasn't exactly wearing s. and ashes,** il n'avait pas tellement l'air désolé *ou* contrit.

sackful ['sækfʊl] *n* plein sac (*de farine etc*).

sacking¹ ['sækɪŋ] *n* **(a)** *F* (*dismissal from job*) renvoi *m* (*d'un employé*); **(b) = SACKCLOTH (a)**; **(c)** (*putting in sack(s)*) mise *f* en sac (*du charbon etc*).

sacking² *n* (*plundering*) sac *m* (*d'une ville etc*).

sacrament ['sækrəmənt] *n Rel* sacrement *m*; **the (Most) Holy S., the Blessed S.,** le saint Sacrement (de l'autel).

sacramental [sækrə'mentəl] **1** *adj* sacramentel. **2** *npl Rel* **the sacramentals,** les sacramentaux *mpl*.

sacred ['seɪkrɪd] *adj* **(a)** (*lieu etc*) sacré; **s. to the memory of ...,** consacré à la mémoire de ...; **(b)** *Rel* sacré, saint; (*musique, procession*) religieux; **s. books,** livres *mpl* d'Église, livres saints; **the S. Heart,** le Sacré-Cœur; **s. cow,** *Rel* vache sacrée; *Fig* institution *f* intouchable; **(c)** (*of promise, duty etc*) sacré, inviolable; **nothing was s. to him,** il ne respectait rien.

sacredness ['seɪkrɪdnɪs] *n* **(a)** caractère sacré (*d'un lieu etc*); **(b)** inviolabilité *f* (*d'un serment etc*).

sacrifice¹ ['sækrɪfaɪs] *n* **(a)** (*act of giving up*) sacrifice *m*, abnégation *f* (*de qch*); (*act of renouncing*) renoncement *m* (*à qch*); *Com* vente *f* à perte; **to make great sacrifices,** faire de grands sacrifices; **to make the supreme s.,** faire le sacrifice suprême; **he succeeded at the s. of his health,** il a réussi au prix de sa santé; **(b)** (*act of offering up*) sacrifice *m*, immolation *f* (*d'une victime*); (*offering*) offrande *f*; **to offer (up) sth as a s.,** offrir qch en sacrifice (**to,** à); **(c)** *Rel* sacrifice *m* (*du Christ*).

sacrifice² **1** *vt* **(a)** sacrifier, renoncer à (*qch*); *Com* vendre à perte (*des marchandises*); **to s. oneself,** se sacrifier (**for,** pour); **(b)** (*offer up*) sacrifier, immoler (*une victime*). **2** *vi* **to s. to idols,** sacrifier aux idoles.

sacrificial [sækrɪ'fɪʃəl] *adj* sacrificatoire.

sacrilege ['sækrɪlɪdʒ] *n Rel & Fig* sacrilège *m*.

sacrilegious [sækrɪ'lɪdʒəs] *adj* sacrilège; **s. person,** sacrilège *mf*.

sacristan ['sækrɪstən] *n Rel* sacristain *m*.

sacristy ['sækrɪstɪ] *n Rel* sacristie *f*.

sacrosanct ['sækrəʊsæŋkt] *adj usu Iron* sacro-saint, *pl* sacro-saint(e)s.

sacrum ['seɪkrəm, 'sæk-] *n Anat* sacrum *m*.

sad [sæd] *adj* (*comp* **sadder,** *superl* **saddest**) **(a)** triste; (*news etc*) affligeant, désolant; (*place etc*) morne, lugubre; **to become s.,** s'attrister; **to look s.,** avoir l'air triste; **to make s.o. s.,** attrister qn, affliger qn; **we were very s. to hear of our friend's death,** nous avons été désolés d'apprendre la mort de notre ami; **that's very s. news,** c'est bien triste; **to be s. at heart,** avoir le cœur gros *ou* serré; **a s. reflection on our society,** une triste réflection sur notre société; **it's s. that no one seems to care about the elderly,** il est triste que personne ne semble se soucier des personnes âgées; **he came to a s. end,** il a eu *ou* fait une triste fin; **(b)** *Culin* (*cake etc*) pâteux, lourd, mal levé.

sadden ['sæd(ə)n] **1** *vt* attrister, affliger (*qn*). **2** *vi* s'affliger, s'attrister.

saddle¹ ['sæd(ə)l] *n* **(a)** selle *f* (*de cheval, de bicyclette etc*); **hunting s.,** selle anglaise; **to rise in the s.,** faire du trot enlevé; **in the s.,** en selle, monté; **to be in the s.,** (*in control*) tenir les reines (du pouvoir); **s. horse,** cheval *m* de selle, monture *f*; **s. room,** sellerie *f*; **(b)** *Culin* selle *f* (*de mouton, de chevreuil*); **(c)** *Tech* support *m* (*d'un cric etc*); (*in engine*) selle *f*, assiette *f* (*de cylindre*); *Geol* col *m* (*de montagne*).

saddle² *vt* seller (*un cheval*); *F* **to s. s.o. with sth,** charger *ou* encombrer qn de qch; **I've been saddled with this project,** on m'a mis ce projet sur les bras; **she's saddled with five children,** elle a cinq enfants sur les bras.

saddleback ['sæd(ə)lbæk] *n Archit* toit *m* en bâtière; (*of hill*) ensellement *m*; (*pig*) cochon noir avec une ceinture blanche.

saddlebag ['sæd(ə)lbæg] *n Horseriding Cycling etc* sacoche *f* (*de selle*).

saddlecloth ['sæd(ə)lklɒθ] *n* couverture *f ou* tapis *m* de selle.

saddler ['sædlər] *n* sellier *m*, bourrelier *m*.

saddlery ['sædlərɪ] *n* (*trade, articles*) sellerie *f*, bourrellerie *f*.

saddle-sore ['sæd(ə)l'sɔːr] *adj* **to be s.,** *Horseriding* avoir mal aux fesses à force d'avoir été en selle; *Cycling* avoir

mal aux fesses à force d'avoir fait du vélo.
saddling ['sædlɪŋ] *n* sellage *m* (*d'un cheval*).
Sadducee ['sædjusiː] *n* Saducéen, -éenne.
sadism ['seɪdɪz(ə)m] *n* sadisme *m*.
sadist ['seɪdɪst] *n* sadique *mf*.
sadistic [sə'dɪstɪk] *adj* sadique.
sadistically [sə'dɪstɪklɪ] *adv* sadiquement, avec sadisme.
sadly ['sædlɪ] *adv* **(a)** tristement, d'un air triste; **(b)** (*deplorably*) déplorablement; **s., this is so,** c'est le cas, ce qui est déplorable; **(c)** (*greatly*) beaucoup; **he is s. missed,** il nous manque beaucoup; **compassion is s. lacking in our society,** la compassion fait tristement défaut dans notre société.
sadness ['sædnɪs] *n* tristesse *f*, mélancolie *f*.
sadomasochism [seɪdəʊ'mæsəkɪz(ə)m] *n Psy* sadomasochisme *m*.
sadomasochist [seɪdəʊ'mæsəkɪst] *n Psy* sadomasochiste *mf*.
sadomasochistic [seɪdəʊmæsə'kɪstɪk] *adj Psy* sadomasochiste.
s.a.e. [eseɪ'iː] *n Com etc* (*abbr* **stamped addressed envelope**) enveloppe timbrée avec son adresse.
safari [sə'fɑːrɪ] *n* safari *m*; **on s.,** en safari; **to go on s.,** faire un safari, aller en safari; **s. jacket,** saharienne *f*; **s. park,** réserve *f* d'animaux sauvages.
safe[1] [seɪf] *n* **(a)** (*strongbox*) coffre-fort *m*, *pl* coffres-forts; *Banking* **night** *or* **deposit s.,** coffre *m* de nuit; **s. deposit,** dépôt *m* en coffre-fort; **(b) (meat) s.,** garde-manger *m inv*; **(c) rifle (set) at s.,** carabine *f* au cran de sûreté.
safe[2] **1** *adj* **(a)** (*not in danger*) en sûreté; **s. from sth,** à l'abri de qch; **at last we are s.,** enfin nous voilà saufs *ou* hors de danger; **to be s. from recognition,** ne pas risquer d'être reconnu; **s. and sound** *or* **well,** sain et sauf; **I'm glad to hear you're s.,** je suis content d'apprendre qu'il ne t'est rien arrivé; **to come home s.,** rentrer sans accident; **your daughter's not s. with him,** votre fille joue avec le feu en le fréquentant;
(b) (*not dangerous*) sans danger, sûr; (*building, bridge etc*) solide; (*conversation, novel etc*) dans lequel on ne prend pas de risque; **not s.,** dangereux; **these toys aren't s.,** ces jouets sont dangereux; **is it s. to leave him alone?,** est-ce qu'il n'y a pas de danger à le laisser seul?; **it's as s. as the Bank of England** *or* **as s. as houses,** c'est de l'or en barres; **it is s. to say that ...,** on peut dire à coup sûr que ...; **better s. than sorry,** deux précautions valent mieux qu'une; **is the meat/water s.?,** (*to eat, drink*) est-ce qu'on peut manger la viande/boire l'eau sans risque?; **it's a pretty s. assumption** *or F* **bet that ...,** il y a fort à parier que ...; **s. beach for children,** plage *f* où les enfants peuvent se baigner en sécurité; **at a s. distance,** à distance respectueuse; *Med* **s. dose,** dose inoffensive; **s. house,** *F* (*for spies, terrorists*) planque *f*; **s. investment,** placement sûr *ou* de tout repos; **to wish s.o. a s. journey,** souhaiter bon voyage à qn; **in s. keeping,** en lieu sûr, en sûreté; **to give sth to s.o. for s. keeping,** confier qch à qn; **it's in his s. keeping,** c'est sous sa garde; *Tech* **s. load,** (*lorry*) charge *f* admissible; (*appliance*) charge de sécurité; **to put s.o./sth in a s. place,** mettre qn/qch en lieu sûr; **s. retreat,** asile assuré *ou* sûr; *Br Parl* **s. seat,** siège assuré; **s. sex,** pratiques sexuelles sans risques; **(in order) to be on the s. side,** pour plus de sûreté, pour être plus sûr.
2 *adv* **to play (it) s.,** ne rien risquer.
safe-breaker ['seɪfbreɪkər] *n* perceur *m* de coffres-forts.
safe-conduct [seɪf'kɒndʌkt] *n* sauf-conduit *m*, *pl* sauf-conduits.
safeguard[1] ['seɪfgɑːd] *n* sauvegarde *f*, garantie *f* (**against,** contre).
safeguard[2] *vt* sauvegarder, protéger (*les intérêts, les droits de qn*).
safely ['seɪflɪ] *adv* **(a) to arrive s.,** arriver sain et sauf *ou* sans accident; (*of parcel*) arriver sans dommage; (*of ship etc*) arriver à bon port; **to put sth s. away,** mettre qch en lieu sûr *ou* en sûreté; **the bomb had been s. defused,** la bombe a été désamorcée en toute sécurité; **(b)** (*with certainty*) avec certitude; **I can s. say that ...,** je puis dire à coup sûr que ...; **you can s. expect her to remember,** vous pouvez vous attendre à coup sûr qu'elle s'en souvienne.
safeness ['seɪfnɪs] *n* **(a) a feeling of s.,** un sentiment de sécurité *ou* de sûreté; **(b)** solidité *f* (*d'un pont*); **(c)** (*certainty*) sûreté *f* (*d'une affaire, d'un placement etc*).
safety ['seɪftɪ] *n* sûreté *f*, sécurité *f* (*de qch, de qn*); salut *m* (*de qn*); **to seek s. in flight,** chercher son salut dans la fuite; **there's s. in numbers,** plus on est nombreux, moins on court de risques; **to guarantee s.o.'s s.,** (*of police etc*) assurer la protection de qn; **for s.'s sake,** pour plus de sûreté; **in a place of s.,** en lieu sûr; **road s.,** prévention routière; **s. first,** mesures *fpl* de prévention des accidents; **s. first!,** la sécurité d'abord!, soyez prudents!; **s. belt,** ceinture *f* de sécurité; **s. chain,** (*of door*) chaîne *f* de sûreté de porte; (*of bracelet etc*) chaînette *f* de sûreté; **s. catch,** (*on gun*) cran *m* de sûreté; *Aut etc* **s. glass,** verre *m* de sécurité; *Min* **s. lamp,** lampe *f* de sûreté; **s. margin,** marge *f* de sécurité; **s. matches,** allumettes *f* de sûreté; **s. measures,** mesures *fpl* de sécurité; **s. net,** filet *m*; *Fig* mesure *f* de sûreté; **s. pin,** épingle *f* de nourrice *ou* de sûreté; **she's very s. conscious,** elle se préoccupe beaucoup de la sécurité; **s. valve,** *Tech* soupape *f* de sûreté; *Fig* soupape.
saffron ['sæfrən] **1** *n* **(a)** *Culin Pharm* safran *m*; **s. (crocus),** (*plant*) safran; **wild** *or* **meadow s.,** safran des prés; **(b)** (*colour*) safran *m*; **s. yellow,** jaune safran. **2** *adj* safran *inv*.
sag[1] [sæg] *n* **(a)** (*act of sagging*) affaissement *m*, fléchissement *m* (*du sol, d'un toit etc*); *Com* baisse *f* (*des valeurs etc*); **(b)** (*shape*) flèche *f*, ventre *m* (*d'une ligne, d'un cordage etc*).
sag[2] *vi* **(-gg-)** (*of platform, roof etc*) s'affaisser, fléchir (*sous un poids etc*); (*of gate etc*) pencher d'un côté; (*of cheek, breast etc*) pendre; (*of cable etc*) se relâcher, se détendre; (*of curtain, rope etc*) fléchir au milieu; *Com* (*of prices*) baisser, fléchir.
saga ['sɑːgə] *n Liter* saga *f*; **s. (novel),** roman-fleuve *m*, *pl* romans-fleuves; *F* **the continuing s. of our washing machine,** le feuilleton de notre machine à laver.
sagacious [sə'geɪʃəs] *adj* (*person, mind*) sagace, avisé; (*action, remark*) plein de sagesse.
sagaciously [sə'geɪʃəslɪ] *adv* avec sagacité.
sagacity [sə'gæsɪtɪ] *n* sagacité *f*, perspicacité *f* (*d'une personne*); sagesse *f* (*d'une remarque etc*).
sage[1] [seɪdʒ] **1** *adj Lit* (*person, conduct etc*) sage, prudent, judicieux. **2** *n* philosophe *m*, sage *m*.
sage[2] *n* (*plant*) & *Culin* sauge *f*; **s. tea,** infusion *f* de sauge; **s. green,** (*colour*) vert cendré *inv*.
sagely ['seɪdʒlɪ] *adv* sagement, prudemment.
sagging ['sægɪŋ] *adj* (*of roof etc*) affaissé, fléchi; (*of gate etc*) penché d'un côté; (*of breast, cheek etc*) tombant, pendant; (*of line etc*) courbe; (*of rope*) lâche; *Com Fin* (*of market*) creux, en baisse.
Sagittarius [sædʒɪ'teərɪəs] *n Astron* le Sagittaire; **I am S.,** je suis Sagittaire *ou* du Sagittaire.
sago ['seɪgəʊ] *n Culin* sagou *m*; **s. palm,** (*tree*) sagoutier *m*; **s. pudding,** sagou au lait.
Sahara [sə'hɑːrə] *n* **the S. (Desert),** le Sahara.
sahib ['sɑːɪb] *n* sahib *m*.
said *see* **SAY**[2].
sail[1] [seɪl] *n* **(a)** *Nau* voile *f*; **square s.,** voile carrée; **to hoist/lower a s.,** hisser/amener une voile; **to make s.,** faire (de la) voile *ou* de la toile; **under s.,** (*of ship*) sous voile(s), à la voile; **under full s.,** toutes voiles dehors; **to set s.,** prendre la mer; **to set s. for ...,** mettre en route pour ...; **s. ho!,** voilier en vue!; **a fleet of twenty s.,** une flotte de vingt voiles *ou* de vingt voiliers; **(b)** aile *f*, volant *m*, toile *f* (*de moulin*); (*of basking shark*) nageoire dorsale.
sail[2] *n* (*journey*) sortie *f* à voile; **it will be a three hours' s.,** ça sera une traversée de trois heures.
sail[3] **1** *vi* (*of sailing ship*) faire voile; (*of any ship*) naviguer, faire route; (*start, voyage*) prendre la mer; (*glide*) planer (*dans l'air etc*); *Av* voler; **to s. round a cape,** contourner un promontoire; **to s. over the seas,** parcourir les mers; **s. on the seas,** naviguer (sur) les mers; **there were clouds sailing by,** des nuages voguaient dans le ciel; *F* **to s. into a room,** entrer majestueusement dans une pièce; **his toupet went sailing out of the open window,** son toupet s'est envolé par la fenêtre ouverte; **to s. through an examination,** réussir un examen sans le moindre effort *ou* les doigts dans le nez.
2 *vt* manœuvrer (*un voilier*); piloter, commander (*un navire*); **to s. a toy boat on a pond,** faire naviguer un petit bateau sur un bassin; **to s. the seas,** naviguer (sur) les mers; (*to travel over, around the seas*) parcourir les mers.
sailboard[1] ['seɪlbɔːd] *n Sp* planche *f* à voile.
sailboard[2] *vi Sp* faire de la planche à voile.
sailboarder ['seɪlbɔːdər] *n Sp* véliplanchiste *mf*.
sailboarding ['seɪlbɔːdɪŋ] *n Sp* véliplanchisme *m*.
sailboat ['seɪlbəʊt] *n Am* voilier *m*, bateau *m* à voile.
sailcloth ['seɪlklɒθ] *n Tex* (*for sails*) toile *f* à voile(s); (*for clothes*) canevas *m*.
sailing ['seɪlɪŋ] *n* **(a)** (*in sailing ship, boat*) navigation *f* à

voile; (*in any ship*) navigation; *Sp* nautisme *m*; **to go s.,** faire de la voile; **it's (all) plain s.,** cela va tout seul; **s. before the wind,** allure *f* du vent arrière; **s. boat,** voilier *m*, bateau *m* à voile; **s. ship,** voilier; **(b)** (*departure*) départ *m*, appareillage *m*; **the 12 o'clock s.,** le bateau de midi.

sailmaker ['seɪlmeɪkər] *n* (*person*) voilier *m*.

sailor ['seɪlər] *n* marin *m* (*officier ou matelot*); **to be a good s.,** avoir le pied marin; **to be a bad s.,** être sujet au mal de mer; **s. suit,** (*garment*) costume marin (*d'enfant*); **s. hat,** canotier *m* (*pour femmes*); chapeau *m* de marin (*de petit garçon*).

sainfoin ['sænfɔɪn] *n* (*plant*) & *Agr* sainfoin *m*.

saint [seɪnt] *n* **(a)** saint, -e; **s.'s day,** fête *f* de saint, fête patronale; **All Saints' (Day),** la Toussaint; **I'm no s.,** je ne suis pas un saint; *F* **to try the patience of a s.,** lasser la patience d'un saint; **(b)** (*usu* [sənt]) **S. George,** Saint Georges; **S. David's Day,** la Saint-David, fête nationale galloise; **S. Bernard,** (chien *m*) saint-bernard *m inv*; *Geog* **S. Helena,** Sainte-Hélène *f*; **S. John the Baptist,** Saint Jean-Baptiste; *Geog* **the S. Lawrence (River),** le (fleuve) Saint-Laurent; **S. Peter's,** (la cathédrale, l'église) Saint-Pierre; **(c) the Communion of Saints,** la Communion des Saints.

sainted ['seɪntɪd] *adj F* **my s. aunt!,** mes aïeux!

sainthood ['seɪnthʊd] *n* sainteté *f*.

saintliness ['seɪntlɪnɪs] *n* sainteté *f*.

saintly ['seɪntlɪ] *adj* (*life, action etc*) (de) saint; *Iron* **to put on a s. air,** prendre un air de petit saint.

sake[1] [seɪk] *n* **(a) to do sth for the s. of s.o.** *or* **for s.o.'s s.,** faire qch dans l'intérêt de qn *ou* par égard pour qn *ou* en considération de qn; **I forgive you for her s.,** je vous pardonne par égard pour elle; **do it for the s. of your family,** faites-le pour (l'amour de) votre famille; **they stayed together for the s. of the children** *or* **for the children's s.,** ils sont restés ensemble à cause des enfants; **for all our sakes, tell no one,** ne le dis à personne dans notre intérêt à tous; **do it for my s.,** faites-le pour moi; (*do it to please me*) faites-le pour me faire plaisir; **for God's s., for goodness' s., for Pete's s.,** pour l'amour de Dieu; **for old times' s.,** en souvenir du passé; **for economy's s.,** par économie; **art for art's s.,** l'art pour l'art; **(b)** *US F* **sakes alive!, sakes!,** grand Dieu!, par exemple!

sake[2] ['sɑːkɪ] *n* (*drink*) saké *m*.

sal [sæl] *n* **s. ammoniac,** sel ammoniac; **s. volatile,** (solution *f* de) sels volatils anglais.

salaam[1] [sə'lɑːm] *n F* salamalec *m*; **salaams to David,** meilleurs vœux à David.

salaam[2] **1** *vt* faire des salamalecs à qn. **2** *vi* faire des salamalecs.

salacious [sə'leɪʃəs] *adj* (*story*) salace; (*person*) lubrique.

salaciousness [sə'leɪʃəsnɪs] *n* (*of story*) salacité *f*; (*of person*) lubricité *f*.

salad ['sæləd] *n* salade *f*; **cheese/ham s.,** salade et fromage/jambon; **green s.,** salade (verte); **fruit s.,** macédoine *f ou* salade de fruits; **s. bar,** (*in restaurant*) comptoir *m* à salade; **s. bowl,** saladier *m*; **s. cream,** assaisonnement *m* pour la salade; *F* **s. days,** années *f* de jeunesse *ou* d'inexpérience; **s. dressing,** (*vinaigrette*) vinaigrette *f*; (*salad cream, mayonnaise etc*) sauce *f* mayonnaise; **s. oil,** huile *f* de table.

salamander ['sæləmændər] *n* (*amphibian*) salamandre *f*.

salami [sə'lɑːmɪ] *n* (*sausage*) salami *m*.

salaried ['sælərɪd] *adj Ind Com* **(a)** (*personnel*) recevant un traitement *ou* des appointements; **s. staff,** = cadres *mpl*; **(b)** (*emploi*) où l'on touche des appointements *ou* un traitement salarié.

salary ['sælərɪ] *n* traitement *m*, appointements *mpl*.

sale [seɪl] *n* **(a)** vente *f*; (*act of selling*) débit *m*, mise *f* en vente (*de marchandises*); **cash/credit s.,** vente au comptant/à crédit; **article for which there is no s.,** article qui ne se vend pas; **house for s.,** maison à vendre; **business for s.,** fonds *m* à céder; **to put sth up for s.,** offrir *ou* mettre qch en vente; *Br* **on s.,** (*available to buy*) en vente; **bill of s.,** acte *m* de vente; **s. by auction, auction s.,** vente à l'enchère *ou* aux enchères; *Br Com* **sales assistant,** vendeur,-euse; *Ind* **sales department,** service commercial, service des ventes; **sales drive,** campagne *f* de vente; **sales pitch** *or* **talk,** boniment *m*; *Jur* **compulsory s.,** adjudication forcée; **s. of work,** vente de charité; **(b)** *Com* **(clearance) s.,** soldes *mpl*; *Br* **in the s.,** *Am* **on s.,** en solde; **I got it in the sales,** je l'ai acheté en solde *ou* dans les soldes; **s. price,** prix *m* de solde.

saleability [seɪlə'bɪlɪtɪ] *n Com* facilité *f* d'écoulement.

saleable ['seɪləb(ə)l] *adj* (*goods etc*) vendable.

saleroom ['seɪlruːm] *n* salle *f* de(s) vente(s).

salesclerk ['seɪlzklɜːk] *n Am* vendeur, -euse *f*.

salesgirl ['seɪlzgɜːl] *n* vendeuse *f*.

salesman, *pl* **-men** ['seɪlzmən] *n Com* **(a)** représentant *m* de commerce; **he's a good s.,** il sait bien vendre, il a une bonne technique de vente; **(b)** (*in shop*) vendeur *m*.

salesmanship ['seɪlzmənʃɪp] *n* technique *f* de vente.

salesperson, *pl* **-people** ['seɪlzpɜːsən, -piːp(ə)l] *n* **(a)** représentant *m* de commerce; **(b)** (*in shop*) vendeur *m*.

saleswoman, *pl* **-women** ['seɪlzwʊmən, -wɪmɪn] *n* **(a)** représentante *f*; **(b)** (*in shop*) vendeuse *f*.

Salic ['seɪlɪk] *adj Hist* **S. law,** loi *f* salique.

salient ['seɪlɪənt] **1** *adj* **(a)** (*angle etc*) saillant; **(b)** (*trait*) saillant, frappant; **the s. points of an argument,** les points forts d'un argument. **2** *n* (*in fortification*) saillant *m*.

saline ['seɪlaɪn] **1** *adj* (*spring, water etc*) salin, salé; *purgatif*) salin; *Med* **s. drip,** goutte-à-goutte *m* de solution saline; **normal s. solution,** solution *f* physiologique. **2** *n Med* purgatif salin, sel purgatif; (*salt solution*) sérum *m* physiologique.

salinity [sə'lɪnɪtɪ] *n* salinité *f*.

saliva [sə'laɪvə] *n* salive *f*.

salivary [sə'laɪvərɪ] *adj* (*glands etc*) salivaire.

salivate ['sælɪveɪt] *vi* saliver.

salivation [sælɪ'veɪʃən] *n* salivation *f*.

sallow[1] ['sæləʊ] *n* (*willow*) saule *m*.

sallow[2] *adj* (*teint*) jaunâtre, olivâtre.

sallowness ['sæləʊnɪs] *n* ton *m* jaunâtre *ou* olivâtre (*du teint*).

sally[1] ['sælɪ] *n* **(a)** *Mil* sortie *f* (*des assiégés*); **(b)** (*excursion*) excursion *f*, sortie *f*; **(c)** saillie *f*, élan *m* (*d'activité etc*); **s. (of wit),** boutade *f*, trait *m* d'esprit.

sally[2] *vi* **(a)** *Mil* **to s. (out),** faire une sortie; **(b)** *Lit* (*go out*) sortir.

Sally ['sælɪ] *n Br F* **the S. Army,** l'armée *f* du salut.

►**sally forth, sally out** *vi* (*go out*) sortir; (*go for walk*) partir en promenade.

salmon ['sæmən] **1** *n* **(a)** (*usu inv in pl*) (*fish*) saumon *m*; **young s.,** saumoneau *m*; **s. ladder** *or* **leap** *or* **pass,** échelle *f* à poissons *ou* à saumon(s); **s. trout,** truite saumonée, truite de mer; *Com* **rock s.,** roussette *f*; **(b)** (*colour*) **s. pink,** saumon *m inv*. **2** *adj* (*colour*) **s. (pink),** saumon *inv*.

salmonella [sælmə'nelə] *n* salmonelle *f*; **to have s. poisoning** *or F* **s.,** avoir attrapé la salmonelle.

salon ['sælɒn] *n* **(a)** salon *m* d'exposition (*d'une modiste etc*); *Art* **the S.,** le Salon; **beauty s.,** institut *m* de beauté; **hairdressing s.,** salon de coiffure; **(b)** *Liter* salon *m* (*littéraire*); **(c)** (*drawing room*) salon *m*.

saloon [sə'luːn] *n* **(a)** salle *f*, salon *m*; *Am* saloon *m*; bar *m*; **billiard s.,** salle de billard; *Am* **s. keeper,** gérant *m* de saloon; *Br* **s. bar,** = bar *m*; **(b)** *Nau* la cabine; salon *m* (*de paquebot*); **(c)** *Br Aut* **s. (car),** conduite intérieure; **two-door s.,** coach *m*; **four-door s.,** berline *f*; **(d)** *Br Rail* **s. (coach** *or* **carriage),** wagon-salon *m*, *pl* wagons-salons, voiture-salon *f*, *pl* voitures-salons.

salopettes [sælə'pets] *npl Ski* (*garment*) combinaison *f*.

salsify ['sælsɪfɪ] *n* (*plant*) salsifis *m*.

salt[1] [sɔːlt] **1** *n* **(a)** (*on roads*) & *Culin* sel *m*; **cake of s.,** salignon *m*; **rock s.,** sel gemme; **sea s.,** sel marin, sel de mer; **table s.,** sel de table; **to take a story with a pinch of s.,** ne pas prendre une histoire au pied de la lettre; **he's not worth his s.,** il ne gagne pas sa nourriture; **any athlete worth his** *or* **her s.,** n'importe quel athlète digne de ce nom, n'importe quel athlète qui se respecte; *Old-fashioned* **to sit (at table) above/below the s.,** être assis au haut bout/au bas bout de la table; **the s. of the earth,** le sel de la terre; **kitchen s.,** gros sel; **s. marsh,** marais salant; **s. mine,** mine *f* de sel; **s. spoon,** cuiller *f* à sel; **s. spring,** source saumâtre *ou* saline; *Hist* **s. tax,** gabelle *f*;
(b) *Ch* sel *m*; **bath salts,** sels de bain;
(c) *F* **old s.,** loup *m* de mer.
2 *adj* **(a)** (*food*) **too s.,** trop salé; **s. water,** eau salée; **s. beef,** bœuf *m* de conserve;
(b) (*concretion etc*) salin; (*rocks, ground*) salifère, saliférien.

salt[2] *vt* **(a)** saler (*un mets*); **(b)** = **SALT AWAY**; **(c)** = **SALT DOWN**; **(d)** *Old-fashioned F* cuisiner, truquer (*des livres de compte etc*).

►**salt away** *vtsep* (*save*) économiser, mettre en lieu sûr (*de l'argent etc*).

►**salt down** *vtsep* (*preserve with salt*) saler (*de la viande, du beurre etc*).

SALT [sɔːlt] *n Mil* (*abbr* **Strategic Arms Limitation Talks**) négociations *fpl* SALT; **S. agreements,** accords *mpl* SALT.

saltbox ['sɔːltbɒks] *n* boîte *f* à sel; *US* (*house*) = maison *f* à toit penchant (*avec deux étages à l'avant et un étage à* *l'arrière*).

saltcellar ['sɔːltselər] *n* **(a)** salière *f* (*de table*); **(b)** *F* salière *f* (*derrière la clavicule*).

salted ['sɔːltɪd] *adj* **(a)** (*beurre etc*) salé; **(b)** *Old-fashioned F* (*campaigner etc*) aguerri, endurci.

salt-free ['sɔːltfriː] *adj* (*régime*) sans sel.

saltine ['sɔːltiːn] *n Am Culin* biscuit salé, craquelin *m*.

saltiness ['sɔːltɪnɪs] *n* salure *f*, salinité *f*.

salting ['sɔːltɪŋ] *n* salaison *f*, salage *m* (*de la viande etc*).

saltmill ['sɔːltmɪl] *n* égrugeoir *m* de table.

saltpetre, *US* **saltpeter** [sɒlt'piːtər] *n* salpêtre *m*.

saltwater ['sɔːltwɔːtər] *adj* **s. fish,** poisson *m* de mer.

saltworks ['sɔːltwɜːks] *n* (*sea salt*) salin *m*; (*rock salt*) saline *f*; (*salt refinery*) raffinerie *f* de sel.

saltwort ['sɔːltwɜːt] *n* (*plant*) **(a)** soude *f*; **prickly s.,** kali *m*; **(b)** (*salicornia*) salicorne *f*.

salty ['sɔːltɪ] *adj* **(a)** (*taste, sauce etc*) salé; (*water*) saumâtre; **(b)** *F* (*anecdote, book*) piquant; (*licentious*) salé, corsé.

salubrious [sə'luːbrɪəs] *n* salubre, sain.

salubrity [sə'luːbrɪtɪ] *n* salubrité *f*.

saluki [sə'luːkɪ] *n* (*dog*) sloughi *m*.

salutary ['sæljʊt(ə)rɪ] *adj* salutaire (**to,** à).

salutation [sæljʊ'teɪʃən] *n* salutation *f*.

salute¹ [sə'luːt] *n* salut *m*, salutation *f*; *Mil Nau* salut; (*at march past*) **to take the s.,** passer les troupes en revue; *Mil Nau* **to fire a s.,** tirer une salve; **to fire a s. of ten guns** *or* **a ten gun s.,** saluer de dix coups.

salute² **1** *vt* saluer (*qn*); *Fml Lit* **to s. s.o.'s greatness/etc,** saluer la grandeur/*etc* de qn; *Mil* faire un salut, faire le salut militaire. **2** *vi Mil* faire un salut, faire le salut militaire.

salvage¹ ['sælvɪdʒ] *n* **(a)** (*salvaging*) sauvetage *m* (*d'un navire etc*); récupération *f* (*de matières pour l'industrie*); **s. tug,** remorqueur *m* de sauvetage; **s. vessel,** navire *m* de relevage; **(b)** (*objects salvaged*) objets sauvés (*d'un naufrage, d'un incendie*); **(c)** (*money*) indemnité *f ou* prime *f* de sauvetage; (*paid to salvage tug*) indemnité de remorquage.

salvage² *vt* sauver, relever (*un navire etc*); sauver, récupérer (*des objets dans un incendie etc*); récupérer (*une voiture etc*); *F* rattraper (*une mayonnaise*); **to s. something from the ruins of one's career,** sauver qch de la ruine de sa carrière; **salvaged goods,** matériel récupéré.

salvation [sæl'veɪʃən] *n* salut *m*; **to work out one's own s.,** travailler à son (propre) salut; **you've been my s.,** vous m'avez sauvé; **S. Army,** Armée *f* du Salut.

salvationist [sæl'veɪʃənɪst] *n* salutiste *mf*.

salve¹ [sælv, sɑːv] *n Pharm* onguent *m*, pommade *f* (*pour les lèvres etc*).

salve² [sælv] *vt* adoucir, apaiser; **to do sth to s. one's conscience,** faire qch par acquit de conscience, faire qch pour avoir la conscience en paix.

salve³ ['sælvɪ] *n Cathol* salvé *m*.

salver ['sælvər] *n* (*tray*) plateau *m* (*d'argent etc*).

salvia ['sælvɪə] *n* (*plant*) sauge (*ornementale*).

salvo ['sælvəʊ] *n Mil Nau & Fig* salve *f*; **to fire a s.,** tirer une salve; **s. of applause,** salve d'applaudissements.

Sam [sæm] *n F* **Uncle S.,** l'oncle Sam, les États-Unis.

SAM [sæm] *n Mil* (*abbr* **surface-to-air missile**) missile *m* sol-air.

Samaritan [sə'mærɪt(ə)n] **1** *adj* samaritain. **2** *n* Samaritain, -aine; *Bible* **the good S.,** le bon Samaritain; **to be a good s.,** être charitable; **the Samaritans,** (*telephone service*) ≈ S.O.S. Amitié.

samba ['sæmbə] *n* (*dance*) samba *f*.

sambo ['sæmbəʊ] *n Offensive Sl* noiraud, -aude.

same [seɪm] **1** *adj* même; **to repeat the s. words,** répéter les mêmes mots; **at the s. time that ...,** au moment même où ...; **he's the s. age as me,** il est du même âge que moi; **in the s. way,** de même, de la même façon; **we are going the s. way,** nous allons dans la même direction; **do you still feel the s. way?,** est-ce que vos sentiments sont toujours les mêmes?; **she's still the s. (old) Sarah,** c'est toujours notre bonne vieille Sarah; **the very s. thing, one and the s. thing,** une seule et même chose, tout à fait la même chose; **it is always/it is no longer the s. thing,** c'est toujours/ce n'est plus la même chose; **it** *or* **all that amounts** *or* **comes to the s. thing,** tout cela revient au même; **at the s. time,** en même temps; (*at once*) à la fois, du même coup; **that s. man is now a millionaire,** ce même homme est maintenant millionnaire.

2 *pron* **(a)** le même, la même, les mêmes; **it's the s. everywhere,** il en est de même partout; **it's all the s., it's just the s.,** c'est exactement la même chose, *F* c'est tout comme; **if it's all the s. to you,** si cela ne vous fait rien, si ça vous est égal; **it's much the s.,** c'est à peu près la même chose; **low-alcohol lager just isn't the s.,** la bière à faible teneur en alcool, ça n'est tout simplement pas la même chose; **the house isn't the s. without her,** la maison n'est pas pareille sans elle; **he had an accident and he's never been the s. since,** il a eu un accident et il n'est plus le même depuis;

(b) (*he, she, it etc*) **the s.,** celui-là, celle-là, *pl* ceux-là, celles-là; **the s. James King was later arrested,** le même James King a été arrêté plus tard; *Com* **s.-day delivery,** livraison le jour même; *F* **the s. again?,** encore un (*verre de whisky etc*)?; **the s. again!,** remettez ça!; *Sl* **s. here!,** et moi aussi!, et moi de même!; **a Happy New Year to you! — (the) s. to you!,** je vous souhaite une bonne année! — vous de même!; **s. to you, you bastard!,** toi aussi, espèce de salaud!; **I would have done the s.,** j'aurais fait de même, j'aurais agi de la même façon.

3 *adv* de même; **to think/feel/act the s.,** penser/sentir/agir de même; **all these houses look the s. to me,** je trouve que ces maisons se ressemblent toutes; **all her songs sound the s.,** toutes ses chansons se ressemblent; **all the s.,** quand même, tout de même; **when I am away things go on just the s.,** quand je suis absent tout marche comme d'habitude.

sameness ['seɪmnɪs] *n* **(a)** identité *f* (**with,** avec); (*ressemblance*) ressemblance *f* (**with,** à); **(b)** (*monotony*) monotonie *f*.

samey ['seɪmɪ] *adj F* **the architecture here's very s.,** ici l'architecture est très monotone.

samovar ['sæməvɑːr] *n* samovar *m*.

sampan ['sæmpæn] *n Nau* sampan(g) *m*.

sample¹ ['sɑːmp(ə)l] *n Com etc* échantillon *m* (*de tissu, de blé etc*); prise *f*, prélèvement *m* (*de minerai, de sang etc*); dégustation *f* (*de vin*); **a s. of one's work,** un échantillon de son travail; **up to s.,** pareil *ou* conforme à l'échantillon; **to take a s. (test),** faire un prélèvement; **s. book/card,** catalogue *m*/carte *f* d'échantillons.

sample² *vt Com* prendre *ou* prélever des échantillons de; goûter à, déguster (*un vin*); goûter (*un mets etc*); essayer (*un nouveau restaurant etc*).

sampler ['sɑːmplər] *n Sewing* = modèle *m* de broderie (*sur canevas*).

sampling ['sɑːmplɪŋ] *n* prise *f* d'échantillons; dégustation *f* (*d'un mets etc*); *Com Ind* **random s.,** prélèvement *m* d'échantillons au hasard.

samurai ['sæmʊraɪ] *n inv* sam(o)uraï *m*.

sanatorium, *pl* **-iums, -ia** [sænə'tɔːrɪəm, -ɪəmz,-ɪə] *n* sanatorium *m*; *Br Sch* infirmerie *f*.

sanctification [sæŋ(k)tɪfɪ'keɪʃən] *n* sanctification *f*.

sanctified ['sæŋ(k)tɪfaɪd] *adj* (*person*) sanctifié, saint; (*thing*) consacré; **s. air,** air confit (*en dévotion*).

sanctify ['sæŋ(k)tɪfaɪ] *vt* **(a)** sanctifier (*qn, qch*); consacrer (*un jour, un terrain etc*); **(b) sanctified by time,** consacré par le temps.

sanctimonious [sæŋ(k)tɪ'məʊnɪəs] *adj* d'une piété suffisante; (*air*) de petit saint.

sanctimoniously [sæŋ(k)tɪ'məʊnɪəslɪ] *adv* d'un air de petit saint.

sanction¹ ['sæŋ(k)ʃən] *n* **(a)** *Jur* **punitive s.,** sanction pénale; *Pol* **to impose sanctions on a country,** prendre des sanctions contre un pays; **(b)** *Fml* (*consent*) sanction *f*, autorisation *f*, consentement *m*; **without their s.,** sans leur consentement; **(c)** *Hist* (*decree*) sanction *f*, décret *m*.

sanction² *vt* **(a)** *Jur* (*penalise*) sanctionner; attacher des sanctions (pénales) à (*une loi etc*); **(b)** *Jur* (*ratify*) ratifier (*une loi etc*); **(c)** (*authorize*) sanctionner, autoriser (*qch*); **sanctioned by usage,** consacré par l'usage.

sanctity ['sæŋ(k)tɪtɪ] *n Rel* **(a)** (*building*) sainteté *f* (*d'une personne, d'une vie etc*); **(b)** caractère sacré (*d'un terrain, d'un serment etc*); inviolabilité *f* (*de la vie privée etc*).

sanctuary ['sæŋ(k)tj(ʊ)ərɪ] *n Rel* **(a)** (*building*) sanctuaire *m*, temple *m*; *Bible* sanctuaire, Saint *m* des Saints; **(b)** (*refuge*) asile *m* (*sacré*); refuge *m*; **to take s.,** chercher asile; **(c)** refuge *m* (*d'oiseaux*); **wild life s.,** réserve *f* zoologique.

sanctum ['sæŋ(k)təm] *n* **(a)** *Rel* sanctuaire *m*; **(b)** *Fig* (*room etc*) sanctuaire *m*.

Sanctus ['sæŋ(k)təs] *n Rel Mus* sanctus *m*.

sand¹ [sænd] *n* sable *m*; **to build on s.,** bâtir sur le sable; **on the sand(s),** (*on the beach*) sur la plage; (*on sandbank*) sur un banc de sable; *Med* **urinary s.,** sable, gravier *m*; **s. bar,** ensablement *m* (*à l'embouchure d'un fleuve*); **s. castle,** = château *m* de sable (*construit par les enfants sur la plage*); **s. dune,** dune *f*; *Met* **s. spout,** trombe *f* de sable; **s. eel,** lançon *m*, ammodyte *f*; **s. flea,** (*insect*) puce pénétrante, chique *f*; (*crustacean*) (*also* **s. hopper**) puce de mer; **s. martin,** (*bird*) hirondelle *f* de rivage; *Am Golf* **s. trap,** bunker *m*.

sand² *vt* **(a)** (*make smoother*) sabler, sablonner; (*remove paint, varnish from*) décaper au papier de verre; **(b)** (*cover with sand*) sabler (*une allée etc*); répandre du sable sur (*le plancher*).

▶**sand down** *vtsep* **(a)** (*make smooth*) poncer (*du bois*); **(b)** (*remove paint, varnish from*) décaper (*du bois*) au papier de verre.

sandal ['sænd(ə)l] *n* sandale *f*.

sandal(wood) ['sænd(ə)l(wʊd)] *n* (bois *m* de) santal *m*.

sandbag¹ ['sændbæg] *n Mil etc* sac *m* à terre; *Av Nau* sac de lest.

sandbag² *vt* (-gg-) **(a)** *Mil* protéger (*un bâtiment etc*) avec des sacs de terre *ou* de sable; **(b)** (*hit*) assommer (*qn*) (*d'un coup de boudin sur la nuque*).

sandbank ['sændbæŋk] *n* banc *m* de sable.

sandblast¹ ['sændblɑːst] *n* (*in glassmaking, metalwork etc*) jet *m* de sable.

sandblast² *vt* passer (*une surface*) au jet de sable, décaper (*une surface*) au jet de sable, sabler (*une surface*).

sandblasting ['sændblɑːstɪŋ] *n* décapage *m ou* décapement *m* au (jet de) sable, sablage *m* (*d'une surface*).

sandboy ['sændbɔɪ] *n* **as happy as a s.,** gai comme un pinson.

sander ['sændər] *n* ponceuse *f*.

sandglass ['sændglɑːs] *n* sablier *m*.

sanding ['sændɪŋ] *n* **(a)** (*smoothing*) sablage *m*, sablonnage *m*; (*removal of paint, varnish*) décapage au papier de verre; **s. disc,** disque *m* en papier de verre; **(b)** (*spreading of sand*) sablage *m* (*d'une allée etc*).

sanding down *n* (*removal of paint, varnish*) décapage *m* au papier de verre; (*smoothing*) ponçage *m*.

sanding up *n* ensablement *m* (*d'un port etc*).

sandman, *pl* **-men** ['sændmæn, -men] *n* marchand *m* de sable.

sandpaper¹ ['sændpeɪpər] *n* papier *m* de verre; *F* **he's got a chin like s.,** il a le menton qui pique.

sandpaper² *vt* poncer *ou* dresser (*une surface*) au papier de verre.

sandpiper ['sændpaɪpər] *n* (*bird*) bécasseau *m*, chevalier *m*.

sandpit ['sændpɪt] *n* sablière *f*, sablonnière *f*, carrière *f* à sable; tas *m* de sable (*pour enfants*).

sandshoes ['sændʃuːz] *npl Old-fashioned* = espadrilles *fpl*.

sandstone ['sændstəʊn] *n* grès *m*; **s. buildings,** bâtiments en grès.

sandstorm ['sændstɔːm] *n* tempête *f* de sable.

sandwich¹ ['sændwɪtʃ] *n* sandwich *m*, *pl* sandwichs, sandwiches; **to bring/take sandwiches,** apporter/prendre des sandwiches; **ham sandwiches,** sandwichs au jambon; **open s.,** canapé *m*, tranche de pain garnie; *US* **hero** *or* **submarine s.,** gros sandwich coupé dans une baguette; **s. board,** panneau *m* (*que porte l'homme-sandwich*); *Culin* **s. (cake),** génoise fourrée; *Sch* **s. course,** cours *m* intercalaire; **the S. Islands,** les îles *fpl* Sandwich; **s. man,** homme-sandwich, *pl* hommes-sandwiches.

sandwich² *vt* coincer, intercaler (**between,** entre); **to be sandwiched between two people,** être (pris) en sandwich entre deux personnes.

sandy ['sændɪ] *adj* **(a)** (*of earth etc*) sableux, sablonneux; (*path*) sablé; *Nau* **s. bottom,** fond *m* de sable; **(b)** (*hair etc*) roux pâle *inv*, blond roux *inv*.

sane [seɪn] *adj* (*person*) sain d'esprit; (*views, speech etc*) raisonnable, sensé; **to be s.,** avoir toute sa raison.

sanely ['seɪnlɪ] *adv* raisonnablement.

sang *see* **SING**.

sang-froid [sɒŋ'frwɑː] *n* sang-froid *m*.

sanguinary ['sæŋgwɪnərɪ] *adj* (*person*) sanguinaire; (*bataille*) sanglant.

sanguine ['sæŋgwɪn] **1** *adj* (*complexion etc*) d'un rouge sanguin, rubicond; (*temperament*) sanguin; (*person, disposition etc*) confiant, optimiste (**about,** quant à); **to be of a s. disposition,** être porté à l'optimisme. **2** *n Art* (*crayon or drawing*) sanguine *f*.

sanguinely ['sæŋgwɪnlɪ] *adv* (*confidently*) avec confiance; (*optimistically*) avec optimisme.

sanitarium [sænɪ'teərɪəm] *n Am* = **SANATORIUM**.

sanitary ['sænɪt(ə)rɪ] *adj* hygiénique, sanitaire; **s. engineer,** technicien *m* en équipement sanitaire; **s. inspector,** inspecteur *m* de la salubrité publique; **s. towel,** *Am* **s. napkin** *or* **pad,** serviette *f* hygiénique.

sanitation [sænɪ'teɪʃən] *n* système *m* sanitaire.

sanitize ['sænɪtaɪz] *vt esp Am* (*clean*) aseptiser; (*sterilize*) stériliser; *Fig* expurger (*roman etc*).

sanity ['sænɪtɪ] *n* **(a)** (*of person*) santé *f* d'esprit; **there are doubts about his s.,** on se demande s'il est sain d'esprit; **(b)** (*of plan, policy etc*) bon sens.

Sanskrit ['sænskrɪt] *adj & n Ling* sanscrit *m*, sanskrit *m*.

Santa (Claus) ['sæntə(klɔːz)] *n* le Père Noël.

Santa Cruz [sæntə'kruːz] *n* **S. C. Island,** l'île *f* Sainte-Croix.

Santo Domingo ['sæntəʊdɒ'mɪŋgəʊ] *n* Saint-Domingue *m*; (*country*) la République Dominicaine.

sap¹ [sæp] *n* **(a)** (*of plant*) sève *f*; *Fig* (*vigour*) vigueur *f*, sève; **(b)** *F* (*gullible person*) niais, -aise; (*idiot*) andouille *f*.

sap² *n Mil etc* sape *f*.

sap³ *v* (-pp-) **1** *vt* **(a)** *Mil* saper, miner (*des fondations etc*); *Mil* approcher (*d'un endroit*) à la sape; **(b)** *Fig* saper, miner (*les fondements d'une doctrine etc*); **the fever has sapped his strength,** la fièvre l'a miné. **2** *vi Mil* saper, miner.

sapless ['sæplɪs] *adj* (*plant, wood*) sans sève, desséché; (*person, character*) sans vigueur; (*saying, idea*) insipide, fade.

sapling ['sæplɪŋ] *n* **(a)** (*young tree*) jeune arbre *m*; **(b)** *Lit* (*young man*) jeune homme *m*; (*young greyhound*) jeune lévrier *m*.

sapper ['sæpər] *n Mil* sapeur *m*; (*in charge of laying mines*) mineur *m*; *F* **the sappers,** le génie.

sapphic ['sæfɪk] *adj* (*in prosody*) saphique; *Lit (lesbian)* saphique, lesbien; **s. vice,** saphisme *m*.

sapphire ['sæfaɪər] **1** *n* **(a)** (*precious stone*) saphir *m*; **(b)** (*colour*) (couleur *f* de) saphir *m*. **2** *adj* (couleur de) saphir *inv*.

sappiness ['sæpɪnɪs] *n* **(a)** (*of tree etc*) abondance *f* de sève, teneur *f* en sève (*du bois*); **(b)** *Old-fashioned F* (*stupidity*) stupidité *f*, bêtise *f*.

sappy ['sæpɪ] *adj* **(a)** (*tree etc*) plein de sève; (*timber*) vert; **(b)** *Old-fashioned F* (*stupid*) bête, stupide.

saraband ['særəbænd] *n* (*dance*) *& Mus* sarabande *f*.

Saracen ['særəs(ə)n] *Hist* **1** *adj* sarrasin. **2** *n* Sarrasin, -ine.

sarcasm ['sɑːkæz(ə)m] *n* **(a)** (*language*) langage *m ou* ton *m* sarcastique; (*sarcastic nature*) esprit *m* sarcastique; **(b)** (*remark*) **(piece of) s.,** sarcasme *m*; **his constant s.,** ses sarcasmes continuels.

sarcastic [sɑː'kæstɪk] *adj* sarcastique; **s. remark,** sarcasme *m*.

sarcastically [sɑː'kæstɪklɪ] *adv* d'une manière sarcastique.

sarcoma [sɑː'kəʊmə] *n Med* sarcome *m*.

sarcophagus, *pl* **-phagi** [sɑː'kɒfəgəs, -fədʒaɪ] *n* sarcophage *m*.

sardine [sɑː'diːn] *n* (*fish*) sardine *f*; **the passengers were packed in like sardines,** les passagers étaient serrés comme des sardines; **s. boat,** sardinier *m*.

Sardinia [sɑː'dɪnɪə] *n* Sardaigne *f*.

Sardinian [sɑː'dɪnɪən] **1** *adj* sarde. **2** *n* **(a)** Sarde *mf*; **(b)** *Ling* sarde *m*.

sardonic [sɑː'dɒnɪk] *adj* (*expression, rire*) sardonique.

sardonically [sɑː'dɒnɪklɪ] *adv* d'une manière sardonique, sardoniquement.

sarge [sɑːdʒ] *n F Mil Av* sergent *m*.

sari ['sɑːrɪ] *n* (*garment*) sari *m*.

sarong [sə'rɒŋ] *n* (*garment*) sarong *m*.

sarsaparilla [sɑːsəpə'rɪlə] *n* salsepareille *f*.

sartorial [sɑː'tɔːrɪəl] *adj* (*trade*) de tailleur; **s. elegance,** élégance *f* vestimentaire.

SAS [eseɪ'es] *n Br Mil* (*abbr* **special air service**) ≈ GIGN *m*.

sash¹ [sæʃ] *n* (*clothing*) (*on dress*) large ceinture *f* à nœud bouffant; écharpe *f*, ceinture (*d'étoffe*) (*portée par les officiers*).

sash² *n Constr* (*of window*) châssis *m* mobile, cadre *m* (*d'une fenêtre à guillotine*); **s. window,** fenêtre *f* à guillotine.

sashay ['sæʃeɪ] *vi Am F* **he sashayed across to the bar,** (*walked affectedly*) il s'est approché du bar avec une nonchalance affectée; **I'll just s. down to Joe's place,** (*go*) je vais juste faire un tour chez Joe.

sashcord ['sæʃkɔːd] *n* corde *f* (d'une fenêtre à guillotine).

Sask *abbr* **Saskatchewan**.

sass [sæs] *vt US Sl* se payer la tête de (*qn*); (*be insolent to*) faire l'insolent avec (*qn*).

Sassenach ['sæsənæk] *n Scot* Anglais, -aise.

sassy ['sæsɪ] *adj US Sl* effronté, qui a du culot.

sat *see* **SIT²**.

Satan ['seɪt(ə)n] *n* Satan *m*.

satanic [sə'tænɪk] *adj* satanique, diabolique.

satanically [sə'tænɪklɪ] *adv* sataniquement,

diaboliquement.

satanism ['seɪtənɪz(ə)m] *n* satanisme *m*.

satanist ['seɪtənɪst] *n* sataniste *mf*.

satchel ['sætʃəl] *n* sacoche *f*; *Sch* cartable *m*.

sate [seɪt] *vt* **(a)** assouvir (*sa faim, ses passions etc*); rassasier (*qn, sa faim*); **(b)** = **SATIATE**.

sateen [sə'tiːn] *n Tex* satinette *f*, satin *m* de coton.

satellite ['sætəlaɪt] *n* **(a)** *Astron etc* satellite *m*; **artificial s.,** satellite artificiel; **manned/unmanned s.,** satellite habité/non habité; **(tele)communications s.,** satellite de télécommunications; **meteorological** *or* **weather s.,** satellite météorologique; *TV* **s. dish,** antenne *f* de télévision par satellite; **s. picture,** *Phot* photo prise par satellite; *Met* animation *f* satellite; *TV* **s. television,** télévision *f* par satellite; **(b) s. (state),** (état *m*) satellite *m*; **s. (town),** ville *f* satellite.

satiate ['seɪʃɪeɪt] *vt* rassasier jusqu'au dégoût (**with,** de).

satiated ['seɪʃɪeɪtɪd] *adj* rassasié (*de manger etc*); gorgé (*de plaisirs etc*).

satiation [seɪʃɪ'eɪʃən] *n* **(a)** (*process*) rassasiement *m*; **(b)** (*state*) satiété *f*.

satiety [sə'taɪɪtɪ] *n* satiété *f*; **to s.,** (*manger*) jusqu'à plus faim, à satiété; (*goûter un plaisir*) jusqu'à satiété.

satin ['sætɪn] *n Tex* satin *m*; **s. finish,** apprêt satiné (*du papier etc*); **s. flower,** stellaire *f*; **s. paper,** papier satiné.

satinette [sætɪ'net] *n Tex* satinette *f*.

satinwood ['sætɪnwʊd] *n* bois *m* de citronnier.

satire ['sætaɪər] *n* satire *f*; **a s. on sth,** une satire de qch.

satiric(al) [sə'tɪrɪk, -ɪk(ə)l] *adj* satirique.

satirically [sə'tɪrɪklɪ] *adv* satiriquement.

satirist ['sætɪrɪst] *n* (*auteur, écrivain*) satirique *m*.

satirize ['sætɪraɪz] *vt* faire la satire de (*qch*); (*in literature*) satiriser.

satisfaction [sætɪs'fækʃən] *n* **(a)** satisfaction *f*, contentement *m* (**at, with,** de); **to have the s. of doing sth,** avoir la satisfaction de faire qch; **it gives me great s. to know that ...,** je suis très heureux d'apprendre que ...; **to one's complete s.,** à sa satisfaction totale; *Com* **s. guaranteed,** (*on label*) satisfaction garantie; **(b)** acquittement *m*, paiement *m* (*d'une dette*); désintéressement *m* (*d'un créancier*); accomplissement *m* (*d'une condition*); réparation *f*, expiation *f* (*d'une offense*); assouvissement *m* (*de la faim, d'une passion*); **to demand s. for an insult,** demander raison d'un affront.

satisfactorily [sætɪs'fækt(ə)rɪlɪ] *adv* d'une manière *ou* de façon satisfaisante.

satisfactory [sætɪs'fækt(ə)rɪ] *adj* **(a)** satisfaisant; (*élève*) qui donne satisfaction; **the result is not very s.,** le résultat laisse à désirer; **to bring negotiations to a s. conclusion,** mener à bien des négociations; **(b)** *Rel* expiatoire.

satisfied ['sætɪsfaɪd] *adj* (*client etc*) content, satisfait.

satisfy ['sætɪsfaɪ] *vt* **(a)** (*make happy with*) satisfaire, contenter (*qn*); **to be satisfied with sth,** se contenter de qch; *Iron* **not satisfied with that she then broke the other chair,** comme ça ne lui suffisait pas, elle a cassé l'autre chaise; *Sch* **to s. the examiners,** être reçu à un examen; **(in order) to s. your curiosity,** pour satisfaire votre curiosité; **(b)** (*convince*) convaincre, assurer, satisfaire (*qn*); **I am satisfied that he was telling the truth,** je suis convaincu qu'il disait la vérité; **(c)** payer, liquider (*une dette*); exécuter (*une promesse*); satisfaire à (*une réclamation*); remplir (*une condition*); désintéresser (*ses créanciers*); *Math* satisfaire à (*une équation*); (*for insult*) satisfaire (*qn*); faire réparation à, satisfaire à (*l'honneur*).

satsuma [sæt'suːmə] *n* **s. (orange),** satsuma *f*.

saturate ['sætʃəreɪt] *vt* **(a)** (*soak*) imprégner, saturer, tremper (**with,** de); **to become saturated with sth,** s'imprégner de qch; **(b)** *Ch Phys* saturer (*une solution etc*); *Com* **to s. the market,** saturer le marché.

saturated ['sætʃəreɪtɪd] *adj* **(a)** (*terrain, vêtement etc*) trempé; **(b)** *Ch Phys* (*solution, compound etc*) saturé, intense; **s. fat,** graisse saturée; **(c)** (*colour*) saturé, intense.

saturation [sætʃə'reɪʃən] *n* imprégnation *f*; *Ch Phys* saturation *f*; *Mil* **s. bombing,** bombardement *m* en masse; **s. point,** point *m* de saturation; *Com* **the market has reached s. point,** le marché est saturé, le marché est arrivé à saturation.

Saturday ['sætədɪ] *n* samedi *m*; **he's coming on S.,** il vient samedi; **he comes on Saturdays,** il vient le samedi; **he comes every S.,** il vient tous les samedis.

Saturn ['sætɜːn] *n Astron Myth* Saturne *m*.

saturnine ['sætənaɪn] *adj* **(a)** (*person*) taciturne, sombre; **(b)** *Med Arch* saturnin.

satyr ['sætər] *n Myth etc* satyre *m*.

sauce [sɔːs] *n* **(a)** *Culin* sauce *f*; (*seasoning*) assaisonnement *m*; (*condiment*) condiment *m*; **tomato s.,** sauce tomate; **white s.,** sauce béchamel; **caper s.,** sauce aux câpres; *Prov* **what's s. for the goose is s. for the gander,** ce qui est bon pour l'un l'est aussi pour l'autre; **(b)** *F* (*impudence*) impertinence *f*; **what s.!, you've got a s.!,** quel toupet!, quel culot!

saucepan ['sɔːspən] *n* casserole *f*; **double s.,** bain-marie *m, pl* bains-marie; **s. lid,** couvercle *m* de casserole.

saucer ['sɔːsər] *n* soucoupe *f*; *F* **flying s.,** soucoupe volante; *F* **eyes like saucers,** yeux en forme de soucoupes.

saucily ['sɔːsɪlɪ] *adv* impertinemment, effrontément, d'un ton *ou* d'un air effronté; (*in risqué manner*) d'un air coquin.

sauciness ['sɔːsɪnɪs] *n F* (*impertinence*) impertinence *f*; (*of joke, nightdress etc*) côté coquin; *Old-fashioned* (*of hat etc*) coquetterie *f*.

saucy ['sɔːsɪ] *adj F* (*impertinent*) impertinent, effronté; (*of joke, nightdress etc*) coquin; *Old-fashioned* **s. little hat,** petit chapeau coquet.

Saudi ['saʊdɪ] **1** *adj* séoudite, saoudite; **S. Arabia,** Arabie *f* séoudite *ou* saoudite; **S. Arabian,** saoudien, -ienne. **2** *n* **(a) S. (Arabian),** Saoudien, -ienne; **(b)** (*country*) Arabie *f* séoudite.

sauerkraut ['saʊəkraʊt] *n Culin* choucroute *f*.

sauna ['saʊnə, 'sɔː-] *n* sauna *m*.

saunter¹ ['sɔːntər] *n* flânerie *f*; **at a s.,** (*arriver*) tout doucement.

saunter² *vi* **to s. (along),** flâner; (*go for a walk*) se balader; **to s. along** *or* **down the street,** descendre la rue en flânant; **she sauntered past as if nothing had happened,** elle est passée d'un pas tranquille comme s'il ne s'était rien passé.

saurian ['sɔːrɪən] *adj & n* (*reptile*) saurien *m*.

sausage ['sɒsɪdʒ] *n* **(a)** *Culin* (*fresh*) saucisse *f*; (*preserved, hard, dry*) saucisson *m*; **s. roll,** = friand *m*; **s. skin,** peau *f* à saucisses, boyau *m*; *Br F* **not a s.,** nib de nib, que dalle; **(b)** *F* **s. dog,** teckel *m*; **(c)** *F* **you silly old s. you!,** que tu es bête!

sausagemeat ['sɒsɪdʒmiːt] *n* chair *f* à saucisse.

sauté¹ ['səʊteɪ] *adj & n Culin* sauté *m*; **s. potatoes,** pommes de terre sautées.

sauté² *vt Culin* (faire) sauter (*des pommes de terre*).

savage¹ ['sævɪdʒ] **1** *adj* (*people, custom etc*) sauvage, barbare; (*animal, coup, critique*) féroce; (*coup*) brutal, -aux; *F* (*person*) en rage, en colère; **to make a s. attack on s.o.,** s'attaquer férocement à qn. **2** *n* sauvage *mf*.

savage² *vt* (*of animal*) attaquer, mordre (*qn, les autres bêtes*); *F* (*of person*) attaquer (*qn*) bec et ongles; (*of critics*) éreinter (*qn, une pièce*).

savagely ['sævɪdʒlɪ] *adv* sauvagement, férocement.

savageness ['sævɪdʒnɪs], **savagery** ['sævɪdʒ(ə)rɪ] *n* sauvagerie *f*, barbarie *f* (*d'une race, d'une coutume etc*); férocité *f* (*d'un animal, d'un coup, d'un critique*); brutalité *f* (*d'un coup*).

savanna(h) [sə'vænə] *n Geog* savane *f*.

save¹ [seɪv] *n* **(a)** *F* économie *f*; **a great s. in heating,** une grande économie de chauffage; **(b)** *Fb* arrêt *m* (*du ballon*) (*par le gardien*).

save² **1** *vt* **(a)** sauver (*qn, une bête*); **to s. s.o.'s life,** sauver la vie à *ou* de qn; **the doctors could not s. him,** les médecins n'ont pas pu le sauver; **to s. s.o. from falling,** empêcher qn de tomber; **this saved us from financial disaster,** ça nous a sauvé d'une catastrophe financière; *Fb etc* **to s. a goal,** arrêter le ballon; *Sp* **to s. the game,** éviter la défaite; *Rel* **to s. one's soul,** sauver son âme; **to s. the situation,** sauver la situation; **to s. sth from a fire,** récupérer qch des décombres d'un incendie; **(God) s. me from my friends!,** Dieu me protège contre mes amis!; **God save the King/the Queen!,** Dieu sauve le Roi/la Reine!;

(b) (*keep for future*) mettre (*qch*) de côté; économiser, épargner, mettre de côté (*de l'argent*); **I'm saving this one for later,** je garde celui-ci pour plus tard; **to s. oneself for sth,** se réserver pour qch; **s. a dance for me,** réservez-moi une danse;

(c) (*not waste*) ménager (*ses vêtements etc*); économiser (*le travail etc*); éviter (*une dépense, de la peine etc*); ménager (*de l'espace*); **to s. time,** gagner du temps; **I am saving my strength,** je me ménage, je ménage mes forces; **I might as well have saved my breath,** j'ai eu beau parler, ça n'a servi à rien; **I saved £10 by buying it there,** j'ai économisé dix livres en l'achetant là; **s. pounds on washing machines,** économisez sur les machines à laver;

(d) (*spare*) **to s. s.o. sth,** éviter *ou* épargner qch à qn; **this has saved him a great deal of expense/trouble,** cela lui a évité beaucoup de dépense/peine; **this will s. us having to do it again,** ça nous évitera de devoir le refaire; **to s. s.o. the trouble of doing sth,** épargner à qn la peine de faire qch; **to s. s.o. from sth,** épargner qch à qn; **to s. s.o. from doing sth,** épargner à qn la peine de faire qch;

(e) *Comptr* sauvegarder; **to s. sth to disk,** sauvegarder qch sur une disquette.

2 *vi* (*save money*) économiser, épargner son argent; **I've never been able to s.,** je n'ai jamais pu économiser; **they are saving for their holiday/a new car,** ils économisent pour leurs vacances/pour acheter une voiture neuve; **s. on heating costs by insulating your house,** économisez sur vos frais de chauffage en isolant votre maison.

save³ 1 *prep Arch & Lit* sauf, excepté, à l'exception de. **2** *conj* **s. that ...,** sauf que ..., excepté que ... .

►save up 1 *vi* (*save money*) économiser (**for,** pour); **we're saving up to go to Canada/buy a new fridge,** nous économisons pour aller au Canada/pour acheter un réfrigérateur. **2** *vtsep* (*save, collect*) économiser, mettre de côté (*de l'argent etc*).

save-as-you-earn ['seɪvəzjuː'ɜːn] *adj Br Fin* **s.-as-y.-e. scheme,** plan *m* d'épargne à contributions mensuelles produisant des intérêts exonérés d'impôts.

saveloy ['sævəlɔɪ] *n Culin* cervelas *m*.

saver ['seɪvər] *n* **(a)** (*rescuer*) sauveur *m*, libérateur, -trice (*de sa patrie etc*); sauveteur *m* (*de vie, de biens*); **(b)** (*device*) appareil permettant d'économiser; **(c)** (*person who saves money*) épargnant, -ante.

saving¹ ['seɪvɪŋ] **1** *adj* **(a)** (*that saves*) qui sauve; (*that protects*) qui protège;

(b) (*redeeming*) **her** *or* **its** *etc* **s. grace,** ce qui la *ou* le *etc* rachète.

2 *n* **(a)** (*rescue*) sauvetage *m*; (*protection*) protection *f* (*de qn, qch*); salut *m* (*de qn, des âmes, des vies*); **this was the s. of him,** cela a été son salut;

(b) (*act of saving money*) économie *f*, épargne *f*; **savings,** économies, *Econ* dépôts *mpl* d'épargne; **to live on one's savings,** vivre de ses épargnes *ou* économies; **to make savings,** faire des économies; **savings account,** compte *m* de dépôt; *US* **savings and loan association,** = coopérative *ou* société immobilière; **(National) Savings Bank,** ≈ Caisse *f* (Nationale) d'Épargne; **(National) savings certificate,** ≈ bon *m* d'Épargne.

saving² 1 *prep & conj Arch* = **SAVE³**. **2** *prep* sauf; **s. your presence,** sauf votre respect.

saviour, *US* **savior** ['seɪvjər] *n* sauveur *m*; *Rel* **Our S.,** Notre Sauveur.

savory ['seɪvərɪ] *n* (*plant*) & *Culin* sarriette *f*.

savour¹, *US* **savor** ['seɪvər] *n* saveur *f*, goût *m* (*d'un mets etc*).

savour², *US* **savor 1** *vt* (*of person*) savourer (*un mets, son succès, l'instant présent etc*). **2** *vi* (*of thing*) **to s. of sth,** (*make suspect*) sentir qch; (*remind of*) tenir de qch.

savoury, *US* **savory** ['seɪvərɪ] **1** *adj* **(a)** (*appetizing*) (*goût, mets*) savoureux, appétissant; *F* **he looked even less s. than the majority of tramps,** il avait l'air encore plus répugnant que la plupart des clochards; **(b)** *Culin* (*not sweet*) (*mets*) piquant, salé; **s. omelette,** omelette salée. **2** *n* entremets non sucré.

Savoy [sə'vɔɪ] *n* **(a)** *Geog* Savoie *f*; **(b) s. (cabbage),** chou frisé de Milan, *pl* choux.

savvy¹ ['sævɪ] *n Sl* jugeote *f*.

savvy² *vt Sl* comprendre; **s.?,** tu piges?

saw¹ [sɔː] *n* (*tool*) scie *f*; **metal s.,** scie à métaux; **circular s.,** scie circulaire; **s. blade,** lame *f* de scie; **s. cut,** trait *m* de scie; **s. tooth,** dent *f* de scie; **s.-tooth(ed) roof,** (toit *m* en) shed *m*.

saw² *vt* (*pt* **sawed**; *pp* **sawn, sawed**) scier (*le bois etc*); sciotter (*la pierre, le marbre*).

saw³ *n* (*saying*) adage *m*, proverbe *m*, dicton *m*.

saw⁴ *see* **SEE¹**.

►saw off *vtsep* couper *ou* enlever (*qch*) à la scie.

►saw up *vtsep* débiter (*du bois*).

sawbones ['sɔːbəʊnz] *n Old-fashioned F* chirurgien *m*, carabin *m*.

sawbuck ['sɔːbʌk] *n Am* **(a)** = **SAWHORSE**; **(b)** *F* (*ten-dollar bill*) billet *m* de dix dollars.

sawdust ['sɔːdʌst] *n* sciure *f* (de bois).

sawfish ['sɔːfɪʃ] *n* (*fish*) (poisson *m*) scie *f*.

sawhorse ['sɔːhɔːs] *n Carp* chevalet *m* de sciage, chèvre *f*.

sawing ['sɔːɪŋ] *n* sciage *m* (*du bois*).

sawing up *n* débitage *m* (*du bois*).

sawmill ['sɔːmɪl] *n* scierie *f*.

sawn-off ['sɔːnɒf] *adj* **s.-o. shotgun,** carabine *f* à canon *ou* fusil scié.

sawyer ['sɔːjər] *n* scieur *m* (de long).

sax [sæks] *n Mus F* saxo(phone) *m*; **s. player,** saxophoniste *mf*, joueur *ou* joueuse de saxophone.

saxe [sæks] *adj & n* **s. blue,** bleu *m* de Saxe.

saxifrage ['sæksɪfreɪdʒ] *n* (*plant*) saxifrage *f*.

Saxon ['sæks(ə)n] **1** *adj Geog etc* saxon; **S. architecture,** architecture anglaise préromane. **2** *n* **(a)** Saxon, -onne; **(b)** *Ling* saxon *m*.

Saxony ['sæksənɪ] *n* Saxe *f*.

saxophone ['sæksəfəʊn] *n Mus* saxophone *m*.

saxophonist [sæk'sɒfənɪst] *n Mus* saxophoniste *mf*.

say¹ [seɪ] *n* **to have one's s.,** dire son mot, dire ce qu'on a à dire; **let me have my s.,** laissez-moi parler; **I have no s. in the matter,** je n'ai pas voix au chapitre.

say² *v* (*pt & pp* **said** [sed], *3rd sing pr* **says** [sez]) **1** *vt* **(a)** (*utter*) dire; **to s. sth to s.o.,** dire qch à qn; **to s. a word,** dire un mot; **you have only to s. the word,** vous n'avez qu'à le dire; **it's for him/not for him to s.,** c'est/ce n'est pas à lui de décider; *Tel* **who shall I s. is calling?,** c'est de la part de qui?; **to s. sth again,** répéter qch, redire qch; **why he did it I can't** *or* **couldn't s.,** (*I have no idea*) pourquoi il l'a fait, je ne sais pas *ou* je n'en sais rien; **I can't s.,** (*I'm not allowed to tell you*) je ne peux pas le dire; **there's no saying what might happen if ...,** on ne sait pas ce qui pourrait se passer si ...; **it goes without saying that ...,** il va de soi *ou* cela va sans dire que ...; **what did you s.?,** (*repeat what you said*) pardon?, qu'avez-vous dit?; **whatever he may s.,** quoi qu'il en dise; **to s. yes/no,** dire (que) oui/(que) non; *F* **I wouldn't s. no to a glass of beer,** je boirais bien *ou* volontiers un verre de bière; **what do you s. to a drink?,** si on prenait un verre?; **'Good morning', she said,** 'bonjour', dit-elle; **he said that you were here,** il a dit que vous étiez ici; **as I said in my letter,** comme je l'ai dit dans ma lettre; **the Bible says** *or* **it says in the Bible that ...,** comme on lit dans la Bible ...; **it says in the newspaper that ...,** on dit dans le journal que ...; **the church clock says ten,** le cadran de l'église marque dix heures; **what does your watch s.?,** quelle heure est-il à ta montre?; **let it be said,** soit dit en passant; **you don't mean to s. he's 86,** vous n'allez pas me dire qu'il a 86 ans; **one might as well s. ...,** autant dire ...; **I must s. ...,** j'avoue ..., je dois dire ...; **it has to** *or* **must be said,** il faut le dire; **that is to s.,** c'est-à-dire; **have you said anything about it to him?,** lui en avez-vous parlé?; **the less said the better, least said soonest mended,** moins nous parlerons, mieux cela vaudra; **he knows no English, to s. nothing of French,** il ne sait pas l'anglais, sans parler du français; **he has very little to s. for himself,** il est peu communicatif; **what have you to s. for yourself?,** eh bien, expliquez-vous!; **there is little/much to be said for beginning now,** on n'a pas/a intérêt à commencer dès maintenant; **there's a lot to be said for it,** c'est une bonne idée; **you're honest, I'll s. that for you,** je dirais en votre faveur que vous êtes honnête; **the way you dress says something about you as a person,** la manière dont on s'habille est très révélatrice du genre de personne que l'on est; **don't s. you've forgotten already!,** ne dis pas que tu as déjà oublié!; *F* **you don't s. (so)!,** pas possible!, vraiment?, ça alors!; **you can s. that again!, you said it!,** vous l'avez dit!, comme vous dites!; **need I s. more?,** est-il besoin d'en dire davantage?; **they s. that ..., it is said that ...,** on dit que ..., on prétend que ...; **I've heard it said that ...,** j'ai entendu dire que ...; **he is said to be rich, they s. he is rich,** on le dit riche, on dit qu'il est riche; **what do you s., Amanda? — should we go?,** qu'en penses-tu Amanda — on y va?; **what d'you s. to that?,** qu'en dites-vous *ou* pensez-vous?; **anyone would s. that he was asleep,** on dirait qu'il dort; **is he tall? — I wouldn't s. that,** est-ce qu'il est grand? — je n'irais pas jusqu'à dire ça; **on the whole I should s. not,** dans l'ensemble, je ne crois pas *ou* je crois que non; **it is difficult to s. (when/where/which/***etc***),** il est difficile de dire *ou* on ne sait pas (quand/où/quel/*etc*); **didn't I s. so!,** je vous l'avais bien dit!; **I should s. so!,** et comment donc!; **what did I s.?,** qu'est-ce que j'avais dit?; **let us** *or* **shall we** *or* **shall I s.,** disons; **if I had, s., £100,000 to spend,** si j'avais, mettons *ou* disons 100000 livres à dépenser; **I should s. not!,** jamais de la vie!; **she didn't accept their offer — I should s. not!,** elle n'a pas accepté leur offre — il ne manquerait plus que ça!;

(b) dire, réciter (*une prière etc*); faire (*ses prières*); **to s. mass,** dire la messe; **to s. grace,** dire le bénédicité.

2 *vi* **I'm not saying,** je ne dis rien; *Sl* **says you!,** que tu dis!; **I mean to s.!,** tout de même!, quand même!; **as they s., as people s.,** comme on dit; **as one might s.,** comme qui dirait; **s., I've got an idea,** écoutez donc, j'ai une idée; *Old-fashioned Br* **I s.!,** *Am* **s.!,** (*exclamatory*) dites donc!; *Old-fashioned Br* **I s.!,** (*expressing surprise*) pas possible!, fichtre!; **I'll s.!,** et comment donc!

SAYE ['cseɪwaɪː] *n Br Fin abbr* **save as you earn.**

saying ['seɪɪŋ] *n* adage *m*, proverbe *m*, dicton *m*; **as the s. goes,** (*according to the proverb*) comme dit le proverbe; (*so people say*) comme on dit.

say-so ['seɪsəʊ] *n F* permission *f*; **I can't do it without her s.-so,** je ne peux pas le faire sans sa permission.

SC [es'siː] (*abbr* **South Carolina**) Caroline *f* du Sud.

scab¹ [skæb] *n* **(a)** (*on wound*) croûte *f*; **(b)** *Vet* (*disease*) gale *f*; **(c)** *Ind Sl* (*person*) renard *m*, jaune *m*; **s. miner/etc,** mineur *m/etc* qui ne fait pas grève.

scab² *vi* (-bb-) **(a)** (*of wound*) former une croûte; **(b)** *Ind Sl* (*replace strikers*) supplanter les grévistes; (*betray workmates*) trahir ses camarades.

►**scab over** *vi* = **SCAB² (a)**.

scabbard ['skæbəd] *n* fourreau *m* (*d'une épée*); gaine *f* (*d'un poignard etc*).

scabby ['skæbɪ] *adj* **(a)** *Vet* (*sheep etc*) galeux; **(b)** (*sore etc*) croûteux, scabieux.

scabies ['skeɪbiːz] *n Med* gale *f*.

scabious ['skeɪbɪəs] *n* (*plant*) scabieuse *f*.

scabrous ['skeɪbrəs] *adj* **(a)** (*surface etc*) rugueux, raboteux; **(b)** (*topic, tale etc*) scabreux, risqué.

scads [skædz] *npl F* grande quantité (**of,** de).

scaffold ['skæf(ə)ld] *n* **(a)** échafaud *m* (*pour exécutions*); **to go to the s.,** monter à *ou* sur l'échafaud; **(b)** *Constr* échafaudage *m*.

scaffolding ['skæfəldɪŋ] *n* échafaudage *m*.

scalawag ['skæləwæg] *n esp Am* = **SCALLYWAG.**

scald¹ [skɔːld] *n* brûlure *f* (*sur la main etc*).

scald² *vt* **(a)** (*burn*) échauder, ébouillanter (*la main etc*); **careful you don't s. yourself,** attention de ne pas t'ébouillanter; **(b)** *Culin* échauder (*un porc etc*); blanchir (*un chou etc*); échauder, ébouillanter (*des fruits etc pour les peler*); faire chauffer (*le lait etc*) juste au-dessous du point d'ébullition; échauder, ébouillanter (*un récipient*).

scalding ['skɔːldɪŋ] **1** *adj* **s. (hot),** (*liquid*) brûlant, tout bouillant; *Lit* **s. tears,** larmes brûlantes. **2** *n* **(a)** (*burning*) échaudage *m*, ébouillantage *m*; **(b)** *Culin* blanchiment *m* (*de la viande etc*); ébouillantage *m* (*de légumes etc*); cuisson *f* (*du lait etc*) juste au-dessous du point d'ébullition.

scale¹ [skeɪl] *n* **(a)** (*on fish, reptile, bud etc*) écaille *f*; *Med* (*on skin*) écaille, squame *f*; **(b)** (*in metalworking*) barbure *f* (*de pièce coulée*); **scale(s),** écailles *fpl* de fer; **(c)** (*incrustation*) battitures *fpl*, incrustation *f*, dépôt *m*; tartre *m* (*des dents*); (*on copper, iron etc*) oxyde *m*; **boiler s.,** tartre; **s. remover,** détartrant *m*.

scale² **1** *vt* écailler (*un poisson*); détartrer (*les dents*); désincruster, détartrer (*une chaudière, un tube*). **2** *vi* **(a)** écailler; (*of skin*) se desquamer; (*of paint*) s'effeuiller; (*of wall, ceiling etc*) se déplâtrer; **(b)** (*become encrusted*) (*of boiler etc*) s'entartrer, s'incruster.

scale³ *n* (*for weighing*) **s. (pan),** plateau *m*, plat *m* (de balance); (*deep*) bassin *m*; **to tip** *or* **turn the scale(s) at 100 kilos,** peser un peu plus de 100 kilos; **to turn the scale(s),** emporter *ou* faire pencher la balance; **(pair of) scales,** balance *f*; **platform scales,** bascule *f*; **letter scales,** pèse-lettres *m inv*; **bathroom scales,** pèse-personne *m*, *pl* pèse-personnes; **baby scales,** pèse-bébé *m*, *pl* pèse-bébés; *Astron* **the Scales,** la Balance.

scale⁴ *vi* (*weigh*) **to s. six kilos,** peser six kilos.

scale⁵ *n* **(a)** échelle *f* (*de thermomètre, de baromètre etc*); graduation(s) *f(pl)* (*d'un thermomètre, d'un système numérique etc*); série *f* (*de nombres etc*); échelle, barème *m* (*de traitements*); échelle, gamme *f* (*de prix*); **sliding s.,** échelle mobile (*des salaires, des prix*); **sliding s. tariff,** tarif dégressif; **at the top of the (social) s.,** en haut *ou* au sommet de l'échelle (sociale);

(b) (*dial*) cadran gradué; (*rule*) règle *f* (*divisée*);

(c) échelle *f* (*d'une carte etc*); **small/large-s. map,** carte à petite/à grande échelle; **to draw sth to s.,** dessiner qch à l'échelle; **to be out of/in s.,** être/ne pas être à l'échelle; **s. model,** maquette *f*, modèle réduit; **on a national s.,** à l'échelle nationale; **the s. of the disaster,** l'étendue *f* du sinistre;

(d) *Mus* gamme *f*; échelle *f*, gamme (*de couleurs*); **major/minor s.,** gamme majeure/mineure; **to practise scales,** faire des gammes.

scale⁶ *vt* (*climb*) escalader (*un mur etc*); faire l'ascension (*d'une montagne*).

►**scale down** *vtsep* **(a)** (*draw to smaller scale*) établir (*un dessin*) à une échelle réduite; **(b)** (*reduce according to sliding scale*) réduire (*des prix etc*) selon une échelle mobile; **to s. down production,** ralentir la production.

►**scale up** *vtsep* (*increase according to sliding scale*) augmenter (*des prix etc*) selon une échelle mobile.

scaling¹ ['skeɪlɪŋ] *n* **(a)** (*removal of scales*) écaillage *m* (*d'un poisson etc*); **(b)** (*removal of incrustation*) détartrage *m* (*des dents*); désincrustation *f*, détartrage (*d'une chaudière, des tubes*); **(c)** (*process of incrustation*) formation *f* du tartre; entartrage *m* (*d'une chaudière*).

scaling² *n* **(a)** (*climbing*) escalade *f*; **(b)** (*grading*) graduation *f* (*des prix, des salaires etc*).

scaling down *n* réduction *f* à l'échelle.

scaling up *n* augmentation *f* à l'échelle.

scallion ['skæljən] *n Bot* échalote *f*.

scallop¹ ['skɒləp, 'skæl-] *n* **(a)** (*mollusc*) **s. (shell),** peigne *m*, coquille *f* Saint-Jacques; *Culin* coquille Saint-Jacques; *Culin* escalope *f* (*de veau etc*); **(b)** *Sewing etc* feston *m*, dentelure *f*.

scallop² *vt* **(a)** *Culin* faire cuire (*du poisson etc*) en coquille(s); **(b)** *Sewing* festonner, découper; **scalloped handkerchief,** mouchoir festonné.

scallywag ['skælɪwæg] *n F* propre à rien *m*; **little s.,** (*child*) petit coquin.

scalp¹ [skælp] *n* **(a)** *Anat* cuir chevelu (*de la tête*); **(b)** (*war trophy*) scalp(e) *m*.

scalp² *vt* (*in war*) scalper (*un ennemi*).

scalpel ['skælp(ə)l] *n Surg* scalpel *m*.

scaly ['skeɪlɪ] *adj* (*fish, skin etc*) écailleux, squameux; (*slate etc*) écailleux; (*metal*) paillé, lamelleux, lamellé; (*boiler*) tartreux.

scam [skæm] *n Sl* arnaque *f*.

scamp¹ [skæmp] *n* fripouille *f*; *F* **little s.,** (*child*) petit coquin.

scamp² *vt F* bâcler, bousiller (*un travail*).

scamper¹ ['skæmpər] *n* (*playful run*) course *f* folâtre *ou* allègre; (*quick run*) course rapide.

scamper² *vi* (*run playfully*) courir allégrement *ou* d'une manière folâtre.

►**scamper away, scamper off** *vi* (*run away*) détaler, décamper.

scampi ['skæmpɪ] *n sing or pl Culin* scampi *mpl*.

scan¹ [skæn] *n* **(a)** (*look*) regard scrutateur; **(b)** *Electron Rad etc* balayage *m*; **(c)** *Med* examen *m* au scanne(u)r; (*in pregnancy*) échographie *f*; **to have a s.,** se faire faire un examen au scanner *ou* une échographie.

scan² *v* (-nn-) **1** *vt* **(a)** (*in prosody*) scander, mesurer (*des vers*); **(b)** (*examine closely*) examiner minutieusement; sonder, scruter (*l'horizon*); (*glance at, over*) jeter un coup d'œil sur (*qch*); feuilleter, parcourir (*un livre etc*); *Electron Rad etc* balayer, explorer (*l'image à transmettre, la piste sonore*); *Med* examiner par scanne(u)r; (*in pregnancy*) examiner par échographie, *Comptr* passer (*un texte*) au scanne(u)r. **2** *vi* **this line doesn't s.,** ce vers est faux.

►**scan in** *vtsep Comptr* insérer (*des graphiques*) par scanne(u)r.

scandal ['skænd(ə)l] *n* **(a)** scandale *m*; **it's a s.,** c'est un scandale; **to create a s.,** faire un scandale, causer du scandale; **(b)** (*gossip*) médisance *f*; **(c)** *Jur* allégations *fpl* diffamatoires.

scandalize ['skændəlaɪz] *vt* scandaliser, choquer, offusquer (*qn*).

scandalmonger ['skænd(ə)lmʌŋgər] *n* cancanier, -ière; colporteur, -euse d'histoires scandaleuses.

scandalous ['skændələs] *adj* **(a)** (*conduct, event, prices etc*) scandaleux; **it's s.!,** c'est scandaleux!; **(b)** *Jur* (*statement, writing*) diffamatoire, calomnieux.

scandalously ['skændələslɪ] *adv* scandaleusement.

Scandinavia [skændɪ'neɪvɪə] *n* Scandinavie *f*.

Scandinavian [skændɪ'neɪvɪən] **1** *adj* scandinave. **2** *n* Scandinave *mf*.

scanner ['skænər] *n Med Comptr* scanne(u)r *m*; **radar s.,** explorateur *m ou* balayeur *m* radar; (*aerial*) antenne *f* (de) radar.

scanning ['skænɪŋ] *n* **(a)** (*in prosody*) scansion *f* (*de vers*); **(b)** (*close examination*) examen minutieux; *Electron Rad etc* balayage *m*, exploration *f* (*de l'image à transmettre, de la piste sonore*); *Comptr* passage *m* au scanne(u)r; **radar s.,** exploration *ou* balayage radar.

scansion ['skænʃən] *n* (*in prosody*) scansion *f*.

scant [skænt] *adj* insuffisant, peu abondant; (*végétation*) pauvre; **they paid s. regard to what he said,** ils ont à peine fait attention à ce qu'il disait.

scantily ['skæntɪlɪ] *adv* peu abondamment; (*insufficiently*) insuffisamment; **s. dressed** *or* **clad,** à peine vêtu; **she came to the party rather s. clad,** elle est venue à la soirée dans une tenue qui ne laissait pas grand-chose à l'imagination.

scantiness ['skæntɪnɪs] *n* insuffisance *f* (*de provisions* *etc*); pauvreté *f* (*de la végétation*); petitesse *f* (*d'un vêtement*).

scanty ['skæntɪ] *adj* (*supply etc*) peu abondant; (*insufficient*) insuffisant, à peine suffisant; **s. meal,** maigre repas *m;* **a s. little dress,** une robe qui ne cache pas grand-chose.

-scape [skeɪp] *suff* **cloud/moon/roof/***etc***-s.,** paysage *m* de nuages/lunaire/de toits/*etc*.

scapegoat ['skeɪpgəʊt] *n* (*who takes the blame*) bouc *m* émissaire; (*on whom frustrations are taken out*) souffre-douleur *m inv*.

scapegrace ['skeɪpgreɪs] *n Old-fashioned* (*good for nothing*) vaurien, -ienne, bon, *f* bonne à rien; (*child*) garnement *m*, galopin *m*.

scapula, *pl* **-ae** ['skæpjʊlə, -iː] *n Anat* omoplate *f*.

scapular ['skæpjʊlər] *adj Anat etc* scapulaire.

scar¹ [skɑːr] *n* **(a)** cicatrice *f*; (*on face*) balafre *f*; **s. tissue,** tissu cicatriciel; **the scars that the old mine workings have left on the hills,** les traces laissées par les anciennes mines qui défigurent les collines; **he carried the (mental) scars for the rest of his life,** il est resté marqué à vie; **(b)** (*on plant*) cicatrice *f*.

scar² *vt* (**-rr-**) marquer (*le visage etc*) d'une cicatrice, balafrer (*le visage*); **to be scarred,** porter *ou* avoir des cicatrices; *Fig* **to be scarred for life,** (*by experience etc*) être marqué à vie; **war-scarred,** (*of country etc*) dévasté par la guerre.

scar³ *n* (*in mountain range etc*) rocher escarpé.

scarab ['skærəb] *n* (*beetle & precious stone*) scarabée *m*.

scarce ['skeəs] **1** *adj* (*commodities*) rare, peu abondant; *F* **to make oneself s.,** s'éclipser, s'esquiver. **2** *adv Arch & Lit* = **SCARCELY**.

scarcely ['skeəslɪ] *adv* à peine, *Fml* guère; **I have s. any left,** il ne m'en reste presque plus, *Fml* il m'en reste guère; **she could s. speak,** c'est à peine si elle pouvait parler, *Fml* elle ne pouvait guère parler; **s. ever,** presque jamais; **he had s. come in** *or* **s. had he come in when the telephone rang,** à peine était-il rentré que le téléphone sonna; **she was s. 21 years old,** elle avait à peine 21 ans; **it is s. likely that ...,** il est peu vraisemblable que ...; **they would s. destroy their own home, would they?,** ils n'iraient quand même pas détruire leur propre maison?

scarceness ['skeəsnɪs] **, scarcity** ['skeəsɪtɪ] *n* (*rarity*) rareté *f*; (*lack*) manque *m*, disette *f* (*de qch*).

scare¹ ['skeər] *n* panique *f*, alarme *f*; *F* **you gave me an awful s.,** vous m'avez fait une drôle de peur; **a bomb s.,** une alerte à la bombe; **a s. over poisoned food,** une panique à propos de nourriture empoisonnée.

scare² **1** *vt* (*alarm*) effrayer, effarer, alarmer; (*frighten*) faire peur à (*qn*). **2** *vi* s'effrayer, s'alarmer; **I don't s. easily,** je ne m'effraie pas facilement *ou* pour rien.

▸scare away, scare off *vtsep* (*frighten*) effaroucher (*le gibier etc*); **her aggressiveness scared boys away,** son agressivité décourageait les garçons; **such high prices will s. off prospective buyers,** des prix aussi élevés décourageront les acheteurs potentiels.

scarecrow ['skeəkrəʊ] *n Agr & Fig* épouvantail *m*; **to be dressed like a s.,** être mis à faire peur.

scared [skeəd] *adj* apeuré; (*regard*) effaré; (*air*) épouvanté; **to be s. of s.o./sth,** avoir peur de qn/qch; **I'm not s. of you,** tu ne me fais pas peur; **to be s. to death** *or* **out of one's wits,** *F* **to be s. stiff,** avoir une peur bleue.

scaredy-cat ['skeədɪkæt] *n* (*in children's language*) froussard, -arde.

scaremonger ['skeəmʌŋgər] *n* alarmiste *mf*.

scaremongering ['skeəmʌŋgərɪŋ] *n* alarmisme *m*.

scarf¹, *pl* **scarfs, scarves** [skɑːf(s), skɑːvz] *n* écharpe *f*, cache-col *m*, *pl* cache-col(s), cache-nez *m inv*; (*in silk*) foulard *m*; **football s.,** écharpe aux couleurs d'une équipe de football.

scarf² *n Carp* **s. (joint),** assemblage *m* à mi-bois, enture *f*.

scarface ['skɑːfeɪs] *n* balafré *m*.

scarification [skærɪfɪ'keɪʃən] *n Agr Med* scarification *f*.

scarify ['skærɪfaɪ] *vt* scarifier (*la peau, le sol*).

scarlatina [skɑːlə'tiːnə] *n Med* scarlatine *f*.

scarlet ['skɑːlɪt] **1** *adj* écarlate; **to blush** *or* **go s.,** devenir cramoisi *ou* écarlate; *Med* **s. fever,** scarlatine *f*; *Cathol* **s. hat,** chapeau *m* de cardinal; **s. pimpernel,** (*plant*) mouron *m* rouge; **s. runner,** haricot *m* d'Espagne; *Iron* **s. woman,** poule *f*. **2** *n* écarlate *m*.

scarp [skɑːp] *n* **(a)** *Geog* escarpement *m* (*d'une colline*); **(b)** *Mil* (*in fortifications*) escarpe *f*.

scarper ['skɑːpər] *vi Br Sl* se tirer, déguerpir.

scary ['skeərɪ] *adj F* **(a)** (*frightening*) effrayant, qui fait peur; **it's s. here,** ça fiche la frousse; **(b)** (*easily frightened*) timide.

scat [skæt] *int F* filez!, fichez le camp!

scathing ['skeɪðɪŋ] *adj* (*remark, sarcasm etc*) acerbe, mordant, cinglant, caustique; **she was s. about security arrangements,** elle a fait des remarques acerbes au sujet des mesures de sécurité.

scathingly ['skeɪðɪŋlɪ] *adv* d'une manière acerbe *ou* caustique; (*to remark*) d'un ton cinglant *ou* acerbe.

scatological [skætə'lɒdʒɪk(ə)l] *adj* scatologique; **s. humour/jokes,** humour *m*/plaisanteries *fpl* scatologique(s).

scatology [skə'tɒlədʒɪ] *n* scatologie *f*.

scatter¹ ['skætər] *n* (*of shot etc*) éparpillement *m*; (*of crowd etc*) dispersion *f*; **s. cushions,** petits coussins que l'on éparpille dans une pièce; **s. rug,** petit tapis; (*by bed*) descente *f* de lit.

scatter² **1** *vt* disperser (*une armée etc*); dissiper (*des nuages etc*); faire envoler (*des oiseaux*); éparpiller (*des feuilles, des papiers etc*); semer (*des graines*) à la volée; *Phys* (*of surface*) diffuser (*la lumière*); **scattered showers,** averses éparses; **scattered light,** lumière diffuse; **scattered over the floor,** éparpillé sur le sol; **houses scattered here and there on the plain,** des maisons çà et là dans la plaine. **2** *vi* (*of crowd etc*) se disperser; (*of birds etc*) s'égailler; (*of army*) se débander; (*of clouds etc*) se dissiper; (*of shot*) s'éparpiller.

scatterbrain ['skætəbreɪn] *n F* étourdi, -ie, écervelé, -ée.

scatterbrained ['skætəbreɪnd] *adj F* étourdi, écervelé.

scattering ['skætərɪŋ] *n* **(a)** (*act of scattering*) dispersion *f* (*d'une armée etc*); éparpillement *m* (*de feuilles etc*); diffusion *f* (*de la lumière*); **(b)** (*small number*) petit nombre; (*small quantity*) petite quantité; **he only has a s. of followers,** ses disciples sont peu nombreux.

scattiness ['skætɪnɪs] *n* (*absent-mindedness*) étourderie *f*; (*craziness*) loufoquerie *f*.

scatty ['skætɪ] *adj F* (*absent-minded*) étourdi, écervelé; (*crazy*) farfelu, loufoque.

scavenge ['skævɪndʒ] **1** *vi* (*hunt through rubbish etc*) fouiller dans les ordures. **2** *vt* **(a)** (*in engine*) balayer, refouler (*les gaz brûlés*); **(b)** *Arch* ébouer (*les rues etc*).

scavenger ['skævɪndʒər] *n* **(a)** (*person, animal*) fouilleur, -euse d'ordures; (*animal*) animal *m* nécrophage; **(b)** *Arch* (*street cleaner*) boueur *m*.

scenario [sɪ'nɑːrɪəʊ] *n Th & Fig* scénario *m*.

scene [siːn] *n* **(a)** *Th* (*place of action*) scène *f*; *Fig* théâtre *m*, lieu *m* (*d'un événement*); *Th* **change of s.,** changement *m* de décor; *Fig* **a change of s. would do him good,** un changement d'air lui ferait du bien; **the s. is set in London,** l'action se passe à Londres; *Fig* **her success set the s. for more women to enter music,** son succès a ouvert la voie pour que plus de femmes entrent dans la musique; **the political s.,** la scène politique; **this athlete is a newcomer to the s.,** cet athlète est nouveau sur la scène; **the s. of the crime,** le(s) lieu(x) du crime; *F* **it's not my s.,** ce n'est pas mon genre; *Sl* **to make the s.,** devenir célèbre;

(b) *Th* (*subdivision of play*) scène *f*; *Fig* (*episode*) scène, spectacle *m*; **act three, s. two,** deuxième scène du troisième acte; **it was a painful s.,** c'était une scène pénible;

(c) *Th* décor *m*; **scenes painted by ...,** décors par ...; **behind the scenes,** (*in theatre*) dans la coulisse; *Fig* dans les coulisses;

(d) (*sight*) vue *f*; **s. from the window,** la vue de la fenêtre;

(e) *F* **now don't make a s.!,** ne fais pas une scène!

scenery ['siːnərɪ] *n* **(a)** *Th* décors *mpl*; *F* **you need a change of s.,** il vous faut du changement, vous avez besoin de changer d'air; **(b)** (*countryside*) paysage *m*; (*view*) vue *f*.

sceneshifter ['siːnʃɪftər] *n Th* machiniste *m*.

scenic ['siːnɪk] *adj* **(a)** (*paysage*) pittoresque; **s. route,** (*for tourists*) route *f* touristique; **area of great s. beauty,** région qui offre de très beaux panoramas; **s. railway,** (*at fair*) montagnes *fpl* russes; **(b)** *Th* scénique; (*theatrical*) théâtral, -aux.

scent¹ [sent] *n* **(a)** (*smell*) parfum *m*, senteur *f*; odeur *f* agréable (*des fleurs etc*); **bottle of s.,** flacon *m* de parfum; **(b)** (*in hunting*) fumet *m*, vent *m* (*de la bête*); **s. gland** *or* **organ,** glande *f* à sécrétion odoriférante; **to pick up the s.,** (*of pack*) trouver la piste; **to be on the right s.,** être sur la piste; **to lose** *or* **be thrown off the s.,** perdre la trace *ou* la piste; **to throw the police off the s.,** dérouter la police; **(c)** (*sense of smell*) odorat *m*, flair *m* (*d'un chien*).

scent² *vt* **(a)** (*of hounds etc*) **to s. game,** flairer *ou* sentir le gibier; *Fig* **to s. dishonesty/***etc*, flairer la malhonnêteté/*etc*; **keen-scented dog,** chien au nez *ou* à l'odorat fin; **(b)**

(*of flower etc*) parfumer, embaumer (*l'air etc*); **to s. sth with sth,** parfumer *ou* imprégner qch de qch.

scented ['sentɪd] *adj* (*soap etc*) parfumé.

scentless ['sentlɪs] *adj* (*fleur*) inodore, sans odeur.

sceptic, *US* **skeptic** ['skeptɪk] *n* sceptique *mf*.

sceptical, *US* **skeptical** ['skeptɪk(ə)l] *adj* sceptique.

sceptically, *US* **skeptically** ['skeptɪklɪ] *adv* sceptiquement.

scepticism, *US* **skepticism** ['skeptɪsɪz(ə)m] *n* scepticisme *m*.

sceptre, *US* **scepter** ['septər] *n* sceptre *m*.

schedule¹ ['ʃedju:l, *US* 'skedju:l] *n* **(a)** (*plan*) plan *m* (*d'exécution d'un travail*); *Rail etc* horaire *m*; **to be behind/ahead of s.,** être en retard/en avance sur les prévisions; **we're on s. (for March),** nous sommes dans les délais (pour mars); **everything went off according to s.,** tout a marché comme prévu; **I work to a very tight s.,** mon temps est très minuté; *Rail etc* **on s.,** (*train, bus etc*) à l'heure; **(b)** *Com* nomenclature *f* (*des pièces etc*); inventaire *m* (*des machines*); barème *m* (*des prix*); *Admin* cédule *f* (*d'impôts*); **(c)** *Jur* annexe *f* (*à une loi, aux statuts d'une société etc*).

schedule² *vt* **(a)** (*plan*) dresser un plan *ou* un programme de (*qch*); inscrire (*un train*) à l'horaire; **the mayor is scheduled to make a speech,** le maire doit prononcer un discours; **to arrive at the scheduled time,** arriver à l'heure indiquée; **it's scheduled for 3.00,** c'est prévu pour 15.00; **(b)** (*class*) **to s. as an ancient monument,** classer (comme) monument historique; **(c)** *Com* inscrire (*un article etc*) sur une liste, sur l'inventaire; **scheduled prices,** prix selon le tarif; **(d)** *Jur* ajouter (*un article*) en annexe (*à une loi etc*).

scheduled ['ʃedju:ld, *US* 'skedju:ld] *adj* **(a) s. services,** services réguliers; *Av* **s. flight,** vol régulier; **(b)** *Fin* **S. Territories,** zone *f* sterling.

schema, *pl* **-ata** ['ski:mə, -ətə] *n* schéma *m*.

schematic [skɪ'mætɪk] *adj* schématique.

scheme¹ [ski:m] *n* **(a)** (*arrangement*) arrangement *m*, combinaison *f*; (*system*) système *m*; **colour s.,** combinaison de(s) couleurs; **I like the colour s. on this carpet,** j'aime les coloris de ce tapis; **where does mankind fit into the s. of things?,** quelle est la place de l'humanité dans l'univers?; **where does it come in your s. of things?,** quelle place cela a-t-il dans votre conception des choses?; **(b)** (*outline*) résumé *m*, exposé *m* (*d'un sujet d'étude*); plan *m* (*d'un ouvrage littéraire*); **(c)** (*plan*) plan *m*, projet *m*; **(d)** *Pej* (*intrigue*) machination *f*, intrigue *f*; **the best laid schemes,** les combinaisons les mieux étudiées; **(e)** *esp Br* **pension s.,** caisse *f* de retraite; **(f) (housing) scheme,** ensemble *m* d'habitations.

scheme² **1** *vi* intriguer. **2** *vt Old-fashioned* machiner, combiner (*une conspiration*).

schemer ['ski:mər] *n Pej* intrigant, -ante, comploteur, -euse.

scheming ['ski:mɪŋ] **1** *adj* intrigant, comploteur. **2** *n* machinations *fpl*, intrigues *fpl*.

scherzo ['skeətsəʊ] *n Mus* scherzo *m*.

schism ['s(k)ɪz(ə)m] *n* schisme *m*.

schismatic [s(k)ɪz'mætɪk] *adj & n* schismatique *mf*.

schist [ʃɪst] *n Miner* schiste *m*; **mica s.,** micaschiste *m*.

schizo ['skɪtsəʊ] *adj & n F* schizo(phrène) *mf*.

schizoid ['skɪtsɔɪd] *adj & n Psy* schizoïde *mf*.

schizophrenia [skɪtsəʊ'fri:nɪə] *n Psy* schizophrénie *f*.

schizophrenic [skɪtsəʊ'frenɪk] *adj & n Psy* schizophrène *mf*, schizophrénique *mf*.

schlock [ʃlɒk] *n Am Sl* camelote *f*, saloperies *fpl*.

schmal(t)z [ʃmɔ:lts] *n F* sensiblerie *f*, sentimentalité doucereuse.

schmaltzy ['ʃmɔ:ltsɪ] *adj F* (*film, novel etc*) à l'eau de rose; (*music*) à la guimauve.

schmuck [ʃmʌk] *n Am Sl* con *m*, conne *f*.

scholar ['skɒlər] *n* **(a)** (*learned person*) savant, -ante, érudit, -ite; **I'm not much of a s.,** je ne suis pas très savant; **Latin s.,** latiniste *mf*; **(b)** *Sch* (*winner of scholarship*) boursier, -ière; **(c)** *Arch* (*pupil*) élève *mf*, écolier, -ière.

scholarly ['skɒləlɪ] *adj* savant, érudit.

scholarship ['skɒləʃɪp] *n* **(a)** (*learning*) savoir *m*, érudition *f*; **(b)** *Sch* (*sum of money*) bourse *f* (*d'études*).

scholastic [skə'læstɪk] **1** *adj* (*philosophie, théologie*) scolastique; (*schools etc*) scolaire. **2** *n Phil Rel* scolastique *m*.

school¹ [sku:l] *n* **(a)** (*for children*) école *f*; **to go to s.,** aller en classe *ou* à l'école; **which s. do you go to?,** quelle école fréquentes-tu, à quelle école vas-tu?; **I went to s. with her,** je suis allé à l'école avec elle; **I'm still at s.,** je vais encore à l'école; **he wasn't at s. today,** il n'était pas à l'école aujourd'hui; **nursery s.,** école maternelle, maternelle *f*; **primary** *or Am* **elementary s.,** école primaire; **comprehensive s.,** école secondaire; **grammar s.,** *Br* ≈ lycée, *Am* ≈ école primaire; **high s.,** ≈ lycée *m*; **independent** *or* **private s.,** ≈ école *ou* collège libre; **public s.,** école privée; *Am* école publique; **state s.,** école publique, établissement public; **approved s.,** centre *m* d'éducation surveillée; **Sunday s.,** catéchisme *m*; **the whole s. knew it,** toute l'école le savait; **the upper/lower s.,** (*the pupils*) les grandes/petites classes; **(of) s. age,** (d')âge scolaire; **s. attendance,** scolarisation *f*; **s. book,** livre *m* de classe, livre scolaire; **s. friend,** camarade *mf ou* copain, -pine d'école; **s. buildings,** bâtiments *mpl* de l'école; **s. leaver,** élève quittant l'école; **s.-leaving age,** âge *m* de fin de scolarité; **s. report,** livret *m* scolaire; bulletin *m* (scolaire); **s. year,** année *f* scolaire;

(b) (*institute*) école *f*, académie *f*, institut *m* (*d'enseignement technique, industriel etc*); *Am* (*college, university*) faculté *f*, université *f*; *Am* **to be at s.,** être à l'université; **art s., s. of art,** école des beaux-arts; **s. of dancing,** académie *ou* école de danse; **fencing s.,** académie *ou* salle *f* d'escrime; **driving s., s. of motoring,** auto-école *f*, *pl* auto-écoles; **summer s.,** cours de vacances;

(c) *Art etc* (*group*) école *f*; disciples *mpl* (*d'un maître*); **the Flemish s.,** l'école flamande; **the Platonic s.,** l'école de Platon; **s. of thought,** école (de pensée); **one of the old s.,** un homme de la vieille école.

school² *vt* **(a)** (*educate*) instruire (*qn*), faire l'éducation de (*qn*); **(b)** (*train*) former (*un enfant, l'esprit de qn etc*); discipliner (*sa voix, son geste etc*); dresser (*un cheval*); **to s. oneself,** se discipliner.

school³ *n* banc voyageur (*de poissons*); bande *f* (*de marsouins*).

schoolboy ['sku:lbɔɪ] *n* écolier *m*; **s. slang,** argot *m* scolaire.

schoolchild, *pl* **-children** ['sku:ltʃaɪld, -tʃɪldrən] *n* écolier, -ière.

schoolday ['sku:ldeɪ] *n* **(a)** jour *m* de classe; **(b) schooldays,** (*period of life*) vie *f* scolaire; **in my schooldays,** quand j'allais à l'école.

schoolfellow ['sku:lfeləʊ] *n Old-fashioned* camarade *mf* de classe *ou* d'école.

schoolgirl ['sku:lgɜ:l] *n* écolière *f*.

schoolhouse ['sku:lhaʊs] *n* **(a)** (*school building*) école *f*; **(b)** (*headmaster's residence*) maison *f* du directeur *ou* de la directrice (*faisant corps avec l'école*).

schooling ['sku:lɪŋ] *n* (*education*) instruction *f*, éducation *f*; (*sending up to school*) scolarisation *f*; dressage *m* (*d'un cheval*); **he paid for his nephew's s.,** il a subvenu aux frais d'études de son neveu; **compulsory s.,** scolarisation obligatoire.

schoolma'am, schoolmarm ['sku:lmɑ:m] *n Old-fashioned F* institutrice *f*; (*still current in*) **she's a real s.,** c'est une pédante.

schoolmaster ['sku:lmɑ:stər] *n Old-fashioned* (*in primary school*) instituteur *m*, maître *m* (d'école); (*in secondary school*) professeur *m*.

schoolmate ['sku:lmeɪt] *n* camarade *mf* de classe.

schoolmistress ['sku:lmɪstrɪs] *n Old-fashioned* (*in primary school*) institutrice *f*, maîtresse *f* (d'école); (*in secondary school*) professeur *m*.

schoolroom ['sku:lru:m] *n* salle *f* de classe.

schoolteacher ['sku:lti:tʃər] *n* (*in primary school*) instituteur, -trice, maître *m*, maîtresse *f* (d'école); (*in secondary school*) professeur *m*.

schooner¹ ['sku:nər] *n Nau* schooner *m*, goélette *f*; **s.-rigged,** gréé en goélette.

schooner² *n* (*glass*) grand verre (*à bière, à xérès*).

sciatic [saɪ'ætɪk] *adj Anat* (*nerf etc*) sciatique.

sciatica [saɪ'ætɪkə] *n Med* sciatique *f*.

science ['saɪəns] *n* science *f*; **pure/applied s.,** science pure/sciences appliquées; **natural s.,** sciences naturelles; **social s.,** sciences sociales; **s. fiction,** science-fiction *f*, *Can* anticipation *f*; **s. teacher,** professeur *m* de sciences; **s. park,** parc *m* scientifique.

scientific [saɪən'tɪfɪk] *n* scientifique; **let's be s. about this,** soyons scientifique là-dessus; **s. research,** recherche *f* scientifique.

scientifically [saɪən'tɪfɪklɪ] *adv* scientifiquement.

scientist ['saɪəntɪst] *n* **(a)** scientifique *mf*, homme *m* de science; **scientists say that ...,** les scientifiques disent que ...; **(b) Christian S.,** scientiste chrétien(ne).

sci-fi ['saɪfaɪ] *F* **1** *n* science-fiction *f*. **2** *adj* de science-fiction.

Scilly [ˈsɪlɪ] *n* **the S. Isles, the Scillies,** les Sorlingues *fpl.*
scimitar [ˈsɪmɪtər] *n* cimeterre *m.*
scintillate [ˈsɪntɪleɪt] *vi* scintiller, étinceler; **scintillating with wit,** qui scintille *ou* pétille d'esprit.
scintillating [ˈsɪntɪleɪtɪŋ] *adj* (*wit, conversation etc*) étincelant, pétillant; *Iron* **it wasn't exactly s.,** ce n'était pas particulièrement brillant.
scintillation [sɪntɪˈleɪʃən] *n* éclat *m,* brillance *f* (*de l'esprit etc*).
scion [ˈsaɪən] *n* **(a)** (*of plant*) scion *m,* greffon *m;* **(b)** (*descendant*) descendant *m,* rejeton *m* (*d'une famille noble etc*).
scissor[1] [ˈsɪzər] *n* **(a) (pair of) scissors,** ciseaux *mpl;* **nail scissors,** ciseaux à ongles; (*wrestling*) *& Gym etc* **scissors,** ciseaux; (*in high jump*) saut *m* en ciseaux; *Swimming* **scissors kick,** les ciseaux; **(b)** (*bird*) **s. bill,** bec-en-ciseaux *m, pl* becs-en-ciseaux.
scissor[2] *vt* (dé)couper (*qch*) avec des ciseaux.
sclerosis, *pl* **-oses** [sklɪəˈrəʊsɪs, -əʊsiːz] *n Med* sclérose *f;* **multiple** *or* **disseminated s.,** sclérose en plaques.
scoff[1] [skɒf] *n* moquerie *f,* raillerie *f.*
scoff[2] *vi* se moquer; **to s. at,** railler (*qn*); se moquer de (*qn, qch*); mépriser (*un danger*); **don't s.,** pas de raillerie!, ne te moque pas!
scoff[3] *n Sl* (*food*) boustifaille *f,* bouffe *f.*
scoff[4] *vt esp Br Sl* (*eat*) bouffer, bâfrer (*de la nourriture*).
scoffing [ˈskɒfɪŋ] *adj* moqueur, -euse.
scold[1] [skəʊld] *n* (*person*) mégère *f,* bougonne *f.*
scold[2] **1** *vi* gronder, criailler (**at s.o.,** contre qn). **2** *vt* gronder, réprimander, attraper (*qn*).
scolding [ˈskəʊldɪŋ] **1** *adj* grondeur, -euse. **2** *n* gronderie *f;* (*reprimand*) réprimande *f,* semonce *f;* **to give s.o. a good s.,** laver la tête à qn; **constant s.,** des criailleries *fpl* sans fin.
scollop [ˈskɒləp] *n & v* = **SCALLOP[1,2]**.
sconce [skɒns] *n* **(a)** (*with handle*) bougeoir *m;* **(b)** (*on wall*) applique *f.*
scone [skɒn, skəʊn] *n Culin* scone *m.*
scoop[1] [skuːp] *n* (*device*) pelle *f* à main; *Nau* (*bailer*) épuisette *f,* écope *f;* cuiller *f,* godet *m* (*de drague*); (*in engine*) cuiller de graissage; **grocer's s.,** main *f;* **ice cream s.,** portionneur *m* à glace; *Fishing* **s. net,** drague *f.*
scoop[2] *n* **(a)** (*act of scooping*) coup *m* de pelle; **at one s.,** d'un seul coup (de pelle); **(b)** (*portion*) cuillerée *f;* **(c)** *F* (*piece of luck*) coup *m* de chance; *Journ F* nouvelle sensationnelle, reportage exclusif *ou* à sensation, scoop *m;* **to make a s.,** réussir un coup; **(d)** *Sewing* **s. neck,** décolleté *m* (arrondi).
scoop[3] *vt* **(a)** (*shovel*) écoper (*l'eau*) (*d'un bateau*); excaver (*la terre*); évider (*du bois etc*); vider (*une tomate etc*); **to s. sth into sth,** se servir d'un récipient pour vider qch dans qch; **(b)** réussir un beau coup; **(c)** *Journ* **to s. the other papers,** publier (*une nouvelle etc*) avant les autres journaux, faire un scoop.
▶**scoop out** *vtsep* évider (*du bois etc*); vider (*une tomate etc*); **to s. the water out of a boat,** écoper un bateau.
▶**scoop up** *vtsep* (*pick up*) épuiser, écoper (*l'eau etc*); ramasser (*du charbon, de la farine etc*) avec la pelle; **she scooped the baby up (in her arms),** elle a saisi le bébé (dans ses bras).
scoot [skuːt] *vi F* **to s. (off, away),** détaler, filer, déguerpir.
scooter [ˈskuːtər] *n* (*for child*) trottinette *f,* patinette *f;* **(motor) s.,** scooter *m.*
scope [skəʊp] *n* portée *f,* étendue *f* (*d'une action etc*); domaine *m* (*d'une science etc*); envergure *f* (*d'une entreprise*); espace *m,* place *f* (*pour les mouvements de qn etc*); **it's beyond** *or* **outside my s.,** cela n'est pas de *ou* ne rentre pas dans ma compétence; **it's outside the s. of this enquiry,** cela n'entre pas dans les limites de cette enquête; **to give full** *or* **free s. to s.o./one's imagination/***etc,* donner libre carrière à *ou* laisser le champ libre à qn/son imagination/*etc;* **there's little s. for people with imagination,** il y a peu de possibilités pour les gens qui ont de l'imagination.
scorch[1] [skɔːtʃ] *n* **s. (mark),** roussissement *m;* brûlure superficielle.
scorch[2] **1** *vt* (*of fire etc*) roussir, brûler légèrement (*le linge etc*); (*of sun*) rôtir, dessécher (*l'herbe etc*); **scorched earth policy,** tactique *f ou* politique *f* de la terre brûlée. **2** *vi* (*of material etc*) roussir.
▶**scorch along** *vi* (*of car, runner*) passer comme un boulet de canon.
scorcher [ˈskɔːtʃər] *n F* (*hot day*) journée *f* torride.
scorching [ˈskɔːtʃɪŋ] **1** *adj* (*sun, wind etc*) brûlant, ardent; (*chaleur*) torride. **2** *adv F* **it's s. hot here,** on rôtit ici. **3** *n* roussissement *m* (*du linge etc*); dessèchement *m* (*de l'herbe etc*).
score[1] [skɔːr] *n* **(a)** *Sp etc* marque *f,* score *m;* **after 20 minutes there was still no s.,** après 20 minutes le score était toujours zéro à zéro; **what's the s.?,** quel est le score *ou* la marque?, où en est le jeu?; **to keep the s.,** marquer *ou* compter les points; *Cards* tenir la marque; **what was your s.?,** combien tu as fait *ou* marqué?; *F* **to know the s.,** être au courant, *F* connaître la musique;
(b) (*mark made by cutting*) rayure *f;* (*deeper*) entaille *f;* (*on skin*) incision *f,* éraflure *f;* (*on rock etc*) strie *f;*
(c) (*to mark level etc*) (trait *m* de) repère *m;*
(d) (*notch*) (en)coche *f;* **to pay one's s.,** régler son compte; **to pay off** *or* **settle old scores,** régler de vieux comptes;
(e) *Mus* partition *f;* **full s.,** partition d'orchestre;
(f) (*pl* **score**) (*twenty*) vingt, une vingtaine; **a s. of people,** une vingtaine de gens; *Arch* **three or four s. people,** entre soixante et quatre-vingt personnes; *F* **you can find them by the s.,** on les ramasse à la pelle; *F* **scores,** (*large number*) un grand nombre; **scores of people,** une foule de gens;
(g) (*matter*) point *m,* compte *m,* question *f,* sujet *m;* **don't worry on that s.,** n'ayez aucune crainte sur ce point.
score[2] **1** *vt* **(a)** *Sp* marquer (*un but, un essai*); faire, marquer (*trente points etc*); **to fail to s.,** ne marquer aucun point; *Fb etc* **to s. a goal,** marquer *ou* enregistrer un but; **to s. a success,** remporter *ou* enregistrer un succès; *F* **to s. points off s.o.,** river son clou à qn;
(b) érafler, couturer (*qch*); inciser (*le cuir etc*); strier (*un rocher etc*); rayer (*un cylindre, la terre, le papier etc*); (*underline in ink*) faire un trait de plume au-dessous de (*qch*); **mountainside scored by torrents,** flanc de montagne sillonné par les torrents; **water had scored grooves into the rock,** l'eau avait creusé des rainures dans le rocher; **to s. a passage in a book,** souligner un passage dans un livre;
(c) (*mark with a notch*) entailler, (en)cocher (*une latte de bois etc*); *Old-fashioned F* = **SCORE UP**; porter (*une dette*) en compte;
(d) *Mus* noter (*un air*); orchestrer (*une composition*); **scored for piano, violin and flute,** arrangé pour piano, violon et flûte.
2 *vi* **(a)** *Sp* (*of player, team*) marquer; (*keep the score*) compter *ou* marquer les points; *Sl Fig* (*have sex*) (*of man*) se faire une nana; (*of woman*) se faire un mec; (*buy drugs*) trouver de la dope; **that's where he scores,** (*that's where he has the advantage*) c'est là qu'il est le plus fort.
(b) (*with knife, scissors*) découper; **s. along the dotted line,** découper le long des pointillés.
▶**score off** **1** *vipo F* (*win point in argument etc*) **to s. off s.o.,** river son clou à qn. **2** *vtsep* (*delete*) rayer; **s. his name off the list,** rayez son nom de la liste.
▶**score out** *vtsep* (*delete*) rayer.
▶**score up** *vtsep Old-fashioned F* (*mark on slate etc*) porter (*une dette*) en compte.
scoreboard [ˈskɔːbɔːd] *n* tableau *m* (*des points etc*).
scorecard [ˈskɔːkɑːd] *n Sp* carte *f ou* fiche *f* de score; *Golf* carte du parcours; (*at shooting range*) carton *m.*
scorer [ˈskɔːrər] *n Sp* **(a)** (*person who keeps score*) marqueur, -euse (*des points*); **(b)** (*person who scores point etc*) celui *ou* celle qui marque; *Fb etc* marqueur, -euse de but; *Fb etc* **the team's top (goal) s.,** le meilleur buteur de l'équipe.
scoring [ˈskɔːrɪŋ] *n* **(a)** *Sp* **to open the s.,** ouvrir la marque; **there was no s., until ...,** rien n'avait été marqué jusqu'à ce que ...; **(b)** (*grooves etc*) éraflement *m* (*de la peau etc*); striation *f* (*d'un rocher*); rayage *m* (*d'un cylindre etc*); **(b)** (*notches on stick*) entaillage *m,* encochage *m* (*d'un bâton etc*) *Old-fashioned F* = **SCORING UP**; *Mus* notation *f* (*d'un air*); orchestration *f* (*d'une composition*), arrangement *m* (*pour divers instruments*).
scoring up *n Old-fashioned F* inscription *f,* enregistrement *m* (*d'une dette*).
scorn[1] [skɔːn] *n* dédain *m,* mépris *m;* **to pour s. on sth,** rejeter qch d'un ton de mépris.
scorn[2] *vt* **(a)** dédaigner, mépriser (*qn, qch*); **she scorned their help,** elle a dédaigné leur aide; **(b) to s. to do sth,** dédaigner de faire qch.
scornful [ˈskɔːnfʊl] *adj* (*person, smile etc*) dédaigneux, méprisant; **to be s. of s.o./sth,** dédaigner *ou* mépriser qn/qch, traiter qn/qch avec mépris.
scornfully [ˈskɔːnfəlɪ] *adv* dédaigneusement, avec mépris.
Scorpio [ˈskɔːpɪəʊ] *n Astron* le Scorpion; **Ian is S.,** Ian est scorpion.

scorpion ['skɔːpɪən] *n* (*animal*) scorpion *m*; *Astron* **the S.**, le Scorpion.
Scot [skɒt] *n* Écossais, -aise; *Hist* **the Scots,** les Scots *mpl*.
scotch [skɒtʃ] *vt* mettre fin à, faire échouer (*un projet etc*).
Scotch [skɒtʃ] **1** *adj* (*not used of persons in Scotland*) écossais; d'Écosse; **S. mist,** bruine *f*, crachin *m*; *Br Culin* **S. egg,** = œuf enrobé de chair à saucisse et pané; **S. pine** *or* **fir,** pin *m* d'Écosse; *esp Am* **S. tape** ®, Scotch *m*; **S. terrier,** scottish-terrier *m*; **S. whisky,** whisky écossais. **2** *n* **(a)** *Ling* l'anglais *m* d'Écosse; **(b)** *F* whisky écossais, scotch *m*; **a (glass of) S.,** un whisky, un scotch; **(c)** *F* (*not used in Scotland*) **the S.,** (*used as pl*) les Écossais *mpl*.
Scotchman, *pl* **-men** ['skɒtʃmən] *n* (*not used in Scotland*) Écossais *m*.
Scotchwoman, *pl* **-women** ['skɒtʃwʊmən, -wɪmɪn] *n* (*not used in Scotland*) Écossaise *f*.
scot-free ['skɒt'friː] *adj F* **to get off s.-f.,** (*unhurt*) s'en tirer indemne; (*unpunished*) s'en tirer sans être puni.
Scotland ['skɒtlənd] *n* Écosse *f*; **S. Yard,** ≈ la Sûreté.
Scots [skɒts] **1** *adj* écossais; **the S. Guards,** la Garde écossaise; **S. pine** *or* **fir,** pin *m* d'Écosse. **2** *n Ling* écossais *m*.
Scotsman, *pl* **-men** ['skɒtsmən] *n* Écossais *m*.
Scotswoman, *pl* **-women** ['skɒtswʊmən, -wɪmɪn] *n* Écossaise *f*.
Scott [skɒt] *int* **Great S.!,** Grand Dieu!
Scottie ['skɒtɪ] *n F* scottish-terrier *m*.
Scottish ['skɒtɪʃ] *adj* écossais; **S. terrier,** scottish-terrier *m*.
scoundrel ['skaʊndr(ə)l] *n* scélérat *m*; (*of child, puppy etc*) canaille *f*.
scour¹ ['skaʊər] *vt* **(a)** lessiver, frotter (*le plancher etc*); (*in metalwork*) décaper (*une surface métallique*); (*of river*) affouiller, dégrader (*les rives*); **to s. a saucepan,** récurer une casserole; **(b)** (*flush out*) donner une chasse d'eau à (*un égout etc*).
scour² **1** *vi* = **SCOUR ABOUT**. **2** *vt* parcourir, battre (*la campagne*); (*of pirates*) balayer, écumer (*la mer*); fouiller (*un bois*); **to s. the country for s.o.,** battre la campagne à la recherche de qn.
►**scour about** *vi* (*search widely*) battre la campagne.
scourer ['skaʊərər] *n* **(pot) s.,** éponge *f ou* tampon *m* à récurer.
scourge¹ [skɔːdʒ] *n* **(a)** (*affliction*) fléau *m*; **(b)** *Arch & Lit* (*whip*) fouet *m*; *Rel* (*for self-flagellation*) discipline *f*; **he was the s. of ...,** il était la terreur de ... .
scourge² *vt* **(a)** (*afflict*) affliger, opprimer (*un peuple etc*); **(b)** *Arch & Lit* fouetter, flageller (*qn*); *Rel* **to s. oneself,** se donner la discipline.
scouring ['skaʊərɪŋ] **(a)** (*rubbing*) récurage *m*, frottage *m*; (*in metalwork*) décapage *m*; **s. pad,** éponge *f ou* tampon *m* à récurer; **s. powder,** poudre *f* à récurer; **(b)** (*flushing out*) nettoyage *m* à grande eau (*d'un fossé*).
scouse [skaʊs] *F* **1** *adj* de Liverpool. **2** *n* **(a)** habitant, -ante de Liverpool; **(b)** *Ling* l'anglais *m* de Liverpool.
scout¹ [skaʊt] *n* **(a)** *Mil* éclaireur *m*, avant-coureur *m*; *Br Aut* dépanneur *m* (*employé par les associations automobiles*); **(boy) s.,** (*Catholic*) scout *m*; (*non-Catholic*) éclaireur *m*; *US* **(girl) s.,** guide *f*, éclaireuse *f*; *Cin Sp etc* **(talent) s.,** recruteur *m* de talent; *Am F* **a good s.,** un bon type; **(b)** *Av* avion *m* de reconnaissance.
scout² *vi Mil etc* aller en reconnaissance; *Cin Sp etc* **to s. for talent,** se mettre à la recherche de futures vedettes.
scout³ *n F* (*search*) **to have a s. around for sth,** chercher qch; **I had a good s. around,** j'ai bien cherché.
scout⁴ *n Univ* garçon *m* de service (*à Oxford etc*).
►**scout about, scout around** *vi* (*search*) chercher (**for sth,** qch).
scoutmaster ['skaʊtmɑːstər] *n Arch* chef *m* de troupe.
scow [skaʊ] *n Nau* chaland *m*.
scowl¹ [skaʊl] *n* air menaçant *ou* renfrogné; froncement *m* de(s) sourcils; **to look at s.o. with a s.,** menacer qn du regard.
scowl² *vi* (*of person*) se renfrogner, froncer les sourcils; **to s. at s.o.,** menacer qn du regard, regarder qn d'un air menaçant.
scowling ['skaʊlɪŋ] *adj* renfrogné, menaçant.
scrabble ['skræb(ə)l] *vi* jouer des pieds et des mains (**for sth,** pour attraper qch).
►**scrabble about, scrabble around** *vi* gratter (ça et là); **I was scrabbling about in the dark trying to find my key,** je farfouillais dans le noir pour trouver ma clef; **beggars scrabbling about in the dirt for coins,** mendiants qui farfouillent dans la saleté pour trouver des pièces.
scrag¹ [skræg] *n* **the s. of the neck,** la nuque; *Culin* **s. (end) of mutton,** collet *m* de mouton.
scrag² *vt* (**-gg-**) *F* tordre le cou à (*qn*).
scraggy ['skrægɪ] *adj* (*person etc*) décharné, maigre.
scram [skræm] *vi* (**-mm-**) *F* filer, décamper, ficher le camp; **s.!,** (allez) ouste!, fiche le camp!
scramble¹ ['skræmb(ə)l] *n* **(a)** (*climbing*) ascension *f* difficile; (*on all fours*) escalade *f* à quatre pattes; **after our s. from the wreckage,** après nous être extirpés des décombres; *Sp* **(motorcycle) s.,** moto-cross *m*; **(b)** (*struggle*) mêlée *f*, lutte *f*; *Av F* décollage immédiat (*en cas d'alerte etc*); **there was a s. for the door,** il y a eu une ruée vers la porte.
scramble² **1** *vi* **(a)** (*move on all fours*) monter *ou* descendre *ou* entrer *ou* sortir *etc* à quatre pattes; *Sp* faire du moto-cross; **to s. up a hill,** grimper une colline à quatre pattes; **(b) to s. for sth,** (*struggle*) se battre *ou* se bousculer pour avoir qch; *Fig* se disputer qch; **(c)** *Av F* décoller rapidement (*en cas d'alerte etc*). **2** *vt* **(a)** *Culin* brouiller (*des œufs*); **(b)** *Tel Electron etc* brouiller (*un message*); **(c) scrambled eggs,** œufs brouillés.
scrambler ['skræmblər] *n* **(a)** *Tel etc* (circuit *m*) brouilleur *m*; **(b)** (*on motorbike*) motocrossman, *pl* -men.
scrambling ['skræmblɪŋ] *n* **(a)** *Tel Electron etc* brouillage *m* (*d'un message*); **(b) (motorcycle) s.,** moto-cross *m*.
scrap¹ [skræp] *n* **(a)** petit morceau; bout *m*, brin *m* (*de papier*); parcelle *f* (*de terrain etc*); bout (*de ruban*); bribe *f* (*de pain etc*); découpure *f* (*pour album*); coupure *f* (*de journal*); **not a s. of evidence,** pas une parcelle de preuve; **to catch scraps of a conversation,** saisir des bouts *ou* des bribes de conversation; **s. paper,** (papier *m*) brouillon *m*; **(b) scraps (left over),** restes *mpl* (*d'un repas*); déchets *mpl* (*de papeterie, d'usine etc*); bouts *mpl*, bribes *fpl* (*de tissu*); **to sell (sth) for s.,** vendre (qch) à la casse; **s. iron,** ferraille *f*; **s. merchant** *or* **dealer,** marchand *m* de ferraille; **s. (metal),** bocage *m*.
scrap² *vt* (**-pp-**) **(a)** mettre (*une pièce etc*) au rebut; mettre (*une machine*) hors service; envoyer *ou* mettre (*une voiture, un camion etc*) à la ferraille *ou* à la casse; **(b)** *F* laisser tomber (*un projet*); **it's been scrapped,** on l'a laissé tomber.
scrap³ *n F* (*fight*) querelle *f*, rixe *f*, bagarre *f*; **to have a s.,** se battre; **to get into a s.,** être mêlé à une bagarre.
scrap⁴ *vi* (**-pp-**) *F* se quereller, se bagarrer.
scrapbook ['skræpbʊk] *n* album *m* (*de découpures*).
scrape¹ [skreɪp] *n* **(a)** (*action with scraper*) coup *m* de grattoir *ou* de racloir; (*wound on skin*) éraflure *f*; (*layer scraped off*) mince couche *f* (*de beurre etc*); (*sound*) grincement *m* (*d'un violon etc*); **(b)** *F* (*difficulty*) embarras *m*, mauvais pas; **to get into a s.,** se mettre dans le pétrin *ou* dans l'embarras, s'attirer des ennuis; **to get out of a s.,** se tirer d'affaire *ou* d'embarras.
scrape² **1** *vt* **(a)** érafler, écorcher (*la peau, une surface polie etc*); **to s. one's shins,** s'érafler les tibias; **to s. the bottom,** (*of ship*) sillonner *ou* talonner le fond;
(b) (*clean*) racler, gratter (*qch*); regratter, ravaler (*un mur*); *Culin* gratter (*des carottes etc*); (*tanning*) racler, dépiler (*une peau*); (*smooth*) riper (*une sculpture etc*); racler, raturer (*le parchemin*); **to s. one's shoes,** se décrotter les chaussures; **to s. one's plate,** gratter le fond de son assiette; *Nau* **to s. a ship's bottom,** nettoyer la carène d'un navire; *Fig* **to s. the (bottom of the) barrel,** (*with money*) racler les fonds de tiroir; (*be reduced to extremes*) être réduit aux dernières extrémités, descendre bien bas;
(c) with her hair scraped back, aux cheveux tirés;
(d) (*laboriously*) **to s. a living,** gagner tout juste sa croûte.
2 *vi* **(a)** gratter; (*of wheel, pen, violin etc*) grincer; **branches that s. against the shutters,** branches qui frottent les volets;
(b) to s. (on the fiddle), racler *ou* gratter du violon;
(c) (*succeed with difficulty*) *F* **to s. home,** gagner tout juste la partie; **to s. into college,** arriver tout juste à entrer à la faculté.
►**scrape along** *vi* (*just manage financially etc*) vivoter, s'en tirer péniblement.
►**scrape by** *vi* **(a)** = **SCRAPE ALONG**; **(b)** (*just succeed*) (*in an exam*) se débrouiller, réussir de justesse.
►**scrape in** *vi* (*just succeed*) (*in entering university etc*) entrer de justesse; (*in winning election*) gagner de justesse; *Sp* (*in qualifying*) se qualifier de justesse.
►**scrape off** *vtsep* (*remove*) racler, enlever (*de la peinture*).
►**scrape out** *vtsep* récurer (*saucepan, boiler*).

►**scrape through 1** *vi* = **SCRAPE BY. 2** *vipo* (*perform just well enough in*) réussir (*un cours*) de justesse; **to s. through an examination,** être reçu de justesse à un examen.

►**scrape together, scrape up** *vtsep* (*save with difficulty*) amasser petit à petit *ou* peu à peu *ou* sou par sou (*une somme d'argent*); *Hum* **he scraped himself up off the floor,** il s'est ramassé peu à peu.

scraper ['skreɪpər] *n* racloir *m*, grattoir *m*; (*implement*) racle *f*, raclette *f*; (*cleaner*) curette *f*; *Aut etc* **(ice) s.,** grattoir (*pour pare-brise etc*); **door/shoe s.,** décrottoir *m ou* gratte-pieds *m inv*.

scrapheap ['skræphiːp] *n* tas *m* de ferraille; **to throw sth on the s.,** mettre qch à la ferraille *ou* au rebut; *Fig* **to throw s.o. on the s.,** (*of person*) laisser tomber qn comme une vieille savate; *Fig* **he ended up on the s.,** (*through redundancy etc*) on l'a mis au rebut; *Fig* **lots of companies are on the s.,** beaucoup d'entreprises sont hors de jeu.

scraping ['skreɪpɪŋ] *n* **(a)** éraflement *m* (*d'un doigt etc*); **(b)** (*cleaning*) raclage *m*, grattage *m* (*de qch*); regrattement *m*, ravalement *m* (*d'un mur*); décrottage *m* (*des souliers etc*); *Culin* grattage (*des carottes*); (*tanning*) dépilage *m*, drayage *m* (*d'une peau*); ripage *m* (*d'un sculpture*); raturage *m* (*du parchemin*); **(c)** (*sound*) grincement *m* (*d'une plume, d'une scie, d'un violon etc*); (*scratching*) grattement *m*; **(d) bowing and s.,** salamalecs *mpl*; **(e)** (*layer scraped off*) mince couche *f* (*de beurre etc*).

scrapman, *pl* **-men** ['skræpmən] *n* marchand *m* de ferraille, ferrailleur *m*.

scrapple ['skræp(ə)l] *n Am Culin* =(genre de) friand fait de farine de maïs et de morceaux de porc que l'on frit à la poêle.

scrappy ['skræpɪ] *adj* (*collection etc*) hétérogène, hétéroclite; (*speech etc*) décousu; (*work*) inégal; **a s. second half,** une seconde mi-temps (de valeur) inégale; **s. knowledge,** bribes *fpl* de connaissances; **s. meal,** (*inadequate meal*) maigre repas *m*; (*meal made up of scraps*) repas composé de restes.

scratch¹ [skrætʃ] *n* **(a)** (*with fingernail*) coup *m* d'ongle; (*with claw*) coup de griffe; (*mark, cut*) égratignure *f*, éraflure *f* (*sur la peau*); (*made by claw*) griffure *f*; rayure *f*, frottis *m* (*sur une surface polie*); égratignure (*sur un film etc*); **he came out of it without a s.,** il s'en est sorti indemne, il s'en est sorti sans la moindre égratignure; **it's nothing, just a s.,** ce n'est rien, juste une égratignure; *Am & Comptr* **s. pad,** bloc-notes *m*, *pl* blocs-notes; **s. paper,** brouillon *m*;

(b) (*repeated action*) grattement *m* (*de la peau*); grincement *m* (*d'une plume*); **to give one's head a s.,** se gratter la tête;

(c) *Sp etc* **s. (line),** scratch *m*; ligne *f* de départ (*d'une course*); **to start (at) s.,** partir scratch; *F* **to start from s.,** partir de zéro; **to build a house from s.,** construire une maison de A à Z; *F* **to come up to s.,** se montrer à la hauteur (*de l'occasion*), faire le poids; *F* **to bring up to s.,** mettre (*qn, qch*) à niveau; (*prepare for exam*) chauffer (*qn*) (*pour un examen*); **he's not up to s.,** il ne fait pas le poids, il n'est pas à la hauteur; **the work was not up to s.,** le travail n'était pas d'un niveau suffisant; *Sp* **s. race,** course *f* scratch; *Sp* **s. player,** scratch *m*; joueur, -euse classé(e) zéro (*dans un tournoi*).

scratch² 1 *vt* **(a)** (*of cat etc*) égratigner, griffer (*qn*); (*of thorn etc*) écorcher, érafler (*la peau*); rayer (*le verre etc*); strier (*la roche etc*); **to s. oneself,** s'égratigner; *Cin* **scratched film,** film rayé; **s. a lawyer and you will find an art-lover,** chez tout juriste se cache un amateur d'art; **to s. the surface,** effleurer (*le problème etc*);

(b) (*rub*) gratter (*le métal, la peau qui démange*); **to s. one's head,** se gratter la tête; **you s. my back and I'll s. yours,** passez-moi la casse et je vous passerai le séné;

(c) (*of bird, animal*) gratter (*le sol*); creuser (*un trou*) avec les griffes;

(d) (*delete*) **to s. s.o. off** *or* **from a list,** rayer *ou* biffer qn d'une liste; *Horseracing* **to s. a horse,** déclarer forfait pour un cheval; (*of stewards*) scratcher un cheval;

(e) (*write*) griffonner, écrire (*quelques mots*).

2 *vi* **(a)** (*of person, animal*) se gratter; (*of bird, animal*) gratter (*dans la terre etc*); **don't s.!,** (*yourself*) arrête de te gratter; (*don't scratch me*) arrête de me griffer; **cat that scratches,** chat qui griffe; **to s. at the door,** gratter à la porte;

(b) (*of pen etc*) grincer, gratter;

(c) *Sp* (*of entrant*) déclarer forfait.

scratch³ *adj* (*repas etc*) improvisé, sommaire; *Sp* **s. team,** équipe improvisée.

►**scratch about, scratch around** *vi* **to s. around for sth,** chercher à dénicher qch; **to s. about for evidence,** dénicher des preuves.

►**scratch out** *vtsep* **(a)** (*remove by scratching*) **to s. s.o.'s eyes out,** arracher les yeux à qn; **(b)** (*delete*) rayer, biffer, raturer (*un mot*); (*with penknife*) gratter, effacer.

►**scratch together** *vtsep* (*assemble with difficulty*) racler les fonds de tiroir pour rassembler (*une somme d'argent*); rassembler à grand peine (*une équipe*).

►**scratch up** *vtsep* **(a)** = **SCRATCH TOGETHER; (b)** (*dig up*) **to s. up a bone,** déterrer un os (*en grattant*).

scratcher ['skrætʃər] *n* **(a)** (*person*) gratteur, -euse; (*cat etc*) chat *etc* qui griffe; **(b)** (*implement*) grattoir *m*, gratteau *m*; **back s.,** gratte-dos *m inv*.

scratching ['skrætʃɪŋ] *n* **(a)** (*with fingernail*) coups *mpl* d'ongle; (*with claw*) coup de griffe; écorchement *m*, éraflement *m* (*de la peau*); rayage *m*, striation *f* (*d'une surface*); **(b)** (*rubbing*) grattement *m* (*de la tête etc*); **(c)** (*deletion*) rayage (*d'un concurrent*); **(d)** (*sound*) grattement *m*; grincement *m* (*d'une plume*); bruit *m* de surface *ou* de fond (*d'un disque*).

scratchy ['skrætʃɪ] *adj* **(a)** (*drawing*) au trait maigre, peu assuré; **s. writing,** pattes *fpl* d'araignée, pattes de mouche; **(b)** (*pen etc*) (*messy*) qui gratte; (*noisy*) qui grince (*sur le papier*); (*material etc*) (*coarse*) rugueux, grossier; (*that irritates skin*) qui gratte la peau; (*record*) rayé, qui craque.

scrawl¹ [skrɔːl] *n* (*writing*) griffonnage *m*, gribouillage *m*, *F* grimoire *m*; (*note*) petit mot écrit à la hâte.

scrawl² 1 *vt* griffonner, gribouiller (*une lettre etc*). **2** *vi* écrire comme un chat.

scrawny ['skrɔːnɪ] *adj F* maigre, décharné.

scream¹ [skriːm] *n* **(a)** (*cry*) cri perçant *ou* aigu; **a s. of pain,** un cri de douleur; **screams of laughter,** de grands éclats de rire; **(b)** *Old-fashioned F* (*amusing thing, person*) **it was a perfect s.,** c'était à se tordre (de rire); **he's a s.,** il est tordant.

scream² 1 *vi* (*once*) pousser un cri perçant *ou* aigu; (*repeatedly*) pousser des cris aigus; (*of rabbit, hare*) couiner; (*of jet, missile*) faire un bruit perçant; **jets screamed overhead,** des jets sont passés au-dessus de nos têtes dans un bruit assourdissant; **to s. with pain,** crier *ou* hurler de douleur; **everyone's screaming about high prices,** tout le monde pousse les hauts cris au sujet des prix élevés; **to s. with laughter,** rire à gorge déployée *ou* aux éclats; **the poster screams at you,** l'affiche vous saute à la figure. **2** *vt* **to s. abuse,** hurler des injures; **to s. oneself hoarse,** s'enrouer à (force de) crier.

screaming ['skriːmɪŋ] **1** *adj* (*person*) criard, brailleur; (*missile, jet*) qui fait un bruit perçant. **2** *n* cris *mpl* (*de terreur etc*); hurlements *mpl*; cris perçants (*d'oiseaux etc*).

screamingly ['skriːmɪŋlɪ] *adv F* **s. funny,** tordant.

scree [skriː] *n Geol* éboulis *m*.

screech¹ [skriːtʃ] *n* cri perçant *ou* aigu; crissement *m* (*de pneus etc*); **a s. of laughter,** un éclat de rire perçant; **there was a s. of brakes,** il y a eu un crissement de freins; **s. owl,** (*bird*) effraie *f*.

screech² *vi* (*of person, parrot etc*) pousser des cris perçants *ou* aigus; (*of tyres*) crisser; **the car screeched to a halt,** la voiture s'est arrêtée dans un crissement de pneus; **she does tend to s. on the high notes,** elle a tendance à hurler dans les notes élevées.

screeching ['skriːtʃɪŋ] **1** *adj* (*rire*) perçant, aigu; (*pneus*) qui crissent. **2** *n* cris perçants *ou* aigus; crissement *m* (*de pneus etc*).

screed [skriːd] *n* **(a)** *Constr* **(floating) s.,** cueillie *f*; guide *m* (*pour plâtrage*); **(b)** (*speech*) harangue *f*; longue liste (*de réclamations etc*); (*long letter*) longue lettre.

screen¹ [skriːn] *n* **(a)** (*in front of fire*) écran *m*; (*against draught*) paravent *m*; (*partition*) cloison *f*; grille *f* (*en fer forgé etc*); rideau *m* (*protecteur*); **choir s.,** (*in church*) grille de chœur; **rood s.,** jubé *m*; **s. of trees,** rideau d'arbres; **to act as a s. for a criminal,** couvrir un criminel; **protective/safety s.,** écran de protection/de sécurité; **fire s.,** écran ignifuge; **(camouflage) s.,** écran (de camouflage);

(b) *Cin etc* écran *m*; **the s.,** le cinéma, l'écran; **television s.,** écran de télévision; **the big s.,** le cinéma; **the small s.,** la télé, le petit écran; **a picture/a face appeared on the s.,** une image/un visage est appparu(e) sur l'écran; *Cin* **s. actor/actress,** acteur/actrice de cinéma; *Cin* **s. rights,** droits *mpl* d'adaptation à l'écran; *Cin* **s. test,** bande *f ou* bout *m* d'essai;

(c) *Comptr* écran *m*; **on s.,** sur l'écran; **to bring up the next s.,** amener l'écran suivant; **this takes you back/forwards a s.** *or* **s. by s.,** ceci vous fait avancer/reculer écran par écran;

(d) *El Electron* écran *m* (*de tube cathodique etc*); **fluorescent s.,** écran fluorescent;

(e) (*for camera*) filtre *m*; (*for dark room work*) écran *m*; (*for colour photography*) réseau *m* mosaïque polychrome; (*in photoengraving*) trame *f*;

(f) *Constr Min etc* crible *m*, tamis *m*, sas *m*; *MecE etc* tamis filtrant, filtre *m*, crépine *f*; *Am* (*ventilation grill*) grille *f* de ventilation (*dans une porte etc*).

screen[2] *vt* **(a)** (*conceal*) cacher (*qch*) derrière un écran *ou* un paravent; *Mil* jalonner (*l'avance de l'ennemi*); (*protect*) abriter, protéger (*qn, qch*); (*from harmful influences etc*) mettre (*qn*) à l'abri (**from**, de); *El Electron* blinder (*un câble, une antenne etc*); **to s. sth from view,** cacher *ou* masquer *ou* dérober qch aux regards *ou* à la vue;

(b) *Cin etc* (*project*) projeter, passer (*un film*); (*show on television*) passer à l'écran (*un film, une émission*); mettre *ou* porter (*une pièce, un roman*) à l'écran;

(c) *Phot* munir (*l'objectif*) d'un filtre correcteur;

(d) (*sieve etc*) cribler, passer au crible (*du gravier, du charbon, du minerai, du grain etc*); sasser (*le grain*); trier, sélectionner (*du personnel*); filtrer (*des immigrants etc*); filtrer, passer au crible (*des nouvelles etc*); *Med* soumettre (*qn*) à une visite de dépistage; **to s. s.o. for a disease,** faire passer à qn une visite de dépistage pour une maladie.

screening ['skri:nɪŋ] *n* **(a)** (*hiding*) dissimulation *f* aux regards; *Mil etc* jalonnement *m* (*de l'avance ennemie*); (*protection*) mise *f* à l'abri; *El Electron* blindage *m* (*d'un câble, d'une antenne etc*); **(b)** *Cin etc* projection *f* (*d'un film*), passage *m* (*d'un film*) à l'écran; (*on television*) passage (*d'un film, d'une émission*) à l'écran; **when the film had its first s.,** quand le film est passé pour la première fois à l'écran; **(c)** (*sieving*) criblage *m* (*du gravier, du charbon etc*); sassement *m* (*du grain*); triage *m*, sélection *f* (*du personnel*); filtrage *m* (*des immigrants, des nouvelles etc*); examen sélectif (*de demandes d'emploi etc*); *Med* triage, dépistage *m* (*des contagieux*); **s. for a disease,** dépistage *m* d'une maladie.

screenplay ['skri:npleɪ] *n Cin* scénario *m*.

screenwriter ['skri:nraɪtər] *n* scénariste *mf*.

screw[1] [skru:] *n* **(a)** vis *f*; **thumb s.,** vis à molette *ou* à tête moletée; *HydE* **Archimedes** *or* **Archimedean s.,** vis d'Archimède; **loose s.,** vis desserrée; *F* **to have a s. loose,** être toqué, avoir une araignée au plafond; *Arch* **the screws,** les poucettes *fpl*; *F* **to put the screws on s.o., to tighten the s.,** serrer la vis à qn; *El* **s. base** *or* **cap,** culot *m* à vis, culot Edison; **s. cap** *or* **top,** couvercle *m ou* bouchon *m* à vis (*d'un bocal, d'une bouteille*); **s. thread,** filet *m* de vis;

(b) *Av Nau* **s. (propeller),** hélice *f* (*d'avion, de bateau*); **twin s.,** hélice double;

(c) (*turn of screw*) tour *m* de vis; (*turn of screwdriver*) coup *m* de tournevis; *Billiards Tennis etc* effet *m*; **give it another s.,** serrez-le encore un peu; **to put (a) s. on the ball,** donner de l'effet (de côté);

(d) (*twist*) papillote *f* (*de tabac etc*); cornet *m*, morceau chiffonné (*de papier*);

(e) *Sl* (*prison officer*) maton *m*;

(f) *Vulg* (*sexual intercourse*) baise *f*; **what she needs is a good s.,** c'est une mal-baisée; **she's a good s.,** elle baise bien;

(g) *Br F* (*salary*) salaire *m*, paye *f*.

screw[2] **1** *vt* **(a)** visser (*qch*); **to s. sth (on) to sth,** visser qch à *ou* sur qch; **screwed together,** assemblé(s) à vis; **to s. one's head round to see sth,** se tordre la tête pour voir qch; **(b)** (*cheat*) avoir, rouler (*qn*); **to s. money from** *or* **out of s.o.,** extorquer de l'argent à qn; **they're out to s. you for every penny you've got,** ils essayent de vous extorquer tout l'argent possible; **(c)** *Billiards* donner de l'effet à (*une bille*); **(d)** *Vulg* (*have sexual intercourse*) s'envoyer, sauter, baiser (*une fille*); **s. you!,** va te faire foutre!; **(e)** *Tech* **to s. (cut),** fileter (*une vis, un boulon*); tarauder (*un tuyau etc*). **2** *vi* **(a)** (*of tap etc*) tourner (*à gauche, à droite*); **the knobs s. into the drawer,** les boutons se vissent sur le tiroir; **(b)** *Billiards* (*of ball*) rebondir de travers, dévier; **(c)** *Vulg* (*have sexual intercourse*) baiser, s'envoyer en l'air.

►**screw around** *vi* **(a)** *F* (*mess around*) glander; **(b)** *Vulg* baiser *ou* coucher avec tout le monde.

►**screw back** *vi Billiards* (*of player*) faire de l'effet rétrograde, faire un rétro; (*of ball*) revenir en arrière.

►**screw down** *vtsep* (*secure*) fixer *ou* assujettir (*qch*) avec des vis.

►**screw off 1** *vtsep* (*unscrew*) dévisser (*un écrou, un couvercle*). **2** *vi* (*become unscrewed*) se dévisser.

►**screw on 1** *vtsep* (*attach*) visser; *F* **he's got his head screwed on, his head's screwed on the right way,** il a la tête solide *ou* la tête sur les épaules. **2** *vi* (*become attached*) se visser.

►**screw up 1** *vtsep* **(a)** (*tighten by screwing*) visser; serrer (*un écrou*); (res)serrer (*un tourniquet, les chevilles d'un violon etc*); **to s. sth (up) tight,** visser qch à bloc; **to s. up a piece of paper,** tortiller du papier; **to s. up one's eyes,** plisser les yeux; **to s. up one's face,** se contorsionner le visage; **to s. up one's courage,** prendre son courage à deux mains; **(b)** *Sl* (*spoil*) gâcher, bousiller, foutre en l'air (*un travail*); **this has screwed up my plans,** ça m'a foutu mes plans en l'air; **he screwed up the interview,** il a complètement merdé à l'entretien; **(c)** (*make neurotic*) **to s. s.o. up,** foutre qn en l'air; **her parents' divorce has really screwed her up,** le divorce de ses parents l'a vraiment foutue en l'air. **2** *vi* **(a)** (*become screwed*) se visser; **(b)** *Sl* (*make a mess of sth*) bousiller.

screwball ['skru:bɔ:l] *adj & n esp Am F* loufoque *mf*.

screwdriver ['skru:draɪvər] *n* **(a)** (*tool*) tournevis *m*; **crossheaded s.,** tournevis cruciforme; **s. blade/handle,** lame *f*/poignée *f* de tournevis; **(b)** (*cocktail*) vodka-orange *f*.

screwed [skru:d] *adj Br F* ivre, soûl.

screw-on ['skru:ɒn] *adj* (*boucles d'oreilles*) à vis; (*objectif*) détachable, mobile.

screwy ['skru:ɪ] *adj F* fou, cinglé, loufoque.

scribble[1] ['skrɪb(ə)l] *n* **(a)** (*act of scribbling*) griffonnage *m*, gribouillage *m*; **(b)** (*bad writing*) écriture *f* illisible, pattes *fpl* de mouche; **that's not drawing, it's just (a) s.,** ce n'est pas du dessin, c'est du gribouillage.

scribble[2] **1** *vt* griffonner, gribouiller (*quelques mots à qn, une note dans son carnet etc*). **2** *vi* barbouiller du papier; **don't s. on the walls,** ne barbouille pas les murs.

►**scribble down** *vtsep* (*write*) = **SCRIBBLE**[2] **1.**

scribbler ['skrɪblər] *n* **(a)** (*person who scribbles*) griffonneur, -euse, *F* gribouilleur, -euse; **(b)** *F* (*inferior writer*) écrivailleur, -euse.

scribbling ['skrɪblɪŋ] *n* (*bad writing*) griffonnage *m*, gribouillage *m*; **scribblings,** (*of writer*) gribouillages, gribouillis *mpl*; **s. paper,** (papier *m*) brouillon *m*; **s. pad,** bloc *m* mémento.

scribe[1] [skraɪb] *n Hist* (*person*) scribe *m*.

scribe[2] *n* **s. (awl),** pointe *f* à tracer.

scribe[3] *vt Carp Constr* tracer (*une ligne*).

scriber ['skraibər] *n* (*tool*) pointe *f* à tracer.

scrimmage[1] ['skrɪmɪdʒ] *n* **(a)** (*struggle*) mêlée *f*, bagarre *f*, bousculade *f*; **(b)** *US Fb* mêlée *f*.

scrimmage[2] **1** *vi* se quereller, se bousculer. **2** *vt US Fb* mettre (*le ballon*) en mêlée.

scrimp [skrɪmp] *vi* **to s. (and save),** faire des économies de bouts de chandelle.

scrimshank ['skrɪmʃæŋk] *vi Mil Sl* tirer au flanc.

scrimshanker ['skrɪmʃæŋkər] *n Mil Sl* tire-au-flanc *m inv*.

scrip [skrɪp] *n Fin* (*shares*) valeurs *fpl*, titres *mpl*, actions *fpl*; **s. (certificate),** certificat *m* d'actions provisoire; **s. (issue),** titres attribués à un actionnaire (*au lieu de dividende etc*).

script [skrɪpt] *n* **(a)** (*manuscript*) manuscrit *m*; *Sch* copie *f* (*d'examen*); *Jur* (document) original *m*, -aux; *Th* texte *m*, script *m*; *Cin* scénario *m*; **to read from a s.,** (*of newsreader, politician etc*) lire ses notes; *Cin TV* **s. girl,** scripte *f*; **(b)** (*as opposed to print*) écriture *f*; **Gothic s.,** écriture gothique; *Typ* **s. (type),** cursive *f*.

scripted ['skrɪptɪd] *adj* (*remark etc*) préparé à l'avance.

scriptural ['skrɪptʃərəl] *adj* scriptural, -aux, biblique.

scripture ['skrɪptʃər] *n* **Holy S., the Scriptures,** l'Écriture sainte, les (saintes) Écritures; *Sch* **s. (lesson),** histoire sainte.

scriptwriter ['skrɪptraɪtər] *n Cin etc* scénariste *mf*.

scrofula ['skrɒfjʊlə] *n Med* scrofule *f*.

scrofulous ['skrɒfjʊləs] *adj* **(a)** *Med* scrofuleux; **(b)** (*corrupt*) dépravé.

scroll[1] [skrəʊl] *n* **(a)** (*roll*) rouleau *m* (*de parchemin, de papier*); **the Dead Sea scrolls,** les manuscrits *mpl* de la Mer morte; **(b)** (*containing inscription*) *Art etc* banderole *f* à inscription; *Her* listel *m*; **(c)** (*decoration*) *Archit etc* spirale *f*; volute *f* (*de chapiteau ionique*); (*in writing*) enjolivement *m*, arabesque *f*; (*in engraving etc*) cartouche *m* (*encadrant un titre*); crosse *f* (*de violon*); **(d)** *Comptr* action *f* de défiler; **s. lock (key),** touche *f* de défilement.

scroll[2] *Comptr* **1** *vi* défiler. **2** *vt* faire défiler.

►**scroll down** *Comptr* **1** *vi* (*of operator*) faire défiler de haut en bas; (*of text*) défiler de haut en bas. **2** *vipo* **to s. down a page,** passer à la page suivante.

►**scroll through** *vipo Comptr* faire défiler (*le texte*) de haut en bas.

▶scroll up *Comptr* **1** *vi* (*of operator*) faire défiler de bas en haut; (*of text*) défiler de bas en haut. **2** *vipo* **to s. up a page,** passer à la page précédente.
Scrooge [skruːdʒ] *n F* **he's a real S.,** c'est un vrai grippe-sou.
scrotal ['skrəʊtəl] *adj Anat* scrotal, -aux.
scrotum ['skrəʊtəm] *n Anat* scrotum *m*.
scrounge [skraʊndʒ] *F* **1** *vt* (*steal*) chiper, chaparder (*qch*); (*sponge*) écornifler (*un dîner, du tabac*). **2** *vi* **to s. round for sth,** aller à la recherche de qch; **to s. on s.o.,** vivre aux crochets de qn.
scrounger ['skraʊndʒər] *n F* (*thief*) chipeur, -euse, chapardeur, -euse; (*sponger*) écornifleur, -euse.
scrounging ['skraʊndʒɪŋ] *n F* **(a)** chipage *m*, chapardage *m*; **(b)** écornifierie *f*, écorniflage *m*.
scrub¹ [skrʌb] **(a)** (*bush*) arbuste rabougri, broussailles *fpl;* brousse *f;* garrigue *f;* **(b)** (*brush*) brosse *f* à soies courtes; **deck s.,** lave-pont *m*, *pl* lave-ponts.
scrub² *n* **(a)** (*rubbing with brush*) **give your hands a good s.,** frottez-vous bien les mains; **to give the table a good s.,** frotter la table à la brosse; *US* **s. brush,** brosse dure *ou* de chiendent; **(b)** *Am* **s. team,** équipe *f* de deuxième ordre.
scrub³ *vt* (**-bb-**) **(a)** (*clean*) récurer (*une casserole*); laver *ou* frotter (*le plancher*) avec une brosse *ou* à la brosse; *Nau* goreter, briquer (*le pont etc*); **(b)** *F* (*cancel*) annuler (*qch*); (*delete*) démagnétiser (*une bande*); **she's been scrubbed from the team,** elle a été virée de l'équipe.
▶scrub up *vi Med* (*wash*) (*of surgeon*) se brosser les mains *etc* (*avant d'opérer*).
scrubber ['skrʌbər] *n* **(a)** (*person who scrubs*) laveur, -euse (à la brosse); **(b)** (*implement*) **pan s.,** tampon *m* à récurer; **(c)** *Br Sl* (*promiscuous woman*) pute *f*, putain *f*, marie-couche-toi-là *f*.
scrubbing ['skrʌbɪŋ] *n* **(a)** (*cleaning*) récurage *m* (*d'une casserole*); (*with brush*) nettoyage *m ou* lavage *m* avec une brosse dure; **s. brush,** brosse dure *ou* de chiendent; **(b)** = **SCRUB² (a)**.
scrubland ['skrʌblænd] *n* terrain broussailleux, brousse *f*.
scruff [skrʌf] *n* **(a)** (*part of neck*) nuque *f;* (*skin*) peau *f* de la nuque; **to take** *or* **seize an animal by the s. of the** *or* **its neck,** saisir un animal par la peau du cou; **(b)** *F* (*scruffy person*) **a s. like you,** quelqu'un d'aussi peu soigné que toi.
scruffily ['skrʌfɪlɪ] *adv* **s. dressed,** débraillé.
scruffy ['skrʌfɪ] *adj F* mal soigné; (*person*) (*badly dressed*) mal habillé, habillé n'importe comment; (*in old, dirty clothes*) habillé salement; (*clothes etc*) sale; (*hôtel*) minable; **his jacket's getting a bit s.,** cette veste commence à s'user; **a s. old van,** un vieux camion tout pourri.
scrum [skrʌm] *n Rugby* mêlée *f; F* (*pushing, shoving*) mêlée, bousculade *f;* **s. cap,** protège-oreilles *m inv;* **s. half,** demi *m* de mêlée.
scrummage ['skrʌmɪdʒ] *n* = **SCRUM**.
scrumptious ['skrʌm(p)ʃəs] *adj F* épatant, fameux.
scrumpy ['skrʌmpɪ] *n Br F* **s. (cider),** cidre fermier.
scrunch¹ [skrʌn(t)ʃ] *n* (*sound*) crissement; grincement *m*.
scrunch² **1** *vt* croquer (*qch*) avec les dents. **2** *vi* craquer, grincer; (*of snow*) crisser.
scruple¹ ['skruːp(ə)l] *n* scrupule *m;* **to have scruples about sth,** avoir des scrupules au sujet de qch; **to have scruples about doing sth,** se faire (un) scrupule de faire qch; **he has no scruples about lying to them,** il n'a aucun scrupule à leur mentir.
scruple² *vi* **not to s. to do sth,** ne pas avoir de scrupules à faire qch.
scrupulous ['skruːpjʊləs] *adj* **(a)** (*person, conscience etc*) scrupuleux; **(b)** (*care, work*) scrupuleux, minutieux.
scrupulously ['skruːpjʊləslɪ] *adv* (*see adj*) **(a)** scrupuleusement; **(b)** méticuleusement, minutieusement; **everything must be s. clean,** tout doit être d'une propreté rigoureuse.
scrupulousness ['skruːpjʊləsnɪs] *n* (*quality*) esprit scrupuleux; scrupulosité *f* (**in doing sth,** à faire qch).
scrutineer [skruːtɪ'nɪər] *n* scrutateur, -trice (*des votes*).
scrutinize ['skruːtɪnaɪz] *vt* scruter, sonder (*qch*); (*examine in depth*) examiner (*qch*) à fond; vérifier (*des suffrages*).
scrutinizing ['skruːtɪnaɪzɪŋ] *adj* scrutateur, -trice; **s. look,** regard pénétrant *ou* scrutateur.
scrutiny ['skruːtɪnɪ] *n* examen minutieux *ou* attentif; investigation *ou* recherche minutieuse; *Pol* vérification minutieuse (*des bulletins de vote*); **to come under s.,** faire l'objet d'un examen.
scuba ['skjuːbə] *n* scaphandre *m* autonome; **s. diver,** plongeur, -euse autonome; **s. diving,** plongée sous-marine autonome.
scud¹ [skʌd] *n* **(a)** (*rapid movement*) course précipitée *ou* rapide; **(b)** (*gust*) rafale *f*.
scud² *vi* (**-dd-**) (*of person, animal etc*) filer comme le vent; **the clouds were scudding across the sky,** les nuages galopaient à travers le ciel.
scuff¹ [skʌf] *vt* frotter, racler, user (*avec les pieds*); érafler (*le cuir etc*).
scuff² *n* **s. (mark),** éraflure *f;* (*on floor*) rayure *f*.
▶scuff up *vtsep* (*push up*) soulever (*la neige, la poussière*) (*en traînant le pas*).
scuffed [skʌft] *adj* (*shoe*) éraflé; (*floor*) rayé.
scuffle¹ ['skʌf(ə)l] *n* mêlée *f*, échauffourée *f*, bagarre *f*.
scuffle² *vi* se battre, se bousculer, se bagarrer.
scull¹ [skʌl] *n* (*oar*) (*one of a pair*) aviron *m* de couple; (*used at stern*) godille *f*.
scull² **1** *vi* (*in rowing*) (*row in pair*) ramer *ou* nager en couple; (*at stern*) godiller. **2** *vt* (*row in pair*) faire avancer (*un bateau*) en couple; (*row at stern*) faire avancer (*un bateau*) à la godille.
sculler ['skʌlər] *n* (*in rowing*) **(a)** (*person rowing*) rameur *m* de couple (*in pair*); godilleur *m* (*at stern*); **(b)** (*boat*) **double s.,** double-scull *m*, *pl* doubles-sculls.
scullery ['skʌlərɪ] *n* arrière-cuisine *f*, *pl* arrière-cuisines; **s. maid,** laveuse *f* de vaisselle.
sculling ['skʌlɪŋ] *n* (*in rowing*) (*in pair*) nage *f* à couple; (*at stern*) nage à la godille.
sculp(t) [skʌlp(t)] *Art* **1** *vt* sculpter (*une statue*). **2** *vi* faire de la sculpture.
sculptor ['skʌlptər] *n Art* sculpteur *m*.
sculptress ['skʌlptrɪs] *n Art* femme sculpteur.
sculptural ['skʌlptʃərəl] *adj Art* (*art*) sculptural, -aux.
sculpture¹ ['skʌlptʃər] *n Art* (*art or object*) sculpture *f*.
sculpture² **1** *vt* **(a)** (*carve*) sculpter (*une statue, la pierre etc*); **she has very sculptured features,** elle a le visage très fin; **(b)** (*decorate with sculpture*) orner (*un fronton etc*) de sculptures *ou* de bas-reliefs. **2** *vi* faire de la sculpture.
scum¹ [skʌm] *n* **(a)** écume *f*, mousse *f;* (*on wine*) chapeau *m; Metal* scories *fpl*, crasse(s) *f(pl)*; **to take the s. off,** écumer (*le pot etc*); **(b)** (*people*) **the s. of society,** le rebut de la société; **he's/they're s.,** c'est une ordure/ce sont des ordures.
scum² *vt* (**-mm-**) écumer (*le bouillon etc*).
scunner ['skʌnər] *n Dial* dégoût *m;* **to take a s. at** *or* **against sth/s.o.,** prendre qch/qn en dégoût.
scupper¹ ['skʌpər] *n Nau* dalot *m* (*de pont*).
scupper² *vt F* couler (*un navire, un projet etc*); saborder (*un navire*); **we're scuppered,** on est fichus.
scurf [skɜːf] *n* pellicules *fpl* (*du cuir chevelu*).
scurfy ['skɜːfɪ] *adj* (*head etc*) pelliculeux.
scurrilous ['skʌrɪləs] *adj* (*language etc*) grossier, injurieux; (*person*) ignoble, vil; **to make a s. attack on s.o.,** se répandre en injures contre qn.
scurrilously ['skʌrɪləslɪ] *adv* (*coarsely*) grossièrement; (*insultingly*) injurieusement.
scurry¹ ['skʌrɪ] *n* **(a)** (*act of scurrying*) course *f* précipitée, débandade *f;* **(b)** tourbillon *m* (*de neige, de poussière etc*).
scurry² *vi* aller *ou* courir à pas précipités.
▶scurry away, scurry off *vi* (*go away*) détaler, décamper.
scurvy ['skɜːvɪ] *n Med* scorbut *m;* **to get s.,** attraper le scorbut.
scutcheon ['skʌtʃən] *n Her* écu *m*, écusson *m*.
scuttle¹ ['skʌt(ə)l] *n* (*container*) **(coal) s.,** seau *m* à charbon.
scuttle² *n Nau* (*hatch*) écoutille *f; Am* (*in ceiling*) trappe *f*.
scuttle³ *vt Nau* saborder (*un navire*).
scuttle⁴ *vi* (*run*) courir à pas précipités.
▶scuttle away, scuttle off *vi* déguerpir, détaler; (*of rabbit etc*) débouler.
scuttling ['skʌtlɪŋ] *n* (*of ship*) sabordage *m*.
scythe¹ [saɪð] *n Agr* faux *f*.
scythe² *vt* faucher (*le blé etc*).
SDI [esdiː'aɪ] *n Mil* (*abbr* **strategic defense initiative**) initiative *f* de défense stratégique.
SDP [esdiː'piː] *n abbr* **Social Democratic Party**.
SE [e'siː] *n* (*abbr* **south east**) S.E. *m*.
sea [siː] *n* **(a)** mer *f*; **at the bottom of the s.,** au fond de la mer; **s. level,** niveau (moyen) de la mer; **by the s.,** au bord de la mer; **by s.,** par (voie de) mer; **beyond** *or* **over the sea(s),** outre-mer, au delà des mers; **to go to s.,** se faire marin; **the open s., the high seas,** le large, la haute mer, la grande mer; **on the high seas, out at s.,** en haute

mer, en pleine mer, au grand large; **to put (out) to s.,** (*of ship*) prendre la mer *ou* le large; *F* **to be all at s.,** être tout dérouté *ou* désorienté *ou* désemparé; **s. air,** air marin; **s. anemone,** actinie *f*, anémone *f* de mer; **s. battle,** bataille navale; **s. bird,** oiseau *m* de mer; **s. breeze,** brise *f* de mer; **s. captain,** capitaine *m* de marine; *Nau* **s. chest,** coffre *m* de marin *ou* de bord; **s. cow,** vache marine; *F* **old s. dog,** vieux loup de mer; **s. eagle,** (*bird*) pygargue *m*, orfraie *f*; **s. elephant,** éléphant *m* de mer; **s. fish,** poisson *m* de mer; **s. fishery** *or* **fishing,** pêche *f* maritime; *Myth* **s. god,** dieu marin *ou* de la mer; **s. horse,** hippocampe *m*; **s. kale,** crambe *m*, chou marin; **s. lane,** couloir *m* maritime; **to find** *or* **get one's s. legs,** (*of person*) s'amariner; **he hasn't found his s. legs,** il n'a pas encore le pied marin; **s. lion,** otarie *f*; **S. Lord,** lord *m* de l'Amirauté; **s. monster,** monstre marin; **s. otter,** loutre marine *ou* de mer; **s. power,** puissance navale; **s. salt,** sel *m* de mer; **s. scout,** scout marin; **s. serpent,** serpent *m* de mer; **s. urchin,** oursin *m* de mer; **room with a s. view,** chambre avec vue sur la mer; **s. voyage,** voyage *m* en mer; **s. wall,** digue *f*; **(b)** (*state of the sea*) (*swell*) lame *f*, houle *f*; **heavy** *or* **strong s.,** grosse mer, mer grosse *ou* houleuse; **there's a heavy s.,** il y a de la mer; **to run before the s.,** avoir la mer de l'arrière; **head s.,** mer debout; mer contraire; **(c)** *Fig* océan *m*, multitude *f*; **a s. of faces,** un océan de visages; **a s. of blood,** une mer de sang; *Lit* **a s. of troubles,** une multitude de soucis.

seaboard ['siːbɔːd] *n* (*coastline*) littoral *m*, -aux; (*coastal region*) bord *m* de la mer, région côtière.

seaboots ['siːbuːts] *npl* bottes *fpl* de marin *ou* de mer.

seaborne ['siːbɔːn] *adj* (*trade*) maritime; (*goods*) transporté par mer.

seafarer ['siːfeərər] *n* **(a)** (*sailor*) homme *m* de mer, marin *m*; **(b)** (*traveller*) voyageur *m* en mer.

seafaring ['siːfeərɪŋ] *adj* (*gens etc*) de mer, qui naviguent; **s. man,** marin *m*.

seafood ['siːfuːd] *n* (*no pl*) fruits *mpl* de mer; **s. restaurant,** restaurant *m* de fruits de mer.

seafront ['siːfrʌnt] *n* **(a)** (*area facing sea*) bord *m* de la mer; **(house) on the s.,** (maison) qui donne sur la mer; **(b)** (*road*) esplanade *f*, front *m* de mer.

seagoing ['siːgəʊɪŋ] *adj* (*navire etc*) de mer; (*commerce*) maritime; (*personnel*) navigant.

seagull ['siːgʌl] *n* (*bird*) mouette *f*, goéland *m*.

seal¹ [siːl] *n* **(a)** (*animal*) phoque *m*, *F* veau marin; **elephant s.,** éléphant *m* de mer; **grey s.,** phoque gris; **eared s.,** otarie *f*; **fur s.,** otarie à fourrure; **s. oil,** huile *f* de phoque; **(b)** (*skin*) (peau *f* de) phoque *m*.

seal² *vi* (*hunt seals*) chasser *ou* pêcher le phoque.

seal³ *n* **(a)** (*on deed etc*) sceau *m*; (*on letter*) cachet *m*; cachet (*de bouteille de vin etc*); *Jur* **given under my hand and s.,** signé et scellé par moi; **under the s. of silence/secrecy,** sous le sceau du silence/du secret; **to give one's s. of approval to sth,** donner son approbation à qch; **to set one's s. to sth,** (*to mark with one's seal*) mettre son sceau sur qch; (*to authorise*) autoriser qch, confirmer qch; (*to give approval to*) donner son approbation à qch; **this event set the s. on their decision,** cet événement a scellé leur décision; *Jur* **official s.,** (*affixed to property etc*) scellé *m*; **under s.,** sous scellés; *Com etc* **lead s.,** plomb *m* (*pour sceller une caisse etc*); capsule *f* (*de bouteille de vin*); **(b)** (*instrument*) sceau *m*, cachet *m*; *Admin* **the Great S.,** le grand sceau (*employé pour les actes publics*); **(c)** *Tech* (*device for making airtight*) dispositif *m* d'étanchéité; (*airtight join*) joint *m* étanche; **in order to get a good s.,** pour obtenir une bonne étanchéité.

seal⁴ *vt* **(a)** (*put seal on*) sceller (*un acte etc*); cacheter (*une lettre, une bouteille*); (*at customs*) (faire) plomber (*des marchandises etc*); *Jur* apposer les scellés sur (*une porte etc*); **his fate is sealed,** son sort est décidé *ou* réglé; **(b)** (*close*) fermer (*une lettre etc*); (*block*) obturer, boucher (*un puits de mine, un tuyau*); (*make airtight*) rendre (*qch*) étanche, étancher (*qch*); (*ensure airtightness of*) assurer l'étanchéité (*d'un joint etc*); *Culin* saisir (*de la viande*); **the frontier has been sealed,** la frontière est fermée; **my lips are sealed,** (*I am not allowed to say*) il m'est défendu de parler; (*I shall not say*) je ne dirai rien.

▶**seal in** *vtsep* (*contain*) enfermer; **the pastry seals the flavour in,** la pâte enferme l'arôme à l'intérieur.

▶**seal off** *vipo* (*isolate*) isoler, cerner; **the area was sealed off by the police,** le quartier a été isolé *ou* cerné par la police.

▶**seal up** *vtsep* = **SEAL⁴ (b).**

sealed [siːld] *adj* (*envelope*) cacheté; *Mil Nau* **s. orders,** ordres cachetés.

sealer ['siːlər] *n* **(a)** (*ship*) phoquier *m*; **(b)** (*seal hunter*) chasseur *m* de phoques.

sealing¹ ['siːlɪŋ] *n* (*seal hunting*) chasse *f* au phoque; **s. fleet,** flotte phoquière.

sealing² *n* **(a)** (*putting on seal*) scellage *m* (*d'un acte etc*); cachetage *m* (*d'une lettre etc*); (*at customs*) plombage *m* (*des marchandises etc*); **s. wax,** cire *f* à cacheter; **(b)** (*closing*) fermeture *f* (*de qch*); obturation *f* (*d'un tuyau etc*); **(c) s. compound,** lut *m*, mastic *m*; *Aut* anti-fuite *m inv* (*de radiateur*).

sealskin ['siːlskɪn] *n* (peau *f* de) phoque *m*; **s. coat,** manteau en (peau de) phoque.

seam¹ [siːm] *n* **(a)** *Sewing* couture *f*; (*in metal pipe, between boards etc*) couture, joint *m*; **flat s.,** couture rabattue *ou* plate; **French s.,** couture double *ou* à l'anglaise; **welded s.,** soudure *f*; **ship's seams,** coutures d'un navire; *F* **room bursting at the seams,** salle pleine à craquer; **to be coming apart at the seams,** (*of garment*) craquer de partout; *Fig* (*of economy, system etc*) aller à la débâcle; **(b)** (*on face etc*) ride *f*; (*crack*) fissure *f*, gerçure *f*; **(c)** *Min etc* veine *f* (*de houille etc*).

seam² *vt* **(a)** *Sewing* faire une couture à (*un vêtement etc*); **(b) face seamed with scars,** visage couturé de cicatrices.

seaman, *pl* **-men** ['siːmən] *n* marin *m*; (*ordinary sailor*) matelot *m*, marin; *Br* **ordinary s.,** matelot de troisième classe *ou* de pont; *Br* **able(-bodied) s.,** matelot de deuxième classe; *Br* **leading s.,** matelot (breveté) de première classe; quartier-maître, *pl* quartier(s)-maîtres.

seamanship ['siːmənʃɪp] *n* habileté *f*; **thanks to his s.,** grâce à son habileté et à son expérience de marin.

seamless ['siːmlɪs] *adj* **(a)** (*bas, tapis etc*) sans couture; **(b)** (*in metalworking*) (*of tube etc*) sans soudure.

seamstress ['semstrɪs] *n* couturière *f*.

seamy ['siːmɪ] *adj* **the s. side of life,** l'envers *m ou* les dessous *mpl* de la vie; **the s. side of politics,** le vilain côté *ou* les dessous de la politique; **one of the city's seamier districts,** l'un des plus bas quartiers de la ville.

seance ['seɪɒns] *n* séance *f* de spiritisme.

seaplane ['siːpleɪn] *n Av* hydravion *m*.

seaport ['siːpɔːt] *n* port *m* maritime *ou* de mer.

sear¹ [sɪər] *adj Lit* (*withered*) flétri, desséché.

sear² *vt* cautériser (*une blessure*); (*brand*) marquer au fer rouge; *Lit* endurcir (*la conscience etc*); dessécher (*le cœur*).

search¹ [sɜːtʃ] *n* recherche(s) *f(pl)*, fouille *f* (*dans un tiroir etc*); *Jur* perquisition *f* (à domicile); (*at customs*) visite *f*; **her s. for her son/the truth,** sa recherche de son fils/la vérité; **in s. of sth,** à la recherche de qch; **to be in s. of sth,** être en quête de qch, être à la recherche de qch; *Comptr* **to do a s. for sth,** rechercher qch; *Comptr* **s. and replace,** recherche *f* et remplacement *m*; **to make a s.,** faire des recherches; **right of s.,** droit *m* de visite; (*at sea*) droit de recherche; **s. party,** expédition *f* de secours; *Jur* **s. warrant,** mandat *m ou* ordre *m* de perquisition.

search² **1** *vt* inspecter (*un endroit*); chercher dans (*un endroit, une boîte*); fouiller dans (*un tiroir*); fouiller (*un suspect, les poches de qn*); scruter (*un visage, Lit sa mémoire*); (*at customs*) visiter (*un navire, la valise de qn*); *Comptr* rechercher dans (*un fichier, un répertoire*); *Comptr* **to s. and replace sth,** rechercher et remplacer qch; *Jur* **to s. a house,** faire une perquisition *ou* une visite domiciliaire; *F* **s. me!,** je n'ai pas la moindre idée! **2** *vi* faire des recherches; *Comptr* effectuer une recherche; **to s. after truth,** rechercher la vérité; **to s. for s.o./sth,** (re)chercher qn/qch.

searcher ['sɜːtʃər] *n* (re)chercheur, -euse.

searching ['sɜːtʃɪŋ] **1** *adj* (*examen*) minutieux; (*regard*) scrutateur; **s. questions,** questions *fpl* qui vont au fond des choses; **the interviewer asked some s. questions,** la personne qui conduisait l'entretien a posé quelques questions approfondies. **2** *n* recherche *f* (**for,** de); inspection *f* (*d'un endroit etc*); fouille *f* (*d'un suspect etc*); (*at customs*) visite *f*; *Jur* perquisition *f*.

searchlight ['sɜːtʃlaɪt] *n* projecteur *m*; (*beam*) projection *f*; **to turn a s. on sth,** donner un coup de projecteur sur qch.

searing ['sɪərɪŋ] *adj* (*pain*) fulgurant.

seascape ['siːskeɪp] *n* **(a)** (*view*) panorama marin; **(b)** *Art* (*picture*) marine *f*.

seashell ['siːʃel] *n* coquille *f* de mer, coquillage *m*.

seashore ['siːʃɔːr] *n* bord *m* de la mer; (*coast*) côte *f*, littoral *m*; (*beach*) plage *f*.

seasick ['siːsɪk] *adj* **to be s.,** avoir le mal de mer; **to be a little/very s.,** avoir un léger/fort mal de mer.

seasickness ['siːsɪknɪs] *n* mal *m* de mer.

seaside ['siːsaɪd] *n* bord *m* de la mer; **at the s.,** au bord de la mer; **s. resort,** station *f* balnéaire.

season[1] ['si:z(ə)n] *n* **(a)** saison *f*; **the four seasons,** les quatre saisons; **the rainy s.,** la saison des pluies; **hunting s.,** saison de la chasse; **close/open s.,** *(in hunting)* chasse fermée/ouverte; *Fishing* pêche fermée/ouverte; **the tourist s.,** la saison touristique; **the high s.,** la haute saison; **the slack s., the off s.,** la morte-saison; **to be in/out of s.,** *(of oysters etc)* être de saison/hors de saison; **strawberries are in s.,** c'est la saison des fraises; **in s.,** *(of animal)* en rut; en chaleur; **S.'s Greetings,** Meilleurs vœux de fin d'année;
(b) *(time)* période *f*, temps *m*; **in due s.,** en temps voulu, en temps et saison; **word in s.,** mot dit à propos; **in s. and out of s.,** à tout propos et hors de propos; à tout bout de champ;
(c) *Rail etc* **s. ticket,** *F* **s.,** carte *f* d'abonnement; **s. ticket holder,** abonné, -ée.

season[2] **1** *vt* assaisonner, apprêter, relever *(un mets)*; dessécher, étuver, conditionner *(le bois)*; aviner *(un tonneau)*; mûrir *(le vin)*; acclimater, endurcir *(qn)*; aguerrir *(un soldat)*. **2** *vi* *(of wood)* se sécher; *(of wine etc)* mûrir, se faire.

seasonable ['si:zənəb(ə)l] *adj* **(a) s. weather,** un temps de saison; **(b)** *(of help, advice)* opportun, à propos.

seasonal ['si:zən(ə)l] *adj* *(changements etc)* des saisons; *(commerce)* saisonnier; **s. worker,** (ouvrier) saisonnier *m*.

seasonally ['si:zən(ə)lɪ] *adv* saisonnièrement; **s. adjusted unemployment figures,** chiffres du chômage corrigés des variations saisonnières.

seasoned ['si:zənd] *adj* **(a)** *Culin* *(dish)* assaisonné; **highly s. dish,** plat relevé *ou* épicé; **(b)** *(wood, cigar etc)* sec, *f* sèche; *(wine)* mûr, fait; *(person)* acclimaté, endurci; *(soldat)* aguerri.

seasoning ['si:zənɪŋ] *n* **(a)** *(act)* *Culin* assaisonnement *m*, apprêt *m* *(d'un mets)*; dessiccation *f*, séchage *m* *(du bois etc)*; avinage *m* *(d'un tonneau)*; maturation *f* *(du vin etc)*; acclimatement *m*, endurcissement *m* *(de qn)*; aguerrissement *m* *(des troupes etc)*; **(b)** *Culin* *(condiment)* assaisonnement *m*, condiment *m*.

seat[1] [si:t] *n* **(a)** siège *m*; banc *m* *(dans un parc etc)*; banquette *f* *(d'autobus, de train etc)*; gradin *m* *(d'amphithéâtre)*; lunette *f*, siège *(de W.C.)*; *Th etc* place *f*; *Parl etc* siège; *Aut* **car s.,** siège de voiture; *Av* **ejection** *or* **ejector s.,** siège éjectable; *F* **to be in the hot s.,** être sur la sellette; *Aut Av* **s. belt,** ceinture *f* *(de sécurité)*; *Aut* **inertia reel s. belt,** ceinture à enrouleur (automatique); **fasten your s. belts,** attachez vos ceintures; *Aut Th etc* **flap** *or* **folding s.,** strapontin *m*;
(b) *(somewhere to sit)* place *f*; **there were no seats left,** il n'y avait plus de places; **to take a s.,** s'asseoir; **to keep one's s.,** rester assis; **keep a s. for me,** gardez une place pour moi, gardez-moi une place; **to have a s. in the House,** être député; **to have a s. on the Council,** être conseiller (municipal);
(c) *(part of chair)* siège *m*, fond *m* *(d'une chaise)*; *F* *(of person)* derrière *m*, fesses *fpl*; fond *m* *(de pantalon)*;
(d) *(centre)* siège *m*, centre *m* *(du gouvernement, d'une industrie)*; chef-lieu *m* *(judiciaire)*; centre *(intellectuel)*; foyer *m* *(de science, d'une maladie etc)*; *Med* **the s. of the trouble,** le siège du mal; **country s., s. in the country,** château *m*;
(e) *Horseriding* assiette *f*; **to have a good s.,** avoir une bonne assiette;
(f) *Tech* siège *m* *(d'une soupape)*; chaise *f* *(d'un coussinet)*; embase *f*, assiette *f* *(d'une machine etc)*; *(in engine)* selle *f*, assiette *(de cylindre)*.

seat[2] **1** *vt* **(a)** (faire) asseoir *(un enfant etc)*; **to remain seated,** rester assis; *Fml* **please be seated** veuillez vous asseoir, je vous prie de vous asseoir; **(b)** placer *(qn)*; disposer, placer *(les invités)*; **bus to s. thirty,** autobus *m* à trente places (assises); **this table seats twelve,** on tient à douze à cette table; **(c)** (re)mettre le siège à *(une chaise)*; remettre un fond à *(une culotte)*; **(d)** fournir *(une salle etc)* en chaises *ou* en sièges; **(e)** *Tech* asseoir, poser *(une machine etc)*; *MecE etc* faire reposer *ou* caler *(une pièce)* sur son siège; *(in engine)* assurer *ou* ajuster l'assise *(d'une soupape)*. **2** *vi* *(of skirt etc)* faire des poches.

-seater ['si:tər] *suff* **two/single/*etc*/-s.,** *Aut* voiture *f* à deux places/une place/*etc*; *Av* un avion *m* biplace *ou* à deux places/à une place/*etc*.

seating ['si:tɪŋ] *n* **(a)** *(allocation of seats)* allocation *f* des sièges *ou* des places; disposition *f* *(des invités)*; *(seats)* sièges *mpl* *(dans une salle etc)*; **there is more s. upstairs,** il y a encore des places en haut; **s. arrangements,** *(at dinner)* plan *m* de table; *(in rail carriage)* disposition *f* des sièges; **s. capacity,** nombre *m* de places (assises) *(dans une salle etc)*; **s. plan,** *(at dinner)* plan de table; **(b)** *(material for making seats of chairs)* matériaux *mpl* pour sièges de chaises; **(c)** *Tech* portage *m*; siège *m* *(de soupape etc)*; embase *f*, lit *m* de pose *(d'une machine)*; assiette *f*, logement *m* *(d'un organe de machine)*; **(d)** *(act of mounting)* montage *m* *(d'une piece, d'une soupape etc)*.

SEATO ['si:təʊ] *n Mil* *(abbr* **Southeast Asia Treaty Organization***)* O.T.A.S.E. *f* (Organisation *f* du Traité de l'Asie du Sud-Est).

seat-of-the-pants [si:tɒvðə'pænts] *adj* **it's a s.-of-the-p. operation,** c'est une opération qui demande de savoir faire face à l'improviste.

seaward ['si:wəd] **1** *adv* *(also* **seawards***)* vers la mer; du côté du large. **2** *adj* **s. breeze,** brise *f* du large. **3** *n* **to s.,** du côté du large; vers le large.

seawater ['si:wɔ:tər] *n* eau *f* de mer.

seaway ['si:weɪ] *n Nau* **(a)** route *f*, sillage *m* *(d'un navire)*; **(b)** *(rough sea)* mer dure; **(b) the St. Lawrence S.,** la voie maritime du Saint-Laurent.

seaweed ['si:wi:d] *n* algue *f*.

seaworthiness ['si:wɜ:ðɪnɪs] *n* (bon état de) navigabilité *f*.

seaworthy ['si:wɜ:ðɪ] *adj* *(of ship)* en (bon) état de navigabilité; *(able to stay afloat)* qui tient la mer.

sebaceous [sɪ'beɪʃəs] *adj* *(gland, cyst etc)* sébacé.

sebum ['si:bəm] *n Physiol* sébum *m*.

sec [sek] *n F* (= **SECOND**[1] **(a)); half a s.!, just a s.!,** un instant!, une seconde!

secant ['si:kənt] *Math* **1** *adj* sécant. **2** *n* sécante *f*.

secateurs [sekə'tɜ:z] *npl* *(in gardening)* sécateur *m*.

secede [sɪ'si:d] *vi* faire scission, faire sécession **(from,** de); se séparer *(d'un parti)*.

secession [sɪ'seʃən] *n* sécession *f*; *US Hist* **the War of S.,** la Guerre de Sécession.

secessionist [sɪ'seʃənɪst] *adj & n* scissionniste *mf*; *US Hist* sécessionniste *mf*.

seclude [sɪ'klu:d] *vt* tenir *(qn, qch)* retiré *ou* éloigné *ou* écarté **(from,** de).

secluded [sɪ'klu:dɪd] *adj* *(endroit)* écarté, retiré; **s. life,** vie retirée *ou* cloîtrée *ou* de reclus; **to live a s. life,** vivre dans la solitude.

seclusion [sɪ'klu:ʒən] *n* solitude *f*, retraite *f*; **in s.,** retiré du monde; **to live in s.,** vivre dans la solitude, vivre en reclus.

second[1] ['sekənd] *n* **(a)** seconde *f* *(de temps)*; **in a split s.,** en une fraction de seconde; **for a s.,** pendant une seconde; **wait a s.!,** attendez une seconde *ou* un instant!; **I won't be a s.,** je reviens dans un instant *ou* une seconde; **s. hand,** *(on clock, watch)* trotteuse *f*; **(b)** *Math Astron* seconde *f* *(de degré)*.

second[2] **1** *adj* **(a)** second, deuxième; **the s. of March,** le deux mars; **twenty-s.,** vingt-deuxième; **thirty-s.,** trente-deuxième; **ninety-s.,** quatre-vingt-douzième; **Charles the S.,** Charles Deux *ou* II; **he is s. to none in intelligence,** pour l'intelligence il ne le cède à personne; **our roads are s. to none,** nos routes sont excellentes; **to be s. in command,** commander en second; **to marry for the s. time,** se marier en secondes noces; **s. best,** deuxième; **it's only a s. best,** ce n'est qu'un pis-aller; **in a fight with him you'll come off s. best,** si tu t'affrontes à lui, tu ne t'en sortiras pas vainqueur; **we're not happy with s. best,** nous ne voulons que ce qu'il y a de mieux; **Spain's s. city,** la deuxième ville d'Espagne *(en importance, par sa population etc)*; *Rail* **to travel s. class,** voyager en seconde; **s. cousin,** petit(e) cousin(e); **to live on the s. floor,** habiter au deuxième (étage) *ou* au second (étage); *Sch* **s. form,** classe *f* de cinquième; *Aut* **s. gear,** deuxième vitesse *f*; **to take a s. helping,** *(at meal)* reprendre; **s. language,** seconde langue; **the s. largest city in the world,** la deuxième ville du monde *(en importance)*; *Gram* **s. person,** deuxième personne; **in (the) s. place,** deuxièmement, en second lieu; **to take s. place,** passer second; **s. rate,** médiocre, inférieur; *(artiste)* de second ordre; *Rugby* **s.-row forward,** avant *m* de deuxième ligne; **on s. thoughts,** tout bien réfléchi; **to have s. thoughts,** avoir des hésitations **(about sth,** au sujet de qch); **are you having s. thoughts?,** est-ce que vous hésitez?; **I've had s. thoughts,** j'ai réfléchi, j'ai changé d'avis; *Mus* **the s. violins,** les seconds violons; **to get one's s. wind,** *(to get one's breath back)* reprendre haleine; *Fig* *(to be ready to continue)* se remettre;
(b) *(another)* **a s. Camus,** un nouveau Camus; *Rel* **the S. Coming,** le second avènement; **s. childhood,** deuxième enfance *f*; **s. nature,** seconde nature; **s. sight,** clairvoyance *f*, seconde vue.

2 *n* **(a)** (le) second, (la) seconde; (le, la) deuxième; *Sp etc*; **to come in a good s.**, arriver bon second; *Mil etc* **s. in command,** commandant *m* en second; *Br Sch* **to get a s.**, (*in degree*) être reçu à la licence avec mention assez bien; *Aut* **to start in s.**, se démarrer en deuxième; *F* **anyone for seconds?**, (*at meal*) qui est-ce qui va en reprendre?;

(b) *Mus* **major/minor s.**, seconde majeure/mineure;

(c) *Com* **seconds,** articles *mpl* de deuxième qualité;

(d) (*in duel*) témoin *m*; *Boxing* second *m*, soigneur *m*.

second³ *vt* **(a)** seconder (*qn*); (*in debate etc*) appuyer (*une proposition*); **to be seconded by s.o.**, être secondé de *ou* par qn; **(b)** [sɪ'kɒnd] *Mil etc* (*detach*) mettre (*un officier*) en disponibilité *ou* hors cadre (*pour fonctions spéciales etc*); **to be seconded,** être mis hors cadre, être détaché (**to,** à; **from,** de).

secondary ['sekənd(ə)rɪ] **1** *adj* secondaire; (*evidence*) indirect; (*rôle etc*) peu important, accessoire; *Sch* **s. education,** enseignement *m* secondaire *ou* du second degré; **s. meaning of a word,** sens dérivé d'un mot; **of s. importance,** d'importance secondaire; **s. road,** route secondaire *ou* départementale; *Sch* **s. school,** école *f* secondaire. **2** *n Astron* planète *f* secondaire.

second-class ['sekənd'klæs] *adj* (*billet, wagon etc*) de deuxième classe; **s.-c. mail,** courrier *m* à tarif réduit; *F* **s.-c. citizen,** citoyen, -enne de seconde classe.

second-degree ['sekənddə'griː] *adj* **s.-d. burn,** brûlure *f* du second degré.

seconder ['sekəndər] *n* **to be the s. of a proposal,** appuyer une proposition.

second-guess ['sekənd'ges] *vt* (*anticipate*) **to s.-g. s.o.,** anticiper ce que qn va dire *ou* faire.

second-hand [sekənd'hænd] **1** *adv* de seconde main; (*to buy*) d'occasion; **to hear news s.-h.**, recevoir des nouvelles de seconde main *ou* d'un tiers. **2** *adj* (*voiture, livre, meubles etc*) d'occasion; (*nouvelle etc*) de seconde main; **s.-h. bookshop,** librairie *f* d'occasion; **s.-h. clothes shop,** friperie *f*; **the s.-h. market,** le marché de l'occasion; **s.-h. dealer,** revendeur, -euse; (*in clothes*) fripier *m*; (*in books*) bouquiniste *m*.

secondly ['sekəndlɪ] *adv* deuxièmement, en second lieu.

secondment [sɪ'kɒndmənt] *n Mil etc* détachement *m* (**to,** à; **from,** de); **to be on s. to another department,** être détaché auprès d'un autre service.

secrecy ['siːkrɪsɪ] *n* **why all the s.?**, pourquoi tous ces secrets?; **there's no s. about it,** ça n'a rien de secret; **business conducted in complete s.**, affaires menées dans le plus grand secret; **can I rely on your s.?**, puis-je compter sur votre discrétion?; **to bid** *or* **swear s.o. to s.**, faire jurer le silence de qn; **in s.**, en secret.

secret ['siːkrɪt] **1** *adj* secret, -ète; (*place*) secret, caché; (*secretive*) secret; **to keep sth s.**, tenir *ou* garder qch secret, cacher qch, taire qch; **he'd kept it s. from me for years,** il me l'avait caché pendant des années; **s. meeting** *or* **assembly,** conciliabule *m*; **s. admirer,** admirateur secret; **s. agent,** agent secret; **the S. Service,** le Deuxième Bureau; **s. police,** police secrète; **s. weapon,** arme secrète; **s. door,** porte cachée *ou* dérobée; **desk with a s. compartment,** bureau *m* à secret.

2 *n* secret *m*; **can you keep a s.?**, est-ce que tu sais garder un secret?; **it can be our little s.**, ça sera notre petit secret à nous; **I make no s. of it,** je n'en fais pas mystère, je ne le cache pas; **to let s.o. into the s.**, mettre qn dans le secret; **the s. is not to press too hard,** l'astuce consiste à ne pas appuyer trop fort; **it's no s.**, ce n'est pas un secret; **an open s.**, le secret de tout le monde *ou* de Polichinelle; **in s.**, en secret.

secretly ['siːkrɪtlɪ] *adv* en secret; (*croire*) secrètement.

secretarial [sekrə'teərɪəl] *adj* (*travail*) de secrétaire; **s. college/course,** école *f*/cours *m* de secrétariat.

secretariat [sekrə'teərɪət] *n* secrétariat *m*.

secretary ['sekrət(ə)rɪ] *n* **(a)** secrétaire *mf*; **private s.**, secrétaire particulier, -ière; **company s.**, secrétaire général; **S. of State,** ministre *m* (à portefeuille), secrétaire d'État; *Br* **Foreign S.**, *US* **S. of State,** ≈ ministre des Affaires étrangères; **(1st, 2nd, 3rd) s.**, ≈ (*to ambassador*) secrétaire d'ambassade; **(b) s. (bird),** serpentaire *m*, secrétaire *m*.

secretary-general ['sekrət(ə)rɪ'dʒenərəl] *n* secrétaire général; **the s.-g. of the United Nations,** le secrétaire général des Nations Unies.

secrete¹ [sɪ'kriːt] *vt* (*of gland etc*) sécréter.

secrete² *vt* (*hide*) cacher (*qn, qch*).

secretion [sɪ'kriːʃən] *n Physiol* sécrétion *f*.

secretive ['siːkrɪtɪv] *adj* (*of person*) réservé; (*hiding things*) dissimulé; (*on particular occasion*) cachottier; **why are you being so s. about it?**, pourquoi fais-tu tant de cachotteries là-dessus?

secretively ['siːkrɪtɪvlɪ] *adv* avec dissimulation.

secretiveness ['siːkrɪtɪvnɪs] *n* (*of person*) réserve *f*; cachotterie *f*.

sect [sekt] *n* secte *f*.

sectarian [sek'teərɪən] **1** *adj* (*esprit, culte*) sectaire; **s. quarrels,** querelles partisanes. **2** *n* sectaire *mf*.

sectarianism [sek'teərɪənɪz(ə)m] *n* sectarisme *m*; (*attitude*) esprit *m* sectaire.

section¹ ['sekʃən] *n* **(a)** section *f*, portion *f* (*de qch*); partie *f*, division *f* (*d'une structure etc*); tronçon *m* (*de tube, de voie ferrée etc*); section, tronçon (*de circuit etc*); quartier *m* (*d'orange etc*); *Com* rayon *m* (*d'un magasin*); *US Rail* compartiment *m* (*d'un wagon-lit*); élément *m* (*constitutif, préfabriqué*); *US* lotissement *m* (*d'un mille carré*); division (*d'un document etc*); article *m* (*d'une loi etc*); *Typ* section, paragraphe *m*, alinéa *m*; *Journ* rubrique *f*; *St Exch* rubrique, compartiment; *Mus* (*in orchestra*) groupe *m* (*de cuivres etc*); *Mil* section (*d'un service*); (*fighting unit*) groupe de combat (*d'une section d'infanterie*); équipe *f* (*de fusiliers, de grenadiers*); *Rail* **block s.**, section de block; *Av* **nose s.**, section avant, nez *m* (*de l'appareil*); *Journ* **sports s.**, rubrique sport; **all sections of the population,** toutes les couches de la population, toutes les catégories sociales;

(b) *Math* section *f*; *Archit Constr etc* coupe *f*, profil *m*, section; (*metalwork*) *&* *Constr etc* profilé *m* (*en métal*); (*thin slice*) tranche *f*, lamelle *f*; **microscopic s.**, mince lame *f*, plaque *f* (*pour examen au microscope*); **conic/plane s.**, section conique/plane; **horizontal s.**, coupe *ou* section horizontale.

section² *vt* couper *ou* diviser (*qch*) en sections; sectionner (*un pays etc*).

sectional ['sekʃənəl] *adj* **(a)** appartenant à une classe *ou* à un parti; **(b)** (*dessin etc*) en coupe, en profil; (*surface*) de section.

sectionalism ['sekʃənəlɪz(ə)m] *n US* régionalisme *m*, esprit *m* de clocher.

sector ['sektər] *n* **(a)** *Math Astron Mil* secteur *m*; **s. of a circle,** secteur circulaire; *Admin* **public/private s.**, secteur public/privé; **public s. spending,** dépenses publiques; **(b)** *MecE* secteur *m*, couronne *f*; **(c)** *Math* compas *m* de proportion.

secular ['sekjʊlər] **1** *adj* **(a)** *Rel* (*history, art etc*) séculier, laïque; (*music*) profane; **s. priest,** (prêtre *m*) séculier *m*; **(b)** (*fête etc*) séculaire. **2** *n* (*priest*) (prêtre *m*) séculier *m*.

secularism ['sekjʊlərɪz(ə)m] *n* **(a)** laïcisme *m*; **(b)** *Phil* sécularisme *m*.

secularization [sekjʊləraɪ'zeɪʃən] *n Rel* sécularisation *f* (*de biens ecclésiastiques etc*); désaffectation *f* (*d'une église*); laïcisation *f* (*d'une école etc*).

secularize ['sekjʊləraɪz] *vt* séculariser (*un domaine etc*); laïciser (*une école etc*); **secularized church,** église désaffectée.

secure¹ [sɪ'kjʊər] *adj* **(a)** (*free from anxiety*) sûr; (*avenir*) assuré; *Fin* (*placement*) sûr, de tout repos; *Psy* (*person*) qui se sent en sécurité; **to feel s. of victory,** être assuré *ou* certain de la victoire; *Fml* **s. in the knowledge that ...**, sachant avec certitude que ...; **(b)** (*safe*) (*valuables*) en sûreté; (*investment*) sûr; (*place*) sûr; **the prisoner is s.**, le prisonnier est en lieu sûr; **(c)** (*door, plank etc*) fixe, assujetti; (*foundations*) solide; (*foothold, grasp*) ferme, sûr; **that rope doesn't look very s.**, cette corde n'a pas l'air très solide; **this nail's not s.**, ce clou ne tient pas; **to make the boat s.**, bien amarrer le canot.

secure² *vt* **(a)** mettre (*qn, qch*) en sûreté *ou* à l'abri (*du danger*); mettre (*un prisonnier*) en lieu sûr; **to s. a pass,** garder un défilé; *Mil* **to s. arms,** mettre l'arme sous le bras gauche; **(b)** (*immobilize*) assujettir (*qch qui a du jeu*); fixer (*un volet qui bat etc*); retenir (*qch à sa place*); accorer (*un tonneau etc*); arrimer (*une cargaison*); *Nau* saisir (*les canots, l'ancre*); **doors and windows should be properly secured,** les portes et les fenêtres doivent être bien fermées; **(c)** *Jur Com* nantir (*un prêteur*) (*par une hypothèque, d'un titre etc*); **to s. a debt by mortgage,** hypothéquer une créance; **(d)** (*obtain*) obtenir, acquérir, se procurer (*qch*); atteindre (*son but*); **to s. sth for s.o.**, procurer qch à qn.

secured [sɪ'kjʊəd] *adj* **(a)** (*avenir etc*) sûr, assuré; **(b)** *Jur* (*emprunt*) garanti, gagé; (*créancier*) garanti, nanti.

securely [sɪ'kjʊəlɪ] *adv* (*see adj*) **(a)** sûrement; **(b)** sans danger; **(c)** solidement; **s. tightened,** bien serré.

security [sɪ'kjʊərɪtɪ] *n* **(a)** sécurité *f*, sûreté *f* (*d'une fermeture etc*); **to live in s.**, vivre en sûreté *ou* en sécurité;

(job) s., sécurité de l'emploi; *Admin* **social s.,** sécurité sociale;

(b) (*at military base, during state visit etc*) sécurité *f*; **s. blanket,** (*for child*) couverture sécurisante; **a s. blanket has been thrown around the airport,** un déploiement de forces de l'ordre a été organisé autour de l'aéroport; *Admin Mil etc* **s. clearance,** contrôle *m* de sécurité (*sur qn*), habilitation *f*; (*pass*) certificat *m* de sécurité; **the United Nations S. Council,** le conseil de sécurité des Nations Unies; **s. device,** dispositif *m* de sûreté; **s. firm,** société *f* de surveillance; **s. forces,** forces *fpl* de sécurité; **s. guard,** garde *m* du sécurité; **he's/it's a s. risk,** il/cela constitue un danger *ou* un risque pour la sécurité;

(c) (*means of protection*) (moyen *m* de) sécurité *f*; (*safeguard*) sauvegarde *f*;

(d) *Com Jur* caution *f*, cautionnement *m*; (*for payment of debt*) gage *m*, garantie *f*; (*collateral*) nantissement *m*; (*person*) (donneur, -euse de) caution; (*for payment of debt*) garant, -ante; **s. for a debt,** garantie d'une créance; **to stand s. for s.o.,** se porter garant pour qn; **to give sth as (a) s.,** donner qch en gage *ou* en cautionnement; **to lend money on s./without s.,** prêter de l'argent sur nantissement/sur gage à découvert;

(e) *Fin* **securities,** titres *mpl*, valeurs *fpl*, fonds *mpl*; (*portfolio*) portefeuille *m* titres, *F* portefeuille; **government securities,** fonds d'État; **the securities market,** le marché des valeurs, la Bourse; *US* **Securities and Exchange Commission,** = Commission *f* des opérations de Bourse.

sedan [sɪ'dæn] *n Aut Am* voiture *f* de tourisme; **four-door s.,** berline *f*; *Arch* **s. (chair),** chaise *f* à porteurs.

sedate¹ [sɪ'deɪt] *adj* (*person*) posé, reposé; (*maintien*) composé, calme; (*esprit*) rassis.

sedate² *vt Med* donner un sédatif à (*qn*).

sedately [sɪ'deɪtlɪ] *adv* posément.

sedation [sɪ'deɪʃən] *n Med* sédation *f*; **to be under s.,** être sous calmants.

sedative ['sedətɪv] *adj & n Med* sédatif *m*, calmant *m*.

sedentary ['sedəntrɪ] *adj* (*posture*) assis; (*emploi etc*) sédentaire; **s. life,** vie *f* sédentaire.

sedge [sedʒ] *n* (*plant*) joncs *mpl*, roseaux *mpl*; **s. warbler,** (*bird*) phragmite *m* des joncs.

sediment ['sedɪmənt] *n* sédiment *m*, dépôt *m*; boue *f* (*d'un accu etc*); lie *f* (*du vin*); *Ch* résidu *m*.

sedimentary [sedɪ'ment(ə)rɪ] *adj Geol* (*couche, roche*) sédimentaire.

sedimentation [sedɪmen'teɪʃən] *n* sédimentation *f*.

sedition [sɪ'dɪʃən] *n* sédition *f*.

seditious [sɪ'dɪʃəs] *adj* séditieux.

seduce [sɪ'djuːs] *vt* séduire (*qn*); **they seduced him away from the company by ...,** ils l'ont convaincu de quitter la société en le séduisant avec ....

seducer [sɪ'djuːsər] *n* séducteur, -trice.

seduction [sɪ'dʌkʃən] *n* **(a)** (*sexually*) séduction *f*; **(b)** (*attractiveness*) attrait *m*, charme *m*, séduction (*de qch*); **the seductions of such a lifestyle,** les attraits *ou* charmes d'un tel style de vie.

seductive [sɪ'dʌktɪv] *adj* séduisant, attrayant; (*sourire*) aguichant; (*discours etc*) suborneur; **s. offer,** offre séduisante *ou* alléchante.

seductively [sɪ'dʌktɪvlɪ] *adv* d'une manière séduisante.

seductiveness [sɪ'dʌktɪvnɪs] *n* caractère séduisant *ou* attrayant (*d'une offre etc*); attraits *mpl*, charmes *mpl* (*d'une femme*); séduction *f* (*du style*).

see¹ [siː] *v* (*pt* **saw** [sɔː]; *pp* **seen** [siːn]) **1** *vt* **(a)** voir; **I saw it with my own eyes,** je l'ai vu de mes (propres) yeux; **the cathedral can be seen from a long way off,** la cathédrale se voit *ou* est visible de loin; **to s. the sights of the town,** visiter les monuments de la ville; **there's nothing to s.,** il n'y a rien à voir; **I can't s. anything,** je ne vois rien; **the moment I saw him,** dès que je l'ai aperçu *ou* vu; **did you s. that programme last night?,** tu as vu cette émission hier soir?; **s. what a mess you've made!,** regardez-moi ce gâchis!; **s. page 50,** voir page 50; **s. above,** se reporter plus haut; **s. (on) the back,** voir au verso; **I'm not fit to be seen,** je ne suis pas présentable; *F* **to s. things,** avoir des hallucinations *ou* des visions; **the quality has to be seen to be believed,** il faut voir la qualité pour y croire; **to s. s.o. do** *or* **doing sth,** voir qn faire qch; **I saw him fall,** je l'ai vu tomber; **to s. s.o. coming,** voir venir qn; *F* **I'll s. you damned** *or* **in hell first!,** va-t-en au diable!, va te faire pendre!; **he has seen a great deal of the world,** (*he has travelled a great deal*) il a beaucoup voyagé; (*he has a great deal of experience*) il a une vaste expérience; **the city hasn't seen such crowds in decades,** la ville n'a pas vu des foules pareilles depuis des dizaines d'années; *Mil* **the first time he saw action,** quand il a reçu le baptême du feu; *Mil* **he saw action in the desert,** il a combattu dans le désert;

(b) (*understand*) comprendre, saisir; reconnaître (*ses erreurs etc*); **they cannot s. the truth,** la vérité leur échappe; **I can't s. the difference,** je ne vois pas la différence; **I don't s. the point,** je ne vois pas à quoi cela servirait; **he can't s. a joke,** il n'entend pas la plaisanterie; **I s. what you mean,** je vois ce que vous voulez dire; **I don't s. it!,** (*I don't agree*) je ne suis pas d'accord!;

(c) (*observe*) observer, remarquer, s'apercevoir de (*qch*); **s. for yourself,** voyez (par) vous-même; **to s. oneself in one's children,** se reconnaître dans ses enfants; **I don't know what you s. in her,** je ne sais pas pourquoi vous l'admirez; **it remains to be seen whether ...,** reste à savoir si ...; **it remains to be seen,** nous verrons bien; **I s.** *or* **saw in the paper that ...,** j'ai vu dans les journaux que ...; **I s. (that) you're a sports fan,** je vois que vous êtes un fan de sport;

(d) (*perceive*) voir, juger, apprécier (*qch d'une certaine manière*); **I s. things differently now,** aujourd'hui je vois les choses autrement; **this is how I s. it,** voici comme j'envisage la chose;

(e) (*envisage*) voir; **what do you s. happening next?,** d'après vous, qu'est-ce qui va se passer en suite?; **how do you s. the situation in a year's time?,** comment voyez-vous la situation dans un an?; **I can't s. them accepting this,** je n'imagine pas qu'ils puissent accepter cela; **they say this will be more efficient but I don't s. it,** ils disent que cela sera plus efficace, mais je n'y crois pas; **I don't s. any chance of that,** à mon avis c'est peu probable; **I can't s. you as a boxer,** je ne te vois pas en boxeur; **I can't s. myself doing this,** je ne me vois pas faisant cela;

(f) (*examine*) examiner (*qch*); (*look at closely*) regarder (*qch*) avec attention; **let me s. that letter again,** repassez-moi cette lettre (pour que je la relise); **I'll s. what I can do,** je vais voir ce que je peux faire;

(g) (*make sure*) **to s. that everything is in order,** s'assurer que tout est en ordre; **I shall s. that he comes,** je me charge de le faire venir; **s. that you don't miss the train!,** faites attention de ne pas manquer le train!;

(h) (*meet*) fréquenter, avoir des rapports avec, voir (*qn*); recevoir (*un visiteur*); **he sees a great deal of the Longs,** il fréquente *ou* voit beaucoup les Long; **we don't s. much of each other,** nous ne nous voyons pas souvent, nous ne nous fréquentons pas beaucoup; **when shall I s. you again?,** quand est-ce que je vais vous revoir?; *F* **s. you soon!, (I'll) be seeing you!,** à bientôt!; **(I'll) s. you Thursday!,** à jeudi!; **to go to** *or* **and s. s.o.,** aller voir qn; **I'd like to s. you on business,** je voudrais vous parler affaires; **to s. a doctor,** consulter *ou* voir un médecin; **I can't s. him today,** je ne peux pas le recevoir aujourd'hui;

(i) (*escort*) **to s. s.o. home,** reconduire qn *ou* accompagner qn jusque chez lui; **I saw him to the station,** je l'ai accompagné jusqu'à la gare; **I'll s. you to the door,** je vous accompagne à la porte.

2 *vi* **(a)** voir; **she can't s. very well,** elle ne voit pas très bien, sa vue n'est pas très bonne; **cats can s. in the dark,** les chats y voient clair la nuit; **as far as the eye can s.,** à perte de vue; *F* **s. here!,** dites donc!, voyons!;

(b) (*understand*) voir; **as far as I can s.,** à ce que je vois, autant que j'en puis juger; **I s.,** je comprends; **ah, I s.!,** ah, je vois!; **do you s.?,** *F* **s.?,** vous comprenez?, vous y êtes?; **you s., I never liked them,** voyez-vous, je ne les ai jamais aimés; **so you s., this is not a rich country,** donc, vous le voyez, ce n'est pas un pays riche;

(c) (*observe*) voir; **s. for yourself,** voyez par vous-même; **wait and s.,** attendre et voir; **we shall s.,** nous verrons; **I'll be a good musician one day, you'll s.,** je serai un bon musicien un jour, vous verrez;

(d) (*examine*) voir; **can I s.?,** je peux voir?; **let me s.!, let's s.!,** faites voir!; **have you got a free room? — let me s.,** est-ce que vous avez une chambre libre? — voyons (voir); **it was, let me s., in 1938,** c'était, voyons (voir), en 1938;

(e) (*consider*) voir; **can we go to the beach, Mummy? — we'll** *or* **I'll s.,** est-ce que nous pouvons aller à la plage, Maman? — vous verrons, je verrai, on verra;

(f) (*make sure*) **to s. to it that ...,** s'assurer que ...; **I shall s. to it that he comes,** je me charge de le faire venir.

see² *n Rel* siège épiscopal; (*of bishop*) évêché *m*; (*of archbishop*) archevêché *m*; **the Holy S.,** le Saint-Siège.

▶**see about** *vipo* **(a)** (*attend to*) voir; **I'll have to s. about that old door,** il faudra que je m'occupe de cette vieille porte; **(b)** (*consider*) voir; **I'll s. about it,** je verrai ça; *Iron* **we'll s. about that!,** nous verrons ça!

►**see across** *vtas* (*escort to other side*) **to s. s.o. across the road,** aider qn à traverser la rue.

►**see in 1** *vi* (*look in*) voir à l'intérieur; **the curtains were drawn, so we couldn't s. in,** les rideaux étaient tirés, nous ne pouvions rien voir à l'intérieur. **2** *vtsep* (*escort in*) faire entrer (*qn*); **to s. the new year in,** faire le réveillon du nouvel an.

►**see into** *vipo* voir *ou* pénétrer dans (*l'avenir etc*).

►**see off** *vtsep* **(a) to s. s.o. off at the station,** accompagner qn jusqu'à la gare (pour lui dire au revoir); **we'll come to s. you off,** nous viendrons vous dire au revoir; **(b) to s. s.o. off (the premises),** (*escort*) accompagner qn jusqu'à la sortie; (*make sure they go*) s'assurer du départ de qn; **she saw off two bigger girls,** (*in fight*) elle a battu deux filles plus grandes; **the dogs saw them off,** les chiens les ont fait fuir.

►**see out** *vtsep* **(a)** (*escort to door*) accompagner (*qn*) jusqu'à la porte; **I'll s. myself out,** je connais le chemin, ne me raccompagnez pas; **(b)** (*stay until end of*) voir la fin de (*qch*); mener (*une entreprise etc*) à bonne fin; **I'll s. another year out here and go home,** je vais passer une autre année ici puis je rentrerai; **I don't think these boots will s. the winter out,** je ne crois pas que ces bottes feront l'hiver; **he'll s. us all out!,** (*will survive*) il nous enterrera tous.

►**see over, see round** *vipo* (*tour*) visiter, voir (*une maison etc*).

►**see through 1** *vipo* (*not be deceived by*) pénétrer les intentions de (*qn*); pénétrer, percer (*un mystère*); **I'm beginning to s. through it,** je commence à y voir clair. **2** *vtas* **(a)** (*stay until end of*) assister à (*un spectacle etc*) jusqu'au bout; mener (*une affaire*) à bonne fin *ou* jusqu'au bout; **I'll s. it through,** je vais tenir jusqu'au bout; **(b)** (*help to cope*) aider; **£20 should s. me through (to Monday),** 20 livres devraient me suffire (jusqu'à lundi); **friends and relatives are seeing her through this bad time,** ses amis et sa famille l'aident à traverser cette période difficile; **200 gallons should s. us through the winter,** 200 gallons devraient nous suffire pour l'hiver.

►**see to** *vipo* (*deal with*) s'occuper de (*qn, qch*); **I'll s. to it,** je vais m'en occuper, je m'en charge; **I'll s. to it that you're not disturbed,** je m'assurerai de ce que vous ne soyez pas dérangé.

►**see up** *vtsep* (*accompany*) accompagner (*qn*) en haut.

seed¹ [siːd] *n* **(a)** (*of fruit*) graine *f*, grain *m*; (*of oyster*) frai *m*; **mustard s.,** grain de moutarde; **s. vessel,** péricarpe *m*; (*gardening*) & *Agr* **seed(s),** semence *f*, graine(s), semis *m*; **to go** *or* **run to s.,** (*of plant*) monter en graine; (*of land*) s'affricher; (*of person*) se laisser aller; *Fig* **the seeds of discord,** les semences *ou* les germes *mpl* de discorde; **to sow (the) seeds of discord/doubt,** semer la discorde/le doute; **s. corn,** grain de semence; **s. potatoes,** pommes *f* de terre à semence; **s. bed,** (couche *f* de) semis *m*, germoir *m*; **s. box/tray,** boîte *f*/terrine *f* à semis; **s. merchant,** grainetier, -ière; **s. oysters,** naissain *m*; **s. pearls,** semence de perles; **(b)** *Arch Lit* = **SEMEN**; **(c)** *Bible Lit* descendance *f*, lignée *f*; **the s. of Abraham,** la descendance d'Abraham; **(d)** *Tennis* tête *f* de série.

seed² 1 *vi* (*of plant*) monter en graine; (*of cereals*) venir à graine. **2** *vt* **(a)** (*sow with seeds*) semer (*un champ etc*); **(b)** (*remove seeds from*) enlever la graine (*d'un fruit*); épépiner (*des melons etc*); égruger (*des raisins etc*); **(c)** *Tennis* **to s. the players,** trier les joueurs; **seeded players,** têtes *f* de série; **she was seeded tenth,** elle était classée dixième.

seedcake ['siːdkeɪk] *n Culin* gâteau parfumé au carvi.

seediness ['siːdɪnɪs] *n F* **(a)** (*of clothes, building*) état *m* minable; **(b)** (*feeling of being unwell*) indisposition *f*.

seedless ['siːdlɪs] *adj* asperme; (*fruit*) sans pépins.

seedling ['siːdlɪŋ] *n* (*plant grown from seed*) (jeune) plant *m*; (*young uncultivated tree*) sauvageon *m*; **seedlings,** semis *m*.

seedsman, *pl* **-men** ['siːdzmən] *n* grainetier *m*.

seedy ['siːdɪ] *adj* **(a)** *F* (*shabby*) (*person*) miteux; (*hotel etc*) moche; **(b)** *F* (*unwell*) mal en train, patraque; **to feel s.,** ne pas être dans son assiette; **(c)** (*plant*) plein de graines; (*épi*) grenu.

seeing ['siːɪŋ] **1** *adj* voyant, qui voit; *Am* **s. eye dog,** chien *m* d'aveugle. **2** *conj* **s. (that) ...,** vu que ..., étant donné que .... **3** *n* vue *f*, vision *f*; **s. is believing,** voir c'est croire.

seek [siːk] *vt* (*pt & pp* **sought** [sɔːt]) **(a)** chercher (*un objet perdu, un emploi etc*); rechercher, quêter (*l'amitié de qn, de l'avancement etc*); **to s. s.o.,** chercher (et trouver) qn; **to s. shelter,** chercher un abri; **they sought shelter under a tree,** ils se sont réfugiés sous un arbre; **to s. s.o.'s help,** rechercher *ou* demander l'aide de qn; **(b)** (*request*) **to s. sth from** *or* **of s.o.,** demander qch à qn; **to s. advice,** demander conseil.

►**seek after** *vipo* (*look for*) chercher (*la vérité etc*); **to be much sought after,** être très recherché *ou* demandé.

►**seek out** *vtsep* (*find*) chercher (et trouver) (*qn*).

seeker ['siːkər] *n* chercheur, -euse; **a s. after truth,** un chercheur de vérité; **pleasure seekers,** gens *mpl* en quête de plaisirs.

seem [siːm] **1** *vi* sembler, paraître; **to s. tired,** paraître *ou* sembler *ou* avoir l'air fatigué; **how does it s. to you?,** qu'en pensez-vous?; **it seems like a dream,** on croirait rêver; **it doesn't s. right, them getting away with it,** ça ne semble pas juste qu'ils s'en tirent à bon compte; **she seems to be** *or* **she seems like a nice person,** elle semble gentille; **I s. to have heard his name,** il me semble avoir entendu son nom; **I seemed to be floating on a cloud,** j'avais l'impression de flotter sur un nuage; **I s. to have dropped your vase,** je crois que j'ai fait tomber votre vase; **she seemed to be trying to say sth,** elle semblait essayer de dire quelque chose.

2 *v impers* **it seems (that) ..., it would s. that ...,** il paraît *ou* il semble que ...; **it seems like only yesterday,** c'est comme si c'était hier; **it seemed to me (that) I was dreaming,** il me semblait *ou* on aurait dit que je rêvais; **it seemed as though** *or* **as if ...,** il semblait que *+sub*, on aurait dit que + *ind*; **it seems so, it would s. so,** à ce qu'il paraît; **it seems not, it wouldn't s. so,** il paraît que non; **it seems to be raining,** on dirait qu'il pleut; **there doesn't s. to be any butter left,** il semblerait qu'il n'y ait plus de beurre.

seemingly ['siːmɪŋlɪ] *adv* apparemment.

seemliness ['siːmlɪnɪs] *n* bienséance *f*.

seemly ['siːmlɪ] *adj* convenable, bienséant.

seen *see* **SEE¹**.

seep [siːp] *vi* suinter; (*into sth*) s'infiltrer; **the water was seeping through the earth,** l'eau filtrait à travers la terre; **information was seeping out,** des renseignements filtraient.

seepage ['siːpɪdʒ] *n* **(a)** (*act*) suintement *m*; **(b)** (*lost liquid*) fuite *f*, déperdition *f* (*par infiltration*).

seer [sɪər] *n Lit* prophète *m*.

seersucker ['sɪəsʌkər] *n Tex* coton gaufré.

seesaw¹ ['siːsɔː] **1** *n* bascule *f*. **2** *adj* (*mouvement*) de bascule; de va-et-vient.

seesaw² *vi* **(a)** (*play on a seesaw*) jouer à la bascule; **(b)** (*of machine part etc*) basculer; (*oscillate*) osciller.

seethe [siːð] *vi* (*of liquid*) bouillonner; (*of crowd etc*) s'agiter; **the street is seething with people,** la rue grouille de monde; **to be seething (with anger),** bouillir de colère; **he's absolutely seething,** il est fou de rage; **the country was seething with rebellion,** l'esprit de rébellion fermentait dans le pays.

seething ['siːðɪŋ] *adj* (*liquid*) bouillonnant; **a s. mass of worms,** une masse grouillante *ou* foisonnante de vers.

see-through ['siːθruː] *adj* transparent.

segment¹ ['segmənt] *n* segment *m* (*d'une sphère, d'un cercle, d'un ver*); quartier *m* (*d'une orange*); **s. of a line,** segment linéaire.

segment² [seg'ment] **1** *vt* couper *ou* partager (*qch*) en segments; segmenter. **2** *vi* (*of worm*) se segmenter.

segmentation [segmən'teɪʃən] *n Biol* segmentation *f*.

segregate ['segrɪgeɪt] **1** *vt* isoler, mettre à part (*qch*); séparer (*deux espèces etc*) l'un(e) de l'autre; soumettre (*des races*) à la ségrégation. **2** *vi* (*become segregated*) se diviser, se désunir (**from,** de); (*form into separate group*) se grouper à part (**from,** de).

segregation [segrɪ'geɪʃən] *n* ségrégation *f*; séparation *f*, isolement *m*; **policy of s.,** ségrégationnisme *m*.

segregationist [segrɪ'geɪʃənɪst] *adj* & *n Pol* ségrégationniste *mf*.

sei [seɪ] *adj* **s. whale,** rorqual boréal.

seism ['saɪz(ə)m] *n* séisme *m*.

seismic ['saɪzmɪk] *adj* s(é)ismique.

seismograph ['saɪzməgræf] *n* s(é)ismographe *m*.

seismologist [saɪz'mɒlədʒɪst] *n* s(é)ismologiste *mf*, s(é)ismologue *mf*.

seismology [saɪz'mɒlədʒɪ] *n* s(é)ismologie *f*.

seize [siːz] **1** *vt* **(a)** saisir; (*take for oneself*) s'emparer de; prendre (*une forteresse*); capturer (*un navire ennemi*); **to s. (hold of),** saisir, empoigner (*qn, qch*); saisir (*une idée*); **to s. s.o. by the throat,** prendre qn à la gorge; **to be seized with fright,** être saisi *ou* frappé d'effroi; **to s. the opportunity of doing sth,** sauter sur *ou* saisir l'occasion de faire qch; **to s. the meaning of sth,** prendre *ou* saisir le sens de qch; **(b)** *Jur* confisquer, arrêter; saisir (*qch*); **to s. s.o.,** arrêter qn; appréhender qn (*au corps*). **2** *vi MecE* (*of part*) = **SEIZE UP**; **the brake is seizing,** le frein prend *ou* mord brutalement.

▶**seize on** *vipo* (*grasp*) saisir (*une idée*); **to s. on a pretext for leaving,** saisir *ou* sauter sur un prétexte pour partir.

▶**seize up** *vi MecE etc* (*become stuck*) (*of part, machine etc*) (se) gripper, coincer; (*engine*) caler; **my knee's seized up,** mon genou est coincé *ou* ankylosé.

▶**seize upon** *vipo* = **SEIZE ON.**

seizing ['siːzɪŋ] *n* **(a)** empoignement *m* (*de qn, de qch*); saisie *f* (*d'une propriété, de marchandises etc*); prise *f* (*d'une forteresse etc*); capture *f* (*d'un navire ennemi etc*); **(b)** *MecE etc* grippage *m*, grippement *m*; calage *m* (*d'un piston etc*).

seizure ['siːʒər] *n* **(a)** prise *f* (*d'une ville etc*); capture *f* (*d'un navire ennemi etc*); *Jur* appréhension *f* au corps (**of s.o.,** de qn); mainmise *f* (**of s.o.,** sur qn); *Jur* saisie *f* (*de marchandises*); **(b)** *Med* crise *f*, attaque *f*; **(apoplectic) s.,** attaque d'apoplexie; **(c)** *MecE* grippage *m*, grippement *m*, calage *m*.

seldom ['seldəm] *adv* rarement, peu souvent; **he is s. seen,** on le voit rarement; **such things are s. seen now,** de telles choses se font rares de nos jours.

select¹ [sɪ'lekt] *adj* **(a)** (*chosen*) choisi; *Parl* **s. committee,** commission *f* d'enquête; **(b)** (*exclusive*) de (premier) choix, d'élite; (*club*) très fermé, select; (*public*) choisi.

select² *vt* choisir (*des objets*); *Comptr Sp* sélectionner; **to s. from ...,** choisir parmi ...

selected [sɪ'lektɪd] *adj* choisi; *Com* de choix; *Lit* **s. passages,** morceaux choisis.

selection [sɪ'lekʃən] *n* **(a)** (*choosing*) choix *m*, sélection *f*; **natural s.,** sélection naturelle; **(b)** (*thing(s) chosen*) **a good s. of wines,** un bon choix de vins; **to make a s.,** faire un choix; **selections from Byron,** morceaux choisis de Byron; *Horseracing* **our selections,** nos pronostics.

selective [sɪ'lektɪv] *adj* sélectif; **s. breeding,** élevage *m* à base de sélection; **to be s.,** (*of person*) savoir choisir, choisir avec discernement; **he's very s. about what he eats,** il est très difficile sur la nourriture; **you should be more s. about your friends,** tu devrais être plus regardant quant au choix de tes amis; **to be s. in the application of a law/***etc*, (*biased*) se montrer sélectif dans l'application d'une loi/*etc*.

selectivity [sɪlek'tɪvɪtɪ] *n* sélectivité *f*.

selectman [sɪ'lektmən] *n US* (*in New England*) = conseiller municipal.

selector [sɪ'lektər] *n* **(a)** (*person*) celui *ou* celle qui choisit *ou* qui sélectionne; *Sp* sélectionneur, -euse (*d'une équipe etc*); **(b)** *Tel* sélecteur *m*; *Aut* (*automatic gearbox*) **s. lever,** levier *m* de sélection; *El* **s. switch,** combinateur *m*.

selenium [sɪ'liːnɪəm] *n* sélénium *m*.

self, *pl* **selves** [self, selvz] **1** *n* **(a)** (*personality*) la personnalité; (*ego*) le moi; **two selves in one body,** deux personnalités dans une seule personne; **that wasn't his real s.,** ce n'était pas vraiment lui; **the notion of the s.,** la notion du moi; **he's quite his old** *or* **former s. again,** (*he has recovered*) il est complètement rétabli; (*his character has returned to normal*) il est tout à fait comme auparavant; **preoccupation with s.,** préoccupation de sa propre personne; *Old-fashioned* **your good selves,** vous-mêmes, vous; **(b)** (*flower*) fleur *f* de couleur uniforme. **2** *pron* (*on cheque*) **pay s.,** payez à moi-même.

self- [self] *pref* **(a)** (*automatic*) automatique; **s.-loading,** à chargement automatique; **(b)** (*by oneself, itself*) auto-; **s.-taught,** autodidacte; **(c)** (*of oneself, itself*) de soi-même; **s.-censorship,** autocensure *f*; **to practise s.-censorship,** s'autocensurer.

self-absorbed [-əb'zɔːbd] *adj* égoïste.

self-addressed [-ə'drest] *adj* **s.-a. envelope,** enveloppe portant sa propre adresse.

self-adhesive [-əd'hiːzɪv] *adj* autocollant.

self-adjusting [-ə'dʒʌstɪŋ] *adj Tech* à autoréglage, à réglage automatique.

self-advocacy [-'ædvəkəsɪ] *n esp Am Admin* (*of mentally handicapped person*) affirmation *f* de soi.

self-apparent [-ə'pærənt] *adj* évident.

self-appointed [-ə'pɔɪntɪd] *adj* (*person*) qui a pris sur lui *ou* sur elle de (faire qch); **s.-a. critic of the régime, William Smith,** William Smith, une personne qui s'érige en critique du régime.

self-assertive [-ə'sɜːtɪv] *adj* décidé; **be more s.-a.,** vous devriez vous affirmer davantage.

self-assured [-ə'ʃʊəd] *adj* sûr de soi, plein d'assurance.

self-catering [-'keɪtərɪŋ] **1** *adj* (*vacances*) en appartement meublé. **2** *adv* **to go s.-c.,** louer un appartement meublé pour ses vacances.

self-centred ['-sentəd] *adj* égocentrique.

self-cleaning ['-kliːnɪŋ] *adj* (*four*) autonettoyant.

self-coloured, *US* **-colored** [-kʌləd] *adj* uni.

self-composed [-kəm'pəʊzd] *adj* (*person*) posé, calme.

self-confessed [-kən'fest] *adj* qui s'accuse soi-même; (*maoïste etc*) avéré; **he is a s.-c. workaholic,** de son propre aveu, il est obsédé par le travail.

self-confidence [-'kɒnfɪdəns] *n* confiance *f* en soi, assurance *f*.

self-confident [-'kɒnfɪdənt] *adj* sûr de soi, plein d'assurance.

self-congratulation [-kəngrætjʊ'leɪʃən] *n* autosatisfaction *f*, fait de chanter ses propres louanges.

self-congratulatory [-kən'grætjʊleɪtərɪ] *adj* autosatisfait, qui aime à chanter ses propres louanges; (*remarks, tone*) d'autosatisfaction, dénotant l'autosatisfaction.

self-conscious [-'kɒnʃəs] *adj* **(a)** (*person*) embarrassé, gêné; (*sourire*) contraint; (*style etc*) affecté; **he's very s.-c. about his large nose,** il est très complexé par son gros nez; **(b)** *Phil* conscient.

self-consciousness [-'kɒnʃəsnɪs] *n* **(a)** (*embarrassment*) contrainte *f*, embarras *m*, gêne *f*; (*of style etc*) affectation *f*; **(b)** *Phil* conscience *f*.

self-contained [-kən'teɪnd] *adj* **(a)** (*person*) réservé; (*uncommunicative*) peu communicatif; **(b)** (*appartement*) indépendant, avec entrée particulière.

self-contradictory [-kɒntrə'dɪktərɪ] *adj* contradictoire.

self-control [-kən'trəʊl] *n* empire *m* sur soi-même, maîtrise *f* de soi; **to exercise s.-c.,** faire un effort sur soi-même; **to have no s.-c.,** ne pas savoir se maîtriser; **to lose one's s.-c.,** perdre tout empire sur soi-même, ne plus se maîtriser *ou* se contrôler; **to regain one's s.-c.,** se ressaisir.

self-controlled [-kən'trəʊld] *adj* **to be s.-c.,** (*of person*) avoir du sang-froid.

self-correcting [-kə'rektɪŋ] *adj* à correction automatique.

self-critical [-'krɪtɪk(ə)l] *adj* **you should be more s.-c.,** tu devrais faire preuve d'un peu plus d'autocritique.

self-criticism [-'krɪtɪsɪz(ə)m] *n* autocritique *f*.

self-deception [-dɪ'sepʃən] *n* aveuglement *m*; **it's pure s.-d. on his part,** il se fait des illusions, c'est pur aveuglement de sa part.

self-defeating [-dɪ'fiːtɪŋ] *adj* **that would be s.-d.,** cela irait à l'encontre du but recherché.

self-defence, *US* **-defense** [-dɪ'fens] *n Jur* légitime défense *f*; **to kill s.o. in s.-d.,** tuer qn en légitime défense; **a course in s.-d.,** un cours de self-défense.

self-denial [-dɪ'naɪəl] *n* abnégation *f* de soi.

self-denying [-dɪ'naɪɪŋ] *adj* qui fait abnégation de soi.

self-deprecation [-deprɪ'keɪʃən] *n* dénigrement *m* de soi-même.

self-deprecatory [-'deprɪkətərɪ] *adj* de dénigrement de soi-même.

self-destruct [-dɪ'strʌkt] *vi* (*of device etc*) s'autodétruire.

self-destruction [-dɪ'strʌkʃən] *n* autodestruction *f*; (*of person*) suicide *m*.

self-destructive [-dɪ'strʌktɪv] *adj* (*behaviour, character*) suicidaire.

self-determination [-dɪtɜːmɪ'neɪʃən] *n Pol* autodétermination *f*.

self-discipline [-'dɪsɪplɪn] *n* autodiscipline *f*.

self-doubt [-'daʊt] *n* manque *m* de confiance en soi.

self-drive [-'draɪv] *adj* **s.-d. cars for hire,** location *f* de voitures sans chauffeur.

self-educated [-'edjʊkeɪtɪd] *adj* autodidacte.

self-effacing [-ɪ'feɪsɪŋ] *adj* qui aime à s'effacer.

self-employed [-ɪm'plɔɪd] *adj* qui travaille à son (propre) compte.

self-esteem [-ɪ'stiːm] *n* estime *f ou* respect *m* de soi, amour-propre *m*.

self-evident [-'evɪd(ə)nt] *adj* évident en soi, qui saute aux yeux.

self-explanatory [-ɪk'splænət(ə)rɪ] *adj* qui s'explique de soi-même.

self-expression [-ɪk'spreʃən] *n* libre expression *f*.

self-fertilization [-fɜːtɪlaɪ'zeɪʃən] *n Biol* autofécondation *f*.

self-fertilizing [-'fɜːtɪlaɪzɪŋ] *adj* autofécondant.

self-financing [-faɪ'nænsɪŋ] **1** *adj* (*entreprise*) qui s'autofinance. **2** *n* autofinancement *m*.

self-fulfilling [-fʊl'fɪlɪŋ] *adj* **s.-f. prophecy,** = prédiction qui se réalise dès qu'on en parle.

self-governing [-'gʌvənɪŋ] *adj* autonome.

self-government [-'gʌv(ə)nmənt] *n* autonomie *f*.

self-help [-'help] *n* efforts personnels; **s.-h. group,** groupe *m* visant à aider les gens à atteindre un but grâce à des efforts personnels.

self-importance [-ɪm'pɔːtəns] *n* suffisance *f*, présomption *f*; **eaten up with s.-i.,** pétri *ou* pourri d'orgueil.

self-important [-ɪm'pɔːtənt] *adj* suffisant, présomptueux.

self-imposed [-ɪm'pəʊzd] *adj* (*tâche etc*) dont on a pris de soi-même la responsabilité; (*exil*) volontaire.

self-induction [-ɪn'dʌkʃən] *n El* self-induction *f*, auto-induction *f*; **s.-i. coil,** bobine *f* de self-induction, *F* self *f*.

self-indulgence [-ɪn'dʌldʒəns] *n* sybaritisme *m*, habitude *f* de ne rien se refuser; **a typical example of the author's stylistic s.-i.,** un exemple typique de la complaisance stylistique de l'auteur envers lui-même.

self-indulgent [-ɪn'dʌldʒənt] *adj* sybarite, qui ne se refuse rien; (*writer, artist etc*) complaisant envers soi-même; (*passage etc*) complaisant.

self-inflicted [-ɪn'flɪktɪd] *adj* (*penance etc*) que l'on s'inflige à soi-même; **s.-i. wound,** mutilation *f* volontaire.

self-interest [-'ɪnt(ə)rɪst] *n* intérêt *m* (personnel); **to act from s.-i.,** agir dans un but intéressé.

selfish ['selfɪʃ] *adj* égoïste, intéressé.

selfishly ['selfɪʃlɪ] *adv* égoïstement, d'une manière intéressée; **to act s.,** agir en égoïste.

selfishness ['selfɪʃnɪs] *n* égoïsme *m*.

self-knowledge [-'nɒlɪdʒ] *n* connaissance *f* de soi.

selfless ['selflɪs] *adj* désintéressé, altruiste.

selflessness ['selflɪsnɪs] *n* désintéressement *m*, altruisme *m*.

self-loading [-'ləʊdɪŋ] *adj* (*gun*) automatique.

self-locking [-'lɒkɪŋ] *adj* **(a)** *MecE* à blocage automatique, auto-bloqueur; (*écrou*) indesserrable; **(b)** (*porte etc*) à verrouillage *ou* fermeture automatique.

self-made ['selfmeɪd] *adj* **s.-m. man,** self-made-man *m*.

self-opinionated [-ə'pɪnjəneɪtɪd] *adj* entêté; **he's very s.-o.,** il veut toujours avoir raison.

self-perpetuating [-pə'petjʊeɪtɪŋ] *adj* qui se reproduit indéfiniment.

self-pity [-'pɪtɪ] *n* attendrissement *m* sur soi-même; **full of s.-p.,** attendri sur soi-même.

self-pollination [-pɒlɪ'neɪʃən] *n Bot* autopollinisation *f*.

self-portrait [-'pɔːtreɪt] *n* portrait *m* de l'artiste par lui-même, auto-portrait *m*.

self-possessed [-pə'zest] *adj* maître de soi, qui a beaucoup de sang-froid, qui a de l'empire sur soi-même; **to remain entirely s.-p.,** rester entièrement maître de soi.

self-possession [-pə'zeʃən] *n* sang-froid *m*, empire *m* sur soi-même.

self-preservation [-prezə'veɪʃən] *n* **(instinct for) s.-p.,** (instinct *m* de) conservation *f* (de soi-même).

self-propelled, -propelling [-prə'peld, -'pelɪŋ] *adj* (*vehicle*) automoteur, -trice, autopropulsé.

self-raising, *Am* **-rising** ['selfreɪzɪŋ, -raɪsɪŋ] *adj Culin* (*farine*) contenant de la levure chimique.

self-regulating [-'regjʊleɪtɪŋ] *adj MecE* autorégulateur, -trice, à autoréglage; (*economy*) qui se régule d'elle-même.

self-reliant [-rɪ'laɪənt] *adj* (*person*) indépendant.

self-respect [-rɪ'spekt] *n* respect *m* de soi, amour propre *m*; **to lose all s.-r.,** tomber dans la dégradation.

self-respecting [-rɪ'spektɪŋ] *adj* qui se respecte, qui a de l'amour-propre; **every s.-r. photographer/***etc*, tout photographe/*etc* qui se respecte.

self-restraint [-rɪs'treɪnt] *n* retenue *f*; **to exercise s.-r.,** se contenir, se retenir.

self-righteous [-'raɪtʃəs] *adj* pharisaïque, qui fait preuve d'autosatisfaction; **stop being so s.-r.!,** cesse d'être aussi content de toi!

self-righteousness [-'raɪtʃəsnɪs] *n* pharisaïsme *m*, autosatisfaction *f*.

self-righting [-'raɪtɪŋ] *adj* (*lifeboat etc*) à redressement automatique, inchavirable.

self-rule [-'ruːl] *n Pol* autonomie *f*.

self-sacrifice [-'sækrɪfaɪs] *n* abnégation *f* (de soi).

selfsame ['selfseɪm] *adj* identique, absolument le même.

self-satisfaction [-sætɪs'fækʃən] *n* contentement *m* de soi, fatuité *f*, suffisance *f*.

self-satisfied [-'sætɪsfaɪd] *adj* (*person*) content de soi; (*person, air*) suffisant; **to look s.-s.,** avoir l'air content de soi-même.

self-seeking [-'siːkɪŋ] *adj* (*personne*) égoïste.

self-service [-'sɜːvɪs] *n Com* libre-service *m*; **s.-s. restaurant,** restaurant *m* libre-service, self *m*; **s.-s. petrol station,** station *f* libre-service.

self-serving [-'sɜːvɪŋ] *adj* égoïste, intéressé.

self-starter [-'stɑːtər] *n Aut* démarreur *m* (automatique).

self-styled ['selfstaɪld] *adj* soi-disant *inv*, prétendu.

self-sufficiency [-sə'fɪʃənsɪ] *n* **(a)** indépendance *f*; *Econ* **national s.-s.,** autarcie *f*; **(b)** (*vanity*) vanité *f*, suffisance *f*.

self-sufficient [-sə'fɪʃənt] *adj* **(a)** (*person, thing*) indépendant, autosuffisant; **the country is s.-s. in foodstuffs,** le pays suffit à ses propres besoins en ce qui concerne les denrées alimentaires; **(b)** (*conceited*) suffisant.

self-supporting [-sə'pɔːtɪŋ] *adj* indépendant; (*person*) qui suffit à ses besoins; (*business*) qui fait *ou* couvre ses frais; *Archit* (*vault*) autoportant.

self-tapping [-'tæpɪŋ] *adj* **s.-t. screw,** vis autotaraudeuse.

self-taught [-'tɔːt] *adj* **(a)** (*person*) autodidacte; **(b)** (*knowledge*) que l'on a appris tout seul.

self-test [-'test] *n* **the printer does a s.-t.,** l'imprimante procède à une vérification de ses fonctions.

selfwilled [-'wɪld] *adj* opiniâtre, obstiné, volontaire.

self-winding [-'waɪndɪŋ] *adj* (*pendule*) à remontage automatique.

sell[1] [sel] *n F* **(a)** vente *f*; **hard s.,** vente par des méthodes agressives; **soft s.,** vente par des méthodes de suggestion *ou* de persuasion; **(b)** (*trick*) déception *f*; attrape-nigaud *m*, *pl* attrape-nigauds; **what a s.!,** on s'est fait avoir!, quel attrape-nigaud!

sell[2] *v* (*pt & pp* **sold** [səʊld]) **1** *vt* **(a)** vendre (*qch*); vendre, placer (*des marchandises*); **to s. s.o. sth, to s. sth to s.o.,** vendre qch à qn; **difficult to s.,** de vente *ou* d'écoulement difficile; **to s. sth by auction,** vendre qch aux enchères; **to s. sth at a loss,** vendre qch à perte; **to sell sth dear/cheap,** vendre qch cher/(à) bon marché; *Lit* **to s. one's life dearly,** donner cher de sa vie; **he sold it to me for £10,** il me l'a vendu (pour) 10 livres; **to s. oneself,** (*in interview etc*) se faire accepter, se faire valoir; *F* **I couldn't s. my father the idea,** je n'ai pas pu faire accepter l'idée à mon père; **you have to s. yourself more to the electorate,** il faudrait vous vendre mieux auprès des électeurs; **to be sold on an idea,** être entiché d'une idée;

(b) (*betray*) vendre, trahir (*un secret, son pays etc*); **to s. oneself,** se vendre;

(c) *F* (*trick*) duper, refaire (*qn*); **you've been sold!,** on vous a refait!

2 *vi* **(a)** (*of person*) vendre, être dans la vente;

(b) goods that s. well, marchandises d'écoulement facile *ou* qui se vendent bien; **big cars don't s. anymore,** les grosses voitures ne se vendent plus; **certain to s.,** d'un débit assuré; **what are plums selling at?,** combien valent *ou* à combien se vendent les prunes?

▶**sell off** *vtsep* (*dispose of at low price*) solder (*des marchandises*); se défaire de (*ses marchandises*); liquider (*son stock etc*).

▶**sell out 1** *vtsep* **(a)** (*sell all stocks of*) *Com* vendre tout son stock de (*qch*); se défaire de (*ses marchandises*); *Fin* réaliser (*tout un portefeuille d'actions*); **the edition is sold out,** l'édition est épuisée; **I'm sold out,** j'ai tout vendu; **the supermarket was sold out of butter,** le supermarché était à court de beurre; **the concert is sold out,** tous les tickets pour le concert sont vendus; **(b)** (*betray*) vendre, trahir (*qn*). **2** *vi* **(a)** (*sell all stocks of something*) **to s. out (of sth),** se trouver à court (*de qch*); **have you got any bread? — no, I'm afraid we've sold out,** est-ce que vous avez du pain? — non, nous n'en avons plus; **the shop has sold out of sunglasses,** la boutique n'a plus de lunettes; **(b)** (*sell a business*) liquider; **(c)** (*betray a cause*) trahir une cause.

▶**sell up 1** *vtsep* vendre, faire saisir (*un failli*). **2** *vi* (*sell business, property*) vendre ses effets; *Com* vendre son fonds; **he sold up and went to Canada,** il a tout vendu et est parti au Canada.

seller ['selər] *n* **(a)** (*person*) vendeur, -euse; (*stockist*) marchand, -ande (**of,** de); *Fin* réalisateur *m* (de titres); *St Exch* **s.'s market,** marché *m* à la hausse; **(b) good/bad s.,** (*thing*) article qui se vend bien/mal; **(c)** *Horseracing* course *f* à réclamer.

selling ['selɪŋ] *n* vente *f*, écoulement *m*, placement *m* (*de marchandises etc*); **the job doesn't involve much s.,** le travail ne fait pas intervenir beaucoup de vente; **s. price,** prix *m* de vente; **the main s. points,** les points forts.

selling off, selling out *n* liquidation *f* (*des stocks*);

Fin (re)vente *f*, réalisation *f* (*de titres etc*).
Sellotape ® [1] ['seləʊteɪp] *n* ruban adhésif, scotch ® *m*.
Sellotape ® [2] *vt* **to s. sth to sth,** scotcher qch à qch.
sellout ['selaʊt] *n F* **(a) this play's a s.,** cette pièce a fait salle comble; **this line has been a s.,** cet article s'est vendu à merveille (et il ne nous en reste plus); **(b)** (*betrayal*) trahison *f*.
selvage, selvedge ['selvɪdʒ] *n Tex* lisière *f*.
semantic [sɪ'mæntɪk] *adj Ling* sémantique.
semantically [sɪ'mæntɪklɪ] *adv* sémantiquement, du point de vue sémantique.
semantics [sɪ'mæntɪks] *npl Ling* sémantique *f*; **that's just s.,** ce ne sont que des discours.
semaphore[1] ['seməfɔːr] *n* sémaphore *m*; *Rail etc* **s. signal,** signal *m* à bras.
semaphore[2] *vt* transmettre (*une communication*) par sémaphore.
semblance ['sembləns] *n* apparence *f*, semblant *m*; (*illusion*) simulacre *m*; **a (mere) s. of friendship,** un semblant d'amitié.
semen ['siːmen] *n Physiol* sperme *m*, semence *f*.
semester [sɪ'mestər] *n Am* semestre *m*.
semi ['semɪ] *n Br F* maison jumelée.
semi- ['semɪ] *pref* semi-; demi-.
semiautomatic [-ɔːtə'mætɪk] **1** *adj* semi-automatique. **2** *n* arme *f* semiautomatique.
semibreve ['semɪbriːv] *n Mus* ronde *f*.
semicircle ['semɪsɜːk(ə)l] *n* demi-cercle *m*, *pl* demi-cercles.
semicircular [-'sɜːkjʊlər] *adj* demi-circulaire, semi-circulaire.
semicolon [-'kəʊlən] *n* point-virgule *m*, *pl* points-virgules.
semiconductor [-kən'dʌktər] *n El* semi-conducteur *m*.
semiconscious [-'kɒnʃəs] *adj* à demi conscient.
semiconsonant [-'kɒnsənənt] *n* semi-consonne *f*, *pl* semi- consonnes.
semidarkness [-'dɑːknɪs] *n* demi-jour *m*, pénombre *f*.
semidetached [-dɪ'tætʃt] **1** *adj* (*house*) jumelé, jumeau, *f* jumelle. **2** *n* maison jumelée.
semifinal [-'faɪn(ə)l] *n Sp* demi-finale *f*, *pl* demi-finales.
semifinalist [-'faɪnəlɪst] *n Sp* demi-finaliste *mf*, semi-finaliste *mf*.
semi-invalid [-'ɪnvəlɪd] *n* maladif, -ive.
seminal ['siːmɪnəl, 'sem-] *adj* **(a)** *Physiol Bot* séminal, -aux; **s. fluid,** sperme *m*, liquide séminal; **(b)** (*event, work*) fructueux.
seminar ['semɪnɑːr] *n Univ* séminaire *m*; (course) cycle *m* d'études.
seminarist ['semɪnərɪst] *n Cathol* séminariste *m*.
seminary ['semɪnərɪ] *n* **(a)** *Cathol* séminaire *m*; **(b)** *Arch* (*girls' school*) pensionnat *m* de jeunes filles.
semi-obscurity [-ɒb'skjʊərɪtɪ] *n* pénombre *f*; *Fig* quasi-obscurité *f*.
semi-official [-ə'fɪʃəl] *adj* semi-officiel.
semi-precious [-'preʃəs] *adj* semi-précieux, fin.
semiquaver ['semɪkweɪvər] *n Mus* double croche *f*.
semi-skilled [-'skɪld] *adj* (*ouvrier*) spécialisé.
Semite ['semaɪt] *n* Sémite *mf*.
Semitic [sɪ'mɪtɪk] *adj* sémitique.
semitone ['semɪtəʊn] *n Mus* demi-ton *m*.
semitropical [-'trɒpɪkəl] *adj* = **SUBTROPICAL.**
semivowel [-'vaʊəl] *n* semi-voyelle *f*, *pl* semi-voyelles.
semolina [semə'liːnə] *n* semoule *f*.
Sen (a) (*abbr* **senator**) sénateur *m*; **(b)** (*abbr* **senior**) aîné, père.
SEN [esiː'en] *n Br Med abbr* **State Enrolled Nurse.**
senate ['senɪt] *n* **(a)** *Pol* sénat *m*; **s. house,** sénat; **(b)** *Univ* conseil *m* de l'université.
senator ['senətər] *n Pol* sénateur *m*.
senatorial [senə'tɔːrɪəl] *adj* sénatorial, -aux.
send [send] *vt* (*pt & pp* **sent** [sent]) **(a)** envoyer, faire parvenir (*qch*); expédier (*une lettre etc*); remettre (*de l'argent etc*); envoyer (*qn*); **to s. word to s.o.,** envoyer un mot à qn, faire savoir qch à qn; **to s. one's love to s.o.,** envoyer *ou* faire ses amitiés à qn; **to s. clothes to the laundry,** donner du linge à blanchir; **to s. a child to school,** envoyer un enfant à l'école; **to s. s.o. to prison,** envoyer qn en prison; **to s. s.o. on an errand,** envoyer qn faire une commission; **to s. s.o. for sth,** envoyer qn chercher qch *ou* à la recherche de qch;

(b) force that sends sth in a certain direction, force qui fait marcher *ou* qui pousse qch dans une certaine direction; **it sends a current down the wire,** il fait passer un courant dans le fil; **it sent a shiver down my spine,** cela m'a fait un frisson dans le dos; **the blow sent him sprawling,** le coup l'a renversé; **that sent him into fits of laughter,** cela l'a fait éclater de rire; **you'll s. me mad,** vous allez me rendre fou;

(c) *Arch* (*grant*) accorder, envoyer (*qch*); **s. him** *or* **her victorious,** que Dieu lui donne *ou* lui accorde la victoire; **what fortune sends us,** ce que la fortune nous envoie;

(d) *Old-fashioned F* **it sends me,** ça me transporte.

►**send along** *vtsep* (*send*) envoyer (*qch*); **s. him along!,** (*send him to see me*) envoyez-le-moi; (*tell to see me*) dites-lui de venir me voir.

►**send away 1** *vtsep* **(a)** (*send to another place*) envoyer (*qn, qch*); **she's too young to be sent away to school,** elle est trop jeune pour être envoyée à l'école; **(b)** (*dismiss*) renvoyer, congédier (*qn*). **2** *vi* (*write to obtain something*) écrire.

►**send away for** *vipo* (*write to obtain*) écrire pour demander (*qch*).

►**send back** *vtsep* (*return*) renvoyer (*qn*).

►**send down** *vtsep* **(a)** (*send to lower place*) faire descendre (*qch*); **(b)** (*cause to fall*) faire descendre (*les prix, la température, etc*); **(c)** *Br Univ* (*expel*) renvoyer, expulser (*un étudiant*) (*de l'université*); **(d)** *Br* (*send to prison*) envoyer (*qn*) en prison; coffrer (*qn*).

►**send for** *vipo* (*summon*) envoyer chercher (*qn, qch*); **we sent for a couple of pizzas,** nous avons fait venir deux pizzas; **we sent for the doctor,** (*we called the doctor*) nous avons appelé *ou* envoyé chercher le médecin; (*we got the doctor to come*) nous avons fait venir le médecin.

►**send in 1** *vtsep* (*send to a place*) livrer, rendre (*un compte*); remettre (*une demande etc*); (faire) servir (*le dîner*); **to s. in one's name,** se faire annoncer; **he has sent in his bill,** il nous a envoyé sa note; **many viewers sent in comments on the programme,** de nombreux spectateurs ont envoyé leurs commentaires sur l'émission; **s. Mrs Jones in,** faites venir Mme Jones; **to s. the army in,** envoyer l'armée. **2** *vi* (*write to obtain sth*) faire une demande écrite; **to s. in for sth,** faire une demande écrite de qch.

►**send off 1** *vtsep* **(a)** (*send by post*) expédier (*une lettre etc*); **(b)** *Fb etc* renvoyer *ou* expulser (*un joueur*) du terrain. **2** *vi* = **SEND AWAY 2.**

►**send on** *vtsep* **(a)** (*forward*) faire suivre (*une lettre*); transmettre (*un ordre*); expédier à l'avance (*des bagages*); **(b)** *Fb etc* envoyer (*un joueur*) sur le terrain.

►**send out** *vtsep* **(a)** envoyer (*qn*) dehors; mettre (*un élève*) à la porte; **(b)** lancer, expédier (*des prospectus*); **(c)** vomir (*des nuages de fumée etc*); émettre (*des signaux, de la chaleur etc*).

►**send up** *vtsep* **(a)** faire monter (*qn, qch*); lancer (*une fusée*); **(b)** faire monter (*les prix, la température etc*); **(c)** *F* se moquer de, parodier (*qn, qch*); *Th* prendre (*une pièce, son rôle*) à la rigolade; **(d)** *F* envoyer (*qn*) en prison, coffrer (*qn*).

sender ['sendər] *n* **(a)** (*person*) envoyeur, -euse; expéditeur, -trice (*d'une lettre, des marchandises*); **(b)** *Telecom Tel* (*device*) manipulateur *m*, transmetteur *m*.
send-off ['sendɒf] *n F* **(a)** fête *f* d'adieu; **to give s.o. a good s.-o.,** assister en nombre au départ de qn (*pour lui souhaiter bon voyage*); **(b)** inauguration réussie; **the press has given the book a good s.-o.,** le livre a eu d'excellentes critiques dans les journaux; **(c)** (*burial*) enterrement *m*.
send-up ['sendʌp] *n F* satire *f*, parodie *f*.
Senegal [senɪ'gɔːl] *n* (République *f* du) Sénégal *m*.
Senegalese [senɪgə'liːz] **1** *adj Geog* sénégalais. **2** *n* Sénégalais, -aise.
senile ['siːnaɪl] *adj* sénile; **s. decay,** dégénérescence *f* sénile, sénilité *f*; **s. dementia,** démence *f* sénile.
senility [sɪ'nɪlɪtɪ] *n* sénilité *f*.
senior ['siːnjər] **1** *adj* (*in age*) aîné; (*in rank, position etc*) plus haut placé; (*longer-serving*) plus ancien; *Mil etc* (*officier, commandement etc*) supérieur; **Bernard Long s.,** Bernard Long père; **he's two years s. to me,** il est mon aîné de deux ans; **s. in rank,** de grade supérieur; *Br* **the S. Service,** la marine; **the s. boys/girls of a school,** les grands/grandes (élèves); **s. citizens,** personnes âgées; **s. partner,** associé principal; **s. management,** la direction; **the s. officer,** l'officier commandant; **I'll report you to your s. officer,** je vais vous signaler à votre supérieur; *Sch* **s. master** *or* **mistress,** professeur *m* en premier; **s. French master** *or* **mistress,** premier professeur de français.

2 *n* **(a)** aîné, -ée; **she is his s. by three years,** elle est son aînée de trois ans; **to be s.o.'s s.,** (*in age*) être l'aîné de qn; (*in rank*) être d'un rang plus élevé que qn; **the seniors,** (*of pupils*) les grand(e)s;

(b) *Sch US* étudiant(e) de quatrième (et dernière) année.
seniority [siːnɪ'ɒrɪtɪ] *n* **(a)** (*age*) priorité *f* d'âge, supériorité *f* d'âge; **chairman by s.,** président d'âge; **(b)** (*rank*) ancienneté *f* (de grade); **to be promoted by s.,** avancer (de grade) *ou* être promu à l'ancienneté.
senna ['senə] *n* (*plant*) *& Pharm* séné *m*.
sensation [sen'seɪʃən] *n* **(a)** sensation *f*; (*feeling*) sentiment *m*, impression *f* (*de malaise, de bien-être etc*); **I had the s. of falling,** j'avais l'impression de tomber; **(b)** (*excitement*) sensation *f*; (*sensational effect*) effet sensationnel; **to create** *or* **make** *or* **cause a s.,** (*of event etc*) faire sensation.
sensational [sen'seɪʃənəl] *adj* **(a)** (*exciting*) sensationnel; (*film*) à sensation; **s. novel,** roman *m* à sensation; **(b)** *F* (*excellent*) sensationnel, fantastique.
sensationalism [sen'seɪʃənəlɪz(ə)m] *n* **(a)** recherche *f* du sensationnel; **(b)** *Phil* sensualisme *m*, sensationnisme *m*.
sensationalist [sen'seɪʃənəlɪst] *n* (*with news*) colporteur *m* de nouvelles à sensation; (*who overdramatizes*) personne ayant tendance à dramatiser.
sensationalize [sen'seɪʃənəlaɪz] *vt* exagérer (*un incident etc*).
sensationally [sen'seɪʃənəlɪ] *adv* (*see adj*) **(a)** d'une manière sensationnelle; **(b)** *F* d'une manière sensationnelle *ou* fantastique.
sense[1] [sens] *n* **(a)** (*faculty*) sens *m*; **the five senses,** les cinq sens; **to have a keen s. of smell/hearing,** avoir l'odorat fin/l'ouïe fine; **she seemed to have a sixth s.,** elle semblait posséder un sixième sens; **to be in possession of all one's senses,** jouir de toutes ses facultés; **pleasures of the senses,** plaisirs sensuels *ou* des sens; **s. impression,** sensation *f*; **s. organs,** organes *mpl* des sens;
(b) to be in one's senses, être sain d'esprit; **have you taken leave of your senses?,** avez-vous perdu l'esprit *ou* la raison?; **to come to one's senses (again),** revenir à la raison; **to bring s.o. to his senses,** ramener qn à la raison; **to lose one's senses,** perdre connaissance; **to come to one's senses,** revenir à soi;
(c) (*feeling*) sensation *f*, sens *m*; (*awareness*) sentiment *m*, conscience *f*; **a s. of pleasure/warmth,** une sensation de plaisir/chaleur; **a s. of belonging,** une impression d'être chez soi; **s. of injustice,** sentiment d'injustice; **s. of colour/beauty,** sentiment des couleurs/de la beauté; **to lose all s. of reality,** perdre la notion de la réalité;
(d) (*rationality*) bon sens; (*judgement*) jugement *m*; **common s.,** sens commun; **good s.,** bon sens; **to talk s.,** parler raison; **there's no s. in that, that doesn't make s.,** cela n'a pas de sens, cela ne rime à rien; **it makes good political/business s. to ...,** il est bon sur le plan politique/commercial de ...; **that makes good s.,** c'est logique, c'est une bonne idée; **where's the s. in that?,** à quoi ça sert?; **there's no s. in doing that,** ça ne sert à rien; **he doesn't make s.,** (*is of contradictory character*) il ne sait pas ce qu'il veut; **to have the (good) s. to do sth,** avoir l'intelligence *ou* le bon sens de faire qch; **to have more s. than to do sth,** avoir trop de bon sens pour faire qch;
(e) (*meaning*) sens *m*, signification *f* (*d'un mot*); **these words don't make s.,** ces mots n'ont pas de sens *ou* sont incompréhensibles; **you're not making s.,** je ne vous comprends pas; **put that way, it makes more s.,** comme ça, c'est plus logique *ou* cohérent *ou* ça a plus de sens; **I can't make s. of it,** je n'arrive pas à le comprendre; **in the literal/figurative s.,** au sens propre/figuré; **in every s. of the word,** dans toute l'acception du mot; **in a s.,** d'une certaine façon, dans un (certain) sens; **in the s. that,** en ce sens que;
(f) *Phys etc* (*direction*) direction *f*, sens *m*; **s. of rotation,** sens de rotation.
sense[2] *vt* **(a)** (*know intuitively*) sentir (*qch*) intuitivement; (*have premonition*) pressentir (*qch*); **I sensed that she was hiding something,** j'avais le pressentiment qu'elle cachait quelque chose; **(b)** (*understand*) comprendre (*qch*); **(c)** *Phil* percevoir (*qch*) par le sens; **(d)** *Electron etc* détecter.
senseless ['senslɪs] *adj* **(a)** (*unconscious*) sans connaissance, inanimé; **to fall s.,** tomber sans connaissance; **to knock s.o. s.,** assommer qn; **(b)** (*stupid*) (*person*) dénué de sens commun; (*action*) insensé, stupide, absurde; **a s. killing,** un meurtre inutile; **a s. remark,** une bêtise; **(c)** (*without sense of touch, sight etc*) dépourvu des facultés des sens.
senselessly ['senslɪslɪ] *adv* absurdement.
senselessness ['senslɪsnɪs] *n* **(a)** (*stupidity*) absurdité *f*; **(b)** (*lack of sense of touch, sight etc*) insensibilité *f*.
sensibility [sensɪ'bɪlɪtɪ] *n* **(a)** (*of person*) sensibilité *f*, émotivité *f*, susceptibilité *f*; **I do not want to offend anyone's sensibilities,** je ne veux pas heurter la susceptibilité de qui que ce soit; **(b)** sensibilité *f* (*d'un organe etc*).
sensible ['sensɪbəl] *adj* **(a)** (*rational*) sensé, raisonnable, judicieux; **be s.,** soyez raisonnable; **s. choice,** choix judicieux; **s. clothes,** vêtements *mpl* commodes *ou* pratiques; **s. person,** personne sensée *ou* pleine de bon sens; **s. shoes,** chaussures *fpl* confortables et pratiques; **(b)** *Arch & Lit* (*aware*) (*person*) conscient (**of,** de); sensible (**of,** à); **to be s. of the fact that ...,** apprécier le fait que ...; **(c)** (*quantity, difference etc*) sensible, appréciable.
sensibly ['sensɪblɪ] *adv* **(a)** (*rationally*) raisonnablement, judicieusement; **(b)** (*perceptibly*) sensiblement, perceptiblement; **to be s. dressed,** porter des vêtements pratiques.
sensitive ['sensɪtɪv] *adj* **(a)** (*person, skin*) sensible; **he's very s. about his accent,** il est très susceptible quant à son accent; **to be s. to noise,** être sensible au bruit; **to be s. to the cold,** (*of person*) être frileux, -euse; **(b)** (*balance, machine, Fin market*) sensible; *Phot* (*plaque*) impressionnable, sensible à la lumière; (*papier*) sensible, sensibilisé; **s. to sth,** sensible à qch; **(c)** (*question, issue etc*) délicat, sensible; (*document, information*) confidentiel.
sensitively ['sensɪtɪvlɪ] *adv* sensiblement; d'une manière sensible; (*écrire etc*) avec sensibilité.
sensitiveness ['sensɪtɪvnɪs] **, sensitivity** [sensɪ'tɪvɪtɪ] *n* sensibilité *f*, sensitivité *f*; (*of person*) susceptibilité *f*; sensibilité (*of machine, instrument etc*); *Phot* impressionnabilité *f*, rapidité *f* (*of emulsion*); caractère délicat (*d'une question etc*); (*of document, information etc*) caractère confidentiel.
sensitization [sensɪtaɪ'zeɪʃən] *n Med Phot* sensibilisation *f*.
sensitize ['sensɪtaɪz] *vt* sensibiliser, rendre sensible; *Phot* **sensitized paper,** papier sensible *ou* sensibilisé.
sensitizer ['sensɪtaɪzər] *n Phot* sensibilisateur *m*.
sensor ['sensər] *n Electron etc* détecteur *m*; *Astronaut* (*in satellite etc*) détecteur, capteur *m*; *Electron Phys* analyseur *m*.
sensory ['sensərɪ] *adj* (*nerf etc*) sensoriel; **s. organs,** organes *mpl* des sens.
sensual ['sensjʊəl] *adj* **(a)** sensuel; (*instinct*) animal; **s. pleasures,** plaisirs *mpl* des sens; **(b)** (*person, art*) sensuel, voluptueux; (*lustful*) libidineux.
sensualism ['sensjʊəlɪz(ə)m] *n* **(a)** sensualité *f*; **(b)** *Phil* sensualisme *m*.
sensualist [sensjʊəlɪst] *n* **(a)** sensualiste, voluptueux, -euse; **(b)** *Phil* sensualiste *mf*.
sensuality [sensjʊ'ælɪtɪ] *n* sensualité *f*.
sensuous ['sensjʊəs] *adj* (*pleasure, life etc*) sybaritique, voluptueux; (*charm etc*) capiteux.
sensuously ['sensjʊəslɪ] *adv* voluptueusement, avec volupté.
sensuousness ['sensjʊəsnɪs] *n* sybaritisme *m*; volupté *f*.
sent *see* **SEND**.
sentence[1] ['sentəns] *n* **(a)** *Gram* phrase *f*; **(b)** *Jur* (*conviction*) sentence *f*, condamnation *f*; (*period in prison*) peine *f*; **life s.,** condamnation à vie; **s. of death, death s.,** arrêt *m ou* peine de mort; **under s. of death,** condamné à mort; **to pass (a) s.,** prononcer une condamnation *ou* une sentence; **while he was serving his s.,** pendant qu'il purgeait sa peine.
sentence[2] *vt Jur* condamner, prononcer une condamnation *ou* une sentence contre (*qn*); **to s. s.o. to a month's imprisonment/to death,** condamner qn à un mois de prison/à mort.
sententious [sen'tenʃəs] *adj* (*person, speech etc*) sentencieux.
sententiousness [sen'tenʃəsnɪs] *n* (*of person*) caractère sentencieux; (*of writing etc*) ton sentencieux.
sentient ['sentɪənt] *adj* sentant, sensible.
sentiment ['sentɪmənt] *n* **(a)** (*opinion*) sentiment *m*, opinion *f*, avis *m*; *Arch & Lit* (*emotion*) sentiment, mouvement *m* de l'âme; **these are my sentiments,** voilà mon sentiment *ou* mon opinion; **my sentiments exactly,** je partage entièrement votre avis; **noble sentiments,** sentiments nobles; **(b)** (*sentimentality*) sentimentalité *f*; (*mawkish*) sensiblerie *f*.
sentimental [sentɪ'mentəl] *adj* sentimental, -aux; **s. value,** valeur sentimentale; **don't be so s.!,** pas tant de sentiment!, ne sois pas si sentimental!
sentimentalism [sentɪ'mentəlɪz(ə)m] *n* sentimentalisme *m*, sensiblerie *f*.
sentimentalist [sentɪ'mentəlɪst] *n* personne sentimentale; **he's** *or* **she's a s.,** c'est un sentimental.
sentimentality [sentɪmen'tælɪtɪ] *n* sentimentalité *f*;

(*mawkishness*) sensiblerie *f*.

sentimentalize [sentɪ'mentəlaɪz] **1** *vi* faire du sentiment. **2** *vt* apporter du sentiment dans (*une œuvre*).

sentimentally [sentɪ'mentəlɪ] *adv* sentimentalement; (*mawkishly*) avec sensiblerie.

sentinel ['sentɪn(ə)l] *n Mil* factionnaire *m*, sentinelle *f*; **to stand s.**, (*to take up post*) monter la garde; (*to be at post*) être de garde.

sentry ['sentrɪ] *n Mil* factionnaire *m*, sentinelle *f*; **to be on** *or* **to do s. duty, to stand s.**, être en sentinelle *ou* de faction; **to relieve a s.**, relever une sentinelle; **s. box**, guérite *f*.

sepal ['sep(ə)l] *n Bot* sépale *m*.

separable ['sep(ə)rəb(ə)l] *adj* séparable.

separate¹ ['sep(ə)rət] **1** *adj* (*parts*) séparé, détaché (**from,** de); (*distinct*) distinct; (*independent*) indépendant; (*room, entrance*) particulier; **the two issues are quite s.**, les deux problèmes sont distincts; **to keep sth s. (from sth else),** garder deux choses séparées; **entered in a s. column,** inscrit dans une colonne particulière; **to sleep in s. rooms,** (*of married couple*) faire chambre à part; **use a s. piece of paper,** utilisez une feuille séparée; **it's now become a s. company,** c'est maintenant une société indépendante. **2** *npl Com* **separates,** coordonnés *mpl*.

separate² ['sepəreɪt] **1** *vt* séparer, dégager, détacher (**from,** de); départir (*les métaux*); dédoubler (*un brin de fil etc*); écrémer (*le lait*); désunir (*les membres d'une famille etc*); détacher (*qn de sa famille etc*); **to s. two boxers,** séparer deux boxeurs; **he is separated (from his wife),** il est séparé (de sa femme); **the Channel separates England from France,** la Manche sépare la France et l'Angleterre; **the gulf that separates him from his colleagues,** l'abîme entre lui et ses collègues, l'abîme qui le sépare de ses collègues; **what separates their language from other African languages is ...,** ce qui distingue leur langue des autres langues africaines c'est ... .

2 *vi* (*become detached*) se séparer, se détacher, se décoller (**from,** de); (*of man and wife*) se séparer; **when we separated for the night,** quand nous nous sommes quittés pour la nuit; **to s. from s.o.,** se séparer de qn, rompre avec qn.

►**separate out 1** *vi Ch* se séparer (*par précipitation*). **2** *vtsep* séparer (**from,** de).

separately ['sep(ə)rətlɪ] *adv* séparément; **are you paying s.?,** (*in shop, restaurant etc*) est-ce que vous payez séparément?; **wash s.,** (*on garment label etc*) laver séparément; **keep this s.,** gardez ceci à part.

separation [sepə'reɪʃən] *n* séparation *f* (**from s.o.,** d'avec qn); écrémage *m* (*du lait*); *Min* classement *m* (*du minerai*); **judicial s.,** séparation (judiciaire); *Mil* **s. allowance,** allocation faite à la femme (*d'un soldat*).

separatism ['sepərətɪz(ə)m] *n* séparatisme *m*.

separatist ['sepərətɪst] *n* séparatiste *mf*.

separator ['sepəreɪtər] *n Tech* séparateur *m*.

sepia ['siːpɪə] *n* (*cuttlefish*) seiche *f*; *Art* sépia; **s. (drawing),** (dessin *m* à la) sépia.

sepoy ['siːpɔɪ] *n Mil* cipaye *m*.

sepsis ['sepsɪs] *n Med* septicité *f*, état *m* septique.

September [sep'tembər] *n* septembre *m*; **in S.**, au mois de septembre, en septembre; **(on) the first/the seventh of S.**, le premier/le sept septembre.

septet [sep'tet] *n Mus* septuor *m*.

septic ['septɪk] *adj Med* septique; **to become** *or* **go s.**, s'infecter; **s. poisoning,** septicémie *f*; **s. tank,** fosse *f* septique.

septicaemia, *US* **septicemia** [septɪ'siːmɪə] *n Med* septicémie *f*.

septuagenarian [septjʊədʒɪ'neərɪən] *n & adj* septuagénaire *mf*.

Septuagesima [septjʊə'dʒesɪmə] *n Rel* **S. (Sunday),** (le dimanche de) la Septuagésime.

Septuagint ['septjʊədʒɪnt] *n* version *f* (de la Bible) des Septante, la Septante.

septum, *pl* **-a** [septəm, -ə] *n Anat* septum *m* (*du nez etc*); *Bot* cloison *f* (*d'une spore*).

sepulchral [sɪ'pʌlkrəl] *adj* sépulcral, -aux.

sepulchre, *US* **sepulcher** ['sepəlkər] *n* sépulcre *m*, tombeau *m*; **the Holy S.**, le Saint Sépulcre.

sequel ['siːkwəl] *n* suite *f* (*d'un roman etc*); **as a s. to these events,** comme suite à ces événements; **action that had an unfortunate s.**, acte qui a entraîné des suites malheureuses.

sequence ['siːkwəns] *n* **(a)** (*order*) ordre *m*; (*in time*) ordre, succession *f*; **what's the s. of events going to be?,** quelle sera la succession des événements?; **in some sort of s.**, dans un ordre quelconque; **in s.**, l'un après l'autre; **logical s.**, enchaînement *m* logique; **(b)** (*series*) suite *f*, série *f* (*d'événements*); **a s. of disasters,** une suite *ou* série de désastres; **(c)** *Cards Mus Cin Comptr* séquence *f*; *Comptr* **s. check(ing),** contrôle *m* de séquence; *Mus* **a chord s.**, une suite d'accords; *Gram* **s. of tenses,** concordance *f* des temps; *Rel* séquence *f* (*chantée avant l'Evangile*).

sequencer ['siːkwənsər] *n Comptr* coordonnateur *m*.

sequential [sɪ'kwenʃəl] *adj* séquentiel; (*teaching, history etc*) continu; *Comptr* **s. computer,** calculateur séquentiel.

sequentially [sɪ'kwenʃəlɪ] *adv* séquentiellement.

sequester [sɪ'kwestər] *vt* confisquer (*qch*); *Jur* séquestrer (*les biens d'un débiteur*); mettre (*un bien*) sous séquestre; *Lit* **to s. oneself (from the world),** se retirer (du monde).

sequestrate [sɪ'kwestreɪt] *vt* confisquer (*qch*); *Jur* séquestrer (*les biens du débiteur etc*); mettre (*un bien*) sous séquestre.

sequestration [siːkwe'streɪʃən] *n* confiscation *f*; *Jur* séquestration *f*, mise *f* sous séquestre.

sequin ['siːkwɪn] *n* paillette *f* (*de robe etc*).

sequoia [sɪ'kwɔɪə] *n* (*tree*) sequoia *m*, wellingtonia *m*.

seraglio [se'rɑːlɪəʊ] *n* sérail *m*, -ails.

seraph, *pl* **seraphs, seraphim** ['serəf, -əfs, -əfɪm] *n* séraphin *m*.

seraphic [sɪ'ræfɪk] *adj* séraphique.

Serb [sɜːb] *n* Serbe *mf*.

Serbia ['sɜːbɪə] *n* Serbie *f*.

Serbian ['sɜːbɪən] **1** *adj* serbe. **2** *n Ling* serbe *m*.

Serbo-Croat [sɜːbəʊ'krəʊæt], **Serbo-Croatian** [sɜːbəʊkrəʊ'eɪʃən] **1** *adj* serbo-croate. **2** *n* **(a)** Serbo-croate *mf*; **(b)** *Ling* serbo-croate *m*.

sere [sɪər] *adj Lit* flétri, desséché.

serenade¹ [serə'neɪd] *n* sérénade *f*.

serenade² *vt* donner une sérénade à (*qn*).

serendipity [serən'dɪpɪtɪ] *n* don *m* de faire des trouvailles.

serene [sɪ'riːn] *adj* **(a)** (*sky, sea, person*) serein, calme, tranquille; (*sky*) clair; **her face wore a s. look,** son visage exprimait le calme *ou* la sérénité; **(b)** (*in title*) sérénissime; **His S. Highness,** son Altesse sérénissime.

serenely [sɪ'riːnlɪ] *adv* calmement, avec sérénité.

serenity [sɪ'renɪtɪ] *n* sérénité *f*, calme *m*.

serf [sɜːf] *n* serf, *f* serve.

serfdom ['sɜːfdəm] *n* servage *m*.

serge [sɜːdʒ] *n Tex* serge *f*; **cotton s.**, sergé *m*.

sergeant ['sɑːdʒənt] *n* (*infantry, air force*) sergent *m*; (*artillery, armoured corps, cavalry*) maréchal *m* des logis; **(police) s.**, brigadier *m*; **quartermaster s., staff s.**, (*infantry, air force*) sergent fourrier *ou* comptable; (*artillery, armoured corps, cavalry*) maréchal des logis fourrier, comptable.

sergeant-major [sɑːdʒənt'meɪdʒər] *n Mil* adjudant *m*; **regimental s.-m.**, adjudant-chef *m*, *pl* adjudants-chefs.

serial ['sɪərɪəl] **1** *adj* **(a)** (*belonging to series*) qui appartient à la série; *Mus* sériel; **s. number,** numéro *m* de série; *Ind* numéro matricule (*d'un moteur*); **s. killer,** meurtrier en série; **(b)** (*arranged in series*) en série; (*forming series*) formant série; **s. rights,** droit *m* de reproduction en feuilleton; **s. story,** roman-feuilleton *m*, *pl* romans-feuilletons; **(c)** *Comptr* (*printer, interface*) en série; **s. port,** port *m* série. **2** *n* (*story published in parts*) roman-feuilleton *m*, *pl* romans-feuilletons; *Rad* radioroman *m*; *TV* téléroman *m*.

serialize ['sɪərɪəlaɪz] *vt Journ* publier (*un roman etc*) en feuilleton; *TV* diffuser (*un roman etc*) en feuilleton; **serialized in six parts,** diffusé en six parties.

serially ['sɪərɪəlɪ] *adv* **(a)** en *ou* par série; **(b)** *Journ* en feuilleton.

sericulture ['serɪkʌltʃər] *n* sériciculture *f*.

series ['sɪəriːz] *n* série *f*; échelle *f*, gamme *f* (*de couleurs etc*); (*of books*) collection *f*; *TV Rad* série; **a s. of terrorist attacks,** une série d'attaques terroristes; **in s.**, en série, en succession; *El* **connection in s., s. connection,** montage *m* en série.

seriocomic [sɪərɪəʊ'kɒmɪk] *adj* moitié sérieux moitié comique; (*of poem*) héroï-comique.

serious ['sɪərɪəs] *adj* **(a)** (*grave*) sérieux, grave; **things are becoming s.**, cela devient sérieux; **s. injury,** blessure *f* grave; **s. mistake,** grosse faute; **(b)** (*person, decision, newspaper*) sérieux; **s. artist,** artiste sérieux; **s. promise,** promesse sérieuse *ou* sincère; **I have never given the subject s. thought,** je n'y ai jamais pensé sérieusement; **s. mood,** humeur sérieuse; **I'm s.**, je ne plaisante pas; **surely you're not s.**, vous n'êtes pas sérieux?, vous plaisantez?; **I was being serious when I said ...,** je ne plaisantais pas quand j'ai dit ... .

seriously ['sɪərɪəslɪ] *adv* **(a)** (*gravely*) sérieusement; **s. ill,** gravement malade; **s. wounded,** grièvement blessé; *Mil* **the s. wounded,** les grands blessés; **(b)** (*parler*) sérieusement; **to take sth s.,** prendre qch au sérieux; **to take oneself s.,** se prendre au sérieux; **if we are to be taken s. as a world class football team,** pour qu'on nous prenne au sérieux en tant qu'équipe de football de classe mondiale; **you can't s. expect them to believe that,** vous ne pouvez pas penser sérieusement qu'ils vont croire ça; **but s., what will you do?,** plaisanterie à part, qu'allez-vous faire?

serious-minded [sɪərɪəs'maɪndɪd] *adj* (*person*) réfléchi, sérieux; **s.-m. people,** les esprits sérieux.

seriousness ['sɪərɪəsnɪs] *n* **(a)** (*gravity*) gravité *f* (*d'une situation, d'une maladie etc*); **(b)** sérieux *m* (*de maintien etc*); **(c) in all s.,** sérieusement.

serjeant ['sɑːdʒənt] *n* **S. at Arms,** *Parl* commandant *m* militaire du Parlement; *Arch* (*attendant*) huisser *m* d'armes.

sermon ['sɜːmən] *n* **(a)** *Rel* sermon *m*; (*Protestant church*) prêche *m*; **collection of sermons,** sermonnaire *m*; *Bible* **the S. on the Mount,** le Sermon sur la montagne; **(b)** *F Fig* sermon, semonce *f*; **the editor does tend to go in for sermons,** le rédacteur en chef a tendance à faire des sermons.

sermonize ['sɜːmənaɪz] *Pej* **1** *vi* sermonner, prêcher. **2** *vt* sermonner (*qn*).

sermonizing ['sɜːmənaɪzɪŋ] *n Pej* prêcherie *f*; **no s.!** (*preaching*) pas de sermons!

serous ['sɪərəs] *adj Anat etc* (*fluide etc*) séreux.

serpent ['sɜːpənt] *n* serpent *m*.

serpentine¹ ['sɜːpəntaɪn] *n Miner* serpentine *f*; **s. (marble),** marbre serpentin.

serpentine² *adj Lit* serpentin; (*sentier*) sinueux, tortueux, serpentant; **s. windings,** sinuosités *fpl*.

serrate ['sereɪt] *adj* denté en scie; *Bot* **s.-leaved,** serratifolié.

serrated [se'reɪtɪd] *adj* denté en scie; **s. edge,** denture *f*; **knife with a s. edge,** couteau *m* à scie.

serried ['serɪd] *adj Lit* serré; **in s. ranks,** en rangs serrés.

serum, *pl* **-ums, -a** ['sɪərəm, -rəms, -rə] *n Physiol* sérum *m*; **blood s.,** sérum sanguin.

servant ['sɜːvənt] *n* serviteur *m*, servante *f*; **the servants,** les serviteurs, les domestiques; **(domestic) s.,** domestique *mf*; (*maid*) servante *f*, bonne *f*; **a large staff of servants,** une nombreuse domesticité; *Fml* **your most humble and obedient s.,** votre très humble serviteur; **civil s.,** fonctionnaire *m*; **public servants,** employés *mpl* d'un service public, employés de la fonction publique.

serve¹ [sɜːv] *n Tennis* service *m*; **(it's) your s.!,** à vous de servir!

serve² **1** *vt* **(a)** (*be of service to*) (*of person*) servir (*un maître, une cause etc*); (*of thing*) être utile à (*qn*); (*be sufficient for*) suffire à (*qn*); **to s. God/one's country,** servir Dieu/sa patrie; **to have served one's country well,** bien mériter de la patrie; **he has served the company faithfully,** il a servi la société fidèlement; **to s. one's own interests,** servir ses propres intérêts; **to s. the purpose,** remplir le but, faire l'affaire; **tool that serves several purposes,** outil qui sert à plusieurs usages; **he** *or* **it has served his** *or* **its purpose and has been discarded,** il a rempli sa fonction et on s'en est débarrassé; **if my memory serves me right,** si j'ai bonne mémoire; *Old-fashioned* **he served me very badly,** (*treated*) il a très mal agi envers moi;

(b) (*carry out*) **to s. one's apprenticeship,** faire son apprentissage; **to s. one's sentence** *or* **one's time,** subir *ou* purger sa peine; **he served a sentence of five years' imprisonment,** il a fait cinq ans de prison;

(c) (*of bus, rail service, TV station etc*) desservir (*une région, population etc*);

(d) (*in shop*) **to s. s.o. with a pound of butter,** servir une livre de beurre à qn; **are you being served?,** est-ce qu'on s'occupe de vous?; **I'm being served, thank you,** on s'occupe de moi, merci; **tradesman who has served us for ten years,** marchand qui fournit chez nous depuis dix ans;

(e) (*at table*) **to s. s.o. with soup/vegetables,** servir du potage/des légumes à qn; **we don't s. (drinks to) people under eighteen,** (*in bar*) nous ne servons pas d'alcool aux moins de dix-huit ans, nous ne servons pas les moins de dix-huit ans; **to s. a dish,** servir un mets; **dinner is served madam,** le dîner est servi, madame; *Old fashioned* madame est servie; **s. chilled,** servir très frais; *Rel* **to s. mass,** servir la messe; **serves four,** (*on packet, in recipe*) pour quatre personnes; *Culin* **beef served in a mushroom sauce,** bœuf dans une sauce aux champignons;

(f) *Tennis* **to s. the ball,** servir; **he served the ball into ...,** il a envoyé la balle de service dans ...; **to s. an ace,** faire un ace;

(g) to s. a writ/a summons on s.o., to s. s.o. with a writ/a summons, délivrer *ou* signifier *ou* notifier une assignation/une citation à qn;

(h) it serves you right!, c'est bien fait, vous n'avez que ce que vous méritez; **it serves him right for not listening to me,** il ne m'a pas écouté, c'est bien fait pour lui; **it would have served you right,** vous l'auriez bien mérité;

(i) (*male animal*) saillir, couvrir (*la femelle*).

2 *vi* **(a)** (*carry out duty etc*) (*in army etc*) **to s. in the army,** servir dans l'armée; **to s. with s.o.,** faire la guerre avec qn; **to have served ten years,** (*in army*) avoir dix ans de service(s); (*in prison*) avoir fait dix ans de prison; **she served under three presidents,** elle a servi sous trois présidents; **to s. (in a government),** servir (dans un gouvernement);

(b) (*meet requirements*) (*of tool, plan etc*) servir; **the boxes s. as tables,** les boîtes tiennent lieu de tables; **to s. as a pretext/as an example,** servir de prétexte/d'exemple;

(c) to s. (in a shop), être vendeur, -euse;

(d) to s. (at table), servir à table;

(e) *Rel* **to s. (at mass),** servir la messe;

(f) *Tennis* servir.

►**serve up 1** *vtsep* (*dinner etc*) servir. **2** *vi* servir.

server ['sɜːvər] *n* **(a)** (*at table*) serveur, -euse; **(b)** *Tennis* serveur, -euse; **(c)** *Rel* (*at mass*) acolyte *m*, répondant *m*; **(d)** (*tray*) plateau *m* (de service); **(e)** (*utensil*) **(set of) salad/fish servers,** service *m* à salade/à poisson; **(f)** *Comptr* **(file) s.,** serveur *m*.

service¹ ['sɜːvɪs] *n* **(a)** service *m*; **in the s. of God/of one's country,** au service de Dieu/de son pays *ou* sa patrie; **to die in the King's/Queen's s.,** mourir au service du roi/de la reine; **I am (entirely) at your s.,** je suis à votre (entière) disposition; **promotion according to length of s.,** avancement selon l'ancienneté; **to give many years of loyal s. to a company/*etc*,** fournir de nombreuses années de bons et loyaux services à une société/*etc*; *Mil* **military** *or Br Hist* **national s.,** service militaire *ou* national; **when I was doing my military s.,** quand j'étais au régiment; **active s.,** service actif; **fit/unfit for s.,** apte/inapte au service; *Nau* **s. afloat,** service à bord; **s. ashore,** service à terre; **domestic s.,** service domestique; *Old-fashioned* **to be in s.,** (*of servant*) être en service; *Old-fashioned* **to go into s.,** (*of servant*) entrer en service; **24-hour s.,** service permanent *ou* 24 heures sur 24; **to bring** *or* **put into s.,** mettre (*un appareil, un véhicule*) en service; **this pen has given me good s.,** ce stylo m'a bien servi; **the s. there is good/slow/*etc*,** (*in restaurant*) le service y est de qualité/lent/*etc*; **s. is included,** le service est compris; **ten per cent s. charge,** service dix pour cent; **s. lift** *or* **hoist,** monte-plats *m inv*; **s. hatch,** guichet *m*; *Br* **s. flat,** appartement *m* avec service compris (et repas à volonté); **rent plus s. charge,** loyer *m* plus charges; *Admin Ind* **s. agreement,** contrat *m* de service; **s. life,** durée *f ou* potentiel *m* d'utilisation; *Av* **s. ceiling,** plafond *m* pratique (*d'un appareil*); *Tech El* **s. test,** essai *m* en charge;

(b) (*use*) utilité *f*; **to be of some s.,** servir à quelque chose; **to be of s. to s.o.,** être utile à qn; **can I be of any s. to you?,** puis-je vous être utile *ou* vous aider en aucune manière?; **to do s.o. a s.,** rendre (un) service à qn; **to offer one's services,** offrir ses services; **his services to education,** les services qu'il a rendus à l'enseignement; **services rendered,** services rendus; *Econ* **goods and services,** biens *mpl* et services;

(c) (*organization*) **the civil s.,** l'administration *f*, la fonction publique; **to be in the civil s.,** être fonctionnaire; **the Foreign** *or* **Diplomatic S.,** le service diplomatique, la diplomatie, *F* la carrière; *F* **the Secret S.,** = le Deuxième Bureau; *Mil etc* **the s.,** (*army*) l'armée *f*; (*navy*) la marine; (*air force*) l'armée de l'air; **the (armed) services,** les forces armées, l'armée, la marine et l'armée de l'air; **when he/she was in the services,** lors qu'il/elle était dans l'armée *ou* la marine *ou* l'armée de l'air; **Joint Services Staff College,** ≈ École *f* d'État-major interarmes; **s. personnel,** personnel *m* militaire; **s. rifle,** fusil *m* réglementaire *ou* de l'armée; **s. vehicle,** véhicule *m* militaire *ou* de l'armée;

(d) (*system*) service *m* (*aérien, ferroviaire*); distribution *f* (*d'eau, de gaz, d'électricité*); **bus s.,** service d'autobus *ou* de cars; **we have a good bus/train s.,** notre ville est bien desservie par les autobus/par le chemin de fer; **goods** *or* **freight s.,** service de marchandises; **passenger s.,** service de voyageurs; **public services,** services publics; **postal/telephone services,** services postaux/téléphoniques; **social/medical services,** services sociaux/médicaux; **the corner shop provides a s. to the community,** la boutique de quartier offre un service à la communauté; **s. area,** zone *f* de desserte; région desservie; *Austr New Zealand* **s. bus** *or* **car,** autocar *m*; *Econ* **s. sector,** secteur *m* tertiaire, tertiaire *m*; **s. industry,** branche *f* du tertiaire;

(e) (*maintenance*) entretien *m*; dépannage *m* (*d'un appareil ménager etc*); *Mil* service *m* (*de la pièce*); **my car needs a complete s.,** ma voiture a besoin d'une révision générale; **services 10 km,** (*on motorway sign*) aire de services, 10 km; **after-sales s.,** service après vente; **s. area,** *Am* **s. centre,** aire *f* de services (au bord d'une autoroute); *Aut* **s. bay,** (*in garage*) zone *f* de travail; **s. engineer,** (*for electrical, gas appliance etc*) ingénieur chargé de l'entretien; **s. manual** *or* **handbook,** manuel *m* d'entretien; *Aut* **s. station,** station-service *f*, *pl* stations-service;

(f) *Rel* office *m*, culte *m*; **morning/evening s.,** office du matin/du soir; **the communion s.,** la sainte communion; **the marriage s.,** la cérémonie du mariage; **open-air s.,** office en plein air; **to attend s.,** assister à l'office *ou* au culte;

(g) *Jur* délivrance *f*, signification *f* (*d'un acte, d'une assignation*);

(h) (*in breeding*) service *m* (*par l'étalon etc*);

(i) tea s., service *m* à thé; **dinner s.,** service de table;

(j) *Tennis* service *m*; **s. court,** rectangle *m* de service; **s. line,** ligne *f* de fond.

service² *vt* **(a)** (*do maintenance work to*) faire la révision de (*une voiture*); faire l'entretien de (*un appareil ménager*); **(b)** (*in breeding*) (*of bull, stallion etc*) couvrir (*la femelle*); **(c)** (*provide services to*) desservir; *Fin* **to s. a debt/loan,** rembourser une dette/un emprunt.

service³ *n* (*plant*) **s. (tree),** sorbier *m*, cormier *m*; **s. apple** *or* **berry,** corme *f*, sorbe *f*.

serviceable ['sɜːvɪsəb(ə)l] *adj* **(a)** (*in functioning state*) en état de fonctionner; (*useable*) utilisable; **(b)** (*useful*) utile; (*vêtement*) pratique.

serviceman, *pl* **-men** ['sɜːvɪsmən, -men] *n* soldat mobilisé; *Hist* **national s.,** appelé *m*; **ex-s.,** ancien combattant; **disabled ex-s.,** mutilé de guerre.

servicewoman, *pl* **-women** ['sɜːvɪswʊmən,-wɪmɪn] *n* soldate *f*, femme *f* soldat.

servicing ['sɜːvɪsɪŋ] *n* entretien *m*.

serviette [sɜːvɪ'et] *n* serviette *f* de table.

servile ['sɜːvaɪl] *adj* (*person, behaviour*) servile.

servility [sɜː'vɪlɪtɪ] *n* servilité *f*.

serving ['sɜːvɪŋ] **1** *adj* (*soldat*) au service; **the longest-s. official,** la personnalité officielle ayant le plus d'ancienneté. **2** *n* **(a)** service *m* (*d'un maître*); **(b)** service *m* (*d'un client*); **(c)** service *m* (*du dîner*); **s. hatch,** guichet *m*; **(d)** *Tennis* service *m* (*d'une balle*); **(e)** *Jur* signification *f*, notification *f* (*d'une citation*); **(f)** (*portion*) portion *f* (*d'un mets*).

servitude ['sɜːvɪtjuːd] *n* **(a)** (*slavery*) servitude *f*, esclavage *m*; **(b)** *Jur* (*imprisonment*) **penal s. for life,** travaux forcés à perpétuité; **(c)** *Jur* servitude *f* (*réelle ou personnelle*).

servo ['sɜːvəʊ] **1** *n F* = **SERVOMECHANISM**. **2** *adj Aut* **s. brake,** servofrein *m*.

servocontrol [sɜːvəʊkən'trəʊl] *n* servocommande *f*.

servomechanism [sɜːvəʊ'mekənɪzm] *n* servomécanisme *m*.

servomotor [sɜːvəʊ'məʊtər] *n* servomoteur *m*.

sesame ['sesəmɪ] *n* **(a)** (*plant*) sésame *m*; **(b) open s.,** (*magic formula*) sésame, ouvre-toi!

session ['seʃən] *n* **(a)** (*period of activity*) séance *f*; **morning/evening s.,** (*at swimming pool etc*) séance du matin/soir; **skiing tuition at £10 per 3-hour s.,** cours *m* de ski à 10 livres par séance de 3 heures; **training s.,** séance d'entraînement; **we had a long s. on the phone,** nous avons passé très longtemps au téléphone; **I've just had a long s. with the lawyers,** je viens d'avoir un long entretien avec les avocats; *F* **she has a complaining s. every morning,** elle se plaint tous les matins; *F* **he had a big kissing s. with ...,** il a eu une longue séance d'embrassade avec ...; **(b)** (*meeting*) session *f*; **to go into secret s.,** se former en comité secret; *Parl* **the autumn s.,** la session d'automne; **the House is now in s.,** la Chambre siège actuellement; **(c)** *US Sch* trimestre *m* scolaire *ou* universitaire; *US & Scot Sch* année *f* universitaire.

set¹ [set] *n* **(a)** (*group*) jeu *m* (*d'outils, de boîtes, de dominos, d'aiguilles etc*); équipage *m*, assortiment *m*, attirail *m* (*d'outils*); série *f* (*de poids, de casseroles, Nau de pavillons*); train *m* (*de pneus, de roues*); batterie *f* (*de turbines, d'ustensiles de cuisine*); suite *f* (*d'estampes*); collection complète (*des œuvres de qn*); service *m* (*de porcelaine*); parure *f* (*de lingerie, de boutons, de pierres précieuses*); groupe *m* (*de personnes*); *Comptr* jeu, ensemble *m* (*de caractères, d'instructions etc*); **s. of teeth,** denture *f*; (*artificial*) dentier *m*; *Math* **s. theory,** théorie *f* des ensembles; **s. of golf clubs,** jeu de crosses; **s. of bells,** sonnerie *f* (*d'église etc*); *Old-fashioned* **toilet s., dressing-table s.,** garniture *f* de toilette; **construction s.,** jeu de construction; **a s. of stamps/postcards/***etc*, collection de timbres/de cartes postales; **to collect the s. (of sth),** rassembler toute la collection (*de qch*), faire la collection (*de qch*); **chairs, the s. of six, £200,** chaises, 200 livres les six; **literary/political s.,** (*people*) coterie *f* littéraire/politique; **the smart s.,** le monde élégant; **I'm not one of their s.,** je ne fais pas partie de leur groupe;

(b) (*act of setting*) couvée *f* (*d'œufs*); (*in hunting*) **(dead) s.,** arrêt *m* (d'un chien);

(c) attitude *f*, posture *f* (*du corps*); disposition *f* des plis (*d'une draperie*); direction *f* (*du courant, de la marée*); tendances *fpl* (*de l'opinion publique*); *MecE* déviation *f*; déformation *f* (*d'une pièce*); (*in hairdressing*) mise *f* en plis; **s. of the features,** modelé *m* des traits, physionomie *f*; **I knew him by the s. of his head,** je l'ai reconnu à son port de tête; (*metalwork*) *& Carp* **s. of a saw,** voie *f ou* chasse *f* d'une scie;

(d) (*firmness of jelly, concrete etc*) prise *f*;

(e) *Rad* **(radio) s.,** poste *m* de radio; **(television) s.,** téléviseur *m*, poste *m* de télévision;

(f) *Constr* **(paving) s.,** pavé *m* d'échantillon;

(g) *Th* (*scenery*) décor *m*; **rehearsal on the s.,** *Th* répétition *f* sur scène; *Cin* répétition sur le plateau;

(h) *Mus etc* (*performance*) **each band will have two sets,** chaque orchestre va jouer deux fois;

(i) (*tool*) **nail s.,** chasse-clou(s) *m inv*; **saw s.,** tourne-à-gauche *m inv*;

(j) *Tennis* manche *f*, set *m*; **s. point,** balle *f* de set;

(k) *Constr* dernière couche (*appliquée à une paroi etc*);

(l) (*of badger*) terrier *m*.

set² *v* (*pt & pp* **set**; *prp* **setting**) **1** *vt* **(a)**(*place*) mettre, poser (*qch sur ou contre qch, devant qch ou qn*); **to s. one's glass on the table,** poser son verre sur la table; **to s. a dish in front of s.o.,** servir un plat; **to s. one's hand/seal to a document,** apposer sa signature/son sceau à un acte; **to s. s.o. on his feet again,** remettre qn sur pied; **to s. one's heart on sth,** avoir qch à cœur, vouloir absolument qch; **the house is set in the heart of the woods,** la maison est située au milieu des bois;

(b) to s. the table, mettre le couvert *ou* la table; **to s. the table for two,** mettre deux couverts;

(c) (*put in ground*) planter (*des graines*); mettre (*une plante*) en terre; **to s. a stake in the ground,** enfoncer *ou* planter un pieu dans la terre;

(d) (*adjust*) régler (*une montre etc*); mettre (*une montre etc*) à l'heure; *MecE* régler, caler; *Phot* caler (*l'obturateur*); régler, ajuster (*le fer d'un rabot*); donner de la voie à (*une scie*); **to s. one's watch by the town clock,** prendre l'heure à l'horloge de la ville; **to s. one's watch to s.o. else's,** régler sa montre d'après la montre de qn d'autre; **to s. the alarm clock for** *or* **at five o'clock,** mettre le réveille-matin sur cinq heures; **to s. the milometer to zero,** ramener *ou* remettre le compteur à zéro; **to s. one's hat straight,** remettre son chapeau droit; **to have one's hair set,** se faire faire une mise en plis;

(e) *Mus* **to s. a melody half a tone higher/lower,** hausser/baisser un air d'un demi-ton; **to s. words to music,** mettre des paroles en musique;

(f) (*mount*) monter (*un papillon*) (*en spécimen*); monter, sertir (*une pierre*); *MecE* loger, mettre en place (*une pièce*); *Nau* déployer, mettre dehors (*une voile*); *Th* **to s. a scene,** monter un décor; **his introduction set the scene for the film,** dans son introduction il a replacé le film dans son contexte; **the second act is set in a street,** le second acte se passe dans une rue; **where is the story/film set?,** où est-ce que l'histoire/le film se passe?; **set with diamonds,** orné *ou* incrusté de diamants; *Nau* **to s. the sails,** déferler les voiles; **(with) all sails set,** toutes voiles dehors;

(g) dresser, tendre (*un piège*); armer (*un piège à loups, Phot un obturateur*);

(h) (*sharpen*) affiler (*un rasoir*); aiguiser, affûter (*un ciseau*); affûter (*une scie*); *Typ* **to s. type,** composer; **to s. a page,** composer une page;

(i) *Surg* remettre (*un os, un membre*); réduire (*une fracture*);

(j) (*fix*) fixer, désigner, arrêter (*une date, un jour*); **to s. limits to sth,** assigner des limites à qch; **to s. prices high/low,** fixer les prix hauts/bas; **to s. an age limit at ...,** fixer une limite d'âge à ...; **to s. the fashion,** mener la mode; donner le ton *ou* la note; **to s. a fashion/trend,** lancer une mode/tendance;

(k) (*of plant*) donner, porter (*des fruits*);

(l) **to s. a good example,** donner un bon exemple; **to s. oneself a task,** s'imposer *ou* entreprendre une tâche; **to s. oneself a target,** se fixer un but; **to s. s.o. a question/a problem,** poser une question/un problème à qn; *Sch* **to s. an essay,** donner un sujet de dissertation; **to s. a book,** mettre (*un livre*) au programme; **to s. an exam(ination) paper,** choisir les questions d'une épreuve écrite;

(m) (*cause to start*) **to s. s.o. to do sth,** mettre qn à faire qch; **to s. a man to work,** mettre un homme au travail; **that set me thinking,** cela m'a fait réfléchir *ou* m'a donné à réfléchir; **to s. the dog barking,** faire aboyer le chien; **to s. people talking,** (*start conversation*) déclencher la conversation; (*provoke comment*) provoquer des commentaires; **to s. (sth) going,** mettre (qch) en train; **to s. a mechanism going,** mettre (*un mécanisme*) en marche;

(n) (*cause to be*) **to s. s.o. free,** libérer qn, rendre sa liberté à qn.

2 *vi* **(a)** (*of sun, moon*) se coucher; *Lit* (*of fame etc*) s'éteindre, pâlir; **we saw the sun setting,** nous avons vu le coucher du soleil;

(b) (*of character*) se former, s'affermir; (*of foundations*) se tasser; (*of the face, eyes*) s'immobiliser; (*of the features*) se figer; (*of broken bone*) se ressouder; (*of blossom, fruit*) se former; (*of tree*) reprendre racine;

(c) (*of white of egg, blood*) se coaguler; (*of blood*) se figer; (*of jelly*) prendre; (*of cement*) prendre, durcir;

(d) (*in hunting*) (*of dog*) tomber en arrêt;

(e) (*of current etc*) **to s. southwards,** porter au sud; **the tide is setting in/out,** la marée commence à monter/à descendre *ou* à se retirer.

set³ *adj* **(a)** (*visage*) immobile, aux traits rigides; (*regard*) fixe; (*sourire*) figé; (*ressort*) bandé, tendu; *Sp* **(get) s.!,** en position, attention!; **to be all s.,** être prêt à commencer; **(hard) s.,** ferme, figé; (*ciment*) bien pris; **well s. person,** personne à la taille cambrée;

(b) **s. piece,** *Culin* pièce montée; (*fireworks*) pièce montée, pièce d'artifice; *Sp* stratégie *f*; *Th* ferme *f*; *Th* **s. scene,** décor *m* (monté);

(c) (*fixed*) **he has a s. way of doing it,** il a une méthode pour le faire; **s. price,** prix *m* fixe; **at s. hours,** à des heures réglées; **s. purpose,** ferme intention *f*; **s. ideas,** idées arrêtées; **s. expression,** (*in language*) expression figée; **s. forms,** les formes prescrites; **s. form of prayer,** prière *f* liturgique; **s. dinner,** (dîner *m* de) table *f* d'hôte; (*at fixed price*) dîner à prix fixe; **s. menu,** menu *m* fixe; **s. speech,** discours composé à l'avance *ou* préparé; **s. time,** heure fix(é)e *ou* prescrite; **he likes having his meals at s. times,** il aime prendre ses repas à heures fixes;

(d) **s. books,** les auteurs *mpl* au programme; *Sch* **s. subject,** sujet imposé aux candidats; **s. task,** tâche assignée;

(e) **the fruit is s.,** le fruit est formé *ou* noué;

(f) **to be s. on sth,** être résolu *ou* déterminé à qch; tenir beaucoup à ce que qch se fasse; **to be (dead) s. on doing sth,** être résolu *ou* déterminé à faire qch; **to be dead s. against s.o.,** s'acharner après *ou* contre *ou* sur qn;

(g) *Journ* **sterling s. to fall,** la livre sterling sur le point de chuter.

►**set about** *vipo* **(a)** (*start*) **to s. about a piece of work,** se mettre à *ou* entreprendre un travail; **to s. about doing sth,** se mettre à faire qch; **they s. about reforming the economy,** ils se sont mis à réformer l'économie; **I don't know how to s. about it,** je ne sais pas comment m'y prendre; **(b)** *F* (*attack*) **to s. about s.o.,** attaquer qn.

►**set against** *vtsep* **(a)** (*cause to oppose*) **to s. against s.o.,** indisposer qn contre qn, monter (la tête à) qn contre qn; **he's trying to s. you against me,** il cherche à me nuire auprès de vous; **something's set him against the idea,** quelque chose l'a monté contre cette idée; **to s. oneself** *or* **one's face against sth,** s'opposer résolument à qch; **(b)** (*compare*) opposer (*qch à qch*); (*weigh against*) contrebalancer (*qch par qch*); **we must s. the government's promises against its actions,** nous devons examiner les promesses du gouvernement à la lumière de ses actions; *Fin* **to s. expenses against taxes,** déduire les dépenses des impôts.

►**set apart** *vtsep* **(a)** (*isolate*) isoler (*qn*); **they set themselves apart,** ils faisaient bande à part; **(b)** (*distinguish*) **what sets them apart from other companies is ...,** ce qui les distingue des autres sociétés c'est ... .

►**set aside** *vtsep* **(a)** (*abandon temporarily*) mettre de côté (*job, task*); **could you s. aside what you're working on for a while?,** pouvez-vous laisser ce que vous êtes en train de faire un moment?; **(b)** (*not consider*) ne pas prendre en ligne de compte; **setting that aspect aside,** sans prendre cet aspect en ligne de compte; **to s. aside one's personal feelings,** mettre de côté tout sentiment personnel; **(c)** (*save*) mettre de côté *ou* en réserve; **I've decided to s. aside some money every week,** j'ai décidé de mettre de l'argent de côté chaque semaine; **(d)** *Jur* casser, infirmer (*un jugement etc*); rejeter (*une réclamation*); annuler (*un testament*).

►**set back** *vtsep* **(a)** *Constr etc* renfoncer (*une façade*); **house set back (from the road),** maison en retrait (de la route); **to s. back its ears,** (*of horse*) coucher les oreilles; **(b)** (*delay*) retarder le progrès de (*qn, qch*); **this will s. him back,** cela retardera sa guérison; **this decision will s. the economy back ten years,** cette décision va faire revenir l'économie dix ans en arrière; **(c)** *F* (*cost*) **it set me back £5,000,** ça m'a coûté 5 000 livres, **that new car must have set her back a bit,** cette nouvelle voiture doit lui avoir coûté un fric fou.

►**set by** *vtsep* = **SET ASIDE (c).**

►**set down** *vtsep* **(a)** (*put down*) déposer (*qch, qn*); **the train stops to s. down passengers only,** le train ne s'arrête que pour déposer des voyageurs; **(b)** **to s. sth down in writing,** coucher qch par écrit; **condition set down in the contract,** condition énoncée dans le contrat; **permissible levels of pollution are set down in the regulations,** les niveaux admissibles de pollution sont fixés dans les réglementations.

►**set forth 1** *vi Arch* (*leave*) se mettre en route, partir. **2** *vtsep* (*present*) présenter, mettre en avant (*a case etc*); **the document sets forth a detailed description of ...,** le document présente une description détaillée de ... .

►**set in 1** *vi* (*begin*) commencer; **before winter sets in,** avant la venue de l'hiver; **night was setting in,** la nuit commençait à tomber; **rain is setting in,** le temps se met à la pluie; **gangrene had not set in,** la gangrène ne s'est pas installée. **2** *vtsep* (*fit*) encastrer, entabler (*une pierre une poutre*); poser (*une vitre*); *Sewing* monter (*une manche, des fronces*).

►**set off 1** *vtsep* **(a)** faire partir (*une fusée etc*);

(b) (*cause*) déclencher (*an argument*);

(c) (*cause to do sth*) **this answer set them off laughing,** cette réponse a déclenché les rires, **if you say anything it'll only s. him off (crying) again,** si tu dis quoi que ce soit, il se remettra à pleurer; **she's so allergic a cut flower will s. her off,** elle est tellement allergique qu'une fleur coupée lui déclenche une crise;

(d) (*enhance*) faire ressortir, faire valoir, rehausser (*les charmes de qn, une couleur*); mettre (*qch*) en relief *ou* en valeur; **those curtains really s. the room off,** ces rideaux mettent vraiment la pièce en valeur;

(e) *Fin* compenser (*une dette*); **to s. off a gain against a loss,** compenser une perte par un gain; **can I s. these expenses off against my tax liability?,** est-ce que je peux déduire ces frais de mes impôts?

2 *vi* (*depart*) se mettre en route, partir; **to s. off on a journey,** se mettre en voyage; **to s. off again,** se remettre en route; **to s. off running,** partir en courant.

►**set on 1** *vipo* **travellers set on by thieves,** voyageurs attaqués par des voleurs. **2** *vtaspo* **(a)** (*cause to follow*) **to s. the police on the tracks of a thief,** mettre la police aux trousses d'un voleur; **to s. s.o. on the wrong track,** aiguiller qn sur la fausse piste; **to s. s.o. on his way,** mettre qn dans le bon chemin; **(b)** (*cause to attack*) **to s. a dog on s.o.,** lâcher un chien contre qn.

►**set out 1** *vtsep* **(a)** (*arrange*) arranger, disposer (*qch*); étaler (*des marchandises*); exposer (*ses idées*); **his work is well set out,** son travail est bien présenté;

(b) *Math etc* faire le tracé de (*une courbe*);

(c) *Typ* espacer (*les caractères, les mots*).

2 *vi* **(a)** (*depart on journey*) se mettre en route, partir; **just as he was setting out,** au moment de son départ; **to s. out for school,** partir pour l'école; **to s. out again,** repartir; **to s. out in pursuit/in search of s.o.,** se mettre à la poursuite/à la recherche de qn;

(b) (*start job etc*) **I didn't realise when I set out how difficult it would be,** je n'avais pas réalisé combien ce serait difficile lorsque je me suis mis au travail;

(c) (*intend*) **I didn't set out to attack the government,** je n'avais aucune intention d'attaquer le gouvernment; **they deliberately set out to cause trouble,** ils avaient l'intention de créer des problèmes; **his theory sets out to prove that ...,** sa théorie a pour objet de prouver que ... .

►**set to 1** *vi* **(a)** (*start working*) se mettre (résolument) au travail *ou* à l'œuvre; **(b)** *F* (*of two people*) (*start arguing*) avoir une prise de bec; (*start fighting*) en venir aux coups *ou* aux mains. **2** *vipo* (*start doing*) **to s. to work,** se mettre au travail *ou* à l'œuvre.

►**set up 1** *vtsep* **(a)** (*erect*) dresser (*un mât, une statue etc*); élever, ériger (*une statue*); élever (*une barrière*); planter (*un drapeau*); installer (*une batterie*); monter (*une machine, une tente etc*); armer (*un appareil*); **to s. sth up again,** (*because it has fallen*) relever qch;

(b) (*arrange*) arranger (*un déjeuner etc*); tramer (*un complot*); agencer (*qch*); **to s. up an appointment with s.o.,** arranger *ou* organiser un rendez-vous avec qn;

(c) (*establish*) établir (*une agence etc*); instituer, constituer (*un comité, un tribunal*); créer, fonder (*une maison de commerce*); monter (*un magasin*); **to s. up house,** s'installer dans une maison; **to s. s.o. up in business,** établir *ou* lancer qn dans une affaire;

(d) (*cause*) *Med etc* occasionner, causer (*une infection, une irritation*);

(e) *F* (*fabricate evidence against*) (*usu passive*) **I've been set up good and proper,** on m'a monté le coup, on m'a bien eu;

(f) to s. up a howl, se mettre à hurler;

(g) (*invigorate*) donner *ou* rendre de la vigueur à (*qn*); **a fortnight in the country will s. you up,** une quinzaine à la campagne va vous remettre d'aplomb;

(h) *Typ* composer (*un manuscrit*).

2 *vi* **(a)** (*establish oneself*) **to s. up in business,** se mettre à son compte; **to s. up as a chemist,** s'établir pharmacien(ne); **he has set up for himself,** il s'est établi à son (propre) compte;

(b) (*claim to be*) **to s. up as a critic,** se poser en critique.

►**set upon** *vipo* attaquer (*qn*); **to be set upon by s.o.,** être attaqué par qn.

setback ['setbæk] *n* **(a)** (*disappointment*) déconvenue *f*, déception *f*; (*stroke of bad luck*) revers *m* de fortune; recul *m* (*dans les affaires etc*); *Fin St Exch* tassement *m*, repli *m*; *Med* rechute *f* (*d'une maladie*); **to suffer a s. in one's plans,** voir ses plans compromis; **(b)** *Archit* décrochement *m*.

set-in ['setɪn] *adj* encastré; *Sewing* **s.-in sleeve,** manche rapportée.

set-off ['setɒf] *n* **(a)** (*contrast*) contraste *m*; **as a s.-o.,** par contraste; **(b)** compensation *f* (*d'une dette*); (*in bookkeeping*) écriture *f* inverse; **as a s.-o. against (sth),** (*as a compensation*) en compensation de (qch); (*as a counterbalance*) en contrepartie de *ou* à (qch).

set-square ['setskweər] *n* équerre *f* (à dessin).

sett [set] *n Constr* **(paving) s.,** pavé *m* d'échantillon.

settee [se'tiː] *n* canapé *m*; **bed s., s. bed,** canapé-lit *m*, *pl* canapés-lits.

setter ['setər] *n* **(a)** *MecE* (*person*) ajusteur *m*; sertisseur *m* (*de diamants etc*); *Typ* **type s.,** compositeur, -trice; *Th* **stage s.,** chef *m* machiniste; **(b)** (*dog*) setter *m*; **Irish s.,** setter irlandais.

setting ['setɪŋ] **1** *adj* **(a)** (*soleil, astre*) couchant; (*astre, gloire*) sur son déclin;

(b) slow-/quick-s. cement, ciment *m* à prise lente/rapide.

2 *n* **(a)** (*act of placing*) mise *f*, pose *f* (*de qch*);

(b) (*act of arranging*) disposition *f*, arrangement *m*; **s. to music,** mise *f* en musique;

(c) (*act of adjusting*) réglage *m*; mise *f* à l'heure (*d'une horloge*); (*in hairdressing*) mise en plis; **s. lotion,** lotion *f* pour mise en plis;

(d) (*act of mounting*) montage *m* (*d'un spécimen*); montage, sertissage *m* (*d'une pierre*);

(e) (*act of laying*) dressage *m* (*d'un piège*);

(f) *Typ* composition *f*; **page s.,** mise *f* en page;

(g) (*act of fixing*) fixation *f*, désignation *f* (*d'une date etc*);

(h) (*act of assigning*) imposition *f* (*d'une tâche*);

(i) (*of sun etc*) coucher *m*;

(j) tassement *m* (*de fondations etc*); recollement *m* (*d'un os brisé*); *Surg* réduction *f* (*d'une fracture*);

(k) (*hardening*) formation *f* (*du fruit*); affermissement *m*, prise *f* (*du ciment*); coagulation *f* (*de l'albumine*);

(l) (*location*) cadre *m* (*d'un récit, d'une fête etc*); *Th* mise *f* en scène;

(m) (*on jewellery*) monture *f* (*d'un diamant*);

(n) (*arrangement*) **s. for violin,** arrangement *m* pour violon; **place s.,** (*at table*) couvert *m*;

(o) (*on washing machine, iron etc*) réglage *m*; **what s. was it on?,** comment était-elle réglée?

setting up *n Typ* composition *f*.

settle¹ ['set(ə)l] *n* (*seat*) banc *m* à dossier.

settle² 1 *vt* **(a)** (*make stable*) rendre stable; (*put firmly in place*) mettre bien en place; établir, installer (*qn, un peuple etc*) (*dans un pays*); coloniser, peupler (*un pays*); régler, mettre ordre à (*ses affaires*); **to s. one's feet in the stirrups,** assurer ses pieds dans les étriers; **she had settled herself in an armchair,** elle s'était installée dans un fauteuil;

(b) (*make arrangements for*) établir (*ses enfants*); marier, caser (*sa fille*); **to s. an invalid for the night,** installer un malade pour la nuit;

(c) laisser se déposer (*un liquide*);

(d) (*calm*) apaiser, calmer (*qn, les nerfs etc*); **give me something to s. my stomach,** donnez-moi quelque chose pour me calmer l'estomac; **to s. s.o.'s doubts,** dissiper les doutes de qn;

(e) (*fix*) fixer, déterminer (*un jour, un endroit etc*); **it's as good as settled,** l'affaire est dans le sac; **everything is settled, it's settled,** c'est une affaire faite, tout est d'accord; **that's settled then,** c'est convenu; **to s. to do sth,** décider de faire qch;

(f) (*resolve*) résoudre, décider (*une question*); trancher, arranger (*un différend*); vider (*une querelle*); arranger, liquider (*une affaire*); (*conclude*) conclure, terminer (*une affaire*); régler, solder (*un compte*); payer (*une dette etc*); **questions not yet settled,** questions en suspens; **that settles it!,** voilà qui tranche la question!, voilà qui décide tout!; **s. it among yourselves,** arrangez cela entre vous; **to s. a matter amicably,** régler une question à l'amiable; *Jur* arranger (*un procès*); **to s. one's bills,** payer ses comptes; *F* **that settled him,** (*that's put a stop to him*) ça lui a réglé son compte; (*that put a stop to his boasting*) ça lui a rabattu le caquet;

(g) (*bestow*) **to s. an annuity on s.o.,** constituer une annuité à qn; **to s. all one's property on one's wife,** mettre tous ses biens sur la tête de sa femme.

2 *vi* **(a)** (*of person, people*) élire domicile, s'établir, se fixer (**in a place,** dans un lieu); (*of bird, insect etc*) se percher, se poser (*sur un arbre etc*); **to s. in an armchair,** s'installer dans un fauteuil; **she had settled in a corner,** elle s'était installée dans un coin; **they settled along the Ohio,** ils se sont installés au bord de l'Ohio; **she lived here a few years, but didn't s.,** elle y a vécu quelques années, mais elle ne s'est pas installée définitivement; (*never felt at home*) elle y a vécu quelques années, mais elle ne s'y est jamais sentie chez elle; **the snow is settling,** la neige ne fond pas; **the wind is settling in the north,** le vent souffle ferme du nord; **to s. to work/to do sth,** se mettre sérieusement au travail/à faire qch; **he can't s. to anything,** il ne se décide pas à choisir une occupation; **I couldn't s.,** (*in bed*) je n'arrivais pas à m'endormir;

(b) (*of liquid*) se clarifier, déposer; (*of sediment*) se déposer; (*of dust*) retomber; **to let s.,** laisser déposer (*un précipité*); laisser rasseoir (*le vin*); laisser reposer (*une solution*);

(c) (*of ground, pillar etc*) prendre son assiette, s'asseoir; (*of foundation etc*) se déniveler, s'affaisser; (*of ship*) couler, (s')enfoncer;

(d) (*of excitement*) s'apaiser, se calmer; **the weather is settling,** le temps se calme.

►**settle down 1** *vi* **(a)** (*make oneself comfortable*) s'installer (*dans un fauteuil etc*); **to s. down to sleep,** se disposer à dormir; **to s. down with a book,** s'installer avec un livre;

(b) (*give serious attention to*) **to s. down to work,** se mettre sérieusement au travail; **to s. down to a job,** attaquer *ou* se mettre à une tâche;

(c) (*adopt regular life*) (*get married*) se ranger, s'assagir; (*of situation*) s'arranger, redevenir normal; (*of excitement*) se calmer; **it's time you settled down and got married,** il est temps que tu te ranges et que tu te maries; **s. down, children!,** calmez-vous, les enfants!; **he's beginning to s. down at school,** il commence à s'habituer à l'école; **things are settling down,** (*become more definite*) les choses commencent à prendre tournure; (*calm down*) l'ordre se rétablit; **as soon as the market settles down,** aussitôt que le marché reprendra son train (ordinaire).

2 *vtsep* **(a)** (*make comfortable*) **to s. the baby down for**

the night, installer le bébé pour la nuit;
(b) (*make calm*) **to s. a class down,** calmer une classe.

▶**settle for** *vipo* (*accept*) accepter (*qch*); **I settled for £100,** j'ai décidé d'accepter 100 livres; **I insist on the best quality — I never s. for (anything) less,** j'insiste sur la meilleure qualité – je n'accepte jamais rien moins; **we haven't got any brandy —will you s. for Scotch?,** nous n'avons pas de cognac – est-ce qu'un whisky fera l'affaire?

▶**settle in 1** *vi* (*become established*) s'installer, s'établir (*dans une nouvelle maison etc*); **to s. in at a job,** s'habituer à un emploi. **2** *vtsep* (*help become established*) (*new employee, person in new home*) aider à s'installer.

▶**settle on** *vipo* (*decide*) décider de (*qch*); **have you settled on a name for the baby/a date for the wedding?,** avez-vous décidé d'un nom pour le bébé/d'une date pour le mariage?; **to s. on a price,** se mettre d'accord sur un prix.

▶**settle up** *vi* **(a)** (*pay bill*) payer; **(b)** (*pay debt*) s'acquitter; **I'll s. up with you tomorrow,** je vous réglerai demain.

▶**settle with** *vipo* **to s. with s.o.,** (*to pay debt*) régler ses comptes avec qn; *F* (*to settle a score with*) régler son compte à qn.

settled ['set(ə)ld] *adj* **(a)** (*state*) invariable, sûr; (*idea, habit*) fixe, enraciné; (*intention*) bien arrêté; (*person, character*) rassis, réfléchi; (*bearing etc*) tranquille, calme; **s. weather,** temps fixe *ou* sûr; (*fine weather*) beau fixe; **I am a man of s. habits,** je suis un homme d'habitudes; **she is s. in her job,** elle est habituée à son emploi; **(b)** (*resolved*) (*affair etc*) arrangé, décidé; **(c)** (*established in home*) (*person*) domicilié, établi; **(d)** (*ground*) tassé; **(e)** (*country*) colonisé.

settlement ['set(ə)lmənt] *n* **(a)** établissement *m* (*d'un peuple dans un pays etc*); installation *f* (*de qn dans une maison etc*); colonisation *f* (*d'un pays*);
(b) clarification *f* (*d'un liquide*); tassement *m*, affaissement *m* (*des terres*);
(c) règlement *m* (*d'une affaire*); arrangement *m* (*d'un différend etc*); résolution *f*, décision *f* (*d'une question*); détermination *f* (*d'une date etc*); conclusion *f* (*d'un traité etc*); *Com* règlement, paiement *m* (*d'un compte*); *St Exch* liquidation *f*; **in (full) s.,** pour règlement de tout compte; **s. day,** jour *m* de (la) liquidation *ou* du règlement;
(d) (*agreement*) accord *m* (*entre deux puissances etc*); **they have reached a s.,** ils sont arrivés à un accord; *Jur* **s. of an annuity,** constitution *f* de rente (**on**, en faveur de); **family s.,** pacte *m* de famille; **marriage s.,** contrat *m* de mariage; (*in favour of daughter*) dot *f*; (*in favour of wife*) douaire *m*;
(e) (*colony*) colonie *f*, **penal s.,** colonie pénitentiaire;
(f) *US* (*small community*) petit village.

settler ['setlər] *n* (*colonist*) colon *m*, immigrant, -ante (*dans un pays nouvellement découvert*).

settling ['setlɪŋ] *n* **(a)** = **SETTLEMENT (a)**; **(b)** clarification *f* (*d'un liquide*); **(c)** apaisement *m* (*d'une agitation, des nerfs etc*); **(d)** précipitation *f*, dépôt *m* (*du sédiment*); tassement *m*; affaissement *m* (*du terrain*); **settlings,** dépôt, sédiment *m*; **(e)** = **SETTLEMENT (c)**; **(f)** conclusion *f*, terminaison *f* (*d'une affaire*); *St Exch* **s. day,** jour *m* de (la) liquidation *ou* du règlement.

set-to ['set'tuː] *n F* (*fight*) bagarre *f*; (*argument*) prise *f* de bec.

setup ['setʌp] *n F* **(a)** (*organization*) organisation *f*; **it's an odd s.,** c'est une drôle de boîte *ou* d'affaire; **(b)** (*arrangement in room, office, factory etc*) installation *f*; **you've got a nice s. here,** vous êtes bien installé ici; **(c)** *esp Am Sl* (*something rigged*) machination *f*, coup monté.

seven ['sev(ə)n] *n* sept *m*; **two sevens are fourteen,** deux fois sept font quatorze; *Cards* **s. of hearts,** le sept de cœur; *F* **the s.-year itch,** la période difficile après sept ans de mariage; **to have the s.-year itch,** commencer à se fatiguer de son mariage; **the s. deadly sins,** les sept péchés capitaux; **s.-league boots,** bottes *fpl* de sept lieues (du Petit Poucet).

sevenfold ['sev(ə)nfəʊld] **1** *adj* septuple. **2** *adv* sept fois autant; **to increase s.,** septupler.

seventeen [sev(ə)n'tiːn] *n* dix-sept *m*; **she's s.,** elle a dix-sept ans.

seventeenth [sev(ə)n'tiːnθ] **1** *adj* dix-septième; **(on) the s. of May,** le dix-sept mai. **2** *n* **(a)** (*of month*) dix-sept *m*; **on the s.,** le dix-sept; **(b)** (*fraction*) dix-septième *m*.

seventh ['sev(ə)nθ] **1** *adj* septième; **to be in s. heaven,** être aux anges *ou* au septième ciel; **Edward the S.,** Edouard Sept; **the s. of May,** le sept mai; *Rel* **S.-day Adventist,** adventiste *mf* du septième jour. **2** *n* **(a)** (*of month*) sept *m*; **(b)** (*fraction*) septième *m*; **(c)** *Mus* (*interval*) septième *f*; (*note*) (note *f*) sensible *f*.

seventieth ['sev(ə)ntɪɪθ] **1** *adj* soixante-dixième; *Belg Swiss* septantième. **2** *n* (*fraction*) soixante-dixième *m*.

seventy ['sev(ə)ntɪ] *n* soixante-dix *m*; *Belg Swiss* septante *mf*; **s.-one,** soixante et onze; **s.-five,** soixante-quinze; **s.-nine,** soixante-dix neuf; **to be in one's seventies,** être septuagénaire.

sever ['sevər] **1** *vt* désunir, disjoindre (*les parties d'un tout*); rompre (*une amitié, une liaison, une relation etc*); **to s. one's connections with s.o.,** couper les liens avec qn; **to s. sth from sth,** séparer qch de qch; **a severed head,** une tête coupée. **2** *vi* (*of rope etc*) (se) rompre.

several ['sev(ə)r(ə)l] **1** *adj* **(a)** (*a number of*) plusieurs; **I've been there s. times,** j'y suis allé plusieurs fois; **he and s. others,** lui et plusieurs autres; **(b)** (*separate*) séparé; (*respective*) respectif; **on three s. occasions,** à trois occasions (différentes); *Lit* **each went his s. way,** ils s'en allèrent, chacun de son côté. **2** *pron* **s. of us/of them/etc,** plusieurs d'entre nous/d'entre eux/*etc*; **s. of our party heard it,** plusieurs membres de notre groupe l'ont entendu.

severally ['sevrəlɪ] *adv* séparément, individuellement.

severance ['sevərəns] *n* séparation *f*, désunion *f*, disjonction *f* (**from,** de); rupture *f* (*des relations etc*); **s. pay,** compensation *f* pour perte d'emploi.

severe [sɪ'vɪər] *adj* **(a)** (*person, measures*) sévère, strict, rigoureux (**with,** envers); **a s. reprimand,** une verte réprimande; **(b)** (*weather*) rigoureux; (*winter, weather*) rigoureux, rude, dur; (*illness, wound*) grave; **s. blow,** coup *m* rude; **to suffer s. hardship,** souffrir de grands malheurs; **s. loss,** grosse *ou* forte perte; **s. pain,** douleur violente *ou* vive; **(c)** (*style etc*) sévère, austère.

severely [sɪ'vɪəlɪ] *adv* (*see adj*) **(a)** sévèrement, strictement; avec sévérité; **(b)** grièvement (*blessé*); gravement (*malade*); **s. tried,** durement éprouvé; **(c)** sévèrement, austèrement.

severity [sɪ'verɪtɪ] *n* **(a)** sévérité *f*, dureté *f*, rigueur *f* (*de qn, d'une punition etc*); **(b)** rigueur *f* (*du temps, du climat etc*); rudesse *f* (*du temps*); gravité *f* (*d'une maladie, d'une perte*); violence *f* (*d'une douleur*); rigueur, caractère rigoureux (*d'un examen etc*); **(c)** sévérité *f*, austérité *f* (*de style*).

Seville [se'vɪl] *n* Séville *f*; **S. orange,** orange amère.

sew [səʊ] *v* (*pt* **sewed** [səʊd]; *pp* **sewn** [səʊn], *occ* **sewed**) **1** *vi* coudre; (*with awl*) piquer. **2** *vt* coudre; (*with awl*) piquer; **hand/machine sewn,** cousu (à la) main/à la machine.

▶**sew on** *vtsep* (*attach by sewing*) **to s. on a button,** (re)coudre un bouton.

▶**sew up** *vtsep* **(a)** (*close by sewing*) fermer par une couture (*hole*); **(b)** *F* **it's all sewn up,** tout est arrangé; **we've got it all sewn up,** l'affaire est dans le sac.

sewage ['suːɪdʒ] *n* eau(x) *f*(*pl*) d'égout(s); effluent urbain; **s. system,** système *m* du tout-à-l'égout; **s. farm** *or* **works,** champs *mpl* d'épandage.

sewer¹ ['səʊər] *n* (*person who sews*) couseur, -euse; **to be a good/bad s.,** être bon/mauvais couturier.

sewer² ['suːər] *n Constr* (*pipe*) égout *m*; **main s.,** égout collecteur; **s. rat,** rat *m* d'égout; *Fig* **s. of vice/***etc*, cloaque *m* de vice/*etc*; **he's got a mind like a s.,** il a l'esprit très sale.

sewerage ['suːərɪdʒ] *n* **(a)** (*system of sewers*) système *m* d'égouts; **(b)** *F* = **SEWAGE.**

sewing ['səʊɪŋ] *n* **(a)** (*activity*) couture *f*; **s. cotton** *or* **thread,** fil *m* à coudre; **s. machine,** machine *f* à coudre; **s. needle,** aiguille *f* à coudre; **(b)** (*work*) ouvrage *m* (à l'aiguille); **the s. on this shirt is terrible,** cette chemise est très mal cousue.

sex¹ [seks] *n* sexe *m*; *F* **to have s. with s.o.,** faire l'amour avec qn; **the fair s.,** le beau sexe; **the sterner s.,** le sexe fort; **the s. act,** l'acte sexuel; **s. appeal,** attrait sexuel, sex-appeal *m*; **to have a s. change,** (*operation*) changer de sexe; **s. crime,** crime sexuel; *Biol* **s. determination,** détermination *f* du sexe; **s. discrimination,** discrimination *f* sexiste; **to have a low/high s. drive,** avoir un appétit sexuel faible/élevé; **s. education,** éducation sexuelle; *esp Journ* **s. fiend,** maniaque sexuel(le); *F* **s. kitten,** nana *f* très sexy; **s. life,** vie sexuelle; **how's your s. life?,** et ta vie amoureuse, comment ça va?; *F* **s. mad,** qui ne pense qu'au sexe; **s. object,** objet sexuel; **s. offender,** délinquant, -ante sexuel(le); **s. organs,** organes sexuels; **s. shop,** sex-shop *m*; **s.-starved,** affamé sexuellement; **s. symbol,** symbole sexuel; *Psy* **the s. urge,** le désir sexuel.

sex² *vt* déterminer le sexe de (*qn, un animal*).

sexagenarian [seksədʒɪ'neərɪən] *adj & n* sexagénaire *mf*.

sexed [sekst] *adj* **(a)** *Biol* sexué; **(b)** *Psy* **highly s.,** à tendances sexuelles très prononcées.
sexiness ['seksınıs] *n* (*appeal*) charme *ou* caractère sexy; (*behaviour*) airs provocants; (*tendency*) tendances sexuelles prononcées.
sexism ['seksız(ə)m] *n* sexisme *m*.
sexist ['seksıst] **1** *adj* sexiste. **2** *n* sexiste *mf*.
sexless ['sekslıs] *adj* **(a)** (*neuter*) asexué; (*fleur*) neutre; **(b)** *F* (*without sexual desire*) froid, frigide; (*unattractive*) asexué.
sexologist [sek'sɒlədʒıst] *n* sexologue *mf*.
sexology [sek'sɒlədʒı] *n* sexologie *f*.
sexploitation [seksplɔı'teıʃən] *n Cin F* **s. movie,** film *m* qui exploite la femme en tant qu'objet sexuel.
sexpot ['sekspɒt] *n F* femme *ou* homme très sexy.
sextant ['sekstənt] *n Math Nau* sextant *m*.
sextet [seks'tet] *n Mus* sextuor *m*; (*jazz*) sextette *f*.
sexton ['sekst(ə)n] *n Rel* sacristain *m* et sonneur *m* de cloches (et fossoyeur *m*).
sextuple ['sekstjʊp(ə)l] *adj & n* sextuple *m*.
sextuplet ['sekstjʊplıt] *n* **(a)** (*child*) sextuplé, -ée; **(b)** *Mus* sextolet *m*, sixain *m*.
sexual ['seksjʊəl] *adj* sexuel; **s. harassment,** harcèlement sexuel; **s. intercourse,** rapports sexuels; **the s. organs,** les organes sexuels; **s. reproduction,** reproduction sexuelle; **s. attraction,** attirance sexuelle.
sexuality [seksjʊ'ælıtı] *n* sexualité *f*.
sexually ['seksjʊəlı] *adv* sexuellement; **to be s. active,** avoir une vie sexuelle, avoir des rapports sexuels; **to be s. attracted to s.o.,** être attiré par qn sur le plan sexuel, éprouver une attirance sexuelle pour qn; **s. transmitted disease,** maladie *f* sexuellement transmissible.
sexy ['seksı] *adj F* (*person, clothes*) sexy; (*book, film*) érotique; *Fig* **skiing has become very s.,** le ski est devenu très chic; **hi there s.!,** bonjour mon mignon!; (*women*) bonjour ma belle!
sez [sez] *int Sl* **s. you!,** (= *says you*) tu parles!, et ta sœur!
SFA [ese'feı] *n Sp abbr* **Scottish Football Association**.
Sgt *Mil abbr* **Sergeant**.
sh [ʃ] *int* chut!
shabbily ['ʃæbılı] *adv* **(a)** pauvrement, piètrement (*meublé, vêtu etc*); **s. dressed,** miteux, râpé; **(b)** (*to behave*) mesquinement.
shabbiness ['ʃæbınıs] *n* **(a)** état râpé *ou* usé (*d'un vêtement etc*); piètre état (*d'un meuble etc*); apparence pauvre *ou F* miteuse (*de qn*); **(b)** mesquinerie *f*, petitesse *f* (*de conduite etc*).
shabby ['ʃæbı] *adj* **(a)** (*vêtement etc*) râpé, usé, élimé; (*mobilier, pièce etc*) pauvre, minable; **s. house,** maison délabrée *ou* minable; **to look s.,** (*of person*) avoir l'air minable *ou* miteux; **to be s. genteel,** s'efforcer de sauver les apparences; **to become s.,** (*of material*) se délustrer, s'élimer; **(b)** (*person, conduct*) mesquin, vilain, petit; **s. excuse,** prétexte mesquin; **s. trick,** mesquinerie *f*.
shack [ʃæk] *n* (*hut*) cabane *f*, hutte *f*; *F* (*old house*) bicoque *f*.
▶**shack up** *vi* (*cohabit*) **to s. up (together),** (*of two people*) se mettre à la colle; **to s. up with s.o.,** se mettre à la colle avec qn.
shackle¹ ['ʃæk(ə)l] *n* **(a) shackles,** fers *mpl* (*d'un prisonnier etc*); *Fig* **the shackles of convention,** les entraves *fpl* des conventions sociales; **(b)** *Tech* maillon *m* de liaison, manille *f* d'assemblage (*d'une chaîne*); anse *f* (*d'un cadenas*); cigale *f* (*d'une ancre*).
shackle² *vt* mettre les fers à, entraver (*un prisonnier*); **shackled by conventions,** entravé par les conventions.
shacktown ['ʃæktaʊn] *n Am F* bidonville *f*.
shade¹ [ʃeıd] *n* **(a)** ombre *f*; *Art* ombre (*dans un tableau*); **in the s. of a tree,** à l'ombre d'un arbre; **a tree provided some s.,** un arbre donnait de l'ombre; **temperature in the s.,** température à l'ombre; *Fig* **to put s.o. in the s.,** éclipser qn, faire de l'ombre à qn; **a s. of annoyance on his face,** une ombre de contrariété sur son visage; *Lit* **the Shades,** les Enfers *mpl*;
(b) nuance *f* (*de couleur, d'opinion*); teinte *f*; (*small amount*) petit peu, tantinet *m*; **different shades of blue,** différentes nuances de bleu; **a s. longer,** un tantinet plus long; **he is a s. better,** il va un tout petit peu mieux; **a s. (too) sweet,** un petit peu (trop) sucré; **a s. of regret,** une nuance de regret;
(c) *Lit* (*ghost*) ombre *f*, fantôme *m* (*d'un mort*); **shades of '1984',** ça rappelle '1984';
(d) (*device*) **(eye) s.,** visière *f*; **(lamp) s.,** abat-jour *m inv*; **(window) s.,** store *m* (de fenêtre); *Sl* **shades,** (*sunglasses*) lunettes *fpl* de soleil.
shade² **1** *vt* **(a)** ombrager (*qch*), donner de l'ombre à (*qch*); obscurcir, assombrir (*le visage etc*); **to s. (sth) from the sun,** abriter (qch) du soleil; **to s. one's eyes with one's hand,** s'abriter les yeux de la main; **to s. a light,** voiler *ou* masquer une lumière; **(b)** *Art* ombrer, mettre des ombres à (*un dessin*); **(c)** (*change by degrees*) nuancer (*un tissu etc*). **2** *vi* **blue that shades into green,** bleu qui se fond en vert; **these categories s. into one another,** ces catégories se confondent.
▶**shade away, shade off** *vtsep* (*change by degrees*) dégrader (*des couleurs*).
shaded ['ʃeıdıd] *adj* **(a)** (*chemin etc*) ombragé; (*lampe etc*) à abat-jour; **(b)** *Art* (*dessin*) ombré; (*area on diagram, map etc*) hachuré; **(c)** (*graduated*) nuancé.
shadeless ['ʃeıdlıs] *adj* **(a)** (*without shade*) sans ombre; **(b)** (*providing no shade*) qui ne donne pas d'ombre.
shadiness ['ʃeıdınıs] *n* **(a)** ombre *f*, ombrage *m* (*d'un sentier etc*); **(b)** *F* (*suspiciousness*) aspect *m* louche (*d'une affaire etc*); réputation suspecte (*de qn*).
shading ['ʃeıdıŋ] *n* **(a)** projection *f* d'une ombre (*sur qch*); protection *f* (*de qch*) contre la lumière *ou* contre le soleil; **(b)** *Art* dessin *m* des ombres; ombres *fpl* (*d'un dessin*); **hill s.,** (*on map*) modelé *m*; **(c)** nuancement *m* (*de couleurs*).
shading away, shading off *n* estompage *m*, dégradation *f* (*d'une couleur*).
shadow¹ ['ʃædəʊ] *n* **(a)** ombre *f*; (*dark area*) obscurité *f*; noir *m* (*d'un tableau, d'une photographie*); **in the s.,** (*in the shade*) à *ou* dans l'ombre; (*in dark place*) dans l'obscurité; **to cast a s.,** jeter une ombre; *Fig* **this cast a s. over the festivities,** cela a jeté une ombre sur la fête; **coming events cast their shadows,** les événements à venir se font pressentir; **to catch at shadows, to run after a s.,** courir après une ombre; **town nestling in the s. of a mountain,** ville nichée à l'ombre d'une montagne; **a figure standing in the shadows,** une silhouette se tenant dans l'ombre; **to be afraid of one's own s.,** avoir peur de son ombre; **not the s. of a doubt,** pas l'ombre d'un doute; **he's worn to a s., he's a mere s. of his former self,** il n'est plus qu'une ombre *ou* que l'ombre de lui-même; **the s. of death,** les ombres de la mort; **under the s. of a terrible accusation,** sous le coup d'une accusation terrible; **a s. on the right lung,** un voile au poumon droit; **to have (dark) shadows round** *or* **under one's eyes,** avoir les yeux cernés; **eye s.,** (*make-up*) ombre à paupières; *F* **five o'clock s.,** la barbe du soir; **s. boxing,** boxe simulée; *Fig* attaque rituelle *ou* de pure forme; *Comptr* **s. printing,** impression ombrée;
(b) (*person*) (*constant companion*) compagnon *m ou* compagne *f* inséparable (*de qn*); (*person following someone*) personne qui prend qn en filature; **to put a s. on s.o.,** faire suivre qn;
(c) *Br Pol* **s. government,** gouvernement *m* fantôme; **s. cabinet,** cabinet *m* fantôme; **the S. Home Secretary,** Ministre de l'Intérieur fantôme.
shadow² *vt* **(a)** ombrager (*qch*); couvrir (*qch*) de son ombre; *Tex* chiner (*un tissu*); **(b)** (*follow*) filer, pister (*qn*); prendre (*un suspect*) en filature.
shadowing ['ʃædəʊıŋ] *n* filature *f*, pistage *m* (*d'un suspect etc*).
shadowy ['ʃædəʊı] *adj* **(a)** (*chemin etc*) ombragé, ombreux; **(b)** (*projet*) indécis, vague; (*contour*) vague, indistinct; **a s. form,** une silhouette vague.
shady ['ʃeıdı] *adj* **(a)** (*tree etc*) qui donne de l'ombre; (*place, lane etc*) ombragé; **(b)** *F* (*suspicious*) (*person, transaction etc*) louche; (*financier*) véreux; **s. business,** (*business activity*) commerce *m* interlope; (*affair*) affaire véreuse; **the s. side of politics,** les dessous *mpl* de la politique.
shaft¹ [ʃɑːft] *n* **(a)** hampe *f*, bois *m* (*d'une lance etc*); manche *m* (*de club de golf, d'un outil*); **(b)** *esp Lit* (*arrow*) flèche *f*, trait *m*; **the shafts of satire,** les traits de la satire; **(c)** (*beam*) rayon *m* (*de lumière*); éclair *m* (*de foudre*); **(d)** fût *m* (*d'une colonne*); souche *f* (*de cheminée d'usine*); tige *f* (*de plume d'oiseau, de candélabre etc*); **(e)** *MecE* arbre *m*; (*stationary*) axe *m*; **connecting/coupling s.,** arbre de liaison/d'accouplement; **driving s.,** arbre moteur; **transmission s.,** arbre de transmission; **propeller s.,** arbre porte-hélice, arbre d'hélice; **(f)** (*on horse-drawn vehicle*) brancard *m*; **s. horse,** cheval *m* de brancard.
shaft² *n* **(a)** *Min* puits *m*; **air** *or* **ventilation s.,** puits d'aérage, conduit *m* d'air; **to sink a s.,** foncer *ou* creuser un puits; **s. sinking,** fonçage *m ou* foncement *m ou* creusage *m* d'un puits; **(b) (lift** *or Am* **elevator) s.,** cage *f* (d'un ascenseur).
shaft³ *vt Sl* (*have sexual intercourse with*) tringler.

shag¹ [ʃæg] *n* **(a)** *Tex* peluche *f*; long poil (*d'un tissu, tapis etc*); **(b)** (*tobacco*) tabac fort (*coupé fin*).
shag² *n* (*bird*) cormoran huppé.
shag³ *n Vulg* (*sex act*) **to have a s.,** tirer un coup.
shag⁴ *Vulg* **1** *vi* (*have sexual intercourse*) baiser. **2** *vt* (*have sexual intercourse with*) baiser.
▶shag out *vtsep Sl* (*exhaust*) crever; **I'm shagged out,** je suis crevé.
shagged [ʃægd] *adj Sl* (*exhausted*) crevé, claqué.
shagginess ['ʃægɪnɪs] *n* rudesse *f*, longueur *f* de poil (*d'un poney etc*); état ébouriffé (*des cheveux*).
shaggy ['ʃægɪ] *adj* poilu; (*poney etc*) à longs poils, à poils rudes; (*cheveux*) ébouriffé; (*barbe*) hirsute, touffu; (*sourcils*) en broussailles; (*terrain*) couvert de broussailles; *Tex* (*drap*) poilu, à long poil; **s. dog story,** = histoire farfelue.
shagreen [ʃæ'griːn] *n* (*leather*) (peau *f* de) chagrin *m*.
shah [ʃɑː] *n* s(c)hah *m* (*de Perse*).
shake¹ [ʃeɪk] *n* **(a)** (*act of shaking*) secousse *f*; (*trembling*) tremblement *m* (*de la main etc*); *US New Zealand* (*earthquake*) tremblement de terre; **to give sth a good s.,** bien secouer *ou* agiter qch; **to give oneself a s.,** se secouer; **a s. of the head,** un hochement de tête; **in two shakes of a lamb's tail,** en un rien de temps, en moins de rien; *F* **to be all of a s.,** trembler dans tous ses membres; **to have the shakes,** (*to be trembling*) avoir la tremblote; (*to have delirium tremens*) avoir le délirium tremens; **with a s. in his voice,** d'une voix tremblotante *ou* mal assurée; **(b)** *Culin* **milk s.** milk-shake *m*; **(c)** (*in wood*) gerçure *f*, crevasse *f*; **(d)** *F* **to be no great shakes,** ne rien casser, ne pas casser des briques.
shake² *v* (*pt* **shook** [ʃʊk]; *pp* **shaken** ['ʃeɪk(ə)n]) **1** *vt* **(a)** secouer (*qn, qch*); agiter (*un liquide*); ébranler, secouer (*un bâtiment etc*); ébranler (*une opinion, la foi de qn etc*); **s. the bottle,** agiter le flacon; **s. well,** (*on carton etc*) bien agiter; **to s. one's head,** secouer *ou* hocher la tête; (*to indicate 'no'*) faire non de la tête; **to s. one's fist at s.o.,** menacer qn du poing; **to s. hands with s.o.,** serrer la main à *ou* de qn; **to s. s.o.'s hand, to s. s.o. by the hand,** donner une poignée de main à qn; **the French s. hands more often,** les Français donnent des poignées de main plus souvent; **they shook hands on it,** ils ont topé; *F* **s.!,** (*congratulations!*) félicitations!; (*to seal bargain*) touchez là!, tope (là)!; **to s. oneself free (from sth),** se dégager (de qch) d'une secousse; **to s. the snow from one's head,** secouer sa tête pour se débarrasser de la neige; **that has shaken my faith in him,** cela m'a fait douter de sa bonne foi; **event that shook the country,** événement qui a bouleversé le pays; **she was badly shaken by the accident,** elle a été très bouleversée par l'accident; **to feel shaken after a fall,** se ressentir d'une chute; *F* **that'll s. him!,** cela le fera tiquer!;
(b) *Austr Sl* (*rob*) voler, cambrioler (*qn*).
2 *vi* **(a)** trembler; (*of door, window*) branler; (*of voice*) trembloter, chevroter; **her hand was shaking,** la main lui tremblait; **the whole building shook,** (*after explosion etc*) le bâtiment entier a tremblé; **the ground shook,** le sol a tremblé; **to s. with fright/rage,** trembler *ou* frémir de crainte/colère; **voice shaking with emotion,** voix émue; **to be shaking like a leaf,** trembler comme une feuille; *F* **to s. in one's shoes,** trembler dans sa peau, grelotter de peur;
(b) *F* **to s. on it,** (*shake hands*) toper.
▶shake down 1 *vtsep* **(a)** (*cause to fall*) secouer, hocher (*des fruits*); **(b)** *Am F* (*extort money from*) **to s. s.o. down for ten dollars,** faire casquer qn de dix dollars; **(c)** *Am F* (*search*) fouiller (*qn, un appartement etc*). **2** *vi* **(a)** (*fall*) (*of fruits etc*) tomber; **(b)** s'habituer (*à une routine, à un travail*); **to s. down (for the night),** se coucher, s'installer pour la nuit.
▶shake off *vtsep* **(a)** (*remove by shaking*) **to s. the dust off sth,** secouer la poussière de qch; Fig **to s. off the dust from one's feet,** secouer la poussière de ses pieds *ou* de ses souliers; **(b)** (*get rid of*) se débarrasser de (*illness, depression etc*); **to s. off a cold,** venir à bout d'un rhume; **I can't seem to s. this cold off,** je n'arrive pas à me débarrasser de ce rhume; **(c)** *F* (*escape from*) débarrasser, se défaire de (*qn*); semer (*un importun, Sp un concurrent*); **I can't s. him off,** il ne me lâche pas d'une semelle; **she's always phoning me up — I can't s. her off,** elle est toujours en train de me téléphoner – je n'arrive pas à m'en débarrasser.
▶shake out *vtsep* **(a)** (*remove dust from*) secouer (*rug, tablecloth etc*); faire sortir (*la poussière etc*); vider (*un sac*) en le secouant; **(b)**(*remove by shaking*) faire sortir (*la poussière etc*); **(c)** (*unfurl*) déferler (*une voile, un drapeau*).
▶shake up *vtsep* **(a)** (*mix by shaking*) secouer (*liquid, container etc*); **don't s. the lemonade up,** ne secoue pas la limonade; **(b)** (*plump up*) secouer, brasser (*un oreiller etc*); **(c)** (*upset*) secouer (*qn*); **(d)** (*arouse from indifference etc*) secouer (*qn*); **he needs shaking up,** il a besoin qu'on le secoue.
shakedown ['ʃeɪkdaʊn] *n* **(a)** *Am F* (*extortion*) chantage *m*, extorsion *f*; **(b)** *Am F* (*search*) fouille *f*; **(c)** *F* (*improvised bed*) lit improvisé.
shaker ['ʃeɪkər] *n* (*person*) secoueur, -euse; (*device*) secoueur; **salad s.,** panier *m* à salade; **cocktail s.,** shaker *m*.
Shakespearian [ʃeɪks'pɪərɪən] *adj* shakespearien.
shake-up ['ʃeɪkʌp] *n F* remaniement *m* (*du personnel*).
shakily ['ʃeɪkɪlɪ] *adv* (*marcher*) à pas chancelants; (*écrire*) d'une main tremblante; (*parler*) d'une voix chevrotante.
shakiness ['ʃeɪkɪnɪs] *n* manque *m* de stabilité *ou* de fermeté *ou* de solidité (*d'un bâtiment, d'une chaise etc*); faiblesse *f* (*de qn, de la santé, des connaissances*); tremblement *m* (*de la main*); chevrotement *m* (*de la voix*); instabilité *f* (*du crédit, d'une position*).
shako ['ʃækəʊ] *n Mil* (*headgear*) s(c)hako *m*.
shaky ['ʃeɪkɪ] *adj* (*meuble etc*) branlant, peu solide; (*santé*) faible, chancelant; (*position*) mal affermi, peu sûr; (*main*) tremblant, vacillant; (*écriture*) tremblé; (*voix*) mal assuré; **to be s. on one's legs** *or F* **one's pins,** ne pas tenir sur ses jambes *ou F* quilles *ou* cannes; **I feel very s.,** (*I am trembling*) je suis tout tremblant; (*I feel unsteady on my feet*) je ne me sens pas bien solide; (*I feel rather unwell*) je suis tout patraque *ou* chose; **his English is s.,** il est faible en anglais.
shale [ʃeɪl] *n* schiste *m* (*argileux, ardoisier*); argile schisteuse; **s. oil,** huile *f* de schiste.
shall [*stressed* ʃæl, *unstressed* ʃəl] *modal aux v* (*pr* **shall,** *Bible & Arch* **shalt** [ʃælt]; **shall**; *pt & cond* **should** [*stressed* ʃʊd, *unstressed* ʃəd]; *Arch* **shouldst** [ʃʊdst]; *no other parts*; **shall not** *and* **should not** *are often contracted into* **shan't** [ʃɑːnt], **shouldn't** ['ʃʊd(ə)nt]) **(a)** (*with full meaning, denotes duty or command*) *Arch* **thou shalt not kill,** tu ne tueras point; *Jur* **ships s. carry three lights,** les navires sont tenus de porter trois feux; **which is as it should be,** ce qui n'est que justice; **he s. do it if I order it,** il devra le faire si je l'ordonne; **he s. not do it,** je défends qu'il le fasse; **he says he won't do it — he s.!,** il dit qu'il ne le fera pas – je l'ordonne!; **you SHALL do it!,** vous le ferez, je le veux!; **you should do it at once,** vous devriez le faire tout de suite; **you should have come earlier,** vous auriez dû arriver plus tôt; **you** *or* **he** *etc* **should not have gone,** il ne fallait pas y aller; **a present? — oh you shouldn't have!,** un cadeau? – vous n'auriez pas dû!; **it was an accident that should have been foreseen,** c'était un accident à prévoir; **you should have seen her!,** il fallait la voir!, si vous l'aviez vue!; **you shouldn't laugh at him,** vous avez tort de vous moquer de lui; **I shouldn't do that if I were you,** je ne ferais pas ça si j'étais toi;
(b) (*expression of opinion*) **she should have arrived by this time,** elle devrait être arrivée à l'heure qu'il est; **that should suit you!,** voilà qui fera sans doute votre affaire!; **this weather should be ideal for anglers,** ce temps doit être ce que les pêcheurs peuvent désirer de mieux; *Iron* **I should worry!,** (*don't worry about it*) ce n'est pas mon affaire!; *Iron* **you should worry about getting fat!,** tu ne risques pas de grossir!; *Iron* **you should complain!,** tu n'as aucune raison de te plaindre!;
(c) (*making suggestion, asking permission*) **s. I open the window?,** voulez-vous que j'ouvre la fenêtre?; **I'll make some coffee, s. I?,** je vais faire du café, d'accord?; **let's go in, s. we?,** rentrons, voulez-vous?; **what should I have said?,** qu'est-ce que j'aurais dû dire?;
(d) (*exclamatory, in rhetorical questions*) **why should you suspect me?,** pourquoi me soupçonner?; **how should I not be happy?,** comment ne serais-je pas heureux?; **whom should I meet but Martin!,** voilà que je rencontre Martin!; **how s. I describe their surprise?,** comment décrire leur surprise!;
(e) (*in subordinate clauses*) **he ordered that they should be released,** il ordonna qu'on les relâchât; **she insisted that he should wear his hair short,** elle a exigé qu'il porte les cheveux courts; **they recommend that classes should be smaller,** ils proposent de réduire le nombre des élèves dans les classes;
(f) (*in conditional clauses*) **if he should come** *or Fml* **should he come, let me know,** (*if he comes*) s'il vient, faites-le-moi savoir; (*if he comes, although it's unlikely*) si

par hasard il vient, faites-le-moi savoir; **should I be free I s. come,** si je suis libre je viendrai; **should the occasion arise, should it (so) happen,** le cas échéant; **in case she should not be there,** au cas *ou* en cas où elle n'y soit pas, dans le cas où elle n'y serait pas;

(g) you shan't have any!, tu n'en auras pas!; **you s. pay for this!,** vous me le payerez!; **tomorrow I s. go and he will arrive,** demain, moi je partirai et lui arrivera; **my holiday was over, the next day I should be far away,** mon congé était fini, le lendemain je serais bien loin; **will you be there? — I s.,** y serez-vous? — oui (j'y serai); **no, I s. not** *or* **I shan't,** non, (je n'y serai pas); **I s. explain the situation to you and you will listen,** je vais vous expliquer la situation et vous allez m'écouter; **as we s. see,** comme nous le verrons, comme nous allons le voir; *Fml & Dial* **s. you come tomorrow?,** vous viendrez demain?;

(h) (*in the main clause of conditional sentences*) **if he comes I s. speak to him,** s'il vient je lui parlerai; **we should come if we were invited,** nous viendrions si on nous invitait; **had you written to me I should have answered you,** si vous m'aviez écrit je vous aurais répondu;

(i) (*in softened affirmation*) **I should like a drink,** je prendrais bien quelque chose; **I should have thought that you would have known better,** j'aurais pensé que vous auriez été plus avisé; **I shouldn't be surprised (if...),** cela ne me surprendrait pas (que ... + *pr sub*).

shallot [ʃə'lɒt] *n* échalote *f*.

shallow ['ʃæləʊ] **1** *adj* (*water, dish etc*) peu profond; (*soil*) superficiel; (*person, mind etc*) superficiel, qui manque de fond; (*amitié*) de surface; **s.-rooted,** (*tree*) à enracinement superficiel; *Med* **s. breathing,** respiration *f* faible. **2** *n* (*in sea etc*) (*often in pl*) bas-fond *m*, *pl* bas-fonds, haut-fond *m*, *pl* hauts-fonds.

shallowness ['ʃæləʊnɪs] *n* **(a)** (le) peu de profondeur (*de l'eau, d'un plat etc*); **(b)** caractère superficiel, superficialité *f* (*de qn, de l'esprit*).

shalt *Arch see* **SHALL.**

shaly ['ʃeɪlɪ] *adj* schisteux.

sham[1] [ʃæm] **1** *adj* faux, truqué; (*illness etc*) simulé, feint; (*piety*) apparent; **s. peace,** paix fourrée. **2** *n* feinte *f*, trompe-l'œil *m inv*, *Sl* chiqué *m*; **that's all s.,** tout ça c'est de la frime; **he's a s.,** c'est un imposteur; **you big s., you're not sad at all!,** espèce d'hypocrite, tu n'es pas triste du tout!; **the elections were a s.,** les élections étaient en trompe-l'œil.

sham[2] *v* (**-mm-**) **1** *vt* feindre, simuler; **to s. sickness,** faire semblant d'être malade. **2** *vi* **he's only shamming,** c'est une comédie qu'il nous joue, il fait semblant; **he shammed dead,** il a fait le mort.

shamateur ['ʃæmətɜːr] *n Sp F* amateur marron.

shamble ['ʃæmb(ə)l] *vi* **to s. (along),** aller à pas traînants; **to s. up to s.o.,** approcher qn d'un pas traînant.

shambles ['ʃæmb(ə)lz] *npl* (*usu with sing verb*) **(a)** *F* (*disorder*) désordre *m*, fouillis *m*; **what a s.!,** quelle pagaille!; **the match was a s.,** le match était totalement nul; **the cupboard was in a s.,** le placard était en désordre; **(b)** (*carnage*) scène *f* de carnage.

shambolic [ʃæm'bɒlɪk] *adj F* chaotique.

shame[1] [ʃeɪm] *n* **(a)** honte *f*; **hooligans are the s. of our country,** les hooligans sont la honte de notre pays; **to bring s. on one's family/country,** jeter la honte sur sa famille/son pays; **to put s.o. to s.,** (*make s.o. ashamed*) faire honte à qn; (*do much better than*) l'emporter sur qn; **to my s.,** à ma honte; **s. (up)on you!,** quelle honte!; **for s.!,** vous n'avez pas honte!; **he hid his face in s.,** il s'est caché la face de honte; **to blush for** *or* **with s.,** (*at one's own behaviour*) rougir de honte; (*at one's nakedness etc*) rougir de pudeur; **without s.,** effronté, éhonté; **to be past or lost to all s.,** avoir perdu toute honte; **to have no s.,** (*no scruples*) n'avoir aucun scrupule; (*no pride*) n'avoir aucune fierté;

(b) (*pity*) dommage *m*; **it would be a s. to ...,** il serait dommage de ...; **what a s.!,** *F Iron* **s.!,** quel dommage!; **it's a s. you can't come,** c'est dommage que vous ne puissiez pas venir.

shame[2] *vt* (*cause to feel ashamed*) faire honte à, mortifier (*qn*); (*bring shame on*) couvrir (*qn*) de honte; **to be shamed into doing sth,** faire qch par amour-propre; **they tried to s. her into donating more,** ils ont essayé de lui faire honte pour qu'elle donne davantage.

shamefaced ['ʃeɪmfeɪst] *adj* **(a)** (à l'air) honteux; (*embarrassed*) embarrassé, décontenancé; **(b)** *Lit* (*timid*) timide; (*modest*) modeste.

shamefacedly [ʃeɪm'feɪsɪdlɪ] *adv* **(a)** d'un air honteux *ou* embarrassé; **(b)** *Lit* (*timidly*) timidement.

shameful ['ʃeɪmfʊl] *adj* honteux, scandaleux, indigne.

shamefully ['ʃeɪmfəlɪ] *adv* honteusement, scandaleusement; **s. ignorant,** honteusement ignorant.

shamefulness ['ʃeɪmfʊlnɪs] *n* honte *f*, infamie *f*.

shameless ['ʃeɪmlɪs] *adj* **(a)** (*without shame*) (*person, conduct*) éhonté, effronté; **he was quite s. about it all,** il ne montrait aucun scrupule; **(b)** (*immodest*) (*person*) sans pudeur, dévergondé; (*conduct*) impudique.

shamelessly ['ʃeɪmlɪslɪ] *adv* (*see adj*) **(a)** effrontément; impudemment; **(b)** impudiquement.

shamelessness ['ʃeɪmlɪsnɪs] *n* **(a)** effronterie *f*, impudence *f*; absence *f* de tout sentiment de honte; **(b)** (*immodesty*) impudeur *f*; impudicité *f*.

shaming ['ʃeɪmɪŋ] *adj* mortifiant.

shammy ['ʃæmɪ] *n* **s. (leather),** peau *f* de chamois.

shampoo[1] [ʃæm'puː] *n* **(a)** (*action*) shampooing *m*; **to give s.o. a s.,** faire un shampooing à qn; **s. and set,** shampooing et mise en plis; **(b)** (*product*) shampooing *m*; **liquid/dry s.,** shampooing liquide/sec; **carpet s.,** shampooing pour moquette.

shampoo[2] *vt* **to s. one's hair,** se faire un shampooing; **to s. s.o.** *or* **s.o.'s hair,** faire un shampooing à qn; **to s. a carpet/***etc*, nettoyer une moquette/*etc*.

shamrock ['ʃæmrɒk] *n* (*plant*) trèfle *m*.

shandy ['ʃændɪ], *US* **shandygaff** ['ʃændɪgæf] *n* mélange *m* de bière et de limonade, panaché *m*; **a lager/bitter s.,** un panaché à la bière blonde/brune.

shanghai [ʃæŋ'haɪ] *vt F Nau* embarquer (*un homme*) de force sur un navire à court d'équipage; (*force*) forcer (**s.o. into doing sth,** qn à faire qch).

Shanghai [ʃæŋ'haɪ] *n* Shanghaï *m*, Changhaï *m*.

Shangri-La [ʃæŋgrɪ'lɑː] *n* paradis *m* terrestre.

shank [ʃæŋk] *n* **(a)** *Culin* jarret *m* (*de bœuf*); jambe *f* (*d'un bas*); (*of horse's leg*) canon *m*; **shanks,** jambes *fpl*, *F* quilles *fpl*; *F* **to go** *or* **ride on Shanks' pony,** y aller à pinces; **s. (bone),** tibia *m*; **(b)** fût *m* (*d'une colonne*); tige *f*, branche *f* (*de clef, de rivet*); hampe *f* (*d'hameçon*); *Typ* corps *m*, tige (*de lettre*); *Nau* verge *f* (*d'ancre*); *Bot* pédoncule *m*; queue *f* (*d'un bouton*).

shan't *see* **SHALL.**

Shantung [ʃæn'tʌŋ] *n Tex* shant(o)ung *m*.

shanty[1] ['ʃæntɪ] *n* (*hut*) hutte *f*, cabane *f*; **s. town,** bidonville *m*.

shanty[2] *n Nau* **(sea) s.,** chanson *f* de bord.

shape[1] [ʃeɪp] *n* **(a)** forme *f* (*de la terre etc*); **what s. is it?,** de quelle forme est-ce?; **they were the same s.,** ils étaient de la même forme *ou* avaient la même forme; **a cake in the s. of a ...,** un gâteau en forme de ...; **oblong in s.,** de forme oblongue; **spherical in s., of spherical s.,** de forme sphérique; **trees of all shapes,** des arbres de toutes les formes; **my hat was knocked out of s.,** mon chapeau a été déformé; **to get out of s., to lose (its) s.,** se déformer; *Journ etc* **to knock an article into s.,** mettre un article au point; *F* **to knock a team into s.,** remettre une équipe sur pied; **to keep in s.,** (*physically*) garder sa forme; **to be in good/poor s.,** (*of person etc*) être en bonne/petite forme; *F* **she was in pretty bad s.,** (*very ill, badly injured*) elle était mal en point; **to give s. to a plan,** faire prendre corps à un projet; **to take s.,** prendre forme *ou* tournure; **our plans are taking s.,** nos projets commencent à prendre forme; **this is the s. of things to come,** c'est ça l'avenir, *esp Pej* c'est ce qui nous attend; **progress, in the s. of bigger roads,** progrès sous forme de routes plus grandes; **no communication in any s. or form,** aucune communication de n'importe quelle sorte; **something in the s. of ...,** une espèce *ou* une sorte de ...; **help arrived in the s. of ...,** l'aide est arrivée sous la forme de ...;

(b) (*figure, human figure*) forme *f*; **two shapes loomed up in the darkness,** deux formes surgirent dans l'obscurité;

(c) (*pattern*) forme *f* (*pour chapeau*);

(d) (*of iron etc*) profil *m*.

shape[2] **1** *vt* façonner, modeler (*de l'argile etc*); tailler (*un bloc de pierre etc*); former (*un plan*); **to s. sth out of sth,** façonner qch avec qch; **to s. the clay into an urn,** donner à l'argile la forme d'une urne; **to s. s.o.'s character,** pétrir le caractère de qn; **to s. the destiny of man,** diriger *ou* régler la destinée de l'homme; *Lit* **to s. one's course,** diriger ses pas, se diriger (**towards,** vers); **to s. the course of public opinion,** imprimer une direction à l'opinion publique. **2** *vi* se développer; **to be shaping well,** promettre; (*of affair etc*) prendre bonne tournure.

►**shape up** *vi* **(a)** (*turn out*) **to s. up well,** promettre; (*of* *affair*) prendre bonne tournure; **let's see how he shapes up in his new job,** voyons comment il va s'en tirer dans son nouvel emploi; **the new player is shaping up well,** le nouveau joueur promet beaucoup; *esp Am F* **s. up or ship out!,** faites des progrès ou prenez la porte!; **(b)** (*advance*) **to s. up to s.o.,** avancer à qn en posture de combat.

SHAPE [ʃeɪp] *n Mil* (*abbr* **Supreme Headquarters Allied Powers, Europe**) quartier général suprême des forces alliées en Europe.

shaped [ʃeɪpt] *adj* **(a)** façonné, taillé; (*metalwork*) (*pièce*) profilé, embouti; **(b) well/badly s.,** bien/mal formé; **s. like an egg,** en forme d'œuf.

-shaped [ʃeɪpt] *suff* **egg/heart/wedge/***etc***-s.,** en forme d'œuf/de cœur/de coin/*etc*.

shapeless ['ʃeɪplɪs] *adj* informe.

shapelessness ['ʃeɪplɪsnɪs] *n* manque *m* de forme.

shapeliness ['ʃeɪplɪnɪs] *n* (*of woman*) beauté *f* de forme, belles proportions; (*of legs*) galbe *m*.

shapely ['ʃeɪplɪ] *adj* bien fait; **a s. leg,** une jambe bien galbée; **to be s.,** (*of woman*) être bien faite *ou F* bien roulée.

shaping ['ʃeɪpɪŋ] *n* façonnement *m*, façonnage *m* (*d'un bloc de pierre etc*); **the s. of his character,** le développement *ou* la formation de son caractère.

shard [ʃɑːd] *n* tesson *m* (*de poterie*).

share¹ [ʃeər] *n Agr* (*of plough*) soc *m* (de charrue).

share² *n* **(a)** (*part*) part *f*, portion *f*; **in equal shares,** par portions égales; **to have a s. in sth,** avoir part à qch; **the lion's s.,** la part du lion; **s. in profits,** (*participation*) participation *f* aux bénéfices; (*amount*) tantième *m*; **to give s.o. a s. in the profits,** mettre qn de part; *F* **to go shares,** partager (**with,** avec); **to go half shares with s.o.,** mettre qn de part à demi; **to come in for a s. of sth,** avoir sa part de qch; **(fair) s.,** portion juste; (*of trouble, work etc*) lot *m*; **she's had more than her fair s. of problems,** elle a eu largement son lot de problèmes; *Jur* **legal s.,** réserve légale (*d'une succession*); **to come in for one's full s. of sth,** avoir sa bonne part de qch; **I've had my s. of worries,** j'ai eu ma bonne part *ou* mon lot de soucis; **s. cropper,** métayer, -ère; *Agr* **s. cropping,** métayage *m*;

(b) (*contribution*) contribution *f*, écot *m*, cotisation *f*, quote-part *f*, *pl* quotes-parts; **to pay one's s.,** payer sa (quote-)part; **to take/bear one's s. of the burden,** prendre/avoir sa part du fardeau; **he doesn't do his s.,** il n'y met pas du sien; **you had a s. in this,** (*you are partly responsible*) vous y êtes pour quelque chose; (*you contributed*) vous y avez mis du vôtre; **to have a s. in an undertaking,** avoir un intérêt *ou* être intéressé dans une entreprise;

(c) *Fin* action *f*, titre *m*; **registered** *or* **personal s.,** action nominative; **fully paid(-up) s.,** action (entièrement) libérée; **ordinary/deferred s.,** action ordinaire/différée; **to hold** *or* **have shares,** détenir des actions, être actionnaire; **s. certificate,** certificat *m* d'action(s) *ou* de titre(s); **s. option,** possibilité *f* d'acheter des actions.

share³ **1** *vt* partager; **to s. sth with s.o.,** partager qch avec qn; **to s. a bathroom,** (*of tenants*) partager une salle de bain; **a shared bathroom,** une salle de bain commune; **to s. s.o.'s opinion,** partager l'avis de qn; **I s. all his secrets,** il me met dans tous ses secrets; **they s. an interest in music,** ils partagent le même intérêt pour la musique. **2** *vi* partager; **to s. and s. alike,** partager entre tous également; **to s. in sth,** prendre part à *ou* avoir part à *ou* participer à qch; **to s. in the profits,** participer *ou* avoir part aux bénéfices; **to s. in s.o.'s grief,** partager la douleur de qn; **I want you to s. in my happiness,** je veux vous associer à mon bonheur.

►share out *vtsep* partager, distribuer, répartir (*le butin etc*); répartir, distribuer (*le travail*).

shareholder ['ʃeəhəʊldər] *n Fin* actionnaire *mf*, sociétaire *mf* (*d'une société anonyme*); **minority s.,** actionnaire minoritaire; **small s.,** petit porteur.

shareholding ['ʃeəhəʊldɪŋ] *n Fin* **(a)** possession *f* d'actions *ou* de titres; **(b) shareholdings,** (*shares*) actions *fpl*.

share-out ['ʃeəraʊt] *n* partage *m*, répartition *f*.

sharing ['ʃeərɪŋ] *n* **(a)** (*distribution*) partage *m* (*du butin, de ses biens etc*); **(b)** (*participation*) participation *f*, partage *m*; **profit s.,** participation aux bénéfices.

shark [ʃɑːk] *n* **(a)** (*fish*) requin *m*; **(b)** *F* (*ruthless person*) requin *m*; **(c)** *Am F* (*talented person*) as *m*; **to be a s. at math,** être calé en maths, être une bête en maths.

sharkskin ['ʃɑːkskɪn] *n* peau *f* de requin.

sharp [ʃɑːp] **1** *adj* **(a)** (*knife, edge*) tranchant, affilé; (*spear, tooth, point*) aigu, pointu;

(b) (*features etc*) anguleux, tiré; (*peak etc*) pointu; (*angle*) saillant, aigu; (*curve*) prononcé; (*ascent, descent*) raide; (*roof*) pointu, en pointe; (*turning*) brusque; (*outline, focus, Phot image*) net, *f* nette; **s. rise/drop in prices,** forte *ou* nette hausse/baisse des prix; **s. contrast,** contraste marqué *ou* net;

(c) (*sight*) perçant; (*hearing*) fin; (*cunning, shrewd*) rusé, malin; (*unscrupulous*) peu scrupuleux; **s. (witted),** (*person*) fin, éveillé; **a s. mind,** un esprit fin; **he's as s. as a needle,** (*quick to understand*) il a l'esprit vif; (*cunning*) il est malin comme un singe; **s. practice(s),** procédés indélicats *ou* peu honnêtes;

(d) (*winter*) rigoureux; (*wind*) vif, perçant; (*cold*) pénétrant, piquant; **s. pain,** douleur vive; **it's a bit s. this morning,** il fait frisquet ce matin; **s. frost,** forte gelée; **s. appetite,** vif appétit;

(e) (*fast*) rapide; (*trot*) vif;

(f) in a s. voice, d'une voix coupante *ou* cinglante; **to make a s. retort,** (*to reply in a sharp tone*) répondre d'une voix cassante; (*to make a cutting reply*) faire une réplique cinglante; **s. reproof,** verte réprimande; **in a s. tone,** d'un ton brusque; **s. tongue,** langue acérée *ou* caustique;

(g) (*taste, sauce*) piquant; (*apple etc*) acide; (*wine*) vert;

(h) (*sound*) perçant, aigu;

(i) *Mus* dièse; **you're s.,** (*to singer, violinist etc*) vous chantez *ou* jouez faux (en haussant le ton); **a semitone s.,** un demi-ton trop haut.

2 *n* **(a)** *Mus* dièse *m*; **double s.,** double dièse;

(b) sharps, (*needles*) aiguilles longues et fines;

(c) = SHARPER.

3 *adv* **(a) s. cut outline,** profil nettement découpé; **s. pointed pencil,** crayon taillé fin; **s. edged,** (*knife etc*) tranchant, affilé; (*beam roof etc*) aux arêtes vives;

(b) (*stop, turn*) brusquement, court; **turn s. right,** prenez à angle droit;

(c) ponctuellement; **at four o'clock s.,** à quatre heures sonnantes *ou* précises *ou F* tapantes;

(d) *F* **look s.!,** dépêchez-vous!, remuez-vous!;

(e) *Mus* (*chanter*) faux (en haussant le ton).

sharpen ['ʃɑːp(ə)n] **1** *vt* **(a)** affiler, aiguiser (*un couteau, un outil etc*); tailler en pointe, aiguiser (*un bâton etc*); tailler (*un crayon*); rendre (*un angle*) plus saillant; aviver (*une arête*); accentuer (*un trait, un contraste*); **to s. its claws,** (*of cat etc*) faire ses griffes; **(b) to s. s.o.'s wits,** éveiller l'esprit de qn, *F* dégourdir qn; **(c)** aviver (*la douleur, l'animosité*); exciter (*une passion, un désir*); (*of walk etc*) aiguiser, ouvrir (*l'appétit*); **(d)** rendre plus sévère (*une loi etc*); **to s. one's voice,** prendre un ton plus acerbe *ou* âpre; **(e)** *Culin* donner du piquant à (*une sauce*); **(f)** *Mus* diéser (*une note*). **2** *vi* **(a)** (*of faculties etc*) s'aiguiser; **(b)** (*of tone*) devenir plus acerbe *ou* âpre; **(c)** (*of sound*) devenir plus perçant *ou* aigu.

sharpener ['ʃɑːp(ə)nər] *n* **(a)** (*person*) aiguiseur *m*; **(b)** (*device*) aiguisoir *m*; **knife s.,** aiguisoir *m* (pour couteaux); **pencil s.,** taille-crayon *m*, *pl* taille-crayon(s).

sharpening ['ʃɑːp(ə)nɪŋ] *n* **(a)** affilage *m*, aiguisage *m* (*d'un outil etc*); accentuation *f* (*d'un contraste*); **(b)** affinage *f* (*de l'intelligence*); **(c)** aggravation *f* (*d'une douleur etc*); **(d)** relèvement *m* (*d'une sauce*); **(e)** haussement *m* (*d'une note*) d'un demi-ton.

sharper ['ʃɑːpər] *n* escroc *m*; *Cards* tricheur, -euse.

sharp-eyed ['ʃɑːpaɪd] *adj* (*good at finding things*) au regard d'aigle; (*keen-sighted*) à la vue perçante.

sharply ['ʃɑːplɪ] *adv* **(a) s. pointed,** (*pencil etc*) pointu, à pointe fine, taillé fin; **(b) this contrasts s. with ...,** ceci contraste nettement avec ...; **s. in focus,** très net; **to bring sth s. home,** mettre qch en relief d'une façon saisissante; **(c)** (*to drop, descend*) raidement, brusquement; (*to turn*) brusquement, court; **(d)** (*regarder, écouter*) attentivement; **he looked s. at her,** il l'a regardée d'un œil pénétrant; **(e)** (*réprimander*) sévèrement; (*répondre*) d'un ton brusque; **(f)** (*sonner*) sec.

sharpness ['ʃɑːpnɪs] *n* **(a)** acuité *f*, finesse *f* (*du tranchant d'un couteau etc*); acuité (*d'une pointe etc*); netteté *f* (*des contours, d'une image photographique*); caractère marqué (*d'un contraste*); *Aut etc* **s. of the turn,** raccourci *m* du virage; **(b)** finesse *f* (*de l'esprit, de l'ouïe*); intelligence *f* (*d'un enfant*); **s. of sight,** acuité visuelle; **(c)** acuité *f* (*de la douleur etc*); **there's a s. in the air,** il fait frisquet; **(d)** sévérité *f*, âpreté *f* (*du ton, d'une réprimande*); brusquerie *f* (*du ton*); aspérité *f* (*du caractère, de la voix*); **(e)** (*goût*) piquant *m* (*d'une sauce*); acidité *f* (*d'une pomme etc*); **(f)** acuité *f*, qualité perçante (*d'un son*).

sharpshooter ['ʃɑːpʃuːtər] *n Mil* tireur *m* d'élite.

sharp-sighted [ʃɑːp'saɪtɪd] *adj* (*keen-sighted*) à la vue perçante; (*observant*) perspicace.

sharp-tongued [ʃɑːp'tʌŋd] *adj* qui a la langue acérée *ou* caustique.

shatter ['ʃætər] **1** *vt* **(a)** fracasser, briser en éclats; **(b)** briser, renverser (*des espérances*); rompre (*le silence*); **(c)** détraquer (*la santé, les nerfs*); *F* **I was absolutely shattered!,** (*I was overcome*) j'étais complètement bouleversé!; (*I was exhausted*) j'étais complètement éreinté! **2** *vi* se briser (en éclats), se fracasser; **the windscreen shattered,** le pare-brise a volé en éclats.

shattering ['ʃætərɪŋ] *adj* (*coup*) écrasant; **s. news,** des nouvelles renversantes.

shatterproof ['ʃætəpruːf] *adj* (*glass, windscreen*) anti-éclats.

shave¹ [ʃeɪv] *n* **(a)** rasage *m*; **to have a s.,** se raser; (*be shaved*) se faire raser; **this razor gives you a really close s.,** avec ce rasoir vous pouvez vraiment vous raser de près; **(b)** *F* **that was a close s.!,** vous l'avez *ou* il l'a *etc* échappé belle!, il était moins une!

shave² **1** *vt* **(a)** (*remove hair*) raser; (*remove hair from face*) faire la barbe à (*qn*); **to s. s.o.'s head,** raser la tête à qn; **to s. one's legs,** se raser les jambes; **(b)** planer (*le bois etc*); rogner (*un angle*); **to s. prices,** rogner les prix; **(c)** (*brush against*) friser, effleurer (*qch*). **2** *vi* se raser, se faire la barbe; **to start shaving,** (*of boy*) commencer à se raser.

shave³ *n* (*tool*) plane *f*, racloir *m*.

▶**shave off** *vtsep* (*remove by shaving*) **to s. off one's moustache,** se raser la moustache; **to s. off a slice of sth,** couper une mince tranche de qch.

shaven ['ʃeɪv(ə)n] *adj* (*monk*) tonsuré; (*head, chin*) rasé; **clean s.,** (*homme*) sans barbe ni moustache; (*visage*) glabre.

shaver ['ʃeɪvər] *n* **(a)** (*person*) barbier *m*; *F* **young s.,** gosse *m*, gamin *m*; **(b) (electric) s.,** rasoir *m* électrique.

Shavian ['ʃeɪvɪən] *adj* de *ou* à la George Bernard Shaw.

shaving ['ʃeɪvɪŋ] *n* **(a)** (*act of shaving face etc*) rasage *m*; **s. brush,** blaireau *m*; **s. cream,** crème *f* à raser; **s. foam,** mousse *f* à raser; **s. soap,** savon *m* à barbe; **s. stick,** bâton *m* de savon pour la barbe; **(b)** (*small piece shaved off*) copeau *m* (*de bois*); rognure *f*.

shawl [ʃɔːl] *n* châle *m*.

she [ʃiː] *pers pron f* **(a)** (*of person, female animal and sometimes motor vehicle, nation and other things personified, esp in literary language*) elle; (*of ship*) il; **s. was running,** elle courait; **what's s. doing?,** qu'est-ce qu'elle fait?; **here s. comes!,** la voici (qui vient)!; **s. sails at ten o'clock,** (*of ship*) il part à dix heures; **she's had it, this old car,** elle est bonne pour la casse, cette vieille voiture; **(b)** (*stressed*) elle; **s. and I,** elle et moi; **SHE knows nothing about it,** elle n'en sait rien, elle; **if I were s.,** si j'étais à sa place; *esp Lit* **s. of whom you speak,** celle dont vous parlez; **(c)** (*substantive*) *F* femelle; **it's a s.,** (*of newborn child*) c'est une petite fille; (*of animal*) c'est une femelle.

she- [ʃiː] *pref* **s.-ass,** ânesse *f*; **s.-bear,** ours *m* femelle, ourse *f*; **s.-cat,** chatte *f*; **s.-devil,** diablesse *f*; **s.-monkey,** singe *m* femelle, guenon *f*.

sheaf, *pl* **-ves** [ʃiːf, -vz] *n* gerbe *f* (*de blé, etc*); gerbe (*de fleurs*); faisceau *m*, botte *f* (*de branchages*); liasse *f* (*de papiers*); **I had a whole s. of letters this morning,** j'ai reçu toute une pile de lettres ce matin.

shear¹ [ʃɪər] *n* **(pair of) shears,** (*large scissors*) cisaille(s) *f(pl)*; (*for sheep, at hairdresser*) tondeuse *f*; **garden shears,** sécateur *m*; *Sewing etc* **pinking shears,** ciseaux *mpl* à denteler.

shear² *v* (*pt* **sheared**; *pp* **shorn** [ʃɔːn], **sheared**) **1** *vt* **(a)** tondre (*un mouton etc*); **to be shorn of sth,** être dépouillé *ou* privé de qch; **(b)** (*cut*) couper (*une branche etc*); (*in metalworking*) cisailler (*une tôle etc*); *Tex* ciseler (*le velours*); **to s. through sth,** trancher qch; **(c)** *Phys etc* cisailler (*qch*). **2** *vi* (*of material*) se fendre.

▶**shear off** *vi* se détacher.

shearer ['ʃɪərər] *n* (*person*) **(a)** tondeur, -euse (*des moutons*); (*in metalworking*) cisailleur *m*; **(b)** (*machine*) tondeuse *f* (*pour moutons*); (*in metalworking*) cisailleuse *f*.

shearing ['ʃɪərɪŋ] *n* **(a)** tonte *f* (*des moutons*); taille *f* (*d'une haie etc*); cisaillement *m* (*d'une tôle*); tondage *m* (*du drap*); **s. machine,** tondeuse *f* (*pour moutons*); **(b) shearings,** tontes *fpl* (*de laine*); tontisse *f*, tonture (*du drap*).

sheath [ʃiːθ] *n* (*pl* [ʃiːðz, ʃiːθs]) (*protective sleeve*) manchon protecteur; fourreau *m* (*d'épée, de parapluie etc*); étui *m* (*de ciseaux etc*); gaine *f* (*de couteau, El d'un câble*); *Anat* enveloppe *f* (*d'une organe*); fourreau (*du cheval, du taureau etc*); gaine (*de muscle etc*); *Bot* gaine; **contraceptive s.,** préservatif *m*, condom *m*; **s. dress,** (*garment*) fourreau; **s. knife,** couteau *m* à gaine.

sheathe [ʃiːð] *vt* **(a)** (re)mettre au fourreau, rengainer (*une épée etc*); engainer (*un couteau etc*); **(b)** envelopper (*qch*) dans une gaine; *El* gainer (*un câble*).

sheathing ['ʃiːðɪŋ] *n* **(a)** (*act of putting in sheath*) mise *f* au fourreau (*d'une épée*); mise dans sa gaine (*d'un couteau etc*); **(b)** (*covering*) revêtement *m* (*de, en métal*); *MecE etc* garniture *f*; chemise *f* (*d'un cylindre etc*); **(c)** gaine *f* (*d'un câble*).

sheave [ʃiːv] *vt* gerber, engerber (*le blé etc*).

Sheba ['ʃiːbə] *n* Saba *f*; **the Queen of S.,** la reine de Saba.

shebang [ʃɪ'bæŋ] *n esp Am Sl* **the whole s.,** tout le bataclan.

shebeen [ʃɪ'biːn] *n Dial* (*Irish*) débit *m* de boissons clandestin.

shed¹ [ʃed] *n* (*larger*) hangar *m*; (*smaller*) remise *f*; **lean-to s.,** appentis *m*; **garden s.,** cabane *f* de jardin; *Rail* **engine s.,** remise *f* de locomotives; **tool s.,** cabane à outils; **bike s.,** (*small*) remise à vélo; (*big*) hangar *m* à vélo; **cattle s.,** étable *f*; *Constr* **s. roof,** toit *m* en appentis.

shed² *v* (*pt & pp* **shed**; *prp* **shedding**) **1** *vt* **(a)** perdre (*ses dents, ses feuilles etc*); (*of animal*) jeter (*sa peau, ses cornes etc*); (*of crab etc*) dépouiller (*sa carapace*); (*of lorry etc*) déverser (*sa charge*); **to s. its leaves,** (*of plant*) s'effeuiller; **to s. labour,** licencier de la main-d'œuvre; *El* **to s. the load,** délester; **he shed 20 pounds in a month,** il a perdu 10 kilos en un mois; **to s. one's clothes,** se dépouiller de ses vêtements; **(b)** répandre, verser (*des larmes, le sang*); (r)épandre (*de la lumière*); déverser (*de l'eau*); **before more blood is shed,** avant que davantage de sang ne coule; **to s. light on sth,** faire *ou* jeter la lumière sur une affaire. **2** *vi* (*of cat*) perdre ses poils.

shedding ['ʃedɪŋ] *n* **(a)** perte *f*, chute *f* (*des feuilles, des dents etc*); *El* **load s.,** délestage *m*; **(b)** effusion *f* (*de sang etc*).

she'd [ʃiːd] **(a) = she had,** *see* **HAVE²**; **(b) = she would,** *see* **WILL³**.

sheen [ʃiːn] *n* reflet *m*; **hair with a s. like gold,** cheveux *mpl* à reflets d'or.

sheep [ʃiːp] *n* (*inv in pl*) mouton *m*; **black s.,** brebis noire; **the black s. (of the family** *etc***),** la brebis galeuse; **lost** *or* **stray s.,** brebis perdue *ou* égarée; **they follow one another like s.,** ce sont les moutons de Panurge; **to separate the s. from the goats** *or* **the s. and the goats,** séparer les brebis d'avec les boucs; **to make s.'s eyes at s.o.,** faire les yeux doux à qn; **s. farmer,** éleveur *m* de moutons; **s. farming,** élevage *m* de moutons; **s. pen,** parc *m* à moutons; bercail *m*; **s. shearer,** (*person*) tondeur, -euse (*de moutons*); (*machine*) tondeuse *f* mécanique; **s. shearing,** tonte *f*.

sheep-dip ['ʃiːpdɪp] *n* **(a)** (*place*) enclos *m* (*avec bain désinfectant*); **(b)** (*disinfectant*) bain désinfectant (*pour les moutons*).

sheepdog ['ʃiːpdɒg] *n* (chien *m* de) berger *m*; **Old English s.,** berger anglais sans queue; **s. trial,** concours *m* de chiens de berger.

sheepfold ['ʃiːpfəʊld] *n* parc *m* à moutons, bercail *m*.

sheepish ['ʃiːpɪʃ] *adj* **(a)** penaud; **to look s.,** rester penaud; **(b)** (*timid*) embarrassé, gauche.

sheepishly ['ʃiːpɪʃlɪ] *adv* (*see adj*) **(a)** d'un air penaud; **(b)** d'un air embarrassé.

sheepishness ['ʃiːpɪʃnɪs] *n* air penaud; (*timidity*) timidité *f*.

sheepskin ['ʃiːpskɪn] *n* **(a)** peau *f* de mouton; (*jacket*) veste *f* en mouton; **(b)** (*parchment*) parchemin *m*; *esp US* diplôme *m* (*sur parchemin*).

sheer¹ [ʃɪər] *n Nau* (*change of course*) embardée *f*.

sheer² *vi Nau* embarder, faire une embardée.

sheer³ **1** *adj* **(a)** (*pur*) pur, véritable, vrai; **it's s. madness,** c'est de la folie pure (et simple), c'est de la pure folie; **with a look of s. disbelief,** avec un air d'incrédulité absolue; **a s. waste of time,** une pure perte de temps; **out of s. malice,** par pure méchanceté; **it was s. stupidity,** c'était franchement stupide; **in s. desperation she wrote to him,** en désespoir de cause elle lui écrivit; **(b)** (*perpendicular*) perpendiculaire; (*rocher, chemin etc*) à pic, abrupt, escarpé; **(c)** *Tex* (*linen etc*) fin, transparent, diaphane; **s. silk stockings,** bas de soie extra-fins. **2** *adv* **(a)** (*completely*) tout à fait, complètement; **the tree was torn s. out by the roots,** l'arbre fut bel et bien déraciné; **(b)** (*drop etc*) perpendiculairement, à pic, à plomb.

▶**sheer away, sheer off** *vi* (*move away*) (*of vehicle, boat*) faire une embardée; *F* **to s. away from a subject,** éviter un sujet.

sheet¹ [ʃiːt] *n* **(a)** drap *m* (*de lit*); **fitted s.,** drap-housse *m*; *F* **to get between the sheets,** se mettre au lit; se pieuter; **what's he like between the sheets?,** comment est-il au lit?; **(b)** feuille *f*, feuillet *m* (*de papier*); *Old-fashioned F* (*newspaper*) journal *m*, -aux; (*bulletin*) feuille; **loose s., fly s.,** feuille volante; *Com* **order s.,** bulletin *m* de commande; *Ind* **time** *or* **work** *or* **job s.,** feuille de présence; **s. music,** partition *f*; **(c)** feuille *f* (*de verre, de plomb etc*); feuille, tôle *f*, plaque *f* (*de métal*); *Culin* **baking s.,** plaque *f* à pâtisserie; **s. copper,** cuivre *m* en tôles; **s. glass,** verre *m* à vitres; **s. metal,** tôle; **s. mill,** laminoir *m* à tôles, tôlerie *f*; **(d)** nappe *f* (*d'eau, d'écume, de feu etc*); couche *f* (*de glace*); **a s. of flames,** un mur de flammes; **the rain was coming down in sheets,** la pluie tombait à verse; **s. lightning,** éclairs *mpl* diffus, éclairs en nappe(s).

sheet² *vt* (*covered with a bed sheet*) couvrir *ou* garnir (*qch*) d'un drap *ou* d'une bâche; **the town was sheeted over with snow,** la ville était recouverte d'un manteau de neige.

sheet³ *n Nau* écoute *f*; **s. bend,** nœud *m* d'écoute; *Old-fashioned F* **to be three sheets in the wind,** être aux trois quarts ivre.

sheet⁴ *n* **s. (anchor),** ancre *f* de veille; *Fig* **our s. anchor,** notre ancre de salut.

▶sheet down *vi* (*of rain*) tomber à verse; **it was sheeting down,** il pleuvait à verse.

sheet-fed [ˈʃiːtfed] *adj Comptr* à alimentation feuille par feuille.

sheetfeed [ˈʃiːtfiːd] *n Comptr* alimentation *f* feuille par feuille; feuille à feuille *m*.

sheeting [ˈʃiːtɪŋ] *n* **(a)** *Tex* (*material*) toile *f* pour draps; **(b)** *Constr Min* blindage *m*; **(c)** (*metal sheets*) tôlerie *f*, tôles *fpl*.

sheik(h) [ʃeɪk, ʃiːk] *n* cheik *m*, s(c)heik *m*.

sheik(h)dom [ˈʃeɪkdəm, ˈʃiːk-] *n* territoire *m* d'un sheik.

shekel [ˈʃek(ə)l] *n* **(a)** *Hist* (*measurement, coin*) sicle *m*; **(b)** *F* **shekels,** argent *m*, galette *f*.

shelf, *pl* **shelves** [ʃelf, ʃelvz] *n* **(a)** tablette *f* (*de rayonnage*); planche *f* (*d'armoire*); rayon *m* (*d'armoire, de bibliothèque*); étagère *f* (*de buffet etc*); plateau *m* (*de four etc*); **set of shelves,** étagères; **s. space,** rayonnage *m*; *Aut* **window s.,** plage *f* arrière; **s. filler,** (*person in supermarket*) réassortisseur, -euse; **they have a s. life of two months,** la durée de conservation avant vente est de deux mois; **these machines can be bought off the s.,** ces machines sont disponibles en stock; **to stay on the shelves,** (*of goods*) (*not get sold*) ne pas se vendre; (*not sell well*) être de vente difficile; *F* **to be on the s.,** (*abandoned*) être laissé pour compte; (*of woman*) être en passe de devenir vieille fille; **(b)** rebord *m*, saillie *f* (*d'un rocher, d'un précipice etc*); (*oceanography*) *& Geog* terrasse *f*, plate-forme *f*, *pl* plates-formes; banc *m* (*de roche, de sable*); **continental s.,** plate-forme continentale.

shell¹ [ʃel] *n* **(a)** coquille *f* (*de mollusque, d'escargot*); carapace *f* (*de homard, de tortue*); écaille *f* (*d'huître, de moule, de tortue*); coquille (*d'œuf, de noix*); écale *f* (*de noix*); gousse *f*, cosse *f* (*de pois etc*); (*in entomology*) enveloppe *f* (*de nymphe*); (*empty shape*) forme *f* vide; (*mere appearance*) simple apparence *f*; **(empty) shells,** coquillages *mpl*; *Fig* **to come out of/retire into one's s.,** sortir de/rentrer dans sa coquille; **s. pink,** (*colour*) rose pâle *m*;

(b) paroi *f*, coque *f* (*de chaudière*); caisse *f*, chape *f* (*de poulie*); caisse (*de tambour*); *Metal* manteau *m* (*de moule*); carcasse *f*, squelette *m*, coque (*de navire etc*); carcasse, cage *f* (*d'un édifice*); **the burnt out s. of a car/house,** la carcasse brûlée d'une voiture/maison;

(c) (*in rowing*) canot *m* de course;

(d) *Mil* obus *m*; **incendiary s.,** obus incendiaire; **live/spent s.,** obus armé/mort; **s. shock,** psychose *f* traumatique, syndrome commotionnel.

shell² **1** *vt* **(a)** écaler, décortiquer (*des noix etc*); écosser, égrener (*des pois etc*); écailler (*des huîtres, des moules*); éplucher (*des crevettes*); **(b)** *Mil* (*bombard*) bombarder. **2** *vi* **nuts that s. easily,** noix *fpl* qui se laissent décortiquer; **peas that s. easily,** pois *mpl* qui se laissent écosser.

▶shell out **1** *vtsep F* (*pay, esp unwillingly*) payer, débourser; **I was shelling out £100 a week on petrol,** je déboursais 100 livres par semaine pour l'essence. **2** *vi* (*pay money, esp unwillingly*) casquer, raquer.

she'll [ʃiːl] = **she will,** *see* **WILL³.**

shellac¹ [ʃeˈlæk] *n* gomme-laque *f*; *Ch* shellac *m*.

shellac² *vt* (**shellacked**) **(a)** traiter à la gomme-laque; **(b)** *US Sp* battre (*qn*) à plate(s) couture(s).

shelled [ʃeld] *adj* **(a)** (*mollusc, reptile etc*) à coquille, à écaille, à carapace; **(b)** (*nuts etc*) écalé; (*peas etc*) écossé, égrené.

shellfire [ˈʃelfaɪər] *n* tir *m* à obus; **to be under s.,** subir un bombardement; **we came under heavy s.,** nous avons subi un bombardement intensif.

shellfish [ˈʃelfɪʃ] *n* **(a)** (*mollusc*) mollusque *m* (comestible), coquillage *m*; (*crustacean*) crustacé *m*; **(b)** (*collectively*) mollusques et crustacés; *Culin* fruits *mpl* de mer.

shelling [ˈʃelɪŋ] *n* **(a)** (*removing shells*) égrenage *m* (*de pois etc*); décorticage *m* (*d'amandes etc*); épluchage *m* (*de crevettes*); écaillage *m* (*d'huîtres*); **(b)** *Mil* bombardement *m*.

shelling out *n F* déboursement *m*.

shell-shaped [ˈʃelʃeɪpt] *adj* conchiforme, en forme de coquillage.

shellshocked [ˈʃelʃɒkt] *adj Med Mil* (*invalide*) commotionné; **s. soldier,** commotionné de guerre; *F* **to feel s.,** se sentir en état de choc.

shellwork [ˈʃelwɜːk] *n* (décoration *f* en) coquillages *mpl*.

shelter¹ [ˈʃeltər] **(a)** lieu *m* de refuge; abri *m* (*contre la pluie, à un arrêt d'autobus etc*); asile *m*, refuge *m* (*pour indigents etc*); abrivent *m* (*pour sentinelles etc*); *Mil* **air raid s.,** abri contre les attaques aériennes, abri de défense passive; **(b)** **under s.,** à l'abri, à couvert; **to take s. under/from sth,** s'abriter *ou* se mettre à l'abri sous/de qch; **to seek s. under a tree,** chercher l'abri d'un arbre; **to find s.,** (*short period of time*) trouver un abri; (*longer period of time*) trouver asile; **to give s. to s.o.,** (*short period of time*) abriter qn; (*longer period of time*) offrir un asile *ou* un refuge à qn.

shelter² **1** *vt* abriter; donner asile à, recueillir (*un malheureux etc*); **to s. s.o./sth from the rain,** abriter qn/qch de la pluie. **2** *vi* s'abriter, se mettre à l'abri *ou* à couvert (**from,** de); **to s. under a tree,** s'abriter sous un arbre; **to s. from the wind,** s'abriter du vent; **to s. from the rain,** se mettre à couvert.

sheltered [ˈʃeltəd] *adj* abrité, protégé (**against, from,** de); *Admin* **s. housing,** foyers *mpl* (*pour personnes handicapées, personnes âgées, femmes battues etc*); *Econ* **s. industry,** industrie garantie contre la concurrence étrangère; **to have had** *or* **led a s. life,** avoir eu *ou* mené une vie protégée; **s. workshop,** atelier *m* pour les handicapés qui ont besoin de conditions spéciales.

shelve [ʃelv] **1** *vt* **(a)** (*fit with shelves*) munir *ou* garnir (*une bibliothèque etc*) de rayons; **(b)** (*put on shelves*) mettre (*des livres etc*) sur les rayons; **(c)** *F* (*postpone*) accrocher, ajourner, enterrer (*une question etc*); mettre (*un projet*) en veilleuse. **2** *vi* (*slope downwards*) aller en pente; **the land shelves down to the sea,** le terrain descend en pente douce jusqu'à la mer.

shelving [ˈʃelvɪŋ] **1** *adj* en pente, incliné. **2** *n* **(a)** (*no pl*) (*shelves*) rayons *mpl*, rayonnage *m*; **adjustable s.,** rayons mobiles; **(b)** *F* enterrement *m*, ajournement *m* (*d'une question etc*); mise *f* au rancart (*de qn*).

shemozzle [ʃɪˈmɒz(ə)l] *n F* (*fight*) bagarre *f*.

shenanigans [ʃɪˈnænɪgənz] *npl esp Am F* manigances *fpl*; **he's been having s. with my wife,** il a une aventure avec ma femme.

shepherd¹ [ˈʃepəd] *n* berger *m*, pâtre *m*; *Rel* **the Good S.,** le bon Pasteur; *Bible* **the Lord is my S.,** l'Éternel est mon berger; **German s.,** berger allemand; **s. dog,** chien *m* de berger; *Bot* **s.'s purse,** capselle *f*, bourse-à-pasteur *f*, *pl* bourses-à-pasteur.

shepherd² *vt* surveiller, garder (*les moutons*); (*of priest*) soigner, guider (*ses ouailles*); conduire, piloter (*des touristes etc*); **we were shepherded into the next room,** nous avons été conduits dans la pièce suivante.

shepherdess [ʃepəˈdes] *n* bergère *f*.

sherbet [ˈʃɜːbət] *n* **(a)** **s. (powder),** limonade sèche (*pour préparer une boisson gazeuse*); **(b)** (*water ice*) sorbet *m*; **(c)** (*fruit drink*) sorbet *m* (*du Levant etc*).

sheriff [ˈʃerɪf] *n* **(a)** *Br Admin* shérif(f) *m* (*représentant de la Couronne dans un comté*); **(b)** *Jur Scot* juge *m* de premier instance; **(c)** *US* chef *m* de la police (*d'un comté*), shérif *m*; **deputy s.,** = citoyen assermenté faisant fonction d'agent de police.

sherry [ˈʃerɪ] *n* vin *m* de Xérès, xérès *m*; **s. glass,** = verre *m* à madère.

she's [ʃiːz] **(a)** = **she is,** *see* **BE**; **(b)** = **she has,** *see* **HAVE².**

Shetland [ˈʃetlənd] *n* **(a)** **the S. Islands, the Shetlands,** les îles *fpl* Shetland; **S. pony,** poney shetlandais *ou* de Shetland; **(b)** *Tex* shetland *m*.

shew [ʃəʊ] *v* (*pt* **shewed** [ʃəʊd]; *pp* **shewn** [ʃəʊn]) *Arch &*

Lit = **SHOW²**.

shibboleth [ˈʃɪbəleθ] *n Bible* s(c)hibboleth *m*; mot *m* d'ordre (*d'un parti etc*); **outworn shibboleths,** doctrines vieux-jeu *ou* désuètes.

shield¹ [ʃiːld] *n* **(a)** (*worn on arm*) bouclier m; *Her* écu *m*, écusson *m*; *Fig* **he used his body as a s. to protect the president,** il a fait un bouclier de son corps pour protéger le président; *Geol* **the Laurentian s.,** le bouclier canadien; **s. bearer,** écuyer *m*; **(b)** (*around nuclear reactor*) bouclier *m*; *Astron* **heat s.,** bouclier thermique; *Aut* **sun s.,** pare-soleil *m inv*; **(c)** (*in spray painting*) masque *m*, cache *m*; **(d)** (*in horticulture*) **s. bud,** écusson *m*; **s. grafting,** écussonnage *m*, greffe *f* en écusson; **s. fern,** (*plant*) aspidie *f*; **(e)** (*police badge*) plaque *f ou* médaille *f* de policier; **(f)** *Sp* (*trophy*) plaque *f*.

shield² *vt* **(a)** protéger (**from, against,** contre); **to s. s.o. from criticism,** soustraire qn à la censure; **to s. s.o. from punishment,** faire échapper qn à la punition; **to s. s.o. from danger,** protéger qn contre le danger; **to s. s.o. with one's (own) body,** faire un bouclier de son corps à qn; **to s. one's eyes,** se protéger les yeux; **(b)** (*in spray painting*) masquer (*les surfaces*); **(c)** *El Rad* blinder.

shieling [ˈʃiːlɪŋ] *n Scot* **(a)** (*land*) pâturage *m*; **(b)** (*shelter*) abri m (*pour moutons, chasseurs etc*).

shift¹ [ʃɪft] *n* **(a)** changement *m* (*de position etc*); renverse *f* (*de la marée, du courant*); décalage *m* (*des joints d'un mur etc*); saute *f*, renversement *m* (*du vent*); **s. in meaning,** glissement *m* de sens; **there has been a s. in public opinion,** il y a eu un glissement de l'opinion publique; *Am Aut* **(gear) s.,** changement de vitesse; *Ling* **consonant s.,** mutation *f* consonantique; *Astron* **red s.,** décalage *m* vers le rouge; **s. key,** (*on typewriter, computer*) touche *f* des majuscules; *Comptr* **s. lock,** (*facility*) dispositif *m* de blocage; (*key*) touche *f* de blocage *ou* fixe-majuscules;

(b) *Ind etc* (*group of workers*) équipe *f*, brigade *f* (*d'ouvriers*); (*work period*) poste *m*; **day/night s.,** (*workers*) équipe de jour/nuit; (*period*) poste de jour/nuit; **to work in shifts,** travailler par équipes, se relayer; **to work eight-hour shifts,** travailler par poste(s) de huit heures; **we stood guard in three-hour shifts,** nous nous sommes relayés à la garde toutes les trois heures;

(c) (*dress*) robe *f* fourreau; *Arch* (*undergarment*) chemise *f* (*de femme*);

(d) (*expedient*) expédient *m*, ressource *f*; (*subterfuge*) échappatoire *f*, faux-fuyant *m*, *pl* faux-fuyants; **to make s.,** s'arranger, se débrouiller.

shift² **1** *vt* **(a)** (*move*) changer (*qch*) de place; (*with difficulty*) remuer, bouger, déplacer (*qch*); *Nau* désarrimer, déplacer (*la cargaison*); **could you s. your car?,** pouvez-vous déplacer votre voiture?; **I can't s. it,** je ne peux pas le bouger; **the drawer's stuck, I can't s. it,** le tiroir est coincé, je ne peux le faire bouger; **they've shifted offices again,** ils ont déménagé de nouveau; **he keeps getting shifted to a different job,** on n'arrête pas de le changer de travail; **he's shifted his position,** (*in negotiations*) il a changé de position; **to s. a stain,** (*of washing powder etc*) enlever une tache; **to s. the responsibility onto s.o.,** (*of person, action*) rejeter la responsabilité sur (le dos de) qn; *Th* **to s. the scenery,** changer le décor; *Am Aut* **to s. the gears,** changer de vitesse;

(b) *F* (*get rid of, sell*) se débarrasser de; **I've got to s. this work by 4.00,** il faut que j'aie terminé ce travail avant 4 heures; **we've been shifting these at 50 a day,** (*selling them*) nous les écoulons au rythme de 50 par jour.

2 *vi* **(a)** (*move*) changer de place; (*with difficulty*) remuer, bouger, se déplacer; *Nau* (*of cargo*) se désarrimer, se déplacer; *F* **this car can really s.!,** cette voiture est un vrai bolide!; **that's really shifting,** ça c'est de la vitesse; **this stain won't s.,** cette tache ne veut pas partir; *Th* **the scene shifts,** la scène change; **the wind has shifted (round),** le vent a tourné *ou* viré; **could you s.?,** (*out of the way*) pouvez-vous dégager?; **excuse me, could you possibly s. a little?,** excusez-moi, pourriez-vous vous déplacer un peu?; **the building is shifting,** l'immeuble bouge; **it won't s.,** ça ne veut pas bouger!; **he wouldn't s.,** (*in negotiations etc*) il est resté ferme sur ses positions;

(b) *F* **to s. (for oneself),** (*manage*) se débrouiller; (*provide for oneself*) se suffire; **she can s. for herself,** elle est débrouillarde.

▶**shift about, shift around** **1** *vtsep* faire changer (*qch*) de place; **he's always being shifted around,** (*in job*) on le change tout le temps d'emploi; (*in location*) on le change tout le temps de place. **2** *vi* **(a)** (*fidget*) bouger; **(b)** (*move around*) changer de place; (*changing jobs*) changer d'emploi.

▶**shift along, shift up** *vi F* (*move on seat etc*) se décaler; **s. along a bit,** pousse-toi *ou* décale-toi.

▶**shift over** *vi* **s. over!,** pousse-toi!

▶**shift up** *vi Aut* passer à une vitesse supérieure.

shifter [ˈʃɪftər] *n Th* **scene s.,** machiniste *m*.

shiftily [ˈʃɪftɪlɪ] *adv* sournoisement.

shiftiness [ˈʃɪftɪnɪs] *n* sournoiserie *f*, manque *m* de franchise, fausseté *f*.

shifting [ˈʃɪftɪŋ] **1** *adj* qui se déplace; (*relationship, scene etc*) changeant; (*wind etc*) inégal, -aux. **2** *n* (*moving*) déplacement *m* (*de qch par qn*); (*movement*) mouvement *m*, déplacement (*de qch*); (*of cargo*) désarrimage *m*; (*change*) changement *m* (*de place, de direction etc*); *Th* **scene s.,** changement des décors; *Am Aut* **(gear) s.,** changement de vitesse.

shiftless [ˈʃɪftlɪs] *adj* **(a)** (*lazy*) paresseux; (*lethargic*) sans énergie; **(b)** (*lacking resourcefulness*) peu débrouillard, qui manque d'initiative *ou* de ressource; (*of action*) inefficace, futile.

shiftlessness [ˈʃɪftlɪsnɪs] *n* **(a)** (*laziness*) paresse *f*; (*lethargy*) manque *m* d'énergie; **(b)** (*lack of resourcefulness*) manque *m* de ressource *ou* d'initiative; futilité *f* (*d'une action*).

shiftwork [ˈʃɪftwɜːk] *n Ind* travail *m* par équipes *ou* par roulement.

shiftworker [ˈʃɪftwɜːkər] *n Ind* ouvrier, -ière posté(e) *ou* qui fait les trois huit; (*nurse etc*) salarié(e) qui travaille par équipes.

shifty [ˈʃɪftɪ] *adj* (*individu*) roublard, retors; (*regard*) faux, sournois; (*conduite*) ambigu; **s. eyes,** regard fuyant; **there is something s. about him,** il y a quelque chose de louche chez lui.

shillelagh [ʃɪˈleɪlə] *n* gourdin irlandais.

shilling [ˈʃɪlɪŋ] *n* (*coin, sum*) shilling *m*; **to cut s.o. off with a s.,** déshériter qn.

shillyshally [ˈʃɪlɪʃælɪ] *vi F* être indécis, hésiter.

shillyshallying [ˈʃɪlɪʃælɪɪŋ] *n* hésitation *f*, indécision *f*.

shimmer¹ [ˈʃɪmər] *n* lueur *f*; (*of sea, silk etc*) miroitement *m*; (*in heat*) reflets *mpl*; **the s. of the moon on the lake,** les reflets *mpl* de la lune sur le lac.

shimmer² *vi* (*of sea, silk etc*) miroiter, luire, chatoyer.

shimmering [ˈʃɪmərɪŋ] *adj* (*sea, silk etc*) miroitant, luisant.

shimmy¹ [ˈʃɪmɪ] *n* **(a)** *US* (*garment*) chemise *f* (*de femme*); **(b)** *Aut* (*movement of front wheels*) flottement *m* des roues avant; **(c)** (*dance*) shimmy *m*.

shimmy² *vi* (*of wheels*) osciller.

shin [ʃɪn] *n Anat* le devant de la jambe, tibia *m*; *Culin* jarret *m* (de veau); **to kick s.o. in the shins,** donner un coup de pied dans les tibias de qn; *Sp* **s. guard** *or* **pad,** jambière *f*.

▶**shin up** *v* **(-nn-)** *F* **1** *vipo* (*climb*) **to s. up a tree,** grimper à un arbre. **2** *vi* (*climb*) grimper.

shinbone [ˈʃɪnbəʊn] *n Anat* tibia *m*.

shindig [ˈʃɪndɪg] *n esp Am* **(a)** (*gathering*) réunion *f* (bruyante), fête *f*; **(b)** = **SHINDY(a)**.

shindy [ˈʃɪndɪ] *n F* **(a)** (*din*) tapage *m*, chahut *m*; **to kick up a s.,** (*make a din*) chahuter, faire du chahut *ou* du tapage; (*protest loudly*) élever des protestations énergiques (**about sth,** contre qch); **(b)** *US* = **SHINDIG(a)**.

shine¹ [ʃaɪn] *n* **(a)** éclat *m*, lumière *f*; (*on shoes etc*) brillant *m*; (*on textiles etc*) luisant *m*; **rain or s.,** par tous les temps; **(b)** (*action*) **to give one's shoes a s.,** cirer ses chaussures; **to take the s. off sth,** défraîchir qch, délustrer qch; **to give the brass a s.,** astiquer les cuivres; **(c)** **to take a s. to s.o.,** s'éprendre *ou* s'enticher de qn.

shine² *v* (*pt & pp* **shone** [ʃɒn]) **1** *vi* (*of sun etc*) briller; (*of polished article*) (re)luire; **the moon/the sun is shining,** il y a un clair de lune/il fait du soleil; **the sun was shining straight into my eyes,** le soleil brillait directement dans mes yeux; **her face was shining with joy,** son visage rayonnait de joie; *Fig* **he doesn't s. in conversation,** il ne brille pas dans la conversation; **the light from the torch shone on a piece of paper,** la lumière de la lampe de poche est tombée sur un morceau de papier. **2** *vt* **(a)** **to s. a light on sth,** (*illuminate*) éclairer qch (*avec une lampe etc*); (*direct at*) braquer une lampe sur qch; **(b)** (*pt & pp* **shined** [ʃaɪnd]) *esp Am* (*polish*) polir, cirer (*les chaussures etc*); astiquer (*les cuivres etc*).

shiner [ˈʃaɪnər] *n* **(a)** *F* (*black eye*) œil poché, *F* œil au beurre noir; **(b)** (*person*) **(shoe) s.,** cireur, -euse.

shingle¹ [ˈʃɪŋg(ə)l] *n* **(a)** *Constr* (*wooden tile*) bardeau *m*, aisseau *m*; **(b)** *Am* (*sign*) plaque *f* (*de cuivre*) (*de médecin, d'avocat etc*); **to put one's s. up,** (*to open business*) s'installer; **(c)** *Arch* (*hairstyle*) coupe *f* à la garçonne.

shingle[2] *vt* **(a)** *Constr* couvrir (*un toit*) de bardeaux; **(b) to s. s.o.** *or* **s.o.'s hair,** couper les cheveux de qn à la garçonne.

shingle[3] *n* (*no pl*) (*on beach*) galets *mpl*; (*large pebbles*) (gros) cailloux *mpl*; **s. beach,** plage *f* de galets.

shingles ['ʃɪŋg(ə)lz] *n Med* zona *m*.

shingly ['ʃɪŋglɪ] *adj* (*covered in pebbles*) couvert de galets, caillouteux; (*plage*) de galets.

shininess ['ʃaɪnɪnɪs] *n* brillance *f*; (*due to wear*) lustrage *m*.

shining ['ʃaɪnɪŋ] *adj* brillant, (re)luisant; **a s. example,** un exemple brillant *ou* insigne (**of sth,** de qch).

►**shinny up** ['ʃɪnɪ] *vi Am F* = **SHIN UP**.

Shintoism ['ʃɪntəʊɪz(ə)m] *n* shintoïsme *m*, shintô *m*.

shiny ['ʃaɪnɪ] *adj* brillant, luisant; **clothes made s. by long wear,** vêtements lustrés par l'usage.

ship[1] [ʃɪp] *n* **(a)** navire *m*; **to go by s.,** aller en bateau; **to send sth by s.,** envoyer qch par voie maritime; (*by river*) envoyer qch par voie fluviale; **is there a doctor/swimming pool on the s.?,** y-a-t-il un docteur/une piscine à bord?; **sailing s.,** voilier *m*, navire *m* à voiles; **passenger s.,** paquebot *m*; **merchant s.,** navire marchand, cargo *m*; **container s.,** navire porte-conteneurs; **depot** *or* **supply s.,** ravitailleur *m*; **training s.,** navire-école *m*, *pl* navires-écoles; **to lay down a s.,** mettre un navire en chantier *ou* sur cale; *Fig* **the s. of State,** le char de l'État; **the s. of the desert,** (*camel*) le chameau; **when my s. comes home** *or* **in,** dès que j'aurai fait fortune; **s.'s boat,** embarcation *f* de bord; **s.'s boy,** mousse *m*; **s.'s carpenter,** charpentier *m* de bord; **the s.'s company,** l'équipage *m*; **(b)** *F* (*aeroplane*) avion *m*.

ship[2] *v* (**-pp-**) **1** *vt* embarquer (*une cargaison etc*); enrôler (*l'équipage*); *Com* (*to send by sea, rail etc*) envoyer, expédier (*des marchandises etc par voie de mer, par chemin de fer etc*); (*to put on board a ship*) mettre des marchandises à bord; **to s. water,** (*of ship*) embarquer de l'eau; **to s. a sea,** (*of ship*) embarquer une lame *ou* un paquet de mer; **to s. oars,** rentrer *ou* border les avirons. **2** *vi* (*of passenger*) s'embarquer; (*of sailor*) armer sur un navire; **to s. as cook,** embarquer comme cuisinier.

►**ship off** *vtsep F* (*send*) (*thing, person*) expédier; **the paper shipped her off to Moscow,** le journal l'a expédiée à Moscou.

►**ship out 1** *vtsep* (*send*) expédier (*goods*); envoyer (*troops etc*). **2** *vi esp Am F* (*leave*) dégager, mettre les voiles; *see* **SHAPE UP**.

shipboard ['ʃɪpbɔːd] *n* **on s.,** à bord d'un navire.

ship-broker ['ʃɪpbrəʊkər] *n* courtier *m* maritime.

shipbuilder ['ʃɪpbɪldər] *n* constructeur *m* de navires, constructeur maritime.

shipbuilding ['ʃɪpbɪldɪŋ] *n* construction navale *ou* maritime; **a s. firm,** une entreprise de construction navale; **the s. industry,** l'industrie de la construction navale.

shipload ['ʃɪpləʊd] *n* chargement *m*, cargaison *f*; *Fig* **by the s., in shiploads,** en masse.

shipmate ['ʃɪpmeɪt] *n* compagnon *m ou* camarade *m* de bord.

shipment ['ʃɪpmənt] *n* **(a)** (*goods shipped*) chargement *m*, expédition *f*; **(b)** (*act of putting on board*) embarquement *m*, mise *f* à bord (*de marchandises etc*); (*sending*) expédition *f*, envoi *m* (*de marchandises*) (*par mer, par chemin de fer etc*).

shipowner ['ʃɪpəʊnər] *n* propriétaire *m* de navire.

shipper ['ʃɪpər] *n* affréteur *m*, chargeur *m*, expéditeur *m*.

shipping ['ʃɪpɪŋ] *n* **(a)** (*taking on board*) embarquement *m*, mise *f* à bord (*d'une cargaison etc*); enrôlement *m* (*d'un équipage*); (*sending*) expédition *f*, envoi *m* (*de marchandises par voie de mer, par chemin de fer etc*); **s. agent,** agent *m* maritime; **s. bill,** connaissement *m*; **(b)** (*ships*) navires *mpl* (*d'un pays, d'un port*); **dangerous to** *or* **for s.,** dangereux pour la navigation; **s. intelligence,** nouvelles *fpl* maritimes; **s. lanes** *or* **routes,** routes *fpl* de navigation.

shipshape ['ʃɪpʃeɪp] **1** *adj* bien tenu, bien rangé; (*documents etc*) en bon ordre; **everything's s.,** tout est à sa place. **2** *adv* comme il faut; **to get a room s.,** ranger une pièce, mettre de l'ordre dans une pièce.

shipwreck[1] ['ʃɪprek] *n* naufrage *m*; **to suffer s.,** (*of ship*) faire naufrage; **the s. of one's fortune,** le naufrage de sa fortune.

shipwreck[2] *vt* (*usu in passive*) **to be shipwrecked,** faire naufrage.

shipwrecked ['ʃɪprekt] *adj* naufragé.

shipwright ['ʃɪpraɪt] *n* constructeur *m* de navires; (*on board ship*) charpentier *m* du bord.

shipyard ['ʃɪpjɑːd] *n* atelier *m ou* chantier *m* de constructions navales, chantier maritime *ou* naval.

shire [ʃaɪər] *n* comté *m*; **s. horse,** = cheval anglais de gros trait.

shirk [ʃɜːk] **1** *vt* manquer à, se soustraire à (*une obligation etc*); renâcler à (*une besogne*); esquiver (*un devoir*); négliger (*son devoir*); **to s. the question,** esquiver *ou* éluder la question. **2** *vi* (*avoid work*) tirer au flanc; **stop shirking!,** arrête de tirer au flanc *ou* de te défiler devant le travail!

shirker ['ʃɜːkər] *n* renâcleur *m*; **she's no s.,** elle ne renâcle à rien.

shirr [ʃɜːr] *vt Sewing* bouillonner.

shirring ['ʃɜːrɪŋ] *n Sewing* bouillonné *m*.

shirt [ʃɜːt] *n* chemise *f*; (*with short sleeves*) chemisette *f*; *Sp* maillot *m*; **sports** *or* **casual s.,** chemise sport; *F* **he's a stuffed s.,** il est guindé; **to change one's s., to put on a clean s.,** changer de chemise; *F* **to put one's s. on a horse,** parier tout ce qu'on possède sur un cheval; *F* **he'd have the s. off your back,** il te prendrait jusqu'au dernier centime; *F* **he'd give you the s. off his back,** il donnerait sa chemise; *F* **to lose one's s.,** (*to lose everything*) tout perdre, être lessivé; *Am* (*to lose one's temper*) s'emporter, prendre la mouche; *F* **keep your s. on!,** ne vous emballez pas!, calmez-vous!; *Hist* **Red/Black/Brown Shirts,** Chemises rouges/noires/brunes; **s. collar,** col *m* de chemise; **s. front,** plastron *m ou* devant *m* de chemise.

shirting ['ʃɜːtɪŋ] *n* toile *f* pour chemises.

shirtmaker ['ʃɜːtmeɪkər] *n* chemisier, -ière.

shirtsleeve ['ʃɜːtsliːv] *n* manche *f* de chemise; **to be in one's shirtsleeves,** être en bras *ou* en manches de chemise.

shirt-tail ['ʃɜːtteɪl] *n* pan *m* de chemise.

shirtwaister, *Am* **shirtwaist** ['ʃɜːtweɪst(ər)] *n* (*dress*) robe *f* chemisier.

shirty ['ʃɜːtɪ] *adj F* irritable; **to get s.,** se fâcher.

shit[1] [ʃɪt] *Sl* **1** *n* **(a)** (*excrement*) merde *f*; **to have a s.,** chier; **bird/dog s.,** merde d'oiseau/de chien; **when the s. hits the fan,** quand la merde me *ou* nous *etc* tombera dessus; **tough s.!,** pas de chance!; **this is a s. record,** c'est un disque de merde; **he doesn't give a s.,** il s'en fout, il n'en a rien à branler; **(b)** (*person*) salaud *m*, merdeux *m*. **2** *int* merde!

shit[2] *v* (*pt & pp* **shat** [ʃæt], **shitted** ['ʃɪtɪd]) *Sl* **1** *vi* chier. **2** *vt* chier; **I was shitting myself,** je chiais dans mon froc.

shite [ʃaɪt] *n & v Sl* = **SHIT**[1,2].

shitless ['ʃɪtlɪs] *adj Sl* **to be scared s.,** chier dans son froc.

shitty ['ʃɪtɪ] *adj Sl* (*weather*) merdique, de merde; **that was a s. thing to say to someone,** c'est dégueulasse de lui avoir dit ça; **he was really s. to her,** il a été vraiment dégueulasse avec elle.

shiver[1] ['ʃɪvər] *n* frisson *m*; **it sent cold shivers down my back,** cela m'a fait froid dans le dos; *F* **to have the shivers,** avoir la tremblote; **it gives me the shivers to think of it,** ça me donne des frissons quand j'y pense.

shiver[2] **1** *vi* **(a)** frissonner, trembler (**with cold, fear,** de froid, de peur); grelotter (*de froid*); **to s. like a leaf** *or* **a jelly,** trembler comme une feuille; **(b)** (*of sail*) faseyer, ralinguer. **2** *vt Nau* faire faseyer, faire ralinguer (*les voiles*).

shiver[3] *n* (*fragment*) éclat *m*, fragment *m*; **to break sth into shivers,** briser qch en éclats.

shiver[4] **1** *vt* (*break*) fracasser (*qch*), briser (*qch*) en morceaux. **2** *vi* (*break*) se fracasser, se briser en morceaux.

shivering ['ʃɪvərɪŋ] **1** *adj* tremblant, grelottant, frissonnant. **2** *n* tremblement *m*, frissonnement *m*; **to have a s. fit,** être pris de frissons.

shivery ['ʃɪvərɪ] *adj* **(a)** = **SHIVERING 1**; **(b) to feel s.,** avoir des frissons; (*to feel feverish*) se sentir fiévreux; **it gives you a s. feeling,** cela donne le frisson.

shoal[1] [ʃəʊl] **1** *adj* (*eau*) peu profond. **2** *n* haut-fond *m*, *pl* hauts-fonds; (*sandbank*) banc *m* de sable.

shoal[2] *n* banc voyageur (*de poissons*); bande *f* (*de marsouins*); *F* foule *f*, multitude *f* (*de personnes*); grande quantité, tas *m* (*de lettres etc*).

shock[1] [ʃɒk] *n* **s. of hair,** tignasse *f*.

shock[2] *n* **(a)** (*impact*) choc *m*, heurt *m*; impact *m* (*d'une collision etc*); (*jolt*) secousse *f*; *Geol* séisme *m*; **to stand the s.,** résister au choc; *Aut etc* **s. absorber,** amortisseur *m*; **slight (earthquake) shocks were felt,** on a senti de petites secousses sismiques; **acoustic s.,** choc acoustique; *Mil* **s. tactics/action,** tactique *f*/action *f* de choc; **s. troops,** troupes *fpl* d'assaut *ou* de choc; (*force*) force *f* de choc; **s. wave,** onde *f* de choc; *Fig* **the news sent s. waves through the financial world,** les nouvelles ont provoqué des ondes de choc à travers le monde des finances;

(b) (*emotional blow*) coup *m*; choc *m* (*porté par une mauvaise nouvelle etc*); *Med* choc, trauma *m*; **it was a s. to find out I'd got no money left/I'd won the competition,** ça m'a fait un choc de découvrir que je n'avais plus d'argent/que j'avais remporté la compétition; **the s. killed him, he died of the s.,** il est mort de saisissement; **be prepared for a s.,** attendez-vous à encaisser un choc; *Med* **post-operative s.,** choc post- opératoire; **in a state of s.,** en état de choc; **electric s.,** commotion *f* électrique, décharge *f*; **to get an electric s.,** recevoir une décharge; *Med* **s. therapy,** électrothérapie *f*; **electric s. treatment,** traitement *m* par électrochocs.

shock³ *vt* (*scandalize*) choquer, scandaliser (*qn*); (*overwhelm*) bouleverser (*qn*); (*make indignant*) frapper (*qn*) d'indignation *ou* d'horreur; (*horrify*) frapper (*qn*); blesser (*l'oreille*); **book that shocked the public,** livre qui a fait scandale; **easily shocked,** qui se choque facilement; **not easily shocked,** qui ne se choque pas facilement; **to be shocked at** *or* **by sth,** (*scandalized*) être choqué de *ou* scandalisé par qch; **I was shocked to hear that ...,** j'ai été bouleversé *ou* atterré *ou* choqué d'apprendre que ...; **millions were shocked by pictures of the famine,** des millions de personnes ont été choquées *ou* bouleversées par les images de la famine; *Med* **to be shocked,** être en état de choc, être commotionné.

shockable ['ʃɒkəb(ə)l] *adj* **he's easily/not easily s.,** il se choque facilement/ne se choque pas facilement.

shocked [ʃɒkt] *adj* (*scandalized*) (*person, voice etc*) choqué, scandalisé; (*stunned*) bouleversé, atterré; **there was a s. silence when she announced her resignation,** un silence atterré se produisit lorsqu'elle annonça sa démission; **to sound s.,** (*scandalized*) sembler outré; (*stunned*) sembler bouleversé.

shocker ['ʃɒkər] *n* **(a)** *F* (*person*) **he really is a s.!,** il est vraiment impossible!; **(b)** *Old-fashioned* roman *m* à gros effets *ou* sensationnel; **(c)** (*shocking news*) **that was a real s.,** ça a été un rude coup.

shocking ['ʃɒkɪŋ] **1** *adj* (*spectacle etc*) (*scandalizing*) choquant; (*revolting*) révoltant, affreux; (*news*) atterrant, bouleversant; (*weather*) abominable, exécrable; (*douleur etc*) atroce; **s. behaviour,** (*scandalizing*) comportement scandaleux; (*unworthy*) conduite indigne; **how s.!,** quelle horreur!; **the s. truth about conditions in our prisons,** la terrible vérité sur les conditions de vie dans nos prisons; **their s. ignorance,** leur scandaleuse ignorance; **s. pink,** rose criard. **2** *adv F* **he carried on something s.!,** il nous a fait une scène abominable!

shockingly ['ʃɒkɪŋlɪ] *adv* **(a)** (*to behave*) scandaleusement; abominablement, outrageusement; **s. deprived,** dans une misère atroce; **s. immoral,** d'une immoralité scandaleuse; **a s. low-cut dress,** une robe outrageusement décolletée; **in s. bad taste,** du dernier mauvais goût; **(b)** *F* (*extremely*) affreusement.

shockproof ['ʃɒkpruːf] *adj* **(a)** (*scientific instrument etc*) antichoc *inv*, à l'épreuve des chocs; **(b)** (*person*) qui ne se choque pas facilement.

shod *see* **SHOE²**.

shoddily ['ʃɒdɪlɪ] *adv* **s. made,** mal fait; **to behave s.,** se conduire mesquinement.

shoddiness ['ʃɒdɪnɪs] *n* mauvaise qualité.

shoddy¹ ['ʃɒdɪ] *n Tex* (*cloth*) drap *m* de laine d'effilochage, laine *f ou* tissu *m* de récupération.

shoddy² *adj* **(a)** (*goods etc*) de camelote, de pacotille; (*conduct*) mesquin; **s. goods,** camelote *f*; **s. workmanship,** fabrication médiocre; **(b)** *Tex* (*cloth*) d'effilochage, de récupération.

shoe¹ [ʃuː] *n* **(a)** chaussure *f*, soulier *m*; **a pair of shoes,** une paire de chaussures; **lace-up shoes,** richelieus *m*; **high-heeled shoes,** chaussures à talons hauts; **to put on/take off one's shoes,** se chausser/se déchausser, mettre/enlever ses chaussures; **to step into s.o.'s shoes,** prendre la place de qn, succéder à qn; **I shouldn't like to be in his shoes,** je ne voudrais pas être à sa place; **to be waiting for dead men's shoes,** attendre la mort de qn (*pour le remplacer*); **s. leather,** cuir *m* pour chaussures; **you might as well save your s. leather,** c'est inutile que vous y alliez; **s. polish,** cirage *m*; **s. rack,** porte-chaussures *m inv*; **s. repairs,** réparations de chaussures; **s. tree,** embauchoir *m* (*pour chaussures*); **(b)** (*horseshoe*) fer *m* (*à cheval*); **to cast** *or* **throw a s.,** perdre un fer, se déferrer; **(c)** *Tech* sabot *m* (*d'un pieu, de frein etc*); patin *m* (*de traîneau etc*).

shoe² *vt* (*pt & pp* **shod** [ʃɒd]; *prp* **shoeing**) **(a)** (*provide with shoes*) chausser (*qn*); **to be well shod,** être bien chaussé; **(b)** (*pt & pp also* **shoed**) ferrer (*un cheval*); **(c)** *Tech* garnir d'une ferrure *ou* d'une semelle *ou* d'un patin *etc*; saboter, armer (*un pieu etc*); embattre, ferrer (*une roue*); **ironshod stick,** bâton ferré.

shoeblack ['ʃuːblæk] *n* cireur *m*.

shoebrush ['ʃuːbrʌʃ] *n* brosse *f* à chaussures *ou* à souliers.

shoehorn ['ʃuːhɔːn] *n* chausse-pied *m*, *pl* chausse-pieds.

shoeing ['ʃuːɪŋ] *n* **(a)** ferrage *m*, ferrure *f* (*d'un cheval*); **s. smith,** maréchal-ferrant *m*, *pl* maréchaux-ferrants; **(b)** *Tech* pose *f* d'une ferrure *ou* d'un patin *etc*; mise *f* d'un sabot (*à un pieu etc*); embattage *m*, ferrage (*d'une roue*).

shoelace ['ʃuːleɪs] *n* lacet *m* (*de soulier*); *Fig* **he's not fit to tie your shoelaces,** il n'est pas digne de cirer vos chaussures.

shoemaker ['ʃuːmeɪkər] *n* (*person who makes shoes*) fabricant *m* de chaussures; (*person who makes and sells shoes*) chausseur *m*; (*shoe repairer*) cordonnier *m*.

shoemender ['ʃuːmendər] *n* cordonnier *m*.

shoeshine ['ʃuːʃaɪn] *n US* **(a)** (*action*) cirage *m* de chaussures; **(b)** (*person*) cireur *m* de chaussures; **s. boy,** petit cireur de chaussures.

shoestring ['ʃuːstrɪŋ] *n* lacet *m* de chaussure; *Fig F* **on a s.,** à peu de frais; **they're doing it on a s.,** ils tirent sur la corde; **a film made on a s. (budget),** un film réalisé à peu de frais.

shone *see* **SHINE²**.

shoo [ʃuː] *int* (*to chickens*) ch-ch!; (*to children etc*) allez!, filez!

►**shoo away, shoo off** *vtsep* (*scare away*) chasser (*les poules etc*).

shook *see* **SHAKE²**.

shoot¹ [ʃuːt] *n* **(a)** *Bot* pousse *f* (*d'une plante*); (*on a plant*) rejet *m*, rejeton *m*, scion *m*; (*of vine*) sarment *m*, pampre *m*; **young** *or* **tender s.,** tendrille *f*, tendron *m*; **(b)** (*in river*) rapide *m*; **(c)** = **CHUTE (a)**; **(d)** (*shooting contest*) concours *m* de tir; *esp Br* (*hunting party*) partie *f* de chasse; *Mil etc* **to carry out a s.,** effectuer un tir; **(e)** (*land*) chasse gardée; **(f)** *F* **the whole (bang) s.,** (*everything*) tout le bataclan.

shoot² *v* (*pt & pp* **shot** [ʃɒt]) **1** *vi* **(a)** (*move rapidly*) se précipiter; (*of star*) filer; **he shot into the room,** il est entré dans la pièce en éclair *ou* en trombe; **to s. forward,** foncer *ou* s'élancer à toute allure; **to s. ahead,** devancer les autres;

(b) (*of pain*) lanciner, élancer; **I've got pains shooting through my shoulder,** j'ai des élancements dans l'épaule;

(c) (*of tree, bud etc*) pousser, bourgeonner; (*of plant*) germer;

(d) (*fire gun*) tirer; **don't s.!,** ne tirez pas!; **to s. straight,** bien viser; **to s. at s.o./sth,** (*with gun*) tirer *ou* faire feu sur qn/qch; **to be shot at,** (*with gun*) se faire tirer dessus; **to s. over an estate,** chasser dans un domaine;

(e) *Cin* tourner; filmer; *Phot* (*take photo*) prendre la *ou* une photo;

(f) *Fb etc* shooter.

2 *vt* **(a)** (*pass rapidly*) franchir (*un rapide*); passer rapidement sous (*un pont*); *Aut* **to s. the (traffic) lights,** griller *ou* brûler le feu rouge;

(b) (*move rapidly*) précipiter, lancer (*qch*); pousser vivement (*un verrou*); déverser, décharger (*du charbon dans la cave*); *Fishing* jeter (*un filet*); **we were shot out of the car,** nous avons été précipités hors de la voiture; **to s. the breeze,** (*chat*) bavarder; (*exaggerate*) plaisanter; *F* **to s. a line,** (*to boast*) exagérer son importance; (*to smooth-talk*) baratiner;

(c) décocher (*une flèche*); lancer, tirer (*un projectile, une balle etc*);

(d) (*hit with bullet*) atteindre (*qn*) d'un coup de feu; (*kill*) tuer (*qn*) d'un coup de feu; abattre (*un espion*); chasser (*le gibier*); tirer (*une perdrix*); (*wound*) blesser (*qn*) d'un coup de feu; **he's been shot,** il a été tué (*d'une balle*); (*of politician etc*) il a été assassiné; (*wounded*) il a reçu une balle *ou* un coup de feu; **to be shot in the arm,** être atteint au bras; **the robbers tried to s. their way out,** les voleurs tentèrent de se frayer un passage à coups de feu; **to s. s.o. dead** *or* **to death,** tuer qn net *ou* raide; **to s. s.o. through the head,** tirer une balle dans la tête de qn, brûler la cervelle de qn; **to s. oneself in the foot,** se tirer dans le pied; *Fig* (*to spoil one's chances*) se faire du tort à soi-même; *Mil* **to be (court-martialled and) shot,** être passé par les armes, être fusillé; *Fig F* **I'll be shot,** je suis foutu; *Fig F* **you'll get me shot,** tu vas me faire des ennuis; **to s. a glance at s.o.,** lancer *ou* décocher un regard à qn;

(e) (*of light*) darder, faire jaillir (*des rayons etc*);

(f) *Cin* tourner; filmer;

(g) **to s. a marble,** lancer une bille; *Fb etc* **to s. the**

ball, shooter; **to s. a goal,** marquer un but; *Golf* **to s. a 64,** faire le parcours en 64 coups;

(h) *esp Am F* **s.!,** *(say what you want to)* allez-y!

►shoot down *vtsep* **(a)** *(cause to fall by gunfire etc)* abattre *(qn)* à coups de fusil *ou* d'un coup de fusil; abattre, descendre *(un avion)*; **(b)** *(show to be wrong or unacceptable)* descendre *(qn)*; **to s. down s.o.'s argument/proposal/***etc*, descendre l'argument/la proposition/*etc* de qn.

►shoot off 1 *vi* **(a)** *(leave quickly)* partir comme une flèche; **(b)** *Sl (to ejaculate)* décharger. **2** *vtsep (remove by gunfire)* emporter *(qch)* par une balle *ou* par un obus; **he had a foot shot off,** il a eu un pied fauché par un obus; *Sl* **to s. one's mouth off,** *(chat indiscreetly)* bavarder; *(to reveal a secret)* révéler un secret, vendre la mèche.

►shoot out 1 *vi (emerge quickly) (of water, flames)* jaillir; **to s. out of a side street,** déboucher brusquement d'une rue latérale. **2** *vtsep* **(a)** *(put out quickly)* lancer *(des étincelles etc)*; **the snake shot out its tongue,** le serpent a dardé sa langue; **(b)** *F* **to s. it out,** régler ses comptes à coups de feu.

►shoot up 1 *vtsep* **they shot the place up,** ils ont mitraillé la pièce; **he was badly shot up in the war,** il a été sérieusement blessé à la guerre; **he's been shot up,** il a reçu des balles (dans la peau). **2** *vi* **(a)** *(of plants, children)* pousser; *(of rocket)* s'élever; *(of prices)* monter en flèche; *(of fountain etc)* jaillir; **he's really shot up!,** *(he's grown)* qu'est-ce qu'il a poussé!; **(b)** *Sl (with drugs)* se shooter.

shooter ['ʃuːtər] *n Sl (gun)* flingue *m*, feu *m*.

shooting ['ʃuːtɪŋ] **1** *adj* qui s'élance; *(water, flame)* jaillissant; **s. star,** étoile filante; **s. pains,** douleurs lancinantes.

2 *n* **(a)** *(rapid movement)* franchissement *m (d'un rapide)*; course *f* rapide; déchargement *m (de charbon etc)*; *Fishing* jet *m (d'un filet)*;

(b) décochement *m (d'une flèche)*; *(gunfire)* coups *mpl* de feu; *(firing of gun)* tir *m (avec une arme à feu)*; *(killing)* meurtre *m (de qn) (avec une arme à feu)*; *(of spies, revolutionaries etc)* mise *f* à mort; *(hunting)* la chasse; **there was no s.,** *(in robbery etc)* aucun coup de feu n'a été tiré; **there was a s. in the main street,** *(person killed)* quelqu'un a été tué d'un coup de feu dans la rue principale; *(person injured)* quelqu'un a reçu une balle dans la rue principale; **pigeon s.,** tir aux pigeons; **s. range,** champ *m* de tir; **s. match,** concours *m* de tir; *F* **the whole s. match,** tout le bataclan; **s. gallery,** (stand *m* de) tir *m*; **the s. season,** la saison de la chasse; **s. party,** partie *f* de chasse; **s. stick,** canne-siège *f*, *pl* cannes-sièges; *Aut* **s. brake,** break *m* de chasse, canadienne *f*; *F* **s. war,** guerre chaude;

(c) *Cin* tournage *m (d'un film)*; **s. starts next week on her new film,** le tournage de son nouveau film commence la semaine prochaine.

shoot-out ['ʃuːtaʊt] *n F* échange *m* de coups de feu; **they settled it with a s.-o.,** ils ont réglé leurs comptes à coups de feu.

shop¹ [ʃɒp] *n* **(a)** magasin *m*; *(small)* boutique *f*; **I'm just going down to the shops,** je sors faire des courses; **the ones you buy in shops,** ceux que l'on achète dans les magasins; **the new book should reach the shops in July,** le nouveau livre devrait être en vente en juillet; **grocer's s.,** épicerie *f*; **baker's s.,** boulangerie *f*; **shoe s.,** magasin de chaussures; **duty-free s.,** boutique hors taxes; **mobile s.,** boutique ambulante; *Old-fashioned* **s.!,** il y a quelqu'un (pour servir)?; **to set up s.,** *(to open a shop)* ouvrir un magasin; *(to set up as shopkeeper)* s'établir comme commerçant, -ante; **to keep (a) s.,** tenir un magasin; **to shut up s.,** *(to close shop)* fermer boutique; *Fig (cease activities)* suspendre ses activités; *F* **you've come to the wrong s.,** vous vous trompez de porte; *F* **all over the s.,** *(in confusion)* dans la confusion; *(in disorder)* en désordre; *(everywhere)* partout, dans tous les coins; **s. assistant,** vendeur, -euse (de magasin), employé(e) de magasin; **s. front,** devanture *f* de magasin; **s. window,** vitrine *f*; *(display)* étalage *m*; **in the s. window,** dans la *ou* en vitrine;

(b) *F (act of shopping)* courses *fpl*, shopping *m*; **I do my big s. on a Friday,** je fais mes grosses courses le vendredi;

(c) *Ind etc* atelier *m*; **assembly s.,** atelier de montage; **pattern s.,** atelier de modelage; **repair s.,** atelier de réparations; **carpenter's s.,** atelier de menuiserie; **closed s.,** entreprise qui n'admet que du personnel appartenant à un certain syndicat; **the s. floor,** l'atelier; *(workforce)* les ouvriers *mpl*; **s. foreman,** chef *m* d'atelier; **s. steward,** porte-parole *m* des ouvriers;

(d) *F* **to talk s.,** parler métier, parler affaires.

shop² *v* **(-pp-) 1** *vi* **to s., to go shopping,** (aller) faire ses courses; *(for food) (to market)* aller faire son marché; aller aux provisions; **to go shopping for clothes,** aller acheter des vêtements; *Can* magasiner. **2** *vt Sl* (faire) coffrer *(qn)*, dénoncer *(qn)*.

shopfitter ['ʃɒpfɪtər] *n* installateur *m ou* agenceur *m* de magasins.

shopgirl ['ʃɒpgɜːl] *n Old-fashioned* vendeuse *f*, employée *f* de magasin; *(saleswoman)* vendeuse.

shop-in-shop ['ʃɒpɪnʃɒp] *n Com* magasin *m* à l'intérieur d'une grande surface.

shopkeeper ['ʃɒpkiːpər] *n* commerçant, -ante.

shoplifter ['ʃɒplɪftər] *n* voleur, -euse à l'étalage.

shoplifting ['ʃɒplɪftɪŋ] *n* vol *m* à l'étalage.

shopman, *pl* **-men** ['ʃɒpmən] *n US* mécanicien *m (dans un atelier de réparations)*.

shopper ['ʃɒpər] *n* **(a)** *(person)* **for the convenience of shoppers,** *(sign in shop)* pour mieux servir nos clients; **streets crowded with shoppers,** des rues pleines de gens qui font leurs courses; **(b)** *F (bag)* sac *m* à provisions.

shopping ['ʃɒpɪŋ] *n* achats *mpl*, courses *fpl*; **to do one's s.,** faire ses courses; *(for food) (at market)* faire son marché, aller aux provisions; **I hate s.,** *(for food etc)* je déteste faire les courses; *(for clothes, wandering round shops)* je déteste faire du shopping; **to do one's Christmas s.,** faire ses achats de Noël; **I had a lot of heavy s.,** j'étais lourdement chargé d'achats; **I haven't got much s. to do.,** je n'ai pas beaucoup de courses à faire; **I've got to do some clothes/food/***etc* **s.,** il faut que j'achète quelques vêtements/un peu de nourriture/*etc*; **s. bag/basket,** sac *m*/panier *m* à provisions; **s. centre,** *(district)* quartier commerçant; *(complex of shops)* centre commercial; **Saturday is my main s. day,** le samedi est le jour où je fais mes grosses courses; **only three s. days to Christmas,** il ne reste plus que trois jours pour faire les courses avant Noël; **s. list,** liste *f* de commissions; **s. mall, s. precinct,** *Can* **s. plaza,** centre commercial; **s. street,** rue commerçante.

shopsoiled, shopworn ['ʃɒpsɔɪld, -wɔːn] *adj (article)* défraîchi, qui a fait l'étalage.

shoptalk ['ʃɒptɔːk] *n* **no s. OK?,** on ne parle pas métier *ou* affaires d'accord?

shopwalker ['ʃɒpwɔːkər] *n* **(a)** chef *m* de rayon; **(b)** inspecteur, -trice, surveillant, -ante *(de magasin)*.

shore¹ [ʃɔːr] *n (coast)* rivage *m*, littoral *m*, côte *f*; bord *m (de la mer, d'un lac, d'un fleuve)*; **on the s.,** sur le rivage; *(by sea)* au bord de la mer; *Nau* **on s.,** à terre; **to go on s.,** se rendre à terre; *(disembark)* débarquer; **off s.,** au large; **in s.,** près de la côte; *Lit* **distant shores,** de lointains rivages; **she rarely visits our shores,** elle visite rarement nos contrées; *Nau* **s. leave,** permission *f* à terre.

shore² *n Constr etc* étai *m*, étançon *m*.

shore³ *vt* = **SHORE UP**.

►shore up *vtsep (support)* étayer, étançonner *(une maison, un mur)*; épontiller *(un navire)*; *Fig* étager, consolider *(un gouvernement)*.

shoreline ['ʃɔːlaɪn] *n* rivage *m*; *(by sea)* côte *f*.

shoreward(s) ['ʃɔːwəd(z)] *adv* vers la terre.

shorn¹ [ʃɔːn] *adj* **(a)** *(head)* rasé; **(b)** *(sheep)* tondu.

shorn² *see* **SHEAR²**.

short¹ [ʃɔːt] **1** *adj* **(a)** *(in space)* court; **to be s.,** *(of person)* être petit; **to be s. in the arm/leg,** *(of person)* avoir les bras courts/les jambes courtes; *(of garment)* court au niveau des bras/des jambes; **s. back and sides,** coupe dégagée; **a s. distance from the station,** à une petite distance de la gare; **to have s. hair,** avoir les cheveux courts; **a s. person,** une personne de petite taille; **to go by the shortest road, to go the shortest way,** prendre par le plus court *ou* au plus court; *Horseracing* **s. price,** faible cote *f*; **at s. range,** à courte portée; *Av* **s. take-off and landing aircraft,** avion à décollage et à atterrissage court;

(b) *(in time)* court, bref; *(breath)* court; *(style)* concis, serré; *(reply, tone etc)* brusque, sec, *f* sèche; **the days are getting shorter,** les jours raccourcissent; **s. and sweet,** court et bon; **in s.,** *(to sum up)* bref, en résumé, en somme; *(in a few words)* en un mot; **Bill is s. for William,** Bill est un diminutif de William; **to be s. with s.o.,** être cassant avec qn; **he was very s. with me,** il s'est montré très brusque envers moi; **the s. answer is 'no',** la réponse est brève, c'est 'non'; *Fin* **s. bills, bills at s. date,** billets *mpl ou* traites *fpl* à courte échéance; **a s. drink,** un alcool fort; **of s. duration,** de peu de durée; **we've just got time for a s. game,** nous avons juste le temps de faire une petite partie; **s. history of France,** précis *m* d'histoire de France; **at s. intervals,** à de courts intervalles; **s. list,** liste choisie *(d'aspirants à un poste etc)*; **to have a s. memory,** avoir la mémoire courte; *US* **in s. order,** peu de temps après; **s. story,** nouvelle *f*, conte *m*; **s. syllable,** syllabe brève; **s. temper,** caractère emporté; **for a s. time,** pour peu de temps; **a s. time ago,** il y a peu de temps; *Ling* **s. vowel,** voyelle brève; **to make s. work of,** expédier (*qch*); trancher (*un problème, une difficulté*); **to make s. work of it,** ne pas y aller par quatre chemins;

(c) (*weight, measure etc*) insuffisant; **water/money/***etc* **is very s. at the moment,** nous manquons d'eau/d'argent/*etc* en ce moment; **it is two francs s.,** il s'en faut de deux francs; **I am twenty francs s.,** il me manque vingt francs; **little** *or* **not far s. of it,** peu s'en faut; **he is not far s. of thirty,** il n'a guère moins de trente ans; **it is little s. of folly,** cela tient de la folie; **it was nothing s. of a masterpiece,** ce n'était rien moins qu'un chef-d'œuvre; **nothing s. of violence would compel him,** la violence seule le contraindrait; **to be s. of sth,** (*of person*) être à court de qch, manquer de qch; **I'm a bit s. of cash,** je suis un peu à court d'argent; **the country is s. of engineers,** le pays manque d'ingénieurs; **he's a bit s. on common sense,** il manque un peu de bon sens; *Cards* **to be s. of** *or* **in spades,** avoir une renonce à pique; **water in s. supply,** approvisionnement d'eau réduit; *Ind* **to be on s. time,** être en chômage partiel;

(d) (*metal, clay*) aigre, cassant; *Cer* (*pâte*) court;

(e) *Culin* **s. pastry,** pâte brisée.

2 *n* **(a) shorts,** short *m*; *Am* (*underwear*) caleçon *m*;

(b) the long and the s. of it, le fin mot de l'affaire; **he knows the long and the s. of it,** il connaît l'affaire à fond;

(c) (*in prosody*) (*syllabe*) brève *f*; *Ling* voyelle brève;

(d) *El F* (*short circuit*) court-circuit *m*, *pl* courts-circuits;

(e) *Cin* (*short film*) court métrage;

(f) (*drink*) alcool fort.

3 *adv* **(a) hair cut s.,** cheveux coupés court;

(b) (*brusquely*) **to stop s.,** s'arrêter (tout) court *ou* net, *F* s'arrêter pile; **to cut s.o. s.,** couper la parole à qn; **to be taken** *or* **caught s.,** *F* (*need to relieve oneself*) être pris d'un besoin pressant; *F* **to be caught s.,** (*not have enough money*) être à court d'argent;

(c) to go s. of sth, se priver de qch; **to run s. of,** venir à bout de (*ses provisions etc*); **we are running s. of provisions, our provisions are running s.,** les vivres commencent à manquer *ou* à s'épuiser; **to fall s. of,** (*of arrow etc*) ne pas atteindre (*le but*), tomber court; **to fall s. of s.o.'s expectations,** être *ou* rester au-dessous de l'attente de qn; **to fall s. of one's duty,** manquer à son devoir; **s. of a miracle we are ruined,** à moins d'un miracle nous sommes perdus; **there's not much we can do s. of selling the house,** il n'y a pas grand chose à faire à part vendre la maison; **it just stops s. of being criminal,** c'est à la limite de la criminalité; **she stopped s. of actually calling him a liar,** pour un peu elle le traitait de menteur;

(d) *St Exch* (*to buy*) à découvert; (*to borrow*) à courte échéance; *Fig* **to sell s.o. s.,** (*trick*) duper qn, *F* avoir qn; rabaisser qn; (*denigrate*) dénigrer qn.

short² *vi El F* = **SHORT-CIRCUIT²**.

shortage ['ʃɔːtɪdʒ] *n* **(a)** insuffisance *f*, manque *m* (*de poids etc*); **to make up** *or* **make good the s.,** (*in money*) combler le déficit; *Com* **shortages,** manquants *mpl*; **(b)** crise *f*, disette *f*; **food s.,** disette; **the paper s.,** la crise du papier; **we have constant staff shortages,** nous manquons constamment de personnel.

short-arse ['ʃɔːtɑːs] *n Sl* **he's a little s.,** il est un peu court sur pattes; *Pej* il a le cul un peu bas.

shortbread, shortcake ['ʃɔːtbred, -keɪk] *n Culin* = sablé *m*.

short-change ['ʃɔːt(t)ʃeɪndʒ] *vt F* (*intentionally*) voler (*qn*) (en lui rendant la monnaie); (*accidentally*) ne pas rendre assez de monnaie à (*qn*).

short-circuit¹ [ʃɔːt'sɜːkɪt] *n El* court-circuit *m*, *pl* courts-circuits.

short-circuit² **1** *vt El & Fig* court-circuiter. **2** *vi El* (*of current*) se mettre en court-circuit.

shortcoming ['ʃɔːtkʌmɪŋ] *n* **(a)** (*flaws*) (*usu pl*) **shortcomings,** défauts *mpl*, imperfections *fpl* (*chez qn*); **(b)** (*lack*) manque *m*, déficit *m*.

short-dated [ʃɔːt'deɪtɪd] *adj Fin* (*billet*) à courte échéance; (*papier*) court.

shorten ['ʃɔːt(ə)n] **1** *vt* raccourcir (*une jupe etc*); abréger (*un texte, une tâche*); écourter (*un séjour*); **Albert is often shortened to Bert,** le diminutif d'Albert est Bert; *Culin* **to s. pastry,** travailler la pâte avec une matière grasse. **2** *vi* (*of days etc*) raccourcir.

shortening ['ʃɔːtnɪŋ] *n* **(a)** raccourcissement *m* (*des jours*); **(b)** *Culin* matière grasse.

shortfall ['ʃɔːtfɔːl] *n* manque *m; (financially)* déficit *m*; **we're going to have a s. of three weeks,** il va nous manquer trois semaines.

shorthaired ['ʃɔːtheəd] *adj* (*homme*) à cheveux courts; (*chat*) à poil court.

shorthand ['ʃɔːthænd] *n* sténo(graphie) *f*; **to take a speech down in s.,** sténographier un discours, noter un discours en sténo; **s. typist,** sténodactylographe *mf*, *F* sténodactylo *mf*; **s. writer** *or* **reporter,** sténographe *mf*; **s. writing,** écriture *f* sténographique.

shorthanded [ʃɔːt'hændɪd] *adj* à court de personnel *ou* de main-d'œuvre; **to be s.,** manquer de personnel.

short-haul ['ʃɔːthɔːl] *adj Av* **s.-h. aircraft,** (avion *m*) court-courrier *m*.

shorthorn ['ʃɔːthɔːn] *n* race bovine shorthorn, shorthorn *m*.

shortish ['ʃɔːtɪʃ] *adj* assez *ou* plutôt court; (*person*) courtaud.

short-legged [ʃɔːt'leg(ɪ)d] *adj* à jambes courtes.

short-list ['ʃɔːtlɪst] *vt* **to s. a candidate,** retenir une candidature (*en vue d'une sélection ultérieure*).

short-lived [ʃɔːt'lɪvd] *adj* (*person, animal*) qui ne vit que peu de temps; (*joy, triumph etc*) bref, éphémère, de courte durée.

shortly ['ʃɔːtlɪ] *adv* **(a)** (*soon*) bientôt, prochainement; (*in a short time*) sous peu; **s. after(wards),** (*soon afterwards*) bientôt après; (*a short time later*) peu (de temps) après; **President Smith who was s. to be** *or* **would s. be reelected,** le président Smith qui allait bientôt être réélu; **(b)** (*répondre etc*) brusquement, sèchement; **(c)** (*raconter qch etc*) brièvement, en peu de mots.

shortness ['ʃɔːtnɪs] *n* **(a)** peu *m* de longueur (*du bras, d'une jupe*); petite taille (*d'une personne*); brièveté *f*, courte durée (*de la vie*); **s. of memory,** manque *m* de mémoire; **(b)** brusquerie *f* (*d'humeur*); **(c)** manque *m*, insuffisance *f* (*de vivres etc*); **(d)** *Culin* (*of pastry*) friabilité *f*.

short-range ['ʃɔːtreɪndʒ] *adj* (*tir, missile etc*) à courte portée; (*prévision*) à court terme.

shortsheet [ʃɔːt'ʃiːt] *vt US* mettre (*un lit*) en portefeuille.

shortsighted [ʃɔːt'saɪtɪd] *adj* **(a)** myope, à la vue basse; **I am getting s.,** ma vue baisse; **(b)** (*approach etc*) imprévoyant; **that was very s. of you** *or* **him** *etc*, ça n'était pas faire preuve de beaucoup de prévoyance.

shortsightedness [ʃɔːt'saɪtɪdnɪs] *n* **(a)** (*myopia*) myopie *f*; **(b)** (*of approach etc*) imprévoyance *f*, manque *m* de perspicacité.

short-staffed [ʃɔːt'stɑːft] *adj* **to be s.-s.,** manquer de personnel.

short-tempered [ʃɔːt'tempəd] *adj* vif, d'un caractère emporté.

short-term ['ʃɔːttɜːm] *adj* (*prisoner*) qui subit un emprisonnement de courte durée; (*contract*) de courte durée; (*solution, memory*) & *Fin* à court terme.

short-time ['ʃɔːttaɪm] *adj* **s.-t. worker/working,** chômeur/chômage partiel.

short-winded [ʃɔːt'wɪndɪd] *adj* au souffle court; **to be s.-w.,** manquer de souffle.

shorty ['ʃɔːtɪ] *n F* petit *m*, petite *f*; **come on s.!,** allez le petit!

shot [ʃɒt] *n* **(a)** (*act of firing, sound*) coup *m* (de feu); **pistol s.,** coup de pistolet; **warning s.,** coup d'avertissement; *Nau* coup de semonce; **to fire a s.,** tirer un coup de feu; **without firing a s.,** sans tirer un (seul) coup de feu; **parting s.,** (*remark*) remarque *f ou* réplique *f* qu'on lance en partant, dernière remarque; **he's a good s.,** il est bon tireur; (*in hunting*) il est bon chasseur; *F* **a big s.,** un type important, un grand manitou, *Sl* une grosse légume;

(b) (*inv in pl*) (*projectile*) (*from shotgun*) plomb *m*; *Arch* boulet(s) *m(pl)*; *Sp* poids *m*; **round s.,** boulet(s) rond(s); **small s.,** menu plomb, petit plomb; **bird s.,** cendrée *f*; *F* **like a s.,** (*partir*) comme une flèche; (*accepter*) d'emblée, sans hésitation; *Metal* **lead s.,** grenaille *f* de plomb; *Sp* **to put the s.,** lancer le poids;

(c) (*stroke etc*) coup *m*; *Phot* photo *f*; *Cin* plan *m*, séquence *f*, prise *f* de vue; *Med F* (*injection*) piqûre *f*; *Sl* (*drugs*) piquouse *f*; *F* (*drink*) petit verre (*d'eau de vie*); **it's your s.,** (*in game*) à vous de jouer; **good s.!,** bien joué!; *Tennis etc* **drop s.,** amortie *f*; **passing s.,** passing-shot *m*; *Fig* **I'll have a s. at it,** je vais essayer *ou* tenter le coup; **it's worth having a s. at,** cela vaut le coup; **her second s. at the presidency,** sa deuxième tentative d'obtenir la présidence; **she made** *or* **had a good s. at it,** elle s'est très bien acquittée; *esp Am F* **give it your best s.,** fais de ton mieux; **to make a long s.,** (*to aim from a distance*) viser de loin; (*to guess wildly*) (*also* **to make a s. in the dark**) deviner au hasard; (*to take a risk*) prendre un (gros) risque; **not by a long s.,** il s'en faut de beaucoup; *Fb etc* **s. (at goal),** shot *m*, shoot *m*; *Phot* **high angle s.,** plongée *f*; **pan s.,** panoramique *f*; **you can get a good s. of the castle from here,** d'ici vous pouvez prendre une bonne photo du château; **s. in the arm,** (*injection*) piqûre au bras; *Fig* (*stimulation*) remontant *m*, coup de fouet; *F* **to call the shots,** prendre les décisions; **THEY call the shots,** c'est eux qui décident.

shotgun ['ʃɒtgʌn] *n* fusil *m* de chasse; *F* **s. wedding,** mariage forcé.

should *see* **SHALL**.

shoulder¹ ['ʃəʊldər] *n* épaule *f*; *Culin* épaule (*de mouton etc*); épaulement *m* (*de colline etc*); contrefort *m* (*de montagne*); **s. blade,** *Anat* omoplate *f*; paleron *m* (*de cheval etc*); **round shoulders,** dos rond *ou* voûté; **he's got broad shoulders,** il est large d'épaules; *Fig* il a bon dos; **coat too tight across the shoulders,** manteau trop étroit de carrure; **off-the-s. dress,** robe dégageant les épaules; **slung across** *or* **over the s.,** en bandoulière; **to look over one's shoulder,** vérifier si on est suivi; *Mil* **to bring the gun to the s.,** épauler le fusil; **to tell s.o. sth straight from the s.,** dire qch carrément *ou* brutalement à qn; **to have a good head on one's shoulders,** avoir de la tête *ou* du bon sens, avoir la tête sur les épaules; **to rub shoulders with millionaires/film stars,** côtoyer les millionnaires/stars du cinéma; **to stand head and shoulders above the rest,** (*to be head and shoulders taller*) dépasser les autres d'une tête; (*to be far better*) surpasser tous les autres; **s. high,** à la hauteur des épaules; **to carry s.o. s. high,** porter qn en triomphe; **s. to s.,** (*side by side*) côte à côte, épaule contre épaule; **to lay the blame on s.o.'s shoulders,** rejeter la faute sur le dos de qn; **to put one's s. to the wheel,** pousser à la roue; *Fig* (*to put effort into one's work*) se mettre à l'œuvre (*avec énergie*); **hard s.,** bas-côté *m* (*d'une route*); **soft s.,** accotement non stabilisé; **s. bag,** sac *m* en *ou* à bandoulière; **s. belt,** baudrier *m*; **s. braid,** fourragère *f*; *Av* **s. harness,** bretelles *fpl*; **s. knot,** aiguillette *f*; **s. pad,** *Sewing* épaulette *f*; *US Fb* protège-épaule *m*, *pl* protège-épaules; **s. strap,** bretelle, bandoulière *f* (*d'un sac etc*); (*on clothes*) épaulette, patte *f* d'épaules; (*on underwear*) bretelle; *Mil etc* **s. strap** *or US* **loop,** patte d'épaule, épaulette.

shoulder² *vt* **(a)** (*push*) pousser (*qn, qch*) avec l'épaule; **to s. one's way through the crowd,** se frayer un passage à travers la foule; **to s. s.o. out of the way** *or* **aside,** écarter *ou* repousser qn d'un coup d'épaule; **(b)** (*put on shoulder*) mettre (*qch*) sur l'épaule; **to s. one's gun,** mettre son fusil sur l'épaule; *Fig* **to s. the responsibility,** endosser la responsabilité; *Mil* **to s. arms,** se mettre au port d'armes; **s. arms!,** portez armes!

shout¹ [ʃaʊt] *n* **(a)** cri *m* (*de joie, de douleur etc*); **shouts of laughter,** éclats *mpl* de rire; **there was a s. of 'no more taxes!',** on cria 'plus d'impôts!'; **(b)** *Br F* (*round of drinks*) tournée *f*.

shout² **1** *vi* crier, pousser un cri *ou* des cris; **to s. for s.o.,** appeler qn de toutes ses forces; **to s. for help,** crier *ou* appeler au secours; **to s. at s.o.,** crier après qn; **don't s. at me,** ne me crie pas après; **there's no need to s.,** ce n'est pas la peine de crier; **to s. to s.o. to do sth,** crier à qn de faire qch. **2** *vt* crier (*qch*); vociférer (*des injures etc*); **to s. oneself hoarse,** s'enrouer à force de crier; **'look out!', he shouted,** 'attention!', cria-t-il.

►shout down *vtsep* (*express disapproval of by shouting*) huer, conspuer (*qn*); conspuer (*une proposition*); **the speaker was shouted down,** l'orateur n'a pas réussi à se faire entendre.

►shout out **1** *vi* (*shout*) **I shouted out in pain,** je hurlais de douleur. **2** *vtsep* (*shout*) crier.

shouting ['ʃaʊtɪŋ] *n* cris *mpl*; (*uproar*) clameur *f*; **there was a lot of s.,** on criait beaucoup; *Fig* **it's all over bar the s.,** c'est dans le sac.

shove¹ [ʃʌv] *n F* poussée *f*; coup *m* (*d'épaule etc*); **to give sth/s.o. a s.,** pousser qch/qn, donner une poussée à qch/à qn; *Fig* **he's lazy, he just needs a little s.,** il est paresseux, il a juste besoin qu'on le pousse un peu.

shove² *F* **1** *vt* pousser (*qn, un objet*); **to s. s.o./sth along** *or* **forward,** pousser qn/qch en avant, faire avancer qn/qch; **to s. sth into a drawer,** fourrer qch dans un tiroir. **2** *vi* **to s. along** *or* **on,** se frayer un chemin; **stop shoving!,** arrêtez de pousser!; **she shoved past me,** elle m'a bousculé en passant.

►shove around *vtsep F* **(a)** (*push*) bousculer (*qn*); **(b)** (*bully*) faire marcher (*qn*).

►shove aside, shove away *vtsep F* (*push away*) écarter (*qn, qch*) d'une poussée.

►shove off **1** *vtsep* (*launch*) pousser (*une embarcation*) au large. **2** *vi F* (*leave*) décamper; **s. off!,** fiche le camp!

shove-halfpenny, -ha'penny ['ʃʌvheɪpnɪ] *n* = (jeu *m* du) galet *m*.

shovel¹ ['ʃʌv(ə)l] *n* pelle *f*; **coal s.,** pelle à charbon *ou* à feu; *Constr etc* **power/steam s.,** pelle mécanique/à vapeur.

shovel² *vt* (**-ll-**) pelleter (*le charbon etc*), prendre *ou* jeter (*le charbon etc*) à la pelle; *F* **to s. food into one's mouth,** s'empiffrer.

►shovel away *vtsep* (*remove with shovel*) déblayer (*la neige etc*).

►shovel up *vtsep* (*collect with shovel*) ramasser, entasser (*le grain etc*) à la pelle.

shovelful ['ʃʌvəlfʊl] *n* pelletée *f* (*de sable etc*).

shovel(l)er ['ʃʌvələr] *n* (*duck*) souchet *m*.

show¹ [ʃəʊ] *n* **(a)** (*act of showing*) **to vote by s. of hands,** voter à mains levées; **to be on s.,** être exposé; **wonderful s. of flowers,** étalage merveilleux de fleurs; **to put up a good s.,** bien s'acquitter; *Old-fashioned F* **good s.!,** très bien!, bravo!; **it was a poor** *or* **bad s.,** c'était plutôt manqué; **s. house/flat,** maison *f*/appartement *m* témoin; **s. window,** vitrine *f* (*de magasin*); (*display*) étalage *m*;

(b) (*exhibition*) exposition *f* (*d'horticulture etc*); exhibition *f* (*de bêtes sauvages etc*); concours *m*, comice *m* (*agricole etc*); **motor/air s.,** salon *m* de l'automobile/de l'aviation; **fashion s.,** présentation *f* de collections; **dog s.,** exposition canine; **s. animal,** animal *m* à concours; *Horse-riding* **s. jumping,** jumping *m*; **s. jumper,** sauteur *m*; **travelling s.,** (*at a fair*) spectacle forain; *F* **to make a s. of oneself,** se donner en spectacle; (*make a fool of oneself*) se rendre ridicule;

(c) (*spectacle*) spectacle, concert *m*; émission *f* (*de radio, de télévision*); **to go to a s.,** aller au spectacle; **to stop the s.,** faire un tabac; *Th & Fig* **the s. must go on,** il faut continuer; **to steal the s.,** (r)emporter la vedette; **film s.,** séance *f* de cinéma; *Rad TV* **talk** *or* **chat s.,** talk-show *m*; **one-man s.,** solo *m*; **s. business,** industrie *f ou* monde *m* du spectacle; **that's s. business!,** c'est ça la vie d'artiste!; **s. bill,** affiche *f* (de spectacle); **s. girl,** girl *f*; *F* **s. stopper,** acteur, -trice *ou* chanteur, -euse *ou* numéro *etc* qui fait un tabac.

(d) (*appearance*) apparence *f*; (*pretence*) semblant *m*, simulacre *m*; (*ostentation*) parade *f*, ostentation *f*; **it's all a s.,** ce n'est qu'une façade; **s. of generosity,** affectation *f* de générosité; **s. of strength,** démonstration *f* de force; **to make a s. of resistance,** faire un semblant de résistance; **to make a s. of being angry,** faire semblant *ou* faire mine d'être fâché; **to make a great s. of friendship,** faire de grandes démonstrations d'amitié; **to be fond of s.,** aimer l'éclat *ou* la parade; **to make a s. of learning,** faire parade d'érudition; **to do sth for s.,** faire qch pour les apparences; **s. trial,** procès-spectacle *m*;

(e) *F* affaire *f*; **to run the s.,** être à la tête de *ou* diriger l'affaire;

(f) *F* occasion *f*, chance *f*; **to give s.o. a (fair) s.,** laisser franc jeu à qn.

show² *v* (*pt* **showed** [ʃəʊd]; *pp* **shown** [ʃəʊn]) **1** *vt* **(a)** montrer; (*let see*) faire voir, laisser voir (*qch*); exposer, exhiber (*ses muscles, ses bijoux*); présenter (*son passeport*); (*of cinema*) passer, projeter (*un film*); représenter, figurer (*qch par la peinture, par le discours etc*); **to s. sth to s.o., to s. s.o. sth,** montrer *ou* faire voir qch à qn; **to s. one's wares,** déployer *ou* étaler ses marchandises; **we're going to s. some films this evening,** nous allons passer *ou* projeter des films ce soir; *TV* **this programme will be shown tomorrow,** cette émission passera sur l'écran demain; **to s. one's cards** *or* **one's hand,** découvrir son jeu; *Fig* (*make one's intentions known*) jouer cartes sur table; **to have sth to s. for one's money,** en avoir pour son argent; **to s. one's legs,** exposer ses jambes; **he won't s. his face here again,** il ne se montrera plus ici; **colour that doesn't s. the dirt,** couleur qui n'est pas salissante; **to s. oneself,** se montrer, se faire voir; (*for inspection etc*) se présenter, s'exhiber; (*at a reception etc*) faire acte de présence; **to s. itself,** devenir visible, se montrer, se manifester, se révéler; **the picture shows three figures,** le tableau représente trois personnes; **a diagram shows how the system works,** un diagramme indique le fonctionnement du système; **place shown on a map,** lieu indiqué sur une carte; **to s. the time/the temperature,** (*of watch, thermometer etc*) indiquer *ou* marquer l'heure/la température; **to s. a profit/**

a loss, faire ressortir un bénéfice/une perte; **to s. great improvement,** montrer *ou* accuser une grande amélioration;

(b) (*point out*) **to s. s.o. the way,** indiquer *ou* montrer le chemin à qn; **to s. s.o. to his room,** conduire qn à sa chambre; **to s. s.o. round the town,** faire visiter *ou* faire voir la ville à qn; **we were shown over the house,** on nous a fait visiter la maison; **to s. s.o. into a room,** introduire *ou* faire entrer qn dans une pièce;

(c) montrer (*des qualités*); manifester (*ses sentiments etc*); témoigner (*sa reconnaissance etc*); laisser voir, laisser paraître (*ses sentiments*); faire preuve de (*courage, zèle*); (*prove*) prouver, démontrer; **to s. a taste for sth,** témoigner d'un goût pour qch; **his face showed his delight,** son visage annonçait sa joie; **these remarks show how worried the government is,** ces remarques témoignent de l'inquiétude du gouvernement; **she showed no sign of having heard anything,** elle n'a manifesté en aucune façon avoir rien entendu; **he shows his age,** il accuse *ou* il fait (bien) son âge; **to s. oneself (to be) a coward,** se montrer lâche; **she showed herself to be a hard worker,** elle s'est révélée être dure à la tâche; **he showed me no mercy,** il n'a fait preuve d'aucune pitié envers moi; **time will s.,** qui vivra verra; **his round shoulders s. his age,** son dos voûté accuse *ou* révèle son âge; **a mere glance will s. that ...,** il suffit d'un coup d'œil pour se rendre compte que ...; **it only** *or* **all goes to s. that ...,** ce qui prouve que ...; **it just shows you how lucky we are,** ça vous montre la chance que nous avons; *F* **I'll s. you!,** je vous apprendrai!; **to s. s.o. how to do sth,** montrer à qn comment faire qch; *Jur* **to s. cause** *or* **reason,** (*set out one's reasons*) exposer ses raisons; (*offer valid reasons*) offrir des raisons valables.

2 *vi* se montrer, paraître, se voir; **the buds are beginning to s.,** les bourgeons commencent à se montrer *ou* à paraître; **your slip's showing,** votre jupon dépasse; **she lets her feelings s. too much,** elle laisse trop voir ses sentiments; **it shows in your face,** cela se voit *ou* se lit sur votre visage; **she's used to getting what she wants — it shows!,** elle a l'habitude d'obtenir ce qu'elle veut – ça se voit!; **it doesn't s.,** ça ne se voit pas, on ne dirait pas; **to s. to advantage,** faire bonne figure; *F* **to s. willing,** faire preuve de bonne volonté; **ah well, it all goes to s.,** eh oui, c'est la vie!

►**show in** *vtsep* (*escort inside*) faire entrer (*qn*).

►**show off 1** *vtsep* **(a)**(*flaunt*) faire parade *ou* montre *ou* étalage de (*qch*); **he likes to s. off his muscles/knowledge,** il aime bien exhiber ses muscles/connaissances; **she was showing off her new car,** elle exhibait sa nouvelle voiture; **(b)** (*show to advantage*) faire valoir, mettre en valeur (*qch*); **coat that shows off the figure well,** manteau qui marque *ou* dessine bien la taille; **wearing white shows off a tan,** porter du blanc met le bronzage en valeur. **2** *vi* (*try to impress*) (*with clothes, possessions etc*) parader, se pavaner; (*with skills*) se donner des airs, *F* faire de l'épate; **to s. off in front of s.o.,** chercher à épater qn; **stop showing off!,** cessez de faire l'important *ou* de vous donner des airs!; **you don't have to drive that fast, you're just showing off,** ce n'est pas la peine de conduire aussi vite, tu cherches juste à nous épater.

►**show out** *vtsep* (*escort out*) reconduire (*qn*), accompagner (*qn*) jusqu'à la porte.

►**show up 1** *vtsep* **(a)** (*reveal*) démasquer, dénoncer (*un imposteur etc*); révéler (*un défaut etc*); **he's been shown up,** le voilà grillé; **(b)** (*shame*) faire honte à, embarrasser; (*deliberately humiliate*) humilier, vexer; **you're always showing me up in front of other people!,** (*embarrassing me*) tu me mets toujours dans l'embarras devant les gens!; **(c)** (*escort upstairs*) accompagner en haut. **2** *vi* **(a)** (*be evident*) se dessiner, se détacher, ressortir (*sur un fond*); **the dirt really shows up on a white carpet,** la saleté ressort vraiment sur une moquette blanche; **(b)** *F* (*arrive*) venir; **they'll s. up at twelve,** ils s'amèneront à midi; **he showed up in a three piece suit,** il est arrivé en costume trois pièces; **you're the boss, you really ought to s. up,** tu es le patron, tu devrais vraiment faire acte de présence.

showbiz ['ʃəʊbɪz] *n F* industrie *f ou* monde *m* du spectacle, showbiz *m*; **s. personality,** personnalité *f* du showbiz *ou* du monde du spectacle.

showboat ['ʃəʊbəʊt] *n US Arch* bateau-théâtre *m*, *pl* bateaux-théâtres (*sur le Mississippi*).

showcase ['ʃəʊkeɪs] *n Com* vitrine *f*, montre *f*; *Fig* **the exhibition will be a s. for Italy's best furniture designers,** l'exposition sera la vitrine de tous les meilleurs créateurs de mobilier d'Italie.

showdown ['ʃəʊdaʊn] *n* **(a)** *F* (*confrontation*) confrontation *f*, déballage *m*; **(b)** *Cards* étalement *m* de son jeu (*sur la table*).

shower[1] ['ʃəʊər] *n* exposant, -ante (*à une exposition etc*).

shower[2] ['ʃaʊər] *n* **(a)** (*of rain*) averse *f*; (*sudden*) giboulée *f*; volée *f* (*de coups, de pierres*); gerbe *f* (*d'étincelles*); avalanche *f* (*d'injures*); **(heavy) s.,** ondée *f*; **(b)** (*act, device*) douche *f*; **to have** *or* **take a s.,** prendre une douche, se doucher; **he was in the s. for half an hour,** il est resté une demi-heure sous la douche; *Old-fashioned* **s. bath,** bain-douche *m*, *pl* bains-douches; **s. cabinet,** cabine *f* de douche; **s. curtain,** rideau *m* de douche; **s. enclosure,** bac *m* à douche; **s. gel,** gel *m* de douche; **s. head,** pommeau *m* de la douche; **s. unit,** bloc-douche *m*, *pl* blocs-douches; **(c)** *Astron* **meteor s.,** essaim *m* (de météores); **(d)** *Am F* (*party*) réception *f* où chacun apporte un cadeau (*de noce etc*); **(e)** *Br F* **what a s.!,** quelle bande *ou* quel tas de crétins!

shower[3] 1 *vt* verser; faire tomber (*de l'eau etc*) par ondées; **to s. blows on s.o.,** faire pleuvoir des coups sur qn; **to s. gifts/honours on s.o.,** combler qn de cadeaux/d'honneurs; **to s. questions on s.o.,** assaillir qn de questions; **to s. invitations on s.o., to s. s.o. with invitations,** accabler qn d'invitations. **2** *vi* (*take a shower*) prendre une douche, se doucher.

►**shower down** *vi* (*of rocks*) tomber; *Fig* (*of compliments, insults*) pleuvoir; **rocks showered down on us,** des pierres s'abattèrent sur nous.

showerproof ['ʃaʊəpruːf] *adj Tex* imperméabilisé.

showery ['ʃaʊərɪ] *adj* (*temps*) pluvieux; **it's s. (weather),** le temps est à l'averse.

showground ['ʃəʊgraʊnd] *n* (*fairground*) champ *m* de foire; (*for equestrian event etc*) terrain *m* de concours hippique *etc*.

showiness ['ʃəʊɪnɪs] *n* faste *m*, ostentation *f*; (*of jewellery*) clinquant *m*; (*of dress, decoration*) luxe criard *ou* tapageur.

showing ['ʃəʊɪŋ] *n* **(a)** (*exhibition*) exposition *f*, manifestation *f*, témoignage *m* (*de ses sentiments etc*); **(b)** (*of film*) projection *f*; **the first s. will be ...,** la première projection aura lieu ...; **(c)** (*performance*) performance *f*; **a poor s. by our team,** une déplorable performance de la part de notre équipe; **on this s. we don't stand a chance,** vu cette performance, on n'a pas une chance; **(d)** *esp Fml* **on your own s.,** (*admission*) comme vous le dites vous-même.

showman, *pl* **-men** ['ʃəʊmən] *n* (*at fair*) forain *m*; **he's a real s.,** il a le sens du spectacle.

showmanship ['ʃəʊmənʃɪp] *n* (*of person*) sens *m* du spectacle; **the s. of the act,** le numéro spectaculaire; **it's just s.,** c'est du cinéma.

shown *see* **SHOW[3]**.

show-off ['ʃəʊɒf] *n F* (*person*) poseur, -euse, m'as-tu-vu(e); **John's a terrible s.-off,** John est un sacré prétentieux; **don't be a s.-off,** (*with clothes, possessions*) arrête de parader; (*with skills*) arrête de te donner des airs *ou F* de faire de l'épate.

showpiece ['ʃəʊpiːs] *n* objet *m ou* monument *m etc* de grand intérêt; (*in exhibition etc*) article *m* d'exposition *ou* de vitrine.

showplace ['ʃəʊpleɪs] *n* (*scenic place*) endroit *m* pittoresque; (*monument*) monument *m* d'intérêt architectural *ou* touristique.

showring ['ʃəʊrɪŋ] *n* (*at exhibition*) arène *f* d'exposition; (*at auction*) arène de vente (*de chevaux etc*); (*at equestrian event*) arène de concours hippique.

showroom ['ʃəʊruːm] *n* salle *f ou* salon *m ou* magasin *m* d'exposition (*d'une maison de commerce*); salle de démonstration (*de voitures etc*).

showy ['ʃəʊɪ] *adj* (*appearance, dress*) voyant; *Pej* tapageur, tape-à-l'œil *inv*; (*jewellery*) clinquant; (*decoration, wallpaper*) criard, tape-à-l'œil.

shrapnel ['ʃræpn(ə)l] *n Mil* **(a)** (*projectile*) shrapnel *m*, obus *m* à balles *ou* à mitraille; **(b)** (*fragments*) éclats *mpl* d'obus; **s. wound,** blessure provoquée par des éclats d'obus.

shred[1] [ʃred] *n* brin *m*; lambeau *m*, fragment *m* (*de tissu etc*); petit morceau (*de viande etc*); **to tear sth (in)to shreds,** (*into small pieces*) déchiqueter qch; (*into strips*) mettre qch en lambeaux; **to tear s.o.'s reputation** *or* **s.o. to shreds,** déchirer qn à belles dents; **to tear s.o.'s argument/a play/*etc* to shreds,** démolir l'argument de qn/une œuvre/*etc*; **his reputation was in shreds,** sa réputation était ruinée; **his argument was in shreds,** son argument était réduit à néant; **her dress was all in shreds,** sa robe était tout en lambeaux; **there isn't a s. of**

evidence, il n'y a pas la moindre preuve; **not a s. of truth,** pas un grain de vérité; **without a s. of clothing on,** complètement nu.
shred² *vt* (**-dd-**) déchirer (*qch*) en lambeaux; déchiqueter (*des documents confidentiels*); (*in papermaking*) effilocher (*des chiffons*).
shredder ['ʃredər] *n* (*device*) (*for confidential documents*) déchiqueteuse *f*.
shredding ['ʃredɪŋ] *n* déchiquetage *m* (*de tissu, de documents confidentiels*); effilochage *m* (*de chiffons*).
shrew [ʃruː] *n* **(a)** (*animal*) musaraigne *f*; **(b)** *Pej* (*woman*) mégère *f*, chipie *f*.
shrewd [ʃruːd] *adj* (*person etc*) sagace, perspicace, fin; (*homme d'affaires*) d'une grande acuité; **he's a s. man,** c'est une fine mouche; **s. answer,** réponse adroite; **I've got a s. idea that ...,** je suis porté à croire que ...; **to make a s. guess,** deviner juste; **I could make a pretty s. guess,** ce n'est pas difficile à deviner.
shrewdly ['ʃruːdlɪ] *adv* avec perspicacité, avec sagacité.
shrewdness ['ʃruːdnɪs] *n* sagacité *f*, perspicacité *f*, acuité *f*, finesse *f*.
shrewish ['ʃruːɪʃ] *adj Pej* (*woman*) acariâtre, querelleux.
shriek¹ ['ʃriːk] *n* cri aigu *ou* perçant (*d'une personne, d'un animal*); **shrieks of laughter,** grands éclats de rire.
shriek² **1** *vi* pousser un cri aigu *ou* des cris aigus; **to s. with laughter,** rire aux éclats, s'esclaffer, pouffer (de rire). **2** *vt* **to s. (out) a warning,** pousser un cri d'avertissement.
shrieking ['ʃriːkɪŋ] *n* cris aigus *ou* perçants.
shrift [ʃrɪft] *n Arch* confession *f* et absolution *f*; *Fig* **to give s.o. short s.,** expédier vite qn, *F* envoyer promener qn; *F* **I got short s. from him,** il m'a envoyé promener; *Iron* il m'a bien reçu.
shrike [ʃraɪk] *n* (*bird*) pie-grièche *f*, *pl* pies-grièches.
shrill¹ [ʃrɪl] *adj* (*voice, sound etc*) aigu, strident, perçant; (*complaint etc*) ardent; **in a s. voice,** d'une voix perçante; **s. whistle,** coup de sifflet strident.
shrill² *vi Lit* pousser *ou* avoir un son aigu *ou* strident; **a whistle shrilled,** un coup de sifflet déchira l'air.
shrillness ['ʃrɪlnɪs] *n* acuité *f*, stridence *f* (*d'un son*).
shrilly ['ʃrɪlɪ] *adv* d'un ton aigu.
shrimp¹ [ʃrɪmp] *n* (*crustacean*) crevette *f* (grise); *F* (*person*) nabot, -ote; **s. boat,** crevettier *m*.
shrimp² *vi* **to go shrimping, to s.,** pêcher la crevette, faire la pêche à la crevette.
shrine [ʃraɪn] *n* **(a)** (*place of pilgrimage*) lieu *m* de pèlerinage; **(b)** (*saint's tomb*) tombeau *m* de saint(e); **(c)** (*reliquary*) chasse *f*, reliquaire *m*.
shrink¹ [ʃrɪŋk] *n* **(a)** (*act of shrinking*) rétrécissement *m* (*d'un tissu*); retrait *m* (*du bois etc*); **(b)** *F* (*psychiatrist*) psy *mf*.
shrink² *v* (*pt* **shrank** [ʃræŋk]; *pp* **shrunk** [ʃrʌŋk], *as adj* **shrunken** ['ʃrʌŋk(ə)n]) **1** *vi* **(a)** (*become smaller*) (se) rétrécir, rapetisser; (*of material etc*) rétrécir; (*of person*) se faire tout petit (*par timidité etc*); **he is beginning to s. (with age),** il commence à se tasser; **to s. in the wash,** rétrécir au lavage; **my income has shrunk,** mon revenu s'est amoindri *ou* a diminué; **to s. into oneself,** rentrer en soi-même; **(b)** (*move away*) reculer; **to s. from sth,** reculer devant *ou* se dérober à qch; **to s. in horror,** reculer d'horreur; **to s. from doing sth,** reculer *ou* répugner à faire qch; **2** *vt* contracter (*du métal*); rétrécir (*un tissu*); **fully shrunk material,** tissu irrétrécissable.
▶shrink back *vi* (*move away*) avoir un mouvement de recul; **to s. back in horror,** reculer d'horreur.
shrinkage ['ʃrɪŋkɪdʒ] *n* retrait *m* (*du bois*); *Tex etc* rétrécissement *m*.
shrinker ['ʃrɪŋkər] *n* **head s.,** (*in anthropology*) réducteur *m* de têtes; *F* (*psychiatrist*) psy *mf*.
shrinking ['ʃrɪŋkɪŋ] *n* **(a)** (*act of becoming smaller*) = **SHRINKAGE**; **s. away,** rétrécissement *m*, rapetissement *m*; **(b)** (*act of moving back*) **s. from sth,** recul *m* devant qch; répugnance *f* à une action.
shrink-wrap [ʃrɪŋk'ræp] *vt* emballer sous pellicule plastique.
shrink-wrapping [ʃrɪŋk'ræpɪŋ] *n* **(a)** (*process*) emballage *m* sous pellicule plastique; **(b)** (*material*) pellicule *f* plastique.
shrive [ʃraɪv] *vt* (*pt* **shrove** [ʃrəʊv]; *pp* **shriven** ['ʃrɪv(ə)n]) *Arch* confesser, absoudre (*un pénitent*).
shrivel ['ʃrɪv(ə)l] *v* (**-ll-**, *US* **-l-**) **1** *vt* rider, ratatiner, recroqueviller (*la peau, une pomme etc*); (*of sun*) brûler, hâler (*les plantes*); **the old man's shrivelled face,** le visage ratatiné *ou* ridé du vieillard. **2** *vi* se rider, se ratatiner, se recroqueviller.
▶shrivel up *vi & vtsep* = **SHRIVEL**.
shroud¹ [ʃraʊd] *n* **(a)** (*for dead body*) linceul *m*, suaire *m*; **in a s. of mystery,** enveloppé de mystère; *Lit* **under a s. of darkness,** sous les voiles de la nuit; **(b)** *MecE etc* bouclier *m*, blindage *m*.
shroud² *n Nau* hauban *m*; **s. (lines),** (*of parachute*) suspentes *fpl*.
shroud³ *vt* ensevelir (*un cadavre*); *Fig* envelopper, voiler (*qch*) (**in,** de); **shrouded in mist/mystery,** enveloppé de brume/mystère; **shrouded in gloom,** (*place*) enténébré; (*person*) plongé dans la tristesse.
shrove [ʃrəʊv] **(a)** *see* **SHRIVE**; **(b)** **S. Tuesday,** Mardi gras.
Shrovetide ['ʃrəʊvtaɪd] *n Rel* les jours gras.
shrub [ʃrʌb] *n* (*plant*) arbrisseau *m*, arbuste *m*.
shrubbery ['ʃrʌbərɪ] *n* massif *m* d'arbustes; **the ball disappeared into the s.,** la balle disparut dans les massifs (d'arbustes).
shrubby ['ʃrʌbɪ] *adj* **(a)** (*resembling a shrub*) qui ressemble à un arbuste *ou* un arbrisseau; **s. tree,** arbrisseau; **(b)** (*covered in shrubs*) couvert d'arbustes.
shrug¹ [ʃrʌg] *n* **s. (of the shoulders),** haussement *m* d'épaules; **with a s. of his shoulders,** en haussant les épaules.
shrug² *v* (**-gg-**) **1** *vt* **to s. one's shoulders,** hausser les épaules. **2** *vi* hausser les épaules.
▶shrug off *vtsep* (*treat as unimportant*) ignorer (*un problème, les sentiments des autres etc*); dédaigner, mépriser (*un danger*).
shrunken ['ʃrʌŋkən] *adj Tex* rétréci; (*features etc*) ratatiné; **s. with age,** tassé par l'âge; **shrunken heads,** (*in anthropology*) têtes réduites.
shuck¹ [ʃʌk] *Am* **1** *n* cosse *f*, gousse *f* (*de petits pois etc*); spathe *f* (*de maïs*); écale *f* (*de noix etc*); coquille *f* (*d'huître, de palourde*). **2** *int F* **shucks!,** mince (alors)!, flûte (alors)!
shuck² *vt Am* **(a)** écosser (*des petits pois etc*); écaler (*des noix*); éplucher (*du maïs*); écailler (*des huîtres*); ôter (*un vêtement*); **(b)** = **SHUCK OFF**.
▶shuck off *vtsep Am* (*rid oneself of*) se défaire de (*une habitude*).
shudder¹ ['ʃʌdər] *n* frisson *m*, frémissement *m*, frissonnement *m*; *F* **it gives me the shudders,** j'en ai des frissons.
shudder² *vi* frissonner (**with cold/horror,** de froid/d'horreur); (*of ship etc*) vibrer; **I s. to think of it** *or* **at the thought of it,** j'ai des frissons rien que d'y penser; **I s. to think what went into this soup,** je tremble à l'idée de ce qu'il peut y avoir dans cette soupe; **I s. to think,** je n'ose y penser; **the bus shuddered to a halt,** le bus s'immobilisa en vibrant.
shuddering ['ʃʌdərɪŋ] *n* **(a)** (*of person*) frisson *m*, frémissement *m*, frissonnement *m*; **(b)** (*of machine, vehicle, ship etc*) vibration *f*.
shuffle¹ ['ʃʌf(ə)l] *n* **(a)** traînement *m* de pieds, marche traînante; (*in dancing*) frottement *m* de pieds; **soft shoe s.,** = danse de music-hall (*exécutée en chaussons*); **(b)** *Cards* battement *m*, mélange *m*; **to give the cards a s.,** battre *ou* mélanger les cartes; **(c)** (*evasiveness*) atermoiement *m*, tergiversations *fpl*; (*evasive act*) faux-fuyant *m*, *pl* faux-fuyants; **(d)** *Pol* **Cabinet s.,** remaniement ministériel.
shuffle² **1** *vt* (*mix*) mêler (*des papiers etc*); *Cards* battre, mélanger (*les cartes*); **to s. one's feet,** traîner les pieds; **he stood there shuffling his feet,** il se tenait là à frotter ses pieds contre le sol. **2** *vi* (*drag one's feet*) traîner les pieds; **she shuffled into the room,** elle entra dans la pièce en traînant les pieds.
▶shuffle along *vi* (*walk dragging one's feet*) avancer lentement *ou* en traînant les pieds.
▶shuffle off **1** *vi* (*walk away dragging one's feet*) s'en aller en traînant les pieds; **the badger shuffled off into the bushes,** le blaireau disparut dans les buissons en trottinant. **2** *vtsep* **(a)** (*set aside*) se débarrasser (*d'une responsabilité*); **(b)** (*take off in a hurry*) ôter (*ses vêtements*) à la hâte.
shuffling ['ʃʌflɪŋ] *adj* (*person*) qui traîne les pieds; (*gait*) traînant.
shun¹ [ʃʌn] *int Mil etc F* (*attention!*) garde à vous!
shun² *vt* (**-nn-**) fuir, éviter (*qn, qch*); fuir (*la publicité*); **to s. society,** fuir le monde; **to s. everybody,** éviter tout le monde.
shunt¹ [ʃʌnt] *n* **(a)** *Rail* garage *m*, manœuvre *f* (*d'un train*); **(b)** *El* shunt *m*, dérivation *f*.
shunt² **1** *vt* **(a)** *Rail* manœuvrer (*un train, des wagons*); **to s. a train onto a siding,** aiguiller un train sur une voie de

garage; *F* **we were shunted into another room,** on nous a parqués dans une autre pièce; **the responsibility was shunted back and forth between departments,** la responsabilité a été renvoyée de service en service; **(b)** *El* shunter, dériver (*un circuit etc*); monter (*un condensateur*) en dérivation; **(c)** *F* (*to push*) pousser; **he just shunted me out of his way,** il m'a poussé hors de son chemin; **s. the salt over, will you?,** envoie-moi le sel! **2** *vi Rail* (*of train*) se garer.

shunting ['ʃʌntɪŋ] *n* **(a)** *Rail* manœuvre *f*; (*changing track*) changement *m* de voie; **s. engine,** locomotive *f ou* machine *f* de manœuvre; **s. operations,** manœuvres de triage; **s. yard,** gare *f* de triage; **(b)** *El* dérivation *f*, shuntage *m*.

shush¹ [ʃʌʃ] *int* chut!

shush² *vt* faire taire (*qn*).

shut¹ [ʃʌt] *adj* fermé.

shut² *v* (*pt & pp* **shut**; *prp* **shutting**) **1** *vt* fermer (*une porte, un magasin, une boîte, un livre etc*); **to s. the door on s.o.** *or* **in s.o.'s face,** fermer la porte au nez de qn; **to find the door shut,** trouver la porte fermée, trouver porte close; **to s. one's eyes,** fermer les yeux; **to s. one's finger in the door,** se pincer le doigt dans la porte; **we're shut in by hills,** nous sommes entourés de collines; *F* **to keep one's mouth shut,** avoir la bouche cousue; **to s. s.o.'s mouth (for him),** faire taire qn; *Sl* **s. your mouth!,** la ferme!, ta gueule! **2** *vi* (*of door*) (se) fermer; (*of shop*) fermer; **the door won't s.,** la porte ne ferme pas; **the door shut to,** la porte s'est fermée (toute seule).

▶**shut down 1** *vtsep* fermer (*une usine, un aéroport etc*); *Tech* couper (*la vapeur, l'électricité*); *Av* arrêter (*le moteur*). **2** *vi* (*of factory etc*) (*through lack of work*) chômer; (*for holiday*) fermer; (*permanently*) fermer ses portes; (*of TV station etc for the night*) arrêter ses programmes.

▶**shut in** *vtsep* (*confine in a place*) enfermer (*qn, qch*).

▶**shut off** *vtsep* **(a)** (*stop*) couper, interrompre, intercepter (*la vapeur*); fermer (*l'eau*); *Aut* couper, arrêter (*le moteur*); **(b)** (*isolate*) séparer, isoler (**from,** de); **she shut herself off from other people,** elle s'isolait du reste des gens; **to be shut off from society,** être exclu du monde; **you shouldn't s. yourself off so,** tu ne devrais pas t'isoler comme ça.

▶**shut out** *vtsep* **(a)** (*exclude*) exclure (*qn, l'air, la lumière*); étouffer (*la concurrence*); chasser (*un souvenir etc*); **the trees s. out the view,** les arbres bouchent la vue; **to s. s.o. out (from sth),** exclure qn (de qch); **I've shut her out of my life,** je l'ai sortie de ma vie; **(b)** (*keep outside*) **to s. s.o. out (of doors),** fermer la porte à qn; **I've s. myself out (of my room),** je me suis enfermé dehors; **he's taken the keys and has shut me out,** il a pris les clefs et du coup je suis enfermé dehors; **(c)** *Am Sp* blanchir.

▶**shut up 1** *vtsep* **(a)** (*confine*) enfermer (*qn, qch*); **to s. oneself up,** s'enfermer chez soi; **to s. s.o. up (in prison),** emprisonner qn; **(b) to s. up shop,** (*close shop at end of day*) fermer le magasin *ou* la boutique; (*close shop permanently*) fermer boutique; (*of theatre etc*) fermer ses portes; **(c)** (*close completely*) condamner (*une porte, une pièce*); obstruer (*un orifice etc*); **to s. up a house,** (*when going away*) boucler une maison; **(d)** *F* (*make quiet*) faire taire (*qn*); réduire (*qn*) au silence; **s. those kids up!,** faites taire ces gamins!; **that ought to s. him up,** (*stop him boasting*) ça devrait lui rabattre son clapet; (*stop him complaining*) ça devrait arrêter ses complaintes. **2** *vi F* se taire; **s. up!,** taisez-vous!; *Sl* la ferme!, ta gueule!

shutdown ['ʃʌtdaʊn] *n* (*of factory*) (*temporary*) chômage *m*; (*permanent*) fermeture *f*.

shut-eye ['ʃʌtaɪ] *n F* somme *m*, roupillon *m*; **to have a bit of s.-e.,** faire un (petit) somme.

shut-in [ʃʌt'ɪn] *adj* **to have a s.-in feeling,** (*in room etc*) se sentir enfermé; (*in relationship*) se sentir prisonnier, -ière.

shut-off [ʃʌt'ɒf] *adj* **to have a s.-off feeling,** se sentir isolé.

shut-out ['ʃʌtaʊt] *n* **(a)** *Ind* lock-out *m inv*; **(b)** *Cards* **s.o. bid,** ouverture préventive; **(c)** *Am Sp* blanchissage *m*.

shutter¹ ['ʃʌtər] *n* **(a)** volet *m*; *Rel* guichet *m* (*de confessionnal*); **slatted shutters,** persiennes *f*; **folding shutters,** volets pliants *ou* brisés; **to open/close the shutters,** ouvrir/fermer les volets; **to put up the shutters,** fermer la *ou* les devanture(s); mettre les volets (*d'un magasin*); *Fig* (*close shop*) fermer boutique; **(b)** *Phot* obturateur *m*; **to set/release the s.,** armer/déclencher l'obturateur; **s. speed,** vitesse *f* d'obturation; **(c)** *Metal* écluse *f*; *HydE* hausse *f* (*de vanne*); **(d)** *Constr* banche *f* (*pour béton*).

shutter² *vt* mettre les volets à (*une fenêtre, une maison*); fermer les volets de (*une maison etc*); **shuttered window,** fenêtre aux volets fermés *ou* clos.

shutting ['ʃʌtɪŋ] *n* (*act of closing*) fermeture *f* (*d'une porte, d'une boîte etc*).

shutting down *n* (*of factory*) (*temporary*) chômage *m*; (*permanent*) fermeture *f*.

shutting off *n* interruption *f* (*de la vapeur*); fermeture *f* (*de l'eau*).

shutting out *n* exclusion *f* (*de qn, de l'air*).

shuttle¹ ['ʃʌt(ə)l] *n* **(a)** *Tex Sewing etc* navette *f*; **(b)** (*train, bus, plane etc*) navette *f*; **s. service,** service *m* de navettes, navette; *Astronaut* **space s.,** navette spatiale; **s. diplomacy,** série *f* de visites diplomatiques; *MecE* **s. (movement),** (mouvement *m* de) va-et-vient *m inv*; *Rail* **s. train,** navette *f*.

shuttle² 1 *vi* faire la navette, aller et venir (**between,** entre). **2** *vt* **to s. s.o. back and forth** *or* **to and fro,** faire aller et venir qn, envoyer qn à droite et à gauche.

shuttlecock ['ʃʌt(ə)lkɒk] *n Sp* volant *m*.

shy¹ [ʃaɪ] *n* (*movement*) écart *m*, faux bond (*d'un cheval*).

shy² *n F* **(a)** (*throw*) jet *m*, lancement *m* (*d'une pierre etc*); (*at fairs*) **5p a s.,** 5p le coup; **(b)** *Old-fashioned* (*attempt*) essai *m*, tentative *f* (*pour atteindre qch*); **to have a s. at doing sth,** s'essayer à faire qch.

shy³ *adj* (*comp* **shyer**, *superl* **shyest**; *occ* **shier, shiest**) **(a)** (*bird, child etc*) sauvage, farouche; (*horse etc*) ombrageux; (*person*) timide; **don't be s., bring your chairs nearer,** ne soyez pas timides, approchez vos chaises; **to make s.o. s.,** intimider qn; **to be s. of people,** être gêné *ou* mal à l'aise parmi les gens; **to fight s. of,** se défier de, se méfier de (*qch*); renâcler à (*une besogne*); **to be s. of doing sth,** hésiter à faire qch; **(b)** *Am* **to be s. of,** (*to be deficient*) manquer de (*qch*); être à court (*d'argent*); **we're still 500 dollars s.,** nous sommes encore à court de 500 dollars.

shy⁴ *vi* (*pt & pp* **shied**; *prp* **shying**) (*of horse*) s'effaroucher; **to s. at sth,** (*of horse*) s'effaroucher devant qch; (*of person*) renâcler devant qch.

shy⁵ *v* (*pt & pp* **shied**; *prp* **shying**) *F* **1** *vi* (*throw*) lancer *ou* jeter qch (**at,** à). **2** *vt* (*throw*) lancer (*une pierre*) (**at s.o.,** à qn).

▶**shy away** *vi* (*retreat in fear, nervousness*) s'effaroucher (**from,** de); **he has shied away from driving since the accident,** il évite de conduire depuis l'accident.

Shylock ['ʃaɪlɒk] *n* usurier *m*.

shyly ['ʃaɪlɪ] *adv* timidement; (*to blush etc*) modestement.

shyness ['ʃaɪnɪs] *n* timidité *f*, réserve *f* (*de qn*); caractère *m* farouche (*d'un animal, de qn*); **to lose one's s.,** s'enhardir.

shyster ['ʃaɪstər] *n esp Am Pej F* (*lawyer*) avocassier *m*; (*businessman*) homme d'affaires véreux.

SI [e'saɪ] *n Tech* (*abbr* **Système International**) SI *m*; **SI units,** unités *fpl* de SI.

si [siː] *n Mus* si *m*.

Siam [saɪ'æm] *n Hist* Siam *m*.

Siamese [saɪə'miːz] **1** *adj Hist* siamois; **S. cat,** siamois *m*; **S. twins,** frères siamois; sœurs siamoises. **2** *n* **(a)** *Hist* (*person*) Siamois, -oise; **(b)** *Ling Hist* siamois; **(c)** (*cat*) siamois *m*.

Siberia [saɪ'bɪərɪə] *n* Sibérie *f*.

Siberian [saɪ'bɪərɪən] **1** *adj* sibérien. **2** *n* Sibérien, -ienne.

sibilant ['sɪbɪlənt] **1** *adj* sifflant. **2** *n Ling* sifflante *f*.

sibling ['sɪblɪŋ] *n* = l'un(e) de deux ou de plusieurs enfants qui ont les mêmes parents ou le même père ou la même mère.

sibyl ['sɪbɪl] *n* sibylle *f*.

sibylline ['sɪbɪlaɪn] *adj* (*livre etc*) sibyllin.

sic [sɪk] *adv* sic, ainsi.

siccative ['sɪkətɪv] *adj & n* siccatif *m*.

Sicilian [sɪ'sɪlɪən] **1** *adj* sicilien. **2** *n* Sicilien, -ienne.

Sicily ['sɪsɪlɪ] *n* Sicile *f*.

sick [sɪk] **1** *adj* **(a)** (*ill*) malade; *F* (*humour*) noir; (*plaisanterie*) macabre; **to be s.,** être malade; **to report s.,** se faire porter malade; **you have to be pretty s. to desecrate s.o.'s grave,** il faut être vraiment malade pour profaner la tombe de qn; **to have a s. mind,** avoir un esprit malade; **s. bay,** infirmerie *f*; *Nau* poste *m* des malades; **s. bed,** lit *m* de malade; **s. benefit,** prestations *fpl* en cas de maladie; **s. call** *or* **parade,** visite *f* des malades; **s. leave,** congé *m* de maladie; *Mil etc* congé de réforme; **s. list,** rôle *m ou* état *m* des malades; **s. note,** mot *m* d'excuse (expliquant qu'on est malade); **s. pay,** allocation *f* de maladie; **(b) to feel s.,** avoir mal au cœur; avoir des nausées; **he**

was as s. as a cat *or* **a dog,** il a été malade comme un chien; *F* **it makes me s.,** cela m'écœure; *Sl* **you make me s.!,** tu m'écœures!; *Am* **to be s. to one's stomach,** avoir mal au cœur; **s. feeling,** malaise *m*; **s. headache,** migraine *f*; *F* **he was very s. at** *or* **about failing his exam,** son échec l'a tout retourné; **she looked pretty s. when she didn't get the prize,** elle avait l'air plutôt écœuré quand elle n'a pas reçu le prix; **to be s. with jealousy,** être malade de jalousie; **to grow s. of sth,** se dégoûter de qch; **to be s. of sth,** être las de qch; **I'm s. of spaghetti every night/your constant complaining,** j'en ai assez de manger des spaghetti tous les soirs/que vous vous plaignez sans cesse; **I'm s. and tired** *or* **I'm s. to death of it,** j'en ai assez, j'en ai plein le dos, j'en ai marre;

(c) (*discouraged*) *Lit* **to be s. at heart,** avoir le cœur navré.

2 *n* **(a) the s.,** (*used as pl*) les malades *mpl*;

(b) *Sl* (*vomit*) vomi *m*.

►**sick up** *vtsep* (*vomit*) vomir, rendre (*qch*).

sicken ['sɪk(ə)n] **1** *vi* tomber malade (**of, with,** de); (*of plants*) languir, dépérir; **to be sickening for an illness/***F* **for sth,** couver une maladie/qch; *Fig* **to s. of sth,** se lasser *ou* se dégoûter de qch. **2** *vt* (*make ill*) rendre (*qn*) malade; (*make nauseous*) donner mal au cœur à (*qn*), donner envie de vomir à (*qn*); *Fig F* **his business methods s. me,** ses procédés me révoltent *ou* m'écœurent *ou* me rendent malade.

sickening ['sɪknɪŋ] *adj* écœurant, dégoûtant; (*odeur*) nauséabond; (*peur*) qui serre le cœur; (*spectacle*) révoltant; *F* **how perfectly s.!,** c'est vraiment écœurant!; **she's so good at maths — I know, it's s.,** elle est tellement bonne en maths — je sais, c'est écœurant; **there was a s. crunch as the boats collided,** il y a eu un craquement sinistre lorsque les bateaux sont entrés en collision.

sickeningly ['sɪknɪŋlɪ] *adv* de façon à vous soulever le cœur *ou* à vous écœurer.

sickle ['sɪk(ə)l] *n Agr* faucille *f*; *Pol* **the hammer and s.,** la faucille et le marteau; *Med* **s. cell anaemia,** drépanocytose *f*.

sickliness ['sɪklɪnɪs] *n* **(a)** état maladif (*de qn*); **(b)** pâleur *f* (*de teint*); **(c)** goût écœurant (*d'un gâteau*).

sickly ['sɪklɪ] *adj* **(a)** (*of child*) maladif, souffreteux, malingre; (*plant*) étiolé; (*colour, light*) faible, pâle; (*complexion*) terreux; (*pallor*) maladif; (*sun*) blafard; (*smile*) pâle; **(b)** (*climate*) malsain, insalubre; **(c)** (*taste, smell etc*) écœurant, nauséabond; (*sentiment*) qui écœure, qui dégoûte; *F* (*story, tune*) d'une sentimentalité outrée; **s. sweet,** douceâtre.

sickness ['sɪknɪs] *n* **(a)** (*illness*) maladie *f*; **sleeping s.,** maladie du sommeil; *Br Admin* **s. benefit,** (*payments*) prestations *fpl* en cas de maladie; (*insurance*) assurance *f* maladie; **(b)** (*nausea*) mal *m* de cœur; **(bouts of) s.,** (*nausea*) nausée(s) *f*(*pl*); (*vomiting*) vomissement(s) *m*(*pl*); **altitude** *or* **mountain s.,** mal des montagnes; **morning s.,** nausées matinales.

sickroom ['sɪkruːm] *n* chambre *f* de malade; (*in school etc*) infirmerie *f*.

side¹ [saɪd] *n* **(a)** (*of person, animal*) côté *m*, flanc *m*; **to be lying on one's s.,** être couché sur le côté; **right/left s.,** côté droit/gauche; **by the s. of s.o.,** à côté de qn; **by** *or* **at my s.,** à côté de moi, à mes côtés; **they were standing s. by s.,** ils se tenaient l'un à côté de l'autre; **they worked s. by s. with their former enemies,** ils ont travaillé en collaboration avec leurs anciens ennemis; *F* **to split** *or* **burst one's sides (with laughing),** se tordre (de rire); **s. of beef,** demi-carcasse *f* de bœuf; **s. of bacon,** flèche *f* de lard; **s. pocket,** poche *f* de côté; **s. whiskers,** favoris *mpl*;

(b) côté *m* (*of house, box, triangle*); pan *m* (*d'un objet taillé, d'un comble*); flanc *m*, versant *m* (*d'une montagne*); paroi *f* (*d'un fossé, d'un vase*); bande *f*, bord *m*, côté (*d'un navire*); *Math* membre *m* (*d'une équation*); *Opt* branche *f* (*de lunettes*); **to put two boxes s. by s.,** mettre deux boîtes l'une à côté de l'autre;

(c) (*surface*) côté *m*; face *f* (*d'un disque*); **the right/wrong s. (of sth),** le bon/mauvais côté (de qch); **the right/wrong s. of a fabric,** l'endroit *m*/l'envers *m* d'un tissu; **the under/upper s. of sth,** le dessous/le dessus de qch; **printed on one s. only,** imprimé d'un seul côté; **buttered s. up,** (*of slice of bread*) le côté beurré vers le haut; **the good/bad s. of the business,** le bon/mauvais côté de l'affaire; **the other s. of the picture,** le revers de la médaille; **to look on the bright s. (of things),** voir les choses du bon côté, prendre les choses par le bon côté; **on this s.,** de ce côté(-ci); **on that s.,** de ce côté-là; **on this s. of sth,** de ce côté(-ci) *ou* en deçà de qch; **on that s. of sth,** de ce côté-là *ou* au delà de qch; **on the other s. (of sth),** de l'autre côté (de qch); **with a dog on either s.,** flanqué de deux chiens; **on both sides,** des deux côtés, de part et d'autre; **on all sides, on every s.,** de tous les côtés; (*everywhere*) partout; **on the left/right hand s.,** à (main) gauche/droite; **on the south s.,** du côté sud; **to be on the wrong s. of forty,** avoir les quarante ans sonnés; **it costs the wrong s. of £1,000,** ça coûte plus de 1 000 livres; **the tower leans on** *or* **to one s.,** la tour penche d'un côté; **to put sth on** *or* **to one s.,** mettre qch de côté; **to take s.o. on** *or* **to one s.,** prendre qn à part *ou* en particulier; **to stand on** *or* **to one s.,** se tenir à l'écart *ou* à part; **from all sides, from every s.,** de tous (les) côtés, de toutes parts; **from s. to s.,** d'un côté à l'autre; **he always looks on the gloomy s. of things,** il voit tout en noir; **to be/to get on the right s. of s.o.,** être/se mettre dans les petits papiers de qn; **to get on the wrong s. of s.o.,** prendre qn à rebrousse-poil; **to hear** *or* **look at both sides (of a question),** (*consider both aspects*) considérer les deux aspects d'une question; (*consider arguments for and against*) entendre *ou* envisager le pour et le contre; **you haven't heard my s. of the story!,** vous n'avez pas entendu ma version de l'histoire!; **there are many sides to her character,** son caractère est très complexe; **his good s.,** ses bons côtés; **her speech was a bit on the long/short s.,** son discours était plutôt long/court; **the weather's on the cool s.,** il fait plutôt froid; **s. aisle,** (*in church, cathedral*) bas-côté *m*; *Th etc* passage latéral *ou* de côté; *Am* **s. chair,** chaise *f* (*de salle à manger etc*); **s. chapel,** (*in church, cathedral*) chapelle latérale; **s. dish,** entremets *m*, hors d'œuvre *m inv*; **s. door,** porte latérale; *F* **to enter a profession by the s. door,** entrer dans une profession par la petite porte; *Mus* **s. drum,** tambour *m*; **s. effect,** effet *m ou* réaction *f* secondaire (*d'un médicament etc*); **s. entry** *or* **entrance,** entrée *f* de côté; **s. face,** profil *m*; **with a s. glance at her,** en la regardant de côté *ou* du coin de l'œil, en lui jetant un regard en coin; *Gym* **s. horse,** cheval *m* d'arçons; **s. issue,** question *f* d'importance *ou* d'intérêt secondaire; **the s. issues of a question,** les à-côtés d'une question; **s. rail,** rambarde *f* (*de navire*); garde-fou *m* (*de pont*); **s. road,** chemin latéral; (*minor road*) route *f* secondaire; **s. salad,** salade *f* (*pour accompagner un plat principal*); **s. street,** rue latérale *ou* transversale; (*small street*) petite rue; **s. table,** petite table, desserte *f*; **s. view,** vue *f* de profil *ou* de côté;

(d) (*in dispute, match, war etc*) parti *m*; *Sp* équipe *f*, camp *m*; **to be on the right s.,** être du bon parti; **to take sides,** se ranger d'un côté; **to take sides with s.o., to take the s. of s.o.,** se ranger avec *ou* du côté de qn; **he's on our s.,** il est avec nous *ou* de notre parti *ou* de notre côté; **whose s. are you on?,** de quel côté êtes-vous?; **to change sides,** changer de camp, virer de bord; *Pol etc* faire volte-face; **they fought on our s.,** ils se sont battus de notre côté; **they were on the other s.,** (*in war etc*) ils étaient de l'autre côté; **time's on our s.,** le temps travaille pour nous; *Jur* **the other s.,** la partie adverse; *Fb* **a club/national s.,** une équipe locale/nationale; **to pick sides,** tirer les camps; **to let the s. down,** trahir *ou* décevoir ses amis *etc*;

(e) (*lineage*) côté *m*; **on his mother's s.,** du côté maternel *ou* de sa mère;

(f) *Old-fashioned Br F* (*affectation*) **to put on s.,** se donner des airs; **there's no s. to her at all,** elle est authentique;

(g) *Billiards* **running s.,** effet *m* en tête *ou* en avant;

(h) to do a bit of gardening on the s., faire un peu de jardinage (pour qn) dans ses heures libres; *F* **to make sth** *or* **a bit on the s.,** se faire des extras; **profits on the s.,** de la gratte; *Sl* **to have a bit on the s.,** (*have lover*) (*of man*) avoir une petite amie *ou* une maîtresse; (*of woman*) avoir un petit ami *ou* un amant; (*have casual sex*) faire un petit écart.

side² *vi* **to s. with s.o.,** (*fight for same thing*) se ranger du côté de qn, faire cause commune avec qn; (*defend*) prendre la parti de qn; **to s. against s.o.,** prendre parti contre qn, se tourner contre qn.

sideboard ['saɪdbɔːd] *n* **(a)** (*piece of furniture*) buffet *m*; **(b)** *Br F* **sideboards,** (*whiskers*) favoris *mpl*.

sideburns ['saɪdbɜːnz] *npl Am F* (*whiskers*) favoris *mpl*.

sidecar ['saɪdkɑːr] *n* **(a)** side-car *m*, *pl* side-cars (*de motocyclette*); **(b)** *esp Am* (*cocktail*) cocktail composé de cointreau, de cognac et de jus de citron.

-sided [-saɪdɪd] *suff* **a four-s. figure,** une figure à quatre côtés; **a many-s. debate,** un débat avec de nombreux participants; **three-s. contract,** contrat *m* à trois parties *ou* tripartite.

sidekick ['saɪdkɪk] *n F* associé, -ée; *Pej* acolyte *mf*.

sidelight ['saɪdlaɪt] *n* **(a)** *Phot etc* lumière *f* oblique *ou* qui vient de côté; *Fig* **to throw a s. on a subject,** éclairer fortuitement un sujet, donner un aperçu indirect sur un sujet; **(b)** *Constr (window)* fenêtre latérale; **(c) sidelights,** *Aut* feux *mpl* de position; *Nau etc* feux de côté.

sideline¹ ['saɪdlaɪn] *n* **(a)** ligne latérale; *Fb etc* ligne de touche; **to be on the sidelines,** ne pas se mêler à une affaire, rester sur la touche; **to watch from the sidelines,** *Sp* regarder de la ligne de touche; *Fig* regarder en spectateur; **(b)** *(secondary job)* occupation *f* secondaire; **it's just a s.,** *(which earns money)* c'est un petit à-côté; **we sell guide books as a s.,** nous vendons aussi des guides (comme activité secondaire).

sideline² *vt Am Sp (usu passive)* **to be sidelined,** être mis sur *ou* rester sur la touche.

sidelong ['saɪdlɒŋ] **1** *adv (se mouvoir)* obliquement, de côté; *(regarder qn)* de côté, du coin de l'œil. **2** *adj (regard)* oblique, de côté; **to give s.o. a s. glance,** regarder qn de côté *ou* du coin de l'œil.

sidereal [saɪ'dɪərɪəl] *adj Astron* sidéral, -aux.

side-saddle ['saɪdsæd(ə)l] **1** *n* selle *f* de dame *ou* de femme. **2** *adv* **to ride s.-s.,** monter en amazone.

sideshow ['saɪdʃəʊ] *n* **(a)** spectacle forain *(à une foire)*; **(b)** *F* affaire *f* d'importance secondaire.

sideslip¹ ['saɪdslɪp] *n* **(a)** *Aut Cycling Ski* dérapage *m*; **(b)** *Av* glissade *f* (sur l'aile), glissement latéral.

sideslip² *vi* **(a)** *Aut Cycling Ski* déraper; **(b)** *Av* glisser sur l'aile.

sidesman, *pl* **-men** ['saɪdzmən] *n Rel* = marguillier adjoint.

side-splitting ['saɪdsplɪtɪŋ] *adj F (joke)* tordant.

sidestep ['saɪdstep] **1** *vi* faire un pas de côté; *Boxing etc* esquiver. **2** *vt* éviter *(qn)*; *Fig* éviter *(une question)*.

sidestroke ['saɪdstrəʊk] *n Swimming* nage *f* sur le côté.

sideswipe¹ ['saɪdswaɪp] *n* coup *m* sur le côté; **to take a s. at s.o.,** frapper qn sur le côté; *Fig* faire une remarque désagréable sur qn en passant; **that was a s. at the Prime Minister,** c'était une allusion malveillante à propos du Premier Ministre.

sideswipe² *vt* donner un coup dans, cogner *(le côté d'une voiture etc)*.

sidetrack¹ ['saɪdtræk] *n Am Rail* voie *f* de garage; voie secondaire.

sidetrack² *vt* **(a)** *Am Rail* garer *(un train)*, aiguiller *(un train)* sur une voie de garage; **(b)** *Fig (divert from aim)* distraire; *(divert from subject)* faire dévier (**from,** de); **they tried to s. him onto something else,** ils ont essayé de le faire dévier sur un autre sujet; **he's easily sidetracked,** il se laisse facilement distraire; **to be** *or* **get sidetracked,** *(be diverted from one's aim)* se détourner de son but; *(digress)* s'écarter de son sujet.

sidewalk ['saɪdwɔːk] *n Am* trottoir *m;* **s. café,** terrasse *f* de café.

sideways ['saɪdweɪz] **1** *adv* latéralement; *(to look)* en biais; *(to turn sth)* en travers, de biais; **to lean/fall s.,** se pencher/se tomber sur le côté; **to slide s.,** *(of door etc)* coulisser latéralement; **to walk s.,** marcher en crabe; **to put sth s. on to sth,** accoler qch à qch. **2** *adj* latéral, -aux; de côté; **s. motion,** mouvement latéral.

sidewinder ['saɪdwaɪndər] *n (snake)* serpent *m* à sonnettes cornu; *US (blow)* coup *m* sur le côté.

siding ['saɪdɪŋ] *n Rail* **(a)** voie *f* de garage *ou* d'évitement; **(b)** *Br (secondary line)* embranchement *m*; voie *f* de raccordement *(d'usine)*; **goods s.,** voie de chargement.

sidle ['saɪd(ə)l] *vi* **to s. along,** s'avancer de côté *ou* de guingois; **to s. up to s.o.,** se couler auprès de qn; **he was trying to s. out of the room,** il essayait de se glisser hors de la salle.

SIDS [sɪdz] *n Med (abbr* **sudden infant death syndrome)** mort subite du nourrisson.

siege [siːdʒ] *n Mil & Fig* siège *m*; **to lay s. to a town,** assiéger une ville; **to raise the s.,** lever le siège; **to declare a state of s.,** déclarer l'état de siège; **there's enough food to last a s.,** il y a assez de nourriture pour tenir un siège; *Hist* **s. gun,** pièce *f* de siège.

Siena [sɪ'enə] *n* Sienne *f*.

sienna [sɪ'enə] **1** *n* terre *f* de Sienne; **raw/burnt s.,** terre de Sienne naturelle/brûlée. **2** *adj (colour)* **s. (brown),** terre de Sienne *inv*.

sierra [sɪ'eərə] *n Geog* sierra *f*.

siesta [sɪ'estə] *n* sieste *f*; **to take a s.,** faire la sieste.

sieve¹ [sɪv] *n (with coarse mesh)* crible *m*; *(with fine mesh)* tamis *m*; *(for grain)* van *m*; *(for powders and liquids)* sas *m*; **to pass sth through a s.,** passer qch au tamis *ou* au crible; *F* **he's got a memory like a s.,** il a une cervelle comme une passoire; **this bucket leaks like a s.,** ce seau fuit comme une passoire.

sieve² *vt* = **SIFT 1**.

sift [sɪft] **1** *vt* passer (qch) au tamis *ou* au crible *ou* au sas; tamiser, bluter *(la farine)*; escarbiller *(des cendres)*; vanner *(le blé)*; cribler *(du sable etc)*; *Fig (examine)* examiner minutieusement, passer par l'étamine *(des preuves)*; approfondir, éplucher *(une question)*; **to s. sugar over a cake,** saupoudrer un gâteau de sucre; **to s. the facts,** passer les faits au crible. **2** *vi (of dust etc)* filtrer (**through,** à travers).

▶**sift out** *vtsep* **(a)** *(remove by sifting)* ôter *(des impuretés)* par tamisage; **(b)** *(eliminate)* éliminer *(unsuitable candidates)*.

sifter ['sɪftər] *n* **(a)** *(sieve)* tamis *m*, crible *m*; **(b)** saupoudroir *m (à sucre)*.

sifting ['sɪftɪŋ] *n* tamisage *m*, criblage *m*, sassement *m*, blutage *m (de qch)*; *Fig (examination)* examen minutieux *(des preuves etc)*; démêlement *m (du vrai et du faux)*.

sigh¹ [saɪ] *n* soupir *m*; **heavy/deep/long(-drawn) s.,** gros/profond/long soupir; **he breathed** *or* **heaved a s. of relief,** il a poussé un soupir de soulagement; **with a s.,** en soupirant, avec un soupir.

sigh² *vi* soupirer, pousser un soupir; *(of wind)* gémir; **to s. with relief,** pousser un soupir de soulagement; *Old-fashioned* **to s. for sth/s.o.,** soupirer pour *ou* après qn/qch.

sighing ['saɪɪŋ] *n* soupirs *mpl*; *Lit* plainte *f (du vent)*.

sight¹ [saɪt] *n* **(a)** *(faculty)* vue *f*; **to have good/bad s.,** avoir une bonne/mauvaise vue; **to have long s.,** avoir la vue longue, être presbyte; **short s.,** myopie *f*; **to lose one's s.,** perdre la vue, devenir aveugle; **to catch s.** *or* **get a s. of s.o./sth,** apercevoir *ou* entrevoir qn/qch; **to lose s. of s.o.,** perdre qn de vue; **to lose s. of the fact that ...,** perdre de vue (le fait) que ...; **I can't bear the s. of him, I hate the very s. of him,** je ne peux pas le sentir *ou* le voir; **to translate at s.,** traduire à vue *ou* à livre ouvert; **to shoot s.o. at** *or* **on s.,** faire feu *ou* tirer sur qn à vue; *Mus* **to play at s.,** jouer à vue, déchiffrer; *Com Fin* **bill payable at s.,** effet *m* payable à vue; *Com* **we need to have s. of it first,** il faut le voir d'abord; **to buy goods s. unseen,** acheter des marchandises sans les avoir vues; **at first s.,** à première vue, au premier abord; **at first s. everything seemed normal,** à première vue tout semblait normal; **to fall in love at first s.,** avoir le coup de foudre (**with,** pour); **it was a case of love at first s.,** c'était le coup de foudre; **to know s.o. by s.,** connaître qn de vue; **to find favour in s.o.'s s.,** trouver grâce aux yeux de qn; *Tech* **s. check,** contrôle *m* à vue, contrôle visuel; mirage *m*; *Med* **to have a s. test,** faire vérifier sa vue;

(b) *(range of vision)* **to come into s.,** (ap)paraître; **to be within s.,** être à portée de la vue, être en vue; **to be (with)in s. of land,** être en vue de (la) terre; **land in s.!,** terre!; **keep him in s.,** ne le perdez pas de vue; **out of s.,** caché aux regards; **to vanish out of s.,** disparaître; **to put sth out of s.,** faire disparaître qch, cacher qch; **keep it out of s. of the kids,** fais attention que les gamins ne le voient pas; **to keep out of s.,** se cacher, se dérober; **out of my s.!,** hors de ma vue!, hors d'ici!; *Prov* **out of s. out of mind,** loin des yeux, loin du cœur;

(c) *(aiming device)* appareil *m* de visée *ou* de pointage *(d'un instrument, d'une arme à feu)*; œilleton *m (de viseur)*; lumière *f (de sextant)*; **angle of s.,** angle *m* de visée *ou* de site, site *m*; **line of s.,** ligne *f* de visée *(d'un instrument d'optique)*; ligne de mire *ou* de tir *(d'une arme à feu)*; **to take a s. on sth,** viser qch, mirer qch; *Mil* **back** *or* **rear s.,** hausse *f*; cran *m* de mire; **fore** *or* **front s.,** guidon *m*; **telescopic s.,** hausse téléscopique, hausse à lunette; **to adjust sights,** prendre *ou* régler la hausse; **to have s.o./sth in one's sights,** avoir qn/qch en vue; *Fig* **to have** *or* **set one's sights on sth,** avoir des vues sur qch; *Fig* **to lower one's sights,** viser moins haut, baisser ses prétentions;

(d) *(spectacle)* spectacle *m*; *(something worth seeing)* chose digne d'être vue; **sad s.,** spectacle navrant; **it's a s. to see,** cela vaut la peine d'être vu; **it was a s. for sore eyes,** c'était réjouissant à voir; *F* **his face was a s.,** si vous aviez vu son visage!; **what a s. you are!, you do look a s.!,** comme vous voilà fait!, de quoi avez-vous l'air!; **the sights,** *(scenic places)* les sites *mpl* pittoresques; *(of a city etc)* les monuments *mpl*, les curiosités *fpl*; **we're going to see the sights,** nous allons visiter la ville *ou* la région etc;

(e) *F* **not by a long s.,** loin de là; *F* **she's a damn s. better,** elle va beaucoup mieux;

(f) s. (hole), *Opt* lumière *f* (*de pinnule etc*); regard *m* (*d'inspection, d'égout etc*).

sight[2] *vt* **(a)** apercevoir (*qn, qch*); viser, observer (*un astre etc*); **a golden eagle has been sighted here twice,** on a aperçu un aigle royal ici à deux reprises; **(b)** pointer (*un fusil*); **to s. a gun,** viser.

sighted ['saɪtɪd] **1** *adj* qui voit. **2** *n* **the s.,** (*used as pl*) les voyants *mpl*.

sighting ['saɪtɪŋ] *n* **(a)** vue *f*; **several sightings of teal have been reported,** on a vu des sarcelles à plusieurs reprises; **(b)** visée *f* (*avec un instrument d'optique, avec une arme à feu*); pointage *m* (*d'une arme à feu etc*).

sightless ['saɪtlɪs] *adj* aveugle; (*yeux*) éteint.

sightlessness ['saɪtlɪsnɪs] *n* cécité *f*.

sightly ['saɪtlɪ] *adj* agréable à voir; **not very s.,** pas très beau à voir.

sight-read ['saɪtri:d] *vi & vt Mus* déchiffrer.

sight-reading ['saɪtri:dɪŋ] *n* déchiffrage *m*.

sight(-)see ['saɪtsi:] *vi* visiter des sites pittoresques *ou* les curiosités (*d'une ville, d'un pays, d'une région etc*).

sightseeing ['saɪtsi:ɪŋ] *n* tourisme *m*; **we spent the day s.,** nous avons passé la journée à visiter le pays *ou* les monuments; **to go s.,** visiter la ville *ou* la région *etc*; **a s. tour of Paris,** un tour de Paris.

sightseer ['saɪtsi:ər] *n* touriste *mf*.

sign[1] [saɪn] *n* **(a)** signe *m*; **to make a s./signs to s.o.,** faire (un) signe/des signes à qn; **s. of the cross,** signe de la croix; **to make the s. of the cross,** se signer; **s. of recognition,** signe de reconnaissance; *Telecom* **call s.,** indicatif *m* d'appel; **s. language,** (langage *m*) mimique *f*; (*of the deaf*) langage par signes; **to use s. language,** (*to deaf person, foreigner etc*) parler par signes;

(b) (*indication*) indice *m*, indication *f*; **sure s.,** indice certain; **it's a good/bad s.,** c'est bon/mauvais signe; **s. of the times,** signe des temps; **as a s. of ...,** en signe de ...; **he gave no s. of having heard anything,** il n'a manifesté en aucune façon avoir entendu quoi que ce soit; **no s. of ...,** nulle *ou* aucune trace de ...; **there is little s. of progress,** il n'y a pas de signe de progrès; **if there's the slightest s. of unrest,** s'il y a le moindre signe d'agitation; **all the signs are that ...,** tout porte à croire que ...; **the room showed signs of having been recently occupied,** la pièce révélait une occupation recente; **to show no s. of life,** ne donner aucun signe de vie, ne pas donner signe de vie; **there was no s. of her,** (*not to be seen*) elle n'était nulle part en vue; (*hadn't arrived*) elle n'était pas encore arrivée; **is there any s. of him yet?,** il ne serait pas arrivé par hasard?;

(c) (*of pub, inn etc*) enseigne *f*; **(shop) s.,** enseigne, écriteau *m*; **s. writer** *or* **painter,** (*of lettering*) peintre *m* en lettres; (*of signs*) peintre d'enseignes; **a s. on the wall said 'no smoking',** un panneau sur le mur indiquait 'prière de ne pas fumer'; **a 'for sale' s.,** un écriteau 'à vendre'; **neon s.,** enseigne *ou* réclame *f* au néon; **(road) s.,** panneau indicateur (de route); **road signs,** (*collectively*) signalisation routière; **follow the signs for Manchester,** suivre les panneaux indiquant Manchester; **traffic s.,** panneau de signalisation (routière); **advance warning s.,** panneau de présignalisation;

(d) (*symbol*) symbole *m*; **positive** *or* **plus s.,** signe positif, (signe) plus *m*; **negative** *or* **minus s.,** signe négatif, (signe) moins *m*; **s. of the zodiac,** signe du zodiaque; **lucky s.,** signe de chance.

sign[2] **1** *vt* **(a)** signer (*son nom, un document, un chèque etc*); viser (*un compte*); accepter (*une traite*); signer, passer (*un contrat*); *Arch* (*mark with sign*) signer (*qn, qch*), marquer (*qn, qch*) d'un signe; **the letter was signed by the president,** la lettre portait la signature du président *ou* était signée de la main du président; *Jur* **signed, sealed and delivered in presence of ...,** fait et signé en présence de ...;

(b) (*indicate by gesture*) *Old-fashioned* **to s. assent,** faire signe que oui; **to s. s.o. to do sth,** faire signe à qn de faire qch;

(c) *Fb etc F* embaucher (*un joueur*); **he was signed to United for £1,000,000,** il a été embauché par United pour 1 000 000 livres, il a signé un contrat de 1 000 000 livres avec United.

2 *vi* **(a)** (*write signature*) signer; **s. here,** signez là; **she refused to s.,** elle a refusé de signer;

(b) (*use sign language*) parler par signes; **many hearing-impaired people can't s.,** de nombreux malentendants ne savent pas parler par signes;

(c) (*indicate by gesture*) **to s. to s.o. to do sth,** faire signe à qn de faire qch.

▶**sign away** *vtsep* (*concede by signing*) signer la cession de (*un droit etc*); **to s. sth away to s.o.,** céder qch par écrit à qn; *Hum* **I get the feeling I'm signing my life away,** j'ai l'impression de signer ma condamnation à mort.

▶**sign for** *vipo* (*acknowledge receipt of*) signer pour accuser réception de (*delivery, registered letter etc*).

▶**sign in 1** *vi* (*sign when entering*) signer à l'entrée; **all visitors must s. in,** tous les visiteurs doivent signer en entrant. **2** *vtsep* (*gain entrance for s.o.*) signer pour faire entrer (*qn*); **I'm a member, so I can s. you in,** je suis membre, donc je peux vous faire entrer.

▶**sign off** *vi* **(a)** *Rad TV* terminer l'émission (*en jouant l'indicatif*); **(b)** (*close letter*) finir une lettre; **I'll s. off now and go to bed,** je vais finir cette lettre maintenant et aller au lit.

▶**sign on 1** *vtsep* engager (*qn*); (*hire*) embaucher (*un ouvrier*). **2** *vi* **(a)** (*of worker*) s'embaucher; (*of soldier*) s'engager; **(b)** *Br F* (*register for unemployment benefit*) s'inscrire au chômage.

▶**sign out 1** *vi* (*sign when leaving*) signer à la sortie; **visitors must s. in and s. out,** les visiteurs doivent signer en entrant et en sortant. **2** *vtsep* (*indicate s.o.'s departure*) **could you s. me out?,** est-ce que vous pouvez noter que je suis parti?

▶**sign up 1** *vi* **(a)** (*register*) s'inscrire à (*un cours etc*); **(b)** (*enlist*) (*of soldier*) s'engager. **2** *vtsep Sp Th etc* (*hire*) donner un contrat à, engager (*qn*); **can I s. you up for fund raising?,** est-ce que je peux vous inscrire pour une collecte?

signal[1] ['sɪgn(ə)l] *n* **(a)** signal *m*, -aux; *Fig* signe *m*; **warning s.,** signal avertisseur *ou* d'avertissement; **alarm s.,** signal d'alarme *ou* d'alerte; **all clear s.,** signal de fin d'alerte; **time s.,** signal horaire; *Sp etc* **starting s.,** signal de *ou* du départ; *Tel* **calling** *or US* **line s.,** indicatif *m* d'appel; *Br* **engaged** *or Am* **busy s.,** signal de ligne occupée; **to give/send/receive a s.,** faire/envoyer/recevoir un signal; **when I give the s. switch on the machine,** quand je donne le signal, mettez la machine en marche; *Fig* **he was putting out a lot of confusing signals,** il donnait beaucoup de signaux contradictoires; *Fig* **the demonstration is a clear s. to the government to change its policy,** la manifestation est un signe manifeste indiquant au gouvernement qu'il devrait changer sa politique; **traffic signals,** feux *mpl* de circulation; **light s.,** signal lumineux; *Nau* **flashing (light) s.,** signal à éclats *ou* par scott; *Mil* **arm/hand s.,** signal à bras; **sempahore s.,** signal sémaphorique *ou Nau* à bras; **flag s.,** *Mil* signal par fanion(s); *Nau* signal à pavillon; *Rail* signal par drapeau; **Morse signals,** signaux Morse; *Rail* **disc s.,** disque *m*; **distant s.,** signal à distance, signal avancé; **home s.,** signal rapproché; **stop s.,** signal d'arrêt immédiat; *Nau* **yeoman of signals,** maître-timonier *m*, *pl* maîtres-timoniers; *Nau* **s. book,** livre *m* des signaux; *Rail* **s. box,** poste *m* d'aiguillage; **s. communications,** télécommunications *fpl*, transmissions *fpl*; **s. flag,** *Mil* fanion *m* de signalisation; *Nau* pavillon *m* pour signaux; **s. flare,** (*rocket*) fusée éclairante; (*stationary*) bengale *m*; **s. lamp,** (*for making signals*) lampe *f ou* projecteur *m* de signalisation; (*serving as a signal*) (lampe) témoin *m*; **s. light,** *Nau* fanal *m*, -aux; *Mil* voyant *m* (lumineux); *Br Mil* **Signals,** transmissions *fpl*; *Mil* **Signals officer,** officier *m* des transmissions; *Am* **s. red,** vermillon chinois; **s. rocket,** fusée de signalisation;

(b) *Electron Rad etc* **input/output s.,** signal *m* d'entrée/de sortie.

signal[2] *v* (**-ll-**, *US* **-l-**) **1** *vi* donner un signal, faire des signaux (**to,** à); **I signalled to him (to stop),** je lui ai fait signe (de s'arrêter); *Aut* **to s. before stopping,** prévenir *ou* avertir avant de s'arrêter. **2** *vt* signaler (*un train, un navire*); transmettre (*un ordre*); *Aut* **to s. that one is turning,** signaler un changement de direction; **this signals the start of the rainy season,** cela indique le début *ou* c'est le signe du début de la saison des pluies; **he signalled the car on,** il a fait signe à la voiture d'avancer.

signal[3] *adj Lit* (*service*) signalé, insigne; (*succès*) éclatant, remarquable; (*faveur*) insigne; (*échec*) notoire.

signalize ['sɪgnəlaɪz] *vt* signaler, marquer (*une victoire, un succès*).

signaller ['sɪgnələr] *n* signaleur *m*.

signalling, *US* **signaling** ['sɪgnəlɪŋ] *n* **(a)** (*act*) signalisation *f*; (*sending signals*) transmission *f* de signaux; (*warning*) avertissement *m*; *Nau* timonerie *f*; balisage *m* (*d'une route etc*); **s. flag,** *Mil* fanion *m* de signalisation; *Nau* pavillon *m* pour signaux; *Rail* drapeau *m*; **(b)** (*signals*) signaux *mpl.*

signally ['sɪgnəlɪ] *adv Lit* remarquablement, d'une façon éclatante.

signalman, *pl* **-men** ['sɪgnəlmən] *n* signaleur *m*; (*using semaphore*) sémaphoriste *m*; *Nau* timonier *m*; *Rail* bloqueur *m*.

signatory ['sɪgnət(ə)rɪ] **1** *n* signataire *mf* (**to a treaty,** d'un traité); **the signatories to the Treaty of Rome,** les pays signataires du Traité de Rome. **2** *adj* (*nation*) signataire.

signature ['sɪgnətʃər] *n* **(a)** signature *f*; *Admin* visa *m*; **to put one's s. to a letter,** apposer sa signature à une lettre; **his s. was on the letter,** la lettre portait sa signature; *Com etc* **for s.,** pour signature; *Rad TV* **s. tune,** indicatif *m* (*d'une émission*); **(b)** *Typ* signature *f* (*d'un cahier*); cahier *m* (*d'imprimerie*); **(c)** *Mus* **key s.,** armature *f*.

signboard ['saɪnbɔːd] *n* enseigne *f* (*d'auberge*).

signet ['sɪgnɪt] *n* cachet *m*; **s. ring,** (bague *f*) chevalière *f*; (*for sealing*) anneau *m* sigillaire.

significance [sɪg'nɪfɪkəns] *n* **(a)** (*importance*) importance *f*, portée *f*; **event of no/of great s.,** événement sans importance/de la plus haute importance; **(b)** (*meaning*) signification *f* (*d'un mot, d'un geste etc*); **what is the s. of this ceremony?,** que signifie cette cérémonie?; **look of deep s.,** regard très significatif.

significant [sɪg'nɪfɪkənt] *adj* **(a)** (*événement, différence, amélioration etc*) important, significatif; (*somme d'argent*) important; **do you think this is s.?,** pensez-vous que cela a de l'importance?; **what's s. about it is that ...,** ce qu'il y a d'important là-dedans c'est que ...; **(b)** (*mot, geste, regard*) significatif.

significantly [sɪg'nɪfɪkəntlɪ] *adv* **(a)** (*appreciably*) **s. cheaper,** sensiblement moins cher; **(b)** (*to look at etc*) d'une manière significative.

signification [sɪgnɪfɪ'keɪʃən] *n* signification *f*, sens *m* (*d'un mot etc*); *Ling* signifié *m*.

significative [sɪg'nɪfɪkətɪv] *adj* significatif (**of,** de).

signify ['sɪgnɪfaɪ] **1** *vt* **(a)** (*indicate*) signifier, être (le) signe de (*qch*); **a broad forehead signifies intelligence,** un front large est (un) signe d'intelligence; **(b)** (*mean*) signifier, vouloir dire; (*make known*) signifier, faire connaître (*ses intentions etc*). **2** *vi* importer; **it doesn't s.,** cela n'a aucune importance, peu importe.

signing ['saɪnɪŋ] *n* **(a)** signature *f* (*d'un document etc*); passation *f* (*d'un acte*); acceptation *f* (*d'une traite*); **(b)** (*act of using sign language*) utilisation *f* du langage par signes.

signpost¹ ['saɪnpəʊst] *n* poteau indicateur; *Fig* indication *f*.

signpost² *vt* signaliser, marquer de poteaux indicateurs; **well/badly signposted road,** route qui est bien/mal signalisée.

signposting ['saɪnpəʊstɪŋ] *n* signalisation *f* des routes.

Sikh [siːk] *adj & n Rel* sikh, -e.

silage ['saɪlɪdʒ] *n Agr* fourrage ensilé.

silence¹ ['saɪləns] *n* silence *m*; **there was a sudden s.,** il s'est fait un silence subit; **to keep s.,** garder le silence, se taire; **to break (the) s.,** rompre le silence; **to reduce s.o. to s.,** réduire qn au silence, faire taire qn; **there's been complete s. from head office,** le siège est resté totalement silencieux; **to suffer in s.,** souffrir en silence; **s.!,** (du) silence!; (*notice in library etc*) défense de parler; **to buy s.o.'s s.,** acheter le silence de qn, payer qn pour le *ou* la faire taire; **to write to s.o. after five years' s.,** écrire à qn après un silence de cinq ans; **to pass over sth in s.,** passer qch sous silence; **the s. of the night,** le silence de la nuit; *Prov* **s. is golden,** le silence est d'or.

silence² *vt* réduire (*qn, l'opposition*) au silence; imposer silence à (*des élèves etc*); faire taire (*qn, sa conscience*); étouffer (*les plaintes*); *Mil* faire cesser, faire taire (*le feu de l'ennemi*); (*muffle*) amortir, étouffer (*un bruit*); *Aut* assourdir (*l'échappement*); **that really silenced him!,** (*made speechless*) ça l'a laissé sans voix!

silencer ['saɪlənsər] *n Aut* (*on exhaust*) silencieux *m*, pot *m* d'échappement; (*on gun*) silencieux.

silent ['saɪlənt] *adj* **(a)** silencieux; (*personne*) silencieux, taciturne, peu loquace; **to keep s.,** observer le silence; (*not reveal information*) garder le silence, se taire (**about,** sur); (*keep low profile*) se tenir coi *ou f* coite; **to remain s.,** rester muet; **be s.!,** taisez-vous!; **they stood a minute in s. memory of ...,** ils ont observé une minute de silence en mémoire de ...; **s. as the grave,** muet comme la tombe; **s. actor/actress,** acteur/actrice de film(s) muet(s); **s. film** *or* **movie,** film muet; **stars of the s. screen,** vedettes *fpl* du cinéma muet; *Rel* **s. orders,** ordres *mpl* (religieux) qui gardent le silence; **s. majority,** majorité silencieuse; **s. sorrow,** douleur muette; *Com* **s. partner,** commanditaire *m*, bailleur *m* de fonds; **(b)** *Ling* (*lettre*) muet; **the k is s.,** le k ne se prononce pas, le k est muet.

silently ['saɪləntlɪ] *adv* silencieusement.

silex ['saɪleks] *n Miner* silex *m*.

silhouette¹ [sɪluː'et] *n* silhouette *f*; **in s.,** en silhouette.

silhouette² *vt* silhouetter, projeter en silhouette; **to be silhouetted against a light background,** se détacher (en silhouette) sur un fond clair; **a tree silhouetted against the sky,** un arbre qui se détachait *ou* qui se découpait sur le ciel.

silica ['sɪlɪkə] *n Ch* silice *f*.

silicate ['sɪlɪkət] *n Ch* silicate *m*.

siliceous [sɪ'lɪʃəs] *adj Ch* siliceux.

silicon ['sɪlɪkən] *n Ch* silicium *m*; **s. chip,** puce *f ou* pastille *f* de silicium; **S. Valley,** Silicon Valley *f*; **s. technology,** technologie *f* du silicium; **amorphous s.,** silicium amorphe; **crystalline s.,** silicium cristallin.

silicone ['sɪlɪkəʊn] *n Ch* silicone *f*; **s. rubber,** caoutchouc *m* silicone.

silicosis [sɪlɪ'kəʊsɪs] *n Med* silicose *f*.

silk [sɪlk] *n* **(a)** soie *f*; **raw s.,** soie grège *ou* écrue; *Tex* **wild s.,** soie sauvage; **artificial s.,** rayonne *f*; **s. culture,** sériciculture *f*; **a black s. dress,** une robe de soie noire; **s. fabric(s), silk(s),** soierie *f*; **s. finish,** similisage *m*; **s. screen printing,** sérigraphie *f*; **s. stockings,** bas *mpl* de *ou* en soie; **s. yarn,** fil *m* de soie; **s. waste, waste s.,** bourre *f* de soie, (fils de) schappe *m or f*; **(b)** *Horseracing* **silks,** casaque *f* (*de jockey*); **(c)** *Br Jur F* (*King's, Queen's Counsel*) conseiller *m* du roi *ou* de la reine; (*collectively*) les conseillers du roi *ou* de la reine; **to take s.,** être nommé conseiller du roi *ou* de la reine.

silken ['sɪlk(ə)n] *adj Lit* **(a)** soyeux; (*boucles*) de soie; **(b)** (*voice, words*) doucereux, mielleux.

silkiness ['sɪlkɪnɪs] *n* **(a)** nature soyeuse (*d'un tissu*); **(b)** moelleux *m* (*de la voix, des paroles*).

silkworm ['sɪlkwɜːm] *n* ver *m* à soie; **s. breeder,** sériciculteur *m*, magnanier, -ière; **s. breeding,** sériciculture *f*, magnanerie *f*; **s. moth,** bombyx *m* (du mûrier); **s. nursery** *or* **farm,** magnanerie.

silky ['sɪlkɪ] *adj* soyeux; **s. voice,** voix moelleuse.

sill [sɪl] *n Constr etc* sole *f*, semelle *f* (*de cadre*); seuil *m* (*de porte*); rebord *m*, appui *m* (*de fenêtre*); *HydE* seuil, radier *m* (*d'écluse*).

sillabub ['sɪləbʌb] *n Culin* = entremets sucré semblable au sabayon.

silliness ['sɪlɪnɪs] *n* sottise *f*, bêtise *f*, niaiserie *f*.

silly ['sɪlɪ] **1** *adj* (*person*) sot, *f* sotte, stupide, bête; (*question, réponse*) stupide; **don't be so s.!,** ne sois pas si bête *ou* si stupide!; **I'll pay — don't be s.,** je vais payer – il n'en est pas question!; **(you) s. fool** *or* **ass!,** imbécile!, idiot!; **it would make me look s.,** j'aurais l'air bête *ou* stupide *ou* ridicule; **that was a s. thing to do!,** ça *ou* ce n'était pas très intelligent!; **to say sth s.,** dire une bêtise; **but that's s., she was here half an hour ago,** mais c'est ridicule, elle était ici il y a une demi-heure; **there was a new manager every week, it was** *or* **things were getting s.,** il y avait un nouveau gérant chaque semaine, ça devenait ridicule; **it was s. of me to ask,** c'était idiot de ma part de demander ça; **he's forgotten his umbrella, (the) s. man,** il a oublié son parapluie, cet idiot; *Journ F* **the s. season,** = l'époque des vacances (*dépourvue de nouvelles sérieuses*); **to laugh oneself s.,** mourir de rire; **to worry s.o. s.,** rendre qn malade d'inquiétude; **she's been worrying herself s.,** elle est morte d'inquiétude; **she will worry herself s.,** elle se rendra malade d'inquiétude (**about,** à cause de); **to knock s.o. s.,** étourdir *ou* assommer qn.

2 *n F* idiot, -ote; **don't be such a s.!,** que tu es bête!

sillybilly [sɪlɪ'bɪlɪ] *n F* (*to child*) idiot, -ote, imbécile *mf*.

silo ['saɪləʊ] *n Agr* silo *m*; **launching s.,** (*for missile*) puits *m ou* silo de lancement.

silt¹ [sɪlt] *n* boue *f*; dépôt *m*, vase *f*, limon *m* (*dans un chenal etc*).

silt² *vt* = **SILT UP 2.**

►silt up 1 *vi* (*of harbour etc*) s'envaser. **2** *vtsep* (*fill with silt*) envaser (*un port, un canal*).

silting ['sɪltɪŋ] *n* **(a)** *Min Petr* embouage *m* (*d'une galerie etc*); **(b)** = **SILTING UP.**

silting up *n* envasement *m*.

silver¹ ['sɪlvər] *n* **(a)** argent *m*; **is that spoon s.?,** est-ce que cette cuiller est en argent?; **s. birch,** bouleau blanc; **s. bromide,** bromure *m* d'argent; **s. fox,** renard argenté; **s. gilt,** vermeil *m*; **s. grey,** gris argenté *inv*; **s. haired,** aux cheveux argentés; **s. inkstand,** encrier *m* en argent; **s. paper,** papier d'étain, papier argenté *ou* d'argent; **s. plate,**

(*layer of silver*) plaqué *m* (d')argent; (*silver-plated objects*) argenterie *f*; **s. plating,** argenture *f*; **stars of the s. screen,** stars *mpl* du grand écran; **s. service,** (*in restaurant*) service *m* de grande classe; **he was born with a s. spoon in his mouth,** il est né coiffé; **s. toned,** (*voice etc*) argentin; **s. wedding,** noces *fpl* d'argent;

(b) s. (money), argent monnayé; **s. coin,** pièce *f* d'argent; (*collectively*) argent; **a pound in s.,** une livre en argent, une livre en pièces *ou* en monnaie d'argent;

(c) (*silverware*) argenterie *f*;

(d) *Sp etc* **s. (medal),** médaille *f* d'argent; **to get a s. in the shot putt,** remporter une médaille d'argent en lancer du poids.

silver² *vt* argenter (*des couverts etc*); étamer (*un miroir*); *Lit* argenter (*les flots etc*).

silverfish ['sɪlvəfɪʃ] *n* **(a)** (*fish*) argentine *f*; **(b)** (*insect*) lépisme *m*, poisson *m* d'argent.

silver-plate [sɪlvə'pleɪt] *vt* argenter (*qch*).

silver-plated [sɪlvə'pleɪtɪd] *adj* argenté.

silverside ['sɪlvəsaɪd] *n Culin* gîte *f* à la noix.

silversmith ['sɪlvəsmɪθ] *n* orfèvre *m*.

silverware ['sɪlvəweər] *n* argenterie *f* (*de table*).

silverwork ['sɪlvəwɜːk] *n* orfèvrerie *f*.

silvery ['sɪlvərɪ] *adj* (*nuage, flot*) argenté; (*écailles etc*) d'argent; (*rire, timbre*) argentin.

simian ['sɪmɪən] **1** *adj* simiesque, simien. **2** *n Zool* anthropoïde *m*; **the simians,** les simiens *mpl*.

similar ['sɪmɪlər] *adj* semblable, pareil (**to,** à), similaire; *Math* (*triangles*) semblables; **your case is s. to mine,** votre cas est semblable au mien; **the two women are s.,** les deux femmes se ressemblent; **there was a s. mistake on page 1,** il y avait une erreur semblable page 1; **something s. happened to me,** il m'est arrivé quelque chose de semblable.

similarity [sɪmɪ'lærɪtɪ] *n* ressemblance *f*; *Math* similitude *f* (*de triangles*).

similarly ['sɪmɪləlɪ] *adv* pareillement, semblablement; **they were s. dressed,** ils étaient habillés de la même façon; **s. ...,** de même ... .

simile ['sɪmɪlɪ] *n* comparaison *f*.

similitude [sɪ'mɪlɪtjuːd] *n* (*resemblance*) ressemblance *f*, similitude *f*; (*comparison*) comparaison *f*; *Arch* allégorie *f*.

simmer¹ ['sɪmər] *n Culin* **to keep sth at a s.** *or* **on the s.,** (faire) mijoter qch, faire cuire qch à petit feu *ou* à feu doux.

simmer² **1** *vi* **(a)** *Culin etc* (*of liquid*) frémir; (*of food in pot*) mijoter, cuire à petit feu *ou* à feu doux; **(b)** (*of revolt etc*) fermenter; **he was simmering with rage,** il bouillonnait de rage. **2** *vt Culin* mijoter, mitonner (*un ragoût etc*).

▶**simmer down** *vi* (*become calmer*) (*of person*) se calmer.

simmering ['sɪmərɪŋ] *n* **(a)** frémissement *m* (*d'un liquide*); *Culin* cuisson *f* à petit feu *ou* à feu doux; **(b)** ferment *m* (*de révolte etc*).

simnel ['sɪmn(ə)l] *n* **s. (cake),** gâteau *m* de Pâques *ou* de la mi-carême.

simony ['saɪmənɪ] *n Rel* simonie *f*.

simper¹ ['sɪmpər] *n* sourire affecté *ou* minaudier.

simper² *vi* minauder, mignarder; (*smile affectedly*) sourire avec affectation.

simpering ['sɪmpərɪŋ] **1** *adj* minaudier, mignard, affecté. **2** *n* minauderie *f*.

simple ['sɪmp(ə)l] **1** *adj* (*méthode etc*) simple, élémentaire; (*caractère*) simple, naturel; (*fleur, Med fracture*) simple; (*naive*) simple, naïf, crédule; (*foolish*) bête, niais; **because I don't want to, it's as s. as that,** parce que je ne veux pas, c'est aussi simple que ça; **I'm not so s. as to believe that,** je n'ai pas la naïveté de croire cela; **to become s.** *or* **simpler,** se simplifier; **the simplest thing to do is to ...,** le plus simple est de ...; **a meal that is s. to prepare,** un repas qui est simple à préparer; **s. envy,** envie pure et simple; **s. hearted,** simple, ingénu, candide; *Com* **s. interest,** intérêts *mpl* simples; *Gram* **s. sentence,** proposition indépendante; **to have s. tastes,** avoir des goûts simples; **that's the plain and s. truth,** c'est la vérité pure et simple. **2** *n Bot Arch* simple *m*, herbe médicinale.

simple-minded [sɪmp(ə)l'maɪndɪd] *adj* simple (d'esprit), simplet, -ète; (*naive*) naïf, candide.

simple-mindedness [sɪmp(ə)l'maɪndɪdnɪs] *n* simplicité *f* (d'esprit, de caractère); (*naiveness*) naïveté *f*, candeur *f*.

simpleness ['sɪmp(ə)lnɪs] *n* candeur *f*, simplicité *f* (*d'un enfant etc*); (*foolishness*) bêtise *f*, niaiserie *f*.

simpleton ['sɪmp(ə)ltən] *n* nigaud, -aude, niais, -aise.

simplex ['sɪmpleks] *n Ling* forme *f* de base (*d'un mot*).

simplicity [sɪm'plɪsɪtɪ] *n* **(a)** (*candour*) candeur *f*, simplicité *f* (*d'un enfant etc*); (*foolishness*) bêtise *f*, sottise *f*; **(b)** simplicité *f* (*d'un problème etc*); absence *f* de recherche, simplicité (*dans la tenue*); **it's s. itself,** c'est simple comme bonjour.

simplification [sɪmplɪfɪ'keɪʃən] *n* simplification *f*.

simplify ['sɪmplɪfaɪ] *vt* simplifier (*un raisonnement, un calcul etc*); apporter des simplifications à (*un procédé*).

simplistic [sɪm'plɪstɪk] *adj* simpliste; **am I being too s.?,** est-ce que je simplifie trop?

simply ['sɪmplɪ] *adv* **(a)** (*in simple manner*) (*parler, agir*) simplement; (*vêtu*) avec simplicité; **(b)** (*absolutely*) absolument; **I s. won't do it,** je refuse absolument de le faire; **I was s. amazed by it,** j'en étais tout à fait abasourdi; **(c)** (*just*) tout simplement; **purely and s.,** purement et simplement; **it's s. a matter of time,** c'est une simple question de temps, c'est tout simplement une question de temps.

simulacrum, *pl* **-a** [sɪmjʊ'leɪkrəm, -ə] *n* simulacre *m*, semblant *m*.

simulate ['sɪmjʊleɪt] *vt* **(a)** (*imitate*) simuler, feindre (*une maladie etc*); affecter (*de l'enthousiasme etc*); imiter l'apparence de, prendre l'aspect de (*qn, qch*); **(b)** *Tech* imiter, simuler; **using a model we can s. the effects of flooding,** à l'aide d'un modèle nous pouvons simuler les effets de la submersion.

simulation [sɪmjʊ'leɪʃən] *n* **(a)** (*imitation*) simulation *f*, feinte *f*; **(b)** *Tech* simulation *f*; **flight s.,** simulation de vol.

simulator ['sɪmjʊleɪtər] *n* simulateur, -trice; *Tech* simulateur; **flight s.,** simulateur de vol.

simultaneity [sɪməltə'neɪɪtɪ] *n* simultanéité *f*.

simultaneous [sɪməl'teɪnɪəs] *adj* simultané; **s. translation,** traduction simultanée; **s. with ...,** qui a lieu en même temps que ...; *Math* **s. equation,** identités *fpl* remarquables.

simultaneously [sɪməl'teɪnɪəslɪ] *adv* simultanément; **s. with,** en même temps (que).

sin¹ [sɪn] *n* péché *m*; *F* offense *f* (*contre le goût etc*); **original s.,** péché originel; **the seven deadly sins,** les sept péchés capitaux; **the forgiveness of sins,** le pardon des offenses; *F* **to live in s.,** vivre en concubinage; **to die in s.,** mourir dans le péché; *F* **for my sins, I was appointed...,** pour mes péchés j'ai été nommé...; *F* **it's a s. to stay indoors on a day like this,** c'est un crime *ou Old fashioned* un péché de rester à l'intérieur par une si belle journée; *F* **if it's not a s. to ask ...,** s'il est permis de poser la question ... .

sin² *vi* (**-nn-**) pécher, commettre un péché *ou* des péchés; **to s. against,** pécher contre, blesser (*les convenances*); manquer à (*une règle etc*); **more sinned against than sinning,** plus à plaindre qu'à blâmer.

Sinai ['saɪnaɪ] *n* Sinaï *m*; **the S. Peninsula,** la presqu'île de Sinaï; **Mount S.,** le mont Sinaï.

since [sɪns] **1** *adv* depuis; **I've not seen him s.,** je ne l'ai pas revu depuis; **he's been in perfect health ever s.,** depuis (lors), sa santé a été parfaite; *Old-fashioned* **many years s.,** (*ago*) il y a bien des années; **long s.,** (*for a long time*) depuis longtemps; (*a long time ago*) il y a longtemps; **not long s.,** il n'y a pas très longtemps; **how long s.?,** depuis combien?

2 *prep* depuis; **s. his death,** depuis sa mort; **s. early June,** dès les premiers jours de juin; **I've been here (ever) s. lunch,** je suis là depuis le déjeuner; **she has lived here s. 1984,** elle vit ici depuis 1984; **she had lived there s. 1933,** elle vivait là depuis 1933; **I haven't seen her s. Christmas,** je ne l'ai pas vue depuis Noël; **s. then, s. that time,** depuis ce temps-là, depuis lors; **s. when?,** depuis quand?; *F* **s. when do you come into a room without knocking?,** depuis quand est-ce qu'on entre sans frapper?; **s. seeing you,** depuis que je vous ai vu.

3 *conj* **(a)** depuis que; **s. I've been here,** depuis que je suis ici; **it's a long time s. I saw her,** il y a longtemps que je ne l'ai vue, ça fait longtemps que je ne l'ai pas vue; **(ever) s. I have lived in London,** depuis que j'habite Londres; **s. he had been there,** depuis qu'il était là;

(b) (*because*) puisque; **I'll do it s. I must,** je le ferai puisqu'il le faut.

sincere [sɪn'sɪər] *adj* (*genuine*) sincère; (*frank*) franc, *f* franche; **he is completely s.,** il est de bonne foi.

sincerely [sɪn'sɪəlɪ] *adv* sincèrement; **yours s.,** *esp Am* **s. yours,** (*letter ending*) veuillez agréer, Monsieur *etc*, l'expression de mes sentiments distingués *ou* les meilleurs.

sincerity [sɪn'serɪtɪ] *n* sincérité *f*, bonne foi; (*of emotions*) sincérité; **in all s.,** de la meilleure foi du monde, en toute sincérité.

sine [saɪn] *n Math* sinus *m* (*d'un angle*).

sinecure ['saɪnɪkjʊər] *n* sinécure *f*.

sine que non ['siːneɪkwɑːnəʊn] *n* **to be a s. q. n.,** être indispensable; (*in thesis, policy etc*) être une condition sine qua non.

sinew ['sɪnjuː] *n* **(a)** *Anat* tendon *m*; *Culin* (*in meat*) croquant *m*, tirant *m*; **(b) sinews,** nerf *m*, force *f*, vigueur *f*; **the sinews of war,** le nerf de la guerre.

sinewy ['sɪnjuːɪ] *adj* **(a)** (*meat*) tendineux; **(b)** (*bras etc*) musclé, nerveux, vigoureux.

sinful ['sɪnfʊl] *adj* (*plaisir, acte*) coupable; (*gaspillage*) scandaleux; **it is s. to ...,** c'est un crime *ou Old-fashioned* un péché de ...; **s. person,** pécheur, *f* pécheresse; **s. world,** monde *m* de pécheurs; **s. life,** vie *f* de péchés; **s. city,** ville *f* de perdition.

sinfully ['sɪnfʊlɪ] *adv* d'une façon coupable; (*scandalously*) scandaleusement.

sinfulness ['sɪnfʊlnɪs] *n* (*of behaviour*) caractère scandaleux; **his/her s.,** son état de pécheur/pécheresse; **a life of s.,** une vie de péché.

sing [sɪŋ] *v* (*pt* **sang** [sæŋ]; *pp* **sung** [sʌŋ]) **1** *vi* **(a)** (*of person, bird*) chanter; **I can't s.,** je ne sais pas chanter; **(b)** (*of the wind etc*) siffler; (*of the ears*) tinter, bourdonner; **the kettle is singing,** la bouilloire chante *ou* siffle; **(c)** *F* (*inform*) moucharder. **2** *vt* chanter (*un air, une chanson*); **s. me a song,** chante-moi une chanson; **Sinatra sings the Beatles,** Sinatra chante les Beatles; *Fig* **to s. another** *or* **a different tune,** changer de ton; **to s. s.o. to sleep,** endormir qn en chantant; **to s. s.o.'s praises,** chanter les louanges de qn.

►**sing along** *vi* **s. along if you like,** chantez avec moi *ou* nous *etc* si vous voulez.

►**sing of** *vipo Lit* chanter.

►**sing out** *vi* **(a)** (*sing loudly*) chanter (plus) fort; **(b)** *F* (*call*) appeler; **s. out if you need me,** appelez si vous avez besoin de moi.

►**sing up** *vi* (*sing louder*) chanter plus fort.

singable ['sɪŋəb(ə)l] *adj* chantable.

Singapore [sɪŋə'pɔːr] *n* Singapour *m*.

singe¹ [sɪndʒ] *n* **s. (mark),** légère brûlure.

singe² *vt* **(a)** brûler (*qch*) légèrement; roussir (*du linge, des poils etc*); **(b)** flamber (*une volaille, les cheveux*).

►**singe off** *vtsep Tex* **to s. (off) cloth,** griller (*l'étoffe*).

singeing ['sɪndʒɪŋ] *n* flambage *m* (*d'une volaille etc*); roussissement *m* (*du linge*); *Tex* grillage *m* (*d'un tissu*).

singer ['sɪŋər] *n* chanteur, *f* chanteuse; **s. songwriter,** auteur-compositeur-interprète *mf*.

Singhalese [sɪŋgə'liːz] *adj & n* = **SINHALESE**.

singing ['sɪŋɪŋ] **1** *adj* qui chante; (*oiseau etc*) chanteur; **s. telegram,** télégramme chanté. **2** *n* **(a)** chant *m* (*de qn, d'un oiseau etc*); **his s. is awful,** il chante atrocement; **s. lesson,** leçon *f* de chant; **(b)** sifflement *m* (*du vent etc*).

single¹ ['sɪŋg(ə)l] *n* **(a)** *Tennis etc* simple *m*, single *m*; **men's/women's singles,** simple messieurs/dames; **(b)** (*record*) disque *m* 45 tours; (*ticket*) billet *m* d'aller, aller *m* simple; (*banknote*) (*one pound*) billet d'une livre; (*one dollar*) billet d'un dollar; *Phot* **don't cut your negatives into singles,** ne pas découper vos négatifs; **(c)** (*unmarried person*) célibataire *mf*; **a package holiday for singles,** des vacances organisées pour célibataires; **singles not admitted tonight,** couples uniquement ce soir; **singles bar,** bar *m* pour célibataires.

single² *adj* **(a)** seul, unique; **(one) s. case,** un cas unique; **every s. day,** tous les jours; **to do sth in a s. movement,** faire qch en un seul mouvement; **not a s. one,** pas un seul, pas un; **s. parts,** pièces détachées (*d'une machine*); **I haven't seen a s. soul,** je n'ai pas vu âme qui vive; **s. sum,** somme payée en une fois; **don't say a s. word,** ne dites pas un (seul) mot *ou* un traître mot;

(b) (*for one person, not double etc*) (*lit*) à une place, pour une personne; (*chambre*) à un lit, pour une personne; *Nau* (*cabine*) individuel; **in s. rank,** sur un rang; *Bot* **s. flower,** fleur simple; **s. seater,** (*car*) monoplace *f*; (*plane*) monoplace *m*;

(c) (*person*) célibataire, non-marié(e); **a s. man/woman,** un/une célibataire; **he/she is s.,** il/elle ne s'est pas marié(e); **he remained s.,** il est resté célibataire *ou Old-fashioned* garçon; **she remained s.,** elle est restée célibataire *ou Old-fashioned* demoiselle; **s. parent,** père *m ou* mère *f* célibataire.

►**single out** *vtsep* (*choose from many*) isoler, choisir; **she was singled out for praise,** elle a été félicitée en particulier; **why s. him out (for praise)?,** pourquoi le féliciter en particulier?; **why s. him out (for blame)?,** pourquoi le blâmer en particulier?

single-breasted [-'brestɪd] *adj* **s.-b. jacket,** veston droit.

single-cylinder [-'sɪlɪndər] *adj Aut etc* **s.-c. engine,** moteur *m* monocylindrique.

single-deck [-'dek] *adj* **s.-d. bus,** autobus *m* sans impériale.

single-decker [-'dekər] *n* autobus *m* sans impériale.

single-density [-'densɪtɪ] *adj Comptr* (*disk*) à simple densité.

single-drive [-'draɪv] *adj Comptr* (*computer*) à un seul lecteur de disquettes.

single-engined [-'endʒɪnd] *adj Av* **s.-e. aircraft,** (avion *m*) monomoteur *m*.

single-handed [-'hændɪd] **1** *adv* **I did it s.-h.,** je l'ai fait tout seul *ou* à moi seul; **to sail s.-h.,** naviguer seul. **2** *adj* **his s.-h. efforts,** ses efforts solitaires.

single-handedly [-'hændɪdlɪ] *adv* seul, tout seul.

single-lens [-'lenz] *adj Phot* **s.-l. reflex,** reflex *m* monoculaire; **s.-l. camera,** appareil-photo *m* monoculaire.

single-line [-'laɪn] *adj Aut* **s.-l. traffic only,** circulation *f* à sens unique.

single-minded [-'maɪndɪd] *adj* (*person*) constant (*dans la poursuite d'un but*); immuable (*dans ses convictions etc*); obstiné, résolu (*dans son attitude, ses actes*).

single-mindedly [-'maɪndɪdlɪ] *adv* (*with constancy*) avec constance; (*obstinately*) obstinément; (*determinedly*) résolument.

single-mindedness [-'maɪndɪdnɪs] *n* (*constancy*) constance *f*; obstination *f*; (*determination*) résolution *f*.

singleness ['sɪŋg(ə)lnɪs] *n* **with s. of purpose,** avec un seul but en vue; **his s. of purpose,** sa détermination.

single-parent [-'peərənt] *adj* **s.-p. family,** famille monoparentale *ou* à parent unique.

single-phase [-'feɪz] *adj El* **s.-p. current,** courant uniphasé *ou* monophasé.

single-sex [-'seks] *adj Sch* **s.-s. school,** école *f* non-mixte.

single-sided [-'saɪdɪd] *adj Comptr* (*disk*) à une seule face.

singlet ['sɪŋglɪt] *n* maillot *m* de corps; gilet *m* (*de coton, de flanelle*); *Sp* maillot.

singleton ['sɪŋg(ə)ltən] *n Cards Math* singleton *m*.

single-track [-'træk] *adj Rail* **s.-t. railway,** chemin *m* de fer à voie unique.

singly ['sɪŋglɪ] *adv* **(a)** séparément, un à un; *Com* **articles sold s.,** articles qui se vendent séparément *ou* à la pièce; **people entered s. or in pairs,** les gens sont entrés seuls ou par deux; **(b)** *Old-fashioned* (*unaided*) seul, sans aide.

singsong ['sɪŋsɒŋ] *n* **(a)** (*tone*) ton chantant; **in a s. voice,** d'un ton chantant; **(b)** *F* (*singing session*) concert improvisé (*entre amis*); **they like a s.,** ils aiment bien chanter.

singular ['sɪŋgjʊlər] **1** *adj* **(a)** *Gram* (*nombre*) singulier; **(b)** (*remarkable*) rare, remarquable; (*strange*) singulier, bizarre. **2** *n* **in the s.,** au singulier.

singularity [sɪŋgjʊ'lærɪtɪ] *n* **(a)** (*state of being single*) singularité *f*; **(b)** (*remarkableness*) particularité *f*; **(c)** (*strangeness*) bizarrerie *f*; **(d)** (*remarkable thing*) exemple *m* unique *ou* remarquable.

singularize ['sɪŋgjʊləraɪz] *vt* singulariser.

singularly ['sɪŋgjʊləlɪ] *adv* (*remarkably*) singulièrement, remarquablement; *Old-fashioned* (*strangely*) bizarrement.

Sinhalese [sɪn(h)ə'liːz] *Geog* **1** *adj* cing(h)alais. **2** *n* **(a)** (*person*) Cing(h)alais, -aise; **(b)** *Ling* cing(h)alais *m*.

sinister ['sɪnɪstər] *adj* **(a)** (*influence, présage, événement, sourire*) sinistre; (*air*) menaçant; **a man of s. appearance,** un homme de mauvaise mine; **(b)** *Her* senestre, sénestre.

sink¹ [sɪŋk] *n* **(a)** (*basin*) évier *m* (*de cuisine*); **to pour (sth) down the s.,** jeter (qch) à l'égout; *Fig* **s. of iniquity,** cloaque *m ou* sentine *f* de tous les vices; **s. unit,** bloc-évier *m*, *pl* blocs-éviers; **(b)** *Geol etc* bétoire *f*.

sink² *v* (*pt* **sank** [sæŋk]; *pp* **sunk** [sʌŋk]; *Arch & as adj* **sunken** ['sʌŋkən]) **1** *vi* **(a)** (*in water*) aller au fond (des eaux); (*of ship*) sombrer, couler; **to s. like a stone,** (*of person*) couler à pic; *Fig* **here goes! s. or swim!,** allons-y! il faut risquer le tout pour le tout!;

(b) to s. into the mud/the snow, s'enfoncer dans la boue/la neige; **to s. into the quicksand,** s'enliser dans des sables mouvants; **to s. into one's memory,** se graver dans la mémoire; **to s. into oblivion,** tomber dans l'oubli; **to s. deep(er) into crime,** s'enfoncer dans le crime; **to s. into a deep sleep,** s'endormir profondément;

(c) (*subside*) **to s. (down),** s'affaisser; (*of wall, building etc*) s'affaisser, se tasser; **to s. (down) into an armchair,** (*of person*) se laisser tomber *ou* s'effondrer dans un fauteuil; **to s. to the ground,** (se laisser) tomber à terre; **her heart sank at the news,** à cette nouvelle son cœur s'est serré; **his spirits sank,** son courage s'est abattu;

(d) *(of ground etc)* s'abaisser; *(subside)* descendre; **the sun is sinking,** le soleil baisse;

(e) *(decrease)* baisser *(en valeur, en puissance)*; *(become weaker)* s'affaiblir, décliner; **prices are sinking,** les cours baissent *ou* sont en baisse; **the pond has sunk,** la livre a chuté *ou* baissé; **they've sunk to the bottom of the league table,** ils sont tombés tout en bas du classement; **the patient is sinking fast,** le malade baisse *ou* décline rapidement; **her voice sank to a whisper,** sa voix s'est réduite à un murmure; **he has sunk in my estimation,** il a baissé *ou* diminué dans mon estime; **how could anyone s. so low?,** comment peut-on tomber si bas?

2 *vt* **(a)** couler, faire sombrer *(un navire)*, envoyer *(un navire)* au fond; mouiller *(une mine)*; *F* **we're sunk,** nous sommes ruinés *ou* fichus; **sunk in thought,** plongé dans ses pensées;

(b) (faire) baisser *(qch à un niveau inférieur)*; enfoncer *(un pieu etc)*; **stone sunk into the wall,** pierre encastrée dans le mur; **to s. one's teeth into sth,** enfoncer ses dents dans qch;

(c) *F* **to s. a drink,** vider un pot; s'envoyer un demi *etc*;

(d) creuser, forer *(un puits)*; supprimer *(une objection etc)*; laisser de côté *(son opinion etc)*; **they sank their differences,** ils ont fait table rase de leurs différends;

(e) *Fin* amortir *(une dette)*;

(f) **to s. money in an undertaking,** *(invest)* placer de l'argent dans une entreprise; *(lose)* engloutir de l'argent dans une entreprise;

(g) **to s. the ball,** *Billiards* mettre la bille dans la blouse; *Golf* envoyer la balle dans le trou.

►sink in *vi* **(a)** *(be absorbed)* pénétrer; **pour syrup on the cake and let it s. in,** verser le sirop sur le gâteau et le laisser pénétrer; **(b)** *(be understood)* **her remark didn't s. in until later,** sa remarque n'a fait effet que plus tard; **his words are beginning to s. in,** ses paroles commencent à faire impression; **the lesson hasn't sunk in,** *(been learnt)* la leçon n'a pas été apprise; *(been understood)* la leçon n'a pas été (bien) comprise; **it was beginning to s. in that things had changed,** je commençais *ou* il commençait *etc* à comprendre que les choses avaient changé.

sinker ['sɪŋkər] *n* **(a)** *(person)* **well s.,** *Min* **shaft s.,** foreur *m*, puisatier *m*; **(b)** plomb *m* *(d'une ligne de pêche)*; *Nau* crapaud *m* d'amarrage *(d'une mine)*; **(c)** *Am Culin F* beignet soufflé.

sinking ['sɪŋkɪŋ] **1** *adj* qui s'enfonce, qui s'affaisse; *(mur etc)* qui se tasse; *(navire)* qui coule; **with a s. heart,** avec un serrement de cœur.

2 *n* **(a)** enfoncement *m*; enlisement *m* *(dans une fondrière etc)*; engloutissement *m* *(d'un navire)*; *(intentional, in war etc)* torpillage *m* *(d'un navire)*;

(b) *(subsiding)* affaissement *m* *(du sol etc)*; tassement *m* *(d'un édifice etc)*; serrement *m* *(du cœur)*; abattement *m* *(des esprits)*; **that s. feeling,** ce sentiment de catastrophe imminente; **I get that s. feeling every time I think about what happened,** à chaque fois que je pense à ce qui s'est passé, j'ai l'estomac qui se serre;

(c) *(weakening)* affaiblissement *m*, déclin *m* *(des forces etc)*; abaissement *m* *(de la voix etc)*;

(d) creusage *m*, forage *m* *(d'un puits)*;

(e) *Fin* amortissement *m*, extinction *f* *(d'une dette)*; placement *m* *(d'une somme)* à fonds perdu; **s. fund,** fonds *m ou* caisse *f* d'amortissement.

sinless ['sɪnlɪs] *adj* sans péché; *(pure)* innocent, pur.

sinner ['sɪnər] *n* pécheur *m*, pécheresse *f*; *F* **I didn't do my homework — you s.!,** je n'ai pas fait mes devoirs – quelle honte!

sinning ['sɪnɪŋ] *n* le péché.

sinologist [saɪ'nɒlədʒɪst, sɪ-] *n* sinologue *mf*.

sinology [saɪ'nɒlədʒɪ, sɪ-] *n* sinologie *f*.

sinuosity [sɪnjʊ'ɒsɪtɪ] *n* sinuosité *f*.

sinuous ['sɪnjʊəs] *adj* **(a)** sinueux, tortueux; **(b)** *(person)* souple, agile.

sinus ['saɪnəs] *n Anat* sinus *m*; *F* **I've got a bit of s. trouble,** j'ai un problème de sinus.

sinusitis [saɪnə'saɪtɪs] *n Med* sinusite *f*.

Sioux [suː] **1** *adj* sioux *inv*. **2** *n inv* **(a)** Sioux *mf*; **(b)** *Ling* sioux *m*.

sip¹ [sɪp] *n* petite gorgée; **to drink sth in sips,** siroter qch, boire qch à petits coups; **try a s.,** prenez un petit coup.

sip² *v* **(-pp-) 1** *vt* boire *(qch)* à petites gorgées *ou* à petits coups, siroter *(qch)*. **2** *vi* **to s. at sth,** boire qch à petites gorgées.

siphon¹ ['saɪf(ə)n] *n* siphon *m*.

siphon² *vt* siphonner *(un liquide)*.

►siphon off *vtsep* **(a)** = **SIPHON²**; **(b)** *Fin* éponger, résorber *(un excédent)*; prendre *(du personnel)*; *(steal etc)* pomper, faucher; *F* **they siphoned off all the profits,** ils ont épongé tous les bénéfices.

sir [sɜːr, sər] *n* **(a)** *(as form of address to a superior, esp Am to an equal)* monsieur *m*; **yes, s.,** oui, monsieur; *Mil etc (to superior officer)* oui, mon capitaine *ou* mon colonel *etc*; *Nau* oui, commandant *ou* amiral *etc*; **dinner is served, s.,** monsieur est servi; **Dear S.,** *(in letter)* Monsieur; *(less formal)* Cher Monsieur; **Dear Sirs,** Messieurs; *Sch Sl* **s. told me,** le maître me l'a dit; **(b)** *(title)* sir (= *titre d'un baronet et d'un knight; ne s'emploie jamais sans le prénom, ainsi Sir Walter Scott, Sir Walter*).

sire¹ ['saɪər] *n* **(a)** *(in breeding)* père *m* (= *en parlant des quadrupèdes*); *(stallion)* étalon *m*; **(b)** *Arch & Lit (father)* père *m*; *Arch (address to sovereign)* sire *m*.

sire² *vt (of stallion, F man)* engendrer, procréer *(un poulain)*.

siren ['saɪərən] *n* **(a)** *Myth & Fig* sirène *f*; **s. song,** chant *m* de sirène; **(b)** *Ind Nau etc* sirène *f* *(d'usine, de navire, d'alarme)*.

sirloin ['sɜːlɔɪn] *n Culin* aloyau *m* *(de bœuf)*; **s. steak,** steak *m* d'aloyau.

sirocco [sɪ'rɒkəʊ] *n Met* siroc(c)o *m*.

sirup ['sɪrəp] *n Am* = **SYRUP**.

sis [sɪs] *n F (sister)* sœurette *F*, frangine *f*.

sisal ['saɪs(ə)l] *n (plant or fibre)* sisal *m*.

sissy ['sɪsɪ] **1** *n Pej (effeminate man, boy)* homme *ou* garçon efféminé; *(cowardly child etc)* enfant *etc* peureux, poule mouillée; **that's a game for sissies!,** c'est un jeu pour les poules mouillées. **2** *adj (cowardly)* lâche, peureux; *(effeminate)* efféminé; **he thinks it's s. to ...,** il pense que ça fait efféminé de ... .

sister ['sɪstər] *n* **(a)** sœur *f*; **sisters unite!,** *(to female workers, feminists)* sœurs, unissez-vous!; **s. company,** société-sœur *f*; **s. nations,** nations *fpl* sœurs; **s. ships,** bâtiments *mpl* identiques, sister-ship *m*; **(b)** *Rel* religieuse *f*, (bonne) sœur *f*; **S. of Mercy,** sœur de la Charité; **come in, S.,** entrez, ma sœur; **(c) (ward) s.,** *(in hospital)* infirmière-chef *f*; **theatre s.,** infirmière-chef qui fait le service de la salle d'opération; **thank you, s.,** merci madame *ou* mademoiselle.

sisterhood ['sɪstəhʊd] *n* **(a)** *Rel* communauté religieuse *(de sœurs)*; **(b)** *(in relationship)* solidarité féminine; **the s.,** la communauté des femmes.

sister-in-law, *pl* **sisters-in-law** ['sɪstərɪn'lɔː] *n* belle-sœur *f*, *pl* belles-sœurs.

sisterly ['sɪstəlɪ] *adj* de sœur; **in a s. fashion,** en sœur.

Sistine ['sɪstiːn, -taɪn] *adj* **the S. chapel,** la chapelle Sixtine.

sit *v (pt & pp* **sat** [sæt]; *prp* **sitting) 1** *vi* **(a)** *(of person)* s'asseoir; **to be sitting,** être assis *(dans un fauteuil, par terre etc)*; **s.!,** *(to dog)* assis!; **we usually s. in the living room,** nous nous tenons d'ordinaire dans le salon; **where would you like me to s.?, where shall I s.?,** où dois-je me mettre *ou* m'asseoir?; **she was sitting reading,** elle était assise à lire *ou* en train de lire; **to s. at home,** se tenir chez soi; **don't just s. there, say something!,** ne restez pas bouche cousue, dites quelque chose!; **to s. at (the) table,** *(take one's seat)* s'asseoir *ou* se mettre à (la) table, s'attabler; **they were sitting at (the) table,** ils étaient assis à table, ils étaient (assis) à (la) table, ils étaient attablés; **we were sitting at lunch/dinner,** nous étions en train de déjeuner/dîner; **he sits for hours over his books,** il passe des heures penché sur ses livres; *F* **to s. tight,** *(not move)* ne pas bouger de sa place; *(not give in)* ne pas céder;

(b) **to s. for one's portrait,** poser pour son portrait; **to s. for an examination,** passer *ou* subir un examen; **to s. in Parliament,** = être député;

(c) *(of assemblies)* siéger, être en séance; **the court is sitting,** la séance est ouverte;

(d) *F (of object)* **the diskette was sitting on the radiator,** la disquette était *ou* se trouvait sur le radiateur; **I found it sitting on the fridge,** je l'ai trouvé sur le frigo;

(e) *(of bird) (alight)* (se) percher; *(be stationary)* être perché; **to s. (on eggs),** *(of hen)* couver (des œufs);

(f) *(of responsibility)* **to s. heavy on s.o.,** peser sur qn;

(g) *(of garment)* tomber (bien, mal).

2 *vt* **(a)** *Horseriding* **to s. a horse well/badly,** se tenir bien/mal à cheval, avoir une bonne/mauvaise assiette;

(b) **to s. a child on the table,** asseoir un enfant sur la table; **to s. a hen (on eggs),** mettre une poule à couver;

(c) *Sch* passer *(un examen)*.

►sit about, sit around *vi (hang around)* traîner; *(do nothing)* ne rien faire.

►sit back *vi* **(a)** *(lean back)* **to s. back in one's chair,**

s'appuyer sur le dossier de sa chaise *ou* son fauteuil; **(b)** *F* (*relax*) se relaxer; **to s. back and let the others do the work,** regarder les autres travailler; **the authorities just sat back and did nothing,** les autorités n'ont pas daigné faire quoi que ce soit; **we can't just s. back and do nothing,** il faut que nous fassions quelque chose.

►sit down 1 *vi* s'asseoir; **I haven't sat down all day,** je ne me suis pas assis de la journée; **please s. down,** asseyez-vous, je vous en prie, veuillez vous asseoir; **to s. down again,** se rasseoir; (*at table*) se remettre à (la) table; **to s. down at (the) table,** se mettre à table, s'attabler; **to s. down to a meal,** se mettre à table pour un repas; **to s. down to a game of bridge,** s'installer pour faire une partie de bridge. **2** *vtas* asseoir (*un enfant etc*); *F* **s. yourself down!,** asseyez-vous donc!

►sit for *vipo* **(a)** (*be candidate in*) passer (*un examen*); **(b)** (*pose for*) **to s. for one's portrait,** poser pour son portrait.

►sit in *vi* **(a)** (*at meeting etc*) assister sans participer; **do you mind if I s. in for a while?,** ça vous ennuie si je reste à écouter un moment?; **(b)** (*occupy building, office etc*) faire grève avec occupation des locaux.

►sit in on *vipo* (*attend as observer*) **to s. in on a rehearsal/a meeting,** assister à une répétition/une réunion (sans y participer).

►sit on *vipo F* **(a)** (*not deal with*) s'asseoir sur; **they sat on it for two months,** ils se sont assis dessus pendant deux mois; **(b)** (*snub*) rembarrer.

►sit out 1 *vi* (*sit outside*) s'asseoir dehors; (*be seated outside*) être assis dehors. **2** *vtsep* **(a)** (*not participate in*) ne pas prendre part à (*un jeu etc*); **to s. out a dance,** manquer une danse; **I'll s. this one out,** je ne veux pas danser celle-ci; **(b)** (*wait until end of*) rester (patiemment) jusqu'à la fin de (*une conférence etc*).

►sit through *vipo* (*wait until end of*) rester pendant toute la durée de; **he sat through the whole play,** il est resté jusqu'à la fin de la pièce; **we had to s. through two hours of Wagner,** nous avons dû nous payer deux heures de Wagner.

►sit up 1 *vi* (*straighten one's back*) se tenir droit; se redresser (*sur sa chaise*); (*from lying position*) se dresser *ou* se mettre sur son séant; **s. up straight!,** tiens-toi droit!; *F* **to make s.o. s. up,** étonner qn, épater qn; **he's beginning to s. up and take notice,** (*of convalescent*) il est en train de se remettre; *Fig* **her competitors are beginning to s. up and take notice,** ses concurrents commencent à prendre conscience de son existence; **to s. up (and beg),** (*of dog*) faire le beau; **to s. up (late),** veiller tard; **to s. up for s.o.,** (rester debout à) attendre qn, veiller en attendant le retour de qn; **to s. up with someone who is ill,** garder *ou* veiller un malade; **to s. up to (the) table,** approcher sa chaise de la table. **2** *vtsep* **to s. s.o. up,** soulever qn pour l'asseoir.

sitcom ['sɪtkɒm] *n TV Rad F* comédie *f* de situation.

sit-down¹ ['sɪtdaʊn] *n* (*act*) **come and have a s.-d.,** venez vous asseoir.

sit-down² *adj* **s.-d. meal,** repas servi à table; *Ind* **s.-d. strike,** grève *f* sur le tas.

site¹ [saɪt] *n* **(a)** emplacement *m*, situation *f* (*d'un édifice etc*); site *m* (*archéologique etc*); **the s. of a battle/a historic meeting,** le site d'une bataille/d'une réunion historique; **camp(ing) s.,** (terrain *m* de) camping *m*; **launching s.,** aire *f* de lancement; **(b) building s.,** chantier *m* (de construction); (*land for building on*) terrain *m* à bâtir; **on s.,** sur place; **to be on s.,** être à pied d'œuvre; **s. manager,** chef *m* de chantier.

site² *vt* placer, situer (*un bâtiment etc*).

sit-in ['sɪtɪn] *n* sit-in *m*; (*strike*) occupation *f* des locaux.

sitter ['sɪtər] *n* **(a)** (*sitting person*) personne assise; **(b)** *Art* personne qui pose (*chez un artiste*); **(c)** *F* **s.(-in),** gardien, -ienne d'enfants; **(d)** (*hen*) couveuse *f*; **(e)** *Sp F* **to miss a s.,** rater un but tout fait.

sitting ['sɪtɪŋ] **1** *adj* assis; (*tribunal etc*) siégeant; (*animal*) au repos; (*lièvre*) au gîte; (*faisan*) au perché; *Art* **s. figure,** figure assise; **s. tenant,** locataire *mf* en possession des lieux; *Parl* **our s. member,** le député qui nous représente actuellement; **s. hen,** poule *f* en train de couver; *Fig* **to be a s. duck,** (*to be easy target for criticism etc*) être une cible facile.

2 *n* (*position*) posture assise; pose *f* (*pour son portrait etc*); (*of hen*) couvaison *f*, incubation *f*; couvée *f* (*d'œufs*); séance *f*, réunion *f* (*d'une commission etc*); **s. still,** immobilité *f*; **s. and standing room,** places assises et places debout; **s. up (late),** veille *f*; **s. room,** (*in house*) salon *m*, salle *f* de séjour; **to paint a portrait in three sittings,** faire un portrait en trois séances; **first/second s.,** (*for meals*) premier/deuxième service; **to serve 500 people in** *or* **at one s.,** servir 500 personnes à la fois; **to write two chapters at one s.,** écrire deux chapitres d'un trait *ou* d'un (seul) jet; **s. of court,** audience *f*; **the sittings,** les (quatre) sessions *fpl* de l'année judiciare.

situate ['sɪtjʊeɪt] *vt* situer (*une maison etc*); **pleasantly situated house,** maison bien située; **awkwardly situated,** (*of person*) dans une situation *ou* une position embarrassante; **he's well situated to know what's going on,** il est bien placé pour savoir ce qui se passe.

situation [sɪtjʊ'eɪʃən] *n* **(a)** situation *f*, emplacement *m* (*d'un édifice, d'une ville*); **(b)** situation *f* (*politique etc*); **to explain the s.,** exposer la situation; **to find oneself in an unfortunate s.,** se trouver dans une déplorable conjoncture; *F* **what's** *or* **how's the coffee s.?,** combien nous reste-t-il de café?; *F* **we're in a high inflation s.,** nous sommes dans une situation d'inflation élevée; **what to do in an emergency s.,** que faire en cas d'urgence; **(c)** *Th* situation *f* (dramatique); **s. comedy,** comédie *f* de situation; **(d)** (*employment*) emploi *m*, position *f*; **to get a s.,** obtenir un emploi; **situations vacant/wanted,** (*in advertisements*) offres *fpl*/demandes *fpl* d'emplois.

sit-upon ['sɪtəpɒn] *n F* derrière *m*, postérieur *m*.

six [sɪks] *n* **(a)** six *m*; **number s.,** (le) numéro six; **twenty-s.,** vingt-six; **s. fours** *or* **four sixes are twenty-four,** six fois quatre *ou* quatre fois six font vingt-quatre; **s. and a half,** six et demi; **at s. (o'clock),** à six heures; **at s. thirty,** à six heures et demie; **to be s. (years old),** avoir six ans; **double s.,** (*at dominoes etc*) double-six *m*, *pl* doubles-six; *Cards* **the s. of hearts,** le six de cœur; *F* **it's s. of one and half a dozen of the other,** c'est blanc bonnet et bonnet blanc, c'est kif-kif; **we're all** *or* **everything's at sixes and sevens,** tout est désorganisé *ou* en pagaille; *F* **to be s. feet under,** être enterré; **s.-cylinder car,** une six cylindres; **s. day bicycle race,** six jours; *Hist* **the S. Day War,** la guerre des six jours; **s.-seater (car),** voiture *f* à six places; **(b)** *Cr* six points (*marqués par le batteur*); *F* **to knock for s.,** (*knock down*) étendre (*qn*); (*stun*) abasourdir (*qn*); battre (*l'ennemi etc*) à plate(s) couture(s); ficher (*un projet etc*) en l'air; **that's knocked everything for s.,** ça a tout fiché en l'air.

sixfold ['sɪksfəʊld] **1** *adj* sextuple. **2** *adv* au sextuple; **to increase s.,** sextupler.

six-foot ['sɪksfʊt] *adj* (*poutre etc*) de six pieds.

six-footer [sɪks'fʊtər] *n* homme *ou* femme mesurant six pieds; **he's obviously going to be a s.-f.,** on voit bien qu'il va atteindre les deux mètres.

six-pack ['sɪkspæk] *n Com* pack *m* de six (*bouteilles, boîtes, cannettes*).

sixpence ['sɪkspəns] *n* **(a)** (*sum*) six pence; **(b)** *Arch* (*coin*) pièce *f* de six pence; **two and s.,** deux shillings et six pence.

sixpenny ['sɪkspənɪ] *adj Old-fashioned* (*bonbon etc*) qui coûte *ou* qui vaut six pence; (*timbre*) de six pence; *Arch* **s. piece** *or* **bit,** pièce *f* de six pence.

sixpennyworth [sɪks'penɪwəθ] *n Old-fashioned* **to buy s. of chocolate,** acheter pour six pence de chocolat.

six-shooter [sɪks'ʃuːtər] *n* revolver *m* à six coups.

six-sided [sɪks'saɪdɪd] *adj* qui a six côtés, hexagone.

sixteen [sɪks'tiːn] *n* seize *m*; **she is s.,** elle a seize ans.

sixteenth [sɪks'tiːnθ] **1** *adj* seizième; **Louis the S.,** Louis Seize; **(on) the s. (of August),** le seize (août); *esp Am Mus* **s. note,** double croche *f*. **2** *n* (*fraction*) seizième *m*.

sixth [sɪksθ] **1** *adj* sixième; **Henry the S.,** Henri Six; **(on) the s. (of December),** le six (décembre); *Eng Sch* **the s. form,** ≈ les classes de première et de terminale; *Eng Sch* **s. form college,** école de préparation aux examens O levels et A levels; *Eng Sch* **s. former,** = élève de la (classe de) première ou de terminale. **2** *n* (*fraction*) sixième *m*; *Mus* sixte *f* (*majeure, mineure*).

sixthly ['sɪksθlɪ] *adv* sixièmement.

sixtieth ['sɪkstɪɪθ] *adj & n* soixantième *mf*.

sixty ['sɪkstɪ] *n* soixante *m*; **s. one,** soixante et un; **s.-third,** soixante-troisième; **about** *or* **some s. books,** une soixantaine de livres; **she's in her sixties,** elle a (dé)passé la soixantaine; **in the sixties,** pendant les années soixante (de notre siècle).

sixty-four [sɪkstɪ'fɔːr] *n* soixante-quatre *m*; *F* **the s.-f. (thousand) dollar question,** la question cruciale.

sizable ['saɪzəb(ə)l] *adj* = **SIZEABLE**.

size¹ [saɪz] *n* **(a)** (*of building, room*) grandeur *f*; (*of town, country, island*) superficie *f*; (*of carpet, machine, car*) dimensions *fpl*, taille *f*; (*of apple, cake, print*) grosseur *f*, taille *f*; (*of problem, undertaking*) importance *f*, taille *f*; **of equal** *or* **the same s., of a s.,** de (la) même grandeur *ou* taille *etc*; **I was surprised by the s. of the bill,** j'ai été étonné par le montant de la note; **bicycles/people come in**

all shapes and sizes, il y a des bicyclettes/des gens de toutes les formes et de toutes les tailles; **books arranged according to s.,** livres disposés par rang de taille; **it's the s. of an egg,** c'est gros comme un œuf; **actual** *or* **full s.,** grandeur nature; **a town of that s.,** une ville de cette importance; *F* **that's about the s. of it,** c'est à peu près cela; **standard s.,** cote *f* d'origine; **to cut a piece to s.,** tailler une pièce à la dimension *ou* à la cote; *F* **to cut s.o. down to s.,** rabattre le caquet à qn, remettre qn à sa place;

(b) (*of person*) taille *f*; *Com* taille (*de vêtements*); encolure *f* (*de chemise*); pointure *f* (*de chaussures, de gants, de coiffures*); format *m* (*d'un livre, de papier*); calibre *m* (*d'un fusil, d'une cartouche*); **a boy half/twice his s.,** un garçon deux fois moins/plus grand que lui; **a s. larger/smaller,** (*shoes*) une pointure au-dessus/en-dessous; (*dresses etc*) une taille au-dessus/en-dessous; **what s. do you take?, what's your s.?, what s. are you?,** (*dresses etc*) quelle est votre taille?; (*in shoes*) quelle pointure chaussez-vous?; **s. ten shoes,** ≈ chaussures *fpl* de pointure 44; **I've nothing in your s.,** je n'ai rien à votre taille *ou* à votre pointure; **to try sth for s.,** essayer qch (*pour voir si cela vous convient*); *F* **try this one for s.,** qu'est-ce que vous pensez de ça?

size[2] *vt* **(a)** (*classify according to size*) classer (*des objets*) par grosseur *ou* par dimension; **(b)** *Ind etc* (*gauge*) calibrer (*une pièce*); (*finish to size*) mettre (*un trou, une pièce*) à la cote *ou* à dimensions.

size[3] *n Tech* apprêt *m*; (*glue*) colle *f*, encollage *m*; *Tex* empois *m*; **animal s.,** colle animale.

size[4] *vt Tech* apprêter, coller, encoller (*le papier etc*); *Tex* parer.

►**size up** *vtsep* (*gauge size of*) jauger *ou* prendre les dimensions de (*qch*); *F* **to s. s.o. up,** évaluer qn, jauger qn; **they soon sized him up,** ils ont eu vite fait de le jauger.

sizeable ['saɪzəb(ə)l] *adj* assez grand, plutôt grand; (*difference*) assez important; (*fine, sum*) assez élevé.

sized [saɪzd] **(a)** (*classified according to size*) classé par ordre de grandeur *ou* de taille; **(b) fair s.,** (*quite large*) assez grand; **large/small s.,** de grande/petite taille; (*livre, papier etc*) de grand/petit format; **medium s.,** de grandeur moyenne, de taille moyenne.

sizing[1] [saɪzɪŋ] *n* **(a)** (*classification by size*) classement *m* par ordre de grandeur *ou* de grosseur *ou* de taille; **(b)** (*gauging*) calibrage *m*; (*finishing to size*) mise *f* à la cote (*d'une pièce*); (*checking*) vérification *f* des dimensions (*d'une pièce*).

sizing[2] *n* **(a)** (*process*) apprêtage *m*; collage *m*, encollage *m* (*du papier etc*); *Tex* parage *m*; **(b)** (*substance*) colle *f*; (*in painting*) apprêt *m*.

sizzle[1] ['sɪz(ə)l] *n* grésillement *m* (*de la friture etc*).

sizzle[2] *vi* (*of frying pan, sausages etc*) grésiller.

sizzling ['sɪzlɪŋ] **1** *adj* grésillant. **2** *adv* **s. hot,** tout chaud; *F* (*jour*) torride. **3** *n* grésillement *m*.

skate[1] [skeɪt] *n* (*fish*) raie *f*.

skate[2] *n* (*runner*) patin *m*; **ice/roller s.,** patin à glace/à roulettes; *F* **to get one's skates on,** se dépêcher.

skate[3] *vi* patiner, faire du patin (*sur glace*); **to roller s.,** faire du patin à roulettes; *F* **to s. round sth,** tourner autour du pot.

► **skate over** *vipo* **(a)** (*skate across surface of*) parcourir en patin; **(b)** (*discuss superficially*) effleurer (*un sujet*); passer rapidement sur (*des difficultés*).

skateboard[1] ['skeɪtbɔːd] *n Sp* planche *f* à roulettes, *F* skate(-board) *m*, *pl* skate(-boards), *Can* rouli-roulant ® *m*, *pl* rouli-roulants.

skateboard[2] *vi Sp* faire de la planche à roulettes *ou F* du skate *ou Can* du rouli-roulant.

skateboarder ['skeɪtbɔːdər] *n Sp* personne *f* pratiquant le skate(-board).

skateboarding ['skeɪtbɔːdɪŋ] *n* skate(-board) *m*; **s. enthusiast,** mordu *m* du skate(-board).

skater ['skeɪtər] *n* patineur, -euse (*sur glace*); **roller s.,** qui fait du patinage à roulettes.

skating ['skeɪtɪŋ] *n* patinage *m* (*sur glace*); **roller s.,** patin *m* à roulettes; **s. rink,** patinoire *f*; (*for roller skating*) piste *f*.

skedaddle [skɪ'dæd(ə)l] *vi F* **(a)** (*run off*) se sauver à toutes jambes, décamper, déguerpir; **(b)** (*of group of people*) s'enfuir à la débandade.

skeet [skiːt] *n Sp* **s. (shooting),** tir *m* au pigeon (d'argile), (genre de) ball-trap *m*.

skein [skeɪn, skiːn] *n* **(a)** écheveau *m* (*de soie, de laine*); *Fig* **(tangled) s.,** confusion *f*, embrouillamini *m*; **(b)** vol *m* (*d'oies sauvages*).

skeletal ['skelɪt(ə)l] *adj* squelettique; *Fig* (*presentation etc*) sommaire.

skeleton ['skelɪt(ə)n] *n* **(a)** squelette *m*, ossature *f* (*d'homme, d'animal, de feuille etc*); *Fig* **s. in the cupboard** *or Am* **in the closet,** secret honteux de la famille; **s. at the feast,** rabat-joie *m inv*, trouble-fête *m inv*; **he's a living s.,** c'est un vrai squelette, il n'a plus que la peau et les os; **(b)** *Fig* charpente *f*, carcasse *f*, squelette *m* (*d'un bâtiment etc*); canevas *m*, esquisse *f* (*d'un roman etc*); **s. key,** (clef *f* à) crochet *m* (de serrurier), fausse clef, rossignol *m*; **s. map,** carte muette; **s. staff/crew,** personnel/équipage réduit.

skeptic, skeptical *etc US* = **SCEPTIC, SCEPTICAL** *etc.*

sketch[1] [sketʃ] *n* **(a)** *Art Liter* croquis *m*, esquisse *f*; (*in surveying*) levé *m* (topographique); **character s.,** portrait *m* littéraire; **first s.,** premier jet; **to make a s. of sth,** faire le croquis de qch, croquer qch; **s. map,** plan *m* sommaire (*d'un terrain*); **s. block,** bloc *m* à croquis; **(b)** *Fig* exposé *m*, ébauche *f* (*d'un projet*); **she drew a brief s. of the situation,** elle a donné un bref résumé de la situation; **(c)** *Th TV* sketch *m*, saynète *f*.

sketch[2] *vt* **(a)** *Art* esquisser, dessiner à grands traits, croquer (*un paysage etc*); faire un *ou* le croquis de (*qch*); **(b)** = **SKETCH OUT (b).**

►**sketch in** *vtsep* dessiner sommairement (*des détails*).

►**sketch out** *vtsep* **(a)** (*draw up outline of*) faire le canevas *ou* l'esquisse de (*un roman*); **(b)** (*provide outline of*) esquisser, tracer (*un projet etc*).

sketchbook ['sketʃbʊk] *n* cahier *m* de croquis.

sketchily ['sketʃɪlɪ] *adv* d'une manière incomplète *ou* vague *ou* sans détails; (*to remember*) vaguement.

sketching ['sketʃɪŋ] *n* (*act*) action *f* de croquer *ou* d'esquisser; (*style*) dessin *m* rapide *ou* à main levée; **s. block** *or* **pad,** bloc *m* à croquis.

sketchy ['sketʃɪ] *adj* (*ouvrage*) qui manque de fini; (*dessin*) qui manque de détails; (*connaissances*) superficiel, sommaire; (*idées*) plutôt vague.

skew[1] [skjuː] *n* biais *m*, obliquité *f* (*d'un pont etc*); **on the s.,** de *ou* en biais, obliquement.

skew[2] **1** *adj* en biais, oblique. **2** *adv* de *ou* en biais.

skew[3] **1** *vi* biaiser, obliquer. **2** *vt* couper en sifflet *ou* en biseau.

skewbald ['skjuːbɔːld] *adj* (*white and chestnut*) (*cheval*) blanc à taches alezanes; (*white and red-brown*) (*cheval*) blanc et roux.

skewer[1] ['skjuːər] *n Culin* brochette *f*, broche *f*.

skewer[2] *vt Culin* brocheter, embrocher (*de la viande etc*).

skew-whiff ['skjuː'wɪf] *adj Br F* de travers, *F* de traviole.

ski[1], *pl* **skis** [skiː, -iːz] *n* ski *m*; **s. binding,** fixation(s) *f(pl)*; **s. boots,** chaussures *fpl* de ski; **s. centre,** station *f* de ski; **s. instructor,** moniteur, -trice de ski; **s. jump,** saut *m* en *ou* à ski; (*structure*) tremplin *m*; **s. jumper,** sauteur *m*; **s. jump(ing),** saut en *ou* à ski(s); **s. lift,** remonte-pente *m*, *pl* remonte-pentes, téléski *m*; **s. pants,** fuseau *m*; **s. pass,** carte *f* de remonte-pente; **s. run** *or* **slope,** piste *f* de ski; **s. stick, s. pole,** bâton *m* de ski; **s. resort,** station *f* de ski; **s. suit,** combinaison *f* de ski; **s. wax,** fart *m*.

ski[2] *vi* (*pt & pp* **skied**) skier, faire du ski; (*move*) aller à *ou* en skis; **he skis well,** il skie bien; **to learn to s.,** apprendre à skier *ou* à faire du ski; **to s. down the slope,** descendre la piste à *ou* en skis; **we skied back,** nous sommes rentrés à *ou* en skis.

skid[1] [skɪd] *n* **(a)** *Aut* (*action*) dérapage *m*; **to go into a s.,** déraper, faire un dérapage; **(b)** (*device*) *Com* palette *f* sur patins; *Av* patin *m* (*d'atterrissage etc*); **tail s.,** béquille *f* (arrière); *Am F* **s. row,** quartier mal famé, bas-fonds *mpl*; **he's heading for s. row,** il va finir clochard; **s.-mounted,** à glissière; sur patins; *F* **to put the skids under s.o.,** (*hurry*) faire se dépêcher qn, presser qn; (*bring about ruin of*) faire échouer qn; *F* **to be on the skids,** (*economy, company, marriage etc*) battre de l'aile; *F* **he's on the skids,** il va mal finir.

skid[2] *v* (-dd-) **1** *vi* (*of car, tyre etc*) déraper; (*of wheel*) patiner; *Av* glisser sur l'aile; **his glasses went skidding across the table,** ses lunettes ont glissé jusqu'à l'autre bout de la table. **2** *vt* faire faire un dérapage à (*une voiture*).

skidding ['skɪdɪŋ] *n* **(a)** dérapage *m* (*d'un pneu, d'une voiture*); patinage *m* (*d'une roue*); *Av* glissement *m* (*sur l'aile*); **(b)** (*applying drag to wheel*) ensabotement *m*, enrayage *m*.

skidlid ['skɪdlɪd] *n Aut Sl* casque *m* de moto.

skidpan ['skɪdpæn] *n Aut* piste savonnée.

skier ['skiːər] *n* skieur, -euse.

skiff [skɪf] *n* esquif *m*, yole *f*; (*in rowing*) skiff *m*.

skiffle ['skɪf(ə)l] *n Mus* skiffle *m*; **s. group,** skiffle-group *m inv*.
ski-flying ['ski:flaɪɪŋ] *n Ski* vol *m* à ski.
skiing ['ski:ɪŋ] *n* ski *m*; **to go s.,** faire du ski; **we went on a s. holiday,** nous sommes allés aux sports d'hiver; **s. instructor,** moniteur, -trice de ski; **s. resort,** station *f* de ski.
skilful, *US* **skillful** ['skɪlfʊl] *adj* adroit, habile; **to be s. at** *or* **in (doing) sth,** être habile *ou* adroit à (faire) qch.
skilfully ['skɪlfʊlɪ] *adv* habilement, adroitement.
skilfulness, *US* **skillfulness** ['skɪlfʊlnɪs] *n* habileté *f*, adresse *f*.
skill [skɪl] *n* **(a)** (*ability*) habileté *f*, adresse *f*, dextérité *f*; **technical s.,** habileté, aptitude *f*; (*competence*) compétence *f*; **s. in doing sth,** talent *m ou* habileté pour faire qch; **lack of s.,** maladresse *f*, inhabileté *f*; **a game involving no s.,** un sport *ou* un jeu n'exigeant aucune aptitude particulière; **repairing pianos requires great s.,** réparer les pianos demande une grande compétence; **(b)** (*trade*) métier *m*; (*learned technique*) art *m* pratique, technique *f*; **learn new skills,** apprenez de nouvelles techniques; **an archaeologist requires many skills,** un archéologue doit posséder de nombreuses aptitudes.
skilled [skɪld] *adj* habile; (*travail*) de spécialiste; **to be s. in doing sth,** être habile *ou* adroit à faire qch; **she's highly s.,** elle est très qualifiée; **s. worker,** ouvrier, -ière qualifié(e); **s. labour,** main-d'œuvre qualifiée.
skillet ['skɪlɪt] *n Am* poêle *f* (à frire).
skillful, skillfully *etc US* = **SKILFUL, SKILFULLY** *etc*.
skim[1] [skɪm] *n* **just give it a quick s.,** (*read through quickly*) jetez-y un coup d'œil rapide.
skim[2] *v* **(-mm-) 1** *vt* **(a)** écumer (*le bouillon etc*); écrémer (*le lait, le verre en fusion etc*); **(b)** (*pass lightly over*) effleurer, raser (*une surface*); **to s. stones on water,** faire des ricochets; *Fig* **the book just skims the surface (of the problem),** le livre se contente de survoler le problème. **2** *vi* **to s. along** *or* **over the ground,** (*fly just above*) voler au ras du sol; (*move on surface*) raser le sol; **to s. over the water,** (*fly just above*) voler à fleur d'eau; (*move on surface*) raser l'eau; *Fig* **the author skims over the real problem,** l'auteur esquive les vrais problèmes; **skimmed milk,** lait écrémé; **skimmed (milk) cheese,** fromage *m* maigre.
►**skim off** *vtsep* (*remove by skimming*) enlever, prélever (*la crème etc*); *Fig* **to s. the cream off sth,** prendre la meilleure partie de qch; **the accounts department skims off the best recruits,** la comptabilité récupère les meilleures nouvelles recrues.
►**skim through** *vipo* (*read superficially*) parcourir rapidement (*un roman etc*).
skimmer ['skɪmər] *n* (*for soup, metals*) écumoire *f*; (*for milk*) écrémeuse *f*; (*for glass*) casse *f*.
skimp [skɪmp] **1** *vt* lésiner sur (*la nourriture, le tissu d'une robe*); *F* bâcler (*son travail*). **2** *vi* lésiner sur tout; (*live parsimoniously*) vivre avec parcimonie; **they skimped on the cost of the new road,** ils lésinaient sur le coût de la nouvelle route.
skimpily ['skɪmpɪlɪ] *adv* parcimonieusement (*meublé etc*); **s. made,** (*dress*) étriqué; **s. dressed,** légèrement vêtu.
skimping ['skɪmpɪŋ] *n* lésine(rie *f*) *f*; parcimonie *f*; *F* bâclage *m* (*d'un travail*).
skimpiness ['skɪmpɪnɪs] *n* insuffisance *f*; aspect étriqué (*d'un vêtement*).
skimpy ['skɪmpɪ] *adj* insuffisant; **s. meal,** maigre repas; **s. skirt,** jupe étriquée; **to be s. with sth,** (*be mean*) lésiner sur qch.
skin[1] [skɪn] *n* **(a)** peau *f*; **outer s.,** épiderme *m*; *Fig* **to have a thin s.,** être susceptible; *Fig* **to have a thick s.,** avoir la peau dure; **to cast** *or* **throw its s.,** (*of snake etc*) muer; **I always wear cotton next to my s.,** je porte toujours du coton sur la peau; **to strip to the s.,** se mettre tout nu; **wet to the s.,** mouillé jusqu'aux os; *F* **she's nothing but** *or* **she's all s. and bone,** elle n'a que la peau et les os; **to sell one's s. dearly,** vendre (bien) cher sa peau; **I nearly jumped out of my s.,** cela m'a fait sursauter; **to escape by** *or* **with the s. of one's teeth,** s'échapper de justesse; **to save one's (own) s.,** sauver sa peau; (*escape criticism, scandal etc*) se tirer d'affaire; *F* **to get under s.o.'s s.,** (*annoy someone*) ennuyer qn; (*get on s.o.'s nerves*) taper sur les nerfs de qn, énerver qn; *F* **I've got her under my s.,** je l'ai dans la peau; *F* **it's no s. off my nose,** ça n'a aucune conséquence pour moi; **s. care,** soins *mpl* de la peau; **s. cream,** crème *f* de beauté; **s. deep,** (*of emotions*) à fleur de peau; (*of wound*) superficiel; **beauty is only s. deep,** la beauté n'est qu'à fleur de peau; **s. diving,** plongée sous-marine autonome; **s. diver,** plongeur, -euse, sous-marin(e) autonome; *F* **s. flick,** film *m* porno; *F* **s. game,** escroquerie *f*, filouterie *f*; *Med* **s. graft(ing),** greffe cutanée; **s. test,** cuti-réaction *f*, *pl* cuti-réactions;
(b) (*of dead animal*) dépouille *f*, peau *f*; **skins,** (*for wine etc*) peausserie(s) *f(pl)*; **fur skins,** pelleterie(s) *f(pl)*; **s. dressing,** peausserie;
(c) *Bot* tunique *f* (*d'une graine*); pellicule *f* (*d'un grain de café etc*); peau *f* (*de fruit, de saucisse*); pelure *f* (*d'oignon*); *Culin* **potatoes (cooked) in their skins,** pommes *fpl* de terre en robe de chambre *ou* en robe des champs;
(d) *Nau* bordé extérieur (*d'un navire, d'un canot*); enveloppe *f*, coque *f* (*d'un navire*); *Av* revêtement *m* (*du fuselage, de la coque*); *El* **s. effect,** effet *m* pelliculaire;
(e) peau *f*, pellicule *f* (*sur le lait etc*); *Metal* croûte *f* (*de la fonte*);
(f) *Sl* (*skinhead*) skin *mf*.
skin[2] *vt* **(-nn-)** écorcher, dépouiller (*un lapin etc*); peler, éplucher (*un fruit etc*); **to s. one's knees,** s'écorcher les genoux; *F* **to s. s.o.,** écorcher qn, estamper qn.
►**skin over** *vi Med* (*of wound*) se recouvrir de peau, se cicatriser.
skinflint ['skɪnflɪnt] *n F* avare *mf*, pingre *mf*, grippe-sou *m*, *pl* grippe-sous.
skinful ['skɪnfʊl] *n Sl* **he's had a s.,** (*of alcohol*) il a pris une (bonne) cuite.
skinhead ['skɪnhed] *n* skinhead *mf*; **s. gang,** bande *f* de skinheads.
skinless ['skɪnlɪs] *adj* (*saucisse etc*) sans peau.
skinned ['skɪnd] *adj* (*rabbit etc*) dépouillé; **to keep one's eyes s. (for sth),** rester à l'affût (de qch).
skinning ['skɪnɪŋ] *n* écorchement *m* (*d'un lapin etc*); épluchage *m* (*d'un fruit*); *Med* **s. over,** cicatrisation *f*.
skinny ['skɪnɪ] *adj F* (*person*) maigre; (*sweater etc*) collant.
skinny-dip[1] [skɪnɪ'dɪp] *n F* baignade *f* tout nu *ou* à poil.
skinny-dip[2] *vi F* nager *ou* se baigner tout nu *ou* à poil.
skint [skɪnt] *adj Br Sl* **to be s.,** être sans le sou, être fauché.
skintight ['skɪntaɪt] *adj* (*vêtement*) collant, moulant.
skip[1] [skɪp] *n* (petit) saut, gambade *f*; *Am* **s. rope,** corde *f* à sauter.
skip[2] *v* **(-pp-) 1** *vi* **(a)** (*of lambs, children*) sauter, sautiller, gambader; (*with rope*) sauter à la corde; **they came skipping out of school,** ils sont sortis de l'école en gambadant; **to s. from one subject to another,** sauter d'un sujet à un autre; **to read without skipping,** lire sans rien sauter; **(b)** *F* **I skipped across to Paris,** j'ai fait un saut à Paris; **he's just skipped out to the shops,** il vient d'aller faire des courses; **if you s. through the work too fast ...,** si vous travaillez à la va-vite ... . **2** *vt* **(a)** omettre (*qch*); sauter (*un repas etc*); *Sch* sauter (*une classe*); omettre, sauter (par-dessus), passer (*un mot etc*); *F* **to s. bail,** se dérober à la justice (*alors qu'on jouit de la liberté provisoire*); *F* **s. it!,** (*that's enough*) ça suffit!; (*forget it*) passons!, laisse courir!; **(b)** *Am* **to s. rope,** sauter à la corde.
skip[3] *n Constr Min etc* benne *f*.
►**skip off** *vi Br F* (*leave*) filer, décamper.
►**skip over** *vipo* (*omit*) omettre, sauter (par-dessus), passer (*un mot etc*).
skipper[1] ['skɪpər] *n Nau* capitaine *m*, patron *m* (*d'un navire*); *Av* commandant *m* de bord; *Sp F* capitaine, chef *m*; *Nau F* **the s.,** le capiston; *Nau F* **s.'s daughters,** vagues *fpl* à crêtes d'écume.
skipper[2] *vt F* être le commandant de (*un navire*); *Av* être le commandant à bord de (*un avion*); *Sp* être le chef de (*une équipe sportive*).
skipping ['skɪpɪŋ] *n* **(a)** (*repeated jumps*) gambades *fpl*, sauts *mpl*; **(b)** (*with rope*) saut *m* à la corde; **s. rope,** corde *f* à sauter; **(c)** (*omission*) omission *f* (*de qch*).
skirl [skɜ:l, *Scot* skɪrl] *n Scot* son aigu (*de la cornemuse*).
skirmish[1] ['skɜ:mɪʃ] *n Mil* escarmouche *f*, échauffourée *f*; *Fig* escarmouche (verbale).
skirmish[2] *vi Mil etc* combattre par escarmouches.
skirmisher ['skɜ:mɪʃər] *n Mil* tirailleur *m*.
skirt[1] [skɜ:t] *n* **(a)** (*garment*) jupe *f*; pan *m*, basque *f* (*de pardessus etc*); *Sl* **(bit of) s.,** nana *f*, gonzesse *f*; **divided s.,** jupe-culotte *f*, *pl* jupes-culottes; *Culin* **s. of beef,** flanchet *m* de bœuf; **(b) (saddle) s.,** petit quartier (de la selle); **(c)** (*of hovercraft*) jupe *f*; **(d)** (*in engine*) jupe *f* (*du piston*).
skirt[2] *vt* contourner (*un village, une colline, un problème*); (*of person*) longer, serrer (*le mur etc*); (*of ship*) côtoyer (*le rivage*); **the path skirts the wood,** le sentier côtoie *ou* contourne le bois.

▶skirt around *vipo* = **SKIRT²**.
skirting ['skɜːtɪŋ] *n* (*edge*) bord *m*, bordure *f*; *Br Constr* **s. (board),** plinthe *f*.
skit [skɪt] *n Liter Mus Th* pièce *f* satirique, satire *f*; **a s. on the current crisis,** une satire sur la crise actuelle.
skittish ['skɪtɪʃ] *adj* **(a)** (*horse*) ombrageux; **(b)** (*person*) (*capricious*) capricieux; (*frivolous*) frivole.
skittishly ['skɪtɪʃlɪ] *adv* (*capriciously*) capricieusement; (*frivolously*) frivolement.
skittishness ['skɪtɪʃnɪs] *n* **(a)** (*of horse*) ombrage *m*; **(b)** (*of person*) (*capriciousness*) caractère capricieux; (*frivolousness*) frivolité *f*.
skittle ['skɪt(ə)l] *n* **(a) s. (pin),** quille *f*; **(b) (game of) skittles,** jeu *m* de quilles; **to play (at) skittles,** jouer aux quilles; **s. alley,** (terrain *m* de) jeu de quilles; *F* **life isn't all beer and skittles,** tout n'est pas rose dans ce monde.
skive [skaɪv] *vi Br F* tirer au flanc.
▶skive off *vi Br F* (*leave work etc*) s'esquiver.
skiver ['skaɪvər] *n F* tire(-)au(-)flanc *m inv*, tire(-)au(-)cul *m inv*.
skiving ['skaɪvɪŋ] *n Br* **there's too much s. here,** on tire trop au flanc ici.
skivvy¹ ['skɪvɪ] *n Pej* bonniche *f*, bonne *f* à tout faire; **I'm not your s.!,** je ne suis pas ta bonne à tout faire!
skivvy² *vi* faire la bonne (à tout faire); **I'm not skivvying for you,** je ne suis pas ta bonne à tout faire.
skua ['skjuːə] *n* (*bird*) stercoraire *m*.
skulduggery [skʌl'dʌgərɪ] *n* procédés *mpl* peu honnêtes, magouilles *fpl*; (*with money*) tripotage *m*.
skulk [skʌlk] *vi* **(a)** (*hide*) se cacher; (*remain hidden*) se tenir caché; **(b)** (*move furtively*) rôder furtivement; **to s. in/out,** entrer/sortir furtivement.
skull [skʌl] *n* crâne *m*; **s. and crossbones,** tête *f* de mort et tibias; **he's got a thick s.,** il a la tête dure; *F* **can't you get that into your thick s.?,** est-ce que tu ne peux pas te rentrer ça dans la crâne?; *F* **I was bored out of my s.,** je crevais d'ennui; *Sl* **to be out of one's s.,** (*be crazy*) débloquer.
skullcap ['skʌlkæp] *n* calotte *f* (*de prêtre etc*).
skunk [skʌŋk] *n* (*animal*) mouffette *f*; (*fur*) scons(e) *m*, skons *m*, skun(k)s *m*; *F* (*person*) mufle *m*, salaud *m*.
sky¹ [skaɪ] *n* ciel *m*, *pl* cieux, *Art Tech* ciels; **under the open s.,** au grand air; **to sleep under the open s.,** dormir à la belle étoile; **the sunny skies of Italy,** les ciels bleus d'Italie; (*climate*) le climat ensoleillé d'Italie; **the sky's the limit,** tout va!; **to praise s.o. to the skies,** porter qn aux nues; **s. blue,** bleu *m* ciel, bleu azur; *Prov* **red s. at night (is the) shepherd's delight,** rouge le soir, l'espoir; **the bridge was blown s. high,** le pont a sauté jusqu'aux cieux; **prices are s. high,** les prix sont astronomiques.
sky² *vt* (*pl & pp* **skied**) *Cr Tennis etc* envoyer (*la balle*) en chandelle.
sky-blue [skaɪ'bluː] *adj* bleu ciel, bleu azur.
skydiver ['skaɪdaɪvər] *n Av Sp* parachutiste *mf* qui pratique la chute libre.
skydiving ['skaɪdaɪvɪŋ] *n Av Sp* parachutisme *m* en chute libre.
Skye [skaɪ] *n* (l'île *f* de) Skye; **S. terrier,** skye-terrier *m*, *pl* skye-terriers.
skyjack¹ ['skaɪdʒæk] *n F* piraterie aérienne.
skyjack² *vt F* pirater, détourner (*un avion*).
skyjacker ['skaɪdʒækər] *n F* pirate *m* de l'air.
skyjacking ['skaɪdʒækɪŋ] *n* piraterie aérienne.
skylark¹ ['skaɪlɑːk] *n* (*bird*) alouette *f* des champs.
skylark² *vi F* (*play about*) rigoler, batifoler; (*play jokes*) faire des farces.
skylarking ['skaɪlɑːkɪŋ] *n F* rigolade *f*; (*jokes*) farces *fpl*.
skylight ['skaɪlaɪt] *n* jour *m* (*dans le toit, le plafond*); (*in attic*) (lucarne *f*) faîtière *f*; (*hinged*) (châssis *m*, fenêtre *f*, lucarne à) tabatière *f*.
skyline ['skaɪlaɪn] *n* (*horizon*) (ligne *f* d')horizon *m*; (*outline of horizon*) profil *m* de l'horizon; le profil, la silhouette (*d'une ville*).
skypilot ['skaɪpaɪlət] *n Sl* (*priest etc*) soutane *f*.
skyrocket¹ ['skaɪrɒkɪt] *n* fusée blanche éclairante.
skyrocket² *vi* (*of prices etc*) monter en flèche.
skyscape ['skaɪskeɪp] *n Art* paysage *m* celeste.
skyscraper ['skaɪskreɪpər] *n* gratte-ciel *m inv*.
skyward(s) ['skaɪwəd(z)] *adv* vers le ciel.
skyway ['skaɪweɪ] *n* **(a)** *Av* route aérienne; **(b)** *Am* (*flyover*) saut-de-mouton *m*; (*raised road*) route surélevée.
sky(-)writing ['skaɪraɪtɪŋ] *n* publicité aérienne.
slab [slæb] *n* **(a)** *Tech* plaque *f*, dalle *f* (*de pierre, marbre etc*); (*of timber*) dosse *f*; pavé *m* (*de pain d'épice*); (grosse) tranche *f* (*de gâteau*); darne *f*, dalle (*de poisson*); plaque, tablette *f* (*de chocolat*); **(b)** *Typ* marbre *m* (*pour broyer les couleurs*); **(c)** (*in mortuary*) table *f*.
slabstone ['slæbstəʊn] *n* dalle *f*, plaque *f* (*de pierre*).
slack¹ [slæk] *n* **(a)** mou *m* (*d'un câble, d'une courroie*); *MecE* jeu *m* (nuisible); **to take up the s. in a cable,** mettre un câble au raide; *Fig* **to take up the s.,** résorber les capacités excédentaires; **(b)** *Nau* mer *f* étale; **(c)** (*garment*) **slacks,** pantalon *m* (*de femme*).
slack² *adj* **(a)** (*cordage etc*) mou, *f* molle, lâche, flasque; (*écrou*) desserré; (*main, prise*) faible; **to be** *or* **hang s.,** (*of rope*) avoir du mou; *Fig* **to have a s. rein on sth,** gouverner qch sans fermeté *ou* mollement;
(b) (*person*) (*careless*) négligent; (*lazy*) *F* flemmard; **to get** *or* **become s.,** (*of person*) se laisser aller; (*of person, attention*) se relâcher; **to be s. in** *or* **about doing sth,** être lent *ou* paresseux à faire qch; **security at the base is very s.,** les mesures de sécurité à la base ne sont pas du tout strictes;
(c) (*not busy*) (*market economy*) peu actif; (*commerce*) stagnant; **business is s.,** les affaires ne marchent pas fort; **we're s. this afternoon,** (*in business etc*) nous ne sommes pas très occupés cet après-midi; **when things are a bit slacker,** quand les choses se calmeront; **s. periods,** moments *mpl* de creux, périodes *fpl* calmes; **s. sea, s. water,** mer *f* étale; **the s. season,** la morte-saison, la saison creuse; **s. time,** période (d')accalmie.
slack³ *vi F* (*of person*) (*to become negligent*) se laisser aller; (*to become lazy*) paresser, fainéanter; (*of attention*) se relâcher; **your pupils are slacking,** vos élèves se laissent aller; **dear me, I must be slacking!,** mon Dieu, je vieillis!
slack⁴ *n* (*coal*) menu charbon, charbonnaille *f*, poussier *m*.
▶slack off *vtsep* (*diminish*) *MecE* **to s. off the pressure,** relâcher la pression.
slacken ['slæk(ə)n] **1** *vt* ralentir (*le pas, ses efforts, son ardeur*); détendre, relâcher (*un cordage*); donner du mou à (*un cordage, une voile*); affaiblir (*l'opposition*); adoucir (*la sévérité*); **to s. speed,** diminuer la vitesse, ralentir (la marche); **to s. the reins,** lâcher la bride *ou* les rênes. **2** *vi* (*of person*) se relâcher, devenir négligent, diminuer d'efforts; (*of rope*) prendre du mou; (*of speed*) ralentir; (*of storm*) se calmer; (*of energy, mind etc*) diminuer (*de force, d'ardeur*); (*of the tide*) mollir; (*of lime*) s'éteindre, s'amortir; **business is slackening,** les affaires deviennent stagnantes.
slackening ['slæk(ə)nɪŋ] *n* ralentissement *m* (*de zèle*); diminution *f* (*de force, de zèle, de vitesse*); relâchement *m* (*d'un cordage, d'ardeur, d'efforts*); **s. of speed,** ralentissement.
slacker ['slækər] *n F* paresseux, -euse, flemmard, -arde.
slackly ['slæklɪ] *adv* **(a)** (*to hang*) mollement; **(b)** (*carelessly*) négligemment.
slackness ['slæknɪs] *n* **(a)** (*lack of energy*) manque *m* d'énergie; (*negligence*) négligence *f*; (*laxity*) mollesse *f*; (*laziness*) paresse *f*, *F* flemme *f*; (*idleness*) désœuvrement *m*; relâchement *m* (*de la discipline*); **(b)** détente *f* (*des muscles etc*); mou *m* (*d'un cordage*); **(c)** *Com* stagnation *f* (*des affaires*).
slag¹ [slæg] *n* **(a)** *Metal* scorie(s) *f(pl)* (*de métal*); crasse *f*, laitier(s) *m(pl)* (*de haut fourneau*); *Geol* **volcanic s.,** scories volcaniques; **s. heap,** crassier; **(b)** *Sl Pej* (*woman*) salope *f*.
slag² *vt Br Sl* = **SLAG OFF**.
▶slag off *vtsep Br Sl* (*denigrate*) dire du mal de; **he is always slagging me off behind my back,** il est toujours en train de dire du mal de moi dernière mon dos.
slain *see* **SLAY**.
slake [sleɪk] *vt* **(a)** *Lit* **to s. one's thirst,** étancher *ou* apaiser sa soif, se désaltérer; **(b)** *Ch* éteindre (*la chaux*); **slaked lime,** chaux éteinte.
slaking ['sleɪkɪŋ] *n* **(a)** étanchement *m*, assouvissement *m* (*de la soif*); **(b)** *Ch* extinction *f* (*de la chaux*).
slalom ['slɑːləm] *n Ski* slalom *m*.
slam¹ [slæm] **1** *n* claquement *m* (*d'une porte etc*). **2** *adv* **s. (bang) in the middle of ...,** en plein dans ... . **3** *int* **s.!,** v'lan!
slam² *v* (**-mm-**) **1** *vt* **(a)** (faire) claquer (*une porte*); envoyer *ou* lancer violemment, *F* flanquer (**against,** contre; **into,** dans); **to s. the door in s.o.'s face,** claquer la porte au nez de qn; **she slammed the book (down) on the table,** elle a flanqué le livre sur la table; **Nixon slammed the phone down,** Nixon raccrocha avec fracas; **he slammed the ball into the back of the net,** il a écrasé la balle dans les filets; **she slammed her fist into his face,** elle lui a flanqué son poing dans la figure; **(b)** *F* (*criticize*

severely) critiquer, éreinter (*qn, qch*); **he was slammed in the press,** il a été éreinté par la presse. **2** *vi* (*of door etc*) claquer; **to s. out of the house,** (*of person*) sortir de la maison en claquant la porte.

slam³ *n Cards* (*at bridge*) chelem *m*, schelem *m*; **grand s.,** grand chelem; **to make a s.,** faire (le) chelem; *Sp* **the grand s.,** le grand chelem.

▶slam on *vtsep F* **to s. on the brakes, to s. the brakes on,** bloquer les freins.

slammer ['slæmər] *n Sl* (*prison*) tôle *f*, taule *f*.

slander¹ ['slɑːndər] *n* calomnie *f*; *Jur* diffamation verbale.

slander² *vt* calomnier; *Jur* diffamer (*qn*).

slanderer ['slɑːndərər] *n* calomniateur, -trice; *Jur* diffamateur, -trice.

slanderous ['slɑːndərəs] *adj* (*propos*) calomnieux, calomniateur; *Jur* diffamatoire.

slanderously ['slɑːndərəslɪ] *adv* calomnieusement.

slang¹ [slæŋ] *n* argot *m*; **theatrical** *or* **stage/police/student s.,** argot des coulisses/de la police/étudiant; **s. phrase** *or* **expression,** expression *f* argotique.

slang² *vt F* (*abuse*) injurier (*qn*); (*reprimand*) réprimander sévèrement (*qn*), *F* engueuler (*qn*).

slangily ['slæŋɪlɪ] *adv* (*s'exprimer*) en argot.

slanging ['slæŋɪŋ] *n F* (*reprimand*) verte réprimande; **after his s. of the government,** après avoir déversé un tombereau d'injures sur le gouvernement; **s. match,** prise *f* de bec, engueulade *f*.

slangy ['slæŋɪ] *adj* **(a)** (*personne*) qui aime à s'exprimer en argot, argotier; **(b)** (*style, langage*) argotique; (*terme*) populaire, d'argot.

slant¹ [slɑːnt] *n* **(a)** (*slope*) pente *f*, inclinaison *f*; **(b)** (*oblique angle*) biais *m*, biseau *m*; **on the** *or* **at a s.,** de biais, obliquement; **(c)** (*opinion*) point *m* de vue; **these historians put a different s. on events,** ces historiens ont envisagé les événements sous un angle différent; **information with a s. on it,** informations tendancieuses *ou* faussées.

slant² *adj* oblique; **s.-eyed,** aux yeux bridés.

slant³ **1** *vi* (*slope*) être en pente, (s')incliner; (*be oblique*) être oblique. **2** *vt* **(a)** (*angle*) incliner (*qch*); **(b)** (*bias*) fausser; **slanted news,** informations tendancieuses *ou* faussées.

slanting ['slɑːntɪŋ] *adj* (*toit*) en pente, incliné; (*direction*) oblique; (*écriture*) couché.

slantwise, slantways ['slɑːntwaɪz, -weɪz] *adv* obliquement; en *ou* de biais.

slap¹ [slæp] **1** *n* coup *m*, claque *f*, tape *f*; **s. in the face,** gifle *f*; *Fig* gifle, affront *m*, soufflet *m*; **s. on the back,** tape dans le dos; *Fig* félicitations *fpl*; *Hum F* **they were having a bit of s. and tickle on the sofa,** ils ont fait un câlin sur le divan. **2** *adv F* **the car went s. into the wall,** la voiture est rentrée en plein dans le mur; *F* **s. bang,** brusquement, de but en blanc; **they ran s. (bang) into each other,** ils se sont rentrés en plein dedans; **s. bang in the middle,** en plein milieu.

slap² *vt* (**-pp-** [slæpt]) (*with open hand*) frapper avec la main (ouverte); (*with flat object*) donner une claque *ou* une tape à (*qn*); (*spank*) donner une fessée à (*qn*); **to s. s.o.'s face,** gifler qn; **to s. s.o. on the back,** donner à qn une tape sur le dos; (*congratulate*) féliciter qn; **she slapped the money on the table,** elle a jeté *ou* flanqué l'argent sur la table.

▶slap down *vtsep* **(a)** (*put down brusquely*) flanquer, balancer; **(b)** *F* (*reprimand*) réprimander (*qn*); (re)mettre (*qn*) à sa place.

▶slap on *vtsep F* **he slapped on some aftershave,** il s'est aspergé de lotion après-rasage; **they slapped on another £50,** ils ont augmenté le prix de 50 livres; **the paint had been just slapped on,** la peinture avait été appliquée n'importe comment.

slapdash ['slæpdæʃ] **1** *adj* sans soin(s); (*travail*) à la six-quatre-deux; **to do sth s.** *or* **in a s. manner,** faire qch à la va-vite *ou* à la six-quatre-deux; **s. worker,** sabreur *m* de besogne. **2** *adv* sans soin(s).

slap(-)happy ['slæp'hæpɪ] *adj F* (*careless*) insouciant; **he's s.-h.,** il fait les choses au petit bonheur (la chance); *US F* (*punch drunk*) groggy, abruti de coups.

slapping ['slæpɪŋ] *n* claques *fpl*, gifles *fpl*; (*on bottom*) fessée *f*.

slapstick ['slæpstɪk] *n Th* **s. (comedy),** comédie bouffonne, farce *f*.

slap-up ['slæpʌp] *adj Br F* (*restaurant etc*) soigné, chic; **s.-up meal,** festin *m*, repas somptueux.

slash¹ [slæʃ] *n* **(a)** (*cut*) estafilade *f*, entaille *f*, taillade *f*; (*on the face*) balafre *f*; **(b)** *Arch* (*in garment*) crevé *m*; **(c)** *Am* (*in forestry*) (*pieces of wood*) déchets *mpl* (d'abattage); (*clearing*) clairière *f*; **(d)** *Typ* barre *f* oblique; **(e)** *Br Sl* **to have a s.,** pisser.

slash² **1** *vt* (*cut*) taillader (*la chair*); balafrer (*le visage*); couper *ou* trancher net (*un cordage etc*); cingler (*un cheval etc*) (d'un coup de fouet); éreinter (*un ouvrage littéraire etc*); écraser (*les prix*); couper (*un texte etc*); **all prices slashed,** nous écrasons les prix; *Arch* **slashed sleeve,** (*of garment*) manche *f* à crevés. **2** *vi* frapper à droite et à gauche; **to s. at s.o. with a knife,** donner des coups de couteau en direction de qn; **they slashed at the undergrowth,** ils ont donné des coups de couteau dans les fourrés.

slashing ['slæʃɪŋ] *adj* (*criticism*) mordant, cinglant.

slat [slæt] *n* lame *f*, lamelle *f*, planchette *f* (*de jalousie etc*); traverse *f* (*de lit*).

slate¹ [sleɪt] *n* **(a)** *Geol* ardoise *f*; *Constr* (feuille *f* d')ardoise; **s. blue,** bleu ardoise *m inv*; **s. colour(ed), s. grey,** ardoisé; (gris *m*) ardoise *inv*; **s. quarry,** ardoisière *f*; **s. roof,** toit *m* d'ardoises; **s. worker** *or* **quarryman,** ardoisier *m*; **(b) (writing) s.,** ardoise *f* (pour *ou* à écrire); *F* **to put sth on the s.,** mettre qch sur la note *ou* sur le compte; **to wipe the s. clean,** faire table rase (du passé); **I have a clean s.,** (*I have no debts*) je n'ai pas de dettes; (*I have committed no offence*) mon casier judiciaire est vierge; **s. pencil,** crayon *m* d'ardoise.

slate² *vt* **(a)** *Constr* couvrir (*un toit*) d'ardoises *ou* en ardoise; **slated roof,** toit *m* d'ardoises; **(b)** *Am Pol* inscrire (*un candidat*) sur la liste.

slate³ *vt F* **(a)** (*reprimand*) réprimander vertement (*qn*); **(b)** (*criticize severely*) critiquer, éreinter (*un auteur, un livre etc*).

slater ['sleɪtər] *n* **(a)** (*person*) couvreur *m* (en ardoises); **(b)** (*crustacean*) cloporte *m*.

slating ['sleɪtɪŋ] *n F* **(a)** (*reprimand*) savon *m*; **he got a s. from the P.M.,** il s'est fait passer un savon par le Premier Ministre; **(b)** (*severe criticism*) critique *f* acerbe; **the play got a s. in the press,** la pièce a été éreintée par la presse.

slatted ['slætɪd] *adj* (*shutters etc*) à lames, à planchettes.

slattern ['slætɜːn] *n* femme mal soignée, souillon *f*.

slatternly ['slætənlɪ] *adj* (*woman*) mal soigné; (*habit, dress*) négligé.

slaty ['sleɪtɪ] *adj* **(a)** *Geol* ardoisier, schisteux; **(b)** (*colour*) ardoisé.

slaughter¹ ['slɔːtər] *n* **(a)** abattage *m* (*d'animaux de boucherie*); **(b)** (*of people*) tuerie *f*, carnage *m*, massacre *m*; **the senseless s. of seal cubs,** le massacre insensé des bébés phoques.

slaughter² *vt* **(a)** abattre (*des animaux de boucherie*); **(b)** tuer, massacrer (*des gens*); *F* battre (*un adversaire*) à plate(s) couture(s).

slaughterer ['slɔːtərər] *n* **(a)** abatteur *m*, tueur *m* (*d'animaux*); **(b)** tueur, -euse (*de gens*).

slaughterhouse ['slɔːtəhaʊs] *n* abattoir *m*.

slaughtering ['slɔːtərɪŋ] *n* **(a)** abattage *m* (*d'animaux de boucherie*); **(b)** (*of people*) tuerie *f*, carnage *m*, massacre *m* (*de gens*).

Slav [slɑːv] **1** *adj* slave. **2** *n* Slave *mf*.

slave¹ [sleɪv] *n* esclave *mf*; **to be s.o.'s s.,** être l'esclave de qn; **to be the s. of** *or* **a s. to a passion,** être l'esclave d'une passion; **to be a s. to duty,** ne connaître que son devoir; **to be a s. to one's work,** être esclave de son travail; **s. driver,** surveillant *m* des esclaves; *Fig F* garde-chiourme *m*, *pl* garde(s)-chiourme(s); **s. labour,** travail *m* d'esclave; *Fig* esclavage *m*; **s. trade,** traite *f* des noirs, commerce *m ou* traffic *m* des esclaves; **white s. trade,** traite des blanches; **s. trader,** marchand *m* d'esclaves.

slave² *vi* travailler comme un nègre, peiner, bûcher; **to s. over a hot stove,** peiner au dessus du fourneau.

▶slave away *vi* (*work hard*) travailler comme un nègre, peiner, bûcher; **to s. away at sth,** s'échiner *ou* s'éreinter à qch.

slaver¹ ['sleɪvər] *n* **(a)** *Nau* (*ship*) (bâtiment *m*) négrier *m*; **(b)** (*person*) marchand *m* d'esclaves; **black s.,** négrier *m*; **white s.,** personne pratiquant la traite des blanches.

slaver² ['slævər] *n* (*saliva*) bave *f*, salive *f*.

slaver³ *vi* (*dribble*) baver (**over,** sur).

slavery ['sleɪvərɪ] *n* **(a)** esclavage *m*; **to sell s.o. into s.,** vendre qn comme esclave; **to reduce to s.,** réduire (*qn*) en esclavage; asservir (*un peuple*); **white s.,** traite *f* des blanches; **(b)** asservissement *m* (**to a passion,** à une passion); **(c)** *F* (*heavy work*) travail tuant; **this work is sheer s.,** ce travail est un véritable esclavage.

Slavic ['slɑːvɪk] *adj & n Ling* slave *m*.

slavish ['sleɪvɪʃ] *adj* (*soumission*) d'esclave; (*imitation*) servile.

slavishly ['sleɪvɪʃlɪ] *adv* servilement.
slavishness ['sleɪvɪʃnɪs] *n* servilité *f*.
Slavonic [slə'vɒnɪk] **1** *adj* slave; **student of S. languages,** slavisant, -ante. **2** *n Ling* slave *m*; **Church S., Old S.,** slavon *m*.
slaw [slɔː] *n esp Am Culin* salade *f* de chou cru.
slay [sleɪ] *vt* (*pt* **slew** [sluː]; *pp* **slain** [sleɪn]) *Lit* tuer; *esp US Journ* assassiner; **the slain,** (*used as pl*) les morts *mpl*; *F* **this one will really s. you,** (*of joke etc*) celle-là va vous faire mourir de rire.
slayer ['sleɪər] *n Lit* (*killer*) tueur, -euse; *esp US Journ* (*murderer*) assassin *m* (**of,** de).
slaying ['sleɪɪŋ] *n Lit* (*killing*) tuerie *f*; *esp US Journ* (*murder*) assassinat *m*, meurtre *m*; massacre *m*.
sleaze [sliːz] *n F* ragots *mpl*.
sleaziness ['sliːzɪnɪs] *n F* apparence *f* louche, aspect *m* sordide (*d'un endroit etc*).
sleazo ['sliːzəʊ] *n F* personne *f* louche; **he's a s.,** c'est un type louche.
sleazy ['sliːzɪ] *adj F* louche.
sled [sled] *n & v Am* = **SLEDGE**[1, 2].
sledge[1] [sledʒ] *n* traîneau *m*.
sledge[2] **1** *vi* aller en traîneau; **to go sledging,** se promener en traîneau, faire une promenade en traîneau. **2** *vt* transporter (*qch*) en traîneau.
sledge[3] *n* = **SLEDGEHAMMER**.
sledgehammer ['sledʒhæmər] *n* (*tool*) marteau *m* à deux mains *ou* à frapper devant; **a film with the subtlety of a s.,** un film aux effets trop appuyés; *F* **s. arguments,** arguments *mpl* massue(s); **a s. blow,** (*punch*) un coup de massue; *Fig* (*to industry etc*) un coup fatal.
sleek[1] [sliːk] *adj* **(a)** (*smooth*) lisse; (*shiny*) luisant; (*of person*) (*well-groomed*) soigné et bien nourri; **s. hair,** cheveux *mpl* lisses; **s. horse,** cheval *m* d'un beau poil; **(b)** (*manner*) mielleux; (*unctuous*) onctueux.
sleek[2] *vt* lisser (*les cheveux, le poil d'un cheval*).
▶**sleek down** *vtsep* **to s. down one's hair,** se lisser les cheveux; (*with oil*) se brillantiner les cheveux.
sleekly ['sliːklɪ] *adv* **(a)** (*to be brushed etc*) avec une apparence lisse; **(b)** (*to talk, act*) mielleusement; (*unctuously*) onctueusement.
sleekness ['sliːknɪs] *n* **(a)** luisant *m* (*d'une peau, du satin etc*); **(b)** onctuosité *f* (*de manières*).
sleep[1] [sliːp] *n* sommeil *m*; **short s.,** somme *m*; **deep** *or* **sound s.,** sommeil profond; **beauty s.,** sommeil avant minuit (*considéré comme le plus réparateur*); **to go** *or* **drop off to s.,** s'endormir, s'assoupir; **to go** *or* **drop off to s. again,** se rendormir; **to put** *or* **send** *or* **lull s.o. to s.,** endormir qn; *Med* **to put s.o. to s.,** endormir qn; *Vet F* **to put an animal to s.,** piquer un animal; **to read oneself to s.,** lire pour s'endormir; **to rouse s.o. from his s.,** réveiller qn, arracher qn au sommeil; **to have a good (night's) s.,** bien dormir; **I need my s.,** il me faut beaucoup de sommeil; **to get two hours' s.,** dormir deux heures; **I didn't get a wink of s. all night,** je n'ai pas fermé l'œil de la nuit; (*stayed up working etc*) j'ai passé une nuit blanche; **a night without s.,** une nuit blanche; **in my s.,** pendant que je dors *ou* que je dormais, en dormant; **to walk in one's s.,** être somnambule; **to talk in one's s.,** rêver tout haut; **to call out in one's s.,** dire quelques mots en dormant; **my foot's gone to s.,** j'ai des fourmis dans le pied, j'ai le pied engourdi.
sleep[2] *v* (*pt & pp* **slept** [slept]) **1** *vi* **(a)** dormir; **to s. like a log** *or* **a top,** dormir à poings fermés, dormir comme un sabot *ou* comme une marmotte; **to s. soundly,** dormir profondément; **to s. the night through,** dormir toute la nuit; **to s. through a noise,** ne pas être réveillé par un bruit; **I haven't slept a wink all night,** je n'ai pas fermé l'œil de (toute) la nuit; **to s. six hours,** dormir six heures; **to try to s.,** chercher le sommeil; **he can't s. for thinking about it,** il n'en dort pas; **I'll s. on it,** la nuit porte conseil; **s. on it,** la nuit porte conseil; *Lit* **to s. the sleep of the just,** dormir du sommeil du juste;
(b) (*spend a night*) coucher; **to s. at an hotel,** coucher dans un hôtel; **to s. rough,** coucher sur la dure; **to s. on the floor/in a bed,** coucher par terre/dans un lit; **the bed had not been slept in,** le lit n'avait pas été défait; **to s. late,** faire la grasse matinée; (*wake up too late*) ne pas se réveiller à l'heure.
2 *vt* **house that sleeps ten people,** maison où dix personnes peuvent coucher; **this room sleeps four,** on peut coucher à quatre dans cette chambre.
▶**sleep around** *vi F* (*be promiscuous*) coucher avec n'importe qui.
▶**sleep away** *vtsep* **to s. the day/the hours away,** passer la journée/les heures à dormir *ou* en dormant.
▶**sleep in** *vi* **(a)** (*sleep until late*) faire la grasse matinée; **(b)** (*of servant*) coucher à la maison.
▶**sleep off** *vtsep F* (*remove by sleeping*) faire passer (*un mal de tête*) en dormant; **to s. off a hangover,** *F* **to s. it off,** cuver son vin *ou* sa bière *etc*.
▶**sleep out** *vi* (*not sleep at home*) découcher; (*of servant*) coucher à domicile, venir en journée.
▶**sleep together** *vi* coucher ensemble; (*in same room*) coucher dans la même chambre.
▶**sleep with** *vipo* **to s. with s.o.,** coucher avec qn.
sleeper ['sliːpər] *n* **(a)** (*person*) dormeur, -euse; **to be a light/a heavy s.,** avoir le sommeil léger/profond; **(b)** *Constr etc* poutre horizontale; lambourde *f* (*de parquet etc*); gîte *m* (*de plancher*); *Br Rail* **(cross) s.,** traverse *f*; **(c)** *Rail* (*carriage*) wagon-lit *m*, *pl* wagons-lits; **I took the s. to London,** j'ai pris le wagon-lit pour Londres; **(d)** *Am* **sleeper(s),** pyjama *m* d'enfant.
sleepily ['sliːpɪlɪ] *adv* d'un air endormi *ou* somnolent.
sleepiness ['sliːpɪnɪs] *n* **(a)** (*desire to sleep*) envie *f* de dormir, somnolence *f*; **(b)** (*apathy*) apathie *f*, indolence *f*, léthargie *f*; **(c)** (*of town etc*) calme *m*, engourdissement *m*; *Pej* apathie *f*.
sleeping ['sliːpɪŋ] **1** *adj* dormant, endormi; *Prov* **let s. dogs lie,** ne réveillez pas le chat qui dort; *Com* **s. partner,** (associé *m*) commanditaire *m*; (*who supplies capital*) bailleur *m* de fonds. **2** *n* sommeil *m*; **s. accommodation,** logement *m*; **the house has s. accommodation for ten,** c'est une maison où dix personnes peuvent coucher; **s. bag,** sac *m* de couchage; *Rail* **s. car(riage),** wagon-lit *m*, *pl* wagons-lits; **s. pill,** (comprimé *m*) somnifère *m*; *F* **s. policeman,** ralentisseur *m*; **s. quarters,** chambre(s) *f(pl)*; dortoir(s) *m(pl)*; *Mil* chambrée *f*; *Med* **s. sickness,** maladie *f* du sommeil; **s. suit,** pyjama *m* (d'enfant).
sleepless ['sliːplɪs] *adj* **(a)** sans sommeil; (*nuit*) d'insomnie; **to have a s. night,** ne pas fermer l'œil de la nuit; **(b)** *Lit* (*esprit*) sans cesse en éveil; (*énergie*) inlassable.
sleeplessly ['sliːplɪslɪ] *adv* sans dormir.
sleeplessness ['sliːplɪsnɪs] *n* insomnie *f*.
sleepwalk ['sliːpwɔːk] *vi* être somnambule; **I sleepwalked last night,** j'ai eu une crise de somnambulisme la nuit dernière.
sleepwalker ['sliːpwɔːkər] *n* somnambule *mf*.
sleepwalking ['sliːpwɔːkɪŋ] *n* somnambulisme *m*.
sleepy ['sliːpɪ] *adj* **(a)** somnolent; **to be** *or* **feel s.,** avoir envie de dormir, avoir sommeil; **to make s.o. s.,** assoupir qn; **s. look,** air endormi; **(b)** (*apathetic*) apathique, indolent, léthargique; (*of fruit*) blet, *f* blette; **(c) s. little town,** petite ville endormie.
sleepyhead ['sliːpɪhed] *n F* endormi, -ie; **wake up, s.!,** debout, paresseux *ou* paresseuse!
sleet[1] [sliːt] *n* **(a)** (*precipitation*) pluie mêlée de neige; **(b)** *Am* (*ice*) verglas *m*.
sleet[2] *v impers* **it's sleeting,** (*of melted snow*) il tombe de la neige fondue; (*of rain turning to snow*) la pluie tourne à la neige.
sleeve [sliːv] *n* **(a)** manche *f*; **short s.,** manche courte, mancheron *m*; **s. hole,** emmanchure *f* (*de robe etc*); *Fig F* **to have something up one's s.,** avoir un expédient en réserve; **to have more than one trick up one's s.,** avoir plus d'un tour dans son sac; **s. board,** jeannette *f*; **(b)** *MecE* chemise *f*, fourreau *m*, gaine *f* (souple); (*tubular casing*) douille *f*; **s. nut,** manchon fileté *ou* taraudé; **(c)** (*of record*) pochette *f*; **s. notes,** annotations *fpl* sur la pochette; **(d)** *Av* **air s.,** manche *f* à air.
sleeved [sliːvd] *adj* (*vêtement*) à manches.
-sleeved [-sliːvd] *suff* **long/short/***etc***-s.,** à manches longues/courtes/*etc*.
sleeveless ['sliːvlɪs] *adj* (*robe etc*) sans manches.
sleigh [sleɪ] *n* traîneau *m*; **s. bell,** grelot *m*, clochette *f*; **s. ride,** promenade *f* en traîneau.
sleight [slaɪt] *n* **s. of hand,** (*skill*) prestidigitation *f*; (*conjuring trick*) escamotage *m*, tour *m* de passe-passe; **by s. of hand,** par un tour de passe-passe.
slender ['slendər] *adj* **(a)** mince, ténu; (*of figure*) svelte, fluet; **s. waist,** taille fine *ou* fluette; **(b)** (*intelligence, hope etc*) faible; (*income etc*) modique, maigre, modeste; **there is a very s. chance,** il y a une chance très faible; **s. means,** ressources médiocres *ou* exiguës; **of s. means,** qui a de petits *ou* maigres moyens.
slenderize ['slendəraɪz] *vt Am* amincir.
slenderly ['slendəlɪ] *adv* **(a) s. built,** d'une taille svelte; **(b)** (*to a slight extent*) maigrement, faiblement.
slenderness ['slendənɪs] *n* **(a)** minceur *f*; sveltesse *f* (*de*

qn, de la taille); **(b)** modicité *f* (*d'une fortune*); exiguïté *f*, faiblesse *f* (*des ressources*).

slept *see* **SLEEP[2]**.

sleuth[1] [ˈsluːθ] *n F* limier *m*, détective *m*.

sleuth[2] *vi F* faire le détective.

sleuthhound [ˈsluːθhaʊnd] *n* (*dog*) limier *m*; *F* (*detective*) limier, détective *m*.

slew[1] [sluː] *n* virage *m*; *Aut* tête(-)à(-)queue *m inv*.

slew[2] **1** *vt* faire pivoter (*qch*). **2** *vi* pivoter; (*of car*) (*to turn right round*) faire un tête(-)à(-)queue; **the car slewed off the track,** la voiture a dérapé hors de la piste.

slew[3] *n Am F* grande quantité.

slew[4] *see* **SLAY**.

►**slew around, slew round** **1** *vtsep* (*to turn right round*) (*rotate*) faire pivoter (*qch*). **2** *vi* (*rotate*) pivoter; (*of car*) faire un tête(-)à(-)queue.

slice[1] [slaɪs] *n* **(a)** tranche *f* (*de pain etc*); côte *f*, tranche (*de melon*); darne *f* (*de gros poisson*); (*thin*) lèche *f* (*de pain, viande etc*); **(round) s.,** rond *m*, rondelle *f* (*de citron, saucisse etc*); **s. of bread and butter,** tartine beurrée; **to take a large s. of the credit for sth,** s'attribuer une large part du mérite de qch; **a. s. of the profits,** une part des bénéfices; **a s. of life,** une tranche de vie; **(b)** (*utensil*) **fish s.,** truelle *f* (à poisson); **cake s.,** tranche *f* de gâteau; **(c)** *Golf* coup *m* qui fait dévier la balle à droite.

slice[2] **1** *vt* **(a)** couper *ou* découper (*qch*) en tranches; **to s. thinly,** couper (*la viande*) en tranches fines; émincer (*les oignons etc*); **to s. sth in two** *or* **in half,** couper qch en deux; **(b)** *Lit* fendre (*l'air, les vagues etc*); **(c)** *Tennis* couper (*la balle*); *Golf Rugby* faire dévier la balle à droite. **2** *vi* **this meat slices easily,** cette viande fait de belles tranches.

►**slice into** *vipo* (*cut easily*) couper sans effort; **the knife sliced into the flesh,** le couteau a pénétré dans la chair.

►**slice off** *vtsep* (*remove by slicing*) trancher, couper, détacher (*un morceau*); **to s. off the tip of one's finger,** trancher le bout du doigt.

►**slice through** *vipo* (*cut easily*) couper sans effort; **the knife sliced through the rope,** le couteau a tranché la corde; *Fig* **the river slices through the city,** la rivière parcourt la ville.

►**slice up** *vtsep* (*cut into slices*) couper *ou* découper (*qch*) en tranches.

sliced [slaɪst] *adj* (*bread, ham etc*) en tranches; *F* **he thinks it's the best thing since s. bread,** il pense que c'est ce qu'on a fait de mieux depuis l'invention de la roue.

slicer [ˈslaɪsər] *n Culin* (*device*) émninceur *m*; **bacon s.,** coupe-jambon *m inv*.

slick[1] [slɪk] *adj F* (*skilful, deft*) habile, adroit; (*smooth*) lisse; (*cunning*) malin, rusé; **s. talker,** beau-parleur *m*; **s. movie/magazine,** film/magazine bien fait.

slick[2] *n* **(a)** **(oil) s.,** nappe *f* d'huile; **(b)** (*of snow*) plaque *f* de neige.

slick[3] *vt Am* mettre (*une chambre*) en ordre.

►**slick back** *vtsep* (*comb back with oil etc*) **to s. back one's hair,** lisser ses cheveux vers l'arrière.

►**slick down** *vtsep* (*comb down with oil etc*) **to s. one's hair down,** lisser ses cheveux.

►**slick up** *vi* (*make oneself attractive*) faire beau.

slicker [ˈslɪkər] *n Am* **(a)** (*raincoat*) imperméable *m*; (*oilskin*) ciré *m*; **(b)** (*person*) **(city) s.,** homme *m* du milieu.

slickly [ˈslɪklɪ] *adv* (*skilfully*) habilement; (*cunningly*) habilement, adroitement.

slickness [ˈslɪknɪs] *n F* (*skill, deftness*) habileté *f*, adresse *f*; (*cunning*) ruse *f*.

slide[1] [slaɪd] *n* **(a)** (*action*) glissade *f*, glissement *m*; éboulement *m*, glissement (*de terrain*); *Mus* (*ornament*) coulé *m*; (*in violin playing etc*) glissade; **to have a s.,** (*of person*) faire une glissade; **the alarming s. of the economy,** le dérapage alarmant de l'économie; **a mud/rock s.,** une coulée de boue/un écoulement rocheux;

(b) (*place*) (*on snow or ice*) glissoire *f*; (*in playground*) toboggan *m*; (*slope*) plan *m* de glissement; **timber s.,** (*in forestry*) glissoir *m*; *Av* **escape s.,** toboggan *m* d'évacuation;

(c) *MecE* glissière *f*, coulisse *f*;

(d) *Tech* (*sliding part*) pièce *f* qui glisse *ou* qui coulisse; curseur *m* (*d'une règle, d'un compas etc*); coulisseau *m*, réglette *f* (*d'une règle à calcul*); *Mus* coulisse (*de trombone etc*); (*in rowing*) glissière *f*; **s. rule,** règle *f* à calcul; *esp Am* **s. fastener,** fermeture *f* éclair *ou* à glissière;

(e) (*microscopy*) **(object) s.,** (plaque *f*, lame *f*) porte-objet *m*, *pl* porte-objet(s);

(f) *Phot* **(colour) s.,** diapositive *f* (en couleur), *F* diapo *f*; **lecture illustrated with slides,** conférence *f* avec projections; **s. projector,** projecteur *m* pour diapositives; **s. show,** présentation *f* de diapositives;

(g) *Br* **(hair) s.,** barrette *f*.

slide[2] *v* (*pt & pp* **slid** [slɪd]) **1** *vi* **(a)** (*slip*) glisser, coulisser; **mechanism that slides between runners,** mécanisme qui glisse *ou* coulisse entre des guides; **to s. (on ice),** (*of person*) glisser (sur la glace), faire une glissade *ou* des glissades; **she slid on the floor,** elle a glissé sur le parquet; **the dish slid off the table/onto the floor,** le plat a glissé de sur la table/sur le sol; **to let things** *or* **everything s.,** laisser tout aller à la dérive *ou* à vau-l'eau; (*lose interest in everything*) se désintéresser de tout; **the country was sliding into anarchy,** le pays glissait vers l'anarchie;

(b) (*move quietly etc*) se glisser (*dans une pièce, derrière un rideau etc*); **the snake slid along the ground,** le serpent a glissé sur le sol; **the pilot slid into the cockpit,** le pilote s'est glissé dans le cockpit; **to s. over a delicate subject,** glisser sur un sujet délicat.

2 *vt* (faire) glisser; **to s. sth into one's pocket,** glisser qch dans sa poche.

►**slide down** **1** *vi* (*go down by sliding*) descendre en glissant. **2** *vipo* (*go down by sliding*) descendre en glissant; **to s. down a rope,** se laisser couler *ou* glisser le long d'une corde; **to s. down the banisters,** glisser le long de la rampe.

►**slide off** *vi* **(a)** (*be removed by sliding*) **the lid slides off,** pour enlever le couvercle il faut le faire glisser *ou* coulisser; **(b)** *F* (*sneak away*) décamper, filer.

►**slide out** *vi* **(a)** (*come out by sliding*) sortir en glissant; **(b)** *F* (*sneak outside*) se glisser dehors; (*slip off*) se défiler.

►**slide out of** *vipo* (*evade*) se tirer de; **to s. out of doing the housework,** échapper aux tâches ménagères; **I'd like to see him s. out of that one,** j'aimerais bien voir comment il va se tirer de cette situation.

sliding [ˈslaɪdɪŋ] **1** *adj* glissant; (*panneau*) coulissant, mobile; *Aut* (*toit*) ouvrant; **s. door,** porte coulissante, porte à coulisse *ou* à glissières; *MecE* **s. parts,** organes *mpl* mobiles; *Econ* **s. scale,** échelle *f* mobile (*des prix etc*); **s. seat,** (*in rowing boat*) banc *m* à coulisses *ou* à glissières; *Aut* siège *m* réglable *ou* mobile. **2** *n* glissement *m*, coulissement *m*.

slight[1] [slaɪt] *adj* **(a)** (*small*) (*pain, mistake etc*) léger, petit; (*intelligence, difference etc*) faible; (*damage*) peu considérable; (*wound*) sans gravité; **a s. accident,** un petit accident; **a s. improvement,** un léger mieux; **not the slightest danger/interest/***etc*, pas le moindre danger/intérêt/*etc*; **to take offence at the slightest thing,** se piquer d'un rien; **on the slightest pretext,** sous un prétexte quelconque; **I haven't the slightest (idea),** je n'en ai pas la moindre idée; **not in the slightest,** pas du tout, pas le moins du monde; **they weren't in the slightest bit interested, they weren't interested in the slightest,** ils n'étaient pas le moins du monde intéressés; **(b)** (*thin*) mince, ténu; (*figure*) frêle.

slight[2] *n* (*affront*) affront *m*; (*lack of consideration*) manque *m* de considération *ou* d'égards.

slight[3] *vt* (*affront*) faire un affront à (*qn*); (*treat without consideration*) traiter (*qn*) sans considération, manquer d'égards pour *ou* à (*qn*); **to feel slighted,** se sentir vexé *ou* froissé.

slighting [ˈslaɪtɪŋ] *adj* (*air*) de mépris, de dédain.

slightingly [ˈslaɪtɪŋlɪ] *adv* dédaigneusement.

slightly [ˈslaɪtlɪ] **(a)** (*to a small degree*) légèrement, un peu; **s. better,** un petit peu mieux; **I know him s.,** je le connais un peu; **(b)** (*weak*) au corps frêle; (*thin*) à la taille mince.

slightness [ˈslaɪtnɪs] *n* **(a)** (*small extent*) légèreté *f* (*d'une faute etc*); faiblesse *f* (*de l'intelligence, d'une différence*); peu *m* d'importance, insignifiance *f* (*des dégâts*); **(b)** (*thinness*) minceur *f* (*d'une pièce de bois, du corps*).

slim[1] [slɪm] *adj* (*comp* **slimmer**, *superl* **slimmest**) (*person*) svelte, élancé, fluet; (*fingers etc*) fuselé, menu; (*book etc*) mince; (*chance, hope etc*) mince, léger; **his first s. volume,** son premier petit opuscule.

slim[2] *v* (**-mm-**) **1** *vt* amincir; **dress that is slimming,** robe amincissante *ou* qui amincit. **2** *vi* maigrir; **to be slimming,** être au régime, suivre un régime amaigrissant.

►**slim down** **1** *vtsep* (*reduce*) réduire (*la main-d'œuvre*); **the company is slimming down its electronics operation,** la société réduit ses activités dans le domaine de l'électronique. **2** *vi* **(a)** (*lose weight*) maigrir; **(b)** (*become smaller in size*) (*of company, army etc*) diminuer de taille.

slime [slaɪm] *n* **(a)** (*mud*) limon *m*, vase *f*; (*gold mining*) boue *f ou* poussier *m* de minerai; **(b)** humeur visqueuse (*sur* *les poissons etc*); bave *f* (*de limace*).

sliminess ['slaɪmɪnɪs] *n* **(a)** état vaseux; (*of fish etc*) viscosité *f*; **(b)** *F* (*servility*) servilité *f*, obséquiosité *f*.

slimly ['slɪmlɪ] *adv* **s. built,** à la taille svelte.

slimmer ['slɪmər] *n* personne *f* qui suit un régime amaigrissant; **ideal for slimmers,** l'idéal pour maigrir.

slimming ['slɪmɪŋ] *n* amincissement *m*; **s. course,** cure *f* d'amaigrissement; **s. diet,** régime amaigrissant; **s. pill,** pilule amaigrissante.

slimness ['slɪmnɪs] *n* (*of person*) minceur *f*, sveltesse *f*; minceur (*d'un livre etc*).

slimy ['slaɪmɪ] *adj* **(a)** (*consistency*) limoneux, vaseux; (*boue*) gras; (*paste etc*) visqueux, gluant; **the frog felt all s.,** la grenouille était toute visqueuse; **(b)** (*covered in slime*) couvert de vase *ou* de limon; (*fish*) couvert d'une sécrétion visqueuse; (*slug etc*) couvert de bave; **(c)** *F* (*person*) servile, obséquieux; **he's a real s. creep,** c'est un vrai lèche-bottes.

sling¹ [slɪŋ] *n* **(a)** *Med* écharpe *f*; bandoulière *f* (*de harpe etc*); bretelle *f* (*de fusil etc*); (*for hoisting*) *Nau etc* élingue *f*; (*for animals*) ventrière *f*; (*for hoisting s.o.*) agui *m*, chaise *f* (*pour charpentier etc*); *Vet* (*pour chevaux*) travail *m*, *pl* travails; **to have one's arm in a s.,** avoir *ou* porter le bras en écharpe; **boat slings,** pattes *fpl* d'embarcation; *Constr* **(rope) s.,** brayer *m* (*de maçon*); **rescue s.,** bridage *m* (*de sauvetage*); **(b)** (*weapon*) fronde *f*.

sling² *vt* (*pt & pp* **slung** [slʌŋ]) **(a)** (*hang*) suspendre; **to s. sth over one's shoulder,** jeter qch sur l'épaule; (*on strap*) mettre qch en bandoulière; **slung rifle,** fusil *m* à la grenadière; **(b)** (*throw*) lancer, jeter; **s. that paper over, will you?,** lance-moi le journal, s'il te plaît; **they were slinging insults at each other,** ils se lançaient des insultes.

►**sling off** *vtsep* **to s. s.o. off a course,** exclure qn d'un cours.

►**sling out** *vtsep F* **(a)** (*dismiss*) flanquer qn dehors; **he was slung out of the army,** il s'est fait jeter dehors de l'armée; **(b)** (*throw away*) jeter, balancer.

►**sling up** *vtsep* (*hoist*) hisser (*avec une grue*).

slingback ['slɪŋbæk] **1** *n* chaussure *f* à talon ouvert, sandale *f*. **2** *adj* (*chaussure*) à talon ouvert.

slingshot ['slɪŋʃɒt] *n esp Am* fronde *f*.

slink [slɪŋk] *vi* (*pt & pp* **slunk** [slʌŋk]) **to s. off** *or* **away,** partir furtivement *ou* en catimini, s'éclipser, filer à l'anglaise; **to s. in/out,** entrer/sortir furtivement.

slinking ['slɪŋkɪŋ] *adj* furtif.

slinky ['slɪŋkɪ] *adj F* (*figure*) svelte, mince; (*clothing*) collant, ajusté; (*walk*) ondulant.

slip¹ [slɪp] *n* **(a)** (*fall*) **he had a s. on the ice,** il a glissé sur la glace; **he had a nasty s.,** il est mal tombé; **it was only a s. of the hand,** sa main a glissé;

(b) (*error*) faute *f ou* erreur *f* d'inattention, faute d'étourderie; (*in speaking*) lapsus *m*; **to make a s.,** faire une erreur; (*in speaking*) faire un lapsus; **s. of the pen,** petite erreur d'orthographe; **she made a s. of the tongue,** la langue lui a fourché; **it was a s., I meant to say ...,** ma langue a fourché, je voulais dire ...;

(c) to give s.o. the s., se dérober à qn, fausser compagnie à qn; **s. stitch,** *Knitting* maille glissée; *Sewing* point perdu;

(d) *Geol* glissement *m*, éboulement *m* (*de terrain*);

(e) (*by thing*) glissement *m*; patinage *m* (*d'une courroie, Aut de l'embrayage*);

(f) *Av Nau* recul *m* (*de l'hélice*);

(g) (*in hunting*) laisse *f*, slip *m* (*de chien de chasse*);

(h) *Rail* **s. carriage** *or* **coach,** voiture *f ou* rame *f* à décrocher en cours de route;

(i) *Br Aut* **s. road,** bretelle *f* (*d'une autoroute*);

(j) (*garment*) combinaison *f* (*de femme*); **half** *or* **waist s.,** jupon *m*; **your slip's showing,** votre jupon dépasse; **gym s.,** tunique *f* (*d'écolière*); **(pillow) s.,** taie *f* d'oreiller;

(k) cale *f* de chargement (*d'un bac*); **building s.,** (*in naval architecture*) cale *ou* chantier *m* de construction; **ship on the slips,** navire sur cale(s) *ou* en construction;

(l) *Th* **the slips,** les coulisses *fpl*;

(m) *Cr* (*player*) chasseur posté à droite du garde-guichet; **the slips,** station *f* à droite du garde-guichet.

slip² *v* (**-pp-**) **1** *vi* **(a)** (*slide*) glisser; (*of knot*) couler, courir; (*of earth etc*) s'ébouler; *MecE etc* (*of belt etc*) patiner, glisser; *El etc* (*of frequency etc*) se décaler; **his foot slipped,** son pied a glissé; **I slipped on a banana skin,** j'ai glissé sur une peau de banane; **to s. from s.o.'s hands or grasp,** (*of vase etc*) glisser des mains *ou* des doigts de qn; **to s. through s.o.'s fingers,** glisser entre les doigts de qn; **to s. into bad habits,** se laisser aller à *ou* prendre de mauvaises habitudes; **error that has slipped into the text,** faute qui s'est glissée dans le texte; **the patient slipped into a coma,** le malade est entré dans le coma; **money just slips through his fingers,** l'argent lui glisse entre les doigts;

(b) (*move quickly etc*) **to s. into bed,** se glisser *ou* se couler dans son lit; **to s. into one's dressing gown,** passer *ou* enfiler sa robe de chambre; **she slipped into the next room,** elle s'est glissé dans la pièce voisine; **just s. round** *or* **over to the post office,** faites un saut jusqu'au bureau de poste;

(c) (*make mistake*) faire une (faute d')étourderie *ou* une bévue; **you're slipping,** (*beginning to make mistakes*) tu perds les pédales; **the quality is slipping,** la qualité n'est plus ce qu'elle était; **he slipped and said 'twenty' by mistake,** sa langue a fourché et il a dit 'vingt' par erreur;

(d) to let s., lâcher (*un lévrier etc*); laisser échapper (*une belle occasion, un mot, un secret*); **to let s. that ...,** laisser échapper que ... .

2 *vt* **(a)** se dégager de (*qch*); *Rail* décrocher (*une voiture en cours de route*); *Aut* **to s. the clutch,** laisser patiner l'embrayage; **to s. its chain** *or* **leash** *or* **lead,** (*of animal*) se détacher; **the dog has slipped its collar,** le chien s'est dégagé de son collier; **his name has slipped my mind,** son nom m'échappe; **to s. s.o.'s attention,** échapper à l'attention de qn;

(b) (*put*) glisser (*qch dans la main de qn, une lettre à la poste*); *Knitting* glisser (*une maille*); **he slipped it into his pocket,** il l'a glissé dans sa poche; **could you s. it in the drawer,** tu peux le mettre dans le tiroir; **to s. sth into the conversation,** glisser qch dans la conversation; **to s. the bolt (home),** pousser le verrou à fond; **I slipped my arm round her waist,** je lui ai passé mon bras autour de la taille; *Med* **to s. a disc,** se faire une hernie discale; *F* **to s. sth** *or* **one over on s.o.,** duper qn;

(c) to s. the hounds, (*in hunting*) lâcher *ou* découpler les chiens; *Nau* **to s. a cable,** larguer *ou* filer une amarre par le bout; **to s. one's moorings,** filer le corps-mort; **to s. its young,** (*of animal*) mettre bas avant terme.

slip³ *n* **(a)** (*piece*) bout *m* (*de papier*); (*docket*) fiche *f*; bande étroite (*de terre etc*); **pay s.,** bulletin *m* de paie; **sales s.,** récépissé *m*; **(b)** *Old-fashioned F* **s. of a girl,** jeune fille fluette; (*young*) fillette *f*; **(c)** (*in horticulture*) bouture *f*; (*for grafting*) scion *m*.

►**slip away** *vi* (*of person*) (*get away*) filer; (*leave work early*) s'esquiver, s'éclipser; **the patient was slipping away,** le malade s'éteignait doucement; **control of the party was slipping away from her,** elle perdait peu à peu son emprise sur le parti.

►**slip back 1** *vi* **(a)** (*return*) revenir, repasser; **(b)** (*get worse*) (*of work*) se dégrader. **2** *vtsep* (*put back*) remettre.

►**slip by** *vi* **(a)** (*of time, years etc*) passer; (*fast*) fuir; **(b)** (*pass unnoticed*) (*of person*) passer inaperçu; **to s. by s.o.,** (*of errors etc*) échapper à qn.

►**slip down** *vi* (*slide down*) descendre en glissant; (*of socks etc*) descendre.

►**slip in 1** *vi* (*enter quickly, inconspicuously*) entrer (en passant); (*enter room, house quickly, inconspicuously*) se glisser dans une pièce *ou* une maison *etc*; **a few mistakes slipped in,** quelques erreurs se sont glissées. **2** *vt* (*insert inconspicuously*) glisser; **she slipped in several references to ...,** elle a glissé plusieurs allusions à ... .

►**slip off 1** *vtsep* (*jacket, shoes*) enlever. **2** *vi* (*of person*) s'éclipser.

►**slip on** *vtsep* (*put on quickly*) enfiler, passer (*un vêtement*).

►**slip out** *vi* **(a)** (*escape*) s'échapper; **the soap slipped out of my hands,** le savon m'a échappé des mains; **to let sth s. out,** laisser échapper qch; **the secret has slipped out,** le secret a transpiré; **it slipped out that ...,** le bruit s'est répandu selon lequel ...; **(b)** (*leave quickly, inconspicuously*) filer (à la dérobée); **I'm just slipping out for a few minutes,** je sors pour quelques minutes.

►**slip through** *vi* (*of errors etc*) échapper à l'attention; **too many mistakes are slipping through,** il y a trop d'erreurs qui nous *ou* leur *etc* échappent.

►**slip up** *vi* **(a)** (*fall*) tomber; **he slipped up on the ice,** il a glissé sur la glace et est tombé; **(b)** (*make mistake*) se tromper; (*socially etc*) faire une gaffe, gaffer.

slipcase ['slɪpkeɪs] *n* (*for books*) étui *m*.

slipcover ['slɪpkʌvər] *n esp Am* **(a)** (*for furniture*) housse *f*; **(b)** (*book cover*) jaquette *f*.

slipknot ['slɪpnɒt] *n* nœud coulant.

slip-on ['slɪpɒn] **1** *n F* **(a) s.-ons,** (*shoes*) mocassins *mpl*; **(b)** *Am* (*sweater*) pull-over *m*, *pl* pull-overs. **2** *adj* **s.-on**

shoes, mocassins *mpl*.

slipover ['slɪpəʊvər] *n* débardeur *m*.

slipper ['slɪpər] *n* **(a)** (*footwear*) (*backless*) pantoufle *f*; (*ladies'*) mule *f*; **(bedroom) s.,** chausson *m*; **(b)** *MecE* patin *m* (*de frein*).

slipperiness ['slɪpərɪnɪs] *n* **(a)** nature glissante (*d'une surface*); **(b)** (*of person*) caractère rusé.

slippery ['slɪpərɪ] *adj* **(a)** (*pavement, fish etc*) glissant; **it's s. (underfoot),** le pavé est glissant; ça glisse; **(b)** (*unstable*) instable, incertain; (*sujet*) délicat, scabreux; *Fig* **to be on s. ground,** être sur un terrain glissant; *Fig* **it's a s. slope,** nous sommes *ou* il est *etc* sur la pente dangereuse; **this was the start of the s. slope that led to alcoholism,** c'est là qu'a commencé la déchéance qui l'a mené à l'alcoolisme; **(c)** (*person*) (*cunning*) fin, rusé; (*devious*) retors; **he's as s. as an eel,** il glisse comme *ou* est aussi insaisissable qu'une anguille; **a s. customer,** une fine mouche.

slipping ['slɪpɪŋ] **1** *adj* glissant, qui glisse. **2** *n* (*on ice etc*) glissement *m*; (*of belt in machinery etc*) patinage *m*; (*of standards*) déclin *m*.

slippy ['slɪpɪ] *adj F* **(a)** (*slippery*) glissant; **(b)** *Br* (*quick*) **you'll have to be pretty s. about it,** il faudra que tu fasses vite *ou* que tu te grouilles; **look s.!,** grouille-toi!

slipshod ['slɪpʃɒd] *adj* (*negligent*) négligent; (*travail*) négligé, bâclé; (*style*) débraillé; **book written in a s. manner,** livre écrit sans soin.

slipstream ['slɪpstriːm] *n* sillage *m*, remous *mpl* (*d'air, d'eau*); *Av* souffle *m ou* vent *m* de l'hélice.

slip(-)up ['slɪpʌp] *n* gaffe *f*, bévue *f*; **there's been a s.-up,** il y a eu une bévue; **to make a s.-up,** faire une bévue.

slipway ['slɪpweɪ] *n* (*naval architecture*) cale *f ou* chantier *m* de construction; slip *m* (*de halage, de carénage*).

slit[1] [slɪt] *n* fente *f*, fissure *f*, rainure *f*; (*between curtains etc*) entrebâillement *m*; (*in wall, of postbox*) fente *f*; (*for shooting through*) meurtrière *f*; **s.-eyed,** aux yeux bridés; **s. pocket,** (*in outer garment*) fente verticale donnant accès aux vêtements de dessous; (*false pocket*) fausse poche; *Mil* **s. trench,** tranchée *f*.

slit[2] *vt* (*pt & pp* **slit**; *prp* **slitting**) fendre; *Surg* faire une incision dans (*la chair*); refendre (*le cuir, le bois etc*); **the blow slit his cheek,** le coup lui a déchiré la joue; **to s. s.o.'s throat,** couper la gorge à qn; **to s. open a sack,** éventrer un sac; **slit skirt,** jupe fendue.

slither[1] ['slɪðər] *n* glissement *m*, glissade *f*.

slither[2] *vi* glisser; (*of snake, worm*) ramper; **the dog was slithering about on the ice,** le chien patinait *ou* dérapait sur la glace; **to s. down a hill,** dégringoler une pente.

sliver[1] ['slɪvər] *n* **(a)** (*thin slice*) tranche *f* (fine); éclat *m* (*de bois, d'obus*); **(b)** *Tex* ruban *m* (*de lin cardé*).

sliver[2] **1** *vt* couper (*qch*) en tranches (fines). **2** *vi* (*of wood, shell*) voler en éclats.

Sloane (Ranger) [sləʊn('reɪndʒər)] *n* jeune fille de la bonne société; **she's rather S.,** elle est très comme il faut.

slob [slɒb] *n F* rustaud *m*; **big fat s.,** gros lard.

slobber[1] ['slɒbər] *n* (*saliva*) bave *f*, salive *f*; *F* (*sentimentality*) sentimentalité larmoyante.

slobber[2] *vi* (*salivate*) baver; (*cry exaggeratedly*) larmoyer.

▶**slobber over** *vipo* **(a)** (*of dog etc*) lécher (*qn*); **to s. (all) over s.o.,** (*be sentimental towards*) témoigner une tendresse exagérée envers qn, s'attendrir exagérément sur qn; **(b)** (*kiss etc*) faire des mamours à (*qn*).

sloe [sləʊ] *n* **(a)** (*fruit*) prunelle *f*; **s. gin,** = (alcool *m* de) prunelle; **(b) s. bush** *or* **tree,** prunellier *m*.

slog[1] [slɒg] *n F* **(a)** (*blow*) coup *m* (violent); **(b)** (*hard work*) corvée *f*, gros boulot; **a hard s.,** (*great effort*) un gros effort; (*walk, ride*) un trajet pénible; **it's a long s. to the top,** (*of hill, organization*) c'est un long et pénible trajet pour arriver en haut.

slog[2] *v* **(-gg-)** *F* **1** *vt* (*hit*) cogner, battre (*qch, qn*); *Cr* frapper fort sur (*la balle*); **he slogged his way through the text,** il a déchiffré le texte avec grande difficulté. **2** *vi* (*work hard*) turbiner, trimer; (*walk, ride*) **they slogged for miles,** ils ont poursuivi leur chemin à grand-peine pendant des kilomètres.

▶**slog along** *vi F* (*keep walking*) marcher d'un pas lourd *ou* péniblement.

▶**slog away** *vi F* (*keep working*) continuer à trimer.

▶**slog away at** *vipo F* **(a)** (*work hard*) travailler avec acharnement à (*qch*); **(b)** (*hit*) continuer à frapper.

▶**slog on** *vi F* **(a)** = **SLOG ALONG**; **(b)** (*keep working*) continuer à trimer; **I think I'll s. on a little longer,** je pense que je vais continuer à bosser encore un peu.

slogan ['sləʊgən] *n Pol Com* slogan *m*; **election/advertising s.,** slogan électoral/publicitaire.

slogger ['slɒgər] *n F* **(a)** *Boxing Cr* cogneur *m* (*qui frappe au hasard*); **(b)** (*hard worker*) bûcheur *m*.

sloop [sluːp] *n Nau* sloop *m*.

slop[1] [slɒp] *n* **(a)** (*spilt drinks*) boissons renversées (*sur la table etc*); *Pej* (*drink*) lavasse *f*; (*liquid food*) aliments *mpl* liquides; (*dirty water*) eaux sales *ou* usées; (*in cup*) fonds *m* de tasse; **s. basin,** vide-tasses *m inv*; **s. pail,** seau *m* de toilette *ou* hygiénique; **(b)** *F* sentimentalité excessive.

slop[2] *v* **(-pp-)** **1** *vt* (*spill*) renverser, répandre (*un liquide*) (**over the table,** sur la table). **2** *vi* (*of liquids*) déborder.

▶**slop about, slop around** *vi* **(a)** *F* (*walk in water, mud etc*) patauger, barboter; **(b)** (*of liquid*) clapoter; **(c)** *Fig* **he just slops around the house all day,** il passe toute la journée à traîner *ou F* à glandouiller chez lui.

▶**slop out** *vi* (*empty toilet buckets in prison*) vider les seaux hygiéniques.

▶**slop over** *vi* = **SLOP**[2] **2.**

slop[3] *n Nau* **slops,** effets *mpl*, frusques *fpl* (*d'un matelot*).

slope[1] [sləʊp] *n* **(a)** pente *f*, inclinaison *f*; **steep/gentle s.,** pente raide/douce; *Mil* **with rifle at the s.,** l'arme sur l'épaule; **(b)** (*hill*) pente *f*; (*ramp*) talus *m*; (*of mountain*) versant *m*; (*in road, railway*) rampe *f*; *Ski* piste *f*; **on the slopes of the Himalayas,** sur les pentes de l'Himalaya; **on the northern s.,** sur le versant nord; **halfway down** *or* **up the s.,** à mi-pente.

slope[2] **1** *vi* (*of ground etc*) être en pente; (*not be straight*) (*of picture etc*) pencher; **to s. forward/backward,** (*of writing*) pencher à droite/à gauche; **the garden slopes down to the river,** le jardin descend (en pente) vers la rivière; **the ground slopes up to the house,** le terrain monte vers la maison. **2** *vt* incliner (*qch*); *Mil* **to s. arms,** mettre l'arme sur l'épaule; **s. arms!,** arme sur l'épaule!

▶**slope away, slope off** *vi F* (*leave furtively*) décamper, filer.

sloping ['sləʊpɪŋ] *adj* en pente; (*leaning*) incliné; (*garden etc*) en talus, en pente; **s. shoulders,** épaules tombantes; **s. (hand)writing,** écriture couchée *ou* penchée.

sloppily ['slɒpɪlɪ] *adv* **(a)** (*carelessly*) sans soin; **(b)** *F* (*sentimentally*) avec sensiblerie; **s. dressed,** habillé sans soin.

sloppiness ['slɒpɪnɪs] *n* **(a)** (*of person*) mollesse *f*; (*carelessness*) manque *m* de soin, négligence *f* (*dans un travail*); négligence *f* (*de style*); ampleur *f* (*d'une robe mal coupée*); **(b)** *F* (*sentimentality*) sentimentalité excessive.

sloppy ['slɒpɪ] *adj* **(a)** (*person*) mou, *f* molle; (*job*) fait sans soin; (*style*) négligé, débraillé; (*dress etc*) ample, (trop) large; (*of guards etc*) coulant, peu strict; *F* **s. joe,** pull-over *m* très ample; **to get s.,** (*of person*) s'amollir; **(b)** *F* (*novel etc*) larmoyant; **to get s.,** (*of person*) devenir (trop) sentimental; **s. sentimentality,** sensiblerie *f*; **(c)** (*floor*) (*plancher*) mouillé; (*untidy*) (*table*) qui n'a pas été essuyé.

slosh [slɒʃ] **1** *vi* (*of liquid*) (*move around*) clapoter. **2** *vt F* **(a)** (*apply liberally*) flanquer (*de la peinture sur un mur etc*); **(b)** (*hit*) flanquer un coup à, tabasser (*qn*).

▶**slosh about, slosh around** *vi* **(a)** (*walk in water, mud etc*) patauger; **(b)** (*of liquid*) clapoter; **the water was sloshing around in the bucket,** l'eau clapotait dans le seau.

sloshed [slɒʃt] *adj Br Sl* (*drunk*) bourré, rond.

slot[1] [slɒt] *n* **(a)** (*groove*) entaille *f*, encoche *f*, rainure *f*; fente *f* (*de la tête d'une vis, d'une tirelire*); **to put a coin in the s.,** introduire une pièce de monnaie dans la fente (*d'un distributeur etc*); **s. machine,** (*vending machine*) distributeur *m* (automatique); (*gambling machine*) machine *f ou* appareil *m* à sous; **s. meter,** compteur *m* dans lequel on introduit des pièces; **(b)** *Rad TV etc* = tranche *f* horaire; (*in programme, production schedule, waiting list etc*) créneau *m*; (*for aircraft in flight control*) créneau; **we've missed our s.,** nous avons raté notre créneau; *Comptr* **expansion s.,** emplacement *m* pour carte d'extension; **prime time s.,** heure *f* de grande écoute.

slot[2] *v* **(-tt-)** **1** *vt MecE etc* tailler une fente *ou* une rainure dans (*qch*), rain(ur)er (*qch*); **to s. sth into sth,** insérer *ou* mettre qch dans qch. **2** *vi* s'introduire, se glisser (**into sth,** dans qch).

slot[3] *n* (*in hunting*) foulées *fpl*, voies *fpl* (*d'une bête*).

▶**slot in** **1** *vtsep* (*fit in*) prendre (*patient, customer etc*); **to s. a book in a space on a shelf,** glisser un livre dans un espace sur une étagère. **2** *vi* (*fit in*) rentrer dans; **the book will s. in here,** le livre rentrera là-dedans; **it slots well into our programme,** cela s'insère bien dans notre programme.

sloth [sləʊθ] *n* **(a)** (*laziness*) paresse *f*, fainéantise *f*, indolence *f*; **(b)** (*animal*) paresseux *m*; **s. bear,** ours jongleur; **s. monkey,** loris lent.

slothful ['sləʊθfʊl] *adj* (*lazy*) paresseux, fainéant, indolent.

slothfully ['sləʊθfəlɪ] *adv* (*lazily*) paresseusement, avec indolence.

slothfulness ['sləʊθfʊlnɪs] *n* = **SLOTH (a)**.

slouch[1] [slaʊtʃ] *n* **(a)** (*way of walking*) démarche *f* mollasse; (*deportment*) allure avachie *ou* molle; **s. of the shoulders,** épaules arrondies; **(b) s. hat,** (grand) chapeau mou *ou* rabattu; **(c)** *F* **he's no s.,** il n'est pas empoté.

slouch[2] *vi* (*hold oneself badly*) être avachi; (*walk badly*) avoir une démarche molasse; **don't s.!**, tenez-vous droit!

►**slouch about, slouch around** *vi* (*walk slowly, carelessly*) traîner le pas; (*do nothing much*) traînasser.

slough[1] [slaʊ] *n* (*bog*) bourbier *m*, fondrière *f*; (*swampy ground*) terrain marécageux.

slough[2] [slʌf] *n* **(a)** (*of reptile, insect*) dépouille *f*, mue *f*; **to cast its s.,** (*of snake*) se dépouiller, muer; **(b)** *Med* croûte *f* (*sur une plaie*).

slough[3] **1** *vi* (*of reptile etc*) se dépouiller, muer. **2** *vt* (*of reptile, insect*) **to s. its skin,** se dépouiller, muer; *Lit* **to s. a bad habit,** se débarrasser d'une mauvaise habitude.

►**slough away** *vi* = **SLOUGH OFF 2**.

►**slough off 1** *vtsep* = **SLOUGH**[3] **2**. **2** *vi* (*become detached*) (*of scab etc*) se détacher, tomber.

Slovak, Slovakian ['sləʊvæk, sləʊ'vækɪən] **1** *adj* slovaque. **2** *n* **(a)** (*person*) Slovaque *mf*; **(b)** *Ling* slovaque *m*.

Slovakia [sləʊ'vækɪə] *n* Slovaquie *f*.

sloven ['slʌv(ə)n] *n* **(a)** (*untidy person*) mal soigné, -ée; (*woman*) souillon *f*; **(b)** *Old-fashioned* (*careless worker*) bousilleur, -euse.

Slovene, Slovenian ['sləʊviːn, -'viːnɪən] **1** *adj* slovène. **2** *n* **(a)** (*person*) Slovène *mf*; **(b)** *Ling* slovène *m*.

slovenliness ['slʌv(ə)nlɪnɪs] *n* **(a)** (*untidiness*) négligence *f* (*de mise*); débraillé *m* (*de la tenue*); **(b)** (*negligence*) négligence *f*; (*lack of care*) manque *m* de soin.

slovenly ['slʌv(ə)nlɪ] *adj* **(a)** (*untidy*) (*person*) mal soigné; (*dress*) débraillé; **(b)** (*negligent*) (*person*) négligent; (*lacking care*) peu soigné; (*work*) négligé, bousillé; (*style*) débraillé; **done in a s. way,** fait sans soin.

slow[1] [sləʊ] **1** *adj* **(a)** lent; (*spectacle etc*) ennuyeux, qui manque d'entrain; **to be s. over (doing) sth,** mettre longtemps à faire qch; **business is s.,** les affaires languissent *ou* ne vont pas fort; **to be s. to do sth,** (*of person*) être lent à faire qch; **s. to act** *or* **to take action, s. in action,** lent à agir; **progress has been s.,** les progrès ont été lents à se manifester; **this method is s. but sure,** cette méthode est lente mais sûre; **he wasn't s. to respond,** il n'a pas été long à répondre; **he's been s. to get it done,** il a mis du temps à le faire faire; **s. (of intellect),** à l'esprit lent *ou* lourd; **you're very s. today,** tu es très lent aujourd'hui; **s. child,** enfant attardé *ou* arriéré; *Aut* **s. lane,** voie lente; *Cin etc* **(in) s. motion,** (au) ralenti *m*; *Culin* **to cook sth in a s. oven,** faire cuire qch à four doux; *MecE* **s. running,** ralenti *m*; **s. steps,** pas lents; *Rail* **s. train,** (train *m*) omnibus *m*; **it's s. work,** ça ne va pas vite; **she's a s. worker,** elle travaille lentement;
(b) (*of clock, watch*) en retard; **my watch is five minutes s.,** ma montre retarde de cinq minutes.
2 *adv* lentement; **to go s.,** aller lentement; *Ind* faire la grève perlée; **to run s.,** (*of engine*) tourner au ralenti; **s.!,** (*on road sign*) ralentir!; *Nau* **s. ahead/astern!,** en avant/en arrière doucement!; **s. moving,** (*traffic*) qui se déplace lentement; (*film*) lent; **s. spoken,** qui parle lentement; **s. burning,** qui brûle lentement, à combustion lente; (*in explosives*) (*poudre*) lent; *US Sl* **to do a s. burn,** avoir la moutarde qui vous monte au nez.

slow[2] *vi & vt* = **SLOW DOWN, SLOW UP**.

►**slow down, slow up 1** *vi* (*go more slowly*) ralentir; *Aut* (*of engine*) prendre le ralenti; **to s. down** *or* **up (to a stop),** s'arrêter; **as he got older he slowed down,** à mesure qu'il prenait de l'âge il a ralenti son rythme. **2** *vtsep* ralentir; *Ind* **to s. down production,** ralentir la production; **her heavy suitcase was slowing her up,** sa valise lourde la ralentissait.

slowcoach ['sləʊkəʊtʃ] *n Br F* lambin, -ine, traînard, -arde.

slowdown ['sləʊdaʊn] *n* **(a)** (*slowing*) ralentissement *m* (*des affaires etc*); **(b)** travail *m* au ralenti.

slowing ['sləʊɪŋ] *n* **s. down,** ralentissement *m*.

slowly ['sləʊlɪ] *adv* lentement; **the time/morning has gone very s.,** le temps/la matinée a passé très lentement; **running s.,** (*moteur*) qui tourne au ralenti; **he's s. realizing that ...,** il se rend compte peu à peu que ...; **to cook sth s.,** faire cuire qch à feu doux.

slowness ['sləʊnɪs] *n* **(a)** lenteur *f*; lourdeur *f*, lenteur (*d'esprit*); manque *m* d'entrain (*d'un spectacle etc*); **(b)** retard *m* (*d'une pendule etc*).

slowpoke ['sləʊpəʊk] *n Am F* lambin, -ine, traînard, -arde.

slow-worm ['sləʊwɜːm] *n* orvet *m*, serpent *m* de verre.

SLR [esel'ɑːr] *n Phot* (*abbr* **single-lens reflex**) reflex *m* monoculaire.

sludge [slʌdʒ] *n* (*mud*) vase *f*, fange *f*; (*snow*) neige à moitié fondue; *Ind* boue *f*; **sewage s.,** vidanges *fpl*.

sludgy ['slʌdʒɪ] *adj* vaseux; *Ind* boueux.

slug[1] [slʌg] *n* (*mollusc*) limace *f*; **s. pellet,** pastille *f* antilimace.

slug[2] *n* **(a)** (*bullet*) balle *f*, plomb *m* (*d'une arme à feu*); **(b)** *esp Am F* goutte *f*, coup *m* (*d'eau-de vie etc*).

slug[3] *n Am F* (*blow*) coup violent.

slug[4] *vt Am F* (*hit*) battre, tabasser (*qn*); *Baseball* frapper fort.

►**slug out** *vtsep* **to s. it out,** se tabasser, se taper dessus, se rentrer dedans; *Fig* (*verbally*) se rentrer dedans.

sluggard ['slʌgəd] *adj & n* paresseux, -euse, fainéant, -ante.

sluggish ['slʌgɪʃ] *adj* **(a)** (*person*) (*lazy*) paresseux, *F* flemmard; (*not energetic*) léthargique; (*mind*) lourd, engourdi; **(b)** (*river, pulse etc*) lent, paresseux; *Aut* (*engine*) mou; (*market*) stagnant; (*sales*) difficile, qui ne va pas fort.

sluggishly ['slʌgɪʃlɪ] *adv* **(a)** (*lazily*) paresseusement; **(b)** (*slowly*) lentement.

sluggishness ['slʌgɪʃnɪs] *n* **(a)** (*of person*) paresse *f*, *F* flemme *f*; (*of mind*) lourdeur *f*; **(b)** (*of river etc*) lenteur *f*; (*of liver, intestine etc*) paresse *f*; *Aut* (*of engine*) mollesse *f*.

sluice[1] [sluːs] *n* **(a)** écluse *f*; canal *m*, -aux de décharge (*du trop-plein d'un réservoir*); **put it down the s.,** versez-le dans les égouts; **(b)** = **SLUICEGATE**; **(c)** *F* **to give sth a s. down,** laver qch à grande eau.

sluice[2] *vt HydE* vanner (*un cours d'eau*); laver à grande eau; débourber (*un égout, Min le minerai*).

►**sluice down** *vtsep* (*wash down*) laver à grande eau; **to s. oneself down with cold water,** s'asperger d'eau fraîche.

►**sluice out 1** *vtsep* (*release*) laisser échapper (*l'eau d'un reservoir*) (par les vannes). **2** *vi* (*of water etc*) (*flow in great quantity*) couler à flots.

sluicegate ['sluːsgeɪt] *n* porte *f* d'écluse, vanne *f*; *Lit* **the sluicegates of heaven have opened,** les écluses du ciel se sont ouvertes.

sluiceway ['sluːsweɪ] *n* canal *m*, -aux à vannes.

slum[1] [slʌm] *n* (*district*) bas quartier, quartier pauvre; (*house*) taudis *m*; **s. clearance,** suppression *f* des taudis.

slum[2] *vi* (-mm-) *F* **to s. it,** vivre pauvrement, *F* manger de la vache enragée; *Fig Hum* **I'm slumming it tonight,** (*different area*) je change de quartier ce soir; (*different pub, restaurant etc*) je change de cantine ce soir.

slumber[1] ['slʌmbər] *n Lit* sommeil *m*; **her s. was** *or* **her slumbers were interrupted by ...,** son sommeil a été interrompu par ...; *Fig* **he awoke from his intellectual slumbers,** il a enfin repris ses activités intellectuelles; *Com* **s. wear,** vêtements *mpl* de nuit.

slumber[2] *vi Lit* sommeiller, dormir (paisiblement).

slummy ['slʌmɪ] *adj* sordide; **s. district,** bas quartier.

slump[1] [slʌmp] *n Com* baisse soudaine, chute *f*, effondrement *m* (*des cours etc*); **the s. in oil prices,** l'effondrement des prix du pétrole; **s. in the pound,** dégringolade *f ou* baisse soudaine de la livre; **the s.,** la crise *ou* dépression économique.

slump[2] *vi* **(a)** tomber lourdement, s'affaisser (**into a chair,** dans un fauteuil); **the editor was slumped unconscious over his desk,** le rédacteur en chef s'est effondré sans connaissance sur son bureau; **(b)** *Com Ind etc* (*of prices etc*) (*fall suddenly*) dégringoler, baisser tout à coup; (*collapse*) s'effondrer, dégringoler.

slung *see* **SLING**[2].

slunk *see* **SLINK**.

slur[1] [slɜːr] *n* **(a)** (*insult*) insulte *f*; (*stain*) tache *f*; **to cast a s. on s.o.'s reputation,** porter atteinte à *ou* ternir la réputation de qn; **(b)** *Typ* macule *f*, maculage *m*; **(c)** *Mus* (*sign*) liaison *f*; (*passage*) coulé *m*; **(d)** (*in speech*) mauvaise articulation.

slur[2] *v* (-rr-) **1** *vt* **(a)** mal articuler (*ses mots*); (*mumble*) bredouiller, escamoter (*un mot*); **his speech was slurred,** il articulait mal, il mangeait la moitié de ses mots; **(b)** *Mus* lier (*deux notes*); couler (*un passage*); **slurred notes,** notes liées coulant. **2** *vi* (*speak indistinctly*) mal articuler ses mots, manger la moitié de ses mots.

►slur over *vtsep* **(a)** (*not deal with fully*) **to s. over a fact,** passer *ou* glisser sur un fait; **(b)** (*mumble*) bredouiller, escamoter (*un mot*).

slurp [slɜːp] **1** *vt* boire (*qch*) avec bruit. **2** *vi* boire avec bruit; **don't s.!,** ne fais pas de bruit en buvant!

slush [slʌʃ] *n* **(a)** (*snow*) neige à moitié fondue; (*mud*) fange *f*, bourbe *f*; **(b)** *F* (*sentimentality*) sensiblerie *f*; **(c)** *Pol F* **s. fund,** caisse noire; **s. (money) payments,** graissage *m* de patte.

slushy ['slʌʃɪ] *adj* **(a)** (*from snow*) détrempé par la neige; (*muddy*) bourbeux, fangeux; **(b)** *F* (*roman, film etc*) d'une sentimentalité excessive, fadasse.

slut [slʌt] *n* **(a)** (*dirty woman*) souillon *f*; **(b)** (*promiscuous woman*) garce *f*, salope *f*.

sluttish ['slʌtɪʃ] *adj* (*woman*) malpropre, sale; (*behaviour etc*) de salope.

sluttishness ['slʌtɪʃnɪs] *n* (*dirtiness*) malpropreté *f*; (*promiscuity*) conduite immorale.

sly [slaɪ] **1** *adj* (*comp* **slyer**, *superl* **slyest**) **(a)** (*cunning*) rusé; **s. dog,** fin matois; **(b)** (*dishonest*) sournois; **(c)** (*mischievous*) malin, *f* -igne, espiègle; **s. grin,** sourire espiègle. **2** *n* **on the s.,** furtivement, à la dérobée, en cachette.

slyboots ['slaɪbuːts] *n F* (*cunning person*) petit malin; (*mischievous child*) espiègle *mf*, petit(e) coquin(e); **you old s.!,** espèce de coquin!

slyly ['slaɪlɪ] *adv* (*see adj*) **(a)** avec finesse; **(b)** sournoisement; **(c)** d'une manière espiègle, avec espièglerie.

slyness ['slaɪnɪs] *n* **(a)** finesse *f*; **(b)** sournoiserie *f*; **(c)** espièglerie *f*.

smack¹ [smæk] **1** *n* **(a)** (*blow*) claque *f*; **s. in the face,** gifle *f*; *Fig F* (*also* **s. in the eye**) affront *m*, rebuffade *f*; **to give a child a s. on the bottom,** donner une fessée à un enfant; **he gave the ball a hard s.,** il a frappé vigoureusement la balle; *F* **to have a s. at sth,** (*attempt*) essayer de faire qch; **(b)** (*sound*) claquement *m* (*d'un fouet etc*); **with a s. of his tongue,** avec un claquement de langue; **the s. of the waves,** le fouettement des vagues; **(c)** *F* (*loud kiss*) gros baiser retentissant, grosse bise. **2** *adv* **(a)** (*make sound*) **to go s.,** faire claquer; **(b) to bump s. into a tree,** rentrer en plein dans un arbre; **s. in the middle,** en plein milieu, au beau milieu; **he caught him s. on the chin,** il l'a frappé en plein sur le menton.

smack² **1** *vt* (*hit*) frapper, taper (*avec le plat de la main*); donner une claque à (*qn*); **to s. s.o.'s face,** donner une gifle à qn, gifler qn; **to s. a child's bottom,** donner une fessée à un enfant. **2** *vi* claquer.

smack³ *n Nau* **(fishing) s.,** bateau *m* de pêche.

smack⁴ *n Sl* (*heroin*) héro *f*, horse *f*.

smack⁵ *n Old-fashioned* (*slight taste*) léger goût, soupçon *m* (*d'ail, Fig de malice etc*).

►smack of *vipo* (*have slight taste of*) avoir un léger goût de qch; **opinions that s. of heresy,** opinions *fpl* qui sentent *ou* qui fleurent l'hérésie.

smacker ['smækər] *n* **(a)** *F* (*blow*) gifle retentissante; *F* (*big kiss*) gros baiser, grosse bise; **(b)** *Sl* (*pound*) livre *f*; (*dollar*) dollar *m*; *Sl* (*franc*) balle *f*.

smacking ['smækɪŋ] *n* (*spanking*) fessée *f*; claquement *m* (*d'un fouet*); **to give s.o. a s.,** donner une fessée à qn.

small [smɔːl] **1** *adj* **(a)** petit; petit, menu (*morceau, brin etc*); petit, faible (*dose etc*); **to make sth smaller,** rapetisser qch; **to make oneself s.,** se faire tout petit; **s. arms,** armes portatives; *Typ* **s. capitals,** *F* **small caps,** petites majuscules; *Typ* **s. letters,** minuscules *fpl*; **s. child,** (*young*) enfant en bas âge, petit enfant; (*small in size*) enfant de petite taille; **s. coffee,** une petite tasse (de café); **a s. white coffee please!,** un petit crème, s'il vous plaît!; **of s. dimensions,** de petites dimensions; **he's a s. eater,** il n'est pas gros mangeur; **s. hours,** heures matinales; *Anat* **s. intestine,** intestin *m* grêle; **in s. numbers,** en petit nombre; **the smallest number of people possible,** le moins de gens possible; **s. party,** (*group*) parti peu nombreux; (*gathering*) réunion peu nombreuse; **the s. print,** (*in contract etc*) le texte en petits caractères; **s. stature,** petite taille; **s. talk,** bavardages *mpl* sans importance; **I'm no good at s. talk,** je ne suis pas très porté sur la conversation; **s. T-shirt/***etc*, T-shirt *m/etc* de petite taille; **s. voice,** voix fluette, petite voix (*que l'on entend à peine*);

(b) of no s. consequence, de très grande importance; **not the smallest difference,** pas la moindre différence; **it was no s. surprise to me,** cela m'a beaucoup surpris; **s. income,** revenu *m* modique; **it's s. wonder that ...,** ce n'est guère étonnant que + *sub*;

(c) (*not important*) peu important, peu considérable; *Journ F* **s. ads,** petites annonces; *Br F* **to be s. beer,** (*of s.o., sth*) être insignifiant; *Com* **s. business,** petite entreprise; **s. businessman,** gérant *m* d'une petite entreprise *ou* d'une PME; **s. change,** petite monnaie; **s. details,** menus détails; **the smallest details,** les moindres détails; **a s. hotel,** un hôtel modeste; **the smaller industries,** la petite industrie; **a s. matter,** une bagatelle; **s. shopkeeper,** petit commerçant; **in a s. way,** (*to a modest extent*) modestement; **he's a farmer in a s. way,** il tient une petite exploitation agricole;

(d) (*petty*) mesquin, chétif; **I felt very s.,** (*ashamed*) je n'étais pas fier; (*humiliated*) je me suis senti très humilié; **to make s.o. look** *or* **feel s.,** humilier qn, rabaisser qn; **only a s. man could behave like that,** il n'y a qu'un esprit mesquin pour agir de la sorte; **s. mind,** esprit mesquin.

2 *n* **(a) s. of the back,** creux *m ou* chute *f* des reins;

(b) (*coal*) menu *m* du charbon, menus, charbonnaille *f*;

(c) *F* **smalls,** lingerie *f*, sous-vêtements *mpl*; **to wash one's smalls,** faire sa petite lessive;

(d) (*small size*) (*in T-shirt etc*) petite taille.

3 *adv* **(a)** (*hacher etc*) menu, fin;

(b) (*écrire*) petit.

smallholder ['smɔːlhəʊldər] *n* petit cultivateur.

smallholding ['smɔːlhəʊldɪŋ] *n Agr* petite ferme.

smallish ['smɔːlɪʃ] *adj* assez *ou* plutôt petit.

small-minded [smɔːl'maɪndɪd] *adj* à l'esprit mesquin *ou* étroit; **a s.-m. man,** un homme à l'esprit mesquin.

smallness ['smɔːlnɪs] *n* **(a)** petitesse *f*, modicité *f* (*de revenus*); faible montant *m* (*d'une somme*); **(b)** (*pettiness*) **the s. of his mind,** sa mesquinerie.

smallpox ['smɔːlpɒks] *n Med* petite vérole, variole *f*; **s. pustules,** pustules *fpl* varioliques; **s. patient,** varioleux, -euse.

small-scale ['smɔːlskeɪl] *adj* **(a)** (*modèle*) réduit; (*carte*) à petite échelle; **(b)** (*entreprise*) peu important; **(c)** *Comptr* **s.-s. integration,** intégration *f* à petite échelle.

small-time ['smɔːltaɪm] *adj F* insignifiant, médiocre; **s.-t. crook,** petit escroc.

small-town ['smɔːltaʊn] *adj F* provincial, de province; **a s.-t. attitude,** une mentalité provinciale.

smarm [smɑːm] *n F Pej* caractère doucereux.

►smarm down *vtsep* **to s. down one's hair,** se brillantiner les cheveux.

►smarm up to *vipo* **(a)** (*flatter*) flatter, flagorner (*qn*); **(b)** (*be obsequious to*) lécher les bottes à (*qn*).

smarminess ['smɑːmɪnɪs] *n F Pej* caractère doucereux.

smarmy ['smɑːmɪ] *adj F Pej* doucereux; **he's a real s. git,** c'est un vrai lèche-bottes; **a s. person,** un lécheur.

smart¹ [smɑːt] *n* (*pain*) douleur cuisante.

smart² *vi* **(a)** (*of wound etc*) cuire, brûler; **my eyes are smarting,** les yeux me brûlent; **(b)** (*of person*) souffrir; **to s. under an insult,** souffrir sous le coup d'une insulte.

smart³ **1** *adj* **(a)** (*clever*) habile, intelligent; (*shrewd*) malin, rusé; (*quick-thinking*) à l'esprit rapide; (*resourceful*) dégourdi, débrouillard; *Comptr* intelligent; **it isn't s. to break the law,** ce n'est pas malin de ne pas respecter la loi; **to be too s. for s.o.,** être trop intelligent pour qn; **trying to be s., eh?,** tu essaies de faire le malin, hein?; **don't try to be s. with me,** n'essaie pas de faire le malin avec moi; **that wasn't very s., was it?,** ce n'était pas très malin, n'est-ce pas?; **s. lad wanted,** on recherche un jeune garçon intelligent; **s. businesswoman,** femme d'affaires habile; **s. answer,** réponse adroite; *esp Am F* **s. aleck,** petit malin; *F* **he's a s. one,** c'est un malin; **a s. move,** une sage décision;

(b) (*dress, person, building etc*) (*elegant*) élégant, chic; (*attractive*) coquet, pimpant; **to make oneself s.,** se faire beau *ou* belle; (*for interview etc*) bien s'habiller; **you do look s.,** comme tu es beau!; **the s. set,** la haute;

(c) (*quick*) vif, rapide; (*prompt*) prompt; (*alert*) alerte; **s. pace,** allure vive *ou* rapide; **that's s. work,** vous allez vite en besogne!; **s. box on the ear,** bonne gifle; **s. reprimand,** verte réprimande.

2 *adv* **look s. (about it)!,** dépêchez-vous!, remuez-vous!

smartarse ['smɑːtɑːs] **1** *n Br Sl* petit malin. **2** *adj* (*answer*) malin, *f* -igne.

►smarten up ['smɑːt(ə)n] **1** *vtsep* **(a)** (*make more elegant*) donner du chic à (*qch*); (*make more presentable*) arranger; **to s. oneself up,** se faire beau; **(b)** (*improve*) **you'd better s. up your ideas!,** tu ferais bien de te reprendre; (*to lazy person*) tu ferais bien de te secouer. **2** *vi* (*make oneself elegant*) se faire beau.

smarting ['smɑːtɪŋ] **1** *adj* (*pain, eyes*) cuisant, brûlant. **2** *n* douleur cuisante.

smartish ['smɑːtɪʃ] *adv Br F* vite fait, en vitesse; **you'd better get ready pretty s.,** tu ferais mieux de te préparer vite fait.

smartness ['smɑːtnɪs] *n* **(a)** (*cleverness*) habileté *f*, intelligence *f*; (*shrewdness*) ruse *f*; (*quickness of thought*) vivacité *f* (d'esprit); (*resourcefulness*) débrouillardise *f*; **(b)** (*elegance*) élégance *f*, chic *m*.

smarty-pants ['smɑːtɪpænts] *n F* petit malin.

smash[1] [smæʃ] **1** *n* **(a)** (*heavy blow*) coup violent; (*loud noise*) bruit *m* de fracas; *Tennis* smash *m*; **(b)** (*act of breaking into pieces*) mise *f* en morceaux *ou* en miettes; (*shattering*) fracassement *m*; **(c)** (*accident*) accident *m* (*de chemin de fer*); (*collision*) collision *f*, tamponnement *m* (*de trains, de voitures*); **(d)** (*failure*) débâcle *f*, faillite *f* (*commerciale*); (*total defeat*) débâcle complète; **(e) s. (hit),** gros succès, succès fou; **(f)** *US* **(brandy) s.,** cognac *m* à la glace et à la menthe. **2** *adv* **(a) to go s.,** (*of firm, bank*) faire faillite, tomber en faillite; **(b) to run s. into sth,** rentrer en plein dans qch, heurter qch de front; (*of car*) rentrer en plein dans (*un mur etc*).

smash[2] **1** *vt* **(a) to s. sth on** *or* **against sth,** heurter *ou* choquer *ou* lancer qch contre qch avec violence; **she smashed him over the head with a chair,** elle lui a cassé une chaise sur la tête; **she smashed her fist into his face,** elle lui a fichu son poing dans la figure;

(b) to s. sth (to pieces), briser qch (en morceaux); (*shatter*) fracasser qch; **to s. the door open,** enfoncer la porte;

(c) (*destroy*) détruire (*qn, qch*); écraser (*une armée etc*); *Sp* pulvériser (*un record*); (*ruin*) ruiner (*qn*); (*bankrupt*) faire faire faillite à (*qn*); faire échouer (*un projet*); **to s. a drugs ring,** démanteler un réseau de trafiquants de drogue.

2 *vi* **(a)** (*strike*) se heurter violemment (**into sth,** contre qch); **the car smashed into the wall,** la voiture est allée s'écraser contre le mur;

(b) to s. (in pieces), éclater en morceaux *ou* en pièces; (*shatter*) se fracasser;

(c) (*of firm etc*) faire faillite.

►**smash down** *vtsep* défoncer (*une porte etc*).

►**smash in** *vtsep* **(a)** (*break open*) enfoncer, défoncer (*un coffre etc*); défoncer (*une porte*); **(b)** *F* **to s. s.o.'s face in,** casser la figure *ou F* la gueule à qn.

►**smash up** *vtsep* briser (*qch*) en morceaux; démolir (*une voiture etc*).

smash-and-grab [smæʃən'græb] *adj* **s.-and-g. raid,** rafle *f* (*de bijoux etc*) après bris de devanture.

smashed [smæʃt] *adj Sl* (*drunk*) bourré, rond; (*on drugs*) camé; **to get s.,** se soûler; (*on drugs*) se camer.

smasher ['smæʃər] *n* **what a s.!,** (*attractive person*) il *ou* elle est vachement bien!, il *ou* elle est super!; **that's a s.!,** (*excellent thing*) c'est génial!

smashing ['smæʃɪŋ] *adj* **(a)** (*coup*) violent; **(b)** *esp Br F* (*excellent*) super; (*impressive*) génial; **she's s.!,** elle est super!, elle est vachement bien!; **we had a s. time,** c'était vachement bien.

smash-up ['smæʃʌp] *n F* (*act of breaking*) destruction complète; *Aut Rail etc* (*collision*) télescopage *m*.

smattering ['smæt(ə)rɪŋ] *n* légère connaissance (*d'une langue etc*); **to have a s. of English,** savoir un peu *ou* quelques bribes d'anglais; **to have a s. of chemistry,** avoir des notions de chimie.

smear[1] [smɪər] *n* **(a)** (*stain*) tache *f*, souillure *f*; (*slander*) diffamation *f*, calomnie *f*; **s. campaign,** campagne *f* de calomnies; **(b)** (*for microscope*) frottis *m* (*vaginal etc*); *Med* **s. test,** frottis vaginal.

smear[2] *vt* **(a)** (*stain*) barbouiller, salir (**with,** de); salir (*la réputation de qn*); enduire (**with,** de); **to s. sth with grease, to s. grease on sth,** étaler de la graisse sur qch; **(b)** maculer, barbouiller (*une page écrite etc*); **to get smeared,** (*of outline*) s'estomper; **the rain has smeared the address,** la pluie a en partie effacé l'adresse; **(c)** (*slander*) calomnier (*qn*); **to smear s.o.'s reputation,** porter atteinte à la réputation de qn.

smeary ['smɪərɪ] *adj* (*stained*) taché, barbouillé; (*with blurred outlines*) aux contours estompés; (*greasy*) graisseux.

smell[1] [smel] *n* **(a) (sense of) s.,** odorat *m*; (*of animals*) flair *m*; **to have a keen sense of s.,** avoir l'odorat fin; (*of dog etc*) avoir beaucoup de flair; **(b)** (*odour*) odeur *f*, parfum *m*, senteur *f* (*des fleurs*); **(bad) s.,** mauvaise odeur; **there's a bad s.,** ça sent mauvais; **what's that s.?,** quelle est cette odeur?; **stale s.,** relent *m* (*de bière etc*); **it has no s.,** ça n'a pas d'odeur; **(pleasant) s. of cooking,** fumet *m* de cuisine; **the s. was unbearable,** l'odeur était intolérable; **to take a s. at,** sentir (*qch*); respirer (*un flacon de sels etc*).

smell[2] *v* (*pt & pp* **smelt,** *occ* **smelled**) **1** *vt* sentir (*qch*); respirer l'odeur (*d'un bouquet*); (*of dog*) flairer, renifler (*qch*); (*perceive smell of*) sentir l'odeur de (*qch*); sentir (*une odeur*); *Fig* sentir, flairer, pressentir (*le danger etc*); **I can s. something burning,** je sens quelque chose qui brûle. **2** *vi* **(a)** (*of flower etc*) sentir; **to s. good/bad/strong(ly),** sentir bon/mauvais/fort; **to s. of violets,** sentir la violette; **to s. of gas,** sentir le gaz; **these flowers don't s.,** ces fleurs n'ont pas d'odeur, ces fleurs ne sentent rien; **(b)** (*have bad smell*) sentir (mauvais); **it smells (awful)!,** ça pue!; **his breath smells,** il a une mauvaise haleine; **why won't you come? — do we s.?,** pourquoi est-ce que tu ne viens pas? – ça te gêne d'être avec nous?; **(c) he can't s.,** il n'a pas d'odorat.

►**smell out** *vtsep* **(a)** (*discover by smelling*) (*of dog*) flairer, dépister (*le gibier*); *Fig* (*of person*) flairer, découvrir (*un secret*); **(b) his cigarettes are smelling the office out,** ses cigarettes empestent *ou* empuantissent le bureau.

smelliness ['smelɪnɪs] *n* mauvaise odeur, puanteur *f*.

smelling ['smelɪŋ] **1** *adj* odorant, odoriférant; **sweet s.,** qui sent bon. **2** *n* **s. salts,** sels (volatils) anglais, sel de vinaigre.

smelly ['smelɪ] *adj* malodorant, puant; **it's s. in here,** ça sent mauvais ici; **he's got s. feet,** il pue des pieds; **am I still s.?,** est-ce que j'empeste encore?

smelt[1] [smelt] *n* (*fish*) éperlan *m*.

smelt[2] *vt* fondre (*le minerai*); extraire (*le métal*) par fusion.

smelting ['smeltɪŋ] *n* fonte *f*, fusion *f* (*d'un minerai, d'un métal*); extraction *f* (*du métal*) par fusion; **s. works,** fonderie *f*.

smidgen ['smɪdʒən] *n F* **a s. of sth,** un tout petit peu de qch.

smile[1] [smaɪl] *n* sourire *m*; **with a s.,** en souriant, avec un sourire; **with a s. on his lips,** le sourire aux lèvres; **to give s.o. a s.,** adresser un sourire à qn, sourire à qn; **she was all smiles,** elle était toute souriante *ou* tout sourire; (*pretence*) elle était tout sucre tout miel; **that'll take** *or* **wipe the s. off his face!,** cela va lui faire passer l'envie de sourire!

smile[2] **1** *vi* sourire; **to s. at s.o.,** sourire à qn, adresser un sourire à qn; **fortune smiles on him,** la fortune lui sourit; **to keep smiling,** *Lit* **to s. in the face of adversity,** garder le sourire; **he always comes up smiling,** il garde toujours le sourire; *Phot* **s.!,** souriez!; **she smiled back,** elle lui rendit son sourire. **2** *vt* **to s. a bitter smile,** sourire amèrement, avoir un sourire amer; **to s. a welcome to s.o.,** accueillir qn avec *ou* par un sourire; **to s. one's gratitude,** exprimer sa gratitude par un sourire.

smiling ['smaɪlɪŋ] *adj* souriant; **s. faces,** visages souriants.

smilingly ['smaɪlɪŋlɪ] *adv* en souriant, avec un sourire.

smirch[1] [smɜːtʃ] *n* tache *f*, salissure *f*, souillure *f*.

smirch[2] *vt* salir, souiller; **smirched reputation,** réputation ternie *ou* salie.

smirk[1] [smɜːk] *n* (*affected smile*) sourire affecté, minauderie *f*; (*mocking*) petit sourire supérieur.

smirk[2] *vi* (*smile affectedly*) sourire d'un air affecté, minauder, mignarder; (*smile mockingly*) sourire d'un air supérieur.

smite [smaɪt] *vt* (*pt* **smote** [sməʊt]; *pp* **smitten** ['smɪt(ə)n]) **(a)** *Arch & Lit* (*strike*) frapper, battre (*l'ennemi*); **my conscience smote me,** j'ai été frappé de remords; **(b) to be smitten with blindness,** être frappé de cécité; **to be smitten with remorse,** être pris *ou* frappé de remords; **to be smitten with a desire to do sth,** être pris d'un *ou* du désir de faire qch; *F* **to be smitten with a girl,** être épris *ou* amouraché d'une jeune fille; **he's totally smitten,** il est sous le charme.

►**smite down** *vtsep Arch & Lit* abattre (*qn*).

smith [smɪθ] *n* forgeron *m*; **shoeing s.,** maréchal ferrant.

smithereens [smɪðə'riːnz] *npl F* **the ship was blown to s.,** l'explosion a réduit le navire en miettes; **to smash sth to s.,** briser *ou* réduire qch en éclats *ou* en mille morceaux.

smithy ['smɪðɪ] *n* forge *f*; **shoeing s.,** (atelier *m* de) maréchalerie *f*.

smitten *see* **SMITE**.

smock[1] [smɒk] *n* (*garment*) blouse *f*, sarrau *m*.

smock[2] *vt Sewing* orner (*une robe etc*) de smocks.

smocking ['smɒkɪŋ] *n* smocks *mpl*.

smog [smɒg] *n* brouillard fumeux, smog *m*.

smoke[1] [sməʊk] *n* **(a)** (*substance*) fumée *f*; **tobacco s.,** fumée de tabac; **s. bomb,** bombe *f* fumigène; **s. detector,** détecteur *m* de fumée; *Mil Nau* **s. screen,** rideau *m ou* écran *m* de fumée; *Fig* (*comments, action etc*) tentative *f* de dissimulation; **s. signals,** signaux *mpl* de fumée; **s. brown/grey,** brun/gris fumée *inv*; *Fig F* **to go up in s.,** (*of building, papers etc*) partir en fumée; *F* **he just about had**

s. coming out of his ears, (*was angry*) il avait les yeux qui lançaient des éclairs; *Prov* **(there's) no s. without fire,** il n'y a pas de fumée sans feu;
(b) (*act of smoking*) **let's have a s.,** si on fumait (une cigarette *ou* une pipe *ou* un cigare)?; **s. room,** fumoir *m*;
(c) *Old-fashioned F* (*cigarette*) cigarette *f*; (*cigar*) cigare *f*; **I always have a s. at about 10,** je me fume toujours ma petite cigarette aux alentours de dix heures;
(d) (*marijuana*) joint *m*.

smoke² **1** *vi* **(a)** (*smoke tobacco*) fumer; **do you s.?,** (est-ce que) vous fumez?; **do you mind if I s.?,** est-ce que ça vous dérange si je fume?; **(b)** (*emit smoke, vapour*) fumer; (*of lamp*) fumer, filer; **the horses' flanks were smoking,** les flancs des chevaux fumaient, les chevaux étaient tout fumants. **2** *vt* **(a)** fumer (*du tabac*); **to s. a pipe/cigarettes,** fumer une pipe/des cigarettes; **to s. twenty a day,** fumer vingt cigarettes par jour; **(b)** *Culin* fumer (*le jambon, la viande, le poisson*); (*in horticulture*) enfumer (*une plante, les pucerons etc*).

►**smoke out** *vtsep* (*flush out with smoke*) enfumer (*des insectes*) pour les chasser; (*fill with smoke*) enfumer.

smoked [sməʊkt] *adj Culin* (*jambon etc*) fumé; **s. glass,** verre *m* de teinte fumée.

smokeless ['sməʊklɪs] *adj* (*houille*) sans fumée; **s. zone,** zone *f* où il est interdit de brûler du charbon afin de limiter la pollution atmosphérique.

smoker ['sməʊkər] *n* **(a)** (*of tobacco*) fumeur, -euse (*de tabac*); **cigarette/pipe s.,** fumeur de cigarette/pipe; **heavy s.,** gros fumeur; **(b)** *Ind* (*person*) fumeur, -euse (*de jambon etc*); **(c)** *Rail etc F* (*compartment*) compartiment *m* fumeurs.

smokestack ['sməʊkstæk] *n* cheminée *f* (*de locomotive, d'usine etc*).

smoking ['sməʊkɪŋ] **1** *adj* fumant, qui fume. **2** *n* **(a)** (*of tobacco*) (*habit*) tabagisme *m*; **the effects of s. on the foetus,** les effets du tabagisme sur le fœtus; **s. can damage your health,** fumer est nuisible à votre santé; **no s. (allowed),** défense de fumer; *Rail* **s. compartment,** compartiment *m* fumeurs; **s. jacket,** veste *f ou* veston *m* d'intérieur; **s. room,** fumoir *m*; **(b)** *Culin* fumage *m* (*de jambon etc*); **(c)** émission *f* de fumée.

smoky ['sməʊkɪ] *adj* **(a)** (*atmosphere, room, town*) enfumé; **(b)** (*ceiling etc*) noirci par la fumée; **s. grey,** gris fumée; **s. blue,** gris bleu *inv*; *Geol* **s. quartz,** quartz *m* fumée; **(c)** (*fire*) qui fume; **s. lamp,** lampe qui fume *ou* qui file; **(d)** (*taste*) de fumée.

smolder, smoldering *US* = **SMOULDER, SMOULDERING.**

smooch [smuːtʃ] *F* **1** *vi* **(a)** (*kiss*) se bécoter; (*cuddle*) se peloter; **(b)** (*dance*) danser un slow. **2** *n* **to have a s.,** (*kiss*) se bécoter; (*cuddle*) se peloter; (*dance*) danser un slow.

smoochy ['smuːtʃɪ] *adj F* (*music etc*) doux et romantique.

smooth¹ [smuːð] *adj* **(a)** (*surface, pâte, papier*) lisse; (*chemin etc*) uni, égal; (*front*) sans rides; (*sans barbe*) glabre; (*drap*) à poil ras; **to make s.,** lisser (*ses cheveux*); aplanir (*une route etc*); *Br F* **as smooth as a baby's bottom,** (*of skin, face etc*) doux comme la peau d'un bébé; **as s. as a millpond,** (*of sea*) d'un calme plat; **s. skin,** peau douce *ou* satinée; **(b)** (*gentle*) doux, *f* douce; (*voyage, vol etc*) (*comfortable*) confortable; (*without problems*) sans anicroches; (*vin*) moelleux; (*style*) uni, coulant; (*personne*) doucereux, mielleux; **s. running,** fonctionnement doux *ou* régulier (*d'une machine*); déroulement *m* (*d'un projet*) sans anicroches; **s. talker,** beau parleur; **s. temper,** humeur égale *ou* facile; **s. tongue,** langue doucereuse; *F* **s. type** *or* **character,** personne mielleuse.

smooth² *n* **(a) to give one's hair a s. (down),** lisser ses cheveux, se lisser les cheveux; **(b)** (*smooth part*) partie *f* lisse (*de qch*); (*land*) terrain uni; **you have to take the rough with the s.,** il faut prendre le bon avec le moins bon.

smooth³ *vt* lisser (*ses plumes, ses cheveux etc*); aplanir (*une planche*); égaliser (*le terrain*); défroisser (*un vêtement*); **to s. one's brow,** dérider son front; **to s. the way for s.o.,** aplanir la voie pour qn.

►**smooth away** *vtsep* (*problems, fears etc*) faire oublier.

►**smooth back** *vtsep* **to s. back one's hair,** se rabattre les cheveux en arrière.

►**smooth down** *vtsep* (*make smooth*) lisser (*ses plumes, ses cheveux etc*).

►**smooth off** *vtsep* (*make smooth*) adoucir (*un angle*).

►**smooth out** *vtsep* **(a)** (*remove by smoothing*) faire disparaître (*un faux pli*); **(b)** = **SMOOTH OVER.**

►**smooth over** *vtsep* (*make easier*) **to s. over difficulties,** aplanir des difficultés; **to s. things over,** arrondir les angles.

smoothbore ['smuːðbɔːr] *n* **s. firearm,** arme *f* à canon lisse.

smoothie ['smuːðɪ] *n F* personne mielleuse; **he's a real s.,** c'est un beau parleur; **you're a bit of a s., aren't you?,** tu n'es qu'un beau parleur, n'est-ce pas?

smoothing ['smuːðɪŋ] *n* lissage *m* (*d'une surface, d'une pâte, du papier*); aplanissement *m*, aplanissage *m* (*du bois*); égalisation *f* (*du terrain*); *Carp* **s. plane,** varlope *f*.

smoothly ['smuːðlɪ] *adv* **(a)** (*marcher, travailler*) doucement; **to work** *or* **go s.,** marcher sans à-coups; **everything's going s.,** tout va comme sur des roulettes; **the journey went s.,** le voyage s'est déroulé sans problème; **(b)** (*with a smooth surface*) sans inégalités, uniment; **the ground stretched away s. in front of us,** le sol se déroulait, uni, devant nous.

smoothness ['smuːðnɪs] *n* **(a)** égalité *f* (*d'une surface*); douceur *f*, satiné *m* (*de la peau*); calme *m* (*de la mer*); **(b)** douceur *f*, régularité *f* (*de la marche d'une machine*); bon fonctionnement (*d'une machine, d'une administration etc*); coulant *m* (*du style*); **(c)** (*of person*) air doucereux.

smooth-running [smuːð'rʌnɪŋ] *adj* (*machine etc*) qui fonctionne régulièrement; (*project*) qui se déroule sans anicroches.

smooth-spoken ['smuːð'spəʊk(ə)n] *adj* doucereux, mielleux.

smooth-talking ['smuːð'tɔːkɪŋ] *adj* doucereux, mielleux.

smooth-tongued ['smuːð'tʌŋd] *adj* doucereux, mielleux.

smoothy ['smuːðɪ] *n* = **SMOOTHIE.**

smote *see* **SMITE.**

smother ['smʌðər] **1** *vt* étouffer (*qn, le feu*); suffoquer (*qn*); éteindre, étouffer (*un son*); retenir (*un cri*); réprimer (*un juron*); faire taire (*son orgueil*); cacher (*ses sentiments*); *F* **to smother s.o. with kisses,** étouffer qn de baisers; **to s. a scandal,** cacher *ou* couvrir un scandale; **strawberries smothered in** *or* **with cream,** fraises recouvertes de crème; **to be smothered in furs,** être emmitouflé de fourrures. **2** *vi* suffoquer, étouffer.

smothered ['smʌðəd] *adj* (*cri*) sourd, étouffé; (*son*) étouffé.

smother-love ['smʌðə'lʌv] *n F* amour étouffant d'une mère.

smoulder, *US* **smolder** ['sməʊldər] *vi* (*of coal etc*) brûler lentement *ou* sans flamme; (*of fire, rebellion etc*) couver (sous la cendre); **to s. with anger/passion/*etc*,** se consumer de colère/passion/*etc*.

smouldering, *US* **smoldering** ['sməʊldərɪŋ] *adj* (*charbon etc*) qui brûle sans flamme; (*feu etc*) qui couve (sous la cendre). **2** *n* combustion lente.

smudge¹ [smʌdʒ] *n* tache *f*, salissure *f*; (*slip with pen*) bavure *f* de stylo; **you've got a s. on your nose,** vous avez une tache (*de suie, d'encre etc*) sur le nez.

smudge² **1** *vt* salir, souiller (*le visage etc*); barbouiller, maculer (*une page d'écriture, un texte*); *Typ* mâchurer (*une épreuve*). **2** *vi* (*of ink, writing*) s'étaler.

smudgy ['smʌdʒɪ] *adj* **(a)** sali, souillé; (*text*) barbouillé, maculé; **(b)** (*contour etc*) estompé.

smug [smʌg] *adj* (*ton, air*) suffisant, satisfait de soi-même; **he has a s. look,** il a l'air suffisant *ou* content de lui; **he was s. about his success,** sa réussite le rendait plein de suffisance.

smuggle ['smʌg(ə)l] **1** *vt* (faire) passer (*des marchandises etc*) en contrebande *ou* en fraude; **to s. sth into/out of a country,** (faire) entrer/sortir qch en contrebande; **to s. sth into a room,** apporter qch subrepticement dans une pièce; **to s. s.o. out of the country,** faire sortir clandestinement qn du pays. **2** *vi* faire de la contrebande.

►**smuggle in** *vtsep* (*introduce by smuggling*) (*into country*) introduire en contrebande; (*into prison, building etc*) introduire illégalement.

►**smuggle out** *vtsep* (*take out by smuggling*) (*from country*) faire sortir en contrebande; (*from building etc*) faire sortir illégalement.

smuggler ['smʌglər] *n* contrebandier, -ière; fraudeur, -euse (*à la douane*).

smuggling ['smʌglɪŋ] *n* contrebande *f*; fraude *f* (*aux droits de douane*); **drug s.,** trafic *m* de stupéfiants; **s. operation,** opération *f* de contrebande.

smugly ['smʌglɪ] *adv* (*to say, look at*) d'un air *ou* d'un ton suffisant.

smugness ['smʌgnɪs] *n* suffisance *f*.

smut [smʌt] *n* **(a)** (*soot*) parcelle *f* de suie; (*mark*) tache *f* de suie (**on the face,** au *ou* sur le visage); **(b)** (*obscenity*) cochonneries *fpl*, grivoiseries *fpl*; **to talk s.,** dire des cochonneries; **that book's/film's just s.,** il n'y a que des cochonneries dans ce livre/film; **(c)** *Agr* charbon *m* (*des céréales*).

smuttiness ['smʌtɪnɪs] *n* (*lewdness*) grivoiserie *f*, grossièreté *f* (*d'une remarque etc*).

smutty ['smʌtɪ] *adj* **(a)** (*of conversation etc*) grossier, grivois; **(b)** (*dirty*) noirci, noir, sali (*de suie*).

snack [snæk] *n* léger repas, casse-croûte *m inv*, collation *f*; **if you eat too many snacks between meals ...,** si vous grignotez (trop) entre les repas ...; **to have a s.,** casser la croûte, manger un morceau sur le pouce; **s. bar,** snack(-bar) *m*.

snaffle[1] ['snæf(ə)l] *n* **s. (bit),** mors brisé; **s. (bridle),** bridon *m*.

snaffle[2] *vt Br F* (*take, steal*) piquer.

►snaffle up *vt sep F* (*bargains, cakes etc*) rafler.

snafu [snæ'fuː] *adj Am Sl* en (grand) désordre, chaotique.

snag[1] [snæg] *n* **(a)** (*protrusion*) chicot *m* (*d'arbre, de dent*); (*in water*) chicot *ou* souche *f* au ras de l'eau *ou* formant écueil; (*hidden obstacle*) écueil *m*, obstacle caché; (*problem*) accroc *m*; **to strike** *or* **hit** *or* **come across a s.,** se heurter à un obstacle *ou* à une anicroche; **that's the s.!,** voilà le hic!; **the s. is that it's too expensive,** le hic c'est que c'est trop cher; **(b)** accroc *m* (*dans un vêtement*).

snag[2] *vt* **(-gg-)** *F* faire un accroc à (*sa robe etc*); accrocher (*un bas etc*).

snail [sneɪl] *n* escargot *m*; **edible s.,** escargot comestible; **at a s.'s pace,** à pas d'escargot.

snake[1] [sneɪk] *n* **(a)** (*reptile*) serpent *m*; **common s., grass s.,** couleuvre *f* à collier; *Lit Fig* **to nourish a s. in one's bosom,** réchauffer un serpent dans son sein; **a s. in the grass,** (*treacherous person*) un faux jeton, un individu louche; (*hidden danger*) un danger caché, une anguille sous roche; *US F* **snakes alive!,** grand Dieu!; **snakes and ladders,** (*game*) le jeu de l'oie; **s. charmer,** charmeur, -euse de serpents; **(b)** *Fin* serpent monétaire.

snake[2] *vi* (*of road etc*) serpenter.

snakebite ['sneɪkbaɪt] *n* morsure *f* de serpent.

snakeskin ['sneɪkskɪn] *n* peau *f* de serpent.

snaky ['sneɪkɪ] *adj* **(a)** (*apparence*) de serpent; (*langue etc*) de vipère; (*homme*) perfide; **(b)** (*of road etc*) serpentant, sinueux; **(c)** (*full of snakes*) infesté de serpents.

snap[1] [snæp] **1** *n* **(a)** (*of teeth*) coup *m* de dents; (*of scissors*) coup de ciseaux; (*sound*) coup sec, claquement *m* (*des dents, d'un fouet etc*); bruit *m* (*d'un bouton pression qui se ferme*); **to make a s. at sth,** essayer de happer qch; **with a s. of the fingers,** claquant ses doigts;

(b) (*sudden breaking*) cassure *f ou* rupture soudaine; **there was a s.,** quelque chose a cassé;

(c) (*cold weather*) **cold s.,** courte période de temps froid, coup *m* de froid;

(d) *F* (*energy*) punch *m*;

(e) *Culin* **ginger s.,** biscuit sec au gingembre;

(f) **s. fastener,** bouton-pression *m*; **s. lock,** serrure *f* à ressort;

(g) (*in metalwork*) **(rivet) s., s. tool,** bouterolle *f*, chasse-rivet(s) *m inv*;

(h) *Phot F* instantané *m*;

(i) *Cards* = (jeu *m* de) bataille *f*;

(j) *US F* **soft s.,** chose *f* facile.

2 *adj* instantané, imprévu; **s. decision,** décision immédiate; *Parl* **s. division,** vote *m* de surprise.

3 *adv* **to go s.,** (*make sound*) faire clac; (*break cleanly*) (se) casser net; **s. went my stick!,** et crac! voilà ma canne cassée!

4 *int Cards F* **s.!,** ≈ bataille!; **I'm going to Paris — s.!,** je vais à Paris — ça par exemple! moi aussi!; **do you like my new tie? — yes, but look, s.!,** tu aimes ma nouvelle cravate? oui, mais regarde, j'ai la même!

snap[2] *v* **(-pp-)** **1** *vi* **(a)** (*of dog etc*) mordre;

(b) (*of teeth, whip etc*) claquer, faire un bruit sec; **to s. (shut),** (*of fastener, door etc*) se fermer avec un bruit sec;

(c) (*of stick, rope etc*) **to s. (in two),** (*break cleanly*) (se) casser net; (*break with sound*) se rompre avec un bruit sec.

2 *vt* **(a)** (*of dog etc*) saisir (*qch*) d'un coup de dents, happer (*qch*);

(b) faire claquer (*un fouet etc*); *Phot F* (*take snapshot of*) prendre un instantané de; **to s. one's fingers,** (faire) claquer ses doigts; **to s. one's fingers at s.o.** *or* **in s.o.'s face,** narguer qn, faire la nique à qn; **she snapped him eating a cake,** elle l'a pris en photo en train de manger un gâteau;

(c) (*break*) casser, rompre (*une canne etc*); **to s. sth in two,** casser qch en deux;

(d) (*say sharply*) **to s. (out),** jeter (*des mots*) d'un ton cassant; donner (*un ordre*) d'un ton sec; **'mind your own business!', he snapped (at me),** 'occupe-toi de ce qui te regarde' m'a-t-il jeté d'un ton cassant.

►snap at *vipo* **(a)** (*try to bite*) (*of dog etc*) chercher à mordre *ou* à happer (*qn, qch*); **(b)** *F* (*speak sharply to*) s'adresser à (*qn*) d'un ton sec *ou* cassant.

►snap back *vi* (*of trigger etc*) revenir brusquement.

►snap off **1** *vtsep* (*break off*) (*with teeth*) enlever (*qch*) d'un coup de dents; (*with hands etc*) arracher; (*accidentally*) casser (*le bout d'une canne etc*); *Fig F* **to s. s.o.'s head off,** rembarrer vivement qn. **2** *vi* (*break off*) se casser.

►snap out **1** *vtsep* (*say sharply*) donner (*un ordre*) d'un ton sec. **2** *vi F* **to s. out of it,** (*return to normal mood*) se ressaisir.

►snap to **1** *vi* (*close with snap*) (*of lid, door etc*) se (re)fermer avec un bruit sec. **2** *vtas* (re)fermer (avec un bruit sec).

►snap up *vtsep* **(a)** (*seize in jaws*) saisir, happer (*qch*); **(b)** (*buy, take quickly etc*) rafler; **to s. up a bargain,** sauter sur *ou* saisir une occasion; **the tickets are being snapped up like hot cakes,** les billets s'enlèvent *ou* s'arrachent comme des petits pains.

snapdragon ['snæpdræg(ə)n] *n* (*flower*) muflier *m*, gueule-de-loup *f*, *pl* gueules-de-loup.

snappish ['snæpɪʃ] *adj* (*person, dog*) hargneux.

snappishness ['snæpɪʃnɪs] *n* humeur hargneuse, ton hargneux.

snappy ['snæpɪ] *adj* **(a)** (*person, tone, reply, dog*) hargneux; **(b)** (*style etc*) vif, plein d'allant; (*prose, translation*) alerte; (*organization*) dynamique; *F* **make it s.!** grouille-toi!, magne-toi!; **he's a s.dresser,** il s'habille chic.

snapshot ['snæpʃɒt] *n Phot F* instantané *m*.

snare[1] ['sneər] *n* **(a)** (*in hunting*) lacet *m*, lacs *m*, collet *m*; *Fig* piège *m*; **to lay** *or* **set a s.,** dresser *ou* tendre un piège *ou* un lacet; **to be caught in a s.,** (*of animal*) être pris au lacet; **to be caught in a** *or* **the s.,** (*of person*) être pris au piège; **(b)** *Mus* **s. drum,** caisse claire.

snare[2] *vt* prendre (*un oiseau*) au filet; prendre (*un lapin*) au collet *ou* au lacet; *Fig* prendre (*qn*) au piège.

snarl[1] [snɑːl] *n* (*of dog, person*) grondement *m*, grognement *m*; (*of tiger*) feulement *m*.

snarl[2] *vi* (*of animal*) (*show teeth*) montrer les dents; (*make sound*) grogner, gronder; (*of tiger*) feuler; **to s. at s.o.,** (*of person*) grogner *ou* gronder contre qn.

snarl[3] *n* (*entanglement*) enchevêtrement *m*, emmêlement *m*, entortillement *m*; **(traffic) s.(-up),** embouteillage *m*.

snarl[4] **1** *vi* (*become entangled*) s'emmêler, s'enchevêtrer. **2** *vt* (*entangle*) emmêler, enchevêtrer.

►snarl up **1** *vtsep* **to s. up the traffic,** provoquer des embouteillages. **2** *vi* (*of traffic*) bouchonner; **the traffic gets snarled up at the traffic lights,** la circulation bouchonne aux feux.

snarling ['snɑːlɪŋ] **1** *adj* grondant, grognant. **2** *n* grondement *m*, grognement *m*.

snarl-up ['snɑːlʌp] *n* (*of traffic*) embouteillage *m*, bouchon *m*; (*in system etc*) paralysie *f*; **there's a s.-up in the switchboard,** le standard est saturé.

snatch[1] [snætʃ] *n* **(a)** (*attempt to grab*) mouvement vif (*pour saisir qch*); *F* (*kidnapping*) kidnapping *m*, enlèvement *m* (*de qn*); (*robbery*) vol *m* à l'arraché (*de bijoux, d'argent etc*); *Sp* (*weight-lifting*) arraché *m*; **to make a s. at sth,** chercher à saisir qch; **s. squad,** = groupe de policiers ou de soldats formés pour arrêter les meneurs etc dans les manifestations; **(b)** (*short period*) courte période; (*small piece*) fragment *m*; **s. of sleep,** petit somme; **in** *or* **by snatches,** (*dormir*) par intervalles; (*travailler*) de façon intermittente, à bâtons rompus; **to overhear snatches of conversation,** surprendre des bouts *ou* des bribes de conversation; **to hear a s. of music,** entendre des bribes de musique; **(c)** *esp US Sl* (*female pubic area*) chatte *f*.

snatch[2] **1** *vt* saisir, empoigner, s'emparer de, se saisir brusquement de (*qch*); kidnapper (*un bébé*); *F* (*steal*) voler (*de l'argent, un sac à main*); *Sp* (*weight-lifting*) arracher (*un poids*); **to s. sth from s.o.,** arracher qch à qn; **to s. sth out of s.o.'s hands,** arracher qch des mains de qn; **to s. an opportunity,** saisir une occasion; **to s. a meal,** manger un morceau sur le pouce *ou* au lance-pierres; **to s. a bit of sleep,** faire un petit somme; **to s. the end of the news,** se débrouiller pour voir les informations de justesse. **2** *vi* saisir brusquement *ou* arracher les objets; **don't s.!,** n'arrache pas les choses (*des mains etc*).

►snatch at *vipo* (*try to grab*) tâcher de saisir (*qch*); **to s. at an opportunity,** saisir une occasion (au vol).

►snatch away *vtsep* (*grab*) arracher, enlever (*qch*); **he**

snatched away the book I was reading, il m'a arraché des mains le livre que je lisais; **he snatched it away from me/George,** il me l'a arraché des mains/il l'a arraché des mains de George.

►**snatch up** *vtsep* (*pick up quickly*) ramasser vivement (*qch*); **she snatched up the baby,** elle s'est emparée vivement du bébé.

snazzy ['snæzɪ] *adj F* chouette, super; **he's a s. dresser,** il s'habille chic; *Pej* il s'habille d'une manière un peu voyante.

sneak¹ [sniːk] *n* **(a)** (*person*) pleutre *m*; **(b)** *Sch F* cafard, -arde, mouchard *m*; **s. thief,** chipeur, -euse, chapardeur, -euse; **(c)** *F* **to have a s. preview of,** voir (*un film, une pièce etc*) en avant-première; avoir la primeur de (*un roman, un produit etc*).

sneak² 1 *vi* (*move furtively*) se déplacer furtivement. **2** *vt* (*steal*) voler, chiper (*qch*); **to s. a glance at s.o.,** glisser un œil vers qn.

►**sneak about, sneak around** *vi* (*move about furtively*) se déplacer furtivement; **I caught him sneaking about in the garden,** je l'ai surpris alors qu'il rôdait dans le jardin.

►**sneak away** *vi* = **SNEAK OFF.**

►**sneak in 1** *vi* (*enter furtively*) se glisser furtivement *ou* se faufiler dans un endroit. **2** *vtsep* (*bring in furtively*) introduire (*qch*) furtivement *ou* subrepticement; **someone must have sneaked it into my suitcase,** quelqu'un a dû le glisser dans ma valise.

►**sneak off** *vi* (*leave, go away furtively*) partir furtivement; **he sneaked off and joined another team,** il a filé en douce et a rejoint une autre équipe.

►**sneak on** *vipo esp Br Sch F* (*tell tales on*) moucharder, cafarder (*qn*).

►**sneak out 1** *vi* (*leave, go out furtively*) se glisser furtivement *ou* se faufiler hors d'un endroit. **2** *vtsep* (*take out furtively*) sortir (*qch*) furtivement.

►**sneak out of** *vipo* (*leave furtively*) se glisser furtivement *ou* se faufiler hors de (*un endroit*).

sneakers ['sniːkəz] *npl Am* tennis *mpl*.

sneaking ['sniːkɪŋ] *adj* furtif; (*underhand*) sournois, dissimulé; **to have a s. liking for sth,** avoir un penchant caché *ou* inavoué pour qch; **to have a s. feeling** *or* **suspicion that ...,** avoir comme une vague impression que ... .

sneaky ['sniːkɪ] *adj* sournois.

sneer¹ ['snɪər] *n* **(a)** (*expression*) sourire *m* de mépris; (*laugh*) ricanement *m*; **(b)** (*remark*) sarcasme *m*.

sneer² 1 *vi* (*smile, laugh*) sourire *ou* rire d'un air moqueur; (*laugh*) ricaner; **to s. at s.o.,** se moquer de qn; (*address scornful remarks to*) lancer des sarcasmes à qn. **2** *vt* **'you couldn't do that', he sneered,** 'tu n'en serais pas capable', a-t-il lancé en ricanant.

sneerer ['snɪərər] *n* moqueur, -euse, ricaneur, -euse.

sneering ['snɪərɪŋ] **1** *adj* (*face, look*) ricaneur, -euse; (*remark, laughter*) sarcastique. **2** *n* (*expression*) ricanement *m*; (*remarks*) sarcasmes *mpl*.

sneeringly ['snɪərɪŋlɪ] *adv* (*contemptuously*) d'un air de mépris; (*sarcastically*) d'un air sarcastique; (*laughing scornfully*) en ricanant.

sneeze¹ [sniːz] *n* éternuement *m*.

sneeze² *vi* éternuer; **she sneezed all over the food,** elle a éternué au-dessus de la nourriture.

►**sneeze at** *vipo F* **that's not to be sneezed at,** cela n'est pas à dédaigner, il ne faut pas cracher dessus.

sneezing ['sniːzɪŋ] *n* éternuement *m*; *Med* sternutation *f*; **s. powder,** poudre *f* à éternuer.

snick¹ [snɪk] *n* **(a)** (*notch*) entaille *f*, encoche *f*; **(b)** (*action*) coup *m* de ciseaux, entaille *f* (*dans l'étoffe, le papier etc*).

snick² *vt* **(a)** entailler, encocher (*le bois etc*); faire une entaille dans (*le drap*); **(b)** *Cr* couper légèrement (*la balle*).

snicker¹ ['snɪkər] *n* **(a)** = **SNIGGER¹**; **(b)** (*of horse*) hennissement *m*.

snicker² *vi* **(a)** = **SNIGGER²**; **(b)** (*of horse*) hennir.

snide [snaɪd] *adj F* (*scornful*) méprisant; (*sarcastic*) sarcastique; **she was very s. about it,** elle s'est montrée très méprisante *ou* très sarcastique à ce sujet.

sniff¹ [snɪf] *n* reniflement *m*; **to take a s. at sth,** renifler qch; **with a s. of disgust,** (*in disgust*) en reniflant d'un air dégoûté; (*to express disgust*) avec un reniflement de dégoût; **I caught a s. of his aftershave,** j'ai senti son after-shave; **there's still a s. of gas,** ça sent toujours le gaz; *F* **to have a little s.,** (*smell*) renifler un petit coup; (*have a slight cold*) avoir un léger rhume.

sniff² 1 *vi* renifler; **he sniffed with disdain,** il a reniflé avec dédain. **2** *vt* **(a)** (*investigate by smelling*) flairer, renifler (*qch*); (*detect*) flairer (*un bon dîner, un danger etc*); **the dog sniffed my hand,** le chien m'a flairé la main; **(b)** humer, renifler (*une prise de tabac etc*); aspirer (*la cocaïne*); sniffer (*de la colle*); *Med* **to be sniffed up the nostrils,** à aspirer par les narines.

►**sniff at** *vipo F* **(a)** (*disdain*) **the offer is not to be sniffed at,** ce n'est pas une proposition à dédaigner; **(b)** (*smell*) flairer, renifler (*qch*); **the dog sniffed at my hand,** le chien m'a flairé la main.

►**sniff out** *vtsep* (*discover by smelling*) (*of dog*) détecter, flairer (*qch, qn*); *Fig* déterrer (*un scandale etc*).

sniffer ['snɪfər] *n* **s. dog,** chien renifleur.

sniffle¹ ['snɪf(ə)l] *n* (*slight cold*) petit rhume (de cerveau).

sniffle² *vi F* **(a)** renifler; **(b)** (*cry*) pleurnicher.

sniffling ['snɪflɪŋ] *adj F* **(a)** (*with cold*) enrhumé; **(b)** (*crying*) pleurnicheur, -euse.

sniffy ['snɪfɪ] *adj F* **(a)** (*disdainful*) dédaigneux; **to be s. about sth,** (*take exception to sth*) voir qch d'un mauvais œil; (*regard with contempt*) regarder qch avec mépris; **(b)** (*bad-smelling*) malodorant; **it's a bit s. in here,** ça pue un peu ici.

snifter ['snɪftər] *n Old-fashioned F* goutte *f*, petit verre (*d'alcool*).

snigger¹ ['snɪgər] *n* (*stifled laughter*) rire *m* en dessous; petit rire contenu; (*wicked laugh*) petit rire méchant; (*at dirty story etc*) petit rire grivois.

snigger² *vi* (*stifle laughter*) rire sous cape, ricaner tout bas; (*laugh wickedly*) lancer un rire méchant; (*at a dirty story etc*) lancer un rire grivois.

sniggering ['snɪgərɪŋ] *n* (*stifled laughter*) rires *mpl* en dessous; (*wicked laughter*) rires méchants; (*at a dirty story etc*) rires grivois.

snip¹ [snɪp] *n* **(a)** (*piece cut off*) morceau coupé, bout *m*, petit morceau (*de papier, de toile*); **(b)** (*cut*) petite entaille; (*act of cutting*) coup *m* de ciseaux; **(c)** *F* (*something certain*) affaire certaine; *Br* (*bargain*) affaire (avantageuse), occasion *f*; **at £25 it's a s.,** à 25 livres c'est une affaire; **(d)** (*in metalworking*) **(tin) snips,** petits morceaux d'étain.

snip² *vt* (**-pp-**) couper (*du papier, du tissu etc*) avec des ciseaux.

►**snip off** *vtsep* (*cut off*) enlever *ou* détacher (*qch*) d'un coup de ciseaux.

snipe¹ [snaɪp] *n inv* (*bird*) bécassine *f*.

snipe² 1 *vi Mil* **to s. at the enemy,** canarder l'ennemi; (*from hiding*) tirer à l'affût *ou* en embuscade sur l'ennemi; **to be sniped at,** se faire canarder; *Fig* **to s. at s.o.,** critiquer qn sournoisement. **2** *vt* canarder (*l'ennemi*).

sniper ['snaɪpər] *n Mil* tireur embusqué; **s. fire,** tir *m* d'embuscade.

sniping ['snaɪpɪŋ] *n Mil* tir *m* d'embuscade; *Fig* critique sournoise (**at s.o.,** de qn).

snippet ['snɪpɪt] *n* (*small piece*) bout *m*, morceau *m* (coupé); court extrait (*d'un livre etc*); bribes *fpl* (de conversation).

snipping ['snɪpɪŋ] *n* morceau coupé; petit coupon (*de tissu*).

snitch¹ [snɪtʃ] *n Sl* (*nose*) pif *m*.

snitch² *Sl* **1** *vi* (*inform*) vendre la mèche; **to s. on s.o.,** dénoncer qn, moucharder qn. **2** *vt* (*steal*) chaparder (*qch*).

snivel¹ ['snɪv(ə)l] *n* (*sniffle*) reniflement larmoyant; (*whine*) pleurnicherie *f*.

snivel² *vi* (**-ll-**, *US* **-l-**) (*sniff*) renifler; (*whine*) pleurnicher, larmoyer.

sniveller, *US* **sniveler** ['snɪv(ə)lər] *n* pleurnicheur, -euse.

snivelling, *US* **sniveling** ['snɪv(ə)lɪŋ] **1** *adj* (*person*) (*whining*) pleurnicheur, -euse. **2** *n* (*sniffling*) reniflement *m*; (*whining*) pleurnicherie *f*.

snob [snɒb] *n* snob *mf*; **she's a bit of a s.,** c'est une snobinarde; **a music s.,** un snob en matière de musique.

snobbery ['snɒbərɪ] *n* snobisme *m*; **inverted s.,** snobisme à rebours; **intellectual s.,** snobisme intellectuel.

snobbish ['snɒbɪʃ] *adj* snob; **he is a bit s.,** il est un peu snob.

snobbishness ['snɒbɪʃnɪs] *n* snobisme *m*.

snog¹ [snɒg] *n Br F* **to have a s.,** se peloter.

snog² *vi Br F* (*of couple*) se peloter.

snogging ['snɒgɪŋ] *n Br F* pelotage *m*.

snood [snuːd] *n* (*hairnet*) résille *f* pour cheveux.

snook [snuːk] *n F* **to cock a s. at s.o.,** (*make gesture at*) faire un pied de nez à qn; *Fig* (*defy*) faire la nique à qn.

snooker¹ ['snuːkər] *n Billiards* (sorte *f* de) jeu *m* de billard.

snooker² *vt Billiards* empêcher (*qn*) de frapper directement la bille; *Fig F* mettre qn dans une impasse; *Fig F* **now I've snookered myself,** maintenant je me suis fourré dans une impasse, maintenant me voilà coincé; **to be snookered,** *Billiards* se trouver dans l'impossibilité de frapper directement la bille; *Fig* être coincé, être dans une impasse.

snoop[1] [snu:p] *n* **(a)** = **SNOOPER; (b) I'll have a s. around,** je vais jeter un petit coup d'œil.

snoop[2] *vi F* fourrer le nez partout, fureter, fouiner; **to s. in s.o.'s papers/desk/***etc*, fouiller dans les papiers/le bureau/*etc* de qn.

▸snoop around = **SNOOP[2]**.

▸snoop on *vipo* (*spy on*) espionner (*qn*).

snooper ['snu:pər] *n F* (*person who asks questions*) inquisiteur *m*; (*person who rummages*) fouine *f*.

snooty ['snu:tɪ] *adj F* arrogant, hautain.

snooze[1] [snu:z] *n F* (*short sleep*) petit somme; **to have a s.,** faire un petit somme, **s. button,** (*on alarm*) bouton *m* de rappel.

snooze[2] *vi F* sommeiller, faire un petit somme.

snore[1] [snɔ:r] *n* ronflement *m* (*d'un dormeur*).

snore[2] *vi* ronfler; **to s. gently,** ronflot(t)er.

snorer ['snɔ:rər] *n* ronfleur, -euse.

snoring ['snɔ:rɪŋ] **1** *adj* ronflant. **2** *n* ronflement *m*.

snorkel[1] ['snɔ:k(ə)l] *n Swimming* tuba *m*; schnorchel *m*, schnorkel *m* (*de sous-marin*).

snorkel[2] *vi* **to go snorkelling,** faire de la plongée avec un tuba.

snort[1] [snɔ:t] *n* **(a)** reniflement *m*; ébrouement *m* (*d'un cheval etc*); **(b)** (*expressing disdain, anger, impatience, disgust*) fort reniflement de dédain *ou* de colère *ou* d'impatience *ou* de dégoût; **s. of laughter,** court éclat de rire; **(c)** *F* (*of drink*) petit coup; (*of cocaine*) prise *f*.

snort[2] **1** *vi* renifler fortement; (*of horse*) s'ébrouer; **to s. with laughter,** rire par courts éclats: *F* **to s. at sth,** dédaigner qch. **2** *vt* grogner (*une réponse*); **'that's preposterous!', she snorted,** 'c'est absurde!', a-t-elle jeté.

snorter ['snɔ:tər] *n Sl* **(a)** (*impressive thing*) chose épatante; **he wrote me back a s.,** il m'a (r)envoyé une lettre carabinée; **that's a real s.,** (*of problem*) ça va nous donner du fil à retordre; **(b)** (*short drink*) goutte *f*, petit verre (*d'alcool*).

snorting ['snɔ:tɪŋ] *n* reniflement *m*; ébrouement *m* (*d'un cheval*).

snot [snɒt] *n Sl* morve *f*; **a bit of s.,** de la morve; **s. rag,** tire-jus *m*.

snotty ['snɒtɪ] *adj Sl* (*handkerchief*) sale, dégoûtant; (*nose*) couvert de morve; (*kid*) morveux; **s. (nosed),** morveux; (*arrogant*) arrogant.

snout [snaʊt] *n* **(a)** museau *m*; groin *m* (*de porc, de hérisson*); boutoir *m* (*de sanglier*); *F* (*nose*) naze *m*, tarin *m*, pif *m*; **(b)** *Sl* (*tobacco*) tabac *m*.

snow[1] [snəʊ] *n* **(a)** neige *f*; **eternal s.,** neiges éternelles; **the s. line,** la limite des neiges (éternelles); **s. fence,** (*on road*) paraneige *m*; **s. tyres** *ou Am* **tires,** pneus *mpl* neige; **s. goggles,** lunettes *fpl* d'alpiniste; **s. blindness,** cécité *f* des neiges; **s. goose,** oie *f* des neiges; **s. leopard,** léopard *m* des neiges, once *f*; **(b)** *TV Rad* neige *f*; *Ind* **carbonic acid s.,** neige carbonique; *Culin* **apple s.,** pommes meringuées; **(c)** *Sl* (*cocaine*) neige *f*.

snow[2] *v impers* neiger; **it's snowing,** il neige, il tombe de la neige.

▸snow in *vtsep* (*usu passive*) (*block with snow*) **to be snowed in,** être bloqué par la neige.

▸snow off *vtsep* (*usu passive*) **the match was snowed off,** le match a été annulé à cause de la neige.

▸snow under *vtsep* **snowed under with work,** débordé de travail.

▸snow up *vtsep* (*usu passive*) **to be snowed up,** être bloqué par la neige.

snowball[1] ['snəʊbɔ:l] *n* **(a)** boule *f* de neige; *Sl* **he hasn't a s.'s chance in hell,** il n'a pas l'ombre d'une chance; **s. fight,** bataille *f* de boules de neige; **(b) s. (tree, bush),** boule-de-neige *f*, *pl* boules-de-neige, obier *m*.

snowball[2] **1** *vi* **(a)** (*of story, debts etc*) faire boule de neige; **(b)** (*fight with snowballs*) se battre à coups de boules de neige. **2** *vt* (*throw snowballs etc*) lancer des boules de neige à (*qn*).

snowboot ['snəʊbu:t] *n* après-ski *m inv*.

snowbound ['snəʊbaʊnd] *adj* retenu *ou* pris *ou* bloqué par la neige.

snowcapped ['snəʊkæpt] *adj* couronné de neige.

snowdrift ['snəʊdrɪft] *n* congère *f*.

snowdrop ['snəʊdrɒp] *n* (*flower*) perce-neige *m inv*.

snowfall ['snəʊfɔ:l] *n* chute *f* de neige.

snowfield ['snəʊfi:ld] *n* champ *m* de neige.

snowflake ['snəʊfleɪk] *n* flocon *m* de neige.

snowman, *pl* **-men** ['snəʊmæn, -men] *n* bonhomme *m* de neige; **the abominable s.,** l'abominable homme des neiges.

snowmobile ['snəʊməʊbi:l] *n Am* (*open*) motoneige *m*; (*enclosed*) autoneige *f*.

snowplough, *US* **-plow** ['snəʊplaʊ] *n Rail Ski etc* chasse-neige *m inv*.

snowshoe ['snəʊʃu:] *n* raquette *f*.

snowstorm ['snəʊstɔ:m] *n* tempête *f* de neige.

snowsuit ['snəʊsu:t] *n* tenue *f* de ski.

snow(-)white ['snəʊwaɪt] **1** *adj* blanc comme la neige; *Old-fashioned Lit* (*pure*) pur, innocent. **2** *n* **S. W.,** Blanche-Neige.

snowy ['snəʊɪ] *adj* neigeux; de neige; (*field etc*) enneigé; (*la saison*) des neiges; **s. (white) hair,** cheveux blancs (comme la neige).

SNP [esen'pi:] *n Pol* (*abbr* **Scottish National Party**) parti nationaliste écossais.

snub[1] [snʌb] *n* rebuffade *f*, affront *m*.

snub[2] *vt* (**-bb-**) faire un affront à (*qn*), rebuffer (*qn*); **I said hello but he just snubbed me,** je lui ai dit bonjour mais il m'a ignoré *ou* m'a snobé.

snub[3] *adj* (*nez*) camard, camus, retroussé.

snub-nosed ['snʌbnəʊzd] *adj* au nez retroussé *ou* camus.

snuff[1] [snʌf] *n* tabac *m* à priser; **to take s.,** priser; **a pinch of s.,** une prise; **s. (coloured),** (couleur) tabac *inv*; **s. taker,** priseur, -euse.

snuff[2] *vi* priser (*du tabac*).

snuff[3] *vt* **(a)** (*extinguish*) moucher (*une chandelle*); éteindre (*un espoir etc*); **(b)** *Sl* **to s. it,** (*die*) clamecer, clamser, passer l'arme à gauche.

▸snuff out *vtsep* = **SNUFF[3](a)**.

snuffbox ['snʌfbɒks] *n* tabatière *f*.

snuffer ['snʌfər] *n* **snuffers,** mouchettes *fpl*.

snuffle[1] ['snʌf(ə)l] *n* **(a)** reniflement *m*; **snuffles,** rhume *m*; **(b)** (*nasal tone*) ton nasillard.

snuffle[2] *vi* **(a)** (*have a cold*) renifler, avoir un rhume; **(b)** (*speak in nasal tone*) nasiller.

snug [snʌg] **1** *adj* (*house etc*) confortable, où l'on est bien; (*person*) (*sheltered*) bien abrité; (*warm*) bien au chaud; (*bed*) douillet; (*jacket*) bien chaud; **to make oneself s.,** se mettre à son aise; **to lie s. in bed,** être bien au chaud dans son lit; *F* **as s. as a bug in a rug,** tranquille comme Baptiste; **to lie s.,** (*to stay hidden*) se tenir caché; être tapi (*dans un trou*); *F* **a s. little job,** un emploi pépère, **s. little fortune,** fortune rondelette; **it's a s. fit,** (*of machine part etc*) ça s'emboîte parfaitement; (*of clothing*) c'est bien ajusté; (*too tight*) c'est un peu trop serré. **2** *n Br* petite arrière-salle (*dans un pub*).

snuggery ['snʌgərɪ] *n* **(a)** petite pièce intime (et confortable); **(b)** petite arrière-salle (*dans un café*).

snuggle ['snʌg(ə)l] **1** *vi* **village snuggling in the valley,** village niché dans la vallée. **2** *vt* **to s. a child close to one,** serrer un enfant dans ses bras.

▸snuggle down *vi* (*make oneself comfortable*) **to s. down in bed,** se blottir (bien au chaud) dans son lit.

▸snuggle up *vi* (*come close*) se pelotonner, se blottir (**to s.o.,** contre qn); **to s. up with a good book,** s'installer bien confortablement avec un bon livre.

snugly ['snʌglɪ] *adv* confortablement; (*warmly*) bien au chaud; **s. wrapped,** douillettement enveloppé (*dans une couverture etc*); **garment that fits s.,** vêtement bien ajusté; **this piece should fit s. into ...,** cette pièce devrait s'emboîter parfaitement *ou* exactement dans ...

so [səʊ] **1** *adv* **(a)** (*to such an extent*) si, tellement; **it's so easy,** c'est si *ou* tellement facile; **I was so disappointed,** j'étais tellement déçu; **we're so pleased you could come,** nous sommes tellement *ou* si contents que vous ayez pu venir; **she isn't so very old,** elle n'est pas tellement *ou* si vieille; **the young and the not so young,** les jeunes et les moins jeunes; **I'm not so sure of that,** je n'en suis pas si sûr; **so serious a wound,** une blessure aussi grave; **what's so important about this case?,** qu'est-ce que cette affaire a de si important?; **he's not so clever as she is,** il n'est pas aussi intelligent qu'elle; **she wouldn't be so stupid as to do that,** elle ne serait pas bête au point de faire cela, elle ne serait pas assez bête pour faire cela; **would you be so kind as to ...?,** voudriez-vous avoir la gentillesse de ...?; **I was so hungry I could have eaten it all,** j'avais si faim que j'aurais pu tout manger; **he's so rich that he doesn't know what he's worth,** il est riche au point d'ignorer sa fortune; **I loved her so (much),** je l'aimais tant; **we enjoyed ourselves so much,** nous nous sommes tellement amusés; **it's not so much that I dislike them, more that I don't LIKE them,** ce n'est pas tant qu'ils me déplaisent, ça serait plutôt qu'ils ne me plaisent pas;

you do exaggerate so!, tu exagères tellement!;

(b) (*in this way*) ainsi, de cette façon, de cette manière; **stand just so,** tenez-vous ainsi *ou* comme ça; **while he was so occupied,** pendant qu'il était ainsi occupé; **as X is to Y, so Y is to Z,** X est à Y ce que Y est à Z; **she so arranged things that ...,** elle a fait en sorte que ... + *sub*; **I have been so informed,** c'est ce que l'on m'a dit; **it so happened that I was there,** le hasard a voulu que je fusse là, il s'est trouvé que j'étais là; **and so on, and so forth,** et ainsi de suite; **so to speak** *or* **say,** pour ainsi dire; **has the train gone? — I think so,** est-ce que le train est parti? — je crois *ou* je pense que oui; **he's clever — do you think so?,** il est intelligent — vous trouvez?; **I suppose so, I expect so,** je le suppose; **I hope so,** je l'espère bien; **I'm afraid so,** j'en ai bien peur, je le crains; **I didn't say so,** moi, je n'ai pas dit cela; **is she really ill? — so it seems,** elle est donc vraiment malade? — à ce qu'il paraît; **so I told him,** c'est ce que je lui ai dit; **there is a train at six, or so I was told,** il y a un train à six heures, ou du moins c'est ce qu'on m'a dit; **I'm not very organised — so I see!,** je ne suis pas très organisé — c'est ce que je vois!; **I told you so!,** je vous l'avais bien dit!; **so much so that...,** à tel point que..., tellement que...; **much more so,** bien plus encore; **that's so,** c'est bien vrai; **is that so?,** vraiment?; **that being so,** (*as this is the case*) puisqu'il en est ainsi; (*should this prove the case*) dans ces conditions; **so be it!,** soit!, qu'il en soit ainsi!; **if so,** s'il en est ainsi; **why so?,** pourquoi cela?; **how so?,** comment cela?; **perhaps so,** cela se peut; **quite so,** parfaitement, absolument; **a hundred pounds or so,** une centaine de livres; **a week or so,** une huitaine de jours; **a little girl so high,** une petite fille grande comme ça; **she's right and so are you,** elle a raison et vous aussi; **and so am I/are we,** et moi/et nous aussi; **he thinks he can do it — so he can,** il pense qu'il peut le faire en effet — il le peut; **you're late! — so I am!,** vous êtes en retard! — c'est vrai!; **it was Mr Smith — so it was!,** c'était Monsieur Smith — en effet!; *Dial* **they aren't French — they are so!,** ils ne sont pas français — si!;

(c) (*purpose*) **so that, so as to,** afin que + *sub*, pour que + *sub*, afin de + *inf*, pour + *inf*; **she stood up so as to** *or* **so that she could see better,** elle s'est levée afin de *ou* pour mieux voir; **she sat down so that I could see better,** elle s'est assise afin que *ou* pour que je puisse mieux voir; **we hurried so as not to be late, we hurried so that we shouldn't be late,** nous nous sommes dépêchés pour ne pas être *ou* afin de ne pas être en retard;

(d) (*consequence*) **so that,** de sorte que; **the flight was cancelled so that we had to stay at home,** le vol a été annulé de sorte que *ou* si bien que nous avons dû rester à la maison; **the crates had fallen over so that we couldn't get past,** comme les caisses étaient tombées nous n'avons pas pu passer.

(e) so so, (*in mediocre fashion*) médiocre(ment), passable(ment); (*not too bad*) comme ci comme ça; **how are you? — so, so,** comment vas-tu?— comme ci comme ça; **the cooking is only so so,** la cuisine est médiocre *ou* quelconque.

2 *conj* **(a)** (*therefore*) donc, c'est pourquoi; **she has a bad temper, so be careful,** elle a mauvais caractère, donc faites attention; **he wasn't there, so I came back again,** il n'était pas là, donc je suis revenu; **so what?,** et alors?; **it's very expensive — so? what am I supposed to do about it?,** c'est très cher — et alors? que voulez-vous que j'y fasse?;

(b) so there you are!, vous voilà donc!; **so, we're a bit late, what difference does that make?,** et alors, nous sommes un peu en retard, quelle différence cela fait-il?; **so that's what it is!,** ah! c'est comme ça!; **so you're not coming?,** vous ne venez donc pas?; **so, what do we do?,** eh bien, qu'est-ce qu'on fait?

So (a) (*abbr* **South**) S.; **(b)** (*abbr* **Southern**) S..

soak[1] [səʊk] *n* **(a) give them a good s.,** mets-les bien à tremper; **to put dirty washing in s.,** (mettre à) tremper le linge sale; **I intend to have a good s. (in the bath),** je vais prendre un bon bain; **(b)** *F* (*drunkard*) ivrogne *m*, soûlard *m*.

soak[2] 1 *vt* **(a)** (*of liquid*) tremper, détremper; (*of person*) tremper qch (**in sth,** dans qch); **the rain soaked me to the skin,** la pluie m'a trempé jusqu'aux os; **(b)** *F* écorcher (*un client*); *F* **to s. the rich,** faire payer les riches. **2** *vi* **(a)** baigner, tremper (**in sth,** dans qch); (*of liquid*) s'infiltrer, s'imbiber (**into sth,** dans qch); **to leave a saucepan to s.,** laisser une casserole tremper; **(b)** *Sl* (*drink heavily*) boire comme un trou.

▶soak in 1 *vi* (*of liquid*) pénétrer; *Fig* **has it soaked in yet?,** est-ce qu'il a *ou* que tu as *etc* pigé? **2** *vtsep* (*be absorbed*) **to s. in water,** s'imprégner d'eau, absorber l'eau; **she went to Europe to s. in the atmosphere,** elle est allée en Europe pour s'imprégner de son atmosphère.

▶soak through *vi* **(a)** (*seep through to other side*) s'infiltrer à travers (*qch*); **(b)** (*be absorbed*) pénétrer, s'infiltrer.

▶soak up *vtsep* absorber, boire, imbiber (*un liquide*); **to s. up water,** s'imprégner d'eau, absorber de l'eau; *Fig* **to s. up the sun,** se rôtir au soleil; **to s. up the local culture,** s'imprégner de la culture locale.

soaked [səʊkt] *adj* trempé; (*ground*) détrempé; **s. to the skin, s. through,** trempé jusqu'aux os.

soaking ['səʊkɪŋ] **1** *n* trempage *m*; **to get a s.,** se faire tremper. **2** *adj* trempé; **you're absolutely s.!,** vous êtes tout trempé! **3** *adv* **s. wet,** trempé.

so-and-so ['səʊ(ə)n(d)səʊ] *n F* **(a)** (*unspecified person*) Untel; Unetelle; **Mr. So-and-so,** Monsieur un tel; **Mrs. So-and-so,** Madame une telle; **(b)** *Pej* (*unpleasant person*) type *m*; **a crafty so-and-so,** une fine mouche, un malin; **the old so-and-so!,** quel sale type!; **you greedy old so-and-so!,** espèce de gourmand!

soap[1] [səʊp] *n* savon *m;* **toilet s.,** savon de toilette; (*small*) savonnette *f*; **shaving s.,** savon à barbe; **soft s.,** savon noir *ou* vert *ou* mou; *F* (*flattery*) flatterie *f*; **to wash with s.,** savonner (*qch*); **soap bubble,** bulle *f* de savon; *US Sl* **no s.,** rien à faire; *TV* **s. (opera),** feuilleton sentimental *ou* à l'eau de rose; **s. powder,** lessive *f* en poudre.

soap[2] *vt* **(a)** savonner (*le linge etc*); **(b)** *F* **to (soft-)s. s.o.,** flatter qn, flagorner qn.

▶soap down *vtsep* se savonner.

soapbox ['səʊpbɒks] *n* caisse *f* à savon, voiture *f* pour enfant; *F* **s. orator,** orateur *m* de carrefour; **to get up on a s.,** faire un discours improvisé.

soapdish ['səʊpdɪʃ] *n* porte-savon *m inv*.

soapflakes ['səʊpfleɪks] *npl* savon *m* en paillettes.

soapiness ['səʊpɪnɪs] *n* caractère savonneux (*de qch*).

soapstone ['səʊpstəʊn] *n Miner* stéatite *f*.

soapsuds ['səʊpsʌdz] *npl* (*lather*) mousse *f* de savon; (*water*) eau savonneuse; (*washing powder*) lessive *f*.

soapy ['səʊpɪ] *adj* **(a)** (*water*) savonneux; (*body*) couvert de savon; (*taste*) de savon; **(b)** *F* (*of person, voice*) doucereux, onctueux.

soar [sɔːr] *vi esp Lit* prendre son essor, monter, s'élever (*dans les airs*); (*glide*) planer (*dans les airs*); (*of spirit*) remonter; **rents have soared,** les loyers ont augmenté de façon vertigineuse.

soaring ['sɔːrɪŋ] **1** *adj* (*bird, arrow*) qui monte *ou* s'élève dans les airs; (*steeple*) élancé; (*price, popularity etc*) qui monte en flèche; **s. flight,** vol plané (*d'un oiseau*). **2** *n* essor *m* (*d'un oiseau*); hausse *f* (*des prix*); (*gliding*) vol plané (*d'un oiseau*).

sob[1] [sɒb] *n* sanglot *m*; **s. story,** histoire *f* à faire pleurer dans les chaumières; **to tell s.o. a s. story,** raconter une histoire pour apitoyer qn; **s. stuff,** sensiblerie *f*, *F* mélo *m*.

sob[2] *v* **(-bb-) 1** *vi* sangloter. **2** *vt* (*say*) dire (*qch*) en sanglotant; **she sobbed herself to sleep,** elle s'est endormie en sanglotant.

▶sob out *vtsep* **(a)** (*say*) dire (*qch*) en sanglotant; **(b) to s. one's heart out,** pleurer à gros sanglots.

sobbing ['sɒbɪŋ] **1** *adj* **in a s. voice,** d'une voix sanglotante *ou* brisée de sanglots. **2** *n* sanglots *mpl*.

s.o.b. [esəʊ'biː] *n esp Am Sl* (*abbr* **son of a bitch**) fils *m* de pute *ou* de putain, salaud *m*.

sober[1] ['səʊbər] *adj* **(a)** sobre; **she was still fairly s.,** elle était encore relativement sobre; **as s. as a judge,** sobre comme un chameau; **when he's s. (again),** quand il sera dégrisé; **(b)** (*moderate*) sobre, modéré, tempéré; (*calm*) calme, posé; (*visage*) grave; **s. colours,** couleurs sobres *ou* peu voyantes; **s. dress,** vêtement discret *ou* sobre; **s. opinion,** opinion réfléchie *ou* sobre; **s. truth,** la simple vérité.

sober[2] *vt* dégriser; **this news sobered him,** cette nouvelle l'a dégrisé; **it's had a sobering effect on him,** ça a eu un effet dégrisant sur lui.

▶sober down 1 *vi* (*become calmer*) s'assagir. **2** *vtsep* dégriser.

▶sober up 1 *vi* (*become less drunk*) se dégriser. **2** *vtsep* = **SOBER[2]**.

sober-minded [səʊbə'maɪndɪd] *adj* (*serious*) sérieux, réfléchi; (*in character*) de caractère sobre, pondéré.

soberness ['səʊbənɪs] *n* (*moderation*) sobriété *f*, modération *f*, tempérance *f*; (*calm*) calme *m*, tranquillité *f*; (*seriousness*) sérieux *m*; **s. of speech,** sobriété de parole.

sobersides ['səʊbəsaɪdz] *n Old-fashioned F* bonnet *m* de nuit.

Soc (a) *abbr* **society; (b)** *abbr* **Socialist.**

so-called [səʊ'kɔːld] *adj* **(a)** appelé ainsi, ainsi nommé; **the so-c. temperate zone,** la zone dite tempérée; **(b)** (*supposed*) **a so-c. doctor,** un soi-disant *ou* un prétendu docteur; **so-c. improvements,** prétendus progrès.

soccer ['sɒkər] *n* football *m*, *F* foot *m*; **s. match,** match *m* de football *ou* de foot; **s. player,** footballeur, -euse.

sociability [səʊʃə'bɪlɪtɪ] *n* sociabilité *f*.

sociable ['səʊʃəb(ə)l] **1** *adj* sociable; **he isn't very s.,** il n'est pas très sociable; **I had a drink with them to be s.,** j'ai pris un verre avec eux pour me montrer sociable; **to become more s.,** (*of person*) (*to become less shy*) s'apprivoiser; (*to become more friendly*) devenir plus sociable; **s. animals,** animaux sociables; *Am* **s. evening,** (*party*) soirée amicale; (*gathering*) réunion *f*. **2** *n Am* (*party*) soirée amicale; (*gathering*) réunion *f*.

sociably ['səʊʃəblɪ] *adv* sociablement.

social ['səʊʃəl] **1** *adj* **(a)** social, -aux; *Pol* **s. democrat,** social-démocrate *mf*; **s. drinking,** consommation *f* d'alcool lors de réunions amicales; **to be s.o.'s s. equal,** être l'égal de qn sur le plan social; **s. evening,** (*party*) soirée *f*; (*gathering*) réunion *f*; **s. ladder,** l'échelle sociale; **to have a busy s. life,** (*see a lot of people*) voir beaucoup de monde; (*go out a lot*) sortir beaucoup; **work is getting in the way of my s. life,** j'ai trop de travail pour pouvoir sortir; **since he's been married he's had to give up his s. life,** depuis son mariage il a dû cesser de sortir; **s. order,** l'ordre social; **s. position,** rang *m* dans la société; **s. reformer,** réformateur, -trice de la société; **s. sciences,** sciences humaines; **to be on** *or* **get s. security,** recevoir des prestations sociales; **the s. services,** les services sociaux *ou* d'assistance sociale; **s. work,** œuvres sociales; **s. worker,** assistant(e) social(e);

(b) *Zool* social; **man is an essentially s. animal,** l'homme est essentiellement sociable.

2 *n* (*party*) soirée *f*; (*gathering*) réunion *f*.

socialism ['səʊʃəlɪz(ə)m] *n* socialisme *m*.

socialist ['səʊʃəlɪst] *adj & n* socialiste *mf*.

socialite ['səʊʃəlaɪt] *n* membre *m* de la haute société, homme *ou* femme du monde, mondain, -aine.

socialize ['səʊʃəlaɪz] **1** *vi* **to s. with s.o.,** frayer avec qn; **he won't s.,** il n'accepte jamais une invitation; **they do a lot of socializing,** ils fréquentent beaucoup de gens. **2** *vt Old-fashioned Econ* nationaliser (*la propriété*); *US* **socialized medicine,** médecine *f* d'État.

socially ['səʊʃəlɪ] *adv* socialement; **to be s. active,** (*go out a lot*) sortir beaucoup; (*see a lot of people*) voir beaucoup de monde; **we don't do much s.,** nous sortons peu, nous fréquentons peu de gens; **I saw her s. for a while, but nothing beyond that,** je l'ai vaguement fréquentée pendant un temps, mais rien de plus; **I don't know him s. at all, just at work,** en dehors du travail je ne le connais pas du tout.

society [sə'saɪətɪ] *n* **(a)** société *f*; **he's a danger to s.,** c'est un danger pour la société; **to avoid the s. of one's colleagues,** éviter la société de ses collègues; **this word isn't used in polite s.,** ce mot n'est pas d'un usage poli, ce mot ne s'utilise pas chez les gens polis; **fashionable s.,** le beau monde; *Journ* **s. news** *or* **column,** mondanités *fpl*, échos mondains; **consumer s.,** société de consommation; **alternative s.,** société alternative; **s. people,** gens *mpl* du monde; **s. wedding,** un mariage dans le grand monde; **(b)** (*body*) société *f*; (*association*) association *f*; **charitable s.,** œuvre *f* de bienfaisance *ou* de charité; **National S. for the Prevention of Cruelty to Children,** organisation *f* de protection de l'enfance.

sociocultural [səʊsɪəʊ'kʌltjər(ə)l] *adj* socioculturel.

socioeconomic [səʊsɪəʊiːkə'nɒmɪk] *adj* socio-économique.

sociolinguistic [səʊsɪəʊlɪŋ'gwɪstɪk] *adj* sociolinguistique.

sociolinguistics [səʊsɪəʊlɪŋ'gwɪstɪks] *n* sociolinguistique *f*.

sociological [səʊsɪəʊ'lɒdʒɪk(ə)l] *adj* sociologique.

sociologist [səʊsɪ'ɒlədʒɪst] *n* sociologue *mf*.

sociology [səʊsɪ'ɒlədʒɪ] *n* sociologie *f*.

sociometry [səʊsɪ'ɒmɪtrɪ] *n* sociométrie *f*.

sock[1] [sɒk] *n* (*Am pl also* **sox**) **(a)** (*garment*) chaussette *f*; **(ankle) socks,** socquettes *fpl*, mi-chaussettes *fpl*; *Br F* **to pull one's socks up,** se reprendre; *Br F* **put a s. in it, will you!,** ferme-la!; **(b)** (*insole*) semelle intérieure (*d'une chaussure*).

sock[2] *n Sl* (*blow*) gnon *m*, beigne *f*; (*in the eye*) cocard *m*; **to give s.o. a s. on the jaw,** flanquer une beigne à qn.

sock[3] *vt* (*hit*) flanquer une beigne à (*qn*); *Sl* **to s. it to s.o.,** (*show what one is made of*) montrer à qn de quel bois on se chauffe; (*show what one can do*) montrer à qn de quoi on est capable.

socket ['sɒkɪt] *n Anat* orbite *f* (*de l'œil*); alvéole *f* (*de dent, de diamant*); cavité *f* articulaire, glène *f* (*d'un os*); (*plumbing*) emboîtement *m*, manchon *m* (*de tuyau*); *El esp Br* douille *f* (*de lampe*); prise *f* (de courant) femelle; **ball and s. joint,** *Anat* énarthrose *f*; *Tech* articulation *f*; *El esp Br* **wall s.,** prise (de courant) murale; **microphone s.,** prise microphone.

Socrates ['sɒkrətiːz] *n* Socrate.

Socratic [sɒ'krætɪk] *adj* socratique.

sod[1] [sɒd] *n* **(a)** (*turf*) gazon *m*; **under the s.,** (*buried*) enterré; **(b)** (*piece of turf*) motte *f* de gazon; **to cut** *or* **turn the first s.,** donner le premier coup de bêche.

sod[2] *n esp Br Sl* **he's a real s.,** c'est un sale con; **you silly s.,** espèce d'imbécile!; **poor s.!,** (*person*) pauvre bougre!; **odds and sods,** petits bouts, bribes *fpl* et morceaux *mpl*; **that's S.'s law,** tout s'en mêle pour vous emmerder!

sod[3] *vt esp Br Sl* **s. you!,** va te faire foutre!; **s. them!,** ils peuvent toujours aller se faire voir!; **s. the party, I'm tired,** la soirée, je m'en fous, je suis fatigué; **s. it!,** merde, alors!

►**sod off** *vi esp Br Sl* (*go away*) foutre le camp; **I told him to s. off,** je lui ai dit d'aller se faire voir.

soda ['səʊdə] *n Ch etc* soude *f*; **caustic s.,** soude caustique; **washing s.,** carbonate *m* de soude; **bicarbonate of s., baking s.,** bicarbonate *m* de soude; **s. bread,** = pain levé au bicarbonate de soude; *Am* **s. cracker,** biscuit *m* au bicarbonate de soude; **s. fountain,** bar *m* pour glaces et boissons (non alcoolisées); **s. (water),** eau *f* de Seltz, soda *m*.

sod-all ['sɒdɔːl] *n esp Br Sl* (*nothing*) que dalle; **they've got s.-a. hope of winning,** ils n'ont aucune chance de gagner; **they do s.-a. all day,** ils n'en fichent pas une rame de la journée.

sodden ['sɒd(ə)n] *adj* (*field*) (dé)trempé; (*clothes etc*) trempé; **s. with drink,** abruti par l'alcool.

sodium ['səʊdɪəm] *n Ch* sodium *m*; **s. chloride,** chlorure *m* de sodium.

Sodom ['sɒdəm] *n* Sodome *f*.

sodomite ['sɒdəmaɪt] *n* sodomite *m*.

sodomize ['sɒdəmaɪz] *vt* sodomiser (*qn*).

sodomy ['sɒdəmɪ] *n* sodomie *f*.

sofa ['səʊfə] *n* sofa *m*, canapé *m*; **s. bed,** canapé-lit *m*, *pl* canapés-lits.

soft [sɒft] **1** *adj* **(a)** (*substance, terrain, fromage etc*) mou, *f* molle; (*roche, crayon etc*) tendre; (*houille*) gras, *f* grasse; (*oreiller etc*) mou, doux, *f* douce, douillet; (*tissu etc*) moelleux; (*chapeau*) mou; (*cuir*) souple; (*personne*) (*lacking in vigour*) mou, qui manque de vigueur; (*easy-going*) doux, malléable; **as s. as butter,** mou comme le beurre *ou* la cire; **as s. as silk,** doux comme de la soie; **s. to the touch,** doux au toucher; **to become** *or* **get s.,** s'amollir; **you mustn't be so s. with** *or* **on them,** il faut les traiter plus sévèrement; **s. skin,** peau douce *ou* veloutée; *Br Com* **s. furnishings,** tissus *mpl* d'ameublement; (*carpets and curtains*) tapis *mpl* et rideaux; **s. mouth,** (*of horse*) bouche *f* tendre *ou* sensible; **s. muscles,** muscles flasques *ou* mous;

(b) (*voice, music, colour, rain, wind etc*) doux, *f* douce; *F* **to be s. on s.o.,** être amoureux *ou* entiché de qn; *Ling* **s. consonant,** consonne douce; **s. drinks,** boissons non alcoolisées; **s. drugs,** drogues douces; *Phot* **s. focus,** flou *m*; **s. fruit,** fruit *m* sans noyau; *F* **a s. job,** un emploi pépère; **s. heart,** cœur *m* tendre; *Av Astronaut* **s. landing,** atterrissage *m* en douceur; **s. life,** vie douce; **s. light,** lumière douce *ou* atténuée; **s. lighting,** éclairage doux *ou* atténué; **s. loan,** prêt *m* offrant des conditions avantageuses; **s. option,** solution *f* de facilité; **s. outline,** contour flou; **s. porn,** pornographie relativement peu explicite; *Com* **s. sell,** publicité discrète; *Aut* **s. shoulder,** accotement non-stabilisé; **to have a s. spot for s.o.,** avoir un faible pour qn; **s. step,** pas feutré *ou* de loup; *F* **to be a s. touch,** (*of person*) (*easy to get a loan from*) être facile à taper; (*easy to win over*) être bonne poire; **s. water,** eau douce *ou* non calcaire; **s. words,** mots doux *ou* tendres;

(c) *Comptr Typ* **s. hyphen,** tiret conditionnel; **s. return,** retour *m* de chariot conditionnel.

(d) *F* (*stupid*) stupide, bête; **don't be s.!,** ne sois pas bête!; **he's gone s. in the head!,** il a perdu la boule!

2 *adv F* doucement; *Sl* **don't talk s.!,** ne dis pas de bêtises!

softback, soft-cover ['sɒftbæk, -kʌvər] *n esp Am* livre *m* de poche.

softball ['sɒftbɔːl] *n Am* = genre de baseball (*joué avec

une balle plus grande et plus molle).
soft-boiled ['sɒftbɔɪld] *adj Culin* (*œuf*) mollet.
soft-core ['sɒftkɔːr] *adj* **s.-c. pornography,** pornographie relativement peu explicite.
soften ['sɒf(ə)n] **1** *vt* amollir, ramollir (*la cire etc*); adoucir (*la peau*); assouplir (*le cuir*); détremper, adoucir (*l'acier*); affaiblir, énerver (*qn*); adoucir (*une couleur, sa voix, l'eau etc*); atténuer (*une couleur, une lumière, un contraste etc*); radoucir (*le ton*); calmer, atténuer (*la colère de qn*); attendrir, émouvoir (*qn*); **troops softened by idleness,** troupes amollies par l'oisiveté. **2** *vi* (*of wax etc*) s'amollir, se ramollir; (*of skin etc*) s'adoucir; (*of meat*) s'attendrir; (*of person*) se radoucir; **the government has softened in its talks with the unions,** le gouvernement s'est radouci dans ses négociations avec les syndicats.
►**soften up 1** *vtsep* **(a)** (*make softer*) adoucir; **(b)** *Mil etc* réduire la résistance de (*qn*); **(c)** (*flatter*) amadouer (*qn*). **2** *vi* (*of material*) = **SOFTEN 2.**
softener ['sɒf(ə)nər] *n* **water s.,** adoucisseur *m* d'eau; **fabric s.,** adoucissant *m*.
softening ['sɒf(ə)nɪŋ] *n* amollissement *m*, ramollissement *m* (*de la cire etc*); assouplissement *m* (*du cuir*); détrempe *f*, adoucissage *m* (*de l'acier*); adoucissement *m* (*du caractère*); adoucissement (*de l'eau*); atténuation *f* (*de la lumière, des contrastes, des contours*); **s. of the brain,** ramollissement du cerveau; **there has been a s. of attitudes,** il y a eu un adoucissement *ou* un fléchissement des attitudes.
soft-focus [sɒft'fəʊkəs] *adj Phot* **s.-f. lens,** objectif *m* pour créer des effets de flou.
softheaded [sɒft'hedɪd] *adj F* bête, niais.
softhearted [sɒft'hɑːtɪd] *adj* au cœur tendre; **he's too s.,** il a trop de cœur.
softie ['sɒftɪ] *n F* = **SOFTY.**
softly ['sɒftlɪ] *adv* doucement; (*to walk*) sans bruit; (*tenderly*) tendrement.
softness ['sɒftnɪs] *n* **(a)** douceur *f* (*de la peau, d'un tissu, du climat etc*); **(b)** mollesse *f* (*de caractère*); (*lack of energy, character*) manque *m* d'énergie *ou* de caractère; flou *m* (*des contours*); **(c)** *F* (*foolishness*) niaiserie *f*; (*simplicity*) simplicité *f*.
soft(-)pedal [sɒft'ped(ə)l] **1** *vi* **(a)** *Mus* appuyer sur la pédale douce (*d'un piano*); **(b)** *F* (*not emphasize strongly*) y aller doucement, ne pas trop insister. **2** *vt F* atténuer, amoindrir (*l'importance d'un incident*).
soft-sectored ['sɒftsektəd] *adj Comptr* **s.-s. disk,** disque *m* à secteurs logiciels.
soft-soap ['sɒftsəʊp] *vt F* flatter, passer la pommade à (*qn*).
softly-softly ['sɒftlɪ'sɒftlɪ] *adj* (*approach etc*) doux, *f* douce.
soft-spoken [sɒft'spəʊk(ə)n] *adj* (*having gentle voice*) à voix douce; (*glib, flattering*) mielleux, doucereux.
software ['sɒftweər] *n Comptr* logiciel *m*, software *m*; **s. company,** fabricant *m* de logiciels; **s.-controlled,** contrôlé par logiciel; **s. package,** logiciel; **all the s. written for ...,** tous les logiciels réalisés pour ...; **a piece of s. that ...,** un logiciel qui ... .
softwood ['sɒftwʊd] *n Carp etc* bois *m* tendre.
softy ['sɒftɪ] *n F* (*person who isn't tough*) mou, molle; (*coward*) couard, -arde; (*fool*) niais, -aise; **to be a terrible s.,** être sentimental à l'excès; **you know I'm a big s.,** tu sais que je suis trop mou avec toi *ou* elle *etc*.
SOGAT ['səʊgæt] *n abbr* **Society of Graphical and Allied Trades.**
soggy ['sɒgɪ] *adj* détrempé, imbibé; (*bread*) pâteux.
soh [səʊ] *n Mus* sol *m inv*.
soil[1] [sɔɪl] *n* sol *m*, terre *f*; **to cultivate the s.,** cultiver la terre; **cover it with s.,** recouvre-le de terre; **alluvial s.,** terrain d'alluvion(s); *Lit* **one's native s.,** le sol natal.
soil[2] *n* **(a)** (*sailing*) souillure *f*, salissure *f*; **(b)** *Old-fashioned* **night s.,** vidanges *fpl*.
soil[3] **1** *vt* souiller, salir; encrasser (*ses habits*); maculer (*son linge*). **2** *vi* **fabric that soils easily,** tissu salissant *ou* qui se salit facilement.
soiled [sɔɪld] *adj* souillé, sali; **s. linen,** linge *m* sale; **if its s. the shop won't exchange it,** si c'est sale la boutique ne fera pas l'échange; **some slightly s. items at reduced prices,** des articles légèrement salis à prix réduits.
soirée ['swɑːreɪ] *n* soirée *f*.
soixante-neuf [swæsɑːnt'nɜːf] *n* soixante-neuf *m*.
sojourn[1] ['sɒdʒɜːn] *n Arch & Lit* séjour *m*.
sojourn[2] *vi Arch & Lit* séjourner.
sol [sɒl] *n Mus* sol *m inv*.
solace[1] ['sɒləs] *n Lit* consolation *f*, soulagement *m*; **to find s. in sth,** trouver une consolation dans qch.
solace[2] *vt Lit* consoler (*qn*); **I solaced myself with this thought,** j'ai trouvé une consolation dans cette pensée.
solar ['səʊlər] *adj* (*système, énergie etc*) solaire; **s. battery,** pile *f* solaire; **s. cell,** cellule *f* solaire; **s. panel,** panneau *m* solaire; *Anat* **s. plexus,** plexus *m* solaire; **s.-powered,** à énergie solaire.
solarium, *pl* **-ia** [səʊ'leərɪəm, -ɪə] *n* solarium *m*.
sold *see* **SELL**[2].
solder[1] ['sɒldər, 'səʊldər] *n* soudure *f*; **hard s.,** soudure forte; **brazing s.,** brasure *f*; **soft s.,** soudure tendre.
solder[2] *vt* (*metalworking*) souder.
solderer ['sɒldərər] *n* soudeur, -euse.
soldering ['sɒldərɪŋ] *n* soudure *f*; **s. iron,** fer *m* à souder.
soldier[1] ['səʊldʒər] *n* **(a)** soldat *m*, militaire *m*; (*commander*) tacticien *m*, stratégiste *m*; **private s.,** simple soldat, (soldat de) deuxième classe *m*; **an old s.,** un ancien soldat, un vétéran; **s. of fortune,** soldat de fortune; **tin s.,** soldat de plomb; **(b) s. (ant),** (fourmi *f*) soldat *m*.
soldier[2] *vi* **(a)** (*be a soldier*) faire le métier de soldat; **(b)** *Am & Nau Arch Sl* (*shirk*) tirer au flanc.
►**soldier on** *vi F* (*persevere*) persévérer; **we soldiered on through the blizzard,** nous avons progressé dans le blizzard; **I'll s. on with this for another half hour,** je vais encore m'escrimer là-dessus pendant une demi-heure.
soldiering ['səʊldʒərɪŋ] *n* la carrière militaire *ou* des armes; **he was tired of s.,** il en avait assez du métier de soldat; **to go s.,** se faire soldat.
soldierlike, soldierly ['səʊldʒəlaɪk, -lɪ] *adj* de soldat; (*allure*) martial, militaire.
soldiery ['səʊldʒərɪ] *n no pl Old-fashioned* soldats *mpl*, militaires *mpl*.
sole[1] [səʊl] *n* **(a)** plante *f* (*du pied*); (*of horse etc*) sole *f*; **(b)** semelle *f* (*de chaussure*); **(c)** semelle *f* (*de rabot, de crosse de golf etc*).
sole[2] *vt* (*fit with sole*) mettre une semelle à (*une chaussure*); (*resole*) ressemeler (*une chaussure*).
sole[3] *n* (*fish*) sole *f*; **Dover s.,** (vraie) sole.
sole[4] *adj* seul, unique; (*légataire*) universel; *Com* **s. agent,** représentant exclusif; **his s. reason,** son unique raison; **s. right,** droit exclusif.
solecism ['sɒlɪsɪz(ə)m] *n* solécisme *m*.
solely ['səʊllɪ] *adv* seulement, uniquement; **I went there s. to see it,** j'y suis allé dans le seul but de le voir.
solemn ['sɒləm] *adj* **(a)** (*oath etc*) solennel; (*duty*) sacré; (*question*) grave; *Jur* **s. agreement,** contrat solennel; **s. ceremony,** solennité *f*, fête solennelle; **s. fact,** réalité sérieuse; **s. warning,** avertissement formel; **(b)** (*person*) grave, sérieux; (*tone*) solennel; **to look s.,** avoir l'air solennel; **as s. as a judge,** sérieux comme un évêque.
solemness ['sɒləmnɪs] *n* = **SOLEMNITY (a)**.
solemnity [sə'lemnɪtɪ] *n* **(a)** solennité *f* (*d'une occasion, d'une cérémonie*); gravité *f*, sérieux *m* (*de l'expression, de l'attitude*); **with all s.,** en toute solennité; **(b)** (*event*) fête solennelle, solennité *f*.
solemnization [sɒləmnaɪ'zeɪʃən] *n* célébration *f* (*d'un mariage*).
solemnize ['sɒləmnaɪz] *vt* solenniser, célébrer (*une fête*); célébrer, bénir (*un mariage*).
solemnly ['sɒləmlɪ] *adv* **(a)** solennellement; **(b)** (*seriously*) gravement; (*to speak*) avec solennité.
solenoid ['sɒlənɔɪd] *n El* solénoïde *m*.
solfa ['sɒlfɑː] *n Mus* **tonic s.,** solfège *m*.
solicit [sə'lɪsɪt] **1** *vt* **(a)** solliciter (*qch de qn*); solliciter, briguer (*des suffrages*); **(b)** (*of prostitute*) racoler (*des clients*). **2** *vi* (*of prostitute*) racoler.
solicitation [səlɪsɪ'teɪʃən] *n* sollicitation *f*.
soliciting [sə'lɪsɪtɪŋ] *n* **(a)** sollicitation *f*; **(b)** (*of prostitute*) racolage *m*.
solicitor [sə'lɪsɪtər] *n* **(a)** *Br Jur* solicitor *m*; **S. General,** conseiller *m* juridique de la Couronne; **(b)** *US* (*seeking trade*) courtier, -ière, placier, -ière.
solicitous [sə'lɪsɪtəs] *adj Lit* soucieux, désireux (**of sth,** de qch); (*concerned*) préoccupé (*de qch*); (*caring*) plein de sollicitude; **s. attention to detail,** soin méticuleux des détails.
solicitously [sə'lɪsɪtəslɪ] *adv* avec sollicitude.
solicitousness [sə'lɪsɪtəsnɪs] **, solicitude** [sə'lɪsɪtjuːd] *n* sollicitude *f*, souci *m*, préoccupation *f*.
solid ['sɒlɪd] **1** *adj* solide; (*or, argent*) massif; (*pneu*) plein; (*mur*) plein, sans ouvertures; (*in a single piece*) en une seule pièce, d'un seul tenant; **pond frozen s.,** étang gelé jusqu'au fond; *Pol etc* **the union was s. behind him,** le syndicat était tout entier derrière lui; **they are s. for Labour,** ils sont acquis aux Travaillistes; **s. food,**

nourriture *f* solide; **to become s.,** (*of fluid*) se solidifier; **s. as a rock,** solide comme le roc *ou* la pierre; **to build on s. foundations,** bâtir sur le solide; **s. fuel,** combustible *m* solide; **on s. ground,** sur un terrain ferme; **man of s. build,** homme bien charpenté; **s. common sense,** solide bon sens; **to have s. reasons for believing sth,** avoir des raisons solides pour croire qch; **a good s. meal,** un solide repas; **some good s. research,** des recherches bien concrètes; *Math* **s. angle,** angle *m* solide; **to sleep/work for nine s. hours,** dormir/travailler neuf heures d'affilée; **three days' s. rain,** trois jours de pluie continue; **s. vote,** vote *m* unanime.

2 *n* solide *m*; **solids,** (*food*) aliments *mpl* solides; **is the baby on solids yet?,** est-ce que le bébé a commencé à manger des aliments solides?; **milk solids,** extrait *m* du lait; **non-fat solids,** solides non gras.

3 *adv* **to sleep/work for nine hours s.,** dormir/travailler neuf heures d'affilée.

solidarity [sɒlɪ'dærɪtɪ] *n* solidarité *f*; **to show s. with s.o.,** faire preuve de solidarité envers qn; **S.,** (*in Poland*) Solidarité *f*.

solidification [səlɪdɪfɪ'keɪʃən] *n* solidification *f*; congélation *f* (*de l'huile*).

solidify [sə'lɪdɪfaɪ] **1** *vt* **(a)** solidifier (*de l'huile*); **(b)** *Fig* (*support fact*) consolider. **2** *vi* **(a)** se solidifier; (*of oil*) se figer, se congeler; **(b)** *Fig* (*of union, fact*) se consolider.

solidity [sə'lɪdɪtɪ] *n* solidité *f*.

solidly ['sɒlɪdlɪ] *adv* **(a)** solidement; (*without interruption*) sans interruption, sans s'arrêter; **s. held,** tenu fermement *ou* solidement; **s. built man,** homme bien charpenté; **(b)** (*to vote*) à l'unanimité; **we're s. behind you,** nous vous soutenons à fond.

solid-state [sɒlɪd'steɪt] *adj* (*physique*) des solides; (*électronique, circuit, dispositif*) à semiconducteurs.

soliloquize [sə'lɪləkwaɪz] *vi* faire un soliloque, soliloquer, monologuer.

soliloquy [sə'lɪləkwɪ] *n* soliloque *m*, monologue *m*.

soling ['səʊlɪŋ] *n* (*of shoe*) pose *f* d'une semelle; (*resoling*) ressemelage *m*.

solitaire [sɒlɪ'teər] *n* **(a)** (*game*) solitaire *m*; *Am Cards* (jeu *m* de) patience *f*; **(b) s. (diamond),** solitaire *m*.

solitary ['sɒlɪt(ə)rɪ] **1** *adj* solitaire; (*on one's, its own*) seul, solitaire; (*isolated*) isolé; **not a s. one,** pas un seul; **s. confinement,** (*in prison*) régime *m* (d'isolement) cellulaire; **to be kept in s. confinement,** être détenu en régime (d'isolement) cellulaire. **2** *n F* régime *m* (d'isolement) cellulaire; **he got three months s.,** il a pris trois mois de cachot.

solitude ['sɒlɪtju:d] *n* solitude *f*; **to live in s.,** vivre dans la solitude.

solo ['səʊləʊ] **1** *n* **(a)** *Mus* solo *m*; **violin s.,** solo de violon; **s. album,** album *m* solo; **(b)** *Cards* **s. (whist),** whist *m* de Gand. **2** *adv* **to fly s.,** voler seul; **to play s.,** jouer en solo; **to go s.,** *Cards* jouer solo; (*of former partner, member of rock group etc*) faire une carrière en solo. **3** *adj* **s. guitar,** guitare *m* solo; **s. flight,** vol *m* en solo.

soloist ['səʊləʊɪst] *n Mus* soliste *mf*.

solstice ['sɒlstɪs] *n Astron* solstice *m*.

solubility [sɒljʊ'bɪlɪtɪ] *n* solubilité *f* (*d'un sel etc*).

soluble ['sɒljub(ə)l] *adj* **(a)** soluble (**in water,** dans l'eau); **(b)** (*problème*) soluble.

solution [sə'lu:ʃən] *n* **(a)** *Ch etc* solution *f*; (*in engraving*) solution, bain *m*; **salt in s.,** sel *m* en solution; **(b)** (*solving*) résolution *f*, solution *f* (*d'une difficulté, d'une équation*); (*answer*) solution, résultat *m* (*d'un problème de mathématique*); **there is no real s. to this,** il n'y a aucune solution dans ce cas.

solvable ['sɒlvəb(ə)l] *adj* (*problème*) soluble.

solve [sɒlv] *vt* résoudre (*un problème, une équation*); éclaircir (*un mystère*); **this question has not yet been solved,** cette question reste toujours en suspens, cette question reste sans réponse; **to s. a riddle,** résoudre une énigme.

solvency ['sɒlvənsɪ] *n Com Jur* solvabilité *f*.

solvent ['sɒlvənt] **1** *adj* **(a)** *Com Jur* solvable; **(b)** (*liquid*) dissolvant, solvant. **2** *n* dissolvant *m*, solvant *m*; **s. abuse/abuser,** utilisation *f* de solvants hallucinogènes/toxicomane *mf* utilisant des solvants hallucinogènes.

Som *abbr* **Somerset**.

Somali [sə'mɑ:lɪ] **1** *adj Geog* somali, somalien. **2** *n* **(a)** Somali, -ie; **the S.,** les Somalis; **(b)** *Ling* somali *m*.

Somalia [sə'mɑ:lɪə] *n* (République *f* démocratique de) Somalie *f*.

Somaliland [sə'mɑ:lɪlænd] *n Hist* Somalie *f*; **French S.,** Côte française des Somalis.

somatic [sə'mætɪk] *adj Biol* somatique.

sombre, *US* **somber** ['sɒmbər] *adj* **(a)** (*colour etc*) sombre; **(b)** (*person, mood etc*) sombre, morne, maussade.

sombrely, *US* **somberly** ['sɒmbəlɪ] *adv* (*to look at s.o. etc*) sombrement, d'un air sombre *ou* morne *ou* maussade; **s. dressed,** habillé de couleurs sombres.

some [sʌm] **1** *adj* **(a)** (*not specified*) **s. (sort of an) excuse,** une excuse quelconque; **he'll come s. day,** il arrivera un de ces jours; **s. days she is better,** certains jours elle va mieux; **s. books are difficult to read,** il y a des livres qui sont difficiles à lire, certains livres sont difficiles à lire; **s. people say...,** il y en a qui disent...; **s. people!,** il y a des gens, vraiment!; **s. fool left the door open,** un imbécile a laissé la porte ouverte; **s. bureaucrat decided the road would be here,** un bureaucrate quelconque a décidé que la route passerait ici; **s. book or other,** un livre quelconque;

(b) (*certain quantity, number*) de; **to drink s. water,** boire de l'eau; **I ate s. fruit,** j'ai mangé des fruits; **s. strange people appeared,** d'étranges personnes *ou* des personnes étranges ont fait leur apparition; **s. people,** des personnes; (*a few*) quelques personnes; **s. people think ...,** il y a des personnes qui pensent ...; **I felt s. uneasiness,** je ressentais quelque inquiétude; **that would be s. help,** cela faciliterait un peu les choses; **in s. measure, to s. degree,** jusqu'à un certain point, dans une certaine mesure; **s. distance away,** à quelque distance, à une certaine distance; **s. days ago,** il y a quelques jours; **for s. time,** pendant quelque temps *ou* un certain temps; **he has been waiting for s. time,** il attend depuis quelque temps *ou* depuis un certain temps; **it will be s. time** *or* **s. little while before it's finished,** ça va prendre un certain temps *ou* un moment avant que ça soit fini; **at s. length,** assez longuement;

(c) *F* (*intensive*) **(that was) s. storm!,** quelle tempête!; **she's s. girl!,** c'est une fille formidable!; **that was s. meal!,** ce que nous avons bien mangé!;

(d) (*Iron*) **s. hope!,** quelle illusion!

2 *pron* **(a)** (*people*) certains, quelques-uns, quelques-unes; **s. or all of them,** tous ou seulement certains d'entre eux; **s. believe that ...,** il y en a qui croient que ..., certains croient que ...; **they went off, s. one way, s. another,** ils se sont dispersés, les uns d'un côté, les autres de l'autre *ou Lit* qui d'un côté, qui de l'autre; **s. of my friends,** certains de mes amis;

(b) (*things, quantity*) (*referring to countable nouns*) quelques-uns, quelques-unes; (*referring to uncountable nouns*) un peu; **I have s.,** j'en ai; **give me s.,** donnez-m'en; **I've s. more,** (*I have some left*) j'en ai encore; (*I have some others*) j'en ai d'autres; **s. of the time,** une partie du temps; **s. of the most beautiful scenery in the world,** un des plus beaux paysages du monde; **at least there's SOME left,** (*not nothing*) au moins il en reste quand même un peu.

3 *adv* **(a)** (*approximately*) environ, quelque *inv*; **s. thirty pounds,** une trentaine de livres, quelque trente livres; **s. fifteen minutes,** un bon petit quart d'heure; **s. few minutes,** quelques minutes;

(b) *esp Am F* (*intensive*) **to go it s.,** y aller en plein; **it annoyed him s.,** il en était pas mal fâché.

somebody ['sʌmbədɪ] **1** *pron* **s. told me so,** quelqu'un *ou* on me l'a dit; **s. I know told me,** quelqu'un que je connais me l'a dit; **he's not s. you can trust,** ce n'est pas quelqu'un à qui on peut faire confiance; **somebody's knocking,** on frappe; **s. is missing,** il manque quelqu'un; **s. (or other) has told him,** quelqu'un lui a dit; **can s. help me, quick?,** est-ce que quelqu'un peut m'aider, vite?; **is this s.'s wallet?,** est-ce que ce portefeuille est à quelqu'un?; **it must belong to s., it must be s.'s,** ça doit bien appartenir à quelqu'un, ça doit bien être à quelqu'un; **Mr S. (or other),** Monsieur Chose; **s. else,** quelqu'un d'autre; **he went and s. else came along,** il est parti et un autre est venu; **s. important,** quelqu'un d'important; **we need s. a bit taller/who speaks Russian,** il nous faut quelqu'un d'un peu plus grand/qui parle russe; **it wasn't John, it was s. else,** ce n'était pas John, c'était quelqu'un d'autre; **s. else has been here today,** quelqu'un d'autre est venu ici aujourd'hui.

2 *pron & n* (*pl* **somebodies** ['sʌmbədɪz]) **he's (a) s.,** c'est un personnage, ce n'est pas le premier venu; **she thinks she's s.,** elle se croit quelqu'un, elle ne se prend pas pour n'importe qui.

somehow ['sʌmhaʊ] *adv* **(a)** d'une façon ou d'une autre, d'une manière ou d'une autre; **we'll manage it s. (or other),** nous y parviendrons tant bien que mal; **s. we got there on time,** nous nous sommes débrouillés pour arriver à l'heure; **(b) I never liked her s.,** pour une raison ou pour une autre elle ne m'a jamais été sympathique; **s. (or other)**

it's different, il y a pourtant une différence.

someone ['sʌmwʌn] *pron* = **SOMEBODY 1**.

someplace ['sʌmpleɪs] *adv Am* = **SOMEWHERE**.

somersault¹ ['sʌməsɔːlt] *n Gym* (*in air*) saut périlleux; (*on ground*) culbute *f*; (*accidental*) culbute; **to turn** *or* **do a s.,** faire le saut périlleux; (*accidentally*) faire la culbute; (*of car*) faire un tonneau *ou* des tonneaux.

somersault² *vi Gym* faire le saut périlleux *ou* des sauts périlleux; (*accidentally*) faire la culbute; (*of car*) faire un tonneau *ou* des tonneaux.

something ['sʌmθɪŋ] **1** *n & pron* **(a)** quelque chose *m*; **I've brought you a little s.,** je vous ai apporté un petit quelque chose *ou* une bricole; **say s.,** dites quelque chose; **s. or other,** une chose ou une autre; **Anne s. (or other),** Anne je ne sais plus quoi; **there's s. about him I don't like,** il y a en lui quelque chose qui me déplaît; **s. tells me she'll come,** quelque chose me dit qu'elle viendra; **s. has happened,** il est arrivé quelque chose; **was it s. I said?,** est-ce que j'ai dit quelque chose qu'il ne fallait pas?; **s. to drink,** quelque chose à boire; **to ask for s. to drink,** demander (quelque chose) à boire; **can I get you s.?,** est-ce que je peux vous offrir quelque chose (à manger, à boire)?; **let's have s. to eat,** mangeons quelque chose; **it must have been s. he ate that made him ill,** ça doit être quelque chose qu'il a mangé qui l'a rendu malade; **s. to live for,** une raison de vivre; **to have s. to be annoyed about,** avoir de quoi se fâcher; **to have s. to hang on to,** avoir quelque chose à quoi se raccrocher; **s. new,** quelque chose de nouveau *ou* de neuf; **I've s. else to do,** j'ai autre chose à faire; **he's s. in a bank,** il travaille dans une banque; **in the year eleven hundred and s.,** en l'an onze cent et quelque chose; **she's eighty s.,** elle a quatre-vingts ans et des poussières, elle a quatre-vingts ans et quelque; **a certain indefinable s.,** un je ne sais quoi d'indéfinissable; **he has seen s. of the world,** il a l'expérience du monde; (*he has travelled*) il a voyagé; **her plan has s. in it, there's s. in her plan,** son projet mérite considération; **there's s. in what you say,** il y a de la vérité dans ce que vous dites; **there's s. in him,** (*depth of character*) il a de l'étoffe; **she has s. to do with it,** elle y est pour quelque chose; **it's s. to do with the law,** ça a à voir avec la loi; **well, that's s.!,** c'est déjà quelque chose!; **that was quite s.!,** c'était vraiment quelque chose!; **she's an accountant or s.,** elle est comptable ou quelque chose comme ça; **is it broken or s.?,** c'est cassé ou quoi?;

(b) there's s. of an improvement, il y a une certaine amélioration; **she's s. of a miser,** elle est un peu *ou* quelque peu avare.

2 *adv* quelque peu, tant soit peu; **it looks s. like a guinea pig,** ça ressemble à un cochon d'Inde; *F* **he treated me s. shocking,** il m'a traité d'une façon abominable; **s. like 500,** 500 environ, quelque chose comme 500, **is this s. like him?,** est-ce que ça lui ressemble un peu?; **s. like that,** quelque chose comme ça.

sometime ['sʌmtaɪm] **1** *adv* (*often written as two words*) **s. (or other),** tôt ou tard; un jour ou l'autre; **s. last year,** au cours de l'année dernière; **s. in August,** pendant le mois d'août; **s. before last Tuesday,** avant mardi dernier; **s. between 1927 and 1931,** entre 1927-1931; **s. soon,** bientôt; *F* **see you s.!,** à bientôt! **2** *adj Lit* **Mr Martin, my s. tutor,** M. Martin, autrefois mon professeur.

sometimes ['sʌmtaɪmz] *adv* quelquefois, parfois; **s. one, s. the other,** tantôt l'un, tantôt l'autre.

someway ['sʌmweɪ] *adv F* **s. (or other),** de façon ou d'autre.

somewhat ['sʌmwɒt] **1** *adv* un peu; **it's s. difficult,** c'est assez *ou* un peu difficile. **2** *n* **he was s. of a coward,** il était quelque peu poltron; **this was s. of a relief,** c'était en quelque sorte un soulagement.

somewhere ['sʌmweər] *adv* **(a)** quelque part; **it's s. in the Bible,** cela se trouve quelque part dans la Bible; **s. near us,** pas bien loin de nous; **s. in the world,** de par le monde; **s. in France,** quelque part en France; **s. else,** ailleurs, autre part; **s. or other,** je ne sais où; **he lives s. near Oxford,** il habite dans les environs d'Oxford; **(b) he is s. around fifty,** il a à peu près cinquante ans; **it costs s. in the region of £500,** cela coûte environ 500 livres; **there were s. around 50 kilobytes left,** il restait environ 50 kilo-octets.

somnambulism [sɒm'næmbjʊlɪz(ə)m] *n* somnambulisme *m*.

somnambulist [sɒm'næmbjʊlɪst] *n* somnambule *mf*.

somnolence ['sɒmnələns] *n* somnolence *f*.

somnolent ['sɒmnələnt] *adj* somnolent.

son [sʌn] *n* fils *m*; *Am F* **s. of a bitch,** (*obnoxious person*) fils de pute *ou* de putain, salaud *m*; **the S. of God,** le fils de Dieu; **the S. of Man,** le fils de l'homme; *Fig* **a s. of the people,** un fils du peuple; **OK, s.?,** OK fiston?

sonar ['səʊnɑːr] *n Nau* sonar *m*.

sonata [sə'nɑːtə] *n Mus* sonate *f*.

sonatina [sɒnə'tiːnə] *n Mus* sonatine *f*.

sonde [sɒnd] *n Met etc* sonde *f*.

song [sɒŋ] *n Mus* **(a)** chanson *f*; *Lit* chant *m*; *Rel* cantique *m*; **marching s.,** chanson de route; **give us a s.,** chantez-nous quelque chose; *F* **to buy sth for a s.,** acheter qch pour rien *ou* pour une bouchée de pain; **it went for a s.,** cela s'est vendu pour rien *ou* pour une bouchée de pain; *F* **he made a great s. and dance about it,** il en a fait tout un plat; *Lit* **s. of victory,** chant de victoire; *Bible* **the S. of Songs, the S. of Solomon,** le Cantique des Cantiques; **s. book,** recueil *m* de chansons, chansonnier *m*; **(b)** (*singing*) chant *m*; **to burst** *or* **break into s.,** se mettre à chanter; **the s. of the birds,** le chant *ou* le ramage des oiseaux.

songbird ['sɒŋbɜːd] *n* oiseau chanteur.

songster ['sɒŋstər] *n* **(a)** (*singer*) chanteur *m*; **(b)** (*poet*) poète *m*, chantre *m*; **(c)** = **SONGBIRD**.

songstress ['sɒŋstrɪs] *n* (*singer*) chanteuse *f*.

songwriter ['sɒŋraɪtər] *n Mus* compositeur, -trice de chansons.

sonic ['sɒnɪk] *adj Phys* acoustique, audible; *Av* (*vitesse*) sonique; **s. barrier,** mur *m* du son; **s. boom,** bang *m*.

son-in-law ['sʌnɪnlɔː] *n* gendre *m*, beau-fils *m*, *pl* beaux-fils.

sonnet ['sɒnɪt] *n* (*in poetry*) sonnet *m*.

sonny ['sʌnɪ] *n F* mon petit, fiston *m*; **look here, s. Jim,** attention petit gars.

sonority [sə'nɒrɪtɪ] *n* sonorité *f*.

sonorous ['sɒnərəs] *adj* sonore; **s. voice,** voix sonore *ou* timbrée.

sonorously ['sɒnərəslɪ] *adv* d'un ton sonore.

sonorousness ['sɒnərəsnɪs] *n* sonorité *f*.

soon [suːn] *adv* **(a)** bientôt; **s. after,** peu après; **s. after four,** (un) peu après quatre heures; **it will s. be three years since ...,** voici bientôt trois ans que ..., cela fera bientôt trois ans que ...; **he'll be here very s.,** il sera ici sous peu, il sera ici très bientôt; **must you leave so s.?,** vous faut-il partir si tôt?; **too s.,** trop tôt, avant l'heure; **an hour too s.,** (*arriver etc*) avec une heure d'avance; **they were s. making friends,** ils se sont bien vite fait des amis; **it ended all too s.,** cela a fini bien trop tôt; **none too s.,** juste à temps;

(b) as s. as, aussitôt que, dès que; **I'll see him as s. as he comes,** je le verrai aussitôt *ou* dès qu'il arrivera; **as s. as I arrived in London,** dès mon arrivée à Londres; **as s. as he saw them,** dès qu'il les a vus; **as s. as possible,** le plus tôt possible, aussitôt que possible, dès que possible;

(c) sooner, plus tôt; **we would have got there sooner, if ...,** nous serions arrivés plus tôt, si ...; **the sooner you begin the sooner you will have finished,** plus tôt vous commencerez plus vite vous aurez fini; **the problem should be dealt with sooner rather than later,** il faut faire face au problème le plus tôt possible; **the sooner the better,** le plus tôt sera le mieux; **sooner or later,** tôt ou tard; **no sooner said than done,** (aus)sitôt dit, (aus)sitôt fait; **no sooner had he finished than he was arrested,** à peine eut-il fini qu'il fut arrêté;

(d) (*preference*) **I would just as s. stay,** j'aime autant rester; **sooner than give in I would die,** je mourrais plutôt que de céder; **I would sooner die,** j'aimerais mieux mourir; **someone will have to do it — sooner you than me!,** quelqu'un devra le faire — il vaudrait mieux que ce soit vous, plutôt que moi;

(e) *F* **soonest,** (*faire qch*) aussitôt que possible; **it will be next week at the soonest,** ce sera la semaine prochaine au plus tôt; *Prov* **least said soonest mended,** moins on en dit, mieux ça vaut.

soot¹ [sʊt] *n* suie *f*.

soot² *vt* enduire *ou* couvrir (*qch*) de suie.

sooth [suːθ] *n Arch* vérité *f*; **in (good) s.,** en vérité.

soothe [suːð] *vt* calmer, apaiser (*la douleur, une brûlure etc*); tranquilliser (*l'esprit*); apaiser (*qn*); **to s. s.o.'s anger,** apaiser la colère de qn.

soothing ['suːðɪŋ] *adj* calmant, apaisant; *Med* lénitif; **in a s. voice,** d'une voix calmante.

soothingly ['suːðɪŋlɪ] *adv* (*to say*) (d'un ton) calmant *ou* apaisant.

soothsayer ['suːθseɪər] *n Arch* devin *m*, *f* devineresse.

soothsaying ['suːθseɪɪŋ] *n Arch* divination *f*.

sooty ['sʊtɪ] *adj* **(a)** (*covered in soot*) couvert de suie; (*black*) noir de suie; **(b)** (*deposit*) de suie; (*ressembling*

soot) fuligineux.
sop¹ [sɒp] *n* **(a)** (*bread*) morceau *m* de pain trempé; **(b)** (*gift*) cadeau destiné à amadouer qn; (*concession*) concession *f*; **he just said that as a s. to her feelings,** il a dit ça seulement pour lui plaire *ou* (*if she is angry etc*) pour l'amadouer; **a concession that was not much more than a s. to the unions,** une concession qui n'avait pour but que d'amadouer les syndicats; **to throw a s. to Cerberus,** jeter le gâteau à Cerbère.
sop² *vt* (-pp-) (faire) tremper (*le pain*).
►**sop up** *vtsep* (*mop up*) éponger (*un liquide*).
sophism ['sɒfɪz(ə)m] *n* sophisme *m*.
sophist ['sɒfɪst] *n* sophiste *mf*.
sophistical [sə'fɪstɪk(ə)l] *adj* sophistique, captieux.
sophisticate [sə'fɪstɪkɪt] *n* personne raffinée; *Pej* personne sophistiquée.
sophisticated [sə'fɪstɪkeɪtɪd] *adj* (*person*) raffiné; *Pej* sophistiqué; (*conversation etc*) raffiné; (*style*) recherché; (*plan*) subtil; (*machinery*) (très) perfectionné; (*style, technology*) sophistiqué; **s. tastes,** goûts raffinés.
sophistication [səfɪstɪ'keɪʃən] *n* **(a)** (*of person*) (*appearance*) sophistication *f*; (*tastes*) goûts raffinés; (*of style, dress*) recherche *f*; (*of machinery*) perfectionnement *m*; **(b)** (*sophistic arguments*) raisonnements *mpl* sophistiques.
sophistry ['sɒfɪstrɪ] *n* **(a)** sophistique *f*; **to indulge in s.,** se laisser aller à la sophistique; **(b)** (*example*) sophisme *m*.
Sophocles ['sɒfəkliːz] *n* Sophocle *m*.
sophomore ['sɒfəmɔːr] *n Sch Am* étudiant, -ante de seconde année.
soporific [sɒpə'rɪfɪk] *adj & n* somnifère *m*, soporifique *m*.
soppiness ['sɒpɪnɪs] *n F* mollesse *f*, fadasserie *f*.
sopping [ʃɒpɪŋ] *adj* trempé; **s. wet,** tout trempé; (*person*) trempé jusqu'aux os.
soppy ['sɒpɪ] *adj* **(a)** (*wet*) (*terrain etc*) détrempé; **(b)** *Br F* (*person*) mou, *f* molle; (*sentiment*) fadasse; (*story etc*) larmoyant; (*silly*) stupide, bête; **don't be s.!,** ne sois pas si bête!
soprano, *pl* **-os, -i** [sɒ'prɑːnəʊ, -əʊz, -iː] *n Mus* soprano *mf*, *pl* soprani, sopranos; **s. voice,** voix *f* de soprano.
sorb [sɔːb] *n* **(a) s. (apple),** (*fruit of service tree*) sorbe *f*, corme *f*, alise *f*, alize *f*; **(b) s. tree,** (*service tree*) sorbier *m*, cormier *m*, alisier *m*, alizier *m*.
sorbet ['sɔːbeɪ] *n Culin* sorbet *m*.
sorbitol ['sɔːbɪtɒl] *n* sorbitol *m*.
sorcerer ['sɔːs(ə)rər] *n* sorcier *m*.
sorceress ['sɔːs(ə)rɪs] *n* sorcière *f*.
sorcery ['sɔːs(ə)rɪ] *n* sorcellerie *f*.
sordid ['sɔːdɪd] *adj* sordide; (*place etc*) sale, crasseux; (*business, motives*) bas, vil.
sordidly ['sɔːdɪdlɪ] *adv* sordidement.
sordidness ['sɔːdɪdnɪs] *n* sordidité *f*; (*of place etc*) saleté *f*; (*of business, motives*) bassesse *f*.
sore¹ [sɔːr] *adj* **(a)** (*painful*) douloureux, endolori; **s. to the touch,** douloureux au toucher; (*inflamed*) enflammé, irrité; **s. eyes,** yeux enflammés; **s. throat,** mal *m* de gorge; **I've (got) a s. throat,** j'ai mal à la gorge; **to have a s. finger,** avoir mal au doigt; **it's still s.,** ça fait toujours mal; **it's a s. point** *or* **subject with him,** il est très sensible sur ce point; **(b)** (*annoyed*) chagriné; *Am F* (*angry*) fâché; **to be** *or* **feel s. about sth,** être chagriné au sujet de qch; *Am F* **to be** *or* **get s.,** se fâcher; **(c)** *Lit* **to be in s. need of sth,** avoir grandement besoin de qch; **s. trial,** cruelle épreuve; **s. temptation,** tentation *f* irrésistible.
sore² *n* plaie *f*, écorchure *f*; **to (re)open an old s.,** raviver une plaie ancienne; **(running) s.,** ulcère *m*.
sorehead ['sɔːhed] *n esp Am* ronchon, -onne.
sorely ['sɔːlɪ] *adv* **(a)** *Lit* gravement, grandement; **s. wounded,** gravement *ou* grièvement blessé; **(b) s. tried,** cruellement éprouvé; **s. distressed,** dans une grande *ou* profonde détresse; **s. needed,** dont on a grandement besoin; **s. tempted,** fortement tenté.
soreness ['sɔːnɪs] *n* **(a)** endolorissement *m*, douleur *f*; **(b)** (*annoyance*) chagrin *m*, contrariété *f*; (*distress*) peine *f*; *esp Am* (*resentment*) rancune *f*; (*anger*) colère *f*.
sorghum ['sɔːgəm] *n* (*plant*) sorg(h)o *m*.
sorrel¹ ['sɒrəl] *n* (*plant*) oseille *f*.
sorrel² **1** *adj* (*cheval*) alezan. **2** *n* (*colour, horse*) alezan *m*; **chestnut s.,** alezan châtain.
sorrow¹ ['sɒrəʊ] *n* douleur *f*, chagrin *m*, tristesse *f*; **to my s.,** à mon (grand) regret; **more in s. than in anger,** avec plus de tristesse que de colère; *Bible* **Man of Sorrows,** l'Homme *m* de douleur.
sorrow² *vi esp Lit* s'affliger, être affligé (**over, at, about sth,** de qch); **to s. for** *or* **after s.o./sth,** pleurer qn/qch.
sorrowful ['sɒrəfʊl] *adj* (*person*) affligé, chagriné; (*sad*) triste; (*news*) attristant, pénible; **s. look,** regard attristé *ou* désolé.
sorrowfully ['sɒrəfəlɪ] *adv* tristement; (*to look at*) d'un air affligé *ou* désolé.
sorrowing ['sɒrəʊɪŋ] *adj* affligé.
sorry ['sɒrɪ] *adj* **(a)** fâché, chagriné, désolé (**about sth,** de qch); **she's s. she did it** *or* **for having done it,** elle est désolée *ou* elle se repent *ou* elle regrette de l'avoir fait; **to be s. not to have done sth,** regretter *ou* avoir du regret de ne pas avoir fait qch; **I'm only s. we couldn't have stayed longer,** je regrette que nous n'ayons pas pu rester plus longtemps; *F* **you'll be s. for it,** il vous en cuira, vous vous en repentirez; **you'll be s. you ever came here!,** vous allez regretter d'être venu ici; **I'm s. I ever let him in the house,** je regrette de l'avoir laissé entrer dans la maison; **I'm (very) s. to hear that ...,** je regrette (infiniment) que, je suis désolé d'apprendre que ...; **you won't be s. you bought a ...,** vous ne regretterez pas d'avoir acheté un ...; **I'm s. to say that ...,** je regrette d'avoir à vous dire que ...; **I'm so s. to keep you waiting,** excusez-moi de vous faire attendre; **(I'm) s.!,** pardon!, excusez-moi!; **so s.!,** vraiment désolé; **s. I can't help,** désolé, je ne peux rien pour vous; **to feel s. for s.o.,** (*take pity on*) avoir pitié de qn; (*feel sympathy for*) plaindre qn; **I'm s. for him,** (*I feel pity for him*) il me fait pitié; (*I sympathize with him*) je le plains; **to look s. for oneself,** avoir l'air piteux;
(b) (*pitiful*) pauvre, misérable, piteux; **to be in a s. plight,** (*to be in bad situation*) être dans une mauvaise passe; (*to be in bad state*) être dans un état piteux; **to cut a s. figure,** faire piètre figure; **the whole s. tale,** toute cette malheureuse affaire.
sort¹ [sɔːt] *n* **(a)** sorte *f*, genre *m*, espèce *f*; **all sorts of people,** des gens de toutes sortes; **it takes all sorts (to make a world),** il faut de tout (pour faire un monde); **what s. of a man is he?,** quelle sorte d'homme est-ce?; **she's a good s.,** c'est une fille sympa; **we don't want your s. here,** nous ne voulons pas de gens comme vous ici; **this** *or F* **these s. of people,** les gens de cette espèce, ces gens-là; **you get all sorts at these parties,** on rencontre toutes sortes de gens dans ces soirées; **what s. of tree is it?,** quelle sorte d'arbre est-ce?; **what s. of day did you have?,** comment c'est passée ta journée?; **I've heard all sorts of things about him,** j'en ai entendu de toutes les couleurs sur son compte; **I can't stand that s. of thing,** je ne peux pas souffrir ce genre de chose; **something of the s.** *or* **of that s.,** quelque chose de pareil *ou* de semblable *ou* dans ce genre-là; **nothing of the s.,** (*nothing of that type*) rien de semblable *ou* de la sorte; (*not in the least*) pas du tout!; **I've a s. of feeling that ...,** *F* **I s. of feel that ...,** j'ai dans l'idée que ..., j'ai comme l'impression que ...; *F* **I s. of expected it,** je m'en doutais un peu; *F* **it's s. of heavy,** c'est un peu lourd, c'est plutôt lourd; *F* **it's getting s. of late,** il commence à se faire tard; **the trees formed a s. of arch,** les arbres formaient comme une arche; **that's my s. of holiday,** c'est des vacances comme je les aime; *Pej* **coffee of a s.,** un soi-disant café; **a peace of sorts,** une paix si l'on peut dire; **some s. of writer, a writer of sorts,** quelque vague écrivain; **to make some s. of (a) reply,** répondre d'une façon quelconque *ou* tant bien que mal; **to be out of sorts,** (*a little unwell*) être mal fichu, ne pas être dans son assiette; (*in a bad mood*) être de mauvaise humeur;
(b) (*manner*) manière *f*, façon *f*; **in some s.,** à un certain degré; jusqu'à un certain point, en quelque sorte;
(c) *Typ* sorte *f*; **sorts,** assortiment *m*.
sort² **1** *vt* faire le tri de (*qch*); (*put together*) assortir; classer (*des papiers etc*); *Comptr* trier; **to s. the letters,** (*in post office*) trier les lettres. **2** *vi Comptr* trier; **s. on this field to a new file,** trier à partir de ce champ et sauvegarder les données réordonnées dans un nouveau fichier.
►**sort out** *vtsep* **(a)** (*eliminate by sorting*) trier, éliminer (par tri); **to s. out the foreign stamps from the British ones,** séparer les timbres étrangers des timbres britanniques;
(b) (*organize*) mettre de l'ordre dans (*papers, desk etc*); arranger (*problem*); débrouiller (*confusion etc*); **to s. oneself out,** (*organize life*) s'organiser; (*get ready*) se préparer; **give me a few minutes to get (myself) sorted out** *or* **to s. myself out,** donnez-moi quelques minutes pour me préparer; **to s. out who's sleeping where,** décider qui dort où; **to s. out a room/some clothes for s.o.,** (*allocate*) préparer une chambre/des vêtements pour qn; **I'll**

go and s. the tickets out, (*make arrangements for, obtain*) je vais m'occuper des billets;

(c) (*establish*) **we never sorted out what really happened,** nous n'avons jamais compris ce qui s'était vraiment passé; **let's s. out how much we owe you,** voyons combien nous vous devons;

(d) *F* (*put a stop to*) régler son compte à (*qn*); **two aspirins ought to s. out that headache,** deux aspirines devraient avoir raison de ce mal de tête.

▸sort through *vipo* (*search among*) faire du tri dans (*old clothes, papers etc*).

sorta ['sɔːtə] *F* = **sort of.**

sorter ['sɔːtər] *n* (*person*) trieur, -euse; (*who classifies*) classeur, -euse; (*device*) trieur (*de minerai etc*); trieuse (*de laine etc*); **(letter) s.,** trieur de lettres.

sortie ['sɔːtiː] *n Mil Av etc* sortie *f*; **I make the occasional s. to the shops,** je sors de temps à autre pour faire des achats.

sorting ['sɔːtɪŋ] *n* triage *m*, tri *m*; (*classifying*) classement *m*; **s. office,** (*in post office*) bureau *m ou* centre *m* de tri.

SOS [esəʊ'es] *n Rad* (*abbr* **save our souls**) S.O.S. *m*; **to send (out) an SOS,** envoyer un SOS; *Fig* **relief organizations are sending out an SOS for food and clothing,** les organisations d'aide demandent d'urgence de la nourriture et des vêtements; **SOS call,** appel *m* de détresse.

sot [sɒt] *n* ivrogne *m*, soûlard, -arde.

sottish ['sɒtɪʃ] *adj* (*person*) abruti par l'alcool; (*behaviour*) d'ivrogne.

sotto voce [sɒtəʊ'vəʊtʃɪ] *adv* (*parler etc*) tout bas.

soufflé ['suːfleɪ] *n Culin* soufflé *m*; **cheese s.,** soufflé au fromage.

sough[1] [saʊ] *n Lit* murmure *m* (*du vent etc*).

sough[2] *vi Lit* (*of wind etc*) murmurer.

sought *see* **SEEK.**

sought-after ['sɔːtɑːftər] *adj* (*job, car etc*) recherché.

soul [səʊl] *n* **(a)** âme *f*; **to throw oneself body and s. into sth,** se donner corps et âme à qch; *Old-fashioned* **upon my s.!,** sur mon âme!; **he's the s. of discretion,** il est la discrétion même; **departed souls,** les âmes des trépassés *ou* des disparus; **to pray for s.o.'s s.,** prier pour l'âme de qn; *Fig* **this music/drama's got no s.,** cette musique/ce théâtre n'a pas d'âme; **God rest her s.!,** que Dieu ait son âme!; **All Souls' Day,** la Fête des Morts;

(b) (*person*) âme *f*; **population of two thousand souls,** population *f* de deux mille âmes; **without meeting a (living) s.,** sans rencontrer âme qui vive; **there wasn't a s. in the street,** il n'y avait pas un chat dans la rue; **he's a good s.,** c'est une bonne âme; **she's a happy s.,** elle a un tempérament heureux *ou* optimiste; **poor s.!** le *ou* la pauvre!; **poor little s.!,** pauvre petit(e)!;

(c) **s. (music),** soul *m*, soul music *f*; *esp US* **s. brother/sister,** frère *m*/sœur *f*; **s. food,** = nourriture traditionnelle des Noirs américains; **s. singer,** chanteur, -euse de blues.

soul-destroying ['səʊldɪstrɔɪŋ] *adj* (*emploi etc*) abrutissant, d'une monotonie mortelle.

soulful ['səʊlfʊl] *adj* plein d'âme; (*musique*) qui touche l'âme; (*sentimental*) sentimental, -aux; **s. eyes,** yeux expressifs.

soulfully ['səʊlfəlɪ] *adv* (*chanter*) avec âme, de façon éloquente; (*sentimentally*) sentimentalement.

soulless ['səʊllɪs] *adj* **(a)** (*person*) sans âme; **(b)** (*emploi*) abrutissant.

soulmate ['səʊlmeɪt] *n* âme *f* sœur.

soul-searching ['səʊlsɜːtʃɪŋ] *n* examen *m* de conscience; **after a lot of s.-s.,** après un profond examen de conscience.

soul-stirring ['səʊlstɜːrɪŋ] *adj* émouvant.

sound[1] [saʊnd] *n Phys Mus etc* son *m*; (*of door, car engine, wind etc*) bruit *m*; **it recognizes the s. of your voice,** il *ou* elle reconnaît le son de votre voix; **there was not a s. to be heard,** on n'entendait pas le moindre bruit; **the s. of a dog barking,** le bruit d'un chien qui aboie; **musical s.,** son musical; **every violin has its own s.,** chaque violon a sa propre sonorité; **vowel s.,** son vocalique; **within (the) s. of ...,** à portée du son de ...; *TV etc* **to turn up/turn down the s.,** augmenter/diminuer le volume; **I don't like the s. of it,** cela ne me dit rien qui vaille; **he's angry by the s. of it,** on dirait bien qu'il est fâché; *F* **today's sounds,** (*music*) les sons d'aujourd'hui; *Phys* **s. wave,** onde *f* sonore; *Av* **s. barrier,** mur *m* du son; **s. recording,** enregistrement *m* du son; **s. effects,** effets *mpl* sonores, bruitage *m*; **s. effects man,** bruiteur *m*; **s. engineer,** ingénieur *m* du son; **s. board,** table *f* d'harmonie (*de piano*); tamis *m* (*d'orgue*); abat-voix *m inv* (*de chaire etc*); **s. box,** caisse *f* de résonance (*d'un instrument à cordes*); diaphragme *m* (*de phonographe*); **s. hole,** ouïe *f* (*de violon, de guitare*); esse *f* (*de violon*).

sound[2] **1** *vi* **(a)** (*make sound*) sonner, résonner; (*resound*) retentir; **the trumpet was sounding,** la trompette sonnait; **there are notes on this piano that don't s.,** ce piano a des notes qui ne sonnent pas;

(b) (*seem*) paraître, sembler; **name that sounds French,** nom qui sonne français; **she sounds French,** elle a l'air d'être française; **the translation still sounds a bit French,** la traduction sent toujours le français *ou* sonne toujours un peu français; **it still sounds a bit wrong,** (*of words, music*) ça sonne encore un peu faux; **that sounds odd!,** voilà qui paraît *ou* semble étrange *ou* bizarre!; **what about an omelette? — that sounds good!,** que dirais-tu d'une omelette? — bonne idée!; **'attractive four-bedroomed house' — how does that s.?,** 'belle maison avec quatre chambres à coucher' — qu'est-ce que tu en penses?; **their suggestion sounds interesting,** leur suggestion semble intéressante; **how does that s. to you?,** (*referring to suggestion*) qu'est-ce que tu en dis?; **she sounded interested/happy,** elle semblait intéressée/heureuse; **the noise sounded a long way off,** le bruit semblait venir de loin; **it sounds like Mozart,** on dirait du Mozart; **he doesn't s. like a man to ...,** d'après ce que vous dites il ne serait pas homme à ... .

2 *vt* **(a)** sonner (*le tocsin etc*); donner (*l'alerte*); **to s. the alarm,** donner l'alerte; **to s. the trumpet,** sonner la trompette; *Aut* **to s. one's horn,** appuyer sur l'avertisseur; *Mil* **to s. the retreat,** sonner la retraite; *Lit* **to s. s.o.'s praises,** chanter les louanges de qn;

(b) (*pronounce*) prononcer (*une lettre*); **the h is not sounded,** l'h ne se prononce pas *ou* est muet;

(c) *Med* ausculter (*qn, la poitrine*); (*by percussion*) percuter (*la poitrine*); *Rail etc* vérifier (*une roue*) au marteau; **he sounded my chest,** il m'a ausculté.

sound[3] *n Med* sonde *f*.

sound[4] **1** *vt* **(a)** *Nau* sonder, prendre *ou* trouver le fond; **(b)** *Med* sonder (*une plaie*); **(c)** = **SOUND OUT**; **to s. public opinion,** sonder l'opinion publique. **2** *vi* **(a)** *Nau* sonder; **(b)** (*of whale*) plonger au fond.

sound[5] *n* (*channel*) détroit *m*, goulet *m*, bras *m* de mer; **the S.,** le Sund.

sound[6] **1** *adj* **(a)** (*person, animal*) sain; (*horse*) sans tare; (*thing*) (*in good condition*) en bon état; (*not damaged*) non endommagé; (*solid*) solide; (*wood*) sans tare; (*fruit*) sain; **s. in body and mind,** sain de corps et d'esprit; **of s. mind,** sain d'esprit; *F* **to be s. in wind and limb,** (*of person*) avoir bon pied bon œil; **I'm as s. as a bell,** je suis en parfaite santé; **s. financial position,** situation financière solide; **s. business,** entreprise saine *ou* solide;

(b) (*argument*) valide, irréfutable; (*politique etc*) sage; (*raisonnement*) juste; (*investissement*) sûr; (*recherches, introduction*) solide, fiable; (*goalkeeper*) bon, fiable; **ecologically s. legislation,** législation *f* juste au point de vue écologique; **s. doctrines,** doctrines saines; (*orthodox*) doctrines orthodoxes; **s. piece of advice,** bon conseil; *Jur* **s. title,** titre valable *ou* valide *ou* légal; **he's pretty s. on his grammar,** il a de bonnes bases en grammaire; **it makes good s. sense,** c'est tout à fait raisonnable;

(c) **s. sleep,** sommeil profond; **I'm a s. sleeper,** je dors bien; **to give s.o. a s. thrashing,** administrer une bonne correction à qn.

2 *adv* **to be s. asleep,** être profondément endormi, dormir à poings fermés.

▸sound off *vi F* **(a)** (*express opinions forcefully, complain*) **to s. off about sth,** faire de grands laïus sur qch; **she's always sounding off about rude shop assistants,** elle est toujours en train de se plaindre des vendeuses peu aimables; **(b)** (*be angry*) **to s. off at s.o.,** engueuler qn.

▸sound out *vtsep* (*ascertain opinion, allegiance of*) sonder (*qn*); (*seek information from*) essayer d'obtenir des renseignements de (*qn*).

sounder ['saʊndər] *n Nau* sondeur *m*.

sounding[1] ['saʊndɪŋ] *n* **(a)** son *m*, résonnement *m*, retentissement *m* (*d'un tambour etc*); *Mil* **the s. of the retreat,** le signal de la retraite; **s. board,** abat-voix *m inv* (*de chaire etc*); table *f* d'harmonie (*de piano*); tamis *m* (*d'orgue*); *Fig* **it's nice to have a s. board sometimes,** quelquefois, c'est bien d'avoir quelqu'un sur qui on peut essayer des idées; **(b)** *Med* auscultation *f*.

sounding[2] *n* **(a)** *Nau* (*act*) sondage *m*; *Met* sondage; **echo s.,** sondage par ultra-sons; **s. line,** (ligne *f* de) sonde *f*; **s. lead** [led], (plomb *m* de) sonde; **(b)** *Nau* **soundings,** (*measurements*) sondages *mpl*; (*bottom*) fonds *mpl*; **to take soundings,** sonder, prendre le fond; *Fig* sonder.

soundless ['saʊndlɪs] *adj* muet, silencieux.

soundlessly ['saʊndlɪslɪ] *adv* silencieusement, sans bruit.

soundly ['saʊndlɪ] *adv* **(a)** sainement; (*wisely*) judicieusement; (*solidly*) solidement; (*to invest*) sûrement; **he argued s.,** son argumentation était solide; **(b)** (*dormir*) profondément; **to thrash s.o. s.,** administrer une bonne correction à qn; *Sp* **we were s. beaten,** on nous a battus à plate(s) couture(s).

soundness ['saʊndnɪs] *n* **(a)** état sain (*de l'esprit*); bon état, bonne condition (*des marchandises etc*); solidité *f* (*d'une entreprise*); (*solvency*) solvabilité *f*; **(b)** solidité (*d'un argument etc*); justesse *f* (*d'un jugement*); sagesse *f* (*d'un conseil, d'une politique*); orthodoxie *f* (*d'une doctrine*).

soundproof¹ ['saʊndpruːf] *adj* (*room etc*) insonorisé; (*material*) insonore.

soundproof² *vt* insonoriser (*une pièce etc*).

soundproofing ['saʊndpruːfɪŋ] *n* insonorisation *f*.

soundtrack ['saʊndtræk] *n Cin* bande *f ou* piste *f* sonore; **s. (album),** (*record*) bande originale.

soup¹ [suːp] *n* soupe *f*; (*thinner*) potage *m*; *F* (*fog*) brouillard *m* (épais); **cream s.,** velouté *m*; **onion s.,** soupe à l'oignon; *F* **to be in the s.,** être dans le pétrin; *F* **to land s.o. in the s.,** mettre qn dans le pétrin; **s. kitchen,** (*for homeless*) soupe populaire; **s. ladle,** louche *f*; **s. plate,** assiette creuse; **s. spoon,** cuillère *f* à soupe; **s. tureen,** soupière *f*.

▶**soup up** *vtsep F* (*make more powerful*) gonfler (*un moteur*).

soupçon ['suːpsɒn] *n* soupçon *m*, pointe *f* (*d'ail, Fig de sarcasme etc*).

souper ['suːpər] *n esp Br F* **pea s.,** (*fog*) purée *f* de pois, brouillard *m* (jaune) à couper au couteau.

sour¹ ['saʊər] *adj* **(a)** (*fruit etc*) aigre, acide; (*lait, crème, pain etc*) aigre; (*vin*) suret, verjuté; (*soil*) trop humide; **to turn s.,** (*of situation, relationship*) tourner à l'aigre, *F* tourner au vinaigre; (*of food*) (s')aigrir, surir; **to turn sth s.,** (faire) aigrir qch; **to smell s.,** sentir l'aigre; **the plan went s. on him,** (*lost its appeal*) le projet a perdu son charme pour lui; (*went wrong*) le projet a mal tourné pour lui; *Culin* **s. cream,** crème *f* aigre; **(b)** (*of person*) revêche, aigre; **he's s. about being left out,** il est amer parce qu'on l'a laissé à l'écart; *F* **it was just s. grapes that made her say that,** elle a simplement dit ça par rancœur.

sour² **1** *vi* surir, (s')aigrir; **her temper has soured,** son caractère s'est aigri. **2** *vt* aigrir (*le lait, le caractère etc*); *Culin* **soured cream,** crème *f* aigre; **soured by misfortune,** (*person*) aigri par le malheur; **these events have soured their relationship,** ces événements ont aigri leur relation.

source [sɔːs] *n* source *f* (*d'un fleuve, de malheurs etc*); foyer *m* (*de chaleur, d'infection etc*); **light s.,** source lumineuse; **a good s. of vitamin C.,** une bonne source de vitamine C; **the book is a good s. of information about ...,** ce livre est une bonne source d'informations sur ...; **the Rhone has its s. in the Alps,** le Rhône prend sa source dans les Alpes; **I have it from a good s.,** je le sais *ou* tiens de bonne source *ou* de source sûre; **a historian's sources,** les sources d'un historien; *Comptr* **s. document,** document *m* de base; *Comptr* **s. language,** langage *m* source; (*in translation, interpreting*) langue *f* de départ; **s. materials,** matériaux *mpl* (*d'un livre etc*); *Comptr* **s. program,** programme *m* source.

sour-dough ['saʊədəʊ] *n* **s.-d. loaf,** pain *m* au levain.

sourface ['saʊəfeɪs] *n F* = **SOURPUSS.**

sourfaced ['saʊəfeɪst] *adj* au visage morose *ou* revêche.

sourly ['saʊəlɪ] *adv* (*répondre*) aigrement; (*regarder qn*) d'un air revêche.

sourness ['saʊənɪs] *n* **(a)** aigreur *f*, acidité *f* (*d'un fruit etc*); aigreur (*du lait*); **(b)** aigreur (*de qn*).

sourpuss ['saʊəpʊs] *n F* personne morose *ou* revêche; (*kill-joy*) rabat-joie *m inv*.

sousaphone ['suːsəfəʊn] *n Mus* sousaphone *m*.

souse¹ [saʊs] *n Culin* saumure *f*, marinade *f*.

souse² *vt* plonger, immerger (**in,** dans); *Culin* faire mariner (*le poisson*); **to s. sth with water,** arroser qch d'eau.

soused *adj* ['saʊst] **(a)** *Culin* mariné; **s. herrings,** harengs marinés; **(b)** *Sl* (*drunk*) rond, bourré.

south [saʊθ] **1** *n* sud *m*, midi *m*; le sud, le midi (*d'un pays*); **house facing (the) s.,** maison (exposée) au sud *ou* au midi; **to the s. (of sth),** au sud (de qch); **the S. of France,** le Midi (de la France); *US Hist* **the S.,** les États *mpl* du sud (des États-Unis).

2 *adv* au sud; (*voyager*) vers le sud; **s. of a place,** (*être situé*) au sud d'un endroit; **to face s.,** (*of building etc*) faire face au sud; **s. by east,** sud-quart-sud-est; **s. by west,** sud-quart-sud-ouest; **to go s.,** aller dans le sud *ou* dans le midi.

3 *adj* sud *inv*; (*vent*) du sud; (*pays*) du sud, méridional, -aux; (*mur, fenêtre*) qui fait face au sud; **S. Africa,** l'Afrique *f* du Sud; **S. African,** sud-africain; (*person*) Sud-africain, -aine; **S. America,** Amérique *f* du Sud; **S. American,** (*climate, flora, tradition etc*) sud-américain, de l'Amérique du Sud; (*person*) Sud-Américain, -aine; **the s. coast,** la côte sud; **the S. Pole,** le pôle sud; **the S. Pacific,** le Pacifique sud; **the S. Seas,** les mers *fpl* du Sud; **the S. Sea Islands,** l'Océanie *f*; **s. side,** côté *m* sud; **on the s. side,** du côté du sud; **on the s. side of sth,** au sud de qch.

southbound ['saʊθbaʊnd] *adj* (*train etc*) allant vers le sud; (*from big city etc*) en direction de la banlieue sud.

southeast [saʊθ'iːst] **1** *n* sud-est *m*; *Nau* suet *m*. **2** *adv* au sud-est; (*voyager*) vers le sud-est; **s. by east,** sud-est-quart-est; **s. by south,** sud-est-quart-sud. **3** *adj* du sud-est; **the S. Asian Treaty Organisation,** Organisation *f* du Traité de l'Asie du Sud-Est, O.T.A.S.E.

southeasterly [saʊθ'iːstəlɪ] **1** *adj* (*vent etc*) du sud-est; (*quartier etc*) (du *ou* au) sud-est; (*direction*) vers le sud-est. **2** *adv* vers le sud-est.

southeastern [saʊθ'iːstən] *adj* (du) sud-est.

southerly ['sʌðəlɪ] **1** *adj* (*vent*) du sud, qui vient du sud; (*direction*) vers le sud; (*courant*) qui se dirige vers le sud; **s. point,** point situé au sud *ou* vers le sud; **the most southerly point of the United States,** le point situé le plus au sud des États-Unis; **s. aspect,** (*of house*) exposition *f* au midi *ou* au sud; *Nau* **to steer a s. course,** faire route au sud; (*change course*) mettre le cap au sud. **2** *adv* vers le sud.

southern ['sʌðən] *adj* **(a)** (*cooking, people, climate*) (du) sud, du midi; (*country, climate, temperament*) méridional, -aux; (*region of the world, hemisphere*) austral, -aux; **S. Italy,** l'Italie *f* du sud; **the countries of S. Europe,** les pays de l'Europe méridionale; **the s. hemisphere,** l'hémisphère sud *ou* austral; **s. lights,** aurore australe; *Astron* **the S. Cross,** la Croix du Sud; **(b)** *US Hist* (*armée etc*) sudiste.

southerner ['sʌðənər] *n* **(a)** habitant, -ante du sud, méridional, -ale; **(b)** *US Hist* sudiste *mf*.

south-facing ['saʊθfeɪsɪŋ] *adj* (*window, building etc*) qui fait face au sud, qui est orienté vers le sud.

southpaw ['saʊθpɔː] *n Boxing etc* gaucher, -ère.

south-south-east, *Nau* **sou'sou'east** [saʊ(θ)-saʊ(θ)'iːst] **1** *adj & n* sud-sud-est *m*. **2** *adv* au sud-sud-est; (*voyager*) vers le sud-sud-est.

south-south-west, *Nau* **sou'sou'west** [saʊ(θ)-saʊ(θ)'west] **1** *adj & n* sud-sud-ouest *m*; *Nau* susuroît *m*. **2** *adv* au sud-sud-ouest; (*voyager*) vers le sud-sud-ouest

southward ['saʊθwəd] **1** *n* sud *m*; **to the s.,** vers le sud. **2** *adj* au *ou* du sud. **3** *adv* **s. bound,** allant vers le sud.

southwards ['saʊθwədz] *adv* vers le sud.

southwest, *Nau* **sou'west** [saʊ(θ)'west] **1** *n* sud-ouest *m*; *Nau* suroît *m*. **2** *adv* au sud-ouest; (*voyager*) vers le sud-ouest; **s. by west,** sud-ouest-quart-ouest; **s. by south,** sud-ouest-quart-sud. **3** *adj* du sud-ouest; **s. wind,** vent *m* (du) sud-ouest.

southwesterly, *Nau* **sou'westerly** [saʊ(θ)'westəlɪ] **1** *adj* (*vent etc*) du sud-ouest; (*quartier etc*) (du *ou* au) sud-ouest; (*direction*) vers le sud-ouest. **2** *adv* vers le sud-ouest.

southwestern [saʊθ'westən] *adj* (du) sud-ouest.

souvenir [suːvə'nɪər] *n* souvenir *m*; **s. shop,** boutique *f* de souvenirs.

sou'wester [saʊ'westər] *n* **(a)** *Nau* (vent *m* du) sud-ouest *m*; **(b)** (*hat*) suroît *m*, ciré *m*.

sovereign ['sɒvrɪn] **1** *adj* souverain, suprême; **the s. good,** le bien souverain; **s. rights,** droits *mpl* de souveraineté. **2** *n* **(a)** (*monarch*) souverain, -aine, monarque *m*; **(b)** *Arch Br* (*coin*) = souverain *m* (*pièce d'or de la valeur d'une livre*).

sovereignty ['sɒvrəntɪ] *n* souveraineté *f*.

soviet ['səʊvɪət] **1** *n* **(a)** (*council*) soviet *m*; **Supreme S.,** Soviet suprême; **(b) the Soviets,** les Soviétiques *mpl*. **2** *adj* soviétique; **the Union of S. Socialist Republics, the S. Union,** l'Union *f* des Républiques socialistes soviétiques, l'Union soviétique.

sovietization [səʊvɪətaɪ'zeɪʃən] *n* soviétisation *f*.

sow¹ [səʊ] *v* (*pt* **sowed** [səʊd]; *pp* **sown** [səʊn], **sowed**) **1** *vt* semer (*des graines, un champ*); **to s. a field with wheat,** ensemencer un champ de blé; **to s. (the seeds of) discord/doubt,** semer la discorde/le doute. **2** *vi* semer.

sow² [saʊ] *n* (*female pig*) truie *f*; (*wild*) laie *f*.

sower ['səʊər] *n* (*person*) semeur, -euse; (*device*) semoir *m*.

sowing ['səʊɪŋ] *n* (*period*) semailles *fpl*; (*result*) semis *m*; (*task*) ensemencement *m*; **s. time** *or* **season,** (saison *f* des) semailles.

sox [sɒks] *npl Am* = **socks,** *see* **SOCK⁴**.

soy [sɔɪ] *n Culin* **s. sauce,** sauce *f* au *ou* de soya.

soya ['sɔɪə] *n* **s. (bean),** soya *m*, soja *m*; **s. flour/oil,** farine *f*/huile *f* de soja; *Culin* **s. sauce,** sauce *f* au soya.

soybean ['sɔɪbiːn] *n Am* graine *f* de soja.

sozzled ['sɒz(ə)ld] *adj Sl* (*drunk*) rond, bourré; **to get s.,** se soûler.

spa [spɑː] *n* (*spring*) source thermale; (*in sports centre, health farm etc*) spa *m*; **s. (town),** station thermale.

space¹ [speɪs] *n* **(a)** espace *m*; (*room*) place *f*; **he sat staring into s.,** il était assis le regard perdu dans le vide *ou* dans l'espace; **open spaces,** (*green*) espaces verts; (*not built on*) étendues non bâties; **wide open spaces,** grands espaces; **living s.,** espace vital; **in a confined s.,** dans un espace restreint; **to sell s. (in a newspaper),** vendre de l'espace (dans un journal); **to take up a lot of s.,** prendre *ou* occuper beaucoup de place; **there's no s. left,** il n'y a plus de place; *esp Am* **s. heater,** chauffage *m* d'appoint; *F* **s. saver,** gagne-place *m*, *pl* gagne-places;

(b) *Astronaut* **the conquest of s.,** la conquête de l'espace; **outer s.,** espace *m* extra-atmosphérique; **s. age,** ère *f* de l'exploration spatiale; **s. blanket,** couverture *f* de survie; **s. flight,** vol *ou* voyage spatial; **s. invaders** ®, envahisseurs venus de l'espace; **s. travel,** voyages *mpl* dans l'espace; (*science*) astronautique *f*; **s. rocket,** fusée spatiale *ou* interplanétaire; **s. shot,** lancement *m* d'engin dans l'espace; **s. shuttle,** navette spatiale; **s. suit,** scaphandre *m* d'astronaute; **s. station,** station spatiale;

(c) (*free area, place*) espace *m* libre; (*interval*) espacement *m*, intervalle *m*; (*between lines of writing etc*) interligne *m*; *Typ* espace blanc; **blank s.,** (*on form etc*) (endroit *m* en) blanc *m*, espace; **a free (parking) space,** une place de parking libre; (*on typewriter*) **s. between letters,** intervalle entre les lettres; **s. bar,** barre *f* d'espacement; **s. rule,** filet *m* maigre;

(d) (*period*) espace *m*, intervalle *m* (*de temps*); **in the s. of a year,** dans *ou* en l'espace d'un an; **after a short s. of time,** après un court intervalle.

space² *vt* espacer (*des arbres, des mots, des visites*); échelonner (*des troupes, des paiements etc*); **evenly spaced,** régulièrement espacés; **the posts are spaced ten feet apart,** les poteaux sont plantés à dix pieds d'intervalle.

►space out *vtsep* **(a)** (*arrange at intervals*) = **SPACE²**; **(b)** *Sl* **to be spaced out,** (*under influence of drugs*) être parti, être déchiré; (*naturally*) planer.

space-age ['speɪseɪdʒ] *adj* de l'an 2000 (*la technologie etc*).

spacecraft ['speɪskrɑːft] *n* véhicule *ou* vaisseau spatial, astronef *m*.

spacelab ['speɪslæb] *n Astronaut* laboratoire spatial.

spaceman, *pl* **-men** ['speɪsmæn, -men] *n* **(a)** (*astronaut*) astronaute *m*; (*cosmonaut*) cosmonaute *m*; **(b)** (*in science fiction*) habitant *m* de l'espace.

spacer ['speɪsər] *n* **(a)** *Typ* espace *f*; **(b)** (*on typewriter*) barre *f* d'espacement; **back s.,** rappel *m* de chariot, rappel arrière; **(c)** *MecE* pièce *f* d'écartement, écarteur *m*.

space-saving ['speɪsseɪvɪŋ] *adj* qui permet de gagner de la place; (*meuble etc*) compact.

spaceship ['speɪsʃɪp] *n* véhicule *ou* vaisseau spatial, astronef *m*.

space-time ['speɪstaɪm] *n Phys* espace-temps *m*.

spacewalk ['speɪswɔːk] *n Astronaut* marche *f* dans l'espace.

spacewoman ['speɪswʊmən] *n* **(a)** (*astronaut*) astronaute *f*; (*cosmonaut*) cosmonaute *f*; **(b)** (*in science fiction*) habitante *f* de l'espace.

spacing ['speɪsɪŋ] *n* espacement *m*, écartement *m* (*des arbres etc*); *Typ* espacement (*des lettres, des lignes*); (*with typewriter*) **in single/double s.,** à simple/double interligne.

spacious ['speɪʃəs] *adj* (*kitchen, house, car boot*) spacieux, vaste; (*clothes*) ample.

spaciousness ['speɪʃəsnɪs] *n* vaste étendue *f*; dimensions spacieuses (*d'une maison, d'un coffre etc*); ampleur *f* (*d'un vêtement*).

spade¹ [speɪd] *n* (*tool*) bêche *f*; (*child's*) pelle *f*; **to call a s. a s.,** appeler les choses par leur nom, appeler un chat un chat.

spade² *vt* bêcher (*la terre etc*).

spade³ *n* **(a)** *Cards* pique *m*; **ace of spades,** as *m* de pique; **to play a s., to play spades,** jouer pique; **(b)** *Offensive Sl* (*negro*) nègre, *f* négresse.

spadeful ['speɪdfʊl] *n* pelletée *f*.

spadework ['speɪdwɜːk] *n* **(a)** (*with spade*) travaux *mpl* à la bêche; **(b)** *Fig* travaux préliminaires.

spaghetti [spə'getɪ] *n Culin* spaghetti *mpl*; *El F* (*cables, wires*) souplisseau *m*; *Br F* **s. junction,** échangeur *m* sur plusieurs niveaux; *Cin* **s. western,** western *m* spaghetti.

Spain [speɪn] *n* Espagne *f*.

span¹ [spæn] *n* **(a)** empan *m* (*de la main*); **wing s.,** (*of bird, aircraft*) envergure *f*; portée *f* (*entre deux appuis*); largeur *f* (*d'une arche*); écartement *m* (*de deux piliers*); volant *m* (*d'une poutre*); travée *f* (*d'un pont, d'un comble*); **single s. bridge,** pont *m* à travée unique; **the vast s. of her knowledge,** la vaste étendue *ou* portée de son savoir; **the whole s. of human activity,** toute l'étendue de l'activité humaine; **(b)** petite étendue (*de terre*); *Lit* court espace de temps.

span² *vt* **(-nn-)** mesurer (*à l'empan*); encercler (*le poignet*) avec la main; (*of bridge etc*) franchir, traverser, enjamber (*une rivière etc*); **his life spans nearly the whole century,** sa vie embrasse presque tout le siècle.

span³ *n* (*pair*) paire *f*, couple *m* (*de chevaux, de bœufs*); (*in Africa*) attelage *m* (*de bœufs*).

spangle¹ ['spæŋg(ə)l] *n Tex etc* paillette *f*; (*large*) paillon *m*; **gold spangles,** paillettes d'or.

spangle² *vt* pailleter (**with,** de); **spangled with silver,** pailleté d'argent.

Spaniard ['spænɪəd] *n* Espagnol, -ole.

spaniel ['spænjəl] *n* épagneul *m*; **cocker/springer s.,** épagneul cocker/springer.

Spanish ['spænɪʃ] **1** *adj* espagnol; *Mus* **S. guitar,** guitare sèche de style espagnol; **S. inquisition,** (*Hist & Fig*) inquisition *f*; *Culin* **S. omelette,** omelette *f* à l'espagnole; **S. onion,** oignon *m* d'Espagne. **2** *n* **(a)** *Ling* espagnol *m*; **S. teacher,** professeur *m* d'espagnol; **(b) the S.,** (*used as pl*) les Espagnols *mpl*.

Spanish-American ['spænɪʃə'merɪkən] *adj* hispano-américain.

spank¹ [spæŋk] *n* claque *f* sur le derrière, fessée *f*.

spank² *vt* fesser (*un enfant*), administrer *ou* donner une fessée *ou* une claque sur le derrière à (*un enfant*).

►spank along *vi* (*go fast*) (*of horse etc*) aller bon train.

spanking ['spæŋkɪŋ] **1** *n* fessée *f*; **to give a child a s.,** donner une fessée à un enfant. **2** *adj* **(a)** *Old-fashioned F* (*excellent*) épatant; **(b) to go at a s. pace,** aller bon train. **3** *adv Old-fashioned F* **brand s. new,** flambant neuf; **a s. good time was had,** ou s'est diablement bien amusé.

spanner ['spænər] *n* clef *f*; **adjustable s.,** clef à molette; **box s.,** clef à douille *ou* à tire-fonds; *F* **to put** *or* **throw a s. in the works,** mettre des bâtons dans les roues.

spar¹ [spɑːr] *n* **(a)** *Nau* espar(t) *m*; *Av* **wing s.,** longeron *m* d'aile.

spar² *n Miner* spath *m*.

spar³ *n* **(a)** *Boxing* combat d'entraînement; (*minor fight*) escarmouche *f*; *F* (*argument*) prise *f* de bec; **(b)** (*cockfight*) combat *m* de coqs.

spar⁴ *vt* **(-rr-)** **(a)** (*of person*) **to s. with s.o.,** *Boxing* s'entraîner avec qn; (*argue*) argumenter avec qn; **(b)** (*of cocks*) se battre.

spare¹ ['speər] **1** *adj* **(a)** (*surplus*) de trop, de reste; (*free*) disponible; **is this bed s.?,** est-ce que ce lit est libre?; **that left a few hours s.,** ça a laissé quelques heures libres; **in my s. time,** à mes heures perdues; **I don't get much s. time,** je n'ai pas beaucoup de temps libre; **s. capital,** fonds *mpl* disponibles; **with the s. cash they bought a table,** avec l'argent qui leur restait ils ont acheté une table; **s. room,** chambre *f* d'ami(s); **we have a s. bed,** on peut vous offrir un lit (*pour la nuit*); *F* **is this cake going s.?,** voulez-vous que je vous débarrasse de ce gâteau?; *F* **if you have any tickets going s.,** si vous avez des tickets en trop;

(b) (*accessoires, vêtements*) de rechange; **s. parts,** pièces *fpl* de rechange, pièces détachées; **have you got a s. plastic bag?,** est-ce que tu as un sac en plastique qui ne te sert pas?; *Aut* **s. wheel,** roue *f* de secours; **s. tyre** *or Am* **tire,** pneu *m* de rechange; *Br F* (*around waist*) bourrelet *m* de graisse, pneu;

(c) (*frugal*) frugal, -aux; (*person*) sec, *f* sèche; **he was tall and s.,** il était grand et mince;

(d) *Br Sl* (*mad*) **to drive s.o. s.,** rendre qn dingue; **he'll go s. if he finds out,** il va être fou s'il apprend ça.

2 *n* (*spare part*) pièce *f* de rechange, pièce détachée; **I've lost my pencil — have you a s.?,** j'ai perdu mon crayon — en as-tu un à me prêter?

spare² *vt* **(a)** (*go without*) épargner, ménager; **to s. no expense,** ne pas regarder à la dépense; **to s. no pains,** se donner beaucoup de mal, ne pas épargner sa peine; **he spared no pains to please me,** il n'a pas épargné ses efforts pour me faire plaisir;

(b) (*go without*) se passer de (*qch*); **can you s. it?,** (*make sacrifice*) pouvez-vous vous en passer?; **we can't s. him,** il nous est indispensable, nous ne pouvons pas nous passer de lui; **to have nothing to s.,** n'avoir que le strict nécessaire, ne rien avoir de superflu; **to have enough and to s. (of sth),** avoir plus qu'il n'en faut (de qch), ne pas manquer de qch; **there is room to s.,** la place ne manque pas; **I cannot s. the time to finish it,** je n'ai pas le temps de le finir; **to have no time to s.,** ne pas avoir de temps de libre; **when I have time to s.,** quand j'ai des loisirs, quand j'ai du temps libre; **I have a minute to s.,** j'ai une minute de libre; **to catch a train with five minutes to s.,** prendre un train avec cinq minutes de battement; **we caught the plane with absolutely no time to s.,** nous avons attrappé l'avion vraiment de justesse; **don't worry, we'll have at least half an hour to s.,** ne t'en fais pas, nous aurons au minimum une demi-heure de battement; **to s. s.o. sth,** donner *ou* céder qch à qn; **can you s. me a hundred francs?,** pouvez-vous me prêter cent francs?; **can you s. a couple of people this afternoon?,** est-ce que je peux vous emprunter quelques personnes cet après-midi?; **can you s. me a few moments?,** pouvez-vous m'accorder quelques minutes?;

(c) (*show mercy towards*) faire grâce à (*qn*); ménager (*qn, son cheval*); **to s. s.o.'s life,** épargner la vie de qn; **s. me!,** grâce!, épargnez-moi!; **if she is spared,** si elle vit; **death spares no one,** la mort n'épargne personne; **the flood spared nothing,** l'inondation n'a rien épargné; **to s. s.o.'s feelings,** ménager qn, épargner qn; **tell me, don't s. my feelings,** dis-moi, n'essaye pas de me ménager; **the report spared no one,** le rapport ne ménageait personne; **s. my blushes!,** ne me faites pas rougir!; **I'll s. you the rest,** je vous fais grâce du reste; **he doesn't s. himself,** il ne se ménage pas;

(d) to s. s.o. the trouble of doing sth, éviter à qn la peine de faire qch; **you could have spared yourself/us the trouble,** vous auriez pu vous/nous éviter cette peine; **s. me the details!,** (*don't tell me*) épargne-moi les détails!

sparing ['speərɪŋ] *adj* (*frugal*) frugal; (*economical*) économe; (*merciful*) clément, miséricordieux; **to be s. with the butter,** ménager le beurre; *Lit* **he is s. of praise,** il est avare de louanges.

sparingly ['speərɪŋlɪ] *adv* frugalement; (*to eat*) sobrement; (*moderately*) modérément; **to use sth s.,** utiliser qch en petites quantités; **apply the cream s. on the affected area,** appliquer la crème en couche fine sur la région touchée.

spark[1] [spɑːk] *n* **(a)** étincelle *f*; (*from fire*) flammèche *f*; **the s. of life,** l'étincelle de la vie; **sparks flew,** des étincelles ont jailli; *Fig* ça a fait des étincelles; **s. of wit,** étincelle *ou* lueur *f* d'esprit; **he hasn't a s. of generosity in him,** il n'a pas la moindre parcelle de générosité; **(b)** *El etc* étincelle *f*; **s. discharge,** décharge disruptive; **s. gap,** *El* distance explosive *ou* d'éclatement; (*in engine*) pont *m* d'allumage; **s. ignition,** (*of engine*) allumage *m* par bougies; **s. plug,** bougie *f* (d'allumage); **(c)** *Nau Av F* **sparks,** le radio; (*electrician*) électricien *m*.

spark[2] *vi* émettre des étincelles; (*of dynamo etc*) cracher; **to s. across the terminals,** (*of current*) jaillir entre les bornes.

spark[3] *n F Iron* **you're a bright s.,** tu es vraiment malin!; *Old-fashioned* **gay s.,** gaillard *m*, noceur *m*.

►**spark off** *vtsep* (*initiate*) déclencher, provoquer (*une révolution, une réaction etc*); donner naissance à (*une idée etc*); **this remark sparked off a discussion about ...,** cette remarque a provoqué *ou* déclenché *ou* donné lieu à une discussion au sujet de ... .

sparking ['spɑːkɪŋ] *n* **(a)** émission *f* d'étincelles; (*accidental*) jaillissement *m* d'étincelles; **(b)** *Br Aut* **s. plug,** bougie *f* (d'allumage).

sparkle[1] ['spɑːk(ə)l] *n* **(a)** (*spot of light*) étincelle *f*; (*lasting only short time*) brève lueur; **not a s. of wit,** pas la moindre parcelle d'esprit; **(b)** (*act, state of sparkling*) étincellement *m*; éclat *m*, pétillement *m* (*des yeux*); feux *mpl* (*d'un diamant*); **wine that has lost its s.,** vin qui ne pétille plus; *Fig* **the s. had gone out of their marriage,** le charme avait disparu de leur mariage; *Fig* **he's got no s. about him,** il est plutôt terne; *Fig* **he's lost his s.,** il a perdu sa joie de vivre; **(c)** (*of mind*) vivacité *f* d'esprit.

sparkle[2] *vi* **(a)** (*of jewel, tinsel, metal, snow etc*) étinceler, scintiller; (*of surface*) miroiter; (*of wine*) pétiller, mousser; **her eyes sparkled (with joy),** ses yeux pétillaient *ou* brillaient (de joie); **sparkling with wit,** (*book*) qui pétille d'esprit; **(b)** (*of fire*) émettre des étincelles, pétiller.

sparkler ['spɑːklər] *n* **(a)** (*firework*) cierge *m* magique; **(b)** *F* (*diamond*) diamant *m*.

sparkling ['spɑːklɪŋ] **1** *adj* étincelant, brillant, miroitant; (*conversation*) brillant; (*vin*) mousseux, pétillant; (*limonade*) gazeux. **2** *n* étincellement *m*, scintillement *m*, pétillement *m*. **3** *adv* **s. clean,** étincelant de propreté, d'une propreté étincelante.

sparring ['spɑːrɪŋ] *n Boxing* entraînement *m*; (*arguing*) échanges verbaux; **it was just a little good-natured s.,** (*verbal*) ce n'était qu'une petite bagarre amicale; *Boxing* **s. partner,** partenaire *mf* d'entraînement, sparring partner *mf*; *Fig* adversaire favori, -ite.

sparrow ['spærəʊ] *n* (*bird*) moineau *m*; **hedge s.,** fauvette *f* d'hiver.

sparrowhawk ['spærəʊhɔːk] *n* (*bird*) épervier *m*.

sparse [spɑːs] *adj* (*trees, population*) clairsemé, épars, peu dense; **s. hair,** cheveux rares *ou* clairsemés; **s. vegetation,** végétation éparse.

sparsely ['spɑːslɪ] *adv* peu abondamment; **s. covered with trees,** aux arbres clairsemés; **s. populated,** peu peuplé.

sparseness ['spɑːsnɪs] *n* faible densité *f* (*de la population*); manque *m* (*de végétation*).

Sparta ['spɑːtə] *n* Sparte *f*.

Spartan ['spɑːtən] **1** *adj* spartiate; **s.,** austère (*environnement*); *Fig* **to lead a s. life,** vivre en spartiate, mener une vie austère *ou* de spartiate. **2** *n Hist* Spartiate *mf*; *Fig* spartiate.

spasm ['spæz(ə)m] *n Med* spasme *m*; *Fig* accès *m* (*de toux, de jalousie*); **to work in spasms,** travailler par à-coups; **after a sudden s. of feverish activity ...,** après un accès *ou* un à-coup soudain d'activité fébrile ... .

spasmodic [spæz'mɒdɪk] *adj Med* spasmodique; *Fig* (*irregular*) irrégulier; (*intermittent*) intermittent; **s. work,** travail fait par à-coups.

spasmodically [spæz'mɒdɪklɪ] *adv Med* spasmodiquement; *Fig* (*irregularly*) irrégulièrement; (*intermittently*) de façon intermittente; (*to work*) par à-coups.

spastic ['spæstɪk] **1** *adj Med* (*paralysie etc*) spasmodique; *Fig Sl* (*performance, attempt etc*) minable, nul. **2** *n* (*person*) handicapé(e) moteur.

spat[1] [spæt] *n* naissain *m* (*d'huîtres etc*).

spat[2] *n* (*on ankle*) demi-guêtre *f*, *pl* demi-guêtres

spat[3] *n Am F* (*quarrel*) querelle *f*.

spat[4] *vi* (**-tt-**) *Am F* (*quarrel*) se quereller avec qn.

spat[5] *see* **SPIT**[4].

spate [speɪt] *n* crue *f* (*d'une rivière*); *Fig* avalanche *f* (*de lettres etc*); torrent *m* (*d'injures*); **river in s.,** rivière en crue; **a s. of burglaries,** une série de cambriolages; **there's been a sudden s. of orders,** il y a eu une soudaine avalanche *ou* un soudain déluge de commandes.

spatial ['speɪʃəl] *adj Math Phys etc* spatial, -aux.

spatiotemporal [speɪʃɪəʊ'tempərəl] *adj* spatio-temporel.

spatter[1] ['spætər] *n* éclaboussure *f* (*de liquide*); (*d'huile, de graisse*) projection *f*; *Ind* projection *f* (*de soudure*).

spatter[2] **1** *vt* éclabousser (**with,** de); **the wall was spattered with grease,** le mur était couvert d'éclaboussures *ou* tout éclaboussé de graisse. **2** *vi* (*of liquid*) jaillir, gicler; **the rain spattering down on the pavement,** la pluie qui gicle sur le trottoir; **the tomato spattered against/all over the wall,** la tomate a giclé contre/partout sur le mur.

-spattered [-spætəd] *suff* **blood/mud/oil/***etc***-s.,** couvert d'éclaboussures de sang/de boue/d'huile *etc*.

spatula ['spætjʊlə] *n Pharm Surg etc* spatule *f*.

spatulate ['spætjʊleɪt] *adj Biol* spatulé.

spavin ['spævɪn] *n Vet* éparvin *m*.

spawn[1] [spɔːn] *n* **(a)** frai *m*, œufs *mpl* (*de grenouille, poisson etc*); *F* (*offspring*) progéniture *f*; **(b) mushroom s.,** blancs *mpl* de champignon, mycélium *m*.

spawn[2] **1** *vi* (*of fish etc*) frayer; *F* (*of person*) se multiplier. **2** *vt* (*of fish, frog etc*) déposer (*son frai, ses œufs*); *F* engendrer, donner naissance à (*qch*); **the organization/movement spawned various offshoots,** l'organisation/le mouvement a donné naissance à plusieurs ramifications.

spawning ['spɔːnɪŋ] *n* (le moment du) frai *m*; **s. ground,** frayère *f*; **s. season,** frai *m*.

spay [speɪ] *vt Vet* châtrer (*une femelle*).

spaying ['speɪɪŋ] *n* castration *f* (*d'une femelle*).

SPCK [espiːsiː'keɪ] *n Br Rel* (**Society for the Promoting of Christian Knowledge**) société *f* visant à promouvoir la connaissance chrétienne.

speak [spiːk] *v* (*pt* **spoke** [spəʊk]; *pp* **spoken** ['spəʊk(ə)n]) **1** *vi* **(a)** parler; (*of gun, organ etc*) parler; (*in* *hunting*) (*of dog*) donner de la voix; **can he s.?**, est-ce qu'il parle?, est-ce qu'il sait parler?; **without speaking,** sans parler, sans rien dire; **to s. to s.o.**, parler à qn (**about sth,** de qch); (*reprimand*) réprimander qn; **he spoke slowly/hesitatingly/too quickly,** il s'est exprimé *ou* il a parlé lentement/avec hésitation/trop rapidement; **she hasn't spoken to me since,** elle ne m'a pas adressé la parole depuis; **I can't give you a rise — you'll have to s. to the boss,** je ne peux pas vous donner une augmentation — il va falloir que vous vous adressiez au patron; **they're not speaking (to each other),** ils ne se parlent pas; **I'll s. to him about it,** je lui en toucherai un mot, je lui en parlerai; **I know her to s. to,** nous nous disons bonjour; **honestly speaking,** franchement; **roughly speaking,** approximativement; **legally/morally speaking,** légalement/moralement parlant; **so to s.**, pour ainsi dire; *Tel* **who's speaking?**, qui est à l'appareil?; (*before transferring call*) c'est de la part de qui?; **Mr Thomas? — yes, speaking,** M. Thomas? — lui-même; **to s. by signs,** (*of deaf, mute etc*) parler par gestes;

(b) (*give a speech*) faire un discours; **he spoke on the subject of ...,** il a parlé *ou* traité de ...; **to have the right to s.**, avoir le droit de se faire entendre, avoir droit à la parole.

2 *vt* **(a)** dire (*un mot, la vérité*); **not to s. a word,** ne pas dire un mot; **she has never spoken a word to me,** elle ne m'a jamais adressé la parole, elle ne m'a jamais dit un mot; **he didn't s. a word about it,** il n'en a pas soufflé mot; **to s. one's mind,** dire ce qu'on pense;

(b) (*show*) indiquer (*qch*), témoigner de (*qch*); **eyes that s. affection,** yeux qui témoignent de l'amitié;

(c) parler (*une langue*); **do you s. French?**, parlez-vous français?; **English is spoken everywhere,** l'anglais se parle partout; **English spoken,** (*on sign*) on parle anglais.

▶**speak against** *vipo* (*in debate*) parler contre.

▶**speak for** *vipo* **(a)** (*speak on behalf of*) parler pour (*qn*); (*speak in support of*) plaider pour (*qn*); (*in debate*) parler pour; **I'm sure I s. for everyone when I say ...,** je suis sûr que j'exprime la pensée générale lorsque je dis ...; **speaking for myself,** pour ma part, en ce qui me concerne; *F* **s. for yourself!**, parle pour toi!; **the facts s. for themselves,** ces faits se passent de commentaires *ou* parlent d'eux-mêmes; **that speaks well for her courage,** cela fait honneur à son courage; **(b) to be spoken for,** (*to be reserved*) être réservé; (*of man, woman*) (*at dance etc*) être accompagné; (*have girlfriend, boyfriend etc*) avoir un(e) petit(e) ami(e).

▶**speak of** *vipo* **(a)** (*talk about*) parler de (*qch*); **speaking of ...,** à propos de ..., en parlant de ...; **it's nothing to s. of,** (*it's nothing much*) ce n'est rien; (*it's not worth talking about*) cela ne vaut pas la peine d'en parler; **there's nothing to s. of on television/in the town,** il n'y a rien de spécial à la télévision/en ville; **to s. well/highly of s.o./sth,** dire du bien/beaucoup de bien de qn/qch; **he is well spoken of,** il a une bonne réputation, on dit du bien de lui; **to s. ill of s.o.**, dire du mal de qn, médire de qn; **(b)** (*indicate*) être significatif de (*qch*); **this speaks of large-scale corruption,** cela est significatif d'une corruption à grande échelle.

▶**speak out** *vi* **(a)** (*speak with courage*) oser parler, oser prendre la parole, ne pas avoir peur de prendre la parole; **(b)** (*speak loudly*) parler fort *ou* à haute voix.

▶**speak up** *vi* **(a)** (*speak louder*) parler plus fort *ou* plus haut; **(b)** (*take active part in discussion etc*) prendre la parole, participer à une discussion; **she speaks up in class/meetings,** elle prend la parole en classe/lors de réunions; **(c)** = **SPEAK OUT (a)**.

▶**speak up for** *vipo* (*speak in favour of*) parler en faveur de (*qn*).

speakeasy [ˈspiːkiːzɪ] *n US* débit *ou* bar clandestin.

speaker [ˈspiːkər] *n* **(a)** parleur, -euse; (*in dialogue*) interlocuteur, -trice; **as a s. of Italian myself ...,** moi qui parle italien ...; **there are very few surviving speakers of the language,** il reste très peu de personnes qui parlent cette langue; **I'm a plain s.**, j'appelle les choses par leur nom, je dis ce que je pense, je dis les choses comme elles sont; **(b)** (*in public*) orateur *m*; **to be a fluent/good s.**, avoir la parole facile/avoir le don de la parole; **the next s. will be ...,** la parole est maintenant à ...; **(c)** *Parl* **the S.**, = le Président (des Communes); **(d)** *Electron* haut-parleur *m*, *pl* haut-parleurs.

speaking [ˈspiːkɪŋ] **1** *adj* (*doll etc*) parlant; *Br Telecom* **s. clock,** horloge parlante. **2** *n* parler *m*, discours *m*, parole *f*; **plain s.**, franchise *f*, franc-parler *m*; **public s.**, l'art *m* oratoire; **unaccustomed as I am to public s.**, bien que je n'aie pas l'habitude de parler en public; **we're no longer on s. terms,** nous sommes brouillés, nous ne nous parlons plus; **s. tube,** tube *m* acoustique; *Nau etc* porte-voix *m inv*; *Av* aviophone *m*.

-speaking *suff* **Chinese/Spanish/Tamil/***etc***-s.**, qui parle le chinois/l'espagnol/le tamoul *etc*; **English-s.**, (*as mother tongue*) de langue anglaise, anglophone; (*as learnt language*) qui parle anglais; **French-s.**, de langue française, francophone; qui parle français; **slow-s.**, qui s'exprime lentement; **plain-s.**, qui appelle les choses par leur nom.

spear[1] [ˈspɪər] *n* **(a)** lance *f*; (*in hunting*) épieu *m*; (*for throwing*) javelot *m*; **(b)** *Fishing* harpon *m*; **s. gun,** fusil *m* à harpon; **s. fishing,** pêche *f ou* chasse *f* (sous-marine) au harpon.

spear[2] *vt* **(a)** transpercer *ou* (*kill*) tuer (*qn*) d'un coup de lance; piquer (*une olive etc, avec une fourchette etc*); **(b)** *Fishing* harponner (*un poisson*).

spear[3] *n* brin *m* (*d'herbe*); jet *m*, tige *f* (*d'osier*); **spears of asparagus, asparagus spears,** pointes *fpl* d'asperges.

spearhead[1] [ˈspɪəhed] *n* (*of spear*) fer *m ou* pointe *f* de lance; *Mil* (*of attack*) pointe *f*; *Fig* (*of organization etc*) fer de lance; **to launch a s. against ...,** pousser une pointe sur ....

spearhead[2] *vt Mil* **they spearheaded the crossing of the river,** ils ont forcé les premiers le passage du fleuve; *Fig* **to s. a movement,** être le fer de lance d'un mouvement.

spearmint [ˈspɪəmɪnt] *n* (*plant, flavour*) menthe verte; (*chewing gum*) chewing gum *m* à la menthe verte.

spec [spek] *n F* **(a) we've got it on s. for a week,** on l'a à l'essai pour une semaine; **to buy sth on s.**, acheter qch à tout hasard; **(b)** *Ind* **specs,** spécifications *fpl*.

special [ˈspeʃəl] **1** *adj* spécial, -aux, particulier (**to,** à); (*ami*) intime; *Com Ind* (*article*) hors série; **nothing s.**, rien de particulier; **the food was OK but nothing s.**, la nourriture était assez bonne mais n'avait rien d'exceptionnel; **what's so s. about the 19th November?**, qu'est-ce que le 19 novembre a de si spécial?; **for someone s.**, (*on card*) pour quelqu'un qui m'est cher; *Journ* **our s. correspondent,** notre envoyé spécial; **s. agent,** (*spy etc*) agent particulier; *Br* **S. Branch,** (*police*) service *m* de renseignements; **s. mission,** mission particulière; **s. feature** *or* **characteristic,** particularité *f*; *Com* **s. price,** prix spécial; **s. delivery,** envoi *m* par exprès; *Fin* **s. drawing rights,** droits de tirage spéciaux; **for s. occasions,** pour les jours de fête, pour les occasions spéciales; **to get s. treatment,** bénéficier d'un traitement de faveur; *Cin TV etc* **s. effects,** trucages *mpl*, effets spéciaux.

2 *n Rail* (*train*) train spécial; édition spéciale (*d'un journal*); *Br* (*constable*) citoyen assermenté faisant fonction d'agent de police; **today's s.**, (*in restaurant*) (*dish*) plat *m* du jour; (*menu*) menu *m* du jour.

specialist [ˈspeʃəlɪst] *n* spécialiste *mf*; **to become a s. in electronics** *or* **an electronics s.**, se spécialiser dans l'électronique; *Med* **heart s.**, cardiologue *mf*; **what are your s. subjects,** dans quels sujets vous spécialisez-vous?; **it requires s. skills,** ça demande les compétences d'un spécialiste; **it's s. work,** c'est un travail de spécialiste; **if you don't have the s. knowledge,** si vous n'avez pas les connaissances spécialisées; **s. dictionary,** dictionnaire spécialisé; **s. bookshop,** librairie spécialisée.

speciality [speʃɪˈælɪtɪ] *n* **(a)** spécialité *f* (*d'un magasin etc*); (*of study*) objet spécial d'étude *ou* de recherches; **that's my s.**, ça c'est mon fort, *ou* c'est ma spécialité; *Iron* c'est ma spécialité; **skiing holidays our s.**, (*in advertisement, window etc*) les sports d'hiver sont notre spécialité; **(b)** (*characteristic*) qualité particulière, particularité *f*; **(c)** *Jur* = **SPECIALTY**.

specialization [speʃəlaɪˈzeɪʃən] *n* spécialisation *f* (**in,** dans).

specialize [ˈspeʃəlaɪz] **1** *vi* **(a)** se spécialiser; **a shop that specializes in large sizes,** un magasin qui se spécialise dans les grandes tailles; **to s. in historical research,** se spécialiser dans les recherches historiques; *Iron* **she specializes in that sort of blunder,** elle est spécialiste de ce genre de gaffes, ce genre de gaffes est sa spécialité; **(b)** *Biol* se différencier. **2** *vt* désigner *ou* adapter à un emploi spécial.

specialized [ˈspeʃəlaɪzd] *adj* (*work, subject*) spécialisé.

specially [ˈspeʃəlɪ] *adv* (*in particular*) spécialement, particulièrement; (*mainly*) surtout; **I went there s. to see them,** j'y suis allé dans le seul but de les voir, j'y suis allé exprès pour les voir; **I waited up s.**, je suis resté debout exprès; **s. designed to ...,** spécialement conçu pour ...; **I s. asked you not to ...,** je t'ai bien demandé de ne pas ...; **it's**

not s. good, ce n'est pas particulièrement bon; **s. at night,** surtout le soir; **they had a cake s. made,** ils ont fait faire un gâteau spécialement.

specialty ['speʃəltɪ] *n* **(a)** *Jur* contrat formel sous seing privé; **(b)** *esp Am* = **SPECIALITY (a).**

specie ['spiːʃiː] *n* (*no pl*) espèces *fpl* (monnayées).

species ['spiːʃiːz] *n inv* **(a)** *Biol* espèce *f*; (*in forestry*) essence *f*; **the human s.,** l'espèce humaine; **the origin of s.,** l'origine *f* des espèces; **(b)** (*type*) espèce *f*, sorte *f*; **(c)** *Rel* **(Eucharistic) s.,** les (saintes) espèces *fpl*.

specific [spɪ'sɪfɪk] **1** *adj* spécifique; (*statement etc*) précis; (*order etc*) explicite; **or, to be s., ...,** ou, pour être précis, ...; **in this s. case,** dans ce cas précis *ou* particulier; **to be s.,** (*of person*) être explicite; **s. aim,** but déterminé; *Phys* **s. gravity,** poids *m* spécifique. **2** *n Med* spécifique *m* (**for,** contre); *US Ind* **specifics,** (*precise description*) description précise; (*characteristics*) caractéristiques *fpl*; *F* **to get down to specifics,** en venir aux faits précis.

specifically [spɪ'sɪfɪk(ə)lɪ] *adv* spécifiquement; (*precisely*) précisément; **your name was mentioned s.,** votre nom a été bien précisément mentionné; **you must state quite s. what the requirements are,** vous devez bien spécifier *ou* établir spécifiquement les conditions requises; **I s. told you not to ...,** je t'ai dit très précisément de ne pas ...; **I s. asked for a small portion,** j'ai bien demandé une petite portion; **we were s. forbidden to ...,** il nous était expressément défendu de ...; **it is s. designed for use in ...,** c'est particulièrement conçu pour une utilisation dans ...; **a book which is s. written for people who ...,** un livre écrit en particulier pour les gens qui ... .

specification [spesɪfɪ'keɪʃən] *n* **(a)** (*act*) spécification *f* (*des détails etc*); **(b)** description précise; caractéristiques *fpl* (*d'une voiture*); prescriptions *fpl* (*des travaux à exécuter*); *Constr Ind* **specifications,** cahier *m* des charges.

specify ['spesɪfaɪ] *vt* spécifier, désigner, déterminer, préciser (*des conditions etc*); **I specified blue,** j'ai spécifié la couleur bleue; **specified load,** charge prévue *ou* prescrite; **unless otherwise specified,** sauf indication contraire.

specimen ['spesɪmɪn] *n* spécimen *m*; (*sample*) spécimen, exemple *m*, échantillon *m*; **the finest specimens in his collection,** les plus belles pièces de sa collection; **that's a magnificent s.,** (*butterfly etc*) c'est un très beau spécimen; **a s. of s.o.'s handwriting,** un échantillon *ou* exemple de l'écriture de qn; *Med* **to take a s. of s.o.'s blood, to take a blood s. from s.o.,** faire une prise de sang à qn; *F* **a s.,** un échantillon d'urine; **to test a urine s.,** faire une analyse d'urine; *F* **odd s.,** (*person*) drôle *m* de type; *F* **you're a pretty pathetic s., aren't you!,** tu es vraiment un lamentable numéro!; **s. copy,** spécimen; **s. page,** page *f* spécimen, page type.

specious ['spiːʃəs] *adj* (*appearance*) spécieux, trompeur; (*argument etc*) captieux, spécieux.

speciousness ['spiːʃəsnɪs] *n* spéciosité *f*; (*appearance*) apparence trompeuse.

speck [spek] *n* **(a)** (*mark*) petite tache; point *m* (*de couleur, d'encre*); *Med* **floating specks (in front of the eyes),** mouches devant les yeux; **(b)** (*small piece*) grain *m*, atome *m* (*de poussière*); brin *m* (*de consolation, de générosité etc*); **the ship was only a s. on the horizon,** le navire n'était qu'un point à l'horizon; **(c)** (*fault*) défaut *m*; tavelure *f* (*sur un fruit*).

specked [spekt] *adj* (*animal, egg*) tacheté, moucheté; (*fruit*) tavelé.

speckle[1] ['spek(ə)l] *n* petite tache; point *m* (*de couleur*); (*on animal, egg*) moucheture *f*, tacheture *f*.

speckle[2] *vt* tacheter, moucheter.

speckled ['spek(ə)ld] *adj* tacheté, moucheté; (*plumage*) grivelé; (*hen*) tacheté; **bird s. with white,** oiseau tacheté de blanc.

specs [speks] *npl F* **(a)** (*spectacles*) binocles *mpl*; **(b)** (*specifications*) spécifications *fpl*.

spectacle ['spektək(ə)l] *n* **(a)** spectacle *m*; **to make a s. of oneself,** se donner en spectacle; **(b)** (paire of) spectacles, (paire *f* de) lunettes *fpl*; **to put on one's spectacles,** mettre *ou* chausser ses lunettes; **s. case,** étui *m* à lunettes.

spectacled ['spektəkld] *adj* à lunettes.

spectacular [spek'tækjʊlər] **1** *adj* spectaculaire; **she fell over in a s. fashion,** elle est tombée de façon spectaculaire; **s. play,** pièce *f* à spectacle. **2** *n Th etc* production *f* à grand spectacle; **an ice-skating s.,** une revue de patinage artistique.

spectacularly [spek'tækjʊləlɪ] *adv* (*to improve, collapse etc*) de façon spectaculaire.

spectate [spek'teɪt] *vi esp Sp* **to s. at,** assister à (*un match etc*); **I prefer to s.,** je préfère être spectateur, -trice.

spectator [spek'teɪtər] *n* spectateur, -trice; **the spectators,** l'assistance *f*; **s. sport,** sport *m* que l'on se contente de regarder en spectateur.

spectral ['spektr(ə)l] *adj* **(a)** *Phys Ch* spectral, -aux; **s. colours,** couleurs spectrales; **(b)** (*ghostly*) spectral.

spectre, *Am* **specter** ['spektər] *n* spectre *m*, fantôme *m*, apparition *f*; (*threat*) **the s. of war/famine** *etc*, le spectre de la guerre/famine *etc*.

spectrogram ['spektrəʊgræm] *n Phys Opt* spectrogramme *m*.

spectrograph ['spektrəʊgræf] *n* spectrographe *m*.

spectrometer [spek'trɒmɪtər] *n* spectromètre *m*.

spectroscope ['spektrəskəʊp] *n* spectroscope *m*.

spectroscopy [spek'trɒskəpɪ] *n* spectroscopie *f*.

spectrum, *pl* **-tra** ['spektrəm, -trə] *n Phys etc* spectre *m*; **the colours of the s.,** les couleurs spectrales *ou* du spectre; **a wide s. of opinions,** toute une gamme d'opinions; **the whole s. of political opinion,** tout l'éventail *ou* toute la gamme des opinions politiques; **across the political s.,** dans l'ensemble des tendances politiques; **s. analysis,** analyse spectrale.

speculate ['spekjʊleɪt] *vi* **(a)** (*wonder*) **to s. on** *or* **about sth,** spéculer *ou* méditer sur qch; (*conjecture*) faire des conjectures sur qch; **(b)** *Fin* spéculer; **to s. on the Stock Exchange,** spéculer en Bourse.

speculating ['spekjʊleɪtɪŋ] *n* spéculation *f*.

speculation [spekjʊ'leɪʃən] *n* **(a)** (*thought*) spéculation *f*, méditation *f* (**on,** sur); (*conjecture*) conjecture *f*; **it was pure s. on his part,** c'était (une) pure conjecture de sa part; **(b)** *Fin* spéculation *f*, entreprise spéculative; **to buy sth on s.,** *St Exch* acheter qch à titre de spéculation; (*on the off chance*) acheter qch à tout hasard.

speculative ['spekjʊlətɪv] *adj* **(a)** spéculatif, contemplatif; (*conjectural*) conjectural, -aux; (*theoretical*) théorique; **these are merely s. assumptions,** ce sont là de pures hypothèses *ou* de pures conjectures; **(b)** *Fin* spéculatif.

speculatively ['spekjʊlətɪvlɪ] *adv* (*to suggest, argue*) à titre d'hypothèse; (*to invest*) spéculativement.

speculator ['spekjʊleɪtər] *n* spéculateur, -trice; *St Exch* joueur, -euse en Bourse.

speculum, *pl* **-ums, -a** ['spekjʊləm, -əmz, -ə] *n* **(a)** *Med* spéculum *m*; **(b)** miroir *m* (*d'un télescope*).

speech [spiːtʃ] *n* **(a)** (**faculty of**) **s.,** la parole; **to lose the power of s.,** perdre la parole; **her s. was slow and deliberate,** elle parlait lentement en pesant ses mots; **to be slow of s.,** parler lentement; **to be abrupt in one's s.,** parler d'une manière brusque; **s. defect** *or* **disorder,** trouble *m* d'élocution; **s. impediment,** défaut *m* d'élocution; *Comptr* **s. recognition,** reconnaissance *f* de la parole; **s. therapist,** orthophoniste *mf*, **s. therapy,** orthophonie *f*;

(b) (*speaking*) paroles, propos *mpl*; **things which people say in everyday s.,** des choses que les gens disent dans la langue de tous les jours;

(c) (*language*) langue *f* (*d'un peuple*); parler *m* (*d'une région etc*); **in the s. of this specific community,** dans le parler de cette communauté particulière; *Ling* **s. community,** communauté *f* de langue;

(d) (*address*) discours *m*, allocution *f*; **to give** *or* **make a s.,** faire *ou* prononcer un discours *ou* une allocution; **s.!, s.!,** un discours!, un discours!; *Br Sch* **s. day,** = distribution *f* des prix; **s. making,** (*speeches*) discours *mpl*;

(e) *Gram* **parts of s.,** parties *fpl* du discours; **direct/indirect s.,** discours *ou* style direct/indirect; **figure of s.,** figure *f* de rhétorique.

speechify ['spiːtʃɪfaɪ] *vi F Pej* discourir, pérorer.

speechifying ['spiːtʃɪfaɪɪŋ] *n F Pej* beaux discours, laïus *m*.

speechless ['spiːtʃlɪs] *adj* **(a)** (*struck dumb*) interdit, interloqué, muet (**with surprise, fright,** de surprise, d'épouvante); **emotion left him s.,** l'émotion l'a laissé muet; **(b)** (*for physiological reasons*) incapable de parler; **I was s.,** (*with anger, surprise etc*) j'étais sans voix; **I'm s.!,** je ne sais pas quoi dire!

speechlessly ['spiːtʃlɪslɪ] *adv* sans voix.

speechwriter ['spiːtʃraɪtər] *n* rédacteur, -trice de discours.

speed[1] [spiːd] *n* **(a)** vitesse *f*, rapidité *f*; (*of vehicle, machine*) vitesse, régime *m*; *Phot* rapidité *f* (*d'une émulsion*); rapidité, luminosité *f* (*d'un objectif*); *Lit* **to make all s.,** faire diligence, se hâter; **with all possible s.,** aussi rapidement *ou* aussi vite que possible; **the s. with which she learnt/the building was completed,** la vitesse à laquelle elle a appris/le bâtiment a été terminé; *Aut etc* **at s.,** (*rouler*) à grande vitesse; **at top** *or* **full s.,** à toute vitesse;

(*of runners*) à toutes jambes; **to drive at top s.**, (*of motorist*) rouler à toute vitesse *ou* à toute allure; *Nau* **full s. ahead/astern!**, en avant/en arrière toute!; **maximum** *or* **top s.**, (*highest possible*) vitesse maximale *ou* maximum; (*highest permitted*) vitesse limite; **car with a maximum s. of 150 km an hour**, voiture qui plafonne à 150 km à l'heure; **cruising s.**, vitesse *ou* régime de croisière; *Av* **take-off s.**, vitesse de décollage; **to gather/lose s.**, prendre/perdre de la vitesse; **to reduce s.**, ralentir; **to pick up s.**, (*of train etc*) prendre de la vitesse, gagner en vitesse; (*of car*) reprendre; **s. bump**, ralentisseur *m*; *F* **s. cop**, motard *m*; **s. indicator**, indicateur *m* de vitesse; *Av* badin *m*; **s. limit**, *Aut* limitation *f* de vitesse; (*of machine*) vitesse maximale *ou* maximum, régime maximal *ou* maximum; **to exceed the s. limit**, dépasser la vitesse autorisée *ou* limite; **exceeding the s. limit**, excès *m* de vitesse; *F* **s. merchant**, chauffard *m*, fou *m* du volant; **s. trap**, contrôle *m* de vitesse-surprise;

(b) (*gear*) vitesse *f*; **three-s. gearbox**, boîte *f* à trois vitesses;

(c) *Arch* **to wish s.o. good s.**, souhaiter bonne chance à qn;

(d) *Sl* (*amphetamine*) amphé(tamine) *f*, speed *m*.

speed² *v* **1** *vi* **(a)** (*pt & pp* **sped** *or* **speeded**) (*hasten*) se hâter, se presser; (*go fast*) aller vite; *Aut etc* (*go fast*) faire de la vitesse; **the car sped into the garage**, la voiture s'enfila rapidement dans le garage; **(b)** (*pt & pp* **speeded**) *Aut* (*exceed speed limit*) dépasser la vitesse autorisée; **I was caught speeding**, j'ai eu une contravention pour excès de vitesse; **(c)** (*pt & pp* **speeded**) *Sl* (*be under effect of amphetamines*) speeder. **2** *vt* (*pt & pp* **sped** *or* **speeded**) *Arch & Lit* **s. the parting guest**, (*wish a good journey*) souhaiter bon voyage à un invité qui part; *F* (*encourage to leave*) encourager *ou* presser un invité à partir plus vite; *Arch* **God s.!**, = bon voyage!

▶**speed along** **1** *vi* (*in car, on bike*) rouler vite, *F* foncer; (*on foot*) marcher *ou* courir vite; **the work is speeding along**, le travail avance à bonne allure. **2** *vtsep* faire avancer *ou* progresser en vitesse (*le travail*).

▶**speed back** **1** *vi* (*person, driver*) rentrer à toute vitesse. **2** *vtsep* ramener (*qn*) à toute vitesse.

▶**speed off** **1** *vi* (*on foot, in car*) partir à toute allure. **2** *vtsep* **they sped him off to hospital**, ils l'ont expédié à l'hôpital.

▶**speed up** **1** *vi* (*of driver, runner etc*) accélérer; (*of work, pace*) s'accélérer; **management are only interested in getting people to s. up**, tout ce qui intéresse la direction, c'est de faire travailler le personnel plus rapidement. **2** *vtsep* (*staff, job, project*) activer; (*job*) accélérer; **do everything you can to s. things up**, faites tout ce que vous pouvez pour accélérer *ou* activer les choses.

speedboat ['spi:dbəʊt] *n* canot *m* automobile; (*faster*) vedette *f*; (*with outboard motor*) hors-bord *m inv*.

speedily ['spi:dɪlɪ] *adv* rapidement.

speediness ['spi:dɪnɪs] *n* rapidité *f*; (*of carrying out a job etc*) rapidité, célérité *f*.

speeding ['spi:dɪŋ] *n* (*exceeding speed limit*) excès *m* de vitesse; **s. fine**, contravention *f* pour excès de vitesse.

speeding up *n* accélération *f*.

speedo ['spi:dəʊ] *n F* = **SPEEDOMETER**.

speedometer [spi:'dɒmɪtər] *n Aut etc* compteur *m* (de vitesse).

speedster ['spi:dstər] *n* (*car*) bolide *m*; (*driver*) fou *m* du volant, *Pej* chauffard *m*.

speed(-)up ['spi:dʌp] *n* accélération *f*.

speedway ['spi:dweɪ] *n* **(a)** *Sp* (*motorcycle racing*) course *f* (de motos); (*track*) circuit *m*; *Am* (*for cars*) circuit automobile; **(b)** *Am* (*fast road*) = autoroute *f*.

speedwell ['spi:dwel] *n* (*plant*) véronique *f*.

speedy ['spi:dɪ] *adj* rapide, prompt; (*car*) rapide; **s. revenge**, prompte vengeance.

speleologist [spi:lɪ'ɒlədʒɪst] *n* spéléologue *mf*.

speleology [spi:lɪ'ɒlədʒɪ] *n* spéléologie *f*.

spell¹ [spel] *n* **(a)** (*words*) charme *m*, incantation *f*, formule *f* magique; **(b)** (*state*) charme, sort *m*, maléfice *m*; **to cast a (magic) s. over s.o., to put a (magic) s. on s.o.**, jeter un sort à *ou* sur qn, ensorceler qn; **to break the s.**, rompre le charme; **under a spell**, sous un charme, ensorcelé.

spell² *v* (*pt & pp* **spelt, spelled** [spelt, speld]) **1** *vt* **(a)** épeler; (*in writing*) orthographier (*un mot*); **how is it spelt?, how do you s. it?**, comment ça s'épelle *ou* s'écrit?, comment écrivez-vous ça?; **how do you s. 'Mississippi'?**, comment écrit-on 'Mississippi'?; **can you s. that for me?**, (*on telephone etc*) pouvez-vous me l'épeler?; **it's spelt** *or* **you spell it with an 'o'**, ça s'écrit avec un 'o'; **(b) what do these letters s.?**, quel mot forment ces lettres; **(c)** (*signify*) signifier; **this spells disaster**, on est perdu; **it would s. disaster**, cela précipiterait un désastre. **2** *vi* orthographier *ou* écrire correctement; **he can't s.**, il ne sait pas l'orthographe.

spell³ *n* **(a)** (*period*) période *f*, temps *m*; *Austr* (*rest period*) repos *m*; **to rest for a (short) s.**, se reposer pendant quelque temps; **a long s. of cold weather**, une longue période de froid; **during the cold s.**, pendant le coup de froid; **we're in for a s. of wet weather**, le temps se met à la pluie; **to suffer from dizzy spells**, être sujet à des vertiges; **(b)** (*turn*) tour *m* (*de travail etc*); (*in system of shifts*) relais *m*; **to do a s. of duty**, faire un tour de service; **to take spells at the pumps**, se relayer aux pompes; **do you want to take a s. at the wheel?**, tu veux me relayer au volant?; **to have another s. of prison**, retâter de la prison.

spell⁴ *vt* **(a)** *Am F* (*relieve*) relayer, relever (*qn*) (*dans son travail*); **(b)** *Austr* laisser reposer (*un cheval*).

▶**spell out** *vtsep* **(a)** (*spell letter by letter*) déchiffrer (*qch*) péniblement; **(b)** (*explain explicitly*) expliquer bien clairement; **do I have to s. it out for you?**, faut-il que je te fasse un dessin *ou* que je mette les points sur les i?; **I'll s. it out for you**, je vais bien tout t'expliquer.

spellbinder ['spelbaɪndər] *n* (*person*) orateur captivant (*qui tient ses auditeurs*).

spellbound ['spelbaʊnd] *adj* **(a)** (*fascinated*) fasciné, magnétisé, envoûté; **to hold s.o. s.**, fasciner qn, envoûter qn; **(b)** (*under magic spell*) sous l'effet d'un charme.

spell-check ['speltʃek] *n Comptr* correction *f* orthographique; **to do** *or* **run a s.-c. on a document**, effectuer une correction orthographique sur un document.

spell-checker ['speltʃekər] *n Comptr* correcteur *m* orthographique.

speller ['spelər] *n* **(a) to be a good/a bad s.**, être fort/faible en orthographe, savoir/ne pas savoir l'orthographe; **(b)** (*book*) alphabet *m*.

spend [spend] *vt* (*pt & pp* **spent** [spent]) **(a)** dépenser (*de l'argent*); **to s. one's money on cigarettes**, dépenser son argent en cigarettes; **her father has spent a great deal on her education**, son père a dépensé beaucoup pour son éducation; **to s. money on s.o.**, faire des dépenses pour qn; **she spends money like water**, l'argent lui fond *ou* glisse entre les mains; *F* **to s. a penny**, aller faire une petite commission, aller faire pipi;

(b) passer (*son temps*); **to s. time on (doing) sth**, consacrer *ou* employer du temps à (faire) qch; **to s. Sunday in the country**, passer le dimanche à la campagne; **haven't you got any better ways of spending your time?**, n'as-tu rien de mieux à faire pour passer *ou* employer ton temps?; **could you please s. a little time talking to her about it?**, pourrais-tu prendre un peu de temps pour lui en parler?; **how do you s. your weekends?**, où passes-tu tes week-ends?;

(c) to spend a lot of effort on a job, se donner beaucoup de mal dans un travail; **if you spent a bit more care on ...**, si tu apportais *ou* mettais un peu plus de soin à ...;

(d) (*use up*) épuiser (*ses forces*); consumer (*son énergie*); **our ammunition was all spent**, nos munitions étaient épuisées.

spender ['spendər] *n* **to be a big s.**, être très dépensier.

spending ['spendɪŋ] *n* dépense *f*; **public s.**, dépenses publiques; **s. power**, pouvoir *m* d'achat; **s. money**, argent *m* pour ses dépenses courantes; (*pocket money*) argent de poche; **s. spree**, vague *f* de dépenses; **to go on a s. spree**, faire des folies.

spendthrift ['spendθrɪft] *n* dépensier, -ière, dissipateur, -trice; **s. habits**, habitudes dépensières.

spent¹ [spent] *adj* épuisé (*de fatigue*); **s. bullet**, balle morte.

spent² *see* **SPEND**.

sperm¹ [spɜ:m] *n Physiol* sperme *m*; **s. bank**, banque *f* de sperme.

sperm² *n* **(a)** (*whale*) **s. whale**, cachalot *m*; **(b) s. oil**, huile *f* de spermaceti.

spermaceti [spɜ:mə'setɪ] *n* spermaceti *m*, blanc *m* de baleine.

spermatozoon, *pl* **-oa** [spɜ:mətəʊ'zəʊɒn, -əʊə] *n Biol* spermatozoïde *m*.

spermicidal [spɜ:mɪ'saɪd(ə)l] *adj* spermicide.

spermicide ['spɜ:mɪsaɪd] *n* spermicide *m*.

spew¹ [spju:] *vt & vi* vomir, *Sl* dégueuler.

spew² *n F* (*vomit*) vomi *m*, *Sl* dégueulis *m*.

►**spew forth, spew out 1** *vi* (*of lava, flames etc*) jaillir, fuser (**from, of,** de); (*of propaganda, lies, etc*) fuser. **2** *vtsep* déverser (*de la lave, de la propagande*).
►**spew up** *vi & vtsep* vomir, *Sl* dégueuler.
sphagnum, *pl* **-a** ['sfægnəm, -ə] *n* (*moss*) sphaigne *f*.
sphere [sfɪər] *n* **(a)** *Astron Math* sphère *f* ; **the celestial s.,** la sphère céleste; **(b)** (*field*) domaine *m*, sphère *f*; (*social circle*) milieu *m*, sphère; **to extend one's s. of activity,** étendre sa sphère d'activité; **that is not within my s.,** cela n'est pas de mon domaine *ou* de mon ressort; **in the political s.,** sur le plan politique; **s. of influence,** sphère *ou* zone *f* d'influence.
spherical ['sferɪk(ə)l] *adj* sphérique.
spheroid ['sfɪərɔɪd] *n* sphéroïde *m*.
sphincter ['sfɪŋktər] *n Anat* sphincter *m*.
sphinx, *pl* **sphinxes** [sfɪŋks, 'sfɪŋksɪz] *n Myth* sphinx *m*.
spice¹ [spaɪs] *n* **(a)** *Culin* épice *f*, aromate *m*; **mixed spice(s),** épices mélangées; **s. rack,** étagère *f ou* présentoir *m* à épices; **(b)** *Fig* sel *m*, piquant *m*; **to give s. to a story,** pimenter un récit; **the s. of life,** le sel *ou* le piquant de la vie; **the s. of adventure,** le piment de l'aventure.
spice² *vt* **(a)** épicer (*un gâteau, une boisson etc*); **(b)** *Fig* pimenter, relever (*un récit etc*).
spiciness ['spaɪsɪnɪs] *n* **(a)** (*of food*) caractère épicé; **(b)** *Fig* piquant *m*, sel *m* (*d'un récit*).
spick ['spɪk] *n* **(a) s. and span,** reluisant de propreté, propre comme un sou neuf; (*person*) tiré à quatre épingles; **(b)** *Am Offensive Sl* (*Spanish-American*) latino *mf*.
spicy ['spaɪsɪ] *adj* **(a)** *Culin* épicé; (*goût*) relevé; **(b)** (*having strong taste*) aromatique, parfumé; **(c)** (*story, conversation etc*) piquant, croustillant; (*risqué*) salé, épicé, poivré; **to tell s. stories,** en dire de vertes.
spider ['spaɪdər] *n* **(a)** (*animal*) araignée *f*; **s.'s web,** *Am* **s. web,** toile *f* d'araignée; **s. crab,** araignée de mer; **s. monkey,** atèle *m*; **(b)** *F* (*wheelbrace*) X *m*.
spiderman, *pl* **-men** ['spaɪdəmæn, -men] *Br n* ouvrier qui travaille au sommet des édifices.
spidery ['spaɪdərɪ] *adj* **(a)** d'araignée; (*resembling a spider*) qui ressemble à une araignée; **s. handwriting,** écriture *f* en pattes d'araignée; **(b)** (*grenier etc*) infesté d'araignées.
spiel¹ [ʃpiːl, spiːl] *n F* boniment *m*, baratin *m*; **he gave me some s. about having been held up at the airport,** il m'a servi tout un baratin comme quoi il avait été bloqué à l'aéroport.
spiel² *vi F* baratiner, faire du baratin.
►**spiel off** *vtsep Am F* (*recite*) débiter.
spieler ['spiːlər] *n F* **(a)** (*talker*) beau parleur, baratineur, -euse; **(b)** *esp Austr* (*cardsharp*) tricheur, -euse aux cartes.
spiffing ['spɪfɪŋ] *adj Old-fashioned Br F* épatant.
spigot ['spɪgət] *n* **(a)** fausset *m*, broche *f* (*de tonneau*); **(b)** (*tap for water etc*) robinet *m*; (*handle of tap*) clef *f* (de robinet).
spike¹ [spaɪk] *n* **(a)** pointe *f* (*de fer*); piquant *m* (*de fil de fer barbelé etc*); (*on railing etc*) lance *f*; **s. heel,** (*on woman's shoes*) talon *m* aiguille; **(b)** *Rail etc* crampon *m* (d'attache); **s. (nail),** clou *m* à large tête *ou* à tête de diamant; **bill s., s. file,** pique-notes *m inv*; *Sp* **spikes,** chaussures *fpl* à pointes; **(c)** *Bot* épi *m*; **s. (lavender),** (lavande) aspic *m*; **(d)** *El* pointe *f ou* crête *f* de tension.
spike² *vt Constr etc* (*nail*) clouer, cheviller; (*fit with spikes*) armer (*qch*) de pointes; *Am* (*thwart*) faire avorter (*une affaire*); contrecarrer, entraver (*des projets*); corser (*une boisson*); **spiked gate,** grille *f* à pointes *ou* garnie de pointes; *Sp* **spiked shoes,** chaussures *fpl* à pointes; *Fig* **to s. s.o.'s guns,** priver qn de ses moyens d'action, mettre qn hors d'action.
spikenard ['spaɪknɑːd] *n* (*ointment*) nard *m* (indien).
spiky ['spaɪkɪ] *adj* **(a)** à pointe(s) aiguë(s); **s. hair,** cheveux hérissés; **(b)** (*fitted with spikes*) armé de pointes; **(c)** (*touchy, short-tempered*) susceptible, chatouilleux.
spill¹ [spɪl] *n* (*fall, roll*) culbute *f*, chute *f* (*de cheval, de voiture*); **to have a s.,** culbuter; (*from bicycle, horse*) tomber, faire une chute, *F* ramasser une pelle.
spill² *v* (*pt & pp* **spilt, spilled** [spɪlt, spɪld]) **1** *vt* répandre, renverser (*un liquide, du sel*); verser (*du sang*); désarçonner (*un cavalier*); verser (*les occupants d'une voiture*); **without spilling a drop,** sans laisser tomber une goutte; *F* **to s. the beans,** vendre la mèche. **2** *vi* (*of liquid*) se répandre, couler; **some wine had spilled on the floor,** du vin s'était répandu sur le tapis.
spill³ *n* (*firelighter*) allume-feu *m inv*; allumette *f* (*de papier etc*).
►**spill out 1** *vi* (*of liquid*) déborder; *Fig* (*of words*) s'écouler; **the crowd started spilling out of the stadium,** la foule commença à s'écouler hors du stade. **2** *vtsep* renverser (*un liquide*); répandre (*une histoire*).
►**spill over** *vi* (*overflow*) (*of liquid*) déborder, se déverser; **the population has spilled over into the surrounding areas,** la population s'est déversée sur les zones avoisinantes; **a bad influence which could s. over into other ...,** une mauvaise influence qui pourrait déborder *ou* se répandre dans d'autres ... .
spillage ['spɪlɪdʒ] *n* (*action*) action *f* de répandre un liquide; (*amount*) quantité (*de liquide*) répandue.
spillover ['spɪləʊvər] *n* surplus *m ou* déversement *m* de population.
spillway ['spɪlweɪ] *n HydE* déversoir *m*.
spin¹ [spɪn] *n* **(a)** tournoiement *m*; (mouvement *m* de) rotation *f* (*d'une balle etc*); *Nucl Phys* spin *m* (*de l'électron etc*); *Av* vrille *f*; *Sp* **to put s. on a ball,** donner de l'effet à une balle; *Aut* **to go into a s.,** faire un tête-à-queue *inv*; *Av* **flat s.,** vrille à plat, tonneau *m*; **to give sth a long/short s.,** (*in washing machine*) mettre qch sur cycle long/court; *Fig F* **to be in a flat s.,** ne pas savoir où donner de la tête; *Cr* **s. bowler,** lanceur *m* qui donne de l'effet à la balle; **(b)** *Old-fashioned* (*short journey*) tour *m*, promenade *f* (*en voiture etc*); **to go for a s.,** aller faire un tour (*en voiture etc*); **(c)** *Austr F* (*luck*) coup *m* de chance; (*bad luck*) malchance *f*.
spin² *v* (*pt & pp* **spun** [spʌn]; *prp* **spinning**) **1** *vt* **(a)** filer (*la laine, le coton etc*); **to s. its web,** (*of spider*) filer sa toile; **to s. a top,** lancer *ou* fouetter une toupie; **to s. a coin,** jouer à pile ou face; **(b)** = **SPIN-DRY. 2** *vi* **(a)** (*of top etc*) tourner; (*of suspended object*) tournoyer; (*of compass*) être affolé, s'affoler; **my head's spinning,** la tête me tourne; **the room's spinning,** (*because I'm dizzy, drunk etc*) la pièce tourne (autour de moi); **the blow sent him spinning,** le coup l'a envoyé rouler; **(b)** (*of wheel*) patiner (*sur place*); **(c)** *Fishing* pêcher à la cuillère; **to s. for fish,** pêcher, lancer.
►**spin out 1** *vtsep* (*prolong*) délayer (*un discours*); faire durer, prolonger (*une discussion*); faire traîner (*une affaire, un récit*) en longueur; **to s. out one's money,** ménager son argent. **2** *vi* **to make one's money s. out,** faire durer son argent.
►**spin round 1** *vi* (*turn*) (*of car*) faire un tête-à-queue; (*of person*) pivoter, virevolter; (*turn around sharply*) se retourner vivement, faire volte-face; **she spun round in her chair,** elle pivota sur sa chaise; **to s. round and round,** tournoyer, tourbillonner. **2** *vtsep* (*turn fast*) (*wheel etc*) faire tourner; faire tourner (*qn*); (*several times*) faire tournoyer (*qn*).
spina bifida [spaɪnə'bɪfɪdə] *n Med* spina-bifida *m*.
spinach ['spɪnɪtʃ] *n* (*plant*) épinard *m*; *Culin* épinards *mpl*.
spinal ['spaɪn(ə)l] *adj Anat* spinal, -aux, vertébral, -aux; **s. column,** colonne vertébrale; **s. cord,** moelle épinière; **s. curvature,** déviation *f* de la colonne vertébrale; **s. injury,** lésion *f* de la colonne vertébrale.
spindle ['spɪnd(ə)l] *n* **(a)** *Tex* fuseau *m*; **s.-shaped,** fusiforme, fuselé; **(b)** *MecE etc* arbre *m*, axe *m*, mandrin *m*; (*of potter's wheel etc*) pivot *m*; (*of axle, shaft*) fusée *f*.
spindleshanks ['spɪnd(ə)lʃæŋks] *npl F* **(a)** (*legs*) jambes *fpl* en fuseau; **(b)** (*with sing verb*) (*person*) type grand et maigre, manche *m* à balai.
spindly ['spɪndlɪ] *adj* (*person*) maigrelet, maigrichon; (*legs*) fuselé; (*furniture etc*) peu solide, peu robuste.
spindrift ['spɪndrɪft] *n* embrun(s) *m(pl)*, poudrin *m*.
spin-dry ['spɪn'draɪ] *vt* (faire) essorer (*du linge*).
spin-dryer ['spɪn'draɪər] *n* essoreuse *f* (centrifuge).
spin-drying ['spɪn'draɪɪŋ] *n* essorage *m*.
spine [spaɪn] *n* **(a)** *Anat* (*backbone*) épine dorsale; (*spinal column*) colonne vertébrale; **s. chiller,** (*story*) histoire *f* à vous glacer le sang; (*novel, film*) roman *m ou* film *m* d'épouvante; **(b)** *Geog* arête *f*; **(c)** (*in bookbinding*) dos *m* (*d'un livre*); **(d)** (*sharp protrusion*) piquant *m*, épine *f* (*d'une plante, d'un poisson, d'un hérisson etc*).
spineless ['spaɪnlɪs] *adj* **(a)** (*person*) (*lacking character*) faible, mou, *f* molle; qui manque de caractère; (*lacking courage*) poltron, lâche; **(b)** (*without spines*) sans épines, sans piquants.
spinet [spɪ'net] *n Mus* épinette *f*.
spinnaker ['spɪnəkər] *n Nau* spinnaker *m*, spi *m*.
spinner ['spɪnər] *n* **(a)** *Tex* fileur, -euse; *Fig* **s. of tales** *or* **yarns,** conteur, -euse d'histoires; **(b)** (*of silkworm etc*) filière *f* ; **(c)** *Fishing* cuillère *f*; **(d)** *Cr* (*spin bowler*) lanceur *m* qui donne de l'effet à la balle; (*ball that spins*) balle *f* avec de l'effet.
spinneret ['spɪnəret] *n* filière *f* (*d'araignée etc*).
spinney ['spɪnɪ] *n* petit bois, bosquet *m*.

spinning ['spɪnɪŋ] **1** *adj* tournant, tournoyant. **2** *n* **(a)** (*making by spinning*) filage *m* (*au rouet*); *Ind* filature *f*; **s. gland,** filière *f* (*de l'araignée, du ver à soie*); *Ind* **s. mill** *or* **factory,** filature; **s. wheel,** rouet *m*; **(b)** (*rotation*) tournoiement *m*, rotation *f*; affolement *m* (*de l'aiguille magnétique*); *Av* vrille *f*; **s. motion** *or* **movement,** mouvement rotatif *ou* de rotation; **s. top,** toupie *f*.

spin(-)off ['spɪnɒf] *n* (*advantage*) retombée *f*, avantage *m ou* bénéfice *m* supplémentaire; (*by-product*) sous-produit *m*, *pl* sous-produits, (produit) dérivé *m*; **the film is a s.-o. from a TV series,** le film est tiré d'une série télévisée; **a s.-o. of the Olympics was meant to be the creation of permanent jobs,** on estimait qu'une des retombées des Jeux Olympiques serait la création d'emplois permanents.

spinster ['spɪnstər] *n* **(a)** *Old-Fashioned* célibataire *f*, femme *ou* fille non mariée; **(b)** *Pej* vieille fille.

spiny ['spaɪnɪ] *adj Biol* épineux; (*covered in spines*) couvert d'épines *ou* de piquants; *Fig* (*problem*) épineux; **s. lobster,** langouste *f*.

spiracle ['spaɪərək(ə)l] *n* (*of whale etc*) évent *m*; (*of insect*) stigmate *m*.

spiral[1] ['spaɪər(ə)l] **1** *n* spirale *f*; (*single curve*) spire *f*, tour *m* (*de spirale*); **in a s.,** en spirale; *Av* **s. (climb/dive),** montée *f*/descente *f* en spirale *ou* en vrille; **wage-price s.,** course *f ou* spirale des prix et des salaires. **2** *adj* spiral, -aux; en spirale; **s. binding,** reliure spirale; **s. staircase,** escalier *m* en spirale *ou* en colimaçon *ou* en hélice *ou* à vis.

spiral[2] *vi* (**-ll-**, *US* **-l-**) (*form a spiral*) former une spirale; (*turn*) tourner en spirale; (*rise*) (*of steam, smoke*) s'élever en spirale.

►**spiral down** *vi* (*of plane*) descendre en spirale *ou* en vrille; (*of steps*) descendre en spirale *ou* en colimaçon.

►**spiral up** *vi* (*of rocket etc*) s'élever *ou* monter en spirale; (*of smoke*) s'élever en spirale; (*of steps*) monter en spirale *ou* en colimaçon; (*of prices*) monter en vrille.

spirally ['spaɪərəlɪ] *adv* en spirale.

spire ['spaɪər] *n Archit* aiguille *f*, flèche *f* (*d'église*).

spirit ['spɪrɪt] *n* **(a)** esprit *m*, âme *f*; **I'll be with you in s.,** je serai avec vous en pensée; *Bible* **the poor in s.,** les pauvres d'esprit;

(b) (*incorporeal being*) esprit *m*; **the Holy S.,** le Saint-Esprit, l'Esprit saint; **evil s.,** esprit malin, mauvais génie; **to raise a s.,** évoquer un esprit; **to believe in spirits,** croire aux esprits *ou* aux revenants; **s. writing,** psychogramme *m*;

(c) (*person*) esprit *m*; **the leading s.,** l'âme *f*, le chef (*d'une entreprise*); le meneur, la meneuse (*d'une révolte*);

(d) (*mood, attitude*) esprit *m*, disposition *f*; **the s. of the age,** l'esprit du siècle; **the s. of liberty,** le génie de la Liberté; **that was not the s. of the agreement,** ce n'était pas l'esprit de cet accord; **to have the party s.,** participer dans la gaieté de la réunion; **to enter into the s. of sth,** entrer dans l'esprit de qch; **to enter into the s. of the thing,** entrer de bon cœur dans la partie; *F* **that's the s.!** à la bonne heure!;

(e) (*character*) caractère *m*, cœur *m*, courage *m*; (*ardour*) ardeur *f*, feu *m*, entrain *m*; **man of unbending s.,** homme d'un caractère inflexible; **woman of s.,** (*having strong character*) femme de caractère; (*brave*) femme courageuse; **to show s.,** montrer du caractère *ou* du courage; **to have s.,** avoir de l'allant; **the pianist played with more s. than skill,** le pianiste jouait avec plus d'ardeur que de talent; **to be in good spirits,** (*to be cheerful*) être gai *ou* dispos; (*to be in a good mood*) être de bonne humeur; **to be in high spirits,** être en train *ou* en verve; **to be in low spirits,** (*to be depressed*) être abattu *ou* accablé; (*to feel sad*) se sentir tout triste; **to keep up one's spirits,** ne pas perdre courage; **to raise** *or* **revive s.o.'s spirits,** relever *ou* remonter le courage *ou* le moral de qn; **their spirits rose,** ils reprenaient courage;

(f) **spirits,** spiritueux *mpl*; **wines and spirits,** vins *mpl* et spiritueux; *Ch* **(volatile) s.,** esprit *m*; **methylated spirits,** alcool dénaturé *ou* à brûler; **surgical s.,** = alcool à 90°; **spirit(s) of salt,** esprit-de-sel *m*; *Th etc* **s. gum,** gomme *f* arabique (*pour coller de faux cheveux*); **s. lamp/stove,** lampe *f*/réchaud *m* à alcool;

(g) *Constr etc* **s. level,** niveau *m*.

►**spirit away, spirit off** *vtsep* (*remove secretly, quickly*) faire disparaître *ou* enlever (*qn*) comme par enchantement; subtiliser, escamoter (*qch*).

spirited ['spɪrɪtɪd] *adj* **(a)** (*person*) (*lively*) vif, animé; (*passionate*) plein de fougue *ou* de verve; (*intrepid*) intrépide; (*horse*) fougueux; **(b)** (*style, reply etc*) chaleureux, plein de verve; **s. attack,** attaque fougueuse; **s. discussion,** discussion vive *ou* ardente; **to give a s. performance,** jouer avec brio *ou* avec verve.

spiritless ['spɪrɪtlɪs] *adj* (*style*) sans vie, qui manque de verve; (*conversation etc*) qui manque d'entrain; (*lacking courage, character*) sans courage, sans caractère; (*cowardly*) lâche; (*lacking vigour, passion*) sans vigueur, sans ardeur; (*weak*) mou, *f* molle.

spiritual ['spɪrɪtjʊəl] **1** *adj Rel* spirituel; (*tribunal*) ecclésiastique; (*not material, physical*) spirituel, immatériel; **s. father,** père *ou* directeur spirituel; **s. features,** traits purs *ou* raffinés; **s. life,** vie spirituelle. **2** *n Mus* **(negro) s.,** (negro-)spiritual *m*, *pl* (negro-)spirituals.

spiritualism ['spɪrɪtjʊəlɪz(ə)m] *n* **(a)** (*belief in spirits*) spiritisme *m*; **(b)** *Phil* spiritualisme *m*.

spiritualist ['spɪrɪtjʊəlɪst] **1** *n* **(a)** (*believer in spirits*) spirite *mf*; **(b)** *Phil* spiritualiste *mf*. **2** *adj* **(a)** (*believing in spirits*) spirite; **(b)** *Phil* spiritualiste.

spirituality [spɪrɪtjʊ'ælɪtɪ] *n* spiritualité *f* (*de l'âme, d'une personne*).

spiritually ['spɪrɪtjʊəlɪ] *adv* spirituellement.

spirituous ['spɪrɪtjʊəs] *adj* spiritueux, alcoolique.

spirt[1,2] [spɜːt] *n & v* = **SPURT**[1,2].

spit[1] [spɪt] *n* **(a)** *Culin* broche *f*; **(b)** *Geog* langue *f* de sable, flèche littorale.

spit[2] *vt* (**-tt-**) *Culin* (*put on a spit*) embrocher, mettre à la broche (*un rôti etc*); *Lit* embrocher (*qn*).

spit[3] *n* **(a)** (*saliva*) crachat *m*, salive *f*; (*act of spitting*) crachement *m*; *F* **he's the dead s. of his father,** c'est son père tout craché; *F* **s. and polish,** astiquage *m*, fourbissage *m*; **(b)** crachin *m* (*de pluie*).

spit[4] *v* (*pt & pp* **spat** [spæt]; *prp* **spitting**) **1** *vi* cracher; **to s. in s.o.'s face, to s. at s.o.,** cracher au visage à qn; (*of cat*) cracher; (*of pen*) cracher, crachoter; (*of fire*) crépiter, pétiller; (*of hot fat*) pétiller, grésiller; *El* (*of collector etc*) cracher; **I wouldn't trust him further than I could s.,** je n'ai pas la moindre confiance en lui; **it's spitting (with rain),** il crachine, il fait du crachin. **2** *vt* cracher (*de la salive, du sang, des injures*).

spit[5] *n* (*depth of spade*) profondeur *f* de fer de bêche; **to dig the ground two spits deep,** labourer la terre à deux fers de bêche.

►**spit back** *vi* (*of engine*) avoir des retours de flamme (au carburateur).

►**spit out** *vtsep* (*expel from mouth*) cracher (*qch*); recracher (*qch de mauvais*); **he spat the words out,** il lança *ou* proféra les mots; *F* **s. it out!,** (*say what you want to*) accouche!, vide ton sac!

►**spit up** *vtsep* cracher (*le sang*).

spite[1] [spaɪt] *n* **(a)** (*malice*) rancune *f*; (*ill will*) malveillance *f*; (*pique*) pique *f*, dépit *m*; **from** *or* **out of s.,** (*out of maliciousness*) par pure malice *ou* méchanceté; **he broke her toy out of pure s.,** il a cassé son jouet par pure méchanceté envers elle; **she went to a different university out of s.,** (*to annoy s.o.*) elle est allée à une autre université pour ennuyer son monde; **to have a s. against s.o.,** avoir de la rancune contre qn; (*bear a grudge*) garder rancune à qn; **(b) in s. of ...,** en dépit de ..., malgré ...; **in s. of everything,** malgré tout; **in s. of the fact that I had warned her, in s. of my having warned her,** en dépit du fait que je l'avais prévenue, bien que je l'aie prévenue.

spite[2] *vt* vexer, contrarier (*qn*); **he does it to s. me,** il le fait pour me tracasser *ou* m'ennuyer.

spiteful ['spaɪtfʊl] *adj* méchant, malveillant; (*because of a grudge*) rancunier, vindicatif; **s. remark,** observation méchante; **s. tongue,** langue *f* de vipère.

spitefully ['spaɪtfəlɪ] *adv* par malveillance, méchamment; par dépit *ou* rancune; **'that's a stupid idea', he said s.,** 'c'est une idée stupide', dit-il méchamment.

spitefulness ['spaɪtfʊlnɪs] *n* méchanceté *f*, malveillance *f*; (*because of grudge*) rancœur *f*.

spitfire ['spɪtfaɪər] *n* furie *f*.

spitroast ['spɪtrəʊst] *vt Culin* cuire à la broche; **spitroast lamb,** agneau à la broche.

spitter ['spɪtər] *n* cracheur, -euse.

spitting ['spɪtɪŋ] *n* crachement *m*; **no s.,** (*on sign*) défense de cracher; *F* **within s. distance of the front door,** à deux pas de la porte d'entrée; *F* **he's the s. image of his father,** c'est son père tout craché.

spitting back *n* retour *m* de flamme (*au carburateur*).

spittle ['spɪt(ə)l] *n* salive *f*, crachat *m*; bave *f* (*du crapaud*).

spittoon [spɪ'tuːn] *n* crachoir *m*.

spitz [spɪts] *n* (*dog*) loulou *m*.

spiv [spɪv] *n Br F* filou *m*; (*on black market*) profiteur *m ou* trafiquant *m* du marché noir.

spivvy ['spɪvɪ] *adj Br F* (*appearance, clothes*) tape-à-l'œil *inv*, tapageur; **do I look a bit s. in this?**, n'ai-je pas l'air un peu filou avec ça?

splash¹ [splæʃ] **1** *n* **(a)** (*action*) éclaboussement *m* (*de l'eau, du métal fondu*); clapotement *m*, clapotis *m* (*des vagues*); **to fall into the water with a s.**, tomber dans l'eau en faisant floc *ou* flac; *F* **to make a (big) s.**, faire sensation; (*on purpose*) faire de l'épate; *Journ* **s. headline**, grosse manchette; **s. back**, panneau protecteur (*d'évier etc*); **(b)** (*mark, amount*) éclaboussure *f* (*de boue, d'encre etc*); tache *f* (*de couleur, de lumière*); *F* **a whisky and s.**, un whisky soda; **just a s., please**, très peu *ou* juste un soupçon (*d'eau etc*), s'il vous plaît; **water s.**, gué *m* (peu profond). **2** *int* floc!, flac!, ploc!

splash² **1** *vt* éclabousser (**s.o. with water**, qn d'eau); **to s. water about**, faire jaillir *ou* faire gicler de l'eau; **to s. water at one another**, se jeter de l'eau; *Journ* **to s. a piece of news**, mettre une nouvelle en manchette; **a photo was splashed across the front page**, une photo s'étalait en première page; **to s. one's way across a field**, traverser un champ en pataugeant; **to s. oneself**, s'éclabousser (*d'eau etc*); se tacher (*de peinture etc*); **to s. oneself** *or* **one's face with water**, s'asperger *ou* s'asperger la figure d'eau. **2** *vi* (*of liquid*) jaillir en éclaboussures; (*of waves*) clapoter; (*of tap*) cracher; (*of person, animal*) barboter, patauger.

►**splash about, splash around** **1** *vtsep* (*spread by splashing*) faire jaillir, faire gicler (*de l'eau*); *F* **to s. one's money about**, prodiguer son argent, dépenser sans compter. **2** *vi* (*of person, animal*) barboter, patauger.

►**splash down** *vi Astronaut* (*land in sea*) amerrir.

►**splash out** **1** *vi* (*spend more money than usual*) faire des frais; **I decided to s. out and buy a really good cooker**, j'ai décidé de casser ma tirelire et de m'acheter une cuisinière qui soit vraiment bonne; **I've splashed out on a new hat**, je me suis payé un nouveau chapeau; **you have been splashing out, haven't you!**, tu as fait des frais *ou* des folies, n'est-ce pas! **2** *vtsep* **we splashed out £500 on a new ...**, nous avons dépensé *ou F* claqué 500 livres dans un nouveau ... .

►**splash up** **1** *vi* (*be thrown up*) (*of liquid, mud etc*) gicler. **2** *vtsep* faire gicler (*de la boue etc*).

splashdown ['splæʃdaʊn] *n Astronaut* amerrissage *m* (*d'un engin spatial*).

splat [splæt] *int* flac! **the fruit landed s. on the ground**, le fruit tomba sur le sol avec un flac.

splatter¹ ['splætər] *n* éclaboussure *f*.

splatter² **1** *vt* **to s. s.o. with mud, to s. mud over s.o.**, éclabousser qn de boue; **blood was splattered everywhere**, tout était éclaboussé de sang. **2** *vi* (*of liquid*) jaillir, gicler; **the tomato splattered against the wall**, la tomate s'est éclatée contre le mur.

splay¹ [spleɪ] *vt* étendre (*ses mains*); *Archit etc* **to s. the sides of a window**, ébraser *ou* évaser une fenêtre; **splayed opening**, ouverture ébrasée *ou* évasée.

splay² *adj* (*knees etc*) tourné en dehors.

►**splay out** **1** *vtsep* (*spread*) étendre (*ses mains*). **2** *vi Archit etc* s'évaser.

splayfooted [spleɪ'fʊtɪd] *adj* (*person*) aux pieds plats tournés en dehors.

spleen [spliːn] *n* **(a)** *Anat* rate *f*; **(b)** (*bad mood*) mauvaise humeur; (*anger*) bile *f*; *Lit* spleen *m*; (*black mood*) humeur noire; **to vent one's s. on s.o.**, décharger sa bile sur qn.

splendid ['splendɪd] *adj* (*gowns, occasion*) superbe, magnifique, splendide; (*meal*) magnifique; (*view*) splendide, magnifique; (*opportunity*) splendide; **we had a s. time**, c'était formidable; **that's s., thanks very much!**, c'est formidable, merci beaucoup!

splendidly ['splendɪdlɪ] *adv* splendidement; magnifiquement; **s. dressed**, superbement vêtu; **they got along s.**, ils s'entendirent magnifiquement bien.

splendiferous [splen'dɪfərəs] *adj F Hum* magnifique.

splendour, *Am* **splendor** ['splendər] *n* splendeur *f*, magnificence *f*; **the mountains in all their s.**, les montagnes dans toute leur splendeur.

splice¹ [splaɪs] *n* (*in rope, cable etc*) épissure *f*; *Carp* enture *f*; (point *m* de) collage *m* (*d'un film*); (*in magnetic tape*) raccord *m*.

splice² *vt Nau etc* épisser (*un cordage, un câble*); *Carp* enter (*deux pièces de bois*); *Cin etc* coller (*un film*); raccorder, faire un raccord à (*une bande magnétique*); *F* **to get spliced**, se marier.

splicing ['splaɪsɪŋ] *n* épissage *m* (*d'un cordage, d'un câble*); *Carp* enture *f* (*de deux pièces de bois*); *Cin etc* collage *m* (*d'un film, d'une bande magnétique*); raccordement *m* (*d'une bande magnétique*).

spliff [splɪf] *n Sl* joint *m*, cigarette *f* de marijuana.

splint¹ [splɪnt] *n Med* attelle *f*, éclisse *f*; **to put a limb in splints**, éclisser un membre.

splint² *vt Med* éclisser (*un membre fracturé*).

splinter¹ ['splɪntər] *n* éclat *m* (*de bois, d'obus etc*); (*in finger etc*) écharde *f* (*de bois*); *Surg* esquille *f* (d'os fracturé); **I've got a s. in my finger**, j'ai une écharde dans le doigt; **a glass s., a s. of glass**, un éclat de verre; *Pol* **s. group**, groupe *m* séparatiste.

splinter² **1** *vt* briser (*qch*) en mille morceaux; (*violently*) faire voler (*qch*) en éclats; craquer (*un aviron, un mât etc*); **2** *vi* (*shatter*) éclater; (*violently*) voler en éclats; (*of oar, mast etc*) craquer, éclater.

splinterproof ['splɪntəpruːf] *adj* (*verre*) se brisant sans éclats.

split¹ [splɪt] *n* **(a)** fente *f* (*dans un mur etc*); fissure *f*, crevasse *f* (*dans une roche etc*); déchirure *f* (*dans une robe etc*); gerçure *f* (*de la peau*); **(b)** (*division*) division *f*; scission *f* (*dans un groupe*); (*in personality*) dédoublement *m*; **there was a s. in the party over ...**, il y avait une division *ou* une scission dans le parti à propos de ...; **to heal the s.**, effacer la division; **they suggested a fifty-fifty s. of the proceeds**, ils ont proposé un partage des indemnités à cinquante-cinquante; **(c)** *F* demi(-bouteille) *f* (*d'eau de Vichy etc*); **(d)** *Culin* **Devonshire s.**, brioche fourrée à la crème; **banana s.**, banana *f* split; **(e)** *Gym* **to do the splits**, faire le grand écart; **(f)** *F* (*share in profits, loot etc*) part *f*; **(g)** (*in meaning of word etc*) distinction *f*.

split² *v* (*pt & pp* **split**; *prp* **splitting**) **1** *vt* fendre (*du bois etc*); (re)fendre (*de l'ardoise*); cliver (*la roche etc*); déliter (*la pierre*); (*tear*) déchirer; (*divide*) diviser, partager (*une somme etc*) (**into equal shares**, en parts égales); **to s. sth in two** *or* **in half**, couper qch en deux; *Nucl Phys* **to s. the atom**, fissionner l'atome; **I've split my skirt**, j'ai déchiré ma jupe; **to s. a bottle**, partager une bouteille (de vin); *F* **can you s. a fiver for me?**, pouvez-vous me donner la monnaie de cinq livres?; *Pol* **to s. the party**, provoquer une scission dans le parti; **this split the party three ways**, ceci a divisé *ou* scindé le parti en trois; **to s. the vote**, partager les voix (*dans un parti*); **to s. one's vote**, *esp US* **to s. the ticket**, partager ses votes entre plusieurs candidats.

2 *vi* **(a)** (*of wood etc*) se fendre; (*of stone*) se déliter; (*of rock*) se cliver; (*of skin etc*) se gercer; (*of dress etc*) se déchirer; (*of seam in dress etc*) craquer; (*of political party etc*) se scinder; *F* **my head's splitting**, j'ai un mal de tête fou;

(b) *Sl* (*leave*) s'en aller, partir; **let's s.!** fichons le camp!

split³ *adj* fendu; **s. ends**, cheveux fourchus; *Gram* **s. infinitive**, infinitif éclaté (*lorsqu'un mot s'intercale entre 'to' et le verbe*); **s. peas**, pois cassées; *Psy* **he has a s. personality**, il souffre d'un dédoublement de personnalité, *Comptr* **s. screen**, écran divisé; **s. second**, quart *m* de seconde.

►**split off** **1** *vi* (*become detached*) se séparer, se détacher (*par clivage*). **2** *vtsep* (*break off*) détacher, séparer, enlever (*qch*) (*par clivage*).

►**split on** *vipo F* (*inform on*) dénoncer (*qn*); donner (*un complice, un camarade*).

►**split open** **1** *vi* (*burst open*) se fendre, s'ouvrir. **2** *vtsep* (*break open*) ouvrir (*qch*).

►**split up** **1** *vtsep* **(a)** (*divide*) répartir, partager (*de l'argent, du travail, le butin*); séparer (*un couple, deux personnes qui se battent*); diviser, scinder (*une organisation, un parti*); (*break up into several parts*) fragmenter (*un parti etc*); **we split the work up amongst ourselves**, nous nous sommes réparti le travail; **I don't want to s. you and Joyce up**, je ne veux pas te séparer de Joyce; **the police tried to s. the crowd up**, la police a essayé de disperser la foule;

(b) (*break down, analyse*) analyser, décomposer (*le sens, d'un mot*); **it should be split up into paragraphs**, il faudrait le décomposer *ou* diviser en paragraphes; *Ch* **to s. up a compound into its elements**, dédoubler un composé en ses éléments.

2 *vi* (*divide*) se fractionner; **the compound had s. up into its elements**, le composé s'était divisé en ses éléments; **the party split up into three groups**, le parti s'est divisé en trois groupes; **Paul and Anne have split up**, Paul et Anne se sont séparés *ou* ont rompu; **the rock group has split up**, le groupe de rock s'est séparé.

split-level ['splɪtlev(ə)l] *adj Archit* (*building, room etc*) à deux niveaux; **s.-l. grill**, grill *m* à deux étages.

split-second ['splɪtsekənd] *adj* **with s.-s. timing**, avec un minutage réglé au dixième de seconde; **trapeze work**

requires s.-s. timing, le trapèze requiert une synchronisation réglée au dixième de seconde.

splitting ['splɪtɪŋ] **1** *adj* qui (se) fend; *F* **to have a s. headache,** avoir un mal de tête fou. **2** *n* **(a)** fendage *m* (*de peaux etc*); refendage *m* (*de bois, d'ardoises etc*); délitement *m*, délitage *m* (*de la pierre*); *Nucl Phys* **s. of the atom,** fission *f* de l'atome; **(b)** (*division*) division *f*, morcellement *m* (*d'une terre etc*); séparation *f* (*de deux personnes etc*); scission *f* (*d'un parti politique etc*).

splitting up *n* **(a)** (*act of breaking up*) fragmentation *f*, division *f*, fractionnement *m* (*de qch*); **(b)** = **SPLITTING 2(b).**

split-up ['splɪtʌp] *n* (*in political party*) division *f*, scission *f*; (*of couple*) séparation *f*, rupture *f*; (*of friends*) séparation.

splodge¹ [splɒdʒ] *n F* (*stain*) tache *f* (*de couleur, d'encre*); (*piece*) plâtrée *f* (*de glace, ketchup etc*).

splodge² *vt F* tacher, barbouiller (**with,** de); **he splodged a great lump of cream on top,** il étala une plâtrée de Chantilly là-dessus.

splotch¹ [splɒtʃ] *n F* tache *f* (*de couleur, d'encre*).

splotch² *vt F* tacher, barbouiller (**with,** de).

splurge¹ [splɜːdʒ] *n F* **(a)** (*ostentation*) esbrouffe *f*, épate *f*; **(b)** (*extravagant spending*) folles dépenses; (*extravagant behaviour*) folie *f*; **let's have a big s. and give the biggest party ever,** soyons extravagants et organisons la plus grande fête qu'on ait jamais vue.

splurge² *vi F* faire de l'esbrouffe *ou* de l'épate.

►**splurge out** *vi F* (*spend extravagantly*) faire des dépenses extravagantes; **to s. out on sth,** faire des folies pour qch.

splutter¹ ['splʌtər] *n* **(a)** (*speech*) bredouillement *m*; **(b)** crachement *m* (*d'un stylo, El d'un collecteur etc*); bafouillage *m* (*d'un moteur*).

splutter² **1** *vt* bredouiller (*une excuse, une menace*). **2** *vi* (*of person*) (*spit*) envoyer des postillons en parlant, postillonner; (*of pen, El of collector*) cracher; (*of engine*) bafouiller.

►**splutter out** *vtsep* = **SPLUTTER² 1.**

spoil¹ [spɔɪl] *n* **(a)** (*usu pl*) dépouilles *fpl*; butin *m*; **to claim one's share of the spoil(s),** demander sa part du gâteau; **(b)** *Min etc* **s. (earth),** déblai(s) *m(pl)*.

spoil² *v* (*pt & pp* **spoiled, spoilt** [spɔɪld, spɔɪlt]) **1** *vt* **(a)** gâcher (*qch*); avarier (*des marchandises*); altérer, gâter (*la viande, le vin*); **this book was spoilt by the rain,** ce livre a été abîmé par la pluie; **the picnic was spoilt by the rain,** le pique-nique a été gâché par la pluie; **to get spoilt** *or* **spoiled,** s'abîmer; **to s. s.o.'s fun,** gâter *ou* gâcher le plaisir de qn; **to s. the beauty of sth,** défigurer qch; *F* **it spoils her,** (*of behaviour*) ça lui fait tort; **to s. s.o.'s appetite,** couper l'appétit *ou* la faim à qn; *Pol* **spoilt paper,** bulletin (de vote) nul; **(b)** gâter (*un enfant etc*); **her husband spoils her,** son mari la gâte; **a spoilt child,** un enfant gâté; **we're spoilt here — not many cities have 20 theatres,** nous sommes gâtés ici – peu de villes comptent 20 théâtres; **to be spoilt for choice,** avoir l'embarras du choix. **2** *vi* **(a)** (*of fruit, fish etc*) s'avarier; **(b) to be spoiling for a fight,** avoir envie de se battre, *F* chercher la bagarre.

spoilage ['spɔɪlɪdʒ] *n Typ* déchets *mpl* de tirage.

spoiler ['spɔɪlər] *n Av* déporteur *m*; *Aut* béquet *m*, becquet *m*.

spoilsport ['spɔɪlspɔːt] *n F* trouble-fête *mf inv*, rabat-joie *mf inv*; **don't be a s.!,** ne joue pas les trouble-fête!; **he's such a s.,** qu'est-ce qu'il est rabat-joie.

spoke¹ [spəʊk] *n* **(a)** rayon *m*, rai *m* (*de roue*); *Nau* poignée *f*, manette *f* (*de roue de gouvernail*); **(b)** échelon *m* (*d'échelle*); bâton *m* (*à enrayer*); **to put a s. in s.o.'s wheel,** mettre des bâtons dans les roues de *ou* à qn.

spoke² *see* **SPEAK.**

spoken ['spəʊk(ə)n] *adj* **s. language,** langue parlée; **the s. word,** la parole.

spoken-voice ['spəʊk(ə)n'vɔɪs] *adj* (*record*) parlé.

spokeshave ['spəʊkʃeɪv] *n Carp* (*tool*) vastringue *f*.

spokesman, *pl* **-men** ['spəʊksmən] *n* porte-parole *m inv* (*d'un parti etc*); **to act as s. for s.o.,** être le porte-parole de *ou* (*on one occasion*) prendre la parole pour qn.

spokesperson ['spəʊkspɜːsən] *n* porte-parole *m inv*.

spokeswoman, *pl* **-women** ['spəʊkswʊmən, -wɪmɪn] *n* (femme) porte-parole *f inv*.

spoliation [spəʊlɪ'eɪʃən] *n* **(a)** (*despoiling*) spoliation *f*, dépouillement *m*; (*plundering*) pillage *m*; **(b)** *Jur* destruction *f*, altération *f* (*de documents probants*).

spondaic [spɒn'deɪɪk] *adj* (*in prosody*) spondaïque.

spondee ['spɒndiː] *n* (*in prosody*) spondée *m*.

sponge¹ [spʌndʒ] *n* **(a)** éponge *f*; **s. bag,** trousse *f* de toilette *ou* de voyage; *Tex* **s. cloth,** tissu *m* éponge; **to throw in** *or* **up the s.,** *Boxing* jeter l'éponge; *Fig* s'avouer vaincu, abandonner la partie; **s. fisher,** pêcheur, -euse d'éponges; **(b)** (*action*) coup *m* d'éponge; **to give sth a s.,** passer l'éponge sur *ou* donner un coup d'éponge à qch; **(c)** *Culin* gâteau *m* mousseline; **s. biscuit** = madeleine *f*.

sponge² **1** *vt* **(a)** éponger (*qch*); passer l'éponge sur (*qch*); laver à l'éponge; **(b)** *Med* lotionner (*une plaie*); **(c)** *F* (*cadge*) écornifler, grappiller (*un repas etc*). **2** *vi F* (*be parasite*) faire le parasite.

►**sponge down** *vtsep* (*wash*) doucher (*qn*) avec une éponge; éponger (*un cheval*); nettoyer (*une voiture*) à l'éponge.

►**sponge off** **1** *vtsep* enlever *ou* effacer (*une tache*) à l'éponge. **2** *vipo F* (*be parasite of*) vivre aux crochets *ou* aux dépens de (*qn*); **they're just sponging off the state!,** ce ne sont que des parasites de l'État!

►**sponge on** *vipo* = **SPONGE OFF 2.**

►**sponge out** *vtsep* enlever *ou* effacer (*une tache*) à l'éponge; nettoyer (*un tiroir, une plaie*) à l'éponge.

►**sponge up** *vtsep* éponger (*un liquide*).

sponger ['spʌndʒər] *n F* parasite *m*.

sponginess ['spʌndʒɪnɪs] *n* spongiosité *f*; moelleux *m*; caractère mou; souplesse *f*.

sponging ['spʌndʒɪŋ] **1** *adj F* (*person*) parasite. **2** *n* **(a)** (*act of cleaning*) nettoyage *m* à l'éponge; *Med* lavage *m* (*d'une plaie*) avec une lotion; **(b)** (*sponge collecting*) pêche *f* des éponges.

spongy ['spʌndʒɪ] *adj* spongieux; (*cake, pastry*) moelleux; (*road surface*) mou, *f* molle; (*soles*) souple.

sponsor¹ ['spɒnsər] *n* (*for athlete, team, festival, programme, giving money*) sponsor *m*; (*introducing new member to club, for student*) parrain *m*; (*at baptism*) parrain *m*, marraine *f*; *Jur* garant *m*, répondant *m* (**for s.o.,** de qn); caution *f*; **to stand s. to a child,** tenir un enfant sur les fonts (baptismaux).

sponsor² *vt* **(a)** *TV Sp etc* sponsoriser, patronner; sponsoriser (*athlete team, festival etc*); parrainer (*student*); *Rad TV* sponsoriser, parrainer (*programme*); sponsoriser (*charity walker etc*); **sponsored walk,** marche sponsorisée (pour aider une œuvre de charité); **(b)** *Jur* (*act as guarantor for*) être le garant de, répondre pour, se porter caution pour (*qn*); (*act as godparent to*) parrainer (*qn*).

sponsorship ['spɒnsəʃɪp] *n* **(a)** *TV Sp etc* (*of athlete, team, festival etc*) parrainage *m*, patronage *m*; (*of student*) parrainage; *Rad TV* (*of programme*) parrainage, patronage; **(b)** *Jur* garantie *f*, caution *f*; (*of child*) parrainage *m*.

spontaneity [spɒntə'niːɪtɪ, -'neɪ-] *n* spontanéité *f*.

spontaneous [spɒn'teɪnɪəs] *adj* spontané; (*mouvement*) automatique; (*acte, aveu*) volontaire; **a s. gesture,** un geste spontané; **s. combustion,** combustion spontanée.

spontaneously [spɒn'teɪnɪəslɪ] *adv* (*see adj*) spontanément; automatiquement; volontairement; **she s. offered to help,** elle a spontanément proposé son aide.

spoof¹ [spuːf] *n F* **(a)** (*play, film etc*) satire *f* (**on,** de); **s. thriller,** satire des films à sensations; **(b)** (*trick*) blague *f*; (*dummy, decoy, mock-up etc*) attrape *f*; **they erected some s. factories to fool the enemy,** ils ont installé des semblants d'usines pour tromper l'ennemi; **he sent round a s. memo about redundancies,** il a fait passer une fausse circulaire *ou F* une circulaire bidon parlant de licenciements.

spoof² *vt F* (*parody, satirize*) parodier, caricaturer.

spook [spuːk] *n F* spectre *m*, fantôme *m*, apparition *f*.

spooky ['spuːkɪ] *adj F* (*histoire etc*) de spectres, de revenants; (*endroit*) hanté; *Sl* (*strange*) dingue; **it's s. here at night,** c'est sinistre ici le soir; **he's a s. sort of person,** il est du genre sinistre.

spool¹ [spuːl] *n* **(a)** *Tex* bobine *f*, can(n)ette *f*; (*of sewing machine*) can(n)ette; **s. of thread,** bobine de coton (à coudre); **(b)** *Fishing* tambour *m* (de moulinet); **(c)** *El* (corps *m* de) bobine *f*; *Phot Cin* bobine (de film); **take-up s.,** bobine enrouleuse; **(ribbon) s.,** (*for typewriter*) bobine du ruban.

spool² *vt Tex etc* bobiner; *Comptr* (*jobs for a printer*) mettre en attente.

spoon¹ [spuːn] *n* **(a)** cuillère *f*, cuiller *f*; **soup s.,** cuillère à soupe; **serving s.,** cuillère de service *ou* à service; **wooden s.,** cuillère en bois; **(b)** *Golf* bois *m* numéro 3, spoon *m*; *Fishing* **s. (bait), trolling s.,** cuillère *f*; **s. net,** épuisette *f*; **(c) s. drill,** cuillère *f*.

spoon² **1** *vt* **(a)** prendre/verser à l'aide d'une cuillère (*liquid*); **to s. syrup/gravy onto sth,** verser un sirop/une sauce sur qch à l'aide d'une cuillère; **to s. one's soup,**

manger sa soupe (avec une cuillère); **(b)** *Fishing* pêcher à la cuillère; *Sp* prendre (*la balle*) en *ou* à la cuillère. **2** *vi Old-fashioned F* (*of couple*) se faire des mamours.

►**spoon out** *vtsep* (*serve*) servir (*la sauce etc*) (avec une cuillère).

►**spoon up** *vtsep* manger (*qch*) à la cuillère.

spoonbill ['spu:nbɪl] *n* (*bird*) spatule *f* (blanche).

spoonerism ['spu:nərɪz(ə)m] *n* contrepèterie *f*.

spoon-feed ['spu:nfi:d] *vt* (*pt & pp* **-fed** [-fed]) nourrir (*qn*) à la cuillère; *Fig* (*spoil*) gâter, dorloter (*child*); ménager (*workforce etc*); mâcher (*le travail*) à (*qn*).

spoonful ['spu:nfʊl] *n* cuillerée *f*.

spoor ['spʊər] *n* (*in hunting*) foulées *fpl*, piste *f* (*d'un cerf*).

sporadic [spə'rædɪk] *adj* sporadique; isolé (*des averses*); intermittent (*des tirs, du travail*).

sporadically [spə'rædɪk(ə)lɪ] *adv* sporadiquement; (*to fire, work*) par intervalles, à intermittence.

spore [spɔ:r] *n* spore *f*.

sporran ['spɒrən] *n Scot* = aumônière en cuir brut (*pendue sur le devant du kilt*).

sport¹ [spɔ:t] *n* **(a)** sport *m*; **aquatic/winter sports,** sports nautiques/d'hiver; **sports car,** voiture *f* de sport; *Sch* **sports day,** fête sportive; **sports ground,** terrain *m* de sport *ou* de jeux; *Br* **sports** *or US* **s. jacket** *or* **coat,** veston *m* sport; *Journ* **sports page,** rubrique sportive; *TV etc* **sports results,** résultats sportifs; **sports shop,** magasin *m* de sport; **(b)** *F* **a (good, real) s.,** (*good loser*) un beau joueur; (*generous, fair, lively person*) un chic type; **come on, be a s.!,** voyons, sois chic!; *esp Austr* **hello, (old) s.!,** salut, mon vieux!; **(c)** (*amusement*) jeu *m*, divertissement *m*, amusement *m*; **in s.,** pour rire, par plaisanterie; *Old-fashioned* **to make s. of sth,** s'amuser *ou* se moquer de qch; **to have good s.,** (*in hunting*) faire bonne chasse; (*in fishing*) faire bonne pêche *ou* bonne prise; **(d)** *Lit* **to be the s. of fortune,** être le jouet *ou* le jeu de la fortune; **(e)** *Biol* variété anormale, type anormal.

sport² **1** *vt* (*wear*) porter, arborer (*qch de très voyant*); exhiber (*un manteau de fourrure etc*). **2** *vi* **(a)** *Old-fashioned* se divertir, s'amuser; **(b)** *Biol* (*of plants, animals*) produire une variété anormale.

sporting ['spɔ:tɪŋ] *adj* **(a)** (*to do with sport*) de sport; sportif; **s. man/woman,** (*sport enthusiast*) amateur de sport; (*horseracing enthusiast*) turfiste; **in a s. spirit,** animé de l'esprit sportif, sportivement; *F* **it's very s. of him,** c'est très chic de sa part; **you've got a s. chance,** il vaut la peine d'essayer; **to give s.o. a s. chance,** donner une bonne chance à qn; **I'll make you a s. offer,** je vais vous faire une offre à laquelle vous ne perdrez rien; **(b)** *Old-fashioned* (*fond of hunting*) amateur de chasse *ou* de pêche.

sportingly ['spɔ:tɪŋlɪ] *adv* sportivement.

sportive ['spɔ:tɪv] *adj Old-fashioned* (*joking*) badin; (*playful*) folâtre.

sportscast ['spɔ:tskɑ:st] *n Rad TV* émission sportive.

sportscaster ['spɔ:tskɑ:stər] *n Rad TV* reporter sportif.

sportsman, *pl* **-men** ['spɔ:tsmən] *n* **(a)** (*player*) sportif *m*; (*hunter*) chasseur *m*; (*angler*) pêcheur *m*; **a keen s.,** un ardent sportif; **(b) he's a real s.,** (*fair-minded person*) il est animé de l'esprit sportif; (*good loser*) il est un beau joueur.

sportsmanlike ['spɔ:tsmənlaɪk] *adj* sportif; **in a s. way,** sportivement.

sportsmanship ['spɔ:tsmənʃɪp] *n* **(a)** (*skill*) habileté *f ou* qualités *fpl* de sportif; **(b)** (*fair-mindedness*) esprit sportif, sportivité *f*.

sportsperson ['spɔ:tspɜ:sən] *n* (*player*) sportif *m*, sportive *f*.

sportswear ['spɔ:tsweər] *n* vêtements *mpl* (de) sport.

sportswoman, *pl* **-women** ['spɔ:tswʊmən, -wɪmɪn] *n* **(a)** (*player*) sportive *f*; **(b) she's a real s.,** (*fair-minded person*) elle est animée de l'esprit sportif; (*good loser*) elle est belle joueuse.

sporty ['spɔ:tɪ] *adj F* **(a)** (*fond of sport*) sportif; **(b)** (*veston etc*) gai; (*car*) sportif; **it's a bit too s.,** c'est un peu trop sport; *Old-fashioned* **it's awfully s. of you to ...,** c'est très chic de votre part de ... .

spot¹ [spɒt] *n* **(a)** (*place*) endroit *m*, lieu *m*; *TV Rad* créneau *m* (*réservé à la publicité, à une personne*); (*for publicity*) spot *m* publicitaire; **remote s.,** endroit écarté *ou* isolé; **a local beauty s.,** une belle vue locale; **a black s.,** (*on road*) un point noir; **X marks the s.,** la croix indique le lieu (*du crime etc*); **the police are on the s.,** la police est sur les lieux; **to have s.o. on the s.,** (*reporter, representative, agent etc*) avoir qn sur place; **our reporter on the s., Mary Smith,** notre correspondante sur place, Mary Smith; *F* **to put s.o. on the s.,** (*put in difficult position*) mettre qn dans une situation difficile; (*force to answer difficult question*) embarrasser qn par des questions; **to be fined on the s.,** recevoir une amende sur les lieux de l'infraction; **to do sth on the s.,** faire qch sur place *ou* sur-le-champ; **to be killed on the s.,** être tué sur le coup, être tué net *ou* raide; *F* **to hit the high spots,** faire la noce; *F* **to be in a (tight) s.,** (*in predicament*) être dans le pétrin; **night s.,** boîte *f* de nuit; **weak s.,** point faible; **to find s.o.'s weak s.,** trouver le défaut dans la cuirasse de qn; **the sore s.,** l'endroit sensible; **blind s.,** *Anat* point *m* aveugle; *Aut* angle *m* aveugle; *F* **that's your blind s.,** c'est là où vous refusez de voir clair; *TV Rad* **s. announcement,** bref message publicitaire; *Com* **s. cash,** (argent) comptant *m*; **s. check,** (*without notice*) contrôle-surprise *m*; (*random check*) contrôle *m* par sondage(s); (*at random intervals*) contrôle à intervalles irréguliers; *Geog* **s. height,** altitude *f*; **s. market,** marché *m* du disponible *ou* du comptant; *St Exch* **s. transaction** *or* **deal,** operation *f* au comptant;
(b) (*stain*) tache *f*, macule *f*; (*on fruit etc*) tavelure *f*; (*on face etc*) bouton *m*; **to come out in spots,** se couvrir de boutons; **it makes me come out in spots,** ça me donne des boutons; **s. remover,** détachant *m*;
(c) (*dot*) pois *m* (*de couleur, de broderie*); point *m* (*sur une carte à jouer etc*); *Billiards* mouche *f*; **blue tie with red spots,** cravate bleue à pois rouges; **a leopard's spots,** la tacheture *ou* la moucheture d'un léopard; *F* **to knock spots off s.o.,** battre qn à plate(s) couture(s); *Med* **a s. on the lung,** un voile au poumon; **s. welding,** soudure *f* par points;
(d) (*small amount*) goutte *f* (*de pluie, de vin*); *F* **a s. of whisky,** deux doigts *mpl* de whisky; **what about a s. of lunch?,** si nous allions déjeuner?; **to do a s. of work,** faire un peu de travail; **a s. of bother** *or* **trouble,** un petit ennui;
(e) (*spotlight*) *Th* projecteur *m*; (*in home, on exhibition stand*) spot *m*.

spot² *vt* (**-tt-**) **1** *vt* **(a)** (*mark with spots*) tacher, moucheter (*qch*); (*stain, mark*) tacher, souiller (*qch*); *Billiards* mettre (*la bille*) sur la mouche; **(b)** *F* (*notice*) repérer, apercevoir (*qn, qch*); **I spotted her in the crowd,** je l'ai repérée au milieu de la foule; *Horseracing etc* prédire, repérer (*le gagnant*); *Mil* repérer, observer (*des emplacements ennemis etc*); repérer (*des différents modèles de trains etc*); dénicher (*du talent*); **to s. a mistake,** détecter une erreur; **I spotted him as a German,** je l'ai reconnu comme étant allemand; **well spotted!,** (*when noticing mistake*) bien vu!; (*when finding s.o. in crowd*) quel œil!; **I'd never have spotted it,** je ne l'aurais jamais remarqué; **she was last spotted in the pub,** c'est au pub qu'on l'a vue en dernier; **(c)** (*metalworking*) *& MecE* marquer, centrer (*un trou*). **2** *vi* **(a)** (*become stained*) **material that spots easily,** tissu qui se tache facilement; **(b) it's spotting (with rain),** il commence à pleuvoir.

spot-check *vt* (*without notice*) faire des contrôles-surprises de; (*randomly*) contrôler (*qch*) par sondage(s); (*at random intervals*) contrôler (*qch*) à intervalles irréguliers.

spotless ['spɒtlɪs] *adj* sans tache, immaculé; (*maison, cuisine*) d'une propreté irréprochable.

spotlessly ['spɒtlɪslɪ] *adv* **s. clean,** d'une propreté irréprochable; **s. white,** d'une blancheur immaculée *ou* parfaite.

spotlessness ['spɒtlɪsnɪs] *n* propreté *f*.

spotlight¹ ['spɒtlaɪt] *n Th Cin* (*beam*) lumière *f* de projecteur; (*device*) projecteur *m* (*orientable, intensif*); (*in home, on exhibition stand*) projecteur directif, spot *m*; *Aut* projecteur auxiliaire orientable; **to hold the s.,** *Th* occuper le centre de la scène (*dans la lumière du projecteur*); *Fig* avoir *ou* tenir la vedette, être la vedette; **she has always been in** *or* **has never been out of the s.,** elle n'a pas cessé de tenir la vedette.

spotlight² *vt Th* diriger les projecteurs sur (*qn, qch*); *Fig* mettre (*qn, qch*) en vedette.

spotlighting ['spɒtlaɪtɪŋ] *n Th Cin &* (*in home*) éclairage *m* à effet.

spot-on ['spɒt'ɒn] *adj F* exact, au point; **that's s.-on,** c'est exact; **his answer was s.-on,** sa réponse était parfaitement exacte *ou* correcte; **the missiles were s.-on,** les missiles ont atterri en plein dans le mille.

spotter ['spɒtər] *n* **(a)** *Mil Av* observateur *m*; **s. plane,** avion *m* d'observation; **(b) train s.,** = personne *f* qui regarde passer des trains (*pour repérer les différents modèles*); **talent s.,** dénicheur, -euse de talent.

spotting ['spɒtɪŋ] *n* **(a)** (*marks, stains*) tacheture *f*; **(b) train/plane** *etc* **s.,** repérage *m* de trains/d'avions/*etc*; **(c)** *MecE* centrage *m* (*d'un trou*).

spotty ['spɒtɪ] **1** *adj* **(a)** (*marked with spots*) moucheté, tacheté; (*covered with stains*) couvert de taches; (*visage*) couvert de boutons, boutonneux; **a s. adolescent,** un adolescent boutonneux; **(b)** *F* (*travail*) qui manque d'ensemble, inégal. **2** *n* **hi there, s.!,** salut, le boutonneux *ou* la boutonneuse!

spot-weld¹ ['spɒtweld] *vt* souder (par fusion) par points.

spot-weld² *n* soudure *f* (par fusion) par points.

spouse [spaʊz] *n Arch & Lit* époux, *f* épouse; *Admin Jur* conjoint, -ointe.

spout¹ [spaʊt] *n* **(a)** bec *m* (*de théière, de bouilloire etc*); canon, goulot *m* (*d'arrosoir*); jet *m* (*de pompe*); **s. (hole),** (*of whale*) évent *m*; *Sl* **up the s.,** perdu, fichu, foutu; (*pregnant*) en cloque; *Constr* **rainwater s.,** tuyau *m* de décharge, gargouille *f*, chantepleure *f* (*de gouttière*); **(b)** (*jet of liquid*) jet *m*; **a s. of water shot up,** un jet d'eau s'éleva en giclant.

spout² 1 *vi* **(a)** (*of liquid*) jaillir, rejaillir; (*more forcefully*) gicler; (*of whale*) lancer un jet d'eau *ou* d'air, souffler; **(b)** *F* (*of person*) parler à jet continu, dégoiser; *F* **what's he spouting on about now?,** qu'est-ce qu'il est en train de débiter maintenant? **2** *vt* **(a)** (*of person*) faire jaillir, lancer (*de l'eau etc*); **(b)** *F* dégoiser *ou* débiter à jet continu (*des discours, des sottises*); **the pipe spouted water everywhere,** de l'eau jaillissait du tuyau.

►spout out 1 *vi* (*of water, lava etc*) jaillir, sortir en giclant; **the liquid was spouting out of the barrel,** le liquide sortait du tonneau en giclant, le liquide jaillissait du tonneau. **2** *vtsep* **(a)** cracher (*de la lave*); **the pipe spouted out water,** de l'eau jaillissait du tuyau; **(b)** (*speaking*) débiter (*une série de chiffres etc*).

sprain¹ [spreɪn] *n Med* entorse *f*; (*less serious*) foulure *f*.

sprain² *vt* se fouler (*la cheville, le poignet*); (*more seriously*) se donner *ou* se faire une entorse au (*pied, poignet*); **sprained ankle,** foulure *f* au pied; entorse *f*.

sprang *see* **SPRING²**.

sprat [spræt] *n* (*fish*) sprat *m*, harenguet *m*.

sprawl [sprɔːl] *vi* **(a)** (*of person*) s'étendre, s'étaler; **to s. on a sofa,** s'étaler *ou* se vautrer sur un divan; **he was lying sprawled out on the sofa,** il était étalé de tout son long sur le divan; **to send s.o. sprawling,** envoyer rouler qn de tout son long; **to go sprawling,** s'étaler par terre; **(b)** (*of town etc*) s'étendre de tous les côtés; (*of plant*) s'étendre, se déployer.

sprawling ['sprɔːlɪŋ] *adj* **(a)** (*person*) vautré; **(b)** (*suburbs etc*) informe, tentaculaire; (*plants*) tentaculaire; **s. handwriting,** écriture informe.

spray¹ [spreɪ] *n* brin *m*, ramille *f*; **s. of diamonds,** aigrette *f* de diamants; **s. of flowers,** branche *f* de fleurs, rameau fleuri; *Archit Sewing etc* chute *f* de fleurs.

spray² *n* **(a)** (*liquid*) (*of seawater, fine snow*) embrun *m*, poudrin *m*; (*foam*) écume *f*; (*water in particles*) poussière *f* d'eau, eau vaporisée; jet atomisé *ou* pulvérisé (*de parfum, d'essence etc*); (*for hair*) spray *m*, laque *f*; **fly s.,** insecticide *f*; **s. paint,** peinture *f* au pistolet;

(b) (*act of spraying*) coup *m* de vaporisateur; jet *m* (*de peinture, de parfum etc*); **to give sth a s.,** arroser (*les champs etc*); peindre (*les murs etc*) au pistolet; mettre du spray *ou* de la laque sur (*les cheveux*);

(c) (*device*) (*for hair spray, paint etc*) bombe *f*; (*for hair, non-gas operated*) spray *m*; (*atomizer*) atomiseur *m*, vaporisateur *m*; **deodorant s.,** désodorisant *m* atomiseur; **perfume s.,** atomiseur à parfum; **fly s.,** atomiseur *ou* bombe insecticide; **s. can,** atomiseur, bombe; *Ind* **s. drying,** séchage *m* (*du lait etc*) par atomisation; **s. gun,** pistolet *m*, pulvérisateur *m* (*à peinture etc*); **s. nozzle,** gicleur *m*.

spray³ 1 *vt* **(a)** atomiser, pulvériser, vaporiser (*un liquide*); **to s. a solution up one's nostrils,** se vaporiser un liquide dans le nez; *Ind* **to s. dry,** sécher par atomisation; **slogan sprayed on a wall,** slogan écrit à la bombe sur un mur; **this liquid is sprayed on the oil slick,** ce liquide est vaporisé sur la marée de pétrole; **three layers of paint are sprayed onto the metal,** trois couches de peinture sont vaporisées sur le métal; **s. the paint on carefully,** vaporisez la peinture avec soin; **she sprays her hair in position,** elle met ses cheveux en place en les vaporisant;

(b) (*cover with spray*) asperger, arroser; bassiner (*des plantes etc*); peindre (*qch*) au pistolet; (*in horticulture*) passer (*un arbre*) au vaporisateur; **to s. sth with machine-gun fire,** arroser qch à la mitrailleuse.

2 *vi* **water sprayed up in our faces,** de l'eau éclaboussait nos visages.

sprayer ['spreɪər] *n* **(a)** vaporisateur *m*, pulvérisateur *m*; (*atomizer*) atomiseur *m*; pistolet *m* (*à peinture*); **foam s.,** extincteur *m* à mousse; **(b)** (*vehicle, plane*) arroseuse *f*.

spread¹ [spred] *n* **(a)** étendue *f* (*de pays etc*); (*of wings, of sails etc*) envergure *f*; *Com* différence *f* (*entre le prix de fabrique et le prix de vente, entre deux tarifs*); *Am* (*ranch*) ranch *m*; *F* **middle-age(d) s.,** embonpoint *m* de la maturité; **we have a good s. of products,** (*range*) nous avons un bel éventail *ou* une belle gamme de produits;

(b) (*expansion*) diffusion *f* (*de l'éducation*); propagation *f* (*d'une doctrin, d'une maladie*); expansion *f*, dissémination *f* (*des idées*); (*in ballistics*) dispersion *f* (*du tir*);

(c) *F* (*big meal*) festin *m*, repas somptueux; **cold s.,** repas froid;

(d) *Journ etc* **double page s.,** (*advertisement*) annonce *f* en double page; (*article*) article *m* sur deux pages; (*picture*) photo *f* en double page;

(e) *Culin* fromage *m ou* pâte *f* de viande *etc* à tartiner; **cheese s.,** fromage à tartiner; **chocolate s.,** chocolat *m* à tartiner.

spread² *v* (*pt & pp* **spread**) **1** *vt* **(a)** étendre (*les bras etc*); tendre (*un filet*); déployer (*les voiles*); écarter (*les doigts*); **a bird with its wings spread,** un oiseau aux ailes déployées; **s. eagle,** *Her* aigle éployée; (*skating*) grand aigle;

(b) (*distribute*) répandre (*du sable, de la paille*); épandre (*du fumier*); semer (*la terreur*); répandre, colporter, rapporter (*des nouvelles*); propager (*une maladie*); **to s. s.o.'s fame (abroad),** faire connaître la réputation de qn; *Fig* **he's in danger of spreading himself too thin,** il risque de faire trop de choses à la fois; **the payments are spread over several months,** les paiements sont échelonnés *ou* étalés *ou* répartis sur plusieurs mois; **if we can s. the work over three months,** si nous pouvons répartir le travail sur trois mois; **could you s. the word?,** voulez-vous passer le mot?;

(c) to s. butter on a slice of bread, étendre *ou* étaler du beurre sur une tranche de pain, tartiner une tranche de pain de beurre; **to s. ointment on a burn,** appliquer de l'onguent sur une brûlure; **s. the paint evenly,** étendre *ou* étaler la peinture en couches égales;

(d) to s. a surface with sth, recouvrir *ou* enduire une surface de qch; *Old-fashioned & Am* **to s. the table,** dresser *ou* mettre la table, mettre le couvert.

2 *vi* **(a)** (*stretch*) s'étendre, s'étaler; **it spreads over a vast area,** cela s'étend *ou* est reparti sur une grande étendue;

(b) (*of rumour, news, ideas etc*) se répandre, se propager; (*of disease, fire, theory etc*) se propager; (*of smell, smoke, sound*) se répandre; (*of evil, epidemic, fame*) s'étendre; (*of evil, cancer*) se généraliser; (*of group of people*) se disperser; **the fire is spreading,** l'incendie gagne (du terrain); **her ideas are spreading,** ses idées font tache d'huile; **the rumour was spreading,** la rumeur grandissait;

(c) (*of butter, paste, cheese etc*) **it spreads easily,** c'est facile à tartiner.

►spread about, spread around *vtsep* répandre (*une rumeur, une maladie etc*); **have you been spreading it around that I ...?,** est-ce que tu as été raconter partout que je ...?

►spread out 1 *vtsep* (*open out*) déployer, étaler (*une carte etc*); **the plain lay spread out in front of us,** la plaine s'étalait *ou* se déployait devant nous; **a bird with its wings spread out,** un oiseau aux ailes déployées; **to s. oneself out,** s'étendre, s'allonger (*sur un divan etc*); **he spread his papers out on the desk,** il étala ses papiers sur le bureau. **2** *vi* (*of person*) s'étendre, s'allonger (*sur un divan etc*); (*of troops etc*) se disperser; **give yourself room to s. out,** (*doing craft work etc*) accordez-vous de l'espace pour vous étaler; **tell the rescue party to s. out more,** dites à l'équipe de sauvetage de se disperser davantage.

spreader ['spredər] *n* **(a)** (*person*) propagateur, -trice (*d'une idée, d'un bruit*); colporteur, -euse, rapporteur, -euse (*de nouvelles, d'un bruit*); semeur, -euse (*de discorde etc*); **(b)** arrosoir *m* (*d'une machine à arroser*); éventail *m* (*d'une lance d'arrosage*); *Agr Constr* épandeur *m*, épandeuse *f*; (*for putty, plaster etc*) spatule *f*.

spreading ['spredɪŋ] **1** *adj* **under a s. chestnut tree,** sous un châtaignier bien déployé. **2** *n* **(a)** (*act of spreading*) déploiement *m*, développement *m*; colportage *m* (*de nouvelles*); propagation *f* (*d'une maladie, d'une doctrine*); dissémination *f* (*d'idées*); diffusion *f* (*de l'éducation*); étendage *m* (*de la peinture etc*); répandage *m* (*du goudron sur la chaussée etc*); **(b)** (*becoming spread*) extension *f* (*de territoire, d'une industrie*); dispersion *f* (*d'un groupe etc*).

spreadsheet ['spredʃiːt] *n Comptr* feuille *f* de calcul; (*software*) tableur *m*.

spree [spriː] *n F* partie *f* de plaisir; (*eating and drinking*) bombe *f*; **to have a s., to go (out) on a s.,** faire la noce *ou* la bombe; **to go on a shopping** *or* **spending s.,** faire des achats extravagants; **a s. of looting and violence,** une explosion de saccage et de violence.

sprig [sprɪg] *n* brin *m*, brindille *f*.

sprightliness ['spraɪtlɪnɪs] *n* vivacité *f*, enjouement *m*; pétillement *m* (*de l'esprit*).

sprightly ['spraɪtlɪ] *adj* éveillé, enjoué, vif; (*esprit*) pétillant; **to be as s. as a two-year-old,** avoir des jambes de vingt ans; **a s. eighty-year-old,** un octagénaire fringant.

spring¹ [sprɪŋ] *n* **(a)** (*of water*) source *f* (d'eau), fontaine *f*; *Fig* source, origine *f* (*d'une coutume etc*); **hot** *or* **thermal s.,** source thermale; **hot** *or* **thermal springs,** eaux thermales; **mineral s.,** source d'eau minérale; **s. water,** eau *f* de source, eau vive;

(b) (*season*) printemps *m*; **in (the) s.,** au printemps; *Culin* **s. chicken,** poussin *m*; *F* **she's no s. chicken,** elle n'est plus toute jeune; **a lovely s. evening,** une belle soirée de printemps; **to have s. fever,** être amoureux, *Can* avoir la fièvre du printemps; **s. flowers,** fleurs printanières; **s. onion,** petit oignon; *Culin* **s. roll,** rouleau *m* de printemps; **s. tide,** (marée *f* de) vives-eaux *fpl*; **s. vegetables,** primeurs *mpl*, *Can* grand ménage;

(c) (*leap*) saut *m*, bond *m*;

(d) (*elasticity*) élasticité *f*; **the s. of a bow,** la force *ou* la souplesse d'un arc; **with a s. in his step,** d'un pas léger; **there's too much s. in this type of wood,** ce type de bois est trop élastique;

(e) (*device*) ressort *m*; **(interior) s. mattress,** matelas *m* à ressorts; *MecE* **spiral s.,** ressort à *ou* en boudin; **springs, s. suspension,** suspension *f* à ressort(s) (*d'une voiture etc*); **s.-loaded,** à ressort; **s. driven,** actionné par ressort; **s. balance,** balance *f* à ressort; **s. gun,** piège *m* à fusil.

spring² *v* (*pt* **sprang** [spræŋ], *pp* **sprung** [sprʌŋ]) **1** *vi* **(a)** (*jump*) bondir, sauter; **to s. to one's feet,** se lever vivement *ou* d'un bond; **to s. into action,** (*of person, device*) entrer en action; **the lid sprang open,** le couvercle a sauté; **one thing that immediately springs to mind is ...,** une chose qui vient immédiatement à l'esprit est ...; **a tear sprang to her eye,** une larme surgit dans ses yeux; **he sprang to fame overnight,** il est devenu célèbre du jour au lendemain; **they sprang to attention,** d'un bond ils se mirent au garde à vous;

(b) (*of water etc*) jaillir, filtrer, sourdre; **hope springs eternal,** l'espérance reste toujours vivace; **to s. into existence,** naître, surgir; *F* **where did you s. from?,** d'où sortez-vous?;

(c) (*of wood*) (*warp*) gauchir, se déformer, se déjeter, (*of mast, pole*) craquer, se fendre.

2 *vt* **(a)** fendre (*une raquette*); faire craquer (*un mât, un aviron*); gauchir, déformer (*une planche etc*); **to s. a leak,** faire une voie d'eau;

(b) (faire) lever (*une perdrix etc*);

(c) faire jouer (*un piège*); faire sauter (*une mine*);

(d) munir (*une voiture*) de ressorts; **sprung carriage,** voiture suspendue;

(e) *F* (*cause to escape from prison*) faire échapper (*qn*) de prison.

▶**spring back** *vi* (*move back suddenly*) se redresser, repartir en arrière; **the branch sprang back,** la branche s'est redressée; **she sprang back in horror,** elle recula d'un bond, horrifiée.

▶**spring forward** *vi* (*rush forward*) s'élancer *ou* se précipiter en avant.

▶**spring on** *vtaspo* (*confront with*) **to s. a question on s.o.,** (*unexpectedly*) poser à qn une question inattendue; (*point-blank*) demander qch à brûle-pourpoint; **to s. a surprise on s.o.,** faire une surprise à qn; **I wish you wouldn't s. things on me like that,** (*not give advance notice*) j'aimerais bien que tu ne me fasses pas de telles surprises.

▶**spring up** *vi* **(a)** (*jump to one's feet*) se lever vivement *ou* d'un bond; **(b)** (*appear suddenly*) **a breeze sprang up,** une brise s'est levée; **an intimacy sprang up between them,** l'intimité s'est établie entre eux; **a doubt sprang up in his mind,** un doute a germé dans son esprit; **the company sprang up almost overnight,** la société s'est montée quasiment du jour au lendemain; (*of plant etc*) **(to begin to) s. up,** (commencer à) pousser; **weeds are springing up all over the garden,** des mauvaises herbes apparaissent dans tout le jardin.

springboard ['sprɪŋbɔːd] *n Gym Swimming & Fig* tremplin *m*.

springbok ['sprɪŋbɒk] *n* (*antelope*) springbok *m*.

spring-clean¹ [sprɪŋ'kliːn] *n* nettoyage *m* de printemps; **to give a house a s.-c.,** faire le nettoyage de printemps dans une maison.

spring-clean² **1** *vt* nettoyer à fond (*une maison*). **2** *vi* faire le nettoyage de printemps, *Can* faire le grand ménage.

spring-cleaning [sprɪŋ'kliːnɪŋ] *n* grand nettoyage de printemps.

springe [sprɪndʒ] *n* (*for rabbits*) lacet *m*, collet *m*.

springer ['sprɪŋər] *n* **(a)** (*person*) sauteur, -euse; **(b) S. (spaniel),** épagneul *m* springer.

springiness ['sprɪŋɪnɪs] *n* effet *m* de ressort; élasticité *f* (*d'un matelas etc*).

springing ['sprɪŋɪŋ] *n* suspension *f* (*d'une voiture, d'un lit*).

springless ['sprɪŋlɪs] *adj* sans ressort(s); **s. step,** démarche lourde.

springlike ['sprɪŋlaɪk] *adj* de printemps; (*dress*) printanier.

springtide ['sprɪŋtaɪd] *n Lit* = **SPRINGTIME**.

springtime ['sprɪŋtaɪm] *n* printemps *m*.

springy ['sprɪŋɪ] *adj* élastique, qui fait ressort; (*flexible*) flexible; (*corps*) à ressort; (*tapis*) moelleux; (*bois*) élastique; (*cheveux*) gonflant; **with a s. step,** (*marcher*) d'un pas leste *ou* léger.

sprinkle¹ ['sprɪŋk(ə)l] *n* **a s. of rain,** quelques gouttes *fpl* de pluie; **a s. of salt,** quelques grains *mpl* de sel, une pincée de sel.

sprinkle² *vt* répandre, jeter (*de l'eau, du sel, du gravier*); asperger, arroser, bassiner (**with water,** d'eau); saupoudrer (**with sugar,** de sucre); **to s. the floor with sand,** répandre du sable par terre; **he should s. a few well-known names in the text,** il devrait introduire quelques noms fameux par-ci par-là dans le texte; **the odd house was sprinkled here and there on the hillside,** quelques maisons étaient éparpillées sur la colline.

sprinkler ['sprɪŋklər] *n* **(a)** (*for lawns etc*) arroseur *m*; (*elongated*) arroseur, rampe *f* d'arrosage; **(rotary) s.,** arroseur (rotatif); **(automatic) fire s.,** (*extinguisher*) extincteur *m* (automatique) d'incendie; **s. system,** noyage *m* en pluie; **(b)** *Rel* goupillon *m*, aspersoir *m*; **(c)** (*for sugar*) saupoudreuse *f*.

sprinkling ['sprɪŋklɪŋ] *n* **(a)** (*action*) aspersion *f*, arrosage *m*; (*with sugar etc*) saupoudrage *m*; *Rel* **s. of holy water,** aspergès *m*, aspersion; *US* **s. can,** arrosoir *m*; **(b)** (*quantity*) **a s. of gravel,** une légère couche de gravier; **a s. of knowledge,** quelques connaissances; **with a liberal s. of literary references,** avec une distribution généreuse de références littéraires; **a s. of new faces in the congregation,** quelques nouvelles têtes parsemées dans la congrégation.

sprint¹ [sprɪnt] *n Sp* sprint *m*; (*acceleration, spurt*) pointe *f* de vitesse; **there was a s. finish,** il y a eu un sprint à l'arrivée; **he has a good s. finish,** il est bon au sprint.

sprint² *vi Sp* sprinter; **I was good at sprinting,** j'étais bon dans les courses de vitesse; **to s. past s.o.,** sprinter pour dépasser qn; **the little boy sprinted off,** le petit garçon s'élança à toutes jambes; **he sprinted upstairs,** il est monté en courant; **he sprinted after her,** il a couru derrière elle; **I had to s. for the bus,** j'ai dû courir *ou F* piquer un sprint pour attraper le bus.

sprinter ['sprɪntər] *n Sp* coureur, -euse de vitesse; (*good at finishing races*) sprinter *m*.

sprit [sprɪt] *n Nau* livarde *f*.

sprite [spraɪt] *n* lutin *m*, esprit *m* (follet), farfadet *m*.

sprocket ['sprɒkɪt] *n MecE* **(a)** (*tooth*) dent *f* (de pignon); **(b) s. (wheel),** pignon *m* de chaîne.

sprog [sprɒg] *n F* (*child*) môme *mf*, gosse *mf*.

sprout¹ [spraʊt] *n Bot* **(a)** (*shoot*) jet *m*, rejeton *m*, pousse *f*; (*bud*) germe *m*, bourgeon *m*; **(b) Brussels sprouts,** *F* **sprouts,** choux *mpl* de Bruxelles.

sprout² **1** *vi* **(a)** (*of plant*) pousser, pointer; (*of branch, shrub*) bourgeonner; (*of seed*) germer; **(b)** *see* **SPROUT UP**. **2** *vt* (*of animal*) **to s. horns,** pousser des cornes; *F* (*of person*) **to s. a moustache,** laisser pousser sa moustache.

▶**sprout up** *vi* (*of plants*) pousser; *Fig* (*of new buildings, towns etc*) pousser comme un champignon *ou* des champignons; *Fig* (*of new community, sect*) surgir, naître.

sprouting ['spraʊtɪŋ] *n* (*process*) germination *f*, bourgeonnement *m*; **s. broccoli,** brocoli *m*.

spruce¹ [spruːs] *adj* (*person*) pimpant, soigné, tiré à quatre épingles; (*house, room*) soigné, bien entretenu.

spruce² *n* (*tree*) **s. (fir),** (sapin *m*) épicéa *m*; **Norway s.,** sapin de Norvège.

▶**spruce up** *vtsep* (*make neat*) donner de l'éclat à, nettoyer (*la maison, une pièce etc*); **to s. oneself up,** se parer, se faire beau *ou* belle; **all spruced up,** sur son trente et un.

spruceness ['spru:snɪs] *n* (*of person*) mise pimpante *ou* soignée; (*of house, room etc*) propreté *f*, bonne tenue.

sprung[1] [sprʌŋ] *adj* (*mattress etc*) à ressorts.

sprung[2] *see* **SPRING**[2].

spry [spraɪ] *adj* (*comp* **spryer**, *superl* **spryest**) vif, actif, (plein d')allant.

spud [spʌd] *n* **(a)** *F* (*potato*) patate *f*; *Mil Sl* **s. bashing,** corvée *f* de patates, (corvée de) pluches *fpl*; **(b)** (*horticulture*) & *Agr* (*spade*) petite bêche; (*weeding hoe*) sarcloir *m*.

spume [spju:m] *n Arch & Lit* écume *f* (*de la mer*).

spun[1] [spʌn] *adj Tex* câblé; **s. silk,** soie filée.

spun[2] *see* **SPIN**[2].

spunk [spʌŋk] *n* **(a)** *F* (*courage*) courage *m*, cran *m*; **to have plenty of s.,** avoir du cran; **(b)** *Br Vulg* (*semen*) foutre *m*.

spunky ['spʌŋkɪ] *adj F* (*brave*) courageux, qui a du cran.

spur[1] [spɜ:r] *n* **(a)** (*for riding*) éperon *m*; *Fig* **to win one's spurs,** faire ses preuves; **the s. of Italy,** l'éperon de la botte (de l'Italie); **(b)** (*action*) coup *m* d'éperon; *Fig* stimulant *m*; **this hope was the s. that drove her on,** cet espoir fut l'aiguillon qui la fit aller de l'avant; **to do sth on the s. of the moment,** faire qch sous l'impulsion *ou* sous l'inspiration du moment *ou* par coup de tête *ou* à l'improviste; **it was a s. of the moment decision,** j'ai pris *ou* il a pris *etc* cette décision sur un coup de tête; **(c)** ergot *m* (*de coq*); éperon *m* (*d'un coq de combat*); **(d)** éperon *m*, contrefort *m* (*d'une chaîne de montagnes*); épi *m* (*de chemin de fer*); **(e) climbing spurs,** grappins *m*, crampons *m*; **(f)** *Bot* éperon *m*; **fruit s.,** dard *m*; **(g)** *MecE etc* **s. gear** *or* **wheel,** (roue *f* d')engrenage cylindrique *ou* droit.

spur[2] *vt* (-rr-) **(a)** éperonner, talonner (*un cheval*); **(b)** (*fit with spurs*) éperonner (*un cavalier, un coq de combat*); **booted and spurred,** botté et éperonné.

▶**spur on** *vtsep* **(a)** éperonner, talonner (*un cheval*); **(b)** (*motivate*) aiguillonner, stimuler (*qn*); **spurred on by a desire to ...,** stimulé *ou* aiguillonné par un désir de ...; **this spurred us on to redouble our efforts,** ceci nous a stimulés et fait redoubler nos efforts.

spurge [spɜ:dʒ] *n* (*plant*) euphorbe *f*, épurge *f*; **s. laurel,** daphné *m*, lauréole *f*, laurier *m* des bois.

spurious ['spjʊərɪəs] *adj* **(a)** (*false*) faux, *f* fausse; (*distinction*) non valide; **(b)** (*writings*) apocryphe; (*edition*) de contrefaçon; **(c)** (*limb etc*) faux.

spuriously ['spjʊərɪəslɪ] *adv* faussement.

spuriousness ['spjʊərɪəsnɪs] *n* **(a)** fausseté *f* (**of,** de); (*of distinction etc*) manque *m* de validité; **(b)** caractère *m* apocryphe (*d'un texte*).

spurn [spɜ:n] *vt* rejeter (*une offre*) avec mépris; repousser (*qn, les avances de qn*) avec mépris; (*treat with contempt*) traiter (*qn*) avec mépris; **she's feeling spurned,** (*by lover, boyfriend*) elle se sent repoussée.

spurt[1] [spɜ:t] *n* **(a)** (*of liquid*) (*act of spurting*) jaillissement *m*, jet *m*, giclée *f*; **(b)** (*sudden effort*) effort soudain; (*burst of energy*) poussée *f* d'énergie; *Sp* (*of speed*) effort de vitesse; (*flat out*) pointe *f* de vitesse; *Cycling* emballage *m*; *Sp* **to put on a s.,** démarrer; *Cycling* emballer; (*in work etc*) mettre un coup de collier; **there's been a sudden s. of activity,** il y a eu un regain d'activité; **final s.,** pointe finale, rush *m*.

spurt[2] **1** *vi* **(a)** (*of liquid*) jaillir, gicler; **(b)** *Sp* démarrer, faire un effort de vitesse. **2** *vt* (*of person*) faire jaillir, faire gicler (*un liquide*); (*of pen*) cracher, gicler (*de l'encre*); **the pipe spurted water everywhere,** de l'eau jaillissait du tuyau.

▶**spurt out 1** *vi* = **SPURT**[2] **1(a)**. **2** *vt sep* **(a)** = **SPURT**[2] **2**; **(b)** lancer (*des paroles*); **'not just yet', he spurted out,** 'pas tout de suite', lança-t-il.

sputnik ['spʊtnɪk] *n Astronaut* spoutnik *m*.

sputter ['spʌtər] **1** *vt* (*mumble*) dire (*qch*) en bredouillant; (*say while spitting saliva etc*) dire (*qch*) en lançant des postillons. **2** *vi* bredouiller; (*talk while spitting saliva etc*) lancer des postillons en parlant; (*of pen, El of electric arc*) cracher; (*of kindling wood*) pétiller; (*of meat on grill*) grésiller; (*of flame*) grésiller, crépiter.

▶**sputter out** *vi* (*stop burning*) **the candle sputtered out,** la bougie s'est éteinte en grésillant.

sputtering ['spʌtərɪŋ] *n* bredouillement *m*; crachement *m* (*d'un stylo*); *El* crachement, crépitement *m* (*d'un arc électrique*); pétillement *m* (*du bois*); grésillement *m* (*de la friture, d'une bougie*).

sputum, *pl* **-a** ['spju:təm, -ə] *n Med* crachat *m*.

spy[1], *pl* **spies** [spaɪ, spaɪz] *n* espion, -onne, *F* mouchard, -arde; *Av* **s. plane,** avion-espion *m*, *pl* avions-espions; **s. master,** chef *m* de réseau; **s. network** *or* **ring,** réseau *m* d'espionnage; **s. satellite,** satellite-espion *m*, *pl* satellites-espions.

spy[2] **1** *vi* espionner; **to s. on s.o.,** épier *ou* espionner qn. **2** *vt* **(a)** (*notice*) apercevoir, voir; **(b)** (*reconnoiter*) reconnaître.

▶**spy out** *vtsep* **to s. out the land,** explorer le terrain.

spyglass ['spaɪglɑ:s] *n* lunette *f* d'approche, longue-vue *f*, *pl* longues-vues.

spyhole ['spaɪhəʊl] *n* trou *m* (*dans un rideau etc*); judas *m*, guichet *m* (*de porte*).

spying ['spaɪɪŋ] *n* espionnage *m*.

sq. *adj* (*abbr* **square**) carré.

Sq. *n* (*abbr* **Square**) place, square.

sq. ft. (*abbr* **square foot** *or* **feet**) pied(s) carré(s).

Sqn. Ldr. *Mil Av abbr* **Squadron Leader**.

squab [skwɒb] *n* **(a)** (*young pigeon*) pigeonneau *m* sans plumes; **(b)** (*cushion*) coussin capitonné; *Aut* coussin (de siège).

squabble[1] ['skwɒb(ə)l] *n* querelle *f*, chamaillerie *f*.

squabble[2] *vi* se quereller, se chamailler (**with,** avec).

squabbler ['skwɒblər] *n* querelleur, -euse, chamailleur, -euse.

squabbling ['skwɒblɪŋ] *n* querelles *fpl*, chamaillerie *f*.

squad [skwɒd] *n* **(a)** brigade *f*, équipe *f* (*de cheminots etc*); *Sp* équipe; **rescue s.,** équipe de secours; **s. car,** voiture *f* de police; **(b)** *Mil* escouade *f*; **firing s.,** peloton *m* d'exécution.

squaddie ['skwɒdɪ] *n Br Sl* (*private soldier*) bidasse *m*.

squadron ['skwɒdrən] *n* **(a)** *Mil* escadron *m*; **armoured s.,** escadron de chars; **(b)** *Mil Av* escadron *m*, escadrille *f*; groupe *m* d'aviation (*d'avions de transport*); **fighter s.,** escadron de chasse; **s. leader,** (*rank*) = commandant *m*; **(c)** *Nau* escadre *f*.

squalid ['skwɒlɪd] *adj* sale; (*sordid*) sordide.

squalidly ['skwɒlɪdlɪ] *adv* sordidement.

squalidness ['skwɒlɪdnɪs] *n* = **SQUALOR**.

squall[1] [skwɔ:l] *n* (*cry*) cri rauque *ou* discordant.

squall[2] **1** *vi* (*cry*) crier, brailler, piailler. **2** *vt* brailler, crier (*qch*).

squall[3] *n* coup *m* de vent, bourrasque *f*, rafale *f*; *Nau* grain *m*.

squalling ['skwɔ:lɪŋ] **1** *adj* criard, piaillard. **2** *n* criaillerie *f*, piaillerie *f*.

squally ['skwɔ:lɪ] *adj* (*temps*) à rafales; *Nau* à grains; **it's s. today,** il y des bourrasques *ou* *Nau* des grains aujourd'hui.

squalor ['skwɒlər] *n* (*dirtiness*) saleté *f*; (*misery*) misère *f*; **to die in s.,** mourir dans la misère.

squander ['skwɒndər] *vt* gaspiller (*de l'argent, son temps*); dissiper, dilapider, *F* claquer (*une fortune*).

squandering ['skwɒndərɪŋ] *n* gaspillage *m* (*d'argent, de temps*); dissipation *f*, dilapidation *f* (*d'une fortune*).

square[1] [skweər] **1** *n* **(a)** *Math etc* carré *m*; **magic s.,** carré magique;

(b) carreau *m* (*de figure, quadrillée etc*); case *f*, compartiment *m* (*d'échiquier etc*); **to divide a map into squares,** quadriller une carte; **framework of squares,** (*for enlargement etc of maps and plans*) graticule *m*; **(reference) s.,** (*on map*) carreau-module *m*, *pl* carreaux-modules; *Fig* **to be back at s. one,** revenir à son point de départ; **let's start again from s. one,** repartons du point de départ; (*in relationship*) repartons à zero; **(silk) s.,** carré *ou* foulard *m* (de soie);

(c) (*of town, village*) place *f*; (*with garden*) square *m*; (*in front of church*) parvis *m*; *Mil* terrain *m* de manœuvre(s); *Am* (*block of buildings*) block *m ou* pâté *m* de maisons (*entre quatre rues*);

(d) (*for drawing, measuring angles*) équerre *f*; **set s.,** équerre à dessin; **to cut sth on the s.,** couper qch à angles droits; **out of s.,** hors d'équerre; *Old-fashioned F* **to be on the s.,** jouer franc jeu, être honnête;

(e) *Math* carré *m* (*d'un nombre etc*);

(f) *F* **he's a s.,** (*old-fashioned*) il est tout à fait vieux jeu.

2 *adj* **(a)** (*figure, shoulders etc*) carré; **nine metres s.,** de neuf mètres sur neuf, de neuf mètres au carré; **nine s. metres,** neuf mètres carrés; **s. dance,** danse *f* à quatre; *Carp* **s. joint,** assemblage *m* à plat; **s. measure,** mesure *f* de surface *ou* de superficie; **s. metre/centimetre,** mètre/centimètre carré; **s. neck,** encolure carrée, décolleté (en) carré; **s. ruler,** carrelet *m*, règle *f* quadrangulaire; *Nau* **s. sail,** voile carrée;

(b) line s. with another, ligne à angle droit avec une autre; **s. corner,** coin *m* en angle droit; **s. thread,** (*of screw*) filet carré; **s.-headed,** à tête carrée; *Electron etc* **s. wave,** onde carrée *ou* rectangulaire;

(c) *Math* **s. number,** nombre carré; **s. root,** racine carrée;
(d) (*refus*) net, catégorique; (*repas*) copieux; **what he needs is a good s. meal,** tout ce dont il a besoin c'est un vrai repas; **to get things s.,** (*arrange*) arranger les choses; (*put in order*) mettre tout en ordre; **to make an account s.,** régler un compte; **to be s. with s.o.,** être quitte envers qn; **to be (all) s.,** être à égalité; (*of two people*) être quittes; **let's call it s.,** je vous tiens quitte; **to get s. with s.o.,** (*get even*) régler son compte à qn; (*settle bills etc*) être quitte envers qn; **a s. deal,** une affaire honnête; **he always gives you a s. deal,** il est toujours loyal en affaires;
(e) *F* (*old-fashioned*) vieux jeu *inv*, ringard; **you're so s.,** qu'est-ce que tu peux être vieux jeu *ou* ringard.
3 *adv* **(a)** à angles droits (**to, with,** avec); d'équerre (**to, with,** avec); **set s. upon its base,** d'aplomb sur sa base; **he hit him (fair and) s. on the jaw,** il l'a frappé en plein menton;
(b) (*agir*) honnêtement; **fair and s.,** loyalement, carrément.

square² **1** *vt* **(a)** carrer, équarrir (*un bloc de marbre, du bois*);
(b) *F* (*buy*) acheter, soudoyer (*qn*); (*bribe*) graisser la patte à (*qn*); balancer, régler (*un compte*); *F* **to s. accounts with s.o.,** régler ses comptes avec qn; (*get revenge*) régler son compte à qn; **to s. matters,** arranger les choses; **to s. one's practice with one's principles,** accorder ses actions avec ses principes; **how do you s. it with your conscience?,** comment arrangez-vous cela avec votre conscience?; **it's OK, I'll s. it with him,** ça va, j'arrangerai ça avec lui;
(c) **to s. the circle,** faire la quadrature du cercle;
(d) *Math* élever *ou* mettre *ou* porter (*un nombre, une expression*) au carré; **four squared,** quatre au carré;
(e) (*divide into squares*) quadriller (*une feuille de papier*); **squared paper,** papier quadrillé *ou* à carreaux;
(f) *Golf etc* **to s. the match,** galiser la marque.
2 *vi* **(a)** **the end and the side should s. with each other,** le bout et le côté doivent se raccorder;
(b) (*coincide*) s'accorder (**with,** avec); **the theory does not s. with the facts,** la théorie ne correspond pas aux faits.

►square away *vtsep Am* (*tidy*) ranger (*des livres*); arranger (*une chambre*).

►square off **1** *vtsep* **(a)** (*divide into squares*) quadriller (*une feuille de papier*); **(b)** *Carp etc* (*make square*) mettre d'équerre, équarrir (*le bout d'une planche*). **2** *vi esp Am* (*assume fighting position*) se mettre en position de combat.

►square up **1** *vi* **(a)** (*settle debts*) régler ses dettes *ou* comptes; **can we s. up later?,** pouvons-nous nous arranger *ou* faire nos comptes plus tard?; **to s. up with s.o.,** régler ses comptes avec qn; *Fig* (*get even with*) se venger de qn, régler son compte à qn; **(b)** (*face with determination*) **to s. up to the difficulties/to s.o.,** faire face aux difficultés/à qn; **(c)** (*assume fighting position*) se mettre en posture de combat. **2** *vtsep Carp etc* (*make square*) mettre d'équerre, équarrir (*le bout d'une planche*).

square-bashing ['skweəbæʃɪŋ] *n Br Mil F* = l'exercice *m*.

square-built ['skweəbɪlt] *adj* bâti en carré; (*person*) aux épaules carrés, de belle carrure.

squarely ['skweəlɪ] *adv* **(a)** carrément; **s. built,** bâti en carré; (*person*) aux épaules carrées; **look me s. in the eyes,** regarde-moi bien dans les yeux; **stand it s. on its base,** placez-le bien en équilibre sur son socle; **(b)** (*honestly*) carrément, honnêtement; (*to act*) loyalement.

squareness ['skweənɪs] *n* **(a)** (*shape*) forme carée; **(b)** (*honesty*) honnêteté *f*, (*dans les affaires*); **(c)** *F* (*of person, views*) conservatisme *m* (*d'une personne vieux-jeu*).

square-shouldered ['skweə'ʃəʊldəd] *adj* aux épaules carrées.

square-toed ['skweətəʊd] *adj* (*shoes*) à bouts carrés.

squaring ['skweərɪŋ] *n* **(a)** équarrissage *m* (*d'un bloc de pierre etc*); **(b)** quadrillage *m* (*d'une carte etc*); **(c)** règlement *m* (*d'un compte*); **(d)** **the s. of the circle,** la quadrature du cercle.

squash¹ [skwɒʃ] *n* **(a)** (*crush*) écrasement *m*, aplatissement *m*; *Old-fashioned* **s. hat,** chapeau mou; **(b)** (*crowd*) cohue *f*; **there was a dreadful s. at the doors,** la foule s'écrasait aux portes; **it was a s., but everyone got in the car,** nous étions serrés comme des sardines mais tout le monde a tenu dans la voiture; **(c)** (*pulp*) pulpe *f*; **orange/lemon s.,** sirop *m* d'orange/de citron; (*drink*) orangeade/limonade non gazeuse; **(d)** *Sp* **s.** *or Fml* **s. rackets,** squash *m*; **s. court,** terrain *m* de squash.

squash² **1** *vt* écraser, aplatir (*qch*); écraser, étouffer (*une révolte etc*); *F* (*put in her or his place*) remettre (*qn*) à sa place, rembarrer (*qn*); *F* **she looked rather squashed,** elle avait l'air plutôt dépité. **2** *vi* s'écraser, s'aplatir; **everyone squashed into the car,** tout le monde s'entassa dans la voiture.

squash³ *n* (*plant, fruit*) gourde *f*; *esp Am* courge *f* (calebasse).

►squash up **1** *vi* (*sit, stand together closely*) se serrer, se presser. **2** *vtsep* écraser (*qch*).

squashy ['skwɒʃɪ] *adj* mou et humide; (*easily squashed*) qui s'écrase facilement; (*fruit*) à pulpe molle; (*terrain*) bourbeux, détrempé.

squat¹ [skwɒt] *n* **(a)** (*action*) accroupissement *m*; (*posture*) posture accroupie; **(b)** *F* (*place*) appartement *etc* occupé par un squatter.

squat² *vi* (**-tt-**) **(a)** s'accroupir; (*in hunting*) (*of game*) se tapir; **she was squatting by the fire,** elle était accroupie au coin du feu; **(b)** (*occupy house illegally*) squatter; **to s. on a piece of land,** occuper un terrain illégalement.

squat³ *adj* (*person*) ramassé, trapu; (*object, building etc*) écrasé; (*arc*) surbaissé.

squatter ['skwɒtər] *n* squatter *mf*.

squaw [skwɔː] *n* squaw *f*.

squawk¹ [skwɔːk] *n* **(a)** cri *m* rauque, couic *m* (*d'un oiseau, F de qn*); **(b)** *F* (*complaint*) rouspétance *f*.

squawk² *vi* **(a)** (*of bird, F of person*) pousser des cris rauques; **(b)** (*complain*) *F* rouspéter.

squeak¹ [skwiːk] *n* **(a)** (*little cry*) petit cri aigu, couinement *m*, couic *m* (*d'un animal*); crissement *m*, grincement *m* (*de choses mal huilées*); *F* **I don't want to hear another s. out of you,** je ne veux pas entendre le moindre murmure; **(b)** *F* **that was a near s.,** nous l'avons échappé belle, il était moins une!

squeak² **1** *vi* **(a)** (*of person*) pousser des cris aigus, couiner; (*of animal*) couiner, faire couic; (*of machine part etc*) crier, grincer; (*of shoes*) craquer, couiner; **(b)** *F* (*inform*) vendre la mèche. **2** *vt* crier (*qch*) d'une petite voix aiguë.

squeaking ['skwiːkɪŋ] *n* (*of animal*) couinements *mpl*; (*of door etc*) grincement *m*.

squeaky ['skwiːkɪ] *adj* criard, qui crie; (*chaussures*) qui crissent; **s. voice,** petite voix aiguë; **s. hinges,** gonds grinçants.

squeaky-clean ['skwiːkɪ'kliːn] *adj F* (*person*) blanc, *f* blanche, à la réputation sans tache.

squeal¹ [skwiːl] *n* cri aigu; cri perçant (*d'un animal*); grincement *m* (*de freins*); crissement *m* (*de pneus*).

squeal² **1** *vi* **(a)** pousser des cris aigus, couiner; (*of tyres, brakes*) grincer, crisser; **to s. like a stuck pig,** crier comme un porc qu'on égorge; **(b)** *F* (*complain*) protester, jeter les hauts cris; **(c)** *F* (*inform*) vendre la mèche; (*of outsider*) moucharder; **to s. on s.o.,** dénoncer qn. **2** *vt* crier (*qch*) d'une voix aiguë *ou* perçante.

squealer ['skwiːlər] *n* **(a)** personne criarde; **(b)** *F* (*informer*) donneur, -euse; (*outsider*) mouchard, -arde.

squealing ['skwiːlɪŋ] **1** *adj* qui crie, qui piaille. **2** *n* cris aigus; (*protestation*) hauts cris; (*of tyres, brakes*) crissement *m*, grincement *m*.

squeamish ['skwiːmɪʃ] **1** *adj* **(a)** (*prone to nausea*) délicat; **to feel s.,** avoir des nausées, avoir mal au cœur; **it makes me feel s.,** ça me donne mal au cœur; **I'm s. about seeing blood,** ça me donne mal au cœur de voir du sang; **(b)** (*excessively scrupulous*) scrupuleux à l'excès; (*excessively prudish*) pudique à l'excès; **don't be so s.!,** pas tant de délicatesses!, ne faites pas le dégoûté! **2** *n* **the s.,** (*used as pl*) les petites natures; **this programme/film** *etc* **is not for the s.,** ce programme/film *etc* est réservé à ceux qui ont l'estomac *ou* le cœur bien accroché.

squeamishness ['skwiːmɪʃnɪs] *n* **(a)** (*proneness to nausea*) délicatesse *f*; **(b)** (*fastidiousness*) délicatesse exagérée.

squeegee ['skwiːdʒiː] *n* **(a)** (*mop*) balai *m* en caoutchouc; (*for window cleaning*) racloir *m* (*avec bordure de caoutchouc*); *Nau* râteau *m* de pont; **(b)** *Phot etc* raclette *f*; **roller s.,** rouleau *m* en caoutchouc.

squeeze¹ [skwiːz] *n* **(a)** (*act of squeezing*) compression *f*; serrement *m* (*de main*); (*hug*) étreinte *f*; *Econ* mesures *fpl* d'austérité; **to give sth a s.,** (*toothpaste*) serrer qch; (*cloth*) essorer qch; (*lemon*) presser qch; **to give s.o.'s, hand a s.,** serrer la main à qn; **to give s.o. a s.,** serrer qn dans ses bras; **credit s.,** restriction *f* du crédit; **it'll be a s. but I think we should all fit in,** on sera serrés mais je crois que tout le monde tiendra; **it's something of a s.**

getting into these jeans, c'est toute une affaire pour entrer dans ces jeans; **(b)** (*crowd*) foule *f*, cohue *f*; **it was a tight s.,** on tenait tout juste; **(c) a. s. of lemon,** quelques gouttes *fpl* de citron; **(d)** (*pressure*) exaction *f*; *F* **to put the s. on s.o.,** forcer la main à qn.

squeeze² **1** *vt* **(a)** presser (*une éponge, un citron*); (*hug*) embrasser, étreindre (*qn*); (*wring*) essorer (*un linge*); **to s. s.o.'s hand,** serrer la main à qn;

(b) (*force*) **to s. sth into a box,** faire entrer qch de force dans une boîte; **to s. the juice out of a lemon,** extraire le jus d'un citron; **to s. money out of s.o.,** extorquer de l'argent à qn; **he squeezed his way under the fence,** il s'est glissé *ou* faufilé sous le grillage; **any room for one more to s. in?,** y a-t-il encore une toute petite place?;

(c) (*put pressure on*) exercer une pression sur (*qn etc*); (*force s.o.'s hand*) forcer la main à qn.

2 *vi* **to s. into a crowded train,** entrer de force dans un train bondé; **to find a little parking space to s. into,** trouver une petite place de parking où se faufiler; **we squeezed under the fence,** nous nous sommes glissés *ou* faufilés sous le grillage.

▶**squeeze out** *vtsep* (*extract*) extraire (*juice etc*); **to s. out a tear,** y aller de sa (petite) larme.

▶**squeeze through** **1** *vi* se faufiler, se glisser. **2** *vipo* **to s. through a narrow window,** se glisser par une fenêtre étroite.

▶**squeeze up** *vi* (*sit, stand together closely*) **to s. up (together),** se serrer (les uns contre les autres); **s. up a bit so Jane can sit down,** serrez-vous un peu pour que Jane puisse s'asseoir.

squeezebox ['skwi:zbɒks] *n F* accordéon *m*, concertina *m*.

squeezer ['skwi:zər] *n* presse *f*; **lemon s.,** presse-citrons *m inv*.

squelch¹ [skweltʃ] *n* **(a)** giclement *m* (*de boue*); gargouillement *m*, gargouillis *m* (*de chaussures détrempées etc*); **(b)** (*heavy fall*) lourde chute (*sur qch de mou*).

squelch² **1** *vt* écraser (*qch*) (*en le faisant gicler*). **2** *vi* **to s. through the mud,** patauger dans la boue; **they squelched across the muddy farmyard,** ils ont traversé la cour de la ferme en pataugeant; **the water squelched in his shoes,** l'eau gargouillait dans ses chaussures.

squib [skwɪb] *n* **(a)** (*firework*) pétard *m*, serpenteau *m*; *Fig* **damp s.,** affaire ratée; **(b)** (*verbal attack*) satire *f*, brocard *m*.

squid [skwɪd] *n* calmar *m*.

squiffy ['skwɪfɪ] *adj Old-fashioned Br F* un peu ivre, gris, éméché.

squiggle ['skwɪg(ə)l] *n F* (*mark, line*) trait *m ou* ligne *f* en paraphe; (*writing*) écriture *f* illisible.

squiggly ['skwɪglɪ] *adj F* tortueux, sinueux.

squint¹ [skwɪnt] *n* **(a)** (*eye defect*) strabisme *m*; **he has a slight s.,** il louche légèrement; **(b)** (*sideways glance*) regard *m* de côté *ou* de travers; **I had a s. at his paper,** j'ai jeté un coup d'œil oblique sur son journal; **(c)** *F* (*look, glance*) regard *m*, coup *m* d'œil; **let's have a s. at it!** faites voir!; **(d)** (*inclination*) inclination *f*, penchant *m* (**to, towards,** vers).

squint² *vi* **(a)** (*have eye defect*) loucher; **they're all squinting because of the sun,** ils font tous la grimace à cause du soleil; **(b) to s. at sth/s.o.,** regarder qch/qn de côté *ou* de travers *ou* furtivement.

squint³ *adj* **(a) s. eyes,** yeux *mpl* louches; **(b)** (*crooked*) de travers; (*table with short leg etc*) bancal, -als; **the plumber had put it on s.,** le plombier l'avait mis de travers.

squint-eyed ['skwɪntaɪd] *adj* au regard louche.

squinting ['skwɪntɪŋ] *n* strabisme *m*.

squire¹ ['skwaɪər] *n* **(a)** *Br* (*local landowner*) châtelain *m*; **(b)** *Hist* (*attendant to knight*) écuyer *m* (*attaché à un chevalier*); **(c)** *Br Sl* **evening, s.,** 'soir, patron.

squire² *vt* servir de cavalier à, escorter (*une dame*).

squirm¹ [skwɜ:m] *n* tortillement *m* (*de douleur etc*).

squirm² *vi* (*of worm etc*) se tordre, se tortiller; (*with embarrassment*) éprouver de l'embarras, être mal à l'aise; **he was squirming with embarrassment,** il se tordait d'embarras; **his over-politeness makes me s.,** sa politesse excessive me met mal à l'aise; **his prose makes me s.,** sa prose est un vrai supplice pour moi, sa prose me donne la nausée; **the sight of all that blood made me s.,** tout ce sang m'a donné la nausée.

squirrel ['skwɪr(ə)l] *n* **(a)** (*animal*) écureuil *m*; **Siberian s.,** petit-gris *m*, *pl* petits-gris de Sibérie; **s. cage,** cage *f* d'écureuil; (*wheel*) tournette *f*; *El* cage d'écureuil; **(b)** *Com* **s. (fur),** petit-gris.

squirt¹ [skwɜ:t] *n* **(a)** (*amount*) jet *m*, giclée *f* (*de liquide*); **to add a s. of soda,** ajouter une giclée d'eau de Seltz; **to give s.o. a s. with a water pistol,** arroser qn avec un pistolet à eau; **(b)** (*device*) seringue *f*; **(c)** *F* (*person*) merdaillon *m*.

squirt² **1** *vt* faire (re)jaillir, faire gicler (*un liquide etc*); injecter (*un liquide etc*) avec une seringue; **to s. soda water into a glass,** mettre une giclée d'eau de Seltz dans un verre; **s. the liquid generously over the petals,** faites gicler le liquide en bonne quantité sur les pétales; **he squirted a little deodorant into each armpit,** il fit gicler un peu de déodorant sur chacune de ses aisselles. **2** *vi* (*of liquid etc*) (re)jaillir, gicler; **water was squirting out everywhere,** de l'eau giclait partout.

squishy ['skwɪʃɪ] *adj F* (*ground*) détrempé; (*fruit etc*) mou, *f* molle; **the ground's s. under foot,** le sol gargouille sous les pas.

Sr (*abbr* **Senior**) Sr.

SRN [esa:r'en] *n Br Med abbr* **State Registered Nurse.**

SS [es'es] *n Nau* (*abbr* **steamship**) SS; **the SS Normandie,** = le Normandie SS.

st. *abbr* **stone.**

St **(a)** *abbr* **Street;** **(b)** (*abbr* **Saint**) S(t), Ste.

stab¹ [stæb] *n* (*with knife etc*) coup *m* de poignard *ou* de couteau; *Fig* **s. in the back,** coup de Jarnac, attaque déloyale; **s. of pain,** élancement *m*; *F* **to have a s. at sth,** essayer de faire qch; *F* **I'll have a s.,** je vais essayer; **s. wound,** blessure *f* de coup(s) de poignard; **he had severe s. wounds in the chest,** il était gravement blessé de coups de poignard dans la poitrine.

stab² *v* **(-bb-)** **1** *vt* (*with dagger, knife etc*) poignarder (*qn*), donner un coup de couteau à (*qn*); **to s. s.o. to death,** tuer qn d'un coup *ou* des coups de poignard; **to s. s.o. in the back,** poignarder qn dans le dos; *Fig* tirer dans le dos de qn; **he's been stabbed,** il a été poignardé; **he stabbed his knife into the tabletop,** il planta son couteau dans la table; **she stabbed a piece of sausage with her fork,** elle piqua un morceau de saucisse avec sa fourchette. **2** *vi* **to s. at s.o.,** porter un coup de couteau *ou* de poignard à qn; **he stabbed at the map with his finger,** il a indiqué un point sur la carte avec son doigt.

stabbing ['stæbɪŋ] **1** *adj* **s. pain,** élancement lancinant, douleur lancinante. **2** *n* (*act of stabbing*) coups *mpl* de poignard *ou* de couteau; (*murder*) assassinat *m* à coups de couteau *etc*; (*attack*) coup(s) de poignard *ou* de couteau; **there was a s. in the pub last night,** quelqu'un s'est fait poignarder au pub hier soir.

stability [stə'bɪlɪtɪ] *n* stabilité *f*, solidité *f* (*d'une construction*); stabilité (*d'un avion, d'un composé chimique etc*); stabilité (*économique etc*); **mental s.,** équilibre mental.

stabilization [steɪbɪlaɪ'zeɪʃən] *n* stabilisation *f* (*du sol, d'un avion, Phys El de phase etc*); *Fin* stabilisation, valorisation *f* (*des cours etc*).

stabilize ['steɪbɪlaɪz] **1** *vt* stabiliser (*le sol, un navire, le cours du change*). **2** *vi* se stabiliser.

stabilizer ['steɪbɪlaɪzər] *n* **(a)** *Nau Av* stabilisateur *m*; *Av* empennage *m*; **(b)** stabilisant *m* (*de produits alimentaires, d'explosifs etc*).

stabilizing ['steɪbɪlaɪzɪŋ] **1** *adj* **(a)** stabilisateur, -trice; **to have** *or* **exert a s. effect on prices,** exercer une action stabilisatrice sur les prix; **her new job had a s. effect on her,** son nouvel emploi a eu un effet stabilisateur *ou* équilibrant sur elle; **(b) s. agent,** agent stabilisant (*pour produits alimentaires etc*). **2** *n* = **STABILIZATION.**

stable¹ ['steɪb(ə)l] *n* **(a)** (*building*) écurie *f*; *Fig* **to lock the s. door after the horse has bolted,** fermer la cage quand les oiseaux se sont envolés; **(b)** (*horses*) chevaux *mpl* (*d'une certaine écurie*); *Horseracing Aut etc* écurie *f*; **racing s.,** écurie de courses; **s. companion** *or* **mate,** (*horse*) cheval *m* de la même écurie; *F* (*person*) personne *f* qui a été à la même école.

stable² *vt* loger (*un cheval*) dans une écurie; **we can s. three horses,** nous avons de la place pour trois chevaux.

stable³ *adj* **(a)** stable; (*firmly in place*) solide, fixe; *Ch Phys* stable; **s. state,** état *m* stable, état de stabilité; **s. currency,** monnaie *f* stable; **the government is becoming more s.,** le gouvernement se consolide; **to be in a s. condition,** (*of patient*) être dans un état stationnaire; **s. job,** emploi stable *ou* permanent; **(b)** (*person*) équilibré; *F* **he's perfectly s.,** il est parfaitement sain d'esprit *ou* équilibré; **he's not s.,** il n'est pas équilibré, il est instable.

stableboy ['steɪblbɔɪ] *n* palefrenier *m*.

stablelad ['steɪbllæd] *n* lad *m*.

stabling ['steɪblɪŋ] *n* **(a)** logement *m* (*de chevaux*) dans une écurie; **(b)** (*space in stables*) écuries *fpl*; **we have plenty of s.,** nous ne manquons pas de place aux écuries.

staccato [stə'kɑːtəʊ] **1** *adj* piqué; (*style*) haché; (*voix*) saccadé; **s. note,** note piquéee. **2** *adv Mus* staccato; **3** *n Mus* staccato *m*; **she replied in a rapid s.,** elle répondit sur un ton rapide et saccadé.

stack[1] [stæk] *n* **(a)** meule *f* (*de foin etc*); pile *f*, tas *m* (*de bois, de charbon, d'assiettes*); faisceau *m* (*d'armes*); *F* **stacks of ...,** des tas de ..., beaucoup de ...; *F* **I've stacks of work to do,** j'ai de quoi faire; *F* **to make stacks of money,** ramasser l'argent à la pelle; *F* **I've got stacks of it,** j'en ai des tas; **stacks,** (*in library*) rayonnages *mpl*; **s. room,** réserve *f*; **(b)** souche *f*, corps *m* (*de cheminée*); cheminée *f* (*d'une locomotive etc*); **s. (pipe),** tuyau *m* de descente, descente *f* d'eau (*d'une gouttière*); **(c)** *Geog* (*rock formation*) haut rocher (*au large d'une côte*); **(d)** *Av* (*aircraft waiting to land*) avions *mpl* en attente (*échelonnés en altitude*).

stack[2] *vt* **(a)** (*put in stacks*) mettre (*le foin*) en meule(s); empiler, entasser (*du bois, du charbon, des assiettes etc*); mettre (*les armes*) en faisceaux; **the odds were stacked against them,** tous les augures s'accumulaient contre aux; *Sl* **how's she stacked?,** comment est-elle roulée?; **(b)** *Am* **to s. the cards,** tricher aux cartes; **to s. the jury,** truquer le jury; **(c)** *Av* échelonner en altitude (*les avions en attente*).

stacking ['stækɪŋ] *n* **(a)** mise *f* en meule (*du foin*); empilement *m*, entassement *m* (*du bois, du charbon etc*); mise *f* en faisceaux (*des armes*); **s. chairs,** chaises *fpl* superposables; **(b)** *Av* échelonnement *m* en altitude (*des avions en attente*).

stadium, *pl* **-iums, -ia** ['steɪdɪəm, -ɪəmz, -ɪə] *n Sp etc* stade *m*.

staff[1] [stɑːf] *n* **(a)** (*stick*) bâton *m*; hampe *f* (*de bannière, de lance*); *Nau* mât *m* (*de pavillon*); (*tool*) crochet *m*, ringard *m*; (*in surveying*) jalon *m*, mire *f*; **pilgrim's s.,** bourdon *m* de pèlerin; *Rel* **pastoral s.,** bâton pastoral; *US* **at half s.,** (*of flag*) en berne;

(b) (*personnel, employees*) personnel *m*; **when he joined the s.,** quand il est entré dans le personnel; **how many people are there on the s.?,** combien de personnes le personnel compte-t-il?; **domestic s.,** domestiques *mfpl*; *Journ* **editorial s.,** la rédaction; **teaching s.,** personnel enseignant; **nursing s.,** les infirmiers, les infirmières; **office s.,** personnel de bureau; **senior** *or* **managerial s.,** les cadres supérieurs; **s. association,** syndicat *m* du personnel; **s. management,** direction *f* du personnel; *Med* **s. nurse,** *F* **s.,** = infirmière diplômée; *Sch* **s. room,** salle *f* des professeurs;

(c) *Mil* état-major *m*, *pl* état-majors; **general s.,** état-major général; **chief of s.,** chef d'état-major; **joint chiefs of s.,** état-major interarmées; **S. College,** = École supérieure de guerre; **s. officer,** officier *m* d'état-major;

(d) *Mus* (*pl* **staves** [steɪvz]) portée *f*.

staff[2] *vt* fournir (*un bureau etc*) de personnel *ou* d'employés; **army staffed with brilliant generals,** armée dont l'état-major se compose de généraux remarquables; **the office is almost entirely staffed by women,** le personnel du bureau est presque entièrement composé de femmes.

staffer ['stɑːfər] *n* membre *m* du personnel.

Staffs. *abbr* **Staffordshire**.

stag [stæg] *n* **(a)** (*animal*) cerf *m*; *Ent* **s. beetle,** lucane *m*, cerf-volant *m*, *pl* cerfs-volants; **(b)** *St Exch F* (*premium hunter*) loup *m*; **(c) s. party** *or* **dinner,** réunion *f* pour hommes seulement, *F* un P.H.S.; **to have a s. party** *or* **night,** (*before wedding*) enterrer sa vie de garçon; **it's John's s. party tomorrow,** John enterre sa vie de garçon demain.

stage[1] [steɪdʒ] *n* **(a)** *Th* scène *f*; *Fig* théâtre *m*; **front of the s.,** avant-scène *f*; **revolving s.,** plateau tournant; **to come on (the) s.,** entrer en scène; **to set the s.,** monter les décors; *Fig* exposer la situation; **s. directions,** indications *fpl* scéniques; **s. door,** entrée *f* des artistes; **s. effects,** effets *mpl* scéniques; **s. fright,** trac *m*; **s. left/right,** côté jardin/cour; **s. manager,** régisseur *m*; **s. name,** nom *m* de théâtre; **s. whisper,** aparté *m*; **the s.,** le théâtre; **to go on the s.,** devenir acteur *ou* actrice;

(b) (*platform*) estrade *f*; (*to work on*) échafaudage *m*; platine *f* (*d'un microscope*); **hanging s.,** *Constr etc* échafaud volant; **landing s.,** débarcadère *m*; embarcadère *f*;

(c) (*phase*) (*duration*) phase *f*, période *f*; (*state, point*) stade *m*, étape *f*; **the stages of an evolution,** les étapes *ou* les stades d'une évolution; *Electron etc* **input s.,** étage *m* d'entrée; **to go through a critical s.,** traverser une phase *ou* période critique; **at this s.,** à ce point, à ce moment; **in the larval s.,** à l'état de larve; **to do sth in (successive) stages,** faire qch par étapes (successives); **at what s. in its development?,** à quel moment *ou* stade de son développement?; **at this s. in the project,** à ce stade du projet; **at a later s. in his life,** à un stade plus avancé de sa vie; **to pay in easy stages,** payer en petits versements; **to do sth one s. at a time,** faire qch étape par étape;

(d) (*part of journey*) étape *f*; *Arch* (*for stagecoach etc*) relais *m*; **s. by s.,** d'étape en étape; **we did the journey in easy stages,** nous avons fait le voyage en petites étapes; *Br* **fare s.,** = (changement *m* de) section *f* (*de l'itinéraire d'un autobus*); **s. (coach),** diligence *f*;

(e) *Astronaut* (*of rocket*) étage *m*.

stage[2] *vt* **(a)** *Th etc* monter (*une pièce*), porter (*une pièce*) à la scène; organiser, faire (*une manifestation etc*); monter (*un coup*); **to s. a comeback,** faire un come-back; **(b)** (*phase*) **carefully staged reduction of nuclear weapons,** réduction soigneusement étagée des armes nucléaires.

stagecraft ['steɪdʒkrɑːft] *n Th* technique *f* de la scène.

stagehand ['steɪdʒhænd] *n Th* machiniste *mf*.

stage-manage ['steɪdʒ'mænɪdʒ] *vt* mettre en scène; *Fig Pej* (*manifestation etc*) organiser depuis les coulisses.

stager ['steɪdʒər] *n* **old s.,** vieux routier.

stage-struck ['steɪdʒstrʌk] *adj* épris *ou* féru du théâtre.

stagey ['steɪdʒɪ] *adj* = **STAGY**.

stagflation [stæg'fleɪʃən] *n Econ* stagflation *f*.

stagger[1] ['stægər] *n* **(a)** chancellement *m*; (*way of walking*) pas chancelant; **(b)** *Vet* **staggers,** vertigo *m*.

stagger[2] **1** *vi* chanceler, tituber; **she staggered beneath the weight,** elle chancela sous le poids; **to s. along,** marcher en chancelant *ou* en titubant; **to s. to one's feet,** se relever en chancelant. **2** *vt* **(a)** (*overwhelm*) confondre, consterner, renverser (*qn*); **to be staggered,** tomber à la renverse; (*emotionally*) être bouleversé; **I'm staggered!,** je n'arrive pas à le croire!; **(b)** échelonner (*les heures de travail, les vacances*); *El* échelonner (*les balais*); *Av* décaler (*les ailes*); *MecE* disposer (*des rivets, des joints etc*) en quinconce *ou* en zigzag; alterner, étager (*des rivets*).

staggering ['stægərɪŋ] **1** *adj* (*news*) renversant, atterrant; **s. blow,** coup *m* de massue *ou* d'assommoir; **s. increase in prices,** hausse vertigineuse des prix; **it cost a s. £4,000,** ça a coûté la somme incroyable de 4000 livres. **2** *n* **(a)** (*on one's feet*) chancellement *m*; **(b)** échelonnement *m* (*des vacances, des heures de travail*); *El* échelonnage *m* (*des balais*); *Av* décalage *m* (*des ailes*); *MecE etc* disposition *f* en quinconce.

staghorn ['stæghɔːn] *n* bois *mpl* de cerf.

staghunt(ing) ['stæghʌnt(ɪŋ)] *n* chasse *f* au cerf.

staging ['steɪdʒɪŋ] *n* **(a)** mise *f* à la scène (*d'une pièce*); **(b)** *Arch* **s. post,** relais *m* (*de diligences*).

stagnant ['stægnənt] *adj* stagnant; (*trade, business*) en stagnation, dans le marasme.

stagnate [stæg'neɪt] *vi* (*of water, trade, business, Fig of person*) stagner.

stagnation [stæg'neɪʃən] *n* stagnation *f*; stagnation, marasme *m* (*des affaires*).

stagy ['steɪdʒɪ] *adj* théâtral, -aux.

staid [steɪd] *adj* posé, sérieux, sage.

staidness ['steɪdnɪs] *n* caractère posé *ou* sérieux *ou* sage.

stain[1] [steɪn] *n* **(a)** tache *f*, souillure *f*; **to remove a s.,** enlever une tache (**from,** de); **s. remover,** détachant *m*; *Fig* **without a s. on his character,** sans atteinte à sa réputation; **a grease/blood s.,** une tache de graisse/sang; **(b)** (*dye*) colorant *m*; **(wood) s.,** teinture *f* (pour bois).

stain[2] **1** *vt* **(a)** tacher, souiller, salir (**with,** de); *Fig* entacher, souiller, ternir (*la réputation de qn*); **hands stained with blood,** mains tachées *ou* souillées de sang; *Fig* **hands stained with the blood of innocent people,** les mains tachées du sang d'innocents; **(b)** teindre, teinter (*le bois*); peindre (*le verre*). **2** *vi* **material that stains easily,** tissu qui se tache facilement.

stained-glass ['steɪndglɑːs] *adj* **s.-g. window,** fenêtre *f* en vitrail.

staining ['steɪnɪŋ] *n* **(a)** souillure *f*; **(b)** (*colouring*) coloration *f*; (*of wood*) teinture *f*.

stainless ['steɪnlɪs] *adj* **(a)** sans tache; (*pure*) immaculé, pur; **(b) s. steel,** acier *m* inoxydable, *F* inox *m*.

stair ['steər] *n* **(a)** (*flight of stairs*) escalier *m*; **she walked up/down the stairs,** elle prit l'escalier; **I met him on the stairs,** je l'ai rencontré dans l'escalier; **back stairs,** escalier de service; **s. carpet,** tapis *m* d'escalier; **(b)** (*step*) marche *f*, degré *m* (*d'un escalier*).

staircase ['steəkeɪs] *n* (*stairs*) escalier *m*; (*structure*) cage *f* d'escalier; **secret s.,** escalier dérobé.

stairway ['steəweɪ] *n* = **STAIRCASE**.

stairwell ['steəwel] *n* cage *f* d'escalier.

stake¹ [steɪk] *n* **(a)** (*piece of wood, metal*) pieu *m*, poteau *m*; (*for marking land*) jalon *m*, fiche *f*; (*for tethering animal*) piquet *m*; (*in horticulture*) tuteur *m*; échalas *m* (*de vigne*); (*in surveying*) jalon, piquet; *F* **to pull up stakes,** (*leave*) partir; (*leave one's home*) déménager; **s. boat,** (*in rowing*) bateau *m* de ligne de départ;

(b) (*for execution*) (poteau *m* du) bûcher *m*; **to die** *or* **be burned at the s.,** mourir sur le bûcher;

(c) (*in gambling*) mise *f*, enjeu *m*; **the stakes are down,** les jeux sont faits; **to play for high stakes,** jouer gros jeu; **our honour is at s.,** il y va de notre honneur, notre honneur est en jeu; **there's a lot at s.,** de lourds intérêts sont en jeu; **to have large sums at s. in an enterprise,** avoir de fortes sommes engagées dans une entreprise; **to have a s. in sth,** avoir des intérêts dans une affaire; *Horseracing* **stakes,** prix *m*.

stake² *vt* **(a)** (*mark out*) jalonner, piqueter (*une concession, etc*); (*in surveying*) jalonner (*une ligne, une route etc*); **to s. a claim,** *Min* jalonner une concession; *Fig* établir *ou* faire valoir ses droits; **(b)** (*support with stakes*) soutenir (*qch*) avec des pieux; échalasser (*une vigne etc*); tuteurer (*des tomates*); **(c)** (*in gambling*) mettre (*une somme*) en jeu, jouer, risquer (*une somme*); **to s. twenty francs,** miser *ou* jouer vingt francs; **to s. everything** *or* **one's all,** jouer son va-tout, mettre tout en jeu; **I'd s. my life on it,** j'y mettrais ma tête à couper; **(d)** *Am F* (*provide with money*) fournir (*qn*) d'argent; (*provide needs of*) fournir aux besoins de (*qn*).

▶stake off *vtsep* = **STAKE² (a)**.

▶stake out *vtsep* **(a)** = **STAKE² (a)**; **(b)** (*keep under observation*) surveiller (*building etc*).

stakeout ['steɪkaʊt] *n* guet *m*, surveillance *f*; **to be on s. duty,** faire le guet.

staking ['steɪkɪŋ] *n* **(a)** (*marking off*) jalonnement *m*, piquetage *m* (*d'une concession etc*); **(b)** (*support*) échalassage *m* (*d'une vigne*); tuteurage *m* (*des tomates*); **(c)** (*in gambling*) mise *f* (en jeu) (*d'une somme*).

stalactite ['stæləktaɪt, *Am also* stə'læktaɪt] *n Geol* stalactite *f*.

stalagmite ['stæləgmaɪt, *Am also* stə'lægmaɪt] *n Geol* stalagmite *f*.

stale¹ [steɪl] *adj* **(a)** qui n'est pas frais *ou f* fraîche; (*bread, cake*) rassis; (*wine*) éventé; (*air*) vicié, croupi; **s. smell,** odeur *f* de renfermé; **(b)** *Fig* (*old*) vieux, *f* vieille; vieilli, passé; **s. joke,** vieille plaisanterie; **s. news,** nouvelle défraîchie; *Fin* (*marché*) lourd, plat; **(c)** (*tired*) fatigué, éreinté; **to go s.,** (*of athlete etc*) se surentraîner; (*of actor, musician etc*) perdre son inspiration; **I'm s.,** (*of athlete, actor etc*) je suis vidé; j'ai perdu mon inspiration; *F* **it's gone s. on me,** ça ne me plaît plus, je n'arrive plus à m'y mettre.

stale² *vi* (*of beer etc*) s'éventer; (*of news etc*) perdre son intérêt; **pleasure that never stales,** plaisir toujours nouveau.

stalemate¹ ['steɪlmeɪt] *n Chess* pat *m*; *Fig* **negotiations have reached a s.,** les négociations sont arrivées *ou* ont abouti à une impasse; **it's s. between them,** ils sont dans une impasse.

stalemate² *vt Chess* faire pat (*son adversaire*).

staleness ['steɪlnɪs] *n* **(a)** état rassis (*du pain*); évent *m* (*de la bière etc*); relent *m* (*d'un aliment, d'une pièce*); (*stale smell*) odeur *f* de renfermé; **(b)** manque *m* de fraîcheur (*d'une nouvelle*).

Stalinism ['stɑːlɪnɪz(ə)m] *n* stalinisme *m*.

Stalinist ['stɑːlɪnɪst] *adj & n* stalinien, -ienne.

stalk¹ [stɔːk] *n* **(a)** (*way of walking*) démarche majestueuse *ou* (*showing disdain*) dédaigneuse; **(b)** (*in hunting*) chasse *f* à l'approche.

stalk² **1** *vi* (*walk haughtily*) marcher *ou* s'avancer d'un pas hautain; **to s. out of a room,** sortir d'une pièce d'un air hautain. **2** *vt* (*of animal*) suivre, être sur les traces de (*une proie*); (*of hunter*) poursuivre (*le gibier*); chasser (*le daim*) à l'approche; suivre furtivement (*qn*); (*of private detective*) filer (*qn*).

stalk³ *n* **(a)** tige *f* (*de plante, de fleur*); queue *f* (*de fruit, de fleur*); chaume *m* (*de blé*); rafle *f*, râpe *f* (*de grappe de raisins*); trognon *m* (*de chou*); *Biol* pédoncule *m*; **s.-eyed,** aux yeux pédonculés; **(b)** pied *m* (*de verre à vin*).

stalk⁴ *vt* égrapper (*des raisins*); équeuter (*des cerises etc*).

stalked [stɔːkt] *adj Bot* (*feuille*) pétiolée; (*champignon*) stipité; *Biol* pédonculé.

stalker ['stɔːkər] *n* (*hunter*) chasseur *m* à l'approche; (*person following s.o.*) personne *f* qui fait une filature.

stalking ['stɔːkɪŋ] *n* (*in hunting*) chasse *f* à l'approche; **s. horse,** (*in hunting*) cheval *m* d'abri; *Fig* prétexte *m*.

stall¹ [stɔːl] *n* **(a)** stalle *f* (*d'écurie*); case *f* (*d'étable*); loge *f*, box *m* (*de porcherie*); **(b)** (*for selling etc*) étalage *m* (en plein vent), éventaire *m*; (*permanent*) échoppe *f*; étal, -aux *m* (*de boucher*); (*at exhibition etc*) stand *m*; **(market) s.,** place *f ou* emplacement *m* (au marché); **newspaper s.,** kiosque *m* à journaux; **(c) choir s.,** stalle *f*; *Th* **(orchestra) stalls,** fauteuils *mpl* d'orchestre; **(d)** *Min* taille *f*; **(e) finger s.,** doigtier *m*; **(f)** *Aut* (*act of stalling*) calage *m* (*du moteur*).

stall² **1** *vt* **(a)** *Aut* caler (*le moteur*); **(b)** (*put in stalls*) mettre à l'étable (*du bétail*); **(c)** (*hold off*) **try and s. them for half an hour,** essaie de les retenir une demi-heure; **I think he's deliberately stalling us,** je crois qu'il nous fait attendre délibérément. **2** *vi* **(a)** (*of engine*) (se) caler; *Av* être en perte de vitesse; **(b) to s. (for time),** chercher à gagner du temps; **stop stalling!,** arrête de tergiverser!; **we'll have to s. on this for another week or so,** il faudra que nous gagnions environ une semaine de plus pour ça.

stall-feed ['stɔːlfiːd] *vt* (*pt & pp* **stall-fed** [-fed]) nourrir, engraisser (*du bétail*) à l'étable.

stallholder ['stɔːlhəʊldər] *n* étalagiste *mf*, marchand, -ande en plein vent; (*at charity bazaar*) vendeuse *f*.

stalling ['stɔːlɪŋ] *n Aut* **to prevent s.,** pour empêcher que le moteur ne cale.

stallion ['stæljən] *n* étalon *m*.

stalwart ['stɔːlwət] **1** *adj* (*strong*) robuste, vigoureux; (*brave*) vaillant; (*resolute*) résolu. **2** *n* **a party s.,** un pilier de parti.

stamen ['steɪmən] *n Bot* étamine *f*.

stamina ['stæmɪnə] *n* résistance *f*; **to lack s.,** manquer de résistance.

stammer¹ ['stæmər] *n* (*permanent*) bégaiement *m*; (*out of nervousness etc*) bégaiement, balbutiement *m*; **man with a s.,** homme qui bégaie, bègue *m*.

stammer² **1** *vi* (*normally*)) bégayer; (*out of nervousness etc*) balbutier. **2** *vt* = **STAMMER OUT**.

stammer out *vtsep* (*say with a stammer*) bégayer, balbutier (*qch*); **to s. out an excuse,** bégayer *ou* balbutier une excuse.

stammerer ['stæmərər] *n* bègue *mf*.

stammering ['stæmərɪŋ] *n* bégaiement *m*; (*through nervousness etc*) balbutiement *m*.

stamp¹ [stæmp] *n* **(a) (postage) s.,** timbre(-poste) *m*, *pl* timbres(-poste); **s. album,** album *m* de timbres-poste (de collectionneur); **s. collector,** philatéliste *mf*; **s. machine,** distributeur *m* automatique de timbres-poste; **s. duty,** impôt *m* du timbre; droit *m* de timbre;

(b) (*device for marking*) tampon *m*, empreinte *f*; (*esp for metal*) estampe *f*, étampe *f*; (*esp for gold etc*) poinçon *m*; (*act of minting*) coin *m*; **signature s.,** griffe *f*; **date s.,** (timbre *m*) dateur *m*; **rubber s.,** tampon *ou* timbre de caoutchouc;

(c) (*mark*) marque *f* (apposée); *Ind* estampille *f ou* marque de contrôle; **(hallmark) s.,** poinçon *m* (de contrôle) (*marquant l'or ou l'argent*); **customs s.,** marque de la douane; *Fig* **it needs his s. of approval,** il faut son approbation; **to bear the s. of genius,** porter la marque du génie; **there are few politicians of her s.,** (*calibre*) il y a peu de politiciens qui aient le même calibre qu'elle; (*type*) il y a peu de politiciens de son espèce;

(d) (*in metalwork*) étampeuse *f*, estampeuse *f*;

(e) (*of foot*) battement *m* de pied (*d'impatience, de colère*); **with a s. of the foot,** en frappant du pied; **ceaseless s. of feet,** piétinement perpétuel, bruit continuel de pas.

stamp² **1** *vt* **(a) to s. one's foot,** frapper *ou* taper du pied;

(b) (*imprint mark on*) frapper *ou* imprimer une marque sur (*qch*); marquer (*du beurre, du papier etc*); contrôler, poinçonner (*l'or, l'argent*); frapper, estamper (*la monnaie, le cuir etc*); gaufrer (*le cuir*); *Fig* **he was determined to s. his mark on the party,** il était déterminé à empreindre le parti de sa marque;

(c) (*mark with ink*) timbrer (*un document etc*); viser (*un passeport*); timbrer, affranchir (*une lettre*); estampiller (*un document, des marchandises*); **they s. the details on your cheque,** ils tamponnent les détails sur votre chèque; **a machine that stamps the date on ...,** une machine qui marque *ou* tamponne la date sur ...;

(d) (*put postage stamp on*) timbrer, affranchir (*letter, parcel*); **this letter is insufficiently stamped,** cette lettre n'est pas suffisamment affranchie;

(e) (*in metalwork*) étamper, estamper (*des objets en métal*);

(f) *Fig* **to s. s.o./sth (as) ...,** donner à qn/qch le caractère de ... .

2 *vi* **to s. upstairs/outside/***etc,* monter l'escalier/sortir à pas bruyants.

►**stamp about** *vi* (*stamp feet*) trépigner, piétiner; (*for warmth*) battre la semelle.

►**stamp on 1** *vipo* **(a)** (*step on*) piétiner (*qch*), fouler (*qch*) aux pieds; **(b)** *Fig* (*repress*) (*person*) écraser, bafouer; (*suggestions*) fouler aux pieds. **2** *vtsep* tamponner, marquer; **the date is automatically stamped on,** la date est tamponnée *ou* marquée automatiquement.

►**stamp out** *vtsep* **(a)** (*eradicate*) écraser (*une rébellion etc*); enrayer (*un abus etc*); étouffer, écraser (*une épidermie etc*); **(b)** éteindre (*un feu*) en piétinant dessus; **(c)** (*in metalwork*) découper (*des tôles*) à la presse *ou* à l'emporte-pièce.

stamped [stæmpt] *adj* **(a)** (*crushed*) broyé, concassé; **s. earth,** terre piétinée *ou* battue; **(b)** (*imprinted*) (*beurre, papier etc*) marqué; (*or, argent*) contrôlé, poinçonné; (*cuir*) gaufré; **(c)** (*marked with ink*) (*document etc*) timbré; **(d)** (*with postage stamp affixed*) timbré; **send a s. addressed envelope,** joindre une enveloppe timbrée (libellée) à votre adresse.

stampede[1] [stæm'piːd] *n* (*rush, flight*) fuite précipitée; (*panic*) panique *f*; débandade *f* (*de troupes, de chevaux etc*); **there was a s. for the door,** tout le monde s'est précipité vers la porte.

stampede[2] **1** *vi* (*rush*) se ruer, se précipiter (**for, towards,** vers, sur); (*flee*) fuir en désordre *ou* à la débandade; (*of cattle etc*) partir à la débandade. **2** *vt* jeter la panique parmi (*des bêtes, des personnes*); **to s. a nation into war,** précipiter un peuple dans la guerre; **to s. s.o. into doing sth,** presser qn à faire qch, bousculer qn pour qu'il fasse qch; **I don't want to s. you into making a decision,** je ne veux pas te presser *ou* te bousculer dans ta décision.

stamping ['stæmpɪŋ] *n* **(a)** (*with feet*) piétinement *m*, trépignement *m*; *F* **it's our favourite s. ground,** c'est notre endroit préféré; *F* **this was one of my old university s. grounds,** c'était l'un de mes anciens coins favoris à l'université; **(b)** poinçonnage *m* (*de l'or etc*); **(c)** timbrage *m* (*des documents etc*); estampillage *m* (*des marchandises etc*); affranchissement *m* (*des lettres*); **(d)** (*in metalwork*) (*process of punching*) estampage *m*, étampage *m*; (*process of punching out*) découpage *m* à la presse *ou* à l'emporte pièce; (*item*) pièce estampée; *Aut* **body s.,** embouti *m ou* pièce emboutie pour carrosserie; **s. press,** estampeuse *f*.

stamping out *n* **(a)** (*eradication*) écrasement (*d'une rébellion etc*); enraiement *m* (*d'un abus etc*); éradication *f* (*d'une maladie*); **(b)** (*in metalwork*) découpage *m* à la presse *ou* à l'emporte-pièce.

stance [stæns] *n Golf Cr* posture *f* (*du joueur*); *Fig* position *f*, attitude *f*; **to take up one's s.,** se mettre en posture (*pour jouer*); **the government's s. on this,** la position *ou* l'attitude du gouvernement là-dessus.

stanch [stɑːntʃ] *vt* = **STAUNCH**[2].

stanchion ['stɑːnʃən] *n* étançon *m*, étai *m*.

stand[1] [stænd] *n* **(a)** (*position*) place *f*, position *f*; **to take one's s. near the door,** se placer *ou* se poster *ou* prendre position près de la porte; **to take one's s. on a principle,** s'en tenir à *ou* se fonder sur un principe; **to take a firm s.,** ne pas transiger; **you should take a firmer s. with them,** tu devrais adopter une attitude plus ferme envers eux;

(b) (*resistance*) résistance *f*; **to make a s. against an abuse,** s'opposer résolument à un abus; **to make a s. (against the enemy),** (*of troops*) faire face (à l'ennemi);

(c) *Th* représentation *f*; (*by band*) concert *m*; **we did a s. in Lancaster,** nous avons donné une représentation *ou* un concert à Lancaster;

(d) station *f* (*de taxis*);

(e) (*support*) support *m*, pied *m* (*de lampe etc*); affût *m* (*de télescope*); râtelier *m* (*pour bouteilles etc*); béquille *f* (*pour moto etc*); **revolving s.,** (*for books, postcards etc*) tourniquet *m*;

(f) (*stall*) étalage *m*, étal *m*, boutique *f* (*en plein air*); (*at exhibition etc*) stand *m*;

(g) *Sp etc* (*at sports ground*) tribune *f*; **the stands,** les tribunes;

(h) *Agr* récolte *f* sur pied; (*of trees*) peuplement *m*;

(i) *US Jur* barre *f* des témoins; **to take the s.,** paraître à la barre.

stand[2] *v* (*pt & pp* **stood** [stud]) **1** *vi* **(a)** (*have, maintain upright position*) être debout; se tenir debout; rester debout; (*assume upright position*) se lever: **she stood with her back to me,** elle se tenait debout en me tournant le dos; **to be/keep standing,** être/rester debout; **I was too weak to s.,** j'étais trop faible pour me tenir debout; **I could hardly s.,** je pouvais à peine me tenir debout; *Fig* **to s. on one's own two feet,** ne dépendre que de soi; *F* **he hasn't a leg to s. on,** il est entièrement dans son tort; **I've lost everything but what I s. up in,** j'ai tout perdu sauf ce que j'ai sur le dos; **to s. six feet high,** (*object*) avoir six pieds de haut, mesurer six pieds; (*person*) mesurer six pieds; **the house is still standing,** la maison tient toujours debout; *Sch* **stand!,** levez-vous!; *Mil* **to s. to attention,** se mettre au garde-à-vous;

(b) (*be situated, be*) se trouver, être; **a chapel stands at the top of the hill,** une chapelle se dresse au sommet de la colline; **a car was standing at the door,** il y avait une voiture à la porte; **I found the door standing open,** j'ai trouvé la porte ouverte; **nothing stands between you and success,** rien ne s'oppose à votre succès; **a man stood in the doorway,** un homme se tenait à la porte; **I'll s. at** *or* **by the window,** je me mettrai à la fenêtre; **I didn't know where to s.,** je ne savais où me mettre; **I stood and looked at him, I stood looking at him,** je suis resté à le regarder; **I was standing a few feet away from him,** je me tenais à quelques pas de lui; **to s. talking,** rester à parler; **don't s. there arguing!,** ne restez pas là à discuter!; **don't just s. there! – do something!,** ne reste pas là les bras ballants! – fais quelque chose!; **don't s. in the passage!,** n'encombrez pas le couloir!; **to leave s.o. standing (there),** laisser qn planté (là); *Sp etc* **to be left standing,** être laissé sur place; *Sp* **to leave a competitor standing,** brûler *ou* griller un concurrent; **s. and deliver!,** la bourse ou la vie!;

(c) (*maintain position*) rester, durer; **to s. fast** *or* **firm,** (*not retreat*) tenir, tenir ferme, tenir bon; **we s. or fall together,** nous sommes solidaires (les uns des autres); **I shall s. or fall by the issue,** je suis prêt à engager ma fortune sur le résultat; **to s. alone,** faire face *ou* tenir tête seul;

(d) (*remain valid*) tenir, se maintenir; **the passage must stand,** le passage doit rester comme il est *ou* sans modification; **the bet stands,** le pari tient; **the objection stands,** cette objection subsiste; **what you said last week, does that still s.?,** à propos de ce que tu as dit la semaine dernière, ça tient toujours?;

(e) (*be in certain position*) être, se trouver; **to s. convicted of ...,** être déclaré coupable de ..., être convaincu de ...; **to s. in need of ...,** avoir besoin de ...; **you s. in danger of getting killed,** vous risquez de vous faire tuer; **to s. to lose £5,000,** risquer de perdre 5 000 livres; **to s. to win a lot of money,** risquer de gagner beaucoup d'argent; **to s. as security for a debt,** assurer une créance; **to s. (as candidate) for Parliament,** se présenter *ou* se porter candidat à la députation; **the thermometer stood at 30°,** le thermomètre marquait 30°; **the house does not s. in his name,** la maison n'est pas portée à son nom; **the balance stands at £50,** le reliquat de compte est de cinquante livres; **the amount standing to your credit,** votre solde créditeur; **how do we s.?,** (*in work etc*) où en sommes-nous?; (*financially*) où en sont nos comptes?; **as matters s., as it stands,** au point où en sont les choses, dans l'état actuel des choses; **to know how things s.,** être au fait de la question; **I don't know where I s.,** j'ignore quelle est ma situation *ou* ma position; **how do you s. with him?,** quelle est votre position vis-à-vis de lui?; **you never know how** *or* **where you s. with her,** on ne sait jamais sur quel pied danser avec elle;

(f) *Nau* **to s. to the south,** avoir *ou* mettre le cap au sud; **to s. inshore,** rallier la terre;

(g) (*remain motionless*) **to allow a liquid to s.,** laisser reposer *ou* laisser déposer un liquide.

2 *vt* **(a)** (*place upright*) mettre, poser, placer; **to s. sth on the table,** mettre *ou* poser qch sur la table; **to s. sth against the wall,** dresser qch contre le mur; **to s. sth upright,** mettre qch debout;

(b) to s. one's ground, tenir bon *ou* ferme; **stand your ground!,** (*don't retreat*) ne reculez pas d'une semelle!; (*don't give up opposition*) tenez ferme!, ne lâchez pas prise!;

(c) (*endure*) supporter, soutenir, subir; **to s. the cold,** supporter le froid; **to s. a shock,** résister à *ou* supporter un choc; **argument that does not s. investigation,** argument qui ne supporte pas l'examen; **he can't stand her,** il ne peut pas la souffrir *ou* la sentir; **I won't stand such behaviour,** je ne supporterai pas une pareille conduite; **I can't s. it any longer,** (*heat, cold, discomfort etc*) je ne tiens plus; (*emotional tension, cruelty etc*) je n'en peux plus;

(d) *F* (*pay for*) payer, offrir; **to s. s.o. a drink,** payer à boire à qn; **to s. s.o. a dinner,** payer un dîner à qn.

►**stand around** *vi* (*be standing, doing nothing*) se tenir là; **there were a lot of people standing around talking,** il y avait beaucoup de monde qui se tenait là à parler.

►**stand aside** *vi* **(a)** (*be standing apart*) se tenir à l'écart; **(b)** (*move aside*) se ranger; **to s. aside to let s.o. pass,** s'effacer pour laisser passer qn; *Fig* **to s. aside in favour of s.o.,** se désister en faveur de qn.

►**stand away** *vi* (*move away*) s'éloigner (**from,** de); *Nau* **to s. away from shore,** s'éloigner de la côte; prendre le large.

►**stand back** *vi* **(a)** (*of person*) (*move away*) (se) reculer; (*keep in background*) se tenir en arrière; **s. well back please!,** reculez-vous bien, s'il vous plaît; **(b)** (*of building etc*) être situé en retrait; **house standing back from the road,** maison située en retrait (de la route).

►**stand by 1** *vi* **(a)** (*be ready*) se tenir prêt; *Nau* se tenir paré; *Mil* **the troops are standing by,** les troupes sont en état d'alerte; *Nau* **s. by!,** paré!, attention!;

(b) (*wait*) attendre, patienter; **viewers were told to s. by for further developments,** on demanda aux téléspectateurs de patienter pour la suite des événements;

(c) (*not get involved*) se tenir là (*sans intervenir*); **people just stood by and watched him being beaten up,** les gens restèrent là à le regarder se faire cogner.

2 *vipo* **(a)** (*stand next, near to*) se tenir près de *ou* à côté de (*qn*);

(b) (*support, defend*) soutenir, défendre (*qn*); (*take side of*) se ranger du côté de (*qn*); **she stood by her friend throughout the trial,** elle a soutenu son amie tout au long du procès;

(c) (*keep, honour*) rester fidèle à (*sa promesse*); **I s. by what I said,** je m'en tiens à ce que j'ai dit.

►**stand down** *vi* (*retire*) se retirer (*d'une équipe, d'un poste etc*); (*of candidate*) retirer sa candidature (**in favour of,** en faveur de); *Mil* quitter son service *ou* la garde; *Jur* (*of witness*) quitter la barre.

►**stand for** *vipo* **(a)** *esp Br* (*present oneself as candidate for*) se présenter; **to s. for parliament,** se présenter au parlement; **to s. for the chairmanship,** se présenter à la présidence; **(b)** (*mean, represent*) signifier, vouloir dire (*qch*); **'tsp' stands for 'teaspoonful',** cu. à c. signifie cuillère à café; **the letters AA s. for 'Alcoholics Anonymous',** les lettres A.A. veulent dire 'Alcooliques Anonymes'; **our party stands for freedom and democracy,** notre parti est celui de la liberté et de la démocratie; **(c)** (*tolerate*) supporter, tolérer (*qch*); **I won't s. for it,** je ne supporterai pas cela.

►**stand in** *vi Nau* **to s. in to land** *or* **for (the) land,** courir *ou* porter à terre.

►**stand in for** *vipo* (*act as replacement for*) remplacer (*qn*); *Cin* doubler (*un acteur*); **Mrs Smith has agreed to s. in for our scheduled speaker,** Mme Smith a accepté de remplacer l'orateur que nous avions prévu; **a little party with fruit juice standing in for champagne,** une petite fête où le jus de fruit tient lieu de champagne.

►**stand off 1** *vi* **(a)** (*remain at a distance*) se tenir éloigné *ou* á l'écart; **(b)** (*move away*) s'éloigner; *Nau* courir au large. **2** *vtsep* (*of employer*) (*dismiss*) congédier (*des ouvriers*).

►**stand out** *vi* **(a)** (*be noticeable*) (*of objects*) ressortir, *Pej* détonner; (*protrude*) faire saillie; (*be protruding*) être en saillie; **to s. out in relief,** ressortir, se détacher; **to s. out against sth,** faire contraste avec qch; **mountains that s. out against the horizon,** montagnes qui se dessinent à *ou* sur l'horizon; **the qualities that s. out in his work,** les qualités marquantes de son œuvre; **she stands out in a crowd,** on la remarque dans la foule; *Fig* **characteristics that make him s. out in the crowd,** traits qui le caractérisent; *F* **that stands out a mile!,** (*is very obvious*) c'est évident!; **it really stands out that he's not a local,** ça se voit *ou* se remarque vraiment qu'il n'est pas d'ici; **(b)** (*adopt firm position*) résister (**against,** à), tenir bon *ou* ferme (**against,** contre); **(c)** *Nau* **to s. out to sea,** (*move*) gagner le large; (*remain*) se tenir au large.

►**stand out for** *vipo* insister sur (*qch*).

►**stand over 1** *vi* (*be postponed*) rester en suspens; **to let a question s. over, to allow a question to s. over,** (*postpone*) remettre une question à plus tard, laisser une question en suspens. **2** *vipo* **to s. over s.o.,** (*lean over*) se pencher sur qn; (*watch*) surveiller qn de près; **if I don't s. over him he does nothing,** si je ne suis pas toujours sur son dos il ne fait rien.

►**stand to 1** *vi* **(a)** *Nau* **to s. to the south,** avoir le cap au sud; **(b)** *Mil etc* être prêt, être en état d'alerte; **s. to!,** aux armes! **2** *vtas Mil etc* mettre en état d'alerte; **the troops were stood to,** les soldats furent mis en état d'alerte.

►**stand up 1** *vi* **(a)** se lever, se mettre debout; **s. up!,** levez-vous!, debout!; **to s. up and be counted,** se déclarer publiquement pour *ou* contre une question discutable; **(b)** (*be valid*) se tenir, être valide; **there isn't enough evidence for the charge to s. up in court,** il n'y a pas suffisamment de preuves pour que l'accusation tienne debout au tribunal. **2** *vtsep* **(a)** *F* (*fail to meet*) planter là, lâcher (*qn*); poser un lapin à (*boyfriend, girlfriend*); **we've been stood up,** on nous a laissés plantés; **(b)** (*put in upright position*) mettre (*qch*) debout; **to s. a child up (again),** (re)mettre un enfant sur ses pieds.

►**stand up for** *vipo* (*defend*) soutenir, défendre (*qn*); **only Chris stood up for her,** seul Chris l'a soutenue *ou* s'est mis de son côté; **s. up for what you believe in,** défendez ce en quoi vous croyez.

►**stand up to** *vipo* (*resist, oppose*) tenir tête à (*qn*); (*endure*) résister à (*qn, qch*); **it won't s. up to that sort of treatment,** ça ne résistera pas à ce genre de traitement; **it doesn't s. up to close analysis,** ça ne résiste pas à une analyse poussée.

stand-alone ['stændələʊn] *n Comptr* poste *m* autonome.

standard¹ ['stændəd] *n* **(a)** (*flag etc*) bannière *f*; *Mil* étendard *m*; *Nau* pavillon *m*; **the Royal S.,** la bannière royale; *Mil* **s. bearer,** porte-étendard *m inv*;

(b) (*accepted length, quantity etc*) étalon *m*; **the metre is the s. of length,** le mètre est le module *ou* l'unité de mesure de la longueur; *Fin* **gold/silver s.,** étalon (d')or/d'argent; *Rail* **s. gauge,** voie normale; **s. model,** (*of car*) voiture *f* de série; (*of machine*) modèle *m* standard *ou* de série;

(c) (*model*) modèle *m*, type *m*, niveau *m*, norme *f*; (*level, quality*) niveau; **s. of living,** niveau de vie; **everyone has his own standards,** tout homme a sa manière de voir; **to aim at/reach a high s.,** viser à/atteindre un niveau élevé; **a high s. of playing/academic achievement,** un niveau de jeu/de réussite académique élevé; **last year's students set very high standards,** les étudiants de l'année dernière ont établi un niveau très haut; **not to come up to s.,** ne pas atteindre le niveau exigé; **my cooking isn't up to your s.,** ma cuisine n'est pas à la hauteur de la vôtre;

(d) *esp Br Sch Arch* classe *f* (*dans une école primaire*);

(e) *Tech;* (*support*) pied *m*, support *m* (*d'un instrument scientifique etc*); montant *m* (*d'une machine etc*); **lamp s.,** (*in house etc*) pied de lampe; (*in street*) pylône *m* d'éclairage; (*street lamp*) réverbère *m* électrique; **s. lamp,** lampadaire *m*;

(f) (*in forestry*) baliveau *m*; (*in horticulture*) **s. (tree),** arbre *m* de plein vent; **s. rose (tree),** rosier *m* sur tige.

standard² *adj* **(a)** (*established by standard*) **s. measure,** mesure *f* étalon; **s. thickness,** épaisseur type *ou* courante (*du fer etc*); **s. weight,** poids normal; **headrests are s. (equipment),** les appuis-têtes sont montés en série; **British s. time,** heure légale anglaise; **(b)** (*habitual*) **the cooking is fairly s.,** la cuisine n'a rien de sensationnel; **s. authors,** auteurs classiques; **s. edition,** édition courante (*d'un auteur*); **s. English,** l'anglais des gens cultivés; **a s. French dictionary,** un dictionnaire général de la langue française; **one of his s. jokes,** une de ses plaisanteries habituelles.

standardization [stændədaɪ'zeɪʃən] *n* standardisation *f*; étalonnage *m*, étalonnement *m* (*des poids etc*); uniformisation *f* (*des méthodes etc*).

standardize ['stændədaɪz] **1** *vt* standardiser; étalonner; uniformiser (*des méthodes, des objets de commerce*); normaliser (*une condition*). **2** *vi* **to s. on sth,** adopter qch comme standard.

stand-by ['stændbaɪ] **1** *n* **(a)** (*reliable person*) personne *f* sur qui l'on peut compter; **(b)** (*sth held in reserve*) réserve *f*; ressource *f*; **to have a sum in reserve as a s.-b.,** avoir une somme en réserve en cas de besoin; **a fruitcake can be a useful s.-b. for unexpected guests,** il est toujours bon d'avoir un cake en réserve pour les invités-surprises; **(c)** *Rail* **s.-b. engine,** locomotive *f* de réserve; **(d)** *Mil etc* (état *m* d')alerte *f*; **to be on s.-b.,** être en état d'alerte; *Fig* (*in reserve*) être en réserve, se tenir prêt; **(e)** *Av etc* **s.-b. (passenger),** passager *m* (en) standby; **s.-b. (ticket),** standby *m*; **to be on s.-b.,** être en standby. **2** *adv* **to fly s.-b.,** voler en standby.

standee [stæn'diː] *n esp Am* (*in bus*) voyageur, -euse debout; *Th* spectateur, -trice debout.

stand-in ['stændɪn] *n* (*person*) remplaçant, -ante; *Th etc* doublure *f*.

standing ['stændɪŋ] **1** *adj* **(a)** (*qui se tient*) debout; **to sell a crop s.,** vendre une récolte sur pied; **s. crops,** récoltes *fpl* sur pied; **s. passengers,** voyageurs *mpl* debout; *Sp* **s. jump,** saut *m* sans élan; *Sp* **s. start,** départ *m* debout; **s. stone,** (*prehistoric monument*) menhir *m*; **s. water,** eau stagnante *ou* dormante; **(b)** (*prix*) fixe; *Mil* **s. army,** armée *f* de métier; *Com* **s. expenses,** frais généraux; **I have a s. invitation,** j'ai mon couvert mis (dans cette famille); **you have a s. invitation,** vous serez toujours le bienvenu; **s. joke,** plaisanterie traditionnelle; **he's become a s. joke,** il est devenu un objet de risée; *Banking* **s. order,** virement *m* automatique; *Com* **to place a s. order for sth,** placer une commande permanente de qch; **s. orders,** règlement *m* des assemblées législatives; *Mil* **s. rule,** règle *f* fixe.

2 *n* **(a)** station *f* debout; **no s.!,** défense de voyager debout; *Rail Th etc* **s. room,** place(s) *f(pl)* debout; **s. (room) only!,** debout seulement;

(b) of long s., (*amis*) de longue date; **friend of twenty years' s.,** ami *m* de vingt ans;

(c) (*position*) rang *m*, position *f*, standing *m*; **social s.,** position sociale; **the firm's s.,** l'importance *f* de la maison; **financial s.,** situation financière; **firm of recognized s.,** entreprise d'une solidité reconnue.

stand-offish [stænd'ɒfɪʃ] *adj* (*person*) peu accessible, distant, réservé; **to be s.-o.,** se mettre *ou* se tenir sur son quant-à-soi.

stand-offishness [stænd'ɒfɪʃnɪs] *n* raideur *f*, réserve *f*.

standpoint ['stændpɔɪnt] *n* point *m* de vue; **from the s. of ...,** du point de vue de ...; **from a late 20th-century s.,** dans une perspective de fin de XXe siècle.

standstill ['stændstɪl] *n* arrêt *m*, immobilisation *f*; **to come to a s.,** s'arrêter, s'immobiliser; **to bring sth to a s.,** arrêter qch; (*railways, production etc*) paralyser qch; **many factories are at a s.,** beaucoup d'usines chôment; **the railways are at a s.,** les chemins de fer sont paralysés.

stand-up ['stændʌp] *adj* **(a)** (*collar*) droit, montant; **(b)** (*meal*) pris debout; **(c)** *Boxing* **s.-up fight,** combat *m* en règle; **they just about had a s.-up fight!,** ils ont failli entrer dans un combat en règle!; **(d) s.-up comedian** *or* **comic,** comique *mf* (de scène).

stank *see* **STINK^{2}**.

stannic ['stænɪk] *adj Ch* stannique.

stanza, *pl* **-as** ['stænzə, -əz] *n* (*in prosody*) stance *f*, strophe *f*.

staphylococcus, *pl* **-cocci** [stæfɪləʊ'kɒkəs, -'kɒksaɪ] *n* (*bacteria*) staphylocoque *m*.

staple^{1} ['steɪp(ə)l] *n* (*for paper*) agrafe *f*; (*for cable etc*) crampon *m*; **wire s.,** (clou *m*) cavalier *m*; **s. gun,** agrafeuse *f*.

staple^{2} *vt* **(a)** agrafer; *Constr etc* fixer *ou* attacher (*qch*) avec un crampon *ou* une agrafe, agrafer, cramponner; **to s. two pieces of paper together,** agrafer deux morceaux de papier; **(b)** (*in bookbinding*) brocher (*des feuilles*).

staple^{3} *n* (*product*) produit principal (*d'un pays*); (*raw material*) matière première, matière brute; **s. commodities,** produits de première nécessité; **s. crop,** culture *f* de base; **s. diet,** régime *m* de base.

staple^{4} *n Tex* brin *m*, fibre *f* (*de laine, de lin*).

stapler ['steɪplər] *n* (*device*) agrafeuse *f*.

stapling ['steɪplɪŋ] *n* **(a)** (*of paper*) fixation *f* à l'aide d'agrafes, agrafage *m*; (*of cables etc*) fixation à l'aide de crochets *ou* crampons; **s. machine,** agrafeuse *f*; **(b)** (*in bookbinding*) brochage *m*; **s. machine,** brocheuse *f* mécanique.

star^{1} [stɑːr] *n* **(a)** *Astron* étoile *f*; astre *m*; **shooting s.,** étoile filante; **the morning s.,** l'étoile du matin; **the pole s.,** l'étoile polaire, la polaire; **he was born under a lucky s.,** il est né sous une bonne étoile; **to reach for the stars,** demander la lune; *F* **to see stars,** voir les étoiles en plein midi, voir trente-six chandelles; *US* **the stars and stripes,** la bannière étoilée; *Mil* **S. Wars,** guerre *f* des étoiles;

(b) (*insignia*) plaque *f* (*d'un ordre*); *Mil* étoile *f* (*sur l'épaule*); **S. of David,** étoile de David; **three s. brandy,** cognac *m* trois étoiles; **three s. hotel,** hôtel *m* trois étoiles;

(c) (*on horse's forehead*) étoile *f*; *Typ* astérisque *m*; *MecE* étoile, croix *f*;

(d) *Cin etc* étoile *f*, vedette *f*, star *f*; **film** *or* **movie s.,** star de cinéma; **rock s.,** star du rock; **to get s. billing,** tenir le haut de l'affiche; **s. mentality,** mentalité *f* de star; **s. part,** rôle *m* de vedette; *Sp* **s. player,** joueur, -euse vedette; **s. turn,** numéro *m* de premier ordre; *F* clou *m* (*d'une fête*).

star^{2} *v* **(-rr-) 1** *vt* **(a)** étoiler (*qch*); (*scatter with stars*) (par)semer (*qch*) d'étoiles; étoiler, fêler (*une glace, une vitre*); *Typ etc* (*asterisk*) marquer (*un mot etc*) d'un astérisque;

(b) *Cin Th TV etc* (*of film, play etc*) mettre (*qn*) en scène dans le rôle principal, avoir (*qn*) pour vedette; **the film/play stars/starred Katherine Hepburn (as** *or* **in the role of),** le film/la pièce met/mettait en scène Katherine Hepburn dans le rôle principal (de); **'The Last Métro' starring Catherine Deneuve and Gérard Depardieu,** 'le Dernier Métro' avec Catherine Deneuve et Gérard Depardieu dans les rôles principaux.

2 *vi* **(a)** (*of glass*) se fêler, s'étoiler;

(b) *Cin Th TV etc* (*of actor, actress*) être en vedette; **he starred as a gangster,** il était la vedette dans un rôle de gangster; **to have a starring role,** avoir un rôle de vedette.

starboard ['stɑːbəd] *n Nau* tribord *m*; **on the s. side, to s.,** à tribord; **on the s. bow,** par tribord devant; **hard a-s.!,** tribord toute!

starch^{1} [stɑːtʃ] *n* amidon *m*; fécule *f* (*de pommes de terre*); amidon (*de riz, maïs, blé etc*); **laundry s.,** empois *m* (d'amidon).

starch^{2} *vt* empeser, amidonner (*le linge*).

starched [stɑːtʃt] *adj* empesé, amidonné.

starching ['stɑːtʃɪŋ] *n* empesage *m*, amidonnage *m*.

starchy ['stɑːtʃɪ] *adj* **(a)** *Ch* amylacé, amyloïde; féculent; **s. foods,** féculents *mpl*; **(b)** *F* (*person, manner*) empesé, guindé.

star-crossed ['stɑːkrɒst] *adj* **s.-c. lovers,** amants maudits du sort.

stardom ['stɑːdəm] *n Cin etc* (*state*) célébrité *f*, vedettariat *m;* **to rise to s.,** devenir une vedette, atteindre la célébrité; **dreams of s.,** rêves de célébrité.

stardust ['stɑːdʌst] *n Astron* amas *m* stellaire.

stare^{1} [steər] *n* regard *m* fixe; **glassy/stony s.,** regard terne/dur; **vacant s.,** regard vague.

stare^{2} 1 *vi* regarder fixement; (*with astonishment*) ouvrir de grands yeux; **to s. into the distance,** regarder au loin; **don't s.!,** ne regarde pas comme ça; **it's rude to s.,** c'est mal poli de dévisager les gens; **to s. at s.o./sth,** (*look at hard*) regarder qn/qch fixement, fixer qn/qch; (*begin to look at*) porter son regard sur qn; (*look at insolently*) regarder qn effrontément; (*attempt to disconcert*) dévisager qn; (*be stupefied by*) regarder qn d'un air hébété; **what are you staring at?,** que regardez-vous comme ça? **2** *vt* **to s. s.o. in the face,** dévisager qn; *F* **it's staring you in the face,** ça vous saute aux yeux; **the answer was staring me in the face all the time,** la réponse était sous mon nez depuis le début.

starfish ['stɑːfɪʃ] *n* (*animal*) astérie *f*, étoile *f* de mer.

stargaze ['stɑːgeɪz] *vi F* **(a)** (*look at stars*) faire de l'astronomie; **(b)** (*daydream*) bayer aux corneilles, rêvasser.

stargazer ['stɑːgeɪzər] *n F* **(a)** (*astronomer*) astronome *mf*; **(b)** (*daydreamer*) rêveur, -euse, rêvasseur, -euse.

stargazing ['stɑːgeɪzɪŋ] *n F* **(a)** (*looking at stars*) astronomie *f*; **(b)** (*daydreaming*) rêvasserie(s) *f(pl)*.

staring ['steərɪŋ] *adj* **s. eyes,** yeux *mpl* fixes; (*with astonishment*) yeux grands ouverts.

stark [stɑːk] **1** *adj* **(a)** (*contrast*) absolu, fort; (*light, neon*) cru; (*furnishing, black and white*) austère, sobre; (*truth, facts*) brut; (*landscape*) nu; **this stands out in s. contrast to ...,** ceci se détache dans un contraste absolu de ...; **then in the s. light of day ...,** puis dans la froide lumière du jour ...; **s. realism,** (*of novel, painting*) réalisme brut; **a very stark flat,** un appartement très nu *ou* sobre; **the s. simplicity of ...,** la sobre *ou* l'austère simplicité de ...; **the s. desolation of the region,** l'absolue désolation de la région; **s. madness,** folie pure; **the s. towns of the North,** les mornes villes du Nord; **(b)** *Lit* (*stiff*) raide, rigide; **he lay s. in death,** il gisait dans la rigidité de la mort. **2** *adv* **s. naked,** tout nu, *F* à poil; **s. staring mad,** complètement fou.

starkers ['stɑːkəz] *adj & adv Br F* tout nu.

starkness ['stɑːknɪs] *n* (*of contrast*) force *f*; (*of furnishing etc*) austérité *f*, sobriété *f*; (*of landscape*) nudité *f*.

starless ['stɑːlɪs] *adj* sans étoiles.

starlet ['stɑːlɪt] *n Cin etc* starlette *f*, starlet *f*.

starlight ['stɑːlaɪt] *n* lumière *f* des étoiles; **in the** *or* **by s.,** à la lumière des étoiles; **s. night,** nuit étoilée.

starling ['stɑːlɪŋ] *n* (*bird*) étourneau *m*.

starlit ['stɑːlɪt] *adj* (*ciel*) étoilé; **s. night,** nuit étoilée.

star-of-Bethlehem ['stɑːrəv'beθlɪhem] *n* (*plant*) ornithogale *m* (*à ombelle*), *F* dame *f* d'onze heures.

starred [stɑːd] *adj* **(a)** *Lit* (*sky*) étoilé, parsemé d'étoiles; **(b)** *Typ* (*asterisked*) marqué d'un astérisque.

-starred [stɑːd] *suff* **ill-s.,** né sous une mauvaise étoile.

starry ['stɑːrɪ] *adj* **(a)** (*ciel*) étoilé, (par)semé d'étoiles; **s. night,** nuit étoilée; **(b)** *Lit* étincelant, brillant.

starry-eyed [stɑːrɪ'aɪd] *adj* extasié, qui voit les choses en rose; **a s.-e. scheme,** un projet utopique; **she was all s.-e. about him until ...,** elle était tout émerveillée par lui jusqu'à ce que ... .

starshell ['stɑːʃel] *n Mil* obus éclairant *ou* à étoiles.

star-spangled ['stɑːspæŋg(ə)ld] *adj* étoilé; **the S.-S. Banner,** (*flag*) la bannière étoilée (*des États-Unis*); (*national anthem*) la Bannière Étoilée.

start[1] [stɑːt] *n* **(a)** (*beginning*) commencement *m*, début *m*; (*of journey*) départ *m*; *Aut* démarrage *m*; *Av* envol *m*; **for a s.,** pour débuter, pour commencer; **at the s.,** au début; **at the very s.,** de prime abord; **from the s. there were problems,** dès le commencement il y a eu des problèmes; **I never liked him — right from the s.,** il m'a toujours déplu — depuis le tout début; **from s. to finish,** du commencement (jusqu')à la fin; **£5 isn't much, but it's a s.,** 5 livres ce n'est pas grand-chose, mais c'est un début; **I've cleaned the kitchen — well, it's a s.,** j'ai nettoyé la cuisine — eh bien c'est déjà ça; **she had a good s. in life,** elle a bien débuté dans la vie; **to give s.o. a s.,** lancer qn (*dans les affaires etc*); **to make a good s.,** bien commencer; **to make a fresh s.,** recommencer (*sa carrière, sa vie*); **to make a s.,** (*begin work*) s'y mettre; (*begin journey*) se mettre en route; **to make a s. on sth,** se mettre à qch; *Sp* **false s.,** faux départ; *Sp* **to give s.o. a s.,** laisser qn partir le premier; donner un peu d'avance à qn; **to give s.o. a 60 metre(s) s.,** donner à qn 60 mètres d'avance;

(b) (*jump*) saut *m*; (*sudden movement*) mouvement *m* brusque; (*with fear, surprise*) tressaillement *m*, sursaut *m*, soubresaut *m*; **to wake with a s.,** se réveiller en sursaut; **he gave a s.,** il a tressailli, il a sursauté; **to give s.o. a s.,** faire tressaillir qn; **you gave me such a s.!,** tu m'as fait peur *ou F* une drôle de frayeur!

start[2] **1** *vi* **(a)** (*begin*) commencer; (*in a job*) débuter; **the story starts with a murder,** l'histoire commence par un meurtre; **to s. at the beginning,** pour commencer depuis le début; **you'd better s. by telling me your name,** vous devriez commencer par me dire votre nom; **let's s. with the cost,** commençons par le coût; **to s. the way one means to go on,** donner la mesure dès le début; **starting Monday,** à partir de lundi; **to s. again,** recommencer; (*make a fresh start in one's life*) refaire sa vie; **she had started as a doctor,** elle avait débuté *ou* commencé en tant que médecin; **to s. in business,** se mettre *ou* se lancer dans les affaires; **there were only six members to s. with,** il n'y avait que six membres au début; **to s. with,** en premier lieu, tout d'abord; **to s. on a job,** commencer *ou* entamer un travail;

(b) *Br F* (*begin crying, fighting etc*) se mettre à pleurer *ou* se battre *etc*; **now don't YOU s.!,** et ne t'y mets pas à ton tour!;

(c) (*move suddenly*) se déplacer brusquement; (*with surprise, fear etc*) tressaillir, tressauter, sursauter; **he started at the sound of my voice,** il a tressailli au son de ma voix; **she started with surprise,** elle a eu un mouvement de surprise; **to s. out of one's sleep,** se réveiller en sursaut; **to s. to one's feet,** se lever d'un bond;

(d) (*begin journey*) partir, se mettre en route; **to s. on a journey,** commencer un voyage; **we s. tomorrow,** nous partons demain; **to s. again,** repartir, se remettre en route;

(e) (*of car*) démarrer; (*of train*) partir, s'ébranler; (*of engine*) partir, démarrer; (*of injector, dynamo*) s'amorcer; **the engine won't s.,** le moteur refuse de partir *ou* de démarrer;

(f) (*of timber*) se déjeter; (*of planks*) se disjoindre; (*of rivets*) se détacher.

2 *vt* **(a)** commencer (*un travail etc*); amorcer (*un sujet etc*); entamer (*une conversation, des négociations etc*); lancer (*une mode, une rumeur etc*); **you started it,** c'est vous qui avez commencé; **to s. doing sth, to s. to do sth,** commencer *ou* se mettre à faire qch; **to s. crying again,** se remettre à pleurer; **it's just started raining,** voilà qu'il commence à pleuvoir; *F* **now you've started something!,** en voilà une affaire!; **if you s. him on this subject he will never stop,** si vous le lancez sur ce sujet il ne tarira pas; **we started him in the sales department,** nous l'avons fait débuter au service des ventes; **to get started,** (*to start*) commencer, s'y mettre; (*on journey*) partir, se mettre en route; (*in career etc*) débuter, démarrer; **to help s.o. get started in life,** aider qn à démarrer dans la vie;

(b) *Sp* donner le signal du départ à (*des coureurs etc*); (*in hunting*) lancer (*un cerf*); lever (*un lièvre*); faire partir (*une perdrix etc*); *Horseriding* **to s. a horse at a gallop,** faire partir un cheval au galop;

(c) (*set up*) lancer (*une entreprise, un journal*); fonder (*un commerce*); ouvrir (*une école*); **to s. s.o. in business,** lancer qn dans les affaires;

(d) (*cause to function*) mettre en marche, lancer (*une machine*); démarrer (*une voiture*); mettre (*un moteur*) en marche; amorcer (*un injecteur, une pompe*); **to s. a fire,** provoquer un incendie.

▶start in on *vipo esp Am* s'attaquer à (*qn*).

▶start off 1 *vi* **(a)** (*begin journey*) = **START**[2] **1(d)**; **(b)** (*begin*) commencer; **you s. off,** (*in discussion etc*) vous commencez, à vous l'honneur; **she started off by talking about ...,** elle commença en parlant de ... .

2 *vtsep* **(a)** (*begin*) commencer; **s. your talk off with a reference to ...,** commencez votre discours en mentionnant ...; **he lent us a couple of thousand pounds to s. us off,** (*in business etc*) il nous a prêté quelques milliers de livres pour nous aider à démarrer; **here are three specimens to s. you off,** (*with your collection*) voici trois spécimens pour commencer; **the pianist played a few bars to s. them off,** (*in singing etc*) le pianiste a joué quelques mesures d'introduction; **what started the whole thing off?,** comment tout a-t-il commencé?;

(b) *F* (*cause s.o. to start doing sth*) (*on a specific subject*) lancer; **the baby's crying again — what started him off this time?,** le bébé s'est remis à pleurer — qu'est-ce qui lui prend cette fois?; **don't s. him off on that!,** (*get him talking about it*) ne le lance pas sur ce sujet!

▶start on *vipo* (*begin quarrelling with, shouting at etc*) commencer à s'en prendre à.

▶start out *vi* **(a)** (*begin*) commencer, débuter; **she started out as a postwoman/driving a van,** elle a commencé comme factrice/conductrice de camion; **he started out to write a novel,** il a eu (d'abord) l'idée d'écrire un roman; **(b)** (*begin journey*) se mettre en route (**for,** pour).

▶start up 1 *vi* **(a)** (*start functioning*) (*of engine*) démarrer, se mettre en marche; (*of injector, dynamo*) s'amorcer; **(b)** (*of business*) se monter, s'installer; **to s. up in business,** se monter en affaires; **he decided to s. up by himself,** il a décidé de se monter *ou* de se lancer tout seul; **(c) he started up,** (*in bed etc*) il se dressa dans un sursaut; **a deer started up in the undergrowth,** un cerf bondit dans le sous-bois. **2** *vtsep* **(a)** (*cause to function*) mettre (*un moteur*) en marche; lancer, mettre (*une machine*) en marche; amorcer (*un injecteur, une pompe*); **(b)** lancer (*une entreprise, un journal*); fonder (*un commerce*); ouvrir (*un restaurant, une école*).

starter ['stɑːtər] *n* **(a)** *Sp* (*competitor*) partant *m*; **to be an early s.,** (*leave, start work early*) partir *ou* commencer son travail de bonne heure; **s. flat,** = appartement convenant à ceux qui achètent pour la première fois; **(b)** *Sp etc* (*official*) starter *m*; **under starter's orders,** sous les ordres du starter; **(c)** (*device*) *Aut* démarreur *m*; *MecE* dispositif *m* de mise en marche; **s. motor,** moteur *m* auxiliaire de démarrage; *El* (rhéostat *m*) démarreur, rhéostat de démarrage; **(d)** *esp Br F* hors-d'œuvre *m inv*, entrée *f*; **what will you have for a s.?,** qu'est-ce que vous prendrez pour commencer? **(e)** *Br F* **for starters,** pour commencer, (tout) d'abord.

starting ['stɑːtɪŋ] *n* **(a)** (*beginning*) commencement *m*, début *m*; (*departure*) départ *m*; *Sp* **s. line/block,** ligne *f*/bloc *m* de départ; *Sp* **s. pistol,** pistolet *m* de starter; **s. point** *or* **place,** point *m* de départ; **s. signal,** signal *m* de *ou* du départ; *Horseracing* **s. price,** dernière cote avant le départ; **s. salary,** salaire initial *ou* de début; **(b)** mise *f* en route *ou* en train (*d'une entreprise etc*); **(c)** mise *f* en marche, démarrage *m* (*d'un moteur etc*); lancement *m* (*d'une machine*); déclenchement *m* (*d'un mécanisme*); amorçage *m* (*d'une dynamo etc*); *Aut* **s. handle,** manivelle *f*; **(d)** (*in hunting*) lancer *m* (*du gibier*).

starting up *n* = **STARTING (b), (c)**.

startle ['stɑːt(ə)l] *vt* (*alarm*) effrayer, alarmer (*qn*); (*cause to jump*) faire sursauter (*qn*); **she was startled to see him so pale,** elle a été saisie de le voir si pâle.

startled ['stɑːt(ə)ld] *adj* effrayé; (*cri*) d'alarme, d'effroi; **he was quite s.,** il est resté tout saisi.

startling *adj* (*noise etc*) effrayant; (*news, event etc*) renversant; **s. resemblance,** ressemblance saisissante.

start-up ['stɑːtʌp] *n* **(a)** (*of machine*) démarrage *m*, mise *f* en marche; **(b)** (*new business*) ouverture *f*, lancement *m*; **there have been 500 s.-ups this year,** il y a eu 500 créations d'entreprises cette année.

starvation [stɑː'veɪʃən] *n* privation *f ou* manque *m* de nourriture; **to die of s.,** mourir de faim; **prisoners were kept on a s. diet,** les prisonniers étaient presque entièrement privés de nourriture; **I'm on a s. diet,** (*to slim*) je suis un régime draconien.
starve [stɑːv] **1** *vi* (*lack food*) manquer de nourriture; (*endure hunger*) endurer la faim; (*of tree, plant*) dépérir, s'étioler; **to s. (to death),** mourir de faim; *F* **I'm starving,** je meurs *ou* je crève de faim. **2** *vt* (*deprive of food*) priver (*qn*) de nourriture; (*cause to die*) faire mourir (*qn*) de faim; **to s. a garrison into surrender,** réduire une garnison par la faim; *Fig* **to s. s.o./sth of sth,** priver qn/qch de qch.
▶**starve out** *vtsep Mil etc* affamer (*une ville, une garnison*).
starved [stɑːvd] *adj* affamé; **she looks half s.,** elle a l'air famélique; **s. of affection,** privé d'affection; **I'm feeling s. of affection,** je suis en manque d'affection.
starving ['stɑːvɪŋ] **1** *adj* affamé; **the s. millions,** tous ceux qui souffrent de la faim. **2** *n* privation *f* de nourriture.
stash¹ [stæʃ] *n F* (*place*) nid *m*, planque *f*; **a s. of drugs was discovered,** de la drogue a été découverte.
stash² *vt F* (*hide*) cacher, planquer (*qch*), mettre au sec; (*put*) ficher.
▶**stash away** *vtsep* = **STASH²**.
state¹ [steɪt] *n* **(a)** (*condition*) état *m*, condition *f*; (*situation*) situation *f*; **in a good s.,** en bon état, en bonne condition; *Iron* **here's a nice** *or* **a pretty s. of affairs,** nous voilà bien!, c'est du joli *ou* du propre!; **body in a s. of rest,** corps à l'état de repos *ou* au repos; **s. of health,** état de santé; **I am not in a fit s. to travel,** je ne suis pas en état de voyager; **the married s.,** le mariage; **the single s.,** le célibat; **s. of mind,** disposition *f* d'esprit; *F* **to be in a terrible s.,** (*of person*) être dans tous ses états; (*of room, papers etc*) être dans un état désastreux; **this reprsents the s. of the art in ...,** c'est la pointe de la technologie en matière de ...;
(b) (*rank*) rang *m*, dignité *f*; (*ceremony*) pompe *f*, parade *f*, apparat *m*; *Admin* représentation *f* (*d'un ambassadeur etc*); **she lived in a style befitting her s.,** elle avait un train de vie digne de son rang; **to live in s.,** mener grand train; **to travel in s.,** voyager en grand apparat; **to dine in s.,** dîner en grand gala; **to lie in s.,** (*of body*) être exposé (sur un lit de parade); **lying in s.,** exposition *f* (d'un corps); **he was in his robes of s.,** il était en costume d'apparat; **s. ball,** grand bal officiel; **s. apartments,** grands appartements; salons *m* d'apparat; **s. ball,** grand bal officiel; **s. carriage, s. coach,** voiture *f* d'apparat;
(c) *Fr Hist* **the States General,** les États généraux; (*Channel Islands*) **the States,** l'Assemblée législative; *Pol* **the S.,** l'État; **Church and S.,** l'Église et l'État; **Secretary of S.,** *Br* secrétaire *m* d'État; *US* = Ministre *m* des Affaires étrangères; **s.-aided industry,** industrie subventionnée par l'État; **affairs of S.,** affaires *fpl* d'État; **s. church,** église *f* d'État; **s. control,** étatisme *m*; **to bring an industry under s. control,** étatiser une industrie; *US* **S. Department,** = Ministère *m* des Affaires étrangères; **s. documents,** documents officiels; **the s. education system,** le système éducatif national; *Br Med* **State Enrolled Nurse,** = infirmier, -ière qualifié(e) par deux ans de pratique; **s.-owned industry,** industrie étatale; **s. papers,** papiers *mpl* d'État; *Br Med* **State Registered Nurse,** infirmier, -ière diplômé(e); **s.-run,** public; **s. school,** école publique; *US* **S. university,** université subventionnée et contrôlée par l'État;
(d) (*administrative region in some countries*) état *m*; **the United States of America,** *F* **the States,** les États-Unis (d'Amérique); *US* **s. police,** police *f* d'État.
state² *vt* **(a)** énoncer, déclarer, affirmer (*qch*); exposer (*une réclamation etc*); *Math* poser, énoncer (*un problème*); **this condition was expressly stated,** cette condition était expressément énoncée; **the receipt should s. the source of payment,** la quittance doit énoncer l'origine de l'argent; **please s. below ...,** veuillez noter en bas...; **I have stated my opinion,** j'ai donné mon opinion; *Jur* **to s. the case,** faire l'exposé des faits; **(b)** (*fix*) arrêter, fixer (*une heure, une date*); **at stated intervals,** à intervalles réglés.
stateless ['steɪtlɪs] *adj* apatride; **s. person,** apatride *mf*.
statelessness ['steɪtlɪsnɪs] *n* apatridie *f*.
stateliness ['steɪtlɪnɪs] *n* **(a)** (*elegance*) majesté *f*; (*grandeur*) aspect imposant, grandeur *f*; **(b)** (*dignity*) dignité *f*.
stately ['steɪtlɪ] *adj* **(a)** (*elegant*) majestueux; (*imposing*) imposant; **the s. homes of England,** les châteaux de l'Angleterre; **(b)** (*dignified*) plein de dignité; (*noble*) noble, élevé; **s. bearing,** allure pleine de majesté.
statement ['steɪtmənt] *n* **(a)** exposition *f*, exposé *m*, énoncé *m* (*des faits, de la situation etc*); (*report, account*) rapport *m*, compte rendu, relation *f*; (*affirmation*) assertion *f*, affirmation *f*; **official s. (to the press),** communiqué *m*; **she made the following s. ...,** elle a déclaré que ...; **bare s. of the facts,** simple énoncé des faits; **according to his own s.,** suivant sa propre déclaration; *Jur* **the statements made by the witnesses,** les dépositions des témoins; **a s. appeared in the press to the effect that ...,** il fut affirmé dans la presse que ...; **(b)** *Com* **s. of account,** état *m* de compte, relevé *m* de compte; **monthly s.,** fin *f* de mois; **bank s.,** relevé de compte; **s. of affairs,** (*in bankruptcy*) bilan *m* de liquidation.
state-of-the-art [steɪtəvðɪ'ɑːt] *adj* (*technology, design etc*) de pointe, très avancé; **it's very s.-of-the-art,** c'est de la technologie de pointe.
stateroom ['steɪtruːm] *n* **(a)** *Nau* cabine *f* de luxe; *Am Rail Old-fashioned* (compartiment *m* de) wagon-lit *m*; **(b)** *esp Br* (*in palace etc*) chambre *f* d'apparat, grand appartement.
statesman, *pl* **-men** ['steɪtsmən] *n* **(a)** homme *m* d'État; **(b)** (*politician*) homme *m* politique.
statesmanlike ['steɪtsmənlaɪk] *adj* (*attitude etc*) d'homme d'État; *Fig* stratégique.
statesmanship ['steɪtsmənʃɪp] *n* l'art *m* de gouverner; **a decision which shows considerable s.,** une décision qui révèle une grande maîtrise de l'art de gouverner.
static ['stætɪk] *adj* **(a)** (*électricité etc*) statique; **(b)** (*not moving*) statique; (*unchangeable*) immuable; *Pej* (*relationship etc*) stagnant; **the situation remains s.,** la situation n'a pas changé.
statics ['stætɪks] *npl* **(a)** *Phys* (*usu with sing verb*) la statique; **(b)** *Rad* parasites *mpl*.
station¹ ['steɪʃən] *n* **(a) (railway) s.,** gare *f*; **(underground) s.,** station *f* de métro; **bus** *or* *Br* **coach s.,** gare routière; *Rail* **passenger/goods s.,** gare de voyageurs/de marchandises; **s. hotel,** hôtel *m* de la gare; *Am Aut* **s. wagon,** break *m*;
(b) (*place*) position *f*, place *f*; (*post*) poste *m*; **to take up one's s.,** (*take one's place*) prendre sa place; (*go to one's post*) se rendre à son poste; *Mil etc* **action stations,** postes de combat; *Mil & Fig* **action stations!,** à vos postes!; **naval s.,** station navale; (*port*) port *m* de guerre; **military s.,** poste militaire; (*garrison*) garnison *f*; **field dressing s.,** poste de secours; *Av* **air s.,** base aérienne *ou* d'aviation; *Nau* **lifeboat s.,** station de sauvetage; *Met* **weather s.,** station météo(rologique); **police s.,** *F* **the s.,** commissariat *m*, poste de police; **fire s.,** poste *ou* caserne *f* de pompiers; **power s.,** centrale *f* électrique; **atomic power s.,** centrale atomique; **radio/television s.,** station *f* de radio/chaîne *f* de télévision; *Aut* **filling s.,** *Br* **petrol s.,** *Am* **gas s.,** poste d'essence, station-service *f*, *pl* stations-service; *Rel* **the stations of the Cross,** le chemin de la Croix;
(c) *Austr NZ* = ferme *f* (et ses dépendances); **sheep s.,** élevage *m* de moutons;
(d) (*social condition*) position *f*, condition *f*; (*rank*) rang *m*; **s. in life,** situation sociale; *Old-fashioned* **to marry below one's s.,** faire une mésalliance, se mésallier.
station² *vt* placer, mettre (*qn dans un endroit*); désigner son poste à (*un soldat*); poster (*des troupes*); **to be stationed at ...,** *Mil* être stationné *ou* être en garnison à ...; *Nau* être en station à ...; **he stationed himself behind a door,** il s'est posté derrière une porte.
stationary ['steɪʃən(ə)rɪ] *adj* **(a)** (*not moving*) immobile; (*voiture*) en stationnement; **to remain s.,** rester immobile; *Mil* **s. target,** cible *f* fixe; **(b)** (*fixed*) fixe; (*permanent*) installé à demeure; *MecE* **s. shaft,** arbre *m* fixe; *Mil* **s. troops,** troupes *fpl* sédentaires.
stationer ['steɪʃənər] *n* papetier *m*; **stationer's (shop),** papeterie *f*.
stationery ['steɪʃən(ə)rɪ] *n* papeterie *f*; **office s.,** fournitures *fpl* de bureau; *Br Admin* **the S. Office,** le Service des fournitures et des publications de l'Administration.
station-master ['steɪʃənmɑːstər] *n Rail* chef *m* de gare.
statistic [stə'tɪstɪk] *n* **(a)** élément *m* d'un tableau statistique; **statistics for 1980,** statistiques *fpl* pour 1980; **to become just another s.,** (*of person etc*) n'être plus qu'un numéro; **he became just another s.,** (*was killed*) il est juste venu s'ajouter aux statistiques (des morts); **vital statistics,** statistiques démographiques; *F* mensurations *fpl* (*d'une femme*); **(b)** (*subject*) **statistics,** (*usu with sing verb*) la statistique.
statistical [stə'tɪstɪk(ə)l] *adj* statistique; **s. tables,**

statistiques *fpl*.

statistically [stə'tɪstɪk(ə)lɪ] *adv* statistiquement; **s., this is unlikely,** statistiquement, ceci est peu probable.

statistician [stætɪs'tɪʃən] *n* statisticien, -ienne.

stator ['steɪtər] *n MecE El* stator *m* (*d'une turbine*).

statuary ['stætjʊərɪ] **1** *adj* (*art, marbre etc*) statuaire. **2** *n* **(a)** (*art*) la statuaire, l'art *m* statuaire; **(b)** (*statues*) statues *fpl*.

statue ['stætjuː] *n* statue *f*; **don't stand there like a s.!,** ne reste pas là comme une souche!

statuesque [stætjʊ'esk] *adj* sculptural, -aux.

statuette [stætjʊ'et] *n* statuette *f*.

stature ['stætjər] *n* stature *f*, taille *f*; **to be short of s.,** être de petite taille; **it will increase her s.,** (*of author etc*) sa réputation y gagnera; **a writer of some international s.,** un écrivain ayant une certaine renommée internationale; **a politician of his s.,** un homme politique de son envergure.

status ['steɪtəs] *n* statut *m*; (*marital*) statut légal (*de qn*); (*prestige, standing*) prestige *m*, standing *m*; **personal s.,** statut personnel; *Admin* **civil s.,** état civil; **social s.,** rang social; **with no official s.,** sans titre officiel; **he's only interested in the job because of the s. that attaches to it,** cet emploi ne l'intéresse qu'en raison du prestige qui y est attaché; *Comptr* **s. line,** ligne *f* d'état *ou* de statut; **s. report,** état *m* des travaux; **s. symbol,** marque *f* de prestige *ou F* de standing.

status-conscious ['steɪtəs'kɒnʃəs] *adj* attaché à son standing.

status quo ['steɪtəs'kwəʊ] *n* statu quo *m inv*; **to maintain the s. q.,** maintenir le statu quo.

statute ['stætjuːt] *n Jur* loi *f*, ordonnance *f*; *Br* acte *m* du Parlement; **the statutes of God,** les ordonnances de Dieu; **s. book,** code *m* (des lois); **to put sth in the s. book,** passer qch à l'état de statut; **s. law,** droit écrit; **statutes,** statuts *mpl*, règlements *mpl* (*d'une société*).

statutory ['stætjʊt(ə)rɪ] *adj* **(a)** (*established by law*) établi *ou* fixé *ou* imposé par la loi; (*by regulations*) réglementaire; (*offence*) prévu par la loi; **s. declaration,** acte *m* de notoriété; attestation *f* (*en lieu de serment*); **s. holiday,** fête légale; *US Jur* **s. rape,** détournement *m* de mineur; **s. regulations,** règlements *mpl* statutaires; **(b)** (*according to law*) statutaire, conforme aux statuts.

staunch[1] [stɔːntʃ] *adj* **(a)** (*person*) sûr, dévoué; (*supporter*) assidu; (*courage*) inébranlable; **s. friend,** ami à toute épreuve; **s. socialist,** socialiste convaincu(e); **s. Catholic,** catholique à tout crin; **(b)** (*ship*) étanche.

staunch[2] [stɔːntʃ, stɑːntʃ] *vt* étancher (*le sang*); **to s. a wound,** étancher le sang d'une blessure.

staunchly ['stɔːntʃlɪ] *adv* avec fermeté; (*with resolve*) avec résolution; **s. Catholic/republican area,** région résolument catholique/républicaine.

staunchness ['stɔːntʃnɪs] *n* **(a)** (*of person*) fermeté *f*; (*loyalty*) dévouement *m*; **(b)** (*of ship etc*) étanchéité *f*.

stave[1] [steɪv] *n* **(a)** (*wooden stick*) bâton *m*; échelon *m* (*d'une échelle*); **barrel staves,** douves *fpl* pour tonneaux; **(b)** (*in prosody*) stance *f*, strophe *f* (*d'un poème*); **(c)** *Mus* portée *f*.

stave[2] *vt* (*pt* **staved**; *pp* **staved**, *esp Nau* **stove** [stəʊv]) (*fit with staves*) garnir (*un tonneau*) de douves.

►**stave in** *vtsep* (*break*) défoncer, enfoncer (*une barrique, un bateau etc*).

►**stave off** *vtsep* (*keep away*) détourner, écarter (*un ennui etc*); prévenir, parer à (*un danger*); conjurer (*un désastre*); **to s. off hunger,** tromper la faim.

stay[1] [steɪ] *n* **(a)** séjour *m* (*dans une ville etc*); visite *f* (*chez un ami*); **fortnight's s.,** séjour de quinze jours; **(b)** *Arch & Lit* (*delay*) retard *m*; *Jur* **s. of execution,** sursis *m*; **s. of proceedings,** suspension *f* d'instances.

stay[2] **1** *vi* **(a)** (*not move*) rester; **s. there!, s. where you are!,** tenez-vous là!; *F* **to s. put,** rester en place; (*refuse to move*) refuser de bouger; **I shall s. put, I'm staying put,** j'y suis, j'y reste; **to s. at home,** rester à la maison *ou* chez soi; **to s. in bed,** rester au lit; (*when ill*) garder le lit; **to s. to** *or* **for dinner,** rester (à) dîner; **computers are here to s.,** les ordinateurs sont entrés dans les mœurs; **this word is here to s.,** ce mot est entré dans la langue; **these changes are here to s.,** ces changements sont passés dans les mœurs; **the weather stayed fine/wet all week,** le temps est resté au beau/à la pluie toute la semaine; **if the weather stays like this,** si le temps se maintient; **it won't s. in position on the wall,** ça ne veut pas rester en place sur le mur; **I can't s. long — I've got a bus to catch,** je ne peux pas rester très longtemps — j'ai un bus à prendre;

(b) (*reside*) (*for short time*) séjourner; **I stayed 5 years in the States,** j'ai passé *ou* habité cinq années aux Etats-Unis; **where are you staying?,** où est-ce que tu es descendu?; **he has come to s.,** (*for a visit*) il est venu passer quelques jours chez nous; (*for good*) il est venu habiter chez nous; **to s. at a hotel,** (*occupy room in*) être installé à un hôtel; **let's s. at that hotel,** descendons à cet hôtel; **to s. with s.o.,** (*visit*) faire une visite à qn; (*spend some time*) passer quelque temps chez qn; **we're staying with relations,** nous sommes chez des parents;

(c) *Sp* **she can s. five kilometres,** elle peut fournir une course de cinq kilomètres; **horse that can s.,** cheval qui a du fond;

(d) *Arch* (*stop*) s'arrêter; (*still used in*) **s.!,** (*to dog*) attendez!;

(e) *Scot* (*live*) habiter, demeurer.

2 *vt* **(a)** *Arch & Lit* (*stop*) arrêter (*le progrès de qn*); enrayer (*une épidémie*); **to s. s.o.'s arm** *or* **hand,** retenir le bras de qn; **to s. one's hand,** se retenir;

(b) *Jur etc* remettre; ajourner (*une décision etc*); suspendre (*son jugement etc*); **to s. judgement,** surseoir à un jugement;

(c) to s. the course, tenir le rythme; *Sp* **will he s. the distance?,** tiendra-t-il la distance?

stay[3] *n* **(a)** (*support*) support *m*, soutien *m*; (*for tree*) tuteur *m*; *Constr MecE etc* support, étai *m*, étançon *m*; **(b)** (*on corset*) **stays,** corset *m*.

stay[4] *vt Constr etc* étayer, étançonner, accorer (*un mur, une maison*).

stay[5] *n Nau* **(a)** étai *m* (*de mât*); **(b) to be in stays,** (*of ship*) être pris vent devant.

stay[6] **1** *vt* **(a)** hauban(n)er (*un mât, un poteau etc*); **(b)** *Nau* faire virer de bord (*un navire*) vent devant. **2** *vi* (*of ship*) virer de bord vent devant.

►**stay away** *vi* (*not approach*) ne pas s'approcher (**from,** de); (*not attend*) ne pas assister (**from,** à); **to s. away from danger,** se tenir à l'écart du danger.

►**stay down** *vi* **(a)** *Sch* (*repeat year*) redoubler (*une classe*); **(b)** (*of hair, lid etc*) tenir en place; **(c) the turtle/diver can s. down for ...,** la tortue/le plongeur peut rester sous l'eau pendant ... .

►**stay in** *vi* **(a)** (*not go out*) ne pas sortir; (*stay in house*) rester à la maison; **(b)** (*of screw, fitting etc*) rester en place.

►**stay off 1** *vi* **(a)** (*not go to work, school*) rester à la maison; **(b)** (*hold off*) (*of bad weather*) ne pas arriver, attendre; **we're hoping the rain will s. off a little longer,** nous espérons que la pluie attendra encore un peu. **2** *vipo* **(a)** (*keep away from*) éviter, ne pas passer par (*main roads, private property etc*); ne pas prendre, éviter (*alcohol, drugs, sweets etc*); **s. off the whisky!,** pas de whisky! **(b)** (*not attend*) ne pas aller à (*l'école etc*).

►**stay on** *vi* **(a)** (*remain longer*) rester plus longtemps; **(b)** (*remain in place*) (*of hat, wig etc*) tenir *ou* rester en place; (*of sticker etc*) tenir.

►**stay out** *vi* **(a)** (*stay outside*) rester dehors; (*not come home*) ne pas rentrer; **to s. out all night,** découcher; **to s. out until all hours of the night,** rester dehors jusqu'à une heure très avancée; **(b)** *Ind* (*continue strike*) poursuivre *ou* continuer la grève; **the women decided to s. out,** les femmes décidèrent de poursuivre la grève.

►**stay up** *vi* **(a)** (*not go to bed*) ne pas se coucher, veiller; **to s. up late,** veiller tard; **to let the children s. up late,** laisser les enfants se coucher *ou* veiller tard; **we stayed up all night talking,** nous sommes restés debout à parler toute la nuit; **(b)** (*remain in place*) (*of picture, shelf, tent, trousers*) tenir; **(c)** (*at university*) **he used to s. up over the vacations,** il restait (travailler) à l'université pendant les vacances.

stay-at-home ['steɪəthəʊm] *adj & n* casanier, -ière.

stayer ['steɪər] *n Sp* (*runner*) coureur *m* de fond; (*horse, cyclist*) stayer *m*; (*horse*) cheval *m* qui a du fond; (*person who perseveres*) personne persévérante; **she's a real s.,** elle a vraiment de l'endurance; **gifted but not a stayer,** doué mais manque de suivi *ou* de persévérance.

staying ['steɪɪŋ] *n* **(a) s. power,** résistance *f*, endurance *f*; **to have good s. power,** (*of horse*) avoir du fond; **(b)** *Arch & Lit* arrêt *m* (*du progrès de qch etc*); enraiement *m* (*d'une épidémie etc*); *Jur* ajournement *m* (*d'une décision etc*).

STD [estiː'diː] *n* **(a)** *Telecom* (*abbr* **subscriber trunk dialling**) **STD code,** indicatif régional; **(b)** *Med* (*abbr* **sexually transmitted disease**) MST *f*.

stead [sted] *n* **(a) to stand s.o. in good s.,** être fort utile à qn; **(b)** *esp Lit* **in s.o.'s s.,** à la place *ou* au lieu de qn.

steadfast ['stedfɑːst] *adj* ferme, stable, inébranlable; **s. in love/in adversity,** constant en amour/dans l'adversité.

steadfastly ['stedfɑːstlɪ] *adv* (*to refuse*) fermement; (*to love, progress etc*) avec constance.

steadfastness ['stedfɑːstnɪs] *n* fermeté *f* (*d'esprit*); constance *f*; ténacité *f* (*de caractère*).

steadily ['stedɪlɪ] *adv* solidement, fermement; (*at regular rate*) régulièrement; (*without stopping*) sans arrêt; (*without jolting*) sans à-coups; (*constantly*) continuellement; (*to work*) assidûment; (*calmly*) d'une manière rangée *ou* posée; **to walk s.,** marcher d'un pas ferme; **s. increasing output,** rendement augmentant de façon soutenue; **his health grows s. worse,** sa santé empire régulièrement; **to work s. at sth,** travailler fermement *ou* assidûment à qch.

steadiness ['stedɪnɪs] *n* fermeté *f*, sûreté *f*; fermeté (*d'esprit*); (*perseverance*) assiduité *f*, persévérance *f*, application *f*; régularité *f* (*de mouvement, d'action*); (*stability*) stabilité *f*; (*of person*) (*calm*) conduite rangée *ou* posée; **s. of hand,** sûreté de main; *St Exch* **s. of prices,** tenue *f* des prix.

steady[1] ['stedɪ] **1** *adj* (*stable, solid*) (*table, ladder etc*) ferme, solide; (*rate, increase, growth*) continu, soutenu; (*income*) régulier; (*pulse*) égal; *Com* (*market*) soutenu; (*person*) (*constant*) constant; (*calm*) rangé, posé; **to make a table s.,** mettre une table en bon équilibre; **to hold sth s.,** bien tenir qch; **to keep s.,** ne pas bouger; **to be s. on one's feet** *or* **legs,** être d'aplomb sur ses jambes; **to be s. in one's affections,** être constant dans ses affections; **s. breeze,** brise étale *ou* franche; *Com* **s. demand for ...,** demande suivie pour ...; *Sp* **to play a s. game,** avoir un jeu régulier; **beneath her s. gaze,** sous son regard soutenu; **s. income,** revenu fixe *ou* régulier; **s. increase,** augmentation régulière; **to have a s. hand,** avoir la main sûre; **with a s. hand,** d'une main assurée *ou* ferme; **s. horse,** cheval calme; **s. pace,** allure modérée; **s. prices,** prix fixes; **s. progress,** progrès ininterrompus; **s. rain,** pluie persistante; **s. weather,** temps établi; **s. worker,** travailleur appliqué *ou* assidu.

2 *adv F* **to go s. with s.o.,** sortir avec qn.

3 *adv & int* **s.!,** (*don't move*) ne bougez pas!; (*watch out you don't fall*) attention (de ne pas tomber)!; *F* **s. (on)!, s. the buffs!,** doucement!

4 *n* **(a)** support *m* (*pour la main etc*); *MecE* **s. (rest),** lunette *f* (*d'un tour etc*);

(b) *F* (*boyfriend, girlfriend*) **my s.,** mon petit ami, ma petite amie.

steady[2] **1** *vt* raffermir, affermir; **to s. one's hand,** assurer sa main; **to s. oneself against sth,** s'étayer contre qch; **to s. the nerves,** calmer *ou* détendre les nerfs; **marriage has steadied him,** le mariage l'a rangé *ou* équilibré. **2** *vi* reprendre son aplomb; (*of boat etc*) retrouver son équilibre; **prices are steadying,** les prix se raffermissent.

►steady down *vi* (*become calmer*) reprendre son aplomb.

steak [steɪk] *n Culin* (*beef*) bifteck *m*, steak *m*; (*cut from the ribs*) entrecôte *f*; tranche *f* (*de viande, de poisson*); darne *f* (*de saumon*); **fillet s.,** tournedos *m*; **s. and chips,** steak frites; **s. tartare,** steak tartare; *Am* **Salisbury s.,** = côtelette de viande hachée accompagnée d'une sauce.

steakhouse ['steɪkhaʊs] *n* steak-grill *m*.

steal[1] [stiːl] *n esp Am F* (*bargain*) affaire *f*; **at $35 it's a s.!,** à 35 dollars c'est une affaire!

steal[2] *v* (*pt* **stole** [stəʊl]; *pp* **stolen** ['stəʊl(ə)n]) **1** *vt* voler, dérober (**sth from s.o.,** qch à qn); prendre, *F* piquer (*s.o.'s idea, husband, girlfriend*); dérober, voler (*un baiser*); **stolen goods,** objets volés; **I've had my purse stolen,** on m'a volé mon porte-monnaie; **to s. money from the till,** (*of employee*) prendre de l'argent *ou* se servir dans la caisse; **to s. s.o.'s heart,** prendre le cœur de qn; **to s. a few hours from one's studies,** dérober quelques heures à ses études; **to s. a glance at s.o.,** jeter un coup d'œil furtif à qn; **to s. a march on s.o.,** prendre les devants sur qn, devancer qn. **2** *vi* **(a)** voler (**from s.o.,** qn); *Bible* **thou shalt not s.,** tu ne voleras point; **to be caught stealing,** être pris en train de voler; **(b)** (*move stealthily*) **to s. away/in/out,** s'en aller/entrer/sortir à la dérobée *ou* furtivement; **she stole into the room,** elle s'est faufilée *ou* glissée dans la pièce.

stealer ['stiːlər] *n* voleur, -euse (**of,** de).

stealing ['stiːlɪŋ] *n* vol *m*; **s. is wrong,** c'est mal de voler.

stealth [stelθ] *n* ruse *f*; **by s.,** par la ruse; (*furtively*) à la dérobée, furtivement; *Mil* **s. bomber,** avion furtif.

stealthily ['stelθɪlɪ] *adv* furtivement, à la dérobée.

stealthiness ['stelθɪnɪs] *n* caractère furtif (*d'une action etc*); manières secrètes *ou* furtives (*d'une personne*).

stealthy ['stelθɪ] *adj* furtif; (*regard*) dérobé, à la dérobée; **with a s. step,** d'un pas furtif, à pas de loup, à pas feutrés.

steam[1] [stiːm] *n* vapeur *f* (*d'eau*); (*condensation*) buée *f*; *Phys* vapeur; **dry s.,** vapeur sèche; *MecE etc* **to get up** *or* **to raise s.,** mettre (une chaudière) sous pression; **to get up s.,** (*of person*) rassembler toutes ses forces *ou* toute son énergie; *Nau* **engine under s.,** machine *f* sous pression *ou* en pression; **at full s.,** à toute vapeur; *Nau* **full s. ahead!,** en avant toute!; **to keep up s.,** tenir (de) la pression; *F* (*of person*) ne pas se relâcher; **to run out of s.,** (*of engine etc*) ne plus être sous pression; *F* (*of project, campaign etc*) s'essouffler; *F* (*of person*) être épuisé; **I'm running out of s.,** je commence à peiner; **to let off** *or* **blow off s.,** lâcher *ou* laisser échapper (de) la vapeur; *F* (*of person*) (*use up excess energy*) dépenser son trop-plein d'énergie; *F* (*of person*) (*emotionally*) donner libre cours à ses sentiments; *F* (*of person*) (*work off anger*) passer sa colère, *F* se défouler; **to proceed under its own s.,** (*of damaged ship etc*) marcher par ses seuls moyens; *Fig* **I can do it under my own s.,** je peux le faire tout seul *ou* sans aide; **s. bath,** bain *m* de vapeur; **s. cooking,** cuisson *f* à la vapeur; **s. engine,** machine *f* à vapeur; **s. iron,** fer *m* à vapeur; **s. power,** la vapeur (en tant qu'énergie); *Hum* **s. radio,** radio *f* de l'an quarante.

steam[2] **1** *vt* passer (*qch*) à la vapeur, étuver (*qch*); *Culin* cuire (*des légumes etc*) à la vapeur *ou* à l'étuvée; **steamed potatoes,** pommes *fpl* vapeur; **to s. open an envelope,** décacheter une lettre à la vapeur. **2** *vi* **(a)** (*give off steam*) jeter *ou* exhaler de la vapeur, fumer; **horses steaming with sweat,** chevaux fumants (de sueur); **(b) to s. ahead,** (*of ship, locomotive*) avancer (à la vapeur); *F* (*make rapid progress*) avancer toutes voiles dedans; **the train steamed out of the station,** le train a quitté la gare (en fumant); **the ferry steamed into port,** le ferry entra dans le port (en fumant).

►steam off **1** *vtsep* décoller (*un timbre*) à la vapeur. **2** *vi* (*of ship*) s'éloigner (en fumant).

►steam up **1** *vi* (*become covered in condensation*) (*of window, windscreen, glasses etc*) s'embuer. **2** *vtsep* (*usu passive*) **to get all steamed up,** (*of windows, glasses etc*) se couvrir de buée, s'embuer; *F* (*of person*) (*lose one's composure*) s'emballer; (*give way to anger*) se laisser emporter (*par la colère*).

steamboat ['stiːmbəʊt] *n* (bateau *m* à) vapeur *m*.

steamer ['stiːmər] *n* **(a)** (*ship*) *Nau* vapeur *m*; **(b)** *Culin* marmite *f* à vapeur.

steaming ['stiːmɪŋ] **1** *adj* fumant; *Fig F* (*angry*) fumant de colère. **2** *adv* **s. hot,** tout chaud. **3** *n* étuvage *m*, injection *f* de vapeur; *Culin* cuisson *f* à la vapeur *ou* à l'étuvée.

steamroller[1] ['stiːmrəʊlər] *n Constr* rouleau *m* compresseur; *Fig* force *f* irrésistible *ou* qui écrase toute opposition.

steamroller[2] *vt Constr Arch* cylindrer (*une route*); *Fig* écraser (*l'opposition etc*); **to s. a bill through parliament,** imposer un projet de loi au parlement; **he steamrollered his plans through the committee,** il a imposé ses plans au comité.

steamship ['stiːmʃɪp] *n* (bateau *m* à) vapeur *m*.

steamy ['stiːmɪ] *adj* (*full of steam*) plein de vapeur; (*covered in steam*) couvert de buée; *Fig* **s. novel/movie** *etc*, roman/film chaud *ou* érotique.

steed [stiːd] *n Lit* coursier *m*, destrier *m*.

steel[1] [stiːl] *n* **(a)** *Metal* acier *m*; **rolled s.,** acier laminé; **s. plated,** cuirassé; **a grip/a will of s.,** une poigne/une volonté de fer; **nerves of s.,** nerfs *mpl* d'acier; **the iron and s. industry,** l'industrie *f* sidérurgique, la sidérurgie; *Mus* **s. band,** steel band *f*; **s. knife/ladder,** couteau *m*/ échelle *f* en acier; **s. mill,** aciérie *f*; **s. wool,** paille *f* de fer; **(b)** *Arch & Lit* (*sword*) fer *m*, épée *f*; (*blade*) lame *f*; **(c)** (*for sharpening knives*) affiloir *m*, fusil *m*; **(d) s. (grey),** (gris *m*) acier.

steel[2] *vt* **to s. oneself/one's heart to do sth,** (*harden oneself*) s'endurcir pour faire qch; s'armer de courage pour faire qch; **to s. oneself against sth,** se cuirasser contre qch.

steelclad ['stiːlklæd] *adj* couvert *ou* revêtu d'acier; (*knight*) bardé de fer.

steelwork ['stiːlwɜːk] *n* **(a)** *Aut etc* tôleries *fpl*; **constructional s.,** profilés *mpl* pour constructions; **(b)** (*usu with sing verb*) **steelworks,** aciérie *f*.

steelworker ['stiːlwɜːkər] *n* ouvrier *m* de l'industrie sidérurgique.

steely ['stiːlɪ] *adj* **(a)** d'acier; **(b)** (*hard*) dur, inflexible; (*regard etc*) d'acier; **his s. determination,** sa détermination inflexible; **(c) s. blue,** (bleu) acier.

steelyard ['stiːljɑːd, 'stɪljəd] *n* (balance) romaine *f*.

steep[1] [stiːp] **1** *adj* **(a)** escarpé, à pic, raide; (*pente*) rapide; (*chemin*) à forte pente; **s. climb,** pente *f* raide; **the plane went into a s. climb/dive,** l'avion monta/descendit à pic; **s. gradient,** forte pente, pente *f* raide *ou* rapide; **s.**

rise in prices, hausse considérable des prix; **(b)** *F* (*excessive*) fort, raide; **that's a bit s.!,** c'est un peu fort!; **s. price,** prix exorbitant. **2** *n Lit* pente *f* rapide, escarpement *m*.

steep² *n Ind* **(a)** = **STEEPING**; **to put sth in s.,** mettre qch en trempe; **(b)** (*liquid*) bain *m* (*de macération*).

steep³ **1** *vt Ind etc* baigner, tremper; mouiller (*le linge*); rouir (*le lin*); (*in tanning*) tremper (*les peaux*); *Culin Fig* saturer, imbiber (*qch de qch*); **terrace steeped in sunshine,** terrasse baignée de soleil; **steeped in prejudice,** imbibé de préjugés; **steeped in history,** imprégné d'histoire; **to s. oneself in the atmosphere of the Middle Ages,** se tremper *ou* se plonger dans l'atmosphère du moyen âge. **2** *vi* tremper; (*of flax*) rouir; *Culin* mariner.

steepen ['stiːp(ə)n] *vi* (*of slope etc*) devenir plus raide; (*of prices*) augmenter.

steeping ['stiːpɪŋ] *n Ind etc* trempage *m*, macération *f*, trempe *f*; mouillage *m* (*du linge*); rouissage *m* (*du chanvre*).

steeple ['stiːp(ə)l] *n* (*bell tower*) clocher *m*; (*spire*) flèche *f* (de clocher).

steeplechase ['stiːp(ə)ltʃeɪs] *n Sp* steeple-chase *m*, *pl* steeple-chases, steeple *m*.

steeplechaser ['stiːp(ə)ltʃeɪsər] *n* (*rider*) cavalier *m* qui monte en steeple-chases; (*horse, athlete*) steeple-chaser *m*.

steeplechasing ['stiːp(ə)ltʃeɪsɪŋ] *n Sp* steeple-chases *mpl*.

steeplejack ['stiːp(ə)ldʒæk] *n* réparateur *m* de clochers *ou* de cheminées d'usines.

steeply ['stiːplɪ] *adv* (*to drop etc*) en pente rapide; (*to drop, climb*) à pic; **road that climbs s.,** route à forte pente; **to rise s.,** (*of prices*) monter en flèche.

steepness ['stiːpnɪs] *n* raideur *f*, escarpement *m* (*d'une pente*).

steer¹ [stɪər] **1** *vt Nau* gouverner (*un navire*); barrer (*un yacht*); *Aut* conduire, diriger (*une voiture*); diriger (*qn*) (**towards,** vers); **to s. a northerly course, to s. north,** faire route au nord; (*turn north*) mettre le cap sur le nord; **to s. clear of sth/s.o.,** éviter qch/qn; **to s. the conversation away from a subject,** détourner la conversation d'un sujet; **to s. the conversation round to another subject,** faire tourner *ou* aiguiller la conversation vers un autre sujet; **to s. a country out of a crisis,** faire sortir un pays de la crise. **2** *vi* (*of person*) conduire, diriger; (*of ship*) gouverner; **ship that steers well,** navire qui gouverne bien; **to s. for sth,** se diriger vers qch; *Fig* **you're steering for trouble,** vous allez droit vers les embêtements.

steer² *n* bœuf *m*.

steerage ['stɪərɪdʒ] *n Nau Arch* (*third-class accommodation*) emménagements *mpl* pour passagers de troisième classe; entrepont *m*.

steerageway ['stɪərɪdʒweɪ] *n* vitesse *f* nécessaire pour gouverner.

steering ['stɪərɪŋ] *n* **(a)** direction *f*, conduite *f* (*d'un bateau, d'une voiture*); **s. (gear),** organes *mpl* de transmission d'un moteur; *Aut* timonerie *f*, (boîte *f* de) direction *f*; *Nau* appareil *m* à gouverner; *Av* direction; **s. wheel,** *Aut* volant *m*; *Nau* roue *f* du gouvernail; *Aut* **s. column,** colonne *f* de direction; **s. lock,** angle *m* de braquage; (*anti-theft*) antivol *m* de direction; **s. committee,** comité *m* d'organisation; **(b)** *Nau* manœuvre *f* de la barre.

steersman, *pl* **-men** ['stɪəzmən] *n Nau* homme *m* de barre, timonier *m*.

stellar ['stelər] *adj* stellaire.

stem¹ [stem] *n* **(a)** *Bot* tige *f* (*de plante, de fleur*); queue *f* (*de fruit, de feuille*); pétiole *m*, pédoncule *m* (*de fleur*); tronc *m*, souche *f* (*d'arbre*); **(b)** pied *m*, patte *f* (*de verre à boire*); tige *f* (*de soupape, de clef*); tuyau *m* (*de pipe*); *Mus* queue *f* (*d'une note*); **(c)** souche (*de famille*); *Ling* radical *m* (*d'un mot*); **(d)** (*naval architecture*) étrave *f*, avant *m*; **from s. to stern,** de l'avant à l'arrière.

stem² *v* (**-mm-**) **1** *vt* égrapper (*des raisins*). **2** *vi* **to s. from sth,** (*of problems, errors, theories etc*) provenir de qch; (*of models, versions, designs etc*) être issu de; **much harm stemmed from this,** il en est résulté beaucoup de mal.

stem³ **1** *vt* (*hold back*) contenir, endiguer (*un cours d'eau*); enrayer (*une épidémie*); lutter contre (*la marée*); remonter (*le courant*); résister à (*une attaque*); **to s. the tide of ...,** arrêter le flot de ... . **2** *vi Ski* faire un stem.

stem⁴ *n Ski* (virage *m* en) stem *m*; **S. Christie,** stem christie; **s. parallel,** stem parallèle.

stemmed [stemd] *adj* (*fleur etc*) à tige, à queue; (*verre*) à pied, à patte.

-stemmed [-stemd] *suff Bot* **long-s.,** longicaule; **thick-s.,** crassicaule.

stench [stentʃ] *n* odeur infecte, puanteur *f*.

stencil¹ ['stens(ə)l] *n* **(a)** (*device*) patron *m* (ajouré), poncif *m*, pochoir *m*; **s. plate,** pochoir; **coloured by s.,** colorié au patron; **cipher s.,** grille *f*; **(b)** (*work*) peinture *f ou* travail *m* au poncif *ou* au pochoir, tracé *m*; **(c)** (*typewritten copy etc*) cliché *m*, stencil *m*; **s. paper,** papier *m* stencil.

stencil² *vt* (**-ll-**, *US* **-l-**) peindre *ou* marquer (*qch*) au poncif *ou* au patron *ou* au pochoir, poncer, patronner (*qch*); *Ind Com* marquer (*une caisse, un ballot*); polycopier (*une circulaire etc*); tirer (*une circulaire*) au stencil.

sten gun ['stengʌn] *n* mitraillette *f*.

stenographer, *US* **stenographist** [stə'nɒgrəfər, -fɪst] *n* sténographe *mf*, *F* sténo *mf*.

stenography [stə'nɒgrəfɪ] *n* sténographie *f*.

stentorian [sten'tɔːrɪən] *adj* (*voix*) de stentor.

step¹ [step] *n* **(a)** pas *m*; **to take a s.,** faire un pas (**back, forward,** en arrière, en avant); **one s. forward, two steps back,** un pas en avant et deux pas en arrière; *esp Lit* **to turn one's steps towards a place,** se diriger *ou* diriger ses pas vers un lieu; **a child's first steps,** les premiers pas d'un enfant; **at every s.,** à chaque pas; **s. by s.,** pas à pas; (*little by little*) petit à petit, graduellement, progressivement; **within a few steps of** *or* **from the house,** à quelques pas de la maison; **it's quite a s.,** (*quite a long way*) c'est un bon bout de chemin; **that's a great s. forward,** c'est déjà un grand pas de fait, c'est déjà un grand progrès; **with quick steps,** d'un pas rapide; **to tread in s.o.'s steps,** marcher sur *ou* suivre les traces de qn; **you'll have to watch your s.,** il va falloir que tu fasses attention où tu mets les pieds; *Fig* fais attention à ce que tu fais; *Fig* **they fought us every s. of the way,** ils nous ont combattu sans répit *ou* sur chaque point; *Fig* **we're behind you every s. of the way,** nous sommes avec vous sur toute la ligne;

(b) (*walking, dancing*) pas *m*; **marching s.,** pas ordinaire; **to be in s.,** marcher au pas, être au pas; **to fall into s.,** se mettre au pas; **to keep s.,** rester au pas; **to change s.,** changer de pas; **to break s.,** rompre le pas; **to be out of s. (with s.o.),** marcher à contre-pas de qn; *Fig* marcher à contre-courant de qn; *Fig* **supply had got out of step with demand,** l'offre ne correspond plus à la demande; *El* **alternators in s.,** alternateurs synchronisés; **alternators out of s.,** alternateurs déphasés; **waltz s.,** pas de valse;

(c) (*action*) démarche *f*, mesure *f*; **a s. in the right direction,** un pas dans la bonne voie; **false s.,** faux pas; **to take the necessary steps,** faire *ou* entreprendre les démarches nécessaires; **to take steps to do sth,** prendre des mesures pour faire qch; **the first s. will be to...,** la première chose à faire, ce sera de...;

(d) marche *f*, degré *m* (*d'un escalier*); échelon *m* (*d'une échelle*); marche (*d'un escabeau*); marchepied *m* (*d'un véhicule*); **flight of steps,** escalier *m*, volée *f* de marches; (*outside building*) perron *m*; **mind the s.,** attention à la marche; *F* **to go up a s.,** (*be promoted*) avancer en grade; **it's a s. up from the old house,** c'est un peu mieux que la vieille maison; *Geol* **rock s.,** ressaut *m*; **to cut steps,** (*in mountaineering*) tailler;

(e) (*stage*) étape *f*; **it is a simple, two-s. procedure,** c'est une procédure simple en deux étapes; **the next s. is to ...,** l'étape suivante consiste à ...;

(f) **(pair of) steps,** escabeau *m*, échelle double; *Av* **steps,** passerelle *f*;

(g) (*in pattern*) cran *m*; **steps of a key,** dents *fpl* d'une clef.

step² *v* (**stepped** [stept]) **1** *vi* (*take a step, steps*) faire un pas *ou* des pas; (*walk*) marcher, aller; **to s. on s.o.'s foot,** marcher sur le pied de qn; **s. this way,** venez par ici; **s. inside for a moment,** entrez pour un moment; **he stepped carefully over the cat,** il enjamba soigneusement le chat; **when I stepped off the ladder,** quand je suis descendu de l'échelle. **2** *vt* **(a)** (*arrange in steps*) disposer en échelons, échelonner; recouper (*un mur, un parapet*); *Nau* dresser, arborer (*un mât*); **(b)** *Old-fashioned F* **to s. it with s.o.,** danser avec qn.

▸**step aside** *vi* s'écarter; **to s. aside to let s.o. pass,** s'écarter pour laisser passer qn; *Fig* se retirer pour laisser la place à qn; **it's time the old chairman stepped aside,** il est temps que le vieux président se retire et laisse la place à quelqu'un d'autre.

▸**step back** *vi* faire un pas en arrière; *Fig* **if we could s. back into the last century,** si nous pouvions repartir au siècle passé; **sometimes it helps to s. back and look at**

things, il est parfois bon de prendre du recul.
►**step down 1** *vtsep* (*decrease*) *El* dévolter (*le courant*); *MecE* **to s. down the gear,** démultiplier la transmission. **2** *vi* **(a)** (*resign*) démissionner; **he stepped down in favour of the other candidate,** (*withdrew*) il s'est retiré en faveur de l'autre candidat; **(b)** (*descend*) descendre; **to s. down from a platform,** descendre d'une plate-forme.
►**step forward** *vi* faire un pas en avant; *Fig* (*volunteer etc*) se désigner, se porter volontaire.
►**step in** *vi* entrer (**to,** dans); (*intervene*) intervenir, s'interposer.
►**step on** *vipo* (*tread on*) marcher sur (*qch*); *F* **to s. on the gas, to s. on it,** *Aut* appuyer sur l'accélérateur *ou F* sur le champignon; (*hurry*) se dépêcher, *F* se grouiller; **to s. on the brakes,** donner un coup de frein brusque.
►**step out** *vi* **(a)** (*go outside house etc*) sortir (*de la maison etc*); **(b)** (*walk faster*) allonger *ou* forcer le pas; **to s. out briskly,** marcher rapidement; **(c)** *Old-fashioned* **to be stepping out with s.o.,** sortir avec qn.
►**step up 1** *vi* **to s. up to s.o./sth,** s'approcher de qn/qch; **s. up!, s. up!, come and see the ...,** approchez! approchez! venez voir ...; **he stepped up onto the platform,** il est monté sur la plate-forme. **2** *vtsep* (*increase, intensify*) accroître, augmenter.
stepbrother ['stepbrʌðər] *n* demi-frère, *pl* demi-frères.
stepchild, *pl* **-children** ['steptʃaɪld, -tʃɪldrən] *n* beau-fils *m*, belle-fille *f*, *pl* beaux-fils, belles-filles.
stepdaughter ['stepdɔːtər] *n* belle-fille, *pl* belles-filles.
stepfather ['stepfɑːðər] *n* (*second mari de la mère*) beau-père, *pl* beaux-pères.
Stephen ['stiːvən] *n* Étienne, Stéphane.
stepladder ['steplædər] *n* escabeau *m*.
stepmother ['stepmʌðər] *n* belle-mère (*seconde femme du père*), *pl* belles-mères.
steppe [step] *n Geog* steppe *f*.
stepped [stept] *adj* à gradins, en gradins; (*in stages*) à étages; (*engrenage*) échelonné, en échelon; *Archit* **s. gable,** pignon *m* à redans.
stepper ['stepər] *n El* **s. motor,** moteur *m* pas-à-pas.
stepping ['stepɪŋ] *n* **(a)** (*walking*) marche *f*, pas *mpl*; **s. stone,** pierre *f* (pour passer une rivière *etc* à gué); *Fig* tremplin *m*; **(b)** (*arrangement in steps*) échelonnement *m*.
stepping down *n El* dévoltage *m* (*de la transmission*); *MecE* démultiplication *f* (*de la transmission*).
stepping up *n El* survoltage *m*; *MecE* multiplication *f* (*d'un engrenage*); augmentation *f* (*de production etc*); intensification *f* (*d'une campagne etc*).
stepsister ['stepsɪstər] *n* demi-sœur, *pl* demi-sœurs.
stepson ['stepsʌn] *n* beau-fils, *pl* beaux-fils.
stereo, *pl* **-os** ['sterɪəʊ, -əʊz; 'stɪə-] **1** *n* **(a)** (*equipment*) (appareil *m*) stéréo *f*; **(b)** (*sound*) stéréo *f*; **to listen to sth in s.,** écouter qch en stéréo; **(c)** *Typ* = **STEREOTYPE**[1] **(a)**. **2** *adj* (*equipment*) stéréo *inv*; (*recording, broadcast*) en stéréo.
stereophonic [sterɪə'fɒnɪk, stɪə-] *adj* stéréophonique.
stereoscope ['sterɪəskəʊp, 'stɪər-] *n Opt* stéréoscope *m*.
stereoscopic [sterɪəʊ'skɒpɪk, 'stɪə-] *adj* stéréoscopique.
stereotype[1] ['sterɪətaɪp, 'stɪə-] *n* **(a)** *Typ* cliché *m*; **(b)** *Fig* stéréotype *m*.
stereotype[2] *vt* **(a)** *Typ* stéréotyper, clicher; **(b)** *Fig* stéréotyper.
stereotyped ['sterɪətaɪpt, 'stɪə-] *adj* **(a)** *Typ* stéréotypé; **(b)** *Fig* **s. phrase,** stéréotype *m*, cliché *m*; **the s. idea of a farmer,** le stéréotype de l'agriculteur.
sterile ['steraɪl] *adj* stérile.
sterility [ste'rɪlɪtɪ] *n* stérilité *f*.
sterilization [sterɪlaɪ'zeɪʃən] *n* stérilisation *f*.
sterilize ['sterɪlaɪz] *vt* stériliser; **sterilized milk,** lait stérilisé.
sterilizer ['sterɪlaɪzər] *n* stérilisateur *m*.
sterilizing ['sterɪlaɪzɪŋ] *n* stérilisation *f*.
sterling ['stɜːlɪŋ] **1** *adj* (*monnaie, or, argent*) de bon aloi; *Fig* de bon aloi, vrai, solide; **s. qualities,** qualités *fpl* solides; **pound s.,** livre *f* sterling; **the s. area,** la zone sterling. **2** *n* (*currency*) (livre *f*) sterling *m* ; **to pay in s.,** payer en livres sterling.
stern[1] [stɜːn] *adj* sévère; **we are made of sterner stuff,** nous, nous sommes d'une autre trempe.
stern[2] *n* **(a)** *Nau* arrière *m*; **s. light,** feu *m* d'arrière *ou* de poupe; **(b)** *F* (*of person*) postérieur *m*, derrière *m*; (*in hunting*) queue *f* (*d'un chien courant*).
sternly ['stɜːnlɪ] *adv* sévèrement.
sternness ['stɜːnnɪs] *n* sévérité *f*.
sternum, *pl* **-a, -ums** ['stɜːnəm, -ə, -əmz] *n Anat* sternum *m*.
steroid ['stɪərɔɪd] *n Bio Ch* stéroïde *m*.
stertorous ['stɜːtərəs] *adj Med & Lit* stertoreux, ronflant.
stet[1] [stet] *n Typ* bon, à maintenir.
stet[2] *vt* (**-tt-**) maintenir (*un mot sur l'épreuve*).
stethoscope ['steθəskəʊp] *n Med* stéthoscope *m*.
stetson ['stets(ə)n] *n* (*hat*) chapeau mou à larges bords.
stevedore ['stiːv(ə)dɔːr] *n* docker *m*, arrimeur *m*.
Steven ['stiːvən] *n* Étienne, Stéphane.
stew[1] [stjuː] *n* **(a)** *Culin* ragoût *m*; **Irish s.,** ragoût de mouton à l'irlandaise; *F* **to be in a s.,** être dans tous ses états; **(b)** *Arch* (*brothel*) bordel *m*.
stew[2] **1** *vt Culin* faire cuire (*la viande*) en ragoût, faire un ragoût de (*qch*); **to s. fruit,** faire une compote de fruits. **2** *vi Culin* (*of meat*) mijoter; *F* **to let s.o. s. in his own juice,** laisser qn cuire *ou* mijoter dans son jus, laisser mariner qn.
steward ['stjʊəd] *n* **(a)** économe *m*, régisseur *m*, intendant *m* (*d'une propriété*); **(b)** économe *m* (*d'un collège*); maître *m* d'hôtel (*d'un cercle etc*); *Nau* distributeur *m*, commis *m ou* agent *m* aux vivres; *Nau Av* steward *m*; *Nau* **steward's mate,** cambusier *m*; **(c)** commissaire *m* (*d'une réunion sportive, d'un bal*); (*at demonstration etc*) responsable *m*, organisateur *m*; (*at dance, disco etc*) portier *m*; **(d)** *Ind* **shop s.,** délégué d'atelier *ou* d'usine *ou* du personnel.
stewardess [stjʊə'des] *n Nau* femme *f* de chambre (*de bord*); *Av* **air s.,** hôtesse *f* de l'air.
stewardship ['stjʊədʃɪp] *n* économat *m*, intendance *f*; **under his s.,** quand il sera *ou* pendant qu'il est *ou* était intendant *ou* économe.
stewed [stjuːd] *adj Culin* **s. beef,** ragoût *m* de bœuf, bœuf *m* (à la) mode; **s. fruit,** compote *f* de fruits; *F* **s. tea,** thé trop infusé.
stewing ['stjuːɪŋ] *n* **s. beef,** bœuf *m* pour ragoût; **s. pears,** poires *fpl* à cuire; **s. pan = STEWPAN.**
stewpan ['stjuːpæn] *n* (grande) casserole *f*.
stewpot ['stjuːpɒt] *n* cocotte *f*, fait-tout *m inv*.
St. Ex. *Fin* (*abbr* **Stock Exchange**) Bourse *f*.
stick[1] [stɪk] *n* **(a)** bâton *m*; manche *m* (*à balai, de parapluie*); *F* levier *m* (*de changement de vitesse*); baguette *f* (*de chef d'orchestre*); (*small piece of wood*) morceau *m* de bois; *Fig* **you're giving him a s. to beat you with,** vous lui donnez des verges pour vous battre; *F* **to take a lot of s.,** être critiqué *ou* éreinté; (*to be mocked*) se faire mettre en boîte; *F* **to give it some s.,** (*exert oneself*) s'y mettre; **the big s.,** la manière forte; (la politique de) la force; **pea sticks,** rames *fpl* de petits pois; **hop sticks, vine sticks,** échalas *mpl*; **(walking) s.,** canne *f*; *Av* **control s.,** *F* **joy s.,** manche à balai; *Sp* **(hockey etc) s.,** crosse *f*; **to gather sticks,** ramasser du bois sec *ou* du petit bois; **cocktail** *or* **cherry s.,** bâtonnet *m* (*pour cerise de cocktail*); **swizzle s.,** agitateur *m* (*pour cocktails etc*); **not a s. was left standing,** tout était rasé; **my few sticks of furniture,** mes quelques meubles; **s. figure,** bonhomme dessiné *ou* composé de bâtonnets; *Ent* **s. insect,** phasme *m*, insecte-brindille *m*, *pl* insectes-brindilles; *Typ* **(setting** *or* **composing) s.,** compositeur *m*; *F* **he lives out in the sticks,** il habite un trou perdu, il vit dans la brousse; *Sl* **to be up the s.,** (*pregnant*) être en cloque;
(b) *F Old-fashioned* (*person*) **he's/she's a funny old s.,** c'est un drôle de personnage; **a dry old s.,** un pince-sans-rire; *Old-fashioned* **Jeremy, old s.!,** Jeremy, vieille branche!;
(c) bâton *m* (*de sucre d'orge, de colle etc*); applicateur *m* (*de déodorant*); bâton, canon *m* (*de soufre*); *El* baguette *f* (*de charbon*); bâtonnet *m* (*de dynamite*);
(d) *Culin* **s. of celery,** branche *f* de céleri; **s. of rhubarb,** tige *f* de rhubarbe; **s. of asparagus,** (pointe *f* d') asperge *f*;
(e) *Mil Av* **s. of bombs,** chapelet *m* de bombes; **s. of parachutists,** stick *m* (de parachutistes).
stick[2] *v* (*pt & pp* **stuck** [stʌk]) **1** *vt* **(a)** (*insert*) piquer, enfoncer (**sth into sth,** qch dans qch); planter, fixer (**sth on a spike,** qch sur une pointe); **to s. a pin into sth,** enfoncer une épingle dans qch; **she stuck the spade into the ground,** elle a planté la bêche dans le sol; **to s. pigs,** (*of butcher*) égorger *ou* saigner les porcs; (*in hunting*) chasser le sanglier à l'épieu;
(b) *F* (*put*) mettre; **to s. one's hat on one's head,** mettre *ou* planter son chapeau sur sa tête; **s. it in your pocket,** fourrez-le dans votre poche; **s. it in the corner,** collez ça dans le coin; **s. it on the table,** mettez ça sur la table;
(c) (*attach with glue etc*) coller, attacher; **to s. sth on(to) sth,** coller qch à *ou* sur qch; **trunk stuck all over with labels,** malle bardée d'étiquettes;
(d) *F* (*endure*) supporter, endurer, souffrir (*qn, qch*); **to s. it,** tenir le coup, tenir bon; **I can't s. it any longer,** je

n'en peux plus; **I can't s. him,** je ne peux pas le sentir;

(e) (*in horticulture*) ramer (*des pois etc*); mettre des tuteurs à (*des plantes*);

(f) to be stuck, to get stuck, (*unable to move*) être coincé; (*in mud etc*) s'embourber, être embourbé; (*mentally, in a problem etc*) être en panne; **to get stuck in a bog,** s'embourber dans un marécage; **there's something stuck in the pipe,** il y a quelque chose de coincé dans le tuyau; **here I am stuck in hospital for six weeks,** me voilà cloué à l'hôpital pour six semaines; **I'm stuck,** (*I can't move*) je suis bloqué; (*in exam, puzzle etc*) je suis en panne; **I was stuck at Heathrow for 6 hours,** j'ai été bloqué six heures à Heathrow; **to be s. in a job,** être coincé dans un emploi; **the book's finished but I'm stuck for a title,** le livre est fini mais je ne trouve pas de titre; **stuck for money,** à court d'argent; **to s., to be stuck,** (*in a speech*) *F* rester en carafe *ou* en panne; *F* **I'm stuck with it/him,** je ne peux pas m'en débarrasser; **we're stuck with it,** il faut s'y résigner;

(g) *F* **you can s. your job,** ton boulot tu peux te le mettre où je pense.

2 *vi* **(a) sewing left with a needle sticking in it,** ouvrage laissé avec une aiguille piquée dedans; **the point was sticking through the lining,** la pointe avait percé la doublure;

(b) (*adhere*) (se) coller, s'attacher, tenir (**to,** à); *Culin* (*of rice etc*) attacher; **the stamp won't s.,** le timbre ne colle pas; **the name stuck,** (*to one person etc*) ce nom lui est resté; (*to several people*) ce nom leur est resté;

(c) (*to be caught, jammed*) être pris, rester pris; (*in sand, bog etc*) s'enfoncer, s'empêtrer; (*of machine parts*) (se) coincer, gommer; *Aut* (*of valve, cut-out*) rester collé; **this drawer sticks,** le tiroir coince; **the words stuck in his throat,** les mots lui restèrent dans la gorge; **it sticks in my throat,** je ne peux pas avaler *ou* digérer ça; **to s. fast,** (*of boat*) s'enliser (sur un banc de sable *ou* dans la vase); **the lift has stuck,** l'ascenseur est coincé *ou* en panne.

►**stick around** *vi F* (*wait*) attendre; (*stay*) rester; **s. around!** restez (si vous voulez)!

►**stick at** *vipo* **(a)** (*persevere with*) s'acharner à (faire) (*qch*); **s. at it!,** persévérez!; **(b)** (*stop in face of*) **to s. at a difficulty,** s'arrêter devant *ou F* rester en panne devant une difficulté; **to s. at doing sth,** se faire scrupule de faire qch; **to s. at nothing,** ne reculer devant rien.

►**stick by** *vipo* **(a)** (*remain loyal to*) **to s. by a friend,** ne pas abandonner un ami; **(b)** (*continue to affirm*) confirmer, maintenir; **I s. by what I said,** je maintiens ce que j'ai dit.

►**stick down** *vtsep* **(a)** *F* (*put down*) **s. it down anywhere,** mettez-le *ou* collez-le n'importe où; **to s. sth down in a notebook,** inscrire qch sur un carnet; **(b)** (*with glue*) coller (*une enveloppe*).

►**stick in 1** *vtsep* **(a)** (*with glue*) coller; **(b)** *F* (*put in*) mettre, *F* coller; enfoncer (*un couteau etc*); **(c)** *F* **to get stuck in,** (*start working*) s'y mettre; (*start eating*) se mettre à manger (**to sth,** qch); **to get stuck into sth,** (*work etc*) se mettre à qch; **let's get stuck in!,** alors, on s'y met! **2** *vi* **(a)** (*of knife etc*) s'enfoncer; **he threw it at the wall and it stuck in,** il l'a lancé au mur et il s'y est enfoncé; **(b)** *F* (*persevere*) **just s. in there!,** tenez bon!

►**stick on 1** *vtsep* coller, fixer (*un timbre etc*); *F* **to s. one on s.o.,** (*hit*) coller *ou* ficher un marron à qn; *F* **to be stuck on s.o.,** être fou de qn; *F* **he is stuck on the idea,** il s'enthousiasme pour cette idée; *F* **to s. it on,** exagérer. **2** *vi* (*adhere*) adhérer; (*remain stuck on*) rester collé.

►**stick out 1** *vtsep* **(a)** (*cause to protrude*) faire dépasser (*qch*), sortir (*qch*); **to s. out one's tongue,** tirer la langue; **to s. out one's chest,** bomber la poitrine; **he stuck his head out (of the window),** il sortit la tête (par la fenêtre); *F* **to s. one's neck out (for s.o.),** prendre des risques (pour qn); **(b)** *F* **to s. it out,** tenir jusqu'au bout. **2** *vi* **(a)** (*protrude*) faire saillie, ressortir; **to s. out (beyond sth),** dépasser (de qch); **his ears s. out,** il a les oreilles décollées; **her teeth s. out,** elle a les dents qui avancent, elle a les dents en avant; **(b)** *F* (*be noticeable*) se voir, se remarquer; **the way she dresses makes her s. out,** la manière dont elle s'habille fait qu'elle ne passe pas inaperçue; **it sticks out a mile,** c'est clair comme le jour; **it sticks out like a sore thumb,** ça se voit comme le nez au milieu de la figure.

►**stick out for** *vipo F* (*insist*) **to s. out for sth,** s'obstiner à demander qch.

►**stick to** *vipo* **(a)** (*like glue*) coller à; **the rice had stuck to the pan,** le riz avait collé *ou* attaché à la casserole; **her shirt stuck to her back,** elle avait la chemise collée au dos; **the name stuck to him,** ce nom lui est resté; **to s. to s.o. like a limpet** *or* **a leech** *or* **like glue,** se cramponner *ou* s'accrocher à qn;

(b) (*remain loyal to*) **to s. to a friend,** ne pas abandonner un ami;

(c) (*remain true to*) **to s. to one's promise,** tenir sa promesse; **s. to it!,** persévérez!, ne lâchez pas!; *F* **to s. to one's guns,** ne pas en démordre; **to s. to an opinion,** maintenir une opinion, ne pas démordre d'une opinion;

(d) (*restrict oneself to*) **to s. to (the) facts,** s'en tenir *ou* s'attacher aux faits; **to s. to the point,** ne pas s'écarter de la question; **to s. to the text,** serrer le texte de près;

(e) (*continue to affirm*) **I s. to what I said,** j'en suis pour ce que j'ai dit; **she's sticking to her version of what happened,** elle maintient sa version des faits; **that's my story and I'm sticking to it,** c'est ma version et je m'y tiens;

(f) (*keep*) **s. to what you've got!,** gardez vos biens!, ne lâchez pas ce que vous avez!;

(g) (*not leave*) **to s. to one's post,** rester à son poste; **he sticks to his room,** il ne sort pas de sa chambre.

►**stick together 1** *vi* **(a)** (*with glue etc*) être collé, adhérer; **(b)** (*of friends etc*) **it's amazing they've stuck together,** c'est incroyable qu'ils soient restés ensemble; **they always s. together,** ils sont inséparables; (*of members of a club etc*) ils sont toujours solidaires. **2** *vtsep* coller (ensemble).

►**stick up 1** *vtsep* **(a)** *F* (*erect*) dresser (*une cible etc*); **(b)** *Sl* (*raise*) **s. 'em up!,** haut les mains!; **(c)** *F* (*attach to wall etc*) afficher (*un avis etc*); **(d)** *F* **to s. up a bank,** attaquer une banque à main armée. **2** *vi* (*point upwards*) se dresser; **his hair sticks straight up,** il a les cheveux qui se dressent sur sa tête; **a table on its back with its legs sticking up in the air,** une table à l'envers avec les pieds dans l'air.

►**stick up for** *vipo* (*defend*) prendre la défense de qn, soutenir qn.

►**stick with** *vipo* **(a)** (*remain loyal to*) rester fidèle à (*qn*); **(b)** (*stay near*) rester avec (*qn*); **the other runners couldn't s. with him,** les autres coureurs ne pouvaient pas le suivre; **(c)** (*persevere with*) persévérer à (*faire qch*); **I'm sticking with my old car for now,** je garde ma vieille voiture pour le moment.

sticker ['stɪkər] *n* **(a)** (*label*) étiquette gommée; *US F* (*poster*) affiche *f*; (*election poster*) affiche électorale; **(b)** (*s.o. who puts up posters*) colleur, -euse (*d'affiches*); **(c)** *F* (*determined person*) personne persévérante; **she's a s.,** elle ne manque pas de persévérance; **(d)** (*butcher's knife*) couteau *m* de boucher; (*hunting knife*) couteau *m* de chasse.

stickiness ['stɪkɪnɪs] *n* (*of substance, hands etc*) moiteur *f*; nature gluante, collante (*d'un produit*).

sticking ['stɪkɪŋ] **1** *adj* collant, adhésif. **2** *n* **(a)** (*adhering*) adhérence *f*, adhésion *f* (**to,** à); **s. plaster,** pansement adhésif, sparadrap *m*; **(b)** (*catching*) arrêt *m*, coincement *m*; bloquage *m* (*d'une soupape*); **s. point,** point *m* de désaccord.

stick-in-the-mud ['stɪkɪnðəmʌd] *F* **1** *n* **he's an old s.-in-the-m.,** c'est un vieux réac, il retarde sur son siècle. **2** *adj* (*attitude etc*) réac, rétro.

stickleback ['stɪklbæk] *n* (*fish*) épinoche *f*.

stickler ['stɪklər] *n* rigoriste *mf* (**for sth,** à l'égard de qch); **to be a s. for etiquette,** être à cheval sur l'étiquette.

stick-on ['stɪkɒn] *adj* (*étiquette*) adhésif; **s.-on soles,** semelles autocollantes.

stick-up ['stɪkʌp] *n F* attaque *f* à main armée, braquage *m*; **this is a s.-up!,** c'est un hold-up!

sticky ['stɪkɪ] *adj* **(a)** (*of substance, hands*) poisseux, gluant; (*label etc*) collant, adhésif; (*climate*) moite; **s. tape,** ruban adhésif; **to have s. fingers,** avoir les doigts poisseux; *F* être voleur; **s. weather,** temps lourd; *Br F* **to be on a s. wicket,** être dans une situation difficile; **(b)** *F* (*awkward*) peu accommodant; (*problème*) difficile; **is he being s. about it?,** est-ce qu'il fait des histoires (à ce sujet)?; **he will come to a s. end,** il finira mal.

stiff [stɪf] **1** *adj* **(a)** raide, rigide, dur; (*brosse*) dure; (*person, manner*) raide, contraint, guindé; (*stubborn*) inflexible, obstiné; *Fin* (*market, commodity*) ferme, raffermi; **s. joint,** articulation ankylosée; **to grow s.,** (*of joint*) s'ankyloser; **to be quite s.,** (*with sitting still*) être engourdi; (*after exercise*) être tout courbaturé; (*through lack of exercise*) être raide, manquer de souplesse; *F* **s. as a poker,** (*person*) raide *ou* droit comme un piquet; **he is very s.,** (*formal*) il est d'un abord difficile; *F* **exams scare me s.,** j'ai une peur bleue des examens; **s. bow,** salut contraint *ou* froid; **book bound in s. cover,** livre relié en carton; **s. neck,** torticolis *m*; **to offer s. resistance,** (*of* *person*) résister opiniâtrement; (*of person, thing*) tenir bon; **s. shirt front,** plastron empesé; **s. style,** style guindé *ou* empesé;

(b) (*door-handle, hinge etc*) qui fonctionne mal; (*paste, batter*) ferme; (*soil, clay*) dur; **the handle is s.,** la poignée est dure; *Nau* **s. wind,** forte brise;

(c) *F* (*examen*) difficile; **s. bill,** note salée; **I had a s. job to get it,** j'ai eu fort à faire pour l'obtenir; *F* **s. price,** prix élevé; **s. sentence,** dure peine; *F* **you need a s. drink,** un bon verre va te remonter; **I need a s. drink,** j'ai besoin d'un remontant; **a s. vodka,** une vodka bien tassée; **that's a bit s.!,** c'est un peu fort!

2 *n* **(a)** *Sl* (*corpse*) macchabée *m*; **(b)** *Old-fashioned F* **big s.,** grand nigaud, grand bêta.

stiffen ['stɪf(ə)n] **1** *vt* **(a)** renforcer (*une plaque, un mur, une poutre etc*); (*make more obstinate*) raidir (*qn*); empeser (*un plastron*); **age has stiffened his joints,** l'âge lui a raidi les articulations; **this action stiffened their resolve,** cette action a raffermi leur résolution; **(b)** rendre ferme, donner de la consistance à (*une pâte*); corser (*une boisson*); **(c)** rendre (*un examen*) plus difficile. **2** *vi* **(a)** (se) raidir, devenir raide; (*of person*) se raidir; **opposition is stiffening,** l'opposition devient de plus en plus intransigeante *ou* se durcit; **(b)** (*of paste etc*) devenir ferme, prendre de la consistance; *Nau* (*of wind*) fraîchir; **(c)** (*of examination*) devenir plus difficile.

stiffener ['stɪf(ə)nər] *n* (pièce *f* de) renfort *m*; **collar s.,** baleine *f* (de col).

stiffening ['stɪf(ə)nɪŋ] *n* **(a)** (*action*) raidissement *m*, renforcement *m* (*de qch*); durcissement *m* (*de la résistance*); **s. of the joints,** ankylose *f*; **(b)** (*substance*) empois *m*; (*for cloth*) amidon *m*; entoilage *m* (*du col d'un habit*).

stiffly ['stɪflɪ] *adv* (*to greet s.o. etc*) raidement, avec raideur; (*to answer, say etc*) d'un air guindé; (*to resist*) obstinément.

stiff-necked ['stɪfnekt] *adj* obstiné, entêté.

stiffness ['stɪfnɪs] *n* **(a)** raideur *f*, rigidité *f* (*d'une poutre, des membres etc*); dureté *f* (*d'un ressort etc*); *Fin* fermeté *f* (*du marché*); **s. of the legs,** (*after exercise*) courbatures *fpl* dans les jambes; (*through lack of exercise*) raideur, manque *m* de souplesse; (*after sitting*) engourdissement *m* des jambes; **s. of manner,** raideur, contrainte *f*, air guindé; **(b)** fermeté *f*, consistance *f* (*d'une pâte*), dureté *f*, fermeté (*du sol*); **(c)** raideur *f* (*d'une pente*); montant élevé (*d'un prix*); difficulté *f* (*d'un examen*).

stiffy ['stɪfɪ] *n F* **to have a s.,** (*erection*) triquer, avoir la trique, tringler.

stifle¹ ['staɪf(ə)l] **1** *vt* étouffer, suffoquer (*qn*); étouffer (*les cris de qn etc*); réprimer (*une émeute*); étouffer (*un bâillement, un rire*); retenir (*un cri*) **2** *vi* suffoquer, étouffer.

stifle² *n* **s. (joint),** grasset *m* (*du cheval etc*).

stifled ['staɪf(ə)ld] *adj* (*cri etc*) étouffé; **with a s. voice,** d'une voix éteinte.

stifling ['staɪflɪŋ] *adj* étouffant, suffocant; (*sensation*) d'étouffement; **it's s. here!,** on étouffe ici!

stigma, *pl* **-as, -ata** ['stɪgmə, -əz, 'stɪgmətə, stɪg'mɑːtə] *n* **(a)** (*pl usu* **stigmas**) (*shame*) stigmate *m*, tache *f*; flétrissure *f* (*morale*); *Arch* (*mark of brand*) flétrissure (*au fer rouge*); **being a single mother no longer has this s.,** il n'y a plus de honte à être mère célibataire; **(b) stigmata,** stigmates *mpl* (*d'un saint*); **(c)** (*pl* **stigmata**) *Biol* stigmate *m* (*d'un insecte etc*); **(d)** *Bot* (*pl* **stigmas**) stigmate *m* (*du pistil*).

stigmatism ['stɪgmətɪz(ə)m] *n Opt* stigmatisme *m*.

stigmatize ['stɪgmətaɪz] *vt* stigmatiser; **stigmatized as a coward,** marqué comme lâche; **stigmatized as illegitimate,** entaché de bâtardise.

stile¹ [staɪl] *n* **(a)** (*in fence, hedge etc*) échalier *m*; **(b)** (*turnstile*) tourniquet *m*, moulinet *m*.

stile² *n* montant *m* (*de porte etc*).

stiletto, *pl* **-os, -oes** [stɪ'letəʊ, -əʊz] *n* **(a)** (*dagger*) stylet *m*; **s. heels, stilettos,** talons *m* aiguille; **(b)** *Sewing etc* poinçon *m*.

still¹ [stɪl] **1** *adj* (*motionless*) immobile; (*calm*) calme; (*silent*) silencieux; (*wine*) non mousseux; (*orange juice, mineral water*) non gazeux; (*water*) plat; *Art* **s. life,** *pl* **s. lifes,** nature morte; **s. water,** eau dormante; *Prov* **s. waters run deep,** il faut se méfier de l'eau qui dort. **2** *adv* **to keep s.,** ne pas bouger, se tenir *ou* rester tranquille; **sit s.!,** restez *ou* tenez-vous tranquille!; **to stand s.,** (*not move*) ne pas bouger, se tenir immobile; (*come to a halt*) s'arrêter, s'immobiliser; (*of science etc*) rester stationnaire; **her heart stood s.,** son cœur cessa de battre. **3** *n* **(a) in the s. of the night,** dans le calme de la nuit; **(b)** *Cin* photo *f* (*empruntée au film*).

still² **1** *vt* tranquilliser, calmer, apaiser; **to s. s.o.'s fears,** calmer les craintes de qn. **2** *vi Liter* se calmer.

still³ **1** *adv* **(a)** encore; **he is s. here,** il est encore *ou* toujours ici; **I s. have 500 francs,** il me reste 500 francs, j'ai encore 500 francs; **I have s. to thank you,** il me reste à vous remercier; **in spite of his faults, I love him s.,** malgré ses fautes je l'aime toujours; **s. more/less,** encore plus/moins; **if you can reduce the price s. further,** si vous pouvez réduire encore le prix;

(b) (*nonetheless, all the same*) pourtant; **he's s. the boss,** c'est pourtant lui le patron; **but that s. doesn't justify ...,** mais cela ne justifie pourtant pas ...; **it s. doesn't make me change my mind,** je ne vais pas pour autant changer d'avis; **s., what else could I have done?,** qu'aurais-je pu faire d'autre, enfin?; **but s., if she DID accept!,** mais enfin, si elle acceptait!

2 *conj* cependant, pourtant, néanmoins, toutefois; **s. the fact remains that...,** toujours est-il que..., il n'en reste pas moins vrai que ... .

still⁴ *n* (*for distilling*) alambic *m*; **water s.,** appareil *m* à eau distillée.

stillbirth ['stɪlbɜːθ] *n* enfant mort-né; **the number of stillbirths,** mortinatalité *f*.

stillborn ['stɪlbɔːn] *adj* mort-né, -ée, *pl* mort-nés, -ées; *Fig* (*project etc*) avorté, mort-né.

stillness ['stɪlnɪs] *n* tranquillité *f*; (*of person*) calme *m*, repos *m*; (*of place, atmosphere*) silence *m*, paix *f*.

stilt [stɪlt] *n* **(a)** (*for walking*) échasse *f*; **to walk on stilts,** marcher sur des échasses; **(b)** *Constr* pilotis *m*, pieu *m*.

stilted ['stɪltɪd] *adj* **(a)** (*style, manner etc*) guindé, raide; **(b)** *Archit* (*arch*) surhaussé, surélevé.

Stilton ['stɪlt(ə)n] *n* fromage *m* de Stilton, stilton *m*.

stimulant ['stɪmjʊlənt] *n* **(a)** excitant *m*; **coffee is a s.,** le café est un excitant; **(b)** *Med* stimulant *m*, remontant *m*; **heart s.,** tonicardiaque *m*.

stimulate ['stɪmjʊleɪt] *vt* **(a)** stimuler (*qn, le zèle de qn*); aiguillonner, activer, exciter (**to,** à); aiguiser (*l'esprit, l'appétit etc*); *Ind* encourager, activer (*la production*); **(b)** *Med* stimuler (*le foie etc*).

stimulating ['stɪmjʊleɪtɪŋ] *adj* **(a)** (*concurrence, travail*) stimulant; (*désir*) aiguillonnant; (*musique*) entraînant; (*livre*) qui donne à penser; **it's s. to work with talented people,** c'est stimulant de travailler avec des gens qui ont du talent; **(b)** *Med* (*régime etc*) stimulant, remontant.

stimulation [stɪmjʊ'leɪʃən] *n* stimulation *f*; **to need s.,** avoir besoin d'être stimulé.

stimulative ['stɪmʊlətɪv] *adj* stimulant.

stimulus, *pl* **-i** ['stɪmjʊləs, -aɪ] *n* **(a)** stimulant *m*, impulsion *f*; **to give a s. to trade,** donner de l'impulsion au commerce; **(b)** *Physiol* stimulus *m*; **to apply a s. to a muscle,** exciter un muscle.

sting¹ [stɪŋ] *n* **(a)** dard *m*, aiguillon *m* (*d'abeille*); poil piquant (*d'ortie*); crochet venimeux (*d'un serpent*); **(b)** (*injury*) piqûre *f* (*de guêpe etc*); *Fig* pointe *f* (*d'une épigramme*); douleur cuisante (*d'une blessure*); vigueur *f*, mordant *m* (*d'une attaque*); **with the s. of the wind in our faces,** le visage fouetté par le vent; **joke with a s. in it,** plaisanterie qui comporte une pointe; *Fig* **to have a s. in the tail,** (*of story etc*) avoir une fin inattendue; *Lit* **the s. of remorse,** l'aiguillon du remords; *Fig* **to take the s. out of sth,** affaiblir qch; **(c)** *US Sl* (*con trick*) arnaque *f*.

sting² *v* (*pt & pp* **stung** [stʌŋ]) **1** *vt* **(a)** (*of bees, nettles etc*) piquer; **a bee stung her finger** *or* **stung her on the finger,** une abeille lui a piqué le doigt; **the blow stung him,** le coup le cingla; **that reply stung her (to the quick),** cette réponse l'a piquée (au vif); **smoke that stings the eyes,** fumée qui picote les yeux; **this stung him into action,** cela l'a aiguillonné; **(b)** *F* (*cheat*) **to s. s.o. for £50,** rouler qn en lui faisant payer 50 livres; **to be stung,** essuyer le coup de fusil; **could I s. you for a tenner?,** (*borrow*) est-ce que je peux te taper de dix livres? **2** *vi* (*of parts of the body*) cuire; (*of cut, graze*) picoter, brûler; **my eyes were stinging,** les yeux me brûlaient; **this is going to s. a bit,** ça va faire un peu mal.

stingily ['stɪndʒɪlɪ] *adv* mesquinement, chichement.

stinginess ['stɪndʒɪnɪs] *n* (*of person*) mesquinerie *f*, ladrerie *f*, pingrerie *f*; (*of portion etc*) insuffisance *f*.

stinging ['stɪŋɪŋ] *adj* (*pain etc*) cuisant; (*blow, answer*) cinglant; **s. plant,** plante piquante; **s. nettle,** ortie *f* qui pique; **s. remark,** remarque blessante *ou* offensante.

stingray ['stɪŋreɪ] *n* (*fish*) pastenague *f*.

stingy ['stɪndʒɪ] *adj* (*person*) mesquin, chiche, ladre, pingre; **a s. portion,** une mini-portion; **to be s. with one's**

money, être avare (de son argent); **to be s. with the cream,** lésiner sur la crème.

stink[1] ['stɪŋk] *n* **(a)** *(smell)* puanteur *f*; **what a s.!,** quelle puanteur!; **(b)** *Sl* *(trouble)* grabuge *m*; **to raise** *or* **kick up a s.,** faire de l'esclandre *ou* du grabuge; **there'll be a s.!,** il y a du grabuge dans l'air.

stink[2] *vi* (*pt* **stank** [stæŋk], **stunk** [stʌŋk]; *pp* **stunk**) *(of place, person etc)* puer, *F* empester; **it stinks in here,** ça pue ici; **to s. of garlic,** puer *ou* empester l'ail; *Sl* **to s. of money,** puer le fric; *Sl* **what do you think of it? — it stinks!,** qu'en dis-tu? — c'est dégueulasse!

►stink out *vtsep* **(a)** *(force out)* chasser *(qn)* par la mauvaise odeur; **(b)** *(fill with bad smell)* empester; **that smoke is stinking the room out,** cette fumée empeste la pièce.

stinkbomb ['stɪŋkbɒm] *n F* boule puante.

stinker ['stɪŋkər] *n F* **(a) to write s.o. a s.,** *(unpleasant letter)* écrire une lettre carabinée à qn; **the algebra paper was a s.,** on a eu une sale composition d'algèbre; **(b)** *(person)* individu *m* méprisable, salaud *m*.

stinkhorn ['stɪŋkhɔːn] *n* phallus *m* impudique.

stinking ['stɪŋkɪŋ] **1** *adj* puant, empesté; *Sl* *(disgusting)* dégueulasse; **a s. cold,** un gros rhume. **2** *adv F* **to be s. rich,** puer le fric.

stinkpot ['stɪŋkpɒt] *n Old-fashioned F* *(unpleasant person)* salaud *m*; **what a s.!,** *(smelly)* qu'est-ce qu'il pue!

stint[1] [stɪnt] *n* **(a)** *(restriction)* restriction *f*; **without s.,** sans limite; *(dépenser)* sans compter; **(b)** *(amount of work)* besogne assignée; **to do one's daily s.,** accomplir sa tâche quotidienne; **if you do a regular s. (with the weights/your clarinette)** si tu travailles régulièrement (tes haltères/ta clarinette); **do you want a s. at the wheel?,** est-ce que tu veux prendre un peu le volant?; **I did the last s.,** c'est moi qui ai pris le dernier tour; **after a long s. at the keyboard,** après être resté longtemps au clavier; **(c)** *(period)* temps *m*, période *f*; **she had a two-year s. in the army,** elle a fait deux ans dans l'armée.

stint[2] *vt* imposer des restrictions à *(qn)*; réduire *(la nourriture)*; épargner *(l'argent, la peine)*; lésiner sur *(qch)*; **to s. oneself,** se refuser le nécessaire; **to s. s.o. of sth,** priver qn de qch, refuser qch à qn; **to give without stinting,** donner sans compter.

stipend ['staɪpend] *n* traitement *m*, appointements *mpl* *(d'un ecclésiastique, d'un magistrat)*.

stipendiary [staɪ'pendjərɪ] **1** *adj* appointé, qui reçoit des appointements fixes; *Br* **s. magistrate,** juge *m* d'un tribunal d'instance *(à Londres et dans les grandes villes)*. **2** *n Br* = **stipendiary magistrate.**

stipple ['stɪp(ə)l] **1** *vt Art* faire *(un dessin)* en pointillé; *(in engraving)* graver *(qch)* au pointillé. **2** *vi Art* pointiller.

stipulate ['stɪpjʊleɪt] *vt* stipuler *(une date, une condition etc)*; **to s. (in writing) that ...,** stipuler (par écrit) que ...; **within the period stipulated,** dans le délai prescrit.

stipulation [stɪpjʊ'leɪʃən] *n* condition *f*; *Jur* stipulation *f*; **the only s. I make is that ...,** la seule condition que je pose c'est que ...; **on the s. that ...,** à condition que ... .

stir[1] [stɜːr] *n* **(a)** *(act of stirring liquid etc)* **to give one's coffee a s.,** remuer *ou* tourner son café; **(b)** *(movement of crowd etc)* mouvement *m*; *(agitation)* agitation *f*, émoi *m*; **there was a great s.,** il y eut un grand remue-ménage; **to make a s.,** faire du bruit, faire sensation; **the news caused a s. in the town,** la nouvelle a mis la ville en émoi.

stir[2] *v* (**-rr-**) **1** *vt* *(set in motion)* remuer, mouvoir; *(move emotionally)* émouvoir, remuer *(qn)*; agiter *(les passions de qn)*; remuer, tourner *(son thé)*; *Culin* tourner *(une sauce, une crème, un civet etc)*; agiter *(un mélange)*; activer, attiser, tisonner *(le feu)*; **not a breath stirs the leaves,** pas un souffle ne remue *ou* ne fait trembler les feuilles; **stirred,** *(moved)* ému; **to s. s.o. to pity,** provoquer la compassion de qn; **events that s. the soul,** événements qui remuent l'âme; **these words stirred her to action,** ces mots l'ont fait agir; *Sl* **s. yourself** *or* **your stumps!,** remue-toi!; *Br F* **to s. it,** *(make trouble)* fomenter la discorde.

2 *vi* **(a)** bouger, remuer; **don't s.!,** ne bougez pas!; **don't s. from here,** ne bougez pas d'ici; **he did not s. out of the house,** il n'est pas sorti de la maison; **she stirred and went back to sleep,** elle a bougé et s'est rendormie; **he is not stirring yet,** il n'est pas encore levé;

(b) *Br F* *(make trouble)* faire des histoires; **she's always stirring,** elle est toujours en train de faire des histoires.

►stir up *vtsep* **(a)** *(stir)* remuer, agiter *(un liquide)*; ranimer, activer *(le feu)*; **(b)** *(cause)* fomenter *(une sédition, les dissensions)*; **(c)** *(arouse)* remuer, ameuter *(le peuple)*; exciter, animer *(la curiosité)*; *F* travailler *(des ouvriers)*; **to s. up hatred,** attiser les haines; **to s. up trouble,** fomenter la discorde; **stirred up,** agité, troublé, en émoi; **he wants stirring up,** il a besoin d'être secoué.

stir[3] *n Sl* *(prison)* taule *f*; **in s.,** en taule.

stir-crazy ['stɜːkreɪzɪ] *adj esp Am F* fou, *f* folle, détraqué *(à cause d'une longue période de détention)*.

stir-fry ['stɜːfraɪ] *vt Culin* frire rapidement; **s.-fried vegetables,** légumes cuits rapidement.

stirrer ['stɜːrər] *n* **(a)** *Br* *(troublemaker)* personne *f* qui sème la pagaille; *(person who pushes people to revolt)* fauteur *m* de troubles, agitateur, -trice; **(b)** *(device)* *Ch Phot* agitateur *m*.

stirring ['stɜːrɪŋ] **1** *adj* *(moving)* émouvant; **s. times,** époque mouvementée. **2** *n* **(a)** remuement *m*; agitation *f*; **(b)** *Br F* *(troublemaking)* **s. is her speciality,** semer la pagaille, c'est sa spécialité.

stirring up *n* excitation *f* *(des émotions)*; mise *f* en émoi *(du peuple)*; fomentation *f* *(de la discorde)*.

stirrup ['stɪrəp] *n* **(a)** *Horseriding* étrier *m*; **to put one's feet in the stirrups,** chausser les étriers; **s. cup,** coup *m* de l'étrier; **s. leather** *or* **strap,** étrivière *f*; **s. pump,** pompe portative; **(b)** *Med* **stirrups,** étriers.

stitch[1] [stɪtʃ] *n* **(a)** *Sewing* point *m*; *(in knitting, crochet)* maille *f*; *Surg* (point de) suture *f*; **(machine) s.,** piqûre *f* (à la machine); *Knitting* **moss s.,** point de riz; **to put a few stitches in a garment,** faire un point à un vêtement; *Nau* **with every s. of canvas set,** toutes voiles dehors; *F* **he hasn't got a dry s. on him,** il est trempé jusqu'aux os; **without a s. on,** nu comme un ver; **to drop a s.,** *(in knitting, crochet)* sauter une maille; **dropped s.,** *(in knitting, crochet)* maille coulée; **to make a s.,** *(in knitting, crochet)* faire une augmentation; **to put stitches in a wound,** suturer *ou* faire une suture à une plaie, recoudre une plaie; **she had to have ten stitches,** ils ont dû lui faire dix points de suture; **when are you having the stitches out?,** quand allez-vous vous faire retirer vos points de suture?; *Prov* **a s. in time saves nine,** un point à temps en épargne cent, un point fait à temps en vaut mille;

(b) s. (in the side), point *m* de côté; **I've got a s.,** j'ai un point de côté;

(c) *F* **we were in stitches,** *(laughing)* on se tordait de rire; **his story/the film had us in stitches,** son histoire était tordante/le film était tordant *ou* à se tordre de rire; **he had us in stitches,** il nous a fait (nous) tordre de rire.

stitch[2] *vt* **(a)** coudre *(un vêtement)*; piquer *(le cuir)*; **to (machine) s.,** piquer (à la machine); **to s. sth onto sth,** coudre qch sur qch; **(b)** *Surg* suturer *(une plaie)*; **(c)** *(in bookbinding)* brocher *(un livre)*.

►stitch down *vtsep* coudre; *(repairing)* recoudre.

►stitch up *vtsep* **(a)** *F* *(repair by sewing)* recoudre *(bag etc)*; **(b)** *F* *(of surgeon)* recoudre *(person, wound)*; **we'll soon have you stitched up,** on va vous faire quelques points de suture et ce sera fini; **(c)** *Sl* *(falsely incriminate)* (faire) accuser *(qn)* à tort.

stitching ['stɪtʃɪŋ] *n* **(a)** *Sewing* *(act)* couture *f*; *(in leather)* piqûre *f*; *Surg* suture *f*; *(in bookbinding)* brochage *m*, brochure *f*; *Sewing* **line of s.,** piqûre; **(b)** *(stitches)* points *mpl*, piqûres *fpl*; **the s.'s coming undone,** les piqûres se sont défaites; **ornamental s.,** broderie *f*.

stoat [stəʊt] *n* hermine *f* *(d'été)*.

stock[1] [stɒk] *n* **(a)** *(supply)* provision *f*, approvisionnement *m*, stock *m*; *(in forestry)* peuplement *m*; *Ind* stock; *(at cards, dominoes)* talon *m*; **s. of wood,** provision de bois; **s. of plays,** répertoire *m*; **to lay in a s. of food,** faire provision de vivres, s'approvisionner en vivres; *Com* **s. (in trade),** marchandises *fpl* (en magasin), stock; *Fig* **double entendre was her s. in trade,** l'ambiguïté était son fonds de commerce; **new/fresh s.,** rassortiment *m*; **old s.,** fonds *mpl* de boutique; **surplus s.,** surplus *mpl*; **s. in hand,** marchandises en magasin, stock; **stocks are low,** il y a peu de marchandises en stock; **while stocks last,** jusqu'à épuisement des stocks; **to take s.,** faire *ou* dresser l'inventaire; *Fig* **to take s. of s.o.,** scruter *ou* toiser qn; **to take s. of the situation,** faire le bilan de la situation, faire le point de la situation; **in s.,** en magasin, en stock; **to be out of s.,** *(of goods)* manquer en magasin; **book temporarily out of s.,** livre qui est temporairement épuisé; **to be out of s. of sth,** *(of trader, firm)* manquer de qch; **grazing s.,** *(livestock)* bétail *m*, animaux *mpl* sur pied; **fat s.,** *(livestock)* bétail de boucherie; *Rail* **locomotive s.,** effectif *m ou* dotation *f* en locomotives; *Cin* **(film) s.,** film *m* vierge, films *ou* bandes *fpl* vierges; **s. control,** gestion *f* des stocks; **s. farm,** élevage *m*; **s. farmer** *or* **breeder,** éleveur *m*; **s. farming** *or* **breeding,** élevage; *Com* **s. keeper,** magasinier *m*; *Com* **s. list,** inventaire *m*; **s. mare,** jument *f* de haras;

Austr **s. rider,** cowboy *m*;

(b) *Fin* fonds *mpl*, valeurs *fpl*, actions *fpl*; **government s.,** fonds d'Etat, fonds *ou* effets publics, rentes *fpl* (sur l'Etat); *Fig* **her s. is going up/down,** ses actions sont en hausse/en baisse; **stocks and shares,** valeurs mobilières, valeurs de bourse, titres *mpl*; **s. exchange,** bourse *f* (*des valeurs*); **the S. Exchange,** la Bourse (*de Londres*); *St Exch* **s. list,** (bulletin *m* de la) cote *f*; **s. market,** marché des titres *ou* des valeurs;

(c) tronc *m* (*d'arbre*); souche *f* (*d'arbre, d'iris*); (*stump*) bûche *f*, bloc *m*; billot *m* (*d'enclume*); (*in horticulture*) sujet *m*, ente *f*, porte-greffe *m inv*; *Fig* (*lineage*) souche *f*; **true to s.,** fortement racé; **he comes of good s.,** il descend d'une bonne famille, il est de bonne souche;

(d) fût *m*, bois *m*, monture *f* (*de fusil*); manche *m* (*de fouet*); macheron *m* (*de charrue*); sommier *m*, mouton *m* (*de cloche*); boîte *f* de bois (*enfermant une serrure*); *Nau* jas *m* (*d'ancre*); **die s.,** porte-filière *m*, *pl* porte-filières;

(e) (*naval architecture*) **stocks,** cales *fpl*; **to be on the stocks,** être sur cales, être en construction; *Fig* (*of new novel etc*) être en chantier;

(f) **stocks,** (*for punishment*) pilori *m*;

(g) *Ind* (*raw materials*) matières premières (*de pâte à papier, de savon*);

(h) *Culin* **soup s.,** consommé *m*; **meat s.,** bouillon *m* (*concentré*); **s. cube,** bouillon-cube *m*, *pl* bouillons-cubes;

(i) (*plant*) matthiole *f*, giroflée *f* des jardins;

(j) (*necktie*) col-cravate *m* (*d'équitation*), *pl* cols-cravates; plastron *m* en soie noire (*des ecclésiastiques anglais*).

stock[2] *adj* normal; **s. answer,** réponse régulière; *Th* **s. company,** troupe *f* à demeure (*dans une ville*); **s. phrase,** expression toute faite *ou* consacrée; *Th* **s. play** *or* **piece,** pièce *f* de *ou* du répertoire; **he has three s. speeches,** il a un répertoire de trois discours.

stock[3] *vt* **(a)** (*supply*) approvisionner (*un magasin*) (**with,** de, en); meubler (*une ferme*) (**with,** de); monter (*une ferme*) en bétail; approvisionner (*une maison*) (**with,** de); empoissonner (*un étang*); peupler (*une forêt*) (**with,** de); **this shop is well stocked,** ce magasin est bien approvisionné; **to have a well-stocked cellar,** avoir une cave bien remplie; **(b)** (*have, keep in stock*) avoir *ou* tenir *ou* garder (*des marchandises*) en magasin *ou* en dépôt; stocker (*des marchandises*); **I don't s. this article,** je ne vends pas cet article; **we s. all leading makes of furniture,** nous faisons toutes les grandes marques de meubles; **(c)** (*fit with a stock*) monter (*un fusil*); *Nau* jaler, enjaler (*une ancre*).

▶**stock up 1** *vi* (*build up a stock*) faire des provisions *ou* des réserves; **to s. up with sth,** bien s'approvisionner en *ou* de qch. **2** *vtsep* (*larder, cellar*) approvisionner.

stockade[1] [stɒ'keɪd] *n* **(a)** (*fort*) palissade *f*, palanque *f*; **(b)** *US Mil* bloc *m*; **to be in the s.,** être au bloc.

stockade[2] *vt* palissader, palanquer.

stockbroker ['stɒkbrəʊkər] *n* agent *m* de change, courtier *m* de bourse; *Br F* **s. belt,** banlieue aisée.

stock-car ['stɒkkɑːr] *n Sp* stock-car *m*; **s.-c. racing,** course *f* de stock-cars.

stockfish ['stɒkfɪʃ] *n* stockfisch *m*, merluche *f*.

stockholder ['stɒkhəʊldər] *n* actionnaire *mf*, porteur *m ou* détenteur *m* de titres.

stockily ['stɒkɪlɪ] *adv* **s. built,** trapu.

stockiness ['stɒkɪnɪs] *n* stature trapue *ou* courtaude.

stockinet(te) [stɒkɪ'net] *n Tex* **wool/cotton s.,** jersey *m* de laine/coton.

stocking ['stɒkɪŋ] *n* **(a)** (*garment*) bas *m*; *Med* **elastic** *or* **support s.,** bas pour varices; **body s.,** combinaison *f* (une pièce); **s. filler,** petit cadeau de Noël supplémentaire; **s. mask,** = bas utilisé comme masque par les bandits; *Knitting* **s. stitch,** point *m* (de) jersey; **(b)** (*of horse*) **white s.,** balzane *f*.

stockinged ['stɒkɪŋd] *adj* **in one's s. feet,** sans chaussures.

stockist ['stɒkɪst] *n Com* stockiste *m*.

stockman, *pl* **-men** ['stɒkmən] *n* **(a)** (*man who works with livestock*) gardeur *m* de bestiaux; (*owner*) bouvier *m*; **(b)** *Am* (*warehouseman*) magasinier *m*.

stockpile[1] ['stɒkpaɪl] *n* stock *m*, stocks *mpl* de réserve *ou* de sécurité; **nuclear s.,** réserve(s) d'armements nucléaires.

stockpile[2] *vt* stocker (*des marchandises*); entasser, accumuler (*le matériel de guerre*).

stockpiling ['stɒkpaɪlɪŋ] *n* stockage *m*, constitution *f* de réserves; (*of nuclear weapons*) accumulation *f*.

stockpot ['stɒkpɒt] *n Culin* marmite *f*.

stockroom ['stɒkruːm] *n* magasin *m*, réserve *f*, resserre *f*.

stock-still ['stɒk'stɪl] *adv* **to stand s.-s.,** rester (complètement) immobile; **he suddenly stood s.-s.,** soudain il s'immobilisa.

stocktaking ['stɒkteɪkɪŋ] *n Com Ind* (établissement *m ou* levée *f* d')inventaire *m*; **s. is in February,** on fait l'inventaire en février.

stocky ['stɒkɪ] *adj* trapu, courtaud; (*cheval*) ragot.

stockyard ['stɒkjɑːd] *n* parc *m* à bétail *ou* à bestiaux.

stodge [stɒdʒ] *n F* (*food*) aliment bourratif; *Fig* (*writing*) littérature *f* indigeste; **the s. we get in the canteen,** les trucs bourratifs qu'on nous donne à la cantine.

stodgy ['stɒdʒɪ] *adj* **(a)** (*repas, aliment*) lourd, *F* bourratif; (*pain*) pâteux; **(b)** (*livre*) indigeste; (*style*) lourd; (*person*) à l'esprit lourd.

stoic ['stəʊɪk] *adj & n* stoïque *mf*; *Antiq* stoïcien, -ienne.

stoical ['stəʊɪk(ə)l] *adj* stoïque.

stoically ['stəʊɪklɪ] *adv* stoïquement.

stoicism ['stəʊɪsɪz(ə)m] *n* stoïcisme *m*.

stoke [stəʊk] *vt* charger (*un foyer*); entretenir le feu (*d'un four*); chauffer le foyer (*d'une machine à vapeur*); *Fig* **the way he stokes his food in,** la façon dont il engouffre sa nourriture.

▶**stoke up 1** *vtsep* = **STOKE**. **2** *vi* **(a)** (*stoke a fire*) pousser les feux; **(b)** *F* (*eat heavily*) bouffer, bâfrer.

▶**stoke up on** *vipo F* (*eat a lot of*) se bourrer de.

stokehole ['stəʊkhəʊl] *n* ouverture *f* de foyer; *Nau* enfer *m* (devant la chaudière).

stoker ['stəʊkər] *n* **(a)** (*person*) chauffeur *m*; chargeur *m* (*d'un foyer*); **(b)** **mechanical s.,** chauffeur automatique, chargeur mécanique.

STOL [stɒl] *n Mil Av* (*abbr* **short takeoff and landing**) **(a)** (*system*) décollage et atterrissage courts; **(b)** (*aircraft*) A.D.A.C. *m*.

stole[1] [stəʊl] *n* **(a)** *Rel* étole *f*; **(b)** (*garment*) étole (*de vison*).

stole[2] *see* **STEAL.**

stolen[1] ['stəʊlən] *adj* (*car, property etc*) volé.

stolen[2] *see* **STEAL.**

stolid ['stɒlɪd] *adj* flegmatique, impassible.

stolidity [stɒ'lɪdɪtɪ] *n* flegme *m*.

stolidly ['stɒlɪdlɪ] *adv* flegmatiquement.

stolidness ['stɒlɪdnɪs] *n* = **STOLIDITY**.

stoma, *pl* **-ata,** ['stəʊmə, -ətə] *n* stomate *m*.

stomach[1] ['stʌmək] *n* (*organ*) estomac *m*; (*tummy*) ventre *m*; **pain in the s.,** mal *m* d'estomac; **upset s., s. upset,** troubles *mpl* de digestion; *Pharm* **to be taken on an empty s.,** à prendre à jeun; **to drink on an empty s.,** boire lorsqu'on a l'estomac vide, boire à jeun; **to turn s.o.'s s.,** soulever le cœur à qn, écœurer qn; **to have a cast iron s.,** avoir un estomac d'autruche; **an army marches on its s.,** une armée ne se bat pas le ventre vide; **first s.,** (*of ruminants*) panse *f*; **second s.,** bonnet *m*; **third s.,** feuillet *m*, mellier *m*; **fourth** *or* **true s.,** caillette *f*; **to have a large s.,** (*be fat*) avoir un gros ventre; **s. ache,** douleurs *fpl* d'estomac, *F* mal de ventre; **to have s. ache,** avoir mal au ventre; **s. pump,** pompe stomacale; *Fig* **to have no s. for sth,** (*not feel like*) ne pas se sentir d'humeur à qch; *Fig* **he had no s. for a fight,** il ne se sentait pas d'attaque pour se battre.

stomach[2] *vt* **(a)** (*eat with pleasure*) manger avec appétit; (*digest well*) bien digérer (*qch*); **I can't s. oysters,** je ne peux pas avaler les huîtres; **(b)** (*support*) endurer, supporter, tolérer (*qch*); supporter (*qn*); *F* avaler, digérer (*une insulte*); **I can't s. it any longer,** j'en ai plein le dos, j'en ai ras le bol.

stomp [stɒmp] *vi* frapper du pied; **to s. out of the room,** quitter la pièce d'un pas lourd.

stone[1] [stəʊn] *n* **(a)** pierre *f*; (*pebble*) caillou, -oux *m*; *Constr* mœllon *m*, pierre de taille; (*flagstone*) dalle *f*; (*gravestone*) pierre tombale; **not to leave a s. standing,** tout raser *ou* démolir; **to throw stones at s.o.,** lancer des pierres sur *ou* à qn; *Fig* **who's going to be the one to cast the first s. at him?,** qui lui jettera la première pierre?; *Fig* **to leave no s. unturned,** mettre tout en œuvre *ou* en jeu, remuer ciel et terre (**to do sth,** pour accomplir qch); **a s.'s throw from here,** à deux pas d'ici;

(b) (*gem*) pierre *f*; *Com F* (*diamond*) diamant *m*; (*in watch*) rubis *m*; **precious stones,** pierreries *fpl*, pierres précieuses;

(c) (*material*) pierre *f* (*à batir etc*); **broken s.,** pierraille *f*, cailloutis *m*; *Typ* **(imposing, press) s.,** marbre *m*; **the Stone Age,** l'âge de la pierre; **s. axe,** hache *f* de pierre; *Constr* marteau *m* à dresser; **s. coloured,** beige; **s. cutter,** tailleur *m ou* équarrisseur *m* de pierres; **s. floor,** sol dallé;

s. jug, cruche *f* de grès; **s. saw,** scie *f* à pierre *ou* de carrier;

(d) *Med* calcul *m*;

(e) noyau *m* (*de fruit*); pépin *m* (*de raisin*); **s. fruit,** fruit *m* à noyau, drupe *f*;

(f) *Br* (*unit of weight*) stone *m* (= 6,348kg);

(g) (*domino*) dé *m*.

stone[2] *vt* **(a)** dénoyauter (*les fruits*); épépiner (*les raisins secs*); **(b)** lapider (*qn*), assaillir (*qn*) à coups de pierres; *Br Sl* **s. the crows!, s. me!,** ça alors!

stone-blind ['stəʊn'blaɪnd] *adj* complètement aveugle.

stonechat ['stəʊntʃæt] *n* (*bird*) traquet *m* pâtre.

stone-cold ['stəʊn'kəʊld] **1** *adj* froid comme (le) marbre; **the tea is s.-c.,** le thé est complètement froid *ou* glacé. **2** *adv* **s.-c. sober,** complètement sobre.

stonecrop ['stəʊnkrɒp] *n* (*plant*) orpin *m*.

stoned [stəʊnd] *adj* **(a)** *Sl* **to be s.,** (*drunk*) être bourré; (*on drugs*) être déchiré; **(b)** (*fruit*) dénoyauté; (*raisins*) épépiné; **(c)** (*chemin*) pavé *ou* revêtu de pierres.

stone-dead ['stəʊn'ded] *adj* raide mort.

stone-deaf ['stəʊn'def] *adj* complètement sourd, *F* sourd comme un pot.

stoneground ['stəʊngraʊnd] *adj* (*flour*) à l'ancienne.

stoneless ['stəʊnlɪs] *adj* (*raisins secs*) sans pépins.

stonemason ['stəʊnmeɪs(ə)n] *n* maçon *m*.

stonewall [stəʊn'wɔːl] *vi* **(a)** *Sp* jouer un jeu prudent pour tenir jusqu'à la fin; **(b)** *Parl & Fig* faire de l'obstruction.

stonewalling [stəʊn'wɔːlɪŋ] *n* **(a)** *Sp* jeu prudent; **(b)** *Parl & Fig* obstructionnisme *m*.

stoneware ['stəʊnweər] *n* poterie *f* de grès.

stonewashed ['stəʊnwɒʃt] *adj* (*jeans etc*) délavé.

stonework ['stəʊnwɜːk] *n* maçonnerie *f*.

stonily ['stəʊnɪlɪ] *adv* froidement; (*regarder qn*) d'un air glacial; (*répondre*) d'un ton glacial.

stoniness ['stəʊnɪnɪs] *n* **(a)** nature pierreuse (*du sol*); **(b)** dureté *f* (*de cœur*); froideur *f* (*du regard*).

stoning ['stəʊnɪŋ] *n* **(a)** dénoyautage *m* (*d'un fruit*); épépinage *m* (*des raisins secs*); **(b)** (*of person*) lapidation *f*.

stony ['stəʊnɪ] *adj* **(a)** (*full of, covered in stones*) pierreux, rocailleux; **(b)** (*made of stone*) de *ou* en pierre; (*hard like stone*) dur comme la pierre; **s. concretion,** concrétion pierreuse; **(c)** (*lacking in emotion*) froid, dur; (*regard*) glacial, -ials; **s. heart,** cœur de pierre; **s. politeness,** politesse glacée; **a s. silence,** un silence glacial; **(d)** *Br F* **s. (broke),** sans le sou, à sec; **I'm s. (broke),** je n'ai pas un sou, je suis fauché.

stony-hearted [stəʊnɪ'hɑːtɪd] *adj* au cœur de pierre.

stood *see* **STAND**[2].

stooge[1] [stuːdʒ] *n F* **(a)** *Th* faire-valoir *m inv* (*d'un comique*); **(b)** *Fig* (*dupe*) nègre *m*; (*being manipulated etc*) pantin *m*.

stooge[2] *vi F* **(a)** *Th* **to s. for a comedian,** servir de faire-valoir à un comique; **(b)** *Fig* **to s. for s.o.,** faire le nègre de qn.

stook[1] [stuːk] *n Agr* tas *m* de gerbes, moyette *f*.

stook[2] *vt Agr* mettre (*les gerbes*) en moyettes.

stool [stuːl] *n* **(a)** tabouret *m*; (*with steps*) escabeau *m*; **folding s.,** pliant *m*; **piano s.,** tabouret de piano; *Fig* **to fall between two stools,** se retrouver le cul à terre; **prayer s.,** prie-Dieu *m inv*; **(b)** (*piece of excrement*) crotte *f*; *Med* **stools,** selles *fpl*, fèces *fpl*; **to go to s.,** aller à la selle; **(c)** (*horticulture*) *& Agr* pied *m* mère, plante *f* mère; **(d) s. pigeon,** mouchard *m*, indicateur, -trice; **(e)** *Constr* tablette *f*, rebord *m* (*de fenêtre*).

stoop[1] [stuːp] *n* **(a)** (*act*) inclination *f* en avant (*du corps*); **(b)** (*posture*) dos rond, épaules voûtées; **to walk with a s.,** marcher le dos voûté.

stoop[2] **1** *vi* (*bend down*) se pencher, se baisser; (*have bent back*) avoir le dos rond, être voûté; *Fig* (*abase oneself*) s'abaisser, s'avilir, descendre (**to do sth,** à *ou* jusqu'à faire qch); (*deign*) daigner (**to do sth,** faire qch); **she stooped to pick up the pin,** elle s'est baissée pour ramasser l'épingle; **man who would s. to anything,** homme prêt à toutes les bassesses; *Lit* **to s. to conquer,** s'abaisser pour triompher; **I never thought they'd s. so low as to ...,** je ne pensais pas qu'ils s'abaisseraient jusqu'à ... . **2** *vt* pencher, incliner (*la tête*); courber, arrondir (*le dos*).

stoop[3] *n Am* porche *m* (*avec perron*); terrasse surélevée (*devant une maison*).

stooping ['stuːpɪŋ] *adj* penché (en avant); (*permanently*) voûté.

stop[1] [stɒp] *n* **(a)** arrêt *m*; (*pause*) arrêt, halte *f*, pause *f*; *Av* (*in flight*) escale *f*; **to put a s. to sth,** arrêter *ou* faire cesser qch, mettre fin à qch; **this must be put a s. to,** il faut y mettre fin; **ten minutes' s.,** dix minutes d'arrêt; **to come to a s.,** s'arrêter; (*of car*) stopper; **to make a s.,** faire halte; (*for short period*) faire une pause; **we made four stops along the way,** nous nous sommes arrêtés *ou* nous avons fait halte quatre fois en chemin; **the bus** *etc* **makes a s. at ...,** le bus *etc* s'arrête à ...; **to bring sth to a s.,** arrêter qch; **let's have a s. for lunch,** faisons une pause pour le déjeuner; **we travelled without a s.,** nous avons voyagé sans escale; **we had a s. at the castle on the way back,** nous nous sommes arrêtés au château sur le chemin du retour; **bus s.,** arrêt d'autobus; **regular s.,** arrêt fixe; **request s.,** arrêt facultatif; **s. sign,** *Aut* stop *m*; **s. signal,** signal *m* d'arrêt; *Am* **s. street,** rue *f* avec un stop au débouché;

(b) (*full stop*) point *m*; **s.,** (*in telegram*) stop *m*;

(c) *Mus* jeu *m*, registre *m* (*d'orgue*); **s. (key** *or* **knob),** bouton *m* d'appel; **to pull out a s.,** tirer un registre; *F* **to pull out all the stops,** faire un effort surhumain (*pour faire qch*);

(d) *Carp MecE etc* dispositif *m* de blocage, arrêt *m*, taquet *m*, butée *f*; heurtoir *m* (*d'une porte*); arrêtoir *m* (*de vis, de boulon*); (*on moving part of machine*) mentonnet *m*; *MecE* butoir *m* (*de bout de course*); *Carp* **bench s.,** crochet *m ou* griffe *f* d'établi; (*on typewriter*) **margin(al) s.,** margeur *m* (*réglable*); **s. valve,** soupape *f ou* robinet *m* d'arrêt;

(e) *Cards* (carte *f* d')arrêt *m*; *Boxing* coup bloqué;

(f) *Opt Phot* diaphragme *m* (*d'objectif*); **s. bath,** bain *m* d'arrêt;

(g) *Comptr* **s. bit,** bit *m* d'arrêt;

(h) *Ling* plosive *f*, explosive *f*;

(i) *Zool* cassure *f* du nez (*d'un chien*).

stop[2] *v* **(-pp-) 1** *vt* **(a)** arrêter; interrompre (*la circulation*); arrêter (*une pendule*); arrêter, stopper (*une machine*); mettre fin à (*un abus*); enrayer (*une grève*); **to s. s.o. short,** arrêter qn (tout) net; **s. thief!,** au voleur!; **to s. an opponent,** *Fb* arrêter un adversaire; *Boxing* mettre son adversaire knock-out; **to s. a blow,** parer un coup; *Boxing* bloquer; *Mil Sl* **to s. a bullet,** prendre une balle; **curtains that s. the light,** rideaux qui interceptent la lumière; **to s. s.o.'s doing sth** *or* **s.o. (from) doing sth,** empêcher qn de faire qch; **I couldn't s. myself,** je n'ai pas pu m'en empêcher; **to s. sth being done,** empêcher que qch (ne) se fasse; **nothing will s. her,** rien ne l'arrêtera; **what's stopping you?,** qu'est-ce qui vous retient?, qu'est-ce qui vous en empêche?; *Com* **to s. (payment of) a cheque,** faire opposition à un chèque; **it ought to be stopped,** on devrait y mettre fin;

(b) (*cease*) cesser (*ses efforts, ses visites, son travail*); *Com* **to s. payment,** cesser ses paiements; **to s. doing sth,** s'arrêter de faire qch; **to s. playing,** cesser de jouer; **he never stops talking,** il n'arrête pas de parler, il parle sans cesse; **s. that noise!,** arrête ce bruit!; **s. it!,** assez!, finissez!; **it has stopped raining,** il a cessé de pleuvoir, la pluie a cessé;

(c) to s. s.o.'s wages, retenir le salaire de qn; **to s. so much out of s.o.'s wages,** faire une retenue de tant sur le salaire de qn; **to s. s.o.'s pension,** rayer *ou* supprimer la pension de qn; *Mil* **all leave is stopped,** toutes les troupes sont consignées, toutes les permissions sont suspendues;

(d) (*block*) boucher, étancher, tamponner (*une voie d'eau*); plomber (*une dent*); boucher, fermer (*un trou*); obstruer, obturer (*un tuyau*); **to get stopped,** (*of pipe*) s'obstruer; **to s. one's ears,** se boucher les oreilles; **to s. a gap,** boucher *ou* combler un trou;

(e) (*in horticulture*) pincer (*une plante*);

(f) *Mus* **to s. a string,** presser une corde; **to s. a flute,** boucher les trous d'une flûte.

2 *vi* **(a)** s'arrêter; (*of ship, car*) s'arrêter, stopper; **to s. short** *or* **dead,** s'arrêter net *ou F* pile *ou* (tout) court; **to s. and talk to s.o.,** s'arrêter pour parler à qn; **to do a hundred kilometres without stopping,** faire cent kilomètres sans s'arrêter *ou* sans arrêt *ou* tout d'une traite; **we stopped in Caen,** nous nous sommes arrêtés à Caen; **all buses s. here,** arrêt fixe; **buses s. by request,** arrêt facultatif; **to pass a station without stopping,** brûler une gare; *Nau* **to s. at a port,** faire escale à un port; **s.!,** (*to engine room*) stop!, stoppez!;

(b) (*cease*) cesser (*de parler, fonctionner*); **my watch has stopped,** ma montre (s')est arrêtée; **to work fifteen hours without stopping,** travailler pendant quinze heures d'arrache-pied *ou* de suite; **to s. for lunch,** faire une pause pour déjeuner; **he/she just doesn't s.,** (*never stops working*) il/elle ne s'arrête pas; **she stopped in the middle of a sentence,** elle s'arrêta au milieu d'une phrase; **he never stops to think,** il ne prend jamais le temps de réfléchir; **she did not s. at that,** elle ne s'en tint pas là; **he'll s. at nothing,** rien ne l'arrêtera; **s. a moment!,** arrêtez un instant!; **the matter will not s. there,** l'affaire n'en demeurera pas là; **the rain has stopped,** la pluie a cessé;

(c) (*stay*) rester; **to s. at home,** rester à la maison; **she's stopping with us for a few days,** elle est venue passer quelques jours chez nous; **he didn't s. long, only half an hour,** il n'est pas resté longtemps, juste une demi-heure; **to s. at a hotel,** descendre *ou* séjourner dans un hôtel.

►**stop away** *vi* (*not come*) ne pas venir; (*not go*) ne pas y aller.

►**stop by** *vi F* (*visit briefly*) faire une petite visite (*chez qn etc*); **I'll s. by at the post office on my way home,** je passerai à la poste en rentrant à la maison; **we'll s. by and see you next week,** nous passerons te voir la semaine prochaine.

►**stop down** *vi Phot* réduire l'ouverture.

►**stop off** *vi* (*stay briefly*) faire étape, faire halte; **they're stopping off at Bali for a couple of days on their way home,** ils font étape à Bali pour quelques jours en rentrant.

►**stop out 1** *vi* (*not come home*) **to s. out all night,** ne pas rentrer de toute la nuit, *F* découcher. **2** *vtsep* (*in etching*) recouvrir de vernis (*un faux trait*); réserver (*certaines parties de la planche*).

►**stop over** *vi* (*stay briefly*) faire escale, faire halte; **we stopped over at Manchester on the flight to Toronto,** nous avons fait escale à Manchester en route vers Toronto.

►**stop up 1** *vtsep* (*block*) boucher (*un trou*); obstruer, obturer (*un tuyau*). **2** *vi* **(a)** (*not go to bed*) **to s. up late,** veiller tard; **(b)** *Phot* augmenter l'ouverture.

stop-(and-)go ['stɒp((ə)n)'gəʊ] *adj* (*politique*) de coups de frein et d'accélérations alternés.

stopcock ['stɒpkɒk] *n* robinet *m* d'arrêt.

stopgap ['stɒpgæp] *n* bouche-trou *m*, *pl* bouche-trous; **s. measure,** pis-aller *m*.

stoplight ['stɒplaɪt] *n* **(a)** (*in street*) feu *m* rouge; **(b)** (*on car*) stop *m*.

stopoff ['stɒpɒf] *n* escale *f*, arrêt *m*.

stopover ['stɒpəʊvər] *n* **(a)** (*break in journey*) escale *f*; (*place*) (lieu *m* d')escale; **a s. for aircraft flying from London to Sydney,** une escale pour un avion qui vole de Londres à Sydney; **(b)** *Rail* faculté *f* d'arrêt; **s. ticket,** billet *m* avec (faculté d')arrêt.

stoppage ['stɒpɪdʒ] *n* **(a)** arrêt *m*, suspension *f*; *Mil etc* suppression *f* (*de solde, des permissions*); **(b)** retenue *f* (*sur les salaires*); arrêt, halte *f*, interruption *f* (*du travail*); (*by discontented employees*) débrayage *m*; **(c)** (*obstruction*) obstruction *f*, engorgement *m* (*d'un tuyau*); *Med* occlusion *f*.

stopper[1] ['stɒpər] *n* **(a)** bouchon *m* (*esp en verre*); obturateur *m* (*de tuyau*); **(ground) glass s.,** bouchon à l'émeri; **(b)** *MecE* taquet *m* (*d'arrêt de mouvement*).

stopper[2] *vt* boucher (*un flacon etc*).

stopping ['stɒpɪŋ] **1** *adj* qui s'arrête; *Rail* **s. train,** train *m* omnibus. **2** *n* **(a)** (*act of coming to halt*) arrêt *m*; **s. place,** (point *m* d')arrêt, halte *f*; **(b)** (*act of ending*) cessation *f*; suppression *f* (*d'un service*); arrêt de paiement (*d'un chèque*), opposition *f* (*à un chèque*); **(c)** (*act of blocking*) obturation *f*, bouchage *m*, obstruction *f* (*d'une voie d'eau*); plombage *m* (*d'une dent*); **(d)** (*thing that blocks*) bouchon *m*, tampon *m*; mastic *m* (*à reboucher*); (*in dentistry*) plombage *m*, mastic.

stopping up *n* = **STOPPING 2 (c)**.

stop-press ['stɒppres] *adj Journ* **s.-p. news,** informations de dernière heure.

stopwatch ['stɒpwɒtʃ] *n* chronomètre *m* (à déclic).

storage ['stɔːrɪdʒ] *n* **(a)** (*act of storing*) emmagasinage *m*, emmagasinement *m*; (*of heat*) accumulation *f*; *El* emmagasinage, emmagasinement; *Comptr* stockage *m*; **to put sth into s.,** mettre qch en dépôt; *El* **s. cell,** élément *m* d'accumulateur; *Comptr* **s. device,** dispositif *m* de stockage; **(night) s. heater,** radiateur *m* à accumulation (*chauffé pendant la nuit*); **the kitchen has plenty of s. space,** la cuisine a beaucoup d'espace de rangement; **s. tank,** réservoir *m* d'emmagasinage *ou* de stockage; **s. unit,** meuble *m ou* élément de rangement; **(b)** (*available space*) espace *m* disponible (*en magasin, pour rangement*); caves *fpl*, greniers *mpl* (*d'une maison particulière*); entrepôts *mpl*, magasins *mpl* (*d'une maison de commerce*); **(c)** (*cost*) frais *mpl* d'entrepôt, magasinage *m*.

store[1] [stɔːr] *n* **(a)** provision *f*, approvisionnement *m*; **to have (a) good s. of wine,** avoir une bonne provision de vin; **a s. of jokes,** un stock d'histoires drôles; **to lay in a s. of sth,** faire une provision de qch, s'approvisionner de *ou* en qch; **to lay in stores,** s'approvisionner; **to hold** *or* **keep sth in s.,** tenir *ou* garder qch en réserve; **what the future holds in s. for us,** ce que l'avenir nous réserve; **I have a surprise in s. for her,** je lui ménage *ou* réserve une surprise; **to set great/little s. by sth,** faire grand/peu de cas de qch; **s. cattle,** bétail *m* à l'engraissage;

(b) stores, provisions *fpl*, approvisionnements *mpl*; (*food and drink*) vivres *mpl*; **marine stores,** (*supplies*) approvisionnements matériels *ou* de navires; (*shop*) magasin *m ou* maison *f* d'approvisionnements de navires;

(c) *Com Ind* entrepôt *m*, magasin *m*; (*for furniture*) garde-meuble *m*, *pl* garde-meubles; *Mil Nau* (*in barracks*) magasin;

(d) *esp Am* boutique *f*, magasin *m*; **general s.,** épicerie *f*; **the village s.,** l'épicerie *ou* l'alimentation *f* du village; **toy/book s.,** magasin de jouets/librairie *f*; **(department or big) store,** grand magasin;

(e) *Comptr* mémoire *f*.

store[2] **1** *vt* **(a)** (*put in a store*) (em)magasiner (*le foin, le blé*); mettre en silo (*des betteraves etc*); (*take into store*) prendre (*des meubles*) en dépôt; (*put in store*) mettre (*des meubles*) en dépôt; **squirrels s. food for the winter,** les écureuils font des provisions pour l'hiver; **(b)** (*accumulate*) amasser, accumuler (*qch*); (*put in reserve*) mettre (*qch*) en réserve; emmagasiner (*l'électricité, la chaleur*); **s. in a cool place,** conserver au frais; **stored furniture,** mobilier *m* au garde-meubles; **(c)** *Comptr* stocker; **(d)** (*supply*) pourvoir, munir, approvisionner (**with,** de). **2** *vi* **goods that don't s. well,** marchandises qui ne se conservent *ou* ne se gardent pas bien.

►**store away** *vtsep* (*put away for future*) emmagasiner; *Fig* **dates stored away in the memory,** dates emmagasinées dans la mémoire.

►**store up** *vtsep* = **STORE**[2] **1 (b)**; **to s. up problems for oneself,** se garantir des problèmes pour l'avenir; **feelings of resentment that have been stored up over the years,** des sentiments d'amertume qui se sont accumulés au fil des ans.

storefront ['stɔːfrʌnt] *n Am* devanture *f* de magasin.

storehouse ['stɔːhaʊs] *n* magasin *m*, entrepôt *m*, dépôt *m*; *Fig* **a s. of information,** une mine de renseignements.

storekeeper ['stɔːkiːpər] *n* magasinier *m*; (*in hospital*) dépensier, -ière; *Am* (*shopkeeper*) marchand, -ande.

storeroom ['stɔːruːm] *n* **(a)** (*in private house*) office *f*, dépense *f*; *Ind* halle *f* de dépôt; *Nau* soute *f* aux vivres *ou* à provisions, magasin *m*, cambuse *f*; **(b)** *Am* (*for old furniture etc*) (chambre *f* de) débarras *m*

storey, *Am* **story** ['stɔːrɪ] *n* étage *m* (*d'un bâtiment*); **on the third s.,** *Am* **on the fourth s.,** au troisième étage; **single** *or* **one s. house,** maison sans étage *ou* de plain-pied

-storeyed, *Am* **-storied** ['stɔːrɪd] *suff* **two-s house,** maison à un étage; **one-s.** *or* **single-s. house,** maison sans étage *ou* de plain-pied.

storing ['stɔːrɪŋ] *n* **(a)** (*putting into store*) emmagasinage *m*, emmagasinement *m* (**of,** de); **(b)** (*accumulation*) accumulation *f* (**of,** de); **(c)** (*stocking*) approvisionnement *m* (**with,** en).

stork [stɔːk] *n* (*bird*) cigogne *f*.

storm[1] [stɔːm] *n* **(a)** orage *m*; (*wind*) tempête *f*; **rain s.,** tempête de pluie; **there's a s. coming,** le temps est à l'orage; *Fig* **a s. in a teacup,** une tempête dans un verre d'eau; **political s.,** ouragan *m ou* tourmente *f* politique; **to bring a s. about one's ears,** s'attirer une véritable tempête d'indignation, soulever un tollé général; **s. cloud,** nuée *f* d'orage; *Fig* nuage à l'horizon *ou* menaçant; **s. cone,** cône *m* de tempête; **s. damage,** dommage causé par l'orage *ou* la tempête; **s. door,** (élément extérieur de la) double-porte *f*; *CivE* **s. drain,** *US* **s. sewer,** égout pluvial; **s. lantern,** lampe-tempête *f*, *pl* lampes-tempêtes;

(b) pluie *f* (*de projectiles*); bordée *f* (*d'injures*); tempête *f* (*d'applaudissements, de protestations*); **to raise a s. of laughter,** déchaîner l'hilarité générale;

(c) *Mil* assaut *m*; **to take a stronghold by s.,** prendre d'assaut une place forte; *Fig* **to take the audience by s.,** emporter *ou* soulever l'auditoire; *Fig* **to take s.o. by s.,** (*emotionally*) bouleverser qn; **s. troops,** troupes *fpl* d'assaut; *German Hist* sections *fpl* d'assaut.

storm[2] **1** *vi* (*of wind, rain*) se déchaîner, faire rage; (*of person*) tempêter, pester; **to s. at s.o.,** s'emporter contre qn; **to s. into/out of the room,** entrer dans/quitter la pièce comme un ouragan. **2** *vt Mil* (*attack*) donner *ou* livrer l'assaut à (*une place forte*); (*capture*) prendre d'assaut, emporter d'assaut, enlever (*une place forte*).

stormbound ['stɔːmbaʊnd] *adj* retenu par une tempête.

storming ['stɔːmɪŋ] *n Mil* (*attack*) assaut *m* (**of,** de);

(*capture*) prise *f* d'assaut (**of,** de).

stormy ['stɔːmɪ] *adj* (*temps, ciel*) orageux, d'orage; (*mer*) démonté; **the weather is s.,** le temps est orageux *ou* à l'orage; *Fig* **s. discussion,** discussion orageuse; **s. life,** vie tumultueuse; **s. meeting,** réunion houleuse; **s. marriage,** mariage orageux; **s. petrel,** (*bird*) pétrel *m.*

story¹ ['stɔːrɪ] *n* **(a)** histoire *f*; **to tell a s.,** raconter *ou* conter une histoire; **there is a s. that ...,** on raconte que ...; **as the s. goes,** à ce que l'on raconte; *F* **that is quite another s.,** ça c'est une autre histoire; *F* **it's the (same) old s.** *or* **the old, old s.,** c'est toujours la même histoire, c'est toujours la même chose; *F* **it's the s. of my life,** c'est le genre de chose qui m'arrive tout le temps; **it's a long s.,** c'est toute une histoire, c'est une longue histoire; **these bruises tell their own s.,** ces meurtrissures en disent long; **each photo tells its** *or* **a s.,** toutes les photos racontent une histoire; **funny/good s.,** bonne histoire; **she can tell a good s.,** elle en connaît de bonnes;
(b) short s., nouvelle *f*, conte *m*; **short s. writer,** nouvelliste *mf*;
(c) (*plot*) **s. (line),** intrigue *f* (*d'un roman, d'une pièce de théâtre*);
(d) *Journ F* article *m*;
(e) *F* (*lie*) histoire *f*, conte *m*; **to tell stories,** raconter des histoires;
(f) *Arch* l'histoire *f*, la légende.

story² *n esp Am* = **STOREY.**

storybook ['stɔːrɪbʊk] *n* livre *m* de contes, livre d'histoires; **it looks like a s. castle,** cela ressemble à un château de conte de fées; **it had a s. ending,** ça c'est terminé comme un conte de fées.

storyteller ['stɔːrɪtelər] *n* **(a)** conteur, -euse; **to be a good/bad s.,** être bon/mauvais conteur; **(b)** *F* (*esp said to children*) (*liar*) menteur, -euse; **you big s.!,** gros menteur!, grosse menteuse!

storytelling ['stɔːrɪtelɪŋ] *n* **(a)** l'art *m* de conter; **to be good at s.,** avoir l'art de raconter des histoires; **(b)** *F* (*telling lies*) mensonges *mpl.*

stoup [stuːp] *n Rel* bénitier *m.*

stout¹ [staʊt] *adj* **(a)** (*person*) (*strong*) fort, vigoureux; (*brave*) brave, vaillant; (*resolute*) ferme, résolu; *Old-fashioned* **s. fellow,** (*brave*) homme vaillant *ou* courageux; (*sturdy*) costaud *m;* **s. heart,** cœur vaillant; **to put up a s. resistance,** se défendre vaillamment; **(b)** (*thing*) fort, solide; (*cloth*) renforcé; (*material*) résistant; **(c)** (*fat*) corpulent, fort; **to grow s.,** engraisser, prendre de l'embonpoint.

stout² *n* (*beer*) stout *m*, bière brune forte.

stouthearted [staʊt'hɑːtɪd] *adj* courageux, intrépide.

stoutly ['staʊtlɪ] *adv* **(a)** (*vigorously*) fortement, vigoureusement; (*nier qch*) fermement; **she s. maintained that ...,** elle affirmait énergiquement que ...; **(b)** (*sturdily*) (*bâti*) solidement.

stoutness ['staʊtnɪs] *n* **(a)** (*vigorousness*) fermeté *f*, vigueur *f* (*de la résistance etc*); **(b)** (*solidity*) solidité *f*; **(c)** (*fatness*) embonpoint *m.*

stove [stəʊv] *n* **(a)** (*cooker*) cuisinière *f*; (*oven*) fourneau *m* de cuisine; (*small, portable*) réchaud *m*; **electric/gas s.,** cuisinière électrique/à gaz; **oil s.,** poêle *m* à pétrole; (*heater*) calorifère *m* à mazout; **(b)** *Ch Ind* étuve *f*, four *m.*

stove-enamelled ['stəʊvɪnæm(ə)ld] *adj* émaillé au four.

stovepipe ['stəʊvpaɪp] *n* **(a)** tuyau *m* de poêle; **(b)** *F Old-fashioned* **s. hat,** chapeau *m* tuyau de poêle.

stow [stəʊ] *vt* **(a)** (*put away*) mettre en place, ranger (*des objets*); *Sl* **s. it!,** (*shut up*) la ferme!; (*that's enough*) ça suffit!; **(b)** *Nau* arrimer (*des marchandises*); saisir (*l'ancre, les canots*); **(c) to s. sth full of sth,** remplir qch de qch.

▶**stow away 1** *vtsep* = **STOW (a)**; *F* **to s. away a huge meal,** s'envoyer un repas énorme. **2** *vi* (*hide on ship, plane*) s'embarquer clandestinement (*à bord d'un navire, d'un avion*).

stowage ['stəʊɪdʒ] *n Nau* arrimage *m*; (*space*) espace *m* utile; (*for goods*) capacité *f* de stockage; (*cost*) frais *mpl* d'arrimage.

stowaway ['stəʊəweɪ] *n Nau Av* passager *ou* voyageur clandestin.

stower ['stəʊər] *n* **(a)** *Nau* arrimeur *m*; **(b)** *Min* remblayeur *m.*

stowing ['stəʊɪŋ] *n* **(a)** (*putting away*) rangement *m*, mise *f* en place; **(b)** *Nau* arrimage *m* (*de la cargaison*).

stowing away *n* **(a)** = **STOWING (a)**; **(b)** (*on ship, plane*) embarquement clandestin.

strabismus [stræ'bɪzməs] *n Med* strabisme *m.*

straddle¹ ['stræd(ə)l] **1** *vt* **(a)** (*be on both sides of*) enfourcher (*un cheval*); se mettre à califourchon sur (*une chaise*); chevaucher (*un mur*); **their empire straddled the Mediterranean,** leur empire couvrait la Méditerranée; **to s. a river,** (*of bridge*) enjamber une rivière; **the village straddles the border,** le village est à cheval sur la frontière; **her life straddled two centuries,** sa vie est à cheval sur deux siècles; **a company that straddles two continents,** une entreprise qui a des intérêts dans deux continents; **(b)** *Am Pol etc* refuser de se compromettre sur (*une question*); **to s. the fence,** ne pas prendre parti, ne pas s'engager. **2** *vi* **(a)** écarter les jambes; **(b)** *Mil* tirer à la fourchette.

straddle² *n Sp* (*in high jump*) saut *m* en ciseaux.

strafe [streɪf] *vt Mil* (*machine-gun*) mitrailler; (*from low-flying aircraft*) mitrailler (*l'ennemi*) en rase-mottes; (*bomb*) bombarder.

straggle ['stræg(ə)l] *vi* **(a)** (*walk in disorderly fashion*) marcher sans ordre *ou* à la débandade; (*not keep up*) rester en arrière, traîner; **other climbers straggled behind and got lost,** d'autres grimpeurs sont restés à la traîne et se sont perdus; **his hair straggled over his jacket collar,** ses cheveux traînaient en désordre sur le col de son veston; **(b)** (*of plants*) pousser en désordre; **the roses are straggling everywhere,** les roses poussent dans tous les sens.

straggler ['stræglər] *n* traînard, -arde; *Nau* (*ship, sailor*) retardataire *m*, lanterne *f* rouge.

straggling ['stræglɪŋ] *adj* **a few s. houses,** quelques maisons éparpillées; **s. hairs,** mèches rebelles.

straggly ['stræglɪ] *adj* (*branches, hair*) épars; **a s. procession of refugees,** un défilé inégal de réfugiés.

straight [streɪt] **1** *adj* **(a)** droit, rectiligne; (*mouvement*) en ligne droite; **s. line,** (ligne) droite *f*; **s. up and down,** (*of figure*) tout d'une venue; **s. back,** dos droit; **s. legs,** jambes droites; **s. edge,** (*tool*) règle *f* (à araser); **s. hair,** cheveux raides; *Boxing* **s. right/left,** direct *m* du droit/gauche; *Tennis* **to win in three s. sets,** gagner par trois sets de suite; *Horseracing Fin* **s. tip,** tuyau sûr *ou* de source sûre;
(b) (*honest*) honnête, loyal, -aux; (*frank*) franc, *f* franche; (*réponse*) sans équivoque, franc; **s. as a die,** d'une droiture absolue; **s. dealings,** procédés *mpl* honnêtes; **to be s. with s.o.,** agir loyalement avec qn *ou* envers qn; **be s. with me, is he ...?,** sois franc avec moi, est-il ...?; **I want a s. answer!,** je veux une réponse honnête; **to play a s. game,** jouer franc jeu;
(c) *Th* **s. part,** rôle sérieux; **s. actor,** comédien *m* dramatique; **s. man,** (*comedian's*) faire-valoir *m inv*;
(d) (*serious, conventional*) normal; *F* (*heterosexual*) hétéro(sexuel); **to keep a s. face,** garder son sérieux; **I couldn't keep a s. face,** je n'ai pas pu m'empêcher de rire;
(e) *Pol* **s. fight,** campagne électorale à deux candidats; *US* **s. ticket,** liste non panachée; **she got s. As in the exam,** (*all As*) elle n'a obtenu que des mentions très bien à l'examen;
(f) *F* (*neat*) **s. whisky,** whisky sec *ou* pur; **to drink one's whisky s.,** boire son whisky sec *ou* pur;
(g) (*aligned*) droit, d'aplomb; (*in order*) en ordre; **to put sth s.,** redresser *ou* ajuster qch; **your tie isn't s.,** votre cravate est de travers; **to put the room s.,** remettre de l'ordre dans la pièce; **to put things** *or* **matters s.,** arranger les choses; (*sort problem out*) débrouiller l'affaire; **let's try to get things s.,** essayons d'y voir clair; **let's get this s., he left at two o'clock?,** mettons les choses au clair, il est parti à deux heures?; *F* **get this s.!,** comprends-moi bien!; *F* **I need five hundred pounds to get me s.,** il me faut cinq cents livres pour me remettre d'aplomb.
2 *n* **(a)** aplomb *m*; **to be out of (the) s.,** n'être pas d'aplomb, être de travers; **to cut a material on the s.,** couper une étoffe de droit fil; **the s. and narrow,** le droit chemin; **to keep on the s. and narrow,** ne pas s'écarter du droit chemin; *F* **to be on the s.,** vivre honnêtement;
(b) *Rail* alignement *m* (droit); *Sp* **the s.,** (*on race track*) la ligne droite; **the back s.** la ligne opposée *ou* d'en face; **the home s.,** la ligne droite; *Fig* **we're on the home s. now,** nous sommes dans la dernière ligne droite;
(c) *Sl* (*honest, old-fashioned person*) personne *f* honnête (et vieux jeu); (*heterosexual*) hétéro *mf.*
3 *adv* **(a)** droit; **to fly s. as a dart** *or* **an arrow,** voler droit comme une flèche; **to shoot s.,** tirer juste; **to go s.,** aller droit; (*of criminal*) vivre honnêtement; (*of drug addict*) se désintoxiquer; **keep s. on,** continuez tout droit; **to read a book s. through,** (*from beginning to end*) lire un livre d'un bout à l'autre; (*without stopping*) lire un livre sans s'arrêter *ou* d'un seul tenant;
(b) (*without delay*) directement; **it comes s. from Paris,**

ça vient directement *ou* tout droit de Paris; **I'll come s. back,** je reviendrai directement, je ne ferai que faire l'aller-retour; **to come/go s. to the point,** aller/venir droit au fait; **to get s. on with one's work,** se mettre directement au travail; **to walk s. in,** entrer sans frapper; **s. away,** immédiatement, aussitôt, tout de suite; *F* **s. off,** sur-le-champ, tout de suite; **I can't tell you s. off,** je ne peux pas vous le dire tout de suite;

(c) (*directly*) directement; **to drink s. from the bottle,** boire à (même) la bouteille; **it is s. across the road,** c'est juste en face; **s. above sth,** juste au-dessus de qch; **to look s.o. s. in the face,** regarder qn bien en face; **he looked s. through me,** il m'a regardé sans me voir; **we drove s. through Nantes,** nous avons traversé Nantes sans nous arrêter; *F* **to let s.o. have it s.,** dire son fait à qn; **I told him s. (out) what I thought of it,** je lui ai dit carrément *ou* franchement *ou* tout net ce que j'en pensais;

(d) (*honestly*) honnêtement; **to deal s. with people,** être loyal en affaires; **to play s.,** jouer beau jeu; *Br Sl* **s. up!,** vraiment!, honnêtement!;

(e) *Th* **to play a part s.,** jouer un rôle à la lettre; **I can't see s.,** je ne vois pas clair; **I can't think s.,** mon cerveau refuse de fonctionner.

straightaway ['streɪtəweɪ] **1** *adv* immédiatement, tout de suite. **2** *adj Am* en ligne droite.

straight-edged ['streɪtedʒd] *adj* à tranchant droit.

straighten ['streɪt(ə)n] **1** *vt* rendre (*qch*) droit; (*put in order*) ranger, mettre en ordre; redresser (*un clou, une tige etc*); défausser (*une barre*); **to s. one's back,** se redresser; **to s. one's hair,** se recoiffer; (*take curls out*) se défriser les cheveux; **to s. one's tie,** arranger sa cravate; **to s. one's affairs,** mettre ses affaires en ordre. **2** *vi* (*of person*) se redresser; (*of thing, road etc*) devenir droit.

►**straighten out 1** *vtsep* **(a)** (*make straight*) redresser; défausser (*une barre*); **he straightened out the crumpled bedclothes,** il a remis de l'ordre dans les draps froissés; **(b)** (*put right*) arranger (*ses affaires*), mettre (*ses affaires*) en ordre; **I will try to s. things out,** je vais essayer d'arranger les choses. **2** *vi* **(a)** (*become straight*) (*of river, road etc*) redevenir droit; **(b)** (*become right*) **I expect things will s. out,** je pense que ça s'arrangera.

►**straighten up 1** *vtsep* **(a)** (*put straight*) redresser (*picture etc*); **(b)** (*put in order*) mettre de l'ordre dans (*room etc*). **2** *vi* (*straighten one's back*) se redresser.

straight-faced ['streɪt'feɪst] *adj* impassible, qui ne perd pas son sérieux.

straightforward [streɪt'fɔːwəd] *adj* **(a)** (*person, conduct*) loyal, -aux, franc, *f* franche, sans détours; **to give a s. answer to a question,** répondre sans détours à une question; **to be quite s. about it,** y aller franc jeu; **(b)** (*simple*) simple; **it's a very s. cooker to use,** c'est une cuisinière très simple à utiliser.

straightforwardly [streɪt'fɔːwədlɪ] *adv* **(a)** (*agir*) avec droiture, loyalement; (*parler*) carrément, franchement, sans détours; **(b)** (*simply*) facilement; **it can be assembled s. enough,** il peut être monté assez facilement, le montage en est assez facile; **you then quite s. remove the lid,** puis vous ôtez le couvercle tout simplement *ou* très facilement.

straightforwardness [streɪt'fɔːwədnɪs] *n* (*of person*) droiture *f*, honnêteté *f*, franchise *f*; (*of matter, question*) simplicité *f*.

straightness ['streɪtnɪs] *n* **(a)** rectitude *f* (*d'une ligne*); **(b)** droiture *f*, rectitude *f* (*de conduite*).

strain¹ [streɪn] *n* **(a)** (*tension*) tension *f*, surtension *f*; (*effort*) effort *m*, contrainte *f*; *Phys* rapport *m* de la déformation, allongement *m* unitaire; **the s. on the rope,** la tension de la corde; **to relieve the s. on** *or* **take the s. off a beam,** soulager une poutre; *MecE* **breaking s.,** force *f* *ou* contrainte à la rupture, effort de rupture; **to take the s.,** (*of beam*) (*be subjected to*) être soumis à la tension; (*to support*) supporter la tension; (*of person*) supporter la tension nerveuse; **it would be** *or* **put too great a s. on my finances,** ce serait trop demander à ma bourse; **the long hours put a s. on her marriage,** ses longs horaires de travail ont occasionné des tensions dans son mariage; **the s. of modern life,** la tension de la vie moderne; **the s. of business life,** la fatigue due à la vie des affaires; **all this driving's getting a bit of a s.,** tous ces déplacements en voiture commencent à me fatiguer; **I find it a s.,** je trouve cela fatigant; **the s. was beginning to tell (on them** *etc***),** la tension commençait à devenir apparente; **mental s.,** surmenage *m* (cérébral); **eye s.,** fatigue *f* des yeux;

(b) *Med* entorse *f*, foulure *f*; **s. in the back,** tour *m* de reins;

(c) *esp Lit* (*usu pl*) (*sounds, music*) accents *mpl*; **sweet strains,** doux accords;

(d) (*tone*) ton *m* (*d'un discours etc*); **he said much more in the same s.,** il s'est étendu longuement dans ce sens.

strain² 1 *vt* **(a)** tendre, surtendre (*un câble*); **to s. one's ears,** tendre l'oreille; **to s. one's eyes,** (*overuse*) se fatiguer *ou* s'abîmer les yeux *ou* la vue (**doing sth,** à faire qch); (*make effort*) s'efforcer (**to see sth,** pour voir qch); **to s. one's voice,** (*overuse*) se fatiguer la voix; (*make effort*) forcer sa voix; **to s. relations,** tendre les rapports (**between,** entre); **to s. one's resources,** grever ses ressources jusqu'à la limite;

(b) *Med etc* fouler, forcer (*un membre*); forcer (*un mât, une poutre*); *MecE* déformer (*une pièce*); **to s. one's back,** se donner un tour de reins; **to s. one's heart,** surmener son cœur; **to s. a muscle,** se froisser un muscle; **to s. oneself,** (*overexert oneself*) se surmener, s'éreinter (**doing sth,** à faire qch); *Iron* **he doesn't (exactly) s. himself,** on ne peut pas dire qu'il se foule (la rate); *Iron* **don't s. yourself, will you!,** surtout ne te foule pas!;

(c) filtrer, passer (*un liquide*); tamiser, passer (*le bouillon*); faire égoutter (*les légumes*); **to s. sth out (of a liquid),** enlever *ou* ôter *ou* extraire qch d'un liquide (*en se servant d'une passoire*).

2 *vi* **(a)** (*make great effort*) faire un grand effort, peiner; **to s. at a rope/at the oars,** tirer sur une corde/sur les rames; **the author doesn't s. after effect,** l'auteur ne s'évertue pas à produire de l'effet; **to s. at the leash,** (*of dog*) tirer sur la laisse; *Fig* (*be restless*) ne pas tenir en place; *Fig* (*be rebellious*) se rebeller;

(b) (*of beam*) fatiguer, travailler; (*of rope*) être trop tendu;

(c) *MecE* (*of machine part*) se déformer; (*of beam, piece of metal*) gauchir, se fausser;

(d) *Lit* **to s. at (doing) sth,** (*be unwilling*) se faire scrupule de (faire) qch, avoir scrupule à (faire) qch;

(e) (*of liquid*) filtrer (**through,** à travers).

strain³ *n* **(a)** *Biol* souche *f* (*d'un virus*); variété *f* (*de graine, de plante*); race *f*, lignée *f* (*d'un animal*); **(b)** (*quantity*) **a s. of weakness,** un fond de faiblesse.

strained [streɪnd] *adj* **(a)** (*rope etc*) tendu; trop tendu; **s. nerves,** nerfs tendus; **s. relations,** rapports tendus; **Anglo-American relations were s.,** les relations anglo-américaines étaient tendues; **(b)** *Med* **s. ankle,** cheville foulée; **s. heart,** cœur surmené; **(c)** (*forced*) (*laughter*) forcé, contraint; (*of language, interpretation*) forcé, exagéré, poussé trop loin; **(d)** (*liquid*) filtré.

strainer ['streɪnər] *n* filtre *m*, tamis *m*; *Culin* passoire *f*; *Ind etc* épurateur *m* (*d'air etc*); **tea s.,** passe-thé *m inv*; **milk s.,** passe-lait *m inv*.

strait [streɪt] *n* **(a)** détroit *m*; **the Straits of Gibraltar,** le détroit de Gibraltar; **the Straits of Dover,** le Pas de Calais; **(b) to be in dire** *or* **desperate straits,** être dans une situation désespérée; (*financially*) être dans la plus grande gêne; **(c) s. jacket,** camisole *f* de force.

straitened ['streɪtənd] *adj* **in s. circumstances,** dans une situation (financière) difficile.

straitlaced ['streɪt'leɪst] *adj* prude, collet monté *inv*.

strand¹ [strænd] *n Lit* (*shore*) rive *f*, plage *f*, grève *f*.

strand² 1 *vt* échouer (*un navire*); **tourists stranded by the air controllers' strike,** touristes laissés en rade à cause de la grève des aiguilleurs du ciel. **2** *vi* (*of ship, whale*) s'échouer.

strand³ *n* **(a)** (*piece*) brin *m*, toron *m* (*de cordage*); *Sewing* brin (*de fil à coudre*); fil *m* (*d'un tissu*); *Fig* (*of plot*) fil; *Fig* **to unravel the strands of a complicated affair,** démêler les fils d'une affaire compliquée; **(b)** fil *m* (*de perles*); mèche *f* (*de cheveux*).

strand⁴ *vt* toronner (*un cordage*); **to s. a coloured thread into a piece of cloth,** introduire un fil de couleur dans la trame d'une étoffe.

stranded ['strændɪd] *adj* **(a)** (*navire*) échoué; **s. whale,** baleine échouée (à la côte); **(b)** (*person*) à bout de ressources; (*left behind*) laissé en arrière; (*abandoned*) abandonné; **to leave s.o. s.,** laisser qn en plan; **to be s.,** être *ou* rester en panne; **s. tourists,** touristes laissés en rade.

-stranded ['strændɪd] *suff* **three-s. rope,** corde à trois torons.

strange [streɪndʒ] *adj* **(a)** (*unusual*) étrange, bizarre; **they didn't write — (that's) s.,** ils n'ont pas écrit — (c'est) bizarre; **s. beasts,** bêtes curieuses; **she wears the strangest clothes,** elle porte les vêtements les plus bizarres; **she's a s. girl,** c'est une fille bizarre; **it's a s. thing,** c'est (une chose) étrange; **s. to say, I've never met**

him, chose étrange (à dire), je ne l'ai jamais rencontré; **it's s. that you should not have** *or* **haven't heard of it,** il est étonnant que vous ne l'ayez pas appris; **it was s. to see her in a dress,** ça faisait bizarre *ou* drôle de la voir en robe; **s. how some faces stick in your mind,** c'est bizarre *ou* drôle comme certains visages restent gravés dans la mémoire; **they've got a s. way of saying thank-you,** ils ont une drôle de façon de dire merci;
(b) (*unfamiliar*) **s. faces,** des visages nouveaux *ou* inconnus; **a strange place/house,** un endroit/une maison qu'on ne connaît pas; **I can't work with s. tools,** je ne peux pas travailler avec des outils qui ne sont pas les miens; **this handwriting is s. to me,** je ne (re)connais pas cette écriture; **I felt s. in those surroundings,** je me sentais dépaysé dans ce milieu; **don't talk to s. men,** ne parle pas aux hommes que tu ne connais pas;
(c) *Arch* (*foreign*) étranger; **in a s. land,** dans un pays étranger; **a s. man,** un étranger.

strangely ['streɪndʒlɪ] *adv* étrangement, bizarrement, singulièrement; **it all seemed s. familiar,** tout (cela) semblait étrangement familier; **he's behaving very s.,** il se conduit de manière très étrange; **s. enough, he felt nothing,** chose étrange, il n'a rien senti.

strangeness ['streɪndʒnɪs] *n* **(a)** (*unusual quality*) étrangeté *f*; singularité *f*, bizarrerie *f*; **(b)** (*unfamiliarity*) étrangeté *f*, nouveauté *f*.

stranger ['streɪndʒər] *n* **(a)** étranger, -ère; (*someone not known*) inconnu, -ue; **don't talk to strangers,** ne parle pas aux inconnus; **I'm a s. here,** je suis étranger ici, je ne suis pas d'ici; **they're strangers (to us),** nous ne les connaissons pas; **you're quite a s. these days!,** vous vous faites rare; *F* **hello, s.!,** tiens! bonjour! ça fait longtemps que l'on ne s'est pas vus!; **to become a s. to s.o.,** devenir étranger à qn; **to become a s. to sth,** perdre l'habitude de qch; **they had become complete strangers to one another,** ils étaient devenus complètement étrangers l'un à l'autre; **he's a s./no s. to fear,** il ne connaît pas/il connaît bien la peur; **I spy strangers!,** (*in House of Commons*) je demande le huis clos!; **(b)** *F* (*in cup of tea*) chinois *m*.

strangle ['stræŋg(ə)l] **1** *vt* étrangler (*qn*); étouffer (*un rire*); réprimer (*un éternuement*); **to s. the press,** étrangler la presse; **strangled voice,** voix étranglée. **2** *vi* s'étrangler.

stranglehold ['stræŋg(ə)lhəʊld] *n* **(a)** (*in wrestling*) étranglement *m*; **(b)** *Fig* **to have a s. on s.o.,** tenir qn à la gorge; **economic s.,** mainmise *f* économique; **to break the s. on a country's economy,** mettre fin à la mainmise sur l'économie d'un pays.

strangler ['stræŋglər] *n* (*person*) étrangleur, -euse.

strangling ['stræŋglɪŋ] *n* étranglement *m*, strangulation *f*.

strangulate ['stræŋgjʊleɪt] *Med* **1** *vt* étrangler (*l'intestin*); **strangulated hernia,** hernie étranglée. **2** *vi* (*of hernia, intestine*) devenir étranglé.

strangulation [stræŋgjʊ'leɪʃən] *n* strangulation *f*; *Fig* **economic s.,** asphyxie *f* économique.

strap¹ [stræp] *n* **(a)** courroie *f*, sangle *f*, bande *f*, lanière *f* (*de cuir, de toile*); (*on clothing*) bande *f*, patte *f* (*d'étoffe*); (*on bra etc*) bretelle *f*; barrette *f*, lanière, patte (*de soulier*); **watch s.,** bracelet *m* de montre; (*horseriding*) **stirrup s.,** étrivière *f*; (*in vehicle*) **window s.,** tirant *m* de fenêtre *ou* de vitre; **(standing passengers') s.,** (*on underground train etc*) poignée *f*; **trouser s.,** (*under foot*) sous-pied *m*, *pl* sous-pieds (*de pantalon*); **to give s.o. the s.,** (*punishment*) fouetter qn (avec une sangle); **(b)** *Tech* attache *f*, lien *m* (*en métal*); armature *f*, étrier *m* (*de renfort*); chape *f*, bride *f* (de bielle); collier *m*, bague *f* (*d'excentrique*); *MecE* bande *f*, ruban *m*.

strap² *vt* (**-pp-** [stræpt]) **(a)** (*attach*) attacher *ou* lier *ou* fixer qch avec une courroie; boucler (*une malle*); ceinturer (*une personne*); sangler (*un paquet*); **to s. sth to sth,** sangler qch à qch; **(b)** (*punish*) administrer une correction à (*un enfant*) avec une courroie; **(c)** *Med* mettre des bandelettes *ou* un pansement adhésif sur (*une blessure*); maintenir (*un membre cassé*) au moyen de bandages.

▸**strap down** *vtsep* arrimer (*des conteneurs etc*); entraver (*un prisonnier, un patient*).

▸**strap in** *vtsep* attacher (*un passager*); **to s. oneself in,** s'attacher.

▸**strap up** *vtsep* **(a)** sangler (*une valise*); **(b)** = **STRAP² (c)**.

straphang ['stræphæŋ] *vi* voyager debout (*en se tenant à la courroie ou à la poignée*).

straphanger ['stræphæŋər] *n* voyageur, -euse debout (*dans le métro etc*); **after 15 years of being a s.,** après avoir passé quinze ans à voyager debout.

strapless ['stræplɪs] *adj* sans bretelles; **s. top,** bustier *m*; **s. bra,** soutien-gorge *m* sans bretelles.

strapped [stræpt] *adj F* **to be s. (for cash),** être à court d'argent, être fauché.

strapping ['stræpɪŋ] *adj* solide, robuste; **s. fellow,** grand gaillard; **tall s. girl,** fille grande et bien faite.

stratagem ['strætədʒəm] *n* stratagème *m*.

strategic [strə'tiːdʒɪk] *adj* stratégique.

strategically [strə'tiːdʒɪk(ə)lɪ] *adv* stratégiquement; **s. placed,** placé à un endroit *ou* aux endroits stratégique(s).

strategist ['strætədʒɪst] *n* stratège *m*.

strategy ['strætɪdʒɪ] *n* stratégie *f*.

stratification [strætɪfɪ'keɪʃən] *n* stratification *f*.

stratified ['strætɪfaɪd] *adj* (*formation, society*) stratifié.

stratify ['strætɪfaɪ] **1** *vt* stratifier. **2** *vi* se stratifier.

stratosphere ['strætəsfɪər] *n* stratosphère *f*.

stratum *pl* **-a** ['strɑːtəm, -ə] *n Geol* strate *f*, couche *f*; couche (*d'air etc*); *Fig* couche; **the various strata of society,** les différentes couches sociales.

straw [strɔː] *n* **(a)** paille *f*; **loose s.,** paille de litière; **rice s.,** paille de riz; *Agr* **s. cutter,** hache-paille *m inv*; **s. hat,** chapeau *m* de paille; *Fig* **man of s.,** *Am* **s. man,** homme *m* de paille; **s. mattress,** paillasse *f*; **s. mat,** paillasson *m*; **it's not worth a s.,** cela ne vaut pas quatre sous; *Fig* **to clutch at any s.,** se raccrocher à n'importe quoi; *Prov* **a drowning man will clutch at a s.,** = quand on se noie on est prêt à se raccrocher à n'importe quoi; *Fig* **straws in the wind,** indications *fpl* de l'opinion publique; *Prov* **it's the last s. that breaks the camel's back,** c'est la goutte d'eau qui fait déborder le vase; **it's the last s.!,** ça c'est le comble!, il ne manquait plus que cela!; **s. vote,** sondage *m* d'opinion publique (*à un meeting etc*);
(b) (*for drinking*) **to drink lemonade through a s.,** boire de la limonade avec une paille;
(c) (*colour*) (jaune *m*) paille *f*.

strawberry ['strɔːb(ə)rɪ] *n* **(a)** (*fruit, flavour*) fraise *f*; **wild s.,** *Am* **field s.,** fraise des bois; **s. bed,** planche *f ou* plant *m* de fraisiers; **s. field,** plantation *f* de fraisiers, fraiseraie *f*; **s. ice cream,** glace *f* à la fraise; **s. jam,** confiture *f* de fraises; **s. (plant),** fraisier *m*; **(b) s. (colour),** fraise *inv*; **s. blond,** blond ardent; **s. mark,** fraise *f* (sur la peau).

straw-bottomed ['strɔːbɒtəmd] *adj* (*chaise*) de paille.

straw-coloured ['strɔːkʌləd] *adj* jaune paille *inv*.

stray¹ [streɪ] **1** *n* **(a)** (*animal*) animal égaré; (*dog*) chien errant; *Jur* animal sans maître; **(b) waifs and strays,** enfants abandonnés; **(c)** *Rad* **strays,** (bruits *mpl*) parasites *mpl*), (bruits de) friture *f*. **2** *adj* **(a)** (*animal*) égaré, perdu; *Jur* sans maître; **(b)** *Fig* égaré; (*example, specimen*) isolé; **s. bullets,** balles perdues; **s. thoughts,** pensées détachées.

stray² *vi* s'égarer, errer; (*of sheep*) s'écarter du troupeau; **the plane had strayed off course,** l'avion s'était écarté de sa route; **the sheep will s. onto the roads,** les moutons vont errer sur les routes; *Fig* **to s. from the right path,** s'écarter du bon chemin; **to let one's thoughts s.,** laisser vaguer *ou* errer ses pensées; **to s. from the point,** sortir du sujet.

streak¹ [striːk] *n* **(a)** (*stripe*) raie *f*, rayure *f*, bande *f*, strie *f*; traînée *f* (*de brume, de vapeur, de saleté*); trait *m*, raie (*de lumière*); filet *m* (*de liquide*); **s. of sunlight,** rayon *m* de soleil; **the first s. of dawn,** la première lueur du jour; **like a s. of lightning,** comme un éclair; **there were streaks of dirt on his face,** il y avait des traînées de saleté sur son visage; **streaks of grey hair,** mèches *fpl* de cheveux gris; **(b)** filon *m* (*de minerai*); *F* **I've had a s. of luck,** je tiens le filon; **winning s.,** suite *f* de victoires; **to be on a winning s., to hit a winning s.,** être en veine; **there's a s. of Irish blood in her,** il y a en elle des traces de sang irlandais; **there was a s. of cowardice in him,** il y avait de la lâcheté dans sa nature; **(c)** *F* (*act of running naked*) **to do a s.,** = courir nu (en public).

streak² **1** *vt* rayer, strier, zébrer; **fur streaked with black,** pelage rayé de noir; **wall streaked with damp,** mur couturé d'humidité; **white marble streaked with red,** marbre blanc veiné de rouge; **to have one's hair streaked,** se faire faire des mèches. **2** *vi* **(a)** (*run, move etc fast*) **to s. along/past,** aller/passer comme un éclair; **to s. off,** (*escape*) se sauver à toute allure; (*starting race etc*) partir à toute allure; **the Ferrari streaked past him,** la Ferrari le dépassa en trombe; **the rocket streaked up into the sky,** la fusée fonça vers le ciel; **(b)** *F* (*run naked*) courir nu (en public).

streaker ['striːkər] *n F* coureur, -euse nu(e) (en public).

streaking ['striːkɪŋ] *n* **(a)** raies *fpl*, rayures *fpl*, bandes *fpl*; (*in hairdressing*) effet *m* de mèches; **(b)** *F* (*running naked*)

= course *f* de nudiste(s) (devant le public).

streaky ['stri:kɪ] *adj* **(a)** (*cloud etc*) en raies, en bandes; **(b)** (*paint*) irrégulier; (*mirror, plates etc*) couvert de traces; **her make-up had gone s.,** son maquillage avait dégouliné; **(c) s. bacon,** bacon entrelardé, ≈ petit salé.

stream¹ [stri:m] *n* **(a)** (*brook*) ruisseau *m*; (*watercourse*) cours *m* d'eau; (*river*) fleuve *m*, rivière *f*; **mountain s.,** torrent *m*; **in a thin s.,** en mince filet; **a s. of water shot out of the tap,** l'eau jaillit à flot du robinet; *Prov* **little streams make great rivers,** les petits ruisseaux font les grandes rivières;

(b) coulée *f* (*de lave*); flot(s) *m(pl)*, jet *m* (*de lumière, de sang*); flux *m*, torrent *m* (*de larmes, de paroles, de félicitations, d'insultes*); flots (*de gens*); **s. of cars,** défilé ininterrompu de voitures; **to hold up the s. of traffic,** arrêter le flot de voitures; **in one continuous s.,** à jet continu; *Liter* **s. of consciousness,** monologue intérieur; **s. feed,** (*on photocopier*) alimentation *f* automatique;

(c) (*current*) courant *m*; **with the s.,** dans le sens du courant, au fil de l'eau; **against the s.,** contre le courant, à contre-courant; *Fig* **to go with the s.,** suivre le mouvement; *Fig* **to go against the s.,** aller à contre-courant; **the main s. of public opinion,** le courant de l'opinion publique;

(d) to come on s., (*of oil*) commencer à couler; (*of new power station etc*) entrer en production; **to go off s.,** (*of oil*) cesser de couler; (*of power station*) cesser de produire;

(e) *Br Sch* niveaux *mpl* (*d'aptitude*); **three-s. school,** école où les classes sont réparties sur trois niveaux différents.

stream² **1** *vi* **(a)** (*of liquid*) couler à flots, ruisseler; **people were streaming over the bridge,** les gens traversaient le pont à flot continu; **people s. out of the stadium,** les gens sortent du stade à flots; **the sunlight streams in(to the room),** le soleil pénètre à flots (dans la chambre); **(b)** (*of surface*) ruisseler (**with,** de); **his eyes were streaming,** (*he was crying*) ses larmes coulaient à flots; (*his eyes were watering*) ses yeux larmoyaient; **(c)** (*of hair, garment, banner*) flotter (au vent). **2** *vt* **(a)** laisser couler (*un liquide*) à flots; **the river streamed blood,** la rivière coulait rouge; **(b)** *Br Sch* répartir (*les élèves*) selon leur niveau d'aptitude.

streamer ['stri:mər] *n* **(a)** (*flag*) banderole *f*; *Nau* flamme *f*; *Journ* titre flamboyant, **(paper) streamers,** serpentins *mpl* (de carnaval); **(b)** *Met* **streamers,** (*at North Pole*) lumière *f* polaire.

streaming ['stri:mɪŋ] **1** *adj* **(a)** (*liquid*) qui coule; *F* **to have a s. cold,** avoir un gros rhume; **(b)** (*surface, umbrella*) ruisselant; **(c)** (*flag*) flottant au vent. **2** *n* *Br Sch* répartition *f* (*des élèves*) par niveaux.

streamline *vt* **(a)** caréner (*une voiture etc*); **(b)** *Fig* rationaliser (*une méthode*); réduire (*l'économie*) à l'essentiel.

streamlined ['stri:mlaɪnd] *adj* **(a)** *Aut Av* caréné; (*fuselage*) aérodynamique; (*fish, ship's hull*) hydrodynamique; **(b)** *Fig* (*system*) rationalisé; (*économie*) réduite à l'essentiel.

streamlining ['stri:mlaɪnɪŋ] *n* **(a)** carénage *m*, profilage *m* (*de la carrosserie*); **(b)** *Fig* rationalisation *f* (*d'un système*); réduction *f* (*de l'économie*) à l'essentiel.

street [stri:t] *n* rue *f*; (*people living in street*) (habitants *mpl* de la) rue; **back s.,** petite rue écartée; *Pej* rue pauvre *ou* (*dangerous*) mal fréquentée; **the High S.,** la Grand-rue; **to turn** *or* **throw s.o. (out) into the s.,** jeter qn à la rue, mettre qn sur le pavé; **to walk the streets,** courir les rues, battre le pavé; (*of prostitute*) (*also* **to be on the streets),** faire le trottoir; **the man in the s.,** Monsieur Tout-le-Monde, l'homme de la rue, le commun des mortels; *F* **she's streets better,** elle est bien meilleure; *F* **she's streets ahead of her competitors,** elle a devancé de beaucoup *ou* dépassé de plusieurs longueurs ses concurrents; **that's right up my s.,** c'est tout à fait mon rayon; *Fig F* **the whole s. heard the row,** toute la rue a entendu la dispute; *F* **the S.,** *Br Journ* (*Fleet Street*) le monde des journalistes; *Fin US* (*Wall Street*) le monde financier; *Old-fashioned* **s. arab,** gamin, -ine des rues; **they're gaining s. credibility** *or* *Sl* **s. cred,** ils sont de plus en plus branchés; **this won't do much for my s. cred,** ça ne va pas arranger ma crédibilité auprès du public; **s. furniture,** mobilier urbain; **s. guide,** indicateur *m* des rues; **s. lamp** *or* **light,** réverbère *m*; **s. level,** rez-de-chaussée *m inv*; **s. life,** (*activity*) animation *f* des rues; **s. map/plan,** plan *m*; **s. market,** marché *m* en plein air (*dans une rue*); *St Exch* marché après Bourse; **s. musician,** musicien, -ienne des rues *ou* de carrefour; **s. theatre,** théâtre *m* de rue; **s. value,** (*of drugs*) valeur *f* au niveau du revendeur.

streetcar ['stri:tkɑ:r] *n Am* tramway *m*.

streetwalker ['stri:twɔ:kər] *n* racoleuse *f*.

streetwise ['stri:twaɪz] *adj* averti, malin.

strength [streŋθ] *n* **(a)** force *f* (*d'un homme, d'un acide*); *Ch* titre *m*, teneur *f* (*d'une solution*); *El* intensité *f* (*d'un courant*); solidité *f*, résistance *f* (*d'une poutre, d'une corde*); solidité *f* (*du papier*); robustesse *f* (*d'un meuble*); force (*d'un joueur, d'une équipe*); force, puissance *f* (*d'une émotion*); **solution at full s., full-s. solution,** solution concentrée; **s. of mind,** force de caractère; **s. of will,** résolution *f*, volonté *f*; **by sheer s.,** de vive force, à force de bras; **to recover** *or* **regain s.,** se rétablir, reprendre des forces; **you must keep up your s.,** il faut garder vos forces; **she doesn't know her own strength,** elle ne connaît pas sa force; **to build up one's s. again,** reprendre des forces; **to lose s.,** s'affaiblir; *Fig* **to do sth on the s. of what one has been told,** faire qch en se fiant à *ou* en s'appuyant sur ce qu'on vous a dit; **convicted on the s. of this evidence,** condamné au vu de cette preuve; **he got a good job on the s. of his qualifications,** il a obtenu un bon emploi grâce à ses diplômes; **s. of a friendship,** solidité d'une amitié; **s. of materials,** résistance des matériaux; **to go from s. to s.,** (*of person's health*) aller de mieux en mieux; (*of project etc*) avancer à pas de géant; (*of company, new writer etc*) connaître une réussite de plus en plus remarquable; **we went from s. to s.,** (*in business or political relationship*) nous avons progressé à pas de géant; (*in personal relationship*) on s'est entendu de mieux en mieux;

(b) (*numbers*) **to be present in great s.,** être présents en grand nombre; **to be there in full s.,** y assister *ou* y être au grand complet;

(c) *Mil* effectif(s) *m(pl)* (*d'une armée*); **war/peace s.,** effectif de guerre/de paix; **under s.,** à effectif insuffisant; **to bring a battalion up to s.,** compléter *ou* recruter un bataillon; **to be on the s.,** figurer sur les contrôles.

strengthen ['streŋθ(ə)n] **1** *vt* consolider (*un mur, une maison, une position, une amitié*); renforcer (*une poutre, un matériau, une loi, la livre sterling*); fortifier (*qn, le corps*); (r)affermir (*l'autorité de qn*); *Ch* augmenter la concentration de (*une solution*); *Typ* charger (*une couleur*); **it would s. my hand** *or* **position,** cela raffermirait ma position; **this merely strengthened their resolve,** ça n'a fait que raffermir leur résolution. **2** *vi* (*of resolve, position etc*) se fortifier, se renforcer, s'affermir; (*of sterling etc*) se raffermir; (*of patient, industry, country etc*) prendre *ou* reprendre des forces.

strengthening ['streŋθ(ə)nɪŋ] **1** *adj* (*tonic*) fortifiant; (*drink*) réconfortant. **2** *n* renforcement *m*, renforçage *m* (*d'un matériau*); consolidation *f* (*d'un mur, d'une maison*); (r)affermissement *m* (*de l'autorité de qn*); armement *m* (*d'une poutre, du béton*); **s. piece,** renfort *m*.

strenuous ['strenjʊəs] *adj* **(a)** (*work, match, day at office*) fatigant; (*effort, opposition*) acharné; (*denial*) formel, énergique; **very s.,** épuisant, très fatigant; **to make s. efforts to get sth done,** faire des efforts acharnés pour accomplir qch; **s. life,** vie toute d'effort; **(b)** (*person*) actif, énergique; (*zealous*) zélé.

strenuously ['strenjʊəslɪ] *adv* vigoureusement; (*to work*) avec acharnement; (*to deny*) formellement, énergiquement.

strenuousness ['strenjʊəsnɪs] *n* (*of work*) dureté *f*; (*of opposition*) acharnement *m*.

strep throat [strep'θrəʊt] *n US* **to have a s. t.,** avoir mal à la gorge.

streptococcal [streptəʊ'kɒk(ə)l] *adj* streptococcique.

streptococcus, *pl* **-cocci** [streptəʊ'kɒkəs, -'kɒk(s)aɪ] *n Med* streptocoque *m*.

streptomycin [streptəʊ'maɪsɪn] *n Med* streptomycine *f*.

stress¹ [stres] *n* **(a)** (*mental*) stress *m*, tension *f*; **to be under a lot of s.,** être en proie au stress, subir un stress important; **how does he react under s.?,** comment réagit-il sous le stress *ou* *F* sous pression?; **this puts our relationship under s.,** ça crée des tensions dans nos relations; **how to cope with s.,** comment vivre avec le stress; **some people thrive on s.,** certaines personnes vivent du stress; **a major s. factor,** un important facteur de stress *ou* de tension; **the stresses and strains of modern life,** les tensions et les contraintes de la vie moderne; **period of storm and s.,** période de trouble et d'agitation;

(b) *MecE etc* (*tension*) tension *f*, travail *m*, contrainte *f*; **to be in s.,** (*of beam*) travailler; **s. limit,** limite *f* de travail *ou* de fatigue;

(c) (*emphasis*) insistance *f*; *Ling* accent *m* tonique; (*in prosody*) temps marqué; **to lay s. on (sth),** insister sur, faire ressortir (*un fait*); insister sur (*un mot*); appuyer sur (*une syllabe*); **the s. falls on the last syllable,** l'accent tonique tombe sur la dernière syllabe; **s. mark,** accent écrit.

stress² *vt* **(a)** (*emphasize*) insister sur (*qch*); faire ressortir (*un fait*); souligner, insister sur (*un mot*); **she stressed that no decision had been taken,** elle a insisté sur *ou* souligné le fait qu'aucune décision n'avait été prise; **(b)** *Ling* appuyer sur (*une syllabe*); **stressed syllable,** syllabe accentuée; **(c)** *MecE* charger, fatiguer, faire travailler (*une poutre*); **to be stressed,** (*of beam*) travailler.

stressful ['stresfʊl] *adj* (*situation, travail*) stressant, qui provoque de la tension nerveuse.

stress-related ['stresrɪleɪtɪd] *adj* dû au stress; **s.-r. illnesses,** maladies dues au stress.

stretch¹ [stretʃ] *n* **(a)** (*act of stretching*) allongement *m*, extension *f*, allongement *ou* élargissement *m* par traction; déploiement *m* (*des ailes*); (*reach*) étendue *f*, portée *f* (*du bras, du sens du mot*); (*elasticity*) élasticité *f*; **with a yawn and a s.,** en bâillant et en s'étirant; *F* **to have a s.,** se dégourdir, s'étirer; *Sp* **at full s.,** à toute allure, ventre à terre; **by no s. of the imagination could I conceive that ...,** il me serait absolument impossible de croire que ...; **by no s. of the imagination could you say they're the same,** même avec beaucoup d'imagination, vous ne pourriez pas dire qu'ils sont pareils; **it's not ready yet, not by a long s.,** ce n'est pas encore prêt, et il s'en faut de beaucoup; *Mus* **s. of the fingers,** écart *m* des doigts (*au piano*); **with two-way s.,** (*of elastic fabric*) extensible dans les deux sens; **s. fabric,** tissu extensible; *Obst* **s. mark,** vergeture *f*;

(b) (*part*) étendue *f* (*de pays, d'eau*); bande *f* (*de terrain*); section *f* (*de route*); **for a long s. of time,** (pendant) longtemps; *F* **at a s., at one s.,** (tout) d'un trait, d'affilée; **she's been working for hours at a s.,** voilà des heures qu'elle travaille sans désemparer; *F* **to do a five-year s.,** (*in prison*) faire cinq ans de prison.

stretch² **1** *vt* **(a)** tendre (*un élastique, une courroie, un câble, un ressort*); étendre, élargir (*des souliers, des gants*); détirer (*le linge*); éprouver, exercer (*la patience de qn*); (*ask great effort of*) demander un effort maximum à (*qn*); grever (*les ressources*) jusqu'à la limite; forcer (*le sens d'un mot*); allonger (*le bras*); tendre, avancer (*la main*); *Art* **to s. the canvas on the frame,** tendre la toile sur le châssis; **to s. oneself,** s'étirer; **to s. one's neck to see sth,** allonger le cou pour voir qch; **to s. one's legs,** (*extend legs*) allonger les jambes; (*take short walk etc*) se dégourdir les jambes; **to s. its wings,** (*of bird*) déployer ses ailes; **he stretched his arm through the broken window,** il allongea le bras à travers le carreau cassé; **to be fully stretched,** (*of person*) donner son plein; (*of resources, services*) être sollicité à fond; **she needs a job that will s. her,** elle a besoin d'un travail qui la pousse à donner le maximum; **to s. the truth,** outrepasser les bornes de la vérité; **to s. a point,** faire une concession *ou* une exception (**for s.o.,** en faveur de qn); *F* **that's stretching it a bit!,** c'est un peu tiré par les cheveux!; **to s. a rope across a room,** tendre une corde à travers une pièce; **to s. an awning over the deck,** établir une tente sur le pont;

(b) tirer au maximum sur, utiliser au maximum (*one's income, food etc*); **how far can I s. this dish?,** pour combien de personnes au maximum ce plat suffira-t-il?

2 *vi* **(a)** (*of person, rope*) s'étirer; (*of elastic*) s'étendre, s'allonger; (*of gloves etc*) s'étendre, s'élargir; **material that stretches,** étoffe extensible; **it's rude to s.!,** il est impoli d'allonger le bras comme ça!; **she stretched across the table,** elle allongea le bras *ou* tout le corps en travers de la table; **he stretched down under the table to pick up ...,** il allongea le bras *ou* le corps sous la table pour ramasser ...; **I have to s. up to reach the top shelf,** il faut que je m'étire pour atteindre l'étagère du haut;

(b) (*of terrain, road etc*) s'étendre; **the road stretches away into the distance,** la route se déroule au loin;

(c) **my resources won't s. to that,** mes moyens (pécuniaires) ne vont pas jusque-là; **the dish will s. to six helpings,** au besoin on peut faire six portions de ce plat; **there is enough material to s. to two books,** il y a assez de matière pour en faire deux livres.

▶**stretch out** **1** *vi* **(a)** (*of person*) (*extend limbs*) s'étirer; (*of racehorses*) aller ventre à terre; (*in rowing*) souquer (sur les avirons); **(b)** (*extend*) (*of road, valley etc*) s'étendre; (*of line of runners*) s'étirer; **a barren future stretched out ahead of her,** un avenir sombre se profilait devant elle. **2** *vtsep* (*extend*) allonger (*le bras*); tendre, avancer (*la main*); **to lie stretched out on the ground,** être allongé par terre de tout son long; **we could s. the meat out till Sunday,** nous pourrions faire durer la viande jusqu'à dimanche.

stretcher ['stretʃər] *n* **(a)** (*for casualty*) brancard *m*, civière *f*; **he was carried** *or* **taken off on a s.,** on l'a emmené sur une *ou* en civière; **s. bearer,** brancardier *m*, ambulancier *m*; **he's a s. case,** *Med* il faut l'emporter sur une civière; *Fig F* (*having been beaten up etc*) il est bon pour l'hôpital; **s. party,** détachement *m ou* équipe *f* de brancardiers; **(b)** (*crosspiece*) bois *m* d'écartement (*de hamac*); traverse *f* (*de tente*); baleine *f* (*d'un parapluie*); barreau *m*, bâton *m* (*de chaise*); **(c)** *Nau* barre *f* des pieds, traversin *m* (*d'une embarcation*); **(d)** (*stretching device*) tendeur *m*, tenseur *m* (*de hauban*); *Art* **canvas s.,** châssis *m* (*de toile d'artiste*).

▶**stretcher off** *vtsep* (*remove on stretcher*) emmener en civière.

stretchy ['stretʃɪ] *adj F* élastique, extensible.

strew [struː] *vt* (*pp* **strewed** [struːd] *or* **strewn** [struːn]) **(a)** **to s. sand over the floor,** jeter *ou* répandre du sable sur le plancher; **toys were strewn over** *or* **around** *or* **on the floor,** des jouets étaient éparpillés sur le plancher; **(b)** **to s. the floor with sand/flowers,** (re)couvrir le plancher de sable/de fleurs; **the ground was strewn with rushes,** une jonchée de roseaux recouvrait le sol, le sol était jonché de roseaux.

strewth [struːθ] *int Sl* ça alors!

striated [straɪ'eɪtɪd] *adj* strié; **striated muscle,** muscle strié.

stricken¹ ['strɪk(ə)n] *adj esp Lit* **(a)** (*person*) (*with disease, injury etc*) affligé, éprouvé, frappé; **s. with grief,** accablé de douleur; **s. with guilt,** frappé de remords; **s. by a disease,** frappé d'une maladie; **the s. city,** la ville sinistrée; **the s. vessel,** le vaisseau en détresse *ou* naufragé; *F* **he's s. with her,** il en pince pour elle; **(b)** (*in hunting*) (*daim*) blessé.

stricken² *see* **STRIKE²**.

strict [strɪkt] *adj* **(a)** (*teacher, boss, parent etc*) strict, sévère; **to be s. with s.o.,** être sévère *ou* strict avec *ou* envers qn; **(b)** (*règlement, étiquette*) strict, péremptoire; (*discipline, régime*) sévère, strict; (*jeûne*) strict, austère; **s. morals,** morale stricte *ou* rigide; mœurs *fpl* sévères *ou* strictes; **s. Moslem,** musulman de stricte obédience; **she gave s. orders,** elle a donné des ordres formels *ou* stricts; **to keep a s. watch over s.o.,** exercer sur qn une surveillance rigoureuse *ou* stricte; **(c)** (*exact*) exact, strict; **the s. minimum,** le strict minimum; **in the s. sense of the word,** au sens précis *ou* strict du mot; **to observe s. neutrality,** observer une neutralité rigoureuse *ou* stricte; **in strictest confidence,** à titre tout à fait *ou* strictement confidentiel.

strictly ['strɪktlɪ] *adv* (*see adj*) **(a)** strictement, sévèrement; (*traité, élevé*) avec rigueur; **(b)** strictement; **smoking (is) s. prohibited,** il est strictement *ou* formellement interdit de fumer; **it is s. forbidden,** c'est absolument *ou* strictement défendu; **to guard s.o. s.,** surveiller étroitement qn; **(c)** exactement, rigoureusement; **s. (speaking),** à proprement parler; **this rule was s. observed,** cette règle a été rigoureusement *ou* strictement observée.

strictness ['strɪktnɪs] *n* **(a)** sévérité *f* (*de la discipline*); **(b)** rigueur *f* (*des règles*); **(c)** exactitude *f*, rigueur *f*, précision *f* (*d'une traduction*).

stricture ['strɪktjər] *n* **(a)** (*usu pl*) **to pass strictures (up)on s.o./sth,** diriger ses critiques *fpl* contre qn/qch; **(b)** restriction *f*, limitation *f*; **(c)** *Med* rétrécissement *m* (*du canal de l'urètre*); étranglement *m* (*de l'intestin*).

stride¹ [straɪd] *n* **(a)** (grand) pas *m*, enjambée *f*; (*when running*) foulée *f*; **to shorten/lengthen one's s.,** raccourcir/allonger le pas *ou Sp* la foulée; *Fig* **to make great strides,** faire de grands progrès *ou* des progrès rapides; *Fig* **to take sth in one's s.** *or US* **in s.,** (*do easily*) faire qch sans le moindre effort; (*not be disconcerted by*) ne pas se laisser troubler par qch; **after 6 months she just turned round and left him, but he took it all in his s.,** après six mois elle l'a quitté brusquement, mais ça ne l'a pas troublé pour autant; **sometimes life is like that, you just have to learn to take it all in your s.,** c'est la vie, il faut savoir la prendre comme elle vient; **eventually you come to take it all in your s.,** on finit par s'y faire; **to get into** *or Sl* **to hit one's s.,** (*in walking*) prendre son allure normale; (*in working*) attraper la cadence; *Fig* **to put s.o. off his s.,** faire perdre la cadence à qn;

(b) *esp Austr F* **strides,** (*trousers*) fute *m*, futal *m*.

stride² *v* (*pt* **strode** [strəʊd]; *pp* **stridden** ['strɪd(ə)n]) **1** *vi* marcher à grands pas *ou* à grandes enjambées; **she strode into the room,** elle est entrée dans la pièce à grande enjambées; **to s. along/away,** avancer/s'éloigner à grands pas; **science is striding further ahead each year,** la science avance *ou* progresse à pas de géant d'année en année; **she just strode straight up to him and said ...,** elle se dirigea droit vers lui à grandes enjambées et dit ...; **Bonaparte strode impatiently up and down the room,** Bonaparte arpentait impatiemment la pièce; **to s. over sth,** enjamber qch. **2** *vt Lit* enjamber (*un fossé etc*).

stridency ['straɪdənsɪ] *n* stridence *f*; (*of protests*) véhémence *f*.

strident ['straɪdənt] *adj* strident; (*colours*) criard; (*protests*) véhément.

stridently ['straɪdəntlɪ] *adv* (*parler*) d'une voix stridente; (*rire, crier*) de façon stridente; (*protester*) avec véhémence.

strife [straɪf] *n* lutte *f*, contestation *f*, différends *mpl*; **domestic s.,** querelles *fpl* de ménage; **after years of industrial s.,** après des années de conflits sociaux; *Lit* **to be at s.,** être en conflit *ou* en lutte (**with,** avec).

strike¹ [straɪk] *n* **(a)** *Ind* grève *f*; **lightning s.,** grève surprise; **sit-down s.,** grève sur le tas; **sympathy s.,** grève de solidarité; **to be on s.,** être en grève; **to go on** *or* **come out on s.,** se mettre en grève, *F* débrayer; **to bring people out on s.,** amener des gens à faire grève; **to go on hunger s.,** (*of prisoner*) faire la grève de la faim; **s. pay,** allocation *f* de grève; **(b)** *Min* rencontre *f* (*de minerai, pétrole*); découverte *f* (*d'un gisement*); **another major oil s.,** nouvelle découverte d'un important gisement de pétrole; *F* **lucky s.,** coup *m* de veine; **(c)** (*blow*) coup *m*; sonnerie *f* (*d'horloge*); *Mil* raid *m* (**on,** sur); *Fishing* (*by angler*) ferrage *m*; (*by fish*) mordage *m*; (*baseball*) balle manquée (*par le batteur*); (*tenpin bowling*) honneur *m* double; *Mil* **first s. weapon,** arme *f* de première frappe; *Mil Av* **air s.,** raid *m*, intervention aérienne; **s. aircraft,** avions *mpl* d'assaut.

strike² *v* (*pt* **struck** [strʌk]; *pp* **struck,** *Arch* **stricken** ['strɪk(ə)n]) **1** *vt* **(a)** (*hit*) frapper (*qn, qch*); frapper (*une monnaie, une médaille*); *Mus* frapper (*les touches du piano*); toucher de (*la harpe*); **to s. s.o. in the face,** frapper qn à la figure; **to s. s.o. a blow,** porter *ou* assener un coup à qn; **without striking a blow,** sans coup férir; **to be struck by a stone,** être frappé d'une pierre; **to be struck by a heavy sea,** (*of ship*) essuyer un coup de mer; **ready to s. a blow for freedom of speech,** prêt à se battre pour défendre la liberté de parole; *Fig* **in his speech he struck a blow for ...,** par son discours, il a fait avancer ...; *Fig* **to s. a blow at sth,** taper sur qch; **to s. a chord,** plaquer un accord; *Fig* **that strikes a familiar note,** cela fait l'effet du déjà vu *ou* du déjà entendu; **the clock strikes the hour,** l'horloge sonne l'heure; **as the clock struck 10,** lorsque l'horloge sonna dix coups;

(b) (*collide with*) frapper *ou* heurter *ou* donner *ou* buter contre (*qch*); **his head struck the pavement,** sa tête a heurté le trottoir; **to s. (the) bottom,** (*of ship*) toucher (le fond), talonner; **struck by lightning,** (*maison*) frappée par la foudre; (*arbre, personne*) foudroyé; **lightning had struck the house,** la foudre était tombée sur la maison; **to s. a mine,** (*of ship*) heurter une mine; **to s. a pedestrian,** (*of car*) heurter un piéton; **a sound struck my ear,** un bruit frappa mon oreille;

(c) to s. terror into s.o., frapper qn de terreur; **it struck fear into their hearts,** cela frappa leurs cœurs de terreur; **to s. s.o. with surprise,** frapper qn d'étonnement; **struck with terror/panic,** saisi d'effroi/pris de panique; **to be struck dumb,** être frappé de mutisme;

(d) allumer, frotter (*une allumette*); faire jaillir (*des étincelles*); *El* **to s. the arc,** produire l'arc (*entre les charbons*); *Br Sl* **s. a light!,** nom de Dieu!;

(e) (*make given impression*) faire une impression sur (*qn*); (*impress*) impressionner (*qn*); frapper (*l'œil, l'imagination*); **how does/did she s. you?,** quelle impression vous fait-elle/vous a-t-elle faite?; **he strikes me as (being) sincere,** il me paraît sincère; **the place struck her as familiar,** l'endroit lui a paru familier; **that is how it struck me,** voilà l'effet que cela m'a fait; **did it never s. you that you weren't wanted there?,** ne vous est-il jamais venu à l'esprit que vous étiez de trop?; **what struck me was his brazen impudence,** ce qui m'a frappé, c'est son effronterie cynique; **the thought struck me that ...,** l'idée m'est venue *ou* il m'est venu à l'idée que ...; **it strikes me that we'd do better to say no,** j'ai la nette impression que nous ferions mieux de dire non;

(f) (*discover*) tomber sur, découvrir (*une piste*); découvrir (*un filon d'or*); **to s. oil,** atteindre une nappe pétrolifère, rencontrer *ou* toucher le pétrole; *Fig* trouver le filon; *F* **she has struck it rich,** elle tient le filon;

(g) (*lower*) démonter (*une tente*); *Nau* amener, caler (*une voile*); abaisser, dépasser, caler (*un mât*); *Th* **to s. the set,** démonter le décor; **to s. camp,** lever le camp; **to s. one's flag** *or* **one's colours,** *Nau* amener *ou* rentrer son pavillon, mettre pavillon bas; *Fig* (*surrender*) se rendre;

(h) to s. an attitude, poser;

(i) to s. an average, établir *ou* prendre une moyenne; **to s. a bargain,** faire *ou* conclure un marché; **to s. a balance between X and Y,** trouver un équilibre entre X et Y; **to s. an agreement,** conclure un accord;

(j) (*remove, delete*) enlever; **that remark must be struck** *or US* **stricken from the record,** cette remarque doit être retirée du procès-verbal;

(k) (*of plant*) **to s. root,** prendre racine.

2 *vi* **(a)** (*attack*) attaquer; (*hit*) frapper; (*of serpent*) foncer; **don't wait for the enemy to s.,** n'attendez pas que l'ennemi attaque; *Fig* **to s. at sth,** menacer qch; **these reforms s. deep at the heart of our traditional way of life,** ces réformes attaquent profondément notre mode de vie traditionnel; **to s. home,** frapper juste; *Prov* **s. while the iron is hot,** il faut battre le fer tant il est chaud; **the terrorists struck twice,** les terroristes ont frappé deux fois; **where the missile struck,** là où le missile a frappé;

(b) (*of clock*) sonner; *Fig* **her hour has struck,** son heure est venue;

(c) *Ind* se mettre en grève, *F* débrayer; **to s. for better conditions,** se mettre en grève pour de meilleures conditions de travail; **striking workers,** ouvriers *mpl* en grève;

(d) (*travel, head*) prendre (*une certaine direction*); **to s. across country,** prendre à travers champs; **they then struck west,** ils sont ensuite partis vers l'ouest;

(e) (*of roots*) s'enfoncer (**into sth,** dans qch); (*of cutting*) prendre (racine);

(f) *Nau* (*to touch bottom*) (*of ship*) toucher (*le fond*), talonner.

►**strike back 1** *vtsep* (*hit return blow*) **to s. s.o. back,** répondre au coup de qn; **if anyone strikes me I s. him back,** si quelqu'un me frappe je rends le coup. **2** *vi* **(a)** (*hit return blow*) rendre un coup; *Fig* (*retaliate*) effectuer des représailles; **to s. back at the enemy,** répliquer à l'ennemi, contre-attaquer; **the government struck back at its critics,** le gouvernement a répliqué à ses critiques; **(b)** (*go back*) rebrousser chemin.

►**strike down** *vtsep* (*knock down*) renverser (*qch, qn*); *Fig* **struck down by disease,** terrassé par la maladie.

►**strike off 1** *vtsep* **(a)** (*remove by hitting*) enlever d'un coup; trancher (*la tête de qn*); **(b)** (*delete*) **to s. off a name from a list, to s. a name off a list,** biffer *ou* rayer un nom d'une liste; **to be struck off,** (*of doctor, solicitor*) être radié (de l'exercice de sa profession); **(c)** *Com* (*deduct*) **to s. off £5,** faire une réduction de *ou* déduire cinq livres; **(d)** *Typ* tirer (*tant d'exemplaires*). **2** *vi* (*travel, head in*) **to s. off to the left,** (*of person*) prendre à gauche; (*of road*) tourner à gauche.

►**strike out 1** *vtsep* (*delete*) rayer, biffer, raturer, barrer (*un mot*); **s. out whichever does not apply,** rayer la mention inutile. **2** *vi* **(a)** (*hit out*) **to s. out at s.o.,** allonger *ou* porter un coup à qn; *Fig* (*criticize, attack*) attaquer qn; **to s. out right and left,** frapper à droite et à gauche; **(b)** (*travel, head*) **I struck out for the shore,** j'ai commencé à nager *ou* (*rowing*) ramer dans la direction du rivage; *Fig* **to s. out in a new direction,** (*in life, thinking etc*) prendre une direction nouvelle; **(c)** (*become independent*) **to s. out for oneself, to s. out on one's own,** voler de ses propres ailes; **(d)** *Baseball* sortir (du jeu).

►**strike up 1** *vtsep* entonner (*une chanson*); commencer de *ou* à jouer (*un morceau*); **to s. up a friendship with s.o.,** se lier d'amitié avec qn, se prendre d'amitié pour qn; **to s. up an acquaintance with s.o.,** lier connaissance avec qn; **to s. up a conversation with s.o.,** entrer en conversation avec qn; **they immediately struck up a conversation,** ils sont immédiatement entrés en conversation. **2** *vi* (*begin*) **on his arrival the band struck up,** à son arrivée la fanfare attaqua un morceau.

strikebound ['straɪkbaʊnd] *adj* paralysé par une *ou* la grève.

strikebreaker ['straɪkbreɪkər] *n Ind* briseur, -euse de grève, *F* renard *m*, jaune *m*.

striker ['straɪkər] *n* **(a)** *Ind* gréviste *mf*; **(b)** *Sp Fb* buteur *m*; *Tennis* relanceur, -euse; *Baseball* batteur *m*; **(c)** (*device*) frappeur *m*; (*of clock*) marteau *m*; (*of firearm*) percuteur *m*.

striking ['straɪkɪŋ] **1** *adj* **(a)** (*spectacle*) frappant, saisissant; (*trait*) saillant; (*situation*) dramatique; **he was**

a s. figure, il était impressionnant; **of s. beauty,** d'une beauté frappante; **a s. similarity,** une ressemblance frappante;

(b) s. clock, pendule *f* à sonnerie;

(c) (*workers*) en grève.

2 *n* **(a)** (*blows*) coups *mpl*; frappe *f* (*de la monnaie*); frottement *m* (*d'une allumette*); *El* amorçage *m* (*de l'arc*); **s. is forbidden,** il est interdit de frapper; **within s. distance,** à portée de la main; **we were within s. distance of the summit,** nous étions à un jet de pierre du sommet; *Mil* **s. power,** puissance *f ou* force *f* de frappe; **s. surface,** frottoir *m*;

(b) (*in horticulture*) **s. (root),** reprise *f* (*d'une bouture*);

(c) *Nau* calage *m* (*d'une voile*); **s. camp,** levée *f* du camp;

(d) établissement *m* (*d'une moyenne*);

(e) sonnerie *f* (*d'une horloge*); **s. mechanism,** sonnerie.

striking down *n* abattage *m*, renversement *m*.

striking off *n* rayure *f* (*d'un nom*); radiation *f* (*d'un avoué, d'un médecin*).

striking out *n* rayure *f*, biffage *m* (*d'un mot*).

strikingly ['straɪkɪŋlɪ] *adv* d'une manière frappante *ou* saisissante; **s. beautiful,** d'une beauté frappante.

strine [straɪn] *n Hum F* (*langue*) anglais australien.

string¹ [strɪŋ] *n* **(a)** ficelle *f*; (*cord*) corde *f*, cordon *m*; (*piece of string*) bout *m* de ficelle; **ball of s.,** pelote *f* de ficelle; *F* **to have s.o. on a s.,** mener qn par le bout du nez; *F* **to keep s.o. on a s.,** tenir qn dans l'incertitude; (*keep control over*) tenir qn en laisse; *Fig* **(with) no strings (attached),** sans conditions, sans condition aucune; **the strings of a marionette,** les fils *mpl* d'une marionnette; *Fig* **to pull the strings,** tirer les ficelles; *Fig* **to pull strings,** faire jouer ses relations *ou F* le piston; **s. bag,** filet *m* (à provisions); *Br* **s. vest,** maillot *m* de corps à grosses mailles;

(b) (*in plant*) fibre *f*, filament *m* (*de plante*); **s. bean,** haricot vert;

(c) *Mus* corde *f* (*de violon, piano*); (*in archery*) corde (*d'un arc*); *Tennis* cordes, cordage *m* (*d'une raquette de tennis*); **the strings of a violin,** la monture d'un violon; **guitar/violin s.,** corde de guitare/de violon; **the strings,** (*in orchestra*) les (instruments *ou* joueurs d'instruments à) cordes; *Sp* **first s.,** meilleur athlète (*sélectionné pour une épreuve*); *Horseracing* premier champion (*d'une écurie*); **second s.,** second athlète sélectionné; *Horseracing* second champion; *Fig* **to touch a s. in s.o.'s heart,** faire vibrer une corde dans le cœur de qn; *Fig* **to have more than one s. to one's bow,** avoir plus d'une corde à son arc; **s. bass,** contrebasse *f*; **s. orchestra, s. band,** orchestre *m* à cordes; **s. quartet,** quatuor *m* à cordes;

(d) chapelet *m* (*d'oignons, d'îles*); brochette *f* (*de décorations*); file *f* (*de véhicules*); rame *f* (*de wagons*); train *m* (*de péniches*); suite *f*, série *f* (*de mots*); **s. of beads,** collier *m*; *Rel* chapelet; **a whole s. of children/of names,** toute une kyrielle d'enfants/de noms; *Horseracing* **Lord Derby's s. (of horses),** l'écurie *f* de Lord Derby;

(e) *Comptr* suite *f*, chaîne *f*; **s. of characters,** suite de caractères.

string² *vt* (*pp & pt* **strung** [strʌŋ]) **(a)** (*fit with strings*) garnir *ou* munir (*qch*) de cordes; corder (*une raquette de tennis etc*); mettre les cordes à, monter (*un violon*); **(b)** bander (*un arc*); **to be highly strung,** (*of person, horse*) être nerveux; (*likely to suffer for emotional reasons*) impressionnable; **(c)** enfiler (*des perles*); **to s. fairy lamps across a garden,** accrocher des guirlandes de lampions dans un jardin; *Fig* **to s. sentences together,** enfiler des phrases; **he can't s. two sentences together,** il est incapable d'aligner trois mots; **(d)** *Culin* **to s. beans,** ôter les fils des haricots.

►**string along** *vtsep F* (*deceitfully encourage*) duper, tromper (*qn*); **they're just stringing you along,** ils sont en train de te faire marcher.

►**string along with** *vipo F* (*accompany*) accompagner, faire route avec (*qn*).

►**string out 1** *vi* (*form long line*) s'espacer; **the field strung out behind,** le peloton des coureurs s'égrenait *ou* s'allongeait derrière. **2** *vtsep* faire traîner (*qch*) en longueur; **the TV series was strung out over six weeks,** le feuilleton (de) télé a traîné pendant six semaines; **troops strung out over two hundred kilometres,** les troupes s'échelonnaient sur 200 kilomètres.

►**string up** *vtsep* **(a)** *F* (*hang*) pendre (*qn*) haut et court; **(b)** *F* (*become nervous*) **to get strung up,** s'en faire, s'énerver (**about sth,** à propos de qch).

stringboard ['strɪŋbɔːd] *n Constr* limon *m* (d'escalier).

stringed [strɪŋd] *adj Mus* (*instrument*) à cordes.

stringency ['strɪndʒənsɪ] *n* **(a)** rigueur *f*, sévérité *f* (*des règles*); **(b)** *Fin* resserrement *m* (*du marché*).

stringent ['strɪndʒənt] *adj* **(a)** (*règlement*) rigoureux, strict; (*économies*) rigoureux; **(b)** *Fin* (*marché*) tendu, serré.

stringently ['strɪndʒəntlɪ] *adv* rigoureusement, strictement.

stringer ['strɪŋər] *n* **(a)** (*person*) monteur *m* de cordes (*de piano*); *Journ* reporter local; **(b)** *Constr* longrine *f*, longeron *m* (*d'une charpente*); *Aut Av* longeron (*du châssis, de l'aile*).

stringing ['strɪŋɪŋ] *n* **(a)** (*act*) montage *m* (*d'un violon*); cordage *m* (*d'une raquette*); bandage *m* (*d'un arc*); enfilement *m* (*de perles*); **(b)** (*strings*) cordage *m*, cordes *fpl* (*d'une raquette*).

stringpiece ['strɪŋpiːs] *n Constr* longeron *m*, longrine *f*.

string-puller ['strɪŋpʌlər] *n F* **he could be a useful s.-p.,** il peut nous *etc* être utile s'il fait jouer ses relations.

stringy ['strɪŋɪ] *adj* (*vegetables*) fibreux, filandreux; **s. meat,** viande filandreuse.

strip¹ [strɪp] *n* **(a)** bande *f* (*de tissu, de papier*); lambeau *m* (*de tissu*); lame *f*, lamelle *f* (*de métal*); bande, langue *f* (*de terrain*); *F* **to tear s.o. off a s.,** laver la tête à qn, donner *ou* passer un savon à qn; **narrow s.,** bandelette *f*; *Med* **dressing s.,** bande à pansement; **feeding** *or* **loading s.,** (*of machine gun*) bande-chargeur *f*, *pl* bandes-chargeurs; *Av* **landing s.,** bande (d'atterrissage), piste *f* (de fortune); **take-off s.,** bande d'envol; **s. cartoon, comic s.,** bande dessinée; **s. light,** rampe *f* au néon fluorescente; **s. lighting,** éclairage *m* au néon *ou* fluorescent; *esp Am Min* **s. mining,** exploitation *f* à ciel ouvert; **(b)** *Sp F* tenue *f*, couleurs *fpl* (*d'une équipe de football*).

strip² *n* **to do a s.,** se déshabiller (*en public*); **s. club,** boîte *f* de strip-tease; *Cards* **s. poker,** strip-poker *m*; **s. show,** (spectacle *m* de) strip-tease.

strip³ *v* (**-pp-**) **1** *vt* **(a)** (*undress*) mettre (*qn*) tout nu, déshabiller, dévêtir (*qn*); **to s. s.o. to the skin, to s. s.o. naked,** mettre qn à poil; **stripped to the waist,** nu jusqu'à la ceinture, torse nu;

(b) to s. s.o. of sth, dépouiller *ou* déposséder qn de qch; **to s. s.o. of his** *or* **her clothes,** dépouiller qn de ses vêtements; **trees stripped of their leaves,** arbres dépouillés de leurs feuilles; **stripped of all his worldly goods,** dépouillé de tous ses biens; **to be stripped of one's title/rank/office,** être dépouillé de son titre/rang/poste;

(c) défaire (*un lit*); *Nau* déshabiller, décapeler (*un mât, une vergue*); *El* dénuder (*un câble*); *Metal* démouler, décocher (*une pièce coulée*); *Phot* pelliculer (*un cliché*); **to s. a tree,** (*of leaves*) effeuiller un arbre; (*of bark*) écorcer un arbre; (*of branches*) ébrancher un arbre; (*of fruit*) défruiter un arbre; **to s. a wall,** arracher le papier d'un mur; **thieves have stripped the house,** des cambrioleurs ont complètement vidé la maison; *Mil F* **to s. an N.C.O.,** dégrader un sous-officier; **to s. an engine/a gun,** démonter un moteur/un fusil; *Aut* **stripped chassis,** châssis nu;

(d) to s. sth from sth, enlever *ou* ôter qch de qch.

2 *vi* **(a)** (*of person*) se déshabiller, se dévêtir; **to s. to the skin,** se mettre tout nu, se mettre à poil; **to s. to the waist,** se mettre nu jusqu'à la ceinture;

(b) (*of bark, negative, film*) **to s. (off),** s'enlever, se détacher.

►**strip down 1** *vtsep* **(a)** (*dismantle*) démonter (*un moteur, un fusil*); **(b)** (*remove non-essential parts from*) enlever les parties non essentielles de (*un vélo etc*); *Fig* **to s. a theory down to essentials,** simplifier une théorie pour n'en garder que l'essentiel. **2** *vi* (*undress*) se déshabiller.

►**strip off 1** *vi* **(a)** (*undress*) se déshabiller; **(b)** (*of wallpaper etc*) se décoller, s'enlever. **2** *vtsep* (*remove*) gratter (*paint*); décoller (*wallpaper*); **to s. the paint off a wall,** enlever *ou* gratter la peinture d'un mur.

stripe¹ [straɪp] *n* **(a)** raie *f*, barre *f* (*d'un tissu*); raie, rayure *f*, zébrure *f* (*du pelage*); bande *f* (*de pantalon*); *Mil* galon *m*; **black with a red s.,** noir à raie rouge; **to mark sth with stripes,** rayer *ou* zébrer qch; *Mil* **long service s.,** chevron *m*; *Mil* **to get/lose a s.,** être promu/dégradé; **(b)** *Am* **a man of that s.,** un homme de ce genre.

stripe² *vt* rayer, barrer (*un tissu*).

striped [straɪpt] *adj* **(a)** (*chaussettes*) à raies, à rayures; (*pelage*) rayé, zébré; **red and blue s. jacket,** veston rayé rouge et bleu; **(b)** *Anat* (*muscle*) strié.

stripling ['strɪplɪŋ] *n* tout jeune homme, adolescent *m*.

strippagram ['strɪpəgræm] *n* = message délivré par une

jeune fille qui fait un strip-tease.

stripped-down [strɪpt'daʊn] *adj* réduit à sa plus simple expression, simplifié; *Comptr* **s.-d. version,** version simplifiée; **a s.-d. version of Shakespeare's play,** une version simplifiée de la pièce de Shakespeare.

stripper ['strɪpər] *n* **(a)** (*person*) (*striptease artist*) strip-teaseuse *f*; *Tex* teilleur, -euse (*de lin, de chanvre*); *Metal* démouleur *m*; **male s.,** strip-teaseur *m*; **(b) (paint) s.,** décapant *m*; **wallpaper s.,** produit *m* pour décoller le papier peint.

stripping ['strɪpɪŋ] *n* **(a)** (*of person*) déshabillage *m*, déshabillement *m*; **(b)** dégarnissement *m* (*d'un lit*); dénudation *f* (*d'un câble*); effeuillage *m* (*d'un arbre*); démontage *m* (*d'un moteur, d'un fusil*); *Ch* grattage *m*, décapage *m* (*d'une surface*); *Nau* décapelage *m*, déshabillage (*d'un mât, d'une vergue*); *Metal* démoulage *m*, décochage *m* (*d'une pièce coulée*); *Phot* pelliculage *m* (*d'un cliché*); **wallpaper s.,** décollage *m* du papier peint.

strip-search[1] ['strɪpsɜːtʃ] *n* fouille *f* d'une personne dévêtue; **to undergo a s.-s.,** devoir se déshabiller afin d'être fouillé.

strip-search[2] *vt* faire déshabiller (*qn*) pour le fouiller.

striptease ['strɪptiːz] *n* (spectacle *m* de) strip-tease *m*; **to do a s.,** faire un strip-tease; **s. artist,** strip-teaseuse *f*.

stripy ['straɪpɪ] *adj F* = **STRIPED (a)**.

strive [straɪv] *vi* (*pt* **strove** [strəʊv]; *pp* **striven** ['strɪv(ə)n]) **(a) to s. to do sth,** s'efforcer de faire qch, faire des efforts pour faire qch; **s. as we might,** quels que soient nos efforts; **to s. for sth,** essayer d'obtenir qch; **to s. after effect,** chercher à faire de l'effet; **(b) to s. against s.o.,** lutter contre qn.

strobe [strəʊb] *n Phys etc F* stroboscope *m*; **s. lighting,** éclairage *m* stroboscopique.

stroboscope ['strəʊbəʊskəʊp] *n* stroboscope *m*.

strode *see* **STRIDE[2]**.

stroke[1] [strəʊk] *n* **(a)** (*blow*) coup *m*; **to receive twenty strokes,** recevoir vingt coups (*de férule*); **to fell a tree at a s.,** abattre un arbre d'un seul coup; **to abolish a practice at a s.,** abolir un usage d'un seul coup; **s. of lightning,** coup de foudre;

(b) coup *m* (*d'aile, d'aviron*); coup, trait *m* (*de lime*); *MecE* mouvement *m*, course *f* (*du piston, du chariot etc*); *Swimming* brasse *f*; **whose s. is it?,** (*at billiards*) à qui de jouer?; *Golf* **s. play competition,** concours *m* par coups; (*in rowing*) **to lengthen the s.,** allonger la nage; **to keep s.,** nager ensemble, garder la cadence; *Fig* **to be off one's s.,** être mal en train; *Fig* **to put s.o. off his or her s.,** déconcerter qn; **the swimming strokes,** les nages *fpl*; **s.'s length,** nagée *f*; **arm s.,** brasse, **not to do a s. of work,** ne rien faire; **s. of (good) luck,** coup de bonheur *ou* de fortune, aubaine *f*; **s. of wit/of genius,** trait d'esprit/de génie; **bold s.,** coup hardi;

(c) coup *m* (*d'horloge etc*); **on the s. of nine,** sur le coup de neuf heures, à neuf heures sonnantes *ou* tapantes; **to arrive on the s. (of time),** arriver à l'heure juste;

(d) *Med* **(apoplectic) s.,** attaque *f* d'apoplexie; **to have a s.,** tomber en apoplexie, avoir une attaque d'apoplexie;

(e) (*mark*) trait *m*; *Typ* barre *f*; (*of pencil, brush*) coup *m* de crayon *ou* de pinceau; (*of pen*) trait de plume; **oblique s.,** barre transversale; **at the s. of a pen,** d'un coup de crayon; **with a few bold strokes of the brush,** de quelques hardis coups de pinceau; *Fig* **to put the finishing strokes to one's work,** apporter les dernières touches *ou* mettre la dernière main à son travail;

(f) (*person*) chef *m* de nage; **to row s.,** donner la nage, être chef de nage; **s. oar,** (*oar*) aviron *m* du chef de nage; (*person*) chef de nage.

stroke[2] (*in rowing*) **1** *vt* être chef de nage de (*un canot*). **2** *vi* être chef de nage (*d'un canot*), donner la nage.

stroke[3] *n* **(a)** (*caress*) caresse *f* (de la main); **to give s.o./sth a s.,** caresser qn/qch; **(b)** *esp Am* (*remark*) **(positive) s.,** encouragement *m*; **to give s.o. a s.,** encourager qn.

stroke[4] *vt* (*caress*) passer la main sur, lisser avec la main, caresser de la main (*une fourrure, les cheveux de qn*); **to s. one's chin,** se flatter le menton de la main; **to s. one's hair down or into place,** lisser ses cheveux; **s. the ointment evenly over the ...,** passer la pommade en couche régulière sur le ...; **he stroked the ball into the net,** il fit glisser le ballon dans le filet.

-stroke [strəʊk] *suff* **two/four-s. engine,** moteur à deux/à quatre temps.

stroking ['strəʊkɪŋ] *n* caresses *fpl* (de la main).

stroll[1] [strəʊl] *n* petit tour, flânerie *f*, *F* balade *f*; **to take or go for a s.,** (aller) faire un tour.

stroll[2] *vi* flâner, *F* se balader; **to s. around town,** flâner en ville; **she strolled in an hour late and didn't even say sorry,** elle est arrivée mine de rien avec une heure de retard et ne s'est même pas excusée; **he strolled across to me,** il s'avança tranquillement vers moi.

stroller ['strəʊlər] *n* **(a)** (*person*) flâneur, -euse, promeneur, -euse; **(b)** *Am* (*pushchair*) poussette *f* (d'enfant).

strolling ['strəʊlɪŋ] *adj* vagabond, errant; **s. player,** comédien ambulant; **s. players,** troupe ambulante.

strong [strɒŋ] **1** *adj* (*comp* **stronger** ['strɒŋgər]; *superl* **strongest** ['strɒŋgɪst]) **(a)** (*physically*) fort, puissant; (*horse*) vigoureux; (*character*) fort, ferme; (*constitution*) fort; **s. nerves,** nerfs bien équilibrés *ou* solides; **he's not very s.,** il n'est pas très fort; **to be s. in the arm,** avoir le bras fort; **she's as s. as a horse or an ox,** elle est forte comme un cheval *ou* un bœuf;

(b) (*healthy*) vigoureux, robuste; **he isn't very s.,** il n'est pas très robuste; **to be getting stronger,** reprendre ses forces; **his eyesight is not as s. as it was,** sa vue a baissé *ou* n'est pas aussi bonne qu'elle a été;

(c) (*forceful, powerful*) (*motives, character, will, argument, consideration*) puissant; (*reasons*) solide; (*attraction*) fort; (*protest, plea*) puissant, énergique; (*food, taste, drink, curry*) fort; (*country*) puissant; (*candidate*) sérieux; *Fin* (*currency*) fort; *Com* (*market*) ferme; *El* (*current*) fort, intense; (*feelings*) fort; **if you have s. feelings about it,** si ça vous tient très à cœur; **the pound is getting stronger,** la livre sterling se raffermit; **not in a very s. position,** pas dans une position très forte; **s. conviction,** ferme conviction; **you've got to be s. and say 'no',** il faut être ferme et dire 'non'; **be s.,** (*be brave*) sois courageux *ou* fort; **s. in numbers,** en grand nombre; **company two hundred s.,** compagnie forte de deux cents personnes; **the wind is growing stronger,** le vent forcit; **the s. arm of the law,** l'autorité publique; *Mus* **s. beat,** temps fort; **a s. chance,** une forte chance; **s. colour,** couleur forte *ou* intense; **a s. drink,** une boisson forte; **s. evidence,** preuves convaincantes; *Nau* **s. gale,** gros vent; **s. light,** lumière forte *ou* vive; **s. likeness,** grande *ou* forte ressemblance; **s. measures,** mesures *fpl* énergiques; *Fig* **I found the book rather s. meat,** j'ai trouvé ce livre plutôt corsé; **politeness is not her s. point,** la politesse n'est pas son fort; **s. reason,** raison majeure; **to have a strong smell,** (*of food*) sentir fort; **s. solution,** solution forte *ou* concentrée; **to give s. support to s.o./a measure,** donner un grand appui à *ou* appuyer fortement qn/une mesure; *Cards* **s. suit,** (*couleur*) longue *f*; *Nau* **s. tide,** grande *ou* forte marée; **s. voice,** voix forte *ou* puissante; **s. wind,** grand vent; **s. wine,** vin corsé;

(d) (*resistant*) (*rope, cloth, shoes*) solide, résistant, (*building*) solide, résistant, robuste;

(e) (*supporter*) ardent, vigoureux; **a s. Protestant community,** une communauté Protestante vigoureuse; **the religion which is strongest in ...,** la religion la plus forte en ...;

(f) to be strong on sth, (*good at*) être fort en qch;

(g) (*accent, syllable, verb*) fort;

(h) s. language, (*forceful*) langage énergique *ou* vigoureux; (*swearwords*) grossièretés *fpl*; **to write in s. terms to s.o.,** écrire une lettre énergique à qn; **to put sth in the strongest possible terms,** exprimer qch dans des termes les plus énergiques possible.

2 *n* **the s.,** (*used as pl*) les forts, les puissants.

3 *adv F* **to be going s.,** (*be in good condition etc*) aller *ou* marcher bien; **she's going s.,** elle est toujours d'attaque *ou* solide au poste; **how's grandfather? — still going s.,** comment va le grandpère? — toujours solide; **you're pitching it a bit s.,** vous y allez un peu fort.

strong-arm[1] ['strɒŋɑːm] *adj* **to use s.-a. tactics,** utiliser la méthode forte; **by s.-a. methods,** de vive force, à la méthode forte.

strong-arm[2] *vt Am F* rouer (*qn*) de coups.

strong-box ['strɒŋbɒks] *n* coffre-fort *m*, *pl* coffres-forts.

stronghold ['strɒŋhəʊld] *n* (*fortress*) forteresse *f*; (*fortified place etc*) place forte, redoute *f*; **s. of trade unionism,** citadelle *f* du syndicalisme.

strongly ['strɒŋlɪ] *adv* (*see adj*) **(a)** fortement, solidement, fermement; **s. built bicycle,** bicyclette (de construction) robuste; **(b)** fortement, vigoureusement, énergiquement; **to be s. in favour of sth,** être fortement en faveur *ou* chaud partisan de qch; **s. worded letter,** lettre en termes énergiques; **I don't feel s. about it,** je n'y attache pas une grande importance; **I feel very s. that they should be punished,** je suis convaincu qu'ils devraient être punis.

strongman ['strɒŋmæn] *n* **(a)** (*powerful man*) homme *m* à poigne; **(b)** *(in circus)* Monsieur Muscle.

strong-minded [strɒŋ'maɪndɪd] *adj* à l'esprit résolu; **s.-m. person,** forte tête.

strong-mindedly [strɒŋ'maɪndɪdlɪ] *adv* avec décision, avec résolution.

strong-mindedness [strɒŋ'maɪndɪdnɪs] *n* force *f* de caractère, résolution *f.*

strongroom ['strɒŋru:m] *n* chambre forte.

strong-willed [strɒŋ'wɪld] *adj* = **STRONG-MINDED.**

strontium ['strɒntɪəm] *n Ch* strontium *m.*

strop¹ [strɒp] *n* **(razor) s.,** cuir *m* *(à repasser, à rasoir)*, affiloir *m.*

strop² *vt* (-pp-) affiler *ou* repasser *(un rasoir)* sur le cuir.

strophe ['strəʊfɪ] *n* *(in prosody)* strophe *f.*

stroppiness ['strɒpɪnɪs] *n Br Sl* *(insolence, awkwardness)* caractère *m* difficile.

stroppy ['strɒpɪ] *adj Br Sl* *(insolent, awkward)* difficile; *(angry)* coléreux; *(aggressive)* agressif, -ive, hargneux; **now don't get s. with me!,** ne monte pas sur tes grands chevaux.

strove *see* **STRIVE.**

struck *see* **STRIKE².**

structural ['strʌktʃər(ə)l] *adj* **(a)** *Phil Geol etc* structural, -aux; *(relating to structure)* structurel; **s. differences,** différences structurelles; **(b)** *Constr* de construction; **s. fault,** défaut *m* de construction; **s. damage,** dommages structurels; **s. engineer,** (ingénieur *m*) constructeur *m*; **s. iron/steel,** *(material)* fer *m*/acier *m* de construction; *(framework)* charpentes *fpl* métalliques.

structuralism ['strʌktʃər(ə)lɪz(ə)m] *n Psy Ling* structuralisme *m.*

structurally ['strʌktʃər(ə)lɪ] *adv* structuralement; structurellement.

structure¹ ['strʌktʃər] *n* **(a)** *(of society, language etc)* structure *f*; structure, agencement *m* *(de vers, d'un récit)*; structure, construction *f* *(d'un bâtiment)*; **(b)** *(building, monument, organization etc)* construction *f*, édifice *m*, bâtiment *m*; **the social s.,** l'édifice social; *Econ* **price s.,** structure *f* des prix; *Mil etc* **command s.,** structure de commandement.

structure² *vt* structurer *(une organisation, une situation)*; structurer, architecturer *(une œuvre d'art)*.

structured ['strʌktʃəd] *adj* structuré; **highly s.,** très structuré.

struggle¹ ['strʌg(ə)l] *n* lutte *f* **(for, against,** pour, contre); **fierce/desperate s.,** lutte acharnée/désespérée; **he gave in without a s.,** il n'a opposé aucune résistance; **the class s.,** la lutte des classes; **s. for freedom,** lutte pour la liberté; **the s. for life/for existence,** la lutte pour la vie/pour l'existence; *F* **it's a s. getting the kids to wash properly,** il est difficile de convaincre les enfants de se laver correctement; **it'll be a s. but I think we'll make it,** ce sera difficile *ou* dur, mais je crois que nous y arriverons; **I had a s. getting him to change his mind,** j'ai eu du mal à le faire changer d'avis; **life is a s.,** la vie est un combat; **the s. that many people have just to make ends meet,** la lutte que livrent beaucoup de gens juste pour joindre les deux bouts.

struggle² *vi* lutter **(with, against, for,** avec, contre, pour); se débattre, se démener; **to s. to do sth,** avoir du mal à faire qch; **she struggled to control her temper,** elle a eu du mal à ne pas s'emporter; **the child struggled and kicked,** l'enfant se débattait des pieds et des mains; **she was struggling with her umbrella,** elle se débattait avec son parapluie; **he struggled to his feet,** il s'est levé avec difficulté; **to s. along,** *(walking etc)* marcher *ou* avancer péniblement; **we are struggling along,** *(in life, with work etc)* nous nous débrouillons tant bien que mal; **he struggled through the hole in the wall,** avec difficulté il réussit à passer par le trou du mur; **the more he struggled the deeper he sank in the mud,** plus il se débattait plus il s'enfonçait dans la boue; **we'll s. on for another month or so,** nous allons continuer tant bien que mal pendant encore un mois environ; **the climbers struggled back to camp,** les grimpeurs sont rentrés au camp tant bien que mal; **we struggled through,** nous avons surmonté tous les obstacles; **to be struggling (badly),** *(in one's job, university course etc)* avoir du mal; **the team is struggling,** *(in match, to retain position in league etc)* l'équipe a des difficultés; **to s. against circumstances,** lutter contre les événements; **to s. with death,** lutter contre la mort, être entre la vie et la mort; **to s. with one's conscience/homework,** être aux prises avec sa conscience/ses devoirs; **we have to s. to make ends meet,** il nous faut lutter pour joindre les deux bouts; **many companies are struggling,** *(financially)* beaucoup d'entreprises ont du mal *ou* sont en difficulté; **I was struggling to make myself understood,** je me débattais pour me faire comprendre; **he was obviously struggling for** *or* **to find the right word,** visiblement il se débattait pour trouver le mot juste.

struggling ['strʌglɪŋ] *adj* *(artiste etc)* qui vit péniblement.

strum¹ [strʌm] *n* son *m*, bruit *m* *(d'une guitare etc)*.

strum² *v* (-mm-) **1** *vt* pincer les cordes de *(une guitare)*; **to s. a tune,** jouer un air *(à la guitare)*; tapoter un air *(au piano)*. **2** *vi* *(on a guitar)* pincer les cordes; **her fingers strummed on the table,** ses doigts pianotaient sur *ou* tapotaient la table.

strumpet ['strʌmpɪt] *n Arch & Lit* prostituée *f.*

strung *see* **STRING².**

strung-up [strʌŋ'ʌp] *adj* *(person)* tendu.

strut¹ [strʌt] *n Constr* *(support)* étai *m*; *(cross-piece)* traverse *f*; *(spur)* arc-boutant *m*, *pl* arcs-boutants; *(in roofing)* jambe *f* de force; *(of roof truss)* contrefiche *f*; *Av* pilier *m*, mât *m.*

strut² *n* *(walk)* démarche affectée.

strut³ *vi* (-tt-) se pavaner, parader; *(after victory, compliment etc)* se rengorger; **to s. in/out,** entrer/sortir en se pavanant.

▶strut about, strut around *vi* **(a)** *(parade oneself)* se pavaner; **(b)** *(walk around self-importantly)* parader.

struth [stru:θ] *int Sl* ça alors!

strychnine ['strɪkni:n] *n* strychnine *f.*

stub¹ [stʌb] *n* **(a)** bout *m* *(de crayon)*; *F* mégot *m* *(de cigarette, de cigare)*; tronçon *m* *(de mât, de queue de chien)*; souche *f* *(d'arbre)*; chicot *m* *(d'arbre, de dent)*; **(b)** *Com* talon *m*, souche *f* *(de chèque)*.

stub² *vt* (-bb-) **to s. one's toe on** *or* **against sth,** se heurter *ou* se cogner le pied contre qch, buter contre qch.

▶stub out *vtsep* écraser *(une cigarette)*.

stubble ['stʌb(ə)l] *n* **(a)** *Agr* chaume *m*, éteule *f*; **to clear a field of s.,** (dé)chaumer un champ; **s. field,** chaume; **(b)** *(on face)* barbe piquante *(de plusieurs jours)*.

stubbly ['stʌblɪ] *adj* **(a)** *Agr* *(field)* couvert de chaume *ou* d'éteule; **s. field,** chaume *m*; **(b) s. beard,** barbe piquante *(de plusieurs jours)*; **s. chin,** menton piquant.

stubborn ['stʌbən] *adj* **(a)** *(personne)* obstiné, opiniâtre, entêté, têtu; *(volonté)* tenace; *(caractère)* buté; **their s. refusal to surrender,** leur refus obstiné de se rendre; *F* **as s. as a mule,** têtu *ou* entêté comme un mulet *ou* une mule; **(b)** *(thing)* réfractaire, rebelle; **s. fever,** fièvre rebelle.

stubbornly ['stʌbənlɪ] *adv* *(awkwardly)* obstinément; *(tenaciously)* avec entêtement; **she s. refused to give up hope,** elle a obstinément refusé d'abandonner espoir.

stubbornness ['stʌbənnɪs] *n* entêtement *m*, obstination *f*, opiniâtreté *f*; ténacité *f* *(de volonté)*.

stubby ['stʌbɪ] *adj* *(plant)* tronqué; *(person)* trapu; **s. fingers,** doigts boudinés.

stucco¹ ['stʌkəʊ] *n* stuc *m*; **s. work,** stucage *m.*

stucco² *vt* *(pt & pp* **stuccoed**; *prp* **stuccoing)** stuquer.

stuck-up ['stʌk'ʌp] *adj F* snob; *(conceited)* prétentieux.

stud¹ [stʌd] *n* **(a)** *(nail)* clou *m* à grosse tête; clou doré *(pour ornement)*; *(on road)* clou *(de passage clouté)*; **studs,** *(on football boots)* crampons *mpl*; **(b)** bouton *m* (double) *(de chemise de soirée)*; **collar s.,** bouton de col; **(c)** *Tech* *(short pin)* goujon *m*, tourillon *m*; *Nau* étai *m* *(d'un maillon de chaîne)*; **s. (bolt),** goujon; **(d)** *Constr* poteau *m*, montant *m*; **s. wall,** mur *m* de séparation.

stud² *vt* (-dd-) **(a)** *(fit with studs)* garnir de clous, clouter; **studded door,** porte garnie de clous *ou* cloutée; *Fig* **studded with stars,** *(sky)* criblé *ou* (par)semé d'étoiles; **her dress was studded with jewels,** sa robe était constellée de pierreries; **(b)** *Constr* établir la charpente *(d'une cloison)*.

stud³ *n* **(a)** *(stable)* écurie *f* *(de chasse)*; **(b) s. (farm),** haras *m* (de pur-sang); **to be at s.,** *(of horse)* être en haras; *(of dog)* faire des saillies; **to put a horse to s.,** utiliser un cheval comme étalon; **s. mare,** (jument-)poulinière *f*; **(c)** *(stallion)* étalon *m*; *Fig Sl* *(man)* mec bien monté; **he's a real s.,** c'est un vrai tombeur; **(d)** *Cards* **s. (poker),** poker *m.*

studbook ['stʌdbʊk] *n* stud-book *m.*

student ['stju:dənt] *n* **(a)** étudiant, -ante; **law/medical/arts s.,** étudiant en droit/en médecine/en lettres; **the s. body,** les étudiants; *US* **s. driver,** apprenti(e) conducteur, -trice; **s. life,** la vie d'étudiant; **s. nurse,** élève infirmière; **s. riots,** émeutes étudiantes; **s. teacher,** professeur *m* en cours de formation; **(b)** *(person who studies sth)* investigateur, -trice *(d'un phénomène)*; **students of Middle**

East politics will know that ..., ceux qui étudient la politique du Moyen-Orient savent que ... .

studhorse ['stʌdhɔːs] *n* étalon *m*.

studied ['stʌdɪd] *adj* (*style, attitude, posture*) étudié, recherché; (*move, act*) prémédité, calculé; (*negligence*) voulue; **s. elegance,** élégance recherchée.

studio ['stjuːdɪəʊ] *n* atelier *m*, studio *m* (*d'artiste, de photographe*); **film/television s.,** studio de cinéma/télévision; **recording s.,** studio d'enregistrement; *Rad* auditorium *m*; *TV* **s. audience,** public *m* (présent lors d'un enregistrement); **s. couch,** lit *m* canapé; *Am* **s. apartment,** *Br* **s. flat,** studio.

studious ['stjuːdɪəs] *adj* **(a)** (*person, atmosphere*) studieux; **person of s. habits,** personne adonnée à l'étude; **(b)** (*careful*) **with s. attention,** avec une attention réfléchie.

studiously ['stjuːdɪəslɪ] *adv* **(a)** (*listen to teacher*) studieusement; **(b)** (*carefully*) attentivement; **she s. avoided me,** elle s'ingéniait à m'éviter; **he was s. polite,** il était d'une politesse étudiée.

studiousness ['stjuːdɪəsnɪs] *n* **(a)** amour *m* de l'étude; **(b)** (*carefulness*) empressement *m*, zèle *m* (**to do sth, in doing sth,** à faire qch).

study[1] ['stʌdɪ] *n* **(a)** (*investigation*) étude *f* (**of,** de); (*report*) étude, rapport *m*; **to make a s. of sth,** s'appliquer à l'étude de qch, étudier qch; **I've made a special s. of ...,** je me suis spécialisé dans ...; **studies,** études; **to neglect one's studies,** négliger ses études; **to finish one's studies,** achever ses études; **s. group,** groupe *m* d'étude; **s. tour,** voyage *m* d'étude; **(b)** (*room*) cabinet *m* de travail, bureau *m*; *Sch* salle *f* d'étude; **(c)** *Old-fashioned* **(brown) s.,** rêverie *f*; **to be (lost) in a brown s.,** être plongé *ou* absorbé dans ses réflexions *ou* dans de vagues rêveries; **(d)** *F* **her face was a s.!,** il fallait voir sa tête!; **(e)** *Art Mus* étude *f*.

study[2] **1** *vt* étudier (*une langue, la musique, un rôle*); observer (*le terrain, les astres*); faire des études de (*français, droit*); examiner, étudier (*des plans*); mettre (*une question*) à l'étude; **she studied history at Yale,** elle a étudié l'histoire à Yale; **he studied her face for signs of emotion,** il examina son visage pour y détecter des signes d'émotion. **2** *vi* faire ses études; étudier; **you ought to s. harder,** tu devrais étudier davantage; **he's studying,** il étudie; (*he's at college etc*) il fait ses études; **she's studying to be a doctor,** elle fait des études de médecine; **to s. for an examination,** préparer *ou* se préparer à un examen.

stuff[1] [stʌf] *n* **(a)** matière(s) *f(pl)*, matériaux *mpl*, substance *f*; **here's some s. to put on that burn,** voici quelque chose à mettre sur cette brûlure; **there's some sticky s. in the saucepan,** il y a quelque chose qui colle dans la casserole; **he is of the s. that heroes are made of,** il est du bois dont sont faits les héros; *F* **she writes good s.,** elle écrit de bons trucs, elle écrit bien; *F* **there was some s. about unions on the news,** ils ont parlé des syndicats aux informations; **dangerous s., acid,** c'est dangereux, l'acide; *F* **this wine is good s.,** ce vin c'est du bon; **I don't like that s. you gave me,** je n'aime pas ce que vous m'avez donné là; **come on, do your s.!,** allons, montre-nous ce que tu sais faire!; **he knows his s.,** il s'y connaît; **that's the s.!** voilà ce qu'il faut!; **old s.,** vieilleries *fpl*; **silly s.,** sottises *fpl*, balivernes *fpl*; *Old-fashioned* **s. and nonsense!,** ça c'est de la bêtise!;

(b) (*possessions*) affaires *fpl*; **her stuff's still in Cardiff,** ses affaires sont encore à Cardiff;

(c) *Arch Tex* étoffe *f*, tissu *m* (*de laine*);

(d) *Sl* (*drug*) came *f*.

stuff[2] *vt* **(a)** bourrer (**with,** de); rembourrer (*un meuble, un coussin*) (**with,** de); *Culin* farcir (*un poulet*); empailler, naturaliser (*un spécimen zoologique*); *Vulg* (*have sex with*) bourrer, se farcir (*qn*); **her pockets are stuffed with sweets,** elle a des bonbons plein les poches; *F* **to s. oneself, to stuff one's face,** s'empiffrer; **head stuffed with romantic ideas,** tête bourrée *ou* farcie d'idées romanesques; *F* **stuffed shirt,** individu suffisant *ou* prétentieux; *Br Sl* **get stuffed!,** va te faire foutre!; *Br Sl* **he can get stuffed,** il peut aller se faire foutre;

(b) (*shove*) **to s. sth into sth,** fourrer qch dans qch; **to s. one's fingers in one's ears,** se boucher les oreilles (avec les doigts); *Br Sl* **you can s. it (up your arse)!,** tu peux te le mettre où je pense!; **s. the job!,** ton/son boulot, tu peux/il peut te/se le mettre où tu penses/il pense; **s. this, I'm going home!,** et puis merde, je rentre!

▶**stuff up** *vtsep* boucher (*un trou etc*); **I'm all stuffed up with a cold,** j'ai le nez complètement bouché avec ce rhume; **my nose is stuffed up,** j'ai le nez bouché.

stuffing ['stʌfɪŋ] *n* **(a)** *Culin* (*filling for meat, poultry etc*) farce *f*; (*for upholstery*) bourre *f*, rembourrage *m*; **horsehair s.,** matelassure *f* de crin; *F* **to knock the s. out of s.o.,** (*defeat heavily*) mettre la pâtée à qn; (*of blow, person, illness*) mettre qn K.O.; **(b)** (*act of stuffing*) bourrage *m*, rembourrage *m*; empaillage *m* (*d'animaux*).

stuffy ['stʌfɪ] *adj* **(a)** (*room etc*) mal ventilé, mal aéré; **to smell s.,** sentir le renfermé; **it's a bit s. in here,** on manque d'air ici; **(b)** *F* (*standoffish*) collet monté; (*overconventional*) vieux jeu; **don't be so s.,** (*don't be offended*) il n'y a pas de quoi te scandaliser; **(c) to feel s.,** (*have blocked nose*) avoir le nez bouché.

stultify ['stʌltɪfaɪ] *vt* **(a)** enlever toute valeur à (*un argument, un témoignage*); invalider, infirmer (*un décret*); (*of work*) abrutir, assommer (*qn*); **(b)** ridiculiser (*qn, qch*); faire ressortir l'absurdité (*d'une action*).

stultifying ['stʌltɪfaɪɪŋ] *adj* (*travail*) abrutissant.

stumble[1] ['stʌmbl] *n* trébuchement *m*; bronchement *m* (*d'un cheval*).

stumble[2] *vi* **(a)** trébucher; (*of horse*) broncher; **to s. off,** partir en trébuchant; **to s. over the carpet,** trébucher dans la moquette; **he stumbled against the filing cabinet,** il a trébuché contre le classeur et s'est cogné; **(b) to s. in one's speech,** (*hesitate*) hésiter en parlant; (*confuse words etc*) s'embrouiller en parlant; **she stumbled through her speech,** elle s'est empêtrée tout au long de son discours.

▶**stumble across** *vipo* rencontrer (*qn, qch*) par hasard, tomber sur (*qn, qch*).

▶**stumble along** *vi* (*walk with difficulty*) avancer en trébuchant.

▶**stumble up(on)** *vi* = **STUMBLE ACROSS.**

stumbling ['stʌmblɪŋ] **1** *adj* qui trébuche; (*horse*) qui bronche; (*speech*) hésitant. **2** *n* trébuchement *m*; bronchement *m* (*d'un cheval*); (*in speech*) hésitation *f*; **s. block,** pierre *f* d'achoppement.

stump[1] [stʌmp] *n* **(a)** tronçon *m*, souche *f*, chicot *m* (*d'arbre*); chicot (*de dent*); moignon *m* (*de bras, de jambe*); bout *m* (*de cigare, de crayon*); *F* mégot *m* (*de cigare*); tronçon (*de queue, de colonne, de mât*); trognon *m* (*de chou*); **(b)** *F* **stumps,** (*legs*) pattes *fpl*, quilles *fpl*; **stir your stumps!,** remuez-vous!, grouillez-vous!; **(c)** *esp Am Pol F* **to be on the s.,** faire des harangues politiques; **s. orator,** *Am* **s. speaker,** orateur *m* de carrefour; **(d)** *Cr* piquet *m* (*du guichet*); **to draw stumps,** enlever les piquets, cesser le match.

stump[2] **1** *vt* **(a)** *F* coller (*un candidat*); faire sécher (*qn*) (*sur un sujet*); **to be stumped,** ne plus savoir que faire, sécher; **it stumped me,** cela m'a désarçonné; **this one has got me stumped,** alors là, suis désarçonné *ou* collé; **(b)** *Cr* mettre hors jeu (*un batteur qui est sorti de son camp*). **2** *vi esp Am Pol F* faire des harangues politiques.

▶**stump along** *vi* (*walk heavily*) marcher *ou* avancer d'un pas lourd *ou* (*limping*) en clopinant.

▶**stump off** *vi* (*annoyed*) partir d'un pas lourd.

▶**stump up** *Br F* **1** *vtsep* (*pay*) payer, aligner. **2** *vi* payer, casquer.

stumpy ['stʌmpɪ] *adj* (*person*) trapu, ragot, ramassé; (*object*) trapu; **s. pencil,** petit bout de crayon.

stun[1] [stʌn] *vt* (**-nn-**) **(a)** (*make unconscious*) étourdir, assommer; **s. grenade,** grenade incapacitante; **s. gun,** (*in science fiction*) pistolet paralysant; (*for animals*) fusil *m* hypodermique; **(b)** *Fig* (*shock*) renverser, abasourdir; **the news stunned us,** ces nouvelles ont été coup de massue *ou* nous ont abasourdis; **we were stunned to hear of your accident,** nous avons été consternés d'apprendre que vous aviez eu un accident; **Sophie, I am stunned,** Sophie, je suis stupéfait; **stunned with surprise,** stupéfié, frappé de stupeur.

stung *see* **STING**[2].

stunner ['stʌnər] *n F* **(a) he's/she's a s.,** il/elle est vachement beau/belle, c'est un vrai canon; **(b)** (*excellent thing*) chose épatante, *F* truc *m* sensas(s).

stunning ['stʌnɪŋ] *adj* **(a)** (*coup*) étourdissant, abrutissant; (*malheur*) accablant, bouleversant; **(b)** *Fig* (*shocking*) renversant; (*amazing, excellent*) formidable, épatant; **she's really s.,** (*beautiful*) elle est vraiment ravissante; **his/her s. good looks,** sa beauté éblouissante.

stunningly ['stʌnɪŋlɪ] *adv* **s. beautiful,** d'une beauté renversante; **s. dressed,** magnifiquement vêtu(e).

stunt[1] [stʌnt] *vt* arrêter (*qn, qch*) dans sa croissance; arrêter, ralentir (*la croissance*); **stunted,** (*arbre*) rabougri; (*esprit*) noué; **to become stunted,** se rabougrir.

stunt[2] *n* **(a)** tour *m* de force; *Cin* cascade *f*; **to do one's own stunts,** (*of actor, actress*) ne pas se faire doubler dans les scènes dangereuses, tourner ses cascades soi-même; *Av*

to perform stunts, faire des acrobaties (*en vol*); *Av* **s. flying,** vol *m* acrobatique; *Cin* **s. man/woman,** cascadeur *m*/cascadeuse *f*; *Av* **s. pilot,** pilote *m* de voltige; **(b)** (*sth done to gain attention*) coup *m* d'épate; (*for publicity*) affaire *f* de publicité *ou* de pure réclame.

stupefaction [stjuːpɪ'fækʃən] *n* stupeur *f*, stupéfaction *f*.

stupefy ['stjuːpɪfaɪ] *vt* **(a)** abasourdir, stupéfier; **I'm absolutely stupefied (by what has happened),** je n'en reviens pas, j'en reste stupéfait; **(b)** (*make insensitive*) hébéter, abrutir; *Med* stupéfier, engourdir.

stupefying ['stjuːpɪfaɪɪŋ] *adj* stupéfiant.

stupendous [stjuː'pendəs] *adj* prodigieux, *F* formidable.

stupendously [stjuː'pendəslɪ] *adv* prodigieusement.

stupid ['stjuːpɪd] **1** *adj* stupide, sot, *f* sotte, bête; **I did a s. thing,** j'ai fait une bêtise *ou* une chose stupide; **don't be s.!,** ne faites pas l'idiot!; **how s. of me!,** que je suis bête!; **I'm not s., you know!,** je ne suis pas idiot quand même!; **what a s. place to put it in!,** c'est idiot de l'avoir mis là!; **a s. record/film/*etc*,** un disque/film/*etc* idiot; **I don't want your s. book!,** je n'en veux pas de ton livre!; *F* **to drink oneself s.,** s'abrutir d'alcool. **2** *n* (*term of address*) **of course not, s.!,** bien sûr que non, grosse bête!

stupidity [stjuː'pɪdɪtɪ] *n* stupidité *f*; (*action, remark*) bêtise *f*.

stupidly ['stjuːpɪdlɪ] *adv* stupidement, bêtement; **rather s., I agreed,** bêtement, j'ai accepté.

stupor ['stjuːpər] *n* stupeur *f*; **in a drunken s.,** abruti par la boisson.

sturdily ['stɜːdɪlɪ] *adv* (*see adj*) **(a)** fortement; **s. built,** solide; (*person, car*) solide, robuste; **(b)** hardiment, résolument.

sturdiness ['stɜːdɪnɪs] *n* **(a)** (*of person, plant etc*) vigueur *f*, robustesse *f*; (*of table, piece of equipment*) solidité *f*; **(b)** (*of resolve, opposition*) résolution *f*, fermeté *f*.

sturdy ['stɜːdɪ] *adj* **(a)** vigoureux, robuste, fort; **s. fellow,** gaillard *m* robuste; **a s. table,** une table solide; **(b)** (*opposition, resistance*) hardi, résolu, ferme.

sturgeon ['stɜːdʒ(ə)n] *n* (*fish*) esturgeon *m*.

stutter¹ ['stʌtər] *n* bégaiement *m*; **he has a s.,** il est bègue.

stutter² **1** *vi* bégayer. **2** *vt* bégayer (*qch*).

stutterer ['stʌtərər] *n* bègue *mf*.

stuttering ['stʌtərɪŋ] **1** *adj* bègue. **2** *n* bégaiement *m*.

sty¹ *pl* **sties** [staɪ, staɪz] *n* porcherie *f*; *Fig* taudis *m*.

sty², stye [staɪ] *n Med* orgelet *m*.

Stygian ['stɪdʒɪən] *adj Lit* **S. gloom,** (*darkness*) nuit noire comme le Styx; (*mood*) humeur noire comme le Styx.

style¹ [staɪl] *n* **(a)** (*manner*) style *m*, manière *f*, façon *f*; type *m*, modèle *f* (*de voiture*); (*of clothes etc*) mode *f*; **s. of living,** style *ou* train *m* de vie; **to live in (grand *or* great) s.,** mener grand train, vivre sur un grand pied; **they arrived in s.,** ils ont fait leur entrée en grande pompe; **let's do things in s.,** faisons bien les choses; **let's travel in s.,** voyageons en grand style; **that's the s.!,** c'est cela!, bravo!; **Gothic/Byzantine s.,** style gothique/byzantin; **building in the classical s.,** bâtiment *m* de style classique; **chicken cooked Kentucky s.,** poulet *m* Kentucky; **that's not my s.,** ce n'est pas mon genre *ou* style; **something in that s.,** quelque chose de *ou* dans ce genre *ou* style; **in the latest s.,** à la (dernière) mode, *F* dernier cri;

(b) (*in writing, speaking*) style *m*, ton *m*; (*way of writing*) manière *f* d'écrire; **written in a humorous s.,** écrit dans un style humoristique; **written in the s. of a 1940s thriller,** écrit dans le style *ou* la veine du roman policier des années 1940; **this writer lacks s.,** (*good style*) cet écrivain n'a pas de style;

(c) (*distinction, class*) chic *m*, cachet *m*, classe *f*; **she has s.,** elle a de l'allure *ou* de la classe;

(d) (*of calendar*) **old/new s.,** vieux/nouveau style;

(e) (*in engraving*) (*of sundial*) style *m*, gnomon *m*; *Bot* style.

style² *vt* **(a)** (*design*) créer; **dress styled by X,** robe créée par X; **hair styled by X,** coiffé(e) par X; **(b)** *Old-fashioned* dénommer (*qch*); appeler (*qch, qn*); **to s. oneself doctor,** se donner le titre de docteur.

styling ['staɪlɪŋ] *n* façon *f*; ligne *f* (*d'une voiture*); **hair s.,** coiffure *f*; **s. mousse/gel,** mousse coiffante/gel coiffant.

stylish ['staɪlɪʃ] *adj* élégant, chic, qui a du cachet *ou* de la classe.

stylishly [staɪlɪʃlɪ] *adv* élégamment, avec chic, avec classe.

stylishness ['staɪlɪʃnɪs] *n* élégance *f*, chic *m*, classe *f*.

stylist ['staɪlɪst] *n* styliste *mf*; **hair s.,** coiffeur, -euse (d'art); (*shop sign*) = coiffure *f* (d'art).

stylistic [staɪ'lɪstɪk] *adj* stylistique, du *ou* de style.

stylistically [staɪ'lɪstɪk(ə)lɪ] *adv* du point de vue de la stylistique.

stylistics [staɪ'lɪstɪks] *npl* (*usu with sing verb*) stylistique *f*.

stylization [staɪlaɪ'zeɪʃən] *n* stylisation *f*.

stylize ['staɪlaɪz] *vt Art* styliser; **stylized flowers,** fleurs stylisées.

stylus, *pl* **-i, -uses** ['staɪləs, -aɪ, -əsɪz] *n* (*in engraving etc*) style *m*; (*on record player*) pointe *f* de lecture; (*made of sapphire*) saphir *m*; (*made of diamond*) diamant *m*.

stymie ['staɪmɪ] *vt F* **this question stymied me,** cette question m'a coincé; **to be stymied,** être dans une impasse.

styptic ['stɪptɪk] *Med* **1** *adj* styptique, astringent; **s. pencil,** pierre *f* d'alun. **2** *n* styptique *m*, astringent *m*.

suasion ['sweɪʒ(ə)n] *n Arch* persuasion *f*; **to subject s.o. to moral s.,** agir sur la conscience de qn, agir sur qn par persuasion.

suave [swɑːv] *adj* affable, courtois, *Lit* urbain; *Pej* doucereux, mielleux.

suavely ['swɑːvlɪ] *adv* affablement; *Pej* doucereusement.

suaveness ['swɑːvnɪs], **suavity** ['swɑːvɪtɪ] *n* affabilité *f*, courtoisie *f*, *Lit* urbanité *f*; *Pej* manières mielleuses.

sub¹ [sʌb] *n F* **(a)** (*subscription*) cotisation *f* (*à un club*); **to pay one's subs,** payer sa cotisation; **(b)** *Sp* (*substitute*) remplaçant *m*; **(c)** *Nau* (*submarine*) sous-marin *m*; **(d)** *Journ* (*subeditor*) secrétaire *mf* de rédaction; **(e)** *Mil* (*subaltern*) subalterne *mf*.

sub² *v* (**-bb-**) *F* **1** *vi* **(a)** (*substitute*) **to s. for s.o.,** remplacer qn; **(b)** *Journ* (*subedit*) mettre un article au point. **2** *vt Journ* mettre (*un article*) au point.

subagent [sʌb'eɪdʒənt] *n* sous-agent *m*.

subalpine [sʌb'ælpaɪn] *adj* subalpin.

subaltern ['sʌbəltən] **1** *adj* subalterne, subordonné. **2** *n Mil* (officier) subalterne *m*.

subaqua [sʌb'ækwə] *adj* (*sport*) subaquatique; **s. diving,** plongée sous-marine; **s. club,** club *m* de plongée sous-marine.

subatomic [sʌbə'tɒmɪk] *adj* subatomique.

subclass ['sʌbklɑːs] *n* sous-classe *f*.

subclause ['sʌbklɔːz] *n esp Jur* paragraphe *m* (*d'un contrat*).

subcommittee ['sʌbkəmɪtɪ] *n* sous-comité *m*; (*in larger organisations*) sous-commission *f*.

subconscious [sʌb'kɒnʃəs] *adj & n Psy* subconscient *m*.

subconsciously [sʌb'kɒnʃəslɪ] *adv* subconsciemment.

subcontinent [sʌb'kɒntɪnənt] *n* sous-continent *m*; **the Indian s.,** le sous-continent indien.

subcontract¹ [sʌb'kɒntrækt] *n* (contrat *m* de) sous-traitance *f*.

subcontract² [sʌbkən'trækt] *vt* sous-traiter (*une affaire, des travaux, une commande*); **to s. a job to s.o.,** sous-traiter un travail à qn.

subcontracting ['sʌbkəntræktɪŋ] *n* sous-traitance *f*.

subcontractor ['sʌbkəntræktər] *n* sous-entrepreneur *m*, sous-traitant *m*; *Constr etc* tâcheron *m*.

subculture ['sʌbkʌltʃər] *n* **(a)** (*in sociology*) groupe *ou* phénomène culturel secondaire; *Pej* sous-culture *f*; **youth s.,** phénomène culturel propre à la jeunesse; **(b)** (*in bacteriology*) repiquage *m*, culture *f* secondaire.

subcutaneous [sʌbkjʊ'teɪnɪəs] *adj* sous-cutané.

subdeacon [sʌb'diːkən] *n Rel* sous-diacre *m*.

subdivide [sʌbdɪ'vaɪd] **1** *vt* subdiviser, sous-diviser. **2** *vi* se subdiviser.

subdivision [sʌbdɪ'vɪʒən] *n* subdivision *f*, sous-division *f*.

subdominant [sʌb'dɒmɪnənt] *n Mus* sous-dominante *f*.

subdue [səb'djuː] *vt* **(a)** subjuguer, soumettre, assujettir (*une tribu*); maîtriser (*un incendie*); dompter, réprimer (*un mouvement de colère*); asservir (*ses passions*); **(b)** adoucir (*la lumière, la chaleur, la voix*); amortir, atténuer (*la lumière, la douleur*).

subdued [səb'djuːd] *adj* (*person*) (*quieter than usual*) inhabituellement calme; (*sad*) triste; (*heat, light, sound*) adouci; **s. colours,** couleurs sobres; **s. conversation,** conversation à voix basse; **s. light,** demi-jour *m*, lumière tamisée; **it's a very s. tone for him,** c'est un ton très modéré qui ne lui ressemble pas; **in a s. tone *or* voice,** à voix basse, à mi-voix.

subedit [sʌb'edɪt] *Journ* **1** *vi* mettre au point un article. **2** *vt* mettre (*un article*) au point.

subeditor [sʌb'edɪtər] *n Journ* secrétaire *m* de rédaction; (*in publishing*) rédacteur, -trice; **assistant s.,** secrétaire adjoint.

subfamily ['sʌbfæmɪlɪ] *n Biol* sous-famille *f*.

sub-frame ['sʌbfreɪm] *n Aut* faux-châssis *m inv*.

subfusc [sʌb'fʌsk] *adj (clothing)* sombre.

subgenus, *pl* **-genera** ['sʌbdʒiːnəs, -dʒenərə] *n Biol* sous-genre *m*.

subgroup ['sʌbgruːp] *n* sous-groupe *m*.

subhead, subheading ['sʌbhed, 'sʌbhedɪŋ] *n* sous-titre *m*.

subhuman [sʌb'hjuːmən] *adj* pas tout à fait humain; *F* **he's positively s.,** il est bête comme ses pieds.

subject¹ ['sʌbdʒɪkt] *n* **(a)** *(topic)* sujet *m (de conversation, d'un livre)*; objet *m (d'un litige, de méditation)*; *Mus* sujet *(d'une fugue)*; *Sch* matière *f*; **this will be the s. of my next lecture,** cela fera l'objet de ma prochaine conférence; **to wander from the s.,** sortir de la question, faire une digression; **while we are on the s.,** à ce propos, pendant que nous sommes sur ce sujet; **on the s. of,** au sujet de; **to change the s.,** parler d'autre chose, changer de sujet; **to change the s., has anyone seen Andy?,** pour changer de sujet, est-ce que quelqu'un a vu Andy?; **don't try to change the s.!,** n'essaie pas de changer de sujet; **what subjects do you teach?,** quelles matières enseignez-vous?; **s. matter,** contenu *m (d'une lettre)*; sujet *(d'un livre)*; objet *m (d'un contrat réel)*; **she prefers science subjects,** elle préfère les matières scientifiques;
(b) sujet *m (d'une expérience)*; *Med* sujet, malade *mf (que l'on traite)*; **to be a s. of an experiment,** servir de sujet d'expérience; **to be a s. for pity,** être un objet de pitié;
(c) *Gram* sujet *(du verbe)*;
(d) *Art Phot* sujet *m*;
(e) sujet, -ette *(d'un souverain)*; **British s.,** sujet britannique.

subject² *adj* **(a)** *(état, pays)* assujetti, soumis (**to,** à); sous la dépendance (**to,** de); **s. to military laws,** justiciable des tribunaux militaires;
(b) *(liable)* sujet *(au rhumatisme)*; porté *(à l'envie)*; **prices s. to 5% discount,** prix bénéficiant d'une remise de 5%; **s. to stamp duty,** soumis au timbre; **the plan is s. to modifications,** ce projet pourra subir des modifications; **all trains will be s. to delays,** tous les trains seront susceptibles d'être en retard; **we're all s. to taxation,** nous sommes tous assujettis à l'impôt; **an area that is s. to avalanches,** zone d'avalanches; **as people become more and more s. to colds,** alors que les gens sont de plus en plus vulnérables au rhume;
(c) *(conditional)* **s. to ...,** sous réserve de ...; **s. to your consent,** sous réserve de votre consentement; **it's all s. to her approval,** tout dépend de *ou* est subordonné à son approbation.

subject³ [səb'dʒekt] *vt* **(a)** soumettre, assujettir, subjuguer *(un peuple)*; **(b)** *(force to undergo)* soumettre, exposer (**s.o./sth to sth,** qn/qch à qch); **to s. s.o. to torture,** mettre qn à la torture, faire subir la torture à qn; **to s. s.o./sth to an examination,** faire subir un examen à qn/qch, soumettre qn/qch à un examen; **to be subjected to much criticism,** être en butte à de nombreuses critiques; **metal subjected to great heat,** métal exposé à une forte chaleur; **to s. oneself to sth,** se soumettre à qch.

subjection [səb'dʒekʃən] *n* soumission *f*, assujettissement *m* (**to,** à); **in a state of s.,** dans la sujétion.

subjective [səb'dʒektɪv] *adj* subjectif.

subjectively [səb'dʒektɪvlɪ] *adv* subjectivement.

subjectivism [səb'dʒektɪvɪz(ə)m] *n* subjectivisme *m*.

subjectivity [sʌbdʒek'tɪvɪtɪ] *n* subjectivité *f*.

subjoin [sʌb'dʒɔɪn] *vt* ajouter, adjoindre *(une liste)*.

sub judice ['sʌb'dʒuːdɪsɪ] *adj Jur* **the case is s. j.,** l'affaire n'est pas encore jugée.

subjugate ['sʌbdʒʊgeɪt] *vt* subjuguer, soumettre, assujettir *(un peuple)*; dompter *(un animal)*.

subjugation [sʌbdʒʊ'geɪʃən] *n* subjugation *f*, assujettissement *m*.

subjunctive [səb'dʒʌŋktɪv] *Gram* **1** *adj* subjonctif. **2** *n* subjonctif *m*; **in the s. (mood),** au (mode) subjonctif.

sublease¹ ['sʌbliːs] *n (document, type of contract)* sous-bail *m*, *pl* sous-baux; *(act)* sous-location *f*; *(of farm)* sous-ferme *f*.

sublease² [sʌb'liːs] *vt* sous-louer *(un appartement)*; sous-affermer *(une terre)*.

sub-lessee [sʌble'siː] *n* sous-locataire *mf (à bail)*.

sub-lessor [sʌb'lesɔːr] *n* sous-bailleur, -bailleresse.

sublet [sʌb'let] *vt (pt & pp* **-let**; *prp* **-letting**) sous-louer *(un appartement)*; sous-affermer *(une terre)*.

sub-letting *n* [sʌb'letɪŋ] sous-location *f*.

sub-lieutenant [sʌblef'tenənt] *n Nau* enseigne *m* (de vaisseau) de première classe.

sublimate¹ ['sʌblɪmeɪt] *n Ch* sublimé *m*.

sublimate² *vt* **(a)** sublimer *(un sentiment, un instinct etc)*; **(b)** *Ch* sublimer *(un solide)*.

sublimation [sʌblɪ'meɪʃən] *n* sublimation *f*.

sublime¹ [sə'blaɪm] **1** *adj (pensée, poète, F petite robe etc)* sublime; **s. indifference,** suprême indifférence *f*. **2** *n* **the s.,** le sublime; **to go from the s. to the ridiculous** *or F* **gor blimey,** passer du sublime au ridicule.

sublime² **1** *vt Ch* sublimer *(un solide)*. **2** *vi Ch (of solid)* se sublimer.

sublimely [sə'blaɪmlɪ] *adv* **(a)** **s. beautiful,** d'une beauté sublime; **(b)** *F (indifferent)* suprêmement; **he remained s. unaware of ...,** il était toujours ignorant au plus haut point de ... .

subliminal [sʌb'lɪmɪn(ə)l] *adj Psy* subliminal, -aux, subliminaire; **s. advertising,** publicité *f* subliminal.

sublimity [sʌb'lɪmɪtɪ] *n* sublimité *f*.

sub-machine-gun [sʌbmə'ʃiːngʌn] *n* mitraillette *f*.

submarine [sʌbmə'riːn] **1** *adj (câble, volcan)* sous-marin. **2** *n* **(a)** sous-marin *m*; **midget** *or* **pocket s.,** sous-marin de poche; **(b)** *Am* gros sandwich.

submariner [sʌb'mærɪnər] *n* sous-marinier *m*.

submediant [sʌb'miːdɪənt] *n Mus* sous-dominante *f*.

submenu ['sʌbmenjuː] *n Comptr* sous-menu *m*.

submerge [səb'mɜːdʒ] **1** *vt* **(a)** submerger, immerger, plonger *ou* enfoncer *(qch)* dans l'eau; **(b)** inonder, noyer *(un champ)*; **submerged in details,** perdu dans les détails. **2** *vi* plonger; *(of submarine)* effectuer sa plongée.

submerged [səb'mɜːdʒd] *adj* submergé, noyé; *(sous-marin)* en plongée; *(écueil)* sous-marin; **wreck s. at high tide,** épave submergée à (la) marée haute; *Fig* **s. in work,** submergé de travail, qui croule sous le travail.

submergence [səb'mɜːdʒəns] *n* submersion *f*.

submersible [səb'mɜːsɪb(ə)l] *Nau* **1** *adj* submersible, sous-marin. **2** *n* (bateau *m*) submersible *m*, sous-marin *m*.

submersion [səb'mɜːʃən] *n* submersion *f*.

submission [səb'mɪʃən] *n* **(a)** soumission *f (à la volonté de qn, à une autorité)*; résignation *f (à une défaite)*; *(in wrestling)* abandon *m*; **to starve s.o. into s.,** réduire qn par la famine; **(b)** *(docility)* soumission *f*, docilité *f*; **(c)** soumission *(d'une question à un arbitre)*; présentation *f (de pièces d'identité)*; **(d)** *Jur* plaidoirie *f*; **in my s. ...,** selon ma thèse ...; **it's my s. that ...,** j'ai la conviction que ... .

submissive [səb'mɪsɪv] *adj (ton, air)* soumis; *(personne)* docile.

submissively [səb'mɪsɪvlɪ] *adv* avec soumission, docilement.

submissiveness [səb'mɪsɪvnɪs] *n* soumission *f*, docilité *f*.

submit [səb'mɪt] *v* **(-tt-)** **1** *vi* se soumettre *(à qn, à la volonté de qn, à une force supérieure)*; se plier *(à une nécessité)*; s'astreindre *(à la discipline)*; se résigner *(à un malheur)*; *(in wrestling)* abandonner; **to s. to authority,** se soumettre à l'autorité. **2** *vt* soumettre; **to s. sth for s.o.'s approval/for s.o.'s inspection,** soumettre *ou* présenter qch à l'approbation/à l'inspection de qn; **to s. proof of identity,** présenter des pièces d'identité; **to s. that...,** représenter *ou* alléguer que...; *Jur* **I s. that there is no case against my client,** je plaide le non-lieu; **I s. that you are not in fact ...,** j'affirme que vous n'êtes pas en fait ...; **the author submits that ...,** l'auteur affirme que ... .

subnormal [sʌb'nɔːməl] *adj* subnormal, -aux; *(température)* au-dessous de la normale; *(person)* faible d'esprit; **educationally s.,** arriéré.

suborder ['sʌbɔːdər] *n Biol* sous-ordre *m*.

subordinate¹ [sə'bɔːdɪnət] **1** *adj (rang)* inférieur, subalterne; *(rôle)* accessoire; **s. to,** subordonné à; *Gram* **s. clause,** proposition subordonnée. **2** *n* subordonné, -ée.

subordinate² [sə'bɔːdɪneɪt] *vt* subordonner (**to,** à); **everything is subordinated to religion,** tout est subordonné à la religion.

subordination [səbɔːdɪ'neɪʃən] *n* **(a)** *(state of being subordinate)* subordination *f* (**to,** à); **(b)** *(act of subordinating)* soumission *f* (**to,** à).

suborn [sʌ'bɔːn] *vt Jur* suborner *(un témoin)*.

suborning [sʌ'bɔːnɪŋ] *n Jur* subornation *f*.

subplot ['sʌbplɒt] *n Liter Th* intrigue *f* secondaire.

subpoena¹ [sə'piːnə] *n Jur* citation *f*, assignation *f (de témoins) (sous peine d'amende)*.

subpoena² *vt (pt & pp* **subpoenaed**) **to s. s.o. to appear,** citer qn à comparaître *(sous peine d'amende)*; **to s. s.o. as witness,** assigner qn comme témoin; **to s. a witness,** signifier une assignation à un témoin; **he has been subpoenaed,** il a été cité à comparaître.

sub-postmaster [sʌb'pəʊstmɑːstər] *n Br* receveur *m* d'un petit bureau de poste *(dans un village)*.

sub-postmistress [sʌb'pəʊstmɪstrɪs] *n Br* receveuse *f* d'un petit bureau de poste (*dans un village*).

sub-post office [sʌb'pəʊstɒfɪs] *n Br* petit bureau de poste (*dans un village*).

sub-prefect [sʌb'priːfekt] *n Fr Admin* sous-préfet *m*.

subroutine ['sʌbruːtiːn] *n Comptr* sous-programme *m*.

subscribe [səb'skraɪb] **1** *vi* **(a)** (*contribute, give money*) souscrire; **to s. to a share issue,** souscrire à une émission d'actions; **to s. to a newspaper,** (*become a subscriber*) s'abonner à un journal; (*be a subscriber*) être abonné à un journal;
(b) to s. to an opinion, souscrire à une opinion; **I don't s. to that theory,** je ne souscris pas à cette théorie; **I cannot s. to that,** je ne peux pas consentir à cela.
2 *vt* **(a) to s. ten pounds,** souscrire pour (la somme de) dix livres; **to s. a thousand francs to a charity,** souscrire mille francs pour une œuvre de charité; *Fin* **to s. shares,** souscrire des actions; **subscribed capital,** capital souscrit; **to s. a book,** (*of publisher*) offrir un livre en souscription; (*of bookseller*) acheter un livre en souscription;
(b) *Fml* souscrire (*son nom*); signer (*un document*); **to s. one's name to a document,** apposer sa signature à un document.

subscriber [səb'skraɪbər] *n* **(a)** abonné, -ée (*à un journal*); **telephone s.,** abonné du *ou* au téléphone; **s. trunk dialling,** (téléphone) automatique *m*; **(b)** souscripteur *m* (*à une œuvre de charité*); **(c)** *Fml* signataire *mf*, souscripteur *m* (*d'un document*); **the s.,** le soussigné.

subscript ['sʌbskrɪpt] *n* indice *m*.

subscription [sʌb'skrɪpʃən] *n* **(a)** abonnement *m* (*à un journal*); **to take out a s. to a paper,** s'abonner à un journal, prendre un abonnement à un journal; **s. to a club,** cotisation *f* à un club; **to pay one's s.,** payer *ou* verser sa cotisation (**to,** à); **(b) s. to a charity,** souscription *f* à une œuvre de bienfaisance; **to get up a s.,** se cotiser; **monument erected by public s.,** monument élevé par souscription publique; *Fin* **s. to a loan,** souscription à un emprunt; **s. list,** liste *f* de souscription *ou* des souscripteurs; **(c)** (*in publishing*) souscription *f*; **(d)** (*to an opinion*) adhésion *f* (**to,** à); (*to an act, a decision etc*) approbation *f* (**to,** de); **(e)** *Fml* souscription *f* (*de son nom*), signature *f*.

subsection ['sʌbsekʃən] *n* subdivision *f*; (*in text*) paragraphe *m*.

subsequent ['sʌbsɪkwənt] *adj* suivant, ultérieur, *Fml & Jur* subséquent; **at a s. meeting,** au cours d'une séance ultérieure; **any s. corrections,** toutes corrections ultérieures; **the investigation and all the s. recriminations,** l'enquête et toutes les plaintes qui s'en sont suivies; **s. events proved us right,** la suite des événements a prouvé *ou* les événements ultérieurs ont prouvé que nous avions raison; **s. to this,** à la suite de ceci, par la suite.

subsequently ['sʌbsɪkwəntlɪ] *adv* plus tard, par la suite; postérieurement (**to,** à); **we s. learnt that ...,** nous avons appris plus tard *ou* par la suite que ... .

subservience [sʌb'sɜːvɪəns] *n* soumission *f*, servilité *f*; assujettissement *m* (*à la mode*).

subservient [sʌb'sɜːvɪənt] *adj* **(a)** (*servile*) obséquieux, servile; **(b)** *Fml* (*useful*) utile, qui aide (**to,** à); **to make sth s. to sth,** subordonner qch à qch.

subset ['sʌbset] *n Math* sous-ensemble *m*.

subside [səb'saɪd] *vi* **(a)** (*ground, building*) s'affaisser, se tasser; *F* **to s. into an armchair,** s'affaler dans un fauteuil; **(b)** (*of water*) baisser, diminuer; (*of blister, bump*) (se) dégonfler; **the flood is subsiding,** la crue diminue; **(c)** (*of storm, excitement, fever*) s'apaiser, se calmer; *F* (*of person*) se taire.

subsidence ['sʌbsɪdəns, səb'saɪdəns] *n* **(a)** affaissement *m* (*d'un édifice, d'une route*); tassement *m* (*du terrain, des fondations*); **(b)** décrue *f*, baisse *f* (*d'une rivière*); *Med* délitescence *f* (*d'une tumeur*); apaisement *m* (*d'une fièvre*); **(c)** *Geol* subsidence *f*, effondrement *m*.

subsidiary [sʌb'sɪdɪərɪ] **1** *adj* subsidiaire, auxiliaire; **s. account,** sous-compte *m*; *Fin* **s. company,** filiale *f*. **2** *n Fin* (*company*) filiale *f*.

subsidize ['sʌbsɪdaɪz] *vt* subventionner (*un projet, une organisation, une industrie, qn*); **to be subsidized by the State** *or* **the government,** recevoir une subvention de *ou* être subventionné par l'État; **subsidized industry,** industrie subventionnée.

subsidy ['sʌbsɪdɪ] *n* subvention *f*; *Ind* prime *f*, subvention; **export/building s.,** prime à l'exportation/à la construction.

subsist [səb'sɪst] *vi* (*stay alive*) tirer sa subsistance, vivre (**on,** de); (*remain in existence*) subsister; **custom that still subsists,** coutume qui existe *ou* subsiste encore (de nos jours).

subsistence [səb'sɪstəns] *n* **(a)** (*staying alive*) subsistance *f*; **means of s.,** moyens *m* de subsistance; **s. (allowance),** frais *mpl* de subsistance; **to live at s. level,** avoir tout juste de quoi vivre; **s. farming,** autoconsommation *f*; **a bare s. wage,** un salaire à peine suffisant pour vivre; **(b)** (*remaining in existence*) subsistance *f*.

subsoil ['sʌbsɔɪl] *n Geol etc* sous-sol *m*.

subsonic [sʌb'sɒnɪk] *adj Av* subsonique.

subspecies [sʌb'spiːʃiːz] *n Biol* sous-espèce *f*.

substance ['sʌbstəns] *n* **(a)** substance *f*, matière *f*; *Rel* substance (*spirituelle, corporelle*); *Ch* **stable s.,** corps *m* stable; **(b)** (*essential element*) substance *f*, fond *m*, essentiel *m* (*d'un article, d'un argument*); **I agree in s.,** je suis d'accord sur le fond; **(c)** (*strength, solidity*) solidité *f*; **book of s.,** livre *m* solide; **his argument has little s.,** son argument n'a rien de solide; **(d)** (*income*) **he's a man of s.,** il a du bien.

substandard [sʌb'stændəd] *adj* de qualité inférieure; **it's s. English/French,** ce n'est pas du bon anglais/français.

substantial [səb'stænʃəl] *adj* **(a)** (*point*) important; (*progrès, Com réduction*) considérable; (*différence*) appréciable; **s. proof,** preuve concluante *ou* valable; **a s. number of ...,** un nombre important de ...; **(b)** (*repas*) substantiel, copieux, solide; (*construction, livre*) solide; (*drap*) résistant; **(c)** *Arch & Fml* (*bourgeois*) qui a du bien; (*maison de commerce*) solide, bien assis; **s. landlord,** gros propriétaire; **(d)** (*real*) substantiel, réel.

substantially [səb'stænʃəlɪ] *adv* **(a)** (*considerably*) fortement, considérablement; **it's now s. improved,** il est maintenant fortement *ou* considérablement amélioré; **they are s. the same,** dans l'ensemble *ou* pour l'essentiel ils sont pareils; **the text is s. unaltered,** le texte est dans l'ensemble *ou* pour l'essentiel resté inchangé; **this contributed s. to our success,** cela a contribué largement *ou* pour une grande part à notre succès; **(b)** (*solidly*) solidement, substantiellement; **(c)** (*really*) substantiellement, réellement, en substance.

substantiate [səb'stænʃɪeɪt] *vt* établir, prouver, justifier (*une affirmation etc*); prouver *ou* établir le bien-fondé de (*une réclamation, une accusation, une affirmation etc*).

substantiation [səbstænʃɪ'eɪʃən] *n* justification *f* (*d'une affirmation*); énumération *f* des faits à l'appui (*d'une accusation*).

substantival [sʌbstən'taɪv(ə)l] *adj Gram* substantivé.

substantive ['sʌbstəntɪv] **1** *adj* réel, indépendant; *Gram* substantif; *Jur* **s. law,** droit positif. **2** *n Gram* substantif *m*.

substantively ['sʌbstəntɪvlɪ] *adv* substantivement.

substation ['sʌbsteɪʃən] *n El etc* sous-station *f*.

substitute[1] ['sʌbstɪtjuːt] *n* **(a)** (*foodstuffs, drugs*) succédané *m*; (*imitation*) contrefaçon *f*; **as a s. for ...,** comme succédané de ...; **coffee s.,** ersatz *m* de café; **there's no s. for parental love,** rien ne remplace l'amour parental; **low-alcohol lager is a poor s. for the real thing,** la bière à faible teneur en alcool n'a rien de comparable à la vraie bière; **beware of substitutes,** méfiez-vous des contrefaçons *ou* imitations; **(b)** (*person*) remplaçant, -ante, suppléant, -ante; *Sp* remplaçant; *Jur Rel* substitut *m*; **as a s. for ...,** en remplacement de ..., pour remplacer ...; **to act as a s. for s.o./sth,** remplacer qn/qch, se substituer à qn/à qch.

substitute[2] **1** *vt* substituer; **to s. margarine for butter,** remplacer le beurre par la margarine. **2** *vi* **to s. for s.o.,** remplacer *ou* suppléer qn.

substitution [sʌbstɪ'tjuːʃən] *n* substitution *f*, remplacement *m*; *Sp* remplacement; *Sp* **to make a s.,** faire un remplacement.

substratum, *pl* **-a, -ums** [sʌb'streɪtəm, -ə, -əmz] *n* couche inférieure; *Geol & Phil* substrat(um) *m*.

substructure ['sʌbstrʌktjər] *n Constr* fondement *m* (*d'un édifice*); infrastructure *f* (*d'une route*).

subsume [sʌb'sjuːm] *vt* subsumer; **to s. X under Y,** incorporer X à Y.

subsystem ['sʌbsɪstəm] *n* sous-système *m*.

subtenancy ['sʌbtenənsɪ] *n* sous-location *f*.

subtenant ['sʌbtenənt] *n* sous-locataire *mf*.

subtend [səb'tend] *vt Math* sous-tendre (*un arc*).

subterfuge ['sʌbtəfjuːdʒ] *n* subterfuge *m*; **to resort to s.,** user de subterfuge; **this was a s. to ...,** c'était un subterfuge pour ... .

subterranean [sʌbtə'reɪnɪən] *adj* souterrain.

subtilize ['sʌtɪlaɪz] *vt* donner de la subtilité à (*une pensée*).

subtitle[1] ['sʌbtaɪt(ə)l] *n Cin TV Typ* sous-titre *m*; **film with English subtitles,** film sous-titré en anglais.

subtitle[2] *vt Cin TV etc* sous-titrer.

subtitled ['sʌbtaɪt(ə)ld] *adj Cin TV* (*film, programme*) sous-titré.

subtitling ['sʌbtaɪtlɪŋ] *n Cin TV* sous-titrage *m*.

subtle ['sʌt(ə)l] *adj* (*personne, esprit, raisonnement, parfum, charme*) subtil; (*cunning*) rusé, astucieux; **s. distinction,** distinction ténue *ou* subtile; **you are being too s.,** vous finassez; **s. irony,** fine ironie; **s. remark,** observation subtile.

subtlety ['sʌt(ə)ltɪ] *n* **(a)** subtilité *f* (*d'une distinction, de l'esprit, d'un raisonnement*); subtilité, raffinement *m*, finesse *f* (*d'une politique*); **(b)** (*subtle thing*) subtilité *f*; (*distinction*) distinction subtile.

subtly ['sʌt(ə)lɪ] *adv* subtilement, avec finesse; (*to argue etc*) avec subtilité; **s. different,** avec une différence à peine perceptible.

subtonic [sʌb'tɒnɪk] *n Mus* note *f* sensible, sensible *f*.

subtotal ['sʌbtəʊt(ə)l] *n* sous-total *m*, total partiel.

subtract [səb'trækt] *vt Math* soustraire, retrancher (**from,** de).

subtraction [səb'trækʃən] *n Math* soustraction *f* (**from,** de).

subtropical [sʌb'trɒpɪk(ə)l] *adj* subtropical, -aux.

subtype ['sʌbtaɪp] *n* sous-type *m*.

suburb ['sʌbɜːb] *n* banlieue *f*; (*nearer city*) faubourg *m*; **the suburbs,** la banlieue; **in the suburbs,** en banlieue; **in the suburbs of Paris,** dans la banlieue de Paris; **garden s.,** cité-jardin *f*, *pl* cités-jardins.

suburban [sə'bɜːbən] *adj* suburbain; (*maison, gare, train*) de banlieue; *Pej* (*personne*) à l'esprit étroit; (*vie*) étriqué; **even the city centre's s.,** même le centre-ville sent la banlieue.

suburbanite [sə'bɜːbənaɪt] *n F* banlieusard, -arde.

suburbia [sə'bɜːbɪə] *n* la banlieue.

subvention [səb'venʃən] *n* subvention *f*.

subversion [səb'vɜːʃən] *n Pol etc* subversion *f*.

subversive [səb'vɜːsɪv] **1** *adj* subversif (**of,** de). **2** *n* individu subversif; **a group of subversives,** un groupe subversif.

subvert [səb'vɜːt] *vt* renverser, subvertir.

subway ['sʌbweɪ] *n* **(a)** *Br* (*walkway under road etc*) passage souterrain, souterrain *m*; **(b)** *Rail esp Am* métro *m*.

sub-zero [sʌb'zɪərəʊ] *adj* au-dessous de zéro; **s.-z. temperatures,** températures inférieures à zéro.

succeed [sək'siːd] **1** *vi* **(a)** réussir; **hard workers always s.,** les grands travailleurs arrivent *ou* réussissent toujours; **how to s.,** le moyen de parvenir; **young man who will s.,** jeune homme qui ira loin; **to s. in doing sth,** réussir *ou* arriver à faire qch; **she always succeeds,** tout lui réussit; **I/the plan only succeeded in making things worse,** je/le projet n'ai/n'a réussi qu'à aggraver la situation; **to s. in one's attempt to ...,** réussir dans sa tentative de ...; *Prov* **nothing succeeds like success,** rien ne réussit comme le succès; **(b) to s. to the throne** *or* **the Crown,** succéder à la couronne; **to s. to an office/estate,** hériter d'une fonction/d'une propriété; *Jur* **right to s.,** droits *mpl* de succession. **2** *vt* succéder à (*qn*); **George III was succeeded by George IV,** George IV succéda à *ou* fut le successeur de George III; **day succeeds day,** les jours se suivent.

succeeding [sək'siːdɪŋ] *adj* **(a)** (*following*) suivant; **(b)** (*future*) futur, à venir; **(c)** (*successive*) successif; **with each s. year,** d'année en année.

success [sək'ses] *n* **(a)** succès *m*, réussite *f*; **we wish you s.,** bonne chance!; **to meet with** *or* **to achieve s.,** avoir *ou* remporter du succès; **without s.,** sans succès, en vain; **to score a s.,** remporter *ou* avoir un succès; **to be a s.,** (*go well, work out well etc*) réussir, être réussi, être un succès; (*be popular*) (*of film, book etc*) être un succès; (*of party, cake*) être une réussite, être réussi; **the cake was a big s.,** (*everyone liked it*) le gâteau a eu un grand succès; **to be a s. with s.o.,** (*be popular etc*) avoir un *ou* du succès auprès de qn; **it was a huge** *or* **great s.,** ça a été un succès fou; **he was the s. of the evening,** il a été le clou de la soirée; **to make a s. of sth,** réussir qch; **it's a s. story,** c'est une réussite; **(b)** *Arch* succès *m* (*d'une affaire*); (*still used in*) **a second attempt met with no better s.,** une seconde tentative n'a pas eu plus de succès.

successful [sək'sesful] *adj* (*projet*) couronné de succès; (*résultat*) heureux; (*portrait*) réussi; (*pièce*) qui a du succès; **to be s. in doing sth,** réussir à faire qch; **were you s.?,** avez-vous réussi?, est-ce que ça a marché?; **he is s. in everything,** tout lui réussit, il réussit dans tout ce qu'il entreprend; **a s. businesswoman,** une femme d'affaires qui a réussi *ou* qui est arrivée; **to be s. at the polls,** sortir victorieux du scrutin; **s. candidates,** candidats élus; *Sch* candidats reçus; **to bring an operation to a s. conclusion,** mener une opération à bonne fin *ou* à bien.

successfully [sək'sesfəlɪ] *adv* avec succès; **when we've s. completed this stage of the operation,** après avoir mené à bien cette partie de l'opération.

succession [sək'seʃən] *n* **(a)** succession *f*, suite *f*; (*series*) série *f*, suite ininterrompue (*de victoires etc*); **in s.,** consécutivement, successivement; **for two years in s.,** pendant deux années successives *ou* consécutives *ou* de suite; **in close s.,** se succédant de près; **in rapid s.,** coup sur coup; **a rapid s. of governments,** une succession rapide de gouvernements; **long s. of kings,** longue suite de rois; **(b)** succession *f* (*à la couronne*); *Jur* succession; (*descendants*) lignée *f*; **to settle the s.,** régler la succession; **at the time of his s. to the throne,** au moment de son avènement *m*; *Hist* **the Wars of S.,** les guerres *fpl* de succession; **law of s.,** droit *m* des successions; **right of s.,** droits de succession.

successive [sək'sesɪv] *adj* successif, consécutif; **on five s. Sundays,** cinq dimanches consécutifs *ou* de suite; **s. generations,** les générations successives.

successively [sək'sesɪvlɪ] *adv* successivement.

successor [sək'sesər] *n* successeur *m* (**to,** à); **the s. to the throne,** le successeur au trône; **my first car and its successors,** ma première voiture et celles qui lui ont succédé *ou* qui sont venues ensuite.

succinct [sʌk'sɪŋ(k)t] *adj* (*récit, écrivain*) succinct.

succinctly [sʌk'sɪŋ(k)tlɪ] *adv* succinctement.

succinctness [sʌk'sɪŋ(k)tnɪs] *n* concision *f*.

succour[1], *US* succor[1] ['sʌkər] *n Lit* secours *m*, aide *f*; **to give s.,** porter secours *ou* assistance.

succour[2], *US* succor[2] *vt Lit* venir en aide à, venir à l'aide de (*qn*); secourir (*les pauvres*).

succulence ['sʌkjʊləns] *n* succulence *f*.

succulent ['sʌkjʊlənt] **1** *adj* **(a)** (*food*) succulent; **(b)** *Bot* **s. leaf,** feuille charnue. **2** *n Bot* plante grasse.

succumb [sə'kʌm] *vi* succomber (**to** à), céder (**to** à); **to s. to one's injuries,** succomber à *ou* mourir de ses blessures; **we have all succumbed to her charm,** son charme nous a tous conquis, nous avons tous succombé à son charme; **I eventually succumbed,** j'ai fini par céder.

such [sʌtʃ] **1** *adj* **(a)** tel, pareil, semblable; **beasts of prey s. as the lion or the tiger,** des bêtes fauves telles que le lion ou le tigre; **s. a man,** un tel homme; **on s. an occasion,** en semblable occasion, en une telle occasion, en une occasion pareille; **why do you ask s. a question?,** pourquoi demander une chose pareille?, pourquoi poser une question pareille?; **did you ever see s. a thing!,** a-t-on jamais vu pareille chose!; **you wouldn't have s. a thing as a corkscrew, would you?,** vous n'auriez pas un tire-bouchon, par hasard?; **s. is not my intention,** ce n'est pas là mon intention; **if s. were the case,** s'il en était ainsi, si tel était le cas; **the village boasts a bus, s. as it is,** le village a un autobus, si l'on peut dire; **s. books as these are always useful,** les livres de ce genre sont toujours utiles; **in s. cases,** en pareils cas; **in s. weather,** par un temps pareil; **how can you tell s. lies?,** comment pouvez-vous mentir de la sorte?, comment pouvez-vous dire des mensonges pareils?; **she has s. ideas!,** elle a de ces idées!; **s. courage,** tant de courage, un tel courage; **some s. plan was in my mind,** j'avais dans l'esprit un projet de ce genre; **s. is life!,** c'est la vie!; **there is no s. thing,** cela n'existe pas; **if there were no s. thing as money,** si l'argent n'existait pas; **I said no s. thing,** je n'ai rien dit de semblable *ou* de la sorte; **no s. thing!,** pas du tout!; *Jur* **persons guilty of s. offences,** personnes coupables des délits susmentionnés;

(b) on s. (and s.) a day in s. (and s.) a place, tel jour en tel endroit; **your letter of s. and s. a date,** votre lettre du tant; **s. a one,** un tel, une telle;

(c) she arranges things in s. a way that she is free on Saturdays, elle s'arrange de manière à être libre le(s) samedi(s); **his kindness was s. as to make us feel ashamed,** sa bonté était telle que nous en étions confus; *Fml* **to take s. steps as shall be considered necessary,** prendre toutes mesures qui paraîtront nécessaires; *Fml* **until s. time as is convenient to me,** jusqu'à ce que cela me convienne.

2 *adv* **s. large houses,** de si grandes maisons; **I had never heard s. good music,** je n'avais jamais entendu d'aussi bonne musique; **he's not s. a good player as you,** ce n'est pas un aussi bon joueur que vous; **s. a clever woman,** une femme si intelligente; **it was s. a long time ago,** il y a si longtemps de cela; **he is s. a liar,** il est si *ou* tellement menteur, c'est un tel menteur; **s. an enjoyable day,** une journée si *ou* tellement agréable; **we had s. a**

good time, on s'est tellement *ou* si bien amusé(s), on s'est tant amusé(s); **don't be in s. a hurry,** ne soyez pas si pressé; **you gave me s. a fright!,** vous m'avez fait une (telle) peur!

3 *pron* **(a) he enjoys cakes, ices and s.,** il mange avec plaisir des gâteaux, des glaces et autres choses de ce genre;

(b) that's not for s. as you, cela n'est pas pour quelqu'un comme toi; **I haven't many, but I will send you s. as I have,** je n'en ai pas beaucoup, mais je vous enverrai ce que j'ai;

(c) she was a very brave woman and well known as s., c'était une femme très courageuse, et elle était bien connue en tant que telle; **history as s. is too often neglected,** l'histoire en tant que telle est trop souvent négligée; **the text as s. is fine but ...,** le texte en soi est bien mais ...; **I wasn't scared as s.,** je n'avais pas vraiment peur.

suchlike ['sʌtʃlaɪk] *F* **1** *adj* semblable, pareil. **2** *pron* **beggars, tramps and s.,** mendiants, chemineaux et autres gens de la sorte; **concerts, theatres and s.,** concerts, théâtres, et autres choses de ce genre.

suck¹ [sʌk] *n* **(a)** action *f* de sucer; *HydE* succion *f*, aspiration *f* (*d'un déversoir, d'une pompe*); **to have** *or* **take a s. at a sweet,** sucer un bonbon; **(b) to give a child s.,** donner à téter *ou* la tétée à un enfant.

suck² **1** *vt* sucer; téter (*le lait*); sucer, suçoter (*une orange, des bonbons*); mordiller (*le coin de son mouchoir*); tirer sur (*sa pipe*); **to s. one's fingers,** se sucer les doigts; **to s. one's thumb,** sucer son pouce; **to s. poison out of a wound,** extraire le poison d'une blessure en la suçant; *Fig* **to s. s.o. dry,** sucer qn jusqu'à la moelle; *F* **you can't teach your grandmother to s. eggs,** ce n'est pas aux vieux singes qu'on apprend à faire des grimaces; **the dust is sucked into the bag,** la poussière est aspirée dans le sac; *Fig* **to get sucked into a conspiracy,** être entraîné dans une conspiration.

2 *vi* **(a)** sucer; (*of child etc*) téter (le lait); *Nau* (*of pump*) super; **the child won't s.,** l'enfant ne prend pas le sein; **to s. at a sweet,** sucer *ou* suçoter un bonbon; **to s. at a pipe,** tirer sur *ou* sucer sa pipe; **to s. on a straw,** boire à la paille;

(b) *esp US Sl* (*be very bad, unpleasant etc*) être merdique; **this city sucks,** cette ville est merdique.

▶**suck down** *vtsep* (*draw down by sucking*) (*of whirlpool etc*) engloutir, entraîner vers le fond.

▶**suck in** *vtsep* (*draw in by sucking*) sucer; (*draw in by vacuum*) aspirer; absorber (*des connaissances*); (*of air pump*) aspirer (*l'air*); engloutir (*dans un tourbillon*); creuser (*ses joues*); **to get sucked in,** (*to conspiracy, plot etc*) se faire entraîner (**to,** dans).

▶**suck off** *vtsep Vulg* (*sexually*) sucer, pomper, faire une pipe à.

▶**suck out** *vtsep* (*remove by sucking*) sucer (*du jus*); **to s. out the poison from the wound,** aspirer *ou* sucer le poison de la blessure.

▶**suck up** *vtsep* sucer, aspirer, pomper (*un liquide, de l'air*); **these gases get sucked up into the upper atmosphere,** ces gaz sont aspirés dans les couches supérieures de l'atmosphère.

▶**suck up to** *vipo F* (*ingratiate oneself with*) faire (de) la lèche à qn, lécher les bottes *ou Sl* le cul à qn.

sucker¹ ['sʌkər] *n* **(a)** (*person who sucks*) suceur, -euse; **(b)** *F* (*gullible person*) niais *m*, nigaud *m*; **to be a s. for a pretty/handsome face,** ne pas savoir résister à un joli visage; **(c)** suçoir *m* (*de pou*); ventouse *f* (*de sangsue, sur une machine*); **(d)** *F* (*sweet*) bonbon *m*; **(e)** (*in horticulture*) rejeton *m*, rejet *m* (*d'une plante*); drageon *m*, surgeon *m* (*d'arbre*); **to throw out suckers,** (*of tree*) drageonner, surgeonner.

sucker² **1** *vt* (*in horticulture*) enlever les drageons (*d'un arbre*). **2** *vi* (*of tree*) drageonner.

sucking ['sʌkɪŋ] **1** *adj* **s. pig,** cochon *m* de lait. **2** *n* (*of baby*) succion *f*; (*of pump*) aspiration *f*.

sucking up *n* **(a)** *F* (*ingratiation*) lèche *f*, flagornerie *f*; **(b)** aspiration (*d'un liquide*).

suckle ['sʌk(ə)l] **1** *vt* allaiter (*un enfant, un petit*); donner le sein *ou* donner à téter à (*un enfant*). **2** *vi* (*of baby etc*) téter.

suckling ['sʌklɪŋ] *n* **(a)** (*act*) allaitement *m*; **(b)** *Arch* (*child*) nourrisson, -onne, enfant *mf* au sein; (*animal*) jeune animal *m* qui tète encore; (*still used in*) **s. pig,** cochon *m* de lait.

sucrose ['suːkrəʊs] *n Ch* saccharose *m*.

suction ['sʌkʃən] *n* succion *f*; aspiration *f* (*de l'eau dans une pompe*); aspiration, appel *m* (*d'air*); **to adhere by s.,** faire ventouse; *Aut etc* **s. cup,** ventouse *f*; **s. pump,** pompe aspirante; **s. stroke,** temps *m* de l'aspiration.

Sudan (the) [ðəsuː'dæn] *n* le Soudan.

Sudanese [suːdə'niːz] **1** *adj* soudanais, soudanien. **2** *n* Soudanais, -aise, Soudanien, -ienne.

sudden ['sʌd(ə)n] *adj* **(a)** soudain, subit; (*mouvement, tournant*) brusque; **this is rather s.,** c'est plutôt inattendu; **it was a very s. decision,** j'ai *ou* il a *etc* pris cette décision très vite; **it's all so s.,** tout est arrivé si vite; **their marriage was rather on the s. side,** leur mariage s'est fait assez soudainement *ou* brusquement; **s. death,** mort soudaine *ou* subite; *Sp* **s. death play-off,** jeu pour décider d'un match nul (*dans lequel celui qui marque le premier point est le gagnant*); **s. shower,** averse subite; **(b) all of a s.,** soudain, tout à coup, *F* tout d'un coup.

suddenly ['sʌd(ə)nlɪ] *adv* soudain, soudainement, subitement, tout à coup, *F* tout d'un coup; (*to move*) brusquement; **she died s.,** elle est morte soudainement *ou* subitement; **it happened so s.,** c'est arrivé si vite; **then s. he was gone,** et puis subitement *ou* soudain il était parti; **she very s. changed her mind,** elle a changé d'avis très soudainement.

suddenness ['sʌd(ə)nnɪs] *n* soudaineté *f*; (*of movement*) brusquerie *f*.

suds [sʌdz] *npl* **(soap) s.,** (*foam*) mousse *f* de savon; (*soapy water*) eau savonneuse; (*washing powder*) lessive *f*.

sue [suː] **1** *vt Jur* **to s. s.o. at law,** intenter un procès à qn, poursuivre qn en justice; **to s. s.o. for damages,** poursuivre qn en dommages-intérêts. **2** *vi* **(a)** *Jur* **to s. for a separation,** plaider en séparation; **to s. for libel,** attaquer en diffamation; **(b) to s. for peace,** demander la paix.

suede, suède [sweɪd] *n* (*for shoes*) daim *m*; (*for gloves etc*) (peau *f* de) suède *m*; **s. cloth,** suédine *f*; **s. gloves,** gants *mpl* de suède; **s. shoes,** chaussures *fpl* en daim.

suet ['suːɪt] *n Culin* graisse *f* de rognon; **beef s.,** graisse (de rognon) de bœuf; **s. pudding,** pouding fait avec de la farine et de la graisse de bœuf.

Suez ['suːɪz, 'sʊɪz] *n* Suez; **the S. Canal,** le canal de Suez.

suffer ['sʌfər] **1** *vt* éprouver, subir, souffrir (*une perte*); endurer, ressentir (*une douleur*); subir, éprouver (*une peine*); (*tolerate*) permettre, supporter, tolérer; **to s. hunger,** souffrir la faim; **to s. defeat,** essuyer *ou* subir une défaite; **she doesn't s. fools gladly,** elle ne peut pas supporter *ou* souffrir les imbéciles.

2 *vi* (*of person, business, marriage, relations, health etc*) souffrir; (*of economy*) être perturbé; (*of profits*) subir une perte; **to s. from rheumatism,** souffrir de rhumatismes; **to s. for one's misdeeds,** supporter les conséquences de ses méfaits; **you'll s. for it,** il vous en cuira, vous allez le payer; **to be made to s. for what others have done,** payer pour les actions d'autrui; **to s. from neglect,** pâtir d'un manque de soins; **country suffering from labour troubles,** pays en proie à l'agitation ouvrière; **his good name has suffered,** sa réputation a souffert; **she started drinking and her work suffered,** elle a commencé à boire et son travail en a pâti; **the vines have suffered from the frost,** les vignes ont souffert de la gelée.

sufferance ['sʌf(ə)rəns] *n* tolérance *f* (**of,** de); **children are admitted on s.,** l'entrée des enfants est tolérée; **I get the feeling I'm just here on s.,** j'ai l'impression de n'être ici que parce qu'on m'y tolère.

sufferer ['sʌf(ə)rər] *n* **to be a s. from ill health,** souffrir d'une mauvaise santé; **sufferers from asthma, asthma sufferers,** personnes sujettes à l'asthme.

suffering ['sʌf(ə)rɪŋ] **1** *adj* souffrant, qui souffre. **2** *n* souffrance *f*; **the depression caused great s.,** la dépression a causé de grandes souffrances; **cheerful in spite of his s.,** gai malgré ses souffrances.

suffice [sə'faɪs] **1** *vi Fml* suffire; **that will s. for me,** cela me suffira; **s. it to say that I got nothing out of it,** suffit que je n'en ai rien obtenu. **2** *vt* suffire à (*qn*), être suffisant pour (*qn*).

sufficiency [sə'fɪʃənsɪ] *n Fml* quantité suffisante, *Arch* suffisance *f*; **to have a s. of sth,** avoir assez de qch; **to have no more than a bare s.,** avoir tout juste assez de qch; (*of food*) avoir tout juste de quoi vivre.

sufficient [sə'fɪʃənt] **1** *adj* assez de, suffisant; **lack of s. food,** insuffisance *f* d'alimentation; **this is s. to feed them,** cela suffit pour les nourrir; **a hundred francs will be s.,** j'aurai assez de cent francs; **one light will be s.,** une lampe suffira; **they didn't have s. warning,** ils n'ont pas été suffisamment prévenus; **is that s. time for you?,** cela vous donne-t-il suffisamment de temps?; **let me know in s. time so that I can ...,** prévenez-moi suffisamment à l'avance pour que je puisse ...; **with s. supplies,** avec des réserves suffisantes, avec suffisamment de réserves; **there was nowhere near s. heating in the building,** l'immeuble était loin d'être suffisamment chauffé. **2** *n* assez; **have you had s. (to eat)?,** avez-vous assez mangé?, êtes-vous rassasié?

sufficiently [sə'fɪʃəntlɪ] *adv* suffisamment, assez; **to be s. tactful to ...,** avoir suffisamment de tact pour ... .

suffix[1] ['sʌfɪks] *n Gram Comptr* suffixe *m*.

suffix[2] ['sʌfɪks, sʌ'fɪks] *vt Gram Comptr* suffixer.

suffixed ['sʌfɪkst] *adj* (*lettre, particule*) suffixe.

suffocate ['sʌfəkeɪt] **1** *vt* (*kill*) étouffer (*qn*); (*of smell*) suffoquer (*qn*); *Fig* **all signs of initiative were suffocated,** toute indication d'initiative était étouffée. **2** *vi* étouffer, suffoquer (**with rage/***etc*, de colère/*etc*).

suffocating ['sʌfəkeɪtɪŋ] *adj* suffocant, étouffant; **it's s. (in) here,** on étouffe ici.

suffocation [sʌfə'keɪʃən] *n* suffocation *f*, étouffement *m*; **to die of s.,** mourir suffoqué *ou* étouffé.

suffragan ['sʌfrəgən] **1** *adj Rel* **bishop s.,** (*évêque*) suffragant. **2** *n* **s. (bishop),** (évêque *m*) suffragant *m*.

suffrage ['sʌfrɪdʒ] *n Pol* suffrage *m*; (*vote*) vote *m*, voix *f*; (*right to vote*) droit *m* de vote; **universal s.,** suffrage universel; **women's s.,** droit de vote pour les femmes.

suffragette [sʌfrə'dʒet] *n Pol Hist* suffragette *f*.

suffuse [sə'fjuːz] *vt esp Lit* se répandre sur (*qch*); **a blush suffused her cheeks,** une rougeur s'est répandue sur ses joues, *Lit* ses joues s'empourprèrent; **eyes suffused with tears,** yeux noyés *ou* baignés de larmes; **suffused with light,** inondé de lumière.

sugar[1] ['ʃʊgər] *n* **(a)** sucre *m*; **granulated s.,** sucre cristallisé; **lump s.,** sucre en morceaux; **lump** *or* **cube of s.,** morceau *m ou* cube *m* de sucre; **caster s.,** sucre semoule; (*finer*) sucre en poudre; **icing s.,** sucre glace; **brown s.,** cassonade *f*; **help yourself to s.,** prenez du sucre; **milk, no s., please,** avec du lait, sans sucre, s'il vous plaît; **s. almond,** dragée *f*; **s. basin** *or* **bowl,** sucrier *m*; **s. beet,** betterave *f* à sucre; **s. cane,** canne *f* à sucre; *F* **s. daddy,** entreteneur *m*; **he's my s. daddy,** (*affectionately*) c'est mon papounet; **she's found herself a s. daddy,** *Pej* elle s'est trouvé un vieux friqué; **I've no intention of being your s. daddy,** je n'ai pas l'intention de t'entretenir; **s. maple,** érable *m* à sucre; **s. mouse,** souris *f* en sucre; **s. pea,** mange-tout *m inv*; **s. shaker,** saupoudroir *m* à sucre, **(pair of) s. tongs,** pince *f* à sucre; **s. refinery,** raffinerie *f* (de sucre), sucrerie *f*;

(b) milk s., sucre de lait, lactose *f*; *Physiol* **blood s.,** glucose sanguin; **blood s. level,** taux *m* de sucre dans le sang;

(c) *F* (*term of address*) (mon) trésor.

sugar[2] *vt* sucrer (*son café etc*); dragéifier, recouvrir (*une pilule*) de sucre; **sugared almond,** dragée *f*; *Fig* **to s. the pill,** dorer la pilule.

sugar-coated [ʃʊgə'kəʊtɪd] *adj* recouvert de sucre; (*almond*) lissé; **s.-c. pill,** pilule dragéifiée.

sugar-free [ʃʊgə'friː] *adj* sans sucre.

sugarloaf ['ʃʊgələʊf] *n* pain *m* de sucre; **s. mountain,** montagne *f* en pain de sucre.

sugarplum ['ʃʊgəplʌm] *n Arch* bonbon *m*.

sugary ['ʃʊgərɪ] *adj* **(a)** (*containing sugar*) sucré; (*sprinkled with sugar*) saupoudré de sucre; **to go s.,** (*of jam*) se cristalliser; **s. taste,** goût sucré; **(b)** (*sourire, ton*) mielleux, sucré; (*ton*) doucereux.

suggest [sə'dʒest] *vt* **(a)** suggérer, proposer (*qch à qn*); *Med Psy* suggérer (*une idée, une action*); **she suggested going for a walk,** elle a suggéré *ou* proposé de faire une promenade; **what do you s. I do?,** que suggérez-vous que je fasse?; **I shall do as you s.,** je ferai comme vous le suggérez; **a solution suggested itself to me,** une solution m'est venue à l'esprit;

(b) inspirer, faire naître (*une idée*); **prudence suggests a retreat,** la prudence conseille la retraite; **which suggests that it was an accident,** ce qui semblerait indiquer qu'il s'agissait d'un accident; **are eggs as scarce as the price would s.?,** les œufs sont-ils aussi rares que le prix le laisse supposer?; **the marks in the sand s. a person of about ...,** les traces sur le sable indiquent la présence d'une personne d'environ ...; *Jur* **I s. that ...,** n'est-il pas vrai que ...?;

(c) (*insinuate*) insinuer; **are you suggesting that I am lying?,** est-ce que vous insinuez que je mens?;

(d) (*evoke*) évoquer; **what do these abstract forms s. to you?,** que vous suggèrent *ou* évoquent ces formes abstraites?

suggestible [sə'dʒestɪb(ə)l] *adj Psy* suggestible, influençable par la suggestion (hypnotique); (*easily influenced*) influençable.

suggestion [sə'dʒestʃən] *n* **(a)** suggestion *f*, proposition *f*; **to be open to s.,** être prêt à accueillir des suggestions; **at her s. I stayed at home,** suivant son conseil je suis resté chez moi; **to make a s.,** faire une suggestion *ou* proposition; **practical s.,** conseil *m* pratique; **suggestions for improvement,** propositions en vue d'une amélioration; **to be full of suggestions,** être fécond en idées *ou* en conseils; **it was only a s.,** ce n'était qu'une suggestion; **suggestions box,** boîte *f* à idées;

(b) *Jur* **my s. is that you were not there at the time,** n'est-il pas vrai que vous étiez absent à ce moment-là?;

(c) *Psy etc* suggestion *f*; **hypnotic s.,** suggestion hypnotique; **adverts work by s.,** les publicités fonctionnent à la suggestion;

(d) (*insinuation*) indication *f*; **there is no s. that he might be guilty,** rien *ou* personne ne suggère *ou* dit qu'il puisse être coupable;

(e) (*hint*) **to speak with just a s. of a foreign accent,** parler avec une pointe d'accent étranger; **s. of regret,** nuance *f ou* pointe *f* de regret.

suggestive [sə'dʒestɪv] *adj* suggestif, évocateur, -trice; (*lyrics, dance etc*) suggestif; **s. of sth,** qui évoque qch; **s. joke,** plaisanterie grivoise.

suggestively [sə'dʒestɪvlɪ] *adv* d'une façon suggestive.

suggestiveness [sə'dʒestɪvnɪs] *n* caractère suggestif (*d'un dessin etc*).

suicidal [sʊɪ'saɪd(ə)l] *adj* suicidaire; **it would be s. (to do it),** ce serait du suicide *ou* ce serait suicidaire (d'agir de la sorte); *Fig* **as far as your career is concerned it would be s.,** sur le plan professionnel, ça serait du suicide; **s. tendencies,** tendances *fpl* au suicide *ou* suicidaires; **to be feeling s.,** se sentir suicidaire; **some absolutely s. driving,** une conduite complètement suicidaire.

suicide ['sʊɪsaɪd] *n* **(a)** suicide *m* ; **to commit s.,** se suicider; **attempted s.,** tentative *f* de suicide; **to commit political s.,** se suicider politiquement; **it would be s. to go there,** ce serait du suicide d'y aller; **mass s.,** suicide collectif; **s. attempt,** tentative de suicide; *Mil* **s. mission,** mission *f* suicide; **s. pact,** pacte *m* de suicide; **s. squad,** équipe *f* (en mission) suicide; **(b)** (*person*) suicidé, ée; **there was an attempted s. in the next bed,** il y avait un suicidé dans le lit d'à côté.

suit[1] [s(j)uːt] *n* **(a)** (*clothing*) ensemble *m*; (*man's*) complet *m*, costume *m*; (*woman's*) tailleur *m*; **two-piece/three-piece s.,** complet en deux/trois pièces; **lounge s.,** complet veston; *Av Astronaut* **flying** *or* **flight s.,** combinaison *f* de vol; **pressure s.,** combinaison pressurisée, **space s.,** combinaison de cosmonaute;

(b) *Cards* **the four suits,** les quatres couleurs; *Fig* **politeness is not his long s.,** la politesse n'est pas son fort; **to follow s.,** fournir à la couleur (demandée); *Fig* en faire autant, faire de même;

(c) *Nau* **s. of sails,** jeu *m* de voiles;

(d) *Jur* **s. at law,** (*lawsuit*) procès *m* (civil); (*act of suing*) poursuites *fpl* (en justice); **criminal s.,** action *f ou* procès criminel(le); **to be a party in a s.,** être en cause;

(e) *Old-fashioned* (*courting*) **to press one's s. with a girl,** faire une cour assidue à une jeune fille;

(f) *Old-fashioned* (*request*) prière *f*, demande *f*.

suit[2] **1** *vt* **(a)** (*of clothes, colours etc*) aller à; (*of arrangement, time, job*) convenir à; **to be suited to** *or* **for sth,** être fait pour qch; **blue suits you,** le bleu te va bien; **this climate/this food does not s. me,** ce climat/cette nourriture ne me convient pas; **this hat suits you,** ce chapeau vous va (bien); **clothes not suited to the climate,** vêtements ne convenant pas au climat; **the premises are not suited for display purposes,** le local ne se prête pas à l'étalage; **he is not suited for** *or* **to be a doctor,** il n'est pas fait pour être médecin; **they are suited to each other,** ils sont faits l'un pour l'autre; **a small job in the country would s. me very well,** un petit emploi en province m'irait *ou* me conviendrait très bien; **she found a house that suited her,** elle a trouvé une maison à son gré; **marriage suits you,** le mariage vous réussit; **that suits me best,** c'est ce qui m'arrange le mieux; **that suits me (just) fine** *or F* **down to the ground,** ça me va à merveille, ça me convient parfaitement; **I shall do it when it suits me,** je le ferai quand cela me conviendra; **you can't just come and go when(ever) it suits you,** tu ne peux pas aller et venir à ta guise; **would that s. you?,** cela ferait-il votre affaire?; **(would) two o'clock s. you?,** est-ce que deux heures vous conviendrait?; **s. yourself,** faites comme vous voudrez;

(b) *Am* habiller (*qn*) d'un costume;

(c) (*adapt*) accommoder, adapter (**sth to sth,** qch à qch); **to s. the action to the word,** adapter les actes à la parole.

2 *vi* **that date does not s.,** cette date ne convient pas; **would tomorrow s.?,** demain conviendrait-il?

suitability [s(j)uːtə'bɪlɪtɪ] *n* convenance *f* (*d'une date*); à-propos *m* (*d'une remarque*); accord *m*, rapport *m* (*de caractères*); **s. of a candidate for a post,** aptitude *f* d'un candidat à un poste.

suitable ['s(j)uːtəb(ə)l] *adj* (*sujet, travail*) convenable, qui convient; (*exemple*) apte; **we have found nothing s.,** nous n'avons rien trouvé qui convienne; **wherever you think s.,** où bon vous semblera; **the most s. date,** la date qui conviendrait le mieux; **is tomorrow s.?,** demain convient-il?; **s. expression,** expression pertinente *ou* appropriée; **s. marriage,** union bien assortie; **the most s. candidate,** le candidat qui convient le mieux; **I've nothing s. to wear,** je n'ai rien de convenable à me mettre; **with a s. note of sarcasm,** avec une touche de sarcasme appropriée; **s. to** *or* **for sth,** bon *ou* propre *ou* approprié à qch; **he's not s. for our Christine,** ce n'est pas l'homme qu'il faut à notre Christine; **is it a book s. for children?,** est-ce un livre pour les enfants?, est-ce que ce livre convient aux enfants?; **s. for children of seven years and under,** pour les enfants de sept ans ou moins; **to make sth s. for sth,** adapter qch à qch.

suitably ['s(j)uːtəblɪ] *adv* convenablement; (*say*) à propos; *Iron* **I hope you're s. impressed,** j'espère bien que vous êtes contents; **s. matched,** bien assortis.

suitcase ['s(j)uːtkeɪs] *n* valise *f*; **I'm still living out of a s.,** je ne suis pas encore installé; **I've been travelling around, living out of a s.,** j'ai voyagé un peu partout sans jamais déballer mes bagages.

suite [swiːt] *n* **(a) s. (of rooms),** appartement *m*; **three piece s.,** (*furniture*) canapé *m* avec deux fauteuils assortis, salon *m* trois pièces; **bedroom s.,** (meubles *mpl* de) chambre *f* à coucher; **bathroom s.,** (meubles de) salle *f* de bains; **(b)** *Mus* suite *f*; **orchestral s.,** suite d'orchestre; **(c)** suite *f* (*d'un prince*).

suiting ['s(j)uːtɪŋ] *n Com* (*cloth*) tissu *m* de confection; **men's suitings,** tissus pour complets.

suitor ['s(j)uːtər] *n* **(a)** *Arch & Hum* soupirant *m*; **(b)** *Jur* plaideur, -euse.

sulfa, sulfate *etc US* = **SULPHA, SULPHATE** *etc.*

sulk¹ [sʌlk] *n* bouderie *f*; **to be in a s.,** bouder; **to have (a fit of) the sulks,** bouder, faire la tête.

sulk² *vi* bouder, faire la tête; **stop sulking,** arrête de bouder.

sulkily ['sʌlkɪlɪ] *adv* en boudant, d'un ton *ou* d'un air boudeur.

sulkiness ['sʌlkɪnɪs] *n* bouderie *f*.

sulky ['sʌlkɪ] *adj* boudeur; **to be s.,** bouder; **to look s.,** avoir un air boudeur, faire la tête.

sullen ['sʌlən] *adj* (*person*) maussade, renfrogné, morose; (*silence*) obstiné, buté; *Lit* (*sky, clouds*) maussade.

sullenly ['sʌlənlɪ] *adv* d'un air maussade *ou* renfrogné; (*obéir*) de mauvaise grâce.

sullenness ['sʌlənnɪs] *n* maussaderie *f*, air renfrogné.

sullied ['sʌlɪd] *adj* souillé, terni.

sully ['sʌlɪ] *vt* souiller, ternir; tacher (*sa réputation*).

sulpha, *US* **sulfa** ['sʌlfə] *n* **s. drug,** sulfamide *f*.

sulphate, *US* **sulf-** ['sʌlfeɪt] *n* **(a)** *Ch* sulfate *m*; **iron s., ferrous s.,** sulfate de fer; **copper s.,** sulfate de cuivre; **(b)** *Com* sulfate *m* de soude.

sulphide, *US* **sulf-** ['sʌlfaɪd] *n Ch* sulfure *m*; **hydrogen s.,** hydrogène sulfuré, acide *m* sulfhydrique.

sulphonamide, *US* **sulf-** [sʌl'fɒnəmaɪd] *n Pharm* sulfamide *m*.

sulphur, *US* **sulf-** ['sʌlfər] *n* soufre *m*; **flowers of s.,** fleur(s) *f(pl)* de soufre; **s. dioxide,** anhydride sulfureux; *Geol* **s. spring,** source sulfureuse; **s. mine,** soufrière *f*.

sulphureous, *US* **sulf-** [sʌl'fjʊərɪəs] *adj* **(a)** sulfureux; **(b)** couleur de soufre *inv*, soufré.

sulphuric, *US* **sulf-** [sʌl'fjʊərɪk] *adj* (*acide*) sulfurique.

sulphurous, *US* **sulf-** ['sʌlfərəs, -fjʊər-] *adj* **(a)** = **SULPHUREOUS**; **(b)** *Ch* (*acide*) sulfureux.

sultan ['sʌltən] *n* sultan *m*.

sultana [sʌl'tɑːnə] *n* **(a)** *Culin* (*fruit*) raisin sec de Smyrne; **(b)** (*woman*) sultane *f*.

sultanate ['sʌltəneɪt] *n* sultanat *m*.

sultriness ['sʌltrɪnɪs] *n* chaleur étouffante; lourdeur *f* (*de l'atmosphère*); *Fig* (*sensuality*) sensualité *f*, volupté *f*.

sultry ['sʌltrɪ] *adj* **(a)** étouffant, suffocant; (*temps*) lourd, orageux; **it is s.,** il fait très lourd; **(b)** (*voice, look*) sensuel, voluptueux.

sum¹ [sʌm] *n* **(a)** (*amount*) somme *f*; (*total*) somme *f*, total *m*; montant *m* (*d'un compte*); **s. total,** somme totale, montant total; **in s.,** en somme, somme toute; **s. (of money),** somme (d'argent); **large s.,** grosse somme; **nice little s.,** somme rondelette; **the s. and substance of the matter,** la substance *ou* l'essence *f* de l'affaire; **(b)** problème *m*, exercice *m* (d'arithmétique); *Sch* **sums,** calcul *m*; **to do a s. in one's head,** faire un calcul de tête; **to do sums,** faire du calcul *ou* de l'arithmétique.

sum² *vt* (**-mm-**) additionner (*des nombres*); *Math* sommer (*une série*).

►**sum up 1** *vtsep* **(a)** (*summarize*) résumer, faire un résumé (*des faits*); **to s. up (what one has said before),** se résumer, résumer les faits; *Jur* **to s. up (the case** *or* **the evidence),** (*of judge*) résumer les débats (*avant la délibération du jury*); **(b)** (*assess quickly*) **to s. up the situation at a glance,** évaluer la situation d'un coup d'œil; **to s. s.o. up,** juger *ou* évaluer qn; **(c)** (*add*) faire la somme de, totaliser (*des nombres*). **2** *vi* (*summarize*) résumer; **to s. up I will say that ...,** en résumé je dirai que ...; **in summing up the judge said ...,** dans son résumé, le juge a dit ... .

sumac(h) ['s(j)uːmæk, 'ʃuː] *n* (*plant*) sumac *m*.

summarily ['sʌmərɪlɪ] *adv* sommairement.

summarize ['sʌməraɪz] *vt* résumer sommairement (*un ouvrage etc*); récapituler (*les débats etc*).

summary ['sʌmərɪ] **1** *adj* sommaire; **s. account,** (*short*) récit sommaire *ou* succinct; (*providing summary*) récit récapitulatif; *Jur* référé *m*; **he was dealt rather s. justice,** on lui a rendu une justice plutôt sommaire; **s. proceedings,** affaire *f* sommaire; **s. offences,** délits qui peuvent être jugés en procédure sommaire. **2** *n* sommaire *m*, résumé *m*, aperçu *m*; argument *m* (*d'un livre*); récapitulation *f*, relevé *m* (*d'opérations commerciales*); **s. of the news, news s.,** nouvelles *fpl* en bref.

summation [sʌ'meɪʃən] *n* **(a)** (*addition*) sommation *f*, addition *f*; **(b)** (*total*) somme *f*, total *m*; **(c)** *Am Jur* résumé *m* des débats (*par le juge*).

summer¹ ['sʌmər] *n* été *m*; **in s.,** en été; **in the s.,** pendant l'été; **in the s. of 1945,** pendant l'été 1945; **a s.('s) day,** un jour d'été; **winter and s. alike, I live in the country,** été comme hiver j'habite la campagne; **next s.,** l'été prochain; **Indian s.,** été de la Saint-Martin, été indien; *Lit* **many summers ago,** il y a bien longtemps; *Lit* **a girl of 12 summers,** une fille de 12 printemps; **s. clothes,** habits *mpl ou* vêtements *mpl* d'été; **the s. holidays,** les grandes vacances; **s. resort,** station estivale; **s. school,** cours *mpl ou* stages *mpl* de vacances; *Admin* **s. time,** heure *f* d'été; **s. visitor,** estivant(e).

summer² 1 *vi* passer l'été (*au bord de la mer etc*); (*of cattle*) estiver. **2** *vt* estiver (*le bétail*).

summerhouse ['sʌməhaʊs] *n* (*in garden*) pavillon *m*; (*second house in the country etc*) maison *f* d'été.

summertime ['sʌmətaɪm] *n* (saison *f* d')été *m*.

summery ['sʌmərɪ] *adj* estival, -aux, d'été.

summing ['sʌmɪŋ] *n Math* addition *f*, sommation *f*.

summing-up [sʌmɪŋ'ʌp] *n* **(a)** (*quick assessment*) évaluation *f* (*de la situation*); **(b)** *Jur* résumé *m* des débats (*par le juge*); **in her s. up the judge said ...,** dans son résumé (des débats), le juge a dit ...; **(c)** = **SUMMING.**

summit ['sʌmɪt] *n* **(a)** sommet *m*, cime *f*, faîte *m* (*d'une montagne*); **the s. of greatness,** le faîte *ou* sommet des grandeurs; **the s. of happiness,** le summum de la félicité; **to be at the s. of one's power/fame,** être à l'apogée du pouvoir/de la gloire; **(b)** *Pol* sommet *m*; **s. conference,** conférence *f* au sommet; **talks will be held at s. level,** des négociations auront lieu au sommet.

summiteer [sʌmɪ'tɪər] *n* participant, -ante à un sommet.

summon ['sʌmən] *vt* **(a)** (*call*) appeler, faire venir (*un domestique, de l'aide, la police*); convoquer (*une assemblée, qn à une réunion*); *Jur* sommer (*qn*) de comparaître; **business summoned him back to London,** les affaires l'ont rappelé à Londres; **to s. help,** appeler au secours; **to s. a defendant/a witness to appear,** citer *ou* assigner un défendeur/un témoin; **s. the next witness!,** faites entrer le témoin suivant; **(b)** = **SUMMON UP.**

►**summon up** *vtsep* faire appel à (*son courage etc*); **to s. up all one's strength,** rassembler toutes ses forces; **summoning up all her courage ...,** en prenant son courage à deux mains ...; (*more serious*) en rassemblant tout son courage ... .

summons¹, *pl* **-ses** ['sʌmənz, -zɪz] *n* **(a)** (*order to attend etc*) appel *m* (*fait d'autorité*); **(b)** *Jur* citation *f* (à comparaître), assignation *f*, sommation *f* (à comparaître), mandat *m* de comparution; **to issue a s.,** lancer une assignation; **to**

serve a s. on s.o., signifier une citation à qn, assigner qn; **to take out a s. against s.o.,** faire assigner qn.

summons² *vt Jur* citer (*qn*) à comparaître, assigner (*qn*), appeler (*qn*) en justice.

sump [sʌmp] *n* **(a) (oil) s.,** carter *m* à huile; *Aut* **to drain the s.,** faire la vidange; **(b)** *Min etc* puisard *m*; **(c)** (*cesspool*) fosse *f* d'aisance.

sumptuous ['sʌm(p)tjʊəs] *adj* somptueux.

sumptuously ['sʌm(p)tjʊəslɪ] *adv* somptueusement.

sumptuousness ['sʌm(p)tjʊəsnɪs] *n* somptuosité *f*.

sun¹ [sʌn] *n* soleil *m*; **the s. is shining,** il fait (du) soleil, le soleil brille; **the s. rises/sets,** le soleil se lève/se couche; **rising/setting s.,** soleil levant/couchant; **against the s.,** dans le soleil; *Fig* **to have a place in the s.,** avoir une place au soleil; **(full) in the s.,** au (grand) soleil, en plein soleil; **just to lie in the s.,** juste pour s'allonger au soleil; **let's get out of the s.,** mettons-nous à l'abri du soleil; **too much s. can be harmful,** de trop longues expositions au soleil peuvent être dangereuses; **to take the s., to bask in the s.,** prendre le soleil; **to catch the s.,** (*get suntanned*) bronzer; (*get sunburnt*) prendre des coups de soleil; **to get a touch of the s.,** prendre *ou* attraper un coup de soleil; **every species/subject under the s.,** toutes les espèces existantes/tous les sujets possibles; **there's nothing new under the s.,** rien de nouveau sous le soleil; **fixed s.,** gloire *f*; **s. awning,** store *m*; **s. helmet,** casque *m* (colonial) (*à couvre-nuque*); *Nau* **s. deck,** pont-promenade *m*, *pl* ponts-promenades; **S. King,** Roi *m* Soleil; **s. lamp,** *Cin* grand projecteur, sunlight *m*; lampe ultra(-)violette (pour le bronzage); **s. lounge** *or Am* **s. parlor** *or* **porch,** solarium *m*; **s. oil/lotion,** huile *f*/lotion *f* solaire; *Aut* **s. visor,** pare-soleil *m inv*.

sun² *vt* (**-nn-**) exposer au soleil; **to s. oneself,** prendre le soleil, *F* faire le lézard.

sunbaked ['sʌnbeɪkt] *adj* (*earth*) brûlé par le soleil; (*tiles*) cuit au soleil.

sunbathe ['sʌnbeɪð] *vi* prendre un bain de soleil, se faire bronzer.

sunbather ['sʌnbeɪðər] *n* personne *f* qui prend un bain *ou* des bains de soleil; **suddenly the park was full of sunbathers,** soudain le parc s'est rempli de gens prenant des bains de soleil.

sunbathing ['sʌnbeɪðɪŋ] *n* bains *mpl* de soleil.

sunbeam ['sʌnbiːm] *n* rayon *m* de soleil.

sunbed ['sʌnbed] *n* table *f* de bronzage par UV.

sunblind ['sʌnblaɪnd] *n* store *m*.

sunblock ['sʌnblɒk] *n* écran total.

sunburn ['sʌnbɜːn] *n* **(a)** *Med* coup *m* de soleil; **suffering from s.,** souffrant de coups de soleil; **(b)** (*suntan*) hâle *m*, bronzage *m*, teint bronzé.

sunburnt, sunburned ['sʌnbɜːnt, -bɜːnd] *adj* (*burnt*) brûlé par le soleil; (*suntannned*) bronzé, hâlé; **to get s.,** (*to get burnt*) attraper *ou* prendre un coup de soleil; (*get suntanned*) (se) (faire) bronzer, se hâler.

sunburst ['sʌnbɜːst] *n* échappée *f* de soleil; (*brooch*) broche *f* (en forme de) soleil.

sundae ['sʌndeɪ] *n Culin* glace aux fruits recouverte de noix *ou* de crème Chantilly/*etc*.

Sunday ['sʌnd(e)ɪ] *n* dimanche *m*; **I expect him on S.** *or* **this (coming) S.,** je l'attends dimanche; **he comes on Sundays,** il vient le dimanche; **she comes every S.,** elle vient tous les dimanches; **in one's S. clothes** *or* **one's S. best,** dans ses habits du dimanche; **to put on one's S. best,** s'habiller en dimanche, s'endimancher; *Br* **S. lunch,** déjeuner dominical; **S. paper,** journal *m* du dimanche; *Rel* **S. school,** catéchisme *m*.

sundial ['sʌndaɪəl] *n* cadran *m* solaire, gnomon *m*.

sundown ['sʌndaʊn] *n* coucher *m* du soleil; **at s.,** au coucher du soleil.

sundowner ['sʌndaʊnər] *n Austr F* (*tramp*) clochard *m*.

sun-drenched ['sʌndren(t)ʃt] *adj* (*beaches etc*) baigné *ou* arrosé de soleil.

sun-dried ['sʌndraɪd] *adj* séché au soleil.

sundry ['sʌndrɪ] **1** *adj* divers; **s. expenses,** frais divers; **on s. occasions,** à différentes occasions. **2** *n* **(a) all and s.,** tous sans exception; **for all and s.,** pour chacun et pour tous; **(b) sundries,** (*items*) articles divers; (*costs*) frais divers.

sunfish ['sʌnfɪʃ] *n* môle *f*, poisson-lune *m*, *pl* poissons-lunes.

sunflower ['sʌnflaʊər] *n* (*plant*) hélianthe *m*, soleil *m*, tournesol *m*; **s. seeds,** graines *fpl* de tournesol; **s. (seed) oil,** huile *f* de tournesol.

sung *see* **SING.**

sunglasses ['sʌnglɑːsɪz] *npl* lunettes *fpl* de soleil.

sun-god ['sʌngɒd] *n* dieu *m* soleil.

sunhat ['sʌnhæt] *n* chapeau *m* de soleil.

sunk *see* **SINK².**

sunken¹ ['sʌŋk(ə)n] *adj* (*rock*) submergé; (*wreck*) sous-marin; (*cheeks*) creux; (*garden etc*) encaissé, en contrebas; **s. eyes,** yeux creux *ou* enfoncés; **s. chest,** poitrine creuse.

sunken² *see* **SINK².**

sunless ['sʌnlɪs] *adj* sans soleil.

sunlight ['sʌnlaɪt] *n* lumière *f* du soleil *m*; **in the s.,** au (grand) soleil, en plein soleil; **to keep out of the s.,** éviter la lumière du soleil; **keep it out of the s.,** protégez-le du soleil, évitez-lui le soleil.

sunlit ['sʌnlɪt] *adj* éclairé par le soleil; (*full of sunlight*) ensoleillé.

sunniness ['sʌnɪnɪs] *n* situation ensoleillée; **the s. of her disposition,** ses bonnes dispositions.

sunny ['sʌnɪ] *adj* **(a)** (*journée, endroit*) ensoleillé; (*bâtiment*) éclairé par le soleil; (*côté*) exposé au soleil; **it's s.,** il fait (du) soleil; *esp Am* **s. side up,** (œuf sur le plat) cuit d'un seul côté; *Fig* **to look on the s. side of things,** voir le bon côté des choses; *F* **to be on the s. side of 40,** ne pas avoir encore atteint la quarantaine; **(b)** (*visage*) radieux, rayonnant; (*caractère*) heureux.

sunray ['sʌnreɪ] *n* rayon *m* de soleil, rayon solaire; **s. lamp,** lampe ultra(-)violette (pour le bronzage); *Med* **s. treatment,** héliothérapie *f*.

sunrise ['sʌnraɪz] *n* lever *m* du soleil; **at s.,** au soleil levant, au lever du soleil; *F* **s. industry,** industrie *f* de l'avenir *ou* du futur.

sunroof ['sʌnruːf] *n Aut* toit ouvrant; (*of hotel etc*) toiture-terrasse *f*, solarium *m*.

sunset ['sʌnset] *n* coucher *m* du soleil; **at s.,** au soleil couchant, au coucher du soleil.

sunshade ['sʌnʃeɪd] *n* ombrelle *f*; (*for table etc*) parasol *m*; (*in car*) pare-soleil *m inv*.

sunshine ['sʌnʃaɪn] *n* (clarté *f ou* lumière *f* du) soleil *m*; **in the s.,** au soleil; **in the bright** *or* **brilliant s.,** au grand soleil; **they need more s.,** il leur faut davantage de soleil; **period of s.,** période d'ensoleillement; *Aut* **s. roof,** toit ouvrant; **hello s.!,** (*to girl, woman*) bonjour ma jolie!; (*to boy, man*) salut mon vieux!; *Iron* **where d'you think you're going, s.?,** et où est-ce que tu avais l'intention d'aller comme ça, mon ami?

sun-soaked ['sʌnsəʊkt] *adj* (*beaches*) baigné de soleil.

sunspot ['sʌnspɒt] *n* **(a)** (*on the sun*) tache *f* solaire, tache du soleil; **(b)** (*holiday resort etc*) (*for summer holiday*) station estivale; **it's our favourite winter s.,** c'est là que nous préférons aller prendre du soleil pendant nos vacances d'hiver.

sunstroke ['sʌnstrəʊk] *n Med* insolation *f*; **to get s.,** attraper une insolation *ou* un coup de soleil.

sunsuit ['sʌns(j)uːt] *n* (costume *m*) bain *m* de soleil.

suntan ['sʌntæn] *n* bronzage *m*, hâle *m*; **to get a s.,** (se faire) bronzer; **she's got a tremendous s.,** elle a un super bronzage; **s. lotion/oil,** lotion *f*/huile *f* solaire.

suntanned ['sʌntænd] *adj* bronzé, hâlé.

suntrap ['sʌntræp] *n* coin très ensoleillé.

sun-up ['sʌnʌp] *n Am* lever *m* du soleil; **at s.-up,** au lever du soleil.

sun-worship ['sʌnwɜːʃɪp] *n* culte *m* du soleil.

sun-worshipper ['sʌnwɜːʃɪpər] *n Rel* adorateur, -trice du soleil; *Fig* (*on beach etc*) amateur *m* de soleil.

sup¹ [sʌp] *n esp Scot & North Eng* petite gorgée; **to take a s. of soup,** prendre une goutte de bouillon.

sup² *v* (**-pp-** [sʌpt]) **1** *vt esp Scot & North Eng* boire à petites gorgées. **2** *vi Old-fashioned* souper (**off, on,** de).

▶**sup up** *esp Scot & North Eng* **1** *vtsep* (*drink up*) finir (*son verre etc*). **2** *vi* finir son verre.

super ['suːpər] **1** *adj F* (*excellent*) superbe, formidable, magnifique, génial. **2** *n* **(a)** *F* = **SUPERINTENDENT**; **(b)** *F* = **SUPERVISOR**; **(c)** *Aut* super *m*.

superable ['suːpərəb(ə)l] *adj* surmontable.

superabundance [suːpərə'bʌndəns] *n* surabondance *f* (**of,** de).

superabundant [suːpərə'bʌndənt] *adj* surabondant.

superabundantly [suːpərə'bʌndəntlɪ] *adv* surabondamment.

superannuate [suːpər'ænjʊeɪt] *vt* mettre (*qn*) à la retraite; *Fig* mettre au rancart, remiser (*qch*).

superannuated [suːpər'ænjʊeɪtɪd] *adj* (*person*) (mis) en *ou* à la retraite, retraité; (*ideas, system*) suranné; (*equipment*) désuet, -ète, démodé.

superannuation [suːpərænjʊ'eɪʃən] *n* retraite *f* par limite d'âge; **s. fund,** caisse *f* des retraites.

superb [suː'pɜːb] *adj* (*athlete, performance, food,*

accommodation) excellent; (*animal, view etc*) superbe.
superbly [suːˈpɜːblɪ] *adv* superbement.
supercargo [ˈsuːpəkɑːgəʊ] *n* subrécargue *m*.
supercharge [ˈsuːpətʃɑːdʒ] *vt Aut Av etc* suralimenter, surcomprimer (*un moteur etc*); **supercharged engine,** moteur suralimenté *ou* surcomprimé *ou* à compresseur.
supercharger [ˈsuːpətʃɑːdʒər] *n Aut Av etc* compresseur *m*, surpresseur *m*.
supercilious [suːpəˈsɪlɪəs] *adj* hautain, dédaigneux.
superciliously [suːpəˈsɪlɪəslɪ] *adv* avec hauteur, dédaigneusement.
superciliousness [suːpəˈsɪlɪəsnɪs] *n* hauteur *f*.
superconductor [suːpəkənˈdʌktər] *n Phys El* supraconducteur *m*.
supercooling [ˈsuːpəˈkuːlɪŋ] *n* sous-refroidissement *m*.
supercritical [suːpəˈkrɪtɪk(ə)l] *adj Nucl Phys* supercritique, surcritique.
superego [ˈsuːpəriːgəʊ] *n Psy* sur-moi *m*.
superelevation [suːpərelɪˈveɪʃən] *n* surhaussement *m*; dévers *m* (*de la voie*).
super-duper [ˈsuːpəˈduːpər] *adj F* super, superchouette.
supererogation [suːpərerəʊˈgeɪʃən] *n Fml* surérogation *f*.
superficial [suːpəˈfɪʃəl] *adj* **(a)** superficiel; **he has a s. charm,** il a un charme superficiel; **to have a s. knowledge of sth,** avoir des connaissances superficielles de qch; **s. learning,** vernis *m* de connaissances; **(b) s. measurement,** mesure *f* de superficie; *Med* **s. wound,** blessure superficielle.
superficiality [suːpəfɪʃɪˈælɪtɪ] *n* superficialité *f*.
superficially [suːpəˈfɪʃəlɪ] *adv* superficiellement.
superfine [ˈsuːpəfaɪn] *adj* **(a)** *Com etc* superfin, surfin; **(b)** (*esprit etc*) raffiné.
superfluity [suːpəˈfluːɪtɪ] *n* superfluité *f*; **s. of good things,** surabondance *f* de biens; **s. of words,** surabondance de paroles.
superfluous [suːˈpɜːflʊəs] *adj* superflu, *Lit* superfétatoire; **s. weight,** excédent *m* de poids; **it would be s. to mention ...,** il serait superflu de mentionner ...; *F* **I'm starting to feel a bit s.,** je commence à me sentir un peu de trop ici.
superfluously [suːˈpɜːflʊəslɪ] *adv* d'une manière superflue.
superfluousness [suːˈpɜːflʊəsnɪs] *n* superfluité *f*.
supergrass [ˈsuːpəgrɑːs] *n Br Sl* super-indic *m*.
superhighway [ˈsuːpəhaɪweɪ] *n Am* autoroute *f*.
superhuman [suːpəˈhjuːmən] *adj* surhumain.
superimpose [suːpərɪmˈpəʊz] *vt* superposer, surimposer; *Phot Cin* faire une surimpression de, surimprimer; *Fig* **Western culture superimposed on an indigenous one,** une culture occidentale venue se superposer à une culture indigène.
superimposition [suːpərɪmpəˈzɪʃən] *n* superposition *f*; *Phot Cin* surimpression *f*.
superintend [suːpərɪnˈtend] *vt* diriger, surveiller; **to s. an election,** présider au scrutin.
superintendence [suːpərɪnˈtendəns] *n* direction *f*, surveillance *f*, contrôle *m*, surintendance *f*.
superintendent [suːpərɪnˈtendənt] *n* **(a)** directeur, -trice; surveillant, -ante, chef *m* (*des travaux etc*); *US F* **sidewalk s.,** passant, -ante qui regarde les travaux de construction; **(b)** (*police officer*) commissaire *m* (de police); **(c)** *Am* (*of apartment block*) concierge *f*.
superior [suːˈpɪərɪər] **1** *adj* (*position, officer, quality*) supérieur (**to,** à); (*person*) orgueilleux; (*air*) de supériorité; *Bot* (*ovary*) supère; *Geog* **Lake S.,** le lac Supérieur; **to be s. in numbers to the enemy,** être supérieur en nombre à l'ennemi, avoir la supériorité du nombre sur l'ennemi; **they were overcome by s. numbers,** ils ont succombé sous le nombre, ils ont été vaincus par le nombre; *Com* **article of s. quality,** article *m* de qualité supérieure; **she felt s. to her colleagues,** elle se sentait supérieure à ses collègues; **with a s. smile,** avec un sourire condescendant; *Astron* **the s. planets,** les planètes supérieures; *Typ* **s. letter,** lettre supérieure; **s. number,** chiffre supérieur.
2 *n* supérieur, -eure; **he is your s.,** il est votre supérieur; **to be s.o.'s s. in courage,** être supérieur en courage à qn; **Father S.,** père supérieur; **Mother S.,** mère supérieure.
superiority [suːpɪərɪˈɒrɪtɪ] *n* supériorité *f*; **s. in men and materials,** supériorité en hommes et en matériel; *Mil Av* **air s.,** supériorité aérienne; **s. complex,** complexe *m* de supériorité.
superlative [suːˈpɜːlətɪv] **1** *adj* **(a)** excellent; **(b)** *Gram* superlatif. **2** *n Gram* superlatif *m*; **to speak in superlatives,** s'exprimer par superlatifs.
superlatively [suːˈpɜːlətɪvlɪ] *adv* extrêmement, au plus haut degré; **s. fit,** dans une forme excellente.
superman, *pl* **-men** [ˈsuːpəmæn, -men] *n* surhomme *m*; *Hum F* superman *m*.
supermarket [ˈsuːpəmɑːkɪt] *n* supermarché *m*; **s. prices,** prix *mpl* dans les supermarchés.
supernatural [suːpəˈnætʃərəl] **1** *adj* surnaturel. **2** *n* surnaturel *m*.
supernaturally [suːpəˈnætʃərəlɪ] *adv* de manière surnaturelle.
supernova [suːpəˈnəʊvə] *n Astron* supernova *f*.
supernumerary [suːpəˈnjuːm(ə)rərɪ] **1** *adj* surnuméraire; (*staff*) en surnombre. **2** *n* surnuméraire *m*; *Th Cin* figurant, -ante.
superphosphate [suːpəˈfɒsfeɪt] *n* superphosphate *m*.
superpose [suːpəˈpəʊz] *vt* superposer (**upon, on,** à); étager (*des planches etc*).
superposition [suːpəpəˈzɪʃən] *n* superposition *f*; application *f* (**of sth on sth,** de qch à *ou* sur qch).
superpower [ˈsuːpəpaʊər] *n* superpuissance *f*; **s. talks,** négociations *fpl* entre les superpuissances.
superscript [ˈsuːpəskrɪpt] *Typ* **1** *adj* (*character*) inscrit au dessus de la ligne. **2** *n* (*number*) exposant *m*; (*other*) caractère inscrit au dessus de la ligne.
superscription [suːpəˈskrɪpʃən] *n* (*on coin*) inscription *f*; (*on letter*) suscription *f*.
supersede [suːpəˈsiːd] *vt* remplacer (*qch, qn*); prendre la place de (*qn*), supplanter (*qn*); **this catalogue supersedes previous issues,** ce catalogue annule les précédents; **method now superseded,** méthode périmée; **to be superseded by s.o.,** être évincé par qn.
supersensitive [suːpəˈsensɪtɪv] *adj* hypersensible.
supersonic [suːpəˈsɒnɪk] *adj* ultrasonique; (*avion, vitesse*) supersonique; **s. boom** *or* **bang,** bang *m*.
superstar [ˈsuːpəstɑːr] *n Cin Sp* superstar *f*.
superstition [suːpəˈstɪʃən] *n* superstition *f*.
superstitious [suːpəˈstɪʃəs] *adj* superstitieux.
superstitiously [suːpəˈstɪʃəslɪ] *adv* superstitieusement.
superstore [ˈsuːpəstɔːr] *n* hypermarché *m*.
superstructure [ˈsuːpəstrʌktʃər] *n* superstructure *f*.
supertanker [ˈsuːpətæŋkər] *n Nau* pétrolier géant, supertanker *m*.
supertax [ˈsuːpətæks] *n* surimposition *f*, surtaxe *f*.
supertonic [suːpəˈtɒnɪk] *n Mus* sus-tonique *f*.
supervene [suːpəˈviːn] *vi* survenir; **if no complications s.,** s'il ne survient pas de complications.
supervise [ˈsuːpəvaɪz] *vt* **(a)** (*keep watch on*) surveiller (*des enfants, des prisonniers*); **(b)** diriger (*un service, une thèse*).
supervision [suːpəˈvɪʒən] *n* **(a)** (*keeping watch on*) surveillance *f*; **children are under the s. of trained instructors at all times,** les enfants se trouvent toujours sous la surveillance de moniteurs formés; **(b)** (*control*) direction *f* (*d'un service, d'une thèse*).
supervisor [ˈsuːpəvaɪzər] *n* **(a)** (*person who keeps watch over s.o./sth*) surveillant, -ante; **(b)** (*manager*) directeur, -trice; **(c)** *US Admin* **(chief) s.,** président *m* du conseil municipal; **(d)** *Univ* (*for PhD etc*) directeur *m* de thèse(s).
supervisory [suːpəˈvaɪz(ə)rɪ] *adj* (*comité etc*) de surveillance; **a s. function,** une fonction de surveillance.
superwoman, *pl* **-women** [ˈsuːpəwʊmən, -wɪmɪn] *n Hum F* superwoman *f*.
supine[1] [ˈsuːpaɪn] *adj* **(a)** (*person*) couché *ou* étendu sur le dos; *Med* en supination; **(b)** (*inactive*) mou, *f* molle, indolent, inerte.
supine[2] *n Gram* supin *m*; **in the s.,** au supin.
supineness [ˈsuːpaɪnnɪs] *n* indolence *f*.
supper [ˈsʌpər] *n* (*dinner*) dîner *m*, souper *m*; (*snack before going to bed*) collation *f*; **to have s.,** souper, dîner; **the Last S.,** la Cène, le dernier repas (du Seigneur); *Rel* **the Lord's S.,** la communion, la cène, l'eucharistie *f*.
suppertime [ˈsʌpətaɪm] *n* heure *f* du souper *ou* dîner; **(it's) s.!,** on dîne!, à table!
supplant [səˈplɑːnt] *vt* supplanter, prendre la place de (*qn*), évincer (*qn*).
supple [ˈsʌp(ə)l] *adj* (*limb, object, material*) souple, pliable, flexible; (*person*) souple; **to become s.,** s'assouplir; **s. figure,** taille souple *ou* déliée; **s. limbed,** aux membres souples; **s. minded,** à l'esprit souple.
supplement[1] [ˈsʌplɪmənt] *n* supplément *m* (*d'un journal*); *Math* supplément (*d'un angle*); *Journ* **colour s.,** supplément en couleurs.
supplement[2] [sʌplɪˈment] *vt* ajouter un supplément à (*un livre*); **to s. one's income by writing articles,** augmenter ses revenus en écrivant des articles.

supplementary [sʌplɪ'ment(ə)rɪ] *adj* supplémentaire (**to,** de), additionnel (**to,** à); **s. income,** revenus *mpl* annexes; *Math* **s. angle,** angle *m* supplémentaire.

suppleness ['sʌp(ə)lnɪs] *n* souplesse *f*.

suppliant ['sʌplɪənt] **1** *adj* (*attitude, gesture*) suppliant, de supplication. **2** *n* suppliant, -ante.

supplicant ['sʌplɪkənt] *n* suppliant, -ante.

supplicate ['sʌplɪkeɪt] **1** *vt* supplier (*qn*) (**to do sth,** de faire qch); solliciter humblement (*la protection de qn*). **2** *vi* supplier.

supplicating ['sʌplɪkeɪtɪŋ] *adj* suppliant, de supplication.

supplication [sʌplɪ'keɪʃən] *n* **(a)** (*act*) supplication *f*; **(b)** (*request*) supplique *f*.

supplier [sə'plaɪər] *n Com* fournisseur, -euse.

supply¹ [sə'plaɪ] *n* **(a)** (*act of supplying*) approvisionnement *m*, fourniture *f*; **electricity s.,** alimentation *f* en électricité; *Parl* **bill of s.,** projet *m* de crédit supplémentaire; **committee of s.,** commission *f* du budget; *Econ* **s. and demand,** l'offre *f* et la demande; **s.-side economics,** théorie *f* économique de l'offre; *Mil* **s. lines,** lignes *fpl* de ravitaillement; *Nau* **s. ship,** ravitailleur *m*;

(b) (*stock*) provision *f*; **to get (in) a fresh s. of sth,** se réapprovisionner en qch; **supplies,** fournitures *fpl* (*de photographie, de bureau*); **supplies of money,** fonds *mpl*, ressources *fpl*; **food supplies,** vivres *mpl*; **to cut off** *or* **stop the enemy's supplies,** couper l'ennemi de ses approvisionnements;

(c) *Sch* **s. teacher,** suppléant, -ante, remplaçant, -ante; **s. teaching,** suppléance *f*, remplacements *mpl*; **to do s. teaching,** faire des remplacements.

supply² **1** *vt* **(a)** fournir, pourvoir, approvisionner (**s.o. with sth,** qn de qch); alimenter (*un marché*); fournir, apporter (*qch*); amener (*l'eau, le gaz etc*); **to s. oneself with sth,** s'approvisionner en qch; **the tradesmen who s. us,** nos fournisseurs *mpl*; *El* **to s. a factory with current,** alimenter une usine en courant; **the arteries that s. the brain,** les artères qui amènent le sang au cerveau; **to s. proof,** fournir des preuves; **(b)** réparer (*une omission*); répondre à (*un besoin*); **to s. s.o.'s needs,** pourvoir *ou* subvenir aux besoins de qn. **2** *vi* **to s. for s.o.,** (*of teacher etc*) assurer l'intérim *ou* la suppléance de qn.

supply³ ['sʌplɪ] *adv* souplement.

support¹ [sə'pɔːt] *n* **(a)** (*act of supporting*) appui *m*, soutien *m*; soutènement *m* (*d'une voûte*); **moral s.,** appui *ou* soutien moral; **to give s. to the proposal,** venir à l'appui de *ou* appuyer la proposition; **the rebels have little s.,** les rebelles bénéficient d'un soutien limité; **there is widespread s. for the government/these policies,** le gouvernement fait/ces politiques font l'objet d'un soutien très étendu; **to produce documents in s. of an allegation,** produire des pièces à l'appui d'une allégation *ou* pour appuyer une allégation; *Jur* fournir les pièces au soutien; **in s. of this theory,** à l'appui de *ou* pour corroborer cette théorie; *Mil* **air s.,** appui *ou* soutien aérien; **with (financial) s. from the council,** avec l'appui (financier) du conseil; **insufficient air for the s. of life,** air en quantité insuffisante pour permettre la vie; **they depended on their son for s.,** ils n'avaient que leur fils pour les faire vivre; **to be without means of s.,** être sans ressources *fpl*; *Mil* **s. unit,** unité *f* de soutien;

(b) (*person, thing supporting*) soutien *m*; appui *m*, support *m*, soutien (*d'une voûte*); pied *m* (*de sustentation*); console *f*, soupente *f* (*de treuil de poulie*); assiette *f* (*d'une poutre*); *Phot Cin* support (*de la couche sensible*); (*in horticulture*) tuteur *m*; **she is the s. of the family,** c'est elle qui fait vivre la famille; *Sp* **(athletic) s.,** slip *m* de soutien (*pour sportifs*); **s. stockings,** bas *mpl* à varices; *US* **price supports,** subventions *fpl*.

support² *vt* **(a)** supporter, soutenir, appuyer, maintenir, buter (*une voûte*); (*in horticulture*) tuteurer (*un arbuste*); *MecE* supporter, résister à (*un effort, une charge*); **I supported him with my arm,** je lui ai prêté l'appui de mon bras;

(b) appuyer (*qn, une pétition*); soutenir (*une théorie*); (*of new discoveries etc*) renforcer (*une théorie*); apporter son soutien à (*un gouvernement, un projet*); seconder les efforts de (*qn*); patronner (*un bal de charité*); faire une donation à (*une œuvre de charité*); *Sp* supporter (*une équipe*); *Mil* soutenir (*des troupes*); **proofs that s. a case,** preuves à l'appui d'une cause; **theory supported by facts,** théorie appuyée sur *ou* corroborée par des faits; *Parl* **to s. the motion,** soutenir la motion; **to be supported by s.o.,** (*in a proposal*) être soutenu par qn; **environmentalists s. the bill,** les écologistes soutiennent le projet de loi; **the mayor, supported by the clergy and the officers of the garrison,** le maire, avec le soutien du clergé et des officiers de la garnison; **his parents supported him in his ambition,** ses parents l'ont appuyé dans son ambition;

(c) entretenir (*la vie, la combustion*); subvenir à l'entretien de (*qn*); faire vivre, faire subsister (*qn*); **to have a wife and three children to s.,** avoir une femme et trois enfants à charge; **hospital supported by voluntary contributions,** hôpital entretenu par les souscriptions volontaires; **to s. oneself,** se suffire (à soi-même), gagner sa vie;

(d) supporter, tolérer, endurer (*une injure*);

(e) *Comptr* permettre l'utilisation de, supporter; **this package, which is supported by all ABC workstations ...,** ce progiciel, qui peut être utilisé sur tous les postes de travail ABC ... .

supportable [sə'pɔːtəb(ə)l] *adj* **(a)** (*bearable*) supportable, tolérable; **(b)** (*theory etc*) soutenable.

supporter [sə'pɔːtər] *n* **(a)** (*person*) défenseur *m*, tenant, -ante (*d'une opinion*); adhérent, -ente (*d'un parti*); partisan, -ane (*d'un homme politique*); *Sp* supporter *m* (*d'une équipe*); **football s.,** amateur *m* de foot(ball); **(b)** (*device*) soutien *m*, support *m*; **athletic s.,** slip *m* de soutien (*pour sportifs*); **(c)** *Her* (*animal*) support *m*; (*human*) tenant *m* (de l'écu).

supporting [sə'pɔːtɪŋ] *adj* (*mur, point*) d'appui, de soutènement; *Mil* (*troupes*) de soutien; *Cin* (*film, programme*) supplémentaire; *Th Mus* **s. act,** première partie; **in the days when the Beatles were one of the s. acts,** quand les Beatles se produisaient en première partie; *Th* **the s. cast,** les seconds rôles.

supportive [sə'pɔːtɪv] *adj* (*parent, friend, ally etc*) qui soutient; **to be s.,** prêter son appui, être un soutien; **she's been very s.,** elle nous *etc* a bien soutenu(s); **you could be more s.!,** vous pourriez me *ou* nous soutenir un peu plus!; **to be s. of s.o.'s efforts,** soutenir qn dans ses efforts.

supportiveness [sə'pɔːtɪvnɪs] *n* soutien *m*, appui *m*.

suppose [sə'pəʊz] *vt* **(a)** supposer; (*imagine*) s'imaginer; (*think*) croire, penser; **you mustn't s. that ...,** il ne faut pas vous imaginer que ...; **what makes you s. that I trust you?,** qu'est-ce qui vous fait croire que j'ai confiance en vous?; **I don't s. he'll do it,** je ne crois pas qu'il le fera; **will you go? — I s. so.,** irez-vous? — probablement; **please can I stay up late? — oh, I s. so.,** s'il te plaît est-ce que je peux veiller tard? — bon si tu veux; **I don't think he'll come — no, I s. not** *or* **I don't s. so,** je ne crois pas qu'il viendra — non, sans doute *ou* probablement pas; **I don't s. you remember me,** vous ne vous souvenez sans doute pas de moi; **I s. you can't remember THAT either!,** tu ne te souviens probablement pas de ça non plus!; **s. ABC an equilateral triangle,** soit ABC un triangle équilatéral; **supposing** *or* **(let us) s. (that) you're right,** supposons *ou* en supposant *ou* mettons que vous ayez raison; **s.** *or* **supposing you were ill,** supposez que vous soyez malade; **supposing** *or* **s. he came back,** si par supposition il revenait, supposons qu'il revienne; **yes, but s. I were to die,** oui, mais si je venais à mourir; *F* **s. we change the subject,** si nous changions de sujet; **just supposing it DID happen,** supposons que ça se produise; **the creation supposes the creator,** la création suppose le créateur;

(b) to be supposed to do sth, être censé faire qch; **she's supposed to be in London,** (*they say she is, she should be*) elle est censée être à Londres; **she's not supposed to be in London,** (*shouldn't be there*) elle n'est pas censée être à Londres; **the film's supposed to be very good,** on dit que ce film est très bon; **it's supposed to have been discovered by ...,** on dit que cela a été découvert par ...; **there is supposed to be a well in the garden,** on dit qu'il y a un puits dans le jardin; **I'm not supposed to do it,** je ne suis pas censé le faire; **you're not supposed to know that,** (*so I won't tell you*) vous n'êtes pas censé le savoir; (*so keep quiet about it*) vous êtes censé ne pas le savoir; **you're not supposed to park here,** vous ne devez pas vous garer ici; **don't ask me! — YOU'RE supposed to be in charge!,** ne me demande pas ça! — je croyais pourtant bien que c'était toi le responsable!; **you're supposed to be my friend!,** je vous croyais mon ami!; **could you lend me the key? — well, I'm not supposed to, but ...,** pourriez-vous me prêter la clef? — eh bien, je ne devrais pas, mais ...; **the computer's not supposed to make a noise like that,** l'ordinateur ne devrait pas faire un tel bruit; **how am I supposed to work in conditions like this!,** comment veut-on que je travaille dans de telles conditions!; **how is anybody supposed to make sense of that!,** comment est-on censé s'y retrouver?

supposition [sʌpə'zɪʃən] *n* supposition *f*, hypothèse *f*; **un-**

founded s., supposition gratuite; **on the s. that...**, supposé que *+sub*, dans l'hypothèse où + *cond*; **on the s. that she had caught the train**, dans l'hypothèse où elle aurait pris le train.

supposititious [sɒpɒzɪ'tɪʃəs] *adj* **(a)** *Fml* (*false*) faux, *f* fausse; **(b)** *Jur* (*enfant, testament*) supposé.

suppository [sə'pɒzɪtrɪ] *n Pharm* suppositoire *m*.

suppress [sə'pres] *vt* **(a)** réprimer, étouffer (*une révolte*); supprimer (*un journal, une association*); faire disparaître (*un abus*); **(b)** étouffer (*une toux, un scandale*); étouffer, ravaler (*un sanglot*); réprimer, refouler (*ses sentiments*); dominer (*une émotion*); **to s. one's feelings**, se contenir, faire taire ses sentiments; **(c)** (*hide*) cacher, dissimuler (*qch*); (*keep silent about*) passer (*qch*) sous silence; ne pas révéler (*un fait*); taire, ne pas donner (*un nom*); *Jur* supprimer (*un état de fait, une circonstance*); **(d)** *Rad El* déparasiter (*un appareil*).

suppressed [sə'prest] *adj* étouffé, réprimé; **s. anger**, colère refoulée; **s. excitement**, agitation contenue.

suppression [sə'preʃən] *n* **(a)** répression *f* (*d'une émeute, d'un abus*); suppression *f* (*d'un livre*); **(b)** étouffement *m* (*d'un scandale*); refoulement *m* (*des émotions*); *Med* suppression (*de transpiration, d'urine*); **(c)** suppression (*d'un état de fait*); dissimulation *f* (*de la vérité*); **(d)** *Rad* antiparasitage *m*.

suppressor [sə'presər] *n* **(a)** (*person*) étouffeur, -euse (*d'une émeute*); dissimulateur, -trice (*d'un fait*); **(b)** *Rad* (*device*) (dispositif *m ou* appareil *m*) antiparasite *m*; **s. grid**, grille *f* de freinage.

suppurate ['sʌpjʊreɪt] *vi* (*of wound, sore*) suppurer.

suppurating ['sʌpjʊreɪtɪŋ] *adj* (*abcès etc*) suppurant.

suppuration [sʌpjʊ'reɪʃən] *n* suppuration *f*.

supranational [suːprə'næʃen(ə)l] *adj* supranational, -aux.

supremacist [sʊ'preməsɪst] *n* = personne croyant en la supériorité d'un groupe, racial ou autre.

supremacy [sʊ'preməsɪ] *n* suprématie *f*.

supreme¹ [sʊ'priːm] *adj* suprême; **to reign s.**, régner en maître *ou* en souverain absolu; **the S. Being**, l'Être suprême; *US Jur* **S. Court**, Cour *f* suprême; *Eng Jur* **S. Court (of Judicature)**, Cour souveraine *ou* suprême; **s. happiness**, bonheur suprême, souverain bonheur; **to make the s. sacrifice**, (*die*) consentir au sacrifice suprême.

supreme² *n Culin* (*sauce*) sauce suprême *ou* veloutée; (*dish*) suprême *m* (*de volaille etc*).

supremely [sʊ'priːmlɪ] *adv* suprêmement; **we are s. happy**, nous jouissons d'un bonheur suprême, nous sommes suprêmement heureux.

supremo, *pl* **-s** [sʊ'priːməʊ, -məʊz] *n Br esp Iron* grand chef, *F* big boss *m*.

Supt *abbr* **superintendent**.

surcharge¹ ['sɜːtʃɑːdʒ] *n* (*additional charge*) droit *m* supplémentaire; majoration *f* d'impôt (*par pénalisation*); **s. on a letter**, surtaxe *f* d'une lettre.

surcharge² *vt* surtaxer (*une lettre etc*); **if motorists were surcharged to ...**, si on surtaxait les automobilistes pour ... .

surd [sɜːd] *n* **(a)** *Math* quantité irrationnelle; **(b)** *Ling* (*consonne*) sourde *f*.

sure [ʃʊər] **1** *adj* sûr, certain; (*infallible*) infaillible; (*jugement, tireur, asile*) sûr; (*remède*) sûr, infaillible; (*bénéfice, succès*) sûr, assuré; **to be s. of** *or* **about sth**, être sûr *ou* certain de qch; **I'm s. of it**, j'en suis sûr *ou* certain; **I'm not so s. of** *or* **about that**, je n'en suis pas bien sûr *ou* certain; **I'm not so s. about that**, (*implying permission won't be given*) ça, ça m'étonnerait; **I can't be s., but I think it was two o'clock**, je n'en suis pas tout à fait sûr, mais je pense qu'il était deux heures; **I'm s. you're mistaken**, je suis sûr que vous vous trompez; **are you quite s. he hasn't left yet?**, êtes-vous bien sûr qu'il n'est pas encore parti?; **I'm s. you must be** *or* **you're very tired**, je suis sûr que vous êtes très fatigué; **I'm s. you don't know the answer**, vous ne savez assurément pas la réponse; **to be s. of oneself**, être sûr de soi; **I don't know, I'm s.**, ma foi, je ne sais pas; **we're all very grateful, I'm s., but ...**, nous sommes certainement très reconnaissants, mais ...; **to make s. of sth**, s'assurer de qch; **make s. (that) the door is shut**, assurez-vous que la porte est fermée, verifiez que la porte est fermée; **I'll just go and make s.**, je vais vérifier; **to make s. of a seat**, s'assurer une place; **don't be too** *or* **so s.!**, vous êtes bien sûr de vous!; **what makes you so s.?**, comment pouvez-vous en être si sûr?; **with a s. hand**, d'une main assurée; **there is only one s. way of doing it**, il n'y a qu'un moyen sûr de le faire; *Iron* **that's a s. way of failing the interview**, c'est un moyen sûr d'échouer à l'entretien; **(it's a) s. thing**, c'est une certitude *ou* une chose certaine; *esp Am F* **s. thing!**, bien sûr!, pour sûr!; **I don't know for s.**, je n'en suis pas bien sûr; **tomorrow for s.**, demain sans faute; **she won't come, that's for s.**, elle ne viendra pas c'est certain; **it's s. to be fine**, il fera sûrement beau; **he's s. to come**, il viendra sûrement *ou* à coup sûr; **be s. to come early**, ne manquez pas d'arriver de bonne heure; **be s. not to lose it, be s. that you don't lose it**, prenez garde de ne pas le perdre.

2 *adv esp Am F* (*really*) vraiment; **it s. is cold**, il fait vraiment froid; **it s. was difficult**, c'était vraiment *ou* bien difficile; **you s. do know your history!**, vous vous y connaissez vraiment *ou F* drôlement bien en histoire!; **as s. as fate, as s. as eggs are** *or F* **is eggs**, aussi vrai qu'il fait jour, aussi sûr que deux et deux font quatre; **s. enough he was there**, il était bien là; **she'll come s. enough**, elle viendra à coup sûr; **no, it's whisky s. enough**, non, c'est bien du whisky; *F* **for s.!**, *esp Am* **s.!**, mais oui!, bien sûr!

surefooted [ʃʊə'fʊtɪd] *adj* au pied sûr; **to be s.**, avoir le pied sûr.

surely ['ʃʊəlɪ] *adv* **(a)** (*in a sure manner*) sûrement; **slowly but s.**, lentement mais sûrement; **(b)** (*certainly*) assurément, sans doute; **he will s. come**, il viendra sûrement; **s. you don't believe that!**, vous ne croyez quand même pas cela!; **s. you're not going to leave us?**, vous n'allez quand même pas nous quitter?; *esp Am* **will you help me? — s.!**, voulez-vous m'aider? — bien sûr!; **it's all gone — s. not?**, il n'y en a plus — c'est pas vrai!

sureness ['ʃʊənɪs] *n* sûreté *f* (*de main, jugement etc*); efficacité *f* (*d'un remède*); (*certainty*) certitude *f*; **the s. of his aim**, la précision de son tir.

surety ['ʃʊərətɪ] *n* **(a)** *Jur* (*person*) caution *f*, garant, -ante; *Com* donneur *m* d'aval; **to stand s. for s.o.**, se porter caution pour qn, se rendre *ou* se porter garant de qn; **s. for a debt**, garant d'une dette; **in his own s. of £5000**, sous (sa propre) caution de cinq mille livres; **(b)** *Arch* **of a s.**, sans aucun doute.

surf¹ [sɜːf] *n* ressac *m*.

surf² *vi Sp* faire du surf.

surface¹ ['sɜːfɪs] *n* **(a)** surface *f*; **the earth's s.**, la surface de la terre; **to rise to the s. of the water**, remonter *ou* revenir à la surface de l'eau; **to rise** *or* **come to the s.**, (*of submarine*) revenir en surface; **to break s.**, faire surface; **smooth/even s.**, surface lisse/unie; **his politeness is only on the s.**, sa politesse est toute de surface; **on the s. she is very calm**, en surface, elle est très calme; **meaning that lies below the s.**, signification cachée; **we're still very much on the s. of the problem**, nous n'avons pas encore attaqué le fond du problème; *Ling* **s. grammar**, grammaire *f* de surface; *Post* **to send a letter by s. mail**, envoyer une lettre par voie de terre *ou* de mer; **s. water**, eau superficielle, eaux de surface; **s. noise**, (*on recording*) bruit *m* de surface; **s. speed**, vitesse *f* en surface (*d'un sous-marin*); *Ling* **s. structure**, structure *f* de surface; *Phys* **s. tension**, tension superficielle *ou* de surface; *Min* **s. work**, travail *m* au jour; **s. worker**, ouvrier *m* du jour;

(b) (*area*) aire *f*, étendue *f*, superficie *f*; *Math* **s. of revolution**, surface *f* de révolution *ou* de rotation; **working s.**, plan *m* de travail; surface utile (*d'un bureau*); *Av* **lifting s.**, surface portante *ou* de sustentation;

(c) *Constr* revêtement *m* (*d'une route*); **temporary s.**, chaussée *f* provisoire.

surface² **1** *vt* apprêter la surface de (*qch*); (*in papermaking*) calandrer (*le papier*); *Constr* revêtir (*une route*) (**with**, de). **2** *vi* **(a)** (*of submarine, whale etc*) faire surface; (*return to surface*) revenir en surface; **(b)** *F* (*of person*) (*reappear, regain consciousness*) refaire surface.

surface-mounted ['sɜːfɪsmaʊntɪd] *adj Comptr* (*chips*) monté en surface.

surfacing ['sɜːfɪsɪŋ] *n* **(a)** apprêtage *m* de la surface (*de qch*); (*in papermaking*) calandrage *m*; *Constr* revêtement *m* (*d'une route*); **(b)** (*of submarine*) réapparition *f* en surface.

surface-to-air ['sɜːfɪstʊ'eər] *adj Mil* **s.-to-a. missile**, missile *m* sol-air.

surface-to-surface ['sɜːfɪstə'sɜːfɪs] *adj Mil* **s.-to-s. missile**, missile *m* sol-sol.

surfboard ['sɜːfbɔːd] *n Sp* planche *f* de surf(ing).

surfboarder, surfboarding ['sɜːfbɔːdər, -ɪŋ] = **SURFER, SURFING**.

surfeit¹ ['sɜːfɪt] *n* surabondance *f*; réplétion *f* (*d'aliments*); (*disgust*) dégoût *m*; (*nausea*) nausée *f*; **to have a s. of oysters/of music**, être rassasié d'huîtres/de musique.

surfeit² **1** *vt* gorger, rassasier (*qn de qch*); **to s. oneself**

with sth, se gorger de qch jusqu'à s'en dégoûter; **surfeited with pleasure,** blasé *ou* écœuré par les plaisirs. **2** *vi Arch* se gorger, se repaître.

surfer ['sɜːfər] *n* surfeur, -euse.

surfing ['sɜːfɪŋ] *n Sp* surfing *m*, surf *m*.

surfrider, surfriding ['sɜːfraɪdər, -ɪŋ] = **SURFER, SURFING.**

surge¹ [sɜːdʒ] *n Nau* houle *f*; irrégularité *f* (*dans la marche d'une machine*); *Fig* poussée *f* (*d'activité*); accès *m* (*d'enthousiasme, colère*); *Fig* **the s. of the crowd,** les remous *mpl* de la foule; **a s. of anger,** un flot *ou* une vague de colère; **there has been a s. of public interest in ...,** il y a eu un mouvement *ou* une poussée de l'intérêt public pour ...; **she felt a s. of fury,** elle sentit une poussée *ou* un flot de fureur; **these seasonal surges in production/sales,** ces poussées saisonnières de la production/des ventes; *El* **s. of current,** à-coup *m ou* impulsion *f* de courant, surintensité *f*.

surge² *vi* **(a)** (*of sea*) être houleux; (*of waters*) se soulever; *Fig* **the crowd surged along the street/onto the pitch,** la foule s'est répandue en flots dans la rue/sur le terrain; **the crowd surged back,** la foule a reflué; *El* **the current surges,** il y a des à-coups de courant; **(b)** *Nau* (*of cable*) choquer brusquement.

▶**surge up** *vi* (*well up*) monter d'un seul coup; **anger surged up within her,** un flot de colère est monté en elle.

surgeon ['sɜːdʒ(ə)n] *n* chirurgien, -ienne; *US Admin* **S. General,** ministre *m* de la santé.

surgery ['sɜːdʒərɪ] *n* **(a)** chirurgie *f*; **major/minor s.,** grande/petite chirurgie; **he'll need s.,** il faudra l'opérer; **heart s.,** chirurgie du cœur; **he's had heart s.,** il a eu une opération du cœur; **the s. was successful,** l'opération a réussi; **a clever piece of s.,** une opération habile; **(b)** *Br* (*place*) cabinet *m* de consultation (*chez un médecin*); cabinet (*de dentiste*); **town councillors hold weekly surgeries,** les conseillers municipaux tiennent des consultations hebdomadaires; **s. (hours),** heures *fpl* de consultation.

surgical ['sɜːdʒɪk(ə)l] *adj* chirurgical, -aux; **s. boot,** chaussure *f* orthopédique; **s. instruments,** instruments *mpl* de chirurgie; **s. spirit,** alcool *m* à 90°; *Fig* **the operation was carried out with s. precision,** cette opération a été réalisée avec une précision mathématique.

surging ['sɜːdʒɪŋ] *adj* **s. sea,** mer houleuse; **a s. mass of people,** un flot pressé de gens.

surliness ['sɜːlɪnɪs] *n* humeur *f* maussade; (*expression*) air bourru; (*of remark*) ton bourru.

surly ['sɜːlɪ] *adj* (*personne*) maussade, revêche; (*ton, air*) bourru; **s. disposition,** humeur *f* maussade.

surmise¹ [sɜː'maɪz] *n* conjecture *f*, supposition *f*.

surmise² [sɜː'maɪz] *vt* conjecturer, soupçonner, deviner; **as you may well have surmised,** comme vous l'avez peut-être deviné, comme vous le soupçonnez peut-être.

surmount [sɜː'maʊnt] *vt* **(a)** surmonter; **column surmounted by a cross,** colonne surmontée d'une croix; **(b)** surmonter (*un obstacle, une difficulté etc*); triompher de (*une passion, une difficulté*).

surmountable [sɜː'maʊntəb(ə)l] *adj* surmontable.

surname ['sɜːneɪm] *n* nom *m* de famille; **s. and Christian** *or* **first names,** nom et prénoms *mpl*.

surpass [sɜː'pɑːs] *vt* **(a)** (*be superior to*) surpasser (*qn*); devancer (*ses rivaux*); **to s. s.o. in kindness,** renchérir sur la bonté de qn; **he has surpassed himself,** il s'est surpassé; *Iron* **you've surpassed yourself this time,** vous vous êtes surpassé cette fois; **(b)** (*exceed*) dépasser, excéder; **the result surpassed my hopes,** le résultat a dépassé mes espérances *ou* mon attente; **this surpasses all previous records,** ceci surpasse tous les records précédents.

surpassing [sɜː'pɑːsɪŋ] *adj* sans égal, sans pareil; **of s. beauty,** d'une beauté incomparable *ou* sans pareille.

surplice ['sɜːplɪs] *n Rel* surplis *m*.

surplus ['sɜːpləs] *n* surplus *m*, excédent *m*; **to have a s. of sth,** avoir qch en excès; **to have a s. of books,** avoir des livres en surnombre; **EEC grain surpluses,** excédents de céréales de la CEE; **s. population/products,** population *f*/produits *mpl* excédentaire(s); *Com* **s. stock,** surstock *m*; **government s. (stock),** les surplus du gouvernement.

surprise¹ [sə'praɪz] *n* surprise *f*; **to take s.o. by s.,** prendre qn à l'improviste *ou* au dépourvu, surprendre qn; *Mil* **to take a town by s.,** enlever une ville par (un coup de) surprise; **the President's s. announcement,** l'annonce surprise du président; **s. party,** surprise-party *f*; **s. visit,** visite *f* à l'improviste, visite-surprise; **to pay s.o. a s. visit,** aller surprendre qn chez lui; **to give s.o. a s.,** faire une surprise à qn; **it was a s. to see her there,** c'était une surprise de la voir là; **what a s. to see you here!,** je m'étonne de vous rencontrer ici; **what a pleasant s.!,** quelle bonne surprise!; **the party was meant to be a s.,** la fête était censée être une surprise; **to spoil the s.,** gâcher la surprise; **it was no s. to learn that he had a criminal record,** ce n'était pas surprenant d'apprendre qu'il avait un casier judiciaire; **he's in for a bit of a s.!,** s'il savait ce qu'on lui prépare!; **s., s.!, it's us!,** surprise!, c'est nous!; **to my great s., much to my s.,** à ma grande surprise, à mon grand étonnement; **imagine my s. when ...,** imaginez comme j'ai été surpris quand ..., imaginez quelle a été ma surprise *ou* quel a été mon étonnement quand ... .

surprise² *vt* **(a)** surprendre, étonner (*qn*); **nothing surprises him,** rien ne l'étonne; **you could s. yourself,** tu pourrais t'étonner toi-même; **to be surprised at sth,** être surpris *ou* étonné de qch; **I am surprised to see you** *or* **at seeing you,** je m'étonne de vous voir, je suis surpris de vous voir; **I should be surprised if he came back,** cela m'étonnerait qu'il revienne; **there can't be many people who don't have a phone — you'd be surprised,** il ne doit pas y avoir beaucoup de gens qui n'ont pas le téléphone — ne crois pas ça; **I wouldn't** *or* **shouldn't be surprised if they know already,** ça ne me surprendrait pas qu'ils le sachent déjà; **it doesn't s. me in the least,** ça ne m'étonne pas du tout; **I was agreeably surprised,** j'ai été agréablement surpris; **I'm surprised at you!,** vous m'étonnez!; **(b)** surprendre (*une armée etc*); prendre (*une place*) par surprise; **to s. s.o. in the act,** surprendre qn en flagrant délit, prendre qn sur le fait, prendre qn la main dans le sac.

surprised [sə'praɪzd] *adj* (*regard*) étonné, surpris; (*air*) de surprise; **don't look so s.,** ne prends pas un air aussi étonné.

surprising [sə'praɪzɪŋ] *adj* surprenant, étonnant; **well, it's not s., is it?,** et bien, ça n'a rien de surprenant, n'est-ce pas?; **it wouldn't be s. if he was in the plot,** ça n'aurait rien de surprenant s'il était du complot; **that's s. coming from him,** cela surprend (venant) de sa part.

surprisingly [sə'praɪzɪŋlɪ] *adv* étonnamment; **I found him s. young,** je lui ai trouvé l'air étonnament jeune; **s. enough, he agreed,** contrairement à toute attente, il a accepté; **not s., she changed her mind,** comme on pouvait s'y attendre, elle a changé d'avis.

surrealism [sə'rɪəlɪz(ə)m] *n Liter Art* surréalisme *m*.

surrealist [sə'rɪəlɪst] *adj & n Liter Art* surréaliste *mf*.

surrealistic [sərɪə'lɪstɪk] *adj Liter Art* surréaliste.

surrealistically [sərɪə'lɪstɪk(ə)lɪ] *adv* d'une manière *ou* dans un style surréaliste.

surrender¹ [sə'rendər] *n* **(a)** (*act of surrendering*) *Mil* reddition *f* (*d'une armée, d'une forteresse*); **no s.!,** nous ne nous rendrons pas!; *Jur* **s. of a defendant to his bail,** décharge *f* de ses cautions par un accusé (*libéré sous caution*); **(b)** *Jur* abandon *m*, cession *f* (*de biens, de droits*); restitution *f* (*d'un droit de propriété*); abdication *f* (*de droits, de l'autorité*); **to make a s. of principle,** transiger avec ses principes; **(c)** (*in insurance*) rachat *m* (*d'une police*); **s. value,** valeur *f* de rachat.

surrender² **1** *vi* se rendre; *Mil* faire (sa) soumission, rendre les armes; **to s. to the police,** se constituer prisonnier, se livrer à la police; **to s. to one's bail,** décharger ses cautions; *Fig* **all right! I surrender!,** ça va! je me rends! **2** *vt* **(a)** *Mil* rendre, livrer (*une forteresse*); **(b)** *Jur* abandonner, céder (*un droit, ses biens*); abdiquer (*un droit*); **to s. all hope of sth,** abandonner *ou* renoncer à tout espoir de qch; **(c)** (*in insurance*) racheter (*une police d'assurances*).

surreptitious [sʌrəp'tɪʃəs] *adj* subreptice, clandestin.

surreptitiously [sʌrəp'tɪʃəslɪ] *adv* subrepticement, clandestinement.

surreptitiousness [sʌrəp'tɪʃəsnɪs] *n* caractère *m ou* nature *f* subreptice, clandestinité *f*.

surrogacy ['sʌrəgəsɪ] *n* maternité *f* de substitution.

surrogate ['sʌrəgɪt] *n* (*person*) suppléant, -ante, substitut *m*; *Rel Jur* subrogé, -ée; (*thing*) succédané *m* (**for, of sth,** de qch); **s. mother,** mère porteuse; **s. motherhood,** maternité *f* de substitution.

surround¹ [sə'raʊnd] *n* encadrement *m*, bordure *f*.

surround² *vt* entourer; *Mil* entourer, cerner (*l'ennemi*); investir (*une ville*); **to s. a town with walls,** entourer *ou* ceinturer une ville de murs; **the crowd surrounded the car,** la foule a assiégé la voiture; **surrounded by** *or* **with dangers,** cerné de dangers; **he likes to be surrounded by ...,** il aime être entouré de ...; **give up!, you're surrounded!,** rendez-vous!, vous êtes cernés!

surrounding [sə'raʊndɪŋ] *adj* entourant, environnant; **the s. country,** le pays alentour *ou* environnant.

surroundings [sə'raʊndɪŋz] *npl* **(a)** milieu *m*, cadre *m*, environnement *m*; **in its natural s.,** dans son milieu naturel; **to be in familiar s.,** être en pays de connaissance; **(b)** environs *mpl*, alentours *mpl* (*d'une ville etc*).

surtax¹ ['sɜːtæks] *n Admin* surtaxe *f*; (*on income*) = surtaxe progressive sur le revenu.

surtax² *vt* surtaxer.

surveillance [sɜː'veɪləns] *n Admin* surveillance *f*, contrôle *m*; **to be under s.,** être sous surveillance.

survey¹ ['sɜːveɪ] *n* **(a)** étude *f* (*d'un sujet, de la situation*); **in a recent s.,** dans une étude récente; **to make a s. of sth,** étudier (*une question*); **(b)** (*inspection*) inspection *f*, visite *f*; **(c)** levé *m* des plans, relevé *m*; *Constr* métrage *m* des travaux; plan *m*, levé (*du terrain, d'un édifice*); *Constr* étude *f*; **aerial s.,** levé aérophotogrammétrique; **to make a s. of an estate,** relever un domaine; **quantity s.,** métrage *m*, métré *m*, toisé *m*.

survey² [sɜː'veɪ] *vt* **(a)** regarder, contempler, promener ses regards sur (*le paysage etc*); étudier, mettre (*une question*) à l'étude; **to s. the situation,** examiner la situation, passer la situation en revue; **(b)** (*inspect*) inspecter, faire l'expertise de l'état (*d'un navire, d'un immeuble*); **to have a house surveyed,** faire inspecter un immeuble par un (architecte) expert; **(c)** (*in surveying*) relever, faire le (re)levé de, lever le(s) plan(s) de (*la ville, la propriété*); hydrographier, faire l'hydrographie (*d'une côte*).

surveying [sɜː'veɪɪŋ] *n* **(a)** *Constr* levé *m* de plans; (*for mapmaking*) géodésie *f*, topographie *f*; **s. instruments,** instruments *mpl* topographiques; **quantity s.,** métrage *m*, métré *m*, toisé *m*; **(b)** (*inspection*) inspection *f*, visite *f*.

surveyor [sə'veɪər] *n* **(a) (land) s.,** géomètre expert; **naval s.,** (ingénieur) hydrographe *m*; **surveyor's table,** planchette *f*; *Admin* **land s. and valuer, district s.,** cadastreur *m*; **quantity s.,** métreur vérificateur; **(b)** *Admin* surveillant, -ante, inspecteur, -trice; *Nau* **marine s.,** visiteur *m ou* inspecteur de navires; **property s.,** (architecte *m*) expert *m*.

survival [sə'vaɪv(ə)l] *n* **(a)** survivance *f* (*d'une tradition*); survie *f* (*d'un accidenté*); **her s. as party leader,** sa survie en tant que tête du parti; **it's a question of s.,** c'est notre *ou* leur *etc* survie qui est en jeu; *Nat Hist* **the s. of the fittest,** la survie des mieux adaptés *ou* du plus apte; **s. bag,** sac *m* de couchage de survie; **s. kit,** équipement *m* de survie; **(b)** (*remaining part*) restant *m* (*d'une ancienne coutume*); **a s. of times past,** une survivance des temps passés.

survivalist [sə'vaɪv(ə)lɪst] *n esp Am* = personne qui se prépare à une catastrophe (nucléaire etc).

survive [sə'vaɪv] **1** *vi* survivre; (*of custom*) survivre, subsister; **those who survived,** les survivants *mpl*; **those toys wouldn't s. two minutes with our kids,** ces jouets ne survivraient pas plus de deux minutes avec nos gamins; **it's not serious, you'll s.,** ce n'est pas grave, tu survivras; *F* **it'll be awful, I don't know how I'll s.!,** ça va être horrible, je ne sais pas comment je vais survivre! **2** *vt* survivre à (*qn*); **he will s. us all,** il nous enterrera tous; **he is survived by a family of four,** il laisse derrière lui une famille de quatre personnes; **to s. an injury,** survivre à une blessure; **to s. an illness,** réchapper d'une maladie; **to s. a recession,** (*of company*) survivre à une récession.

surviving [sə'vaɪvɪŋ] *adj* survivant; **there is one s. sister,** une des sœurs est encore en vie, il y a une sœur encore en vie.

survivor [sə'vaɪvər] *n* survivant, -ante; **he is the sole s. of his family,** il est le seul qui reste de sa famille; **the survivors of the disaster,** les rescapé(s); **earthquake/flood s.,** rescapé d'un tremblement de terre/d'une inondation; **she's a s.,** (*in politics, business etc*) elle ne se laisse pas abattre, *Pej* c'est une rescapée.

Susan ['suːz(ə)n] *n* Suzanne *f*.

susceptibility [səseptɪ'bɪlɪtɪ] *n* **(a)** susceptibilité *f*; **s. to a disease,** prédisposition *f* à une maladie; **s. to pain,** sensibilité *f* à la douleur; **(b)** (*sensitivity*) sensibilité *f*, susceptibilité *f*; **words that wound susceptibilities,** mots qui blessent *ou* heurtent les susceptibilités, mots blessants.

susceptible [sə'septɪb(ə)l] *adj* sensible (**to,** à); (*touchy*) susceptible, qui se froisse facilement; **s. to media influences,** sensible à l'influence des média; **s. to a disease,** prédisposé à une maladie; **this will make you less s. to colds,** ceci vous rendra plus résistant au rhume; **s. to cold,** frileux; *Fml* **s. of proof,** prouvable, démontrable.

suspect¹ ['sʌspekt] **1** *adj* suspect. **2** *n* suspect, -e.

suspect² [sə'spekt] *vt* **(a)** soupçonner, s'imaginer (*qch*); se douter de (*qch*); flairer, subodorer (*un danger*); **to s. s.o. of a crime,** soupçonner qn d'un crime, suspecter qn; **to be suspected by s.o. of sth/of doing sth,** être soupçonné par qn de qch/de faire qch; **he suspects nothing,** il ne se doute de rien; **does your husband s. anything?,** est-ce que ton mari se doute de quelque chose?;

(b) (*doubt*) avoir des doutes sur; **to s. the authenticity of a work,** avoir des doutes sur l'authenticité d'une œuvre; **I never suspected it for a moment,** je n'en avais pas le moindre soupçon, je ne m'en suis jamais douté;

(c) (*consider likely*) croire, penser; **I suspected as much,** je m'en doutais; **I s. that what she really means is ...,** je pense que ce qu'elle veut vraiment dire, c'est ... ; **I s. you're right,** je crois bien que vous avez raison.

suspected [sə'spektɪd] *adj* **a s. person,** un(e) suspect(e); *Med* **s. case of typhoid,** cas présumé de typhoïde; **he has a s. fracture,** on craint qu'il (n')ait une fracture.

suspend [sə'spend] *vt* **(a)** (*hang*) suspendre, pendre (*qch*); **to s. sth from the ceiling,** suspendre *ou* pendre qch au plafond; **(b)** (*stop*) suspendre (*un service d'autobus, le travail*); *Jur* **to s. judgment,** surseoir au jugement; **to s. proceedings,** suspendre les poursuites; *Com* **to s. payment,** suspendre ses paiements; **(c)** suspendre (**s.o. from his** *or* **her office,** qn de ses fonctions); interdire (*qn*); mettre (*un officier*) en non-activité; mettre (*un jockey*) à pied; suspendre (*un journal*); **to s. a pupil (from school),** renvoyer un élève (provisoirement); *Admin* **suspended on full pay,** suspendu sans suppression de traitement *ou Mil* de solde.

suspended [sə'spendɪd] *adj* suspendu; (*particules*) en suspension; *Jur* en suspens, suspendu; **she was given a s. prison sentence of six months,** elle a été condamnée à six mois de prison avec sursis; **to be in a state of s. animation,** (*of person, animal*) *& Fig Hum* être en hibernation; **the scheme is in a state of s. animation,** le projet est en suspens.

suspender [sə'spendər] *n* suspensoir *m*; (*women's*) jarretelles *fpl*; **s. belt,** porte-jarretelles *m inv*; (*men's*) supports *mpl* pour chaussettes; *Am* **(pair of) suspenders,** (paire *f* de) bretelles *fpl*.

suspense [sə'spens] *n* **(a)** suspens *m*; **to keep** *or* **hold s.o. in s.,** tenir *ou* garder qn en suspens *ou* en haleine; **the s. is killing me,** ce suspens me rend fou; *Iron* quel suspens!; **(b)** *Liter* suspens *m*, suspense *m*; **author who has used s. to good effect,** auteur qui s'est bien servi du suspens(e); **(c)** *Jur* **the question remains in s.,** la question reste posée *ou* en suspens; **s. account,** (*in bookkeeping*) compte *m* d'ordre.

suspension [sə'spenʃən] *n* **(a)** (*of car etc*) suspension *f*; **spring s.,** suspension par ressorts; *Ch* **(substance in) s.,** (substance *f* en) suspension; *Constr* **s. bridge,** pont suspendu; **s. cable,** câble porteur; *MecE* **s. chain/hook,** chaîne *f*/croc *m* de suspension; **(b)** suspension *f* (*de la circulation, des hostilités*); *Jur* surséance *f* (*de jugement*); *Com* (*of payment*) suspension de paiements; *Typ Gram* **s. points,** points *mpl* de suspension; **(c)** suspension *f* (*d'un fonctionnaire etc*); mise *f* en non-activité (*d'un officier*); mise à pied (*d'un jockey*).

suspensory [sə'spensərɪ] *adj Anat* (*ligament*) suspenseur; *Med* **s. bandage,** suspensoir *m*.

suspicion [sə'spɪʃən] *n* **(a)** soupçon *m*; *Jur* suspicion *f*; (*characteristic, quality*) méfiance *f*, défiance *f*, suspicion *f*; **not the shadow** *or* **ghost of a s.,** pas l'ombre d'un soupçon; **to look at s.o. with s.,** regarder qn avec défiance; **the s. in her eyes/voice,** la défiance dans ses yeux/sa voix; **to be under s.,** être soupçonné; **to have (one's) suspicions about s.o.,** avoir des doutes sur qn, soupçonner qn; **to arouse s.,** éveiller *ou* faire naître les soupçons; **to arouse** *or* **awaken s.o.'s suspicions,** éveiller les soupçons de qn; **above s.,** au-dessus de tout soupçon; **praise free from any s. of flattery,** louanges aucunement suspectes de flatterie; **to be right in one's suspicions,** soupçonner juste; *Jur* **to arrest/detain s.o. on s.,** arrêter/détenir qn préventivement; **on s. of arson,** sous la présomption d'incendie volontaire; **detention on s.,** détention préventive; **I had my suspicions about it,** je m'en doutais, j'avais mes soupçons là-dessus; **I had no s. of it,** je n'en avais pas le moindre soupçon;

(b) (*hint*) très petite quantité, soupçon *m* (**of,** de); pointe *f* (*d'ironie, de malice*).

suspicious [sə'spɪʃəs] *adj* **(a)** (*arousing suspicions*) suspect; (*conduct*) louche, équivoque, suspect; **it looks s.,** cela me paraît louche *ou* suspect; **s. character,** individu louche *ou* suspect; *Admin* sujet noté; **he died in s. circumstances,** il est mort dans des circonstances suspectes; **(b)** (*having suspicions*) méfiant, soupçonneux; **she has a very**

s. mind, elle est très soupçonneuse *ou* méfiante; **to be** *or* **feel s. about s.o./sth** *or* **of s.o./sth,** avoir des soupçons à l'endroit *ou* à l'égard de qn/sur qch; **her behaviour made me s.,** sa conduite a éveillé mes soupçons.

suspiciously [sə'spɪʃəslɪ] *adv* **(a)** (*to act*) d'une manière suspecte *ou* louche; **he was s. eager to leave,** l'empressement qu'il avait de partir était suspect; **it sounded s. as though she had lost it,** on aurait dit qu'elle l'avait perdu; **it looks s. like the one I lost,** il ressemble étrangement à celui que j'ai perdu; **two texts that are s. similar,** deux textes qui sont étrangement similaires; **it looks s. like measles (to me),** cela ressemble étrangement à la rougeole; **(b)** (*to watch*) d'un air méfiant, avec méfiance.

suspiciousness [sə'spɪʃəsnɪs] *n* **(a)** (*of behaviour, parcel etc*) (*causing suspicion*) caractère suspect *ou* louche; **(b)** (*of person, in voice etc*) (*feeling suspicion*) caractère soupçonneux, méfiance *f*.

suss [sʌs] *vt* = **SUSS OUT**.

▶**suss out** *vtsep F* (*work out*) savoir ce que vaut (*qn*), *Sl* cataloguer (*qn*); *F* piger (*system, technique*); **to s. out how a machine works,** comprendre comment une machine fonctionne; **I finally sussed out what she was doing,** j'ai fini par comprendre ce qu'elle faisait; **to have sth sussed out,** *F* avoir pigé qch.

sustain [sə'steɪn] *vt* **(a)** soutenir, supporter; **enough oxygen to s. life,** suffisamment d'oxygène pour entretenir la vie; **to s. the body,** sustenter le corps; **evidence to s. an assertion,** témoignages pour appuyer une affirmation; *Mus* **to s. a note,** tenir *ou* prolonger une note; *Jur* **to s. an objection,** (*of court*) admettre une objection; **objection sustained,** objection admise; **(b)** (*suffer, receive*) éprouver, essuyer, subir (*une perte*); soutenir (*une attaque*); **to s. an injury,** recevoir une blessure, être blessé.

sustainable [sə'steɪnəbl] *adj* (*growth, lifestyle*) que l'on peut maintenir.

sustained [sə'steɪnd] *adj* soutenu; **s. applause,** applaudissements prolongés; *Mil* **s. fire,** feu soutenu *ou* nourri; *Mus* **s. note,** tenue *f*.

sustaining [sə'steɪnɪŋ] *adj* (*power*) soutenant; (*food*) nourrissant.

sustenance ['sʌstɪnəns] *n* **(a) necessary for the s. of our bodies,** nécessaire à notre subsistance *f*; **means of s.,** moyens de subsistance; **(b)** (*food*) aliments *mpl*, nourriture *f*; (*nutritional value*) valeur nutritive.

suttee [sʌ'tiː] *n* (*in Hindu religion*) **(a)** (*practice*) satî *m*; **(b)** (*widow*) satî *f*.

suture¹ ['suːtʃər] *n* **(a)** *Anat Bot* suture *f*; **(b)** *Surg* (*action*) suture *f*; (*stitch*) point *m* de suture; (*thread*) fil *m* pour sutures.

suture² *vt Surg* suturer (*une plaie*).

suzerain ['suːzəreɪn] *n* suzerain.

suzerainty ['suːzəreɪntɪ] *n* suzeraineté *f*.

svelte [svelt] *adj* svelte.

swab¹ [swɒb] *n* (*mop*) torchon *m*; (*for floors*) serpillière *f*; *Nau* vadrouille *f*; *Mil* écouvillon *m*; *Med* (*material*) tampon *m*; (*specimen*) prélèvement *m*; (*smear*) frottis *m*; **s. of cotton wool,** tampon d'ouate; **to take a s. of s.o.'s throat,** faire un prélèvement dans la gorge de qn.

swab² *vt* **(-bb-) (a)** nettoyer, essuyer (*avec un torchon*); **(b)** = **SWAB DOWN**; **(c)** = **SWAB OUT**.

▶**swab down** *vtsep* (*clean*) laver (*la cour*) à grande eau; *Nau* essarder (*le pont*).

▶**swab out** *vtsep* (*clean*) *Mil* écouvillonner (*une pièce*); *Med* nettoyer (*une plaie*) avec un tampon.

swaddle ['swɒd(ə)l] *vt* emmailloter (**with,** de).

swaddling ['swɒdlɪŋ] *n Arch* **s. clothes,** maillots *mpl*, langes *mpl*.

swag [swæg] *n F* rafle *f*, butin *m* (*d'un cambrioleur*); *Austr* baluchon *m* (*de chemineau*).

swagger¹ ['swægər] *n* **(a)** air important; (*carefree*) air cavalier *ou* désinvolte; **to walk with a s.,** marcher avec un air avantageux, se pavaner; *Mil* **s. stick** *or* **cane,** jonc *m*, stick *m*; (*short*) badine *f*; **(b)** (*boasting*) rodomontades *fpl*, crâneries *fpl*, fanfaronnades *fpl*.

swagger² *vi* **(a)** crâner, se pavaner; **to s. about,** se promener d'un air conquérant *ou* en se rengorgeant; **to s. in/out,** entrer/sortir d'un air conquérant; **(b)** (*boast*) faire de l'esbrouffe; **to s. about sth,** se vanter de qch.

swaggering ['swægərɪŋ] **1** *adj* (*air*) important, crâneur. **2** *n* **(a)** air important; **(b)** (*boasting*) rodomontades *fpl*.

swagman, *pl* **-men** ['swægmən] *n Austr F* chemineau *m* (*qui porte son baluchon*).

Swahili [swɑː'hiːlɪ] **1** *adj* souahéli, swahéli, swahili. **2** *n* **(a)** (*pl* **Swahili(s)**) Souahéli, -ie, Swahéli, -ie, Swahili, -ie; *pl* -i(s); **(b)** *Ling* souahéli *m*, swahéli *m*, swahili *m*.

swain [sweɪn] *n* **(a)** (*poetry*) & *Arch* jeune berger *m*; *Hum Old-fashioned* (*suitor*) soupirant *m*.

SWALK ['swɔːlk] (*abbr* **sealed with a loving kiss**) = scellée d'un tendre baiser.

swallow¹ ['swɒləʊ] *n* **(a)** (*act of swallowing*) déglutition *f*; (*mouthful*) gorgée *f* (*d'eau*); **at one s.,** d'un seul coup *ou* trait; **(b)** *Geol* **s. hole,** aven *m*.

swallow² **1** *vt* avaler, ingurgiter; *Physiol* déglutir (*qch*); gober (*une huître*); gober, avaler (*une histoire*); avaler (*un affront*); (r)avaler (*ses larmes*); retenir (*sa colère*); mettre (*son orgueil*) dans sa poche (et son mouchoir par dessus); **to s. sth whole,** avaler qch tout rond; **to s. the bait,** (*of fish*) avaler l'appât; *F* (*of person*) se laisser prendre à l'appât; **I told her a lie and she swallowed it,** je lui ai raconté un mensonge et elle l'a gobé *ou* avalé; **he swallowed it hook, line and sinker,** il a tout gobé; **her story is hard to s.,** son histoire est difficile à avaler; **to s. one's words,** (*speak indistinctly*) manger ses mots; (*deny what one has said*) se dédire, revenir sur ses paroles. **2** *vi* avaler; **to s. hard,** avaler sa salive (*pour faire passer une émotion*).

swallow³ *n* **(a)** (*bird*) hirondelle *f*; *Prov* **one s. doesn't make a summer,** une hirondelle ne fait pas le printemps; **(b)** *Swimming* **s. dive,** saut *m* de l'ange.

▶**swallow down** *vtsep* avaler (*une boisson, une pilule*).

▶**swallow up** *vtsep* (*engulf*) dévorer, avaler (*qn, qch*); (*of the sea*) engloutir, engouffrer (*qn, qch*); *Fig* **they walked away and were soon swallowed up by** *or* **in the mist,** ils sont partis à pied et ont vite été engloutis par le brouillard; **the small country/company was swallowed up,** le petit pays/la petite société à été englouti(e).

swallow-dive ['swɒləʊdaɪv] *vi Swimming* faire le saut de l'ange.

swallowing ['swɒləʊɪŋ] *n* **(a)** *Physiol* déglutition *f*; **(b)** = **SWALLOWING UP**.

swallowing up *n* engloutissement *m*, engouffrement *m*.

swallowtail ['swɒləʊteɪl] *n* **(a)** (*forked tail*) queue fourchue; (*of swallow*) queue d'hirondelle; **(b)** *F Old-fashioned* (*often pl*) (*coat*) queue-de-morue *f*, *pl* queues-de-morue; **(c) s. (butterfly),** machaon *m*.

swallow-tailed ['swɒləʊteɪld] *adj* **(a)** à queue fourchue; **(b) s.-t. coat = SWALLOWTAIL (b)**.

swamp¹ [swɒmp] *n* marais *m*, marécage *m*.

swamp² *vt* inonder; submerger (*un pré*); remplir d'eau (*une embarcation*); **F to be swamped with sth,** (*work, orders, requests*) être débordé *ou* submergé de; (*letters, offers of help*) être submergé de.

swampy ['swɒmpɪ] *adj* (*terrain*) marécageux.

swan¹ [swɒn] *n* cygne *m*, **mute s.,** cygne commun *ou* muet; **black s.,** cygne noir; *Am Swimming* **s. dive,** saut *m* de l'ange; *MecE* **s. neck,** cou *m ou* col *m* de cygne; *Fig* **s. song,** chant *m* du cygne.

swan² *vi* **(-nn-)** *F* **to s. around,** se balader, musarder; **he just sort of swans around the office all day,** il ne fait que musarder dans le bureau toute la journée; **he seems to have swanned off early,** on dirait qu'il a pris le large de bonne heure; **don't think you can come swanning back just when you feel like it, she said,** ne crois pas que tu peux revenir en te pavanant juste quand tu en as envie, dit-elle; **a swanning sort of job,** un boulot plutôt tranquille *ou F* peinard.

swank¹ [swæŋk] *F* **1** *n* **(a)** (*ostentation*) épate *f*; **(b)** (*ostentatious person*) épateur, -euse; (*boastful person*) crâneur, -euse. **2** *adj esp Am* = **SWANKY**.

swank² *vi F* se donner des airs, faire de l'épate.

swanky ['swæŋkɪ] *adj F* (*person*) prétentieux, poseur; (*restaurant, dinner, hotel*) superchic; (*car*) tapageur.

swan-necked ['swɒnnekt] *adj* au cou de cygne.

swannery ['swɒnərɪ] *n* réserve *f* de cygnes.

swan's-down ['swɒnzdaʊn] *n* duvet *m* de cygne (*pour garnitures*); cygne *m*; *Tex* molleton *m*.

swap¹ [swɒp] *n* (*exchange*) troc *m*, échange *m*; objet *m ou* article *m* à échanger *ou* qu'on a échangé; **to do a s.,** faire un troc *ou* un échange; **it wasn't a very good s.,** ce n'était pas un échange très équitable; **it's a good s.,** c'est un échange avantageux; **she took my old car as a s. for this one,** elle a pris ma vieille voiture en échange de celle-ci; **swaps,** (*in stamp collecting etc*) doubles *mpl*.

swap² *v* **(-pp-)** **1** *vt F* **to s. sth for sth,** échanger *ou* troquer qch contre *ou* pour qch; **I'll s. you mine for yours,** je t'échange le mien contre le tien; **(I'll) s. you!,** je te l'échange!; **to s. places with s.o.,** changer de place avec qn; **to s. stories,** échanger ses impressions. **2** *vi F* faire du troc; **shall we s.?,** si nous faisions un échange?

swapping ['swɒpɪŋ] *n F* échange *m*, troc *m*.

SWAPO ['swɑːpəʊ] *n Pol* (*abbr* **South-West Africa People's Organization**) SWAPO *f*.

sward [swɔːd] *n Lit* gazon *m*, pelouse *f*.

swarm[1] [swɔːm] *n* essaim *m* (*d'abeilles, de gens*); vol *m* (*de sauterelles*); nuée *f* (*de moucherons, de gens*); fourmillement *m* (*de petits bateaux*); essaim, troupe *f* (*d'enfants*); **there were swarms of tourists,** il y avait des nuées de touristes.

swarm[2] **1** *vi* **(a)** (*of bees*) essaimer; (*of people*) accourir en foule, se presser (**round, in,** autour de, dans); **the crowd swarmed over the pitch,** la foule a inondé *ou* a fait irruption sur le terrain; **(b)** (*of place*) fourmiller, grouiller, pulluler (**with,** de); **the roads were swarming with people,** les rues grouillaient *ou* regorgeaient *ou* fourmillaient de monde. **2** *vt* = **SWARM UP**.

▶**swarm up** *vipo* (*climb*) grimper à (*un arbre, un mât*).

swarming *n* (*in beekeeping*) essaimage *m*.

swarthiness ['swɔːðɪnɪs] *n* teint basané *ou* bistré.

swarthy ['swɔːðɪ] *adj* (*complexion*) basané, bistré; (*person*) noiraud.

swash[1] [swɒʃ] *n* clapotis *m* (*des vagues*).

swash[2] *vi* (*of water*) clapoter.

swashbuckler ['swɒʃbʌklər] *n* bravache *m*.

swashbuckling ['swɒʃbʌklɪŋ] **1** *adj* fanfaron, bravache; **s. film,** film *m* d'aventures bravache; **s. tale,** fanfaronnade *f*; **s. fellow,** fanfaron *m*. **2** *n* fanfaronnades *fpl*, rodomontades *fpl*.

swastika ['swɒstɪkə] *n* svastika *m*, croix gammée.

swat[1] [swɒt] *n* tape *f*; **fly s.,** tapette *f* tue-mouches.

swat[2] *v* (**-tt-**) *vt F* frapper, taper (*qn, qch*); **s. that fly!,** écrasez donc cette mouche!

swath [swɔːθ] *n Agr* = **SWATHE[1]**.

swathe[1] [sweɪð] *n Agr* andain *m*; *Fig* **the cannons had cut great swathes through the troops,** les canons avaient beaucoup entamé les effectifs des troupes.

swathe[2] *vt* emmailloter, envelopper; **head swathed in bandages,** tête enveloppée de bandages; **swathed in mist,** entouré *ou* baigné de brume.

swatter ['swɒtər] *n* **fly s.,** tapette *f* tue-mouches.

sway[1] [sweɪ] *n* **(a)** (*movement*) balancement *m*, oscillation *f*, mouvement *m* de va-et-vient; *Rail* mouvement de lacet (*des wagons*); *Aut* roulis *m* (*de la voiture*); **(b)** (*control, power*) empire *m*, domination *f*; **under her s.,** sous son empire, sous son influence; **to have** *or* **hold s. over a people,** régner sur un peuple; **to hold s. over a country,** tenir un pays en souveraineté, régner sur un pays; **emotions that no longer hold any s. over me,** des émotions qui n'ont plus aucun empire sur moi.

sway[2] **1** *vi* se balancer, osciller; (*of drunkard*) vaciller; (*remain undecided*) rester indécis, vaciller; **to s. in the wind,** (*of trees*) se balancer au vent; **he swayed back up to the bar,** il revint au bar en vacillant; **public opinion is prone to s. this way and that,** l'opinion publique est encline à osciller de part et d'autre.

2 *vt* **(a)** faire osciller, balancer, agiter (*les arbres*); **she sways her hips when she walks,** elle balance *ou* roule les hanches en marchant;

(b) (*influence*) **considerations that s. our opinions,** considérations qui influencent nos opinions; **to s. s.o. from his** *or* **her course,** détourner qn de ses projets; **to refuse to be swayed,** ne pas se laisser influencer; **what can we say or do to s. you?,** que pouvons-nous dire ou faire pour vous convaincre *ou* (*make you change your mind*) vous faire changer d'avis?; **what finally swayed them was ...,** ce qui les a finalement convaincu a été ...; **it was close but one thing swayed it ...,** (*in vote etc*) la lutte était serrée mais une chose a tout fait balancer;

(c) *Arch* (*rule*) gouverner, diriger.

swaying ['sweɪɪŋ] **1** *adj* qui se balance de ci de-là, oscillant; **s. motion,** balancement *m*, mouvement *m* de va-et-vient. **2** *n* balancement *m*, oscillation *f*, mouvement *m* de va-et-vient; *Rail* mouvement de lacet (*des wagons*); *Aut* roulis *m* (*de la voiture*).

Swazi ['swɑːzɪ] **1** *adj* souazi. **2** *n* **(a)** Souazi(e); **(b)** *Ling* le dialecte souazi.

Swaziland ['swɑːzɪlænd] *n* le Souaziland.

swear [sweər] *v* (*pt* **swore** [swɔːr]; *pp* **sworn** [swɔːn]) **1** *vt* **(a)** jurer; (*on oath*) déclarer (*qch*) sous (*la foi du*) serment; **to s. an oath,** faire un serment, jurer; **to s. sth on the Bible,** jurer qch sur la Bible; **to s. to do sth,** jurer de faire qch; **I could have sworn I heard a shout,** j'aurais juré entendre un cri; **it wasn't me, I s. (it)!,** ce n'était pas moi, je le jure!; **to s. allegiance to s.o./sth,** prêter serment d'allégeance à qn/qch; **to s. revenge,** jurer *ou* faire serment de se venger; **to s. s.o. to secrecy,** faire jurer le secret à qn; **(b)** (*utter swearwords*) **'bloody idiot!' she swore,** 'espèce d'abruti!' a-t-elle juré.

2 *vi* **(a)** (*use swearwords*) jurer, proférer *ou* lâcher un juron *ou* des jurons; **to s. at s.o.,** injurier qn; **to s. like a trooper,** jurer comme un charretier;

(b) (*give one's word*) jurer.

▶**swear by** *vipo* **(a)** (*invoke*) jurer par (*qn, qch*); **to s. by one's honour,** jurer sur l'honneur; **to s. by all that one holds sacred,** jurer ses grands dieux, jurer sur tout ce qu'il y a de plus sacré; **(b)** (*have confidence in*) se fier à (*qn, qch*); **she swears by her boss/those vitamin tablets,** elle ne jure que par son patron/par ces vitamines; **it's marvellous stuff, we all s. by it,** c'est merveilleux, nous ne jurons plus que par ça!

▶**swear in** *vtsep* faire jurer (*le jury, un témoin*) sur l'honneur.

▶**swear off** *vipo* jurer de renoncer à (*l'alcool etc*).

▶**swear to** *vipo* attester *ou* certifier (*qch*) sous serment; **I s. to it,** je l'atteste; **I would s. to it,** j'en jurerais, *F* j'en mettrais la main au feu, j'en mettrais ma tête à couper; **I couldn't** *or* **wouldn't s. to it,** je n'en mettrais pas la main au feu, je n'en mettrais pas ma tête à couper.

swearing ['sweərɪŋ] *n* **(a)** (*use of swearwords*) jurons *mpl*, gros mots; **there's too much s. on television,** il y a trop de grossièretés à la télévision; **(b)** = **SWEARING IN**.

swearing in *n* assermentation *f* (*du jury*).

swearword ['sweəwɜːd] *n* gros mot, juron *m*.

sweat[1] [swet] *n* **(a)** sueur *f*, transpiration *f*; **covered in s.,** (*of people, clothes*) couvert *ou* trempé de sueur; **by the s. of one's brow,** à la sueur de son front; **the s. was pouring off him,** il dégoulinait de sueur; **to be in a s.** *or* **all of a s.,** suer, être tout en nage; *Fig* (*to be excited*) être tout en émoi; *Fig* **to be in a s. about sth,** s'inquiéter de qch; *Fig* **to work oneself (up) into a s.,** s'énerver (**about sth,** de qch); **to break into a s.,** se mettre à transpirer; **to be in a cold s.,** avoir des sueurs froides; **it's an awful s.,** c'est une suée *ou* un drôle de travail; **it was a real s. getting this piano up the stairs,** monter le piano par l'escalier, c'était vraiment tuant; *F* **no s.,** pas de problème; *Mil Sl* **old s.,** vieux troupier; *Anat* **s. duct,** conduit *m* sudorifère; **s. gland,** glande *f* sudoripare; *Sp* **s. shirt,** sweat-shirt *m*, *pl* sweat-shirts, sweat *m*;

(b) (*condensation*) condensation *f*; suintement *m* (*d'un mur etc*).

sweat[2] **1** *vi* suer, transpirer; *Fig F* (*work hard*) peiner, turbiner; *Fig F* (*worry*) se faire de la bile, se faire un sang d'encre; (*of walls*) suinter; **to s. profusely,** suer à grosses gouttes, *F* être en nage; **schoolboy sweating over his lessons,** élève qui bûche *ou* potasse ses leçons. **2** *vt* suer; faire suer (*qn, un cheval*); exploiter (*la main-d'œuvre*); *Am Fig F* cuisiner (*un suspect*); *F* **to s. blood,** suer sang et eau; *F* **to s. buckets,** être en nage; *Sl* **to s. one's guts out,** s'échiner.

▶**sweat off** *vtsep* (*lose by exercise*) perdre (*du poids*) en faisant de l'exercice; (*in sauna*) perdre (*du poids*) en transpirant.

▶**sweat out** *vtsep* **(a)** (*cure*) chasser *ou* guérir (*un rhume*) en transpirant; **(b)** *F* **to s. it out,** (*endure*) prendre son mal en patience, tenir jusqu'au bout.

sweatband ['swetbænd] *n* (*of hat*) cuir intérieur (*d'un chapeau*); *Sp* bandeau *m* en éponge.

sweated ['swetɪd] *adj* **s. labour,** (*work*) travail exténuant et mal rétribué, travail d'esclave; (*people*) main-d'œuvre exploitée; **s. goods,** articles produits par des ouvriers exploités.

sweater ['swetər] *n* (*garment*) pullover *m*, chandail *m*.

sweatiness ['swetɪnɪs] *n* moiteur *f* (*du corps etc*).

sweating ['swetɪŋ] **1** *adj* (*person*) en sueur; (*hand, body*) moite; (*wall*) suintant. **2** *n* transpiration *f*; suintement *m* (*d'un mur*); exploitation *f* (*de la main-d'œuvre*); *Am Fig F* cuisinage *m* (*d'un prisonnier*); *Med* suée *f*; **s. room,** étuve *f*, salle *f* de sudation (*d'un hammam*).

sweatshop ['swetʃɒp] *n* atelier *m* où les ouvriers sont exploités; *Fig Hum* **it's a real s. here,** c'est le bagne ici.

sweaty ['swetɪ] *adj* (*person*) en sueur; (*work*) qui fait transpirer; (*shirt etc*) imprégné de sueur *ou* de transpiration; (*smell*) de sueur, de transpiration; **s. hands,** mains moites; **s. afternoon,** après-midi d'une chaleur humide; **to get s.,** (*of person*) suer, transpirer.

swede [swiːd] *n* (*plant*) rutabaga *m*.

Swede [swiːd] *n* (*person*) Suédois, -oise.

Sweden ['swiːd(ə)n] *n* Suède *f*.

Swedish ['swiːdɪʃ] **1** *adj* suédois. **2** *n Ling* suédois *m*.

sweep¹ [swiːp] *n* **(a)** (*single stroke of broom, paintbrush, scythe*) coup *m* de balai *ou* de pinceau *ou* de faux; (*cleaning*) balayage *m*; **at one s.,** d'un seul coup; **to give a room a good s. (out),** balayer une chambre à fond; **to make a clean s.,** (*replace staff etc*) faire table rase; (*in gambling*) rafler le tout; **the thieves made a clean s.,** les voleurs ont tout enlevé *ou* raflé;

(b) (*movement*) mouvement *m* circulaire (*du bras*); *Mil Av* balayage *m*, opération offensive de chasse en territoire ennemi; **with a wide s. of the arm,** d'un geste large; **s. of the eye,** regard *m* circulaire; *Fishing* **within the s. of the net,** dans le cercle du filet;

(c) zone *f* de jeu (*d'une manivelle*); *Mil* portée *f* (*d'une pièce*); balayage *m*, portée (*d'un phare*); *Mil* envergure *f* (*des ailes, d'un génie*);

(d) *Rad Electron* **scan(ning) s.,** balayage *m*;

(e) (*rapid flow*) course *f ou* flot *m* rapide (*d'un fleuve*);

(f) (*curve*) courbe *f*, courbure *f*; boucle *f* (*d'une rivière*); *Archit* courbure (*d'un arc*); **to make a wide s. to take a bend,** prendre du champ pour effectuer un virage; **s. of a car's lines,** galbe *f* d'une voiture; **a fine s. of grass/of country,** une belle étendue de gazon/de pays;

(g) aviron *m* de queue (*d'une embarcation*); bascule *f* (*pour tirer l'eau d'un puits*);

(h) s. second hand, (*on clock face*) trotteuse centrale;

(i) *Nau* câble balayeur; drague *f* (*des mines*);

(j) (chimney) s., (*person*) ramoneur *m*;

(k) *F* sweepstake *m*.

sweep² *v* (*pt & pp* **swept** [swept]) **1** *vt* balayer (*une pièce, les rues, la poussière etc*); ramoner (*une cheminée*); *Nau* draguer (*un chenal*); **dress that sweeps the ground,** robe qui balaie le sol; **a storm swept the town,** un orage ravagea la ville; **the deck was swept by a huge wave,** une grosse vague balaya le pont; **to s. the horizon with a telescope,** parcourir *ou* scruter *ou* balayer l'horizon avec un télescope; **to s. the seas,** parcourir *ou* balayer les mers; **to s. the board,** (*in gambling*) faire rafle, rafler le tout; *Fig* remporter un succès complet; **the latest craze to s. the country,** la dernière mode qui balaie le pays; **to s. for mines,** draguer des mines; *Fig* **to s. a matter under the carpet,** enterrer une question; **a wave swept him overboard,** une lame l'a entraîné par dessus bord; **she was swept to power by a wave of nationalism,** elle a été propulsée au pouvoir par une vague de nationalisme; **the victorious army swept all before it,** l'armée victorieuse a tout balayé sur son passage.

2 *vi* **(a)** (*with broom*) balayer;

(b) (*extend widely*) s'étendre, s'étaler; (*move rapidly*) avancer avec un mouvement rapide et uni; **she swept into/out of the room,** elle est entrée dans/sortie de la salle d'un air majestueux; **to s. round the corner,** (*of car*) tourner le coin de la rue en décrivant un large virage; **the plague swept over Europe,** la peste a balayé toute l'Europe; **the beam swept across the sea,** le faisceau lumineux balaya la mer; **rolling prairies s. away into the distance,** les prairies ondoyantes se perdent dans le lointain; **the road sweeps round the lake,** la route décrit une courbe autour du lac.

▶**sweep along 1** *vi* (*move rapidly*) avancer rapidement. **2** *vtsep* (*carry forward*) (*of current etc*) entraîner, emporter (*qch*); **we were swept along by a tide of nationalism,** nous avons été balayés par une marée de nationalisme.

▶**sweep aside** *vtsep* (*move aside*) écarter d'un geste large; **to s. aside opposition,** écarter l'opposition.

▶**sweep away** *vtsep* balayer (*la neige, les nuages*); supprimer (*un abus*); **bridge swept away by the torrent,** pont emporté *ou* entraîné *ou* balayé par le torrent.

▶**sweep by** *vi* (*move past rapidly*) (*of cars*) passer à toute vitesse; (*of person*) (*majestically*) passer majestueusement; (*disdainfully*) passer dédaigneusement.

▶**sweep down 1** *vtsep* (*bring down rapidly*) **the current sweeps the logs down with it,** le courant emporte *ou* entraîne le bois. **2** *vi* **(a)** (*attack*) **the enemy swept down upon us,** l'ennemi s'abattit *ou* fonça sur nous; **(b)** (*curve downwards*) **hills sweeping down to the sea,** collines qui descendent *ou* qui dévalent vers la mer.

▶**sweep in** *vi* (*approach, enter rapidly*) **the wind sweeps in,** le vent s'engouffre; **she swept in,** elle a fait son entrée d'un air majestueux.

▶**sweep off** *vtsep** enlever *ou* emporter avec violence; **the plague swept off thousands,** la peste emporta des milliers de personnes; **he swept her off to Paris for the weekend,** il l'a emmenée en week-end à Paris; *F* **to be swept off one's feet by s.o.,** s'emballer pour qn, être emballé par qn.

▶**sweep on** *vi* (*advance rapidly*) (*of flood*) avancer d'un flot régulier; (*continue*) continuer d'avancer (irrésistiblement).

▶**sweep out 1** *vtsep* (*clean*) balayer (*une pièce*) (à fond). **2** *vi* (*leave majestically*) **she swept out (of the room),** elle est sortie (de la pièce) d'un air majestueux.

▶**sweep past** *vi* = **SWEEP BY.**

▶**sweep up 1** *vtsep* (*collect by sweeping*) balayer, ramasser (*la poussière*); (*sweep into a pile*) ramasser (*la poussière*) en tas; **with her hair swept up into a chignon,** avec ses cheveux relevés en chignon; **she swept up her two babies and ...,** en toute hâte, elle prit ses deux bébés dans ses bras et ... . **2** *vi* **(a)** (*clean up*) balayer; **(b)** (*arrive rapidly*) **the car swept up to the door,** la voiture a roulé jusqu'à la porte.

sweepback ['swiːpbæk] *n Av* (angle *m* de) flèche *f*.

sweeper ['swiːpər] *n* **(a)** (*person*) balayeur, -euse; *Fb F* arrière volant; **(b)** (*machine*) (*for industrial use*) balayeuse *f*; (*for domestic use*) balai *m* (mécanique).

sweeping ['swiːpɪŋ] **1** *adj* (*ruisseau*) rapide, impétueux; (*geste*) large; (*mouvement*) circulaire; **s. changes,** changements de fond en combles *ou* radicaux; **s. curtsy,** révérence profonde; **s. generalization,** généralisation hâtive *ou* par trop absolue; *Art* **s. line,** ligne allongée *ou* élancée; **low s. lines,** (*of car*) lignes basses et allongées; **s. plain,** vaste plaine; **s. reform,** réforme complète *ou* radicale; **s. statement,** généralisation hâtive, déclaration par trop générale. **2** *n* balayage *m* (*d'une chambre, d'une rue*); ramonage *m* (*d'une cheminée*); ébouage *m* (*d'une rue*); balayage (*d'un projecteur*); *Mil* fauchage *m* (*d'une arme à feu*); **s. machine,** balayeuse *f*; (*for roads*) éboueuse *f*; **sweepings,** balayures *fpl*, ordures *fpl*.

sweeping away *n* balayage *m* (*de la neige*).

sweeping up *n* balayage *m*, ramassage *m*.

sweepingly ['swiːpɪŋlɪ] *adv* **(a)** (*rapidly*) rapidement; **(b)** (*to make changes*) sans distinction; (*to describe things etc*) d'une façon par trop générale.

sweepstake ['swiːpsteɪk] *n Horseracing* sweepstake *m*.

sweet [swiːt] **1** *adj* **(a)** doux, *f* douce; (*cream, cake, fruit*) sucré; **as s. as honey,** doux comme le miel; **to taste s.,** avoir une saveur douce; *Culin* **s. corn,** maïs doux; *Culin* **s. and sour sauce,** sauce aigre-douce; **to have a s. tooth,** aimer les sucreries;

(b) (*of flower*) parfumé, odorant; **to smell s.,** avoir une douce odeur, sentir bon; (*of rose*) embaumer; **s. violet,** violette odorante;

(c) *Bot* **s. cherry,** merisier *m*; **s. pea,** pois *m* de senteur; **s. william,** œillet *m* de(s) poète(s);

(d) s. breath, haleine fraîche;

(e) (*son*) doux, *f* douce, mélodieux, (*chanteur*) à la voix douce; **flattery that sounds s.** *or* **is s. to hear,** flatteries douces à l'oreille;

(f) (*pleasant*) agréable; (*sourire*) doux, *f* douce; **revenge is s.,** la vengeance est douce; *F* **to keep s.o. s.,** cultiver la bienveillance de qn; **my s.!,** ma chérie!; **s. old lady,** vieille dame charmante; **that's very s. of you,** c'est bien gentil à vous; **a s. little dress,** une gentille petite robe, une petite robe exquise; **s. girl,** gentille jeune fille; **what a s. kitten!,** quel petit chat adorable!; **to say s. nothings to s.o.,** conter fleurette à qn, dire des mots doux à qn; **s. repose,** doux repos; *Am F* **s. talk,** flatterie *f*, boniment *m*; **s. temper,** caractère doux *ou* aimable;

(g) *F* **to be s. on s.o.,** avoir un béguin pour qn;

(h) s. running, fonctionnement régulier *ou* sans à-coups (*d'une machine*); *F* **to fit together** *etc* **as s. as a nut,** s'assembler *etc* tout seul *ou* sans problème.

2 *n esp Br* (*piece of confectionery*) bonbon *m*; (*dessert*) dessert *m*; **sweets,** sucreries *fpl*, confiseries *fpl*, friandises *fpl*; **s. shop,** confiserie *f*.

sweetbread ['swiːtbred] *n Culin* ris *m* (*de veau, d'agneau*).

sweeten ['swiːt(ə)n] *vt* sucrer (*un plat, une boisson*); épurer (*l'eau*); désodoriser (*l'air, l'haleine etc*); adoucir, rendre plus agréable (*un son, la vie*); (*flatter*) flatter, passer de la pommade à (*qn*); (*bribe etc*) graisser la patte à (*qn*).

sweetener ['swiːt(ə)nər] *n* **(a)** *Culin* édulcorant *m*; **artificial s.,** édulcorant de synthèse; **(b)** *F* (*bribe*) pot-de-vin *m*; **to give s.o. a s.,** graisser la patte à qn, verser un pot-de-vin à qn.

sweetening ['swiːt(ə)nɪŋ] *n* **(a)** (*act*) sucrage *m*; purification *f*, assainissement *m* (*de l'air*); désodorisation *f* (*de l'air, de l'haleine*); adoucissement *m* (*du travail, de l'humeur de qn*); **(b)** (*substance*) édulcorant *m*; **what s. did you use?,** avec quoi (l')avez-vous sucré?

sweetheart ['swiːthɑːt] *n* amoureux, -euse; **(my) s.!,** mon amour!, mon cœur!; **they have been sweethearts since childhood,** ils s'aiment depuis leur enfance; **a childhood s.,** un amour d'enfance; *Ind* **s. agreement,** = accord officieux.

sweetie ['swi:tɪ] *n F* **(a)** *Br* (*confectionery*) bonbon *m;* **(b)** **s. (pie),** (*term of endearment*) chéri, -e; **he's such a s.,** il est si gentil, c'est vraiment un chéri.

sweetish ['swi:tɪʃ] *adj* assez doux; (*unpleasantly*) douceâtre.

sweetly ['swi:tlɪ] *adv* **(a)** avec douceur; (*chanter*) mélodieusement; **the engine's running s.,** le moteur tourne bien rond; **(b)** (*pleasantly*) agréablement, gentiment; **to smile s.,** sourire gentiment.

sweetmeat ['swi:tmi:t] *n Arch* bonbon *m*; **sweetmeats,** sucreries *fpl*, confiseries *fpl*, douceurs *fpl*

sweetness ['swi:tnɪs] *n* **(a)** douceur *f* (*du miel etc*); **(b)** (*of person, gesture etc*) gentillesse *f*, charme *m*; **she's all s. when you are there,** elle fait la sucrée quand vous êtes là; **s. and light,** amabilité *f* et raison *f*; **now the little boy was all s. and light,** à présent le petit garçon était toute douceur.

sweet-scented, sweet-smelling [swi:t'sentɪd, -'smelɪŋ] *adj* qui sent bon, odorant.

sweet-talk ['swi:ttɔ:k] *vt Am F* flagorner, flatter (*qn*); **you can't s.-t. your way around me this time,** cette fois, tu ne m'auras pas par la flatterie.

sweet-tempered [swi:t'tempəd] *adj* doux, *f* douce, au caractère doux *ou* agréable.

swell¹ [swel] **1** *n* **(a)** *Nau* houle *f*; **(b)** (*protuberance*) (*on head, body*) bosse *f*; (*on surface*) bombement *m*; renflement *m* (*d'une colonne*); gros *m* (*de l'avant-bras*); saillie *f* (*du mollet*); augmentation *f* (*d'un son*); *Lit* **the majestic s. of the organ,** les accents majestueux de l'orgue; **(c)** *Mus* soufflet *m* (*d'un orgue*); **s. box,** boîte expressive; **s. organ,** (jeux *mpl* de) récit *m*; **(d)** *F Old-fashioned* (*well-dressed man*) élégant *m*; (*aristocrat*) aristo *m*. **2** *adj F Old-fashioned* (*fashionable*) chic *inv*, élégant; *Am F* (*excellent*) épatant; *Iron* **that's just s.!,** ça, c'est la meilleure!; **a s. guy,** un chic type.

swell² *v* (*pt* **swelled**; *pp* **swollen** ['swəʊl(ə)n], *occ* **swelled**) **1** *vt* (r)enfler, gonfler; *Mus* enfler (*une note*); **river swollen by the rain,** rivière grossie *ou* enflée par la pluie; **eyes swollen with tears,** yeux gonflés de larmes; **all this has helped to s. the ranks of the unemployed,** tout cela est venu grossir le nombre de chômeurs. **2** *vi* (s')enfler, se gonfler; (*of part of the body*) se tuméfier; (*of earth, lime*) foisonner; (*of number, crowd*) augmenter, grossir; (*of sea*) se soulever; **her arm is swelling,** son bras enfle; **his heart swelled with pride,** son cœur se gonflait d'orgueil; **the problem had swollen to massive proportions,** le problème avait pris des proportions énormes.

►**swell out** *vi* (*be swollen*) être bombé; (*expand*) bomber; **the sails s. out,** les voiles se gonflent.

►**swell up** *vi* (*of injured part of body etc*) enfler; *esp Lit* **all swollen up with pride,** tout bouffi d'orgueil.

swellheaded [swel'hedɪd] *adj* vaniteux, suffisant.

swelling ['swelɪŋ] **1** *adj* qui s'enfle *ou* se gonfle; (*sail*) gonflé; *Med* tumescent; (*numbers*) croissant; **s. with importance,** (*of person*) gonflé d'importance. **2** *n* **(a)** enflement *m*, gonflement *m* (*d'un fleuve*); crue *f* (*d'un fleuve*); gonflement (*des voiles*); augmentation *f* (*d'un nombre*); renflement *m* (*d'une colonne*); **(b)** *Med* tuméfaction *f*, gonflement *m*, enflure *f* (*du visage*); bosse *f*, enflure (*au front*); (*growth*) tumescence *f*, tumeur *f*.

swelter ['sweltər] *vi* étouffer *ou* être accablé de chaleur.

sweltering ['sweltərɪŋ] *adj* (*chaleur*) étouffant, accablant; **s. (hot) day,** journée étouffante *ou* d'une chaleur accablante; **it's s. in here,** on étouffe ici.

swept *see* **SWEEP².**

sweptwing ['sweptwɪŋ] *adj Av* (*aircraft*) à ailes en flèche.

swerve¹ [swɜ:v] *n* écart *m*, déviation *f*; *Fb* crochet *m*; *Aut* embardée *f*; *Sp* courbe latérale (*décrite par la balle*).

swerve² **1** *vi* faire un écart, un crochet; (*of horse*) se dérober; (*of car*) embarder, faire une embardée; (*of footballer*) crocheter; *Fig* (*from truth etc*) s'écarter; **to s. to avoid s.o./sth,** (*of car, driver*) faire une embardée pour éviter qn/qch; *Fig* **she never swerves from her duty,** elle ne s'écarte *ou* s'éloigne jamais de son devoir. **2** *vt* faire dévier (*une balle*); faire faire une embardée à (*une voiture*).

swift [swɪft] **1** *adj* rapide; (*reaction etc*) prompt; **as s. as an arrow,** vif *ou* rapide comme l'éclair; *Lit* **s. of foot,** rapide à la course; **s. to anger,** toujours prêt à s'emporter, irascible. **2** *n* (*bird*) martinet *m*.

swift-flowing ['swɪftfləʊɪŋ] *adj* (*rivière*) au cours rapide.

swift-footed ['swɪftfʊtɪd] *adj* rapide à la course.

swiftly ['swɪftlɪ] *adv* (*to run etc*) vite, rapidement; (*to react etc*) promptement.

swiftness ['swɪftnɪs] *n* (*speed*) rapidité *f*, vitesse *f*; promptitude *f* (*d'une réplique etc*).

swig¹ [swɪg] *n F* lampée *f*; **to take a s. at the bottle,** boire un coup à la bouteille; **he took a s. of whisky,** il a bu une lampée *ou* gorgée de whisky; **fancy a s.?,** (*passing bottle etc*) un petit coup?

swig² (-**gg**-) *F vt* boire à grands traits *ou* à grands coups (*beer, lemonade etc*).

►**swig down** *vtsep* boire *ou F* descendre d'un seul trait (*une bière, sa potion*).

swill¹ [swɪl] *n* **(a)** (*for pigs*) pâtée *f*; (*dirty water*) eaux grasses; *Fig Pej* **this horrible s.,** (*food, drink*) cette saloperie; **(b)** (*act of rinsing*) lavage *m* à grande eau; **to give sth a s. out,** laver *ou* rincer qch à grande eau.

swill² *vt* **(a)** *F* (*drink*) boire avidement (*qch*); **(b)** = **SWILL OUT.**

►**swill out** *vtsep esp Br* (*rinse*) laver (*qch*) à grande eau; **to s. out a basin,** rincer une cuvette à grande eau.

swim¹ [swɪm] *n* **(a)** **to have** *or* **take a s.,** nager; **to go for a s.,** aller se baigner; **coming for a s.?,** tu viens nager?, tu viens te baigner?; **did you enjoy your s.?,** vous vous êtes bien baigné(s)?; **it was a long s. to the shore,** il a fallu nager longtemps pour atteindre le rivage; **after my morning s. ...,** après ma séance de natation matinale; **that's a long s.!,** c'est loin!; **s. bladder,** (*of fish*) vessie *f* natatoire; **(b)** *F* **to be in the s.,** être dans le mouvement *ou* dans le train *ou* à la page.

swim² *v* (*pt* **swam** [swæm]; *pp* **swum** [swʌm]; *prp* **swimming**) **1** *vi* nager; (*float*) surnager, flotter; *Fig* (*of head*) tourner; *Fig* (*of eyes, vision*) se brouiller; *F* **to s. like a fish,** nager comme un poisson; **to s. to the shore,** gagner le rivage à la nage; **to s. over** *or* **across a stream,** traverser une rivière à la nage; **they swam under the net,** ils sont passés sous la filet (en nageant); **let's s. back,** rentrons (à la nage)!; *also Fig* **to s. with the tide,** suivre le courant; *Sp* **to s. for one's country,** faire partie de l'équipe nationale de natation; **to go swimming,** aller se baigner; **meat swimming in gravy,** viande nageant dans la sauce; **eyes swimming with tears,** yeux noyés *ou* baignés de larmes; **to make s.o.'s head s.,** faire tourner la tête à qn; **my head is swimming,** la tête me tourne, j'ai la tête qui tourne; **everything swam before my eyes,** tout semblait tourner autour de moi.

2 *vt* traverser *ou* passer (*une rivière*) à la nage; **to s. the Channel,** traverser la Manche à la nage; **to s. a stroke,** faire une brasse; **to s. the breast stroke,** nager (à) la brasse; **to s. a race,** faire une course de natation (**with s.o.,** contre qn).

swimmer ['swɪmər] *n* (*person*) nageur, -euse.

swimming ['swɪmɪŋ] **1** *adj* (*animal*) nageant, qui nage; **s. eyes,** yeux noyés *ou* baignés de larmes; **s. head,** tête qui tourne. **2** *n* nage *f*; *esp Sp* natation *f*; **s. of the head,** vertige *m*, étourdissement *m*; **s. bladder,** vessie *f* natatoire; **s. costume,** maillot *m* de bain; **s. pool,** piscine *f*; **s. match,** concours *m* de natation; **s. trunks,** slip *m* de bain.

swimmingly ['swɪmɪŋlɪ] *adv F* au mieux, à merveille; **everything is going s.,** tout va comme sur des roulettes.

swimsuit ['swɪms(j)u:t] *n* maillot *m* de bain.

swindle¹ ['swɪnd(ə)l] *n* escroquerie *f*, filouterie *f*, *Lit* duperie *f*; **it's a s.,** c'est une escroquerie; **these tickets were a s.,** on nous a remis *ou F* refilé des faux tickets.

swindle² *vt* escroquer, filouter (*qn*), *F* rouler (*qn*); **to s. s.o. out of sth,** escroquer qch à qn; **I'm afraid you've been swindled,** j'ai (bien) peur que vous n'ayez été roulé(s).

swindler ['swɪndlər] *n* filou *m*, escroc *m*.

swine [swaɪn] *n inv in pl* **(a)** *Sl* (*man*) salaud *m*; (*woman, translation, problem, nail etc*) saloperie *f*; **dirty s.!,** sale cochon!; **(b)** *Arch & Dial* (*pig*) cochon *m*, porc *m*, *Arch & Lit* pourceau *m*; *Vet* **s. fever,** peste porcine.

swineherd ['swaɪnhɜ:d] *n Arch & Lit* porcher *m*, gardeur *m* de cochons.

swing¹ [swɪŋ] *n* **(a)** (*movement*) balancement *m*; tour *m* (*de manivelle*); *Boxing Golf* swing *m*; **to give a child a s.,** pousser un enfant sur une balançoire; *F* **to take a s. at s.o.,** balancer un coup de poing à qn; **he took a wild s. at the ball and missed by a mile,** il prit un grand élan pour frapper la balle, et la rata d'un kilomètre; **he took a huge s. at the ball and landed right on the green,** il prit un grand élan pour frapper la balle, et atterrit sur le gazon;

(b) oscillation *f*, va-et-vient *m* (*d'un pendule*); *Fig* **the s. of the pendulum,** le jeu de bascule (*entre les partis etc*);

Fig **to give full s. to one's imagination,** donner libre cours à son imagination; **to be in full s.,** (*of fete*) battre son plein; (*of organization*) être en pleine activité; **when the season is in full s.,** quand la saison bat son plein; **single s. of a pendulum,** oscillation simple *ou* battement *m* d'un pendule; *Fig* **sudden s. of public opinion,** revirement inattendu de l'opinion publique; *Pol* **s. to the left,** glissement *m* à gauche *ou* vers la gauche; *Econ* **seasonal swings,** variations saisonnières; **s. bridge,** pont tournant *ou* pivotant; **s. door,** porte battante; **s. glass** *or* **mirror,** miroir *m* à bascule; (*full length*) psyché *f*; *Am Ind* **s. shift,** (*workers*) équipe *f* (*d'ouvriers*) assurant la relève (*esp celle de mi-journée*); (*period*) journée *f* de travail mi-jour mi-nuit;

(c) amplitude *f* (*d'une oscillation*); *Nau* évitage *m* (*d'un navire à l'ancre*); **s. of a door,** ouverture *f* d'une porte;

(d) (*rhythmic movement*) mouvement rythmé; **to walk with a s.,** marcher d'un pas rythmé *ou* d'un pas cadencé; **song that goes with a s.,** chanson très rythmée; *F* **everything went with a s.,** tout a très bien marché; *F* **to get into the s. of things,** se mettre au courant *ou* dans le bain; *Mus* **s. (music),** swing *m*;

(e) (*in playground, hanging from tree etc*) balançoire *f*; *F* **what you gain on the swings, you lose on the roundabouts,** ce qu'on gagne d'un côté on le perd de l'autre; *F* **it's a swings and roundabouts situation,** c'est une situation où on n'a rien à perdre ni à gagner;

(f) **s. boat,** balançoire *f* (en forme de bateau).

swing[2] *v* (*pt & pp* **swung** [swʌŋ]) **1** *vi* (*on child's swing*) se balancer (*sur la balançoire*); (*change direction*) changer de direction; *Mus* jouer du *ou* un swing; *Old-fashioned F* (*be up to date*) être dans le mouvement *ou* dans le vent; être dynamique; **to s. to and fro,** se balancer; (*of bell*) se balancer; (*of pendulum*) osciller; **shop sign that swings to and fro in the wind,** enseigne de magasin qui ballotte au vent; *Sl* **to s. for a crime,** être pendu pour un crime; **to s. on** *or* **round an axis,** tourner *ou* pivoter sur un axe; (*of mirror*) basculer; **the door swings on its hinges,** la porte tourne sur ses gonds; **to s. open,** (*of door*) s'ouvrir; **to s. to,** (*of door*) se refermer; **to s. (at anchor),** (*of ship*) éviter (sur l'ancre); *Mil* **the whole line swung to the left,** toute la ligne fit une conversion vers la gauche; **to s. along,** marcher d'un pas balancé; **to s. into the saddle,** sauter à cheval *ou* en selle; **to s. from branch to branch,** se balancer d'une branche à une autre; **to s. into action,** passer (vivement) à l'action.

2 *vt* (faire) balancer (*qch*); faire osciller (*un pendule etc*); (*turn*) faire tourner (*qch*); *Av* lancer (*l'hélice*); suspendre (*qch*); pendre, accrocher (*un hamac*); *Mus* interpréter (*une mélodie etc*) en swing; **to s. one's arms,** balancer les bras (*en marchant*); **to s. one's hips (in walking),** se dandiner; *Boxing* **to s. a blow,** balancer un coup; **to s. oneself into the saddle,** sauter à cheval *ou* en selle; *Nau* **boat swung out,** embarcation parée au dehors; *Cr* **to s. the ball,** faire dévier la balle en l'air; **to s. the voting in favour of s.o.,** faire pencher la balance en faveur de qn; *F* **to s. a deal,** (*bring it off*) mener une affaire à bien; *F* **to s. it so that ...,** (*arrange things*) arranger les choses de manière (à ce) que ... .

▶**swing at** *vipo* (*aim blow at*) **to s. at s.o.,** balancer un coup de poing à qn; **he swung wildly at the ball,** il prit un grand élan pour frapper la balle.

▶**swing back** *vi* (*of door*) se rabattre; (*of pendulum*) revenir; **public opinion swung back,** il y eut un revirement d'opinion.

▶**swing out** *vi* (*of car, driver*) faire un écart; (*from side road*) déboucher.

▶**swing round 1** *vi* (*turn around suddenly*) (*of person*) se retourner vivement; (*of public opinion, person etc*) faire volte-face; (*of car*) virer (brusquement), faire un brusque virage; **the car swung right round,** la voiture a fait un tête-à-queue. **2** *vtsep* (*turn round suddenly*) faire faire un brusque virage à (*une auto*); **to s. a car right round,** faire faire un tête-à-queue à une auto.

swingeing ['swɪndʒɪŋ] *adj* énorme; **s. majority,** majorité écrasante; **s. damages,** forts dommages-intérêts; **s. blow,** coup bien envoyé.

swinger ['swɪŋər] *n F* (*lively, trendy person*) **to be a s.,** être dans le vent.

swinging ['swɪŋɪŋ] **1** *adj* balançant; (*miroir*) à bascule; *Old-fashioned F* (*person*) dans le vent; **with s. arms,** les bras ballants; **s. blow,** coup balancé; **s. door,** porte battante; **s. London,** le Londres branché des années soixante; **the s. Sixties,** les folles années soixante; *Old-fashioned* **s. party,** réception endiablée; **s. stride,** allure rythmée *ou* cadencée *ou* dégagée; **s. tune,** air enlevant *ou* entraînant. **2** *n* **(a)** balancement *m*, oscillation *f*; **s. motion,** mouvement *m* pendulaire; **(b)** (*turning*) mouvement *m* de bascule *ou* de rotation; **(c)** *Nau* évitage *m*; **(d)** *Av* lancement *m* (*de l'hélice*).

swinish ['swaɪnɪʃ] *adj F* (*behaviour*) dégueulasse; **that s. brother of yours,** ton dégueulasse de frère.

swingle[1] ['swɪŋg(ə)l] *n* **(a)** *Tex* écang *m*; **(b)** battoir *m* (*d'un fléau*).

swingle[2] *vt Tex* teiller, écanguer (*le lin*).

swing-wing ['swɪŋ'wɪŋ] *adj Av* (*aircraft*) à géométrie variable.

swipe[1] [swaɪp] *n F* coup *m* de poing *ou* de bâton; *Cr Golf* coup à toute volée; **I gave myself a s. round the head with it,** je me suis donné un coup sur la tête avec; **to take a s. at s.o.,** (*aim blow at*) lâcher un coup (de poing) à qn; *Fig* (*in satire etc*) taper sur qn.

swipe[2] **1** *vi* **to s. at the ball,** lancer un coup à la balle à toute volée. **2** *vt F* **(a)** (*hit*) donner un coup de poing *ou* de bâton à (*qn*); *Cr Golf* frapper (*la balle*) à toute volée; **I managed to s. myself in the eye,** j'ai réussi à me donner un coup dans l'œil; **(b)** (*steal*) chiper (*qch, sa petite amie*).

swirl[1] [swɜːl] *n* remous *m* (*de l'eau*); tourbillonnement *m* (*d'un mélange gazeux*); spirale *f* (*de Chantilly etc*); **a s. of dust,** un tourbillon de poussière.

swirl[2] **1** *vi* tournoyer, tourbillonner. **2** *vt* faire tournoyer (*qch, qn*).

swirling ['swɜːlɪŋ] **1** *adj* tourbillonnant, tournoyant. **2** *n* tourbillonnement *m*.

swish[1] [swɪʃ] *n* **(a)** (*sound*) bruissement *m* (*de l'eau*); froufrou *m* (*d'une robe*); sifflement *m* (*d'un fouet*); crissement *m* (*d'une faux*); **(b)** (*blow*) coup *m* de fouet.

swish[2] **1** *vi* (*of water*) bruire; (*of silk*) froufrouter; (*of whip*) siffler. **2** *vt* faire siffler (*sa canne, une badine*); **to s. its tail,** (*of animal*) battre l'air de sa queue.

swish[3] *adj esp Br F* (*elegant*) élégant, chic, rupin.

Swiss [swɪs] **1** *adj* suisse; **the S. government,** le gouvernement helvétique; **S. cheese,** emmenthal *m*; **S. cheese (plant),** caoutchouc *m*; **S. French,** suisse romand; **S. German,** suisse alémanique; **S. roll,** roulé *m*. **2** *n inv in pl* Suisse *m*, Suissesse *f*.

switch[1] [swɪtʃ] *n* **(a)** *El* commutateur *m*, interrupteur *m*, *F* bouton *m*; **two-way s.,** commutateur à deux directions, interrupteur; **s. gear,** appareillage *m* de commutation *ou* de distribution; **(b)** (*change*) passage *m*; **to make the s. from gas to electricity,** passer du gaz à l'électricité; **(c)** *Am Rail* (*point*) aiguille *f* (*de changement de voie*); (*siding*) voie *f* de raccordement *ou* de garage; **(d)** (*stick*) baguette *f*, badine *f*; (*blow*) coup *m* de baguette; (*for caning pupil*) canne *f*; **riding s.,** petite cravache; **(e)** (*false hair*) postiche *m*.

switch[2] **1** *vt* **(a)** *El* commuter (*le courant*); **(b)** (*change*) changer de (*places etc*); (*exchange*) échanger; changer la position de (*une manette, un levier*); **to s. the conversation to another subject,** détourner la conversation (sur un autre sujet); **can I s. it for another one?,** puis-je l'échanger contre un autre?; **he's been switched to another department,** il a été muté dans un autre service; **(c)** *Am Rail* aiguiller (*un train*); **to s. a train onto a branch line,** aiguiller un train sur un embranchement; **(d)** (*hit with stick*) donner un coup de badine à (*qn, qch*); **to s. its tail,** (*of cow*) battre l'air de sa queue. **2** *vi* (*change*) **to s. (from gas/etc) to electricity,** passer (du gaz/*etc*) à l'électricité; **she later switched to teaching,** elle s'est réorientée vers l'enseignement par la suite.

▶**switch back** *vi* (*revert to*) **to s. back (from electricity/etc) to gas,** repasser (de l'électricité *etc*) au gaz; **we switched back to gas,** nous sommes revenus au gaz.

▶**switch off 1** *vtsep* couper, éteindre (*la radio, la lumière, le chauffage etc*); (*disconnect*) interrompre, couper (*le courant*); **s. the light off when you go out!,** éteignez l'électricité *ou* n'oubliez pas d'éteindre quand vous sortez!; *Aut* **to s. off the ignition** *or* **the engine,** couper l'allumage. **2** *vi* (*of appliance etc*) se couper, s'éteindre; **where does it s. off?,** où est l'interrupteur, où est-ce qu'on coupe (le courant *etc*); *F* **to s. off (completely),** (*of person*) cesser d'écouter.

▶**switch on** *vtsep* mettre (*la radio, la télévision, le chauffage etc*) (en marche); mettre (*la lumière*); allumer (*l'électricité*); donner (*du courant*); *Aut* **to s. on the ignition** *or* **the engine,** mettre le contact (d'allumage); **to be switched on,** (*of person*) *F* (*be up to date*) être bien au courant de ce qui se passe; *Sl* (*be under influence of drugs*) être chargé (par des drogues); *F* **they switched me on to new ideas,** ils m'ont initié aux idées nouvelles.

▶**switch over** *vi* **(a)** *Rad TV* (*change channels*) **to s. over (to another channel),** changer de chaîne; **(b) to s. over to modern languages,** réorienter ses études vers les langues vivantes; **we switched over to gas,** nous sommes passés au gaz.
▶**switch round 1** *vtsep* (*exchange one for the other*) (é)changer; **someone's switched these photos round,** quelqu'un a échangé ces photos; **why don't we s. the desks round?,** pourquoi est-ce qu'on ne change pas les bureaux? **2** *vi* (*change places*) changer de place.
switchback ['swɪtʃbæk] *n* (*road, railway*) route *ou* voie ferrée en lacets; (*bend*) virage *m* en lacet; (*at fair*) montagnes *fpl* russes.
switchblade ['swɪtʃbleɪd] *n Am* couteau *m* à cran d'arrêt.
switchboard ['swɪtʃbɔːd] *n* **(a)** *Tel* central *m* (téléphonique); (*in office*) standard *m*; **s. operator,** standardiste *mf*; **(b)** *El* tableau *m* (commutateur *ou* de distribution).
switchman, *pl* **-men** ['swɪtʃmən, -men] *n Am Rail* aiguilleur *m*.
Switzerland ['swɪtsələnd] *n* Suisse *f*; **German S.,** la Suisse alémanique; **French(-speaking) S.,** la Suisse romande; **Italian(-speaking) S.,** la Suisse italienne.
swivel¹ ['swɪv(ə)l] *n* pivot *m*; **s. chair** *or* **seat,** siège tournant; **s. joint,** (joint *m* à) rotule.
swivel² *v* (**-ll-**, *US* **-l-**) **1** *vi* pivoter, tourner. **2** *vt* faire pivoter (*qch*).
▶**swivel round 1** *vi* (*turn*) pivoter, tourner; **to s. round on one's heels,** pivoter sur ses talons. **2** *vtsep* faire pivoter; **to s. one's eyes round,** tourner les yeux de coté.
swivelling, *US* **swiveling** *adj* pivotant, tournant; *Comptr etc* (*screen, arm etc*) pivotant, mobile.
swiz(z) [swɪz] *n Br Sch Sl* **(a)** (*trick*) **it's a s.!,** c'est pas juste!; **(b)** (*disappointment*) déception *f*.
swizzle ['swɪz(ə)l] *n* **(a)** *Am F* (*cocktail*) cocktail *m*; **s. stick,** fouet *m ou* marteau *m* à champagne; **(b) = SWIZ(Z).**
swollen ['swəʊl(ə)n] *adj* enflé, gonflé; (*visage*) bouffi; (*ventre*) ballonné; **his arm was very s.,** il avait le bras très enflé; **s. glands,** glandes enflées; **the river is s.,** la rivière est en crue; (*also* **swelled**) *F* **to suffer from** *or* **to have a s. head,** avoir la grosse tête.
swollen-headed [swəʊlən'hedɪd] *adj* vaniteux, -euse, *F* qui a la grosse tête.
swoon¹ [swuːn] *n Old-fashioned* évanouissement *m*, défaillance *f*; **to fall into a s.,** s'évanouir, se pâmer.
swoon² *vi Old-fashioned* **(a)** (*faint*) s'évanouir; **(b)** (*in rapture*) se pâmer.
swoop¹ [swuːp] *n* abat(t)ée *f* (*d'un avion*) (**upon,** sur); descente *f* (*du faucon qui fond sur sa proie*); **police s.,** descente de police (*sur une boîte de nuit*); *F* **at one (fell) s.,** d'un seul coup.
swoop² *vi* **the hawk swooped down on the rabbit,** (*dived*) le faucon a plongé sur le lapin; (*caught it*) le faucon s'est abattu sur le lapin; **the gunship swooped down over the village,** l'hélicoptère de combat a plongé *ou* piqué sur le village; **a swallow swooping and whirling,** une hirondelle tourbillonnante; **the police swooped on the district,** la police a fait une descente sur le quartier.
swoosh [swuːʃ] **1** *vi* **the water swooshes round the toilet then ...,** l'eau inonde la cuvette des toilettes et puis ...; **the waves swooshed over the deck,** les vagues ont déferlé sur le pont; **you could hear the liquid swooshing around in the tank,** on entendait le liquide clapoter dans le réservoir; **the rocket/whip swooshes through the air,** la fusée/le fouet siffle dans l'air. **2** *vt* **he swooshed it down the loo,** il l'a fait disparaître dans les toilettes; **she then swooshed it out with clean water,** (*rinsed*) elle l'a ensuite rincé à l'eau propre; **swoosh the detergent all over the stain,** répandre le détergent généreusement sur la tache.
swop [swɒp] *n & vt* =**SWAP¹,².**
sword [sɔːd] *n* épée *f*; (*poetic*) *& Arch* glaive *m*; *Mil Nau* sabre *m*; **to draw one's s.,** tirer son épée; dégainer; **to cross swords with s.o.,** croiser l'épée *ou* le fer avec qn; *Fig* (*argue*) se disputer avec qn; (*in debate*) se mesurer avec qn; **to put the inhabitants to the s.,** passer les habitants au fil de l'épée; **those that live by the s. shall die by the s.,** ceux qui ont vécu par le fer *ou* par l'épée périront par le fer *ou* par l'épée; *Lit* **the S. of Justice,** le glaive de la Justice; **s. arm,** bras droit; **s. cut,** (*blow*) coup *m* de sabre; (*wound*) blessure faite avec le sabre; (*on face*) balafre *f*; **s. dance,** danse *f* du sabre.
swordbearer ['sɔːdbeərər] *n* officier *m* (*esp municipal*) qui porte le glaive.
swordbelt ['sɔːdbelt] *n* ceinturon *m*.
swordfish ['sɔːdfɪʃ] *n* espadon *m*.
swordplay ['sɔːdpleɪ] *n* (*technique*) escrime *f* (*à l'épée*); **the very realistic s. in the fight scenes,** le réalisme des scènes de combat à l'épée; **verbal s.,** joute *f* oratoire.
swordsman, *pl* **-men** ['sɔːdzmən] *n* épéiste *m*, tireur *m* d'épée; **good** *or* **fine s.,** fine lame, bonne épée.
swordsmanship ['sɔːdsmənʃɪp] *n* habileté *f* à l'épée, talents *mpl* d'escrimeur.
swordstick ['sɔːdstɪk] *n* canne *f* à épée.
sword-swallower ['sɔːdswɒləʊər] *n* avaleur *m* de sabres.
swore *see* **SWEAR.**
sworn¹ [swɔːn] *adj* (*agent*) assermenté; (*déclaration*) sous serment; (*témoin*) qui a prêté serment; **s. enemies,** ennemis jurés *ou* acharnés.
sworn² *see* **SWEAR.**
swot¹ [swɒt] *n Br Sch F* (*person*) bûcheur, -euse.
swot² *vi* (**-tt-**) *Br Sch F* bûcher, *Pej* bachoter.
▶**swot up** *Br Sch F* **1** *vtsep* potasser, piocher, bûcher (*les maths etc*). **2** *vi* = **SWOT².**
▶**swot up on** *vipo Br Sch F* potasser, piocher, bûcher (*les maths etc*).
swotting ['swɒtɪŋ] *n Br Sch F* bachotage *m*; **I'd better do some s.,** je ferais mieux de bûcher.
swum *see* **SWIM².**
swung *see* **SWING².**
sybarite ['sɪbəraɪt] *adj & n* sybarite *mf*.
sybaritic [sɪbə'rɪtɪk] *adj* sybaritique, sybarite.
sycamore ['sɪkəmɔːr] *n* (*maple*) (érable *m*) sycomore *m*, faux platane; *Am* (*plane tree*) platane.
sycophancy ['sɪkəfənsɪ] *n* flagornerie *f*.
sycophant ['sɪkəfənt] *n* flagorneur *m*.
sycophantic [sɪkə'fæntɪk] *adj* adulateur, -trice.
syllabic [sɪ'læbɪk] *adj* syllabique.
syllabification [sɪlæbɪfɪ'keɪʃən] *n* syllabisation *f*.
syllabify [sɪ'læbɪfaɪ] *vt* syllabiser (*un mot*).
syllable ['sɪləb(ə)l] *n* syllabe *f*; **short s.,** (*in prosody*) brève *f*; **long s.,** longue *f*; **to explain sth in words of one s.,** expliquer qch en termes très simples.
syllabub ['sɪləbʌb] *n Culin* = sabayon *m*.
syllabus, *pl* **-i, -uses** ['sɪləbəs, -aɪ, -əsɪz] *n* programme *m* (*d'un cours*); **to take a subject off the s.,** enlever une matière du programme.
syllogism ['sɪlədʒɪz(ə)m] *n* (*in logic*) syllogisme *m*.
syllogistic [sɪlə'dʒɪstɪk] *adj* (*in logic*) syllogistique.
sylph [sɪlf] *n* **(a)** *Myth* sylphe *m*, sylphide *f*; **(b)** *Lit* (*of woman*) sylphide *f*; *F* **she's no s.,** elle prend de la place; **(c)** *Am* (*hummingbird*) (espèce *f* de) colibri *m*.
sylph-like ['sɪlflaɪk] *adj* (*taille etc*) de sylphide; (*femme*) à la taille de sylphide.
sylvan ['sɪlvən] *adj* sylvestre.
symbiosis, *pl* **-ses** [sɪmb(a)ɪ'əʊsɪs, -iːz] *n Biol & Fig* symbiose *f*.
symbiotic [sɪmb(a)ɪ'ɒtɪk] *adj Biol & Fig* symbiotique.
symbol¹ ['sɪmb(ə)l] *n* symbole *m* (**of, for,** de); *Am* **road symbols,** pictogrammes routiers.
symbol² *vt Am* = **SYMBOLIZE.**
symbolic [sɪm'bɒlɪk] *adj* symbolique; **s. logic,** logique *f* symbolique.
symbolically [sɪm'bɒlɪklɪ] *adv* symboliquement.
symbolism ['sɪmbəlɪz(ə)m] *n* symbolisme *m*.
symbolist ['sɪmbəlɪst] *adj & n* symboliste *mf*.
symbolization [sɪmbəlaɪ'zeɪʃən] *n* symbolisation *f*.
symbolize ['sɪmbəlaɪz] *vt* symboliser.
symmetrical [sɪ'metrɪk(ə)l] *adj* symétrique.
symetrically [sɪ'metrɪklɪ] *adv* symétriquement.
symmetry ['sɪmɪtrɪ] *n* symétrie *f*.
sympathetic [sɪmpə'θetɪk] *adj* **(a)** (*kind, understanding*) (*person*) compréhensif, -ive; (*stronger*) compatissant; (*lettre*) de sympathie, qui marque la sympathie; (*regard, sourire*) de sympathie; **he's always very s.,** il est toujours prêt à vous écouter; **I didn't find him very s. (about it),** je ne l'ai pas trouvé très compréhensif; **you could try to be more s. (towards her),** tu pourrais essayer de te montrer plus compréhensif (envers elle); **to be s. to a proposal,** être en sympathie avec une proposition; **s. audience,** auditoire bien disposé; **her novel got a very s. reception,** son roman a été très bien accueilli; **(b)** (*pain*) sympathique; *Phys* (*vibration*) due à la résonance; **the s. nerve,** le grand sympathique; *Mus* **s. string,** corde *f* qui vibre par résonance.
sympathetically [sɪmpə'θetɪklɪ] *adv* **(a)** (*showing understanding*) avec bienveillance; (*showing pity*) avec compassion; **the new play was s. received,** la nouvelle pièce a été bien accueillie; **(b)** *Med* par sympathie; *Phys* (*vibrer*) par résonance.

sympathize ['sɪmpəθaɪz] *vi* **(a)** (*show sympathy*) compatir; (*have understanding*) comprendre; **I s. because I used to have similar problems,** je compatis car j'ai connu des problèmes du même genre; **I s. with your point of view but ...,** je comprends votre point de vue mais ...; **I do s.,** (*feel pity etc*) je compatis; (*feel understanding*) je (vous) comprends très bien; **(b)** (*agree*) **those who s. with Professor Smith in his view that ...,** ceux qui s'associent au Professeur Smith pour dire que ...; **to s. with the IRA/*etc*,** sympathiser avec l'IRA/*etc*.

sympathizer ['sɪmpəθaɪzər] *n* **(a)** (*person in agreement*) sympathisant, -ante (**with a cause,** d'une cause); **a rebel s.,** un sympathisant des rebelles; **(b)** (*person who shows sympathy, understanding*) **to be a s. in s.o.'s grief,** compatir au chagrin de qn; **we have received many letters from sympathizers,** nous avons reçu de nombreuses lettres de personnes compatissantes.

sympathy ['sɪmpəθɪ] *n* **(a)** (*compassion*) compassion *f*; **to have s. for s.o.,** éprouver de la compassion pour qn; **to show s. to s.o.,** faire preuve de compassion envers qn; **you have my deepest s.,** *Fml* (*on bereavement etc*) je vous présente toutes mes condoléances; *Hum* (*on your new girlfriend etc*) je te souhaite bien du plaisir; **a letter of s.,** une lettre de condoléances; **we'd all like to express our s. on this tragic loss,** nous aimerions tous exprimer notre sympathie à l'égard de cette perte tragique; **our sympathies are with the families of the dead,** nous compatissons avec les familles des victimes; **I don't need s. I need help,** ce n'est pas de compassion que j'ai besoin, c'est d'aide; **if you do catch a cold don't expect any s. from me!,** si tu attrapes un rhume, n'espère pas que je te plaigne;

(b) (*understanding etc*) sympathie *f* (**for s.o.,** pour qn); **to feel a s. for s.o.,** éprouver de la sympathie pour qn; **popular sympathies are on his side,** il a l'opinion pour lui; **to view a proposal with s.,** regarder une proposition d'un bon œil; **to be in s. with s.o.'s ideas,** être en sympathie avec les idées de qn; **my s. is** *or* **my sympathies are with the opposition,** je partage les opinions de l'opposition; **to have sympathies with a terrorist organization,** sympathiser avec une organisation terroriste; **to strike** *or* **come out (on strike) in s.,** se mettre en grève de solidarité (**with,** avec); **prices went up in s.,** les prix sont montés par contrecoup; *Phys* **string that vibrates in s.,** corde qui vibre par résonance; *Physiol* **the temperature of the other hand falls in s.,** la température de l'autre main tombe par réaction; *Ind* **s. strike,** grève *f* de solidarité.

symphonic [sɪm'fɒnɪk] *adj Mus* symphonique.

symphony ['sɪmfənɪ] *n Mus* **(a)** symphonie *f*; **s. orchestra,** orchestre *m* symphonique; **s. concert,** concert *m* symphonique; **(b)** *Am* (*orchestra*) orchestre *m* symphonique.

symposium, *pl* **-ia, -iums** [sɪm'pəʊzɪəm, -ɪə, -ɪəmz] *n* colloque *m*, symposium *m*; conférence *f* (académique); (*collection*) recueil *m* d'articles (*sur un sujet du jour*).

symptom ['sɪm(p)təm] *n Med & Fig* symptôme *m*; **to show all the symptoms of ...,** présenter tous les symptômes de ... .

symptomatic [sɪm(p)tə'mætɪk] *adj* symptomatique.

symptomatically [sɪmptə'mætɪklɪ] *adv* symptomatiquement.

synagogue ['sɪnəgɒg] *n* synagogue *f*.

sync [sɪŋk] *n* (*abbr* **synchronization**) **in s.,** (*of film etc*) synchronisé; **out of s.,** (*of film etc*) non synchronisé; **the engine is a bit out of s.,** le moteur ne tourne pas très rond; **to be in s. with the times,** être en harmonie avec son temps; **to be out of s. with the times,** être déphasé; **he's somehow out of s. with the others,** (*not in tune, not thinking the same way etc*) il est un peu décalé *ou* déphasé par rapport aux autres; **her ideas are out of s. with ...,** ses idées sont en décalage par rapport à ...; **the translation is a bit out of s.,** il y a comme un décalage dans cette traduction.

synchromesh ['sɪŋkrəʊmeʃ] *n Aut* synchronisation *f*; **s. on all gears,** boîte *f* de vitesses avec rapports synchronisés.

synchronic [sɪŋ'krɒnɪk] *adj* (*synchronous*) synchrone; *Ling* (*descriptive*) synchronique.

synchronism ['sɪŋkrənɪz(ə)m] *n* synchronisme *m*.

synchronization [sɪŋkrənaɪ'zeɪʃən] *n* synchronisation *f*.

synchronize ['sɪŋkrənaɪz] **1** *vt* synchroniser (*deux montres*; **sth with sth,** qch avec qch); *El* coupler (*deux générateurs*) en phase; établir le synchronisme de (*différents événements*). **2** *vi* (*of events*) arriver *ou* avoir lieu simultanément; **clocks that s.,** horloges qui marquent la même heure; **we'll try to s. with you,** nous essaierons de nous synchroniser avec vous.

synchronized ['sɪŋkrənaɪzd] *adj* synchronisé; *El* **s. generators,** générateurs synchronisés *ou* en phase; **s. swimming,** natation synchronisée.

synchronizer ['sɪŋkrənaɪzər] *n* synchronisateur *m*.

synchronizing ['sɪŋkrənaɪzɪŋ] *n* synchronisation *f*.

synchronous ['sɪŋkrənəs] *adj* synchrone (**with,** de).

syncline ['sɪŋklaɪn] *n Geol* synclinal *m*.

syncopate ['sɪŋkəpeɪt] *vt* syncoper; **syncopated music,** musique syncopée.

syncopation [sɪŋkə'peɪʃən] *n Mus* syncope *f*.

syncope ['sɪŋkəpɪ] *n Med Gram* syncope *f*.

syncretic [sɪŋ'kretɪk] *adj* syncrétique.

syncretism ['sɪŋkrətɪz(ə)m] *n* syncrétisme *m*.

syndic ['sɪndɪk] *n* syndic *m*.

syndicalism ['sɪndɪkəlɪz(ə)m] *n* syndicalisme *m*.

syndicalist ['sɪndɪkəlɪst] *n & adj* syndicaliste *mf*.

syndicate[1] ['sɪndɪkət] *n* **(a)** *Com Fin* syndicat *m*, consortium *m*; *Am* (*criminal organization*) association *f* de malfaiteurs; *Am* (*news agency*) agence *f* de presse spécialisée; *US* (*chain of newspapers*) chaîne *f* de journaux; **financial s.,** syndicat financier; **member of a s.,** syndicataire *m*; **(b)** (*board of syndics*) conseil *m* de syndics.

syndicate[2] ['sɪndɪkeɪt] **1** *vt* publier (*un article*) simultanément dans plusieurs journaux. **2** *vi* se syndiquer.

syndication [sɪndɪ'keɪʃən] *n* publication simultanée (*d'un article*) dans plusieurs journaux.

syndrome ['sɪndrəʊm] *n Med & Fig* syndrome *m*.

synergy ['sɪnədʒɪ] *n* synergie *f*.

synod ['sɪnəd] *n* **(a)** *Rel* synode *m*, concile *m*; **the General S.,** le conseil d'administration de l'Église anglicane; **(b)** (*council*) assemblée *f*, convention *f*.

synodic [sɪ'nɒdɪk] *adj Rel* synodique, synodal, -aux; *Astron* (*période etc*) synodique.

synonym ['sɪnənɪm] *n* synonyme *m*.

synonymous [sɪ'nɒnɪməs] *adj* synonyme (**with,** de); **their name is s. with quality,** leur nom est synonyme de qualité.

synonymously [sɪnɒnɪməslɪ] *adv* (*employer un mot*) comme synonyme (**with,** de); **if two words can be used s.,** si deux mots peuvent être employés comme synonymes.

synonymy [sɪ'nɒnɪmɪ] *n* synonymie *f*.

synopsis, *pl* **-pses** [sɪ'nɒpsɪs, -psiːz] *n* résumé *m*, sommaire *m*; synopsis *f* (*d'une science, d'un film*).

synoptic [sɪ'nɒptɪk] *adj* synoptique.

synovia [sɪ'nəʊvɪə, saɪ-] *n Physiol Anat* synovie *f*.

syntactic(al) [sɪn'tæktɪk, -ɪk(ə)l] *adj Gram Comptr* syntactique, syntaxique.

syntax ['sɪntæks] *n Gram Comptr* syntaxe *f*; **s. error,** *Comptr* erreur *f* de syntaxe.

synthesis, *pl* **-es** ['sɪnθɪsɪs, -iːz] *n* synthèse *f*.

synthesize ['sɪnθəsaɪz] *vt* synthétiser (*des éléments*); faire la synthèse (*d'un produit*).

synthesizer ['sɪnθəsaɪzər] *n* synthétiseur *m*.

synthetic [sɪn'θetɪk] **1** *adj* (*produit, fibre*) synthétique; **s. rubber,** caoutchouc *m* synthétique; *F* **s. smile,** sourire artificiel *ou* factice. **2** *n* (*usu pl*) **synthetics,** matières *fpl* plastiques.

synthetically [sɪn'θetɪklɪ] *adv* synthétiquement.

syph [sɪf] *n F* = **SYPHILIS**.

syphilis ['sɪfɪlɪs] *n Med* syphilis *f*.

syphilitic [sɪfɪ'lɪtɪk] *adj & n Med* syphilitique (*mf*).

syphon ['saɪf(ə)n] *n & v* = **SIPHEN**[1,2].

Syria ['sɪrɪə] *n* Syrie *f*.

Syrian ['sɪrɪən] **1** *adj* syrien. **2** *n* Syrien, -ienne.

syringe[1] ['sɪrɪndʒ, sɪ'rɪndʒ] *n* seringue *f*.

syringe[2] *vt* seringuer (*une plaie etc*); **to s. (out) the ears,** laver les oreilles avec une seringue.

syrup ['sɪrəp] *n* **(a)** sirop *m*; **red currant s.,** sirop de groseilles; *Med* **cough s.,** sirop pectoral, sirop pour *ou* contre la toux; **(b) (golden) s.,** mélasse raffinée; **(c)** (*sentimentality*) douceur affectée.

syrupy ['sɪrəpɪ] *adj* **(a)** sirupeux; **(b)** *Fig* (*ton*) mielleux, doucereux; **s. music/prose,** musique/prose qui sent la guimauve.

system ['sɪstəm] *n* **(a)** système *m*; **the feudal s.,** le régime féodal; *F* **the s.,** (*established order*) l'ordre établi; **to challenge the s.,** défier l'ordre établi; *Sch* **block s.,** enseignement groupé; *Astron* **the solar s.,** le système solaire; *Anat* **nervous/muscular s.,** système nerveux/musculaire; **the digestive s.,** l'appareil digestif; **bad for the s.,** mauvais pour l'organisme; **it's a bit of a shock to the s.,** ça secoue un peu (l'organisme); *F* **to get sth out of one's s.,** se libérer *ou* se purger de qch; *F* **to get s.o. out of**

one's s., (*after romance*) se sortir qn de la tête;
(b) (*network*) réseau *m* (*télégraphique*); réseau ferré (*d'un chemin de fer*); **road/river s.,** réseau routier/fluvial; **s. of pulleys,** système *m* de poulies; **central heating s.,** installation *f* de chauffage central;
(c) *Comptr* **the XYZ is an excellent s.,** le XYZ est un excellent ordinateur; **operating s.,** système *m* d'exploitation; **to return to s.,** retourner *ou* revenir au système; **s. disk,** disque *m* système; **s. software,** logiciel *m* d'exploitation;
(d) (*usu with sing verb*) *Comptr* **systems, systems analysis,** analyse fonctionnelle; **systems analyst,** analyste-programmeur *m*; **systems disk,** disque *m* système; **s. software,** logiciel *m* de base;
(e) (*methodicalness*) méthode *f* (*de travail*); **to lack s.,** manquer de méthode *ou* d'organisation.

systematic [sɪstə'mætɪk] *adj* systématique, méthodique; **the s. destruction of the forest,** la destruction systématique de la forêt; **she's very s.,** elle a de l'ordre *ou* de la méthode.

systematically [sɪstə'mætɪklɪ] *adv* systématiquement, avec méthode; (*to destroy etc*) systématiquement.

system(at)ization [sɪstəm(ət)aɪ'zeɪʃən] *n* systématisation *f*.

system(at)ize ['sɪstəm(ət)aɪz] *vt* systématiser.

systemic [sɪs'tiːmɪk] *adj* (*insecticide*) & *Ling* systémique.

T

T, t [tiː] *n* (la lettre) T, t *m*; **to cross one's t's,** barrer ses t; *Fig* (*spell things out*) mettre les points sur les i; **to a T,** (*in every detail*) exactement; (*perfectly*) à la perfection; **that's you to a T,** c'est absolument vous; **my job suits me to a T,** mon poste me va à merveille *ou* comme un gant.

ta [tɑː] *n & int Br F* merci *m*.

TA [tiː'eɪ] *n* **(a)** *Br Mil abbr* **Territorial Army**; **(b)** *Am Univ abbr* **teaching assistant.**

tab [tæb] *n* **(a)** (*flap, strip*) (*on garment*) patte *f*; *Mil* patte du collet, écusson *m*; (*on package, tin*) languette *f*; (*on boot*) tirant *m*; (*on lace*) ferret *m*;
(b) (*loop*) attache *f*;
(c) (*label*) étiquette *f*;
(d) (*for identification*) (*on file*) patte *f*; (*on book*) onglet *m*; *Fig* **to keep tabs on s.o./sth,** avoir qn/qch à l'œil, ne pas perdre qn/qch de vue; **to keep tabs on expenses,** contrôler les dépenses;
(e) *Am* (*bill*) (*in restaurant*) addition *f*; (*in hotel*) note *f*; *F* **to pick up the t.,** (*for meal, accommodation*) régler l'addition *ou* la note; (*for government programme, research etc*) payer; (*for damage done by others*) *F* casquer, raquer;
(f) (*on typewriter, word processor etc*) (*position*) colonne *f*; (*mechanism*) **t. (key),** tabulateur *m*; **how many tabs should I put in?,** combien de colonnes est-ce que je dois mettre?; **to set tabs,** régler *ou* positionner les tabulateurs **(at,** à).

TAB [tæb] *n Med* (*abbr* **typhoid-paratyphoid A and B**) vaccin *m* TAB; **he has had a TAB injection,** on lui a fait le vaccin de la TAB.

tabard ['tæbəd] *n* (*garment*) tabar(d) *m*.

Tabasco ® [tə'bæskəʊ] *n* Tabasco ® *m*.

tabbouleh ['tæbʊleɪ] *n Culin* taboulé *m*.

tabby ['tæbɪ] *n* **t. (cat),** chat tigré *ou* moucheté; *F* (*female cat*) chatte *f*.

tabernacle ['tæbənæk(ə)l] *n Rel* **(a)** (*receptacle*) tabernacle *m*; **(b)** (*place of worship*) temple *m*.

table¹ ['teɪb(ə)l] *n* **(a)** (*piece of furniture*) table *f*; (*small and round*) guéridon *m*; **card** *or* **gaming t.,** table de jeu; **changing/ironing/***etc* **t.,** table à langer/repasser/*etc*; **hall/telephone/***etc* **t.,** table de l'entrée/du téléphone/*etc*; **bedside/card/operating/***etc* **t.,** table de nuit/de jeu/d'opération/*etc*; **nest of tables,** table gigogne; **to book** *or* **reserve a t.,** réserver une table; **to set** *or Br* **lay the t.,** mettre *ou* dresser la table *ou* le couvert; **to clear the t.,** desservir, débarrasser la table, ôter le couvert; **to sit down to t.,** se mettre à table; **to be at t.,** être attablé *ou* à table; **to be (sitting) at the breakfast/dinner t.,** être à table pour le petit déjeuner/(le) dîner; **to leave the t.,** se lever *ou* sortir de table, quitter la table; **may I leave the t.?,** puis-je sortir de table?; **he has awful t. manners,** il se tient très mal à table; **mind your t. manners!,** tiens-toi bien à table!; *F* **to drink s.o. under the t.,** mieux tenir l'alcool que qn; (*deliberately*) faire rouler qn sous la table; *F* **two drinks and I'm under the t.,** deux verres et je roule sous la table; *Parl* **to lay a bill on the t.,** *Br & Can* déposer un projet de loi; *US* ajourner la discussion d'un projet de loi; *Fig* **to give s.o. money under the t.,** donner un dessous de table *ou* un pot-de-vin à qn; *Fig* **to get back to the negotiating t.,** reprendre les pourparlers; *Fig* **management has nothing new to put on the t.,** la direction n'a rien de nouveau à proposer; *Fig* **the offer is still on the t.,** la proposition tient toujours; *Fig* **to turn the tables on s.o.,** retourner la situation, renverser les rôles; *Fig* **the tables have been turned,** les rôles sont renversés; **high** *or F* **top t.,** (*at banquet etc*) table d'honneur; *Rel* **the Lord's T., the communion t.,** la sainte table; *Geog* **T. Bay/Mountain,** la baie/montagne de la Table; **t. knife/linen/wine/***etc*, couteau *m*/linge *m*/vin *m*/*etc* de table; **t. leg/top,** pied *m*/dessus *m* de table; **t. mat,** (*of fabric*) napperon individuel, set *m*; (*hard*) dessous-de-plat *m inv*; **t. napkin,** serviette *f* de table; **t. runner,** chemin *m* de table; **t. salt,** sel fin *ou* de table; **t. tennis,** tennis *m* de table, ping-pong *m*; **t.-tennis player,** joueur, -euse de ping-pong, pongiste *m*; **t.-tennis ball/bat/***etc*, balle *f*/raquette *f*/*etc* de ping-pong;
(b) (*group of diners*) table *f*, tablée *f*; **she kept the entire t. amused,** elle a distrait tout le monde à table; *Am* **to wait (on) t.,** travailler comme serveur *ou* serveuse; **I'm not going to wait t. all my life,** je ne vais pas être serveur *ou* serveuse toute ma vie; **t. talk,** menus propos;
(c) (*food*) table *f*; **she keeps a good t.,** on mange bien chez elle; **the restaurant has a hot and cold t.,** le restaurant propose des plats chauds et des plats froids;
(d) (*list*) (*of facts, figures etc*) table *f*, tableau *m*; (*of fares*) liste *f*; **t. of contents,** table des matières; *Math* **twelve times t.,** table de (multiplication par) douze; *Sp* **league t.,** classement *m*; **where is the team in the league t.?,** quel est le classement de l'équipe?; *Ch* **periodic t.,** (*of the elements*) tableau de la classification périodique; *Nau* **tide t.,** annuaire *m ou* indicateur *m* des marées;
(e) (*plateau*) plateau *m*;
(f) (*slab*) (*of stone etc*) plaque *f*, tablette *f*; *Rel* **the Tables of the Law,** les Tables de la Loi;
(g) *Mus* (*sounding board*) table *f* d'harmonie.

table² *vt* **(a)** *Br & Can Parl* (*submit*) présenter (*une proposition, une résolution*); déposer (*un projet de loi*); **to t. a motion of confidence,** poser la question de confiance; **(b)** *US* (*suspend*) ajourner la discussion de (*proposition, résolution, projet de loi etc*); ajourner (*une enquête*).

tableau, *pl* **-eaux** *or* **-eaus** ['tæbləʊ, -əʊz] *n Th* tableau *m*; **t. vivant,** tableau vivant.

tablecloth ['teɪb(ə)lklɒθ] *n* nappe *f*.

table d'hôte ['tɑːbl'dəʊt] *n* table *f* d'hôte; **who wants the t. d'h.?,** qui prend le menu à prix fixe?; **t. d'h. dinner,** dîner *m* à prix fixe.

table-hop ['teɪb(ə)lhɒp] *vi Am* aller (faire des grâces) de table en table.

tableland ['teɪb(ə)llænd] *n Geog* plateau *m*.

table-rapping ['teɪb(ə)lræpɪŋ] *n* (*in spiritualism*) (phénomène *m* des) coups frappés au guéridon.

tablespoon ['teɪb(ə)lspuːn] *n* **(a)** (*utensil*) cuiller *f ou* cuillère *f* de service; **(b)** (*quantity*) cuillerée *f* à soupe **(of,** de).

tablespoonful ['teɪb(ə)lspuːnfʊl] *n* cuillerée *f* à soupe **(of,** de).

tablet ['tæblɪt] *n* **(a)** (*pill*) (*for swallowing*) comprimé *m*, cachet *m*; (*for sucking*) pastille *f*; **(b)** (*slab*) (*of clay, slate etc*) tablette *f*; **(c)** (*inscribed stone*) plaque commémorative; *Rel* **votive t.,** ex-voto *m inv*; **(d)** (*bar*) (*of soap*) pain *m*; (*of chocolate*) tablette *f*; **(e)** *Scot* (*sweet*) fondant *m* au caramel.

table-turning ['teɪb(ə)ltɜːnɪŋ] *n* (phénomène *m* des) tables tournantes.

tableware ['teɪb(ə)lweər] *n* vaisselle *f*.

tabloid ['tæblɔɪd] **1** *n* **t. (newspaper),** tabloïd *m*. **2** *adj* **t., in t. form,** (*news etc*) en condensé *ou* raccourci; **the t. press,** la presse petit format; *Pej* la presse à scandale.

taboo, tabu¹ [tə'buː] *Rel & Fig* **1** *n* tabou *m*, *pl* -ous; **there is a t. on the subject/place/***etc*, le sujet/l'endroit/*etc* est tabou. **2** *adj* (*subject, place etc*) tabou (*often inv in pl*); **to declare s.o./sth t.,** déclarer qn/qch tabou; **these subjects are t.,** ces sujets sont tabou(s).

taboo, tabu² *vt Rel & Fig* interdire (*qch*); déclarer (*qn, qch*) tabou.

tabular ['tæbjʊlər] *adj* (*information, statistics etc*) tabulaire, disposé en table(s) *ou* tableau(x); **in t. form,** (*information, statistics etc*) sous forme de table(s) *ou* tableau(x).

tabulate ['tæbjʊleɪt] *vt* (*arrange in table*) présenter (*des chiffres, des faits*) sous forme de table(s) *ou* de tableau(x); (*on typewriter etc*) mettre (*des chiffres etc*) en colonnes.

tabulation [tæbjʊ'leɪʃən] *n* (*of figures etc*) présentation *f* sous forme de table(s) *ou* tableau(x); (*on typewriter*) mise *f* en colonnes.

tabulator ['tæbjʊleɪtər] *n* **(a)** (*mechanism*) (*on typewriter, word processor etc*) tabulateur *m*; **(b)** (*machine*) tabulatrice *f*.
tacheometer [tækɪ'ɒmɪtər] *n* tachéomètre *m*.
tachograph ['tækəʊgræf] *n Aut* tachygraphe *m*.
tachometer [tæ'kɒmɪtər] *n Aut* tachymètre *m*.
tachycardia [tækɪ'kɑːdɪə] *n Med* tachycardie *f*.
tachycardiac [tækɪ'kɑːdɪæk] *adj Med* tachycardiaque.
tachymeter [tæ'kɪmɪtər] *n* tachéomètre *m*.
tacit ['tæsɪt] *adj* (*admission, consent etc*) tacite.
tacitly ['tæsɪtlɪ] *adv* (*to admit, consent etc*) tacitement.
taciturn ['tæsɪtɜːn] *adj* (*person*) taciturne.
taciturnity [tæsɪ'tɜːnɪtɪ] *n* (*of person*) taciturnité *f*.
Tacitus ['tæsɪtəs] *n Hist* Tacite *m*.
tack¹ [tæk] *n* **(a)** (*fastener*) (*for carpet*) clou *m*; (*for upholstery*) broquette *f*, semence *f*; *Am* (*for poster, notice etc*) (*Br* = **drawing pin**) punaise *f*; *F* **to get down to brass tacks,** en venir aux faits; **(b)** *Sewing* (*stitch*) point *m* de bâti; **to take out the tacks,** retirer le bâti; **(c)** (*course*) *Nau* bord *m*, bordée *f*; *Fig* voie *f*; **to make a t.,** faire *ou* courir *ou* tirer un bord *ou* une bordée; **to be/run/sail on the starboard/port t.,** être/courir/faire route tribord amures/bâbord amures; *Fig* **to be on the right t.,** être sur la bonne voie; *Fig* **to be on the wrong t.,** être sur la mauvaise voie, faire fausse route; *Fig* **let's try another t.,** essayons une autre tactique; *Fig* **to go off on a fresh t.,** (*in career*) changer de voie; (*in conversation*) passer à un autre sujet.
tack² **1** *vt* **(a)** (*fasten*) **to t. (down),** clouer (*qch*); punaiser (*une affiche*) (**to,** à); *Fig* **to t. sth on,** (*add*) rajouter qch (**to,** à); **(b)** *Sewing* **to t. (down** *or* **in** *or* **on** *or* **together),** bâtir, faufiler; **to t. up a hem,** faire le bâti d'un ourlet; *Fig* **to t. sth on,** (*add*) rajouter qch (**to,** à). **2** *vi* (*of ship*) louvoyer, faire *ou* courir *ou* tirer un bord *ou* une bordée; **to t. to port,** virer (de bord) sur bâbord.
tack³ *n Horseriding* (*harness*) sellerie *f*; **t. room,** sellerie.
tack⁴ *n F* (*food*) nourriture *f*, aliment *m*.
tackiness ['tækɪnɪs] *n* **(a)** (*stickiness*) (*of paint, varnish*) adhésivité *f*; (*of glue*) visquosité *f*; **(b)** *F* (*shabbiness*) (*of shop, neighbourhood etc*) apparence *f* minable; (*vulgarity*) (*of remark, joke etc*) goût douteux; (*of clothes, jewellery*) aspect *m* bon marché; (*of person*) vulgarité *f*.
tacking ['tækɪŋ] *n* **(a)** (*of carpet*) clouage *m*; **(b)** *Sewing* bâti *m*, faufilage *m*; **to take out the t.,** retirer le bâti (**from,** de); **t. stitch,** point *m* de bâti; **t. thread,** fil *m* à bâtir, faufil *m*; **(c)** (*of ship*) **t. (about),** louvoiement *m*.
tackle¹ ['tæk(ə)l] *n* **(a)** (*equipment*) (*for hobby, sport*) attirail *m*, matériel *m*, équipement *m*; *Nau etc* (*for lifting*) appareil *m* de levage; **fishing t.,** articles *mpl* de pêche; **(b)** (*challenge*) (*in hockey etc*) interception *f*; *Fb* arrêt *m*, tacle *m*; *Rugby* plaquage *m*, placage *m*; *Rugby* **late t.,** plaquage à retardement.
tackle² *vt* **(a)** (*deal with*) attaquer, s'attaquer à (*un problème, une tâche, un dessert etc*); aborder (*un sujet*); se mettre à (*ses devoirs*); **I don't know how to t. it,** je ne sais pas comment m'y prendre; **(b)** (*speak to*) entreprendre (*qn*), attaquer (*qn*) (**about,** sur); **(c)** (*challenge*) (*in hockey etc*) intercepter (*qn*); *Fb* tacler (*qn*); *Rugby* plaquer (*qn*); **to t. a thief,** saisir un voleur.
tackler ['tæklər] *n* (*in hockey etc*) intercepteur, -trice; *Fb* tacleur *m*; *Rugby* plaqueur *m*.
tackling ['tæklɪŋ] *n* **(a)** (*of opponent*) (*in hockey etc*) interception *f*; *Fb* arrêt *m*; *Rugby* plaquage *m*, placage *m*; **(b)** (*of task etc*) entreprise *f*.
tacky ['tækɪ] *adj* **(a)** (*paint, varnish*) collant, qui n'est pas sec *ou f* sèche; (*glue*) qui commence à prendre; (*surface*) collant, poisseux; **(b)** *F* (*shop, neighbourhood etc*) minable, moche; (*vulgar*) (*remark, joke etc*) d'un goût douteux; (*clothes, jewellery*) à deux sous; (*person*) vulgaire, commun.
taco ['tɑːkəʊ] *n Culin* crêpe *f* de maïs.
tact [tækt] *n* (*of person*) (*innate*) tact *m*; (*acquired*) doigté *m*; (*in difficult situation*) délicatesse *f*; **a matter requiring t.,** une question qui demande du doigté; **to show a lack of/great t.,** faire preuve de peu/beaucoup de tact.
tactful ['tæktfʊl] *adj* **(a)** (*person*) plein de tact, diplomate; (*in difficult situation*) délicat; **to be t.,** avoir du tact; **that wasn't very t. of him,** il a manqué de tact, ce n'était pas très délicat de sa part; **she was her usual t. self,** elle a fait preuve de son tact habituel; **(b)** (*answer, remark*) plein de tact, diplomatique; (*question*) discret, -ète; (*reference*) discret, délicat; **the t. thing would have been to say nothing,** le plus délicat aurait été de ne rien dire; **that wasn't very t.,** cela manquait de tact, ce n'était pas très délicat.
tactfully ['tæktfəlɪ] *adv* (*to behave, act*) avec tact *ou* doigté *ou* délicatesse; **I t. refrained from asking him,** par tact *ou* délicatesse, je me suis retenu de lui poser la question.
tactfulness ['tæktfʊlnɪs] *n* = **TACT**.
tactic ['tæktɪk] *n Mil & Fig* tactique *f*, manœuvre *f*; **tactics,** la tactique; **to use delaying tactics,** utiliser une tactique pour gagner du temps.
tactical ['tæktɪk(ə)l] *adj Mil & Fig* **(a)** (*move, voting, weapon etc*) tactique; **t. mistake,** erreur *f* (de) tactique; **t. withdrawal,** retrait *m* stratégique; **(b)** (*person, conduct*) adroit.
tactically ['tæktɪklɪ] *adv* (*to behave, act*) adroitement; *Mil* **t. (speaking),** du point de vue de la tactique; *Fig* du point de vue tactique.
tactician [tæk'tɪʃən] *n Mil & Fig* tacticien, -ienne.
tactile ['tæktaɪl] *adj* (*organ, reflex etc*) tactile.
tactless ['tæktlɪs] *adj* **(a)** (*person*) qui manque de tact; **that was a bit t. of you,** tu as fait preuve d'un certain manque de tact, ce n'était pas très délicat de ta part; **(b)** (*answer, remark*) dépourvu de tact, qui manque de tact; (*question, reference*) indiscret, -ète.
tactlessly ['tæktlɪslɪ] *adv* (*to behave, act*) sans tact *ou* doigté *ou* délicatesse.
tad [tæd] *n Am* **(a)** (*of milk, sugar etc*) **a t.,** un peu; **(b)** (*child*) gosse *mf*.
Tadjik ['tɑːdʒɪk, tɑː'dʒiːk] *n* = **TADZHIK**.
tadpole ['tædpəʊl] *n* têtard *m*.
Tadzhik ['tɑːdʒɪk, tɑː'dʒiːk] *n* Tadjik *mf*; **T. Soviet Socialist Republic,** République socialiste soviétique du Tadjikistan.
Tadzhiki [tɑː'dʒɪkɪː, -'dʒiːkɪː] **1** *n Ling* tadjik *m*. **2** *adj* tadjik.
Tadzhikistan [tɑːdʒɪkɪ'stɑːn] *n* Tadjikistan *m*.
taffeta ['tæfɪtə] *n* (*fabric*) taffetas *m*; **t. dress/skirt/***etc*, robe *f*/jupe *f*/*etc* en taffetas.
taffrail ['tæfreɪl] *n Nau* (*structure*) couronnement *m*; (*rail*) lisse *f* de couronnement.
taffy ['tæfɪ] *n* **(a)** (*sweet*) *US* caramel *m* (dur); *Can* tire *f*; **(b)** *Am* (*flattery*) *Sl* flagornerie *f*.
Taffy ['tæfɪ] *n F* Gallois *m*; **hey, T!,** hé, toi le Gallois!
tag¹ [tæg] *n* **(a)** (*for identification*) (*on garment*) marque *f*; (*label*) étiquette *f*; (*on animal*) agrafe *f*; (*on file*) onglet *m*; *Comptr* (*of data*) préfixe *m*; (*of program*) étiquette; *US Aut* **license t.,** plaque *f* d'immatriculation *ou* minéralogique;
(b) (*end piece*) (*on cord, shoelace*) ferret *m*; (*of material etc*) bout *m*; *esp Am* **t. end,** (*of day, speech, procession etc*) fin *f*; (*of conversation*) bribes *fpl*; (*of supplies, sale goods etc*) restes *mpl*; **t. line,** (*in play*) mot *m* de la fin; (*in poem*) dernier vers; (*of entertainer etc*) slogan *m*; *Gram* **t. (question),** question-tag *f*;
(c) (*epithet, nickname*) surnom *m*;
(d) (*quotation*) citation *f*; (*trite saying*) lieu commun, cliché *m*; **she's always coming out with Latin tags,** elle est toujours en train de sortir des citations latines;
(e) *Am* (*paper etc flag*) insigne *m*, cocarde *f*; **t. day,** jour *m* de quête;
(f) (*game*) jeu *m* de chat (perché); **to play** *or* **have a game of t.,** jouer à chat *ou* au chat perché.
tag² *v* **(-gg-)** **1** *vt* **(a)** marquer (*un vêtement*), étiqueter (*des marchandises, un programme informatique*); mettre une agrafe à (*un cochon*); mettre un onglet à (*un dossier*); préfixer (*une donnée*); **(b)** (*term*) qualifier, traiter (*qn*) (**as,** de); (*nickname*) surnommer (*qn*); **(c)** *Am* (*for traffic offence*) attacher une contravention *ou F* un papillon à (*une voiture*); mettre une contravention à (*qn*); **(d)** toucher (*qn*) au jeu de chat; *Baseball* **to t. s.o. (out),** mettre un coureur hors jeu; **(e)** *esp Am F* suivre (*qn*); (*of police etc*) filer (*qn*). **2** *vi* **to t. after s.o.,** suivre qn.
▶**tag along** *vi* (*follow*) suivre; **mind if I t. along?,** est-ce que je peux venir avec vous?; **to t. along behind,** (*lagging*) traîner derrière.
▶**tag on** **1** *vi* **to t. on to s.o.,** coller (aux talons de) qn. **2** *vtsep* **to t. sth on,** (*add*) rajouter (**to,** à).
tagboard ['tægbɔːd] *n Am* carton *m*.
tagine [tæ'dʒiːn, tæ'ʒiːn] *n Culin* tajine *m*.
tagliatelle [tæljə'telɪ] *n Culin* tagliatelles *fpl*.
Tahiti [tə'hiːtɪ] *n* Tahiti *m*; **in T.,** à Tahiti.
Tahitian [tɔː'hiːʃən] **1** *adj* tahitien. **2** *n* Tahitien, -ienne.
tai chi ['taɪtʃiː] *n* taïchi *m*; **t. c. class/teacher/***etc*, cours *m*/professeur *m*/*etc* de taïchi.
taiga ['taɪgɑː] *n Geog* taïga *f*.
tail¹ [teɪl] *n* **(a)** (*of animal, bird, fish, reptile*) queue *f*; **to spread its t.,** (*of peacock*) faire la roue; *Fig* **the tail's wagging the dog,** les subordonnés l'emportent sur les

chefs; *Fig* **the t. of the hostages is wagging the dog of foreign policy,** le problème des otages dicte la politique étrangère; **with his t. between his legs,** (*of dog*) la queue entre les jambes; *Fig* (*of person*) la queue entre les jambes, l'oreille basse; *Fig* **to turn t.,** prendre ses jambes à son cou, montrer les talons; *Fig* **to keep one's t. up,** ne pas se laisser abattre; **t. feather,** (penne) rectrice *f*;

(b) (*of person*) *F* derrière *m*; (*of shirt*) pan *m*; (*of coat*) basque *f*, pan; **tails, t. coat,** habit *m*, queue-de-pie *f*; **tails will be worn,** l'habit sera de mise; **to look at s.o. out of the t. of one's eye,** regarder qn de côté;

(c) (*of comet, kite, plane*) queue *f*; (*of lock*) aval *m*; (*of ski*) arrière *m*; (*of coin*) pile *f*, revers *m*; **story with a sting in the t.,** histoire qui se termine sur une pointe de méchanceté; *Aut F* **to sit on s.o.'s t.,** coller qn; **tails!,** pile!; **t. end,** (*of material*) bout *m*; (*of procession*) queue; (*of storm*) fin *f*, queue; (*of conversation, film etc*) fin, toutes dernières minutes; **t. gate,** (*of lock*) porte *f* d'aval; *Av* **t. assembly,** dérive *f*; **t. unit,** empennage *m*;

(d) *F* (*someone following*) fileur *m*; **we've got a t.,** quelqu'un nous file, nous sommes suivis; **to put a t. on s.o.,** faire filer qn;

(e) (*trail*) piste *f*; **to be on s.o.'s t.,** suivre qn de près; (*of detective*) filer qn;

(f) *Vulg* (*woman in sexual terms*) femme *f* baisable; **she's a great piece of t.,** elle est très baisable; **he's looking for some t.,** il cherche une fille à baiser.

tail² **1** *vt* **(a)** couper la queue à (*un agneau*); enlever les queues, équeuter (*des cerises etc*); **(b)** *F* (*follow*) filer (*qn*), prendre (*qn*) en filature. **2** *vi* **to t. after s.o.,** suivre qn de près; (*of several persons*) suivre qn à la queue leu leu.

▶tail away *vi* (*of attendance, clientele etc*) diminuer, décroître; (*of voice*) se faire petit, s'affaiblir; (*of book etc*) se terminer en queue de poisson; (*of competitors in race etc*) s'espacer, s'égrener; (*of column on the march*) s'allonger.

▶tail back *vi* (*of traffic*) bouchonner.

▶tail off *vi* = **TAIL AWAY.**

tailback ['teɪlbæk] *n Aut* (*queue*) bouchon *m*.

tailboard ['teɪlbɔːd] **, tailgate** ['teɪlgeɪt] *n* (*on lorry*) porte *f* à rabattement arrière; (*on car*) hayon *m* arrière.

-tailed [teɪld] *suff* **short/long/*etc*-t.,** à queue courte/longue/*etc*.

tailgate ['teɪlgeɪt] *vt Aut F* coller (*qn*).

tailhopping ['teɪlhɒpɪŋ] *n Ski* ruade *f*.

tailings ['teɪlɪŋz] *npl* (*from mining*) déchets *mpl*.

taillamp ['teɪllæmp] *n Am Aut* (*Br* = **rear light**) feu *m* arrière.

tailless ['teɪllɪs] *adj* sans queue.

taillight ['teɪllaɪt] *n Am Aut* (*Br* = **rear light**) feu *m* arrière.

tailor¹ ['teɪlər] *n* (*for men*) tailleur *m*; (*for women*) couturière *f*; **t.'s chalk,** craie *f* de tailleur; **t.'s dummy,** mannequin; *Fig* **he looks like a t.'s dummy,** il a l'air d'un fantoche.

tailor² *vt* faire, façonner (*un complet*); *Fig* adapter (*un discours*) (**to, to suit,** à); **(woman's) tailored suit,** (costume *m*) tailleur *m*; **the tailored look is back,** le style bien structuré est de retour; **tailored shirt,** chemise cintrée; **tailored skirt,** jupe évasée.

tailoring ['teɪlərɪŋ] *n* **(a)** (*profession*) métier *m* de tailleur; **(b)** (*work*) ouvrage *m* de tailleur; **to do dressmaking and t.,** faire le flou et le tailleur.

tailor-made ['teɪləmeɪd] *adj* (*suit etc*) fait sur mesure; **t.-m. for,** (*specially designed*) conçu pour; (*suited*) fait pour; **it's t.-m. for me, I'm t.-m. for it,** c'est du sur mesure *ou* juste ce qu'il me faut.

tailpiece ['teɪlpiːs] *n* (*to document, speech etc*) appendice *m*; (*to letter*) post-scriptum *m inv*; (*on stringed instrument*) cordier *m*; *Typ* cul-de-lampe *m*, *pl* culs-de-lampe.

tailpipe ['teɪlpaɪp] *n Aut* tuyau *m* d'échappement.

tailplane ['teɪlpleɪn] *n Av* stabilisateur *m*.

tailrace ['teɪlreɪs] *n* (*for mill*) bief *m* d'aval.

tailskid ['teɪlskɪd] *n Av* béquille *f* de queue.

tailspin ['teɪlspɪn] *n Av* (descente *f* en) vrille *f*; *Av* **to go into a t.,** vriller; *Fig* **to go** *or* **get into a t.,** s'affoler, paniquer (**about,** de); **the news sent her into a t.,** la nouvelle l'a affolée *ou* paniquée.

tailwind ['teɪlwɪnd] *n* vent *m* arrière; *Av* **we've picked up a t.,** nous profitons d'un vent arrière.

taint¹ [teɪnt] *n* (*of food*) corruption *f*; (*of air, water*) infection *f*, pollution *f*; *Fig* (*of madness*) tare *f*; *Fig* (*of reputation*) souillure *f*; *Fig* **the t. of sin,** la tache *ou* souillure du péché; **book with no t. of bias,** livre *m* sans trace de préjugés.

taint² *vt* (*contaminate*) gâter (*la nourriture*); infecter, polluer (*l'air, l'eau*); infecter, vicier, corrompre (*les esprits, les mœurs*); *Fig* souiller (*une réputation*).

tainted ['teɪntɪd] *adj* (*air, water*) infecté, pollué; (*food*) gâté; (*meat*) avarié; *Fig* (*reputation*) souillé; (*heredity*) lourd, chargé; (*money*) mal acquis.

Tajik ['tɑːdʒɪk, tɑː'dʒiːk] *n* = **TADZHIK.**

take¹ [teɪk] *n* **(a)** (*recording*) (*of film, scene*) prise *f* de vue(s); (*of record*) enregistrement *m*; **we'll do that t. again,** on va refaire cette prise *ou* cet enregistrement; **(b)** (*catch*) (*of fish, game*) prise *f*; **(c)** (*money*) (*of restaurant, shop*) recette *f*, produit *m*; **our t. is up this week,** nos recettes sont en hausse cette semaine; *F* **to be on the t.,** toucher des pots de vin.

take² *v* (*pt* **took** [tʊk]; *pp* **taken** ['teɪk(ə)n]) **1** *vt* **(a)** (*grasp*) prendre (*un couteau, la main de qn*); **to t. sth again,** reprendre qch; **to t. sth in one's hand,** prendre qch dans la main; **you're taking your life in your hands doing that,** tu risques ta vie à faire ça; **to t. s.o.'s arm,** (*lean on*) prendre le bras de qn; **to t. s.o. by the arm, to t. s.o.'s arm,** (*to prevent escape*) attraper qn par le bras; **to t. s.o. in one's arms,** prendre qn dans ses bras; **to t. (hold of) s.o./sth,** se saisir *ou* s'emparer de *ou* saisir *ou* empoigner qn/qch; **to take s.o. by the throat/collar,** prendre qn à la gorge/au collet; **to t. the opportunity to do** *or* **of doing sth,** profiter de l'occasion pour faire qch; **t. your partners,** (*at dance*) invitez vos partenaires;

(b) (*remove*) prendre (*un livre, une plume*); **to t. sth (away) from s.o.,** enlever *ou* prendre *ou* ôter qch à qn; (*steal*) prendre *ou* voler qch à qn; **to t. one number from another,** soustraire *ou* ôter un chiffre d'un autre; **to t. sth from the table/out of a drawer,** prendre qch sur la table/dans un tiroir; **to t. a saucepan off the heat,** ôter *ou* retirer une casserole du feu; **to t. sth out of s.o.'s hands,** prendre qch des mains de qn; *Fig* **to t. the food out of s.o.'s mouth,** retirer le pain de la bouche de qn;

(c) (*hold*) (*of container, building etc*) contenir, avoir une capacité de (*quantité*); **this bus takes fifty passengers,** cinquante personnes peuvent tenir dans ce car;

(d) (*tolerate*) supporter (*la chaleur etc*); **she can't t. a joke,** elle ne comprend pas la plaisanterie; **I can't t. any more,** je n'en peux plus; **I can't t. any more of him,** je ne peux plus le supporter; **I can't t. much more of this,** je commence à en avoir assez, je ne vais pas pouvoir supporter cela bien longtemps encore; **I can't t. whisky,** je ne supporte pas le whisky; *esp Am* **I'm not taking any!,** je ne marche pas!; **he can t. it,** il sait encaisser;

(e) (*lead*) amener (*qn*) (**to,** à); (*away*) emmener (*qn*); (*in car*) conduire (*qn*) (**to,** à); (*of road*) mener (*qn*) (**to,** à); **to t. the dog for a walk,** promener le chien; **to t. oneself to bed,** aller se coucher; *Hum* **I can't t. you anywhere,** tu n'es pas sortable; **to t. s.o. home,** (*on foot, by car etc*) raccompagner *ou* ramener qn; (*to meet parents*) (r)amener qn à ses parents *ou* la maison; **he's taking me (out) tonight,** je sors avec lui ce soir; **he's taking me (out) to dinner/the theatre,** il m'emmène au restaurant/au théâtre; **to t. s.o. (along) with one,** emmener qn avec soi; **to t. s.o. round a museum,** faire visiter un musée à qn; **to t. s.o. across the road,** faire traverser la rue à qn; **to t. s.o. along** *or* **over** *or* **round,** amener qn; **her job takes her all over the world,** elle voyage dans le monde entier pour son travail; **the scandal has taken her to the top of the best-seller list,** le scandale l'a propulsée en haut de la liste des best-sellers; **whatever took him there?,** qu'allait-il faire là-bas?; **to t. s.o. to court,** intenter un procès contre qn;

(f) (*carry*) apporter (*des fleurs*) (**to,** à); prendre (*son manteau*); **will this train t. me to Cambridge?,** est-ce que ce train va à *ou* passe par Cambridge?; **to t. s.o. to hospital,** transporter qn à l'hôpital; **to t. sth along** *or* **over** *or* **round,** (ap)porter qch (**to s.o.,** à qn); **to t. sth with one,** emporter qch; **t. some food with you,** emportez des provisions; **to t. sth down(stairs),** descendre qch; *F* **you can't t. it with you,** vous n'emporterez pas votre fortune avec vous; **to t. a problem/matter to s.o.,** soumettre un problème/une affaire à qn;

(g) (*go by*) prendre (*l'autobus, un raccourci, une route*); **t. the turning on the left,** prenez à gauche;

(h) (*require*) (*of journey, work etc*) prendre (*du temps*); (*of engine, machine*) user, consommer (*du charbon*); **it takes an army/courage/*etc*,** il faut une armée/du courage/*etc* (**to do,** pour faire); **it took four of us to carry him,** il a fallu s'y mettre *ou* nous avons dû nous y mettre à quatre pour le porter; **that will t. some explaining,** voilà qui va demander des explications; **the work took some doing,** le travail a été difficile; **it will t. him two hours,** il en aura pour deux heures; **how long does it t. to go there?**, combien de temps faut-il pour y aller?; **how long does it t.?**, (*for journey, job to be done etc*) combien de temps est-ce que ça prend?; **I took an hour to do** *or* **over it,** j'ai mis une heure à *ou* ça m'a pris une heure pour le faire; **it takes a clever man to do that,** bien malin *ou* habile qui peut le faire; *F* **she's got what it takes to be a leader,** elle a l'étoffe d'un chef; **she's got what it takes,** (*for job etc, F sexually*) elle a tout ce qu'il faut; **not to have what it takes,** ne pas avoir les qualités *ou* capacités requises (**to do,** pour faire); *Gram* **verb that takes a preposition,** verbe qui veut la préposition; **noun that takes an 's' in the plural,** nom qui prend un 's' au pluriel;

(i) (*adopt*) prendre (*des précautions, des mesures*); **to t. legal advice,** consulter un avocat; **to t. the veil,** prendre le voile; **to t. holy orders,** entrer dans les ordres; **to t. a dislike to s.o.,** prendre qn en aversion *ou* en grippe; **to t. a decision about sth,** prendre une décision quant à *ou* touchant qch; **to t. the view that ...,** penser *ou* estimer *ou* considérer que...;

(j) (*occupy*) louer (*un appartement, une maison*); prendre (*un siège*); **all the seats are taken,** toutes les places sont prises; **please t. a seat,** veuillez vous asseoir; **t. your seats!,** prenez vos places!;

(k) (*consume*) prendre (*un cachet, du sucre*); **to t. something to drink,** prendre quelque chose à boire; **how do you t. your coffee?,** que prenez-vous dans votre café?; **to t. drugs,** se droguer; (*in hospital etc*) prendre des médicaments; **not to be taken internally,** médicament pour usage externe; **are you taking anything for that cold?,** est-ce que vous soignez ce rhume?, est-ce que vous prenez quelque chose pour ce rhume?;

(l) (*do, perform*) faire (*une promenade, un voyage*); prendre (*un congé*); **t. a look at this!,** regarde-moi ça!; **t. your pick,** faites votre choix; **to t. a bath,** (*wash*) prendre un bain; *Am F* (*lose money*) perdre gros; *Fb* **penalty shot taken by Smith,** penalty botté par Smith; **to t. a print from a negative,** tirer une épreuve d'un négatif; **to t. a photograph of s.o./sth,** prendre qn/qch en photo; **to have one's photograph taken,** se faire photographier *ou* prendre en photo; *Rel* **to t. a service,** célébrer un office; *Sch* **he takes them for** *or* **in English,** il fait la classe d'anglais, il leur enseigne l'anglais; **to t. the part of Hamlet,** jouer (le rôle d') Hamlet;

(m) (*record*) prendre (*la température, une lettre, des notes*); prendre, relever (*une adresse*);

(n) (*capture*) s'emparer de (*pouvoir, une ville*); gagner, remporter (*un prix*); **to t. a woman,** prendre une femme; **t. him alive!,** prenez-le vivant; **to t. s.o. prisoner,** faire qn prisonnier; **to t. s.o. by surprise,** prendre qn à l'improviste, surprendre qn; *Chess etc* **to t. a piece,** prendre une pièce; *Cards* **to t. a trick,** faire une levée;

(o) (*experience, feel*) prendre, attraper (*froid*); prendre (*peur, un refroidissement*); **to be taken ill,** tomber malade;

(p) (*assume*) prendre (*qn, qch*) (**for,** pour); **I took you for an Englishman,** je vous croyais anglais; **what do you t. me for?,** pour qui me prenez-vous?; **to t. the news as** *or* **to be true,** tenir la nouvelle pour vraie; **how old do you t. her to be?,** quel âge lui donnez-vous?; **I t. it that you agree,** je présume que vous êtes d'accord; **she took your silence to mean refusal,** elle a interprété votre silence comme *ou* a pris votre silence pour un refus;

(q) (*negotiate*) prendre (*un virage*); sauter (*un obstacle*);

(r) (*consider*) prendre (*un cas*); **t. (for example) the pensioners,** prenez (par exemple) les *ou* le cas des retraités; **taking one thing/year with another,** l'un/une année dans l'autre;

(s) (*accept, receive*) prendre (*un client, un pensionnaire*); accepter (*un chèque*); **t. five!,** cinq minutes de pause!, reposez-vous cinq minutes!; **to t. sth well/ badly,** bien/mal prendre qch; **he took the news better than I thought he would,** il a pris la nouvelle mieux que je ne l'aurais cru; **to t. s.o./sth the wrong way,** (*misunderstand*) mal comprendre qn/qch; **don't t. this the wrong way, but ...,** (*be offended*) ne le prenez pas mal, mais...; **I wonder how she'll t. it,** je me demande quelle tête elle fera *ou* comment elle va le prendre; **I'll t. it here,** (*of phone call*) je le prendrai ici; **I took a phone call for her yesterday,** j'ai eu un coup de fil pour elle hier; *Old-fashioned* **to t. a wife,** prendre femme; **do you t. this man ...?,** (*in wedding ceremony*) consentez-vous à prendre M. ...?; **to t. a chance,** risquer le coup; *Com etc* **to t. so much a week,** faire (une recette de) tant par semaine; **what will you t. for it?,** combien en voulez-vous?; **does this machine t. pound coins?,** cette machine accepte-t-elle les pièces d'une livre?; **to t. the hook** *or* **bait,** (*of fish*) mordre à l'hameçon; *Fig* tomber dans le panneau; **t. it or leave it!,** c'est à prendre ou à laisser; **to t. a beating,** (*be punched*) recevoir une rossée; (*be defeated*) essuyer une défaite; **to t. a bet,** tenir un pari; **to t. all responsibility,** assumer toute la responsabilité; **we must t. things as we find them** *or* **as they come,** il faut prendre les choses comme elles sont *ou* comme elles viennent; **t. it from me!,** croyez-moi!; **to t. s.o. seriously,** prendre qn au sérieux; **nylon does not t. dyes well,** le nylon est réfractaire à la teinture *ou* ne se teint pas bien; **surface that will t. a high polish,** surface qui prend un beau poli; **to t. heavy loads,** (*of crane, engine etc*) supporter de lourdes charges;

(t) (*buy*) prendre (*un billet*); **what paper do you t.?,** quel journal achetez-vous?;

(u) *Scol* (*sit*) se présenter à, passer (*un examen*); (*study*) faire (*de la philosophie*); suivre (*un cours*); **I didn't t. Latin at school,** je n'ai pas fait de latin au lycée; **she took her degree last year,** elle a obtenu son diplôme l'an dernier;

(v) (*copy, quote*) (*from author*) emprunter (*un passage*) (**from,** à); (*from book, report etc*) tirer (*une citation, des chiffres*) (**from,** de); **word taken from the Latin,** mot emprunté au latin;

(w) (*use*) prendre (*des œufs, de la farine etc*); **t. the scissors/brush/***etc* **to it,** vas-y avec les ciseaux/la brosse *etc*; **t. the hammer to it,** vas-y à coups de marteau; **he took a red pen to my dissertation,** il y est allé au stylo rouge pour corriger mon mémoire; **I'll have to t. bleach to this stain,** il faudra que je nettoie cette tache à l'eau de javel; **his father took a stick to him,** son père lui a donné des coups de bâton.

2 *vi* (*be successful*) (*of fire, graft, plant cutting, vaccine*) prendre; **to t. a good photo(graph),** (*be photogenic*) être photogénique.

▶**take aback** *vtas* (*surprise*) décontenancer, interloquer (*qn*) (**with,** par).

▶**take after** *vipo* (*be like*) (*in looks*) ressembler à (*son père*); (*in personality*) tenir de (*son père*).

▶**take apart 1** *vtsep* (*dismantle*) démonter (*une machine etc*); *Fig* démolir (*un projet etc*); *Fig* **to t. s.o. apart,** (*in fight*) démolir qn; (*scold*) passer un savon à qn. **2** *vi* (*of machine, furniture etc*) se démonter.

▶**take away 1** *vtsep* **(a)** (*remove*) (*from person*) enlever (*qn, qch*) (**from,** à); (*from place*) enlever (*qch*) (**from,** de); *Math* soustraire, ôter (*un chiffre*) (**from,** de); **to t. a child away from school,** retirer un enfant de l'école; **(b)** (*lead, carry*) emmener (*qn*); emporter (*qch, un blessé*); **what takes you away so soon?,** qu'est-ce qui vous fait partir de si bonne heure?; *Br* **sandwiches to t. away,** sandwich(e)s à emporter; **not to be taken away,** (*on book in library*) exclu du prêt. **2** *vi* **to t. away from the pleasure/value of sth,** diminuer le plaisir/la valeur de qch.

▶**take back** *vtsep* **(a)** (*lead*) reconduire, ramener, raccompagner (*qn*); ramener (*un cheval*); **(b)** (*return*) rapporter (*un livre etc*) (**to,** à); **that takes me back to my childhood,** cela me rappelle mon enfance; **it takes you back a bit, doesn't it?,** ça ne nous rajeunit pas tout ça, hein?; **(c)** (*accept*) reprendre (*un ancien employé, les invendus*); **she's a fool to t. him back,** elle est idiote d'accepter son retour; **(d)** (*withdraw*) retirer (*ce qu'on a dit*); retirer, reprendre (*sa parole*); reprendre (*un cadeau*); **I t. it (all) back,** je n'ai rien dit.

▶**take down** *vtsep* **(a)** (*remove*) enlever (*une affiche etc*); (*from cupboard, shelf etc*) descendre (*une assiette*); (*from hook*) décrocher (*un manteau, un tableau etc*); **(b)** (*lower*) baisser (*son pantalon, sa culotte*); **(c)** (*destroy*) démolir (*un mur etc*); *F* **to t. s.o. down a peg** *or* **two,** remettre qn à sa place, rabattre son caquet à qn; **(d)** (*dismantle*) démonter (*l'échafaudage*); **(e)** (*record*) noter, inscrire (*un nom, une adresse etc*); prendre (*des notes*); **to t. down a letter in shorthand,** prendre une lettre en sténo.

▶**take in** *vtsep* **(a)** (*lead, carry*) faire entrer (*qn*); rentrer (*le linge, la moisson etc*);

(b) (*admit, receive*) recueillir (*un orphelin*); héberger, loger, recevoir (*qn*); prendre (*des locataires, un journal*); **to t. in sewing/washing,** faire la couture/la lessive à domicile;

(c) (*reduce*) reprendre (*une jupe*); serrer (*une manche*); *Nau* **to t. in sail,** diminuer de voile(s); **to t. in the slack,** (*on rope*) reprendre du mou;

(d) (*cover*) comprendre, englober (*plusieurs pays*); embrasser (*des questions, des possibilités*); **tour which takes in all the important towns,** excursion qui passe par toutes les villes importantes;

(e) (*understand*) (*intellectually*) comprendre, se rendre compte de (*qch*); (*emotionally*) se faire à (*une mauvaise nouvelle*); **I didn't quite t. it in at first,** je n'ai pas très bien compris au début; **to t. in the situation,** juger la situation; **to t. it all** *or* **everything in,** (*listen*) être tout oreilles; **to t. in everything at a glance,** tout embrasser d'un coup d'œil;

(f) (*deceive*) tromper, rouler (*qn*) (**with,** avec); **to be taken in,** se faire avoir; **I've been taken in,** on m'a eu *ou* roulé; **to allow oneself to be taken in,** se laisser avoir *ou* duper *ou* tromper; **to be taken in by appearances,** se laisser tromper par les apparences *fpl*;

(g) (*see, visit*) *Am* visiter (*une musée*); **to t. in the sights,** visiter la ville; **to t. in a movie/show,** aller au cinéma/théâtre.

►**take off 1** *vtsep* **(a)** (*remove*) enlever; ôter, retirer (*un vêtement*); enlever (*une tache, un couvercle*); amputer (*une jambe*); *Math* déduire (*une quantité*) (**from,** de); **t. your feet off the table!,** retire tes pieds de sur la table!; **to t. s.o.'s attention off sth,** détourner l'attention de qn; **he never took his eyes off us,** il ne nous quittait pas des yeux; **to t. something off,** (*reduce price*) baisser le prix, faire un rabais; **to t. a couple of pounds off,** (*price*) baisser le prix *ou* faire un rabais de quelques livres; (*weight*) perdre du poids; **to t. s.o. off a list,** rayer qn d'une liste; **to t. sth off s.o.'s hands,** débarrasser qn de qch; **I'll t. the baby off your hands for a few hours,** je vais te libérer du bébé pour quelques heures; **t. your hands off me!,** bas les pattes!; **to t. a load off s.o.'s mind,** ôter un poids à qn *ou* de la poitrine de qn; **to t. years off s.o.,** (*of clothes, diet etc*) rajeunir qn; **to t. passengers off a ship,** (*by boat*) débarquer les voyageurs; (*by helicopter, in emergency etc*) recueillir les voyageurs;

(b) (*lead*) emmener (*qn*) (**to,** à, chez, en); **to t. oneself off,** s'en aller, *F* décamper;

(c) (*cancel*) supprimer (*un train, un autobus etc*);

(d) (*mimic*) imiter (*qn*), copier les gestes *ou* manières de (*qn*);

(e) (*rest*) **to t. some time off,** prendre un congé; **to t. three days off,** prendre trois jours de congé.

2 *vi* **(a)** (*leave*) (*of plane*) décoller; s'envoler (**for,** pour); (*of athlete*) prendre son élan, s'élancer (**from,** de); (*of person*) partir (**for,** pour); (*hurriedly*) *F* s'en aller, décamper, filer; **she's taken off for two weeks in the Caribbean,** elle est partie passer deux semaines aux Caraïbes;

(b) (*succeed*) (*of company etc*) prendre un grand essor, être en plein essor.

►**take on 1** *vtsep* **(a)** (*accept*) se charger de, (en-tre)prendre (*un travail*); assumer (*une responsabilité*); accepter le défi de (*qn*); **to t. it on oneself to do,** prendre sur soi de faire; **to t. s.o. on at tennis,** engager une partie de tennis avec qn; **to t. on passengers,** (*of train etc*) prendre *ou* embarquer des voyageurs; **(b)** (*hire*) engager, embaucher, prendre (*un employé*); **(c)** (*assume*) prendre, revêtir, affecter (*une couleur, une apparence*) (**of,** de); **the word takes on another meaning,** le mot prend une autre signification; **(d)** (*escort*) (*further*) mener (*qn*) plus loin, (*too far*) mener (*qn*) au-delà de sa destination. **2** *vi* **(a)** *Br F* (*be upset*) s'en faire; **(b)** (*become popular*) (*of idea, tune etc*) prendre.

►**take out** *vtsep* **(a)** (*remove*) sortir (*qch*) (**of,** de); arracher (*une dent*); ôter, enlever (*une tache*); *Fig F* **to t. it out of s.o.,** (*tire*) épuiser, éreinter qn; *Fig* **to t. it out on s.o.,** passer sa colère sur qn; *Fig* **to t. s.o. out of herself** *or* **himself,** remonter le moral *ou* faire oublier ses problèmes à qn, changer les idées de qn; **(b)** (*carry*) sortir (*des chaises, le linge*); *Am* **sandwiches to t. out,** sandwich(e)s à emporter; **(c)** (*to theatre, restaurant etc*) faire sortir (*qn*); promener, sortir (*le chien*); **he's been taking her out for a couple of months,** il sort avec elle depuis quelques mois; **(d)** (*obtain*) prendre, obtenir (*un brevet, un permis*); souscrire (*une police d'assurance, un abonnement*); **(e)** *esp Am* (*destroy*) anéantir (*une ville, des troupes*).

►**take over 1** *vtsep* **(a)** (*be responsible for*) prendre la direction de (*restaurant, société etc*); **to t. over s.o.'s job,** remplacer qn; **to rent a flat and t. over the furniture,** louer un appartement avec une reprise de meubles; **(b)** (*buy out*) racheter (*une compagnie*); **(c)** (*overrun*) envahir (*un pays*); **she takes the place over,** (*of bossy person etc*) elle joue les despotes; **(d) to t. over the lead,** (*in race, polls*) prendre la tête. **2** *vi* **(a)** *Mil Pol* prendre le pouvoir; (*of new manager etc*) prendre la direction; **(b)** (*relieve*) prendre la relève (**from,** de); **(c)** (*succeed*) prendre la succession (**from,** de).

►**take to** *vipo* **(a)** (*go to*) prendre (*la fuite, la route*); **to t. to one's bed,** prendre le lit, s'aliter; **to t. to the mountains,** se réfugier dans les montagnes; **(b)** (*adopt*) prendre (*de mauvaises habitudes*); **to t. to drink** *or* **drinking,** se mettre à boire *ou* à la boisson; **(c)** (*like*) éprouver de la sympathie pour (*qn*); **I didn't t. to him/it,** il/ça ne m'a pas plu; **to t. to a game,** prendre goût à un jeu.

►**take up 1** *vtsep* **(a)** (*lead*) faire monter (*qn*); **there's a lift to t. you up,** vous pouvez monter en ascenseur; **the lift took us up to the 25th floor,** l'ascenseur nous a amenés au 25e étage;

(b) (*carry*) monter (*une valise*);

(c) (*lift*) relever, ramasser (*qch*); enlever, déclouer (*un tapis*); enlever (*des pavés, des rails*); dépaver, défoncer (*une rue*); *Rail etc* prendre (*des voyageurs*); **to t. up a book from the table,** prendre un livre sur la table;

(d) (*shorten*) raccourcir (*une jupe*); **to t. up the slack in a cable,** retendre un câble;

(e) (*accept*) relever (*un défi*); accepter (*une offre*); *St Exch* souscrire à (*des actions*); **to t. up a bet,** tenir un pari; **to t. s.o. up on sth,** (*offer, promise etc*) prendre qn au mot; **I'll t. you up on that one day,** je te prendrai au mot un de ces jours;

(f) (*discuss*) parler de, discuter (de) (*un sujet, problème etc*); **to t. s.o. up on sth,** (*in discussion, argument etc*) reprendre qn sur qch;

(g) (*absorb*) absorber (*de l'eau*);

(h) (*adopt*) adopter (*une idée etc*); **to t. up an attitude on sth,** prendre *ou* adopter une attitude à l'égard de qch;

(i) (*begin*) embrasser, suivre (*une carrière*); se mettre à (*un passe-temps, une étude*); (*again*) reprendre, se remettre à (*un travail, une lecture etc*); **to t. up one's duties,** entrer en fonctions; **to t. up (the thread of) the conversation,** reprendre le fil de la conversation;

(j) (*occupy*) occuper, prendre (*de la place, du temps*); absorber, occuper (*l'attention*); **he is entirely taken up with his business,** il est entièrement absorbé dans son commerce.

2 *vi* **to t. up with s.o.,** se lier avec qn.

takeaway ['teɪkəweɪ] *Br* **1** *adj* (*meal, sandwich etc*) à emporter. **2** *n* **(a)** café *m ou* restaurant *m* qui fait des plats à emporter; **(b)** sandwich *m ou* plat *m ou* repas *m* à emporter.

take-home ['teɪkhəʊm] *adj* **t.-h. pay,** salaire net.

taken ['teɪkən] *adj* **(a)** (*seat, table*) occupé, pris; **(b)** (*impressed*) impressionné (**with,** par); **he was very much t. with the idea,** l'idée l'enchantait; **I was not t. with her,** elle ne m'a pas fait bonne impression.

takeoff ['teɪkɒf] *n* **(a)** (*mimicry*) imitation *f*, caricature *f*; **to do a t. of s.o.,** imiter *ou* caricaturer qn; **(b)** (*departure*) (*of plane*) décollage *m*, envol *m*; (*of athlete*) élan *m*; **to step back to get a better t.,** prendre du recul pour mieux sauter; **(c)** (*success*) (*of country, industry etc*) essor *m*.

takeout ['teɪkaʊt] *adj & n Am* = **TAKEAWAY**.

takeover ['teɪkəʊvər] *n* **(a)** (*of company*) prise *f* de contrôle, rachat *m*; **t. bid,** offre publique d'achat; **(b)** *Pol* prise *f* de pouvoir.

taker ['teɪkər] *n* (*of lease*) preneur *m*; (*at auction etc*) acheteur *m*, preneur; **any takers?,** (*to go to cinema etc*) est-ce qu'il y a des amateurs?; **I asked but there were no takers,** j'ai demandé mais il n'y avait pas d'amateurs

take-up ['teɪkʌp] *n* **(a)** (*of benefits*) reclamation *f*; **(b)** *Cin* enroulement *m*; **t.-up spool/reel,** bobine réceptrice/enrouleuse *f*.

taking ['teɪkɪŋ] **1** *adj* (*person*) attirant, séduisant; (*smile, manners, ways*) engageant. **2** *n* **(a)** (*of city etc*) prise *f*; (*of criminal*) arrestation *f*; **the money/job is his for the t.,** il n'a qu'à accepter l'argent/le poste; **(b)** *Med* (*of blood*) prélèvement *m*; (*of blood pressure*) prise *f*; **(c)** *Com* **takings,** recette *f*; **(d)** *Old-fashioned* **to be in a t.,** être agité.

talc [tælk] *n* (*toiletry*) (poudre *f* de) talc *m*; (*mineral*) talc.

talcum ['tælkəm] *n* **t. (powder),** (poudre *f* de) talc *m*.

tale [teɪl] *n* **(a)** (*story*) conte *m*; (*legend*) légende *f*; **The Winter's T.,** Le Conte d'Hiver; **thereby hangs a t.,** il y a toute une histoire là-dessous; **his drawn face told the t. of his sufferings,** ses traits tirés en disaient long sur ses souffrances; **she lived to tell the t.,** elle a survécu; **(b)** (*lie*) histoire *f*; **to tell tales,** (*exaggerate, lie*) raconter des histoires; **(c)** (*account, report*) récit *m*; **to tell tales,** (*sneak*) rapporter, cafarder; *Fig* **you mustn't t. tales out of school,** (*be indiscreet*) il ne faut pas raconter ce que tu devais taire.

talebearer ['teɪlbeərər] *n* (*sneak*) rapporteur, -euse, cafard *m*.

talebearing ['teɪlbeərɪŋ] *n* (*sneaking*) rapportage *m*, cafardage *m*.

talent ['tælənt] *n* **(a)** (*ability*) talent *m*, don *m*; **to have a t. for sth,** être doué en *ou* pour qch, avoir du talent pour qch; **to have a t. for annoying everyone,** avoir le talent *ou* don d'agacer tout le monde; **he has no t. for business,** il n'a pas le don des affaires; **a woman of** *or* **with t.,** une femme talentueuse *ou* de talent; **(b)** (*person with ability*) talent *m*; *F* **t. scout** *or* **spotter,** dénicheur, -euse de talent(s) *ou* de vedettes; **(c)** *Br F* (*people of the opposite sex*) (*women*) nanas *fpl*, nénettes *fpl*, minettes *fpl*; (*men*) types *mpl*, mecs *mpl*, gars *mpl*; **what's the local t. like?,** comment sont les nénettes *ou* les mecs par ici?; **where does the t. hang out?,** où est-ce qu'on trouve des nénettes *ou* des mecs?; **(d)** (*coin*) talent *m*.

talented ['tæləntɪd] *adj* (*artist, writer*) talentueux, de talent, doué; (*portrait, play, film etc*) plein de talent.

taleteller ['teɪltelər] *n* (*sneak*) rapporteur, -euse.

taletelling ['teɪltelɪŋ] *n* rapportage *m*, cafardage *m*.

talisman ['tælɪzmən] *n* talisman *m*.

talk¹ [tɔːk] *n* **(a)** (*conversation*) entretien *m*, conversation *f*; (*informal*) causerie *f*; **to have a t. with s.o.,** (*chat*) s'entretenir *ou* avoir un entretien avec qn; (*about problem etc*) dire deux mots *ou* en toucher deux mots à qn (**about,** à propos de):

(b) (*discussion*) discussion *f*; **it's time we had a t. about your behaviour,** il est temps que nous discutions *ou* parlions de votre conduite; **there is some t. of his returning,** il est question qu'il revienne; **there has been t. of it,** on en a parlé, il en a été question; *Pol etc* **talks,** dialogue *m*, pourparlers *mpl*; **to start talks,** engager le dialogue, entrer en pourparlers; **peace talks,** négociations *ou* pourparlers de la paix;

(c) (*gossip*) bavardages *mpl*, bruit *m*, dires *mpl*; **there is some t. of his returning,** le bruit court qu'il va revenir; **it's the t. of the town,** on ne parle que de cela; **she's the t. of the town,** elle défraie la chronique; **their behaviour is causing a lot of t.,** leur conduite fait jaser; **it's just t.,** ce n'est que des racontars; **t. show,** (*on radio, television*) causerie *f*;

(d) (*speech*) langage *m*, propos *mpl*; **idle t.,** paroles en l'air, balivernes *fpl*; **small t.,** banalités *fpl*, conversation banale, propos sans importance; **to make** *or* **indulge** *or* **engage in small t.,** parler de choses et d'autres *ou* à bâtons rompus; **I'm no good at small t.,** je ne suis pas doué pour faire la conversation; **that was just sales t.,** tout ça ce n'était que des boniments; **double t.,** (*unclear*) propos ambigus; (*false*) propos insincères; **baby t.,** babil enfantin;

(e) (*bravado*) paroles *fpl*; **to be all t.,** (*person*) être fort en paroles; **he's all t. and no action,** il parle beaucoup, mais quand il s'agit de passer à l'action, il n'y a plus personne;

(f) (*lecture*) exposé *m* (**on,** sur); (*informal*) causerie *f* (**on,** sur); **to give a t. on** *or* **about sth,** faire un exposé *ou* une causerie sur qch.

talk² **1** *vi* **(a)** (*converse*) parler; (*chat*) bavarder (**of, about,** de; **with,** avec); **to t. of one thing and another** *or* **this and that,** parler de choses et d'autres *ou* à bâtons rompus; **to t. to** *or* **with s.o.,** s'entretenir avec qn, parler à *ou* avec qn; **she never talked to me the whole evening,** elle ne m'a pas dit un mot de la soirée;

(b) (*about problem, in reprimanding way*) **to t. (severely) to s.o.,** réprimander *ou* gronder qn; **I'LL t. to him!,** je vais lui dire *ou* lui en toucher deux mots!;

(c) (*gossip*) cancaner, jaser; **people will t.,** on va jaser, le monde est cancanier; **you know how people t.,** tu sais comme les gens sont cancaniers *ou* comme les langues vont bon train; **we don't want people to t.,** il ne faut pas faire jaser; **this will give them something to t. about,** voilà quelque chose qui va les faire jaser; **the whole town was talking about it,** toute la ville en parlait; **to get oneself talked about,** faire parler de soi;

(d) (*speak*) parler; **to learn to t.,** apprendre à parler; **can he t.?,** (*of bird*) est-ce qu'il parle?; **is the baby talking yet?,** est-ce que le bébé parle?; **to t. and t.,** parler sans arrêt; **don't all t. at the same time,** ne parlez pas tous en même temps; *Hum* surtout, ne parlez pas tous en même temps; **to t. of** *or* **about doing sth,** parler de faire qch; **you're the only one I can t. to,** tu es le seul auquel je puisse parler *ou* me confier; *F* **that's no way to t.!,** il ne faut pas dire des choses pareilles!; (*referring to bad language*) en voilà un langage!; **he likes to hear himself t.,** il s'écoute parler; **to t. through one's hat,** dire *ou* débiter des sottises; **now you're talking!, that's the way to t.!,** à la bonne heure!; **YOU can** *or* **can't t.!,** tu peux (bien) parler!; **to make a prisoner t.,** faire parler *ou* avouer un prisonnier; **his accomplices are afraid he'll t.,** ses complices craignent qu'il ne vende la mèche; **he talks big,** il est courageux en paroles; **money talks,** l'argent veut tout dire; **t. of the devil!,** quand on parle du loup on en voit la queue!; **what are you talking about?,** (*asking question*) de quoi parlez-vous?; (*expressing disbelief*) *F* qu'est-ce que vous racontez?; **I don't know what you're talking about,** (*in answer to accusation*) je ne sais pas ce que vous voulez dire; **she knows what she is talking about,** elle s'y connaît, elle sait ce qu'elle dit; *F* **t. about luck/laugh,** tu parles d'une chance/d'un fou-rire; *Hum* **t. about interesting!,** tu parles comme c'était intéressant!; **to t. to oneself,** parler tout seul, monologuer; **who do you think you are talking to!,** à qui croyez-vous donc parler?;

(e) (*lecture*) **to t. on the radio,** faire un discours *ou* parler à la radio;

2 *vt* (*speak*) parler (*le français etc*); dire (*des bêtises*); **to t. politics,** parler politique; **to t. (common) sense,** tenir des propos raisonnables; **do t. sense!,** tu radotes!; **to t. oneself hoarse,** s'enrouer à force de parler; **to talk oneself into a job,** obtenir un emploi à force de belles paroles; **he talked himself into trouble,** ses discours imprudents finirent par le mettre dans le pétrin; **she can talk her way out of anything,** avec son bagou elle arrive toujours à se tirer d'affaires; **to t. s.o. into/out of doing sth,** persuader/dissuader qn de faire qch; **to t. s.o. into a better frame of mind,** remonter le moral à qn en lui parlant; **to t. s.o. out of a bad mood,** rendre à qn sa bonne humeur en lui parlant, faire passer sa mauvaise humeur à qn.

►**talk away** **1** *vtsep* passer (*le temps, la nuit*) à parler; **to t. a child's fears away,** chasser les craintes d'un enfant avec des paroles réconfortantes. **2** *vi* parler sans arrêter.

►**talk back** *vi* (*answer*) (*on two-way radio*) répondre; (*cheekily*) répondre avec insolence (**to,** à), répliquer; **don't t. back to me!,** je te défends de me répondre.

►**talk down** **1** *vi* **to t. down to s.o.,** parler avec condescendance *ou* comme à un inférieur à qn. **2** *vtsep* **(a)** donner des instructions d'atterrissage à (*un avion*); **the priest talked the man down from the parapet,** le prêtre a persuadé l'homme de descendre du parapet; **(b)** réduire (*qn*) au silence en parlant.

►**talk out** *vtsep* **to t. things out,** discuter la chose à fond; *Parl* **to t. a bill out,** prolonger les débats de façon qu'un projet de loi ne puisse être voté avant la clôture.

►**talk over** *vtsep* discuter (de), débattre (*une question*); **let's t. it over,** discutons la chose.

►**talk round** **1** *vtas* persuader, enjoler (*qn*), faire changer d'avis à (*qn*); **I talked them round to my way of thinking,** je les ai amenés à partager mon avis. **2** *vipo* **to t. round a problem/an issue,** tourner autour du pot, ne pas entrer dans le vif du sujet.

►**talk up** **1** *vtsep* vanter (*un film, un livre etc*). **2** *vi Am* (*speak openly, without hesitation*) parler franchement.

talkathon ['tɔːkəθɒn] *n Am* (*in Congress, on television etc*) débat-marathon *m*.

talkative ['tɔːkətɪv] *adj* (*person*) (*chatty*) causant, loquace; (*chatterbox*) bavard; (*gossip*) jaseur; **he's very t.,** il a la langue déliée *ou* bien pendue, il n'a pas sa langue dans sa poche.

talkativeness ['tɔːkətɪvnɪs] *n* (*of person*) loquacité *f*; (*chatter*) bavardage *m*.

talker ['tɔːkər] *n* **(a)** (*conversationalist*) causeur, -euse; *Pej* parleur, -euse; **to be a good t.,** bien parler; **brilliant t.,** personne *f* qui brille dans la conversation; (*in Parliament etc*) brillant orateur; **(b)** (*chatterbox*) bavard, -e; **to be a great t.,** avoir la langue déliée *ou* bien pendue, ne pas avoir sa langue dans sa poche.

talkie ['tɔːkɪ] *n Cin F Old-fashioned* film parlant *ou* parlé.

talking ['tɔːkɪŋ] **1** *adj* parlant; **t. book,** (*for the blind*) livre enregistré; **t. doll,** poupée *f* qui parle; *Cin* **t. film,** film parlant *ou* parlé. **2** *n* **(a)** (*discussion*) discours *mpl*, propos *mpl*, paroles *fpl*; **that's enough t.,** assez parlé; **the United Nations is accused of being a t. shop,** on accuse les Nations Unies de ne faire que de la parlotte; **t. point,** sujet *m* de discussion, argument *m*; **(b)** (*conversation*) conversation *f*; **to do all the t.,** faire tous les frais de la conversation; **(c)** (*chatter*) bavardage *m*; **no t., please!,** pas de bavardage!

talking-to ['tɔːkɪŋtuː] *n F* (*scolding*) réprimande *f*, semonce *f*; **to give s.o. a t.-to,** passer un savon à qn, vertement réprimander qn (**about,** sur; **for,** pour); **he needs a good t.-to,** il a besoin d'un bon savon.

talky ['tɔ:kɪ] *adj Am* (*book, film etc*) verbeux.

tall [tɔ:l] *adj* (*person*) grand, de haute taille; (*building etc*) grand, haut, élevé; **how t. are you?**, combien mesurez-vous?; **she's taller than I am,** elle est plus grande que moi; **he was taller by a head** *or* **stood a (whole) head taller than me,** il me dépassait d'une tête; **she's growing taller,** elle se fait grande; **he has grown t.,** il a grandi; *F* **to walk t.,** marcher la tête haute; **how t. is that mast?,** quelle est la hauteur de ce mât?; **tree five metres t.,** arbre de cinq mètres de hauteur; **I'd love a t. glass of something cold,** j'aimerais bien un grand verre de quelque chose de bien frais; *Fig* **a t.** *Br* **story** *or Am* **tale,** une histoire invraisemblable *ou* à dormir debout; *Fig* **that's a t. order,** voilà qui va être difficile *ou* compliqué.

tallboy ['tɔ:lbɔɪ] *n Br* (*Am* = **highboy**) grande commode *f*.

tallness ['tɔ:lnɪs] *n* (*of person*) grande taille; (*of building etc*) hauteur *f* considérable.

tallow ['tæləʊ] *n* (*fat*) suif *m*; **t. candle,** chandelle *f*.

tally¹ ['tælɪ] *n* **(a)** (*record*) (*of merchandise*) pointage *m*; **to keep a t. of goods/names,** pointer des marchandises/des noms; **t. clerk,** pointeur *m*, contrôleur *m*; **(b)** (*calculation*) compte *m*; *Am* (*in match*) (nombre *m* de) points *mpl*; **to keep (a) t. of one's score/spending/***etc*, noter son score/ses dépenses/*etc*; **who's keeping t.?,** qui fait les comptes *ou* compte les points?

tally² **1** *vt* pointer (*des marchandises*). **2** *vi* (*of figure, report etc*) correspondre (**with,** à), concorder (**with,** avec); **these accounts do not t.,** ces comptes ne concordent pas.

tally-ho [tælɪ'həʊ] *int & n* (*in hunting*) taïaut *m*, tayaut *m*.

Talmud ['tælmʊd] *n Rel* Talmud *m*.

Talmudic ['tælmʊdɪk] *adj* (*scholar etc*) talmudique.

Talmudist ['tælmʊdɪst] *n* Talmudiste *m*.

talon ['tælən] *n* **(a)** (*claw*) (*of bird*) serre *f*, griffe *f*; *Fig* (*of person*) griffe *f*; **(b)** (*pile of cards*) talon *m*.

tam [tæm] *n* béret écossais.

tamable ['teɪməb(ə)l] *adj* = **TAMEABLE**.

tamarind ['tæmərɪnd] *n* **(a)** (*fruit*) tamarin *m*; **(b) t. (tree),** tamarinier *m*.

tamarisk ['tæmərɪsk] *n* (*plant*) tamaris *m*.

tambour ['tæmbʊər] *n* **(a)** *Sewing* **t. (frame),** tambour *m* à broder; **t. lace,** dentelle *f* (brodée) sur tulle; **(b)** tambour *m* (*de vestibule, Archit de colonne*); **(c)** *Mus* tambour *m*.

tambourine [tæmbə'ri:n] *n Mus* tambourin *m*.

tame¹ [teɪm] *adj* **(a)** (*animal*) (*unafraid*) apprivoisé, domestiqué; (*domesticated*) domestique; *Am* (*plant, land*) cultivé; **to grow** *or* **become t.,** (*of animal*) s'apprivoiser; **(b)** *F* (*person*) soumis, docile; (*story etc*) anodin, insipide; **the circus was a very t. affair,** le cirque n'avait rien de sensationnel; *Hum* **we have a t. builder,** nous disposons d'un entrepreneur complaisant; **the story has a t. ending,** l'histoire se termine sur une note banale.

tame² *vt* **(a)** apprivoiser; domestiquer (*une bête*); *Am* cultiver (*une plante, un terrain*); mater (*qn, une passion*); dompter (*un lion*).

tameable ['teɪməb(ə)l] *adj* (*animal etc*) apprivoisable; (*lion etc*) domptable.

tamely ['teɪmlɪ] *adv* (*se soumettre*) sans résistance, docilement; **the story ends very t.,** l'histoire se termine très anodinement *ou* banalement; **t. worded,** platement écrit.

tamer ['teɪmər] *n* apprivoiseur, -euse (*d'oiseaux etc*); dompteur, -euse (*de lions etc*).

Tamil ['tæmɪl] **1** *adj* tamoul, tamil (*no f*). **2** *n* **(a)** (*person*) Tamoul, -e, Tamil *m*; **(b)** *Ling* tamoul *m*, tamil *m*.

taming ['teɪmɪŋ] *n* apprivoisement *m*; domestication *f* (*d'une bête*); domptage *m* (*d'un lion, Fig de qn*); **the T. of the Shrew,** la Mégère Apprivoisée.

tammy ['tæmɪ] *n F* béret écossais.

tam-o'-shanter [tæmə'ʃæntər] *n* béret écossais.

tamp [tæmp] *vt Constr* damer, pilonner (*la terre etc*); bourrer (*une pipe, le tabac*); *Min* bourrer (*un fourneau de mine*).

tampax ® ['tæmpæks] *n* tampax *m*.

▶**tamper with** ['tæmpər] *vipo* (*interfere with*) toucher à, *F* trifouiller (*un mécanisme etc*); altérer (*un document etc*); falsifier (*un registre*); fausser, brouiller (*une serrure*); truquer, tripatouiller (*des comptes etc*); spolier (*une lettre, un colis*); *Horseracing* **to t. with a horse,** doper un cheval; **to t. with a witness,** suborner un témoin.

tampering ['tæmpərɪŋ] *n* **t. with (sth),** altération *f*, adultération *f* (*de documents*); falsification *f* (*de registres*); trucage *m*, tripatouillage *m* (*de comptes etc*); spoliation *f* (*de colis etc*); **t. with witnesses,** subornation *f* de témoins.

tamping ['tæmpɪŋ] *n Constr* damage *m*, pilonnage *m*; *Min* (*act*) bourrage *m* (*d'un fourneau de mine*); (*substance*) bourre *f* (*d'un fourneau de mine*).

tampon ['tæmpɒn] *n Surg* tampon *m* (*d'ouate, de gaze*); (*to absorb menstrual flow*) tampon (périodique).

tan¹ [tæn] **1** *n* **(a)** (*on skin*) bronzage *m*, hâle *m*, teint hâlé (*de la peau*); **to get a (good) t.,** bronzer; **to have a t.,** être bronzé *ou* hâlé; **to lose one's t.,** débronzer; **(b)** (*colour*) couleur *f* du tan, tanné *m*; **leather goods in t.,** maroquinerie *f* en havane; **(c)** = **TANBARK**. **2** *adj* (*colour*) tanné, tan *inv*; (*shoes*) en cuir jaune; (*gloves*) en tanné; **black and t. dog,** chien noir et feu *inv*.

tan² (-nn-) **1** *vt* tanner (*les peaux*); (*of sun*) hâler, bronzer (*la peau*); *F* **to t. s.o.** *or* **s.o.'s hide,** tanner le cuir à qn. **2** *vi* (*of complexion*) se hâler, bronzer; **I t. easily,** je bronze facilement.

tanbark ['tænbɑ:k] *n* écorce *f* à tan; **spent t.,** tannée *f*.

tandem ['tændəm] **1** *n* (*bicycle*) tandem *m* (de tourisme); (*carriage*) tandem; **to harness two horses in t.,** atteler deux chevaux en tandem *ou* en flèche; *Tech* **t. engine,** machine *f* à cylindres en tandem; **t. working,** fonctionnement *m* en tandem. **2** *adv* **to drive t.,** conduire en flèche *ou* en tandem.

tang [tæŋ] *n* **(a)** (*flavour*) saveur piquante, piquant *m*, montant *m*; **a t. of irony,** une pointe d'ironie; **the t. of the morning air,** le piquant de l'air matinal; **(b)** soie *f* (*d'un couteau*); queue *f* (*d'une lime*).

tangent ['tændʒənt] **1** *adj* tangent, tangentiel (**to,** à); *Math* **t. line,** ligne tangentielle, tangente *f*. **2** *n Math* tangente *f*; **at a t. to a curve,** tangentiellement à une courbe; *F* **to fly** *or* **go off at a t.,** changer de sujet; (*in order to hide sth etc*) prendre la tangente.

tangential [tæn'dʒenʃəl] *adj Math etc* tangentiel; *Fig* **to be t. to sth,** toucher à le périphérie de qch.

tangerine [tændʒə'ri:n, 'tænd-] *n* mandarine *f*.

tangibility [tæn(d)ʒɪ'bɪlɪtɪ] *n* tangibilité *f*.

tangible ['tæn(d)ʒɪb(ə)l] *adj* **(a)** tangible, palpable; **the t. world,** le monde sensible; *Jur* **t. assets,** valeurs matérielles; **(b)** (*real*) réel; **t. difference,** différence *f* sensible.

tangibly ['tæn(d)ʒɪblɪ] *adv* (*see adj*) **(a)** tangiblement; **(b)** sensiblement.

Tangier(s) [tæn'dʒɪər, -'dʒɪəz] *n* Tanger *m*.

tanginess ['tæŋɪnɪs] *n* saveur piquante, piquant *m*.

tangle¹ [tæŋg(ə)l] *n* (*bundle, confusion*) embrouillement *m* (*de fils, d'affaires*), emmêlement *m* (*de fils, de cheveux*); fouillis *m* (*de broussailles*); enchevêtrement *m* (*de branches, de barbelés, de routes*); entrelacs *m* (*de ronces*); **to be (all) in a t.,** (*of string etc*) être (tout) embrouillé; (*of wool, hair*) être (tout) emmêlé; *Fig* (*of person*) ne savoir plus où on en est; **his finances are in such a t.,** ses finances sont tellement embrouillées; **to get into a t.,** (*of string, business*) s'embrouiller; (*of wool, hair*) s'enchevêtrer; (*making speech, explaining sth*) s'embrouiller, s'emmêler; **to get into an emotional t.,** entrer dans une relation embrouillée *ou* compliquée.

tangle² **1** *vt* = **TANGLE UP**. **2** *vi* (*of string etc*) s'embrouiller, s'emmêler, s'enchevêtrer.

▶**tangle up** *vtsep* **(a)** (*make confused*) embrouiller, (em)mêler (*des fils, des cheveux*); embrouiller (*une affaire*); **to get tangled up,** (*of things*) s'emmêler; (*of things, people*) s'embrouiller; **she got tangled up in some barbed wire,** elle a été prise dans des barbelés; **(b)** (*involve*) impliquer, mêler; **they got tangled up in something dishonest,** ils ont été mêlés à une affaire malhonnête.

▶**tangle with** *vipo F* (*quarrel, fight with*) se brouiller avec qn; **don't t. with her,** ne te brouille pas avec elle.

tangled ['tæŋg(ə)ld] *adj* (*hair, love life etc*) embrouillé, emmêlé.

tango¹ ['tæŋgəʊ] *n* (*dance*) tango *m*.

tango² *vi* danser le tango; *Fig F* **it takes two to t.,** il faut être deux pour ces choses-là.

tangy ['tæŋɪ] *adj* qui a un goût piquant, relevé.

tank [tæŋk] *n* **(a)** (*container*) réservoir *m*; **water t.,** réservoir à eau *ou* d'eau; *Nau* caisse *f* à eau; *Rail* caisse à eau, soute *f* (à eau); (*along track*) château *m* d'eau; **(live) fish t.,** vivier *m*; **storage t.,** réservoir de stockage; **a full t. (of fuel),** un plein réservoir (de carburant); *Aut Av* **fuel** *or* **petrol** *or Am* **gas(oline) t.,** réservoir de carburant; *Br* **t. lorry** *or esp Am* **truck,** camion-citerne *m*, *pl* camions-citernes; *Rail* **t. wagon** *or Am* **car,** wagon-citerne *m*, *pl* wagons-citernes; **(b)** *Ind etc* cuve *f*, bac *m*; compartiment *m* (*d'un réservoir etc*); *HydE* bassin *m*; *Phot* **developing t.,** cuve *f* pour développement; *Pol* **think t.,** comité *m* *ou* groupe *m* d'experts; *Nau* **(water) ballast t.,** ballast *m*; **air/buoyancy t.,** (*on lifeboat etc*) caisson *m* à air/de flottabilité;

(c) *Mil* char *m*; **the tanks,** les blindés *mpl;* **t. trap,** obstacle *m* antichar; **(d) t. top,** (*garment*) débardeur *m*.

▶**tank along** *vi F* (*go fast*) (*of driver, car etc*) foncer.

▶**tank up 1** *vi Aut* (*fill fuel tank*) faire le plein (*d'essence*). **2** *vtsep* (*usu passive*) *Sl* **to get tanked up,** se soûler; **to be tanked up,** être bourré *ou* bituré.

tankard ['tæŋkəd] *n* pot *m*, chope *f*; **a t. of ale,** un pot de bière.

tanker ['tæŋkər] *n Nau* navire-citerne *m*, *pl* navires-citernes; *Rail* wagon-citerne *m*, *pl* wagons-citernes; **oil t.,** (navire) pétrolier *m*; **t. (aircraft),** avion-citerne *m*, *pl* avions-citernes; (*for refuelling*) avion *m* de ravitaillement; **t. (lorry** *or Am* **truck),** camion-citerne *m*, *pl* camions-citernes.

tanned [tænd] *adj* (*cuir*) tanné; (*teint, visage*) hâlé, bronzé; (*deeply, naturally*) basoné.

tanner¹ ['tænər] *n* (*person*) tanneur *m*.

tanner² *n Br Sl Arch* (*coin*) (pièce *f* de) six anciens pence.

tannery ['tænərɪ] *n* tannerie *f*.

tannic ['tænɪk] *adj Ch* (*acide*) tannique.

tannin ['tænɪn] *n Ch* tan(n)in *m*.

tanning ['tænɪŋ] *n* **(a)** (*act of tanning*) tannage *m*; **t. (trade),** tannerie *f*; **(b)** *F* (*beating*) raclée *f*; **to give s.o. a good t.,** donner une belle *ou* une bonne raclée à qn.

tannoy ® ['tænɔɪ] *n* système *m* de haut-parleurs; **an announcement came over the t.,** une annonce a été passée par les haut-parleurs.

tansy ['tænzɪ] *n* (*plant*) tanaisie *f*.

tantalize ['tæntəlaɪz] *vt* tourmenter, torturer (*qn*), mettre (*qn*) au supplice.

tantalizing ['tæntəlaɪzɪŋ] *adj* tentant (*mais hors de portée*); **it's t.,** c'est un vrai supplice de Tantale.

tantalizingly ['tæntəlaɪzɪŋlɪ] *adv* cruellement; (*to look at s.o.*) d'un air provocant; **we came t. close to solving it,** c'était exaspérant *ou* rageant de voir à quel point nous étions près de la solution.

tantamount ['tæntəmaʊnt] *adj* équivalent (**to,** à); **to be t. to sth,** équivaloir à qch; **that's t. to saying I'm a liar,** cela revient à dire que je mens.

tantrum ['tæntrəm] *n* accès *m* de colère; **to get into** *or* **to throw a t.,** se mettre en colère, piquer une colère.

Tanzania [tænzə'nɪə] *n* Tanzanie *f*.

Tanzanian [tænzə'nɪən] **1** *adj* tanzanien. **2** *n* Tanzanien, -ienne.

Taoism ['taʊɪz(ə)m] *n Phil* taôisme *m*.

Taoist ['taʊɪst] *n Phil* taôiste *mf*.

tap¹ [tæp] *n* **(a)** robinet *m*; (*of cask*) cannelle *f*, cannette *f*; **to turn on/turn off the t.,** ouvrir/fermer le robinet; *F* **to turn on the t.,** (*cry*) pleurer; **on t.,** (*of beer etc*) à la pression; **to be on t.,** (*of person, thing*) être (toujours) disponible; **they've got cheap labour on t.,** ils ont de la main d'œuvre pas chère à volonté; **t. water,** eau *f* du robinet; **(b)** = **TAPROOM; (c)** *esp Am El* prise *f* (intermédiaire); **(d)** branchement *m*; captage *m* (clandestin) (*d'une communication téléphonique*); **who authorized the t.?,** qui a autorisé la mise sur écoute?; **(e)** (*for cutting screw thread*) **(screw) t.,** taraud *m*; **t. auger** *or* **borer,** tarière *f*; foret *m*, mèche *f*.

tap² *vt* (**-pp-**) **(a)** percer, mettre en perce (*un fût*); inciser, entailler (*un arbre*); gemmer (*un pin*); tirer (*du vin*); exploiter (*des ressources naturelles etc*); capter (*un cours d'eau*); faire un branchement sur (*une conduite de gaz, d'eau*); **to t. a telephone conversation,** capter une communication téléphonique; **the phones are tapped,** les téléphones sont sur écoute; *F* **to t. s.o. for fifty francs,** taper qn de cinquante francs; **(b)** tarauder, fileter (*un écrou*).

tap³ *n* **(a)** (*light blow, sound*) petit coup; (*with head*) tape *f*; **t. at the door,** coup léger *ou* discret à la porte; **there was a t. on the window,** on a frappé à la fenêtre; **a t. on the shoulder,** une tape sur l'épaule; **(b)** *Mil* **taps,** (sonnerie *f* de) l'extinction *f* des feux; **(c) t. dance** *or* **dancing,** (danse *f* à) claquettes *fpl*; **t. dancer,** danseur, -euse à claquettes; **to do t.,** faire des claquettes.

tap⁴ *v* (**-pp-**) **1** *vt* (*strike lightly*) frapper légèrement, taper légèrement, tapoter; **she tapped me on the shoulder,** elle m'a tapé sur l'épaule. **2** *vi* **(a) to t. at** *or* **on the door,** frapper doucement à la porte; **(b) to t. (dance),** faire des claquettes.

▶**tap out** *vtsep* **(a) to t. out the rhythm,** marquer le rythme; **to t. out a message,** émettre un message (*en morse*); (*on central heating pipes etc*) taper un message; **(b) to t. out one's pipe,** débourrer sa pipe.

tape¹ [teɪp] *n* **(a)** (*ribbon*) ruban *m* (*de coton*); bande *f* (*de toile, de papier*); *Sp* bande d'arrivée; **masking t.,** ruban-cache *m*; **((self-)adhesive** *or F* **sticky) t.,** ruban adhésif; *Pharm* **adhesive t.,** sparadrap *m*; *El* **insulating t.,** ruban isolant, chatterton *m*; *Sp* **to breast the t.,** arriver le premier; *Horseracing* **the tapes,** (*at start*) les rubans; **t. (measure),** mètre *m* (ruban); centimètre *m* (*de couturière*); **(b)** (*in recording*) (*length of tape*) bande *f*; (*cassette*) cassette *f* (*audio*); **magnetic** *or* **recording t.,** bande magnétique; **(video) t.,** vidéocassette *f*; **pre-recorded t.,** bande enregistrée; **a Frank Sinatra t., a t. of Frank Sinatra,** une cassette de Frank Sinatra; **to get sth on t.,** enregistrer qch; **t. deck,** lecteur *m* de cassettes; **t. recorder,** magnétophone *m*; **t. recording,** enregistrement *m* sur bande; **(c)** *Comptr* **t. reader,** lecteur *m* de bande; **t. streamer,** streamer *m*.

tape² *vt* **(a)** attacher (*un paquet*) avec un ruban adhésif; *Sewing etc* border (*un vêtement*); guiper (*un fil électrique*); **to t. sth to sth,** attacher qch à qch au ruban adhésif; **(b)** mesurer (*un terrain etc*) au cordeau; *Fig* **I've got him taped,** j'ai pris sa mesure, je sais ce qu'il vaut; **(c)** (*record*) enregistrer (*qch*) (sur bande); **she was taped talking to them,** elle a été enregistrée en train de leur parler; **taped music,** musique enregistrée (sur bande).

▶**tape up** *vtsep* fermer (*un paquet*) au ruban adhésif; recoller (*un objet brisé*) au ruban adhésif.

taper¹ ['teɪpər] *n* (*candle*) bougie filée; *Rel* cierge *m*.

taper² *n Archit Constr etc* (*shape*) conicité *f*, cône *m*.

taper³ 1 *vt* tailler en pointe *ou* en cône; effiler (*les cheveux*); *MecE* ajuster en cône, côner (*une fusée etc*); *Archit* fuseler, diminuer (*une colonne*). **2** *vi* s'effiler, s'amincir, aller en diminuant; **column that tapers upwards,** colonne qui diminue vers le haut; **her hair tapers in to the neck,** ses cheveux sont effilés sur son cou; **it tapers to a point,** ça s'amincit jusqu'à se terminer en pointe.

▶**taper off 1** *vi* (*of line, long thin object*) s'amincir, se rétrécir, diminuer; (*get smaller gradually*) (*of production, numbers etc*) diminuer, se réduire. **2** *vtsep* (*long thin object*) réduire, diminuer.

tape-record ['teɪprɪkɔːd] *vt* enregistrer sur bande.

tapered ['teɪpəd] *adj* (*hair*) effilé; (*column, candle*) en fuseau; **t. trousers,** fuseaux *mpl*.

tapering ['teɪpərɪŋ] **1** *adj* en pointe; (*doigt*) effilé, fuselé; *Archit* (*colonne*) en fuseau, diminué. **2** *n* (*act of tapering*) taille *f* en pointe; (*in hairdressing*) effilement *m*.

tapestry ['tæpɪstrɪ] *n* tapisserie *f*; **t. maker** *or* **weaver,** tapissier, -ière.

tapeworm ['teɪpwɜːm] *n* ténia *m*; (*in human*) ver *m* solitaire.

taping ['teɪpɪŋ] *n* **(a)** bordage *m* (*d'une robe etc*); *El* guipage *m* (*de câbles etc*); **(b)** (*recording*) enregistrement *m* (sur bande).

tapioca [tæpɪ'əʊkə] *n* tapioca *m*.

tapir ['teɪpər] *n* (*often inv in pl*) (*animal*) tapir *m*.

tappet ['tæpɪt] *n MecE* poussoir *m*; **t. guide,** guide *m* de poussoir; **t. lever,** basculeur *m*; **t. rod,** tige-poussoir *f*, *pl* tiges-poussoirs.

tapping¹ ['tæpɪŋ] *n* **(a)** perçage *m* (*d'un tonneau*); incision *f*, gemmage *m* (*d'un arbre*); tirage *m* (*du vin*); prise *f* d'eau (*sur une rivière*); branchement *m* (*sur une conduite d'eau*); prise, branchement (*de gaz, d'électricité*); *Tel Telecom* branchement d'écoute; exploitation *f* (*des ressources naturelles*); **telephone t.,** captage *m* (clandestin) de communications téléphoniques; **(b)** *MecE* (*of screws*) taraudage *m*.

tapping² *n* (*knocking*) petits coups; (*with hand*) tapotement *m*.

taproom ['tæpruːm] *n* bar *m*.

taproot ['tæpruːt] *n Bot* racine pivotante, pivot *m*.

tar¹ [tɑːr] *n* **(a)** goudron *m*; *F* **to spoil the ship for a ha'porth of t.,** tout gâcher pour des économies de bouts de chandelle; **t. paper,** papier goudronné; **(b)** *Nau F* **(Jack) t.,** loup *m* de mer.

tar² *vt* (**-rr-**) goudronner (*une route, le bois etc*); bitumer (*un trottoir, du carton*); *Nau* goudronner, brayer (*un navire*); **to t. and feather s.o.,** passer qn au goudron et aux plumes; *Fig* **to be tarred with the same brush,** être à mettre dans le même panier *ou* sac.

tarantella [tærən'telə] *n* (*dance*) & *Mus* tarentelle *f*.

tarantula [tə'ræntjʊlə] *n* (*spider*) tarentule *f*.

tardily ['tɑːdɪlɪ] *adv Fml* **(a)** (*late*) tardivement; (*too late*) en retard; **(b)** (*slowly*) lentement.

tardiness ['tɑːdɪnɪs] *n Fml* **(a)** (*lateness*) retard *m*; tardivité *f* (*d'un fruit etc*); **(b)** (*slowness*) lenteur *f*, nonchalance *f* (**in doing sth,** à faire qch).

tardy ['tɑːdɪ] *adj Fml* **(a)** (*late*) (*payment, reaction*) tardif;

(b) (*slow*) nonchalant; (*unhurried*) peu empressé.

tare[1] [teər] *n* **(a)** (*weed*) vesce *f*; **(b)** *Bible* **tares,** ivraie *f*.

tare[2] *n Com* tare *f*; poids net (*d'un camion*).

target[1] ['tɑːgɪt] *n* **(a)** *Mil etc & (in production etc)* cible *f*, objectif *m*; **moving t.,** objectif mobile *ou* mouvant; **to land on t.,** (*of bomb etc*) toucher la cible *ou* l'objectif; *Fig* **we're on t. (to meet the deadline),** nous sommes à jour *ou* dans les temps (pour respecter la date limite); **the project is/we're behind t.,** le projet est/nous sommes en retard sur le programme; **to set oneself a t.,** se fixer un but *ou* un objectif; **sitting t,** cible facile; **t. area,** zone *f* des objectifs; *Rad TV* **t. audience,** public *m* cible; **t. cost,** coût *m* de référence; *Com etc* **t. date,** date *f* limite (*de livraison etc*); **t. figure,** objectif; **t. group,** groupe *m* cible; **t. language,** langue *f* d'arrivée, langue cible; **t. market,** marché *m* cible; **t. practice,** exercices *mpl* de tir; **(b)** (*in surveying*) voyant *m*; (*over a bench mark*) signal *m*, -aux; *Am Rail* disque *m*; **position t.,** signal de position.

target[2] *vt Mil & Fig* viser, prendre pour cible; **to t. a sum of £0.5 m,** prendre pour objectif une somme de 0,5 million de livres.

targetting ['tɑːgɪtɪŋ] *n* **(a)** (*of group etc*) ciblage *m* (**of,** sur); **(b)** (*setting targets*) détermination *f* d'objectifs; **because of unrealistic t.,** en raison d'objectifs non réalistes.

tariff[1] ['tærɪf] *n* **(a)** (*customs*) *& Rail etc* tarif *m*; **reduced t.,** tarif réduit; **full t.,** plein tarif; **t. barrier** *or* **wall,** barrière douanière; **(b)** (*post office*) *& Rail etc* tableau *m ou* liste *f* des prix.

tariff[2] *vt* tarifer (*des marchandises etc*).

tarmac ®[1] ['tɑːmæk] *n* **(a)** *Constr* macadam goudronné; **(b)** *Av* (*runway*) piste *f*; **planes waiting on the t.,** avions attendant sur la piste.

tarmac[2] *vt* (*pt & pp* **tarmacked**) macadamiser (*une route etc*).

tarmacadam [tɑːmə'kædəm] *n Constr* macadam goudronné, macadam *m*.

tarn [tɑːn] *n* petit lac (*de montagne*).

tarnish[1] ['tɑːnɪʃ] *n* ternissure *f*.

tarnish[2] **1** *vt* ternir (*la surface d'un métal, la réputation de qn*). **2** *vi* (*of metal etc*) se ternir.

tarnishing ['tɑːnɪʃɪŋ] *n* ternissure *f* (*d'un métal*).

tarot ['tærəʊ] *n Cards* tarot *m*; **t. cards,** tarots.

tarpaulin [tɑː'pɔːlɪn] *n* (*fabric*) toile goudronnée; (*sheet*) bâche *f*, prélart *m*.

tarragon ['tærəgən] *n* (*plant*) *& Culin* estragon *m*.

tarring ['tɑːrɪŋ] *n* goudronnage *m* (*d'une route, du bois etc*); bitumage *m* (*d'un trottoir, du carton*).

tarry[1] ['tɑːrɪ] *adj* **(a)** (*made of tar*) goudronneux, bitumineux; **(b)** (*covered, stained with tar*) couvert *ou* souillé de goudron.

tarry[2] ['tærɪ] *vi Lit* **(a)** (*stay*) rester, demeurer (**at, in a place,** dans un endroit); **(b)** (*delay*) tarder, s'attarder.

tarsus, *pl* **-i** ['tɑːsəs, -aɪ] *n Anat* tarse *m*.

tart[1] [tɑːt] *n* **(a)** *esp Br Culin* tarte *f*; (*small*) tartelette *f* aux confitures; **(b)** *Sl* (*prostitute*) putain *f*, poule *f*; (*promiscuous woman*) traînée *f*; *Pej* (*woman*) taupe *f*; *Pej* **the silly old t.,** la vieille taupe crétine.

tart[2] *adj* au goût âpre, aigrelet; (*tone*) acerbe, aigre.

►tart up *vtsep Sl Pej* **to t. oneself up,** s'affubler, s'attifer; **to t. sth up,** (*room etc*) retaper qch; **it's just a tarted up version of the old one,** ce n'est qu'une version rafistolée de l'ancien.

tartan ['tɑːt(ə)n] *n Tex* (*cloth or plaid*) tartan *m*, écossais *m*; **t. shirt,** chemise écossaise.

tartar ['tɑːtər] *n* (*on teeth*) *& Ch* tartre *m*.

Tartar ['tɑːtər] **1** *adj* tatar, tartare. **2** *n* **(a)** Tatar *m*, Tartare *mf*; **(b)** *Fig* (*man*) homme *m* intraitable; (*woman*) mégère *f*.

tartaric [tɑː'tærɪk] *adj Ch* (*acide etc*) tartrique.

tartly ['tɑːtlɪ] *adv* avec aigreur; (*to say*) d'un ton acerbe.

tartness ['tɑːtnɪs] *n* acerbité *f*; goût *m* âpre (*d'un fruit*); verdeur *f* (*d'un vin*); aigreur *f* (*du ton*).

tarty ['tɑːtɪ] *adj Sl Pej* (*woman*) **to look t.,** avoir l'air d'une putain *ou* d'une poule; (*clothes etc*) tapageur, tape-à-l'œil.

task [tɑːsk] *n* **(a)** travail, -aux *m*, tâche *f*; *Sch* devoir *m*; **these are your tasks,** voici votre travail; **their task is to ...,** leur travail *ou* tâche consiste à ...; **the unpleasant t. of informing the parents,** la tâche désagréable d'informer les parents; **it's an endless t.,** c'est un travail sans fin; **to set s.o. a t.,** imposer une tâche à qn; **(b) to take s.o. to t. for (doing) sth,** prendre qn à partie *ou* réprimander qn pour avoir fait qch; **(c)** *Mil etc* **t. force,** corps *m* expéditionnaire.

taskmaster, taskmistress ['tɑːskmɑːstər, -mɪstrɪs] *n* **hard t.,** véritable tyran *m*.

Tasmania [tæz'meɪnɪə] *n* Tasmanie *f*.

Tasmanian [tæz'meɪnɪən] **1** *adj* tasmanien. **2** *n* Tasmanien, -ienne.

TASS [tæs] *n* (*abbr* **telegraphic news agency of the Soviet Union**) TASS *f*.

tassel ['tæs(ə)l] *n* **(a)** (*on furniture, clothing etc*) gland *m*; (*in bookbinding etc*) signet *m*; **(b)** *Bot* épi *m* mâle (*du maïs*).

tasselled ['tæs(ə)ld] *adj* à glands, orné de glands.

taste[1] [teɪst] *n* **(a)** (*flavour*) saveur *f*, goût *m*; **it has a burnt t.,** cela a un goût de brûlé; **this drink has no t.,** cette boisson n'a pas de goût *ou* est insipide; **a t. of cheese/***etc*, un petit peu de fromage/*etc*; **a t. of wine/***etc*, une petite gorgée (de vin etc); **have a t. of this claret,** goûtez donc à ce bordeaux; **he gave us a t. of his bad temper,** il nous a donné un échantillon de sa mauvaise humeur; **to give s.o. a t. of the whip,** faire tâter du fouet à qn; **my first t. of freedom,** mon premier contact avec la liberté; **she's already had a t. of prison,** elle a déjà tâté de la prison; **is this a t. of things to come?,** est-ce là un avant-goût de ce qui nous attend?; **the film gives a t. of what life is like for ...,** le film donne un aperçu *ou* une petite idée de ce qu'est la vie des ...;

(b) (sense of) t., goût *m*; **t. bud,** papille gustative;

(c) (*liking*) goût *m*, penchant particulier, prédilection *f* (**for,** pour); **to have a t. for sth,** avoir du goût pour qch, avoir le goût de (*la musique etc*); **to have expensive tastes,** avoir des goûts de luxe; **to acquire** *or* **develop a t. for sth,** prendre goût à qch; **to find sth to one's t.,** trouver qch à son goût; *Culin* **add sugar to t.,** on ajoute du sucre à volonté; **it's a matter of t.,** c'est (une) affaire de goût; *Prov* **everyone to his t.,** des goûts et des couleurs on ne discute pas, chacun ses goûts;

(d) she has excellent t. in dress, elle s'habille avec (beaucoup de) goût; **in perfect t.,** d'un goût parfait; **in bad t.,** de mauvais goût; **it would be bad t. to refuse,** il serait de mauvais goût de refuser.

taste[2] **1** *vt* **(a)** percevoir la saveur de (*qch*), sentir (*qch*); **I can't t. anything when I have a cold,** je n'ai pas de goût quand je suis enrhumé; **can't you t. the garlic?,** tu ne trouves pas que ça a un goût d'ail?; **(b)** (*of cook*) goûter (*un mets*); déguster (*des vins, des thés etc*); sonder (*un fromage*); **(c)** (*get a little taste of*) goûter de *ou* à (*qch*); *Fig* tâter de (*le fouet, le prison etc*); boire une petite gorgée (*d'un liquide*); **I haven't even tasted it,** je n'y ai pas même goûté; **he had not tasted food for three days,** il n'avait pas mangé depuis trois jours; **to t. happiness,** connaître le bonheur. **2** *vi* **the meat tasted of garlic,** la viande avait un goût d'ail; **it tastes like spinach,** ça a un goût d'épinard; **to t. good/bad,** être bon/mauvais, avoir un bon/mauvais goût; **it tastes fine to me,** moi je trouve ça bon.

tasteful ['teɪstfʊl] *adj* **(a)** (*remark, action*) de bon goût; (*decoration*) fait avec goût; **that wasn't a very t. thing to say,** cette remarque n'était pas de très bon goût; **(b)** (*person*) de goût.

tastefully ['teɪstfəlɪ] *adv* avec goût.

tastefulness ['teɪstfʊlnɪs] *n* bon goût.

tasteless ['teɪstlɪs] *adj* **(a)** (*mets etc*) sans goût, sans saveur, fade, insipide; **(b)** (*vêtement etc*) qui manque de goût; (*remarks*) de mauvais goût.

tastelessly ['teɪstlɪslɪ] *adv* (*s'habiller etc*) sans goût.

tastelessness ['teɪstlɪsnɪs] *n* **(a)** insipidité *f*, fadeur *f* (*d'un mets etc*); **(b)** (*of person, clothes, remark etc*) manque *m* de goût.

taster ['teɪstər] *n* **(a)** (*person*) dégustateur, -trice (*de vins, de thés etc*); **(b)** (*foretaste*) **this is just a t. (of what's to come),** ce n'est qu'un avant-goût (de ce qui va se passer).

tastiness ['teɪstɪnɪs] *n* saveur *f ou* goût *m* agréable.

tasting ['teɪstɪŋ] *n* **(a)** *Physiol* gustation *f*; **(b)** dégustation *f* (*de vins*).

tasty ['teɪstɪ] *adj* **(a)** (*mets, repas*) savoureux; **t. morsel,** morceau succulent; **(b)** *Br F* (*good-looking*) bien foutu; **she's a t. piece,** c'est un beau morceau.

tat[1] [tæt] *n see* **TIT[2]**.

tat[2] *n F* (*junk*) camelote *f*.

ta-ta [tæ'tɑː] *int Br Sl & children's language* au revoir!

Tatar ['tɑːtər] **1** *adj* tatar, tartare; **T. Republic,** République *f* de Tatarie. **2** *n* Tatar *m*, Tartare *mf*.

Tatary ['tɑːtərɪ] *n* Tatarie *f*.

tater ['teɪtər] *n Br Sl* (*potato*) patate *f*.

tatter ['tætər] *n* lambeau *m*, loque *f*; **in tatters,** en lambeaux, en loques; **to tear s.o.'s reputation to tatters,** éreinter qn, déchirer qn à belles dents.

tattered ['tætəd] *adj* (*vêtement*) en loques, en lambeaux; (*homme*) déguenillé, loqueteux.
tattie ['tætɪ] *n esp Scot F* (*potato*) patate *f*.
tattle¹ ['tæt(ə)l] *n* (*gossiping*) commérage *m*; (*gossip, rumour*) cancans *mpl*, potins *mpl*.
tattle² *vi* (*gossip*) commérer, cancaner, faire des cancans.
tattler ['tætlər] *n* **(a)** (*chatterbox*) bavard, -arde; **(b)** (*gossip, rumour-monger*) cancanier, -ière.
tattoo¹ [tə'tuː] *n Mil* **(a)** (*drum signal*) retraite *f* (du soir); **to beat** *or* **sound the t.,** battre *ou* sonner la retraite; **(b)** (*parade*) carrousel *m* militaire; **torchlight t.,** retraite *f* aux flambeaux.
tattoo² *n* (*design*) tatouage *m*; **a t. of an anchor, an anchor t.,** un tatouage représentant une ancre; **t. artist,** tatoueur *m*.
tattoo³ *vt* tatouer.
tattooing [tə'tuːɪŋ] *n* tatouage *m*.
tattooist [tə'tuːɪst] *n* tatoueur *m*.
tatty ['tætɪ] *adj F* (*in poor condition*) miteux; (*of poor quality*) minable.
taught *see* **TEACH²**.
taunt¹ [tɔːnt] *n* injure *f* (*en paroles*); sarcasme *m*.
taunt² *vt* accabler de sarcasmes; **to t. s.o. with sth,** railler qn à propos de qch; **to t. s.o. with cowardice,** traiter qn de lâche.
taunting ['tɔːntɪŋ] *adj* sarcastique, railleur.
tauntingly ['tɔːntɪŋlɪ] *adv* d'un ton sarcastique *ou* railleur.
Taurus ['tɔːrəs] *n Astron* le Taureau.
taut [tɔːt] *adj* (*rope*) tendu, raide, raidi; (*muscle*) tendu, étiré; (*prose, style*) incisif, nerveux; **she looked t.,** elle avait l'air tendu; **t. situation,** situation tendue.
tauten ['tɔːt(ə)n] *vt* raidir, tendre (*un câble etc*).
tautness ['tɔːtnɪs] *n* raideur *f* (*d'un câble etc*); tension *f* (*des muscles*); caractère incisif (*d'une prose*).
tautological [tɔːtə'lɒdʒɪk(ə)l] *adj* tautologique.
tautology [tɔː'tɒlədʒɪ] *n* tautologie *f*.
tavern ['tæv(ə)n] *n* (*in proper names*) *& Arch* taverne *f*, cabaret *m*.
tawdriness ['tɔːdrɪnɪs] *n* clinquant *m*; faux brillant (*d'un bijou*).
tawdry ['tɔːdrɪ] *adj* (*vêtement, ornement*) d'un mauvais goût criard; **t. jewellery,** clinquant *m*, toc *m*.
tawny ['tɔːnɪ] *adj* fauve; tirant sur le roux; **t. eagle,** aigle ravisseur; **t. owl,** chouette *f* hulotte; **old t. port,** porto *m* qui a jauni dans le fût.
tax¹ [tæks] *n* **(a)** *Admin* impôt *m*, taxe *f*; contribution *f*; **you pay out a small fortune in t.,** on paye une petite fortune en impôts; **direct/indirect t.,** impôt direct/indirect; **income t.,** impôt sur le revenu; **capital gains t.,** impôt sur les plus-values; **value added t.,** *US* **processing t.,** taxe à la valeur ajoutée; **inspector of taxes,** inspecteur *m* des contributions directes; **to levy a t. on sth,** frapper qch d'un droit; **t. authorities,** autorités fiscales; **t. avoidance,** évasion fiscale; **t. bracket,** tranche *f* d'imposition; **t. burden,** charge fiscale; **t. code,** barème fiscale; **t. collector,** percepteur *m* d'impôt; **t. disc,** (*on vehicle*) vignette *f*; **t. evasion,** fraude fiscale; **t. free,** exempt d'impôts; **t. haven,** refuge *ou* paradis fiscal; **t. incentive,** incitation fiscale; **t. office,** (bureau *m* de) perception *f*; **t. paid,** net d'impôt; **t. rebate,** abattement *m* d'impôt; **t. return,** (*form*) déclaration *f* d'impôt; **to make one's t. return,** faire sa déclaration d'impôt; **t. revenue,** recettes fiscales; **t. year,** année *f* d'imposition; **(b)** (*burden*) charge *f*; fardeau *m* (*imposé à qn*).
tax² *vt* **(a)** *Admin* taxer (*les objets de luxe etc*); frapper (*qch*) d'un impôt; imposer (*qn*); **to t. income,** imposer (des droits sur) le revenu; **to be heavily taxed,** être lourdement imposé; **if businesses are taxed out of existence ...,** si on fait disparaître les entreprises à force d'impôts ...; **we're being taxed out of existence,** on nous accable d'impôts; *Br Aut* **taxed,** avec vignette; **(b)** (*put under strain*) mettre à l'épreuve; **to t. s.o.'s intellect/imagination,** éprouver l'intelligence/l'imagination de qn; **to t. s.o.'s patience to the limit,** pousser la patience de qn à bout; **(c) to t. s.o. with sth/with doing sth,** taxer *ou* accuser qn de qch/ d'avoir fait qch.
taxable ['tæksəbl] *adj* **(a)** (*revenu, terrain etc*) imposable; **to make sth t.,** imposer qch; **(b)** *Jur* **costs t. to s.o.,** frais *mpl* à la charge de qn.
taxation [tæk'seɪʃən] *n* (*imposing taxes*) imposition *f* (*sur la propriété*); (*charges*) charges fiscales, prélèvement fiscal; (*revenue*) revenu réalisé par les impôts; **the t. authorities,** l'administration fiscale, le fisc, les impôts *mpl*.
taxi¹ ['tæksɪ] *n* taxi *m*; **to go by t.,** aller en taxi; **t. driver,** chauffeur, -euse de taxi; **t. rank** *or esp Am* **stand,** station *f* de taxis.
taxi² *vi* (*pt & pp* **taxied**; *prp* **taxying**) *Av* (*of aircraft*) rouler au sol; **the plane taxied back to the terminal,** l'avion regagna le terminal en roulant.
taxicab ['tæksɪkæb] *n* taxi *m*.
taxidermist ['tæksɪdɜːmɪst] *n* taxidermiste *mf*, empailleur, -euse.
taxidermy ['tæksɪdɜːmɪ] *n* taxidermie *f*, naturalisation *f* des animaux.
taxiing ['tæksɪɪŋ] *n Av* roulement *m* (au sol).
taximeter ['tæksɪmiːtər] *n* taximètre *m*, compteur *m* (de taxi).
taxing ['tæksɪŋ] *adj* (*job, course*) ardu; **these long hours are very t.,** ces longues journées sont complètement éreintantes.
taxonomic [tæksə'nɒmɪk] *adj* taxonomique.
taxonomy [tæk'sɒnəmɪ] *n* taxonomie *f*.
taxpayer ['tækspeɪər] *n* contribuable *mf*.
TB [tiː'biː] *n Med abbr* **tuberculosis.**
T-bar ['tiːbɑːr] *n Ski* téléski *m*, tire-fesses *m* à deux places.
T-bone ['tiːbəʊn] *n Culin* **T-b. steak,** steak *m* d'aloyau.
tbs, tbsp *n Culin* (*abbr* **tablespoonful**) cuillerée *f* à soupe.
TCP® [tiːsiː'piː] *n* (*antiseptic*) ≈ Merchryl ® *m*.
TD [tiː'diː] *n Br Sch* (*abbr* **technical drawing**) dessin *m* technique.
tea [tiː] *n* **(a)** (*plant*) thé *m*; **t. plant,** arbre *m* à thé, théier *m*; **t. plantation,** plantation *f* de thé; **t. planter,** planteur *m* de thé; **t. rose,** rose *f* thé;
(b) (*leaves, drink*) thé *m*; **to drink t.,** boire *ou* prendre du thé; **a cup of t.,** une tasse de thé; **China t.,** thé de Chine; **black/green t.,** thé noir/vert; **t. bag,** sachet *m* de thé; **t. blending,** mélange *m* des thés; **t. break,** pause-thé *f*, = pause-café *f*; **t. chest,** caisse *f* à thé; **t. caddy,** boîte *f* à thé; **t. cosy,** couvre-théière *m*; **t. leaf,** feuille *f* de thé; *Br Sl* (*thief*) voleur *m*; **to read the t. leaves,** lire le marc de thé; **(used) tea leaves,** marc *m* de thé; **t. strainer,** passe-thé *m inv*;
(c) *esp Br* (*meal*) **(afternoon) t.,** thé *m*, = goûter *m*; **high t.,** repas *m* du soir; *Scot* **t.,** dîner *m*; **to ask s.o. to t.,** inviter qn à (venir) prendre le thé; **to give a t. party,** donner un thé; (*for children*) organiser un goûter d'enfants; **t. table,** table *f* à thé; **t. service** *or* **set,** service *m* à thé; *Br* **t. towel** *or* **cloth,** torchon *m*; **t. urn,** fontaine *f* à thé;
(d) (*infusion*) tisane *f*, infusion *f*; **mint t.,** infusion de menthe;
(e) *Old-fashioned Sl* marijuana *f*.
teacake ['tiːkeɪk] *n Culin* (genre *m* de) brioche plate.
teach¹ [tiːtʃ] *n Sl* (*teacher*) prof *mf*.
teach² *v* (*pt & pp* **taught** [tɔːt]) **1** *vt* enseigner (*qch*); **to t. s.o. sth,** enseigner *ou* apprendre qch à qn; **your Japanese is very good, who taught you?,** ton japonais est très bon, avec qui as-tu appris?; **I taught myself,** j'ai appris tout seul; **who taught you to drive!,** où as-tu appris à conduire!; **who taught you that trick?,** qui t'a appris *ou* enseigné ce tour?; **can you t. me the butterfly stroke?,** est-ce que tu peux m'apprendre la nage papillon?; **he teaches the young pupils,** il fait la classe *ou* l'école aux petits; **she teaches the piano,** elle est professeur de piano; **he teaches French,** il enseigne le français, il est professeur de français; **the way history is taught,** la manière dont on enseigne l'histoire; **to t. s.o. (how) to do sth,** apprendre à qn à faire qch; **to t. oneself sth,** apprendre qch tout seul; *F* **to t. s.o. a lesson,** donner une leçon à qn; *F* **that'll t. him!,** ça lui apprendra!; *F* **to t. s.o. a thing or two,** dégourdir qn; *F* **I'll t. you to speak to me like that!,** je vous apprendrai à me parler comme ça!
2 *vi* **to t.,** *Am* **to t. school,** enseigner; (*as profession*) être dans l'enseignement; **she has taught abroad,** elle a enseigné à l'étranger; **when you've been teaching for 25 years ...,** quand tu as passé 25 ans dans l'enseignement ...; **I normally t. all afternoon,** normalement j'enseigne tout l'après-midi.
teachable ['tiːtʃəb(ə)l] *adj* **(a)** (*person*) qui apprend facilement; **(b)** (*subject*) enseignable.
teacher ['tiːtʃər] *n* (*at primary school*) instituteur, -trice, maître, *f* maîtresse (*d'école*); (*at secondary school*) professeur *m*, enseignant, -ante; **history t.,** professeur d'histoire; **to become a t.,** entrer dans l'enseignement; **t. training,** formation *f* pédagogique; **to do one's t. training,** suivre une formation pédagogique; **to get one's t. training certificate,** obtenir son certificat d'aptitude pédagogique; **t. training college,** école normale.
teach-in ['tiːtʃɪn] *n* colloque *m*.
teaching ['tiːtʃɪŋ] *n* **(a)** enseignement *m*; **a low/high**

standard of maths/language t., un niveau élevé/bas dans l'enseignement des maths/des langues; to go into t., entrer dans l'enseignement; t. aids, matériel m ou équipement m pédagogique; Med t. hospital, centre hospitalier universitaire, CHU m; t. method, méthode f d'enseignement; the t. profession, (teachers) le corps enseignant; (activity) l'enseignement; the t. staff, les professeurs mpl, les instituteurs mpl (d'un lycée, d'une école); (b) (what is taught) enseignement m; leçons fpl; the teachings of experience, les leçons de l'expérience; (c) doctrine f; teachings, préceptes mpl.

teacup ['tiːkʌp] n tasse f à thé.

teacupful ['tiːkʌpful] n (measure) tasse f (of, de).

teak [tiːk] n (wood) teck m, tek m; (tree) tectona m.

teal [tiːl] n (pl usu teal) (duck) sarcelle f.

team¹ [tiːm] n (a) équipe f (de joueurs, d'ouvriers); football t., équipe de football; member of a t., t. member, one of the t., équipier m; t. games, jeux mpl d'équipe; the t. spirit, l'esprit m d'équipe; t. sports, sports mpl d'équipe; (b) attelage m (de chevaux, de bœufs).

team² vt & vi = TEAM UP.

►**team up** 1 vtsep to t. (up), associer (qch) (with, avec); mettre (qn) en collaboration (with, avec). 2 vi s'associer, entrer en collaboration; to t. up with s.o., se joindre à qn (pour faire qch).

team-mate ['tiːmmeɪt] n Sp coéquipier m.

teamster ['tiːmstər] n (a) conducteur m (d'attelage), charretier m; (b) US (trucker) camionneur m, routier m.

teamwork ['tiːmwɜːk] n (combined effort) travail m d'équipe; (ability to work together) collaboration f; Sp jeu m d'ensemble ou d'équipe; success due to t., réussite due à un travail d'équipe.

teapot ['tiːpɒt] n théière f.

tear¹ [tɪər] n (a) larme f; to shed bitter tears/tears of joy, verser des larmes amères/larmes de joie; on the verge of tears, au bord des larmes; to burst into tears, fondre en larmes; to bring tears to s.o.'s eyes, faire venir des larmes aux yeux de qn; in tears, (tout) en larmes; crocodile tears, larmes de crocodile; Anat t. duct, conduit lacrymal; t. gas, gaz m lacrymogène; t. (gas) bomb, bombe f lacrymogène; (b) (drop) larme (de résine etc).

tear² [teər] n (rip) déchirure f; (in cloth) accroc m.

tear³ v (pt tore [tɔːr]; pp torn [tɔːn]) 1 vt déchirer; I've torn my dress, j'ai déchiré ma robe; to t. sth in two or in half, déchirer qch en deux; to t. (sth) open, ouvrir (qch) en le déchirant; to t. s.o.'s character to shreds, déchirer qn à belles dents; to t. a hole in sth, faire un trou ou un accroc à qch; to t. a muscle, (of person) se déchirer un muscle; torn tendon, tendon déchiré; F that's torn it, il ne manquait plus que ça; country torn by civil war, pays déchiré par la guerre civile; torn between two feelings, tiraillé entre deux émotions; F to t. one's hair, s'arracher les cheveux. 2 vi (a) to t. at sth, déchirer ou arracher qch avec des doigts impatients; (b) material that tears easily, tissu qui se déchire facilement.

►**tear about, tear around** 1 vi (rush around) courir ou aller de tous les côtés. 2 vipo I've been tearing around the house all morning, j'ai couru dans tous les sens dans la maison toute la matinée; a sales rep spends most of his time tearing around the country, un représentant commercial passe la plupart de son temps à parcourir le pays dans tous les sens.

►**tear along** 1 vi (go fast) aller à toute vitesse ou à fond de train; (of horseman) aller à bride abattue. 2 vipo (a) (go fast on) he was tearing along the road, il dévorait la route; (b) t. along the dotted line, déchirer selon les pointillés.

►**tear away** 1 vtsep (remove by tearing) arracher (qch) (from, de). 2 vtas (leave reluctantly) to t. oneself away, se décider à partir; I couldn't t. myself away from the place, je ne pouvais pas m'arracher de ou à cet endroit; if you can t. yourself away from the television for five minutes, si tu peux te décider à quitter la télé cinq minutes. 3 vi F (leave at high speed) partir à toute vitesse; (of car) démarrer en trombe.

►**tear down** vtsep (take down forcefully) arracher (un poster etc); he tore down the poster from the wall, il a arraché l'affiche du mur; to t. down a wall/statue/etc, abattre un mur/une statue/etc.

►**tear into** vipo (a) (attack physically) attaquer, assaillir (qn); the lion tore into the deer's flesh, le lion déchira la chair du cerf; (b) (attack verbally) lapider (qn).

►**tear off** 1 vtsep (detach by tearing) arracher (qch) (from, de); F to t. s.o. off a strip, donner ou passer un savon à qn. 2 vi F = TEAR AWAY 3.

►**tear out** 1 vtsep (remove by tearing) arracher qch (from, de); to t. s.o.'s eyes out, arracher les yeux à qn; to t. a page out of a book, arracher une page d'un livre. 2 vi (leave at high speed) partir en trombe; she tore out of the house after them, elle sortit de la maison en trombe derrière eux.

►**tear up** 1 vtsep (a) (tear into small pieces) déchirer (une lettre etc); Fig she threatened to t. up her contract, elle a menacé de déchirer son contrat; (b) (pull up) to t. up a plant by the roots, déraciner une plante. 2 vipo F (go up fast) to t. up the stairs, monter l'escalier quatre à quatre.

tearaway ['teərəweɪ] F n casse-cou m.

teardrop ['tɪədrɒp] n larme f.

tearful ['tɪəful] adj tout en pleurs; in a t. voice, avec des larmes dans la voix; Pej d'un ton pleurnicheur.

tearfully ['tɪəfəlɪ] adv (crying) en pleurant; (on verge of tears) les larmes aux yeux.

tearing ['teərɪŋ] n déchirement m (d'un tissu etc); F to be in a t. hurry, être terriblement pressé.

tearjerker ['tɪədʒɜːkər] n F (film, play, book) mélo m.

tearless ['tɪəlɪs] adj t. eyes, yeux secs; t. grief, chagrin m sans larmes.

tear-off ['teərɒf] adj (label etc) perforé; t.-off calendar, calendrier m éphéméride.

tearoom ['tiːruːm] n salon m de thé.

tearstained ['tɪəsteɪnd] adj (visage) portant des traces de larmes, barbouillé de larmes.

tease¹ [tiːz] n taquin, -ine; he's a t., il est taquin.

tease² 1 vt (a) taquiner, tourmenter (qn); exciter (un chien etc); don't t. the cat, ne tourmente pas le chat; (b) effiler, effilocher (un tissu etc); démêler (de la laine); (c) = TEASEL². 2 vi être taquin, user de taquineries.

►**tease out** vtsep = TEASE² 1 (b).

teasel¹ ['tiːz(ə)l] n (a) (plant) cardère f; (b) Tex carde f.

teasel² vt (pt & pp teaseled) Tex lainer, chardonner.

teaser ['tiːzər] n (a) = TEASE¹; (b) F (problem) question f difficile, colle f; that really was a t.!, ça m'a donné du fil à retordre!

teashop ['tiːʃɒp] n salon m de thé.

teasing ['tiːzɪŋ] 1 adj (ton etc) railleur. 2 n (a) (provoking) taquinerie f; (b) effilage m, effilochage m (d'un tissu); démêlage m (de la laine).

teasing out n = TEASING 2 (b).

teasingly ['tiːzɪŋlɪ] adv (in a teasing tone) d'un ton railleur; (in order to tease) pour taquiner.

teaspoon ['tiːspuːn] n cuillère f ou cuiller f à café.

teaspoonful ['tiːspuːnful] n cuillerée f à café.

teat [tiːt] n mamelon m, bout m de sein (de femme); tette f, trayon m (de vache etc); tétine f (de biberon).

teatime ['tiːtaɪm] n l'heure f du thé.

teazel, teazle ['tiːz(ə)l] n & vt = TEASEL¹,².

Tech [tek] n Br F = technical college.

technical ['teknɪk(ə)l] adj (a) (terme, dictionnaire etc) technique; (difficulté) d'ordre technique; Br t. college, = école f d'enseignement technique; t. drawing, dessin m technique; t. hitch, incident m technique; (b) Jur t. offence, quasi-délit m, pl quasi-délits; Boxing t. knockout, victoire f sur un adversaire qui ne peut pas continuer.

technicality [teknɪ'kælɪtɪ] n (a) technicité f (d'un terme); (b) (detail) détail m technique; (technical term) terme m technique; Jur she was acquitted on a t., elle a été acquittée sur un point de droit.

technically ['teknɪklɪ] adv (a) techniquement; (s'exprimer) en termes techniques; (b) t. (speaking), du point de vue technique, techniquement parlant.

technician [tek'nɪʃən] n technicien, -ienne.

Technicolor ® ['teknɪkʌlər] adj & n Cin Technicolor m.

technique [tek'niːk] n technique f (d'un art, d'un artiste etc); his t. is poor, il manque de technique.

technocracy [tek'nɒkrəsɪ] n technocratie f.

technocrat ['teknəkræt] n technocrate mf.

technological [teknə'lɒdʒɪk(ə)l] adj technologique.

technologist [tek'nɒlədʒɪst] n technologue mf, technologiste mf.

technology [tek'nɒlədʒɪ] n technologie f; the police have all the lastest t., la police dispose de la technologie la plus avancée; t. transfer, transfert m de technologie.

techy ['tetʃɪ] adj = TETCHY.

tectonic [tek'tɒnɪk] adj tectonique.

tectonics [tek'tɒnɪks] n tectonique f.

ted [ted] vt (-dd-) Agr faner (le foin).

Ted [ted] n (a) = TEDDY (a); (b) F ≈ blouson noir.

tedder ['tedər] n Agr (machine) faneuse f.

tedding ['tedɪŋ] n fanage m; t. machine, faneuse f.

Teddy ['tedɪ] n (a) (dimin of Edward, Theodore) Edouard,

Théodore; **(b)** *F* **t. boy,** ≈ blouson noir; **(c) t. bear,** (*toy*) ours *m* en peluche.

tedious ['tiːdɪəs] *adj* (*work etc*) fatigant, pénible; (*speech etc*) ennuyeux, fastidieux.

tediously ['tiːdɪəslɪ] *adv* d'une manière ennuyeuse.

tediousness, tedium ['tiːdɪəsnɪs, -dɪəm] *n* ennui *m*; manque *m* d'intérêt (*d'un travail, de l'existence*).

tee¹ [tiː] *n Golf* **(a)** (*support for ball*) tee *m*; **(b)** (*piece of ground*) tertre *m ou* point *m* de départ.

tee² *vt Golf* mettre (*la balle*) sur un tee.

tee³ *n Sp* (*curling*) but *m*.

▶**tee off** *vi Golf* jouer sa balle (*du tertre de départ*).

▶**tee up** *vi Golf* placer la balle sur le tee.

teem [tiːm] *vi* **(a)** foisonner, fourmiller (**with,** de); (*with ideas*) abonder (**with,** en); **(b) the rain was teeming down,** la pluie tombait à verse; **it's teeming with rain,** il tombe des cordes.

teeming ['tiːmɪŋ] *adj* **(a)** grouillant; **(b) in the t. rain,** sous la pluie battante.

teen [tiːn] *adj F* = **TEENAGE**; **t. idol,** idole *f* des jeunes.

teenage ['tiːneɪdʒ] *adj* (*boy, girl etc*) adolescent, jeune.

teenager ['tiːneɪdʒər] *n* adolescent(e).

teens [tiːnz] *npl F* l'adolescence *f*; **to be in one's t.,** être adolescent(e); **to be hardly out of one's t.,** être à peine sorti de l'adolescence; avoir juste vingt ans.

teen(s)y(-ween(s)y) ['tiːn(z)ɪ('wiːn(z)ɪ)] *adj F* minuscule, tout petit; **just a t.(-w.) drop, please,** juste une toute petite goutte, s'il vous plaît.

teeny-bopper ['tiːnɪbɒpər] *n* minet, minette.

teeshirt ['tiːʃɜːt] *n* tee-shirt *m*, T-shirt *m*.

teeter¹ ['tiːtər] *n esp Am* (*seesaw*) bascule *f*, balançoire *f*.

teeter² *vi* (*be unsteady*) chanceler; *Fig* **to t. on the brink of ruin,** être à deux doigts de la ruine.

teethe [tiːð] *vi* (*used only in prp and progressive tenses*) faire ses (premières) dents.

teething ['tiːðɪŋ] *n* dentition *f*, poussée *f* dentaire; **t. ring,** anneau *m* de dentition; *Fig* **t. troubles,** difficultés initiales.

teetotal [tiː'təʊt(ə)l] *adj* (*person*) qui ne prend pas de boissons alcooliques, qui ne boit pas.

teetotalism [tiː'təʊtəlɪz(ə)m] *n* abstention *f* des boissons alcooliques.

teetotaller, *US* **teetotaler** [tiː'təʊt(ə)lər] *n* abstinent, -ente.

TEFL ['tef(ə)l] *n* (*abbr* **Teaching of English as a Foreign Language**) Enseignement *m* de l'Anglais Langue Étrangère; **TEFL course,** formation *f* en Anglais Langue Étrangère.

tegument ['tegjʊmənt] *n Biol* tégument *m*.

tel (*abbr* **telephone**) tél. .

telecast¹ ['telɪkɑːst] *n TV* émission *f* de télévision.

telecast² *vt* (*pt & pp* **telecast**) téléviser.

telecommunication [telɪkəmjuːnɪ'keɪʃən] *n* télécommunication *f*; **telecommunications engineer,** ingénieur *m* des télécommunications.

telecommute ['teləkəmjuːt] *vi* télétravailler.

telecommuter ['teləkəmjuːtər] *n* télétravailleur, -euse.

telecommuting ['teləkəmjuːtɪŋ] *n* télétravail *m*.

telefilm ['telɪfɪlm] *n* téléfilm *m*, film télévisé.

telegenic [telɪ'dʒenɪk] *adj* télégénique.

telegram ['telɪgræm] *n* télégramme *m*, dépêche *f* (télégraphique); **greetings t.,** télégramme de félicitations; **radio t.,** radiotélégramme *m*.

telegraph¹ ['telɪgrɑːf] *n* **(a)** télégraphe *m*; *F* **bush t.,** téléphone *m* arabe; **t. pole/wire,** poteau *m*/fil *m* télégraphique; **(b)** *Sp* **t. (board),** tableau *m* d'affichage (des résultats).

telegraph² **1** *vt* télégraphier (*une nouvelle*). **2** *vi* télégraphier.

telegrapher [tɪ'legrəfər] *n US* télégraphiste *mf*.

telegraphese [telɪgrə'fiːz] *n* langage *m ou* style *m* télégraphique.

telegraphic [telɪ'græfɪk] *adj* télégraphique.

telegraphically [telɪ'græfɪk(ə)lɪ] *adv* **(a)** télégraphiquement; **(b)** (*in telegraphic style*) en style télégraphique.

telegraphist [tɪ'legrəfɪst] *n* télégraphiste *mf*.

telegraphy [tɪ'legrəfɪ] *n* télégraphie *f*.

telekinesis [telɪkɪ'niːsɪs] *n* télékinésie *f*.

Telemessage ® ['telɪmesɪdʒ] *n Br* télégramme *m*.

telemeter¹ ['telɪmiːtər] *n* appareil *m* de télémesure; (*in surveying*) *& Mil etc* télémètre *m*.

telemeter² *vt* (*in surveying*) *& Mil etc* télémesurer.

teleological [telɪə'lɒdʒɪk(ə)l] *adj Phil* téléologique.

teleology [telɪ'ɒlədʒɪ] *n Phil* téléologie *f*.

telepathic [telɪ'pæθɪk] *adj* télépathique; (*personne*) télépathe; **you must be t.!,** tu dois avoir des dons de télépathie!; **tell me, I'm not t.!,** dis-le moi, je ne suis pas médium!

telepathically [telɪ'pæθɪklɪ] *adv* télépathiquement.

telepathy [tɪ'lepəθɪ] *n* télépathie *f*.

telephone¹ ['telɪfəʊn] *n* téléphone *m*; **t. subscriber,** abonné *m* du téléphone; **public t., coin-operated t.,** téléphone public; **t. box,** cabine *f* téléphonique; *Mil* **field t.,** téléphone de campagne; *Nau* **ship-to-shore t.,** téléphone bâtiment-terre; **t. line/network,** ligne *f*/réseau *m* téléphonique; **t. operator,** téléphoniste *mf*, standardiste *mf*; **t. directory** *or* **book,** annuaire *m* (du téléphone); **to be on the t.,** être abonné au téléphone; (*be speaking on it*) être au téléphone; **what's your t. number?,** quel est votre numéro de téléphone?; **to speak to s.o. on the t.,** parler à qn au téléphone; **come on, get off the t.!,** allez, raccroche!; **t. call,** appel *m* téléphonique; **you're wanted on the t.,** on vous demande au téléphone; **to have a good t. manner,** avoir un bon contact téléphonique.

telephone² **1** *vi* téléphoner (**to,** à); **to t. for a taxi,** appeler un taxi (par téléphone). **2** *vt* téléphoner (*un message*); téléphoner à (*qn*).

telephonic [telɪ'fɒnɪk] *adj* téléphonique.

telephonist [tɪ'lefənɪst] *n* téléphoniste *mf*.

telephony [tɪ'lefənɪ] *n* téléphonie *f*; **wireless t.,** téléphonie sans fil, radiotéléphonie *f*.

telephoto [telɪ'fəʊtəʊ] *adj* téléphotographique; **t. lens,** téléobjectif *m*.

telephotography [telɪfə'tɒgrəfɪ] *n* téléphotographie *f*.

teleprinter ['telɪprɪntər] *n* téléimprimeur *m*, téléscripteur *m*, télétype *m*; **t. operator,** télétypiste *mf*.

Teleprompter ® ['telɪprɒm(p)tər] *n TV* télésouffleur *m*.

telescope¹ ['telɪskəʊp] *n* **(reflecting) t.,** télescope *m* (à réflexion, à miroir); **(refracting) t.,** lunette *f* (d'approche), longue-vue *f*, *pl* longues-vues; *Astron* réfracteur *m*; **radio t.,** radiotélescope *m*.

telescope² **1** *vt* télescoper (*un train etc*). **2** *vi* (*of train etc*) (se) télescoper; **parts made to t.,** pièces qui s'emboîtent.

telescopic [telɪs'kɒpɪk] *adj* **(a)** télescopique; (*visible with telescope*) visible au télescope; *Phot* **t. lens,** téléobjectif *m*; **t. sight,** (*of firearm*) appareil *m* de visée à lunette, hausse *f* télescopique; **(b)** (*expanding*) télescopique; (*passerelle etc*) coulissant; **t. tripod,** trépied *m* télescopique; **t. ladder,** échelle *f* à coulisse; **t. umbrella,** parapluie *m* télescopique.

teletext ['telɪtekst] *n TV* téléaffichage *m*.

telethon ['telɪθɒn] *n TV* téléthon *m*.

teletype¹ ['telɪtaɪp] *n* télétype *m*, téléscripteur *m*; **t. operator,** télétypiste *mf*.

teletype² *vt* envoyer (*un message*) par télétype *ou* par téléscripteur.

teletypewriter [telɪ'taɪpraɪtər] *n US* = **TELEPRINTER**.

televiewer ['telɪvjʊər] *n* téléspectateur, -trice.

televise ['telɪvaɪz] *vt* téléviser; **televised programme,** programme télévisé *ou* télédiffusé.

television [telɪ'vɪʒən] *n* télévision *f*; **t. (set),** téléviseur *m*, (poste *m* de) télévision; **closed-circuit t.,** télévision à *ou* en circuit fermé; **colour t.,** télévision (en) couleur; **pay t.,** télévision à péage; **colour t. (set),** téléviseur couleur; **what's on t.?,** qu'est-ce qu'il y a à la télévision?; **have you been on t.?,** êtes-vous passé à la télévision?; **to watch t.,** regarder la télévision; **I saw it on t.,** je l'ai vu à la télévision; **from a t. point of view,** d'un point de vue télévisuel; **it makes/doesn't make good t.,** ça a/n'a pas un bon impact télévisuel; **t. camera,** caméra *f* de télévision; **it's my first time in front of the t. cameras,** c'est la première fois que je suis devant les caméras; **t. commentary,** téléreportage *m*; **t. film,** téléfilm *m*; **t. interview, interview on t.,** interview télévisée *ou* à la télévision; **t. personality,** personnalité *f* de la télévision; **t. play,** pièce *f* pour la télévision; **t. programme,** émission *f* de télévision, programme télévisé; **t. rights,** droits *mpl* de télédiffusion; **t. screen,** écran *m* de télévision; **t. studio,** studio *m* de télévision.

telex¹ ['teleks] *n* télex *m*; **to send by t.,** télexer (*qch*); **t. operator,** télexiste *mf*; **t. subscriber,** abonné *m* du télex.

telex² *vt* télexer (*un message*); **I'll t. you,** je vous enverrai un télex.

tell [tel] *v* (*pt & pp* **told** [təʊld]) **1** *vt* **(a)** dire; raconter (*une histoire etc*); annoncer, proclamer (*un fait etc*); révéler (*un secret*); **to t. the truth,** dire la vérité; **to t. a lie,** dire *ou* faire un mensonge; **to t. s.o. sth,** dire *ou* apprendre qch à qn; **I know — Dennis told me,** je sais — Dennis me l'a dit; **she doesn't t. me anything,** elle ne me dit *ou* raconte rien; **to t. s.o. a joke,** raconter une blague à qn; **to t. s.o. a lie,** dire *ou* raconter un mensonge à qn; **can you t. me**

the way to the station?, pouvez-vous m'indiquer le chemin de la gare?; **I can't t. you how pleased I am**, je ne saurais vous dire combien je suis content; **we are told that ...**, on nous informe *ou* dit que ...; **I told you no!**, je vous ai dit que non!; **it's just as I told you**, c'est tout comme je vous l'ai dit; **I told you so!, didn't I t. you!, what did I t. you!**, je vous l'avais bien dit!; **you're telling me!**, à qui le dites-vous?; **are you telling me (that) you spent £50 on THAT?**, est-ce que tu es en train de me dire que tu as payé 50 livres pour ça?; **t. me another!**, à d'autres!; *esp US F* **t. him goodbye (for me)!**, dites lui au revoir de ma part!; **I'll t. you what happened**, je vais vous raconter ce qui est arrivé; **t. me something about yourself**, parlez-moi un peu de vous(-même); *F* **to hear t. of ...**, entendre parler de ...; **to hear t. that ...**, entendre dire que ...; *F* **that would be telling!**, ça c'est mon secret!; *F* **to t. teacher**, rapporter; **to t. the time**, (*of clock*) marquer l'heure; **to t. s.o. the time**, (*of person*) dire l'heure qu'il est *ou* donner l'heure à qn; **to t. s.o. about s.o.**, parler de qn à qn; **she wrote to t. me of her father's death**, elle m'a écrit pour m'annoncer la mort de son père; **t. me what you know about it**, dites-moi ce que vous en savez; **let me t. you ...**, permettez-moi de vous dire ...; **it's not so easy, let me t. you!**, ce n'est pas si facile, je vous assure *ou* je vous le dis!;

(b) (*discern*) **to t. good from bad** *or* **right from wrong**, discerner le bien du mal; **you can hardly t. him from his brother**, c'est à peine si on peut le distinguer de son frère; **in the dark it was hard to t. friend from foe**, dans l'obscurité il était difficile de distinguer ses amis de ses ennemis; **one can t. him by his voice**, on le reconnaît à sa voix; **she can't t. the time**, elle ne sait pas lire l'heure; **one** *or F* **you can t. (that) she's lived abroad**, on voit bien qu'elle a vécu à l'étranger; **I can t. it from the look in your eyes**, je le lis dans vos yeux; **I could t. they were lying**, je voyais bien qu'ils mentaient; **we couldn't t. if he was angry or not**, nous ne pouvions pas dire s'il était en colère ou non; **nobody can t. what the future has in store for us**, on ne peut pas savoir ce que l'avenir nous réserve; **there's no telling what he might do!**, je ne sais pas comment il va réagir!;

(c) (*order etc*) **to t. s.o. to do sth**, dire à qn de faire qch; **you can't t. me what to do!**, tu n'as pas à me dire ce que je dois faire!; **t. him to come**, dites-lui de venir; **do as you are told**, faites comme on vous dit; **she'll do as she's told**, elle marchera;

(d) *Arch* compter, énumérer (*les voix*); *Rel* **to t. one's beads**, égrener son chapelet; **all told**, tout compris; somme toute; **I made £100 out of it all told**, tout compte fait j'en ai retiré 100 livres.

2 *vi* **(a) please don't t.**, ne dis rien, s'il te plaît; **time will t.**, qui vivra verra; **it's difficult** *or* **hard to t.**, c'est difficile à dire; **it's too early to tell**, il est trop tôt pour se prononcer; **who can t.?, there's no telling!**, qui sait?; **you never can t.**, on ne sait jamais; **it's a male — how can you t.?**, c'est un mâle — comment le sais-tu?; **more than words can t.**, plus qu'on ne saurait dire;

(b) (*have effect*) (*of drug etc*) produire son effet; (*of sleepless nights etc*) porter coup; **breeding will t.**, bon sang ne peut mentir; **it will t. against you**, cela vous nuira.

►**tell apart** *vtas* (*distinguish*) **I can't t. them apart**, je n'arrive pas à les distinguer l'un de l'autre *ou* à les différencier.

►**tell of** *vipo* (*indicate, reveal*) annoncer, accuser, révéler (*qch*); **rings under her eyes told of sleepless nights**, des cernes sous ses yeux révélaient des nuits blanches.

►**tell off 1** *vtas F* (*scold*) dire son fait à (*qn*); **he told them off in no uncertain terms**, il leur a dit leurs quatre vérités. **2** *vtsep Mil etc* (*assign*) désigner (*qn pour une corvée*).

►**tell on** *vipo* **(a)** (*affect badly*) **the heat is telling on him**, il commence à souffrir de la chaleur; **his age is beginning to t. on him**, il commence à accuser son âge; **(b)** *F* (*inform on*) rapporter sur le compte de (*qn*); **I'll t. on you!**, je le dirai!, tu seras dit!

teller ['telər] *n* **(a)** (*of story etc*) conteur, -euse, narrateur, -trice; **(b)** (*in bank etc*) guichetier, -ière (*de banque etc*); *Parl* scrutateur *m*.

telling ['telɪŋ] **1** *adj* **(a) t. blow**, coup bien asséné *ou* qui porte; **with t. effect**, avec un effet marqué; **(b)** (*revealing*) révélateur, -trice; **her remarks were very t.**, ses remarques étaient très révélatrices. **2** *n* narration *f* (*d'une histoire*); divulgation *f*, révélation *f* (*d'un secret etc*); *Arch* énumération *f* (*des votes etc*); **it loses nothing in the t.**, ça ne perd rien à être raconté.

telling off *n* réprimande *f*; **to give s.o. a t. off**, réprimander qn, faire une remontrance à qn.

telltale ['telteɪl] *n* (*person*) rapporteur, -euse, cafard, -arde; **t. sign**, signe révélateur.

tellurium [te'luərɪəm] *n Ch* tellure *m*.

telly ['telɪ] *n esp Br F* télé *f*.

telpher ['telfər] *n* **t. (line** *or* **railway)**, (ligne *f*) téléphérique *m*; **t. car** *or* **carrier**, télébenne *f*, télécabine *f*.

temerity [tɪ'merɪtɪ] *n* témérité *f*, audace *f*; **she had the t. to accuse me!**, elle a eu l'audace de m'accuser!

temp[1] [temp] *n F* (*temporary worker*) secrétaire *mf*; (*typist*) dactylo *mf* intérimaire; **to do t. work**, faire des intérims.

temp[2] *vi F* travailler comme intérimaire, faire des intérims (*surtout comme secrétaire*).

temp[3] *abbr* **temperature**.

temper[1] ['tempər] *n* **(a)** (*anger*) colère *f*, irritation *f*; (*bad mood*) mauvaise humeur; **in an outburst of t.**, dans un éclat d'humeur; **to be in a t.**, être en colère; **to put s.o. in a t.**, mettre qn en colère; *F* **t.!**, du calme!, on se calme!; **to keep one's t.**, rester calme, garder son sang-froid; **to lose one's t.**, se mettre en colère, s'emporter; **to be out of t.**, être de mauvaise humeur; **(b)** (*character*) caractère *m*, tempérament *m*; (*state of mind*) état *m* d'esprit; (*habitual*) **good t.**, placidité *f*; **fiery/even t.**, caractère fougueux/égal; **she's got (quite) a t.**, elle a un sacré caractère; **to be in a good/bad t.**, être de bonne/mauvaise humeur; **(c)** *Metal* coefficient *m* de dureté (*de l'acier*); trempe *f*; **soft t.**, trempe douce.

temper[2] *vt Tech* **(a)** donner la trempe à (*l'acier, une lame*); recuire, adoucir (*un métal*); délayer (*le mortier etc*); broyer (*les couleurs etc*); **(b)** (*moderate*) modérer, adoucir (*une action etc*); retenir, maîtriser (*son chagrin etc*); tempérer, modérer (*son ardeur etc*); **(c)** accorder (*un piano*) par tempérament.

tempera ['tempərə] *n Art* **to paint in t.**, peindre à tempera; **t. painting**, peinture *f* à tempera.

temperament ['temp(ə)rəmənt] *n* **(a)** (*character*) caractère *m*, tempérament *m*; (*moodiness*) caractère fantasque; (*excitability*) caractère émotif; *Arch* (*physical*) tempérament *m*, constitution *f*; **(b)** *Mus* tempérament *m*; **equal** *or* **even t.**, tempérament égal.

temperamental [temp(ə)rə'ment(ə)l] *adj* **(a)** (*difference etc*) du tempérament; **(b)** (*person*) (*excitable*) impétueux, fougueux; (*moody*) capricieux, fantasque; (*machine*) capricieux; (*player, runner*) inconstant.

temperamentally [temp(ə)rə'ment(ə)lɪ] *adv* naturellement, de nature; **they were t. unsuited**, (*of couple*) leurs caractères étaient incompatibles.

temperance ['temp(ə)rəns] *n* **(a)** (*moderation*) tempérance *f*, modération *f*, retenue *f* (*dans les plaisirs etc*); **(b)** (*abstinence from alcohol*) tempérance *f*, sobriété *f*; antialcoolisme *m*; **t. society**, ligue *f* antialcoolique.

temperate ['temp(ə)rət] *adj* **(a)** (*climate, zone etc*) tempéré; **(b)** (*language etc*) modéré, mesuré.

temperature ['temp(ə)rətʃər] *n* température *f*; **fall in t., t. drop**, chute *f* de température; **room t.**, température ambiante; **at room t.**, (*of wine*) chambré; **the t. was in the thirties**, le thermomètre marquait plus de trente degrés; *Med* **to take s.o.'s t.**, prendre la température de qn; **to have a raised t., to have** *or* **to run a t.**, avoir de la température *ou* de la fièvre; **he's got a t. of forty**, il a quarante de fièvre; **to judge the t. of a meeting**, prendre la température d'une réunion; **to raise/lower the political t.**, faire monter/faire baisser la température politique.

tempered ['tempəd] *adj* **(a)** (*acier*) trempé, recuit; **(b)** *Mus* **equally t. scale**, gamme tempérée.

-tempered [-tempəd] *suff* **to be bad-t.**, avoir un mauvais caractère; (*to be in a bad mood*) être de mauvaise humeur; **good-t.**, d'une humeur égale.

tempest ['tempɪst] *n Lit* tempête *f*, tourmente *f*.

tempestuous [tem'pestjuəs] *adj* **(a)** (*weather etc*) orageux; **(b)** (*meeting etc*) orageux, tempétueux; (*person, mood, relationship etc*) turbulent, agité, violent.

tempestuously [tem'pestjuəslɪ] *adv* (*see adj*) **(a)** orageusement; **(b)** violemment.

tempestuousness [tem'pestjuəsnɪs] *n* **(a)** violence *f* (*du temps*); **(b)** caractère orageux (*d'une réunion*); turbulence *f*, agitation *f* (*de la foule*).

Templar ['templər] *n Hist* **(Knight) T.**, Templier *m*, chevalier *m* du Temple.

template ['templɪt] *n* **(a)** (*metalworking*) & *Carp etc* gabarit *m*, calibre *m*, patron *m*; **(b)** *Constr* sablière *f*.

temple[1] ['temp(ə)l] *n* **(a)** temple *m* (*grec etc*); **(b)** *Hist* **the Knights of the T.**, les chevaliers *mpl* du Temple, les

Templiers *mpl*.
temple[2] *n Anat* tempe *f*; larmier *m* (*du cheval*).
templet ['templɪt] *n* = **TEMPLATE**.
tempo, *pl* **-i** ['tempəʊ, -iː] *n Mus* tempo *m*; *Fig* **strikes that upset the t. of production,** grèves qui perturbent le rythme de la production.
temporal[1] ['tempər(ə)l] *adj* **(a)** (*pouvoir etc*) temporel; **(b)** *Gram* (*argument etc*) temporel.
temporal[2] *adj Anat* (*os etc*) temporal, -aux.
temporarily ['temp(ə)rərɪlɪ, tempə'reərɪlɪ] *adv* temporairement, provisoirement; (*to work*) par intérim; (*for the present time*) momentanément, pour le moment.
temporary ['temp(ə)rərɪ] *adj* provisoire; (*office, entrance etc*) temporaire; (*hearing loss etc*) momentané, passager; **the improvement is only t.,** l'amélioration n'est que passagère *ou* momentanée; **t. appointment,** emploi *m* (à titre) temporaire; *Admin* emploi amovible; **on a t. basis,** provisoirement; (*to work*) par intérim; **to exercise t. command,** commander par intérim; *Jur* **t. injunction,** injonction *f* temporaire; **this will at least give you t. relief,** cela vous soulagera pour le moment.
temporize ['tempəraɪz] *vi* **(a)** temporiser, chercher à gagner du temps; **(b)** (*adapt to circumstances*) se plier aux circonstances.
tempt [tem(p)t] *vt* tenter; **to t. s.o. to do sth,** tenter qn pour lui faire faire qch; **to let oneself be tempted,** se laisser tenter, céder à la tentation; **I'm tempted to try,** je suis tenté *ou* j'ai envie d'essayer; **the fine weather tempts us to go out,** le beau temps nous invite à sortir; **to t. providence/fate,** tenter la providence/le sort; **don't t. me!,** arrête! je risque de me laisser tenter!
temptation [tem(p)'teɪʃən] *n* tentation *f*; **to throw t. in s.o.'s way,** exposer qn à la tentation; **to yield to t.,** succomber *ou* céder à la tentation; **there's a great t. to say that ...,** on est très tenté de dire que ... .
tempter ['tem(p)tər] *n* tentateur *m*.
tempting ['tem(p)tɪŋ] *adj* tentant, alléchant; (*offer*) séduisant, attrayant; (*meal*) appétissant.
temptingly ['tem(p)tɪŋlɪ] *adv* d'une manière tentante.
temptress ['tem(p)trɪs] *n* tentatrice *f*.
ten [ten] *num adj & n* dix *m*; **number t.,** le numéro dix; **some** *or* **about t. years ago,** il y a une dizaine d'années; **three tens are thirty,** trois fois dix font trente; **tens of thousands,** des dizaines de milliers; *Rugby* **t. metre line,** ligne *f* des dix mètres; **t. to one he'll find out,** je vous parie dix contre un qu'il le découvrira; **the top t.,** (*in record charts*) palmarès *m* des dix meilleurs.
tenable ['tenəb(ə)l] *adj* **(a)** (*position, forteresse*) tenable; (*théorie*) soutenable; **(b) appointment t. for three years,** poste auquel on est nommé pour trois ans.
tenacious [te'neɪʃəs] *adj* tenace; (*stubborn*) opiniâtre, obstiné; **t. memory,** mémoire sûre; **to be t. in** *or Fml* **of one's opinion,** (*of person*) s'obstiner dans *ou* tenir à son opinion; **to be t.,** s'opiniâtrer (*dans un projet etc*).
tenaciously [te'neɪʃəslɪ] *adv* avec ténacité; (*stubbornly*) obstinément.
tenaciousness, tenacity [te'neɪʃəsnɪs, -'næsɪtɪ] *n* ténacité *f*; sûreté *f* (*de la mémoire*); attachement *m* (*à ses idées*); (*obstinacy*) obstination *f*, opiniâtreté *f*.
tenancy ['tenənsɪ] *n* location *f*; **expiration of t.,** expiration *f* de bail, échéance *f* de location; **during my t.,** pendant la période de ma location; **to hold a life t. of a house,** jouir viagèrement d'une maison.
tenant[1] ['tenənt] *n* locataire *mf*; **t. in possession, sitting t.,** occupant(e); **t. farmer,** cultivateur *m* à bail.
tenant[2] *vt* habiter, occuper (*une maison etc*) comme locataire.
tenantry ['tenəntrɪ] *n no pl* locataires *mpl*; (*farmers*) fermiers *mpl* et tenanciers *mpl* (*d'un domaine*).
tench [tenʃ] *n* (*fish*) tanche *f*.
tend[1] [tend] *vt* soigner (*un malade etc*); surveiller (*une machine etc*); garder (*les moutons etc*); entretenir (*un jardin*); soigner (*le feu*).
tend[2] *vi* **(a)** tendre, se diriger, aller (**towards,** vers); **doctrine that tends towards socialism,** doctrine socialisante, doctrine qui penche vers le socialisme; **blue tending to green,** bleu tirant sur le vert; **examples that t. to undermine morality,** exemples qui tendent à ébranler les mœurs; **(b) to t. to do sth,** avoir tendance à *ou* être sujet à faire qch; **to t. to skid,** (*of car*) déraper facilement; **she tends to exaggerate,** elle a tendance à exagérer; **we t. to think of cats as ...,** nous avons tendance à penser aux chats comme ...; **some do, but I t. not to,** certains le font, mais moi plutôt pas.
tendency ['tendənsɪ] *n* tendance *f*, inclination *f*, disposition *f*, penchant *m* (**to,** à); **t. to drink,** penchant à la boisson; **to have a t. to (do) sth,** avoir (une) tendance à (faire) qch; **a growing t.,** une tendance de plus en plus marquée; *Fin* **tendencies of the market,** tendances du marché.
tendentious [ten'denʃəs] *adj* tendancieux.
tendentiously [ten'denʃəslɪ] *adv* tendancieusement.
tendentiousness [ten'denʃəsnɪs] *n* caractère tendancieux.
tender[1] ['tendər] *n* **(a)** *Nau* (*boat*) navire *m* annexe; (*for supplies*) ravitailleur *m*; *Rail* tender *m*; **(b)** (*person*) **bar t.,** barman *m*.
tender[2] *adj* **(a)** (*soft*) tendre; *Culin* **t. meat,** viande *f* tendre; **to make meat t.,** attendrir la viande; **(b)** (*sensitive*) tendre, sensible; **t. conscience,** conscience délicate *ou* susceptible; **t. to the touch,** sensible *ou* douloureux au toucher; **t. heart,** cœur *m* tendre *ou* sensible; **to touch s.o. on a t. spot,** toucher qn à un endroit sensible; *Fig* toucher à un point sensible chez qn; **(c)** (*plant etc*) délicat, fragile; **child of t. years,** enfant en bas âge; **t. youth,** la tendre *ou* verte jeunesse; **(d)** (*light etc*) tendre, doux, *f* douce; **the t. green of the first leaves,** le vert tendre des premières feuilles; **(e)** (*person, sentiment etc*) tendre, affectueux; **t. look,** regard doux *ou* tendre.
tender[3] *n* **(a)** *Com* soumission *f*, offre *f*; **to invite tenders for a piece of work, to put a piece of work out to t.,** mettre un travail en adjudication; **to make** *or* **put in a t. for sth,** soumissionner *ou* faire une soumission pour qch; **a call for t.,** un appel d'offres; **by t.,** par voie d'adjudication; **t. documents,** documents *mpl* d'appel d'offres; **t. price,** prix *m* d'offre; **(b)** *Jur* **t. of payment,** offre *f* de paiement; **(c)** *Jur Com* **legal t.,** cours légal, monnaie *f* libératoire; **to be legal t.,** (*of money*) avoir cours, avoir force libératoire.
tender[4] **1** *vt* offrir (*ses services, une somme etc*); **to t. one's resignation,** présenter sa démission; **to t. one's apologies,** faire *ou* présenter ses excuses; *Jur* **to t. money in discharge of debt,** faire une offre réelle; *Jur* **to t. an oath to s.o.,** déférer le serment à qn. **2** *vi Com* **to t. for sth,** soumissionner (pour) qch, faire une soumission pour qch; **to t. for a contract,** soumissionner à une adjudication.
tenderfoot, *pl* **-foots, -feet** ['tendəfʊt(s), -fiːt] *n esp Am* nouveau venu (*dans un lieu sauvage*).
tenderhearted [tendə'hɑːtɪd] *adj* au cœur tendre *ou* sensible; **to be too t.,** avoir trop de cœur.
tenderheartedness [tendə'hɑːtɪdnɪs] *n* (*compassion*) compassion *f*; (*sensitivity*) sensibilité *f*.
tenderize ['tendəraɪz] *vt Culin* attendrir (*la viande*).
tenderizer ['tendəraɪzər] *n* attendrisseur *m*.
tenderloin ['tendəlɔɪn] *n Culin* filet *m* (*de bœuf etc*).
tenderly ['tendəlɪ] *adv* **(a)** (*to touch, hold sth*) doucement, délicatement; **(b)** (*to look at, feel*) tendrement, avec tendresse.
tenderness ['tendənɪs] *n* **(a)** tendreté *f* (*de la viande*); **(b)** délicatesse *f*, fragilité *f* (*d'une plante*); délicatesse (*de conscience*); **(c)** douceur *f* (*de la lumière etc*); **(d)** (*affection*) tendresse *f*, affection *f* (**for,** pour).
tendon ['tendən] *n Anat* tendon *m*.
tendril ['tendrɪl] *n Bot* vrille *f*, cirre *m*.
tenement ['tenɪmənt] *n* **(a) t. (house),** immeuble *m* d'habitation; **(b)** *Jur* fonds *m* de terre.
tenet ['tenet, 'tiː-] *n* (*dogma*) doctrine *f*, dogme *m*; (*opinion*) opinion *f*; (*belief*) croyance *f*.
tenfold ['tenfəʊld] **1** *adj* décuple. **2** *adv* au décuple; **to increase t.,** décupler.
Tenn *abbr* **Tennessee**.
tenner ['tenər] *n F Br* (*ten pound note*) billet *m* de dix livres; *US* (*ten-dollar bill*) billet de dix dollars; **it cost a t.,** ça a coûté dix livres *ou US* dix dollars.
tennis ['tenɪs] *n Sp* **(lawn) t.,** (lawn-)tennis *m*; **to play t.,** jouer au tennis; **table t.,** tennis de table; **deck t.,** deck-tennis *m*; **(real** *or* **royal** *or US* **court) t.,** (jeu *m* de) paume *f*; **t. ball,** balle *f* de tennis; **t. club,** club *m* de tennis; **t. court,** court *m* de tennis; (*in real tennis*) jeu de paume; *Med* **t. elbow,** synovite *f* du coude; **t. player,** joueur, -euse de tennis.
tenon ['tenən] *n Carp* tenon *m*; **t. saw,** tenonneuse *f*.
tenor ['tenər] *n* **(a)** *Mus* (*voice, singer*) ténor *m*; **t. clef,** clé *f* d'ut quatrième ligne; **t. sax(ophone),** saxo(phone *m*) *m* ténor, ténor; **t. voice,** voix *f* de ténor; **(b)** contenu *m*, sens général (*d'une lettre etc*); *Jur* copie *f* conforme.
tenpence ['tenpəns, -pens] *n Br* (pièce *f* de) dix pence *m*.
tenpenny ['tenpənɪ] *adj Br* de *ou* à dix pence; **t. stamp,** timbre *m* de dix pence.
tenpin ['tenpɪn] *n* quille *f*; **tenpins, t. bowling,** jeu *m* de quilles; (*in bowling alley*) bowling *m*.
tense[1] [tens] *n Gram* temps *m*; **verb in the present/the**

future t., verbe au (temps) présent/futur.

tense² *adj* **(a)** (*nerves, situation etc*) tendu; **t. moment,** moment *m* de forte tension; **t. silence,** silence tendu; **t. voice,** voix étranglée (par l'émotion); **to be t.,** (*of person*) être contracté *ou* tendu; **the situation is getting rather t.,** la situation commence à être plutôt tendue; **(b)** (*cord etc*) tendu, raide.

tense³ 1 *vt* tendre. **2** *vi* **to t. up,** se raidir.

►**tense up** *vtsep & vi* = **TENSE³**.

tensely ['tenslɪ] *adv* (*see adj*) **(a)** (avec) les nerfs tendus *ou* l'esprit tendu; **we watched t. as ...,** nous avons regardé, très tendus, tandis que ...; **(b)** raidement.

tenseness ['tensnɪs] *n* **(a)** tension *f* (*des nerfs, d'une situation etc*); **(b)** (*stiffness*) rigidité *f*; (état *m* de) tension *f* (*des muscles etc*).

tensile ['tensaɪl] *adj* **(a)** extensible, élastique; (*metal*) ductile; **(b)** (*effort, force*) de traction; **t. strength,** limite *f* d'élasticité.

tension ['tenʃən] *n* **(a)** tension *f* (*de l'esprit, des nerfs, dans région etc*); **(b)** tension *f* (*d'une corde etc*); *Phys* tension, force *f* élastique (*d'un fluide*); pression *f* (*de la vapeur*); *El* tension, voltage *m*; **muscular t.,** tension musculaire; **cable under t.,** câble sous tension; **(c)** (force *f* de) traction *f*; tension *f* (*d'un ressort*); **to be in t.,** être en traction; **(d)** (*of sewing machine etc*) tendeur *m*.

tent [tent] *n* tente *f*; **bell t.,** tente conique; **oxygen t.,** tente à oxygène; **to pitch/strike tents,** monter/démonter les tentes; **t. peg,** piquet *m* de tente; **t. pole,** mât *m* de tente.

tentacle ['tentək(ə)l] *n Biol & Fig* tentacule *m*.

tentative ['tentətɪv] **1** *adj* d'essai; (*hesitant*) hésitant; (*conclusion*) provisoire; **t. move,** démarche expérimentale; **t. offer,** offre *f* préliminaire *ou* d'essai; **it was just a t. suggestion,** ce n'était qu'une suggestion.

tentatively ['tentətɪvlɪ] *adv* à titre d'essai; (*hesitantly*) avec hésitation; provisoirement.

tenterhook ['tentəhʊk] *n* **to be on tenterhooks,** être au supplice *ou* sur le gril *ou* sur des charbons ardents; **to keep s.o. on tenterhooks,** faire languir qn, mettre qn sur des charbons ardents.

tenth [tenθ] **1** *num adj & n* dixième *mf*; **in the t. place,** (*in grading*) en dixième position; (*in enumeration*) dixièmement. **2** *n* **(a)** (*fraction*) dixième *m*; **(b)** *Mus* (intervalle *m* de) dixième *f*.

tenthly ['tenθlɪ] *adv* (*in enumeration*) dixièmement; (*in grading*) en dixième position.

tenting ['tentɪŋ] *n* toile *f* à tentes.

tenuity [te'njuːɪtɪ] *n* (*of argument, link etc*) ténuité *f*; (*of material*) finesse *f*.

tenuous ['tenjʊəs] *adj* (*argument, link etc*) ténu; (*of material*) très fin.

tenure ['tenjər] *n* **(a)** *Hist Jur* (*of property*) tenure *f*; **system of land t.,** régime foncier; **(b)** *Jur* (période *f* de) jouissance *f ou* (d')occupation *f* (*d'un office, d'une propriété etc*); **during his t. of office,** pendant qu'il exerçait ses fonctions.

tepee ['tiːpiː] *n* tipi *m*, wigwam *m*.

tepid ['tepɪd] *adj* (*water etc*) tiède; (*feeling, welcome etc*) tiède, qui manque d'ardeur.

tepidness ['tepɪdnɪs] *n* tiédeur *f*.

tercentenary [tɜːsen'tiːnərɪ], **tercentennial** [tɜːsen'tenɪəl] *adj & n* tricentenaire *m*.

tercet ['tɜːsɪt] *n* (*in prosody*) tercet *m*.

term¹ [tɜːm] *n* **(a)** (*word, expression*) terme *m*, expression *f*; **technical/scientific t.,** terme *ou* expression technique/scientifique; **he spoke of him in the most flattering terms,** il a parlé de lui en des termes les plus flatteurs; **I told her in no uncertain terms,** je le lui ai dit carrément *ou* sans mâcher mes mots;

(b) (*relations*) **friendly terms,** relations amicales; **to be on good/bad terms with s.o.,** être bien/mal *ou* être en bonne/mauvaise intelligence avec qn; **to be on the best of terms with s.o.,** être au mieux avec qn, être dans les meilleurs termes avec qn; **to come to terms with sth,** accepter qch, se faire à qch;

(c) (*logic*) & *Math* terme *m*; **to express one quantity in terms of another,** exprimer une quantité en fonction d'une autre; **in terms of financial risk,** en ce qui concerne les risques financiers; **in terms of salary/pollution/*etc*,** en termes de salaire/de pollution/*etc*; **in financial terms,** financièrement parlant, en matière de finance; **terms of a problem,** énoncé *m* d'un problème;

(d) *Com etc* **terms,** (*conditions*) conditions *fpl;* clauses *fpl*, termes *mpl* (*d'un contrat*); *Fin* **terms and conditions of an issue,** modalités *fpl* d'une émission; **on these terms I accept,** à ces conditions j'accepte; **make** *or* **name your own terms,** fixez vos conditions; **under the terms of the clause,** sous le bénéfice de la clause; **to dictate terms,** imposer des conditions; **to come to** *or* **make terms,** s'arranger, s'accorder, prendre un arrangement (**with,** avec); **terms of reference,** attributions *fpl*, mandat *m* (*d'une commission etc*); **terms of payment,** conditions de paiement; **terms strictly cash,** payable au comptant; **weekly terms,** (*in hotel etc*) pension *f* par semaine; **on easy terms,** avec facilités de paiement; **not on any terms,** à aucun prix;

(e) (*period*) terme *m*, période *f*, durée *f*; *Sch* trimestre *m*; *Jur* session *f*; **to serve a t. of five years (in prison),** faire cinq ans de prison; **during her t. of office,** pendant qu'elle exerçait ses fonctions; *Com* **long-/short-t. transaction,** opération *f* à long/court terme; **a long-t. policy,** une politique à longue échéance; **in the long t.,** à la longue; **in the short t.,** dans l'immédiat; *Jur Scot* **t. day,** (jour *m de*) terme; *Sch* **in t. time, during t.,** pendant le trimestre; *Sch* **half t. (holiday),** congé *m* de mi-trimestre; *US* **t. paper,** dissertation trimestrielle;

(f) (*limit*) terme *m*, fin *f*, limite *f*; *Com* (terme d')échéance *f* (*d'une lettre de change*); **to set** *or* **put a t. to sth,** fixer une limite à qch; **to have reached (full) t.,** (*of pregnancy*) être à terme.

term² *vt* designer, appeler; **that is what I would t. a stupid answer,** voilà ce que j'appelle une sotte réponse.

termagant ['tɜːməgənt] *n* mégère *f*, virago *f*.

terminal ['tɜːmɪn(ə)l] **1** *adj* **(a)** (*line, mark*) qui borne, qui termine (*une région etc*); **(b)** *Bot* terminal, -aux; *Rail etc* (*gare etc*) terminus, de tête de ligne; (*word, market etc*) final, -als, dernier; *Med* (*maladie*) en phase terminale; **I'm afraid it's t.,** je crains que vous ne soyez *ou* qu'il ne soit condamné; **t. bonus,** (*in insurance*) = bonus versé au titulaire d'une assurance-vie au terme de celle-ci; **t. case,** malade *mf ou* cas *m* condamné(e); *Rail* **t. point,** terminus *m*; *Geol* **t. moraine,** moraine frontale; **(c)** *Sch etc* trimestriel. **2** *n* **(a)** *El* borne *f* (*de prise de courant*); borne d'attache, cosse *f* (*d'un conducteur*); tête *f*, extrémité *f* (*de câble*); **t. voltage,** tension *f* aux bornes; **(b)** *Am Rail etc* terminus *m*, gare *f* terminus; *Av* **air t.,** aérogare *f* (terminale); **(c)** *Comptr* (poste *m*) terminal *m*; **(d)** *Gram* terminaison *f*.

terminally ['tɜːmɪn(ə)lɪ] *adv Med* **to be t. ill,** être en phase terminale; **the t. ill,** (*used as pl*) les malades incurables *ou* condamnés.

terminate ['tɜːmɪneɪt] **1** *vt* terminer, mettre un terme à; (*of boundary line etc*) délimiter (*une région etc*); résilier (*un contrat etc*); mettre fin *ou* un terme à (*un engagement etc*); **to have one's pregnancy terminated,** se faire avorter. **2** *vi* (*of word etc*) se terminer, finir (**in,** en, par); (*of line etc*) se terminer, aboutir (**in, at,** à); (*of train*) avoir son terminus (**at,** à) **this train is terminating here,** ce train s'arrête ici.

termination [tɜːmɪ'neɪʃən] *n* **(a)** fin *f*, conclusion *f* (*d'un procès etc*); cessation *f* (*de relations, d'affaires etc*); *Jur* résolution *f*, résiliation *f* (*d'une obligation etc*); **t. of pregnancy,** avortement provoqué; **(b)** *Gram* terminaison *f*, désinence *f*.

terminological [tɜːmɪnə'lɒdʒɪk(ə)l] *adj* terminologique.

terminologist [tɜːmɪ'nɒlədʒɪst] *n* terminologue *mf*.

terminology [tɜːmɪ'nɒlədʒɪ] *n* terminologie *f*.

terminus, *pl* **-i, -uses** ['tɜːmɪnəs, -aɪ, -əsɪz] *n Rail etc* (gare *f*) terminus *m*, (gare de) tête *f* de ligne.

termite ['tɜːmaɪt] *n* (*insect*) termite *m*.

tern [tɜːn] *n* (*bird*) sterne *f*; **arctic t.,** sterne arctique.

ternary ['tɜːnərɪ] *adj Ch Math etc* ternaire.

terra firma ['terə'fɜːmə] *n* terre *f* ferme, *F* le plancher des vaches; **to be back on t. f. again,** être de retour sur le plancher des vaches; *Fig* (*in known area etc*) se retrouver en terrain connu.

terrace¹ ['terɪs] *n* **(a)** *Constr Geol Agr* terrasse *f*; *Fb etc* **the terraces,** les gradins *mpl*; **(b)** *Br* **t. (of houses),** rangée *f* de maisons (attenantes).

terrace² *vt* disposer (*un jardin etc*) en terrasse(s); terrasser (*un flanc de colline etc*).

terraced ['terɪst] *adj* **(a)** (*jardin*) en terrasse; **t. hillsides,** collines cultivées en terrasses; **(b)** *Br* **t. houses,** rangée *f* de maisons (attenantes).

terracotta ['terə'kɒtə] *n* terre cuite, terra-cotta *f*; *Art* **a t.,** une terre cuite.

terrain [tə'reɪn] *n Mil Geog* terrain *m*.

terrapin ['terəpɪn] *n* (*reptile*) tortue *f* d'eau douce.

terrarium, *pl* **-ia, -iums** [te'reərɪəm, -ɪə, -ɪəmz] *n* terrarium *m*.

terrestrial [tɪ'restrɪəl] **1** *adj* (*globe, plant etc*) terrestre;

(*life etc*) terrestre. **2** *n* (*inhabitant of the Earth*) terrien, -ienne.

terrible ['terɪb(ə)l] *adj* terrible; (*accident, crime, shock*) affreux, épouvantable; *F* (*film, teacher etc*) nul, lamentable; (*coffee etc*) horrible, atroce; **he's a t. talker,** (*talks a lot*) c'est un terrible bavard; **I'm t. at maths,** je suis nul en math; **going without a meal isn't so t.,** ce n'est pas si terrible que de sauter un repas.

terribly ['terɪblɪ] *adv* **(a)** terriblement, affreusement, atrocement; **(b)** *F* (*very*) **t. busy,** terriblement occupé; **t. worried,** terriblement *ou* affreusement inquiet; **t. important,** de la dernière importance; **that's t. kind of you,** vous êtes vraiment trop aimable; **not t. interesting,** pas excessivement intéressant; **are you interested? — not t.,** ça vous intéresse? — pas terriblement *ou* excessivement.

terrier ['terɪər] *n* **(a)** (*dog*) (chien *m*) terrier *m*; **bull t.,** bull-terrier *m*, *pl* bull-terriers; **(b)** *Br Mil F* = **TERRITORIAL 2.**

terrific [tə'rɪfɪk] *adj* **(a)** *F* (*excellent*) terrible; (*enormous*) énorme; **t.!,** magnifique!, splendide!; **a t. noise,** un bruit énorme; **t. pace,** allure vertigineuse; **(b)** (*terrifying*) terrifiant, épouvantable;

terrifically [tə'rɪfɪklɪ] *adv* **(a)** *F* **it was t. hot,** il faisait terriblement chaud; **(b)** (*terrifyingly*) d'une manière terrifiante.

terrified ['terɪfaɪd] *adj* (*look, person*) terrifié; **to be t. of s.o.,** avoir une peur bleue de qn; **they're t. of losing their jobs,** ils tremblent à l'idée de perdre leurs emplois; **to be t. (that),** être terrifié *ou* mort de peur (à l'idée que + *sub*).

terrify ['terɪfaɪ] *vt* terrifier, effrayer, affoler (*qn*), frapper (*qn*) de terreur; **this remark terrified me,** cette remarque m'a terrifié; **it terrifies me what he'll do next,** je suis terrifié à la pensée de ce qu'il pourrait faire.

terrifying ['terɪfaɪɪŋ] *adj* terrifiant, terrible, épouvantable.

terrifyingly ['terɪfaɪɪŋlɪ] *adv* (*close*) épouvantablement; (*to scream*) d'une manière terrifiante.

terrine [te'riːn] *n* terrine *f*.

territorial [terɪ'tɔːrɪəl] **1** *adj* (*possessions, tax, claim etc*) territorial, -aux; **the T. Army,** l'armée territoriale, la territoriale; **t. waters,** eaux territoriales; **the male deer then becomes very t.,** le cerf commence alors à beaucoup protéger son territore. **2** *n Mil* territorial *m*.

territoriality [terɪtɔːrɪ'ælɪtɪ] *n* territorialité *f*.

territory ['terɪt(ə)rɪ] *n* territoire *m* (*d'un état, d'un animal & Fig*); région assignée (*à un représentant*); **the Northern T.,** le Territoire du Nord (*de l'Australie*).

terror ['terər] *n* **(a)** terreur *f*, effroi *m*, épouvante *f*; **a look of t.,** un regard épouvanté; **to be in (a state of) t.,** être terrorisé *ou* dans la terreur; **to be in t. of one's life,** craindre pour sa vie; **to go in t. of s.o.,** avoir une peur bleue de qn; *F* **to have a holy t. of sth,** craindre qch comme la peste; **a reign of t.,** un régime de terreur; *Fr Hist* **the T.,** la Terreur; **t. campaign, campaign of t.,** campagne *f* de terreur; **(b) he was the t. of the countryside,** c'était la terreur du pays; *F* **she's a little** *or* **a holy t.,** c'est un enfant terrible *ou* un petit diable; **he's a t. for being late,** il est terrible à être toujours en retard.

terrorism ['terərɪz(ə)m] *n* terrorisme *m*.

terrorist ['terərɪst] *n* terroriste *mf*; **there have been several t. attacks,** les terroristes ont effectué plusieurs attaques; **t. bombing,** attentat *m* à la bombe.

terrorize ['terəraɪz] *vt* terroriser.

terror-stricken, terror-struck ['terəstrɪk(ə)n, -strʌk] *adj* saisi de terreur, sous le coup de la terreur.

terry ['terɪ] *adj & n Tex* **t. towelling,** tissu *m* éponge; **t. towel,** serviette *f* éponge.

terse [tɜːs] *adj* (*concise*) concis, net; (*abrupt*) abrupt, brusque.

tersely ['tɜːslɪ] *adv* (*see adj*) d'une façon concise, avec concision; (*abruptly*) abruptement, brusquement.

terseness ['tɜːsnɪs] *n* concision *f* (*du style, du langage*); netteté *f* (*de style*); (*brusqueness*) brusquerie *f*.

tertiary ['tɜːʃərɪ] *adj & n* tertiaire *m*; **t. education,** enseignement *m* du troisième cycle.

Terylene ® ['terɪliːn] *n Tex* térylène *m*; **T. skirt,** jupe en térylène.

TESL ['tes(ə)l] *n* (*abbr* **Teaching English as a Second Language**) Enseignement *m* de l'Anglais Langue Étrangère.

tessellated ['tesɪleɪtɪd] *adj Constr* en mosaïque.

tessellation [tesɪ'leɪʃən] *n* mosaïque *f*.

test¹ [test] *n* **(a)** épreuve *f*; (*esp scientific*) test *m*; **to put sth to the t.,** mettre qch à l'épreuve *ou* à l'essai, éprouver qch; **to undergo a t.,** subir une épreuve; **to pass** *or* **stand the t.,** soutenir *ou* supporter l'épreuve; **method that has stood the t. of time,** méthode éprouvée; **it was a t. of our friendship,** ça a mis notre amitié à l'épreuve; **endurance t.,** épreuve d'endurance; **field t.,** essai *m* sur le terrain; *Aut etc* **road t.,** essai sur route; *Nucl Phys* **nuclear t.,** test nucléaire; **Wassermann t.,** réaction *f* de Wassermann; **t. ban,** prohibition *f* des essais nucléaires; **t. ban treaty,** traité *m* de prohibition des essais nucléaires; *Jur* **t. case,** affaire *f* qui fait jurisprudence; **t. drive** *or* **run,** course *f* d'essai; **to take a car for a t. drive,** prendre une voiture pour l'essayer *ou* en faire l'essai; *Av* **t. flight,** vol *m* d'essai; *Ch etc* **t. paper,** papier réactif; *TV* **t. pattern, t. card,** mire *f*; *Av* **t. pilot,** pilote *m* d'essai; *Comptr* **t. run,** essai de programme, passage *m* d'essai; **t. tube,** éprouvette *f*, tube *m* à essai;

(b) (*examination*) examen *m*; **eye t.,** examen des yeux; *Med etc* **blood t.,** examen du sang, *F* prise *f* de sang; *Aut* **driving t.,** (examen du) permis *m* de conduire; **hearing t.,** examen de l'ouïe; *Sch* **French/Maths t.,** examen *ou* interrogation *f* de français/math; **oral t.,** épreuve orale; *Cin etc* **screen t.,** bout *m* d'essai; *Br Sch* **t. paper,** (*questions*) libellé *m* d'examen; (*answers*) copie *f*; *Mus* **t. piece,** morceau imposé (*dans un concours etc*);

(c) *Cr Rugby* **t. (match),** match international.

test² **1** *vt* **(a)** éprouver (*qn, qch*), mettre (*qn, qch*) à l'épreuve *ou* à l'essai; essayer (*un ciment, une machine etc*); contrôler, vérifier (*des poids et mesures etc*); examiner (*la vue de qn etc*); expérimenter (*un procédé*); sonder (*une poutre etc*); analyser (*l'eau etc*); *Med* **to t. s.o. for Aids,** faire les examens *ou* les tests du sida à qn; **to t. an athlete for steroids,** contrôler un athlète en vue d'un dépistage de stéroïdes; **to t. a drug on s.o./animals,** expérimenter un médicament sur qn/des animaux; **(b)** *Sch* **to t. a class in algebra,** examiner une classe en algèbre; **(c)** coupeller (*l'or*); *Ch* déterminer la nature (*d'un corps*) au moyen d'un réactif. **2** *vi* (*of scientist etc*) expérimenter; **one, two, testing,** (*when testing microphone*) un, deux, essai; **to t. for alkaloids,** faire la réaction des alcaloïdes.

▶**test out** *vtsep* (*person, idea etc*) mettre à l'épreuve; **to t. out a scheme,** essayer un projet.

testament ['testəmənt] *n* **(a) to make one's (last will and) t.,** tester, faire son testament; **(b)** *Bible* **the Old/the New T.,** l'Ancien/le Nouveau Testament.

testamentary [testə'ment(ə)rɪ] *adj* testamentaire; **t. capacity,** habilité *f* à tester.

testate ['testeɪt] **1** *adj Jur* (*personne*) qui a testé, qui est mort en laissant un testament valable. **2** *n Jur* personne qui a testé *ou* qui est morte en laissant un testament valable.

testator, *f* **testatrix,** *pl* **-trices, -trixes** [tes'teɪtər, -'teɪtrɪks, -trɪsiːz, -trɪksɪz] *n* testateur, -trice.

test-bed ['testbed] *n* banc *m* d'essai.

test-drive ['testdraɪv] *vt Aut* faire l'essai de (*une voiture*).

tester¹ ['testər] *n* **(a)** (*person*) contrôleur, -euse; (*device*) appareil *m* de contrôle; **battery t.,** appareil de contrôle de piles *ou* (*car battery*) de batterie; **(b)** (*sample*) échantillon *m* (*de cosmétique*).

tester² *n* (*canopy*) baldaquin *m*, ciel *m* (*de lit*).

testicle ['testɪk(ə)l] *n Anat* testicule *m*.

testify ['testɪfaɪ] **1** *vi Jur* témoigner, rendre témoignage; **to t. in s.o.'s favour,** rendre témoignage en faveur de qn; **to t. against s.o.,** déposer contre qn; **to t. to a fact,** (*of things*) témoigner d'un fait; (*of person*) attester *ou* affirmer un fait, témoigner d'un fait. **2** *vt* **(a)** témoigner (*son regret, sa foi etc*); **(b)** *Jur* déclarer, affirmer (*qch*) (*sous serment*).

testily ['testɪlɪ] *adv* d'un air irrité, avec humeur.

testimonial [testɪ'məʊnɪəl] *n* **(a)** (*character reference*) certificat *m* (*délivré par une maison, un chef*); (*letter of recommendation*) (lettre *f* de) recommandation *f*; (*affirmation*) attestation *f*; **(b)** (*tribute*) témoignage *m* d'estime (*offert en reconnaissance de services*).

testimony ['testɪmənɪ] *n* témoignage *m* (*des sens etc*); *Jur* attestation *f*; déposition *f* (*d'un témoin*); **to bear t. to sth,** témoigner de qch, rendre témoignage de qch; **in t. whereof,** en foi de quoi.

testing ['testɪŋ] **1** *adj* (*problème etc*) difficile. **2** *n* essai *m*, épreuve *f* (*d'une machine, d'un pont etc*); contrôle *m*, vérification *f* (*des poids et mesures etc*); examen *m* (*de la vue de qn etc*); expérimentation *f* (*of drug, cosmetic*); **animal t.,** expérimentation sur les animaux.

testis, *pl* **testes** ['testɪs, 'testiːz] *n* testicule *m*.

testosterone [tes'tɒstərəʊn] *n* testostérone *f*.

test-tube ['testtjuːb] *adj F* **t.-t. baby,** bébé-éprouvette *m*, *pl* bébés-éprouvette.

testy ['testɪ] *adj* irritable.

tetanus ['tetənəs] *n Med* tétanos *m*; **t. injection,** piqûre *f* antitétanique.

tetchily [ˈtetʃılı] *adv* sur un ton irrité.
tetchiness [ˈtetʃınıs] *n* irritation *f*, mauvaise humeur.
tetchy [ˈtetʃı] *adj* irritable.
tête-à-tête [ˈteıtɑːˈteıt] **1** *adv* tête-à-tête. **2** *n* (*pl* **tête-à-têtes**) tête-à-tête *m inv* ; **t.-à-t. dinner,** dîner *m* en tête-à-tête.
tether¹ [ˈteðər] *n* (*for tying horse etc*) longe *f*, attache *f* (*d'un cheval etc*); **to be at the end of one's t.,** (*of person*) (*exhausted*) être à bout de forces; (*unable to cope*) être à bout de ressources, *F* être au bout du rouleau.
tether² *vt* attacher (*un cheval etc*).
tetrachloride [tetrəˈklɔːraıd] *n* tétrachlorure *m*.
tetragon [ˈtetrəgən] *n Math etc* quadrilatère *m*.
tetragonal [teˈtrægən(ə)l] *adj Math* quadrilatère.
tetrahedron [tetrəˈhiːdrən, -ˈhed-] *n Math* tétraèdre *m*.
tetrameter [teˈtræmıtər] *n* (*in prosody*) tétramètre *m* .
tetrasyllable [tetrəˈsıləb(ə)l] *n* (mot *m ou* vers *m*) tétrasyllabe *m*.
Teutonic [tjuːˈtɒnık] *adj* teuton, teutonique; *Hist* **the T. Order (of Knights),** l'ordre *m* Teutonique.
Tex *abbr* **Texas.**
Texan [ˈteks(ə)n] **1** *adj* texan. **2** *n* Texan, -ane.
text [tekst] *n* **(a)** texte *m* (*d'un manuscrit, d'un auteur*); *Sch* **set texts,** textes imposés; **(b)** (*passage from Bible*) citation tirée de l'Écriture sainte; **(c)** *Comptr* texte *m*; **t. editor,** éditeur *m* de texte; **t. input,** entrée *f ou* introduction *f* de texte; **t. processing,** traitement *m* de texte; **t. processing capabilities,** potentiel *m* de traitement de texte; **t. processor,** (unité *f* de) traitement de texte.
textbook [ˈtekstbʊk] *n Sch etc* manuel *m*; **t. on physics/on algebra,** manuel de physique/d'algèbre; **t. definitions,** définitions exactes *ou* exemplaires; **a t. example,** un exemple classique *ou* modèle (**of,** de); **a t. landing,** un atterrissage modèle.
textile [ˈtekstaıl] **1** *adj* textile. **2** *n* (*fabric*) tissu *m*; (*raw material*) textile *m*; **the t. industries,** l'industrie *f* textile.
textual [ˈtekstjʊəl] *adj* textuel; **t. error,** erreur *f* de texte.
textually [ˈtekstjʊəlı] *adv* textuellement.
texture [ˈtekstʃər] *n* tissage *m* (*d'un tissu*); texture *f*, grain *m* (*de la peau, du bois etc*); contexture *f* (*des muscles*); *Fig* (*of prose etc*) texture *f*; **close/loose t.,** tissage serré/lâche; **it'll improve the t. of your life,** ça améliorera la qualité de votre vie.
TGWU [tiːdʒiːdʌbljuːˈjuː] *n Br* (*abbr* **Transport and General Worker's Union**) = syndicat *m* des transports et des travailleurs confédérés.
Thai [taı] **1** *adj* thaïlandais; *Ling* thaï. **2** *n* **(a)** Thaïlandais, -aise; **(b)** *Ling* thaï *m*.
Thailand [ˈtaılænd] *n* Thaïlande *f*.
thalidomide [θəˈlıdəmaıd] *n Pharm* thalidomide *f*; **t. baby,** victime *f* de la thalidomide.
Thames [temz] *n* **the T.,** la Tamise; **he'll never set the T. on fire,** il n'a pas inventé le fil à couper le beurre.
than [ðæn; *unstressed* ð(ə)n] *conj* (*in comparison of inequality*) que; (*with numbers*) de; **I have more/less t. you,** j'en ai plus/moins que vous; **more t. twenty,** plus de vingt; **more t. once,** plus d'une fois; **he's taller t. me** *or* **t. I am** *or Fml* **t. I,** il est plus grand que moi; **I know her better t. you,** je la connais mieux que toi; **I feel better t. ever,** je me sens mieux que jamais; **she would do anything rather t. let him suffer,** elle ferait n'importe quoi plutôt que de le laisser souffrir; **no sooner had we entered t. the music began,** nous étions à peine entrés que la musique a commencé; **any person other t. himself,** tout autre que lui; **it was none other t. her old friend,** ce n'était nul autre que son vieil ami.
thane [θeın] *n Eng & Scot Hist* ≈ baron *m*.
thank [θæŋk] *vt* **(a)** remercier (*qn*); rendre grâce(s) à (*Dieu*); **to t. s.o. for sth,** remercier qn de *ou* pour qch; **t. God!, t. heaven(s)!, t. goodness!,** Dieu merci!, grâce au ciel!; **t. you,** *F* **thanking you,** merci, je vous remercie; **will you have some tea? — no, t. you,** prenez-vous *ou* voulez-vous du thé? — (non) merci!, (non) je vous remercie; **(yes,) t. you,** oui, merci; **t. you very much,** merci beaucoup, merci bien; **t. you for coming,** merci d'être venu; *F* **t. you for nothing!,** merci de rien!; **t. you note,** mot *m* de remerciement; **(b)** *often Iron* **I'll t. you to mind your own business!,** occupez-vous donc de ce qui vous regarde!; **(c) to have s.o. to t. for sth,** devoir qch à qn; *Iron* **you have only yourself to t. for it,** c'est à vous seul qu'il faut vous en prendre; **the curtains are torn — we've got the cat to t. for that,** les rideaux sont déchirés — c'est le chat qui a fait ce beau travail.
thankful [ˈθæŋkfʊl] *adj* reconnaissant; **to be t. to s.o. for sth,** être reconnaissant à qn de qch, *esp Fml* avoir gré à qn de qch; **to be t. that ...,** être bien content que ...; **you should be t. you weren't charged extra,** vous pouvez vous estimer heureux *ou* vous devriez être content qu'on ne vous ait pas fait payer de supplément; **it's something to be t. for,** il y a de quoi nous féliciter.
thankfully [ˈθæŋkfəlı] *adv* avec reconnaissance, avec gratitude; **t. no one was hurt,** heureusement *ou* Dieu merci, personne n'a été blessé.
thankfulness [ˈθæŋkfʊlnıs] *n* reconnaissance *f*, gratitude *f*.
thankless [ˈθæŋklıs] *adj* **(a)** (*travail etc*) mal récompensé, ingrat; **(b)** (*person*) ingrat.
thanks [θæŋks] **1** *npl* remerciement(s) *m(pl)*; **give him my t.,** remerciez-le de ma part; **t.!,** merci!; **(very) many t.!, t. very much!, t. awfully!,** merci beaucoup!, merci bien!; *F* **t. for your letter,** merci de *ou* pour votre lettre; *F* **t. for coming,** merci d'être venu; *F* **no t.,** (non,) merci; *F* **t. for nothing!,** merci de rien!; **to give t. to s.o. for sth,** remercier qn de *ou* pour qch; **to offer** *or* **give t. to God,** rendre grâce à Dieu; **to propose a vote of t. to s.o.,** voter des remerciements à qn; **t. be to God!** (rendons) grâce à Dieu!; **that's all the t. I get!,** voilà comme on me remercie! **2** *prep* **t. to him/to his help,** grâce à lui/à son aide; **no t. to you/them/***etc***!,** ce n'est pas grâce à vous/eux *etc*!
thanksgiving [θæŋksˈgıvıŋ] *n* action *f* de grâce(s); **T. Day,** = *US* fête célébrée le 4e jeudi de novembre; *Can* fête célébrée le 2e lundi d'octobre, *Can* le jour de l'action de grâces.
thank you [ˈθæŋkjʊ] *n* remerciement *m*; **t. y. note,** mot *m* de remerciement; **t. y. letter,** lettre *f* de remerciement; **a big t. y. from all of us,** un grand merci de nous tous; **say t. y.,** dis merci.
that¹ [ðæt] **1** *dem pron* (*pl* **those** [ðəʊz]) **(a)** cela, *F* ça; ce; **give me t.,** donnez-moi cela *ou* ça; **what's t.?** qu'est-ce (que c'est) que cela *ou* que ça?; **who's t.?,** qui est-ce?; **that's Mr Thomas,** c'est M. Thomas; **is t. you, Anne?,** est-ce vous *ou* c'est vous Anne?; **those are my things,** ce sont mes affaires; **those are my orders,** voilà mes ordres; **is t. all the luggage you're taking?,** c'est tout ce que vous emportez comme bagages?; **that's where he lives,** c'est là qu'il habite; **after/before t.,** après/avant cela; **t. was two years ago,** il y a deux ans de cela; **with t. she took out her handkerchief,** là-dessus, elle a sorti son mouchoir; **what do you mean by t.?,** qu'entendez-vous par là?; **t. is** *or* **that's to say,** c'est-à-dire; **so THAT'S settled,** bon, ça c'est réglé, voilà qui est réglé; **it needs a good actor and an experienced one at t.,** cela demande un bon acteur, et qui plus est, un acteur expérimenté; **that's right!, that's it!,** c'est cela!, ça y est!; **that's all,** voilà tout; **that's strange!,** voilà qui est curieux!; *F* **good stuff, t.!,** ça c'est du bon!, voilà du bon!; **and that's t.!, so that's t.!,** et voilà!, alors voilà qui est fini!; **t. will do,** cela *ou* ça suffit; **that's enough of t.!,** en voilà assez!;
(b) (*opposed to* **this, these**) celui-là, *f* celle-là; *pl* ceux-là, *f* celles-là; **this is new and that's old,** celui-ci est neuf et celui-là est vieux;
(c) (*indefinite, as antecedent to a relative*) celui, *f* celle, *pl* ceux, *f* celles; **what's t. (that) you're holding?,** qu'est-ce que (c'est que) vous avez dans la main?; **all those that I saw,** tous ceux que j'ai vus; **one of those who were present,** (l')un de ceux qui étaient présents; **I'm not one of those who ...,** je ne suis pas de ceux qui ...; (*with relative understood*) **all those present at the wedding,** tous ceux qui ont assisté au mariage.
2 *dem adj* (*pl* **those**) ce, (*before vowel or h mute*) cet, *f* cette, *pl* ces; (*for emphasis and in opposition to* **this, these**) ce ... -là, cet ... -là, cette ... -là, ces ... -là; **t. book, those books,** ce livre(-là), ces livres(-là); **compare t. edition with these two,** comparez cette édition-là avec ces deux-ci; **t. one,** celui-là, celle-là; **at t. time, in those days,** en ce temps-là, à cette époque; **everybody is agreed on t. point,** tout le monde est d'accord là-dessus; **t. fool of a gardener,** cet imbécile de jardinier; *Dial* **t. there table,** cette table-là; **well, how's t. leg of yours?,** eh bien, et cette jambe?; **it's t. wife of his who's to blame,** c'est la faute de sa femme; **all those flowers that you have there,** toutes ces fleurs que vous avez là; **I don't have t. much confidence in him to believe all he says,** je n'ai pas assez confiance en lui pour croire tout ce qu'il dit; **what about t.** *or* **those five pounds you owe me?,** et ces cinq livres que vous me devez?
3 *dem adv* **(a)** (*with adj or adv of quantity*) aussi ... que cela; **t. high,** aussi haut que ça; **can you run t. far** *or* **as far as t.?,** peux-tu courir aussi loin (que ça)?;

(b) (*so*) tellement, si; **is she t. tall?**, est-elle si grande (que ça)?; **he's t. stupid he'd ...**, il est tellement stupide qu'il ... .

that² [ðæt; *unstressed* ðət] *rel pron sing & pl* (*sometimes omitted*) **(a)** (*for subject*) qui; (*for object*) que; **the letter t. came yesterday**, la lettre qui est arrivée hier; **the letter t. I sent you**, la lettre que je vous ai envoyée; **you're the only person t. can help me**, vous êtes la seule personne qui puisse m'aider; **miser t. he was, he would not pay**, avare comme il était, il n'a pas voulu payer;

(b) (*governed by prep which always follows* **that**) lequel, *f* laquelle, *pl* lesquels, *f* lesquelles; **the envelope t. I put it in**, l'enveloppe dans laquelle je l'ai mis; **the woman t. we're talking about**, la femme dont nous parlons; **the person t. I gave it to**, la personne à laquelle *ou* à qui je l'ai donné; **no one has come t. I know of**, personne n'est venu que je sache;

(c) (*after expression of time*) où; que; **the time t. I saw him**, la fois *ou* le jour où je l'ai vu; **during the years t. she had spent in prison**, pendant les années qu'elle avait passées en prison.

that³ [ðæt; *unstressed* ðət] *conj* **(a)** (*introducing subordinate clause; often omitted*) que; **she said t. she would come**, elle a dit qu'elle viendrait; **I'll see to it t. everything is ready**, je veillerai à ce que tout soit prêt; **he's so ill t. he can't work**, il est si malade qu'il est incapable de travailler; **to wish/hope/*etc* t.**, souhaiter/espérer/*etc* que +*sub or ind*; **I wish t. it had never happened**, je voudrais que cela ne soit jamais arrivé; **I hope t. you'll come**, j'espère que vous viendrez;

(b) so t., in order t., (afin) que, pour que + *sub*; (*same subject in both clauses*) afin de + *inf*, pour + *inf*; **they kept quiet so t. he could sleep**, ils ont gardé le silence pour *ou* afin qu'il puisse dormir; **come nearer so t. I can see you**, approchez, que je vous voie; **put it there so t. it won't be forgotten**, mettez-le là pour qu'on ne l'oublie pas; **I sold it so t. I would have the money**, je l'ai vendu afin d'avoir *ou* pour avoir l'argent;

(c) *esp Lit* (*exclamatory*) **t. he should behave like this!**, dire qu'il se conduit comme cela!; (*expressing desire + sub*) **oh t. it were possible!**, oh, si c'était possible!

thatch¹ [θætʃ] *n* chaume *m* (*de toiture*); *F* (*hair*) crinière *f*; **under this great t. of hair**, sous cette épaisse crinière, sous cette épaisse masse de cheveux.

thatch² *vt* couvrir (*un toit*) de *ou* en chaume; **thatched cottage**, chaumière *f*; **thatched roof**, toit *m* de chaume.

thatcher ['θætʃər] *n* couvreur *m* en chaume.

Thatcherism ['θætʃərɪz(ə)m] *n* thatcherisme *m*.

Thatcherite ['θaetʃəraɪt] *adj & n* thatcherien, -ienne.

thaw¹ [θɔː] *n* dégel *m*; fonte *f* des neiges; **the t. is setting in**, le temps est *ou* se met au dégel; *Fig* **a t. in relations**, un dégel *ou* une détente des relations.

thaw² **1** *vt* dégeler (*la neige etc*); décongeler (*des aliments congelés*); *Fig* **to t. s.o.**, dégeler qn; **to t. s.o.'s reserve**, tirer qn de sa réserve. **2** *vi* (*of snow, ice*) fondre; (*of frozen food etc*) se décongeler; *Fig* (*of lake etc*) dégeler; (*of person*) (*relax*) se dégeler; **it's thawing**, il dégèle.

▸**thaw out** **1** *vi* (*of frozen food etc*) se décongeler; (*of lake etc*) dégeler; *F* **come in and t. out**, entrez et réchauffez-vous. **2** *vtsep* décongeler (*des aliments congelés*).

thawing ['θɔːɪŋ] *n* dégel *m* (*d'un cours d'eau etc*); fonte *f* (*des neiges*); décongélation *f* (*d'aliments congelés*); **a t. in relations**, un dégel *ou* une détente des relations.

the¹ [ðiː; *unstressed before consonant* ðə; *unstressed before vowel* ðɪ] *def art* **(a)** le, *f* la; (*before vowel or h mute*) l', *pl* les; **at/to the ...**, au, à la, *pl* aux; **of/from the ...**, du, de la, *pl* des; **t. father and (t.) mother**, le père et la mère; **I spoke to t. driver**, j'ai parlé au chauffeur; **t. roof of t. house**, le toit de la maison; **t. arrival of t. guests**, l'arrivée des invités; **at t. corner**, au coin; **on t. other side**, de l'autre côté; **on t. Monday he fell ill**, le lundi il est tombé malade; **I'll see him in t. summer**, je le verrai cet été; **in t. summer of 1946**, pendant l'été 1946, en été 1946; **(in) t. year 1939**, (en) l'an 1939; **t. Greeks**, les Grecs; **t. Martins**, les Martin; **Edward t. Seventh**, Édouard Sept; **t. England of today**, l'Angleterre d'aujourd'hui; **he's t. best-looking man I know**, c'est le plus bel homme que je connaisse; *F* **well, how's t. throat then?**, eh bien, et cette gorge?; *F* **t. wife**, ma femme; **Mrs Long, t. manager of the firm**, Mme. Long, directeur de la maison; **t. impudence of it!**, quelle audace!; **I didn't have t. heart to tell him**, je n'ai pas eu le courage de le lui dire; **the concept of t. beautiful**, le concept du beau; **words borrowed from t. French**, mots empruntés au français; **t. poor**, les pauvres; **Catherine t. Great.**, Catherine la Grande; *F* **she's got t. measles**, elle a la rougeole; **t. Golden Eagle lives in mountainous regions**, l'aigle royal vit dans les régions montagneuses; **who invented t. wheel?**, qui a inventé la roue?; **to be paid by t. hour**, être payé à l'heure; **eight apples to t. kilo**, huit pommes au kilo; **thirty miles to t. gallon** = dix litres aux cent kilomètres; **to play the trumpet/drums**, jouer de la trompette/de la batterie; **I was absent at t. time**, j'étais absent à cette époque *ou* à ce moment-là; **do leave t. child alone!**, mais laissez la donc, cette enfant!; **she's giving up her job — t. woman's mad!**, elle quitte son emploi — elle est folle!;

(b) (*stressed*) [ðiː] **her father is Professor Smith, THE Professor Smith**, son père est le professeur Smith, le grand *ou* le célèbre professeur Smith; **Maurice's is THE shop for furniture**, pour les meubles, la maison Maurice est la meilleure qui soit.

the² *adv* **I am all t. more/the less surprised that ...**, j'en suis d'autant plus/d'autant moins surpris que ...; **he ran all t. faster**, il a couru d'autant plus vite; **t. sharper the point t. better the needle**, les aiguilles sont d'autant meilleures que leur pointe est fine; **t. sooner t. better**, le plus tôt sera le mieux; **t. less said about it t. better**, moins on en parlera mieux cela vaudra; **t. more he drinks the thirstier he gets**, plus il boit, plus il a soif.

theatre, *US* **theater** ['θɪətər] *n* **(a)** théâtre *m*; **open air t.**, théâtre en plein air; **to go to the t.**, aller au théâtre *ou* au spectacle; **news t.**, cinéma où l'on passe des actualités; **the t.**, le théâtre; **the English t.**, le théâtre anglais; **t. bill**, affiche *f* de théâtre; **t. critic**, critique théâtral *ou* de théâtre; **(b) (lecture) t.**, amphithéâtre *m*; *Br Med* **(operating) t.**, salle d'opération; **(c) the t. of war**, le théâtre de la guerre.

theatre(-)goer, *US* **theater-** ['θɪətəgəʊər] *n* amateur, -trice de théâtre.

theatre(-)going, *US* **theater-** ['θɪətəgəʊɪŋ] **1** *adj* **the t.(-)g. public**, ceux qui vont au théâtre. **2** *n* fréquentation *f* des théâtres.

theatrical [θɪ'ætrɪk(ə)l] *adj* **(a)** théâtral, -aux; **t. company**, compagnie théâtrale; **(b)** (*attitude etc*) théâtral, histrionique.

theatrically [θɪ'ætrɪklɪ] *adv* (*see adj*) **(a)** théâtralement; **(b)** théâtralement, avec affectation.

theatricals [θɪ'ætrɪkəlz] *npl* **amateur t.**, théâtre *m* d'amateurs; *Fig* **we don't need all the t.!**, épargnez-nous toute cette mise en scène *ou* toute cette comédie!

thee [ðiː] *pers pron objective case Arch & Lit* **(a)** (*unstressed*) te; (*before a vowel or h mute*) t'; **we beseech t.**, nous te supplions; **sit t. down**, assieds-toi; **(b)** (*stressed*) **he thinks of t.**, il pense à toi.

theft [θeft] *n* vol *m*; *Jur* **petty t.**, larcin *m*.

theftproof ['θeftpruːf] *adj* (*véhicule etc*) muni d'un dispositif antivol; (*serrure etc*) antivol, de sécurité.

their ['ðeər] *poss adj* **(a)** leur, *f* leur, *pl* leurs; **t. neighbour(s)**, leur(s) voisin(s); **t. father and mother**, leur père et leur mère, leurs père et mère; **t. eyes are blue**, ils ont les yeux bleus; **they have a car of t. own**, ils ont leur propre voiture; **T. Majesties**, Leurs Majestés; **(b)** *F* (*after indef pron or to replace his/her*) son, *f* sa, *pl* ses; **someone's left t. umbrella**, quelqu'un a laissé son parapluie; **each candidate should bring t. ...**, chaque candidat doit amener son ... .

theirs ['ðeəz] *poss pron* le leur, la leur, *pl* les leurs; **this house is t.**, cette maison est la leur *ou* est à eux *ou* à elles *ou* leur appartient; **a friend of t.**, un ami à eux *ou* à elles, un de leurs amis; **that damn dog of t.!**, leur sacré chien!; **I'm interested in them and (in) t.**, (*their family*) je m'intéresse à eux et aux leurs; *Fml* **t. is not to reason why**, il ne leur revient pas d'en questionner la raison.

theism ['θiːɪz(ə)m] *n Rel* théisme *m*.

theistic(al) [θiː'ɪstɪk(əl)] *adj Rel* théiste.

them [ðem, ðəm] **1** *pers pron pl objective case* **(a)** (*unstressed*) (*direct*) les *mf*; (*indirect*) leur *mf*; (*after prepositions*) eux, *f* elles; **I like t.**, je les aime bien; **have you seen t.?**, les avez-vous vu(e)s?; **give t. some**, donnez-leur-en; **speak to t.**, parlez-leur; **look at t.**, regardez-les; **they took the keys away with t.**, ils ont emporté les clefs avec eux;

(b) (*stressed*) eux, *f* elles; **I'm thinking of t.**, c'est à eux *ou* à elles que je pense;

(c) (*other prep combinations*) **every one of t. was killed**, ils ont tous été tués; **there were three of t.**, (*of people*) ils *ou* elles étaient trois; (*of objects*) il y en avait trois; **give me half of t.**, donnez-m'en la moitié; **several/many/most of t.**, plusieurs/beaucoup/la plupart d'entre eux; **neither of t.**, ni l'un ni l'autre; **none of t.**, aucun d'entre eux;

(d) (*disjunctive nom*) **it's t.!**, c'est eux *ou* elles, ce sont eux *ou* elles!, les voilà!; **we're not as rich as t.**, nous ne sommes pas si riches qu'eux;

(e) *F* (*after indef pron*) **when anyone comes she says to t ....**, quand quelqu'un vient elle lui dit ... .

2 *adj* (*incorrect usage*) (*those*) ces.

thematic [θiːˈmætɪk] *adj Mus etc* thématique.

theme [θiːm] *n* **(a)** sujet *m*, thème *m* (*d'un discours etc*); **t. park**, parc *m* à thème; **(b)** *Sch & Am* dissertation *f*; (*exercise*) exercice *m* littéraire; **(c)** *Art Lit Mus etc* thème *m*, motif *m*; **t. with variations**, air varié; **t. music/song/tune**, *Rad TV* (*of programme*) thème de générique; *Th* (*in film, play*) thème principal *ou* leitmotiv.

themselves [ðəmˈselvz, *stressed* ðem-] *pers pron pl* (*emphatic*) eux-mêmes, *f* elles-mêmes; (*reflexive*) se; **they did it t.**, ils l'ont fait eux-mêmes; **they t. are resigned to it**, eux, pour leur part, s'y sont résignés; **they've hurt t.**, ils se sont fait mal; **they were standing in a corner by t.**, ils étaient tout seuls dans un coin; **they were whispering among t.**, ils chuchotaient entre eux.

then [ðen] **1** *adv* **(a)** (*at that time*) alors, en ce temps-là, à cette époque; **what were you doing t.?**, que faisiez-vous alors?; **the t. existing system**, le système qui existait à cette époque *ou* en ce temps-là; **there and t.**, séance tenante, sur-le-champ;

(b) (*after, next*) puis, ensuite, alors; (*in space*) puis; **we'll have soup first (and) t. some fish**, on prendra d'abord du potage (et) ensuite du poisson; **what t.?**, et puis (quoi)?, et (puis) après?; **on the left the church, t. a few old houses**, à gauche l'église, puis quelques vieilles maisons;

(c) (*in addition*) d'ailleurs; et aussi, et puis; **and t. there are the children to be considered**, et puis *ou* et aussi il faut penser aux enfants;

(d) but t., mais; **she lost her temper, but t. that's hardly surprising**, elle s'est énervée, mais à vrai dire ce n'est pas étonnant; **it's beautiful material, but t. it is expensive**, c'est une belle étoffe, mais aussi elle coûte cher;

(e) before t., avant cela; **will you have finished by t.?**, est-ce que vous aurez fini d'ici là?; **until t.**, (*referring to past time*) jusqu'alors; (*until future time*) jusque-là; **by t. it will be too late**, alors *ou* à ce moment-là il sera trop tard; **(ever) since t., from t. on**, dès lors, depuis ce temps-là, **between now and t.**, d'ici là; **(every) now and t.**, de temps en temps, de temps à autre;

(f) (*in that case*) en ce cas, donc, alors; **if you want to go, well t. go!**, si vous voulez partir, eh bien (alors) partez!; **well t., you're coming?**, alors vous viendrez?; **(but) t. you should have told him so**, en ce cas vous auriez dû le lui dire; **you knew all the time t.?, t. you knew all the time?**, vous le saviez donc depuis le début?

2 *adj* (*in front of noun*) **the t. Foreign Secretary**, le Ministre des Affaires Étrangères d'alors *ou* de l'époque.

thence [ðens] *adv Arch & Lit* **(a)** (*from there*) de là; **we went to Paris and (from) t. to Rome**, nous sommes allés à Paris et de là à Rome; **(b)** = **THENCEFORTH**; **(c)** (*as a result of that*) pour cette raison, par conséquent.

thenceforth, thenceforward [ˈðensˈfɔːθ, -ˈfɔːwəd] *adv Arch & Lit* **(from) t.**, dès lors.

theocracy [θiːˈɒkrəsɪ] *n* théocratie *f*.

theocratic [θiːəˈkrætɪk] *adj* théocratique.

theodolite [θiːˈɒdəlaɪt] *n* (*in surveying*) théodolite *m*.

theologian [θiːəˈləʊdʒ(ɪ)ən] *n* théologien *m*.

theological [θiːəˈlɒdʒɪk(ə)l] *adj* théologique; **t. college**, séminaire *m*.

theologically *adv* [θiːəˈlɒdʒɪklɪ] théologiquement.

theology [θiːˈɒlədʒɪ] *n* théologie *f*.

theorem [ˈθɪərəm] *n Math Phys etc* théorème *m*.

theoretical [θiːəˈretɪk(ə)l] *adj* (*raisonnement etc*) théorique; (*doctrine etc*) théorétique; **it's only t.**, ce n'est que de la théorie.

theoretically [θiːəˈretɪklɪ] *adv* théoriquement; **t. individuals can travel where they like**, théoriquement *ou* en théorie, les individus peuvent voyager où ils le désirent.

theoretician [θiːərɪˈtɪʃən] *n* théoricien, -ienne.

theorist [ˈθiːərɪst] *n* théoricien, -ienne.

theorize [ˈθiːəraɪz] *vi* théoriser.

theorizing [ˈθiːəraɪzɪŋ] *n* théorisation *f*.

theory [ˈθiːərɪ] *n* théorie *f*; **in t.**, en théorie.

theosophical [θiːəˈsɒfɪk(ə)l] *adj* théosophique.

theosophist [θiːˈɒsəfɪst] *n* théosophe *mf*.

theosophy [θiːˈɒsəfɪ] *n* théosophie *f*.

therapeutic [θerəˈpjuːtɪk] *adj Med & Fig* thérapeutique.

therapeutically [θerəˈpjuːtɪklɪ] *adv* thérapeutiquement.

therapeutics [θerəˈpjuːtɪks] *npl* (*usu with sing verb*) *Med* thérapeutique *f*.

therapist [ˈθerəpɪst] *n* thérapeute *mf*.

therapy [ˈθerəpɪ] *n Med* thérapie *f*; **speech t.**, orthophonie *f*.

there [ðeər, *unstressed* ðər] **1** *adv* **(a)** là, y; **the keys aren't t.**, les clefs ne sont pas là *ou* n'y sont pas; **put it t.**, mettez-le là; **she's still t.**, elle est encore là, elle y est toujours; **does he work t.?**, c'est là qu'il travaille?; **we're t.!**, nous voilà arrivés!; **who's t.?**, qui est là?; *F* **to be all t.**, (*alert, shrewd*) être malin *ou* avisé *ou* dégourdi; (*in full possession of one's faculties*) avoir toute sa raison; **she's not all t.**, elle a un (petit) grain, elle est un peu marteau; **I'm going t.**, j'y vais; **t. and back**, aller et retour; **I've been t.**, je suis passé par là, j'ai connu ça; **give me that book t.**, donnez-moi ce livre-là; **that man t.**, cet homme-là; **your friend t.**, votre ami; **hey! you t.!**, hé, vous là-bas!; **move along t., please!**, circulez, s'il vous plaît; **there's the bell ringing**, voilà la cloche qui sonne; **t. they are!**, les voilà!; **t. she comes!**, la voilà qui arrive!; **there's a dear!**, tu seras bien gentil!; **t. you are!**, (et) voilà!; **just press the button and t. you are!**, vous n'avez qu'à appuyer sur le bouton et ça y est!;

(b) t. is *or* **are**, il y a; **t. was** *or* **were**, il y avait, il était; **t. will be**, il y aura; **t. was once a king**, il était *ou* il y avait une fois un roi; **t. was singing and dancing**, on a chanté et dansé; **will t. be food?**, est-ce qu'il y aura à manger?; **there's a page missing**, il manque une page; **t. is only one**, il n'y en a qu'un; **there's one slice left**, il reste une tranche; **there are** *or* *F* **there's two slices left**, il reste deux tranches; **t. isn't any**, il n'y en a pas; **there's someone at the door**, il y a quelqu'un à la porte; **t. comes a time when ....**, il arrive un moment où ...;

(c) (*in that matter*) quant à cela; dans ce domaine, sur ce sujet; **there's** *or* **t. lies the difficulty**, voilà la difficulté, c'est là qu'est la difficulté; *F* **t. you have me!, you've got me t.!**, ça, ça me dépasse;

(d) (*that place*) **we go to Paris and from t. to Rome**, nous allons à Paris et de là à Rome; **somewhere round t.** *or* **near t.**, quelque part par là; **put it over t.**, mettez-le là-bas *ou* par là; **down t.**, en bas; **up t.**, là-haut; **in t.**, là-dedans; **under t.**, là-dessous.

2 *int* voilà!; **t. now, that's done!**, là! voilà qui est fait!; **t. now that wasn't too painful, was it?**, alors, ça n'a pas été trop douloureux, hein?; **t. (you are), I told you so**, là! je vous l'avais bien dit!; **t.!, t.! (now) don't worry!**, là là, ne vous inquiétez pas!; **I'll do as I like, so t.!**, je ferai comme il me plaira, et puis c'est tout!

thereabouts [ˈðeərəˈbaʊts] *adv* **(a)** (*with place*) (*nearby*) près de là; (*in that area*) dans le voisinage; **in Brighton or t.**, à Brighton ou quelque part par là; **(b)** (*with number, quantity, distance etc*) (*approximately*) à peu près, environ; **the parcel weighs two kilos or t.**, le colis pèse environ deux kilos.

thereafter [ðeərˈɑːftər] *adv Arch & Fml* après (cela), par la suite.

thereby [ðeəˈbaɪ *when at the end of clause*; ˈðeəbaɪ *when preceding verb*] *adv* ainsi, de cette façon; **t. hangs a tale!**, c'est toute une histoire!

therefore [ˈðeəfɔːr] *adv* donc, par conséquent, aussi; **I think, t. I am**, je pense, donc je suis; **I should t. be grateful if you would ....**, par conséquent je vous serais reconnaissant *ou* aussi vous serais-je reconnaissant de vouloir bien ...; **they had t. decided to ....**, par conséquent ils avaient décidé de ...; **you are his friend and t. mine**, vous êtes son ami et donc vous êtes aussi le mien.

therefrom [ðeəˈfrɒm] *adv Arch & Fml* de là; **it follows t. that ....**, il suit de là que ... .

therein [ðeərˈɪn] *adv Arch & Fml* **(a)** (*in that matter*) en cela; **t. you are mistaken**, en cela vous vous trompez; **(b)** (*in that place*) (là-)dedans; **and all the furniture t.**, et tous les meubles qu'elle contient.

thereof [ðeərˈɒv] *adv Arch & Fml* de cela; en; **in lieu t.**, au lieu de cela; **he drank t.**, il y but; **the building and the owner t.**, l'immeuble et le propriétaire de celui-ci.

there's [ðeəz] = **THERE IS, THERE HAS**.

thereto [ðeəˈtuː] *adv Arch & Fml* à cela; y; **the house and the garden pertaining t.**, la maison et le jardin qui y appartient.

theretofore [ˈðeətuːfɔːr] *adv Arch & Fml* jusqu'alors, avant cela.

thereupon [ˈðeərəˈpɒn] *adv* **(a)** (*at which point*) sur ce, sur quoi, là-dessus; **t. he left**, sur quoi il est parti; **(b)** *Lit* **there is much to be said t.**, il y aurait beaucoup à dire là-dessus *ou* à ce sujet.

therewith [ðeəˈwɪð, -ˈwɪθ] *adv Arch & Fml* **(a)** (*with that*) avec cela; **(b)** = **THEREUPON (a)**.

therm [θɜːm] *n Br Phys etc* 100 000 btu (*unités britanniques de chaleur*).

thermal[1] ['θɜːm(ə)l] *adj* **(a)** thermal, -aux; **t. springs,** eaux *ou* sources thermales; *Comptr* **t. paper,** papier *m* thermique *ou* thermosensible; *Comptr* **t. printer,** imprimante *f* thermique *ou* thermoélectrique; *Comptr* **t. transfer,** transfert *m* thermique; **t. underwear,** sous-vêtements *mpl* en thermolactyl ®; **(b)** *Phys* thermal, thermique, calorifique; **t. energy,** énergie *f* thermique *ou* calorifique; *Nucl Phys* **t. reactor,** pile *f ou* réacteur *m* à neutrons thermiques; **t. unit,** unité *f* thermique *ou* de chaleur.

thermal[2] *n* **(a)** *Met Av* thermique *m*, ascendance *f* thermique; **(b)** *F* **thermals,** (*underwear*) (sous-vêtements *mpl* en) thermolactyl *m* ®.

thermic ['θɜːmɪk] *adj Phys etc* thermique, calorifique.

thermionic [θɜːmɪ'ɒnɪk] *adj Electron* thermoélectronique, thermionique.

thermistor [θɜː'mɪstər] *n El* résistance *f* thermique.

thermocouple ['θɜːməʊkʌp(ə)l] *n El* couple *m* thermoélectrique, thermocouple *m*.

thermodynamic [θɜːməʊdaɪ'næmɪk] *adj* thermodynamique.

thermoelectric [θɜːməʊɪ'lektrɪk] *adj* thermoélectrique.

thermometer [θə'mɒmɪtər] *n* thermomètre *m*.

thermonuclear [θɜːməʊ'njuːklɪər] *adj Nucl Phys* thermonucléaire.

thermopile ['θɜːməʊpaɪl] *n El* pile *f* thermoélectrique.

thermoplastic [θɜːməʊ'plæstɪk] *adj & n* thermoplastique *m*.

Thermos ® ['θɜːməs] *n* **T. (flask),** (bouteille *f*) Thermos *m or f inv* ®.

thermostat ['θɜːməstæt] *n* thermostat *m*.

thermostatic [θɜːmə'stætɪk] *adj* thermostatique; **t. control,** réglage *m* (de la température) par thermostat.

thermostatically [θɜːmə'stætɪklɪ] *adv* **t. controlled,** réglé par thermostat.

thesaurus, *pl* **-i** [θɪ'sɔːrəs, -aɪ] *n* dictionnaire *m* de synonymes.

these *see* **THIS**.

thesis, *pl* **theses** ['θiːsɪs, -iːz] *n* (*logic*) *& Univ etc* thèse *f*; **to uphold/defend a t.,** soutenir/défendre une thèse; **PhD t.,** thèse de doctorat.

Thespian ['θespɪən] *Arch & Hum* **1** *adj* tragique, dramatique. **2** *n* acteur, -trice.

thew [θjuː] *n Lit* tendon *m*, muscle *m*; *Fig* **thews,** ardeur *f*, vigueur *f*.

they [ðeɪ] **1** *pers pron nom pl* (*unstressed*) ils, *f* elles; (*stressed*) eux, *f* elles; (*with dem force*) ceux, *f* celles; **t. are dancing,** ils *ou* elles dansent; **here t. come,** les voici (qui arrivent); **t. alone can ...,** eux seuls *ou* elles seules peuvent ...; **we are as rich as t. are,** nous sommes aussi riches qu'eux *ou* qu'elles; *Lit* **t. who believe,** ceux *ou* celles qui croient. **2** *indef pron* **(a)** on; **t. say that ...,** on dit que ...; **(b)** *F* (*after indef pron or to replace he/she*) **nobody ever admits they're wrong,** on ne veut jamais reconnaître qu'on a tort; **each candidate must be told that t. should ...,** chaque candidat doit être informé qu'il doit ... .

they'd [ðeɪd] = **(a) they had,** *see* **HAVE**[2]; **(b) they would,** *see* **WILL**[3].

they'll [ðeɪl] = **they will,** *see* **WILL**[3].

they're [ðeər] = **they are,** *see* **BE**.

they've [ðeɪv] = **they have,** *see* **HAVE**[2].

thiamine ['θaɪəm(a)ɪn] *n Bio Ch* thiamine *f*.

thick [θɪk] **1** *adj* **(a)** (*walls, material etc*) épais, *f* épaisse; (*book, thread, lips etc*) gros, *f* grosse; **wall one metre t.,** mur d'un mètre d'épaisseur; *F* **to give s.o. a t. ear,** arranger le portrait de qn; **the t. end of a stick,** le gros bout d'un bâton; *Fig* **to have a t. skin,** (*of politician etc*) avoir la peau dure; *F* **can't you get it into your t. skull** *or* **head that ...?,** tu ne peux pas te rentrer dans ta petite tête que ...?;

(b) (*wheat, forest*) épais, *f* épaisse, dru, serré, touffu; (*hair*) abondant, épais; (*crowd*) compact, serré; (*voice*) étouffé; **t. eyebrows,** sourcils touffus *ou* épais;

(c) (*liquid*) épais, *f* épaisse, visqueux; (*mist*) dense, épais; (*darkness*) profond; **t. mud,** boue grasse; **air t. with smoke,** air épaissi par la fumée;

(d) *F* **to be very t. with s.o.,** être très lié *ou* être à tu et à toi avec qn; **they're as t. as thieves,** ils s'entendent comme larrons en foire;

(e) *F* (*excessive*) excessif, fort; **that's a bit t.!,** ça c'est un peu raide *ou* un peu fort!;

(f) *F* (*stupid*) abruti, bouché; **to be as t. as two short planks,** être bête comme ses pieds.

2 *n* **(a) in the t. of the forest,** au beau milieu de la forêt; **in the t. of it** *or* **of things,** en plein dedans; **in the t. of the fight,** au (plus) fort *ou* au vif de la mêlée; **to go through t. and thin for s.o.,** courir tous les risques *ou* aller contre vents et marées pour qn; **to follow s.o.** *or* **stick to s.o. through t. and thin,** rester fidèle à qn à travers toutes les épreuves;

(b) (*fleshy part*) partie charnue, gras *m* (*de la jambe etc*).

3 *adv* **(a)** (*in a thick layer*) en couche épaisse; **snow lay t. on the ground,** une neige épaisse *ou* une épaisse couche de neige couvrait le sol; **to cut the bread t.,** couper le pain en tranches épaisses; *F* **to lay it on a bit t.,** exagérer;

(b) his blows fell t. and fast, il frappait à coups redoublés, les coups pleuvaient dru; **insults were falling t. and fast,** les insultes pleuvaient dru; **letters came in t. and fast,** les lettres pleuvaient *ou* affluaient.

thicken ['θɪk(ə)n] **1** *vt* épaissir (*un mur etc*); épaissir, lier (*une sauce*). **2** *vi* (*of tree trunk, figure, air etc*) (s')épaissir; (*of sauce*) épaissir; (*of plot*) se compliquer, se corser.

thickening ['θɪk(ə)nɪŋ] *n* épaississement *m* (*d'un mur, de la taille, d'un liquide*); complication *f* (*d'une intrigue*).

thicket ['θɪkɪt] *n* bosquet *m*, hallier *m*, fourré *m*.

thickhead ['θɪkhed] *n F* abruti *m*.

thickheaded [θɪk'hedɪd] *adj F* (*stupid*) bête, stupide, bouché.

thickie ['θɪkɪ] *n Br Sl* bêta, *f* bêtasse, andouille *f*.

thick-lipped ['θɪk'lɪpt] *adj* lippu.

thickly ['θɪklɪ] *adv* **(a)** (*in thick layer(s)*) en couche(s) épaisse(s); (*couper qch*) en tranches épaisses; **to spread butter t.,** étaler généreusement du beurre; **(b)** dru; **the snow fell t.,** la neige tombait dru; **t. wooded,** très boisé; **(c) to speak t.,** parler d'une voix étouffée; (*when drunk*) avoir la langue pâteuse.

thickness ['θɪknɪs] *n* **(a)** épaisseur *f* (*d'un mur etc*); grosseur *f* (*des lèvres etc*); **(b)** épaisseur *f* (*d'une forêt etc*); abondance *f* (*de la chevelure etc*); **(c)** consistance *f* (*d'un liquide*); épaisseur *f* (*du brouillard*); étouffement *m* (*de la voix*); **(d)** couche *f* (*de papier etc*); **roll the pastry out to a t. of 1/2 inch,** étaler la pâte sur une épaisseur d'un peu plus d'un centimètre.

thicko ['θɪkəʊ] *n Br Sl* = **THICKIE**.

thickset ['θɪk'set] *adj* (*person*) trapu.

thick-skinned [θɪk'skɪnd] *adj* (*animal etc*) à la peau épaisse; *Fig* (*person*) qui a la peau dure.

thick-sliced ['θɪkslaɪst] *adj* (*bread*) coupé en tranches épaisses.

thief, *pl* **thieves** [θiːf, θiːvz] *n* voleur, -euse; **horse t.,** voleur de chevaux; **stop t.!,** au voleur!; *Prov* **set a t. to catch a t.,** à fripon, fripon et demi.

thieve [θiːv] **1** *vi* être voleur, -euse. **2** *vt* voler.

thieving ['θiːvɪŋ] **1** *adj* voleur, -euse. **2** *n* vol *m*; **petty t.,** larcin *m*.

thievish ['θiːvɪʃ] *adj* voleur, -euse.

thigh [θaɪ] *n* cuisse *f*; **t. boots,** (bottes) cuissardes *fpl*.

thighbone ['θaɪbəʊn] *n Anat* fémur *m*.

thigh-length ['θaɪleŋθ] *adj* (*dress, coat*) qui descend jusqu'à mi-cuisse; **t.-l. boots,** (bottes) cuissardes *fpl*.

thimble ['θɪmb(ə)l] *n Sewing* dé *m* (à coudre); **hunt the t.,** (*game*) = cache-tampon *m inv*.

thimbleful ['θɪmb(ə)lfʊl] *n* doigt *m* (*de cognac etc*).

thin[1] [θɪn] (*comp* **thinner;** *superl* **thinnest**) **1** *adj* **(a)** (*paper etc*) mince, fin; (*thread etc*) ténu, fin; (*material*) fin, mince, léger; (*person*) maigre, mince; (*air*) raréfié; **to grow** *or* **become thinner,** maigrir; **to get** *or* **become thinner,** (*of air*) se raréfier; **as t. as a rake,** maigre comme un clou; **long t. fingers,** doigts effilées; *Typ* **t. stroke,** délié *m*;

(b) (*wheat, hair etc*) clairsemé, rare; (*population, audience*) clairsemé; **his hair was getting t.,** ses cheveux s'éclaircissaient; **t. on the ground,** peu nombreux; **t. beard,** barbe peu fournie;

(c) (*liquid*) clair, peu consistant; (*blood*) appauvri; **t. soup,** potage clair; **t. voice,** voix fluette *ou* grêle;

(d) my patience is wearing t., je suis presque à bout de patience; **t. excuse,** pauvre excuse; **to have a t. time (of it),** (*not enjoying oneself*) s'ennuyer, s'embêter; (*have a hard time*) manger de la vache enragée.

2 *adv* **t. sown,** (*wheat etc*) clairsemé; **to spread sth t.,** étaler qch en couche fine *ou* mince.

3 *n see* **THICK 2 (a)**.

thin[2] (-nn-) **1** *vt* **(a)** amincir (*qch*); diluer, délayer (*la peinture*); allonger, éclaircir (*une sauce*). **2** *vi* s'amincir, s'effiler; (*of trees, crowd, hair etc*) s'éclaircir; (*of liquid*) devenir clair; **his hair is thinning,** il perd ses cheveux.

►thin down *vtsep* **(a)** (*make thinner*) amincir (*qch*); **(b)** (*dilute*) diluer, délayer (*la peinture*); allonger, éclaircir (*une sauce*).

►thin out 1 *vi* (*become less dense*) (*of hair*) s'éclaircir; **he's thinning out on top,** il se dégarnit sur le dessus du crâne. **2** *vtsep* (*make less dense*) éclaircir, démarier (*des jeunes plants*); éclaircir, désépaissir (*les cheveux*).

thine [ðaɪn] *Arch & Lit* **1** *poss pron* le tien, la tienne; *pl* les tiens, les tiennes; **for thee and t.,** pour toi et les tiens; **what is mine is t.,** ce qui est à moi est à toi. **2** *poss adj* (*used instead of* **THY** *before a noun or adj beginning with a vowel or h mute*) **when I look into t. eyes,** quand je regarde dans tes yeux.

thing [θɪŋ] *n* **(a)** chose *f*, *F* truc *m*; **a t. of beauty,** une belle chose; **the things of this world,** les choses de ce monde; **to go the way of all things,** mourir; **things to be washed,** du linge à laver; **chocolate, sweets, and things (like that),** le chocolat, les bonbons, et autres choses du style; *F* **what's that t.?,** qu'est-ce que c'est que ce machin-là?; **tea things,** service *m* à thé; **where's that scraper t.?,** où est ce machin à gratter?; **my things,** (*clothes etc*) mes vêtements *mpl*, mes effets *mpl*; (*belongings*) mes affaires *fpl*; **winter things,** (*clothes*) vêtements d'hiver; **bring along your swimming things,** apportez vos affaires de bain; **I forbid you to touch my things,** je vous défends de toucher à mes affaires; **to pack (up) one's things,** faire ses malles *ou* ses valises; **I didn't bring a lot of things,** (*on holiday*) je n'ai pas apporté beaucoup d'affaires; *Jur* **things personal/real,** biens *mpl* meubles/immeubles;

(b) *F* (*person*) (*with adj expressing pity, contempt etc*) être *m*, créature *f*; **poor t.!,** le *ou* la pauvre!; **you silly t.!,** sot *ou* sotte que tu es!; **poor little things!,** pauvres petits!; **she's a dear old t.,** c'est une bonne vieille très sympathique;

(c) (*action, remark, fact etc*) **that was a silly t. to do,** quelle bêtise!; **what a silly/nasty t. to say!,** comme c'est bête/méchant d'avoir dit ça!; **the things you say!,** les choses que tu peux dire!; **how could you do such a t.?,** comment avez-vous pu faire une chose pareille?; **how could you say such a t.!,** comment avez-vous pu dire une chose pareille!; **did you ever hear of such a t.?,** on n'a pas idée d'une chose pareille!; **you take things too seriously,** vous prenez les choses trop au sérieux; **she gets things done,** elle fait marcher les choses; **to think things over,** réfléchir; **it's just one of those things,** ce sont des choses qui arrivent; **it's a t. you need to give careful consideration to,** c'est une chose à laquelle tu dois porter une grande attention; **to talk of one t. and another,** parler de choses et d'autres; **it's been one t. after the other,** (*problems*) ça a été un truc après l'autre; **what with one t. and another we haven't had time,** plein de trucs ont fait que nous n'avons pas eu le temps; **that's the very t.,** c'est juste ce qu'il faut; **the t. is this,** voici ce dont il s'agit; **the t. is, I haven't got any money,** le problème, c'est que je n'ai pas d'argent; **the only t. left is to ...,** il ne reste plus qu'à ...; **the important t. is that ...,** l'important c'est que ...; **the t. to remember is that ...,** ce dont il faut se souvenir est que ...; **that's quite another t.,** ça c'est tout autre chose; **neither one t. nor another,** ni l'un ni l'autre; **and another t.,** en plus; *F* **he's on to a good t.,** il est sur un bon filon *ou* un bon coup; **I don't know a t. about algebra,** je n'y connais absolument rien en algèbre; **it doesn't mean a t. to me,** (*I don't understand it at all*) je n'y comprends (absolument) rien; (*it isn't at all familiar to me*) ça ne me dit absolument rien; (*it doesn't concern me at all*) ça ne me concerne pas; **there isn't a t. we can do about it,** il n'y a absolument rien que nous puissions y faire; **to know a t. or two,** (*to know a few tricks etc*) avoir plus d'un tour dans son sac; (*to be well informed*) en savoir long; *F* **she's got a t. about French,** (*loves it*) le français, c'est son truc; (*hates it*) le français, ce n'est pas son truc; *F* **he's got a t. about that, it's a t. with him,** c'est son idée fixe; *F* **do your (own) t.!,** fais comme il te plaira!; **things are going badly,** les affaires vont mal; **as things are,** les choses étant comme elles sont; *F* **how are things?, how's things?,** comment vont les affaires?; (*how are you*) comment ça va?;

(d) the latest t. in shoes, chaussure(s) dernier cri; **it's the (very) latest t.,** c'est tout ce qu'il y a de plus moderne; **he looks quite the t.,** il est vraiment très chic; **the t. (to do),** l'usage *m*, l'étiquette *f* ; **it's not the done t.,** cela ne se fait pas;

(e) *F* (*sex organ*) machin *m*.

thingummy, thingamy, thingumajig, thingumabob ['θɪŋəmɪ, -dʒɪg, -bɒb] *n F* chose *m*, machin *m*, truc *m*.

think¹ [θɪŋk] *n* **to have a (quiet) t.,** réfléchir; **what do you say?, — I'll have a t. about it,** qu'en dis-tu? — je vais réfléchir; *F* **you've got another t. coming!,** tu peux toujours courir!

think² *v* (*pt & pp* **thought** [θɔːt]) **1** *vi* penser, réfléchir; **to t. aloud,** penser tout haut; **to t. hard,** réfléchir profondément, se creuser la tête; *F* **to t. big,** être ambitieux; **I did it without thinking,** je l'ai fait sans réfléchir *ou* sans y penser; **I'm sorry, I wasn't thinking,** désolé, je l'ai fait *ou* dit sans réfléchir; **t. before you speak,** pesez vos paroles; **t. before you act,** réfléchissez avant d'agir; **just t. a minute!,** réfléchissez un peu!; **give me time to t. (and remember),** laissez-moi me reprendre; **you t. too much,** tu réfléchis trop; **to t. again,** se raviser; **you just don't t., do you!,** (*are inconsiderate, careless etc*) jamais tu ne réfléchis, hein!; **you can (just) t. again!,** tu peux toujours courir!; **it makes you t.,** ça vous fait réfléchir; **I'd t. twice about that, if I were you,** je réfléchirais si j'étais toi.

2 *vt* **(a)** (*imagine, suppose*) **what are you thinking?,** à quoi pensez-vous?; **I know what you're thinking,** je sais ce que vous pensez *ou* ce que vous vous dites; **I was just thinking 'I wonder where he is' when ...,** j'étais justement en train de me dire 'je me demande où il est' lorsque ...; **I (really) can't t. why/what/where ...,** je me demande bien pourquoi/ce que/où ...; **I can't t. what you mean,** je n'arrive pas à comprendre *ou* voir ce que vous voulez dire; **what will people t.?,** que vont penser les gens?; **he thinks he knows everything,** il s'imagine tout savoir; **one would have thought that ...,** c'était à croire que ...; **anyone would t. she was asleep,** on dirait qu'elle dort; **who'd have thought it!,** qui l'aurait dit?; **just t.!,** songez donc!; **to t. that he's only twenty!,** et dire qu'il n'a que vingt ans!; **and to t. it used to cost just ...!,** quand je pense qu'avant ça ne coûtait que ...; **I have been thinking that ...,** l'idée m'est venue que ...; *esp Lit* **I only thought to help you,** ma seule pensée était de vous aider; **did you t. to bring any money?,** avez-vous pensé *ou* songé à apporter de l'argent;

(b) (*believe, have as opinion*) **do you t. you could do it — I t. I could,** pensez-vous que cela vous serait possible? — je pense que oui; **it's better, don't you t., to get it over with?,** il vaut mieux en finir, vous ne croyez pas?; **I thought I heard her,** j'ai cru l'entendre; **I thought it was all over,** je croyais que tout était fini; **everyone asked him what he thought,** chacun lui a demandé son avis; **what do you t. Jenny?,** et toi, que penses- *ou* dis-tu, Jenny?; **well what do you t.? does it suit me?,** alors, qu'est-ce que tu en penses, ça me va?; **I t. she's pretty,** je la trouve jolie; **everyone thought he was mad,** on le tenait pour fou; **I rather t. it's going to rain,** j'ai dans l'idée qu'il va pleuvoir; **it is thought that ...,** on suppose que + *ind*; **I t. so,** je pense que oui; **I don't t. so, I think not,** je pense que non; **yes, that's what I t. (too),** c'est ce qu'il me semble; **so I thought, I thought so, I thought as much,** je le pensais bien; **I (should) hardly t. so,** c'est peu probable; **I should t. so!,** je crois bien!; **do you t. they'll agree? — I should t. so.,** croyez-vous qu'ils accepteront? — je pense que oui; **Smith finally apologized — I should t. so (too)!,** Smith a enfin présenté ses excuses — j'espère bien!; **I shouldn't t. so,** je ne crois pas; *F* **that's what you t.!,** tu peux toujours y croire!;

(c) (*judge*) juger, considérer, croire, trouver, penser; **if you t. it necessary to ...,** si vous jugez nécessaire de ...; **I hardly t. it likely that ...,** il n'est guère probable que + *sub*; **to t. proper** *or* **fit to ...,** juger bon de ...; **you thought her (to be) a fool,** vous l'avez prise pour une sotte; **they were thought to be rich,** on les disait *ou* supposait riches; (*they passed for rich*) ils passaient pour (être) riches;

(d) (*expect*) s'attendre à (*qch*); **I little thought I would see him again,** je ne m'attendais guère à le revoir.

►think about *vipo* **(a)** (*reflect on*) penser à (*qn, qch*); **what are you thinking about?,** à quoi penses-tu?; **do you still t. about her?,** pensez-vous encore à elle; **he can't sleep for thinking about it,** il perd le sommeil à force d'y penser, *F* il n'en dort pas; **that's worth thinking about,** cela mérite réflexion; **quite cheap when you t. about it,** plutôt bon marché quand on y pense;

(b) (*consider*) réfléchir à (*qch*); **what do you say? — I'll t. about it,** qu'en dites-vous? — j'y songerai *ou* réfléchirai; **I've thought about your proposal,** j'ai réfléchi à votre proposition; **that will give them sth to t. about,** ça va leur donner à réfléchir; **to t. about doing sth,** envisager de *ou* songer à faire qch;

(c) (*take into account*) penser à (*qn, qch*); **I've got my family/future to t. about,** il faut que je pense à ma famille/mon avenir;

(d) (*have opinion about*) **what do you t. about it?,** qu'en pensez-vous?

▶**think back** *vi* (*reflect on past events*) repenser; **to t. back on past events,** repenser à des événements passés; **when I t. back,** quand j'y repense; **t. back to what you were doing in 1975,** songer à *ou* rappelez-vous ce que vous faisiez en 1975; **thinking back, I suppose I never really liked him,** à la réflexion, je crois que je ne l'ai jamais vraiment aimé.

▶**think of** *vipo* **(a)** (*be attentive to*) penser à, songer à (*qn*); **to t. of others,** penser aux autres; **I've got the children/the children's education to t. of,** il faut que je songe aux enfants/à l'éducation des enfants; **I can't t. of everything!,** je ne peux pas penser à tout!;

(b) (*reflect on*) penser à (*qn, qch*); **we're thinking of you,** nous pensons à toi; **I was thinking of how much times have changed,** je pensais à combien les temps ont changé; **when I t. of what might have happened!,** quand je pense à ce qui aurait pu arriver!; **it's rather silly, when you (come to) t. of it,** c'est plutôt bête, quand on y pense; **come to t. of it, I DID see her that night,** maintenant que j'y pense, je l'ai vue cette nuit-là; **what am I thinking of?,** où ai-je la tête?; **what were you thinking of, letting the child out on his own?,** où avais-tu la tête, pour laisser cet enfant sortir seul?; **we wouldn't t. of letting our daughter travel alone,** nous ne songerions même pas à laisser notre fille voyager seule; **I couldn't t. of it!,** c'est impossible!;

(c) (*recall, bring to mind*) se rappeler (de) (*name etc*); **I can't t. of their number at the moment,** je n'arrive pas à me rappeler leur numéro là tout de suite; **I can't t. of the right word,** le mot juste m'échappe;

(d) (*imagine*) imaginer, se figurer; **just t. of it — a holiday in the Caribbean!,** imagine, des vacances aux Caraïbes!; **and it weighs two tons, (just) t. of that!,** et ça pèse deux tonnes, imagine *ou* figure-toi un peu!;

(e) (*have opinion about*) penser de; **what do you t. of it?,** qu'en pensez-vous?; **what do you t. of this picture?,** que dites-vous de ce tableau?; **I don't t. much of the idea/her taste,** je ne trouve pas que cette idée soit très bonne/qu'elle ait très bon goût; **to t. a lot of** *or* **highly of s.o.,** avoir une haute opinion de qn; **to t. a great deal of oneself, to t. too much of oneself,** avoir une haute idée de sa personne; **to t. too much of sth.,** attacher trop d'importance à qch; **I told her what I thought of her,** je lui ai dit son fait; **to t. well/badly of s.o.,** avoir une bonne/mauvaise opinion de qn; **he is well thought of,** il est bien vu *ou* considéré;

(f) to t. of doing sth, envisager *ou* projeter de faire qch, songer à faire qch; **what were you thinking of giving her?,** que pensais-tu lui donner?;

(g) (*have idea*) imaginer, penser à, avoir l'idée de; (*solution*) imaginer; **the longest word I could t. of,** le plus long mot que je puisse imaginer *ou* auquel je puisse penser; **I've thought of a way of persuading her,** j'ai pensé à *ou* imaginé un moyen de la persuader; **try every method you can t. of.,** essayer toutes les méthodes que vous puissiez imaginer; **who thought of coming to this restaurant?,** qui a eu l'idée de venir dans ce restaurant?; **why didn't you telephone? — I didn't t. of it,** pourquoi n'avez-vous pas téléphoné? — je n'y ai pas pensé; **who thought of the idea?,** qui a eu cette idée?; **what a clever idea! — now why didn't I t. of that?,** quelle idée géniale! — pourquoi n'y ai-je pas pensé *ou* songé?; **t. of a number,** pensez à un chiffre; **I thought of him as being tall,** je le voyais grand.

▶**think out** *vtsep* imaginer (*un plan, une solution*); **he likes to t. things out for himself,** il aime juger des choses par lui-même; **see if you can t. something out,** essaie d'imaginer *ou* de trouver une solution; **well thought out plan,** projet bien étudié; **carefully thought out answer,** réponse bien pesée.

▶**think over** *vtsep* réfléchir sur (*une question etc*); **I'll t. it over,** j'y réfléchirai; **t. it over (carefully),** réfléchissez-y *ou* songez-y bien; **on thinking it over,** à la réflexion.

▶**think through** *vtas* bien considérer (*un plan etc*); **I thought it through all night,** je l'ai ressassé toute la nuit; **the scheme has not been properly thought through,** le plan n'a pas été considéré suffisamment en détail.

▶**think up** *vtsep* imaginer (*un projet, une méthode*); **who thought that idea up?,** qui a eu *ou* imaginé cette idée?

thinkable ['θɪŋkəb(ə)l] *adj* concevable, imaginable; **is it t. that ...?,** peut-on imaginer que + *sub*.

thinker ['θɪŋkər] *n* penseur, -euse.

thinking ['θɪŋkɪŋ] **1** *adj* pensant, qui pense; **the paper for t. people,** le journal pour les gens qui réfléchissent; **the t. man's pin-up,** la pin-up des intellectuels; **any t. person would agree that ...,** n'importe qui réfléchissant un tant soit peu serait d'accord pour dire que ... . **2** *n* pensée(s) *f(pl)*, méditation(s) *f(pl)*, réflexion(s) *f(pl)*; (*opinion*) pensée, opinion *f*, avis *m*; **he did some hard t.,** il a réfléchi profondément; **we'd better do a bit of quick t.,** nous ferions mieux de réfléchir un peu en vitesse; **to put on one's t. cap,** méditer une question; **to my (way of) t.,** à mon avis; **I hope to bring you round to my way of t.,** j'espère vous amener à mon opinion *ou* à mon point du vue.

think-tank ['θɪŋktæŋk] *n* comité *m ou* groupe *m* d'experts.

thin-lipped ['θɪnlɪpt] *adj* aux lèvres minces; **he was rather t.-l.,** (*displeased*) il avait les lèvres plutôt pincées.

thinly ['θɪnlɪ] *adv* **(a)** (*in thin layers*) en couche(s) mince(s); (*in thin slices*) en tranches minces; (*not densely*) clair; **t. sown wheat,** blé clairsemé; **t. populated,** (*pays*) de population peu dense; **(b) t. clad,** (*lightly*) vêtu légèrement; (*inadequately*) vêtu insuffisamment; **t. veiled allusion,** allusion à peine voilée.

thinner ['θɪnər] *n* (*occ* **thinners**) diluant *m*, dissolvant *m* (*pour peinture etc*) .

thinness ['θɪnnɪs] *n* **(a)** minceur *f* (*d'une feuille de papier etc*); légèreté *f* (*d'un tissu etc*); maigreur *f*, minceur (*d'une personne*); **(b)** état clairsemé (*du blé, des cheveux etc*); **(c)** fluidité *f* (*d'un liquide*); raréfaction *f*, légèreté *f* (*de l'air*); caractère grêle *ou* fluet (*d'une voix*).

thinning ['θɪnɪŋ] **1** *n* amincissement *m*; délayage *m* (*de la peinture*); (*dilution*) dilution *f*; démariage *m* (*des jeunes plants*); **t. agent,** dissolvant *m*, diluant *m*. **2** *adj* **his t. hair,** ses cheveux qui commencent à se clairsemer.

thin-skinned [θɪn'skɪnd] *adj* (*animal etc*) à la peau mince; *Fig* (*person*) susceptible, trop sensible.

thin-sliced ['θɪnslaɪst] *adj* (*bread*) coupé en tranches minces, finement coupé.

third [θɜːd] **1** *num adj & n* troisième (*jour, étage etc*); tiers (*état etc*); **Edward the T.,** Édouard Trois; **(on) the t. (of May),** le trois (mai); **every t. day,** tous les trois jours; *F* **t. degree,** interrogatoire serré; **to give s.o. the t. degree,** faire subir un interrogatoire serré à qn; (*treat roughly*) malmener qn; *Jur* **t. party,** (*person*) tiers *m*, tierce personne *f*; **t. party cover,** *F* assurance *f* aux tiers; *Gram* **t. person,** troisième personne; **in (the) t. place,** en troisième lieu, troisièmement; **a t. rate pianist,** un pianiste de troisième ordre; **the T. World,** le tiers monde.

2 *n* **(a)** (*fraction*) tiers *m*; **to lose a t./two thirds of one's money,** perdre le tiers/les deux tiers de son argent; **one t. full,** plein au tiers;

(b) *Mus* tierce *f*;

(c) *Br Univ* **to get a t. (class honours degree) in history,** obtenir la mention 'passable' en histoire;

(d) *Aut* **to go into t.,** passer en troisième *f*.

thirdly ['θɜːdlɪ] *adv* troisièmement, en troisième lieu.

thirst¹ [θɜːst] *n* soif *f*; *Fig esp Lit* **the t. for** *or* **after knowledge,** la soif de connaître *ou* de connaissances; **to satisfy one's t. for adventure,** satisfaire sa soif d'aventures.

thirst² *vi Arch & Lit* être altéré *ou* avide (**for,** de); *Fig Lit* **to t. for blood/revenge,** être altéré de sang/de vengeance.

thirstily ['θɜːstɪlɪ] *adv* avidement.

thirsty ['θɜːstɪ] *adj* **(a)** assoiffé; (*earth etc*) desséché, sec, *f* sèche; *F* (*car*) qui consomme énormément; **to be/feel t.,** avoir soif; **I'm t.,** j'ai soif; *F* **all this talking is t. work,** de tant parler, cela donne soif *ou* cela vous sèche le gosier; *Fig Lit* **t. for blood/for riches,** assoiffé *ou* altéré *ou* avide de sang/de richesses.

thirteen [θɜː'tiːn] *num adj & n* treize *m*; **she's t. (years old),** elle a treize ans; **at t. hundred hours,** à treize heures.

thirteenth [θɜː'tiːnθ] **1** *num adj & n* treizième *mf*; **(on) the t. (of May),** le treize (mai); **Friday the t.,** vendredi treize. **2** *n* (*fraction*) treizième *m*.

thirtieth ['θɜːtɪɪθ] *num adj & n* trentième *mf*; **(on) the t. (of June),** le trente (juin).

thirty ['θɜːtɪ] *num adj & n* trente *m*; **t.-three,** trente-trois; **t.-first,** trente et unième, **t.-second,** trente-deuxième; **(on) the t.-first (of May),** le trente et un (mai); **about t. guests,** une trentaine d'invités; **to be t. (years old),** avoir trente ans; **the thirties,** les années trente; **he leaves at two-t.,** il part à deux heures trente.

this [ðɪs] **1** *dem pron pl* **these** [ðiːz] **(a)** ceci; ce; **what's t.?, what are these?,** qu'est-ce que c'est (que ceci, *F* que ça)?; **who's t.?**, qui est-ce?; *Tel* **who is t.?**, qui est à l'appareil?; **you'll be sorry for t.**, vous le regretterez; **at** *or* **upon t.**, sur ce, là-dessus; **it ought to have come before t.**, cela devrait être déjà arrivé; **after t.**, après cela, ensuite; **t. is curious,** c'est curieux, voilà qui est curieux; **t. is what she told me,** voici ce qu'elle m'a dit; **t. is Mr Ford,** je vous présente M. Ford; **these are my children,** voici mes enfants; **t. is where she lives,** c'est içi qu'elle habite; **these are things we cannot do without,** ce sont des choses dont on ne peut se passer; **listen to t.**, écoutez bien ceci; **eat/drink some of t.**, mangez-/buvez-en un peu; **what's t. (that) I hear?**, qu'est-ce que j'apprends?; **do it like t.**, fais comme ceci; **what's all t.?**, qu'est-ce qu'il y a?, qu'est-ce qui se passe?;

(b) (*opposed to* **that**) **will you have t. or that?**, voulez-vous ceci ou cela?; *F* **they were talking about t. and that,** ils parlaient de choses et d'autres;

(c) (*referring to sth already mentioned*) celui-ci, *f* celle-ci, *pl* ceux-ci, *f* celles-ci; **I prefer these to those,** je préfère ceux-ci à ceux-là.

2 *dem adj pl* **these** ce, (*before vowel or h mute*) cet, *f* cette, *pl* ces; (*for emphasis and in opposition to* **that, those**) ce... -ci, cet... -ci, cette... -ci, ces... -ci; **t. book,** ce livre(-ci); **these books,** ces livres(-ci); **t. morning,** ce matin, **this afternoon,** cet après-midi, **this week,** cette semaine; **one of these days,** un de ces jours; **(in) these days, in t. day and age,** de nos jours; **by t. time,** à l'heure qu'il est; **to run t. way and that,** courir de-ci de-là; **he will tell you that in t. or that case you should...,** il vous dira qu'en tel ou tel cas il faut...; **for t. reason,** voilà pourquoi, pour cette raison; *F* **t. here house,** cette maison(-ci); *Pej* **she's one of these artist women,** c'est une de ces artistes; *Dial* **I've known him these three years,** je le connais depuis trois ans.

3 *dem adv* aussi ... que ceci; **t. high, as high as t.**, aussi haut que ceci *ou* que cela *ou* que ça; **t. far,** jusqu'ici, jusque-là; **can you eat t. much?**, pourras-tu manger tout cela?; **t. much is certain ...**, ceci au moins est sûr ....

thistle ['θɪs(ə)l] *n* (*plant*) chardon *m*.

thistledown ['θɪs(ə)ldaʊn] *n* duvet *m* de chardon.

thither ['ðɪðər] *adv Arch & Lit* (*expressing motion*) là, y; **to run hither and t.**, courir çà et là.

tho' [ðəʊ] *conj & adv F & Lit* = **THOUGH**.

thole, tholepin ['θəʊl(pɪn)] *n Nau* tolet *m*.

thong [θɒŋ] *n* lanière *f* de cuir; lanière, longe *f* (*de fouet*).

thoracic [θɔː'ræsɪk] *adj* thoracique.

thorax, *pl* **thoraces** ['θɔːræks, θɔː'reɪsiːz] *n Anat Ent* thorax *m*

thorn [θɔːn] *n* **(a)** *Bot* épine *f*; *Fig* **a t. in one's flesh** *or* **in one's side,** une épine au pied; *Fig* **to be a t. in s.o.'s flesh** *or* **side,** être un sujet continuel d'irritation à qn; **(b)** (*tree*) épine *f*; **t. apple,** pomme épineuse.

thornback ['θɔːnbæk] *n* (*fish*) raie bouclée.

thornbush ['θɔːnbʊʃ] *n* (arbrisseau) épineux *m*.

thornless ['θɔːnlɪs] *adj* sans épines.

thorny ['θɔːnɪ] *adj* épineux; **t. devil,** moloch *m*; *Fig* **t. question,** question épineuse.

thorough ['θʌrə] *adj* (*search etc*) minutieux; (*knowledge*) profond; (*work*) consciencieux; **to be t. in one's work,** travailler consciencieusement; **to give a room a t. cleaning,** nettoyer une pièce à fond; **it needs a t. revision,** il a besoin d'une profonde révision *ou* d'une révision en profondeur; **a t. scoundrel,** un fieffé coquin; **to make a t. nuisance of oneself,** se rendre complètement empoisonnant.

thoroughbred ['θʌrəbred] **1** *adj* (*cheval*) pur sang *inv*; (*chien etc*) de race; (*person*) qui a de la race. **2** *n* (*animal*) animal, -aux *m* de race; (*horse*) pur-sang *m inv*; (*person*) **she's a real t.**, elle est très racée.

thoroughfare ['θʌrəfeər] *n* voie *f* de communication; **public t.**, voie publique; **one of the main thoroughfares of the town,** une des rues principales *ou* une des artères de la ville; **busy t.**, (*street*) rue très passante; (*road*) route très passagère *ou* à circulation intense; **no t.**, (*on sign*) (*no through road*) rue barrée; (*no access*) passage interdit (au public).

thoroughgoing ['θʌrəgəʊɪŋ] *adj* (*search, inspection etc*) minutieux; (*knowledge, changes, revision, reform etc*) profond; (*work, worker etc*) consciencieux; (*moralist etc*) intransigeant; **such a t. rogue as him,** un tel fieffé coquin.

thoroughly ['θʌrəlɪ] *adv* complètement; (*savoir une langue etc*) parfaitement; (*renouveler*) entièrement; (*nettoyer, savoir qch*) à fond; **to be t. bored,** s'ennuyer mortellement; **t. honest,** d'une honnêteté à toute épreuve; **t. untrustworthy,** absolument indigne de confiance.

thoroughness ['θʌrənɪs] *n* (*of work*) perfection *f*, minutie *f*; (*of knowledge, revision*) profondeur *f*.

those *see* **THAT**[1].

thou [ðaʊ] *pers pron Arch & Bible & Dial* (*unstressed*) tu; (*stressed*) toi; **t. seest,** tu vois; **t. art,** tu es; **hearest t.?**, entends-tu?; **t. and I,** toi et moi.

though [ðəʊ] **1** *conj* **(a)** quoique, bien que + *sub*; **t. she is poor she is generous,** quoiqu'elle soit pauvre elle est généreuse; **I respect him t. I don't like him,** je le respecte, bien qu'il ne me soit pas sympathique; **t. I am a father,** tout père que je suis; **t. not handsome, he was attractive,** sans être beau il avait du charme;

(b) this statement, terrible t. it be, cette déclaration, pour terrible qu'elle soit; **strange t. it may seem,** si étrange que cela semble; **even t. you'll laugh at me,** même si vous vous moquez de moi;

(c) as t., comme si; **it looks as t. she's gone,** il semble qu'elle soit partie; **as t. nothing had happened,** comme si de rien n'était.

2 *adv* cependant, pourtant; **it's not what I want t.**, mais ce n'est pas ce que je veux; **I didn't mean it t.**, mais je ne disais pas ça sérieusement; **he had promised to go — he didn't t.**, il avait promis d'y aller — cependant il n'en a rien fait; **did she t.!**, elle a dit *ou* fait cela?

thought[1] [θɔːt] *n* **(a)** (*thinking*) pensée *f*; **contemporary t.**, la pensée contemporaine; **capable of t.**, capable de penser;

(b) (*idea*) pensée *f*, idée *f*; **he hasn't a t. in his head,** il n'a pas une idée dans la tête; **happy t.**, heureuse idée; **dark** *or* **gloomy thoughts,** idées *ou* pensées sombres; *F* **a penny for your thoughts,** à quoi pensez-vous?; **to read s.o.'s thoughts,** lire dans la pensée de qn; **t. reading,** lecture *f* de la pensée; **t. reader,** liseur, -euse de pensées; **I'm not a t. reader, I can't read your thoughts,** je ne suis pas devin; **the mere t. of it,** rien que d'y penser; **have you ever given it a single t.?**, y avez-vous jamais pensé?; **I didn't give it another t.**, je n'y ai pas repensé; **what are your thoughts on the matter?**, quelle est votre opinion sur ce sujet?; **to collect one's thoughts,** rassembler ses idées *ou* ses esprits; **her thoughts were elsewhere,** son esprit était ailleurs;

(c) (*reflection*) réflexion *f*, considération *f*; (*meditation*) pensées *fpl*, rêverie *f*, méditation *f*; **after much t.**, après mûre réflexion; **to give a great deal of t. to sth,** réfléchir beaucoup à qch; **on second thoughts,** (toute) réflexion faite, à la réflexion; **to be deep** *or* **lost in t.**, être perdu *ou* absorbé dans ses pensées, être plongé dans ses réflexions;

(d) (*intention*) intention *f*, dessein *m*; **I had no t. of offending you,** je n'avais pas l'intention de vous offenser; **you must give up all thought(s) of seeing him,** il faut renoncer à le voir, il ne faut plus penser à le voir; **his one t. is to get money,** il ne pense qu'à l'argent; *Old-fashioned* **I had no t. of meeting you here,** je ne m'attendais pas à vous rencontrer ici;

(e) *Old-fashioned F* **a t. too sweet,** un tout petit peu trop sucré.

thought[2] *see* **THINK**[2].

thoughtful ['θɔːtfʊl] *adj* **(a)** (*pensive*) (*person, expression*) pensif, méditatif; **to look t.**, avoir l'air pensif; **(b)** (*considered, prudent*) réfléchi, prudent; **(c)** (*considerate*) prévenant, attentionné (**of,** pour); **he was t. enough to warn me,** il a eu la prévenance *ou* l'attention de m'avertir; **it was very t. of her to ...**, c'était très attentionné de sa part de ...; **that wasn't very t.**, ce n'était pas très attentionné; **(d)** (*book, writer*) profond.

thoughtfully ['θɔːtfəlɪ] *adv* **(a)** (*pensively*) pensivement, d'un air pensif *ou* méditatif; **(b)** (*with careful thought*) d'une manière réfléchie *ou* prudente; **(c)** (*considerately*) avec prévenance.

thoughtfulness ['θɔːtfʊlnɪs] *n* **(a)** (*meditation*) méditation *f*, recueillement *m*; **(b)** (*prudence*) réflexion *f*, prudence *f*; **(c)** (*consideration*) prévenance *f*; égards *mpl* (**of,** pour, envers).

thoughtless ['θɔːtlɪs] *adj* **(a)** (*ill-considered*) irréfléchi, étourdi; **t. action,** acte inconsidéré; **(b)** (*inconsiderate*) **t. of others,** qui manque d'égards *ou* de prévenance pour les autres.

thoughtlessly ['θɔːtlɪslɪ] *adv* **(a)** (*without reflection*) étourdiment, sans réfléchir; **(b)** (*inconsiderately*) **to treat s.o. t.**, manquer d'égards envers qn; **he very t. left it locked,** il l'a très inconsidérément laissé fermé; **they t. took the whole lot,** sans aucun égard ils ont pris le tout.

thoughtlessness ['θɔːtlɪsnɪs] *n* **(a)** (*lack of forethought*) irréflexion *f*, étourderie *f*; **(b)** (*lack of consideration*) manque d'égards *ou* de prévenance (**of,** pour, envers).

thought-out ['θɔːt'aʊt] *adj* **well/poorly t.-o. plan,** projet bien/mal étudié *ou* conçu; **carefully t.-o. answer,** réponse bien pesée.

thought-provoking ['θɔːtprəvəʊkɪŋ] *adj* qui invite à la réflexion, qui donne à *ou* fait réfléchir.

thousand ['θaʊz(ə)nd] **1** *num adj* mille *m inv*; **the year 4000 B.C.,** l'an quatre mille av. J.-C.; *Jur Admin* **the year one t. nine hundred and thirty,** l'an mil neuf cent trente; *Culin* **T. Island dressing,** mayonnaise *f* au ketchup et aux cornichons; **about a t. men,** un millier d'hommes; **three hundred t. people,** trois cent mille personnes; *F* **I've got a t. and one things to ask you,** j'ai mille et une choses à vous demander; **no, no, a t. times no!,** non, non, et cent fois non!; **a t. years,** mille ans. **2** *n* mille *m*; millier *m*; **thousands of people,** des milliers de gens; **in thousands,** par milliers; **in hundreds of thousands,** par centaines de mille; **she's one in a t.,** c'est une femme entre mille; **a t.,** mille, un millier; **a. t. and one,** mille un.

thousandfold ['θaʊz(ə)n(d)fəʊld] **1** *adj* multiplié par mille. **2** *adv* mille fois autant.

thousandth ['θaʊz(ə)n(t)θ] *num adj & n* millième *mf*.

thraldom ['θrɔːldəm] *n Lit* esclavage *m*, assujetissement *m*, servitude *f*.

thrall [θrɔːl] *n Lit* **(a)** esclave *mf*, serf *m* (**of, to,** de); **(b) kept in t.,** maintenu en esclavage *m*.

thrash [θræʃ] **1** *vt* (*beat*) battre (*qn, une bête*); rosser, tanner le cuir à (*qn*); battre (*le blé*); (*defeat heavily in game etc*) battre (*un adversaire*) à plate(s) couture(s); **to t. s.o. soundly,** donner une bonne raclée à qn; **to t. the water,** battre l'eau; **to t. one's arms and legs in the air,** se débattre des mains et des pieds. **2** *vi* (*of water*) battre, clapoter (**against,** contre); **a sea of thrashing limbs,** un océan de bras et de jambes battant l'air.

▶**thrash about, thrash around 1** *vtsep* (*wave, move furiously*) **to t. one's arms and legs about,** se débattre des mains et des pieds. **2** *vi* (*move limbs, body furiously*) (*of person*) se débattre des mains et des pieds; (*of fish*) remuer, se débattre; **the fish thrashed about in the net,** le poisson se débattait dans le filet.

▶**thrash out** *vtsep* **(a)** (*discuss thoroughly*) débattre, creuser (*une question*), discuter (*une question*) à fond; **to t. it out with s.o.,** en débattre avec qn; **(b)** (*reach*) arriver à (*une solution, la vérité etc*).

thrashing ['θræʃɪŋ] *n* (*beating*) volée *f* (de coups), *F* raclée *f*, *F* rossée *f*; *Sp etc* défaite *f*; battage *m* (*du blé*); **to give s.o. a t.,** donner une raclée à qn; **to give one's opponent a sound t.,** battre son adversaire à plate(s) couture(s).

thread[1] [θred] *n* **(a)** filament *m*, fil *m* (*de soie, d'une plante etc*); filet *m* (*d'eau, de fumée, de lumière, d'un billet de banque etc*); **his life hung by a t.,** sa vie ne tenait qu'à un fil; **t. mark,** (*in papermaking*) filigrane *m* (des billets de banque); **(b)** *Sewing* fil *m* (*de coton, de nylon etc*); *Tex* fil (*de trame, de chaîne*); **(length of) t.,** brin *m*, bout *m* (*de coton, de soie etc*); **gold t.,** fil d'or; **button t.,** fil à boutons; *Sewing* **drawn t. work,** ouvrage *m ou* travail *m* à jour(s); **the t. of life,** la trame de la vie; **to lose the t. of the conversation,** perdre le fil de la conversation; **to gather up the threads of a story,** reprendre les fils d'une histoire; **(c)** *Tech* filet *m* (*d'une vis, d'un boulon etc*).

thread[2] **1** *vt* **(a)** enfiler (*une aiguille*); enfiler (*des perles*) (**on,** sur); enfiler (*une ficelle, un élastique*) (**through sth,** dans qch); **to t. one's way between the cars,** se faufiler *ou* s'insinuer entre les voitures; **(b)** *Tech* fileter (*une vis etc*); tarauder (*un tuyau, un écrou etc*). **2** *vi* **(a) we threaded through the crowd,** nous nous sommes faufilés à travers la foule; **(b) to t. into sth,** (*of screw etc*) se visser dans qch.

threadbare ['θredbeər] *adj* (*clothes etc*) râpé *ou* élimé *ou* usé (jusqu'à la corde); *Fig* (*subject, argument, joke etc*) usé (jusqu'à la corde), rebattu.

threading ['θredɪŋ] *n* **(a)** enfilage *m* (*d'une aiguille etc*); **(b)** *Tech* filetage *m* (*d'une vis etc*); taraudage *m* (*d'un tuyau etc*).

threadworm ['θredwɜːm] *n* oxyure *m*.

threat [θret] *n* menace *f*; **to make threats,** faire des menaces; **to utter a t.,** proférer une menace; **idle t.,** menace en l'air; **there is a t. of rain,** la pluie menace; **to see s.o. as a t.,** voir une menace en qn; **is that a t. or a promise?,** est-ce un bien on un mal?; **if we exist under the t. of nuclear war,** si nous vivons sous la menace d'une guerre nucléaire.

threaten ['θret(ə)n] **1** *vt* menacer (*qn*); *Jur* intimider (*qn*); **to t. s.o. with sth,** menacer qn de qch; **(to be) threatened with sth,** (être) menacé de qch; **race threatened with extinction,** race en voie de disparition; **the threatened strike didn't come off,** cette menace de grève n'a pas abouti; **the sky threatened rain,** la pluie menaçait, le ciel était menaçant de pluie; **to t. to do sth,** menacer de faire qch; **this situation threatens to become dangerous,** cette situation menace de devenir dangereuse. **2** *vi* **a storm is threatening,** l'orage menace, un orage s'annonce.

threatening ['θret(ə)nɪŋ] *adj* (*ton, air*) menaçant; (*lettre*) de menaces *ou Jur* d'intimidation; **the weather looks t.,** le temps est menaçant; **t. language,** menaces *fpl* (verbales).

threateningly ['θret(ə)nɪŋlɪ] *adv* d'une manière menaçante.

three [θriː] *num adj & n* trois *m*; **every t. months,** tous les trois mois; **twenty-t.,** vingt-trois; **t. and a half,** trois et demi; **to be t. (years old),** avoir trois ans; **he leaves at t. thirty** *or* **at half past t.,** il part à trois heures trente *ou* à trois heures et demie; **to come in t. by t.** *or* **in threes,** entrer (trois) par trois; *Pol* **the Big T.,** les Trois (Grands); **t.-bladed propeller,** hélice *f* tripale; *Av* **t.-engine(d) aircraft,** trimoteur *m*; *Cards* **t. of diamonds,** trois de carreau; **double t.,** (*at dominoes etc*) double-trois *m*, *pl* doubles-trois; *Th* **t. act play,** pièce *f* en trois actes; **t.-pointed,** à trois pointes; **t. seater,** triplace *m*; **t. sided** *or* **t. party conversations,** conversations tripartites *ou* triparties; **t. star hotel/brandy,** hotel *m*/cognac *m* trois-étoiles; **t.-stranded rope,** corde à trois cordons.

three-colour(ed), *US* **three-color(ed)** [θriː'kʌlər, -'kʌləd] *adj* tricolore; *Phot* trichrome; **t.-colour process,** trichromie *f*.

three-cornered [θriː'kɔːnəd] *adj* triangulaire; **t.-c. discussion,** débat *m* à trois; **t.-c. hat,** tricorne *m*.

three-course ['θriːkɔːs] *adj* (*repas*) à trois plats.

three-D [θriː'diː] **1** *adj F* = **THREE-DIMENSIONAL**. **2** *n* **in t.-D.,** en trois dimensions.

three-dimensional [θriːd(a)ɪ'menʃənəl] *adj* tridimensionnel.

threefold ['θriːfəʊld] **1** *adj* triple. **2** *adv* trois fois autant; **to increase t.,** tripler.

three-four [θriː'fɔːr] *adj Mus* **t.-f. time,** mesure *f* à trois temps.

three-handed [θriː'hændɪd] *adj Cards etc* **t.-h. game,** partie *f* à trois.

three-legged [θriː'legɪd] *adj* (*tabouret etc*) à trois pieds; **t.-l. race,** (*game*) course *f* à trois pieds.

threepence ['θrep(ə)ns] *n* trois pence *mpl*.

threepenny ['θrep(ə)nɪ] *adj* coûtant trois pence, à *ou* de trois pence; *Arch* **t. (bit),** pièce *f* de trois pence.

three-piece ['θriːpiːs] *adj* en trois pièces; **t.-p. suit,** (*clothes*) (costume *m*) trois-pièces *m inv*; **t.-p. suite,** (*furniture*) canapé et deux fauteuils assortis, salon *m* trois pièces.

three-ply ['θriːplaɪ] *adj* (*wool etc*) à trois fils; (*rope*) en trois brins; (*tissue paper*) à trois épaisseurs.

three-point ['θriːpɔɪnt] *adj Av* **t.-p. landing,** atterrissage *m* trois points; *Aut* **t.-p. turn,** demi-tour *m* en trois manœuvres.

three-quarter [θriː'kwɔːtər] **1** *adj* **t.-q. face portrait,** portrait *m* de trois quarts; **t.-q. length coat,** trois-quarts *m inv*. **2** *n Rugby* **t.-q. (back),** trois-quarts *m*; **the t.-q. line,** la ligne des trois-quarts.

three-ring ['θriːrɪŋ] *adj* **t.-r. circus,** cirque *m* contenant trois arènes et montrant plusieurs numéros à la fois; *Fig* cirque, chantier *m*, chaos *m*.

threescore ['θriːskɔːr] *adj Arch & Lit* soixante; **t. (years) and ten,** soixante-dix ans.

threesome ['θriːsəm] *n* (*three people*) groupe *m* de trois personnes; *Golf* partie *f* à trois; **do you want to make up a t.?,** (*in games*) veux-tu faire le troisième?; (*going out etc*) veux-tu te joindre à nous (deux)?; **we went as a t.,** nous y sommes allés à trois.

three-speed ['θriːspiːd] *adj* à trois vitesses.

three-storey(ed), *US* **-story, -storied** [θriː'stɔːrɪ(d)] *adj* (*maison*) à trois étages.

three-way ['θriːweɪ] *adj* (*division etc*) en trois; (*discussion etc*) à trois.

three-wheeler [θriː'wiːlər] *n Aut* (petite) voiture *f* à trois roues; (*tricycle*) tricycle *m*.

threnody ['θrenədɪ] *n* chant *m* funèbre.

thresh [θreʃ] *vt* battre (*le blé*); *Fig* **to t. the water,** (*of ship's screw, of whale's tail etc*) battre l'eau.

thresher ['θreʃər] *n* (*person*) batteur, -euse en grange; (*machine*) batteuse.

threshing ['θreʃɪŋ] *n* battage *m* (*du blé*); **t. floor,** aire *f* de battage; **t. machine,** batteuse *f*.

threshold ['θreʃəʊld] *n* **(a)** seuil *m*, pas *m* (*d'une porte etc*); **on the t.,** sur le seuil; **to cross the t.,** franchir le seuil; *Fig* **to be on the t. of life,** être au seuil *ou* au début de la vie; **(b)** *Phys etc* seuil *m* (*de fission, de réaction*); **to have a low boredom t.,** être prédisposé à l'ennui, s'ennuyer facilement; *Physiol* **t. of audibility** *or* **of hearing,** seuil d'audibilité; **to have a low/high pain t.,** mal tolérer/bien tolérer la douleur.

threw *see* **THROW[2]**.

thrice [θraɪs] *adv Arch & Lit* trois fois.

thrift [θrɪft] *n* économie *f*, épargne *f*; **t. shop,** = magasin spécialisé dans la vente des articles de seconde main.

thriftily ['θrɪftɪlɪ] *adv* avec économie; (*vivre*) frugalement.

thriftiness ['θrɪftɪnɪs] *n* économie *f*, épargne *f*.

thriftless ['θrɪftlɪs] *adj* (*spendthrift*) dépensier; (*improvident*) imprévoyant.

thriftlessness ['θrɪftlɪsnɪs] *n* gaspillage *m*; (*improvidence*) imprévoyance *f*.

thrifty ['θrɪftɪ] *adj* économe, épargnant.

thrill[1] [θrɪl] *n* (*exciting feeling*) (vive) émotion *f*; (*trembling*) frisson *m*, tressaillement *m*; **t. of pleasure,** frisson de plaisir; **the t. of riding a motorbike,** le frisson que donne la moto; **the crowd had the t. of their lives,** la foule était électrisée; **to get a t. out of sth,** se donner des sensations fortes avec qch; **it gave me quite a t.,** ça m'a fait quelque chose; **all the thrills of the big wheel,** tous les frissons que procure la grande roue; **all the thrills and spills of the circus,** toutes les joies et les frissons du cirque; *F* **go on, give us a t. let's see you dance!,** allez, montre-nous ce que tu sais faire, danse!

thrill[2] **1** *vt* (*experience, thought, prospect*) exalter; (*s.o.'s touch*) faire frémir *ou* frissonner, donner des frissons à; (*conjuror etc*) faire vibrer (*l'auditoire, les enfants*); **a novel/film that will t. you,** un roman/film qui vous fera frémir; **he was so thrilled with his present,** son cadeau le transportait tellement de joie *ou* le ravissait tellement; **she's thrilled with her new car,** elle est ravie de sa nouvelle voiture; *F* **I'm thrilled for you,** je suis très heureux pour vous; (*excite*) (*of scenery, danger, ride*) **to be thrilled at the sight of sth,** être fou de joie à la vue de qch; **to be thrilled to bits,** être fou de joie; **we were absolutely thrilled (to bits) to hear your news/to have won the holiday,** nous étions ravis *ou* électrisés par vos nouvelles/d'avoir gagné les vacances. **2** *vi esp Lit* tressaillir, frissonner (de joie).

thriller ['θrɪlər] *n* (*film, novel, play*) pièce *f ou* film *m ou* roman *m* à suspense, thriller *m*.

thrilling ['θrɪlɪŋ] *adj* sensationnel, passionnant; (*sight*) saisissant; *Sp* **t. finish,** arrivée palpitante; *Iron* **how t. for you!,** c'est passionnant, ce qui t'arrive!

thrive [θraɪv] *vi* (*pt & pp* **thrived** [θraɪvd]; *Arch & US pt* **throve** [θrəʊv] ; *pp* **thriven** ['θrɪvn]) (*grow well*) (*of child, plant*) (bien) se développer; (*of child*) *F* profiter; (*of adult*) bien se porter; (*of business etc*) bien marcher, bien aller; (*prosper*) (*of person*) prospérer (**on sth,** de qch); (*develop potential*) s'épanouir; **children who t. on milk,** enfants à qui le lait profite bien; **plant that thrives in all soils,** plante qui s'accommode de tous les sols; **to t. on danger/***etc*, se nourrir de danger/*etc*; **to t. on other people's misfortunes,** s'engraisser de la misère d'autrui; **some people t. on stress,** certaines personnes s'épanouissent dans le stress; **do I object? I t. on it!,** si je suis contre? j'adore ça!

thriving ['θraɪvɪŋ] *adj* (*person, plant etc*) vigoureux; (*person*) bien portant; (*person, business*) prospère, florissant.

thro' [θruː] *prep F* = **THROUGH**.

throat [θrəʊt] *n Anat* gorge *f*; (*gullet*) gorge, gosier *m*; **to cut s.o.'s t.,** couper la gorge à qn; *Fig* **he's cutting his own t.,** il travaille à sa propre ruine; *Fig* **they were cutting each other's** *or* **one another's throats,** ils se faisaient une concurrence désastreuse; **the back of the t.,** le fond de la gorge, l'arrière-gorge *f*, *pl* arrière-gorges; **to grab s.o. by the throat,** attraper *ou* saisir qn à la gorge; **to have a sore t.,** avoir mal à la gorge; **to clear one's t.,** s'éclaircir la voix *ou* la gorge, se racler la gorge; *Fig F* **she's always ramming it down my t.,** elle m'en rabat toujours les oreilles; *F* **if you pour enough wine down his t. ...,** si tu arroses son gosier de suffisamment de vin ...; **t. microphone,** laryngophone *m*; *Med* **t. spray,** insufflateur *m*.

throatiness ['θrəʊtɪnɪs] *n* qualité gutturale (*de la voix*).

throaty ['θrəʊtɪ] *adj* (*voice*) d'arrière-gorge, guttural, -aux; (*cough*) caverneux.

throb[1] [θrɒb] *n* palpitation *f*, pulsation *f* (*du pouls, du cœur etc*); vrombissement *m* (*d'une machine*).

throb[2] *vi* (-bb-) (*of heart etc*) battre fort, palpiter; (*of engine etc*) vrombir; **a city throbbing with activity,** une ville palpitante d'activité; **my finger is throbbing,** mon doigt lancine; **my head is throbbing,** ça me tape dans la tête.

throbbing ['θrɒbɪŋ] **1** *adj* (*heart etc*) palpitant; (*engine*) vrombissant; **t. pain,** douleur lancinante. **2** *n* battement fort, palpitations *fpl*, pulsations *fpl* (*du cœur etc*); vrombissement *m* (*d'une machine*); élancements *mpl* (*d'un panaris*).

throes [θrəʊz] *npl* douleurs *fpl*, angoisse *f*, agonie *f*; **the t. of death,** les affres *fpl* de la mort, l'agonie; **a country in the t. of revolution,** un pays en proie à la révolution *ou* dans la tourmente de la révolution; *F* **we're in the t. of moving house,** nous sommes en plein déménagement; *F* **don't disturb him while he's in the t. (of writing** *etc***),** ne le dérange pas pendant qu'il est sous le coup de l'inspiration; **in the t. of a divorce,** dans la tourmente d'un divorce.

thrombosis [θrɒm'bəʊsɪs] *n Med* thrombose *f*; **coronary t.,** infarctus *m* du myocarde.

throne [θrəʊn] *n* trône *m*; *F* (*lavatory*) trône; **to come to** *or* **ascend** *or Lit* **mount the t.,** monter sur le trône; **the heir to the t.,** l'héritier au trône; (*of king etc*) *& Fig* **the power behind the t.,** l'Éminence grise.

throneroom ['θrəʊnruːm] *n* salle *f* du trône; *F Hum* **in the t.,** (*on the toilet*) sur le trône.

throng[1] [θrɒŋ] *n* foule *f*, affluence *f*; **a t. of angels,** une multitude d'anges.

throng[2] **1** *vi* (*gather*) s'assembler en foule; (*go to*) affluer (*à ou dans un endroit*); **to t. round s.o.,** se presser autour de qn; **they thronged into the square,** ils arrivèrent en foule sur la place. **2** *vt* encombrer, emplir; **the room was thronged with people,** la pièce était bondée.

thronging ['θrɒŋɪŋ] *adj* **a t. mass,** une foule grouillante (de gens).

throttle[1] ['θrɒt(ə)l] *n* **(a)** *Aut etc* étrangleur *m*, obturateur *m*; *MecE* (*in steam engine*) régulateur *m*, prise *f* de vapeur; *Aut* **to open/to close the t.,** ouvrir/fermer les gaz; **t. (control** *or* **lever),** (*on motorbike, speedboat, plane*) manette *f* des gaz; **at full t.,** à pleins gaz; **(b)** (*throat*) gosier *m*.

throttle[2] *vt* **(a)** (*strangle*) étrangler (*qn*); (*seize, grip by the throat*) saisir *ou* serrer (*qn*) à la gorge; **(b)** *Aut MecE* étrangler (*le moteur, la vapeur*).

►**throttle back, throttle down** **1** *vi* (*slow engine*) mettre le moteur au ralenti; (*cut, close off fuel*) couper *ou* fermer les gaz; **the pilot/rider gradually throttles back,** le pilote/motard coupe les gaz progressivement. **2** *vtsep* mettre (*le moteur*) au ralenti.

throttling ['θrɒt(ə)lɪŋ] *n* **(a)** (*strangling*) étranglement *m*, *Jur* strangulation *f* (*de qn*); **(b)** *Aut etc* obturation *f*.

through [θruː] **1** *prep* **(a)** à travers; par; (*time*) pendant, durant; **t. a hedge,** au travers d'une haie; **to go t. a tunnel,** passer dans un tunnel; **the nail/arrow went t. the wood/wall/***etc*, le clou/la flèche traversa le bois/le mur/*etc*; **the path goes** *or* **leads t. the forest,** le sentier traverse *ou* passe par la forêt; **I'm on my way t. Paris,** je suis de passage à Paris; **to look t. the window/a telescope/a hole,** regarder par la fenêtre/dans un télescope/par un trou; **she came in t. the window,** elle est entrée par la fenêtre; **to go t. someone's pockets,** fouiller qn; *Aut* **to go t. a red light,** brûler un feu (rouge); **he's been t. it** *or* **t. a lot,** il en a vu de dures, il a mangé de la vache enragée; **to speak t. one's nose,** parler du nez; **she got t. her exam,** elle a été reçue à son examen; *F* **to put s.o. t. it,** (*question*) faire subir à qn un interrogatoire très serré; (*test*) faire subir à qn un examen très serré; **I'm halfway t. this book,** j'ai lu la moitié de ce livre; **all t. his life,** durant *ou* pendant toute sa vie; **t. the ages,** à travers les âges; *esp Am* **Monday t. Friday,** de lundi à vendredi, du lundi au vendredi;

(b) (*by means of*) **t. s.o.,** par qn, par l'entremise *ou* l'intermédiaire de qn; **t. sth,** par le moyen de qch; (*as a result of*) en conséquence de, par suite de, à cause de, par (*qch*); par l'action de (*qn, qch*); **to send sth t. the post,** envoyer qch par la poste; **t. ignorance,** par ignorance; **absent t. illness,** absent par suite *ou* pour cause de maladie; **to act t. fear,** agir sous le coup de la peur; **it's (all) t. me that he missed his train,** c'est à cause de moi qu'il a manqué son train; **t. failing to lock the door ...,** pour n'avoir pas fermé la porte à clé ...;

(c) *esp Am* **to be t. doing sth,** avoir fini de faire qch; **are you t. telling me what to do?,** tu as fini de me dire ce que j'ai à faire?

2 *adv* **(a)** à travers; **the water poured t.,** l'eau coulait à travers; **the nail has come t.,** le clou est passé à travers; **to let s.o. t.,** laisser passer qn; **her trousers are t. at the knees,** son pantalon est percé aux genoux; **he's t. in the living-room,** il est de l'autre côté dans le salon; **England are t. to the semi-final,** l'Angleterre jouera dans la demi-finale; **France are not t.,** la France n'est pas qualifiée; **to be good/bad t. and t.,** (*of person*) être bon/mauvais de bout en bout *ou* de part en part; **to know a district t. and t.,** connaître un quartier comme (le fond de) sa poche; **to be soaked t.,** être trempé jusqu'aux os;

(b) d'un bout à l'autre; jusqu'au bout, jusqu'à la fin; **to read a book (right) t.,** lire un livre d'un bout à l'autre; **to see** *or* **carry sth t.,** mener qch à bien *ou* à bonne fin; **I slept all night t.,** j'ai dormi tout d'une traite cette nuit; **we'll stay t. until Friday,** nous resterons jusqu'à vendredi; **I was aware all t. that ...,** j'étais conscient tout du long du fait que ...; **we must go t. with it,** il faut aller jusqu'au bout; **to be t. with sth,** (*to have finished with*) avoir fini qch; (*with scissors etc*) avoir fini avec qch; (*to have had enough of*) en avoir (eu) assez; **are you t. with your work?,** avez-vous fini votre travail?; **I'm t. with you,** j'en ai fini avec toi; **we're t.,** c'est fini entre nous; **to be t.,** *esp Am* (*to have stopped talking etc*) avoir terminé *ou* fini (*de parler etc*); *F* (*to be done for*) être fichu;

(c) to book t. to Paris, prendre un billet direct pour Paris; *Tel* **to get t. to s.o.,** obtenir la communication avec qn; *F* (*make s.o. understand*) faire comprendre qch à qn; *Tel* **I'll put you t. to the secretary,** je vous passe la *ou* le secrétaire; *Tel* **you're t.,** vous avez la communication.

3 *adj* **(a)** (*train, road, ticket*) direct; *Rail* **t. coach,** wagon *m* de groupage; **t. carriage for Paris,** voiture directe pour Paris; **t. freight,** marchandises *fpl* en transit; **t. passenger to Paris,** voyageur, -euse direct(e) pour Paris; **no t. road,** (*on sign*) voie sans issue; **t. traffic,** transit *m*;

(b) *Tech etc* (*bolt etc*) traversant.

throughout [θruːˈaʊt] **1** *prep* **t. the country,** dans tout le pays; **t. the world,** à travers le monde; **t. the year,** pendant toute l'année; **t. her life,** durant *ou* pendant toute sa vie. **2** *adv* partout; (*time*) tout le temps; **the coat is lined t.,** le manteau est entièrement doublé; **they remained loyal t.,** ils sont restés loyaux du début à la fin.

throughput [ˈθruːpʊt] *n* débit *m*.

throughway [ˈθruːweɪ] *n Am* autoroute *f*.

throve *see* **THRIVE**.

throw[1] [θrəʊ] *n* **(a)** jet *m*, lancement *m* (*de qch*); *Sp* lancer *m* (*du javelot etc*); **his longest t. so far,** son meilleur jet jusqu'à présent; (*in wrestling*) mise *f* à terre (*de l'adversaire*); **3 throws for 50p,** (*at fair etc*) 3 essais pour 50 pence; **it's your t.,** (*javelin, dice etc*) à toi de lancer; **t. of dice,** coup *m* de dés; **long t.,** jet de longue portée; **(b)** *MecE* volée *f* (*du piston*); **(c)** maneton *m* (*de vilebrequin*); *Am* (*cover*) couvre-lit *m*, *pl* couvre-lits; (*scarf*) écharpe *f*.

throw[2] *v* (*pt* **threw** [θruː] ; *pp* **thrown** [θrəʊn]) **1** *vt* **(a)** lancer, jeter (*une balle etc*); *Sp* lancer (*le disque etc*); **to t. s.o. a kiss,** envoyer un baiser à qn; **to t. the dice,** jeter les dés; **to t. a five/a six,** (*at dice*) amener cinq/six; **to t. stones at s.o./at a dog,** lancer *ou* jeter des pierres sur *ou* à qn/à un chien; **to t. sth in s.o.'s face,** jeter qch à la figure de qn; *Fig* **don't t. that in my face,** ne me faites pas de reproches à ce sujet; **to t. a glance at s.o.,** jeter un coup d'œil à *ou* sur qn; **to t. oneself forwards,** se jeter en avant; **to t. oneself backwards,** se rejeter en arrière; **to t. oneself into sth,** se jeter dans (*la rivière etc*); se lancer à corps perdu dans (*une entreprise*); **to t. oneself on s.o.'s mercy** *or* **generosity,** s'en remettre à la merci *ou* la générosité de qn; *Fig* **she threw herself at him,** (*in relationship*) elle s'est jetée à sa tête; **to t. temptation in s.o.'s way,** exposer qn à la tentation; **to t. the blame on s.o.,** rejeter la faute sur qn; **to t. a sheet over sth,** couvrir qch d'un drap; **to t. a shawl over one's shoulders,** jeter un châle sur ses épaules; **to t. s.o. into prison,** jeter *ou* mettre qn en prison; **to t. s.o. to the lions,** jeter qn aux lions; **to t. s.o. into confusion,** jeter qn dans l'embarras; **to t. a switch,** basculer un interrupteur; **to t. open the door,** ouvrir la porte toute grande; **to t. open one's house to s.o.,** ouvrir sa maison à qn; **to t. s.o. out of work,** mettre qn au chômage;

(b) projeter (*de l'eau, une image, une ombre*) **(on,** sur); *Fig* **to t. light on the matter,** jeter la lumière sur la question, éclairer la question;

(c) to t. a fit, tomber en convulsions, *F* piquer une crise de nerfs; *F* **to t. a party,** organiser une soirée;

(d) renverser (*un adversaire*); **to t. its rider,** (*of horse*) désarçonner son cavalier; **to be thrown,** (*of rider*) vider les arçons, être désarçonné;

(e) to t. its skin, (*of reptile*) muer;

(f) (*of animals*) (*have litter*) mettre bas;

(g) tourner, façonner (*un pot*);

(h) *F* (*disconcert*) étonner, déconcerter (*qn*); **his question threw me for a moment,** pendant un moment je n'ai su que répondre à sa question; **I was completely thrown,** j'étais complètement déconcerté;

(i) *Sp* (*deliberately lose*) *F* perdre délibérément (*un match*).

2 *vi* **she can t. a hundred metres,** elle est capable de lancer à cent mètres; **I can't t. straight,** je n'arrive pas à lancer droit.

▶**throw about, throw around** *vtsep* jeter (*des objets*) çà et là; (*scatter*) éparpiller, disséminer (*des objets*); **to t. a ball around,** jouer à la balle; **to t. one's money about** *or* **around,** gaspiller son argent; **to t. one's arms about** *or* **around,** faire de grands gestes; **to t. oneself about,** se démener; **to be thrown about,** être ballotté; **to like to t. one's weight around,** aimer faire sentir sa force.

▶**throw aside** *vtsep* (*throw to one side*) jeter (*qch, qn*) de côté; (*discard*) écarter (*qch*); jeter, balancer (*qn*); se dépouiller de (*toute haine etc*).

▶**throw away** *vtsep* **(a)** (*discard*) jeter (*sa cigarette etc*); (*put in rubbish*) jeter, mettre (*qch*) au rebut; **(b)** (*waste*) gaspiller; **to t. away a chance,** laisser passer une occasion; **to t. away one's life,** (*waste*) gâcher sa vie; (*sacrifice for nothing*) se sacrifier inutilement; **don't t. yourself away on a waster like him,** ne gâche pas ta vie pour un tel bon à rien; **you're just throwing money away buying that stuff,** tu gaspilles vraiment ton argent en achetant ce truc; **to t. away a line,** (*of actor*) énoncer une phrase avec une indifférence calculée.

▶**throw back** *vtsep* **(a)** (*return by throwing*) jeter (*un poisson dans l'eau etc*); renvoyer, relancer (*une balle etc*); **(b)** (*reflect*) (*of mirror*) refléter, réfléchir (*l'image etc*); réverbérer (*la lumière, la chaleur*); **(c)** (*open forcefully*) repousser (*les volets etc*); **(d) to t. one's head back,** rejeter la tête en arrière; **(e)** (*delay*) retarder (*un travail etc*); **(f) to be thrown back upon s.o./sth,** être forcé de se rabattre sur qn/qch.

▶**throw down** *vtsep* (*throw from height*) jeter (*qch*) de haut en bas; (*throw to the ground*) jeter (*qch*) à terre *ou* par terre; abattre (*ses cartes etc*); **to t. oneself down,** se jeter sur le sol; **to t. down one's arms,** jeter ses armes; *Fig* (*surrender*) se rendre; *F* **it's throwing it down,** (*raining*) qu'est-ce qui descend!

▶**throw in** *vtsep* **(a)** (*throw into a place*) jeter (*qn, qch*) dedans; *Fb* **to t. in the ball,** remettre la balle en touche *ou* jeu; **(b)** (*add*) ajouter (*qch*); (*give as extra*) donner (*qch*) en plus; *F* **if you buy that table I'll t. in the bookcase,** si vous achetez cette table je vous donne la bibliothèque en supplément; **(c)** intercaler, insérer (*une observation, un mot*); placer (*un mot*); **(d) to t. in one's lot with s.o.,** partager le sort de qn; **(e) to t. in one's hand** *or* **one's cards,** (*leave game*) abandonner *ou* quitter la partie; *Fig* (*admit defeat*) s'avouer vaincu; **to t. in the towel,** *Boxing* jeter l'éponge; *Fig* (*admit defeat*) s'avouer vaincu, jeter l'éponge.

▶**throw off** *vtsep* **(a)** (*remove hastily*) enlever, ôter (*ses vêtements*); lever (*le masque*); **(b)** (*get rid of*) guérir (*d'un rhume etc*); se débarrasser de (*pursuer etc*); se libérer de (*oppressive regime*); secouer, se débarrasser de (*old image*); **(c)** (*write hastily*) composer (*un poème etc*) au pied levé; **(d) to t. s.o. off his bicycle,** faire tomber qn de sa bicyclette; **to t. off its rider,** (*of horse*) désarçonner son cavalier; **(e)** (*put off*) **to t. the dogs/the police off the scent,** dépister *ou* semer les chiens/la police.

▶**throw on** *vtsep* (*put on hastily*) mettre *ou* passer (*ses vêtements*) à la hâte; jeter (*du bois dans le feu*).

▶**throw out** *vtsep* **(a)** (*eject*) jeter (*qn, qch*) dehors; mettre (*qn*) à la porte; *Cr* mettre (*le batteur*) hors jeu en lançant la balle sur le guichet; **(b)** (*discard*) jeter *ou* mettre (*qch*) au rebut; (*reject*) rejeter, repousser (*un projet de loi etc*); **the takeover will t. a lot of people out of work,** le rachat va mettre beaucoup de monde au chômage; **(c)** (*give out*) jeter, émettre (*des rayons etc*); répandre (*de la chaleur etc*); **to t. out roots,** pousser des racines; **(d) to t. out one's chest,** bomber la poitrine; **(e)** lancer (*un défi etc*); **to t. out a suggestion,** émettre une proposition (*sans insister*); **(f)** (*disconcert*) troubler, déconcerter (*un orateur etc*); **to t. s.o. out in his calculations,** tromper les calculs de qn.

▶**throw over** *vtsep* **(a)** (*abandon*) abandonner (*un ami *etc*); lâcher, plaquer (*un amant etc*); **(b)** (*operate*) renverser (*un levier*).

►**throw together** *vtsep* **(a)** *F* (*make hurriedly*) préparer en vitesse (*un repas*); **(b)** (*gather together hurriedly*) assembler (*qch*) à la hâte; **a few paintings/facts thrown together,** quelques tableaux/faits assemblés à la hâte; **the film/book is a bit thrown together,** ce film/livre sent un peu l'assemblage à la hâte; **chance had thrown us together,** le hasard nous avait réunis.

►**throw up 1** *vtsep* **(a)** (*throw upwards*) jeter (*qch*) en l'air; **volcano that throws up lava,** volcan qui vomit de la lave; **(b)** (*raise high*) lever haut, mettre haut (*les mains etc*); **(c)** *F* (*vomit*) vomir, rendre; **(d)** (*build hurriedly*) construire (*une maison etc*) à toute vitesse; **(e)** (*abandon*) renoncer à, abandonner (*une affaire etc*); **to t. up one's job,** quitter son emploi; **to feel like throwing everything up,** avoir envie de tout plaquer; **(f)** (*reveal*) révéler, indiquer; (*produce*) **recent events have thrown up anomalies in the law,** les derniers événements ont révélé des anomalies contenues dans la loi; **the discussion threw up some new ideas,** la discussion a amené *ou* soulevé de nouvelles idées. **2** *vi F* (*vomit*) vomir, rendre.

throwaway[1] [ˈθrəʊəweɪ] *adj* **(a)** (*disposable*) (*couche etc*) à jeter, jetable; **(b)** *F* **a t. line** *or* **remark,** un aparté.

throwaway[2] *n esp Am F* (*leaflet*) prospectus *m*.

throwback [ˈθrəʊbæk] *n* **(a)** *Biol* régression *f*; **he's a t. to his great-grandfather,** il a hérité (des caractéristiques) de son arrière-grand-père; **(b)** *Fig* retour *m* (en arrière); **it's a t. to the 16th century,** c'est un retour au 16ème siècle.

thrower [ˈθrəʊər] *n* **(a)** lanceur, -euse (*de javelot etc*); **discus t.,** discobole *m*; **(b)** *Cer* potier *m*.

throw-in [ˈθrəʊɪn] *n Fb* rentrée *f* en touche, remise *f* en jeu (*du ballon*).

throwing [ˈθrəʊɪŋ] *n* **(a)** (*act of throwing*) jet *m*, lancement *m*; *Sp* lancer *m* (*du disque etc*); **(b)** projection *f* (*d'une image*); **(c)** renversement *m* (*d'un cavalier*); **(d)** tournage *m* (*d'un pot*).

throw-out [ˈθrəʊaʊt] *n Com* **t.-outs,** rebuts *mpl*.

thru [θruː] *prep US & F* = **THROUGH.**

thrum [θrʌm] **1** *vt* pincer (*la guitare*). **2** *vi* pincer de la guitare; (*on window etc*) tambouriner.

thrush[1] [θrʌʃ] *n* (*bird*) grive *f*.

thrush[2] *n Med* muguet *m*.

thrust[1] [θrʌst] *n* **(a)** (*push*) poussée *f*; (*with knife etc*) coup *m* de pointe; *Fencing* coup d'estoc; *Mil* poussée (*d'une armée*); *Fencing* **t. and parry,** la botte et la parade; **the cut and t. of political debate,** le jeu d'attaques et de ripostes des débats politiques; **that was a t. at you,** c'était une attaque à votre adresse; **the (general) t. of an argument,** l'idée générale d'une argumentation; **(b)** *MecE* poussée *f*, butée *f*; *Archit* poussée (*d'une voûte*); *Av Nau* poussée (*d'une hélice*).

thrust[2] *v* (*pt & pp* **thrust**) **1** *vt* pousser (*qn, qch*) (avec force); **to t. sth into sth,** enfoncer *ou* fourrer qch dans qch; **to t. one's hands into one's pockets,** fourrer *ou* plonger les mains dans ses poches; **to be t. into a position of responsibility,** être parachuté à un poste à responsabilités; **to t. oneself** *or* **one's way through the crowd,** se frayer un chemin à travers la foule. **2** *vi* **to t. at s.o.,** porter un coup à qn (*du bout de sa canne etc*); *Fencing* porter un coup d'estoc à qn; **to cut and t.,** frapper d'estoc et de taille; *Fig* **to t. and parry,** riposter, répondre du tac au tac.

►**thrust aside, thrust away** *vtsep* (*reject*) repousser, écarter (*qn, qch*); *Lit* **to t. temptation aside,** repousser *ou* écarter la tentation.

►**thrust forward** *vtas* (*push forward*) pousser (*qch, qn*) en avant; *Fig* **to t. oneself forward,** se mettre en avant.

►**thrust on, thrust upon** *vtaspo* (*force on*) **to. t. sth on s.o.,** forcer qn à accepter qch; **to t. an opinion on s.o.,** imposer son opinion à qn; **the responsibility was t. upon me,** la responsabilité m'a été incombée; **and some have greatness t. upon them,** et à certains la grandeur *ou* la noblesse s'impose; **to t. oneself (up) on s.o.,** s'imposer à qn *ou* chez qn.

►**thrust out** *vtsep* allonger brusquement (*son bras, sa jambe*); bomber (*la poitrine*); **he t. his head out of the car window,** il tendit brusquement la tête par la vitre de la voiture.

thruster [ˈθrʌstər] *n* **(a)** *F* (*person*) arriviste *mf*; **(b)** *Astronaut* (*rocket engine*) propulseur *m*.

thrustful [ˈθrʌstfʊl] *adj* = **THRUSTING.**

thrusting [ˈθrʌstɪŋ] *adj* **(a)** (*dynamic*) entreprenant, dynamique; **(b)** (*socially climbing*) arriviste.

thruway [ˈθruːweɪ] *n Am* autoroute *f*.

thud[1] [θʌd] *n* bruit sourd.

thud[2] *vi* (**-dd-**) tomber *ou* frapper avec un bruit sourd; **his feet went thudding along the corridor,** ses pas résonnaient sourdement dans le couloir; **my heart was thudding against my ribs,** mon cœur cognait sourdement dans ma poitrine; **the missile thudded into its target,** le missile frappa sa cible avec un bruit sourd.

thug [θʌg] *n* **(a)** (*violent person*) brute *f* sanguinaire; **(b)** *Hist* = en Inde, bandit qui étranglait ses victimes.

thumb[1] [θʌm] *n* pouce *m*; *F* **he's all thumbs,** il est maladroit de ses mains; **to be under s.o.'s t.,** être sous la domination de qn; **she's got him right under her t.,** elle le mène à la baguette, elle le fait marcher comme elle veut; *F* **to stick out like a sore t.,** choquer la vue; *F* **thumbs up!,** bravo!; *F* **to give the thumbs up/down to a proposal,** accepter/rejeter une proposition; **t. index,** onglets *mpl*.

thumb[2] *vt* **(a) to t. a book,** feuilleter *ou* parcourir un livre; **well thumbed book,** livre qui a fait beaucoup d'usage; **(b) to t. one's nose at s.o.,** faire un pied de nez à qn; **(c)** *F* **to t. a lift** *or* **ride, to t. it,** faire de l'auto-stop *ou* du stop; **I thumbed a lift with a Dutch motorist,** un conducteur hollandais m'a pris en stop.

thumb-indexed [ˈθʌmˈɪndekst] *adj* (*edition etc*) à onglets.

thumbmark [ˈθʌmmɑːk] *n* marque *f* de pouce.

thumbnail [ˈθʌmneɪl] *n* ongle *m* du pouce; **t. sketch,** *Art* croquis minuscule *ou* hâtif; (*description*) description concise.

thumbprint [ˈθʌmprɪnt] *n* empreinte *f* de pouce.

thumbscrew [ˈθʌmskruː] *n* vis *f* à oreilles; (*for torture*) = instrument de torture utilisé pour écraser les pouces des prisonniers.

thumbstall [ˈθʌmstɔːl] *n* poucier *m* (*de cordonnier etc*); *Med* doigtier *m* pour pouce.

thumbtack [ˈθʌmtæk] *n Am* punaise *f*.

thump[1] [θʌmp] *n* **(a)** (*sound*) coup sourd; cognement *m* (*d'un mécanisme etc*); **to fall with a t.,** tomber avec un bruit sourd; **(b)** (*blow with fist*) coup *m* de poing; **he's given himself a t. on the head,** il s'est donné un coup sur la tête.

thump[2] **1** *vt* cogner (*qn*); (*repeatedly*) bourrer (*qn*) de coups; cogner sur (*la table*); **they began to t. one another,** ils ont commencé à se cogner; **don't t. it down like that, be careful!,** ne le cogne pas comme ça en le posant, fais attention!; **he thumped his fist on the table,** il cogna du poing sur la table. **2** *vi* cogner (*sur la table etc*); **my heart was thumping,** mon cœur battait à grands coups.

►**thump out** *vtsep* (*play heavily*) **to t. out a tune,** marteler un air (*sur le piano*).

thumping [ˈθʌmpɪŋ] *adj F* énorme; **a t. big lie,** un gros mensonge.

thunder[1] [ˈθʌndər] *n* tonnerre *m*; **clap** *or* **peal of t.,** coup *m* de tonnerre; **roll of t.,** roulement *m ou* grondement *m* de tonnerre; **there's t. in the air,** le temps est à l'orage; *Fig* l'atmosphère est orageuse; **t. of applause,** tonnerre d'applaudissements; **voice of t.,** voix de tonnerre; **voice like t.,** voix tonnante; *Fig* **to steal s.o.'s t.,** couper l'herbe sous le pied à qn.

thunder[2] *vi* **(a)** tonner; (*of guns, waves*) retentir dans un bruit de tonnerre; **it's thundering,** il tonne; **the avalanche thundered down,** l'avalanche roula dans un bruit de tonnerre; **the train thundered past,** le train est passé avec un bruit de tonnerre; **(b)** (*of speaker*) tonitruer; donner (*un ordre*) d'une voix tonnante; **'get out!' he thundered,** 'dehors!' tonitrua-t-il *ou* dit-il d'une voix tonitruante; **to t. against s.o./sth,** tonitruer contre qn/qch.

thunderbolt [ˈθʌndəbəʊlt] *n* coup *m* de foudre; *Fig* (*astounding event etc*) coup d'eclat; (*piece of news*) nouvelle foudroyante; **the news came like a t.,** cette nouvelle m'a *ou* l'a *etc* foudroyé.

thunderclap [ˈθʌndəklæp] *n* coup *m* de tonnerre.

thundercloud [ˈθʌndəklaʊd] *n* nuage orageux.

thundering [ˈθʌnd(ə)rɪŋ] **1** *adj* (*sound etc*) tonnant, tonitruant; **t. applause,** tonnerre *m* d'applaudissements; **to be in a t. rage,** être dans une rage à tout casser; *Old-fashioned F* **what a t. nuisance!,** ce que c'est embêtant!; *Old-fashioned F* **what a t. (great) lie!,** quel gros mensonge! **2** *n* (*thunder*) tonnerre *m*; (*loud sound*) bruit retentissant; (*sound of thunder*) bruit de tonnerre.

thunderous [ˈθʌnd(ə)rəs] *adj* (*voice etc*) tonnant, tonitruant; **t. applause,** tonnerre *m* d'applaudissements, applaudissements *mpl* à tout rompre.

thunderstorm [ˈθʌndəstɔːm] *n* orage *m*.

thunderstruck ['θʌndəstrʌk] *adj* abasourdi, foudroyé; **I was t. by the news,** cette nouvelle m'a foudroyé.

thundery ['θʌndərɪ] *adj* (*temps, ciel*) orageux; (*temps, pluie*) d'orage; **the weather's t.,** le temps est à l'orage; **t. shower,** averse accompagnée de tonnerre.

thurible ['θjuː(ə)rɪb(ə)l] *n Rel* encensoir *m*.

Thursday ['θɜːzdɪ] *n* jeudi *m*; **Maundy T.,** jeudi saint; **he's coming on T.,** il viendra jeudi; **every T. morning,** tous les jeudis matins.

thus [ðʌs] *adv* **(a)** *esp Lit* (*in this way*) ainsi, de cette façon, de cette manière; **t. prepared,** ainsi préparé, préparé de cette façon; **(b)** (*therefore*) ainsi, donc; **t., when he arrived,** donc, lorsqu'il est arrivé; **(c) t. far,** (*as far as this*) jusqu'ici; (*as far as that*) jusque-là; **t. much,** autant que cela (et pas davantage).

thwack¹ [θwæk] *n* coup *m*; (*with hand*) claque *f*, taloche *f*; (*noise*) claquement *m*; **I gave myself a t. on the shin,** je me suis donné un coup dans le tibia.

thwack² *vt* frapper, cogner; (*with hand*) gifler; **I thwacked my head on the beam,** je me suis cogné la tête contre la poutre.

thwart¹ [θwɔːt, *Nau* θɔːt] *n* banc *m* de nage.

thwart² *vt* contrarier (*qn*); déjouer (*une intrigue, les projets de qn*); **to be thwarted,** essuyer un échec.

thy [ðaɪ] *poss adj* (**thine,** *before a vowel*) *Arch & Lit* ton, *f* ta, *pl* tes; **thine own son,** ton propre fils.

thyme [taɪm] *n* (*plant*) *& Culin* thym *m*; **wild t.,** serpolet *m*.

thyroid ['θaɪərɔɪd] *adj & n* thyroïde *f*.

thyself [ðaɪ'self] *pers pron Arch & Lit* toi(-même).

ti [tiː] *n Mus* si *m*.

tiara [tɪ'ɑːrə] *n* **(a)** diadème *m*; **(b)** *Rel* tiare *f*.

Tiber (the) [ðə'taɪbər] *n* le Tibre.

Tiberius [taɪ'bɪərɪəs] *n* Tibère *m*.

Tibet [tɪ'bet] *n* Tibet *m*.

Tibetan [tɪ'bet(ə)n] **1** *adj* tibétain. **2** *n* **(a)** Tibétain, -aine; **(b)** *Ling* tibétain *m*.

tibia ['tɪbɪə] *n Anat etc* tibia *m*.

tic [tɪk] *n Med* tic *m*.

tich [tɪtʃ] *n Br F* **a (little) t.,** (*person*) un (petit) bout de chou.

tichy ['tɪtʃɪ] *adj Br F* minuscule.

tick¹ [tɪk] *n* **(a) t.(-tock),** (*sound*) tic-tac *m* (*d'une pendule*); **(b)** *Br F* (*moment*) moment *m*, instant *m*; **just a t.!, half a t.!,** un moment!, une seconde!; **(c)** (*mark*) marque *f*, pointage *m*, coche *f*; **to put a t. against a name,** cocher un nom.

tick² **1** *vi* (*of clock*) **to t.,** *F* **to t. tock,** faire tic-tac, tictaquer; **the minutes are ticking by,** le temps passe; *F* **I'd like to know what makes him t.,** je voudrais bien savoir ce qui le pousse. **2** *vt* = **TICK OFF (a)**.

tick³ *n* (*parasite*) tique *f* (*du bétail etc*).

tick⁴ *n Br F* (*credit*) crédit *m*; **to buy** *or* **get sth on t.,** acheter qch à crédit.

tick⁵ *n* enveloppe *f*, toile *f* (*à matelas*).

►**tick off** *vtsep* **(a)** (*mark with tick*) pointer (*un article sur une liste etc*); cocher (*un nom*); **(b)** *Br F* (*reprimand*) attraper, enguirlander (*qn*); **to get ticked off,** se faire rembarrer; **(c)** *Am F* **to t. s.o. off,** embêter qn; **he's really ticked off,** il est drôlement en rogne.

►**tick over** *vi* (*of engine*) tourner au ralenti; **the engine is ticking over nicely,** le moteur tourne bien; **my business is just ticking over,** mes affaires vont doucement; **business is ticking over nicely,** les affaires tournent bien; **it keeps my brain ticking over,** ça fait travailler ma cervelle.

ticker ['tɪkər] *n* **(a)** *Sl* (*watch*) montre *f*; (*clock*) pendule *f*; (*heart*) palpitant *m*; **(b)** *Am St Exch* téléimprimeur *m*; **t. tape,** bande *f* de téléimprimeur.

ticket¹ ['tɪkɪt] *n* **(a)** billet *m* (*de chemin de fer, d'avion, de théâtre, de loterie etc*); ticket *m* (*de métro, d'autobus etc*); *Th etc* **complimentary t.,** billet de faveur; **single t.,** billet simple, (billet d')aller *m*; **return t.,** billet d'aller et retour, aller-retour *m inv*; **left-luggage t., cloakroom t.,** bulletin *m ou* ticket de consigne; **platform t.,** ticket de quai; **season t.,** carte *f* d'abonnement; **season-t. holder,** abonné(e); *Aut F* **(parking) t.,** papillon *m*, P.V. *m*; **to get a (parking) t.,** attraper un P.V.; **t. collector** *or* **inspector,** contrôleur, -euse (de billets); **t. holders only,** (*on sign*) réservé aux personnes munies de billets; *Rail* **t. office,** billetterie *f*; **t. tout,** revendeur *m* de billets;
(b) *Com* **(price) t.,** étiquette *f*;
(c) *Am Pol* (*list of candidates*) liste *f* des candidats; *F* **the democratic t.,** le programme du parti démocrate;
(d) *Mil* **to get one's t.,** être libéré (*du service*); *Nau F* **to get one's (master's) t.,** passer (son brevet de) capitaine;
(e) *Old-fashioned Sl* **that's the t.!,** voilà qui fera l'affaire!, à la bonne heure!

ticket² *vt* (**ticketed**) étiqueter (*des marchandises*).

ticketing ['tɪkɪtɪŋ] *n* (*issuing of tickets*) billetterie *f*.

ticking¹ ['tɪkɪŋ] *n* tic-tac *m* (*d'une pendule*).

ticking² *n Tex* toile *f ou* coutil *m* à matelas.

ticking off *n* **(a)** (*marking*) pointage *m*; **(b)** *Br F* (*reprimanding*) engueulade *f*, savon *m*; **to get a t. o.,** prendre un savon; **to give s.o. a t. o.,** passer un savon à qn.

tickle¹ ['tɪk(ə)l] *n* chatouillement *m*; **he gave her a t.,** il lui a fait des chatouilles; **to have a t. in one's throat,** avoir un chatouillement dans le gosier.

tickle² **1** *vt* chatouiller (*qn*); *Fishing* pêcher (*la truite etc*) à la main; *F* (*amuse*) amuser (*qn*); **to t. the palate,** (*of food, wine*) chatouiller le palais; *F* **to t. s.o.'s fancy,** amuser qn; *F* **to be tickled to death** *or* **tickled pink at** *or* **by sth,** (*be amused*) s'amuser beaucoup de qch; (*be delighted*) être enchanté *ou* ravi de qch. **2** *vi* **you're tickling,** tu me chatouilles.

tickler ['tɪklər] *n esp Br F* (*problem*) os *m*; (*delicate subject*) sujet délicat.

tickling ['tɪklɪŋ] **1** *adj* qui chatouille; **t. cough,** toux *f* d'irritation. **2** *n* chatouillement *m*; *Fishing* pêche *f* à la main (*de la truite*).

ticklish ['tɪklɪʃ] *adj* **(a)** (*person, place*) chatouilleux, -euse; **to be t.,** être chatouilleux; **(b)** (*touchy*) chatouilleux; (*subject, task etc*) délicat; **to be in a t. situation,** se trouver dans une situation délicate.

ticktack ['tɪktæk] *n Br* = signaux utilisés entre les bookmakers; **t. man,** aide *m* de bookmaker (qui fait des signaux à bras).

tick-tack-toe [tɪktæk'təʊ] *n Am* jeu *m* des petites croix.

tidal ['taɪd(ə)l] *adj* **(a)** (*energy etc*) marémoteur, -trice; **t. power station,** usine marémotrice; **t. wave,** raz *m* de marée; (*on river*) barre *f* de flot; *Fig* vague *f* (*d'enthousiasme etc*); **(b)** (*river etc*) à marée; **t. basin,** bassin *m* à flot.

tidbit ['tɪdbɪt] *n* = **TITBIT**.

tiddler ['tɪdlər] *n Br F* (*small fish*) petit poisson; (*minnow*) épinoche *f*; (*child*) bambin *m*, mioche *mf*.

tiddl(e)y¹ ['tɪdlɪ] *adj Br F* (*small*) minuscule.

tiddl(e)y² *adj Br F* (*drunk*) gris, pompette.

tiddlywinks ['tɪdlɪwɪŋks] *n* jeu *m* de (la) puce.

tide [taɪd] *n* **(a)** marée *f*; **rising t., flood t.,** marée montante, flux *m*; **ebb t.,** marée descendante, jusant *m*; **high t.,** marée haute; **low t.,** marée basse; **neap t.,** marée de morte-eau; **spring t.,** grande marée, marée de vive eau; *Nau* **to go out with the t.,** partir à la marée; **rise/fall of the t.,** montée *f*/baisse *f* de l'eau; **against the t.,** à contre-marée; *Fig* à contre-courant; *Fig* **the rising t. of discontent,** la vague croissante de mécontentement; *Fig* **borne along by the t. of events,** entraîné par la marée d'événements; *Fig* **when the t. of the battle turned,** quand le vent de la bataille a tourné; *Fig* **for us the t. has turned,** pour nous le vent a tourné; **t. gate,** porte *f* à flot; **t. race,** raz *m* de marée; **(b)** *Arch* (*season*) temps *m*, saison *f*; *Rel* **Ascension t.,** temps *ou* semaine *f* de l'Ascension.

►**tide over** *vtas* aider (*qn*) à surmonter une difficulté, *F* dépanner (*qn*); **can you lend me five pounds to t. me over till Monday?,** pourrais-tu me prêter cinq livres pour me dépanner jusqu'à lundi?

tidemark ['taɪdmɑːk] *n* **(a)** (*marker*) ligne *f* de marée haute *ou* des hautes eaux; (*mark left by tide*) laisse *f* de haute mer; **(b)** *Br F* (*line of dirt*) ligne *f* de crasse (*dans une baignoire etc*).

tidewater ['taɪdwɑːtər] *n* eau *f* de marée.

tideway ['taɪdweɪ] *n* lit *m* de la marée.

tidily ['taɪdɪlɪ] *adv* avec ordre; (*habillé*) avec soin; **he puts everything away t. in a drawer at night,** il range tout bien en ordre *ou* soigneusement dans un tiroir le soir.

tidiness ['taɪdɪnɪs] *n* (*of room, files etc*) bon ordre; (*of person*) goût *m* de l'ordre; (*in appearance, dress, of handwriting*) soin *m*.

tidings ['taɪdɪŋz] *npl Lit* nouvelle(s) *f(pl)*.

tidy¹ ['taɪdɪ] **1** *adj* **(a)** (*desk, room*) bien rangé, en (bon) ordre; (*handwriting*) net, soigné; (*hair*) soigné; **to have a t. mind,** avoir la tête bien ordonnée *ou* les idées bien en place; **a clean and t. room,** une pièce propre et nette; **he's very t.,** (*in habits*) il est très ordonné; (*in appearance*) il est très soigné; **(b)** *F* (*considerable*) assez bon; **to cost a t. penny,** coûter chaud; **a t. sum,** une somme rondelette.

tidy² *n* vide-poches *m inv*; **sink t.,** coin *m* d'évier.

tidy³ *vt* ranger, mettre de l'ordre dans (*une chambre*); **to t. one's hair,** s'arranger les cheveux.

►**tidy away** *vtsep* (*put away*) ranger (*des livres etc*).

►**tidy up 1** *vi* (*clear things away*) ranger. **2** *vtsep* ranger, mettre de l'ordre dans (*une chambre*); **to t. things up,** ranger; **to t. oneself up,** faire un bout de toilette.

tie¹ [taɪ] *n* **(a)** (*link*) lien *m*; **not to have any ties,** ne pas avoir d'attaches; **family ties,** liens de famille; **ties of friendship,** liens de l'amitié; **(b)** lien *m* (*de corde, de paille, d'osier etc*); *Nau* itague *f*; lacet *m*, cordon *m* (*de soulier*); (*for plastic bag*) cordon; **(c)** (*neck tie*) cravate *f*; **bow t.,** nœud *m* papillon; **black t.,** (*on invitation*) = smoking *m*; **old school t.,** cravate portée par les anciens élèves d'une école; **it's the old school t.,** (*that's why he got the job etc*) c'est les vieilles relations *ou* amitiés d'école; **t. clip,** fixe-cravate *m*, *pl* fixe-cravates; **(d)** *Constr etc* crampon *m*; *Am Rail* traverse *f*; *Constr* **t. beam,** longrine *f*; **(e)** *Mus* liaison *f*; **(f)** *Sp* match *m ou* course *f* à égalité; **(cup) t.,** = match de championnat; **the election ended in a t.,** les candidats obtinrent un nombre égal de suffrages.

tie² (*pt & pp* **tied**; *prp* **tying**) **1** *vt* lier, nouer (*un lacet, une ficelle etc*); faire (*un nœud, sa cravate*); attacher, nouer (*les brides de son capuchon*); *Mus* lier (*deux notes*); attacher (*un chien à sa niche etc*); lier, attacher, ligoter (*qn à un poteau*); **to t. two things together,** lier deux choses (ensemble); *Fig* **to t. s.o.'s hands,** lier les mains à qn; **to be tied hand and foot,** être ligoté; *Fig* **to have one's hands tied,** avoir les mains liées, être pieds et poings liés; **to be tied to one's bed,** être cloué au lit (*par la maladie etc*). **2** *vi Sp etc* être *ou* arriver à égalité (**with,** avec); (*of candidates*) obtenir un nombre égal de suffrages; *Sch* **to t. for first place,** être premier ex æquo (**with,** avec).

►**tie back** *vtsep* attacher (*ses cheveux, les rideaux*).

►**tie down** *vtsep* **(a)** (*prevent from moving by tying*) immobiliser (*qn*) en l'attachant; assujettir (*un objet qui pourrait se déplacer*); **(b)** (*restrict*) assujettir (*qn*) à certaines conditions; **children t. you down,** les enfants représentent une contrainte; **this ticket doesn't t. you down to specific dates,** ce billet vous laisse libre de changer vos dates de départ; **to t. s.o. down to facts,** obliger qn à ne pas s'écarter des faits; **tied down to one's job,** assujetti à ses fonctions.

►**tie in** *vi* (*correspond*) (*of facts, story*) concorder, cadrer, *F* coller; **the two versions don't t. in,** les deux versions ne concordent *ou F* ne collent pas.

►**tie in with** *vipo* (*fit in with*) concorder *ou* cadrer *ou F* coller avec; **that ties in with what we know,** ça cadre avec ce que nous savons.

►**tie on** *vt* (*attach by tying*) attacher (*une étiquette etc*) avec une ficelle.

►**tie up 1** *vtsep* **(a)** (*tie together*) attacher, ficeler (*un paquet etc*); se nouer, s'attacher (*les cheveux*); lier, ficeler (*le haut d'un sac*); bander, panser (*un bras blessé etc*);

(b) (*prevent moving*) attacher (*un animal*); ligoter (*qn*); amarrer (*un bateau*);

(c) (*prevent from being spent*) immobiliser (*ses capitaux*); **my capital is tied up in stocks and shares,** mon capital est immobilisé sous forme d'actions *ou* en actions;

(d) *F* **to be tied up,** (*busy*) être très occupé, avoir beaucoup à faire; **he's going to be tied up all afternoon,** il va être pris tout l'après-midi; *Am* **the traffic was all tied up,** il y avait un embouteillage, la circulation était complètement bloquée;

(e) (*be connected*) **to be tied up with sth,** être lié à qch; **it's tied up with the increase in the bank rate,** c'est lié à l'augmentation des taux d'intérêt; **our firm is tied up with theirs,** notre maison a des accords avec la leur; **I'm getting pretty tied up with her,** (*involved*) je commence à être drôlement attaché à elle; **he's much too tied up with his work,** son travail l'accapare vraiment.

2 *vi* **(a)** (*of boat*) jeter l'ancre; **(b)** (*connect, make sense*) avoir des rapports; **that ties up with what I was just saying,** cela rejoint ce que je viens de dire.

►**tie up with** *vipo* (*fit in with*) concorder *ou* cadrer *ou F* coller avec.

tie-break, tie-breaker ['taɪbreɪk, -breɪkər] *n Tennis* tie-break *m*, *pl* tie-breaks; (*in TV game etc*) question *f* visant à départager les candidats.

tied [taɪd] *adj* **(a)** assujetti (*à son service etc*); **(b)** *Br* **t. cottage** *or* **house,** = logement *m* de fonction; **t. house,** débit de boissons astreint par bail à vendre la bière d'une certaine brasserie; **(c)** *Mus* **t. notes,** notes liées.

tie-in ['taɪɪn] *n* rapport *m*, association *f*; (*film from book*) film tiré d'un livre; **we've got a film t.-in,** nous avons vendu les droits pour le cinéma.

tie-on ['taɪɒn] *adj* **t.-on label,** étiquette *f* à œillets.

tiepin ['taɪpɪn] *n* épingle *f* de cravate.

tier [tɪər] *n* étage *m*; rangée *f* (*de sièges, de barriques etc*); **tiers of an amphitheatre,** gradins *mpl* d'un amphithéâtre; **two-t. postal service system,** courrier *m* à deux vitesses; **to arrange sth in tiers,** disposer qch par étages, étager qch; **to rise in tiers,** s'étager.

tiered ['tɪəd] *adj* à gradins, à étages; **three-t. cake,** pièce montée à trois étages; **three-t. stand,** (*for cakes etc*) étagère *f* à trois tablettes.

Tierra del Fuego [tɪ'ɛərədel'fweɪgəʊ] *n* la Terre de Feu.

tie-up ['taɪʌp] *n* **(a)** amarrage *m* (*pour un canot*); *Am Aut* (*traffic jam*) embouteillage *m*; suspension forcée (*du travail*); **(b)** (*connection*) rapport *m* (*entre deux choses*).

tiff [tɪf] *n* petite querelle.

tiffin ['tɪfɪn] *n* (*Anglo-Indian*) déjeuner *m*.

tig [tɪg] *n* (*game*) (jeu *m* de) chat *m*.

tiger ['taɪgər] *n* (*animal*) *& Fig* tigre *m*; **t. lily,** lis tigré; **t. moth,** écaille *f*.

tiger's-eye [taɪgəz'aɪ] *n* (*stone*) œil *m* de tigre.

tight [taɪt] **1** *adj* **(a)** (*clothes*) serré; (*skintight*) collant, moulant; (*mortise etc*) bien ajusté; (*knot, screw*) serré; (*cord etc*) raide, tendu; **to draw a cord t.,** serrer un cordon; **to keep a t. hand** *or* **hold over s.o.,** tenir qn serré, tenir la bride haute à qn; **too t.,** (*clothes*) étriqué, trop serré, trop juste; **t. shoes,** chaussures trop petites *ou* (trop) étroites; **it's a bit t.,** (*of clothes*) c'est un peu juste; *F* **to be in a t. corner** *or* **a t. spot,** être dans une mauvaise passe, être dans le pétrin; **t. schedule,** horaire minuté; **I work to a very t. schedule,** mon temps est très minuté; **t. rules,** règles strictes; **it should be a t. finish,** (*in race*) l'arrivée devrait être serrée; **it's going to be t. but we should just make it,** ça va être juste mais nous devrions arriver; **there was just room to park, but it was t.,** il y avait juste la place pour se garer;

(b) (*money, credit*) resserré, rare; *Sp* (*race*) serré, chaudement disputé; *F* **money's a bit t. with me,** je suis un peu à court (d'argent);

(c) *F* **to be t.,** (*drunk*) être pété *ou* soûl; **to get t.,** prendre une cuite;

(d) (*partition etc*) imperméable (*à l'eau, à l'air etc*); (*ship, container*) étanche; (*joint*) hermétique.

2 *adv* **(a)** (*firmly*) fortement; **to hold sth t.,** tenir qch fermement serré; **to hold s.o. t.,** serrer qn fort; **hold t.!,** tenez bon!, tenez ferme!; **to screw a nut up t.,** serrer un écrou à fond *ou* à bloc; **to squeeze sth t.,** serrer qch étroitement *ou* fort;

(b) (*to seal, shut*) hermétiquement; (*properly*) bien; **shut t., t. shut,** (*porte, yeux*) bien fermé.

tight-assed ['taɪtɑːst] *adj esp Am Sl* coincé.

tighten ['taɪt(ə)n] **1** *vt* serrer, resserrer (*une vis, un nœud etc*); bloquer (*un écrou*), bander, tendre (*un ressort*); tendre, raidir (*un cordage etc*); renforcer (*un blocus, des restrictions*); **to t. one's belt,** serrer sa ceinture; *Fig* se serrer la ceinture. **2** *vi* se (res)serrer; (*of spring, cable etc*) se tendre; **her lips tightened,** elle a serré les lèvres.

►**tighten up 1** *vtsep* **(a)** (*make tighter*) resserrer (*screw etc*); refaire (*shoelaces*); **(b)** (*make more stringent*) renforcer (*un blocus, des restrictions, des régulations*); **the company has tightened up (it's) security,** la société a renforcé ses mesures de sécurité. **2** *vi* (*in discipline, security etc*) devenir plus ferme *ou* strict.

tightening ['taɪt(ə)nɪŋ] *n* serrage *m*, (res)serrement *m* (*d'une vis etc*); tension *f* (*d'un ressort*); raidissement *m* (*d'un cordage*); renforcement *m* (*d'un blocus etc*); *Fin* resserrement (*du crédit etc*).

tightfisted [taɪt'fɪstɪd] *adj F* radin; **to be t.,** être près de ses sous.

tight-fitting [taɪt'fɪtɪŋ] *adj* (*clothes*) (*dress, trousers*) moulant; (*suit*) bien ajusté; (*joint etc*) bien ajusté; (*door, lid*) qui ferme bien.

tightknit ['taɪt'nɪt] *adj* (*community*) uni, dont les membres sont étroitement liés.

tight-lipped ['taɪtlɪpt] *adj* les lèvres serrées; **to be t.-l.,** ne rien dire (**about sth,** au sujet de qch); **they kept a t.-l. silence,** ils ont gardé un silence de mort, *F* ils sont restés bouche cousue; **you're very t.-l. about this,** tu es très peu loquace là-dessus.

tightly ['taɪtlɪ] *adv* **(a)** fortement, fermement; **to hold on t. to sth,** se cramponner à qch; **to squeeze sth t.,** serrer qch étroitement *ou* fort; **to fit t.,** être bien ajusté; **to fit too t.,** être (trop) serré *ou* (trop) juste; **we were t. packed,** nous étions serrés comme des sardines; **don't screw it on too t.,** ne le serre pas trop fort *ou* à fond; **(b)** (*to close*) hermétiquement; **eyes t. shut,** yeux bien fermés.

tightness ['taɪtnɪs] *n* **(a)** raideur *f* (*d'un cordage*); *Med* oppression *f* (*de la poitrine*); étroitesse *f* (*d'un lien*); force *f* (*d'une étreinte*); étroitesse (*d'un vêtement*); **(b)** (*of container etc*) herméticité *f*; (*of joint*) étanchéité *f*; **(c)** (*of regulations, security*) rigueur *f*.

tightrope ['taɪtrəʊp] *n* corde raide; **to walk a t.,** marcher sur une corde raide; *Fig* être sur une corde raide; **t. walker,** funambule *mf*; *Fig* **political t. walking,** acrobatie *f* politique; **we're walking a diplomatic t.,** nous sommes sur une corde raide diplomatique.

tights [taɪts] *npl* (*garment*) collant *m*; *Th* maillot *m*.

tightwad ['taɪtwɒd] *n Am F* avare *m*, radin, -ine.

tigress ['taɪgrɪs] *nf* (*animal*) *& Fig* (*fierce woman*) tigresse *f*.

Tigris (the) [ðə'taɪgrɪs] *n* le Tigre.

tike [taɪk] *n* = **TYKE**.

'til [tɪl] *prep & conj Lit* = **UNTIL**.

tilde ['tɪldə] *n Gram* tilde *m*.

tile¹ [taɪl] *n* tuile *f* (*de toiture etc*); (*on ground, floor*) carreau *m*; **crest** *or* **ridge t.,** tuile faîtière; *F* **to spend a night on the tiles,** traîner dehors toute la nuit; **floor(ing) t.,** carreau de pavage *ou* de revêtement de sol; **wall t.,** carreau de revêtement mural; **t. kiln,** tuilerie *f* (*four*); **t. works,** tuilerie.

tile² *vt* couvrir (*un toit*) de tuiles; carreler (*un sol*).

tiled [taɪld] *adj* (*toit*) de *ou* en tuiles; (*pavage*) carrelé, en carrelage; (*paroi*) carrelé, revêtu de carrelage.

tiler ['taɪlər] *n* (*layer of roof tiles*) couvreur *m* (en tuiles); (*layer of floor tiles*) carreleur *m*.

tiling ['taɪlɪŋ] *n* **(a)** (*activity*) (*on roof*) pose *f* des tuiles; (*on floor*) carrelage *m*, pose des carreaux; **(b)** (*covering*) (*of roof*) (couverture *f* en) tuiles *fpl*; (*of floor*) carrelage *m*.

till¹ [tɪl] *vt* labourer, cultiver (*un champ etc*).

till² *n Com* tiroir-caisse *m*, *pl* tiroirs-caisses; **pay at the t.,** payer à la caisse; *Fig F* **to be caught with one's hand in the t.,** être surpris la main dans le sac; **t. money,** encaisse *f*.

till³ 1 *prep* jusqu'à; **t. tomorrow,** jusqu'à demain; **t. now,** jusqu'ici; **t. then,** jusque-là, jusqu'alors; **from morning t. night,** du matin au soir; **(goodbye) t. Thursday!,** à jeudi!; **wait t. after the holidays,** attendez jusqu'après les vacances; **not t. Monday,** pas avant lundi; **he won't come t. after dinner,** il ne viendra qu'après le dîner; **I'd never heard of it t. now,** c'est la première fois que j'en entends parler.

2 *conj* jusqu'à ce que + *sub*; **we won't go t. all the doors are shut,** nous ne partirons pas tant que toutes les portes ne seront pas fermées; **I have to wait t. all the doors are shut,** je dois attendre jusqu'à ce que toutes les portes soient fermées; **t. I met you ...,** avant de te rencontrer ...; **to laugh t. one cries,** rire aux larmes; **I'm not going t. I get my money,** je ne sortirai d'ici que lorsque j'aurai mon argent.

tillage ['tɪlɪdʒ] *n* **(a)** (*activity*) labour *m*, labourage *m*, culture *f*; **(b)** (*land*) terres *fpl* en labour.

tiller¹ ['tɪlər] *n Nau* barre franche (de direction); **who was at the t.?,** qui était à la barre?

tiller² *n* (*ploughman*) laboureur *m*; *Lit* **a t. of the soil,** un homme de la terre.

tilling ['tɪlɪŋ] *n* (*ploughing*) labour *m*; (*farming*) culture *f*.

tilt¹ [tɪlt] *n* (*canopy*) (*for vehicle*) bâche *f*, banne *f*.

tilt² *n* **(a)** (*angle*) inclinaison *f*, pente *f*; (*in dancing*) tilt *m*; **to wear one's cap at a t.,** porter sa casquette légèrement de côté; **(b)** *Arch* (*joust*) joute *f*; *Arch* (*lance blow*) coup *m* de lance; *Fig* **to have a t. at s.o.,** lancer une pointe à qn; **(at) full t.,** à toute vitesse, *F* à fond de train; **to run full t. into sth,** donner en plein contre qch, rentrer en plein dans qch.

tilt³ 1 *vi* **(a)** (*incline*) (*state*) pencher; (*act*) s'incliner, pencher; **to t. backwards/forwards,** s'incliner *ou* pencher vers l'arrière/vers l'avant; **(b)** *Arch* (*joust*) jouter (**with s.o.,** avec qn); (*still used in*) *Fig* **to t. at s.o.,** lancer une pointe à qn (*dans un débat etc*). **2** *vt* pencher, incliner (*un tonneau, sa chaise* etc); **to t. one's hat over one's eyes,** rabattre son chapeau sur ses yeux; **to t. one's chair back,** se balancer sur sa chaise.

▶**tilt over** *vi* (*fall*) se renverser.

tilted ['tɪltɪd] *adj* incliné, penché.

tilth [tɪlθ] *n Agr* **(a)** (*ploughing*) labour *m*; **(b)** (*soil turned up*) couche *f* arable; (*tilled land*) cultures *fpl*.

tilting ['tɪltɪŋ] **1** *adj* **(a)** (*at an angle*) incliné, penché; **(b)** (*able to be tilted*) inclinable; (*truck*) qui bascule, à benne. **2** *n* **(a)** (*angle, slope*) inclinaison *f*, pente *f*; **(b)** (*act of tilting*) basculement *m*; *Arch* (*jousting*) joute *f*.

timber¹ ['tɪmbər] **1** *n* **(a)** bois *m* d'œuvre; **building t.,** bois de construction *ou* de charpente; **standing t.,** bois sur pied, arbres *mpl*; **to fell t.,** abattre *ou* couper du bois; **to put an area under t.,** boiser une région; **t. merchant,** marchand *m* de bois; **the t. trade,** le commerce du bois; **t. yard,** chantier *m* de bois (de charpente); **t. line,** limite *f* des arbres; **(b)** (*beam*) poutre *f*, madrier *m*; (*in naval architecture*) membre *m*; *Nau* **t. hitch,** nœud *m* de bois *ou* d'anguille; **(c)** *esp Am* trempe *f* (de qn). **2** *int* **t.!,** attention à l'arbre (qui tombe)!

timber² *vt* boiser, cuveler (*un puits de mine etc*).

timbered ['tɪmbəd] *adj* **(a)** (*house etc*) en bois; **half t.,** à *ou* en colombage; **(b)** (*land*) boisé.

timbering ['tɪmbərɪŋ] *n* **(a)** boisage *m*, boisement *m* (*d'une région*); **(b)** boisage *m*, cuvelage *m* (*d'un puits de mine*); (*frame*) armature *f* (*de bois*); **half t.,** colombage *m*.

timberwork ['tɪmbəwɜːk] *n* **(a)** (*activity*) charpenterie *f*; **(b)** (*framework*) charpente *f*.

timbre [tæ̃mbr(ə), 'tæmbər] *n* timbre *m* (*de la voix*).

Timbuktu [tɪmbʌk'tuː] *n* Tombouctou *m*.

time¹ [taɪm] *n* **(a)** temps *m*; **t. will tell** *or* **show,** qui vivra verra; **in (the course of) t.,** avec le temps, à la longue; **it's just a matter of t.,** ce n'est qu'une question de temps; **a race against t.,** une course contre la montre; *Prov* **t. is money,** le temps c'est de l'argent; **my t. is my own,** je suis libre de mon temps; **when I have the t.,** quand j'aurai le temps; **to have t. on one's hands,** avoir du temps à perdre; **to have no t. to do sth,** ne pas avoir le temps de faire qch; *F* **I've no t. for him,** il m'embête; *F* **I've got no** *or* **little t. for people like that!,** les gens comme ça me cassent les pieds; **to gain t.,** gagner du temps; **to play for t.,** chercher à gagner du temps; **you've got plenty** *or F* **heaps of t.,** vous avez tout le temps qu'il vous faut; **there's no t. to be lost** *or* **to lose,** il n'y a pas de temps à perdre; **to make up for lost t.,** rattraper le temps perdu; **to lose no t. doing sth,** s'empresser *ou* se hâter à faire qch; **to waste t.,** perdre du temps; **to make t. to do sth,** trouver le temps de faire qch; **I can always make t. for you,** pour vous je suis toujours là; *Am Sl* **to make t. with s.o.,** (*chat up*) draguer qn; (*have sex with*) se faire qn, s'envoyer qn; **it takes t.,** cela prend du temps; **t.'s up!,** l'heure a sonné!, c'est l'heure!; *Br* **t., gentlemen, please!,** (*in pub*) on ferme!; *Fb etc* **to play extra t.,** jouer les prolongations *fpl*; *Fb etc* **two minutes into extra t.,** deux minutes de prolongations; **(that was) before my t.,** c'était avant que je sois né; **convict nearing the end of his t.,** prisonnier qui a bientôt fait *ou* fini son temps; *F* **to do t.,** faire de la taule; **if I had my t. over again,** si j'avais à recommencer (ma vie); **she's seen a few things in her t.,** elle a vu pas mal de choses dans sa vie; *Fin* **t. bill,** échéance *f* à terme; **t. bomb,** bombe *f* à retardement; *Fig* **you're sitting on a t. bomb in this city,** vous êtes assis sur une poudrière dans cette ville; *Sp* **t. trial,** épreuve *f* contre la montre; *Tel* **t. unit,** unité *f*; *Gram* **t. clause,** proposition temporelle; *Phot* **t. exposure,** pose *f*; *El* **t. switch,** minuterie *f* (d'escalier);

(b) (*period*) **in a short t.,** (*quickly*) en peu de temps; (*soon*) sous peu; **in three weeks' t.,** dans trois semaines; **in a month's t.,** dans un mois; **in no t. (at all), in next to no t.,** en un rien de temps, en moins de rien; **within the required t.,** dans le délai prescrit; **to take a long t. over sth,** mettre longtemps à faire qch; **to take t. over sth/to do sth properly,** prendre le temps qu'il faut pour qch/pour faire qch; **take your t.!,** prenez (tout) votre temps!; **you took your t.!,** tu as pris ton temps!, tu en as mis *ou* pris un temps!; **what a (long) t. he is taking!,** il n'en finit pas!, il prend son temps!; **to take the t. and trouble to check the facts,** ne ménager ni son temps ni sa peine pour vérifier les faits; **she took the t. to explain it to us,** elle a pris le temps de nous l'expliquer; **we haven't seen him for a long t.,** voilà longtemps que nous ne l'avons vu; **for some t. past,** depuis quelque temps; **for some t. (to come),** pendant quelque temps; **a short t. after, after a short t.,** peu (de temps) après; **after a t.,** après quelque temps, au bout d'un certain temps; **after a long t.,** longtemps après; **all this t.,** pendant tout ce temps; **she does it all the t.,** elle le fait toujours *ou* tout le temps; *Sp* **1 minute 34 seconds is her best/a good t.,** 1 minute 34 secondes, c'est son meilleur temps/c'est un bon temps; *Sp* **to keep the t.,** chronométrer; *Cin* **running t.,** durée *f* de projection (*d'un film*);

(c) (*age*) époque *f*; **sign of the times,** signe de l'époque; **in times past, in former times,** autrefois, jadis, dans le temps (passé); **the good old times,** le bon vieux temps; **in happier times,** en un *ou* des temps plus heureux; **in times to come,** à l'avenir, dans l'avenir; **in our times** *or* **these times,** de nos jours; **to be ahead of** *or* **in advance of one's t.,** être en avance sur son temps; **it was a very popular car in its t.,** c'était une voiture très populaire à l'époque (où elle est sortie); **she was probably a good singer in her t.,** c'était sûrement une bonne chanteuse dans son temps; **very advanced for its t.,** très en avance sur son temps *ou* sur l'époque; **to move with the times,** *F* être à la page; **to be behind the times,** retarder *ou* être en retard sur son siècle, *F* ne pas être à la page; **times are bad,** les temps sont difficiles *ou* durs; **hard times,** temps difficiles; **to be on hard times,** connaître des temps difficiles; **t. machine,** machine *f* à remonter le temps; **t. travel,** voyage *m* dans le temps; **t. warp,** (*in science fiction*) brèche *f* dans le temps; **it's like going into a t. warp,** c'est comme être transporté dans le passé/le futur;

(d) (*moment*) moment *m*; **at the t. of delivery,** au moment de la livraison; **I didn't know it at the t.,** (*at that moment*) je n'en savais rien à ce moment-là; (*at that period*) je n'en savais rien à cette époque; **at that t.,** en ce temps-là; **at the present t.,** à l'heure qu'il est, actuellement, à présent; **at a given t.,** à un moment donné *ou* déterminé; **at the t. fixed,** à l'heure convenue *ou* dite; **at one t. it was different,** autrefois *ou* dans le temps, ce n'était pas comme ça *ou* c'était différent; **at no t.,** jamais, à aucun moment; **at no t. did I say that ...,** je n'ai jamais dit que ..., à aucun moment je n'ai dit que ...; **at times,** parfois, quelquefois, par moments; **at all times,** toujours; **between times,** entre temps; **(at) any t. (you like),** n'importe quand, quand vous voudrez; **if at any time ...,** si à l'occasion ...; **some t. or other,** un jour ou l'autre; **some t. next month,** dans le courant du mois prochain; **this t. next year,** l'an prochain à pareille époque *ou* à la même date; **this t. tomorrow,** demain à la même heure; **by the t. (that) I got there,** lorsque je suis arrivé; **from t. to t.,** de temps en temps, de temps à autre; **from that t. (onwards),** dès lors, à partir de ce moment-là; **at the proper t.,** en temps utile; **we shall see when the t. comes,** nous verrons (cela) quand le moment sera venu; **now is the t.** *or* **our t.** *or* **your t. to ...,** c'est le (bon) moment pour ...; **to choose one's t.,** choisir son heure *ou* le moment; **this is no t.** *or* **this is not the t. to ...,** ce n'est pas le moment de ...; **in due t. and place,** en temps et lieu; **all in good t.,** chaque chose en son temps; **in her own good t.,** à son heure;

(e) (*time of day etc*) heure *f*; **Greenwich mean t.,** l'heure de Greenwich; **standard t.,** heure du fuseau; **(standard) t. belt** *or* **t. zone,** fuseau *m* horaire; **summer t.,** *Am* **daylight saving t.,** heure d'été, *Can* heure avancée; **do you have the t.?,** vous avez l'heure?; **what's the t.?,** quelle heure est-il?; **what t. do you make it?,** quelle heure avez-vous?; **t. signal,** signal *m* horaire; **to look at the t.,** regarder l'heure; (*look at one's watch*) regarder (à) sa montre; **watch that keeps (good) t./that loses t.,** montre qui est toujours à l'heure/qui retarde; **t. of day,** heure du jour; **to pass the t. of day with s.o.,** parler de la pluie et du beau temps avec qn; **at any t. of the day or night,** à n'importe quelle heure du jour ou de la nuit; **dinner t.,** l'heure du dîner; **(dead) on t.,** à l'heure (exacte); **to run on t.,** (*of trains etc*) être à l'heure; **to be ahead of/behind t.,** être en avance/en retard; **I was just in t. to see it,** je suis arrivé juste à temps pour le voir; **to start in good t.,** s'y prendre (bien) à temps; (*on journey*) se mettre en route de bonne heure; **it is t. we left,** il est temps de songer à partir; **it's t. he understood,** il est temps qu'il comprenne; *F* **it's high t.!, and about t. too!,** ce n'est pas *ou* c'est pas trop tôt!; **t. of (the) year,** époque *f* de l'année; **at my/her/their/***etc* **t. of life,** à mon/son/leur/*etc* âge; **it was holiday t.,** c'était l'époque des vacances; **before one's** *or* **its t.,** prématurément; **his t. had not yet come,** son heure n'était pas encore venue; **to be nearing her t.,** (*of pregnant woman*) approcher de son terme; **the t. for talking is past,** ce n'est plus le moment de parler;

(f) *Ind etc* **to be paid by t.,** être payé à l'heure; **to put in t.,** faire des heures; **to work** *or* **to be on short t.,** être en chômage partiel; **to be on t. and a half/double t.,** être payé une fois et demie/deux fois le taux horaire; **t. and motion study,** étude *f* des temps et mouvements; **t. and motion expert,** spécialiste *mf* des temps et mouvements; **t. card,** fiche *f* de pointage; **t. clock,** (*in factory etc*) pendule *f* de pointage; **t. sheet,** feuille *f* de présence; (*weekly*) semainier *m*;

(g) to have a good t. (of it), bien s'amuser; (*lead a pleasant life*) mener une vie agréable; *F* **to have a high old t.,** faire la noce; **to have the t. of one's life,** s'amuser comme un fou; **to have a bad** *or* **hard** *or* **rough t. (of it),** (*long period*) manger de la vache enragée, en voir de dures; (*shorter period*) passer un mauvais quart d'heure; **to have an easy t. of it,** se la couler douce, passer du bon temps; **to give s.o. a hard** *or* **rough** *or* **tough t.,** en faire voir de dures à qn, en faire voir de toutes les couleurs à qn;

(h) (*occasion*) fois *f*; **five times,** cinq fois; **this is the third t.,** c'est la troisième fois; **next t.,** la prochaine fois; **another t.,** une autre fois; **the first t. I saw her,** la première fois que je l'ai vue; **to do sth several times over,** faire qch à plusieurs reprises *ou* plusieurs fois; **four times running,** quatre fois de suite, à quatre reprises; **t. and t. again, t. after t.,** à maintes reprises, maintes et maintes fois; **he succeeds every t.,** il réussit à chaque coup; **every t. that ...,** chaque fois que ...; **to do two things at a t.,** faire deux choses à la fois; **to run upstairs four at a t.,** monter l'escalier quatre à quatre; **for weeks at a t.,** des semaines durant *ou* d'affilée; **it costs me £6 a t. to have my hair cut,** une coupe de cheveux me coûte six livres; **four times two is eight,** quatre fois deux font huit; **three times as big as the other,** trois fois plus grand que l'autre; **six times as much,** six fois autant;

(i) at the same t., en même temps; (*to do two things*) à la fois; *Prov* **you can't be in two places at the same t.,** on ne peut être à la fois au four et au moulin; **at the same t., you mustn't forget that ...,** en même temps *ou* tout de même *ou* néanmoins il ne faut pas oublier que ...;

(j) *Mus* mesure *f*; **t. (value),** valeur *f* (*d'une note*); **duple/triple t.,** mesure à deux/trois temps; **to beat t.,** battre la mesure; **in strict t.,** en mesure; **to keep t., to be in t.,** être en mesure; **to get out of t.,** perdre la mesure; **to quicken/slow the t.,** presser/ralentir le tempo *ou* le mouvement; *Gym etc* **in quick t.,** au pas accéléré; **t. signature,** fraction *f* indiquant la mesure;

(k) *F* **the big t.,** le haut de l'échelle; **to be in the big t., to have made the big t.,** être en haut de l'échelle, être arrivé; **big-t. operator,** gros trafiquant; **small-t. crook,** petit escroc.

time² *vt* **(a)** fixer l'heure de (*qch*); régler (*une horloge*); *Aut etc* régler, ajuster (*l'allumage, les soupapes*); caler (*le distributeur, une soupape*); mettre (*le moteur*) au point; *Phot* calculer (*le temps de pose*); **to t. one's arrival to coincide with one's friend's,** s'arranger pour arriver en même temps que son ami; **to t. a blow/a remark,** choisir le moment de porter un coup/de placer un mot; **well timed,** (*of remark etc*) opportun, à propos; **badly timed,** inopportun, mal à propos;

(b) (*measure time of*) *Sp etc* chronométrer (*qn, une course*); prendre le temps (*d'un coureur*); *Mil etc* minuter (*une opération etc*); **to t. a journey,** calculer la durée d'un voyage; **to t. how long it takes s.o. to do sth,** mesurer le temps que qn met à faire qch; **t. yourself doing one batch of work,** mesure le temps que tu mets à faire un paquet de travail; *Sp* **timed race,** course *f* contre la montre

time consuming ['taɪmkənsjuːmɪŋ] *adj* (*travail etc*) qui prend beaucoup de temps.

time-honoured ['taɪmɒnəd] *adj* (*custom etc*) consacré (par l'usage), vénérable, séculaire.

timekeeper ['taɪmkiːpər] *n* **(a)** (*official*) *Ind* contrôleur *m* (de présence); *Sp* chronométreur *m*; **(b) to be a good t.,** (*of person, watch*) être toujours à l'heure.

timekeeping ['taɪmkiːpɪŋ] *n* **(a)** *Ind* (*regulation*) contrôle *m ou* pointage *m* de présence; **(b)** *Sp etc* (*calculation of time*) chronométrage *m*; **(c) good t.,** (*punctuality*) ponctualité *f* (*de qn*); exactitude *f* (*d'une montre*); **her t. was poor,** elle ne respectait pas les horaires.

time-lapse ['taɪmlæps] *adj* **t.-l. photography,** accéléré *m*.

timeless ['taɪmlɪs] *adj* (*scene, appeal, novel etc*) intemporel; (*eternal*) éternel.

timeliness ['taɪmlɪnɪs] *adj* opportunité *f*, à-propos *m* (*d'une intervention etc*).

timely ['taɪmlɪ] *adj* opportun, à propos; **I made a t. escape,** je me suis échappé juste à temps.

time-out ['taɪmaʊt] *n Am* **(a)** *Sp* pause *f*; **(b) to take t.-o.,** (*pause*) faire une pause.

timepiece ['taɪmpiːs] *n* (*clock*) pendule *f*; (*watch*) montre *f*.

timer ['taɪmər] *n* **(a)** (*person*) chronométreur *m*; **(b)** (*device*) *Aut etc* commutateur *m* d'allumage; (*on electric appliance etc*) minuterie *f*; *Culin* compte-minutes *m inv*; **egg t.,** sablier *m*.

time(-)saving ['taɪmseɪvɪŋ] **1** *adj* (*device, method*) qui permet de gagner du temps. **2** *n* gain *m* de temps.

timescale ['taɪmskeɪl] *n* délais *mpl*; **4½ years is a very different t.,** quatre ans et demi représentent une tout autre échelle *ou* de tout autres délais; **the t. of a novel,** la période sur laquelle s'échelonne un roman.

time-sensitive ['taɪmsensɪtɪv] *adj* qui requiert un minutage très précis.

time-served ['taɪmsɜːvd] *adj* (*toolmaker etc*) qui a fait son apprentissage.

timeserver ['taɪmsɜːvər] *n Pej* opportuniste *mf*.

timeserving ['taɪmsɜːvɪŋ] *n Pej* opportunisme *m*.

time-share ['taɪmʃeər] **1** *adj* (*flat, house*) en multi-propriété. **2** *n* appartement *m*/maison *f* en multi-propriété.

time-sharing ['taɪmʃeərɪŋ] *n* (*of house*) multi-propriété *f*; *Comptr* temps partagé.

timespan ['taɪmspæn] *n* intervalle *m* de temps.

timetable ['taɪmteɪb(ə)l] *n* **(a)** horaire *m*; *Rail* horaire *m*, indicateur *m* (*des chemins de fer*); **(b)** *Sch* emploi *m* du temps; *Ind* plan *m* de mise en exécution; **to work to a t.,** travailler selon un emploi du temps.

time-wasting ['taɪmweɪstɪŋ] *n esp Sp* **penalized for t.-w.,** pénalisé pour avoir cherché à gagner du temps.

timework ['taɪmwɜːk] *n* travail *m* à l'heure; **to be on t.,** travailler à *ou* être payé à l'heure.

timeworn ['taɪmwɔːn] *adj* (*worn*) usé (par le temps).

timid ['tɪmɪd] *adj* timide, peureux.

timidity [tɪ'mɪdɪtɪ] *n* timidité *f*.

timidly ['tɪmɪdlɪ] *adv* timidement.

timing ['taɪmɪŋ] *n* **(a)** *Sp etc* rythme *m* (*d'un mouvement*); **error of t.,** mauvais calcul; **good/bad t.,** à-propos *m*/manque *m* d'à-propos (*d'une observation*); opportunité *f*/inopportunité *f* (*d'une démarche*); **good t., we've just started dinner!,** juste à temps, nous venons juste de commencer à dîner!; **the actors' t. was awful,** la synchronisation entre les acteurs était terrible; **a comedian with a perfect sense of t.,** un comédien qui contrôle parfaitement le rythme de son débit; **he has no sense of t.,** (*of what is suitable*) il n'a aucun sens de l'à-propos; **we must get the t. right between us,** il faut que nous nous synchronisions; **how's that for t!, we've finished one day before the deadline,** quel minutage!, nous avons terminé un jour avant la date limite; **they're still discussing the t. of the election,** ils sont encore en train de discuter de la date des élections; **the t. of the announcement was criticized,** on a critiqué le manque d'à-propos de cette annonce;
(b) *Phot* calcul *m* (*du temps de pose*);
(c) (*measuring of time*) *Sp etc* chronométrage *m*; *Mil etc* minutage *m* (*d'une opération*);
(d) *Aut etc* distribution *f*; réglage *m* (*de l'allumage*); calage *m* (*d'une soupape*).

timorous ['tɪmərəs] *adj* timoré, timide.

timorously ['tɪmərəslɪ] *adv* timidement.

Timothy ['tɪməθɪ] *n* Timothée.

timpani ['tɪmpənɪ] *npl Mus* timbales *fpl*.

timpanist ['tɪmpənɪst] *n Mus* timbalier *m*.

tin[1] [tɪn] *n* **(a)** (*metal*) étain *m*; **t.-bearing,** stannifère; **t. mine,** mine *f* d'étain; **(b) t. (plate),** fer-blanc *m*; *Mil etc F* **t. hat,** casque *m*; **t. mug,** timbale *f*; *F* **t. pan alley,** = le monde de la musique populaire; **t. roof,** toit *m* en tôle; **t. whistle,** flûte *f* en métal; **(c)** (*container*) (*for cake*) moule *m*; (*for tart*) tourtière *f*; **(d)** *esp Br* **t. (can),** boîte *f* (*en fer-blanc*); (*containing food*) boîte de conserves; **t. of sardines,** boîte de sardines; *Br* **t. loaf,** pain cuit au moule; **t. opener,** ouvre-boîte(s)*m*, *pl* ouvre-boîtes.

tin[2] *vt* **(-nn-) (a)** (*put in can*) mettre (*des sardines etc*) en boîtes; **(b)** (*coat with tin*) étamer.

tincture[1] ['tɪŋ(k)tjər] *n* **(a)** teinture *f* (*d'iode etc*); **(b)** (*colour*) teinte *f*, nuance *f*.

tincture[2] *vt* teindre, colorer.

tinder ['tɪndər] *n* amadou *m*.

tinderbox ['tɪndəbɒks] *n* briquet *m* (à silex); **the country is like a t.,** le pays est une poudrière.

tine [taɪn] *n* **(a)** dent *f*, fourchon *m* (*de fourche*); dent, pointe *f* (*de herse etc*); **(b)** (*of antler*) andouiller *m*.

tinfoil ['tɪn'fɔɪl] *n* (*aluminium*) papier *m* (d')étain, papier (d')aluminium.

ting[1] [tɪŋ] *n* tintement *m* (*d'une cloche*).

ting[2] **1** *vi* tinter. **2** *vt* faire tinter.

ting-a-ling ['tɪŋəlɪŋ] *n & adv* drelin drelin *m*.

tinge[1] [tɪn(d)ʒ] *n* nuance *f*, soupçon *m*; **a t. of irony,** une pointe *ou* une note d'ironie.

tinge[2] *vt* teinter, colorer; **sky tinged with pink,** ciel teinté de rose; **words tinged with malice,** paroles teintées de malice; **memories tinged with sadness,** souvenirs empreints de tristesse.

tingle[1] ['tɪŋg(ə)l] *n* **(a)** (*feeling*) picotement *m*, fourmillement *m* (*de la peau*); **to have a t. in one's legs,** avoir des fourmis dans les jambes; **to feel a t. of excitement,** ressentir une pointe d'exaltation; **(b)** (*sound*) **t. in the ears,** tintement *m* d'oreilles.

tingle[2] **1** *vi* **(a)** picoter; **my hand tingles,** j'ai des picotements dans la main; **to t. with impatience,** vibrer d'impatience; **breeze that makes the blood t.,** brise qui fouette le sang; **champagne that makes your mouth t.,** champagne qui vous chatouille la bouche; **(b)** (*of ears*) tinter. **2** *vt* **(a)** faire picoter (*la peau*); **(b)** faire tinter (*les oreilles*).

tingling ['tɪŋglɪŋ] **1** *adj* **(a) t. sensation,** picotement *m*; **(b)** (*oreilles*) qui tintent. **2** *n* = **TINGLE**[1].

tingly ['tɪŋglɪ] *adj* **t. sensation,** picotement *m*; **my arm has gone all t.,** j'ai des picotements dans tout le bras, tout mon bras me picote; **the sauna made me (feel) t. all over,** le sauna m'a donné des picotements partout.

tininess ['taɪnɪnɪs] *n* petitesse *f* (extrême).

tinker[1] ['tɪŋkər] *n* (*pot repairer*) chaudronnier ambulant, rétameur ambulant; *Dial* (*gypsy*) bohémien *m*; *Br F* **you little t.!,** espèce de petit coquin!; *F* **he doesn't give a t.'s cuss,** il s'en moque *ou* s'en fiche comme de sa première chemise *ou* comme de l'an quarante.

tinker[2] *vi* bricoler (**with,** avec); (*with text etc*) trafiquer; **to t. with the radio,** passer du temps à rafistoler le poste de radio; **someone's been tinkering with the water heater,** quelqu'un a trafiqué *ou* tripoté le chauffe-eau.

tinkering ['tɪŋkərɪŋ] *n* bricolage *m*; rafistolage *m*

tinkle[1] ['tɪŋk(ə)l] *n* tintin *m*, tintement *m* (*de clochettes, de verres*); *Br F* **I'll give you a t.,** (*telephone*) je vous passerai un coup de fil.

tinkle[2] **1** *vi* tinter; **tinkling bells,** cloches argentines; **to t. on the piano,** tapoter sur le piano, pianoter. **2** *vt* faire tinter (*une sonnette, des grelots*).

tinkling ['tɪŋklɪŋ] *n* tintement *m* (*de clochettes, de verres*).

tinned [tɪnd] *adj* **(a)** *Br* (*meat etc*) en boîte; **t. foods,** conserves *fpl*; **to eat t. fruit,** manger des fruits en conserve; **(b)** (*fer etc*) étamé.

tinning ['tɪnɪŋ] *n* **(a)** *Br* mise *f* en boîte(s) (*de conserves*); **(b)** (*of metal*) étamage *m*.

tinnitus [tɪn'aɪtəs] *n Med* acouphène *m*.

tinny ['tɪnɪ] *adj* (*son*) grêle, fêlé; (*loudspeaker, radio*) qui rend un son grêle *ou* fêlé; **to sound t.,** rendre un son métallique *ou* fêlé *ou* grêle; *Pej* **a t. car,** une boîte de conserve; **food with a t. taste,** aliment *m* qui a un goût d'étain *ou* de boîte de conserve.

tin-opener ['tɪnəʊp(ə)nər] *n esp Br* ouvre-boîte(s) *m*, *pl* ouvre-boîtes.

tinplate ['tɪnpleɪt] *n* fer-blanc *m*.

tinpot ['tɪnpɒt] *adj F* de rien du tout, misérable; **a t. dictator,** un dictateur en carton-pâte.

tinsel ['tɪns(ə)l] **1** *n* clinquant *m*; (*Christmas decorations*) guirlandes *fpl*. **2** *adj* (*fil etc*) de clinquant; *Fig* d'un faux brillant, clinquant.

tinsmith ['tɪnsmɪθ] *n* (*coats with tin*) étameur *m*; (*makes tin objects*) ferblantier *m*.

tint[1] [tɪnt] *n* **(a)** (*shade*) teinte *f*, nuance *f*; (*in hairdressing*) colorant *m*, couleur *f*; **red with a blue t.,** teinte rouge avec une nuance de bleu; **warm tints,** tons chauds; **half t.,** demi-teinte *f*, *pl* demi-teintes; **(b)** (*in line engraving*) grisé *m*.

tint[2] *vt* **(a)** (*colour*) teinter, colorer; *Opt* **tinted glasses,** verres teintés; **to have one's hair tinted,** se faire faire une coloration, se faire teinter les cheveux; **(b)** (*in engraving*) ombrer, hachurer (*une gravure*).

tintack ['tɪntæk] *n* broquette *f*, clou *m* de tapisserie.

tinting ['tɪntɪŋ] *n* coloration *f*.

tintinnabulation [tɪntɪnæbjʊ'leɪʃən] *n* tintinnabulement *m*.

tinware ['tɪnweər] *n* (*no pl*) ferblanterie *f*.

tiny ['taɪnɪ] *adj* minuscule; **a t. bit,** un tout petit peu; **a t. little house,** une toute petite maison; **in a t. voice,** d'une toute petite voix.

tip[1] [tɪp] *n* **(a)** bout *m*, extrémité *f*; (*pointed*) pointe *f*; **on the tips of the toes,** sur la pointe des pieds; **to have sth on the t. of one's tongue,** avoir qch sur le bout de la langue; **from t. to toe,** de la tête aux pieds; *Culin* **asparagus tips,** pointes d'asperge; **(b)** bout ferré, embout *m* (*d'une canne etc*); *Billiards* procédé *m* (*de queue*); bout *m* (filtre) (*de cigarette*); **steel t.,** fer *m* (*de bout de chaussure*).

tip[2] *vt* **(-pp-) (a)** mettre un bout à (*un soulier*); embouter (*une canne etc*); **arrow tipped with poison,** flèche à bout empoisonné; **(b)** (*cut tip from*) couper le bout de (*qch*).

tip[3] *n* **(a)** (*payment*) pourboire *m*; **to give s.o. a t.,** donner un pourboire à qn; **(b)** *Horseracing St Exch* (*advice*) tuyau *m*; **if you take my t. ...,** si vous m'en croyez ..., si vous suivez mon conseil ...; **to give s.o. a t.,** tuyauter *ou* renseigner qn; **to take a t. from s.o.,** suivre le conseil de qn; **a book full of useful tips on how to save energy,** un livre plein de tuyaux utiles pour économiser l'énergie; **(c)** *Constr etc* chantier *m* de versage; *Min* terri(l) *m*; **(rubbish) t.,** dépotoir *m*; *F* **this room's a t.!,** cette pièce est un vrai dépotoir!; **t. car** *or* **truck,** wagon *ou* wagonnet basculant *ou* à bascule; **t. cart,** tombereau *m* (*à bascule*); **(d)** (*slope*) pente *f*, inclinaison *f*; **(e)** (*light blow*) coup léger; (*with hand*) tape *f*.

tip[4] **(-pp-)** *vt* **(a)** (*give money to*) donner un pourboire à (*qn*); **to t. s.o.,** donner un pourboire à qn; **(b)** *Horseracing St Exch etc* tuyauter (*qn*), donner un tuyau à (*qn*); **to t. a certain horse to win,** pronostiquer qu'un certain cheval sera le gagnant; *F* **she's widely tipped for the job,** on lui donne toutes les chances pour le poste; **(c)** verser, déposer (*des immondices*); (*cause to lean*) faire pencher, faire incliner; **to t. sth into sth,** verser qch dans qch; **to t. sth on the ground,** déverser qch par terre; **to t. one's hat over one's eyes,** rabattre son chapeau sur ses yeux; **to t. one's hat to s.o.,** tirer son chapeau à qn; **(d)** (*touch lightly*) toucher légèrement, effleurer (*qch*).

▶tip off *vtsep* (*inform*) informer (*la police*); tuyauter (*un journaliste*); **to be tipped off about sth,** être tuyauté sur qch.

▶tip out *vtsep* (*pour out*) déverser, décharger (*le contenu de qch*); **to t. sth out on the ground,** déverser qch par terre.

▶tip over 1 *vtsep* (*overturn*) renverser (*qch*); chavirer (*un canot etc*). **2** *vi* (*overturn*) se renverser, basculer; (*of boat etc*) chavirer.

▶tip up 1 *vtsep* (*tilt upwards*) soulever (*un strapontin*); faire basculer (*une charrette*); *Min* verser (*un wagon*). **2** *vi* (*tilt upwards*) (*of plank etc*) se soulever, basculer.

tip-off ['tɪpɒf] *n* tuyau *m*; (*warning*) avertissement *m*; **to give s.o. a t.-o.,** tuyauter *ou* renseigner qn; **the police received a t.-o.,** la police a été informée.

tipped [tɪpt] *adj* **(filter) t. cigarettes,** cigarettes à bout filtre; **t. or plain?,** filtre *ou* sans filtre?

-tipped [tɪpt] *suff* **gold/silver/***etc***-t.,** à bout doré/d'argent/*etc*.

tipper ['tɪpər] *n* **(a) t. (truck** *or Br* **lorry),** camion *m* à benne; **(b) to be a good t.,** (*of person*) donner des pourboires généreux.

tippet ['tɪpɪt] *n* pèlerine *f*, collet *m* (*de fourrure*).

Tippex ® ['tɪpeks] *n* tippex ® *m*.

▶Tippex ® **out** *vtsep* passer (*qch*) au tippex ®.

tipping ['tɪpɪŋ] **1** *adj* (*wagon etc*) basculant, à bascule. **2** *n* **(a)** (*giving money*) distribution *f* de pourboires; (*system*) (système *m* des) pourboires *mpl*; **is t. normal?,** est-ce qu'il est normal de distribuer *ou* donner des pourboires?; **(b)** *Horseracing* tuyautage *m*; **(c)** (*tilting*) inclinaison *f*; versage *m*, déversement *m* (*du contenu d'un wagon etc*); **t. apparatus,** culbuteur *m* (*pour wagons etc*); **no t.,** (*on sign*) dépôt d'ordures interdit, décharge interdite.

tipping out *n* déversement *m* (*du contenu d'un wagon etc*).

tipping over *n* renversement *m* (*de qch*); chavirement *m* (*d'un canot*).

tipple[1] ['tɪp(ə)l] *n F* boisson *f* alcoolique; **what's your t.?,** qu'est-ce que vous prenez habituellement?; **gin was my t.,** je buvais du gin à l'époque.

tipple[2] *vi F* boire à droite à gauche, picoler.

tipple[3] *n Am Min* (*apparatus*) basculeur *m* de wagons; (*place*) décharge *f*.

tippler ['tɪplər] *n F* picoleur, -euse.

tippy-toe ['tɪpɪtəʊ] *n, adv, vi Am* = **TIPTOE.**

tipsily ['tɪpsɪlɪ] *adv* (*d'une voix*) qui accuse l'ivresse; (*marcher*) en titubant.

tipsiness ['tɪpsɪnɪs] *n* (légère) ivresse *f*.

tipstaff, *pl* **-staffs** ['tɪpstɑːf, -stɑːfs] *n Br Jur* huissier *m*.

tipster ['tɪpstər] *n Horseracing etc* pronostiqueur *m*.

tipsy ['tɪpsɪ] *adj* gris, *F* pompette; **slightly t.,** un peu éméché; **to get t.,** se griser, s'enivrer.

tiptoe[1] ['tɪptəʊ] **1** *n* **on t.,** sur la pointe des pieds. **2** *adv* sur la pointe des pieds.

tiptoe[2] *vi* marcher sur la pointe des pieds; **to t. into/out of the room,** entrer/sortir sur la pointe des pieds.

tiptop ['tɪptɒp] *adj* excellent; (*hôtel etc*) de premier ordre; **I feel t.,** je me sens à merveille.

tip-up ['tɪpʌp] *adj* (*charrette, cuvette etc*) à bascule; **t.-up seat,** strapontin *m*.

tirade [taɪ'reɪd] *n* tirade *f*, diatribe *f* (**against,** contre); **t. of invective,** tirade *ou* bordée *f* d'injures.

tire[1] ['taɪər] **1** *vt* fatiguer; (*to weary*) lasser; **to t. oneself doing sth,** se fatiguer à faire qch. **2** *vi* se fatiguer; (*to weary*) se lasser (**of s.o./sth,** de qn/de qch); **he never tires of telling me,** il ne se lasse pas de me le dire; **they tired of his complaining** *or* **complaints,** ils se sont fatigués *ou* lassés de ses plaintes.

tire[2] *n US* = **TYRE.**

▶tire out *vtsep* (*exhaust*) épuiser *ou* briser (*qn*) de fatigue; (*complaints etc*) excéder (*qn*); (*exhaust patience of*) lasser la patience de (*qn*); **to t. oneself out,** se fatiguer jusqu'à n'en plus pouvoir; **she was t. out,** elle n'en pouvait plus de fatigue.

tired ['taɪəd] *adj* fatigué; (*weary*) las, *f* lasse; **to get t.,** se fatiguer; *F* **you make me t.,** tu me fatigues, tu m'ennuies *ou* m'embêtes; *F Hum* **t. and emotional,** (*drunk*) dans les vignes du Seigneur; **to be t. of sth,** être las de qch; **to grow** *or* **get t. of s.o./sth,** se lasser de qn/qch; **to grow** *or* **get t. of doing sth,** se lasser de faire qch; *F* **I'm t. of you,** j'en ai assez de vous; **t. of arguing, he consented,** de guerre lasse, il a donné son consentement; *F* **t. carpet,** tapis usé; **t. phrase,** expression usée; **in a t. voice,** d'une voix lasse *ou* fatiguée.

tiredly ['taɪədlɪ] *adv* avec lassitude.

tiredness ['taɪədnɪs] *n* fatigue *f*; lassitude *f*.

tireless ['taɪəlɪs] *adj* infatigable, inlassable.

tirelessly ['taɪəlɪslɪ] *adv* infatigablement, inlassablement.

tiresome ['taɪəsəm] *adj* (*boring*) assommant, ennuyeux; (*irritating, annoying*) fatigant, exaspérant; **how t.!,** que c'est ennuyeux *ou* assommant!

tiring ['taɪərɪŋ] *adj* (*work etc*) fatigant, lassant; (*person, speech etc*) ennuyeux.

tiro, *pl* **-o(e)s** ['taɪrəʊ, -əʊz] *n* = **TYRO.**

'tis [tɪz] = **it is,** *see* **BE.**

tissue ['tɪsjuː] *n* (*cloth*) & *Biol* tissu *m*; (*paper handkerchief*) mouchoir *m* en papier; **t. (paper),** papier *m* de soie; *Fig* **t. of lies,** tissu de mensonges.

tiswas ['tɪzwɒz] *n F* = **TIZZY.**

tit[1] [tɪt] *n* (*bird*) mésange *f*; **blue t.,** mésange bleue; **coal t.,** mésange noire; **great t.,** (mésange) charbonnière *f*.

tit[2] *n* **t. for tat,** un prêté pour un rendu; **to give s.o. t. for tat,** rendre la pareille à qn; (*verbally*) riposter, répondre du tac au tac.

tit[3] *n Sl* **(a)** (*breast*) néné *m*, nichon *m*; **to get on s.o.'s tits,** (*annoy, irritate*) porter sur le système à qn; **(b)** (*idiot*) imbécile *mf*; **I felt a right t.,** je me suis senti vraiment bête *ou* un parfait imbécile.

▶tit up *vtsep Vulg* (*feel breasts of*) peloter les nichons à (*une femme*).

Titan ['taɪt(ə)n] *n Myth* Titan *m*; *Fig* **t.,** titan.

titanic [taɪ'tænɪk] *adj* titanesque.

titanium [taɪ'teɪnɪəm] *n Ch* titane *m*.

titbit ['tɪtbɪt] *n* morceau friand; (*sweet*) friandise *f*; (*of gossip*) potin *m*.

titch, titchy [tɪtʃ, 'tɪtʃɪ] = **TICH, TICHY.**

titfer ['tɪtfər] *n Br Sl* (*hat*) galurin *m*, bitos *m*.

tit-for-tat [tɪtfə'tæt] *adj* (*killing, expulsions etc*) fait en représailles *ou* en riposte.

tithe [taɪð] *n Hist* dîme *f*; **t. barn,** grange *f* de la dîme *ou* aux dîmes.

Titian ['tɪʃɪən] **1** *n* (*the painter*) le Titien. **2** *adj* (*hair*) acajou *inv*.

titillate ['tɪtɪleɪt] **1** *vt* émoustiller (*les lecteurs, les téléspectateurs*); émoustiller, titiller (*les sens*); chatouiller (*le palais*). **2** *vi* (*of film, book etc*) titiller les sens.

titillating ['tɪtɪleɪtɪŋ] *adj* chatouillant; titillant, émoustillant.

titillation [tɪtɪ'leɪʃən] *n* titillation *f*.

titivate ['tɪtɪveɪt] **1** *vt* faire (*qn*) beau, pomponner (*qn*); pomponner, bichonner (*qch*). **2** *vi* se faire beau.

title[1] ['taɪtl] *n* **(a)** titre *m* (*d'un livre, d'un chapitre*); intitulé *m* (*d'un journal, d'un acte*); **the story that gives the collection its t.,** l'histoire qui donne son titre à la collection; **the t. is taken from ...,** le titre est tiré de ...; *Typ* **t. page,** (page *f* de) titre; (*with embellishments*) frontispice *m*; **to publish fifty titles a year,** publier cinquante titres par an; **t. piece,** (*of anthology*) conte *m ou* morceau *m* qui donne le titre au recueil; *Th* **t. rôle,** rôle *m* qui donne le titre à la pièce; *Mus* **t. track,** (*of album*) morceau *m* qui donne son titre à l'album;

(b) (*of person*) titre *m*; **to give s.o. a t.,** donner un titre à *ou* titrer qn; **... to give her her full t. ...,** ... pour lui donner *ou* lui conférer son titre complet ...; **t. (of nobility),** titre de noblesse; **to have a t.,** avoir un titre de noblesse, être titré;

(c) *Sp* titre *m*; **to hold the t.,** détenir le titre (de champion); *Boxing* **t./non t. fight,** combat *m* comptant/ne comptant pas pour le titre;

(d) t. to property, titre *m* de propriété; **t. (deed),** titre (constitutif) de propriété;

(e) *Cin TV* (*credits*) générique *m*.

title² *vt* intituler (*un livre etc*).

titled ['taɪtld] *adj* (*person*) titré; **to be t.**, avoir un titre (de noblesse).

titleholder ['taɪtlhəʊldər] *n Sp* tenant, -ante du titre.

titmouse ['tɪtmaʊs] *n* (*bird*) mésange *f*.

titrate ['taɪtreɪt] *vt Ch Ind* titrer (*une solution*).

titter¹ ['tɪtər] *n* (*suppressed laughter*) rire étouffé; (*nervous laughter*) petit rire nerveux *ou* bête.

titter² *vi* avoir un petit rire étouffé; (*laugh nervously*) rire nerveusement *ou* bêtement.

tittering ['tɪtərɪŋ] *n* petits rires.

tittie ['tɪtɪ] *n* = **TITTY**.

tittle ['tɪt(ə)l] *n* **not one t.**, pas un iota.

tittle-tattle¹ ['tɪtltætl] *n* **(a)** (*chatter*) bavardage *m*; **(b)** (*gossip*) cancans *mpl*.

tittle-tattle² *vi* **(a)** (*chatter*) bavarder; **(b)** (*gossip*) potiner, cancaner.

titty ['tɪtɪ] *n Sl* (*breast*) nichon *m*, roploplo *m*; **that's tough t., that's his tough t.**, c'est tant pis pour lui, (c'est) tant pis.

titular ['tɪtjʊlər] **1** *adj* titulaire; (*function, office etc*) nominal; **t. possessions**, terres attachées à un titre. **2** *n Jur* titulaire *mf* (*d'un droit etc*).

tizzy ['tɪzɪ] *n F* **to be in a t.**, ne (pas) savoir où donner de la tête.

TNT [ti:en'ti:] *n* (*abbr* **trinitrotoluene**) TNT *m*.

to [tu:; *unstressed* tə] **1** *prep* **(a)** à; **to go to church/to school**, aller à l'église/à l'école; **what school do you go to?**, à quelle école allez-vous?; **I'm off to Paris**, je pars pour Paris; **he went to France/to Japan**, il est allé en France/au Japon; **she returned home to her family**, elle est rentrée auprès de sa famille; **I am going to the grocer's**, je vais chez l'épicier; **from town to town**, de ville en ville; **flights to the Continent**, vols à destination du Continent; **the road to London**, la route de Londres; **journey to Paris**, voyage à Paris; **the shortest way to the station**, le plus court chemin pour aller à la gare; **to bed!**, (*go to bed*) allez vous coucher!; (*I'm off to bed*) je vais me coucher;

(b) (*towards*) vers, à; **to the east**, vers l'est; **to the trains**, (*on sign*) accès aux quais; **to the station**, direction de la gare; **to the right**, à droite; **to the left**, à gauche; **the rooms to the back**, les chambres de derrière;

(c) **elbow to elbow**, coude à coude; **I told him so to his face**, je le lui ai dit en face; **to clasp s.o. to one's heart**, serrer qn sur son cœur; **to fall to the ground**, tomber à *ou* par terre;

(d) (*of time*) **from morning to night**, du matin au soir; **from day to day**, de jour en jour; **ten minutes to six**, six heures moins dix; **it's ten to**, il est moins dix;

(e) (*until*) jusqu'à; **to this day**, jusqu'à ce jour; **to count up to ten**, compter jusqu'à dix; **moved to tears**, ému jusqu'aux larmes; **fight to the death**, bataille *ou* combat à mort; **to a high degree**, à un haut degré; **generous to a fault**, généreux à l'excès; **accurate to a millimetre**, exact à un millimètre près; **a year to the day**, un an jour pour jour; **to cut sth down to a minimum**, réduire qch au minimum;

(f) (*purpose*) **to this end**, à cet effet, dans ce but; **to sit down to dinner**, se mettre à table (pour dîner);

(g) (*result*) **to my despair**, à mon grand désespoir; **to everyone's surprise**, à la surprise de tous; *Bot* **to run to seed**, monter en graine; **to put to flight**, mettre en fuite; **to pull to pieces**, mettre en pièces;

(h) **what tune is it sung to?**, sur quel air cela se chante-t-il?;

(i) **heir to s.o./to an estate**, héritier de qn/d'une propriété; **ambassador to the King of Sweden**, ambassadeur auprès du roi de Suède; **apprentice to a joiner**, apprenti chez un menuisier; **the key to the door**, la clef de la porte; **the answer to a question**, la réponse à une question;

(j) (*in comparisons*) **superior to**, supérieur à; **compared to this**, comparé à *ou* en comparaison de celui-ci; **that's nothing to what I have seen**, cela n'est rien à côté de ce que j'ai vu;

(k) (*expressing a proportion*) **three is to six as six is to twelve**, trois est à six ce que six est à douze; **six votes to four**, six voix contre quatre; **three goals to nil**, trois buts à zéro; **to bet ten to one**, parier dix contre un; **it's a thousand to one (that) it won't happen**, il y a mille à parier contre un que cela n'arrivera pas;

(l) **to all appearances**, selon les apparences; **not to my taste**, pas à mon goût; **to the best of my recollection**, (pour) autant que je m'en souvienne;

(m) **to drink to s.o.**, boire à la santé de qn;

(n) (*concerning*) **what did she say to my suggestion?**, qu'est-ce qu'elle a dit de ma proposition?; **is that all there is to it?**, c'est tout?; **there's nothing to it**, (*it's easy*) ce n'est rien du tout, c'est simple comme bonjour; **there's nothing/there isn't a lot to these cameras — just a lens and box**, ce n'est rien du tout/ce n'est pas grand chose, ces appareils-photo — juste un objectif et une boîte;

(o) (*used to form the dative*) **to give sth to s.o.**, donner qch à qn; **who did you give it to?**, à qui l'avez-vous donné?; **to speak to s.o.**, parler à qn; **to whom?**, à qui?; **what's it to you?**, qu'est-ce que cela vous fait?; **to keep sth to oneself**, garder qch pour soi; **to allude to sth**, faire allusion à qch; **he has been a father to me**, il a été un père pour moi; **known to the ancients**, connu des anciens; **used to doing sth**, accoutumé à faire qch.

2 (*with the infinitive*) **(a)** (*purpose, result*) pour; **he came to help me**, il est venu (pour) m'aider; **we must eat (in order) to live**, il faut manger pour vivre; **so to speak**, pour ainsi dire; **born to rule**, né pour régner; **happy to do it**, heureux de le faire; **ready to listen**, prêt à écouter; **old enough to go to school**, d'âge à aller *ou* en âge d'aller à l'école; **built to house 10 people**, construit pour loger 10 personnes; **too hot to drink**, trop chaud pour qu'on puisse le boire; **to hear her speak, you'd think she owned the place!**, à l'entendre, on dirait que c'est elle le propriétaire des lieux!; **he left the house never to return to it again**, il quitta la maison pour n'y plus revenir;

(b) **to have a letter to write**, avoir une lettre à écrire; **to have a lot to do**, avoir beaucoup à faire; **there was not a sound to be heard**, on n'entendait pas le moindre bruit; **he isn't one to forget his friends**, il n'est pas homme à oublier ses amis; **tendency to do sth**, tendance à faire qch; **desire to do sth**, désir de faire qch;

(c) **to lie is shameful, it is shameful to lie**, il est honteux de mentir; **to be or not to be**, être ou ne pas être; **it is better to do nothing**, il vaut mieux ne rien faire; **to learn to do sth**, apprendre à faire qch; **to refuse to do sth**, refuser de faire qch;

(d) (*inf in finite clause*) **I want him to know**, je veux qu'il sache; **it seemed to grow**, il semblait croître;

(e) (*in headline*) **a hundred employees to go**, cent employés vont recevoir leur congé; **Bush to meet Major**, entretiens entre Mr Bush et Mr Major;

(f) (*with ellipsis of verb*) **you ought to**, vous devriez le faire; **I want to**, j'ai envie de le faire; (*I would like to*) je voudrais bien; **take it — it would be absurd not to**, prenez-le — ce serait absurde de ne pas le faire *ou* de manquer l'occasion; **we shall have to**, il le faudra bien, nous serons bien obligés.

3 *adv* (*stressed*) **(a)** **to pull the door to**, fermer la porte; **to turn to** *or* **set to with a will**, se mettre résolument à l'ouvrage; **to come to**, (*to one's senses*) reprendre connaissance; **ship moored head to**, (*to the wind*) navire amarré vent debout;

(b) **to go to and fro**, aller et venir; (*of shuttle bus etc*) faire la navette.

toad [təʊd] *n* **(a)** (*animal*) crapaud *m*; *F Pej* (*person*) type répugnant, sale type; **(b)** *Culin* **t. in the hole**, = saucisses cuites au four dans de la pâte à crêpes.

toadstool ['təʊdstu:l] *n F* champignon vénéneux.

toady¹ ['təʊdɪ] *n* lécheur *m* (de bottes).

toady² *vi* **to t. to s.o.**, lécher les bottes à qn, flagorner qn.

to-and-fro [tu:ən'frəʊ] *adj MecE* **t.-a.-f. movement**, mouvement *m* de va-et-vient.

toast¹ [təʊst] *n* **(a)** (*toasted bread*) pain grillé, toast *m*; **piece** *or* **slice** *or* **round of t.**, rôtie *f*, toast; **t. rack**, porte-rôties *m inv*, porte-toasts *m inv*; **as warm as t.**, bien chaud; **(b)** toast *m*; **to give** *or* **propose a t.**, porter un toast; **to drink a t. to s.o.**, boire à la santé de qn; **the t. was the future**, on a porté un toast à l'avenir; **t. master**, annonceur *m* des toasts; **to be the t. of the town**, être la célébrité de la ville.

toast² **1** *vt* **(a)** rôtir, griller (*du pain*); *F* **to t. one's feet (in front of the fire)**, se chauffer les pieds; **toasted sandwich**, sandwich grillé; **(b)** **to t. s.o.**, porter un toast à (la santé de) qn, boire à la santé de qn. **2** *vi* (*of bread, people*) rôtir, griller.

toaster ['təʊstər] *n* grille-pain *m inv*; **sandwich t.**, grill *m* (électrique).

toastie ['təʊstɪ] *n F* sandwich grillé.

toasting *n* rôtissage *m*, grillage *m*; **t. fork**, fourchette *f* à rôties.

toasty ['təʊstɪ] *n* = **TOASTIE**.

tobacco, *pl* **-os** [tə'bækəʊ, -əʊz] *n* **(a)** tabac *m*; **chewing t.**, tabac à chiquer *ou* mâcher; **t.-coloured,** tabac *inv*; **t. tin,** boîte *f* à tabac; **(b) t. (plant),** tabac *m*.

tobacconist [tə'bækənɪst] *n Br* débitant, -ante (de tabac); **tobacconist's (shop),** (bureau *m ou esp Fml* débit *m* de) tabac *m*.

toboggan¹ [tə'bɒgən] *n* toboggan *m*; **(Swiss) t.**, luge *f*; *Sp* **t. run,** piste *f* de toboggan.

toboggan² *vi* faire du toboggan; **to t. down a slope,** descendre une côte en toboggan.

tobogganing [tə'bɒgənɪŋ] *n* (sport du) toboggan *m*; **to go t.**, aller faire du toboggan.

toby ['təʊbɪ] **t. (jug),** = pot *m* à bière (*en forme de gros bonhomme à tricorne*).

tocsin ['tɒksɪn] *n* tocsin *m*.

tod [tɒd] *n Br Sl* **on my/his/etc t.**, tout seul.

today [tə'deɪ] **1** *adv* aujourd'hui; **a week ago t.**, il y a aujourd'hui huit jours; **t. week,** (d')aujourd'hui en huit; *F* **he's here t. and gone tomorrow,** il est comme l'oiseau sur la branche. **2** *n* aujourd'hui *m*; **today's paper,** le journal d'aujourd'hui *ou* du jour; *Com* **today's date/price** la date/le prix du jour; **the young people of t.**, les jeunes d'aujourd'hui *ou* de nos jours.

toddle¹ ['tɒd(ə)l] *n* (*short walk*) petite promenade, balade *f*; **I'm going for a t.**, je vais faire un tour *ou* une balade.

toddle² *vi* **(a)** (*of young child*) marcher à petits pas chancelants; **(b)** *F* (*of adult*) trottiner; **to t. along,** aller *ou* faire son petit bonhomme de chemin; **I'd better be toddling,** (*leaving*) il faut que je bouge *ou* parte; **I'm just going to t. up to the shops,** je vais juste faire un tour en courses.

►**toddle off** *vi F* (*leave*) partir, lever le camp.

toddler ['tɒdlər] *n* enfant qui commence à marcher.

toddy ['tɒdɪ] *n* grog *m*.

to-do [tə'duː] *n F* bruit *m*, remue-ménage *m inv*; **what a to-do!**, quelle affaire!; **there was a great to-do about it,** l'affaire a fait grand bruit.

toe¹ [təʊ] *n* **(a)** orteil *m*, doigt *m* de pied; **big/little t.**, gros/petit orteil; **on the tips of one's toes,** sur la pointe des pieds; **to tread on s.o.'s toes,** marcher sur les pieds de qn; *Fig* **I hope I'm not treading on any toes,** j'espère que je n'empiète sur les plates-bandes de personne; *Fig* **to be on one's toes,** être alerte; *Fig* **to keep people on their toes,** maintenir les gens en alerte; **(b)** bout *m*, pointe *f* (*de soulier etc*); *Golf* pointe (*de la crosse*).

toe² *vt* **(a)** *Fb* botter (*le ballon*) avec la pointe du pied; *Golf* frapper (*la balle*) avec la pointe de la crosse; **(b)** *Sp* **to t. the line** *or* **the mark,** s'aligner; *Fig* **to t. the party line,** s'aligner sur son parti; **to t. the line,** obéir, s'exécuter.

toecap ['təʊkæp] *n* bout rapporté.

-toed [-təʊd] *suff* **two/three/***etc***-t.**, à deux/trois/*etc* orteils; **square/pointed/***etc***-t.**, (*souliers*) à bouts carrés/pointus/*etc*.

toehold ['təʊhəʊld] *n* **(a)** (*in climbing*) prise *f* de pied; **(b)** *Fig* prise précaire.

toenail ['təʊneɪl] *n* ongle *m* d'orteil.

toepiece ['təʊpiːs] *n* (*on ski*) butée *f*.

toerag ['təʊræg] *n Br Sl* merdeux, -euse.

toff [tɒf] *n Old-fashioned F* aristo *mf*; **the toffs,** le gratin.

toffee, toffy ['tɒfɪ] *n* caramel *m* au beurre; *F* **he can't sing for t.**, il ne sait pas chanter pour deux sous; **t. apple,** pomme *f* d'amour.

toffee-nosed ['tɒfɪnəʊzd] *adj esp Br F* snob *inv*, snobinard.

tofu ['tɒfuː] *n* tofu *m*, tofou *m*.

►**tog out, tog up** [tɒg] *vtsep* (*dress smartly*) *F* **to t. s.o. up** *or* **out,** fringuer qn; **to t. (oneself) up,** bien se fringuer, se mettre sur son trente et un; **to be (all) togged up,** être en grand tralala; (*in special clothing*) être en tenue.

toga ['təʊgə] *n* (*garment*) toge *f*.

together [tə'geðər] **1** *adv* ensemble; **to go** *or* **belong t.**, aller ensemble; **we stand or fall t.**, nous sommes tous solidaires; **t. with,** (*as well as*) avec (*qn, qch*), ainsi que (*qn, qch*); (*at the same time as*) en même temps que (*qn, qch*); **t. with the French, the Swedes objected,** les Suédois émirent une objection, de même que les Français; **to gather** *or* **collect t.**, (*bring together*) réunir, rassembler; (*come together*) se réunir, se rassembler; **to add t.**, additionner; **to bring t.**, rassembler, réunir; **to act t.**, agir de concert; **to be/get t. again,** (*of couple, partners*) être de nouveau ensemble/se remettre ensemble; **the family will all be t. at Christmas,** la famille sera réunie à Noël; **all t.**, tout le monde ensemble; (*at the same time*) tous à la fois; **now all t.!**, (*sing*) tous en chœur!; **all t. now! – push!**, tous ensemble maintenant! – poussez!; **all t. it cost us £480,** l'ensemble nous a coûté 480 livres; **for hours t.**, des heures durant, pendant des heures et des heures; **she's really got it t.**, (*in life*) c'est une femme accomplie, elle a sa vie bien en mains; (*in business etc*) elle connaît bien son affaire.
2 *adj esp Am F* (*person*) équilibré; **the band weren't very t.**, le groupe n'était *ou* ne jouait pas vraiment ensemble.

togetherness [tə'geðənɪs] *n* **(a)** (*unity*) unité *f*, harmonie *f*; **(b)** (*solidarity*) solidarité *f*.

toggle¹ ['tɒg(ə)l] *n* **(a)** (*on duffel coat etc*) olive *f*, barrette *f*; *Nau* **t. (pin),** cabillot *m* (*d'amarrage*); **(b)** *El* **t. switch,** interrupteur *m* à bascule, basculeur *m*; *Comptr* **t. key,** touche *f* à deux positions.

toggle² *vi Comptr* alterner (**between,** entre); **to t. sth on/off,** sélectionner/déselectionner qch.

Togo ['təʊgəʊ] *n* Togo *m*.

Togolese [təʊgəʊ'liːz] **1** *adj* togolais. **2** *n* Togolais, -aise.

togs [tɒgz] *npl F* (*clothes*) fringues *fpl*, frusques *fpl*.

toil¹ [tɔɪl] *n* travail dur *ou* pénible, dur labeur, peine *f*; **t. and trouble,** peine et ennuis *mpl*.

toil² *vi* travailler dur, peiner (**at,** à); **to t. and moil,** peiner, travailler dur; **to t. up a hill,** gravir péniblement une colline; **to t. on,** (*continue work*) continuer péniblement son travail; (*continue journey*) continuer péniblement sa route.

toiler ['tɔɪlər] *n* travailleur, -euse.

toilet ['tɔɪlɪt] *n* **(a)** (*lavatory*) (*device*) cabinets *mpl*; (*room*) cabinet *m* de toilette; **toilets,** toilettes *fpl*; **to go to the t.**, aller aux cabinets; **he's still in/on the t.**, il est encore aux toilettes; **to throw sth down the t.**, jeter qch dans les toilettes; **t. paper,** papier *m* hygiénique; **t. roll,** rouleau *m* de papier hygiénique; **t. seat,** siège *m* des toilettes; **t. training,** apprentissage *m* de la propreté; **(b)** *Old-fashioned* (*washing*) toilette *f*; **to make one's t.**, faire sa toilette; (*still used in*) **t. case,** nécessaire *m ou* trousse *f* de toilette; **t. soap/water,** savon *m*/eau *f* de toilette; **t. table,** (table *f* de) toilette, coiffeuse *f*.

toiletries ['tɔɪlɪtrɪz] *npl* articles *mpl* de toilette.

toils [tɔɪlz] *npl Lit & Fig* (*net*) filets *mpl*.

toilsome ['tɔɪlsəm] *adj Lit* pénible, laborieux.

toing ['tuːɪŋ] *n* **t. and froing,** va-et-vient *m*.

Tokay [tə'kaɪ] *n* (*wine*) tokai *m*, tokaï *m*, tokay *m*.

token ['təʊk(ə)n] *n* **(a)** (*indication*) indication *f*, marque *f*, témoignage *m* (*d'identité, de respect etc*); **in t.** *or* **as a t. of sincerity,** en signe *ou* en témoignage de bonne foi; **by this** *or* **by the same t.**, (*therefore*) donc; (*equally*) pareillement; **a t. black person,** un noir qui est là pour la forme; *Mil etc* **a t. force,** une force symbolique; **t. money,** monnaie *f* fiduciaire; **t. payment/strike,** paiement *m*/grève *f* symbolique *ou* d'avertissement; **(b)** (*disc etc*) jeton *m* (*pour distributeur automatique etc*); (*proof of attendance*) jeton (*de présence*); **gift t.**, bon *m* d'achat; **book t.**, chèque-livre *m*, *pl* chèques-livres; **record t.**, chèque-disque *m*, *pl* chèques-disques; **(c)** *Old-fashioned* signe *m*; **love t.**, gage *m* d'amour.

Tokyo ['təʊkɪəʊ] *n* Tokyo.

told *see* **TELL**.

Toledo [tɒ'leɪdəʊ] *n* Tolède.

tolerable ['tɒlərəb(ə)l] *adj* **(a)** (*pain etc*) tolérable, supportable; **(b)** (*acceptable*) passable; (*quite good*) assez bon; **we're in t. health,** nous nous portons assez bien.

tolerably ['tɒlərəblɪ] *adv* passablement; **I'm t. well,** je me porte assez bien; **it was t. well done,** c'était passablement bien fait.

tolerance ['tɒlərəns] *n* **(a)** tolérance *f* (*religieuse etc*); **to show great t.**, faire preuve de beaucoup de tolérance *ou* d'une grande indulgence; **(b)** tolérance *f* (*à une drogue*); **increasing t.**, accoutumance *f* (*à une drogue*); *MecE etc* tolérance, écart *m* admissible; (*minting*) tolérance.

tolerant ['tɒlərənt] *adj* **(a)** tolérant; (*parent etc*) tolérant, indulgent; **(b)** *Med* **t. of a drug,** (*patient*) qui tolère une drogue.

tolerate ['tɒləreɪt] *vt* **(a)** tolérer, supporter (*la douleur, la contradiction etc*); **I will not t. this behaviour,** je ne supporterai pas une telle conduite; *F* **I can't t. him,** je ne peux pas le souffrir *ou* le sentir; **(b)** *Med* tolérer (*une drogue*).

toleration [tɒlə'reɪʃən] *n* tolérance *f*.

toll¹ [təʊl] *n* **(a)** (*charge*) péage *m*, droit *m* de passage; droit de place (*au marché*); **t. bridge,** pont *m* à péage, pont payant; **t. gate** *or* **bar,** barrière *f* (de péage); **t. house,** (bureau *m* de) péage; **t. road,** route *f* à péage; *Fig* **to take its t.**, (*of disease etc*) faire beaucoup de victimes; (*have *severe effect*) laisser ses traces (**of s.o.,** sur qn); **accident that takes a heavy t. of human life,** accident qui cause beaucoup de morts; **the t. of the road,** les accidents de la route; **(b)** *Am Tel* **t. call,** communication interurbaine; **to call t. free,** faire un libre-appel.

toll[2] *n* tintement *m*, son *m* (*de cloche*); (*for death*) glas *m*.

toll[3] **1** *vt* tinter, sonner (*une cloche*); (*of bell, clock*) sonner (*l'heure*); **to t. s.o.'s death,** sonner le glas pour la mort de qn. **2** *vi* (*of bell*) tinter, sonner; (*for death*) sonner le glas; **to t. for the dead,** sonner pour les morts.

tolling ['təʊlɪŋ] *n* tintement *m* (*de cloche*); (*for death*) glas *m*.

tollway ['təʊlweɪ] *n Am* autoroute *f* à péage.

Tom [tɒm] *n* **(a)** (*dimin of* **Thomas**) Thomas, Tom; *F* **any T., Dick or Harry,** n'importe qui, le premier venu; **T. Thumb,** le petit poucet, Tom Pouce; **(b) t. (cat),** matou *m*; *Am* **t. (turkey),** dindon *m*.

tomahawk ['tɒməhɔːk] *n* hache *f* de guerre (*des Peaux-Rouges*), tomahawk *m*.

tomato, *pl* **-oes** [tə'mɑːtəʊ, -əʊz; *Am* tə'meɪtəʊ] *n* tomate *f*; **t. juice,** jus *m* de tomate; **t. ketchup,** ketchup *m*; **t. sauce,** sauce *f* tomate.

tomb [tuːm] *n* tombe *f*, tombeau *m*.

tombac ['tɒmbæk] *n Metal* tombac *m*.

tombola [tɒm'bəʊlə] *n* tombola *f*.

tomboy ['tɒmbɔɪ] *n* **she's a real t.,** c'est un vrai garçon manqué.

tomboyish ['tɒmbɔɪɪʃ] *adj* (*manières etc*) de garçon manqué.

tombstone ['tuːmstəʊn] *n* pierre tombale.

tome [təʊm] *n* (*volume*) tome *m*; (*large book*) gros livre; *F* (*book*) bouquin *m*.

tomfool [tɒm'fuːl] *F* **1** *n* idiot *m*, niais *m*. **2** *adj* idiot; **t. scheme,** projet insensé.

tomfoolery [tɒm'fuːlərɪ] *n F* bêtises *fpl*.

Tommy ['tɒmɪ] *n* (*dimin of* **Thomas**) Thomas, Tom; **t.,** simple soldat *m* (de l'armée britannique), *F* troufion *m*; *Mil* **T. gun,** mitraillette *f*.

tommyrot ['tɒmɪrɒt] *n Old-fashioned F* bêtises *fpl*, inepties *fpl*; **that's all t.,** tout ça c'est de la blague.

tomorrow [tə'mɒrəʊ] **1** *adv* demain; **t. morning,** demain matin; **t. week,** (de) demain en huit; **the day after t.,** après-demain; *Prov* **never put off till t. what you can do today,** il ne faut pas remettre au lendemain ce qu'on peut faire le jour même; *Fig* **what will the world be like t.?,** à quoi ressemblera le monde demain? **2** *n* demain *m*; **t.'s breakfast,** le petit déjeuner de demain; **who knows what t. holds?,** qui sait ce que demain nous réserve?; **t. never comes,** c'est maintenant ou jamais; **t. is another day,** demain tout peut changer, ça ira mieux demain; **the cities of t., t.'s cities,** les villes de demain; *F* **she was eating like there was no t.,** elle mangeait comme si son dernier jour était arrivé.

tomtit ['tɒmtɪt] *n* (*bird*) mésange bleue.

tom-tom ['tɒmtɒm] *n* tam-tam *m*, *pl* tam-tams.

ton [tʌn] *n* **(a)** tonne *f*; *Br* **(long) t.,** tonne longue (= 1 016 kg); *US* **(short** *or* **net) t.,** tonne courte (= 907 kg); **metric t.,** tonne (métrique) (= 1 000 kg); *F* **tons of ...,** des tonnes de ...; *F* **we've tons of time,** nous avons tout notre temps; *F* **there's tons of it,** il y en a des tas; *F* **this suitcase weighs a t.,** cette valise est rudement lourde *ou* pèse une tonne; **(b)** *Nau* **(gross** *or* **register) t.,** tonneau *m* de jauge; **t. of displacement,** tonne *f* de déplacement; **(c)** *esp Br Sl (100 mph)* vitesse *f* de 100 milles à l'heure; (*score of 100*) cent *m*; (*£100*) = cent livres; **to do a t.,** (*of vehicle, driver etc*) faire du cent milles à l'heure.

tonal ['təʊn(ə)l] *adj* tonal, -aux.

tonality [təʊ'nælɪtɪ] *n* tonalité *f*.

tone[1] [təʊn] *n* **(a)** (*sound*) son *m*; (*quality*) sonorité *f*; **t. (colour),** timbre *m* (*de la voix, d'un instrument de musique*); **this radio has a good t.,** ce poste a une bonne sonorité; *Tel* **ringing t.,** tonalité *f* d'appel; **t. arm,** bras *m* de lecture (*d'un tourne-disque*); **t. control,** (*on radio etc*) touche *f* de tonalité; **t. quality,** timbre (*d'un instrument etc*);

(b) (*sound of voice*) ton *m*, voix *f*; intonation *f*; *Med* tonicité *f*, tonus *m* (*des muscles etc*); **t. of voice,** accent *m*; **in an impatient t.,** d'un ton impatient; **I don't like your t. (of voice), don't take that t. with me,** je vous prierai de ne pas me parler sur ce ton; **in a low t.,** sur un ton bas, d'une voix basse; **to give a serious t. to a discussion,** donner un ton sérieux à une discussion; **the t. of her remarks,** le ton de ses remarques; **it was the t. of the letter I didn't like,** c'est le ton de cette lettre qui ne m'a pas plu; *Fin etc* **the t. of the market,** l'allure *f ou* l'atmosphère *f* du marché;

(c) (*acoustics*) & *Mus* ton *m*; **whole t.,** ton entier; **quarter t.,** quart *m* de ton; *Mus* **t. poem,** poème *m* symphonique;

(d) *Art etc* ton *m*, nuance *f* (*d'une couleur*); *Phot* ton (*d'une épreuve*); **warm tones,** tons chauds; *Art* **half t.,** similigravure *f*, *F* simili *f*;

(e) *Ling* ton *m*, accent *m* tonique, accent de hauteur; *Ling* **t. language,** langue *f* à ton.

tone[2] *vt* adoucir les tons (*d'un tableau*); *Phot* virer (*une épreuve*); **toned paper,** papier teinté; papier crémé.

►**tone down 1** *vtsep* **(a)** (*make less bright*) adoucir, atténuer (*une couleur etc*); (*on painting*) estomper (*des details trop crus*); **(b)** (*moderate*) modérer, adoucir (*remarks etc*); **the editor had to t. down the article,** le rédacteur a dû atténuer les termes de l'article. **2** *vi* (*of voice etc*) s'adoucir.

►**tone in** *vi* (*of colour etc*) s'harmoniser (**with,** avec).

►**tone up 1** *vtsep* (*make stronger*) tonifier (*les muscles*). **2** *vi* (*become stronger*) (*of person, muscles*) se tonifier.

►**tone with** *vipo* (*match, nearly match*) (*of colour, wallpaper etc*) s'harmoniser avec (*qch*).

tone-deaf [təʊn'def] *adj* incapable de reconnaître les notes; (*not appreciating music*) qui n'a aucun sens musical.

tone-deafness [təʊn'defnɪs] *n* incapacité *f* à reconnaître les notes; manque *m* de sens musical.

toneless ['təʊnlɪs] *adj* **(a)** (*couleur*) sans éclat; **(b)** (*voix*) blanc, atone.

tonelessly ['təʊnlɪslɪ] *adv* (*to say*) d'une voix blanche *ou* atone.

toner ['təʊnər] *n* **(a)** (*cosmetic*) astringent *m*, lotion astringente; **(b)** (*for photocopier, laser*) toner *m*; **t. cartridge/cassette,** cartouche *f* de toner.

tongs [tɒŋz] *npl* **(pair of) t.,** pince(s) *f(pl)*, tenailles *fpl*; (*in glassmaking*) morailles *fpl*; **fire t.,** pincettes *fpl*; (*Culin*) **sugar t.,** pince à sucre.

tongue[1] [tʌŋ] *n* **(a)** langue *f*; *Med* **coated t.,** langue pâteuse; **to put out** *or* **stick out one's t.,** tirer la langue (**at s.o.,** à qn); *Fig* **to have one's t. hanging out,** (*be exhausted*) tirer la langue; (*from thirst*) avoir soif; (*in expectation*) s'attendre à qch; **to have a ready or glib t.,** avoir la langue déliée *ou* bien pendue; **hold your t.!,** taisez-vous!; **to find one's t.,** retrouver la parole *ou* sa langue; *Fig* **with one's t. in one's cheek,** en plaisantant, avec une ironie masquée; **she was being t. in cheek,** elle plaisantait, elle faisait de l'ironie; **it's hard to get your t. round these words,** ces mots sont difficiles à prononcer; **to give t.,** (*of hounds*) donner de la voix, aboyer; **t. twister,** mot *m ou* phrase *f* difficile à prononcer, mot *ou* phrase à décrocher la mâchoire;

(b) *esp Lit* (*language*) langue *f*, idiome *m* (*d'un peuple*); **the German t.,** la langue allemande; *esp Bible* **the gift of tongues,** le don des langues;

(c) langue *f* (*de terre, de feu*); patte *f*, languette *f* (*de chaussure*); battant *m* (*de cloche*); aiguille *f* (*d'une balance*); *Mus* anche *f* (*de hautbois*); *Carp* languette.

tongue[2] *vt Mus* **to t. a passage,** (*on wind instrument*) détacher les notes d'un passage avec la langue.

tongue-and-groove [tʌŋən'gruːv] **1** *n* (*joint, edge*) assemblage *m* à languette; (*wood*) lattes *fpl* à languette. **2** *vt* pratiquer des languettes et des rainures sur (*des planches, des lattes*).

tongue-in-cheek [tʌŋɪn'tʃiːk] *adj* (*remark, article*) fait pour plaisanter, ironique.

tongue-lash ['tʌŋlæʃ] *vt Old-fashioned* tancer (*qn*) vertement.

tongue-lashing ['tʌŋlæʃɪŋ] *n Old-fashioned* **to give s.o. a t.-l.,** tancer qn vertement.

tongue-tied ['tʌŋtaɪd] *adj* muet, -ette (*de timidité etc*); interdit (*de stupeur etc*); **it's not like her to be t.-t.,** ça ne lui ressemble pas de rester sans mot dire.

tonguing ['tʌŋɪŋ] *n Mus* (*on wind instrument*) coup *m* de langue.

tonic ['tɒnɪk] **1** *adj* **(a)** *Med etc* tonique *m*, remontant, fortifiant; **t. lotion,** (lotion *f*) tonique *m*; **(b)** *Gram* (*accent*) tonique; *Mus* (*note*) tonique. **2** *n* **(a)** *Med* tonique *m*, remontant *m*, fortifiant *m*; **to act as a t. on s.o.,** (*of news etc*) réconforter *ou* remonter qn; **he's a t.,** il vous remonte le moral, il est stimulant *ou* énergisant; **skin t.,** (*lotion*) tonique; **(b) t. (water),** eau *f* tonique; **gin and t.,** gin-tonic *m*, *pl* gin-tonics; **(c)** *Mus* tonique *f*; **t. solfa,** solfège *m*.

tonicity [təʊ'nɪsɪtɪ] *n* tonicité *f* (*des muscles etc*).

tonight [tə'naɪt] **1** *adv* (*evening*) ce soir; (*night*) cette nuit. **2** *n* (*evening*) ce soir; (*night*) cette nuit; **t.'s main news,** les nouvelles principales de la soirée.

toning ['təʊnɪŋ] *n Phot* virage *m (des épreuves)*.
toning down *n (of colour, remarks)* atténuation *f*, adoucissement *m*.
toning in *n (with environment etc)* harmonisation *f*.
toning up *n* tonification *f*.
tonnage ['tʌnɪdʒ] *n* tonnage *m*; **register(ed) t.**, tonnage net.
tonne [tʌn] *n* tonne *f* (métrique).
tonsil ['tɒns(ə)l] *n Anat* amygdale *f*; **to have one's tonsils out,** se faire opérer des amygdales.
tonsillectomy [tɒnsɪ'lektəmɪ] *n* amygdalectomie *f*.
tonsillitis [tɒnsɪ'laɪtɪs] *n Med* amygdalite *f*, angine *f*; **to have t.**, avoir *ou* faire une amygdalite.
tonsure¹ ['tɒnʃər] *n* tonsure *f*.
tonsure² *vt* tonsurer *(un ecclésiastique)*.
tontine [tɒn'tiːn] *n (in insurance)* tontine *f*.
ton-up ['tʌnʌp] *adj Br F* **t.-up boys,** = motards *mpl* en furie, fous *mpl* de la moto (qui font du cent milles à l'heure).
tonus ['təʊnəs] *n Med* tonicité *f*, tonus *m*.
Tony ['təʊnɪ] *n (dimin of* **Anthony, Antony***)* Toine.
too [tuː] *adv* **(a)** trop; **it's t. difficult,** c'est trop difficile; **t. difficult a job,** un travail trop difficile; **t. many people,** trop de gens; **t. far,** trop loin; **to work t. much** *or* **t. hard,** travailler trop, trop travailler; **50p t. much,** 50p de trop; **this job's t. much for me,** ce travail est au-dessus de mes forces; **I've listened to him t. long,** je l'ai trop écouté; **I know her all t. well,** je ne la connais que trop; **you're t. kind,** vous êtes très *ou* trop gentil; **he's not t. well today,** il ne va pas très bien aujourd'hui; *Austr Br F* **t. right!,** et comment!, vous l'avez dit!; **(b)** *(also)* aussi, également; **you're coming t.,** vous venez aussi; **she t. is a painter,** elle aussi est peintre; **(c)** *(moreover)* en *ou* de plus; **30° in the shade and in September t.,** 30° à l'ombre et en septembre en plus.
toodle-oo, toodle-pip ['tuːdl'uː, -pɪp] *int Old-fashioned Br F* salut!
took *see* **TAKE²**.
tool¹ [tuːl] *n* **(a)** outil *m*; **(set of) tools,** outillage *m*; **garden** *or* **gardening tools,** outils de jardinage; **power t.**, outil à moteur; **t. bag,** sac *m* à outils; *(Cycling)* sacoche *f*; **t. box,** boîte *f ou* coffre *m* à outils; **t. holder,** *(for one tool)* porte-outil *m*; *(for several tools)* manche spécial pour divers outils; **t. kit,** outillage, jeu *m* d'outils; **t. rack,** râtelier *m* à outils; **t. set,** jeu *m* d'outils; **t. shed,** reserre *f*, remise *f*; **you have to learn the tools of your trade,** on ne peut pratiquer un métier sans apprentissage; **(b)** *Fig* instrument *m*; **to make a t. of s.o.,** se servir de qn *(dans un but intéressé)*; **he was a mere t. in their hands,** il n'était qu'un instrument entre leurs mains; **(c)** *Sl (penis)* bite *f*.
tool² *vt* **(a)** ciseler *(le cuir, une reliure)*; *MecE* usiner, travailler *(une pièce de fonte)*; **tooled leather,** cuir repoussé; **(b)** =**TOOL UP**.
▶tool up 1 *vtsep (equip with tools)* outiller *(une usine etc)*. **2** *vi (become equipped with tools)* s'outiller.
tooling ['tuːlɪŋ] *n* **(a)** *(of leather, binding)* ciselage *m*; *MecE* usinage *m*; **(b)** *(providing of tools)* outillage *m*.
tool-maker ['tuːlmeɪkər] *n* fabricant *m* d'outils, outilleur *m*.
toot¹ [tuːt] *n* son *m ou* appel *m* de clairon *etc*; *Nau* coup *m* de sirène; *Aut* coup *ou* appel de klaxon; **to give s.o. a t.**, donner un coup de klaxon à qn, klaxonner qn.
toot² 1 *vt* **to t. a horn/a trumpet,** sonner du cor/de la trompette; *Aut* **to t. the horn,** klaxonner; *F* **to toot s.o.,** klaxonner qn. **2** *vi (of person)* sonner du cor; *(of instrument)* sonner; *Aut (of driver)* klaxonner.
tooth¹, *pl* **teeth** [tuːθ, tiːθ] *n* **(a)** dent *f*; **(set of) teeth,** denture *f*, dentition *f*; **first** *or* **milk teeth,** dents de lait; **buck teeth,** dents proéminentes; **(set of) false teeth,** dentier *m*, *F* râtelier *m*; **to have a fine set of teeth,** avoir de belles dents; **to cut one's teeth,** faire *ou* percer ses dents; *Fig* **to cut one's teeth on sth,** se faire les dents sur qch; **to have a t. out,** se faire arracher une dent; **to kick s.o. in the teeth,** donner un coup de pied dans les dents à qn; *Fig* traiter qn avec mépris; *Fig* **to cast** *or* **fling sth in s.o.'s teeth,** reprocher qch à qn; **in the teeth of all opposition,** malgré *ou* en dépit de toute opposition; **to show** *or* **bare one's teeth,** montrer les dents; **armed to the teeth,** armé jusqu'aux dents; **to give a law teeth,** renforcer une loi; **to fight t. and nail,** se battre avec acharnement; **a meal/book you can get your teeth into,** un repas/livre consistant; *F* **a job you can get your teeth into,** un boulot dans lequel on peut s'en donner à cœur joie; **I want to get my teeth into the problem,** je veux m'attaquer à ce problème; **to grit** *or* **set one's teeth,** serrer les dents; *F* **I'm fed up to the back teeth with it,** j'en ai plein le dos de ça; *F* **she's a bit long in the t.,** elle n'est plus dans sa première jeunesse; *F* **I'm getting a bit long in the t. for that,** je commence à me faire un peu trop vieux pour ça; **t. glass** *or* **mug,** verre *m* à dents; **t. powder,** poudre *f* dentifrice;
(b) dent *f (de scie, de peigne, de roue d'engrenage)*; **teeth of a wheel,** denture *f*; *MecE* **gear teeth,** dents d'engrenage.
tooth² 1 *vt* denter *(une roue)*. **2** *vi (of cogwheels)* s'engrener.
toothache ['tuːθeɪk] *n* mal *m ou* rage *f* de dents; **to have t.**, avoir mal aux dents.
toothbrush ['tuːθbrʌʃ] *n* brosse *f* à dents.
toothed [tuːθt] *adj* **(a)** *(animal)* denté; *(leaf etc)* dentelé; **(b)** *MecE etc* **t. wheel,** roue dentée.
toothless ['tuːθlɪs] *adj* sans dents, édenté.
toothpaste ['tuːθpeɪst] *n* pâte *f* dentifrice, dentifrice *m*.
toothpick ['tuːθpɪk] *n* cure-dent(s) *m*, *pl* cure-dents.
toothsome ['tuːθsəm] *adj (tasty)* savoureux.
toothy ['tuːθɪ] *adj* à dents saillantes; **to give a big t. grin,** sourire à pleines *ou* belles dents; **t. pegs,** *(in children's language)* dents.
tooting ['tuːtɪŋ] *n* sonnerie *f (de la trompette etc)*; *Aut* coups *mpl* de klaxon.
tootle¹ ['tuːt(ə)l] *vi (toot)* corner, klaxonner *(de façon continue)*.
tootle² *vi Br F (go)* *(in car)* rouler tranquillement; *(on foot)* se balader.
▶tootle along *vi Br F (go)* aller *ou* suivre son petit bonhomme de chemin; **well, I'll t. along now,** bon, je vais me mettre en route.
toots [tʊts] *n F* **are you ready t.?**, *(to woman)* tu es prête, poupée?; *(to toddler)* tu es prêt(e), doudou?
tootsy ['tʊtsɪ] *n F (in children's language) (foot)* peton *m*; *(toe)* doigt *m* de pied.
top¹ [tɒp] **1** *n* **(a)** haut *m*, sommet *m*, cime *f*, faîte *m (d'un arbre, d'une montagne)*; sommet *(d'une tour, de la tête)*; **at the t. of the stairs,** en haut de l'escalier; **at the t. of the tree,** en haut de l'arbre; *Fig* au premier rang de sa profession; **from t. to bottom,** de haut en bas; *(to search a flat etc)* de fond en comble; **from t. to toe,** de la tête aux pieds; **to put sth on (the) t. of sth,** mettre qch sur qch *ou* (tout) en haut de qch; **the green book was on (the) t. (of the pile),** le livre vert était sur le dessus *ou* en haut (de la pile); **a cake with a cherry on t.**, un gâteau avec une cerise dessus; **to be on t.**, *(be in control)* avoir le dessus; **to be on t. of the situation,** maîtriser la situation; **you mustn't let things get on t. of you,** il ne faut pas te laisser dépasser par les événements; **to come out on t.**, prendre le dessus; **it's just one thing on t. of another,** ça n'arrête jamais; **on t. of it all,** et pour comble (de malheur), et en plus de tout cela; **to be** *or* **to feel on t. of the world,** être *ou* se sentir en pleine forme; *Mil* **to go over the t.**, (sortir des tranchées pour) aller à l'assaut; *F* **over the t.**, excessif; **I find her a bit over the t.**, je trouve qu'elle exagère un peu.
(b) surface *f*, dessus *m (d'une table etc)*; impériale *f (d'un autobus)*; **t. of the milk,** crème *f (séparée du lait)*;
(c) dessus *m (d'une chaussure)*; revers *m (d'une botte à revers, d'un bas)*; couvercle *m (d'une boîte, d'une casserole etc)*; bouchon *m*, capsule *f (d'une bouteille etc)*; capuchon *m (de stylo etc)*; haut *m*, corsage *m (d'une robe)*; *(separate garment)* haut; *F* **to blow one's t.**, s'emporter, sortir de ses gonds; **t. boots,** bottes *fpl* à revers;
(d) tête *f (de page, de carte etc)*; haut *m (d'une page, etc)*;
(e) haut bout *(de la table)*; **at the t. of the street,** au bout de la rue; *Sch* **to be (at) the t. of the class,** être le premier *ou* la première de la classe; **to be (at) the t. of the bill,** *(of actor, singer etc)* faire tête d'affiche; **to make it to the t.**, *(in profession, sport, music etc)* faire sa place parmi les grands; *F* **he's (the) tops!,** c'est le dessus du panier!; *F* **he's tops with me,** pour moi c'est le meilleur;
(f) **to shout/sing at the t. of one's voice,** crier/chanter à tue-tête *ou* à pleine gorge; **to be on t. of one's form,** être *ou* se sentir en pleine forme; *Irish F* **(the) t. of the morning (to you),** bien le bonjour!;
(g) **turnip/carrot tops,** fanes *fpl* de navets/de carottes;
(h) *Nau* hune *f*; **main t.**, grand-hune *f*;
(i) **the Big T.**, *(in circus)* le chapiteau;
(j) *Aut* **in t.**, en quatrième; en cinquième.
2 *adj* **(a)** *(highest)* supérieur, du dessus, du haut, d'en haut; **the t. floor** *or* **storey,** le dernier étage; **t. stair** *or* **step,** dernière marche (en montant); **t. hat,** chapeau *m* haut de forme; **car with a t. speed of 150 km.p.h.,**

voiture avec un plafond de 150 km/h; **t. people,** personnalités *fpl*; (*superior people*) gagnants *mpl*; (*in an organization*) gros bonnets *mpl*; *F* **the t. brass,** les officiers supérieurs; (*in company etc*) les gros bonnets; **t. coat,** (*of paint*) couche *f* de finition; *F* **t. dog,** le chef; *F* **to be t. dog,** (*have the advantage*) avoir le dessus; **to pay t. dollar,** payer le mieux; **he was given t. security,** on lui a accordé le maximum de sécurité; **t. shelf,** étagère *f* du dessus *ou* du haut; **to be/to feel on t. form,** être/se sentir en pleine forme; *Aut* **t. gear,** quatrième *ou* cinquième vitesse; prise *f* (directe);

(b) (*best, major*) premier; **she got the t. mark** *or F* **came t. in history,** elle a eu la meilleure note en histoire; **the country's t. ten companies,** les dix premières sociétés du pays; **one of the world's t. ten players,** un des dix meilleurs joueurs du monde; **t. pupil,** premier, -ère de la classe; **t. ten** *or* **twenty,** (*hit records*) hit-parade *m*; **in the t. ten,** au hit-parade.

top² *vt* (-pp-) **(a)** (*remove top*) écimer (*un arbre, une plante*); étêter (*un arbre*); **to t. and tail blackcurrants/gooseberries/*etc*,** éplucher des cassis/des groseilles à maquereau; **(b)** (*place on top of*) surmonter, couronner, coiffer (**with,** de); *Culin* garnir (*un dessert etc*) (**with,** de); **and to t. it all,** et pour comble (de malheur), et en plus de tout cela; **(c)** (*exceed*) excéder, surpasser; **the takings have topped a thousand pounds,** les recettes dépassent mille livres; **to t. s.o. by a head,** dépasser qn d'une tête; **(d)** atteindre le sommet (*d'une colline etc*); **(e) to t. a list/a class,** être à la tête d'une liste/de la classe; **topping the bill tonight we have ...,** le clou de cette soirée est ...; **(f)** *Golf* calotter (*la balle*); **(g)** *Sl* **to t. oneself,** (*commit suicide*) se foutre en l'air.

▶**top off** *vtsep* (*complete*) couronner (*une soirée*); **you can t. off this dessert with a cherry,** vous pouvez surmonter ce dessert d'une cerise.

▶**top out 1** *vtsep Br Constr* célébrer (*l'achèvement de la construction d'un immeuble*). **2** *vi Br Constr* célébrer l'achèvement de la construction d'un immeuble.

▶**top up 1** *vtsep* (*add more*) remplir un verre (*à ras bords*); *F* **let me t. you up,** encore un peu?; *Aut* **to t. up the battery/the oil/the tank/*etc*,** ajouter de l'eau/de l'huile/de l'essence/*etc*; **the government tops up the rest,** (*pays the balance*) le gouvernement met un appoint pour compléter. **2** *vi Aut* (*with oil*) ajouter de l'huile; (*with petrol*) faire le plein.

top³ *n* **(spinning** *or* **peg) t.,** toupie *f*; **humming t.,** toupie d'Allemagne.

topaz ['təʊpæz] *n* (*gem*) topaze *f*.

top-bracket ['tɒpbrækɪt] *adj* de première catégorie.

topcoat ['tɒpkəʊt] *n* pardessus *m*, manteau *m*.

top-dress ['tɒpdres] *vt Agr* fumer en surface.

tope [təʊp] *vi Old-fashioned F* boire (*avec excès*), picoler.

topee ['təʊpɪ] *n* casque colonial.

toper ['təʊpər] *n Old-fashioned F* picoleur, -euse.

top-flight ['tɒpflaɪt] *adj* de premier ordre, excellent.

top-heavy [tɒp'hevɪ] *adj* trop lourd du haut, mal équilibré, peu stable; *Fig* (*organization*) dont les dirigeants sont trop nombreux; *Nau* (*ship*) trop chargé dans les hauts.

top-hole ['tɒphəʊl] *adj Old-fashioned Br F* épatant, au poil.

topi ['təʊpɪ] *n* = **TOPEE**.

topic ['tɒpɪk] *n* matière *f* (*d'un écrit, d'une discussion*); sujet *m*, thème *m* (*de conversation*).

topical ['tɒpɪk(ə)l] *adj* **(a)** (*question*) d'actualité; **matters of t. interest,** des affaires d'un intérêt d'actualité; **it's very t.,** c'est tout à fait d'actualité; **a few t. references in the text,** quelques références à l'actualité dans le texte; **(b)** (*index*) (organisé) par matières.

topicality [tɒpɪ'kælɪtɪ] *n* actualité *f*.

topically ['tɒpɪklɪ] *adv* (*to write etc*) sur des thèmes d'actualité.

topknot ['tɒpnɒt] *n* huppe *f* (*d'un oiseau*); (*hair*) petit chignon.

topless ['tɒplɪs] *adj* (*danseuse*) aux seins nus; **t. beach,** plage seins nus; **to go t.,** aller torse nu.

top-level ['tɒplevəl] *adj* (*talks etc*) au plus haut niveau.

top-loader ['tɒpləʊdər] *n* (*washing machine*) machine *f* à laver à chargement par le haut.

topmast ['tɒpməst] *n Nau* mât *m* de hune.

topmost ['tɒpməʊst] *adj* le plus haut, le plus élevé.

topnotch ['tɒpnɒtʃ] *adj Old-fashioned F* de premier ordre *ou* rang.

topographer [tə'pɒgrəfər] *n* topographe *m*.

topographic(al) [tɒpə'græfɪk(əl)] *adj* topographique.

topographically [tɒpə'græfɪklɪ] *adv* topographiquement.

topography [tɒ'pɒgrəfɪ] *n* topographie *f*.

topologic(al) [tɒpə'lɒdʒɪk(əl)] *adj* topologique.

topology [tə'pɒlədʒɪ] *n* topologie *f*.

-topped [-tɒpt] *suff Lit* **cloud-t. peaks,** sommets couronnés de nuages; **ivory-t. walking stick,** canne à pomme d'ivoire.

topper ['tɒpər] *n F* (*top hat*) haut *m* de forme.

topping ['tɒpɪŋ] **1** *adj Old-fashioned Br F* excellent, formidable. **2** *n* **(a)** (*act of removing top*) écimage *m*, étêtement *m* (*d'un arbre*); **(b)** *Culin* garniture *f* (*pour un dessert, une pizza etc*); **ice-cream with raspberry t.,** glace recouverte d'un coulis de framboises.

topple ['tɒp(ə)l] **1** *vi* (*fall*) tomber, culbuter, dégringoler; (*wobble, be unsteady*) chanceler; **to bring the government toppling,** faire tomber *ou* renverser le gouvernement; **he toppled into the pool/over the edge of the cliff,** il est tombé *ou* a culbuté dans la piscine/par-dessus la falaise. **2** *vt* faire tomber, faire dégringoler (*qch*); faire écrouler (*un édifice etc*); renverser (*un gouvernement etc*).

▶**topple down, topple over** *vi & vtsep* = **TOPPLE**.

top-rank(ing) ['tɒpræŋk(ɪŋ)] *adj* de premier rang; **t.-r. civil servant,** haut fonctionnaire.

topsail ['tɒps(ə)l] *n Nau* hunier *m*; (*of cutter*) flèche *f*.

top-secret ['tɒpsiːkrɪt] *adj* (*information etc*) top secret, -ète.

top-security [tɒpsɪ'kjʊrɪtɪ] *adj* **t.-s. prison/wing,** prison *f*/aile *f ou* quartier *m* de haute surveillance.

topside ['tɒpsaɪd] *n* **(a)** *Culin* tende *f* de tranche (*de bœuf*); **(b)** *Nau* **topsides,** accastillage *m* (*d'un navire*).

topsoil ['tɒpsɔɪl] *n* couche *f* arable.

topsy-turvy [tɒpsɪ'tɜːvɪ] **1** *adj* sens dessus dessous; **everything's t.-t.,** (*of organization etc*) tout est en désordre, c'est la confusion totale. **2** *adv* **the whole world's turned t.-t.,** c'est le monde renversé, c'est le monde à l'envers.

top-up ['tɒpʌp] *n Aut F* (remplissage *m* d')appoint *m*; **let me give you a t.-up,** (*when serving drinks*) encore un peu?; **t.-up loan/finance,** prêt *m*/fonds *m* complémentaire.

toque [təʊk] *n* (*hat*) toque *f*.

tor [tɔːr] *n* (*hill*) pic *m*, butte rocheuse.

torch [tɔːtʃ] *n* **(a)** torche *f*, flambeau *m*; **to carry a** *or* **the t. for a cause,** embrasser *ou* épouser une cause; **to carry a torch for s.o.,** porter qn dans son cœur; **(b)** (*for welding*) chalumeau *m*; **(c)** *Br* **(electric) t.,** lampe *f* (électrique) (de poche), torche *f* électrique.

torchbearer ['tɔːtʃbeərər] *n* porte-flambeau *m inv*.

torchlight ['tɔːtʃlaɪt] *n* lumière *f* de torche(s) *ou* de flambeau(x); **t. procession,** retraite *f* aux flambeaux.

tore *see* **TEAR³**.

toreador ['tɒrɪədɔːr] *n* toréador *m*, torero *m*.

torment¹ ['tɔːment] *n esp Lit* tourment *m*, torture *f*, supplice *m*; **the torments of jealousy,** les tourments de la jalousie; **he suffered torments,** il souffrait le martyre; **to be in t.,** être au supplice.

torment² [tɔː'ment] *vt* tourmenter, torturer (*qn*); harceler (*qn, un animal etc*); **tormented with remorse,** tourmenté par les remords, en proie aux remords; **tormented soul,** âme tourmentée.

tormentor [tɔː'mentər] *n* bourreau *m*; **if you continue to be my t.,** si tu continues à me tourmenter.

torn *see* **TEAR³**.

tornado, *pl* **-oes** [tɔː'neɪdəʊ, -əʊz] *n* tornade *f*.

torpedo¹, *pl* **-oes** [tɔː'piːdəʊ, -əʊz] *n* **(a)** *Nau etc* torpille *f*; **t. boat,** vedette *f* lance-torpilles; **t. tube,** (tube *m*) lance torpilles *m inv*; **(b) t. (fish),** (poisson *m*) torpille *f*.

torpedo² *vt* torpiller (*un navire, Fig la paix*).

torpid ['tɔːpɪd] *adj* engourdi, torpide; **t. state,** engourdissement *m* (*d'un animal*).

torpidity [tɔː'pɪdɪtɪ], **torpor** ['tɔːpər] *n* torpeur *f*, engourdissement *m*.

torque [tɔːk] *n MecE Phys etc* moment *m* de torsion *ou* de rotation; **starting t.,** couple *m* de *ou* au démarrage; **t. wrench,** clé *f* dynamométrique.

torrent ['tɒrənt] *n* torrent *m*; **it's raining in torrents,** il pleut à torrents *ou* à verse; **t. of abuse/of tears,** torrent *ou* déluge *m* d'injures/de larmes.

torrential [tɒ'renʃəl] *adj* torrentiel; **t. rain,** une pluie diluvienne *ou* torrentielle.

torrid ['tɒrɪd] *adj* (*chaleur, zone, relation amoureuse*) torride.

torsion ['tɔːʃən] *n* torsion *f*; *Aut etc* **t. bar,** barre *f* de torsion.

torso, *pl* **-os** ['tɔːsəʊ, -əʊz] *n* torse *m*.

tort [tɔːt] *n Jur* acte *m* dommageable, préjudice *m*, délit civil.

tortoise ['tɔːtəs] *n* tortue *f*.

tortoiseshell ['tɔːtəsʃel] *n* écaille *f* (de tortue); **t. cat,** chat *m* écaille de tortue; **t. comb,** peigne *m* en écaille.

tortuous ['tɔːtjʊəs] *adj* (*sentier, moyen*) tortueux; **to have a t. mind,** avoir l'esprit tortu *ou* retors.

tortuously ['tɔːtjʊəslɪ] *adv* tortueusement.

tortuousness ['tɔːtjʊəsnɪs] *n* tortuosité *f* (*d'un sentier, de la pensée etc*).

torture1 ['tɔːtʃər] *n* **(a)** torture *f*; **instrument of t.,** instrument *m* de torture; **t. chamber,** chambre *f* de torture; **t. victim,** victime *mf* de torture; **(b)** *Fig* (*physical, mental pain*) torture *f*, tourment *m*, supplice *m*; **wearing these shoes is t.,** c'est un vrai supplice de porter ces chaussures.

torture2 *vt* torturer (*qn*); *Fig* (*by making s.o. wait etc*) mettre (*qn*) au supplice; *Fig* torturer (*un texte etc*); **tortured by remorse,** tenaillé par le remords.

torturer ['tɔːtʃərər] *n* tortionnaire *m*; *Hist* bourreau *m*.

torturing ['tɔːtʃərɪŋ] **1** *adj Lit* (*remords etc*) torturant. **2** *n* (mise *f* à la) torture *f*.

Tory ['tɔːrɪ] *adj & n Br Pol* tory *m*.

Toryism ['tɔːrɪɪz(ə)m] *n Br Pol* torysme *m*.

tosh [tɒʃ] *n Old-fashioned Br F* bêtises *fpl*, blague(s) *f(pl)*.

toss1 [tɒs] *n* **(a)** lancée *f*, lancement *m* (*d'une balle etc*); **t. (of a coin),** coup *m* de pile ou face; **to win/lose the t.,** gagner/perdre à pile ou face; **to argue the t.,** discuter inutilement *ou* pour rien; **(b) t. of the head,** brusque mouvement de tête; **(c) to take a t.,** faire une chute (*de cheval etc*); **(d)** *Br Sl* **he doesn't give a toss (what happens/***etc***),** il n'en a rien à ficher *ou* à taper (de ce qui arrivera/*etc*).

toss2 (-ss-)) **1** *vt* lancer, jeter (*une balle etc*) en l'air; (*of bull*) lancer (*qn*) en l'air; (*of sea etc*) agiter, secouer, ballotter; **to t. sth to s.o.,** jeter qch à qn; **to t. s.o. in a blanket,** faire sauter qn en l'air sur une couverture; **to t. the salad,** mélanger *ou F* fatiguer *ou* tourner la salade; **to t. a coin,** jouer à pile ou face; **who's going to pay? — I'll t. you for it,** qui va payer? – décidons-le à pile ou face; **to t. one's head,** relever la tête (*d'un air dédaigneux*). **2** *vi* **(a) to t. for sth,** jouer qch à pile ou face; **(b) to t. and turn, to t. in bed,** se tourner et se retourner dans son lit; **(c)** (*of waves*) s'agiter; **to t. on the waves,** être ballotté par les flots; **to pitch and t.,** (*of ship*) tanguer.

▸**toss about, toss around** *vtas* lancer, taper dans (*une balle*); **the ship, tossed about by the waves, ...,** le bateau, agité *ou* secoué *ou* ballotté par les vagues, ..., **let's t. the idea around for a while,** retournons un peu cette idée.

▸**toss across** *vtsep* envoyer; **t. the salt across, will you?,** envoie le sel, s'il te plaît.

▸**toss away** *vtsep* (*get rid of*) jeter.

▸**toss back** *vtsep* renvoyer (*la balle*); rejeter (*ses cheveux*) en arrière; **they tossed the report back and asked for a rewrite,** ils ont simplement renvoyé le rapport et demandé à ce qu'il soit réécrit.

▸**toss off 1** *vtsep* **(a)** (*drink quickly*) avaler d'un trait (*un verre de vin*); **(b)** (*complete quickly*) expédier (*une tâche, un essai, un article*); **(c)** *Br Vulg* (*masturbate*) branler. **2** *vi Br Vulg* (*masturbate*) se branler.

▸**toss out** *vtsep* jeter, *F* balancer (*des ordures*); **to t. s.o. out of a club,** (*physically, cancel membership*) mettre qn à la porte *ou F* jeter qn d'un club.

▸**toss up 1** *vtsep* (*throw up*) lancer, envoyer; **t. that brush up, will you,** lance-moi *ou* envoie-moi la brosse s'il te plaît; **to t. sth up into the air,** lancer *ou* envoyer qch en l'air. **2** *vi* (*with coin*) tirer à pile ou face; **let's t. up for it,** jouons-le *ou* décidons-le à pile ou face.

tossing ['tɒsɪŋ] *n* **(a)** lancement *m* en l'air (*d'une balle etc*); **t. of a coin,** jeu *m* de pile ou face; **(b)** (*of boat etc*) agitation *f*, ballottement *m*.

toss-up ['tɒsʌp] *n* (*of coin*) coup *m* de pile ou face; *F* **it's a t.-up,** c'est impossible à dire.

tot [tɒt] *n* **(a) (tiny) t.,** tout(e) petit(e) enfant; **books for tiny tots,** livres *mpl* pour les tout petits; **(b)** (*small quantity*) goutte *f*, petit verre (*de whisky etc*).

▸**tot up 1** *vtsep* (*add*) additionner; (*total*) faire le total de; **she has totted up 2,500 hours flying time,** elle totalise 2 500 heures de vol. **2** *vi* (*of expenses etc*) s'élever **(to,** à).

total1 ['təʊt(ə)l] **1** *adj* total, -aux, global, -aux; **t. amount,** somme totale *ou* globale; **t. eclipse,** éclipse totale; **t. failure,** échec complet; **they were in t. ignorance of it,** ils l'ignoraient complètement; **the t. population,** la population totale; **t. war,** guerre totale. **2** *n* total *m*; (*sum of money*) montant *m*; **grand t.,** total global; **there are a t. of thirteen inspectors in the whole country,** il y a un total de treize inspecteurs dans l'ensemble du pays; **sum t.,** somme totale; **the t. amounts to £100,** la somme *ou* le montant s'élève à 100 livres; **a t. of 102 hours/people/***etc*, un total de 102 heures/personnes/*etc*; **in t.,** au total.

total2 (*pt & pp* **totalled,** *Am* **totaled**) *vt* **(a)** (*add up*) additionner, totaliser (*les dépenses*); **(b)** (*amount to*) **to t. £100,** s'élever à *ou* se monter à 100 livres; **(c)** *US F* (*write off*) bousiller, déglinguer, fusiller (*une voiture*).

totalitarian [təʊtælɪ'teərɪən] *adj Pol* totalitaire.

totalitarianism [təʊtælɪ'teərɪənɪz(ə)m] *n Pol* totalitarisme *m*.

totality [təʊ'tælɪtɪ] *n* totalité *f*.

totalization [təʊtəlaɪ'zeɪʃən] *n* totalisation *f*.

totalizator ['təʊtəlaɪzeɪtər] *n Horseracing* totalisateur *m*, totaliseur *m* (*des paris*).

totalize ['təʊtəlaɪz] *vt* additionner, totaliser.

totally ['təʊtəlɪ] *adv* totalement.

tote1 [təʊt] *n Horseracing F* = **TOTALIZATOR.**

tote2 *vt esp Am* transporter (*des marchandises etc*); porter (*un sac, un revolver etc*); **t. bag,** sac fourre-tout *m inv*.

totem ['təʊtəm] *n* totem *m*; **t. pole,** mât *m* totémique.

totemism ['təʊtəmɪz(ə)m] *n* totémisme *m*.

t'other, tother ['tʌðər] *adj & pron Dial & F* = **the other.**

totter1 ['tɒtər] *n* (*act of tottering*) chancellement *m*.

totter2 *vi* **(a)** (*of person*) chanceler, tituber; **to t. in/out,** entrer/sortir d'un pas mal assuré *ou* chancelant. **(b)** (*of building, government*) chanceler, branler.

tottering ['tɒtərɪŋ] *adj* (*person, building, regime*) chancelant; (*person*) titubant; **t. steps,** pas chancelants *ou* mal assurés.

tottery ['tɒtərɪ] *adj* chancelant, titubant.

toucan ['tuːkæn] *n* (*bird*) toucan *m*.

touch1 [tʌtʃ] *n* **(a)** (*act of touching*) toucher *m*, contact *m*; **I felt a t. on my arm,** j'ai senti qu'on me touchait le bras; **the engine starts at the first t. of the starter,** le moteur démarre du premier coup;

(b) (*sense*) (*le sens du*) toucher *m*; **hard/soft to the t.,** dur/mou au toucher;

(c) (*feel*) toucher *m*; **the cold t. of marble,** le contact froid du marbre;

(d) (*light blow*) léger coup; touche *f* (*de pinceau*); coup (*de crayon*); **t. of** *or* **with a stick,** léger coup de baguette; **to give one's horse a t. of the spurs,** toucher son cheval de l'éperon; **to add a few touches to a picture,** faire quelques retouches à un tableau; **to put the finishing touch(es)** *or* **to add the final t. to sth,** mettre la dernière main *ou* la dernière touche à qch; **sculptor with a bold/light t.,** sculpteur au ciseau hardi/délicat; **to have a light t. (on the piano),** avoir un toucher délicat; **delicate t. (with** *or* **of the brush),** coup de pinceau délicat; *Fig* **there were some nice touches in the film,** il y avait quelques notes bien vues dans le film; **he's lost his t.,** il a perdu la main; **this room needs a woman's t.,** toute influence féminine fait défaut dans cette pièce;

(e) (*hint*) pointe *f*, nuance *f*, soupçon *m*; **t. of garlic,** pointe *ou* soupçon d'ail; **a t. of bitterness,** une nuance d'amertume; **there's a t. of colour in her cheeks,** ses joues ont pris un peu de couleur; **the first touches of autumn,** les premières teintes de l'automne; **a t. of originality,** une note d'originalité; **t. of flu,** petite grippe;

(f) (*contact*) contact *m*; **to be in t. with s.o.,** être *ou* se tenir en contact avec qn, être en rapport avec qn; **they're still in t.,** ils ont maintenu le contact *ou* sont toujours en rapport; **to get in t. with s.o.,** joindre *ou* contacter qn, prendre contact *ou* se mettre en contact avec qn; **to get in t. with the police,** se mettre en communication avec la police; **I'll be in t.,** je vous ferai signe; **to put s.o. in t. with s.o.,** mettre qn en relations *ou* en rapport avec qn; **to keep** *or* **stay in t. with s.o.,** rester en contact avec qn; **keep in t.!,** on reste en contact!; **to keep s.o. in t. with sth,** tenir qn au courant de qch; **to be out of t. with foreign affairs,** ne plus être au courant des affaires étrangères; **to be out of t.** *or* **to have lost t. with s.o.,** ne plus être en communication avec qn; **to lose t. with reality,** avoir perdu le contact avec la réalité; **the President has lost t. with the electorate,** le Président a perdu le contact avec son électorat;

(g) *Sp* touche *f*; **kick into t.,** envoi *m* de touche; **the ball had gone into t.,** le ballon est sorti en touche;

(h) it was t. and go whether we would catch the train, nous courions grand risque de manquer le train; **it was t. and go with him,** il revient de loin; (*he almost died*) il a frôlé la mort;

(i) (*financially*) **to make a t.,** emprunter de l'argent à qn, taper qn; **easy** *or* **soft t.,** personne *f* à qui on emprunte de l'argent facilement; **she's no easy** *or* **soft t.,** elle ne lâche pas l'argent facilement.

touch² **1** *vt* **(a)** toucher; (*be in contact with*) toucher (à) (*qch*); toucher, effleurer (*les cordes de la harpe*); *Fencing* toucher, boutonner (*son adversaire*); **to t. sth with one's finger,** toucher qch du doigt; **to t. s.o. on the shoulder,** toucher qn à l'épaule; **to t. s.o. on the arm,** toucher le bras à qn; **he touched his hat to me,** il m'a salué en touchant son chapeau; **t. wood!,** touche du bois!; **I wouldn't t. it with a bargepole** *or Am* **a ten foot pole,** je ne voudrais pas y toucher avec des pincettes; **to t. the bottom,** (*of ship*) toucher le fond; **her garden touches mine,** son jardin touche au mien *ou* le mien; **he touched the bell,** il a appuyé sur (le bouton de) la sonnette; **the curtains t. the floor,** les rideaux descendent jusqu'au plancher; *Horseriding* **to t. one's horse with the spur,** piquer son cheval de l'éperon; **the law can't t. her,** la loi ne peut rien contre elle; **there's no one to t. him in comedy,** il n'y a personne qui l'égale dans la comédie; **I never t. wine,** je ne bois jamais de vin; **you haven't touched your meat!,** tu n'as pas touché à ta viande!; **stains that other detergents won't t.,** des taches contre lesquelles les autres détergents ne peuvent rien; **when it comes to reliability, there's nothing to t. it,** quand il s'agit de fiabilité, elle est sans égal; **there's only one other company that can t. them,** il n'y a qu'une entreprise qui puisse rivaliser avec eux *ou* qui soit à leur niveau; **you haven't really touched the problem of ... in your essay,** vous n'avez pas vraiment abordé le problème de ... dans votre essai; **if it's in any way against the law, we won't t. it,** si c'est en quelque point que ce soit illégal, nous ne nous en mêlerons pas; **stolen, are they, sorry, can't t. them,** elles sont volées, hein, désolé, je ne veux rien avoir à faire avec ça;
(b) (*produce an effect on*) produire de l'effet sur (*qch*); *F* **to t. the spot,** (*of remedy etc*) aller à la racine du mal; **to t. s.o. on a raw** *or* **tender spot,** toucher qn à l'endroit sensible; **flowers touched by the frost,** fleurs atteintes par la gelée;
(c) (*move*) toucher, émouvoir, attendrir (*qn*); **to be touched by s.o.'s kindness,** être touché de *ou* par la bonté de qn; **to t. s.o. to the quick,** toucher qn au vif;
(d) *esp Fml* (*concern*) toucher, regarder (*qn*); **the question touches you closely,** la question vous touche de près;
(e) *F* **to t. s.o. for a fiver,** taper *ou* faire casquer qn de cinq livres.
2 *vi* **(a)** (*of two people, things*) se toucher; (*to be in contact*) être en contact; (*to come into contact*) venir en contact; **don't t.!,** n'y touchez pas!; **please do not t.,** (*on notice*) prière de ne pas toucher; **the two ships touched,** les deux navires ont touché; *Nau* **to t. at a port,** faire escale à un port; **the (two) wires are touching,** les deux câbles se touchent;
(b) *Nau* (*to touch bottom*) toucher.

▶**touch down** **1** *vi* **(a)** *Rugby US Fb* faire un touché-en-but, toucher dans les buts; **(b)** *Astronaut & Av* (*land*) atterrir; (*in mid-journey*) faire escale. **2** *vtsep Rugby US Fb* toucher (*le ballon*) dans les buts.

▶**touch off** *vtsep* (*detonate*) décharger (*un canon etc*); faire partir, faire exploser (*une mine*); déclencher (*une révolte, une querelle*).

▶**touch on** *vipo* (*make brief reference to*) aborder, effleurer (*un sujet*); **her speech didn't even touch on this problem,** elle n'a même pas abordé *ou* effleuré ce problème dans son discours.

▶**touch up** *vtsep* **(a)** (*add paint etc to*) faire des retouches à (*un tableau*); aviver, rafraîchir (*les couleurs de qch*); enjoliver (*un récit*); retaper, fignoler (*un ouvrage*); **to t. up (the paint on) a window frame/etc,** donner un coup de pinceau à un châssis de fenêtre/*etc*; **to t. up one's make-up,** rafraîchir son maquillage; **to t. up a photograph,** retoucher une photo; **(b)** *Br Sl* (*touch sexually*) toucher, peloter (*qn*); **(c)** *Horseriding* toucher (*un cheval*) du fouet.

▶**touch upon** = **TOUCH ON.**

touch-and-go [tʌtʃən'gəʊ] *adj* (*affair*) très risqué, hasardeux; **it's t.-and-go whether we'll have time,** il n'est pas du tout sûr que nous aurons le temps; **it's t.-and-go whether he'll live,** il a une chance sur deux de s'en sortir; **right up to the minute they signed it was t.-and-go,** jusqu'au moment où ils ont signé rien n'était sûr.

touchdown ['tʌtʃdaʊn] *n* **(a)** *Rugby US Fb* touché-en-but *m*, touché-à-terre *m*; **(b)** *Astronaut & Av* atterrissage *m*.

touché ['tu:ʃeɪ] *int* touché!

touched [tʌtʃt] *adj* **(a)** (*moved*) touché, ému; **(b)** *F* **t. (in the head),** toqué, timbré.

touchiness ['tʌtʃɪnɪs] *n* susceptibilité *f*, irascibilité *f*.

touching ['tʌtʃɪŋ] **1** *adj* touchant, émouvant, attendrissant. **2** *n* **t. is not allowed,** il est défendu de toucher. **3** *prep Fml* concernant.

touchingly ['tʌtʃɪŋlɪ] *adv* d'une manière touchante *ou* émouvante.

touching up *n* **(a)** (*in painting*) retouches *fpl*; avivage *m* (*d'une couleur*); **(b)** *Br Sl* (*sexual*) pelotage *m*.

touch-judge ['tʌtʃdʒʌdʒ] *n Rugby* juge *m* de touche.

touchline ['tʌtʃlaɪn] *n Fb etc* ligne *f* de touche.

touch-sensitive ['tʌtʃsensɪtɪv] *adj Comptr* (*screen etc*) tactile.

touchstone ['tʌtʃstəʊn] *n* pierre *f* de touche.

touch-type ['tʌtʃtaɪp] *vi* taper au toucher.

touch-typing ['tʌtʃtaɪpɪŋ] *n* dactylographie *f* au toucher.

touchwood ['tʌtʃwʊd] *n* amadou *m*.

touchy ['tʌtʃɪ] *adj* (*person*) susceptible (**about,** sur); (*subject*) délicat; **to be t.,** se froisser *ou* s'offusquer facilement; **she's very t. on that point,** elle est très susceptible *ou* chatouilleuse là-dessus.

tough [tʌf] **1** *adj* **(a)** (*meat etc*) dur, coriace; (*material, metal*) dur, résistant;
(b) (*resistant, strong*) (*person*) fort, solide; **you have to be t. to ...,** il faut être solide *ou* résistant *ou F* costaud pour ...; **to become t.,** s'endurcir; *F* **a tough guy,** un dur (à cuire);
(c) (*mentally*) fort; (*stubborn*) opiniâtre; (*strict*) dur, sévère; **she's a t. customer,** (*not easy to deal with*) elle n'est pas commode; (*mentally resistant*) c'est une dure (à cuire); **is he t. enough to be sales director?,** a-t-il la force de caractère nécessaire à un directeur des ventes?; **we'll have to get t. with them,** il faudra que nous nous montrions plus durs avec eux;
(d) (*difficult*) (*question, job, climb*) dur, ardu; **it's t. at the top,** (*in job etc*) c'est dur au sommet; **it was a t. job,** c'était une rude besogne; **they had a t. time when their parents died,** ils en ont connu de dures quand leurs parents sont morts;
(e) (*unfortunate*) dur; **that's t. on the rest of them,** c'est dur pour ceux qui restent; **it's t. for him, great for us,** c'est dur pour lui, mais génial pour nous; **well, isn't that just t.!,** quel dommage!; **t. luck!,** pas de chance!; **that's your t. luck!,** ce n'est pas de chance pour toi!, c'est tant pis pour toi.
2 *n* voyou *m*.

toughen ['tʌf(ə)n] **1** *vt* durcir; endurcir (*qn*); **toughened glass,** verre trempé. **2** *vi* durcir; (*of person*) s'endurcir.

▶**toughen up** = **TOUGHEN.**

toughly ['tʌflɪ] *adv* **(a) t. made,** robuste; **(b)** (*to fight*) vigoureusement; **(c)** (*to argue, refuse*) avec opiniâtreté.

▶**tough out** *vtas* **to t. it out,** faire front.

toughness ['tʌfnɪs] *n* **(a)** dureté *f*; (*of wood etc*) résistance *f*; (*of meat*) coriacité *f*; **(b)** (*of person*) (*physical strength*) force *f*, solidité *f*; (*resistance to fatigue*) résistance *f* à la fatigue; (*mentally*) force *f* de caractère; **(c)** (*of person*) (*inflexibility*) inflexibilité *f*, ténacité *f*, opiniâtreté *f*; (*awkwardness*) caractère *m* peu commode (*de qn*); difficulté *f* (*d'un travail*).

toupee, toupet ['tu:peɪ] *n* (mèche *f*) postiche *m*.

tour¹ [tʊər] *n* **(a)** (*visit to different places*) voyage *m*; (*excursion*) excursion *f*; **conducted** *or* **guided t.,** voyage organisé; (*of museum, city, factory, premises etc*) visite *f* (guidée); **to go on a t. of the Highlands,** partir en voyage dans les Highlands; **to go on a bus t. of Paris,** faire une visite guidée de Paris en bus; **the PM was taken on a t. of the factory/hospital,** le Premier Ministre a fait la visite de l'usine/l'hôpital; *esp Hum* **would you like a t. of the new offices?,** vous aimeriez-vous visiter nos nouveaux bureaux?; **package t.,** *Am* **all-expense t.,** voyage à forfait *ou* à prix forfaitaire; **cycle t.,** excursion *f ou* randonnée *f* à bicyclette; **t. guide,** (*person*) accompagnateur, trice; **t. operator,** voyagiste *mf*; **walking t.,** excursion *ou* randonnée à pied;
(b) (*short walk, ride etc*) tournée *f*; **t. of inspection,** tournée d'inspection; **t. of duty,** *Mil etc* service *m*; (*working day*) journée *f* (de travail); *Mil* **to do a t. of duty,** servir;
(c) *Mus, Th etc* (*by orchestra, theatre company etc*) tournée *f*; **during their European t.** *or* **t. of Europe,** pendant leur tournée européenne *ou* en Europe; **concert t.,** tournée de concerts; **to go on t.,** partir en tournée; **to take a play on t.,** jouer une pièce en tournée.

tour² **1** *vt* voyager dans (*un pays*); visiter (*un hôpital, une usine etc*); **(b)** *Mus Th* **to t. the provinces,** (*of company*) faire une tournée en province; (*of play*) passer en province. **2** *vi* **(a) we're just touring around,** nous ne faisons que visiter la région; **we decided to t. through the Loire Valley down to ...,** nous avons décidé de visiter *ou* faire *ou* descendre la Vallée de la Loire jusqu'à ...; **(b)** (*of theatre company etc*) **we spend most of the year touring,** nous passons la plus grande partie de l'année en tournée; **we go touring every summer,** nous partons en tournée *ou* nous tournons tous les étés.

tourer ['tʊərər] *n* (*car*) voiture *f* de tourisme; (*cycle*) vélo *m* de randonnée.

touring ['tʊərɪŋ] *adj Cycling* **t. bike** *or* **cycle,** vélo *m* de randonnée; **t. car,** voiture *f* de tourisme; *Th* **t. company,** troupe *f* en tournée; **we had a t. holiday in the North of Italy,** pour nos vacances nous avons visité le Nord de l'Italie.

tourism ['tʊərɪz(ə)m] *n* tourisme *m*.

tourist ['tʊərɪst] *n* touriste *mf*; **t. agency,** agence *f ou* bureau *m* de tourisme; **t. centre,** centre *m ou* ville *f* touristique; *Av etc* **t. class,** classe *f* touriste; **t. information,** renseignements *mpl* touristiques; **t. information office,** syndicat *m* d'initiative, office *m* du tourisme; **t. season,** saison *f* touristique; **the t. trade,** le tourisme; **t. restaurant/pub/***etc*, restaurant/pub/*etc* pour les touristes; *F* **t. trap,** attrape-touristes *m inv*.

touristy ['tʊərɪstɪ] *adj Pej* (trop) touristique.

tournament ['tʊənəmənt] *n Sp etc* tournoi *m* (*de tennis, de bridge*); *Hist* tournoi.

tourniquet ['tʊənɪkeɪ] *n Med* tourniquet *m*, garrot *m*.

tousle ['taʊz(ə)l] *vt* ébouriffer, écheveler (*les cheveux de qn*); **tousled hair,** cheveux ébouriffés.

tout¹ [taʊt] *n* **(a)** (*for hotels*) rabatteur, -euse; (*for shops, shows etc*) racoleur *m*; **(ticket) t.,** revendeur, -euse de billets (au marché noir); **(b) (racing) t.,** (*person who secretly watches horses*) individu qui suit secrètement l'entraînement des chevaux, à l'affût de tuyaux; (*person who sells tips*) donneur, -euse de tuyaux.

tout² **1** *vi* **(a)** *Horseracing* (*secretly watch horses*) suivre secrètement les chevaux de course à l'entraînement, espionner dans les écuries; (*sell tips*) vendre des tuyaux; **(b) to t. for custom,** racoler des clients. **2** *vt* **to t. s.o. for his custom,** importuner qn avec des offres de service; **to t. a product (around),** faire l'article d'un produit.

touting ['taʊtɪŋ] *n* **(a)** *Horseracing* espionnage *m*; **(b)** (*of product*) racolage *m*, démarchage *m*.

tow¹ [təʊ] *n* **(a)** (*act of towing*) **to give s.o./sth a t.,** remorquer qn/qch; **to take a car in t.,** prendre une voiture en remorque; **to be taken in t.,** se mettre en remorque; **to be on** *or* **in t.,** être en remorque; (*of boat*) être à la traîne; *F* **he always has his family in t.,** il trimbale toujours toute sa famille avec lui; **with six assistants in t.,** avec six assistants dans son sillage; **t. hook,** croc *m* de remorque; *Am* **t. truck,** dépanneuse *f*; **(b)** (*rope etc*) (câble *m* de) remorque *f*.

tow² *vt* remorquer (*un navire, une voiture*); prendre (*un navire, une voiture*) en remorque; touer (*un chaland*); (*from towpath*) haler (*une péniche, un chaland*); **my car's been towed away by the police,** la police a saisi ma voiture *ou* a mis ma voiture à la fourrière.

tow³ *n* étoupe *f* (blanche), filasse *f*.

▶**tow away** *vtsep* remorquer, prendre en remorque; (*police*) emmener (*une voiture*) à la fourrière, saisir.

towage ['təʊɪdʒ] *n* **(a)** remorquage *m*, touage *m*; (*on canal*) halage *m*; **(b)** (*charge*) (frais *mpl* de) remorquage *m*.

toward [tə'wɔːd, twɔːd] *prep esp Am* = **TOWARDS**.

towards [tə'wɔːdz, twɔːdz] *prep* **(a)** vers, du côté de; **t. the town,** vers la ville, du côté de la ville; **he came t. me,** il est venu vers moi; **(b)** (*with feelings, behaviour, attitude*) envers *ou* à l'égard de (*qn*); **her feelings t. me,** ses sentiments envers *ou* pour moi, ses sentiments à mon égard; **they behaved strangely t. us,** ils se sont conduits d'une manière étrange envers nous *ou* à notre égard; **(c)** (*contributing to*) pour; **to save t. the children's education,** économiser pour *ou* en vue de l'éducation des enfants; **to contribute (something) t. the cost of ...,** cotiser pour l'achat de ...; **would you like to give something t. it?,** voudriez-vous y contribuer quelque chose?; **(d)** (*of time*) vers; **t. evening,** vers le soir; **t. the end of his life,** vers *ou* sur la fin de sa vie.

towbar ['təʊbɑːr] *n Aut* timon *m* de remorque; barre *f* de remorquage (*d'un planeur*).

towel¹ ['taʊəl] *n* **(a)** serviette *f* (de toilette); **hand t.,** essuie-main(s) *m*, *pl* essuie-mains; *Fig* **to throw in the t.,** jeter l'éponge; **roller t.,** essuie-main(s), serviette sans fin (*pour rouleau*); **tea t.,** *Am* **dish t.,** torchon *m* (à vaisselle); **t. rail,** porte-serviettes *m inv*; **(b) sanitary t.,** serviette *f* hygiénique *ou* périodique.

towel² *vt* (**-ll-**, *US* **-l-**) essuyer *ou* frotter (*qn*) avec une serviette; **to t. oneself (dry),** s'essuyer (*après le bain etc*).

towelling, *US* **toweling** ['taʊəlɪŋ] *n* **(a)** (*act of rubbing with towel*) friction *f* avec une serviette; **(b)** (*fabric*) tissu-éponge *m*; **t. robe,** peignoir *m* en tissu-éponge.

tower¹ ['taʊər] *n* **(a)** *Archit Constr* tour *f*; **the T. of Babel,** la tour de Babel; **the T. of London,** la Tour de Londres; **church t.,** clocher *m*; **clock t.,** tour de l'horloge; *HydE* **water t.,** château *m* d'eau; *Av* **control t.,** tour de contrôle; *Ind Ch* **fractionating t.,** tour de fractionnement; *Br* **t. block,** tour, immeuble-tour *m*, *pl* immeubles-tours; **she's a t. of strength,** c'est un puissant appui *ou* un puissant secours; **(b)** *Constr etc* pylône *m*; *Rail US* **signal t.,** cabine *f* de signaux; **(c)** *Comptr* boîtier vertical; **t. system,** système *m* à boîtier vertical.

tower² *vi* (*climb very high*) monter très haut (*en l'air*).

▶**tower above, tower over** *vipo* (*be much higher than*) dominer (*qch*); dépasser (*qn, qch*) de beaucoup, être beaucoup plus grand que (*qn, qch*).

towering ['taʊərɪŋ] *adj* **(a)** très haut, très élevé; (*ambitions*) sans bornes; **(b) in a t. rage,** au paroxysme de la colère.

towheaded ['təʊhedɪd] *adj* aux cheveux (blond) filasse.

towing *n* remorque *f*, remorquage *m*; (*of narrowboat*) touage *m*; (*from towpath*) halage *m*.

towline ['təʊlaɪn] *n* (câble *m* de) remorque *f*.

town [taʊn] *n* **(a)** ville *f*; **fortified t.,** place forte; **to go out on the t.,** faire la bombe *ou* la noce; **t. centre,** centre *m* de la ville, centre(-)ville; **t. clerk,** secrétaire *mf* de mairie, secrétaire de municipalité; **t. council,** conseil municipal; **t. hall,** hôtel *m* de ville, mairie *f*; **t. house,** (*house in town*) maison *f* de ville; (*town residence*) résidence urbaine; **t. life,** vie urbaine; **t. planner/planning,** urbaniste *mf*/urbanisme *m*; **the whole t. is talking about it,** toute la ville en parle;

(b) (*without article*) **to go into t.,** aller *ou* se rendre à la *ou* en ville; **she's in t. shopping,** elle fait ses courses en ville; **he's out of t.,** il est à la campagne *ou* en voyage; **the best pizzas in town,** les meilleures pizzas de la ville; **man/woman about t.,** mondain, -aine; *F* **to go to t.,** (*make great effort*) se mettre en quatre; **they really went to t.,** (*on redecoration, doing a job etc*) ils ont vraiment mis le paquet; (*preparing a party etc*) ils ont vraiment fait les choses en grand; **I really went to t. on the third question,** je me suis vraiment foulé pour le troisième question; **no need to go to t. on it,** (*on essay etc*) ce n'est pas la peine d'aller chercher très loin; (*doing sth*) ce n'est pas la peine d'en faire trop *ou* de se fouler; *Sch* **t. and gown,** les habitants de la ville et les étudiants; **to live in T.,** (*in London*) habiter Londres.

townee, townie ['taʊnɪ] *n Pej* habitant, -ante de la ville.

townsfolk ['taʊnzfəʊk] *npl* habitants *mpl ou* gens *mpl* de la ville, citadins *mpl*.

township ['taʊnʃɪp] *n* **(a)** (*small town*) commune *f*, bourg *m*; **(b)** *Am* municipalité *f*, *Can* canton *m*; *US* (*in New England*) commune *f*; **(c)** (*in S Africa*) banlieue noire.

townsman, *pl* **-men** ['taʊnzmən] *n* habitant *m* de la ville, citadin *m*.

townspeople ['taʊnzpiːp(ə)l] *npl* habitants *mpl ou* gens *mpl* de la ville, citadins *mpl*.

townswoman, *pl* **-women** ['taʊnzwʊmən, -wɪmɪn] *n* habitante *f* de la ville, citadine *f*.

towpath ['təʊpɑːθ] *n* chemin *m* de halage.

towrope ['təʊrəʊp] *n* (câble *m* de) remorque *f*.

toxaemia, *Am* **toxemia** [tɒk'siːmɪə] *n Med* toxémie *f*.

toxic ['tɒksɪk] *adj* (*substance, waste etc*) toxique.

toxicologic(al) [tɒksɪkə'lɒdʒɪk, -ɪk(ə)l] *adj Med* toxicologique.

toxicologist [tɒksɪ'kɒlədʒɪst] *n* toxicologue *mf*.

toxicology [tɒksɪ'kɒlədʒɪ] *n Med* toxicologie *f*.

toxin ['tɒksɪn] *n Bio Ch* toxine *f*.

toy [tɔɪ] *n* jouet *m*; **this computer is just a t.,** cet ordinateur n'est qu'un jouet; **he's like a child with a new t.,** il est comme un enfant avec un nouveau jouet; *F* **t. boy,** jeune amant; **she's got herself a t. boy,** elle s'est déniché un petit jeune *ou* un jeune amant; **t. dog,** chien *m* de manchon, bichon *m*; **t. poodle,** caniche nain; **t. soldier,** soldat *m* de plastique *ou* de plomb; **t. shop,** magasin *m* de jouets; **t. trumpet,** trompette *f* d'enfant.

▶**toy with** *vipo* (*play with*) jouer avec (*qch*); **to t. with one's food,** manger du bout des lèvres *ou* des dents; **to t. with an idea,** caresser une idée; **to t. with s.o.,** badiner *ou* flirter avec qn; **to t. with s.o.'s affections,** jouer avec le cœur de qn.

trace¹ [treɪs] *n* **(a)** trace *f*, vestige *m*; **they could find no t. of him,** ils n'ont pas pu retrouver trace de lui; **there's not a t. of it,** (*there's nothing left of it*) il n'en reste pas trace; (*it isn't to be found*) cela ne se voit plus; **he has disappeared without (a) t.,** il a disparu sans laisser trace; **(b)** *usu pl* trace(s) *f(pl)* (*de qn, d'un animal*); empreinte *f* (*d'un animal*); **(c)** (*small amount*) trace *f*, quantité *f* infime; (*hint*) soupçon *m*; **traces of cyanide,** des traces de cyanure; **a t. of sarcasm,** un soupçon de sarcasme; *Ch* **t. element,** oligo-élément *m*, *pl* oligo-éléments.

trace² *vt* **(a)** (*outline*) tracer (*un plan, une ligne de conduite etc*); **(b)** (*draw*) faire le tracé de (*un plan, un diagramme*); (*copy*) calquer (*un dessin*); **(c)** (*follow tracks of*) suivre la trace *ou* la piste (*de qn, d'une bête*); (*locate*) recouvrer (*des objets perdus*); retrouver les vestiges, relever les traces (*d'un ancien édifice etc*); retracer, retrouver (*une influence etc*); **they traced him as far as Paris** *or* **to Paris,** on a suivi sa piste jusqu'à Paris; **to t. the evil to its source,** remonter à la source du mal.

trace³ *n* (*part of harness*) trait *m*; **in the traces,** attelé; *F* **to kick over the traces,** (*of person*) (*rebel*) ruer dans les brancards; (*break free*) s'émanciper.

►**trace back** *vtsep* (*uncover origins of*) **to t. sth back to its source,** remonter jusqu'à l'origine de qch; **to t. one's family back to William the Conqueror,** faire remonter sa famille à Guillaume le Conquérant.

►**trace out** *vtsep* = **TRACE² (a)**.

tracer ['treɪsər] *n* **(a)** (*person*) (*drawer*) traceur, -euse (*d'un plan etc*); (*copier*) calqueur, -euse; **(b)** *Mil etc* **t. bullet,** (balle) traçante *f*; **t. shell,** traçant *m*; **(c)** *Med* traceur *m*.

tracery ['treɪsərɪ] *n* **(a)** *Archit* réseau *m*, remplage *m* (*d'une rosace*); **(b)** nervures *fpl* (*d'une feuille etc*).

trachea, *pl* **-eae** [trə'kiːə, -iiː] *n Anat* trachée *f*.

tracheal [trə'kiːəl] *adj Anat* trachéal, -aux.

tracheotomy [trækɪ'ɒtəmɪ] *n Surg* trachéotomie *f*.

trachoma [trə'kəʊmə] *n Med* trachome *m*.

tracing ['treɪsɪŋ] *n* **(a)** (*act of drawing*) tracement *m*; (*copying*) calquage *m*; **t. paper,** papier *m* calque *ou* à calquer; *Sewing etc* **t. wheel,** roulette *f* (à patron); **(b)** (*copy*) calque *m*.

track¹ [træk] *n* **(a)** (*left by animal*) voie *f*, foulées *fpl*, trace(s) *f(pl)*, piste *f* (*d'un animal*); trace(s), piste (*de qn*); sillage *m* (*d'un navire*); sillon *m* (*d'une roue*); **to follow the t.,** suivre la piste; **to follow in s.o.'s tracks,** suivre la voie tracée par qn; **to be on s.o.'s t.,** suivre la piste de qn; **to throw s.o. off the t.,** dépister qn; *F* **to be off the t.,** divaguer; **to be on the right t.,** être sur la (bonne) voie; **to be on the wrong t.,** avoir perdu la piste; *Fig* (*in search, guess etc*) être sur une mauvaise piste; **to keep t. of s.o./sth,** suivre les progrès de qn/qch; **I've lost t. of her,** je l'ai perdue de vue; **I've lost track of all the times I've ...,** j'ai perdu de compte du nombre de fois où j'ai ...; *F* **to make tracks,** (*leave*) partir, filer; **to stop in one's tracks,** s'arrêter net;

(b) (*path*) piste *f*, chemin *m*, sentier *m*; *Rail* voie *f* (ferrée); *MecE etc* (*in which sth slides etc*) chemin de roulement *ou* de glissement; piste (*de disque*); voie, piste (*de bande magnétique*); **cart t.,** chemin de terre; **mule t.,** sentier muletier; **cycle t.,** piste cyclable; *Sp* **(running, racing) t.,** piste; *Sp* **t. and field events,** épreuves *fpl* d'athlétisme; *Sp* **t. event,** course *f* sur piste; **race** *or* **racing t.,** piste de vitesse; **single-t./double-t. line,** ligne *f* à une voie/à deux voies; **the train left the t.,** le train a déraillé; *Sp* **t. racing,** courses *fpl* de *ou* sur piste; *Sp* **t. record,** (*of racehorse, car, person*) carrière *f*, antécédents *mpl*; **he doesn't have a very good t. record for punctuality,** il n'est pas réputé pour sa ponctualité; **in view of his t. record of getting home late every Friday night ...,** vu l'habitude qu'il a de rentrer tard tous les vendredis soirs ...; **a company with a good/poor t. record in winning export orders,** une entreprise avec un bon/mauvais palmarès sur le plan des commandes à l'exportation; **no wonder the insurance is high with your t. record!,** pas étonnant que l'assurance soit chère avec ton palmarès; **given the government's t. record in the field of cutting benefits,** vu les antécédents du gouvernement en matière de réduction des prestations sociales; *Sp* **t. shoe,** chaussures *fpl* de course; **sound t.,** piste sonore;

(c) (*route*) route *f*, chemin *m*; cours *m* (*d'une comète*);

(d) (*of tracked vehicle*) chenille *f*; **t./half-t. vehicle,** véhicule chenillé/semi-chenillé;

(e) (*distance between wheels*) écartement *m* des roues, voie *f*.

track² **1** *vt* suivre (*une bête, un voleur etc*) à la piste, pister; traquer (*un malfaiteur*); suivre (*un missile*) à la trace; tracer (*une voie etc*). **2** *vi* (*of gear wheels etc*) être en alignement; (*of stylus on record player*) suivre la piste; (*of camera*) se déplacer en travelling; **the band of rain that is tracking across the country,** le front de pluie qui se déplace à travers le pays.

►**track down** *vtsep* (*discover*) dépister (*game, criminal etc*); dépister, découvrir (*information*); retrouver (*missing object*); **they tracked her down to her hide-out,** ils ont remonté sa trace *ou* sa piste jusqu'à sa cachette.

tracked [trækt] *adj* (*véhicule*) chenillé; **half-t.,** semi-chenillé.

tracker ['trækər] *n* traqueur *m* (*de gibier*); **t. dog,** chien policier.

tracking ['trækɪŋ] *n* **(a)** pistage *m* (*d'un animal, de qn*); **t. (down),** dépistage *m* (*du gibier, d'un criminel, d'une erreur etc*); **(b)** *Electron Astronaut* poursuite *f*; **t. station,** station *f* de dépistage; **t. systems,** systèmes *mpl* de repérage et poursuite; **(c)** *Cin* **t. shot,** travelling *m* en poursuite.

tracklayer ['trækleɪər] *n Rail* (*person*) poseur *m* de voie.

tracklaying ['trækleɪɪŋ] *n Rail* pose *f* de voie; **t. vehicle,** véhicule *m* à chenilles.

trackless ['træklɪs] *adj* **(a)** sans chemins, sans sentiers; (*forêt*) vierge; **(b)** *Am* **t. trolley,** trolleybus *m*.

tracksuit ['træks(j)uːt] *n Sp* survêtement *m*.

tract¹ [trækt] *n* **(a)** étendue *f* (*de pays, de sable, d'eau*); nappe *f* (*d'eau*); région *f* (*montagneuse etc*); **(b)** *Anat* appareil *m* (*respiratoire, digestif*).

tract² *n* (*treatise*) petit traité; (*pamphlet*) brochure *f*, tract *m*.

tractable ['træktəb(ə)l] *adj* (*person, character*) docile, traitable; (*material*) facile à ouvrer.

traction ['trækʃən] *n* traction *f*, tirage *m*; *Med* traction; **steam t.,** traction à vapeur; **t. cable,** câble tracteur; **t. engine,** tracteur *m*; **t. wheels,** roues motrices (*d'une locomotive etc*).

tractive ['træktɪv] *adj* tractif; (*force*) de traction.

tractor ['træktər] *n* **(a)** (*vehicle*) tracteur *m*; **t.-drawn,** tracté; **t. driver,** conducteur *m*, -trice *f* de tracteur; **(b)** *Comptr* **t. feed,** (*device*) dispositif *m* d'alimentation par entraînement; (*facility*) alimentation *f* par entraînement.

trad [træd] *n Br F* jazz traditionnel.

trade¹ [treɪd] *n* **(a)** (*commerce*) commerce *m*, affaires *fpl*, négoce *m*; *Am* (*commercial transaction*) transaction *f* (commerciale); (*swap*) échange *m*; **to be in t.,** être dans le commerce, être commerçant, -ante; **wholesale/retail t.,** commerce de gros/de détail; **balance of t.,** balance commerciale; **the tea t.,** le commerce du thé; **it's good for t.,** cela fait marcher le commerce; **we don't get much t. nowadays,** les affaires ne marchent pas très bien ces temps-ci; **she's doing a roaring t.,** elle fait des affaires en or; **the t. in animal skins,** le commerce des peaux; **(illicit) t.,** trafic *m*; **t. barriers,** barrières douanières; *Br* **T. Descriptions Act,** ≈ loi *f* sur la publicité mensongère; **t. embargo,** embargo commercial; **t. gap,** déséquilibre commercial; **t. winds, trades,** (vents) alizés *mpl*;

(b) (*profession*) métier *m*; (*as a body*) (corps *m* de) métier; **to follow** *or* **carry on a t.,** exercer un métier; **to learn a t.,** apprendre un métier; **he's a plumber by t.,** il est plombier de son métier; **everyone to his t.,** chacun son métier; **it's what, in the t., we call a ...,** c'est ce que, dans le métier, on appelle un ...; **the building t.,** le bâtiment; **the publishing t.,** l'édition *f*; **the printing t.,** l'imprimerie *f*; **to be in the t.,** être du métier; **t. name,** (*product*) appellation commerciale; (*firm*) raison commerciale; **t. association,** syndicat professionel; **t. discount,** remise *f*, escompte *m*; **t. journal,** journal professionnel; **t. secret,** secret *m* de fabrique; *Br Aut* **t. plate,** plaque *f* d'immatriculation provisoire (du garage); **t. press,** presse spécialisée; **t.** *or* **trades union,** syndicat *m* (ouvrier); **to form a t. union,** (*of workers*) se syndiquer; **t.** *or* **trades unionism,** syndicalisme *m* (ouvrier); **t.** *or* **trades unionist,** syndicaliste *mf*, (ouvrier, -ière) syndiqué(e).

trade² **1** *vi* **(a)** faire le commerce *ou* le négoce (**in sth,** de qch; **with s.o.,** avec qn); faire des affaires, entretenir des relations commerciales (**with s.o.,** avec qn); *Am* (*to shop*) se ravitailler (**at, with,** chez); **(b)** (*exchange*) **to t. with s.o.,** faire un troc avec qn. **2** *vt* **to t. sth for sth,** échanger *ou* troquer qch contre qch; *Am* **to t. places with s.o.,** changer de place avec qn.

►**trade down** *vi St Exch* acheter des valeurs basses.

►**trade in** *vtsep* (*give in part exchange*) donner (*une voiture etc*) en reprise.

►**trade off** *vtsep* (*exchange*) échanger (*qch contre qch*).

►**trade on** *vipo* (*exploit*) exploiter, tirer profit de (*l'ignorance de qn*).

►**trade up** *vi St Exch* acheter des valeurs hautes.

trade-in ['treɪdɪn] *n* objet donné en reprise; **will you take**

my old car as a t.-in?, est-ce que vous reprendrez ma vieille voiture?; **what's its t.-in value?**, quelle est sa valeur de reprise?

trademark ['treɪdmɑːk] *n* marque *f* de fabrique; **registered t.**, marque déposée; *Fig* **these close-up shots are her t.**, ces gros-plans sont sa marque *ou* sa signature.

trade-off ['treɪdɒf] *n esp Am* échange *m*; (*compromise*) compromis *m*; **you're going to have a t.-o. between speed and quality**, si vous allez plus vite, ce sera au detriment de la qualité.

trader ['treɪdər] *n* **(a)** (*person*) négociant, -ante, commerçant, -ante, marchand, -ande; **(b)** *Nau* (*ship*) navire marchand.

tradesman, *pl* **-men** ['treɪdzmən] *n* marchand *m*, fournisseur *m*; **tradesmen's entrance,** entrée *f* des fournisseurs.

trading ['treɪdɪŋ] *n* commerce *m*, négoce *m*; **(illicit) t.**, trafic *m*; **t. company,** société commerciale; *Br Com Ind* **t. estate,** zone industrielle; *St Exch* **t. floor,** parquet *m*, corbeille *f*; **t. loss,** perte *f*; **France is our most important t. partner,** la France est notre principal partenaire commercial; **t. results,** résultats *mpl* de l'exercice; **t. stamp,** timbre-prime *m*, *pl* timbres prime(s); **t. year,** année *m* d'exploitations, exercice *m* (financier).

tradition [trə'dɪʃən] *n* tradition *f*; **t. has it that ...,** selon la tradition ...; **it has become a t.** c'est passé dans la tradition; **the t. is to ...,** la tradition veut que l'on + *sub*.

traditional [trə'dɪʃənəl] *adj* traditionnel.

traditionalism [trə'dɪʃənəlɪz(ə)m] *n* traditionalisme *m*.

traditionalist [trə'dɪʃənəlɪst] *n* traditionaliste *mf*.

traditionally [trə'dɪʃənəlɪ] *adv* traditionnellement.

traduce [trə'djuːs] *vt Fml Lit* calomnier, diffamer (*qn*).

traffic¹ ['træfɪk] *n* **(a)** circulation *f*, trafic *m*; **road t.**, circulation routière; **heavy t.**, circulation intense; **through t.**, circulation directe; **southbound t. should avoid ...,** les conducteurs se dirigeant vers le sud ont intérêt à éviter ...; **ocean t.**, navigation *f* au long cours; **rail(way) t.**, trafic ferroviaire; **goods/passenger t.**, trafic marchandises/voyageurs; *Am* **t. circle,** sens *m* giratoire; **t. control,** régulation *f* de la circulation; *F* **t. cop,** = **T. POLICEMAN**; **t. island,** refuge *m*; **t. jam,** embouteillage *m*, encombrement *m*, bouchon *m*; *Br* **t. lights,** *US* **t. light, t. signals,** feux *mpl* de circulation *ou* de signalisation routière; **at the next (set of) t. lights,** au(x) prochain(s) feu(x); **t. police,** (*in town*) police *f* de la circulation; (*out of town*) gendarmerie routière; **t. policeman,** (*in town*) agent *m* de la circulation; (*out of town*) gendarme *m*; **t. regulations,** règlements *mpl* sur la circulation; *Br* **t. warden,** contractuel, -elle;

(b) *Pej* (*trade*) trafic *m*, commerce *m*, négoce *m* (**in,** de); **the drug t.**, le trafic des stupéfiants.

traffic² *vti* (*pt & pp* **trafficked** ['træfɪkt]) *Pej* trafiquer (**in drugs,** en stupéfiants).

trafficator ['træfɪkeɪtər] *n Old-fashioned Aut* flèche *f* de direction.

trafficker ['træfɪkər] *n Pej* trafiquant, -ante, trafiqueur, -euse (**in,** de, en); **drug t.**, trafiquant de drogue.

tragedian [trə'dʒiːdɪən] *n* (*dramatist*) auteur *m* tragique; *Th f* **tragedienne** [trədʒiːdɪ'en] (*actor*) tragédien, -ienne.

tragedy ['trædʒɪdɪ] *n* (*accident, disaster*) *& Th* tragédie *f*; **to make a t. out of sth,** prendre qch au tragique; **the t. of his death,** sa mort tragique; **it will be a t.**, ce sera un drame; **the real t. was that ...,** ce qu'il y avait de vraiment tragique, c'est que ... .

tragic ['trædʒɪk] *adj* tragique; **t. actor/actress,** tragédien, -ienne; *F* **to put on a t. act,** jouer la tragédie; **t. event,** événement *m* tragique; **the t. side of the story is that...,** le tragique de l'histoire c'est que ...; *Iron* **how t. for you!,** c'est bête ce qui t'arrive!

tragically ['trædʒɪklɪ] *adv* tragiquement; **he died at a t. early age,** c'est tragique qu'il soit mort si jeune.

tragicomedy [trædʒɪ'kɒmɪdɪ] *n* tragi-comédie *f*, *pl* tragicomédies.

tragicomic(al) [trædʒɪ'kɒmɪk, -ɪk(ə)l] *adj* tragicomique.

trail¹ [treɪl] *n* **(a)** traînée *f* (*de sang, de fumée etc*); panache *m* (*de fumée*); queue *f* (*d'un météore*); *Mil* flèche *f*, crosse *f* (*d'affût*); **a t. of broken promises,** une série de promesses non tenues; *Fishing* **t. net,** traîneau *m*, traîne *f*; chalut *m*; **(b)** piste *f*, trace *f* (*d'une bête, de qn*); trace (*d'un colimaçon*); (*in hunting*) voie *f* (*d'une bête*); **to pick up the t.**, (*of hounds*) retrouver la trace; **false t.**, fausse piste; **to be on the t. of s.o.**, être sur la piste de qn; **the criminals left with the police hot on their t.**, les criminels sont partis avec la police sur leurs talons; **to leave ruin in one's t.**, laisser la ruine sur son passage; **(c)** (*path*) sentier *m* (battu); piste *f* (*dans une forêt, de ski de fond*); **t. bike,** moto *f* de cross; **t. mix,** (*dried fruit & nuts*) fruits secs.

trail² **1** *vt* **(a)** (*pull*) traîner (*qch*) après soi; (*of car etc*) remorquer (*une caravane etc*); **(b)** (*track*) traquer, suivre à la piste (*une bête, un criminel*); (*of crook*) suivre, filer (*une victime*). **2** *vi* **(a)** traîner; **your skirt is trailing (on the ground),** votre jupe traîne (par terre); **to let one's dress t. in the dust,** laisser sa robe traîner dans la poussière; **(b)** (*of plant*) grimper, ramper; **(c)** = **our team is trailing at the bottom of the league,** notre équipe se traîne au fin fonds du classement; *see also* **TRAIL BEHIND (a)**.

▶**trail away** *vi* (*become silent*) **his voice trailed away in embarrassment,** la gêne a étouffé sa voix; **her voice trailed away in the distance,** sa voix se perdit dans le lointain.

▶**trail behind** *vi* **(a)** (*linger*) traîner derrière (les autres), être à la traîne; *Fig* (*of team etc*) être en retard sur les autres; **(b)** (*be pulled*) se faire remorquer, être en remorque; **with a boat trailing behind,** avec un bateau à la traîne *ou* en remorque.

▶**trail off** *vi* = **TRAIL AWAY**.

trailblazer ['treɪlbleɪzər] *n* pionnier, -ière.

trailer ['treɪlər] *n* **(a)** *Aut etc* (*vehicle*) remorque *f*; *Am* caravane *f* (de camping); **(b)** *Cin TV* bande-annonce *f*, *pl* bandes-annonces (**for,** de); **(c)** (*person*) traqueur *m*.

trailing ['treɪlɪŋ] **1** *adj* **(a)** (*skirt etc*) traînant; **(b)** (*plant*) grimpant, rampant; **(c)** *Av* **t. edge,** bord *m* de fuite (de l'aile). **2** *n* **(a)** (*pulling*) traînement *m*; **(b)** (*following*) poursuite *f* (*de qn*) à la piste, pistage *m*.

train¹ [treɪn] *n* **(a)** *Rail* train *m*; rame *f* (*du métro*); **passenger/goods t.**, train de voyageurs/de marchandises; **fast t.**, (train) rapide *m*; **express t.**, train express; **slow** *or* **stopping t.**, train omnibus; **relief t.**, train supplémentaire; **excursion t.**, train d'excursion *ou* à prix réduit; **the 5 o'clock t.**, le train de 5 heurs; **the Cardiff train, the t. to Cardiff,** le train de Cardiff; **she wasn't on the t.**, elle n'était pas dans le train; **by t.**, (*voyager*) par *ou* en chemin de fer, en train; **to the trains,** (*on sign*) accès aux quais; **t. ferry,** ferry(-boat) *m*; **t. journey,** voyage *m* en *ou* par chemin de fer, voyage en train; **t. station,** gare *f* de chemin de fer;

(b) train *m*, convoi *m* (*de wagons, de péniches*); succession *f*, série *f*, enchaînement *m* (*d'événements, de circonstances*); *Min* traînée *f* (de poudre); **t. of thought,** chaîne *f* d'idées; **to set sth in t.**, mettre qch en train;

(c) *Tech* système *m* d'engrenages; rouage(s) *m(pl)* (*d'une montre, d'une horloge*); **wheel t.**, train *m* de roues;

(d) suite *f*, cortège *m*, équipage *m* (*d'un prince etc*); *Mil* équipage, train *m*; **the evils that follow in the t. of war,** les maux que la guerre traîne à sa suite;

(e) traîne *f*, queue *f* (*d'une robe*); queue (*d'un paon, d'une comète*); **t. bearer,** porte-queue *m inv*; caudataire *m* (*d'un cardinal etc*).

train² **1** *vt* **(a)** former, instruire (*qn*); dresser (*un animal*); former (*le caractère, l'esprit*); exercer (*l'oreille*); *Sp* entraîner (*un coureur, un cheval de course etc*); **he was trained at the Academy of Dramatic Art,** il sort de l'Académie des Arts Dramatiques; **to t. s.o. for sth/to do sth,** exercer qn à qch/à faire qch; **to t. s.o. in the use of a machine/weapon,** instruire qn à se servir d'une machine/d'une arme; **to t. oneself to do sth,** s'exercer à faire qch; **(b)** (*in horticulture*) palisser, mettre en espalier (*un arbre fruitier, une vigne*); (*Mil*) pointer (*un canon*); braquer, diriger (*une lunette, un projecteur etc*) (**on,** sur); *Nau* orienter (*un canon*). **2** *vi* s'exercer; *Mil* faire l'exercice; *Sp* s'entraîner; **to t. for sth,** s'exercer *ou* se préparer à qch; **to t. as a typist,** suivre un cours de dactylographie.

▶**train up** *vtsep* donner une formation complémentaire à (*des employés*).

trained [treɪnd] *adj* (*personne, ouvrier etc*) formé; (*chien etc*) dressé; (*œil*) exercé; *Sp* entraîné; **highly/poorly t.**, très bien/peu entraîné; **t. nurse,** infirmière diplômée; *Hum* **her husband is very well t.**, son mari est très bien dressé.

trainee [treɪ'niː] *n* stagiaire *mf*; **t. manager,** stagiaire de direction.

trainer ['treɪnər] *n* **(a)** (*person*) dresseur *m* (*d'animaux*); *Sp Horseracing* entraîneur *m* (*d'athlètes, d'équipe de football, de chevaux de course*); *Mil US* pointeur *m*; **(b)** *Av* **t. (aircraft),** avion-école *f*, *pl* avions-écoles; **(c) trainers,** (*shoes*) chaussures *fpl* de sport.

training ['treɪnɪŋ] *n* **(a)** instruction *f*, formation *f*; *Sp* entraînement *m*; dressage *m* (*d'un animal*); **physical t.**, éducation *f* physique; **vocational t.**, éducation professionnelle; **I'm a historian by t.**, je suis historien de formation; **she had received a good t.**, elle avait fait un bon apprentissage; *Fig* **it's good t. for when you're a parent,** ça vous prépare pour quand vous aurez des enfants; *Mil* **military t.,** dressage *m* militaire; *Sp* **to go into t.,** s'entraîner; **to be in t.,** (*being trained*) être à l'entraînement; (*fit*) être bien entraîné; **to be out of t.,** ne plus être en forme; **t. base,** base *f* école; **t. centre,** centre *m* de formation; **t. college,** école *f* (de formation) professionnelle; **t. course,** cours professionnel *ou* de formation professionnelle; **t. manual,** manuel *m* d'utilisation; *Nau* **t. ship,** navire-école *m*, *pl* navires-écoles;

(b) (*in horticulture*) palissage *m* (*d'une plante, d'un arbre fruitier*); *Mil* orientation *f* (*d'une pièce*).

trainload ['treɪnləʊd] *n* **t. of coal,** train chargé de houille; **t. of tourists,** plein train de touristes.

train-spotter ['treɪnspɒtər] *n* = personne dont le passe-temps est de repérer les numéros des trains.

traipse [treɪps] *vi* **to t. through the streets,** battre le pavé; **to t. around,** traîner ça et là; **to t. around the shops,** traîner dans les magasins; **we had to t. all the way back to the ...,** il a fallu que nous nous trainions sur tout le chemin du retour au ... .

trait [treɪt] *n* trait *m* (*de caractère etc*).

traitor ['treɪtər] *n* traître *m* (**to,** à); **to turn t.,** passer à l'ennemi, se vendre.

traitorous ['treɪt(ə)rəs] *adj* traître, *f* traîtresse, fourbe, perfide.

traitorously ['treɪt(ə)rəslɪ] *adv* traîtreusement, en traître.

traitress ['treɪtrɪs] *n Old-fashioned* traîtresse *f*.

trajectory [trə'dʒekt(ə)rɪ] *n* trajectoire *f*.

tram[1] [træm] *n* **(a)** (*vehicle*) tramway *m*; **to go by t.,** aller en tramway; **t. driver,** conducteur *m* de tramway; **(b)** *Min* benne *f*, berline *f*.

tram[2] *n Tex* **t. (silk),** trame *f*.

tramcar ['træmkɑːr] *n Old-fashioned* tramway *m*.

tramline ['træmlaɪn] *n* **(a)** ligne *f* de tramways; **(b) tramlines,** voie *f* de tramway; *Tennis* couloir *m*.

trammel[1] ['træm(ə)l] *n* **the trammels of superstition,** les entraves *fpl* de la superstition.

trammel[2] *vt* (**-ll-**, *US* **-l-**) entraver, empêtrer (**with,** de); **trammelled by prejudices,** entravé par les préjugés.

tramp[1] [træmp] *n* **(a)** (*person*) chemineau *m*, vagabond, -onde, clochard, arde; **(b)** *Nau* **(ocean) t., t. steamer,** tramp *m*; **(c)** (*sound*) bruit *m* de pas marqués; **I heard the (heavy) t. of the guard,** j'ai entendu le pas lourd du gardien; **(d)** (*walk*) promenade *f* à pied; **(e)** *F Pej* (*loose woman*) traînée *f*.

tramp[2] **1** *vi* **(a)** (*walk with firm steps*) marcher à pas marqués; (*heavily*) marcher lourdement; **to t. on sth,** piétiner *ou* écraser qch; **(b)** (*travel on foot*) se promener *ou* voyager à pied; (*be a tramp*) vagabonder; **to t. wearily along,** suivre péniblement son chemin. **2** *vt* **to t. the streets,** battre le pavé; **to t. the country,** parcourir le pays à pied.

trample ['træmp(ə)l] **1** *vi* **to t. on sth/s.o.,** piétiner *ou* écraser qch/qn; **to t. on s.o.'s feelings,** fouler aux pieds les susceptibilités de qn. **2** *vt* piétiner (*le sol*); **to t. s.o./sth under foot,** fouler qn/qch aux pieds; **to t. down the grass,** fouler l'herbe; **child trampled to death (by the crowd),** enfant écrasé (sous les pieds de la foule) *ou* piétiné (par la foule).

trampoline [træmpə'liːn] *n Gym etc* trempoline *m*.

tramway ['træmweɪ] *n* (voie *f* de) tramway *m*.

trance [trɑːns] *n Med* (*ecstasy*) extase *f*; (*catalepsy*) catalepsie *f*; **(hypnotic) t.,** transe *f*, hypnose *f*; **to send s.o. into a t.,** hypnotiser qn; **to go into a t. (state),** (*in spiritualism etc*) se mettre en transe; **he's been wandering around in a t. ever since ...,** il erre en transe depuis que ... .

tranny ['trænɪ] *n esp Br F* transistor *m*.

tranquil ['træŋkwɪl] *adj* tranquille, serein, calme.

tranquillity, *US also* **tranquility** [træŋ'kwɪlɪtɪ] *n* tranquillité *f*, calme *m*, sérénité *f*.

tranquillization, *US* **tranquilization** [træŋkwɪlaɪ'zeɪʃən] *n* tranquillisation *f*.

tranquillize, *US* **tranquilize** ['træŋkwɪlaɪz] *vt* tranquilliser, calmer, apaiser (*qn, l'esprit etc*).

tranquillizer, *US* **tranquilizer** ['træŋkwɪlaɪzər] *n Med etc* tranquillisant *m*, calmant *m*; **to be on tranquillizers,** être sous calmants.

transact [træn'zækt] *vt* **to t. business with s.o.,** faire des affaires avec qn; **the business was successfully transacted,** la transaction *ou* l'affaire a été conclue à notre satisfaction.

transaction [træn'zækʃən] *n* **(a)** (*act of transacting*) conduite *f* (*d'une affaire*); **business transactions,** les affaires *fpl*, le commerce; *esp Fml* **open for the t. of business from ...,** ouvert au commerce à partir de ...; **(b)** (*instance of transacting*) opération *f* (commerciale); affaire *f* (faite); **cash t.,** opération *ou* marché *m* au comptant; **(c) transactions,** mémoires *mpl*, procès verbaux *mpl*, comptes rendus des séances (*d'une société savante*).

transalpine [trænz'ælpaɪn] *adj* transalpin.

transatlantic [trænzət'læntɪk] *adj* transatlantique.

transceiver [træn'siːvər] *n Rad* émetteur-récepteur *m*, *pl* émetteurs-récepteurs.

transcend [træn'send] *vt* **(a)** (*go beyond*) transcender; dépasser les bornes de (*la raison etc*); aller au delà de (*ce que l'on peut concevoir*); **(b)** (*be superior to*) surpasser (*qn*).

transcendence, transcendency [træn'sendəns(ɪ)] *n* transcendance *f*.

transcendent [træn'sendənt] *adj* transcendant.

transcendental [trænsen'dent(ə)l] *adj Phil* transcendental, -aux.

transcendentalism [trænsen'dentəlɪzm] *n Phil* transcendentalisme *m*.

transcontinental [trænzkɒntɪ'nent(ə)l] *adj* transcontinental, -aux.

transcribe [træns'kraɪb] *vt* **(a)** copier, transcrire; traduire (*des notes sténographiques*); **(b)** *Mus* transcrire (*un morceau pour un autre instrument*).

transcript ['trænskrɪpt] *n* transcription *f*, copie *f*; traduction *f* (*de notes sténographiques*).

transcription [træns'krɪpʃən] *n* **(a)** = **TRANSCRIPT**; **(b)** *Mus* transcription *f*.

transducer [trænz'djuːsər] *n* transducteur *m*.

transect [træn'sekt] *vt* couper transversalement.

transept ['trænsept] *n* (*in church architecture*) transept *m*; **(arm of the) t.,** croisillon *m*.

transfer[1] ['trænsfɜːr] *n* **(a)** transfert *m*; transport *m* (*de qch à un autre endroit*); déplacement *m*, mutation *f* (*d'un fonctionnaire etc*); *Jur* transfert, transmission *f* (*d'un droit etc*); translation *f*, mutation (*de biens*); *Fin* transfert (*d'actions*); *Banking etc* transport *m* (*d'une somme d'un compte à un autre*); *Sp* **the new striker has asked for a t.,** le nouveau buteur a demandé son transfert; *Banking* **t. of funds,** virement *m* de fonds; *Av* **t. desk/lounge,** (*at airport*) guichet *m*/salle *f* de transit; *Fb etc* **t. fee,** prix *m* de transfert (*d'un joueur*); *Av* **t. passengers,** voyageurs *mpl* en transit; *Comptr* **t. speed,** vitesse *f* de transfert; *Br* **(capital) t. tax,** droits *mpl* de succession; droit de mutation (*entre vifs*); *Can* **t. (ticket),** correspondance *f*;

(b) (*document*) *St Exch* (feuille *f* de) transfert *m*; *Jur* **(deed of) t.,** acte *m* de cession;

(c) (*in lithography*) report *m*; transport *m* (*sur la pierre*); *Cer Sewing etc* décalque *m*.

transfer[2] [træns'fɜːr] *v* (**-rr-**) **1** *vt* **(a)** transférer (*qch, qn, d'un endroit à un autre*); déplacer, muter (*un fonctionnaire etc*); muter (*un militaire etc*); *Jur* transmettre (*des droits etc*); céder (*un privilège etc*); *Banking etc* virer (*une somme*); *Phot* reporter (*un plan etc*); **let's t. this desk into the blue room,** mettons ce bureau dans la pièce bleue; *Tel* **transfer(red) charge call,** communication *f* en PCV;

(b) *Typ Sewing etc* calquer, décalquer (*un dessin*).

2 *vi* **(a) to t. to a different department,** (*of person*) être transféré dans un autre service; **to t. from one course to another,** changer de cours; **to t. mentally to a different culture,** s'adapter mentalement à une autre culture; *Fb* **to t. to a different team,** obtenir son transfert dans une équipe différente;

(b) (*to change trains etc*) changer; **to t. to a different plane/***etc*, changer d'avion/*etc*; **we then t. back to the train at ...,** puis on reprend le train à ... .

transferable [træns'fɜːrəb(ə)l] *adj* transmissible; *Jur* (*droit, bien*) cessible; (*droit*) communicable, transférable; **non t.,** (*on ticket etc*) non cessible.

transference ['trænsfərəns] *n Psy* transfert *m*; **thought t.,** transmission *f* de pensée.

transfiguration [trænsfɪgjə'reɪʃən] *n* transfiguration *f*.

transfigure [træns'fɪgər] *vt* transfigurer; **to become transfigured,** se transfigurer.

transfix [træns'fɪks] *vt* **(a)** transpercer (*qn avec une lance etc*); **(b)** *Fig* rendre (*qn*) immobile; **transfixed with fear,** pétrifié *ou* cloué par la peur.

transform [træns'fɔːm] *vt* transformer (**into,** en); métamorphoser, transformer (*qn*); *MecE El* transformer (*le courant*).

transformation [trænsfə'meɪʃən] *n* transformation *f* (**into,** en); métamorphose *f* (**into,** en); *MecE El* transformation (*du courant*).

transformational [trænsfə'meɪʃ(ə)nl] *adj Ling* transformationnel.

transformer [træns'fɔːmər] *n El* transformateur *m*; **t. station,** station transformatrice.

transfuse [træns'fjuːz] *vt Med* transfuser (*du sang*); faire une transfusion de sang (*à qn*).

transfusion [træns'fjuːʒ(ə)n] *n Med* **blood t.,** transfusion *f* de sang, transfusion sanguine.

transgress [trænz'gres] **1** *vt* transgresser *ou* violer *ou* enfreindre (*la loi etc*). **2** *vi* transgresser, violer, enfreindre (la loi *etc*); (*sin*) pécher.

transgression [trænz'greʃən] *n* transgression *f*, violation *f* (*d'une loi*); infraction *f* (*à la loi*); (*sin*) péché *m*.

transgressor [trænz'gresər] *n* transgresseur *m*; (*sinner*) pécheur, *f* pécheresse.

tranship [træn'ʃɪp] **1** *vt* transborder (*des voyageurs, des marchandises*). **2** *vi* changer de bateau.

transhipment [træn'ʃɪpmənt] *n* transbordement *m*.

transience ['trænzɪəns] *n* nature passagère *ou* transitoire (*d'un phénomène etc*).

transient ['trænzɪənt] **1** *adj* transitoire; (*bonheur etc*) passager, -ère; (*beauté etc*) éphémère; *Am* **t. visitor,** client, -ente de passage. **2** *n Am* client, -ente de passage.

transistor [træn'zɪstər] *n Electron* transistor *m*; **t. (set** *or* **radio),** poste *m* à transistors, transistor.

transistorize [træn'zɪstəraɪz] *vt* transistoriser.

transit ['trænsɪt] *n* **(a)** transit *m*; (*transport*) transport *m* (*de marchandises etc*); **goods lost in t.,** marchandises perdues en cours de route; **t. freight,** merchandises transportées; **goods in t.,** marchandises en transit; **t. duty,** droit *m* de transit; **t. visa,** acquit *m* de transit; **(b)** passage *m*, voyage *m* (*à travers un pays etc*); *Astron* passage (*d'une planète sur le disque du soleil, d'un astre au méridien*); **t. circle,** cercle méridien; **t. camp,** camp *m* provisoire.

transition [træn'zɪʃ(ə)n] *n* transition *f*; **t. from day to night/from fear to hope,** passage *m* du jour à la nuit/de la crainte à l'espoir; *Ch* **t. element,** élément *m* de transition; **t. period,** période *f* de transition, période transitoire.

transitional [træn'zɪʃən(ə)l] *adj* transitionnel, de transition; *Archit Art* **t. style,** style *m* de transition.

transitive ['trænzɪtɪv] *Gram* **1** *adj* transitif. **2** *n* (*verbe*) transitif *m*; **in the t.,** à la forme transitive, transitivement.

transitively ['trænsɪtɪvlɪ] *adv* transitivement.

transitory ['trænsɪt(ə)rɪ] *adj* transitoire, passager, -ère; (*bonheur etc*) fugitif; (*désir etc*) momentané; (*gloire etc*) de courte durée.

translatable [træns'leɪtəb(ə)l] *adj* traduisible.

translate [træns'leɪt] **1** *vt* **(a)** traduire (*un livre etc*) **(from,** de; **into,** en); **to t. words into action(s)** *or* **deeds,** passer des paroles à l'acte; *F* **can you t. that (into plain English), please?,** tu peux traduire (en langage de tous les jours), s'il te plaît; **we can now t. these figures into a graph,** nous pouvons maintenant traduire ces dessins en un graphe; **to t. a novel into film terms,** adapter un roman à l'écran; **(b)** *Rel* transférer (*un évêque*) **(to,** à); *Bible* **Enoch was translated (to heaven),** Énoch fut enlevé au ciel; **(c)** *MecE* déplacer (*qch*) par translation. **2** *vi* (*of person*) faire de la traduction; (*of writing*) se traduire; **this expression translates literally as ...,** la traduction littérale de cette expression est ... .

translation [træns'leɪʃən] *n* **(a)** traduction *f*; *Sch* version *f* (*latine, russe etc*); (*of novel into film etc*) adaptation *f*; **lost in t.,** perdu dans la traduction; **a t. problem,** un problème de traduction; **simultaneous t.,** traduction simultanée; **(b)** *Rel* translation *f* (*d'un évêque*); *Bible* enlèvement *m* (au ciel); **(c)** *MecE etc* **movement of t.,** mouvement *m* de translation.

translator [træns'leɪtər] *n* traducteur, -trice.

transliterate [trænz'lɪtəreɪt] *vt* translit(t)érer, transcrire (*en caractères différents ou phonétiques*).

transliteration [trænzlɪtə'reɪʃən] *n* translit(t)ération *f*, transcription *f* (*en caractères différents ou phonétiques*).

translucence [trænz'luːsəns] *n* translucidité *f*.

translucent [trænz'luːsənt] *adj* translucide.

transmigrate [trænzmaɪ'greɪt] *vi* (*of people*) migrer; (*of souls*) transmigrer.

transmigration [trænzmaɪ'greɪʃən] *n* (*of people*) migration *f*; (*of souls*) transmigration *f*.

transmissible [trænz'mɪsɪb(ə)l] *adj* transmissible.

transmission [trænz'mɪʃən] *n* **(a)** *Rad TV Phys* transmission *f*; **(b)** *Aut* **the t.,** la transmission; **t. shaft,** arbre *m* de transmission; **(c)** (*programme*) *TV* programme télévisé; *Rad* programme radiodiffusé.

transmit [trænz'mɪt] *vt* (-tt-) transmettre (*un colis, un ordre, une maladie etc*) *& Rad Phys*; *MecE* **to t. a motion to sth,** imprimer *ou* communiquer un mouvement à qch.

transmitter [trænz'mɪtər] *n Telecom etc* transmetteur *m*; *Rad TV* (poste *m*) émetteur *m*, poste d'émission; *Telecom Rad* **t. receiver,** emetteur-récepteur *m*.

transmogrify [trænz'mɒgrɪfaɪ] *vt Hum* transformer, métamorphoser **(into,** en).

transmutation [trænzmjuː'teɪʃən] *n* transmutation *f* **(into,** en).

transmute [trænz'mjuːt] *vt* transformer, changer **(into,** en); (*in alchemy*) transmuer.

transom ['trænsəm] *n* **(a)** *Archit* traverse *f*, linteau *m* (*de fenêtre, de porte*); **(b)** *Am* (*window over door*) imposte *f*.

transparence [træns'pær(ə)ns] *n* transparence *f*; clarté *f* (*du verre etc*).

transparency [træns'pærənsɪ, -'peər-] *n* **(a)** (*quality*) transparence *f*; limpidité *f* (*de l'eau etc*); **(b)** (*picture*) transparent *m*; *Phot* diapositive *f*; *Phot* **colour t.,** diapositive en couleur.

transparent [træns'pærənt, -'peər-] *adj* **(a)** (*verre etc*) transparent; (*eau, quartz etc*) limpide; **(b)** (*obvious*) évident, clair, qui saute aux yeux.

transparently [træns'pærəntlɪ, -'peər-] *adv* (*obviously*) de toute évidence; **that's t. obvious,** c'est clair comme de l'eau de roche.

transpiration [trænspɪ'reɪʃən] *n* transpiration *f*.

transpire [træns'paɪər] **1** *vi* **(a)** (*of news, secret*) transpirer, se répandre; **it transpired that...,** on a appris que...; **(b)** (*happen*) arriver, se passer; **(c)** *Physiol Bot* transpirer. **2** *vt* (*of body, plant etc*) exsuder (*un fluide*); exhaler (*une odeur*).

transplant¹ ['trænsplɑːnt, 'trɑː-] *n* **(a)** *Surg* (*act of transplanting*) transplantation *f*, greffe *f*; (*transplanted organ etc*) transplant *m*, greffon *m*; **heart t.,** greffe du cœur; **(b)** (*in horticulture*) plant repiqué.

transplant² [træns'plɑːnt, trɑː-] *vt* **(a)** *Surg* transplanter, greffer (*un organe*); **(b)** transplanter, transporter (*une population etc*); **(c)** (*in horticulture*) transplanter (*des arbres etc*); repiquer (*des plants*).

transplantation [trænsplɑːn'teɪʃən, -trɑː-] *n* transplantation *f*.

transport¹ ['trænspɔːt] *n* **(a)** transport *m* (*de marchandises, de voyageurs, de troupes etc*); **public t.,** les transports en commun; **to use/rely on public t.,** utiliser les/se fier aux transports en commun; **road/rail t.,** transport routier/ferroviaire; *Br* **t. café,** routier *m*; **t. costs,** frais *mpl* de transport; **(b)** (*means of transport*) moyen *m* de transport; *Nau* **(troop) t.,** (bâtiment *m* de) transport *m*; *Av* **t. (aircraft** *or* **plane),** (avion *m* de) transport; (*for cargo*) avion cargo; *F* **have you got t.?** est-ce que vous avez une *ou* votre voiture?; **(c)** (*emotion*) transport *m* (de joie).

transport² [træns'pɔːt] *vt* **(a)** transporter (*des voyageurs, des marchandises*); **(b)** (*usu passive*) **to be transported with joy,** être transporté de joie.

transportable [træns'pɔːtəb(ə)l] *adj* transportable.

transportation [trænspɔː'teɪʃən] *n* **(a)** (*transport*) transport *m*; (*means of transport*) moyen *m* de transport; **(b)** *Jur Arch* (*to colonies*) transportation *f*.

transporter [træns'pɔːtər] *n* (*vehicle*) transporteur *m*, transporteuse *f*; (*person*) entrepreneur *m* de transports; **car t.,** (*lorry*) camion *m* transporteur de voitures; *Rail* wagon *m* transporteur de voitures; **t. bridge,** (pont) transbordeur *m*.

transpose [træns'pəʊz] *vt* **(a)** transposer (*des mots, les termes d'une équation etc*); **(b)** *Mus* transposer.

transposing [træns'pəʊzɪŋ] *n Mus* transposition *f*.

transposition [trænspə'zɪʃən] *n* **(a)** transposition *f*, inversion *f* (*de lettres etc*); **(b)** *Mus* transposition *f*; **(c)** *Tel* croisement *m* (technique) des fils.

transputer [trans'pjuːtər] *n Comptr* transputeur *m*.

transsexual [træn(z)'seksjʊəl] *adj & n* transsexuel, -elle.

transship [træn(z)'ʃɪp] = **TRANSHIP**.

Trans-Siberian [træn(z)saɪ'bɪərɪən] *adj* **T.-S. Railway,** chemin de fer transsibérien, Transsibérien *m*.

transubstantiate [trænsəb'stænʃɪeɪt] *vt Rel* transsubstantier.

transubstantiation [trænsəbstænʃɪ'eɪʃən] *n Rel* transsubstantiation *f*.

Transvaal ['trɑːnzvɑːl] *n* **the T.,** le Transvaal; **a T. farmer,** un fermier transvaalien.

transversal [trænz'vɜːs(ə)l] **1** *adj* transversal, -aux. **2** *n Math* transversale *f*.

transversally [trænz'vɜːsəlɪ] *adv* transversalement.

transverse ['trænzvɜːs] *adj* (*section, muscle*) transversal, -aux; *Anat* (*colon*) transverse; *Math* **t. line,** transversale *f*; *Constr* **t. beam,** traverse *f*.

transversely ['trænzvɜːslɪ] *adv* transversalement, en

travers.

transvestism [trænz'vestɪz(ə)m] *n* tra(ns)vestisme *m*.

transvestite [trænz'vestaɪt] *n* travesti, -ie.

trap¹ [træp] *n* **(a)** (*in hunting etc*) piège *m*; (*pit*) trappe *f*; (*for hares etc*) panneau *m*; *Nucl Phys* piège (à particules); *Fig* (*deception*) piège, ruse *f*, attrape *f*; **to set a t.,** dresser *ou* tendre un piège (**for,** à); **to catch an animal in a t.,** prendre une bête au piège; *Mil* **tank t.,** (obstacle *m*) antichar *m*; **police t.,** souricière *f*; **radar/speed t.,** zone *f* de contrôle de vitesse; **she's fallen into her own t.,** elle est prise à son propre piège; **he fell into the t.,** il s'y laissa prendre, il tomba dans le piège; **to walk** *or* **fall straight into the t.,** donner *ou* tomber en plein dans le piège *ou* dans le lac;

(b) (*opening*) trappe *f*; trappe (*de colombier*); *Sl* (*mouth*) gueule *f*; **shut your t.!,** ta gueule!, la ferme!; **you would have to go and open your big t.!,** il a fallu que tu y ailles et ouvres ta grande gueule!; **t. (door),** trappe; *Min* porte *f* d'aérage;

(c) *Sp* (projecteur *m*) ball-trap *m*, *pl* ball-traps (*pour pigeons artificiels*); boîte *f* de lancement (*pour pigeons vivants*); (*in dog racing*) box *m* (de départ);

(d) *Tech* collecteur *m* (*d'eau, d'huile etc*); (*plumbing*) *& Constr* siphon *m*; **sink t.,** puisard *m*;

(e) (*horse-drawn vehicle*) cabriolet *m*;

(f) *esp Am Mus* **traps,** instruments *mpl* à percussion.

trap² *v* (**-pp-**) **1** *vt* **(a)** prendre (*une bête, qn*) au piège, piéger; **to t. one's finger in the door,** se coincer le doigt dans la porte; **she trapped him into marriage,** elle l'a obligé à se marier avec elle en usant de ruse; **to t. s.o. into saying sth,** piéger qn pour qu'il dise qch; **to t. s.o. into making a false move,** piéger qn pour qu'il fasse un faux pas; **I was trapped in the lift for two hours,** je suis resté coincé dans l'ascenseur pendant deux heures; **the climbers were trapped by an avalanche,** les alpinistes ont été bloqués par une avalanche; **trapped by the flames,** cerné par les flammes; **to feel trapped (in a relationship),** se sentir enfermé *ou F* coincé (dans une relation); **(b)** *Tech* arrêter (*un gaz etc*) au moyen d'un siphon; **(c)** *Sp* (*stop*) bloquer (*le ballon*). **2** *vi* **(a)** (*set traps*) tendre des pièges; **(b)** *Can* trapper.

trapeze [trə'piːz] *n* trapèze *m*; **to perform on the flying t.,** faire du trapèze volant *ou* de la voltige; **t. artist,** trapéziste *mf*, voltigeur, -euse.

trapezist [trə'piːzɪst] *n* trapéziste *mf*.

trapezium [trə'piːzɪəm] *n Math* trapèze *m*.

trapezoid ['træpɪzɔɪd] *n Math* trapézoïde *m*.

trapper ['træpər] *n* (*hunter*) trappeur *m*.

trapping ['træpɪŋ] *n* (*in hunting*) (*activity*) piégeage *m*; (*profession*) métier *m* de trappeur.

trappings ['træpɪŋz] *npl* **(a)** (*of power, success etc*) signes *mpl*, apparat *m*; **the t. of authority,** l'apparat de l'autorité; **(b)** (*for horses*) harnachement *m*, caparaçon *m*.

Trappist ['træpɪst] *adj & n Rel* trappiste *m*.

traps [træps] *npl Old-fashioned F* effets *mpl* (personnels).

trapshooting ['træpʃuːtɪŋ] *n Sp* ball-trap *m*.

trash [træʃ] *n* (*worthless objects*) camelote *f*; *Am* (*refuse*) détritus *mpl*, déchets *mpl*, ordures *fpl*; littérature *f* de camelote; (*people*) vermine *f*, racaille *f*; **she's t.,** elle ne vaut rien; **to talk a lot of t.,** dire des tas d'imbécilités; *Am* **t. can,** poubelle *f*, boîte *f* à ordures.

trashy ['træʃɪ] *adj* (*marchandises etc*) de pacotille; (*littérature*) de camelote.

trauma, *pl* **-as, -ata** ['trɔːmə, -əz, -ətə] *n Med Psy* trauma *m*.

traumatic [trɔː'mætɪk] *adj Med* traumatique; *Fig* (*experience, journey, exam*) traumatisant.

traumatism ['trɔːmətɪz(ə)m] *n Med* traumatisme *m*.

traumatize ['trɔːmətaɪz] *vt Med & Fig* traumatiser (*qn*).

travail¹ ['træveɪl] *n* **(a)** *Lit* (*labour, hard work*) dur labeur; *esp Hum* **after all your travails,** après tout vos durs labeurs; **(b)** *Arch & Lit* douleurs *fpl* de l'enfantement, travail *m*; **woman in t.,** femme en travail.

travail² *vi Arch & Lit* (*labour, work hard*) œuvrer dur; (*of woman*) être en travail (*d'enfantement*).

travel¹ ['træv(ə)l] *n* **(a)** voyages *mpl*; **t. was slower in those days,** on voyageait plus lentement à cette époque; **what do you spend on t. (to and from work)?,** à combien vous reviennent vos déplacements (pour aller et revenir du travail)?; **when are you next off on your travels?,** quand repartez-vous en voyage?; **I met him on my** *or* **in the course of my travels,** j'ai fait sa connaissance en voyage; **t. agency/agent,** agence *f*/agent *m* de voyages; **t. book,** (*account*) récit *m* de voyage; (*guide*) guide *m* de voyage; **t. bureau,** agence *f* de voyage; **t. company** *or* **firm,** voyagiste *mf*; **t. goods,** articles *mpl* de voyage; **t. insurance,** assurance *f* (en) voyage; **t. writer,** auteur *m* de récit(s) de voyage(s); **(b)** *MecE etc* course *f* (*du piston, du chariot*); déplacement *m* (*d'une pièce mécanique*); (*in ballistics*) course, trajet *m* (*d'un mobile, d'un projectile*).

travel² *v* (**-ll-**, *US* **-l-**) **1** *vi* **(a)** voyager; (*travel around*) faire des voyages; (*of news*) circuler, se répandre; **he has travelled a great deal** *or* **widely,** il a beaucoup voyagé; **to t. round the world,** faire le tour du monde; **to t. all over the world,** courir le monde; **to t. through a country,** parcourir *ou* traverser un pays; **light travels faster than sound,** la lumière voyage *ou* se propage plus vite que le son; **news travels fast round here,** les nouvelles vont vite par ici; **the train was travelling at 150 km an hour,** le train marchait à 150 km à l'heure; **thats travelling!,** (*is fast*) ça c'est de la vitesse!; **this wine won't t.,** ce vin ne voyage pas;

(b) to t. (for a firm), voyager (pour une maison), représenter une maison; **to t. in wine,** voyager pour les vins;

(c) *MecE* (*of part*) se mouvoir, se déplacer; (*of electric current*) se déplacer.

2 *vt* parcourir (*country*); **to t. the length and breadth of the country,** parcourir le pays de long en large; **I t. this road every day,** je fais *ou* parcours cette route tous les jours.

travelator ['trævəleɪtər] *n* trottoir *ou* tapis roulant.

travelled, *US* **traveled** ['trævəld] *adj* **much** *or* **well t.,** (*person*) qui a beaucoup voyagé; **much t.,** (*road*) très fréquenté.

traveller, *US* **traveler** ['træv(ə)lər] *n* (*person*) voyageur, -euse; (*salesperson*) représentant, -ante; *Br* (*living in caravan etc*) nomade *mf*; **I'm not a good t.,** je supporte mal les voyages; **a frequent t.,** personne *f* qui est souvent en voyage; *Br* **t.'s cheque,** *US* **traveler's check,** chèque *m* de voyage.

travelling, *US* **traveling** ['træv(ə)lɪŋ] **1** *adj* (*cirque*) ambulant; (*prédicateur*) itinérant; *MecE* (*trottoir etc*) roulant; (*grue*) mobile; **t. salesman,** voyageur *m* de commerce. **2** *n* voyages *mpl*; **to do a lot of t.,** beaucoup voyager; **there isn't a lot of t. in this job,** on ne voyage pas beaucoup dans ce travail; **t. companion,** compagnon *m* de voyage; **t. clock,** réveil *m* de voyage; **t. expenses,** (*cost of journey*) frais *mpl* de voyage *ou* de route; *Com etc* frais de déplacement; **t. people,** nomades *mfpl*; *Cin* **t. platform,** travelling *m*; **t. rug,** couverture *f* de voyage; **t. scholarship,** bourse *f* de voyage; *Cin* **t. shot,** prise *f* de vues en travelling.

travelogue, *US* **travelog** ['trævəlɒg] *n* documentaire *m* de voyage.

travel-sick ['træv(ə)lsɪk] *adj* qui souffre du mal de la route *ou* de l'air *ou* de mer; **to feel t.-s.** avoir le mal de la route *ou* de l'air *ou* de la mer.

travel-sickness ['træv(ə)lsɪknɪs] *n* mal *m* de la route *ou* de l'air *ou* de mer; **t.-s. pill,** cachet *m* contre le mal de la route *ou* de l'air *ou* de mer.

travelstained ['træv(ə)lsteɪnd] *adj* sali par le voyage.

travel-weary ['træv(ə)lwɪərɪ] *adj* fatigué par le(s) voyage(s).

traverse¹ ['trævəs] *n* **(a)** *MecE Constr etc* traverse *f*, entretoise *f* (*de châssis, de cadre etc*); **(b)** *Math* (ligne) transversale *f*; (*in surveying*) cheminement *m*; **(c)** (*in mountaineering, skiing*) traverse *f* (*sur la face d'un escarpement*), vire *f*.

traverse² **1** *vt* **(a)** *MecE* charioter (*une pièce*); **(b)** *Lit* traverser, passer à travers (*une région, le corps*); passer (*un pont, la mer*); **(c)** (*in surveying*) faire un cheminement (*d'une région*). **2** *vi* (*in mountaineering, skiing*) traverser, prendre une traverse; (*of horse*) se traverser.

traversing ['trævəsɪŋ] *n* **(a)** (*in surveying*) (levé *m* par) cheminement *m*; **(b)** (*in mountaineering, skiing*) prise *f* d'une traverse.

travesty¹ ['trævəstɪ] *n* travestissement *m* (*d'une pièce de théâtre etc*); **a t. of the truth,** un travestissement de la vérité; **it was a t. of justice,** c'était un travestissement *ou* une parodie de justice.

travesty² *vt* parodier, travestir (*une histoire, un personnage etc*).

trawl¹ [trɔːl] *n Fishing* **t. (line),** palangre *f*; **t. (net),** chalut *m*, traille *f*.

trawl² *Fishing* **1** *vi* pêcher à la traille *ou* au chalut. **2** *vt* traîner (*un chalut*); prendre (*le poisson*) à la traille *ou* au chalut; *Fig* **to t. for business,** chercher des clients.

trawler ['trɔːlər] *n* **(a)** (*ship*) chalutier *m*; **(b)** (*person*) (*also* **trawlerman**) pêcheur *m* au chalut, chalutier *m*.

trawling ['trɔːlɪŋ] *n* pêche *f* au chalut, chalutage *m*.
tray [treɪ] *n* **(a)** plateau *m*, *Can* cabaret *m*; casier *m*, châssis *m* (*d'une malle etc*); (*in office etc*) corbeille *f* (à correspondance); (*for selling ice-cream etc*) éventaire *m*; **tea t.**, plateau à thé; *Surg etc* **instrument t.**, plateau à instruments; **to bring/take sth in on a t.**, apporter/prendre qch sur un plateau; **a t. of sandwiches,** un plateau de sandwiches; **in-t.**, (*in office etc*) corbeille de la correspondance reçue; **out-t.**, (*in office etc*) corbeille du courrier à expédier *ou* des documents à classer; **(b)** *Phot etc* cuvette *f*.
traycloth ['treɪklɒθ] *n* napperon *m* (*de plateau*).
treacherous ['tretʃərəs] *adj* (*homme, caractère*) traître, -esse, déloyal, -aux; (*action*) déloyal; (*routes, montagnes, glace*) traître.
treacherously ['tretʃərəslɪ] *adv* (*agir*) en traître, traîtreusement, perfidement; **we drove in t. bad conditions,** nous avons conduit dans des conditions terriblement mauvaises; **it can get t. icy up there,** il y a parfois un verglas traître par là-haut.
treachery ['tretʃərɪ] *n* trahison *f*, perfidie *f*; **act of t.**, trahison, perfidie.
treacle [triːk(ə)l] *n* mélasse *f*; **t. tart,** tarte *f* à la mélasse.
treacly ['triːklɪ] *adj* sirupeux; *Fig* doucereux, mielleux.
tread¹ [tred] *n* **(a)** pas *m*; (*sound*) bruit *m* de pas; **I heard his familiar t. on the path,** j'ai entendu son pas familier sur le chemin; **heavy t.**, pas lourd; *esp Lit* **to walk with measured t.**, marcher à pas mesurés; **(b)** giron *m* (*de marche d'escalier*); semelle *f* (*d'une chaussure*); fourchon *m*, étrier *m* (*d'échasse*); échelon *m* (*d'échelle etc*); *Rail* surface *f ou* table *f* de roulement (*d'un rail*); *Aut* (*outer layer of tyre*) bande *f* de roulement, chape *f*; (*pattern on tyre*) sculpture *f*; **there isn't much t. left,** (*on tyre*) il ne reste presque plus de chape; **non-skid t.**, (*on tyre*) roulement antidérapant; **the t. marks of a heavy vehicle on the sand,** les empreintes de pneus d'un véhicule lourd sur le sable.
tread² *v* (*pt* **trod** [trɒd]; *pp* **trodden** ['trɒd(ə)n]) **1** *vi* marcher; **watch where you t.**, regarde ou tu mets les pieds; **to t. in sth,** marcher dans qch; **to t. on sth,** marcher sur qch; *Fig* **we shall have to t. carefully** *or* **warily,** nous marchons sur des œufs. **2** *vt* marcher sur (*le sol*); (*of male bird*) couvrir, côcher (*la femelle*); **to t. sth under foot,** écraser qch du pied, fouler qch aux pieds; **don't t. it into the carpet!**, ne l'écrase pas sur la moquette!; **well-trodden path,** chemin battu; (*much used*) chemin (très) fréquenté; *Old-fashioned* **to t. a path,** suivre un chemin; **to t. grapes,** fouler la vendange; *Swimming* **to t. water,** nager debout.
▶**tread down** *vtas* (*push down with feet*) piétiner (*le sol etc*).
treading ['tredɪŋ] *n* piétinement *m*; foulage *m* (*des raisins*); *Swimming* **t. water,** nage *f* debout.
treadle ['tred(ə)l] *n* pédale *f* (*de machine à coudre etc*); **t. machine,** machine *f* à pédale.
treadmill ['tredmɪl] *n Arch* (*in prisons*) moulin *m* de discipline; (*routine*) besogne (quotidienne) ingrate.
treason ['triːz(ə)n] *n Jur* trahison *f*; **high t.**, haute trahison.
treasonable ['triːz(ə)nəb(ə)l] *adj* (*remarks etc*) traître, -esse, perfide; (*act*) de trahison.
treasure¹ ['treʒər] *n* trésor *m*; **art treasures,** trésors *ou* richesses *fpl* artistiques; *F* **my home help's a real t.**, ma femme de ménage est une perle; **t. hunt,** chasse *f* au(x) trésor(s).
treasure² *vt* (*prize*) estimer (*qn*); priser, faire beaucoup de cas de (*qch*); (*save*) garder (*qch*) soigneusement; **to t. sth in one's memory,** garder précieusement le souvenir de qch; **a memory I shall always t.**, un souvenir que je chérirai toute ma vie.
treasure(-)house ['treʒəhaʊs] *n Old-fashioned* trésor *m*.
treasurer ['treʒərər] *n* trésorier, -ière.
treasure-trove ['treʒətrəʊv] *n* **(a)** *Jur* trésor *m* (qu'on a découvert); **(b)** *F* **the book was a t.-t. of anecdotes,** le livre était une mine d'anecdotes.
treasury ['treʒərɪ] *n* **(a)** (*funds*) trésor *m* (public); (*place*) trésorerie *f*; trésor (*d'une cathédrale etc*); **the T.** (*in England*) = le Ministère des finances; *Fin* **t. bonds** *or* **bills,** bons *mpl* du Trésor; **(b)** (*anthology*) trésor *m* (*de poésie*).
treat¹ [triːt] *n* **(a)** (*gift*) cadeau *m*; (*meal, delicacy*) régal *m*, -als, festin *m*; **it's my t.**, (*it's my round*) c'est ma tournée; (*I'm paying*) c'est moi qui paie; **(b)** (*pleasure*) plaisir *m*; **it would be a great t. to go to the theatre,** ce serait une véritable fête d'aller au théâtre; **to give s.o. a t.**, gâter qn; **it's a t. seeing you look so well!**, c'est un plaisir de te voir aussi en forme!; **to give oneself a t.**, faire un petit extra, se faire plaisir; **a t. in store,** un plaisir en réserve; **(c)** *F* **a (fair) t.**, à merveille; **that whisky went down a t.!**, ce whisky m'a fait du bien; **it worked a t.**, (*of plan etc*) ça a marché comme sur des roulettes.
treat² **1** *vt* **(a)** (*behave towards, use*) traiter (*qn, qch*); **to t. s.o. well,** bien traiter qn; **to t. s.o./an animal roughly,** malmener *ou* maltraiter qn/un animal; **my father still treats me like a child,** mon père me traite toujours en enfant; **he doesn't t. things seriously,** il ne prend pas les choses au sérieux; **to t. sth as a joke,** considérer qch comme une plaisanterie;
(b) traiter (*un métal*); *Med* traiter (*un malade, une maladie*); **to t. s.o. for rheumatism,** soigner qn pour le rhumatisme; **she was treated in hospital,** elle a reçu des soins à l'hôpital; **to t. wood with creosote,** traiter le bois à la créosote;
(c) *Lit Mus etc* traiter (*un sujet, un thème*);
(d) **to t. s.o. to the theatre,** inviter qn au théâtre; **I'll t. you to an ice-cream,** je t'offre une glace; **to t. oneself to oysters,** s'offrir des huîtres; *F* **I'll t. you,** je t'invite; *Iron* **he treated us to a fair old display of petulance,** nous avons eu droit à une belle démonstration de mauvaise humeur.
2 *vi Fml* (*negotiate*) **to t. with s.o.**, traiter *ou* négocier avec qn; **to t. with the enemy,** pactiser avec l'ennemi.
▶**treat of** *vipo Fml* (*deal with*) **to t. of a subject,** (*of book*) traiter d'un sujet.
treatise ['triːtɪz] *n* traité *m* (**on,** de).
treatment ['triːtmənt] *n* **(a)** traitement *m* (*de qn*); **to give special/preferential t. to s.o.**, réserver un traitement spécial/le traitement de faveur à qn; **to receive good/ill t.**, (*of person, thing*) recevoir un bon/mauvais traitement; *F* **to give s.o. the (full) t.**, faire la totale à qn; **(b)** (*of metal, paper etc*) & *Med* traitement *m*; **(c)** *Lit Mus etc* façon *f* de traiter (*un sujet, un thème*).
treaty ['triːtɪ] *n* **(a)** (*international*) traité *m* (*de paix, de commerce*); convention *f*; **(b)** (*between individuals*) accord *m*; (*contract*) contrat *m*; **to sell sth by private t.**, vendre qch de gré à gré *ou* à l'amiable.
treble¹ ['treb(ə)l] **1** *adj* **(a)** (*triple*) triple; **(b)** *Mus* **t. voice,** (voix *f* de) soprano *m* (*masculin*); **t. clef,** clef *f* de sol. **2** *adv* trois fois autant. **3** *n* **(a)** triple *m*; **(b)** *Mus* (*person, voice*) soprano *m*, *Electron* **t. (control)**, touche *f* de tonalité aiguë; **(c)** (*crochet*) **simple t.**, brides *fpl* simples.
treble² **1** *vt* tripler (*la valeur, le nombre*). **2** *vi* (se) tripler.
trebly ['treblɪ] *adv* trois fois autant; **this makes it t. important,** ça le rend triplement important.
tree¹ [triː] *n* **(a)** arbre *m*; **fruit t.**, arbre fruitier; **timber t.**, arbre de haute futaie; *Fig* **to be at the top of the t.**, être au sommet, être au haut de l'échelle; *Fig* **to get to the top of the t.**, arriver; *F* **to be up a (gum) t.**, être dans une impasse *ou* dans le pétrin; *F* **money doesn't grow on trees!**, l'argent ne pousse pas sur les arbres; *F* **good trainers don't grow on trees,** les bons entraîneurs ne courent pas les rues; *esp Am Sl* **to be out of one's t.**, (*be crazy*) débloquer; **the t. of life,** l'arbre de la vie; **t. creeper,** (*bird*) grimpereau *m* des bois; **t. fern,** fougère arborescente; **t. frog,** rainette verte; *Geog* **the t. line,** la limite des arbres; **above/below the t. line,** au-dessus/en-dessous de la limite des arbres; **t. pipit,** (*bird*) pipit *m* des arbres; **t. surgeon,** arboriculteur, -trice (qui s'occupe de la régénération des arbres); **t. trunk,** tronc *m* d'arbre;
(b) **family t.**, arbre *m* généalogique;
(c) *Arch* **gallows t.**, gibet *m*, potence *f*;
(d) **(shoe) t.**, embauchoir *m* (pour chaussures);
(e) *Comptr* **t. structure,** arborescence *f*.
tree² *vt* (*chase up a tree*) obliger (*un animal, une proie*) à se réfugier sur un arbre.
treeless ['triːlɪs] *adj* sans arbres.
treetop ['triːtɒp] *n* cime *f* d'un arbre; *Av* **to skim the treetops,** voler en rase-mottes.
trefoil ['triːfɔɪl, 'tref-] *n* **(a)** *Bot* trèfle *m*; **bird's foot t.**, lotier *m*; **(b)** *Archit Her* trèfle *m*; *Archit* trilobe *m*.
trek¹ [trek] *n* **(a)** **a long t.**, un trajet long et pénible (*surtout à pied*); **it's a long t. back up from the beach,** le chemin est long et pénible pour remonter de la plage; **(b)** (*in S Africa*) (*journey by ox cart*) voyage *m* en chariot (*à bœufs*); (*stage*) étape *f* (*d'un voyage*); *Hist* migration *f*.
trek² *vi* (**-kk-**) **(a)** (*make long journey*) faire un trajet long et pénible (*surtout à pied*); *F* **to t. to the shops/***etc*, aller péniblement en courses/*etc*; **(b)** (*in S Africa*) (*travel by ox cart*) voyager en chariot (*à bœufs*).
trekking ['trekɪŋ] *n* (*as holiday activity*) randonnée *f*, trekking *m*; **a t. holiday in Nepal,** des vacances de

trekking au Népal.

trellis¹ ['trelɪs] *n* treillis *m*, treillage *m*; **t. window,** fenêtre treillissée.

trellis² *vt* **(a)** treillisser, treillager (*une fenêtre etc*); **(b)** échalasser (*une vigne*).

trelliswork ['trelɪswɜːk] *n* treillis *m*, treillage *m*.

tremble¹ ['tremb(ə)l] *n* tremblement *m*; (*in voice*) tremblotement *m*; **to be all of a t.,** être tout tremblant.

tremble² *vi* (*vibrate*) trembler, vibrer; (*shiver*) trembler, frissonner; (*with emotion*) frémir; **to t. like a leaf,** trembler comme une feuille; **to t. with fear,** trembler de peur; **where are they?, I t. to think!,** où sont-ils?, je n'ose y penser!

trembler ['tremblər] *n* **(a)** (*person*) trembleur, -euse; **(b)** *El* trembleur *m*.

trembling ['tremblɪŋ] **1** *adj* tremblant, tremblotant. **2** *n* tremblement *m*; tremblotement *m* (*d'une feuille, de la voix*); **in fear and t.,** tout tremblant.

tremendous [trɪ'mendəs] *adj* **(a)** *F* (*enormous*) immense, énorme; (*excellent*) formidable; **there was a t. crowd,** il y avait un monde fou; **a t. difference,** une énorme différence; **a. t. lot of sth,** une quantité énorme de qch; **thanks, that's t.,** merci, c'est formidable; **(b)** *Arch* (*dreadful*) terrible, épouvantable.

tremendously [trɪ'mendəslɪ] *adv* **(a)** (*enormously*) énormément; **it was t. successful/funny/difficult,** c'était un succès fou/énormément drôle/terriblement difficile; **(b)** *Arch* (*dreadfully*) terriblement.

tremolo ['tremələʊ] *n Mus* tremolo *m*, trémolo *m*.

tremor ['tremər] *n* **(a)** tremblement *m*, frémissement *m*; frisson *m* (*de peur*); *Med* tremblement, trémulation *f*; **(b)** trépidation *f* (*des vitres etc*); **earth t.,** tremblement *m* de terre; secousse *f* sismique.

tremulous ['tremjʊləs] *adj* tremblotant, frémissant; (*sourire*) timide, craintif; **t. voice,** voix tremblante *ou* chevrotante.

tremulously ['tremjʊləslɪ] *adv* en tremblant, en tremblotant; timidement.

trench¹ [tren(t)ʃ] *n* **(a)** (*horticulture*) *& Agr* tranchée *f*, fossé *m*; (*for draining*) rigole *f*; **water** *or* **irrigation t.,** fossé d'irrigation; **t. plough,** rigoleuse *f*; **(b)** *Mil* tranchée *f*; **communication t.,** boyau *m*, -aux; **t. coat,** trench-coat *m*, *pl* trench-coats; **t. warfare,** guerre *f* de tranchées.

trench² **1** *vt* creuser un fossé *ou* une tranchée dans (*le sol*). **2** *vi* creuser des fossés *ou* des tranchées.

trenchant ['tren(t)ʃənt] *adj* **(a)** (*style, tone*) tranchant, net, incisif; (*reply, epigram*) mordant, caustique; **(b)** *Arch Lit* (*sword etc*) tranchant.

trencher ['tren(t)ʃər] *n Arch* tranchoir *m*, tailloir *m*.

trencherman, *pl* **-men** ['tren(t)ʃəmən] *n Old-fashioned* **good** *or* **stout t.,** grand *ou* gros mangeur.

trend¹ [trend] *n* tendance *f*, marche *f* (*de l'opinion publique etc*); (*fashion*) mode *f*; direction *f* (*d'un cours d'eau etc*); **to set a t.,** lancer une mode *ou* une tendance; **a t. towards ...,** une tendance vers ...; **current trends,** tendances actuelles; **if present trends continue,** si les tendances actuelles se poursuivent.

trend² *vi* se diriger, s'orienter (**to, towards,** vers).

trendiness ['trendɪnɪs] *n Br F* (*of clothes*) style branché *ou* mode; (*of person, views etc*) modernité *f*.

trendsetter ['trendsetər] *n* lanceur, -euse de modes *ou* de nouvelles tendances/*etc*.

trendsetting ['trendsetɪŋ] **1** *adj* (*innovation, design etc*) qui donne le ton. **2** *n* lancement *m* de nouvelles modes *ou* tendances.

trendy ['trendɪ] *Br F* **1** *adj* (*clothes, person, views etc*) branché. **2** *n Pej* (*person*) personne branchée.

trepan¹ [trɪ'pæn] *n Surg Min* trépan *m*.

trepan² *vt* **(-nn-)** *Surg* trépaner.

trepanning [trɪ'pænɪŋ] *n Surg* trépanation *f*.

trepidation [trepɪ'deɪʃən] *n* (*anxiety*) trépidation *f*, agitation nerveuse; **he stood there in t. before the headmaster,** il se tenait tout trépidant devant le directeur de l'école; **he opened the letter with t.,** il ouvrit la lettre avec trépidation; **he picked up the phone and, not without t., dialled,** il saisit l'écouteur et composa le numéro d'une main trépidante.

trespass¹ ['trespəs] *n Jur* **(a)** (*unlawful act*) contravention *f* de la loi; *Rel* offense *f*, péché *m*; **forgive us our trespasses,** pardonne-nous nos offenses; **(b)** *Jur* violation *f* de propriété (*sur un bien foncier*).

trespass² *vi* **(a)** *Jur* **to t. (on s.o.'s property),** entrer *ou* passer sans autorisation sur la propriété de qn; **to t. (up)on s.o.'s rights,** violer *ou* enfreindre les droits de qn; *Old-fashioned* **I don't wish to t. on your time,** je ne veux pas abuser de votre temps; **(b)** *Arch & Lit* (*break the law*) transgresser la loi; *Rel* pécher (**against,** contre); **as we forgive them that t. against us,** comme nous pardonnons à ceux qui nous ont offensés.

trespasser ['trespəsər] *n* **(a)** *Jur* (*on s.o.'s land*) auteur *m* d'une violation de propriété (foncière); (*on s.o.'s privacy*) intrus *m*; **trespassers will be prosecuted,** (*on sign*) défense d'entrer sous peine d'amende; **(b)** *Rel* pécheur, *f* pécheresse.

trespassing ['trespəsɪŋ] *n* **t. on s.o.'s land,** violation *f* de propriété (foncière); **no t.,** (*on sign*) défense d'entrée.

tress [tres] *n* tresse *f*, boucle *f* (*de cheveux*); *Lit* **tresses,** chevelure *f*, cheveux *mpl* (*d'une femme*).

trestle ['tres(ə)l] *n* tréteau *m*, chevalet *m*; **t. bed,** lit *m* de sangle; **t. bridge,** pont *m* de *ou* sur chevalets; **t. table,** table *f* à tréteaux.

trews [truːz] *npl Scot* (*trousers*) pantalon *m* en tartan; *Br F* pantalon.

triad ['traɪæd] *n* **(a)** triade *f*; **(b)** *Ch* élément trivalent; **(c)** *Mus* accord *m* parfait.

trial ['traɪəl] *n* **(a)** *Jur* (*proceedings*) procès *m*; (*trying*) jugement *m* (*d'un litige, d'un accusé*); **to bring s.o. to t.,** faire passer qn en jugement; **to be on t. for a crime/for one's life,** passer en jugement pour un crime/pour un crime qui entraîne la peine de mort; **they were sent for t.,** ils furent renvoyés en jugement; **t. by jury,** jugement par jury; *Hist* **t. by combat,** combat *m* judiciaire; **criminal t.,** procès criminel; **famous trials,** causes *fpl* célèbres; **t. court,** tribunal *m* de première instance; *US* **t. judge** = juge *m* d'instance;

(b) (*test*) épreuve *f*; essai *m* (technique) (*d'un appareil, d'un véhicule etc*); **t. of strength,** épreuve de force; *Sp* **t. (game),** match *m* de sélection; **to give sth a t.,** faire l'essai de qch; **on t.,** à l'essai; **to proceed by t. and error,** procéder par tâtonnements *ou* par approximations successives; **sheepdog trials,** concours *m* de chiens de berger; **speed t.,** essai de vitesse; **t. balance,** (*in bookkeeping*) balance *f* de vérification; *Av* **t. flight,** vol *m* d'essai; *Com* **t. order,** commande *f* d'essai; **t. period,** période *f* d'essai; **to be on a t. period,** (*of employee*) faire une période d'essai; **t. run,** (*of machine*) essai; (*of car*) essai sur route;

(c) (*ordeal*) épreuve *f* (douloureuse); (*adversity*) peine *f*, adversité *f*; **that child is a great t. to his parents,** cet enfant fait le martyre de ses parents; **despite the trials and tribulations,** en dépit des ennuis.

triangle ['traɪæŋg(ə)l] *n* **(a)** *Math etc* triangle *m*; *Phys* **t. of forces,** triangle des forces; *F* **the eternal t.,** l'éternel triangle; **(b)** *Mus* triangle *m*; (*drawing instrument*) équerre *f* (en triangle).

triangular [traɪ'æŋgjʊlər] *adj* (*shape etc*) triangulaire, en triangle; (*contest, relationship etc*) triangulaire.

triangulate [traɪ'æŋgjʊleɪt] *vt* (*in surveying*) trianguler.

triangulation [traɪæŋgjʊ'leɪʃən] *n* (*in surveying*) triangulation *f*.

tribal ['traɪb(ə)l] *adj* (*society, war*) tribal; (*leader*) de tribu; (*people etc*) qui vit en tribus; **t. system,** système tribal.

tribalism ['traɪbəlɪz(ə)m] *n* tribalisme *m*.

tribe [traɪb] *n* **(a)** tribu *f*; *F* tribu, smala *f*; **the twelve tribes of Israel,** les douze tribus d'Israël; **(b)** *Biol* tribu *f*.

tribesman, *pl* **-men** ['traɪbzmən] *n* membre *m* d'une *ou* de la tribu; **Bedouin t.,** membre d'une tribu bédouine.

tribulation [trɪbjʊ'leɪʃən] *n* tribulation *f*, affliction *f*.

tribunal [tr(a)ɪ'bjuːnəl] *n* tribunal *m*, -aux.

tribune¹ ['trɪbjuːn] *n* (*platform*) tribune *f* (*d'orateur*).

tribune² *n* (*officer in ancient Rome etc*) tribun *m*.

tributary ['trɪbjʊt(ə)rɪ] **1** *adj* tributaire. **2** *n* **(a)** *Geog* affluent *m* (*d'un fleuve*); **(b)** (*person, country*) tributaire *m*.

tribute ['trɪbjuːt] *n* **(a)** tribut *m*, hommage *m* ; **to pay a t. to s.o.,** rendre hommage à qn; **it is a t. to her (determination) that the work was finished at all,** ce n'est que grâce à elle (*ou* à sa détermination) que le travail a été terminé; **to pay a last t. to s.o.,** rendre à qn les derniers devoirs; **floral tributes,** gerbes *fpl* et couronnes *fpl* (de fleurs); **(b)** *Hist* **t. (money),** tribut *m*; **to pay t.,** payer tribut (**to,** à).

trice¹ [traɪs] *n* **in a t.,** en un clin d'œil, en moins de rien.

trice² *vt* = **TRICE UP.**

▶trice up *vtsep Nau* (*hoist*) hisser (*une voile*).

tricentenary, *esp US* **tricentennial** [traɪsen'tiːnərɪ, -'tenɪəl] *adj & n* tricentenaire *m*.

triceps ['traɪseps] *n Anat* **t. (muscle),** triceps *m*.

trichinosis [trɪkɪ'nəʊsɪs] *n Med* trichinose *f*.

trick¹ [trɪk] *n* **(a)** tour *m*, ruse *f*, finesse *f*; (*dishonest*) supercherie *f*; (*practical joke*) farce *f*, tour; (*knack*) truc *m*; (*taught to animal, child etc*) tour d'adresse; **by a t.,** (*obtain sth*) par ruse; **to play a t. on s.o.,** faire une farce *ou* une blague à qn; **my eyes must have been playing tricks on me** *or* **playing me tricks,** mes yeux ont dû me jouer des tours, j'ai dû avoir la berlue; **a t. of the light,** effet *m* de lumière; **that was a nasty** *or* **mean** *or* **dirty t.,** ça c'était un vilain tour!; **you've been up to your tricks again,** vous avez encore fait des vôtres; **the car's up to it's old tricks again,** la voiture recommence à faire des siennes; **the tricks of the trade,** les trucs *ou* les astuces *fpl* du métier; **that should do the t.,** ça fera l'affaire, ça devrait marcher; **to teach a dog tricks,** apprendre des tours à un chien; **card t.,** tour de cartes; **conjuring t.,** tour de prestidigitation *ou* de passe-passe; *F* **the whole bag of tricks,** tout le bataclan, tout le tremblement; **she doesn't miss a t.,** rien ne lui échappe; *F* **how's tricks?,** (*how are you?*) comment vas-tu?; (*what's the news?*) quoi de neuf?; **t. cigarette,** cigarette piégée; **t. cyclist,** cycliste *mf* acrobate; *Sl* (*psychiatrist*) psy *mf*; *Phot Cin* **t. photography,** truquage *m*, trucage *m*; **t. riding,** voltige *f* (*à cheval*);

(b) (*mannerism*) manie *f*; (*habit*) habitude *f*; (*tic*) tic *m*; **he has a t. of repeating himself,** il se répète toujours;

(c) *Cards* levée *f*; **to take a t.,** faire une levée *ou* un pli;

(d) *Sl* (*of prostitute*) passe *f*.

trick[2] *vt* attraper, duper (*qn*); **I've been tricked,** on m'a refait, on m'a eu; **to t. s.o. into doing sth,** amener qn à faire qch en usant de ruse; **you won't t. me into doing that again!,** tu ne m'y reprendras pas!; **to t. s.o. out of sth,** (*of opportunity etc*) frustrer qn de qch; (*of money etc*) escroquer qch à qn.

►trick out *vtsep* (*dress*) parer, attifer (*qn*).

trickery ['trɪkərɪ] *n* tricherie *f*, duperie *f*; **piece of t.,** supercherie *f*; **by t.,** par ruse.

trickiness ['trɪkɪnɪs] *n* **(a)** (*of person, behaviour*) fourberie *f*; **(b)** (*of mechanism, situation*) complication *f*, délicatesse *f*.

trickle[1] ['trɪk(ə)l] *n* filet *m* (*d'eau etc*); **sales were down to a t.,** il n'y avait presque plus de ventes; **emigration is down to a t.,** l'émigration ne se fait plus qu'au compte-gouttes; **we've had a slow but steady t. of contributions,** les contributions nous arrivaient assez lentement mais de manière régulière; *El* **t. charge,** charge *f* en régime lent; *El* **t. charger,** chargeur *m* à régime lent.

trickle[2] **1** *vi* couler (goutte à goutte); **water was trickling down the wall,** l'eau dégoulinait *ou* coulait le long du mur; **tears were trickling down her cheeks,** les larmes coulaient le long de ses joues; **news is beginning to t. through** *or* **out from the devasted area,** on commence à recevoir peu à peu des nouvelles de la région sinistrée; **refugees are still trickling across the border,** les réfugiés continuent à passer la frontière au compte-gouttes; **the ball just trickled into the hole,** la balle a roulé tout doucement dans le trou. **2** *vt* laisser goutter, laisser tomber (*un liquide*) goutte à goutte.

trickling ['trɪklɪŋ] *n* gouttement *m*, écoulement *m* goutte à goutte.

trickster ['trɪkstər] *n* escroc *m*; **confidence t.,** voleur, -euse à l'américaine.

tricky ['trɪkɪ] *adj* **(a)** (*difficult*) difficile; (*awkward*) compliqué, délicat; **(b)** (*deceitful*) rusé; *F* **he's a t. customer,** c'est un rusé *ou* un malin.

tricolour, *US* **tricolor** ['trɪkələr] *n* drapeau *m* tricolore (*français*).

tricorn(e) ['traɪkɔːn] **1** *adj* (*chapeau*) tricorne. **2** *n* tricorne *m*.

tricuspid [traɪ'kʌspɪd] *adj* tricuspide.

tricycle ['traɪsɪk(ə)l] *n* tricycle *m*.

trident ['traɪdənt] *n* trident *m* (*de Neptune etc*).

tried [traɪd] *adj* **well t.,** (*remedy*) éprouvé, qui a fait ses preuves; **t. and trusted,** (*friend*) à toute épreuve.

triennial [traɪ'enɪəl] *adj* triennal, -aux; (*plant*) trisannuel.

triennially [traɪ'enɪəlɪ] *adv* tous les trois ans.

trier ['traɪər] *n* **to be a t.,** (*persevere*) ne pas se laisser décourager; (*do one's best*) toujours faire de son mieux.

trifle[1] ['traɪf(ə)l] *n* **(a)** (*insignificant thing*) chose *f* sans importance, bagatelle *f*, vétille *f*; (*money*) petite somme d'argent; **to quarrel over a mere t.,** se quereller pour un oui pour un non, se quereller sur des riens; **it's not exactly a t.,** ce n'est pas une petite affaire; **it was sold for a mere t.,** on l'a vendu pour un rien; **a t.,** un tout petit peu, (un) tant soit peu; **a t. too wide/too short,** trop large/trop court d'un doigt; **(b)** *Br Culin* diplomate *m*.

trifle[2] *vi* (*waste time*) s'amuser *ou* s'occuper à des futilités ou à des riens.

►trifle away *vtsep* (*waste*) gaspiller; **to t. one's time away,** gaspiller son temps.

►trifle with *vipo* (*toy with*) jouer *ou* badiner (**with,** avec); **to t. with sth,** manier nonchalamment (*sa canne etc*); jouer avec (*son lorgnon etc*); **she's not a woman to be trifled with,** on ne joue pas *ou* ne plaisante pas avec elle; **to t. with one's food,** manger du bout des dents, grignoter.

trifling ['traɪflɪŋ] **1** *adj* (*unimportant*) insignifiant, peu important, sans importance; (*negligible*) négligeable; **t. incidents,** menus incidents; **that's a t. matter,** ce n'est qu'une bagatelle; *Iron* **the t. sum of 10,000 francs,** la bagatelle de 10 000 francs. **2** *n* **(a)** (*toying*) badinage *m* (**with,** avec); **(b)** (*wasting*) gaspillage *m* du temps (*en futilités*).

triforium, *pl* **-ia** [traɪ'fɔːrɪəm, -ɪə] *n* triforium *m*.

trigger[1] ['trɪgər] *n* (*on gun*) détente *f*, gâchette *f*; *MecE &* (*on cine-camera*) déclencheur *m*; poussoir *m* (*à ressort*); **to be quick on the t.,** *F* **to be t. happy,** ne pas hésiter à tirer; *F* avoir la gâchette facile; **t. action,** déclenchement *m*; **t. finger,** index *m* (*avec lequel on presse sur la détente*); **my t. finger's itching,** la gâchette me démange; **t. mechanism,** mécanisme *m* de déclenchement.

trigger[2] *vt* **(a)** déclencher (*le départ du coup d'une arme à feu*); **(b)** déclencher, provoquer (*une explosion, une révolution, une réaction etc*).

►trigger off *vtsep esp Br* = **TRIGGER[2] (b)**.

trigonometric(al) [trɪgənə'metrɪk, -ɪk(ə)l] *adj* trigonométrique.

trigonometrically [trɪgənə'metrɪklɪ] *adv* trigonométriquement.

trigonometry [trɪgə'nɒmɪtrɪ] *n* trigonométrie *f*.

trike ['traɪk] *n* (*abbr* **tricycle**) tricycle *m*.

trilateral [traɪ'læt(ə)rəl] *adj* trilatéral, -aux.

trilby ['trɪlbɪ] *n* **t. (hat),** chapeau mou, feutre *m*.

trilingual [traɪ'lɪŋgw(ə)l] *adj* trilingue.

trill[1] [trɪl] *n* **(a)** *Mus* trille *m*; **(b)** chant perlé, trille (*des oiseaux*); **(c)** *Ling* consonne roulée.

trill[2] **1** *vi Mus etc* faire des trilles; **trilling laugh,** rire perlé. **2** *vt Mus etc* triller (*une note*); *Ling* **trilled consonant,** consonne roulée; **'I'm up here', trilled Penelope,** 'je suis en haut' dit Pénélope d'une voix flûtée.

trillion ['trɪljən] *n* **(a)** *Br* trillion *m* (10^{18}); **(b)** *Am* billion *m* (10^{12}).

trilogy ['trɪlədʒɪ] *n* trilogie *f*.

trim[1] [trɪm] *n* **(a)** (*of hair etc*) coupe *f* d'entretien; **just a t.,** (*said to hairdresser*) c'est simplement pour rafraîchir; **(b) in good t.,** en bon ordre; (*of person*) (*in good health*) en bonne santé; (*fit*) en (bonne) forme; **in fighting t.,** prêt pour le combat; **(c)** *Nau* assiette *f* (*sur l'eau*); *Av* équilibrage *m*; *Nau* orientation *f* (*des voiles*); **in t.,** équilibré; **out of t.,** déséquilibré; **sailing t.,** allure *f*; **(d)** (*on car*) garniture *f*; **interior t.,** garniture intérieure.

trim[2] *adj* soigné; *Nau* (*navire*) bien voilé; **a t. little yacht,** un petit yacht fringant; **to have a t. figure,** (*of person*) avoir une silhouette svelte; **a t. little garden,** un petit jardin coquet *ou* bien tenu.

trim[3] *vt* **(-mm-) (a)** (*cut*) tailler (*une haie, un arbre*); ébarber, rogner (*les tranches d'un livre*); égaliser, rafraîchir (*la barbe etc*); couper, rafraîchir (*les cheveux de qn*); **(b)** (*cut back, reduce*) **to t. (the wick of) a lamp,** moucher une lampe; *Culin* **to t. meat,** habiller *ou* parer la viande; **(c)** équilibrer (*un navire, un avion*); arrimer (*le chargement*); *Nau* orienter, appareiller (*les voiles*); **(d)** *Sewing etc* orner, garnir, agrémenter (*une robe etc*) (**with,** de); garnir (*un chapeau*); *Am* décorer (*l'arbre de Noël*); **trimmed with lace,** garni de dentelles.

►trim away *vtsep* (*excess growth, the unnecessary details, verbiage*) élaguer.

►trim down **1** *vtsep* (*growth, hedge etc, text, size of company, expenditure, budget*) réduire. **2** *vi* (*spend less*) réduire ses dépenses; (*get trimmer*) (*of company*) réduire ses effectifs.

►trim off *vtsep Culin etc* (*remove by cutting*) enlever (*le gras*); **to t. the fat off the meat,** dégraisser la viande; *Fig* **I think we could t. a couple of hours off the journey,** je pense que nous pourrions réduire ce voyage de quelques heures.

►trim up *vtsep* (*beard, hair*) rafraîchir.

trimaran ['traɪmərən] *n Nau* trimaran *m*.

trimester [tr(a)ɪ'mestər] *n* trimestre *m*.

trimmer ['trɪmər] *n* machine *f* à trancher (*le bois etc*); (*in papermaking, bookbinding etc*) massicot *m*; *Av* (dispositif) compensateur *m*; *Av Nau* équilibreur *m*.

trimming ['trɪmɪŋ] *n* **(a)** (*cutting*) taille *f* (*des haies, des arbres*); ébarbage *m* (*des tranches d'un livre, des pièces coulées*); **t. machine,** *Metal etc* ébarbeuse *f*; (*in bookbinding*) rogneuse *f*; **trimmings,** rognures *fpl*, ébarbures *fpl* (*de fer, de bois, de papier etc*); **(b)** (*cutting back, reduction*) réduction *f* (*des dépenses etc*); **(c)** *Nau Av* équilibrage *m* (*d'un navire, d'un avion*); arrimage *m* (*du chargement*); *Nau* orientation *f* (*des voiles*); **(d)** garnissage *m* (*de chapeaux, de linge etc*); *Culin* apprêt *m* (*d'un mets*); garniture *f*, ornement *m* (*de vêtements, de rideaux etc*); (*often pl*) passementerie *f* (*pour vêtements etc*); *Culin F* **the (usual) trimmings,** accompagnements *mpl*, garniture (*d'un plat*); **roast beef and all the trimmings,** du rosbif et tout ce qui l'accompagne; *Fig* **with all the trimmings,** avec tout le tralala.

trimness ['trɪmnɪs] *n* air soigné (*de qn, de qch*); sveltesse *f* (*de la silhouette*); apparence bien tenue (*d'un jardin etc*).

Trinidad ['trɪnɪdæd] *n* (île de) Trinidad *f*, (île de) la Trinité.

Trinity ['trɪnɪtɪ] *n* **(a)** *Rel* **the (Holy) T.,** la (sainte) Trinité; **T. Sunday,** (fête *f* de) la Trinité; **(b)** *Univ* **T. term,** troisième trimestre *m* (universitaire).

trinket ['trɪŋkɪt] *n* petit objet de parure; (*jewellery*) petit bijou, breloque *f*; (*worthless object*) bibelot *m*.

trinomial [traɪ'nəʊmɪəl] *adj & n Math* trinôme *m*.

trio, *pl* **-os** ['triːəʊ(z)] *n Mus etc* trio *m*.

trip[1] [trɪp] *n* **(a)** voyage *m*; (*outing*) excursion *f*; **business t.,** vogage d'affaires; **honeymoon t.,** voyage de noces; **to go on a shopping t.,** aller faire des courses; **the t. takes two hours,** on fait le trajet en deux heures; **he's away on a t. to Italy,** il est en voyage en Italie; **I'm afraid I'm going to have to make another t. to the loo,** je crois que je vais devoir refaire un tour aux cabinets; *Nau* **maiden t.,** premier voyage; **round t.,** (*circular journey*) voyage circulaire; *Nau* croisière *f*; (*journey there and back*) voyage d'aller et retour; *Br Sch* **school t.,** voyage *ou* excursion scolaire; *Br Sch* **geography field t.,** excursion *ou* (*longer*) voyage d'études de géographie;
(b) **(drug) t.,** voyage *m*, trip *m*; **to be on a t.,** faire un voyage *ou* un trip;
(c) (*stumble*) faux pas *m*; *Fig* (*mistake*) faute *f*, faux pas;
(d) *Sp* (*deliberate tripping up*) croc-en-jambe *m*, *pl* crocs-en-jambe, croche-pied *m*, *pl* croche-pieds; **t. wire,** = fil tendu (*en guise de traquenard ou d'avertisseur*); **that was a t.!,** il lui a fait un croc-en-jambe!
(e) *MecE* **t. gear,** déclic *m*; culbuteur *m* (*de bennes*).

trip[2] **(-pp-) 1** *vi* **(a)** (*step lightly*) aller d'un pas léger; **he tripped merrily into the room,** il entra dans la pièce d'un pas léger; **(b)** (*stumble*) trébucher, faire un faux pas; (*of horse*) broncher; **(c)** *MecE* (*of catch etc*) se déclencher; (*of part of mechanism*) basculer, culbuter; **(d)** *Sl* (*on drugs*) faire un voyage; **to be tripping,** être en voyage; **(e) to t. off the tongue,** (*of name, jingle etc*) bien couler. **2** *vt* **(a)** =**TRIP UP**[1]; **(b)** *MecE* déclencher (*une pièce de machine*); culbuter (*un levier etc*).

▸**trip over 1** *vi* trébucher et tomber. **2** *vipo* trébucher sur, buter contre (*qch*); *Fig* **you can't go anywhere here without tripping over celebrities,** par ici on ne peut pas faire un pas sans rentrer dans une célébrité.

▸**trip up 1** *vtsep* **(a)** (*cause to fall*) faire un croc-en-jambe *ou* un croche-pied à (*qn*); (*of obstacle*) faire trébucher, faire tomber (*qn*); **(b)** *Fig* (*catch out*) prendre (*qn*) en défaut *ou* en erreur. **2** *vi* **(a)** (*stumble*) trébucher, faire un faux pas; **(b)** (*be mistaken*) faire un faux pas, se tromper; **the robbers/fugitives finally tripped up,** les voleurs/fugitifs ont fini par faire un faux pas *ou* une erreur; **to t. up over a word,** trébucher sur un mot; **that's where we tripped up,** c'est là que nous avons fait erreur.

tripartite [traɪ'pɑːtaɪt] *adj* tripartite; (*divided into three*) divisé en trois, en trois parties.

tripe [traɪp] *n Culin* tripes *fpl*; *F* (*nonsense*) bêtises *fpl*; **that's all** *or* **a lot of t.,** tout ça c'est des sottises.

triphammer ['trɪphæmər] *n MecE* marteau *m* à bascule *ou* à soulèvement.

triphase ['traɪfeɪz] *adj El* (*courant*) triphasé.

triple[1] ['trɪp(ə)l] *adj* triple; *Constr* **t. glazing,** triple vitrage *m*; *Sp* **t. jump,** triple saut *m*; *Mus* **t. time,** mesure *f* ternaire *ou* à trois temps; *Hist* **the T. Alliance,** la Triplice, la triple Alliance.

triple[2] **1** *vt* tripler. **2** *vi* (se) tripler.

triplet ['trɪplɪt] *n* (*child*) triplé, -ée; *Mus* triolet *m*; (*in prosody*) tercet *m*.

triplex ['trɪpleks] *adj* (*planche*) en trois épaisseurs; (*machine*) à trois cylindres.

triplicate[1] ['trɪplɪkət] **1** *adj* triplé; (*copies*) triple. **2** *n* triple *m*, triplicata *m*; **invoice in t.,** facture *f* en triplicata *ou* en trois exemplaires.

triplicate[2] ['trɪplɪkeɪt] *vt* **(a)** tripler; **(b)** rédiger (*un document*) en trois exemplaires.

triply *adv* triplement.

tripod ['traɪpɒd] *n* trépied *m*.

tripos ['traɪpɒs] *n Eng Univ* = licence *f* ès lettres *ou* ès sciences (*à Cambridge*).

tripper ['trɪpər] *n esp Br* (*person*) excursionniste *mf*; **they're (just) day trippers,** ils sont (juste) venus passer la journée.

triptych ['trɪptɪk] *n Art* triptyque *m*.

trisect [traɪ'sekt] *vt Math etc* diviser, couper (*une ligne, un angle*) en trois.

trisyllabic [traɪsɪ'læbɪk] *adj* (*in prosody*) tris(s)yllabe, tris(s)yllabique.

trisyllable [traɪ'sɪləb(ə)l] *n* (*in prosody*) tris(s)yllabe *m*.

trite [traɪt] *adj* banal, -als; (*theme*) rebattu; **t. remarks,** (*banal remarks*) banalités *fpl*; (*commonplaces*) lieux communs.

tritely ['traɪtlɪ] *adv* banalement.

triteness ['traɪtnɪs] *n* banalité *f*.

tritium ['trɪtɪəm] *n Ch* tritium *m*.

triton ['traɪt(ə)n] *n (mollusc) & Myth* triton *m*.

triturate ['trɪtjəreɪt] *vt* triturer, broyer.

trituration [trɪtjə'reɪʃən] *n* trituration *f*.

triumph[1] ['traɪəmf] *n* triomphe *m* (**over,** sur); **to achieve great triumphs,** remporter de grands succès; **she came home in t.,** elle est rentrée chez elle en triomphe; **a look of t.,** un air triomphant; **the t. in his voice/eyes,** le triomphe dans sa voix/ses yeux.

triumph[2] *vi* triompher; **to t. over one's enemies,** (*defeat*) triompher de ses ennemis; **now it was my turn to t.,** c'était alors à moi de chanter *ou* crier victoire.

triumphal [traɪ'ʌmf(ə)l] *adj* triomphal, -aux; **to get a t. reception,** faire une arrivée triomphale.

triumphant [traɪ'ʌmfənt] *adj* triomphant; **the Church T.,** l'Église triomphante; **a t. expression,** un air de triomphe; **to be t. over s.o./sth.** triompher de qn/qch.

triumphantly [traɪ'ʌmfəntlɪ] *adv* en triomphe; (*to look at etc*) d'un air de triomphe; (*to say*) d'un ton triomphant.

triumvirate [traɪ'ʌmvɪrɪt] *n Hist* triumvirat *m*; *Fig* trio *m* (*de personnes*).

triune ['traɪjuːn] *adj Rel* d'une unité triple; en trois parties, trin.

trivet ['trɪvɪt] *n Culin* trépied *m*, chevrette *f*.

trivia ['trɪvɪə] *npl* vétilles *fpl*, petits riens; **to get bogged down in t.,** s'embarrasser de questions *fpl* sans importance.

trivial ['trɪvɪəl] *adj* **(a)** insignifiant, sans importance; (*person*) superficiel, frivole; **he's just being t.,** il plaisante; **t. matter,** bagatelle *f*; **t. offence,** peccadille *f*; **(b)** (*banal*) banal, -als, dépourvu d'orginalité.

triviality [trɪvɪ'ælɪtɪ] *n* **(a)** caractère insignifiant *f* (*d'une perte, d'une offense etc*); banalité *f*, manque *m* d'intérêt (*d'une observation etc*); **(b) to talk polite trivialities,** dire des futilités *ou* des banalités pour être poli.

trivialization [trɪvɪəlaɪ'zeɪʃən] *n* banalisation *f*.

trivialize ['trɪvɪəlaɪz] *vt* banaliser (*qch d'important*).

trochaic [trəʊ'keɪɪk] *adj & n* (*in prosody*) trochaïque *m*.

trochee ['trəʊkiː] *n* (*in prosody*) trochée *m*, chorée *m*.

trod, trodden *see* **TREAD**[2].

troglodyte ['trɒglədaɪt] *n* troglodyte *m*.

troilism ['trɔɪlɪz(ə)m] *m* amour *m ou* sexe *m* à trois.

Trojan ['trəʊdʒən] **1** *adj Hist* troyen; de Troie; **the T. War,** la guerre de Troie; **the T. Horse,** le cheval de Troie. **2** *n Hist* Troyen, -enne; **like a T.,** (*se battre*) vaillamment, avec courage; (*travailler*) sans relâche.

troll[1] [trəʊl] *n Fishing* cuiller *f*; moulinet *m* (*de canne à pêche*).

troll[2] **1** *vi Fishing* **to t. for pike,** pêcher le brochet à la cuiller. **2** *vt Arch* (*sing*) chantonner (*un air, une chanson*).

troll[3] *n Myth* troll *m*.

trolley ['trɒlɪ] *n* **(a)** *Br* (*cart*) chariot *m*; (*two wheeled*) diable *m*; **luggage t.,** chariot à bagages; **shopping t.,** (*in supermarket etc*) chariot, caddie *m*; **dinner** *or* **tea t.,** table roulante; **(b)** *Ind* **overhead t.,** chariot *m* (*de pont roulant etc*); **(c) t. (wheel),** (poulie *f* de) trolley *m*; *Am* **t. car,** tramway *m* à trolley; *F* **he's off his t.,** (*mad*) il débloque.

trolleybus ['trɒlɪbʌs] *n* trolleybus *m*.

trolling *n* pêche *f* à la cuiller.

trollop ['trɒləp] *n Old-fashioned* **(a)** (*dirty woman*) souillon *f*; **(b)** (*promiscuous woman*) putain *f*.

trombone [trɒm'bəʊn] *n Mus* trombone *m*.

trombonist [trɒm'bəʊnɪst] *n* tromboniste *mf*.

troop¹ [tru:p] *n* **(a)** groupe *m*, bande *f* (*de personnes*); **(b)** *Mil* (*unit*) peloton *m* (*de cavalerie, de l'arme blindée*); **troops,** troupes *fpl*; **to raise troops,** lever des troupes; **shock troops,** troupes de choc; **t. carrier,** (*vehicle*) véhicule blindé de transport de troupes; (*aircraft*) avion *m* de transport de troupes; **t. train,** train *m* militaire; **(c)** (*in scouting*) troupe *f*.

troop² **1** *vi* **to come trooping up,** s'attrouper, s'assembler; **to t. in/off/out/past,** entrer/partir/sortir/passer en groupe *ou* en bande. **2** *vt esp Br Mil* **to t. the colour,** faire la parade *ou* le salut du drapeau, présenter le drapeau.

trooper ['tru:pər] *n* **(a)** *Mil* (*soldier*) cavalier *m*, soldat *m* de la cavalerie; *US Austr* (*mounted police officer*) membre *m* de la police montée; (*horse*) cheval *m* de cavalerie; *US* **(state) t.,** ≈ C.R.S. *m*; *F* **to swear like a t.,** jurer comme un charretier; **(b)** = **TROOPSHIP**.

trooping ['tru:pɪŋ] *n esp Br Mil* **t. (of) the colour,** parade *f ou* salut *m* du drapeau, présentation *f* du drapeau.

troopship ['tru:pʃɪp] *n* (navire *m* de) transport *m* de troupes.

trophy ['trəʊfɪ] *n* (*hunting*) *& Sp Fig* trophée *m*.

tropic ['trɒpɪk] *n Astron Geog* tropique *m*; **the tropics,** les tropiques.

tropical ['trɒpɪk(ə)l] *adj* (*climat etc*) tropical, -aux; (*maladie etc*) des tropiques; **t. fish,** poissons tropicaux; **t. heat,** chaleur tropicale; **it's absolutely t. in here!,** il fait une chaleur torride ici!

tropism ['trəʊpɪz(ə)m] *n Biol* tropisme *m*.

troposphere ['trɒpəsfɪər] *n Met* troposphère *f*.

trot¹ [trɒt] *n* **(a)** *Horseriding etc* trot *m*; **at a brisk t.,** au grand trot; **to set off at a t.,** partir au trot; *F* **they've had 22 wins on the t.,** ils ont gagné la partie vingt-deux fois à la file *ou* de suite; **for five days on the t.,** pendant cinq jours de suite; *F* **to keep s.o. on the t.,** ne laisser aucun repos à qn; **(b)** *Sl* **to have the trots,** (*diarrhoea*) avoir la chiasse *ou* la courante.

trot² (-tt-) **1** *vi* **(a)** *Horseriding* trotter, aller au trot; (*of person*) trotter; (*of child etc*) trottiner; *F* **I must be trotting (along),** il faut que je file; *F* **I'll just t. up to the post office,** je vais juste faire un saut à la poste; *F* **he trotted off down the road,** il s'éloigna en trottinant dans la rue. **2** *vt* trotter (*un cheval*)

▸**trot out** *vtsep* **(a)** (*produce*) débiter (*excuses*); faire étalage de, débiter (*ses connaissances etc*); désenterrer (*de vieux griefs*); *F* **he can always t. out excuses,** il est toujours prêt à débiter des excuses; **(b)** (*parade*) faire trotter, faire parader (*un cheval*) (*devant un client*).

▸**trot round** **1** *vtas* **(a)** (*give guided tour of town etc*) faire voir la ville/*etc* à (*qn*); **(b)** (*escort*) **to t. s.o. round to the boss**/*etc*, accompagner qn chez le patron. **2** *vi* **I'll just t. round to the shops,** je vais faire un saut *ou* un tour en courses.

Trot [trɒt] *n Pol Sl* trotskyste *mf*.

troth [trəʊθ] *n Arch & Lit* **(a)** foi *f*; **by my t.!,** sur ma foi!; **(b) in t.,** en vérité.

Trotskyite ['trɒtskɪaɪt] *adj & n* trotskyste *mf*.

trotter ['trɒtər] *n* **(a)** (*horse*) cheval *m* de trot, trotteur, -euse; **(b)** *Culin* **sheep's/pigs'/trotters,** pieds *mpl* de mouton/de porc; *F* **trotters,** (*feet*) pieds.

trotting ['trɒtɪŋ] *n* trot *m*; **t. race,** course *f* de trot (attelé).

troubadour ['tru:bədʊər] *n Lit* troubadour *m*.

trouble¹ ['trʌb(ə)l] *n* **(a)** (*difficulty, problem*) ennui *m*, difficulté *f*, problème *m*; **he told me his troubles,** il m'a raconté ses malheurs *ou* ses problèmes; **her troubles are over,** elle est au bout de ses malheurs *ou* de ses ennuis; **in one's time of t.,** quand on a des ennuis; **money troubles,** soucis *mpl* d'argent; **what's the t.?,** qu'est-ce qu'il y a?, quel est le problème?; **we must get to the root of the t.,** il faut chercher la source du mal; **the t. is that...,** l'ennui *ou* le problème c'est que...; **the t. with you** *or* **your t. is you don't think,** ton problème *ou* le problème chez toi c'est que tu ne réfléchis pas; **their t. was (that) they didn't have enough time,** le problème c'est qu'ils n'ont pas eu assez de temps; **the t. with these machines is (that) they're too complicated,** le problème avec ces machines c'est qu'elles sont trop compliquées; **you'll have t. with him,** il va vous causer des difficultés *ou* des ennuis; **this new machine's/system's more t. than it's worth,** cette nouvelle machine/ce nouveau système pose plus de problèmes qu'elle/qu'il n'en résoud; **this machine's been** *or* **given nothing but t.,** cette machine ne nous a apporté que des problèmes; **to be in t.,** avoir des ennuis *ou* des difficultés; **to get into t.,** s'attirer des ennuis *ou* des désagréments; *Old-fashioned F* (*of unmarried woman*) tomber enceinte; **to get into t. with the police,** avoir affaire à la police; **to get s.o. into t., to make t. for s.o.,** créer *ou* susciter des ennuis à qn; *F* **to get a girl into t.,** mettre une fille enceinte; **to get s.o. out of t.,** tirer qn d'affaire; **to keep out of t.,** éviter des ennuis; **to be looking** *or* **asking for t.,** (*cause problems for the future*) se préparer des ennuis; *F* **he was asking for t., the way he drank,** il cherchait des ennuis à boire comme ça; **are you looking for t.?,** (*said aggressively*) tu cherches les ennuis *ou* la casse?; **that's asking for t. not locking it,** ne pas la fermer, c'est tenter le diable; **to make** *or* **cause t.,** semer la discorde; **to make t. for oneself,** se créer des ennuis; **there will be t.,** il va y avoir du vilain *ou* *F* de la casse;

(b) (*disorder, unrest*) désordre *m*; **there was t. in the streets,** il y a eu des désordres dans la rue; **labour troubles,** conflits ouvriers; **the Troubles,** (*in N. Ireland*) les troubles;

(c) (*physical, medical, mechanical*) **eye t.,** affection *f* de l'œil; (*sight disorder*) troubles *mpl* de vision; **stomach t.,** troubles digestifs; **to have heart t.,** être malade du cœur; **to locate** *or* **trace the t.,** (*in machine, engine etc*) trouver la source de la panne; **my eyes have been giving me some t.,** j'ai des problèmes avec mes yeux; **the car/engine hasn't given me any t.,** je n'ai eu aucun problème avec la voiture/le moteur; *Aut etc* **engine t.,** panne de moteur; *F* **he's/she's got woman/man t.,** il/elle a des problèmes de cœur; **t. spot,** point *m* névralgique;

(d) (*disturbance, bother*) dérangement *m*, peine *f*, mal *m*; **to take the t. to do sth, to go to the t. of doing sth,** prendre *ou* se donner la peine de faire qch; **to go to** *or* **put oneself to** *or* **to take a great deal of t.,** se donner beaucoup de mal *ou* de peine; **it's not worth the t.,** cela n'en vaut pas la peine *ou* le dérangement; **nothing's too much t. for him,** rien ne lui coûte; **(it's) no t.,** (ça ne pose) aucun problème; **to have had all one's t. for nothing,** en être pour sa peine, s'être donné de la peine *ou* du mal pour rien.

trouble² **1** *vt* **(a)** (*afflict*) affliger, chagriner (*qn*); (*worry*) inquiéter, préoccuper (*qn*); affliger, faire souffrir (*qn*); **I'm troubled about his future,** son avenir me préoccupe *ou* m'inquiète; **don't let it t. you!,** que cela ne vous inquiète pas!, ne vous tourmentez pas à ce sujet!; **how long has this cough been troubling you?,** depuis combien de temps souffrez-vous de cette toux?; **her conscience troubled her,** sa conscience la troublait, elle avait des problèmes de conscience;

(b) (*disturb, put out*) déranger, incommoder (*qn*); (*put to trouble*) donner de la peine à (*qn*); **I'm so sorry to t. you,** excusez-moi de vous déranger; *usu Iron* **may I t. you to shut the door?,** cela vous dérangerait-il de fermer la porte?

2 *vi* (*put oneself out*) se déranger, se mettre en peine; **don't t. to write,** ne vous donnez pas la peine d'écrire; **don't t.!, you needn't t.!,** ne vous dérangez pas!; **he didn't even t. to ...,** il n'a même pas pris la peine de ... .

troubled ['trʌbld] *adj* **(a)** (*worried*) inquiet, -ète, troublé; **t. period,** (*of history*) époque *f* de troubles; **t. sleep,** sommeil agité; **a t. soul,** une âme agitée *ou* troublée; **(b)** (*liquid*) trouble.

trouble-free ['trʌb(ə)lfri:] *adj* sans problèmes.

troublemaker ['trʌb(ə)lmeɪkər] *n* fomentateur, -trice de troubles, agitateur, -trice.

troubleshooter ['trʌb(ə)lʃu:tər] *n Pol Ind etc* médiateur, -trice, conciliateur, -trice; (*for machinery etc*) dépanneur *m*.

troubleshooting ['trʌb(ə)lʃu:tɪŋ] *n Pol Ind etc* médiation *f*, conciliation *f*.

troublesome ['trʌb(ə)lsəm] *adj* ennuyeux; (*enfant*) énervant; (*rival*) gênant; (*toux*) pénible.

troubling ['trʌblɪŋ] *adj* inquiétant.

troublous ['trʌbləs] *adj Arch* troublé, agité.

trough [trɒf] *n* **(a) (feeding) t.,** auge *f*, mangeoire *f*; **drinking t.,** abreuvoir *m*; **(b)** *Tech* auge *f* (*de meule*); *Ch Phys* cuve *f*, cuvette *f* (*à mercure, à eau*); *El* **accumulator t.,** bac *m* d'accumulateur; **kneading t.,** pétrin *m* (*de boulanger*); **(c)** *Geol* auge *f*; **(d)** *Phys Math* creux *m* (*d'une onde, d'un graphique*); *Met* dépression *f* (*barométrique*), zone *f* dépressionnaire; **t. of the sea,** creux de la lame.

trounce [traʊns] *vt* **(a)** *Old-fashioned* (*beat*) rosser (*qn*); **(b)** *Sp* (*defeat heavily*) écraser, battre à plate(s) couture(s).

trouncing ['traʊnsɪŋ] *n* **(a)** *Old-fashioned* (*beating*) raclée *f*; **(b)** *Sp* (*heavy defeat*) défaite écrasante; **Wales gave France a t.,** le pays de Galles a battu la France à plate(s) couture(s).

troupe [tru:p] *n* troupe *f* (*de comédiens etc*).

trouper ['tru:pər] *n Th* membre *m* d'une *ou* de la troupe;

Fig **he's an old t.,** c'est un vieux de la vieille; *Fig* **a good reliable t. like her,** un bon vieux soldat comme elle.

trouser ['traʊzər] *n esp Br* **(pair of) trousers,** pantalon *m*; *F* **she's the one who wears the trousers,** c'est elle qui porte la culotte; *F* **to be caught with one's trousers down,** être pris au dépourvu; **short trousers,** shorts *mpl*; **when I was still in short trousers,** quand j'étais encore en culottes courtes; **t. press,** presse-pantalon *m*, *pl* presse-pantalons; **t. suit,** tailleur-pantalon *m*, *pl* tailleurs-pantalons.

trousseau ['truːsəʊ] *n* trousseau *m*.

trout [traʊt] *n* **(a)** (*inv in pl*) (*fish*) truite *f*; **rainbow t.,** truite arc-en-ciel; **salmon t.,** truite saumonée; **t. fishing,** pêche *f* à la truite; **(b)** *Sl* (*woman*) **old t.,** vieille bique.

trove [trəʊv] *n* = **TREASURE-TROVE (a)**.

trowel ['traʊəl] *n Constr* truelle *f*, gâche *f*; (*in gardening*) déplantoir *m*, houlette *f*.

troy [trɔɪ] *n* **t. (weight),** poids *m* troy (pour l'or et l'argent); **t. ounce,** once *f* troy (31,1 g,).

Troy [trɔɪ] *n* Troie *f*.

truancy ['truːənsɪ] *n Sch* absentéisme *m* scolaire.

truant ['truːənt] *n Sch* élève absent (*de l'école*) sans permission; **to play t.,** faire l'école buissonnière.

truce [truːs] *n* trêve *f*; **let's call it a t.!,** faisons une trêve!

truck¹ [trʌk] *n* **(a)** (*lorry*) camion *m*; (*small vehicle*) chariot *m*, fardier *m*; *Min* berline *f*, benne *f*, bac *m*; **fork-lift t.,** chariot élévateur à fourche; *Aut* **heavy t.,** gros camion, poids lourd; *Am* **wrecking t.,** camion de dépannage, dépanneuse *f*; **(b)** *Rail* wagon *m* (*à marchandises*); **cattle t.,** fourgon *m* à bestiaux.

truck² **1** *vt* camionner (*des marchandises*). **2** *vi esp Am* (*drive a truck*) être conducteur de camion, être camionneur.

truck³ *n* **(a)** (*barter*) troc *m*, échange *m*; **(b)** *Hist* **t. (system),** paiement *m* des ouvriers en nature; **(c)** *F* (*relations*) rapports *mpl*, relations *fpl* (*avec qn*); **I'll have no t. with him,** je ne veux rien avoir à faire avec lui; **(d)** *Am* produits maraîchers; **t. gardener** *or* **farmer,** maraîcher *m*.

truckdriver ['trʌkdraɪvər], **trucker** ['trʌkər] *n Am* camionneur *m*, routier *m*.

trucking ['trʌkɪŋ] *n esp Am* camionnage *m*; **t. company,** entreprise *f* de transports routiers.

truckle¹ ['trʌk(ə)l] *n* **t. bed,** lit *m* gigogne.

truckle² *vi Lit* ramper, s'abaisser (**to,** devant).

truckstop ['trʌkstɒp] *n esp Am* café *m* de routiers, routier *m*.

truculence ['trʌkjʊləns] *n* agressivité *f*.

truculent ['trʌkjʊlənt] *adj* agressif.

truculently ['trʌkjʊləntlɪ] *adv* agressivement.

trudge¹ [trʌdʒ] *n* marche *f* pénible; **a long t.,** un trajet long et pénible.

trudge² *vi* marcher lourdement *ou* péniblement, se traîner; **we trudged across the sodden fields,** nous nous sommes traînés à travers les champs détrempés; **I've been trudging around the shops all day,** je me suis traîné péniblement dans les magasins toute la journée.

►trudge along *vi* (*walk heavily, with difficulty*) cheminer *ou* avancer péniblement, se traîner.

true [truː] **1** *adj* **(a)** vrai; (*accurate*) exact; **t. account,** récit fidèle *ou* exact; **t. adventures,** aventures vécues; **it's only too t.,** ce n'est que trop vrai; **it is t. that ...,** il est vrai que ...; **if it were t. that ...,** s'il était vrai que ... *+sub.*; **to come t.,** (*of wish etc*) se réaliser; **this also holds t. for ...,** il en est de même pour ...; **how t.!, how very t.!,** c'est bien vrai!; **that's all too t. I'm afraid,** ce n'est que trop vrai, malheureusement; **I can't believe it's t.,** je n'arrive pas à le croire; **it's getting late — t.,** il se fait tard — tu as raison;

(b) (*genuine*) véritable; (*real*) vrai, réel; **t. repentance,** repentir *m* sincère *ou* véritable; **her t. nature,** son véritable caractère; **he's a t. Scot,** c'est bien un Écossais; **to get a t. idea of the situation,** se faire une idée juste de la situation; **t. horizon,** horizon réel; **t. north,** nord *m* géographique; *Tech* **t. time,** temps vrai, heure vraie; **t. centre,** centre réel;

(c) *MecE Carp* juste, droit, rectiligne; (*terrain*) égal, uni; **to make a piece t.,** ajuster une pièce; *Lit* **his aim was t.,** (*was a good shot*) il était bon tireur; (*hit target*) il a visé juste; **the table isn't t.,** la table n'est pas d'aplomb;

(d) (*faithful*) fidèle, loyal; **to be t. to a friend,** être loyal envers *ou* fidèle à un ami; **to be t. to oneself,** ne pas se démentir; **to be t. to one's** *or* **a promise,** rester fidèle à une promesse; **t. to life,** qui correspond bien à la réalité; **t. to form he ...,** typiquement, il ...; *Old-fashioned* **he's a t. blue,** c'est un homme loyal *ou* fidèle; **t. friend,** ami loyal; **t. love,** grand amour, amour véritable; **a jury of twelve good men and t.,** un jury de douze citoyens de bonne renommée;

(e) (*of voice, instrument*) juste.

2 *adv* **(a)** *F Old-fashioned* (*truthfully*) vraiment;

(b) (*chanter, viser*) juste; **to run t.,** (*of wheel*) tourner rond *ou* sans balourd; **the wheel is not running t.,** la roue est désaxée *ou* faussée.

3 *n MecE etc* **out of t.,** (*of vertical post, member etc*) hors d'aplomb; (*of horizontal member etc*) dénivelé; (*of metal plate etc*) gauchi, gondolé; (*of wheel rim*) voilé; (*of axle etc*) faussé, dévoyé; (*of timber*) déjeté; (*of wheel*) décentré, excentré, désaxé.

►true up *vtsep* mettre (*qch*) bien en place.

trueborn ['truːbɔːn] *adj Old-fashioned* vrai, véritable; **a t. Englishman,** un vrai Anglais d'Angleterre.

truehearted [truː'hɑːtɪd] *adj Old-fashioned* fidèle, loyal, -aux.

true(-)love ['truːlʌv] *n* bien-aimé(e); **t. knot** (*also* **true lover's knot**), lacs *m* d'amour (en 8 couché).

truffle ['trʌf(ə)l] *n* truffe *f*; *Br* **(rum) t.,** truffe *f* au rhum; **t. hound,** chien truffier.

trug [trʌg] *n* panier *m ou* corbeille *f* de jardinier.

truism ['truːɪz(ə)m] *n* truisme *m*, vérité *f* de La Palice, lapalissade *f*; **it is a t. that...,** c'est un lieu commun de dire que ... .

truly ['truːlɪ] *adv* **(a)** vraiment, véritablement; **a t. difficult situation,** une situation vraiment difficile; **I am t. grateful to her,** je lui suis sincèrement reconnaissant; **it may t. be called tragic,** on peut bien le qualifier de tragique; **I t. believe that ...,** je crois vraiment *ou* sincèrement que ...; **yours t.,** (*letter ending*) = je vous prie d'agréer *ou* de croire à mes sentiments distingués; *F* **yours t.,** votre serviteur; *F* **meanwhile yours t. had left,** entretemps mézigue *ou* votre serviteur était parti; **(b)** (*in truth*) en vérité, à vrai dire; *F* **(really and) t.?,** vrai de vrai?; **(c)** (*servir qn*) fidèlement, loyalement.

trump¹ [trʌmp] *n Arch & Lit* trompette *f*; **the last t.,** la trompette du jugement dernier.

trump² *n Cards* **t. (card),** atout *m*; **spades are trumps,** c'est pique atout; **to play trumps,** jouer l'atout; **to call no trumps,** appeler *ou* demander sans-atout; *F* **she turned up trumps,** elle a fait des miracles; *Fig* **to play one's t. card,** jouer son atout.

trump³ *vt Cards* couper (*une carte*) avec l'atout.

►trump up *vtsep* (*invent*) inventer, forger (*une excuse*); **to t. up a charge against s.o.,** forger *ou* fabriquer une accusation contre qn; **trumped-up story,** histoire inventée.

trumpery ['trʌmpərɪ] **1** *n* (*worthless objects*) friperie *f*, camelote *f*; (*nonsense*) absurdités *mpl*. **2** *adj esp Lit* (*marchandises*) de camelote; (*argument etc*) spécieux.

trumpet¹ ['trʌmpɪt] *n* **(a)** *Mus* trompette *f*; *Fig* **to blow one's own t.,** chanter ses propres louanges; **t. call,** coup *m ou* sonnerie *f* de trompette; **first t.,** (*in orchestra*) première trompette; *Mil* **t. major,** trompette-major *m*, *pl* trompettes-majors; **t. player,** joueur, -euse de trompette, trompettiste *mf*, trompette *m*; **(b)** pavillon *m* (*de phonographe, de cornet avertisseur etc*); **(ear) t.,** cornet *m* acoustique.

trumpet² *v* (-t-) **1** *vi* trompeter, sonner de la trompette; (*of elephant*) barrir. **2** *vt esp Lit* publier (*qch*) à cor et à cri; célébrer (*un succès*) à grand bruit.

trumpeter ['trʌmpɪtər] *n Mil* trompette *m*; (*by profession*) trompettiste *mf*, trompette *m*.

trumpeting ['trʌmpɪtɪŋ] *n* sonnerie *f* de trompette; (*of elephant*) barrit *m*, barrissement *m*.

truncate [trʌŋ'keɪt] *vt* tronquer (*un corps, un texte etc*).

truncated ['trʌŋkeɪtɪd] *adj* (*crystals etc*) tronqué; *Math* **t. cone,** tronc *m* de cône, cône tronqué.

truncheon ['trʌn(t)ʃən] *n* matraque *f*, casse-tête *m inv*; (*esp for directing traffic*) bâton *m*; **rubber t.,** matraque en caoutchouc.

trundle¹ ['trʌnd(ə)l] *n* **t. bed,** lit *m* gigogne.

trundle² **1** *vt* faire rouler, faire courir (*un cerceau etc*); pousser (*une brouette, une voiture à bras*); **they trundled him in on the stretcher,** ils l'ont amené en le faisant rouler sur un brancard. **2** *vi* (*of hoop etc*) rouler.

trunk [trʌŋk] *n* **(a)** tronc *m* (*d'arbre*, du corps); *Art* torse *m*; *Anat* tronc (*d'artère etc*); *Archit* fût *m* (*d'une colonne*); **t. call,** appel interurbain; **t. line,** *Rail* ligne principale, grande ligne; *Tel* l'inter *m*; **t. roads,** grandes routes; **(b)** (*luggage*) malle *f*; **(c)** *Am Aut* coffre *m*; **(d)** trompe *f* (*d'éléphant*); **(e)** **trunks,** maillot *m* (de bain), slip *m* de bain (*pour hommes*); (*underpants*) *slip m*.

trunnion ['trʌnjən] *n Mil MecE* tourillon *m*.

truss¹ [trʌs] *n* **(a)** *Med* bandage *m* herniaire; **(b)** *Constr* armature *f* (*de poutre etc*); ferme *f* (*de comble, de pont*); cintre *m* (*de voûte*); *Constr* treillis *m* (*métallique*); **t. girder,** poutre armée; (*assembly*) ferme *f*; **(c)** touffe *f* (*de fleurs*).

truss² *vt* **(a)** *Constr Tech* armer, renforcer (*une poutre etc*); **trussed beam** *or* **girder,** poutre armée *ou* renforcée; **(b)** *Culin* trousser, brider (*une volaille*).

►truss up *vtsep* (*tie up*) ligoter (*qn*); **trussed up like a chicken,** ficelé comme un poulet.

trust¹ [trʌst] *n* **(a)** confiance *f* (**in,** en); **to put one's t. in s.o.,** mettre sa confiance en qn, se reposer sur qn; **to put one's t. in sth,** se reposer sur qch; **I took what you said on t.,** je t'ai cru sur parole, je t'ai fait confiance;
(b) (*hope*) espérance *f*, espoir *m*; **it is my firm t. that ...,** j'espère avec confiance que ...; j'ai le ferme espoir que ...;
(c) (*responsibility*) responsabilité *f*, charge *f*; **to be in a position of t.,** occuper un poste de confiance; **he committed it to my t.,** il l'a confié à mes soins *ou* à ma garde; **a sacred t.,** un dépôt sacré;
(d) *Jur* fidéicommis *m*, fiducie *f*; **to hold in t.,** tenir (*qch*) par fidéicommis; administrer (*un bien etc*) par fidéicommis; *Br* **National T.,** = société *f* pour la conservation des sites et monuments;
(e) *Ind etc* trust *m*, syndicat *m*, cartel *m*; **brains t.,** brain-trust *m*, *pl* brain-trusts; *Fin* **investment t.,** trust *ou* société *f* de placement; **unit t.,** société d'investissement à capital variable;
(f) *Pol* **t. territories,** territoires *mpl* sous tutelle.

trust² **1** *vt* **(a)** se fier à; **she's not to be trusted,** on ne peut pas se fier à elle; **are the figures to be trusted?,** est-ce que ces chiffres sont fiables?; **I don't t. you with money,** je ne te confierais pas mon argent; **you can't t. anyone nowadays,** on ne peut faire confiance *ou* **se fier à personne de nos jours; I don't t. you with her!,** je ne la laisserais pas seule avec toi!; **I couldn't t. myself not to say anything,** je ne pourrais pas résister à l'envie de dire quelque chose; **to t. s.o. with sth,** confier qch à qn; **to t. s.o. to do sth,** se fier à qn du soin de faire qch; *F* **t. him to say that!,** c'est bien de lui!; *F* **I've lost it – t. you!,** je l'ai perdu – ça c'est tout toi!; **I couldn't t. myself to speak,** j'étais trop ému pour me risquer à rien dire; *F* **she won't t. him out of her sight,** elle le surveille tout le temps;
(b) (*entrust*) **to t. sth to s.o.,** confier qch à qn *ou* aux soins de qn *ou* à la garde de qn;
(c) **to t. (that) ...,** (*hope*) espérer que; (*express wish that*) exprimer le vœu (que + *sub*); **I t. he is not ill,** j'espère bien qu'il n'est pas malade.
2 *vi* **to t. to luck,** s'en remettre au hasard.

►trust in *vipo* (*put one's hopes in*) mettre ses espérances *ou* son espoir en (*qch*); **to t. in God,** s'abandonner à Dieu; **I want someone I can t. in,** (*have confidence in*) il me faut une personne de confiance.

trusted ['trʌstɪd] *adj* (*personne*) de confiance; **tried and t.,** (*friend, remedy, method*) éprouvé; (*ami*) à toute épreuve.

trustee [trʌs'tiː] *n* **(a)** *Jur* fidéicommissaire *m*, fiduciaire *m*; (*with powers of attorney*) mandataire *m*; **the Public T.,** le curateur de l'État aux successions; **(b)** administrateur *m*, curateur *m* (*d'un musée etc*); **board of trustees,** conseil *m* d'administration.

trusteeship [trʌs'tiːʃɪp] *n* **(a)** *Jur* fidéicommis *m*; **(b)** (*of museum etc*) administration *f*, curatelle *f*; **(c)** *Pol* tutelle *f*.

trustful ['trʌstfʊl] *adj* plein de confiance, confiant.

trustfully ['trʌstfəlɪ] *adv* avec confiance.

trustfulness ['trʌstfʊlnɪs] *n* confiance *f*.

trustiness ['trʌstɪnɪs] *n* fidélité *f*, loyauté *f*.

trusting ['trʌstɪŋ] *adj* plein de confiance, confiant.

trustingly ['trʌstɪŋlɪ] *adv* avec confiance.

trustworthiness ['trʌstwɜːðɪnɪs] *n* (*person*) loyauté *f*, honnêteté *f*; (*of testimony, account etc*) crédibilité *f*, véracité *f*.

trustworthy ['trʌstwɜːðɪ] *adj* (*person*) digne de confiance *ou* de foi; (*information*) digne de foi; (*testimony*) irrécusable; **a t. person,** une personne de confiance.

trusty ['trʌstɪ] *adj Arch & Lit* sûr, fidèle, loyal, -aux; *Hum* **my t. typewriter,** ma bonne vieille machine à écrire.

truth [truːθ, *pl* truːðz] *n* vérité *f*; **to speak** *or* **tell the t.,** dire la vérité; *Jur* **the t., the whole t., and nothing but the t.,** la vérité, toute la vérité, rien que la vérité; **the real** *or* **plain** *or* **unvarnished** *or* **honest t.,** la pure vérité, la vérité pure et simple; **in t.,** en vérité; **the t. (of the matter) is** *or* **to tell the t., I forgot it,** pour dire la vérité *ou* à dire vrai je l'ai oublié; **... and that's the t.,** ... et voilà la vérité; **there's some t. in what you say,** il y a du vrai dans ce que vous dites; **there's not a word of t. in it,** il n'y a pas un brin de vérité là-dedans; *Prov* **t. will out,** la vérité finit toujours par se découvrir; **I told him a few home truths,** je lui ai dit son fait *ou* ses quatre vérités; **t. drug,** sérum *m* de vérité.

truthful ['truːθfʊl] *adj* (*person*) sincère, honnête, véridique; (*témoignage etc*) vrai; (*portrait etc*) fidèle; **to be t.,** dire la vérité, être sincère *ou* honnête.

truthfully ['truːθfəlɪ] *adv* (*to speak, answer, claim etc*) sincèrement, honnêtement, véridiquement; (*to portray etc*) fidèlement.

truthfulness ['truːθfʊlnɪs] *n* véracité *f* (*d'une personne, d'une assertion etc*); fidélité *f* (*d'un portrait etc*).

try¹ [traɪ] *n* **(a)** essai *m*, tentative *f*; **to have a t. at (doing) sth,** essayer de faire qch; (*experiment with*) s'essayer à qch; **I had a t. at skin-diving,** je me suis essayé à la plongée sous-marine; **let's have a t.!,** essayons toujours!; **can I have a t.?,** (est-ce que) je peux essayer?; **I think I'll have a t. for this job,** je crois que je vais me présenter pour ce travail; **you've already had three tries,** vous avez déjà essayé trois fois *ou* eu trois chances; **ok you can have one more t.,** bon d'accord, tu as encore une chance; **go on, give it a t.,** (*activity*) allez, essaie; (*food*) allez, goûte; **at the first t.,** du premier coup; **it won't be easy but it's worth a. t.,** ça ne va pas être facile mais ça vaut la peine *ou* le coup d'essayer; **worth a t.?,** ça vaut le coup d'essayer?;
(b) *Rugby* essai *m*; **to score a t.,** marquer un essai.

try² *v* (*pt & pp* **tried** [traɪd]) **1** *vt* **(a)** (*try out*) essayer; **here, t. my pen,** tenez, essayez avec mon stylo; **to t. a dish,** goûter (à) un mets; **t. some,** (*food*) goûtes-y; **I'll t. anything once,** il faut tout essayer dans la vie;
(b) essayer, tenter; **to t. an experiment,** tenter une expérience; **to t. one's strength against s.o.,** se mesurer avec qn; **to t. the door/the window,** essayer (d'ouvrir) la porte/la fenêtre;
(c) **t. (asking) Jane,** demande à Jane; **have you tried the chemist's?,** tu as essayé le pharmacien?; **t. washing them by hand,** essayez de les laver à la main; **to t. to do** *or F* **and do sth,** tâcher *ou* essayer de faire qch; **she tried to smile,** elle a essayé de sourire; **he was trying hard to keep back the tears,** il faisait de grands efforts pour retenir ses larmes; **it's worth trying,** cela vaut la peine d'essayer;
(d) vérifier (*un mécanisme*); essayer (*un cordage, une voiture*);
(e) *Jur* juger (*une cause, un accusé*); *US* (*of advocate*) plaider (*une cause*); **to be tried for theft,** passer en correctionnelle pour vol;
(f) (*test*) éprouver (*qn*); mettre (*qn, qch*) à l'épreuve; faire l'épreuve de (*qch*); *Lit* (*afflict*) éprouver, affliger; **to t. s.o.'s courage,** mettre à l'épreuve le courage de qn; **a people sorely tried,** une nation fort *ou* durement éprouvée; **to t. s.o.'s patience,** mettre la patience de qn à l'épreuve; **to t. one's eyes (reading),** se fatiguer les yeux (à lire).
2 *vi* faire un effort *ou* des efforts; **to t. again,** essayer de nouveau; **you must t. harder,** il faut faire de plus grands efforts; **at least you tried;** au moins tu as *ou* auras essayé; **he didn't really t.,** il n'a pas vraiment essayé; **you weren't really trying,** tu n'as pas vraiment fait d'efforts; **go on then, t.!,** alors vas-y, essaie!; **... and she wasn't even trying,** ... et elle l'a fait sans même s'efforcer; **just you t.!,** essaie un peu pour voir!; **I'd like to see you t.!,** je voudrais bien t'y voir!

►try for *vipo* (*attempt to obtain*) tâcher d'obtenir (*qch*); **to t. for a job,** poser sa candidature à un emploi; **he's trying for a place at music school,** il essaie d'obtenir une place à l'école de musique; *Sp etc* **she's trying for the record,** elle essaie de battre le record.

►try on *vtsep* **(a)** (*test clothes, shoes for size, appearance*) essayer; **(b)** *F* **to t. it on (with s.o.),** bluffer; **they're just trying it on,** ils bluffent, c'est du bluff; **you're (just) trying it on!,** ça ne marche pas *ou* ne prend pas!; **she tried it on with my husband,** elle a essayé de lever mon mari.

►try out *vtsep* (*test*) faire l'essai de (*qch*); essayer, expérimenter (*un nouveau procédé*); **to t. sth out on s.o.,** essayer *ou* expérimenter qch sur qn; **they're trying him out in goal,** ils l'essaient *ou* l'ont mis à l'essai comme gardien de but.

trying ['traɪɪŋ] **1** *adj* (*difficult*) difficile, pénible; (*hard*) dur; (*vexing*) vexant, contrariant, *F* agaçant; **t. light,** lumière fatigante (*pour les yeux*). **2** *n Jur* jugement *m* (*d'une cause, d'un accusé*).

trying on *n* essayage *m* (*de vêtements*).

try-on ['traɪɒn] *n Br F* bluff *m*; **it's just a t.-on,** c'est du bluff.

try-out ['traɪaʊt] *n* premier essai, essai préliminaire (*d'une machine etc*); *Am Th* audition *f*; *Sp* épreuve *f* de sélection; **to give s.o./sth a t.-o.,** mettre qn à l'essai/essayer qch.
tryst [trɪst] *n Lit* rendez-vous amoureux.
tsar [tsɑːr] *n* tsar *m*, czar *m*.
tsarevitch ['tsɑːrəvɪtʃ] *n* tsarévitch *m*, czarévitch *m*.
tsarina [tsɑː'riːnə] *n* tsarine *f*, czarine *f*.
tsarist ['tsɑːrɪst] *adj & n* tsariste *mf*.
tsetse ['t(s)etsɪ] *n* **t. (fly),** (mouche *f*) tsé-tsé *f*.
tsp *Culin* (*abbr* **teaspoon, teaspoonful**) cu. à cu; **2 tsp sugar,** (*in recipe*) 2 cu. à c. de sucre.
TT [tiː'tiː] *n* **(a)** *Sp* (*abbr* **Tourist Trophy**) = course *f* motocycliste; **(b)** (*abbr* **teetotal**) **I'm TT,** je ne bois pas d'alcool.
tub [tʌb] *n* **(a)** (*container*) baquet *m*, bac *m*; bac, caisse *f* (*à fleurs, à arbustes*); (*in papermaking*) bac, cuve *f*; baquet (*à lessive*); (*in washing machine*) cuve; carton *m* (*de glaces, de crème etc*); **a t. of ice-cream,** (*individual*) un pot de glace; **t. chair,** (fauteuil *m*) crapaud *m*; **(b)** (*bathtub*) baignoire *f*; **a hot t.,** un bain chaud; **(c)** *Nau F* **old t.,** vieux sabot; **(d)** *F* (*in rowing*) canot *m* d'entraînement.
tuba ['tjuːbə] *n Mus* tuba *m*.
tubby ['tʌbɪ] *adj F* (*person*) dodu, boulot, -otte.
tube [tjuːb] *n* **(a)** tube *m*; (*pipe*) tuyau *m*; tube (*de couleur, de dentifrice*); *Austr F* boîte *f* (*de bière*); *Med etc* drain *m* (*pour plaie profonde*); tube, canule *f*, sonde *f* (*pour tubage*); **angle** *or* **bent t.,** tube coudé; **seamless t.,** tube sans soudure; *MecE etc* **boiler t.,** tube de chaudière; *Aut etc* **inner t.,** chambre *f* à air (*d'un pneu*); *Ch Phys etc* **test t.,** éprouvette *f*; **stomach t.,** sonde pour tubage gastrique; *Br F* **the t.,** (*London underground*) ≈ le métro; *Br F* **t. station,** ≈ station *f* de métro; **Fallopian tubes,** trompes *fpl* de Fallope; **bronchial tubes,** les bronches *fpl*; *F* **that's £500 down the tubes,** voilà 500 livres de foutues en l'air *ou* qui s'envolent en poussière; *F* **that's all our efforts gone down the tubes,** et voilà tous nos efforts qui s'envolent en poussière; *F* **he watched his marriage/life's work go down the tubes,** il a vu son mariage/le travail de toute une vie tourner en eau de boudin;
(b) *El Electron TV etc* tube *m* (*électronique, thermionique*); **cathode-ray t.,** tube cathodique *ou* à rayons cathodiques; **picture** *or* **television t.,** tube cathodique pour télévision; *F* **the t.,** la télé.
tubeless ['tjuːblɪs] *adj* (*pneu*) sans chambre (à air).
tuber ['tjuːbər] *n* (*root*) racine tubéreuse; (*on potato*) tubercule *m*.
tubercle ['tjuːbɜːk(ə)l] *n Anat Med* tubercule *m*.
tubercular [tjuː'bɜːkjʊlər] *adj Med Bot* tuberculeux.
tuberculin [tjʊ'bɜːkjʊlɪn] *n Med* tuberculine *f*; **t. test,** épreuve *f* de la tuberculinisation; tuberculino-diagnostic *m*.
tuberculin-tested [tjʊbɜːkjʊlɪn'testɪd] *adj* **t.-t. milk,** lait garanti exempt de tuberculose, = lait cru certifié.
tuberculosis [tjʊbɜːkjʊ'ləʊsɪs] *n Med* tuberculose *f*; **t. of the lungs,** tuberculose pulmonaire.
tuberculous [tjʊ'bɜːkjʊləs] *adj Med* tuberculeux.
tubful ['tʌbfʊl] *n* cuvée *f*, plein baquet (**of,** de).
tubing ['tjuːbɪŋ] *n* (*no pl*) tubes *mpl*; (*pipework*) tuyauterie *f*; **copper t.,** tubes de cuivre; **rubber t.,** tuyau(x) *m(pl)* en caoutchouc.
tub-thumper ['tʌbθʌmpər] *n F* harangueur *m*, orateur *m* de carrefour.
tubular ['tjuːbjʊlər] *adj* tubulaire; *Mus* **t. bells,** carillon *m* (*d'orchestre*).
TUC [tiːjuː'siː] *n Br Ind* (*abbr* **Trades Union Congress**) = confédération des syndicats britanniques.
tuck¹ [tʌk] *n* **(a)** *Sewing* (petit) pli *m*, rempli *m*, plissé *m*; **(b)** *Br Sch F* gâteaux *mpl*, friandises *fpl*, sucreries *fpl*; **t. box,** boîte *f* à provisions; **t. shop,** annexe *f* de la cantine où se vendent les friandises.
tuck² *vt* **(a)** *Sewing* faire des plis à (*un vêtement*); **(b)** (*put in, under*) passer, mettre; (*fold*) replier; **to t. one's legs under one,** replier les jambes sous soi; **she tucked her arm in(to) mine,** elle a passé son bras sous le mien; **he tucked his briefcase under his arm,** il mit *ou* cala son porte-documents sous son bras; **to t. one's trousers into one's socks,** mettre son pantalon dans ses chaussettes; **to t. a rug round s.o.,** envelopper qn d'une couverture; **the bird tucked its head under its wing,** l'oiseau a replié *ou* caché sa tête sous son aile; **to t. sth into a drawer,** serrer qch dans un tiroir.
▶tuck away *vtsep* (*put away*) ranger; (*hide*) cacher, mettre à l'abri; **he tucked it away in his bag,** il l'a rangé dans son sac; **village tucked away in the valley,** village blotti au fond de la vallée; **you are** *or* **your house is a bit tucked away,** vous êtes *ou* votre maison est un peu à l'écart; *F* **she really can t. it away!,** (*eat a lot*) qu'est-ce qu'elle peut en mettre à l'abri!
▶tuck in 1 *vtsep* (*put in, under*) serrer, rentrer (*qch*); replier (*le bord d'un vêtement etc*); **to t. in the bedclothes,** border le lit; **to t. s.o. in,** border qn (*dans son lit*). **2** *vi F* (*eat heartily*) manger à belles dents; **t. in!,** allez-y!, mangez!
▶tuck into *vipo F* (*eat heartily*) attaquer (*un repas*).
▶tuck up *vtsep* **(a)** relever, retrousser (*sa jupe, ses manches*); **(b)** border (*qn*) (*dans son lit*).
tucker¹ ['tʌkər] *n* **(a)** *Arch* (*garment*) fichu *m*, guimpe *f*; (*still used in*) *F* **in one's best bib and t.,** endimanché; **(b)** *esp Austr F* (*food*) mangeaille *f*.
tucker² *vt esp Am F* (*tire out*) fatiguer (*qn*); **tuckered (out),** épuisé, éreinté.
tuck-in ['tʌkɪn] *n F* **to have a good t.-in,** (*eating session*) s'envoyer un bon repas.
Tudor ['tjuːdər] **1** *n* **the Tudors,** la maison des Tudors. **2** *adj* des Tudors; *Archit* **T. house,** maison de style Tudor, maison élisabéthaine; *Archit* **T. style,** style Tudor *ou* élisabéthain.
Tuesday ['tjuːzdɪ] *n* mardi *m*; **he comes on Tuesdays,** il vient le mardi; **every T.,** tous les mardis.
tufa ['t(j)uːfə] *n Geol* tuf *m* calcaire *ou* volcanique.
tuft [tʌft] *n* **(a)** touffe *f* (*d'herbe, de plumes, de cheveux*); huppe *f*, aigrette *f* (*d'un oiseau*); **t. of bristles,** (*in brush*) loquet *m* de soies; **(b)** (*small beard*) barbiche *f*; (*under lip*) mouche *f*.
tufted ['tʌftɪd] *adj* (*bird*) huppé; **t. duck,** morillon *m*; **t. heron,** héron *m* à aigrette, aigrette *f*.
tug¹ [tʌg] *n* **(a)** (*pull*) traction *f*; (*jerky*) saccade *f*; **to give a good t.,** tirer fort; **he gave a t. at the bell,** il a tiré (sur) la sonnette; **I felt a t. at my sleeve,** j'ai senti qu'on me tirait par la manche; *Journ* **t. of love,** déchirement familial; **t.-of-love parents/child,** parents/enfant déchiré(s); **t. of war,** *Sp* lutte *f* de traction à la corde; *Fig* (*protracted, fierce struggle*) lutte acharnée et prolongée; *Fig* **to feel a t. at one's heartstrings,** avoir un serrement de cœur; **(b)** *Nau* remorqueur *m*.
tug² *v* (-gg-) **1** *vi* **to t. at sth,** tirer (sur) qch; **to t. at one's moustache,** tirer (sur) *ou* tourmenter sa moustache. **2** *vt* **(a)** tirer (*qch*) avec effort; **(b)** *Nau* remorquer (*un navire*).
tugboat ['tʌgbəʊt] *n Nau* remorqueur *m*.
tuition [tjʊ'ɪʃən] *n* instruction *f*, enseignement *m*; **maths t., t. in maths,** enseignement de math; **private t.,** leçons particulières.
tulip ['tjuːlɪp] *n* tulipe *f*; **t. tree,** tulipier *m*; **t. glass,** (verre *m*) tulipe.
tulle [tjuːl] *n Tex* tulle *m*.
tum [tʌm] *n* (*in children's language*) *& F* ventre *m*.
tumble¹ ['tʌmb(ə)l] *n* **(a)** (*fall*) chute *f*; (*head over heels*) culbute *f*; **she had a nasty t.,** elle a fait une mauvaise chute; **(b)** *Gym* culbute *f* (*d'acrobate*); **(c)** (*disorder*) désordre *m*; **everything was in a t.,** tout était en désordre.
tumble² 1 *vi* tomber (par terre), faire une chute; culbuter, faire la culbute; (*of acrobat*) faire des culbutes; **to t. into bed,** se jeter dans son lit; **to t. into one's clothes,** sauter dans ses vêtements; **to t. out of the window,** tomber par la fenêtre; **they were tumbling over one another,** ils se bousculaient. **2** *vt* **(a) to t. sth/s.o. down** *or* **over,** culbuter *ou* renverser *ou* faire tomber qch/qn; **(b)** (*put in disorder*) bouleverser, déranger; mettre en désordre (*un lit*); **(c)** (*in tumble dryer*) mettre (*les vêtements*) dans le séchoir à linge; **(d)** *F* (*make love to*) culbuter.
▶tumble about *vi* (*of children, kittens*) gambader.
▶tumble down *vi* (*fall, collapse*) s'écrouler; **the wall came tumbling down,** le mur s'est écroulé; **building that is tumbling down,** édifice qui s'écroule *ou* qui tombe en ruine.
▶tumble out *vi* (*from box etc*) **the suitcase came open and everything tumbled out,** la valise s'est ouverte et tout est tombé par terre; **the van doors flew open and the kids came tumbling out,** les portes de la camionnette se sont ouvertes et les enfants sont sortis en désordre.
▶tumble to *vipo F* (*understand*) piger; **eventually she tumbled to it,** elle a fini par piger.
tumbledown ['tʌmb(ə)ldaʊn] *adj* croulant, délabré; (*mur*) à moitié écroulé; (*maison*) qui tombe en ruine(s).
tumble-drier [tʌmb(ə)l'draɪər] *n* séchoir *m* à linge (à mouvement rotatif).
tumble-dry ['tʌmb(ə)l'draɪ] *vt* faire sécher (*des vêtements*).
tumbler ['tʌmblər] *n* **(a)** (*glass*) verre *m* (*à boire*) sans pied; **(b)** gorge *f* (*de serrure*); *El* culbuteur *m*

(*d'interrupteur etc*); **t. lock,** serrure *f* à gorge(s); **(c) t. (pigeon),** (pigeon *m*) culbutant *m*; **(d)** (*toy*) poussa(h) *m*; **(e)** (*acrobat*) acrobate *mf*; **(f)** (*tumble drier*) séchoir *m* à linge (à mouvement rotatif).

tumblerful ['tʌmbləfʊl] *n* plein verre (**of,** de).

tumbleweed ['tʌmb(ə)lwiːd] *n* herbes roulées par le vent.

tumbrel ['tʌmbrəl], **tumbril** ['tʌmbrɪl] *n Hist* = charrette *f* (des condamnés).

tumefaction [tjuːmɪ'fækʃən] *n* tuméfaction *f*.

tumefy ['tjuːmɪfaɪ] **1** *vt* tuméfier. **2** *vi* se tuméfier.

tumescent [tjuː'mesənt] *adj* tumescent.

tumid ['tjuːmɪd] *adj* **(a)** *Med* enflé, gonflé; **(b)** (*style etc*) enflé.

tummy ['tʌmɪ] *n* (*in children's language*) *& F* ventre *m*; **t. ache,** mal *m* de ventre; **t. button,** boudine *f*; **to have t. trouble,** avoir l'estomac dérangé.

tumour, *US* **tumor** ['tjuːmər] *n Med* tumeur *f*.

tumult ['tjuːmʌlt] *n* tumulte *m*; tumulte, agitation *f*, trouble *m*, émoi *m* (*des passions*).

tumultuous [tjʊ'mʌltjʊəs] *adj* tumultueux; **t. meeting,** réunion orageuse; **t. session,** séance mouvementée.

tumultously [tjʊ'mʌltjʊəslɪ] *adv* tumultueusement.

tumulus, *pl* **-i** ['tjuːmjʊləs, -aɪ] *n* tumulus *m*.

tun [tʌn] *n* tonneau *m*, fût *m*; (*in brewing*) cuve *f*.

tuna ['tjuːnə] *n* (*fish*) thon *m*; **t. sandwich,** sandwich *m* au thon.

tundra ['tʌndrə] *n Geog* toundra *f*.

tune[1] [tjuːn] *n* **(a)** *Mus* (*melody*) air *m*, mélodie *f*; *F* **give us a t.!,** faites-nous un peu de musique!, jouez-nous un air!; **it's got no t.,** il n'y a pas de mélodie; *Fig* **to call the t.,** donner la note; **to the t. of the Marseillaise,** sur l'air de la Marseillaise; *Fig* **to change one's t.,** changer de ton *ou* de gamme *ou* de note; *Fig* **to be fined to the t. of £50,** avoir une amende de 50 livres;

(b) the piano is in/out of t., le piano est d'accord *ou* accordé/désaccordé; **to get out of t.,** se désaccorder; **to be out of t.,** (*of singer, player*) détonner; **to sing in/out of t.,** chanter juste/faux; **the trumpet isn't in t.** *or* **is out of t. with the other instruments,** la trompette n'est pas en harmonie *ou* en accord avec les autres instruments; *Fig* **to be in t. with s.o./with one's surroundings,** être en harmonie avec qn/avec son milieu; *Fig* **the government's out of t. with the people,** le gouvernement n'est pas en harmonie avec le peuple; **in perfect t.,** (*moteur*) au point.

tune[2] **1** *vt* **(a)** *Mus* accorder, mettre d'accord (*un instrument*); **to t. a string to ...,** accorder une corde sur ...; **(b)** *El Rad etc* **to t. one circuit to another,** accorder un circuit sur un autre; **stay tuned to this channel,** restez avec nous; **(c)** *Aut etc* régler, (re)mettre au point (*un moteur*); **to be tuned,** (*of engine*) être au point. **2** *vi Mus* **to t. to a note,** s'accorder sur une note.

►**tune in** *vi esp Rad* **don't forget to t. in again tomorrow ...,** n'oubliez pas de nous réjoindre *ou* de vous mettre à l'écoute demain ...; **to t. in to a station/programme,** se brancher sur une station *ou TV* chaîne/une émission.

►**tune up 1** *vi Mus* (*get in tune*) (*of orchestra*) s'accorder. **2** *vtsep Aut etc* = **TUNE**[2] **1(c)**.

tuned-in [tjuːnd'ɪn] *adj Sl* branché.

tuneful ['tjuːnfʊl] *adj* mélodieux, harmonieux.

tunefully ['tjuːnfəlɪ] *adv* mélodieusement.

tunefulness ['tjuːnfʊlnɪs] *n* qualité mélodieuse (*d'un air etc*).

tuneless ['tjuːnlɪs] *adj* (*unpleasant*) discordant; (*without melody*) sans mélodie.

tuner ['tjuːnər] *n* **(a)** *Mus* (*person*) accordeur *m* (*de pianos etc*); **(b)** *Rad etc* syntonisateur *m*, tuner *m*.

tungsten ['tʌŋstən] *n Ch* tungstène *m*; **t. steel,** acier *m* au tungstène.

tunic ['tjuːnɪk] *n* tunique *f*.

tuning ['tjuːnɪŋ] *n* **(a)** *Mus* accord *m*; **fine t.,** accord précis; **t. fork,** diapason *m*; **(b)** *Aut etc* réglage *m*, (re)mise *f* au point; **(c)** *esp Rad* réglage *m* de la tonalité *ou* des tonalités; **t. into a station,** accrochage *m* d'un poste; **t. dial,** cadran *m* d'accord.

Tunisia [tjuː'nɪzɪə] *n* Tunisie *f*.

Tunisian [tjuː'nɪzɪən] **1** *adj* tunisien. **2** *n* Tunisien, -ienne.

tunnel[1] ['tʌn(ə)l] *n* **(a)** tunnel *m*; galerie *f* (*creusée par une taupe etc*); **to drive a t. through a mountain,** percer un tunnel à travers *ou* sous une montagne; *Fig* **at last we can see (some, the) light at the end of the tunnel,** enfin on voit la lumière au bout du tunnel; *MecE etc* **wind t.,** tunnel aérodynamique, soufflerie *f* (aérodynamique); **t. vision,** rétrécissement *m* du champ visuel; *Fig* vision limitée des choses; *Fig* **to suffer from t. vision,** avoir une vision limitée des choses; **(b)** (*fishing*) **t. net,** verveux *m*.

tunnel[2] *v* (**-ll-**, *US* **-l-** ['tʌn(ə)ld]) **1** *vi* creuser *ou* percer un tunnel; **to t. through/into a hill,** percer un tunnel à travers *ou* dans *ou* sous une colline; **rats had tunnelled under the foundations,** les rats avaient creusé des galeries sous les fondements. **2** *vt* **to t. one's way out (of a prison/*etc*),** creuser un tunnel pour s'échapper (d'une prison/*etc*).

tunnelling, *US* **tunneling** ['tʌn(ə)lɪŋ] *n* percement *m* d'un tunnel *ou* de tunnels.

tunny ['tʌnɪ] *n* (*fish*) **t. (fish),** thon *m*.

tuppence ['tʌp(ə)ns] *n Old-fashioned F* = **TWOPENCE**.

tuppenny ['tʌp(ə)nɪ] *adj Old-fashioned F* = **TWOPENNY**; **t. halfpenny** = **TWOPENNY-HALFPENNY**.

turban ['tɜːbən] *n* turban *m*.

turbid ['tɜːbɪd] *adj* **(a)** (*liquide*) trouble, bourbeux; **(b)** (*esprit*) trouble, brouillon.

turbidity [tɜː'bɪdɪtɪ] *n* turbidité *f*.

turbine ['tɜːbaɪn] *n* turbine *f*; **gas/steam t.,** turbine à gaz/à vapeur; **t. engine,** turbomoteur *m*.

turbo-charged ['tɜːbəʊtʃɑːdʒd] *adj* à turbo.

turbo-charger ['tɜːbəʊtʃɑːdʒər] *n* turbocompresseur *m* à suralimentation.

turbo-electric [tɜːbəʊɪ'lektrɪk] *adj* turbo-électrique.

turbofan ['tɜːbəʊfæn] *n Av* turboréacteur *m* à double flux.

turbogenerator [tɜːbəʊ'dʒenəreɪtər] *n El* turbogénérateur *m*, turbogénératrice *f*.

turbojet ['tɜːbəʊdʒet] *n Av* **t. (aircraft),** avion *m* à turbopropulseur; **t. (engine),** turboréacteur *m* (*à simple flux*).

turboprop ['tɜːbəʊprɒp] *Av* **t. (aircraft),** avion *m* à turbopropulseur; **t. (engine),** turbopropulseur *m*.

turbot ['tɜːbət] *n* (*fish*) turbot *m*.

turbulence ['tɜːbjʊləns] *n* turbulence *f*, agitation *f*; *Met Av* turbulence.

turbulent ['tɜːbjʊlənt] *adj* turbulent, tumultueux; *Met Av* turbulent, agité.

turbulently ['tɜːbjʊləntlɪ] *adv* d'une manière turbulente.

turd [tɜːd] *n Sl* **(a)** merde *f*, crotte *f*; **(b)** (*person*) couillon, -onne.

tureen [tjʊə'riːn] *n* **(soup) t.,** soupière *f*.

turf[1], *pl* **turves, turfs** [tɜːf, tɜːvz, tɜːfs] *n* (*grass-covered earth*) gazon *m*; (*piece*) motte *f* de gazon; (*peat*) tourbe *f*; *Am Sl* (*territory*) territoire *m*; *Sp* **the t.,** le turf, les courses *fpl* de chevaux; *esp Br Sp* **t. accountant,** bookmaker *m*; **t. cutting,** extraction *f* de la tourbe.

turf[2] *vt* **(a)** gazonner (*un terrain*); **(b)** *F* (*throw*) balancer.

►**turf out** *vtsep F* (*eject*) flanquer (*qn*) à la porte; (*throw away*) foutre (*qch*) en l'air; (*reject*) rejeter (*un plan etc*).

turgid ['tɜːdʒɪd] *adj* **(a)** enflé, gonflé, *Lit* turgide; **(b)** (*style etc*) boursouflé, ampoulé.

turgidly ['tɜːdʒɪdlɪ] *adv* (*written etc*) emphatiquement, pompeusement.

Turk [tɜːk] *n* Turc, *f* Turque; *esp Pol* **he's a young T.,** c'est un jeune turc.

turkey ['tɜːkɪ] *n* **(a)** *Culin* dinde *f*, dindonneau *m*; **t. (cock),** dindon *m*; **hen t.,** dinde; **t. buzzard,** vautour *m* aura; **(b)** *esp Am F* **to talk t.,** parler franchement; *Sl* **cold t.,** état *m* de manque de drogue(s); **(c)** *esp Am Sl* (*failed play, film*) bide *m*, four *m*; (*ineffectual person*) abruti, -ie, crétin, -ine.

Turkey ['tɜːkɪ] *n* Turquie *f*.

Turkish ['tɜːkɪʃ] **1** *adj* turc, *f* turque; **t. bath,** bain turc; **T. delight,** rahat-lo(u)koum *m*; *Hist* **the T. Empire,** l'Empire *m* ottoman *ou* du Croissant; **T. towel,** serviette *f* éponge. **2** *n Ling* turc *m*.

turmeric ['tɜːmərɪk] *n* curcuma *m*.

turmoil ['tɜːmɔɪl] *n* trouble *m*, tumulte *m*, agitation *f*; remous *m* (*des eaux*); **the whole town is in (a) t.,** toute la ville est agitée *ou* est en ébullition; **my mind was in a t.,** la confusion régnait dans mon esprit.

turn[1] [tɜːn] *n* **(a)** tour *m*, révolution *f* (*d'une roue*); **with a t. of the wrist,** avec un tour de poignet; *Fig* **to give another t. to the screw,** serrer la vis (*à qn*); **the meat is done to a t.,** la viande est cuite à point;

(b) (*act of changing direction*) changement *m* de direction; (*skiing*) virage *m*; tournant *m* (*d'un chemin etc*); tour *m* (*d'une corde*); tour, spire *f* (*d'une spirale*); **the second t. on the left,** la prochaine (rue, route) à gauche; **twists and turns,** tours et détours *mpl*; (*of events*) tournure *f* (*des affaires*); *Aut* **sharp t.,** virage à la corde; **no right/left t.,** défense de tourner à droite/à gauche; **U turn,** demi-tour *m*; **three-point t.,** demi-tour *m* en trois manœuvres; *Ski* **kick t.,** virage en plaine, conversion *f*; *Fig* **at every t.,** à tout bout de champ; **to take a tragic t.,** (*of events*) tourner au tragique; **the patient has taken a t. for the better/the worse,** l'état du malade s'est amélioré/a empiré; **t. of the tide,** changement *ou* renversement *m* de la marée; **the milk is on the t.,** le lait est en train de tourner; **at the t. of the century,** au tournant du siècle; **t.-of-the-century London/fashions/***etc*, le Londres/les modes/*etc* du début du siècle; *Fin* **jobbers' t.,** écart *m* entre le prix d'achat et celui de vente;

(c) *F* (*surprise, shock*) choc *m*, coup *m*; **it gave me quite a t.,** ça m'a donné un (vrai) coup; **you gave me such a t.!,** vous m'avez donné une belle peur!;

(d) *Méd F* **she had one of her turns,** elle a eu une de ses crises *ou* attaques;

(e) (*short walk*) tour *m*, petite promenade; **to take a t. in the garden,** faire un tour *ou* quelques pas dans le jardin;

(f) (*at activity*) tour *m* (de rôle); *Th* numéro *m* (*de music-hall etc*); **it's your t.,** c'est votre tour, c'est à vous (de jouer); **each in (his) t., t. and t. about,** chacun (à) son tour; **in t.,** tour à tour, à tour de rôle; **they, in t., contributed food,** à leur tour, ils donnèrent de la nourriture; **to speak out of (one's) t.,** parler mal à propos; **to take turns with s.o.,** se relayer avec qn; **they take it in turns to drive,** ils se relaient au volant;

(g) to do s.o. a good t., rendre (un) service à qn; **to do s.o. a bad t.,** jouer un mauvais tour à qn; *Prov* **one good t. deserves another,** à beau jeu beau retour, un service en vaut un autre;

(h) it will serve my t., cela fera mon affaire (pour le moment);

(i) t. of mind, tournure *f* d'esprit; **humorous t. of mind,** esprit *m* humoristique; **t. of phrase,** tournure *f* de phrase; **to have a good t. of speed,** (*of car*) être rapide; (*of horse*) être capable de fournir un effort à grande allure.

turn² **1** *vt* **(a)** (faire) tourner (*une roue, une manivelle*); (faire) tourner, faire jouer (*une clef dans la serrure*); *Fig* **to t. the knife in the wound,** retourner le fer *ou* le couteau dans la plaie; **to t. the gas low,** mettre le gaz en veilleuse;

(b) tourner (*une page etc*); retourner (*un matelas, le foin etc*); **to t. a garment inside out,** retourner un vêtement; **to t. everything upside down,** mettre tout sens dessus-dessous; *F* **he didn't t. a hair,** il n'a pas bronché *ou* sourcillé; **onions t. my stomach,** les oignons m'écœurent *ou* me soulèvent le cœur; **the sight/story turned my stomach,** cette vue/histoire m'a soulevé le cœur;

(c) she turned her steps towards home, elle a dirigé ses pas vers la maison; **he never turned anyone from his door,** il n'a jamais fermé sa porte à personne; **to t. the conversation,** donner un autre tour à la conversation; **to t. one's thoughts to God,** tourner ses pensées vers Dieu; **to t. one's attention to ...,** tourner son attention vers *ou* **sur ...;**

(d) tourner, retourner (*la tête*); tourner, diriger (*les yeux*) (*vers qch*); **t. your face this way,** tournez-vous de ce côté; (*look this way*) regardez de ce côté; **t. your desk this way,** tournez votre bureau dans cette direction;

(e) to t. the corner, tourner le coin; *Fig* passer le moment critique; **she's turned forty,** elle a quarante ans passés, elle a passé la quarantaine; **it's turned seven,** il est sept heures passées;

(f) (*change*) changer, convertir, transformer (**into,** en); **to t. the water into wine,** changer l'eau en vin; **his love had been turned to hate,** son amour s'est changé *ou* s'est transformé en haine; **to t. a theatre into a cinema,** convertir un théâtre en cinéma; **the witch turned him into a scarecrow,** la sorcière l'a transformé en corbeau; **we've turned the attic into a study,** nous avons transformé *ou* converti le grenier en bureau;

(g) (*cause to become*) faire devenir; **the heat has turned the milk sour,** la chaleur a fait tourner le lait; **autumn turns the leaves yellow,** l'automne fait jaunir les feuilles; **to t. sth green/black,** rendre qch vert/noir; **the blood turned the water red,** le sang a rougi l'eau; **June Smith, athlete turned politician,** June Smith, athlète passée femme politique; **success has turned her head,** le succès lui a tourné la tête;

(h) (*make on lathe*) tourner, façonner au tour (*un pied de table etc*); *Fig* **well turned sentence,** phrase bien tournée; *Knitting* **to t. a heel,** faire le talon.

2 *vi* **(a)** tourner; **the wheel turns,** la roue tourne; **to t. a complete circle,** virer un cercle complet; **it won't t.,** ça ne marche pas *ou* ne tourne pas; **my head's turning,** la tête me tourne; **everything turns on your answer,** tout dépend de votre réponse;

(b) to toss and t., (*in bed*) se tourner et se retourner (dans son lit); **to t. upside down,** se retourner;

(c) (*turn head, body*) se tourner, se retourner; **he turned to look at the landscape,** il s'est retourné pour regarder le paysage; *Mil* **right t.!,** à droite!; **left t!,** à gauche!;

(d) (*change direction*) tourner, se diriger; **the path turns to the left,** le chemin tourne à gauche; **she turned to the left,** elle a tourné à gauche; **he turned towards home,** il s'est dirigé vers la maison; **the wind is turning,** le vent tourne *ou* change; **she turned to me — what do YOU think?,** elle se tourna vers moi – qu'est-ce que tu en penses, toi?; **my thoughts often t. to this subject,** mes réflexions se portent souvent sur ce sujet; **to t. to another subject,** passer à une autre question; **to t. to the dictionary,** consulter le dictionnaire; **I don't know where** *or* **which way to t.,** je ne sais pas où donner de la tête; **to t. to s.o. (for help/advice),** s'adresser à *ou* consulter qn (pour obtenir de l'aide/du conseils); **I didn't know who to t. to,** je ne savais pas à qui m'adresser;

(e) the tide is turning, la marée change; **her luck has turned,** sa chance a tourné;

(f) (*change*) se transformer, se changer (**into,** en); **caterpillars t. into butterflies,** la chenille se transforme en papillon; **she's turned into a very hard-headed businesswoman,** elle s'est transformée en une femme d'affaire à la tête froide; **it is turning to rain,** le temps se met à la pluie; **everything he touches turns to gold,** tout ce qu'il touche se change en or; **to t. acid,** tourner au vinaigre; **to t. (sour),** (*of milk*) tourner; **it's turning cold,** le temps tourne au froid, il commence à faire froid; **the crowd turned nasty,** la foule est devenue agressive; **the leaves are beginning to t.,** les feuilles commencent à jaunir; **he turned red,** il a rougi; *Ch* **to t. red/blue,** virer au rouge/bleu; **to t. sulky,** devenir maussade; **to t. socialist,** devenir socialiste.

►turn against **1** *vipo* se retourner contre (*qn*). **2** *vtaspo* (*make opposed to*) retourner (*qn, qch*) contre; **she turns everyone against her,** elle se met tout le monde à dos; **they turned the laughter/his argument against him,** ils ont retourné les rires/son argument contre lui.

►turn around *vi & vtsep* = **TURN ROUND.**

►turn aside *vtsep* (*deflect*) **to t. aside a blow,** détourner *ou* faire dévier un coup.

►turn away **1** *vtsep* **(a)** (*direct elsewhere*) détourner (*la tête, les yeux*); **police were turning drivers/people away (from the scene of the accident),** la police détournait *ou* écartait les conducteurs/les gens (du lieu de l'accident); **(b)** (*refuse entry, help etc to*) (*of hospital, hotel etc*) refuser, refluer; *Th etc* **to t. people away,** refuser du monde; **we've been turning business away,** nous avons refusé du travail. **2** *vi* (*look away*) se détourner, détourner son regard; (*go away*) s'écarter; **to t. away from s.o.,** (*turn one's back on*) tourner le dos à qn; (*abandon*) délaisser *ou* abandonner qn.

►turn back **1** *vi* **(a)** (*return in same direction*) rebrousser chemin, faire demi-tour; *Fig* **there's no turning back now,** on ne peut plus faire demi-tour maintenant; **(b)** (*in book*) **t. back to page ...,** revenez à la page ... . **2** *vtsep* **(a)** (*cause to return in same direction*) faire faire demi-tour à (*qn*), faire revenir (*qn*) sur ses pas; **refugees were turned back at the border,** des réfugiés ont été refoulés *ou* reflués à la frontière; **(b)** (*fold*) replier (*les draps*); **(c)** (*adjust to earlier time*) mettre en arrière (*sa montre etc*); **to t. the clocks back an hour,** reculer les pendules d'une heure; *Fig* **you can't t. the clock back,** on ne peut pas repartir en arrière.

►turn down *vtsep* **(a)** (*fold down*) rabattre (*un col*); plier, corner (*la page d'un livre*); **to t. down the bed,** ouvrir le lit; **(b)** *Cards* renverser (*une carte*) (*face à la table*); **(c)** (*reduce heat, sound etc*) baisser (*le gaz, la radio etc*); **(d)** (*refuse, reject*) repousser, rejeter (*une offre*); refuser (*un candidat etc*); écarter (*une réclamation*); **I've been turned down for that job,** j'ai été refusé pour cet emploi; **she turned me down flat,** elle a refusé catégoriquement, *F* elle m'a envoyé promener; **they offered him a job but he turned them down,** ils lui ont proposé un emploi mais il a rejeté leur offre.

►turn in **1** *vtsep* **(a) to t. in one's toes,** tourner les pieds en dedans; **(b)** *F* (*hand in*) rendre, rapporter (*qch*); (*betray to police*) livrer, vendre (*qn*) à la police; **(c)** *F* quitter, abandonner (*son emploi*); **(d)** *Sp Th etc* **to t. in a good score/performance/***etc*, faire un bon score/une belle performance/*etc*. **2** *vi* **(a)** (*point inwards*) **his toes t. in,** il a les pieds tournés en dedans; **(b)** (*go through entrance off road etc*) **he turned in at the gate,** arrivé à la porte, il est entré; **(c)** *F* (*go to bed*) se mettre au pieu, se pieuter.

►turn off **1** *vtsep* **(a)** (*switch off*) fermer (*l'eau, le robinet, le gaz, l'électricité*); éteindre (*la lumière, la radio, la télé etc*); **(b)** *Sl* (*disgust*) écœurer, dégoûter; (*take away en-*

thusiasm from) rebuter, refroidir; (*sexually*) couper l'envie à. **2** *vi* (*leave road, street*) changer de route; **I turned off to the left,** j'ai pris (la route, la rue) à gauche, j'ai tourné à gauche; **he turned off onto the motorway,** il s'est engagé sur l'autoroute. **3** *vipo* **we turned off the main road,** nous avons quitté la grande route; **a small street turning off the High Street,** une petite rue qui fait coin *ou* fait angle avec la Grande Rue.

►**turn on 1** *vtsep* **(a)** (*switch on*) ouvrir (*l'eau, le robinet, le gaz, l'électricité*); allumer (*la lumière, la radio, la télé etc*); **shall I t. on the light?,** voulez-vous que j'allume?; **(b)** *Sl* (*excite*) brancher (*qn*); (*sexually*) exciter *ou* allumer (*qn*); **she turned me on to Zen Buddhism,** elle m'a branché sur le Bouddhisme Zen. **2** *vipo* **(a)** (*attack physically or verbally*) s'attaquer à; **(b)** (*depend on*) reposer, dépendre; **everything turns on your answer,** tout dépend de votre réponse. **3** *vi* (*of heater etc*) se mettre en route *ou* en marche.

►**turn out 1** *vtsep* **(a)** (*eject*) mettre *ou F* flanquer (*qn*) à la porte; déloger, évincer (*un locataire*); mettre (*le bétail*) au vert; *Nau* réveiller (*les hommes*); *Mil* alerter (*les troupes*);

(b) (*empty*) vider, retourner (*ses poches etc*); *Culin* démouler (*une crème etc*); **to t. out a drawer,** (*empty*) vider un tiroir; (*empty and tidy*) mettre de l'ordre dans un tiroir; **to t. out a room,** nettoyer une pièce à fond;

(c) (*switch off*) couper, éteindre (*le gaz, la lumière*);

(d) (*produce*) produire, fabriquer (*des marchandises*); **turned out by the dozen,** confectionnés à la douzaine; **the sort of students that we aim to t. out here,** le type d'étudiants que nous nous fixons de produire ici;

(e) well turned out, (*person*) élégant, soigné;

(f) (*point outwards*) **to t. one's toes out,** tourner les pieds en dehors.

2 *vi* **(a)** (*attend*) sortir; (*get out of bed*) se lever, sortir du lit; (*of doctor, fire brigade etc*) sortir en service; **the whole town turned out to see it,** toute la ville est sortie pour le voir *ou* le regarder; *F* **not many people turned out for his funeral/the march/the carnival,** il n'est pas venu beaucoup de monde à son enterrement/à la manifestation/au carnaval;

(b) (*point outwards*) **his toes t. out,** il a les pieds tournés en dehors;

(c) (*end*) **to t. out well/badly,** bien/mal tourner; **it will t. out all right,** cela s'arrangera; **how did the cake t. out?,** le gâteau était-il réussi?; **I don't know how it will t. out,** je ne sais pas comment cela finira; **things don't t. out that way,** ce n'est pas comme ça que ça se passe; **as it turned out,** comme il est apparu, en l'occurrence; **she's turned out (to be) beautiful,** elle est devenue belle;

(d) (*transpire*) **he turned out to be the son of an old friend of mine,** il s'est trouvé qu'il était le fils d'un de mes anciens amis; **it turns out that ...,** il se trouve que ...; **as it turns out, we would have had time,** en fait, nous aurions eu le temps.

►**turn over 1** *vtsep* **(a)** (*turn*) retourner (*qch*); tourner (*une page*); **to t. over the pages of a book,** feuilleter un livre; **she turned the body over,** elle a retourné le corps; *Agr* **to t. over the soil,** retourner la terre; **to t. an idea/a plan over in one's mind,** ruminer *ou* retourner une idée/retourner un projet dans sa tête;

(b) (*surrender*) **to t. sth over to s.o.,** remettre qch entre les mains de qn; **the thief was turned over to the police,** on a remis le voleur entre les mains de la police;

(c) (*of business*) rapporter; **he must be turning over a good £1,000 a week,** il doit gagner *ou F* se faire au moins 1 000 livres par semaine;

(d) *Sl* (*rob*) faucher, piquer, truander; *Fig* **£500? — you've been turned over!,** 500 livres? — tu t'es fait rouler!

2 *vi* **(a)** (*change position by turning*) se tourner, se retourner; **to t. over in bed,** se retourner dans son lit; **to t. right over,** (*of car etc*) capoter;

(b) *TV F* (*change channel*) changer de chaîne;

(c) (*in reading*) **please t. over,** tournez s'il vous plaît.

►**turn round 1** *vi* tourner; (*of crane etc*) virer, pivoter; (*face other way*) tourner, se retourner; (*abruptly*) faire volte-face; (*in one's opinions etc*) tourner casaque, virer de bord; **she turned round in her chair,** elle se retourna sur sa chaise; **t. round and let me see your face,** tournez-vous (un peu) que je voie votre visage; *F* **he just turned round and hit me,** (*without warning*) tout d'un coup il m'a frappé; **after eight years of marriage she turned round and said she was leaving,** (*without warning*) après huit années de mariage elle annonça soudain qu'elle partait.

2 *vt* **(a)** (*move to face other way*) retourner (*qch, qn*); **she turned the chair round,** elle retourna la chaise;

(b) (*reverse*) renverser, retourner (*une mauvaise situation*); **to t. the economy/a company round,** remettre l'économie/une entreprise sur pied;

(c) *Com* (*process, deal with*) traiter, s'occuper de (*une commande*).

3 *vipo* (*go around*) tourner (*le coin*).

►**turn round on** *vipo* (*attack verbally or physically*) s'attaquer à, s'en prendre à.

►**turn up 1** *vi* **(a)** (*arrive*) arriver, se présenter; **he turned up ten minutes late,** il est arrivé *ou F* s'est amené dix minutes en retard; **she turned up at the party with a new boyfriend,** elle est arrivée *ou F* a débarqué à la soirée avec un nouvel ami; **he'll t. up one of these days,** il reparaîtra un de ces jours;

(b) (*be found*) se retrouver; **it's bound to t. up,** il finira bien par repparaître *ou* se retrouver; **the pen turned up in his jacket,** on a retrouvé le stylo dans sa veste; *Fig* **something is sure to t. up,** il se présentera sûrement une occasion; **until something better turns up,** en attendant mieux;

(c) (*turn upwards*) se relever, se replier; **her nose turns up,** elle a le nez retroussé.

2 *vtsep* **(a)** (*fold upwards*) relever (*le col de son pardessus*); retrousser (*ses manches*); *F* **to t. one's nose up** *or* **to t. up one's nose at sth,** snober qch;

(b) (*uncover*) retourner (*le sol, une carte*);

(c) (*unearth*) déterrer (*qch*); (*find*) trouver (*qch*);

(d) (*increase, make louder etc*) augmenter (*le volume*); monter (*le gaz*); **to t. the radio/radiator up,** mettre la radio/le radiateur plus fort;

(e) *Br Sl* **t. it up!,** (*stop that*) c'est fini, oui!

turnabout ['tɜːnəbaʊt] *n* retournement *m*, revirement *m*.

turnaround ['tɜːnəraʊnd] *n* retournement *m*, revirement *m*; rotation *f* (*d'un navire, d'un avion etc*); *Com* (*of an order*) traitement *m*; **they offer a faster t.,** leurs délais sont plus courts; **t. time,** *Com* (*for order*) délai *m* de livraison.

turncoat ['tɜːnkəʊt] *n Pol etc* renégat *m*.

turndown ['tɜːndaʊn] *adj* (*collar etc*) rabattu.

turned [tɜːnd] *adj* **(a) (lathe, machine) t.,** façonné *ou* fait au tour; **t. work,** tournage *m*; **(b)** retourné; *Typ* **t. letter,** caractère retourné; **t. down,** (*collar etc*) rabattu; **t. up,** (*col etc*) relevé; (*nez*) retroussé.

turner ['tɜːnər] *n Ind* tourneur *m*.

turnery ['tɜːnərɪ] *n* atelier *m* de tourneur.

turning ['tɛːnɪŋ] *n* **(a)** mouvement *m* giratoire *ou* rotatoire; (*act of turning sth*) rotation *f*, giration *f*; (*changing direction*) changement *m* de direction; (*skiing*) virage *m*; *Aut etc* **t. circle,** rayon *m* de braquage; *Fig* **t. point,** point décisif, moment *m* critique; **at the t. point of her career,** au tournant de sa carrière;

(b) retournage *m* (*de la terre, d'un vêtement etc*);

(c) (*on lathe*) tournage *m*, travail *m* au tour; **turnings,** tournures *fpl*, copeaux *mpl* de tour;

(d) (*off road etc*) tournant *m* (*d'une route*); (*bend*) virage *m*; **the first t. to the right,** la première route *ou* rue à droite; *Fig* **it's a long road that has no t.,** il n'est de situation qui dure toujours.

turnip ['tɜːnɪp] *n* (*plant, vegetable*) navet *m*; *Hum* (*pocket watch*) montre *f* de poche *ou* de gousset.

turnkey ['tɜːnkiː] **1** *n Arch* (*jailer*) geôlier, -ière. **2** *adj* **t. project,** projet *m* clés en main; *Comptr* **t. system,** système *m* clés en main.

turn-off ['tɜːnɒf] *n* **(a)** sortie *f* (*d'autoroute etc*); **the Leeds t.-o.,** la sortie pour Leeds; **(b)** *Sl* **it's a t.-o.,** c'est dégoûtant *ou* dégueulasse; **it's a t.-o. for me,** (*sexually*) cela me coupe l'envie.

turn-on ['tɛːnɒn] *n Sl* **it's/he's a real t.-o.,** (*exciting thing, person*) c'est/il est vraiment craquant; (*sexual*) c'est/il est vachement excitant.

turnout ['tɜːnaʊt] *n* assistance *f*; **a good/poor t.,** une belle/maigre assistance; **there was a large** *or* **good t. at his funeral/the wedding/meeting,** il y avait foule à son enterrement/au mariage/à la réunion; **low turnouts at elections,** faible participation aux élections; **(b)** (*cleaning*) nettoyage *m* à fond (*d'une pièce etc*); **(c)** *Ind* (*production*) production *f*, rendement *m*; **(d)** (*dress*) tenue *f*.

turnover ['tɜːnəʊvər] *n* **(a)** *Com* chiffre *m* d'affaires; (*of stock*) écoulement *m*, rotation *f*; **t. of staff,** changement *m* de personnel; **our annual t.,** notre chiffre d'affaires annuel; **the (staff) t. there is very high,** le taux de renouvellement du personnel y est très élevé; **t. tax,** impôt *m ou* taxe *f* sur le chiffre d'affaires; **(b)** *Culin* **apple t.,** chausson *m* aux pommes.

turnpike ['tɜːnpaɪk] *n US* autoroute *f* (à péage); *Br Hist* barrière *f* de péage.
turnround ['tɜːnraʊnd] *n esp Br* = **TURNAROUND**.
turnstile ['tɜːnstaɪl] *n* tourniquet(-compteur) *m* (pour entrées).
turntable ['tɜːnteɪb(ə)l] *n* **(a)** *Rail* plaque tournante; *Mil* plate-forme tournante; **(b)** (*on record player*) platine *f* (*de tourne-disques*).
turn(-)up ['tɜːnʌp] *n* **(a)** revers *m* (*de pantalon*); **(b)** *F* **what a t. (for the book)!**, ça c'est une sacrée surprise!
turpentine ['tɜːp(ə)ntaɪn] *n* térébenthine *f*; *Tech* **(oil of) t.**, essence *f* de térébenthine; **t. substitute,** white-spirit *m*, *pl* white-spirits.
turpitude ['tɜːpɪtjuːd] *n* turpitude *f*.
turps [tɜːps] *n Br F* essence *f* de térébenthine; **t. substitute,** white-spirit *m*, *pl* white-spirits.
turquoise ['tɜːkwɔɪz, -kwɑːz] **1** *n* **(a)** (*stone*) turquoise *f*; **(b)** (*colour*) **t. (blue),** (bleu *m*) turquoise *m*. **2** *adj* **t. (blue),** (bleu) turquoise *inv*.
turret ['tʌrɪt] *n* **(a)** *Archit* tourelle *f*; **(b)** *Mil Nau* **(gun) t.**, tourelle *f* (*de pièce d'artillerie, de mitrailleuse*); **(c)** *MecE* tourelle *f*.
turreted ['tʌrɪtɪd] *adj Archit* (*château*) à tourelles.
turtle ['tɜːt(ə)l] *n* **(a)** tortue *f* de mer; **t. soup,** consommé *m* à la tortue; *F* **to turn t.**, *Nau* chavirer; (*of motor car etc*) capoter; **t. neck,** col montant *ou* roulé; **t. necked-sweater,** chandail *m* à col montant *ou* roulé; **(b) t. dove,** tourterelle *f* des bois; *F* **a pair of t. doves,** un couple d'amoureux *ou* de tourtereaux.
Tuscan ['tʌskən] **1** *adj Geog Archit* toscan. **2** *n* **(a)** *Geog* Toscan, -ane; **(b)** *Ling* toscan *m*.
Tuscany ['tʌskənɪ] *n* Toscane *f*.
tush [tʌʃ] *int Old-fashioned* bah!, taratata!
tusk [tʌsk] *n* défense *f* (*de sanglier, d'éléphant etc*).
tussle¹ ['tʌs(ə)l] *n* lutte *f*, mêlée *f*, corps-à-corps *m*; *Fig* lutte, bataille *f*; **to have a t.**, en venir aux mains (**with s.o.**, avec qn).
tussle² *vi* **to t. with s.o.**, lutter avec qn; **to t. over sth,** se disputer qch.
tussock ['tʌsək] *n* touffe *f* d'herbe.
tut¹ [tʌt] *int* **t. (t.)!**, allons donc!
tut² *vi* **to t. (t.) at sth,** faire un bruit désapprobateur, émettre une exclamation désapprobatrice; **don't you t. t. at me!**, je n'ai pas besoin de tes petits bruits désapprobateurs!
tutelage ['tjuːtɪlɪdʒ] *n* (*period*) tutelle *f*; **child in t.**, enfant en tutelle.
tutelar, tutelary ['tjuːtɪlər, -lərɪ] *adj* tutélaire.
tutor¹ ['tjuːtər] *n* **(a)** *Br Univ* directeur, -trice d'études; **(b) private t.**, précepteur *m*; **music t.**, professeur *mf* de musique; **(c)** *Jur* tuteur, -trice (*d'un mineur etc*).
tutor² *vt* instruire (*qn*); **to t. a child in French,** donner à un enfant des leçons particulières de français.
tutorial [tj'tɔːrɪəl] **1** *adj* (*fonctions etc*) de répétiteur, de préparateur; **the t. system,** = le système d'enseignement où les étudiant(e)s sont supervisé(e)s par un directeur d'études. **2** *n* cours (individuel) fait par le directeur d'études; **I've got a t. at 3 o'clock,** j'ai un cours avec mon directeur d'études à trois heures.
tutti-frutti ['tʊtɪ'frʊtɪ] *n Culin* plombières *f*.
tutu ['tuːtuː] *n* (*garment*) tutu *m*.
tu-whit, tu-whoo [tʊ'wɪtʊ'wuː] *int* hou hou!
tux [tʌks] *n Am F* smoking *m*.
tuxedo [tʌk'siːdəʊ] *n Am* smoking *m*.
TV [tiː'viː] *n* (*abbr* **television**) télé *f*, TV *f*; **TV dinner,** plateau-repas surgelé; **TV programme,** programme *m* télé.
TVP [tiːviː'piː] *n Culin* (*abbr* **textured vegetable protein**) proteine végétale texturée.
twaddle¹ ['twɒd(ə)l] *n F* fadaises *fpl*; **to talk t.**, dire *ou* débiter des balivernes *ou* des sottises.
twaddle² *vi F* dire des fadaises *ou* des balivernes.
twain [tweɪn] *adj & n Lit* deux; *Hum* **and ne'er the t. shall meet,** et ils resteront à jamais inconciliables.
twang¹ [twæŋ] *n* **(a)** bruit sec (*de la corde d'un arc*); son aigu (*d'une guitare*); **(b)** (*in voice*) **nasal t.**, ton nasillard, nasillement *m*; **to speak with a t.**, nasiller, parler d'une voix nasillarde.
twang² **1** *vt* lâcher (*la corde de l'arc tendu*); faire résonner (*les cordes d'une harpe*); **to t. a guitar,** pincer de la guitare. **2** *vi* **(a)** (*of string etc*) résonner; **to t. on a guitar,** pincer de la guitare; **(b)** (*speak with twang*) nasiller.
'twas [twɒz] *Lit* = **it was**.
twat [twæt] *n Br Sl* **(a)** (*vagina*) moule *f*, chatte *f*; **(b)** (*idiot*) crétin, -ine.
tweak¹ [twiːk] *n* pinçon *m*; **he gave her nose a t.,** il lui a doucement tordu le nez.
tweak² *vt* **(a)** (*pinch*) pincer; (*twist*) serrer entre les doigts (*en tordant*); **to t. a boy's ear,** tirer l'oreille à un gamin; **(b)** *F* (*adjust*) régler (*un moteur*); arranger (*un texte*).
twee [twiː] *adj F Pej* gentillet, mignard.
tweed [twiːd] *n Tex* tweed *m*; **t. jacket,** veste *f* en *ou* de tweed; **tweeds,** (*suit, outfit*) complet *m ou* costume *m* de *ou* en tweed.
tweedy ['twiːdɪ] *adj F* (*tissu*) qui tient du tweed; *Pej* (*person*) qui affecte la tenue d'un propriétaire rural.
'tween [twiːn] *adv & prep Arch & Lit* entre.
'tween decks ['twiːndeks] *Nau* **1** *n* faux-point *m*, entrepont *m*. **2** *adj* dans l'entrepont.
tweet¹ [twiːt] *n* pépiement *m*, gazouillement *m* (*d'un oiseau*).
tweet² *vi* (*of bird*) pépier, gazouiller.
tweeter ['twiːtər] *n* (*loudspeaker*) haut-parleur aigu, tweeter *m*.
tweezers ['twiːzəz] *npl* brucelles *fpl*; (*for hairs*) pince *f* à épiler.
twelfth [twelfθ] **1** *adj* douzième; **Louis the T.**, Louis Douze; **T. Night,** le jour des Rois. **2** *n* **(a)** douzième *mf*; **(b)** (*fraction*) douzième *m*.
twelve [twelv] *n* douze *m*; **t. o'clock,** (*midday*) midi *m*; (*midnight*) minuit *m*.
twelvemonth ['twelvmʌnθ] *n Old-fashioned & Lit* année *f*; **this day t.**, (*in a year from today*) d'aujourd'hui en un an; (*a year ago today*) il y a un an aujourd'hui.
twelve-tone ['twelvtəʊn] *adj Mus* dodécaphonique; **t.-t. system,** dodécaphonisme *m*.
twentieth ['twentɪɪθ] **1** *adj* vingtième; **(on) the t. of June,** le vingt juin. **2** *n* **(a)** vingtième *mf*; **(b)** (*fraction*) vingtième *m*.
twenty ['twentɪ] *n* vingt *m*; **t.-one,** vingt et un; **t.-two,** vingt-deux; **about t. people,** quelque vingt personnes, une vingtaine de personnes; **the twenties,** les années vingt; **to be in one's twenties,** avoir entre vingt et trente ans; **t.-four hour service,** service vingt-quatre heures sur vingt-quatre; **we've been working t.-four hours a day,** nous avons travaillé jour et nuit; **t.-t. vision,** vue parfaite; *Rugby* **t.-two metre line,** ligne *f* des vingt-deux mètres.
twerp [twɜːp] *n Sl* andouille *f*.
twice [twaɪs] *adv* deux fois; **t. as big as sth,** deux fois plus grand que qch; **t. as slow,** deux fois plus lent; **t. over,** à deux reprises; **to think t. before doing sth,** y regarder à deux fois avant de faire qch; **to think twice before saying something,** tourner la langue sept fois dans la bouche avant de parler; **she didn't have to think t. before accepting,** elle a accepté sans hésiter; **he did not have to be asked t.**, il ne se fit pas prier.
twiddle¹ ['twɪd(ə)l] *n F* **to give sth a t.**, tourner *ou* faire tournoyer qch.
twiddle² **1** *vt F* jouer avec, tripoter (*qch*); **to t. a knob,** tripoter un bouton; **to t. one's thumbs,** se tourner les pouces. **2** *vi* **to t. with sth,** jouer avec *ou* tripoter qch.
twig¹ [twɪg] *n* ramille *f*; **(dowser's hazel) t.**, baguette *f* (divinatoire).
twig² *vt & vi* (-gg-) *F* piger; **I soon twigged his little game,** je n'ai pas tardé à voir dans son jeu.
twilight ['twaɪlaɪt] *n* crépuscule *m*, demi-jour *m*; **in the (evening) t.**, au crépuscule, entre chien et loup, à la brune; *Fig* **in the t. of life,** au crépuscule de la vie; **the t. hours,** les heures crépusculaires; *Fig* **a t. zone of mediums and the paranormal,** l'entre-deux-mondes des médiums et du paranormal.
twill [twɪl] *n Tex* (tissu *m*) croisé *m*, sergé *m*.
'twill [twɪl] *Lit* = **it will**.
twin¹ [twɪn] **1** *n* jumeau, -elle; **t. brother,** frère jumeau; **t. sister,** sœur jumelle; *Astron* **the Twins,** les Gémeaux *mpl*. **2** *adj* jumeau, jumelé; **t. beds,** lits jumeaux; *Med* **t. birth,** accouchement *m* de jumeaux; **t. columns,** colonnes géminées; **t.-engine(d) aircraft,** avion bimoteur; **t. towns,** villes jumelées; **Watford's t. town is Nanterre,** Watford est jumelée avec Nanterre.
twin² *v* (-nn-) **1** *vt* jumeler (*des villes*); **Paisley is twinned with ...,** Paisley est jumelée avec ... . **2** *vi* **to t. with sth,** s'apparier à qch.
twine¹ [twaɪn] *n* (*string*) ficelle *f*, fil retors.
twine² **1** *vt* tordre, tortiller (*des fils*); entrelacer (*une guirlande, les doigts etc*). **2** *vi* se tordre, se tortiller.
►twine about, twine (a)round **1** *vtaspo* (*wrap around*) **to t. sth about** *or* **(a)round sth,** (en)rouler qch autour de qch; **he twined his arms around me,** il m'a entouré(e) de ses bras. **2** *vipo* (*wrap, coil oneself, itself around*) s'enrouler *ou* s'enlacer autour de (*qch*).
twinge [twɪn(d)ʒ] *n* élancement *m* (*de douleur*); légère

crise (*de goutte etc*); **t. of conscience,** remords *m*; *F* **my tooth/knee still gives the odd t.,** ma dent/mon genou m'élance toujours de temps en temps.

twining ['twaınıŋ] *adj* (*plante, tige*) volubile; (*sentier etc*) sinueux.

twinkle¹ ['twıŋk(ə)l] *n* scintillement *m*, clignotement *m* (*des étoiles, de feux lointains*); clignement *m* (*des paupières*); pétillement *m* (*du regard*); **a mischievous t. in the eye,** un éclair de malice dans les yeux; *F* **when you were just a t. in your father's eye,** quand tu n'étais pas encore de ce monde; **in a t. (of an eye),** en un clin d'œil.

twinkle² **1** *vi* (*of light, star*) scintiller, étinceler, clignoter; (*of object in motion*) papillonner; **her eyes twinkled (with amusement/mischief),** ses yeux pétillaient (de rire/malice). **2** *vt* **to t. one's eyes,** clignoter des yeux.

twinkling ['twıŋklıŋ] **1** *adj* (*star etc*) scintillant, étincelant, clignotant; **t. eyes,** yeux pétillants de rire *ou* de malice. **2** *n* scintillement *m*, étincellement *m*, clignotement *m*; **in the t. of an eye,** en un clin d'œil.

twinning ['twınıŋ] *n* jumelage *m* (*de deux villes etc*); **t. arrangements,** arrangements *mpl* en vue de jumelage.

twinset ['twınset] *n Br* (*garments*) twin-set *m*, *pl* twin-sets.

twirl¹ [twɜːl] *n* **(a)** (*movement*) tournoiement *m*; (*of dancer etc*) pirouette *f*; **(b)** volute *f* (*de fumée etc*); *Archit* enroulement *m*, volute; (*of seashell*) spire *f*; (*in writing*) enjolivure *f* en spirale; (*in music*) fioriture *f*; **with a t. of cream on top,** avec une spirale de crème dessus.

twirl² **1** *vt* **(a)** faire tournoyer (*sa cavalière, un lasso*); faire des moulinets avec (*une canne etc*); tortiller (*sa moustache*). **2** *vi* tournoyer; (*of dancer*) pirouetter.

twist¹ [twıst] *n* **(a)** (*act of twisting*) (effort *m* de) torsion *f*; tors *m*, torsion (*des brins d'un cordage*); *Sp* effet *m* (*donné à une balle*); contorsion *f* (*des traits, du visage*); **to give one's ankle a t.,** se fouler la cheville; (*more serious*) se faire une entorse; **with a t. of the wrist,** avec un tour de poignet; **give the lid another t.,** donne encore un tour au couvercle;

(b) (*of coil*) spire *f*; tournant *m*, coude *m* (*d'une rue etc*); **t. of rope round a post,** tour de corde autour d'un poteau; **road full of twists and turns,** route pleine de tours et de détours; **final t. in a story,** tour inattendu à la fin d'un récit; *Br F* **to be round the t.,** être fou *ou* cinglé;

(c) (*distortion*) déformation *f*; gauchissement *m* (*d'une pièce de bois*); perversion *f* (*du sens d'un texte*); perversion (*d'esprit*);

(d) (*something twisted*) torsade *f*, tortillon *m* (*de cheveux*); écheveau *m* (*de laine*); tortillon, cornet *m* (*de papier*); **sweet in a t. of paper,** bonbon *m* dans une papillote; **t. (tobacco),** tabac mis en corde; **t. of tobacco,** rouleau *m ou* boudin *m* de tabac;

(e) (*thread*) fil retors; cordon *m*, cordonnet *m*;

(f) (*dance*) twist *m*.

twist² **1** *vt* tordre, tortiller (*ses cheveux, un cordage etc*); tirebouchonner (*son mouchoir*); *Tex etc* retordre (*le fil*); se tordre (*le bras etc*); se déboîter (*le genou*); dénaturer (*les paroles de qn, le sens d'un texte*); altérer (*la vérité, le sens de qch*); donner de l'effet à (*une balle*); **to t. together,** torsader; câbler (*des fils métalliques*); **to t. one's ankle,** se faire une entorse; (*less serious*) se fouler la cheville; **to t. s.o.'s arm,** tordre *ou* retourner le bras à qn; *Fig* exercer une pression sur qn; *Hum* **if you t. my arm,** si tu me forces, si tu insistes.

2 *vi* (*of worm etc*) se tordre; se tortiller; (*spiral*) former une spirale; (*of smoke*) former des volutes; (*of road etc*) tourner, faire des tours; (*dance*) twister; **to get all twisted,** s'entortiller; **to t. and turn,** (*of road etc*) serpenter.

►**twist off** **1** *vi* (*of lid*) se dévisser. **2** *vtsep* dévisser (*le couvercle*).

►**twist round** **1** *vtaspo* (*wrap around*) **to t. sth round sth,** rouler *ou* entortiller qch autour de qch; *F* **he can t. her round his little finger,** il la mène par le bout du nez. **2** *vi* (*turn round*) **to t. round in one's seat,** se tourner sur son siège.

►**twist up** **1** *vi* (*of smoke*) s'élever en spirale. **2** *vtsep* emmêler, entortiller; **to get all twisted up,** (*of cables etc*) s'emmêler, s'entortiller.

twisted ['twıstıd] *adj* tordu, tors; (*wire etc*) retors; (*tree*) tortueux; (*limb*) contourné; (*meaning etc*) perverti, dénaturé, altéré; **t. mind,** esprit tordu *ou* retors; **he's so bitter and t.,** il est tellement amer et tordu; **face t. with pain,** traits contractés *ou* tordus par la douleur; *Archit* **t. pillar,** colonne torse; **the t. wreckage of the plane/car,** l'épave enchevêtrée de l'avion/de la voiture.

twisted-pair ['twıstıd'peər] *adj* **t.-p. cable,** câble torsadé.

twister ['twıstər] *n* **(a)** *F* (*swindler*) escroc *m*; **(b)** *Am F* (*tornado*) tornade *f*.

twisting ['twıstıŋ] *adj* (*sentier*) tortueux.

twisty ['twıstı] *adj* (*road etc*) tortueux.

twit¹ [twıt] *n esp Br Sl* andouille *f*, imbécile *m*.

twit² *vt esp Lit* narguer, taquiner (*qn*); **to t. s.o. with sth,** railler qn de qch.

twitch¹ [twıtʃ] *n* **(a)** (*jerk*) saccade *f*, petit coup sec; **(b)** élancement *m* (*de douleur*); **(c)** contraction soudaine (*du visage*); crispation nerveuse (*des mains*); mouvement convulsif (*d'un membre*); **facial t.,** tic *m* (nerveux).

twitch² **1** *vt* **(a)** tirer vivement, donner une saccade à (*qch*); **(b)** contracter (*ses traits*); crisper (*les mains, le visage*); **to t. its tail,** (*of cat*) faire de petits mouvements de la queue. **2** *vi* (*of face*) se contracter nerveusement; (*of eyelids*) clignoter; (*of hands*) se crisper nerveusement.

twitter¹ ['twıtər] *n* **(a)** (*of birds*) gazouillement *m*, gazouillis *m*; **(b)** *F* **to be in a t.,** (*of person*) être tout en émoi *ou* dans tous ses états.

twitter² *vi* (*of bird*) gazouiller.

twittering ['twıtərıŋ] *n* gazouillement *m*.

'twixt [twıkst] *prep Arch & Lit* entre.

two [tuː] *n* deux *m*; **twenty-t.,** vingt-deux; *Gym etc* **one t.! one t.!,** une deux! une deux!; **no t. men are alike,** il n'y a pas deux hommes qui se ressemblent; **to break/fold sth in t.,** casser/plier qch en deux; **to walk in twos** *or* **t. by t.** *or* **t. and t.,** marcher deux à deux *ou* (deux) par deux; *Fig* **to put t. and t. together,** tirer ses conclusions (*après avoir rapproché les faits*); *F* **that makes t. of us,** on est deux; **t. fours** *or* **four twos are eight,** deux fois quatre *ou* quatre fois deux font huit; **at t. (o'clock),** à deux heures; **a mother of t.,** la mère de deux enfants; **the t. of us/them,** nous/eux deux; *Cards* **t. of spades,** deux de pique; **t.-engine(d),** bimoteur; **t.-horse carriage,** voiture *f* à deux chevaux; *Aut* **t.-door,** (*voiture*) à deux portes; *Mus* **t. part song,** chanson *f* à deux voix; **t.-headed,** bicéphale; *Her* (*aigle*) double, à deux têtes; *Mus* **t. part song,** chanson *f* à deux voix; *Pol* **t.-party system,** système biparti(te); *El* **t.-phase,** (*courant*) bi-phasé; **t.-seater,** voiture *ou* avion *m* à deux places; (*plane*) biplace *m*; **t.-wheeler,** deux-roues *m inv*; **t.-yearly,** biennial.

two-bit ['tuːbıt] *adj Am F* de quatre sous, de rigolo; (*person*) à la noix.

two-colour ['tuːkʌlər] *adj* de deux couleurs, bicolore; (*print ribbon*) bicolore; *Typ* **t.-c. process,** bichromie *f*.

two-dimensional [tuːd(a)ı'menʃən(ə)l] *adj* bidimensionnel; *Fig Pej* (*character, film etc*) simpliste, superficiel.

two-edged ['tuːedʒd] *adj* (*épée, argument*) à deux tranchants, à double tranchant; (*ambiguous*) ambigu, -uë.

two-faced ['tuːfeıst] *adj* (*person*) hypocrite.

twofer ['tuːfər] *n US* deux billets *etc* vendus pour le prix d'un.

twofold ['tuːfəʊld] **1** *adj* double; (*cordage*) à deux brins. **2** *adv* doublement; **kindness returned t.,** bontés rendues au double.

two-four ['tuː'fɔːr] *adj Mus* **t.-f. time,** mesure *f* à deux quatre; **in t.-f. time,** en deux quatre.

two-handed [tuː'hændıd] *adj* **(a)** **t.-h. sword,** épée *f* à deux mains, espadon *m*; **(b)** *Zool etc* bimane; **(c)** *Cards etc* (*jeu*) qui se joue à deux.

two-legged [tuː'legd, -'legıd] *adj* bipède.

twopence ['tʌpəns] *n Br* deux pence *m*; *Fig F* **it isn't worth t.,** ça ne vaut pas chipette *ou* pas un sou.

twopenny ['tʌp(ə)nı] *adj Br* à *ou* de deux pence.

twopenny-halfpenny ['tʌp(ə)nı'heıpnı] *adj Br* **(a)** **a t.-h. stamp,** un timbre de deux pence et demi; **(b)** *Fig F* de quatre sous; (*person*) à la noix; **all that fuss over a t.-h. ring!,** tout ça pour une méchante bague de quatre sous!

two-piece ['tuːpiːs] **1** *adj* (*suit, swimwuit*) en deux pièces. **2** *n* **t.-p. (suit/swimsuit),** complet *m ou* tailleur *m*/maillot *m* de bain en deux pièces, deux-pièces *m*.

two-pin ['tuːpın] *adj* **t.-p. plug,** prise *f* à deux fiches; **t.-p. socket,** prise à deux douilles.

two-ply ['tuːplaı] *adj* (*cordage*) à deux brins; (*laine*) deux fils; (*papier*) double épaisseur.

two-sided [tuː'saıdıd] *adj* **(a)** (*contract etc*) bilatéral; **(b)** (*question, argument etc*) qui comporte deux points de vue.

twosome ['tuːsəm] *n* **(a)** (*game*) jeu *m ou* partie *f* à deux joueurs; (*dance*) danse *f* par couples; **(b)** (*pair*) paire *f*, couple *m* (*d'amis etc*); **let's just go as a t.,** allons-y rien que tous les deux.

two-step ['tuːstep] *n Mus* pas *m* de deux.

two-stroke ['tuːstrəʊk] *adj* (*moteur, cycle*) à deux temps; **t.-s. mixture,** (mélange *m*) deux-temps *m*.

two-time ['tu:taɪm] *vt F* tromper *(qn)*.
two-timer [tu:'taɪmər] *n F* mari *ou* copain *ou* femme *ou* copine infidèle.
two-timing ['tu:taɪmɪŋ] *adj esp Am F* infidèle.
two-tone ['tu:təʊn] *adj (peinture, voiture)* deux tons; *(klaxon etc)* à deux notes.
two-way ['tu:weɪ] *adj (rue)* à double sens; *(miroir)* sans tain; *El (commutateur)* à deux directions; *Telecom* bilatéral; *F* **a relationship is a t.-w. thing,** une relation amoureuse ne peut exister qu'à double sens; **t.-w. radio,** poste émetteur-récepteur; **t.-w. trade,** commerce *m* dans les deux sens.
tycoon [taɪ'ku:n] *n F* magnat *m*, grand manitou.
tying up *n* **(a)** ficelage *m (d'un paquet etc)*; **(b)** mise *f* à l'attache *(d'un cheval etc)*; **(c)** ligotage *m (de qn)*; **(d)** immobilisation *f (de ses capitaux)*.
tyke [taɪk] *n F* **(a)** *(dog)* vilain chien; **(b)** *(person)* **(dirty) t.,** salaud *m*; **(c)** *(small child)* môme *mf*; *(mischievous child)* diablotin *m*.
tympanum, *pl* **-a, -ums** ['tɪmpənəm, -ə, -əmz] *n Anat Archit* tympan *m*.
type¹ [taɪp] *n* **(a)** type *m*; **people/books of this t.,** des personnes/des livres de ce genre; **people of every t.,** des gens de toutes sortes; *F* **he's/she's not my t.,** il/elle n'est pas mon genre; **she's not the t. to ...,** elle n'est pas du genre à ...; *F* **the t. with the red beard,** *(person)* le type à barbe rousse; *Biol* **t. genus,** genre type; **(b)** *Typ (letters)* caractères *mpl*; **to print in large t.,** imprimer en gros caractères; **in t.,** composé; **wait till you see it in t.,** attend de le voir imprimé *ou* de voir ce que ça rend imprimé; **t. face,** œil *m* (de caractère).
type² **1** *vt (write on typewriter)* écrire *ou* taper à la machine, dactylographier; *F* taper *(une lettre etc)* (à la machine). **2** *vi* écrire *ou* taper à la machine, dactylographier; **can you t.?,** savez-vous taper à la machine?; **he types well,** il tape bien.
type³ *vt Med* déterminer le groupe *(sanguin etc)*.
►**type out** *vtsep* taper *(qch)* à la machine.
►**type up** *vtsep* taper *(qch)* au propre.
typecast ['taɪpkɑ:st] *vt Th Cin (pt & pp* **typecast***)* donner toujours les mêmes rôles à *(un acteur)*; **she was being typecast as a dumb blonde,** elle était cantonnée aux rôles de blondes écervelées.
typescript ['taɪpskrɪpt] *n* texte dactylographié.
typeset ['taɪpset] *vt (pt & pp* **typeset***)* composer; **typeset by MWP,** composition MWP.
typesetter ['taɪpsetər] *n (person)* compositeur *m*; *(machine)* machine *f* à composer.
typesetting ['taɪpsetɪŋ] *n Typ* composition *f*; **who did the t.?,** qui a fait la composition?; **t. machine,** machine *f* à composer; **t. techniques,** techniques *fpl* de composition.
typewriter ['taɪpraɪtər] *n* machine *f* à écrire; **to write sth on a t.,** écrire *ou* taper qch à la machine.
typewriting ['taɪpraɪtɪŋ] *n* dactylographie *f*.
typewritten ['taɪprɪt(ə)n] *adj (document etc)* écrit *ou* tapé à la machine, dactylographié.
typhoid ['taɪfɔɪd] **1** *adj Med* typhoïde; *(bacille)* typhoïdique; **t. fever,** (fièvre *f*) typhoïde *f*. **2** *n* (fièvre *f*) typhoïde *f*.
typhoon [taɪ'fu:n] *n Met* typhon *m*.
typhus ['taɪfəs] *n Med* typhus *m*.
typical ['tɪpɪk(ə)l] *adj* typique; **the t. Frenchman,** le Français typique; **in a t. day you can earn £300,** en une journée normale vous pouvez gagner 300 livres; *F* **isn't that t. (of him/her)!,** c'est bien de lui/d'elle!; **t. male/woman/** *etc***!,** c'est bien un homme/une femme/*etc*!; **your letter took six days to get here - t.!,** ta lettre a mis six jours pour arriver — ça c'est typique! *ou* ça ne m'étonne pas!
typically ['tɪpɪklɪ] *adv* typiquement; **he's t. French,** c'est le vrai type français; *F* **she was t. late,** conformément à son habitude elle était en retard; **t. employees work a 40-hour week,** l'employé moyen travaille 40 heures par semaine.
typify ['tɪpɪfaɪ] *vt* **(a)** *(of symbol etc)* représenter *(qch)*, symboliser *(qch)*; **(b)** *(of specimen etc)* être caractéristique de *(sa classe etc)*; *(of person)* être le type de, personnifier *(l'officier etc)*.
typing ['taɪpɪŋ] *n* dactylographie *f*, *F* dactylo *f*; **t. error,** faute *f* de frappe; **t. paper,** papier *m* machine; **t. pool,** pool *m* de dactylos; **t. speed,** vitesse *f* de frappe.
typist ['taɪpɪst] *n* **(copy) t.,** dactylographe *mf*, *F* dactylo *mf*; **audio t.,** dactylo audio-magnéto; **t.'s error,** faute *f* de frappe.
typo ['taɪpəʊ] *n Typ F* coquille *f*.
typographer [taɪ'pɒgrəfər] *n* typographe *mf*.
typographic(al) [taɪpə'græfɪk, -ɪk(ə)l] *adj* typographique.
typographically ['taɪpə'græfɪklɪ] *adv* typographiquement.
typography [taɪ'pɒgrəfɪ] *n* typographie *f*.
tyrannical [tɪ'rænɪk(ə)l] *adj* tyrannique.
tyrannically ['tɪrænɪklɪ] *adv* tyranniquement.
tyrannize ['tɪrənaɪz] **1** *vi* faire le tyran; **to t. over s.o.,** tyranniser *(qn)*; **2** *vt* tyranniser *(qn)*.
tyranny ['tɪrənɪ] *n* tyrannie *f*.
tyrant ['taɪrənt] *n* tyran *m*.
tyre ['taɪər] *n* **(a)** *esp Br* pneu *m*, *pl* pneus, pneumatique *m*; **cross ply/radial ply t.,** pneu à carcasse croisée/radiale; **t. lever,** démonte-pneu *m*, *pl* démonte-pneus; **t. marks,** *(in mud, snow etc)* empreintes *fpl ou* traces *fpl* de pneu.
tyro ['taɪrəʊ] *n* novice *mf*, débutant, -ante.
Tyrol (the) [ðətɪ'rəʊl] *n* le Tyrol.
Tyrolean [tɪrə'li:ən] *adj* tyrolien; **T. hat,** chapeau tyrolien.
tzar, tzarist *etc* = **TSAR, TSARIST** *etc*.

U

U, u [juː] *n* (la lettre) U, u *m*; *Old-fashioned F* **U and non U,** ce qui est bien *ou* comme il faut, et ce qui ne l'est pas; **U bend,** (*in pipe*) coude *m*; (*in road*) virage *m* en épingle à cheveux; **U boat,** sous-marin allemand; *MecE* **U bolt,** étrier *m*; *Cin* **U film,** film *m* pour tout le monde; *Geog* **U-shaped valley,** vallée *f* (à profil) en U; *Aut* **U turn,** demi-tour *m*, *pl* demi-tours; *Fig* revirement *m*; **no U turns,** demi-tour interdit; **to do a (complete) U turn on sth,** procéder à un revirement *ou* à un virage à 180 degrés sur qch.

UAE [juːeɪ'iː] *n* (*abbr* **United Arab Emirates**) Émirats Arabes Unis, E.A.U..

UB40 [juːbiː'fɔːtɪ] *n* (*abbr* **unemployment benefit form 40**) = carte justifiant la condition de chômeur.

ubiquitous [juː'bɪkwɪtəs] *adj* (*person, divinity*) doué d'ubiquité; (*substance, theme*) omniprésent; **the u. hamburger restaurant,** le restaurant de hamburgers qu'on trouve partout.

ubiquity [juː'bɪkwɪtɪ] *n* ubiquité *f*; omniprésence *f*.

UCCA ['ʌkə] *n abbr* **Universities Central Council on Admissions**.

UDA [juːdiː'eɪ] *n abbr* **Ulster Defence Association**.

UDI [juːdiː'aɪ] *n abbr* **Unilateral Declaration of Independence**.

UDR [juːdiː'ɑː] *n abbr* **Ulster Defence Regiment**.

UFO ['juːfəʊ] *n* (*abbr* **unidentified flying object**) OVNI *m*.

udder ['ʌdər] *n* mamelle *f*, pis *m* (*de vache etc*).

UEFA [juː'eɪfə] *n abbr* **Union of European Football Associations**.

ufologist [juː'fɒlədʒɪst] *n* ovniologue *mf*.

Uganda [juː'gændə] *n* Ouganda *m*.

Ugandan [juː'gændən] **1** *adj* ougandais. **2** *n* Ougandais, -aise.

ugh [ʌχ] *int* pouah! beuh!

ugli, *pl* **ugli(e)s** ['ʌglɪ, -ɪz] *n* (*fruit*) tangelo *m*.

uglify ['ʌglɪfaɪ] *vt* enlaidir.

ugliness ['ʌglɪnɪs] *n* laideur *f*.

ugly ['ʌglɪ] *adj* (*person*) laid; (*building, furniture, pattern, hat, colour*) affreux, horrible, laid; (*word*) horrible; (*threatening*) (*sky, look*) menaçant; (*incident, scene*) regrettable; **she's as u. as sin,** elle est laide comme les sept péchés capitaux; **u. person,** laideron *m*; **to grow u.,** (s')enlaidir; **u. duckling,** vilain petit canard; *F* **an u. customer,** un sale type; **to turn** *or* **cut up u.,** devenir agressif; **the situation was starting to turn u.,** la situation commençait à mal tourner; **u. piece of furniture,** meuble laid *ou* horrible *ou* affreux; **u. wound,** vilaine blessure; **u. rumour,** bruit sinistre.

uh-huh *int* [ʌ'hʌ] (*agreeing, yes*) hmm hmm, oui oui; ['ʌhʌ] (*disagreeing, no, don't*) tut-tut, non non.

UHF [juːeɪtʃ'ef] *n* (*abbr* **ultra-high frequency**) fréquence ultra-haute.

UHT [juːeɪtʃ'tiː] *adj* (*abbr* **ultra high temperature**) **UHT milk,** lait *m* UHT.

UK [juː'keɪ] *n* (*abbr* **United Kingdom**) Royaume-Uni, R.-U..

Ukraine [juː'kreɪn] *n* Ukraine *f*

Ukrainian [juː'kreɪnɪən] **1** *adj* ukrainien. **2** *n* **(a)** Ukrainien, -ienne; **(b)** *Ling* ukrainien *m*.

ukulele [juːkə'leɪlɪ] *n Mus* guitare hawaïenne.

ulcer ['ʌlsər] *n* ulcère *m*; *Fig* cancer *m*; (*ugly building etc*) atrocité *f*; **peptic u.,** ulcère simple de l'estomac *ou* du duodénum.

ulcerate ['ʌlsəreɪt] *Med* **1** *vt* ulcérer; **ulcerated wound,** blessure ulcérée *ou* ulcéreuse. **2** *vi* s'ulcérer.

ulceration [ʌlsə'reɪʃən] *n* ulcération *f*.

ulcerative ['ʌls(ə)rətɪv] *adj Med* ulcératif.

ulcerous ['ʌls(ə)rəs] *adj Med* ulcéreux.

ullage ['ʌlɪdʒ] *n* creux *m* du tonneau.

ulna ['ʌlnə] *n Anat* cubitus *m*.

Ulster ['ʌlstər] *n* **(a)** Ulster *m*; **(b)** (*coat*) **u.,** ulster *m*.

Ulsterman, *pl* **-men** ['ʌlstəmən] *n* Ulstérien *m*.

Ulsterwoman, *pl* **-women** ['ʌlstəwʊmən, -wɪmɪn] *n* Ulstérienne *f*.

ult [ʌlt] *abbr* **ultimo**.

ulterior [ʌl'tɪərɪər] *adj* ultérieur **u. designs,** desseins secrets; **u. motive,** motif secret *ou* caché, arrière pensée *f*; **without u. motive,** sans arrière pensée.

ultimate ['ʌltɪmət] **1** *adj* **(a)** (*final*) final, -als, définitif; **is that your u. position on this?,** est-ce là votre opinion définitive?; **the u. decision is his,** c'est à lui qu'appartient la décision finale; **u. goal,** but final; **certain of u. success,** certain du succès final; **they made the u. sacrifice,** ils ont fait l'ultime sacrifice;

(b) (*basic, fundamental*) fondamental, -aux; **the u. constituents of matter,** les constituants fondamentaux de la matière; **is this the u. physical particle?,** ceci est-il la particule physique fondamentale *ou* première?;

(c) (*supreme, best etc*) absolu; **the u. double-glazing/laser printer/***etc*, le double-vitrage/l'imprimante laser/*etc* absolu(e); **the u. deterrent,** l'arme de dissuasion absolue; **that really is the u. cheek!,** c'est vraiment le comble du culot!; **he really is the u. incompetent!,** il est l'incompétence portée à son comble;

(d) (*furthest*) le plus lointain; **the u. ends of the universe,** les extrémités les plus lointaines *ou* les limites externes de l'univers; **we trace our u. origins back to ...,** nous avons établi nos origines les plus lointaines à ... .

2 *n* **(a)** *Rel Phil* **the u.,** l'absolu *m*; **(b) the u.,** le fin du fin; **the u. in luxury,** le summum du luxe; **it's the u. in vulgarity,** c'est du dernier vulgaire, c'est le comble de la vulgarité.

ultimately ['ʌltɪmɪtlɪ] *adv* **(a)** (*finally, in the end*) finalement; **when he u. gets here,** quand finalement il arrivera; **the events which led u. to his downfall,** les événements qui ont finalement conduit à sa chute; **(b)** (*at bottom, basically*) en fin de compte; **u. it's the same thing,** en fin de compte *ou* au fond c'est la même chose.

ultimatum, *pl* **-tums, -ta** [ʌltɪ'meɪtəm, -təmz, -tə] *n* ultimatum *m*; **to deliver an u. to s.o., to present s.o. with an u.,** adresser un ultimatum à qn.

ultimo ['ʌltɪməʊ] *adv Old-fashioned Com* du mois dernier; **on the tenth u.,** le dix du mois dernier.

ultra- ['ʌltrə] *pref* extrême.

ultrafashionable ['ʌltrəfæʃənəb(ə)l] *adj* à la pointe de la mode, *F* hyper-mode *inv*.

ultrahigh [ʌltrə'haɪ] *adj Phys* **u. frequency,** très haute fréquence.

ultramarine [ʌltrəmə'riːn] *adj & n* **u. (blue),** (bleu d')outremer *m*.

ultramodern [ʌltrə'mɒd(ə)n] *adj* ultramoderne.

ultramontane [ʌltrə'mɒnteɪn] *adj & n* ultramontain, -aine.

ultrasensitive [ʌltrə'sensɪtɪv] *adj* ultrasensible.

ultrashort [ʌltrə'ʃɔːt] *adj Phys* ultra-court.

ultrasonic [ʌltrə'sɒnɪk] **1** *adj* ultrasonique. **2** *n* (*usu with sing verb*) **ultrasonics,** science *f* des ultrasons.

ultrasound (scan) ['ʌltrəsaʊnd (skæn)] *n Med* échographie *f*.

ultraviolet [ʌltrə'vaɪələt] *adj Phys* ultra(-)violet; **u. rays,** rayons ultra(-)violets; *Med* **u. treatment,** traitement *m* aux (rayons) ultra(-)violets.

ultra vires [ʌltrə'vaɪəriːz, ʊltrə'viːreɪz] *adj & adv Jur* au delà de ses pouvoirs.

ululate ['juːljʊleɪt] *vi* (*of owl etc*) ululer, huer; (*of jackal etc*) hurler; (*of person, mourner*) se lamenter.

ululation [juːljʊ'leɪʃən] *n* ululation *f*, ululement *m* (*du hibou etc*); hurlement *m* (*du chacal etc*); lamentation *f* (*d'une personne*).

Ulysses ['juːlɪsiːz] *n* Ulysse.

um [ʌm] **1** *int* (*hesitating in speaking*) heu. **2** *vi* **to u. and err,** bafouiller.

umber ['ʌmbər] **1** *n Art* terre *f* d'ombre *ou* de Sienne, ombre *f*; **burnt u.**, terre d'ombre brûlée. **2** *adj* couleur *inv* d'ombre.

umbilical [ʌm'bɪlɪk(ə)l, ʌmbɪ'laɪk(ə)l] *adj Anat* ombilical, -aux; **u. cord**, cordon ombilical.

umbilicus [ʌm'bɪlɪkəs, ʌmbɪ'laɪkəs] *n* ombilic *m*, nombril *m*.

umbrage ['ʌmbrɪdʒ] *n* ombrage *m*, ressentiment *m*; **to take u. at sth**, prendre ombrage de qch, se froisser de qch .

umbrella [ʌm'brelə] *n* **(a)** parapluie *m*; **to put up one's u.**, ouvrir son parapluie; **to put down** *or* **to fold (up) one's u.**, fermer *ou* replier son parapluie; **telescopic u.**, parapluie télescopique; **beach u.**, parasol *m*; **u. stand**, porte-parapluies *m inv*; **(b) under the u. of the United Nations**, sous la protection des Nations Unies; **u. organization**, organisation *f* qui en regroupe plusieurs autres; **(c)** *Mil Av* **air** *or* **aerial u.**, parapluie aérien, ombrelle *f* de protection aérienne; **nuclear u.**, parapluie nucléaire; **(d)** ombrelle *f* (*de méduse*).

umlaut ['ʊmlaʊt] *n Ling* **(a)** inflexion *f* vocalique, métaphonie *f*; **(b)** (*sign*) tréma *m*.

umph [hm] *int* (*disbelieving, not pleased*) hum!, hmm!

umpire¹ ['ʌmpaɪər] *n Sp etc* arbitre *m*, juge *m*; **to be an u. at a match**, arbitrer un match.

umpire² *Sp etc* **1** *vt* arbitrer (*un match*). **2** *vi* arbitrer (le *ou* un match).

umpteen [ʌmp'tiːn] *adj F* je ne sais combien; **I've told you u. times not to ...**, je t'ai dit mille *ou* je ne sais combien de fois de ne pas ...; **she's got u. books on Africa**, elle a des tas de livres sur l'Afrique; **to have u. reasons for doing sth**, avoir trente-six raisons de faire qch.

umpteenth [ʌmp'tiːnθ] *adj F* **that's the u. time I've told you**, c'est la (é)nième fois que je te le dis.

UN [juː'en] *n* (*abbr* **United Nations**) Nations Unies, O.N.U..

'un [ən] *pron Sl* (= *one*) **a little 'un**, un petit, une petite; **he's a bad 'un**, c'est un sale type.

un- [ʌn] *pref* (*with adjectives*) in; non; peu, mal; dé; (*with nouns*) in; sans; manque *m* de, absence *f* de; dé; (*with verbs*) dé; ne pas.

unabashed [ʌnə'bæʃt] *adj* aucunement ébranlé *ou* décontenancé *ou* déconcerté.

unabated [ʌnə'beɪtɪd] *adj* qui n'a pas diminué, non diminué; **for three days the storm continued u.**, pendant trois jours l'orage a continué sans répit; **the riots went on u.**, les émeutes continuèrent sans faiblir.

unabbreviated [ʌnə'briːvɪeɪtɪd] *adj* non abrégé.

unable [ʌn'eɪb(ə)l] *adj* incapable; **to be u. to do sth**, ne pas pouvoir faire qch; (*because of external factor*) être dans l'impossibilité de faire qch, ne pas pouvoir faire qch; **he seems u. to understand you**, il semble être incapable de vous comprendre; **we are u. to help you**, nous ne sommes pas en mesure de vous aider; **I was u. to persuade him**, je n'ai pas pu le persuader.

unabridged [ʌnə'brɪdʒd] *adj* non abrégé, intégral, -aux; **u. edition**, édition intégrale.

unaccented, unaccentuated [ʌnək'sentɪd, ʌnək'sentjʊeɪtɪd] *adj* inaccentué; *Ling* (*of syllable etc*) non accentué, atone; *Mus* **u. beat**, temps *m* faible.

unacceptable [ʌnək'septəb(ə)l] *adj* inacceptable; (*théorie*) irrecevable; (*conduite*) inadmissible; **conditions u. to us**, conditions que nous ne pouvons pas agréer; **it's quite u. for so many people to be homeless**, il est tout à fait inacceptable *ou* inadmissible que tant de gens soient sans foyer.

unacceptably [ʌnək'septəblɪ] *adv* **an u. high level of ...**, un niveau inadmissible *ou* intolérable de ...; **what they are, quite u., demanding is ...**, l'objet tout à fait inadmissible de leur demande est ... .

unaccommodating [ʌnə'kɒmədeɪtɪŋ] *adj* (*person*) peu accommodant, désobligeant.

unaccompanied [ʌnə'kʌmp(ə)nɪd] *adj* **(a)** (*person, baggage*) non accompagné; **(b)** *Mus* sans accompagnement; **passage for u. violin**, passage pour violon seul.

unaccomplished [ʌnə'kʌmplɪʃt] *adj* **(a)** (*project*) inaccompli, non réalisé; (*work*) inachevé; **(b)** (*person, performance etc*) médiocre.

unaccountable [ʌnə'kaʊntəb(ə)l] *adj* **(a)** (*phénomène*) inexplicable; **(b)** (*conduite*) bizarre, étrange.

unaccountably [ʌnə'kaʊntəblɪ] *adv* inexpliquablement.

unaccounted [ʌnə'kaʊntɪd] *adj* **these £10 are u. for in the balance sheet**, ces 10 livres ne figurent pas au bilan; **five of the passengers are still u. for**, on reste sans nouvelles de cinq passagers; **two books are still u. for**, il manque toujours deux livres.

unaccustomed [ʌnə'kʌstəmd] *adj* **(a)** inaccoutumé, inhabituel; **(b)** (*person*) **u. to sth/to doing sth**, peu habitué à qch/à faire qch; **u. as I am to public speaking**, n'ayant pas l'habitude de faire des discours.

unacknowledged [ʌnək'nɒlɪdʒd] *adj* **(a)** *esp Jur* (*enfant*) non reconnu; (*talents*) non reconnu; **(b)** (*citation*) sans nom d'auteur; **(c)** (*lettre*) resté sans réponse; **you shouldn't let his letter go u.**, tu ne devrais pas laisser sa lettre sans réponse.

unacquainted [ʌnə'kweɪntɪd] *adj* **to be u. with s.o.**, ne pas connaître qn; **to be u. with sth**, ignorer qch; **we are not u. with pressure**, nous n'ignorons pas ce que c'est que le stress.

unadaptable [ʌnə'dæptəb(ə)l] *adj* (*person*) qui ne s'adapte pas aux circonstances.

unadapted [ʌnə'dæptɪd] *adj* mal adapté, peu adapté (**to sth**, à qch).

unaddressed [ʌnə'drest] *adj* (*colis etc*) sans adresse, qui ne porte pas d'adresse.

unadopted [ʌnə'dɒptɪd] *adj* non adopté; **to remain u.**, (*of measure*) rester en souffrance; *Br* **u. road**, rue non prise en charge par la municipalité.

unadorned [ʌnə'dɔːnd] *adj* sans ornement, sans parure; *esp Lit* **her u. beauty**, sa beauté sans parure *ou* sans fard; **the u. truth**, la vérité pure *ou* toute nue.

unadulterated [ʌnə'dʌltəreɪtɪd] *adj* pur, sans mélange; (*vin*) non frelaté; **u. joy**, joie *f* sans mélange; **the u. truth**, la vérité pure et simple; **u. by Western influences**, non corrompu par les influences occidentales; **this is pure u. garbage!**, ceci est purement et simplement de la foutaise!

unadventurous [ʌnəd'ventʃərəs] *adj* (*life, person*) peu aventureux; (*style, performance, director, prose etc*) peu audacieux; **we went to Spain again — that's very u. of you**, nous sommes retournés en Espagne — ce n'était pas très aventureux de votre part.

unadventurously [ʌnəd'ventʃərəslɪ] *adv* (*produced, designed*) peu audacieusement; (*to decide, choose*) sans prendre des risques; **we very u. chose beige carpets again**, nous n'avons pas été très aventureux et avons encore choisi des moquettes beiges.

unadvertised [ʌn'ædvətaɪzd] *adj* (*product, meeting etc*) sans publicité; (*action etc*) discret, -ète.

unadvisable [ʌnəd'vaɪzəb(ə)l] *adj* (*action*) peu sage, imprudent; **alcohol is u. for people suffering from heart complaints**, l'alcool est à déconseiller aux cardiaques.

unadvised [ʌnəd'vaɪzd] *adj esp Lit* imprudent.

unaesthetic [ʌniːs'θetɪk] *adj* inesthétique.

unaffected [ʌnə'fektɪd] *adj* **(a)** (*person, behaviour*) sans affectation, naturel, simple; (*style*) sans recherche, sans apprêt; **u. joy**, joie qui n'a rien de simulé; **u. modesty**, modestie simple; **to be u. by sth**, (*of person*) ne pas être influencé par qch; (*by s.o.'s tears*) rester impassible *ou* insensible à qch; (*of thing*) (*by rain, cold, heat etc*) ne pas être altéré par qch; **we were u. by the strike/recession**, nous n'avons pas été affectés par la grève/récession; **there's snow everywhere, but the north-west is u.**, il y a de la neige partout, mais le nord-ouest n'est pas touché; **u. by air or water**, inaltérable à l'air ou à l'eau.

unaffectedly [ʌnə'fektɪdlɪ] *adv* (*to behave, speak*) sans recherche, simplement, sans affectation; (*dressed*) sans recherche, sans apprêt.

unaffiliated [ʌnə'fɪlɪeɪtɪd] *adj* non affilié (**to**, à).

unafraid [ʌnə'freɪd] *adj* sans peur.

unaided [ʌn'eɪdɪd] **1** *adv* sans aide, sans assistance; **he did it u.**, il l'a fait tout seul *ou* à lui seul. **2** *adj* **by my own u. efforts**, par mes propres moyens.

unaired [ʌn'eəd] *adj* non aéré.

unalike [ʌnə'laɪk] *adj* dissemblable, différent; **they are not u.**, ils se ressemblent un peu, ils ne sont pas totalement dissemblables.

unalleviated [ʌnə'liːvɪeɪtɪd] *adj* sans soulagement; **u. boredom**, ennui mortel.

unallocated [ʌn'æləʊkeɪtɪd] *adj* (*rooms, places*) non assigné *ou* affecté; (*money, grants*) non alloué.

unalloyed [ʌnə'lɔɪd] *adj Lit* (*bonheur*) parfait.

unalterable [ʌn'ɔːlt(ə)rəb(ə)l] *adj* immuable; (*character*) inaltérable.

unalterably [ʌn'ɔːlt(ə)rəblɪ] *adv* immuablement.

unaltered [ʌn'ɔːltəd] *adj* inchangé, toujours le même; **let's leave it u.**, n'y touchons pas.

unambiguous [ʌnæm'bɪgjʊəs] *adj* non équivoque; (*réponse*) sans ambiguïté; **what he meant was quite u.**, il a été tout à fait clair; **u. terms**, termes clairs.

unambiguously [ʌnæm'bɪgjʊəslɪ] *adv* (*worded etc*) sans équivoque, sans ambiguïté; **he told us quite u. to ...**, il nous a dit tout à fait clairement de ... .

unambitious [ʌnæm'bɪʃəs] *adj* (*person*) sans ambition, peu ambitieux; (*project, undertaking*) modeste.

un-American [ʌnə'merɪk(ə)n] *adj* antiaméricain; contraire à l'esprit américain.

unamiable [ʌn'eɪmɪəb(ə)l] *adj* peu aimable, désagréable.

unamused [ʌnə'mju:zd] *adj* **she was distinctly u.,** visiblement, cela ne l'amusait pas.

unanimity [ju:nə'nɪmɪtɪ] *n* unanimité *f*, accord *m*.

unanimous [jʊ'nænɪməs] *adj* unanime; **they were u. in accusing him,** ils étaient unanimes à l'accuser; **to reach a u. decision,** se prononcer à l'unanimité; **u. vote,** résolution adoptée à l'unanimité.

unanimously [jʊ'nænɪməslɪ] *adv* à l'unanimité; **u. elected,** élu à l'unanimité.

unannounced [ʌnə'naʊnst] *adj* sans être annoncé; **he marched in u.,** il est entré sans se faire annoncer.

unanswerable [ʌn'ɑ:ns(ə)rəb(ə)l] *adj* (*argument*) incontestable, irréfutable; **u. question,** question à laquelle on ne peut pas répondre.

unanswered [ʌn'ɑ:nsəd] *adj* **(a)** sans réponse; **u. letter,** lettre sans réponse; **I had to leave two questions u.,** j'ai dû laisser deux questions sans réponse; **our letter has remained u.,** notre lettre est restée sans réponse; **(b)** (*argument*) irréfuté.

unappealing [ʌnə'pi:lɪŋ] *adj* peu attrayant.

unappeased [ʌnə'pi:zd] *adj* (*hunger, desire, lust*) inassouvi.

unappetizing [ʌn'æpɪtaɪzɪŋ] *adj* peu appétissant.

unappreciated [ʌnə'pri:ʃɪeɪtɪd] *adj* peu apprécié, peu estimé; (*contribution etc*) peu apprécié; (*difficulty, scope of task etc*) sous-estimé.

unappreciative [ʌnə'pri:ʃɪətɪv] *adj* (*audience*) insensible; (*report etc*) peu favorable; **she was very u. of everything we had done for her,** elle ne montrait aucune gratitude pour tout ce qu'on avait fait pour elle, elle était tout à fait inconsciente de tout ce que nous avons fait pour elle; **don't be so u.!,** ne sois pas si ingrat!

unapproachable [ʌnə'prəʊtʃəb(ə)l] *adj* (*person, place*) inaccessible; **an u. sort of person,** une personne d'un abord difficile.

unarguable [ʌn'ɑ:gjʊəb(ə)l] *adj* (*case, theory etc*) indéfendable.

unarguably [ʌn'ɑ:gjʊəblɪ] *adv* (*undisputably*) incontestablement.

unarmed [ʌn'ɑ:md] *adj* (*person*) non armé, désarmé; **u. combat,** combat sans armes; **I am u.,** je n'ai pas d'armes; **I'm not going in there u.,** je n'entre pas là-dedans sans armes.

unashamed [ʌnə'ʃeɪmd] *adj* **to be u. about doing sth,** ne pas avoir honte de faire qch; **his u. nationalism,** son nationalisme éhonté; **with u. relief,** avec un soulagement qu'il *ou* qu'elle *etc* ne cherchait pas à cacher, avec un soulagement non dissimulé.

unashamedly [ʌnə'ʃeɪmɪdlɪ] *adv* sans honte; **he was u. open about it all,** il s'est exprimé sur cette affaire avec une franchise non dissimulée; **she was quite u. relieved about not having to ...,** elle ne cacha pas son soulagement à l'idée de ne pas devoir ...; **he is u. outspoken in his support of ...,** il affiche (tout à fait ouvertement) son soutien à ... .

unasked [ʌn'ɑ:skt] **1** *adv* (*faire qch*) spontanément; **she came to help us quite u.,** elle est venue nous aider sans qu'on le lui ait demandé. **2** *adj* **u. (for),** (*cadeau etc*) spontané, qu'on n'a pas demandé.

unaspirated [ʌn'æspɪreɪtɪd] *adj Ling* non aspiré.

unassailable [ʌnə'seɪləb(ə)l] *adj* (*fortress, position*) inattaquable; (*conclusion, argument*) irréfutable; **his reputation is u.,** sa réputation est hors d'atteinte.

unassimilated [ʌnə'sɪmɪleɪtɪd] *adj* inassimilé; **u. knowledge,** connaissances mal assimilées.

unassisted [ʌnə'sɪstɪd] **1** *adv* sans aide, sans assistance; **he did it u.,** il l'a fait tout seul. **2** *adj* **by her own u. efforts,** sans l'aide de personne.

unassuming [ʌnə'sju:mɪŋ] *adj* sans prétention(s), modeste.

unassumingly [ʌnə'sju:mɪŋlɪ] *adv* modestement, sans prétention(s).

unattached [ʌnə'tætʃt] *adj* **(a)** (*part, wire etc*) qui n'est pas attaché (**to,** à); **(b)** (*journalist, group etc*) indépendant (**to,** de); *Mil* (*officier*) disponible, en disponibilité; **(c)** (*not married etc*) **to be u.,** être libre *ou* sans attaches.

unattainable [ʌnə'teɪnəb(ə)l] *adj* inaccessible (**by,** à).

unattended [ʌnə'tendɪd] *adj* **(a)** (*shop, printer etc*) sans surveillance; **to leave one's car u.,** laisser sa voiture sans surveillance; **do not leave your luggage u.,** surveillez toujours vos bagages; **(b) u. to,** négligé; **don't leave the guests u. to,** ne négligez pas les invités, occupez-vous des invités; **the bad road surface/leaking pipe/***etc* **had been left** *or* **had gone u. to for months,** le revêtement de la route/le tuyau percé/*etc* n'a pas été entretenu pendant des mois; **(c)** (*person, child*) seul; (*queen etc*) sans escorte.

unattractive [ʌnə'træktɪv] *adj* peu attrayant, sans attrait, peu séduisant; (*character*) peu sympathique; **she is not u.,** elle ne manque pas de charme.

unauthenticated [ʌnɔ:'θentɪkeɪtɪd] *adj* dont l'authenticité n'est pas établie; *Jur* (*document*) non légalisé.

unauthorized [ʌn'ɔ:θəraɪzd] *adj* non autorisé, sans autorisation; **no entry to u. persons, no u. access,** accès interdit à toute personne étrangère au service.

unavailability [ʌnəveɪlə'bɪlɪtɪ] *n* indisponibilité *f*.

unavailable [ʌnə'veɪləb(ə)l] *adj* (*person, goods*) indisponible, pas disponible; (*sold out etc*) épuisé; **this reduced-price ticket is u. on certain trains,** ce billet à tarif réduit n'est pas valable pour certains trains.

unavailing [ʌnə'veɪlɪŋ] *adj* inutile; (*tears*) vain, inefficace; (*efforts*) infructueux.

unavailingly [ʌnə'veɪlɪŋlɪ] *adv* inutilement, en vain.

unavenged [ʌnə'vendʒd] *adv* **it won't go u.,** cela ne restera pas impuni; **the u. death of ...,** la mort de ... qui n'a pas été vengée.

unavoidable [ʌnə'vɔɪdəb(ə)l] *adj* inévitable; (*sort*) auquel on ne peut échapper; (*événement*) qu'on ne peut prévenir; **my absence was u.,** mon absence a été due à un cas de force majeure; **it is u. that ...,** il est inévitable que ... + *sub*.

unavoidably [ʌnə'vɔɪdəblɪ] *adv* inévitablement; **u. detained,** retenu pour raison majeure.

unaware [ʌnə'weər] *adj* ignorant, non informé, pas au courant (**of sth,** de qch); **to be u. of sth,** ignorer qch; **her husband was totally u. of what was going on,** son mari ne se rendait absolument pas compte de ce qui se passait; **he was u. that he was being watched,** il ne se rendait pas compte qu'on l'observait; **we are not u. of the need for reform,** nous n'ignorons pas la nécessité d'une réforme; **is that so?, I was u. of that,** ah oui?, je n'étais pas au courant; **you will surely not be u. of the importance of ...,** l'importance de ... ne vous a certainement pas échappé; **if there are any other problems I am u. of them,** s'il y a d'autres problèmes, je ne suis pas au courant; **he is sexually/politically/***etc* **quite u.,** il vit dans un monde où la sexualité/la politique/*etc* n'existe pas.

unawares [ʌnə'weəz] *adv* (*without realizing*) inconsciemment, sans s'en rendre compte; **to take** *or* **catch s.o. u.,** (*by surprise*) prendre qn au dépourvu.

unbalance¹ [ʌn'bæləns] *n* déséquilibre *m*.

unbalance² *vt* déséquilibrer; déranger, déséquilibrer (*l'esprit de qn*).

unbalanced [ʌn'bælənst] *adj* **(a)** (*volant*) mal équilibré; **(b)** (*esprit etc*) déséquilibré, dérangé; **(c)** *Fin* (*compte*) non soldé.

unbandage [ʌn'bændɪdʒ] *vt* débander (*une plaie*).

unbaptized [ʌnbæp'taɪzd] *adj* non baptisé.

unbar [ʌn'bɑ:r] *vt* débarrer (*une porte*).

unbearable [ʌn'beərəb(ə)l] *adj* insupportable, intolérable; **in this heat, the office is u.,** par cette chaleur le bureau n'est pas tenable.

unbearably [ʌn'beərəblɪ] *adv* insupportablement, intolérablement; **it's u. hot,** il fait une chaleur étouffante; **he's u. arrogant,** son arrogance est insupportable.

unbeatable [ʌn'bi:təb(ə)l] *adj* imbattable; (*army*) invincible.

unbeaten [ʌn'bi:t(ə)n] *adj* invaincu; (*champion, record*) qui n'a pas encore été battu.

unbecoming [ʌnbɪ'kʌmɪŋ] *adj* peu convenable, malséant (**to,** à); (*garment*) peu seyant; (*facial hair*) peu esthétique; **it's u. of him to act in this manner,** il lui sied mal d'agir de la sorte.

unbeknown [ʌnbɪ'nəʊn] **1** *adj Lit* inconnu (**to,** de). **2** *adv* (*also esp Am* **unbeknownst**) **u. to me/her/***etc*, à mon/son/*etc* insu; **to do sth u. to anyone,** faire qch à l'insu de tous.

unbelief [ʌnbɪ'li:f] *n* incrédulité *f*; **he looked at me in u.,** il me regarda avec incrédulité.

unbelievable [ʌnbɪ'li:vəb(ə)l] *adj* incroyable; **it's u. that ...,** il est incroyable que + *sub*.

unbelievably [ʌnbɪ'li:vəblɪ] *adv* incroyablement; **u. stupid,** d'une sottise incroyable.

unbeliever [ʌnbɪ'li:vər] *n* incrédule *mf*.

unbelieving [ʌnbɪ'li:vɪŋ] *adj* incrédule.

unbelievingly [ʌnbɪ'li:vɪŋlɪ] *adv* (*to say, look*) d'une manière incrédule.

unbend [ʌn'bend] *v* (*pt & pp* **unbent** [ʌn'bent]) **1** *vt* détendre (*un arc*); redresser (*une tige d'acier etc*); déplier (*la jambe*). **2** *vi* **(a)** (*relax*) se détendre; **(b)** (*straighten out*) se redresser; (*of limb*) se déplier.

unbending [ʌn'bendɪŋ] *adj* (*caractère*) inflexible, rigide; **u. attitude,** attitude intransigeante.

unbias(s)ed [ʌn'baɪəst] *adj* impartial, -aux.

unbidden [ʌn'bɪd(ə)n] *adv Old-fashioned* **to do sth u.,** faire qch spontanément *ou* sans y avoir été invité.

unbind [ʌn'baɪnd] *vt* (*pt & pp* **unbound** [ʌn'baʊnd]) **(a)** délier (*un prisonnier, les mains*); **(b)** débander (*une plaie*).

unbleached [ʌn'bliːtʃt] *adj* écru; **u. linen,** toile bise *ou* écrue; **(b)** (*cheveux*) non oxygénés.

unblemished [ʌn'blemɪʃt] *adj* sans défaut; (*reputation*) sans tache.

unblinking [ʌn'blɪŋkɪŋ] *adj* (*person*) impassible; (*gaze, look*) fixe; **with u. eyes,** sans ciller (des yeux).

unblock [ʌn'blɒk] *vt* dégager, désencombrer (*un passage*); déboucher (*un tuyau etc*); *Comptr* débloquer.

unblushing [ʌn'blʌʃɪŋ] *adj* sans vergogne, éhonté.

unblushingly [ʌn'blʌʃɪŋlɪ] *adv* sans rougir.

unbolt [ʌn'bəʊlt] *vt* déverrouiller (*une porte*); déboulonner (*un rail etc*).

unborn ['ʌnbɔːn] *adj* qui n'est pas (encore) né; **u. child,** enfant à naître; **generations yet u.** [ʌn'bɔːn], générations à venir, générations futures.

unbosom [ʌn'buzəm] *vt* **to u. oneself to s.o.,** ouvrir son cœur à qn.

unbound [ʌn'baʊnd] *adj* (*book*) non relié, broché; (*hands*) libre; (*prisoners*) pas attaché.

unbounded [ʌn'baʊndɪd] *adj* sans bornes, illimité; (*conceit ambition etc*) démesuré.

unbowed [ʌn'baʊd] *adj* invaincu, insoumis; **defeated but u.,** vaincu, mais non soumis.

unbreakable [ʌn'breɪkəb(ə)l] *adj* incassable; (*promise, rule etc*) sacré, inviolable; *Sp* (*record*) imbattable; (*habit*) immuable.

unbreathable [ʌn'briːðəb(ə)l] *adj* (*air*) irrespirable.

unbribable [ʌn'braɪbəb(ə)l] *adj* incorruptible.

unbridled [ʌn'braɪd(ə)ld] *adj* **(a)** (*passion, greed, capitalism etc*) débridé, effréné; **(b)** (*horse*) débridé, sans bride.

unbroken [ʌn'brəʊk(ə)n] *adj* **(a)** (*things*) non brisé, non cassé, intact; **(b)** intact; **u. spirit,** courage inébranlé; **(c)** (*rule*) toujours observé *ou* respecté; (*promise*) inviolé; **the peace remained u. for ten years,** la paix n'a pas été troublée pendant dix ans; *Sp* **record still u.,** record qui n'a pas été battu; **(d)** (*silence*) ininterrompu, continu; (*line of descent, ground*) non accidenté; **u. sheet of ice,** nappe de glace continue; **(e)** (*horse*) non rompu, non dressé; **(f)** *Agr* **u. ground,** terre vierge.

unbrotherly [ʌn'brʌðəlɪ] *adj* peu fraternel.

unbuckle [ʌn'bʌk(ə)l] *vt* déboucler (*une ceinture*).

unbudgeted [ʌn'bʌdʒɪtɪd] *adj* non prévu au budget.

unbuilt [ʌn'bɪlt, 'ʌnbɪlt] *adj* **u. plot, plot of u. ground,** terrain vague *ou* non construit.

unbundle [ʌn'bʌndl] *vt US* (*itemize*) détailler.

unburden [ʌn'bɜːd(ə)n] *vt* **(a) to u. the mind,** soulager *ou* alléger l'esprit; **to u. oneself** *or* **one's heart,** s'épancher; **to u. oneself to s.o.,** se confier à qn; **to u. oneself of a secret,** se soulager du poids d'un secret; **to u. one's sorrows to s.o.,** épancher ses chagrins dans le sein de qn.

unburied [ʌn'berɪd] *adj* non enseveli, non enterré.

unbusinesslike [ʌn'bɪznɪslaɪk] *adj* (*person*) peu commerçant, qui n'a pas le sens des affaires; (*procedure, handling*) peu professionnel; **to conduct one's affairs in an u. way,** mal conduire ses affaires.

unbutton [ʌn'bʌt(ə)n] *vt* déboutonner (*son manteau*); **to come unbuttoned,** se déboutonner.

uncalled-for [ʌn'kɔːldfɔːr] *adj* (*remark*) déplacé; (*rebuke*) immérité, injustifié; (*insult*) gratuit; **that was quite u.-f.,** c'était tout à fait injustifié.

uncannily [ʌn'kænɪlɪ] *adv* étrangement; (*accurate*) mystérieusement.

uncanny [ʌn'kænɪ] *adj* **(a)** (*strange, weird, inexplicable*) étrange, mystérieux; **it's u. how he knows where I am,** c'est vraiment étrange *ou* bizarre qu'il sache où je suis; **with u. accurary,** avec une exactitude surprenante; **(b)** (*eerie*) inquiétant; **it can be u. here late at night,** ici, tard la nuit, on a presque l'impression qu'il y a une présence surnaturelle.

uncared-for [ʌn'keədfɔːr] *adj* négligé; **to leave a garden u.-f.,** laisser un jardin à l'abandon.

uncaring [ʌn'keərɪŋ] *adj* qui ne se soucie pas (des autres), indifférent.

uncarpeted [ʌn'kɑːpɪtɪd] *adj* sans tapis; sans moquette.

uncatalogued [ʌn'kætəlɒgd] *adj* qui n'est pas catalogué, qui ne figure pas dans le catalogue.

unceasing [ʌn'siːsɪŋ] *adj* incessant, continu, continuel; (*travail*) assidu; (*effort*) soutenu.

unceasingly [ʌn'siːsɪŋlɪ] *adv* sans cesse, sans arrêt.

uncensored [ʌn'sensəd] *adj* (*scene, version etc*) non expurgé; (*version, edition*) intégral, -aux.

unceremonious [ʌnserɪ'məʊnɪəs] *adj* **he was packed off in a very u. way to stay with his uncle in Australia,** on l'a envoyé très cavalièrement *ou* sans aucune cérémonie chez son oncle en Australie; **after his u. departure from politics,** après qu'il eut peu glorieusement abandonné la politique; **the rather u. treatment that the visiting delegation received,** le traitement plutôt cavalier réservé à la délégation visiteuse.

unceremoniously [ʌnserɪ'məʊnɪəslɪ] *adv* sans cérémonie, brusquement; **he was u. bundled into the back of a van,** sans plus de cérémonie, on le jeta à l'arrière d'une camionnette.

uncertain [ʌn'sɜːt(ə)n] *adj* incertain; **it's u. who will win,** on ne sait pas au juste qui gagnera; **I feel u. about him,** j'ai des doutes à son sujet; **he told him in no u. terms,** il lui a dit sans mâcher ses mots; **to be u. what to do,** être incertain du parti à prendre, hésiter sur le parti à prendre.

uncertainly [ʌn'sɜːt(ə)nlɪ] *adv* d'une façon incertaine; (*to look at s.o.*) avec hésitation.

uncertainty [ʌn'sɜːt(ə)ntɪ] *n* incertitude *f*; **there is some u. about...,** l'incertitude règne au sujet de...; **u. about** *or* **as to the future,** incertitude quant à l'avenir; **to be in a state of u.,** être dans l'incertitude; **to remove any u.,** pour dissiper toute équivoque; **there's still some u. as to what was actually said,** il reste quelque incertitude sur ce qui s'est réellement dit; **there are still too many uncertainties for my liking,** il y a encore trop d'incertitudes à mon goût.

uncertified [ʌn'sɜːtɪfaɪd] *adj* non certifié.

unchain [ʌn'tʃeɪn] *vt* (*dog*) désenchaîner; (*passions*) déchaîner.

unchallengeable [ʌn'tʃælɪndʒəb(ə)l] *adj* (*affirmation*) indiscutable; (*argument*) irréfutable; (*right*) incontestable; (*evidence, proof*) irrécusable; **to be in an u. position,** (*of runner, team, politician etc*) être hors de portée.

unchallenged [ʌn'tʃælɪn(d)ʒd] *adj* **(a)** (*speaker*) que personne ne vient contredire; **to continue u.,** continuer sans être contredit; **(b)** (*right*) indisputé, incontesté; **to let (sth) go** *or* **pass u.,** ne pas relever (*une affirmation*); ne pas contester (*un droit*); ne pas récuser (*un témoignage*); **I can't let that go u.,** je ne peux pas laisser passer cela; **his record stayed u. for several years,** son record est resté imbattu pendant plusieurs années; **(c)** *Mil* **to let s.o. pass u.,** laisser passer qn sans interpellation.

unchangeable [ʌn'tʃeɪndʒəb(ə)l] *adj* inchangeable, immuable.

unchanged [ʌn'tʃeɪn(d)ʒd] *adj* inchangé; *Med* **his condition remains u.,** son état est stationnaire.

unchanging [ʌn'tʃeɪn(d)ʒɪŋ] *adj* invariable, immuable.

uncharacteristic [ʌnkærəktə'rɪstɪk] *adj* inhabituel; **it's u. of her,** cela ne lui ressemble pas; **it's u. for her to make a mistake like that,** ce n'est pas dans son habitude de faire une erreur pareille.

uncharacteristically [ʌnkærəktə'rɪstɪklɪ] *adv* (*rude, late, reticent etc*) inhabituellement, anormalement.

uncharitable [ʌn'tʃærɪtəb(ə)l] *adj* peu charitable; **that's rather u. of you,** ce n'est pas très charitable de ta part.

uncharted [ʌn'tʃɑːtɪd] *adj* non porté sur la carte; inexploré; *Fig* **these are u. areas,** (*of a science etc*) ce sont des domaines inexplorés.

unchaste [ʌn'tʃeɪst] *adj esp Lit* (*person, thoughts*) non chaste.

unchastened [ʌn'tʃeɪs(ə)nd] *adj* (*person*) aucunement ravalé; **he was u. by his experience,** son expérience n'a rien rabattu de ses prétentions.

unchecked [ʌn'tʃekt] *adj* **(a)** (*not stopped*) (*avance*) sans (la moindre) opposition; (*passion*) effréné; (*colère*) non contenu; **we can't allow this abuse to go u.,** nous ne pouvons pas permettre que cet abus continue sans rencontrer d'opposition; **if Aids were to spread u. ...,** si le sida se propageait sans qu'ou lui oppose de résistance ...; **the enemy advanced u.,** l'ennemi s'est avancé sans qu'on lui oppose de résistance; **(b)** (*not verified*) (*compte rendu, bilan*) non vérifié.

unchivalrous [ʌn'ʃɪvəlrəs] *adj* peu courtois.

unchristian [ʌn'krɪstjən] *adj* **(a)** peu chrétien; **(b)** *F* **at**

this u. hour, à cette heure indue; **that's very u. of you,** ce sont là des paroles *ou* des pensées peu chrétiennes.

uncial ['ʌnsɪəl] **1** *adj* (*of letters*) oncial, aux. **2** *n* (écriture) onciale *f*.

uncircumcised [ʌn'sɜːkəmsaɪzd] *adj* incirconcis.

uncivil [ʌn'sɪv(ɪ)l] *adj* incivil, impoli.

uncivilized [ʌn'sɪvɪlaɪzd] *adj* non civilisé, barbare; *F* **at this u. hour,** à cette heure indue; *F* **very u. of you not to have any whisky in the flat!,** pas du tout civilisé de ta part de ne pas avoir une goutte de whisky dans tout l'appartement!, *F* **it's very u. of him to keep us waiting like this,** ce n'est pas permis de nous faire attendre comme ça.

unclaimed [ʌn'kleɪmd] *adj* non réclamé; (*droit*) non revendiqué.

unclasp [ʌn'klɑːsp] **1** *vt* défaire (*un bracelet*); desserrer (*le poing*). **2** *vi* (*of hands*) se desserrer.

unclassifiable [ʌn'klæsɪfaɪəb(ə)l] *adj* inclassable.

unclassified [ʌn'klæsɪfaɪd] *adj* (*information*) non (classé) secret, -ète.

uncle ['ʌŋk(ə)l] *n* **(a)** oncle *m*; *Fig* **rich u.,** oncle d'Amérique; *US* **to cry u.,** (*give up*) crier grâce; *US* **U. Sam,** l'oncle Sam; *US F* **U. Tom,** noir *m* qui s'insinue dans les bonnes grâces des blancs; **(b)** *Old-fashioned F* **my watch is at my u.'s,** (*at pawnbroker's*) ma montre est chez ma tante.

unclean [ʌn'kliːn] *adj Rel* impur, immonde; (*thoughts*) impur; *Iron* (*cup etc*) souillé; *Bible* **u. spirit,** esprit *m* immonde.

unclear [ʌn'klɪər] *adj* (*statement*) peu clair, vague; (*result*) incertain; (*prose, text*) obscur; **it's still u. what has happened,** ce qui est arrivé n'est pas encore très clair; **I'm u. about what is wanted,** je ne suis pas sûr de ce qu'on demande.

uncleared [ʌn'klɪəd] *adj* **(a) u. ground,** terrain non défriché; **(b)** (*debt*) non liquidé; **(c) u. goods,** marchandises non dédouanées; **(d)** (*cheque*) non compensé.

unclench [ʌn'klen(t)ʃ] *vt* desserrer (*le poing*).

unclimbable [ʌn'klaɪməb(ə)l] *adj* (*mountain*) impossible à escalader.

unclimbed [ʌn'klaɪmd] *adj* (*mountain, peak*) vierge.

uncloak [ʌn'kləʊk] *vt esp Lit* découvrir (*des projets*); démasquer, dévoiler (*une imposture*).

unclog [ʌn'klɒg] *vt* (**gg-**) débloquer (*une machine*); déboucher, décrasser (*une conduite*).

unclothed [ʌn'kləʊðd] *adj* nu, sans vêtements.

unclouded [ʌn'klaʊdɪd] *adj* (*sky, future, bliss*) sans nuage(s); (*vision*) clair; (*liquid*) clair.

uncluttered [ʌn'klʌtəd] *adj* **(a)** (*desk, room*) qui n'est pas encombré; **(b)** (*style*) dépouillé; **an u. mind,** un esprit clair.

unco ['ʌŋkəʊ] *adv Scot Arch* très.

uncoil [ʌn'kɔɪl] **1** *vt* dérouler; *Hum* **to u. oneself from s.o.'s arms,** se dégager des bras de qn; **2** *vi* (*snake, rope*) **to u. (itself),** se dérouler.

uncollectable [ʌnkə'lektəb(ə)l] *adj* (*tax*) non percevable.

uncollected [ʌnkə'lektɪd] *adj* (*luggage*) non réclamé; **u. taxes,** impôts non perçus.

uncoloured [ʌn'kʌləd] *adj* non coloré; *Fig* **u. account of sth,** rapport impartial de qch.

uncombed [ʌn'kəʊmd] *adj* (*hair, wool*) non peigné; (*hair*) mal peigné.

uncomely [ʌn'kʌmlɪ] *adj* peu joli.

uncomfortable [ʌn'kʌmf(ə)təb(ə)l] *adj* **(a)** inconfortable; (*fauteuil*) peu confortable; (*vêtement*) gênant; **this is a very u. armchair,** on est très mal (assis) dans ce fauteuil; **I feel u. in this collar,** je ne suis pas à l'aise avec ce col; **(b) to make things u. for s.o.,** attirer *ou* créer des ennuis à qn; **(c) to feel** *or* **be u.,** (*ill at ease*) être mal à l'aise; (*embarrassed*) se sentir gêné; **to be** *or* **feel u. about sth,** être inquiet au sujet de qch; **to make s.o. feel u.,** mettre qn mal à l'aise; **it's a very u. feeling, knowing you could easily have been killed,** c'est un sentiment très déplaisant *ou* inconfortable de savoir que tu aurais très bien pu mourir; **there was an u. silence,** il y eut un silence gêné.

uncomfortably [ʌn'kʌmf(ə)təblɪ] *adv* **(a)** (*be sitting*) inconfortablement; (*dressed*) de mainière inconfortable; **it was u. stuffy in the plane,** il y avait une atmosphère étouffante dans l'avion; **(b) to come u. close to sth,** (*to bankruptcy, war, disaster etc*) s'approcher dangereusement de qch; **we came u. close to meeting them on holiday!,** nous avons échappé de peu à les rencontrer pendant les vacances; **I was u. aware of him watching me,** j'étais désagréablement conscient du fait qu'il me regardait.

uncommitted [ʌnkə'mɪtɪd] *adj* **(a)** (*person*) non engagé; **to be u. to any course of action,** n'être engagé à aucune ligne de conduite; **to remain u.,** ne pas s'engager; **(b)** *Pol* neutraliste, non aligné.

uncommon [ʌn'kɒmən] **1** *adj* peu commun; **u. word,** mot peu usité; **not u.,** assez fréquent. **2** *adv F Arch* singulièrement.

uncommonly [ʌn'kɒmənlɪ] *adv* **(a) not u.,** assez souvent; **(b)** *Old-fashioned* (*very*) singulièrement; **u. good,** excellent.

uncommunicative [ʌnkə'mjuːnɪkətɪv] *adj* peu communicatif, renfermé, taciturne; **he was very u. about it,** il s'est montré très peu communicatif à ce sujet.

uncomplaining [ʌnkəm'pleɪnɪŋ] *adj* qui ne se plaint pas; patient, résigné.

uncomplainingly [ʌnkəm'pleɪnɪŋlɪ] *adv* sans se plaindre.

uncomplicated [ʌn'kɒmplɪkeɪtɪd] *adj* (*style, person*) peu compliqué, simple; (*task*) facile.

uncomplimentary [ʌnkɒmplɪ'ment(ə)rɪ] *adj* peu flatteur, -euse; **he was very u. about you,** il ne s'est pas montré flatteur du tout à ton égard.

uncomprehending [ʌnkɒmprɪ'hendɪŋ] *adj* qui ne comprend pas; **to give s.o. an u. look,** regarder qn sans comprendre; **in u. amazement,** ahuri.

uncomprehendingly [ʌnkɒmprɪ'hendɪŋlɪ] *adv* sans comprendre.

uncompromising [ʌn'kɒmprəmaɪzɪŋ] *adj* intransigeant; **a man of u. principles,** un homme aux principes intransigeants *ou* inflexibles; **we took an u. stance on this,** nous avons adopté une position inflexible à ce sujet; **u. honesty,** honnêteté irréductible *ou* intransigeante; **u. insistence on quality,** notre intransigeance quant à la qualité.

uncompromisingly [ʌn'kɒmprəmaɪzɪŋlɪ] *adv* irréductiblement; **u. honest,** d'une honnêteté intransigeante.

unconcealed [ʌnkən'siːld] *adj* non dissimulé; **u. dislike,** aversion non dissimulée.

unconcern [ʌnkən'sɜːn] *n* insouciance *f*, indifférence *f*; **to show u. in the face of danger,** se montrer indifférent en face du danger.

unconcerned [ʌnkən'sɜːnd] *adj* insouciant, indifférent; **u., he went on speaking,** sans se (laisser) troubler, il a continué de parler; **they were quite u. about her well-being,** ils ne se soucient pas du tout de son bien-être; **he seems entirely u. about his results,** il ne semble pas du tout s'inquiéter au sujet de ses résultats.

unconcernedly [ʌnkən'sɜːnɪdlɪ] *adv* d'un air indifférent, sans se (laisser) troubler.

unconditional [ʌnkən'dɪʃənəl] *adj* inconditionnel, sans réserve; **u. surrender,** reddition sans condition.

unconditionally [ʌnkən'dɪʃənəlɪ] *adv* incondition nellement; (*accepter*) sans réserve; **to surrender u.,** se rendre sans condition.

unconfirmed [ʌnkən'fɜːmd] *adj* non confirmé; **the report remains u.,** le rapport n'a pas encore été confirmé.

uncongenial [ʌnkən'dʒiːnɪəl] *adj* (*person*) peu sympathique, antipathique; (*climate*) peu favorable **(to,** à); (*work, atmosphere*) peu agréable.

unconnected [ʌnkə'nektɪd] *adj* **(a)** sans rapport **(with,** avec); **the two events are totally u.,** les deux événements n'ont aucun rapport entre eux; **this reaction was not u. with the recent ...,** cette réaction n'était pas sans rapport avec le récent ...; **(b)** (*style*) décousu.

unconquerable [ʌn'kɒŋkərəb(ə)l] *adj* (*ennemi*) invincible; (*courage*) indomptable; (*curiosité*) irrésistible; (*désir*) irrépressible; (*difficulté*) insurmontable.

unconquered [ʌn'kɒŋkəd] *adj* (*peuple, pays*) inconquis; (*passion*) indompté; (*difficulté*) insurmontable; (*sommet*) vierge.

unconscionable [ʌn'kɒnʃənəb(ə)l] *adj* déraisonnable, excessif; **to take an u. time doing sth,** mettre un temps invraisemblable à faire qch .

unconscious [ʌn'kɒnʃəs] **1** *adj* **(a)** sans connaissance; **to become u.,** perdre connaisance; **to knock s.o. u.,** assommer qn raide; **(b)** (*unaware*) (*movement etc*) inconscient; (*joke, insult*) involontaire; **to be u. of doing sth,** ne pas se rendre compte qu'on fait qch; **to be u. of sth,** ne pas avoir conscience de qch, ne pas se rendre compte de qch; **the u. mind,** l'inconscient. **2** *n Psy* **the u.,** l'inconscient *m*.

unconsciously [ʌn'kɒnʃəslɪ] *adv* inconsciemment, sans s'en rendre compte; **if I u. insulted you,** si je vous ai offensé sans m'en rendre compte.

unconsciousness [ʌn'kɒnʃəsnɪs] *n* **(a)** inconscience *f*; (*fainting*) évanouissement *m*; **(b)** (*unawareness*) inconscience *f* (**of,** de).

unconsecrated [ʌn'kɒnsɪkreɪtɪd] *adj* non consacré.

unconsidered [ʌnkən'sɪdəd] *adj* (*remark, opinion*) inconsidéré; *Lit* **u. trifle,** vétille *f*

unconstitutional [ʌnkɒnstɪ'tjuːʃənl] *adj* inconstitutionnel, anticonstitutionnel.

unconstitutionally [ʌnkɒnstɪ'tjuːʃnəlɪ] *adv* inconstitutionnellement, anticonstitutionnellement.

unconstrained [ʌnkən'streɪnd] *adj* non contraint; (*person*) sans contrainte, libre; (*act*) spontané; **u. laughter,** hilarité débordante.

unconsummated [ʌn'kɒnsəmeɪtɪd] *adj* **u. marriage,** mariage non consommé.

uncontaminated [ʌnkən'tæmɪneɪtɪd] *adj* (*by disease, radiation & Fig*) non contaminé.

uncontested [ʌnkən'testɪd] *adj* (*right*) incontesté; *Pol* **u. seat,** siège (à la Chambre) qui n'est pas disputé; **the championship has been u. for ...,** le titre n'a pas été contesté depuis ... .

uncontrollable [ʌnkən'trəʊləb(ə)l] *adj* (*enfant, peuple*) ingouvernable; (*mouvement*) irrépressible; (*désir*) irrésistible, irrépressible; (*inflation*) irrésistible; **u. laughter,** fou rire, rire irrépressible; **fits of u. temper,** violents accès de colère.

uncontrollably [ʌnkən'trəʊləblɪ] *adv* irrésistiblement; **she sobbed u.,** elle ne pouvait s'arrêter de sangloter; **as inflation rises u.,** alors que l'inflation augmente irrésistiblement.

uncontrolled [ʌnkən'trəʊld] *adj* (*anger, weeping, laughter*) incontrôlé; (*style*) débridé; **u. passions,** passions effrénées; **u. inflation,** inflation rampante.

uncontroversial [ʌnkɒntrə'vɜːʃəl] *adj* (*sujet*) qui ne soulève *ou* ne provoque pas de controverses.

unconventional [ʌnkən'venʃənəl] *adj* peu conventionnel; non-conformiste.

unconventionally [ʌnkən'venʃənlɪ] *adv* de manière peu conventionnelle, non conventionnellement.

unconvinced [ʌnkən'vɪnst] *adj* sceptique (**of,** au sujet de); **I am still u.,** je ne suis toujours pas convaincu.

unconvincing [ʌnkən'vɪnsɪŋ] *adj* (*témoignage etc*) peu convaincant; (*excuse*) peu convaincant *ou* vraisemblable; **he was very u. as Tartuffe,** il n'était pas convaincant du tout en Tartuffe.

unconvincingly [ʌnkən'vɪnsɪŋlɪ] *adv* d'une manière peu convaincante.

uncooked [ʌn'kʊkt] *adj* non cuit, cru.

uncool [ʌn'kuːl] *adj Sl* ringard.

uncooperative [ʌnkəʊ'ɒp(ə)rətɪv] *adj* peu coopératif; **he's being very u.,** il se montre très peu coopératif.

uncooperatively [ʌnkəʊ'ɒp(ə)rətɪvlɪ] *adv* de manière peu coopérative.

uncooperativeness [ʌnkəʊ'ɒp(ə)rətɪvnɪs] *n* manque *m* de coopération; **as a result of their u.,** en conséquence de leur refus à coopérer *ou* manque de coopération.

uncoordinated [ʌnkəʊ'ɔːdɪneɪtɪd] *adj* non coordonné; (*manœuvre*) qui manque de coordination; **to be u.,** (*of person, dancer*) ne pas être coordonné.

uncork [ʌn'kɔːk] *vt* déboucher (*une bouteille*).

uncorrected [ʌnkə'rektɪd] *adj* (*exercise, proof*) non corrigé; (*error*) non rectifié; *Phys* **result u. for temperature/for pressure,** résultat brut.

uncorroborated [ʌnkə'rɒbəreɪtɪd] *adj* non corroboré, non confirmé.

uncorrupted [ʌnkə'rʌptɪd] *adj* non corrompu, intègre.

uncountable [ʌn'kaʊntəb(ə)l] *adj Gram* indénombrable.

uncountably [ʌn'kaʊntəblɪ] *adv Gram* **nouns which can only be used u.,** noms qu'on ne peut dénombrer.

uncounted [ʌn'kaʊntɪd] *adj* (*innumerable*) innombrable.

uncouple [ʌn'kʌp(ə)l] *vt* dételer, découpler (*des wagons, une locomotive*).

uncouth [ʌn'kuːθ] *adj* (*person, behaviour*) grossier; **u. manner,** manières gauches *ou* frustes.

uncover [ʌn'kʌvər] *vt* **(a)** découvrir; **(b)** *Chess* découvrir, dégarnir (*une pièce*).

uncovered [ʌn'kʌvəd] *adj* **(a)** découvert; **to remain u.,** (*without a hat*) rester la tête découverte; **(b)** *Fin* (*achat, vente*) à découvert.

uncreasable [ʌn'kriːsəb(ə)l] *adj* (*tissu*) infroissable.

uncritical [ʌn'krɪtɪk(ə)l] *adj* dépourvu de sens *ou* d'esprit critique; (*approach, acceptance*) sans discernement; (*audience*) peu exigeant; **to be u. of s.o./sth,** ne faire preuve d'aucun sens *ou* esprit critique à l'égard de qn/qch.

uncross [ʌn'krɒs] *vt* décroiser (*les jambes*).

uncrossed [ʌn'krɒst] *adj* (*chèque*) non barré.

uncrowded [ʌn'kraʊdɪd] *adj* (*beaches*) presque vide; (*roads*) peu encombré; **I'd never seen Heathrow so u.,** je n'avais jamais vu aussi peu de monde à Heathrow.

uncrowned [ʌn'kraʊnd] *adj* sans couronne; *Fig* **the u. king of ...,** le roi de ... .

uncrushable [ʌn'krʌʃəb(ə)l] *adj* (*tissu*) infroissable.

unction ['ʌŋkʃən] *n* onction *f*.

unctuous ['ʌŋktjʊəs] *adj* onctueux.

unctuously ['ʌŋktjʊəslɪ] *adv* onctueusement, d'un air *ou* d'un ton onctueux.

unctuousness ['ʌŋktjʊəsnɪs] *n* onctuosité *f*.

uncultivated [ʌn'kʌltɪveɪtɪd] *adj* (*terrain*) inculte; (*personne*) inculte, sans culture.

uncultured [ʌn'kʌltʃəd] *adj* (*mind*) inculte; (*person*) peu lettré, sans culture, inculte; (*accent*) peu raffiné.

uncurbed [ʌn'kɜːbd] *adj* (*autorité*) sans restriction; (*passion*) déchaîné; **if these tendencies are allowed to go u.,** si on ne met pas un frein à ces tendances.

uncurl [ʌn'kɜːl] **1** *vt* défriser, déboucler (*les cheveux*); déplier (*ses jambes*). **2** *vi* (*of cat*) s'étirer; (*of snake*) se dérouler.

uncut [ʌn'kʌt] *adj* **(a)** (*hedge*) non coupé; (*diamond*) brut, non taillé; **(b)** (*play, edition*) sans coupures, intégral.

undamaged [ʌn'dæmɪdʒd] *adj* non endommagé, intact; (*reputation*) intact.

undamped, undampened [ʌn'dæmpt, ʌn'dæmpənd] *adj* (*courage*) non affaibli.

undated [ʌn'deɪtɪd] *adj* non daté, sans date.

undaunted [ʌn'dɔːntɪd] *adj* intrépide; **to be u. by sth,** n'être aucunement intimidé *ou* aucunement ébranlé par qch; (*by difficulty*) n'être aucunement découragé par qch; **we carried on u.,** nous avons continué sans nous laisser intimider *ou* décourager.

undeceive [ʌndɪ'siːv] *vt* désabuser (**of,** de), détromper, désillusionner (*qn*).

undecided [ʌndɪ'saɪdɪd] *adj* **(a)** (*question, problem*) indécis, non résolu; **that's still u.,** aucune décision n'a encore été prise; **(b)** (*person*) indécis, irrésolu; **he was u. whether he would go or not,** il se demandait s'il irait ou non; **to be u. how to act,** ne pas savoir quel parti prendre.

undeclared [ʌndɪ'kleəd] *adj* (*war*) non déclaré; (*at Customs*) **u. goods,** marchandises non déclarées.

undefeated [ʌndɪ'fiːtɪd] *adj* invaincu.

undefended [ʌndɪ'fendɪd] *adj* **(a)** sans défense; (*goal, king at chess*) non défendu; **(b)** *Jur* (*accusé*) qui n'est pas représenté par un avocat; **u. case/trial,** débats non contentieux; **u. suit,** cause où le défenseur s'abstient de plaider.

undefiled [ʌndɪ'faɪld] *adj* sans souillure, immaculé; **u. by any contact with Western society,** non contaminé par un contact avec la civilisation occidentale.

undefinable [ʌndɪ'faɪnəb(ə)l] *adj* indéfinissable.

undefined [ʌndɪ'faɪnd] *adj* (*term etc*) non défini; (*vague*) (*feeling etc*) indéterminé, vague.

undelivered [ʌndɪ'lɪvəd] *adj* non livré, non remis; (*colis*) en souffrance; **if u. return to sender,** en cas de non-délivrance prière de retourner à l'expéditeur.

undemanding [ʌndɪ'mɑːndɪŋ] *adj* peu exigeant.

undemocratic [ʌndemə'krætɪk] *adj* antidémocratique.

undemonstrative [ʌndɪ'mɒnstrətɪv] *adj* (*person*) peu expansif, peu démonstratif, réservé.

undeniable [ʌndɪ'naɪəb(ə)l] *adj* indéniable, incontestable; (*témoignage*) irrécusable; **of u. worth,** d'une valeur indéniable.

undeniably [ʌndɪ'naɪəblɪ] *adv* incontestablement.

undenominational [ʌndɪnɒmɪ'neɪʃənəl] *adj* non confessionnel.

undependable [ʌn'dɪpendəb(ə)l] *adj* (*machine, trains, person*) peu fiable; (*person, weather*) imprévisible.

under ['ʌndər] **1** *prep* **(a)** (*beneath*) sous; au-dessous de; **the dog is u. the table,** le chien est sous la table; **u. water,** sous l'eau; **he hid u. it,** il se cacha dessous; **you have to crawl u. it,** il faut ramper par en-dessous; **put it u. that,** mettez-le là-dessous; **to wear a waistcoat u. one's jacket,** porter un gilet sous son veston; **he pulled a stool out from u. the table,** il a tiré un tabouret de sous la table; **to look for/to file sth u. ...,** chercher/classer qch sous la rubrique ...; **visible u. the microscope,** visible au microscope;

(b) (*less than*) **all their books were u. £5,** tous leurs livres coûtaient moins de 5 livres; **salaries u. £5000,** salaires inférieurs à *ou* au-dessous de 5000 livres; **he's u. thirty,** il a moins de trente ans; **people u. thirty, the u. thirties,** les moins de trente ans; **children u. ten,** les enfants au-dessous de dix ans; **in u. ten minutes,** en moins de dix minutes; **to speak u. one's breath,** parler à mi-voix;

(c) (*according to*) **u. the terms of the agreement,** aux termes de la convention; **u. his father's will,** d'après le testament de son père;

(d) (*under control of, subordinate to etc*) **he had a hundred men u. him,** il avait cent hommes sous ses ordres; **to be u. s.o.,** être sous les ordres de qn; **to be** *or* **to come u. the authority of the Home Office,** relever du Ministère de l'Intérieur; **u. government control,** soumis au contrôle de l'État; **to be u. the influence of alcohol,** *F* **to be u. the influence,** être sous l'empire de la boisson; **u. Louis XIV,** sous Louis XIV; **to study u. s.o.,** étudier sous la direction de qn; *F* **to be u. the doctor,** obéir aux ordres du médecin; **she wrote it u. a pseudonym,** elle l'a écrit sous un pseudonyme; **to be u. sentence of death,** être condamné à mort; **to be u. orders to do sth,** avoir reçu l'ordre de faire qch; **u. these conditions,** dans ces conditions; **u. the circumstances,** vu les circonstances; **u. lock and key,** sous clef;

(e) u. repair, en (voie de) réparation; **u. construction,** en construction; **patient u. observation,** malade en observation; **the question is u. examination,** le problème a été pris en considération;

(f) field u. wheat, champ mis en blé.

2 *adv* **(a)** (*underneath*) (au-)dessous; **to stay u. for two minutes,** (*underwater*) rester deux minutes sous l'eau; **to be u.,** (*anaesthetic*) être sous anesthésiant; *F* **to get out from u.,** se tirer d'affaire; *Com etc* **as u.,** comme ci-dessous;

(b) (*less*) au-dessous; **children of seven years old and u.,** des enfants (âgés) de sept ans et au-dessous.

underachieve [ʌndərə'tʃiːv] *vi esp Sch* ne pas concrétiser ses possibilités.

underachiever [ʌndərə'tʃiːvər] *n esp Sch* élève *ou* personne qui n'obtient pas des résultats conformes à ses possibilités.

under-age [ʌndər'eɪdʒ] *adj* mineur; **u.-a. drinking,** consommation *f* d'alcool par les mineurs.

underarm ['ʌndərɑːm] **1** *adv Cr Tennis* **to bowl/to serve u.,** lancer/servir la balle par en-dessous. **2** *adj* **(a)** *Cr Tennis* (*lancement, coup etc*) par en-dessous; **(b) u. deodorant,** désodorisant *m* pour les aisselles.

underbelly ['ʌndəbelɪ] *n* **(a)** bas-ventre *m*, *pl* bas-ventres (*d'un animal*); poitrine *f* (*de porc*); **(b)** *Fig* point *m* vulnérable *ou* faible; **the soft u. of Europe,** le ventre mou de l'Europe.

underbid [ʌndə'bɪd] *vt & vi* (*pt* **underbid;** *pp* **underbid(den)** [-'bɪd(n)]) **(a)** faire des soumissions *ou* offrir des conditions plus avantageuses que celles de (*qn d'autre*); **(b)** *Cards* **to u. (one's hand),** demander au-dessous de son jeu.

underblanket ['ʌndəblæŋkɪt] *n* protège-matelas *m inv*.

underbody ['ʌndəbɒdɪ] *n Aut* dessous *m* de caisse.

underbrush ['ʌndəbrʌʃ] *n* sous-bois *m*.

undercapitalization [ʌndəkæpɪtəlaɪ'zeɪʃən] *n Econ* sous-capitalisation *f*.

undercapitalized [ʌndə'kæpɪtəlaɪzd] *adj* (*industry*) sous-capitalisé.

undercarriage ['ʌndəkærɪdʒ] *n Av* train *m* d'atterrissage.

undercharge [ʌndə'tʃɑːdʒ] **1** *vt* **they undercharged him,** on ne lui a pas *ou* on ne l'a pas fait assez payer; **they undercharged her** *or* **she was undercharged by £5,** on aurait dû lui faire payer 5 livres de plus. **2** *vi* demander trop peu (**for sth,** pour qch).

underclass ['ʌndəklɑːs] *n* (*of society*) classe inférieure, basses classes.

underclothes ['ʌndəkləʊðz] *npl*, **underclothing** ['ʌndəkləʊðɪŋ] *n* sous-vêtements *mpl*; (*women's*) lingerie *f*, dessous *mpl*.

undercoat ['ʌndəkəʊt] *n* **(a)** (*of paint*) couche *f* de fond, première couche; **(b)** *Am Aut* couche *f ou* revêtement *m* antirouille; **(c)** duvet *m* (*d'un chien*).

undercoating ['ʌndəkəʊtɪŋ] *n* = **UNDERCOAT (a)**.

undercook [ʌndə'kʊk] *vt* ne pas assez cuire.

undercover ['ʌndəkʌvər] *adj* secret, -ète, clandestin; **u. agent,** agent secret.

undercurrent ['ʌndəkʌrənt] *n* (*in sea*) courant sous-marin; *Fig* **u. of discontent,** vague *f* de fond de mécontentement; *Fig* **but there are undercurrents,** (*in relationship etc*) mais il y a des tensions sous-jacentes.

undercut¹ ['ʌndəkʌt] *n Culin* filet *m* (de bœuf).

undercut² *vt* (*pt & pp* **undercut;** *prp* **undercutting) (a)** *Sp* couper, lifter (*la balle*); **(b)** *Com* vendre (*qch*) moins cher que (*qn*).

underdeveloped [ʌndədɪ'veləpt] *adj* **(a)** *Phot* insuffisamment développé; **(b)** (*enfant*) retardé; (*muscle*) pas assez développé; **u. countries,** pays sous-développés; **u. area,** région sous-exploitée.

underdog ['ʌndədɒg] *n Sp* perdant, -ante; (*socially etc*) (*oppressed*) opprimé, -ée; (*through bad luck*) défavorisé, -ée; **to side with the underdog(s),** plaider la cause des opprimés; **the underdogs won 5-2,** ceux qui étaient donnés perdants à l'avance ont gagné 5-2.

underdone [ʌndə'dʌn] *adj Culin* (*undercooked*) pas assez cuit; (*lightly done*) pas trop cuit; (*bifteck*) saignant.

underdrawers ['ʌndədrɔːəz] *npl US* caleçon *m* (d'homme).

underdressed [ʌndə'drest] *adj* **to be u.,** (*not warm enough*) ne pas être assez habillé *ou* couvert; (*not formal enough*) ne pas avoir fait d'effort de toilette; **I feel u.,** (*at party etc*) je me sens un peu déplacé.

underemployed [ʌndərem'plɔɪd] *adj* sous-employé; (*resources*) sous-exploité.

underemployment [ʌndərem'plɔɪmənt] *n* sous-emploi *m* (*de qn*); sous-exploitation *f* (*de ressources*).

underestimate¹, underestimation [ʌndər'estɪmɪt, -estɪ'meɪʃən] *n* sous-estimation *f*, sous-évaluation *f*.

underestimate² [ʌndər'estɪmeɪt] *vt* sous-estimer, sous-évaluer (*les dépenses*); méconnaître, mésestimer (*les difficultés, un concurrent*); sous-estimer (*une personne*).

underexpose [ʌndəreks'pəʊz] *vt Phot* sous-exposer (*un film*).

underexposure [ʌndəreks'pəʊʒər] *n Phot* sous-exposition *f* (*d'un film*).

underfed [ʌndə'fed] *adj* sous-alimenté, mal nourri.

underfeeding [ʌndə'fiːdɪŋ] *n* sous-alimentation *f*.

underfelt ['ʌndəfelt] *n* thibaude *f* (*pour moquette*).

underfinance [ʌndə'faɪnæns] *vt* financer insuffisamment.

underfloor ['ʌndəflɔːr] *adj* **u. heating,** chauffage *m* par le sol.

underfoot [ʌndə'fʊt] *adv* sous les pieds; **it's wet u.,** le sol est mouillé; **the snow crunched u.,** la neige crissait sous les pieds; **to trample** *or* **tread sth u.,** fouler qch aux pieds.

underfunded [ʌndə'fʌndɪd] *adj* (*project etc*) insuffisamment financé *ou* doté.

underfunding [ʌndə'fʌndɪŋ] *n* (*of industry*) insuffisance *f* de financement *ou* de dotation; **the project suffered from u.,** le projet a souffert d'un financement insuffisant.

under(-)gardener ['ʌndəgɑːdnər] *n* aide-jardinier *m*, *pl* aides-jardiniers.

undergarment ['ʌndəgɑːmənt] *n* sous-vêtement *m*.

undergo [ʌndə'gəʊ] *vt* (*pt* **underwent** [-'went]; *pp* **undergone** [-'gɒn]) **(a)** passer par, subir (*un changement, de dures épreuves etc*); **to u. a complete change,** subir une métamorphose complète; **undergoing repairs,** en (voie de) réparation; **(b)** subir (*une épreuve, un examen*), **to u. an operation,** subir une opération, *Med* **to u. treatment,** suivre un traitement.

undergrad [ʌndə'græd] *n F* = **UNDERGRADUATE**.

undergraduate [ʌndə'grædjʊɪt] *n* étudiant, -ante (*qui prépare la licence*); **in my u. days,** lorsque j'étais étudiant; **u. life,** la vie d'étudiant.

underground ['ʌndəgraʊnd] **1** *adv* **(a)** sous (la) terre; **to work u.,** travailler sous (la) terre; **(b)** *Fig* (*secretly*) clandestinement, secrètement; **to go u.,** passer dans la clandestinité. **2** *adj* **(a)** (*travail*) sous (la) terre; (*tuyau, lac, câble*) souterrain; **u. railway,** chemin de fer souterrain; **u. gallery** *or* **passage,** souterrain *m*; **u. workings,** chantier souterrain, travaux souterrains; **(b)** (*organization, press*) clandestin, secret, -ète; **u. movement,** mouvement clandestin; (*in occupied country*) résistance *f*. **3** *n* **(a)** chemin de fer souterrain; **the u.** = le métro; **(b)** (*in occupied country etc*) **the u.,** la résistance.

undergrowth ['ʌndəgrəʊθ] *n* broussailles *fpl*, sous-bois *m*.

underhand ['ʌndəhænd] *adj* clandestin; (*person*) sournois; **to behave in an u. way,** agir en sous-main; **u. dealings,** agissements clandestins.

underhanded [ʌndə'hændɪd] *adj* **(a)** = **UNDERHAND;** **(b)** *US* à court de personnel *ou* de main-d'œuvre.

underhandedly [ʌndə'hændɪdlɪ] *adv* en sous-main.

underinsured [ʌndərɪn'ʃɔːd] *adj* sous-assuré.

underinvestment [ʌndərɪn'vestmənt] *n* insuffisance *f* d'investissement.

underlay¹ ['ʌndəleɪ] *n* thibaude *f* (*pour moquette*); assise *f* (*pour carrelage*).

underlay² [ʌndə'leɪ] *vt* (*pt & pp* **underlaid** [-'leɪd]) **to u. sth with sth,** mettre qch sous qch; **carpet underlaid with felt,** moquette sur thibaude.

underlie [ʌndə'laɪ] *vt* (*pt* **underlay** [-'leɪ] ; *pp* **underlain**

[-ˈlcɪn]; *prp* **underlying** [-ˈlaɪɪŋ] **(a)** être sous *ou* en dessous de *(qch)*; **(b)** *Fig* être à la base *ou* à l'origine de *(qch)*; servir de base à *(qch)*.

underline [ʌndəˈlaɪn] *vt* souligner *(un mot)*; *Fig* souligner, appuyer sur, insister sur *(un fait)*.

underling [ˈʌndəlɪŋ] *n Pej* subalterne *mf*, subordonné, -ée.

underlining [ʌndəˈlaɪnɪŋ] *n* soulignement *m*, soulignage *m*.

underlying [ʌndəˈlaɪɪŋ] *adj* **1** au-dessous; *(rock)* sous-jacent; **(b)** *(principles, causes etc)* sous-jacent.

undermanager [ˈʌndəmænɪdʒər] *n* sous-chef *m*, sous-directeur *m*.

undermanned [ʌndəˈmænd] *adj* à court de personnel *ou* de main-d'œuvre; **to be u.**, manquer de personnel.

undermanning [ʌndəˈmænɪŋ] *n* manque *m ou* pénurie *f* de personnel.

undermentioned [ˈʌndəmenʃənd] *adj* (cité, mentionné) ci-dessous; **the u. persons,** les personnes dont les noms suivent.

undermine [ʌndəˈmaɪn] *vt* **(a)** miner, saper *(la côte, une muraille)*; *(of sea, river)* affouiller *(les falaises, les berges)*; **foundations undermined by water,** fondements minés par l'eau; **(b)** saper *(un principe, l'autorité de qn)*; miner *(la santé de qn)*; ébranler *(la confiance de qn)*; **to u. the foundations of society,** attaquer les bases de la société.

undermost [ˈʌndəməʊst] *adj* le plus bas, *f* la plus basse.

underneath [ʌndəˈniːθ] **1** *prep* au-dessous de, sous; **he pushed the letter u. the door,** il a glissé la lettre sous la porte; **he pulled it (out) from u. the blanket,** il l'a tiré de dessous la couverture. **2** *adv* au-dessous; dessous; **he picked up the book and found the ticket u.**, il a soulevé le livre et a trouvé le billet en dessous. **3** *n* dessous *m*; **the u. of the box is black,** la boîte est noire en dessous. **4** *adj* d'en dessous.

undernourished [ʌndəˈnʌrɪʃt] *adj* sous-alimenté.

undernourishment [ʌndəˈnʌrɪʃmənt] *n* sous-alimentation *f*.

underpaid [ʌndəˈpeɪd] *adj* *(travail, ouvrier)* sous-payé, sous-rémunéré.

underpants [ˈʌndəpænts] *npl* *(for men)* slip *m*; *(with legs)* caleçon *m*; **a pair of u.**, un caleçon.

underpart [ˈʌndəpɑːt] *n* partie inférieure.

underpass [ˈʌndəpɑːs] *n* *(for cars)* passage inférieur; *(for pedestrians)* (passage) souterrain *m*.

underpay [ʌndəˈpeɪ] *vt* *(pt & pp* **underpaid** [-ˈpeɪd]) sous-payer, sous-rémunérer *(un ouvrier etc)*.

underpin [ʌndəˈpɪn] *vt* **(-pp-)** **(a)** étayer *(un mur, Fig une organisation etc)*.

underpinning [ʌndəˈpɪnɪŋ] *n* étai *m*; *(of project etc)* soutien *m*.

underplay [ʌndəˈpleɪ] *vt* **(a)** minimiser l'importance de *(qch)*; **(b)** *Th* **to u. a part,** ne pas faire assez ressortir un rôle; **(c)** *Fig* **to u. one's hand,** mal exploiter ses possibilités; *(deliberately)* cacher son jeu.

underpopulated [ʌndəˈpɒpjʊleɪtɪd] *adj* sous-peuplé.

underprice [ʌndəˈpraɪs] *vt* mettre un prix trop bas à *(un article)*; **you've underpriced them,** vous les proposez à un prix trop bas.

underpriced [ʌndəˈpraɪst] *adj* trop bon marché; **at £15.99 it's definitely u.** à 15,99 livres c'est vraiment donné.

underprivileged [ʌndəˈprɪvɪlɪdʒd] **1** *adj* déshérité, défavorisé; économiquement faible. **2** *n* **the u.**, *(used as pl)* les défavorisés (sociaux); les économiquement faibles.

underproduce [ʌndəprəˈdjuːs] *vi Ind* être en situation de sous-production.

underproduction [ʌndəprəˈdʌkʃən] *n Ind* sous-production *f*.

underproductive [ʌndəprəˈdʌktɪv] *adj Ind* sous-productif.

underqualified [ʌndəˈkwɒlɪfaɪd] *adj* sous qualifié.

underrate [ʌndəˈreɪt] *vt* sous-estimer *(un adversaire, les difficultés, l'importance de qch)*.

underscore [ˈʌndəskɔːr] *vt* souligner *(un titre etc)*; *Fig* faire ressortir, mettre en évidence *(un fait)*; souligner *(l'importance de qch)*.

undersea [ˈʌndəsiː] *adj* sous-marin.

underseal¹ [ˈʌndəsiːl] *n Aut* couche *f* antirouille (pour dessous de châssis).

underseal² *vt* **to u. (the chassis of) a car,** traiter contre la rouille le châssis d'une voiture.

undersecretary [ʌndəˈsekrɪt(ə)rɪ] *n* sous-secrétaire *mf*; **permanent u.**, directeur général (d'un ministère).

undersell [ʌndəˈsel] *vt* *(pt & pp* **undersold** [-ˈsəʊld]) vendre moins cher que *(la concurrence etc)*; vendre *(qch)* au-dessous de sa valeur; **don't u. yourself at the interview,** essaie de bien te vendre lors de l'entretien.

undersexed [ʌndəˈsekst] *adj* de *ou* à faible libido; **he's u.**, il a une sexualité peu exigeante.

undershirt [ˈʌndəʃɜːt] *adj Am (for men)* maillot *m*.

undershoot [ʌndəˈʃuːt] *vt & vi* *(pt & pp* **undershot** [-ˈʃɒt]) *Av* **to u. (the runway),** se présenter *ou* atterrir trop court (sur la piste); *Fig* **to u. a production target,** ne pas atteindre ses objectifs de production.

underside [ˈʌndəsaɪd] *n* dessous *m*.

undersigned [ʌndəˈsaɪnd] *adj & n* **I, the u.,** je soussigné(e); **the u. declare that...,** les soussignés déclarent que... .

undersize(d) [ʌndəˈsaɪz(d)] *adj* de (trop) petite taille, trop petit; *(premises etc)* sous-dimensionné.

underskirt [ˈʌndəskɜːt] *n* jupon *m*.

underslung [ʌndəˈslʌŋ] *adj* *(ressort)* sous l'essieu; *Aut (châssis)* surbaissé; *(voiture)* à carrosserie surbaissée.

understaffed [ʌndəˈstɑːft] *adj* à court de personnel; **the office is u.**, le bureau manque de personnel.

understaffing [ʌndəˈstɑːfɪŋ] *n* manque *m ou* pénurie *f* de personnel.

understand [ʌndəˈstænd] *v* *(pt & pp* **understood** [-ˈstʊd]) **1** *vt* **(a)** comprendre; **I don't u. French,** je ne comprends pas le français; **he can't make himself understood in German,** il ne peut pas se faire comprendre en allemand; **he understands business matters,** il s'y connaît *ou* s'y entend en affaires; **this sentence can be understood in several ways,** cette phrase peut s'interpréter de plusieurs façons; **no one understands me,** personne ne me comprend; **to u. each other** *or* **one another,** se comprendre; *(have same ideas etc)* s'entendre; **I quite u. that he must be tired,** je comprends très bien qu'il soit fatigué; **I don't u. why he did it,** je ne comprends pas pourquoi il l'a fait; **do you u. what he's talking about?** comprenez-vous quelque chose à ce qu'il raconte?; **what I can't u. is that...,** ce que je ne comprends pas, c'est que + *sub*; **I can u. your being angry,** je comprends que vous soyez fâché; **I can't u. it,** je ne (le) comprends pas; **I'm at a loss to u. it, I can't u. a word of it, I don't u. the first thing about it,** je n'y comprends (absolument) rien; **(is that) understood?** (vous avez *ou* c'est bien) compris?, (c'est) entendu? **that's easily understood,** cela se comprend facilement;

(b) *(believe)* **I understood that I was to be paid for my work,** j'ai cru comprendre que je devais être payé pour mon travail; **I u. (that) you're coming to work here,** si j'ai bien compris vous venez travailler ici; **am I to u. that...?** ai-je bien compris que...?; **he is understood to be abroad, it is understood that he is abroad,** il paraît *ou* on croit qu'il est à l'étranger; **it must be understood** *or* **you must u. that...,** il doit être (bien) entendu *ou* il faut (bien) comprendre que...; **to give s.o. to u. that...,** laisser entendre à qn que...; **I have made it understood** *or* **I have let it be understood that...,** j'ai laissé entendre que...;

(c) sous-entendre *(un mot)*; présumer, supposer *(une condition)*; **in this sentence the verb is understood,** dans cette phrase le verbe est sous-entendu; **that's understood,** cela va sans dire, cela va de soi.

2 *vi* comprendre; **now I u.!** je comprends *ou* j'y suis maintenant!; **you don't u.**, vous n'y êtes pas; **do you u.?** vous comprenez?; **he left yesterday, I u.**, il est parti hier, si j'ai bien compris *ou* si je ne me trompe (pas); **to u. about sth,** comprendre qch.

understandable [ʌndəˈstændəb(ə)l] *adj* *(in speech, prose etc)* compréhensible, intelligible; *(normal, natural)* compréhensible; **that's u.**, cela se comprend (facilement), c'est bien normal; **it's quite u. that she should be ...,** il est tout à fait compréhensible qu'elle soit ... .

understandably [ʌndəˈstændəblɪ] *adv* de manière compréhensible; **he was u. disappointed,** il était compréhensible qu'il soit déçu.

understanding [ʌndəˈstændɪŋ] **1** *adj* compréhensif, bienveillant (**about sth,** au sujet de qch); **u. parents,** parents compréhensifs *ou* qui comprennent; **u. smile,** sourire d'intelligence; *(seeing through sth)* sourire entendu; **he behaved in a very u. way,** il a agi avec beaucoup de discernement.

2 *n* **(a)** compréhension *f*, entendement *m*, intelligence *f*; **the age of u.**, l'âge de discernement *m*; **it's beyond all u.**, c'est incompréhensible, c'est à n'y rien comprendre; **it's beyond my u.**, cela dépasse mon entendement, je n'y comprends rien; **lacking in u.**, *(unsympathetic)* incompréhensif; **to be lacking in u. of a problem,** ne pas bien comprendre un problème; **according to my u. of it,** si j'ai *ou* je l'ai bien compris;

(b) *(between nations etc)* entente *f*, accord *m*; **spirit of u.**, esprit d'entente; *(agreement)* accord, arrangement *m*; **they had an u., there was an u. between them,** ils étaient d'intelligence; **to come to** *or* **to reach an u. with s.o.**, s'entendre *ou* s'arranger avec qn;

(c) condition *f*; **on the u. that he gives it me back,** à (la) condition qu'il me le rende; **on the firm u. that...,** à la condition expresse que... .

understandingly [ʌndə'stændɪŋlɪ] *adv (to act)* avec compréhension; **to write** *or* **speak u. about a problem,** s'exprimer avec bienveillance sur un problème.

understate [ʌndə'steɪt] *vt* minimiser; **understated,** *(make-up etc)* discret, -ète; *(theme etc)* atténué; **the deliberately understated figures in the foreground,** les silhouettes volontairement estompées au premier plan.

understatement [ʌndə'steɪtmənt] *n* **(a)** minimisation *f (des faits)*; **(b)** *Ling* litote *f*; **with typical British u.,** avec un euphémisme typiquement britannique; **to say it's expensive is an u.,** dire que c'est cher est bien au-dessous de la vérité; **that's an u. if I ever heard one!,** c'est un des plus beaux euphémismes que j'aie entendus; *F* **that's the u. of the year!,** si tu crois que c'est assez dire!

understudy[1] ['ʌndəstʌdɪ] *n Th* doublure *f*.

understudy[2] *vt Th* doubler; servir de doublure pour *(un rôle)*.

undertake [ʌndə'teɪk] *vt (pt* **undertook** [-'tʊk]; *pp* **undertaken** [-'teɪk(ə)n]) **(a)** entreprendre *(un voyage etc)*; **(b)** se charger de, entreprendre *(une tâche)*; assumer *(une responsabilité)*; **to u. to do sth,** se charger de *ou* s'engager à faire qch; **(c) to u. that ...,** garantir *ou* assurer que ... .

undertaker ['ʌndəteɪkər] *n* entrepreneur *m* des pompes funèbres, *F* croque-mort *m*, *pl* croque-morts; **ring the undertaker's,** appelle les pompes funèbres!

undertaking [ʌndə'teɪkɪŋ] *n* **(a)** *(enterprise)* entreprise *f*; **it's quite an u.,** c'est toute une affaire, c'est une grande entreprise; **the u. of this project meant that ...,** la mise en œuvre de ce projet signifiait que ...; **(b)** *(promise etc)* engagement *m*, promesse *f*; *Jur* soumission *f*; **he gave an u. to do it** *or* **that he would do it,** il s'est engagé à *ou* il a promis de le faire; **I give you my solemn u. never to ...,** je vous promets solennellement de ne jamais ...; **I can't give you that u.,** je ne peux vous faire cette promesse; **(c)** *(profession of undertaker)* métier *m* d'entrepreneur des pompes funèbres.

undertax [ʌndə'tæks] *vt* taxer insuffisamment *(qch)*; ne pas faire payer assez d'impôts à *(qn)*.

under-the-counter [ʌndəðə'kaʊntər] *adj (sales etc)* clandestin.

undertone ['ʌndətəʊn] *n* **(a) in an u.,** *(parler)* à mi-voix *ou* à voix basse; **(b) u. of discontent,** courant sourd de mécontentement; **grey with blue undertones,** gris nuancé de bleu.

undertow ['ʌndətəʊ] *n (in water)* courant *m* (sous-marin); *Fig (in relationship etc)* tension sous-jacente.

underuse[1] [ʌndə'juːs] *n* sous-utilisation *f*.

underuse[2] [ʌndə'juːz] *vt* sous-utiliser.

underutilization [ʌndəjuːtɪlaɪ'zeɪʃən] *n (of facilities etc)* sous-utilisation *f*.

underutilize [ʌndə'juːtɪlaɪz] *vt (facilities, equipment)* sous-utiliser.

undervalue [ʌndə'væljuː] *vt* sous-évaluer *(des marchandises)*; sous-estimer, mésestimer *(qn, qch)*.

undervest ['ʌndəvest] *n esp Am (for men)* maillot *m ou* tricot *m* de corps; *(for women)* chemise américaine, *Can* camisole *f*.

underwater 1 ['ʌndəwɔːtər] *adj* sous-marin; **u. camera/ photography,** caméra/photographie sous-marine; **u. fishing,** pêche sous-marine *ou* subaquatique. **2** [ʌndə'wɔːtər] *adv* sous l'eau; *(under sea)* sous la mer.

underwear ['ʌndəweər] *n* sous-vêtements *mpl*; *(for women)* lingerie *f*, dessous *mpl*.

underweight [ʌndə'weɪt] *adj (article)* d'un poids insuffisant; **to be u.,** *(of person)* ne pas peser assez; **I'm 10lbs u.,** il me manque cinq kilos, je devrais peser cinq kilos de plus.

underwhelm [ʌndə'welm] *vt Iron* **your generosity underwhelms me,** votre générosité me renverse; **he was obviously underwhelmed by his present,** le cadeau l'avait laissé manifestement indifférent; **the critics were underwhelmed by his next film,** son nouveau film fut accueilli avec un enthousiasme très relatif par la critique.

underworld ['ʌndəwɜːld] *n* **(a)** *Myth* **the u.,** les enfers *mpl*; **(b)** *(of criminals)* pègre *f*, milieu *m*.

underwrite ['ʌndəraɪt] *vt (pt* **underwrote** [-rəʊt] ; *pp* **underwritten** [-rɪtn]) **1** *Fin* garantir *(un emprunt, une nouvelle émission, une police, un risque)*; **policy underwritten at Lloyd's,** police garantie par Lloyd.

underwriter ['ʌndəraɪtər] *n* **(a)** *Fin* syndicataire *mf*; **the underwriters,** le syndicat de garantie; **(b)** *(in insurance)* assureur *m*; **marine u.,** assureur maritime; **Lloyd's underwriters,** assureurs de Lloyd.

underwriting ['ʌndəraɪtɪŋ] *n Fin* garantie *f (d'émission, d'une police, d'un risque)*; **marine u.,** assurance *f* maritime.

undeserved [ʌndɪ'zɜːvd] *adj (praise, reproach)* immérité.

undeservedly [ʌndɪ'zɜːvɪdlɪ] *adv* à tort, injustement; *(être décoré etc)* sans le mériter, sans l'avoir mérité.

undeserving [ʌndɪ'zɜːvɪŋ] *adj (person)* sans mérite; *(cause etc)* peu méritoire; **u. of attention,** qui ne mérite pas l'attention, indigne d'attention.

undesirable [ʌndɪ'zaɪərəb(ə)l] **1** *adj* indésirable; **an u. character,** un personnage peu désirable; **if you think this is u.,** si vous pensez que ce n'est pas souhaitable *ou* acceptable; **it is u. that he should be sent to an adult prison,** il est inadmissible qu'on l'envoie dans une prison pour adultes. **2** *n* indésirable *mf*.

undetected [ʌndɪ'tektɪd] *adj* non détecté, non décelé; **to go u.,** passer inaperçu.

undetermined [ʌndɪ'tɜːmɪnd] *adj (quality, date)* indéterminé, incertain; *(question)* indécis; *esp Lit (person)* irrésolu, indécis.

undeterred [ʌndɪ'tɜːd] *adj* **to carry on u.,** continuer sans se laisser décourager **(by,** par); **we remained u.,** nous ne nous sommes pas laissé décourager; **u. by the weather, he went out for a walk,** en dépit du mauvais temps, il est sorti se promener.

undeveloped [ʌndɪ'veləpt] *adj* **(a)** non développé; *(land, resources)* inexploité, non exploité; *(mind)* non formé; **(b)** *(film)* non développé.

undeviating [ʌn'diːvɪeɪtɪŋ] *adj (cours, chemin)* droit, direct; *(fidélité)* qui ne se dément pas.

undies ['ʌndɪz] *npl F (esp for women)* lingerie *f*, dessous *mpl*.

undigested [ʌnd(a)ɪ'dʒestɪd] *adj (food)* non digéré, mal digéré; *(facts)* mal assimilé.

undignified [ʌn'dɪgnɪfaɪd] *adj* peu digne, qui manque de dignité; **to be u.,** manquer de dignité; **what an u. way to sit!,** quelle manière peu digne *ou* peu convenable de s'asseoir!

undiluted [ʌndaɪ'luːtɪd] *adj* non dilué, non délayé, *(vin)* pur; *(acide)* concentré; *(joie)* sans mélange.

undiminished [ʌndɪ'mɪnɪʃt] *adj* non diminué; **my respect for him remains u.,** mon respect pour lui n'a pas diminué *ou* est resté intact.

undiplomatic [ʌndɪplə'mætɪk] *adj* peu diplomatique, peu diplomate.

undiplomatically [ʌndɪplə'mætɪklɪ] *adv* de manière peu diplomate *ou* peu diplomatique.

undipped [ʌn'dɪpt] *adj Aut* **to drive with u. headlights,** ne pas se mettre en code.

undiscernible [ʌndɪ'sɜːnəb(ə)l] *adj* indiscernable.

undiscerning [ʌndɪ'sɜːnɪŋ] *adj (esprit)* sans discernement, peu pénétrant; **to be u.,** manquer de discernement.

undischarged [ʌndɪs'tʃɑːdʒd] *adj* **(a)** *(fusil)* non déchargé. **(b)** *(débiteur)* non libéré (d'une obligation); *Jur* **u. bankrupt,** failli non réhabilité; **u. debt,** dette non liquidée; **(c)** *(devoir)* inaccompli.

undisciplined [ʌn'dɪsɪplɪnd] *adj* indiscipliné.

undisclosed [ʌndɪs'kləʊzd] *adj* non révélé.

undiscovered [ʌndɪs'kʌvəd] *adj* non découvert; **u. country,** terre inconnue; **the ruins of Troy went u. for ...,** l'emplacement des ruines de Troie est resté ignoré pendant ... .

undiscriminating [ʌndɪs'krɪmɪneɪtɪŋ] *adj* sans discernement, qui manque de discernement.

undiscriminatingly [ʌndɪs'krɪmɪneɪtɪŋlɪ] *adv* sans discernement.

undisguised [ʌndɪs'gaɪzd] *adj* non déguisé; *(feelings)* non dissimulé.

undisguisedly [ʌndɪs'gaɪzɪdlɪ] *adv* ouvertement.

undismayed [ʌndɪs'meɪd] *adj* non découragé; **he was quite u. by the incident,** l'incident ne l'a nullement consterné.

undisputed [ʌndɪs'pjuːtɪd] *adj* incontesté, indiscuté.

undistinguished [ʌndɪs'tɪŋgwɪʃt] *adj* médiocre; *(appearance)* peu distingué.

undisturbed [ʌndɪs'tɜːbd] *adj (sleep)* paisible, calme; *(peace)* que rien ne vient troubler; *(papers)* non dérangé, non déplacé; **please leave us u. for fifteen minutes,**

veuillez ne pas nous déranger pendant quinze minutes; **I could do with an u. night's sleep,** une bonne nuit de sommeil me ferait du bien; **he was apparently u. by the news,** la nouvelle ne l'a apparemment pas troublé.
undivided [ʌndɪ'vaɪdɪd] *adj* non divisé; (*love, affection*) non partagé; (*loyalties*) sans partage; **he gave her his u. attention,** il lui a donné toute son attention; **u. opinion,** opinion unanime.
undo [ʌn'du:] *v* (*pt* **undid** [-'dɪd]; *pp* **undone** [-'dʌn]) **1** *vt* détruire **(a)** (*une œuvre*); réparer (*une faute*); *Comptr* annuler (*une instruction*); **you can't u. the past,** ce qui est fait est fait; **(b)** défaire (*un nœud, un bouton, un tricot*); enlever (*une agrafe*); ouvrir (*un fermoir*); desserrer (*une vis*); défaire, déficeler (*un paquet*); délacer (*ses chaussures*); dégrafer, déboutonner (*sa robe*). **2** *vi* (*of dress etc*) se défaire.
undoing [ʌn'du:ɪŋ] *n* ruine *f*, perte *f*; **drink was his u.,** l'alcool a causé sa perte.
undone [ʌn'dʌn] *adj* **(a)** défait; **to come u.,** (*of knot, button*) se défaire; (*of hair*) se dénouer; (*of screw*) se desserrer; (*of shoe*) se délacer; (*of dress*) se dégrafer; (*of seam*) se découdre, se défaire; (*of parcel*) se déficeler; **(b)** *Hum Arch* **I am u.!** je suis perdu!; **(c)** (*not finished, not done*) **we had to leave it u.,** nous n'avons pas pu le terminer; *Lit* **we have left u. those things which we ought to have done,** nous n'avons pas fait les choses que nous aurions dû faire.
undomesticated [ʌndə'mestɪkeɪtɪd] *adj* **he's completely u.,** il ne sait rien faire dans la maison.
undoubted [ʌn'daʊtɪd] *adj* (*fait*) incontestable, indubitable.
undoubtedly [ʌn'daʊtɪdlɪ] *adv* indubitablement, incontestablement.
undramatic [ʌndrə'mætɪk] *adj* (*ouvrage, style*) peu dramatique, qui manque de sens dramatique.
undrawn [ʌn'drɔ:n] *adj* **the curtains were still u.,** les rideaux n'étaient toujours pas tirés.
undreamed-of, undreamt-of [ʌn'dri:mdɒv, ʌn'dremtɒv] *adj* (*unsuspected*) insoupçonné; (*beyond one's dreams*) inimaginable.
undress¹ [ʌn'dres] **1** *vi* se déshabiller. **2** *vt* **(a)** déshabiller; **to get undressed,** se déshabiller; **(b)** ôter les pansements (*d'une plaie*).
undress² *n F* **in a state of u.,** en petit tenue.
undressed [ʌn'drest] *adj* **(a)** déshabillé; (*in nightdress*) en déshabillé; **(b)** (*cloth*) inapprêté; (*wood*) en grume; **u. stone,** pierre non taillée; **(c)** *Culin* (*meat*) non accommodé; (*lobster*) nature *inv*; (*salad*) non assaisonné; **(d) u. wound,** blessure non pansée.
undrinkable [ʌn'drɪŋkəb(ə)l] *adj* (*because unpleasant*) imbuvable; (*because poisonous etc*) non potable.
undue [ʌn'dju:] *adj* **(a)** (*demand*) injuste, injustifiable; (*reward*) immérité; **(b)** (*haste*) exagéré, indu; **u. optimism,** optimisme peu justifié.
unduly [ʌn'dju:lɪ] *adv* **(a)** (*unfairly*) injustement; **(b)** (*excessively*) à l'excès, trop; **u. high price,** prix excessif; **to be u. optimistic,** faire preuve d'un optimisme peu justifié; **he worries u.** *or* **he's u. worried about his health,** sa santé le préoccupe trop.
undulate ['ʌndjʊleɪt] **1** *vt* onduler. **2** *vi* onduler, ondoyer.
undulating ['ʌndjʊleɪtɪŋ] *adj* ondulé, onduleux; (*blé*) ondoyant; **u. country,** pays vallonné.
undulation [ʌndjʊ'leɪʃən] *n* ondulation *f*.
undying [ʌn'daɪɪŋ] *adj* immortel; (*love*) éternel.
unearned [ʌn'ɜ:nd] *adj* **(a)** (*reward, punishment*) immérité; **(b)** (*money*) qui ne provient pas du travail; **u. income,** rentes *fpl*.
unearth [ʌn'ɜ:θ] *vt* **(a)** déterrer, exhumer; **(b)** (*find*) découvrir, dénicher (*qn, qch*); **wherever did you u. that?,** où diable as-tu déniché ça?; **(c)** faire sortir (*un animal*) de son trou *ou* de son terrier.
unearthly [ʌn'ɜ:θlɪ] *adj* **(a)** (*supernatural etc*) surnaturel; mystérieux; **u. pallor,** pâleur mortelle; **u. light,** lueur sinistre; **(b)** *F* **at an u. hour,** à une heure impossible; **u. din,** vacarme de tous les diables; **for some u. reason,** pour une raison absurde.
unease [ʌn'i:z] *n* malaise *m*.
uneasily [ʌn'i:zɪlɪ] *adv* (*with embarrassment*) d'un air gêné; (*worried*) avec inquiétude; (*dormir*) d'un sommeil agité.
uneasy [ʌn'i:zɪ] *adj* (*ill at ease*) mal à l'aise, gêné; (*worried*) inquiet, -ète; (*sommeil*) agité; (*calme*) troublé; **an u. truce,** une trêve précaire *ou* incertaine; **there was an u. silence,** il y a eu un silence gêné; **to be u.,** être inquiet *ou* anxieux (**about,** au sujet de); **to be u. in one's mind about sth,** ne pas avoir l'esprit tranquille au sujet de qch; **I've just an u. feeling that it won't work,** j'ai justement le sentiment désagréable que çe ne marchera pas.
uneatable [ʌn'i:təb(ə)l] *adj* (*unpleasant to eat*) immangeable; (*not possible to eat*) non comestible.
uneaten [ʌn'i:t(ə)n] *adj* non mangé; **u. food,** restes *mpl*.
uneconomic [ʌni:kə'nɒmɪk] *adj* non économique; (*travail*) pas rentable.
uneconomical [ʌni:kə'nɒmɪk(ə)l] *adj* (*method, car*) peu économique; **it's u. to do it that way,** il est anti-économique d'agir ainsi.
unedifying [ʌn'edɪfaɪɪŋ] *adj* peu édifiant.
unedited [ʌn'edɪtɪd] *adj* (*text*) qui n'a pas été rédigé définitivement, à l'état brut; (*film*) non monté; (*recording*) à l'état brut.
uneducated [ʌn'edjʊkeɪtɪd] *adj* (*person*) sans instruction; (*no manners*) sans éducation; (*speech, accent*) populaire; (*handwriting*) qui dénote un manque d'instruction.
unemotional [ʌnɪ'məʊʃən(ə)l] *adj* (*person*) peu émotif, peu émotionnable; (*not showing emotion*) impassible, qui ne montre aucune émotion; (*reaction*) peu émotionnel; (*style*) neutre, dépourvu de passion.
unemotionally [ʌnɪ'məʊʃən(ə)lɪ] *adv* (*to react, look at things*) sans passion.
unemployable [ʌnɪm'plɔɪəb(ə)l] *adj* (*person*) (*because of illness etc*) inapte à travailler; (*because of criminal record etc*) non employable.
unemployed [ʌnɪm'plɔɪd] **1** *adj* (*person*) en chômage, sans travail; (*time*) inemployé; (*machine*) inutilisé; **u. capital,** fonds inactifs. **2** *n* **the u.,** (*used as pl*) les chômeurs *mpl*.
unemployment [ʌnɪm'plɔɪmənt] *n* chômage *m*; **as the u. rate rises ...,** alors que le taux de chômage est en augmentation ...; **u. benefit,** *Am* **u. compensation,** allocation *f ou* indemnité *f* de chômage; **u. figures,** statistiques *fpl* du chômage.
unencumbered [ʌnɪn'kʌmbəd] *adj* non encombré (**by, with,** de); *Jur* **u. estate,** propriété franche d'hypothèques.
unending [ʌn'endɪŋ] *adj* interminable, qui n'en finit plus; (*in positive use*) éternel.
unendurable [ʌnɪn'djʊərəb(ə)l] *adj* insupportable.
unenforceable [ʌnɪn'fɔ:səb(ə)l] *adj* inapplicable.
unengaged [ʌnɪn'geɪdʒd] *adj* libre.
un-English [ʌn'ɪŋglɪʃ] *adj* peu anglais, indigne d'un Anglais, contraire à l'esprit anglais.
unenlightened [ʌnɪn'laɪt(ə)nd] *adj* (*peuple, siècle*) peu éclairé; **I remained completely u.,** je suis resté dans l'ignorance la plus totale.
unenlightening [ʌnɪn'laɪtnɪŋ] *adj* (*remarque*) qui jette peu de lumière (sur une question).
unenterprising [ʌn'entəpraɪzɪŋ] *adj* (*person*) peu entreprenant, qui manque d'initiative; (*plan*) qui manque d'audace; **that was very u. of you,** vous avez vraiment manqué d'initiative, vous avez fait preuve d'une absence d'initiative totale.
unenthusiastic [ʌnɪnθ(j)u:zɪ'æstɪk] *adj* peu enthousiaste; **he seems rather u. about it,** ça n'a pas l'air de l'enthousiasmer.
unenthusiastically [ʌnɪnθ(j)u:zɪ'æstɪklɪ] *adv* sans enthousiasme.
unenviable [ʌn'envɪəb(ə)l] *adj* peu enviable.
unequal [ʌn'i:kwəl] *adj* **(a)** (*size, amount*) inégal, -aux; **(b) he was u. to the job,** il n'était pas à la hauteur de la tâche; **to be u. to doing sth,** ne pas être de force à faire qch.
unequalled [ʌn'i:kwəld] *adj* inégalé.
unequally [ʌn'i:kwəlɪ] *adv* inégalement.
unequivocal [ʌnɪ'kwɪvək(ə)l] *adj* sans équivoque.
unequivocally [ʌnɪkwɪvəklɪ] *adv* sans équivoque.
unerring [ʌn'ɜ:rɪŋ] *adj* infaillible, sûr; **with u. aim, he hit the target,** visant avec precision, il a touché la cible.
unerringly [ʌn'ɜ:rɪŋlɪ] *adv* infailliblement, sûrement.
UNESCO [ju:'neskəʊ] *n* (*abbr* **United Nations Educational, Scientific and Cultural Organization**) U.N.E.S.C.O. *f*.
unescorted [ʌnɪ'skɔ:tɪd] *adj* non accompagné.
unessential [ʌnɪ'senʃəl] **1** *adj* non essentiel. **2** *npl* **unessentials,** le superflu.
unesthetic [ʌnɪ:s'θetɪk] *adj US* = **UNAESTHETIC.**
unethical [ʌn'eθɪk(ə)l] *adj* (*conduite*) immoral.
uneven [ʌn'i:v(ə)n] *adj* **(a)** inégal, -aux; (*chemin*) raboteux; (*terrain*) accidenté; **the floorboards are u.,** les planches ne sont pas de niveau; **u. breathing,** respiration irrégulière; **u. temper,** humeur inégale; **(b)** (*nombre*) impair.

unevenly [ʌn'iːv(ə)nlɪ] *adv* inégalement; (*to breathe*) irrégulièrement; **the opponents were u. matched,** les adversaires étaient de force inégale; **u. distributed load,** charge répartie inégalement.

unevenness [ʌn'iːv(ə)nnɪs] *n* inégalité *f*; irrégularité *f* (*de la respiration*).

uneventful [ʌnɪ'ventfʊl] *adj* (*voyage*) sans incidents, calme; **u. life,** vie calme *ou* peu mouvementée.

uneventfully [ʌnɪ'ventfəlɪ] *adv* **to pass u.,** se passer sans incidents.

unexceptionable [ʌnɪk'sepʃənəb(ə)l] *adj* (*conduite*) irréprochable; (*personne*) tout à fait convenable.

unexceptional [ʌnɪk'sepʃən(ə)l] *adj* qui n'a rien d'exceptionnel.

unexciting [ʌnɪk'saɪtɪŋ] *adj* (*histoire*) plat; (*conte, film, travail*) insipide, peu passionnant; (*personne*) terne, insipide; (*vie*) monotone; **u. day,** journée calme; (*boring*) journée ennuyeuse; **this restaurant serves very u. food,** on sert des repas très ordinaires dans ce restaurant.

unexpected [ʌnɪks'pektɪd] **1** *adj* (*visiteur, résultat*) inattendu; (*événement*) imprévu; (*départ*) inopiné; (*secours, bonheur*) inespéré; **u. meeting,** rencontre inopinée; **it was completely u.,** on ne s'y attendait pas du tout; **this is all so u.!,** tout est si inattendu! **2** *n* **you must allow for the u.,** il faut parer à l'imprévu.

unexpectedly [ʌnɪks'pektɪdlɪ] *adv* de manière inattendue; **to arrive u.,** arriver à l'improviste.

unexpired [ʌnɪks'paɪəd] *adj* (*bail*) non expiré; (*passeport, billet*) non périmé, encore valable.

unexplained [ʌnɪks'pleɪnd] *adj* inexpliqué.

unexploded [ʌnɪks'pləʊdɪd] *adj* (*bomb*) non explosé, non éclaté.

unexploited [ʌnɪks'plɔɪtɪd] *adj* inexploité.

unexplored [ʌnɪks'plɔːd] *adj* (*pays etc*) inexploré.

unexposed [ʌnɪks'pəʊzd] *adj* **(a)** *Phot* (*film*) vierge; **(b)** (*criminel*) non démasqué.

unexpressed [ʌnɪks'prest] *adj* inexprimé.

unexpurgated [ʌn'ekspɜːgeɪtɪd] *adj* (*livre, texte*) non expurgé; **u. edition,** édition intégrale.

unfading [ʌn'feɪdɪŋ] *adj* (*souvenir*) ineffaçable, impérissable; (*espoir, amour*) impérissable.

unfailing [ʌn'feɪlɪŋ] *adj* **(a)** qui ne se dément pas; (*moyen, remède*) infaillible, certain, sûr; (*courage*) inlassable; (*zèle*) infatigable; (*mémoire*) sans défaillance; (*bonté*) inaltérable; (*espoir*) inébranlable; **to be u. in one's duty,** ne jamais faillir à son devoir; **(b)** (*source, réserve*) intarissable, inépuisable.

unfailingly [ʌn'feɪlɪŋlɪ] *adv* infailliblement, immanquablement.

unfair [ʌn'feər] *adj* injuste (**to s.o.,** envers qn), (*marché, arrangement*) peu équitable; **to be u. to s.o.,** défavoriser qn; **it's u.!** ce n'est pas juste!; **to have an u. advantage over everybody else,** être injustement avantagé par rapport à tous les autres; **he has been put at an u. disadvantage,** il a été injustement défavorisé *ou* désavantagé; **u. competition,** concurrence déloyale.

unfairly [ʌn'feəlɪ] *adv* injustement; peu équitablement; (*jouer*) déloyalement; **he has been u. treated,** il est victime d'une injustice; **to act u.,** agir deloyalement *ou* avec mauvaise foi.

unfairness [ʌn'feənɪs] *n* injustice *f*; déloyauté *f*, mauvaise foi.

unfaithful [ʌn'feɪθfʊl] **1** *adj* **(a) to be u. to (s.o.),** tromper, être infidèle à (*sa femme, son mari*); **(b)** (*compte rendu*) inexact, infidèle. **2** *n Rel* **the u.,** (*used as pl*) les infidèles *mpl*.

unfaithfully [ʌn'feɪθfəlɪ] *adv* infidèlement.

unfaithfulness [ʌn'feɪθfʊlnɪs] *n* infidélité *f*.

unfaltering [ʌn'fɔːltərɪŋ] *adj* sans défaillance; **u. voice,** voix ferme; **u. steps,** pas assurés.

unfalteringly [ʌn'fɔːltərɪŋlɪ] *adv* sans défaillir; (*parler*) d'une voix ferme; (*marcher*) d'un pas bien assuré.

unfamiliar [ʌnfə'mɪlɪər] *adj* peu familier, peu connu; **u. face,** visage étranger *ou* inconnu; **to be u. with sth,** ne pas connaître *ou* mal connaître qch; ne pas être au fait de qch; **I'm totally u. with this town,** je ne connais pas du tout cette ville; **he is quite u. with this subject,** il ne sait absolument rien de ce sujet.

unfamiliarity [ʌnfəmɪlɪ'ærɪtɪ] *n* **(a)** caractère étranger (*d'un lieu*); **(b)** ignorance *f* (**with,** de); **my u. with legal procedure,** mon inexpérience *f* de la procédure.

unfashionable [ʌn'fæʃənəb(ə)l] *adj* (*clothes*) démodé, passé de mode; (*restaurant, author*) qui n'est pas *ou* plus à la mode; **I know these ideas are u. but ...,** je sais que ces idées sont démodées mais ... .

unfashionably [ʌn'fæʃ(ə)nəblɪ] *adv* (*to dress etc*) sans se préoccuper de la mode.

unfasten [ʌn'fɑːs(ə)n] **1** *vt* défaire, dégrafer (*un vêtement, un bracelet*); desserrer (*une ceinture*); défaire (*une cravate, un nœud*); ouvrir, déverrouiller (*une porte*); **to come unfastened,** (*of garment*) se dégrafer; se déboutonner; (*of knot*) se défaire, se dénouer; (*of belt*) se desserrer; **to u. sth from sth,** détacher *ou* délier qch de qch. **2** *vi* se détacher; (*of dress etc*) se dégrafer.

unfathomable [ʌn'fæðəməb(ə)l] *adj* (*abîme, mystère*) insondable; (*visage*) impénétrable, inscrutable.

unfathomed [ʌn'fæðəmd] *adj* (*gouffre, mystère*) insondé; **u. depths,** profondeurs inexplorées.

unfavourable, *US* **unfavorable** [ʌn'feɪv(ə)rəb(ə)l] *adj* défavorable, peu favorable (**to,** à); (*moment*) peu propice, inopportun; (*vent*) contraire; (*critique*) adverse; **u. weather/report,** temps/compte rendu défavorable; **to appear in an u. light,** se montrer sous un jour désavantageux.

unfavourably, *US* **unfavorably** [ʌn'feɪv(ə)rəblɪ] *adv* défavorablement; **to be u. disposed towards s.o./sth,** être mal disposé envers qn/qch; **his work compares u. with his brother's,** son travail supporte mal la comparaison avec celui de son frère.

unfeeling [ʌn'fiːlɪŋ] *adj* (*person*) insensible, impitoyable; dur; **u. heart,** cœur froid *ou* indifférent.

unfeelingly [ʌn'fiːlɪŋlɪ] *adv* (*agir*) sans pitié, impitoyablement; (*répondre*) froidement, durement.

unfeigned [ʌn'feɪnd] *adj* non simulé, sincère.

unfeignedly [ʌn'feɪnɪdlɪ] *adv* sans simulation, sincèrement.

unfeminine [ʌn'femɪnɪn] *adj* peu féminin.

unfenced [ʌn'fenst] *adj* (*terrain etc*) sans clôture.

unfermented [ʌnfə'mentɪd] *adj* non fermenté.

unfertilized [ʌn'fɜːtɪlaɪzd] *adj* (*œuf*) non fécondé.

unfettered [ʌn'fetəd] *adj Lit* sans entrave(s).

unfilial [ʌn'fɪlɪəl] *adj* peu filial, -aux.

unfinished [ʌn'fɪnɪʃt] *adj* **(a)** inachevé, incomplet, -ète; **u. game,** partie interrompue; **to have some u. business,** avoir quelques affaires pendantes; (*esp menacing*) avoir une affaire à régler; **(b)** *Ind* non façonné; non usiné.

unfit [ʌn'fɪt] *adj* **(a)** impropre, peu propre (**for,** à); **u. for (human) consumption/u. to eat,** impropre à la consommation/non comestible; **u. to drink,** (*unpleasant*) imbuvable; (*harmful*) non potable; **u. for publication,** impubliable; **this house is u. for habitation,** cette maison est inhabitable; **road u. for heavy traffic,** route impraticable aux poids lourds; **(b)** (*person*) (*not suitable*) **u. for military service,** inapte au service militaire; **to be u. for one's job,** ne pas convenir à son poste; **u. to rule,** indigne de régner; **(c)** (*physically*) **to be u.,** ne pas être en forme; **he's u. to travel,** il n'est pas en état de voyager; **u. for duty,** incapable de faire son service; *Mil* **to be discharged as u.,** être réformé.

unfitness [ʌn'fɪtnɪs] *n* **(a)** (*unsuitability*) **u. for sth/to do sth,** inaptitude *f* à qch/à faire qch; **(b)** (*bad health*) mauvaise santé; (*lack of form*) mauvaise forme.

unfitted [ʌn'fɪtɪd] *adj* **to be u. for sth,** (*of equipment*) être impropre à qch; (*of person*) ne pas convenir à qch; (*morally*) être indigne de qch.

unfitting [ʌn'fɪtɪŋ] *adj* peu convenable; (*remark*) mal à propos, déplacé.

unfittingly [ʌn'fɪtɪŋlɪ] *adv* (*to behave etc*) peu convenablement.

unfix [ʌn'fɪks] *vt* détacher, défaire; *Mil* **to u. bayonets,** remettre la baïonnette.

unflagging [ʌn'flægɪŋ] *adj* (*intérêt*) soutenu; (*courage, vigueur*) inlassable; (*optimisme*) inébranlable.

unflaggingly [ʌn'flægɪŋlɪ] *adv* inlassablement, infatigablement.

unflappability [ʌnflæpə'bɪlɪtɪ] *n F* imperturbabilité *f*.

unflappable [ʌn'flæpəb(ə)l] *adj F* imperturbable; **he is completely u.,** il garde toujours son calme.

unflattering [ʌn'flætərɪŋ] *adj* peu flatteur (**to,** pour); **her hat was most u.,** son chapeau était loin de la mettre en valeur; **it shows him in an u. light,** ça le montre sous un jour défavorable; **he was rather u. about your playing,** il ne s'est pas montré très flatteur quant à votre jeu.

unflatteringly [ʌn'flætərɪŋlɪ] *adv* d'une manière peu flatteuse.

unfledged [ʌn'fledʒd] *adj* (*bird*) sans plumes; *esp Lit* (*person*) sans expérience (de la vie).

unflinching [ʌn'flɪnʃɪŋ] *adj* qui ne bronche pas; (*resolute*) résolu; (*resolve, courage*) inébranlable.

unflinchingly [ʌn'flɪnʃɪŋlɪ] *adv* sans broncher *ou*

sourailler; résolument.

unfold [ʌn'fəʊld] **1** *vt* **(a)** déplier (*un journal, une serviette*); déployer (*une carte*); **to u. one's arms,** décroiser les bras; **(b)** (*reveal*) révéler; exposer (*ses intentions, un projet*); dévoiler, découvrir (*ses plans, un secret*). **2** *vi* se déployer, se dérouler; (*of flower*) s'ouvrir, s'épanouir; (*of story, action*) se dérouler.

unforced [ʌn'fɔːst] *adj* qui n'est pas forcé; spontané; **u. laugh,** rire franc.

unforeseeable [ʌnfɔː'siːəb(ə)l] *adj* imprévisible.

unforeseen [ʌnfɔː'siːn] *adj* imprévu, inattendu; **unless something u. happens,** sauf imprévu; **u. circumstances,** circonstances imprévues; *Jur* force majeure.

unforgettable [ʌnfə'getəb(ə)l] *adj* inoubliable.

unforgivable [ʌnfə'gɪvəb(ə)l] *adj* impardonnable, inexcusable; **it's u. of me,** je suis impardonnable.

unforgivably [ʌnfə'gɪvəblɪ] *adv* **he was u. rude,** il s'est montré d'une impolitesse impardonnable.

unforgiven [ʌnfə'gɪv(ə)n] *adj* impardonné.

unforgiving [ʌnfə'gɪvɪŋ] *adj* implacable, impitoyable.

unforgotten [ʌnfə'gɒt(ə)n] *adj* inoublié.

unformed [ʌn'fɔːmd] *adj* (*os*) qui n'est pas (encore) formé; (*masse*) informe; (*esprit*) inculte.

unformulated [ʌn'fɔːmjʊleɪtɪd] *adj* informulé.

unforthcoming [ʌnfɔːθ'kʌmɪŋ] *adj* réservé; **to be u. about sth,** être *ou* se montrer réticent au sujet de qch.

unfortified [ʌn'fɔːtɪfaɪd] *adj* non fortifié, sans fortifications; **u. town,** ville ouverte.

unfortunate [ʌn'fɔːtjənɪt] **1** *adj* **(a)** malheureux, malchanceux; **he's been most u.,** il n'a pas eu beaucoup de chance; **(b)** (*accident, événement*) malheureux, malencontreux; (*erreur*) regrettable; **u. state of affairs,** situation regrettable *ou* fâcheuse; **u. consequences,** suites malheureuses; **u. choice of words,** choix de mots peu heureux; **in u. circumstances,** dans de tristes circonstances; **it's u. that she has to leave today,** il est dommage qu'elle soit obligée de partir aujourd'hui; **how (very) u.!** quel malheur!, quel dommage! **2** *n* malheureux, -euse; **the u.,** (*used as pl*) les infortunés *mpl*.

unfortunately [ʌnfɔːtjənɪtlɪ] *adv* malheureusement; **an u. worded statement,** déclaration formulée d'une façon regrettable; **u. for him,** malheureusement pour lui.

unfounded [ʌn'faʊndɪd] *adj* sans fondement; **u. rumour,** bruit dénué de tout fondement; **u. criticism,** critique injustifiée.

unframed [ʌn'freɪmd] *adj* sans cadre.

unfreeze [ʌn'friːz] *v* (*pt* **unfroze** [ʌn'frəʊz] ; *pp* **unfrozen** [ʌn'frəʊz(ə)n]) **1** *vt* **(a)** (faire) dégeler; (*food*) décongeler; **(b)** dégeler, débloquer (*des crédits*). **2** *vi* (se) dégeler.

unfrequented [ʌnfrɪ'kwentɪd] *adj* peu fréquenté; **u. spot,** endroit peu fréquenté *ou* écarté.

unfriendliness [ʌn'frendlɪnɪs] *n* manque *m* d'amitié (**towards,** pour); froideur *f* (**towards,** envers, à l'égard de); hostilité *f* (**towards,** envers, contre).

unfriendly [ʌn'frendlɪ] *adj* (*person*) peu sympathique; (*tone, feeling*) peu amical, -aux, inamical, -aux; **u. action,** action inamicale *ou* hostile; **to be u. to(wards) s.o.,** traiter qn avec froideur; **u. reception,** accueil froid; **environmentally u.,** nuisible à l'environnement; **a very u. user-interface,** une interface utilisateur très rébarbative; **written in an u. style,** écrit dans un style rébarbatif.

unfrock [ʌn'frɒk] *vt* défroquer (*un prêtre etc*).

unfrozen [ʌn'frəʊz(ə)n] *adj* **(a)** (*terrain*) dégelé; non gelé; (*produit alimentaire*) décongelé; (*never was frozen*) non congelé; **(b)** (*crédit*) dégelé, débloqué.

unfruitful [ʌn'fruːtfʊl] *adj* stérile, infertile; **u. research,** recherche infructueuse *ou* improductive.

unfulfilled [ʌnfʊl'fɪld] *adj* (*prophecy, duty*) inaccompli; (*promise*) non tenu; (*desire*) non satisfait, inassouvi; (*prayer*) inexaucé; **to feel u.,** éprouver un sentiment d'insatisfaction.

unfunny [ʌn'fʌnɪ] *adj* qui n'est pas drôle; **I find that distinctly u.,** je ne trouve pas ça drôle du tout.

unfurl [ʌn'fɜːl] **1** *vt* déployer, déferler (*une voile, un drapeau*); ouvrir (*un parapluie*). **2** *vi* se déployer.

unfurnished [ʌn'fɜːnɪʃt] *adj* non meublé.

ungainliness [ʌn'geɪnlɪnɪs] *n* gaucherie *f*.

ungainly [ʌn'geɪnlɪ] *adj* gauche.

ungallant [ʌn'gælənt] *adj* peu galant, discourtois.

ungenerous [ʌn'dʒen(ə)rəs] *adj* peu généreux.

ungentlemanly [ʌn'dʒentlmənlɪ] *adj* peu galant, discourtois; **u. behaviour,** manque *m* de savoir-vivre.

ungetatable [ʌnget'ætəb(ə)l] *adj F* inaccessible.

ungird [ʌn'gɜːd] (*pt & pp* **ungirt** [ʌn'gɜːt]) *vt* (*sword*) détacher.

unglazed [ʌn'gleɪzd] *adj* **(a)** (*window*) non vitré, sans vitres; **(b)** (*paper*) mat, non glacé; *Phot* **u. print,** épreuve mate; **(c)** *Cer* non verni, non émaillé; (*brick*) non vitrifié; **u. porcelain,** biscuit *m*; **(d)** (*cake*) non glacé.

ungodliness [ʌn'gɒdlɪnɪs] *n* impiété *f*.

ungodly [ʌn'gɒdlɪ] *adj* **(a)** impie, irréligieux; **(b)** *F* **an u. row,** un bruit de tous les diables; **he got up at an u. hour,** il s'est levé à une heure impossible *ou* indue.

ungovernable [ʌn'gʌv(ə)nəb(ə)l] *adj* **(a)** (*peuple, pays*) ingouvernable; **(b)** (*désir, passion*) irrésistible; **he has fits of u. temper,** il a des emportements de colère incontrôlables.

ungraceful [ʌn'greɪsfʊl] *adj* sans grâce; gauche.

ungracefully [ʌn'greɪsfəlɪ] *adv* sans grâce; gauchement.

ungracious [ʌn'greɪʃəs] *adj* peu gracieux, peu aimable; **it would be u. of me to refuse,** j'aurais mauvaise grâce de refuser.

ungraciously [ʌn'greɪʃəslɪ] *adv* (*to refuse*) de manière peu aimable *ou* peu gracieuse.

ungraciousness [ʌn'greɪʃəsnɪs] *n* mauvaise grâce.

ungrammatical [ʌngrə'mætɪk(ə)l] *adj* non grammatical, -aux, incorrect.

ungrammatically [ʌngrə'mætɪklɪ] *adv* incorrectement.

ungrateful [ʌn'greɪtfʊl] *adj* **(a) to be u. to s.o.,** être peu reconnaissant envers qn **(for sth,** de qch), se montrer ingrat envers qn; **don't be so u.!,** ne sois pas si ingrat!; **(b) u. task,** tâche ingrate.

ungratefully [ʌn'greɪtfəlɪ] *adv* avec ingratitude.

ungratefulness [ʌn'greɪtfʊlnɪs] *n* ingratitude *f*.

ungratified [ʌn'grætɪfaɪd] *adj* (*désir*) inassouvi.

ungrudging [ʌn'grʌdʒɪŋ] *adj* donné de bon cœur; (*admiration*) (très) sincère.

ungrudgingly [ʌn'grʌdʒɪŋlɪ] *adv* de bon cœur; généreusement.

unguarded [ʌn'gɑːdɪd] *adj* **(a)** non gardé; (*prisonnier etc*) sans surveillance; (*ville*) sans défense; *Cards* (*roi*) sec; *Chess* (*pièce*) non gardée; **to leave the goal u.,** dégarnir le but; **(b)** (*remarque*) inconsidéré, irréfléchi; **in an u. moment,** dans un moment d'inattention; **(c)** (*précipice*) sans garde-fou; (*mécanisme*) sans dispositif protecteur.

unguent ['ʌŋgwənt] *n* onguent *m*.

ungulate ['ʌŋgjʊleɪt] *adj & n Zool* ongulé *m*.

unhallowed [ʌn'hæləʊd] *adj* non béni, non consacré.

unhampered [ʌn'hæmpəd] *adj* non entravé (**by,** par); libre (*de ses mouvements*); **u. by rules,** sans être gêné par des règles.

unhand [ʌn'hænd] *vt Arch & Hum* lâcher (*qn*).

unhandy [ʌn'hændɪ] *adj* maladroit, gauche.

unhappily [ʌn'hæpɪlɪ] *adv* **(a)** (*unfortunately*) malheureusement; **(b)** (*sadly, miserably*) tristement, d'un air triste; **they're u. married,** c'est un ménage malheureux; **(c) u. phrased,** rédigé de manière malheureuse *ou* maladroite.

unhappiness [ʌn'hæpɪnɪs] *n* chagrin *m*, tristesse *f*.

unhappy [ʌn'hæpɪ] *adj* **(a)** malheureux, triste; **to make s.o. u.,** causer du chagrin à qn; (*esp intentionally*) rendre qn malheureux; **to be u. at leaving s.o.,** avoir du chagrin de quitter qn; **to be u. with s.o./sth,** être mécontent de qn/qch; **(b)** (*worried*) inquiet, -ète; **I'm u. about leaving the house empty,** je n'aime pas laisser *ou* ça m'inquiète de laisser la maison vide; **(c)** (*not pleased*) pas satisfait; **we're u. with the quality,** nous ne sommes pas satisfaits de la qualité, la qualité ne nous satisfait pas; **(d)** (*remark*) malheureux, malencontreux; **an u. state of affairs,** une situation regrettable.

unharmed [ʌn'hɑːmd] *adj* (*person*) sain et sauf, indemne; (*thing*) intact, non endommagé.

unharness [ʌn'hɑːnɪs] *vt* dételer (*un cheval*).

unhealthiness [ʌn'helθɪnɪs] *n* mauvaise santé; insalubrité *f* (*de l'air, d'un endroit*).

unhealthy [ʌn'helθɪ] *adj* (*person*) maladif; (*state of mind, influence*) malsain; (*air, place*) malsain, insalubre; (*engine*) détraqué; **u. curiosity,** curiosité morbide; *F* **it can be u. to ask too many questions,** (*dangerous*) il peut être malsain de poser trop de questions.

unheard [ʌn'hɜːd] *adj* non entendu; **to condemn s.o. u.,** condamner qn sans l'avoir entendu.

unheard-of [ʌn'hɜːdɒv] *adj* (*incredible*) inouï; (*unknown*) inconnu; **that's u.-of!** c'est vraiment incroyable!

unheated [ʌn'hiːtɪd] *adj* non chauffé.

unheeded [ʌn'hiːdɪd] *adj* négligé, ignoré; **his warning went u.,** on n'a pas tenu compte de son avertissement.

unheeding [ʌn'hiːdɪŋ] *adj* inattentif (**of,** à), insouciant

(**of,** de).
unhelpful [ʌn'helpful] *adj* (*person*) peu secourable, peu obligeant; (*criticism*) peu utile; (*advice*) vain, futile; **don't be so u.!,** tâche donc un peu de nous aider!
unhelpfully [ʌn'helpfəlɪ] *adv* futilement; **someone very u. left the disk on a radiator,** il y a quelqu'un de très négligent qui a laissé la disquette sur un radiateur.
unheralded [ʌn'herəldɪd] *adj esp Lit* qui n'est pas annoncé; (*unexpected*) imprévu, inattendu.
unhesitating [ʌn'hezɪteɪtɪŋ] *adj* qui n'hésite pas; **u. reply,** réponse faite sans hésitation, réponse prompte; **my u. reaction,** ma réaction spontanée; **you can count on our u. support,** vous pouvez compter sur notre soutien sans faille.
unhesitatingly [ʌn'hezɪteɪtɪŋlɪ] *adv* sans hésiter, sans hésitation.
unhindered [ʌn'hɪndəd] *adj* sans obstacle; (*not disturbed*) sans être dérangé (**by,** par); **to go u.,** passer librement; **u. by all that luggage,** sans être encombré par tous ces bagages; **u. by petty regulations,** sans se laisser gêner par des règlements tatillons.
unhinge [ʌn'hɪndʒ] *vt* enlever (*une porte etc*) de ses gonds; déranger, détraquer (*l'esprit de qn*).
unhinged [ʌn'hɪndʒd] *adj* dérangé; **she's a bit u.,** elle est un peu dérangée.
unhitch [ʌn'hɪtʃ] *vt* détacher, décrocher (*qch*); dételer (*un cheval*).
unholy [ʌn'həʊlɪ] *adj Rel* (*place etc*) profane; *F* **u. muddle,** désordre affreux; **there was an u. row,** il y a eu un charivari de tous les diables.
unhook [ʌn'hʊk] **1** *vt* décrocher (*un tableau*); décrocher, dételer (*une remorque*); dégrafer (*un vêtement*); **to come unhooked,** (*of dress*) se dégrafer. **2** *vi* se décrocher; se dégrafer.
unhoped-for [ʌn'həʊptfɔːr] *adj* inespéré.
unhorse [ʌn'hɔːs] *vt* désarçonner.
unhurried [ʌn'hʌrɪd] *adj* lent; **in an u. way,** sans se presser.
unhurt [ʌn'hɜːt] *adj* (*person*) sans mal, sans blessure, sain et sauf; **to escape u.,** sortir indemne.
unhygienic [ʌnhaɪ'dʒiːnɪk] *adj* non hygiénique; **it's u. to ...,** il est peu hygiénique de ..., ... est contraire à l'hygiène.
UNICEF ['juːnɪsef] *n* (*abbr* **United Nations International Children's Emergency Fund**) Fonds international de secours à l'enfance, FISE.
unicellular [juːnɪ'seljʊlər] *adj Biol* unicellulaire.
unicorn ['juːnɪkɔːn] *n Myth Her* licorne *f*.
unicycle ['juːnɪsaɪkl] *n* monocycle *m*.
unidentifiable [ʌnaɪ'dentɪfaɪəb(ə)l] *adj* non identifiable.
unidentified [ʌnaɪ'dentɪfaɪd] *adj* non identifié; **u. flying object,** objet volant non identifié.
unidirectional [juːnɪd(a)ɪ'rekʃən(ə)l] *adj Phys etc* unidirectionnel.
unification [juːnɪfɪ'keɪʃən] *n* unification *f*.
uniform ['juːnɪfɔːm] **1** *adj* (*colour, style*) uniforme; (*temperature*) constant; **these boxes are all of u. size,** ces boîtes sont toutes de la même grandeur; **to make u.,** uniformiser. **2** *n Mil Sch* uniforme *m*; **in u.,** en tenue, en uniforme; **out of u.,** en civil; (*air hostess etc*) sans son uniforme.
uniformed ['juːnɪfɔːmd] *adj* en uniforme, en tenue.
uniformity [juːnɪ'fɔːmɪtɪ] *n* uniformité *f*, unité *f* (*de style*); constance *f* (*d'un courant*).
uniformly ['juːnɪfɔːmlɪ] *adv* uniformément.
unify ['juːnɪfaɪ] **1** *vt* unifier (*un parti politique*). **2** *vi* s'unifier.
unifying ['juːnɪfaɪɪŋ] *adj* unificateur, -trice.
unilateral [juːnɪ'lætərəl] *adj* unilatéral, -aux; **u. disarmament,** désarmement unilatéral.
unilaterally [juːnɪ'lætərəlɪ] *adv* unilatéralement.
unilingual [juːnɪ'lɪŋgwəl] *adj* unilingue.
unimaginable [ʌnɪ'mædʒɪnəb(ə)l] *adj* inimaginable, inconcevable.
unimaginative [ʌnɪ'mædʒɪnətɪv] *adj* qui manque d'imagination; (*person*) qui manque d'imagination, peu imaginatif; **you're so u.,** vous n'avez aucune imagination!
unimaginatively [ʌnɪ'mædʒɪnətɪvlɪ] *adv* sans imagination, d'une manière peu imaginative.
unimaginativeness [ʌnɪ'mædʒɪnətɪvnɪs] *n* manque *m* d'imagination.
unimpaired [ʌnɪm'peəd] *adj* (*health, hearing*) toujours bon; (*force, quality*) non diminué; **his mind is u.,** il conserve toute sa vigueur d'esprit.
unimpeachable [ʌnɪm'piːtʃəb(ə)l] *adj* **(a)** inattaquable; (*droit*) incontestable; **I have it from an u. source,** je le tiens de source sûre; **(b)** (*témoignage, témoin*) irrécusable; (*conduite*) irréprochable, impeccable.
unimpeded [ʌnɪm'piːdɪd] *adj* sans entrave; **u. by ...,** sans être entravé par ... .
unimportant [ʌnɪm'pɔːtənt] *adj* sans importance, peu important; **it's quite u.,** cela n'a pas la moindre importance; **it's u. what THEY think,** leur opinion ne compte pas *ou* est sans importance.
unimposing [ʌnɪm'pəʊzɪŋ] *adj* (*air, aspect*) peu imposant, peu impressionnant.
unimpressed [ʌnɪm'prest] *adj* qui n'est pas impressionné, peu impressionné (**by,** par); **I was u. by his speech,** son discours ne m'a fait aucune impression; **we were all very u.,** nous étions tous très peu impressionnés.
unimpressive [ʌnɪm'presɪv] *adj* peu impressionnant; (*discours*) peu convaincant; (*paysage*) peu frappant.
uninflammable [ʌnɪn'flæməb(ə)l] *adj* ininflammable.
uninfluential [ʌnɪnflʊ'enʃəl] *adj* sans influence.
uninformed [ʌnɪn'fɔːmd] *adj* mal informé, mal renseigné (**about,** sur); (*ignorant*) ignorant; (*mind*) inculte.
uninhabitable [ʌnɪn'hæbɪtəb(ə)l] *adj* inhabitable.
uninhabited [ʌnɪn'hæbɪtɪd] *adj* inhabité, désert, sans habitants.
uninhibited [ʌnɪn'hɪbɪtɪd] *adj* sans inhibitions, qui n'a pas d'inhibitions; (*emotion etc*) non refréné; **she's so u.,** elle est si naturelle.
uninitiated [ʌnɪ'nɪʃɪeɪtɪd] **1** *adj* non initié (**in,** à). **2** *n* **the u.,** (*used as pl*) les profanes *mpl*, les non-initiés *mpl*.
uninjured [ʌn'ɪndʒəd] *adj* sans blessure, sans mal, sain et sauf, indemne.
uninspired [ʌnɪn'spaɪəd] *adj* qui manque d'inspiration; (*architecture, suggestion, style*) banal, -als.
uninspiring [ʌn'ɪnspaɪrɪŋ] *adj* qui n'est pas inspirant; (plutôt) médiocre.
uninsured [ʌnɪn'ʃʊəd] *adj* non assuré (**against,** contre).
unintelligent [ʌnɪn'telɪdʒənt] *adj* inintelligent.
unintelligible [ʌnɪn'telɪdʒɪb(ə)l] *adj* inintelligible.
unintelligibly [ʌnɪn'telɪdʒɪblɪ] *adv* inintelligiblement.
unintended [ʌnɪn'tendɪd] *adj* involontaire, non intentionnel; (*résultat*) non voulu; **the pun was quite u.,** le calembour était tout à fait involontaire.
unintentional [ʌnɪn'tenʃən(ə)l] *adj* involontaire, non intentionnel; **it was quite u.,** ce n'était pas fait exprès.
unintentionally [ʌnɪn'tenʃən(ə)lɪ] *adv* involontairement, sans intention; (*froisser qn*) sans le vouloir; **he did it quite u.,** il ne l'a pas fait exprès.
uninterested [ʌn'ɪnt(ə)restɪd] *adj* indifférent (**in,** à); **to be u. in sth,** ne pas s'intéresser à qch.
uninteresting [ʌnɪnt(ə)restɪŋ] *adj* inintéressant, non intéressant, sans intérêt.
uninterrupted [ʌnɪntə'rʌptɪd] *adj* ininterrompu, sans interruption, continu; **u. correspondence,** correspondance suivie.
uninterruptedly [ʌnɪntə'rʌptɪdlɪ] *adv* sans interruption.
uninvited [ʌnɪn'vaɪtɪd] *adj* **u. guest,** visiteur, -euse inattendu(e); (*intruder*) intrus, -use; **to come u.,** venir sans invitation; **to do sth u.,** faire qch sans y avoir été invité.
uninviting [ʌnɪn'vaɪtɪŋ] *adj* peu attirant, peu attrayant; (*food*) peu appétissant.
union ['juːnjən] *n* **(a)** union *f* (**with,** avec); **(b)** *esp Fml* (*marriage*) mariage *m*; **(c)** (*harmony*) concorde *f*; **in perfect u.,** (*vivre ensemble*) en parfaite harmonie; **(d) the (American) U.,** les États-Unis, l'Union *f* (américaine); **customs u.,** union douanière; **U. Jack,** pavillon *m* britannique; **(e)** (*trade union*) syndicat *m* (ouvrier); **to form/join a u.,** se syndiquer; **u. member,** syndiqué(e), membre *m* du *ou* d'un syndicat; **increasing/decreasing u. membership,** syndicalisation croissante/décroissante; **u. regulations,** règles syndicales; **non-u. workers,** ouvriers, -ières non syndiqué(e)s; **unions and management,** les syndicats et la direction, les partenaires sociaux; **u. shop,** atelier *m* d'ouvriers syndiqués; **(f)** *MecE* **u. (joint),** raccord *m*; **(g)** *US* **u. suit,** combinaison *f*.
unionism ['juːnjənɪz(ə)m] *n* **(a)** *Ind* syndicalisme *m* (ouvrier); **(b)** *Pol* unionisme *m*.
unionist ['juːnjənɪst] *n* **(a)** *Ind* syndicaliste *mf*; **(b)** *Pol* unioniste *mf*; *Hist* **the u. party,** le parti unioniste.
unionize ['juːnjənaɪz] **1** *vt* syndiquer (*des ouvriers*). **2** *vi* se syndiquer.
uniparous [juː'nɪpərəs] *adj Biol* unipare.
unique [juː'niːk] *adj* unique; **a u. opportunity,** une occasion unique *ou* exceptionnelle.
uniquely [juː'niːklɪ] *adv* d'une manière unique; (*extremely well*) exceptionnellement; **he is u. placed to get this information,** il est exceptionnellement bien placé pour obtenir ce renseignement.

uniqueness [juːˈniːknɪs] *n* caractère unique *ou* exceptionnel.

unisex [ˈjuːnɪseks] *adj* (*boutique*) unisexe.

unison [ˈjuːnɪs(ə)n] *n Mus* unisson *m*; **in u.,** à l'unisson (**with,** de); *Fig* **they all replied in u.,** ils ont tous répondu en même temps; *Fig* **to be in u. with s.o.,** être en accord avec qn; **to act in u.,** agir à l'unisson.

unit [ˈjuːnɪt] *n* **(a)** unité *f*; *Math* **units and tens,** unités et dizaines; *Com Ind* **each box contains a hundred units,** chaque boîte contient cent unités; **u. price,** prix *m* unitaire *ou* à l'unité; **standard u.,** module *m*; *Phys* **u. of mass,** unité de masse; **thermal u.,** unité thermique; *Mec* **u. of energy/of work,** unité d'énergie/de travail; **u. of velocity,** unité de vitesse; *Tel* **u. charge,** taxe *f* unitaire; *Fin* **monetary u.,** unité monétaire; *Fin* **u. trust,** société d'investissement à capital variable;
(b) in England the county is the largest administrative u. for local government, en Angleterre le comté est la plus grande division administrative; **information u.,** service *m* d'informations; *Med* **intensive care u.,** centre *m* de soins intensifs; **X-ray u.,** service de radiologie; *Mil* **administrative u.,** unité administrative; **auxiliary units,** formations *f* auxiliaires; **fighting u.,** *US* **combat u.,** unité combattante; **air force u.,** unité *ou* groupe *m* de l'armée de l'air;
(c) *MecE* unité *f*, élément *m*; **control u.,** élément de contrôle *ou* de réglage; **construction u.,** élément de construction; **standardized units,** éléments normalisés; *Aut* **motor u.,** bloc-moteur *m*; **the engine forms a u. with the transmission,** le moteur fait bloc avec la transmission; *Comptr* **central processing u.,** unité centrale; **input/output u.,** élément *ou* dispositif *m* (d')entrée-sortie; **(visual) display u.,** console *f* de visualisation, visuel *m*; **u. construction,** préfabrication *f*; **u. furniture,** mobilier *m* par éléments; **kitchen u.,** élément *m* de cuisine;
(d) *Austr* appartement *m*.

Unitarian [juːnɪˈteərɪən] *adj & n Rel* unitarien, -ienne, unitaire *mf*.

Unitarianism [juːnɪˈteərɪənɪz(ə)m] *n Rel* unitarisme *m*.

unitary [ˈjuːnɪt(ə)rɪ] *adj* (*système etc*) unitaire.

unite [juːˈnaɪt] **1** *vt* **(a)** unir; **to u. one country with another,** unir un pays à un autre; **to u. idealism with common sense,** allier l'idéalisme au bon sens; **(b)** mettre (*les gens*) d'accord; unifier (*un parti*); **common interests that u. two countries,** intérêts communs qui allient deux pays; **(c)** unir (en mariage). **2** *vi* s'unir, s'unifier (**with,** à); (*of two or more persons or things*) s'unir; (*of party*) s'unifier; (*of states*) se confédérer; *Ch* (*of atoms*) s'unir, se combiner; **to u. against s.o./sth,** s'unir contre qn/qch; *Pol* faire bloc contre (*un parti*); **to u. in doing sth,** se mettre d'accord pour faire qch.

united [juːˈnaɪtɪd] *adj* uni; (*unified*) unifié; **u. efforts,** efforts conjugués; **u. we stand, divided we fall,** l'union fait la force; **to present a u. front,** présenter un front uni; **the U. Kingdom (of Great Britain and Northern Ireland),** le Royaume-Uni (de Grande-Bretagne et de l'Irlande du Nord); **the U. States (of America),** les États-Unis (d'Amérique); **the U. Arab Emirates,** les Émirats Arabes Unis; **the U. Arab Republic,** la République Arabe Unie; **the United Nations,** les Nations Unies.

unity [ˈjuːnɪtɪ] *n* **(a)** unité *f*; **national/political u.,** unité nationale/politique; *Prov* **u. is strength,** l'union fait la force; **(b) there is no u. in his work,** ses œuvres manquent d'unité *ou* d'harmonie; **u. of time, place, action,** unité de temps, de lieu, d'action.

univ *abbr* **university**.

univalent [juːnɪˈveɪlənt] *adj Ch* univalent.

universal [juːnɪˈvɜːs(ə)l] **1** *adj* **(a)** universel; **u. suffrage,** suffrage universel; **he's a u. favourite,** tout le monde l'aime; **(b)** *MecE* **u. joint,** joint universel; *US* **u. product code,** code *m* barres. **2** *n Phil* universel *m*.

universality [juːnɪvɜːˈsælɪtɪ] *n* universalité *f*.

universalize [juːnɪˈvɜːsəlaɪz] *vt* universaliser.

universally [juːnɪˈvɜːsəlɪ] *adv* universellement.

universe [ˈjuːnɪvɜːs] *n* univers *m*; **the wonders of the u.,** les merveilles de l'univers.

university [juːnɪˈvɜːsɪtɪ] *n* université *f*; **to go to u.,** aller à l'université; **he's been to u., he's had a u. education,** il a fait des études supérieures; **to get a place at u.,** être admis à l'université; **when I was at u.,** quand j'étais à l'université *ou* à la faculté; **London U.,** l'université de Londres; **u. professor,** professeur de faculté; **u. student,** étudiant, -ante à l'université; **u. town,** ville universitaire; **the Open U.** = le centre de télé-enseignement universitaire; **the great u. of life,** la grande école de la vie.

unjust [ʌnˈdʒʌst] *adj* injuste (**to,** envers, avec); **my suspicions were u.,** mes soupçons étaient mal fondés.

unjustifiable [ʌndʒʌstɪˈfaɪəb(ə)l] *adj* injustifiable.

unjustifiably [ʌndʒʌstɪˈfaɪəblɪ] *adv* sans justification.

unjustified [ʌnˈdʒʌstɪfaɪd] *adj* **(a)** injustifié; **he was absolutely u. in doing that,** il était absolument dans son tort en faisant cela; **(b)** (*text*) non justifié.

unjustly [ʌnˈdʒʌstlɪ] *adv* injustement.

unkempt [ʌnˈkem(p)t] *adj* (*hair*) mal peigné; (*appearance*) négligé, débraillé; (*person*) dépeigné; débraillé; (*garden*) mal tenu.

unkind [ʌnˈkaɪnd] *adj* dur, méchant; (*less strong*) peu aimable, pas gentil; (*weather*) peu favorable; **u. fate,** sort impitoyable *ou* cruel; **that's very u. of him,** ce n'est pas du tout gentil de sa part; **to say u. things to s.o.,** dire des méchancetés à qn; **to be u. to animals,** être cruel avec les animaux; **to be u. to s.o.,** être méchant envers *ou* avec qn.

unkindly [ʌnˈkaɪndlɪ] **1** *adv* méchamment, durement; (*less strong*) peu aimablement; **to take u. to sth,** mal accepter qch; **don't take it u. if I say it frankly,** ne le prenez pas en mauvaise part si je vous le dis franchement. **2** *adj* peu aimable, peu gentil.

unkindness [ʌnˈkaɪndnɪs] *n* manque *m* de gentillesse; (*stronger*) méchanceté *f*; rigueur *f* (*du climat*).

unknot [ʌnˈnɒt] *vt* (**-tt-**) dénouer; défaire les nœuds (*d'une ficelle etc*).

unknowing [ʌnˈnəʊɪŋ] *adj* inconscient (**of,** de); **I was an u. accomplice,** j'étais accomplice sans le savoir.

unknowingly [ʌnˈnəʊɪŋlɪ] *adv* inconsciemment, sans le savoir.

unknown [ʌnˈnəʊn] **1** *adj* inconnu (**to,** de); **u. person,** inconnu, -ue; **the U. Soldier,** le Soldat inconnu; *Jur* **verdict against person or persons u.,** verdict contre inconnu; **this is a process u. to us, this process is u. to us,** c'est un procédé qui nous est inconnu; *Math etc* **u. quantity,** (quantité) inconnue *f*; **he's an u. quantity,** on ne sait pas ce qu'il vaut. **2** *adv* **he did it u. to me,** il l'a fait à mon insu; **u. to us, the bus had already gone,** nous ne le savions pas, mais le bus était déjà parti. **3** *n* **(a)** (*person*) inconnu(e) *mf*; **(b)** *Math* inconnue *f*; **(c) the u.,** l'inconnu *m*.

unlace [ʌnˈleɪs] *vt* délacer, défaire (*ses chaussures*).

unladen [ʌnˈleɪd(ə)n] *adj* (*ship, lorry*) sans charge; **u. weight,** poids à vide.

unladylike [ʌnˈleɪdɪlaɪk] *adj* indigne d'une femme bien élevée, mal élevée; (*manners*) peu distingué; **it's u. to ...,** ce n'est pas distingué de ..., ce ne sont pas des manières de dame de ... .

unlaid [ʌnˈleɪd] *adj* **(a)** (*carpet*) **still u.,** pas encore posé; **(b) the table was still u.,** la table n'était pas encore mise; **(c)** *Sl* (*virgin*) **to be u.,** être puceau; (*of woman*) être pucelle.

unlamented [ʌnləˈmentɪd] *adj* non regretté; **he passed away u.,** il est mort dans l'indifférence générale.

unlatch [ʌnˈlætʃ] *vt* ouvrir (*une porte*).

unlawful [ʌnˈlɔːf(ʊ)l] *adj* illégal, -aux; (*moyen*) illicite; (*acte*) irrégulier, illégitime.

unlawfully [ʌnˈlɔːf(ʊ)lɪ] *adv* illégalement; illicitement; irrégulièrement, illégitimement.

unleaded [ʌnˈledɪd] **1** *adj* (*petrol*) sans plomb. **2** *n* essence *f* sans plomb.

unlearn [ʌnˈlɜːn] *vt* (*pt & pp* **unlearnt** [-ˈlɜːnt] *occ* **unlearned** [-lɜːnd]) désapprendre (*qch*).

unlearned [ʌnˈlɜːnɪd] *adj* inculte.

unleash [ʌnˈliːʃ] *vt* **(a)** lâcher (*des chiens*); **(b)** déchaîner (*la force d'une armée etc*); **to u. a nuclear war,** déclencher une guerre nucléaire.

unleavened [ʌnˈlevənd] *adj* (*pain*) sans levain, azyme.

unless [ʌnˈles] *conj* à moins que + *sub*; **he will do nothing u. you ask him to,** il ne fera rien à moins que vous ne le lui demandiez; **u. I'm mistaken,** à moins que je (ne) me trompe; **will you do it? — not u. you pay me,** le ferez-vous? — seulement si vous me payez; **there aren't any left, not u. you want this one,** il n'y en a plus, à moins que vous ne vouliez celui-ci; **u. I hear to the contrary,** sauf avis contraire.

unlettered [ʌnˈletəd] *adj* peu lettré, inculte.

unliberated [ʌnˈlɪbəreɪtɪd] *adj* (*woman*) non libéré, non émancipé; **they're very u. here,** on n'est pas du tout émancipé par ici; **that's very u. of you,** la libération de la femme, tu connais?

unlicensed [ʌnˈlaɪsənst] *adj* **(a)** non autorisé, illicite; **u. premises,** établissement où la vente des boissons alcooliques n'est pas autorisée; **u. taxi,** taxi marron; **(b)** (*car*) = sans vignette.

unlike [ʌnˈlaɪk] **1** *adj* différent, dissemblable; **they're**

completely u. ils ne se ressemblent pas du tout. **2** *prep* **u. s.o./sth,** différent de qn/qch; **he's not u. his sister,** il ressemble assez à la sœur; **he, u. his father,** lui, à la différence de *ou* contrairement à son père; **it's u. him to do such a thing,** cela ne lui ressemble pas de faire une chose pareille; **that was very u. him!,** on ne s'attendait pas à ça de sa part!

unlikeable [ʌn'laɪkəb(ə)l] *adj* (*person*) antipathique, peu sympathique; (*thing*) peu agréable.

unlikelihood, unlikeliness [ʌn'laɪklɪhʊd, -'laɪklɪnɪs] *n* improbabilité *f*.

unlikely [ʌn'laɪklɪ] *adj* improbable, peu probable; (*explanation*) invraisemblable; **that's most** *or* **very u.,** c'est fort improbable; **it's not (at all) u.,** c'est très probable, cela se pourrait bien; **it's u. to happen,** il y a peu de chances pour que ça arrive; **in the u. event that they do come,** au cas peu probable où ils viendraient vraiment; **he's u. to do it,** il est peu probable qu'il le fasse; **he's an u. man for the job,** il ne semble pas être destiné à ce travail; **we found the ring in a most u. place,** nous avons retrouvé la bague dans un endroit auquel nous n'aurions jamais pensé; *F* **she wears the most u. clothes,** elle s'habille d'une façon invraisemblable.

unlimited [ʌn'lɪmɪtɪd] *adj* (*time*) illimité; (*patience*) sans borne(s); **u. mileage,** (*of hired car*) = kilométrage illimité; **there were u. supplies of beer,** la bière était à discrétion.

unlined [ʌn'laɪnd] *adj* **(a)** (*visage*) sans rides; (*papier*) non réglé; **(b)** (*without lining*) sans doublure.

unlisted [ʌn'lɪstɪd] *adj* qui ne figure pas sur une liste; *St Exch* non inscrit à la cote (officielle); *US* (*not in phone directory*) qui n'est pas sur l'annuaire.

unlit [ʌn'lɪt] *adj* non éclairé.

unload [ʌn'ləʊd] **1** *vt* **(a)** décharger (*un bateau, une voiture, des marchandises*); *Fig* se débarrasser *ou* se défaire de (*qch*); *St Exch* **to u. stock on the market,** se décharger d'un paquet d'actions; **(b)** décharger (*un fusil, un appareil*). **2** *vi* (*of lorry, ship*) décharger.

unloaded [ʌnləʊdɪd] *adj* **(a)** (*lorry, ship*) déchargé; (*without a load*) non chargé, sans chargement; **(b)** (*gun*) non armé, non chargé; (*camera*) non chargé.

unloading [ʌn'ləʊdɪŋ] *n* déchargement *m*.

unlock [ʌn'lɒk] *vt* **(a)** ouvrir (*une porte*); **(b)** révéler, découvrir (*un secret*); **(c)** débloquer (*une roue, un écrou*), **(d) to u. the steering wheel/keyboard,** déverrouiller le mécanisme de direction/le clavier.

unlocked [ʌn'lɒkt] *adj* (*door*) qui n'est pas fermé à clef.

unlooked-for [ʌn'lʊktfɔːr] *adj* inattendu, imprévu.

unloose(n) [ʌn'luːs(n)] *vt* délier, détacher; **to u. one's grip,** lâcher prise; **to u. s.o.'s tongue,** délier la langue à qn.

unlovable [ʌn'lʌvəb(ə)l] *adj* peu attachant.

unloved [ʌn'lʌvd] *adj* qui n'est pas aimé; **to be feeling u.,** ne pas se sentir aimé.

unlovely [ʌn'lʌvlɪ] *adj* (*person*) sans charme; (*sight*) désagréable.

unloving [ʌn'lʌvɪŋ] *adj* peu affectueux, peu aimant; froid.

unluckily [ʌn'lʌkɪlɪ] *adv* malheureusement, par malheur; **u. for me ...,** malheureusement pour moi.

unlucky [ʌn'lʌkɪ] *adj* **(a)** (*person*) malchanceux; **to be u.,** ne pas avoir de chance, *F* avoir de la déveine; **it was u. for him that she arrived just at that moment,** malheureusement pour lui, elle est arrivée à cet instant précis; **(b)** (*coincidence, decision*) malheureux, malencontreux; **u. day,** jour de malheur; **that's u.,** ce n'est pas de chance; **(c)** (*bringing bad luck*) (*number, colour etc*) qui porte malheur; **u. star,** étoile maléfique; **don't walk under a ladder, it's u.,** ne passez pas sous une échelle, ça porte malheur.

unmade ['ʌnmeɪd] *adj* qui n'est pas fait; (*lit*) défait.

unmade-up ['ʌnmeɪdʌp] *adj* (*road*) non goudronné; (*face*) non maquillé.

unmake [ʌn'meɪk] *vt* (*pt & pp* **unmade** [-'meɪd]) défaire.

unman [ʌn'mæn] *vt* (**-nn-**) **(a)** (*made less virile*) déviriliser; *esp Lit* (*castrate*) émasculer; **(b)** (*cause to lose courage*) décourager, démoraliser (*qn*).

unmanageable [ʌn'mænɪdʒəb(ə)l] *adj* (*person*) intraitable; (*child, horse*) indocile; (*vehicle, ship*) difficile à manœuvrer; (*of large book*) difficile à manier, peu maniable; (*company*) difficile à diriger; **u. hair,** cheveux difficiles à coiffer.

unmanly [ʌn'mænlɪ] *adj* **(a)** (*effeminate*) efféminé; **(b)** (*cowardly*) lâche.

unmanned [ʌn'mænd] *adj* (*vehicle*) sans équipage; (*counter*) non occupé; *Rail* (*level crossing*) non géré; *Astronaut* **u. flight,** vol inhabité *ou* non habité; **the reception desk must never be left u.,** il doit toujours y avoir quelqu'un au bureau de réception.

unmannerliness [ʌn'mænəlɪnɪs] *n Lit* manque *m* de savoir-vivre, impolitesse *f*.

unmannerly [ʌn'mænəlɪ] *adj Lit* qui manque de savoir-vivre, impoli, mal élevé.

unmapped [ʌn'mæpt] *adj* (*territory*) dont la carte n'a pas été dressée.

unmarked [ʌn'mɑːkt] *adj* **(a)** sans marque(s); (*no stains etc*) sans tache(s); **u. (police) car,** voiture (de police) banalisée; **(b)** *Sp* (*joueur*) démarqué; **(c) my essay was still u.,** ma dissertation n'était toujours pas corrigée; **(d) he slipped through u.,** il est passé inaperçu.

unmarketable [ʌn'mɑːkɪtəb(ə)l] *adj* invendable.

unmarriageable [ʌn'mærɪdʒəb(ə)l] *adj* immariable.

unmarried [ʌn'mærɪd] *adj* célibataire, qui n'est pas marié; **he remained u.,** il est resté célibataire; **u. mother,** mère célibataire; **u. state,** célibat *m*.

unmask [ʌn'mɑːsk] **1** *vt* démasquer (*qn*); *esp Lit* dévoiler (*un complot*). **2** *vi* se démasquer.

unmatched [ʌn'mætʃt] *adj* sans égal, sans pareil, incomparable (**for courage,** pour son courage; **as a boxer,** comme boxeur).

unmentionable [ʌn'menʃənəb(ə)l] **1** *adj* (*événement, chose*) dont il ne faut pas parler; (*mot, nom*) qu'il ne faut pas prononcer. **2** *npl Old-fashioned Hum* **unmentionables,** sous-vêtements *m*.

unmerciful [ʌn'mɜːsɪfʊl] *adj* impitoyable, sans pitié.

unmercifully [ʌn'mɜːsɪfəlɪ] *adv* impitoyablement, sans pitié.

unmerited [ʌn'merɪtɪd] *adj* immérité.

unmethodical [ʌnmɪ'θɒdɪk(ə)l] *adj* peu méthodique.

unmindful [ʌn'maɪndf(ʊ)l] *adj esp Lit* **to be u. of sth,** être peu soucieux de qch; **u. of one's own interests,** sans penser à ses propres intérêts.

unmistakable [ʌnmɪs'teɪkəb(ə)l] *adj* (*preuve*) indubitable; (*sentiment*) clair; (*personne, bâtiment*) facilement reconnaissable; **u. difference,** différence marquée *ou* manifeste.

unmistakably [ʌnmɪs'teɪkəblɪ] *adv* (*superior etc*) clairement, nettement; (*French etc*) sans aucun doute.

unmitigated [ʌn'mɪtɪgeɪtɪd] *adj* (*mal*) non mitigé, que rien ne vient adoucir; (*used as intensifier*) véritable; **u. lie,** pur mensonge; **an u. disaster,** un échec total.

unmixed [ʌn'mɪkst] *adj* sans mélange, pur.

unmolested [ʌnmə'lestɪd] *adj* sans être molesté; **to leave s.o. u.,** (*not bother*) laisser qn en paix.

unmortgaged [ʌn'mɔːgɪdʒd] *adj* non hypothéqué.

unmotivated [ʌn'məʊtɪveɪtɪd] *adj* sans motif(s), non motivé; (*person*) non motivé; (*without ambition*) dépourvu d'ambition.

unmounted [ʌn'maʊntɪd] *adj* **(a)** (*gem*) non serti; (*photo*) non encadré; **(b)** (*not on horseback*) à pied.

unmourned [ʌn'mɔːnd] *adj* non pleuré; **he died u.,** personne n'a pleuré sa mort.

unmoved [ʌn'muːvd] *adj* impassible; **u. by sth,** aucunement ému de *ou* par qch; **he remained u. by all our arguments, all our arguments left him quite u.,** tous nos arguments le laissaient indifférent *ou* froid.

unmusical [ʌn'mjuːzɪk(ə)l] *adj* peu mélodieux; (*person*) peu musicien, -ienne; **to my u. ear it sounds like ...,** pour mon oreille peu musicienne ça ressemble à ... .

unnameable [ʌn'neɪməb(ə)l] *adj* innommable.

unnamed [ʌn'neɪmd] *adj* (*person*) anonyme; (*thing*) innommé.

unnatural [ʌn'nætjərəl] *adj* **(a)** anormal, -aux; (*vice*) contre nature; **it's u. for him,** ce n'est pas normal venant de lui; **it's u. for him to say no,** ce n'est pas normal qu'il dise non; **(b)** (*style, person*) peu naturel, artificiel, affecté; **u. laugh,** rire forcé.

unnaturally [ʌn'nætjərəlɪ] *adv* **(a)** (*develop etc*) anormalement; **she was u. shy,** elle était anormalement timide; **not u. we turned the offer down,** comme on pouvait s'y attendre nous rejetâmes cette offre; **(b)** (*affectedly*) (*speak*) avec affectation; (*act, walk*) peu naturellement; **the text reads very u.,** ce texte est très forcé.

unnavigable [ʌn'nævɪgəb(ə)l] *adj* non navigable.

unnecessarily [ʌnnesɪ'serɪlɪ] *adv* inutilement; **you're being u. hard on yourself,** tu te fais du mal pour rien.

unnecessary [ʌn'nesɪs(ə)rɪ] *adj* (*costs, delay, trouble*) inutile; **that was quite u. of you!,** (*to say or do that*) ce n'était vraiment pas la peine (que tu dises ou fasses cela)!; **it's u. to change it,** il n'est pas nécessaire *ou* ce n'est pas la peine *ou* il est inutile de le changer; **it's totally u. for**

you to come too, il est absolument inutile *ou* il n'est absolument pas nécessaire que tu viennes aussi.

unneeded [ʌn'ni:dɪd] *adj* inutile.

unneighbourly, *US* **unneighborly** [ʌn'neɪbəlɪ] *adj* désobligeant, peu obligeant; **to behave in an u. manner,** se conduire en mauvais voisin; **that was very u. of them,** c'était vraiment désobligeant de leur part.

unnerve [ʌn'nɜ:v] *vt* faire perdre son courage *ou* son sang-froid à (*qn*); (*disconcert*) déconcerter.

unnerving [ʌn'nɜ:vɪŋ] *adj* déconcertant, déroutant.

unnoticed [ʌn'nəʊtɪst] *adj* inaperçu, inobservé; **to pass u.,** passer inaperçu; **to let an insult pass u.,** ne pas relever une injure.

unnumbered [ʌn'nʌmbəd] *adj* **(a)** (*page*) non numéroté; (*house*) sans numéro; **(b)** *Lit* innombrable.

unobjectionable [ʌnəb'dʒekʃənəb(ə)l] *adj* (*personne*) à qui on ne peut rien reprocher; (*chose*) à laquelle on ne peut trouver à redire; **it/he seems u. enough,** il n'y a rien à redire.

unobservant [ʌnəb'zɜ:vənt] *adj* peu perspicace, peu observateur, -trice.

unobserved [ʌnəb'zɜ:vd] *adj* inaperçu, inobservé; **he went out u.,** il est sorti sans être vu.

unobstructed [ʌnəb'strʌktɪd] *adj* (*pipe etc*) non bouché, non obstrué; (*road*) non encombré; **u. view,** vue dégagée *ou* libre; **they marched on u. to ...,** ils ont poursuivi leur chemin librement *ou* sans rencontrer d'obstacle(s) jusqu'à ... .

unobtainable [ʌnəb'teɪnəb(ə)l] *adj* impossible à obtenir, impossible à se procurer; *Tel* **the number is u.,** il est impossible d'avoir le numéro.

unobtrusive [ʌnəb'tru:sɪv] *adj* discret, -ète; **he always tried to remain u.,** il cherchait toujours à s'effacer.

unobtrusively [ʌnəb'tru:sɪvlɪ] *adv* discrètement; d'une manière effacée.

unoccupied [ʌn'ɒkjʊpaɪd] *adj* **(a)** (*not busy*) inoccupé, désœuvré; **(b)** (*house*) inoccupé, inhabité; **(c)** *Mil* **u. zone,** zone libre; **the town was still u.,** la ville n'était toujours pas occupée; **(d)** (*table, seat*) libre, disponible.

unofficial [ʌnə'fɪʃəl] *adj* (*meeting*) non officiel; (*information*) officieux; **u. strike,** grève *f* sauvage; **in an u. capacity,** à titre non officiel; **from an u. source,** de source officieuse; **it's still u.,** on ne l'a pas encore confirmé.

unofficially [ʌnə'fɪʃ(ə)lɪ] *adv* non officiellement, officieusement, à titre officieux.

unopened [ʌn'əʊpənd] *adj* non ouvert, qui n'a pas été ouvert.

unopposed [ʌnə'pəʊzd] *adj* sans opposition; (*avancer*) sans rencontrer d'opposition *ou* de résistance; *Pol* **u. candidate,** candidat unique; *Parl* **the bill was given an u. second reading,** le projet de loi a été accepté sans opposition à la deuxième lecture.

unorganized [ʌn'ɔ:gənaɪzd] *adj* **(a)** mal organisé; **he's so u.,** il est si désorganisé; **(b)** *Pol* **u. labour,** main-d'œuvre inorganisée.

unoriginal [ʌnə'rɪdʒɪn(ə)l] *adj* sans originalité, peu original, -aux, qui manque d'originalité.

unorthodox [ʌn'ɔ:θədɒks] *adj* peu orthodoxe.

unostentatious [ʌnɒsten'teɪʃəs] *adj* (*person, dress*) peu fastueux, sans ostentation; (*dress*) sobre; (*behaviour*) peu ostentatoire; (*ceremony*) sans faste.

unostentatiously [ʌnɒsten'teɪʃəslɪ] *adv* (*agir*) sans ostentation; (*vêtu*) simplement, sobrement.

unostentatiousness [ʌnɒsten'teɪʃəsnɪs] *n* manque *m* d'ostentation; simplicité *f*.

unpack [ʌn'pæk] **1** *vt* déballer, dépaqueter (*des objets*); défaire (*une valise*). **2** *vi* défaire sa valise.

unpacking [ʌn'pækɪŋ] *n* déballage *m*; **the u. didn't take long,** nous n'avons pas été longtemps à défaire nos bagages.

unpaid [ʌn'peɪd] *adj* **(a)** (*work*) non payé, bénévole; (*person*) qui ne reçoit pas de rémunération; (*post*) non rétribué, non rémunéré; **u. services,** services à titre gracieux; **u. workers,** (travailleurs) bénévoles; **I'll work u.,** je vais traviller bénévolement; **(b)** (*bill*) impayé; (*debt*) non acquitté; **to leave an account u.,** laisser arrérager un compte; **(c)** (*money*) non versé.

unpalatable [ʌn'pælətəb(ə)l] *adj* **(a)** (*food*) d'un goût désagréable; **(b)** (*truth, facts*) désagréable.

unparalleled [ʌn'pærəleld] *adj* (*beauty*) incomparable, sans égal; (*action, event*) sans précédent.

unpardonable [ʌn'pɑ:d(ə)nəb(ə)l] *adj* impardonnable, inexcusable.

unpardonably [ʌn'pɑ:d(ə)nəblɪ] *adv* inexcusablement; **he was u. harsh,** il a été d'une dureté impardonnable.

unparliamentary [ʌnpɑ:lə'ment(ə)rɪ] *adj* (*language, action*) peu parlementaire.

unpatented [ʌn'peɪtəntɪd, -'pæ-] *adj* non breveté.

unpatriotic [ʌnpeɪtrɪ'ɒtɪk, -pæ-] *adj* (*person*) peu patriote; (*action*) peu patriotique; **to be u.,** être mauvais patriote.

unpatriotically [ʌnpeɪtrɪ'ɒtɪklɪ, -pæ-] *adv* (*agir*) en mauvais patriote.

unpaved [ʌn'peɪvd] *adj* non pavé, sans pavés.

unperceived [ʌnpə'si:vd] *adj* inaperçu.

unperforated [ʌn'pɜ:fəreɪtɪd] *adj* sans perforations.

unperson ['ʌnpɜ:sən] *n Pol* non-personne *f*.

unperturbable [ʌnpə'tɜ:bəb(ə)l] *adj* imperturbable.

unperturbed [ʌnpə'tɜ:bd] *adj* impassible; **to be u. by sth,** ne pas se laisser perturber par qch.

unpick [ʌn'pɪk] *vt* défaire (*une couture*).

unpin [ʌn'pɪn] *vt* **(-nn-)** détacher (*qch*) **(from,** de); enlever les épingles de (*ses cheveux*).

unplaced [ʌn'pleɪst] *adj* (*cheval etc*) non placé; (*candidat*) non classé.

unplanned [ʌn'plænd] *adj* (*événement*) imprévu; (*enfant*) non prévu.

unplayable [ʌn'pleɪəb(ə)l] *adj* (*pitch etc*) impraticable, inutilisable; (*service, shot etc*) impossible à rattrapper; **the ball was in an u. position,** la balle n'était pas jouable.

unpleasant [ʌn'plezənt] *adj* désagréable, déplaisant; **u. weather,** mauvais temps; **he made some u. remarks,** il a dit des choses désobligeantes; **she was very u. with me,** elle a été très désagréable avec moi; **things are getting rather u. between them,** la situation est en train de se dégrader entre aux.

unpleasantly [ʌn'plezəntlɪ] *adv* désagréablement; **we had an u. close escape,** nous en avons réchappé d'un cheveu, nous avons frisé la catastrophe.

unpleasantness [ʌn'plezəntnɪs] *n* **(a)** caractère *m* désagréable (*de qch*); aspect déplaisant (*d'un endroit*); **(b)** différend *m*; (*argument*) dispute *f*; **there was some u.,** il y a eu un différend *ou* une dispute; **there's still some u. between them,** il y a toujours du tirage entre eux.

unpleasing [ʌn'pli:zɪŋ] *adj* déplaisant.

unplug [ʌn'plʌg] *vt* **(-gg-)** **(a)** débrancher (*une télévision*); **(b)** déboucher (*une ouverture, un tuyau*).

unplumbed [ʌn'plʌmd] *adj* **u. depths,** profondeurs insondées.

unpoetic(al) [ʌnpəʊ'etɪk(əl)] *adj* peu poétique.

unpolished [ʌn'pɒlɪʃt] *adj* **(a)** non poli; (*stone*) brut; (*floor, furniture*) non ciré, non astiqué; (*shoes*) non ciré; **(b)** (*person*) fruste, rude; (*style*) fruste, non poli.

unpolluted [ʌnpə'lu:tɪd] *adj* non pollué.

unpopular [ʌn'pɒpjʊlər] *adj* impopulaire; **he makes himself u. with everybody,** il se fait mal voir de tout le monde; **he's u. with his employees,** ses employés ne l'aiment pas (beaucoup); **this decision was very u.,** cette décision a été très mal accueillie *ou* très impopulaire.

unpopularity [ʌnpɒpjʊ'lærɪtɪ] *n* impopularité *f*.

unpopulated [ʌn'pɒpjʊleɪtɪd] *adj* non peuplé.

unpractical [ʌn'præktɪk(ə)l] *adj* **(a)** (*person*) peu pratique; **(b)** (*plan*) impracticable, irréalisable.

unpractised, *US* **unpracticed** [ʌn'præktɪst] *adj* inexercé, inexpérimenté; **u. in the art of ...,** sans expérience dans l'art de ... .

unprecedented [ʌn'presɪdentɪd] *adj* sans précédent.

unpredictable [ʌnprɪ'dɪktəb(ə)l] *adj* imprévisible; (*weather*) incertain; **she's u.,** on ne sait jamais ce qu'elle va faire *ou* comment elle va réagir.

unprejudiced [ʌn'predʒʊdɪst] *adj* impartial, -aux, sans parti pris, sans préjugés, sans prévention(s).

unpremeditated [ʌnprɪ'medɪteɪtɪd] *adj Jur* (*délit*) non prémédité.

unprepared [ʌnprɪ'peəd] *adj* **(a)** non préparé; (*discours*) improvisé, impromptu; **to find everything u.,** ne rien trouver de prêt; **(b) to be u. for sth,** ne pas s'attendre à qch; **to go u. into an undertaking,** se lancer à tête perdue dans une entreprise; **I took the exam quite u.,** j'ai passé l'examen sans l'avoir suffisamment préparé.

unpreparedness [ʌnprɪ'peədnɪs, -'peərɪdnɪs] *n* impréparation *f* **(for,** à).

unprepossessing [ʌnpri:pə'zesɪŋ] *adj* (*person*) peu engageant, peu avenant; (*building*) repoussant; **a man of u. appearance,** un homme à l'apparence peu engageante *ou* peu avenante.

unpresentable [ʌnprɪ'zentəb(ə)l] *adj* peu présentable.

unpretentious [ʌnprɪ'tenʃəs] *adj* sans prétention(s), modeste; (*tastes*) simple.

unpretentiously [ʌnprɪ'tenʃəslɪ] *adv* modestement; simplement.

unpriced [ʌn'praɪst] *adj* (*article*) dont le prix n'est pas marqué.

unprincipled [ʌn'prɪnsɪp(ə)ld] *adj* (*person*) sans principes; (*person, behaviour*) peu scrupuleux, sans scrupules.

unprintable [ʌn'prɪntəb(ə)l] *adj* (*comment, reply*) qu'on n'oserait pas *ou* qu'on ne peut répéter; **what he actually said is u.**, on ne saurait répéter ce qu'il a vraiment dit, ce qu'il a vraiment dit n'est pas répétable.

unproductive [ʌnprə'dʌktɪv] *adj* improductif; (*terre*) ingrat, stérile.

unprofessional [ʌnprə'feʃən(ə)l] *adj* (*person, thing to do*) peu professionnel; **it's u. not to reply to your letters,** ça ne fait pas très professionnel de ne pas répondre à vos lettres; **it looks u. not to ...,** ça ne fait pas très professionnel de ne pas ...; **it's u. to leave a job unfinished,** il est contraire aux usages de la profession de laisser un travail inachevé; **he's rather u. in his approach,** il a une approche d'amateur.

unprofessionally [ʌnprə'feʃən(ə)lɪ] *adv* (*to do job, work, carry out contract*) de manière peu professionnelle; (*to behave, react*) en amateur, de manière peu professionnelle.

unprofitable [ʌn'prɒfɪtəb(ə)l] *adj* peu fructueux, peu rentable; (*meeting*) peu fructueux.

unprofitably [ʌn'prɒfɪtəblɪ] *adv* sans profit, peu fructueusement, peu rentablement.

unpromising [ʌn'prɒmɪsɪŋ] *adj* peu prometteur, -euse; **the weather looks u.**, le temps s'annonce mal; **that's an u. start!**, c'est un mauvais départ *ou* un départ qui augure mal de la suite.

unprompted [ʌn'prɒmptɪd] *adj* spontané; **that was quite u. by any self-interest,** ce n'était motivé par aucun intérêt personnel.

unpronounceable [ʌnprə'naʊnsəb(ə)l] *adj* imprononçable.

unprotected [ʌnprə'tektɪd] *adj* sans protection, sans défense; *Tech* (*moving part*) sans garde-fou; **don't leave the wood u. against the weather,** ne laissez pas le bois sans protection contre les intempéries; **to have u. sex,** avoir des relations sexuelles sans utiliser de préservatif.

unproved, unproven [ʌn'pruːvd; -'pruːv(ə)n] *adj* non prouvé.

unprovided-for [ʌnprə'vaɪdɪdfɔːr] *adj* (*family*) sans ressources; (*eventuality*) non prévu; **he left his family u.-f in his will,** il a oublié sa famille dans son testament.

unprovoked [ʌnprə'vəʊkt] *adj* non provoqué; fait sans provocation; **an u. attack,** une agression gratuite.

unpublicized [ʌn'pʌblɪsaɪzd] *adj* non publié, inédit.

unpublished [ʌn'pʌblɪʃt] *adj* inédit, non public; **the u. facts,** les faits qui n'ont pas été révélés au public.

unpunctual [ʌn'pʌŋktjʊəl] *adj* inexact, peu ponctuel.

unpunctuality [ʌn'pʌŋktjʊælɪtɪ] *n* inexactitude *f*, manque *m* de ponctualité.

unpunished [ʌn'pʌnɪʃt] *adj* impuni; **to go u.**, rester impuni.

unputdownable [ʌnpʊt'daʊnəbl] *adj F* **(a)** (*book*) captivant, prenant; **(b)** (*person*) indestructible.

unqualified [ʌn'kwɒlɪfaɪd] *adj* **(a)** non qualifié; (*médecin, professeur*) sans diplôme(s), non diplômé; **she's u. for the job,** elle n'est pas qualifiée pour le poste; **I'm quite u. to talk about it,** je ne suis nullement qualifié pour en parler; **to be u. for sth,** (*not be suitable*) ne pas avoir les qualités requises pour qch; **to be u. to do sth,** être incompétent à faire qch; **(b)** (*accusation*) sans réserve; **u. denial,** dénégation *f* catégorique; **u. praise,** éloges sans réserve; **it was an u. success,** c'était un succès formidable; **(c)** (*adjective*) non modifié.

unquenchable [ʌn'kwenʃəb(ə)l] *adj* (*soif, feu*) inextinguible; (*soif, curiosité*) insatiable.

unquenched [ʌn'kwenʃt] *adj* (*feu*) non éteint; (*désir*) inassouvi; **u. thirst,** soif non étanchée.

unquestionable [ʌn'kwestjənəb(ə)l] *adj* indiscutable; (*droit*) incontestable; **u. fact,** fait indiscutable.

unquestionably [ʌn'kwestjənəblɪ] *adv* incontestablement, sans aucun doute; **she is u. guilty,** elle est indiscutablement coupable.

unquestioned [ʌn'kwestjənd] *adj* indiscuté, incontesté; **to let a statement pass u.**, laisser passer une affirmation sans la relever.

unquestioning [ʌn'kwestjənɪŋ] *adj* (*obéissance*) aveugle; **u. trust,** confiance absolue.

unquestioningly [ʌn'kwestjənɪŋlɪ] *adv* aveuglément, sans poser de question.

unquiet [ʌn'kwaɪət] *adj esp Lit* inquiet, -ète; **u. times,** époque troublée.

unquote ['ʌnkwəʊt] *vi* (*used only in imp*) (*in dictation*) fermez les guillemets; (*in report*) fin de citation.

unquoted [ʌn'kwəʊtɪd] *adj* **u. securities,** valeurs non cotées.

unratified [ʌn'rætɪfaɪd] *adj* qui n'a pas été ratifié.

unravel [ʌn'ræv(ə)l] *v* (**-ll-**, *US* **-l-**) **1** *vt* **(a)** effiler, effilocher (*un tissu*); défaire (*du tricot*); **(b)** débrouiller, démêler (*de la ficelle*); dénouer, démêler (*une intrigue*); débrouiller (*un mystère*). **2** *vi* **(a) to u. (itself), to come unravelled,** (*of cloth*) s'effiler, s'effilocher; (*of knitting*) se défaire; (*of rope*) se détordre; **(b)** (*of facts*) s'éclaircir.

unread [ʌn'red] *adj* qui n'a pas été lu; **to leave sth u.**, ne pas lire qch; **he left the magazine on the table u.**, il a laissé la revue sur la table sans l'avoir lue.

unreadable [ʌn'riːdəb(ə)l] *adj* (*livre, écriture*) illisible.

unreadiness [ʌn'redɪnɪs] *n* impréparation *f*, manque *m* de préparation; **in a state of u.**, dans un état d'impréparation.

unready [ʌn'redɪ] *adj* **to be u. for sth,** ne pas être prêt à qch.

unreal [ʌn'rɪəl] *adj* **(a)** irréel; **everything seemed u. to him,** il avait l'impression de rêver; **(b)** *F* (*very good, very bad, unbelievable*) dingue.

unrealistic [ʌnrɪə'lɪstɪk] *adj* irréaliste.

unreality [ʌnrɪ'ælɪtɪ] *n* irréalité *f*.

unrealizable [ʌnrɪə'laɪzəb(ə)l] *adj* irréalisable.

unrealized [ʌn'rɪəlaɪzd] *adj* **(a)** (*espoir, désir*) irréalisé; **(b)** *Fin* (*capital*) non réalisé.

unreasonable [ʌn'riːz(ə)nəb(ə)l] *adj* **(a)** (*person*) déraisonnable; **don't be u.!**, soyez raisonnable!; **you are being very u.**, vous n'êtes pas raisonnable; **they were quite u. in their demands,** leurs exigences étaient tout à fait déraisonnables; **(b)** (*thing to suppose*) déraisonnable; (*demand*) immodéré; (*price*) excessif; **at this u. hour,** à cette heure indue.

unreasonably [ʌn'riːz(ə)nəblɪ] *adv* d'une manière peu raisonnable; **that's u. expensive,** c'est excessivement cher; **they asked, and not altogether u, that ...,** ils ont demandé, plutôt légitimement, que ... .

unreasoning [ʌn'riːz(ə)nɪŋ] *adj* (*person*) qui ne raisonne pas; **u. hatred,** haine irraisonnée *ou* aveugle.

unrecognizable [ʌnrekəg'naɪzəbl] *adj* méconnaissable, impossible *ou* difficile à reconnaître.

unrecognized [ʌn'rekəgnaɪzd] *adj* **(a)** (*government*) non reconnu; (*writer etc*) méconnu; **(b)** non reconnu; **he mingled u. in the crowd,** il s'est mêlé dans la foule sans être reconnu.

unrecorded [ʌnrɪ'kɔːdɪd] *adj* **(a)** (*fact, comment*) non enregistré, non mentionné; **(b)** (*music, tape*) non enregistré; (*tape*) vierge.

unredeemed [ʌnrɪ'diːmd] *adj* **(a)** (*pécheur*) non racheté; (*mauvais caractère*) non compensé (**by,** par); **he led a life of u. evil,** il a toujours vécu dans le mal; **(b)** (*promesse*) non rempli, non tenu; **(c)** (*objet*) non dégagé (*du prêteur à gages*); **(d)** *Fin* (*emprunt*) non amorti, non remboursé; (*traite*) non honoré; (*hypothèque*) non purgé.

unreel [ʌn'riːl] **1** *vt* dérouler (*un film, un câble*). **2** *vi* se dérouler.

unrefined [ʌnrɪ'faɪnd] *adj* **(a)** brut, non raffiné; **(b)** (*person, taste*) peu raffiné, grossier; **u. manners,** manières frustes.

unreformed [ʌnrɪ'fɔːmd] *adj* (*person*) qui ne s'est pas corrigé; (*law*) non amendé.

unrefreshed [ʌnrɪ'freʃt] *adj* encore fatigué, non reposé.

unregistered [ʌn'redʒɪstəd] *adj* (*person*) non inscrit; (*luggage*) non enregistré; (*parcel*) non recommandé; (*voiture*) non immatriculé; **u. birth,** naissance non déclarée.

unregretted [ʌnrɪ'gretɪd] *adj* que l'on ne regrette pas; **she died u.**, personne n'a pleuré sa mort.

unrehearsed [ʌnrɪ'hɜːst] *adj* (*play*) (joué) sans répétition(s); (*speech*) improvisé.

unrelated [ʌnrɪ'leɪtɪd] *adj* **(a)** (*events*) sans rapport (**to each other,** l'un avec l'autre); **these facts are totally u.**, il n'y a aucun rapport entre ces faits; **(b)** (*people*) **they are u.**, il n'y a aucun lien de parenté entre eux.

unrelenting [ʌnrɪ'lentɪŋ] *adj* **(a)** (*person*) implacable (**towards,** à l'égard de), inexorable (**towards,** à); **he was u.**, il restait inflexible; **(b)** (*struggle*) acharné; (*pain*) sans rémission.

unreliability [ʌnrɪlaɪə'bɪlɪtɪ] *n* manque *m* de sérieux (*d'une entreprise, de qn*); inexactitude *f* (*d'un résultat*); manque de fiabilité (*d'une machine*).

unreliable [ʌnrɪ'laɪəb(ə)l] *adj* (*person*) auquel *ou* à qui on ne peut pas se fier, sur lequel *ou* sur qui on ne peut pas compter; (*character*) instable; (*information*) sujet à caution; (*result*) incertain; (*machine*) non fiable; (*clock*) auquel on ne peut se fier; **an u. source,** une source douteuse; **u. map,** carte peu fiable.

unrelieved [ʌnrɪ'liːvd] *adj* **(a)** (*pain*) non soulagé, sans répit; **(b)** qui manque de relief *ou* de variéte; **she was dressed in u. black,** elle était vêtue tout de noir; **the u. monotony of the concrete walls,** la monotonie absolue des murs de béton; **news of u. gloom,** nouvelles uniformément désolantes; **u. boredom,** ennui mortel.

unremarkable [ʌnrɪ'mɑːkəb(ə)l] *adj* médiocre, (qui ne sort pas de l')ordinaire, quelconque.

unremitting [ʌnrɪ'mɪtɪŋ] *adj* (*travail*) ininterrompu, sans relâche; **u. efforts,** efforts soutenus; **he was u. in his attentions,** son assiduité ne s'est pas démentie un instant.

unremittingly [ʌnrɪ'mɪtɪŋlɪ] *adv* sans cesse, inlassablement; (*to work*) sans relâche.

unremunerative [ʌnrɪ'mjuːnərətɪv] *adj* peu rémunérateur, -trice.

unrepealed [ʌnrɪ'piːld] *adj* (*law etc*) non abrogé.

unrepeatable [ʌnrɪ'piːtəb(ə)l] *adj* **(a)** (*remarque*) qu'on ne peut *ou* qu'on n'oserait pas répéter; **(b)** *Com* (*prix*) exceptionnel; (*offre*) unique.

unrepentant [ʌnrɪ'pentənt] *adj* impénitent; **to die u.,** mourir dans le péché; **she was u. about what she had done,** elle ne s'était pas repentie de ce qu'elle avait fait.

unreported [ʌnrɪ'pɔːtɪd] *adj* (*accident*) non signalé.

unrepresentative [ʌnreprɪ'zentətɪv] *adj* peu représentatif; **it's completely u. of ...,** ce n'est pas du tout représentatif de ... .

unrepresented [ʌnreprɪ'zentɪd] *adj* non représenté; (*nation*) sans représentant, sans délégué.

unrequited [ʌnrɪ'kwaɪtɪd] *adj* **u. love,** amour non payé de retour *ou* non partagé.

unreserved [ʌnrɪ'zɜːvd] *adj* **(a)** (*person*) non réservé; **(b)** (*approval*) entier; **u. praise,** éloges sans réserve; **(c) u. seats,** places non réservées.

unreservedly [ʌnrɪ'zɜːvɪdlɪ] *adv* sans réserve; **to trust s.o. u.,** avoir pleine confiance en qn.

unresisting [ʌnrɪ'zɪstɪŋ] *adj* soumis, docile.

unresolved [ʌnrɪ'zɒlvd] *adj* **(a)** (*person*) irrésolu, indécis; **(b)** (*problem etc*) non résolu.

unresponsive [ʌnrɪ'spɒnsɪv] *adj* **(a)** (*physically*) (*injured arm etc*) insensible; (*engine*) qui manque de nervosité; (*steering*) qui ne répond pas bien; **u. to treatment,** qui ne réagit pas au traitement; **she complained that her husband was u. in bed,** elle s'est plainte du fait que son mari était inerte au lit; **(b)** (*mentally*) (*to suggestion*) indifférent (**to,** à); (*audience etc*) inerte, passif; **when we suggested ... they were completely u.,** quand nous avons suggéré ... ils n'ont pas du tout réagi *ou* ils sont restés totalement indifférents.

unrest [ʌn'rest] *n* troubles *mpl*; **social u.,** malaise social; **labour** *or* **industrial u.,** agitation ouvrière; **there was u. among the workers,** il y avait de l'agitation *ou* du malaise parmi les ouvriers.

unrestrained [ʌnrɪ'streɪnd] *adj* non réprimé, effréné; **u. laughter,** rires non réprimés *ou* immodérés.

unrestrainedly [ʌnrɪ'streɪnɪdlɪ] *adv* librement, sans contrainte.

unrestricted [ʌnrɪ'strɪktɪd] *adj* sans restriction, illimité; (*pouvoir*) absolu; (*accès*) libre.

unrevealed [ʌnrɪ'viːld] *adj* non révélé.

unrevenged [ʌnrɪ'vendʒd] *adj* invengé; **to go u.,** (*of murder etc*) rester invengé.

unrewarded [ʌnrɪ'wɔːdɪd] *adj* non récompensé, sans récompense; **they shouldn't go u.,** on ne peut pas les laisser sans récompense.

unrewarding [ʌnrɪ'wɔːdɪŋ] *adj* **(a)** (*financially*) peu rémunérateur, -trice; **(b)** (*travail, sujet etc*) ingrat.

unrhythmical [ʌn'rɪðmɪk(ə)l] *adj* (*person*) qui n'a pas le sens du rythme; (*music*) peu rythmé.

unrig [ʌn'rɪg] *vt* **(-gg-)** *Nau* dégréer (*un navire*); désappareiller (*une grue*).

unrighteous [ʌn'raɪtʃəs] *adj* (*person, action*) inique, injuste.

unripe [ʌn'raɪp] *adj* vert, qui n'est pas mûr; (*wheat*) en herbe.

unrivalled, *US* **unrivaled** [ʌn'raɪv(ə)ld] *adj* sans rival, hors pair; **our goods are u.,** nos articles sont sans concurrence.

unroadworthy [ʌn'rəʊdwɜːðɪ] *adj* (*vehicle*) qui n'est pas en état de rouler.

unroll [ʌn'rəʊl] **1** *vt* dérouler (*une carte, du tissu*); déferler (*une bannière*). **2** *vi* se dérouler.

unromantic [ʌnrə'mæntɪk] *adj* peu romantique; **how very u. of you!,** comme tu es peu romantique!, comme tu manques de romantisme!

unrope [ʌn'rəʊp] *vi* (*in mountaineering*) se détacher (de la cordée).

unruffled [ʌn'rʌf(ə)ld] *adj* **(a)** (*person*) calme, serein; **u., he continued to speak,** sans se troubler, il a continué de parler; **(b)** (*sea*) calme, uni; (*hair, feathers*) lisse.

unruled [ʌn'ruːld] *adj* (*paper*) uni, non réglé.

unruliness [ʌn'ruːlɪnɪs] *n* indiscipline *f*, turbulence *f* (*d'un enfant*); caractère fougueux (*d'un cheval*).

unruly [ʌn'ruːlɪ] *adj* (*enfant*) indiscipliné, insoumis, turbulent; (*cheval*) fougueux; (*cheveux*) difficile à coiffer; **the crowd started getting u.,** la foule commença à devenir turbulente.

unsaddle [ʌn'sæd(ə)l] *vt* **(a)** desseller (*un cheval*); débâter (*un âne*); **(b)** désarçonner (*un cavalier*).

unsafe [ʌn'seɪf] *adj* **(a)** (*dangerous*) dangereux; (*bridge, structure*) peu sûr; (*undertaking*) hasardeux; (*chair*) peu solide; (*rope*) mal assujetti; **it's u. to leave it near the fire,** c'est dangereux de le laisser près du feu; **(b)** (*in danger*) exposé au danger; **to feel u.,** éprouver un manque de sécurité.

unsaid [ʌn'sed] *adj* non prononcé; **to leave sth u.,** passer qch sous silence; **it's better left u.,** mieux vaut ne rien dire.

unsalaried [ʌn'sælərɪd] *adj* non rémunéré; (*person*) non salarié.

unsaleable [ʌn'seɪləb(ə)l] *adj* (*goods*) invendable.

unsalted [ʌn'sɔːltɪd] *adj* (*meat, fish*) non salé; **u. butter,** beurre frais.

unsatisfactorily [ʌnsætɪs'fækt(ə)rɪlɪ] *adv* d'une manière peu satisfaisante.

unsatisfactory [ʌnsætɪs'fækt(ə)rɪ] *adj* peu satisfaisant, qui laisse à désirer; (*explanation*) peu convaincant; (*system*) défectueux; **it's most u.,** cela laisse beaucoup à désirer.

unsatisfied [ʌn'sætɪsfaɪd] *adj* **(a)** peu satisfait (**with,** de); **(b)** (*not convinced*) **to be u. about sth,** avoir des doutes sur qch; **I'm still u. about it,** je n'en suis pas encore convaincu; **(c)** (*appetite*) non rassasié; (*desire, lust*) insatisfait, inassouvi; **the meal left us u.,** le repas ne nous a pas rassasiés.

unsatisfying [ʌn'sætɪsfaɪɪŋ] *adj* **(a)** peu satisfaisant; **(b)** (*unconvincing*) peu convaincant; **(c)** (*meal etc*) insuffisant.

unsavoury, *US* **unsavory** [ʌn'seɪv(ə)rɪ] *adj* **(a)** (*taste*) désagréable; (*meal*)) d'un goût désagréable; **u. smell,** mauvaise odeur, odeur désagréable; **(b)** (*scandal, district, bar*) répugnant; (*reputation*) équivoque; (*characters*) déplaisant.

unsay ['ʌn'seɪ] (*pt & pp* **unsaid** [ʌn'sed]) *vt* rétracter, retirer; **you can't u. it,** tu ne peux pas faire comme si tu ne l'avais pas dit.

unscathed [ʌn'skeɪðd] *adj* indemne, sain et sauf.

unscented [ʌn'sentɪd] *adj* (*savon etc*) sans parfum, non parfumé.

unscheduled [ʌn'ʃedjuːld] *adj* (*departure, meeting*) imprévu; (*plane, train*) qui n'est pas indiqué dans l'horaire.

unscholarly [ʌn'skɒləlɪ] *adj* peu savant; (*piece of writing*) peu scientifique; **he looks so u.,** il n'a pas du tout l'air d'un intellectuel.

unschooled [ʌn'skuːld] *adj* **(a)** *Old-fashioned* (*person*) sans instruction; **(b)** (*cheval*) non dressé.

unscientific [ʌnsaɪən'tɪfɪk] *adj* non scientifique; peu scientifique; **isn't that rather u.?,** ce n'est pas très scientifique.

unscientifically [ʌnsaɪən'tɪfɪklɪ] *adv* peu scientifiquement.

unscramble [ʌn'skræmb(ə)l] *vt* déchiffrer.

unscrew [ʌn'skruː] **1** *vt* dévisser (*un boulon etc*). **2** *vi* se dévisser.

unscripted [ʌn'skrɪptɪd] *adj* sans préparation, non préparé; **that was quite u.,** c'était complètement improvisé.

unscrupulous [ʌn'skruːpjʊləs] *adj* peu scrupuleux, sans scrupules; (*dealings etc*) peu scrupuleux.

unscrupulously [ʌn'skruːpjʊləslɪ] *adv* peu scrupuleusement.

unscrupulousness [ʌn'skruːpjʊləsnɪs] *n* (*of person*) manque *m* de scrupules; (*of dealings*) malhonnêteté *f*.

unsealed [ʌn'siːld] *adj* descellé; (*letter*) décacheté.

unseasonable [ʌn'siːz(ə)nəb(ə)l] *adj* (*fish, fruit*) hors de saison; **this weather's very u.,** ce temps n'est pas normal pour la saison.

unseasoned [ʌn'siːz(ə)nd] *adj* (*food*) non assaisonné; (*timber*) vert, non conditionné.

unseat [ʌn'siːt] *vt* **(a)** désarçonner (*un cavalier*); **(b)** *Parl* faire perdre son siège à (*un député*).
unseaworthy [ʌn'siːwɜːðɪ] *n* (*navire*) innavigable, en mauvais état de navigabilité.
unsecured [ʌnsɪ'kjʊəd] *adj* (*loan*) non garanti, à découvert; (*debt*) sans garantie.
unseeded [ʌn'siːdɪd] *adj Tennis* (*player*) non classé.
unseeing [ʌn'siːɪŋ] *adj* qui ne voit pas, aveugle; **to look at s.o./sth with u. eyes,** regarder qn/qch sans (le) voir.
unseemliness [ʌn'siːmlɪnɪs] *n* inconvenance *f*.
unseemly [ʌn'siːmlɪ] *adj* inconvenant.
unseen [ʌn'siːn] **1** *adj* **(a)** inaperçu; invisible; **to do sth u.,** faire qch sans être vu; **(b) to buy sth (sight) u.,** acheter qch sans l'avoir vu; *Sch* **u. translation,** version *f*. **2** *n Sch* version *f*.
unselfconscious [ʌnself'kɒnʃəs] *adj* naturel; qui ne ressent pas de gêne *ou* d'embarras.
unselfconsciously [ʌnself'kɒnʃəslɪ] *adv* naturellement; sans aucune gêne.
unselfish [ʌn'selfɪʃ] *adj* généreux; sans égoïsme; (*motif*) désintéressé.
unselfishly [ʌn'selfɪʃlɪ] *adv* généreusement.
unselfishness [ʌn'selfɪʃnɪs] *n* désintéressement *m*.
unsentimental [ʌnsentɪ'ment(ə)l] *adj* peu sentimental, -aux.
unserviceable [ʌn'sɜːvɪsəb(ə)l] *adj* inutilisable.
unsettle [ʌn'set(ə)l] *vt* ébranler (*les idées de qn*); (*less deeply*) troubler (*qn*).
unsettled [ʌn'set(ə)ld] *adj* **(a)** (*pays*) troublé, instable; (*temps*) variable, changeant; (*esprit*) inquiet, -ète, troublé; **the u. state of the weather,** l'incertitude *f* du temps; **I'm still u. in my mind about it,** je ne suis pas encore décidé là-dessus; **(b)** (*question, dispute*) indécis; **(c)** (*bill*) impayé, non réglé.
unsettling [ʌn'setlɪŋ] *adj* troublant, dérangeant.
unsex [ʌn'seks] *vt* déviriliser (*un homme*); déféminiser (*une femme*); (*castrate*) émasculer.
unshackle [ʌn'ʃæk(ə)l] *vt* ôter les fers à (*un prisonnier*).
unshackled [ʌn'ʃæk(ə)ld] *adj* sans entraves, libre; **u. by ...,** non entravé par ..., libre de ... .
unshakeable [ʌn'ʃeɪkəb(ə)l] *adj* inébranlable.
unshaken [ʌn'ʃeɪk(ə)n] *adj* inébranlé, ferme.
unshaved, unshaven [ʌn'ʃeɪvd, -'ʃeɪv(ə)n] *adj* non rasé; **you're looking very u.,** ça fait combien de temps que tu ne t'es pas rasé?
unsheathe [ʌn'ʃiːð] *vt* dégainer (*une épée etc*).
unsheltered [ʌn'ʃeltəd] *adj* sans abri, non abrité, sans protection (**from,** contre).
unship [ʌn'ʃɪp] *vt* (-pp-) *Nau* décharger, débarquer.
unshod [ʌn'ʃɒd] *adj* **(a)** (*person*) sans chaussures; (*having removed shoes*) déchaussé; **(b)** (*horse*) déferré.
unshrinkable [ʌn'ʃrɪŋkəb(ə)l] *adj* irrétrécissable.
unsighted [ʌn'saɪtɪd] *adj* invisible, qui n'est pas en vue.
unsightliness [ʌn'saɪtlɪnɪs] *n* laideur *f*.
unsightly [ʌn'saɪtlɪ] *adj* laid; (*scar*) désagréable à voir; **landscape marred by u. advertisements,** paysage déparé par des panneaux qui offusquent la vue.
unsigned [ʌn'saɪnd] *adj* non signé, sans signature.
unsinkable [ʌn'sɪŋkəb(ə)l] *adj* insubmersible.
unskilful, *US* **unskillful** [ʌn'skɪlf(ʊ)l] *adj* malhabile, inhabile, maladroit (**in, at,** à).
unskilled [ʌn'skɪld] *adj* (*person*) inexpert (**in,** dans, en); **u. in** *or* **at doing sth,** inexpert dans l'art de faire qch; **u. worker,** ouvrier non qualifié; **u. labour,** main-d'œuvre non spécialisée.
unslept-in [ʌn'sleptɪn] *adj* (*lit*) non défait.
unsling [ʌn'slɪŋ] *vt* (*pt & pp* **unslung** [-'slʌŋ]) dégréer, décrocher (*un hamac etc*).
unsmiling [ʌn'smaɪlɪŋ] *adj* sérieux; qui ne sourit pas.
unsmoked [ʌn'sməʊkt] *adj* non fumé.
unsociability [ʌnsəʊʃə'bɪlɪtɪ], **unsociableness** [ʌn'səʊʃəblnɪs] *n* insociabilité *f*.
unsociable [ʌn'səʊʃəb(ə)l] *adj* sauvage, peu sociable.
unsocial [ʌn'səʊʃəl] *adj* **(a)** insocial, -aux; **to work u. hours,** travailler à des heures indues *ou* quand la plupart des gens sont libres; **(b)** = **UNSOCIABLE**.
unsold [ʌn'səʊld] *adj* invendu.
unsoldierly [ʌn'səʊldʒəlɪ] *adj* peu militaire.
unsolicited [ʌnsə'lɪsɪtɪd] *adj* (*comment*) non sollicité; (*contribution*) volontaire; **u. manuscript,** manuscrit non commandé; **to do sth u.,** faire qch spontanément.
unsolvable [ʌn'sɒlvəb(ə)l] *adj* insoluble.
unsolved [ʌn'sɒlvd] *adj* (*problème*) non résolu.
unsophisticated [ʌnsə'fɪstɪkeɪtɪd] *adj* (*person, tastes, pleasures*) simple; (*wine*) sans prétention; *Tech* peu évolué; primitif.
unsound [ʌn'saʊnd] *adj* **(a)** (*kidney etc*) malsain; (*health*) précaire, chancelant; (*timber*) avarié; (*fruit*) gâté; (*foundations, bridge*) peu solide, en mauvais état, dangereux; **to be of u. mind,** ne pas avoir toute sa raison; **to commit suicide while of u. mind,** se suicider en état de démence temporaire; **(b)** (*theory, argument*) mal fondé; (*doctrine, opinion*) faux; discutable; (*decision*) peu judicieux; (*investment*) peu sûr, hasardeux; (*politician*) incompétent; **it is financially u.,** c'est de la mauvaise finance; **he's still rather u. on the basics,** ses bases ne sont pas encore très solides.
unsparing [ʌn'speərɪŋ] *adj* prodigue, qui ne regarde pas à la dépense; **to be u. in one's efforts,** ne pas ménager ses efforts.
unsparingly [ʌn'speərɪŋlɪ] *adv* (*to give, donate*) sans compter, sans regarder à la dépense; (*to work*) sans ménager ses efforts.
unspeakable [ʌn'spiːkəb(ə)l] *adj* (*douleur*) indicible; (*joie*) indicible, ineffable; *F* détestable, exécrable; **it's u.!** ça n'a pas de nom!; **he's really u.!** il est au dessous de tout!
unspeakably [ʌn'spiːkəblɪ] *adv* indiciblement; *F* **u. bad,** exécrable.
unspecified [ʌn'spesɪfaɪd] *adj* non spécifié; **certain u. persons,** certaines personnes, dont on taira les noms.
unspent [ʌn'spent] *adj* (*money*) non dépensé; (*of cartridge*) qui n'a pas servi.
unspoilt [ʌn'spɔɪlt], *occ* **unspoiled** [ʌn'spɔɪld] *adj* **(a)** intact; (*paysage*) qui n'a pas été défiguré; **(b)** (*enfant*) qui n'a pas été gâté; **he has remained u. despite his success,** son succès ne lui a pas tourné la tête.
unspoken [ʌn'spəʊk(ə)n] *adj* non prononcé; (*agreement*) tacite.
unsporting [ʌn'spɔːtɪŋ], **unsportsmanlike** [ʌn'spɔːtsmənlaɪk] *adj* peu loyal, -aux, déloyal; **that's u.,** ce n'est pas fair-play; **MacEnroe was fined for u. behaviour,** MacEnroe a été pénalisé pour manque de fair-play.
unstable [ʌn'steɪb(ə)l] *adj* instable.
unstained [ʌn'steɪnd] *adj* sans tache; *esp Lit* (*reputation*) sans souillure; **(b)** (*wood*) non teint.
unstamped [ʌn'stæmpt] *adj* (*silver, gold*) non poinçonné; (*letter*) sans timbre, non affranchi; *Admin Jur* (*document*) non estampillé.
unstatesmanlike [ʌn'steɪtsmənlaɪk] *adj* peu digne d'un homme d'État; peu diplomatique.
unsteadily [ʌn'stedɪlɪ] *adv* (*marcher*) d'un pas chancelant, en titubant; (*tenir qch*) d'une main tremblante; (*écrire*) d'une main tremblante.
unsteadiness [ʌn'stedɪnɪs] *adj* manque *m* d'aplomb (*d'une table, d'une personne*); manque de sûreté (*de la main*); démarche chancelante (*d'un ivrogne*); instabilité *f* (*du dollar etc*).
unsteady [ʌn'stedɪ] *adj* (*table*) instable, peu stable, branlant; (*legs, footsteps*) chancelant; (*hand, voice*) mal assuré; (*position, foothold*) mal assuré, incertain; (*flame*) tremblant, vacillant; (*economy, the dollar etc*) instable; **to be u. on one's legs** *or* **feet,** marcher d'un pas chancelant; tituber.
unsterilized [ʌn'sterɪlaɪzd] *adj* non stérilisé.
unstick [ʌn'stɪk] *vt* (*pt & pp* **unstuck** [-'stʌk]) décoller (*qch*); **to come unstuck,** se décoller; *F* (*plan*) s'effondrer; *F* **that's where they came unstuck,** c'est là qu'ils ont cafouillé.
unstinted [ʌn'stɪntɪd] *adj* **(a)** (*supplies*) abondant, sans restriction; **(b)** = **UNSTINTING**.
unstinting [ʌn'stɪntɪŋ] *adj* généreux, prodigue; (*compliments, appui*) sans réserve; (*admiration*) sans bornes; **u. efforts,** efforts illimités; **to give u. praise,** ne pas ménager ses louanges.
unstintingly [ʌn'stɪntɪŋlɪ] *adv* généreusement; (*louer qn*) sans réserve; (*aider qn, travailler*) sans se ménager.
unstitch [ʌn'stɪtʃ] *vt* dépiquer, découdre (*une couture*); **to come unstitched,** se découdre.
unstop [ʌn'stɒp] *vt* (-pp-) (*remove stopper from*) déboucher.
unstoppable [ʌn'stɒpəb(ə)l] *adj* (*shot*) imparable; **he's u. now,** on a l'impression que désormais tout va lui réussir.
unstressed [ʌn'strest] *adj* inaccentué, atone.
unstring [ʌn'strɪŋ] *vt* (*pt & pp* **unstrung** [-'strʌŋ]) **(a)** débander (*un arc*); **to u. a violin,** ôter les cordes d'un violon; **(b)** défiler, désenfiler (*des perles etc*); **(c) to be unstrung,** (*of person*) avoir les nerfs à fleur de peau.
unstudied [ʌn'stʌdɪd] *adj* spontané, naturel.
unsubdued [ʌnsəb'djuːd] *adj* indompté.
unsubmissive [ʌnsəb'mɪsɪv] *adj* insoumis, rebelle.

unsubsidized [ʌn'sʌbsɪdaɪzd] *adj* non subventionné.

unsubstantial [ʌnsəb'stænʃəl] *adj* non substantiel, qui manque de substance; (*repas*) peu substantiel, peu nourrissant.

unsubstantiated [ʌnsəb'stænʃɪeɪtɪd] *adj* (*accusation*) non prouvé; (*rumour*) non corroboré.

unsubtle [ʌn'sʌt(ə)l] *adj* peu subtil; **how can anyone be s. u.!,** comment peut-on manquer de subtilité à ce point!

unsuccessful [ʌnsək'sesfʊl] *adj* (*effort, attempt*) vain, infructueux; (*application*) refusé; (*outcome, marriage*) malheureux; **u. outcome,** insuccès *m*, échec *m*; **it was completely u.,** cela a été un échec complet; **to be u.,** (*of person, plan, marriage*) ne pas réussir; **the festival was u.,** le festival a été un échec; **I've tried but have been u. up till now,** j'ai essayé mais je n'ai encore abouti à rien; **u. candidate,** candidat refusé; (*at election*) candidat non élu.

unsuccessfully [ʌnsək'sesfəlɪ] *adv* sans succès, en vain.

unsuitability [ʌns(j)uːtə'bɪlɪtɪ] *n* inaptitude *f* (*de qn à qch*); caractère *m* impropre (*de qch à qch*); (*of time*) inopportunité *f*; (*of phrase etc*) caractère malencontreux; **the u. of the clothes he was wearing,** les vêtements inadéquats qu'il portait.

unsuitable [ʌn's(j)uːtəb(ə)l] *adj* (*tools*) impropre, mal adapté (**for,** à); (*time*) inopportun; (*clothes, conditions, diet*) inadéquat, non approprié; (*climate, environment*) qui ne convient pas; (*choice of words*) malencontreux; (*couple, partners*) mal assorti; **I thought Wednesday was u.,** je pensais que mercredi ne vous *ou* lui *etc* convenait pas; **they're u. for each other,** ils ne vont pas ensemble; **he's u. for her,** ce n'est pas l'homme qu'il lui faut; **he's quite u. for the job,** ce n'est pas l'homme qu'il faut pour ce poste; **u. for the occasion,** qui ne convient pas à la circonstance; **you have chosen a most u. time to...,** vous avez mal choisi le moment de...; **film u. for children,** film à déconseiller aux enfants; **the climate is u. for wheat,** le climat ne convient pas au blé.

unsuitably [ʌn's(j)uːtəblɪ] *adv* inadéquatement; **u. dressed,** habillé d'une façon qui ne convient pas à l'occasion; **they're u. matched,** (*of couple*) ils sont mal assortis.

unsuited [ʌn's(j)uːtɪd] *adj* (*person*) inapte (**for, to sth,** à qch); **they are u. (to each other),** ils s'accordent mal.

unsullied [ʌn'sʌlɪd] *adj* sans souillure, sans tache.

unsung [ʌn'sʌŋ] *adj esp Lit* (*deed*) non célébré; (*hero*) méconnu.

unsupported [ʌnsə'pɔːtɪd] *adj* **(a)** (*statement*) sans preuves; **(b)** (*person*) non appuyé, non soutenu; (*structure, wall*) sans support, sans appui; **to leave one's family u.,** ne pas subvenir aux besoins de sa famille.

unsure [ʌn'ʃʊər] *adj* (*position*) peu sûr, précaire; (*person*) incertain (**about,** de); **to be u. of oneself,** manquer de confiance en soi-même, ne pas être sûr de soi; **I'm u. about it/him,** j'ai des doutes là-dessus/en ce qui le concerne.

unsurmountable [ʌnsə'maʊntəb(ə)l] *adj* insurmontable; **our difficulties are not u.,** il nous sera possible de surmonter nos difficultés.

unsurpassable [ʌnsə'pɑːsəb(ə)l] *adj* insurpassable.

unsurpassed [ʌnsə'pɑːst] *adj* sans égal, -aux.

unsuspected [ʌnsəs'pektɪd] *adj* insoupçonné (**by,** de); dont on ne soupçonnait pas l'existence.

unsuspecting [ʌnsəs'pektɪŋ] *adj* qui ne se doute de rien; **u. by nature,** peu soupçonneux; **he's so u.,** il est si peu soupçonneux; **when he later, all u., ...,** quand plus tard, sans se douter de rien, il ... .

unsuspicious [ʌnsəs'pɪʃəs] *adj* peu soupçonneux.

unsweetened [ʌn'swiːtnd] *adj* non sucré.

unswerving [ʌn'swɜːvɪŋ] *adj* (*loyalty*) constant, ferme; **they have been u. in their support,** ils nous ont prêté un appui constant.

unswervingly [ʌn'swɜːvɪŋlɪ] *adv* sans s'écarter du but; **u. loyal,** d'une loyauté inébranlable.

unsympathetic [ʌnsɪmpə'θetɪk] *adj* **(a)** peu compatissant; indifférent; **they were very u. about our problems,** ils se sont montrés très indifférents en ce qui concerne nos problèmes; **the idea met with an u. reception,** l'idée a reçu un accueil plutôt froid; **(b)** (*unlikeable*) antipathique; **I find the characters of this novel u.,** les personnages de ce roman me sont peu sympathiques.

unsympathetically [ʌnsɪmpə'θetɪklɪ] *adv* froidement; d'un ton *ou* d'un air indifférent.

unsystematic [ʌnsɪstə'mætɪk] *adj* non systématique, sans méthode; **you're too u.,** tu n'es pas assez systématique.

unsystematically [ʌnsɪstə'mætɪklɪ] *adv* sans méthode.

untainted [ʌn'teɪntɪd] *adj* non corrompu; (*food*) non gâté; (*reputation*) sans tache, sans souillure.

untalented [ʌn'tæləntɪd] *adj* peu doué.

untam(e)able [ʌn'teɪməb(ə)l] *adj* (*animal*) inapprivoisable, indomptable; (*spirit*) indomptable.

untamed [ʌn'teɪmd] *adj* (*animal*) inapprivoisé, indompté; (*spirit*) indompté.

untangle [ʌn'tæŋg(ə)l] *vt* démêler (*de la laine, une ficelle, ses cheveux*); éclaircir (*un mystère*); débrouiller (*une affaire compliquée*).

untapped [ʌn'tæpt] *adj* (*resources*) inexploité.

untarnished [ʌn'tɑːnɪʃt] *adj* (*metal*) *& Fig* non terni, sans tache.

untasted [ʌn'teɪstɪd] *adj* auquel on n'a pas goûté; **to send a dish away u.,** renvoyer un plat sans y goûter.

untaught [ʌn'tɔːt] *adj* (*person*) sans instruction; (*skill*) naturel.

untaxable [ʌn'tæksəb(ə)l] *adj* non imposable.

untaxed [ʌn'tækst] *adj* exempt *ou* exempté d'impôts; (*produit*) non imposé, non taxé; (*car*) = sans vignette.

unteachable [ʌn'tiːtʃəb(ə)l] *adj* (*person*) à qui l'on ne peut rien apprendre, incapable d'apprendre; (*subject, art*) impossible à enseigner.

untenable [ʌn'tenəb(ə)l] *adj* (*position*) intenable; (*théorie*) insoutenable.

untenanted [ʌn'tenəntɪd] *adj* sans locataire(s).

untended [ʌn'tendɪd] *adj* (*malade*) non soigné, sans soins; (*jardin*) non entretenu.

untested [ʌn'testɪd] *adj* inéprouvé, qui n'a pas (encore) été mis à l'épreuve; (*invention, drug*) non essayé; (*water etc*) non analysé.

unthinkable [ʌn'θɪŋkəb(ə)l] *adj* inconcevable, impensable; **it's u. that...,** il est inconcevable que + *sub*; **if the u. should happen,** si l'inconcevable se produisait.

unthinking [ʌn'θɪŋkɪŋ] *adj* (*person*) étourdi.

unthinkingly [ʌn'θɪŋkɪŋlɪ] *adv* (*faire qch*) sans réfléchir, étourdiment.

unthought-of [ʌn'θɔːtɒv] *adj* auquel on n'a pas pensé.

unthread [ʌn'θred] *vt* désenfiler, défiler.

untidily [ʌn'taɪdɪlɪ] *adv* en désordre; **she's always u. dressed,** elle a toujours l'air débraillé.

untidiness [ʌn'taɪdɪnɪs] *n* (*of room, appearance*) désordre *m*; (*of person*) (*characteristic*) manque *m* d'ordre *ou* de soin.

untidy [ʌn'taɪdɪ] *adj* **(a)** (*room*) en désordre, mal rangé; (*hair*) ébouriffé; (*writing*) brouillon; **u. appearance,** tenue débraillée; *Mus* **his playing is u.,** son jeu manque de netteté; **(b)** (*as characteristic*) désordonné, qui manque d'ordre; **he's such an u. sort of person,** il est tellement désordonné.

untie [ʌn'taɪ] *v* (*pt & pp* **untied;** *prp* **untying**) **1** *vt* défaire (*les lacets, un ruban*); dénouer (*un nœud*)); défaire, délier (*un nœud, un paquet*); déficeler (*un paquet*); détacher (*ses cheveux, un chien*). **2** *vi* (*of knot*) **to u. itself, to come untied,** se défaire, se dénouer.

until [ʌn'tɪl] **1** *prep* **(a)** jusqu'à; **u. tomorrow,** jusqu'à demain; **u. now,** jusqu'ici, jusque-là; **she didn't arrive u. yesterday,** elle n'est arrivée qu'hier; **u. then we'll just have to make do,** en attendant il va falloir se débrouiller;
(b) not u. (after) eight o'clock, pas avant huit heures (passées); **not u. tomorrow,** pas avant demain; **it wasn't u. Easter that ...,** ce n'est qu'après Pâques que ...; **I've never seen it u. now,** c'est la première fois que je le vois.
2 *conj* **(a)** jusqu'à ce que + *sub*; **u. all the windows are open,** jusqu'à ce que toutes les fenêtres soient ouvertes; **we'll wait u. you're ready,** nous attendrons que vous soyez prêt; **we waited u. the rain stopped,** nous avons attendu jusqu'à ce que la pluie cesse; **wait u. the bus stops,** attends que le bus soit arrêté; (*as sign*) attendre jusqu'à l'arrêt du bus; **he drank u. he was ill,** il a bu jusqu'à s'en rendre malade; **we worked u. we dropped,** nous avons travaillé jusqu'à n'en plus pouvoir; **he laughed u. he cried,** il a pleuré de rire;
(b) he won't come u. he's invited, il ne viendra pas avant d'être invité *ou* sans qu'on l'invite; **I won't leave him u. he's completely recovered,** je ne le quitterai pas tant qu'il n'est pas tout à fait guéri; **don't do anything u. I say so,** ne fais rien avant que je te le dise; **don't sign u. you've checked everything,** ne signe rien avant d'avoir tout vérifié.

untilled [ʌn'tɪld] *adj* non cultivé, non labouré.

untimely [ʌn'taɪmlɪ] *adj* (*death*) prématuré; (*snow*) hors de saison; (*question, action*) inopportun, intempestif, mal à propos; **to come to an u. end,** mourir avant l'âge.

untiring [ʌn'taɪərɪŋ] *adj* infatigable, inlassable.

untiringly [ʌn'taɪərɪŋlɪ] *adv* infatigablement, inlassablement.

unto ['ʌntʊ, 'ʌntə] *prep Arch & Lit* **to liken sth u. sth,** comparer qch à *ou* avec qch; *Bible* **suffer little children to come u. me,** laissez venir à moi les petits enfants; **u. us a child is born,** un enfant nous est né; **and I say u. you ...,** et je vous dis ...; **to turn u. s.o.,** se tourner vers qn.

untold [ʌn'təʊld] *adj* (*richesse*) immense, énorme; **u. suffering,** souffrances inouïes; **u. joy,** joie indicible.

untouchable [ʌn'tʌtʃəb(ə)l] **1** *adj* intouchable. **2** *n* (*in India*) intouchable *mf*, paria *m*.

untouched [ʌn'tʌtʃt] *adj* **(a)** non touché; **food product u. by (human) hand,** produit alimentaire non manié; **(b) he'd left the meal u.,** il n'avait pas touché à son repas; **(c)** (*safe*) (*person*) indemne, sain et sauf; (*thing*) intact; **(d)** (*unmoved*) (*person*) indifférent, insensible (**by,** à); **(e)** (*without equal*) sans égal, incomparable; **they're u. when it comes to sth/doing sth,** ils sont incomparables sur le plan de qch/quand il s'agit de faire qch.

untoward [ʌntə'wɔːd; *Am* ʌn'tɔːd] *adj* fâcheux, malencontreux, malheureux; **I hope nothing u. has happened,** j'espère qu'il n'est pas arrivé un malheur *ou* qu'il ne s'est rien produit de fâcheux.

untraceable [ʌn'treɪsəb(ə)l] *adj* introuvable.

untrained [ʌn'treɪnd] *adj* qui n'a pas reçu de formation professionnelle; (*cheval*) non dressé; **u. ear,** oreille inexercée.

untrammelled [ʌn'træməld] *adj* non entravé (**by,** par), libre (**by,** de).

untransferable [ʌntræns'fɜːrəb(ə)l] *adj* non transmissible; *Jur* (*droit, propriété*) incessible.

untranslatable [ʌntræns'leɪtəb(ə)l] *adj* intraduisible.

untravelled [ʌn'trævəld] *adj* (*person*) qui n'a pas beaucoup voyagé; qui n'a jamais voyagé; (*pays*) inexploré, peu fréquenté.

untried [ʌn'traɪd] *adj* qui n'a pas été essayé, non essayé; **(b)** (*untested*) (*moteur, système*) qui n'a pas été mis à l'épreuve; **u. troops,** troupes qui n'ont pas encore vu le feu; **(c)** *Jur* (*détenu, cas*) qui n'a pas encore été jugé.

untrodden [ʌn'trɒd(ə)n] *adj esp Lit* (*chemin*) peu fréquenté; **u. snow,** neige immaculée *ou* vierge.

untroubled [ʌn'trʌbəld] *adj* calme, tranquille; **he seemed u. by the news,** la nouvelle ne semblait nullement le troubler.

untrue [ʌn'truː] *adj* **(a)** faux, *f* fausse, erroné; *Tech* faux, qui n'est pas juste; **it's absolutely u.,** c'est complètement faux; **(b)** (*unfaithful*) (*to wife, principles etc*) infidèle (**to,** à); (*to comrades*) déloyal, -aux (**to,** envers).

untrustworthiness [ʌn'trʌstwɜːðɪnɪs] *n* (*of person*) manque *m* d'honnêteté; manque de fiabilité.

untrustworthy [ʌn'trʌstwɔːðɪ] *adj* (*person*) indigne de confiance, à qui on ne peut pas se fier; (*reference book, software, information*) peu fiable; (*evidence*) récusable.

untruth [ʌn'truːθ, *pl* -'truːðz] *n* mensonge *m*; **to tell an u.,** dire *ou* commettre un mensonge.

untruthful [ʌn'truːθfʊl] *adj* (*person*) menteur; (*story*) mensonger, faux, *f* fausse; **he's an u. boy,** c'est un garçon qui ne dit jamais la vérité.

untruthfully [ʌn'truːθfəlɪ] *adv* mensongèrement, en mentant.

untruthfulness [ʌn'truːθfʊlnɪs] *n* (*of person*) manque *m* d'honnêteté; fausseté *f* (*d'un témoignage*).

untuned [ʌn'tjuːnd] *adj* (*instrument*) mal accordé; (*moteur*) qui n'est pas réglé.

untuneful [ʌn'tjuːnfʊl] *adj* peu mélodieux.

untutored [ʌn'tjuːtəd] *adj esp Lit* (*person*) peu instruit; (*mind, taste*) non formé.

untwine [ʌn'twaɪn] *vt* détordre, détortiller.

untwist [ʌn'twɪst] **1** *vt* détordre, détortiller (*des fils*); dévisser (*le couvercle d'un bocal etc*). **2** *vi* **to u. (itself), to come untwisted,** se détordre.

untypical [ʌn'tɪpɪk(ə)l] *adj* inhabituel; **it's very u. of her,** c'est très inhabituel de sa part, cela ne lui ressemble pas.

untypically [ʌn'tɪpɪk(ə)lɪ] *adj* inhabituellement.

unusable [ʌn'juːzəb(ə)l] *adj* inutilisable.

unused [ʌn'juːzd] *adj* **(a)** dont on ne se sert pas; inutilisé; (*talent*) non employé; (*bâtiment*) désaffecté; **(b)** (*never yet used*) qui n'a pas encore servi; (*clothes*) neuf; **(c)** [ʌn'juːst] (*person*) peu habitué (**to sth,** à qch); **to be u. to doing sth,** ne pas avoir l'habitude de faire qch; **I'm still u. to you being here,** je ne suis pas encore habitué à ce que tu sois là; **we're not u. to it,** on commence à y être habitué.

unusual [ʌn'juːʒʊəl] *adj* (*not common*) inhabituel, peu commun *ou* ordinaire; (*colour, style, thing to happen*) inhabituel, insolite; (*strange, out of the ordinary*) inhabituel; **an u. case of ...,** un cas peu commun *ou* peu ordinaire de ...; **an u. lapse,** une défaillance inhabituelle; **a very u. exception,** une exception très inhabituelle; **what do you think of the design? — well, it's u.,** que pensez-vous du design? — eh bien, c'est inhabituel *ou* insolite; **he has some rather u. tastes,** il a des goûts plutôt inhabituels *ou* insolites; **it's u. for her not to notice these things,** c'est rare qu'elle ne remarque pas ces choses-là; **you don't want a drink?, that's u. for you,** tu ne veux pas prendre un verre?, c'est étrange *ou* rare de ta part; **the sort of information which is u. in most dictionaries,** le type d'information qui est rare dans la plupart des dictionnaires; **it's u. to see him at the theatre,** il est rare qu'on le voie au théâtre; **nothing u.,** rien d'anormal; **of u. interest,** d'un intérêt exceptionnel.

unusually [ʌn'juːʒʊəlɪ] *adv* inhabituellement; (*exceptionally*) exceptionnellement; **she stayed u. quiet,** elle est restée inhabituellement calme; **u. tall,** exceptionnellement grand; **it's very u. designed,** c'est conçu de manière très insolite *ou* inhabituelle; **he was u. attentive,** il s'est montré plus attentif que d'habitude.

unutterable [ʌn'ʌt(ə)rəb(ə)l] *adj* inexprimable, indicible; *F* **u. fool,** parfait idiot.

unutterably [ʌn'ʌt(ə)rəblɪ] *adv* d'une façon inexprimable; **u. lazy,** d'une paresse inimaginable.

unvaried [ʌn'veərɪd] *adj* non varié; (*nourriture*) qui manque de variété.

unvarnished [ʌn'vɑːnɪʃt] *adj* (*surface*) non verni; (*pottery*) non vernissé; *Fig* **the plain u. truth,** la vérité pure et simple.

unvarying [ʌ'veərɪɪŋ] *adj* invariable, constant.

unveil [ʌn'veɪl] **1** *vt* inaugurer (*une statue, une nouvelle voiture etc*); dévoiler (*un secret*). **2** *vi* se dévoiler.

unveiled [ʌn'veɪld] *adj* sans voile.

unveiling [ʌn'veɪlɪŋ] *n* inauguration *f* (*d'une statue, d'une nouvelle voiture etc*); **u. ceremony,** cérémonie *f* d'inauguration.

unverifiable [ʌn'verɪfaɪəb(ə)l] *adj* invérifiable.

unverified [ʌn'verɪfaɪd] *adj* non contrôlé, non vérifié.

unversed [ʌn'vɜːst] *adj Lit* peu versé (**in,** dans).

unvoiced [ʌn'vɔɪst] *adj* **(a)** (*vowel, consonant*) sourd, muet; **(b)** (*opinion*) non exprimé.

unwanted [ʌn'wɒntɪd] *adj* non voulu; **u. child,** enfant non désiré; **u. hair,** poils superflus; **to give away all one's u. books,** se débarrasser de tous les livres dont on n'a plus besoin; **to be feeling u.,** (*in the way*) se sentir de trop; (*unloved*) se sentir mal-aimé.

unwarlike [ʌn'wɔːlaɪk] *adj* non belliqueux.

unwarrantable [ʌn'wɒrəntəb(ə)l] *adj* injustifiable.

unwarrantably [ʌn'wɒrəntəblɪ] *adj* injustifiablement.

unwarranted [ʌn'wɒrəntɪd] *adj* injustifié, **u. insult,** injure gratuite; **u. familiarity,** familiarité indue.

unwary [ʌn'weərɪ] *adj* imprudent, imprévoyant.

unwashed [ʌn'wɒʃt] **1** *adj* non lavé. **2** *n* (*used as pl*) *F Hum* **the great u.,** les prolétaires *mpl*, les prolos *mpl*.

unwavering [ʌn'weɪvərɪŋ] *adj* constant, ferme; (*determination*) inébranlable; (*gaze*) soutenu.

unwaveringly [ʌn'weɪvərɪŋlɪ] *adv* résolument; sans faiblir.

unweaned [ʌn'wiːnd] *adj* (*enfant, chaton*) non sevré.

unwearable [ʌn'weərəb(ə)l] *adj* (*vêtement*) immettable.

unwearying [ʌn'wɪərɪɪŋ] *adj* inlassable, infatigable.

unwed [ʌn'wed] *adj* qui n'est pas marié.

unweighted [ʌn'weɪtɪd] *adj Econ* (*index*) non pondéré; **u. figures,** chiffres bruts.

unwelcome [ʌn'welkəm] *adj* (*visitor*) importun; (*news, development*) fâcheux; **u. visits,** visites importunes; **a not u. visit,** une visite opportune; **to make s.o. feel u.,** faire en sorte que qn se sente importun; **the extra £50 was not u.,** les 50 livres supplémentaires ne tombaient pas mal du tout.

unwell [ʌn'wel] *adj* indisposé, souffrant; **are you feeling u.?,** êtes-vous souffrant?

unwholesome [ʌn'həʊlsəm] *adj* malsain.

unwieldy [ʌn'wiːldɪ] *adj* (*tool, object*) peu maniable; difficile à manier; (*method, approach*) trop complexe; (*system*) lourd; (*person*) lourd et gauche.

unwilling [ʌn'wɪlɪŋ] *adj* (*consentement*) donné à contrecœur; (*complice*) malgré lui; **to be u. to do sth,** ne pas vouloir faire qch; **they were very u. to ...,** ils étaient très réluctants à ...; **I was u. that my wife should know** *or* **for my wife to know,** je ne voulais pas que ma femme le sache.

unwillingly [ʌn'wɪlɪŋlɪ] *adv* à contrecœur.

unwillingness [ʌn'wɪlɪŋnɪs] *n* réluctance *f*; **they showed such an u. to accept the terms that ...,** ils ont fait preuve d'une telle réluctance à accepter les conditions que **our continuing u. to compromise on this issue,** notre refus persistant à tout compromis pour ce qui regarde ce problème.

unwind [ʌn'waɪnd] *v* (*pt & pp* **unwound** [-'waʊnd]) **1** *vt* dérouler; dépelotonner (*une pelote de laine*). **2** *vi* **(a)** se dérouler; (*ball of wool*) se dépelotonner; **(b)** *F* (*relax*) se détendre, se relaxer.

unwise [ʌn'waɪz] *adj* (*person*) imprudent; peu prudent, peu sage; (*action*) peu judicieux; **that was very u. of you,** c'était très imprudent de votre part.

unwisely [ʌn'waɪzlɪ] *adv* imprudemment.

unwitting [ʌn'wɪtɪŋ] *adj* accidentel, non intentionnel.

unwittingly [ʌn'wɪtɪŋlɪ] *adv* sans le savoir; sans le vouloir.

unwomanly [ʌn'wʊmənlɪ] *adj* peu féminin.

unwonted [ʌn'wəʊntɪd] *adj esp Lit* inaccoutumé.

unworkable [ʌn'wɜːkəb(ə)l] *adj* (*plan*) impraticable; (*gisement*) inexploitable.

unworldliness [ʌn'wɜːldlɪnɪs] *n* détachement *m* de ce monde; simplicité *f*, candeur *f*.

unwordly [ʌn'wɜːldlɪ] *adj* détaché de ce monde; (*naive*) simple, candide; *esp Lit* (*beauty*) qui n'est pas de ce monde.

unworthiness [ʌn'wɜːðɪnɪs] *n* indignité *f*.

unworthy [ʌn'wɜːðɪ] *adj* indigne (**of sth, s.o.,** de qch, de qn); **u. of notice,** qui ne mérite pas qu'on y fasse attention; **that's u. of you,** c'est indigne de vous.

unwounded [ʌn'wuːndɪd] *adj* non blessé, indemne.

unwrap [ʌn'ræp] *vt* (**-pp-**) défaire (*un paquet*); déballer (*un bonbon*); **to come unwrapped,** (*of parcel*) se défaire; (*of contents*) sortir de l'enveloppe.

unwritten [ʌn'rɪt(ə)n] *adj* non écrit; (*tradition*) oral, -aux; (*agreement*) verbal, -aux; **an u. law,** une convention toujours respectée; **according to the u. law,** selon la tradition (établie); **it's an u. law in this office that ...,** dans ce bureau on respecte la convention selon laquelle ...; **this is an u. rule of the game,** c'est une des conventions du jeu.

unyielding [ʌn'jiːldɪŋ] *adj* qui ne cède pas, qui résiste; (*person, determination*) inébranlable, ferme; **u. grip,** prise de fer.

unyoke [ʌn'jəʊk] *vt* dételer, découpler.

unzip [ʌnzɪp] *v* (**-pp-**) **1** *vt* ouvrir la fermeture éclair ® de; **will you u. me?,** tu veux bien ouvrir ma fermeture éclair? **2** *vi* (*of garment*) **it unzips at the side,** ça s'ouvre sur le côté.

up¹ [ʌp] **1** *adv* **(a)** (*at the top*) en haut; (*to the top*) vers le haut; **all the way up, the whole way up, right up (to the top),** jusqu'en haut (*de l'escalier, de la colline*); **half way up,** jusqu'à mi-hauteur; **to live three flights up,** habiter au troisième *ou Am* au quatrième (étage); **to throw sth up in the air,** jeter qch en l'air; **to put one's hand up,** lever la main; **hands up!** haut les mains!; **what are you doing up there?** qu'est-ce que vous faites là-haut?; **up above,** en haut; **up above sth,** au-dessus de qch; **before the sun was up,** avant le lever du soleil; **would you like the window up a bit?,** (*in car*) voulez-vous que je remonte un peu la vitre?; **Comet with Thomas up,** (*in horseracing*) Comet monté par Thomas; **the cat's back was up,** le chat faisait le gros dos; **the river's up,** la rivière est en crue; **to lay sth face up,** placer qch face en dessus; **this side up,** (*on packing case*) haut, dessus; **put it the other way up,** retournez-le;

(b) **to walk up and down,** se promener de long en large; **to go up north,** aller dans le nord; **to go up to London for the day,** aller passer la journée à Londres; **he's going up to Oxford,** il va faire ses études à l'université d'Oxford; **up in London,** à Londres; **up in Yorkshire,** au nord dans le Yorkshire; **up at Oxford,** à l'université d'Oxford; **to come up before the judge,** être cité devant les magistrats;

(c) **from £10 up,** à partir de 10 livres; **sizes from 4 up,** tailles à partir du 4; **all ranks from sergeant up,** tous les rangs au-dessus de sergent;

(d) (*on display, finished, operating*) **to put up the results,** afficher les résultats; **are the results up yet?,** les résultats sont-ils déjà affichés?; **there's a big notice up at the station saying ...,** il y a un grand panneau à la gare disant ...; **the curtains still aren't up,** les rideaux ne sont pas encore accrochés; **the new building is up,** le nouveau bâtiment est terminé; **when the tent's up,** quand la tente sera montée; **to be up and running,** (*of new machine etc*) être en service; (*of project*) être en route; **to get sth up and running,** (*new machine*) mettre qch en service; (*project*) mettre en route;

(e) (*for repair etc*) **the road's always up,** cette route est toujours en réparation; **careful, we've got some of the floorboards up,** attention au plancher, il manque des lattes; **when we've got the carpet up ...,** quand nous aurons enlevé la moquette ...;

(f) (*in phrases*) **prices are 10% up on last year's,** les prix ont augmenté de dix pour cent depuis l'année dernière; **bread is up again,** le pain a encore augmenté; **the temperature is going up,** la température monte; **business is looking up,** les affaires sont à la hausse; **he's something quite high up in the civil service,** il est haut placé dans l'administration; **up with France!,** vive la France!; **to be up in arms,** être en révolte; *Sp* **to be one goal up,** mener par un but; *Golf* **to be one hole up,** avoir un trou d'avance; **to be one up on s.o.,** (*in point, score*) avoir un point d'avance sur un adversaire; (*have advantage*)) avoir l'avantage sur qn; **steam is up,** nous sommes sous pression; **his blood was up,** le sang lui bouillait; **to be up and coming,** (*person, team etc*) être plein d'avenir, promettre; **speak up!** parlez plus fort!;

(g) (*knowledgeable*) **to be well up in a subject,** connaître un sujet à fond; **how are you up in German?,** tu t'y connais en allemand?;

(h) **lean it up against the wall,** appuyez-le contre le mur; **they were standing close up to each other,** ils se tenaient tout près l'un de l'autre; **to be up against difficulties,** se heurter à des difficultés; **to be up against it,** être dans le pétrin;

(i) (*out of bed*) debout, levé; **to be up late,** veiller tard; **to be up all night,** ne pas se coucher de la nuit; **isn't he up yet!,** il n'est pas encore levé *ou* debout!; **I was up late this morning,** je me suis levé tard ce matin; **he's always up and about by seven,** à sept heures il est toujours levé et au travail; **to be up and about again,** (*after illness*) être de nouveau sur pied;

(j) (*wrong*) *F* **what's up?,** qu'est-ce qui se passe?, qu'y a-t-il? **what's up with you/him?,** qu'est-ce qui vous/lui prend?; **something's up,** il y a quelque chose qui ne va pas *ou* (*brewing*) qui se mijote; **there's something up with him,** il y a quelque chose qui ne va pas chez lui;

(k) (*finished*) **time is up,** il est l'heure (*de fermer, de finir etc*); **your time's up,** c'est fini; **his leave is up,** sa permission est expirée; **his time is up,** (*of prisoner*) son temps est fini, il a fini son temps; *F* **the game's up, it's all up,** tout est perdu, c'est fichu; **I thought it was all up with me,** j'ai cru que ma dernière heure était venue; **it's all up with him,** c'en est fait de lui, il a son compte;

(l) **up to,** (*as far as*) **to go up to s.o.,** s'approcher de qn; **covered in mud up to the ears,** couvert de boue jusqu'aux oreilles; **where** *or* **what page are you up to?,** où en êtes-vous (du livre que vous lisez)?; **we're up to page 50,** nous en sommes à la page 50; **up to now, up to here,** jusqu'ici; **up to then,** jusqu'alors, jusque-là; **to be up to date,** être moderne *ou* à la mode *ou F* à la page; **up to £100 a week,** jusqu'à 100 livres par semaine; **up to what age?,** jusqu'à quel âge?;

(m) **up to,** (*good enough*) **to be up to one's job,** être à la hauteur de sa tâche; **he's not up to it,** il n'est pas capable de le faire; **he's not up to the journey,** il n'est pas à même de faire le voyage; **I don't feel up to it,** je ne m'en sens pas le courage; **I don't feel up to much,** je ne me sens pas bien; **it's not up to much,** ça ne vaut pas grand-chose;

(n) **up to,** (*doing, esp Pej*) **he's up to something,** il a quelque chose en tête, il mijote quelque chose; **what are the children up to?** qu'est-ce que font les enfants?; **hoy you, what do you think you're up to?,** vous là, qu'est-ce qui vous prend *ou* qu'est-ce que vous faites?; **what's that guy over there up to?,** qu'est-ce qu'il fabrique ce type là-bas?; **what's he up to with that ladder?,** qu'est-ce qu'il a l'intention de faire *ou* qu'est-ce qu'il fabrique avec cette échelle?; **what are you up to with my girlfriend?,** qu'est-ce que tu lui veux à ma copine?;

(o) **up to,** (*to be decided by etc*) **it's up to him to do it,** c'est à lui de le faire; **what shall I do? — that's up to you,** qu'est-ce que je fais? — c'est à toi de décider; **it's entirely up to you whether you go or not,** il ne tient qu'à toi de rester ou de partir; **it's up to you to accept,** (*you should*) il ne tient qu'à vous d'accepter.

2 *prep* **to go up the stairs,** monter l'escalier; **to climb up a hill,** monter *ou* grimper une colline; **the cat is up a tree,** le chat est (perché) sur un arbre; **the cat went up a tree,** le chat a grimpé à un arbre; **to go up the street,** remonter la rue; **further up the street,** plus loin dans la rue; **they live further up the street,** ils habitent plus loin *ou* plus haut dans cette rue; **the smoke went up my nose,**

la fumée m'est montée par le nez; **the gas goes up this pipe,** le gaz monte par ce tuyau; **it's up river from here,** c'est en amont d'ici; **to walk up and down the platform,** aller et venir sur le quai; (*nervously etc*) arpenter le quai; **he lives up your way,** il habite par chez vous *ou* du côté de chez vous; *Br F* **he's up the pub,** il est au pub; *Br F* **I'm going up the shops,** je vais faire un tour en courses; *Vulg* **up yours!,** va te faire enculer!

3 *adj* ascendant, montant; *Rail* **up line,** voie en direction de Londres (ou d'un terminus important); **up train,** train montant.

4 *n* **(a) ups and downs,** ondulations *fpl* (*du terrain*); les hauts et les bas, les vicissitudes *fpl* (*de la vie*); avatars *mpl* (*de la politique*); *Com* oscillations *fpl* (*du marché*); **life is full of ups and downs,** la vie est faite de hauts et de bas;

(b) *F* **to be on the up and up,** (*be improving*) être en train de monter *ou* de faire son chemin; (*be honest*) être clair *ou* fiable. NOTE: *When* **up** *is an integral part of a verb eg* **come up, go up, get up, take up,** *the user should consult the verb in question.*

up[2] *v* (-pp-) **1** *vt* **(a) to up the swans,** recenser les cygnes; **(b)** *F* augmenter (*les prix etc*); **to up sticks,** déménager. **2** *vi F* se lever d'un bond; **they upped and went,** ils sont partis très soudainement; **he just upped and hit him,** tout à coup il (s'est levé et) l'a frappé; **one day he just upped and left her,** un beau jour il l'a quittée sans crier gare.

up-and-coming ['ʌpənd'kʌmɪŋ] *adj* (*person*) qui est plein d'avenir, qui promet, prometteur; (*town*) plein d'avenir; (*progressive*) progressif.

up-and-down ['ʌpən'daʊn] *adj* **up-and-d. movement,** mouvement *m* de haut en bas.

up-and-over ['ʌpənd'əʊvər] *adj* **u.-and-o. door,** porte basculante (*d'un garage etc*).

up-and-under ['ʌpənd'ʌndər] *n Rugby* up and under *m*, chandelle *f*.

upbeat ['ʌpbiːt] **1** *n Mus* levé *m*. **2** *adj* (*optimistic, cheerful*) optimiste.

upbraid [ʌp'breɪd] *vt* reprocher, faire des reproches à (*qn*), réprimander (*qn*).

upbringing ['ʌpbrɪŋɪŋ] *n* éducation *f*; **what sort of (an) u. has she had?,** comment a-t-elle été élevée?

upchuck ['ʌptʃʌk] *vt & vi US F* (*vomit*) rendre.

upcoming ['ʌpkʌmɪŋ] *adj Am* prochain.

upcountry [ʌp'kʌntrɪ] *esp Am Austr* **1** *n* intérieur *m* (*du pays*). **2** *adj* de l'intérieur (*du pays*). **3** *adv* **to go u.,** aller vers l'intérieur.

update[1] ['ʌpdeɪt] *n* mise *f* à jour; (*of software package*) mise *f* à jour, actualisation *f*; **to give s.o. an u. on sth,** mettre qn au courant de qch; **a dictionary should have an u. at least every 5 years,** un dictionnaire devrait être remis à jour au minimum tous les 5 ans.

update[2] [ʌp'deɪt] *vt* mettre (*un fichier*) à jour, actualiser (*un fichier*); moderniser (*le matériel etc*); **could you u. me on what's been happening?,** pourriez-vous me mettre au courant de ce qui s'est passé; **it needs regular updating,** une remise à jour régulière est nécessaire; **it hasn't been updated since 1933,** il n'a pas été remis à jour depuis 1933.

up-draught, *US* **up-draft** ['ʌpdrɑːft] *n Av* courant d'air ascendant.

upend [ʌp'end] *vt* mettre (*qch*) debout; **to u. s.o.,** (*turn upside down*) mettre qn les pieds en l'air, mettre qn à l'envers.

up-front [ʌp'frʌnt] **1** *adj* **(a)** (*honest, frank*) franc, *f* franche, direct, honnête; **to be very up-f. about sth,** être très franc *ou* honnête au sujet de qch; **(b)** (*payment*) à l'avance. **2** *adv* (*in advance*) à l'avance.

upgrade[1] ['ʌpgreɪd] *n* **(a)** pente ascendante; montée *f* (*d'une ligne de chemin de fer*); **(b) to be on the u.,** (*of prices*) monter; (*of business*) reprendre, se relever; (*of invalid*) être en voie de guérison; **(c)** (*for software package etc*) mise *f* à jour, actualisation *f*; (*for equipment*) extension *f*.

upgrade[2] [ʌp'greɪd] **1** *vt* **(a)** améliorer (*un produit*); actualiser (*un logiciel*); ajouter une *ou* des extension(s) à (*un système*); **(b)** monter en grade (*un fonctionnaire*); nommer (*qn*) *ou* élever (*qch*) à un niveau supérieur. **2** *vi* ajouter une *ou* des extension(s).

upgrad(e)able [ʌp'greɪdəb(ə)l] *adj* (*computer system*) extensible.

upgrading [ʌp'greɪdɪŋ] *n* **(a)** amélioration *f*; actualisation *f*; ajout *m* d'une *ou* de plusieurs extension(s) **(of,** à); **(b)** montée *f* en grade; avancement *m*.

upheaval [ʌp'hiːv(ə)l] *n* bouleversement *m*; **political u.,** commotion *f ou* agitation *f* politique; **an emotional u.,** un bouleversement émotionnel; **moving house is such an u.,** déménager est un tel bouleversement *ou* chamboulement *ou* tumulte; **the u. of moving office,** le tumulte qu'entraîne un déménagement dans d'autres bureaux.

uphill ['ʌphɪl] **1** *adj* (*road*) montant; (*struggle*) pénible, difficile; **it's u. all the way,** ça monte tout le long du chemin; *Fig* c'est une lutte permanente; **u. ski,** ski *m* amont. **2** *adv* **to go u,** monter; **to ski u.,** skier en amont.

uphold [ʌp'həʊld] *vt* (*pt & pp* **upheld** [-'held]) soutenir (*une opinion*); prêter son appui à (*qn*); confirmer (*une décision*); **to u. the law,** faire observer la loi.

upholder [ʌp'həʊldər] *n* défenseur *m* (*d'une cause*).

upholster [ʌp'həʊlstər] *vt* (*pad*)) capitonner, rembourrer; (*cover*) tapisser, couvrir (*un canapé*) **(with, in,** de).

upholstered [ʌp'həʊlstəd] *adj* (*padded*)) capitonné, rembourré; (*covered*) tapissé, couvert; **u. in velvet,** garni de velours; *F* **she's well u.,** elle est bien rembourrée.

upholsterer [ʌp'həʊlstərər] *n* tapissier *m* en ameublement.

upholstery [ʌp'həʊlstərɪ] *n* **(a)** (*padding*) capitonnage *m*, rembourrage *m* (*d'un fauteuil*); (*covering*)) garniture *f*; garniture intérieure (*d'une voiture*); **leather u.,** garniture en cuir; **(b)** (*trade*) tapisserie *f* d'ameublement.

upkeep ['ʌpkiːp] *n* (frais *mpl* d')entretien *m*.

upland ['ʌplənd] **1** *n usu pl* **the uplands,** le haut pays, les hautes terres. **2** *adj* (*village*) des montagnes.

uplift[1] ['ʌplɪft] *n* **moral u.,** inspiration *f* (morale); **u. bra,** soutien-gorge *m* au maintien parfait.

uplift[2] [ʌp'lɪft] *vt* **(a)** élever (*l'âme, le cœur*); **(b)** *Scot* (*collect*) passer prendre.

uplifted [ʌp'lɪftɪd] *adj* **(a)** (*of hand*) levé; **(b)** (*morally, spiritually*) exalté, inspiré.

uplifting [ʌp'lɪftɪŋ] *adj* (*experience, sermon etc*) édifiant, enrichissant.

up-market ['ʌpmɑːkɪt] **1** *adj* (*product*) haut de gamme; (*district, person, accent*) bourgeois. **2** *adv* **to go up-m.,** (*of company*) passer au haut de gamme; (*go to expensive restaurant etc*) donner dans le luxe.

upmost ['ʌpməʊst] *adj* = **UPPERMOST 1**.

upon [ə'pɒn] *prep* sur; **on** *and* **upon** *are interchangeable in meaning; in modern English* **upon** *is used more formally; in certain phrases, however,* **upon** *is preferable* **u. my word!,** ma foi!, mon Dieu!; **the enemy was u. us,** l'ennemi nous attaquait; **I came u. it by accident,** je l'ai trouvé par hasard; **you brought it u. yourself,** ne t'en prends qu'à toi-même!

upper ['ʌpər] **1** *adj* **(a)** supérieur; **the u. atmosphere,** les couches supérieures de l'atmosphère; **u. jaw/lip,** mâchoire/lèvre supérieure; **the u. branches,** les hautes branches; **u. storey,** étage supérieur; **u. deck,** pont supérieur; *Th* **u. circle,** deuxième balcon *m*; **temperature in the u. twenties,** température qui dépasse 25 degrés;

(b) u. reaches, amont *m* (*d'une rivière*); **the u. Rhine,** le haut Rhin; **U. Canada,** le haut Canada; **U. Egypt,** la Haute-Égypte;

(c) u. end of the table, haut bout de la table; *Parl* **the U. House,** la Chambre haute; **the u. classes,** la haute société; **the u. middle classes,** la haute bourgeoisie; *Sch* **the u. school,** les grandes classes; *Br Sch* **the u. sixth,** ≈ la terminale; **to gain the u. hand,** prendre le dessus; **to let s.o. get the u. hand,** laisser qn prendre le dessus, laisser qn dominer;

(d) *Mus* (*clavier*) du côté droit; (*registre*) aigu, -uë.

2 *n* **(a)** (*of shoe*) empeigne *f*; *F* **to be down on one's uppers,** être dans la gêne;

(b) *Sl* (*drug*) amphétamine *f*, amphète *f*.

upper-case ['ʌpəkeɪs] *adj Typ* (*letters*) majuscule.

upper-class ['ʌpə'klɑːs] *adj* (*accent, person*) aristocratique; **to be very u-c.,** être très aristocrate *ou* distingué.

upper-crust ['ʌpə'krʌst] *adj F* (*accent, person*) aristo, de la haute; **they're frightfully u.-c.,** ils sont terriblement distingués.

upper-cut ['ʌpəkʌt] *n Boxing* uppercut *m*.

uppermost ['ʌpəməʊst] **1** *adj* **(a)** (*in position*) le plus haut, le plus élevé; **(b)** (*in importance*) de la plus grande importance; **to be u.,** tenir le premier rang; **the problem (which is) u. in our minds,** le problème qui nous préoccupe le plus. **2** *adv* (le plus) en dessus; **face u.,** face en dessus.

upping ['ʌpɪŋ] *n* **swan u.,** recensement *m* des cygnes.

uppish ['ʌpɪʃ], **uppity** ['ʌpɪtɪ] *adj F* présomptueux, arrogant; **he's getting very u.,** il se croit quelqu'un; **don't you get u. with me!,** ne joue pas les arrogants avec moi!

upright ['ʌpraɪt] **1** *adj* **(a)** (*line*) vertical, aux; (*wall, writing*) droit; **u. piano,** piano droit; **u. freezer,** congélateur *m* armoire; **(b)** (*honest*) droit, juste, honnête. **2**

adv debout; **to stand u.,** se tenir droit; **sitting u. on his chair,** assis raide sur sa chaise; **to put** *or* **stand sth u.,** mettre qch debout *ou* d'aplomb. **3** *n* **(a)** *Carp etc* montant *m*; **uprights of a ladder,** montants d'une échelle; *Fb* **the uprights,** les montants de but; **(b)** piano droit.

uprightly ['ʌpraɪtlɪ] *adv* droitement, honnêtement.

uprightness ['ʌpraɪtnɪs] *n* droiture *f*, honnêteté *f*.

uprising [ʌp'raɪzɪŋ] *n* soulèvement *m* (du peuple), insurrection *f*.

uproar ['ʌprɔːr] *n* (*noise*) tapage *m*, vacarme *m*; (*agitated*) tummulte *m*; **the town was in an u.,** la ville était en tumulte; **his suggestion caused an u.,** (*shouting, protests*) sa suggestion a provoqué un tollé; **the recent u. in the press about ...,** la tempête qui a récemment éclaté dans la presse au sujet de ... .

uproarious [ʌp'rɔːrɪəs] *adj* tumultueux; **u. laughter,** grands éclats de rire.

uproariously [ʌp'rɔːrɪəslɪ] *adv* tumultueusement; (*rire*) à grands éclats; **u. funny,** désopilant.

uproot [ʌp'ruːt] *vt* déraciner, extirper (*une plante, un mal*); **to u. s.o. from his home,** arracher qn de son foyer; **to feel uprooted,** se sentir déraciné.

upsadaisy ['ʌpsədeɪzɪ] *int F* houp là!

upset¹ ['ʌpset] *n* **(a)** renversement *m* (*d'un bateau*); **(b)** (*disturbance*) dérangement *m*; (*emotional*) perturbation *f*; **the bad news caused quite an u.,** les mauvaises nouvelles ont provoqué une grande consternation; **with the fewest possible number of upsets to our plans,** avec le plus petit nombre de dérangements possible de nos plans; **he can't stand upsets in his routine,** il ne supporte pas que sa routine soit dérangée; **have you had an u. with her?,** (*difficulty, argument etc*) est-ce que tu t'es disputé *ou* as eu un problème avec elle?; **they've had a bit of an u.,** (*a quarrel*) ils se sont un peu disputés; **he's had a bit of an u., his girl-friend has ...,** il a eu des problèmes *ou* a été un peu perturbé, sa petite amie a ...; **losing 25-3 was something of an u.,** perdre 25 à 3 était une catastrophe contraire à toutes les prévisions; **after the u. at the last match,** après la déception du dernier match; **that's going to cause a bit of an u.,** cela va causer des difficultés; **(c)** dérangement *m* (d'estomac); **to have a stomach u.,** avoir l'estomac dérangé.

upset² [ʌp'set] *v* (*pt & pp* **upset**; *prp* **upsetting**) **1** *vt* **(a)** (*knock over, spill*) renverser; (faire) chavirer (*un bateau*); **(b)** bouleverser, déranger (*les projets, l'horaire, les calculs etc*); **(c)** (*emotionally*) troubler, émouvoir, bouleverser (*qn*); **the least thing upsets him,** il s'impressionne pour un rien; **don't u. yourself,** ne vous en faites pas, ne vous frappez pas; **(d)** déranger (*l'estomac*); troubler (*la digestion*); **beer upsets me,** la bière me rend malade. **2** *vi* (*of cup, contents*) se renverser; (*of boat*) chavirer.

upset³ [*before noun* 'ʌpset, *otherwise* ʌp'set] *adj* **(a)** renversé; (*boat*) chaviré; **(b)** (*offended*) vexé; (*annoyed*) fâché, ennuyé; (*sad*) triste; **she's u. because you called her a ...,** elle est vexée parce que tu l'as traitée de ...; **are you still u. or are we friends again?,** est-ce que tu es toujours fâché *ou* vexé ou sommes nous amis à nouveau?; **we'd be very u. if we missed the deadline,** nous serions très ennuyés si nous rations la date limite; **you'd be u. too if you'd just paid ...,** tu serais aussi fâché que moi si tu venais juste de payer ...; **I'm u. about losing it/her,** ça me fait mal au cœur de le/la perdre; **your mother's very u. about what you said,** ce que tu as dit a fait très mal au cœur à ta mère; **we're u. about losing the order,** ça nous contrarie de perdre cette commande; **I'd be very u. if you didn't come,** je serais très triste *ou* ça me ferait très mal au cœur si tu ne venais pas; **he was so u. he couldn't speak,** il était tellement bouleversé qu'il ne pouvait pas parler; **come on now, there's nothing to be u. about,** allons, il n'y a pas de quoi en faire un drame; **don't be** *or* **get u.,** ne vous en faites pas; **(c)** (*estomac*) dérangé; **(d) u. price,** (*at auctions*) mise *f* à prix.

upsetting [ʌp'setɪŋ] **1** *adj* bouleversant, inquiétant. **2** *n* renversement *m*; désorganisation *f*; dérangement *m* (*de projets*).

upshot ['ʌpʃɒt] *n* résultat *m*; **what will be the u. of it?,** cela finira comment?; **the u. of it all was that he resigned,** en fin de compte il a donné sa démission.

upside down ['ʌpsaɪd'daʊn] **1** *adv* **(a)** sens dessus dessous; la tête en bas; **to hold sth u. d.,** tenir qch à l'envers; **(b)** en désordre; **to turn everything u. d.,** tout bouleverser, tout mettre sens dessus dessous. **2** *adj* **u.-d.,** renversé; **pineapple u.-down cake,** gâteau renversé à l'ananas.

upstage¹ [ʌp'steɪdʒ] **1** *n Th* arrière-scène *f*. **2** *adj Th* de l'arrière-scène; **3** *adv* à l'arrière-scène.

upstage² *vt* reléguer (*qn*) au second plan, souffler la vedette à (*qn*).

upstairs ['ʌpsteəz] **1** *adv* en haut; **he's u.,** il est en haut; **she has a second living room u.,** elle a un deuxième salon en haut *ou* à l'étage; **I'll take your things u.,** je vais monter tes affaires; **to come/go u.,** monter (l'escalier); *F* **to kick s.o. u.,** donner de l'avancement à qn (pour s'en débarrasser); *F* **he hasn't got much u.,** il n'est pas très intelligent. **2** *adj* (*room*) d'en haut, du haut; à l'étage (supérieur); **we have an u. sitting room,** nous avons un salon au premier. **3** *n F* **(the) u.,** les pièces *fpl* d'en haut; **the house has no u.,** la maison n'a pas d'étage.

upstanding [ʌp'stændɪŋ] *adj* (*person*) **(a)** droit, qui se tient bien; **a fine u. man,** un gars solide; **(b)** (*honest*) honnête; **(c)** *Fml* **please be u. for the toast,** veuillez vous lever pour porter le toast.

upstart ['ʌpstɑːt] *n* parvenu, -ue.

upstate ['ʌpsteɪt] *US* **1** *adj* du nord (d'un État); **u. New York,** la région prospère de L'État de New York. **2** *adv* (*aller*) vers le nord (d'un État).

upstream ['ʌpstriːm] **1** *adv* **(a)** (*to be*) en amont (**from,** de); **(b)** (*to row etc*) en remontant le courant, à contre-fil de l'eau. **2** *adj* d'amont.

upstroke ['ʌpstrəʊk] *n* (*in writing*) délié *m*; course montante *ou* ascendante (*du piston*).

upsurge ['ʌpsɜːdʒ] *n* poussée *f* (*de fièvre*); vague *f* (*d'enthousiasme, de haine*); regain *m* (*d'activité, d'intérêt*).

upswept ['ʌpswept] *adj Aut Av* profilé; **u. hair(style),** coiffure relevée.

upswing ['ʌpswɪŋ] *n* **(a)** mouvement ascendant; **(b)** *Fig* amélioration *f* sensible; **business is on the u.,** les affaires sont à la hausse *ou* en progression constante.

uptake ['ʌpteɪk] *n F* **to be quick on the u.,** avoir la compréhension facile, avoir l'esprit vif; **he's a bit slow on the u.,** il est un peu lent à comprendre *ou* à la détente.

uptight [ʌp'taɪt] *adj F* **(a)** (*nervous*) nerveux, tendu; **he's u. about the exams/about meeting them,** il est nerveux *ou* tendu à cause des examens/à l'idée de les rencontrer; **(b)** (*inhibited*) coincé; (*on particular occasion*) crispé; **relax, don't be so u., everyone else is enjoying themselves,** relaxe-toi, ne sois pas aussi crispé, tous les autres s'amusent; **(c)** (*conventional*) (*parents, attitude*) dur, strict; **(d)** (*upset, irritated*) énervé, fâché; **listen, no need to be u. about it,** écoute, ce n'est pas la peine de s'énerver là-dessus.

up-to-date [ʌptə'deɪt] *adj* très récent; (*method, equipment, technology*) moderne, sophistiqué; (*person*) qui est dans le vent *ou* à la mode; (*information, views*) à jour; *see also* **DATE² (a)**.

up-to-the-minute [ʌptəðə'mɪnɪt] *adj* (*news, information*) de dernière minute; (*style*) du dernier cri.

uptown ['ʌp'taʊn] *esp US* **1** *adv* dans/vers les quartiers résidentiels de la ville. **2** *n* les quartiers résidentiels; **u. society,** les milieux bourgeois.

upturn¹ ['ʌptɜːn] *n* amélioration *f*; progression *f* (*dans les affaires*).

upturn² [ʌp'tɜːn] *vt* retourner, mettre à l'envers; (*esp accidentally*) renverser.

upturned ['ʌptɜːnd] *adj* **(a)** retourné; renversé; **(b)** (*nez*) retroussé; (*yeux*) tourné vers le ciel.

upward ['ʌpwəd] **1** *adj* montant, ascendant; **u. movement,** (*of piston etc*) mouvement ascensionnel; **u. slope,** pente ascendante; **u. tendency** *or* **movement,** (*of prices etc*) tendance *f* à la hausse, mouvement de hausse; **u. mobility,** (*in society*) mobilité sociale vers le haut. **2** *adv* = **UPWARDS**.

upwardly ['ʌpwədlɪ] *adv* **to be u. mobile,** (*in society*) avoir la possibilité de s'élever dans la société.

upwards ['ʌpwədz] *adv* (*to move, climb etc*) vers le haut; **to look u.,** regarder en haut; **to put sth face u. on the table,** mettre qch à l'endroit sur la table; **lying face u.,** (*person*) couché sur le dos; **£100 and u.,** 100 livres et au-dessus; **it costs u. of £100,** ça coûte plus de 100 livres; **u. of 500 pupils,** plus de 500 élèves; **children from ten (years) u.,** des enfants à partir de dix ans.

upwind ['ʌpwɪnd] *adv* (*aller*) contre le vent; (*être*) contre le vent, au vent; **to be u. of an animal,** être au vent d'un animal.

Ural ['jʊərəl] *n* **the U. (river),** l'Oural *m*; **the U. mountains, the Urals,** les monts Ourals, l'Oural.

uranium [jʊ'reɪnɪəm] *n Ch* uranium *m*.

Uranus [jʊ'reɪnəs] *n Myth Astron* Uranus *m*.

urban ['ɜːbən] *adj* urbain; **u. areas,** agglomérations urbaines; **u. guerilla,** guerillero *m* des villes; **u. renewal,** rénovations urbaines; **u. sprawl,** urbanisation incontrôlée *ou* sauvage.

urbane [ɜː'beɪn] *adj* courtois, d'une politesse raffinée.

urbanely [ɜː'beɪnlɪ] *adv* courtoisement, avec urbanité.

urbanism ['ɜːbənɪz(ə)m] *n* urbanisme *m*.

urbanite ['ɜːbənaɪt] *n* citadin, -ine.

urbanity [ɜː'bænɪtɪ] *n* urbanité *f*, courtoisie *f*.

urbanization [ɜːbənaɪ'zeɪʃən] *n* urbanisation *f*.

urbanize ['ɜːbənaɪz] *vt* urbaniser.

urchin ['ɜːtʃɪn] *n* **(a)** **(street) u.**, galopin *m*; (*kid*) gosse *mf*; **(b) sea u.**, oursin *m*.

Urdu ['ʊəduː] *n Ling* ourdou *m*.

urea [jʊ'rɪːə] *n Ch* urée *f*.

ureter [jʊ'riːtər] *n Anat* uretère *m*.

urethra [jʊ'riːθrə] *n Anat* urètre *m*.

urge¹ [ɜːdʒ] *n Psy* pulsion *f*; (*desire*) envie *f*; **I get this irresistible u. to jump off, doctor,** je ressens cette impulsion irrésistible à sauter, docteur; **to have a powerful u. to succeed,** éprouver le désir ardent de réussir; **he's lost the u. to win,** il a perdu l'envie *ou* la rage de gagner; **I had an u. to hit him,** j'ai eu envie de le frapper; *F* **when I get the u.**, (*feel sexy*) quand j'ai envie; *F* **the bottle's there, help yourself if you get the u.,** la bouteille est là, servez-vous si ça vous dit.

urge² *vt* **(a)** (*plead with, try to persuade etc*) **to u. s.o. to do sth,** presser qn à faire *ou* pour qu'il fasse qch; **to u. s.o. not do sth,** presser qn à ne pas faire qch; **I urged him to accept,** je lui ai vivement conseillé d'accepter; **they urged us to give up, but in vain,** ils ont insisté pour que nous abandonnions, mais ce fut en vain; **I u. you not to do it,** je te supplie de ne pas le faire; **to u. a horse forward,** pousser un cheval; **(b)** (*recommend earnestly*) **to u. caution,** recommander *ou* conseiller la prudence; **to u. peace on the nations of the world,** exhorter les nations du monde à la paix; **to u. that sth be done,** recommander *ou* conseiller de faire qch; **I u. that you should abandon this plan,** je vous conseille *ou* recommande vivement d'abandonner ce projet.

►**urge on** *vtsep* (*person, team, runner*) encourager; (*horse*) pousser; (*work*) stimuler; **to u. s.o. on to do sth,** pousser qn à faire qch.

urgency ['ɜːdʒənsɪ] *n* urgence *f*; **it's a matter of u.,** il y a urgence, c'est urgent; **could you do this as a matter of the utmost u.?,** pourriez-vous faire ceci de toute urgence?; **the u. in her voice,** l'instance *f* dans sa voix; **what's all the u.?,** qu'est-ce qu'il y a de si urgent?; **there's no u.,** ce n'est pas urgent *ou* pressé; **he shows no sense of u.,** il ne se presse pas.

urgent ['ɜːdʒənt] *adj* (*needs, case, delivery*) urgent; (*meeting, treatment, solution, tone*) d'urgence; **u. need,** besoin pressant; **u. case,** cas urgent *ou* pressant; **the matter is u.,** l'affaire presse, c'est urgent; **this is u.,** c'est une urgence, c'est urgent; **is it u.?** est-ce que c'est urgent?, est-ce que ça presse?; **just how u. is it?,** mais est-ce vraiment urgent?; **just how u. is it that you should be there tomorrow?,** mais est-il vraiment essentiel que tu y sois demain?; **the doctor had an u. call,** on a appelé le médecin d'urgence; **at their u. request,** sur leurs instances pressantes.

urgently ['ɜːdʒəntlɪ] *adv* d'urgence; **a doctor is u. required,** on demande d'urgence un médecin; **to press u. for sth,** réclamer qch de façon urgente *ou* instamment; **they u. called a meeting,** ils ont convoqué une réunion d'urgence.

uric ['jʊərɪk] *adj* (*acide*) urique.

urinal ['jʊərɪn(ə)l, jʊː'raɪn(ə)l] *n* urinoir *m*, *F* pissotière *f*; **(bed) u.,** urinal *m*, -aux.

urinary ['jʊərɪnərɪ] *adj Anat* urinaire; **u. tract infection,** infection *f* urinaire.

urinate ['jʊərɪneɪt] *vi* uriner.

urine ['jʊərɪn] *n* urine *f*.

urn [ɜːn] *n* urne *f*; **tea u.,** fontaine *f* à thé.

urogenital [jʊərəʊ'dʒenɪt(ə)l] *adj Anat* urogénital, -aux.

urological [jʊərəʊ'lɒdʒɪk(ə)l] *adj* urologique.

urologist [jʊ'rɒlədʒɪst] *n* urologue *mf*.

urology [jʊ'rɒlədʒɪ] *n Med* urologie *f*.

Ursa ['ɜːsə] *n Astron* **U. Major/U. Minor,** la Grande/la Petite Ourse.

urticaria [ɜːtɪ'keərɪə] *n Med* urticaire *f*.

Uruguay ['jʊərəgwaɪ] *n* Uruguay *m*.

Uruguayan [jʊərə'gwaɪən] **1** *adj* uruguayen. **2** *n* Uruguayen, -enne.

us *person pron objective case* **(a)** (*unstressed*) [əs] nous; **he sees us,** il nous voit; **in front of/behind us,** devant/derrière nous; **he gave it to us,** il nous l'a donné; **tell us,** dites-nous; **he wrote us a letter,** il nous a écrit une lettre; **he stayed with us a month,** il est resté un mois chez nous; **there are three of us,** nous sommes trois; **(b)** (*stressed*) [ʌs] nous; **that concerns us alone,** cela ne regarde que nous; **between them and us,** entre eux et nous; **as for us Englishmen,** quant à nous autres Anglais; **he couldn't believe that it was us,** il ne pouvait pas croire que c'était nous; **(c)** *F* (*me*) **let's have a look,** laissez-moi regarder; **give us a bit of it,** donnez-m'en un peu.

US [juː'es] *n* (*abbr* **United States**) É.-U. *mpl*.

USA [juːes'eɪ] *n* **(a)** (*abbr* **United States of America**) U.S.A. *mpl*; **(b)** *abbr* **United States Army**.

usable ['juːzəb(ə)l] *adj* utilisable, employable.

USAF [juːeseɪ'ef] *n abbr* **United States Air Force**.

usage ['juːsɪdʒ] *n* **(a)** (*treatment*) traitement *m*; **this book has had some rough u.,** ce livre a été maltraité; **(b)** (*custom*) usage *m*; **an old u.,** une vieille coutume; **sanctified by u.,** consacré par l'usage; **(c) words in everyday u.,** mots d'usage courant; **it's not in current u.,** ce n'est pas dans l'usage courant; **a book on modern English u.,** un livre sur les usages de l'anglais moderne; **it's not a u. I'm familiar with,** ce n'est pas une utilisation *ou* un emploi que je connais.

use¹ [juːs] *n* **1 (a)** emploi *m*, utilisation *f*; **the u. of steel in building,** l'emploi de l'acier dans la construction; **one of the main uses of steel,** un des principaux emplois de l'acier; **to make u. of sth,** (*tool, equipment*) se servir de qch; (*word, material*) utiliser qch, employer qch; **to make good u. of sth, to put sth to good u.,** bien employer qch; **everything has a** *or* **its u.,** il y a un emploi pour tout; **I'll find a u. for it,** je lui trouverai bien un emploi, je trouverai un moyen de m'en servir; **word in everyday u.,** mot d'usage courant; **not in u., out of u.,** hors d'usage; (*mot*) desuet, -ète, tombé en désuétude; (*on door of lift*) hors (de) service; **for u. in case of fire,** à employer en cas d'incendie; **for u. in schools,** à l'usage des écoles; **directions** *or* **instructions for u.,** mode *m* d'emploi; *Pharm* **for external u.,** pour usage externe; **to improve with u.,** s'améliorer à l'usage;

(b) (*ability to use*) jouissance *f*, usage *m*; *Jur* usufruit *m*; **to have full u. of one's faculties,** jouir de toutes ses facultés; **to lose the u. of a leg,** perdre l'usage d'une jambe; **to have the u. of the bathroom,** avoir le droit de se servir de la salle de bain; **you can have the u. of my car while I'm in London,** tu peux te servir de ma voiture pendant que je suis à Londres; *Jur* **full right and u. (of sth),** plein usufruit *ou* pleine jouissance (de qch);

(c) (*usefulness*) utilité *f*; **to be of u.,** être utile (**for sth,** à qch); **can I be of any u. (to you)?** puis-je vous être utile à quelque chose?; **it's of no u. to me,** je n'en ai pas besoin; **it's not much u.,** cela ne sert pas à grand-chose; *F* **a fat lot of u. that'll be to you!,** si tu crois que ça va t'avancer!; *F Iron* **you're a lot of u.!** je vous retiens!; *F* **he's no u.,** c'est un incapable; **to have no u. for sth,** ne savoir que faire de qch; **I've no further u. for it,** je n'en ai plus besoin; *F* **I haven't much u. for him,** il ne me dit rien; **it was no u.,** c'était inutile; **it's no u. discussing the question,** inutile de discuter la question; **it's no u. crying,** ce n'est pas la peine de pleurer; **it's no u. my talking,** je perds ma peine à parler; **it's no u.(, I can't do it)!,** c'est peine perdue(, je ne peux pas le faire)!; **is it any u. writing to him?,** est-ce que ça servirait à quelque chose de lui écrire?; **what u. would that be?,** à quoi cela servirait-il?; **what's the u. of doing it/of going there?,** à quoi bon le faire/y aller?; **what's the u.!, I give up!,** à quoi bon! j'abandonne!;

(d) *Arch* (*custom*) usage *m*, coutume *f*.

use² [juːz] **1** *vt* employer, se servir de (*qch*), utiliser; **are you using this knife?,** est-ce que vous vous servez de ce couteau?; **u. your head!,** ne sois pas si bête!; **u. your eyes!,** ouvrez les yeux! **to be used for sth,** servir à qch; **I used the money to rebuild my garage,** j'ai utilisé *ou* employé l'argent à reconstruire mon garage; **this word is no longer used,** ce mot est désuet; **word used figuratively,** mot employé au (sens) figuré; **to u. force,** avoir recours à la force; **to u. discretion,** agir avec discrétion; **to u. one's influence,** user de son influence; **to u. every means (at one's disposal),** employer tous les moyens (à sa disposition); **I could u. some coffee,** je prendrais volontiers du café; **this tool has been roughly used,** cet outil a été maltraité; **it will last a long time if you u. it carefully,** cela vous servira longtemps si vous le traitez avec soin; *F* **how's the world been using you?,** comment ça va?; **I feel I've been used,** (*exploited*) j'ai l'impression qu'on s'est servi de moi.

2 (*as aux pt*) [ju:st] **when we were children we used to play together,** quand nous étions enfants nous jouions ensemble; **my father used to tell me that...,** mon père m'a souvent raconté que...; **it used to be a pleasant town to live in,** c'était autrefois une ville agréable à habiter; **things aren't what they used to be,** les choses ne sont plus ce qu'elles étaient, ce n'est plus comme autrefois; **she used not** *or* **use(d)n't to like oysters,** autrefois elle n'aimait pas les huîtres; **I used not to like him, I didn't use to** ['ju:stə] **like him,** autrefois je ne l'aimais pas; **do you smoke? — I do now, but I didn't u. to,** est-ce que vous fumez? — je ne fumais pas mais je m'y suis mis; **do you smoke? — I used to,** est-ce que vous fumez? — j'ai arrêté; **do you travel much? — I used to,** vous voyagez beaucoup? — autrefois, oui.

►**use up** *vtsep* (*food, milk*) finir; (*paint, hot water, ideas, money, resources, time allowance, holiday entitlement etc*) utiliser la totalité de; (*strength, energy*) dépenser la totalité de; **u. up the leftovers to make a ...,** utiliser les restes pour faire un ..., accommoder les restes en faisant un ...; **it's all used up,** (*is gone*) il n'y en a *ou* reste plus.

used [ju:zd] *adj* **(a)** usé, usagé; (*timbre-poste*) oblitéré; (*nappe*) sale; qui a déjà servi; **u. car,** voiture *f* d'occasion; **hardly u.,** presque neuf; **(b)** [ju:st] (*accustomed*) **u. to (doing) sth,** habitué *ou* accoutumé à (faire) qch; **I'm not u. to it,** je n'en ai pas l'habitude; **to get u. to sth/s.o.,** s'habituer *ou* se faire à qch qn; **you'll get u. to it in time,** vous vous y ferez à la longue; **to get s.o. u. to sth,** habituer qn à qch; **I'm not u. to being spoken to like that!,** je n'ai pas l'habitude qu'on me parle comme ça!

useful ['ju:sfʊl] *adj* utile; **this book was very u. to me,** ce livre m'a été très utile *ou* m'a rendu grand service; **it's u. to know,** c'est utile *ou* bon à savoir; **it will come in very u.,** cela rendra bien service; **a u. man to know,** une relation utile, un homme qu'il est bon d'avoir dans ses relations; **to make oneself u.,** se rendre utile; **this machine has a u. life of ten years,** cette machine donnera dix ans de service; **he played a u. game,** il s'est acquitté honorablement; **to be u. with one's fists,** savoir se servir de ses poings; **to be u. with a gun,** savoir manier un fusil; *Iron* **that's u.!,** formidable!

usefully ['ju:sfəlɪ] *adv* utilement; **one might u. write a book on...,** il serait fort utile qu'on écrive un livre sur...; **is there anything I can u. do?,** y a-t-il quoi que ce soit que je puisse faire pour me rendre utile?

usefulness ['ju:sfʊlnɪs] *n* utilité *f*; **it has/he has outlived its/his u.,** cela ne sert plus à rien/il a fait son temps.

useless ['ju:slɪs] *adj* inutile; (*unusable*) inutilisable; (*no good*) nul; (*person*) bon à rien, incompétent, nul; (*remedy*) inefficace; **I hope I haven't been completely u. to you,** j'espère que je ne vous ai pas été totalement inutile; **to be full of u. information,** être riche en informations inutiles; **a map without a key is u.,** une carte sans légende est inutilisable; **it would be u. to make further requests,** d'autres demandes seraient inutiles; **give up, it's u.!,** laisse tomber, ça ne sert à rien!; **it's u. even trying to discuss it,** (*no point*) ce n'est même pas la peine d'essayer d'en discuter; **I'm u. at languages,** je suis nul en langues; **he's u. in bed,** au lit il est nul; **a u. person,** un(e) bon(ne) à rien; *F* **to be worse than u.,** être au-dessous de tout.

uselessly ['ju:slɪslɪ] *adv* inutilement.

uselessness ['ju:slɪsnɪs] *n* inutilité *f*; (*of person*) incompétence *f*; **his general u.,** sa nullité.

user ['ju:zər] *n* usager, -ère (*de la route, d'un moyen de transport*); utilisateur, -trice (*d'un appareil*); abonné, -ée (*du téléphone*).

user-definable [ju:zədɪ'faɪnəb(ə)l] *adj Comptr* (*characters, keys*) définissable par l'utilisateur.

user-defined [ju:zədɪ'faɪnd] *adj Comptr* (*characters, keys*) défini par l'utilisateur.

user-friendliness [ju:zə'frendlɪnɪs] *n* (*see adj*) convivialité *f*; facilité *f* d'utilisation.

user-friendly [ju:zə'frendlɪ] *adj* (*software, computer*) convivial, -aux; (*machine, technology, instruction manual*) facile à utiliser.

user-interface [ju:zər'ɪntəfeɪs] *n Comptr & Fig* interface *f* utilisateur.

usher¹ ['ʌʃər] *n* **(a)** *Jur* **court u.,** (huissier) audiencier *m*; **(b)** *Th Cin* placeur *m*; (*at wedding*) garçon *m* d'honneur.

usher² **1** *vt* précéder (*un roi*) comme huissier; **to u. s.o. into the presence of s.o.,** introduire qn en présence de qn; **they hastily ushered him away/out,** ils le firent s'éloigner/sortir à la hâte; **2** *vi* (*at wedding*) servir de garçon(s) d'honneur.

►**usher in** *vtsep* introduire, faire entrer (*qn*); **to u. in a new epoch,** inaugurer une époque; **the invention which ushered in a new age of ...,** l'invention qui a marqué le début d'une nouvelle époque de ... .

usherette [ʌʃə'ret] *n Th Cin* ouvreuse *f*.

USM [ju:es'em] *n* **(a)** *abbr* **United States Mail**; **(b)** *Mil abbr* **United States Marines**; **(c)** *Fin abbr* **United States Mint**.

USN [ju:es'en] *n abbr* **United States Navy**.

USS [ju:es'es] *abbr* **United States Ship**.

USSR [ju:eses'ɑ:r] *n* (*abbr* **Union of Soviet Socialist Republics**) U.R.S.S. *f*.

usual ['ju:ʒʊəl] **1** *adj* habituel; **at the u. time,** à l'heure habituelle; **it's the u. practice,** c'est la pratique courante; **the u. terms,** les conditions d'usage; **I didn't get my u. bus this morning,** je n'ai pas pris le bus que je prends d'habitude ce matin; **it wasn't the u. postman,** ce n'était pas notre facteur habituel *ou F* de d'habitude; **u. time, u. place, OK?,** même heure, même endroit, d'accord?; **she's her u. self again,** elle est redevenue elle-même; **you're not your u. cheery self today,** tu n'es pas aussi souriant que d'habitude aujourd'hui; **it's quite u. for that sort of thing to happen,** ces choses-là arrivent régulièrement; **it's u. with these machines,** ça arrive régulièrement avec ces machines; **it's not u. to have to wait this long,** d'habitude on ne nous fait pas attendre si longtemps; **it's u. to pay in advance,** il est d'usage de payer d'avance; **earlier/later than u.,** plus tôt/plus tard que d'habitude; **more than u.,** plus que d'habitude; **as u.,** *F* **as per u.,** comme d'ordinaire *ou* d'habitude; **business as u.,** les affaires continuent *ou* la vente continue; (*on sign*) ouvert pendant les réparations.

2 *n F* (*in bar*) **(are you having) your u.?,** (votre demi, votre whisky *etc*) comme d'habitude?; **the u. please Jim,** comme d'habitude s'il te plaît, Jim.

usually ['ju:ʒʊ(ə)lɪ] *adv* habituellement, d'habitude; **I u. get up at seven,** j'ai l'habitude de me lever *ou* d'habitude je me lève à sept heures; **he was more than u. polite,** il s'est montré encore plus poli que d'habitude; **it's not u. that difficult,** ce n'est pas aussi difficile que ça d'habitude *ou* habituellement.

usufruct ['ju:zjʊfrʌkt] *n Jur* usufruit *m* (**of,** de).

usufructuary [ju:zjʊ'frʌktjərɪ] *adj & n Jur* usufruitier, -ière; **u. right,** droit *m* usufructuaire.

usurer ['ju:ʒərər] *n* usurier, -ière.

usurious [ju:'zjʊərɪəs] *adj* (*intérêt etc*) usuraire.

usurp [ju:'zɜ:p, -'sɜ:p] *vt* usurper (*un trône, un titre*) (**from,** sur).

usurpation [ju:zə'peɪʃən, -sɜ:-] *n* usurpation *f*.

usurper [jʊ'zɜ:pər, -sɜ:-] *n* usurpateur, -trice.

usury ['ju:ʒʊrɪ] *n* usure *f*; **that's u.!,** c'est de l'usure *ou* du vol!

Ut *abbr* **Utah**.

utensil [ju:'tens(ə)l] *n* ustensile *m*; **(set of) kitchen utensils,** batterie *f* de cuisine.

uterine ['ju:təraɪn] *adj* utérin.

uterus ['ju:tərəs] *n Anat* utérus *m*.

utilitarian [ju:tɪlɪ'teərɪən] *adj & n* utilitaire *mf*.

utilitarianism [ju:tɪlɪ'teərɪənɪz(ə)m] *n* utilitarisme *m*.

utility [ju:'tɪlɪtɪ] *n* **(a)** utilité *f*; **u. vehicle/car,** véhicule/voiture utilitaire *ou* tous usages; *Com* **u. goods,** articles *m* utilitaires *ou* de consommation courante; *Comptr* **u. program,** programme *m* utilitaire; **u. room,** pièce réservée à la lessive *ou* au repassage; **(b) public utilities, public u. services,** *Am* **utilities,** services publics; **(c)** *Am* entreprise *f* de service public.

utilizable [ju:tɪ'laɪzəb(ə)l] *adj* utilisable.

utilization [ju:tɪl(a)ɪ'zeɪʃ(ə)n] *n* utilisation *f*; mise *f* en valeur; *Banking* réalisation *f;* **better u. of resources,** meilleure utilisation *ou* meilleur emploi des ressources.

utilize ['ju:tɪlaɪz] *vt* utiliser, se servir de (*qn, qch*); (*take advantage of*) tirer profit de, mettre en valeur (*qch*).

utmost ['ʌtməʊst] **1** *adj* **(a)** (*greatest*) le plus grand; **the u. poverty,** la misère la plus profonde; **with the u. contempt,** avec le plus grand mépris; **it is of the u. importance that he should be present,** il est de la dernière importance qu'il soit présent; **with the u. ease,** avec la plus grande facilité *ou* une extrême facilité;

(b) (*furthest*) **the u. ends of the earth,** les confins *mpl ou* les extrémités *fpl* de la terre.

2 *n* **that's the u. we can offer,** c'est le maximum que nous puissions offrir; **$50,000 at the u.,** 50 000 dollars au grand maximum; **to the u.,** (*to work etc*) le plus possible; (*to live, love etc*) au suprême degré; **to enjoy oneself to the u.,** s'amuser au plus haut point; **to do sth to the u. of**

one's abilities, faire qch au maximum de ses capacités; **I'll help you to the u. of my ability,** je vous aiderai autant qu'il est en mon pouvoir; **to do one's u. to achieve sth,** faire tout son possible pour arriver à un but.

Utopia [juːˈtəʊpɪə] *n* utopie *f*.

Utopian [juːˈtəʊpɪən] **1** *adj* utopique, d'utopie. **2** *n* utopiste *mf*.

utter¹ [ˈʌtər] *adj* complet, -ète, absolu; **he's an u. stranger to me,** il m'est complètement étranger; **it's u. madness,** c'est de la folie totale *ou* pure; **we were in u. darkness,** il faisait noir comme dans un four; **u. rubbish,** (*goods*) de la pure camelote; (*nonsense*) des absurdités; **he's an u. fool,** il est complètement idiot; **u. poverty,** la misère la plus profonde; **to my u. horror,** à ma grande horreur.

utter² *vt* **(a)** jeter, pousser (*un cri*); proférer (*un mot*); lancer (*un juron*); **never u. his name in her presence,** il ne faut jamais prononcer son nom devant elle; **I didn't u. a word,** je n'ai pas desserré les dents; **(b)** dire; débiter (*des mensonges*); émettre, mettre en circulation (*de la fausse monnaie*).

utterance [ˈʌtərəns] *n* **(a)** (*what is said*) paroles *fpl*, propos *mpl*, mots *mpl*; *Ling &* (*act of uttering*) articulation *f*; **what was his last u.?,** quels ont été ses derniers mots?; **they taped the child's first utterances,** ils ont enregistré les premiers sons produits par l'enfant *ou* les premiers mots de l'enfant; **his recent utterances in the national press,** ses récentes déclarations dans la presse nationale; **(b)** (*expression*) expression *f* (*des sentiments*); émission *f* (*d'un son*); **on her u. of his name,** au moment où elle prononça son nom; **to give u. to one's feelings,** exprimer ses sentiments.

utterly [ˈʌtəlɪ] *adv* complètement, absolument; **u. stupid,** d'une bêtise extrême.

uttermost [ˈʌtəməʊst] *adj & n* = **UTMOST**; **the u. ends of the earth,** les derniers confins, les extrémités *fpl* de la terre.

UV [juːˈviː] (*abbr* **ultra-violet**) U.V..

uvula, *pl* **-as, -ae** [ˈjuːvjələ, -əs, -iː] *n Anat* uvule *f*, luette *f*.

uvular [ˈjuːvjələr] *adj* uvulaire.

uxorious [ʌkˈsɔːrɪəs] *adj* (*mari*) trop dévoué à sa femme.

uxoriousness [ʌkˈsɔːrɪəsnɪs] *n* attachement exagéré (*d'un mari*) pour sa femme.

V

V, v [viː] *n* (la lettre) V, v *m*; **to fly in a V formation,** (*of birds*) voler en formant un V; **V-shaped,** en (forme de) V; **V-neck (sweater),** pull *m* à col en V; **V-neck(ed),** (*sweater*) à col en V; **V-necked dress,** robe à encolure en pointe *ou* en V; **V-sign,** *Hist* (*1939-45*) le V de la victoire; (*insult*) bras *m* d'honneur; **to give s.o. the V-sign,** faire un bras d'honneur à qn.

v *abbr* **(a) verse**; **(b)** *Jur Sp* **versus**; **(c) very**.

V *Elec abbr* **(volt(s))** V.

Va *abbr* **Virginia**.

vac [væk] *n Br F Univ & Sch* vacances *fpl*.

vacancy ['veɪkənsɪ] *n* **(a)** (*position*) place vacante, poste vacant; (*for dignitary, professional*) vacance *f*; **we have a v. for ...,** (*job advert*) nous recherchons ...; **to fill a v.,** pourvoir un poste vacant; **(b)** (*at hotel*) chambre *f* libre; (*at camp site*) place *f* libre; **no vacancies,** complet; **(c)** (*lack of thought*) absence *f* d'idées; **(d)** (*emptiness*) espace *m* vide, lacune *f*.

vacant ['veɪkənt] *adj* **(a)** (*empty*) vacant, vide; (*lavatory, seat etc*) libre; **to be v.,** (*of official post*) être à pourvoir; **situations v.,** (*newspaper column*) offres *fpl* d'emploi; **v. room/seat,** chambre/place libre *ou* inoccupée; **v. possession,** jouissance immédiate (*d'un immeuble*); **v. site,** *Am* **v. lot,** terrain *m* vague; (*for sale*) terrain à vendre; **v. space,** place *f* vide; **(b)** (*unthinking*) (*mind*) inoccupé; (*look*) distrait, vague, sans expression; **with a v. expression,** le regard perdu.

vacantly ['veɪkəntlɪ] *adv* (*vaguely*) d'un air distrait; d'un regard perdu; (*stupidly*) d'un air stupide.

vacate [və'keɪt] *vt* **(a)** quitter (*un emploi*); **(b)** quitter (*un siège, un appartement, une chambre d'hôtel*); déménager de (*une maison*); (*in emergency*) évacuer (*une maison, un appartement, une boutique*); *Jur* **to v. the premises,** vider les lieux.

vacating [və'keɪtɪŋ] *n* **(a) v. of office,** démission *f*; **(b)** déménagement *m*; départ *m* (*d'une maison*); (*in emergency*) évacuation *f*.

vacation¹ [və'keɪʃən] *n* **(a)** (*holiday*) vacances *fpl*; **the long v.,** *Jur* les vacances judiciaires, la vacation; *Univ* les grandes vacances; **v. work,** travail effectué pendant les vacances; *Am* **to take a v.,** prendre des vacances; **to be on v.,** être en vacances; *Am Admin* **v. leave,** congé annuel; **(b)** (*leaving*) départ *m* (*d'une maison*); (*in emergency*) évacuation *f*; **v. of office,** démission *f*.

vacation² *vi Am* prendre *ou* passer ses vacances (**at, in,** à, en).

vacationist, vacationer [veɪ'keɪʃənɪst, -ər] *n Am* vacancier, -ière; (*in summer*) estivant, -ante.

vaccinate ['væksɪneɪt] *Med* **1** *vt* vacciner (**against,** contre); **to get vaccinated,** se faire vacciner. **2** *vi* faire une vaccination *ou* des vaccinations.

vaccination [væksɪ'neɪʃən] *n Med* vaccination *f*; **smallpox v.,** vaccination contre la variole.

vaccine ['væksiːn] *n Med* vaccin *m*.

vaccinee [væksɪ'niː] *n US* personne vaccinée.

vacillate ['væsɪleɪt] *vi* **(a)** (*sway*) vaciller, chanceler; **(b)** (*be indecisive*) hésiter (entre deux opinions).

vacillating ['væsɪleɪtɪŋ] **1** *adj* **(a)** (*swaying*) vacillant, chancelant; **(b)** (*undecided*) irrésolu, indécis. **2** *n* (*swaying*) vacillation *f*; (*indecision*) indécision *f*, irrésolution *f*.

vacillation [væsɪ'leɪʃən] *n* (*swaying*) vacillation *f*; (*indecision*) indécision *f*, irrésolution *f*.

vacuity [væ'kjuːɪtɪ] *n* **(a)** (*lack of intelligence*) vacuité *f*; **vacuities,** bêtises *fpl*, niaiseries *fpl*; **(b)** (*emptiness*) vacuité *f*, vide *m*.

vacuous ['vækjʊəs] *adj* vide d'expression; (*observation, rire*) bête; **he's completely v.,** c'est un parfait idiot; **v. look,** air hébété *ou* vide d'expression.

vacuously ['vækjʊəslɪ] *adv* (*fixer*) avec des yeux vides d'expression; (*rire*) bêtement.

vacuousness ['vækjʊəsnɪs] *n* (*of look*) absence *f* d'expression; (*of remark, laugh*) bêtise *f*.

vacuum, *pl* **-ua, -uums** ['vækjʊm, -jʊə, -jʊmz] *n* **(a)** *Phys* vide *m*, vacuum *m*; *Fig* vide; **to produce** *or* **create a v. in a vessel,** faire le vide dans un récipient; **nature abhors a v.,** la nature a horreur du vide; *Fig* **to live in a v.,** vivre en vase clos; **v.** *Br* **flask** *or Am* **bottle,** bouteille isolante; (bouteille) thermos ® *mf inv; El* **v. lamp,** lampe *f* à vide; *Am Electron* **v. tube,** tube *m* à vide électronique; **v. pump,** pompe *f* à vide; *Ind Com* **v. packing,** emballage *m* sous vide; **(b) v. (cleaner),** aspirateur *m*; **to give the carpet a v.,** passer l'aspirateur sur le tapis.

vacuum(-clean) ['vækjʊm(kliːn)] *vt* passer (*une moquette*) à l'aspirateur; passer l'aspirateur dans (*une pièce*).

vacuum-packed [vækjʊm'pækt] *adj* emballé sous vide.

VAD [viːeɪ'diː] *n Br Med* (*abbr* **Voluntary Aid Detachment**) = organisation d'aides-soignantes bénévoles; **she was a VAD during the war,** elle était aide-soignante bénévole pendant la guerre.

vade mecum [veɪdɪ'miːkəm, vɑːdɪ'meɪkəm] *n* vade-mecum *m inv*, aide-mémoire *m inv*.

vagabond ['vægəbɒnd] **1** *n* (*tramp*) vagabond, -onde, chemineau *m*. **2** *adj* vagabond, errant.

vagary ['veɪgərɪ] *n* caprice *m*; **the vagaries of fashion/the weather,** les caprices de la mode/du temps.

vagina [və'dʒaɪnə] *n Anat* vagin *m*.

vaginal [və'dʒaɪn(ə)l] *adj Anat* vaginal; **v. douche,** douche vaginale; **v. examination,** examen vaginal; **v. smear,** frottis vaginal; **to have a v. smear taken,** se faire faire un frottis vaginal.

vagrancy ['veɪgrənsɪ] *n Jur* vagabondage *m*; **to be arrested for v.,** être arrêté pour vagabondage.

vagrant ['veɪgrənt] **1** *n Jur* vagabond, -onde. **2** *adj* errant.

vague [veɪg] *adj* (*person, look*) vague; (*impression, memory*) vague, imprécis, confus; (*colour*) indéterminé, indécis; (*shape, outline*) estompé, flou; **the conditions were left deliberately v.,** les conditions ont été laissées vagues délibérement; **I haven't the vaguest idea,** je n'en ai pas la moindre idée; **I had a v. idea that he was dead,** j'avais vaguement l'idée qu'il était mort; **he was rather v. about the date,** il s'est montré assez vague à propos de la date; **she was v. (about it),** elle est restée vague là-dessus.

vaguely ['veɪglɪ] *adv* (*to look*) d'un air vague; (*to remember, express*) vaguement, confusément; (*faintly*) vaguement; (*slightly*) légèrement.

vagueness ['veɪgnɪs] *n* caractère *m* vague, vague *m*, imprécision *f*; (*of shape, outline, photograph*) manque *m* de netteté; (*of story, report, memory etc*) manque de précision.

vain [veɪn] *adj* **(a)** (*conceited*) vaniteux, orgueilleux; **she was v. about her beauty,** elle était fière de sa beauté; **as v. as a peacock,** fier comme Artaban; **(b)** (*unavailing*) vain, inutile, stérile; **v. efforts,** efforts vains *ou* inutiles; **(c)** (*hope*) vain; (*pleasure*) futile; **v. promises,** vaines promesses, promesses vaines; **(d) in v.,** en vain, vainement; **to labour in v.,** travailler en vain, perdre sa peine; **her efforts were in vain,** ses efforts ont été inutiles; **it was all in v.,** c'était peine perdue; **to take God's name in v.,** invoquer le nom de Dieu en vain; *F* **who's taking my name in v.?** qui est-ce qui parle de moi?

vainglorious [veɪn'glɔːrɪəs] *adj Fml* vaniteux, orgueilleux.

vaingloriously [veɪn'glɔːrɪəslɪ] *adv Fml* vaniteusement, orgueilleusement.

vainglory [veɪn'glɔːrɪ] *n Fml* vanité *f*, orgueil *m*.

vainly ['veɪnlɪ] *adv* **(a)** (*uselessly*) vainement, en vain, inutilement; **(b)** (*conceitedly*) vaniteusement, avec vanité.

valance ['væləns] *n* **(a)** (*on side of bed*) frange *f* de lit; **(b)** (*pelmet*) cantonnière *f*, lambrequin *m*.

vale [veɪl] *n Arch & Lit* vallée *f*; (*small*) vallon *m*; **this v. of tears,** cette vallée de larmes.

valediction [vælɪ'dɪkʃən] *n* **(a)** (*farewell*) adieu(x) *m(pl)*;

(b) *US* = **VALEDICTORY 2.**

valedictorian [vælɪdɪk'tɔːrɪən] *n Am Univ & Sch* membre *m* d'une promotion qui prononce le discours d'adieu.

valedictory [vælɪ'dɪktərɪ] **1** *adj* (*allocution, dîner*) d'adieu. **2** *n Am Univ & Sch* discours *m* d'adieu (*à la sortie d'une promotion etc*).

valence ['veɪləns] *n Am* = **VALENCY.**

valency ['veɪlənsɪ] *n Br Ch* valence *f*.

valentine ['væləntaɪn] *n* **(a) v. (card),** = carte envoyée le jour de la Saint-Valentin; **(b)** (*recipient of card*) celui *ou* celle qui reçoit une carte envoyée le jour de la Saint-Valentin; **Robert is my v.,** c'est Robert que j'aime.

Valentine ['væləntaɪn] *n* Valentin *m*, Valentine *f*; **(Saint) V.'s Day,** la Saint-Valentin (*le 14 février*).

valerian [və'leərɪən] *n Bot Pharm* valériane *f*.

valet[1] ['vælei, 'vælɪt] *n* (*servant*) valet *m* de chambre; (*in hotel*) = employé qui s'occupe de l'entretien des vêtements des clients; *Am* = employé d'un hôtel ou d'un restaurant qui se charge de garer les voitures des clients; **v. service,** service *m* de nettoyage des vêtements.

valet[2] *vt* (**valeted** ['vælɪtɪd]) **(a)** (*of servant*) servir (*qn*) comme valet de chambre; **(b) to v. a car,** laver et nettoyer une voiture; **valeting service,** service *m* de nettoyage des vêtements; **can I have my suit valeted?,** puis-je faire nettoyer mon costume?

valetudinarian [vælɪtjuːdɪ'neərɪən] *adj & n* valétudinaire *mf*.

Valhalla [væl'hælə] *n Myth* Walhalla *m*.

valiant ['vælɪənt] *adj* courageux, vaillant, valeureux; **to make a v. effort,** faire un courageux effort (**to do,** pour faire).

valiantly ['vælɪəntlɪ] *adv* courageusement, vaillamment, valeureusement.

valid ['vælɪd] *adj* (*contrat, document etc*) valide, valable; (*passeport*) en règle; **v. argument,** argument *m* valable *ou* solide; **ticket v. for three months,** billet bon pour trois mois; **no longer v.,** périmé.

validly ['vælɪdlɪ] *adv* validement, valablement.

validate ['vælɪdeɪt] *vt* valider, rendre valable (*un acte*); *US* **to v. an election,** valider une élection.

validation [vælɪ'deɪʃən] *n* validation *f*.

validity [və'lɪdɪtɪ] *n* validité *f*, justesse *f*; force *f* (*d'un argument*).

valise [və'liːs, -iːz] *n Old-fashioned Am* valise *f*, sac *m* de voyage.

Valium ® ['vælɪəm] *n* Valium ® *m*; **to be on V.,** prendre du Valium; **the doctor has put her on V.,** le docteur l'a mise au Valium.

Valkyrie ['vælkɪrɪ] *n Myth* Walkyrie *f*, Valkyrie *f*.

valley ['vælɪ] *n* **(a)** vallée *f*; (*small*) vallon *m*; **the Rhone V.,** la vallée du Rhône; **(b)** *Constr* noue *f*; cornière *f* (*de toit*).

valor ['vælər] *n US* = **VALOUR.**

valorization [væləraɪ'zeɪʃən] *n* valorisation *f*.

valorize ['væləraɪz] *vt Com Fin* valoriser.

valorous ['vælərəs] *adj Fml* valeureux, vaillant.

valour, *US* **valor** ['vælər] *n* courage *m*, valeur *f*, vaillance *f*, bravoure *f*; **to be decorated for v.,** (*of soldier, police officer etc*) être décoré pour son courage.

valuable ['væljʊəb(ə)l] **1** *adj* **(a)** (*object, help, time*) précieux; (*object*) de valeur, de prix; **v. gift,** cadeau de valeur; **she has given years of v. service,** elle a donné des années de bons et loyaux services; **(b)** (*assessable*) évaluable. **2** *npl* **valuables,** objets *mpl* de valeur *ou* de prix.

valuation [væljʊ'eɪʃən] *n Fin* **(a)** (*action*) évaluation *f*, estimation *f*, appréciation *f*; *Jur* prisée *f* et estimation; (*by expert*) expertise *f*; **to get a v. of sth,** faire expertiser qch; **to make a v. of the goods,** faire l'expertise des marchandises; **(b)** (*amount*) valeur estimée; **the v. on the house was £50,000,** la valeur estimée de la maison était de 50 000 livres; **to set too high/too low a v. on goods,** surestimer/sous-estimer des marchandises; *Fig* **to take** *or* **accept s.o. at their own v.,** estimer qn selon l'opinion qu'il a de lui-même.

valuator ['væljʊeɪtər] *n Am* = **valuer.**

value[1] ['væljuː] *n* **(a)** (*worth, usefulness*) valeur *f*, prix *m*; **to be of v.,** (*of jewellery etc*) avoir de la valeur; **of great v.,** de grande *ou* haute valeur; **your help/contribution was of great v.,** votre aide/contribution a été très précieuse; **to be of great sentimental v.,** avoir une grande valeur sentimentale; **of little v.,** de peu de valeur; **to be of little v.,** être sans grande valeur; **of no v.,** sans valeur; **it is nothing of any v.,** ce n'est rien qui ait une quelconque valeur; **to lose v., to fall in v.,** s'avilir; *Fin* se dévaloriser; **loss of v., fall in v.,** dévalorisation *f*; **to have a certain v.,** valoir son prix; **to set a high/low v. on sth,** attribuer une haute/faible valeur à qch; **to set a v. upon sth,** (*prize*) priser qch; (*evaluate*) évaluer qch; *Com* attribuer une cote de valeur à qch; **goods to the v. of,** marchandises d'une valeur de; **to set too high a v. on sth,** attacher trop de valeur *ou* de prix à qch, surestimer qch; **what will this do to the v. of property?,** quel effet est-ce que ça va avoir sur le prix de l'immobilier?; **v. judgment,** jugement *m* de valeur; **commercial** *or* **market v.,** (*worth*) valeur marchande; (*price*) cours *m*; **replacement v.,** valeur de remplacement; **it's good v.,** c'est très avantageux; **at £2 it's very good v.,** à 2 livres, c'est une bonne affaire *ou* c'est intéressant; **v. for money,** (*heading on restaurant or wine review*) rapport *m* qualité/prix; **to get (good) v. for one's money,** en avoir pour son argent; **the large size gives you better v. (for your money),** le grand format est plus avantageux; **get better v. for your money with XYZ,** (*advertising slogan*) XYZ vous en donne plus pour votre argent; **he gives you v. for money,** il vous en donne pour votre argent; **it's v. for money,** cela vaut le coup, cela n'est pas cher;

(b) *Math Mus Ling* valeur *f*; **let y have the v. 15,** soit y égale 15; *Th* **to give full v. to each word,** donner du poids à chaque mot;

(c) values, (*standards*) valeurs *fpl*; **sense of values,** sens *m* des valeurs; **moral values,** valeurs morales; **according to a set of values,** selon certains principes.

value[2] *vt* **(a)** (*evaluate*) *Com* évaluer, estimer, apprécier (*des marchandises*); faire l'expertise de (*mobilier*); **to v. a house at £50,000,** évaluer une maison à 50 000 livres; **to get sth valued,** faire expertiser qch, faire évaluer qch; **(b)** (*prize*) estimer, tenir à, faire grand cas de (*qn, qch*); **to v. s.o. as a friend,** tenir à *ou* apprécier qn en tant qu'ami; **if you v. your life,** si vous tenez à la vie.

value-added [væljuː'ædɪd] *adj Fin* (*product, service etc*) à valeur ajoutée; **high v.-a. product,** produit à haute valeur ajoutée; **v.-a. tax,** taxe à la valeur ajoutée.

valued ['væljuːd] *adj* estimé, précieux; **my v. friend Mr Martin,** M. Martin dont l'amitié m'est si précieuse; **a v. employee,** un employé estimé.

valueless ['væljʊlɪs] *adj* sans valeur.

valuer ['væljʊər] *n* (*of antique etc*) expert *m*; **official v.,** commissaire-priseur *m*, *pl* commissaires-priseurs.

valuing ['væljʊɪŋ] *n* évaluation *f*, estimation *f*, appréciation *f*.

valve [vælv] *n* **(a)** soupape *f*; (*tap, cock*) robinet *m*; **(clack** *or* **flap) v.,** (soupape à) clapet *m*, valve *f*; *Aut* **inlet/outlet v.,** soupape d'admission/d'échappement; **(b)** *Aut Cycling* valve *f* (*de chambre à air*); **v. cap,** capuchon *m ou* chapeau *m* de valve; **(c)** vanne *f*; **gas/water v.,** vanne à gaz/d'eau; **(sluice) v.,** vanne de communication; **(d)** *Mus* piston *m* (*d'un instrument en cuivre*); **(e)** *Anat* valvule *f* (*du cœur*); **(f)** *Electron* lampe *f* (*de radio*), valve *f*.

valved [vælvd] *adj* à valve(s), à soupape(s); *Mus* (*instrument*) à pistons; **two-v.,** (*mollusc*) bivalve.

valvular ['vælvjʊlər] *adj Med etc* valvulaire.

vamoose [və'muːs] *vi Old-fashioned Am F* décamper, filer.

vamp[1] [væmp] *n* (*on shoe*) claque *f*, empeigne *m*.

vamp[2] *n Mus F* accompagnement tapoté *ou* improvisé.

vamp[3] *vt & vi Mus F* tapoter au piano (*un accompagnement improvisé*); improviser (*un accompagnement*).

vamp[4] *n Old-fashioned Br F* femme fatale, vamp *f*.

vamp[5] *Old-fashioned Br F* **1** *vt* (*of woman*) vamper (*un homme*). **2** *vi* jouer la femme fatale.

►**vamp up** *vtsep F* rafistoler (*qch*).

vampire ['væmpaɪər] *n* **(a)** *Myth & Fig* vampire *m*; **(b)** (*animal*) **v. (bat),** vampire.

vampirism ['væmpaɪərɪz(ə)m] *n Myth & Fig* vampirisme *m*.

van[1] [væn] *n Mil & Fig* avant-garde *f*; *Mil* front *m* (*de bataille*); *Fig* **to be in the v.,** être à l'avant-garde.

van[2] *n* **(a)** *Br* (*small*) camionnette *f*; (*large*) camion *m*; **furniture** *or* **removal v.,** camionnette de déménagement; **delivery v.,** camion *m ou* camionnette de livraison; **outside broadcasting v.,** car *m* de radio-reportage; **v. driver,** chauffeur *m* de camionnette; *Am* **v. pool,** = coopérative *f* de transport (*en vertu de laquelle les employés d'une société se rendent sur leur lieu de travail dans une camionnette souvent payée par la société en question*); **(b)** *Br Rail* wagon *m*, fourgon *m*; **goods v.,** wagon de marchandises; **luggage v.,** fourgon à bagages.

van[3] *n esp Br Tennis* avantage *m*; **v. in,** avantage dedans *ou* au servant; **v. out,** avantage dehors *ou* au relanceur.

vanadium [və'neɪdɪəm] *n Ch* vanadium *m*.

V & A [viːən'eɪ] *n Br abbr* **Victoria and Albert Museum.**

vandal ['vænd(ə)l] *n* vandale *mf.*

vandalism ['vændəlɪz(ə)m] *n* vandalisme *m*; **act of v.,** acte *m* de vandalisme.

vandalize ['vændəlaɪz] *vt* saccager (*un bâtiment etc*); **the telephone's been vandalized again,** le téléphone a été saccagé une fois de plus; **several pictures have been vandalized,** plusieurs tableaux ont été mutilés (par des vandales).

vane [veɪn] *n* **(a)** (*for indicating wind direction*) girouette *f*; **(b)** moulinet *m* (*d'un anémomètre*); turbine *f* (*d'un compteur à eau*); bras *m* (*de moulin à vent*); pale *f* (*d'hélice de ventilateur*); aube *f*, ailette *f*, palette *f* (*de turbine*); aube (*de tunnel aérodynamique*); **the vanes,** l'aubage *m* (*d'une turbine, d'un tunnel aérodynamique*); **(c)** ailette *f* (*d'une bombe, d'une torpille*); **the vanes,** l'empennage *m.*

vanguard ['vængɑːd] *n Mil* tête *f* d'avant-garde; *Fig* **to be in the v. of a movement,** être un des pionniers d'un mouvement; **to be in the v. of technological progress,** être à la pointe du progrès technologique.

vanilla [və'nɪlə] *n* **v. (plant),** vanille *f*, vanillier *m*; **v. pod,** gousse *f* de vanille; **v. flavouring,** vanille; **flavoured with v., v. flavoured,** vanillé, (parfumé) à la vanille; **v. essence,** extrait *m* de vanille; **v. ice,** glace *f* à la vanille; **v. sugar,** sucre vanillé.

vanillin [və'nɪlɪn] *n Ch* vanilline *f.*

vanish ['vænɪʃ] *vi* disparaître; (*of visions, suspicions*) se dissiper, s'évanouir; (*of difficulties*) s'aplanir; **to make sth v.,** faire disparaître qch; (*of magician*) escamoter qch; **elephants are vanishing from the earth,** les éléphants sont en voie de disparition; **to v. from sight,** disparaître aux yeux de qn; **to v. without trace,** disparaître sans laisser de trace; **to v. into thin air,** se volatiliser; **he's vanished,** il a disparu; *F* (*to avoid sth, s.o.*) il s'est éclipsé; **she saw her last hope v.,** elle a vu s'évanouir son dernier espoir.

vanishing ['vænɪʃɪŋ] **1** *adj* qui disparaît; *Old-fashioned* **v. cream,** crème *f* de jour. **2** *n* disparition *f*; *Art* **v. point,** point *m* de fuite; *Fig* **profits have dwindled to v. point,** les bénéfices se sont trouvés réduits à néant; **to do a v. trick,** (*of magician*) faire un tour de passe-passe; *F* (*disappear from sight*) s'éclipser.

vanitory ['vænɪtərɪ] *n esp Am* (*Br* = **vanity unit**) table *f* de toilette avec lavabo encastré.

vanity ['vænɪtɪ] *n* **(a)** (*conceit*) vanité *f*, orgueil *m*; **to do sth out of v.,** faire qch par vanité *ou* pour la gloriole; **v. bag,** (petit) sac *m* de dame (pour le soir); **v. case,** (*make-up bag*) nécessaire *m* de maquillage; (*small case*) mallette *f* de toilette, vanity-case *m*; **v. (unit),** table *f* de toilette avec lavabo encastré; *Am* **v. press,** maison *f* d'édition qui publie des livres à compte d'auteur; **(b)** (*uselessness*) vanité *f*, vide *m* (*des grandeurs humaines*); futilité *f* (*d'une tentative*).

vanquish ['væŋkwɪʃ] **1** *vt* vaincre, triompher de (*qn, ses passions*). **2** *vi* être vainqueur, vaincre.

vanquisher ['væŋkwɪʃər] *n* vainqueur *m.*

vantage ['vɑːntɪdʒ] *n* **(a) (point of) v., v. point,** terrain avantageux, position avantageuse; **to take up a v. point,** choisir une position avantageuse; **from our v. point we could see ...,** de notre position avantageuse nous pouvions voir ...; *Fig* **from the v. point of the twentieth century, it is easy to ...,** avec le recul qui nous est possible au vingtième siècle, il est facile de ...; **(b)** *Tennis* avantage *m.*

vapid ['væpɪd] *adj* insipide, plat; **v. style,** style *m* fade.

vapidity [və'pɪdɪtɪ] *n* évent *m* (*d'une boisson*); fadeur *f*, insipidité *f* (*d'une boisson, de la conversation*); platitude *f* (*du style*).

vapor ['veɪpər] *n US* = **VAPOUR.**

vaporization [veɪpəraɪ'zeɪʃən] *n* **(a)** vaporisation *f*; **(b)** pulvérisation *f* (*d'un liquide*); *Aut* carburation *f* (*du combustible*).

vaporize ['veɪpəraɪz] **1** *vt* vaporiser, gazéifier; (*atomize*) pulvériser, vaporiser (*un liquide*); *Aut* carburiser (*le combustible*). **2** *vi* se vaporiser, se gazéifier; (*of liquid*) se pulvériser.

vaporizer ['veɪpəraɪzər] *n* **(a)** (*evaporator*) vaporisateur *m*; *Aut etc* réchauffeur *m*; **(b)** *Med* atomiseur *m*, vaporisateur *m.*

vaporous ['veɪpərəs] *adj Fml* (*ciel, style*) vaporeux.

vapour, *US* **vapor** ['veɪpər] *n* **(a)** vapeur *f*; buée *f* (*sur les vitres*); *Phys* vapeur (*d'eau, d'alcool*); **v. laden,** (*atmosphère*) humide; **v. bath,** *Med* bain *m* de vapeur; étuve *f* humide (*de hammam*); *Constr* **v. barrier,** coupe-vapeur *m*; *Av* **v. trail,** traînée *f* de condensation; **(b)** *Med Arch* **to have the vapours,** avoir des vapeurs.

variability [veərɪə'bɪlɪtɪ] *n* variabilité *f* (*du temps etc*); *Biol* inconstance *f* (*de type*).

variable ['veərɪəb(ə)l] **1** *adj* variable, changeant, inconstant; *Astron* **v. star,** étoile *f* variable; **v. motion,** mouvement varié; *Math* **v. quantity,** quantité *f* variable; **v. (at will),** réglable. **2** *n Math Comptr* variable *f*; *Econ* **random v.,** variable aléatoire.

variably ['veərɪəblɪ] *adv* variablement.

variance ['veərɪəns] *n* **(a)** (*disagreement*) désaccord *m*; discorde *f*; **to be at v. with s.o.,** être en désaccord *ou* en contradiction avec qn; (*argue*) avoir un différend avec qn; **his views are totally at v. with mine,** ses opinions sont totalement différentes des miennes; **historians are at v. on this point,** les historiens diffèrent entre eux *ou* ne sont pas d'accord sur ce point; **theory at v. with the facts,** théorie incompatible *ou* en contradiction avec les faits; **(b)** (*difference*) variation *f* (*de température, volume etc*); *Ch* variance *f.*

variant ['veərɪənt] **1** *adj* différent (**from,** de); **v. reading,** variante *f*; **v. spelling,** variante (orthographique). **2** *n* variante *f.*

variation [veərɪ'eɪʃən] *n* **(a)** (*difference*) variation *f*, changement *m*; **magnetic v.,** déclinaison *f* magnétique (locale); **(b)** (*disagreement*) différence *f*, écart *m*; **v. between two readings,** écart entre deux lectures (*d'un appareil scientifique*); **(c)** *Mus* variation *f* (**on,** sur); **theme and variations,** thème et variations.

varicoloured, *US* **-colored** ['veərɪkʌləd] *adj Fml* aux couleurs variées, versicolore.

varicose ['værɪkəʊs] *adj Med* variqueux; **v. vein,** varice *f*; **v. stockings,** bas *m* à varices.

varied ['veəriːd] *adj* **(a)** varié, divers; **the scenery was very v.,** le paysage était très varié; **(b)** *Biol* multicolore, versicolore.

variegated ['veərɪgeɪtɪd] *adj* **(a)** (*different*) varié, divers; **(b)** (*multi-coloured*) bigarré, bariolé, diapré, versicolore; *Bot* panaché; **to become v.,** (*of flower, leaf*) se panacher.

variegation [veərɪ'geɪʃən] *n* diversité *f* de couleurs, bigarrure *f*; *Bot* panachure *f*, diaprure *f.*

varietal [və'raɪətəl] *n* (*wine*) = vin produit entièrement ou principalement à partir d'une seule variété de raisin.

variety [və'raɪətɪ] *n* **(a)** (*diversity*) variété *f*, diversité *f*; **hillocks that give v. to the landscape,** petites collines qui accidentent le paysage; *Prov* **v. is the spice of life,** le changement donne du piquant à la vie; **(b)** (*assortment*) **a v. of patterns,** un assortiment de modèles; **a large** *or* **wide v. of materials,** un grand *ou* vaste choix de tissus; **for a v. of reasons,** pour des raisons diverses; **in a v. of ways,** de diverses manières, diversement; *Am* **v. meat,** abats *mpl*; *Am* **v. store,** grand magasin; **(c)** *Bot* variété *f* (*de fleur etc*); **(d)** *Th* variétés *fpl*; **v. show/theatre,** spectacle *m*/théâtre *m* de variétés; **v. turns,** numéros *mpl* de music hall; **v. artist,** artiste *mf* de variétés; **to work in v.,** travailler dans le monde des variétés.

variola [və'raɪələ] *n Med* variole *f*, petite vérole.

various ['veərɪəs] *adj* divers; **of v. kinds,** de diverses sortes; **to talk about v. things,** parler de chose(s) et d'autre(s) *ou* de choses diverses; **her skills are many and v.,** ses aptitudes sont nombreuses et diverses; **known under v. names,** connu sous des noms divers; **v. people saw it,** plusieurs personnes l'ont vu; **for v. reasons,** pour des raisons diverses; **at v. times,** à diverses reprises, en diverses occasions; **in v. ways,** de diverses *ou* plusieurs manières, diversement.

variously ['veərɪəslɪ] *adv* diversement, de diverses *ou* plusieurs manières; **v. estimated at ...,** estimé par diverses sources à ... .

varlet ['vɑːlɪt] *Arch* coquin *m*, vaurien *m.*

varmint ['vɑːmɪnt] *n Arch F* **young v.,** petit polisson.

varnish¹ ['vɑːnɪʃ] *n* vernis *m*; **spirit v.,** vernis à l'alcool; **transparent** *or* **clear v.,** vernis incolore; *esp Br* **nail v.,** vernis à ongles; **v. remover,** *Ind etc* décapant *m* pour vernis; (*for nails*) dissolvant *m*; **(coat of) v.,** (couche *f* de) vernis.

varnish² *vt* vernir (*du bois, un tableau*); vernir, vernisser (*de la poterie*).

► **varnish over** *vtsep Fig* déguiser (*les faits*); glisser sur, jeter un voile complaisant sur (*les défauts de qn*); maquiller, déguiser (*la vérité*).

varnisher ['vɑːnɪʃər] *n* vernisseur *m.*

varnishing ['vɑːnɪʃɪŋ] *n* vernissage *m*; **v. day,** vernissage (*d'une exposition*).

varsity ['vɑːsɪtɪ] **1** *n* **(a)** *Br F* université *f*, *F* fac *f*; **the V. match,** match *m* entre Oxford et Cambridge; **(b)** *US* équipe *f* universitaire. **2** *adj* universitaire.

vary ['veərɪ] **1** *vt* varier, diversifier (*son style*); apporter de la variété à (*un programme*); **to v. one's methods,** changer de méthodes; **to v. one's route,** changer d'itinéraire de temps en temps. **2** *vi* varier, changer; *Biol* s'écarter du type, présenter une variation; **it varies from day to day,** cela change d'un jour sur l'autre; **it varies with the weather,** ça change en fonction du temps; **it varies,** ça dépend; **to v. in quality,** varier en qualité; **to v. from sth,** dévier de *ou* s'écarter de *ou* différer de qch; **as to the date, authors v.,** les auteurs ne sont pas d'accord *ou* varient quant à la date.

varying ['veərɪɪŋ] **1** *adj* qui varie, variable, changeant; **with v. results,** avec des résultats plus ou moins satisfaisants. **2** *n* variation *f*, changement *m*.

vascular ['væskjʊlər] *adj Biol* vasculaire.

vas deferens [vaez'defərenz] *n Anat* canal déférent.

vase [vɑːz, *Am* veɪz] *n* vase *m*; **flower v.,** vase à fleurs.

vasectomy [və'sektəmɪ] *n Surg* vasectomie *f*; **to have a v.,** se faire faire une vasectomie.

Vaseline ® ['væsəliːn] *n* vaseline *f*.

vasoconstriction [veɪzəʊkən'strɪkʃən] *n Med* vasoconstriction *f*.

vasoconstrictor [veɪzəʊkən'strɪktər] *Med* **1** *n* vasoconstricteur *m*. **2** *adj* vasconstricteur, -trice.

vasodilation [veɪzəʊdaɪ'leɪʃən] *n Med* vasodilatation *f*.

vasodilator [veɪzəʊdaɪ'leɪtər] *Med* **1** *n* vasodilatateur *m*. **2** *adj* vasodilateur, -trice.

vasomotor ['veɪzəʊməʊtər] *adj Anat* vasomoteur, -trice.

vassal ['væs(ə)l] *adj & n Hist* vassal *m*, -aux; *Fig* subordonné, -ée, vassal; **v. state,** pays vassal.

vassalage ['væsəlɪdʒ] *n Hist* vassalité *f*, vasselage *m*; *Fig* sujétion *f*.

vast [vɑːst] *adj* vaste, immense; **a v. number of people,** un extrêmement grand nombre de gens; **a v. expanse of territory,** une grande étendue de territoire; **his v. knowledge,** son immense savoir; **to spend a v. amount** *or* **v. sums (of money),** dépenser de grosses sommes d'argent; **there's a v. difference between them,** il y a une différence énorme entre eux.

vastly ['vɑːstlɪ] *adv* vastement, immensément; **they're not v. different,** ils ne sont pas très différents.

vastness ['vɑːstnɪs] *n* immensité *f*, vaste étendue *f*.

vat [væt] *n* **(a)** (*container*) cuve *f*, bac *m*; **v. dyes,** colorants *mpl* de cuve; **v. for carrying grapes,** bouge *m*; **(b)** (*contents*) cuvée *f*.

VAT [viːeɪ'tiː, væt] *n* (*abbr* **value added tax**) TVA *f*.

vatful ['vætfʊl] *n* (*quantity*) cuvée *f*.

Vatican ['vætɪkən] *n* **the V.,** le Vatican; **the V. library,** la bibliothèque vaticane, la Vaticane; **the V. City,** la cité du Vatican; **the V. Council,** le concile du Vatican; *Hist* **the V. State,** les Etats pontificaux.

vaudeville ['vɔːdəvɪl] *n Am Th* variétés *fpl*.

vault¹ [vɔːlt, vɒlt] *n* **(a)** *Archit* voûte *f*; **tunnel v.,** voûte cylindrique; **fan v.,** voûte en éventail; **ribbed v.,** voûte d'ogives *ou* à nervures; *Fig* **the v. of heaven,** la voûte céleste; **(b)** *Constr* chapelle *f* (*de four de boulangerie*); voûte *f* (*d'un fourneau*); **(c)** *Anat* **cranial v.,** voûte cranienne; **(d)** (*under ground*) souterrain *m*; **bank v.,** chambre forte; **(wine) v.,** cave *f*, cellier *m*; **(wine) vaults,** débit *m* de boissons; **family v.,** caveau *m* de famille.

vault² **1** *vt* **to v. (over),** voûter (*une cave*). **2** *vi* (*of roof*) former une voûte.

vault³ *n Gym* saut *m* (*en s'aidant de la main*); saut au cheval d'arçons; **pole v.,** saut à la perche.

vault⁴ **1** *vi* sauter (*en s'aidant de la main ou des mains*); **he vaulted over the gate,** il a sauté la barrière; **to v. into the saddle,** sauter en selle. **2** *vt* sauter (*une barrière*), franchir (*une barrière*) d'un saut (*en s'aidant de la main ou des mains*).

vaulted ['vɔːltɪd, vɒl-] *adj* voûté, en (forme de) voûte.

vaulter ['vɔːltər, 'vɒl-] *n* sauteur, -euse; (*acrobatic*) voltigeur, -euse; **pole v.,** sauteur *m* à la perche.

vaulting¹ ['vɔːltɪŋ, vɒl-] *n* voûte(s) *f(pl)*; **barrel v.,** voûte(s) en berceau.

vaulting² **1** *n Gym* exercice *m* de saut; voltige *f* (*sur le cheval d'arçons*); **v. horse,** cheval *m* d'arçons, cheval-arçons *m*, *pl* chevaux-arçons; **pole v.,** saut *m* à la perche. **2** *adj Fig* **v. ambition,** ambition démesurée.

vaunt [vɔːnt] *vt* vanter (*qch*), se vanter de (*qch*), se faire gloire de (*qch*); **our much vaunted justice,** notre justice tant vantée *ou* dont on fait tant l'éloge.

vaunting ['vɔːntɪŋ] *n* jactance *f*, fanfaronnade *f*.

VC [viː'siː] *n Br Mil* (*abbr* **Victoria Cross**) = la plus haute distinction britannique, accordée pour récompenser le courage de quelqu'un; **to be awarded the VC,** recevoir la Victoria Cross; **John Smith VC,** = John Smith, titulaire de la Victoria Cross.

VCR [viːsiː'ɑːr] *n abbr* **video cassette recorder**.

VD [viː'diː] *n Med* (*abbr* **venereal disease**) **VD clinic,** centre *m* de traitement des maladies vénériennes.

VDT [viːdiː'tiː] *n Comptr abbr Br* **visual** *or Am* **video display terminal**.

VDU [viːdiː'juː] *n Comptr* (*abbr* **visual display unit**) visu *f*.

veal [viːl] *n Culin* veau *m*; **v. cutlet,** côtelette *f* de veau; **v. olive,** alouette *f* sans tête.

vector ['vektər] *n Math Phys Med* vecteur *m*; **v. function,** fonction vectorielle; *Med* **v.-borne disease,** maladie transmise par (agent) vecteur; *Comptr* **v. generator,** générateur *m* de vecteurs; **v. processing,** traitement *m* de vecteurs.

vectorial [vek'tɔːrɪəl] *adj Math* vectoriel.

veep [viːp] *n US F* vice-président, -ente, *pl* vice-président(e)s.

veer¹ ['vɪər] *n* (*of wind*) changement *m* de direction; (*of ship*) virement *m* de bord; *Fig* (*of opinion*) revirement *m*.

veer² **1** *vi* (*of wind*) tourner; (*of ship*) virer de bord; (*of car, road*) tourner abruptement, virer; **to v. at anchor,** rôder sur son ancre; **to v. off course,** dévier du cap fixé, dévier de sa route; *Aut* **he veered to the right,** il a viré à droite; *Aut* **the car veered off the road,** la voiture a fait une embardée et a quitté la route; *Fig* **the conversation veered to politics,** la conversation a tourné à la politique. **2** *vt* (faire) virer (*un navire*) de bord.

veer³ **1** *vt Nau* **to v. (away, out),** filer (*du câble*). **2** *vi* **to v. and haul,** *Nau* filer et haler (un cordage) alternativement; *Fig* manœuvrer avec adresse.

►**veer round** *vi* (*of person*) changer d'opinion; **to v. round to an opinion,** se ranger à une opinion.

veg [vedʒ] *n(pl) Br F* légume(s) *m(pl)*; **meat and two v.,** plat comportant de la viande et deux légumes.

vegan ['viːgən] *n* végétalien, -ienne.

veganism ['viːgənɪz(ə)m] *n* végétalisme *m*.

vegetable ['vedʒtəb(ə)l] **1** *adj* végétal, -aux; **the v. kingdom,** le règne végétal; **v. life,** la vie végétale; **v. oils,** huiles végétales; *Fig* **to lead a v. existence,** mener une existence végétative. **2** *n* **(a)** *Culin* légume *m*; **to grow vegetables,** cultiver *ou* faire pousser des légumes; **green vegetables,** légumes verts; **early vegetables,** primeurs *fpl*; *Fig* **to live like a v.,** végéter, mener une vie végétative; *Fig* **the accident has left her a v.,** l'accident l'a privée de toutes ses facultés; **v. dish,** (*container*) légumier *m*; (*meal*) plat *m* de légumes; **v. garden,** (jardin) potager *m*; **v. knife,** couteau *m* à légume; **v. marrow,** courge *m*; *F* **v. oyster,** salsifis *f*; **v. slicer,** coupe-légumes *m inv*; **v. soup,** soupe *f* aux *ou* de légumes; **(b)** *Bot* végétal *m*.

vegetal ['vedʒɪt(ə)l] *adj Bot* végétal, -aux.

vegetarian [vedʒɪ'teərɪən] *adj & n* végétarien, -ienne; **to be a v.,** être végétarien; **v. food,** nourriture végétarienne; **v. restaurant,** restaurant végétarien.

vegetarianism [vedʒɪ'teərɪənɪz(ə)m] *n* végétarisme *m*.

vegetate ['vedʒɪteɪt] *vi Pej* végéter; **to v. in an office,** végéter *ou* moisir dans un bureau.

vegetation [vedʒɪ'teɪʃən] *n* végétation *f*.

vegetative ['vedʒɪtətɪv, -teɪtɪv] *adj* végétatif; *Fig* **v. existence,** existence végétative.

veggie [vedʒɪ] *n F* **(a)** végétarien *m*; **(b)** *esp Am* légume *m*.

vehemence ['viːɪməns] *n* véhémence *f* (*du vent, d'un orateur*); impétuosité *f*, ardeur *f* (*de la jeunesse*).

vehement ['viːɪmənt] *adj* (*vent, orateur*) véhément; (*vent*) impétueux; (*amour*) passionné; (*attaque, effort*) violent.

vehemently ['viːɪməntlɪ] *adv* (*see adj*) avec véhémence; impétueusement.

vehicle ['viːɪk(ə)l] *n* **(a)** véhicule *m*; **(extra) long v.,** convoi *m* grande longueur, convoi exceptionnel; **heavy goods v.,** poids *m* lourd; **v. check-in,** (*at ferry*) contrôle *m* des véhicules; **(b)** *Fig* véhicule *m* (*de la pensée*); **the newspaper as a v. for advertising,** le journal comme moyen de publicité; **the play is merely a v. for his talents,** la pièce n'est qu'un moyen de mettre ses talents en valeur; **(c)** *Med* (agent) vecteur *m* (*d'un maladie*); **(d)** (*for paint*) véhicule *m*; **(e)** *Pharm* excipient *m*.

vehicular [vɪ'hɪkjʊlər] *adj* des véhicules, des voitures; **v. traffic,** circulation *f*; **closed to v. traffic,** interdit aux véhicules.

veil¹ [veɪl] *n* voile *m* (*de religieuse, de deuil*); voilette *f* (*de chapeau*); *Fig* voile, déguisement *m*; **bridal v.,** voile de mariée; *Rel* **to take the v.,** prendre le voile; *Jew Rel* **the v. of the temple,** le voile du temple; *Lit* **beyond the v.,** au delà de la tombe; **under the v. of anonymity/secrecy,**

sous le voile de l'anonymat/du secret; **to draw** *or* **throw a v. over sth,** jeter un voile sur qch.

veil² *vt* voiler (*son visage, un tableau*); voiler, cacher, dissimuler (*ses sentiments, desseins*); **their plans were veiled in secrecy,** leurs plans étaient gardés secrets; **to v. oneself,** se voiler; **to v. one's face,** se voiler la face.

veiled [veɪld] *adj* voilé, couvert d'un voile; *Fig* voilé, caché, dissimulé; **v. threats,** menaces déguisées; **to express oneself in v. terms,** s'exprimer en termes voilés; **v. hostility,** hostilité sourde; **a thinly v. reference to,** une référence à peine voilée à; **scarcely v. hostility,** hostilité à peine déguisée.

veiling ['veɪlɪŋ] *n* **(a)** (*action*) action *f ou* fait *m* de voiler (*la face*) *ou* de dissimuler (*la vérité etc*); **(b)** (*veils*) voile(s) *m(pl)*.

vein [veɪn] *n* **(a)** *Anat* veine *f*; *Bot Ent* nervure *f* (*de feuille, d'aile*); veine (*de feuille*); **he has noble blood in his veins,** il a du sang bleu dans les veines; **(b)** *Geol Min* veine *f*, filon *m*; (*in wood, marble*) veine; *Fig* **a v. of melancholy/humour,** une pointe de mélancolie/d'humour; **(c)** *Fig* (*manner, style*) veine *f*, disposition *f*, humeur *f*; **the poetic v.,** la veine poétique; **other remarks in the same v.,** d'autres observations faites dans le même esprit.

veined [veɪnd] *adj* veiné, à veines; *Bot Ent* nervuré.

veining ['veɪnɪŋ] *n* **(a) v. brush,** veinette *f*; **(b)** (*veins*) veinure *f*, marbrure *f*; **(c)** *Bot Ent* nervures *fpl*.

velar ['viːlər] *adj & n Ling* vélaire *f*.

Velcro ® ['velkrəʊ] *n* Velcro ® *m*; **V. fastener,** (*on shoe*) patte *f* Velcro; (*on coat*) fermeture *f* Velcro.

veld(t) [velt] *n* veld(t) *m*.

vellum ['veləm] *n* vélin *m*; **v. paper,** papier *m* vélin.

velocipede [vɪ'lɒsɪpiːd] *n Arch* vélocipède *m*.

velocity [vɪ'lɒsɪtɪ] *n* vélocité *f*, vitesse *f*.

velodrome ['viːlədrəʊm] *n* vélodrome *m*.

velour(s) [və'lʊər] *n Tex* (*velvet*) velours *m* de laine; (*felt*) feutre taupé; **v. (hat),** chapeau (en feutre) taupé.

velum, *pl* **-la** ['viːləm, -ə] *n Anat* voile *m* du palais.

velvet ['velvɪt] *n Tex* velours *m*; **black v.,** (*drink*) mélange *m* de champagne et de stout; **v. skirt/collar,** jupe *f*/col *m* de velours; **to have (a) skin like v.,** avoir une peau de pêche; **as smooth as v.,** (*skin*) doux comme du *ou* le velours; (*drink*) velouté; *Fig* **to be on v.,** (*in pleasant situation*) mener la vie de château; *Fig* **with v. tread,** à pas feutrés; *Fig* **an iron hand in a v. glove,** une main de fer dans un gant de velours.

velveteen [velvɪ'tiːn] *n Tex* velours *m* de coton; **v. jacket/***etc*, veste *f*/*etc* en velours de coton.

velvety ['velvɪtɪ] *adj* (*to appear, taste*) velouté; (*to the touch*) velouteux, doux comme du *ou* le velours; (*vin*) velouté, qui a du velouté.

venal ['viːn(ə)l] *adj* vénal, -aux.

venality [vɪ'nælɪtɪ] *n* vénalité *f*.

vend [vend] *vt esp Jur Admin* vendre; **machine that vends coffee,** distributeur automatique payant de café.

vendee [ven'diː] *n Jur* acquéreur *m*.

vendetta [ven'detə] *n* vendetta *f*; **to wage a v. against s.o.,** mener une vendetta contre qn.

vending ['vendɪŋ] *n* vente *f*; **v. machine,** distributeur *m* automatique payant.

vendor ['vendɔːr] *n* **(a)** *Com Jur* vendeur, -euse; *Comptr* fournisseur *m*; **street v.,** marchand ambulant; **(b)** (*machine*) distributeur *m* automatique.

veneer¹ [və'nɪər] *n* **(a)** (*covering*) placage *m*, revêtement *m*; (*material*) bois *m* de placage, bois à plaquer; **(b)** *Fig* masque *m*, apparence extérieure; vernis *m* (*de connaissances, de culture*); **a v. of politeness,** un vernis de politesse; **beneath the v. of politeness,** sous le masque de politesse.

veneer² *vt* plaquer (*le bois*) (**with,** avec).

venerable ['ven(ə)rəb(ə)l] *adj* (*vieillard etc*) vénérable.

venerate ['venəreɪt] *vt* avoir de la vénération pour (*qn*); *Lit* vénérer (*qn, qch*).

veneration [venə'reɪʃən] *n* vénération *f* (**for,** pour); **to hold s.o. in v.,** avoir de la vénération pour qn.

venereal [vɪ'nɪərɪəl] *adj Med* vénérien; **v. disease,** maladie *f* vénérienne.

venereology [vɪnɪərɪ'ɒlədʒɪ] *n Med* vénéréologie *f*.

venery ['venərɪ] *n Arch* **(a)** (*hunting*) vénérie *f*; **(b)** (*sexual gratification*) débauche sexuelle.

Venetian [vɪ'niːʃən] **1** *adj* vénitien; **V. blinds,** stores vénitiens; **V. glass,** verre *m* de Venise; *Sewing* **V. lace,** point *m* de Venise. **2** *n* Vénitien, -ienne.

Venezuela [vene'zweɪlə] *n* le Vénézuéla.

Venezuelan [vene'zweɪl(ə)n] **1** *adj* vénézuélien. **2** *n* Vénézuélien, -ienne.

vengeance ['ven(d)ʒəns] *n* vengeance *f*; **to take v. on s.o.,** tirer vengeance de qn, se venger de qn; **to take v. for sth,** tirer vengeance de qch; venger (*la mort de qn*); *Fig* **with a v.,** furieusement; à outrance; (*pleuvoir*) pour de bon; (*travailler*) d'arrache-pied.

vengeful ['ven(d)ʒfʊl] *adj* (*person*) vindicatif.

vengefulness ['ven(d)ʒfʊlnɪs] *n* caractère vindicatif, esprit *m* de vengeance.

venial ['viːnɪəl] *adj* **(a)** *Rel* (*péché*) véniel; **(b)** (*faute*) sans gravité, véniel.

veniality [viːnɪ'ælɪtɪ] *n* **(a)** *Rel* caractère véniel (*d'un péché*); **(b)** caractère excusable *ou* véniel (*d'une faute*).

Venice ['venɪs] *n* Venise *f*.

venison ['venɪs(ə)n] *n Culin* venaison *f*; **haunch of v.,** quartier *m* de chevreuil.

venom ['venəm] *n* (*poison*) & *Fig* venin *m*; **to say with v.,** dire avec méchanceté *ou* malveillance.

venomous ['venəməs] *adj* (*snake*) venimeux; (*plant*) vénéneux; *Fig* (*criticism*) venimeux, envenimé; **v. look,** regard venimeux; **v. tongue,** langue *f* de vipère.

venomously ['venəməslɪ] *adv* d'une manière venimeuse, avec méchanceté.

venous ['viːnəs] *adj* (*système, sang*) veineux.

vent¹ [vent] *n* **(a)** trou *m*, orifice *m* (*pour laisser entrer l'air, sortir un gaz*); évent *m* (*d'échappement de gaz, d'une fusée spatiale*); prise *f* d'air (*d'un réservoir à essence*); soupirail *m*, -aux (*d'un puits d'aérage*); trou d'air *ou* d'évent (*d'un moule*); *El* trou d'aération (*d'un élément de pile*); tuyau *m* (*de cheminée*); *Geol* cheminée *f* (*de volcan*); *Av* cheminée (*de parachute*); **v. hole,** évent; **(b)** *Fig* **to give v. to one's grief/anger/indignation,** donner libre cours à sa douleur/sa colère/son indignation; **to give v. to one's spleen,** décharger sa bile.

vent² *vt* **(a)** décharger, vider (*une canalisation*) des gaz; évacuer (*les gaz d'une canalisation, la vapeur d'une chaudière*); munir (*un réservoir*) d'un évent *ou* d'une prise d'air; **(b)** *Fig* donner libre cours à, laisser éclater, exhaler (*sa colère*); **to v. one's spleen/anger on s.o.,** décharger sa bile/épancher sa colère sur qn.

vent³ *n* fente *f* (*dans la basque d'un veston*).

ventilate ['ventɪleɪt] *vt* **(a)** aérer (*une chambre*); ventiler (*un tunnel*); éventer (*une mine*); **(b)** *Fig* mettre (*une question*) au grand jour; soumettre (*une question*) à la discussion.

ventilation [ventɪ'leɪʃən] *n* **(a)** (*of room*) aération *f*; (*of machine*) ventilation *f*; (*of mine*) aérage *m*; *Min* **v. shaft,** puits *m* de ventilation *ou* d'aération *ou* d'aérage; **v. system,** système *m* d'aération *ou* de ventilation; **(b)** *Fig* discussion *f* publique (*d'une question*).

ventilator ['ventɪleɪtər] *n* **(a)** ventilateur *m*, aérateur *m*; *Nau* manche *f* à air; **v. shaft,** puits *m* de ventilation *ou* d'aération; **(b)** (*in window, over door*) vasistas *m*; **(c)** *Aut* volet *m* d'aération; persienne *f* (*de capot*); (*window*) déflecteur *m*; **(d)** *Med* respirateur *m*, poumon artificiel; **to be on a v.,** être sur respirateur.

ventral ['ventr(ə)l] *Anat Biol* **1** *n* (*on fish*) nageoire ventrale. **2** *adj* ventral, -aux; **v. fins,** nageoires ventrales.

ventricle ['ventrɪk(ə)l] *n Anat* ventricule *m*.

ventriloquism [ven'trɪləkwɪz(ə)m] *n* ventriloquie *f*.

ventriloquist [ven'trɪləkwɪst] *n* ventriloque *mf*; **v.'s dummy,** marionnette *f* de ventriloque.

venture¹ ['ventʃər] *n* **(a)** (*risk*) risque *m*; entreprise hasardeuse *ou* risquée; **my v. into advertising,** mon incursion *f* dans la publicité; **desperate v.,** tentative désespérée; **V. Scout,** routier *m*; **(b)** *Com* entreprise *f*; **joint v.,** (*undertaking*) affaire *f* en participation; (*company*) entreprise en participation; **v. capital,** capital risque *m*; **v. capitalist,** personne *f* qui apporte le capital risque; **(c)** *Old-fashioned* **at a v.,** (*at random*) au hasard; (*tirer*) au jugé.

venture² **1** *vt* hasarder, aventurer, risquer (*sa vie, son argent*); **to v. to do sth,** se hasarder à faire qch, se risquer à faire qch; **I v. to affirm he knew nothing about it,** j'ose affirmer qu'il n'en savait rien; **I ventured to go in,** je me hasardai à entrer; **to v. a remark,** hasarder une remarque; **I ventured the remark that ...,** je me suis hasardé à faire la remarque que ...; **to v. an opinion,** se hasarder *ou* se risquer à donner une opinion; *Prov* **nothing venture(d) nothing gain(ed),** qui ne risque rien n'a rien. **2** *vi* se risquer (**on sth,** à faire qch); prendre le risque (*de faire qch*); **to v. into unknown territory,** s'aventurer en terre inconnue; **to v. out (of doors),** se risquer à sortir; **to v. too far,** aller trop loin.

►**venture on, venture upon** *vipo* se risquer à, se hasarder à (*qch*); **he refused to v. on any criticism of the book,** il a refusé de se risquer à critiquer le livre.

venturer ['ventʃʊrər] *n* aventurier *m*.
venturesome ['ventʃəsəm] *adj* **(a)** (*person*) aventureux, entreprenant; **(b)** (*action*) risqué, hasardeux.
venue ['venjuː] *n* **(a)** (*meeting place*) lieu *m* de réunion, rendez-vous *m inv*; **the v. for the concert will be the Albert Hall,** le concert se déroulera à l'Albert Hall; **what is the v. for the match?,** où est-ce que le match aura lieu?; **there has been a change of v.,** ça n'a plus lieu au même endroit, ça se tiendra ailleurs; **(b)** *Jur* lieu *m* du jugement; **to change the v. of a trial,** renvoyer une affaire devant une autre cour.
Venus ['viːnəs] *n* Vénus; *Anat* **mount of V.,** mont *m* de Vénus; *Bot* **V. flytrap,** dionée *f*, attrape-mouches *m inv*.
VER [viːiː'ɑːr] *n Com* (*abbr* **voluntary export restraint**) **VER agreement,** accord *m* d'autolimitation des exportations.
veracious [və'reɪʃəs] *adj* (*person, account*) véridique.
veraciously [və'reɪʃəslɪ] *adv* véridiquement, avec véracité.
veracity [və'ræsɪtɪ], **veraciousness** [və'reɪʃəsnɪs] *n* véracité *f*, véridicité *f* (*de qn, d'un rapport*).
veranda(h) [və'rændə] *n Archit* véranda *f*.
verb [vɜːb] *n Gram* verbe *m*.
verbal¹ ['vɜːb(ə)l] **1** *adj* **(a)** (*agreement, promise*) verbal, -aux, oral, -aux; **v. note,** note verbale; **(b)** (*communication, skills*) verbal; **v. abuse,** paroles insultantes; **v. dispute,** dispute *f* de mots; *F* **v. diarrhoea,** logorrhée *f*; **v. noun,** nom verbal. **2** *n Gram* nom verbal.
verbal² *vt Br Sl* (*of police*) = impliquer (*qn*) dans un crime en citant devant la cour un aveu prétendu.
verbalize ['vɜːbəlaɪz] *vt* **(a)** *Gram* employer (*un nom*) comme verbe; **(b)** exprimer (*une idée*) par des mots; *Psy* verbaliser (*une expérience*).
verbally ['vɜːbəlɪ] *adv* **(a)** verbalement, oralement, de vive voix; **(b)** (*as a verb*) en tant que verbe.
verbatim [vɜː'beɪtɪm] **1** *adv* mot à mot, textuellement; **to report a speech v.,** rendre compte mot à mot d'un discours. **2** *adj* (*reprint*) reproduit exactement, exact, mot à mot; **v. report,** compte rendu sténographique (*des débats*); **to give a v. account of sth,** faire un compte-rendu mot à mot de qch.
verbena [vɜː'biːnə] *n Bot* verveine *f*; **lemon(-scented) v.,** citronnelle *f*.
verbiage ['vɜːbɪɪdʒ] *n* verbiage *m*.
verbose [vɜː'bəʊs] *adj* (*écrivain, style*) verbeux, diffus, prolixe.
verbosely [vɜː'bəʊslɪ] *adv* avec verbosité, verbeusement.
verbosity [vɜː'bɒsɪtɪ] *n* verbosité *f*, prolixité *f*.
verdant ['vɜːdənt] *adj Fml* vert, verdoyant.
verdict ['vɜːdɪkt] *n* **(a)** *Jur* verdict *m*; **to bring in a v. of guilty/not guilty,** rendre un verdict de culpabilité/de non-culpabilité; **to return a v.,** prononcer *ou* rendre un verdict; **to reach a v.,** conclure, décider; **the jury returned a v. of suicide,** (*in coroner's court*) le jury a conclu au suicide; **open v.,** (*at inquest*) = un jugement qui ne formule aucune conclusion sur les circonstances dans lesquelles la mort a eu lieu; (*at trial*) = un jugement qui conclut au crime sans désigner le coupable; **(b)** *Fig* jugement *m*, avis *m*; **to give one's v.,** se prononcer (**on,** sur); **what's your v.?,** qu'est-ce que tu en penses?
verdigris ['vɜːdɪgrɪs] *n* vert-de-gris *m*.
verdure ['vɜːdʒər] *n Lit* (*colour*) verdure *f*; (*foliage*) verdure, feuillage *m*.
verge [vɜːdʒ] *n* **(a)** (*edge*) bord *m* (*d'un fleuve*); orée *f* (*d'une forêt*); bordure *f* (*d'une plate-bande*); **(b)** *Aut* (*of road*) bas-côté *m*, accotement *m*; **sitting on the grass v. of the road,** assis sur l'herbe du bord de la route; **soft verges,** (*road sign*) accotement instable; **(c)** *Fig* **to be on the v. of doing sth,** être sur le point de faire qch; **on the v. of manhood,** au seuil de l'âge viril; **he is on the v. of ruin,** il est à deux doigts de la ruine; **on the v. of tears,** au bord des larmes; **(d)** *Rel* verge *f* (*portée devant l'évêque*).
verge on *vipo* toucher à, être contigu, -uë à, être voisin de, côtoyer (*qch*); *Fig* **courage verging on foolhardiness,** courage qui confine à la témérité; **colour verging on red,** couleur qui tire sur le rouge; **he was verging on sixty,** il frisait la soixantaine.
verger ['vɜːdʒər] *n Br* **(a)** *Rel* bedeau *m*; **(b)** (*official*) huissier *m* à verge.
Vergil ['vɜːdʒɪl] *n Antiq Liter* Virgile *m*.
verifiable [verɪ'faɪəb(ə)l] *adj* vérifiable.
verification [verɪfɪ'keɪʃən] *n* vérification *f*, contrôle *m*.
verify ['verɪfaɪ] *vt* **(a)** (*confirm*) confirmer (*une affirmation, un fait*); **this verifies my suspicions/my fears,** cela confirme mes soupçons/mes craintes; **I can v. that Mr Smith was present,** je peux confirmer que M. Smith était bien là; **(b)** (*check*) vérifier, contrôler (*des renseignements, des comptes*).
verily ['verɪlɪ] *adv Arch & Bible* en vérité, vraiment.
verisimilitude [verɪsɪ'mɪlɪtjuːd] *n Fml* vraisemblance *f*; **beyond the bounds of v.,** au-delà du vraisemblable.
veritable ['verɪtəb(ə)l] *adj* véritable, vrai; **this is a v. disaster,** c'est un véritable *ou* vrai désastre.
veritably ['verɪtəblɪ] *adv* véritablement.
verity ['verɪtɪ] *n Fml* vérité *f*.
vermicelli [vɜːmɪ'tʃelɪ] *n Culin* vermicelle(s) *m(pl)*.
vermicide ['vɜːmɪsaɪd] *n Pharm* vermicide *m*.
vermiculite [vɜː'mɪkjʊlaɪt] *n* vermiculite *f*.
vermiform ['vɜːmɪfɔːm] *adj* vermiforme.
vermifugal ['vɜːmɪfjuːg(ə)l] *adj* vermifuge.
vermifuge ['vɜːmɪfjuːdʒ] *n* vermifuge *m*.
vermilion [və'mɪljən] **1** *n* vermillon *m*. **2** *adj* (de) vermillon *inv*, vermeil, -eille.
vermin ['vɜːmɪn] *n* **(a)** (*insects*) & *Fig* vermine *f*; **(b)** (*animals*) les animaux *mpl* nuisibles.
verminous ['vɜːmɪnəs] *adj* couvert de vermine.
vermouth ['vɜːməθ] *n* vermout(h) *m*.
vernacular [və'nækjʊlər] **1** *adj Ling* vernaculaire, indigène. **2** *n* **(a)** (*native language, everyday speech*) langue *f* vulgaire; **in the v.,** dans la langue vulgaire; **to translate the Bible into the v.,** traduire la Bible dans la langue vulgaire; **(b)** (*dialect*) langue *f* vernaculaire *ou* indigène; **(c)** (*jargon*) jargon *m*; **the sporting v.,** le jargon sportif.
vernal ['vɜːn(ə)l] *adj Fml* printanier, du printemps; *Astron Bot* vernal, -aux; **v. equinox,** équinoxe *m* de printemps.
veronal ['verən(ə)l] *n Pharm* véronal *m*.
veronica [və'rɒnɪkə] *n* **(a)** *Bot* véronique *f*; **(b)** *Rel* véronique *f*, suaire *m*; **(c)** (*in bullfighting*) véronique *f*.
Veronica [və'rɒnɪkə] *n* Véronique.
verruca, *pl* **-ae** [ve'ruːkə, -kiː] *n* verrue *f*.
versant ['vɜːsənt] *n* versant *m* (*d'une montagne*).
versatile ['vɜːsətaɪl] *adj* **(a)** (*person*) aux talents variés, polyvalent; (*dress, jacket*) passe-partout; (*tool, machine etc*) polyvalent, d'une grande souplesse d'emploi, universel; **he's v.,** il a des talents variés, il est polyvalent; **v. mind,** esprit souple *ou* universel; **(b)** *Biol* versatile.
versatility [vɜːsə'tɪlɪtɪ] *n* **(a)** variété *f* de talents *ou* d'aptitudes (*d'une personne*); (*adaptability*) faculté *f* d'adaption; souplesse *f*, universalité *f* (*d'esprit*); polyvalence *f*, grande souplesse d'emploi (*d'un outil, d'une machine*); **his v.,** la variété de ses talents; **(b)** *Biol* versatilité *f* (*d'un organe*).
verse [vɜːs] *n* **(a)** (*poem*) vers *m*; **free v.,** vers libres; **light v.,** poésie légère; **(b)** (*of song*) couplet *m*; (*of poem, hymn*) strophe *f*, stance *f*; (*of Bible*) verset *m*.
versed [vɜːst] *adj* versé (**in,** en, dans); **v. in the arts,** versé dans les arts; **to be well v. in mathematics,** être fort instruit dans les mathématiques; **I am well v. in his ways,** je le connais bien, je sais bien comment il est.
versification [vɜːsɪfɪ'keɪʃən] *n* **(a)** (*art*) versification *f*; **(b)** (*metre*) facture *f* (*du vers*); métrique *f* (*d'un auteur*).
versify ['vɜːsɪfaɪ] **1** *vt* versifier, mettre (*un récit etc*) en vers. **2** *vi* versifier, faire des vers.
version ['vɜːʃən] *n* **(a)** (*account*) version *f* (*des faits*); interprétation *f* (*d'un fait*); **he gave us a very different v. of the affair,** il nous a donné de cette affaire un récit très différent; **according to his v.,** d'après sa version des faits; **her v. differs from mine,** sa version des faits diffère de la mienne; **(b)** (*type, model*) version *f*; **the military v. of this aircraft,** la version militaire de cet avion; **the TV version of a novel,** l'adaptation *f* d'un roman pour la télévision; **(c)** (*translation*) version *f*, traduction *f*; **the English v. of the Bible,** la version anglaise de la Bible.
verso ['vɜːsəʊ] *n* **(a)** verso *m* (*d'une page*); **(b)** revers *m* (*d'une médaille*).
versus ['vɜːsəs] *prep Jur Sp* contre; **Martin v. Thomas,** Martin contre Thomas; **the advantage of a higher salary v. the loss of security,** l'avantage d'un salaire plus élevé en contrepartie d'une sécurité moindre.
vertebra, *pl* **-ae** ['vɜːtɪbrə, -iː] *n* vertèbre *f*.
vertebral ['vɜːtɪbrəl] *adj Anat* vertébral, -aux; **v. column,** colonne vertébrale.
vertebrate ['vɜːtɪbreɪt, -brɪt] **1** *adj* (*animal*) vertébré; (*caractéristique*) des vertébrés. **2** *n* vertébré *m*.
vertex, *pl* **-ices** ['vɜːteks, -tɪsiːz] *n* **(a)** *Math* sommet *m* (*d'un angle, d'une courbe*); **(b)** *Anat* vertex *m*.
vertical ['vɜːtɪk(ə)l] **1** *adj* vertical, -aux; *Mil* (*écart etc*) en hauteur; **v. line,** (ligne *f*) verticale *f*; **v. elevation,** altitude *f*; **v. cliff,** falaise *f* à pic; **v. integration,** (*of oil company etc*) intégration verticale; **v. takeover,** prise de contrôle

verticale; *Av* **v. take-off/landing,** décollage/atterrissage vertical; **v. take-off aircraft,** avion *m* à décollage vertical; *TV* **v. blanking,** suppression *f* de trame; *TV* **v. hold,** bouton *m* de commande de synchronisme vertical. **2** *n Math* verticale *f*; *Astron* (*cercle*) vertical *m*.

verticality [vɜːtɪ'kælɪtɪ] *n* verticalité *f*.

vertically ['vɜːtɪklɪ] *adv* verticalement, à la verticale; *Av* **to take off/land v.,** décoller/atterrir à la verticale.

vertiginous [vɜː'tɪdʒɪnəs] *adj* vertigineux.

vertigo ['vɜːtɪgəʊ] *n Med* vertige *m*; **to get v.,** avoir le vertige; **I had an attack of v.,** j'ai été pris de vertige.

verve [vɜːv] *n* verve *f*, brio *m*; **to play** *or* **act with v.,** jouer avec verve *ou* brio.

very ['verɪ] **1** *adv* **(a)** très; fort, bien; **v. good,** (*adj phrase*) très bon, fort bon; (*adv phrase*) très bien, fort bien; **v. good, captain,** fort bien mon capitaine; **he is v. well known in Paris,** il est très connu à Paris; **that's v. kind of you,** c'est très gentil à vous; **you are v. kind,** vous êtes bien bon; **so v. little,** si peu; **there's v. little one can do to help,** on ne peut pas faire grand-chose pour aider; **I took only a v. little,** j'en ai pris très peu; **it isn't so v. difficult,** ce n'est pas tellement difficile, ce n'est pas si difficile que ça; **he was not v. pleased,** il n'était pas très content; **v. (v.) few,** très (très) peu; **are you hungry? – yes, v.,** avez-vous faim? – oui, très; **he wore a v. pleased expression,** il avait l'air très satisfait; (*with comparatives*) **I feel v. much better,** je me sens beaucoup mieux; **it is v. much better to wait,** il vaut bien mieux attendre; *Petr* **v. large crude carrier,** pétrolier géant; *Rad TV* **v. high frequency,** hyperfréquences *fpl*; **v. low frequency,** très basse fréquence; *Comptr* **v. high level language,** langage très évolué; **v. large scale integration,** intégration *f* à très grande échelle;

(b) (*emphatic use*) **the v. first,** le tout premier; **we were the v. first to arrive,** nous étions les tout premiers à arriver; **the v. last,** le tout dernier; **the v. best,** tout ce qu'il y a de mieux *ou* de meilleur; **I v. nearly died,** j'ai bien failli mourir; **it was the v. last thing I expected,** c'était vraiment la dernière chose à laquelle je m'attendais; **the v. next day,** dès le lendemain; **in the v. front row,** au tout premier rang; **at the v. most/least,** tout au plus/au moins; **at the v. latest,** au plus tard; **the v. same,** exactement le même; **a room of my v. own,** une pièce rien qu'à moi; **it's my v. own,** c'est à moi tout seul.

2 *adj* **(a)** (*emphatic use*) même; **he lives in this v. house,** il habite dans cette maison même; **sitting in this v. room,** assis dans cette pièce même; **by its v. nature,** par sa nature même; **you are the v. man I wanted to see,** vous êtes justement l'homme que je voulais voir; **come here this v. minute!,** venez ici à l'instant!; **this v. day,** aujourd'hui même; **it was a year ago to the v. day,** c'était il y a un an jour pour jour; **these are his v. words,** ce sont là ses propres paroles; **at the v. beginning,** au tout début; **he knows our v. thoughts,** il connaît jusqu'à nos pensées; **the v. idea frightens me,** cette pensée suffit à m'effrayer; **I shudder at the v. thought of it,** je frémis rien que d'y penser;

(b) *Arch* (*real, true*) vrai, véritable; parfait.

Very ['vɪərɪ] *n Mil* **V. light,** fusée éclairante; **V. (light) pistol,** pistolet *m* lance-fusée(s).

vesical ['vesɪk(ə)l] *adj Anat & Med* vésical, -aux.

vesicle ['vesɪk(ə)l] *n Biol Med* vésicule *f*.

vesper ['vespər] *n Rel* **vespers,** vêpres *fpl*; **to attend vespers,** aller aux vêpres; **the v. bell,** la cloche des vêpres *ou* du soir.

vessel ['ves(ə)l] *n* **(a)** *Nav* bateau *m*; (*large*) navire *m*; (*warship*) bâtiment *m*; **(b)** (*receptacle*) récipient *m*; *Phys* **communicating vessels,** vases communicants; **(c)** *Anat & Bot* vaisseau *m*; **(d)** *Arch* **the weaker v.,** le sexe faible.

vest¹ [vest] *n* **(a)** *Br* (*Am* = **undershirt**) (*for men*) maillot *m* de corps; (*knitted*) tricot *m* de corps; (*for women*) chemise américaine; *Can* camisole *f*; (*for baby*) brassière *f*; **string v.,** gilet *m* en point noué *ou* en filet maille (aérée); *Sp* **running** *or* **boxing** *or* **rowing v.,** maillot; **(b)** *Am* (*Br* = **waistcoat**) gilet *m*; **v. pocket,** poche *f* de gilet.

vest² **1** *vt* **(a) to v. s.o. with authority,** investir *ou* revêtir qn d'autorité; **to v. property in s.o.,** assigner des biens à qn; **right vested in the Crown,** droit dévolu à la Couronne; **by the authority vested in me,** en vertu de l'autorité dont je suis investi; **authority vested in the people,** autorité exercée par le peuple; **(b)** *Rel* vêtir, revêtir (*un dignitaire, le prêtre*). **2** *vi* **(a)** (*of priest*) revêtir ses vêtements sacerdotaux, se revêtir; **(b)** (*of property*) **to v. in s.o.,** être dévolu à qn.

vestal ['vest(ə)l] *adj Antiq* **v. virgin,** vestale *f*.

vested ['vestɪd] *adj* **v. interests,** *Jur* droits acquis; *Fig* les personnes qui ont un interêt matériel; **to have a v. interest in sth,** *Fin* avoir des capitaux *ou* être intéressé dans qch; *Fig* avoir un intérêt matériel à qch.

vestibule ['vestɪbjuːl] *n* **(a)** (*entrance hall*) vestibule *m*, antichambre *f*; (*of public building*) hall *m*; **(b)** *Am Rail* soufflet *m*; **v. train,** train *m* à soufflets; **(c)** *Anat* vestibule *m* (*de l'oreille*).

vestige ['vestɪdʒ] *n* **(a)** (*trace*) vestige *m*, trace *f* (*de civilisation*); **not a v. of common sense,** pas un sou de bon sens; **without a v. of clothing,** complètement nu; **(b)** *Biol* organe *m* qui persiste à l'état rudimentaire.

vestigial [ves'tɪdʒɪəl] *adj* **(a)** résiduel; **some v. sense of decency prevented him from doing it,** le peu de décence qui lui restait l'a empêché de le faire; **(b)** *Biol* (*organe*) qui persiste à l'état rudimentaire.

vestment ['vestmənt] *n* vêtement *m* (de cérémonie); *Rel* chasuble *f*; **(church) vestments,** vêtements sacerdotaux.

vest-pocket ['vestpɒkɪt] *adj Am* (*camera, dictionary etc*) de poche, miniature; **a v.-p. version of Fontainebleau,** une version miniature de Fontainebleau; **v.-p. park,** parc *m* miniature.

vestry ['vestrɪ] *n Rel* **(a)** (*in church*) sacristie *f*; **(b)** (*parish council*) conseil paroissial.

Vesuvius [vɪ'suːvɪəs] *n* le Vésuve.

vet¹ [vet] *n F* véto *mf*; **to take an animal to the vet('s),** emmener un animal chez le véto.

vet² *vt* (-tt-) **(a)** *Admin* effectuer un contrôle de sécurité sur (*un candidat*); **she's been positively vetted,** le contrôle de sécurité dont elle a fait l'objet s'est avéré satisfaisant; **(b)** revoir, mettre au point (*l'œuvre littéraire de qn*); **(c)** examiner, traiter (*un animal*); examiner (*qn*) médicalement.

vet³ *n Am F* ancien combattant.

vetch [vetʃ] *n Bot* vesce *f*.

veteran ['vet(ə)r(ə)n] **1** *n* vétéran *m*; *F* vieux *m* de la vieille; *Fig* **I have a real old v. of a typewriter,** j'ai une machine à écrire, c'est une antiquité!; **(war) v.,** ancien combattant; **a v. of the First World War, a First World War v.,** un ancien combattant de la Première Guerre Mondiale; *US* **Veterans Day,** *Fr* ≈ l'Armistice *f*; *Can* ≈ le Jour du Souvenir. **2** *adj* de vétéran, des vétérans, vieux, *f* vieille, ancien; **this ten-year-old boy is a v. traveller,** ce petit garçon de dix ans est un voyageur aguerri; **she is a v. campaigner for human rights,** elle a fait campagne pour les droits de l'homme depuis très longtemps; **v. soldier,** vieux soldat; **v. army,** armée *f* de vétérans; *Aut* **v. car,** (*in England*) voiture *f* d'époque (*vieille voiture d'avant 1905*); (*in international categories*) vétéran *m*.

veterinarian [vet(ə)rɪ'neərɪən] *n esp Am* vétérinaire *mf*.

veterinary ['vet(ə)rɪn(ə)rɪ] *adj* vétérinaire; **she has a v. practice in the country,** elle a un cabinet de vétérinaire à la campagne; **v. medicine,** médecine *f* vétérinaire; **v. surgeon,** vétérinaire *mf*.

veto¹, *pl* **-oes** ['viːtəʊ, -əʊz] *n* veto *m*; **right of v.,** droit *m* de veto; **to have the right** *or* **power of v.,** avoir le droit de veto; **to put a v. on sth,** mettre *ou* opposer son veto à qch; **to use one's v.,** exercer son droit de veto.

veto² *vt* mettre *ou* opposer son veto à (*qch*); **he vetoed it,** il y a mis *ou* opposé son veto.

vetting ['vetɪŋ] *n* **(a)** contrôle *m* de sécurité (*sur un candidat*); **v. procedure,** procédure *f* de contrôle; **(b)** examen *m* (médical).

vex [veks] *vt* vexer, fâcher, ennuyer, chagriner (*qn*).

vexation [vek'seɪʃən] *n* **(a)** (*action*) action *f* de se tourmenter; **(b)** (*cause*) contrariété *f*, ennui *m*; (*state*) chagrin *m*, dépit *m*.

vexatious [vek'seɪʃəs] *adj* **(a)** *Old-fashioned* (*person, thing*) contrariant, irritant, ennuyeux; (*thing*) fâcheux; **(b)** *Jur* vexatoire.

vexed [vekst] *adj* **(a)** (*cross*) fâché, ennuyé, chagriné; **(b) v. question,** question controversée *ou* très débattue *ou* non résolue.

vexing ['veksɪŋ] *adj* contrariant, irritant, ennuyeux.

VFCR [viːefsiː'ɑːr] *n Econ abbr* **voluntary foreign credit restraint.**

VGA [viːdʒiː'eɪ] *n Comptr* (*abbr* **video graphics adaptor**) VGA *m*.

VHF [viːeɪtʃ'ef] *adj Rad TV* (*abbr* **very high frequency**); **VHF radio,** radio *f* en hyperfréquences; **to broadcast on VHF,** émettre en hyperfréquences.

via ['vaɪə, viːə] *prep* via, par la voie de; par (*une route*); **to Paris v. Lyon,** à Paris via Lyon *ou* par Lyon.

viability [vaɪə'bɪlɪtɪ] *n* (*of foetus, seed etc*) viabilité *f*; (*of project etc*) viabilité, chances *fpl* de succès.

viable ['vaɪəb(ə)l] *adj* (*foetus, seed etc*) viable; (*project etc*) viable, qui a des chances de réussir; **I can see no v. alternative,** je ne vois pas d'autre moyen d'y parvenir.
viaduct ['vaɪədʌkt] *n* viaduc *m*.
vial ['vaɪəl] *n Fml* fiole *f*; ampoule *f*.
viands ['vaɪəndz] *npl Arch* aliments *mpl*; **choice v.,** mets délicats.
viaticum [vaɪ'ætɪkəm] *n Rel* viatique *m*.
vibes [vaɪbz] *npl F* **(a)** *Mus* vibraphone *m*; **(b)** (*atmosphere*) ambiance *f*; **the v. are good,** ça marche, ça gaze; **this place gives me bad v.,** cet endroit me fait un effet désagréable; **I get good v. from it,** ça me branche; **I get good v. from him/her,** il/elle me plaît.
vibrancy ['vaɪbrənsɪ] *n* vibrance *f*, qualité vibrante.
vibrant ['vaɪbrənt] *adj* vibrant; **city v. with activity,** ville palpitante d'activité; **v. personality,** nature émotive; **v. colours,** couleurs vives.
vibraphone ['vaɪbrəfəʊn] *n Mus* vibraphone *m*.
vibrate [vaɪ'breɪt] **1** *vi* vibrer; *Phys* vibrer, osciller; **voice vibrating with emotion,** voix vibrante d'émotion; *Fig* **you're making the house v.,** tu fais trembler les murs; **to v. with activity,** vibrer d'activité. **2** *vt* faire vibrer, faire osciller.
vibrating [vaɪ'breɪtɪŋ] **1** *adj* vibrant; (*mouvement*) vibratoire, oscillant. **2** *n Tech* vibrage *m*.
vibration [vaɪ'breɪʃən] *n* vibration *f*; *Phys etc* oscillation *f*, pulsation *f*; *Fig* **vibrations,** ambiance *f*.
vibrato [vɪ'brɑːtəʊ] *n Mus* vibrato *m*.
vibrator [vaɪ'breɪtər] *n* **(a)** *El* vibrateur *m*, vibreur *m*; **(b)** *Mus* anche *f* (*d'harmonium etc*); **(c)** (*for massage*) **(electric) v.,** vibromasseur *m*; **(d)** *Petr* **v. truck,** camion vibrateur.
vibratory [vaɪ'breɪtərɪ] *adj Phys etc* vibratoire.
viburnum [vaɪ'bɜːnəm] *n Bot* viorne *f*.
vicar ['vɪkər] *n Rel* **(a)** *Church of Eng* pasteur *m*; = curé *m*; **(b)** *Cathol* **v. apostolic,** vicaire *m* apostolique; **v. general,** vicaire général, grand vicaire; **the V. of Christ,** le vicaire de Jésus-Christ.
vicarage ['vɪkərɪdʒ] *n Church of Eng* presbytère *m* (*d'un vicar*).
vicarious [vaɪ'keərɪəs, vɪ-] *adj* **(a)** (*at second hand*) **v. punishment** (*suffered indirectly*) châtiment souffert par un autre; (*suffered on s.o.'s behalf*) châtiment souffert pour un autre; **v. pleasure,** (*enjoyed by chance*) plaisir donné par le plaisir d'un autre; (*actively sought*) plaisir procuré indirectement; **to take v. pleasure in sth,** retirer indirectement du plaisir de qch; **(b)** (*delegated*) (*power, authority*) délégué.
vicariously [vaɪ'keərɪəslɪ, vɪ-] *adv* **(a)** (*on s.o.'s behalf*) à la place d'un autre; (*indirectly*) indirectement; **(b)** (*by delegation*) par délégation, par procuration.
vice¹ [vaɪs] *n* **(a)** (*immorality*) vice *m*; **to sink into v.,** sombrer dans le vice; **avarice is a v.,** l'avarice est un vice; **the V. Squad,** la brigade des mœurs, *F* les Mœurs; **(b)** (*defect*) défaut *m*, défectuosité *f*; *Hum* **it's my only v.,** c'est mon seul vice; **there's no v. in him,** (*of person*) il n'est pas méchant; (*of animal*) il n'est pas vicieux.
vice², *US* **vise** *n* étau *m*; **bench v.,** étau *ou* servante *f* d'établi; **v. clamp** *or* **jaw,** mâchoire *f*; **he had a grip like a v.,** il avait une poigne aussi forte qu'un étau.
vice³ *n* (*F* = **vice-chairman, vice president;** *Univ* = **vice-chancellor**) **v. admiral,** *Fr* vice-amiral *m* d'escadre; *Can* vice-amiral; **v. chancellor,** *Pol* vice-chancelier *m*, *pl* vice-chanceliers; *Univ* recteur *m*; **v. president,** vice-président, -ente, *pl* vice-président(e)s.
vice-chairman, *pl* **-men** [vaɪs'tʃeəmən] *n* vice-président, *pl* vice-présidents.
vice-chairmanship [vaɪs'tʃeəmənʃɪp] *n* vice-présidence *f*, *pl* vice-présidences.
vice-chancellorship [vaɪs'tʃɑːnsələʃɪp] *n Pol* fonction *f ou* dignité *f* de vice-chancelier; *Univ* rectorat *m*.
vice-consul [vaɪs'kɒns(ə)l] *n* vice-consul *m*, *pl* vice-consuls.
vice-consulate [vaɪs'kɒnsjʊlət] *n* (*post or premises*) vice-consulat *m*, *pl* vice-consulats.
vicelike ['vaɪslaɪk] *adj* **held in a v. grip,** serré dans une poigne de fer *ou* comme dans un étau.
vice-marshal [vaɪs'mɑːʃəl] *n Mil Av* **air v.-m.,** général *m* de division aérienne.
vice-presidency [vaɪs'prezɪdənsɪ] *n* vice-présidence *f*; **a candidate for the v.-p.,** un candidat à la vice-présidence.
vice-presidential [vaɪsprezɪ'denʃəl] *adj* **v.-p. candidate,** candidat *m* à la vice-présidence.
viceroy ['vaɪsrɔɪ] *n* vice-roi *m*, *pl* vice-rois.
vice versa [vaɪs'vɜːsə] *adv* vice versa.
vicinity [vɪ'sɪnɪtɪ] *n* **(a)** (*nearness*) voisinage *m*, proximité *f* (**to, with,** de); **(b)** (*neighbourhood*) alentours *mpl*, environs *mpl*; **in the v.,** dans les alentours, dans le coin; **in the v. of Dover,** à proximité de *ou* dans les environs de Douvres; **in the immediate v. of the factory,** aux abords de l'usine; **in the v. of five thousand pounds,** environ cinq mille livres, dans les cinq mille livres.
vicious ['vɪʃəs] *adj* **(a)** (*harsh, violent*) rageur, violent; (*combat*) acharné; **v. blow/wind,** coup/vent violent; **a v. attack,** une attaque brutale; **(b)** (*malicious*) méchant, haineux; **to make a v. attack on s.o.'s character,** lancer une attaque haineuse contre le caractère de qn; **v. gossip,** commérages méchants; **she has a v. tongue,** c'est une mauvaise langue; **(c)** (*person*) vicieux, dépravé; (*horse*) vicieux, méchant; **(d) v. circle,** cercle vicieux.
viciously ['vɪʃəslɪ] *adv* (*see adj*) **(a)** rageusement, violemment; **(b)** méchamment, haineusement; **(c)** vicieusement.
viciousness ['vɪʃəsnɪs] *n* **(a)** (*of wind, blow*) violence *m*; **(b)** (*of criticism*) méchanceté *f*; **(c)** (*of person, horse*) nature vicieuse.
vicissitude [vɪ'sɪsɪtjuːd] *n* vicissitude *f*.
victim ['vɪktɪm] *n* **(a)** (*of fire*) incendié, -ée; (*of flood*) inondé, -ée; (*of fire, flood, shipwreck etc*) sinistré, -ée; **to be the v. of s.o.,** être la victime de qn; **to be the v. of an attack,** être victime d'une attaque; **v. of s.o.'s trickery,** dupe *f* de la fourberie de qn; **v. of an accident,** accidenté, -ée; **to die a v. to smallpox,** mourir victime de la petite vérole; **to fall a v. to s.o.'s charm,** succomber au charme de qn; **to fall v. to a disease,** être frappé d'une maladie; **(b)** (*sacrifice*) victime *f*.
victimization [vɪktɪmaɪ'zeɪʃən] *n* représailles *fpl*.
victimize ['vɪktɪmaɪz] *vt* exercer des représailles contre (*les meneurs d'une grève etc*); **he felt that he was being victimized,** il se croyait brimé (**for doing,** parce qu'il faisait); **I'm being victimized,** on s'en prend à moi.
victimless ['vɪktɪmlɪs] *adj* **v. crime,** = délit dans lequel les parties impliquées sont consentantes.
victor ['vɪktər] *n* vainqueur *m*, triomphateur, -trice.
victoria [vɪk'tɔːrɪə] *n* **(a) v. (plum),** (variété *f* de) grosse prune rouge; **(b)** (*carriage*) victoria *f*.
Victoria [vɪk'tɔːrɪə] *n* Victoria; *Hist* **Queen V.,** la reine Victoria; *Mil* **V. Cross,** = la plus haute distinction britannique, accordée pour récompenser le courage de quelqu'un; *Can* **V. Day,** fête *f* de la Reine; **V. Falls,** Chutes *fpl* Victoria.
Victorian [vɪk'tɔːrɪən] **1** *adj* victorien, du règne de la reine Victoria. **2** *n* Victorien, -ienne.
Victoriana [vɪktɔːrɪ'ɑːnə] *n* bric-à-brac *m ou* antiquités *fpl* de l'ère victorienne.
victorious [vɪk'tɔːrɪəs] *adj* **(a)** (*army, team etc*) victorieux, vainqueur *m*; **to be v. over s.o.,** remporter la victoire sur qn; **(b)** (*journée etc*) de victoire.
victoriously [vɪk'tɔːrɪəslɪ] *adv* victorieusement, en vainqueur.
victory ['vɪktərɪ] *n* **(a)** victoire *f*; **to claim v.,** revendiquer la victoire; **to snatch v. from the jaws of defeat,** arracher la victoire; **he described the decision as a v. for common sense,** il a décrit la décision comme étant une victoire du bon sens; **to gain a** *or* **the v.,** remporter la victoire (**over,** sur), être victorieux; **v. celebrations,** réjouissances occasionnées par une victoire, réjouissances pour célébrer la victoire; **v. parade,** parade *f* pour célébrer la victoire; **(b)** *Art* **(statue of) v.,** victoire *f*; **the Winged V. of Samothrace,** la Victoire ailée de Samothrace.
victual ['vɪt(ə)l] *v* (**-ll-,** *US* **-l-** ['vɪt(ə)ld]) **1** *vt* approvisionner; ravitailler (*un navire, une garnison*). **2** *vi* s'approvisionner, se ravitailler.
victualling, *US* **victualing** ['vɪt(ə)lɪŋ] *n* approvisionnement *m*, ravitaillement *m*.
victualler, *US* **victualer** ['vɪtlər] *n* fournisseur *m* de vivres; *Br Fml* **licensed v.,** débitant *m* de boissons.
victuals ['vɪt(ə)lz] *npl* (*food*) vivres *mpl*, victuailles *fpl*.
vicuna [vɪ'kjuːnə] *n* (*animal*) vigogne *f*; **v. coat/jacket/** *etc*, manteau *m*/veste *f*/*etc* en vigogne.
video¹ ['vɪdɪəʊ] *n TV* (*medium*) vidéo *f*; (*cassette*) vidéocassette *f*, cassette *f* vidéo; (*recorder*) magnétoscope *m*; **a v. of the World Cup,** une vidéo sur la Coupe du Monde; **to show a v.,** passer une vidéo; **to have sth on v.,** avoir qch sur vidéo; **v. camera,** caméra *f* vidéo; **v. cassette,** cassette *f* vidéo, vidéocassette *f*; **v. (cassette) recorder,** magnétoscope *m*; **v. clip,** vidéo-clip *m*, *pl* vidéo-clips, clip *m* (vidéo); **v. conference** *or* **conferencing,** vidéoconférence *f*, visioconférence *f*; *Am* **v. display terminal,** console *f* de visualisation; **v. frequency,** vidéo-

fréquence *f*; **v. game,** jeu *m* vidéo; *F* **v. nasty,** = film sur vidéocassette à contenu violent et/ou pornographique; **v. recording,** enregistrement *m* sur magnétoscope; **v. shop,** ≈ vidéoclub *m*; **v. tape,** bande *f* vidéo.

video[2] *vt* enregistrer (*qch*) sur magnétoscope; **I forgot to v. it,** j'ai oublié de l'enregistrer.

videodisc, *US* **videodisk** ['vɪdɪəʊdɪsk] *n* disque *m* vidéo, vidéodisque *m*; **v. player,** lecteur *m* de vidéodisque.

videophone ['vɪdɪəʊfəʊn] *n* vidéophone *m*, visiophone *m*.

videotape ['vɪdɪəʊteɪp] *vt* enregistrer (*un film*) sur magnétoscope.

videotex ['vɪdɪəʊteks] *n Comptr* vidéotex *m*.

vie [vaɪ] *v* (**vied** [vaɪd], **vying** ['vaɪɪŋ]) *vi* rivaliser (**with s.o.,** avec qn); **they are vying for the championship,** ils se disputent le championnat; **to v. with each other in doing sth,** faire qch à l'envi l'un de l'autre *ou* les uns des autres; faire qch à qui mieux mieux; **they were vying with one another to impress her,** ils rivalisaient l'un avec l'autre pour la séduire.

Vienna [vɪ'enə] *n* Vienne *f*.

Viennese [vɪə'niːz] **1** *adj* viennois. **2** *n* Viennois, -oise.

Vietcong [vɪet'kɒŋ] *n* Viêt-cong *mf*; **V. army/guerrillas/** *etc*, armée *f*/guérilleros *mpl*/*etc* Viêt-cong; **a prisoner of the V.,** un prisonnier des Viêt-congs.

Vietnam [vɪet'nɑːm, -'næm] *n* Vietnam *m*.

Vietnamese [vɪetnə'miːz] **1** *adj* vietnamien. **2** *n* **(a)** Vietnamien, -ienne; **(b)** *Ling* vietnamien *m*.

Viet Vet [vɪet'vet] *n US* ancien *m* du Vietnam.

view[1] [vjuː] *n* vue *f* **(a)** (*sight*) vue *f* (**of,** de); **exposed to/hidden from v.,** exposé/caché aux regards; **to pass out of** *or* **be lost to v.,** disparaître de vue; **in v.,** en vue; **in full v. of the crowd,** sous les regards de la foule; **at last a hotel came into v.,** enfin j'ai *ou* il a *etc* aperçu un hôtel; **we were in v. of land,** nous étions en vue de la terre; **to keep sth in v.,** ne pas perdre qch de vue; **field of v.,** (*of telescope*) champ *m*; **angle of v.,** angle *m* de champ;
(b) (*scene, prospect*) vue *f*, perspective *f*; **room with a v.,** chambre *f* avec vue; **front v.,** vue de face; **from here you have a good v. of the castle,** d'ici on a une très belle vue du château; **you will get a better v. from here,** vous verrez mieux d'ici; **views of Paris,** vues de Paris; *Fig* **to take the long v.,** adopter une perspective à long terme; *Archit* **front/back v.,** élévation *f* du devant/du derrière; **sectional v.,** vue en coupe, profil *m*.
(c) (*inspection*) regard *m*, coup *m* d'œil; **on v. (to the public),** (*of collection*) ouvert au public; **private v.,** avant-première *f*, *pl* avant-premières (*d'une exposition etc*); vernissage *m* (*d'une exposition de peinture*);
(d) (*opinion*) opinion *f*, idée *f*, avis *m* (**about,** au sujet de; **on,** sur); **point of v.,** point *m* de vue; **to express a v.,** exprimer une opinion *ou* un avis; **I support the v. that,** je partage l'opinion selon laquelle; **to have very decided views on sth,** avoir des idées arrêtées au sujet de qch; **what is your v. on the matter?,** quelle est votre opinion sur la question?; **in my v.,** à mon avis; **our views differ,** nos opinions diffèrent; **to share s.o.'s views,** partager les opinions de qn;
(e) (*intention*) vue *f*, intention *f*, but *m*, dessein *m*; **to have sth in v.,** avoir qch en vue; **with this in v.,** à cette fin; **they bought the house with a v. to letting it,** ils ont acheté la maison en vue de *ou* dans le but de *ou* avec l'idée de la louer;
(f) (*prep phrase*) **in v. of what has happened,** en considération de *ou* en raison de ce qui est arrivé; **in v. of these facts,** prenant ces faits en considération; **in v. of the great heat,** vu la grande chaleur.

view[2] **1** *vt* **(a)** (*look at, watch*) regarder, porter sa vue sur (*qn, qch*); visionner (*des diapositives*); *TV* regarder (*une émission*); **(b)** (*inspect*) inspecter, examiner (*qch*); visiter (*une maison à vendre*); **(c)** (*consider*) envisager, regarder (*qch*); **to v. sth with horror/delight/***etc*, envisager qch avec horreur/ravissement/*etc*; **the proposal was viewed unfavourably by the authorities,** la proposition était considérée d'un œil peu favorable par les autorités. **2** *vi TV* regarder la télévision.

viewdata ['vjuːdeɪtə] *n Comptr* vidéotex *m*.

viewer ['vjuːər] *n* **(a)** (*person*) spectateur, -trice; *TV* téléspectateur, -trice; *TV* **I'm a a regular v. of your programme,** je suis un de vos fidèles téléspectateurs; **(b)** (*device*) visionneuse *f*; *Phot* **slide v.,** visionneuse *f*.

viewership ['vjuːəʃɪp] *n Am TV* public *m*.

viewfinder ['vjuːfaɪndər] *n Phot* viseur *m*.

viewing ['vjuːɪŋ] *n* **(a)** (*inspection*) examen *m*, inspection *f*; **open for v. from seven to nine,** (*of house etc*) visites de sept à neuf heures; **v. is by arrangement with the owner,** visite sur accord préalable du propriétaire; **(b)** *Opt Electron* vision *f*, visualisation *f*; *Phot* visée *f*; **v. window,** fenêtre *f* d'observation; **(c)** *TV* **v. audience,** public *m*; **v. figures,** indice *m* d'écoute; **the v. public,** les téléspectateurs *mpl*; **v. time,** temps *m* d'antenne.

viewpoint ['vjuːpɔɪnt] *n* **(a)** (*opinion*) point *m* de vue; **from the international v.,** du point de vue international; **(b)** (*lookout*) point *m* de vue.

vigil ['vɪdʒɪl] *n* veille *f*; (*over sick person or corpse*) veillée *f*; *Rel* vigile *f*; **to keep v.,** veiller.

vigilance ['vɪdʒɪləns] *n* vigilance *f*; *US Pej* **v. committee,** milice privée, comité *m* d'autodéfense.

vigilant ['vɪdʒɪlənt] *adj* vigilant, éveillé, alerte.

vigilante [vɪdʒɪ'læntɪ] *n Pej* membre *m* d'une milice privée; **v. justice,** justice *f* sommaire, autodéfense *f*.

vigilant(e)ism [vɪdʒɪ'lænt(ɪ)ɪz(ə)m] *n esp US Pej* = tendance au développement de l'autodéfense ou des milices privées.

vigilantly ['vɪdʒɪləntlɪ] *adv* vigilamment, avec vigilance.

vignette[1] [vɪ'njet] *n* (*illustration*) vignette *f*; *Phot* buste *m* sur un fond dégradé; **this ten-minute v. of city life,** cette esquisse de dix minutes de la vie dans une grande ville.

vignette[2] *vt* peindre (*qn*) en buste sur un fond dégradé; *Phot* dégrader (*un portrait*).

vigor ['vɪgər] *n US* = **VIGOUR.**

vigorous ['vɪgərəs] *adj* (*strong*) vigoureux, robuste; (*blow*) solide; (*style, opposition*) vigoureux; **v. in body and mind,** robuste de corps et d'esprit; **a v. defence of their case,** une défense énergique de leur affaire; **v. denial,** dénégation vive *ou* vigoureuse; **v. growth,** forte croissance; **v. plant,** plante vigoureuse.

vigorously ['vɪgərəslɪ] *adv* vigoureusement; **she v. denied the allegation,** elle a très vivement *ou* vigoureusement dénié l'allégation.

vigour, *US* **vigor** ['vɪgər] *n* **(a)** vigueur *f*, énergie *f*; vitalité *f*; **the v. of youth,** la sève de la jeunesse; **man of v.,** homme énergique; **v. of style,** vigueur (de style); **(b)** *US* **laws in v.,** lois en vigueur.

Viking ['vaɪkɪŋ] *Hist* **1** *n* Viking *m*. **2** *adj* viking; **V. ship,** drakkar *m*.

vile [vaɪl] *adj* **(a)** *F* (*nasty*) abominable, exécrable; **the soup was v.,** la soupe était infecte; **he's in a v. temper,** il est d'une humeur exécrable; **v. weather,** un sale temps; **(b)** (*infamous*) vil, bas, infâme, ignoble; **a v. calumny,** une calomnie infâme; **the vilest of men,** le dernier des hommes.

vilely ['vaɪlɪ] *adv* (*see adj*) **(a)** d'une manière abominable *ou* exécrable; **(b)** vilement, bassement.

vileness ['vaɪlnɪs] *n* **(a)** *F* caractère *m* exécrable; **the v. of the weather,** le temps abominable; **(b)** (*infamy*) bassesse *f*, caractère *m* ignoble (*de qn, d'un sentiment*).

vilification [vɪlɪfɪ'keɪʃən] *n* dénigrement *m*.

vilify ['vɪlɪfaɪ] *vt* diffamer, dénigrer (*qn*), calomnier (*qn*).

villa ['vɪlə] *n* (*in country*) maison *f* de campagne; (*in town*) pavillon *m* de banlieue; (*at seaside*) villa *f*; **Roman v.,** villa romaine; **to rent a v. in Spain,** louer une villa en Espagne.

village ['vɪlɪdʒ] *n* **(a)** village *m*; (*large*) bourg *m*; **I'm going into the v.,** je vais au village; **the whole v. was talking about it,** tout le village en parlait; **the v. church/grocer/***etc*, l'église/l'épicier/*etc* du village; **v. inn,** auberge *f* de campagne; **v. life,** vie *f* de village; **(b)** *US* petite municipalité.

villager ['vɪlɪdʒər] *n* villageois, -oise.

villain ['vɪlən] *n* scélérat *m*; *Br F* (*criminal*) voyou *m*; *Br F* **the big London villains,** les grands criminels de Londres; *F* **you little v.!,** petit garnement!, petit coquin!; *Th* **the v. (of the piece),** le traître; *Fig* **so you are the v. of the piece!,** alors c'est vous qui êtes responsable de tout ça!; *Fig* **why am I always the v. of the piece?,** pourquoi est-ce que c'est toujours moi que l'on blâme?

villainous ['vɪlənəs] *adj* (*behaviour etc*) vil, infâme; **v. deed,** infamie *f*.

villainously ['vɪlənəslɪ] *adv* d'une manière infâme; *F* abominablement.

villainy ['vɪlənɪ] *n* infamie *f*.

villein ['vɪlən] *n Hist* vilain *m*, serf *m*.

vim [vɪm] *n F* vigueur *f*, énergie *f*; **full of v.,** plein d'entrain; **put a bit more v. into it!,** mets-y un peu plus d'entrain!

vinaigrette [vɪnɪ'gret] *n Culin* vinaigrette *f*.

vindaloo [vɪndə'luː] *n* = plat indien très épicé.

vindicate ['vɪndɪkeɪt] *vt* **(a)** (*exonerate*) disculper (*qn*); **she has been vindicated,** elle a été disculpée; **(b)** (*justify*) défendre, soutenir (*qn*); justifier, faire l'apologie de (*qn, sa conduite*); prouver, maintenir (*son dire*); **to v. one's char-**

acter, se justifier; **(c)** (*uphold*) **to v. one's rights,** revendiquer ses droits, faire valoir son bon droit.

vindication [vɪndɪ'keɪʃən] *n* défense *f*, justification *f*; **in v. of his conduct,** pour justifier *ou* en justification de sa conduite.

vindicator ['vɪndɪkeɪtər] *n* défenseur *m*.

vindictive [vɪn'dɪktɪv] *adj* **(a)** vindicatif; (*acte*) de vengeance; **(b)** (*spiteful*) vindicatif, rancunier.

vindictively [vɪn'dɪktɪvlɪ] *adv* par rancune, par esprit de vengeance.

vindictiveness [vɪn'dɪktɪvnɪs] *n* caractère vindicatif; esprit *m* de vengeance; esprit rancunier; **she did it out of v.,** elle a fait cela par esprit de vengeance.

vine [vaɪn] *n* **(a)** (*grapevine*) vigne *f*; **v. growing,** viticulture *f*; **v. grower,** viticulteur *m*, vigneron, -onne; **v.-growing country/region,** pays/région viticole *ou* vinicole; **v. harvest,** vendange *f*; **v. leaf,** feuille *f* de vigne; **(b)** *Am* plante grimpante; **(c)** (*stem*) sarment *m*, tige *f*; **to wither on the vine,** se gâter sur pied.

vinegar ['vɪnɪgər] *n* **(a)** (*condiment*) vinaigre *m*; **wine/cider v.,** vinaigre de vin/de cidre; **tarragon v.,** vinaigre à l'estragon; *Culin* **oil and v. dressing,** vinaigrette *f*; **(b)** *Am F* vigueur *f*, allant *m*.

vinegary ['vɪnɪg(ə)rɪ] *adj* **(a)** (*goût etc*) de vinaigre; **(b)** *F* (*ton*) acerbe, aigre.

vinery ['vaɪnərɪ] *n* **(a)** (*hothouse*) serre *f* où l'on cultive la vigne; **(b)** (*vineyard*) vigne *f*, vignoble *m*.

vineyard ['vɪnjəd] *n* (*field*) clos *m ou* champ *m* de vigne; (*establishment*) vignoble *m*; **the best vineyards,** les meilleurs crus.

viniculture [vɪnɪkʌltʃər] *n* viticulture *f*.

vino ['viːnəʊ] *n F* (*wine*) pinard *m*.

vintage ['vɪntɪdʒ] **1** *n* **(a)** (*harvest*) récolte *f* du raisin; vendanges *fpl*; (*crop*) vendange; (*season*) temps *m* de vendange, les vendanges; **the 1964 v.,** le cru de 1964; **(b)** (*year*) année *f* (de belle récolte); **what v. is it?,** quelle année est-ce que c'est?; **of the 1964 v.,** de l'année 1964; **guaranteed v.,** appellation contrôlée; *Fig* **bicycle of 1920 v.,** bicyclette du modèle de 1920. **2** *adj* **(a)** (*wine*) de grand cru; **v. year,** année de bon vin, grande année; **v. champagne,** champagne *m* d'origine; **(b)** (*film*) classique; *Aut* **v. car,** = voiture construite entre 1916 et 1930; **(c)** *F* (*of high quality*) excellent; **the play is v. Shaw/***etc*, la pièce est du meilleur Shaw/*etc*; **it's been a v. year for comedy,** ça a été une excellente année pour ce qui est de la comédie.

vintner ['vɪntnər] *n* négociant *m* en vins.

vinyl ['vaɪnɪl] *n* vinyle *m*; *Mus F* **the album is available on v. and cassette,** l'album existe en disque et en cassette; **v. (book) jacket/***etc*, couverture/*etc* en vinyle; **v. acetate,** acétate *m* de vinyle; **v. chloride,** chlorure *f* de vinyle; **v. resin,** résine *f* vinylique.

viol ['vaɪəl] *n Mus* viole *f*; **bass v.,** basse *f* de viole; *US* contrebasse *f*.

viola[1] [vɪ'əʊlə] *n Mus* **(a)** (*violin*) alto *m*; **v. player,** altiste *mf*; **(b)** (*viol*) viole *f*; **v. da gamba,** viole de gambe; **v. d'amore,** viole d'amour.

viola[2] *n* **(a)** *Bot* violacée *f*; **(b)** (*flower*) pensée *f* (unicolore); violette *f* (de jardin).

violate ['vaɪəleɪt] *vt* **(a)** (*disregard*) violer (*un secret*); profaner (*un sanctuaire*); manquer à (*une règle*); violer, enfreindre (*la loi*); **to v. s.o.'s privacy,** faire intrusion auprès de qn; **(b)** *Old-fashioned* (*rape*) violer, outrager (*une femme*).

violation [vaɪə'leɪʃən] *n* **(a)** violation *f* (*d'un serment, d'une loi*); viol *m*, profanation *f* (*d'un sanctuaire*); manquement *m*, infraction *f* (*à une règle*); infraction (*à un ordre*); *Am* **traffic v.,** infraction à la circulation; **v. of human rights,** violation des droits de l'homme; **v. of territorial waters,** dépassement *m* des eaux territoriales; **v. of s.o.'s privacy,** intrusion *f* auprès de qn; **(b)** *Old-fashioned* viol *m* (*d'une femme*).

violator ['vaɪəleɪtər] *n* **(a)** violateur, -trice (*des lois*); **(b)** *Old-fashioned* violateur *m*, violeur *m* (*d'une femme*).

violence ['vaɪələns] *n* **(a)** (*roughness*) violence *f*; **v. on television,** la violence à la télévision; **to use v.,** user de violence; **to resort to v.,** recourir *ou* en venir à la violence; *Jur* **to commit acts of v.,** se livrer à des voies de fait; **robbery with v.,** vol avec agression *f ou* avec coups et blessures; **he had struck his victim with great v.,** il avait frappé sa victime avec une grande violence; **to do v. to sth,** (*distort*) faire violence à qch; **the translation does considerable v. to the original,** la traduction trahit considérablement le texte original; **(b)** (*intensity*) violence *f*, intensité *f*; **the v. of the impact,** la violence du choc.

violent ['vaɪələnt] *adj* **(a)** (*fierce*) violent, (*freinage*) brutal; **v. storm,** orage violent, tempête *f*; **to die a v. death,** mourir de mort violente; **to be in a v. temper,** être furieux; **to become v.,** (*of person*) devenir violent *ou* agressif; **(b)** (*intense*) violent, vif, fort; (*coughing, fever, pain*) violent; **hair of a v. red,** cheveux d'un roux violent; **v. colours,** couleurs criardes *ou* crues; **v. dislike,** aversion violente, vive aversion; **to take a v. dislike to s.o.,** se prendre d'une aversion violente *ou* d'une vive aversion à l'égard de qn.

violently ['vaɪələntlɪ] *adv* **(a)** violemment, avec violence; **his heart was beating v.,** son cœur battait à se rompre; **(b)** vivement, extrêmement; **after supper I became v. ill,** après le souper j'ai été terriblement malade; **she was v. sick,** elle a été prise de vomissements violents; **to fall v. in love with s.o.,** tomber follement amoureux de qn.

violet ['vaɪələt] **1** *n* **(a)** (*plant*) violette *f*; **Parma v.,** violette de Parme; *Fig* **shrinking v.,** personne *f* timide; **she is no shrinking v.,** elle est loin d'être timide; **(b)** (*colour*) violet *m*. **2** *adj* **v. (-coloured),** violet, de couleur violette.

violin [vaɪə'lɪn] *n* violon *m*; **first v.,** premier violon, violon principal; **second v.,** second violon; **v. case,** étui *m* à violon; **v. concerto,** concerto *m* pour violon; **v. maker,** luthier *m*.

violinist [vaɪə'lɪnɪst] *n* violoniste *mf*.

violoncellist [vaɪələn'tʃelɪst] *n Fml* violoncelliste *mf*.

violoncello [vaɪələn'tʃeləʊ] *n Fml* violoncelle *m*.

VIP [viːaɪ'piː] *n* (*abbr* **very important person**) personnage *m* de marque, V.I.P. *mf inv*; **VIP lounge,** (*in airport*) salon réservé aux personnages de marque; **to get the VIP treatment,** être traité comme un personnage de marque.

viper ['vaɪpər] *n* (*snake*) *& Fig* vipère *f*; **to cherish a v. in one's bosom,** réchauffer un serpent dans son sein.

viperish ['vaɪpərɪʃ] *adj* vipérin, de vipère; *Fig* **v. tongue,** langue venimeuse *ou* de vipère.

virago [vɪ'rɑːgəʊ] *n Pej* virago *f*, mégère *f*.

viral ['vaɪrəl] *adj Med* viral; **v. pneumonia,** pneumonie virale.

Virgil ['vɜːdʒɪl] *n Antiq Liter* Virgile *m*.

virgin ['vɜːdʒɪn] **1** *n* vierge *f*; **he/she is a v.,** il/elle est vierge; **the (Blessed) V.,** la Sainte Vierge; *F* **a V. Mary,** (*drink*) un jus de tomate; *Astron* **the V.,** la Vierge; *Hist* **the V. Queen,** (*Elizabeth I*) la Reine Vierge; **the V. Islands,** les îles *fpl* Vierges. **2** *adj* de vierge, virginal, -aux; *Rel* **v. birth,** (la) maternité divine; **v. forest/soil/wool,** forêt *f*/sol *m*/laine *f* vierge; **v. snow,** neige virginale; **v. (vegetable) oil,** huile vierge *ou* naturelle; *Fig* **this market is v. territory for the company,** ce marché constitue un territoire vierge pour la société.

virginal ['vɜːdʒɪn(ə)l] **1** *adj* virginal, -aux, de vierge. **2** *n Mus* **virginal(s), pair of virginals,** virginal *m*.

Virginia [və'dʒɪnɪə] *n* **(a)** (*name*) Virginie; **(b)** (*state*) la Virginie; *Bot* **V. creeper,** vigne *f* vierge; **V. (tobacco),** tabac *m* de Virginie, virginie *m*.

virginity [və'dʒɪnɪtɪ] *n* virginité *f*; **to lose one's v.,** perdre sa virginité.

Virgo ['vɜːgəʊ] *n Astron* la Vierge; *Astrol* **I'm a V.,** je suis Vierge; *Astrol* **Virgos should be careful this week,** Vierges, soyez prudents cette semaine.

virile ['vɪraɪl, *Am* 'vɪrəl] *adj* viril, mâle; *Fig* (*leadership, performance etc*) viril; (*voice*) viril; *Anat* **the v. member,** le membre viril.

virility [vɪ'rɪlɪtɪ] *n* virilité *f*; **he's just trying to prove his v.,** il essaye simplement de prouver sa virilité.

virologist [vaɪ'rɒlədʒɪst] *n* virologiste *m*, virologue *m*.

virology [vaɪ'rɒlədʒɪ] *n* virologie *f*.

virtual ['vɜːtjʊəl] *adj* **(a) it's a v. certainty that,** de fait, c'est une certitude que; **he's the v. head of the business,** c'est lui le vrai chef de la maison; **it was a v. failure,** ce fut en fait un échec; **this was a v. admission of guilt,** de fait c'était un aveu de culpabilité; **(b)** *Phys Comptr* virtuel; **v. image,** image virtuelle; **v. memory** *or* **storage,** mémoire virtuelle.

virtually ['vɜːtjʊəlɪ] *adv* virtuellement, pratiquement; **I'm v. certain of it,** j'en suis virtuellement *ou* pratiquement certain; **v. all of them came,** ils sont pratiquement tous venus.

virtue ['vɜːtjuː] *n* **(a)** (*goodness, chastity*) vertu *f*; **Christian virtues,** vertus chrétiennes; **the four cardinal virtues,** les quatre vertus cardinales; *Old-fashioned* **woman of easy v.,** femme de petite vertu *ou* de mœurs faciles; *Prov* **v. is its own reward,** = la récompense de la vertu est la vertu elle-même; **to make a v. of necessity,** faire de la nécessité une vertu; **(b)** (*advantage*) avantage *m*; **the hotel has the v. of being cheap,** l'hôtel a l'avantage d'être bon marché; **there's no v. in arriving early,** il n'y a aucun mérite à arriver en avance; **(c)** vertu *f* (*de certaines drogues, de certaines eaux*); **plants that have healing virtues,** plantes qui ont des vertus curatives; **(d)** (*prep phrase*) **by** *or* **in v. of,** en vertu de; **by v. of one's office,** à titre d'office.

virtuosity [vɜːtjʊ'ɒsɪtɪ] *n Mus etc* virtuosité *f.*

virtuoso, *pl* **-sos, -si** [vɜːtjʊ'əʊzəʊ, -zəʊz, -ziː] *n Mus etc* virtuose *mf*; **he gave a v. performance,** (*of musician, actor*) il a joué en victuose.

virtuous ['vɜːtjʊəs] *adj* vertueux; **to feel v. about doing,** se sentir vertueux en faisant; **he's got that oh-so-v. look on his face,** il a son petit air de ne pas y toucher.

virtuously ['vɜːtʊəslɪ] *adv* vertueusement.

virulence ['vɪr(j)ʊləns] *n* virulence *f.*

virulent ['vɪr(j)ʊlənt] *adj* virulent; *Fig* (*colour*) criard; **a particularly v. strain of flu,** un type de grippe particulièrement violent; **to make a v. attack on s.o.,** lancer une attaque virulente contre qn; **she was v. in her criticism of the system,** elle était virulente dans sa critique du système; **v. satire,** satire venimeuse.

virulently ['vɪr(j)ʊləntlɪ] *adv* avec virulence.

virus, *pl* **-uses** ['vaɪrəs, -əsɪz] *n* **(a)** *Med* virus *m*; **there's a v. going round,** il y a un virus qui sévit *ou* qui se promène; **I've got a v. of some kind,** j'ai un virus quelconque; **v. disease,** maladie virale *ou* à virus; **(b)** *Comptr* virus *m*; **to disable a v.,** désactiver un virus; **to write a v.,** concevoir un virus; **v. attack,** infection virale; **v. author,** créateur *m* de virus.

visa¹ ['viːzə] *n* (*on passport, document*) visa *m*; **a v. for Poland,** un visa pour la Pologne; **transit v.,** visa de transit.

visa² *vt* (**visaed** ['viːzəd]) viser, apposer un visa à (*un passeport*).

Visa ® ['viːzə] *n* Visa ®, *F* carte bleue; **to pay by V.,** payer par Carte Visa *ou* carte bleue.

visage ['vɪzɪdʒ] *n Fml* visage *m*, figure *f.*

vis-à-vis ['viːzɑːviː] **1** *n* vis-à-vis *m.* **2** *adv* vis-à-vis (**to** *or* **with s.o.,** de qn). **3** *prep* **v.-à-v. the economic situation,** par rapport à la situation économique.

Vis(c) (*abbr* **Viscount**) vicomte *m.*

viscera ['vɪsərə] *npl Anat* viscères *mpl.*

visceral ['vɪsər(ə)l] *adj Anat & Fig* viscéral, -aux.

viscid ['vɪsɪd] *adj* visqueux, gluant.

viscidity [vɪ'sɪdɪtɪ] *n* viscosité *f.*

viscose ['vɪskəʊs] *n Ch Ind* viscose *f.*

viscosity [vɪs'kɒsɪtɪ] *n* viscosité *f.*

viscount ['vaɪkaʊnt] *n* vicomte *m.*

viscountcy ['vaɪkaʊntsɪ] *n* vicomté *f.*

viscountess ['vaɪkaʊntɪs] *n* vicomtesse *f.*

viscounty ['vaɪkaʊntɪ] *n* vicomté *f.*

viscous ['vɪskəs] *adj* visqueux.

vise [vaɪs] *n US* = **VICE².**

visibility [vɪzɪ'bɪlɪtɪ] *n* visibilité *f*; **good/bad v.,** bonne/ mauvaise visibilité; **v. was down to a few yards,** la visibilité était réduite à quelques mètres; **v. is one hundred yards,** la visibilité est de cent mètres; **car with good front and rear v.,** voiture avec une bonne visibilité avant et arrière.

visible ['vɪzɪb(ə)l] *adj* visible; *Jur* **to have no v. means of support,** n'avoir aucun moyen apparent de subvenir à ses propres besoins; **to become v.,** apparaître; **with v. satisfaction,** avec une satisfaction évidente; **v. horizon,** horizon visuel.

visibly ['vɪzɪblɪ] *adv* visiblement, manifestement; (*grandir etc*) à vue d'œil; **she was v. moved,** elle était visiblement émue.

Visigoth ['vɪzɪgɒθ] *n Hist* Wisigoth, -e.

vision ['vɪʒən] *n* **(a)** (*sight*) vision *f*, vue *f*; **to have good/ poor v.,** avoir une bonne/une mauvaise vue; **the accident had impaired his v.,** cet accident avait affaibli sa vue; **within the range of v.,** à portée de vue; **beyond our v.,** au delà de notre vue; **field/angle of v.,** champ/angle visuel; **man/woman of v.,** homme/femme d'une grande perspicacité *ou* qui voit loin dans l'avenir; *Med* **double v.,** double vision, diplopie *f*; **(b)** (*dream*) imagination *f*, vision *f*; (*apparition*) vision, apparition *f*; **visions of wealth,** visions de richesse(s); **to have visions of doing,** se voir faire; **I had visions of having to walk all the way into town,** je me suis vu devoir aller jusqu'en ville à pied; **he has** *or* **sees visions,** il a des visions; **(c)** *TV* image *f*; **a temporary loss of v.,** une perte momentanée de l'image; **v. control,** contrôle de l'image.

visionary ['vɪʒənərɪ] **1** *adj* (*leader*) visionnaire; (*impractical*) rêveur. **2** *n* visionnaire *mf.*

visit¹ ['vɪzɪt] *n* (*call, tour*) visite *f*; (*stay*) séjour *m*; *Am* causerie *f*, causette *f* (**with s.o.,** avec qn); **(social) v.,** visite *f*; **courtesy v.,** visite de politesse; **I had a v. from your aunt last week,** j'ai eu la visite de ta tante la semaine dernière; **to pay s.o. a v.,** faire (une) visite à qn, rendre visite à qn; **to return s.o.'s v.,** rendre sa visite à qn; *F* **to pay a v.,** (*go to lavatory*) aller au petit coin; **to be on a v.** *Br* **to** *or Am* **with friends,** être en visite chez des amis; **I'm here on a v.,** je suis ici en visite, je suis de passage ici; **this is my first v. to your country,** c'est la première fois que je viens dans votre pays; *Jur* **v. to the scene of a crime,** descente *f* sur les lieux; *Nau* **right of v. (and search),** droit *m* de visite (*en mer*).

visit² **1** *vt* **(a)** (*of doctor*) visiter (*un malade*); (*of representative*) passer chez (*un client*); **to v. s.o.,** (*call on*) rendre visite à qn; (*stay with*) faire un séjour chez qn; **we visited the museums,** nous avons visité les musées; **worth visiting,** (*museum etc*) qui vaut la visite; **(b)** (*of official*) visiter, aller voir (*un endroit*); *Jur* **to v. the scene of a crime,** faire une descente sur les lieux; **(c)** *Bible* punir (*qn, un péché*); **to v. the sins of the fathers upon the children,** punir les enfants pour les péchés des pères. **2** *vi* **(a)** être en visite; **I don't live here, I'm only visiting,** je n'habite pas ici, je ne suis que de passage; **(b)** *Am* **stay and v. a while,** reste à bavarder un petit moment.

▶**visit with** *vipo Am* **(a)** (*stay with*) être en visite chez; **(b)** (*talk with*) bavarder avec.

visitation [vɪzɪ'teɪʃən] *n* **(a)** (*of bishop*) visite pastorale; *F* visite fâcheuse *ou* trop prolongée; *Hum* **we're having a v. from the managing director next week,** le directeur général nous fait l'honneur de sa visite la semaine prochaine; **v. of the sick,** visite des malades; **v. rights,** (*of divorced parent*) droit *m* de visite; **(b)** *Rel* **(Feast of) the V.,** (fête *f* de) la Visitation; **v. (of God),** châtiment *m.*

visiting ['vɪzɪtɪŋ] **1** *adj* en visite; *Sp* **the v. team,** les visiteurs; **v. lecturer,** conférencier, -ière de l'extérieur; **v. professor,** professeur (*de faculté*) invité; *US* **v. fireman,** = un personnage de marque en visite; *US* **v. nurse,** infirmière visiteuse. **2** *n* visites *fpl*; **to go v.,** aller en visites; *Br* **v.** (*Am* = **calling) card,** carte *f* de visites; **v. hours,** heures *f* de visite (*dans un hôpital*); **v. hours are (from) five to seven,** les visites ont lieu de cinq à sept heures.

visitor ['vɪzɪtər] *n* **(a)** visiteur, -euse; (*guest*) invité, -ée; (*in hotel*) client, -ente; (*in hospital, prison*) visiteur, -euse; **to have visitors,** (*at the moment*) avoir du monde *ou* des invités; (*in general*) recevoir des visites; **I rarely have visitors,** c'est rare que j'ai de la visite; **you have a v.,** tu as la visite; **London will have half a million visitors this summer,** 500 000 personnes visiteront Londres cette année; **she is a frequent v. to our country,** elle se rend regulièrement dans notre pays; **a v. from Mars,** un voyageur venu de Mars; *Br* **health v.,** infirmière visiteuse; **visitors' book,** livre des voyageurs (*à un hôtel*); livre d'or (*d'un hôtel de ville*); **to sign the visitors' book,** signer le livre des voyageurs *ou* d'or; **v. centre,** (*in park, at tourist attraction etc*) centre *m* pour les visiteurs; *Br* **v.'s passport,** = un passeport temporaire; **visitors' tax,** taxe *f* de séjour;

(b) (*bird*) oiseau migrateur; **this species is a winter v. to Britain,** cette espèce vient passer l'hiver en Grande Bretagne.

visor ['vaɪzər] *n* visière *f* (*de casque, casquette*); **to raise/ lower one's v.,** soulever/baisser sa visière; *Aut* **sun v.,** pare-soleil *m inv*; (*over windscreen*) parasol *m.*

vista ['vɪstə] *n* échappée *f* de vue; (*in forest*) percée *f*, éclaircie *f*; *Fig* perspective *f*; *Fig* **to open up new vistas,** ouvrir de nouvelles perspectives *ou* de nouveaux horizons.

vistadome ['vɪstədəʊm] *n Am Rail* vistadôme *m.*

visual ['vɪzjʊəl, 'vɪʒ-] *adj* **(a)** visuel; **the v. arts,** les arts visuels; *Br Comptr* **v. display unit,** console *f* de visualisation; **to have a v. memory,** avoir une mémoire visuelle; **his comedy is very v.,** son comique repose sur les effets visuels; **his fabrics have great v. appeal,** ses tissus sont très attrayants visuellement; *Mil Nau* **v. signal/signalling,** signal *m*/signalisation *f* optique; *Sch* **v. methods (of teaching),** enseignement *m* par l'image; **v. aid,** (*in teaching*) support visuel; **(b)** (*visible*) perceptible à l'œil; **(c)** *Anat* **v. nerve,** nerf *m* optique.

visually ['vɪzjʊəlɪ] *adv* visuellement; **v. handicapped,** malvoyant; **the v. handicapped,** les malvoyants; **v. impaired,** qui a des problèmes de vue; **the v. impaired,** les personnes qui ont des problèmes de vue.

visualization [vɪzjʊəlaɪ'zeɪʃən] *n* visualisation *f.*

visualize ['vɪzjʊəlaɪz, 'vɪʒ-] *vt* (*imagine*) se représenter (*qch*); évoquer l'image de (*qch*); (*foresee*) envisager (*qch*).

vital ['vaɪt(ə)l] **1** *adj* **(a)** (*essential to life*) vital, -aux, essentiel à la vie; **v. organ,** organe vital; **v. force,** force vitale; *Med* **v. signs,** signes *fpl* de vie; **(b)** (*decisive,* *indispensable*) essentiel, capital, -aux, vital; **question of v. importance,** question d'une importance vitale *ou* de toute première importance; **it is v. that ...,** il est indispensable *ou* essentiel que ...+ *sub*; **v. statistics,** (*of births, deaths etc*) statistiques *fpl* démographiques; *F* (*of woman*) mensurations *fpl*; **(c)** (*full of life, vigorous*) vif, plein d'entrain; **Soviet cinema was once v. and innovative,** le cinéma soviétique était autrefois vigoureux et novateur. **2** *n Anat etc* **vitals,** organes vitaux.

vitally ['vaɪt(ə)lɪ] *adv* d'une manière vitale; **supplies are v. needed,** on a un besoin vital de vivres; **v. important question,** question d'une importance vitale *ou* de toute première importance; **it is v. important that ...,** il est essentiel que ..., il faut absolument que ... + *sub*.

vitality [vaɪ'tælɪtɪ] *n* **(a)** vitalité *f* (*d'un organisme*); vitalité, vigueur *f* (*d'une institution*); **(b)** vie *f*, vigueur (*de qn, de style*); **I wish I had her v.,** j'aimerais bien avoir son énergie *f*.

vitalize ['vaɪtəlaɪz] *vt* vitaliser, vivifier.

vitamin ['vɪtəmɪn, *Am* vaɪ-] *n Biol Ch* vitamine *f*; **have you taken your vitamins?,** est-ce que tu as pris tes vitamines?; **v. C/D/***etc*, la vitamine C/D/*etc*; *Med* **v. deficiency,** carence *f* vitaminique *ou* en vitamines; (*disease*) avitaminose *f*; **with added vitamins,** vitaminé; **v. tablet,** comprimé *m* des vitamines.

vitiate ['vɪʃɪeɪt] *vt* **(a)** *Fml* (*spoil, weaken*) vicier (*le sang, l'air*); **(b)** *Jur* vicier (*un contrat*).

vitiated ['vɪʃɪeɪtɪd] *adj Fml* (*air etc*) vicié.

vitiation [vɪʃɪ'eɪʃən] *n Fml* viciation *f*.

viticulture ['vɪtɪkʌltʃər] *n* viticulture *f*.

vitreous ['vɪtrɪəs] *adj* **(a)** *Ch Geol* vitreux; **v. enamel,** émail vitrifié; **(b)** *Anat* **v. body,** corps vitré (*de l'œil*).

vitrification [vɪtrɪfɪ'keɪʃən] *n* vitrification *f*.

vitrified ['vɪtrɪfaɪd] *adj* vitrifié.

vitrify ['vɪtrɪfaɪ] **1** *vt* vitrifier. **2** *vi* se vitrifier.

vitriol ['vɪtrɪəl] *n Ch & Fig* vitriol *m*; **to throw v. at s.o.,** lancer du vitriol sur qn, vitrioler qn; **v. attack,** attaque *f* au vitriol.

vitriolic [vɪtrɪ'ɒlɪk] *adj* (*acide*) vitriolique; *Fig* (*attack, speech*) au vitriol; **v. criticism,** critique mordante.

vitriolize ['vɪtrɪəlaɪz] *vt* vitrioler.

vituperate [vɪ'tjuːpəreɪt] *Fml* **1** *vt* injurier, vitupérer (*qn*). **2** *vi* deblatérer, vitupérer (**against s.o./sth,** contre qn/qch).

vituperation [vɪtjuːpə'reɪʃən] *n Fml* vitupération *f*.

vituperative [vɪ'tjuːpərətɪv] *adj Fml* injurieux.

Vitus ['vaɪtəs] *n Rel* (Saint) Guy; *Med F* **Saint V.'s dance,** danse *f* de Saint-Guy.

viva[1] ['viːvə] *int & n* vivat *m*.

viva[2] ['vaɪvə] *n Univ F* = **VIVA VOCE 3**.

vivacious [vɪ'veɪʃəs] *adj* (*esp woman, girl*) vif, animé, enjoué; **she has a v. laugh,** elle a un rire enjoué; **she is v.,** elle a de la vivacité; **she was very v. last evening,** elle avait beaucoup d'entrain *ou* s'est montrée pleine d'entrain hier soir.

vivaciously [vɪ'veɪʃəslɪ] *adv* avec vivacité *ou* entrain.

vivacity [vɪ'væsɪtɪ] *n* vivacité *f*; verve *f*, entrain *m*.

vivarium, *pl* **-iums, -ia** [vaɪ'veərɪəm, -ɪəmz, -ɪə] *n* (*for animals, plants*) vivarium *m*; (*for fish*) vivier *m*.

vivat ['vaɪvæt] *int & n* vivat *m*.

viva voce ['vaɪvə'vəʊsɪ, -'vəʊtʃɪ] **1** *adv* de vive voix, oralement. **2** *adj* oral, -aux. **3** *n Univ* (*often shortened to* **viva**) examen oral, *F* (l')oral *m*; **to take a v. v.,** passer un oral.

vivid ['vɪvɪd] *adj* **(a)** (*light, colour*) vif, éclatant, brillant; **v. flash of lightning,** éclair aveuglant; **v. imagination,** imagination vive; **it left a v. impression on me,** ça m'a laissé une forte impression; **I have a v. recollection of the scene,** j'ai un souvenir très vif *ou* très net de la scène; **v. description of sth,** description vivante de qch.

vividly ['vɪvɪdlɪ] *adv* vivement, avec éclat; **to describe sth v.,** décrire qch d'une manière vivante *ou* sous de vives couleurs.

vividness ['vɪvɪdnɪs] *n* vivacité *f*, éclat *m* (*de la lumière, des couleurs*); **the v. of his style,** la vigueur *ou* le pittoresque de son style.

vivify ['vɪvɪfaɪ] *vt Fml* vivifier, (r)animer.

viviparous [vɪ'vɪpərəs] *adj Bot Zool* vivipare.

vivisect [vɪvɪ'sekt, 'vɪvɪsekt] *vt Fml* pratiquer des vivisections sur (*des animaux*).

vivisection [vɪvɪ'sekʃən] *n* vivisection *f*; **the v. debate,** le débat sur la vivisection.

vivisectionist [vɪvɪ'sekʃənɪst] *n* **(a)** (*practitioner*) personne qui pratique la vivisection; **(b)** (*advocate*) partisan, -ane de la vivisection.

vixen ['vɪks(ə)n] *n* (*animal*) renarde *f*; *Fig* mégère *f*.

viz [vɪz] *adv* (*when reading aloud usu* **namely** ['neɪmlɪ]) (*abbr* **videlicet**) à savoir, c'est-à-dire.

vizier [vɪ'zɪər] *n Hist* vizir *m*; **grand v.,** grand vizir.

vizor ['vaɪzər] *n* = **VISOR**.

VLCC [viːelsiː'siː] *n Petr abbr* **very large crude carrier.**

VLF [viːel'ef] *n Rad abbr* **very low frequency.**

VLSI [viːele'saː] *n Comptr abbr* **very large scale integration.**

vocab ['vəʊkæb] *n F* vocabulaire *m*.

vocabulary [və'kæbjʊlərɪ] *n* **(a)** (*glossary*) vocabulaire *m*; (*at end of book*) lexique *m*; (*technical*) glossaire *m*; **(b)** vocabulaire *m* (*d'une langue, d'un auteur*); lexique *m* (*d'une langue*); **a large v.,** un vocabulaire étendu; **to enlarge one's v.,** enrichir son vocabulaire.

vocal ['vəʊk(ə)l] **1** *adj* (*music*) vocal, -aux; (*communication*) verbal, oral; *Ling* (*vowel*) voisé; (*consonant*) sonore; *Fig* **the most v. member of the audience,** le membre de l'auditoire qui s'est fait le plus entendre; *Fig* **he is very v. about ...,** il parle beaucoup de, il se fait entendre souvent au sujet de ...; **v. score,** partition *f* de chant; *Anat* **v. cords,** cordes vocales. **2** *n Ling* son vocal; *Mus* **vocals,** musique vocale, chant *m*; **who did the vocals?,** qui a fait la partie vocale?

vocalic [və'kælɪk] *adj Ling* vocalique.

vocalist ['vəʊkəlɪst] *n* chanteur, -euse.

vocalization [vəʊkəlaɪ'zeɪʃən] *n* prononciation *f*, articulation *f*; *Mus Ling* vocalisation *f*.

vocalize ['vəʊkəlaɪz] **1** *vt* **(a)** (*articulate*) prononcer, articuler (*un mot*); chanter (*un air*); sonoriser (*une consonne*); *Mus* vocaliser (*un air*); **(b)** *Ling* vocaliser (*une consonne*). **2** *vi Mus* faire des vocalises, vocaliser; *F* chanter, chantonner; *Fig* se faire entendre.

vocally ['vəʊk(ə)lɪ] *adv* vocalement, oralement; (*to protest*) à haute voix.

vocation [vəʊ'keɪʃən] *n* **(a)** (*aptitude*) vocation *f* (**for teaching,** d'enseignant); **to have a v.,** avoir une vocation; **teaching is a v.,** l'enseignement, c'est une vocation; **(b)** (*profession*) vocation *f*, profession *f*, métier *m*; **to miss one's v.,** manquer sa vocation.

vocational [vəʊ'keɪʃənəl] *adj* (*enseignement, cours, formation*) professionnel; **v. guidance,** orientation professionnelle; **v. adviser,** *Am* **v. guidance counselor,** orienteur professionnel.

vocative ['vɒkətɪv] *adj & n Gram* **v. (case),** (cas) vocatif *m*; **in the v.,** au vocatif.

vociferate [və'sɪfəreɪt] *vi & vt* **(a)** (*protest*) vociférer, crier (**against,** contre); **(b)** (*shout*) crier à pleins poumons.

vociferation [vəsɪfə'reɪʃən] *n* **(a)** vocifération *f*, cris *mpl*, clameurs *fpl*; **(b)** cri *m*, clameur *f*.

vociferous [və'sɪfərəs] *adj* vociférant, bruyant.

vociferously [və'sɪfərəslɪ] *adv* bruyamment; (*to protest*) à haute voix.

vodka ['vɒdkə] *n* vodka *f*.

vogue [vəʊg] *n* vogue *f*, mode *f* (**for,** de, des); **to be in v.,** être en vogue *ou* à la mode; **to come into v.,** devenir à la mode; **v. word,** mot à la mode.

voice[1] [vɔɪs] *n* **(a)** (*of person*) voix *f*; **to raise/lower one's v.,** hausser/baisser la voix; **to keep one's v. down,** parler à voix basse; **his v. has broken,** sa voix a mué; **his v. broke,** (*with emotion*) sa voix s'est brisée; **in a low v.,** à voix basse, à mi-voix; **he's got a deep v.,** il a une voix grave; **to speak in a loud v.,** parler à haute voix *ou* à voix haute; **at the top of one's v.,** à tue-tête; **to make one's v. heard,** se faire entendre; **he likes the sound of his own v.,** il aime à s'entendre parler; **she's not in (good) v.,** (*of singer*) elle n'est pas en voix; **to lose one's v.,** perdre sa voix; **to give v. to one's indignation/***etc*, exprimer son indignation/*etc*; *Fig* **the v. of conscience/reason,** la voix de la conscience/de la raison; **a little v. inside her told her it was wrong,** (*her conscience told her*) une petite voix en elle lui dit que c'était mal; **the v. of the people,** la voix du peuple; **with one v.,** tout d'une voix, à l'unanimité; **v. test,** audition *f*; **v. box,** larynx *m*; *Comptr* **v. input,** entrée vocale; **v. recognition,** reconnaissance vocale; **v. response,** réponse vocale;

(b) (*vote*) voix *f*, suffrage *m*; **we have no v. in the matter,** nous n'avons pas voix au chapitre; **proportional representation would give small parties greater v.,** la représentation proportionnelle donnerait davantage voix au chapitre aux petits partis;

(c) *Gram* voix *f* (*du verbe*); **in the active/passive v.,** à la voix active/passive, à l'actif/au passif;

(d) *Ling* son voisé.

voice[2] *vt* **(a)** exprimer (*une opinion, sa colère etc*); **to v.**

the general feeling, exprimer le sentiment général *ou* l'opinion générale; **(b)** *Ling* sonoriser (*une consonne*).

voice-activated ['vɔɪsæktɪveɪtɪd] *adj* (*device etc*) commandé par la voix, à commande vocale.

voiced [vɔɪst] *adj Ling* (*consonne*) sonore.

-voiced [vɔɪst] *suff* **low/loud/***etc***-v.,** à la voix basse/forte/*etc.*

voiceless ['vɔɪslɪs] *adj Ling* sourd, non voisé.

voice-over ['vɔɪsəʊvər] *n Cin TV* voix *f* hors champ; **who did the v.-o.?,** qui a fait la voix hors champ?

void[1] [vɔɪd] **1** *adj* **(a) v. of,** (*lacking in*) dépourvu *ou* dénué de; **proposal v. of reason,** proposition dénuée *ou* dépourvue de raison; **(b)** *Jur* (*of deed, contract*) **(null and) v.,** nul; **to make v.,** annuler, frapper de nullité; **v. ballot,** bulletin nul; **(c)** *Lit* vide. **2** *n* vide *m*; **to fill the v.,** combler le vide; **the aching v. in his heart,** le vide douloureux qu'il y avait dans son cœur.

void[2] *vt* **(a)** *Jur* résoudre, annuler (*un contrat etc*); **(b)** évacuer (*des matières fécales etc*).

voile [vɔɪl] *n Tex* voile *m*.

vol (a) *Phys* (*abbr* **volume**) vol; **(b)** (*abbr* **volume**) tome *m*, t(om).

volatile ['vɒlətaɪl] *adj* **(a)** (*person*) versatile, changeant; (*situation*) explosif; (*prices, market*) volatile; **(b)** *Ch Comptr etc* volatil; **v. oil,** huile volatile.

volatility [vɒlə'tɪlɪtɪ] *n* **(a)** (*of person*) caractère changeant; (*of situation*) caractère explosif; (*of prices, market*) volatilité *f*; **(b)** *Ch* volatilité *f*.

volatilize [vɒ'lætɪlaɪz] *Ch* **1** *vt* volatiliser (*un liquide*). **2** *vi* se volatiliser.

vol-au-vent ['vɒləʊvɒn] *Culin* vol-au-vent *m inv*.

volcanic [vɒl'kænɪk] *adj & Fig* volcanique.

volcano, *pl* **-oes** [vɒl'keɪnəʊ, -əʊz] *n* volcan *m*.

vole [vəʊl] *n* (*animal*) campagnol *m*.

volition [və'lɪʃən] *n* volition *f*, volonté *f*; **to do sth of one's own v.,** faire qch de son propre gré.

volley[1] ['vɒlɪ] *n* **(a)** (*of gunfire*) volée *f*, salve *f*; (*of blows, stones etc*) volée, grêle *f*; *Fig* (*of insults*) volée, bordée *f*; **to fire** *or* **discharge a v.,** tirer une volée *ou* une salve; **(b)** *Sp* (balle prise de) volée *f*; **half v.,** demi-volée *f*, *pl* demi-volées.

volley[2] **1** *vt* **(a)** *Mil* tirer une volée *ou* une salve de (*projectiles*); **(b) to v. the ball** *or* **a return,** (*in tennis*) relancer la balle à la volée; **to half v. the ball,** prendre la balle à la demi-volée. **2** *vi* **(a)** (*of guns*) partir ensemble; **(b)** (*in tennis*) relancer la balle à la volée; **to half v.,** prendre la balle à la demi-volée.

volleyball ['vɒlɪbɔːl] *n Sp* volley-ball *m*; **v. player,** volleyeur, -euse.

volt [vəʊlt] *n El* volt *m*.

voltage ['vəʊltɪdʒ] *n El* tension *f*; **high/low v.,** haute/basse tension.

voltaic [vɒl'teɪɪk] *adj El* voltaïque.

volte-face[1] ['vɒltfɑːs] *n* volte-face *f inv*; **to make a (complete) v.-f.,** faire volte-face.

volte-face[2] *vi* faire volte-face.

voltmeter ['vəʊltmiːtər] *n El* voltmètre *m*.

volubility [vɒljʊ'bɪlɪtɪ] *n* volubilité *f*.

voluble ['vɒljʊb(ə)l] *adj* volubile; **to be a v. talker,** parler avec beaucoup de volubilité.

volubly ['vɒljʊblɪ] *adv* avec volubilité.

volume ['vɒljuːm] *n* **(a)** (*book*) volume *m*, tome *m*; **work in six volumes, six-v. work,** ouvrage en six volumes; **v. one,** volume *ou* tome premier, premier volume; *Fig* **to speak volumes,** (*of action, remark etc*) être révélateur **(about,** de), en dire long **(about,** sur); **(b)** (*amount*) volume *m*; **volumes of smoke,** nuages *mpl ou* tourbillons *mpl* de fumée; **volumes of water,** flots *mpl ou* torrents *mpl* d'eau; **(c)** *Mus Rad* volume *m*; **to turn the v. up/down,** augmenter/diminuer le volume; *Rad* **at full volume,** à fond, à plein volume; **turn the radio up full v.,** mets la radio à fond; **v. control,** réglage *m* de volume; (*knob, switch*) bouton *m* de (réglage de) volume.

volumetric [vɒljʊ'metrɪk] *adj Ch Phys* volumétrique.

voluminous [və'ljuːmɪnəs] *adj* **(a)** (*author*) volumineux, prolifique; **(b)** (*jacket etc*) ample.

voluminously [və'ljuːmɪnəslɪ] *adv* abondamment.

voluntarily [vɒlʌn'teərɪlɪ] *adv* **(a)** (*willingly*) volontairement, de son plein gré; **(b)** (*unpaid*) bénévolement.

voluntary ['vɒlənt(ə)rɪ] **1** *adj* **(a)** volontaire; (*offer*) spontané; **v. service,** service *m* volontaire; **v. confession of guilt,** confession *f* volontaire, aveu spontané; **v. export restraint,** autolimitation *f* des exportations; **v. foreign credit restraint,** restriction facultative *ou* volontaire de crédit à l'étranger; **(b)** *Admin Econ* non-gouvernemental, -aux; **v. organization,** organisation *f* bénévole; **v. work,** bénévolat *m*; **v. worker,** bénévole *mf*; **(c)** *Physiol* volontaire. **2** *n Rel Mus* (*on organ*) morceau *m* pour orgue; (*on trumpet*) morceau pour trompette.

volunteer[1] [vɒlən'tɪər] **1** *n Mil* volontaire *m*; (*for charity etc*) bénévole *mf*; **to call for volunteers,** demander des volontaires; **can I have a v. from the audience?,** y a-t-il une personne dans la salle qui voudrait bien venir sur scène?; **as a v.,** *Mil* en volontaire; (*for charity*) en bénévole; **v. army,** armée de volontaires; **v. service,** service volontaire. **2** *adj* (*teacher etc*) bénévole.

volunteer[2] **1** *vt* offrir volontairement *ou* spontanément (*ses services*); donner spontanément (*des renseignements*); **to v. advice,** offrir des conseils; **to v. to do sth,** se porter volontaire *ou* se proposer pour faire qch; **he's always volunteering other people,** il propose toujours les services des autres sans leur demander leur avis; **they volunteered their son to look after the neighbours' dog,** ils ont proposé que leur fils s'occupe du chien des voisins.

2 *vi Mil* s'engager comme volontaire **(for,** pour); (*for charitable work etc*) proposer ses services **(for,** pour); **why don't you v.?,** pourquoi est-ce que tu ne te portes pas volontaire?; (*as audience participant*) pourquoi est-ce que tu n'y vas pas?; **I wish I'd never volunteered to help,** si seulement je ne m'étais pas porté volontaire pour aider!; **I wish I'd never volunteered for this,** si seulement je ne m'étais pas porté volontaire!

voluptuary [və'lʌptʊərɪ] *n* voluptueux, -euse.

voluptuous [və'lʌptjʊəs] *adj* **(a)** (*figure*) sensuel; **(b)** (*pleasure*) voluptueux.

voluptuously [və'lʌptʊəslɪ] *adv* voluptueusement, avec sensualité.

voluptuousness [və'lʌptjʊəsnɪs] *n* **(a)** (*of figure*) sensualité *f*; **(b)** (*of pleasure*) volupté *f*.

vomit[1] ['vɒmɪt] *n* vomissure *f*, vomi *m*; **to choke on one's own v.,** s'étouffer avec son propre vomi.

vomit[2] *vt & vi* vomir, rendre; **to v. blood,** vomir du sang; **he vomits up everything he eats,** il vomit *ou* rejette *ou* rend tout ce qu'il mange; **to v. (forth) smoke,** (*of chimney*) vomir de la fumée.

vomiting ['vɒmɪtɪŋ] *n* vomissement *m*.

vomitory ['vɒmɪtərɪ] *adj & n Med* vomitif *m*.

voodoo[1] ['vuːduː] *n* vaudou *m*; **v. priest,** prêtre *m* vaudou.

voodoo[2] *vt* ensorceler.

voodooism ['vuːduɪz(ə)m] *n* vaudou *m*.

voracious [və'reɪʃəs, vɒr-] *adj* (*person, appetite*) vorace; (*hunger*) vorace, de loup; **v. reader,** lecteur avide.

voraciously [və'reɪʃəslɪ, vɒr-] *adv* (*to eat*) voracement, avec voracité; (*to read*) avidement; **to be v. hungry,** avoir une faim de loup.

voracity [vɒ'ræsɪtɪ] *n* voracité *f*.

vortex, *pl* **-ices, -exes** ['vɔːteks, -ɪsiːz, -eksɪz] *n* (*of dust, smoke*) tourbillon *m*; (*whirlpool*) gouffre *m*; *Fig* **the v. of politics,** le tourbillon de la politique.

votary ['vəʊtərɪ] *n* fervent, -ente **(of,** de); *Rel* dévot, -ote **(of,** à).

vote[1] [vəʊt] *n* **(a)** (*by several people*) vote *m*, scrutin *m*; (*of individual*) vote, voix *f*, suffrage *m*; (*right to vote*) droit *m* de vote; **popular v.,** consultation *f* populaire; **to put a question to the v.,** soumettre une question au vote; **let's put it to the v.,** votons; **to take the v.,** procéder au scrutin; **to take a v. on sth,** voter sur qch; **to give one's v. to s.o.,** donner son vote *ou* sa voix à qn; **to count** *or* **tell the votes,** compter les votes, dépouiller le scrutin; **they've got my v.,** je vote pour eux; **can I count on your v.?,** puis-je compter sur votre vote?; **to be elected by one v.,** être élu à une voix de majorité; **the motion was adopted by six votes to two,** la motion a été adoptée par six voix contre deux; **how many votes did she get?,** combien de voix est-ce qu'elle a obtenu?; **to record one's v.,** voter; **the v. went against her,** le vote a été en sa défaveur; **one man, one v.,** suffrage universel; **to have the v.,** avoir le droit de vote; **votes for women!,** le droit de vote aux femmes!; **British women got the v. in 1928,** les femmes britanniques ont obtenu le droit de vote en 1928; **the Republicans got 52% of the v.,** les républicains ont remporté 52% du scrutin; **to lose the trade union/black v.,** perdre les suffrages des syndicalistes/des Noirs.

(b) (*of assembly*) motion *f*, résolution *f*; **v. of censure** *or* **no confidence,** motion de censure; **v. of confidence,** vote *m* de confiance; **to propose a v. of thanks,** faire un discours de remerciement.

vote[2] **1** *vi* voter **(for,** pour; **against,** contre); **to v. by (a) show of hands,** voter à mains levées; **to v. Communist,** voter communiste; **v. for Thomas!,** votez Thomas!; *Fig* **to**

v. with one's feet, voter avec ses pieds, indiquer sa désapprobation en quittant un pays *ou* une région *etc.* **2** *vt* voter (*une somme, un crédit*); **to v. £50,000 for the victims of the disaster,** voter 50 000 livres pour les sinistrés; **the senators voted themselves a pay rise,** les sénateurs se sont voté une augmentation de salaire; **I v. (that) we go,** je propose que nous y allions; **they voted the holiday a success,** ils ont décidé d'un commun accord que les vacances avaient été une réussite.

►**vote down** *vtsep* rejeter (*une motion*); ne pas élire *ou* ne pas réélire (*un candidat*).

►**vote in** *vtsep* élire (*un candidat*) (**as,** en tant que).

►**vote on** *vipo* mettre au vote.

►**vote out** *vtsep* (*decision, bill etc*) rejeter; (*person*) ne pas réélire.

►**vote through** *vtsep* ratifier, approuver, accepter.

voter ['vəʊtər] *n* (*taking part in vote*) votant, -ante; (*with right to vote*) électeur, -trice; **the voters,** l'électorat; **French voters go to the polls tomorrow,** les Français vont aux urnes demain; **v. registration,** inscription *f* sur les registres électoraux; **v. turnout,** (*at election*) taux *m* de participation électorale.

voting ['vəʊtɪŋ] **1** *adj* (*assembly, member*) votant; (*elector*) voteur, -euse. **2** *n* (participation *f* au) vote *m*; (*polling*) scrutin *m*; **result of the v.,** résultat *m* du vote; **v. booth,** isoloir *m*; *US* **v. machine,** machine *f* à voter; **v. paper,** bulletin *m* de vote; *Comm* **v. rights,** droits *mpl* de vote; **v. shares,** actions *fpl* donnant droit au vote.

votive ['vəʊtɪv] *adj* votif; **v. offering,** ex-voto *m inv.*

vouch [vaʊtʃ] *vi* **to v. for the truth of sth,** témoigner de *ou* répondre de *ou* attester la vérité de qch; **I can v. for it,** je m'en porte garant; **to v. for s.o.,** répondre de qn, se porter garant de qn; **I can v. for his honesty,** je peux me porter garant de son honnêteté.

voucher ['vaʊtʃər] *n* **(a)** (*receipt*) pièce justificative; *Com* pièce comptable; **(b)** (*giving price reduction*) coupon *m*; **(luncheon) v.,** chèque-repas *m*, *pl* chèques-repas, chèque-restaurant *m*, *pl* chèques-restaurant.

vouchsafe [vaʊtʃ'seɪf] *vt Lit* **to v. s.o. sth,** accorder *ou* octroyer qch à qn; **to v. to do sth,** daigner faire qch.

vow[1] [vaʊ] *n* vœu *m*, serment *m*; **to take the vows,** prononcer *ou* faire ses vœux; **to make a v.,** faire un vœu (**to do,** de faire); **to take a v. of poverty,** faire vœu de pauvreté; **to break a v.,** rompre *ou* transgresser un vœu, rompre un serment; **to keep a v.,** respecter un serment.

vow[2] *vt* vouer, jurer; **to v. obedience,** jurer obéissance; **to v. revenge on s.o.,** faire vœu de se venger sur qn; **to v. to do sth,** faire vœu *ou* jurer de faire qch.

vowel ['vaʊəl] *n Ling* voyelle *f*; **v. sound,** son *m* vocalique.

voyage[1] ['vɔɪɪdʒ] *n* **(sea) v.,** voyage *m* en mer; **v. by air,** voyage en avion; **v. in space,** voyage dans l'espace.

voyage[2] *vi Lit* voyager.

voyager ['vɔɪɪdʒər] *n Lit* voyageur, -euse.

voyeur [vwɑː'jɜːr] *n* voyeur, -euse.

voyeurism [vwɑː'jɜːrɪz(ə)m] *n* voyeurisme *m*.

voyeuristic [vwɑːjɜː'rɪstɪk] *adj* **it's just v.,** ce n'est que du voyeurisme.

VP [viː'piː] *n abbr* **Vice-President.**

VR [viː'ɑːr] (*abbr* **Victoria Regina**) la Reine Victoria.

vs (*abbr* **versus**) contre, c.

VSO [viːes'əʊ] *n abbr* **Voluntary Service Overseas.**

Vt *abbr* **Vermont.**

VTOL [viːtiːəʊ'el] *n* (*abbr* **vertical take-off and landing (aircraft)**) A.D.A.V..

vulcanite ['vʌlkənaɪt] *n* ébonite *f*.

vulcanization [vʌlkənaɪ'zeɪʃən] *n Ind* vulcanisation *f*.

vulcanize ['vʌlkənaɪz] *vt Ind* vulcaniser (*le caoutchouc*).

vulgar ['vʌlgər] *adj* **(a)** (*coarse*) vulgaire, commun; **don't be v.!,** ne sois pas vulgaire!; **v. expressions,** expressions *fpl* vulgaires; **to make v. remarks,** dire des vulgarités *fpl*; **to be v. in one's speech,** s'exprimer vulgairement; **(b)** (*widespread*) vulgaire, commun; **v. errors,** erreurs très répandues; **the v. tongue,** la langue commune, la langue vulgaire; **(c)** *Math* **v. fraction,** fraction *f* ordinaire.

vulgarian [vʌl'geərɪən] *n* **(a)** personne *f* vulgaire; **(b)** (*upstart*) parvenu(e) mal décrassé(e).

vulgarism ['vʌlgərɪz(ə)m] *n* expression *f* vulgaire; (*swearword*) vulgarité *f*, grossièreté *f*.

vulgarity [vʌl'gærɪtɪ] *n* vulgarité *f*, grossièreté *f*.

vulgarization [vʌlgəraɪ'zeɪʃən] *n* vulgarisation *f*.

vulgarize ['vʌlgəraɪz] *vt* vulgariser (*une science etc*); vulgariser, trivialiser (*son style etc*).

vulgarly ['vʌlgəlɪ] *adv* (*coarsely*) vulgairement.

vulgate ['vʌlgɪt, -eɪt] *n Rel* **the V.,** la Vulgate.

vulnerability [vʌln(ə)rə'bɪlɪtɪ] *n* vulnérabilité *f*.

vulnerable ['vʌln(ə)rəb(ə)l] *adj* vulnérable; **he's at a v. age,** il est à un âge vulnérable; **v. to criticism,** sensible à la critique; **that's her v. spot,** c'est son point faible *ou* son talon d'Achille; **this left them v. on their eastern border,** cela les a laissés dans une position vulnérable sur leur frontière est.

vulture ['vʌltʃər] *n* vautour *m*; *Fig* vautour, rapace *m*.

vulva ['vʌlvə] *n Anat* vulve *f*.

vulvitis [vʌl'vaɪtɪs] *n Med* vulvite *f*.

vv *abbr* **verses.**

vying *see* **VIE.**

W

W, w ['dʌb(ə)ljuː] *n* (la lettre) W, w *m*.

W (a) *El* (*abbr* **watt(s)**) W; **(b)** (*abbr* **west**) O..

wacky ['wækɪ] *adj esp Am F* farfelu; **the film is a w. comedy about ...,** ce film est une comédie farfelue sur ...; **she has a w. sense of humour,** elle a un sens de l'humour farfelu.

wad[1] [wɒd] *n* **(a)** tampon *m*, bouchon *m* (*d'ouate*); boulette *f* (*de chewing gum*); **(b)** liasse *f* (*de billets de banque*); *Am* **to shoot one's w.,** *F* (*spend all one's money*) claquer tout son fric; *Vulg* (*of man, have orgasm*) décharger, envoyer la sauce; **(c)** *Br Mil Sl* sandwich *m*; **(d)** *Mil* bourre *f* (*de cartouche*).

wad[2] *vt* (**-dd-**) **(a)** bourrer (*une arme à feu*); **(b)** *Sewing* ouater, capitonner.

▸**wad up** *vtsep* **he wadded up his cap,** il fit un bourrelet de sa casquette.

wadding ['wɒdɪŋ] *n* **(a)** (*action*) ouatage *m*, capitonnage *m*; rembourrage *m*; **(b)** (*material*) ouate *f* (*pour vêtements*); bourre *f* (*pour armes à feu*).

waddle[1] ['wɒd(ə)l] *n* dandinement *m*; **to walk with a w.,** (*of person*) marcher en se dandinant.

waddle[2] *vi* se dandiner, marcher en se dandinant; **to w. along,** avancer en se dandinant.

wade [weɪd] **1** *vi esp Am* (*of child*) patauger dans l'eau *ou* dans la vase; **to w. across a stream,** passer un cours d'eau à gué. **2** *vt* passer (*un cours d'eau*) à gué.

▸**wade in** *vi* **(a)** entrer dans l'eau; **(b)** *F* (*become involved*) **when the fight started, everybody waded in,** quand la bagarre a commencé tout le monde s'en est mêlé.

▸**wade into** *vipo F* (*attack*) s'attaquer à, s'en prendre à (*qn*); s'attaquer à, se mettre à (*une tâche*).

▸**wade through** *vipo* (*tackle*) faire (*qch*) lentement *ou* laborieusement; **to w. through a book,** venir péniblement à bout d'un livre; **I'm wading through his latest novel,** j'avance péniblement dans son dernier roman.

wader ['weɪdər] *n* **(a)** (*bird*) échassier *m*; **(b) waders,** bottes cuissardes imperméables.

wadi ['wɒdɪ] *n Geog* oued *m*.

wading ['weɪdɪŋ] **1** *adj* **w. bird,** échassier *m*. **2** *n esp Am* pataugeage *m*; **w. pool,** petite piscine (*pour enfants*).

wafer ['weɪfər] *n* **(a)** *Culin* gaufrette *f*; **(b)** *Electron* tranche *f*; **(c)** *Rel* hostie *f*; **(d)** *Jur* cachet *m* de papier rouge.

waferboard ['weɪfəbɔːd] *n Constr* panneaux gaufrés.

wafer-thin [weɪfə'θɪn] *adj* (*slice, sandwich*) mince comme du papier à cigarettes; *Fig* (*majority*) infime; **to cut sth w.-t.,** couper qch en tranches très fines.

waffle[1] ['wɒf(ə)l] *n Culin* gaufre *f*; **w. iron,** gaufrier *m*.

waffle[2] *n F* verbiage *m*; **her speech was just the usual w.,** son discours n'était que du verbiage, comme d'habitude.

waffle[3] *vi F* parler pour ne rien dire; (*in writing*) faire du remplissage; **he just waffles on,** (il n'a rien à dire mais) il ne sait pas s'arrêter.

waft[1] [wɑːft, wɒft] *n* bouffée *f* (*de vent, de parfum*).

waft[2] **1** *vt* (*of wind*) **to w. a sound/a scent through the air,** porter *ou* transporter un son/un parfum dans les airs; **music wafted on the breeze,** musique qui flotte *ou* qui arrive sur la brise. **2** *vi* (*of scent etc*) flotter; **to w. along,** être transporté par le vent, flotter sur la brise; **her voice wafted down the stairs,** sa voix flottait jusqu'en bas de l'escalier.

wag[1] [wæg] *n* agitation *f*; hochement *m* (*de la tête*); **with a w. of his tail,** (*of dog*) en remuant la queue.

wag[2] *v* (**-gg-**) 1 *vt* agiter, remuer (*le doigt*); **to w. its tail,** (*of dog*) remuer *ou* agiter la queue; (*of bird*) hocher la queue; **to w. one's finger at s.o.,** menacer qn du doigt; **to w. one's head,** hocher la tête. **2** *vi* s'agiter, se remuer; **his tail was wagging,** (*of dog*) sa queue frétillait; **to set (people's) tongues wagging,** faire marcher les langues; **tongues are wagging,** les langues vont bon train (**about,** sur, au sujet de); **tongues are beginning to w.,** les langues se délient.

wag[3] *n Old-fashioned F* plaisantin *m*, farceur, -euse.

wage[1] [weɪdʒ] *n* **(a) wage(s),** salaire *m*; paie *f*; gages *mpl* (*de domestique*); **basic w.,** salaire de base; **living w.,** minimum vital; **to get one's weekly w.,** recevoir son salaire de la semaine, *F* toucher sa semaine; **to earn good wages,** être bien payé; **w. bargaining,** négociations salariales; **w. bill,** dépenses salariales; **w. claim** *or* **demand,** revendication salariale; **w.-cost inflation,** inflation *f* par les salaires; **w. earner,** salarié, -iée; (*breadwinner*) soutien *m* de famille; **w. freeze,** blocage *m* des salaires; **w. increase** *or* **rise,** augmentation *f* de salaire; **w. packet,** (*envelope*) enveloppe *f* de paie; (*net pay*) paie, salaire; *F* **w. slave,** = une personne qui dépend entièrement de son salaire pour vivre; **(b)** *Fml* salaire *m*, récompense *f*; **the wages of sin is death,** la mort est le prix du péché.

wage[2] *vt* **to w. war,** faire la guerre (**with, on, against,** à); **to w. a campaign against smoking,** mener une campagne contre le tabagisme.

wager[1] ['weɪdʒər] *n* pari *m*, gageure *f*; **to lay** *or* **make a w.,** faire un pari *ou* une gageure, parier, gager; **he did it for a w.,** il l'a fait pour tenir un pari.

wager[2] *vt* parier, gager (*cent livres etc*); **to w. that ...,** parier que ...; **to w. one's reputation,** mettre sa réputation en jeu.

wagging [wægɪŋ] *n* agitation *f* (*de la queue*); hochement *m* (*de la tête*); **there was a lot of tongue w.,** on jasait beaucoup.

waggish ['wægɪʃ] *adj F* plaisant, badin; (*sense of humour*) blagueur.

waggle ['wæg(ə)l] *vt & vi* remuer; **to w. one's eyebrows/ears,** faire remuer ses sourcils/ses oreilles.

wag(g)on ['wægən] *n* (*the spelling* **waggon** *is now rare except for* **(a)**) **(a)** (*horse-drawn*) charrette *f* (à quatre roues), chariot *m*; *Am* (*child's toy*) chariot miniature; (*for drinks etc*) chariot; *Fig* **to be on the w.,** être au régime sec; *Fig* **to fall off the w.,** (*temporarily*) faire un écart; (*permanently*) se remettre à la boisson; *US Hist* **w. train,** convoi *m* de chariots bâchés; **(b)** *Aut Am* (*Br* = **station w.**) break *m*; *US* **patrol w.,** voiture *f* cellulaire, *F* panier *m* à salade; **(c)** *Rail* wagon *m* (découvert); **goods w.,** wagon à marchandises; **covered goods w.,** fourgon *m*.

Wag(g)on ['wægən] *n Astron* la Grande Ourse.

wag(g)oner ['wægənər] *n* roulier *m*, charretier *m*.

wag(g)onette [wægə'net] *n* (*carriage*) break *m*.

wag(g)onload ['wægənləʊd] *n* charretée *f* (*de foin etc*); *Rail* (charge *f* de) wagon *m*.

Wagnerian [vɑːg'nɪərɪən] *adj & n Mus* wagnérien, -ienne.

wagtail ['wægteɪl] *n* (*bird*) bergeronnette *f*, hochequeue *m*, lavandière *f*.

waif [weɪf] *n* enfant abandonné; **waifs and strays,** enfants abandonnés.

wail[1] [weɪl] *n* cri plaintif, plainte *f*; vagissement *m* (*de nouveau-né*); hurlement *m* (*de sirène etc*); **the child gave a w.,** l'enfant poussa un vagissement.

wail[2] *vi* gémir; (*of new-born child*) vagir; (*of siren*) hurler; **to w. over sth,** se lamenter *ou* pleurer sur qch.

wailing ['weɪlɪŋ] **1** *adj* (*cri, chant*) plaintif. **2** *n* plainte(s) *f(pl)*, lamentation(s) *f(pl)*; **the W. Wall,** (*in Jerusalem*) le mur des Lamentations.

wain [weɪn] *n Arch* charrette *f*; **hay w.,** charrette à foin; *Astron* **Charles's W.,** la Grande Ourse.

wainscot[1] ['weɪnskɒt] *n* lambris *m*, boiseries *fpl*.

wainscot[2] *vt* (**-t(t)-**) lambrisser, boiser.

wainscot(t)ing ['weɪnskɒtɪŋ] *n* **(a)** (*material*) lambris *m*, boiseries *fpl*; **(b)** (*action*) lambrissage *m*, boisage *m*.

waist [weɪst] *n* **(a)** (*of person, dress*) taille *f*, ceinture *f*; **down** *or* **up to the w.,** jusqu'à la ceinture, jusqu'à mi-corps; **stripped to the w.,** nu jusqu'à la ceinture, torse nu; **it's too tight at the w.,** ça serre à la taille; **what w. are these trousers?,** quel est le tour de taille de ce pantalon?;

to put one's arm round s.o.'s w., prendre qn par la taille; **w. lock,** (*in wrestling*) ceinture; **w. measurement,** tour *m* de taille; **(b)** étranglement *m* (*d'un sablier, d'un violon*); rétrécissement *m* (*d'un tuyau*); **(c)** *Nau* embelle *f*, passavant *m* (*d'un navire*); **(d)** *Old-fashioned Am* corsage *m*.

waistband ['weɪstbænd] *n* ceinture *f*.

waistcoat ['weɪskəʊt] *n Br* (*Am* = **vest**) gilet *m*.

waisted ['weɪstɪd] *adj* (*coat, jacket*) cintré; (*vase*) au goulot resserré.

-waisted ['weɪstɪd] *suff* **long-/short-w.,** long/court de taille; **slim-w.,** à taille fine, qui a la taille fine; **wasp-w.,** à taille de guêpe, qui a une taille de guêpe.

waist-deep [weɪs'diːp] *adj* (*water etc*) à hauteur de la taille; **to be w.-d. in water,** avoir de l'eau jusqu'à la taille; *Fig* **I'm w.-d. in work/files/***etc*, je croule sous le travail/les dossiers/*etc*.

waist-high [weɪst'haɪ] *adj* (*grass etc*) à hauteur de la taille.

waistline ['weɪstlaɪn] *n Sewing* taille *f*; **low waistlines are back,** les tailles basses reviennent à la mode; **to watch** *or* **think of one's w.,** surveiller sa ligne.

wait[1] [weɪt] *n* **(a)** attente *f*; **we had a long w.,** nous avons dû attendre longtemps; **it was worth the w.,** ça valait la peine d'attendre; **it will be a long w. before the next train,** il va falloir attendre longtemps avant que le prochain train arrive; **to lie in w.,** (*ambush*) se tenir en embuscade; être à l'affût; **to lie in w. for s.o.,** (*ambush*) tendre un guet-apens à qn; attendre qn au passage; **(b)** *Old-fashioned* **waits,** chanteurs *mpl* de noëls (*qui vont de porte en porte à l'approche de Noël*).

wait[2] **1** *vi* attendre; **w. a moment/a minute/a bit,** attendez un moment/un instant/un peu; **to keep s.o. waiting,** faire attendre qn; **to w. for s.o./sth,** attendre qn/qch; **what are you waiting for?,** qu'attendez-vous?; **we're waiting to be served,** nous attendons qu'on nous serve; **w. until tomorrow,** attendez jusqu'à demain; **I shall w. until she's ready,** j'attendrai qu'elle soit prête; **(just) you w.!,** (*threat*) attends un peu!; **just w. till I tell you what's happened!,** attends que je te dise ce qui s'est passé!; **w. for it!,** (*not yet, guess what*) attends!; **I can't w. to ...,** j'ai hâte de ...; **I can't w. to see him,** je brûle d'impatience de le voir; **I can't w. for the weekend,** vivement le weekend, j'ai hâte que le weekend arrive; **I can hardly w.,** je meurs d'impatience; *Com* **repairs while you w.,** réparations à la minute; *Prov* **everything comes to him** *or* **to he who waits,** tout vient à point à qui sait attendre; **we must w. and see,** il faudra voir; **w. and see!,** attends voir!; **w.-and-see policy,** politique *f* attentiste, attentisme *m*; **to w. at table,** servir (à table), faire le service; *Comptr* **w. state,** état *m* d'attente.

2 *vt* attendre, guetter (*une occasion, un signal*); **w. your turn!,** attendez votre tour!; **don't w. dinner for me,** ne m'attendez pas pour vous mettre à table.

►**wait about** *vi* attendre; **don't keep me waiting about,** ne me fais pas attendre.

►**wait behind** *vi* (*stay*) rester.

►**wait in** *vi* (*stay at home*) rester à la maison; **to w. in for s.o.,** rester à la maison pour attendre qn.

►**wait on 1** *vipo* (*serve*) servir (*qn*); *Arch* présenter ses respects à (*qn*); *Am* **to w. on table,** servir (à table), faire le service; **to w. on s.o. hand and foot,** être aux petits soins auprès de *ou* pour qn. **2** *vi* (*continue to wait*) continuer à attendre.

►**wait out** *vtsep* **to w. it out,** attendre que qch arrête *ou* soit fini.

►**wait up** *vi* **(a)** (*not go to bed*) ne pas aller se coucher; **I'll w. up for you,** j'attendrai que tu arrives *ou* rentres avant d'aller me coucher; **I'll be late so don't w. up for me,** je rentrerai tard, tu n'auras qu'à te coucher; **(b)** *esp Am* attendre; **w. up, I can't walk as fast as you,** attends-moi, je ne peux pas marcher aussi vite que toi.

waiter ['weɪtər] *n* garçon *m* (de restaurant); **head w.,** maître *m* d'hôtel; **w.!,** garçon!

waiting ['weɪtɪŋ] *n* attente *f*; *Aut* **no w.,** stationnement interdit; **to play a w. game,** jouer un jeu d'attente; **w. (at table),** service *m* (à table); **gentleman-in-w.,** gentilhomme-servant *m*, *pl* gentilshommes-servants, gentilhomme *m* de service (**to,** auprès de); **lady-in-w.,** dame *f* d'honneur; *Hum* femme enceinte; **w. list,** liste *f* d'attente; **there's a two-month w. list for an operation,** il faut attendre deux mois pour une opération; **to be on the w. list,** être sur la liste d'attente; **w. period,** période *f* d'attente; **w. room,** salle *f* d'attente, hall *m* (*de gare*); antichambre *f* (*chez un médecin*).

waitlist ['weɪtlɪst] *vt esp Am* mettre (*qn*) sur une liste d'attente; **I'm waitlisted for the next flight,** je suis sur la liste d'attente pour le prochain vol.

waitperson ['weɪtpɜːs(ə)n] *n Am* (*male*) garçon *m*, serveur *m*; (*female*) serveuse *f*; **w. wanted,** (*notice in café etc*) on cherche du personnel de service.

waitress ['weɪtrɪs] *n* serveuse *f*; **w.!,** mademoiselle!

waive [weɪv] *vt* renoncer à, abandonner (*ses prétentions, ses droits*); déroger à (*un principe*); ne pas insister sur (*une condition*).

waiver ['weɪvər] *n Jur* **w. of a right,** renonciation *f* à un droit; **w. of a claim,** désistement *m* de revendication.

wake[1] [weɪk] *n Nau* sillage *m*; *Fig* **in the w. of,** dans le sillage de, à la suite de; *Fig* **in the w. of the storm,** à la suite de la tempête; *Fig* **in the w. of last week's decision,** à la suite de la décision de la semaine dernière; *Fig* **to follow in s.o.'s w.,** marcher sur les traces de qn.

wake[2] *n* **(a)** (*in Ireland*) veillée *f* de corps; **to have a w. for s.o.,** organiser une veillée de commémoration en souvenir de qn; **(b) wakes week,** (*in northern England*) semaine *f* de congé annuel.

wake[3] *v* (*pt* **woke** [wəʊk], **waked** [weɪkt]; *pp* **woke, waked, woken** ['wəʊk(ə)n]) **1** *vi* se réveiller; **to w. with a start,** se réveiller en sursaut. **2** *vt* éveiller (*une émotion, un souvenir*); **to w. s.o.,** (*from sleep*) réveiller qn; (*from inaction*) tirer qn de sa torpeur; **w. me at six,** réveillez-moi à six heures; **to be hard to w.,** avoir le sommeil lourd; **to w. the dead,** réveiller les morts; *Fig* **to make enough noise to w. the dead,** faire un bruit à réveiller les morts.

►**wake up 1** *vi* **(a)** se réveiller; **come on, w. up!,** allons, réveillez-vous!; (*be more alert*) remuez-vous!, secouez-vous!; **(b)** *Fig* prendre conscience; **she is waking up to the truth,** la vérité se fait jour dans son esprit. **2** *vtsep* **(a)** réveiller (*qn*); (*from inaction*) tirer (*qn*) de sa torpeur; *Fig* **this country needs waking up,** ce pays a besoin de se réveiller; **(b)** *Fig* faire réaliser *ou* comprendre; **that woke her up to what was going on,** ça lui a ouvert les yeux sur ce qui se passait.

wakeful ['weɪkfʊl] *adj* **(a)** (*not sleepy*) bien éveillé, peu disposé à dormir; (*not sleeping*) sans sommeil; **w. night,** nuit blanche; **to have a w. night,** passer une nuit blanche; **(b)** (*vigilant*) vigilant.

wakefulness ['weɪkfʊlnɪs] *n* **(a)** (*insomnia*) insomnie *f*; **(b)** (*vigilance*) vigilance *f*.

waken ['weɪk(ə)n] **1** *vt* **(a)** éveiller, réveiller (*qn*); **noise fit to w. the dead,** bruit à réveiller les morts; **(b)** éveiller (*une émotion*). **2** *vi esp Lit* se réveiller, s'éveiller.

wakening ['weɪk(ə)nɪŋ] *n* réveil *m*.

wake-up ['weɪkʌp] *adj esp Am* **w.-up call,** réveil *m* téléphonique; **to ask for a w.-up call,** (*in hotel etc*) demander à être réveillé par téléphone.

wakey ['weɪkɪ] *int F* **w. (w.)!,** debout!, réveillez-vous!

waking ['weɪkɪŋ] *n* **(a)** veille *f*; **between sleeping and w.,** entre la veille et le sommeil; **w. hours,** heures *fpl* de veille; **to spend (all) one's w. hours doing sth,** passer tout son temps à faire qch; **(b)** réveil *m*.

waking up *n* = **WAKING (b)**.

wale [weɪl] *n Fml* marque *f*, trace *f* (*d'un coup de fouet*).

Wales [weɪlz] *n* le pays de Galles; **New South W.,** (*in Australia*) la Nouvelle-Galles du Sud; **the Prince of W.,** le Prince de Galles.

walk[1] [wɔːk] *n* **(a)** (*action*) marche *f*; **it's half an hour's w. from here,** c'est à une demi-heure d'ici à pied *ou* une demi-heure de marche d'ici; **it's only a short w. (from here),** ce n'est qu'une petite promenade;

(b) (*stroll*) promenade *f* (à pied), tour *m*; **to go for a w.,** (aller) se promener, faire un tour *ou* une promenade; **it's a lovely w. from here to the village,** c'est une promenade très agréable d'ici jusqu'au village; *Am* **take a w.!,** (*get lost!*) va te faire voir!; **to take s.o. for a w.,** emmener qn en promenade; **to take the dog for a w.,** sortir *ou* promener le chien;

(c) (*gait*) manière *f* de marcher, démarche *f*, allure *f*; **I know him by his w.,** je le reconnais à sa démarche; **to go** *or* **move at a w.,** aller *ou* avancer *ou* marcher au pas; **to drop into a w.,** (*of horse*) se mettre au pas; (*of person*) se remettre au pas (*après avoir couru*);

(d) (*path*) allée *f* (*de jardin*); avenue *f*, promenade *f*;

(e) *Am* trottoir *m*; **covered w.,** allée couverte; *Archit* péristyle *m*, ambulatoire *m*; *Am* **cross w.,** passage clouté (pour piétons);

(f) *Fig* **w. of life,** (*social class*) milieu *m*; (*profession*) métier *m*, carrière *f*; **people from all walks of life,** des gens de toutes sortes de milieux.

walk[2] **1** *vi* **(a)** (*move on foot*) marcher; *Br Sl* (*of suspected* *criminal*) partir; **to w. on** *or* **in the road,** marcher sur la chaussée; **to w. two paces forward,** faire deux pas en avant; **to w. on all fours,** marcher à quatre pattes; **is the baby walking yet?,** est-ce que le bébé marche maintenant?; **to w. in one's sleep,** être somnambule; **I'll w. a little way with you,** je vais vous accompagner un bout de chemin; **to w. with a limp,** boiter (en marchant); *esp Am* **w.!/don't w.!,** (*traffic sign*) (piétons) passez!/attendez!; **to w. up/down the street/the stairs,** monter/descendre la rue/l'escalier; **to w. up and down,** (*stairs*) monter et descendre à pied; (*pace the floor*) se promener de long en large, faire les cent pas; **to w. up to s.o.,** s'approcher de qn; **to w. across** *or* **over the street to speak to s.o.,** traverser la rue pour parler à qn; **please w. in,** entrez sans frapper; **to w. through the town/the crowd,** traverser la ville/la foule (à pied);

(b) (*as opposed to ride, drive etc*) aller à pied; (*for exercise, pleasure*) se promener (à pied); **to w. home/back,** rentrer/retourner à pied; **I had to w.,** j'ai dû faire le trajet à pied; **w.!,** (*don't run*) ne cours pas!; **he walks five kilometres every day,** il fait 5 kilomètres à pied tous les jours;

(c) (*of horse, rider*) aller au pas;

(d) (*of ghost*) revenir.

2 *vt* **(a)** (*move along*) **to w. the streets,** (*wander*) courir les rues, battre le pavé; (*of prostitute*) faire le trottoir; **to w. one's beat** *or* **one's round,** (*of sentry*) faire sa faction; *Th* **to w. the boards,** être sur les planches;

(b) (*make move*) faire marcher, faire promener (*un malade*); **to w. s.o. home,** raccompagner qn; **to w. s.o. to the bus stop,** accompagner qn jusqu'à l'arrêt d'autobus; **to w. s.o. off their feet,** exténuer *ou* éreinter qn à force de le faire marcher; **to w. a horse,** (*lead along*) conduire *ou* promener un cheval (au pas); (*bring to a walk*) mettre un cheval au pas; **to w. the dog,** promener le chien.

►**walk away** *vi* s'en aller, partir; *Sp* **to w. away from a competitor,** distancer facilement *ou* semer un concurrent.

►**walk away with** *vipo* **(a)** (*take*) prendre; **(b)** (*steal*) faucher.

►**walk in on** *vipo* (*disturb*) déranger (*qn*).

►**walk into** *vipo* **(a)** (*enter*) entrer dans (*une pièce*); **(b)** (*collide with*) rentrer dans (*qn*).

►**walk off 1** *vi* s'en aller, partir. **2** *vtsep* **to w. off one's lunch,** faire une promenade de digestion.

►**walk off with** *vipo* **(a)** (*win easily*) gagner (*qch*) haut la main; **(b)** (*take*) prendre; **who's walked off with the scissors?,** qui est-ce qui a pris les ciseaux?; **(c)** (*steal*) faucher.

►**walk on** *vi* **(a)** continuer à marcher; **(b)** *Th* figurer (*sur la scène*), faire *ou* remplir un rôle de figurant(e).

►**walk out** *vi* sortir (**in a rage,** en colère); *Ind* débrayer, se mettre en grève; **delegates walked out of the meeting,** les délégués ont quitté la réunion (en signe de protestation); *F* **to w. out on s.o.,** (*desert*) abandonner qn, plaquer qn; (*leave in anger*) quitter qn en colère, partir en claquant la porte.

►**walk over** *vipo* **(a)** (*beat*) gagner (*qn*) d'office; **(b)** (*treat badly*) **you shouldn't let him** *or* **her** *or* **people** *etc* **w. all over you,** tu ne devrais pas te laisser marcher sur les pieds; **(c)** *Sp* **to w. over the course,** inspecter le terrain (avant l'épreuve).

►**walk round** *vipo* faire le tour de (*un musée etc*).

►**walk through 1** *vi* (*succeed*) réussir les doigts dans le nez. **2** *vipo* réussir (*ses examens etc*) sans effort.

walkabout ['wɔːkəbaʊt] *n Austr* (*of aborigines*) voyage *m* dans le désert; *Fig* bain *m* de foule; **to go w.,** (*of aborigines*) aller faire un voyage dans le désert; *Fig* prendre un bain de foule.

walkaway ['wɔːkəweɪ] *n Sp* victoire *f* facile.

walker ['wɔːkər] *n* **(a)** (*person*) marcheur, -euse; (*stroller*) promeneur, -euse; **he's a fast/slow w.,** il marche vite/lentement; **(b)** (*aid*) (*for infirm*) (dé)ambulateur *m*; (*for baby*) bébé-trotte *m*; **(c)** *Th* **w. on,** figurant, -ante.

walkie-talkie [wɔːkɪ'tɔːkɪ] *n Rad* talkie-walkie *m*, *pl* talkies-walkies.

walk-in ['wɔːkɪn] *adj* (*cupboard etc*) assez grand pour qu'on puisse y entrer; **w.-in fridge,** armoire réfrigérante; **the flat is in w.-in condition,** l'appartement est immédiatement habitable.

walking ['wɔːkɪŋ] **1** *adj* (*voyageur, spectre*) ambulant; **at a w. pace,** au pas; **to slow (down) to a w. pace,** se remettre au pas (*après avoir couru*); **she's a w. dictionary,** c'est un dictionnaire ambulant; *Mil* **w. wounded,** blessés *mpl* sur pied *ou* en état de marcher.

2 *n* marche *f*; **w. is the best form of exercise,** la marche est le meilleur des exercices; **two hour's w.,** deux heures de marche *ou* de promenade; **I like w.,** j'aime bien marcher; **it's within ten minutes' w. distance,** c'est à moins de dix minutes à pied; **it's within w. distance,** on peut aisément s'y rendre à pied; *esp Am F* **to give s.o. their w. orders** *or* **papers,** congédier qn, donner son congé à qn; *Br* **w. frame,** (*Am* = **walker**) (dé)ambulateur *m*; **w. holiday,** vacances passées à la randonnée; *Sp* **w. race,** concours *m* de marche; **w. shoes,** chaussures *fpl* de marche; **w. shorts,** short *m* de randonnée; **w. stick,** canne *f*.

Walkman ® ['wɔːkmən] *n* (*personal stereo*) walkman *m*, baladeur *m*.

walk-on ['wɔːkɒn] **1** *n Th* **w.-on (part),** rôle *m* de figurant(e). **2** *adj Av* (*flight, service*) pour lequel il n'est pas nécessaire d'effectuer de réservation.

walkout ['wɔːkaʊt] *n Ind etc* débrayage *m*, mise *f* en grève; (*from meeting*) départ *m*; **to cause a w.,** (*at meeting etc*) provoquer le départ d'un groupe *ou* d'une faction.

walkover ['wɔːkəʊvər] *n Sp* victoire *f* facile; **it was a w.!,** c'était facile *ou F* fastoche!

walk-through ['wɔːkθruː] *n Th* répétition *f*.

walk-up ['wɔːkʌp] *adj & n Am* (immeuble *m*) sans ascenseur *m*; **third-floor w.-up,** appartement au troisième étage sans ascenseur.

walkway ['wɔːkweɪ] *n* allée *f* (couverte), passage *m* (couvert); **moving w.,** tapis roulant.

wall[1] [wɔːl] *n* **(a)** mur *m*; **to leave only the four walls standing,** ne laisser que les quatre murs; **between these four walls,** entre ces quatre murs; **the town walls,** les murs *ou* les murailles *fpl* de la ville; **the Great W. of China,** la grande muraille de Chine; **W. Street,** la Bourse *ou* le centre financier de New York; **according to W. Street ...,** selon la bourse de New York ..., selon Wall Street ...; **a W. Street broker,** un courtier de la bourse de New York; **w. bars,** (*in gym*) espalier *m*; **w. bracket,** console murale; **w. clock,** pendule murale; **w. game,** (*at Eton*) = sorte de football pratiqué contre un mur; **w. lamp,** (lampe *f* d')applique *f*; **w. map,** carte murale; **w. paintings,** peintures murales;

(b) muraille *f*, paroi *f* (*de rochers*);

(c) paroi *f* (*d'une chaudière, d'une cellule*); flanc *m* (*d'un pneu*);

(d) *Fig* muraille *f* (*de glace*); rideau *m* (*de fumée*); mur *m* (*de silence*); barrage *m* (*d'agents de police*); **to break down a w. of silence,** abattre un mur de silence; **to come up against a blank** *or* **brick w.,** se heurter à un mur; **to have one's back to the w.,** en être réduit à la dernière extrémité, être au pied du mur; **to drive** *or* **push s.o. to the w.,** acculer qn, mettre qn au pied du mur; **to go to the w.,** être ruiné *ou* acculé à la faillite; **the company has gone to the w.,** la société a fait faillite; **the weakest always go(es) to the w.,** le plus faible est toujours battu; **to bang** *or* **beat one's head against a (brick) w.,** se cogner la tête contre un mur; *F* **you might as well talk to a brick w.,** autant parler à un sourd *ou* au mur; *F* **you're driving me up the w.,** tu vas me rendre fou.

wall[2] *vt* murer, entourer de murs.

►**wall in** *vtsep* murer, entourer de murs.

►**wall off** *vtsep* séparer par un mur *ou* une paroi.

►**wall up** *vtsep* murer, maçonner (*une fenêtre, une porte*); *Arch* emmurer (*un prisonnier*).

wallaby ['wɒləbɪ] *n* (*animal*) wallaby *m*.

wallah ['wɒlə] *n* **(a)** (*in India*) employé *m*, garçon *m*; **punkah-w.,** tireur *m* de panka; **(b)** *Old-fashioned F* type *m*.

wallcovering ['wɔːlkʌvərɪŋ] *n* tapisserie *f*.

walled [wɔːld] *adj* (*garden*) muré, clos de murs *ou* d'une enceinte; **w. city,** ville fortifiée.

-walled [wɔːld] *suff* **double-w.,** à double paroi; **brick-w. house,** maison *f* en brique.

wallet ['wɒlɪt] *n* portefeuille *m*.

wall-eyed ['wɔːlaɪd] *adj* (*horse, person*) vairon; (*person*) à strabisme divergent.

wallflower ['wɔːlflaʊər] *n* (*plant*) giroflée *f* jaune; *Fig* **to be a w.,** (*at a dance*) faire tapisserie.

walling ['wɔːlɪŋ] *n* **(a)** murage *m* (*d'une ville, d'un jardin*); **(b)** (*walls*) murs *mpl*, maçonnerie *f*.

walling in *n* = **WALLING (a)**.

walling up *n* murage *m*, maçonnage *m* (*d'une fenêtre*); *Arch* emmurement *m* (*de qn*).

wall-mounted ['wɔːlmaʊntɪd] *adj* (*clock, telephone*) mural.

Walloon [wɒ'luːn] **1** *adj* wallon. **2** *n* **(a)** Wallon, -onne; **(b)** *Ling* wallon *m*.

wallop[1] ['wɒləp] *n F* **(a)** gros coup; (*spanking*) fessée *f*; **I'll give you a w. in a minute,** je vais te coller une beigne dans une minute; **she gave him a real w. across the face,** elle lui a flanqué une sacrée beigne à travers la figure; **give it a w. with the hammer,** mets-y un coup de marteau; **to pack quite a w.,** (*of boxer etc*) frapper dur; (*of drink*) être fort; **(b)** *Br F* bière *f* (brune).

wallop[2] *vt F* rosser (*qn*), tanner le cuir à (*qn*); *Sp* battre (*qn*) à plate(s) couture(s); **w. it with the hammer,** tape-le à coup(s) de marteau.

walloping ['wɒləpɪŋ] *F* **1** *adj* énorme; **a w. great lie,** un gros mensonge. **2** *n* rossée *f*; **to give s.o. a w.,** rosser qn; *Sp* battre qn à plate(s) couture(s); **he got a w. from his mother,** il s'est fait coller une raclée par sa mère; *Sp* **we gave them a w. they'll never forget,** on leur a flanqué une pâtée qu'ils ne sont pas près d'oublier.

wallow[1] ['wɒləʊ] *n* trou bourbeux, mare bourbeuse.

wallow[2] *vi* (*of animal*) se vautrer; (*of ship*) être ballotté (par les flots); **to w. in blood,** se baigner *ou* se plonger dans le sang; **to w. in self-pity,** s'apitoyer sur son propre sort; **to w. in a bath,** se prélasser dans un bain; **to be wallowing in luxury,** baigner dans le luxe.

wallpaper[1] ['wɔːlpeɪpər] *n* papier peint.

wallpaper[2] **1** *vt* tapisser (*une pièce*). **2** *vi* poser du papier peint.

wallpapering ['wɔːlpeɪpərɪŋ] *n* **w. is easy,** poser du papier peint est facile.

wall-to-wall ['wɔːltəwɔːl] *adj* **the room was w.-to-w. with people,** la pièce était bondée; **w.-to-w. carpet(ing),** moquette *f*; *esp US F* **w.-to-w. grin,** sourire *m* énorme.

wally ['wɒlɪ] *n Br F* (*idiot*) andouille *f*, imbécile *mf*; **I felt a bit of a w.,** je me suis senti un peu idiot; **he looked a real** *or* **right w.,** il avait l'air d'une véritable andouille.

walnut ['wɔːlnʌt] *n* **(a)** (*fruit*) noix *f*; **w. oil,** huile *f* de noix; **w. stain,** brou *m* de noix; **(b) w. (tree),** noyer *m*; **(c)** (*wood*) (bois *m* de) noyer *m*; **w. desk/bookcase/***etc*, bureau *m*/bibliothèque *f*/*etc* en noyer.

walrus ['wɔːlrəs] *n* (*animal*) morse *m*; *F* **w. moustache,** moustache *f* à la gauloise.

waltz[1] [wɔːls] *n* valse *f*; **to play a w.,** jouer une valse; **to dance a w.,** danser une valse, valser; **may I have this w.?,** voulez-vous danser cette valse avec moi?

waltz[2] *vi & vt* valser; **to w. with s.o.,** faire valser qn.

▶**waltz off** *vi F* (*leave*) partir, s'en aller; **to w. off with first prize,** remporter le premier prix haut la main.

waltzer ['wɔːlsər] *n* valseur, -euse.

waltzing ['wɔːlsɪŋ] *n* valse *f*.

wan [wɒn] *adj* pâlot, -otte, blême; **to grow w.,** pâlir, blêmir; **w. light,** lumière blafarde; **w. smile,** sourire triste.

wand [wɒnd] *n* **(a)** baguette *f* (*de fée, de magicien*); **(b)** bâton *m* (*de commandement*); verge *f* (*d'huissier*); **(c)** (*for bar codes*) lecteur *m* de codes barres.

wander[1] ['wɒndər] *n* balade *f*; **to go for a w. in the woods,** aller se promener dans les bois.

wander[2] **1** *vi* **(a)** errer (sans but), se promener au hasard; **to w. about,** se balader; **to w. (about) aimlessly,** errer à l'abandon; **to w. about the world,** rouler sa bosse (un peu partout); **his eyes wandered over the scene,** ses regards se promenaient sur cette scène;

(b) (*stray*) **to w. from the subject,** sortir du sujet, digresser; **my thoughts were wandering,** j'avais l'esprit ailleurs; **to let one's thoughts w.,** laisser vaguer ses pensées; **his mind wanders at times** *or* **is apt to w.,** il a des absences;

(c) *Med* **to w. (in one's mind),** divaguer; (*in speaking*) radoter;

(d) *F* (*go*) **I think I'll be wandering off now,** je crois que je vais y aller *ou* me mettre en route maintenant; **I'll just w. down to the beach later,** j'irai faire un tour *ou* je descendrai à la plage plus tard; **could you w. round to the post office for me?,** pourriez-vous passer à la poste pour moi?; **he just wandered in to the office at about 10.30,** il est tranquillement arrivé au bureau à 10h30; **shall we start wandering back then?,** alors, on prend doucement le chemin du retour?

2 *vt* **to w. the streets,** errer dans les rues; *Arch* **to w. the world,** errer de par le monde.

wandering ['wɒndərɪŋ] **1** *adj* **(a)** errant, vagabond; (*tribe*) nomade; *Hum* **w. hands,** mains baladeuses; **w. Jew,** (*plant*) misère *f*; **W. Jew,** Juif éternel; **w. minstrels,** ménestrels ambulants; **(b)** (*esprit*) distrait; **w. attention,** attention vagabonde; **(c)** *Med* qui délire, qui divague; **(d)** (*discours, récit*) incohérent. **2** *n* **(a)** vagabondage *m*; **wanderings,** pérégrinations *fpl*; **(b)** *Med* égarement *m* (*de l'esprit*), délire *m*; **in his wanderings,** dans ses divagations.

wanderer ['wɒndərər] *n* vagabond, -onde.

wanderlust ['wɒndəlʌst] *n* manie *f ou* passion *f* des voyages.

wane[1] [weɪn] *n* **to be on the w.,** (*of moon*) décroître; (*of person, civilization*) être à *ou* sur son déclin; (*of beauty*) être sur le retour; *Fig* **his star is on the w.,** son étoile pâlit.

wane[2] *vi* décroître, décliner; (*of beauty*) être sur le retour; (*of enthusiasm*) s'affaiblir, s'attiédir; *Fig* **his star/his glory is waning,** son étoile pâlit/sa gloire diminue.

wangle[1] ['wæŋg(ə)l] *n F* combine *f*, embrouille, truc *m*.

wangle[2] *vt F* **(a)** (*arrange*) obtenir (*qch*) par subterfuge, carotter, resquiller (*qch*); **I wangled myself a trip to ...,** je me suis débrouillé pour obtenir un voyage à ...; **I'll w. it somehow,** je me débrouillerai, je me démerderai; **how did you w. that?,** comment est-ce que tu t'es débrouillé pour faire ça?; **(b)** (*falsify*) cuisiner (*des comptes*).

wangler ['wæŋglər] *n F* resquilleur, -euse.

wangling ['wæŋglɪŋ] *n* resquillage *m*, carottage *m*; **it just needs a bit of w.,** il suffit de resquiller un peu.

waning ['weɪnɪŋ] **1** *adj* décroissant, déclinant; (*light*) défaillant, faiblissant; **w. moon,** lune décroissante. **2** *n* décroissance *f*, décroissement *m* (*de la lune*); déclin *m* (*de la beauté*); décadence *f* (*d'un empire*); attiédissement *m* (*de l'enthousiasme*).

wank [wæŋk] *vi Br Vulg* (*masturbate*) se branler.

wanker [wæŋkər] *n Br* **(a)** *Vulg* branleur *m*; **(b)** *Sl* (*fool*) branleur *m*.

wanly ['wɒnlɪ] *adv* (*briller*) faiblement; (*sourire*) tristement.

wanness ['wɒnnɪs] *n* pâleur *f*.

want[1] [wɒnt] *n* **(a)** (*need*) besoin *m*; **to minister** *or* **attend to s.o.'s wants,** pourvoir aux besoins de qn; *F Journ* **w. ad,** demande *f* (**for,** de); (*for job*) offre *f* d'emploi; **to go through the w. ads,** parcourir les annonces d'offre d'emploi;

(b) (*poverty*) misère *f*, besoin *m*; **to be in w.,** être dans le besoin *ou* la gêne; **war on w.,** lutte *f* contre la misère;

(c) (*lack*) manque *m*, défaut *m*; **w. of imagination/respect,** manque d'imagination/de respect; **for w. of sth,** faute de qch, à défaut de qch; **for w. of foresight,** par manque de prévoyance; **for w. of money,** faute d'argent; **for w. of something better to do,** faute de mieux; **for w. of a better word,** faute d'un mot plus approprié; *Prov* **for w. of a nail the shoe was lost, for w. of a shoe the horse was lost,** faute d'un point Martin perdit son âne; *Old-fashioned* **to be in w. of sth,** (*now usu* **need**) avoir besoin de qch.

want[2] **1** *vt* **(a)** (*desire*) vouloir; **she knows what she wants,** elle sait ce qu'elle veut; **the more you get the more you w.,** plus on en a, plus on en veut; **do you w. any?,** en voulez-vous?; **is that all you w.?,** est-ce tout ce que vous voulez?; **what more do you w.?,** que voulez-vous de plus?; **what** *or* **how much do you w. for this armchair?,** combien vendez-vous ce fauteuil?; *Iron* **you don't w. much, do you!,** tu es bien exigeant!; **you're wanted,** on vous demande; **we're not wanted here,** nous sommes de trop ici; **they don't w. to have me,** ils ne veulent pas de moi; **what does he w. with me?,** que me veut-il?; **what does he w. me for?,** qu'est-ce qu'il me veut?; **to w. sth from s.o.,** vouloir qch de qn; **what do you w. of her?,** que voulez-vous d'elle?; **I w. to tell you that ...,** je voudrais vous dire que ...; **to w. to see** *or* **speak to s.o.,** demander qn; **he could have done it if he had wanted to,** il aurait pu le faire s'il avait voulu; **don't come if you don't w. to** *or* **unless you w. to,** ne venez pas si ça ne vous dit pas; **I don't w. it known,** je ne veux pas que cela se sache; **what do you w. done?,** que désirez-vous qu'on fasse?; **I don't w. you turning everything upside down,** je ne veux pas que vous mettiez tout sens dessus dessous;

(b) (*need*) (*of person*) avoir besoin de (*qch*); (*of thing*) exiger, réclamer, demander (*qch*); **to w. rest,** avoir besoin de repos; **situation that wants tactful handling,** situation qui demande à être maniée avec tact; **I shall w. you,** j'aurai besoin de vous; **have you everything you w.?,** avez-vous tout ce qu'il vous faut?; **we've more than we w.,** nous en avons plus qu'il n'en faut; **you shall have as much as you w.,** vous en aurez autant que vous voudrez; **I've had all I want(ed),** j'en ai eu assez; **the goods can be supplied as (and when) they are wanted,** on peut fournir les articles au fur et à mesure des besoins; **that's the very thing I w., that's just what I w.,** c'est juste ce qu'il me faut, cela fera parfaitement mon affaire; **I have the very thing you w.,** j'ai juste ce qu'il vous faut; **the very man we w.,** l'homme de la circonstance; **what does she w. with a house?,** qu'est-ce qu'elle veut faire d'une maison?; **wanted, a good cook,** (*advertisement*) on demande *ou* recherche une bonne cuisinière; **he's wanted by the police,** il est recherché par la police; **you w. to be on your guard,** il faut vous méfier; **he wants a new hat,** il lui faut un nouveau chapeau; **your hair wants cutting,** tu as besoin de te faire couper les cheveux; **the lawn wants cutting,** la pelouse a besoin d'être tondue; **it wants some doing,** ce n'est pas (si) facile à faire;

(c) *Old-fashioned* (*be without*) manquer de, ne pas avoir (*qch*); **I w. one card,** il me manque une carte; *Am* **it still wanted an hour to dinnertime,** il y avait encore une heure à passer avant le dîner.

2 *vi* manquer (**for,** de); *Old-fashioned* **to w. for bread,** manquer de pain; **to w. for nothing,** ne manquer de rien; **her family will see to it that she doesn't w.,** sa famille veillera à ce qu'elle ne manque de rien.

wanted ['wɒntɪd] *adj* désiré, voulu; (*criminel*) recherché par la police; **to feel w.,** sentir qu'on vous aime; *Journ* **w. ad,** demande *f*; (*for job*) offre *f* d'emploi.

wanting ['wɒntɪŋ] **1** *adj* **(a)** manquant, qui manque; **to be w.,** faire défaut; **there is something w.,** le compte n'y est pas; **(b) to be w. in sth,** (*of person*) manquer de qch; **w. in intelligence,** pauvre en intelligence; *Lit* **to be found w.,** se trouver en défaut; **he was tried and found w.,** il a été mis à l'épreuve et cela n'a pas été concluant. **2** *prep Old-fashioned* sans; **he arrived w. both money and luggage,** il est arrivé sans argent ni bagages.

►want in *vi F* (*of cat, dog*) vouloir entrer; *Fig* (*to be part of something*) vouloir être inclus.

►want out *F vi* (*of cat, dog*) vouloir sortir; *Fig* (*to no longer be part of something*) vouloir retirer ses cartes du jeu.

wanton ['wɒntən] **1** *adj* **(a)** (*unjustified*) gratuit, sans motif; **w. cruelty,** cruauté gratuite; **w. destruction,** destruction pour le simple plaisir de détruire; **(b)** *Old-fashioned* (*woman*) licencieux, impudique; **w. thoughts,** pensées *fpl* impudiques. **2** *n Old-fashioned* femme *f* impudique.

wantonly ['wɒntənlɪ] *adv* **(a)** (*blesser, insulter*) sans motif; **(b)** *Old-fashioned* impudiquement.

wantonness ['wɒntənnɪs] *n* **(a)** gratuité *f* (*d'une insulte etc*); **(b)** *Old-fashioned* libertinage *m*.

wapiti ['wɒpɪtɪ] *n* (*deer*) wapiti *m*.

war¹ [wɔːr] *n* **(a)** guerre *f*; **state of w.,** état *m* de guerre; **in (time of) w.,** en temps de guerre; **in w. they would have been stretcher bearers,** en temps de guerre ils auraient été brancardiers; **w. establishment** *or* **strength,** effectif(s) *m(pl)* de guerre; **to set a unit on a w. footing,** mettre une unité sur pied de guerre; **preparations for w.,** préparatifs *mpl* de guerre; *Lit* **to let loose the dogs of w.,** déchaîner les fureurs de la guerre; **to start a w.,** déclencher une guerre; **to be at w. with a country,** être en état de guerre avec un pays; **to make** *or* **wage w. on** *or* **against a country,** faire la guerre à *ou* contre un pays; **to go to w.,** se mettre en guerre (**over territory,** pour un territoire); **to go to the war(s),** partir à la guerre; **I did my w. work in a hospital,** pendant la guerre j'ai travaillé dans un hôpital; *Fig* **you look as if you've been in the wars,** te voilà dans un drôle d'état; **w. cemetery,** cimetière *m* militaire; *Am Pol* **w. chest,** fonds spécial (*pour une campagne*); **w. correspondent,** correspondant, -ante de guerre; **w. crimes,** crimes *mpl* de guerre; **w. criminal,** criminel, -elle de guerre; **w. cry,** (*of Amerindian*) *& Fig* cri *m* de guerre; **w. dance,** danse guerrière; **w. film,** film *m* de guerre; **w. game,** exercice *m* sur la carte; (*with model soldiers*) jeu *m* de stratégie militaire; **w. grave,** sépulture *f* militaire; **w. hero,** héros *m* de guerre; **w. memorial,** monument *m* aux morts; *Br Hist* **W. Office,** Ministère *m* de la Guerre; **w. paint,** (*of Amerindian*) peinture *f* de guerre; *Old-fashioned Pej* (*of woman*) maquillage *m*; **w. widow,** veuve *f* de guerre; **w. zone,** zone *f* de guerre; *Hist* **the Wars of the Roses,** la guerre des Deux Roses; **the American Civil W.,** *US* **the W. Between the States,** la guerre de Sécession; **the Great W.,** (*1914 - 1918*) la Grande Guerre;

(b) *Fig* guerre *f*, lutte *f*; **w. of nerves,** guerre des nerfs; **class w.,** lutte des classes; *Econ* **price w.,** guerre des prix; **w. of words,** dispute *f*, altercation *f*; **to wage w. on** *or* **against s.o./sth,** faire la guerre à *ou* contre qn/à qch, lutter *ou* militer contre qn/qch; **the w. on drugs,** la lutte contre la drogue.

war² *vi* (**-rr-**) **to w. against s.o./sth,** mener une campagne contre qn/qch, lutter contre qn/qch; **to w. against abuses,** faire la guerre aux abus.

War *abbr* **Warwickshire**.

warble¹ ['wɔːb(ə)l] *n* gazouillement *m*, gazouillis *m*.

warble² **1** *vi* gazouiller; (*of lark*) grisoller; *Fig* (*of person*) chanter. **2** *vtr* chanter (*qch*) en gazouillant; *Fig* (*of person*) roucouler (*une chanson*).

warbler ['wɔːblər] *n* (*bird*) fauvette *f*.

warbling ['wɔːblɪŋ] **1** *adj* (*oiseau*) gazouillant; (*son*) mélodieux. **2** *n* = **WARBLE¹**.

ward [wɔːd] *n* **(a)** (*person*) pupille *mf*; *Jur* **w. in Chancery, w. of court,** pupille sous tutelle judiciaire; **to be made a w. of court,** être placé sous tutelle judiciaire; **(b)** *Med* salle *f* d'hôpital; **which w. is she in?,** dans quelle salle est-elle?; **to walk the wards,** (*of medical student*) assister aux leçons cliniques; **(c)** *Pol* (*electoral division*) circonscription électorale.

►ward off *vtsep* parer, écarter (*un coup*); détourner, écarter (*un danger*); prévenir (*une maladie*).

warden ['wɔːd(ə)n] *n* directeur, -trice (*d'une institution, d'une prison*); gardien, -ienne (*d'un parc national*); gouverneur *m* (*d'une ville*); (*in freemasonry*) surveillant *m*; **w. of a hostel,** directeur, -trice d'un foyer; (*of youth hostel*) directeur, -trice d'auberge de jeunesse; *Br* **Lord W. of the Cinque Ports,** gouverneur des Cinq Ports.

warder ['wɔːdər] *n* gardien, -ienne (*de prison, de musée*).

wardress ['wɔːdrɪs] *n* gardienne *f* (*de prison, de musée*).

wardrobe ['wɔːdrəʊb] *n* **(a)** (*cupboard*) armoire *f*, garde-robe *f*, *pl* garde-robes; **w. drawer/mirror/***etc*, tiroir *m*/miroir *m*/*etc* d'armoire; **(b)** (*clothes*) (ensemble *m* de) vêtements *mpl*, *garde-robe f*; **Miss Smith's w. by ...,** (*on film credits*) les costumes de Miss Smith ont été fournis par ...; **to have a large w.,** avoir une garde-robe importante; **she brought half her w. with her,** elle a emporté la moitié de sa garde-robe; *Th* **w. mistress,** costumière *f*; **w. trunk,** = très grosse malle à l'intérieur de laquelle on peut pendre les vêtements; **(c)** *Th* **she's worked in w. for years,** elle s'occupe des costumes depuis des années.

wardroom ['wɔːdruːm] *n Nau* carré *m* des officiers.

wardship ['wɔːdʃɪp] *n* tutelle *f*.

ware [weər] *n* **(a)** articles fabriqués; **aluminium w.,** ustensiles *mpl* en aluminium; **cast-iron w.,** poterie *f* en fonte; **(b)** *Cer* faïence *f*; **(c) wares,** marchandise(s) *f(pl)*; *Arch* **to cry one's wares,** faire l'article de *ou* vanter sa marchandise.

warehouse¹ ['weəhaʊs] *n* entrepôt *m*, magasin *m*; (*for furniture*) garde-meuble *m*, *pl* garde-meubles; **bonded w.,** entrepôt de la douane; *Com* **ex w.,** sortie *f* d'entrepôt.

warehouse² ['weəhaʊz] *vt* (em)magasiner; (*in bond*) entreposer (*des marchandises*).

warehouseman, *pl* **-men** ['weəhaʊsmən] *n* magasinier *m*.

warehousing ['weəhaʊzɪŋ] *n* (em)magasinage *m*; (*in bond*) entreposage *m* (*de marchandises*).

warfare ['wɔːfeər] *n* guerre *f*.

warhead ['wɔːhed] *n* ogive *f*; tête *f* (*de fusée*); cône *m* de charge (*d'une torpille*).

warhorse ['wɔːhɔːs] *n* **(a)** *Fig* **an old w.,** *Mil* un vieux soldat; *Pol* un vétéran de la politique; **(b)** *Arch* destrier *m*, cheval *m* de bataille.

warily ['weərɪlɪ] *adv* avec précaution.

wariness ['weərɪnɪs] *n* circonspection *f*, prudence *f*.

warlike ['wɔːlaɪk] *adj* (*exploit, maintien*) guerrier; (*peuple*) belliqueux; (*air*) martial.

warlock ['wɔːlɒk] *n* sorcier *m*, magicien *m*.

warlord ['wɔːlɔːd] *n* seigneur *m* de la guerre.

warm¹ [wɔːm] **1** *adj* **(a)** (*garment, colour etc*) chaud; (*iron, oven*) moyen; **to be w.,** (*of water*) être chaud; (*of person*) avoir chaud; **the water's only just w.,** l'eau n'est que tiède; **to get w.,** (*of person, room*) se réchauffer; (*of food, water*) chauffer; **you're getting warmer,** (*in guessing game etc*) tu chauffes; **you're really w.,**(*in guessing game etc*) tu brûles; **to keep w.,** se tenir chaud; **to keep a dish w.,** garder un plat au chaud; *Fig* **to keep a place w. for s.o.,** garder un emploi pour qn; **I'll do it once the w. weather is here,** je le ferai quand il commencera à faire chaud; **it's getting warmer,** (*of weather*) il commence à faire plus chaud; **it was w. work,** c'était une rude besogne; *Fig* **to make things** *or* **it w. for s.o.,** en faire voir de dures à qn; *Fig* **things were getting a bit too w.,** (*dangerous*) ça commençait à chauffer; *Met* **w. front,** front chaud; *Aut Comptr* **w. start,** démarrage *m* à chaud; **w. tints,** tons chauds;

(b) (*enthusiastic, kind*) chaleureux; **to meet with a w. reception,** être accueilli chaleureusement; **w. heart,** cœur généreux; *Prov* **cold hands w. heart,** mains froides, cœur chaud; **w. smile,** sourire accueillant.

2 *n* **to have a w.,** se réchauffer.

warm² **1** *vt* (faire) chauffer (*qch*); **to w. oneself by the fire/in the sun,** se chauffer près du feu/au soleil; **wine/**

news that warms the heart, vin/nouvelle qui réchauffe le cœur; **that will w. the cockles of your heart,** voilà qui vous réchauffera; **it warms the cockles of my heart to see ...,** ça me réchauffe le cœur de voir .... **2** *vi* (se) chauffer, s'échauffer, se réchauffer; **to w. to s.o.,** (commencer à) ressentir de la sympathie pour qn.

►**warm over** *vtsep* **(a)** *esp Am* (faire) réchauffer (*du potage*); **(b)** *Fig* réchauffer (*un roman*).

►**warm up 1** *vi* **(a)** (*of weather*) faire plus chaud; *Fig* (*of party etc*) s'animer, *Fig* (*of person*) devenir plus cordial *ou* plus animé, *F* se dégeler; *Fig* (*of discussion*) s'échauffer, s'animer; **(b)** *Sp* s'échauffer, se mettre en train; (*of engine, radio etc*) se mettre en route. **2** *vtsep* faire chauffer (*qch*); réchauffer (*qn*); *Fig* animer (*une soirée*); *Aut* **to w. up the engine,** (faire) chauffer le moteur; **to w. up the soup,** (faire) réchauffer le potage; *Fig* **to w. an audience up,** chauffer le public, mettre un public en train.

warm-blooded [wɔːm'blʌdɪd] *adj* (*animal*) à sang chaud; (*person*) passionné, au sang chaud.

warm-hearted [wɔːm'hɑːtɪd] *adj* au cœur généreux; (*accueil*) chaleureux; **she is very w.-h.,** elle est pleine de cœur.

warm-heartedly [wɔːm'hɑːtɪdlɪ] *adv* chaleureusement, avec chaleur.

warming ['wɔːmɪŋ] **1** *adj* chauffant; qui réchauffe. **2** *n* chauffage *m*; **w. drawer,** (*of oven*) chauffe-plats *m inv*; **w. pan,** bassinoire *f*.

warming over *n esp Am* (*of food*) & *Fig* réchauffage *m*.

warming up *n* **(a)** (*of food*) réchauffage *m*; **(b)** *Sp* échauffement *m*; **w. up exercises,** exercices *mpl* d'échauffement.

warmly ['wɔːmlɪ] *adv* **(a)** (*vêtu*) chaudement; **(b)** (*applaudir*) chaudement; (*accueillir qn, remercier qn*) chaleureusement; **(c)** (*répondre*) avec chaleur.

warmonger ['wɔːmʌŋgər] *n* belliciste *mf*.

warmongering ['wɔːmʌŋg(ə)rɪŋ] *n* bellicisme *m*, propagande *f* de guerre.

warmth [wɔːmθ] *n* **(a)** chaleur *f* (*du soleil, du feu*); **we huddled together for w.,** nous nous sommes blottis les uns contre les autres pour nous tenir chaud; **(b)** (*enthusiasm*) ardeur *f*, chaleur *f*; cordialité *f*, chaleur (*d'un accueil*); **(c)** (*anger*) emportement *m*, vivacité *f*; **... she said with some w.,** ... dit-elle d'un ton vif.

warm-up ['wɔːmʌp] *n* **(a)** réchauffement *m*; **come and have a w.-up by the fire,** viens te réchauffer auprès du feu; **(b)** *Sp* échauffement *m*; **they get a ten-minute w.-up,** ils ont dix minutes d'échauffement; **w.-up match,** match *m* préparatoire *ou* d'entraînement; *esp US* **w.-up suit,** survêtement *m*; **(c)** *TV etc* **w.-up man,** chauffeur *m* de salle.

warn [wɔːn] *vt* **(a)** (*caution*) avertir, prévenir (**that,** que); **to w. s.o. of a danger,** avertir qn d'un danger; **to w. s.o. against sth,** mettre qn en garde contre qch; **they warned me about you,** on m'avait mis en garde contre toi, on m'avait prévenu à ton égard; **he warned her against going, he warned her not to go,** il lui a conseillé (fortement) de ne pas y aller; **you have been warned!,** vous voilà averti *ou* prévenu!; **I'm warning you for the last time,** je te préviens pour la dernière fois; **I shan't w. you again,** tenez-vous-le pour dit; **(b)** (*alert, inform*) informer, donner l'éveil à (*qn*); **to w. the police,** alerter la police.

►**warn off** *vtsep* **(a)** (*tell to leave*) exiger le départ de (*qn*); *Horseracing* exclure (*qn*) des champs de course; **he warned them off his land,** il leur demanda instamment de quitter ses terres; **(b)** (*advise against*) déconseiller; **to w. s.o. off sth,** déconseiller qch à qn.

warning ['wɔːnɪŋ] *n* avertissement *m*; (*advance notice*) avis *m*, préavis *m*; (*alarm*) alerte *f*; **this is your last w.,** (*to criminal*) dernier avertissement; (*to child*) c'est la dernière fois que je te le dis; **without w.,** sans préavis, sans déclaration préalable; **he just left without w.,** il est parti sans crier gare; **it just broke down without w.,** elle est tombée en panne d'un seul coup; **to sound a note of w.,** (*announce danger*) donner l'alarme; (*advise caution*) recommander la prudence; **she gave him a w. glance,** elle lui lança un regard d'avertissement *ou* pour l'avertir; **he was let off with a w.,** il en a été quitte pour un avertissement; **I'm giving you fair w.,** vous voilà averti!; **let this be a w. to you,** que cela vous serve de leçon *ou* d'exemple *ou* d'avertissement; **strike w.,** préavis de grève; **w. strike,** grève *f* d'avertissement; **w. signal,** signal avertisseur, signal d'alarme; **w. device,** (appareil *m ou* dispositif *m*) avertisseur *m*; **w. bell,** sonnette *ou* sonnerie avertisseuse *ou* d'alarme; **w. light,** avertisseur lumineux, voyant *m* (lumineux); *Nau* feu *m* d'avertissement; *Aut* **hazard w. lights,** feux *mpl* de détresse; *Nau* **w. shot,** coup *m* de semonce; **w. sign,** (*indication*) signe avertisseur, signe précurseur; (*notice*) pancarte *f ou* plaque *f* d'avertissement; **w. system,** système *m ou* dispositif *m* d'avertissement; *Mil* **early w. system,** système de surveillance avancée.

warning off *n Horseracing* (*of jockey*) exclusion *f*.

warp¹ [wɔːp] *n* **(a)** (*distortion*) voilure *f*, courbure *f*, gauchissement *m* (*d'une planche*); **(b)** *Tex* chaîne *f*; (*for tapestry*) lisse *f*, lice *f*.

warp² 1 *vt* **(a)** (*distort*) déjeter, (faire) fausser, gauchir (*le bois, une tôle*); faire travailler (*le bois*); *Fig* fausser, pervertir (*l'esprit, le caractère*); **(b)** *Tex* ourdir (*un tissu*). **2** *vi* se déformer; (*of timber*) se déjeter, gauchir; (*of sheet metal*) se fausser, (se) gondoler.

warped [wɔːpt] *adj* (*bois*) gauchi, gondolé; *Fig* (*esprit*) perverti, faussé; **that's a very w. way of thinking,** c'est une drôle de manière de voir les choses; **w. mind/sense of humour,** esprit/sens de l'humour tordu; **w. nature,** caractère mal fait.

warpath ['wɔːpɑːθ] *n* **to be on the w.,** (*of Amerindian*) être sur le sentier de la guerre; *Fig* en vouloir à tout le monde; *Fig* **the boss is on the w.,** le patron est d'une humeur massacrante.

warping ['wɔːpɪŋ] *n* **(a)** gauchissement *m* (*d'une planche*); gondolement *m* (*d'une tôle*); voilure *f*, voilement *m* (*d'une roue*); *Fig* perversion *f* (*de l'esprit, du caractère*); **(b)** *Tex* ourdissage *m*.

warplane ['wɔːpleɪn] *n* avion *m* de guerre.

warrant¹ ['wɒrənt] *n* **(a)** (*guarantee*) garantie *f*; **a w. for s.o.'s good behaviour,** une garantie pour la bonne conduite de qn; **(b)** (*justification*) justification *f*; **(c)** *Jur* mandat *m*, ordre *m*; *Admin* mandat; **w. of arrest,** mandat d'arrêt *ou* d'arrestation, mandat d'amener; **there's a w. out against him** *or* **for his arrest,** il est sous le coup d'un mandat d'amener; **warehouse w.,** certificat *m* d'entrepôt, warrant *m*; **w. for payment,** ordonnance *f* de paiement; **travel w.,** feuille *f* de route; **(d)** *Mil* **w. officer,** adjudant *m*.

warrant² *vt* **(a)** (*guarantee*) garantir, certifier (*qch*); répondre de (*qch*); **it won't happen again, I w. you!,** cela n'arrivera pas deux fois, je vous en réponds!; **(b)** (*justify*) justifier; **nothing can w. such conduct,** rien ne justifie une pareille conduite, rien ne peut excuser une telle conduite.

warrantable ['wɒrəntəb(ə)l] *adj* **(a)** que l'on peut garantir; **(b)** justifiable.

warrantee [wɒrən'tiː] *n* receveur, -euse d'une garantie.

warrantor ['wɒrəntɔːr] *n Jur* garant, -ante.

warranty ['wɒrəntɪ] *n* **(a)** *Com* garantie *f*; **breach of w.,** rupture *f* de garantie; **the iron has a five-year w.,** le fer à repasser est garanti cinq ans; **is it still under w.?,** est-ce que c'est encore sous garantie?; **(b)** (*justification*) justification *f* (**for doing sth,** pour faire qch, pour avoir fait qch).

warren ['wɒrən] *n* **(rabbit) w.,** garenne *f*, clapier *m*; *Fig* labyrinthe *m*.

warring ['wɔːrɪŋ] *adj* (*countries*) en guerre; *Fig* (*ideologies*) en conflit.

warrior ['wɒrɪər] *n* guerrier, -ière; **the Unknown W.,** le Soldat inconnu; **w. tribes,** tribus guerrières.

Warsaw ['wɔːsɔː] *n* Varsovie *f*; *Pol* **W. Pact,** pacte *m* de Varsovie; **W. Pact nations,** les nations *fpl* du pacte de Varsovie.

warship ['wɔːʃɪp] *n* navire *m ou* vaisseau *m* de guerre.

wart [wɔːt] *n* verrue *f*; *Fig* **to paint s.o. warts and all,** faire le portrait de qn sans en omettre les défauts; *Fig* **a biography of Mary Smith, warts and all,** une biographie de Mary Smith qui ne fait pas de cadeau.

warthog ['wɔːthɒg] *n* (*animal*) phacochère *m*.

wartime ['wɔːtaɪm] *n* temps *m* de guerre; **in w.,** en temps de guerre; **w. conditions,** conditions *fpl* de guerre.

warty ['wɔːtɪ] *adj* verruqueux.

wary ['weərɪ] *adj* avisé, prudent, circonspect; **to keep a w. eye on s.o.,** guetter qn, surveiller qn attentivement; **to be w. of sth,** se méfier de qch; **be w. of strangers,** méfiez-vous des étrangers; **I'm still w. about signing it,** j'hésite encore à le signer.

warily ['weərɪlɪ] *adv* avec circonspection, prudemment.

was *see* **BE**.

wash¹ [wɒʃ] *n* **(a)** lavage *m*; (*laundry*) lessive *f*, blanchissage *m*; **to have a w.,** se laver; **give your face a w.,** lave-toi le visage; **to have a w. and brush up,** faire un brin *ou* un bout de toilette; **to give sth a w.,** laver qch; **to do the w.,** faire la lessive; **to send clothes to the w.,** donner du linge à laver *ou* à blanchir; **your jeans are in**

the w., (*being washed*) ton jean est au lavage; **it'll come out in the w.,** ça partira au lavage; *Fig* **it will all come out in the w.,** (*become clear*) les faits se révèleront un jour ou l'autre; (*be all right*) ça se tassera; *Old-fashioned* **w. house,** buanderie *f*, lavanderie *f*; (*public*) lavoir *m*; *US* blanchisserie *f*;

(b) *Med Vet* lotion *f* (*pour plaies*); (*for plants*) lessive *f* (insecticide); (*against mildew*) bouillie *f*;

(c) couche légère (*de couleur sur une surface*); *Art* lavis *m* (*d'aquarelle, d'encre de Chine*); **colour w.,** (*for walls*) badigeon *m*; **w. drawing,** dessin *m* au lavis;

(d) remous *m* (*des vagues, d'un navire*).

wash² **1** *vt* **(a)** laver (*qch*); blanchir, lessiver, laver (*le linge*); **w. in cool/hot water,** à laver à l'eau tiède/chaude; **hand w. only,** laver à la main seulement; **to w. sth in cold w.,** laver qch à l'eau froide; **to w. oneself,** se laver; **to w. one's face/hands,** se laver le visage/les mains; *Br Euph* **would you like to w. your hands?,** (*go to lavatory*) voulez-vous que je vous montre où est la salle de bain?; *Fig* **to w. one's hands of sth/s.o.,** se laver les mains de qch/qn; **I w. my hands of the affair,** je ne suis plus pour rien dans l'affaire, je me lave les mains de cette affaire; *Rel* **to be washed of one's sins,** être lavé de ses péchés;

(b) *Med* lotionner, déterger (*une plaie*);

(c) *Ind* débourber (*le minerai, le charbon*); épurer (*le gaz*);

(d) *Art* laver (*un dessin*); **to w. the walls,** badigeonner les murs (**with,** de);

(e) (*of sea*) baigner (*une côte*); **to w. s.o./sth ashore,** rejeter qn/qch sur le rivage; **sailor washed overboard,** matelot enlevé par une lame.

2 *vi* **(a)** (*of person*) se laver; (*of fabric*) supporter le lavage; **material that washes well,** tissu qui se lave bien; **you w. and I'll dry,** (*doing dishes*) tu laves et j'essuie; *Br F* **that won't w.!,** ça ne prend pas!;

(b) waves washing against the cliff, vagues qui viennent lécher la falaise.

►**wash away** **1** *vtsep* **(a)** enlever (*une tache*) par le lavage; **to w. one's sins away,** se laver de ses péchés; **(b)** (*of running water*) **to w. away the gravel from a river bed,** enlever le gravier du lit d'une rivière; **the flood washed away part of the river bank,** l'inondation a dégradé la berge; **(c)** (*of sea*) emporter, entraîner; **washed away by the tide,** emporté *ou* enlevé par la mer. **2** *vi* (*of mark, stain*) se nettoyer à l'eau; s'en aller à la lessive, partir au lavage.

►**wash down** *vtsep* **(a)** laver (*les murs*) à grande eau; **(b)** (*of the rain*) emporter, entraîner (*le sol, le gravier*); *Fig* **to w. down one's dinner with a glass of beer,** arroser son dîner d'un verre de bière.

►**wash off** **1** *vtsep* enlever *ou* faire partir (*qch*) par le lavage. **2** *vi* (*of mark, stain*) se nettoyer à l'eau; s'en aller à la lessive, partir au lavage.

►**wash out** **1** *vtsep* **(a)** enlever (*une tache*); **(b)** laver, rincer, nettoyer (*une tasse, une bouteille*); **to w. out a few clothes** *or* **things,** faire une petite lessive; *Fig* **to be completely washed out,** (*tired*) être complètement lessivé *ou* vanné *ou* à plat; **(c)** *Art* dégrader (*une couleur*); **washed out,** (*of colour, material*) délavé, déteint; **(d)** *Min* **to w. out the gold,** extraire l'or (*en lavant le sable etc*); **(e)** (*of football match etc*) **to be washed out,** être décommandé à cause de la pluie; **(f)** *Geol* éroder. **2** *vi* (*of stain, colour*) partir au lavage; **it will w. out,** cela s'en ira à la lessive.

►**wash over** *vipo* (*of waves*) balayer; *Fig* ne faire aucun effet à; **anything I say just washes over her,** rien de ce que je lui dis ne lui fait le moindre effet.

►**wash up** **1** *vtsep* **(a) to w. up the dishes,** laver *ou* faire la vaisselle; **(b)** (*of sea*) rejeter (*qn, qch*) sur le rivage; **wreckage washed up by the sea,** débris rejetés par la mer; **(c)** *Fig* **to be (all) washed up,** (*of person*) être fini *ou F* fichu; (*of plan*) être tombé à l'eau; **he's all washed up,** c'est un homme fini *ou* liquidé; **he's all washed up as a boxer,** il est fini comme boxeur. **2** *vi* **(a)** *Br* (*do dishes*) faire la vaisselle; **(b)** *US* se laver (les mains et la figure); **(c) the water washed up on the bank,** l'eau refluait sur la berge.

Wash *abbr* **Washington**.

washable ['wɒʃəb(ə)l] *adj* lavable.

wash-and-wear [wɒʃənd'weər] *adj* lavé-repassé.

washbasin ['wɒʃbeɪs(ə)n] *n* (cuvette *f* de) lavabo *m*.

washboard ['wɒʃbɔːd] *n* planche *f* à laver.

washbowl ['wɒʃbəʊl] *n* cuvette *f*; (*large*) bassine *f*.

washcloth ['wɒʃklɒθ] *n* **(a)** *Br* (*for washing dishes*) torchon *m* à laver la vaisselle; (*for drying dishes*) torchon à essuyer la vaisselle; **(b)** *Am* = gant de toilette.

washday ['wɒʃdeɪ] *n* jour *m* de la lessive.

washed-out ['wɒʃd'aʊt] *adj* **(a)** *Fig* (*tired*) lessivé; **(b)** (*faded*) délavé.

washed-up [wɒʃd'ʌp] *adj Fig F* **(all) w.-up,** (*person, plan*) fichu.

washer¹ ['wɒʃər] *n* **(a)** (*person*) laveur, -euse; **w. up,** *F* **w. upper,** laveur, -euse de vaisselle; (*in restaurant*) plongeur, -euse; **(b)** *F* (*for clothes*) machine *f* à laver; (*for dishes*) lave-vaisselle *m inv*.

washer² *n Tech* rondelle *f*, bague *f*; **the tap needs a new w.,** il faut changer la bague du robinet.

washer-dryer [wɒʃə'draɪər] *n* machine à laver séchante.

washerwoman, *pl* **-women** ['wɒʃəwʊmən, -wɪmɪn] *n Arch* blanchisseuse *f*.

wash(-)hand ['wɒʃhænd] *adj* **w. basin,** (cuvette *f* de) lavabo *m*.

washing ['wɒʃɪŋ] *n* **(a)** lavage *m*; toilette *f*, ablutions *fpl* (*du corps*); *Rel* lavement *m* (*des pieds, des mains*); ablution (*du calice*); **(b)** lessive *f*, blanchissage *m* (*du linge*); (*dirty clothes*) linge *m* à laver; (*clean clothes*) linge lavé; **to do the w.,** faire la lessive; *Fig* **to take in one another's (dirty) w.,** se rendre mutuellement service; **w. day,** jour *m* de la lessive; **Monday is w. day,** le lundi est le jour de la lessive; **w. machine,** machine *f* à laver; **w. powder,** lessive (en poudre), détergent *m*; **w. soda,** cristaux *mpl* de soude; **(c)** *Ind* débourbage *m* (*du charbon, du minerai*); épurage *m* (*du gaz*); **(d)** *Art* lavis *m* (*d'un dessin*); badigeonnage *m* (*d'une surface*).

washing-up [wɒʃɪŋ'ʌp] *n* vaisselle *f*; **to do the w.-up,** faire la vaisselle; (*in restaurant*) faire la plonge; **w.-up bowl,** cuvette *f*, bassine *f*; **w.-up liquid,** liquide *m* pour la vaisselle; **w.-up machine,** machine *f* à laver la vaisselle, lave-vaisselle *m inv*; *Can* laveuse *f* à vaisselle; **w.-up water,** eau *f* de vaisselle.

washleather ['wɒʃleðər] *n* peau *f* de chamois; **w. gloves,** gants *mpl* chamois.

washout ['wɒʃaʊt] *n* **(a)** *F* fiasco *m*; (*person*) raté, -ée, zéro *m*; **the whole thing's a w.,** c'est une perte sèche; **the match was a w.,** le match fut un fiasco; **(b)** *Geol* érosion causée par l'action de l'eau.

washrag ['wɒʃræg] *n US* = gant de toilette.

washroom ['wɒʃruːm] *n* **(a)** *esp Am* (*in hotel etc*) toilettes *fpl*; **where's the w.?,** où sont les toilettes?; **(b)** salle *f* d'eau, cabinet *m* de toilette.

washstand ['wɒʃstænd] *n* (*table*) table *f* de toilette; *Am* lavabo *m*.

washtub ['wɒʃtʌb] *n* baquet *m* (à lessive).

washup ['wɒʃʌp] *n* **(a)** *Med F* stérilisation *f* des mains (*avant une opération*); **(b)** *Am* **to have a w.,** se laver (les mains et la figure).

washy ['wɒʃɪ] *adj F* **(a)** (*thin, watery*) fade, fadasse; **w. tea** *or* **coffee,** de la lavasse; **(b)** (*colour*) délavé.

wasn't ['wɒz(ə)nt] = **was not,** *see* **BE**.

wasp [wɒsp] *n* (*insect*) guêpe *f*; **wasps' nest,** guêpier *m*; **w. waist,** (*of person*) taille *f* de guêpe.

Wasp [wɒsp] *n Am esp Pej* = Américain blanc protestant d'origine anglo-saxonne.

waspish ['wɒspɪʃ] *adj F* méchant, acerbe; (*ton*) aigre.

waspishly ['wɒspɪʃlɪ] *adv* (*to do*) d'une manière acerbe; (*to say*) d'un ton aigre.

wastage ['weɪstɪdʒ] *n* **(a)** (*loss*) gaspillage *m*; (*of heat*) déperdition *f*, perte *f*; **(b)** (*waste*) déchets *mpl*, rebuts *mpl*; **buy enough material to allow for w.,** acheter suffisamment de tissu pour compenser les pertes; **(c)** *Ind* départ *m* d'employés; **we hope to achieve this by natural w.,** nous pensons y parvenir grâce à des départs volontaires.

waste¹ [weɪst] *adj* **(a)** (*uncultivated*) **w. land** *or* **ground,** terre *f* inculte *ou* en friche; (*in town*) terrains *mpl* vagues; **to lie w.,** (*of ground*) rester en friche; **to lay w.,** dévaster, ravager, piller (*un pays*); **(b)** (*product*) non utilisé, perdu; **w. products,** déchets *mpl*; **w. heat,** chaleur perdue; **w. heat recovery,** récupération *f* de la chaleur perdue; **w. water,** (*domestic*) eaux ménagères; *Ind* eaux résiduaires *ou* usées; **w. water treatment,** traitement *m* des eaux usées.

waste² *n* **(a)** gaspillage *m* (*d'argent, d'efforts*); **it's a terrible w. of food,** c'est un terrible gâchis *ou* gaspillage de nourriture; **it's a w. of their skills,** c'est gaspiller leurs talents; **w. of time,** perte *f* de temps; **it's a w. of time,** c'est du temps perdu; **it's a w. of time trying to convince her,** je *ou* tu *etc* perds mon *ou* ton *etc* temps à essayer de la convaincre; **that film is a real w. of time,** ce film ne vaut rien, ce film est nul; **to run** *or* **go to w.,** (*of liquid*) se perdre, se gaspiller; (*of land, garden*) être envahi par de mauvaises herbes;

(b) (*rubbish*) déchets *mpl*; (*household waste*) ordures ménagères; *Min* déblais *mpl*; **radioactive w.,** déchets *ou* résidus radioactifs; **w. collection,** ramassage *m* des ordures; **w. disposal,** élimination *f ou* destruction *f* des déchets *ou* des résidus; **w. disposal site,** dépôt *m* d'ordures; **w. disposal unit,** broyeur *m* d'ordures; **w. pipe,** tuyau *m* d'écoulement (*du trop-plein*); écoulement *m* (*d'une baignoire*);

(c) (*loss*) déperdition *f* (*de force, d'énergie*); détérioration *f*, dépérissement *m* (*de tissus*); *Ind* freinte *f*;

(d) (*desert*) région *f* inculte; désert *m*.

waste³ 1 *vt* **(a)** (*make excessive use of*) gaspiller (*les provisions, son argent*); gâcher (*du papier*); dissiper, dilapider (*une fortune*); perdre, gaspiller (*du temps*); **nothing is wasted,** rien ne se perd; **I hate wasting food,** j'ai horreur de gâcher la nourriture; **to w. one's life,** gâcher sa vie; **she's wasted in that job,** cet emploi est bien audessous de ses capacités; **to w. one's words** *or* **breath,** parler en pure perte; **you're wasting your energy,** vous vous dépensez inutilement; **I haven't any time to w. on him,** je n'ai pas de temps à perdre pour lui; **we're wasting time,** nous perdons notre temps; **we've already wasted too much time on this,** nous avons déjà perdu trop de temps là-dessus; **to w. no time doing sth,** ne pas perdre de temps pour faire qch; *Iron* **you didn't w. any time, did you!,** tu n'as pas perdu de temps, hein?; **that would be wasted on me,** ce serait trop beau pour moi; **sherry is wasted on me,** (*not appreciated by*) je suis incapable d'apprécier le sherry; **a beautiful house like that is wasted on such people,** une belle maison comme ça, c'est trop beau pour des gens pareils; **the joke was wasted on him,** il n'a pas compris la plaisanterie;

(b) (*consume*) consumer, épuiser, faire dépérir (*qn, le corps*); **patient wasted by a disease,** malade miné par une maladie;

(c) *Am Sl* (*murder*) tuer (*qn*);

(d) (*lose*) perdre (*une occasion*).

2 *vi* se perdre; *Prov* **w. not, want not,** qui épargne gagne.

►**waste away** *vi* (*of person*) dépérir, s'affaiblir.

wastebasket ['weɪstbɑːskɪt] *n esp Am* = **WASTEBIN**.

wastebin ['weɪstbɪn] *n* corbeille *f* à papier.

wasted ['weɪstɪd] *adj* **(a)** (*pays*) dévasté, ravagé; **(b)** (*malade, corps*) affaibli, amaigri; (*through drug use*) dévasté, ravagé; (*membre*) atrophié; **(c)** (*argent*) gaspillé; (*effort*) inutile; **it was a w. journey,** c'était un voyage pour rien, **w. life,** vie manquée; **w. time,** temps perdu; (*in mechanical movement*) temps mort.

wasteful ['weɪstfʊl] *adj* gaspilleur, -euse; (*dépense*) en pure perte; (*procédé*) peu économique; **don't be so w. with the hot water!,** ne gaspillez pas l'eau chaude!

wastefully ['weɪstfəlɪ] *adv* prodigalement, avec prodigalité; (*dépenser*) en pure perte.

wastefulness ['weɪstfʊlnɪs] *n* gaspillage *m*.

wasteland ['weɪstlænd] *n* région *f* inculte, désert *m*; *Fig* désert; **an industrial/cultural w.,** un désert industriel/culturel.

wastepaper [weɪst'peɪpər] *n* papier *m* à jeter *ou* de rebut; **w. basket,** corbeille *f* à papier.

waster ['weɪstər] *n* **(a)** gaspilleur, -euse; **time w.,** personne qui perd son temps; **(b)** (*ne'er-do-well*) propre *mf* à rien.

wasting ['weɪstɪŋ] **1** *n* **(a)** gaspillage *m* (*de ses ressources, de son temps*); dissipation *f*, dilapidation *f* (*de sa fortune*); **(b)** dépérissement *m*, amaigrissement *m* (*du corps*); atrophie *f* (*d'un membre*). **2** *adj* **w. disease,** une maladie qui ronge.

►**wasting away** *n* = **WASTING 1 (b)**.

wastrel ['weɪstrəl] *n* vaurien, -ienne, propre *mf* à rien.

watch¹ [wɒtʃ] *n* **(a)** (*observation*) garde *f*, surveillance *f*; **to keep w.,** monter la garde; **to keep (a) good** *or* **close w.,** faire bonne garde; **to keep a close w. on** *or* **over s.o.,** surveiller qn de près; **to keep a w. on one's tongue,** (*not swear*) surveiller son langage; (*keep one's own counsel*) savoir se taire; **to put** *or* **set a w. on s.o.,** faire surveiller qn; **to be on the w. for s.o.,** épier *ou* guetter qn;

(b) (*timepiece*) montre *f*; **it's six o'clock by my w.,** il est six heures à ma montre; **w. chain,** chaîne *f* de montre *ou* de gilet; **w. spring,** ressort *m* de montre;

(c) *Nau* (*shift*) quart *m*; (*men*) bordée *f*; **to be on w.,** être de quart; **to keep/come on w.,** faire/prendre le quart; **the officer of the w.,** l'officier *m* du quart; **the port/starboard w.,** la bordée de bâbord/de tribord;

(d) *Hist* (*guard*) **the w.,** la garde, le guet; *Admin* **w. committee,** comité *m* qui veille au maintien de l'ordre de la commune;

(e) (*vigil*) veille *f*; *Lit* **in the watches of the night,** pendant les heures de veille; **to keep w. at s.o.'s bedside,** veiller au chevet de qn; *Rel* **w. night service,** veillée *f* du 31 décembre.

watch² 1 *vi* **(a)** (*look on*) regarder;

(b) (*keep vigil*) veiller; **I watched all night,** j'ai veillé jusqu'au jour; **to w. by a sick person,** veiller auprès d'un malade.

2 *vt* **(a)** (*observe*) observer, regarder attentivement; *Prov* **a watched pot never boils,** plus on désire une chose plus elle se fait attendre; **to w. s.o. closely,** surveiller qn de près, ne pas quitter qn des yeux; **to have s.o. watched,** faire surveiller qn; **we are being watched,** on nous observe; **to w. birds,** observer les oiseaux; **you can't do this — w. me,** tu peux pas faire ça — tu vas voir;

(b) (*look at, monitor*) regarder (*qn, qch*); **I watched her working,** je la regardais travailler; **to w. a football match,** (*attend*) assister à un match de football; (*on television*) regarder un match de football; **to w. the course of events/s.o.'s career,** suivre le cours des événements/la carrière de qn; *Jur* **to w. a case,** veiller (en justice) aux intérêts de qn; *Pej* **to w. the clock,** avoir les yeux rivés à *ou* fixés sur sa montre; **to w. the world go by,** regarder passer le monde;

(c) (*be careful of*) avoir l'œil sur (*qch*); **we shall have to w. the expenses,** il nous faudra avoir l'œil sur les dépenses; **we'll have to w. the time,** (*so as not to be late*) il va falloir que nous fassions attention à l'heure; **w. what you say about ...,** fais attention à ce que tu dis au sujet de ...; **w. your language!,** surveille ton langage!; **w. the step!,** attention à la marche!; **w. your step!,** (*don't fall*) fais attention de ne pas tomber!; (*step carefully*) fais attention où tu mets les pieds!; (*be careful*) fais attention!; *F* **w. it!,** attention!;

(d) (*keep an eye on*) surveiller (*les enfants, mes valises etc*);

(e) veiller (*un mort*);

(f) (*be mindful of*) **to w. one's opportunity/time,** guetter l'occasion/le moment propice.

►**watch out** *vi* faire attention; **w. out!,** attention!, prenez garde!

►**watch out for** *vipo* **(a)** (*look for*) **ask the garage to w. out for a decent second-hand car,** demande au garage d'essayer de trouver une bonne voiture d'occasion; **(b)** *Am* (*take care of*) s'occuper de (*qn*); **(c)** (*keep watch*) (*for return of*) attendre; (*for approach of*) guetter; **(d)** (*be careful of*) faire attention à; **w. out for Ronnie!,** gare à Ronnie!

►**watch over** *vipo* (*guard, protect*) veiller sur.

watchband ['wɒtʃbænd] *n* bracelet *m* de montre.

watchdog ['wɒtʃdɒg] *n* chien *m* de garde; *Fig* groupe *m* qui surveille; *Fig* **w. committee,** comité *m* qui veille à la dépense.

watcher ['wɒtʃər] *n* **(a)** observateur, -trice; **to be a weight w.,** surveiller son poids; **(b)** veilleur, -euse (*d'un mort, d'un malade*).

watchful ['wɒtʃfʊl] *adj* vigilant, alerte, attentif; **to be w.,** être sur ses gardes; **to keep a w. eye on** *or* **over s.o.,** surveiller qn de près; **to be w. of s.o.,** observer *ou* épier qn d'un œil méfiant *ou* jaloux.

watchfully ['wɒtʃfəlɪ] *adv* avec vigilance, d'un œil attentif.

watching ['wɒtʃɪŋ] *n* **(a)** (*of birds*) observation *f*; **(b)** (*vigil, guard*) surveillance *f*; veillée *f* (*d'un mort*).

watchmaker ['wɒtʃmeɪkər] *n* horloger *m*.

watchmaking ['wɒtʃmeɪkɪŋ] *n* horlogerie *f*.

watchman, *pl* **-men** ['wɒtʃmən] *n* gardien *m*; *Nau* homme *m* de garde.

watchstrap ['wɒtʃstræp] *n* bracelet *m* de montre.

watchtower ['wɒtʃtaʊər] *n* tour *f* d'observation *ou* de guet; (*in prison camp*) mirador *m*.

watchword ['wɒtʃwɜːd] *n* mot *m* d'ordre.

water¹ ['wɔːtər] *n* **(a)** eau *f*; **is the w. safe to drink?,** est-ce que l'eau est potable?; **to take** *or* **drink the waters,** (*mineral springs*) prendre les eaux; faire une cure; *Fig* **to get into hot w.,** se mettre dans de mauvais draps; **to drink a glass of cold w.,** boire un verre d'eau fraîche; *Fig* **to pour cold w. on a scheme,** se montrer très négatif à l'égard d'un projet; **to put w. in one's wine,** couper son vin d'eau; **the wine flowed like w.,** le vin a coulé à flots; *Fig* **to spend money like w.,** jeter l'argent par les fenêtres; *Prov* **you can lead a horse to w. but you cannot make him drink,** on ne saurait faire boire un âne qui n'a pas soif; *Fig* **to hold w.,** (*of argument etc*) tenir debout; **my shoes let in w.,** mes chaussures prennent l'eau; **to take in w.,** (*of ship*) embarquer son eau, faire de l'eau; (*of locomotive*) faire de l'eau; **the waters of the**

Danube, les eaux du Danube; **to feel like a fish out of w.,** se sentir perdu *ou* hors de son élément; *Prov* **still waters run deep,** il faut se méfier de l'eau qui dort; **above w.,** à flot, surnageant; **to keep oneself** *or* **one's head above w.,** se maintenir à la surface *ou* sur l'eau; *Fig* arriver à subvenir à ses besoins; (*financially*) faire face à ses engagements; **on land and w.,** sur terre et sur mer; **by w.,** en bateau; (*transporter des marchandises*) par voie d'eau; **under w.,** (*land, roots*) inondé; (*submarine*) en plongée; (*swim*) sous l'eau; *Fig* **that's all w. under the bridge now,** c'est du passé tout ça; *Fig* **a lot of w. has flowed under the bridge since then,** il y a de l'eau qui a coulé sous les ponts depuis; *Fig* **to get into deep w.,** avoir des gros ennuis; **she's a real w. baby,** c'est un vrai petit poisson; **high/low w.,** marée haute/basse; **w. bed,** matelas *m* à eau; **w. bird,** oiseau *m* aquatique; **w. biscuit** *or Am* **cracker,** = petit biscuit croustillant; *Br Admin* **w. board,** service *m* des eaux; **w. boatman,** (*insect*) notonecte *mf*; **w. bottle,** gourde *f*, bidon *m* (à eau); **hot w. bottle,** bouillotte *f*; **w. buffalo,** kérabu *m*; **w. butt,** tonneau *m* pour recueillir l'eau de pluie; **w. cannon,** canon *m* à eau; **police turned w. canons on the crowd,** la police a arrosé la foule avec des canons à eau; **w. carrier,** porteur, -euse d'eau; *Astron* le Verseau; **w. chestnut,** châtaigne *f* d'eau; **w. chute,** (*in swimming pool*) cascade *f*; *Old-fashioned* **w. closet,** water-closet *m*, *pl* water-closets; toilettes *fpl*; **w. hammer,** (*in pipes*) marteau *m* d'eau; **w. heater,** chauffe-eau *m inv*; **w. hen,** poule *f* d'eau; **w. hole,** (*for animals*) mare *f*; *Culin* **w. ice,** sorbet *m*; *Tech* **w. jacket,** chemise *f* d'eau; *Sp* **w. jump,** douve *f*, brook *m*; **w. level,** niveau *m* piézométrique; **w. lily,** nénuphar *m*; **w. line,** laisse *f*; **w. main,** conduite *f* d'eau; **w. mattress,** matelas *m* à eau; **w. meadow,** champ souvent inondé; **w. mill,** moulin *m* à eau; **w. pipe,** tuyau *m* d'eau; **w. pistol** *or Am* **gun,** pistolet *m* à eau; **w. plant,** plante *f* aquatique; *Sp* **w. polo,** water-polo *m*; **w. power,** énergie *f* hydraulique; **w. rat,** rat *m* d'eau; *Admin* **w. rate,** taxe *f* d'abonnement à l'eau; **w. shortage,** pénurie *f* d'eau; *Sp* **w. skiing,** ski *m* nautique; *Sp* **to w. ski,** faire du ski nautique; **w. snail,** hélice *f* aquatique; *Ch* **w. soluble,** hydrosoluble; **w. sports,** sports *mpl* nautiques; *Myth* **w. sprite,** ondin, -ine; **w. supply,** alimentation *f* en eau; (*intake point*) arrivée *f* d'eau; **w. table,** niveau *m* hydrostatique; **w. tank,** réservoir *m* d'eau; **w. tower,** château *m* d'eau; **w. transport,** transport *m* par voie d'eau; **w. wheel,** roue *f* à eau, roue hydraulique; **w. wings,** (*for swimming*) flotteurs *mpl*;

(b) *Med* **w. on the brain,** hydrocéphalie *f*; **w. on the knee,** hydarthrose *f* du genou, épanchement *m* de synovie; **w. blister,** cloque *f*; *Obst* **breaking of the waters,** perte *f* des eaux; **her waters have broken,** elle perd les eaux; **to pass** *or* **make w.,** uriner;

(c) transparence *f*, eau *f* (*d'un diamant*); **diamond of the first w.,** diamant de première eau; *Old-fashioned Fig* **a liar of the first w.,** un menteur de premier ordre.

water² 1 *vt* **(a)** arroser (*une plante, un jardin*); **an area watered by many rivers,** une région arrosée par de nombreuses rivières; **(b)** diluer, délayer (*un liquide*); **to w. one's wine,** couper son vin; **(c)** faire boire, donner à boire à, abreuver (*des bêtes*); **(d)** *Tex* **watered silk,** soie moirée. **2** *vi* **(a)** (*of eyes*) pleurer, larmoyer; **it makes my mouth w.,** cela me fait venir l'eau à la bouche; **(b)** (*of animals*) s'abreuver.

►**water down** *vtsep* diluer, délayer (*un liquide*); *Fig* atténuer (*une expression, une affirmation*); *Fig* **to w. down one's claims,** en rabattre, mettre de l'eau dans son vin; *Fig* **to w. down an article,** rendre un article moins virulent; *Fig* **a watered-down version of sth,** une version édulcorée de qch.

waterborne ['wɔːtəbɔːn] *adj* **(a)** (*vessel*) à flot, flottant; **(b)** (*goods*) transporté par voie d'eau; **(c)** (*disease*) d'origine hydrique.

water-cool ['wɔːtə'kuːl] *vt Aut* **w.-cooled engine,** moteur *m* à refroidissement d'eau.

watercourse ['wɔːtəkɔːs] *n* cours *m* d'eau.

watercolor ['wɔːtəkʌlər] *n US* = **WATERCOLOUR**.

watercolour, *US* **watercolor** ['wɔːtəkʌlər] *n* (*picture*) aquarelle *f*; (*paint*) couleur *f* pour aquarelle, peinture *f* à l'eau; **to paint in watercolours,** faire de l'aquarelle.

watercress ['wɔːtəkres] *n Bot Culin* cresson *m* de fontaine.

waterfall ['wɔːtəfɔːl] *n* chute *f* d'eau, cascade *f*.

waterfowl ['wɔːtəfaʊl] *n* **(a)** (*bird*) oiseau *m* aquatique; **(b)** (*no pl*) gibier *m* d'eau, sauvagine *f*.

waterfront ['wɔːtəfrʌnt] *n* bord *m* de l'eau; (*docks*) les quais *mpl*; (*at seaside*) bord de mer; **to live on the w.,** vivre au bord des quais; **w. house,** maison construite au bord des quais.

waterglass ['wɔːtəglɑːs] *n Com* silicate *m* de soude.

wateriness ['wɔːtərɪnɪs] *n* insipidité *f*, fadeur *f* (*d'un potage, de qch cuit à l'eau*).

watering ['wɔːtərɪŋ] *n* **(a)** arrosage *m* (*d'une plante*); irrigation *f* (*des champs*); **w. can,** arrosoir *m*; **(b)** abreuvage *m* (*des bêtes*); **w. place,** (*for cattle*) abreuvoir *m*; (*for ships*) aiguade *f*; *Old-fashioned Br* (*spa*) ville *f* d'eau, station thermale; (*resort*) station balnéaire, plage *f*; **w. hole,** (*for animals*) mare *f*, point *m* d'eau; *Fig* (*pub*) bar *m*; **(c)** (*of eyes*) larmoiement *m*; **(d)** *Tex* moirage *m* (*de la soie*).

waterlogged ['wɔːtəlɒgd] *adj* **(a)** (*navire*) plein d'eau, entre deux eaux; **(b)** (*bois*) alourdi par absorption d'eau; (*terrain*) détrempé, envahi par les eaux, imbibé d'eau; (*sous-sol*) aqueux.

Waterloo [wɔːtə'luː] *n* **the Battle of W.,** la bataille de Waterloo; *Fig* **to meet one's W.,** arriver au désastre.

watermark¹ ['wɔːtəmɑːk] *n* **(a)** *Nau* laisse *f* (*de haute ou basse mer*); **(b)** (*on paper, bank note*) filigrane *m*.

watermark² *vt* filigraner.

watermelon ['wɔːtəmelən] *n* pastèque *f*.

waterproof¹ ['wɔːtəpruːf] **1** *adj* imperméable; (*montre*) étanche; **w. sheet,** bâche *f*. **2** *n* imperméable m.

waterproof² *vt* imperméabiliser.

waterproofing ['wɔːtəpruːfɪŋ] *n* imperméabilisation *f*; (*substance*) imperméabilisant *m*.

water-repellent ['wɔːtərɪpelənt] *adj* hydrofuge.

water-resistant ['wɔːtərɪsɪstənt] *adj* qui résiste à l'eau.

watershed ['wɔːtəʃed] *n* **(a)** *Geog* ligne *f* de partage des eaux; *Am* bassin *m* hydrographique; **(b)** *Fig* point décisif; tournant *m*; **at this w. in her life,** à ce moment critique de sa vie; **the decision proved to be a w.,** la décision s'est avérée être un tournant décisif.

waterside ['wɔːtəsaɪd] *n* bord *m* de l'eau; (*quays*) les quais *mpl*; **on the w.,** au bord de l'eau, sur la rive; **w. flowers,** fleurs *fpl* du bord de l'eau; *US* **w. workers,** dockers *mpl*.

waterspout ['wɔːtəspaʊt] *n* **(a)** *Met* trombe *f*; **(b)** (*pipe*) tuyau *m*, descente *f* (d'eau).

watertight ['wɔːtətaɪt] *adj* **(a)** étanche (à l'eau); imperméable (à l'eau); **to be w.,** (*of vessel*) retenir l'eau; *Nau* **w. bulkhead,** cloison *f* étanche; **(b)** *Fig* (*argument*) irréfutable; (*regulation*) qui a prévu tous les cas; **we have a w. case against him,** nous avons des arguments irréfutables contre lui.

waterway ['wɔːtəweɪ] *n* voie *f* navigable.

waterworks ['wɔːtəwɜːks] *npl* **(a)** usine *f* de distribution d'eau; **(b)** *Med F* voies *fpl* urinaires; **he's having a bit of trouble with his w.,** il a des problèmes de vessie; **(c)** *F* **to turn on the w.,** se mettre à pleurer, ouvrir la fontaine.

watery ['wɔːtərɪ] *adj* **(a)** (*terrain*) humide; **(b)** aqueux; qui contient de l'eau; **(c)** noyé d'eau; **she gave a w. smile,** elle eut un sourire mouillé de larmes; **w. eyes,** (*because of wind, dust etc*) yeux *mpl* qui pleurent; **w. soup,** potage trop clair; **w. tea** *or* **coffee,** lavasse *f*; **(d)** (*couleur*) déteint, délavé; **(e)** (*ciel*) chargé de pluie; **w. moon,** lune entourée d'un halo; **(f)** *Lit* **to find a w. grave,** être enseveli par les eaux.

watt [wɒt] *n El* watt *m*.

wattage ['wɒtɪdʒ] *n El* puissance *f ou* consommation *f* en watts.

watt-hour ['wɒtaʊə] *n El* wattheure *m*.

wattle¹ ['wɒt(ə)l] *n* **(a)** (*covering*) clayonnage *m*; **w.-and-daub wall,** mur en clayonnage revêtu de boue *ou* d'argile; **(b)** *Austr* (*tree*) acacia *m*.

wattle² *n* caroncule *f* (*d'un oiseau*); barbillon *m* (*d'un poisson*).

wave¹ [weɪv] *n* **(a)** *Nau & Fig* vague *f*; *Nau* lame *f*; *Art* **new w.,** nouvelle vague; **w. of crime/refugees/enthusiasm,** vague de criminalité/de réfugiés/d'enthousiasme; **w. of anger,** bouffée *f* de colère; **a w. of bitterness swept over her,** un flot d'amertume l'envahit; *F* **to make waves,** (*cause trouble*) créer des remous; **w. machine,** machine *f* à vagues; **w. power,** énergie *f* des vagues;

(b) *Phys* onde *f* (*électrique, magnétique*); *Rad Electron* **hertzian w.,** onde hertzienne; **long waves,** grandes ondes; **medium/short waves,** ondes moyennes/courtes;

(c) (*in hair*) ondulation *f*; **to have a natural w. (in one's hair),** avoir les cheveux qui ondulent naturellement;

(d) (*movement*) balancement *m*, ondoiement *m*; (*of hand, hat*) geste *m*, signe *m*; **with a w. of his hand,** d'un geste *ou* d'un signe de la main; **with a w. of her magic wand,** d'un coup de baguette magique.

wave[2] **1** *vi* **(a)** s'agiter; (*of flag*) flotter (au vent); (*of corn, grass, plume*) ondoyer, onduler; **to w. to s.o.,** (*signal to*) faire signe à qn (en agitant le bras *ou* un mouchoir *etc*); (*greet*) saluer qn de la main; **I waved to him to stop,** je lui ai fait signe d'arrêter;

(b) my hair waves naturally, mes cheveux ondulent naturellement.

2 *vt* **(a)** agiter (*le bras, un mouchoir*); brandir (*un parapluie, une canne*); **to w. a flag,** agiter un drapeau; *Fig* **to w. the flag,** être cocardier; **to w. one's hand,** faire signe de la main; **to w. one's arms about,** agiter les bras; **to w. goodbye to s.o.,** agiter la main en signe d'adieu; **w. Mummy goodbye,** fais signe au revoir à maman; *Fig* **you can w. your money goodbye,** tu peux abandonner tout espoir de récupérer ton argent;

(b) onduler (*les cheveux*); **to have one's hair waved,** se faire faire une mise en plis.

►**wave aside, wave away** *vtsep* faire signe à (*qn*) de s'écarter; **to w. aside an objection,** écarter une objection.

►**wave down** *vtsep* faire signe à (*une voiture*) de s'arrêter.

►**wave on** *vtsep* faire signe à (*une voiture*) de continuer; **he waved us on,** de la main il nous a fait signe de continuer.

waveband ['weɪvbænd] *n Rad* gamme *f* d'ondes, plage *f* (d'ondes).

wavelength ['weɪvleŋθ] *n Rad & Fig* longueur *f* d'onde; *Fig* **we weren't on the same w.,** nous n'étions pas sur la même longueur d'onde.

waver ['weɪvər] *vi* **(a)** (*falter*) (*of person*) vaciller; (*of voice*) se troubler; (*of courage*) défaillir; (*of troops*) fléchir; (*of gaze*) flotter; **they never wavered in their support, their support never wavered,** leur soutien n'a jamais faibli; **to w. in one's resolution,** chanceler dans sa résolution; **(b)** (*of flame*) trembloter.

waverer ['weɪvərər] *n* indécis, -ise, irrésolu, -ue; **we must convince the waverers,** il nous faut convaincre les indécis.

wavering ['weɪvərɪŋ] **1** *adj* **(a)** (*homme, esprit*) irrésolu, indécis, vacillant; (*voix, courage*) défaillant; **(b)** (*flamme*) vacillant, tremblotant. **2** *n* **(a)** vacillement *m*, irrésolution *f* (*de l'esprit*); trouble *m* (*de la voix*); défaillance *f* (*du courage*); **(b)** tremblement *m*, vacillement *m* (*d'une flamme*).

waviness ['weɪvɪnɪs] *n* caractère onduleux *ou* ondulé (*d'une surface*); ondulations naturelles (*des cheveux*).

waving ['weɪvɪŋ] *n* **(a)** (*movement*) agitation *f* (*d'un mouchoir*); ondoiement *m*, ondulation *f* (*du blé*); **w. of the hand,** geste *m ou* mouvement *m* de la main; **(b)** (*curling*) ondulation *f* (*des cheveux*).

wavy ['weɪvɪ] *adj* onduleux, ondulé; **w. hair,** cheveux ondulés; **w. line,** ligne tremblée.

wax[1] [wæks] *n* cire *f*; (*for skis*) fart *m*; (*in ears*) cérumen *m*; **to mould s.o. like w.,** façonner *ou* former (le caractère de) qn comme de la cire; **he's w. in her hands,** elle fait de lui ce qu'elle veut; *Petr* **(paraffin) w.,** cire (minérale), paraffine *f*; *esp Am* **w. beans,** haricots *mpl* beurre; **w. doll,** poupée *f* de cire; **w. paper,** papier paraffiné; *Rel* **w. taper,** cierge *m*.

wax[2] *vt* cirer, encaustiquer (*un plancher, un meuble*); astiquer (*un meuble*); *Ski* farter; (*of shoemaker*) empoisser (*le fil*).

wax[3] *vi* **(a)** (*of the moon*) croître; **to w. and wane,** croître et décroître; **(b)** *Fml* (*be, become*) devenir, se faire; **to w. eloquent in support of sth,** déployer toute son éloquence en faveur de qch; **he waxed indignant,** il s'indigna; **to w. lyrical,** se faire lyrique (**about,** à propos de).

waxed [wækst] *adj* ciré; (*parquet*) frotté à la cire; (*fil*) poissé; **w. moustache,** moustache cosmétiquée.

waxing[1] ['wæksɪŋ] *n* (*of floor*) cirage *m*, encaustiquage *m*; (*of thread*) empoissage *m*; (*of skis*) fartage *m*.

waxing[2] *n* croissance *f* (*de la lune*).

waxcloth ['wæksklɒθ] **(a)** (*oilcloth*) toile cirée; **(b)** (*linoleum*) linoléum *m*.

waxen ['wæks(ə)n] *adj* **(a)** (*of wax*) de cire, en cire; **(b)** (*like wax*) cireux; (*teint*) de cire; **w. pallor,** pâleur cireuse.

waxwing ['wækswɪŋ] *n* (*bird*) jaseur *m*.

waxwork ['wækswɜːk] *n* **w. (dummy),** figure *f* de cire; **waxworks,** (*place*) musée *m* de cire.

waxy ['wæksɪ] *adj* cireux; (*teint*) de cire.

way[1] [weɪ] *n* **(a)** (*street, path*) chemin *m*, route *f*, voie *f*; **over** *or* **across the w.,** de l'autre côté de la route *ou* du chemin *ou* de la rue; **the house/the people over** *or* **across the w.,** la maison/les gens d'en face; *Rail US* **w. train,** (train *m*) omnibus *m*; **w. station,** halte *f*;

(b) (*route*) chemin *m*; **the w. to the station,** le chemin qui mène *ou* qui conduit à la gare, le chemin de la gare; **to show s.o. the w.,** montrer la route à qn; **to ask one's w.,** demander son chemin; **to lose one's w.,** s'égarer, se perdre; **that's the w. to ruin,** c'est le chemin de la ruine; **the right w.,** le bon chemin, la bonne route; **to go the wrong w.,** se tromper de chemin, faire fausse route; **to go the nearest** *or* **shortest w.,** prendre le plus court chemin; **to know one's w. about a house,** connaître les êtres; *Fig* **he knows his w. about** *or* **around,** il sait se débrouiller, il est débrouillard; **to prepare the w.,** préparer la voie; **to start on one's w.,** se mettre en route; **on the w.,** en cours de route, en chemin, chemin faisant; **to stop on the w.,** s'arrêter en chemin; **to be on one's** *or* **the w. to Paris,** être en route pour *ou* sur la route de Paris; **on my** *or* **the w. home,** en revenant chez moi, en rentrant; **I must be on my w.,** il faut que j'y aille; **I'm on my w.,** (*coming*) j'arrive; (*going*) je pars; **he's well on the w. to doing it,** il est en bonne voie de le faire; **the building is well on the w. to completion,** l'édifice est bien avancé; **to lead the w. in research,** être à la pointe de la recherche, être le chef de file dans la recherche; **to lead the w. in fighting inflation,** être le chef de file dans la lutte contre l'inflation; *F* **there's a baby on the w.,** elle attend un bébé; **to go the w. of all things** *or* **of all flesh,** aller où va toute chose, mourir; **to go one's w.,** passer son chemin; **to go one's own w.,** (*follow own wishes*) faire à sa guise; (*differ from others*) se désolidariser d'avec ses collègues, faire bande à part; **to go out of one's w.,** s'écarter de son chemin, dévier de sa route, faire un détour; **to go out of one's w. to oblige s.o.,** se donner de la peine pour être agréable à qn; **the w. to a man's heart is through his stomach,** = pour conquérir le cœur d'un homme, il faut lui faire de bons petits plats; **the village is rather out of the w.,** le village est un peu isolé; **that's nothing out of the w.,** rien d'extraordinaire à cela; *Rel* **the W. of the Cross,** le chemin de la Croix; **w. in/out,** entrée *f*/sortie *f*; **w. through,** passage *m*; **to find a w. out/in,** trouver moyen de sortir/d'entrer; **to find a w. out of a deadlock,** trouver une issue à une impasse; **to find a w. out of a problem,** trouver une solution à un problème; **to leave s.o. a w. out,** laisser à qn le moyen de sortir d'une difficulté; **easy w. out,** solution *f* de facilité; **to find one's w. to a place,** parvenir à un endroit; **can you find your w. out?,** vous connaissez le chemin pour sortir?; **I can find my own w. out,** (*of house etc*) je trouverai mon chemin; **however did it find its w. into print?,** comment en est-on venu à l'imprimer?; **to make one's w. towards a place,** se diriger vers *ou* se rendre dans un endroit; **to make one's w. towards s.o.,** se diriger vers qn; **to make** *or* **work** *or* **push one's w. through the crowd,** se frayer un chemin à travers la foule; **she made her w. into the house,** elle a pénétré dans la maison; **to make one's w. back/out/home,** retourner, revenir/sortir/rentrer; **how to make one's w. (in the world),** le moyen de parvenir; **to work one's w. up,** s'élever (à force de travail); **to pay one's w.,** (*not get into debt*) se suffire; (*contribute to expenses*) payer sa part; **firm that pays its w.,** entreprise qui fait *ou* qui couvre ses frais; **to see one's w. to doing sth,** se croire à même de faire qch; **couldn't you see your w. (clear) to doing it?,** ne trouveriez-vous pas moyen de le faire?; **to stand in s.o.'s w.,** être dans le chemin de qn, barrer le passage à qn; **I don't wish to stand in the w. of your happiness,** je ne voudrais pas faire obstacle à votre bonheur; **to stand in the w. of a scheme,** s'opposer à un projet; **the obstacles that stand in our w.,** les obstacles qui se dressent sur notre chemin; **to put difficulties in s.o.'s w.,** opposer *ou* créer des difficultés à qn; **to get in one another's w.,** se gêner (les uns les autres); **work gets in the w. of my social life,** le travail m'empêche de sortir autant que je voudrais; **to be in s.o.'s w.,** gêner qn; **this table is in the w.,** cette table gêne *ou* est encombrante; **you're in the w.,** tu gênes; **to get out of the w.,** se ranger, s'ôter du chemin, s'écarter (*pour laisser passer qn*); **(get) out of the w.!,** rangez-vous!, ôtez-vous de là *ou* de mon chemin!; **to get out of s.o.'s w.,** s'ôter *ou* s'écarter du chemin de qn; *Fig* (*in relationship*) s'écarter du chemin de qn; laisser le champ libre à (*un rival*); **to get s.o. out of the w.,** se débarrasser de qn, écarter *ou* éloigner qn; **to get sth out of the w.,** écarter *ou* éloigner qch; **to keep out of the w.,** se tenir à l'écart; **to keep out of s.o.'s w.,** éviter qn; **to make w. for s.o.,** laisser passer qn, faire place à qn; **clear the w.!,** poussez-vous!; *Fig* **the agreement will clear the w. for the company's expansion,** l'entente déblaiera le terrain pour permettre l'expansion de la société; *Fig* **the w. is clear,** la voie est libre; **he is retiring to make w. for a younger man,** il prend sa retraite pour céder la place à un plus jeune; **the cinema is being demolished to make w. for a motorway,** le cinéma va être démoli pour la construction d'une autoroute;

(c) (*distance*) **to go a little w.** *or* **part of the w. with s.o.,** faire un bout de chemin avec qn; **all the w.,** tout le long du chemin; (*to the end*) jusqu'au bout; **he talked the entire** *or* **whole w.,** il a parlé pendant tout le trajet; *F* **to go the whole w.** *or* **all the w.,** (*sexually*) aller jusqu'au bout; *Fig* **I'm with you all the w.,** (*agree*) je suis tout à fait d'accord; **I flew most of the w.,** j'ai fait la plupart du voyage en avion; **I've come a long w.,** j'ai fait un long voyage, j'arrive de loin; *Fig* **she's come a long w.,** (*been successful*) elle a bien réussi (dans la vie); *Fig* **she'll go a long w.,** elle ira loin; **it's a long w. to London, London's a long w. from here,** Londres est bien loin; **it's a long w. from Paris to Rome,** il y a loin de Paris à Rome; **to have a long w. to go,** avoir beaucoup de chemin à faire; **a little** *or* **short w. off,** à peu de distance, pas trop loin; **it's only a short w. (off),** c'est assez proche; **Christmas is still a long w. off,** Noël est encore loin; **a little sympathy goes a long w.,** un peu de sympathie fait grand bien; **a little of it goes a long w.,** (*it's very economical*) on en use très peu, il en faut très peu; **I like it but a little goes a long w.,** (*of rich food*) je l'aime mais à petites doses; **a little of him goes a long w.,** on en a vite assez de lui; **you can make a little meat go a long w. by doing this,** utilisez au mieux un petit morceau de viande en faisant ceci; **to make one's money go a long w.,** savoir ménager ses sous; **by a long w.,** de beaucoup; **not by a long w.,** il s'en faut de beaucoup; **you're a long w. out** *or* **out by a long w.,** vous êtes loin de compte, vous vous trompez de beaucoup;

(d) (*direction*) côté *m*, direction *f*, sens *m*; voie *f* (*d'un robinet*); **which w. is the wind blowing?,** d'où vient *ou* souffle le vent?; *Fig* **so that's the w. the wind's blowing!,** ça se passe donc comme ça!; **this w.,** de ce côté-ci, par ici; **that w.,** de ce côté-là, par là; **(step) this w.!,** (venez *ou* passez) par ici!; **is this the w.?,** c'est par ici?; **which w. is the library from here?,** par où faut-il passer pour aller à la bibliothèque?; **which w. did you come?,** par où êtes-vous venu?; **which w. did she go?,** par où est-elle passée?; **which w. do we go?,** de quel côté *ou* par où allons-nous?; **this w. and that,** de-ci de-là, de tous (les) côtés; **he didn't know which w. to look,** il était tout décontenancé; **to look the other w.,** détourner les yeux; **I've nothing to say one w. or the other,** je n'ai rien à dire pour ou contre; **they set off, each going his own w.,** ils sont partis chacun de leur côté; **I'm going your w.,** je vais de votre côté; **the next time you're that w.,** la prochaine fois que vous passerez par là; *F* **down our w.,** chez nous; **she lives Hampstead w.,** elle habite du côté de Hampstead; **if the chance comes your w.,** si l'occasion se présente à vous; **that works both ways,** ça vaut *ou* marche dans les deux sens; *Fig F* **to go both ways,** (*be bisexual*) marcher à voile et à vapeur; **the wrong w.,** à contre-sens; **to brush s.o. the wrong w.,** prendre qn à rebrousse-poil; **the wrong w. up,** sens dessus dessous, à l'envers; **to hold sth (the) right w. up,** tenir qch dans le bon sens; **to split a sum of money three ways,** partager une somme en trois; *Am* **every which w.,** dans tous les sens;

(e) (*means*) moyen *m*; **to find a w. of doing sth,** trouver (le) moyen de faire qch; *Admin* **ways and means,** voies et moyens; **there are ways and means,** il y a des moyens; *Parl* **Committee of Ways and Means,** Commission *f* du Budget;

(f) (*fashion*) façon *f*, manière *f*; **in this w.,** de cette façon; **in a friendly w.,** amicalement; (*treat s.o.*) en ami; **speaking in a general w.,** (parlant) d'une manière générale; **in such a w. as to ...,** de façon à ..., de telle sorte que ...; *esp Am F* **no w.!,** jamais de la vie!, pas question!, *F* des clous!; *F* **there's no w. he'll ...,** il est absolument impossible qu'il ... + *sub*; *F* **there's no w. that's Jeanne Moreau!,** tu rigoles?, ce n'est pas Jeanne Moreau!; **without in any w. wishing to criticize,** sans aucunement vouloir critiquer; **either w.,** (*whatever you decide*) quoi que tu décides; (*whatever happens*) quoi qu'il arrive; **that's the w.!,** ça y est!, voilà!, à la bonne heure!; **in such and such a w.,** de telle et telle façon; **to go** *or* **set about it the right w.,** s'y prendre de la bonne manière *ou* comme il faut; **you're going the right w. to make her angry,** ça, c'est la meilleure manière de la mettre en colère; **the best w. is to say nothing,** le mieux est de ne rien dire; **in one w. or another,** d'une façon ou d'une autre; **there are no two ways about it,** il n'y a pas à discuter; **to go on in the same old w.,** aller toujours son train; **I don't like the w. things are going,** je n'aime pas la tournure que prennent les choses; **they'll never finish it the w. things are going,** ils n'en finiront jamais, au train où vont les choses; **w. of doing sth,** manière *ou* façon de faire qch; **w. of speaking/writing,** façon de parler/d'écrire; **w. of living,** style *m* de vie; **her w. of looking at things,** sa manière de voir (les choses); **it isn't what he says, it's the w. he says it,** ce n'est pas ce qu'il dit mais la manière dont il le dit; **I don't like the w. you talk to her,** je n'aime pas la manière dont tu lui parles; **to my w. of thinking,** selon moi, à mon sens; **that's not my w. (of doing things),** ce n'est pas ma manière de faire; **that's her w.,** c'est sa manière de faire; **that's always the w. when you're in a hurry,** c'est toujours comme ça quand on est pressé; **that's always the w. with him,** il est toujours comme ça, c'est toujours comme ça avec lui; **to do things in one's own w.,** faire les choses à sa guise *ou* à sa façon *ou* à sa manière; **to have a w. of one's own** *or* **one's own w. of doing sth,** avoir une façon à soi de faire qch, avoir sa méthode; **he's a genius in his w.,** c'est un génie dans son genre; **she does what she can for them in her small w.,** elle les aide dans la mesure de ses moyens; **to be doing quite well in a small w.,** aller (toujours) son petit bonhomme de chemin; **one's ways,** (*behaviour*) ses manières; **you'll soon get into our ways,** vous vous ferez bientôt à nos habitudes; **to get** *or* **fall into the w. of doing sth,** (*through habit*) prendre l'habitude de faire qch; s'habituer à faire qch; (*through practice*) apprendre à faire qch; **you'll get into the w. of it,** vous vous y ferez; **that's one w. of looking at it!,** c'est une manière de voir!; **engaging ways,** petites façons engageantes; **I know his little ways,** je connais ses petites manies; **he has a w. with children,** il sait prendre les enfants; **to have one's (own) w.,** faire à sa tête; **to get one's (own) w.,** (en) faire à sa volonté, arriver à ses fins; **she wants her own w.,** elle veut n'en faire qu'à sa tête; **if I had my w.,** si on me laissait faire; **have it your own w.,** (*do as you like*) faites ce que vous voulez *ou* à votre guise; (*if you insist*) soit; **she had it all her own w.,** elle a fait exactement ce qu'elle a voulu; **you can't have it both ways,** on ne peut pas avoir le beurre et l'argent du beurre;

(g) (*respect*) égard *m*; **in many ways,** à bien des égards; **in some ways,** à certains points de vue; **in every w.,** sous tous les rapports, en tous points; **in one w.,** d'un certain point de vue; **you're right in a w.,** d'une certaine manière vous avez raison; **this should in no w. be regarded as a victory,** ça ne devrait en aucun cas être considéré comme une victoire; **in no w.,** en aucune façon, nullement; **she is in no w.** *or* **not in any w. to blame,** elle n'est aucunement *ou* elle n'est en aucune façon responsable;

(h) (*sphere*) cours *m*, course *f*; **I met him in the ordinary w. of business,** je l'ai rencontré dans le courant de mes affaires;

(i) (*progress*) *Nau* erre *f*; **the flood is making w.,** l'inondation fait des progrès; **ship under w.,** navire *m* en marche *ou* en route; **to get under w.,** se mettre en route; (*of ship*) appareiller; (*of meeting*) commencer; (*of campaign etc*) démarrer; **an important experiment is under w.,** une expérience importante est en cours; **the project is well under w.,** le projet est bien avancé;

(j) (*state, condition*) état *m*; **to be in a good/bad w.,** être bien/mal en point; **things seem in a bad w.,** les choses ont l'air d'aller mal; **his business is in a bad w.,** ses affaires vont mal *ou* périclitent; **to be in a good w. of business,** faire de bonnes affaires; **to be in a fair w. to do sth,** être en voie de *ou* en (bonne) passe de faire qch; **to put s.o. in the w. of earning a few pounds,** donner à qn l'occasion de gagner quelques livres;

(k) to mention sth by the w., mentionner qch en passant *ou* incidemment; **(let it be said) by the w.,** soit dit en passant; **all this is by the w.,** tout ceci est entre parenthèses; **by the w., did you see him yesterday?,** à propos, l'avez-vous vu hier?; **by the w.!,** ah, j'y pense!; **by w. of,** (*via*) par (la voie de); (*with the intention of*) à titre de; **by w. of introduction/warning,** à titre d'introduction/d'avertissement; **he asked after her dog by w. of changing the conversation,** il a demandé des nouvelles de son chien, histoire de changer de sujet; **what do you have by w. of** *or* **in the w. of fruit?,** (*what kind do you have*) qu'est-ce que vous avez comme fruits?; **he's by w. of**

being a socialist, il se dit *ou* il fait profession d'être socialiste.

way² *adv F (a lot)* très; **w. ahead,** très avancé (**of,** sur); **it was w. back in the twenties,** cela remonte aux années vingt; **Mary and I go w. back** *or* **are friends from w. back,** Mary et moi sommes amies de longue date; **w. down south,** là-bas dans le sud; **to be w. out,** *(mistaken)* faire une grosse erreur, se tromper sérieusement; **your guess was w. out,** vous étiez très loin de la vérité; **it's w. more than I can afford,** c'est beaucoup plus que je ne peux me permettre de payer.

waybill ['weɪbɪl] *n Com* feuille *f* de route; bulletin *m ou* bordereau *m* d'expédition.

wayfarer ['weɪfeərər] *n* voyageur, -euse (à pied).

wayfaring ['weɪfeərɪŋ] *n* voyages *mpl* (à pied); **w. man,** voyageur *m* (à pied).

waylay [weɪ'leɪ] *vt (pt & pp* **waylaid** [weɪ'leɪd]) **(a)** *(attack)* attirer *(qn)* dans une embuscade, tendre un guet-apens à *(qn)*; **to be waylaid,** tomber dans un guet-apens; **(b)** arrêter *(qn)* au passage *(pour lui parler)*.

way-out [weɪ'aʊt] *adj F (hairstyle, clothes etc)* excentrique; **to be w.-o,** être original *ou* excentrique.

wayside ['weɪsaɪd] *n* bord *m* de la route; **to fall by the w.,** *(not keep up)* rester en chemin; *(become dishonest) & Hum* s'écarter du droit chemin; **w. chapel/inn,** chapelle *f*/auberge *f* au bord de la route; **w. flowers,** fleurs *fpl* qui poussent en bordure de route.

wayward ['weɪwəd] *adj* **(a)** *(wanting one's way)* entêté; **(b)** *(capricious)* capricieux; **to be w.,** avoir des caprices.

waywardness ['weɪwədnɪs] *n* **(a)** entêtement *m*; **(b)** caractère capricieux.

WC [dʌb(ə)lju:'si:] *n (abbr* **water closet**) WC *mpl*; **where is the WC?,** où sont les WC?

we [wi:] *pers pron pl* **(a)** *(unstressed)* nous; **we were playing,** nous jouions; **here we are!,** nous voilà!; **we both thank you,** nous vous remercions tous (les) deux; **(b)** *(stressed)* nous; **we are English, they are French,** nous, nous sommes anglais, eux, ils sont français; **you don't think that we did it!,** vous ne pensez pas que c'est nous qui l'avons fait?; **we English,** nous autres Anglais; **(c)** *(indefinite)* on; **how are we this morning, Mrs Smith?,** comment ça va ce matin Mme Smith?; **as we say in England,** comme on dit en Angleterre; **we all make mistakes sometimes,** tout le monde se trompe parfois; **(d)** *(plural of majesty, editorial* **we**) nous; **we are convinced that ...,** nous sommes convaincus que ... .

w/e *(abbr* **week ending**) semaine se terminant ... .

weak [wi:k] *adj* **(a)** *(person, currency)* faible; *(in character)* inefficace; *(health)* débile; *(body)* infirme; *(argument)* faible, peu solide; *(style)* sans vigueur; *(decision)* qui dénote de la faiblesse; **w. in body,** faible de corps; **to have a w. heart,** être cardiaque; **to have w. (eye-)sight,** avoir la vue faible; *Fig* **I feel all w. at the knees,** j'ai les jambes en coton; *Fig* **he makes me go all w. at the knees,** j'ai les jambes en coton rien que de le voir; **to grow w.,** s'affaiblir; **to have a w. stomach,** avoir l'estomac fragile; **w. with hunger,** affaibli par la faim; **to feel as w. as a kitten,** se sentir mou comme une chiffe; *F* **to be w. in the head,** être faible d'esprit; *F* **you must be w. in the head if you believe that,** tu dois avoir l'esprit dérangé pour croire ça; **the weaker sex,** le sexe faible; **in a w. moment,** dans un moment de faiblesse; **his w. side/spot,** son côté/point faible; **she gave a w. smile,** elle a eu un faible sourire; **the weaker pupils,** les élèves moins doués; **to be w. in French,** être faible en français; **the play is w. in character analysis,** la pièce est faible du point de vue de l'analyse des personnages; **to have a w. chin/mouth,** avoir le menton fuyant/la bouche molle; *Rad* **w. signal,** signal *m* faible; *Mus* **w. beat,** temps *m* faible;

(b) *(solution)* dilué, étendu; **w. tea,** thé léger; *Pej* thé pas assez fort; *Aut* **w. mixture,** mélange *m* pauvre;

(c) *Gram (conjugaison)* faible; *Ling (syllabe)* non accentué.

weaken ['wi:k(ə)n] **1** *vt* affaiblir; amollir *(l'esprit, le courage)*; appauvrir *(la constitution de qn)*; **the floods have weakened the foundations of the house,** les inondations ont miné les fondations de la maison; *Aut* **to w. the mixture,** appauvrir le mélange. **2** *vi* s'affaiblir, faiblir, s'amollir; *(of sound)* fléchir; *Aut (of mixture)* s'appauvrir; **don't w.,** ne faiblis pas; **her courage weakened,** son courage a fléchi *ou* faibli; **the dollar has weakened,** le dollar a baissé.

weakening ['wi:k(ə)nɪŋ] **1** *adj (makes lose strength)* affaiblissant; *(losing strength)* faiblissant. **2** *n* affaiblissement *m*, amollissement *m*; fléchissement *m (de la volonté, des résistances)*; défaillance *f (du courant, du dollar)*; *Aut* appauvrissement *m (du mélange)*.

weakhearted [wi:k'hɑ:tɪd] *adj* sans courage.

weak-kneed [wi:k'ni:d] *adj Fig* sans caractère, mou, *f* molle, lâche; **a w.-k. decision,** une décision lâche.

weakling ['wi:klɪŋ] *n* être *m* faible *ou* débile; enfant chétif; **he's a w.,** c'est un faible *ou* un mou.

weakly ['wi:klɪ] **1** *adj (person)* débile, chétif. **2** *adv* **(a)** *(lacking strength)* faiblement; **(b)** *(lacking energy)* sans énergie.

weak-minded [wi:k'maɪndɪd] *adj* **(a)** *(unintelligent)* faible d'esprit; **(b)** *(lacking character)* irrésolu, indécis, qui manque de résolution.

weakness ['wi:knɪs] *n* **(a)** faiblesse *f (de corps, de caractère, d'un lien)*; débilité *f (de corps)*; *Aut* pauvreté *f (du mélange)*; **the w. of his argument,** la faiblesse de son argument; **(b)** *(fault)* point *m* faible; **to have a w. for sth/s.o.,** *(like)* avoir un faible pour qch/qn.

weak-willed [wi:k'wɪld] *adj* faible, sans volonté.

weal¹ [wi:l] *n* marque *f*, trace *f (d'un coup de fouet)*.

weal² *n Arch* bien *m*, bien-être *m*, bonheur *m*; **the common w.,** le bien commun.

wealth [welθ] *n* **(a)** *(riches)* richesse(s) *f(pl)*; **he was a man of great w.,** il était très riche; **(b)** *(abundance)* abondance *f*, profusion *f (de détails etc)*; **the job offers a w. of opportunity for travel,** cet emploi offre de nombreuses occasions de voyage.

wealthy ['welθɪ] **1** *adj* riche, opulent; **w. heiress,** riche héritière. **2** *n* **the w.,** *(used as pl)* les riches *mpl*.

wean [wi:n] *vt* sevrer *(un nourrisson)*.

►wean from *vtaspo Fig* **to w. s.o. (away) from a bad habit,** détacher *ou* détourner qn d'une mauvaise habitude.

►wean on *vtaspo Fig* **youngsters today are being weaned on computers,** les jeunes d'aujourd'hui sont complètement influencés par l'informatique.

weaner ['wi:nər] *n* = porcelet venant d'être sevré et pesant moins de 40 kgs.

weaning ['wi:nɪŋ] *n* sevrage *m*.

weapon ['wepən] *n Mil & Fig* arme *f*; **the carrying of weapons is illegal,** le port d'armes est prohibé; **he was carrying a w.,** il avait une arme sur lui.

weaponry ['wepənrɪ] *n (weapons)* armes *fpl*, armement *m*.

wear¹ [weər] *n* **(a)** *(clothing)* vêtements *mpl*; **children's w.,** vêtements pour enfants; **for country w.,** pour la campagne;

(b) *(use, deterioration)* usure *f*, détérioration *f* (par usure); fatigue *f (d'une machine)*; dégradation *f (d'une route)*; **to stand hard w.,** *(of material)* être d'un bon usage; **those shoes still have some w. in them,** ces chaussures sont toujours portables; **my shoes are showing signs of w.,** mes chaussures commencent à s'user; **you'll get lots of w. out of it,** *(it will last for long time)* vous le porterez longtemps; *(it is versatile, can be worn often)* vous le porterez beaucoup; **they get very heavy w.,** *(of shoes etc)* ils ont la vie dure; **w. and tear,** usure; dégradation *(d'un immeuble)*; **the cost of w. and tear,** les frais *mpl* d'entretien; *Jur* **fair w. and tear,** usure naturelle *ou* normale *(du mobilier loué etc)*; **to be the worse for w.,** *(of garment)* être usé *ou* défraîchi; *(of machine)* être abîmé; *Fig (tired)* être épuisé; *(bruised)* être amoché; *(hung over)* avoir la gueule de bois; **to be looking worse for w.,** avoir l'air en travers.

wear² *v (pt* **wore** [wɔ:r]; *pp* **worn** [wɔ:n]) **1** *vt* **(a)** *(have on)* porter *(un vêtement)*; avoir *(air, sourire)*; *(put on)* mettre *(un vêtement)*; **men who w. aftershave,** les hommes qui utilisent de la lotion après-rasage; **she was wearing a blue dress,** elle portait une robe bleue; **why not w. your blue dress?,** pourquoi ne pas mettre ta robe bleue?; **blue is being worn,** le bleu se porte (beaucoup) actuellement; **to w. black,** porter du noir; **I've nothing (fit) to w.,** je n'ai rien à me mettre sur le dos, je n'ai rien de mettable; **he was wearing his slippers,** il était en pantoufles; **to w. one's hair long,** porter les cheveux longs; **you must w. your seat belt,** tu dois attacher ta ceinture de sécurité; **she wears her age well,** elle porte bien son âge; *Fig* **I won't w. it,** je ne marche pas; *Fig* **she won't w. that argument,** on ne lui fera pas gober cet argument; *Fig* **to w. one's heart on one's sleeve,** ne pas chercher à dissimuler son amour pour qn;

(b) *(use)* user; **to w. holes in sth,** faire des trous à qch (à force d'usage); **worn with anxiety,** usé par les soucis; **to be worn to a shadow,** *(of person)* ne plus être que l'ombre de soi-même; **to w. a surface flat,** araser une surface; **to w. a path in the lawn,** tracer une allée dans la pelouse à force de passer au même endroit.

2 *vi* s'user; **to w. into holes,** (*of garment*) se trouer; **to w. smooth,** (*of stone*) se lisser par le frottement; **to w. well,** (*of material*) être de bon usage, faire bon usage; (*of person*) bien porter son âge; **this coat has worn well,** ce manteau m'a bien servi *ou* m'a fait de l'usage; **the film has not worn well,** le film n'a pas bien vieilli; **jeans w. well,** les jeans s'usent en beauté; **it will w. for ever,** c'est inusable.

►**wear away 1** *vtsep* user, ronger; effacer (*des couleurs, motifs*). **2** *vi* (*of material*) s'user; (*of colours, patterns*) s'effacer; (*of person*) se consumer (*de chagrin, d'inquiétude etc*).

►**wear down** *vtsep* user; **to w. one's heels down,** user ses talons; **to w. down the enemy's resistance,** user *ou* épuiser peu à peu la résistance de l'ennemi; *Fig* **to w. s.o. down,** briser la résistance de qn.

►**wear off** *vi* s'effacer, disparaître; (*of pain*) se calmer; (*of anaesthetic*) cesser de faire effet; **the novelty soon wore off,** la nouveauté a vite passé.

►**wear on** *vi* (*of time*) s'écouler (lentement), s'avancer (lentement); **as the evening wore on,** à mesure que la soirée avançait.

►**wear out 1** *vtsep* **(a)** user (*ses vêtements etc*); **(b)** (*exhaust*) épuiser (*la patience de qn*); **I'm worn out,** je suis crevé; **to w. oneself out,** s'user, s'épuiser, se consumer; **to w. oneself out with work,** se tuer au travail *ou* à travailler. **2** *vi* **(a)** (*of material*) s'user; **this material will never w. out,** ce tissu ne s'use pas *ou* est inusable; **(b)** (*of patience*) s'épuiser.

wearable ['weərəb(ə)l] *adj* (*garment*) mettable.

wearer ['weərər] *n* **clothes too heavy for the w.,** vêtements trop lourds pour celui *ou* celle qui les porte.

wearied ['wɪəri:d] *adj* lassé, fatigué.

wearily ['wɪərɪlɪ] *adv* **(a)** (*répondre etc*) d'un ton *ou* d'un air las *ou* fatigué; **(b)** (*marcher etc*) péniblement.

weariness ['wɪərɪnɪs] *n* **(a)** (*tiredness*) fatigue *f*, lassitude *f*; **(b)** (*discontent*) dégoût *m*, ennui *m*.

wearing ['weərɪŋ] **1** *adj* fatigant, lassant; (*stronger*) épuisant; **a very w. day,** une journée très fatigante. **2** *n* **(a)** *Fml* **w. apparel,** vêtements *mpl*, habits *mpl*; **(b)** usure *f*; **w. quality,** résistance *f* à l'usure, durabilité *f*; **w. surface,** surface *f* de frottement *ou* d'usure.

wearisome ['wɪərɪs(ə)m] *adj* fatigant, ennuyeux.

weary¹ ['wɪərɪ] *adj* **(a)** (*tired*) fatigué, las, *f* lasse; **to feel w.,** se sentir las; **w. of the war,** las de la guerre; **w. smile,** sourire las; *F* **a w. Willie,** un fainéant, un traîne-la-patte; **(b)** (*discontented*) las, *f* lasse, dégoûté (**of,** de); **to be w. of life,** être dégoûté de la vie; **to grow w. of waiting,** se lasser d'attendre; **(c)** (*tiring*) fatigant, ennuyeux; **a w. day,** une journée fatigante; **it was a w. climb,** la montée était pénible.

weary² **1** *vi* se lasser, se fatiguer; **to w. of (doing) sth,** se lasser de (faire) qch; **to w. of s.o.,** se fatiguer de la compagnie de qn. **2** *vt* lasser, fatiguer (*qn*); **he wearies me with all his complaints,** je suis las de l'entendre se plaindre.

wearying ['wɪərɪɪŋ] *adj* fatigant, ennuyeux; **I find it very w.,** cela me fatigue beaucoup.

weasel ['wi:z(ə)l] *n* (*animal*) belette *f*; *Fig F* fouine *f*; *esp US* **w. word,** parole ambiguë.

►**weasel out** *esp Am* **1** *vtsep* **to w. information out of s.o.,** soutirer des informations à qn. **2** *vi* **to w. out of an obligation,** se débrouiller pour éviter une obligation.

weather¹ ['weðər] *n* temps *m* (qu'il fait); **in all weathers,** par tous les temps; **in (the) hot/cold w.,** par temps chaud/froid; **the w. is settled, we're in for a spell of fine w.,** le temps est au beau; **what kind of w. did you have on your holiday?,** quel temps avez-vous eu pendant vos vacances?; **what's the w. like?,** quel temps fait-il?; **in spite of bad w.,** en dépit du mauvais temps; **in this** *or* **such w.,** par un temps pareil; **w. permitting,** si le temps le permet; *Nau* **heavy w.,** gros temps; **to make heavy w.,** (*of ship*) bourlinguer; *Fig* **to make heavy w. (of sth),** (*make a fuss*) faire un tas d'histoires (pour faire qch); (*find difficulty*) avoir toutes les peines du monde (à faire qch); *Fig* **to keep one's w. eye open,** veiller au grain; *Fig* **to be under the w.,** (*ill*) être indisposé *ou* souffrant; (*depressed*) être déprimé; **w. (situation), state of the w.,** état *m* du temps; **w. forecast,** prévisions *fpl* météorologiques, météo *f*; **what's the w. forecast for tomorrow?,** quelle est la météo pour demain?; **w. map** *or* **chart,** carte *f* météorologique; **w. report** *or* **bulletin,** bulletin *m* météorologique; **w. ship,** navire-météo *m*, *pl* navires-météo; **w. side,** (*of house etc*) côté exposé au vent; *Nau* bord *m* du vent; **w. station,** station *f* météorologique; **w. strip,** (*for door, window*) bourrelet isolant, calfeutrage *m*; **w. vane,** (*on roof*) girouette *f*; **w. window,** accalmie *f*; **w. warning,** (*announcement*) alerte *f* météorologique; **to issue a w. warning,** lancer une alerte météorologique.

weather² **1** *vt* (*usu passive*) *Geol* **weathered rocks,** roches désagrégées; *Nau* **to w. a storm,** étaler une tempête; *Fig* **to w. the** *or* **a storm,** se tirer d'affaire; *Pol* se maintenir contre des attaques. **2** *vi* **(a)** (*of rock*) se désagréger, s'altérer; **(b)** (*of copper, building*) se couvrir de patine, se patiner.

weatherbeaten ['weðəbi:t(ə)n] *adj* battu par le vent; battu par la tempête; (*person, face*) hâlé, basané; (*thing*) dégradé par le temps.

weatherboarding ['weðəbɔ:dɪŋ] *n Constr* planches *fpl* à recouvrement.

weatherbound ['weðəbaʊnd] *adj* retenu *ou* arrêté par le mauvais temps.

weathercock ['weðəkɒk] *n* (*on roof*) & *Fig* girouette *f*; *Fig* **to be a w.,** tourner *ou* virer à tous les vents.

weathering ['weðərɪŋ] *n* **(a)** désagrégation *f*, altération *f* (*des roches*); **(b)** patine *f*.

weatherman, *pl* **-men** ['weðəmæn, -men] *n TV Rad Hum* monsieur *m* météo.

weatherproof¹ ['weðəpru:f] *adj* **(a)** à l'épreuve du gros temps, étanche; **(b)** (*equipment, machinery etc*) qui résiste aux intempéries.

weatherproof² *vt* protéger contre les intempéries.

weatherstrip ['weðəstrɪp] *vt* calfeutrer (*une fenêtre*).

weave¹ [wi:v] *n Tex* (*pattern*) armure *f*; **plain w.,** armure toile.

weave² *v* (*pt* **wove** [wəʊv]; *pp* **woven** ['wəʊv(ə)n]) **1** *vt Tex* tisser; tresser (*une guirlande, un panier*); entrelacer (*des fils, des rameaux*); **to w. yarn into cloth,** tisser du fil; **to w. a garland out of flowers,** tresser une guirlande de fleurs; *Fig* **skilfully woven plot,** intrigue bien tissée *ou F* ficelée; **to w. a spell,** composer un charme; **to w. ideas into a story,** lier des idées pour en faire une histoire; (*add in*) intégrer des idées à une histoire. **2** *vi* **(a)** *Tex* être tisserand, -ande (de métier), **I want to learn how to w.,** je veux apprendre à tisser; **(b)** *Fig* **to w. through the traffic,** se frayer un chemin parmi les voitures; **to w. in and out of a crowd,** se faufiler; **(c)** *F* **to get weaving,** s'y mettre; **get weaving!,** vas-y!

weaver ['wi:vər] *n* **(a)** *Tex* tisserand, -ande, tisseur, -euse; **(b)** (*bird*) tisserin *m*.

weaverbird ['wi:vəbɜ:d] *n* tisserin *m*.

weaving ['wi:vɪŋ] *n Tex* tissage *m*; entrelacement *m* (*de rameaux etc*).

web [web] *n* **(a)** tissu *m*; **w. of lies,** tissu de mensonges; **(b)** (*of spider*) toile *f*; **(c)** *Biol* palmure *f* (*d'un palmipède*); **(d)** rouleau *m* (*de papier*).

webbed [webd] *adj* palmé; **w. foot,** pied palmé.

webbing ['webɪŋ] *n* **(a)** sangles *fpl* (*de chaise, de lit etc*); **(b)** toile *f* à sangles; ruban *m* à sangles.

web-footed [web'fʊtɪd], **web-toed** [web'təʊd] *adj* palmipède, aux pieds palmés.

wed [wed] *v* (*pt & pp* **wedded**; *occ* **wed**; *prp* **wedding**) **1** *vt* **(a)** (*marry*) épouser (*qn*); *Fig* **to be wedded to one's work,** faire passer son travail avant tout; **(b)** (*of priest*) marier (*un couple*); (*of parent*) marier (*sa fille*). **2** *vi* se marier.

we'd [wi:d] **(a)** = **we had,** *see* **HAVE²**; **(b)** = **we would,** *see* **WILL³**.

wedded ['wedɪd] *adj* marié; **my (lawful) w. wife/husband,** mon épouse/époux légitime; **w. bliss,** le bonheur conjugal.

wedding ['wedɪŋ] *n* mariage *m*, noce(s) *f(pl)*; **I've been invited to a w.,** j'ai été invité à un mariage; **w. anniversary,** anniversaire *m* de mariage; **w. breakfast,** repas *m* de noces; **w. cake,** gâteau *m* de noces; **w. day,** jour *m* de mariage; **on my w. day,** le jour de mon mariage; **w. dress,** robe *f* de mariée; **the w. guests,** les invités *mpl* (au mariage); **w. invitation,** invitation *f* au mariage; **w. list,** liste *f* de mariage; *Mus* **w. march,** marche nuptiale; **w. night,** nuit *f* de noces; **w. present,** cadeau *m* de mariage; **w. ring** *or* **band,** alliance *f*.

wedge¹ [wedʒ] *n* **(a)** *Tech* cale *f* (*de fixation*); coin *m* (*de serrage*); **to drive in a w.,** enfoncer un coin; *Fig* **it has driven a w. between them,** ça a mis une distance entre eux; *Fig* **it's the thin end of the w.,** c'est s'engager sur une mauvaise pente; **w. heeled shoes,** chaussures *fpl* à semelles compensées; **(b) w. of cake,** morceau *m* (triangulaire) de gâteau.

wedge² *vt Tech* coincer; caler (*des rails*); **to w. a door open,** maintenir une porte ouverte avec une cale; **to w. sth**

in sth, insérer *ou* enfoncer *ou* serrer qch dans qch; **I was wedged (in) between two large women,** je me suis trouvé coincé entre deux grosses femmes.

wedge-shaped ['wedʒʃeɪpt] *adj* en (forme de) coin.

wedlock ['wedlɒk] *n Jur* mariage *m*; *Lit* la vie conjugale; **to be born out of w.,** être un enfant illégitime.

Wednesday ['wenzdɪ] *n* mercredi *m*; **on Wednesdays,** le mercredi; **every W.,** tous les mercredis.

wee¹ [wiː] *adj F* tout petit, minuscule; **a w. bit,** un tout petit peu; **a w. drop of whisky,** un doigt *ou* une larme de whisky.

wee² *n & vi F* = **WEE(-)WEE¹,²**.

weed¹ [wiːd] *n* **(a)** (*in garden*) mauvaise herbe; **garden running to** *or* **overgrown with weeds,** jardin envahi par les mauvaises herbes; **(b)** *Old-fashioned F* **the w.,** (*tobacco*) le tabac; (*marijuana*) la marijuana, l'herbe; **to give up the w.,** arrêter de fumer; **(c)** *Pej* (*in build*) personne étique *ou* chétive; (*in character*) mauviette *f*; **don't be such a w.!,** arrête de faire la mauviette!

weed² **1** *vt* désherber (*un jardin*); arracher les mauvaises herbes de (*l'allée*). **2** *vi* arracher *ou* enlever les mauvaises herbes.

►**weed out** *vtsep Fig* éliminer (*les candidats faibles*); **to w. out the bad (from the good),** éliminer *ou* rejeter ce qui est de mauvaise qualité.

weeding ['wiːdɪŋ] *n* désherbage *m*; (*with hoe*) sarclage *m*.

weedkiller ['wiːdkɪlər] *n* herbicide *m*, désherbant *m*.

weeds [wiːdz] *npl Old-fashioned* vêtements *mpl* de deuil (*d'une veuve*).

weedy ['wiːdɪ] *adj* **(a)** (*garden etc*) couvert de mauvaises herbes; **(b)** *Pej* (*person*) étique, chétif, à l'air malingre.

week [wiːk] *n* **(a)** semaine *f*; **what day of the w. is it?,** quel jour de la semaine sommes-nous?; **next/last w.,** la semaine prochaine/dernière; **the w. before last,** pas la semaine dernière, celle d'avant; **the w. after next,** pas la semaine prochaine, celle d'après; **w. in w. out,** toutes les semaines que Dieu nous envoie; **I haven't seen her for** *or Am* **in weeks,** je ne l'ai pas vue depuis des semaines; *Rel* **Holy W.,** la semaine sainte; **once/twice a w.,** une/deux fois par semaine; **every w.,** tous les huit jours; **within a w.,** sous huitaine; **a w. from now, today w., in a w.'s time,** (d')aujourd'hui en huit, dans une huitaine; **tomorrow/Tuesday w.,** demain/mardi en huit; **yesterday w.,** il y a eu hier huit jours; **in a w. or so,** dans une huitaine; **in six weeks' time,** dans six semaines; **a w. ago today,** il y a (aujourd'hui) huit jours; **I'm taking a w.'s holiday** *or* **a w. off,** je vais prendre huit jours de congé; *Ind etc* **forty-hour w.,** semaine de quarante heures; **a w.'s wages,** le salaire d'une semaine, une semaine de salaire, *F* une semaine; **this dress cost me a w.'s wages,** cette robe m'a coûté une semaine de salaire; **to be paid by the w.,** être payé à la semaine;

(b) (*opposed to weekend*) semaine *f*; **what I can't get done in the w. I do on Sundays,** ce que je n'arrive pas à faire en semaine je le fais le dimanche.

weekday ['wiːkdeɪ] *n* jour *m* ouvrable; **on weekdays,** en semaine; **weekdays only,** en semaine uniquement, tous les jours sauf samedi et dimanche; **what time does the library open on weekdays?,** à quelle heure est-ce que la bibliothèque ouvre en semaine?

weekend¹ [wiːk'end] *n* week-end *m*, *pl* week-ends; *Can* fin *f* de semaine; **to have one's weekends free,** être libre le week-end; **have a good w.!,** bon week-end!; *Can* bonne fin de semaine!; **I'll do it at** *or Am* **on the w.,** je le ferai pendant le week-end; **what do you do (on) weekends?,** qu'est-ce que vous faites pendant le week-end?; **to make a w. visit to relations,** rendre visite à de la famille pendant le week-end; **w. break,** séjour *m* qui dure un week-end; **to take a w. break in Paris,** passer un week-end à Paris; **w. cottage,** résidence *f* secondaire (*où on passe le week-end*); *Rail* **w. return,** = aller (et) retour valable du vendredi soir jusqu'au lundi.

weekend² *vi* passer le week-end *ou* la fin de semaine.

weekender [wiːk'endər] *n* **they're weekenders,** ils viennent *ou* vont y passer le week-end.

weekly ['wiːklɪ] **1** *adj* (*revue, visite, paiement*) hebdomadaire; (*salaire*) de la semaine; (*locataire*) à la semaine; *Sch* **w. boarder,** = demi-pensionnaire *mf*. **2** *n* (journal *m*, revue *f*) hebdomadaire *m*. **3** *adv* par semaine; tous les huit jours; **twice w.,** deux fois par semaine; **to be paid w.,** être payé à la semaine.

weeknight ['wiːknaɪt] *n* soir *m* de semaine; **at seven on weeknights,** à sept heures les soirs de semaine; **I'm not letting you go to a party on a w.,** je ne vais pas te permettre d'aller à une soirée en semaine.

weenie ['wiːnɪ] = **WIENER**.

weeny ['wiːnɪ] *adj F* minuscule.

weep¹ [wiːp] *n* **to have a good w.,** pleurer un bon coup; **a good w. would help you,** pleure un bon coup, ça ira mieux; **to have a little w.,** verser quelques larmes.

weep² *v* (*pt & pp* **wept** [wept]) **1** *vi* **(a)** (*of person*) pleurer; **to w. bitterly,** pleurer à chaudes larmes; **to w. for joy,** pleurer de joie; **to w. for s.o.,** (*mourn*) pleurer (la mort de) qn; (*feel sorry for*) pleurer sur les malheurs de qn; **to w. for one's lost youth,** pleurer sa jeunesse perdue; **it's enough to make you w.,** c'est à faire pleurer; **I could have wept to see it,** j'en aurais pleuré de voir ça; **(b)** (*of wall, rock*) suinter, suer; (*of tree*) pleurer; (*of sore*) couler, exsuder; **the smoke was making my eyes w.,** la fumée m'a fait venir les larmes aux yeux. **2** *vt* **to w. tears of joy,** pleurer de joie; **to w. one's heart** *or* **one's eyes out,** pleurer à chaudes larmes.

weeping ['wiːpɪŋ] **1** *adj* **(a)** (*child*) qui pleure; **(b)** (*rock*) suintant, humide; *Med* (*eczema*) suintant; **w. willow,** (*tree*) saule pleureur. **2** *n* **(a)** pleurs *mpl*, larmes *fpl*; **a fit of w.,** une crise de larmes; **(b)** suintement *m* (*d'un mur*); exsudation *f* (*d'une plaie*).

weepy ['wiːpɪ] **1** *adj Fig* (*book, film*) larmoyant; **the book has a w. ending,** le livre a une fin larmoyante; **to feel w.,** se sentir une envie de pleurer. **2** *n F* (*book, film*) mélo *m*, film *m ou* livre *m* à faire pleurer dans les chaumières.

weevil ['wiːvɪl] *n* (*pest*) charançon *m*.

wee(-)wee¹ ['wiːwiː] *n F* (*in children's language*) pipi *m*; **to have a w.-w.,** faire pipi; **do you want to go w.-w.?,** tu veux faire pipi?

wee(-)wee² *vi F* (*in children's language*) faire pipi.

weft [weft] *n Tex* **(a)** trame *f*; **(b) w. (yarn),** fil *m* de trame.

weigh [weɪ] **1** *vt* **(a)** peser (*un paquet*); faire la pesée de (*qch*); **to w. sth in one's hand,** soupeser qch; **to w. oneself,** se peser;

(b) (*consider*) peser, mesurer, ménager (*ses paroles*); **to w. sth in one's mind,** considérer qch; **to w. the consequences,** calculer les conséquences **(of sth,** de qch); **to w. the pros and (the) cons,** peser le pour et le contre; **to w. the risks/the evidence,** évaluer les risques/les preuves; **to w. one thing against another,** mettre deux choses en balance;

(c) *Nau* **to w. anchor,** lever l'ancre, appareiller.

2 *vi* **(a)** peser, avoir du poids; **to w. heavy/light,** peser lourd/peu; **it weighs two kilos,** ça pèse deux kilos; *F* **this case weighs a ton,** cette valise pèse une tonne; **how much do you w.?,** combien est-ce que tu pèses?;

(b) it's weighing on my mind, cela me trouble *ou* me tracasse;

(c) (*have influence*) **that doesn't w. with me,** je ne fais pas grand cas de cela; **her qualifications weighed in her favour,** ses qualifications ont fait pencher la balance en sa faveur *ou* ont joué en sa faveur; **his record weighed against him,** son passé a joué en sa défaveur.

►**weigh down** *vtsep* surcharger; **branch weighed down with fruit,** branche surchargée de fruits; *Fig* **weighed down by heavy responsibilities,** accablé de grosses responsabilités; *Fig* **to be weighed down by** *or* **with grief,** être accablé par la tristesse.

►**weigh in** *vi* **(a)** (*of jockey, boxer*) se faire peser avant la course *ou* le match; (*of air traveller*) faire peser ses bagages; **(b)** *F* (*enter conversation*) se mêler; **to w. in (with an argument),** intervenir avec un argument.

►**weigh out** *vtsep* peser; **w. out 200 grams of flour for me,** pèse-moi 200 grammes de farine.

►**weigh up** *vtsep* **to w. up the situation,** peser la situation; **to w. s.o. up,** (*their character*) estimer la valeur de qn; (*their intentions*) estimer les intentions de qn.

weighbridge ['weɪbrɪdʒ] *n* pont-bascule *m*, *pl* ponts-bascules.

weigh-in ['weɪɪn] *n Boxing Horseracing* pesée *f*.

weighing ['weɪɪŋ] *n* **(a)** pesée *f* (*de qch*); **w. machine,** machine *f* à peser; **(b)** *Nau* levage *m* (*de l'ancre*), appareillage *m*.

weighing in *n* pesage *m* (*d'un jockey, d'un boxeur*); **w.-in room,** le pesage.

weight¹ [weɪt] *n* **(a)** (*of person, thing*) poids *m*; **to try** *or* **feel the w. of sth,** soupeser qch; **that case must be quite a w.,** cette valise doit être drôlement lourde; **to sell by w.,** vendre au poids; **to give good/short w.,** faire bon/faux poids; **it's ten pounds in w.,** cela pèse dix livres; **it's twice the w. of the other one,** ça pèse deux fois plus que l'autre; **they're the same w.,** ils font le même poids; **it's worth its w. in gold,** cela vaut son pesant d'or; **what a w.!,** que ça pèse lourd!, que c'est lourd!; **to lose w.,** perdre du poids; **to gain** *or* **put on w.,** prendre du poids; **to watch one's w.,** surveiller son poids; **to have a w. problem,** avoir un problème de poids; *Fig* **to pull one's w.,** y mettre du sien; *Fig* **you're not pulling your w.,** tu ne fais pas assez d'effort; *Horseracing* **to carry w.,** être handicapé;

(b) (*for weighing*) poids *m* (en cuivre); **set of weights,** série *f* de poids; **weights and measures,** poids et mesures *fpl*;

(c) (*object*) poids *m* (*d'une horloge*); olive *f* (*de plomb*); gueuse *f* (*d'athlétisme*); lest *m* (*d'un filet*); **weights and dumb bells,** poids et haltères *mpl*; **to do w. training,** faire des haltères; **don't lift any heavy weights,** ne soulève pas de poids trop lourds;

(d) (*load*) charge *f*; **this pillar bears the w. of the whole building,** cette colonne soutient tout le bâtiment; **to give way under the w. of sth,** fléchir sous le poids de qch; **he feels the w. of his responsibilities,** sa responsabilité lui pèse; **that is** *or* **takes a w. off my mind,** cela me soulage, ça m'ôte un poids; *F* **I'm going to take the w. off my feet for a bit,** je vais m'asseoir *ou* me reposer un peu;

(e) force *f* (*d'un coup*); **blow with no w. behind it,** coup sans force;

(f) *Fig* importance *f*; **to give w. to an argument,** donner du poids à un argument; **what he says carries w.,** sa parole a du poids *ou* de l'autorité; **she doesn't carry much w. with the committee,** elle n'a pas beaucoup d'influence auprès du comité; **the w. of the evidence was against him,** les témoignages pesaient contre lui; *F* **to throw one's w. about** *or* **around,** faire l'important; **they won the battle by sheer w. of numbers,** ils ont gagné la bataille parce qu'ils étaient nombreux.

weight² *vt* **(a)** attacher un poids à (*qch*); lester, plomber (*un filet, une corde*); plomber (*une canne*); **(b)** *Econ* pondérer (*un indice etc*); *Fig* **the circumstances are weighted in his favour,** les circonstances pèsent en sa faveur *ou* lui sont favorables.

►weight down *vtsep* retenir *ou* maintenir (*qch*) avec un poids.

weighted ['weɪtɪd] *adj* **(a)** chargé d'un poids; lesté; (*walking stick*) plombé; **(b)** (*average, index*) pondéré.

weightily ['weɪtɪlɪ] *adv* (*raisonner*) puissamment, avec force.

weighting ['weɪtɪŋ] *n* **(a)** lestage *m*, plombage *m* (*d'un filet*); plombage (*d'une canne*); **(b)** *Econ* (*of index etc*) pondération *f*; *Admin* **London w.,** indemnité *f* de résidence pour Londres.

weightless ['weɪtlɪs] *adj Astronaut* **w. conditions,** état *m* d'apesanteur.

weightlessness ['weɪtlɪsnɪs] *n Astronaut* apesanteur *f*.

weightlifter ['weɪtlɪftər] *n* haltérophile *mf*.

weightlifting ['weɪtlɪftɪŋ] *n* haltérophilie *f*.

weighty ['weɪtɪ] *adj* **(a)** (*heavy*) pesant, (très) lourd; **(b)** *Fig* (*motif*) grave, important, sérieux; (*raisonnement*) puissant, d'un grand poids; (*argument*) de poids; (*personne*) qui exerce une grande influence.

weir [wɪər] *n* **(a)** barrage *m* (*dans un cours d'eau*); **w. keeper,** barragiste *m*; **(b)** déversoir *m* (*d'un étang*).

weird [wɪəd] *adj* **(a)** (*eerie*) d'une étrangeté inquiétante; **(b)** (*odd*) étrange, bizarre; **that's w.,** c'est bizarre.

weirdie ['wɪədɪ] *n F* excentrique *mf*, drôle d'oiseau *m*; (*frightening etc*) type *m* bizarre.

weirdly ['wɪədlɪ] *adv* **(a)** étrangement inquiétant; **(b)** étrangement, bizarrement.

weirdness ['wɪədnɪs] *n* **(a)** étrangeté inquiétante (*d'un spectacle etc*); **(b)** caractère *m* étrange *ou* bizarre (*de qn, des vêtements*).

weirdo, weirdy ['wɪədəʊ, -dɪ] *n F* = **WEIRDIE**.

welcome¹ ['welkəm] *adj* **(a)** (*person*) bienvenu; **to make s.o. w.,** faire bon accueil à qn; **you're always w.,** vous êtes toujours le bienvenu; **I did not feel w.,** je ne me suis pas senti le bienvenu; **w.!,** soyez le bienvenu (chez nous)!; **w. to England!,** soyez le bienvenu en Angleterre!; **w. back!,** nous sommes heureux de vous retrouver!; *Rad TV* (*after commercial*) re-bonsoir!; **w. home!,** bienvenue à la maison!;

(b) (*agreeable*) agréable; **this is w. news,** nous nous réjouissons de cette nouvelle; **the hotel was a w. sight,** on a aperçu l'hôtel avec plaisir; **this cheque is most w.,** ce chèque est vraiment bienvenu *ou* tombe à merveille;

(c) (*free*) **you're w. to borrow any of my books,** ma bibliothèque est à votre disposition; **they're w. to stay with us,** ils peuvent certainement venir faire un séjour chez nous; **you're w. to it,** c'est à votre service *ou* à votre disposition; *Iron* je ne vous l'envie pas; **you're w. to try,** libre à vous d'essayer; **you're w.!,** (*on being thanked*) je vous en prie!, de rien!, ce n'est rien!; **tell her she's w.,** dis-lui que ce n'est rien.

welcome² *n* **(a)** (*of person*) bienvenue *f*; **to outstay** *or* **overstay one's w.,** s'incruster; **to extend a w. to s.o.,** souhaiter la bienvenue à qn; **(b)** (*reception*) accueil *m*; **to give s.o. a hearty w.,** faire bon accueil à qn; **he gave us a very poor** *or* **cold w.,** il nous a reçus froidement, il nous a mal reçus; *Am* **w. mat,** paillasson *m*; *Fig* **to put out the w. mat for s.o.,** accueillir qn à bras ouverts.

welcome³ *vt* **(a)** (*wish welcome*) souhaiter la bienvenue à (*qn*); (*greet*) faire bon accueil à (*qn*), bien accueillir (*qn*), accueillir *ou* recevoir (*qn*) avec plaisir; *Rad TV* **I am pleased to w. back Mary Smith,** j'ai le plaisir d'accueillir à nouveau Mary Smith; **to w. the** *or* **an opportunity to do sth,** se réjouir de *ou* saluer l'occasion de faire qch; **his efforts weren't welcomed,** ses efforts ont reçu peu d'encouragement; **(b)** (*receive*) accueillir; **to w. s.o. warmly,** faire un accueil chaleureux à qn; **the announcement was welcomed with indifference,** la nouvelle a été accueillie avec indifférence.

welcoming ['welkəmɪŋ] *adj* (*sourire etc*) accueillant; (*discours, comité*) d'accueil.

weld¹ [weld] *n* soudure *f*.

weld² *vt* **to w. (together),** souder (*deux pièces de métal*); unir (*deux pièces de plastique*) à chaud; *Fig* unir, joindre étroitement; **to w. employees into a team,** réunir des employés en une équipe bien soudée.

welder ['weldər] *n* soudeur, -euse.

welding ['weldɪŋ] *n* (*process*) soudure *f*, soudage *m*; **arc w.,** soudure à l'arc; **w. torch,** chalumeau soudeur.

welfare ['welfeər] *n* bien-être *m*; **to have s.o.'s w. at heart,** avoir à cœur le bonheur *ou* le bien-être de qn; *Am* **to be on w.,** toucher les allocations; *Am* **w. benefits,** allocations *fpl* de sécurité sociale; **w. centre,** = centre d'assistance sociale; *Am* **w. check,** chèque *m* d'allocations; **w. work,** = assistance sociale; **w. worker,** = assistant(e) social(e); **the W. State,** l'État *m* providence.

well¹ [wel] *n* **(a)** (*of water, oil*) puits *m*; **we get our water from a w.,** notre eau vient d'un puits; **to drive/sink a w.,** forer/creuser un puits; **w.-digger,** puisatier *m*; **w. water,** eau *f* de puits; **(b)** (*shaft*) puits *m*, cage *f* (*d'un ascenseur*); cage, jour *m* (*d'un escalier*); fond *m* de carter (*formant réservoir d'huile*); vivier *m*, réservoir *m* (*d'un bateau de pêche*); *Br Jur* **the w. of the court,** le barreau; *Culin* **make a w. in the flour,** faire une fontaine dans la farine; **(c)** *Arch* (*spring*) source *f*, fontaine *f*.

well² (*comp* **better**; *superl* **best**) **1** *adj* **(a)** (*in good health*) **to be w.,** être bien portant *ou* en bonne santé, se porter *ou* aller bien; **how are you? — w., thank you,** comment allez-vous?— bien, merci; **he's not very w.,** il est indisposé *ou* souffrant; **to get w.,** guérir, se rétablir, se remettre; **you look w.,** tu as l'air en forme; **he's not a w. man,** il ne se porte pas bien, il n'a pas une bonne santé;

(b) it is w. to ..., (*advisable*) il est opportun de ...; **it would be w. to ...,** il serait bon *ou* utile *ou* recommandable de ...; **it would be just as w. if you were present,** il y aurait avantage à ce que vous soyez présent; **it is just as w. we did leave without her,** c'est aussi bien que nous soyons partis sans elle; **it might be as w. to ...,** il faudrait peut-être ..., il serait peut-être bon de ...; **it was w. for him that nobody saw him,** heureusement pour lui personne ne l'a vu; **all's w. that ends w.,** tout est bien qui finit bien; **all's w.!,** tout va bien!; **that's all very w., but ...,** c'est bien beau *ou* tout cela est bel et bon mais ...; **it is all very w. for you to say that,** tu peux bien dire ça, toi; **w. and good!,** soit!, bon!; **that's all very w. and good, but ...,** tout ça c'est très bien, mais ... .

2 *adv* **(a)** bien; **to work w.,** bien travailler; **to do as w. as one can,** faire de son mieux; **this boy will do w.,** ce garçon ira loin; **to be doing w.,** (*after operation etc*) aller bien; **mother and baby are both doing w.,** la mère et l'enfant se portent bien; **w. done!,** bravo!, très bien!; **w. played!,** bien joué!; *Fig* **the government hasn't come out of it very w.,** le gouvernement n'en est pas sorti grandi; *Fig* **to do oneself w.,** (*indulge oneself*) bien se soigner; (*in restaurant etc*) bien manger (et bien boire); **it wouldn't look w. if we refused,** si on refusait cela ferait mauvaise impression; **you would do w. to be quiet (about it),** vous feriez bien *ou* le mieux serait de vous taire; **I know her w.,** je la connais bien; **I know only too w. what patience it needs,** je ne sais que trop quelle patience cela exige; **I can't very w. do it,** il ne m'est guère possible de le faire; **he accepted, as w. he might,** il a accepté et cela n'a rien d'étonnant; **one might as w. say that black**

is white, autant dire que blanc est noir; **you might (just) as w. stay,** (*there's no point in going now*) tu ferais aussi bien de rester; (*you're not intruding*) tu peux rester; **I might (just) as w. do it myself,** je ferais aussi bien de le faire moi-même; **very w.!,** (très) bien!, entendu!; **everyone speaks w. of him,** tout le monde dit du bien de lui; **she is very w. thought of,** on pense beaucoup de bien d'elle; **to do w. by s.o.,** se montrer généreux envers qn; **she deserves w. of you,** elle mérite bien votre reconnaissance; **he meant it w.,** il l'a fait *ou* l'a dit avec une bonne intention; **he means w.,** ses intentions sont bonnes; **you're w. out of it,** soyez heureux d'en être quitte; **the fête went off w.,** la fête s'est bien passée; *Old-fashioned* **w. met!,** heureuse rencontre!, vous arrivez bien à propos!;

(b) (*intensive*) bien; **it's w. worth trying,** cela vaut bien la peine *ou F* le coup d'essayer; **she's w. able to look after herself,** elle est bien capable de se débrouiller toute seule; **I can w. believe it,** je veux bien le croire; **I am w. aware of that,** j'en suis bien conscient; **we'll be w. away by the time she wakens,** nous serons déjà loin quand elle se réveillera; *Br F* **w. away,** (*drunk*) parti; **it's w. after six,** il est six heures bien sonnées; **buy your tickets w. ahead of time** *or* **w. in advance,** achetez vos billets bien à l'avance; **he's w. over fifty,** il a largement dépassé la cinquantaine; **to be w. up in a subject,** bien posséder un sujet; **leave w. enough alone,** ne t'en mêle pas; *Br F* **w. and truly,** bel et bien;

(c) pretty w. all, presque tout; **it's pretty w. finished,** c'est presque *ou* pratiquement terminé; *F* **it serves him damn w.** *or* **jolly w. right!,** il l'a bien cherché *ou* mérité!, c'est bien fait pour lui!;

(d) as w., aussi; **take me as w.,** emmenez-moi aussi; **I need some as w.,** il m'en faut également; **as w. as,** (*in addition to*) de même que, comme, ainsi que; **by day as w. as by night,** de jour comme de nuit, le jour comme la nuit;

(e) (*introducing remark*) eh bien, donc; (*exclamatory*) ça alors!, pas possible!; **w., as I was telling you,** eh bien *ou* donc comme je vous disais; **w., who was it?,** eh bien, qui était-ce?; **w., here we are (at last)!,** enfin nous voilà!; **you told her? — (oh) w.!, (ah) w.!,** vous le lui avez dit? — eh bien!; **w., w.!,** (*expressing resignation*) tant pis!; (*resigned*) (eh bien,) que voulez-vous!; (*surprise*) tiens, tiens!; **w. I never!,** ça alors!; **w., that's life!,** c'est la vie!; **w. then,** eh bien, alors; **w. then, why worry about it?,** eh bien alors, pourquoi se faire du mauvais sang?;

(f) (*used as combining form with participles to give a virtual adj; a hyphen is incorrect if the adj is predicative, and permissible but not obligatory if it precedes the noun*) **w. advised,** sage, prudent, judicieux; **you would be w. advised to do it,** il serait prudent que tu le fasses; **w. appointed,** (*flat etc*) bien aménagé; **w. balanced,** équilibré; **I think she's fairly w. balanced,** je pense qu'elle est plutôt bien équilibrée; **w. behaved,** (*child*) bien élevé, sage; (*animal*) bien dressé; **w. built,** bien construit, bien bâti; (*person*) solide; **w. chosen,** bien choisi; **a few w. chosen words,** quelques mots bien choisis; **to be w. connected,** avoir des relations; **w. disposed,** (*person*) bien disposé (**towards,** envers); (*objects*) bien arrangé, bien disposé; **w. done,** (*beef, lamb etc*) bien cuit; **w. educated,** instruit, cultivé; **w. fed,** bien nourri; *Am* **w. fixed,** riche; **w. founded,** (*suspicion*) bien fondé; **w. groomed,** (*person*) d'aspect soigné; (*horse*) bien entretenu; **w. heeled,** riche; *Austr F* **w. in,** riche; *Br F* **to be w. in with s.o.,** être bien avec qn; **w. informed,** bien renseigné; (*person, mind*) averti; **to be w. informed on a subject,** bien connaître un sujet; **w. intentioned,** bien intentionné; **w. kept,** (*garden*) bien (entre)tenu, soigné; (*hands*) soigné; (*secret*) bien gardé; **w. known,** (bien) connu, célèbre; (*expert*) réputé; **it is w. known that ...,** tout le monde sait que ...; **w. made,** bien fait, bien fini, de fabrication soignée; (*garment*) de coupe soignée; **w. mannered,** poli, bien élevé; **w. matched,** bien assorti; (*teams*) de force égale; **w. meaning,** bien intentionné; **she's very w. meaning,** elle est pleine de bonnes intentions; **w. meant,** fait avec une bonne intention *ou* avec les meilleures intentions; *Br* **w. off,** riche; **to be very w. off,** avoir de la fortune, *F* avoir de quoi; **you don't know when you're w. off,** vous ne connaissez pas votre bonheur; **to be w. off for books/cupboards/paper/***etc*, avoir beaucoup de livres/placards/papier/*etc*; **w. oiled,** (*machinery*) bien graissé; *F* (*drunk*) soûl; **w. paid,** bien payé, bien rétribué; *Hum* **w. padded** *or* **upholstered,** (*plump*) bien rembourré; **w. preserved,** bien conservé; *Fig* **she's w. preserved,** elle est bien conservée; **w. read,** (*person*) instruit, cultivé; **w. spent,** (*money, time*) bien utilisé, bien employé; **it was time w. spent,** c'était du temps bien employé; **w. spoken,** qui parle bien, qui a un accent cultivé; **w. stacked,** (*woman*) bien balancé, bien roulé, bien foutu; **w. stocked,** bien approvisionné; (*shop*) bien achalandé; **w. thought out,** (*plan etc*) bien pensé; **w. thumbed,** (*book, magazine*) qui a fait de l'usage, écorné; **w. timed,** opportun, bien calculé; **w. turned,** (*speech*) bien tourné; (*ankle*) galbé; **w. worn,** (*garment*) usé, fortement usagé; (*book*) qui a beaucoup servi; (*argument*) rebattu, usé jusqu'à la corde.

3 *n* **(a) the w. and the sick,** (*used as pl*) les bien portants et les malades;

(b) to wish s.o. w., vouloir du bien à qn; (*in attitude*) être bien disposé envers qn.

►**well out** *vi* (*of liquid*) jaillir.

►**well over** *vi* (*of tears*) jaillir; **her eyes welled over,** des larmes jaillissaient de ses yeux.

►**well up** *vi* (*of water, spring*) jaillir, *Lit* sourdre; **tears welled up in her eyes,** les larmes lui sont montées aux yeux.

we'll [wi:l] = **(a) we shall,** *see* **SHALL**; **(b) we will,** *see* **WILL³**.

wellbeing ['welbi:ɪŋ] *n* bien-être *m;* **physical and moral w.,** santé *f* physique et morale.

wellbred [wel'bred] *adj* (*polite*) bien élevé; (*of good family*) de bonne famille.

wellhead ['welhed] *n Petr* tête *f* de puits.

wellies ['welɪz] *npl Br F* bottes *fpl* en caoutchouc.

wellington ['welɪŋtən] *n Br* **wellingtons, w. boots,** bottes *fpl* en caoutchouc.

well-nigh ['welnaɪ] *adv Lit* presque.

well-to-do [weltə'du:] **1** *adj* aisé, riche, cossu. **2 the w.-to-do,** (*used as pl*) les riches, les fortunés.

wellwisher ['welwɪʃər] *n* partisan, -ane (*d'une cause etc*); **a w.,** (*at end of anonymous letter*) quelqu'un qui vous veut du bien; **surrounded by wellwishers,** entouré d'admirateurs.

Welsh [welʃ] **1** *adj* gallois; du pays de Galles; **W. dresser,** vaisselier *m*; **W. rabbit** *or* **rarebit,** ≈ croque-monsieur *m*. **2** *n* **(a) the W.,** les Gallois *mpl*; **(b)** *Ling* gallois *m*.

►**welsh on** *vipo F* **to w. on s.o.,** manquer à une obligation envers qn; **to w. on a bet,** ne pas tenir un pari.

Welshman, -woman, *pl* **-men, -women** ['welʃmən, -wumən, -mən, -wɪmɪn] *n* Gallois, -oise.

welt [welt] *n* **(a)** trépointe *f* (*de semelle*); **(b)** marque *f*, trace *f* (*d'un coup*).

welter¹ ['weltər] *n* **(a)** confusion *f*, désordre *m*; **(b)** masse confuse, fouillis *m* (*de choses disparates*).

welter² *vi Lit* se vautrer, se rouler (*dans la boue*); nager, baigner (*dans le sang*).

welterweight ['weltəweɪt] *n Boxing* poids *m* mi-moyen, poids welter; **to fight as a** *or* **at w.,** boxer dans la catégorie des poids welters; **w. match,** match *m* de poids welters.

wen [wen] *n Med* kyste sébacé, *F* loupe *f*.

wench¹ [wentʃ] *n* **(a)** *F & Hum* (jeune) fille *f*, jeune femme *f*; **great strapping w.,** grande gaillarde; **(b)** *Arch* **(serving) w.,** serveuse *f* (*dans une auberge*); **kitchen w.,** fille *f* de cuisine.

wench² *vi F* **to go wenching,** courir le jupon.

wend [wend] *vt Lit* **to w. one's way,** porter *ou* diriger ses pas, se diriger, s'acheminer (**to,** vers); **to w. one's way homeward,** s'acheminer vers la maison.

Wendy ['wendɪ] *n Br* **W. house,** = maison en modèle réduit dans laquelle les enfants jouent.

Wensleydale ['wenzlɪdeɪl] *n* fromage *m* de Wensleydale.

went *see* **GO²**.

wept *see* **WEEP²**.

were *see* **BE**.

we're [wɪər] = **we are,** *see* **BE**.

weren't [wɜ:nt] = **were not,** *see* **BE**.

werewolf, *pl* **-wolves** ['wɪəwulf, -wulvz] *n Myth* loup-garou *m*, *pl* loups-garous.

Wesleyan ['weslɪən] *adj & n* wesleyen, -enne.

west [west] **1** *n* ouest *m*; **house facing (the) w.,** maison exposée à l'ouest; **on the w., to the w.,** à l'ouest (**of,** de); **the W.,** l'Occident; (*in United States*) les États occidentaux; (*in Canada*) les provinces *fpl* de l'ouest; *US* **the Far W.,** le Far-West; *US* **the Mid(dle) W.,** les États de la Prairie.

2 *adv* à l'ouest; **to travel w.,** voyager vers l'ouest; **to go w.,** partir pour l'ouest; *Old-fashioned F* (*die*) casser sa pipe, passer l'arme à gauche; *F* **there's another plate gone w.!,** encore une assiette de cassée!

3 *adj* ouest *inv*; (*vent*) d'ouest; (*mur*) qui fait face *ou* qui est exposé à l'ouest; **W. Bank,** (*in Middle East*) Cisjordanie *f*; *US* **W. Coast,** côte *f* ouest; **she lives on the W. Coast,** elle habite sur la côte ouest; *Br* **the W. Country,** le sud-ouest de l'Angleterre; *Br* **the W. End,** le quartier du centre-ouest de Londres; *Br F* **to go up the W. End,** sortir en ville (à Londres); **W. End theatres,** les théâtres du centre-ouest de Londres, les théâtres des quartiers chics de Londres; *US* **W. Point,** = collège militaire; *US* **the W. Side,** les quartiers ouest de New York; **W. Africa,** l'Afrique occidentale; **W. Berlin,** Berlin Ouest; **W. Germany,** l'Allemagne de l'Ouest; **W. German,** ouest-allemand, -ande; **the W. Indies,** les Antilles *fpl*; **W. Indian,** *adj* des Antilles; antillais; *n* Antillais, -aise.

westbound ['westbaʊnd] *adj* allant vers l'ouest; (*on underground*) en direction de la banlieue ouest; **w. traffic,** véhicules qui se dirigent vers l'ouest; **w. traffic is subject to delays,** on prévoit des embouteillages dans la direction ouest; **the w. lane of the motorway,** la voie de l'autoroute qui va vers l'ouest.

westerly ['westəlɪ] **1** *adj* (*vent*) d'ouest, qui vient de l'ouest; (*courant*) qui se dirige vers l'ouest; **w. point,** point situé à *ou* vers l'ouest. **2** *adv* vers l'ouest. **3** *npl Met* **westerlies,** vents *mpl* d'ouest.

western ['westən] **1** *adj* ouest, de l'ouest; occidental, -aux; **W. Europe,** l'Europe occidentale; *Pol* **the W. powers,** les puissances occidentales; **W. Australia,** l'Australie occidentale; **W. Isles** *or* **Islands,** (*of Scotland*) les Hébrides *fpl*. **2** *n Cin* western *m*.

westerner ['westənər] *n* **(a)** occidental, *pl* -aux; **(b)** *US* habitant, -ante des États occidentaux.

westernization [westənaɪ'zeɪʃən] *n* occidentalisation *f*.

westernize ['westənaɪz] *vt* occidentaliser (*un peuple*); **to become westernized,** s'occidentaliser.

westernmost ['westənməʊst] *adj* le plus à l'ouest.

westward ['westwəd] **1** *adj* **(a)** (*journey*) vers l'ouest; **(b)** (*place*) (du côté) de l'ouest. **2** *adv* = **WESTWARDS.**

westwards ['westwədz] *adv* à l'ouest; (*to travel*) vers l'ouest.

wet¹ [wet] *adj* (*comp* **wetter**; *superl* **wettest**) **(a)** (*soaked*) mouillé; (*damp*) humide; **to get w.,** se mouiller; **to get one's feet w.,** se mouiller les pieds; **to be w. through** *or* **w. to the skin** *or* **dripping w.,** être trempé *ou* mouillé jusqu'aux os; **sopping** *or* **soaking w.,** (*clothes*) mouillé à tordre; (*person*) trempé jusqu'aux os; **cheeks w. with tears,** joues baignées de larmes; **ink still w.,** encre encore fraîche; **three w. days,** trois jours de pluie; **the wettest summer on record,** l'été le plus humide dont on se souvienne; **when it's w.,** quand il pleut; **the w. season,** la saison des pluies; **w. blanket,** rabat-joie *m inv*, trouble-fête *mf inv*; *El* **w. cell,** pile *f* à élément humide; *Petr* **w. Christmas tree,** tête de puits immergée; **w. dream,** éjaculation *f* nocturne; *Br* **w. fish,** poisson frais; **w.-fish shop,** poissonnerie *f*; **w. nurse,** nourrice *f*; **w. paint,** (*notice*) peinture fraîche; **w. suit,** combinaison *f* de plongée; **w. weather,** temps humide *ou* pluvieux, temps de pluie;

(b) *F* bête, idiot; *Pol* modéré; **don't be so w.!,** ne sois pas aussi bête!; **he's (still) w. behind the ears,** on lui pincerait le nez qu'il en sortira encore du lait;

(c) *F* (*country, state*) qui permet la vente des boissons alcooliques.

wet² *n* **(a)** (*dampness*) humidité *f*; **(b)** (*rain*) pluie *f*; *Austr* **the w.,** la saison des pluies; **to go out in the w.,** sortir sous la pluie; **(c)** *Pol F* poule mouillée, modéré, -ée.

wet³ *vt* (**-tt-**) mouiller, humecter; imbiber (*une éponge*); arroser (*de la pâte*); **to w. the bed,** (*of child*) faire pipi au lit; **to w. one's pants** *or* **oneself,** mouiller sa culotte, faire pipi dans sa culotte; *Fig F* pisser dans sa culotte; *Hum F* **to w. one's whistle,** boire un coup.

wetback ['wetbæk] *n US Pej* = ouvrier agricole mexicain entré illégalement aux États-Unis.

wether ['weðər] *n* (*ram*) bélier châtré.

wetlands ['wetlənd] *npl* marais *mpl*.

wetness ['wetnɪs] *n* **(a)** (*dampness*) humidité *f*; **(b)** *F* bêtise *f*.

wetting ['wetɪŋ] *n* mouillage *m*, mouillement *m*; arrosage *m* (*de la pâte*); **to get a w.,** se faire tremper; **w. the bed can be a sign that ...,** l'incontinence nocturne peut indiquer que ...; *Ch* **w. agent,** (agent *m*) mouillant *m*.

WEU [dʌb(ə)ljuːiː'uː] *n Pol* (*abbr* **Western European Union**) UEO *f*.

we've [wiːv] = **we have,** *see* **HAVE².**

WFP [dʌb(ə)ljuːef'piː] *n* (*abbr* **World Food Programme**) PAM *m*.

whack¹ [wæk] *F* **1** *n* **(a)** (*blow*) coup (*de bâton*) retentissant *ou* bien appliqué; (*with hand*) claque *f*, taloche *f*; *Fig* **to have a w. at sth,** essayer de faire qch, tenter le coup; **(b)** (*portion*) part *f*, portion *f*, (grand) morceau *m*; **he didn't get his w.,** il n'a pas eu sa part; **she did/paid more than her w.,** elle a fait/payé plus que sa part; **you're already earning the top w. for this job,** tu gagnes déjà le maximum pour ce travail; **we can offer you £50,000, top w.,** (*no more*), nous pouvons vous offrir 50 000 livres, dernier prix. **2** *int* v'lan!, vlan!

whack² **1** *vt F* **(a)** battre (*qn*) (à coups retentissants), rosser (*qn*); **(b)** *Sp* battre (*ses adversaires*) à plate(s) couture(s). **2** *vi* **to w. at sth with a stick,** donner un coup de baton à qch.

►**whack off** *vi Sl* (*masturbate*) se branler.

whacked [wækt] *adj F* (*exhausted*) épuisé, éreinté.

whacker [wækər] *n F* **(a)** quelque chose de colossal; **what a w.!, isn't it a w.!,** quel gros pépère, celui-là!; **(b)** *Old-fashioned* (*lie*) gros mensonge; **what a w.!,** en voilà une forte!

whacking ['wækɪŋ] *F* **1** *adj & adv* énorme; **a w. great cabbage,** un fameux chou; **a w. great lie,** un mensonge de taille. **2** *n* **(a)** rossée *f*, raclée *f*; **his father gave him a w.** son père lui a donné une raclée; **(b)** *Sp* **we gave them a w.,** on leur a mis une pâtée.

whacko [wæ'kəʊ] *int Old-fashioned Br Sl* magnifique!

whacky ['wækɪ] *adj* = **WACKY.**

whale¹ [weɪl] *n* **(a)** baleine *f*; **blue w.,** baleine bleue; **white w.,** bél(o)uga *m*; **w. calf,** baleineau *m*; **w. oil,** huile *f* de baleine; **w. hunter,** = **WHALER**; **(b)** *F* **we had a w. of a time,** on s'est drôlement bien amusé.

whale² *vi* faire la pêche à la baleine.

whaleboat ['weɪlbəʊt] *n* baleinier *m*.

whalebone ['weɪlbəʊn] *n* busc *m*, baleine *f* (*d'un corset*).

whaler ['weɪlər] *n* (*person, vessel*) baleinier *m*.

whaling ['weɪlɪŋ] *n* pêche *f ou* chasse *f* à la baleine; **w. ship,** baleinier *m*.

wham¹ ['wæm] *int F* v'lan!, vlan!

wham² **1** *vi* **the car whammed into a lampost,** la voiture est rentrée dans le réverbère avec un fracas retentissant. **2** *vt* **to w. a ball into the net,** envoyer une balle dans le filet à toute volée.

wharf, *pl* **-s, wharves** [wɔːf, -s, wɔːvz] *n* appontement *m*, quai *m*; *Com* **ex w.,** à prendre sur quai.

wharfage ['wɔːfɪdʒ] *n* droits *mpl* de quai *ou* de bassin.

what [wɒt] **1** *adj* **(a)** (*rel*) **he took w. little I had left,** il m'a pris le peu qui me restait; **I'll give you w. money I have,** je vais vous donner ce que j'ai comme argent;

(b) (*interr, direct or indirect*) quel, quelle, *pl* quels, quelles; **w. time is it?,** quelle heure est-il?; **tell me w. books you want,** dites-moi quels livres vous désirez; **w. right has she to give orders?,** de quel droit donne-t-elle des ordres?; **w. good** *or* **w. use is this?,** à quoi cela sert-il?; **w.'s the date (today)?,** quelle est la date (aujourd'hui)?; **w. sort of (a) book is it?,** quelle sorte de livre est-ce?; **w. colour/size is it?,** c'est de quelle couleur/de quelle taille?;

(c) (*exclamatory*) **w. an idea!,** quelle idée!; **w. a fool he is!,** qu'il est bête!, comme il est bête!; **w. a fuss about nothing!,** voilà bien du bruit pour rien!; **w. a question!,** quelle question!; **w. a man!,** quel homme!; **w. a pity!,** quel dommage!; **w. a (long) time you are getting dressed!,** comme vous êtes longtemps à vous habiller!; **w. a lot of people!,** que de gens!, que de monde!

2 *pron* **(a)** (*rel*) (*subject*) ce qui; (*object*) ce que; **w. is done cannot be undone,** ce qui est fait est fait; **I don't know w. has happened,** je ne sais pas ce qui est arrivé; **w. I like is a detective story,** ce que j'aime c'est un roman policier; **w. is most remarkable is that ...,** ce qu'il y a de plus remarquable c'est que ...; **this is w. it's all about,** voici ce dont il s'agit; **but that's not w. I said,** mais ce n'est pas ce que j'ai dit; **come w. may,** advienne que pourra; **he never speaks of w. he has gone through,** il ne parle jamais de ce qu'il a enduré; **w. with golf and tennis I have no time to write,** entre le golf et le tennis je n'ai pas le temps d'écrire; *Sl* **to give s.o. w. for,** (*scold*) laver la tête à qn; (*beat*) flanquer une bonne raclée à qn;

(b) (*direct, interr*) (*subject*) qu'est-ce qui; (*object*) qu'est-ce que, que; quoi; **w. has happened?,** qu'est-ce qui est arrivé?; **what's happening?,** que se passe-t-il?; **w. on earth are you doing here?,** qu'est-ce que vous pouvez bien faire ici?; **w. is it?,** (*identify it*) qu'est-ce?, qu'est-ce que c'est?; (*what is wrong*) qu'est-ce qu'il y a?; **what's that?,** (*identify it*) qu'est-ce que c'est que ça?; (*what did you say*) quoi?; **what's that you're telling me?,** qu'est-ce que vous me dites?; **w. will become of her?,** que deviendra-t-elle?; **what's the matter?,** qu'est-ce qu'il y a?, qu'y a-t-il?; **what's her address?,** quelle est son adresse?; **what's his**

name?, quel est son nom?, comment s'appelle-t-il?; **what's that to you?,** qu'est-ce que cela vous fait?, est-ce que ça vous regarde?; **w. is she to you that you're so concerned about her?,** qu'est-ce qu'elle est à tes yeux pour que tu sois aussi inquiet à son sujet?; **w. is there to see in this town?,** qu'y a-t-il à voir dans cette ville?; **what's the good** *or* **the use?,** à quoi bon?; **w. do you want?,** qu'est-ce que vous voulez?; **what's to be done?,** que faire?; **tell me what's to be done,** dis-moi ce qu'il y a à faire; **w. did I tell you?,** qu'est-ce que je vous avais dit?, je vous l'avais bien dit!; **w. will people say?,** que dira-t-on?, que vont dire les gens?; **what's the French for 'dog'?,** comment dit-on 'dog' en français?; **w. else could bring me here?,** quoi d'autre pourrait m'amener ici?; **w. could be more beautiful?,** quoi de plus beau?; **w. do seven and eight make?,** combien font sept plus huit?; **w. is the rent?,** à combien s'élève le loyer?; **w. do I owe you?,** qu'est-ce que je vous dois?; (*in shop*) c'est combien?, ça fait combien?; **w. is he like?,** comment est-il?; **w. do you take me for?,** pour qui me prenez-vous?; **what's it made of?,** en quoi est-ce que c'est fait?, c'est fait en quoi?; **w. are you thinking of?,** à quoi pensez-vous?; **w. were you thinking of, letting her go out on her own?,** qu'est-ce qui t'a pris de la laisser sortir toute seule?; **w. about the ten pounds I lent you?,** et les dix livres que je vous ai prêtées?; **w. about a game of bridge?,** si on faisait une partie de bridge?; **w. about you?,** et vous?; **w. about that coffee?,** et ce café?; **what's that for?,** à quoi cela sert-il?, à quoi ça sert?; **w. did he do that for?,** pourquoi a-t-il fait cela?; **w. (on earth) for?,** mais pourquoi donc?; **and w. if she hears about** *or* **of it?,** et si elle l'apprend?; **w. then?,** et après?; *F* **so w.?,** et alors?; *F* **d'you think I'm mad or w.?,** tu crois que je suis fou ou quoi?; *F* **paper, pens, pencils, and w. not** *or* **and w. have you,** du papier, des stylos, des crayons et d'autres choses encore *ou* et je ne sais quoi encore; **w. did you say?,** vous disiez?, pardon?; **w. of it?,** qu'est-ce que cela fait?, eh bien, et puis après?;

(c) (*indirect, interr*) (*subject*) ce qui; (*object*) ce que; **tell me what's happened,** dites-moi ce qui s'est passé; **I don't know w. you want,** je ne sais pas ce que vous désirez; **he didn't know w. to say/do,** il ne savait que dire/faire; **there were books and I don't know w.,** il y avait des livres et je ne sais quoi d'autre *ou* encore; **tell me w. you're crying for,** dites-moi pourquoi vous pleurez; **I'll tell you w.,** je vais vous dire, écoutez; **he knows what's w.,** il s'y connaît; **I'll show you what's w.!,** tu verras de quel bois je me chauffe!;

(d) (*exclamatory*) **w. she has suffered!,** ce qu'elle a souffert!; **w. next!,** par exemple!; et puis quoi encore!; **w.! you can't come!,** comment! vous ne pouvez pas venir!; **w.! no eggs!,** quoi! pas d'œufs!; *Old-fashioned* **nice girl, w.!,** joli brin de fille, hein!

what-d'ye-call-'em, -her, -him, -it ['wɒtjəkɔːləm, -ər, -ɪm, -ɪt] *n F* machin *m*, truc *m*; (*person*) chose *mf*; **Miss W.-d'ye-c.-her,** mademoiselle Chose.

whate'er [wɒt'eər] *pron Lit* = **WHATEVER**.

whatever [wɒt'evər] **1** *pron* **(a)** (*relative*) (*subject*) tout ce qui; (*object*) tout ce que; **w. you like,** tout ce qui vous plaira, tout ce que vous voudrez;

(b) (*no matter what*) quoi que +*sub*; **w. it is** *or* **may be,** quoi que ce soit; **w. happens, keep calm,** quoi qu'il survienne, restez calme; **he shall have w. he wants,** quoi qu'il désire, il l'aura; **w. she says** *or* **may say,** en dépit de ce qu'elle dit; **use w. you can find,** utilise ce que tu trouveras; **w. can she have said to make him so angry?,** qu'est-ce qu'elle a bien pu dire pour le mettre dans une telle colère?;

(c) *F* **pens, pencils, paper and w.,** des stylos, des crayons, du papier et tout ce que vous voulez; **... or w.,** (*something similar*) ... ou quelque chose de ce genre; (*anything you like*) ... ou tout ce que vous voulez.

2 *adj* **(a)** (*no matter what*) **w. price they are asking,** quel que soit le prix qu'ils demandent; **w. mistakes I (may) have made,** quelles que soient les erreurs que j'ai faites;

(b) (*emphatic*) **under any pretext w.,** sous quelque prétexte que ce soit; **no hope w.,** pas le moindre espoir, pas l'ombre d'un espoir; **is there any hope w.?,** y a-t-il l'ombre d'un espoir?; **none w.,** pas un seul; **nothing w.,** absolument rien.

what-ho [wɒt'(h)əʊ] *int Old-fashioned Br* **(a)** eh bien!, tiens!; **(b)** (*in greeting*) bonjour!, salut!

whatnot ['wɒtnɒt] *n* **(a)** (*for ornaments*) étagère *f*; **(b)** *F* (*thing*) machin *m*, truc *m*.

what's-her-, -his-, -its-name ['wɒtsə, -ɪz-, -ɪts-, neɪm] *n F* = **WHAT-D'YE-CALL-'EM** *etc*.

whatsit ['wɒtsɪt] *n F* machin *m*, truc *m*.

whatsoever [wɒtsəʊ'evər] **1** *pron Lit* **w. it may be,** quoi que ce soit. **2** *adj* (*emphatic*) = **WHATEVER 2 (b)**.

wheat [wiːt] *n* blé *m*, froment *m*; **to plant land with w.,** mettre une terre en blé; *Agr & Fig* **to divide the w. from the chaff,** séparer le bon grain de l'ivraie; **w. germ,** germes *mpl* de blé; **w. field,** champ *m* de blé.

wheatear ['wiːtɪər] *n* (*bird*) traquet *m* (motteux), cul-blanc *m*.

wheaten ['wiːt(ə)n] *adj* (*pain*) de froment, de blé.

wheatmeal ['wiːtmiːl] *n* farine grossière, grosse farine de froment; **w. bread,** pain *m* de froment.

wheatsheaf ['wiːtʃiːf] *n* gerbe *f* de blé.

wheedle ['wiːd(ə)l] *vt* enjôler, embobeliner (*qn*); **to w. s.o. into doing sth,** amener qn à faire qch à force de cajoleries; **to w. money from** *or* **out of s.o.,** soutirer de l'argent à qn; **he wheedled his way into the old lady's confidence,** il s'est assuré la confiance de la vieille dame à force de cajoleries.

wheedling ['wiːd(ə)lɪŋ] **1** *adj* (*manner etc*) enjôleur; **w. voice,** voix pateline. **2** *n* cajolerie *f ou* câlinerie *f* destinée à enjôler.

wheel¹ [wiːl] *n* **(a)** (*on car, printer etc*) roue *f*; (*small*) roulette *f*; **on wheels,** sur roues *ou* roulettes; **to run on wheels,** marcher sur des roues *ou* roulettes; *Br* **meals on wheels,** repas livrés à domicile (*aux personnes âgées etc*); *F* **my wheels,** (*my car*) ma bagnole; *Fig* **the fifth w.,** la cinquième roue du carrosse; *Am F* **to feel like a fifth w.,** (*Br* = **to play gooseberry**) se sentir de trop; *Av* **landing wheels,** roues (du train) d'atterrissage; *Av* **nose w.,** roue (d'atterrisseur) avant; **hydraulic w.,** roue hydraulique; **bucket w.,** roue (hydraulique) à augets *ou* à godets; **the wheels,** les rouages *mpl* (*d'un mécanisme, d'une montre*); *Fig* **the wheels of government,** les rouages de l'administration; *Fig* **there are wheels within wheels,** c'est une affaire très compliquée *ou* dont il faut connaître les dessous; c'est plus compliqué que cela n'en a l'air; *Hist* **to condemn a criminal to the w.,** condamner un criminel à la roue; **to break s.o. on the w.,** rouer qn; **big w.,** (*at fair*) grande roue; *Am F* gros bonnet, grosse légume; **the w. of fortune,** la roue de la fortune; **w. alignment,** parallélisme *m* des roues; *Br* **w. clamp,** (*Am* = **Denver boot**) sabot *m* de Denver; *Aut* **w. disc,** enjoliveur *m*;

(b) (*for steering*) *Aut* volant *m* (de direction); *Nau* roue *f* du gouvernail; barre *f*; **to be at the w.,** *Aut* etre au volant; *Nau* tenir la barre *ou* le gouvernail; *Fig* tenir la barre, être à la tête de l'entreprise *ou* des affaires; **the man at the w.,** *Aut* le conducteur, l'homme au volant; *Nau* l'homme de barre, le timonier; *Fig* l'homme à la tête des affaires, *F* le grand patron;

(c) *Mil etc* (mouvement *m* de) conversion *f*; **left/right w.,** conversion à gauche/à droite.

wheel² **1** *vt* **(a)** rouler (*une brouette etc*); pousser (*une bicyclette*); **to w. sth in a barrow,** transporter qch en brouette; **to w. a child in a pram,** promener un enfant dans son landau; **(b)** *Mil* **to w. a line of men,** faire faire une conversion à une ligne d'hommes. **2** *vi* **(a)** tournoyer; **(b)** *Mil* opérer *ou* effectuer une conversion; **left w.!,** par file à gauche, gauche!; **(c)** *F* **to w. and deal,** brasser des affaires (plus ou moins louches).

▶wheel about, wheel around **1** *vi* **(a)** (*turn*) faire demi-tour *ou* se retourner (brusquement), faire volte-face; **she wheeled around to face him,** elle s'est retournée brusquement pour lui faire face; **(b)** (*circle*) tourner en rond *ou* en cercle, tournoyer; **vultures wheeling about in the sky,** des vautours qui tournoient dans le ciel. **2** *vtsep* tourner (*qch*); (*on axis*) faire pivoter (*qch*).

▶wheel in *vtsep* faire entrer (*qn*) en fauteuil roulant; *Br F* faire entrer (*qn*); **w. him in as soon as he arrives,** faites-le entrer dès qu'il arrive.

▶wheel round *vi & vtsep* = **WHEEL ABOUT**.

wheelbarrow ['wiːlbærəʊ] *n* brouette *f*.

wheelbase ['wiːlbeɪs] *n Aut* empattement *m*.

wheelchair ['wiːltʃeər] *n* fauteuil roulant; **she'll be in a w. for the rest of her life,** elle sera dans un fauteuil roulant pour le reste de ses jours; **access is difficult for people in wheelchairs,** l'accès est difficile pour les personnes en fauteuil roulant.

wheeled [wiːld] *adj* à roues; (*on castors*) à roulettes.

-wheeled [wiːld] *suff* **two/three/***etc***-w.,** à deux/trois/*etc* roues.

-wheeler [wiːlər] *suff* **two/three-w.,** voiture *f ou* bicyclette *f* à deux/trois roues, véhicule *m* à deux/trois roues.

wheeler-dealer ['wiːlə'diːlər] *n* brasseur *m* d'affaires (plus ou moins louches).

wheelhouse ['wi:lhaʊs] *n Nau* abri *m* de navigation, timonerie *f*.

wheelie ['wi:lɪ] *n Br F* **to do a w.,** = rouler sur la roue arrière d'une bicyclette ou d'une moto.

wheeling ['wi:lɪŋ] *n* **(a)** tournoiement *m* (*des oiseaux etc*); **(b)** *Mil* conversion *f*; **(c)** *F* **w. and dealing,** brassage *m* d'affaires (plus ou moins louches); **there's a lot of w. and dealing involved,** il y a tout un brassage d'affaires (plus ou moins louches) là-dessous.

wheelwright ['wi:lraɪt] *n* charron *m*.

wheeze¹ [wi:z] *n* **(a)** (*noise*) respiration asthmatique *ou* sifflante; **(b)** *Old-fashioned* ruse *f*, truc *m*; **a good w.,** une bonne astuce.

wheeze² **1** *vi* respirer péniblement *ou* comme un asthmatique; (*of horse*) corner. **2** *vt* dire (*qch*) d'une voix d'asthmatique.

▶wheeze out *vtsep* = **WHEEZE²**.

wheezing ['wi:zɪŋ] *n* (*of person*) respiration *f* d'asthmatique; sifflement gras (*d'asthmatique*); (*of horse*) cornage *m*.

wheezy ['wi:zɪ] *adj* (*person*) asthmatique, poussif; (*horse*) cornard, poussif; **she's still a little bit w. after her cold,** elle a encore un peu de mal à respirer après son rhume; *Fig* **a w. old barrel organ,** un vieil orgue de Barbarie asthmatique.

whelk [welk] *n* (*mollusc*) buccin *m*.

whelp¹ [welp] *n* jeune chien *m*, chiot *m*; petit *m* (*d'un fauve*); *Old-fashioned F* (*youth*) mauvais garnement; (*child*) petit morveux.

whelp² *vi* (*of animals*) mettre bas (*des petits*).

when [wen] **1** *adv* **(a)** (*interr*) quand; **w. will you come?,** quand viendrez-vous?; **w. will the wedding be?,** à quand le mariage?; **w. ever** *or* **w. on earth will he come?,** quand donc *ou* quand diable viendra-t-il?; *F* **say w.!,** (*when pouring drinks*) arrêtez-moi!;

(b) (*rel*) **the day w. I first met her,** le jour où je l'ai rencontrée pour la première fois; **one day w. I was on duty,** un jour que j'étais de service; **at the very time w. ...,** au moment même où ..., alors même que ... .

2 *conj* **(a)** (*at the time that*) quand, lorsque; **w. I came into the room,** quand *ou* lorsque je suis entré dans la pièce; **w. I think of what she must have suffered!,** quand je pense à ce qu'elle a dû souffrir!; **w. writing I get very tired,** quand j'écris je me fatigue beaucoup; *Culin* **w. cool, turn out onto a dish,** une fois refroidi, démouler sur un plat;

(b) (*at which time*) **the prince will arrive on the 10th, w. he will open the new university,** le prince arrivera le dix et inaugurera la nouvelle université;

(c) (*though*) **he walked there w. he could have taken the car,** il y est allé à pied, alors qu'il aurait pu prendre la voiture;

(d) (*since*) **what's the good of telling you w. you won't listen to me?,** à quoi bon vous le dire puisque vous ne voulez pas m'écouter?

3 *pron* **(a)** (*interr*) **until w. can you stay?,** jusqu'à quand pouvez-vous rester?; **since w. have you been living in Paris?,** depuis quand habitez-vous Paris?; *Iron* **since w. have you been interested in opera?,** depuis quand est-ce que tu t'intéresses à l'opéra?;

(b) (*rel*) **since w. I have always bought a car of that make,** depuis lors j'achète toujours cette marque de voiture; **until w. I shall stay in Paris,** d'ici là je reste à Paris.

4 *n* **the w. and the how of it,** quand et comment cela s'est-il passé *ou* se passera-t-il.

whence [wens] *adv Arch & Lit* d'où; **no one knows w. he comes,** personne ne sait d'où il vient; **w. I conclude that ...,** d'où je conclus que ... .

whenever, *Lit* **whene'er** [wen'evər, -'eər] *conj & adv* **(a)** (*every time*) toutes les fois *ou* chaque fois que; **w. I see it I think of you,** chaque fois que je le vois je pense à vous; **I go w. I can,** j'y vais aussi souvent que possible; **(b)** (*any time*) à n'importe quel moment (que); **come w. you like,** venez quand vous voudrez *ou* à n'importe quel moment; **Sunday, Monday, or w.,** dimanche, lundi, ou n'importe quel jour; **next month or w.,** le mois prochain ou n'importe quand; **(c)** (*interr*) quand; **w. did you find (the) time to do all that?,** quand avez-vous trouvé le temps de faire tout cela?

where [weər] **1** *interr adv* **(a)** (*in what place or direction*) où; **w. am I?,** où suis-je?; **tell me w. she is,** dites-moi où elle est; **w. did you put it?,** où l'avez-vous mis?; **w. are you going to?,** où allez vous?; **w. does he come from?,** d'où vient-il?; **w. have you got to?, w. are you?,** (*in work, book etc*) où en êtes-vous?; (*when looking for someone*) où êtes-vous passé, où êtes-vous?; **w. should I be if I had followed your advice?,** qu'est-ce que je serais devenu si j'avais suivi vos conseils?;

(b) w. is the use *or* **the good of it?,** à quoi bon (faire) cela?

2 *rel conj & adv* (*in, at, to the place which*) (là) où; **I'll stay w. I am,** je resterai (là) où je suis; **go w. you like,** allez où vous voudrez; **that's w. we've got to,** voilà où nous sommes; **that is w. you are mistaken,** c'est là que vous vous trompez, voilà où vous vous trompez; **he came to (the place) w. I was fishing,** il est venu à l'endroit où je pêchais; **I can see it from w. we are,** je le vois d'où nous sommes; **delete w. inapplicable,** (*on form*) rayer les mentions inutiles; **the house w. I was born,** la maison où *ou* dans laquelle je suis né; **they went to Paris, w. they stayed a week,** ils sont allés à Paris et y sont restés huit jours.

3 *n* **the w. and the when,** le lieu et la date, le lieu et l'heure.

whereabouts **1** [weərə'baʊts] *adv & conj* où, de quel côté; **do you know w. the town hall is?,** savez-vous de quel côté se trouve l'hôtel de ville?; **w. in France do you live?,** où est-ce que tu habites en France? **2** ['weərəbaʊts] *npl* **nobody knows her w., her w. are unknown,** personne ne sait où elle est; **the precise w. of the control centre,** le lieu précis où se trouve le centre de contrôle.

whereafter [weə'rɑ:ftər] *rel adv Arch & Lit* après quoi, à la suite de quoi.

whereas [weə'ræz] *conj* **(a)** *Jur etc* (*introducing preamble*) attendu que, vu que, puisque; **(b)** (*on the other hand*) alors que, tandis que.

whereat [weə'ræt] *adv & conj Arch & Lit* à quoi, sur quoi *etc*; **w. he replied that ...,** (ce) à quoi il a répondu que ... .

whereby [weə'baɪ] *adv Arch & Fml* par quoi, par quel moyen; **we have a situation here w. ...,** nous sommes ici en présence d'une situation dans laquelle ...; **a scheme w. we can ...,** un plan par lequel nous pouvons ... .

wherefore ['weəfɔ:r] **1** *adv Arch & Lit* **(a)** (*interr*) pourquoi, pour quelle raison; **(b)** (*rel*) donc; pour cette raison. **2** *n* **the why and the w.,** le pourquoi et le comment.

wherein [weə'rɪn] *adv Arch & Lit* en quoi; **w. have we offended you?,** en quoi vous avons-nous offensé?; **w. the difficulty lies,** où se trouve la difficulté.

whereof [weə'rɒv] *Arch & Lit adv* (*interr*) en quoi, de quoi; (*rel*) dont; **a matter w. I know nothing,** une affaire dont j'ignore tout.

whereon [weə'rɒn] *adv Arch & Lit* sur quoi; sur lequel; **the day w. ...,** le jour où ...; **w. he left us,** sur quoi il nous a quittés.

wheresoever, wheresoe'er [weəsəʊ'evər, -'eər] *adv & conj esp Lit* = **WHEREVER**.

whereupon [weərə'pɒn] *adv & conj Lit* **(a)** *Arch* sur quoi, sur lequel; **(b)** (*at which point*) sur quoi, après quoi; **w. he left us,** sur quoi il nous a quittés.

wherever [weə'revər] *conj & adv* **(a)** (*every place*) partout où; n'importe où; **I shall remember it w. I go,** où que j'aille, je m'en souviendrai; **I'll go w. you want (me to),** j'irai partout où vous voudrez (que j'aille); **w. possible,** partout où cela est possible; *F* **at home, in the office, or w.,** à la maison, au bureau ou n'importe où; **(b)** (*whichever place*) **w. they come from,** d'où qu'ils viennent; **he comes from Glossop, w. that may be,** il est originaire d'un endroit qui s'appellerait Glossop; **(c)** (*interr*) où; **w. can he be?,** où peut-il bien être?

wherewith [weə'wɪθ] *adv & conj Arch* **(a)** (*rel*) avec lequel; avec quoi; **(b)** = **WHEREUPON (b)**.

wherewithal ['weərwɪðɔ:l] *n F* **the w.,** l'argent *m*, le nécessaire, les moyens *mpl*; **I haven't the w. to buy it,** je n'ai pas de quoi l'acheter.

whet [wet] *vt* (**-tt-**) **(a)** (*sharpen*) aiguiser, affûter, repasser (*un outil, un couteau etc*); **(b)** (*stimulate*) stimuler, aiguiser (*l'appétit, les désirs etc*).

whether ['weðər] *conj* **(a)** (*indirect question*) si; **I don't know w. it's true,** je ne sais pas si c'est vrai; **it's doubtful** *or* **uncertain w. ...,** il est douteux *ou* peu certain que + *sub* ...; **I doubt w. he'll come,** je doute qu'il vienne; **I want to know w. ... or w. ...,** je voudrais savoir si ... ou si ...; **it depends on w. you're in a hurry or not,** cela dépend (de) si vous êtes pressé ou non;

(b) (*conditional*) **w. it rains or (w. it) snows, he always goes out,** qu'il pleuve ou qu'il neige, il sort toujours; **w. she comes or not** *or* **no we shall leave,** qu'elle vienne ou non *ou* qu'elle vienne ou qu'elle ne vienne pas nous partirons; **w. or not ...,** qu'il en soit ainsi ou non ...; **everyone, w. rich or poor, needs it,** chacun, qu'il soit riche ou pauvre, en a besoin; **you'll listen to me w. you like it or not,** tu vas m'écouter, que tu le veuilles ou non.

whetstone ['wetstəʊn] *n* pierre *f* à aiguiser *ou* à repasser.

whew [hjuː] *int* **(a)** (*relief, fatigue*) ouf!; **(b)** (*astonishment*) mon Dieu!

whey [weɪ] *n* petit lait.

which [wɪtʃ] **1** *adj* **(a)** (*interr*) quel, *f* quelle, *pl* quels, quelles; **w. colour do you like best?,** quelle couleur aimez-vous le mieux?; **w. way do we go?,** par où allons-nous?; **w. way is the wind blowing?,** d'où vient le vent?; **w. one?,** lequel?, laquelle?; **w. ones?,** lesquels?, lesquelles?; **I know w. one you want,** je sais lequel vous désirez;

(b) (*rel*) lequel, laquelle, *pl* lesquels, lesquelles; **he stayed here two weeks, during w. time he never left the house,** il est resté ici deux semaines, pendant lesquelles il n'a pas quitté la maison; **she came at noon, at w. time I'm usually in the garden,** elle est venue à midi, heure à laquelle je suis habituellement au jardin.

2 *pron* **(a)** (*interr*) lequel, laquelle, *pl* lesquels, lesquelles; **w. have you chosen?,** lequel *ou* laquelle *ou* lesquels *ou* lesquelles avez-vous choisi(e)(s)?; **w. of you?,** lequel d'entre vous?; **w. of the two (girls) is the prettier?,** laquelle des deux (filles) est la plus jolie?; **w. would you rather have?,** lequel préférez-vous?; **I can never tell w. is w.,** je ne sais jamais les distinguer, je ne sais jamais lequel est l'un et lequel est l'autre; **I don't know w. to choose,** je ne sais (pas) lequel choisir; **I don't mind w.,** n'importe (lequel);

(b) (*rel*) (*subject*) qui; (*object*) que; (*referring to whole clause*) ce qui; ce que; **the house w. is for sale,** la maison qui est à vendre; **the book w. I bought yesterday,** le livre que j'ai acheté hier; **he looked like a retired colonel, w. in fact he was,** il avait l'air d'un colonel en retraite, ce qu'il était en effet; **she was back in London, w. I didn't know,** elle était de retour à Londres, fait que *ou* ce que j'ignorais;

(c) (*with prepositions*) lequel, laquelle, *pl* lesquels, lesquelles; **to w., at w.,** auquel, à laquelle, *pl* auxquels, auxquelles; **of w., from w.,** duquel, de laquelle, *pl* desquels, desquelles, dont; **the house of w. I am speaking,** la maison dont je parle; **the countries to w. we are going** *or* **w. we're going to,** les pays où nous irons; **the pen w. I'm writing with,** le stylo avec lequel j'écris; **the town in w. we live,** la ville où nous demeurons *ou* que nous habitons *ou* dans laquelle nous habitons; **he insists that actors should have talent, in w. he is right,** il exige que les acteurs aient du talent, (ce) en quoi il a raison; **there are no trains on Sunday, w. I hadn't thought of,** il n'y a pas de trains le dimanche, ce à quoi je n'avais pas pensé; **after w. he went out,** après quoi il est sorti.

whichever [wɪtʃ'evər] **1** *pron* **(a)** (*any*) (*subject*) celui qui, *f* celle qui, *pl* ceux qui, celles qui; (*object*) celui que *etc*; **take w. you like best,** prenez celui que vous préférez; **w. of you comes in first,** celui (d'entre vous) qui arrive le premier; **the 30th or the last Friday in the month, w. comes first,** le 30 ou le dernier vendredi du mois, suivant lequel de ces deux jours survient le premier;

(b) (*no matter which*) n'importe lequel *etc*; **w. you choose, you will have a good bargain,** quel que soit celui que vous choisirez, vous ferez une bonne affaire;

(c) (*interr*) lequel, laquelle *etc*; **w. shall I choose?,** lequel vais-je choisir?

2 *adj* **(a)** (*any*) le ... que; **take w. book you prefer,** prenez le livre que vous préférez;

(b) (*no matter which*) n'importe quel; quelque ... que + *sub*; **w. way he turned he saw nothing but sand,** de quelque côté qu'il se tourne, il ne voyait (rien) que du sable.

whicker ['wɪkər] *vi* (*of horse*) hennir doucement.

whiff [wɪf] *n* bouffée *f* (*de vent, de fumée, d'air etc*); odeur *f* (*de vin etc*); *Fig* **a w. of scandal,** un parfum de scandale; **there mustn't be the slightest w. of suspicion that I'm involved,** rien ne doit laisser penser que je trempe dans cette affaire; **to take a few whiffs of a cigar,** tirer quelques bouffées de cigare; **to go out for a w. of fresh air,** sortir pour respirer un peu *ou* pour prendre l'air; **what a w.!,** qu'est-ce que ça pue!

whiffy ['wɪfɪ] *adj Br F* puant, qui pue; **the dog's a bit w.,** le chien pue un peu; **it's a bit w. in here, don't you think?,** ça pue un peu ici, tu ne trouves pas?

Whig [wɪg] *n Pol Hist* whig *m*.

while[1] [waɪl] *n* **(a)** (*time*) (espace *m* de) temps *m*; **after a w.,** au bout de quelque temps, quelque temps après; **after a little w., a little w. later,** peu de temps après; **for a (short) w.,** pendant un moment; **in a short** *or* **little w.,** sous peu, avant peu; **a short** *or* **little w. ago,** il n'y a pas bien longtemps; **a long w.,** longtemps; **a long w. ago,** il y a longtemps; **a good w.,** pas mal de temps; **it will be a good w. before you see him again,** vous ne le reverrez pas de si tôt; **it will take me quite a w.,** cela me prendra un certain temps *ou* pas mal de temps; **stay a little w. longer,** restez encore un peu; **all the w.,** tout le temps; **once in a w.,** de temps en temps, de temps à autre; *Arch* **the w.,** en attendant, pendant ce temps;

(b) **to be worth (one's) w.,** valoir la peine, *F* valoir le coup; **it's not worth our w. waiting,** cela ne vaut pas *ou* ce n'est pas la peine que nous attendions; **it is perhaps worth w. pointing out that ...,** cela vaut peut-être la peine de faire remarquer que ...; **I'll make it worth your w.,** vous serez bien récompensé de votre peine.

while[2] *conj* **(a)** (*during the time that*) pendant que, tandis que; **w. (he was) here,** pendant qu'il était ici; **w. in Paris,** pendant mon *ou* son *etc* séjour à Paris; **w. reading I fell asleep,** tout en lisant, je me suis endormi; **w. this was going on,** sur ces entrefaites; **w. you're at it, could you photocopy this too?,** pendant que tu y es, peux-tu aussi me photocopier cela?; **(b)** (*as long as*) tant que; **w. there's life there's hope,** tant qu'il y a de la vie il y a de l'espoir; **(c)** (*concessive*) quoique + *sub*, bien que + *sub*; **w. I admit** *or* **w. admitting it's difficult,** quoique j'admette *ou* tout en reconnaissant que c'est difficile; **(d)** (*whereas*) tandis que; **one of the sisters was (dressed) in white, w. the other was all in black,** une des sœurs était vêtue de blanc, tandis que l'autre était tout en noir.

►**while away** *vtsep* faire passer (*le temps*); tuer (*une heure, le temps*); **I played patience to w. away the time,** j'ai fait des réussites pour me désennuyer.

whilst [waɪlst] *conj esp Br* = **WHILE[2] (d)**.

whim [wɪm] *n* caprice *m*, fantaisie *f*, lubie *f*; **passing w.,** toquade *f*; **a sudden w. of his,** un caprice qui lui a pris; **she indulges his every w.,** elle lui passe tous ses caprices; **it was just a w.,** ce n'était qu'un caprice; **I bought it on a w.,** je l'ai acheté sur un coup de tête.

whimper[1] ['wɪmpər] *n* **(a)** (*crying*) pleurnicherie *f*, pleurnichement *m*; (*complaint*) geignement *m*, plainte *f*; **(b)** (*of dog*) petit cri plaintif.

whimper[2] **1** *vi* **(a)** (*of person*) pleurnicher, geindre; **(b)** (*of dog*) pousser de petits cris plaintifs; **the dog's whimpering to be let in,** le chien gémit pour qu'on le laisse entrer. **2** *vt* dire (*qch*) en pleurnichant.

whimpering ['wɪmpərɪŋ] **1** *adj* pleurnicheur, geignard; (*chien*) qui pousse de petits cris plaintifs. **2** *n* **(a)** (*crying*) pleurnichement *m*, pleurnicheries *fpl*; **(b)** (*complaints*) plaintes *fpl*; **(c)** petits cris plaintifs (*d'un chien*).

whimsey ['wɪmzɪ] *n* = **WHIMSY**.

whimsical ['wɪmzɪk(ə)l] *adj* **(a)** (*capricious*) capricieux, fantasque; **(b)** (*playful*) malicieux; **(c)** (*unusual*) bizarre, baroque.

whimsicality [wɪmzɪ'kælɪtɪ] *n* **(a)** caractère capricieux *ou* fantasque; **(b)** malice *f*; **(c)** bizarrerie *f* (*de caractère*).

whimsically ['wɪmzɪklɪ] *adv* (*see adj*) **(a)** capricieusement; **(b)** malicieusement; **(c)** bizarrement.

whimsy ['wɪmzɪ] *n* **(a)** (*capricious idea*) fantaisie *f*; **(b)** (*playfulness*) malice *f*.

whin [wɪn] *n* (*plant*) ajonc *m*, genêt épineux.

whine[1] [waɪn] *n* **(a)** (*crying*) plainte *f*; pleurnicherie *f*, geignement *m* (*d'un enfant*); gémissement *m*, geignement (*d'un chien*); **(b)** (*complaint*) jérémiade *f*; **(c)** (*of engine etc*) bruit monocorde et strident.

whine[2] *vi & vt* **(a)** (*cry*) (*of child*) pleurnicher; (*of dog*) gémir, geindre; **(b)** (*complain*) se plaindre; **you've nothing to w. about,** il n'y a pas de quoi vous plaindre; **stop whining!,** assez de jérémiades!

whining ['waɪnɪŋ] **1** *adj* geignard; (*enfant*) pleurnicheur; (*ton*) plaintif; **w. voice,** voix dolente. **2** *n* **(a)** gémissement *m*, geignement *m*; **(b)** jérémiades *fpl*, plaintes *fpl*; **stop your w.!,** assez de jérémiades!; **I've had enough of his w.,** j'en ai assez de ses jérémiades.

whinge [wɪndʒ] *v F* = **WHINE[2]**; *Austr F* **whingeing pom,** Anglais pleurnicheur.

whinny[1] ['wɪnɪ] *n* hennissement *m* (*de cheval*).

whinny[2] *vi* (*of horse*) hennir; *Fig* (*of person*) brailler.

whinnying ['wɪnɪɪŋ] *adj* **a w. laugh,** un rire qui ressemble à un hennissement; **he gave a w. laugh,** il a henni.

whip[1] [wɪp] *n* **(a)** (*lash*) fouet *m*; *Fig F* **to give s.o. a fair crack of the w.,** donner toutes ses chances à qn; *Fig* **to get a fair crack of the w.,** (*have fair chance*) avoir toutes ses chances; (*have good go*) avoir (sa bonne) part; *Fig* **to have**

or **hold the w. hand,** avoir l'avantage, avoir le dessus; **to have the w. hand over s.o.,** avoir barre(s) sur qn; **(b)** *Parl (person)* chef *m* de file, whip *m*; *(order)* appel *m* aux membres d'un groupe; **three-line w.,** appel urgent; **(c)** fouettement *m*, coup *m* de fouet *(d'un câble etc)*; **(d)** *Culin* = mousse *f*; **strawberry/raspberry/***etc* **w.,** mousse aux fraises/framboises/*etc*.

whip² *v* **(-pp-) 1** *vt* **(a)** fouetter *(un cheval)*; donner le fouet à *(un enfant)*; *Culin* battre *(des œufs)*; fouetter *(de la crème)*; *F* battre *(qn)* à plate(s) couture(s); **to w. a top,** fouetter *ou* faire aller un sabot; **the rain was whipping the window panes,** la pluie fouettait *ou* cinglait les vitres; *F* **I know when I'm whipped,** je sais quand déclarer forfait; **whipped cream,** crème fouettée;

(b) *Nau* surlier, garnir *(un cordage)*; ligaturer *(un brancard, une canne à pêche)*; *Sewing* **to w. a seam,** surjeter une couture, faire un surjet;

(c) *F* **she whipped it out of sight,** elle l'a caché d'un mouvement rapide;

(d) *F (steal)* faucher, piquer; **someone's whipped my wallet,** on m'a piqué mon portefeuille.

2 *vi* fouetter; **the rain was whipping against the panes,** la pluie fouettait *ou* cinglait les vitres.

▶whip away *vtsep F* **(a)** *(remove)* ôter, enlever *(qch)* brusquement *ou* d'un geste rapide; **(b)** *(hide)* cacher *(qch)*; **he whipped it away,** il l'a caché d'un mouvement brusque.

▶whip back *vi* **(a)** *F (return)* revenir rapidement, retourner rapidement; **w. back and get it,** retournez-y en vitesse le chercher; **(b)** *(of cable)* fouetter.

▶whip in *vtsep (of huntsman)* rassembler.

▶whip in(to) *vi F* entrer brusquement; **w. into the butcher's on your way home,** passe en vitesse chez le boucher en rentrant à la maison; **she's been whipped into hospital,** elle a été transportée à l'hôpital à toute vitesse.

▶whip off *vtsep F (remove)* ôter *ou* enlever *(qch)* d'un geste rapide.

▶whip out 1 *vtsep F (extract)* **he whipped out a revolver,** il a sorti vivement *ou* brusquement un revolver *(de sa poche)*. **2** *vi* sortir brusquement; **I'm just whipping out to the library,** je file à la bibliothèque.

▶whip round 1 *vi F* **(a)** *(turn)* se retourner vivement; **(b)** *(go quickly)* **w. round to the chemist's for me,** fais un saut à la pharmacie pour moi; **(c)** *Br (collect money)* faire une collecte; **we whipped round to get a present for her,** nous avons fait une collecte pour lui acheter un cadeau. **2** *vipo* **to w. round the corner,** tourner vivement le coin.

▶whip up *vtsep* **(a)** toucher *(un cheval)* (du fouet); **to w. up an audience,** galvaniser *ou* exalter un public; **(b)** *Parl* faire passer un appel urgent à *(des membres d'un parti)*; **to w. up support for sth,** susciter un soutien en faveur de qch; **(c)** battre *(des œufs, la crème etc)*; **I'll w. you up something to eat,** je vais te préparer quelque chose à manger en vitesse; **I'll see what I can w. up,** je vais voir ce que je peux préparer en vitesse.

whipcord ['wɪpkɔːd] *n* **(a)** *(on whip)* mèche *f* de fouet; *(for making whip)* corde *f* à fouet; **(b)** *Tex* whipcord *m*; **w. trousers,** pantalon *m* en whipcord.

whiplash ['wɪplæʃ] *n* **(a)** coup *m* de fouet; *Fig* **tongue like a w.,** langue cinglante; **(b)** *Med* **w. (injury),** lésion *f* traumatique des cervicales.

whipper-in [wɪpər'ɪn] *n (of hounds)* piqueur *m*.

whippersnapper ['wɪpəsnæpər] *n F* jeune homme suffisant *ou* qui fait l'important.

whippet ['wɪpɪt] *n (dog)* whippet *m*.

whippoorwill ['wɪpʊwɪl] *n Am (bird)* engoulevent *m* de Virginie; *Can* engoulevent bois-pourri.

whipround ['wɪpraʊnd] *n Br F* quête *f*, collecte *f*; **to have a w. for s.o.,** organiser une collecte en faveur de qn.

whir [wɜːr] *n & vi* = **WHIRR**.

whirl¹ [wɜːl] *n* **(a)** mouvement *m* giratoire, giration *f* *(d'une roue etc)*; *Fig F* **to give sth a w.,** essayer de faire qch; *Fig F* **I'll have a w. at it,** je vais tenter le coup; **(b)** *(of leaves, dust)* tourbillon *m*, tourbillonnement *m*, tournoiement *m*; **the social w.,** la vie mondaine; **a w. of pleasure,** un tourbillon de plaisirs; **my head's in a w.,** la tête me tourne.

whirl² 1 *vi* tourbillonner, tournoyer; **whirling dervish,** derviche tourneur; **my head's whirling,** la tête me tourne; **the thoughts that were whirling through my head,** les pensées qui tourbillonnaient dans mon cerveau. **2** *vt* faire tournoyer, faire tourbillonner *(les feuilles mortes etc)*; **he whirled her onto the dance floor,** il l'a entraînée en tournoyant sur la piste de danse.

▶whirl along 1 *vi* filer à toute vitesse *ou* à toute allure. **2** *vtsep* entraîner (à toute vitesse *ou* à fond de train); **the train whirled us along,** le train nous emportait à toute vitesse.

▶whirl round 1 *vi* **(a)** *(turn)* se retourner vivement; *(of dancer)* pirouetter; **(b)** *(of leaves etc)* tourbillonner, tournoyer. **2** *vtsep* **he whirled her round the dance floor,** il l'a fait tournoyer tout autour de la piste de danse.

whirligig ['wɜːlɪgɪg] *n* **(a)** *(top)* tourniquet *m*; **(b)** *(merry-go-round)* manège *m* de chevaux de bois.

whirlpool ['wɜːlpuːl] *n* tourbillon *m* (d'eau), gouffre *m*; *(produced by boat)* remous *m* d'eau.

whirlwind ['wɜːlwɪnd] *n* tourbillon *m* (de vent), trombe *f* (de vent); **to come in like a w.,** entrer en trombe *ou* en coup de vent; *F* **w. romance,** aventure enivrante.

whirlybird ['wɜːlɪbɜːd] *n Old-fashioned F (helicopter)* hélico *m*.

whirr¹ [wɜːr] *n* bruissement *m (d'ailes)*; ronflement *m*, ronronnement *m (de machines)*; vrombissement *m (d'une hélice d'avion etc)*.

whirr² *vi (of machinery etc)* ronfler, ronronner; *(of propeller)* vrombir.

whisk¹ [wɪsk] *n* **(a)** *(rapid movement)* **a w. of the tail/a duster,** un coup de queue/de torchon; **(b)** *(for dusting)* époussette *f*, plumeau *m*; *(for beating eggs)* fouet *m*, batteur *m*; **fly w.,** chasse-mouches *m inv*.

whisk² *vt* **(a) to w. its tail,** *(of cow etc)* agiter sa queue; **to w. a duster over the table,** donner un coup de chiffon sur la table; **(b)** entraîner, emporter *(qn)* à toute vitesse; **he was whisked to hospital,** il a été transporté à l'hôpital à toute vitesse; **she whisked it out of sight,** elle l'a caché d'un mouvement rapide; **(c)** *Culin* battre *(des œufs)*; fouetter *(de la crème)*.

▶whisk away, whisk off 1 *vi* partir comme un trait *ou* comme une flèche. **2** *vtsep* enlever *(qch)* d'un geste rapide; entraîner *ou* emporter *(qn)* à toute vitesse; **to w. away a fly,** chasser une mouche *(d'un revers de main)*; **the president was whisked away in a helicopter,** le président a été emmené à toute vitesse en hélicoptère; **he was whisked away to hospital in an ambulance,** il a été transporté à l'hôpital à toute vitesse en ambulance.

▶whisk past 1 *vi (of day, weekend etc)* passer comme l'éclair, filer. **2** *vipo* **she whisked past me,** elle est passée devant moi comme un éclair.

▶whisk up *vtsep Culin* battre *(des œufs)*; fouetter *(de la crème)*.

whisker ['wɪskər] *n* **whiskers,** favoris *mpl (d'homme)*; moustache(s) *f(pl) (de chat, de souris etc)*; *Fig F* **he thinks he's the cat's whiskers,** il ne se prend pas pour rien; *Sp Fig* **to win by a w.,** gagner dans un mouchoir; *Fig* **to escape death by a w.,** frôler la mort, échapper de justesse à la mort.

whiskered ['wɪskəd] *adj (homme)* qui a des favoris *ou* des moustaches.

whisky, *Irish or US* **whiskey** ['wɪskɪ] *n* whisky *m*; **a w. and soda,** un whisky soda; **w. on the rocks,** whisky frappé; *Can* whisky sur glace *ou* aux glaçons; **two whiskies,** deux whiskies; **w. company,** société *f* de fabrication de whisky; **w. distillery,** distillerie *f* de whisky; *esp Br* **w. mac,** = whisky mélangé à du vin de gingembre; *esp Am* **w. sour,** = whisky avec du jus de citron ou de citron vert.

whisper¹ ['wɪspər] *n* **(a)** chuchotement *m*; *Lit* bruissement *m (des feuilles)*; **to speak in a w.** *or* **in whispers,** parler en chuchotant; **to say sth in a w.,** chuchoter qch, dire qch tout bas; **(b)** *(rumour)* rumeur *f*, bruit *m*; **I've heard whispers** *or* **a w. that ...,** j'ai entendu des rumeurs selon lesquelles ... .

whisper² 1 *vi* chuchoter, parler bas; *(of leaves)* bruire; *(of water)* murmurer; **the wind was whispering in the trees,** le vent susurrait dans les arbres; **to w. to s.o.,** chuchoter à l'oreille de qn, dire *ou* souffler à l'oreille de qn. **2** *vt* **(a) to w. sth to s.o.,** susurrer qch à l'oreille de qn; **what were you whispering to her?,** qu'est-ce que tu lui disais à l'oreille?; **whispered conversation,** conversation *f* à voix basse; **(b)** faire circuler secrètement *(une nouvelle)*; **it is whispered that ...,** le bruit court que ... .

whispering ['wɪspərɪŋ] *n* **(a)** chuchotement *m*; *Lit* bruissement *m (de feuilles)*; murmure *m (d'eaux)*; *Archit* **w. gallery,** voûte *f* acoustique, galerie *f* à écho; **(b)** *Pej* chuchoterie(s) *f(pl)*; **w. campaign,** campagne sournoise *ou* de chuchoteries.

whist [wɪst] *n Cards* whist *m*; **to have a game of w.,** faire une partie de whist; **to play w.,** jouer au whist; **w. drive,** tournoi *m* de whist; **w. player,** joueur, -euse de whist.

whistle¹ ['wɪs(ə)l] *n* **(a)** *(noise)* sifflement *m*; *(blow on a whistle)* coup *m* de sifflet; *Sp* **she gave a w. of surprise,**

elle a émis un sifflement de surprise; **final w.,** coup de sifflet final; **(b)** *(object)* sifflet *m*; **to blow a w.,** donner un coup de sifflet; *Sp* **to blow the w. for a foul/half time,** siffler une faute/la mi-temps; *Fig F* **to blow the w. on sth,** révéler *ou* dévoiler qch; *Fig F* **to blow the w. on s.o.,** dénoncer qn; *Fig F* **who blew the w.?,** qui est-ce qui a vendu la mèche?; **tin** *or Arch* **penny w.,** flageolet *m*.

whistle² **1** *vi (of person, bird, wind etc)* siffler; *(on whistle)* donner un coup de sifflet; **to w. for one's dog/a taxi,** siffler son chien/un taxi; *F* **he can w. for his money,** il peut courir après son argent; *F* **you can w. for it!,** tu peux toujours courir!; **she whistled in surprise,** elle a émis un sifflement de surprise; **the bullet whistled past his ear,** la balle a passé en sifflant tout près de son oreille; *Fig* **to w. in the dark** *or* **past the graveyard,** essayer de se rassurer. **2** *vt* siffler, siffloter *(un air)*; *Sp* **to w. half-time,** siffler la mi-temps.

►**whistle up** *vtsep F* **I'll w. up a few friends to help us,** je vais trouver quelques amis pour nous aider; **can you w. up some more sandwiches?,** peux-tu nous avoir encore quelques sandwichs?

whistle-blower [ˈwɪs(ə)lbləʊər] *n Fig F* personne qui vend la mèche; **we need a few more w.-blowers like her,** il faudrait d'autres personnes comme elle pour tirer sur la sonnette d'alarme.

whistler [ˈwɪslər] *n* **(a)** *(person)* siffleur, -euse; **(b)** *(bird)* oiseau siffleur; **(c)** *(animal)* siffleur *m*, marmotte canadienne, *Can* siffleux *m*.

whistling [ˈwɪslɪŋ] **1** *adj (oiseau etc)* siffleur; **w. sound,** sifflement *m*; *Nau* **w. buoy,** bouée *f* à sifflet. **2** *n* sifflement *m*.

whistle-stop¹ [ˈwɪs(ə)lstɒp] *n Am* **(a)** *Rail* halte *f* (à arrêt facultatif); **w.-s. tour,** tour rapide; *Pol* tournée électorale rapide *(faite par train spécial)*; **(b)** *F (village)* patelin *m*, bled *m*.

whistle-stop² *vi Am Pol* faire une tournée électorale par train spécial.

whit [wɪt] *n (usu in neg)* brin *m*; **he's not a w. the better for it,** il ne s'en porte nullement mieux; **I don't care a w,** je m'en moque comme de ma première chemise *ou* comme de l'an quarante.

Whit [wɪt] *adj & n* **W. Sunday,** (le dimanche de) la Pentecôte; **W. Monday,** le lundi de la Pentecôte.

white¹ [waɪt] **1** *adj (bread, hair, wine etc)* blanc, *f* blanche; **as w. as snow,** blanc comme la neige; **w. Christmas,** Noël blanc; **we had a w. Christmas,** on a eu un Noël blanc; **to turn** *or* **go w.,** *(of face)* devenir blanc *ou* pâle *ou* blême, blanchir, blêmir; *(of hair)* blanchir; **he's going w.,** il commence à blanchir; **he went w. overnight,** ses cheveux sont devenus blancs en l'espace d'une nuit, **w. ant,** fourmi blanche, termite *m*; **w. area,** *(of water)* mers *fpl* ne se trouvant sur aucune carte; *(of land)* terrain pour lequel aucun projet de planification n'a été adopté; **w. (blood) cell,** globule blanc; **w. coffee,** café *m* au lait; **do you take your coffee w.?,** tu prends du lait dans ton café?; **w. with fear,** blanc de peur; *Br Hist* **w. feather,** = symbole de lâcheté; **to show the w. feather,** se dégonfler; *Br* **w. fish,** *(generic term)* poisson *m* à chair blanche et non huileuse; **w. flag,** drapeau blanc; **w. flour,** farine *f* de ménage; **w. as a ghost/sheet,** pâle comme la mort/un linge; **w. gold,** *(platinum)* or blanc; *Com* **w. goods,** *(linen)* articles *mpl* de blanc; *(réfrigérateurs, machines à laver etc)* appareils ménagers; *Sp* **w. hope,** espoir *m*; **she's our w. hope for the Olympics,** elle est notre espoir pour les jeux Olympiques; **w. horses,** *(waves)* moutons *mpl*; *US* **the W. House,** la Maison Blanche; *St Exch* **w. knight,** chevalier blanc; **w. lie,** pieux mensonge; **I told a w. lie,** j'ai dit un pieux mensonge; **w. magic,** magie blanche; **a w. man,** un blanc; *esp US* un homme loyal; **the w. man's burden,** = obligation pour les blancs d'assurer l'instruction des habitants noirs de leurs colonies; **w. meat,** chair blanche, blanc *m (de poulet)*; *(as opposed to red)* viande blanche; **w. metal** *or* **alloy,** métal blanc, antifriction *f*; *Br* **w. meter,** *(heating)* = système de chauffage permettant d'accumuler la chaleur pendant les heures creuses; *Pol* **w. paper,** livre blanc; **W. Russia,** Russie Blanche; *Am* **w. sale,** solde *m* des articles de blanc; *Culin* **w. sauce,** sauce blanche; **w. slavery,** traite *f* des blanches; **w. slave market,** proxénétisme *m*; **w. spirit,** white-spirit *m*, *pl* white-spirits; **w. stick,** canne blanche; **w. tie,** habit *m*; **w.-tie occasion,** occasion pour laquelle l'habit est de rigueur; **w. water,** eau vive; **w.-water rafting,** descente *f* en eau vive; *Av Sl* **w. tail, w.-tail plane,** avion n'appartenant encore à aucune compagnie aérienne; **w. wedding,** mariage *m* en blanc; **she's having a w. wedding,** elle se marie en blanc. **2** *n* **(a)** *(colour)* blanc *m*; **zinc w.,** blanc de zinc; **dressed in w.,** habillé en blanc *ou* de blanc; **whites,** *Com* linge blanc; *Sp* tenue blanche ; **wash your whites with X,** lavez votre linge avec X;
(b) *(person)* blanc, *f* blanche;
(c) *(of egg, eyes)* blanc *m*.

white² *vt Rel & Fig* **whited sepulchre,** sépulcre blanchi.

►**white out** *vtsep* masquer au vernis correcteur blanc.

whitebait [ˈwaɪtbeɪt] *n Culin* blanchaille *f*; **a dish of w.,** un plat de friture.

whitecap [ˈwaɪtkæp] *n (usu pl)* **whitecaps,** *(waves)* moutons *mpl*.

white-collar [ˈwaɪtˈkɒlər] *adj* **w.-c. worker,** employé *m* de bureau; **w.-c. union,** syndicat *m* d'employés de bureau; **w.-c. crime,** délits financiers.

white-faced [ˈwaɪtˈfeɪst] *adj* au visage pâle.

whitefish [ˈwaɪtfɪʃ] *n* corégone *m*, poisson *m* à chair blanche et non huileuse.

white-haired [ˈwaɪtˈheəd] *adj* aux cheveux blancs; *Am Fig* **w.-h. boy,** chouchou *m*.

Whitehall [ˈwaɪthɔːl] *n* l'Administration *f* britannique.

white-headed [waɪtˈhedɪd] *adj* **(a)** *(animal)* à tête blanche; **(b)** *(person)* aux cheveux blancs; *Am Fig* **w.-h. boy,** chouchou *m*.

white-hot [ˈwaɪtˈhɒt] *adj* chauffé *ou* porté à blanc.

white-knuckle [ˈwaɪtnʌk(ə)l] *adj F* **I'm a w.-k. flyer,** j'ai la trouille en avion.

white-livered [ˈwaɪtlɪvəd] *adj Fig (person)* poltron, pusillanime.

whiten [ˈwaɪt(ə)n] **1** *vt* **(a)** blanchir *(les cheveux, le linge, les chaussures)*; **(b)** *(with whitewash)* blanchir à la chaux, badigeonner en blanc. **2** *vi* **(a)** blanchir; **(b)** *(of person)* pâlir, blêmir.

whiteness [ˈwaɪtnɪs] *n* **(a)** blancheur *f (de la neige, de la peau)*; **(b)** pâleur *f (du visage)*; **(c)** *Arch & Lit* innocence *f*, pureté *f*.

whitening [ˈwaɪt(ə)nɪŋ] *n* **(a)** blanchiment *m (d'un mur)*; **(b)** blanchissement *m (des cheveux)*.

whiteout [ˈwaɪtaʊt] *n* tempête *f* de neige aveuglante.

white-slaver [waɪtsleɪvər] *n* proxénète *mf*.

whitethorn [ˈwaɪtθɔːn] *n (tree)* aubépine *f*.

whitethroat [ˈwaɪtθrəʊt] *n (bird)* fauvette grisette.

whitewall [ˈwaɪtwɔːl] *n* **w. (tyre** *or US* **tire),** pneu *m* avec une bande blanche peinte sur le côté extérieur.

whitewash¹ [ˈwaɪtwɒʃ] *n* **(a)** *(paint)* blanc *m ou* lait *m* de chaux, badigeon *m* à la chaux, **to give a wall a coat of w.,** badigeonner un mur (en blanc); **(b)** *Fig* blanchiment *m (d'une réputation)*; **a w. (job),** une opération de blanchiment; **(c)** *Sp F* défaite *f* à zéro.

whitewash² *vt* **(a)** peindre *ou* blanchir à la chaux, badigeonner en blanc; **(b)** *Fig* blanchir, disculper *(qn)*; **(c)** *Sp F* battre *(ses adversaires)* sans qu'ils aient marqué un point.

whitewashing [ˈwaɪtwɒʃɪŋ] *n* **(a)** *(painting)* peinture *f* à la chaux, badigeonnage *m*; **(b)** *Fig* blanchiment *m (d'une réputation)*.

whitewood [ˈwaɪtwʊd] *n Com* bois blanc.

whitey [ˈwaɪtɪ] *n US Pej* blanc, *f* blanche; *(used as pl)* les blancs.

whither [ˈwɪðər] *adv & conj Arch & Lit* **(a)** *(interr)* où, vers quel lieu; **(b)** *(rel)* (là) où; **I shall go w. fate leads me,** j'irai là où me mènera le destin.

whiting [ˈwaɪtɪŋ] *n (fish)* merlan *m*.

whitish [ˈwaɪtɪʃ] *adj* blanchâtre.

whitlow [ˈwɪtləʊ] *n Med* panaris *m*.

Whitsun(tide) [ˈwɪtsən(taɪd)] *n* (fête *f ou* saison *f* de) la Pentecôte.

whittle [ˈwɪt(ə)l] *vt* amenuiser, parer *(un bâton, une cheville)*.

►**whittle away** *vtsep* rogner *(son capital)*; faire tomber petit à petit *(la résistance)*.

►**whittle down** *vtsep* rogner *(son capital)*; **we've whittled down the number of candidates,** nous avons réussi à réduire le nombre des candidats.

whiz(z) [wɪz] *n F* **w. kid,** jeune prodige *m*.

whizz¹ [wɪz] **1** *int* pan! **2** *n* **(a)** sifflement *m (d'une balle)*; **(b)** *esp US F* as *m*, crack *m* **(at,** en).

whizz² *vi (of bullet etc)* siffler.

►**whizz by** *vi (of traffic)* passer à toute vitesse; *(of holiday, time etc)* passer à toute vitesse, filer.

►**whizz through** *vipo* faire *(qch)* à toute vitesse.

who [huː] *pron* **(a)** *(interr) (subject)* qui, qui est-ce qui; *(object)* qui, qui est-ce que; **w. is it?,** qui est-ce?; **w. with?,** avec qui?; **w. is that woman?,** qui *ou* quelle est cette femme?; **w. on earth told you that?,** qui diable vous a dit cela?; *Tel* **who's speaking?**, qui est à l'appareil?; *Tel* **may I ask who's speaking?**, c'est de la part de qui?; **w. is this?**, (*on telephone*) qui êtes-vous?; **w. did you say?**, qui ça?; **w. does he think he is?**, pour qui se prend-il?; **w. of us can still remember it?**, qui *ou* lesquels d'entre nous se le rappelle(nt) encore?; **w. do you want?**, qui voulez-vous?; **w. were you talking to?**, à qui parliez-vous?; *Br* **Who's W.**, ≈ Bottin Mondain; **to know who's w.**, (*the right people*) avoir des relations; **you'll soon find out who's w.**, (*who people are*) tu connaîtras très vite tout le monde; **tell me who's w.**, dites-moi qui sont tous ces gens-là;

(b) (*rel*) qui; (*to avoid ambiguity*) *Fml* lequel *etc*; (*independent rel*) (celui *etc*) qui; **the friends w. came yesterday**, les amis qui sont venus hier; **Louise's father, w. is very rich**, le père de Louise, *Fml* lequel *ou* qui est très riche; **deny it w. will**, le nie qui voudra.

WHO [dʌb(ə)ljuːeɪtʃ'əʊ] *n* (*abbr* **World Health Organization**) OMS *f*.

whoa [wəʊ] *int* (*to horse*) ho!, holà!; *F* (*to person*) doucement!, attendez!

whodun(n)it [huː'dʌnɪt] *n F* roman *ou* film policier.

whoever [huː'evər] *pron* **(a)** (*anyone that*) celui qui, *f* celle qui *etc*, quiconque; **w. finds it may keep it**, celui qui le trouvera pourra le garder; **(b)** (*no matter who*) qui que + *sub*; **w. you are, speak!**, qui que vous soyez, parlez!; **w. wrote that letter**, qui que ce soit qui ait écrit cette lettre; *F* **... or w.**, ou qui que ce soit; **w. she marries**, qui qu'elle épouse; celui qu'elle épousera; **w. you like**, qui vous voudrez; **(c)** (*intensive*) **w. can that be at this time of night?**, qui cela peut-il bien être à cette heure tardive?

whole [həʊl] **1** *adj* **(a)** (*entire*) entier, complet, -ète; (*emphatic*) tout, entier, tout entier; **ox roasted w.**, bœuf rôti entier; **he swallowed it w.**, (*food*) il l'a avalé sans le mâcher; *Fig* il a pris ça pour de l'argent comptant; **cook the fish w.**, faites cuire le poisson entier; **a w. loaf**, un pain entier; **w. milk**, lait entier; *Math* **w. number**, nombre entier; **to tell the w. truth**, dire toute la vérité; **the w. world**, le monde entier; **do you have to tell the w. world?**, est-ce que tu tiens à ce que tout le monde le sache?; **to last a w. week**, durer toute une semaine; **I never saw her the w. evening**, je ne l'ai pas vue de (toute) la soirée; **w. families died of it**, des familles entières en sont mortes; *F* **the w. lot of you**, vous tous; *F* **to go the w. hog**, aller jusqu'au bout; *F* **there's still a w. lot left**, il en reste encore plein; *F* **for a w. lot of reasons**, pour tout un tas de raisons.

(b) *Arch* sain; (*person*) en bonne santé, sain, sain et sauf; (*thing*) intact; *Bible* **his hand was made w.**, sa main fut guérie.

2 *n* tout *m*, totalité *f*, ensemble *m*; **the w. of the school**, l'école entière, toute l'école; **nearly the w. of our resources**, la presque totalité de nos ressources; **he spent the w. of that year in London**, il a passé toute cette année-là à Londres; **the w. amounts to ...**, le total se monte à ...; **to buy/sell sth as a w.**, acheter/vendre qch en bloc; **taken as a w.**, pris dans sa totalité; **on the w.**, dans l'ensemble.

wholefood ['həʊlfuːd] *n* aliments complets; **w. restaurant**, restaurant *m* qui sert des plats à base d'aliments complets.

wholehearted [həʊl'hɑːtɪd] *adj* (qui vient) du cœur; (*rire*) épanoui.

wholeheartedly [həʊl'hɑːtɪdlɪ] *adv* de bon *ou* de grand *ou* de tout cœur; (*to agree*) de tout cœur; **I admire you w.**, je vous admire de tout cœur.

wholemeal ['həʊlmiːl] *adj Br* (*Am* = **whole-wheat**) **w. bread**, pain complet.

wholeness ['həʊlnɪs] *n* intégralité *f*, intégrité *f*.

wholesale ['həʊlseɪl] **1** *n* (vente *f* en) gros *m*; **w. and retail**, gros et détail. **2** *adj* **(a)** de gros, en gros; **w. dealer** *or* **merchant**, grossiste *mf*, commerçant, -ante en gros; **w. price**, prix *m* de *ou* en gros; **w. trade**, commerce *m* de gros *ou* en gros; **(b)** *Fig* **by w. borrowing**, en empruntant de tous côtés; **a w. slaughter**, un massacre, une tuerie en masse. **3** *adv* **(a) to sell/buy w.**, vendre/acheter en gros; **I can get it for you w.**, je peux vous l'avoir au prix de gros; **(b)** *Fig* en masse, en bloc.

wholesaler ['həʊlseɪlər] *n* grossiste *mf*, commerçant, -ante en gros.

wholesome ['həʊlsəm] *adj* (*aliment*) sain; (*air, climat*) salubre; (*remède*) salutaire; **she has a w. appearance**, elle a l'air rangé, elle a l'air bien comme il faut.

wholesomeness ['həʊlsəmnɪs] *n* nature saine (*de la nourriture*); salubrité *f* (*de l'air*); **the w. of her appearance**, le côté rangé *ou* bien comme il faut de son apparence.

whole-wheat ['həʊlwiːt] *adj Am* (*Br* = **wholemeal**) **w. bread**, pain complet.

wholly ['həʊllɪ] *adv* **(a)** (*completely*) tout à fait, complètement, entièrement; **(b)** (*without exception*) intégralement, en totalité.

whom [huːm] *pron* (*objective case*) *often Fml* **(a)** (*interr*) qui, qui est-ce que; **w. did you see?**, qui avez-vous vu?, qui est-ce que vous avez vu?; **to w./of w. are you speaking?**, à qui/de qui parlez-vous?; **I don't know to w. to turn**, je ne sais à qui m'adresser; **(b)** (*rel*) (*direct object*) que; lequel, laquelle, *pl* lesquels, lesquelles; (*indirect object and after prep*) qui; **the woman w. you saw**, la femme que vous avez vue; **somebody to w. he could talk**, quelqu'un à qui il pouvait parler; **the friend of w. I speak**, l'ami dont je parle; **these two men, both of w. were quite young**, ces deux hommes, qui tous deux étaient tout jeunes; **(c)** (*independent rel*) celui que *etc*, qui; **those w. the gods love die young**, qui est aimé des dieux meurt jeune.

whomsoever [huːmsəʊ'evər] *pron Fml* **(a)** (*any person whom*) celui (quel qu'il soit) que; **w. they choose**, celui qu'ils choisiront; **(b)** (*no matter whom*) qui que ce soit que.

whoop¹ **(a)** [wuːp] cri *m* (de joie); *Am* (h)ululement *m* (*d'un hibou*); **(b)** [huːp] *Med* quinte *f* (*de la coqueluche*).

whoop² *vi* **(a)** [wuːp] crier, pousser des cris (de joie); *Am* (*of owl*) (h)ululer; *F* **to w. it up**, (*have good time, celebrate*) faire la noce; **(b)** [huːp] *Med* tousser convulsivement à cause d'une coqueluche; **she's been whooping all night**, elle a eu des quintes de toux toute la nuit; **whooping cough**, la coqueluche.

whoopee [wʊ'piː] **1** *int* youpi. **2** *n Old-fashioned F* **to make w.**, (*enjoy oneself*) faire la noce *ou* la bombe; (*sexually*) faire l'amour.

whooper ['huːpər] *n* **w. swan**, cygne chanteur *ou* sauvage.

whoops [wuːps] *int* houp-là!

whop [wɒp] *vt* **(-pp-)** *F* **(a)** battre, rosser (*qn*); **(b)** battre, massacrer (*une équipe*).

whopper ['wɒpər] *n F* **(a)** quelque chose de colossal *ou* d'énorme; **a w. of a fish**, un poisson énorme *ou* balaise; **(b)** (*lie*) mensonge *m* de taille.

whopping ['wɒpɪŋ] *F* **1** *adj* énorme; **w. great lie**, mensonge *m* de taille; **a w. big fish**, un poisson énorme *ou* balaise. **2** *n* rossée *f*, raclée *f*.

whore¹ [hɔːr] *n* prostituée *f*, *Sl* putain *f*; *Sl* **w. house**, bordel *m*.

whore² *vi* **(a)** (*of man*) **to w., to go whoring**, fréquenter les prostituées; **(b)** (*of woman*) se prostituer.

whoremonger ['hɔːmʌŋgər] *n* homme *m* à femmes de petite vertu.

whoring ['hɔːrɪŋ] *n* **(a)** prostitution *f*; **(b)** débauche *f*.

whorl [wɜːl] *n* **(a)** *Bot* verticille *m*; **(b)** tour *m* d'une spirale, spire *f*, volute *f*; vortex *m* (*d'une coquille*); **(c)** sillon *m* (*d'une empreinte digitale*).

whorled [wɜːld] *adj Bot* (*flower*) verticillé; (*shell*) convoluté, turbiné; *Archit* voluté.

whortleberry ['wɜːt(ə)lberɪ] *n* (*fruit*) airelle *f* myrtille.

whose [huːz] *poss pron* **(a)** (*interr*) de qui; (*ownership*) à qui; **w. are these gloves?**, à qui sont ces gants?; **w. daughter are you?**, de qui êtes-vous la fille?; **w. fault is it?**, à qui la faute?; **w. book did you borrow?**, à qui avez-vous emprunté un livre; **w. is this?**, à qui est-ce?; **(b)** (*rel*) dont; (*after prep*) de qui; duquel, de laquelle, *pl* desquels, desquelles; **the pupil w. work I showed you**, l'élève dont je vous ai montré le travail; **the man to w. wife I gave the money**, l'homme à la femme de qui *ou* duquel j'ai donné l'argent.

whosoever [huːsəʊ'evər] *pron Arch* = **WHOEVER**.

why [waɪ] **1** *adv & conj* **(a)** (*interr*) pourquoi, pour quelle raison; **w. (ever) didn't you say so?**, pourquoi ne l'avez-vous pas dit?; **w. not?**, pourquoi pas?; **w. not agree?**, pourquoi ne pas accepter?; **w. bother?**, à quoi bon (s'en donner la peine)?; **w. get upset?**, à quoi bon se rendre malade?;

(b) (*rel*) pourquoi; **that is (the reason) w. ...**, voilà pourquoi ...; **w. he should always be late I do not understand**, qu'il soit toujours en retard, je ne me l'explique pas; **I'll tell you w.**, je vais vous dire pourquoi.

2 *n* (*pl* **whys**) pourquoi *m*, raison *f*; **I like to know the whys and wherefores of a thing**, j'aime à savoir le pourquoi et le comment d'une chose.

3 *int* **(a)** (*surprise*) **w., it's David!**, tiens, mais c'est David!;

(b) (*protest*) **w., you're not afraid, are you?**, voyons, vous n'avez pas peur?; **w., it's simple**, allons, c'est simple; **w., what's the harm?**, mais quel mal y a-t-il?;

(c) *(hesitation)* **w., I really don't know,** vraiment *ou* franchement je ne sais pas;

(d) *(introducing consequence)* **if this doesn't do, w. we must try something else,** si ceci ne réussit pas, alors *ou* eh bien il faudra essayer autre chose.

WI [dʌb(ə)lju:'aɪ] **(a)** *abbr* **Women's Institute**; **(b)** *abbr* **West Indies**.

wick [wɪk] *n* **(a)** mèche *f* *(d'une lampe, d'une bougie)*; **(b)** *Br Sl* **she gets on my w.,** elle me tape sur les nerfs; **it gets on my w. that he's always there,** ça me tape sur les nerfs qu'il soit toujours là.

wicked ['wɪkɪd] **1** *adj* **(a)** *(evil)* mauvais, méchant; *(crime)* atroce, affreux; **a w. lie,** un affreux mensonge;

(b) *Fig* *(weather)* affreux, atroce; *(pain)* cruel, atroce; *(mischievous)* malicieux, espiègle; **he's got a w. temper,** il a très mauvais caractère; **it's w. to waste so much food,** c'est un crime de gaspiller tant de nourriture; **they're asking a w. price for their house,** ils ont mis leur maison en vente à un prix exorbitant; **it's a w. shame that ...,** il est scandaleux que ... + *sub*; *F* **you w. little thing!,** *(to child)* petit vilain!, petite vilaine!;

(c) *Sl* *(good)* génial, super.

2 *n* **the w.,** *(used as pl)* les méchants; *Hum* **(there's) no rest for the w.,** pas de répit pour les braves.

wickedly ['wɪkɪdlɪ] *adv* **(a)** méchamment; **(b)** *Fig* terriblement, affreusement, malicieusement; **w. expensive,** hors de prix; **she was smiling w.,** elle souriait d'un air malicieux.

wickedness ['wɪkɪdnɪs] *n* méchanceté *f*; perversité *f*; atrocité *f* *(d'un crime)*.

wicker ['wɪkər] *n* **(a)** osier *m*; **(b)** = **WICKERWORK**.

wickerwork ['wɪkəwɜ:k] *n* vannerie *f*, objet *m* en osier (tressé); **w. chair,** chaise *f* en osier (tressé) *ou* en vannerie.

wicket ['wɪkɪt] *n* **(a)** guichet *m* *(d'une porte etc)*; **(b) w. (door),** porte *f* à piétons; **w. (gate),** petite porte à claire-voie; portillon *m* *(de passage à niveau)*; **(c)** *Am* *(in bank)* guichet *m*; **(d)** *Cr* guichet *m*; *(area)* le terrain entre les guichets; **the bowler took three wickets,** le lanceur a pris trois guichets; **Australia lost four wickets before lunch,** l'Australie a perdu quatre guichets avant le déjeuner; **to keep w.,** garder les guichets; **soft w.,** terrain mou; *Fig* **to be on a good/sticky w.,** être dans une position avantageuse/difficile; **(e)** *Am* *(at croquet)* arceau *m*.

wicketkeeper ['wɪkɪtki:pər] *n* gardien *m* de guichet.

wide [waɪd] **1** *adj* **(a)** *(broad)* large; **the roads gets wider after the village,** au-delà du village la route s'élargit; **to be five metres w.,** faire cinq mètres de large *ou* de largeur; **how w. is the room?,** quelle est la largeur de la pièce?, combien est-ce que la pièce fait de large?; **to give a w. yawn,** bâiller en ouvrant largement la bouche; *Aut* **w. load,** *(notice on vehicle)* = convoi exceptionnel; *Cin* **w. screen,** grand écran;

(b) *(extensive)* *(desert, ocean)* vaste; *(range, experience, knowledge)* étendu, vaste, ample; *(influence)* répandu; **the w. world,** le vaste monde; **there is a w. difference between ...,** il y a une grande différence entre ...; **in a wider sense,** dans un sens plus large, par extension; *Phot* **w. angle of view,** grand angle de champ;

(c) *(unrestricted)* *(vêtement)* ample, large; **w. views/opinions,** vues/opinions larges *ou* libérales; **in the widest sense of the word,** dans l'acception la plus large du mot;

(d) *(remote)* éloigné, loin; **to be w. of the mark,** être loin du compte; *Cr* **w. ball,** balle écartée *ou* qui passe hors de la portée du batteur;

(e) *Br F* **a w. boy,** un malin, un débrouillard.

2 *adv* **(a)** loin; **far and w.,** de tous côtés, partout; **w. apart,** espacé; **with one's legs w. apart,** les jambes très écartées;

(b) *(ouvrir etc)* largement, grandement; **to fling the door open w.** *or* **w. open,** ouvrir la porte toute grande; **w.-open door,** porte toute grande ouverte; **to open one's eyes w.,** ouvrir les yeux tout grands; **to be w. awake,** être complètement *ou* bien éveillé; *Fig* *(of baby, child)* être éveillé; *(of adult)* avoir l'esprit vif; *Boxing* **to leave oneself w. open,** se découvrir; *Fig* **to leave oneself w. open to criticism,** prêter le flanc à *ou* s'exposer à la critique; **this town is w. open (to attack),** cette ville est très exposée (aux attaques); *Aut* **to take a bend w.,** prendre un virage large;

(c) *(tomber, tirer)* loin du but.

3 *n Cr* balle écartée *ou* qui passe hors de la portée du batteur.

wide-angle ['waɪdæŋg(ə)l] *adj Phot* **w.-a. lens,** objectif *m* grand angulaire.

wide-body ['waɪdbɒdɪ] *adj Av* **w.-b. plane,** avion *m* à fuselage élargi.

wide-eyed ['waɪdaɪd] *adj* les yeux grands ouverts, les yeux écarquillés; **he looked at me in w.-e. amazement,** il m'a regardé avec des yeux comme des soucoupes *ou* comme des portes cochères.

widely ['waɪdlɪ] *adv* **(a)** *(extensively)* largement; **w. read newspaper,** journal très lu *ou* à grande circulation; **w. known,** très connu, connu partout; **to be w. read,** *(of author)* avoir un public très étendu; *(of person)* avoir beaucoup lu; **she has travelled w.,** elle a beaucoup voyagé; **it is w. thought** *or* **believed that ...,** on pense généralement que ...; **(b)** *(at a distance)* *(planter)* à de grands intervalles; **(c)** *(very)* extrêmement, très; **w. different versions of what happened,** versions très différentes de ce qui est arrivé.

widen ['waɪd(ə)n] **1** *vt* **(a)** élargir; donner plus d'ampleur à *(un vêtement)*; **(b)** évaser *(un trou)*; **(c)** étendre *(l'influence, les limites de qch)*. **2** *vi* **(a)** s'élargir; *(of skirt)* s'évaser; **the breach is widening,** la rupture s'accentue; **(b)** *(of influence)* s'étendre.

►widen out *vi* *(of road, river, valley etc)* s'élargir.

wideness ['waɪdnɪs] *n* largeur *f*.

widening ['waɪd(ə)nɪŋ] *n* **(a)** élargissement *m*; **(b)** extension *f* *(d'une influence)*.

widespread ['waɪdspred] **(a)** *(plain, wings)* étendu; **(b)** *(extensive)* répandu; **w. opinion,** opinion largement répandue *ou* généralement admise; **w. damage,** des dégâts importants.

widgeon ['wɪdʒən] *n* *(bird)* canard siffleur.

widget ['wɪdʒɪt] *n Br F* truc *m*.

widow¹ ['wɪdəʊ] *n* veuve *f*; **she was left a w. at (the age of) thirty,** elle a été laissée veuve à l'âge de trente ans; **black w. (spider),** veuve noire; *Bible & Fig* **w.'s mite,** denier *m* de la veuve; **w.'s peak,** pointe *f* sur le front que forme la racine des cheveux; **w.'s pension,** pension *f* de veuve; **w.'s weeds,** deuil *m* de veuve.

widow² *vt* **to be widowed,** devenir veuf *ou* veuve.

widowed ['wɪdəʊd] *adj* *(homme)* veuf; *(femme)* veuve; **his w. mother,** sa mère qui est veuve; **w. life,** veuvage *m*.

widower ['wɪdəʊər] *n* veuf *m*.

widowhood ['wɪdəʊhʊd] *n* veuvage *m*.

width [wɪdθ] *n* **(a)** largeur *f* *(d'une route, de la poitrine)*; ampleur *f* *(d'un vêtement)*; grosseur *f* *(d'un pneu)*; **to be three metres in w.,** avoir trois mètres de large; **to swim six widths (of the pool),** nager six largeurs; **(b)** largeur *f* *(d'idées)*; **(c)** lé *m*, laize *f*, largeur *f* *(de tissu, de papier peint)*; **double w.,** grande largeur.

widthways ['wɪdθweɪz] , **widthwise** ['wɪdθwaɪz] *adv* dans la largeur.

wield [wi:ld] *vt* *(handle)* manier *(l'épée, la plume)*; *(brandish)* brandir *(une arme)*; *Fig* **to w. power,** exercer le pouvoir, avoir l'autorité; **she wields a lot of influence,** elle exerce beaucoup d'influence.

wiener ['wi:nər] *n Am* saucisse *f* de Frankfort; **w. roast,** barbecue *m* de saucisses de Frankfort.

Wiener ['vi:nər] *n Culin* **W. schnitzel,** escalope viennoise.

wife, *pl* **wives** [waɪf, waɪvz] *n* **(a)** femme *f* (mariée); *esp Admin* épouse *f*; **Mr Martin and his w.,** M. Martin et sa femme; **she was his second w.,** c'était sa deuxième femme; **the baker's/butcher's/grocer's w.,** *(who is also a baker, butcher, grocer)* la boulangère/la bouchère/l'épicière; *(who is not a baker, butcher, grocer)* la femme du boulanger/du boucher/de l'épicier; **his common-law w.,** sa concubine notoire; **battered wives,** femmes battues; *Br F* **the w.,** la bourgeoise; *Br F* **I'd better ask the w. if she wants to come,** je ferais mieux de demander à ma bourgeoise si elle veut venir; **w. swapping,** échangisme *m*; **w.-swapping party,** soirée *f* échangiste; **(b)** *Arch* femme *f*; *(gossip)* commère *f*; **old wives' remedy/tale,** remède *m*/conte *m* de bonne femme.

wifely ['waɪflɪ] *adj* de bonne épouse.

wig [wɪg] *n* *(full length)* perruque *f*; *(hair piece)* postiche *m*; *Br* *(for lawyers)* perruque *f*; **she's wearing a w.,** elle porte une perruque; **w. block** *or* **stand,** tête *f* à perruque, champignon *m*.

wigeon ['wɪdʒən] *n* *(bird)* canard siffleur.

wigged [wɪgd] *adj* *(juge etc)* à perruque.

wigging ['wɪgɪŋ] *n Old-fashioned F* verte semonce; **to give s.o. a good w.,** tancer vertement qn; **to get a good w.,** se faire laver la tête, se faire passer un savon.

wiggle¹ ['wɪg(ə)l] *n* tortillement *m* *(du corps etc)*; **to give sth a w.,** agiter *ou* remuer qch.

wiggle² **1** *vt* agiter, remuer *(qch)*; **to w. one's toes,** remuer ses orteils; **to w. one's hips,** tortiller les hanches; **to w. one's way out of a difficulty,** se tirer *ou* s'extraire d'une position difficile. **2** *vi* se remuer, se tortiller; (*of fish*) frétiller; **stop wiggling!**, arrête de te tortiller!; **to try to w. out of it**, chercher une échappatoire; **to w. out of a difficulty**, se tirer *ou* s'extraire d'une position difficile.

wiggly ['wɪglɪ] *adj F* qui se remue *ou* se tortille; **w. line**, trait ondulé.

wigmaker ['wɪgmeɪkər] *n* perruquier, -ière.

wigwam ['wɪgwæm] *n* wigwam *m*.

wilco ['wɪlkəʊ] *int esp Rad* (= **will comply**) j'exécute.

wild¹ [waɪld] **1** *adj* **(a)** (*animal, plant*) sauvage; **w. flowers**, fleurs *fpl* des champs *ou* sauvages; **w. country**, pays *m* inculte *ou* sauvage; *Fig* **w. horses wouldn't drag it out of me**, rien au monde ne me le ferait dire; *Fig* **to sow one's w. oats**, jeter sa gourme; **the W. West**, le Far West; **W. West show**, spectacle *m* ayant le Far West pour thème; **w. and woolly**, (*untamed*) frustre, rustre; (*not thought out*) irréfléchi; **w. dog**, (*dingo*) chien *m* sauvage; **w. man**, sauvage *m*; *Pol* extrémiste *m*; **w. rice**, riz *m* sauvage;

(b) (*wind*) furieux, violent; (*torrent*) impétueux; **w. sea**, mer agitée; **a w. (and stormy) night**, une nuit de tempête;

(c) (*shy*) (*animal*) farouche, inapprivoisé;

(d) (*unrestrained*) (*person*) dissipé, dissolu; (*adolescent*) indiscipliné; (*behaviour*) déréglé; (*idea*) fantasque; (*project*) insensé, extravagant; **I'm worried by all his w. talk**, tous ses propos irréfléchis m'inquiètent; **having so much money is beyond my wildest dreams**, même dans mes rêves les plus fous je n'aurais jamais espéré posséder autant d'argent; **to make a w. guess (at the answer)**, répondre à tout hasard *ou* à l'aveuglette; **to make a w. rush at sth**, se ruer sur qch; **w. applause**, applaudissements *mpl* frénétiques; **w. enthusiasm**, enthousiasme délirant *ou* débordant; **w. eyes**, yeux égarés; **w. with joy/ rage**, fou de joie/rage; **it makes me w. to think that ...**, j'enrage *ou* cela me met en rage quand je pense que ...; **to drive s.o. w.**, mettre qn en fureur; **w. rumour**, bruit extravagant *ou* sans fondation; **w. promises**, promesses extravagantes;

(e) *Cards* libre;

(f) *F* (*excited*) **to be w. about s.o./sth**, être emballé par qn/qch; **I'm not w. about it**, ça ne m'emballe pas.

2 *adv* **to grow w.**, (*of plant*) retourner *ou* pousser à l'état sauvage; **to run w.**, (*of children*) mener une vie sans discipline; (*of hooligans*) se livrer à des actes de violence; (*of escaped bull etc*) s'emballer; (*of garden*) devenir inculte.

3 *n* **in the w.**, (*of animal*) à l'état sauvage; **the call of the w.**, l'appel de la jungle; **in the wilds**, dans une région sauvage *ou* déserte; dans la brousse; **he lives in the wilds of Africa/Ealing**, il habite au fin fond de l'Afrique/d'Ealing.

wild² *vi Am Sl* = effectuer, en bande, des actes de violence extrême contre les personnes.

wildcard ['waɪldkɑːd] *adj Comptr* **w. character**, caractère *m* joker.

wildcat¹ ['waɪldkæt] *n* **(a)** chat *m* sauvage; *Fig* **she's a w.**, c'est une sauvageonne; *Am Fig* **w. scheme**, projet insensé *ou* extravagant; spéculation risquée; *Fig* **w. strike**, grève *f* sauvage; **(b)** *Am Petr* **w. (well)**, puits creusé dans un but d'exploration.

wildcat² *vi Am Petr* faire un forage d'exploration.

wildcatter ['waɪldkætər] *n Am Petr* (*company*) entrepreneur *m* de forage d'exploration; (*driller*) ouvrier *m* qui effectue des forages d'exploration.

wildebeest ['wɪldɪbiːst, 'vɪl-] *n* (*animal*) gnou *m*.

wilder ['waɪldər] *n Am Sl* = membre d'une bande de jeunes voyous effectuant des actes de violence extrême contre les personnes.

wilderness ['wɪldənɪs] *n* **(a)** désert *m*; **a voice in the w.**, *Bible* **the voice of one crying in the w.**, une voix qui prêche dans le désert; *Fig* **to be in the w.**, (*of politician, party*) faire une traversée du désert; *Fig* **she spent six months in the w.**, sa traversée du désert a duré six mois; **(b)** friche *f*, partie inculte *ou* laissée à l'état sauvage (*d'un jardin*); **the garden is turning into a w.**, le jardin est en train de se transformer en jungle.

wildfire ['waɪldfaɪər] *n* **to spread like w.**, (*of report etc*) se répandre comme une traînée de poudre; (*of disease*) se propager très rapidement.

wildfowl ['waɪldfaʊl] *n* gibier *m* d'eau, sauvagine *f*.

wildfowler ['waɪldfaʊlər] *n* chasseur *m* au *ou* de gibier d'eau, chasseur à la sauvagine.

wildfowling ['waɪldfaʊlɪŋ] *n* chasse *f* au gibier d'eau *ou* à la sauvagine.

wild-goose [waɪld'guːs] *adj* **w.-g. chase**, fausse piste; **to go on a w.-g. chase**, faire fausse piste; **to send s.o. on a w.-g. chase**, mettre qn sur une fausse piste.

wilding ['waɪldɪŋ] *n Am Sl* = actes de violence extrême effectués par une bande de voyous contre les personnes.

wildlife ['waɪldlaɪf] *n* faune *f* (et flore *f*); *esp Br* **w. park**, parc naturel; **w. sanctuary**, réserve naturelle.

wildly ['waɪldlɪ] *adv* **(a)** (*écrire, parler*) d'une manière extravagante; **to talk w.**, dire des folies; **to rush about w.**, courir çà et là comme un fou; **w. happy**, follement heureux; **to be w. excited**, être dans les nues; *F* **I'm not w. enthusiastic about it**, ça ne m'emballe pas; **(b)** (*vivre, se comporter*) d'une manière déréglée; (*répondre*) au hasard, au petit bonheur; **to hit out w.**, lancer des coups au hasard.

wildness ['waɪldnɪs] *n* **(a)** état *m* sauvage (*d'un pays, d'un animal*); état inculte (*d'une région*); **(b)** fureur *f*, impétuosité *f* (*du vent, des vagues*); déchaînement *m* (*de la tempête*); **(c)** nature *f* farouche (*du gibier*); **(d)** dérèglement *m* (*de mœurs*); égarements *mpl* (*de conduite*); **(e)** frénésie *f* (*d'applaudissements*); extravagance *f* (*d'idées, de paroles*).

wile [waɪl] *n* (*usu pl*) **wiles**, ruse *f*, artifice *m*; **to fall a victim to s.o.'s wiles**, succomber aux séductions de qn.

wilful, *US* **willful** ['wɪlfʊl] *adj* **(a)** (*person*) obstiné, entêté, volontaire; **(b)** (*action*) intentionnel, de propos délibéré, à dessein, fait exprès; *Jur* **w. murder**, homicide volontaire *ou* prémédité; **w. damage**, bris *m*, dommage délibéré; **with w. intent**, délibérément.

wilfully, *US* **willfully** ['wɪlfəlɪ] *adv* (*see adj*) **(a)** obstinément, avec entêtement; **(b)** exprès, à dessein; **are you being w. obtuse?**, est-ce que tu fais exprès de faire l'idiot?

wilfulness, *US* **willfulness** ['wɪlfʊlnɪs] *n* **(a)** (*of person*) obstination *f*, entêtement *m*; **(b)** (*of action*) préméditation *f*.

wiliness ['waɪlɪnɪs] *n* astuce *f*, caractère rusé.

will¹ [wɪl] *n* **(a)** (*intention*) volonté *f*; **to have a strong/ weak w.**, avoir beaucoup/peu de volonté; **w. of iron, iron w.**, volonté de fer; **he has a w. of his own**, il sait ce qu'il veut, il est volontaire; **strength of w.**, force *f* de volonté; **the w. to live**, la volonté de vivre; *Prov* **where there's a w. there's a way**, vouloir c'est pouvoir; **with the best w. in the world**, avec la meilleure volonté du monde; **to work with a w.**, travailler de bonne volonté *ou* de bon cœur; **to show good w.**, faire preuve de bonne volonté;

(b) (*desire, wish*) volonté *f*, désir *m*; *Bible* **Thy w. be done**, que ta volonté soit faite; **to impose one's w. on s.o.**, imposer sa volonté à qn; **at w.**, (*to choose, fire*) à volonté; (*to depart etc*) quand on veut; **free w.**, libre arbitre *m*; **to do sth of one's own free w.**, faire qch de son plein gré; **to do sth against one's w.**, faire qch contre son gré *ou* à contrecœur; **good/ill w.**, bienveillance *f*/ malveillance *f*; **I bear her no ill w.**, (*have no wish for revenge*) je ne lui en veux pas; (*do not dislike her*) je ne lui veux aucun mal;

(c) *Jur* testament *m*; **the last w. and testament of ...**, les dernières volontés de ..., **to make one's w.**, faire son testament; **to mention s.o. in one's w.**, mettre *ou* coucher qn sur son testament.

will² *vt* **(-ll-)** **(a)** **to w. s.o. to do** *or* **into doing sth**, faire faire qch à qn par un acte de volonté *ou* en lui imposant sa volonté; (*by hypnotism*) suggestionner qn; **I willed him to agree**, je l'ai supplié intérieurement d'accepter; **she willed her child to live**, elle a espéré de toutes ses forces que son enfant vivrait; **to w. oneself to do sth**, faire un effort de volonté pour faire qch; *Arch & Lit* **God so willed it**, Dieu l'a voulu ainsi; **(b)** *Jur* léguer (*qch*), disposer de (*qch*) par testament.

will³ *modal aux v* (*I* **will**, *you he we etc* **will**; *Arch thou* **wilt**; *pt & cond* **would** [wʊd]; *I will, he will etc are often contracted into* **I'll** [aɪl], **he'll** [hiːl] *etc*; *I would, they would etc to* **I'd** [aɪd], **they'd** [ðeɪd] *etc; will not and would not to* **won't** [wəʊnt], **wouldn't** ['wʊd(ə)nt])

(a) (*expressing future*) **I'll do it tomorrow**, je le ferai demain; **he won't do it again**, il ne le fera plus; **w. he be there? — he w.**, y sera-t-il? – oui(, il y sera); **no, he won't**, non(, il n'y sera pas); **but I shall starve! — no you won't**, mais je mourrai de faim! – mais non!; **you won't forget, w. you?**, vous n'oublierez pas, hein?; **you'll write to me, won't you?**, vous m'écrirez, n'est-ce pas?; **she told me she would be there**, elle m'a dit qu'elle serait là; **we w. be there**, nous serons là; **Mr Long w. explain the situation to you**, (*immediate future*) M. Long va vous expliquer la situation;

(b) (*consent*) **I w. not do it**, je refuse de le faire; **I w. not have that said of me**, je ne veux pas qu'on dise cela de moi; **I wouldn't do it for anything**, je ne le ferais pour rien au monde; *F* **w. do!**, d'accord!; **the wound wouldn't heal**, la blessure ne voulait pas se cicatriser; **the engine**

won't start, le moteur ne veut pas démarrer; **it won't open,** ça ne s'ouvre pas, ça ne veut pas s'ouvrir; **just wait a moment, w. you?,** pouvez-vous attendre un instant?; (*emphatic*) voulez-vous bien attendre un instant?; **would you pass the mustard please?,** voudriez-vous bien me passer la moutarde?; **won't you sit down?,** asseyez-vous, je vous en prie;

(c) (*emphatic*) **accidents WILL happen,** on ne peut pas éviter les accidents; **she WILL go out in spite of her cold,** elle persiste à sortir malgré son rhume; **he WILL get in my way,** il est toujours dans mon chemin; **the doctor WILL have his little joke,** il aime (à) plaisanter, le docteur; **I quite forgot! — you WOULD!,** j'ai oublié! — c'est bien de vous!, ça ne m'étonne pas de vous!; **you WOULD insist on going,** évidemment, il a fallu que tu insistes pour y aller; *F* **I wouldn't know,** je ne saurais dire; **I W. NOT have it!,** je ne permettrai pas cela!; **WILL you be quiet!,** voulez-vous bien vous taire!;

(d) (*habit*) **this hen w. lay up to six eggs a week,** cette poule pond jusqu'à six œufs par semaine; **she would often return home exhausted,** elle rentrait souvent très fatigué;

(e) (*conjecture*) **that would be your cousin?,** ça c'est sans doute votre cousin?; **you'll be tired,** vous devez être fatigué;

(f) (*wish*) vouloir; **do as you w.,** faites comme vous voudrez; **what would you have me do?,** que voulez-vous que je fasse?; **say what you w., you won't be believed,** quoi que vous disiez, on ne vous croira pas; **he would if he could,** il le ferait s'il le pouvait; *Lit* **would (that) I were a bird!,** je voudrais être un oiseau!; **would to God it wasn't true!,** plût à Dieu que cela ne fût pas vrai!;

(g) (*injunction*) **you'll be here at three,** soyez ici à trois heures;

(h) (*conditional*) **she would come if you invited her,** elle viendrait si vous l'invitiez; **had he** *or* **if he had let go he would have fallen,** s'il avait lâché prise il serait tombé.

William ['wɪljəm] *m* Guillaume *m*; **W. the Conqueror,** Guillaume le Conquérant; **W. pear,** poire *f* Williams.

willie ['wɪlɪ] *n Br F* (*penis*) zizi *m*.

willies ['wɪlɪz] *npl F* **to have the w.,** avoir le trac *ou* la frousse; **this place gives me the w.,** cet endroit me fiche la frousse; **I had a bad case of the w.,** j'avais une frousse incroyable.

willing ['wɪlɪŋ] *adj* **(a)** (*compliant*) de bonne volonté, bien disposé; **w. men,** hommes *mpl* de bonne volonté; **w. hands,** mains empressées; *Fig* **w. horse,** bonne poire; **(b)** (*ready*) **to be w. to do sth,** bien vouloir faire qch, être disposé à faire qch; **w. to help,** prêt à rendre service, serviable; **I am more than w. to come with you,** je ne demande pas mieux que de vous accompagner; **I am able and w. to help them,** je peux les aider et je le ferai très volontiers; **w. or not,** bon gré mal gré; **God w.,** s'il plaît à Dieu; *F* **to show w.,** faire preuve de bonne volonté.

willingly ['wɪlɪŋlɪ] *adv* **(a)** (*volontarily*) volontairement, de plein gré; **(b)** (*with pleasure*) de bonne volonté, de bon cœur, volontiers, avec plaisir.

willingness ['wɪlɪŋnɪs] *n* **(a)** (*compliance*) bonne volonté; **with the utmost w.,** de très bon cœur; **(b)** (*readiness*) consentement *m*; **to express one's w. to do sth,** accepter de faire qch, consentir à faire qch; **his** *or* **her w. to do sth,** son empressement à faire qch.

will-o'the-wisp [wɪləðə'wɪsp] *n* feu follet.

willow ['wɪləʊ] *n* **(a) w. (tree),** saule *m*; **w. pattern plate,** assiette à décoration à la chinoise en teinte bleue *ou* à motif de saule pleureur; **(b)** *Old-fashioned Cr F* **the w.,** la batte.

willowy ['wɪləʊɪ] *adj* souple, svelte, élancé.

willpower ['wɪlpaʊər] *n* volonté *f*; **lack of w.,** manque *m* de volonté.

willy-nilly ['wɪlɪ'nɪlɪ] *adv* **(a)** (*without order, randomly etc*) n'importe comment; **the editor just altered a few words w.-n.,** le rédacteur a simplement changé quelques mots au hasard; **(b)** (*willingly or not*) bon gré mal gré.

wilt¹ [wɪlt] **1** *vi* **(a)** (*of plant*) se flétrir, se faner; **(b)** *Fig* (*with heat, fatigue*) dépérir, languir; perdre contenance (*devant des reproches*); (*lose courage*) se dégonfler. **2** *vt* (*of heat*) flétrir (*les fleurs*).

wilt² *see* **WILL³**.

Wilts *abbr* **Wiltshire**.

wily ['waɪlɪ] *adj* rusé, astucieux, malin, -igne, roublard; **he's a w. old bird,** c'est un vieux roublard.

wimp [wɪmp] *n Br F* poule mouillée.

wimpish ['wɪmpɪʃ] *Br F* (*behaviour, attitude*) de poule mouillée.

wimple ['wɪmp(ə)l] *n* guimpe *f* (*de religieuse*).

win¹ [wɪn] *n Sp* victoire *f*; **to have three wins in succession,** emporter trois victoires consécutives, **to back a horse for a w.,** jouer un cheval gagnant.

win² *v* (*pt & pp* **won** [wʌn]; *prp* **winning**) **1** *vt* **(a)** (*be successful in*) gagner (*une bataille, une course, un pari*); (*obtain*) remporter, gagner (*un prix*); **to w. money from s.o.,** gagner de l'argent à qn; **the Greens have won ten seats,** les verts ont gagné dix sièges; **they won the seat from Labour,** ils ont gagné le siège précédemment détenu par les travaillistes; **to w. an argument,** avoir le dessus dans une dispute; *F* **you can't w. them all,** on ne peut pas plaire à tout le monde;

(b) (*acquire*) acquérir (*de la popularité, la bienveillance de qn*); captiver (*l'attention de qn*); gagner (*la confiance de qn*); **to w. s.o.'s love,** se faire aimer de qn; **to w. all hearts,** gagner *ou* conquérir tous les cœurs; **to w. recognition,** parvenir à être reconnu; **you've just won yourself a friend,** tu viens juste de te faire un ami; **to w. s.o. away from sth,** détourner *ou* détacher qn de qch; **she won her way to the top of her profession,** elle a réussi à atteindre le sommet de sa profession.

2 *vi* gagner; *Sp* **to w. by a length,** gagner d'une longueur; **to back a horse to w.,** jouer un cheval gagnant; *F* **you (just) can't w.,** j'aurai *ou* on aura toujours tort; *F* **to w. hands down,** gagner les doigts dans le nez; **w. or lose, I'm sure I'll enjoy this match,** que je gagne ou que je perde je suis certain que je vais m'amuser pendant ce match.

▶**win back** *vtsep* (*territory, championship*) reprendre (**from,** à), reconquérir (**from,** sur); (*esteem, friendship*) reconquérir; (*money*) recouvrer.

▶**win out** = **WIN THROUGH**.

▶**win over, win round** *vtsep* **see whether you can w. him over,** essayez de le persuader de se mettre avec nous; **I won him round to my point of view,** j'ai réussi à le gagner à mon point de vue.

▶**win through** *vi* y arriver, réussir.

wince¹ [wɪns] *n* crispation *f* (*de douleur etc*).

wince² *vi* faire une grimace de douleur; **the remark made him w.,** à cette observation il s'est crispé.

winceyette [wɪnsɪ'et] *n Br Tex* flanelle *f* de coton, flanellette *f*, pilou *m*; **w. sheet,** drap *m* en flanelle de coton.

winch [wɪntʃ] *n* **(a)** (*crank*) manivelle *f*; **(b)** treuil *m* (*de hissage*).

▶**winch in** *vtsep* amener *ou* rentrer (*qch*) à l'aide d'un treuil.

▶**winch up** *vtsep* soulever *ou* hisser *ou* monter (*qch, qn*) à l'aide d'un treuil; **the crew was winched up by helicopter,** l'équipage a été hissé à l'aide d'un hélicoptère.

wind¹ [wɪnd] *n* **(a)** (*air*) vent *m*; **there's quite a w.,** il fait beaucoup de vent; **house exposed to all the winds,** maison exposée à tous les vents; *Fig* **my friends are all scattered to the four winds,** mes amis sont dispersés aux quatre coins du monde; *Fig* **to throw caution to the w.,** oublier toute prudence; *Fig* **to see** *or* **find out which way the w. blows,** voir de quel côté vient le vent; *Fig* **there's something in the w.,** il se prépare *ou* se mijote quelque chose; *Fig* **to go like the w.,** aller comme le vent; **to sow the w. and reap the whirlwind,** semer le vent et récolter la tempête; *Old-fashioned F* **to raise the w.,** rassembler des fonds; *F* **to have** *or* **get the w. up,** avoir le trac *ou* la frousse; (*stronger*) avoir une peur bleue; *F* **to put the w. up s.o.,** faire une peur bleue à qn; **head w.,** vent debout; **following w.,** vent arrière; *Nau* vent de poupe; *Nau* **to sail against the w.,** avoir le vent droit debout; *Nau* **to sail** *or* **run before the w.,** courir vent arrière; *Nau* **to sail with w. and tide,** avoir vent et marée; **in the teeth of the w.,** contre le vent; **to sail into the w.,** venir *ou* aller au lof; *Fig* **to sail close to the w.,** (*when telling joke*) friser l'indécence; (*in business dealings*) friser la malhonnêteté; *Fig* **to take the w. out of s.o.'s sails,** déjouer les projets de qn, couper l'herbe sous le pied à qn; **w. chimes,** carillon éolien; **w. energy** *or* **power,** energie éolienne; **w. gauge,** anémomètre *m*; *Av* **w. indicator,** indicateur *m* de direction du vent; *Th Cin* **w. machine,** machine *f* à faire le vent; *Av* **w. sleeve,** manche *f* à air, *F* biroute *f*;

(b) (*scent*) vent *m*; *Fig* **to get w. of sth,** avoir vent de qch;

(c) *Med* (*flatulence*) vent(s) *m(pl)*, flatuosité *f*; **to break** *or* **pass w.,** (*upwards*) roter; (*downwards*) péter; **to have w.,** avoir des gaz; **beans give you w.,** les haricots donnent des gaz; **the baby's got w.,** le bébé n'a pas fait son rot; **to get the baby's w. up,** faire faire son rot au bébé; *F* **to be full of w.,** (*useless talk*) parler à tort et à travers *ou* pour ne rien dire; (*boastful talk*) être vantard;

(d) (*breath*) souffle *m*, respiration *f*; **to get one's second w.,** trouver son deuxième souffle; **let me get my w.,** laissez-moi souffler *ou* reprendre haleine;

(e) *Mus* **w. instrument,** instrument *m* à vent; **the w.,** (*in orchestra*) les instruments à vent; **w. ensemble,** ensemble *m* d'instruments à vent;

(f) *Ind* vent *m*; air *m ou* vent de soufflerie; *Mus* **w. chest,** laie *f*, sommier *m* (*d'un orgue*); **w. tunnel,** soufflerie *f*, tunnel *m* aérodynamique.

wind² *vt* **(a)** couper la respiration *ou* le souffle à (*qn*); essouffler (*qn, un cheval*); **(b)** (*of hounds*) avoir vent de.

wind³ [waɪnd] *vt* (*pt & pp* **winded** ['waɪndɪd] *or* **wound** [waʊnd]) **to w. the horn,** sonner du cor *ou* de la trompe.

wind⁴ *n* **to give the clock a w.,** remonter la pendule.

wind⁵ *v* (*pt & pp* **wound** [waʊnd]) **1** *vi* tourner; (*of path, river*) serpenter; (*of staircase*) monter ne colimaçon; **the road winds up/down the hill,** le chemin monte/descend en serpentant. **2** *vt* **(a)** enrouler; *Tex* dévider (*le fil, la soie*); **to w. wool into a ball,** enrouler de la laine en pelote; **to w. cotton on a reel,** bobiner du coton; **to w. in the line,** ramener la ligne; **to w. a bobbin,** enrouler le fil sur une bobine; *El* **to w. a dynamo,** armer une dynamo; **(b)** remonter (*l'horloge*); **(c)** tourner (*une manivelle*).

▶**wind down 1** *vtsep* **(a)** (*car window*) baisser; **(b)** *F* réduire graduellement; **the company has decided to w. down its operations in France,** la société a décidé de réduire progressivement ses activités en France. **2** *vi* **(a)** (*of party, meeting etc*) tirer à sa fin; **(b)** (*relax*) décompresser, se détendre; **I'm taking a bath to w. down,** je prends un bain pour décompresser.

▶**wind round 1** *vtaspo* **to w. scarf round one's neck,** enrouler une écharpe autour de son cou; **she would her arms round the child,** elle a entouré l'enfant de ses bras. **2** *vipo* (*of thread*) s'enrouler autour de (*qch*).

▶**wind up 1** *vtsep* **(a)** (*car window*) remonter;

(b) enrouler (*un cordage etc*);

(c) remonter (*une horloge*); bander (*un ressort*); *Fig* **to be all wound up,** (*of person*) être excité *ou* énervé;

(d) *F* finir, terminer (*qch*); *Com* liquider (*une société*); régler, clôturer (*un compte*); **she wound up her speech by announcing that ...,** elle a terminé son discours en faisant savoir que ...;

(e) *Br F* faire marcher (*qn*), mettre (*qn*) en boîte; **he really wound her up with those remarks about her dress,** il l'a vraiment mise en boîte avec ses remarques à propos de sa robe; **don't you know when you're being wound up?,** tu ne te rends même pas compte quand on te fait marcher?

2 *vi F* **(a)** (*end speech etc*) conclure;

(b) (*end up*) **he'll w. up in prison,** il finira en prison; **we usually w. up back at my place,** généralement nous finissons chez moi; **we wound up working for the same company,** nous nous sommes retrouvés à travailler pour la même compagnie.

windbag ['wɪndbæg] *n F* moulin *m* à paroles; **what a w.!,** quel bavard!

windblown ['wɪndbləʊn] *adj* **w. hair,** cheveux ébouriffés par le vent.

wind-borne ['wɪndbɔːn] *adj* porté par le vent.

windbreak ['wɪndbreɪk] *n* **(a)** (*in garden, for beach etc*) brise-vent *m inv*; **(b)** (*damage to tree*) volis *m*.

windcheater ['wɪndtʃiːtər] *n* (*jacket*) blouson *m*; *Can* coupe-vent *m inv*.

wind-chill ['wɪndtʃɪl] *adj* **w.-c. factor,** facteur d'abaissement de la température provoqué par le vent.

winded ['wɪndɪd] *adj* hors d'haleine, essoufflé.

winder ['waɪndər] *n* **(a)** (*device*) *Tex* bobinoir *m*, dévidoir *m*; remontoir *m* (*d'une horloge, d'une montre*); **(b)** *Aut* lève-glace(s) *m inv* (*de portière*); **(c)** (*person*) *Tex* bobineur, -euse, dévideur, -euse; remonteur, -euse (*d'horloges*).

windfall ['wɪndfɔːl] *n* **(a)** (*in garden, orchard etc*) fruit abattu par le vent, fruit tombé; **(b)** *Fig* aubaine *f*, bonne fortune; (*legacy*) héritage inattendu; **I've had a bit of a w. from my aunt,** j'ai eu la chance d'hériter d'un peu d'argent de ma tante; **w. profits,** (*of company*) bénéfices inattendus.

winding ['waɪndɪŋ] **1** *adj* (*chemin, cours d'eau*) sinueux, qui serpente; (*chemin*) anfractueux; (*route*) en lacets; **w. streets,** rues tortueuses; **w. staircase,** escalier tournant *ou* en vis *ou* en colimaçon. **2** *n* **(a)** mouvement sinueux; cours sinueux, serpentement *m*; **windings,** replis *mpl* (*d'une rivière*); **(b)** *Tex* bobinage *m*, embobinage *m*; *El* enroulement *m*, bobinage; *Arch* **w. sheet,** linceul *m*, suaire *m*; **(c)** *Min* remonte *f*, remontée *f*; **w. gear,** treuil *m* (*d'un ascenseur*); *Min* appareils *mpl ou* machine *f* d'extraction; **(d)** remontage *m* (*d'une horloge, d'une montre*); bandage *m* (*d'un ressort*); **(e) windings,** méandres *mpl* (*d'une rivière*); zigzags *mpl* (*d'une route*); **(f)** enroulement *m* (*d'une bobine etc*); *El* **armature w.,** enroulement d'induit.

winding-up ['waɪndɪŋ'ʌp] *n* (*of business etc*) liquidation *f*, dissolution *f*; (*of speech*) fin *f*, conclusion *f*; (*of account*) clôture *f*.

windjammer ['wɪnd'dʒæmər] *n Nau* grand voilier.

windlass ['wɪndləs] *n* treuil *m*; *Nau* guindeau *m*.

windmill ['wɪndmɪl] *n* moulin *m* à vent; **to tilt at windmills,** se battre contre des moulins à vent.

window ['wɪndəʊ] *n* **(a)** fenêtre *f*; **to look in at/out of the w.,** regarder par/à la fenêtre; **to break a w.,** casser une vitre *ou* un carreau; *F* **to throw money out of the w.,** jeter l'argent par les fenêtres; *F* **that's my holiday out of the w.,** voilà mes vacances de fichues en l'air; *Fig* **a w. on sth,** un aperçu de qch; **w. of opportunity,** ouverture *f*; **bay w.,** fenêtre en saillie; *Rel Arch* **stained glass w.,** vitrail *m*, -aux; **w. box,** (*for flowers*) jardinière *f*; **w. cleaner,** (*person*) laveur *m* de vitres *ou* de carreaux; (*product*) produit *m* pour nettoyer les vitres; **w. frame,** formant *m* de fenêtre; (*around glass*) châssis *m* de fenêtre; **w. ledge,** (*outside*) rebord *m* de fenêtre; (*inside*) appui *m ou* tablette *f* de fenêtre; **w. seat,** (*in house*) banquette située dans l'embrasure d'une fenêtre; (*in aircraft*) place *f* côté hublot;

(b) *Comptr* fenêtre *f*;

(c) (*of ticket office*) guichet *m*;

(d) (*of shop*) vitrine *f*, devanture *f*; **w. display,** étalage *m*;

(e) *Aut Rail* vitre *f*, glace *f*;

(f) (*on envelope*) fenêtre *f*, panneau transparent;

(g) *Anat* fenêtre *f* (*du tympan*).

window-dresser ['wɪndəʊdresər] *n* étalagiste *mf*.

window-dressing ['wɪndəʊdresɪŋ] *n* (l'art *m* de l') étalage *m*; *Fig* façade *f*, décor *m* de théâtre, camouflage *m*; **it's just w.-d.,** ce n'est qu'une façade.

windowing ['wɪndəʊɪŋ] *n Comptr* fenêtrage *m*.

windowless ['wɪndəʊlɪs] *n* sans fenêtres.

windowpane ['wɪndəʊpeɪn] *n* vitre *f*, carreau *m*.

window-shop ['wɪndəʊʃɒp] *vi* faire du lèche-vitrines; **to w.-s. for a coat,** faire du lèche-vitrines pour trouver un manteau.

window-shopper ['wɪndəʊʃɒpər] *n* personne qui fait du lèche-vitrines; **the streets were full of w.-shoppers,** les rues étaient pleines de gens en train de faire du lèche-vitrines.

window-shopping ['wɪndəʊʃɒpɪŋ] *n* lèche-vitrines *m*; **to go w.-s.,** faire du lèche-vitrines.

windowsill ['wɪndəʊsɪl] *n* (*outside*) rebord *m* de fenêtre; (*inside*) appui *m ou* tablette *f* de fenêtre.

windpipe ['wɪndpaɪp] *n Anat* trachée *f*.

wind-pollinated ['wɪnd'pɒlɪneɪtɪd] *adj* (*flower etc*) pollinisé par le vent.

wind-pollination ['wɪndpɒlɪ'neɪʃən] *n* pollinisation *f* par le vent.

windscreen ['wɪndskriːn] *n* **(a)** *Br Aut* parebrise *m inv*; **w. wiper,** essuie-glace *m*, *pl* essuie-glaces; **w. washer,** lave-glace *m*, *pl* lave-glaces; **(b)** (*on chimney etc*) abat-vent *m inv*; (*to protect crop*) abrivent *m*, brise-vent *m inv*.

windshield ['wɪndʃiːld] *n Am* = **WINDSCREEN (a)**.

windsnap ['wɪndsnæp] *n* (*damage to tree*) volis *m*.

windsock ['wɪndsɒk] *n Av* manche *f* à air, *F* biroute *f*.

windstorm ['wɪndstɔːm] *n* tempête *f* de vent.

windsurf ['wɪndsɜːf] *vi* faire de la planche à voile.

windsurfer ['wɪndsɜːfər] *n Sp* **(a)** (*board*) planche *f* à voile; **(b)** (*person*) véliplanchiste *mf*.

windsurfing ['wɪndsɜːfɪŋ] *n* **to go w.,** faire de la planche à voile.

windswept ['wɪndswept] *adj* balayé par le vent; **w. hair,** cheveux ébouriffés.

wind-up ['waɪndʌp] *n Br F* mise *f* en boîte; **it was just another of her w.-ups,** c'était encore une de ses mises en boîte; **he's a real w.-up artist,** c'est un vrai spécialiste de la mise en boîte.

windward ['wɪndwəd] **1** *adj* au vent; **the W. Islands,** les îles *fpl* du Vent. **2** *n* côté *m* au vent; **lying to (the) w. of ...,** situé au vent de ... .

windy¹ ['wɪndɪ] *adj* **(a)** (*journée*) de grand vent; **it's very w.,** il fait beaucoup de vent; **(b)** (*place*) venteux, balayé par le vent; exposé au vent *ou* aux quatre vents; **(c)** *Old-fashioned Br F* **to be w.,** avoir le trac *ou* la frousse.

windy² ['waɪndɪ] *adj* (*road etc*) sinueux.

wine¹ [waɪn] *n* **(a)** vin *m*; **wines and spirits,** (*shop sign*) vins et spiritueux; **w. producing district,** pays *m* vinicole *ou* de vignobles; **w. bar,** bar *m* à vin; **w. box,** cubitainer *m* de vin; **w. bottle,** bouteille *f* à vin; **w. cellar,** cave *f* (à vin); **w. cooler,** rafraîchissoir *m*, rafraîchisseur *m* (à vin); **w. list,** (*in restaurant*) carte *f* des vins; **w. merchant,** négociant *m* en vins, marchand *m* de vins; **w. tasting,** dégustation *f*; **I'm going to a w. tasting,** je vais à une dégustation de vins; **w. vinegar,** vinaigre *m* de vin; **w. waiter,** sommelier, -ière; **(b)** (*colour*) lie *f* de vin *inv*.

wine² *vt* **to w. and dine s.o.,** fêter qn.

wine-coloured ['waɪnkʌləd] *adj* lie de vin *inv*.

wineglass ['waɪnglɑːs] *n* verre *m* à vin.

winepress ['waɪnpres] *n* pressoir *m*.

wing¹ [wɪŋ] *n* **(a)** aile *f* (*d'oiseau, d'insecte, d'avion*); *Fig* **to take s.o. under one's w.,** prendre qn sous son aile *ou* sous sa protection; *Lit* **fear lent him wings,** la peur lui donnait des ailes; **to shoot a bird on the w.,** tirer un oiseau au vol *ou* à la volée; **to be on the w.,** (*of bird*) voler; **to take w.,** s'envoler, prendre son vol *ou* son essor; *Fig* **to spread** *or* **stretch one's wings,** élargir son horizon; *Mil Av* **wings,** insigne *m* de pilote; **w. flap,** (*of plane*) volet *m* (d'aile);

(b) battant *m* (*d'une porte*); aile *f* (*d'un bâtiment*); pavillon *m* (*d'un hôpital*); *Th* **the wings,** la coulisse, les coulisses; **to be standing** *or* **waiting in the wings,** *Th* attendre dans les coulisses *ou* la coulisse; *Fig* rester dans les coulisses *ou* la coulisse;

(c) *Mil* aile *f*, flanc *m* (*d'une armée*); *Sp* aile; (*player*) ailier *m*; **the w. halves,** les demis *mpl* aile; *Rugby* **w. forward,** avant-aile *m*, *pl* avant-ailes; *Rugby* **w. three-quarter,** trois-quarts *m inv* aile; **she plays on the w.,** elle est ailier; *Pol* **the left w. (of the party),** l'aile gauche (du parti);

(d) aile *f* (*d'un moulin à vent, d'une selle*); oreille *f*, ailette *f* (*d'une vis*); **w. bolt/screw,** boulon *m*/vis *f* à oreilles; **w. chair,** fauteuil *m* à oreillettes;

(e) *Br* aile *f* (*d'une voiture*); **w. mirror,** rétroviseur *m* de côté;

(f) *Mil Av* escadre aérienne; *US* brigade aérienne; *Br* **w. commander,** (*Am* = **lieutenant colonel**) lieutenant-colonel *m* (de l'armée de l'air).

wing² *vt* **(a)** (*injure*) frapper, blesser (*un oiseau*) à l'aile; **I've winged him,** je lui ai mis du plomb dans l'aile; **(b)** *esp Am* **to w. it,** improviser; **(c) to w. its way,** (*of bird*) voler; **(d)** (*attach wings to*) empenner (*une flèche*).

winged [wɪŋd, *Lit often* 'wɪŋɪd] *adj* ailé; **w. game,** gibier *m* à plumes.

-winged [wɪŋd] *suff* **red/white/*etc*-w.,** aux ailes rouges/blanches/*etc*.

wingding ['wɪŋdɪŋ] *n US F* **w. (party),** soirée *f*, fête *f*, surprise-partie *f*.

winger ['wɪŋər] *n Fb etc* ailier *m*.

wingless ['wɪŋlɪs] *adj* sans ailes, aptère.

wingspan ['wɪŋspæn] , **wingspread** ['wɪŋspred] *n* (*of bird, plane*) envergure *f*; **the eagle has a w. of two metres,** l'aigle a une envergure de deux mètres.

wink¹ [wɪŋk] *n* clignement *m* d'œil, clin *m* d'œil; **to give s.o. a w.,** faire un clin d'œil à qn; **with a w.,** en clignant de l'œil; *Fig* **to tip s.o. the w.,** prévenir *ou* avertir qn (**about,** de); **to have forty winks,** faire un petit somme *ou* une petite sieste; **I didn't sleep a w.** *or* **didn't get a w. of sleep all night,** je n'ai pas fermé l'œil *ou* dormi de toute la nuit; **a nod's as good as a w. to him,** il comprend à demi-mot.

wink² **1** *vi* cligner de l'œil *ou* des yeux; (*of star, light*) clignoter. **2** *vt* **she winked an eye,** elle a cligné de l'œil.

►**wink at** *vipo* faire *ou* lancer un clin d'œil à (*qn*); *Fig* **to w. at an abuse,** fermer les yeux sur un abus.

►**wink away** *vtsep* cligner des yeux pour chasser (*une larme, une poussière*).

winker ['wɪŋkər] *n Aut F* clignotant *m*.

winking ['wɪŋkɪŋ] **1** *adj* (*light*) clignotant. **2** *n* **(a)** clignement *m* de l'œil; *Fig* **as easy as w.,** simple comme bonjour; **(b)** clignotement *m* (*d'une lumière*).

winkle ['wɪŋk(ə)l] *n* **(a)** (*mollusc*) bigorneau *m*; **(b)** *Br F* **w. pickers,** chaussures *fpl* à bout pointu.

►**winkle out** *vtsep F* **(a)** extraire (*qch*); **I finally winkled the information out of him,** j'ai fini par lui tirer les vers du nez; **it's no good trying to w. any money out of me,** ce n'est pas la peine d'essayer de me soutirer de l'argent; **(b)** déloger (*qn*); **go and w. them out of the pub,** va les déloger du pub.

winner ['wɪnər] *n* **(a)** vainqueur *m*, gagnant, -ante; *Horse-racing* (cheval *m*) gagnant; **the w. of the big prize,** (*in lottery*) le gagnant du gros lot; **to back a w.,** *Horseracing* jouer un cheval gagnant; *Fig* jouer gagnant, bien miser; **every time a w.!,** (*at fair*) à tous les coups l'on gagne!; **(b)** *Fig* roman *m ou* pièce *f* à grand succès; **this book will be a w.,** ce livre a un succès assuré.

winning ['wɪnɪŋ] **1** *adj* **(a)** (*victorious*) gagnant; **w. number,** (*in lottery*) numéro gagnant *ou* sortant; **w. post,** poteau *m* d'arrivée; **he was first past the w. post,** il était le premier à atteindre le poteau d'arrivée; **the w. side,** les vainqueurs; *Sp* **w. streak,** série *f* de victoires; **to be on a w. streak,** (*gambling*) être dans une série gagnante; **(b)** (*attractive*) attrayant, séduisant; (*sourire*) engageant; **that child has a w. way with her,** cette enfant a des manières engageantes. **2** *n* **(a)** acquisition *f* (*de qch*); **(b)** (*usu pl*) **winnings,** gains *mpl* (*aux courses*); **(c)** *Min* extraction *f* (*du charbon*).

winnow ['wɪnəʊ] *vt Agr* vanner (*le grain*); **to w. the chaff from the grain,** séparer le bon grain de l'ivraie; *Fig* **to w. the evidence,** passer les témoignages au crible *ou* au peigne fin.

winnower ['wɪnəʊər] *n* **(a)** (*person*) vanneur, -euse; **(b)** (*machine*) vanneuse *f*, tarare *m*.

winnowing ['wɪnəʊɪŋ] *n Agr* vannage *m*; *Fig* examen minutieux; **w. basket,** van *m*; **winnowings,** (*of grain*) vannure *f*.

wino ['waɪnəʊ] *n F* ivrogne *mf*, soûlard, -arde.

winsome ['wɪnsəm] *adj* captivant, séduisant.

winsomely ['wɪnsəmlɪ] *adv* d'une manière captivante.

winsomeness ['wɪnsəmnɪs] *n* charme *m*, attrait *m*.

winter¹ ['wɪntər] *n* hiver *m*; **in w.,** en hiver; *Lit* **he has seen sixty winters,** il compte soixante hivers; **W. Olympic Games,** Jeux *mpl* Olympiques d'hiver; **w. clothing,** vêtements *mpl ou Can* linge *m* d'hiver; **w. garden,** (*conservatory*) jardin *m* d'hiver; **w. quarters,** quartiers *mpl* d'hiver; **w. resort,** station *f* de sports d'hiver; **w. solstice,** solstice *m* d'hiver; **w. sports,** sports *mpl* d'hiver; **w. visitors,** hivernants *mpl*.

winter² **1** *vi* hiverner, passer l'hiver (**at,** à). **2** *vt* hiverner (*le bétail*).

winter-flowering [wɪntə'flaʊərɪŋ] *adj* (*plant*) hibernal, -aux, hiémal, -aux.

wintergreen ['wɪntəgriːn] *n* (*plant*) gaulthérie *f*; *Pharm* **oil of w.,** essence *f* de wintergreen.

wintering ['wɪntərɪŋ] *n* hivernage *m*.

winterize ['wɪntəraɪz] *vt esp Am* mettre (*une voiture, une maison etc*) en état pour passer l'hiver, *Can* hivériser.

wintertime, *Lit* **wintertide** ['wɪntətaɪm, -taɪd] *n* hiver *m*.

winterweight ['wɪntəweɪt] *adj* (*coat etc*) d'hiver.

wint(e)ry ['wɪnt(ə)rɪ] *adj* d'hiver; (*cold*) hivernal, -aux; **w. weather,** temps *m* d'hiver; **because of the w. conditions,** parce qu'il faisait un temps d'hiver; **w. smile,** sourire glacial.

wipe¹ [waɪp] *n* coup *m* de torchon *ou* de mouchoir *ou* d'éponge; **to give sth a w. (over),** essuyer qch, donner un coup de torchon *ou* d'éponge à qch.

wipe² **1** *vt* **(a)** essuyer (*une table, une assiette*); **to w. one's face/hands/eyes,** s'essuyer la figure/les mains/les yeux; *Fig F* **we wiped the floor with them,** nous n'en avons fait qu'une bouchée; **(b)** effacer; **the tape has been wiped,** la bande a été effacée. **2** *vi* **(a)** (*when washing up*) essuyer; **I'll wash if you'll w.,** je vais laver si tu veux bien essuyer (la vaisselle); **(b) the windscreen wiper isn't wiping,** l'essuie-glace ne marche pas.

►**wipe away** *vtsep* essuyer (*ses larmes*); enlever, ôter (*une tache*); *Fig* effacer (*des souvenirs*).

►**wipe off** **1** *vtsep* **(a)** enlever, essuyer (*une éclaboussure*); **(b)** effacer (*qch du tableau*); *F* **that'll w. the smile off his face,** ça va lui enlever le sourire; **w. that smile off your face!,** arrête de sourire comme ça!; **to w. a town off the map** *or* **off the face of the earth,** rayer une ville de la carte. **2** *vi* (*of stain etc*) s'enlever.

►**wipe out** *vtsep* **(a)** essuyer (*une baignoire etc*); **(b)** liquider, amortir (*une dette*); **his gambling debts wiped out his entire fortune,** ses dettes de jeu ont eu raison de toute sa fortune; **(c)** effacer (*un souvenir, son passé*); passer l'éponge sur (*qch*); **(d)** exterminer (*une armée*); **whole families were wiped out by the disease,** des familles entières ont été exterminées par la maladie; **the fire wiped out the whole district,** l'incendie a rasé tout le quartier; **(e)** *F* épuiser (*qn*); **I feel wiped out,** je me sens lessivé.

►**wipe up** **1** *vtsep* nettoyer, enlever (*une saleté*); essuyer (*la vaisselle*). **2** *vi* essuyer la vaisselle.

wiper ['waɪpər] *n* essuyeur, -euse; *Aut* (*for windscreen*) essuie-glace(s) *m*.

wiping ['waɪpɪŋ] *n* **(a)** essuyage *m*; **(b)** (*of recording*) effacement *m*.

wiping out *n* **(a)** liquidation *f*, amortissement *m* (*d'une dette*); **(b)** effacement *m* (*d'un souvenir*).

wire¹ ['waɪər] *n* **(a)** fil *m* métallique, fil de fer; *El* fil (électrique); **cheese w.,** fil à couper le beurre; **the high w.,** (*in circus*) la corde raide; *US Tel* **party w.,** ligne partagée; *Fig* **to get one's wires crossed,** se tromper, s'embrouiller; *esp Am F* **to pull the wires,** tirer les ficelles, faire jouer ses pistons; **w. brush,** brosse *f* en fil de fer; **w. drawing,** tréfilage *m*, étirage *m*; *Mil* **w. entanglements,** barbelés *mpl*; **w. fence,** clôture *f* en fil de fer; **w. glass,** verre armé; **w. mattress,** sommier *m* métallique; **w. netting,** trellis *m ou* treillage *m* métallique *ou* en fil de fer; *Am* **w. service,** agence *f* de presse; **w. wool,** paille *f* de fer;
(b) *esp Am* (*finishing line*) ligne *f* d'arrivée; *Fig* **down to the w.,** jusqu'à la dernière minute; **to get an application in under the w.,** soumettre une demande juste à temps; *Fig* **to (just) get in under the w.,** (*of application etc*) arriver de justesse;
(c) *Old-fashioned* télégramme *m*, dépêche *f*.

wire² **1** *vt* **(a)** rattacher (*qch*) avec du fil de fer; monter (*des fleurs*) sur fil de fer; grillager (*une ouverture*); **(b)** *El* faire l'installation électrique de (*une maison*); **to w. a hall for sound,** sonoriser une salle; **(c)** *esp Am F* munir (*un policier*) d'un micro; **(d)** télégraphier à (*qn*); **he wired that he would arrive at twelve,** il a télégraphié qu'il arriverait à midi. **2** *vi* télégraphier.

►**wire up** *vtsep* (*équipement*) brancher.

wirecutter ['waɪəkʌtər] *n* coupe-fil *m inv*; **(pair of) wirecutters,** pince(s) coupante(s).

wire-haired ['waɪəheəd] *adj* (*chien terrier*) à poil dur.

wireless ['waɪəlɪs] **1** *adj* sans fil. **2** *n Old-fashioned* télégraphie *f ou* téléphonie *f* sans fil, radio *f*; **w. (set),** poste *m* de T.S.F., radio.

wirepuller ['waɪəpʊlər] *n esp Am* intrigant, -ante; *F* personne qui fait jouer ses pistons.

wirepulling ['waɪəpʊlɪŋ] *n* intrigues *fpl*.

wiretap¹ ['waɪətæp] *n* **they've put a w. on him** *or* **his telephone,** on a mis sa ligne sur écoute.

wiretap² *vt* mettre (*une ligne téléphonique*) sur écoute.

wiretapping ['waɪətæpɪŋ] *n* mise *f* sur écoute d'une ligne téléphonique.

wireworm ['waɪəwɜːm] *n* (*pest*) larve *f* de taupin; (*millipede*) iule *m*.

wiring ['waɪərɪŋ] *n* **(a)** (*action*) montage *m* (*de fleurs etc*) sur fil de fer; *El* pose *f* (*de fils électriques*); *Mil* pose des barbelés; **(b)** (*system*) installation *f* électrique (*d'une maison etc*); **the w. is in very poor condition,** l'installation électrique est en très mauvais état.

wiry ['waɪərɪ] *adj* **(a)** (*hair*) raide; **(b)** (*person*) vigoureux, (sec et) nerveux.

Wis *abbr* **Wisconsin**.

wisdom ['wɪzdəm] *n* (*knowledge*) sagesse *f*; (*advisability*) sagesse, prudence *f*; **w. tooth,** dent *f* de sagesse; **to question the w. of a decision,** mettre en cause la sagesse d'une décision.

wise¹ [waɪz] *adj* (*knowledgeable*) sage; (*advisable*) prudent; **a w. man,** un sage; **the Three W. Men,** les (Rois) Mages *mpl*; **to get** *or* **grow wise(r),** (*learn more*) s'assagir; (*gain experience*) acquérir de l'expérience; **it wouldn't be w. to do it,** il ne serait pas sage *ou* prudent de le faire; **w. after the event,** sage après coup; **to look w.,** prendre un (petit) air entendu; **I'm no wiser than you,** je n'en sais pas plus long que vous; **she's none** *or* **not any the wiser (for it),** elle n'en sait pas plus long pour autant; **without anyone being (any) the wiser,** à l'insu de tout le monde, sans que personne ne sache; **no one will be any the wiser,** personne n'en saura rien; *F* **to get w. to a fact,** se rendre compte d'un fait; *F* **to get w. to s.o.,** se rendre compte de *ou* réaliser ce que quelqu'un fait; *F* **I'm w. to his tricks,** je connais ses combines; *F* **to put s.o. w.,** mettre qn au courant *ou* à la page; *F* **to put s.o. w. to sth,** avertir qn (de qch); *F* **w. guy,** petit malin.

wise² *n Lit* manière *f*, façon *f*; **in no w.,** en aucune manière *ou* façon, nullement, aucunement.

►**wise up** *F* **1** *vtsep* mettre (*qn*) à la page; **w. me up about it,** mets-moi au courant. **2** *vi esp Am* **to w. up to s.o.,** se rendre compte du petit jeu de qn; **to w. up to the fact that ...,** se rendre compte du fait que ...; **w. up!,** ouvre les yeux!

-wise [waɪz] *suff* **(a)** (*indicating direction*) dans le sens de ...; **lengthw.,** dans le sens de la longueur; **(b)** *F* (*with reference to*) en ce qui concerne ...; **healthw./salaryw.,** en ce qui concerne la santé/le salaire.

wiseacre ['waɪzeɪkər] *n* **(a)** (*smart alec*) petit malin; **(b)** *Old-fashioned Am* prétendu sage, pédant *m*.

wisecrack¹ ['waɪzkræk] *n F* blague *f*, vanne *f*; **to make a w.,** faire *ou* lancer une vanne; **I don't want any more wisecracks,** je ne veux plus entendre une seule vanne.

wisecrack² *vi* dire des bons mots, faire de l'esprit.

wisecracking ['waɪzkrækɪŋ] *adj* blagueur.

wisely ['waɪzlɪ] *adv* **(a)** sagement, prudemment; **(b) to shake one's head w.,** secouer la tête d'un air entendu.

wish¹ [wɪʃ] *n* **(a)** (*desire*) désir *m*; **I have no w. to go/to see it,** je n'ai pas envie d'y aller/de le voir; **to express a w. to do sth,** exprimer le désir de faire qch; **the w. to please,** le désir de plaire; **by my father's w.,** sur le désir de mon père; *Hum* **your w. is my command,** vos désirs sont des ordres; **it was done against** *or* **contrary to my wishes,** cela s'est fait à l'encontre de mon désir *ou* contre mon gré; **to make a w.,** faire un vœu; **your w. will come true,** ton vœu se réalisera; *Psy* **w. fulfilment,** réalisation *f* du désir;
(b) (*what is desired*) **you shall have your w.,** votre vœu sera exaucé;
(c) (*greeting*) souhait *m*, vœu *m*; **to send all good wishes to s.o.,** présenter ses souhaits à qn; **New Year's wishes,** vœux de bonne année; **with best wishes,** (*at end of letter*) (bien) amicalement; **with best wishes for a speedy recovery,** avec tous mes *ou* nos meilleurs vœux de prompt rétablissement.

wish² **1** *vi* **to w. for sth,** désirer *ou* vouloir *ou* souhaiter qch; **to w. for happiness/peace,** désirer *ou* souhaiter le bonheur/la paix; **to have everything one can** *or* **could w. for,** avoir tout à souhait *ou* tout pour être heureux; **I couldn't w. for anything better,** je ne pourrais désirer mieux; **what more can you** *or* **do you w. for?,** que voudriez-vous de plus?; **as you w.,** comme vous voulez.
2 *vt* **(a)** (*want*) vouloir; **to w. to do sth,** désirer *ou* vouloir faire qch; **I w. it to be done,** je désire *ou* je veux bien que cela soit fait; **I w. you to be here tomorrow,** je désire *ou* je souhaite que vous soyez là demain; **it is to be wished that ...,** il est à souhaiter que ...;
(b) (*want sth impossible, unlikely*) **I w. I were a bird!,** je voudrais être un oiseau!; **I w. I were in your place,** je voudrais bien être à votre place; **I w. I had seen it!,** j'aurais bien voulu voir cela!; **I w. I hadn't left so early,** je regrette d'être parti si tôt; **I w. she would come,** j'aimerais bien qu'elle vienne; **how I w. I could (do it)!,** si seulement je pouvais (le faire)!;
(c) (*greet*) **he wishes me well,** il est bien disposé envers moi; **he wishes nobody ill,** il ne veut de mal à personne; **w. me luck,** souhaite-moi bonne chance; **to w. s.o. a pleasant journey,** souhaiter bon voyage à qn; **to w. s.o. goodnight,** souhaiter bonne nuit à qn, dire bonsoir à qn.

►**wish away** *vtsep* faire disparaître comme par enchantement; **you can't wish your problems away,** tu ne peux pas te débarrasser de tes problèmes comme par enchantement; **to w. one's life away,** vivre dans le futur.

►**wish on** *vtaspo* obliger à accepter; **it was wished on me,** j'ai été obligé de l'accepter; **I wouldn't w. this on my worst enemy,** je ne souhaiterais pas cela à mon pire ennemi; **can we w. the children on you for the day?,** est-ce que nous pouvons vous imposer les enfants pour la journée?

wishbone ['wɪʃbəʊn] *n* fourchette *f*, bréchet *m*; (*esp Am on surfboard*) wishbone *m*; **to pull a w. with s.o.,** = tirer au sort avec qn avec un bréchet de poulet en essayant de le briser, la personne ayant le morceau le plus long devant voir son vœu se réaliser.

wishful ['wɪʃfʊl] *adj* **that's a bit of w. thinking,** c'est prendre ses désirs pour des réalités.

wishy-washy ['wɪʃɪwɒʃɪ] *adj F* (*style, look*) fade, insipide; (*person*) qui ne sait pas ce qu'il veut, indécis.

wisp [wɪsp] *n* **(a)** (*strand*) bouchon *m*, poignée *f* (*de paille, d'herbe*); **w. of smoke,** trainée *f* de fumée; **w. of hair,** mèche folle; **little w. of a girl,** tout petit bout de fillette; **a w. of cloud,** un filet de nuage; **(b)** (*twist*) tortillon *m*, toron *m* (*de paille*).

wispy ['wɪspɪ] *adj* (*beard, hair*) fin; (*cloud*) vaporeux.

wisteria [wɪs'tɪərɪə] *n* (*plant*) glycine *f*.

wistful ['wɪstfʊl] *adj* plein d'un vague désir *ou* regret; (*regard, air*) mélancolique; **w. smile,** sourire *m* de regret.

wistfully ['wɪstfəlɪ] *adv* avec un regard plein d'un vague désir *ou* regret; d'un air songeur et triste.

wit¹ [wɪt] *n* **(a)** (*intelligence*) (*often pl*) esprit *m*, entendement *m*, intelligence *f*; **he hasn't the w.** *or* **the wits to see it,** il n'est pas assez intelligent pour s'en apercevoir; **to have quick wits,** avoir l'esprit vif; **to have lost one's wits,** avoir perdu l'esprit *ou* la raison; **to collect** *or* **gather one's wits,** se ressaisir, reprendre ses esprits; **to have/**

keep one's wits about one, avoir/conserver toute sa présence d'esprit; **you need your wits about you in this job,** il faut avoir de la présence d'esprit dans ce métier; **she has all her wits about her,** c'est une maligne; **to be at one's w.'s end,** ne plus savoir que faire; **to have** *or* **engage in a battle of wits,** jouer au plus fin; **to live by one's wits,** vivre d'expédients; **to scare s.o. out of their wits,** faire une peur bleue à qn; **to put one's wits to work on a problem,** s'attaquer à un problème;

(b) (*humour*) esprit *m*, vivacité *f* d'esprit; **flash of w.,** trait *m* d'esprit; **sparkling with w.,** étincelant d'esprit.

wit² *n* bel esprit, homme *ou* femme d'esprit.

wit³ *vt Jur* **to w.,** à savoir ..., c'est-à-dire ... .

witch [wɪtʃ] *n* sorcière *f*; **the witches of Salem,** les sorcières de Salem; *Pej F* **old w.,** vieille sorcière; **w. doctor,** sorcier guérisseur; **w. hazel,** (*plant*) hamamélis *m*.

witchcraft ['wɪtʃkrɑːft] *n* **(a)** (*use of powers*) sorcellerie *f*; **to practise w.,** pratiquer la sorcellerie; **(b)** *F* magie *f*; **as if by w., like w.,** comme par magie *ou* enchantement.

witchery ['wɪtʃərɪ] *n* **(a)** (*practice*) ensorcellement *m*, enchantement *m*; **(b)** (*influence, charm*) fascination.

witch-hunt ['wɪtʃhʌnt] *n Pol* chasse *f* aux sorcières.

witching ['wɪtʃɪŋ] *adj* **(a)** enchanteur, -eresse; **(b)** magique; *Lit & Hum* **the w. hour,** minuit *m*, l'heure *f* du crime.

with [wɪð] *prep* **(a)** (*expressing accompaniment*) avec; (*having*) à; **to travel/work w. s.o.,** voyager/travailler avec qn; **he is staying w. friends,** il est chez des amis; **to mingle w. the crowd,** se mêler à la foule; **the king (together) w. his courtiers,** le roi accompagné de ses courtisans; **I have nobody to go out w.,** je n'ai personne avec qui sortir; **there I am w. nobody to talk to,** me voilà sans personne à qui parler; **I'll be w. you in a moment,** je serai à vous dans un moment; **some cheese to eat w. it,** du fromage pour manger avec; **question that is always w. us,** question qui est toujours d'actualité; **knife w. a silver handle,** couteau à manche d'argent; **girl w. blue eyes,** jeune fille aux yeux bleus; **child w. a cold,** enfant enrhumé; **w. his** *or* **her hat on,** le chapeau sur la tête; **w. his (over)coat on,** en pardessus; **w. your intelligence you'll easily guess what followed,** intelligent comme vous l'êtes vous devinerez facilement la suite; *Arch* **w. child,** (*of woman*) enceinte; **w. young,** (*of animal*) pleine; **she came in w. a suitcase,** elle est entrée avec une valise; **have you a pencil w. you?,** avez-vous un crayon sur vous?; **to leave a child w. s.o.,** laisser un enfant à la garde de qn; **the decision rests** *or* **lies w. you,** c'est à vous de décider; **what will happen to her w. both her parents dead?,** (*now that they are dead*) que va-t-elle devenir maintenant que son père et sa mère sont morts?;

(b) (*expressing association*) avec; **to correspond w. s.o.,** correspondre avec qn; **to have to do w. s.o.,** avoir à faire avec qn; **to have nothing to do w. s.o.,** n'avoir rien à faire avec qn; **to part w. sth,** se dessaisir *ou* se défaire de qch; **the next move is w. him,** c'est à lui d'agir maintenant; **w. him all men are equal,** tous les hommes sont égaux à ses yeux; **to be patient w. s.o.,** être patient avec qn; **to be honest w. oneself,** être honnête envers *ou* avec soi-même; **it's a habit w. me,** c'est une habitude chez moi; **to use one's influence w. s.o.,** agir auprès de qn; **all is well w. her,** elle va bien; **I sympathize w. you,** je vous plains; **I don't agree w. you,** je ne suis pas d'accord avec vous; **I'm w. you,** (*I support you*) je suis de votre côté; *F* (*I understand*) je vous suis, je comprends; **I'm not w. you,** (*I don't understand*) je ne (vous) suis pas, je ne comprends pas; *Old-fashioned F* **to be w. it,** être à la page *ou* dans le vent; **I am not w. it today,** je n'y suis pas aujourd'hui; **to rise w. the lark,** se lever au chant du coq; **w. these words** *or* **w. that he dismissed me,** sur ces mots *ou* là-dessus, il m'a congédié; **she said this w. a smile,** elle a dit ça avec un sourire; **w. a cry,** en poussant un cri; **to compete w. s.o.,** concourir avec qn; **to fight w. s.o.,** se battre contre *ou* avec qn; *F* **get w. it,** (*waken up*) réveille-toi; (*realize what's happening*) ouvre les yeux;

(c) (*despite*) **w. all his faults,** malgré tous ses défauts;

(d) (*expressing instrument, agent*) **to cut sth w. a knife,** couper qch avec un couteau *ou* au couteau; **to walk w. (the aid of) a stick,** marcher avec une canne; **to fight w. swords,** se battre à l'épée; **to take sth w. both hands,** prendre qch à deux mains; **to strike w. all one's might,** frapper de toutes ses forces; **to tremble w. rage,** trembler de rage; **to be stiff w. cold,** être engourdi par le froid; **to be ill w. measles,** être malade de la rougeole; **to fill a vase w. water,** remplir un vase d'eau; **lorry loaded w. timber,** camion chargé de bois; **it's pouring w. rain,** il pleut à verse;

(e) (*forming adv phrase*) **to work w. a will,** travailler avec courage; **to advance w. great strides,** avancer à grands pas; **to receive s.o. w. open arms,** recevoir qn à bras ouverts; **w. all due respect,** avec tout le respect que je vous dois; **w. your permission,** avec votre permission; **w. this object (in view),** dans ce but; **I say it w. regret,** je le dis à regret; **w. a few exceptions,** à part quelques exceptions, quelques exceptions mises à part;

(f) (*elliptical*) **away w. care!,** bannissons les soucis!; *F* **down w. the police!,** à bas les flics!; *F* **to hell w. him!,** qu'il aille au diable!

withal [wɪ'ðɔːl] *adv Arch* de plus.

withdraw [wɪð'drɔː] *v* (*pt* **withdrew** [-'druː]; *pp* **withdrawn** [-'drɔːn]) **1** *vt* **(a)** retirer (*sa main*); retirer, enlever (*un étai*);

(b) ramener (*des troupes*) en arrière, faire replier (*des troupes*); lever (*une sentinelle*);

(c) *Banking* retirer (*une somme d'argent*); **I've withdrawn all my savings,** j'ai retiré toutes mes économies; **to w. coins from circulation,** retirer des pièces de la circulation;

(d) retirer (*une offre, une promesse, une remarque, sa candidature*); revenir sur (*une promesse*); renoncer à (*une réclamation*); **to w. a charge,** se rétracter; **to w. an order,** *Com* annuler une commande; *Admin* rapporter un décret; *Jur* **to w. an action,** retirer sa plainte; *Fml* **to w. one's labour,** faire la grève.

2 *vi* **(a)** se retirer (**from,** de); **he withdrew ten paces,** il a reculé de dix pas; **to w. in favour of s.o.,** (*of candidate*) se désister en faveur de qn;

(b) to w. into oneself, se replier sur soi-même; **to w. into silence,** se renfermer dans le silence;

(c) *Mil* se retirer; (*of outpost*) se replier.

withdrawn [wɪð'drɔːn] *adj* (*person*) replié sur soi-même.

withdrawal [wɪð'drɔː(ə)l] *n* **(a)** retrait *m* (*de troupes, d'une somme d'argent*); *Banking* **I can make only one w. a week,** je ne peux effectuer qu'un seul retrait (d'argent) par semaine; *Banking* **w. of capital,** retrait de fonds; *Banking* **w. notice,** avis *m* de retrait de fonds; **(b)** *Psy* repli *m* sur soi; **the boy is showing signs of w.,** le jeune garçon présente des signes de repli sur lui-même; *Med* **w. symptoms,** (*from alcohol*) symptômes *mpl* d'abstinence; (*from drugs*) (état *m ou* crise *f* de) manque *m*; **to suffer w. symptoms,** (*of alcoholic, drug addict*) être en manque; *Fig* se sentir perdu; **(c)** rappel *m* (*d'un décret, d'un ordre*); rétractation *f* (*d'une promesse, d'une accusation*); retrait *m* (*d'une plainte*); **(d)** (*action*) retraite *f*; *Mil* repli *m*, repliement *m* (*des troupes*); **w. of a candidate,** désistement *m* d'un candidat.

withe [wɪθ] *n* brin *m ou* lien *m* d'osier.

wither ['wɪðər] **1** *vi* (*of plant etc*) se dessécher, se flétrir, se faner; *Fig* (*of beauty*) passer; *Fig* (*of hope*) s'évanouir; *Fig* (*of person*) dépérir. **2** *vt* (*of wind, heat*) dessécher, flétrir, faner (*une plante etc*); *Fig* **to w. s.o. with a look,** foudroyer qn du *ou* d'un regard.

▶**wither away, wither up** *vi* = **WITHER 1**.

withered ['wɪðəd] *adj* desséché, flétri, fané; **w. arm,** bras atrophié.

withering ['wɪðərɪŋ] **1** *adj* qui dessèche, qui flétrit; *Fig* (*regard*) foudroyant, écrasant; (*ton*) de souverain mépris; **w. sarcasm,** sarcasme cinglant; **to give s.o. a w. look,** foudroyer qn du regard. **2** *n* (*of plant*) dessèchement *m*.

withering away *n* dépérissement *m* (*d'une plante, Fig d'une personne*); dessèchement *m* (*d'une plante*); *Fig* amenuisement *m* (*d'un parti politique etc*).

witheringly ['wɪðərɪŋlɪ] *adv* (*to look at*) d'un regard foudroyant; (*to say*) d'un ton méprisant.

withers ['wɪðəz] *npl* garrot *m* (*du cheval, du bœuf*).

withershins ['wɪðəʃɪnz] *adv Scot* à contre-sens.

withhold [wɪð'həuld] *vt* (*pt & pp* **withheld** [-'held]) **(a)** (*not give*) refuser (*son consentement, son aide*); retenir (*de l'argent*); **(b)** (*suppress*) taire, supprimer (*un fait etc*); **I managed to w. my indignation/laughter,** j'ai réussi à contenir mon indignation/rire; **to w. the truth from s.o.,** cacher la vérité à qn; **(c)** *Jur* détenir (*des biens*).

within [wɪð'ɪn] **1** *adv* **(a) from w.,** de l'intérieur; **seen from w.,** vu de l'intérieur *ou* du dedans; **staff required — apply w.,** (*notice in shop window*) on recherche du personnel — se présenter à l'intérieur;

(b) *Th* à la cantonade;

(c) *Arch* à l'intérieur; (*at home*) chez soi.

2 *prep* **(a)** (*not beyond*) **w. reason,** dans des limites raisonnables; **to keep w. the law,** rester dans (les bornes de) la légalité; **to keep** *or* **live w. one's income,** vivre selon ses moyens; **w. sight,** en vue; **to be w. sight of the shore,** avoir la côte en vue; **w. call,** à portée de (la) voix; **w. two miles of the town,** à moins de deux milles de la ville; **w. a radius of ten kilometres,** dans un rayon de dix kilomètres; **we were w. an inch of death,** nous étions à deux doigts de la mort;

(b) (*in expressions of time*) **w. an hour,** en moins d'une heure; **it will be ready w. an** *or* **the hour,** ça sera prêt d'ici une heure; **w. a week,** (*in the space of*) en moins d'une semaine; (*by the time a week has passed*) d'ici une semaine; **w. the week,** avant la fin de la semaine, dans la semaine; **w. a year of his death,** (*after he died*) moins d'un an après sa mort; (*before he died*) moins d'un an avant sa mort; **w. the next week,** dans le courant de la semaine prochaine; **w. the next five years, w. five years from now,** d'ici cinq ans; **w. the required time,** dans le délai prescrit; **w. twenty-four hours,** dans les vingt-quatre heures; **w. ten days of receipt of your order,** dans un délai de dix jours à compter de la réception de votre commande; **w. a short time,** (*soon*) à court délai; (*soon after*) peu de temps après; **her time was w. a few seconds of the world record,** son temps était à quelques secondes du record du monde;

(c) *Old-fashioned & Lit* à l'intérieur de, en dedans de; **w. four walls,** entre quatre murs; **the enemy is w. our frontiers,** l'ennemi est dans nos frontières; **he thought w. himself that ...,** il pensait dans son for intérieur que ...; **a voice w. me,** une voix intérieure.

without [wɪð'aʊt] **1** *prep* **(a)** sans; **w. a tail,** sans queue; **to be w. food,** manquer de nourriture; **he came back w. any money,** il est revenu sans argent; **w. any difficulty,** sans aucune difficulté; **rumour w. foundation,** bruit dénué de fondement; **not w. difficulty,** non sans difficulté; **w. end,** sans fin; **he passed by w. seeing me/being seen,** il est passé sans me voir/être vu; **it goes w. saying that ...,** il va sans dire *ou* de soi que ...; **can you do it w. her knowing about it?,** pouvez-vous le faire sans qu'elle le sache?; **they are w. any knowledge of French,** ils n'ont aucune connaissance du français; **to do** *or* **go w. sth,** se passer de qch; **I don't want her to go w. anything,** je ne veux pas qu'elle manque de quoi que ce soit; **w. so much as saying goodbye/asking permission/***etc*, sans même dire au revoir/demander la permission/*etc*;

(b) *Arch* en dehors de;

2 *adv Arch* à l'extérieur, au dehors; **from w.,** de l'extérieur; **seen from w.,** vu de l'extérieur *ou* du dehors.

withstand [wɪð'stænd] *vt* (*pt & pp* **withstood** [-'stʊd]) résister à (*qn, la douleur, la pression etc*); **to w. the heat,** supporter la chaleur; *Mil etc* **to w. an attack,** soutenir une attaque.

withy ['wɪðɪ] *n* brin *m ou* lien *m* d'osier.

witless ['wɪtlɪs] *adj* (*silly*) sans intelligence, sot, *f* sotte; (*retarded*) imbécile, faible d'esprit; *F* **to scare s.o. w.,** faire une peur bleue à qn.

witness[1] ['wɪtnɪs] *n* **(a)** (*person*) témoin *m*; **will you act as a w. at our wedding?,** est-ce que vous voulez bien être témoin à notre mariage?; **I gave my name as a w.,** j'ai donné mon nom en tant que témoin; *Jur* **w. to a document** *or* **a deed,** témoin instrumentaire, témoin à un acte; *Jur* **to call s.o. as w.,** citer qn comme témoin; *Jur* **w. for the defence/prosecution,** témoin à décharge/charge; *Br Jur* **w. box,** (*US* = **stand**) barre *f* des témoins; *Br Jur* **to go into the w. box,** (*US* = **to take the stand**) paraître à la barre;

(b) (*testimony*) témoignage *m*; **to give w. on behalf of the accused,** rendre témoignage pour l'accusé; **to bear w. to sth,** rendre *ou* porter témoignage de qch, témoigner de qch, attester qch; **this situation bears w. to the need to ...,** cette situation témoigne de la nécessité de ...; *Rel* **to bear false w.,** porter un faux témoignage; **I call you to w.,** j'en appelle à votre témoignage.

witness[2] **1** *vt* être spectateur *ou* témoin de (*une scène*); assister à (*une entrevue etc*); *Jur* attester (*un acte*); *Jur* certifier (*une signature*); **I witnessed the whole thing,** j'ai assisté à tout ce qui s'est passé; **the house has witnessed many deaths,** cette maison a vu de nombreux décès; **we are witnessing a historic event,** nous assistons à un événement historique. **2** *vi Jur* **to w. to sth,** témoigner de qch; **to w. against/for s.o.,** témoigner contre/en faveur de qn.

-witted ['wɪtɪd] *suff* **slow/quick/***etc***-w.,** qui a l'esprit vif/lent/*etc*.

witter[1] ['wɪtər] *n* = **WITTERING**.

witter[2] *vi Br F* **to w. (on),** parler sans arrêt pour ne rien dire, papoter.

wittering ['wɪtərɪŋ] *n Br F* bavardage incessant et sans intérêt, papotage *m*; **his constant w. gets on my nerves,** son papotage me tape sur les nerfs.

witticism ['wɪtɪsɪz(ə)m] *n* trait *m* d'esprit, bon mot.

wittily ['wɪtɪlɪ] *adv* spirituellement, avec esprit.

wittiness ['wɪtɪnɪs] *n* esprit *m*; sel *m* (*d'une observation etc*).

wittingly ['wɪtɪŋlɪ] *adv* (*intentionally*) sciemment.

witty ['wɪtɪ] *adj* spirituel, plein d'esprit.

wizard ['wɪzəd] **1** *n* sorcier *m*, magicien *m*; *Fig* génie *m*; **to be a financial w.,** avoir le génie de la finance *ou* des affaires; **she's a w. on the violin,** c'est une violoniste géniale *ou* de génie; **to be a w. with a sewing needle,** avoir des doigts de fée pour les travaux d'aiguille. **2** *adj Old-fashioned Br F* épatant, excellent; **to be a w. cook,** être une fée du fourneau.

wizardry ['wɪzədrɪ] *n* sorcellerie *f*, magie *f*; *Fig* génie *m*; **her financial w.,** son habileté géniale en matières financières.

wizened ['wɪzənd] *adj* ratatiné; (*cheeks*) parcheminé; (*apple*) ratatiné, ridé; **to become w.,** se ratatiner; se parcheminer; **a w. old man,** un viellard tout ratatiné.

wk *abbr* **week.**

WO *Br Mil abbr* **warrant officer.**

wo(a) ['wəʊ(ə)] *int* (*to horse*) ho!, holà!

woad [wəʊd] *n* guède *f*.

wobble[1] ['wɒb(ə)l] *n* **(a)** vacillation *f*, branlement *m*, oscillation *f*, tremblement *m*; *Aut* **front-wheel w.,** shimmy *m*; **(b)** chevrotement *m* (*de la voix*).

wobble[2] *vi* **(a)** vaciller, osciller; (*of table*) branler; (*of person*) chanceler; (*of wheel*) tourner à faux; **(b)** (*of voice etc*) chevroter.

wobbly ['wɒblɪ] *adj* **(a)** branlant, vacillant; (*unbalanced*) hors d'aplomb; **w. chair,** chaise boiteuse *ou* branlante; **my legs feel w.,** j'ai les jambes en coton; **(b)** (*voice etc*) chevrotant.

wodge [wɒdʒ] *n Br F* gros morceau (*de pain etc*).

woe [wəʊ] *n Lit* malheur *m*, chagrin *m*, peine *f*; **to tell a tale of w.,** faire le récit de ses malheurs; **w. is me!,** pauvre de moi!, malheureux que je suis!; *F* **w. betide you if you're late,** malheur à toi si tu es en retard.

woebegone ['wəʊbɪgɒn] *adj* (*air, visage*) désolé, abattu; **to look w.,** avoir l'air désolé.

wo(e)ful ['wəʊfʊl] *adj* **(a)** (*bad*) déplorable; **w. standard of workmanship,** qualité *f* de travail déplorable; **(b)** *Lit* (*look*) affligé, malheureux; (*news*) attristant; **the Knight of the W. Countenance,** (*Don Quixote*) le chevalier à la Triste Figure.

wo(e)fully ['wəʊfəlɪ] *adv* (*see adj*) **(a) w. low standard,** niveau *m* déplorablement faible; **(b)** tristement.

wog [wɒg] *n Br Offensive Sl* barbouillé *m*.

wok[1] [wɒk] *n* poêle *f* à frire chinoise.

wok[2] *vt* cuire (*qch*) dans une poêle à frire chinoise.

wold [wəʊld] *n Geog* (petite) chaîne *f* de collines crayeuses *ou* calcaires.

wolf , *pl* **wolves** [wʊlf, wʊlvz] *n* **(a)** (*animal*) loup *m*; **she w.,** louve *f*; **w. cub,** louveteau *m*; **to be as hungry as a w.,** avoir une faim de loup; **that will keep the w. from the door,** (*prevent financial hardship*) cela vous *ou* nous *etc* mettra à l'abri du besoin; (*stop you feeling hungry*) voilà quelque chose pour écarter la faim; *Fig* **to throw s.o. to the wolves,** sacrifier qn; **a w. in sheep's clothing,** un loup déguisé en brebis; **to cry w.,** crier au loup; **she's a bit of a lone w.,** elle est plutôt du genre solitaire; **(b)** *F* (*womanizer*) coureur *m* de jupons; **w. whistle,** = sifflement admiratif (*au passage d'une jolie fille*); **he gave her a w. whistle,** il l'a sifflée.

▶**wolf down** *vtsep* engloutir, dévorer.

wolfhound ['wʊlfhaʊnd] *n* chien *m* de loup; **Irish w.,** lévrier *m* d'Irlande.

wolfish ['wʊlfɪʃ] *adj* de loup; *Fig* vorace; *Fig* **w. appetite,** appétit énorme.

wolfram ['wʊlfrəm] *n Miner* wolfram *m*.

wolfsbane ['wʊlfsbeɪn] *n* (*plant*) aconit *m*.

wolf-whistle ['wʊlfwɪs(ə)l] *vi* siffler; **he w.-whistled at her,** il l'a sifflée.

wolverine ['wʊlvəriːn] *n* (*animal*) glouton *m*.

woman, *pl* **women** ['wʊmən, 'wɪmɪn] *n* femme *f*; **single w.,** femme célibataire; **a young w.,** une jeune femme; **now listen here, young w.!,** écoute un peu, ma petite demoiselle!; **an old w.,** une vieille (femme); *F* (*man*) un chipoteur; **the other w.,** l'autre femme; **they have a w. in once a week to do the cleaning,** ils ont quelqu'un qui vient faire leur ménage une fois par semaine; *Old-fashioned*

F **the little w.,** ma femme; **get in the car, w.!,** allez la grosse, monte en voiture!; **she's his w.,** c'est sa gonzesse; **he's got women all over the place,** il a des maîtresses partout; **to run after women,** courir le jupon; **it was a w. driver,** il y avait une femme au volant; **a w.'s place is in the home,** une femme doit rester à la maison; *Prov* **a w.'s work is never done,** = les femmes sont constamment occupées (à la maison); **women's movement,** *F* **women's lib,** le Mouvement pour la libération de la femme (M.L.F.); *F Pej* **women's libber,** (*member*) membre *m* du M.L.F.; (*supporter*) partisan, -ane du M.L.F.; *Journ* **women's page,** page *f* des lectrices; **women's magazines,** revues féminines, magazines féminins; **women's problems,** ennuis *ou* problèmes de femmes *ou* féminins; **w. doctor/women doctors,** femme médecin/femmes médecins; **w. artist,** femme peintre; **w. friend,** amie *f*.

womanhater ['wʊmənheɪtər] *n* misogyne *m*.

womanhood ['wʊmənhʊd] *n* **to grow to w.,** devenir femme.

womanish ['wʊmənɪʃ] *adj Pej* (*woman*) de femme; (*man*) efféminé.

womanize ['wʊmənaɪz] *vi* courir les femmes, courir le jupon.

womanizer ['wʊmənaɪzər] *n* coureur *m* de femmes.

womankind ['wʊmənkaɪnd] *n* (*no pl*) les femmes *fpl*.

womanliness ['wʊmənlɪnɪs] *n* féminité *f*.

womanly ['wʊmənlɪ] *adj* féminin; de femme; **she has a very w. nature,** elle est très femme *ou* féminine; **w. wiles,** artifices *mpl* de femme(s).

womb [wuːm] *n Anat* matrice *f*, utérus *m*.

wombat ['wɒmbæt] *n* (*animal*) wombat *m*, phascolome *m*.

womenfolk ['wɪmɪnfəʊk] *n* (*no pl*) les femmes *fpl*; **the settlers brought their w.,** les colons ont amené leurs femmes et leurs filles.

won *see* **WIN**[2].

wonder[1] ['wʌndər] *n* **(a)** (*miracle*) merveille *f*, miracle *m*, prodige *m*; **to work** *or* **do wonders,** faire *ou* accomplir *ou* opérer des merveilles *ou* des miracles, faire des prodiges, faire merveille; **the seven wonders of the world,** les sept merveilles du monde; **a nine-day(s') w.,** la merveille d'un jour; **it's a w. (that) he hasn't lost it,** c'est un miracle qu'il ne l'ait pas perdu; **no** *or* **little** *or* **small w. that the plan failed,** il n'est guère *ou* pas étonnant que le projet n'ait pas réussi; **she's angry and no** *or* **little w.,** elle est en colère et ce n'est pas étonnant; *F* **w. products,** produits *mpl* miracle;

(b) (*astonishment*) étonnement *m*, surprise *f*; (*admiration*) émerveillement *m*, admiration *f*; **to fill s.o. with w.,** émerveiller qn; **expression of w.,** air émerveillé; **sense of w.,** sentiment *m* d'émerveillement.

wonder[2] **1** *vi* s'étonner, s'émerveiller (**at,** de); **I don't w. at it,** cela ne m'étonne pas *ou* ne me surprend pas; **I w. about her sometimes,** je me pose des questions à son sujet parfois; **I was wondering about buying a new car,** je songeais à acheter une nouvelle voiture; **it's not to be wondered at that she left,** il n'est pas étonnant qu'elle soit partie, rien d'étonnant à ce qu'elle soit partie; **she knows a lot more, I shouldn't w.,** cela ne m'étonnerait pas qu'elle en sache beaucoup plus long que ça.

2 *vt* **(a) to w. that ...,** s'étonner que ... + *sub*; **I w. that nobody thought of it before,** je m'étonne du fait que personne n'y ait pensé avant; **can you w. that he refused?,** comment s'étonner qu'il ait refusé?;

(b) se demander, vouloir savoir; **I w.,** (*if he, she etc will do that*) je me le demande; **one wonders!,** c'est à se demander!; **it makes you w. how safe these power stations are,** on en vient à se demander si ces centrales électriques sont vraiment sûres; **I w. whether he'll come,** je me demande *ou* je voudrais bien savoir s'il viendra; **one wonders whether ...,** c'est à se demander si...; **I shouldn't w. if he were already married,** cela ne m'étonnerait pas *ou* ne me surprendrait pas qu'il soit déjà marié; **I w. who invented that,** je suis curieux de savoir qui a inventé cela; **I w. why!,** je voudrais bien savoir pourquoi!; **their son will help them — I w.!,** leur fils leur viendra en aide — vous croyez?; **I was wondering if you were free tonight,** je me demandais si vous étiez libre ce soir; **oh, I just wondered,** (*answering question 'why do you ask?'*) oh, pour rien!, juste pour savoir; **I was just wondering where you'd got to,** j'étais en train de me demander où tu étais passé.

wonderful ['wʌndəfʊl] *adj* merveilleux, prodigieux, admirable; **she's a w. mother,** c'est une mère merveilleuse; **it was w.!,** c'était merveilleux *ou* magnifique!; **we had a w. time,** nous nous sommes très bien amusés.

wonderfully ['wʌndəfəlɪ] *adv* merveilleusement; **w. well,** merveilleusement bien, à merveille.

wondering ['wʌndərɪŋ] *adj* étonné, émerveillé; **the child's w. eyes,** les yeux émerveillés de l'enfant.

wonderland ['wʌndəlænd] *n* pays *m* des merveilles; **Alice in W.,** Alice au Pays des Merveilles.

wonderment ['wʌndəmənt] *n Lit* émerveillement *m*; **she looked at him with w.,** elle l'a regardé avec émerveillement.

wondrous ['wʌndrəs] *Arch & Lit* **1** *adj* merveilleux. **2** *adv* **w. wise,** très sage.

wondrously ['wʌndrəslɪ] *adv Arch & Lit* merveilleusement.

wonky ['wɒŋkɪ] *adj F* (*machine*) détraqué; (*gadget, zip, switch etc*) qui débloque; (*collar, picture etc*) de travers; (*wardrobe, shelves*) branlant; (*one leg short*) (*chair, table*) boiteux; **to feel w.,** se sentir patraque; **this sentence is a bit w.,** il y a quelque chose qui cloche dans cette phrase; **my grammar's a bit w.,** ma grammaire cloche un peu.

wont[1] [wəʊnt] *adj Lit* **to be w. to do sth,** avoir coutume *ou* l'habitude de faire qch.

wont[2] *n Lit* coutume *f*, habitude *f*; **according to his w., as is** *or* **was his w.,** selon sa coutume, à *ou* selon *ou* suivant son habitude.

won't [wəʊnt] = **will not,** *see* **WILL**[3].

wonted ['wəʊntɪd] *adj Lit* habituel, accoutumé.

woo [wuː] *vt* **(a)** *Fig* rechercher (*la fortune, la célébrité*); **they wooed voters with promises of reforms,** (*tried*) ils ont essayé d'attirer des électeurs avec des promesses de réforme; (*succeeded*) ils se sont assuré les voix des électeurs avec des promesses de réforme; **(b)** *Arch & Lit* (*court*) faire la cour à, courtiser (*une femme*).

wood [wʊd] *n* **(a)** bois *m*; (*in forestry*) peuplement *m*; **a walk in the woods,** une promenade dans les bois; **pine w.,** pinède *f*; *Fig* **you can't see the w. for the trees,** les arbres cachent la forêt; *Fig* **his problem is that he can't see the w. for the trees,** son problème, c'est que les arbres lui cachent la forêt; *Fig* **we're not out of the w. yet,** nous ne sommes pas encore tirés d'affaire; **w. anemone,** anémone *f* des bois; **w. pigeon,** (pigeon *m*) ramier *m*; *Myth* **w. nymph,** dryade *f*;

(b) (*material*) bois *m*; **box made of w.,** boîte faite de bois, boîte en bois; *Fig* **touch w.!,** *US* **knock on w.!,** touche *ou* touchons du bois!; **w. alcohol,** alcool *m* méthylique; **w. ash,** cendre *f* de bois; **w. block,** planche *f*, bois; **w. carving/carver,** sculpture *f*/sculpteur *m* sur bois; **w. engraving,** gravure *f* sur bois debout; **w. fire,** feu *m* de bois; **w. floor,** plancher *m* en bois; **w. pulp,** pâte *f* à papier; **w. stove,** poêle *m* à bois;

(c) (*in wine making*) **the w.,** le tonneau, le fût; **wine in the w.,** vin en tonneau *ou* en fût; **beer (drawn) from the w.,** bière tirée au fût;

(d) *Golf* bois *m*; **a number 4 w.,** un bois numéro 4;

(e) *Bowls* boule *f*;

(f) *Mus* = **WOODWIND.**

woodbine ['wʊdbaɪn] *n* (*plant*) **(a)** chèvrefeuille *m* des bois; **(b)** *US* vigne *f* vierge.

woodchuck ['wʊdtʃʌk] *n* (*animal*) marmotte *f* d'Amérique.

woodcock ['wʊdkɒk] *n* (*usu inv in pl*) (*bird*) bécasse *f* (des bois).

woodcraft ['wʊdkrɑːft] *n* **(a)** (*knowledge of forest*) connaissance *f* de la forêt; **(b)** (*woodwork*) (pratique *f* du) travail *m* sur bois.

woodcut ['wʊdkʌt] *n* gravure *f* sur bois.

woodcutter ['wʊdkʌtər] *n* bûcheron *m*.

woodcutting ['wʊdkʌtɪŋ] **(a)** gravure *f* sur bois; **(b)** (*in forest*) abattage *m* du bois.

wooded ['wʊdɪd] *adj* boisé; **w. country,** pays boisé *ou* couvert.

wooden ['wʊd(ə)n] *adj* **(a)** (*made of wood*) de bois, en bois; *Myth* **W. Horse,** Cheval *m* de Troie; **w. shoes,** sabots *mpl*; *Culin & Fig* **w. spoon,** cuiller *f* en *ou* de bois; **(b)** *Fig* (*movement, manner*) raide, gauche; **w. face,** visage fermé; **(c)** *F* **w.(-headed),** stupide, bouché.

woodenness ['wʊdənnɪs] *n* raideur *f*.

woodland ['wʊdlənd] *n* pays boisé; bois *m(pl)*; **w. scenery,** paysage boisé; **w. flowers,** fleurs *fpl* de bois.

woodlark ['wʊdlɑːk] *n* (*bird*) alouette *f* des bois.

woodlouse, *pl* **-lice** ['wʊdlaʊs, -laɪs] *n* cloporte *m*.

woodman, *pl* **-men** ['wʊdmən] *n* **(a)** (*logger*) bûcheron *m*; **(b)** = **WOODSMAN.**

woodpecker ['wʊdpekər] *n* (*bird*) pic *m*; **green w.,**

pivert *m*.
woodpile ['wʊdpaɪl] *n* tas *m ou* monceau *m* de bois.
woodshed ['wʊdʃed] *n* bûcher *m*; *Fig* **there's something nasty in the w.,** il se passe du vilain.
woodsman, *pl* **-men** ['wʊdzmən] *n esp US* chasseur *m* (en forêt); (*for skins*) trappeur *m*.
woodstack ['wʊdstæk] *n* = **WOODPILE.**
woodwind ['wʊdwɪnd] *n Mus* **the w.,** les bois *mpl*; **w. instrument,** instrument *m* à vent en bois.
woodwork ['wʊdwɜːk] *n* **(a)** (*action*) travail *m* du bois; (*smaller scale*) menuiserie *f*, ébénisterie *f*; (*school subject*) menuiserie *f*; **(b)** (*object(s)*) bois travaillé; (*ornamental*) boiserie *f*; (*structural*) charpente *f*; **that's a fine piece of w.,** c'est de la belle menuiserie; *Fig* **to come out of the w.,** sortir d'on ne sait où; *Sp* **to hit the w.,** heurter les bois *mpl*.
woodworking ['wʊdwɜːkɪŋ] *n* (*carpentry*) travail *m* du bois; **w. tools,** outils *mpl* pour le travail du bois; **w. magazine,** magazine *m* sur le travail du bois.
woodworm ['wʊdwɜːm] *n* (*insect*) ver *m* à bois; **this table's got w.,** cette table est vermoulue; **it's full of w.,** c'est rongé par les vers.
woody ['wʊdɪ] *adj* **(a)** (*countryside*) boisé; **(b)** *Bot* ligneux; **(c)** (*smell, texture*) de bois; **w. carrots,** carottes dures.
wooer ['wuːər] *n Arch & Lit* prétendant *m*.
woof¹ [wuːf] *n Tex* trame *f*.
woof² [wʊf] *n F* (*of dog*) aboiement *m*; **the doggie goes w.(w.),** (*in children's language*) le toutou fait oua-oua; **to give a w.,** lancer un aboiement, faire oua-oua.
woof³ [wʊf] *vi* (*of dog*) aboyer, faire oua-oua.
woofer ['wʊfər] *n* (*in stereo equipment*) haut-parleur *m* de basses, boomer *m*, woofer *m*.
wool [wʊl] *n* **(a)** (*material*) laine *f*; **the w. industry,** l'industrie lainière; **the w. trade,** le commerce des laines; **combed w.,** laine peignée; **pure w. suit,** complet *m* pure laine; **a ball of w.,** une pelote de laine; *Fig* **to pull the w. over s.o.'s eyes,** jeter de la poudre aux yeux de qn; *Fig* **you can't pull the w. over my eyes,** tu ne peux pas me faire croire n'importe quoi; **w. cloth,** tissu *m* de laine; **w. grower,** éleveur, -euse de moutons; **w. shop,** magasin *m* de laines; **(b)** pelage *m* (*d'animal*); **(c)** *Bot* laine *f*, duvet *m*; **(d)** *F* (*hair*) cheveux crépus; **(e)** *Tech* **mineral w.,** laine minérale; **steel** *or* **wire w.,** paille *f* de fer.
woolen, wooly *etc US* = **WOOLLEN, WOOLLY** *etc*.
woolgathering ['wʊlgæð(ə)rɪŋ] *n F* **(a)** *n* rêvasserie *f*; **(b)** (*used as a verb*) **to be w.,** rêvasser; **he's always w.,** il a toujours l'esprit ailleurs.
woollen, *US* **woolen** ['wʊlən] **1** *adj* (*dress etc*) en laine; **w. materials,** laines *fpl*, lainages *mpl*. **2** *npl* **woollens,** laines *fpl*, lainages *mpl*.
woolliness, *US* **wooliness** ['wʊlɪnɪs] *n* **(a)** *Fig* imprécision *f* (*de raisonnement, du style*); nébulosité *f* (*d'idées*); manque *m* de netteté, flou *m* (*des contours*); **(b)** nature laineuse (**of,** de).
woolly, *US* **wooly** ['wʊlɪ] **1** *adj* **(a)** laineux; de laine; **w. clouds,** nuages ouatés; **w. hair,** cheveux crépus; **(b)** *Fig* peu net; (*outline*) flou; **w. ideas,** idées vagues *ou* nébuleuses; **w.-minded,** aux idées imprécises *ou* vagues; **w. style,** style *m* qui manque de précision; **a w. thinking liberal,** un libéral aux idées vagues; **(c)** (*fruit*) farineux. **2** *n F* tricot *m*, laine *f*; **winter woollies,** vêtements chauds d'hiver.
woolsack ['wʊlsæk] *n Br Parl* **the W.,** = le siège du Lord Chancellor (à la Chambre des Lords).
woozy ['wuːzɪ] *adj F* tout chose, patraque; **I feel a bit w.,** je me sens un peu patraque, je me sens tout chose.
wop [wɒp] *n Offensive Sl* macaroni *m*, rital *m*.
Worcs *abbr* **Worcestershire.**
word¹ [wɜːd] *n* **(a)** mot *m*; **w. for w.,** (*répéter qch*) mot pour mot; (*traduire qch*) mot à mot, textuellement; **a play on words,** un jeu de mots; **in a** *or* **one w.,** en un mot, bref; **in a w., no,** en un mot, non; **in a few words,** en quelques mots; **in other words,** en d'autres termes, autrement dit; **those were her very words,** ce sont ses propres mots; **I told him in so many words that ...,** je lui ai dit en termes propres *ou* en termes exprès que ...; **did she say you could take it?— well not in so many words,** est-ce qu'elle a dit que tu pouvais le prendre? — eh bien, pas exactement; **in the strict sense of the w.,** au sens strict du mot; **he doesn't know a w. of German,** il ne sait pas un mot d'allemand; **'robbery' would be a better w. for it,** 'vol' serait un mot plus approprié; **bad isn't the w. for it,** mauvais n'est pas assez dire; **that's the wrong** *or* **not the right w. (for it),** ce n'est pas le mot qui convient; **there's a w. for it in Russian,** il y a un mot pour exprimer cela en russe; **the Spanish w. for 'mouse',** 'mouse' en espagnol; **he was reserved — that's one w. for it!,** il était réservé — c'est le moins qu'on puisse dire!; **there's a w. for people like you, it's 'thief',** les gens dans ton genre, on les appelle des voleurs; **she used a less flattering w.,** elle a utilisé un terme moins flatteur; **what's the w. I'm looking for?,** quel est le mot que je cherche?; **there's no other w. for it,** il n'y a pas d'autre mot; **the spoken/written w.,** la parole/les écrits *mpl*; **in the words of Voltaire,** selon (l'expression *f* de) Voltaire, comme l'a dit Voltaire; **that is your w., not mine,** c'est toi qui as dit cela, pas moi; **in your own words,** selon tes propres mots; **a 600-w. article,** un article de 600 mots; **I can't put it into words,** je n'arrive pas à l'exprimer par des mots; **I have been asked to say a few words of introduction,** on m'a demandé de dire quelques mots d'introduction; **he's a man of few words,** c'est un homme qui parle peu *ou* qui ne parle pas beaucoup; **I can't get a w. out of her,** je ne peux pas en tirer un mot; **I couldn't get a w. in (edgeways),** je n'ai pas pu placer un mot; **he didn't say a w.,** il n'a rien dit, il n'a pas soufflé mot; **not a w.!,** pas un mot!, bouche cousue!; **without a w.,** sans mot dire; **no w.** *or* **without the w. of a lie,** sans mentir; **she was here, no w.** *or* **without a w. of a lie,** elle était là, je ne mens pas; **with these words, he went,** ce disant *ou* sur ces mots *ou* là-dessus, il est parti; **you're putting words into my mouth,** vous me faites dire des choses que je ne veux pas dire; **you've taken the words (right) out of my mouth,** tu me l'as retiré de la bouche; **words fail me!,** j'en perds la parole!; **too ridiculous for words,** d'un ridicule sans nom; **too beautiful for words,** d'une beauté ineffable; **hard words,** paroles dures; **fine words, but we'll see if their actions match them,** belles paroles, mais nous verrons si l'on peut en dire de même de leurs actes; **may I have a w. with you?, I'd like a w. with you,** puis-je vous parler un instant?; **I'll have a w. with her about it,** je lui en toucherai deux mots; **to put in a good w. for s.o.,** dire *ou* glisser un mot en faveur de qn; **he never has a good w. for anyone,** il ne peut pas s'empêcher de dire du mal de son prochain; **a w. in/out of season,** un conseil opportun/inopportun; **a w. of warning,** une mise en garde; **I gave him a w. of warning,** je l'ai mis en garde; **can I offer you a w. (or two) of advice?,** puis-je vous donner un petit conseil?; **they had few words of comfort for her,** ils ne lui ont pas dit grand-chose pour la consoler; **a w. of sympathy,** un mot de condoléances; **kind words,** des mots aimables; **war of words,** guerre *f* oratoire; **w. association,** association *f* de mots; *Psy* **w. blindness,** dyslexie *f*; **w. group,** groupe *m* de mots; membre *m* de phrase; *Gram* **w. order,** ordre *m* des mots; **w. picture,** description imagée *ou* pittoresque; portrait *m* en prose (*de qn*); **words per minute,** (*of printer, typist*) mots par minute; **to be w. perfect,** (*of actor*) savoir son rôle sur le bout du doigt; *Comptr* **w. processing,** traitement *m* de texte; *Comptr* **w. processor,** (machine *f* à) traitement de texte;

(b) (*message*) nouvelle *f*; (*official etc*) avis *m*; **to send s.o. w. of sth,** faire part à qn de qch; (*officially, formally*) faire savoir qch à qn; **they sent w. that ...,** ils ont fait savoir que ...; **we received w. that ...,** on nous a apporté la nouvelle que ...; **have you had any w. yet?,** (*of how they are etc*) est-ce que tu as eu des nouvelles?; **there's (been) no w. from Moscow,** on n'a pas de nouvelles de Moscou; **by w. of mouth,** de vive voix, verbalement; **the w. is that he's retiring,** on raconte qu'il va prendre sa retraite; **the w. on the street is that Johnny Razor did it,** le bruit court que c'est Johnny Razor qui l'a fait; **she left w. with Fred for them to join her,** elle a demandé à Fred de leur dire de la rejoindre; **if you want any more paper just say the w.,** si tu veux encore du papier, dis-le;

(c) (*promise*) parole *f*; **one's w. of honour,** sa parole d'honneur; **to give s.o. one's w.,** donner sa parole à qn; **to keep one's w.,** tenir (sa) parole; **to break one's w.,** manquer à sa parole; **to go back on one's w.,** revenir sur sa parole; **I give you my w., (you can) take my w. for it,** je vous en donne ma parole, je vous en réponds; **I'll take your w. for it,** je vous crois sur parole, je m'en rapporte à vous; **we've only got her w. for it,** du moins, c'est ce qu'elle nous a dit: **it's your w. against his,** c'est votre parole contre la sienne; **he's a man of his w.,** c'est un homme de parole; **she's as good as her w.,** elle tient parole; **she was better than her w.,** elle a fait mieux que tenir ses promesses; **his w. is as good as his bond,** sa parole vaut sa signature; **they took her at her w.,** ils l'ont prise au mot; **we will hold you to your w.,** nous vous obligerons à tenir parole; **my w.!,** ma parole!;

(d) to have words with s.o., (*argue*) se disputer *ou* se quereller avec qn; **they had words,** ils ont eu des mots;

(e) w. of command, ordre *m*; **to give the w. to do sth,** (*give order*) donner l'ordre de faire qch; (*give signal*) donner le signal de faire qch;

(f) *Rel* **the w. of God,** la parole de Dieu; **the W.,** (*Christ*) le Verbe; **to spread the w.,** (*proselytize*) annoncer la bonne parole;

(g) *Comptr* mot *m* (machine); **key w.,** mot-clef *m*, *pl* mots-clefs;

(h) (*lyrics*) **words and music by Ian Smith,** paroles *fpl* et musique *f* par Ian Smith; **listen to the words,** écoute les paroles.

word² *vt* formuler, rédiger (*un document etc*); **it might have been differently worded,** on aurait pu l'exprimer autrement *ou* en d'autres termes; **be careful how you w. it,** fais attention à la manière dont tu le formules; **a cleverly worded contract,** un contrat habilement formulé.

wordbook ['wɜːdbʊk] *n* vocabulaire *m*, lexique *m*.

wordiness ['wɜːdɪnɪs] *n* verbosité *f*, prolixité *f*.

wording ['wɜːdɪŋ] *n* **(a)** formulation *f*; (choix *m* de) termes *mpl* (*d'un article, d'un acte etc*); **the w. was ambiguous,** les termes étaient ambigus, la formulation était ambiguë; **it is important to get the w. right,** il est important de choisir les termes appropriés; **(b)** rédaction *f* (*d'un document*); libellé *m* (*d'une traite, d'une lettre de change*); énoncé *m* (*d'un acte, d'un problème*).

wordless ['wɜːdlɪs] *adj* sans paroles, muet.

wordlessly ['wɜːdlɪslɪ] *adv* sans dire un mot.

word-process ['wɜːdprəʊses] *vt* rédiger par traitement de texte.

wordsmith ['wɜːdsmɪθ] *n* = personne qui a l'art des mots ou qui sait manier les mots.

wordy ['wɜːdɪ] *adj* verbeux, prolixe, diffus.

work¹ [wɜːk] *n* **(a)** (*labour*) travail *m*, -aux; **to be at w.,** être au travail; **they are at w. on a new book,** ils sont en train de travailler à un nouveau livre; **the forces at w.,** les forces en jeu; **there are evil forces at w.,** des forces maléfiques sont à l'œuvre; **to be hard at w.,** être en plein travail; **he was hard at w. gardening,** il était en plein jardinage; **to start w., to set** *or* **get to w.,** se mettre au travail; **they set to w. digging the hole/rebuilding their relationship,** ils se sont mis à creuser le trou/rebâtir leur relation; **they put him to w. in the kitchen,** ils l'ont mis au travail dans la cuisine; **she was set to w. cataloguing the collection,** on lui a donné pour tâche de répertorier la collection; **to stop w.,** cesser le travail; suspendre le travail (*pour la journée*); **w. environment,** milieu *m* de travail; **w. permit,** permis *m* de travail; *Comptr* **w. station,** poste *m* de travail;

(b) (*task*) travail *m*, ouvrage *m*, besogne *f*, tâche *f*; **I've (got) w. to do,** j'ai (du travail) à faire; **to have too much w. to do,** avoir trop de travail à faire; **to get through a lot of w.,** abattre de la besogne; **to give s.o. some w. to do,** donner du travail à faire à qn; **there's a lot of w. to be done,** il y a beaucoup (de travail) à faire; **it will take a lot of w. to make a team out of them,** ça va être un drôle de travail de faire d'eux une équipe; **she put a lot of w. into her exams,** elle a beaucoup travaillé à ses examens; **they're doing some w. for an American firm,** (*of subcontractor*) ils travaillent pour une firme américaine; **very little w. has been done on this disease,** peu de travail a été effectué sur cette maladie; **let's get down to w.!,** mettons-nous au travail!; **a fine piece of w.,** un beau travail; **the brandy had done its w.,** l'eau de vie avait fait son effet; **I'll have my w. cut out to finish in time,** je vais en baver pour finir à l'heure; **you'll have your w. cut out with him,** il vous donnera du fil à retordre; **she made short w. of her opponent,** elle a vaincu son adversaire sans peine; **he made quick** *or* **short w. of the ironing,** il est rapidement venu à bout du repassage; **day's w.,** (travail d'une) journée *f*; **it's all in a day's w.,** ça n'a rien d'exceptionnel; **good w.!,** bien fait!; **it was thirsty w.,** c'était un travail qui donnait soif; **the w. of a professional,** le travail *ou* l'œuvre *f* d'un professionnel; **this break-in is the w. of a professional,** cette effraction est l'œuvre d'un professionnel;

(c) (*product, achievement*) ouvrage *m*, œuvre *f*; **the works of God,** les œuvres de Dieu; **good works,** bonnes œuvres; **the (complete) works of Shakespeare,** les œuvres *fpl ou* l'œuvre *m or f* de Shakespeare; **a w. of art/genius,** une œuvre d'art/de génie; **his early works,** ses premières œuvres; **w. of fiction,** ouvrage de fiction; **is this all your own w.?,** est-ce que vous avez fait ça tout seul?; **her w. sells well,** ses ouvrages se vendent bien; **very detailed** *or* **delicate w.,** ouvrage très détaillé *ou* délicat;

(d) (*employment*) travail *m*, emploi *m*; **I need w.,** il me faut du travail; **what kind of w. are you looking for?,** quel genre de travail recherchez-vous?; **office w.,** travail de bureau; **manual w.,** travail manuel; **skilled w.,** travail qualifié; **the factory will provide w. for a hundred people,** l'usine fournira du travail à cent personnes; **to be off w.,** ne pas travailler (*parce qu'on est malade*); **to be out of w.,** (*unemployed*) être en *ou* au chômage; (*not have anything to do*) chômer; **she's not in w. at the moment,** elle ne travaille pas en ce moment; *F* **nice w. if you can get it,** il y en a qui ne s'embêtent pas!; *F* **he's a nasty bit of w.,** c'est un sale type; *F* **their daughter is a nasty bit of w.,** leur fille est une sale gosse;

(e) (*workplace*) (lieu *m* de) travail *m*; **he's not at w. today,** il ne travaille pas aujourd'hui; **on my way to w.,** en allant travailler *ou* au travail; **someone at w. told me,** quelqu'un au travail me l'a dit; **someone from w.,** quelqu'un du travail; **someone from your w. called,** quelqu'un de ton travail a appelé;

(f) *Mil* (*usu pl*) **works,** ouvrages *mpl*, travaux *mpl*; **defensive works,** ouvrages défensifs; **field works,** travaux de campagne;

(g) *Constr* (*usu pl*) **works,** travaux *mpl*; **public works,** travaux publics; **road works ahead!,** attention travaux!; *US* **w. zone!,** travaux!, chantier!;

(h) (*mechanism*) *usu pl* **works,** rouages *mpl*, mécanisme *m* (*d'une montre etc*); *F* **eggs, bacon, toast — the works,** des œufs, du bacon, du pain grillé — tout, quoi!; *F* **the whole works,** tout le bataclan, tout le tralala; *Sl* **to give s.o. the works,** (*a beating*) passer qn à tabac; (*full treatment*) recevoir qn avec la croix et la bannière; *esp US F* **to shoot the works,** (*spend all one's money*) claquer tout son fric; **to be in the works,** (*in preparation*) être en cours;

(i) (*factory*) (*usu pl*) **works,** usine *f*; **works council,** comité *m* d'entreprise.

work² *v* (*pt & pp* **worked** [wɜːkt]; *Arch and in a few expressions* **wrought** [rɔːt]) **1** *vi* **(a)** (*of person*) travailler; (*for good of other people*) œuvrer; **to w. hard,** travailler dur; **to w. like a slave** *or* **a dog** *or* **a Trojan** *or* **a beaver,** travailler comme un forçat; **to w. a 40-hour week,** faire une semaine de 40 heures; **to w. long hours,** avoir des horaires astreignants; *Ind* **to w. to rule,** faire la grève du zèle; **to w. in leather/brass,** travailler dans le cuir/cuivre; **she works in publishing,** elle travaille dans l'édition; **to w. on** *or* **for a newspaper,** collaborer à un journal; **to w. for a good cause,** travailler pour une bonne cause; **he worked with the poor and the sick,** il travaillait avec les pauvres et les malades; **the city council — working to improve the quality of life,** le conseil municipal — à l'œuvre pour l'amélioration de la qualité de la vie; **all her life she worked for peace/to bring the two countries together,** toute sa vie elle a œuvré pour la paix/pour unir les deux pays; **we are working towards a peaceful solution,** nous œuvrons en vue d'une solution pacifique; **to w. for an end,** travailler pour atteindre un but; **to w. against s.o.,** intriguer *ou* travailler contre qn; **their earlier popularity was now working against them,** leur popularité des débuts jouait maintenant en leur défaveur; **let your body weight w. for you rather than against you,** laisse ton poids jouer en ta faveur plutôt que contre toi; **her age worked in her favour,** son âge a joué en sa faveur; **working from the principle that ...,** partant du principe que ...; **I am working on the assumption that you can type,** je pars du principe que vous savez taper à la machine;

(b) (*be employed*) travailler, avoir un emploi; **who do you w. for?,** chez qui est-ce que vous travaillez?; **she works for Smith and Wilson,** elle travaille chez Smith and Wilson; **she works for the water board,** elle travaille au service des eaux;

(c) (*function*) (*of machine, system*) fonctionner, marcher; **the pump isn't working,** la pompe ne marche *ou* ne fonctionne pas; **the lift isn't working,** l'ascenseur est hors de service *ou* est en panne; **system that works well,** système qui fonctionne bien; **I can't get this machine to w.,** je n'arrive pas à faire marcher cette machine; **they soon got** *or* **had it working,** ils sont vite parvenus à le faire fonctionner; **can you show me how the photocopier works?,** est-ce que tu peux me faire voir comment marche la photocopieuse?; **it works like this, here's how it works,** (*of machine, system*) cela marche de la façon suivante, voilà comment ça marche; **it works both ways,** ça marche dans les deux sens; **the clock works off elec-**

tricity, la pendule marche à l'électricité; **these tools w. by compressed air,** ces outils sont actionnés par *ou* marchent à l'air comprimé;

(d) (*have effect, succeed*) (*of drug, cleaning product*) faire effet; (*of plan, method*) marcher, y faire; (*of yeast*) fermenter; **the drug works in most cases,** le médicament fait de l'effet dans la plupart des cas; **rubbing the stain won't w.,** ça n'y fera rien de frotter la tache; **she tried everything she could think of but nothing worked,** elle a essayé tout ce à quoi elle pouvait penser mais rien n'y a fait; **this isn't working,** (*not succeeding*) ça ne marche pas; **his plan didn't w.,** son projet a échoué *ou* n'a pas réussi; **that/flattery won't w. with me,** ça/la flatterie ne prend pas avec moi;

(e) (*of face, features*) remuer;

(f) (*move*) **to w. to windward,** (*of sailing ship*) chasser dans le vent, louvoyer; **to w. upstream,** (*of angler*) remonter le courant; **to w. loose,** (*of nut etc*) se desserrer, se détacher.

2 *vt* **(a)** faire travailler (*qn, un cheval etc*); **he works his employees/himself very hard,** il exige beaucoup de travail de son personnel/lui-même; **to w. oneself to death,** se tuer à force de travailler; **don't w. yourself to death!,** ne va pas te tuer à la tâche *ou* à l'ouvrage!; *Iron* ne te fais pas trop mal, surtout!;

(b) (*operate*) faire travailler, faire fonctionner, faire marcher (*une machine etc*); *Nau etc* manœuvrer (*un navire, les voiles, une pompe*); **it is worked by steam/electricity,** cela marche à la vapeur/à l'électricité;

(c) (*bring about*) opérer (*un miracle, une guérison*); exercer (*une influence*); amener (*un changement*); produire (*un effet*); **the beauty of the place was beginning to w. its magic on her,** la beauté de l'endroit commençait à exercer sa magie sur elle; **the destruction wrought by the fire,** la dévastation causée par l'incendie; **I'll try to w. it** *or* **things so that they pay in advance,** je ferai de sorte qu'ils paient à l'avance; **his keys had worked a hole in his pocket,** ses clefs avaient fini par faire un trou dans sa poche;

(d) (*move*) **to w. one's hands free,** parvenir à dégager ses mains; **she worked the ropes loose,** elle a réussi à desserrer les cordes petit à petit; **to w. one's way down/up,** descendre/monter petit à petit *ou* avec précaution; **his fingers worked their way along the ledge,** ses doigts se sont déplacés petit à petit le long du rebord; **he worked his way towards her,** il s'est avancé vers elle petit à petit; **they worked their way through the crowd,** ils se sont frayé un chemin à travers la foule;

(e) exploiter (*une mine, une carrière*); travailler (*la terre*); *Com* **to w. the south-east,** (*of representative*) couvrir le sud-est;

(f) *Nau* **to w. one's passage,** payer son passage par son travail; **he worked his passage to Rio,** il a payé son passage à Rio en travaillant; **to w. one's way through university,** (*of student*) travailler pour payer ses études;

(g) broder (*un dessin, des initiales*); **the flowers are worked in silk,** les fleurs sont brodées à la soie.

▶**work in** *vtsep* (*include, introduce*) introduire (*un incident dans un roman etc*); incorporer, mélanger (*qch à qch*); **w. in a reference to unemployment,** introduire une allusion au chômage; **w. the other ingredients in,** incorporer les autres ingrédients; **gently w. the cream into your hands,** massez-vous doucement les mains pour y faire pénétrer la crème.

▶**work off** *vtsep* évacuer (*sa colère, sa mauvaise humeur*) (**by doing,** en faisant); **to w. off one's anger on s.o.,** passer sa colère sur qn; **I'm doing some gardening to try to w. off fat,** je fais du jardinage pour essayer de brûler de la graisse.

▶**work on 1** *vi* (*continue to work*) continuer à travailler. **2** *vipo* **(a)** (*be involved in*) travailler à *ou* sur (*qch*); **he's working on an edition of Hamlet,** il travaille à *ou* prépare une édition de Hamlet; **we're working on it,** nous travaillons là-dessus; **a detective is working on this case,** un détective est sur cette affaire; **he's been working on his breaststroke/emotional problems,** il a travaillé sa brasse/essayé de résoudre ses problèmes sentimentaux; **(b)** (*use as basis*) **have you any data to w. on?,** avez-vous des données sur lesquelles vous fonder?; **(c)** (*persuade*) influencer (*qn*), agir sur (l'esprit de) (*qn*); (*attempt to persuade*) travailler (*qn*).

▶**work out 1** *vtsep* **(a)** (*calculate*) calculer (*le coût, la distance*); **from this information, w. out the answer,** à partir de cette information, déduisez la réponse; **I w. it out at £22,** d'après mes calculs, ça fait 22 livres; **the dog had worked out how to open the door,** le chien avait compris comment ouvrir la porte; **he's a strange person — I'd worked that out!,** il est bizarre — je m'en étais rendu compte!;

(b) (*devise*) élaborer (*une methode etc*); organiser, monter (*un cambriolage*);

(c) (*resolve*) résoudre, arranger; faire (*un calcul*); résoudre (*un problème*); **we must try to w. out our differences,** nous devons essayer de résoudre nos désaccords; **I'm sure we can w. this thing out,** (*your problem*) je suis sûr que nous pouvons arranger ça; (*our argument*) je suis sûr que nous finirons par nous mettre d'accord;

(d) (*understand*) comprendre (*qn, qch*); **I can't w. her out,** je n'arrive pas à la comprendre; **she couldn't w. it out,** elle n'y comprenait rien;

(e) (*of mine, seam*) **to be worked out,** être épuisé.

2 *vi* **(a)** (*be resolved*) **I wonder how it will all w. out,** je me demande comment cela finira *ou* va finir; **it** *or* **things worked out very well for me,** ça a *ou* les choses ont très bien marché pour moi; **it worked out well** *or* **all right for us,** ça s'est bien passé pour nous, les choses ont bien tourné pour nous; **but it didn't w. out that way,** mais il en a été tout autrement; **it worked out badly for them,** les choses ont mal tourné pour eux;

(b) (*succeed*) (*of marriage, arrangement*) marcher; **they started a business together, but it didn't w. out,** ils ont monté une affaire ensemble, mais ça n'a pas marché; **I don't like my job, but things may w. out,** je n'aime pas mon travail, mais ça va peut-être s'arranger; **how is the new system working out?,** est-ce que le nouveau système marche?;

(c) (*amount to*) **how much does it all w. out at?,** ça fait combien en tout?; **it** *or* **the cost works out at £150 a head,** cela fait 150 livres par personne;

(d) *Sp* s'entraîner.

▶**work up 1** *vtsep* **(a)** (*develop*) **to w. up an appetite,** s'ouvrir l'appétit; **I can't w. up much enthusiasm/interest for the idea,** j'ai du mal à m'enthousiasmer pour/à m'intéresser à cette idée; **(b)** (*arouse*) **he worked the crowd up into a frenzy,** petit à petit, il a déchaîné la frénésie de la foule; **she had worked herself up into a dreadful rage,** elle s'était mise dans une rage terrible; **to be** *or* **get worked up,** (*upset*) se rendre malade (**about,** au sujet de); (*angry*) se fâcher (**about,** au sujet de); (*excited*) se mettre dans tous ses états (**about,** au sujet de). **2** *vi* (*of skirt*) remonter.

▶**work up to** *vipo* (*move towards*) avancer par degrés à (*qch*); **what are you working up to?,** où voulez-vous en venir?; **he was working up to a discussion of his salary,** il amenait progressivement une discussion concernant son salaire; **the symphony was working up to its finale,** la symphonie approchait sa finale.

workability [wɜːkə'bɪlɪtɪ] *n* maniabilité *f*.

workable ['wɜːkəb(ə)l] *adj* **(a)** *Tech* (*matériel*) maniable; **(b)** (*mine*) exploitable; **(c)** (*projet*) réalisable; **it isn't a w. proposition,** ce n'est pas une proposition réalisable.

workaday ['wɜːkədeɪ] *adj* de tous les jours; **w. clothes,** habits *mpl* de tous les jours.

workaholic [wɜːkə'hɒlɪk] *n F* bourreau *m* de travail, drogué, -ée de travail.

workbag ['wɜːkbæg] *n Sewing* sac *m* à ouvrage.

workbasket ['wɜːkbɑːskɪt] *n Sewing* corbeille *f* à ouvrage.

workbench ['wɜːkbentʃ] *n* établi *m*.

workbox ['wɜːkbɒks] *n Sewing* boîte *f* à ouvrage.

workday ['wɜːkdeɪ] **1** *n* (*weekday*) jour *m* ouvrable; (*day of work*) journée *f* de travail. **2** *adj* = **WORKADAY**.

worker ['wɜːkər] *n* **(a)** travailleur, -euse; *Ind* ouvrier, -ière; **heavy w.,** travailleur de force; **hard w.,** travailleur assidu; **to be a hard w.,** travailler dur; **'Workers of the world unite!',** 'travailleurs de tous pays, unissez-vous!'; **the workers,** (*as opposed to management*) le personnel; **w. of miracles,** faiseur, -euse de miracles; **w. participation,** participation *f* des ouvriers; **w. director,** ouvrier siégeant au conseil d'administration; **(b)** *Ent* **w. (bee** *or* **ant),** ouvrière *f*.

worker-priest ['wɜːkəpriːst] *n* prêtre-ouvrier *m*, *pl* prêtres-ouvriers.

workflow ['wɜːkfləʊ] *n* rythme *m* de travail; **w. schedule,** plan *m* de travail.

workforce ['wɜːkfɔːs] *n* main-d'œuvre *f*.

workhorse ['wɜːkhɔːs] *n* cheval *m* de labour; *Fig* **to be a w.,** travailler comme un cheval *ou* une bête; **she's a willing w.,** elle est toujours prête à faire n'importe quelle tâche.

workhouse ['wɜːkhaʊs] *n* **(a)** *Arch* asile *m* des pauvres; **(b)** *Old-fashioned US* maison *f* de correction.

working ['wɜːkɪŋ] **1** *adj* **(a)** (*person*) qui travaille; **w. man/woman/people,** ouvrier/ouvrière/ouvriers; **w. wife/mother,** femme mariée/mère *f* de famille qui travaille; **the w. classes,** la classe ouvrière; **he's very hard w.,** il est très travailleur, il travaille très dur; **w. party,** *Pol Ind* groupe *m* de travail; *Mil* atelier *m*, équipe *f*;
(b) (*machine etc*) qui fonctionne; **w. parts of a machine,** mécanisme *m* d'une machine;
(c) **w. agreement,** modus vivendi *m*; **to have a w. knowledge of French/the law,** posséder une connaissance suffisante du français/du droit; **w. majority,** majorité suffisante; **w. theory,** théorie *f* qui donne des résultats.
2 *n* **(a)** travail *m*; **a relaxed w. environment,** un milieu professionnel détendu; **throughout her w. life,** tout au long de sa vie active *ou* de sa vie professionnelle; **the two leaders have a good w. relationship,** les deux dirigeants ont une bonne relation de travail; **w. clothes,** vêtements *mpl* de travail; *Comptr* **w. file,** fichier *m* de travail; **w. hours,** heures *fpl* de travail; **w. day,** (*weekday*) jour *m* ouvrable; (*day of work*) journée *f* (de travail); **w. lunch,** déjeuner *m* d'affaires; **the w. week,** la semaine de travail;
(b) exploitation *f* (*d'une mine, d'une forêt*); *Min* **workings,** chantiers *mpl* d'exploitation; **old mine workings,** anciens chantiers d'exploitation d'une mine; *Fin* **w. capital,** capital *m* d'exploitation, fonds *m* de roulement; *Fin* **w. expenses,** frais généraux, frais d'exploitation; *Min* **w. face,** front *m* de taille;
(c) (*operation*) manœuvre *f* (*d'une machine etc*); **in w. order,** en état de fonctionnement *ou* marche; **to be in good w. order,** bien fonctionner; **w. speed,** vitesse *f* de régime;
(d) (*mechanism*) (*usu pl*) **workings,** mécanisme *m*, rouages *mpl*; (*of organization or system*) rouages; **I can't fathom the workings of her mind,** je ne comprends pas ce qui se passe dans sa tête.

working out *n Math* résolution *f* (*d'une problème*); **show all w. out,** faire apparaître un raisonnement.

working-class ['wɜːkɪŋ'klɑːs] *adj* (*family etc*) ouvrier; (*accent*) prolétaire, *F* prolo; **he's very w.-c.,** il fait très prolétaire, **w. c. district,** quartier *m* populaire.

workload ['wɜːkləʊd] *n* quantité *f* de travail; **to have a heavy w.,** avoir beaucoup de travail.

workman, *pl* **-men** ['wɜːkmən] *n* ouvrier *m*; **he's a bad w.,** c'est un mauvais ouvrier; *Prov* **a bad w. blames his tools,** à méchant ouvrier point de bons outils; **workmen's compensation,** indemnité *f* d'invalidité (pour les ouvriers).

workmanlike ['wɜːkmənlaɪk] *adj* (*job*) bien fait, de professionnel; **that looks a w. knife,** ça ressemble à un couteau de professionnel; **to do sth in a w. manner,** faire qch en professionnel; **she took the tent down in a w. manner,** elle a démonté la tente comme une vraie professionnelle; **w. performance,** représentation honnête.

workmanship ['wɜːkmənʃɪp] *n* exécution *f*; travail *m*, façon *f*; **sound w.,** fabrication *ou* exécution soignée; **fine (piece of) w.,** beau travail; **the w. on this furniture is superb,** ce meuble est fait de façon superbe; **poor w.,** travail de mauvaise qualité; **Swiss w. is second to none,** la fabrication suisse est la meilleure du monde.

workmate ['wɜːkmeɪt] *n esp Br* collègue *m* de travail.

work-out ['wɜːkaʊt] *n Sp* séance *f* d'entraînement.

workpeople ['wɜːkpiːp(ə)l] *npl* ouvriers *mpl*.

workplace ['wɜːkpleɪs] *n* lieu *m* de travail.

workroom ['wɜːkruːm] *n* atelier *m ou* salle *f* de travail.

work-sharing ['wɜːkʃeərɪŋ] *n* partage *m* du travail; **we have a w.-s. arrangement,** nous avons un système de partage du travail; **w.-s. is becoming popular,** le système de partage du travail est de plus en plus fréquemment utilisé.

workshop ['wɜːkʃɒp] *n* atelier *m*; **a music/acting w.,** un atelier de musique/de théâtre.

workshy ['wɜːkʃaɪ] *adj* fainéant; **to be w.,** bouder *ou* renâcler à la besogne.

worktable ['wɜːkteɪb(ə)l] *n* table *f* de travail; *Sewing* table à ouvrage.

worktop ['wɜːktɒp] *n* (*in kitchen*) plan *m* de travail.

work-to-rule [wɜːktə'ruːl] *n Ind* grève *f* du zèle; **to operate a w.-to-r.,** faire une grève du zèle.

workweek ['wɜːkwiːk] *n esp Am* semaine *f* de travail; **a four-day w.,** une semaine (de travail) de quatre jours; **the forty-hour w.,** la semaine de quarante heures.

world [wɜːld] *n* **(a)** monde *m*; **in this w.,** en ce monde; **the other** *or* **next w., the w. to come,** l'autre monde; *Rel* **the w., the flesh and the devil,** le monde, la chair et le diable; **he's not long for this w.,** il n'en a pas pour longtemps à vivre; **to bring a child into the w.,** (*of mother, midwife, doctor*) mettre un enfant au monde; **she came into the w. on 25th May 1925,** elle est venue au monde le 25 mai 1925; **he wants the best of both worlds,** il veut tout avoir; **the end of the w.,** la fin du monde; *F* **it's not the end of the w.,** ce n'est pas la fin du monde, ce n'est pas une catastrophe; *Rel* **w. without end,** jusqu'à la fin des siècles; éternellement; **the whole w.,** le monde entier; **there isn't a nicer spot in the whole w.,** il n'y a pas d'endroit plus agréable au monde; **to be alone in the w.,** être seul au monde; **you're not the only person in the w.!,** tu n'es pas seul au monde!; **the happiest man in the w.,** l'homme le plus heureux du monde; **he's the w.'s worst letter-writer,** il n'y a pas pire correspondant que lui au monde; **you're the w.'s worst!,** il n'y a pas pire que toi!; **she lives in a w. of her own,** elle vit dans un monde à part; **you live in a dream** *or* **fantasy w.,** tu vis dans un monde imaginaire; **the w. we live in is not like that,** le monde dans lequel nous vivons n'est pas comme ça; **it's a different w. up north,** c'est complètement différent au nord; **the book takes us into a w. of corruption and intrigue,** le livre nous entraîne dans un monde de corruption et d'intrigues; *F* **it's out of this w.,** c'est (quelque chose d')extraordinaire *ou* épatant; *F* **it was out of this w.,** (*of experience, holiday etc*) c'était fabuleux; *F* **the mountains were out of this w.,** les montagnes étaient d'une beauté extraordinaire; **what in the w. is the matter with you?,** que pouvez-vous bien avoir?; **where in the w. is that?,** où est-ce que ça peut bien être?; **I wouldn't do it for (anything in) the w.,** je ne le ferais pour rien au monde; **nothing in the w. could make me leave,** rien au monde ne pourrait me faire partir; **what I want most of all in the w. is for you to be happy,** ce que je souhaite le plus au monde, c'est que tu sois heureux; **it's been happening ever since the w. began,** ça se passe comme ça depuis que le monde est monde; **to go round the w.,** faire le tour du monde; **(round-the-)w. trip** *or* **tour,** voyage *m* autour du monde; **he has seen the w.,** il a vu du pays; **map of the w.,** carte *f* du monde; (*in two hemispheres*) mappemonde *f*; **(all) the w. over, all over the w.,** dans le monde entier; **people are the same the w. over,** les gens sont partout pareils; **to the end of the w.,** jusqu'au bout du monde; **it's a small w.!,** (que) le monde est petit!; **the Old/New W.,** l'ancien/le nouveau monde; **the ancient** *or* **classical w.,** l'antiquité *f*; **the English-speaking w.,** le monde anglophone; **the richest nation in the w.,** la nation la plus riche au monde; **the W. Bank,** la Banque Mondiale; **w. champion,** champion *m* du monde; **w. championship,** championnat *m* du monde; **the W. Cup,** (*in soccer*) la coupe du monde; **W. Fair,** exposition internationale; **W. Health Organization,** Organisation mondiale de la santé; **w. history,** histoire universelle; **w. politics,** politique mondiale; *Pol* **w. power,** puissance mondiale; **w. record,** record mondial; *US* **W. Series,** = championnat du monde de base-ball; **w. war,** guerre mondiale; **W. War One/Two,** première/deuxième guerre mondiale;
(b) (*society*) monde *m*; **it's the way of the w.,** ainsi va le monde; **what is the w. coming to?,** où allons-nous?; **man of the w.,** homme qui connaît la vie *ou* qui a l'expérience du monde; **she doesn't care what the w. thinks,** elle se moque de ce que les gens pensent; **he's gone up in the w.,** il a fait du chemin; **to come down in the world,** déchoir; **all the w. knows,** c'est bien connu, tout le monde le sait; *F* **the w. and his wife seemed to be there,** tout le monde sans exception semblait être présent; **the singer had the w. at her feet,** la chanteuse avait tout le monde à ses pieds;
(c) (*circle, field*) **the w. of literature** *or* **of letters, the literary w.,** le milieu *ou* monde littéraire; **the theatrical w.,** le milieu *ou* monde du théâtre;
(d) *F* (*great deal*) **that will do you a w. of good,** cela vous fera le plus grand bien; **there's a w. of difference between ...,** il y a une différence énorme entre ...; **their opinions are worlds apart,** leurs opinions sont totalement différentes; **she thinks the w. of him,** elle l'admire énormément; **she means the w. to them,** elle compte énormément à leurs yeux; **I'd give the w. to know what he's thinking,** je donnerais n'importe quoi pour savoir ce qu'il pense; **they kept on talking, for all the w. as if nothing had happened,** ils ont continué à parler comme s'il ne s'était rien passé.

world-beater ['wɜːldbiːtər] *n* le meilleur *ou* la meilleure du monde.

world-famous ['wɜːld'feɪməs] *adj* de renommée mondiale, célèbre dans le monde entier.

worldliness ['wɜːldlɪnɪs] *n* **(a)** (*knowledge of world*) mondanité *f*; **the child's surprising w.,** la surprenante expérience du monde dont fait preuve la petite fille; **there was an air of w. about her,** elle avait l'air de quelqu'un qui a l'expérience du monde; **(b)** (*materialism*) matérialisme *m*, attachement *m* aux biens de ce monde.

worldly ['wɜːldlɪ] *adj* **(a)** (*of this world*) de ce monde, matériel; **all his w. goods,** toute sa fortune; **w. matters,** les choses matérielles; **he's a child in w. matters,** il n'a aucune expérience du monde; **w. pleasures,** les plaisirs de ce monde; **w. wisdom,** la sagesse du monde *ou* du siècle; **(b)** (*knowledgeable*) qui a l'expérience du monde, qui connaît le monde; **she was very w. for one so young,** elle avait une bien grande expérience du monde pour quelqu'un d'aussi jeune; **(c)** (*materialistic*) matérialiste; **w. clerics,** clergé attaché aux biens matériels.

worldly-minded ['wɜːldlɪ'maɪndɪd] *adj* attaché aux choses matérielles *ou* aux biens de ce monde.

worldly-wise ['wɜːldlɪ'waɪz] *adj* qui a l'expérience du monde, qui connaît le monde; **with a w.-w. air,** avec l'air de quelqu'un qui connaît le monde.

world-weary ['wɜːldwɪərɪ] *adj* las *ou f* lasse de ce monde.

worldwide ['wɜːldwaɪd] **1** *adj* universel, mondial, -aux; **the w. problem of ...,** le problème mondial de ... . **2** *adv* dans le monde entier; **the Olympics are watched w.,** on regarde les Jeux Olympiques dans le monde entier.

worm¹ [wɜːm] *n* **(a)** ver *m*; (*maggot*) asticot *m*; *Fig* **the w. has turned,** j'en ai *ou* elle en a *etc* assez de se laisser mener par le bout du nez; *Fig* **even a w. will turn,** il y a une limite à tout; **he's a w.,** c'est un minable; **w.'s-eye view,** (*from below*) perspective vue d'en bas; (*from lowly position*) perspective au ras des pâquerettes; **to get a w.'s-eye view of the theatre/catering/***etc* **industry,** voir le monde du théâtre/de la restauration/*etc* au ras de pâquerettes *ou* d'un point du vue restreint; *F* **that's opening a real can of worms,** nous allons nous fourrer dans un véritable guêpier; *Med Vet* **to have worms,** avoir des vers; *Hum* **I think you've got worms,** tu dois avoir des vers; *F* **to be food for worms,** bouffer les pissenlits par la racine; **meal w.,** ver de farine; *Pharm* **w. powder,** poudre *f* à vers, poudre vermifuge; **(b)** *Tech* filet *m* (*de vis*); **w. (screw),** vis *f* sans fin.

worm² *vt* **(a) he wormed himself** *or* **his way along the tunnel,** il a avancé dans le tunnel en rampant *ou* en se tortillant; *Fig* **to w. one's way out of/into sth,** se faufiler hors de/dans qch; *Fig* **I'd like to see her w. her way out of that one,** j'aimerais bien voir comment elle va s'en tirer; **to w. oneself into s.o.'s favour/confidence,** s'insinuer dans les bonnes grâces de qn/la confiance de qn; **to w. a secret out of s.o.,** tirer un secret de qn, arracher un secret à qn; **I'll w. it out of him,** je saurai lui tirer les vers du nez; **(b)** *Vet* **to w. a dog,** débarrasser un chien de ses vers.

wormcast ['wɜːmkɑːst] *n* déjection *f* de ver de terre.

wormeaten ['wɜːmiːtən] *adj* mangé aux vers; (*wood*) vermoulu; (*fruit*) véreux.

wormhole ['wɜːmhəʊl] *n* (*in wood, ground*) trou *m* de ver; (*in cloth, wood*) piqûre *f* (de ver).

wormwood ['wɜːmwʊd] *n Bot* armoise *f* (amère); *Lit* **life to him was gall and w.,** la vie pour lui n'était qu'amertume et dégoût.

wormy ['wɜːmɪ] *adj* **(a)** (*furniture*) infesté *ou* plein de vers; (*fruit*) véreux; (*wood, cloth*) piqué des vers; **(b)** (*worm-like*) vermiforme, vermiculaire.

worried ['wʌrɪd] *adj* tourmenté, tracassé, soucieux; **I'm w. about this,** cela m'inquiète *ou* me tracasse; **he was w. by these developments,** ces développements l'inquiétaient; **she's w. about the car,** elle est inquiète au sujet de la voiture; **they're w. sick about her,** ils sont malades d'inquiétude à son sujet; **he looks w.,** il a l'air préoccupé *ou* soucieux, **a w. expression,** une expression inquiète.

worriedly ['wʌrɪdlɪ] *adv* anxieusement, soucieusement, avec inquiétude.

worrier ['wʌrɪər] *n* = personne qui se tracasse ou qui se fait de la bile; **he's such a w.,** il se fait tellement de soucis.

worrisome ['wʌrɪsəm] *adj* tracassant, inquiétant.

worry¹ ['wʌrɪ] *n* ennui *m*, souci *m*, tracas *m*; **financial worries,** soucis d'argent; **it's causing me a lot of w.,** cela m'inquiète beaucoup; **that's the least of my worries,** c'est le moindre *ou* le dernier de mes soucis; *F* **what's your w.?,** qu'est-ce qui ne va pas?; **w. beads,** chapelet *m* (*pour s'occuper les mains*).

worry² **1** *vt* **(a)** (*cause anxiety to*) inquiéter (*qn*); **these events worried her greatly,** ces événements l'ont beaucoup inquiétée; **that boiler worries me — suppose it blows up?,** la chaudière m'inquiète — si elle explosait?; **Janet worries me sometimes, she's not like other little girls,** Janet m'inquiète parfois, elle n'est pas comme les autres petites filles; **something is worrying her,** il y a quelque chose qui la préoccupe *ou* qui la travaille; **tell me what's worrying you,** dites-moi ce qui vous préoccupe; **it doesn't w. me what other people think,** je ne me soucie pas de ce que les autres pensent; **it worried him that he was getting older,** le fait de vieillir le préoccupait; **it doesn't seem to w. you if other people get hurt,** que d'autres souffrent ne semble pas te préoccuper; **doesn't it w. you, your daughter out this late?,** ça ne vous inquiète pas que votre fille ne soit pas rentrée à cette heure tardive?; **it doesn't w. her who she upsets,** elle ne se préoccupe pas des gens qu'elle froisse; **it worries me to think of them all on their own,** ça m'inquiète de penser qu'ils sont tout seuls; **to w. oneself sick** *or* **to death about sth/s.o.,** se rendre malade d'inquiétude *ou* mourir d'inquiétude au sujet de qch/qn;

(b) (*of dog, wolf*) attaquer, harceler (*les moutons*); (*of person*) tourmenter, tracasser, harceler, importuner (*qn*); **don't w. him,** laissez-le tranquille; **don't w. your little head about it,** ne te casse pas la tête pour ça.

2 *vi* se tourmenter, se tracasser, s'inquiéter, se faire du souci *ou* de la bile *ou* du mauvais sang; **don't tell them, they'll only w.,** ne le leur dis pas, ça ne fera que les inquiéter; **he keeps worrying about that business,** cette affaire lui travaille l'esprit; **don't (you) w.!,** *F* **not to w.!,** ne vous tracassez *ou* inquiétez pas!, ne vous en faites pas!; **sorry, I forgot the milk — don't w., not to w.,** je suis désolée, j'ai oublié le lait — ne vous inquiétez pas; **don't (you) w. about me,** ne t'inquiète pas pour moi; **there's plenty more beer, don't you w.,** il reste plein de bière, ne t'en fais pas; **you'll find out soon enough, don't you w.,** vous n'allez pas tarder à le savoir, ne vous en faites pas; **there's** *or* **it's nothing to w. about,** ce n'est rien d'inquiétant; **it's only a scratch, nothing to w. about,** ce n'est qu'une égratignure, pas de quoi s'inquiéter; **what's the use of worrying?,** à quoi bon se tourmenter?; *F* **I should w.!,** ce n'est pas mon affaire!

worryguts ['wʌrɪgʌts] *n Br F* bileux *m*, bileuse *f*; **don't be such a w.,** arrête de te tracasser autant.

worrying ['wʌrɪɪŋ] **1** *adj* tracassant, inquiétant. **2** *n* tracasserie *f*, tracas *m*, tourment *m*, inquiétude *f*; **all this w. will get you nowhere,** à quoi bon se tourmenter?

worrywart ['wʌrɪwɔːt] *n Am F* = **WORRYGUTS.**

worse [wɜːs] **1** *adj* (*comp of* **bad**) pire, plus mauvais; **I'm a w. player than he is** *or* **him** *or Fml* **he,** je joue plus mal que lui; **your problems are w. than ours,** vos problèmes sont pires que les nôtres; **the situation was w. than (it had been) before,** la situation était pire qu'avant; **there's nothing w. than arriving too early,** il n'y a rien de pire que d'arriver trop tôt; **you're bad at French but he's w.,** tu es mauvais en français mais il est pire; **in w. condition,** dans un plus mauvais état; **this is getting w. and w.,** c'est *ou* ça va de mal en pis; **how are things? — no w. than before,** comment ça va? — pas plus mal qu'avant; **things could be w.,** ça pourrait être pire; **you're only making things** *or* **matters w.,** vous ne faites qu'empirer les choses; **to make things** *or* **matters w. ...,** par *ou* pour surcroît de malheur...; **it'll just make it w. if you tell them,** ça ne va faire qu'empirer les choses si tu le leur dis; **you'll only make matters w. for yourself by offending them,** tu ne feras qu'aggraver ton cas en les offensant; **it will be the w. for them if she finds out,** ça va être encore pire pour eux si elle l'apprend; **it might have been w.,** il n'y a que demi-mal; **he escaped with nothing w. than a fright,** il en fut quitte pour la peur; **what is w ....,** ce qui est plus grave ...; **to go from bad to w.,** aller de mal en pis; **to get w.,** (*deteriorate*) s'altérer; (*of illness*) s'aggraver, empirer; **the situation is getting w.,** la situation s'aggrave; **how do you feel today? — w.,** comment ça va aujourd'hui? — pire; **things** *or* **it will get w. before they get** *or* **it gets better,** les choses iront plus mal avant d'aller mieux, ça ira plus mal avant d'aller mieux; **I am none the w. for it,** je ne m'en trouve pas plus mal; **his memory's got a lot w.,** sa mémoire s'est beaucoup amoindrie; **I think none the w. of him because he accepted,** je n'ai pas moins bonne opinion de lui parce qu'il a accepté; **so much the w. for them!,** tant pis pour eux!; **she was the w. for drink,** elle était éméchée; **a sofa somewhat the w. for wear,** un sofa un peu défraîchi; *F* **w. things happen at sea,** ce n'est pas la fin du monde; **w. luck!,** hélas!

2 *n* **there was w. to follow** *or* **to come,** le pire était encore à venir; **I have seen w.,** j'en ai vu bien d'autres; **to change for the w.,** s'altérer; **change for the w.,** changement *m* en mal, altération *f*; **he has taken a sudden turn for the w.,** son état s'est subitement aggravé.

3 *adv* (*comp of* **badly**) plus mal; *Lit* pis; **he has been taken w.,** il va plus mal; **w. still,** pire encore; **you could do (a lot) w.,** (*than accept offer*) ce n'est vraiment pas si mal; (*than marry him or her*) tu aurais pu tomber plus mal; **he could do w. than take their offer,** il pouvait faire pire que d'accepter leur proposition; **to think w. of s.o. for doing sth,** estimer qn moins pour avoir fait qch; **he is w. off than before,** (*in worse situation*) sa situation a empiré; (*even poorer*) il est encore plus pauvre qu'avant; **the noise went on w. than ever,** le vacarme a recommencé de plus belle.

worsen ['wɜːs(ə)n] **1** *vt* empirer, aggraver (*un mal*); rendre pire. **2** *vi* empirer, devenir pire; (*of health*) s'aggraver; **the situation has since worsened,** la situation a empiré depuis; **the worsening situation,** la situation qui est en train de s'aggraver; **her worsening memory,** sa mémoire faiblissante.

worsening ['wɜːs(ə)nɪŋ] *n* aggravation *f*.

worship¹ ['wɜːʃɪp] *n* **(a)** *Rel* culte *m*; **divine w.,** le culte divin; **freedom of w.,** liberté *f* du culte; **forms of w.,** formes *fpl* de culte; **hours of w.,** heures *fpl* des offices; **place of w.,** lieu consacré au culte; **to be an object of w.,** être un objet d'adoration; **nature w., the w. of nature,** le culte de la nature; **(b)** (*love, adoration*) adoration *f*.

worship² *v* (**-pp-**) **1** *vt* **(a)** rendre *ou* vouer un culte à, adorer (*un dieu, une idole*); **to w. the golden calf,** adorer le veau d'or; **(b)** adorer (*qn*); vouer un culte à (*qn*); **she worshipped her mother,** elle adorait sa mère; **he worships Elvis Presley,** il voue un culte à Elvis Presley; **he worships the ground she treads on,** il vénère jusqu'au sol qu'elle foule; **to w. money,** vouer un culte à l'argent. **2** *vi* **the church where his family had worshipped for years,** l'église où sa famille a fait ses dévotions pendant des années; **where does he w.?,** à quelle église *ou* à quel temple va-t-il?

Worship ['wɜːʃɪp] *n* (*title*) **His W. the Mayor,** monsieur le maire, **yes, your W.,** oui, Votre Honneur.

worshipful ['wɜːʃɪpfʊl] *adj* honorable (*titre des membres des Corporations de Londres, des juges de paix*).

worshipper ['wɜːʃɪpər] *n* adorateur, -trice; **the worshippers,** (*in church*) les fidèles *mpl*.

worst¹ [wɜːst] **1** *adj* (*superl of* **bad**) (le) pire, (le) plus mauvais; **that was his w. mistake,** c'était sa plus grave erreur; **his w. enemy,** son pire ennemi; **the w. thing about it was the heat,** le pire c'était la chaleur; **the w. weather was in England,** c'était en Angleterre qu'il faisait le plus mauvais temps.

2 *n* **the w. that could happen,** le pire *ou* la pire chose qui puisse arriver; **the w. of it is that ...,** le pire c'est que ...; **that's the w. of cheap shoes,** c'est l'inconvénient des chaussures bon marché; **when things are at their** *or* **the w.,** quand les choses vont au plus mal; **even at her w. she is still a brilliant player,** même dans ses plus mauvais jours, elle reste une joueuse fantastique; **I'm at my w. in the morning,** le matin est mon plus mauvais moment de la journée; **you haven't seen her at her w.,** tu ne l'as pas vue dans un de ses plus mauvais jours; **to get the w. of it,** (*in a fight*) avoir le dessous; **he's prepared for the w.,** il s'attend au pire; **at the w., if it comes to the w., if the w. comes to the w.,** *US* **if the worse comes to the w.,** au pire, au pis aller; **if it comes to the w., we can always take the train,** dans le pire des cas, nous pouvons toujours prendre le train; **at the w. there's still the possibility of finding another actor,** au pire, il y a toujours la possibilité de trouver un autre acteur; **the w. is yet to come,** on n'a pas encore vu le pire, et ce n'est pas fini; **do your w.!,** allez-y!, essayez toujours!; **the w. is over,** le plus mauvais moment est passé; **the w. of the storm is over,** le plus fort de l'orage est passé; **the w. has happened!,** c'est la catastrophe!; **and that's not the w. of it!,** et ce n'est pas le pire!, et il y a pire encore!

3 *adv* (*superl of* **badly**) (le) plus mal; *Lit* (le) pis; **out of all of us I played w.,** j'ai joué le plus mal de nous tous; **that frightened me w. of all,** c'est cela qui m'a effrayé le plus; **the w. possible situation,** la pire situation possible; **the elderly are the w. off,** les personnes âgées sont les plus mal loties; **they are the w. paid,** ce sont les plus mal payés; **the w. dressed men in Europe,** les hommes les plus mal habillés d'Europe.

worst² *vt* battre, vaincre, défaire (*qn*); **to be worsted,** avoir le dessous.

worst-case ['wɜːstkeɪs] *adj* **w.-c. scenario/projection,** scénario *m*/prévision *f* qui envisage le pire; **what's the w.-c. scenario?,** quel est le pire qui puisse se produire?

worsted ['wʊstɪd] *n Tex* laine peignée, peigné *m*.

worth [wɜːθ] **1** *adj* **(a)** (*having a value of*) valant; **to be w. ...,** valoir ...; **this ring is w. $500,** cette bague vaut 500 dollars; **a ring w. $500,** une bague valant 500 dollars; **how much** *or* **what is this painting w.?,** combien vaut ce tableau?; **it's not w. anything,** cela ne vaut pas quatre sous; **the house isn't w. what they paid for it,** la maison ne vaut pas le prix qu'ils ont payé pour l'avoir; **the money isn't w. the paper it's printed on,** cet argent ne vaut pas le papier sur lequel il est imprimé; **she's w. ten of you,** elle en vaut dix comme toi; **to be w. so much/nothing,** valoir tant/ne rien valoir; **what is the franc w.?,** combien vaut le franc?; **it's not w. much,** cela ne vaut pas grand-chose; **to be w. sth to s.o.,** valoir qch pour qn; **this old book is w. a lot to me,** ce vieux livre a beaucoup de valeur pour moi; **what's my silence w. to you?,** tu donnerais combien pour que je me taise?; **whatever it may be w.,** quoi que cela vaille; **I tell you this for what it's w.,** je vous passe ce renseignement pour ce qu'il vaut *ou* sans y attribuer grande valeur; **she's a lawyer, for what that's w.,** elle est avocate, pour ce que cela vaut; **for what it's w. I think they're wrong,** pensez-en ce que vous voulez mais je crois qu'ils ont tort; **that's my advice, for what it's w.,** c'est mon conseil, faites-en ce que vous voulez; **it would be as much as my life is w.,** ce serait risquer ma vie; **it would be more than my job's w.,** ça me coûterait mon emploi;

(b) (*meriting*) **it's not w. the trouble,** cela ne *ou* n'en vaut pas la peine; **is it w. while?, is it w. it?,** cela (en) vaut-il la peine?; **it's not w. my/your/***etc* **while doing it,** ça ne vaut pas la peine que je le fasse/tu le fasses/*etc*; **it isn't w. it,** ça ne vaut pas le coup; **don't get upset, he isn't w. it,** ne te rends pas malade, il n'en vaut pas la peine; **this novel is not w. reading,** ce roman ne vaut pas la peine *ou* ne mérite pas d'être lu; **it's so late, it's not w. going,** il est si tard, ça ne vaut pas la peine *ou F* le coup d'y aller; **something w. having,** une chose précieuse; **life wouldn't be w. living,** la vie serait intolérable; **it's w. thinking about,** cela mérite réflexion; **it's w. knowing,** c'est bon à savoir; **the castle is w. a visit,** le château vaut la visite; **your friendship/opinion is w. a lot to me,** ton amitié/ton opinion représente beaucoup pour moi;

(c) (*having money*) **he's w. millions,** il est riche à millions; **that is all I am w.,** voilà toute ma fortune; *Fig* **he was pulling for all he was w.,** il tirait de toutes ses forces.

2 *n* valeur *f*; **of great/little/no w.,** de grande/de peu de/d'aucune valeur; **give me £4 w. of petrol,** donnez-moi pour 4 livres d'essence; **to have/want one's money's w.,** en avoir/en vouloir pour son argent; **she has no sense of her own w.,** elle n'est pas consciente de sa propre valeur.

worthily ['wɜːðɪlɪ] *adv* (*see adj*) **(a)** dignement; **(b)** à juste titre.

worthiness ['wɜːðɪnɪs] *n* mérite *m*.

worthless ['wɜːθlɪs] *adj* **(a)** (*object*) sans valeur, qui ne vaut rien; **(b) he's completely w.,** c'est un vaurien.

worthlessness ['wɜːθlɪsnɪs] *n* **(a)** (*of object*) peu *m* de valeur; **(b)** (*of person*) nature *f* méprisable.

worthwhile [wɜːθ'waɪl] *adj* qui en vaut la peine *ou F* le coup; **at last I've found a w. job,** j'ai enfin trouvé un poste qui me donne satisfaction; **she didn't think it w. replacing the van,** elle ne pensait pas que cela vaille la peine de changer de camionnette.

worthy ['wɜːðɪ] **1** *adj* **(a)** (*distinguished, meriting respect*) digne; **a w. man,** un homme respectable *ou* estimable; **a w. life,** une vie honorable *ou* vertueuse; **(b) w. of,** (*deserving, meriting*) digne de; **w. of respect,** digne de respect; **you're not w. of your father,** tu n'es pas digne de ton père; **her remarks are w. of contempt,** ses remarques sont dignes de mépris; **to be w. to do sth,** être digne de faire qch; **I am not w. to kiss your hand,** je ne suis pas digne de te baiser la main; **it is w. of note that ...,** il est à noter que ...; **the town has no museum w. of the name,** la ville n'a aucun musée digne de ce nom. **2** *n* personnage *m* (*de l'endroit*); *Hum* **the village worthies,** les notables *mpl* du village.

wotcher ['wɒtʃər] *int Br Sl* **w.!,** (*hello!*) salut!

would *see* **WILL³**.

would-be ['wʊdbiː] *adj* prétendu, soi-disant; (*housebuyer, student*) potentiel; (*musician, actor*) en herbe; **w.-be assassin,** prétendu assassin.

wound¹ [wuːnd] *n* **(a)** *Med* blessure *f*; **w. in the arm,** blessure au bras; **bullet w.,** blessure par balle; **(b)** *Fig* plaie *f*; **to reopen a w.** *or* **an old w.,** rouvrir une plaie; **to rub salt in the w.,** retourner le fer *ou* le couteau dans la plaie.

wound² **1** *vt* **(a)** blesser, faire une blessure à (*qn*); **wounded in the shoulder,** blessé *ou* atteint à l'épaule; **(b)** *Fig* (*of accusation etc*) blesser (*qn*); **to w. s.o.'s pride,** blesser qn dans son amour-propre; **to w. s.o.'s feelings,** blesser les susceptibilités de qn, froisser *ou* heurter qn. **2** *vi* causer une blessure; *Fig* **was it your intention to w.?,** est-ce que tu avais l'intention de me *ou* la *etc* froisser?

wound³ [waʊnd] *see* **WIND³.**

wounded ['wuːndɪd] **1** *adj* blessé; **the w. man,** le blessé; *Fig* **w. pride,** orgueil froissé; *Fig* **my feelings were w.,** j'ai été froissé *ou* heurté. **2** *n* **the w.,** (*used as pl*) les blessés.

wounding ['wuːndɪŋ] *adj* blessant; **he found it w. to his pride,** cela a blessé son amour-propre.

wow¹ [waʊ] *F* **1** *int* oh là là! **2** *n* succès fou; **it's a w.,** c'est sensationnel; **this is a w. of a show,** c'est un spectacle sensationnel.

wow² *vt F* emballer (*qn*).

wow³ *n* (*in sound system*) pleurage *m*.

wp (*abbr* **weather permitting**) si le temps le permet.

WP [dʌb(ə)ljuː'piː] *n Comptr* **(a)** *abbr* **word processing**; **(b)** *abbr* **word processor.**

wpb [dʌb(ə)ljuːpiː'biː] *n abbr* **waste paper basket.**

WPC [dʌb(ə)ljuːpiː'siː] *n* (*abbr* **woman police constable**) femme-agent *f*, *pl* femmes-agents.

wpm [dʌb(ə)ljuːpiː'em] *abbr* **words per minute.**

WRAC [ræk] *n* (*abbr* **Women's Royal Army Corps**) ≈ A.F.A.T..

wrack¹ [ræk] *n* (*seaweed*) varec(h) *m*, goémon *m*.

wrack² *n* = **RACK¹.**

WRAF [ræf] *n Br Mil* (*abbr* **Women's Royal Air Force**) = section féminine de l'armée de l'air britannique.

wraith [reɪθ] *n* apparition *f*; **a w. of her former self,** l'ombre *f* d'elle-même.

wraithlike ['reɪθlaɪk] *adj* (*appearance*) semblable à une apparition *ou* un spectre, spectral.

wrangle¹ ['ræŋg(ə)l] *n* dispute *f*, querelle *f*.

wrangle² **1** *vi* se disputer, se quereller, se chamailler (**over,** à propos de). **2** *vt Am* garder (*le bétail*).

wrangler ['ræŋglər] *n* **(a)** querelleur, -euse; **(b)** *Am* cowboy *m*.

wrangling ['ræŋglɪŋ] *n* disputes *fpl*, querelles *fpl*; **there has been a lot of w. over who to give the job to,** il y a eu beaucoup de querelles pour décider à qui donner le poste.

wrap¹ [ræp] *n* (*blanket*) couverture *f* (*de voyage*); (*shawl*) châle *m*; (*cloak*) pèlerine *f*, manteau *m*; **evening w.,** manteau du soir, sortie *f* de bal; *F* **to keep sth under wraps,** garder qch secret; *F* **the wraps were taken off the new car today,** la voiture a été montrée au public pour la première fois aujourd'hui.

wrap² *v* **(-pp-)** **1** *vt* envelopper, emballer (*qch*); **to w. sth in paper,** envelopper *ou* empaqueter qch dans du papier; **the cheese was wrapped in plastic,** le fromage était emballé *ou* enveloppé sous plastique; *El* **to w. a cable,** guiper un câble (**in,** de); **to w. a parcel** *or* **gift,** faire un paquet; **would you like it wrapped?,** (*of gift*) c'est pour offrir?; **to w. a baby in a shawl,** emmitoufler un bébé dans un châle; **mountain wrapped in mist,** montagne enveloppée de brouillard; *Fig* **wrapped in mystery,** enveloppé *ou* entouré de mystère. **2** *vi Comptr* se boucler.

▶**wrap round** *vtaspo* **to w. sth round sth,** enrouler *ou* entortiller qch autour de qch; **w. this blanket round you/your shoulders,** enroule cette couverture autour de toi/de tes épaules; **he wrapped the bandage round my finger,** il a enroulé le bandage autour de mon doigt; **the cable wrapped itself round the capstan,** le câble s'est enroulé sur le cabestan; *F* **he wrapped his car round a tree,** il a encadré un arbre.

▶**wrap up** **1** *vtsep* **(a)** envelopper (*un paquet, un cadeau*); **to w. sth up in sth,** envelopper qch dans qch; **to be wrapped up in sth,** (*absorbed*) être uniquement préoccupé de qch; **he is wrapped up in his work,** il est entièrement absorbé par son travail; **she is too wrapped up in herself/in her own problems,** elle est trop préoccupée par elle-même/par ses propres problèmes; **they are wrapped up in each other,** ils sont uniquement préoccupés l'un par l'autre;

(b) **w. yourself up well,** emmitoufle-toi bien; **wrapped up,** bien enveloppé; (*person*) emmitouflé;

(c) *F* (*bring to an end*) conclure (*une affaire, des négociations, une discussion*); **well that about wraps it up for today,** voilà, c'est à peu près tout pour aujourd'hui.

2 *vi* **(a)** (*put on warm clothes*) (bien) s'emmitoufler; **(b)** *Br F* (*stop talking*) se taire; **w. up!,** ferme-la!, écrase!

wraparound ['ræpəraʊnd] *n* = **WRAPROUND.**

wrapover ['ræpəʊvər] **1** *n* (*skirt*) jupe *f* portefeuille. **2** *adj* **w. top,** cache-cœur *m inv*.

wrapped [ræpt] *adj* (*bread*) préemballé; (*sweet*) emballé.

wrapper ['ræpər] *n* **(a)** (*packaging*) feuille *f* de papier d'emballage; papier *m* (*de bonbon*); emballage *m* (*de cigare*); **her pocket was full of old sweet wrappers,** sa poche était pleine de vieux papiers de bonbons; **(b)** (*of book*) couverture *f*, couvre-livre *m*, *pl* couvre-livres; (*to protect jacket*) liseuse *f*; (*of newspaper*) bande *f*; **(c)** *Old-fashioned* (*dressing gown*) saut-de-lit *m*, *pl* sauts-de-lit.

wrapping ['ræpɪŋ] *n* **(a)** (*process*) emballage *m*, mise *f* en paquet; **w. paper,** papier *m* d'emballage; **(b)** (*material*) enveloppe *f*, couverture *f*, papier *m ou* toile *f* d'emballage.

wrapround ['ræpraʊnd] **1** *n* (*in word processing*) bouclage *m*, renouement *m* (des mots). **2** *adj Aut* **w. rear window,** lunette *f* arrière panoramique; **w. windscreen,** pare-brise *m* panoramique; **w. skirt,** jupe *f* portefeuille.

wrath [rɒθ, rɔːθ] *n Lit* courroux *m*; **the w. of God,** la colère de Dieu.

wrathful ['rɒθfʊl] *adj Lit* courroucé, en colère.

wreak [riːk] *vt* assouvir (*sa colère, haine*); **to w. one's rage (up)on s.o.,** décharger *ou* passer sa colère sur qn; **to w. (one's) vengeance upon s.o.,** exercer *ou* assouvir sa vengeance sur qn; **the hurricane wreaked terrible destruction on the island,** l'ouragan a entraîné de terribles destructions sur l'île.

wreath [riːθ, *pl* riːðz, riːθs] *n* **(a)** (*of flowers*) couronne *f*, guirlande *f*; **(funeral) w.,** couronne mortuaire; **w. of poppies,** couronne de coquelicots; **he laid a w. on her grave,** il a déposé une couronne sur sa tombe; **(b)** (*of smoke*) volute *f*, panache *m*.

wreathe [riːð] **1** *vt* **(a)** (*encircle*) enguirlander; couronner (*la tête de qn*); **mountain wreathed with mist,** montagne entourée de brouillard; **face wreathed in smiles,** visage rayonnant; **(b)** (*form a wreath of*) tresser (*des fleurs*); **to w. sth round sth,** enrouler *ou* entortiller qch autour de qch. **2** *vi* (*of smoke*) tourbillonner.

wreck¹ [rek] *n* **(a)** (*ship*) navire naufragé, épave *f*; **total w.,** navire entièrement perdu; *Jur* **w. of the sea,** épaves *fpl* de mer; *Fig* **my car's a total w.,** ma voiture est bonne pour la casse; **the burnt-out w. of a bus,** les restes calcinés d'un bus; **human wrecks,** épaves humaines; *Fig* **to be a physical/nervous w.,** avoir la santé détraquée/les nerfs détraqués; **after two hours with those kids I was a (total) w.,** après deux heures avec ces gamins j'étais complètement épuisé; **(b)** (*destruction*) naufrage *m* (*d'un navire*); **to suffer w.,** faire naufrage; **to be saved from the w.,** échapper au naufrage.

wreck² *vt* **(a)** faire faire naufrage à, causer le naufrage de (*un navire*); **to be wrecked,** (*of ship, person*) faire naufrage; **the ship was wrecked on these rocks,** le bateau a fait naufrage sur ces rochers; **(b)** faire dérailler (*un train*); démolir (*une voiture*); démolir, détruire, ruiner (*un bâtiment*); **vandals have wrecked the building/train,** les vandales ont abîmé le bâtiment/le train; **to w. one's health,** se ruiner la santé; **(c)** *Fig* faire échouer, saboter (*une entreprise*); détruire, ruiner, briser (*les espérances de qn*); **to w. s.o.'s plans,** faire échouer les projets de qn; **this defeat has wrecked the team's chances,** cette défaite a anéanti les chances de l'équipe; **the accident had wrecked her hopes,** l'accident a anéanti ses espoirs; **you wrecked his life/career,** tu as brisé sa vie/sa carrière.

wreckage ['rekɪdʒ] *n* **(a)** (*act*) naufrage *m* (*d'un navire, de la fortune de qn*); **(b)** *no pl* (*remnants*) (*of ship*) épave *f*; (*of aircraft, train, car*) débris *mpl*; **documents were found in the w.,** on a trouvé des documents parmi les débris; *Fig* **she hoped to salvage something from the w. of her career,** elle espérait sauver quelque chose de ce qui restait de sa carrière; **piece of w.,** épave.

wrecker ['rekər] *n* **(a)** (*of ship*) naufrageur *m*, pilleur *m* d'épave; **(b)** (*of city, civilisation*) destructeur, -trice; *Constr* démolisseur *m* (*de bâtiments*); **(c)** *Am Nau* (*salvager*) sauveteur *m* d'épaves; (*plunderer*) exploiteur *m* d'épaves; **(d)** *Am Aut* (*vehicle*) dépanneuse *f*, camion *m* de dépannage; (*person*) membre *m* d'une équipe de secours.

wren [ren] *n* (*bird*) troglodyte *m*.

Wren [ren] *n Br F* = membre du Women's Royal Naval Service; **the Wrens,** = section féminine de la marine britannique.

wrench¹ [rentʃ] *n* **(a)** (*twist*) mouvement violent de torsion; **to give sth a w.,** tordre qch violemment; **he gave his ankle a w.,** il s'est fait une entorse; (*less serious*) il s'est foulé la cheville; *Fig* **the separation was a terrible w.,** la séparation fut un déchirement affreux; **it will be a w. to leave the old house,** il m'en *ou* nous *etc* en coûtera de quitter la vieille maison; **(b)** (*tool*) clef *f*; **adjustable w.,** clef à ouverture variable, clef universelle; **pipe w.,** clef à pipes.

wrench² *vt* (*twist*) tordre *ou* tourner violemment; **to w. the lid open,** forcer le couvercle; **to w. off** *or* **out,** arracher *ou* enlever (avec un violent effort de torsion); **to w. sth (away) from s.o.,** arracher qch à qn; **she wrenched herself free,** d'une secousse elle se dégagea; *Fig* **nothing could w. her away from her book,** rien ne pouvait l'arracher à son livre; **to w. one's ankle/shoulder,** se fouler la cheville/l'épaule.

wrest [rest] *vt* arracher (**from,** à); **she wrested the knife from him** *or* **his grip,** elle lui a arraché le couteau; **to w. a confession from s.o.,** arracher un aveu à qn; **we could w. no meaning from the coded message,** nous n'avons pu tirer aucun sens du message codé; **I managed to w. her attention away from the tennis,** j'ai réussi à l'arracher au tennis qui occupait toute son attention.

wrestle¹ ['res(ə)l] **1** *vi* lutter; *Fig* **to w. with,** lutter contre (*les difficultés*); résister à (*la tentation*); être aux prises avec (*l'adversité*); s'attaquer à (*un problème*); **to w. with s.o.,** lutter avec *ou* contre qn; **to w. together,** lutter, se prendre corps à corps; **the two men wrestled briefly,** les deux hommes ont brièvement lutté; **to w. with one's umbrella,** se (dé)battre avec son parapluie; **he wrestled with the zip/knot in the darkness,** il s'est débattu avec la fermeture éclair ®/le nœud dans le noir; *Fig* **they've been wrestling with the problem for years,** ils sont aux prises avec ce problème depuis des années; *Fig* **to w. with one's conscience,** être aux prises avec sa conscience. **2** *vt* lutter avec *ou* contre (*qn*); **he wrestled his attacker to the ground,** il a jeté son attaquant au sol dans la lutte.

wrestle² *n* (*fight*) & *Fig* lutte *f* (corps à corps) (**with,** contre); *Fig* **after a w. with his conscience, he agreed,** après une lutte avec sa conscience il a accepté; **after a w. with the knot she was free,** après s'être débattue avec le nœud, elle était libre.

▶**wrestle down** *vtsep* terrasser (*son adversaire*) (*à la lutte*).

wrestler ['reslər] *n* lutteur *m*.

wrestling ['reslıŋ] *n* lutte *f*; **professional w.,** catch *m*; **Sumo w.,** lutte Sumo; **w. match,** match *m* de catch; **w. championship,** championnat *m* de catch.

wretch [retʃ] *n* **(a)** (*pitiable person*) malheureux, -euse, infortuné, -ée; **poor w.,** pauvre diable *m*; **(b)** (*despicable person*) misérable *mf*; **you w.!,** misérable!; **you little w.!,** petit fripon!

wretched ['retʃıd] *adj* **(a)** (*person*) misérable, malheureux, infortuné; **to feel w.,** (*ill*) être mal en train; (*depressed*) avoir le cafard; **to lead a w. existence,** mener une existence misérable; **to be in w. poverty,** être dans une misère affreuse; **(b)** (*bad*) pitoyable, lamentable; triste, pauvre (*repas*); **the animal/house was in a w. state,** l'animal/la maison était dans un état lamentable; **this coffee is w.,** ce café est abominable; **what w. weather!,** quel temps abominable!, quel temps de chien!; **it's a w. business,** c'est une affaire *ou* une histoire lamentable; **w. hovel,** taudis *m*; **w. lodgings,** appartement *m* minable; **(c)** *F* (*intensifier*) fichu, sacré; **I can't find that w. umbrella,** je ne retrouve pas ce fichu *ou* sacré parapluie.

wretchedly ['retʃıdlı] *adv* (*see adj*) **(a)** misérablement; **to be w. poor,** être dans une misère affreuse; **to be w. ill,** être malade à faire pitié; **(b)** de façon pitoyable *ou* lamentable.

wretchedness ['retʃıdnıs] *n* **(a)** (*misfortune*) misère *f*, malheur *m*; **(b)** (*sadness*) tristesse *f*; **(c)** (*inferiority*) mauvaise qualité.

wrick¹ [rık] *n* **to give oneself a w.,** se faire un froissement; **w. in the neck,** torticolis *m*.

wrick² *vt* **to w. oneself** *or* **a muscle,** se froisser un muscle; **to w. one's ankle,** se fouler la cheville; (*more serious*) se faire une entorse.

wriggle¹ ['rıg(ə)l] *n* tortillement *m* du corps; **to give a w.,** se tortiller, se trémousser; **she gave a little w. in her chair,** elle s'est un peu trémoussée sur sa chaise.

wriggle² **1** *vi* (*of worm*) se tortiller; (*of fish*) frétiller; (*of person*) se tortiller, s'agiter; **stop wriggling!,** arrête de t'agiter!; **to w. through a hedge,** se faufiler à travers une haie (en se tortillant); **he managed to w. into the sweater,** il a réussi à enfiler le pull en se tortillant; **to w. free,** se libérer en se faufilant; *Fig* **to w. out of a difficulty,** se tirer *ou* s'extraire d'une position difficile par des moyens évasifs; *Fig* **to try to w. out of it,** chercher une échappatoire; *Fig* **he tried to w. out of our date,** il a essayé d'échapper à notre rendez-vous.
2 *vt* tortiller (*les doigts*); agiter (*les jambes*); **to w. one's way into,** se faufiler dans; **she wriggled her way along the tunnel,** elle s'est faufilée le long du tunnel; *Fig* **he wriggled his way into my confidence,** il s'est débrouillé pour gagner ma confiance; *Fig* **I'd like to see him w. his way out of that!,** j'aimerais bien voir comment il va se sortir de cette situation!

wriggler ['rıglər] *n* **(a)** gigoteur, -euse; **he's a terrible w.,** il est incapable de rester assis tranquillement; **(b)** (*insect*) larve *f* de moustique.

wriggling ['rıg(ə)lıŋ] **1** *adj* = **WRIGGLY**. **2** *n* tortillement *m*; **a w. movement,** mouvement *m* de tortillement.

wriggly ['rıglı] *adj* qui se tortille *ou* gigote; (*because excited*) frétillant; **the fish was wet and w.,** le poisson était humide et frétillant; **a w. worm,** un ver qui se tortille.

wring¹ [rıŋ] *n* (mouvement *m* de) torsion *f*, action *f* de tordre; **to give the clothes a w.,** tordre le linge, passer le linge à l'essoreuse; **he gave my hand a w.,** il m'a donné une vigoureuse poignée de main.

wring² *vt* (*pt & pp* **wrung** [rʌŋ]) tordre (*qch*); tordre, essorer (*le linge*); **do not w.,** (*on garment label*) ne pas essorer; **to w. s.o.'s hand,** étreindre la main de qn; **to w. one's hands (in despair),** se tordre les mains *ou* les bras (de désespoir); **to w. a bird's neck,** tordre le cou à une volaille; *F* **I'd like to w. his neck,** j'ai envie de lui tordre le cou; **to w. a secret from s.o.,** arracher un secret à qn; **to w. money from s.o.,** arracher *ou* extorquer de l'argent à qn; **to w. tears from s.o.,** arracher des larmes à qn.

▶**wring out** *vtsep* tordre, essorer (*le linge*); **to w. the water out,** (*from clothes*) extraire *ou* faire sortir l'eau.

wringer ['rıŋər] *n* essoreuse *f* (à rouleaux).

wringing ['rıŋıŋ] **1** *adj* **w. (wet),** (*clothes*) mouillé à tordre; (*person*) trempé jusqu'aux os. **2** *n* tordage *m*, essorage *m*; **she told us the news, with much w. of hands,** elle nous a annoncé la nouvelle, non sans se tordre les mains.

wrinkle¹ ['rıŋk(ə)l] *n* **(a)** (*on skin*) ride *f*; (*in cloth, paper, carpet*) faux pli; **(b)** *F* (*tip*) renseignement *m* utile, tuyau *m*.

wrinkle² **1** *vt* rider, plisser (*la peau*); plisser, froisser, chiffonner (*une robe*); **to w. one's forehead,** froncer le(s) sourcil(s); **her stockings were wrinkled,** ses bas faisaient des plis. **2** *vi* (*of skin*) se rider, se plisser; (*of dress*) se plisser, faire des plis; (*of apple*) se rider.

wrinkled ['rıŋk(ə)ld] *adj* (*forehead*) ridé, plissé; (*skin*) ridé; (*dress*) froissé, chiffonné; (*fruit*) ridé, ratatiné.

wrinkly ['rıŋklı] *n esp Br F* (*old person*) croulant, -ante.

wrist [rıst] *n* (*of hand, dress etc*) poignet *m*.

wristband ['rıstbænd] *n* **(a)** poignet *m*, manchette *f* (*de chemise*); **(b)** (*sweatband*) bracelet *m* en éponge; *Gym* bracelet de force (en cuir).

wristbone ['rıstbəʊn] *n Anat* os *m* du carpe.

wristlet ['rıstlıt] *n* bracelet *m*.

wristlock ['rıstlɒk] *n* (*in wrestling*) clef *f* de poignet; **to put a w. on s.o.,** faire une clef de poignet à qn.

wristwatch ['rıstwɒtʃ] *n* montre-bracelet *f*, *pl* montres-bracelets, bracelet-montre *m*, *pl* bracelets-montres.

writ¹ [rıt] *n* **(a)** *Jur* acte *m* judiciaire, mandat *m*, ordonnance *f*; (*summons*) assignation *f*; **w. of attachment,** ordre *m* de saisie; **w. of possession,** envoi *m* en possession; **to serve a w. on s.o., to issue a w. against s.o.,** assigner qn (en justice), signifier *ou* faire donner une assignation à qn; **(b)** *Rel* **Holy** *or* **Sacred W.,** les saintes Écritures, l'Écriture sainte.

writ² *see* **WRITE**.

write [raıt] *v* (*pt* **wrote** [rəʊt]; *pp* **written** ['rıt(ə)n], *Arch* **writ** [rıt]) **1** *vt* **(a)** écrire (*son nom, un roman, une lettre*); rédiger (*un article*); faire, remplir, libeller (*un chèque*); **w. the answer in the space provided,** écrivez la réponse dans l'espace réservé à cet effet; **that was not written by me,** cela n'est pas écrit de ma main; **do you w. it with a capital?,** ça s'écrit avec une majuscule?, ça prend une majuscule?; **the paper is written all over,** le papier est couvert d'écriture; **his guilt was written on his face,** on lisait sur son visage qu'il était coupable; **embarrassment was written all over her (face),** la gêne se lisait sur son visage; *F* **he's got copper written all over him,** on voit tout de suite que c'est un flic; **writ large,** écrit en gros, écrit en grosses lettres; **it is written,** c'est écrit; **she wrote two pages,** elle a écrit deux pages; **he writes a good hand,** il a une belle écriture; *Comptr* **to w. sth to disk,** écrire qch sur un disque;
(b) *esp Am* (*write a letter to*) écrire à (*qn*).

2 *vi* écrire; **to w. legibly,** écrire lisiblement; **he can w. in Italian,** il sait écrire l'italien; **they can read and w.,** ils savent lire et écrire; **please w. in black ink,** prière d'écrire à l'encre noire; **this pen won't w.,** ce stylo ne marche pas; **she writes,** (*is an author*) elle écrit; **to w. for children,** écrire des livres pour enfants; **to w. for a paper,** écrire dans *ou* collaborer à un journal; **he writes on** *or* **about gardening,** il écrit des articles sur le jardinage; **to w. to s.o.,** écrire à qn; **I wrote (to them) to complain,** je leur ai écrit pour me plaindre; **we still w.,** (*to each other*) nous nous écrivons toujours; **he writes home every Sunday,** il écrit à sa famille tous les dimanches; *Fig* **that's nothing to w. home about,** il n'y a pas de quoi s'en relever la nuit *ou* s'extasier; **w. for our catalogue,** demandez notre catalogue en nous écrivant.

►**write away for** *vipo* écrire pour demander (*qch*), faire une demande écrite pour (*qch*).

►**write back** *vi* répondre (à une lettre); **she wrote back to say that ...,** elle a répondu (à la lettre) pour dire que ... .

►**write down** *vtsep* **(a)** (*in order to remember*) noter; écrire (*son nom*); **to w. down one's thoughts/ideas,** mettre ses pensées/ses idées par écrit; **(b)** *Fin* réduire (*le capital*).

►**write in 1** *vtsep* (*enter in writing*) insérer (*une correction, un mot*); *Am* **to w. in a complaint,** envoyer une plainte à la direction; *US Pol* **to w. s.o. in,** inscrire qn. **2** *vi* (*send letter*) écrire; **many (of our) viewers wrote in with suggestions,** de nombreux téléspectateurs nous ont envoyé leurs suggestions; **to w. in for,** faire une demande écrite de (*un catalogue*), demander (*un catalogue*) par écrit.

►**write off 1** *vtsep* **(a)** *Fin* réduire, amortir (*le capital*); **to w. so much off for wear and tear,** déduire tant pour l'usure; *Com* **to w. off a bad debt,** défalquer une mauvaise créance, passer une créance aux profits et pertes; *F* **my car can be written off,** ma voiture est bonne pour la casse; *F* **she wrote her father's car off,** elle a bousillé la voiture de son père; *F* **the critics wrote the play off,** les critiques ont démoli la pièce; **(b)** (*compose quickly*) écrire rapidement, écrire (*un article*) d'un trait. **2** *vi* (*send letter*) écrire; **she wrote off straight away,** elle a écrit immédiatement; **to w. off for a catalogue,** demander *ou* commander un catalogue par écrit.

►**write out** *vtsep* **(a)** (*write in full*) transcrire (*qch*); mettre (*une copie*) au net; **w. this out neatly,** récris *ou* recopie cela au propre; **to w. sth out in full,** écrire qch en toutes lettres; **(b)** (*write*) faire, remplir, libeller (*un chèque*); *Med* rédiger (*une ordonnance*); **(c)** *TV Rad* (*remove from script*) supprimer (*un personnage*) d'une série.

►**write up** *vtsep* **(a)** (*prepare*) écrire, rédiger (*un fait-divers, un compte rendu*); *Sch* **w. up your notes,** recopiez vos notes, mettez vos notes au propre; **(b)** (*praise*) faire l'éloge de, *F* prôner (*qn, qch*); **(c)** (*update*) mettre (*son agenda, sa comptabilité*) à jour; **(d)** *Fin* augmenter (*la valeur des stocks*).

write-down ['raɪt'daʊn] *n Fin* dépréciation *f*.

write-off ['raɪtɒf] *n Fin* annulation *f* par écrit; *F* perte sèche; *F* **my car was a (complete) w.-o.,** ma voiture a été complètement démolie; **the project is a complete w.-o.,** le projet s'avère être une perte sèche *ou* un échec total.

write-protected ['raɪtprətektɪd] *adj Comptr* protégé en écriture.

writer ['raɪtər] *n* **(a)** écrivain *m*; auteur *m* (*d'un roman, du scénario*); scripteur *m* (*d'un document, d'un manuscrit*); **woman w.,** femme *f* écrivain; **w.'s block,** vertige *m* de la page blanche; **w.'s cramp,** crampe *f* des écrivains; **the present w., the w. (of this letter),** celui qui écrit, l'auteur (de cette lettre); **I'm not a good letter w.,** je ne suis pas très bon correspondant; **to be a good/bad w.,** bien/mal écrire; **(b)** *Scot Jur* notaire *m*; **W. to the Signet,** = avoué *m*.

write-up ['raɪtʌp] *n* **(a)** *Journ* article *m*; **the play got a good w.-up,** la pièce a eu une bonne critique; **(b)** *Fin* augmentation *f* de la valeur comptable (*du stock*).

writhe [raɪð] *vi* se contorsionner; se tordre (*de douleur*); (*of snakes, worms*) grouiller; **to w. in agony,** se tordre dans des souffrances atroces; **she writhed under the insult,** elle a tressailli à cette injure; **the remark made him w.,** (*with shame/embarrassment*) la remarque l'a fait pâlir de honte/de gêne; (*with indignation/anger*) la remarque l'a fait frémir *ou* tressaillir d'indignation/de colère.

writhing ['raɪðɪŋ] *n* contorsions *fpl*.

writing ['raɪtɪŋ] *n* **(a)** (*action*) écriture *f*; **the art of w.,** l'art de l'écriture; **I'm very bad about letter w.,** je suis très mauvais correspondant; **at the time of w.,** au moment où j'écris *ou* il écrit *etc*; *Journ* **at the time of w.,** à l'heure où nous rédigeons ceci; **that's my w.,** (*handwriting*) c'est mon écriture; **his w. is bad,** (*illegible*) il écrit mal; *Fig* **the w. on the wall,** un avertissement (*d'une catastrophe imminente*); **the w. is on the wall,** la catastrophe est imminente; **the w. was on the wall for the Roman Empire,** la fin de l'empire romain était imminente; **in w.,** (*coucher, répondre*) par écrit; **agreement in w.,** convention par écrit; **to put sth in w.,** mettre qch par écrit; **can I have that in w.?,** est-ce que vous pouvez me mettre cela par écrit?; **to commit the facts to w.,** consigner les faits par écrit; **to take up w.,** (*of author*) se mettre à l'écriture; **w. case,** correspondancier *m*; **w. desk** *or* **table,** pupitre *m*, bureau *m*, secrétaire *m*; **w. pad,** bloc correspondance *m*, *pl* blocs correspondance; **w. paper,** papier *m* à lettres;
(b) (*work*) ouvrage *m* littéraire; **the writings of an author,** les écrits *mpl ou* l'œuvre *m* d'un auteur; **a fine piece of w.,** (*passage*) un beau morceau; (*work*) une œuvre bien écrite;
(c) (*style*) style *m*, manière *f* d'écrire; **his w. has matured,** son style a mûri.

written ['rɪt(ə)n] *adj* écrit; (*in writing*) par écrit; **the w. word,** le mot écrit; **w. consent,** consentement *m* par écrit; **w. law,** loi écrite.

WRNS [renz] *n Br Mil* (*abbr* **Women's Royal Naval Service**) = section féminine de la marine britannique.

wrong¹ [rɒŋ] **1** *adj* **(a)** (*morally bad*) mauvais (*jugement etc*); **it is w. to steal, stealing is w.,** c'est mal de voler; **that was very w. of you!,** c'était très mal de votre part!; **it is w. for people to have to pay for hospital care,** il n'est pas normal que les gens doivent payer les soins hospitaliers; **it's w. that they should suffer because of other people's incompetence,** il n'est pas normal qu'ils pâtissent de l'incompétence des autres;
(b) (*incorrect, mistaken*) incorrect, inexact, erroné, faux, *f* fausse; **he gave the w. answer,** il a donné une mauvaise réponse *ou* une réponse incorrecte; **the calculations were w.,** les calculs étaient faux; **my watch is w.,** ma montre n'est pas à l'heure; **w. use of a word,** emploi abusif d'un mot; **a w. expression,** une expression impropre; **his ideas are all w.,** il a des idées tout de travers; **to be w.,** (*of person*) avoir tort; se tromper, être dans l'erreur; **they were w. to assume** *or* **in assuming that ...,** ils ont eu tort de supposer que ...; **that's just where you are w.,** c'est justement ce qui vous trompe; **to be w. about sth/s.o.,** se tromper sur qch/sur le compte de qn; **you were w. about the price,** tu avais tort en ce qui concerne le prix; **I was w. about her,** je me suis trompé sur son compte; **you were w. to contradict him,** vous avez eu tort de le contredire; **to be in the w. place,** ne pas être à sa place; **to drive on the w. side of the road,** conduire du mauvais côté de la route; *Fig* **to get out of bed on the w. side,** se lever du pied gauche; *esp Br Fig* **to get on the w. side of s.o.,** se faire mal voir de qn; **your sock is w. side out,** votre chaussette est à l'envers; **to be (the) w. side up,** être à l'envers; **to be on the w. side of forty,** avoir (dé)passé la quarantaine; **to stroke a cat the w. way,** caresser un chat à rebrousse-poil; **you are setting about it in the w. way,** vous vous y prenez mal *ou* de travers; **to take sth the w. way,** prendre quelque chose à contre-pied; **it went down the w. way,** (*of food*) je l'ai avalé de travers; **to take the w. train,** se tromper de train; **to back the w. horse,** miser sur le mauvais cheval; **to take the w. road,** se tromper de chemin *ou* de direction; **this is the w. road for Munich,** ce n'est pas la bonne route pour aller à Munich; **we went the w. way,** nous nous sommes trompés de chemin; **I was sent the w. way,** on m'a mal dirigé; **she gave me the w. address,** elle ne m'a pas donné la bonne adresse, elle m'a donné une mauvaise adresse; **to put s.o. on the w. track,** mettre qn sur une fausse piste; **to be on the w. scent** *or* **track,** suivre une mauvaise piste, faire fausse piste; **you've got the w. man, Jack Taylor isn't a murderer,** vous faites erreur, Jack Taylor n'est pas un meurtrier; **to come at the w. time,** venir à un mauvais moment *ou* mal à propos; **to do** *or* **say the w. thing,** commettre un impair, *F* faire une gaffe, mettre les pieds dans le plat; **I'm the w. person to ask,** il ne faut pas me demander ça à moi; **you're talking to the w. person,** (*ask s.o. else*) ce n'est pas à moi qu'il faut demander ça; *Tel* **w. number,** erreur *f* de numéro; **to dial the w. number,** composer un faux numéro; **I think you've got the w. number,** je crois que vous avez fait un faux numéro; **it was a w. number,** c'était un faux numéro; *Mus* **w. note,** fausse note; *Typ* **w. fo(u)nt,** lettre *f* d'un autre œil *ou* d'un œil étranger;

(c) (*amiss*) **what's w.?,** qu'est-ce qui ne va pas?; **what's w. with you?,** qu'avez-vous?, qu'est-ce qu'il y a qui ne va pas?, qu'est-ce qui ne va pas?; **there's something w. with me,** j'ai quelque chose, il y a quelque chose qui ne va pas; *F* **he's w. in the head,** il a quelque chose qui ne tourne pas rond dans sa tête, il est un peu timbré; **there was something w. with our car,** nous avons eu des ennuis avec la voiture; **there's nothing w. with the engine,** le moteur fonctionne normalement; **there's something w. somewhere,** il y a quelque chose qui cloche *ou* qui ne tourne pas rond; **I hope there's nothing w.,** j'espère qu'il n'est rien arrivé (de malheureux); *F* **what's w. with that?,** qu'avez-vous à redire à cela?; **what's w. with going to France?,** quel mal y a-t-il à aller en France?; **what's w. with my idea?,** en quoi est-ce que mon idée vous déplaît?

2 *n* **(a)** (*immoral action*) mal *m*; **to know right from w.,** distinguer le bien du mal; **two wrongs do not make a right,** deux noirs ne font pas un blanc; **in her eyes he can do no w.,** il trouve toujours grâce à ses yeux; **the king can do no w.,** le roi ne peut pas mal faire;

(b) (*unjust action*) tort *m*, injustice *f*; *Jur* (*tort*) dommage *m*, préjudice *m*; **to acknowledge one's wrongs,** reconnaître ses torts; **to do s.o. w., to do w. to s.o.,** faire tort à qn; **you do her great w. in accusing her of not caring,** tu lui as fait beaucoup de tort en l'accusant de s'en moquer;

(c) (*mistake*) tort *m*; **to be in the w.,** (*because of an action*) être dans son tort; (*be mistaken*) avoir tort; **he wouldn't apologize even though he knew he was in the w.,** il ne voulait pas s'excuser bien qu'il sache qu'il était dans son tort; **she's the one who's in the w., not you,** c'est elle qui a tort, pas toi; **to put s.o. in the w.,** mettre qn dans son tort.

3 *adv* (*see adj*) **(a)** mal, à tort; **you did w.,** vous avez mal agi;

(b) mal, inexactement, incorrectement; **to guess w.,** mal deviner; **you have spelt my name w.,** vous avez mal orthographié mon nom; **she got the time/address/name w.,** (*was mistaken about*) elle s'est trompée d'heure/d'adresse/de nom; (*misunderstood*) elle a mal compris l'heure/l'adresse/le nom; *F* **don't get me w., I'm not saying ...,** comprenez-moi bien, je ne dis pas ...; *F* **you've got me w.,** vous m'avez mal compris; *esp Am* **to get in w. with s.o.,** se faire mal voir de qn;

(c) to go w., (*of mechanism*) se déranger, se dérégler, se détraquer; (*of business*) aller mal, aller de travers; (*mistake route*) se tromper de chemin; *Fig* se fourvoyer, faire fausse route; (*go morally astray*) se dévoyer, mal tourner; (*be mistaken*) se tromper, commettre une erreur; **his son went w.,** son fils a mal tourné; **we went w. at that crossroads,** nous nous sommes trompés à ce carrefour; **it's at the end of this road, you can't go w.,** c'est au bout de cette route, vous ne pouvez pas vous tromper; **where I went w. was in being too kind to him,** là où j'ai commis une erreur, c'est en me montrant trop gentil avec lui; **you can't go w. buying secondhand,** vous faites forcément le bon choix en achetant d'occasion; **the clock's gone w. again,** la pendule s'est déréglée encore une fois; **something went w. with the lighting,** nous avons eu un problème avec l'éclairage; **all our plans went w.,** tous nos projets ont échoué; **things have gone w.,** les choses ont mal tourné; **she used to be a normal, happy little girl, but something went w.,** c'était une petite fille normale et heureuse mais quelque chose a mal tourné; **the space flight went disastrously w.,** le vol dans l'espace a tourné à la catastrophe.

wrong² *vt* **(a)** (*treat badly*) faire (du) tort à (*qn*), faire injure à (*qn*), léser (*qn*); **(b)** (*treat unfairly*) être injuste pour *ou* envers (*qn*).

wrongdoer ['rɒŋduːər] *n* **(a)** (*of immoral action*) auteur *m* d'une injustice; **(b)** (*of illegal action*) malfaiteur *m*.

wrongdoing ['rɒŋduːɪŋ] *n* **(a)** (*injustice*) injustice *f*; **(b)** (*immoral actions*) (*usu pl*) **wrongdoings,** méfaits *mpl*; **(c)** (*illegal action*) infraction *f* à la loi.

wrong-foot ['rɒŋ'fʊt] *vt Sp* prendre (*son adversaire*) à contre-pied; *Fig* prendre (*qn*) à l'improviste *ou* au dépourvu *ou* au pied levé.

wrongful ['rɒŋfʊl] *adj* **(a)** (*unjust*) injuste; **w. arrest,** arrestation injustifiée; **w. dismissal,** renvoi injustifié (*d'un employé*); **(b)** *Jur* (*illegal*) illégal, -aux; préjudiciable, dommageable; **(c)** (*incorrect*) faux (*héritier, roi*).

wrongfully ['rɒŋfəlɪ] *adv* injustement, à tort.

wrong-headed [rɒŋ'hedɪd] *adj* qui a l'esprit pervers *ou* de travers.

wrongly [rɒŋlɪ] *adv* **(a)** (*unjustly*) à tort, à faux; **I've been w. accused,** on m'a accusé injustement *ou* à tort *ou* à faux; **rightly or w.,** à tort ou à raison; **(b)** (*incorrectly*) mal; **to choose w.,** mal choisir.

wrongness ['rɒŋnɪs] *n* **(a)** erreur *f*, inexactitude *f*; **(b)** (*injustice*) injustice *f* (*d'une accusation etc*).

wrought [rɔːt] *adj* travaillé, ouvré, ouvragé, façonné; (*metal*) ouvré, forgé, battu; **w. iron,** fer forgé; **w.-iron gate,** portail *m* en fer forgé.

wrought-up ['rɔːt'ʌp] *adj* agité, excité; **she's very w.-up about it,** elle est très agitée à ce sujet.

WRVS [dʌb(ə)ljuːɑːrviː'es] *n abbr* **Women's Royal Voluntary Service**.

wry [raɪ] *adj* (*comp* **wrier**; **wryer**) tordu, tors, de travers; (*sourire*) forcé, pincé; **to pull a w. face,** faire la grimace; **he gave a w. smile,** il a grimacé un sourire.

wryly ['raɪlɪ] *adv* avec un sourire forcé; en grimaçant.

wt (*abbr* **weight**) p..

wulfenite ['wʊlfənaɪt] *n* wulfénite *f*.

wunderkind ['wʌndəkɪnd, 'vʊ-] *n* enfant *m* prodige.

wuzzy ['wʌzɪ] *adj F* **I feel w.,** j'ai la tête qui tourne.

WVa *abbr* **West Virginia**.

WW *abbr* **world war**.

wych-elm ['wɪtʃelm] *n* (*tree*) orme blanc *ou* de(s) montagne(s).

wynd [waɪnd] *n Scot* venelle *f*.

Wyo *abbr* **Wyoming**.

WYSIWYG ['wɪzɪwɪg] *Comptr* (*abbr* **what you see is what you get**) = représentation fidèle, sur l'écran d'un microordinateur, de la présentation imprimée ultérieure; **this package offers true W.,** avec ce logiciel ce qui apparaît sur l'écran correspond exactement à ce qui sera imprimé.

X

X, x [eks] *n* (la lettre) X, x *m*; **for x number of years,** pendant x années; *Math* **x-axis,** abscisse *f*; *Cin Arch* **X (certificate) film,** = film interdit aux moins de 18 ans; **the film was x-rated,** le film a été interdit aux moins de 18 ans; *Biol* **X-chromosome,** chromosome *m* x.
xenon ['zenɒn] *n Ch* xénon *m*.
xenophobe ['zenəfəʊb] *n* xénophobe *mf*.
xenophobia [zenə'fəʊbɪə] *n* xénophobie *f*.
xenophobic [zenə'fəʊbɪk] *adj* xénophobe.
xerography [zɪə'rɒgrəfɪ] *n* xérographie *f*.
Xerox®[1] ['zɪərɒks] *n* photocopie *f*.
Xerox®[2] *vt* photocopier (*qch*).
XL ['ek'sel] *n* (*abbr* **extra large**) XL *m*.
Xmas ['krɪsməs, 'eksməs] *n* (*abbr* **Christmas**) Noël *m*.
X-ray[1] ['eksreɪ] *n* **(a)** (*radiation*) rayon *m* X; **X-r. examination,** examen *m* radiographique *ou* radioscopique, radioscopie *f*; **X-r. diagnosis,** radiodiagnostic *m*; **X-r. photograph,** radio(graphie) *f*, cliché *m* radiographique; **X-r. photography,** radio(graphie); **X-r. treatment,** radiothérapie *f*; **(b)** (*picture*) radio *f*; *Med* **to have/take an X-r.,** passer/faire une radio; **to take an X-r. of s.o.'s chest,** faire une radio du thorax de qn.
X-ray[2] *vt Med* radiographier (*qn, le thorax*); **to be X-rayed,** se faire radiographier, *F* passer à la radio.
xylograph ['zaɪləʊgrɑːf] *n* xylographie *f*.
xylographic [zaɪləʊ'græfɪk] *adj* xylographique.
xylography [zaɪ'lɒgrəfɪ] *n* xylographie *f*.
xylophone ['zaɪləfəʊn] *n Mus* xylophone *m*.
xylophonist [zaɪ'lɒfənɪst] *n Mus* joueur, -euse de xylophone.

Y

Y, y, *pl* **y's, ys** [waɪ, waɪz] *n* (la lettre) Y, y *m*, i grec; *Math* **y-axis,** ordonnée *f*; *Biol* **Y-chromosome,** chromosome *m* y; **Y-shaped,** en fourche, en Y; **(a pair of) Y-fronts** ®, (*men's underwear*) slip ouvert.

yacht[1] [jɒt] *n* yacht *m*; **sailing y.,** voilier *m*; **motor y.,** yacht à moteur; **racing y.,** yacht de course; **y. club,** yacht-club *m*, *pl* yacht-clubs.

yacht[2] *vi* faire du yachting.

yachting ['jɒtɪŋ] *n* navigation *f* de plaisance, yachting *m*; **to go y.,** faire du yachting *ou* de la navigation de plaisance; **y. cap,** casquette *f* de yachtman.

yachtsman, *pl* **-men** ['jɒtsmən] *n* plaisancier *m*, yacht(s)man *m*, *pl* yacht(s)men.

yack(ety-yack)[1] ['jæk(ətɪ'jæk)] *n F* jacasserie *f*; **to have a y. about sth/s.o.,** jacasser au sujet de qch/qn.

yack(ety-yack)[2] *vi F* jacasser.

yah [jɑː] *int* **(a)** (*expressing disgust*) pouah!, berk!; **(b)** (*expressing derision*) na-na-nè-re!

yahoo [jə'huː] *n F* brute *f*.

yak[1] [jæk] *n* (*animal*) ya(c)k *m*.

yak[2] *n F* jacasserie *f*.

yak[3] *vi F* jacasser.

yam [jæm] *n* (*plant, tuber*) igname *f*.

yang [jæŋ] *n Phil* yang *m*.

yank[1] [jæŋk] *n F* secousse *f*, saccade *f*; **to give sth a y.,** donner une secousse à qch; **she gave the rope a good y.,** elle a donné une bonne secousse à la corde.

yank[2] *vt F* tirer (d'un coup sec); **to y. sth loose** *or* **out** *etc*, arracher qch d'un coup sec; **to y. out a tooth,** arracher une dent d'un seul coup; *Fig* **her parents yanked her off to the seaside,** ses parents l'ont emmenée de force au bord de la mer.

Yank, Yankee [jæŋk, 'jæŋkɪ] **1** *n F* **(a)** Ricain, -e, Amerloque *mf*, Yankee *mf*; **(b)** *US esp Pej* habitant, -ante des États du Nord. **2** *adj* **(a)** ricain, -e, amerloque; **(b)** *US esp Pej* qui habite les États du Nord.

yap[1] [jæp] *n* jappement *m* (*d'un chien*).

yap[2] *vi* (**-pp-**) **(a)** (*of dog*) japper; **(b)** *Fig* (*of person*) jacasser.

yapping ['jæpɪŋ] **1** *adj* jappeur. **2** *n* (*no pl*) **(a)** jappement *m* (*d'un chien*); **I wish that dog would stop its y.,** si ce chien pouvait arrêter ses jappements!; **(b)** *Fig* (*of person*) jacasserie *f*.

yappy ['jæpɪ] *adj F* jappeur.

yarborough ['jɑːbərə] *n Cards* = main qui ne contient aucune carte au-dessus du neuf.

yard[1] [jɑːd] *n* **(a)** (*measurement*) yard *m* (*0,914m*); (*in Canada*) verge *f*; **square y.,** yard carré (*0,765m²*); *Fig* **face a y. long,** figure longue d'un kilomètre; **yards of statistics, statistics by the y.,** des statistiques à n'en plus finir; **(b)** *Nau* vergue *f*; **main y.,** grand-vergue *f*.

yard[2] *n* **(a)** cour *f* (*de maison, de ferme, d'écurie etc*); *Am* jardin *m* (*autour d'une maison*); *Sch* cour, préau *m*; *Austr* (*cattle enclosure*) parc *m* à bétail *ou* à bestiaux; **(b)** *Ind* chantier *m*; **timber** *or* **lumber y.,** chantier de bois; **builder's y.,** chantier (de construction); *Nau* **repair y.,** chantier de radoub; **ship-building y.,** chantier de construction(s) navale(s); **naval (dock) y.,** *US* **navy y.,** chantier naval de l'État, arsenal *m* maritime *ou* de la marine; **(c)** (*for storage*) dépôt *m* de marchandises; **(d)** *Br* **New Scotland Y.,** *F* **the Y.,** ≈ la Sûreté.

yardage ['jɑːdɪdʒ] *n* = métrage *m*.

yardarm ['jɑːdɑːm] *n Nau* bout *m* de vergue.

yardstick ['jɑːdstɪk] *n* (*ruler*) yard *m* (*en bois, en métal*); *Fig* (*as standard of comparison*) critère *m*, point *m* de référence; **to measure others by one's own y.,** mesurer les autres selon ses propres valeurs.

yarn[1] [jɑːn] *n* **(a)** *Tex* fil *m*; filé *m* (*de coton*); **woollen y.,** fil de laine; **(b)** *Nau* **(rope) y.,** fil *m* de caret; **spun y.,** bitord *m*; **(c)** *F* histoire merveilleuse; longue histoire; **to spin a y.,** raconter *ou* débiter une histoire.

yarn[2] *vi F* débiter des histoires, bavarder.

yarrow ['jærəʊ] *n* (*plant*) achillée *f*, mille-feuille *f*.

yashmak ['jæʃmæk] *n* (*Muslim veil*) litham *m*.

yaw[1] [jɔː] *n* **(a)** *Nau* embardée *f*; **(b)** *Av etc* (mouvement *m* de) lacet *m*.

yaw[2] *vi* **(a)** *Nau* faire une embardée; **(b)** *Av etc* faire un (mouvement de) lacet.

yawl [jɔːl] *n Nau* **(a)** (*sailing vessel*) sloop *m*, yawl *m*; **(b)** (*small boat*) yole *f*.

yawn[1] [jɔːn] *n* bâillement *m*; **to give a y.,** bâiller; *F* **the book is one long y.,** le livre est ennuyeux à mourir.

yawn[2] **1** *vi* **(a)** bâiller (*de sommeil etc*); **(b)** *Fig* (*of chasm etc*) être béant, béer; **the gulf yawned at his feet,** le gouffre s'ouvrait *ou* béait à ses pieds. **2** *vt F* **to y. one's head off,** bâiller à se décrocher la mâchoire.

yawning [jɔːnɪŋ] **1** *adj* **(a)** qui bâille d'ennui; **(b)** *Fig* (*gouffre*) béant, ouvert. **2** *n* bâillement *m*.

yaws [jɔːz] *npl Med* pian *m*.

ye[1] [jiː] *def art* (*pseudo-archaic*) & *Arch* le, la, les; **Ye Olde Shoppe,** la Vieille Boutique.

ye[2] *pers pron* **(a)** *pl Arch & Lit* vous; **seek and ye shall find,** cherchez et vous trouverez; *F* **ye gods!,** grand Dieu!; **(b)** *sing F Dial* tu, vous; **how d'ye do?,** comment vas-tu?, comment allez-vous?

yea [jeɪ] **1** *adv Bible & Lit* **(a)** (*yes*) oui; **(b)** (*truly, indeed*) en vérité; voire. **2** *n* oui *m*; *US Pol* **yeas and nays,** voix *fpl* pour et contre.

yeah [jeə] *adv F* ouais; *Iron* **oh y.?,** vraiment?

year [jɪər] *n* **(a)** an *m*; année *f*; **in the y.** (*Arch* **of our Lord** *or* **of grace) 1850,** en l'an *ou* en l'année (du Seigneur *ou* de grâce) 1850; **a ticket valid for one** *or* **a y.,** billet *m* valable (pour) un an; **I have known him for ten years,** je le connais depuis dix ans; *Hist* **the Thirty Years' War,** la Guerre de Trente Ans; **sentenced to ten years' imprisonment,** condamné à dix ans de prison; **he got five years,** (*prison sentence*) il en a pris pour cinq ans; **a y.'s work/salary,** un an de travail/de salaire; **a y. last/next September,** il y a eu/il y aura un an en septembre, **it will be a y. in April,** (*answering question 'how long'*) ça va faire un an en avril; **we're going/we went to Greece this y.,** nous allons/nous sommes allés en Grèce cette année; **last y.,** l'an dernier, l'année dernière; **next y.,** l'an prochain, l'année prochaine; **this day next y.,** dans un an jour pour jour; **every y.,** tous les ans, chaque année; *Fml* annuellement; **twice a y.,** deux fois par an; **to earn £10,000 a y.,** gagner 10 000 livres par an; **a y.-old child, a one-y.-old (child),** un enfant (âgé) d'un an; **to be ten years old,** avoir dix ans; *Fml* **she's in her eightieth y.,** elle est dans sa quatre-vingtième année; **new y.,** nouvel an; **we'll see you in the new y.,** nous vous verrons au début de l'année prochaine; **New Y.'s Day,** le jour de l'An, le 1er de l'An; *Am* **New Years,** (*New Year's Day*) le jour de l'An, le 1er de l'An; (*New Year's Eve*) le 31 décembre, la Saint-Sylvestre; **Happy New Y.!,** bonne année!; **to see the old y. out** *or* **the new y. in,** faire la veillée *ou* le réveillon de la Saint-Sylvestre, réveillonner; **for many long years,** pendant de longues années; **for many years now we have been promised a new road,** ça fait maintenant de nombreuses années qu'on nous promet une nouvelle route; **all (the) y. round,** (pendant) toute l'année; **y. in (and) y. out,** une année après l'autre; **y. by y.,** d'année en année; **over the years,** au fil des années; **in the early years of the century/their marriage,** au cours des premières années de ce siècle/de leur mariage; **years ago,** il y a bien des années; **this is where I met him, all those years ago,** c'est ici que je l'ai rencontré il y a tant d'années; **it's years since I saw him, I haven't seen him for** *or* **in years,** (*for many years*) ça fait des années que je ne l'ai pas vu, je ne l'ai pas vu depuis des années; *F* (*for a long time*) il y a une éternité que je ne l'ai vu; **it seemed like years rather than hours,** ça m'a semblé durer des années plutôt que des heures;

years and years, des années et des années; **the best years of our life,** les plus belles années de notre vie; **from his earliest years,** dès son plus jeune âge; **old for his years,** plus vieux que son âge; (*enfant*) précoce; **young for his years,** jeune pour son âge; **to be getting on in years,** prendre de l'âge; **advanced in years,** âgé; **smoking can take years off your life,** le tabagisme peut raccourcir la durée de votre vie; **those kids have taken years off my life!,** ces gamins m'ont fait prendre dix ans d'un coup!; **working there put years on him,** le fait de travailler là l'a vieilli; **that dress takes years off her,** cette robe la fait paraître des années plus jeune *ou* la rajeunit beaucoup; **calendar** *or* **civil y.,** année civile; **financial** *or* **fiscal** *or* **tax y.,** année budgétaire, exercice *m* (financier); **half y.,** semestre *m*; **leap y.,** année bissextile; *Astron* **light y.,** année-lumière *f*, *pl* années-lumière, année de lumière; **school y.,** année scolaire; **solar/lunar y.,** année solaire/lunaire;

(b) (*at school, university etc*) **third-y. student,** étudiant(e) de troisième année; **he was in my y.,** (*at school*) il était dans ma classe; (*at university*) il est de ma promotion; **she was in the y. above/below me,** elle était dans la classe au dessus/en dessous de la mienne;

(c) (*of wine*) millésime *m*, année *f*; **a good y. for claret,** une bonne année *ou* un bon millésime pour le bordeaux rouge; *Fig* **it was a good y. for apples/French cinema/*etc*,** ça a été une bonne année pour les pommes/le cinéma français/*etc*.

yearbook ['jɪəbʊk] *n* annuaire *m*, almanach *m*; recueil annuel (*de jurisprudence etc*).

yearling ['jɪəlɪŋ] *adj & n* (animal *m*) d'un an; **y. (colt),** poulain *m* d'un an; (*thoroughbred*) yearling *m*.

yearlong ['jɪəlɒŋ] *adj* qui dure un an *ou* toute l'année.

yearly ['jɪəlɪ] **1** *adj* annuel. **2** *adv* annuellement; (*once a year*) une fois par an; (*every year*) tous les ans.

yearn [jɜːn] *vi* **to y. for** *or* **after sth,** languir *ou* soupirer pour *ou* après qch; **they y. for their own country,** ils ont la nostalgie de leur propre pays; **to y. to do sth,** avoir très envie de faire qch, brûler de faire qch, aspirer à faire qch; **she yearned to do great things/to return to her native village,** elle brûlait de faire de grandes choses/de retourner dans son village natal.

yearning ['jɜːnɪŋ] **1** *adj* (*désir*) vif, ardent; (*regard*) plein d'envie *ou* de désir. **2** *n* extrême envie *f* (**for,** de); **he felt a great y. to ...,** il ressentait un désir ardent de ... .

yearningly ['jɜːnɪŋlɪ] *adv* avec envie.

yeast [jiːst] *n* levure *f*; **brewer's y.,** levure de bière.

yell¹ [jel] *n* **(a)** hurlement *m*, grand cri; **to give a y.,** pousser un cri *ou* un hurlement; **yells of laughter,** hurlements de rire; **(b)** *Am* cri *m* de guerre *ou* de bataille (*des étudiants etc*).

yell² **1** *vi* hurler, crier à tue-tête; **to y. with pain/laughter,** hurler de douleur/de rire. **2** *vt* **to y. (out),** hurler, beugler (*une chanson*); hurler, *F* gueuler (*un ordre*).

yelling ['jelɪŋ] *n* hurlements *mpl*, grands cris.

yellow¹ ['jeləʊ] **1** *adj* **(a)** jaune; **to turn** *or* **go y.,** jaunir; **y. metal,** cuivre *m* jaune, laiton *m*; *Fb* **y. card,** carton *m* jaune; *Br Aut* **y. line,** ligne *f* jaune; **to park on a double y. line,** = se garer sur une zone de stationnement interdit; **the y. pages,** les pages *fpl* jaunes (*de l'annuaire téléphonique*); **(b)** *F* (*cowardly*) trouillard, lâche; **to turn** *or* **go y.,** se dégonfler; **to have a y. streak,** être un peu trouillard sur les bords; **(c)** *Old-fashioned Pej* **the y. peril,** le péril jaune. **2** *n* jaune *m*.

yellow² **1** *vt* jaunir (*qch*); **papers yellowed with age,** papiers jaunis par le temps. **2** *vi* jaunir.

yellowbelly ['jeləʊbelɪ] *n* *F* (*coward*) froussard *m*, trouillard *m*.

yellowhammer ['jeləʊhæmər] *n* (*bird*) bruant *m* jaune.

yellowish ['jeləʊɪʃ] *adj* jaunet, *Pej* jaunâtre.

yellowness ['jeləʊnɪs] *n* ton *m* jaune, teinte *f* jaune (*de qch*); teint *m* jaune (*de qn*).

yelp¹ [jelp] *n* jappement *m*, glapissement *m*.

yelp² *vi* japper, glapir; **to y. with pain,** gémir.

yelping ['jelpɪŋ] **1** *adj* jappant, glapissant. **2** *n* (*no pl*) jappement *m*, glapissement *m*; clabaudage *m* (*des chiens*).

Yemen (the) [ðə'jemən] *n* le Yémen.

Yemeni(te) ['jemənɪ, -aɪt] **1** *adj* yéménique, yéménite. **2** *n* Yéménite *mf*.

yen¹ [jen] *n* (*currency*) yen *m*.

yen² *n* *F* envie *f*; **to have a y. for sth/to do sth,** avoir envie de qch/de faire qch.

yen³ *vi* *F* = **YEARN.**

yeoman, *pl* **-men** ['jəʊmən] *n* **(a)** *Arch* petit propriétaire; *Hist* franc-tenancier, *pl* francs-tenanciers; *Fig* **to do y. service,** rendre des services inestimables; **(b)** *Mil Hist* soldat *m* du yeomanry; **Y. of the Guard,** = hallebardier à la Tour de Londres.

yeomanry ['jəʊmənrɪ] *n* (*no pl*) **(a)** *Arch* petits propriétaires; *Hist* francs-tenanciers; **(b)** *Mil Hist* = corps de cavalerie composé de volontaires.

yep [jep] *adv esp Am F* ouais.

yes [jes] **1** *adv* **(a)** oui; (*contradicting negation*) si; **to answer y. or no,** répondre par oui ou non; **to say y.,** dire oui, dire que oui; **y., certainly!, oh y.!,** mais oui!; **are you hungry? — y. (I am),** avez-vous faim? – oui; **you didn't hear me? — y., I did,** vous ne m'avez pas entendu? – (mais) si; **(would you like) some cake? — y. please** *or* *Am* **thanks,** est-ce que vous voulez du gâteau? – oui, s'il vous plaît; **could I have a glass of water? — y., of course,** est-ce que je pourrais avoir un verre d'eau? – oui, bien sûr; **y. sir/madam,** (*I'm coming*) voilà, monsieur/madame; **(b)** (*interrogatively*) **y.?,** (*are you sure?*) vraiment?; (*go on*) et puis après?; (*to s.o. waiting to speak*) oui?, vous désirez? **2** *n* (*pl* **yeses** ['jesɪz]) oui *m inv*; **an emphatic y.,** un oui énergique.

yes-man, *pl* **-men** ['jesmæn, -men] *n* *F* béni-oui-oui *m inv*.

yesterday ['jestədeɪ] *adv & n* hier *m*; **the day before y.,** avant-hier; **a week ago y.,** il y a eu hier huit jours; **y. week, a week (from) y.,** d'hier en huit; **y.'s paper/milk,** le journal/le lait d'hier; **y. morning/evening,** hier (au) matin/(au) soir; **I can remember it as clearly as if it had happened y.,** je m'en souviens comme si c'était hier; **y.'s heroes,** les héros *mpl* de jadis; *Lit* **our yesterdays,** les jours *mpl* d'autrefois *ou* d'antan.

yesteryear [jestə'jɪər] *n* *Lit* **the snows of y.,** les neiges *fpl* d'antan.

yet [jet] **1** *adv* **(a)** (*still*) encore; **we've got ten minutes yet,** nous avons encore dix minutes; **jobs y. to be done,** tâches *fpl* encore à faire; **y. more,** encore plus; **y. again,** encore une fois; **y. greater advantages,** des avantages encore plus grands; **y. another mistake,** encore une erreur; **y. one more,** encore un autre;

(b) (*in neg phrases*) encore; (*in questions*) déjà; **I haven't finished y.,** je n'ai pas encore fini; **we're not ready y.,** nous ne sommes pas encore prêts; **have they decided y.?,** est-ce qu'ils ont déjà décidé?; **are you ready y.?,** tu es prêt?; **not y.,** pas encore; **don't go y.,** ne partez pas encore; **it will not happen just y.,** cela n'arrivera pas tout de suite; **we're not going just y.,** nous ne partons pas tout de suite; **as y. nothing has been done,** jusqu'à maintenant *ou* jusqu'à présent *ou* jusqu'ici on n'a rien fait; **not as y.,** pas encore; **as y. unexplored jungle,** jungle pas encore explorée;

(c) (*in spite of everything*) malgré tout; **I shall catch him y.!,** je finirai bien par l'attraper!; **I'll do it y.!,** j'y arriverai!;

(d) (*even*) **not finished nor y. started,** pas achevé ni même commencé; **not me nor y. you,** ni moi ni vous non plus.

2 *conj* néanmoins, cependant, tout de même; **and y. I like him,** et cependant *ou* et malgré tout *ou* néanmoins il me plaît, mais il me plaît tout de même.

yeti ['jetɪ] *n* yeti *m*.

yew [juː] *n* **(a) y. (tree),** if *m*; **(b)** (*wood*) (bois *m* d')if *m*.

Yid [jɪd] *n* *Offensive Sl* youpin, -ine.

Yiddish ['jɪdɪʃ] *adj & n Ling* yiddish *m*.

yield¹ [jiːld] *n* rendement *m* (*d'un champ, d'une machine*); rapport *m* (*d'un arbre fruitier, d'une mise de fonds, d'une terre etc*); production *f*, produit *m*, débit *m* (*d'une mine*); **this tree gives a better/poor y.,** cet arbre donne un meilleur/un faible rapport; *Fin* **the y. on these shares is large,** ces actions rapportent beaucoup; **net y.,** revenu net.

yield² **1** *vt* **(a)** (*give*) rapporter, produire, donner; **ground that yields well,** terre qui donne un bon rendement *ou* qui rend bien; **shares that y. high interest,** actions à gros rendement; **to y. a 10% dividend,** produire *ou* rapporter *ou* rendre un dividende de 10%; **to y. a profit,** rapporter un bénéfice; **these remarks y. an insight into his motives,** ces remarques donnent une idée de ses motifs; **further investigations yielded no new information,** des recherches supplémentaires n'ont fourni aucune information nouvelle;

(b) (*concede*) céder (*une forteresse à l'ennemi, un droit etc*); **to y. ground,** céder le terrain; **to y. a point to s.o.,** céder à qn sur un point, concéder un point à qn; *Sp* concéder un point à qn; **divers have made the ocean y. (up) its treasures,** les plongeurs ont fait livrer ses trésors à l'océan; *Lit* **to y. (up) the ghost** *or* **one's soul,** rendre l'âme.

2 *vi* **(a)** (*surrender*) se rendre, céder (**to,** à); **to y. to force,** céder devant la force; **to y. to reason,** se rendre à la raison; **we shall not y. to threats,** nous ne céderons pas aux menaces; **I had to y. to them on that point,** j'ai dû leur céder sur ce point; **to y. to temptation,** succomber *ou* céder à la tentation; **to y. to s.o.'s wishes,** consentir *ou* céder aux désirs de qn;

(b) (*of rope etc*) céder; (*of beam etc*) s'affaisser, fléchir; **the plank yielded under our weight,** la planche a manqué *ou* cédé sous notre poids;

(c) *Am Aut* **y.!,** (*on sign*) cédez la priorité!

yielding ['jiːldɪŋ] *adj* **(a)** (*person*) facile, complaisant, accommodant; **the management hasn't been very y.,** la direction n'a pas été très accommodante; **in a y. moment,** dans un moment de faiblesse; **(b)** (*substance*) souple, élastique, flexible.

yin [jɪn] *n Phil* yin *m*.

yippee [jɪ'piː] *int F* hourra!, bravo!

YMCA [waɪemsiː'eɪ] *n* (*abbr* **Young Men's Christian Association**) Union chrétienne de jeunes gens.

yob [jɒb], **yobbo** ['jɒbəʊ] *n Br Sl* voyou *m*, loubar(d) *m*.

yodel[1] ['jəʊd(ə)l] *n Mus* (chant *m* à la) tyrolienne *f*.

yodel[2] *vi* (**-ll-**, *US* **-l-**) *Mus* jodler, iodler.

yod(el)ler, *US* **yod(e)ler** ['jəʊd(ə)lər] *n* jodleur, -euse, iodleur, -euse.

yoga ['jəʊgə] *n* yoga *m*.

yog(h)urt ['jɒgət, 'jəʊ-] *n* yaourt *m*, yog(h)urt *m*; **y. drink, drinking y.,** yaourt à boire.

yogi ['jəʊgɪ] *n* yogi *m*.

yoke[1] [jəʊk] *n* **(a)** (*for ox*) *& Fig* joug *m*; *Fig* **the y. of convention,** le joug des conventions; *Fig* **to throw off** *or* **cast off the y.,** secouer le joug, s'affranchir du joug; **(b)** (*for carrying*) palanche *f*; **(c)** *Sewing* empiècement *m*; **(d)** *El* carcasse *f*, bâti *m* (*de dynamo*).

yoke[2] *vt* **(a)** accoupler, atteler (*des bœufs*) (**to the plough,** à la charrue); *Fig* **to y. together,** unir (*deux personnes en mariage*); **(b)** *Tech* accoupler (*les pièces d'un appareil*).

yokel ['jəʊk(ə)l] *n Pej* rustre *m*, campagnard *m*.

yolk [jəʊk] *n* **(a)** jaune *m* (d'œuf); *Culin* **take the y. of an egg** *or* **one egg y.,** prenez un jaune d'œuf; **(b)** *Biol* vitellus *m*; **y. bag** *or* **sac,** membrane vitelline.

yon [jɒn] *adj & adv Arch & Dial* = **YONDER**.

yonder ['jɒndər] *Lit* **1** *adv* **down** *or* **over y.,** là-bas. **2** *adj* ce ... -là, cette ... -là, *pl* ces ... -là; **y. elms,** ces ormes *mpl* là-bas, ces ormes-là.

yonks [jɒŋks] *npl F* une éternité; **I haven't been there in y.,** ça fait une paye que je n'y suis pas allé; **that was y. ago,** ça fait une paye.

yoohoo ['juːhuː] *int* ohé!

yore [jɔːr] *n Arch & Lit* **of y.,** (d')autrefois; **in days of y.,** au temps jadis, autrefois.

Yorkshire ['jɔːkʃɪər] *n* le comté d'York; *Culin* **Y. pudding,** = pâte à choux cuite servie avec du rosbif.

you [juː] *pers pron* **(a)** (*subject*) *sing & pl* vous; *sing* (*when addressing relatives, intimate friends, children, animals, deities*) tu; **y. are very kind,** vous êtes bien aimable(s), tu es bien aimable; **how are y.?,** comment allez-vous?, comment vas-tu?; **there y. are,** vous voilà, te voilà; **y. all,** vous tous;

(b) (*as object of verb*) vous, te; **I hope to see y. tomorrow,** j'espère vous *ou* te voir demain; **I'll give y. some,** je vous en *ou* t'en donnerai; **I told y. so!,** je vous *ou* te l'avais bien dit!;

(c) (*after preposition*) vous, toi; **between y. and me,** (*when confiding*) entre vous et moi, entre toi et moi, entre nous soit dit; **I gave them to y.,** je te *ou* vous les ai donnés; **away with y.!,** allez-vous-en!, va-t'en!; **all of y.,** vous tous; **now there's a singer for y.!,** ah, voilà un chanteur!; **now there's a typical politician for y.,** voilà un politicien type;

(d) (*stressed*) vous, toi; **y. and I will go by train,** vous et moi *ou* toi et moi nous irons par le train; **is that y.?,** c'est vous *ou* toi?; **oh, it's y.,** ah, c'est vous *ou* toi; **I am older than y.,** je suis plus âgé que vous *ou* que toi; **it's y.,** c'est vous *ou* toi; **if I were y.,** (si j'étais) à votre *ou* ta place; **hey! y. there!,** eh! dites donc, là-bas!; **poor old y.!,** mon pauvre vieux!, ma pauvre vieille!; **that jacket/job wasn't y.,** cette veste/ce travail n'était pas ton style; **y. two are very different,** vous êtes très différents tous les deux; **y. four! come with me,** vous quatre! venez avec moi; **how long have y. two been married?,** cela fait combien de temps que vous êtes mariés tous les deux?;

(e) (*in the imperative*) **don't y. cry!,** ne pleure pas!; **y. sit down and eat your lunch!,** toi, assieds-toi et mange ton déjeuner!; **never y. mind!,** ne t'occupe pas de ça, toi!; **now you tell a joke,** à ton tour *ou* à toi de raconter une blague maintenant; **(just) y. try!,** essaye un peu!;

(f) (*in apposition*) **y. lawyers/Englishmen,** vous autres avocats/Anglais; **y. idiot (,y.)!,** idiot que tu es!, espèce d'idiot!; **y. darling (,y.)!,** tu es un amour!;

(g) (*indefinite*) on; **y. never can tell,** on ne sait jamais; **the joy y. feel when ...,** la joie qu'on ressent quand ...; **exercise is good for y.,** (prendre de) l'exercice est bon pour la santé.

you-all [j(ə)'ɑːl] *pers pron Southern US F* vous tous; (*speaking to one person*) vous.

you'd [juːd] **(a)** = **you had,** *see* **HAVE**[2]; **(b)** = **you would,** *see* **WILL**[3].

you-know-who [juːnəʊ'huː] *n* qui-vous-savez *mf*; **yesterday I had a telephone call from y.-k.-w.,** hier, j'ai reçu un coup de téléphone de qui-vous-savez.

you'll [juːl] **(a)** = **you will,** *see* **WILL**[3]; **(b)** = **you shall,** *see* **SHALL**.

young [jʌŋ] **1** *adj* **(a)** jeune; (*animal*) petit; **younger,** plus jeune; **younger son/daughter,** fils cadet/fille cadette; **my younger brother,** mon frère cadet; **youngest,** le *ou* la plus jeune, le cadet, la cadette; **this is my youngest, Vicki,** voici ma cadette *ou* ma dernière, Vicki; **he's younger than me** *or* **I (am),** il est plus jeune *ou* moins âgé que moi, il est mon cadet; **she's two years younger than me,** elle est plus jeune que moi, elle est ma cadette de deux ans; **they wanted someone younger,** ils voulaient quelqu'un de plus jeune; **when I was twenty years younger,** quand j'avais vingt ans de moins; **if I were twenty years younger!,** si j'avais vingt ans de moins!; **you're only y. once,** on n'est jeune qu'une fois, la jeunesse ne dure qu'un temps; **she's too y. for alcohol/to get married,** elle est trop jeune pour boire de l'alcool/se marier; **don't be too hard on him, he's only y.,** ne sois pas trop sévère avec lui, il est encore bien jeune; **I am not as y. as I was,** je n'ai plus mes jambes de vingt ans; **y. man,** jeune homme; **y. woman,** jeune femme; **now you listen to me, y. man/woman** *or* **lady!,** écoute-moi un peu jeune homme/ma petite demoiselle!; **he's her y. man,** c'est son petit ami; **y. couple/mother,** un jeune couple/une jeune mère; **a y. family,** des enfants en bas âge; **y. offenders' institution,** maison *f* de correction; **y. people,** jeunes gens *mpl*, jeunes *mpl*; **Pliny the Younger,** Pline le Jeune; **the younger generation,** la jeune génération; **in his younger days,** dans son jeune temps, dans sa jeunesse; **in my y. days,** dans ma jeunesse; **a y. country/company,** un pays/une société de création récente; **a y. wine,** un vin vert; **the night is y.!,** j'ai *ou* nous avons toute la soirée devant moi *ou* nous!;

(b) (*youthful*) jeune; **y. for his years,** jeune pour son âge; **y. in mind,** jeune d'esprit; **to grow** *or* **get y. again, to grow younger,** rajeunir; **you look younger than ever!,** tu parais plus jeune que jamais!; **she's a y. forty,** elle a quarante ans mais elle en paraît moins; **thirty's still y.!,** trente ans est encore jeune!

2 *n* **the y.,** (*used as pl*) les jeunes (gens) *mpl*, la jeunesse; **books for the y.,** livres pour la jeunesse; **old and y.,** les grands et les petits; **y. and old,** tout le monde; **it appeals to y. and old alike,** ça plaît aux jeunes comme aux moins jeunes; **animal and its y.,** animal et ses petits; **mare with y.,** (*pregnant*) jument pleine.

youngish ['jʌŋɪʃ] *adj* assez jeune, *F* jeunet, -ette.

youngster ['jʌŋstər] *n* **(a)** (*young person*) jeune personne *f*, *esp* garçon *m*; **(b)** (*child*) petit, -ite, *F* gosse *mf*.

your [jɔːr] *poss adj* **(a)** *sing & pl* votre, *pl* vos; *sing* (*when addressing relatives, intimate friends, children, deities*) ton, ta, *pl* tes; **y. house,** votre maison, ta maison; **y. friends,** vos ami(e)s, tes ami(e)s; **y. father and mother,** votre père et votre mère, ton père et ta mère; (*in official style*) vos père et mère; **the most recent of y. books, y. most recent book,** votre *ou* ton livre le plus récent; **have you hurt y. hand?,** vous vous êtes *ou* tu t'es fait mal à la main?; **turn y. head(s),** tournez la tête; **y. turn!,** (*to play etc*) à vous *ou* toi!; **Y. Majesty,** votre Majesté; **I like y. London buses,** j'aime bien les bus que vous avez à Londres; **I object to y. visiting the children,** je m'oppose à ce que tu rendes visite aux enfants;

(b) (*indefinite*) son, sa, *pl* ses; **you cannot alter y. nature,** on ne peut pas changer son caractère;

(c) *F* **y. typical** *or* **average Frenchman,** le Français typique; **of course y. kings and queens don't do that,** bien sûr, les rois et les reines ne font pas ça.

you're [jɔːr] = **you are,** *see* **BE**.

yours [jɔːz] *poss pron sing* le vôtre, la vôtre, *pl* les vôtres; *sing* (*when addressing relatives, intimate friends, children*) le tien, la tienne, *pl* les tiens, les tiennes; **this is y.,** ceci est à vous *ou* à toi, c'est le tien *ou* le vôtre; **these are y.,** ceux-ci sont à toi *ou* à vous, ceux-ci sont les tiens *ou* les vôtres;

you and y., vous et les vôtres, toi et les tiens; **the bathroom's all y.,** la salle de bains est libre maintenant; **can I use your telephone? — go right ahead, it's all y.,** est-ce que je peux utiliser ton téléphone? — vas-y; **y. (sincerely),** (*in informal letter*) bien amicalement; (*in formal letter*) veuillez agréer l'expression de mes sentiments distingués *ou* respectueux; **y. is a nation of travellers,** vous êtes une nation de voyageurs; **he is a friend of y.,** c'est un de vos *ou* tes amis, c'est un ami à vous *ou* toi; **that's no business of y.,** cela ne vous *ou* te regarde pas, ce n'est pas votre *ou* ton affaire; **that dog of y.,** votre *ou* ton sacré *ou* fichu *ou* foutu chien.

yourself [jɔː'self], *pl* **yourselves** [jɔː'selvz] *pers pron* **(a)** (*emphatic*) *sing & pl* vous-même(s); *sing* (*when addressing relatives, intimate friends, children, deities*) toi-même; **you said y.** *or* **you y. said it was cheap,** tu as dit toi-même *ou* vous avez dit vous-même que ce n'était pas cher; **tell her y.,** dis-lui toi-même, dites-lui vous-même; **you don't look quite y.,** vous avez *ou* tu as l'air mal en train; **just be y.,** contente-toi d'être toi-même, contentez-vous d'être vous-même;

(b) (*reflexive*) vous, te; **are you enjoying y.?,** tu t'amuses bien?, vous amusez-vous bien?; **have you hurt y.?,** vous êtes-vous fait mal?, tu t'es fait mal?; **I see you've got y. a wife/you've bought y. a car,** je vois que tu t'es trouvé une femme/que tu t'es acheté une voiture; *F* **have y. a good time,** amuse-toi bien;

(c) (*after preposition*) **see for y./yourselves,** vois toi-même, voyez vous-même/vous-mêmes; **tell us something about y.,** parle-nous de toi, parlez-nous de vous; **speak for y.!,** parle pour toi!, parlez pour vous!; **keep it for y.,** garde-le pour toi, gardez-le pour vous; **do you live by y.?,** vous vivez *ou* tu vis (tout) seul?; **did you do this by y.?,** est-ce que vous avez *ou* tu as fait ça tout seul?; **among yourselves,** (*reciprocal*) entre vous;

(d) (*used impersonally*) soi-même; (*reflexive*) se; **you have to do it y.,** il faut le faire soi-même; **you can't take y. too seriously,** il ne faut pas se prendre trop au sérieux.

youth [juːθ, *pl* juːðz] *n* **(a)** (*no pl*) jeunesse *f*, adolescence *f*, jeune âge *m*; **in his early y.,** dans sa première jeunesse; **she is not in the first blush of y., she is past her first y.,** elle n'est pas de la première jeunesse; **lost y.,** jeunesse perdue; *Myth* **the fountain of Y.,** la Fontaine de Jouvence; **y. will have its way** *or* **its fling,** il faut que jeunesse se passe; **(b)** (*male teenager*) jeune homme *m*, adolescent *m*; **(c)** (*no pl*) jeunes gens *mpl*, jeunesse *f* (*du village etc*); **inner-city y.,** la jeunesse des quartiers déshérités; **the y. of today,** la jeunesse d'aujourd'hui *ou* actuelle, les jeunes d'aujourd'hui; **y. club,** centre *m* (de loisirs) pour les jeunes; **y. hostel,** auberge *f* de jeunesse; **y. orchestra,** orchestre *m* de jeunes.

youthful ['juːθfʊl] *adj* **(a)** (*person, face, fashion etc*) jeune; **to look y.,** avoir l'air jeune; **y. good looks,** (*of men*) air *m* de jeune homme; **a y. fifty-two,** une personne de cinquante-deux ans qui a l'air jeune; **(b)** (*erreur, enthousiasme*) de jeunesse.

youthfully [juːθfəlɪ] *adv* en jeune homme, en jeune fille.

youthfulness ['juːθfʊlnɪs] *n* jeunesse *f*; (*youthful appearance*) air *m* de jeunesse, air jeune.

you've [juːv] = **you have,** *see* **HAVE**[2].

yowl[1] [jaʊl] *n* hurlement *m* (*de chien*); miaulement *m* (*de chat*).

yowl[2] *vi* (*of dog*) hurler; (*of cat*) miauler.

yo-yo ® ['jəʊjəʊ] *n* yo-yo ® *m*; *Fig* **he was jumping up and down like a yo-yo,** il sautait sur place sans arrêt.

YTS [waɪtiː'es] *n Br* (*abbr* **Youth Training Scheme**) (*person, job*) TUC *mf*.

yucca ['jʌkə] *n* (*plant*) yucca *m*; **a y. plant,** un yucca.

yuck [jʌk] *int F* pouah!, berk!

yucky ['jʌkɪ] *adj F* dégoûtant; **to feel y.,** (*not well*) se sentir patraque.

Yugoslav ['juːgəʊslɑːv] **1** *adj* yougoslave. **2** *n* Yougoslave *mf*.

Yugoslavia [juːgəʊ'slɑːvɪə] *n* Yougoslavie *f*.

Yugoslavian [juːgəʊ'slɑːvɪən] *adj* yougoslave.

yule [juːl] *n Arch & Lit* Noël *m*; **y. log,** bûche *f* de Noël.

yuletide ['juːltaɪd] *n Arch & Lit* l'époque *f* de Noël; **y. festivities,** fêtes *fpl* de Noël.

yummy ['jʌmɪ] *adj F* délicieux.

yum-yum [jʌm'jʌm] *int F* miam-miam!

yup [jʌp] *adv US F* ouais.

yuppie ['jʌpɪ] *n usu Pej* (*abbr* **young upwardly mobile professional**) yuppie *mf*, = jeune homme ou femme à la carrière brillante, prometteuse et hautement rémunératrice; **y. area/restaurant,** quartier/restaurant chic et branché.

YWCA [waɪdʌb(ə)ljuːsiː'eɪ] *n* (*abbr* **Young Women's Christian Association**) Union chrétienne de jeunes femmes.

Z

Z, z *pl* **zs, z's** [zed, *US* ziː, *pl* zedz, *US* ziːz] *n* (la lettre) Z, z *m*.
Zaire [zɑːˈɪər] *n* Zaïre *m*.
Zambezi (the) [ðəzæmˈbiːzɪ] *n* le Zambèze.
Zambia [ˈzæmbɪə] *n* Zambie *f*.
Zambian [ˈzæmbɪən] **1** *adj* zambien. **2** *n* Zambien, -ienne.
zaniness [ˈzeɪnɪnɪs] *n F* loufoquerie *f*.
zany [ˈzeɪnɪ] *adj F* loufoque.
zap[1] [zæp] *F* **1** *int* (*esp in comic books*) paf! **2** *n* claquement *m*.
zap[2] **1** *F vt* **(a)** (*with ray gun, by bombing etc*) détruire (*qch*); tuer (*qn*); **(b)** (*put, send*) **z. it in the microwave,** balance-le au micro-ondes; **we'll z. it across to you by courier,** on vous l'enverra *ou* expédiera vite fait par courrier; **they zapped him off to the TV studios,** ils l'ont emmené vite fait *ou* sur les chapeaux de roues aux studios de la télé; **(c)** *Comptr* (*delete*) effacer; **(d)** (*hit*) donner un coup à, cogner (*qch*); nettoyer (*un adversaire*). **2** *vi* **(a)** (*change channel on TV*) zapper, *Can* pitonner; **(b)** (*move fast*) **the project's really zapping along,** le projet avance vraiment à fond de train; **z., z. and it's done!,** tac tac et c'est fini!
►**zap up** *vtsep* (*make more exciting*) **to z. up one's style,** rendre son style plus coloré *ou* vivant; **to z. up the colour scheme,** (*in house etc*) rehausser les couleurs.
zapped [zæpt] *adj F* (*exhausted*) crevé, claqué.
zappy [ˈzæpɪ] *adj F* (*fast*) (*car, computer*) rapide; (*very responsive*) nerveux; (*stylish, punchy*) (*prose, manager, style*) énergique, qui a du punch.
zeal [ziːl] *n* zèle *m*, ardeur *f*; **religious z.,** zèle, ferveur *f*; **to make a show of z.,** faire du zèle; **to show excessive z.,** faire preuve d'un zèle excessif.
Zealand [ˈziːlənd] *n* (l'île *f* de) Seeland *f*.
zealot [ˈzelət] *n* **(a)** *Bible & Hist* zélote *mf*; **(b)** *Fig* fanatique *mf*, *Lit* zélateur, -trice (**for,** de).
zealotry [ˈzelətrɪ] *n* **(a)** *Hist* zélotisme *m*; **(b)** *Fig* fanatisme *m*, ferveur *f*.
zealous [ˈzeləs] *adj* zélé, empressé; **z. for sth,** plein de zèle pour qch; **z. to do sth,** empressé de faire qch.
zealously [ˈzeləslɪ] *adv* avec zèle.
zebra [ˈziːbrə, ˈzebrə] *n* (*animal*) zèbre *m*; **z. markings** *or* **stripes,** zébrures *fpl*; *Br Aut* **z. crossing,** passage clouté *ou* pour piétons.
zebu [ˈzɪːbuː] *n* (*animal*) zébu *m*.
zed [zed] *n* (la lettre) z *m*.
zee [ziː] *n US* (la lettre) z *m*.
Zen [zen] *n Rel* **Z. (Buddhism),** (bouddhisme *m*) zen *m*.
zenith [ˈzenɪθ] *n Astron & Fig* zénith *m*; *Fig* **at the z. of his fame,** à l'apogée *m ou* au sommet *ou* au zénith de sa gloire.
zephyr [ˈzefər] *n Lit* zéphyr *m*.
zeppelin [ˈzepəlɪn] *n Av Hist* zeppelin *m*.
zero[1] [ˈzɪərəʊ] **1** *n Math* zéro *m*; **z. point two (0.2),** zéro virgule deux (0,2); **z. hour,** l'heure *f* H; **I'd put your chances at z.,** je dirais que tes chances sont nulles; **z. (point),** (point *m*) origine *f*, zéro (*d'une échelle graduée etc*); **the thermometer is at z./four below z.,** le thermomètre est à zéro/à quatre au-dessous de zéro; **the temperature fell below z.,** la température est tombée au-dessous de zéro; *Admin* **z. rating,** imposition nulle; **exports are down to z.,** les exportations sont tombées à zéro; **z. economic growth,** croissance économique nulle; **z. altitude,** altitude *f* zéro; *Pol* **z. option,** option *f* zéro. **2** *adj F* **he's got z. intelligence,** il a une intelligence nulle, il n'a aucune intelligence.
zero[2] *vt* (re)mettre (*un instrument etc*) à zéro.
►**zero in 1** *vtsep US Mil* régler le tir de (*une pièce*). **2** *vi* (*of missile etc*) se régler sur une *ou* la cible.
►**zero in on** *vipo Mil* régler le tir sur (*un objectif*); (*of missile etc*) se régler sur; *Fig* (*concentrate on*) se centrer sur (*un thème, un problème*); (*attack*) s'attaquer à (*qch*); **they zeroed in on the one weak point of the argument,** ils ont attaqué le seul point faible de l'argument.
zero-rated [ˈzɪərəʊreɪtɪd] *adj* (*no VAT*) exempt de TVA.
zest [zest] *n* **(a)** (*enjoyment*) enthousiasme *m*, entrain *m*; (*in speaking*) verve *f*; **with z.,** (*combattre etc*) avec élan, avec entrain; (*manger*) avec appétit, de bon appétit; **her z. for life,** son appétit pour la vie; **(b)** (*interest*) saveur *f*, goût *m*; **to add z. to the adventure,** donner du piquant à l'aventure; **(c)** zeste *m* (*d'orange, de citron*).
zestful [ˈzestfʊl] *adj* plein d'enthousiasme *ou* de verve.
zigzag[1] [ˈzɪgzæg] **1** *n* zigzag *m*; **in zigzags,** en zigzag. **2** *adj* **z. path,** sentier *m* en zigzag; **z. pattern,** dessin *m* à zigzags. **3** *adv* **the road runs z.,** la route fait des zigzags.
zigzag[2] *vi* (**-gg-**) (*of road, line*) zigzaguer, faire des zigzags.
zigzagging [ˈzɪgzægɪŋ] *n* zigzags *mpl*, déplacement *m* en zigzag.
zilch [zɪltʃ] *n Sl* zéro *m*, que dalle.
zillion [ˈzɪljən] *n F* des millions *mpl* (et des millions).
Zimbabwe [zɪmˈbɑːbweɪ] *n* Zimbabwe *m*.
zimmer ® [ˈzɪmər] *n* déambulateur *m*.
zinc [zɪŋk] *n* zinc *m*; **z.(-)bearing,** zincifère; **z. oxide,** oxyde *m* de zinc; **z. white,** (*paint*) blanc *m* de zinc; *Pharm* **z. ointment,** pommade *f* à l'oxyde de zinc; **z. works** *or* **trade,** zinguerie *f*.
zincblende [ˈzɪŋkblend] *n Miner* blende *f*.
zing [zɪŋ] *n F* **(a)** (*zest*) vitalité *f*, entrain *m*; **(b)** (*sound*) bruit perçant, sifflement *m*.
zinnia [ˈzɪnɪə] *n* (*flower*) zinnia *m*.
Zion [ˈzaɪən] *n* Sion *m*.
Zionism [ˈzaɪənɪzm] *n Pol* sionisme *m*.
Zionist [ˈzaɪənɪst] *adj & n Pol* sioniste *mf*.
zip[1] [zɪp] *n* **(a)** *Br* **z. (fastener),** fermeture *f* éclair ® *inv ou* à glissière; *Belg* tirette *f*; **(b)** *F* énergie *f*, vitesse *f*; **put some z. into it!,** mets-y du nerf!; **your style needs more z.,** ton style a besoin d'un peu plus de punch; **(c)** *US Admin* **z. code,** code postal; **(d)** sifflement *m* (*d'une balle*).
zip[2] *vi* (**-pp-**) siffler (*comme une balle*); **to z. past,** (*of car etc*) passer en trombe.
►**zip in** *vtsep* attacher (*une doublure*) à l'aide d'une fermeture éclair ® *ou* à glissière.
►**zip through** *vipo* faire (*qch*) à toute vitesse.
►**zip up** *vtsep* (*clothes*) remonter *ou* fermer la fermeture éclair ® *ou* à glissière; **z. me up,** remonte ma fermeture.
zipper [ˈzɪpər] *n esp Am* fermeture *f* éclair ® *inv ou* à glissière; **z. bag,** (sac *m*) fourre-tout *m inv* à fermeture éclair ® *ou* à glissière.
zippy [ˈzɪpɪ] *adj F* plein d'énergie *ou* d'entrain *ou* de punch; **a z. little car,** une petite voiture nerveuse; **look z.!,** grouille-toi!
zircon [ˈzɜːkɒn] *n Miner* zircon *m*.
zit [zɪt] *n esp Am F* (*pimple*) bouton *m*.
zither [ˈzɪðər] *n Mus* cithare *f*.
zizz [zɪz] *n Br F* somme *m*; **to have a z.,** faire un petit somme.
zodiac [ˈzəʊdɪæk] *n Astrol* zodiaque *m*; **the signs of the z.,** les signes *mpl* du zodiaque.
zodiacal [zəʊˈdaɪək(ə)l] *adj* zodiacal, -aux; **z. light,** lumière zodiacale.
zombi(e) [ˈzɒmbɪ] *n Rel & Fig* zombi *m*; **he walks about like a z.,** il a tout le temps l'air abruti *ou* l'air d'un zombi; **I feel like a z.,** je me sens complètement abruti.
zonal [ˈzəʊn(ə)l] *adj* zonal, -aux.
zone[1] [zəʊn] *n* **(a)** zone *f*; *Admin* **no parking z.,** zone d'interdiction de stationner; **parking meter z.,** ≈ zone bleue; *Mil* **battle z.,** zone de l'avant; **danger z.,** zone dangereuse; **(b)** *US* **(postal delivery) z.,** zone (de distribution) postale.
zone[2] *vt* répartir (*une ville etc*) en zones.
zoning [ˈzəʊnɪŋ] *n* répartition *f* en zones; (*town planning*) zonage *m*.

zonked (out) [zɒŋkt('aʊt)] *adj F* (*drugged*) défoncé; (*drunk*) pété, bourré; (*exhausted*) crevé, vanné.
zoo [zuː] *n* jardin *m* zoologique, *F* zoo *m*.
zookeeper ['zuːkiːpər] *n* gardien *m* de zoo.
zoological [zəʊə'lɒdʒɪk(ə)l, zuːə-] *adj* zoologique; **z. garden(s),** jardin *m* zoologique.
zoologist [zəʊ'ɒlədʒɪst, zuː-] *n* zoologiste *mf*.
zoology [zəʊ'ɒlədʒɪ, zuː-] *n* zoologie *f*.
zoom¹ [zuːm] *n* **(a)** (*noise*) bourdonnement *m*; (*louder*) vrombissement *m*; **(b)** *Av F* (montée *f* en) chandelle *f*; **(c)** *Cin* zoom *m*; *Phot* **z. lens,** zoom.
zoom² *vi* **(a) to z. along** *or* **past** *or* **through,** passer *ou* traverser en trombe *ou* comme une flèche; **the cars are zooming along the road,** les voitures passent en trombe sur la route; **children were zooming around on skateboards,** des enfants passaient à toute vitesse sur des planches à roulettes; **(b)** *Av* (*climb steeply*) monter en chandelle.
►**zoom in** *vi Cin TV* faire un zoom avant.
►**zoom in on** *vipo* faire un zoom avant sur (*qch*); *Fig* se concentrer sur (*qch*); **the camera zoomed in on her face,** la caméra a pris son visage en zoom avant.
►**zoom out** *vi Cin TV* faire un zoom arrière.
►**zoom up** *vi* (*of plane*) monter en chandelle; (*of rocket etc*) s'élever; (*of hit record etc*) monter comme une flèche; (*of prices etc*) monter en flèche.
zoophyte ['zəʊəfaɪt] *n Biol* zoophyte *m*.
Zoroaster [zɒrəʊ'æstər] *n* Zarathustra *m*, Zoroastre *m*.
zounds [zaʊndz] *int Arch* morbleu!, sacrebleu!
zucchini [zʊ'kiːnɪ, zuː-] *n Am* courgette *f*; **z. bread/ lasagne,** gâteau *m*/lasagnes *fpl* aux courgettes.
Zulu ['zuːluː] **1** *adj* zoulou *inv in f*, *pl* zoulous. **2** *n* **(a)** Zoulou *mf*; **(b)** *Ling* zoulou *m*.
Zululand ['zuːluːlænd] *n* le Zoulouland.
zwieback ['zwiːbæk] *n* (genre *m* de) biscotte *f*.
zygote ['zaɪgəʊt] *n Biol* zygote *m*.

Grammaire anglaise

Guide de conversation pratique

TABLE DES MATIERES

1. GLOSSAIRE DES TERMES GRAMMATICAUX

ABSTRAIT Un nom abstrait est un nom qui ne désigne pas un objet physique ou une personne, mais une qualité ou un concept. *Bonheur, vie, longueur* sont des exemples de noms abstraits.

ACTIF L'actif ou la voix active est la forme de base du verbe, comme dans *je le surveille*. Elle s'oppose à la forme passive (*il est surveillé par moi*).

ADJECTIF C'est un mot qui décrit un nom. Parmi les adjectifs on distingue les adjectifs qualificatifs (*une **petite** maison*), les adjectifs démonstratifs (***cette** maison*), les adjectifs possessifs (***ma** maison*), etc.

ADJECTIF SUBSTANTIVE C'est un adjectif employé comme nom. Par exemple l'adjectif *jeune* peut aussi s'employer comme nom, comme dans *il y a beaucoup de jeunes ici*.

ADVERBE Les adverbes accompagnent normalement un verbe pour ajouter une information supplémentaire en indiquant **comment** l'action est accomplie (adverbe de manière), **quand**, **où** et **avec quelle intensité** l'action est accomplie (adverbes de temps, de lieu et d'intensité), ou **dans quelle mesure** l'action est accomplie (adverbes de quantité). Certains adverbes peuvent aussi s'employer avec un adjectif ou un autre adverbe (par exemple *une fille **très** mignonne, **trop** bien*).

APPOSITION On dit qu'un mot ou une proposition est en apposition par rapport à un autre mot ou une autre proposition lorsque l'un ou l'autre est placé directement après le nom ou la proposition, sans y être relié par aucun mot (par exemple *M. Duclos, **notre directeur**, a téléphoné ce matin*).

ARTICLE DEFINI Les articles définis sont *le, la, les* en français. Ils correspondent tous à **the** en anglais.

ARTICLE INDEFINI Les articles indéfinis sont *un, une* en français. Ils correspondent à **a** (ou **an**) en anglais.

ASPECT L'aspect correspond à la manière dont on envisage l'action et son déroulement dans le temps. On distingue l'aspect simple, l'aspect progressif (ou continu) et le "perfect".

ATTRIBUT Groupe nominal placé juste après le verbe "être". Dans la phrase *he is a school teacher, a school teacher* est l'attribut.

AUXILIAIRE Les auxiliaires sont employés pour former les temps composés d'autres verbes, par exemple dans **he has gone** (il est parti), **has** et "est" sont les auxiliaires. En anglais on distingue les "auxiliaires ordinaires" (**have**, **be**, **do**), et les "auxiliaires modaux", ou "défectifs" (**can**, **could**, **may**, etc.). Voir MODAL.

CARDINAL Les nombre cardinaux sont *un, deux, trois*, etc. On les oppose aux nombres ordinaux. Voir ORDINAL.

COLLECTIF Un collectif est un nom qui désigne un groupe de gens ou de choses, mais qui est au singulier. Par exemple **flock** (troupeau) et **fleet** (flotte) sont des collectifs.

COMPARATIF Le comparatif des adjectifs et des adverbes permet d'établir une comparaison entre deux personnes, deux choses ou deux actions. En français on emploie *plus ... que, moins ... que* et *aussi ... que* pour exprimer une comparaison.

COMPLEMENT D'OBJET DIRECT Groupe nominal ou pronom qui accompagne un verbe sans préposition entre les deux. Par exemple *j'ai rencontré* **un ami**.

COMPLEMENT D'OBJET INDIRECT Groupe nominal ou pronom qui suit un verbe, normalement séparé de ce dernier par une préposition (en général **à**) : *je parle **à mon ami.*** Vous noterez qu'en français comme en anglais on omet souvent la préposition devant un pronom. Par exemple dans *je lui ai envoyé un cadeau, lui* est l'équivalent de *à lui* : c'est le complément d'objet indirect.

CONDITIONNEL Mode verbal employé pour exprimer ce que quelqu'un ferait ou ce qu'arriverait si une condition était remplie, par exemple : ***il viendrait** s'il le pouvait; la chaise* **se serait cassée** *s'il s'était assis dessus.*

CONJONCTION Les conjonctions sont des mots qui relient deux mots ou propositions. On distingue les conjonctions de coordination, comme *et, ou, or*, et les conjonctions de subordination comme *parce que, après que, bien que*, qui introduisent une proposition subordonnée.

CONJUGAISON La conjugaison d'un verbe est l'ensemble des formes d'un verbe à des temps et des modes différents.

CONTINU Voir FORME PROGRESSIVE.

DEFECTIF Voir MODAL.

DEMONSTRATIF Les adjectifs démonstratifs (*ce, cette, ces*, etc.) et les pronoms démonstratifs (*celui-ci, celui-là*, etc.) s'emploient pour désigner une personne ou un objet bien précis.

DENOMBRABLE Un nom est dénombrable s'il peut avoir un pluriel et si on peut l'employer avec un article indéfini. Par exemple **house** (maison), **car** (voiture), **dog** (chien).

EXCLAMATION Mots ou phrases employés pour exprimer une surprise, une joie ou un mécontentement, etc. (*quoi !, comment !, quelle chance !, ah non !*).

FAMILIER Le langage familier est le langage courant d'aujourd'hui employé dans la langue parlée, mais pas à l'écrit, comme dans les lettres officielles, les contrats, etc.

FORME PROGRESSIVE La forme progressive d'un verbe se forme avec **to be** + **participe présent**, comme dans : *I am thinking, he has been writing all day, will she be staying with us?*. On l'appelle aussi forme continue.

GERONDIF Le gérondif est aussi appelé "verbe substantivé". En anglais, il a la même forme que le **participe présent** d'un verbe, c.-à-d. radical + **ing**. Par exemple : ***skiing is fun*** : *le ski, c'est amusant*, ***I'm fed up with waiting*** : *j'en ai assez d'attendre*.

IDIOMATIQUE Les expressions idiomatiques (ou idiomes) sont des expressions qui ne peuvent normalement pas se traduire mot à mot dans une autre langue. Par exemple *he thinks he's the cat's whiskers* correspond en français à *il se croit sorti de la cuisse de Jupiter*.

IMPERATIF On emploie ce mode pour exprimer un ordre (par exemple : *va-t'en, tais-toi !*) ou pour faire des suggestions (*allons-y*).

INDENOMBRABLE Les noms indénombrables sont des noms qui n'ont normalement pas de pluriel, par exemple *le beurre, la paresse*.

INDICATIF C'est le mode le plus courant, celui qui décrit l'action ou l'état, comme dans *j'aime, il est venu, nous essayons*. Il s'oppose au subjonctif, au conditionnel et à l'impératif.

INFINITIF L'infinitif en anglais est la forme de base, comme on la trouve dans les dictionnaires précédée ou non de **to** : **to eat** ou **eat**. On appelle cette forme sans **to** le radical.

INTERROGATIF Les mots interrogatifs sont employés pour poser des questions, par exemple *qui ? pourquoi ?*. La forme interrogative d'une phrase est la question, par exemple *le connaît-il ?, dois-je le faire ? peuvent-ils attendre un peu ?*

MODAL Les auxiliaires modaux en anglais sont **can/could, may/might, must/had to, shall/should, will/would**, de même que **ought to, used to, dare** et **need**. Une de leurs caractéristiques est qu'aux formes interrogative et négative, ils se construisent sans **do**.

MODE Le mode représente l'attitude du sujet parlant vis-à-vis de l'action dont il est question dans la phrase. Voir INDICATIF, SUBJONCTIF, CONDITIONNEL, IMPERATIF.

NOM Mot servant à désigner une chose, un être animé, un lieu ou des idées abstraites. Par exemple *passeport, chat, magasin, vie*. On distingue aussi les dénombrables, les indénombrables et les collectifs. Voir DENOMBRABLE, INDENOMBRABLE et COLLECTIF.

NOMBRE Le nombre d'un nom indique si celui-ci est **singulier** ou **pluriel**. Un nom singulier fait référence à une seule chose ou une seule personne (*train, garçon*), et un nom pluriel à plusieurs (*trains, garçons*).

OBJET DIRECT Voir COMPLEMENT.

OBJET INDIRECT Voir COMPLEMENT.

ORDINAL Les nombres ordinaux sont *premier, deuxième, troisième*, etc.

PARTICIPE PASSE En français c'est la forme *mangé, vendu*, etc. Le participe passé anglais est la forme verbale employée après *have*, comme dans *I have **eaten**, I have **said**, you have **tried**, it has been **rained on***.

PARTICIPE PRESENT Le participe présent en anglais est la forme verbale qui se termine en *-ing*.

PASSIF Un verbe est au passif ou à la voix passive lorsque le sujet ne fait pas l'action mais la subit : *les tickets sont vendus à l'entrée*. En anglais, la voix passive est formée avec le verbe **to be** et le participe passé du verbe, par exemple : ***he was rewarded*** *il fut récompensé*.

PAST PERFECT Voir PERFECT.

PERFECT C'est l'aspect qui peut exprimer une action accomplie ou une action du passé qui se poursuit dans le présent. On distingue le *present perfect*, comme dans **I have seen** (j'ai vu), le *past perfect* (ou *pluperfect*) comme dans **I had seen** (j'avais vu).

PERSONNE Pour chaque temps, il y a trois personnes du singulier (1ère : *je*, 2ème : *tu*, 3ème : *il/elle/on*) et trois personnes du pluriel (1ère : *nous*, 2ème : *vous*, 3ème : *ils/elles*).

PHRASE Une phrase est un groupe de mots qui peut être composé d'une ou plusieurs propositions (voir PROPOSITION). La fin d'une phrase est en général indiquée par un point, un point d'exclamation ou un point d'interrogation.

PLUPERFECT Voir PERFECT.

PLURIEL Voir NOMBRE.

POSSESSIF Les adjectifs ou les pronoms possessifs s'emploient pour indiquer la possession ou l'appartenance. Ce sont des mots comme *mon/le mien, ton/le tien, notre/le nôtre*, etc.

PRESENT PERFECT Voir PERFECT.

PRONOM Un pronom est un mot qui remplace un nom. Il en existe différentes catégories :

* **pronoms personnels** (*je, me, moi, tu, te, toi, etc.)*
* **pronoms démonstratifs** (*celui-ci, celui-là*, etc.)
* **pronoms relatifs** (*qui, que*, etc.)
* **pronoms interrogatifs** (*qui ?, quoi ?, lequel ?*, etc.)
* **pronoms possessifs** (*le mien, le tien*, etc.)
* **pronoms réfléchis** (*me, te, se*, etc.)
* **pronoms indéfinis** (*quelque chose, tout*, etc.)

PROPOSITION Une proposition est un groupe de mots qui contient au moins un sujet et un verbe : *il chante* est une proposition. Une phrase peut être composée de plusieurs propositions : *il chante/quand il prend sa douche/et qu'il est content*.

PROPOSITION SUBORDONNEE Une proposition subordonnée est une proposition qui dépend d'une autre. Par exemple dans : *il a dit qu'il viendrait*, *qu'il viendrait* est la proposition subordonnée.

QUESTIONS Il existe deux types de questions : les questions au style **direct**, qui sont des questions telles qu'elles ont été posées, avec une point d'interrogation (par exemple, *quand viendra-t-il ?*) ; les questions au style **indirect**, qui sont introduites par une proposition et ne nécessitent pas de point d'interrogation (par exemple : *je me demande quand il viendra*).

RADICAL Voir INFINITIF.

REFLECHI Les verbes réfléchis "renvoient" l'action sur le sujet (par exemple *je me suis habillé*). Ils sont moins nombreux en anglais qu'en français.

SINGULIER Voir NOMBRE.

SUBJONCTIF Par exemple : *il faut que je* ***sois*** *prêt*, ***vive*** *le Roi*. Le subjonctif est un mode qui n'est pas très souvent employé en anglais.

SUJET Le sujet d'un verbe est le nom ou le pronom qui accomplit l'action. Dans les phrases *je mange du chocolat* et *Pierre a deux chats*, *je* et *Pierre* sont des sujets.

SUPERLATIF C'est la forme d'un adjectif ou d'un adverbe qui, en français, se construit avec *le plus ...*, *le moins ...*

TEMPS Le temps d'un verbe indique quand l'action a lieu, c'est-à-dire le présent, le passé, le futur.

TEMPS COMPOSE Les temps composés sont les temps qui se construisent avec plus d'un élément. En anglais, ils sont formés par l'**auxiliaire** et le participe **présent** ou **passé** du verbe conjugué. Par exemple : *I am reading, I have gone.*

VERBE Le verbe est un mot qui décrit une action (*chanter, marcher*). Il peut aussi décrire un état (*être, paraître, espérer*).

VERBE COMPOSE Un verbe composé (en anglais) est un verbe comme *ask for* ou *run up*. Son sens est généralement différent de la somme des sens des deux parties qui le composent, par exemple : ***he goes in for skiing in a big way*** *il adore faire du ski* (différent de : ***he goes in for a medical next week*** *il va se faire examiner la semaine prochaine*), ***he ran up an enormous bill*** *ça lui a fait une note énorme* (différent de : ***he ran up the road*** *il a monté la rue en courant*).

VOIX Il existe deux voix pour les verbes : la voix active et la voix passive. Voir ACTIF et PASSIF.

2. LES ARTICLES

A. LES FORMES

a) L'article indéfini "un/une" se traduit par **a** devant une consonne et **an** devant une voyelle :

a cat un chat
an owl une chouette
a dog un chien
an umbrella un parapluie

Il est cependant important de se souvenir que l'on emploie **a/an** selon que l'initiale du mot qui suit se prononce comme une voyelle ou non. Ainsi le "h" muet est précédé de **an** :

an hour une heure
an heir un héritier
an honest man un honnête homme

Il en est de même pour les abréviations commençant phonétiquement par une voyelle :

an MP un membre du Parlement

En revanche, la diphtongue se prononçant "iou" et qui s'écrit "eu" ou "u" est précédée de **a** :

a university une université
a eucalyptus tree un eucalyptus
a union un syndicat

Avec le mot **hotel** on peut employer soit **a** ou **an**, bien que dans le langage parlé, on préfère l'emploi de **a**.

b) L'article défini "le", "la", "les" se traduit toujours par **the** :

the cat le chat
the owl la chouette
the holidays les vacances

On peut prononcer le **e** de **the** un peu comme un "i" français lorsque le mot qui suit commence phonétiquement par une voyelle (voir a) ci-dessus), comme pour **the owl**, ou lorsqu'il est accentué :

he's definitely *the* man for the job
voilà vraiment l'homme qu'il faut pour ce travail

B. LA POSITION DE L'ARTICLE

L'article précède le nom et tout adjectif (avec ou sans adverbe) placé devant un nom :

a smart hat/the smart hat
un chapeau élégant/le chapeau élégant

a very smart hat/the very smart hat
un chapeau très élégant/le chapeau très élégant

Cependant **all** et **both** précèdent l'article défini :

they had all the fun
ce sont eux qui se sont bien amusés

both the men (= both men) were guilty
les deux hommes étaient tous les deux coupables

Et les adverbes **quite** et **rather** précèdent normalement l'article :

it was quite/rather a good play
c'était une assez bonne pièce

it was quite the best play I've seen
c'était vraiment la meilleure pièce que j'aie jamais vue

Cependant, **quite** et **rather** se placent parfois *après* l'article indéfini comme dans :

that was a rather unfortunate remark to make
c'était une remarque plutôt regrettable

that would be a quite useless task
ce serait une tâche tout à fait inutile

Les adverbes **too**, **so** et **as** précèdent l'adjectif et l'article indéfini. On a donc la construction :

too/so/as + adjectif + article + nom :

if that is not too great a favour to ask
si ce n'est pas trop vous demander

never have I seen so boring a film
je n'ai jamais vu de film aussi ennuyeux

I have never seen as fine an actor as Olivier
je n'ai jamais vu d'acteur aussi bon qu'Olivier

On peut aussi trouver **many a** (plus d'un), **such a** (un tel) et **what a** (quel !) :

many a man would do the same
plus d'un homme ferait la même chose

she's such a fool
elle est tellement idiote

what a joke!
quelle blague !

Remarquez qu'avec **such** l'adjectif suit l'article indéfini, tandis qu'avec **so** il le précède (voir aussi ci-dessus) :

I have never seen such a beautiful painting
je n'ai jamais vu une peinture aussi belle

I have never seen so beautiful a painting
je n'ai jamais vu une peinture aussi belle

Half (la moitié de) aussi précède habituellement l'article :

half the world knows about this
presque tout le monde est au courant

I'll be back in half an hour
je serai de retour dans une demi-heure

Mais si **half** et le nom forment un mot composé, l'article se place en premier :

why don't you buy just a half bottle of rum?
pourquoi n'achètes-tu pas juste une bouteille de rhum d'un demi-litre ?

C'est-à-dire une petite bouteille de rhum. Comparez :

he drank half a bottle of rum
il a bu la moitié d'une bouteille de rhum

C. L'EMPLOI DES ARTICLES

1. L'ARTICLE INDEFINI (a, an)

Normalement l'article défini s'emploie uniquement pour les noms dénombrables, mais comme nous le verrons p A9, on peut discuter le fait qu'un nom soit dénombrable ou pas.

a) Devant un nom générique, pour faire référence à une catégorie ou une espèce :

a mouse is smaller than a rat
une souris est plus petite qu'un rat

A mouse et **a rat** représentent les souris et les rats en général. Avec une légère différence de sens, l'article défini peut aussi s'employer devant un terme générique. Voir ci-dessous p A6.

Remarquez que le terme générique **man** représentant l'humanité (à la différence de **a man, a male human being** "un homme") ne prend pas l'article :

a dog is man's best friend
le chien est le meilleur ami de l'homme

b) Avec des noms attributs du sujet ou dans des appositions, ou bien après **as**, en particulier avec des noms de métiers à la différence du français :

he is a hairdresser
il est coiffeur

she has become a Member of Parliament
elle est devenue membre du Parlement

Miss Behrens, a singer of formidable range, had no problems with the role
Miss Behrens, chanteuse au registre de voix extraordinaire, n'avait aucun problème à tenir le rôle

John Adams, a real tough guy, was leaning casually on the bar
John Adams, un vrai dur, était appuyé négligemment au bar

he used to work as a skipper
il travaillait comme capitaine

L'article indéfini s'emploie dans de tels cas lorsque le nom fait partie d'un groupe. S'il n'y a pas appartenance à un groupe, on omet l'article, comme dans l'exemple suivant, où la personne mentionnée est unique :

she is now Duchess of York
elle est maintenant duchesse d'York

Professor Draper, head of the English department
le Professeur Draper, chef du département d'anglais

Si le nom fait référence à une caractéristique plutôt qu'à une appartenance à un groupe, on omet aussi l'article (on l'omet toujours après **turn**) :

he turned traitor
il s'est vendu à l'ennemi

surely you're man enough to stand up to her
tu es sûrement homme à lui tenir tête

mais : be a man!
sois un homme !

Si on a une liste de mots en apposition, on peut omettre l'article :

Maria Callas, opera singer, socialite and companion of Onassis, died in her Paris flat yesterday
Maria Callas, cantatrice, membre de la haute société et compagne d'Onassis, est morte hier à Paris, dans son appartement

On emploie l'article défini **the** pour une personne célèbre (ou pour distinguer une personne d'une autre ayant le même nom) :

Maria Callas, the opera singer ...
Maria Callas, la cantatrice ...

c) Comme préposition

L'article indéfini peut s'employer dans le sens de "par", comme dans les exemples suivants :

haddock is £1.80 a kilo
le haddock fait 1,80 livres le kilo

take two tablets twice a day
prenez deux comprimés deux fois par jour

d) Avec **little** (peu de + *sing.*) et **few** ("peu de" + *pl.*)

L'article indéfini qui accompagne ces deux mots indique un sens positif (un peu de). Employés seuls, **little** et **few** ont un sens négatif :

she needs a little attention (= some attention)
elle a besoin d'un peu d'attention

she needs little attention (= hardly any attention)
elle a besoin de peu d'attention

they have a few paintings (= some)
ils ont quelques tableaux

they have few paintings (= hardly any)
ils ont peu de tableaux

Cependant **only a little/few** signifient plus ou moins la même chose que **little/few** qui sont moins courants :

I have only a little coffee left (= hardly any)
il ne me reste presque plus de café

I can afford only a few books (= hardly any)
je ne peux me permettre d'acheter que quelques livres

Remarquez aussi l'expression **a good few** qui équivaut à "pas mal de" en français :

there are a good few miles to go yet
il y a encore pas mal de miles à parcourir

he's had a good few (to drink)
il a pas mal bu

2. L'ARTICLE DEFINI (the)

a) L'article défini s'emploie avec des noms dénombrables et des noms indénombrables :

the butter (indénombrable)	le beurre
the cup (sing. dénombrable)	la tasse
the cups (pl. dénombrable)	les tasses

b) Comme l'article indéfini, l'article défini peut s'employer devant un nom générique. Il paraît alors plus scientifique :

the mouse is smaller than the rat (comparez avec 1a) ci-dessus)
la souris est plus petite que le rat

when was the potato first introduced to Europe?
quand est-ce que la pomme de terre fut introduite en Europe pour la première fois ?

c) Un groupe prépositionnel après un nom peut avoir pour fonction soit de définir ou préciser le nom, soit de le décrire. S'il définit le nom, il faut employer l'article défini :

I want to wear the trousers on that hanger
je veux mettre le pantalon qui est sur ce cintre

she has just met the man of her dreams
elle vient juste de rencontrer l'homme de sa vie

the parcels from Aunt Mary haven't arrived yet
les paquets de tante Mary ne sont pas encore arrivés

Si par contre le groupe prépositionnel sert à décrire ou à classifier plutôt qu'à définir, on omet normalement l'article :

everywhere we looked we saw trousers on hangers
partout où nous regardions nous voyions des pantalons sur des cintres

knowledge of Latin and Greek is desirable
des connaissances en latin et en grec sont souhaitées

presence of mind is what he needs
ce qu'il lui faut, c'est de la présence d'esprit

I always love receiving parcels from Aunt Mary
j'aime toujours recevoir des paquets de tante Mary

Dans la phrase :

the presence of mind that she showed was extraordinary
la présence d'esprit dont elle a fait preuve était extraordinaire

l'emploi de **the** est obligatoire parce que l'on fait référence à un exemple de présence d'esprit bien précis, comme le fait apparaître la proposition relative qui suit.

Cependant quand le complément du nom introduit par **of** sert à la fois à décrire et à définir le nom, c'est-à-dire que le nom n'est ni totalement général, ni totalement spécifique, on emploie l'article défini :

the women of Paris (= women from Paris, in general)
les femmes de Paris

the children of such families (= children from such families)
les enfants de telles familles

d) L'omission de l'article défini

A la différence du français, l'omission de l'article défini en anglais est très fréquente. Ainsi un grand nombre de noms ne sont pas précédés de l'article s'ils font référence à une fonction ou à des caractéristiques en général, plutôt qu'à l'objet. Ces catégories de noms comprennent :

i) les institutions, par exemple :

church	l'église
prison	la prison
college	le collège d'enseignement supérieur
school	l'école
court	le tribunal
university	l'université
hospital	l'hôpital

Exemples:

do you go to church?
tu vas à la messe (tous les dimanches) ?

she's in hospital again and he's in prison
elle est encore une fois à l'hôpital et il est en prison

aren't you going to school today?
tu ne vas pas à l'école aujourd'hui ?

Joan is at university
Joan est à l'université

Cependant en anglais américain on préfère l'emploi de l'article défini devant **hospital** :

Wayne is back in the hospital
Wayne est de retour à l'hôpital

Si le nom fait référence à un objet physique (le bâtiment) plutôt qu'à sa fonction, on emploie alors **the** :

walk up to the church and turn right
allez jusqu'à l'église, puis tournez à droite

the taxi stopped at the school
le taxi s'est arrêté devant l'école

The s'emploie aussi pour désigner un nom défini ou précisé par le contexte :

at the university where his father studied
à l'université où son père a étudié

she's at the university
elle est à l'université (dans cette ville, etc.)

Pour faire référence à l'institution en général on emploie l'article :

the Church was against it
l'Eglise était contre

ii) les moyens de transport précédés de **by** :

we always go by bus/car/boat/train/plane
nous partons toujours en bus/en voiture/en bateau/par le train/par avion

iii) les repas :

can you meet me before lunch?
tu peux me voir avant le déjeuner ?

buy some haddock for tea, will you?
achète du haddock pour le dîner, veux-tu ?

Mais si l'on fait référence à une occasion précise, on emploie l'article. Ainsi il existe une grande différence entre :

I enjoy lunch j'aime le déjeuner
et :
I am enjoying the lunch j'apprécie ce déjeuner

Dans le premier cas on fait référence au plaisir de manger à midi ; dans le second cas à un repas particulier.

iv) les moments de la journée et de la nuit après une préposition autre que **in** et **during** :

I don't like going out at night
je n'aime pas sortir le soir/la nuit

these animals can often be seen after dusk
on peut souvent voir ces animaux après le crépuscule

they go to bed around midnight
ils vont se coucher vers minuit

mais :

see you in the morning!
à demain matin !

if you feel peckish during the day, have an apple
si tu as faim dans la journée, mange une pomme

v) les saisons, en particulier pour exprimer un contraste par rapport à une autre saison plutôt que pour faire référence à une période de l'année. Ainsi :

spring is here! (winter is over)
le printemps est là (l'hiver est fini)

it's like winter today
on se croirait en hiver aujourd'hui

mais :

the winter was spent at expensive ski resorts
on passait l'hiver dans des stations de ski chères

he needed the summer to recover
il avait besoin de l'été pour récupérer

Après **in** on emploie parfois l'article défini, avec très peu de différence de sens entre les deux cas :

most leaves turn yellow in (the) autumn
la plupart des feuilles deviennent jaunes en automne

En anglais américain, on préfère l'emploi de **the**.

vi) dans les combinaisons **next/last** dans les expressions de temps :

Si de telles expressions sont envisagées par rapport au présent, on n'emploie normalement pas l'article :

can we meet next week?
est-ce qu'on peut se voir la semaine prochaine ?

he was drunk last night
il était ivre hier soir/la nuit dernière

Dans les autres cas on emploie l'article :

we arrived on March 31st and the next day was spent relaxing by the pool
nous sommes arrivés le 31 mars et on a passé le jour suivant à se relaxer près de la piscine

vii) avec des noms abstraits :

a talk about politics
un discours sur la politique

a study of human relationships
une étude sur les relations humaines

suspicion is a terrible thing
le soupçon est une chose terrible

Mais, bien sûr, lorsque le mot est précisé on emploie l'article (voir 2c) ci-dessus) :

the politics of disarmament
la politique de désarmement

viii) avec certaines maladies :

he has diabetes il a du diabète	**I've got jaundice** j'ai la jaunisse

Cependant pour certaines maladies communes, on peut employer l'article dans un anglais un peu plus familier :

she has (the) flu elle a la grippe	**he's got (the) measles** il a la rougeole

ix) avec les noms de couleurs :

red is my favourite colour
le rouge est ma couleur préférée

x) avec les noms de matériaux, d'aliments, de boissons, et de corps chimiques, etc. :

oxygen is crucial to life
l'oxygène est indispensable à la vie

concrete is used less nowadays
on emploie moins le béton de nos jours

I prefer corduroy
je préfère le velours côtelé

it smells of beer
ça sent la bière

xi) devant les noms de langues et de matières scolaires :

German is harder than English
l'allemand est plus difficile que l'anglais

Remarquez ici l'emploi des majuscules en anglais.

I hate maths
je déteste les maths

xii) devant les noms pluriels à sens général :

he loves antiques il adore les antiquités	**he's frightened of dogs** il a peur des chiens

e) L'article défini n'est normalement pas employé lorsque l'on fait référence à des noms de pays, de comtés, d'états :

Switzerland	la Suisse
England	l'Angleterre
Sussex	le Sussex
Texas	le Texas
in France	en France
to America	en Amérique

i) mais il existe quelques exceptions :

the Yemen	le Yémen
(the) Sudan	le Soudan
(the) Lebanon	le Liban

et lorsque le nom du pays est qualifié :

the People's Republic of China
la République Populaire de Chine

the Republic of Ireland
la République d'Irlande

ii) les noms de lieux au pluriel prennent l'article :

the Philippines	les Philippines
the Shetlands	les Shetlands
the Azores	les Açores
the Midlands	les Midlands
the Borders	la région des Borders
the Netherlands	les Pays-Bas
the United States	les Etats-Unis

Il en est de même pour les noms de famille :

the Smiths
les Smith

iii) les fleuves, les rivières et les océans prennent l'article :

the Thames	la Tamise
the Danube	le Danube
the Pacific	le Pacifique
the Atlantic	l'Atlantique

iv) les noms de régions prennent l'article :

the Tyrol	le Tyrol
the Orient	l'Orient
the Ruhr	la Ruhr
the Crimea	la Crimée
the City (of London)	la Cité de Londres
the East End	le East End

v) les noms de montagnes et de lacs ne prennent pas l'article :

Ben Nevis	le Ben Nevis
K2	le K2
Lake Michigan	le lac Michigan

mais les chaînes de montagnes sont précédées de l'article :

the Himalayas	l'Himalaya
the Alps	les Alpes

Il existe cependant des exceptions :

the Matterhorn	le mont Cervin
the Eiger	l'Eiger

vi) les noms de rues, de parcs et de places, etc. ne prennent normalement pas l'article :

he lives in Wilton Street
il habite Wilton Street

they met in Hyde Park
ils se sont rencontrés à Hyde Park

there was a concert in Trafalgar Square
il y avait un concert à Trafalgar Square

Mais il existe des exceptions. Parfois l'article fait partie intégrante du nom :

the Strand	le Strand

et parfois on trouve des exceptions fondées sur un usage purement local :

the Edgware Road	l'Edgware Road

f) On omet l'article dans les énumérations (même à deux termes) :

the boys and girls
les garçons et les filles

the hammers, nails and screwdrivers
les marteaux, les clous et les tourne-vis

g) Les noms d'hôtels, de pubs, de restaurants, de théâtres, de cinémas, de musées sont normalement précédés de **the** :

the Caledonian (Hotel), the Red Lion, the Copper Kettle, the Old Vic, the Odeon, the Tate (Gallery)

Mais vous noterez **Covent Garden** (l'opéra royal) et **Drury Lane** (un théâtre du West End à Londres).

h) Les journaux et quelques magazines prennent **the** :

the Observer, the Independent, the Daily Star

et par exemple les magazines :

the Spectator, the Economist

Cependant la plupart des magazines ne sont pas précédés de l'article :

Woman's Own, Punch, Private Eye, etc.

et les deux magazines de télévision et de radio, que l'on appelait autrefois **The Radio Times** et **The TV Times** (et que certains appellent encore ainsi) sont aujourd'hui mentionnés sans article lorsqu'on en fait la publicité à la télévision :

Radio Times et **TV Times**

i) Les instruments de musique

L'article défini s'emploie lorsqu'on fait référence à une aptitude :

she plays the clarinet
elle joue de la clarinette

Cependant lorsqu'on fait référence à une occasion précise plutôt qu'à une aptitude d'ordre général, on omet l'article :

in this piece he plays bass guitar
il joue de la basse dans ce morceau

j) Les noms de titres sont normalement précédés de l'article défini :

the Queen	la reine
the President	le président

Cependant lorsque le titre est suivi du nom de la personne on omet l'article défini :

Doctor MacPherson	le docteur MacPherson
Queen Elizabeth	la reine Elizabeth
Prime Minister Churchill	le Premier Ministre Churchill
Remarquez : **Christ**	le Christ

k) L'omission de l'article défini pour produire un effet spécial :

i) On omet parfois l'article défini pour produire un effet particulier ; soit pour dénoter une importance, un statut ou parfois dans un jargon :

all pupils will assemble in hall
tous les élèves se rassembleront dans le hall

the number of delegates at conference
le nombre des délégués à la conférence

ii) les gros titres de journaux (omission de l'article indéfini aussi) :

Attempt To Break Record Fails
Tentative de pulvériser le record échoue

New Conference Centre Planned
Projet pour un nouveau Palais des Congrès

iii) les instructions (omission de l'article indéfini aussi) :

break glass in emergency
casser la vitre en cas d'urgence

Pour la traduction de l'article partitif voir p A34-5.
Pour les articles avec les parties du corps voir p A30.

3. LES NOMS

A. LES TYPES DE NOMS

Les noms anglais n'ont pas de genre grammatical ("le/la" est toujours **the**).

1. LES NOMS CONCRETS ET LES NOMS ABSTRAITS

On peut classer les noms de différentes manières. On peut ainsi les diviser en (1) noms "concrets", c'est-à-dire des noms faisant référence à des êtres animés ou à des choses : **woman** (femme), **cat** (chat), **stone** (pierre) et en (2) noms "abstraits", c'est-à-dire des noms qui expriment un concept qui n'est pas physique, des caractéristiques ou des activités : **love** (l'amour), **ugliness** (la laideur), **classification** (la classification).

Un grand nombre de noms abstraits sont formés en ajoutant une terminaison (suffixe) à un adjectif, un nom ou un verbe. Cependant beaucoup de noms abstraits ne prennent pas cette terminaison. C'est la cas de **love** (l'amour), **hate** (la haine), **concept** (le concept) par exemple. Voici quelques terminaisons de noms abstraits couramment employées (certaines peuvent aussi s'employer pour des noms concrets).

a) *Les noms abstraits formés à partir d'autres noms*

-age	**percent + -age**	**percentage**	pourcentage
-cy	**democrat + -cy**	**democracy**	démocratie
-dom	**martyr + -dom**	**martyrdom**	martyre
-hood	**child + -hood**	**childhood**	enfance
-ism	**alcohol + -ism**	**alcoholism**	alcoolisme
-ry	**chemist + -ry**	**chemistry**	chimie

b) *Les noms abstraits formés à partir d'adjectifs*

-age	**short + -age**	**shortage**	pénurie
-cy	**bankrupt + -cy**	**bankruptcy**	faillite
	normal + -cy	**normalcy**	normalité (anglais américain)
-hood	**likely + -hood**	**likelihood**	probabilité
-ism	**social + -ism**	**socialism**	socialisme
-ity	**normal + -ity**	**normality**	normalité
-ness	**kind + -ness**	**kindness**	gentillesse

c) *Les noms abstraits formés à partir de verbes*

-age	**break + -age**	**breakage**	rupture
-al	**arrive + -al**	**arrival**	arrivée
-ance	**utter + -ance**	**utterance**	déclaration
-(at)ion	**starve + -ation**	**starvation**	famine
	operate + -ion	**operation**	opération
-ing	voir p A39 le gérondif		
-ment	**treat + -ment**	**treatment**	traitement

Remarquez que la terminaison du nom, de l'adjectif ou du verbe doit parfois subir quelques changements avant d'ajouter le suffixe.

2. LES NOMS COMMUNS ET LES NOMS PROPRES

On peut aussi classer les noms en noms "communs" et en noms "propres", ces derniers faisant référence à des noms de personnes ou à des noms géographiques, de jours et de mois.

communs		*propres*	
cup	tasse	**Peter**	Pierre
palace	palais	**China**	la Chine
cheese	fromage	**Wednesday**	mercredi
time	le temps	**August**	août
love	l'amour	**Christmas**	Noël

Remarquez que les noms propres s'écrivent avec une majuscule en anglais.

3. LES NOMS DENOMBRABLES ET INDENOMBRABLES

Une classification, déterminante pour l'absence ou la présence de l'article indéfini, permet de distinguer les noms en "dénombrables" et "indénombrables". Un nom dénombrable à part entière peut bien sûr être considéré comme une unité (c'est-à-dire qu'il peut être précédé d'un nombre), et doit avoir une forme au singulier aussi bien qu'au pluriel. Les noms indénombrables à part entière ne sont quant à eux ni au singulier, ni au pluriel, puisque par définition on ne peut les compter, bien qu'ils soient suivis d'un verbe au singulier. On dit qu'ils représentent une "totalité" :

dénombrables

a/one pen/three pens	un crayon/trois crayons
a/one coat/three coats	un manteau/trois manteaux
a/one horse/three horses	un cheval/trois chevaux
a/one child/three children	un enfant/trois enfants

indénombrables

furniture	les/des meubles
spaghetti	les/des spaghettis
information	les/des informations
rubbish	les/des ordures
progress	les/des progrès
fish	les/des poissons
fruit	les/des fruits
news	les/des nouvelles
violence	la violence

Lorsque l'on veut faire référence à une unité de chacun de ces noms indénombrables, il faut faire précéder le nom indénombrable d'un autre nom qui soit dénombrable. Ainsi on emploie, par exemple, **piece** pour indiquer une ou plusieurs unités :

a piece of furniture/two pieces of furniture
un meuble/deux meubles

De même on dira **an act of violence** (un acte de violence), **an item of news** (une nouvelle), **a strand of spaghetti** (un spaghetti) où **act**, **item** et **strand** sont des dénombrables tout à fait normaux. Le dénombrable qui accompagne **cattle** est **head**, qui ne prend jamais **-s** dans ce sens : **ten head of cattle** (dix têtes de bétail).

Voici d'autres exemples de noms indénombrables à part entière : **baggage** (les bagages), **luggage** (les bagages), **garbage** (les ordures), **advice** (les conseils). Pour un mot comme **knowledge** (la/les connaissance(s)), voir p A10. Pour **accommodation**, voir p A11.

a) *Les noms qui sont soit dénombrables, soit indénombrables*

i) Certains noms peuvent être dénombrables ou indénombrables, suivant que leur sens fait référence à une "unité" ou une "totalité". De tels noms font souvent référence à la nourriture ou aux matériaux :

dénombrables	*indénombrables*
that sheep has only one lamb ce mouton n'a qu'un agneau	**we had lamb for dinner** nous avions de l'agneau pour le dîner
what lovely strawberries! quelles belles fraises !	**there's too much strawberry in this ice cream** cette glace a trop le goût de fraise
do you like my nylons? tu aimes mes bas ?	**most socks contain nylon** la plupart des chaussettes contiennent du nylon
he bought a paper il a acheté un journal	**I'd like some writing paper** je voudrais du papier à lettres
she's a beauty c'est une beauté	**love, beauty and truth** l'amour, la beauté et la vérité
she has a lovely voice elle a une jolie voix	**she has no voice in the making of decisions** elle n'a pas voix au chapitre lorsqu'il s'agit de prendre des décisions

ii) Comme en français, les noms indénombrables deviennent dénombrables lorsqu'ils représentent "une partie de" ou "une variété de" :

I'd like a coffee
je voudrais un café

two white wines, please
deux vins blancs, s'il vous plaît

Britain has a large selection of cheeses
la Grande-Bretagne a une grande sélection de fromages

a very good beer
une très bonne bière

iii) Certains noms dénombrables sont parfois employés au pluriel pour indiquer une immensité, en général dans un style littéraire :

The Snows of Kilimanjaro
les Neiges du Kilimanjaro

still waters run deep (proverbe)
il faut se méfier de l'eau qui dort

Cependant il est tout à fait normal d'employer **waters** pour faire référence aux eaux territoriales d'un pays (**the territorial limit of Danish waters**), ou aux eaux ayant une vertu médicale : **he has been to take the waters at Vichy** (il a pris les eaux à Vichy).

Weather est considéré comme une "totalité", sauf dans l'expression **in all weathers** (par tous les temps).

b) *Quelques problèmes que posent les dénombrables*

Un nom totalement dénombrable peut être précédé de l'article indéfini, ou de tout adjectif numéral, d'un adjectif démonstratif pluriel (**these**), ou d'un adjectif indéfini (**few**, **many**), et peut être accompagné d'un verbe au pluriel :

a/one table
three/these/those/few/many tables are ...

Mais certains mots ont un statut ambigu :

i) Par exemple, le mot **data**, "données" (du latin **datum** (sing.), **data** (pl.)). On peut dire **these/those data are** mais rarement **many/few data** (on préfère **much/little data**) et en aucun cas **seven data** car on ne peut pas compter les "**data**". **Data** n'a donc pas de singulier, et l'on devra dire **seven pieces of data**. En fait, ce mot est en passe de devenir indénombrable : **this/that/much/little data is** s'entend et s'écrit aujourd'hui plus fréquemment que **these/those/many/few data are**.

ii) **Vegetable** est un autre cas intéressant. En effet on peut dire **many vegetables** (et **a/one vegetable**). Cependant on peut aussi dire **much vegetables** lorsque l'on fait référence à l'ensemble de la catégorie d'aliments "légumes" et non pas à des légumes en particulier :

the Japanese still eat twice as much vegetables, including beans, as the British
les Japonais mangent encore deux fois plus de légumes, dont des haricots, que les Britanniques

Dans cette phrase, on a choisi **much** et non pas **many**, car **many** aurait mis l'accent sur chacun des légumes : **many vegetables** tend à signifier "beaucoup de sortes de légumes" (**many kinds of vegetables**), alors que l'on se réfère ici à la quantité. On aurait aussi pu éviter ce problème en écrivant **a lot of vegetables**. **Much** accompagne donc certains noms au pluriel, indiquant clairement que l'on insiste sur la totalité.

iii) Les mots qui modifient la "quantité" de noms pluriels posent aussi un problème : les plus courants d'entre eux étant **less** et **fewer** (moins de). Nombreux sont ceux qui n'emploient plus **fewer** à l'oral avec les noms au pluriel. Ainsi l'usage le plus répandu du comparatif de **few** à l'oral (et souvent à l'écrit) est **less**. **Fewer** a tendance à être soutenu et trop précis, et il est parfaitement normal d'entendre par exemple **less books/students/crimes** (moins de livres/d'étudiants/de crimes) dit par n'importe qui, quel que soit leur niveau d'éducation.

iv) l'article indéfini et le pluriel avec des indénombrables

Certains noms abstraits sont dénombrables à part entière (**possibility**) et certains sont normalement indénombrables à part entière (**indignation, hate, anger**). Certains de ces noms abstraits indénombrables prennent souvent l'article indéfini, en particulier s'ils sont accompagnés par un adjectif ou un groupe adjectival, tel qu'un groupe prépositionnel ou une proposition relative. C'est parce que le groupe adjectival individualise le nom :

candidates must have a good knowledge of English
les candidats doivent avoir des bonnes connaissances en anglais

he expressed an indignation so intense that people were taken aback
il exprima une indignation si véhémente que les gens en ont été stupéfaits

On peut parfois trouver des noms abstraits comme ceux-ci au pluriel. Ainsi **fears** et **doubts** sont fréquents :

he expressed his fears
il exprima ses craintes

I have my doubts
j'ai mes doutes

Dans d'autres cas, le pluriel indique des manifestations individuelles d'un concept abstrait :

the use of too many adjectives is one of his stylistic infelicities
l'une de ses maladresses stylistiques réside dans l'emploi d'un trop grand nombre d'adjectifs

c) *Les noms en -ics*

Lorsque ces noms sont considérés comme des concepts abstraits, ils sont suivis d'un verbe au singulier :

mathematics is a difficult subject
les mathématiques sont un sujet difficile

On préférera en revanche un verbe au pluriel lorsque l'on met l'accent sur les manifestations pratiques du concept :

his mathematics are very poor
ses mathématiques sont très faibles (son travail pratique)

what are your politics?
quelles sont vos opinions politiques ?

d) *Les maladies, les jeux et les nouvelles*

Certains noms se terminant par ce qui semble être le **-s** du pluriel sont indénombrables. Le mot **news** par exemple, les maladies telles que **measles** (rougeole), **mumps** (oreillons), **rickets** (rachitisme), **shingles** (zona) et quelques noms des jeux :

the news hasn't arrived yet
la nouvelle n'est pas encore arrivée

mumps is not a dangerous disease
les oreillons ne sont pas une maladie dangereuse

darts is still played in many pubs
on joue encore aux fléchettes dans beaucoup de pubs

billiards is preferred to dice in some countries
on préfère jouer au billard plutôt qu'aux dés dans certains pays

Il en est de même pour **bowls** (boules), **dominoes** (dominos), **draughts** (dames) et **checkers** ("dames" en anglais américain).

e) *Noms de "paires"*

Certain noms au pluriel faisant référence à des objets composés de deux parties égales n'ont pas de forme au singulier, et doivent être précédés de **a pair of** si l'on veut mettre l'accent sur leur nombre :

my trousers are here
mon pantalon est ici

this is a good pair of trousers
c'est un bon pantalon

two new pairs of trousers
deux pantalons neufs

de même :

bellows (soufflet), **binoculars** (jumelles), **glasses** (lunettes), **knickers** (culotte, slip), **pants** (culotte), **pincers** (tenailles), **pyjamas** (**pajamas** en anglais américain) (pyjama), **pliers** (pinces, tenailles), **scales** (balance), **scissors** (ciseaux), **shears** (cisailles), **shorts** (short), **spectacles** (lunettes), **tights** (bas), **tongs** (fer à friser), **tweezers** (pince à épiler)

f) *Noms que l'on ne trouve normalement qu'au pluriel et qui sont suivis d'un verbe au pluriel :*

i) **arms** (armes), **arrears** (arriéré(s)), **auspices** (auspices), **banns** (bans (de mariage)), **clothes** (vêtements), **customs** (douane(s)), **dregs** (la lie), **earnings** (revenus), **entrails** (entrailles), **goods** (marchandise(s)), **greens** (légumes verts), **guts** (boyaux, courage), **lodgings** (logement(s)), **looks** (apparence(s)), **manners** (manières), **means** (moyens (financiers)), **odds** (cote(s)), **outskirts** (environs, banlieue(s)), **pains** (peine, effort), **premises** (locaux), **quarters** (résidence(s)), **remains** (restes), **riches** (richesse(s)), **spirits** (humeur, alcool), **(soap) suds** (mousse de savon), **surroundings** (environs, cadre), **tropics** (tropiques), **valuables** (objets de valeur)

et le nom italien au pluriel **graffiti** (qui est aussi accompagné d'un verbe au singulier)

Ces noms sont normalement accompagnés d'un verbe au pluriel, mais ils ont parfois aussi une forme au singulier, qui entraîne souvent un changement de sens :

ashes (cendres en général) mais **cigar(ette) ash, tobacco ash** (la cendre de cigar(ette)/tabac)

contents (le contenu) mais **content** (la quantité qui peut être contenue) :

show me the contents of your purse
montre-moi le contenu de ton porte-monnaie

mais :

what exactly is the lead content of petrol?
quelle est la teneur exacte de l'essence en plomb ?

funds (des fonds) mais **fund** (un fonds), par exemple :

I'm short of funds
je suis à court de fonds

mais :

we started a church roof repair fund
nous avons commencé à faire une collecte pour réparer le toit de l'église

stairs : plus courant que **stair** au sens de **flight of stairs** ((volée d')escalier). **Stair** peut aussi faire référence à une marche dans un escalier.

thanks : vous noterez la possibilité d'employer l'article indéfini devant un adjectif (pas de singulier dans ce cas) :

a very special thanks to ...
un grand merci à ...

wages: souvent au singulier aussi, particulièrement lorsqu'il est précédé d'un adjectif :

all we want is a decent wage
tout ce que nous voulons c'est un salaire correct

Accommodations (logement) est employé en anglais américain. En anglais britannique, on emploie **accommodation** comme indénombrable représentant une totalité.

ii) Quelques noms ne portent jamais la marque du pluriel :

cattle (bétail), **clergy** ((membres du) clergé), **livestock** ((têtes de) bétail), **police** (police, policiers), **vermin** (vermine, parasites)

Mais même **clergy** et **police** peuvent parfois être accompagnés d'un article indéfini, s'ils sont qualifiés par un adjectif, un groupe prépositionnel ou une proposition relative. Dans de tels cas il existe une différence de sens importante entre **clergymen** (ecclésiastiques) et **body of clergymen** (ensemble du clergé), et **policemen** (policiers) et **police force** (la police). Comparez :

seventy-five clergy were present
75 membres du clergé étaient présents

the problem is whether the country needs a clergy with such old-fashioned views
le problème est de savoir si le pays a besoin d'un clergé aux opinions aussi dépassées

at least thirty police were needed for that task
on a eu besoin d'au moins 30 policiers pour cette tâche

the country needed a semi-military police
le pays avait besoin d'une police semi-militaire

Folk dans le sens de "gens", "personnes", ne prend normalement pas de **-s** en anglais britannique :

some folk just don't know how to behave
certaines personnes ne savent pas se tenir

tandis qu'en anglais américain on dit **folks**, ce qui en anglais britannique est normalement employé lorsqu'on s'adresse familièrement à des personnes et qui signifie aussi "famille, parents" :

sit down, folks (anglais britannique)
asseyez-vous mes amis

I'd like you to meet my folks (anglais britannique)
j'aimerais que vous rencontriez ma famille

Youth "la jeunesse" (génération) peut être suivi aussi bien d'un verbe au singulier que d'un verbe au pluriel :

our country's youth has/have little to look forward to
la jeunesse de notre pays a peu de perspectives d'avenir

mais il est dénombrable dans le sens de "jeune homme" :

they arrested a youth/two youths
ils ont arrêté un jeune/deux jeunes

g) *Les noms collectifs*

i) Ce sont des noms qui, au singulier, sont accompagnés d'un verbe au singulier quand le nom désigne un totalité, ou d'un verbe au pluriel si on désire mettre l'accent sur les membres du groupe :

the jury is one of the safeguards of our legal system (sing.)
le jury est garant de notre système législatif

the jury have returned their verdict (pluriel)
le jury a rendu son verdict

Remarquez **their** (leur) dans le second exemple. Les pronoms faisant référence à de tels noms s'accordent normalement en nombre avec le verbe

as the crowd moves forward it becomes visible on the hill-top
alors que la foule avance, on l'aperçoit au sommet de la colline

the crowd have been protesting for hours; they are getting very impatient
la foule a protesté pendant des heures ; elle commence à s'impatienter

L'emploi du verbe au pluriel est plus répandu en anglais britannique qu'en américain.

Les mots suivants sont des exemples typiques de noms collectifs :

army (armée), **audience** (public), **choir** (chorale), **chorus** (refrain, chœur), **class** (classe), **committee** (comité), **enemy** (ennemi), **family** (famille), **firm** (firme), **gang** (gang), **(younger and older) generation** (génération (jeune, ancienne)), **government** (gouvernement), **group** (groupe), **majority** (majorité), **minority** (minorité), **orchestra** (orchestre), **Parliament** (Parlement), **proletariat** (prolétariat), **public** (public), **team** (équipe).

Les noms de nations faisant référence à une équipe (sportive) sont normalement accompagnés d'un verbe au pluriel en anglais britannique :

France have beaten England
la France a battu l'Angleterre

bien que le singulier et le pluriel soient tout aussi corrects.

ii) Remarquez que les noms de pays au pluriel se comportent comme des noms collectifs :

the Philippines has its problems like any other country (sing.)
les Philippines ont leurs problèmes comme tout autre pays

the Philippines consist of a group of very beautiful islands (pluriel)
les Philippines se composent d'un groupe de très belles îles

Il en est de même pour **the Bahamas, the United States**, etc.

iii) Les mots **crew** (équipage), **staff** (personnel), **people** (peuple) sont souvent des noms collectifs, comme dans :

the crew is excellent (sing.)
l'équipage est excellent

the crew have all enjoyed themselves (pluriel)
l'équipage s'est bien amusé

the staff of that school has a good record (sing.)
le personnel de cette école a obtenu de bons résultats

the staff don't always behave themselves (pluriel)
le personnel ne se conduit pas toujours bien

it is difficult to imagine a people that has suffered more (sing.)
il est difficile d'imaginer un peuple qui ait plus souffert

the people have not voted against the re-introduction of capital punishment (pluriel)
le peuple n'a pas voté contre le rétablissement de la peine capitale

Ces trois mots diffèrent des autres noms collectifs par le fait qu'ils peuvent être des dénombrables à part entière, avec ou sans la terminaison **-s** au pluriel, suivant leur sens. Si le pluriel est en **-s**, il est le même que le pluriel en -s d'autres noms collectifs :

five crews/staffs/peoples (nations)/**armies/governments**, etc.

Cependant, le pluriel sans -s fait référence à des membres individuels :

the captain had to manage with only fifteen crew
le capitaine devait se débrouiller avec seulement quinze membres d'équipage

the English Department had to get rid of five staff
le département d'anglais a dû renvoyer cinq personnes

he spoke to six people about it
il a parlé à six personnes à ce sujet

On peut tout aussi bien dire **crew members, staff members** or **members of staff** au pluriel.

Pour **clergy** et **police**, voir **f) ii)** ci-dessus.

B. LES FORMES

1. LES PLURIELS EN -(E)S

a) La marque du pluriel est normalement **-(e)s** en anglais :

soup : soups	soupe(s)
peg : pegs	pince(s) à linge
bus : buses	bus
quiz : quizzes	jeu(x) télévisé(s)
bush : bushes	buisson(s)
match : matches	allumette(s)
page : pages	page(s)

-es s'emploie pour des mots en **-s**, **-z**, **-ch** ou **-sh**. On le prononce alors /ɪz/.

b) Pour les noms se terminant par une consonne plus **-y**, le **-y** se transforme en **-ies** :

lady : ladies	dame(s), demoiselle(s)
loony : loonies	cinglé(s)

Mais le pluriel régulier en **-s** s'emploie lorsque le **-y** est précédé par une voyelle :

trolley : trolleys	chariot(s)

Une exception à cela : l'usage de **monies** (sommes d'argent) dans un registre soutenu ou juridique :

all monies currently payable to the society
toutes les sommes d'argent maintenant dues à la société

Pour plus de détails, voir la section **L'Orthographe**, p A74.

c) Les noms en **-o** prennent parfois un **-s**, parfois **-es** au pluriel. Il est difficile d'établir des règles précises dans ce cas, cependant on peut dire que l'on ajoute seulement un **-s** si (1) le **-o** suit une autre voyelle (**embryo – embryos** embryons, **studio – studios** studios) ; ou si (2) le nom est une abréviation (**photo – photos, piano – pianos** (de **pianoforte**)). Dans d'autres cas, il est difficile de généraliser, bien que l'on puisse observer une préférence pour le **-s** avec des mots qui ont encore une connotation étrangère pour les britanniques :

(avec **-es**) **echo, cargo** (cargaison), **hero, mosquito** (moustique), **negro, potato** (pomme de terre), **tomato, torpedo** (torpille)

(avec **-s**) **canto** (chant), **memento, proviso** (stipulation), **quarto, solo, zero, zoo**

(avec **-s** or **-es**) **banjo, buffalo** (buffle), **commando, flamingo** (flamand rose), **motto, volcano**

d) Pour certains noms en **-f(e)**, le **-f** se transforme en **-ve** au pluriel :

calf : calves	veau(x)

Il en est de même pour : **elf, half** (moitié), **knife** (couteau), **leaf** (feuille d'arbre), **life** (vie), **loaf** (pain), **self** (soi), **sheaf** (gerbe), **shelf** (étagère), **thief** (voleur), **wife** (épouse), **wolf** (loup).

Certains peuvent avoir un pluriel en **-ves** ou en **-s** :

dwarf : dwarfs/dwarves	nain(s)
hoof : hoofs/hooves	sabot(s)
scarf : scarfs/scarves	écharpe(s)
wharf : wharfs/wharves	quai(s)

Un grand nombre de ces mots conservent le **-f** :

belief : beliefs	croyance(s)

Il en est de même pour **chief** (chef), **cliff** (falaise), **proof** (preuve), **roof** (toit), **safe** (coffre-fort), **sniff** (reniflement), etc.

e) Quelques mots français se terminant avec un –**s** muet au singulier ne changent pas leur pluriel à l'écrit, on ajoute cependant le son /z/ au pluriel à l'oral :

corps - le pluriel se prononce avec /z/.

f) Les mots français en **-eu** ou **-eau** prennent un **-s** ou un **-x** (que l'on prononce tous les deux /**z**/), par exemple :

adieu, bureau, tableau

gateau prend normalement un **-x**.

g) *Les noms d'animaux*

Certains noms d'animaux, notamment les noms de poissons, se comportent (ou se comportent presque toujours) comme les noms mentionnés dans la section 3a) ci-dessous, c'est-à-dire qu'ils ne prennent pas de marque du pluriel :

cod (morue), **hake** (colin), **herring** (hareng), **mackerel** (maquereau), **pike** (brochet), **salmon** (saumon), **trout** (truite) (mais on dit **sharks** (requins)), **deer** (cerf), **sheep** (mouton), **grouse** (coq de bruyère).

D'autres noms d'animaux prennent un **-s** ou rien. Dans le contexte de la chasse, on omet souvent le **-s**. Comparez :

these graceful antelopes have just been bought by the zoo
le zoo vient juste d'acheter ces antilopes gracieuses

they went to Africa to shoot antelope
ils sont allés en Afrique pour chasser l'antilope

Il en est de même pour :

buffalo (buffle), **giraffe, lion, duck** (canard), **fowl** (volaille), **partridge** (perdrix), **pheasant** (faisan), et bien d'autres.

Le pluriel régulier de **fish** est **fish**, mais **fishes** s'emploie pour faire référence à des espèces de poissons.

h) *Les adjectifs numéraux*

i) **hundred** (cent), **thousand** (mille), **million, dozen** (douzaine), **score** (vingt) et **gross** (douze douzaines) n'ont pas de pluriel en -s lorsqu'ils sont précédés par un autre adjectif numéral. Remarquez la différence de construction avec le français pour "million" "milliard" et "douzaine" :

five hundred/thousand/million people
cinq cents/mille/millions *de* gens

two dozen eggs
deux douzaines *d*'œufs

we'll order three gross
nous commanderons trente-six douzaines

mais :

there were hundreds/thousands/millions of them
il y en avait des centaines/milliers/millions

I've told you dozens of times
je te l'ai dit des dizaines de fois

Peter and Kate have scores of friends
Peter et Kate ont des tas d'amis

ii) Les unités de mesure le **foot** et le **pound** peuvent être soit au pluriel, soit au singulier :

Kate is five foot/feet eight
Kate mesure un mètre soixante-douze

that comes to three pound(s) fifty
ça fait trois livres cinquante

2. LES PLURIELS AVEC UN CHANGEMENT DE VOYELLE

Il existe un petit groupe de mots dont le pluriel se forme au moyen d'un changement de voyelle :

foot : feet	pied(s)
goose : geese	oie(s)
louse : lice	pou(x)
man : men	homme(s)
mouse : mice	souris
tooth : teeth	dent(s)
woman : women /wɪmɪn/	femme(s)

3. LES PLURIELS INVARIABLES

a) *singulier et pluriel sans -s* :

(air)craft (avion), **counsel** (avocat), **offspring** (progéniture), **quid** ("balle" (argent)), par exemple :

we saw a few aircraft
nous avons vu quelques avions

both counsel asked for an adjournment
les deux avocats ont demandé un renvoi

these are my offspring
c'est ma progéniture

this will cost you ten quid (familier = pound(s))
ça te coûtera cent balles

(Mass) media prend parfois un verbe au singulier, parfois un verbe au pluriel, sans qu'il y ait de différence de sens.

Les mots **kind, sort, type** (genre, sorte, type) apparaissant dans une phrase du type **these/those** + nom + **of** très souvent ne prennent pas de **-s** :

these kind of people always complain
ce genre de personne se plaint toujours

she always buys those sort of records
elle achète toujours ce genre de disque

Il est aussi possible de dire :

this kind of record

où les deux noms sont au singulier.

b) *singulier et pluriel en* **-s**

barracks (caserne), **crossroads** (carrefour), **innings** (tour de batte), **means** (moyens, ressources) (comparez avec **means** (= moyens financiers) p A10), **gallows** (potence), **headquarters** (quartier général), **series** (série), **shambles** (désordre), **species** (espèce), **-works** (usine), par exemple :

every means was tried to improve matters
on a usé de tous les moyens pour améliorer les choses

this is a dreadful shambles
c'est un désordre abominable

they have built a new gasworks north of here
ils ont construit une nouvelle usine à gaz au nord d'ici

Certains de ces noms, en particulier **barracks, gallows, headquarters, -works** peuvent aussi s'employer dans un sens singulier avec un verbe au pluriel :

these are the new steelworks
c'est la nouvelle aciérie

On fait référence ici à une seule usine.

c) ***dice et pence***

Ce sont à proprement parler les pluriels irréguliers de **die** (dé) et **penny**, mais ils commencent à remplacer rapidement le singulier.

Die ne s'emploie pratiquement jamais que dans les expressions figées telles que **the die is cast** (les dés sont jetés) ou **straight as a die** (d'une grande honnêteté). Et il est normal d'entendre **one pence** (un pence) plutôt que **one penny** (un penny) lorsque l'on parle du coût de quelque chose. En revanche on parle encore de la pièce de monnaie en disant **a penny**, donnant au pluriel plusieurs **pennies**, comme dans la phrase suivante : **these are 18th-century pennies** (ce sont des pennies du XVIIIe siècle). Comme **die**, on emploie **penny** dans certaines expressions figées : **to spend a penny** (aller aux toilettes).

4. LES PLURIELS EN -EN

Il n'en existe que trois, et un seul est commun :

child : children enfant(s)

Les autres sont :

ox : oxen bœuf(s)
brother : brethren frère(s)

ce dernier faisant référence aux membres d'une congrégation religieuse, comme dans :

our Catholic brethren from other countries
nos frères catholiques d'autres pays

Le pluriel normal de **brother** est bien entendu, **brothers**.

5. LES PLURIELS EN -A OU -S

Ce sont des noms latins au singulier en **-um** ou des noms grecs au singulier en **-on**. Beaucoup d'entre eux ont un pluriel en **-s**, en particulier s'ils sont employés couramment, par exemple :

museum (musée), **stadium** (stade), **demon, electron**

Certains, souvent employés dans un langage scientifique et dont le singulier est **-um/-on**, ont un pluriel en **-a**, par exemple :

an addendum un addenda (*ou* addendum)

numerous addenda de nombreux addenda

De même on a : **bacterium** (bactérie), **curriculum** (programme d'étude), **erratum, ovum** (ovule), **criterion** (critère), **phenomenon**

Certains varient entre le pluriel en **-s** et en **-a** :

memorandum, millennium (millénaire), **symposium, automaton** (automate)

Le pluriel de **medium** est toujours **mediums** lorsque ce mot fait référence à un extra-lucide. Lorsqu'il signifie "moyen", le pluriel est soit **media** ou **mediums**. Pour **(mass) media**, voir **Les Pluriels invariables**, ci-dessus, section **3.** Pour **data**, voir p A9.

Il apparaît que **strata** (pluriel de **stratum**) remplacera bientôt **stratum** au singulier.

6. LES PLURIELS EN -E OU -S

Ces noms sont latins ou grecs et ont une terminaison en **-a** au singulier. Ceux qui sont fréquemment employés ont un pluriel en **-s**, comme **arena** et **drama**. Les noms plus techniques ou scientifiques ont tendance à avoir un pluriel en **-e** (on obtient alors la terminaison **-ae** prononcée /i:/ ou /aɪ/), par exemple **alumna** et **larva**. La terminaison de certains varie selon le niveau de langue employé dans le contexte. Ainsi **antenna** prend toujours un **-e** lorsqu'il fait référence aux insectes, mais un **-s** lorsqu'il signifie antenne de télévision en américain. Il en est de même pour **formula** et **vertebra**.

7. LES PLURIELS EN -I OU -S (mots italiens)

Quelques mots empruntés de l'italien, notamment **libretto, tempo** et **virtuoso**, conservent parfois leur pluriel italien en **-i** /i:/. C'est plus particulièrement le cas de **tempo**. Parfois ils prennent le **-s** du pluriel régulier anglais. Vous noterez que **confetti** et les pâtes **macaroni, ravioli, spaghetti** et d'autres, sont des indénombrables, c'est-à-dire qu'ils sont suivis d'un verbe au singulier. Pour **graffiti**, voir p A10.

8. LES PLURIELS EN -I OU -ES (mots latins)

Ceux qui sont courants prennent normalement la terminaison **-es** au pluriel, comme :

campus, chorus (refrain, chœur), **virus**

Ceux qui appartiennent au langage plus érudit, gardent en général leur pluriel latin en **-i** (que l'on prononce /i:/ ou /aɪ) comme par exemple :

alumnus, bacillus, stimulus.

D'autres prennent les deux formes au pluriel : **cactus, fungus** (champignon, fongus), **nucleus, syllabus** (programme d'université). Il en est de même pour les noms grecs latinisés : **hippopotamus** et **papyrus**. Le pluriel de **genius** est **geniuses** au sens de "personne extrêmement intelligente", mais **genii** lorsqu'il signifie "(bon/mauvais) esprit".

9. LES PLURIELS DES NOMS EN -EX OU -IX

Ces noms latins peuvent conserver leur pluriel d'origine, leur singulier en **-ex**/**-ix** se transforme alors en **-ices** au pluriel, ou bien ils prennent **-es**, par exemple :

index : pluriel **indices** ou **indexes**

Il en est de même pour **appendix**, **matrix**, **vortex.**

Mais remarquez que **appendixes** est le seul pluriel pour la partie du corps, tandis que **appendixes** et **appendices** peuvent s'employer pour désigner les parties d'un livre ou d'une thèse.

10. LE PLURIEL DES NOMS GRECS EN -IS

Ces derniers changent le **-is** /ɪs/ en **-es** /i:z/ au pluriel, par exemple :

an analysis — une analyse
various different analyses — différentes analyses

Il en est de même pour : **axis**, **basis**, **crisis**, **diagnosis**, **hypothesis**, **oasis**, **parenthesis**, **synopsis**, **thesis**.

Mais remarquez : **metropolis** : **metropolises**

11. LES PLURIELS EN -IM OR -S

Les trois mots hébreux **kibbutz**, **cherub** (chérubin) et **seraph** (séraphin) peuvent soit prendre **-(e)s** (pluriel régulier) ou **-im** au pluriel.

12. LES PLURIELS DES NOMS COMPOSES

a) *Le pluriel porte sur le deuxième élément*

Lorsque le deuxième élément est un nom (et qu'il n'est pas précédé d'une préposition) :

boy scouts, **football hooligans**, **girl friends** (petites amies), **road users** (usagers de la route), **man-eaters** (mangeurs d'hommes, cannibales) (comparez **menservants.**dans c) ci-dessous)

et lorsque le mot composé est formé d'un verbe + adverbe :

lay-bys (aires de stationnement), **lie-ins** (grasses matinées), **sit-ins**, **stand-bys**, **tip-offs** (tuyaux)

Remarquez que les noms de mesures se terminant par **-ful** peuvent avoir un **-s** à la fin de l'un ou l'autre de leurs éléments : **spoonfuls** ou **spoonsful**.

b) *Le pluriel porte sur le premier élément*

Lorsque le deuxième élément est un groupe prépositionnel :

editors-in-chief — rédacteurs en chef
fathers-in-law — beaux-pères
men-of-war — bâtiments de guerre
aides-de-camp

Mais si le premier élément n'est pas considéré comme une personne, on place le **s** en final, comme dans :

will-o'-the-wisps — feux follets
jack-in-the-boxes — diables à ressort

Les noms composés formés à partir d'un verbe et d'un adverbe prennent eux aussi un **-s** à la fin du premier élément (à la différence de ceux composés d'un verbe + adverbe, qui ont un **-s** en finale. voir a) ci-dessus) :

carryings-on — façons de se conduire
hangers-on — suite (de gens)
passers-by — passants

Les noms composés avec **-to-be** prennent un **-s** à la fin du premier élément :

brides-to-be — futures mariées
mothers-to-be — futures mamans

Le premier élément porte aussi la marque du pluriel si le second élément est un adjectif :

Lords temporal and spiritual
membres laïques et ecclésiastiques de la Chambre des Lords

Mais beaucoup peuvent aussi porter la marque du pluriel sur le deuxième élément (ce qui est de plus en plus courant) :

attorneys general ou **attorney generals** (Procureurs Généraux)
directors general ou **director generals**
poets laureate ou **poet laureates**
courts-martial ou **court-martials**

c) *Les deux éléments portent la marque du pluriel*

Lorsque le nom composé avec **man** ou **woman** sert à distinguer le genre (mais le premier élément peut aussi être au singulier) :

menservants — domestiques (comparez **man-eaters** dans a) ci-dessus)
gentlemen farmers — gentlemen-farmers
women doctors — docteurs (femmes)

C. USAGE : PLURIEL OU SINGULIER ?

a) *Le pluriel distributif*

i) type 1, dans un groupe nominal

Dans beaucoup de cas l'anglais préfère le pluriel :

between the ages of 30 and 45
entre l'âge de 30 et 45 ans

the reigns of Henry VIII and Elizabeth I
le règne d'Henri VIII et celui d'Elisabeth Ire

ii) type 2, dans une proposition

Dans ce cas, le nom au pluriel (souvent précédé d'un adjectif possessif) fait référence à un nom ou pronom possessif au pluriel mentionné auparavant, par exemple :

we changed our minds
nous avons changé d'avis

many people are unhappy about their long noses
beaucoup de gens ne sont pas satisfaits de leur long nez

cats seem to spend their lives sleeping
les chats semblent passer leur vie à dormir

they deserve a kick up their backsides
ils méritent un coup de pied au derrière

we respectfully removed our hats
nous avons retiré notre chapeau par respect

can we change places?
on peut changer de place ?

Mais ce n'est pas une règle bien définie. Certaines personnes ont de l'eau jusqu'à la ceinture : **up to their waists** ou **up to the waist**, et ils ont de l'eau ou des dettes jusqu'au cou : **up to their necks** and **up to the neck**. Les conducteurs changent de vitesse (**change gear** ou **gears**) et ils peuvent risquer la vie de leurs passagers : **the death** ou **deaths of their passengers**.

Il y a des situations où des gens **have egg on their face** ou **faces**, c'est-à-dire l'air ridicule, mais seul **faces** est employé s'il s'agit d'un vrai œuf !

Et il y a des choses que certains **turn their nose(s) up at**, c'est-à-dire qu'ils considèrent inférieures. Il semble que si l'expression est employée dans un sens figuré, on emploie le plus souvent le singulier, parfois précédé d'un article défini plutôt que d'un pronom possessif. Ainsi **we pay through the nose** (payer quelque chose la peau des fesses), **we take children under our wing** (on prend des enfants sous son aile), et **we are sometimes at the end of our tether** (on est parfois à bout de nerfs) – autant d'exemples dans lesquels aucune image concrète n'apparaît.

b) *Le complément du nom placé avant ou après le nom*

Lorsqu'un nom est déterminé par une préposition + un nom au pluriel placés après ce nom, comme dans :

a collection of bottles
une collection de bouteilles

le nom au pluriel se transformera en singulier lorsqu'il est placé devant le nom qu'il détermine :

a bottle collection
une collection de bouteilles

Il existe beaucoup d'exemples de ce genre : **record dealer** (disquaire), **letter box** (boîte à lettres), **foreign language teaching** (enseignement des langues étrangères).

Cependant, il y a des cas où l'on préfère un complément du nom au pluriel placé avant le nom, parfois parce que le singulier aurait un sens différent. Ainsi on dirait :

a problems page courrier du cœur

parce que le mot **problem** au singulier signifie normalement "qui cause des problèmes", comme dans :

a problem student
un étudiant à problèmes/qui pose des problèmes

a problem case
un cas à problèmes/problématique

Il en est de même pour :

a singles bar
un bar pour les célibataires

an explosives investigation
une enquête sur les explosifs

étant donné que :

a single bar un seul bar
an explosive investigation une enquête explosive

signifient quelque chose de complètement différent.

Mais souvent ou le singulier ou le pluriel est possible :

in this noun(s) section	dans cette section des noms
a Falkland(s) hero	un héros des Falkland
a call for job(s) cuts	un appel à des réductions d'emplois

D. LE GENITIF

1. LES FORMES

a) Le génitif singulier se forme en ajoutant **-'s** après le nom :

the cat's tail la queue du chat

et le génitif pluriel en ajoutant seulement l'apostrophe au pluriel :

the cats' tails la queue des chats

Il y a souvent confusion au sujet de la position de l'apostrophe. Comparez ces deux exemples :

the boy's school l'école du garçon
the boys' school l'école de garçons

Dans le premier exemple, **boy** est au singulier, on parle donc de l'école d'un garçon. Dans le deuxième exemple le nom **boys** est au pluriel, on parle donc de l'école où vont plusieurs garçons.

Si le pluriel ne se termine pas en **-s**, le génitif pluriel se forme avec le -'s comme le singulier :

the men's toilet les toilettes des hommes
the children's room la chambre des enfants

b) *Exceptions* :

i) Beaucoup de noms classiques (en particulier les noms grecs) se terminant en **-s** prennent normalement juste une apostrophe, en particulier s'ils sont formés de plus d'une syllabe :

Socrates' wife, Aeschylus' plays
l'épouse de Socrate, les pièces d'Eschyle

On pourrait même trouver des noms modernes ayant la même caractéristique, comme dans :

Dickens' (ou **Dickens's**) **novels**
les romans de Dickens

ii) Avant le mot **sake** (amour de/nom de) le génitif singulier est normalement indiqué par l'apostrophe seule avec des noms se terminant en **-s** :

for politeness' sake par politesse

c) Pour les types de noms composés mentionnés p A14, on ajoute le **-'s** du génitif au deuxième élément, même si c'est le premier élément qui porte la marque du pluriel **-s** :

she summoned her ladies-in-waiting
elle convoqua ses dames de compagnie

the lady-in-waiting's mistress
la maîtresse de la dame de compagnie

2. LE GENITIF ET LA CONSTRUCTION AVEC OF

a) *Les êtres animés (personnes, animaux)*

Le génitif est plus courant avec les personnes qu'avec les objets :

John's mind l'esprit de John
my mother's ring la bague de ma mère

Of n'est normalement pas employé dans ces deux exemples, mais on peut l'employer pour faire référence à des animaux :

the wings of an insect/the insect's wings
les ailes d'un insecte/de l'insecte

the movements of the worm/the worm's movements
les mouvements du ver de terre

Cependant, les animaux supérieurs sont considérés comme des personnes pour ce qui concerne la formation du génitif :

the lion's paw shot out from the cage
la patte du lion surgit de la cage

b) *Les objets inanimés*

La construction normale se forme avec **of** :

the size of the coat
la taille du manteau

the colour of the telephone
la couleur du téléphone

Mais avec certains noms d'inanimés, le génitif est aussi possible :

the mind's ability to recover
la capacité de l'esprit à guérir

the poem's capacity to move
la capacité du poème à émouvoir

en particulier si de tels noms font référence à des lieux ou à des institutions :

England's heritage (= the heritage of England)
l'héritage de l'Angleterre

the University's catering facilities (= the catering facilities of the University)
le service de restauration de l'université

Les noms faisant référence au temps et à la valeur sont souvent accompagnés du génitif :

today's menu	le menu du jour
two months' work	deux mois de travail
you've had your money's worth	tu en as eu pour ton argent

Remarquez que la construction avec **of** pour des noms faisant référence au temps implique souvent une qualité de premier ordre ou une distinction particulière, comme dans :

our actor of the year award goes to ...
le prix du meilleur acteur de l'année est attribué à ...

ou bien elle peut impliquer que la durée ne doit pas être prise littéralement, comme dans :

the University of tomorrow
l'université de demain

Ici **tomorrow** ne peut signifier que l'avenir.

Un génitif peut avoir un sens ou littéral ou métaphorique :

Tomorrow's World (métaphorique)
le monde de demain

tomorrow's phone call (littéral)
le coup de téléphone de demain

tomorrow's food (soit littéral, soit métaphorique)
la nourriture de demain

Les mesures de distances sont parfois au génitif, en particulier dans des expressions figées :

a stone's throw (away)	**at arm's length**
à deux pas (d'ici)	à distance

3. LE GENITIF SANS NOM

a) Si le nom que le génitif détermine est assez clair de par le contexte, on peut alors l'omettre :

it's not my father's car, it's my mother's
ce n'est pas la voiture de mon père, c'est celle de ma mère

b) Le "double génitif" (c'est-à-dire la construction avec **of** et le génitif dans la même phrase) est fréquent si le génitif fait référence à une personne *bien définie*. Mais le premier nom est normalement précédé d'un article *indéfini*, d'un pronom *indéfini* ou d'un adjectif numéral :

he's a friend of Peter's
c'est un ami de Peter

he's an acquaintance of my father's
c'est une connaissance de mon père

he's no uncle of Mrs Pitt's
ce n'est pas l'oncle de Madame Pitt

here are some relatives of Miss Young's
voici des parents de Mademoiselle Young

two sisters of my mother's came to visit
deux sœurs de ma mère sont venues nous rendre visite

Un pronom démonstratif peut parfois précéder le premier nom. Ceci implique un certain degré de familiarité :

that car of your father's – how much does he want for it?
cette voiture, ton père, combien est-ce qu'il la vend ?

L'article défini ne peut normalement pas s'employer avec le premier nom, à moins qu'une proposition relative (ou autre déterminatif) ne suive le génitif :

the poem of Larkin's (that) we read yesterday is lovely
le poème de Larkin que nous avons lu hier est magnifique

this is the only poem of Larkin's to have moved me
c'est le seul poème de Larkin qui m'ait ému

c) Le nom sous-entendu après un génitif fait souvent référence à des locaux :

at the baker's (= baker's shop)
chez le boulanger

at Mary's (= at Mary's place)
chez Mary

Il est important de souligner que si un établissement (commercial) est particulièrement bien connu, on omet souvent l'apostrophe. Ainsi on a tendance à écrire **at Smiths** (chez Smiths) ou **in Harrods** (chez Harrods), le premier représentant une chaîne de magasins qui couvre la Grande-Bretagne, le second étant le célèbre grand magasin de Londres. Mais on trouverait habituellement **he bought it at Bruce Miller's** (il l'a acheté chez Miller's), étant donné que cet établissement n'est pas fermement implanté dans l'esprit des gens sur une échelle nationale.

d) On trouve souvent le "groupe génitif" dans deux types de constructions : (1) nom + déterminatif introduit par une préposition, et (2) noms reliés par **and**. Dans de telles combinaisons, on peut ajouter le **-'s** au dernier élément :

the Queen of Holland's yacht
le yacht de la reine de Hollande

the head of department's office
le bureau du chef de département

John and Kate's new house
la nouvelle maison de John et Kate

an hour and a half's work
un travail d'une heure et demie

Si le nom est au pluriel, on emploie normalement la construction avec **of** :

the regalia of the Queens of Holland
les insignes royaux des reines de Hollande

Cependant, si les deux noms ne forment pas une unité, ils prennent chacun la marque du génitif **-'s** :

Shakespeare's and Marlowe's plays
les pièces de Shakespeare et de Marlowe

E. LE FEMININ

En anglais, il est courant de ne pas employer de mot ou de terminaison distincts pour déterminer le genre d'un nom. Beaucoup de noms s'emploient à la fois pour un homme et une femme :

artist (artiste), **banker** (banquier(-ère)), **cousin** (cousin(e)), **friend** (ami(e)), **lawyer** (avocat(e)), **neighbour** (voisin(e)), **novelist** (romancier(-ère)), **teacher** (enseignant(e)), **zoologist** (zoologiste).

Mais il existe certains cas où l'on emploie différentes terminaisons pour distinguer le féminin du masculin :

féminin	*masculin*
actress (actrice)	**actor** (acteur)
duchess (duchesse)	**duke** (duc)
goddess (déesse)	**god** (dieu)
heroine (héroïne)	**hero** (héros)
princess (princesse)	**prince** (prince)
widow (veuve)	**widower** (veuf)
businesswoman (femme d'affaires)	**businessman** (homme d'affaires)

bien que dans beaucoup de cas il s'agisse d'une distinction de *termes*, tout comme **daughter/son** (fille/fils), **cow/bull** (vache/taureau), etc.

Mais on peut aussi dire **she is a good actor** (elle est très bonne actrice), ou bien **she was the hero of the day** (elle était le héros du jour).

S'il est nécessaire d'identifier le sexe d'une personne, on emploie soit :

a female friend (une amie)	**a male friend** (un ami)
a female student (une étudiante)	**a male student** (un étudiant)

soit : **a woman doctor** (une femme docteur)
a man doctor (un docteur)

Lorsqu'il n'est pas nécessaire ou pas possible de distinguer ou d'identifier le sexe d'une personne, il est courant d'employer le mot **person** :

a chairperson	un(e) président(e)
a salesperson	un(e) représentant(e) de commerce
a spokesperson	un porte-parole

bien que certaines femmes soient satisfaites d'être **chairman**.

L'emploi du mot **person** devient de plus en plus courant, par exemple dans les petites annonces :

security person required
on cherche garde de sécurité

4. LES ADJECTIFS

1. GENERALITES

★ Les adjectifs anglais ne s'accordent jamais avec le nom.

★ L'adjectif se place toujours devant le nom en dehors de certaines exceptions (voir **3. b)** ci-dessous).

2. EPITHETE ET ATTRIBUT

Les termes "épithète" et "attribut" font référence à la position de l'adjectif par rapport au nom. Si l'adjectif est placé devant le nom, il est épithète (***this old car*** cette vieille voiture). S'il est placé tout seul après un verbe, il est attribut (***this car is old*** cette voiture est vieille).

Si un adjectif a plusieurs sens, chacun de ces sens peut entrer dans une catégorie différente.

a) *Epithète seulement*

i) Certains adjectifs qui ont un rapport fort avec le nom auquel ils se rapportent dans des constructions toutes faites sont uniquement épithètes, comme dans :

he's a moral philosopher
c'est un philosophe spécialiste en éthique

ii) Les participes passés sont parfois employés de cette manière :

a disabled toilet (toilet for disabled people)
des toilettes pour handicapés

iii) Très souvent en anglais on emploie des noms avec une fonction d'adjectif :

a cardboard box
une boîte en carton

a polystyrene container
un emballage en polystyrène

a foreign affairs correspondent
un correspondant étranger

a classification problem
un problème de classification

b) *Attribut seulement*

Les adjectifs qui sont uniquement attributs qualifient généralement une condition physique ou un état mental, comme ***afraid*** (effrayé), ***ashamed*** (honteux), ***faint*** (= sur le point de perdre conscience), ***fond*** (attaché), ***poorly*** (souffrant), ***(un)well*** (en mauvaise/bonne santé) :

the girl is afraid
la fille a peur

the children need not feel ashamed
les enfants n'ont pas besoin d'avoir honte

my uncle is fond of me
mon oncle m'aime bien

he suddenly felt faint
il se sentit tout à coup sur le point de s'évanouir

our mother has been unwell for some time
notre mère ne se sent pas bien depuis un certain temps

Mais remarquez l'expression :

he's not a well man
il n'est pas dans le meilleur de sa forme (= il est très malade)

De même, ***ill*** et ***glad*** sont le plus souvent attributs, mais sont parfois épithètes lorsqu'ils ne font pas référence à une personne :

his ill health may explain his ill humour
cette mauvaise santé peut expliquer sa mauvaise humeur

these are glad tidings (vieilli)
ce sont de bonnes nouvelles

3. LA POSITION

a) Si plus d'un adjectif précède le nom, celui ou ceux qui peuvent aussi être attributs se placent en premier. Les adjectifs qui peuvent être épithètes uniquement ont un rapport trop étroit avec le nom pour qu'un autre mot puisse se placer entre eux et le nom :

he is a young parliamentary candidate
c'est un jeune candidat parlementaire

they have employed a conscientious social worker
ils ont employé une assistante sociale consciencieuse

a big old red brick house
une grande et vieille maison de brique rouge

Remarquez que les adjectifs ***old*** et ***little*** changent de sens selon leur position. Comparez (a-d) avec (e-h) :

(a) **they only have old worn-out records**
ils n'ont que des vieux disques usés
(b) **up the path came a very old (and) dirty man**
sur le chemin est apparu un homme très vieux et très sale
(c) **I think I left a little black book behind**
je crois que j'ai laissé un petit cahier noir
(d) **I want the little round mirror over there**
je veux le petit miroir rond par ici
(e) **silly old me!**
suis-je donc bête !
(f) **you dirty old man, you!**
eh vous, vieux cochon !
(g) **this is my cute little sister**
c'est mon adorable petite sœur
(h) **what an adorable, sweet little cottage!**
quelle petite maison adorable et mignonne

En (a-d) ***old*** et ***little*** ont leur premier sens et pourraient, avec ces sens, prendre une position d'attribut. Mais en (e-h) le caractère littéral des expressions est perdu : ***a dirty old man*** (un obsédé sexuel) n'est pas forcément âgé. On fait plus une allusion au comportement qu'à l'âge de la personne. ***My little sister*** en (g) signifie "ma sœur plus jeune", on ne s'intéresse pas du tout à la taille de la personne. Et ***little*** en (h) donne plus une description des émotions du locuteur que des dimensions de la maison. De même, en (e), ***old*** ne veut pas du tout dire "vieux".

b) Parfois, quand il est mis en apposition, l'adjectif se place après le nom sans qu'un verbe soit nécessaire. Ces adjectifs (et toute qualification supplémentaire éventuelle) sont similaires en fonction et en usage aux propositions relatives :

this is a custom peculiar to Britain
c'est une coutume propre à la Grande-Bretagne

this is a man confident of success
c'est un homme sûr de réussir

Les adjectifs ne peuvent être en apposition que s'ils peuvent aussi être attributs, et sont très fréquents lorsqu'ils sont qualifiés par un groupe prépositionnel, comme on le voit dans les exemples ci-dessus. Mais on trouve aussi des adjectifs en apposition employés dans un but emphatique, toujours employés par deux et plus :

her jewellery, cheap and tawdry, was quickly removed
ses bijoux, pas chers et clinquants, furent rapidement enlevés

he looked into a face sympathetic but firm
il vit un visage sympathique mais décidé

books, new or secondhand, for sale
livres, neufs ou d'occasion, à vendre

Cette fonction est assez fréquente (mais non obligatoire) après des mots imprécis comme ***things*** (choses, etc.) et ***matters*** (questions, etc.) :

his interest in matters linguistic
son intérêt pour tout ce qui touche à la linguistique

she has an abhorrence of things English
elle a en horreur tout ce qui est anglais

et pour les adjectifs en ***-able*** ou ***-ible***, surtout si le nom est précédé de ***only*** (seul, unique) ou d'un superlatif :

they committed the worst atrocities imaginable
ils commirent les pires atrocités imaginables

he's the only person responsible
il est la seule personne responsable

this is the most inexpensive model available
c'est le modèle disponible le moins cher

c) Certains adjectifs d'origine française ou latine se placent après le nom auquel ils se rapportent comme en français, et dans des expressions toutes faites comme ***poet laureate*** (le poète lauréat), ***the Princess Royal*** (la Princesse Royale), ***Lords Spiritual*** (membres ecclésiastiques de la Chambre des Lords), ***Lords Temporal*** (membres temporels), ***letters patent*** (lettres patentes), ***lion rampant*** (lion rampant), ***devil incarnate*** (diable incarné).

4. LA COMPARAISON

LES FORMES

a) Il y a trois degrés de comparaison : ***la forme de base***, ***le comparatif*** et ***le superlatif*** :

sweet	***beautiful***	(forme de base)
doux	beau	
sweeter	***more beautiful***	(comparatif)
plus doux	plus beau	
sweetest	***the most beautiful***	(superlatif)
le plus doux	le plus beau	

Pour les changements d'orthographe résultant de l'addition de ***-er***, ***-est*** (***happy –happier*** ou ***big – bigger***) voir p A74.

b) ***-er/-est ou more/most ?***

i) Plus l'adjectif est court, plus il est probable que son comparatif et son superlatif se formeront en ajoutant ***-er*** et ***-est***. Ceci concerne particulièrement les adjectifs monosyllabiques, comme ***keen***, ***fine***, ***late***, ***wide***, ***neat***, etc. Des adjectifs très courants comme ***big*** ou ***fast*** prennent toujours la forme ***-er/-est***.

Si les adjectifs ont deux syllabes, on trouve ***-er/-est*** et ***more/most***, ***-er/-est*** étant particulièrement courants avec les adjectifs qui se terminent en ***-y***, ***-le***, ***-ow***, ***-er*** :

(noisy) ***this is the noisiest pub I've been in***
c'est le pub le plus bruyant que j'aie jamais vu

(feeble) ***this is the feeblest excuse I've heard***
c'est la plus mauvaise excuse que j'aie entendue

(shallow) ***the stream is shallower up there***
le ruisseau est moins profond en amont

(clever) ***she's the cleverest***
c'est la plus intelligente

On tend à employer ***more*** et ***most*** d'une façon de plus en plus générale au lieu de ***-er/-est***. ***Commoner*** et ***pleasanter*** étaient plus courants qu'ils ne le sont maintenant ; de même que ***politer*** et ***handsomer*** par rapport à ***more polite*** et ***more handsome***, ces derniers étant maintenant tout à fait acceptés.

ii) Les adjectifs de plus de deux syllabes utilisent ***more*** et ***the most*** :

this is the most idiotic thing I ever heard!
c'est la chose la plus idiote que j'aie entendue !

I prefer a more traditional Christmas
je préfère un Noël plus traditionnel

she's getting more and more predictable
il devient de plus en plus facile de deviner ce qu'elle va faire

Mais il existe des exceptions à cette règle :

she's unhappier than she has ever been
elle est plus malheureuse que jamais

he's got the untidiest room in the whole house
il a la chambre la plus désordonnée de toute la maison

Dans ces cas, on peut aussi employer ***more/the most***.

iii) Les adjectifs qui sont formés à partir des participes passés prennent ***more*** au comparatif et ***the most*** au superlatif :

she's more gifted than her sister
elle est plus douée que sa sœur

the most advanced students
les étudiants les plus avancés

that's the most bored I've ever been!
je ne me suis jamais autant ennuyé !

Tired peut prendre les terminaisons ***-er/-est***.

iv) Si la comparaison se fait entre deux adjectifs (comme choix de mots) on ne peut employer que ***more*** :

this sauce is more sweet than sour
cette sauce est plus douce qu'aigre

c) *Les comparaisons irrégulières*

Quelques adjectifs ont un comparatif et un superlatif irréguliers.

bad	**worse**	**worst**
mauvais	pire	le pire
far	**further/farther**	**furthest/ farthest**
loin	plus loin	le plus loin
good	**better**	**best**
bon	meilleur	le meilleur
little	**less/lesser**	**least**
peu	moins	le moins
many	**more**	**most**
beaucoup	plus	le plus
much	**more**	**most**
beaucoup	plus	le plus

Remarquez aussi ***late, latter, last*** (dernier, deuxième, le dernier) (mais ***later*** (plus tard), ***latest*** (le dernier)) et ***old***, ***elder***, ***eldest*** (vieux, plus vieux, aîné) (mais ***older*** (plus vieux), ***oldest*** (le plus vieux)).

Pour l'emploi du comparatif et du superlatif (et les variantes), voir ci-dessous et p A19.

d) *La comparaison d'infériorité*

Pour former les comparatifs d'infériorité, on place les adverbes ***less/the least*** devant les adjectifs :

it's less interesting than I thought it would be
c'est moins intéressant que je ne le pensais

this was the least interesting of his comments
c'était son commentaire le moins intéressant

Il existe une autre façon d'exprimer le comparatif :

it's not as/so interesting as I thought it would be
ce n'est pas aussi intéressant que je ne le pensais

L'EMPLOI

i) Dans les comparaisons ***than*** se traduit par "que" et ***in*** par "de" :

there isn't a bigger building than this in the world
il n'y a pas de construction plus grande que celle-ci dans le monde

ii) Le comparatif est employé quand deux personnes ou deux choses sont comparées :

of the two she is the cleverer
des deux, elle est la plus intelligente

Dans l'anglais parlé d'aujourd'hui, certains emploient aussi le superlatif :

of the two she is the cleverest
des deux, elle est la plus intelligente

sauf, bien sûr, quand ***than*** suit (***she is cleverer than her brother*** elle est plus intelligente que son frère).

iii) Quand plus de deux personnes ou choses sont comparées on emploie le superlatif :

she is the cleverest in the class
elle est la plus intelligente de la classe

iv) Dans les annonces publicitaires, il n'y a souvent qu'un terme dans la comparaison :

Greece – for a better holiday
La Grèce – pour de meilleures vacances

v) Dans certains cas, le comparatif est employé non pas pour marquer le degré, mais le contraste. Cela s'applique surtout pour les adjectifs qui n'ont pas de forme de base

former: latter	***inner: outer***
premier : dernier	intérieur : extérieur
upper: nether	***lesser: greater***
supérieur : inférieur	petit : grand

Ces adjectifs dans ce sens sont toujours épithètes.

Nether est maintenant remplacé dans la plupart des cas par ***lower*** et il est limité essentiellement au registre de la plaisanterie :

he removed his nether garments
il a enlevé son pantalon

f) Le superlatif absolu : il exprime que quelque chose est à un "très haut degré" au lieu d'être au "plus haut degré". Habituellement, on emploie ***most*** au lieu de ***-est***, même avec des adjectifs monosyllabiques :

this is most kind!
c'est très gentil !

I thought his lecture was most interesting
j'ai trouvé que sa conférence était des plus intéressantes

mais parfois un superlatif en ***-est*** est employé comme épithète :

she was rather plain but could suddenly produce the sweetest smile
elle était d'une beauté plutôt ordinaire, mais pouvait tout à coup avoir un sourire ravissant

please accept my warmest congratulations!
acceptez, je vous en prie, mes très chaleureuses félicitations

g) *Cas particuliers*

i) ***further/farther*** *et* ***furthest/farthest***

Further est d'un usage plus courant que ***further*** quand on fait référence à la distance (et lorsqu'il est employé comme adverbe) :

this is the furthest (farthest) point
c'est le point le plus éloigné

(En tant qu'adverbe : ***I can't go any further (farther)*** je ne peux pas aller plus loin)

Si on fait référence au temps, à un nombre, on ne peut employer que ***further*** :

any further misdemeanours and you're out
une autre incartade et tu sors

this must be delayed until a further meeting
ceci doit être reporté à un prochain meeting

anything further can be discussed tomorrow
on peut parler du reste demain

et comme un adverbe :

they didn't pursue the matter any further
ils ont décidé d'en arrêter là pour cette affaire

ii) ***later/latter*** *et* ***latest/last***

Later et ***latest*** font référence au temps, ***latter*** et ***last*** à l'ordre, à la série :

(a) ***his latest book is on war poetry***
son dernier livre en date est sur la poésie en temps de guerre
(b) ***his last book was on war poetry***
son dernier livre était sur la poésie en temps de guerre

Latest en (a) a le sens de "le plus récent", alors que ***last*** en (b) fait référence au dernier d'une série de livres.

Pour ***latter***, voir à ***Les Nombres***, p A72. Notez, de plus, que ***latter*** sous-entend une division en deux, comme dans ***the latter part of the century*** (la dernière moitié du siècle).

iii) ***less/lesser***

Less est quantitatif, ***lesser*** est qualitatif :

use less butter
prenez moins de beurre

the lesser of two evils
le moindre de deux maux

you'll lose less money if you follow my plan
tu perdras moins d'argent si tu suis mes plans

there's a lesser degree of irony in this novel
il y a moins d'ironie dans ce roman

Mais remarquez ***the lesser*** (opposé à ***the great(er)***) comme un adjectif de catégorie dans un registre technique ou scientifique :

the Lesser Black-backed Gull (nom scientifique)
le goéland à tête noire

Pour ***less*** avec les noms dénombrables, voir ***Les Noms***, p A10.

iv) ***older/elder*** *et* ***oldest/eldest***

Elder et ***eldest*** font en général référence aux liens familiaux uniquement :

this is my elder/eldest brother
c'est mon frère aîné

bien que ***older*** soit aussi utilisable dans ce contexte. Si ***than*** (que) suit, seul ***older*** est possible :

my brother is older than I am
mon frère est plus vieux que moi

Remarquez l'emploi de ***elder*** comme nom :

listen to your elders
écoute tes aînés

she is my elder by two years
elle est mon aînée de deux ans

the elders of the tribe
les anciens de la tribu

5. LES ADJECTIFS EMPLOYES COMME NOMS

a) Les adjectifs peuvent s'employer comme noms. Cet emploi concerne en général les ***concepts abstraits*** et les ***classes ou groupes de gens*** (en général ou dans un contexte particulier) :

i) Concepts abstraits :

you must take the rough with the smooth
il faut prendre les choses comme elles viennent

the use of the symbolic in his films
l'utilisation du symbolique dans ses films

ii) Classes ou groupes de gens :

we must bury our dead
nous devons enterrer nos morts

the poor are poor because they have been oppressed by the rich
les pauvres sont pauvres parce qu'ils ont été opprimés par les riches

the blind, the deaf	***the young, the old***
les aveugles, les sourds	les jeunes, les vieux

Et la célèbre description des chasseurs de renards par Oscar Wilde

the unspeakable in full pursuit of the uneatable
l'innommable à la poursuite de l'immangeable

Remarquez qu'en anglais ces mots ont un sens de pluriel collectif. Pour désigner une personne dans un groupe, on ajoute ***man***, ***woman***, ***person***, etc. selon le cas :

a blind woman	***three deaf people***
une aveugle	trois sourds

b) Normalement, un adjectif ne peut pas remplacer un nom singulier dénombrable. Dans ce cas, il est nécessaire d'employer *one* (mais voir aussi *one*, p A37) :

I don't like the striped shirt; I prefer the plain one
je n'aime pas la chemise à rayures, je préfère l'unie

of all the applicants the French one was the best
de tous les candidats, le français était le meilleur

Cependant, il existe un certain nombre de participes passés que l'on peut utiliser (avec l'article défini) pour remplacer un nom dénombrable. Par exemple :

the accused
l'accusé/les accusés

the deceased/the departed
le mort/les morts

the deceased's possessions were sold
les biens du mort furent vendus

Ces adjectifs substantivés ne prennent pas de *-s* au pluriel.

c) Pour les exemples au pluriel en a), on n'ajoutait pas de *-s* à l'adjectif, mais parfois la conversion d'un adjectif en nom est totale et l'adjectif prend un *-s* au pluriel :

the blacks against the whites in South Africa
les Noirs contre les Blancs en Afrique du Sud

the Reds
les Rouges (les Communistes)

here come the newly-weds
voilà les nouveaux mariés

please put all the empties in a box
s'il te plaît, mets les vides dans un carton (les bouteilles vides)

d) *Nationalités*

i) On peut rendre la nationalité de quatre façons différentes :

(1) adjectif ordinaire
(2) nom et adjectif identiques
(3) comme le groupe (2) mais le nom prend un *-s* au pluriel
(4) nom et adjectif différents (mais, au pluriel, le nom + *-s* est aussi possible)

Groupe 1

adjectif : ***English Literature***
la littérature anglaise

employé comme nom (lorsqu'il se réfère à la nation) :

the English are rather reserved
les Anglais sont plutôt réservés

Les adjectifs du Groupe 1 ne peuvent pas être utilisés comme noms pour faire référence à des individus. Dans ce cas, la terminaison ***-man*** (ou ***-woman***) est utilisée :

we spoke to two Englishmen/Englishwomen
nous avons parlé à deux Anglais/Anglaises

D'autres exemples appartenant au groupe Groupe 1 sont ***Irish*** (irlandais), ***Welsh*** (gallois), ***French*** (français), ***Dutch*** (hollandais).

Groupe 2

adjectif : ***Japanese art***
l'art japonais

employé comme nom lorsqu'il se réfère à une nation :

the Japanese are a hardworking nation
les Japonais sont un peuple de travailleurs

et lorsqu'il se réfère à des individus (sans *-s* au pluriel) :

it's hard to interpret the smile of a Japanese
il est difficile d'interpréter le sourire d'un Japonais

I've got six Japanese in my class
il y a six Japonais dans ma classe

D'autres adjectifs comme ***Japanese*** se terminent en ***-ese*** : ***Chinese*** (chinois), ***Burmese*** (birman), ***Vietnamese*** (vietnamien), ***Portuguese*** (portugais), et aussi ***Swiss*** (suisse).

Groupe 3

adjectif : ***German institutions***
les institutions allemandes

employé comme nom (au pluriel avec un *-s*) lorsqu'il fait référence à une nation :

the Germans produce some fine cars
les Allemands produisent de belles voitures

et lorsqu'il se réfère à des individus (avec un *-s* au pluriel) :

he was having a conversation with a German
il était en conversation avec un Allemand

we met quite a few Germans on our holiday
nous avons rencontré un bon nombre d'Allemands pendant nos vacances

De même, ceux qui se terminent en ***-an***, par exemple :

African (africain), ***American*** (américain), ***Asian*** (asiatique), ***Australian*** (australien), ***Belgian*** (belge), ***Brazilian*** (brésilien), ***Canadian*** (canadien), ***European*** (européen), ***Hungarian*** (hongrois), ***Indian*** (indien), ***Iranian*** (iranien), ***Italian*** (italien), ***Norwegian*** (norvégien), ***Russian*** (russe)

(mais notez que ***Arabian*** (arabe) appartient au Groupe 4 ci-dessous) et ceux qui se terminent en ***-i*** :

Iraqi (iraquien), ***Israeli*** (israélien), ***Pakistani*** (pakistanais).

Remarquez que l'on emploie ***Bangladesh*** comme adjectif (***the Bangladesh economy*** l'économie bengalaise), et ***Bangladeshi*** pour les personnes (***a Bangladeshi/three Bangladeshis came to see me*** un Bengalais est venu me voir/trois Bengalais sont venus me voir).

On trouve aussi dans ce groupe ***Czech*** (tchèque), ***Cypriot*** (chypriote), ***Greek*** (grec).

Groupe 4

adjectif : ***Danish furniture***
les meubles danois

employé comme nom lorsqu'il fait référence à une nation :

the Danish know how to eat
les Danois savent bien manger

Mais il y a un nom différent qui peut aussi être utilisé pour faire référence à la nation :

the Danes know how to eat
les Danois savent bien manger

et qui est la *seule* forme admise pour désigner les individus :

a Dane will always ask you what something costs
un Danois vous demandera toujours combien ça coûte

there were two Danes in the cast
il y avait deux Danois sur le plateau

De même pour : ***British/Briton*** (Britannique), ***Finnish/Finn*** (Finlandais), ***Polish/Pole*** (Polonais), ***Spanish/Spaniard*** (Espagnol), ***Swedish/Swede*** (Suédois).

Remarquez ***Arabian/Arab*** : l'adjectif courant est ***Arabian*** (***Arabian Nights*** les Milles et Une Nuits) sauf si on parle de la langue ou des chiffres :

the Arabic language is difficult – do you speak Arabic?
la langue arabe est difficile – parlez-vous l'arabe ?

thank God for Arabic numerals, I can't cope with the Roman ones
heureusement qu'il y a les chiffres arabes, je ne m'en sors pas avec les chiffres romains

Arab est employé pour désigner les individus, sauf si ***Saudi*** le précède. Dans ce cas ***Saudi Arabian*** ou ***Saudi*** est employé :

he's worked a lot with Arabs
il a beaucoup travaillé avec des Arabes

the hotel has been hired by Saudi Arabians (ou ***Saudis***)
l'hôtel a été loué par des Saoudiens

ii) Remarques sur ***Scottish, Scots*** et ***Scotch*** (écossais) :

Aujourd'hui ***Scotch*** est d'un usage rare, sauf dans des locutions (concernant souvent la nourriture ou les boissons), par exemple ***Scotch egg*** (= une sorte de rissole qui contient un œuf dur), ***Scotch whisky***, ***Scotch broth*** (potage d'orge, de légumes et d'agneau) et ***Scotch terrier***.
Dans les autres cas, l'adjectif est normalement ***Scottish*** comme dans ***a Scottish bar*** (un bar écossais), ***Scottish football supporters*** (supporters de football écossais), même si ***Scots*** est parfois utilisé pour les personnes : ***a Scots lawyer*** (un avocat écossais). Les linguistes font maintenant la distinction entre le ***Scottish English*** (= l'anglais parlé avec un accent écossais) et le ***Scots*** (= le dialecte écossais).

Pour désigner la nation, on emploie ***the Scots*** (les Ecossais) (parfois ***the Scottish***). L'individu est ***a Scot*** (au pluriel ***Scots***) ou ***a Scotsman*** (au pluriel ***Scotsmen***).

5. LES ADVERBES

Par adverbe on entend un seul mot (par exemple ***happily***) et par groupe adverbial ou proposition adverbiale on entend un groupe de mots ayant une fonction adverbiale.

A. LES DIFFERENTS TYPES

1. LES ADVERBES

a) *Adverbes en tant que tels et dérivés*

On peut distinguer deux sortes d'adverbes suivant leur forme : les adverbes "en tant que tels" ou les adverbes "dérivés".

Les adverbes "dérivés" sont ceux dérivés d'une autre classe de mots, par exemple :

happily (heureusement)	de l'adjectif ***happy***
hourly (par heure, etc.)	du nom ***hour*** ou de l'adjectif ***hourly***
moneywise (en ce qui concerne l'argent)	du nom ***money***

Parmi les adverbes en tant que tels on trouve :

here ici	***often*** souvent
there là-bas	***never*** jamais
now maintenant	***soon*** bientôt
then alors	***very*** très

b) *Sens*

Les adverbes peuvent se diviser en divers types selon leur sens. Les adverbes suivants sont particulièrement courants :

i) Adverbes de temps :

now (maintenant), ***then*** (alors), ***once*** (une fois), ***soon*** (bientôt), ***always*** (toujours), ***briefly*** (brièvement)

I saw her once	je l'ai vue une fois
you always say that	tu dis toujours ça

ii) Adverbes de lieu :

here (ici), ***there*** (là-bas), ***everywhere*** (partout), ***up*** (en haut), ***down*** (en bas), ***back*** (derrière)

come here
viens ici

iii) Adverbes de manière :

well (bien), ***clumsily*** (maladroitement), ***beautifully*** (merveilleusement)

what's worth doing is worth doing well
ce qui vaut la peine d'être fait vaut la peine d'être bien fait

iv) Adverbes d'intensité :

rather (plutôt), ***quite*** (assez), ***very*** (très), ***hardly*** (à peine), ***extremely*** (extrêmement)

this gravy is rather good
cette sauce est plutôt bonne

B. LES DIFFERENTES FORMES

a) *Les adverbes en* ***-ly***

On ajoute normalement cette terminaison directement à l'adjectif correspondant :

sweet : sweetly
gentil : gentiment

Mais si l'adjectif se termine en ***-ic***, on ajoute ***-ally*** :

intrinsic : intrinsically
intrinsèque : intrinsèquement

drastic : drastically
radical : radicalement

Les seules exceptions sont :

public : publicly
publique : publiquement

et ***politic* : *politicly*** (judicieux : judicieusement) employé assez rarement.

Pour les changements d'orthographe (comme dans ***happy* : *happily*** heureux : heureusement ou ***noble: nobly*** noble : noblement), voir p A74.

Remarquez que l'on prononce toujours la voyelle de ***-ed*** à l'intérieur d'un adverbe, qu'on la prononce dans l'adjectif correspondant ou pas :

assured : assuredly (*-e* prononcé dans l'adverbe)
assuré : assurément

offhanded : offhandedly (*-e* prononcé dans les deux cas)
désinvolte : avec désinvolture

b) *Même forme que l'adjectif*

Certains adverbes ont la même forme que l'adjectif correspondant, par exemple :

a fast car une voiture rapide	***he drives too fast*** il conduit trop vite
a hard punch un coup dur	**he hit him hard** il l'a frappé fort

D'autres adverbes peuvent soit avoir la même forme que l'adjectif soit avoir la terminaison ***-ly*** :

why are you driving so slow(ly)?
pourquoi conduis-tu si lentement ?

he speaks a bit too quick(ly) for me
il parle un peu trop vite pour moi

La forme sans ***-ly*** est parfois considérée comme appartenant au langage familier.

c) *La comparaison*

On forme le comparatif et le superlatif des adverbes ayant un degré de signification (voir 1b) ci-dessus) avec ***-er/-est*** ou ***more/the most*** de la même manière que les adjectifs.

Les adverbes formés à partir de l'adjectif + ***-ly*** ont un comparatif et un superlatif construits avec ***more*** et ***the most*** :

the most recently published works in this field
les ouvrages publiés le plus récemment dans ce domaine

Mais ***early***, qui n'est pas dérivé d'un adjectif sans ***-ly***, prend ***-er/-est*** :

he made himself a promise to get up earlier in future
il s'est promis de se lever plus tôt à l'avenir

Les adverbes qui ont la même forme que l'adjectif correspondant prennent ***-er/-est*** :

I can run faster than you think
je peux courir plus vite que tu crois

we arrived earlier than we expected
nous sommes arrivés plus tôt que prévu

Aux adjectifs ***slow*** et ***quick*** on peut ajouter soit ***-ly*** ou ne pas ajouter de terminaison du tout (ce que certains considèrent familier) pour former l'adverbe. Ils ont donc deux types de comparatifs :

you ought to drive more slowly
tu devrais conduire plus lentement

could you drive a little slower please
pourriez-vous conduire un peu plus lentement, s'il vous plaît ?

letters are arriving more quickly than they used to
les lettres arrivent plus vite qu'avant

letters are getting through quicker than before
les lettres arrivent plus vite qu'avant

Les adverbes suivants sont irréguliers :

badly mal	**worse** pire	**worst** le pire
far loin	**further, farther** plus loin	**furthest, farthest** le plus loin
little peu	**less** moins	**least** le moins
much beaucoup	**more** plus	**most** le plus
well bien	**better** mieux	**best** le mieux

Le comparatif de ***late*** est ***later*** (régulier) ; le superlatif est ***latest*** (régulier = le plus récent) et ***last*** (irrégulier = le dernier). Pour les différences de sens et d'usage entre ***latest*** et ***last***, ***further/furthest*** et ***farther/farthest***, comparez les adjectifs correspondants, p A19.

d) *Pour exprimer l'idée de "plus/moins ... plus/moins ..."*

the hotter it gets the more she suffers
plus il fait chaud, plus elle souffre

the less I see of him the better!
moins je le vois, mieux je me porte !

the sooner the better
le plus tôt sera le mieux

the more the merrier
plus on est de fous, plus on rit

e) ***-wise***

On peut ajouter le suffixe ***-wise*** à des noms pour former un adverbe qui a le sens général de "en ce qui concerne" (quel que soit le nom) :

how's he feeling? – do you mean mentally or healthwise?
comment se sent-il ? – tu veux dire mentalement ou en ce qui concerne sa santé ?

Bien que cette construction soit très courante, elle a tendance à être employée à l'oral plus qu'à l'écrit, et elle n'est pas toujours considérée comme particulièrement élégante, surtout pour un usage plus "créatif" :

things are going quite well schedule-wise
les choses se passent assez bien en ce qui concerne nos prévisions

we're not really short of anything furniture-wise
nous ne manquons pas de grand-chose en ce qui concerne les meubles

the town's quite well provided restaurant-wise
la ville a pas mal de restaurants

C. USAGE

1. FONCTIONS DE L'ADVERBE ET DES CONSTRUCTIONS ADVERBIALES

Les adverbes et les groupes adverbiaux s'emploient pour modifier

(1) des verbes :

he spoke well il a bien parlé	**he spoke in a loud voice** il a parlé d'une voix forte

(2) des adjectifs :

that's awfully nice of you c'est vraiment gentil à vous	**this isn't good enough** ça n'est pas assez bien

(3) d'autres adverbes :

she didn't sing well enough
elle n'a pas assez bien chanté

it happened extremely quickly
ça s'est passé extrêmement vite

(Remarquez que ***enough*** suit l'adjectif ou l'adverbe qu'il modifie.)

(4) des noms qui sont employés comme des adjectifs attributs :

this is rather a mess c'est plutôt en désordre	**he's quite a hero** c'est un vrai héros

(5) toute la phrase :

fortunately they accepted the verdict
par bonheur ils ont accepté le verdict

this is obviously a problem
c'est de toute évidence un problème

amazingly enough, it was true
aussi incroyable que cela puisse paraître, c'était vrai

2. LES ADVERBES AYANT LA MEME FORME QUE L'ADJECTIF

Parmi ceux-ci on trouve :

far (lointain – loin), ***fast*** (rapide – vite), ***little*** (petit – peu), ***long*** (long – longtemps), ***early*** (en avance – tôt), ***only*** (seul, unique – seulement)

et un certain nombre en *-ly* dérivés de noms (faisant souvent référence au temps), par exemple :

daily (quotidien – tous les jours), ***monthly*** (mensuel – tous les mois), ***weekly*** (hebdomadaire – toutes les semaines), ***deathly*** (cadavérique – comme la mort), ***leisurely*** (tranquille – sans se presser)

he travelled to far and distant lands (adjectif)
il a voyagé dans des pays lointains

he travelled far and wide (adverbe)
il a voyagé par monts et par vaux

this is a fast train (adjectif)
c'est un train rapide

you're driving too fast (adverbe)
vous roulez trop vite

he bought a little house (adjectif)
il a acheté une petite maison

little do you care! (adverbe)
ça t'importe peu

Churchill loved those long cigars (adjectif)
Churchill aimait ces longs cigares

have you been here long? (adverbe)
vous êtes ici depuis longtemps ?

you'll have to catch the early plane (adjectif)
il faudra que tu prennes le premier avion

they arrived early (adverbe)
ils sont arrivés tôt

she's an only child (adjectif)
elle est fille unique

I've only got 10p (adverbe)
j'ai seulement 10p.

do you get a daily newspaper? (adjectif)
vous achetez un quotidien ?

there's a flight twice daily (adverbe)
il y a un vol deux fois par jour

you'll receive this in monthly instalments (adjectif)
vous le recevrez en versements mensuels

the list will be updated monthly (adverbe)
la liste sera mise à jour tous les mois

a deathly silence fell on the spectators (adjectif)
un silence de mort s'abattit sur les spectateurs

she was deathly pale (adverbe)
elle avait le teint blafard

we took a leisurely stroll after dinner (adjectif)
nous avons fait une promenade tranquille après le dîner

his favourite pastime is travelling leisurely along the Californian coast (adverb)
son passe-temps favori est de voyager à loisir le long de la côte californienne

3. LA POSITION DE L'ADVERBE

a) *Les adverbes de temps*

i) S'ils font référence à un moment précis, on les place normalement en fin de phrase :

the shops close at 8 tonight
les magasins ferment à 8 heures ce soir

tonight the shops close at 8
ce soir les magasins ferment à 8 heures

will I see you tomorrow?
est-ce que je te vois demain ?

tomorrow it'll be too late
demain il sera trop tard

Mais le mot ***now*** (maintenant) précède souvent le verbe :

I now see the point
je vois maintenant ce que vous voulez dire

now I see the point
maintenant je vois ce que vous voulez dire

I see the point now
je vois ce que vous voulez dire maintenant

now is the time to make a decision
c'est maintenant le moment de prendre une décision

ii) Si l'on fait référence à un moment imprécis, on place normalement l'adverbe avant le verbe principal :

I always buy my shirts here
j'achète toujours mes chemises ici

we soon got to know him
on a bientôt appris à le connaître

we have often talked about it
on en a souvent parlé

they have frequently discussed such matters
ils ont fréquemment discuté de tels sujets

Mais de tels adverbes suivent normalement les formes du verbe ***to be*** :

he's never late
il n'est jamais en retard

he was frequently in trouble with the police
il avait souvent des problèmes avec la police

S'il y a plus d'un auxiliaire, ces adverbes ont tendance à précéder le deuxième. Pour les accentuer on peut les placer après le deuxième auxiliaire :

she has frequently been visited by distant relatives
des parents lointains lui ont fréquemment rendu visite

she has been frequently visited by distant relatives
fréquemment des parents lointains lui ont rendu visite

b) *Les adverbes de lieu*

Ils suivent le verbe (et le complément d'objet) :

they travelled everywhere
ils/elles ont voyagé partout

they have gone back
ils/elles sont retourné(e)s

I saw you there
je vous ai vu là-bas

Mais remarquez la position à l'initiale devant ***be*** :

there's the postman
le facteur arrive

here are your books
voici tes livres

et devant des pronoms personnels employés avec ***be***, ***come*** et ***go*** :

there he is — le voilà
here she comes — la voilà

c) *Les adverbes de manière*

i) Très souvent la position d'un adverbe de manière ne changera aucunement le sens de la phrase. On peut donc le placer où bon nous semble, suivant les nuances, où le ton que l'on veut donner au discours :

they stealthily crept upstairs
they crept stealthily upstairs
they crept upstairs stealthily
ils ont monté les escaliers furtivement

steathily, they crept upstairs
furtivement, ils ont monté les escaliers

she carefully examined the report
she examined the report carefully
elle examina le rapport avec attention

it was beautifully done
it was done beautifully
ce fut très bien fait

Mais, dans certains cas, si l'on veut mettre l'accent sur l'adverbe, la position où il aura plus d'impact est en fin de phrase. Comparez par exemple :

he quickly wrote a postcard (and left)
il a rapidement écrit une carte (et il est parti)

he wrote a postcard quickly (which nobody could read)
il a écrit une carte en vitesse (qui était illisible)

Plus on met l'accent sur la manière, plus l'adverbe a des chances de suivre le verbe.

Dans la phrase suivante, une seule position est possible :

they fought the war intelligently
ils ont mené la guerre avec intelligence

ii) Si le complément d'objet direct est extrêmement long, on évite de placer l'adverbe en fin de phrase :

she carefully examined the report sent to her by the Minister
elle examina attentivement le rapport envoyé par le Ministre

iii) La position en tête de phrase est très descriptive et emphatique :

clumsily he made his way towards the door
maladroitement, il se dirigea vers la porte

iv) Les adverbes modifiant les phrases et les adverbes modifiant les verbes :

Suivant la place qu'il a dans la phrase, l'adverbe va modifier la phrase entière ou bien le verbe seul :

Comparez les phrases suivantes :

she spoke wisely at the meeting
elle a parlé avec sagesse durant la réunion

she wisely spoke at the meeting
elle a eu la sagesse de parler à la réunion

Voici des exemples analogues :

she spoke naturally and fluently (modifie le verbe)
elle parla avec naturel et aisance

she naturally assumed it was right (modifie la phrase)
elle supposa naturellement que c'était vrai

naturally she assumed it was right (modifie la phrase)
naturellement elle supposa que c'était vrai

she understood it clearly (modifie le verbe)
elle comprit cela clairement

she clearly understood it (modifie la phrase ou le verbe)
de toute évidence elle comprit cela
elle comprit cela clairement

clearly she understood it (modifie la phrase)
de toute évidence elle le comprit

Le mot ***enough*** peut aussi s'employer après un adverbe pour marquer le fait que l'adverbe est employé pour modifier la phrase :

funnily (enough), they both spoke at the meeting
aussi drôle que cela puisse paraître, ils ont parlé tous les deux à la réunion

d) *Les adverbes d'intensité*

i) Si ceux-ci modifient des adverbes, des adjectifs ou des noms, ils précèdent ces mots :

she played extremely well
elle a joué extrêmement bien

this is very good
c'est très bien

it's too difficult to define
c'est trop difficile à définir

it's rather a shame
c'est bien dommage

ii) Sinon ils précèdent normalement le verbe principal :

I nearly forgot your anniversary
j'ai failli oublié ton anniversaire

I could hardly remember a thing
je pouvais à peine me souvenir de quoi que ce soit

I merely asked
j'ai tout simplement demandé

we just want to know the time of departure
nous voulons juste connaître l'heure du départ

we very much enjoyed your book
nous avons beaucoup apprécié votre livre

they also prefer white wine
ils/elles préfèrent aussi le vin blanc

Mais *too* (dans le sens de "aussi") suit normalement les mots qu'il modifie :

you too should go and see the exhibition
toi aussi tu devrais aller voir cette exposition

you should try to see that exhibition too
tu devrais aussi aller voir cette exposition

iii) ***only*** (seulement)

Cet adverbe pose rarement des difficultés en anglais parlé, car l'accentuation et l'intonation révèlent son sens :

(a) ***Bill only saw Bob today***
Bill a seulement vu Bob (mais il ne lui a pas parlé)

(b) ***Bill only saw Bob today***
Bill n'a vu que Bob aujourd'hui (il n'a vu personne d'autre)

(c) ***Bill only saw Bob today***
Bill n'a vu Bob qu'aujourd'hui (il l'a vu seulement aujourd'hui/aujourd'hui seulement)

Mais de telles différences sont obscures dans la langue écrite, à moins que le contexte ne soit clair. Ainsi dans (b) dans la langue écrite on changerait la place de l'adverbe de la façon suivante :

Bill saw only Bob today
Bill n'a vu que Bob aujourd'hui

et (c) deviendrait :

it was only today that Bill saw Bob
ce n'est qu'aujourd'hui que Bill a vu Bob

Dans (a) on écrirait probablement le mot accentué en italique :

Bill only *saw Bob today*
Bill n'a fait que voir Bob aujourd'hui

iv) ***very*** ou ***much*** ? (très/beaucoup)

★ Devant des adjectifs dans leur forme de base on emploie ***very*** :

these are very fine
ils sont très beaux

ainsi que devant des superlatifs en ***-est*** :

these are the very finest copies I've seen
ce sont les plus belles copies que j'aie jamais vues

Cependant dans la construction au superlatif qui suit, ***much*** s'emploie devant ***the*** du superlatif :

this is much the best example in the book
c'est de loin le meilleur exemple du livre

★ Le comparatif est accompagné de ***much*** :

she's much taller than you
elle est bien plus grande que toi

she's much more particular
elle est beaucoup plus pointilleuse

★ Il en est de même avec les adverbes :

you do it very well, but I do it much better
tu le fais très bien, mais je le fais bien mieux

★ Les verbes sont accompagnés de ***much*** (qui est lui-même modifié par ***very***) :

I love you very much
je t'aime énormément

★ Avant les participes passés :

S'ils ont la fonction d'adjectif, on emploie ***very*** :

I'm very tired
je suis très fatigué

we're very interested in this house
nous sommes très intéressés par cette maison

they became very offended
ils se sont beaucoup offensés

they sat there, all very agitated
ils étaient assis là, tous très agités

I'm very pleased to meet you
je suis très heureux de vous rencontrer

these suitcases are looking very used
ces valises paraissent très usagées

Mais s'ils ne sont pas considérés comme adjectifs en tant que tels, ou s'ils gardent leur fonction verbale, on emploie alors ***much*** :

this has been much spoken about (pas ***very***)
on en a beaucoup parlé

these suitcases haven't been much used (pas ***very***)
ces valises n'ont pas été très utilisées

he has been much maligned (pas ***very***)
on l'a beaucoup diffamé

they were much taken aback by the reception they received (aussi ***very***)
ils ont été époustouflés par l'accueil qu'on leur a réservé

his new house is much admired by people round here (pas ***very***)
sa nouvelle maison est très admirée par ici

Dans un langage familier, on préfère employer ***a lot*** que ***much***, en particulier à la forme affirmative :

these haven't been used a lot
ceux-ci n'ont pas été beaucoup utilisés

v) ***enough*** :

Lorsqu'il est employé comme adverbe, ***enough*** se place après l'adjectif :

he isn't big enough for that yet
il n'est pas encore assez grand pour ça

On l'emploie aussi après un nom employé comme adjectif attribut :

he isn't man enough for the job
il n'a pas la carrure suffisante pour ce travail

Remarquez que ***enough*** peut séparer l'adjectif du nom :

it's a decent enough town
c'est pas mal comme ville

e) *Les adverbes modifiant toute la phrase*

i) On a beaucoup de choix quant à la position dans la phrase. Voir plus haut sous ***les adverbes de manière***, p A23-4. Voici quelques exemples de phrases modifiées par des adverbes qui ne sont pas des adverbes de manière :

probably that isn't true
that probably isn't true
ceci n'est probablement pas vrai

fortunately he stopped in time
heureusement, il s'est arrêté à temps

he fortunately stopped in time
il s'est heureusement arrêté à temps

he stopped in time, fortunately
il s'est arrêté à temps, heureusement

f) *La place de **not*** :

i) ***Not*** précède le groupe adverbial qu'il modifie :

is he here? – not yet
est-il ici ? – pas encore

do you mind? – not at all
ça ne te fais rien ? – pas du tout

he speaks not only English, but also French
il parle non seulement anglais, mais aussi français

he lives not far from here
il n'habite pas loin d'ici

Dans l'exemple suivant, c'est ***absolutely*** (absolument) qui qualifie ***not***, et pas le contraire :

have you said something to her? – absolutely not
tu lui a dit quelque chose ? – absolument pas

ii) ***Not*** suit le verbe ***be*** :

he is not hungry
il n'a pas faim

iii) Puisque ***do*** s'emploie lorsque le verbe principal est à la forme négative, il y a au moins toujours un auxiliaire à cette forme. ***Not*** (ou ***-n't***) suit normalement le premier auxiliaire :

he does not smoke/he doesn't smoke
il ne fume pas

they would not have seen her/they wouldn't have seen her
ils ne l'auraient pas vue

Mais dans des questions la forme complète de ***not*** suit le sujet, tandis que ***-n't*** le précède, étant lié à l'auxiliaire :

did they not shout abuse at her?
didn't they shout abuse at her?
est-ce qu'ils ne lui ont pas lancé des insultes ?

have they not shouted abuse at her?
haven't they shouted abuse at her?
est-ce qu'ils ne lui ont pas lancé des insultes ?

iv) En américain, ***not*** peut précéder un subjonctif :

it is important that he not be informed of this
il est important qu'il ne soit pas informé de cela

v) Remarquez aussi ce qui suit :

did you do it? – not me
tu l'as fait ? – non, c'est pas moi

will she come? – I hope not
est-ce qu'elle viendra ? – j'espère que non

Ici ***not*** est la négation de ***will come*** (***I hope she won't come*** j'espère qu'elle ne viendra pas)

6. LES PRONOMS PERSONNELS

	singulier	*pluriel*
1ère	**I/me**	**we/us**
2ème	**you**	**you**
3ème	**he/him, she/her, it**	**they/them**

Voir p A73 pour l'ordre des pronoms personnels dans une phrase.

Dans le tableau ci-dessus la première forme de chaque paire est la forme du sujet, la seconde celle des autres emplois :

she's not here yet (sujet)
elle n'est pas encore là

Jane didn't see her (complément d'objet direct)
Jane ne l'a pas vue

Jane wrote her a letter (complément d'objet indirect)
Jane lui a écrit une lettre

it's her! — c'est elle !
with/for her — avec/pour elle

You correspond à toutes les formes de la deuxième personne française "tu, vous" au singulier et au pluriel.

a) *Sujet ou complément ?*

i) Habituellement, les formes sujets (**I, you, he, she, we, they**) sont utilisées comme sujets. Des phrases comme :

me and the wife are always there
ma femme et moi, nous sommes toujours là

sont incorrectes, bien qu'elles soient souvent entendues. Mais en anglais, on utilise souvent la forme complément (**me, him, her, us, them**) là où en français on utilise les formes "moi, toi", etc. :

who is it? – it's me
qui est-ce ? – c'est moi

who did it? – me (ou **I did**)
qui a fait cela ? – moi

It is I/he/she, etc. seraient considérés d'une politesse presque ridicule.

Cependant, si une proposition relative suit, les formes sujets sont assez courantes à condition que le pronom relatif ait une fonction de sujet : on dira :

it was I who did it
ou :
it was me that did it (familier)
c'est moi qui l'ai fait

mais toujours :

it was me (that) you spoke to
c'est à moi que vous avez parlé

La forme sujet **I** est fréquente dans la phrase **between you and I** (entre vous et moi). Cet emploi extrêmement correct est décrié par certains qui lui préfèrent **between you and me**. Voir plus loin à **Pronoms réfléchis**, p A29.

ii) On place généralement la forme complément après **than** et **as** (si aucun verbe ne suit) :

she's not as good as him, but better than me
elle n'est pas aussi bonne que lui, mais meilleure que moi

mais, si un verbe suit :

she's not as good as he is, but better than I am
elle n'est pas aussi bonne que lui, mais meilleure que moi

Cependant, dans un style plus soutenu, la forme sujet peut être placée en position finale après **than** et **as**, et surtout après **than** :

he is a better man than I
c'est un homme meilleur que moi

b) *Omission du pronom sujet*

En général on n'omet pas le pronom sujet en anglais – il existe cependant, comme partout, quelques exceptions :

i) Omission de **it** :

Dans un registre familier, le pronom à troisième personne du singulier **it** peut être omis dans des usages comme :

looks like rain this afternoon
on dirait qu'il va pleuvoir cet après-midi

what do you think of it? – sounds/smells good
qu'est-ce que tu en penses ? – ça a l'air/sent bon

Mais ce n'est pas une caractéristique que l'on peut appliquer à n'importe quel autre exemple.

ii) Emplois particuliers :

Les pronoms peuvent être omis quand plus d'un verbe suivent le sujet :

I know the place well, go there once a week, even thought about moving there
je connais bien cet endroit, j'y vais une fois par semaine, j'ai même pensé m'y installer

iii) Impératif :

A l'impératif, bien sûr, on omet les pronoms sujets :

don't do that!
ne fais pas cela !

Mais on peut les utiliser pour renforcer le sens de l'impératif (par exemple, pour proférer une menace) :

don't you do that!
ne fais donc pas ça, toi !

c) ***He, she** ou **it** ?*

He (him, his) ou **she (her)** sont parfois employés pour désigner autres choses que des personnes, c.-à-d. des animaux et certains objets. Dans ce cas, on montre que le locuteur a une relation assez intime avec la chose ou l'animal en question, ou qu'il montre un intérêt tout particulier envers cette chose ou cet animal. Autrement, on emploie **it**.

i) Animaux :

Fluffy is getting on: she probably won't give birth to any more kittens
Fluffy vieillit, elle n'aura sans doute plus de chatons

the poor old dog, take him for a walk, can't you!
le pauvre vieux toutou, tu veux bien l'emmener faire une promenade ?

mais :

a dog's senses are very keen; it can hear much higher frequencies than we can
les sens des chiens sont très développés, ils peuvent percevoir des fréquences bien plus élevées que nous

ii) Moyens de transport :

On utilisera en général le féminin **she**, à moins d'une raison particulière (qui peut être tout à fait personnelle) :

she's been a long way, this old car
elle en a fait du chemin, cette vieille voiture

there she is! – the Titanic in all her glory!
le voilà – le Titanic dans toute sa splendeur ! (à propos d'un bateau)

mais :

this ship is larger than that one, and it has an extra funnel
ce bateau est plus grand que celui-là, et il a une cheminée de plus

The Flying Scotsman will soon have made his/her last journey
le "Flying Scotsman" fera bientôt son dernier voyage (à propos d'un train)

iii) Pays :

and Denmark? – she will remember those who died for her
et le Danemark ? – il se souviendra de ceux qui sont morts pour lui

mais :

Denmark is a small country; it is almost surrounded by water
le Danemark est un petit pays ; il est presque entièrement entouré d'eau

d) ***It** sans référence*

i) Comme en français, on peut utiliser en anglais le pronom impersonnel **it** pour parler du temps, donner des jugements et décrire des situations, etc. :

it's raining
il pleut

it's freezing in here
on se gèle ici

what's it like outside today?
il fait comment dehors aujourd'hui ?

it's very cosy here
c'est très confortable ici

it's wrong to steal
il ne faut pas voler

it's not easy to raise that sort of money
ce n'est pas facile de trouver une telle somme d'argent

it's clear they don't like it
il est clair que ça ne leur plaît pas

it looks as if/seems/appears that they've left
on dirait qu'ils sont partis

Et aussi pour faire référence à un point précis dans l'espace ou dans le temps :

it's ten o'clock
il est dix heures

it's June the tenth
c'est le 10 Juin

it's time to go
il est temps de partir

it's at least three miles
ça fait au moins 4 kilomètres

Mais si on évoque la durée, on emploie **there** :

there's still time to mend matters
il reste du temps pour réparer les choses

Remarquez aussi la phrase **it says** (on dit) pour faire référence à un texte :

it says in today's Times that a hurricane is on its way
on dit dans le "Times" d'aujourd'hui qu'un ouragan arrive

ii) **It** peut aussi être utilisé d'une façon impersonnelle, surtout dans des expressions toutes faites :

that's it! (that's right)
c'est ça !

she thinks she's it (familier)
elle s'y croit

beat it! (familier)
vas-t'en !

she has it in for him (familier)
elle a une dent contre lui

e) *Emploi collectif*

You, we et **they** sont souvent employés d'une façon collective pour désigner "les gens en général". La différence entre ces trois termes se résume au fait que si **you** est employé, la personne à laquelle on s'adresse fait normalement partie des "gens", alors que si le locuteur emploie **we**, il renforce le fait qu'il est lui-même inclus dans ces "gens". **They** fait référence aux *autres* gens en général :

you don't see many prostitutes in Aberdeen any more
on ne voit plus beaucoup de prostituées à Aberdeen

I'm afraid we simply don't treat animals very well
j'ai bien peur qu'on ne traite pas les animaux très bien

they say he beats his wife
on dit qu'il bat sa femme

i) **You** employé pour faire une remarque sur une situation :

you never can find one when you need one
on n'en trouve jamais quand on en a besoin

you never can be too careful
on est jamais trop prudent

ii) **You** employé pour donner des instructions :

you first crack the eggs into a bowl
cassez d'abord les œufs dans un saladier

you must look both ways before crossing
il faut regarder des deux côtés de la route avant de traverser

Voir aussi **one** p A28.

f) *Emplois particuliers de **we***

En dehors de l'emploi collectif de **we** (voir **e)** ci-dessus), il convient de noter deux autres emplois :

i) le "nous" de souveraineté (= je), comme on le trouve dans la célèbre remarque de la Reine Victoria :

we are not amused
nous ne trouvons pas cela drôle

ii) le "nous" de condescendance ou ironique (= tu, vous), très fréquemment utilisé par les professeurs et les infirmières :

and how are we today, Mr Jenkins?, could we eat just a teeny-weeny portion of porridge?
et comment nous portons-nous aujourd'hui, M.Jenkins ? allons-nous manger un tout petit peu de porridge ?

I see, Smith, forgotten our French homework, have we?
alors, Smith, on a oublié ses exercices de français, n'est-ce pas ?

g) *Emploi de **they***

i) L'emploi de **they** collectif est devenu très courant, pour renvoyer à **somebody, someone, anybody, anyone, everybody, everyone, nobody, no one**. Le **they** collectif évite le **he or she** maladroit (parfois écrit **s/he**).

Certains considèrent malheureux l'emploi de **he** seul comme pronom collectif mis pour "les gens". Le **they (their, them(selves))** collectif est maintenant courant dans l'anglais parlé et parfois écrit (même si on ne fait référence qu'à un sexe) et offre un moyen pratique d'éviter de s'exprimer d'une façon qui pourrait être jugée sexiste :

if anybody has anything against it, they should say so
si certains sont contre, qu'ils le disent

everybody grabbed their possessions and ran
tout le monde a ramassé ses affaires et s'est enfui

somebody has left their bike right outside the door
quelqu'un a laissé son vélo juste devant la porte

Cet emploi est de plus en plus courant avec des noms précédés non seulement par **any, some** ou **no** mais aussi par l'article indéfini collectif :

some person or other has tampered with my files – they'll be sorry
quelqu'un a touché à mes dossiers sans permission – il va le regretter

no child is allowed to leave until they have been seen by a doctor
aucun enfant ne pourra sortir avant qu'il ait été examiné par un médecin

a person who refuses to use a deodorant may find themselves quietly shunned at parties, etc
les gens qui refusent de se mettre du déodorant risquent de se trouver un peu seul pendant des soirées, etc

Pour l'emploi de **one**, voir **h)** ci-dessous.

ii) **They** est employé pour faire référence à une (ou plusieurs) personne(s) que l'on ne connaît pas, mais qui représente(nt) l'autorité, le pouvoir, le savoir :

they will have to arrest the entire pit
on va devoir arrêter la mine toute entière

they should be able to repair it
ils devraient pouvoir le réparer

they will be able to tell you at the advice centre
on pourra vous renseigner au bureau d'information

when you earn a bit of money they always find a way of taking it off you
quand on gagne un peu d'argent, ils trouvent toujours un moyen pour vous en prélever

De cet emploi est née l'expression "them and us" (eux et nous) qui fait référence à ceux qui ont le pouvoir (eux), et ceux qui ne l'ont pas (nous).

h) ***One collectif***

One est employé comme un sujet et comme un complément d'objet. La forme possessive est **one's**.

i) Si **one** est collectif, le locuteur s'inclut dans "les gens en général" :

well what can one do?
eh bien, qu'est-ce qu'on peut faire ?

one is not supposed to do that
on ne doit pas faire ça

One offre un moyen pratique pour éviter les erreurs d'interprétation du sens (habituel) de **you** comme dans :

you need to express yourself more clearly
tu dois t'exprimer plus clairement

Si le locuteur parle de ce qu'on doit faire en général opposé à ce qu'une personne en particulier doit faire, il pourrait dire pour plus de précision :

one needs to express oneself more clearly
il faut s'exprimer plus clairement

Cependant, on évite habituellement d'employer ce pronom d'une façon excessive ou répétitive.

ii) L'emploi de **one** pour la première personne, c.-à-d. à la place de **I** (je) ou **we** (nous), est maintenant considéré précieux :

seeing such misery has taught one to appreciate how lucky one is in one's own country
le spectacle de tant de misère nous apprend à apprécier la chance de vivre dans notre pays

one doesn't like to be deprived of one's little pleasures, does one?
on ne se prive de rien, n'est-ce pas ?

En anglais américain, le pronom à la troisième personne au masculin peut suivre un **one** collectif :

one shouldn't take risks if he can avoid it
on ne devrait pas prendre de risques si on peut l'éviter

i) ***It ou so ?***

Comparez :

(a) **she managed to escape – I can quite believe it**
elle a réussi à s'échapper – je le crois bien

(b) **did she manage to escape? – I believe so**
est-elle parvenue à s'échapper ? – oui, je le pense

La conviction est plus forte en (a) où on est presque convaincu. En (b) la croyance est plus vague et on pourrait remplacer **believe** (croire) par **think** (penser). De même, **it** représente quelque chose de précis, mais **so** est plus vague. Voici d'autres exemples où **it/so** font référence à une affirmation précédente :

it's a difficult job, but I can do it
c'est difficile, mais je peux le faire

you promised to call me but didn't (do so)
tu avais promis de m'appeler, mais tu ne l'as pas fait

you're a thief! there, I've said it
tu es un voleur ! voilà, je l'ai dit

you're a thief! – if you say so
tu es un voleur ! – puisque tu le dis

D'autres verbes qui prennent souvent **so** : **expect**, **hope**, **seem**, **suppose**, **tell** :

has he left? – it seems so
il est parti ? – on dirait bien

I knew it would happen, I told you so
je savais que ça arriverait, je vous l'avais dit

7. LES PRONOMS REFLECHIS

	singulier	*pluriel*
1ère	**myself** (moi-même)	**ourselves**
2ème	**yourself**	**yourselves**
3ème	**himself, herself, itself, oneself**	**themselves**

a) Employé comme attribut, complément d'objet direct, complément d'objet indirect et après des prépositions pour renvoyer au sujet :

I am not myself today (attribut)
je ne me sens pas bien aujourd'hui

she has burnt herself (complément d'objet direct)
elle s'est brûlée

we gave ourselves a little treat (complément d'objet indirect)
nous nous sommes offert une petite gâterie

why are you talking to yourself? (après une préposition)
pourquoi parles-tu tout seul ?

Mais lorsqu'on évoque l'espace ou la direction, (au sens propre ou au sens figuré) les pronoms personnels sont souvent préférés après une préposition :

we have a long day in front of us
nous avons une longue journée devant nous

she put her bag beside her
elle a posé son sac à côté d'elle

have you got any cash on you?
avez-vous du liquide sur vous ?

she married beneath her
elle s'est déclassée en se mariant

he has his whole life before him
il a toute la vie devant lui

mais toujours **beside** + **-self** dans un sens figuré :

they were beside themselves with worry
ils étaient dévorés d'inquiétude

b) *Emploi d'intensité*

Lorsque le locuteur souhaite donner une certaine intensité à quelque chose dont il parle, il emploie souvent un pronom réfléchi :

you're quite well-off now, aren't you? – you haven't done so badly yourself
tu es plutôt riche, n'est-ce pas ? – tu ne t'es pas si mal débrouillé toi-même

only they themselves know whether it is the right thing to do
eux seuls savent si c'est la bonne chose à faire

get me a beer, will you? – get it yourself
tu vas me chercher une bière, s'il te plaît ? – va te la chercher tout seul

for the work to be done properly, one has to do it oneself
pour bien faire ce travail, il faut le faire soi-même

La position du pronom réfléchi peut modifier le sens de la phrase :

the PM (Prime Minister) wanted to speak to him herself
le Premier Ministre a voulu lui parler elle-même

mais :

the PM herself wanted to speak to him
le Premier Ministre elle-même a voulu lui parler (c.-à-d. que pas moins qu'elle a voulu lui parler)

c) *Après **as**, **like**, **than** et **and***

Après ces mots, il est très courant qu'on utilise les pronoms réfléchis au lieu des pronoms personnels, parfois parce qu'on hésite entre la forme de sujet ou de complément (voir **Les Pronoms Personnels** p A26) :

he's not quite as old as myself
il n'est pas aussi âgé que moi

like yourself I also have a few family problems
comme vous, j'ai aussi mes problèmes familiaux

this job needs people more experienced than ourselves
ce travail demande des gens plus qualifiés que nous

he said it was reserved specially for you and myself
il a dit que ça nous était spécialement réservé, a toi et à moi

d) *Verbes réfléchis*

i) Certains (rares) verbes ne sont que réfléchis, par exemple : **absent oneself** (s'absenter), **avail oneself** (utiliser), **betake oneself** (se rendre), **demean oneself** (s'abaisser), **ingratiate oneself** (se faire bien voir), **perjure oneself** (se parjurer), **pride oneself** (se fier).

ii) D'autres ont des significations totalement différentes lorsqu'ils sont réfléchis et lorsqu'ils ne le sont pas :

he applied for the post
il a posé sa candidature pour le poste

he should apply himself more to his studies
il devrait se consacrer davantage à ses études

iii) Et il existe plusieurs verbes dont le sens demeure le même que le verbe soit réfléchi ou non :

they always behave (themselves) in public
ils se conduisent toujours bien en public

we found it very difficult to adjust (ourselves) to the humid climate
nous avons trouvé très difficile de nous adapter au climat humide

Notez que l'élément réfléchi peut ajouter un sens de détermination. Comparez :

(a) **he proved to be useful**
il a fini par être utile

(b) **so as not to face redundancy, he'll have to prove himself more useful**
pour éviter le licenciement, il devra se montrer plus utile

(c) **the crowd pushed forward**
la foule avançait

(d) **the crowd pushed itself forward**
la foule s'avançait

Dans l'exemple (d), il y a plus de détermination que dans l'exemple (c).

8. LES POSSESSIFS

a) *Les adjectifs*

	singulier	*pluriel*
1ère	**my** (mon, ma, mes)	**our** (notre, nos)
2ème	**your** (ton, ta, tes; votre, vos)	**your** (votre, vos)
3ème	**his** (son, sa, ses)	**their** (leur, leurs)
	her (son, sa, ses)	**its** (son, sa, ses)

Les pronoms

	singulier	*pluriel*
1ère	**mine** (le mien, etc.)	**ours**
2ème	**yours**	**yours**
3ème	**his, hers, its**	**theirs**

Remarquez qu'à la troisième personne du singulier il y a trois formes que l'on utilise selon que le possesseur est du sexe masculin ou féminin ou qu'il est neutre. Il est important de se souvenir qu'il n'existe pas de genres grammaticaux en anglais et que le choix entre **his/her** dépend uniquement du sexe du possesseur. Pour les objets et les animaux on emploie **its** (voir ci-dessous) :

who is that man? what is his name?
qui est cet homme ? quel est son nom ?

who is that woman? what is her name?
qui est cette femme ? quel est son nom ?

what street is this? what is its name?
quelle est cette rue ? quel est son nom ?

Dans les cas où l'on emploie **he** ou **she** pour des animaux ou des objets (voir **Les Pronoms Personnels** p A26-7) on emploie les possessifs correspondants :

our dog's hurt his/its paw
notre chien s'est fait mal à la patte

the lion is hunting its prey
le lion chasse sa proie

Voici d'autres exemples :

they've bought their tickets/they've bought theirs
ils/elles ont acheté leurs tickets/ils/elles ont acheté les leurs

ours is much older/ours are much older
le/la nôtre est beaucoup plus vieux/vieille/les nôtres sont beaucoup plus vieux/vieilles

Remarquez le "double génitif" (comparez p A16) :

he's an old friend of mine
c'est un de mes anciens amis

that mother of hers is driving me mad
sa mère à elle me rend fou

b) *Adjectif possessif ou article ?*

On utilise en anglais un adjectif possessif où, très souvent, en français on préfère utiliser l'article défini. C'est souvent le cas lorsqu'on parle du corps ou des vêtements :

he put his hands behind his back
il a mis les mains derrière le dos

she's broken her leg — elle s'est cassé la jambe
my head is spinning — j'ai la tête qui tourne

what have you got in your pockets?
qu'est-ce que tu as dans les poches ?

Dans une phrase utilisant une préposition, l'article défini est généralement employé (bien que l'adjectif possessif soit aussi possible) :

he grabbed her by the waist
il l'a attrapée par la taille

he was punched on the nose
il a reçu un coup de poing dans le nez

Mais si le mot qui désigne une certaine partie du corps est lui-même qualifié par un adjectif, alors l'adjectif possessif, et non l'article, est utilisé :

he grabbed her by her slim little waist
il l'a attrapée par sa petite taille mince

Voir aussi **Le Pluriel Distributif** dans la section **Les Noms**, p A14.

9. LES DEMONSTRATIFS

singulier	*pluriel*
this, that	**these, those**

Les formes sont les mêmes pour l'adjectif démonstratif (ce, cette, ces, etc.) et le pronom démonstratif (celui-ci, celle-ci, celle-là, etc.).

a) **This** et **these** renvoient à quelque chose qui se trouve **près** du locuteur, ou qui a un rapport **immédiat** avec le locuteur, alors que **that** et **those** ont un rapport plus distant avec lui. **This/these** sont à **here/now** ce que **that/those** sont à **there/then** :

(a) **this red pen is mine; that one is yours**
ce crayon rouge-ci est le mien ; celui-là est le tien

(b) **that red pen is mine; this one is yours**
ce crayon rouge-là est le mien ; celui-ci est le tien

En (a) le crayon rouge se trouve plus près du locuteur que l'autre crayon ; en (b) c'est le contraire.

Autres exemples :

I want to go – you can't mean that
je veux partir – tu ne veux pas dire ça !

this is what I want you to do ...
voici ce que je veux que tu fasses ...

in those days it wasn't possible
à cette époque-là ce n'était pas possible

what are these (knobs) for?
à quoi servent ceux-ci/ces boutons ?

this is Christine, is that Joanna? (au téléphone)
ici Christine, c'est Joanna ?

Quand ils sont pronoms les démonstratifs ne peuvent pas renvoyer à des personnes, sauf s'ils sont sujets ou attributs :

this is Carla — c'est Carla
who is this? — qui est-ce ?

Ainsi dans :

would you take this?
tu veux bien prendre ça ?

this ne peut pas désigner une personne.

b) ***this/these** indéfinis*

L'emploi de **this/these** comme pronoms indéfinis est très courant en l'anglais familier parlé, quand on raconte une histoire, une blague par exemple :

this Irishman was sitting in a pub when ...
un Irlandais était assis dans un pub quand ...

the other day these guys came up to me ...
l'autre jour, des types se sont approchés de moi ...

c) ***that/this** adverbes*

En anglais parlé **that/this** sont souvent utilisés comme des adverbes, dans un sens proche de **so** (si), avant un adjectif ou un autre adverbe :

I like a red carpet but not one that red
j'aime bien les tapis rouges, mais pas aussi rouge que ça

I don't like doing it that/this often
je n'aime pas le faire si souvent

now that we've come this far, we might just as well press on
puisqu'on est allé jusque là, autant continuer

I don't want that/this much to eat !
je veux pas manger autant que ça !

she doesn't want to marry him, she's not that stupid
elle ne veut pas se marier avec lui, elle n'est pas si stupide

10. LES INTERROGATIFS

who/whom/whose, which, what et toutes les formes combinées avec **-ever**, par exemple : **whichever**

On distingue l'emploi adjectif et l'emploi pronom :

which do you want? (pronom)
lequel veux-tu ?

which flavour do you want? (adjectif)
quel parfum veux-tu ?

Remarquez qu'ils sont invariables. Le premier exemple pourrait tout aussi bien se traduire par "laquelle/lesquels/lesquelles veux-tu ?"

a) ***Who et whom***

Who et **whom** sont toujours des pronoms (c.-à-d. qu'ils ne sont jamais suivis par un nom) et ils renvoient à des personnes :

who are you?
qui êtes-vous ?

to whom were your remarks addressed?
à qui s'adressaient vos remarques ?

Whom est utilisé dans un style soutenu, lorsqu'il est complément d'objet (direct ou indirect) ou suit une préposition :

whom did she embrace?
qui a-t-elle embrassé ?

to whom did he give his permission?
à qui a-t-il donné la permission ?

I demanded to know to whom he had spoken
ou :
I demanded to know whom he had spoken to
j'ai exigé de savoir à qui il avait parlé

En anglais parlé d'aujourd'hui, **who** est normalement utilisé pour toutes les fonctions. (**Whom** est obligatoire directement **après** une préposition, mais ce genre de tournure n'est pas très employé en anglais parlé d'aujourd'hui.) Par exemple :

who did you see at the party?
qui as-tu vu à la soirée ?

I want to know who you spoke to just now
I want to know to whom you spoke just now (style soutenu)
je veux savoir avec qui tu étais en train de parler

b) ***whose***

C'est la forme au génitif de **who**. Il peut être pronom ou adjectif :

whose are these bags? **whose bags are these?**
à qui sont ces sacs ? ce sont les sacs de qui ?

c) ***which/what***

Au contraire de **who(m)**, **which** peut être adjectif ou pronom, et peut renvoyer à une personne ou à un objet :

which actor do you mean?
de quel acteur parles-tu ?

which of the actors do you mean?
duquel des acteurs parles-tu ?

of these two recordings, which do you prefer?
de ces deux enregistrements, lequel préfères-tu ?

which recording do you prefer?
quel enregistrement préfères-tu ?

La différence entre **which** et **who/what** est que **which** est limitatif : il invite celui à qui on parle à faire un choix parmi un certain nombre de choses précises.

Comparez :

what would you like to drink?
qu'est-ce que tu veux boire ?

I've got coffee or tea – which would you like?
j'ai du café ou du thé – qu'est-ce que tu veux ?

Si l'objet du choix n'est pas identifié avant la question, on ne peut employer que **what** :

what would you like to drink? I've got sherry or vermouth or Campari
qu'est-ce que tu veux boire ? j'ai du sherry, du vermouth ou du Campari

d) ***what***

Lorsqu'il est un pronom, **what** ne renvoie jamais à une personne :

what is this object?
qu'est-ce que c'est que cet objet ?

don't ask me what I did
ne me demande pas ce que j'ai fait

sauf si on fait référence à des caractéristiques personnelles :

and this one here, what is he? – he's German
et celui-ci, qu'est-ce qu'il est ? – c'est un Allemand

Lorsqu'il est adjectif, **what** peut renvoyer à une personne, un animal ou à une chose :

what child does not like sweets?
quel enfant n'aime pas les bonbons ?

what kind of powder do you use?
quelle sorte de lessive utilisez-vous ?

Pour la différence entre **what** et **which**, voir c) ci-dessus.

Remarquez l'emploi de **what** dans les exclamations :

what awful weather!
quel temps affreux !

what a dreadful day!
quelle journée épouvantable !

what must they think!
ce qu'ils doivent penser !

e) *Avec* ***-ever***

Le suffixe **-ever** exprime la surprise, la confusion ou l'ennui, l'agacement :

whatever do you mean? (confusion ou ennui)
qu'est-ce que tu veux dire ?

whoever would have thought that? (surprise)
qui donc aurait pu penser cela ?

whatever did you do that for? (ennui, agacement)
pourquoi as-tu donc fait ça ?

Which quand il est interrogatif ne se combine normalement pas avec **-ever**.

11. LES RELATIFS

who/whom/whose, **which**, **what**, **that** et toutes les formes combinées avec **-ever**, par exemple : **whichever**.

a) Les pronoms relatifs (sauf **what**) ont en général un antécédent auquel ils se rapportent. Dans :

she spoke to the man who/that sat beside her
elle a parlé à l'homme qui s'était assis à côté d'elle

who/that est le pronom relatif et **the man** l'antécédent.

b) *Déterminative et explicative*

Une proposition relative peut être déterminative ou explicative. Si elle est déterminative, elle est **nécessaire** au sens de la phrase complète par le lien qui l'unit à l'antécédent. Si elle est explicative, elle a un rapport moins étroit avec l'antécédent. Une proposition explicative a un rôle similaire à une parenthèse. Par exemple :

he helped the woman who had called out
il aida la femme qui avait appelé au secours

Cette phrase peut vouloir dire deux choses : (1) "il aida la femme qui avait appelé au secours et non celle qui ne l'avait pas fait" ; ou (2) "il aida la femme (qui, par ailleurs avait appelé au secours)".

Dans le sens (1) on a une proposition relative déterminative : on définit la femme comme celle qui avait appelé au secours.

Dans le sens (2) la femme a déjà été évoquée et définie dans la conversation, et la proposition relative n'apporte pas d'éléments majeurs à la phrase ; elle ne fait que donner une information supplémentaire, mais pas nécessaire.

Il n'est pas tout à fait exact, cependant, de dire que la phrase comme on l'a donnée plus haut peut avoir deux significations : les propositions relatives explicatives *devraient* être précédées d'une virgule, les propositions relatives déterminatives jamais. Ainsi, dans cette phrase, la proposition relative est déterminative. La proposition explicative serait :

he helped the woman, who had called out
il aida la femme, qui avait appelé au secours

Il est évident que l'emploi des propositions déterminatives n'a de sens que s'il existe deux possibilités ou plus. C'est-à-dire qu'une proposition relative qui a un antécédent exclusif comme **my parents** (je n'ai que deux parents, et je n'ai pas besoin de préciser ou déterminer lesquels) est toujours explicative :

my parents, who returned last night, are very worried
mes parents, qui sont rentrés hier soir, sont très inquiets

he went to Godalming, which is a place I don't much care for
il est allé à Godalming, qui n'est pas un endroit que j'apprécie particulièrement

Le pronom relatif **that** est employé uniquement avec des propositions relatives déterminatives. **Who** et **which** peuvent être utilisés dans les deux cas.

c) ***who/whom/that***

Who ou **that** sont utilisés comme sujets (qui) :

the girl who/that rescued him got a medal
la fille qui l'a sauvé a reçu une médaille

Who(m) ou **that** sont utilisés comme compléments (que) :

the man who(m)/that she rescued was a tourist
l'homme qu'elle a sauvé était un touriste

Whom est utilisé dans un style plus soutenu. Pour plus de renseignements, voir **Les Interrogatifs**, p A31.

d) ***who/which/that***

i) **who/that**

Ces formes renvoient à des personnes ou des animaux dont il a été question dans la section **Les Pronoms Personnels** (c) ci-dessus, p A26 :

we ignored the people who/that were late
nous n'avons pas tenu compte des gens qui étaient en retard

the mouse did not get past Fluffy, who had it in her jaws in no time
la souris ne put pas passer devant Fluffy, qui la prit dans sa gueule en un éclair

Remarquez que **who** uniquement et non **that** peut être employé dans le second exemple, qui est une proposition relative explicative, voir b) ci-dessus.

Pour les noms collectifs, si on veut leur donner un caractère individuel, on emploie **who** ou **that**. Si on considère le groupe d'une manière moins personnelle, on emploie **which** ou **that** :

the crowd who/that had gathered were in great spirits (aspect personnalisé) la foule qui s'était rassemblée était très enthousiaste

the crowd which/that had gathered was enormous (aspect collectif)
la foule qui s'était rassemblée était énorme

De même pour les noms de sociétés et les grands magasins :

try Harrods who, I'm sure, will order it for you (aspect personnalisé)
va voir chez Harrods qui, j'en suis sûr, le commandera pour toi

you'll find it in Harrods, which is a gigantic store (aspect non personnalisé)
tu le trouveras chez Harrods, qui est un magasin gigantesque

ii) **which/that** :

Which ou **that** ne sont pas utilisés pour désigner des personnes :

the car which/that drove into me
la voiture qui m'est rentrée dedans
the disks which/that I sent you
les disquettes que je t'ai envoyées

Attention : bien que les pronoms personnels puissent être utilisés pour des moyens de transport, comme on l'a vu p A26-7, cette possibilité de personnalisation ne s'applique pas aux pronoms relatifs.

e) ***whose***

La forme au génitif **whose** renvoie à des personnes et à des animaux. Elle est souvent employée, quand elle renvoie à une chose, à la place de **of which** :

this is the girl whose mother has just died
c'est la fille dont la mère vient juste de mourir

oh, that's that new machine whose cover is damaged
oh, c'est la nouvelle machine dont le couvercle est abîmé

the department, whose staff are all over 50, is likely to be closed down
le service, dont le personnel a plus de 50 ans, risque de fermer

these are antiques whose pedigree is immaculate
ce sont des objets anciens dont l'authenticité est irréprochable

the vehicles, the state of which left a good deal to be desired, had been in use throughout the year
les véhicules, dont l'état laissait à désirer, avaient été en service pendant toute l'année

f) ***which***

i) **Which** ne renvoie jamais aux personnes :

I received quite a few books for Christmas, which I still haven't read
j'ai reçu un bon nombre de livres pour Noël, que je n'ai pas encore lus

sauf quand on évoque un trait de caractère :

she accused him of being an alcoholic, which in fact he is
elle l'accusait d'être alcoolique, ce qu'il est en réalité

ii) Lorsque **which** est un adjectif, normalement on ne le trouve qu'après une préposition et s'il a un antécédent chose ou objet. **Which** quand il est adjectif est d'un style un peu soutenu, même après une préposition :

he returned to Nottingham, in which city he had been born and bred
il revint à Nottingham, ville dans laquelle il avait grandi

et il est très soutenu quand il n'est pas accompagné d'une préposition :

he rarely spoke in public, which fact only added to his obscurity
il parlait très peu en public, particularité qui contribuait à le laisser dans l'ombre

ou archaïque ou légal si l'antécédent est une personne :

Messrs McKenzie and Pirie, which gentlemen have been referred to above ...
MM. McKenzie et Pirie, lesquels messieurs ont été évoqués plus haut ...

g) ***what***

i) **What** est le seul relatif qui ne prend pas d'antécédent. Il peut être pronom ou adjectif. Quand il est pronom, il fait référence normalement à une chose, et a souvent le sens de **that which** (ce qui/que), ou, au pluriel, **the things which** (les choses qui/que) :

show me what did the damage
montre-moi ce qui a causé les dégâts

Quand il est adjectif, il peut renvoyer à une personne ou à une chose, et il correspond à **the** (+ nom) **who/which** :

show me what damage was done
montre-moi quels dégâts ont été faits

with what volunteers they could find they set off for the summit
avec les volontaires qu'ils ont pu trouver, ils sont partis à la conquête du sommet

what money they had left, they spent on drink
l'argent qu'il leur restait, ils le dépensèrent en boisson

ii) **what** ou **which?**

Seul **which** peut renvoyer à une proposition complète alors que **what** n'a pas d'antécédent. Mais **what** peut annoncer ou anticiper une proposition. Comparez :

she left the baby unattended, which was a silly thing to do
elle laissa le bébé tout seul, ce qui était une chose idiote

mais :

she left the baby unattended and what's more, she smacked it when it cried
elle laissa le bébé tout seul, et ce qui est pire encore, elle lui donna une fessée quand il se mit à pleurer

h) *Avec -ever*

Au contraire des pronoms interrogatifs, (voir ci-dessus, p A31) **-ever** n'exprime pas la surprise, la confusion ou l'agacement quand il est associé avec un relatif ; il permet seulement de les renforcer dans le sens de **no matter (who, which, what)** (qui que ce soit qui/que) :

tell it to whoever you want to
dis-le à qui tu veux

take whichever (tool) is best
prend celui (des outils) qui convient le mieux

do whatever you like
fais ce que tu veux

I'll do it whatever happens
je le ferai quoi qu'il arrive

whatever problems we may have to face, we'll solve them
quels que soient les problèmes que nous devions affronter, nous les résoudrons

i) *Omission du relatif*

Le pronom relatif peut être omis (et il l'est très souvent en anglais parlé) dans les propositions relatives déterminatives sauf s'il est sujet ou s'il est précédé par une préposition :

these are the things (which/that) we have to do
ce sont les choses que nous devons faire

I saw the boy (who/that) you met last night
j'ai vu le garçon que tu as rencontré hier soir

is this the assistant (who/that) you spoke to?
est-ce à cette assistante que tu as parlé ?

who's the girl you came to the party with?
qui est la fille avec qui tu es venu à la soirée ?

she's not the woman (that) she was
elle n'est plus la femme qu'elle était

Remarquez que **that** seulement pourrait être utilisé dans cette dernière phrase.

Remarquez aussi que la construction assez soutenue :

who are the people with whom you are doing business?
qui sont les gens avec qui vous travaillez ?

peut être évitée si l'on change de place la préposition (**with**) :

who are the people you are doing business with?

En anglais familier parlé, le pronom relatif sujet est souvent omis après **there is, here is, it is, that is** :

there's a man wants to speak to you
il y a un monsieur qui veut te parler

here's a car will make your eyes pop out
voilà une voiture qui va te faire baver d'envie

it isn't everybody gets a chance like that
ce n'est pas tout le monde qui a une chance comme ça

that was her husband just walked by
c'est son mari qui vient juste de passer

12. LES PRONOMS ET LES ADJECTIFS INDEFINIS

a) ***some** et **any***

i) Lorsqu'ils sont combinés avec **-body**, -**one**, -**thing** ce sont des pronoms alors que **some** et **any** seuls peuvent être pronoms ou adjectifs, singulier ou pluriel :

did you speak to anybody?
as-tu parlé à quelqu'un ?

tell me something
dis-moi quelque chose

I have some (sugar)
j'ai du sucre/j'en ai

do you have any (friends)?
avez-vous des amis ?/en avez-vous ?

ii) Si le locuteur emploie **some**, il considère que la chose, l'animal ou la personne dont il parle existe ou, au moins, il s'attend à ce qu'ils existent. S'il emploie **any**, il ne formule aucune condition concernant cette éventualité d'existence. C'est pourquoi **any** est utilisé dans les propositions négatives, et avec des mots qui ont un sens négatif, comme **hardly** (à peine) :

I haven't got any money, but you have some
je n'ai pas d'argent, mais toi, tu en as

I have got hardly any money
je n'ai presque pas d'argent

De même, **any** est fréquent dans les propositions interrogatives et conditionnelles, car ces propositions sont par définition non-affirmatives :

have you got any money?
avez-vous de l'argent ?

if you have any money, give it to me
si tu as de l'argent, donne-le-moi

Cependant, c'est une erreur de dire (comme le font d'autres grammaires) que **some** est rare dans les propositions interrogatives et conditionnelles. L'emploi dépend de ce que veut dire ou sous-entend le locuteur. Comparez :

(a) **have you got some brandy for the pudding?**
avez-vous du brandy pour le pudding ?

(b) **did you bring some sweets for the kids?**
avez-vous apporté quelques bonbons pour les enfants ?

(c) **if you had some milk, you'd feel better**
si vous preniez du lait, vous vous sentiriez mieux

(d) **if they leave some ice-cream behind, can I have it?**
s'ils laissent de la glace, je peux en avoir ?

(e) **have we got any brandy in the house?**
y a-t-il du brandy dans la maison ?

(f) **did you give any sweets to that donkey?**
avez-vous donné des bonbons à cet âne ?

(g) **if you've had any milk, please tell me**
si vous avez pris du lait, dites-le-moi

(h) **if they left any ice-cream behind, I didn't see it**
s'ils ont laissé de la glace, je ne l'ai pas vue

En (a)-(d) **some** veut dire "un peu de" ou "quelques", alors que en (e)-(h) **any** veut dire "du tout". Par exemple, en (e) le locuteur veut savoir s'il y a du brandy dans la maison ou s'il n'y en a pas. Il ne s'intéresse pas à la quantité, comme c'est le cas du locuteur en (a), qui en veut juste assez pour le pudding.

De même, **some milk** en (c) veut dire "un verre de lait" ou une quantité semblable, alors que le médecin qui parle en (g) veut savoir si le malade a pris la moindre quantité de lait (parce que le lait pourrait expliquer certains symptômes).

iii) **Some/any** et leur combinaisons :

Comparez :

(a) **have they produced any?**
est-ce qu'ils en ont fait ?

(b) **have they produced anything?**
est-ce qu'ils ont fait quelque chose ?

En (a) le nom auquel **any** fait référence est sous-entendu et a été évoqué un peu plus tôt ; mais en (b) on ne fait pas de référence directe à quelque chose en particulier. Un exemple typique pour (a) serait :

they're always going on about how much they like children – have they produced any yet?
ils disent toujours qu'ils adorent les enfants – est-ce qu'ils en ont fait un déjà ?

et pour (b) :

the think-tank have been locked away for a week – have they produced anything yet?
le groupe de réflexion est enfermé depuis une semaine – est-ce qu'ils ont trouvé quelque chose ?

Some et **any** pronoms peuvent aussi renvoyer à des noms indénombrables (dans l'exemple ci-dessus, **any** fait référence à un nom dénombrable (**children**), qui doit être au pluriel) :

I've run out of coffee, have you got any?
j'ai fini le café, tu en as ?

Mais remarquez que **some** est pronom quand il a le sens de "les gens qui" ou "ceux qui" :

there are some who will never learn
il y a des gens qui n'apprendront jamais

iv) **some(thing)/any(thing)** + **of** + nom :

Some/any avant une locution qui commence par **of** est **quantitatif** par son sens, alors que **something/anything** + locution qui commençe par **of** est **qualitatif**. Comparez :

(a) **give me some of that cheese**
donne-moi (un peu) de ce fromage

(b) **he hasn't got any of her qualities**
il n'a aucune de ses qualités

(c) **he hasn't got anything of her qualities**
il n'a en rien ses qualités

(d) **there is something of the artist in her**
il y a quelque chose d'artistique chez elle

En (a) et en (b) **some** et **any** font référence à "une part de, un peu de" alors que en (c) et en (d) ils renvoient à "quelque chose dans la manière de" ou "quelque chose qui relève de".

v) **some** = un(e) certain(e) :

On a vu plus haut (en ii ci-dessus) que **some** est utilisé dans un contexte positif avec des noms au pluriel (**would you like some biscuits?**) ou des noms indénombrables (**he stayed here for some time**). Lorsqu'il est placé devant un nom dénombrable au **singulier**, il veut souvent dire "un certain" :

some person (or other) must have taken it
quelqu'un l'aura pris

he's got some fancy woman in London, it seems
il semble qu'il a une certaine bonne amie à Londres

come and see me some time
viens me voir un jour (emploi de **time** différent de l'exemple ci-dessus)

vi) **some** = "un mauvais" ou "un bon, excellent" :

En anglais familier, on utilise souvent **some** avec ces deux sens :

some husband you are! – always in the pub with your mates!
quel mauvais mari tu fais, toujours au pub avec tes copains !

this really is some party!
c'est vraiment une soirée fantastique !

vii) **some/any, something, anything** adverbes :

Some : devant des nombres = à peu près, autour de :

some fifty people were present
une cinquantaine de personnes étaient présentes

avec **more** :

talk to me some more
parle-moi encore un peu

en anglais américain :

we talked some
on a un peu parlé

Any est utilisé comme un adverbe devant les comparatifs :

he isn't any less of a friend in spite of this
il n'est pas moins un ami pour cela

I refuse to discuss this any further
je refuse de parler de cela davantage

Avant **like**, **something** ou **anything** sont aussi employés comme adverbes dans le sens de "plutôt" ou "environ" (**something**) et "rien" (**anything**) :

it looks something like a Picasso
ça ressemble à du Picasso

something like fifty or sixty people were present
environ cinquante à soixante personnes étaient présentes

it wasn't anything like I had imagined
ça n'avait rien à voir avec ce que j'avais imaginé

Autrement **something** employé comme adverbe d'intensité est familier ou régional :

ooh, that baby howls something terrible!
ce bébé hurle d'une façon terrible

he fancies her something rotten
elle lui plaît un maximum

b) ***no et none***

i) **No** est adjectif :

he has no house, no money, no friends
il n'a pas de maison, pas d'argent, pas d'amis

sauf s'il est employé comme un adverbe, dans le sens de "pas" devant les comparatifs :

we paid no more than 2 pounds for it
nous n'avons pas payé plus de deux livres

I want £2 for it, no more, no less
j'en veux deux livres, ni plus, ni moins

La différence entre **not** et **no** dans ce cas est que **not** est plus précis, **no** ayant un caractère émotionnel. **No more than** peut être remplacé par **only** (seulement). Mais si le locuteur dit :

I wish to pay not more than £2
j'espère payer pas plus de deux livres

il précise que le prix ne doit pas dépasser deux livres.

ii) **None** est un pronom :

do you have any cigarettes? – no, I've none left
avez-vous des cigarettes ? – non, je n'en ai plus

I tried a lot but none (of them) fitted
j'en ai essayé beaucoup, mais aucune ne m'allait

Remarquez qu'en anglais parlé courant, une phrase comme :

I have none
je n'en ai pas

peut paraître formelle ou d'un ton dramatique ou est employé pour marquer l'emphase. La construction normale serait :

I don't have any
je n'en ai pas

Quand on fait référence à des gens, **none of them/us/you** (aucun d'eux/de nous/de vous) est plus courant que **none** (aucun, personne) en anglais parlé :

none of us knew where he had filed it
aucun de nous ne savait où il l'avait classé

I waited for them for hours, but none of them came
je les ai attendus pendant des heures, mais aucun d'eux n'est venu

many have set out to climb this mountain but none have ever returned
nombreux sont ceux qui sont partis à la conquête de cette montagne, mais aucun n'en est jamais revenu

Quand on veut donner à une phrase un ton emphatique, on peut employer la construction **not one** :

not one (of them) was able to tell me the answer!
pas un (d'eux) n'a été capable de me répondre

iii) **none** : singulier ou pluriel ?

Le sens littéral de **none** étant **no one** (pas un), on trouve souvent logique de le faire suivre par un verbe au singulier, comme :

none of them has been here before
aucun d'eux n'est venu ici avant

Cependant, un verbe au pluriel est d'un emploi tout à fait courant en anglais parlé (et écrit) d'aujourd'hui :

none of them have been here before

iv) **None** est un adverbe :

Il est utilisé devant **the** + un comparatif (comparez avec **any** en a) vii ci-dessus) :

none the less (= nevertheless) neanmoins

you can scratch a CD and they are none the worse for it
on peut rayer les CD, et ils ne s'abîment pas pour autant

he took the medicine but is feeling none the better
il a pris les médicaments, mais il ne se sent pas mieux pour autant

after his explanation we were all none the wiser
après ses explications, nous n'étions pas plus avancés

c) ***every et each***

i) **Each** peut être un pronom ou un adjectif ; **every** est toujours un adjectif. Ils font référence tous les deux à des noms dénombrables uniquement :

each (of them) was given a candle
on a donné une bougie à chacun (d'eux)

each (child) was given a candle
on a donné une bougie à chacun (chaque enfant)

every child needs a good education
tous les enfants doivent recevoir une bonne éducation

Every et **each** sont différents car **every** sous-entend la totalité (il n'y a pas d'exception) alors que **each** individualise. Dans les deux premiers exemples, **each** implique "l'un après l'autre". C'est pourquoi **each** fait souvent référence à un plus petit nombre qu'**every**, qui est plus général, comme on le voit dans le dernier exemple.

Remarquez que **every** peut être précédé d'une forme au génitif (nom ou pronom) :

Wendy's every move was commented on
tous les mouvements de Wendy furent commentés

her every move was commented on
le moindre de ses mouvements fut commenté

et notez son emploi avec les nombres :

she goes to the dentist every three months
elle va chez le dentiste tous les trois mois

every other day there's something wrong
un jour sur deux, il y a quelque chose qui ne va pas

the clock seems to stop every two days
l'horloge semble s'arrêter tous les deux jours

La différence entre **every other** et **every two** est que **every other** sous-entend une irritation devant le fait que quelque chose est répétitif tandis que **every two** est plus objectif et précis.

Remarquez aussi son emploi adverbial :

every now and then
every now and again
every so often

qui veulent tous dire "de temps en temps".

Everybody/everyone et **everything** sont des pronoms, et ils sont toujours suivis d'un verbe au singulier mais, comme les autres pronoms indéfinis, **everybody** peut être suivi par **they, them(selves)** ou **their** (voir **Les Pronoms Personnels**, p A26).

d) ***all***

i) **All** est un adjectif ou un pronom et renvoie à des noms dénombrables ou indénombrables. Remarquez que lorsqu'un article défini ou un pronom personnel est utilisé, il se place entre **all** et le nom :

all coins are valuable to me
toutes les pièces ont de la valeur pour moi

I want all the/those/their coins
je veux toutes les/ces/leurs pièces

all his energy was spent
il a dépensé toute son énergie

I want them all/all of them
je les veux tous

I want it all/all of it
je le veux en entier

ii) **all** et **everything** :

La différence entre ces deux mots est souvent assez légère. **All** sera employé si le locuteur évoque quelque chose qui n'est pas précis. Seul **all** peut renvoyer à des noms indénombrables.

we ate everything that was on the table
nous avons mangé tout ce qui était sur la table

all that was on the table was a single vase
tout ce qu'il y avait sur la table était un vase

did you eat the ice-cream? – not all (of it)
as-tu mangé la glace ? – pas tout

they believed everything/all he said
ils croyaient tout ce qu'il disait

did he say anything? – all that he said was 'do nothing'
a-t-il dit quelque chose ? – tout ce qu'il a dit fut "ne faites rien"

iii) **all** et **whole** :

La différence principale entre **all** et l'adjectif **whole** réside dans le fait que **whole** accentue parfois un aspect précis de ce que l'on exprime :

don't interrupt me all the time
ne m'interromps pas tout le temps

he sat there the whole time without moving
il s'est assis là pendant tout le temps sans bouger

he ate all of the pie
il a mangé tout le gâteau

he ate the whole pie
il a mangé le gâteau en entier

Mais l'emploi de **whole** est limité aux noms dénombrables :

the whole town (ou **all the town**)
toute la ville

mais seulement :

all the butter (indénombrable)
tout le beurre

Remarquez que **whole** ne s'emploie pas avec un nom au pluriel. On emploie alors, par exemple :

all the books in their entirety
tous les livres en entier

iv) **all** adverbe :

L'emploi adverbial de **all** est clair dans les exemples ci-dessous, où **all** signifie **completely** (complètement) :

he was all covered in mud
il était complètement couvert de boue

should we teach her a lesson? – I'm all in favour (of that)
on devrait lui donner une leçon ? – je suis tout à fait d'accord (avec ça)

it's all over, honey
c'est fini, mon chéri

Voici d'autres exemples de **all** adverbe :

I've told you all along not to eat the cat's food
je t'ai toujours dit de ne pas manger la nourriture du chat

he was covered in mud all over
il était couvert de boue de la tête aux pieds

Devant des comparatifs :

I've stopped smoking and feel all the better for it
j'ai arrêté de fumer et je m'en sens tellement mieux

your remark is all the more regrettable since the Principal was present
votre remarque est d'autant plus regrettable que le Directeur était présent

e) ***other(s) et another***

i) **Another** est suivi de, ou remplace, un nom singulier dénombrable. Un nom pluriel peut suivre **other** uniquement, tandis que **others** est toujours un pronom :

I want another (hamburger)
j'en veux un autre/je veux un autre hamburger

other children get more money
les autres enfants ont plus d'argent

I like these colours – don't you like the others?
j'aime ces couleurs – tu n'aimes pas les autres ?

ii) Si **than** suit un nom, **other** suivra, et ne précédera pas, ce nom :

there are difficulties other than those mentioned by the government
il y a d'autres difficultés que celles qui sont mentionnées par le gouvernement

Dans cette phrase, **other** pourrait aussi précéder **difficulties**, mais il est toujours placé après **none** :

who should arrive? none other than Jimbo himself
et qui est arrivé ? Jimbo en personne

iii) Parfois **no other** est utilisé à la place de **not another** :

he always wears that coat; he has no other (coat)
il porte toujours ce manteau ; il n'en a pas d'autre

iv) Remarquez la construction avec **some** et ses combinaisons, quand **some** veut dire "un(e) certain(e) ..." (comparez avec a) v ci-dessus). On ajoute **or other** pour intensifier l'aspect vague de la chose dont on parle :

somebody or other must have betrayed her
quelqu'un a dû la trahir

we'll get there somehow or other (emploi adverbial)
on y arrivera d'une manière ou d'une autre

he married some girl or other from the Bahamas
il s'est marié avec je ne sais quelle fille des Bahamas

v) Avec **one** :

One ... another et **one ... the other** ont habituellement la même signification :

one week after another went by
one week after the other went by
les semaines sont passées les unes après les autres

Mais si le locuteur ne fait référence qu'à deux choses, alors **one ... the other** est préféré :

the two brothers worked well together: one would sweep the yard while the other chopped the wood
les deux frères travaillaient bien ensemble : l'un nettoyait la cour pendant que l'autre coupait le bois

bien que si le second élément est précédé d'une préposition, **one ... another** est aussi employé dans ce cas :

they would sit there and repeat, one after another, every single word of the lesson
ils s'asseyaient là et répétaient, l'un après l'autre, chaque mot de la leçon

On trouve parfois la combinaison **the one ... the other**, qui aurait pu être employée dans l'exemple des deux frères ci-dessus. Dans la locution utilisant **hand**, **the one** est obligatoire :

on the one hand, you'd earn less, on the other your job satisfaction would be greater
d'un côté tu gagnerais moins d'argent, mais d'un autre côté, tu aurais une plus grande satisfaction professionnelle

f) ***either** et **neither***

i) **Either** a souvent le sens de "l'un ou l'autre" en parlant de deux choses (on utilisera **any** s'il y en a plus de deux). Il peut être adjectif ou pronom :

'bike' or 'bicycle': either (word) will do
"vélo" ou "bicyclette" : l'un ou l'autre ira

either parent can look after the children
l'un ou l'autre des parents peut s'occuper des enfants

Either peut aussi vouloir dire "chaque" ou "les deux", et dans ce cas, c'est un adjectif :

he was sitting in a taxi with a girl on either side
il était assis dans un taxi, une fille de chaque côté

ii) **Neither** est la forme négative de **either** :

he's in love with both Tracy and Cheryl, but neither of them fancies him
il est amoureux de Tracy et de Chéryl, mais il ne plaît à aucune des deux

neither kidney is functioning properly
aucun des reins ne fonctionne correctement

iii) **Either** et **neither** prennent souvent un verbe au pluriel, s'ils sont suivis de **of** et d'un nom au pluriel :

(n)either of the boys are likely to have done it

bien qu'on emploie un verbe au singulier dans un langage soutenu :

neither of the boys is likely to have done it
ni l'un ni l'autre des garçons n'a pu faire cela

either of the boys is likely to have done it
l'un ou l'autre des garçons a pu faire cela

iv) **(N)either** adverbe :

Either adverbe n'est utilisé que dans des propositions négatives. Il correspond à **too** dans les propositions affirmatives :

I can't do it either
je ne peux pas le faire non plus (comparez avec **I can do it too**)

Neither adverbe (= **nor**) est utilisé dans une proposition **qui suit** une proposition négative :

I can't swim and neither can she
je ne sais pas nager, et elle non plus

I can't swim – neither can I
je ne sais pas nager – moi non plus

ou dans un style familier :

I can't swim – me neither
je ne sais pas nager – moi non plus

Voir aussi **Les Conjonctions**, p A68.

g) ***Both***

Both fait référence à deux choses ou à deux personnes, mais dans le sens de "l'un et l'autre". Comme pour **all**, l'article défini ou le pronom personnel (éventuel) suit **both**, qui peut être un pronom ou un adjectif :

I like both (those/of those) jackets
j'aime ces deux vestes ; j'aime l'une et l'autre de ces vestes

we love both our parents
nous aimons l'un et l'autre de nos parents

I love both (of them)/them both
je les aime tous les deux

both (the/of the) versions are correct
l'une et l'autre de ces versions sont correctes

h) ***One***

i) Ce pronom est employé dans le sens de "une seule chose/personne" en référence à ce qui a été évoqué dans une phrase ou une proposition précédente :

do you like dogs? I bet you haven't ever owned one
vous aimez les chiens ? je suis sûr que vous n'en avez jamais eu un

we've a lot of records of Elvis – we have only one
nous avons beaucoup de disques d'Elvis – nous n'en avons qu'un

his case is a sad one
son cas est triste

this solution is one of considerable ingenuity
cette solution est d'une intelligence remarquable

Il peut aussi être employé au pluriel (**ones**) :

I like silk blouses, especially black ones
j'aime bien les chemisiers de soie, surtout ceux qui sont noirs

ii) L'emploi restrictif :

which girl do you prefer? – the tall one
quelle fille préférez-vous ? – la grande

I prefer the pen you gave me to the one my aunt gave me
je préfère le stylo que vous m'avez donné à celui que ma tante m'a donné

these are the ones I meant
ce sont celles dont je parlais

these burgers are better than the ones you make
ces hamburgers sont meilleurs que ceux que tu fais

iii) **One(s)** est habituellement employé après des adjectifs qui font référence à des noms dénombrables :

I asked for a large whisky and he gave me a small one
je lui ai demandé un grand whisky, et il m'en a donné un petit

which shoes do you want? the grey ones?
quelles chaussures voulez-vous ? les grises ?

Cependant, si deux adjectifs en contraste sont placés près l'un de l'autre, on peut parfois se dispenser d'utiliser **one(s)** :

I like all women, both (the) tall and (the) short
j'aime toutes les femmes, les grandes et les petites

she stood by him in good times and bad
elle fut à ses côtés pour le meilleur et pour le pire

today I wish to talk about two kinds of climate, the temperate and the tropical
aujourd'hui je vous parlerai de deux sortes de climats, le tempéré et le tropical

Si aucun nom n'a été mentionné ou évoqué, l'adjectif fonctionne comme un nom, et **one(s)** n'est pas employé :

the survival of the fittest
la persistance du plus apte

fortune favours the brave
la chance sourit aux braves

Il est évident que **one** ne peut pas référer à un nom indénombrable :

do you want white sugar or brown?
voulez-vous du sucre blanc ou du brun ?

iv) **One** est parfois employé dans un sens proche de "quelqu'un" ou "une personne", comme dans :

she screamed her head off like one possessed
elle hurlait comme une (femme) possédée

I'm not one for big parties
je ne suis pas quelqu'un qui aime les grandes soirées

I'm not one to complain
je ne suis pas du genre à me plaindre

v) **One** collectif, voir p A28.

13. LES VERBES

A. LES DIFFERENTS TYPES

On peut distinguer trois types de verbes : les verbes réguliers, irréguliers et les auxiliaires.

1. LES VERBES REGULIERS

Ces verbes forment leur prétérit et leur participe passé en ajoutant **-(e)d** au radical du verbe :

		prétérit	*participe passé*
seem	(sembler)	**seemed**	**seemed** /d/
kiss	(embrasser)	**kissed**	**kissed** /t/
plant	(planter)	**planted**	**planted** /ɪd/
manage	(diriger)	**managed**	**managed** /d/

Voir p A74 pour les changements d'orthographe.

2. LES VERBES IRREGULIERS

Les verbes irréguliers se caractérisent par leurs formes particulières au prétérit et au participe passé, qui font apparaître parfois un changement de voyelle :

(parler)	**speak, spoke, spoken**
(voir)	**see, saw, seen**
(aller)	**go, went, gone**
(gâter)	**spoil, spoilt, spoilt**
(couper)	**cut, cut, cut**

Vous trouverez une liste des verbes irréguliers p A61.

3. LES AUXILIAIRES

Un auxiliaire modifie le verbe principal dans la phrase. Dans **he can sing** (il peut chanter) l'auxiliaire est **can** et le verbe principal est **sing**. On fait la distinction entre les auxiliaires "ordinaires" et les auxiliaires modaux (ou défectifs).

a) *Les auxiliaires ordinaires*

Ce sont :

be (être), **have** (avoir) et **do** (faire).

Voir aussi sections 9, 17 et 23.

On les appelle "ordinaires" parce qu'ils peuvent parfois avoir fonction de verbe ordinaire :

he does not sing (does = auxiliaire, **sing** = verbe principal) il ne chante pas

he does the washing up (does = verbe principal) il lave la vaisselle

b) Les **auxiliaires modaux** sont appelés ainsi car ils remplacent le mode du subjonctif dans de nombreux cas (voir p A51-2). En voici la liste :

can – could	pouvoir (capacité)
may – might	pouvoir (possibilité – permission)
shall – should	futur – devoir (moral), conseil, etc.
will – would	futur – conditionnel, ordre, etc.
must	devoir (obligation)
ought to	devoir (moral)

Lorsqu'ils ne sont pas accompagnés d'un verbe ordinaire, ce dernier est sous-entendu :

can you get some time off? – yes, I can
est-ce que tu peux te libérer ? – oui

Vous trouverez l'emploi des auxiliaires p A55.

B. LES FORMES

1. L'INFINITIF

On distingue l'infinitif complet (avec **to** : **to be**) et l'infinitif sans **to** :

he can sing
il sait chanter

he is trying to sing
il essaie de chanter

Dans ces deux phrases le mot **sing** est à l'infinitif. Pour l'infinitif passé et la voix passive, voir p A40.

2. LE PARTICIPE PRESENT

Il se forme à partir du radical + **-ing** :

they were whispering
ils murmuraient

Voir **Notes sur l'Orthographe** p A74.

3. LE PARTICIPE PASSE

Le participe passé des verbes réguliers est identique à leur prétérit (radical du verbe + **-ed**) :

they have gone
ils/elles sont parti(e)s

Les verbes irréguliers ont un grand nombre de formes différentes au participe passé. Voir A2 ci-dessus, ainsi que la liste des verbes irréguliers p A61.

4. LE GERONDIF

Le gérondif a la même forme que le participe présent :

I don't like *picking* strawberries
je n'aime pas cueillir les fraises

***sailing* is a very popular sport in Greece**
la voile est un sport très populaire en Grèce

5. LE PRESENT

Il se construit avec le radical + **-(e)s** à la 3ème personne du singulier (pour les changements d'orthographe, voir p A74) :

	singulier		
1ère	*I*	**sing**	je chante
2ème	*you*	**sing**	tu chantes
3ème	*he/she/it*	**sings**	il/elle chante
	pluriel		
1ère	*we*	**sing**	nous chantons
2ème	*you*	**sing**	vous chantez
3ème	*they*	**sing**	ils/elles chantent

Les auxiliaires modaux ne changent pas de forme à la troisième personne du singulier. Il en est de même pour les verbes **dare** et **need** lorsqu'ils sont employés comme auxiliaires :

he may come	**how dare he come here!**
il se peut qu'il vienne	comment ose-t-il venir ici ?!

Les auxiliaires ordinaires ont des formes irrégulières, voir la liste p A63.

6. LE PRETERIT

Le prétérit des verbes réguliers est identique à leur participe passé (radical du verbe + **-ed**) :

they kicked the ball
ils ont donné un coup de pied dans le ballon

Pour les verbes irréguliers et les auxiliaires, voir A2 et 3 ci-dessus, ainsi que la liste des verbes irréguliers et des auxiliaires de la page A61 à la page A63. La forme du verbe est la même à toutes les personnes :

		régulier (embrasser)	*irrégulier* (chanter)	*auxiliaire* (pouvoir)
	singulier			
1ère	*I*	**kissed**	**sang**	**could**
2ème	*you*	**kissed**	**sang**	**could**
3ème	*he/she/it*	**kissed**	**sang**	**could**
	pluriel			
1ère	*we*	**kissed**	**sang**	**could**
2ème	*you*	**kissed**	**sang**	**could**
3ème	*they*	**kissed**	**sang**	**could**

7. LES TEMPS ET LES ASPECTS

L'infinitif, le présent et le passé peuvent avoir différents aspects, considérant un événement dans le temps de trois manières différentes.

Dans la liste ci-dessous les traductions sont données A TITRE INDICATIF.

simple, progressif et perfect (ou passé) :

infinitif	**(to) watch** (regarder)
infinitif progressif	**(to) be watching** (être en train de regarder) (**be** + participe présent)
infinitif passé	**(to) have watched** (avoir regardé) (**have** + participe passé)
infinitif passé progressif	**(to) have been watching** (avoir été en train de regarder)
présent simple	**(I/you/he,** etc.**) watch(es)** (je/tu/il, etc.) regarde(s)
passé simple (ou prétérit)	" **watched** (regardai, etc.)
présent progressif	" **am/are/is watching** (" suis/es/est en train de regarder)
passé progressif	" **was/were watching** (j'étais, etc. en train de regarder)
present perfect	" **have/has watched** (j'ai regardé, etc.)
past perfect	" **had watched** (j'avais regardé, etc.)
present perfect progressif	" **have/has been watching** (j'ai, etc. été en train de regarder)
past perfect progressif	" **had been watching** (j'avais, etc. été en train de regarder)

Pour les formes employées au futur, voir p A49.

8. LES MODES

Les modes font référence à l'attitude d'une personne par rapport aux propos qu'elle rapporte. Il existe trois modes :

. "l'indicatif" pour exprimer des faits réels

le "subjonctif" pour exprimer un souhait, une incertitude ou une possibilité, etc.

"l'impératif" pour exprimer des ordres et des suggestions.

La seule différence de forme entre l'indicatif et le subjonctif réside dans la présence de **-(e)s** à la 3ème personne du singulier au présent de l'indicatif :

God save the Queen! Vive la reine !

Le subjonctif de **to be** est **be** à toutes les personnes du présent et **were** à toutes les personnes du passé :

be they for or against, they all have to pay
qu'ils soient pour ou qu'ils soient contre, ils doivent tous payer

if I were you, I'd leave him
si j'étais toi, je le quitterais

Pour le mode impératif on emploie le radical du verbe seul :

ring the bell!	**somebody go and get it!**
sonne (la cloche) !	que quelqu'un aille le chercher

9. LES VOIX

Les deux "voix" sont la voix active et la voix passive. Elles indiquent si c'est le sujet d'un verbe qui fait l'action de ce verbe :

we always listen to him
nous l'écoutons toujours (voix active)

ou si le sujet subit l'action :

he was always listened to
il a toujours été écouté (voix passive)

Le passif se forme avec le verbe **be** + participe passé :

infinitif	**(to) be watched** (être regardé)
infinitif passé	**(to) have been watched** (avoir été regardé)
présent simple	**are/is watched** (es/est, etc. regardé)
passé simple (ou prétérit)	**was/were watched** (j'étais, etc. regardé)
présent progressif	**am/are/is being watched** (suis/es/est, etc. en train d'être regardé)
passé progressif	**was/were being watched** (j'étais, etc. en train d'être regardé)
present perfect	**have/has been watched** (a/ont, etc. été regardé)
past perfect	**had been watched** (j'avais, etc. été regardé)
present perfect progressif	**have/has been being watched** (j'ai, etc. été en train d'être regardé)
past perfect progressif	**had been being watched** (j'avais, etc. été en train d'être regardé)

Le passif de l'infinitif progressif (par exemple **to be being driven**) est assez inhabituel en anglais (bien que parfaitement possible) :

I wouldn't like to be being filmed looking like this
je ne voudrais pas être filmé dans cet état

Il en est de même pour le passif du present perfect progressif :

he may have been being operated on by then
il se peut qu'on l'ait opéré à ce moment-là

C. EMPLOIS

1. L'INFINITIF

a) *Sans to*

i) après les auxiliaires modaux et **do** :

I must go il faut que je m'en aille
I don't know je ne sais pas

ii) après **dare** et **need** lorsqu'ils sont employés comme auxiliaires :

how dare you talk to me like that!
comment oses-tu me parler ainsi !

you needn't talk to me like that
tu n'as pas besoin de me parler comme ça

iii) après **had better** et **had best** (aussi **would best** en anglais américain) :

you had better apologize
tu ferais mieux de t'excuser

you had (you'd) best ask the porter
tu ferais mieux de demander au portier

iv) avec ce que l'on appelle la construction "accusatif avec infinitif" (nom/pronom + infinitif ayant fonction de complément d'objet direct). Comparez avec b)ii ci-dessous :

★ après **let** (laisser), **make** (faire) et **have** (faire *dans ce cas*) (voir aussi p A55) :

we let him smoke
nous l'avons laissé fumer

I made him turn round
je l'ai fait tourner

we had him say a few words
nous lui avons fait dire quelques mots

★ après les verbes de perception suivants :

feel (sentir), **hear** (entendre), **see** (voir), **watch** (regarder) :

I felt the woman touch my back
j'ai senti la femme me toucher le dos

we heard her tell the porter
on l'a entendu le dire au portier

they saw him die
ils l'ont vu mourir

we watched the train approach the platform
on a regardé le train s'approcher du quai

Pour **feel** (sembler à quelqu'un), voir b) ii ci-dessous.

Ces verbes peuvent aussi être suivis du participe présent pour mettre l'accent sur la durée de l'action :

I felt her creeping up behind me
je sentais qu'elle s'approchait sans bruit derrière moi

we heard her crying bitterly in the next room
nous l'avons entendue pleurer amèrement dans l'autre pièce

she saw smoke coming from the house
elle a vu de la fumée venir de la maison

they watched him slowly dying
ils l'ont vu mourir petit à petit

★ on peut trouver deux formes de l'infinitif après **help** :

we helped him (to) move house
nous l'avons aidé à déménager

L'infinitif sans **to** est aussi particulièrement employé dans le langage publicitaire :

our soap helps keep your skin supple and healthy-looking
notre savon aide à garder votre peau souple et vous donnera bonne mine

Pour les constructions passives correspondantes employées avec ces verbes, voir b) ii ci-dessous.

v) après **why (not)** (pourquoi (pas)) :

why stay indoors in this lovely weather?
pourquoi rester à l'intérieur par ce beau temps ?

why not try our cream cakes?
pourquoi ne pas essayer nos gâteaux à la crème ?

b) *Avec to*

i) L'infinitif avec **to** peut s'employer comme sujet, attribut ou complément d'objet direct dans une phrase. La phrase suivante contient les trois emplois (dans cet ordre) :

to die is to cease to exist
mourir est cesser d'exister

ii) Comme complément d'objet direct, comparez a) iv ci-dessus.

★ Après des verbes exprimant un désir ou une antipathie, en particulier **want** (vouloir), **wish** (souhaiter), **like** (aimer), **prefer** (préférer), **hate** (ne pas aimer/haïr) :

I want/wish you to remember this
je veux/souhaite que tu te souviennes de cela

John would like you to leave
John aimerait que vous partiez

we prefer your cousin to stay here
nous préférons que votre cousin reste ici

we would hate our cat to suffer
nous n'aimerions pas que notre chat souffre

★ Dans un langage assez soutenu, après des verbes exprimant des points de vue, des croyances, un jugement, une supposition ou une affirmation :

we believe this to be a mistake
nous pensons que c'est une erreur

we supposed him to be dead
nous supposions qu'il était mort

we considered/judged it to be of little use
nous considérions/jugions cela peu utile

I felt/knew it to be true
je pensais/savais que cela était vrai

these accusations he maintained to be false
il soutenait que ces accusations étaient fausses

Un langage moins soutenu préférerait une proposition introduite par **that** :

we believe (that) this is a mistake
nous croyons que c'est une erreur

I know (that) it's true
je sais que c'est vrai

he maintained that these accusations were false
il a soutenu que ces accusations étaient fausses

★ Dans la construction passive correspondante, on garde **to** :

this was believed to be a mistake
on pensait que c'était une erreur

★ Remarquez l'expression courante **be said to**, pour laquelle il n'existe pas d'équivalent à la voix active en anglais :

it is said to be true
il paraît que c'est vrai

he's said to be rich
on dit qu'il est riche

★ La forme **to** + infinitif doit aussi être employée dans des constructions passives avec les verbes mentionnés dans a) iv ci-dessus :

she was made to do it
on l'a forcée à le faire

he was seen to remove both jacket and tie
on l'a vu enlever sa veste et sa cravate

iii) Employé à la suite de noms, de pronoms et d'adjectifs :

she has always had a tendency to become hysterical
elle a toujours eu tendance à avoir des crises d'hystérie

we shall remember this in days to come
on se rappellera de cela dans les jours à venir

there are things to be done
il y a des choses à faire

there is that to take into consideration
il y a ça à prendre en considération

glad to meet you!
heureux de faire votre connaissance !

we were afraid to ask
nous avions peur de demander

this game is easy to understand
ce jeu est facile à comprendre

De telles constructions sont particulièrement courantes après des superlatifs et après **only** :

this is the latest book to appear on the subject
c'est le livre le plus récent qui soit paru sur le sujet

she's the only person to have got near him
elle est la seule personne à avoir pu l'approcher

iv) Correspondant à une proposition subordonnée :

★ Exprimant un but ou une conséquence (parfois accompagnés de **in order** ou **so as** (but) ou **only** (conséquence) pour souligner ses propos) :

he left early (in order/so as) to get a good seat for the performance
il est parti tôt pour (afin d') avoir une bonne place au spectacle

they arrived (only) to find an empty house
ils sont arrivés pour trouver une maison vide

try to be there
essaie d'être là

Remarquez qu'en anglais parlé, on peut remplacer **to** après **try** par **and** :

try and be there

★ dans des propositions interrogatives indirectes :

tell me what to do
dis-moi quoi faire

I didn't know where to look
je ne savais pas où regarder

we didn't know who to ask
nous ne savions pas à qui demander

we weren't sure whether to tell him or not
nous ne savions pas si nous devions lui dire ou non

★ Pour exprimer le temps ou la circonstance :

I shudder to think of it
j'en tremble (rien que) d'y penser

to hear him speak, one would think he positively hates women
à l'entendre parler on penserait qu'il déteste les femmes

v) Equivalent d'une principale, dans des exclamations exprimant la surprise :

to think she married him!
dire qu'elle l'a épousé !

vi) Dans des phrases elliptiques exprimant des événements à venir. On les trouve particulièrement dans le langage journalistique :

MAGGIE TO MAKE GREEN SPEECH
MAGGIE FERA UN DISCOURS VERT

GORBACHEV TO VISIT DISASTER ZONE
GORBACHEV VISITERA LA ZONE SINISTREE

vii) On peut aussi trouver l'infinitif avec césure, où un adverbe est placé entre **to** et le radical du verbe. Cette forme est devenue très courante, mais peu appréciée de beaucoup, qui soutiennent qu'il ne faut jamais séparer **to** de l'infinitif :

nobody will ever be able to fully comprehend his philosophy
personne ne sera jamais capable de comprendre complètement sa philosophie

Cela peut cependant être la place que l'on choisirait instinctivement pour un adverbe :

the way out of this is to really try and persuade him
le moyen de s'en sortir c'est de vraiment essayer de le persuader

Ici **really** signifie "beaucoup" et il modifie **try**, tandis que dans la phrase suivante, **really** signifie "en fait", et modifie ainsi toute la phrase :

the way out of this is really to try and persuade him
le moyen de s'en sortir c'est en fait d'essayer de le persuader

viii) On emploie souvent **to** sans le radical du verbe dans une répétition plutôt que l'infinitif complet :

why haven't you tidied your room? I told you to
pourquoi n'as-tu pas rangé ta chambre ? je t'ai dit de le faire

I did it because she encouraged me to
je l'ai fait parce qu'elle m'y a encouragé

ix) **For** + nom/pronom et l'infinitif avec **to** :

there has always been a tendency for our language to absorb foreign words
notre langue a toujours eu tendance à absorber des mots étrangers

he waited for her to finish
il attendit qu'elle ait fini

La construction idiomatique qui suit exprime souvent une condition ou un but :

for the university to function properly, more money is needed
afin que l'université fonctionne bien il faut plus d'argent

ou elle peut exprimer une circonstance et même être le sujet de la phrase :

for me to say nothing would be admitting defeat
ne rien dire serait admettre ma défaite

for a man to get custody of his children used to be difficult
c'était difficile à l'époque pour un homme d'obtenir la garde de ses enfants

2. LE GERONDIF

Le gérondif (ou le verbe substantivé) possède des caractéristiques propres aux noms et aux verbes.

a) *Caractéristiques nominales*

i) Un gérondif peut être sujet, attribut ou complément d'objet :

skating is difficult (sujet)
le patin à glace, c'est difficile

that's cheating (attribut)
c'est de la triche

I hate fishing (complément)
je déteste pêcher

Comme on l'a vu, ce sont des fonctions qui sont communes à l'infinitif ; pour les différences d'emploi, voir 4 ci-dessous.

ii) Il peut être placé après une préposition :

he's thought of leaving
il a pensé partir

L'infinitif ne peut pas occuper cette place.

iii) Il peut être modifié par un article, un adjectif ou un possessif, ou par une proposition commençant par **of** :

he has always recommended the reading of good literature
il a toujours recommandé la lecture des bons livres

there was a knock on the door
on frappa à la porte

careless writing leaves a bad impression
une écriture peu soignée donne une mauvaise impression

the soprano's singing left us unmoved
le chant du soprano nous a laissé totalement froid

there was no end to his trying to be difficult
il se faisait un malin plaisir à créer des problèmes

the timing of his remarks was unfortunate
il a mal choisi son moment pour faire des remarques

b) *Caractéristiques verbales*

i) Un gérondif peut être suivi d'un complément d'objet ou d'un attribut :

hitting the dog was unavoidable
il était inévitable de rentrer dans le chien

becoming an expert took him more than twenty years
il lui a fallu plus de vingt ans pour devenir expert en la matière

ii) Il peut être modifié par un adverbe :

she was afraid of totally disillusioning him
elle avait peur de lui enlever toute illusion

iii) Il peut avoir un sujet :

the idea of John going to see her is absurd
l'idée de John allant la voir est absurde

3. LE POSSESSIF ET LE GERONDIF

Il existe souvent une incertitude concernant la présence ou l'absence d'un adjectif possessif :

do you remember him/his trying to persuade her?
tu te souviens qu'il a essayé de la persuader ?

Les deux formes sont correctes. Mais cela ne signifie pas qu'il n'existe pas parfois des différences d'emploi entre les deux. Il faut noter les exemples suivants :

a) *Le gérondif sujet ou attribut*

Dans ce cas, l'emploi du possessif est normal :

your trying to persuade me will get you nowhere
tes tentatives de me persuader ne te mèneront nulle part

it was John's insisting we went there that saved the situation
c'est grâce à l'insistance de John qui voulait que nous y allions que la situation fut sauvée

b) *Le gérondif complément ou placé après une préposition*

Dans ces cas, les deux emplois sont possibles :

they spoke at great length about him/his being elected president
ils parlèrent longtemps de son élection comme président

you don't mind me/my turning up so late, do you?
ça ne te dérange pas que j'arrive si tard, n'est-ce pas ?

they spoke at great length about Richard/Richard's being elected president
ils parlèrent longtemps de l'élection de Richard comme président

Mais il y a des cas où l'emploi du possessif présenterait un problème de style dans un langage parlé ou familier :

they laughed their heads off at him falling into the river
ils riaient à n'en plus pouvoir parce qu'il était tombé dans la rivière

L'emploi de l'adjectif possessif **his** serait ici d'un langage trop soutenu dans cet exemple.

Dans ces constructions, le gérondif ne doit pas être confondu avec le participe présent. La phrase :

I hate people trying to get in without paying
je déteste les gens qui essaient d'entrer sans payer

est ambiguë. Si **trying** est un gérondif, le sens de la phrase est : **I hate the fact that (some) people try to get in without paying** (je déteste le fait que certaines personnes essaient d'entrer sans payer). Si c'est un participe présent, le sens devient : **I hate people who try to get in without paying** (je déteste les gens qui essaient d'entrer sans payer).

Mais la forme en **-ing** est, bien sûr, très clairement un gérondif dans une phrase comme :

I hate their trying to get in without paying
je déteste qu'ils essaient d'entrer sans payer

On a plus tendance à employer le possessif devant le gérondif en anglais américain qu'en anglais britannique.

c) *Le facteur d'emphase*

Si le sujet du gérondif est particulièrement accentué, le possessif a moins de chance d'être employé :

just to think of HER marrying John!
t'imagine ? ELLE épousant John !

4. COMPARAISON ENTRE LE GERONDIF ET L'INFINITIF

a) *Peu ou pas de différence*

On a vu que l'infinitif et le gérondif ont des caractéristiques nominales du fait que l'un et l'autre peuvent fonctionner comme sujet, complément d'objet ou attribut. Il y a souvent peu ou pas de différence de sens entre eux :

we can't bear seeing you like this
we can't bear to see you like this
nous ne pouvons pas supporter de vous voir comme ça

bien que dans les dictons ou les citations, les expressions soient "figées", comme dans les exemples suivants :

seeing is believing
voir c'est croire

to err is human, to forgive divine
l'erreur est humaine, le pardon est divin

b) *Différents sens*

i) Le général contre le particulier : le gérondif indique souvent un fait général, l'infinitif indique un fait plus particulier :

I hate refusing offers like that (général)
je déteste refuser des offres comme ça

I hate to refuse an offer like that (particulier)
je déteste refuser une offre comme celle-ci

Mais il existe des exceptions :

I prefer being called by my Christian name
I prefer to be called by my Christian name
je préfère être appelé par mon prénom

En anglais américain, l'infinitif est souvent utilisé dans des cas où en anglais britannique on emploierait un gérondif :

I like cooking (anglais britannique)
I like to cook (anglais américain)
j'aime faire la cuisine

Ces deux exemples font référence à un penchant général. Si on voulait faire référence à une occasion particulière, on dirait en anglais britannique et en anglais américain :

I'd like to cook something for you
je voudrais vous préparer un repas

ii) Si le verbe **try** signifie "tenter, essayer", on peut employer l'infinitif ou le gérondif :

I once tried to make a film, but I couldn't
I once tried making a film, but I couldn't
j'ai essayé de faire un film une fois, mais je n'ai pas réussi

try to speak more slowly
try speaking more slowly
essaie de parler plus lentement

Mais si **try** est employé avec le sens de "connaître par l'expérience", alors seul le gérondif est employé :

I've never tried eating shark
je n'ai jamais mangé du requin

Comparez avec ceci :

I once tried to eat shark, but couldn't
j'ai essayé de manger du requin une fois, mais je n'ai pas pu

iii) Après **forget** (oublier) et **remember** (se souvenir) l'infinitif fait référence au futur, le gérondif au passé, en relation avec "l'oubli" ou "le souvenir" :

I won't forget to dance with her (dans le futur)
je n'oublierai pas de danser avec elle

I won't forget dancing with her (dans le passé)
je n'oublierai pas que j'ai dansé avec elle

will she remember to meet me? (dans le futur)
se souviendra-t-elle de son rendez-vous avec moi ?

will she remember meeting me? (dans le passé)
se souviendra-t-elle d'avoir fait ma connaissance ?

c) *L'infinitif seulement ou le gérondif seulement*

i) L'infinitif seulement :

Certains verbes ne peuvent être suivis que de l'infinitif, par exemple **want** (vouloir), **wish** (souhaiter), **hope** (espérer), **deserve** (mériter) :

I want/wish to leave
je veux/souhaite partir

we hope to be back by five
nous espérons être de retour vers cinq heures

he deserves to be punished
il mérite d'être puni

ii) Le gérondif seulement

D'autres verbes ne sont suivis que du gérondif, par exemple : **avoid** (éviter), **consider** (considérer), **dislike** (ne pas aimer), **enjoy** (apprécier), **finish** (finir), **keep** (continuer), **practise** (faire, pratiquer), **risk** (risquer) :

he avoided answering my questions
il évitait de répondre à mes questions

won't you consider travelling by air?
ne veux-tu pas envisager de voyager par avion ?

I dislike dressing up for the theatre
je n'aime pas m'habiller pour aller au théâtre

we enjoy having friends round to dinner
nous apprécions de recevoir des amis pour le dîner

she finished typing her letter
elle a fini de taper sa lettre

why do you keep reminding me?
pourquoi continues-tu à me le rappeler ?

would you mind stepping this way, Sir?
voulez-vous bien venir par ici, Monsieur ?

you must practise playing the piano more often
tu dois travailler ton piano plus souvent

I don't want to risk upsetting Jennifer
je ne veux pas risquer d'inquiéter Jennifer

iii) Dans les exemples des deux sections ci-dessus, l'infinitif et le gérondif sont les compléments d'objet direct des verbes précédents. Il en est de même pour le gérondif dans la phrase suivante :

I stopped looking at her
je me suis arrêté de la regarder

Mais l'infinitif n'est pas complément d'objet direct dans :

I stopped to look at her
je me suis arrêté pour la regarder

Ici, l'infinitif fonctionne comme un complément circonstanciel de but, ce qui explique la différence considérable de sens entre les deux phrases. La différence est de la même importance entre :

he was too busy talking to her
il était trop occupé à lui parler

et :

he was too busy to talk to her
il était trop occupé pour lui parler

Il faut noter ici que les adjectifs **worth** et **like** ne peuvent être suivis que par le gérondif :

that suggestion is worth considering
cette proposition vaut la peine d'être considérée

that's just like wishing for the moon
c'est comme demander la lune

iv) Il est aussi important de faire la distinction entre **to** marque de l'infinitif et **to** préposition. Le gérondif doit suivre une préposition, comme dans :

I'm tired of watching television
j'en ai assez de regarder la télévision

what do you think about getting a loan?
qu'est-ce que tu dirais de faire un emprunt ?

Ceci, bien sûr, concerne aussi la préposition **to** :

they are committed to implementing the plan
ils se sont engagés à réaliser le projet

we're looking forward to receiving your letter
nous attendons votre lettre avec impatience

I object to raising money for that purpose
je désapprouve qu'on rassemble des fonds pour ce but

we're not used to getting up at this hour
nous ne sommes pas habitués à nous lever à cette heure

Be accustomed to est parfois employé avec l'infinitif, bien qu'on le trouve aussi avec le gérondif :

they've never been accustomed to pay(ing) for anything
ils n'ont jamais eu l'habitude de payer pour quoi que ce soit

5. LE PARTICIPE PRESENT

Le participe présent fonctionne normalement comme une forme verbale ou comme un adjectif.

a) *Comme une forme verbale*

i) Le participe présent est employé avec **be** pour former le progressif :

he is/was/has been/had been running
il court/courait/a couru/avait couru

ii) Le participe présent fonctionne fréquemment comme une proposition relative sans pronom relatif :

they went up to the people coming from the theatre (= who were coming)
ils allèrent vers les gens qui venaient du théâtre

iii) Cependant, le participe présent peut partager son sujet avec le verbe au présent ou au passé. A l'écrit, un lien plus lâche est souvent indiqué par une virgule, à l'oral, par une intonation :

she turns/turned towards the man, looking shy and afraid
elle se tourne/tourna vers l'homme, timide et effrayée

Ici, le sujet de **looking** est **she** ; mais si on omet la virgule, on comprendra que le sujet de **looking** est **the man**, et la phrase appartient alors au type ii) ci-dessus.

Ce participe présent relativement lâche peut précéder son sujet :

looking shy and afraid, she turned towards the man
timide et effrayée, elle se tourna vers l'homme

Il exprime souvent une cause, une condition ou le temps, étant équivalent à une proposition subordonnée :

living alone, she often feels uneasy at night (= because/since/as she lives alone ...)
vivant seule, elle se sent souvent inquiète le soir

you'd get more out of life, living alone (= ... if you lived alone)
tu profiterais plus de la vie, si tu vivais seule

driving along, I suddenly passed a field of tulips (= as/while I was driving along ...)
en conduisant, je suis passé tout à coup devant un champ de tulipes

Mais parfois aussi il est équivalent à une proposition indépendante :

she went up to him, asking for his advice (= ... and (she) asked for his advice)
elle s'approcha, pour lui demander conseil

living in the Scottish Highlands, he is a sensitive musician who helped organize the Bath Orchestra (= he lives in the Highlands and (he) is ...)
vivant dans les Highlands en Ecosse, c'est un musicien sensible qui contribua à l'organisation de l'Orchestre de Bath

iv) Le participe présent "non-rattaché" :

Un participe présent est considéré comme "non-rattaché" si son sujet est différent de celui du verbe de la principale au présent ou au passé :

coming down the staircase carrying an umbrella, one of the mice tripped him up
descendant les escaliers et portant un parapluie, une des souris le fit trébucher

Il est assez peu probable que le sujet de **coming** soit **one of the mice** ! Les participes présents "non-rattachés" doivent normalement être évités car ils causent souvent un amusement non intentionnel. Cependant, si un sujet indéfini est sous-entendu comme le **we** indéfini ou le "on" français, alors un participe présent est acceptable :

generally speaking, British cooking leaves a good deal to be desired
d'une manière générale, la cuisine britannique laisse à désirer

judging by the way she dresses, she must have a lot of confidence
à voir sa façon de s'habiller, elle doit avoir une grande confiance en elle

the work will have to be postponed, seeing that only two of us have tools
le travail devra être remis à plus tard, puisque seulement deux d'entre nous ont des outils

v) Dans les autres circonstances, pour éviter un participe présent "non-rattaché", le sujet du participe (différent du sujet de l'autre verbe) peut le précéder dans ce qu'on appelle la "construction absolue" :

the lift being out of order, we had to use the stairs
l'ascenseur étant en panne, nous avons dû monter par les escaliers

she being the hostess, any kind of criticism was out of the question
elle étant l'hôtesse, il était hors de question de faire quelque critique que ce soit

we'll do it on Sunday, weather permitting
nous le ferons dimanche, si le temps le permet

God willing, we can do it
si Dieu le veut, nous pouvons le faire

b) *Comme un adjectif*

she has always been a loving child
elle a toujours été une enfant aimante

her appearance is striking
son allure est frappante

she finds Henry very charming
elle trouve Henry vraiment charmant

De cette fonction dérive la fonction adverbiale :

he is strikingly handsome
il est remarquablement beau

Remarquez que cette structure est bien plus courante en anglais qu'en français :

a self-adjusting mechanism
un mécanisme à auto-réglage

the falling birthrate
le taux de natalité en baisse

increasing sales
des ventes en hausse

6. COMPARAISON DU PARTICIPE PRESENT ET DU GERONDIF

a) *La phrase suivante* :

I can't get used to that man avoiding my eyes all the time

est ambiguë, car **avoiding** peut être compris comme un gérondif ou un participe présent.

Si c'est un gérondif, la phrase équivaut à **I can't get used to the fact that that man is avoiding my eyes** (je ne peux pas m'habituer au fait que cet homme fuit mon regard).

Mais si c'est un participe présent, le sens est **I can't get used to that man who is avoiding my eyes** (je ne peux pas m'habituer à cet homme qui fuit mon regard).

Dans la phrase suivante, il ne fait aucun doute que la forme en **-ing** est un gérondif :

children suffering like that is on our conscience (= the suffering of children)
la souffrance des enfants pèse sur notre conscience

et il n'y a pas de d'ambiguité sur le participe présent dans :

children suffering like that are on our conscience (= children who suffer)
les enfants qui souffrent comme cela pèsent sur notre conscience

b) Quand un gérondif modifie un nom, seul le gérondif est accentué dans le discours, et non pas le nom :

a living room un salon

mais quand l'élément modificateur est un participe présent, celui-ci et le nom sont accentués de la même manière :

a living animal un animal vivant

7. LE PARTICIPE PASSE

Beaucoup d'emplois suivants peuvent être comparés avec ceux du participe présent. Voir 5 ci-dessus.

a) *Comme forme verbale*

i) Le participe passé s'emploie avec **have** pour former le present perfect et le past perfect :

he has/had arrived
il est/était arrivé

et avec **be** pour former la voix passive :

she is/was admired
elle est/était admirée

et avec les deux auxiliaires pour former le passif au present perfect et au past perfect :

she has/had been admired
elle a/avait été admirée

ii) Le participe passé est fréquemment employé pour former une proposition relative elliptique :

they ignore the concerts given by the local orchestra (= which are given)
ils ne vont pas aux concerts donnés par l'orchestre local

they ignored the concerts given by the local orchestra (= which were/had been given)
ils ne sont pas allés aux concerts donnés par l'orchestre local

Il peut aussi avoir la fonction d'une subordonnée de cause, de condition ou de temps. Une conjonction (en particulier **si** et **quand**) peut parfois rendre son sens explicite :

watched over by her family, Monica felt safe but unhappy
surveillée par sa famille, Monica se sentait en sécurité, mais malheureuse

(if) treated with care, records should last for years and years
si l'on en prend soin, les disques devraient durer des années et des années

records should last for years and years if treated with care
les disques devraient durer des années et des années si l'on en prend soin

(when) asked why this was so, he refused to answer
quand on lui demanda pourquoi c'était comme ça, il refusa de répondre

he refused to answer when asked why this was so
il refusa de répondre lorsqu'on lui demanda pourquoi c'était ainsi

Ou il peut avoir valeur de principale :

born in Aberdeen, he now lives in Perth with his wife and children
né à Aberdeen, il habite maintenant à Perth avec sa femme et ses enfants

iii) La phrase est parfois déséquilibrée de manière inacceptable lorsque le participe passé n'est pas rattaché au sujet de la phrase :

told to cancel the meeting, his project was never discussed

On pourrait exprimer ceci de manière plus élégante :

his project was never discussed as he was told to cancel the meeting
son projet ne fut jamais examiné étant donné qu'on lui demanda d'annuler la réunion

iv) La "construction absolue" (voir 5a) v ci-dessus) :

the problems solved, they went their separate ways
les problèmes résolus, ils sont partis chacun de leur côté

that done, he left
une fois fait, il est parti

b) *Comme adjectif*

I am very tired je suis très fatigué(e)	**the defeated army retreated** l'armée vaincue battit en retraite

Remarquez que dans le premier exemple l'adverbe est **very**, puisqu'il se place devant un adjectif. Si l'adverbe est **much**, c'est que l'on insiste plus sur le caractère verbal du participe passé :

I am much obliged
je vous suis très obligé(e)

Lorsque **aged** (âgé), **beloved** (bien-aimé), **blessed** (sacré), **cursed** (maudit) et **learned** (érudit) sont des adjectifs, on prononce normalement **-ed** /ɪd/. Mais lorsque ce sont des verbes, on adopte la prononciation régulière /d/ et /t/ :

he has aged il a vieilli	**an aged man** /ɪd/ un homme âgé

8. LES QUESTIONS

a) *Phrases complètes*

i) **Do** s'emploie pour des questions à moins que (a) la phrase ne contienne un autre auxiliaire (**have, will,** etc.), auquel cas l'auxiliaire précède le sujet, ou que (b) le sujet est un pronom interrogatif. **Do** est au présent ou au passé, le verbe conjugué à l'infinitif :

do you come here often?
tu viens souvent ici ?

how do we get to Oxford Street from here?
comment on fait pour aller d'ici à Oxford Street ?

did you see that girl?
tu as vu cette fille ?

what did you say?
qu'est-ce que tu as dit ?

mais (quand d'autres auxiliaires sont employés) :

are they trying to speak to us?
est-ce qu'ils essaient de nous parler ?

where are you taking me?
où est-ce que tu m'emmènes ?

have they seen us?
est-ce qu'ils nous ont vu(e)s ?

can you come at eight?
tu peux venir à huit heures ?

will you help?
tu pourras nous aider ?

et quand on a un pronom interrogatif sujet :

who said that? qui a dit ça ?	**what happened?** qu'est-ce qui s'est passé ?

what have they said to you?
qu'est-ce qu'ils t'ont dit ?

what shall we write about?
sur quoi est-ce qu'on va écrire ?

Pour **dare** et **need**, voir p A59. Pour **have**, voir p A54.

ii) En anglais parlé, où l'on distingue une proposition interrogative d'une proposition affirmative par l'intonation, on peut employer l'ordre des mots d'une affirmative dans une interrogative (bien que ce soit un emploi moins fréquent en anglais qu'en français) :

you just left him standing there?
tu l'as laissé de planton là-bas ?

you're coming tonight?
tu viens ce soir ?

Dans des propositions interrogatives indirectes, on emploie normalement l'ordre des mots de la proposition affirmative directe :

when are you leaving? (style direct)
quand est-ce que tu pars ?

et :

he asked her when she was leaving (style indirect)
il lui a demandé quand elle partirait

b) *Les question-tags*

Ce sont des phrases courtes qui suivent une phrase affirmative ou négative, et qui normalement ont pour but d'ammener une confirmation.

i) Une proposition affirmative est suivie d'un tag à la forme négative et vice versa :

you can see it, can't you?
tu le vois, n'est-ce pas ?

you can't see it, can you?
est-ce que tu peux le voir ?

à moins que le tag n'exprime une attitude emphatique plutôt qu'une question. Dans de tels cas, un tag à la forme affirmative suit une proposition affirmative :

so you've seen a ghost, have you? (incrédulité ou ironie)
alors, tu as vu un fantôme ?

you think that's fair, do you? (ressentiment)
tu crois que c'est juste, hein ?

you've bought a new car, have you? (surprise ou intérêt)
alors, tu as acheté une nouvelle voiture ?

Remarquez que le question-tag reprend le temps employé dans la principale :

you want to meet him, don't you?
tu veux le rencontrer, n'est-ce pas ?

you wanted to meet him, didn't you?
tu voulais le rencontrer, n'est-ce pas ?

you'll want to meet him, won't you?
tu voudras le rencontrer, n'est-ce pas ?

ii) Si la proposition qui précède a un auxiliaire, il faut le répéter dans le tag :

you have seen it before, haven't you?
tu l'as déjà vu, n'est-ce pas ?

they aren't sold yet, are they?
ils ne sont quand même pas vendus ?

you will help me, won't you?
tu m'aideras, n'est-ce pas ?

you oughtn't to say that, ought you?
tu ne devrais pas dire ça, d'accord ?

Dans ce dernier cas, cependant, on pourrait aussi employer l'auxiliaire "did" dans le tag :

he oughtn't to have said that, did he?
il n'aurait pas dû dire ça, n'est-ce pas ?

L'emploi de "ought he" pourrait paraître assez ampoulé.

S'il n'y a pas d'auxiliaire dans la proposition précédente, on emploie normalement **do** dans le tag :

he sleeps in there, doesn't he?
il dort là, n'est-ce pas ?

your cousin arrived last night, didn't she?
ta cousine est arrivée hier soir, n'est-ce pas ?

à moins que le tag ne suive un impératif, auquel cas on emploie un auxiliaire à la forme affirmative (en particulier **will/would**). Ces tags permettent souvent de nuancer l'impératif :

leave the cat alone, will you?
laisse le chat tranquille, d'accord ?

take this to Mrs Brown, would you?
tu veux bien apporter ça à Mme Brown ?

Dans de tels cas la forme négative **won't** indique une invitation :

help yourselves to drinks, won't you?
servez-vous en boisson, je vous en prie

9. LES NEGATIONS

a) *La négation des formes conjuguées*

i) **Do** avec **not** s'emploie à moins que la proposition ne contienne un autre auxiliaire (**should**, **will**, etc.). En anglais courant à l'oral ou à l'écrit, il est normal de trouver la contraction de l'auxiliaire (**don't, won't, can't**, etc.) :

we do not/don't accept traveller's cheques
nous n'acceptons pas de chèques de voyage

mais (avec un autre auxiliaire) :

the matter should not/shouldn't be delayed
il ne faudrait pas retarder cette affaire

ii) Dans la question négative **not** suit le sujet, à moins qu'il ne soit contracté :

do they not accept traveller's cheques?
(mais : **don't they accept ...?**)
est-ce qu'ils n'accèptent pas les chèques de voyage ?

should you not try his office number?
(mais : **shouldn't you try ...?**)
tu ne devrais pas essayer son numéro au bureau ?

iii) Les verbes exprimant un point de vue **believe, suppose, think**, etc. sont normalement à la forme négative, même si la négation porte logiquement sur le verbe dans la proposition complément d'objet :

I don't believe we have met
je ne crois pas que nous nous soyons déjà rencontrés

I don't suppose you could lend me a fiver?
je suppose que tu ne pourrais pas me prêter un billet de 5 livres ?

I didn't think these papers were yours
je ne pensais pas que ces papiers étaient à toi

mais **hope** est plus logique :

I hope it won't give me a headache
j'espère que ça ne me donnera pas un mal de tête

et il n'est même pas accompagné de **do** lorsqu'il est employé seul :

is she ill? – I hope not
elle est malade ? – j'espère que non

De nombreuses formes sont possibles pour des réponses courtes avec **believe, suppose** et **think** :

will she marry him?
va-t-elle l'épouser ?

I don't believe/think so (couramment employé)
je ne crois pas/ne pense pas
I believe/think not (moins courant, plus soigné)
I don't suppose so (couramment employé)
I suppose not (couramment employé)

b) *La négation des infinitifs et des gérondifs*

On la forme en plaçant **not** devant l'infinitif ou le gérondif :

we tried not to upset her
nous avons essayé de ne pas la contrarier

I want you to think seriously about not going
je veux que tu songes sérieusement à ne pas partir

not eating enough vegetables is a common cause of ...
ne pas manger assez de légumes est une cause commune de ....

L'exemple avec l'infinitif ci-dessus a bien sûr un sens différent de :

we didn't try to upset her
nous n'avons pas essayé de la contrarier

où l'auxiliaire est à la forme négative.

Remarquez l'expression idiomatique **not to worry = don't worry** :

I won't manage to finish it by tomorrow – not to worry
je n'arriverai pas à terminer avant demain – ce n'est pas grave

En anglais de tous les jours, on peut intercaler **not** entre le **to** de l'infinitif et le verbe (**we tried to not upset her**), bien que cela soit considéré incorrect par beaucoup, voir p A41.

c) *La négation des impératifs*

i) Avec **do. Do not** a pour forme contractée **don't** :

don't worry ne t'inquiète pas
don't be silly ne sois pas bête

L'emploi de la forme complète **do not** est couramment employé dans des déclarations officielles, sur des modes d'emploi, des panneaux, etc. :

do not fill in this part of the form
ne pas remplir cette partie du formulaire

do not feed the animals
défense de nourrir les animaux

do not exceed the stated dose
ne pas dépasser la dose prescrite

La forme complète peut aussi s'employer pour rendre un impératif plus emphatique en anglais parlé :

I'll say it again – do not touch!
je le redis encore – ne touche pas !

Dans la forme de l'impératif **let's**, employée pour des suggestions, l'ordre des mots est le suivant :

don't let's wait any longer
n'attendons pas plus longtemps

ii) Il existe une autre manière d'exprimer la négation à l'impératif, en employant **not** seul après le verbe. Ceci est de l'anglais comme il est employé, par exemple, dans la Bible ou dans les œuvres de Shakespeare. Il peut aussi être employé pour produire un effet comique ou sarcastique :

worry not, I'll be back soon
ne t'inquiète pas, je reviendrai bientôt

fear not, the situation is under control
n'aie pas peur, je maîtrise la situation

Mais cet emploi est tout à fait normal avec **let's** :

let's not wait any longer
n'attendons plus

d) *Never* n'est normalement pas accompagné de **do** :

we never accept traveller's cheques
nous n'acceptons jamais les chèques de voyage

I never said a word
je n'ai jamais dit un mot

Mais si l'on veut mettre l'accent sur **never**, on peut alors employer **do** ou **did** :

you never did like my cooking, did you?
tu n'as jamais aimé ma cuisine, hein ?

S'il y a une inversion auxiliaire/sujet, on emploie **do** :

never did it taste so good!
ça n'a jamais été aussi bon !

never did their courage waver
à aucun moment leur courage n'a faibli

Dans le premier de ces deux exemples, la phrase est plus une exclamation qu'une négation, et dans la seconde, le style est poétique ou rhétorique.

e) *La traduction des formes négatives en français*

i) ne ... jamais

he never speaks to me/he doesn't ever speak to me
il ne me parle jamais

ii) ne ... rien

I saw nothing/I didn't say anything
je n'ai rien vu

iii) ne ... personne

she agrees with nobody (no-one)/she doesn't agree with anybody (anyone)
elle n'est d'accord avec personne

iv) ne ... plus

I don't smoke any more/any longer
je ne fume plus

words which are no longer used/word which aren't used any longer
des mots qui ne sont plus employés

10. POUR EXPRIMER LE PRESENT

On peut exprimer le présent de différentes façons selon que l'on se réfère à des événements habituels ou généraux, ou à des événements précis, et selon que ceux-ci sont considérés comme des actions en cours ou comme des événements ponctuels. Cette section décrit les emplois des formes verbales appropriées.

a) *Le présent simple*

i) Pour des événements habituels ou généraux, ou pour des vérités universelles :

I get up at seven o'clock every morning
je me lève à sept heures tous les matins

Mrs Parfitt teaches French at the local school
Madame Parfitt enseigne le français dans l'école locale

the earth revolves round the sun
la terre tourne autour du soleil

ii) Avec des verbes qui n'impliquent pas d'idée de progression dans le temps. Ces verbes sont parfois appelés "statiques" et ils expriment souvent le désir, le dégoût, l'opinion ou font référence aux sens :

I (dis)like/love/hate/want that girl
j'aime (je n'aime pas)/j'adore/je déteste/je veux cette fille

I believe/suppose/think you're right
je crois/suppose/pense que vous avez raison

we hear/see/feel the world around us
nous entendons/voyons/sentons le monde autour de nous

it tastes good/it smells good
c'est bon/ça sent bon

Remarquez que ces verbes "statiques" peuvent devenir de "dynamiques", si le sens sous-entend le "déroulement" ou qu'une action dure. Dans de tels cas, on emploie le présent progressif :

what are you thinking about?
à quoi penses-tu ?

we're not seeing a lot of him these days
on ne le voit pas beaucoup ces jours-ci

are you not feeling well today?
est-ce que vous ne vous sentez pas bien aujourd'hui ?

we're tasting the wine to see if it's all right
nous goûtons le vin pour voir s'il est bon

b) *Le présent progressif*

i) Le présent progressif est employé avec des verbes "dynamiques", c.-à-d. des verbes qui renvoient à des événements en cours et normalement temporaires :

don't interrupt while I'm talking to somebody else
ne m'interromps pas pendant que je parle à quelqu'un

please be quiet; I'm watching a good programme
tais-toi, s'il te plaît ; je regarde une émission intéressante

he's trying to get the car to start
il essaie de faire démarrer la voiture

not now, I'm thinking
pas maintenant, je réfléchis

Comparez :
I live in London (présent simple)
je vis à Londres

I'm living in London (présent progressif)
je vis à Londres (maintenant)

La deuxième phrase implique que le locuteur n'est pas installé à Londres d'une façon permanente, que c'est d'une manière temporaire qu'il vit à Londres.

ii) Si l'on fait référence à a) i ci-dessus, il est clair que les adverbes de temps absolu ou d'habitude sont fréquents avec le présent simple, comme dans :

he always goes to bed after midnight
il va toujours se coucher après minuit

Cet emploi du présent simple s'applique pour donner les états de fait. Mais on emploie parfois le présent progressif avec de tels adverbes, en particulier avec **always** et **forever**, lorsque l'on souhaite exprimer non seulement le fait lui-même, mais une attitude vis-à-vis de celui-ci, en particulier une attitude d'irritation, d'amusement ou de surprise :

you're always saying that! (irritation)
tu dis toujours ça !

he's always criticizing me (ressentiment)
il me critique tout le temps

John is forever forgetting his car keys (légère ironie)
John oublie toujours ses clés de voiture

I'm always finding you here at Betty's (surprise)
tiens, je te trouve toujours ici chez Betty !

11. POUR EXPRIMER LE PASSE

a) *Le prétérit*

On l'emploie lorsque l'on veut mettre l'accent sur l'accomplissement d'une action, souvent à un moment précis indiqué par un adverbe :

he caught the train yesterday
il a pris le train hier

he didn't say a word at the meeting
il n'a pas dit un mot pendant la réunion

Maria Callas sang at the Lyric Opera only a few times
(c'est-à-dire alors qu'elle était vivante)
Maria Callas ne chanta/n'a chanté à l'Opéra Lyrique que quelques fois

b) ***used to/would***

Lorsque l'on veut faire référence à un événement habituel et du passé, on emploie souvent **used to** ou **would** :

on Sundays we used to go to my grandmother's
on Sundays we would go to my grandmother's
le dimanche on allait chez ma grand-mère

c) *Le passé progressif*

Ce temps a pour but d'insister sur la continuité d'une action ou d'un événement :

what were you doing last night around 9 o'clock? – I was repairing the garage door
qu'est-ce que tu faisais hier soir vers 9 heures ? – je réparais la porte du garage

I was watching my favourite programme when the phone rang
je regardais mon émission préférée, quand le téléphone a sonné

Dans le deuxième exemple, **was watching** (passé progressif) s'oppose à **rang** (prétérit). Les deux verbes sont en contraste de manière différente dans l'exemple suivant, où les formes des verbes ont été inversées :

I watched his face while the phone was ringing
j'ai regardé son visage pendant que le téléphone sonnait

Ici le locuteur insiste sur le fait que "regarder" s'est produit à un certain moment. Il ne prend donc pas en compte l'idée de continuité que le verbe pourrait exprimer, en revanche il met l'accent sur la continuité de "sonner". Les deux exemples illustrent l'emploi du passé progressif pour des événements servant de toile de fond à d'autres événements de courte durée, pour lesquels on préfère l'aspect simple.

d) *Le present perfect (progressif)*

On emploie le present perfect pour des actions du passé ou des événements qui ont un lien avec le présent :

she has read an enormous number of books
(c'est-à-dire qu'elle est érudite)
elle a lu un nombre énorme de livres

Comparez le present perfect avec le prétérit dans les deux phrases qui suivent :

have you heard the news this morning? (c'est encore la matinée)
tu as entendu les informations ce matin ?

did you hear the news this morning? (c'est maintenant l'après-midi ou le soir)
tu as entendu les informations ce matin ?

he has just arrived (il est là maintenant)
il vient d'arriver

he arrived a moment ago (accent sur le moment du passé)
il est arrivé il y a un instant

Mrs Smith has died (elle est morte maintenant)
Mme Smith est morte

Mrs Smith died a rich woman (au moment où elle est morte, elle était riche)
Mme Smith est morte riche

Pour insister sur le fait qu'une action est continue, on peut employer l'aspect progressif :

I've been living in this city for 10 years
cela fait dix ans que je vis dans cette ville

Cependant, ici on peut aussi employer la forme simple dans le même sens :

I've lived in this city for 10 years

Remarquez que l'on emploie **since** pour traduire "depuis" pour faire référence à un moment précis dans le temps :

I've been living here since 1971
je vis ici depuis 1971

Dans certains cas cependant, l'emploi de l'aspect progressif et l'emploi de la forme simple impliquent des idées différentes. Comparez :

I've been waiting for you for three whole hours!
cela fait trois heures que je t'attends !

I've waited for you for three whole hours!
je t'ai attendu pendant trois heures !

On ne dirait pas la deuxième phrase directement à la personne que l'on attend lorsque cette personne finit par arriver. Mais on pourrait le dire à cette personne au téléphone, sous-entendant ainsi que l'on va maintenant cesser d'attendre.

On pourrait aussi bien dire la première phrase à la personne lorsqu'elle arrive qu'au téléphone.

e) *Le past perfect (progressif)*

Le past perfect permet de décrire des actions et des événements passés survenus avant d'autres événements passés. Il exprime un passé par rapport à un autre passé :

she had left when I arrived
elle était partie lorsque je suis arrivé

she left when I arrived
elle est partie lorsque je suis arrivé

L'aspect progressif permet d'insister sur le fait que l'action est continue :

she had been trying to get hold of me for hours when I finally turned up
cela faisait des heures qu'elle essayait de me contacter lorsque je suis enfin arrivé

I had been meaning to contact him for ages
cela faisait très longtemps que j'avais l'intention de le contacter

Pour le past perfect dans les propositions conditionnelles, voir p A51.

12. POUR EXPRIMER LE FUTUR

a) ***will et shall***

i) Lorsque le locuteur fait référence au futur à la 1ère personne, on peut employer **will** ou **shall**. Ces deux formes se contractent en **'ll**. Cependant l'emploi de **shall**, est peu fréquent ailleurs qu'en Grande Bretagne :

I will/I'll/I shall inform Mr Thompson of her decision
je ferai part de sa décision à Mr Thomson

we won't/shan't be long
ça ne nous prendra pas longtemps

I will/I'll/I shall be in Rome when you're getting married
je serai à Rome quand vous vous marierez

ii) Aux autres personnes, on emploie **will** :

you will/you'll be surprised when you see him
vous serez surpris quand vous le verrez

he will/he'll get angry if you tell him this
il se mettra en colère si tu lui dis cela

Remarquez qu'après **when** l'anglais emploie un present pour faire reference au futur, comme dans l'exemple ci-dessus. Ceci s'applique aussi pour d'autres conjonctions de temps, par exemple :

I'll do it as soon as I get home
je le ferai dès que j'arriverai à la maison

life will be easier once you learn to accept ... (ou **once you have learnt to accept ...**)
la vie sera plus facile une fois que tu auras appris à accepter ...

iii) Si le locuteur exprime une intention à la deuxième ou à la troisième personne (souvent une promesse ou une menace), on rencontre alors parfois **shall**, mais cet emploi n'est plus de nos jours aussi courant que celui de **will** :

you shall get what I promised you
tu auras ce que je t'ai promis

they shall pay for this!
ils/elles vont me le payer !

Si l'intention ou la volonté n'est pas celle du locuteur, on emploie alors **will ('ll)** :

he will/he'll do it, I'm sure
il le fera, j'en suis sûr(e)

iv) On emploie **shall** pour exprimer des suggestions :

shall we go?
on y va ?

shall I do it for you?
tu veux que je te le fasse ?

Dans ces deux exemples, on n'emploierait pas **will**.

v) On emploie **will** pour demander à quelqu'un de faire quelque chose :

will you step this way, please?
pouvez-vous venir par ici, s'il vous plaît ?

vi) pour proposer de faire quelque chose, pour affirmer quelque chose en ce qui concerne l'avenir immédiat :

Dans les exemples suivants, en emploie **will** de préférence à **shall** (bien que la forme contractée soit de loin la plus courante) :

leave that, I'll do it
laisse ça, je vais le faire

what's it like? – I don't know, I'll try it
c'est bon ? – je ne sais pas, je vais y goûter

try some, you'll like it
goûtez-y, vous aimerez ça

there's the phone – ok, I'll answer it
le téléphone sonne – bon, je réponds

b) *Le futur simple et le futur progressif*

i) la continuité de l'action :

Will et **shall** peuvent être suivis de la forme progressive, si le locuteur veut insister sur l'aspect continu de l'action :

I'll be marking essays and you'll be looking after the baby
je corrigerai des dissertations et tu t'occuperas du bébé

ii) les demandes ou les questions ? :

On peut aussi employer la forme progressive pour indiquer que le locuteur parle de façon neutre d'un état de choses et souhaite atténuer la nuance de volonté que pourrait sous-entendre l'aspect simple. C'est pourquoi on rencontre souvent **will/shall** + forme progressive de l'infinitif dans des phrases qui sous-entendent un arrangement préalable :

she'll be giving two concerts in London next week (= she is due to give ...)
elle donnera deux concerts à Londres la semaine prochaine

will you be bringing that up at the meeting?
est-ce que tu comptes en parler à la réunion ?

La question :

will you bring that up at the meeting?
tu en parleras à la réunion ?

est plus susceptible d'être interprétée comme une demande ou une prière que comme une question quant à ce que vous avez l'intention de faire.

c) ***be going to***

i) Bien souvent, il n'y a aucune différence entre **be going to** et **will** :

I wonder if this engine is ever going to start (... will ever start)
je me demande si le moteur va finir par démarrer

you're going to just love it (you'll just love it)
tu vas adorer ça

what's he going to do about it? (what'll he do about it?)
qu'est-ce qu'il va faire ?

ii) Pour indiquer une intention, **be going to** est plus couramment employé que **will** ou **shall** :

we're going to sell the house after all
après tout, nous allons vendre la maison

he's going to sue us
il va nous faire un procès

I'm going to go to London tomorrow
je vais aller à Londres demain

Mais dans une phrase plus longue comprenant d'autres locutions adverbiales et d'autres propositions, on peut aussi employer **will** :

look, what I'll do is this, I'll go to London tomorrow, talk to them about it and ...
écoute, voilà ce que vais faire, je vais aller à Londres demain, je vais leur en parler et ...

iii) **be going to** s'emploie de préférence à **will** lorsque les raisons justifiant les prévisions sont directement liées au présent :

it's going to rain (look at those clouds)
il va pleuvoir (regarde ces nuages)

I know what you're going to say (it's written all over your face)
je sais ce que tu vas dire (ça se voit à ta tête)

d) *Le présent simple*

i) Dans les principales, le présent simple exprime le futur lorsque l'on fait référence à un programme établi, en particulier lorsque l'on fait référence à un horaire :

when does university start? – classes start on October 6th
quand a lieu la rentrée universitaire ? – les cours reprennent le 6 octobre

the train for London leaves at 11 am
le train qui va à Londres part à 11 heures

ii) On emploie généralement le présent simple dans les propositions temporelles ou conditionnelles :

you'll like him when you see him
il te plaira quand tu le verras

if he turns up, will you speak to him?
tu lui parleras s'il vient ?

Ne confondez pas les propositions de ce type commençant par **when** et **if** et les propositions compléments d'objet interrogatives. Dans ces dernières, **when** signifie "quand ?, à quel moment ?" et **if** signifie "si" (adverbe interrogatif), et la forme du verbe est la même que celle du verbe de l'interrogation directe correspondante :

do you know when dad's taking the dog out?
est-ce que tu sais quand Papa va sortir le chien ? (quand est-ce que Papa va sortir le chien ?)

I wonder if she'll be there
je me demande si elle sera là (est-ce qu'elle sera là ?)

e) *Le présent progressif*

i) Le présent progressif est souvent très semblable à **be going to** servant à exprimer l'intention :

I'm taking this book with me (I'm going to take this book with me)
j'emporte ce livre (je vais emporter ce livre)

what are you doing over Christmas? (what are you going to do over Christmas?)
qu'est-ce que tu fais à Noël ? (qu'est-ce que tu vas faire ... ?)

ii) Mais lorsque l'idée d'intention est moins importante, le présent progressif a tendance à sous-entendre l'idée d'arrangement préalable, et son usage est alors similaire à celui de **will** + infinitif progressif ou du présent simple :

she's giving two concerts in London next week
elle donne deux concerts à Londres la semaine prochaine

the train for London is leaving soon
le train pour Londres part bientôt

f) ***be to***

On emploie souvent **be to** pour faire référence à des projets d'avenir spécifiques, en particulier des projets qu'ont pour nous d'autres personnes, le hasard ou la destinée :

the President is to visit the disaster zone (pour le style employé dans les grands titres voir p A41)
le président doit visiter la zone sinistrée

we are to be there by ten o'clock
nous devons y être pour dix heures

are we to meet again, I wonder?
nous reverrons-nous un jour, je me le demande ?

g) ***be about to***

Be about to exprime le futur très proche :

you are about to meet a great artist (very shortly you will meet a great artist)
vous êtes sur le point de rencontrer un grand artiste

the play is about to start (any second now)
la pièce est sur le point de commencer

Be about to peut aussi s'employer pour exprimer des intentions quant au futur, mais c'est là un usage plus courant en anglais américain :

I'm not about to let him use my car after what happened last time
je ne vais pas lui laisser prendre ma voiture après ce qui s'est produit la dernière fois

En anglais britannique on aurait davantage tendance à employer **be going to**.

h) *Le futur antérieur (progressif)*

On emploie le futur antérieur pour faire référence à une action qui aura été achevée avant une autre action dans le futur :

by the time we get there he will already have left
d'ici à ce que nous arrivions, il sera déjà parti

by then we'll have been working on this project for 5 years
nous aurons alors travaillé pendant cinq ans sur ce projet

On emploie aussi le futur antérieur pour exprimer des suppositions quant au présent ou au passé :

you'll have been following developments on this, no doubt
vous aurez, sans aucun doute, suivi les développements de cette affaire

13. POUR EXPRIMER LA CONDITION

Dans les phrases conditionnelles, on exprime la condition dans une proposition subordonnée placée avant ou après la proposition principale et commençant normalement par **if** :

if the train is late, we'll miss our plane
si le train a du retard, nous raterons notre avion

we'll miss our plane if the train is late
nous raterons notre avion si le train a du retard

Pour les conditions négatives **unless** (si...ne, à moins que) est parfois employé :

unless the train is on time, we'll miss our plane
if the train isn't on time, we'll miss our plane
si le train n'est pas à l'heure, nous raterons notre avion

Etant donné que l'action de la principale dépend de la condition de la subordonnée, cette action doit être au futur (pour les exceptions voir a)i ci-dessous). L'auxiliaire qui se rapproche le plus d'un futur pur est **will**, qui, de même que sa forme du passé **would**, est employé dans les exemples illustrant les emplois des phrases au conditionnel.

a) *Pour faire référence au présent/futur*

i) possibilité vraisemblable :

Le verbe de la proposition subordonnée est au présent ou au present perfect. La proposition principale comprend la construction **will** + infinitif : (quelquefois **shall** + infinitif à la 1ère personne) :

if you see her, you will not recognize her
si tu la vois, tu ne la reconnaîtras pas

if you are sitting comfortably, we will begin
si vous êtes assis confortablement, nous allons commencer

if you have completed the forms, I will send them off
si vous avez/tu as rempli les formulaires, je les enverrai

if he comes back, I shall ask him to leave
s'il revient, je lui demanderai de partir

Il y a trois exceptions importantes :

★ Si le verbe de la principale est aussi au présent, cela sous-entend généralement un résultat automatique ou habituel. Dans ces phrases, **if** a presque le sens de **when(ever)** (lorsque, à chaque fois que) :

if the sun shines, people look happier
quand le soleil brille, les gens ont l'air plus heureux

if people eat rat poison, they often die
souvent, quand les gens mangent de la mort-aux-rats, ils en meurent

if you're happy, I'm happy
si ça te va, ça me va

if you don't increase your offer, you don't get the house
si vous n'offrez pas plus, vous n'aurez pas la maison

★ Lorsque **will** est aussi employé dans la subordonnée, le locuteur fait alors référence à la bonne volonté d'une personne ou à son intention de faire quelque chose :

if you will be kind enough to stop singing, we will/shall be able to get some sleep
si vous voulez bien arrêter de chanter, nous pourrons dormir

if you will insist on eating all that fatty food you will have to put up with the consequences
si tu continues à manger aussi gras, tu devras en supporter les conséquences

Lorsque cette forme est employée pour demander à quelqu'un de faire quelque chose, on peut ajouter à la phrase un nuance de politesse en employant **would** :

if you would be kind enough to stop playing the trombone, we would/should be able to get some sleep
si vous aviez la bonté d'arrêter de jouer du trombone, nous pourrions dormir

★ Lorsque l'on emploie **should** dans la subordonnée (à toutes les personnes), cela sous-entend que la condition est moins probable. Ces propositions avec **should** sont souvent suivies de l'impératif, comme cela est le cas dans les deux premiers exemples :

if you should see him, ask him to call
au cas où vous le verriez, demandez lui de m'appeler

if he should turn up, try and avoid him
s'il venait, essayez de l'éviter

if they should attack you, you will have to fight them
s'ils en venaient à vous attaquer, il vous faudrait vous défendre

Dans un style légèrement plus soutenu, on peut omettre **if** et faire commencer la phrase par la proposition subordonnée avec **should** :

should the matter arise again, telephone me at once
si le problème devait se présenter de nouveau, téléphonez-moi immédiatement

ii) possibilité peu probable ou irréelle :

L'expression "possibilité peu probable ou irréelle" signifie que l'on s'attend à ce que la condition ne se réalise pas ou qu'on l'oppose à des faits connus. Le verbe de la proposition subordonnée est au passé ; la principale comprend la construction **would** (également **should** à la première personne) + infinitif :

if you saw her, you would not recognize her
si tu la voyais, tu ne la reconnaîtrais pas

if she had a car, she would visit you more often
si elle avait une voiture, elle te rendrait visite plus souvent

if I won that amount of money, I would/should just spend it all
si je gagnais une telle somme d'argent, je dépenserais tout

if the lift was working properly, there would not be so many complaints
si l'ascenseur marchait correctement, il n'y aurait pas autant de réclamations

Ce type de phrase n'exprime pas nécessairement une possibilité peu probable ou irréelle. Elle présente souvent peu de différence par rapport à la construction du type a)i ci-dessus :

if you tried harder, you would pass the exam (if you try harder, you will pass the exam)
si tu faisais plus d'efforts, tu réussirais ton examen

L'emploi du passé peut donner à la phrase un ton un peu plus "amical" et poli.

b) *Pour faire référence au passé*

i) Dans ces cas-là la condition n'est pas réalisée, puisque ce qui est exprimé dans la proposition commençant par **if** ne s'est pas produit. Le verbe de la subordonnée est au past perfect ; la principale comprend la construction **would** (également **should** à la première personne) + infinitif passé :

if you had seen her, you would not have recognized her
si tu l'avais vue, tu ne l'aurais pas reconnue

if I had been there, I would/should have ignored him
si j'avais été là, j'aurais fait semblant de ne pas le voir

Dans un style légèrement plus soutenu, on peut omettre **if** et faire commencer la subordonnée par **had** :

had I been there, I would/should have ignored him

ii) exceptions :

★ Si la proposition principale fait référence à la non réalisation dans le présent d'une condition dans le passé, on peut aussi employer **would** + infinitif :

if I had studied harder, I would be an engineer today
si j'avais étudié davantage, je serais ingénieur maintenant

★ On emploie le passé dans les deux propositions si, comme cela est le cas dans a) i ci-dessus, on sous-entend un résultat automatique ou habituel (**if** = when(ever)) :

if people had influenza in those days, they died
si les gens attrapaient la grippe en ce temps-là, ils en mouraient

if they tried to undermine the power of the Church, they were burned at the stake
s'ils essayaient de saper le pouvoir de l'Eglise, ils mouraient au bûcher

★ Si on s'attend à ce que la condition se soit réalisée, les restrictions quant à la concordance des temps indiquées dans a) et b) ci-dessus ne s'appliquent plus. Dans ces cas-là, **if** signifie souvent "comme" ou "puisque". Remarquez par exemple la diversité des formes verbales employées dans les propositions principales qui suivent les propositions commençant par **if** (qui sont toutes au passé) :

if he was rude to you, why did you not walk out?
s'il a été grossier avec toi, pourquoi est-ce que tu n'es pas parti(e) ?

if he was rude to you, why have you still kept in touch?
if he was rude to you, why do you still keep in touch?
s'il a été grossier avec toi, pourquoi est-ce que tu es resté(e) en contact avec lui ?

if he told you that, he was wrong
s'il t'a dit ça, il a eu tort

if he told you that, he has broken his promise
s'il t'a dit ça, il a manqué à sa promesse

if he told you that, he is a fool
s'il t'a dit ça, c'est un imbécile

14. LE SUBJONCTIF

Par opposition à l'indicatif, qui est le mode du réel, le subjonctif est le mode du non-réel, et exprime par exemple le souhait, l'espoir, la possibilité, etc. (Voir **Les Modes** p A39).

Le présent du subjonctif est identique par sa forme à l'infinitif (sans **to**) aux trois personnes du singulier et du pluriel. Autrement dit, la seule différence entre les formes du présent du subjonctif et celles du présent de l'indicatif est l'omission du **-s** à la troisième personne du singulier.

L'imparfait du subjonctif n'est marqué du point de vue de la forme qu'à la première et à la troisième personne du singulier du verbe **to be**, qui est **were**. Cependant, dans le langage de tous les jours, on emploie de préférence **was** (voir aussi b) vi ci-dessous).

a) *Le subjonctif dans les propositions principales*

Ici, l'emploi du subjonctif est limité à des locutions fixes exprimant l'espoir ou le souhait, par exemple :

God save the Queen!
Vive la reine !

Long live the King!
Vive le roi !

Heaven be praised!
Dieu soit loué !

b) *Le subjonctif dans les propositions subordonnées*

i) Dans les propositions conditionnelles, le subjonctif passé est d'un emploi très courant; voir 13a) ii ci-dessus. L'emploi du présent du subjonctif appartient à un niveau de langue très soutenu ou à un style littéraire :

if this be true, old hopes are born anew
si c'était vrai, tous les espoirs renaîtraient

sauf dans l'expression consacrée **if need be** = "s'il le faut, si besoin est" :

if need be, we can sell the furniture
s'il le faut, nous pouvons vendre les meubles

Remarquez aussi l'emploi dans les tournures concessives :

they are all interrogated, be they friend or foe
ils sont tous interrogés, qu'ils soient amis ou ennemis

ii) Les propositions comparatives, introduites par **as if** ou **as though** contiennent souvent, mais certainement pas dans tous les cas, un subjonctif passé :

he looks as though he took his work seriously (= ... as though he takes ...)
il semble prendre son travail très au sérieux

he treats me as if I was/were a child
il me traite comme si j'étais un gamin

iii) Le subjonctif passé est employé après **if only** et dans les propositions compléments d'objet direct après **wish** et **had rather**, toutes ces propositions exprimant le souhait ou le désir :

if only we had a bigger house, life would be perfect
si seulement nous avions une maison plus grande, tout serait parfait

are you going abroad this year? – I wish I were/was
est-ce que tu pars à l'étranger cette année ? – si seulement je pouvais !

I wish he was/were back at school
si seulement il avait repris l'école

where's your passport? – I wish I knew
où est ton passeport ? – si je le savais !

do you want me to tell you? – I'd rather you didn't
tu veux que je te dise ? – je n'aime mieux pas !

iv) Dans un langage soutenu (par exemple, le langage juridique), on rencontre parfois le présent du subjonctif dans les propositions compléments d'objet directs après les verbes ou les expressions impersonnelles (telles que : "il est souhaitable", "il est important") indiquant une suggestion ou un souhait :

we propose that the clause be extended to cover such eventualities
nous proposons que la clause soit élargie pour couvrir ces éventualités

it is important that he take steps immediately
il est important qu'il prenne des mesures immédiatement

it is imperative that this matter be discussed further
il est impératif de discuter davantage de cette affaire

Dans ces propositions, le subjonctif est d'un emploi plus courant en anglais américain qu'en anglais britannique et n'est en aucun cas rare en dehors du langage des négociations ou du langage juridique. Bien que l'anglais américain influence rapidement l'anglais britannique, ce dernier préfère toujours l'emploi de **should** + infinitif :

we suggest that the system (should) be changed
nous suggérons que le système soit changé

I am adamant that this (should) be put to the vote
j'insiste pour que cela soit soumis au vote

it is vital that he (should) start as soon as possible
il est primordial qu'il commence aussi tôt que possible

v) Après **it's time**, lorsque le locuteur veut insister sur le fait que quelque chose devrait être fait, on emploie le subjonctif passé :

it's time we spoke to him
il est temps que nous lui parlions

it's high time they stopped that
il est temps qu'ils arrêtent cela

tandis que dans les exemples suivants, on ne fait qu'exprimer l'opportunité du moment :

it's time to speak to him about it
c'est le moment de lui en parler

vi) **if I was/if I were**

Les confusions sont fréquentes quant à l'emploi correct de **if I was/if I were**.

Il existe des cas dans lesquels on ne peut employer que **if I was**, c'est-à-dire les cas dans lesquels la condition à laquelle on fait référence n'est en aucun cas une condition irréelle :

if I was mistaken about it then it certainly wasn't through lack of trying
si je me suis trompé(e), ce n'est certainement pas faute d'avoir fait de mon mieux

Le locuteur ne met pas en cause le fait que l'erreur soit réelle, mais il se contente d'en expliquer la cause.

Par contre dans la phrase suivante :

if I were mistaken about it, surely I would have realized
si je m'étais trompé(e), je m'en serais certainement aperçu(e)

le locuteur exprime un doute quant à la réalité de l'erreur et l'emploi du subjonctif **were** est donc approprié. Mais il ne serait pas non plus faux d'employer **was** dans ce contexte, il s'agit simplement là d'une expression appartenant à un langage moins soutenu.

15. UN EMPLOI PARTICULIER DU PASSE

Nous avons vu dans les sections 13 et 14 comment le subjonctif passé peut faire référence au présent dans des propositions conditionnelles ou autres. Outre ces emplois du subjonctif passé, le passé peut faire référence au présent dans les propositions principales exprimant une attitude plus hésitante et donc plus polie et respectueuse. Ainsi :

did you want to see me?
vous vouliez me voir ?

est plus poli, plus hésitant, ou moins sec que :

do you want to see me?
vous voulez me voir ?

Mais dans l'expression usuelle :

I was wondering if you could help me do this
est-ce que vous pourriez m'aider à faire cela ?

l'emploi du passé exprime maintenant toujours la nuance de politesse et n'est pour ainsi dire pas différent de :

I wonder if you could help me with this

L'expression usuelle :

I was hoping you could help me here
est-ce que vous pourriez m'aider ici ?

pour formuler une demande polie, n'a pas de construction correspondante au présent.

16. LA VOIX PASSIVE

En ce qui concerne les différences de forme entre la voix active et la voix passive, voir p A40.

a) *Le passif direct et indirect*

Dans la phrase à la voix active :

they sent him another bill
ils lui ont envoyé une autre facture

another bill est le complément d'objet direct et **him** est le complément d'objet indirect. Si dans une construction correspondante à la voix passive, le complément d'objet direct de la phrase à la voix active devient le sujet de la phrase à la voix passive, on a alors un "passif direct" :

another bill was sent (to) him
une autre facture lui a été envoyée

alors qu'un "passif indirect" aurait pour sujet le complément d'objet indirect de la phrase à la voix active :

he was sent another bill
on lui a envoyé une autre facture

b) *Le passif d'état et le passif d'action*

Dans la phrase suivante, le verbe exprime un état :

the shop is closed
la boutique est fermée

tandis que dans l'exemple suivant, cela ne fait aucun doute qu'il exprime une action :

the shop is closed by his mother at 4 pm every day
la boutique est fermée par sa mère tous les jours à 16 heures

Dans la première phrase le verbe est appelé "verbe d'état", dans la deuxième phrase le verbe est appelé "verbe d'action". C'est le contexte qui nous l'apprend et non pas la forme. La forme du verbe reste la même. L'absence de formes distinctes peut parfois donner lieu à des ambiguïtés comme par exemple :

his neck was broken when they lifted him

signifiant soit (passif d'état) "son cou était cassé quand ils l'ont soulevé" soit (passif d'action) "son cou fut cassé quand ils l'ont soulevé". Cependant si l'on souhaite insister sur l'aspect de passif d'action (souvent plus vivant), on peut employer **get** comme auxiliaire à la place de **be**, dans le language de tous les jours en particulier :

his neck got broken when they lifted him
son cou s'est trouvé cassé quand ils l'ont soulevé

they finally got caught
ils ont fini par se faire prendre

he got kicked out of the pub
il s'est fait mettre à la porte du pub

On peut aussi employer le verbe **have** pour exprimer un passif d'action :

he had his neck broken when they lifted him
il a eu le cou cassé quand ils l'ont soulevé

they've had their house burgled three times
ils se sont fait cambrioler trois fois

c) *Voix passive ou voix active ?*

i) Si ce qui fait l'action est moins important que l'action accomplie, on préfère souvent la voix passive à la voix active. Ainsi dans :

his invitation was refused
son invitation a été refusée

d'après le locuteur l'identité de la personne qui refuse n'a évidemment pas d'importance. Si, dans le langage scientifique en particulier, on emploie de très nombreuses tournures passives, c'est parce que l'on considère que mentionner l'agent ou celui qui fait l'action manque d'objectivité. On écrit :

the experiment was conducted in darkness
l'expérience a été effectuée dans le noir

plutôt que :

I conducted the experiment in darkness
j'ai effectué l'expérience dans le noir

ii) Si celui qui fait l'action n'a aucune importance ou si on ne le connaît pas, de nombreux verbes apparaissent à la voix active mais ont un sens passif. Il y a peu de différence entre :

the theatre runs at a profit
le théâtre fait des bénéfices

et :

the theatre is run at a profit

ou entre :

ses yeux étaient remplis de larmes (sens de passif d'action)

et :

ses yeux se sont remplis de larmes

Ces formes actives à sens passif sont d'un emploi relativement fréquent en anglais ; et souvent l'emploi d'une forme passive serait maladroit, voire impossible :

a cloth which feels soft
un tissu qui est doux au toucher

silk blouses do not wash well
les chemisiers en soie ne se lavent pas bien

this essay reads better than your last one
cette dissertation se lit mieux que la dernière que vous avez écrite

it flies beautifully
il se pilote très bien

where is the film showing?
où est ce que le film passe ?

he photographs well
il est photogénique

iii) Quelquefois, la voix active à sens passif se limite à l'infinitif :

the house is to let	**I am to blame**
la maison est à louer	je suis à blâmer

mais de tels cas sont rares. Cependant, dans les constructions du type **there is** + (pro)nom avec infinitif, l'infinitif actif à sens passif est courant :

there is work to do (= ... to be done)
il y a du travail à faire

when we get home there'll be suitcases to unpack
quand nous rentrerons à la maison, il y aura les valises à défaire

there was plenty to eat
il y avait beaucoup de choses à manger

have you got anything to wash?
est-ce que tu as quelque chose à laver ?

have you got anything to mend?
est-ce que tu as quelque chose à réparer ?

Dans certains cas, on peut employer indifféremment l'infinitif actif ou l'infinitif passif :

there's nothing else to say/to be said
il n'y a rien d'autre à dire

is there anything to gain/to be gained from it?
est-ce qu'il y a quelque chose à y gagner ?

Mais quelquefois dans ces constructions après les pronoms **something**, **anything**, **nothing**, il peut y avoir une différence entre l'infinitif actif (à sens passif) et l'infinitif passif de **do**. Par exemple :

there is always something to do

signifie généralement (mais pas nécessairement) "il y a toujours quelque chose pour s'occuper ou pour s'amuser", tandis que :

there is always something to be done

signifie "il y a toujours du travail à faire".

iv) "on"

Le passif est bien plus employé en anglais qu'en français. Souvent le français préfère une construction avec "on" :

he was spotted leaving the bar
on l'a vu sortant du bar

that's already been done
on l'a déjà fait

I hadn't been told that
on ne m'avait pas dit ça

17. BE, HAVE, DO

a) ***be***

i) **Be** est employé comme auxiliaire avec le participe passé afin de former un passif et avec le participe présent pour exprimer l'aspect progressif du passif (p A40). Parfois **be** peut remplacer **have** en tant qu'auxiliaire pour l'aspect "perfect" (ou passé) (p A40), comme dans :

are you finished?	**our happiness is gone**
est-ce que tu as fini ?	notre bonheur s'est enfui

Dans ces cas-là, on insiste particulièrement sur l'état actuel plutôt que sur l'action.

ii) Comme les autres auxiliaires modaux, **be** n'est pas accompagné de **do** dans les négations et les interrogations. Cependant, lorsque **be** se comporte comme un verbe indépendant et non pas comme un auxiliaire, on emploie **do** dans des interdictions :

don't be silly
ne sois pas sot

iii) Lorsque **be** est un verbe ordinaire (c'est-à-dire pas un auxiliaire), il n'est pas employé à l'aspect progressif, sauf lorsqu'il fait exclusivement référence au comportement. Ainsi il y a une différence entre :

he is silly
il est sot (= de nature)

et :

he is being silly
il fait le sot

et entre :

he's American
il est américain

et :

if you said it that way, I'd assume you were deliberately being American
si tu disais ça de cette façon, je penserais que tu t'exprimes exprès à l'américaine

b) ***have***

i) **Have** est employé avec le participe passé pour former l'aspect "perfect" (p A39).

En tant que verbe ordinaire, il exprime quelquefois une activité ou une expérience, comme dans les expressions suivantes :

have dinner	**have difficulty**
dîner/ déjeuner	avoir du mal à
have a chat	**have a good time**
bavarder	s'amuser/passer un bon moment

Lorsque **have** n'exprime pas une activité, il fait normalement référence à la possession, à un état, ou à quelque chose organisé à l'avance :

have a farm	**have an appointment**
avoir une ferme	avoir un rendez-vous
have toothache	**have time (for or to do something)**
avoir mal aux dents	avoir le temps (de faire quelque chose)

Donc :

she'll have the baby in August

appartient au premier type si la phrase signifie qu'elle donnera naissance au bébé. Par contre, si la phrase signifie qu'elle "recevra" le bébé (si elle l'adopte, par exemple), elle appartient au deuxième type.

On peut appeler les types **have 1 (activité +)** et **have 2 (activité -)**.

ii) **have 1** :

★ Il se comporte comme les verbes ordinaires normaux dans les interrogations et les négations, c'est-à-dire qu'il est accompagné de **do**, ainsi que dans les question-tags :

did you have the day off yesterday?
est-ce que tu a pris un jour de congé hier ?

we don't have conversations any more
nous ne nous parlons plus

we had a marvellous time, didn't we?
nous avons vraiment passé un très bon moment, n'est-ce pas ?

★ **Have 1** peut s'employer à l'aspect progressif :

he telephoned as we were having lunch
il a téléphoné pendant que nous déjeunions

I'm having trouble with Carol these days
j'ai des problèmes avec Carol ces temps-ci

iii) **have 2** :

★ Au lieu de **have 2**, l'anglais britannique emploie souvent **have got**, particulièrement dans le langage parlé, et surtout au présent :

he has/he has got/he's got a large garden
il a un grand jardin

Au passé, on emploie normalement **had** ou **used to have**, ce dernier insistant sur l'idée de possession prolongée, la répétition ou l'habitude :

they all had flu in July last year
ils ont tous eu la grippe en juillet l'année dernière

he had/used to have a large garden once
autrefois, il avait un grand jardin

we had/used to have lots of problems in those days
en ce temps-là, nous avions beaucoup de problèmes

★ Dans les interrogations, le sujet et **have** peuvent être inversés :

have you any other illnesses?
avez-vous d'autres maladies ?

Dans les négations, **not** peut s'employer sans **do** :

he hasn't a garden
il n'a pas de jardin

On considère parfois ces phrases comme appartenant à un niveau de langue plutôt soutenu, et dans le langage de tous les jours, on préfère employer **have ... got** ou une construction avec **do** :

have you got/do you have any other illnesses?
he hasn't got/doesn't have a garden

La tournure en **do** est récemment devenue d'un emploi plus fréquent du fait de l'influence de l'anglais américain où il est normal de l'employer. Notez que si le locuteur souhaite faire passer l'idée de quelque chose qui se produit habituellement, régulièrement ou de façon générale, alors on emploie particulièrement fréquemment la tournure en **do** :

have you got/do you have any food for the dog?
est-ce que tu as de la nourriture pour le chien ?

mais :

do you always have dog-food in the sideboard ?
est-ce que tu as toujours de la nourriture pour chien dans ton buffet ?

lorsque **have** a un sens très voisin de "avoir en permanence". De même :

have you got/do you have a pain in your chest?
est-ce que vous ressentez une douleur dans la poitrine ?

mais :

do you frequently have a pain in your chest?
est-ce que vous ressentez souvent une douleur dans la poitrine ?

Dans les question-tags après **have**, on peut employer **have** ou **do** puisque, comme nous l'avons vu, **have** peut s'employer avec ou sans **do** dans les interrogations. **Do**, de plus en plus fréquemment employé à cause de l'usage américain, est particulièrement courant au passé :

he has a Rolls, hasn't/doesn't he?
il a une Rolls, n'est-ce pas ?

they had a large garden once, hadn't they/didn't they?
ils avaient un grand jardin autrefois, n'est-ce pas ?

Mais après **have got** on ne peut employer que **have** dans les questions-tags :

he's got a Rolls, hasn't he?
il a une Rolls, n'est-ce pas ?

Remarquez la différence suivante entre l'anglais britannique et l'anglais américain :

have you a minute? – no, I haven't (britannique)
have you a minute? – no, I don't (américain)
tu as une minute? – non

★ L'aspect progressif n'est pas possible avec **have 2** à moins qu'il fasse référence au futur. Ainsi :

they are having a fridge

ne signifie en aucun cas "ils ont un frigidaire", mais "ils vont avoir un frigidaire". Dans la phrase :

today I'm having the car
aujourd'hui je prends la voiture

am having = type **have 1**.

iv) L'emploi causatif de ***have*** :

Le verbe **have** est employé dans des constructions du type "faire faire quelque chose". Par exemple :

they're having a new porch built
ils se font construire une nouveau porche

could you have these photocopied?
est-ce que vous pouvez faire photopier cela ?

I'll have it done immediately
je vais le faire faire immédiatement

we'll have to have the loo fixed
il va falloir que nous fassions réparer les W.-C.

what on earth have you had done to your hair!
qu'est-ce qui est arrivé à tes cheveux !

Remarquez que **get** peut s'employer à la place de **have** dans tous les exemples ci-dessus, sauf le dernier.

★ Dans une construction américaine, l'idée de "faire faire quelque chose" a en majeure partie disparu :

Mr Braithwaite is here – ah, have him come in
M. Braithwaite est là – ah, faites-le entrer

Ceci équivaut simplement à prier quelqu'un de demander à M. Braithwaite d'entrer.

★ On peut aussi employer le verbe **have** ou **get** avec un complément d'objet direct :

I'll have the kitchen send it up to your room, madam
je vais demander à la cuisine de vous le monter à votre chambre, madame

Notez que **have** est employé sans **to**. Cependant avec **get**, qui a le même sens, on emploi **to** :

I'll get the kitchen to send it up to your room, madam

v) Constructions à la voix passive :

Le verbe **have** s'emploie aussi pour former un type de construction passive, particulièrement pour sous-entendre que le sujet de la phrase a souffert d'une manière ou d'une autre (voir aussi 16 b) :

he's had all his money stolen
il s'est fait voler tout son argent

he's had both his wives killed in car crashes
ses deux femmes se sont fait tuer dans des accidents de voiture

c) ***do***

On a déjà vu l'emploi de **do** dans les interrogations et les négations – voir p A46. Voir p A72 son emploi dans les autres cas d'inversion (par exemple **never did I once dream he would !**).

i) Le **do** emphatique :

Dans les phrases qui ne sont ni des interrogations, ni des négations, on peut, pour marquer l'emphase, employer un **do** (que l'on accentue à l'oral) avant le verbe principal :

oh, I do like your new jacket!
oh, j'aime beaucoup ta nouvelle veste !

do try to keep still !
essaye de rester tranquille

he doesn't know any German but he does know a little French
il ne sait pas l'allemand, mais par contre il sait un peu de français

I didn't manage to get tickets for ... but I did get some for...
je n'ai pas réussi à avoir de billets pour ... mais par contre, j'en ai pour ...

Et le verbe **do** lui-même peut s'employer avec **do** en tant qu'auxiliaire emphatique :

well, if you don't do that, what do you do?
bon, si tu ne fais pas ça, qu'est-ce que tu fais, alors ?

we don't do much skiing, but what we do do is go hill-walking
nous ne faisons pas beaucoup de ski, mais par contre nous faisons des promenades en montagne

ii) **do** pour remplacer le verbe :

On a déjà donné des exemples de cet emploi dans la section traitant des question-tags (voir p A46). En voici d'autres exemples :

she never drinks! – oh yes, she does
elle ne boit jamais ! – bien sûr que si

can I help myself to another cream cake? – please do
est-ce que peux avoir un autre gâteau à la crème ? – je vous en prie !

do you both agree? – I do, but she doesn't
vous êtes tous les deux d'accord ? – moi oui, mais elle, non

18. LES AUXILIAIRES MODAUX

Ce sont les auxiliaires **will-would, shall-should, can-could, may-might, must-had to, ought to.**

a) ***will-would***

Les formes négatives contractées sont **won't-wouldn't**.

i) Pour les phrases au conditionnel voir p A50-1.

ii) Pour une étude générale de l'expression du futur, voir p A49.

iii) Pour exprimer les ordres plutôt qu'un futur pur :

you will do as you are told!
tu feras ce qu'on te dit !

new recruits will report to headquarters on Tuesday at 8.30 am
les jeunes recrues se présenteront au quartier général mardi à 8 heures 30

will you stop that right now!
arrête tout de suite !

iv) Pour faire appel, sur un ton plutôt cérémonieux, aux souvenirs ou aux connaissances de quelqu'un :

you will recall last week's discussion about the purchase of a computer
vous vous souvenez certainement de notre discussion de la semaine dernière concernant l'achat d'un ordinateur

you will all know that the inspector has completed his report
vous savez certainement tous que l'inspecteur a terminé son procès-verbal

v) Pour exprimer une supposition, plutôt qu'un futur :

there's the telephone, Mary! – oh, that will be John
le téléphone sonne, Mary ! – oh, ça doit être John

they'll be there by now
ils/elles doivent être arrivé(e)s maintenant

how old is he now? – he'll be about 45
quel âge a-t-il maintenant ? – il doit avoir à peu près 45 ans

vi) Pour insister sur la notion de capacité ou d'inclination naturelle ou inhérente, ou sur la notion de comportement caractéristique, plutôt que pour exprimer un futur :

cork will float on water
le liège flotte sur l'eau

the Arts Centre will hold about 300 people
le centre culturel peut contenir environ 300 personnes

John will sit playing with a matchbox for hours
John peut rester assis à jouer avec une boîte d'allumettes pendant des heures

it's so annoying, he will keep interrupting! (accent sur "will" à l'oral)
c'est énervant, il n'arrête pas de m'interrompre !

the car won't start
la voiture ne veut pas démarrer

well, if you will drive so fast, what do you expect?
ben ! il fallait t'y attendre, à conduire aussi vite !

De même **would**, pour faire référence au passé :

when he was little, John would sit playing with a matchbox for hours
quand il était petit, John restait assis à jouer avec une boîte d'allumettes pendant des heures

she created a scene in public – she would!
elle a fait une scène en public – c'est bien son genre !

vii) Pour poser des questions, proposer :

will you have another cup?
vous en voulez une autre tasse ?

won't you try some of these?
vous ne voulez pas y goûter ?

viii) Pour demander à quelqu'un de faire quelque chose :

will you move your car, please?
est-ce que vous pouvez déplacer votre voiture, s'il vous plaît ?

On peut poser la même question d'une façon légèrement plus polie :

would you move your car, please?
est-ce que vous pourriez déplacer votre voiture, s'il vous plaît ?

ix) Pour exprimer la détermination :

I will not stand for this!
je ne le supporterai pas !

I will be obeyed!
je veux qu'on m'obéisse !

b) *shall-should*

Les formes négatives contractées sont **shan't-shouldn't**.

i) Pour les phrases au conditionnel, voir p A50.
ii) Pour **should**, équivalent du subjonctif, voir p A52.
iii) Pour **shall** exprimant le futur, voir p A49.
iv) (**shall** uniquement) Dans le langage juridique ou officiel **shall** s'emploie fréquemment pour exprimer une obligation. Ce sens de **shall** est très semblable à celui de **must** :

the committee shall consist of no more than six members
le comité sera constitué de six membre au plus

the contract shall be subject to English law
le contrat sera régi par la loi anglaise

v) (**should** uniquement) obligation (souvent obligation morale) :

you should lose some weight
tu devrais perdre du poids

he shouldn't be allowed to
jl ne devrait pas y être autorisé

you really should see this film
tu devrais essayer de voir ce film

is everything as it should be?
est-ce que tout va comme il faut ?

something was not quite as it should be
il y avait quelque chose de bizarre

vi) (**should** uniquement) déduction, probabilité :

it's ten o'clock, they should be back any minute
il est dix heures, ils devraient rentrer d'un moment à l'autre

John should have finished putting up those shelves by now
John devrait avoir fini d'installer ces étagères maintenant

are they there? – I don't know, but they should be
ils/elles sont là ? – je ne sais pas, mais ils/elles devraient

vii) (**should** uniquement) affirmations hésitantes :

I should just like to say that ...
j'aimerais simplement dire que ...

I should hardly think that's right
je ne pense pas que ça soit vrai

will he agree? – I shouldn't think so
est-ce qu'il sera d'accord ? – je ne pense pas

viii) **Should** est souvent employé pour faire référence à la **notion** (par opposition à la **réalité concrète**) d'une action. Cet emploi de **should** est quelquefois qualifié de "putatif" :

that she should want to take early retirement is quite understandable
il est tout à fait compréhensible qu'elle veuille prendre sa retraite anticipée

Comparez ce dernier exemple avec :

it is quite understandable that she wanted to take early retirement
il est tout à fait compréhensible qu'elle ait voulu prendre sa retraite anticipée

La différence est subtile. Dans le premier exemple, on insiste sur l'idée selon laquelle elle a voulu prendre sa retraite anticipée ; dans la deuxième phrase on insiste sur le fait qu'elle l'ait fait.

Il est important de remarquer que ce **should** est neutre pour ce qui est du temps. Le premier exemple ci-dessus pourrait tout aussi bien faire référence au passé (**she has taken early retirement**) ou au futur (**she will be taking early retirement**) suivant le contexte. Le second exemple ne peut bien sûr que faire référence au passé.

L'emploi putatif de **should** peut être comparé à l'emploi de **should** lorsqu'il est employé après les constructions ou verbes impersonnels de suggestion, de souhait ou d'ordre, dont il est question dans la section sur le subjonctif, p A51-2.

Dans l'exemple ci-dessus, l'emploi putatif de **should** est apparu dans une proposition subordonnée, mais il peut aussi apparaître dans des propositions principales :

where have I put my glasses? – how should I know?
où est-ce que j'ai mis mes lunettes ? – comment veux-tu que je le sache ?

as we were sitting there, who should walk by but Joan Collins!
nous étions assis, là, et devine qui passe ? ... Joan Collins !

there was a knock at the door, and who should it be but ...
on frappe à la porte, et qui c'est ? ...

c) ***can-could***

Les formes négatives contractées de **can-could** sont **can't-couldn't**. La forme négative non contractée au présent est **cannot**.

i) capacité (= be able to) :

I can't afford it — **I can swim**
je ne peux me le permettre — je sais nager

when I was young, I could swim for hours
quand j'étais jeune, je pouvais nager pendant des heures

La troisième phrase fait référence à une capacité passée. Cependant, dans les propositions conditionnelles **could** + infinitif fait référence au présent et au futur (comparez avec **would** dans la section **Pour Exprimer la Condition** p A50-1) :

if you try/tried harder, you could lose weight
si tu faisais plus d'efforts, tu arriverais à perdre du poids

ii) permission :

can/could I have a sweet?
je peux avoir un bonbon ?

Remarquez que **could** fait autant référence au présent ou au futur que **can**. La seule différence est que **could** est un peu plus hésitant ou poli. Cependant, **could** peut quelquefois s'employer pour exprimer une permission au passé lorsque le contexte est incontestablement passé :

for some reason we couldn't smoke in the lounge yesterday; but today we can
pour une raison ou une autre, nous ne pouvions pas fumer dans le salon hier, mais aujourd'hui nous pouvons

Il existe souvent une légère nuance de sens entre **can** et **may** lorsqu'ils signifient "avoir le droit de", dans la mesure où **can** est moins cérémonieux que **may**.

iii) possibilité :

what shall we do tonight? – well, we can/could watch a film
qu'est-ce qu'on va faire ce soir ? – ben ... on pourrait voir un film

Là encore, on peut remarquer que **could** ne fait pas référence au passé mais au présent ou au futur. Pour faire référence au passé on doit employer **could** suivi de l'infinitif passé :

instead of going to the pub we could have watched a film
au lieu d'aller au pub, nous aurions pu voir un film

I could have (could've) gone there if I'd wanted to, but I didn't
j'aurais pu y aller si j'avais voulu, mais je ne voulais pas

Il y a quelquefois une différence importante entre **can** et **may** quant à la façon dont ils font référence à la possibilité : **can** exprime fréquemment la possibilité logique pure et simple, tandis que **may** sous-entend souvent l'incertitude, le hasard ou un certain degré de probabilité d'un événement :

(a) **your comments can be overheard**
on peut entendre vos remarques
(b) **your comments may be overheard**
on pourrait entendre vos remarques

Dans (a) on dit qu'il est possible d'entendre les remarques, par exemple parce qu'elles sont faites à voix très haute, qu'il soit ou non probable que quelqu'un les entende effectivement. Dans (b) on dit qu'il est dans une certaine mesure probable que quelqu'un entende effectivement les remarques.

On peut aussi voir la différence dans les propositions à la forme négative :

he can't have heard us (= it is impossible for him to have heard us)
il ne peut pas nous avoir entendus

he may not have heard us (= it is possible that he did not hear us)
il se peut qu'il ne nous ait pas entendus

iv) suggestions (**could** uniquement) :

you could always try Marks & Spencers
tu peux toujours essayer à Marks & Spencers

he could express himself more clearly
il pourrait s'exprimer plus clairement

Cette construction peut parfois traduire une sorte de reproche :

you could have let us know!
tu aurais pu nous le dire !

he could have warned us!
il aurait pu nous prévenir !

d) ***may-might***

La forme négative contractée **mayn't** exprimant la permission négative, c'est à dire l'interdiction, disparaît progressivement et est remplacée par **may not** ou **must not/mustn't** ou encore **can't**. La forme négative contractée de **might** est **mightn't**, mais elle n'est pas employée pour exprimer l'interdiction.

i) permission :

you may sit down (comparer avec **can** dans c) ii ci-dessus, ici langage plutôt soutenu)
vous pouvez vous asseoir

may I open a window? – no, you may not!
est-ce que je peux ouvrir une fenêtre ? – non, pas question

you must not/mustn't open the windows in here
tu ne dois pas ouvrir les fenêtres ici

Il est extrêmement poli d'employer **might** pour exprimer la permission :

I wonder if I might have another wee glass of sherry
pourrais-je avoir un autre petit verre de sherry ?

might I suggest we adjourn the meeting?
puis-je me permettre de suggérer que nous ajournions la réunion ?

Notez que **might** fait référence au présent et au futur, et fait très rarement référence au passé lorsqu'il est employé dans une proposition principale. Comparez :

he then asked if he might smoke (langage plutôt soutenu)
he then asked if he was allowed to smoke
il a alors demandé s'il pouvait fumer

et :

he wasn't allowed to smoke
il n'avait pas le droit de fumer, il ne pouvait pas fumer

On ne peut pas employer **might** dans le dernier exemple. On ne peut employer **might** comme passé dans une principale que dans certains cas spéciaux :

in those days we were told not to drink; nor might we smoke or be out after 10 o'clock
en ce temps-là, nous n'avions pas le droit de boire, pas plus que de fumer ou de rentrer après dix heures

Une manière plus courante et moins littéraire de formuler cette phrase serait :

in those days we were told not to drink; nor were we allowed to smoke or be out after 10 o'clock

ii) possibilité :

it may/might rain
il pleuvra peut-être

they may/might be right
il se peut qu'ils aient raison

it mayn't/mightn't be so easy as you think
ce ne sera peut-être pas aussi facile que vous le pensez

she may/might have left already
elle est peut-être déjà partie

Might exprime généralement un moindre degré de possibilité.

Remarquez la tournure idiomatique :

and who may/might you be?
et pour qui est-ce que tu te prends ?

dans laquelle l'emploi de **may/might** introduit une nuance de surprise, d'amusement ou peut-être d'ennui dans la question :

and who *may/might* you be to give out orders?
et pour qui est-ce que tu te prends pour donner des ordres ?

iii) Notez l'emploi de **might** pour formuler des suggestions :

you might help me dry the dishes
tu pourrais m'aider à essuyer la vaisselle

well, you might at least try!
tu pourrais au moins essayer, enfin !

you might have a look at chapter 2 for next Wednesday
vous voudrez bien lire le chapitre 2 pour mercredi prochain

he might be a little less abrupt
il pourrait être un peu moins brusque

L'usage suivant exprime souvent une pointe de reproche :

you might have warned us what would happen!
vous auriez pu nous prévenir de ce qui allait se produire

he might have tried to stop it!
il aurait pu essayer d'arrêter cela

iv) souhaits :

may the best man win!
que le meilleur gagne !

may you be forgiven for telling such lies!
que le Bon Dieu te pardonne de dire de tels mensonges !

might I be struck dumb if I tell a lie!
que le diable m'emporte si je mens !

Cet usage est normalement réservé à des expressions consacrées (comme dans les deux premiers exemples) ou considéré comme étant d'un style quelque peu ampoulé ou littéraire (comme dans le dernier).

e) ***must-had to***

i) obligation :

you must try harder
tu dois faire un effort

we must park the car here and walk the rest of the way
il faut que nous garions la voiture ici et que nous fassions le reste du chemin à pied

Remarquez que l'on emploie **had to** pour le passé. On ne peut employer **must** pour le passé qu'au discours indirect, et même alors **had to** est beaucoup plus courant :

you said the other day that you had to/must clean out the garden shed
tu as dit l'autre jour qu'il faudrait que tu nettoies la cabane du jardin

On peut aussi employer **have to**, ou **have got to** dans un niveau de langue moins soutenu, au présent. La différence entre **must** et **have (got) to** réside généralement dans le fait que **must** exprime des sentiments personnels d'obligation ou de contrainte tandis que **have (got) to** exprime une obligation extérieure. Comparez :

I must go and visit my friend in hospital
il faut que je rende visite à mon amie à l'hôpital (= je pense qu'il est nécessaire que j'y aille)

you must go and visit your friend in hospital
il faut que tu rendes visite à ton ami à l'hôpital (je pense qu'il est nécessaire que tu y ailles)

I have (got) to be at the hospital by 4 pm
je dois être à l'hôpital pour 4 heures de l'après-midi (c'est-à-dire j'y ai un rendez-vous)

ii) négations :

Les tournures négatives exigent une vigilance toute particulière. On ne peut employer **must not/mustn't** que pour exprimer l'interdiction (= une obligation de ne pas faire quelque chose) :

we mustn't park the car here (= we're not allowed to park here)
nous ne devons pas nous garer ici (= nous n'avons pas le droit de nous garer ici)

you mustn't take so many pills (= do not take so many pills)
il ne faut pas que tu prennes autant de cachets

Mais si l'obligation négative signifie, non pas par exemple qu'il est interdit de faire quelque chose, mais qu'il n'est pas nécessaire ou obligatoire de faire quelque chose, alors ont doit employer **don't have to** ou **haven't got to** :

we don't have to park here, we could always drive a little further
nous ne sommes pas obligés de nous garer ici, nous pourrions aller un peu plus loin

you don't have to take so many pills (= you needn't take ...)
tu n'as pas besoin de prendre autant de comprimés

we haven't got to be there before 9
nous n'avons pas besoin d'y être avant neuf heures

iii) déduction, probabilité :

if they're over 65, they must be old age pensioners
s'ils ont plus de 65 ans, ils doivent être retraités

you must be joking!
tu veux rire !

they must have been surprised to see you
ils ont dû être surpris de te voir

Have to s'emploie souvent dans ce sens :

you have to be kidding!
c'est une blague !

de même que **have got to**, en anglais britannique en particulier :

well if she said so, it's got to be true (it's = it has)
si elle l'a dit, c'est que c'est vrai

A la forme négative, on emploie **can** :

he can't be that old!
il ne peut pas être si vieux que ça !

f) ***ought to***

La forme négative contractée de **ought to** est **oughtn't to**, et l'infinitif placé après **ought** est précédé de **to**, ce qui n'est pas le cas des autres auxiliaires modaux.

i) obligation :

Ought to et **should**, lorsqu'ils expriment l'obligation, ont des significations similaires :

you oughtn't to speak to her like that
tu ne devrais pas lui parler de cette façon

I ought to be going now
il faudrait que je m'en aille maintenant

I know I really ought (to), but I don't want to
je sais bien que je devrais, mais je n'en ai pas envie

ii) déduction, probabilité :

they ought to have reached the summit by now
ils devraient avoir atteint le sommet maintenant

20 square metres? – that ought to be enough
20 mètres carrés ? – ça devrait suffire

Comparez la différence entre **ought to** et **must** dans la phrase suivante :

if they possess all these things, they must be rich (déduction logique)
ils doivent être riches s'ils possèdent tout ça

if they possess all these things, they ought to be happy (prévision ou probabilité logique – ou obligation morale)
ils devraient être heureux s'ils possèdent tout ça

g) ***used to***

Puisqu'il est possible de former des phrases interrogatives et négatives contenant **used to** sans employer **do**, certains considèrent **used to** comme une sorte de semi-auxiliaire. Cependant l'emploi de **do** est au moins aussi courant que le fait de l'omettre :

he used not/usedn't to visit us so often
he didn't use to visit us so often
(autrefois), il ne nous rendait pas visite aussi souvent

A la forme interrogative, la forme sans **do** est moins courante et appartient davantage au langage écrit qu'au langage parlé :

used you to live abroad?
did you use to live abroad?
est-ce que vous habitiez à l'étranger (autrefois) ?

On emploie souvent **never** à la place de **not** :

he never used to visit us so often
(autrefois), il ne nous rendait pas visite aussi souvent

Used to exprime une action habituelle dans le passé, mais sans cependant exprimer l'idée de comportement typique ou caractéristique que traduirait **would** (voir a) vi ci-dessus) :

John used to play badminton when he was younger
John jouait au badminton lorsqu'il était plus jeune

I used to live abroad
autrefois, je vivais à l'étranger

do you smoke? – I used to
est-ce que tu fumes ? – plus maintenant

19. DARE, NEED

Ces verbes peuvent se comporter soit comme des verbes ordinaires, soit comme des auxiliaires modaux. Lorsqu'ils sont auxiliaires :

- ils ne prennent pas de -s à la troisième personne du singulier du présent
- on n'emploie pas **do** dans les phrases interrogatives ou négatives
- s'ils sont suivis d'un infinitif, celui-ci n'est pas précédé de **to**.

a) *Lorsqu'ils sont verbes ordinaires*

he didn't dare to speak
il n'osait pas parler/il n'a pas osé parler

does he really dare to talk openly about it?
est-ce qu'il ose vraiment en parler ouvertement ?

I dare you
je t'en défie

he needs some money
il a besoin d'argent

you don't need to pay for them now
ce n'est pas la peine que tu les paies maintenant

all he needs to do now is buy the tickets
tout ce qu'il a à faire maintenant, c'est d'acheter les billets

Cependant, **dare** peut être en partie un verbe ordinaire (par exemple avec **do** dans les phrases interrogatives ou négatives) et en partie un auxiliaire (suivi d'un infinitif sans **to**) :

does he really dare talk openly about it?
est-ce qu'il ose vraiment en parler ouvertement ?

mais on doit employer l'infinitif avec **to** après le participe présent

not daring to speak to her, he quietly left the room
n'osant pas lui parler, il est sorti de la pièce silencieusement

Dans les propositions **principales** à la forme affirmative (c'est-à-dire les propositions principales qui ne sont ni interrogatives ni négatives) **need** ne peut qu'avoir le statut de verbe ordinaire :

the child needs to go to the toilet
l'enfant a besoin d'aller aux toilettes

b) *Lorsqu'ils sont auxiliaires modaux*

he dared not speak
il n'osait pas parler/il n'a pas osé parler

dare he talk openly about it?
est-ce qu'il ose en parler ouvertement ?

this is as much as I dare spend on it
c'est tout ce que j'ose dépenser pour cela

you needn't pay for them right now
ce n'est pas la peine que tu les paies maintenant

need I pay for this now?
est-ce qu'il faut que je le paie maintenant ?

all he need do now is buy the tickets
tout ce qu'il a à faire maintenant, c'est d'acheter les billets

Notez que **I dare say** = "probablement" :

I dare say he's going to fail
il va probablement échouer

is it going to rain, do you think? – I dare say it will
est-ce que tu crois qu'il va pleuvoir ? – probablement

20. LES VERBES COMPOSES

a) *Les verbes composés inséparables*

i) Il est important de faire une distinction entre un "verbe + préposition introduisant un complément" ((a) et (c) ci-dessous) et un "verbe composé + complément d'objet direct" ((b) et (d)). Dans le dernier cas, la préposition fonctionne comme une **particule** faisant partie du verbe, c'est-à-dire comme un prolongement du verbe. Comparez les deux phrases :

(a) **they danced after dinner**
ils ont dansé après le dîner
(b) **they looked after the child**
ils se sont occupé de l'enfant

Au premier abord, ces deux phrases semblent avoir la même structure, et cependant, lorsqu'on y regarde de plus près, on se rend compte que les deux mots

look after forment une seule unité verbale (comparez avec **they nursed the child** ils ont soigné l'enfant), tandis que cela n'est pas le cas pour **danced after** : **after dinner** est un complément introduit par une préposition distincte du verbe et qui fonctionnent comme groupe adverbial de temps dans (a), tandis que **the child** est le complément d'objet direct de **look after** dans (b). On peut observer la même différence dans les deux exemples suivants :

(c) **they went through Germany**
ils sont passés par l'Allemagne
(d) **they went through the accounts** (= examined)
ils ont examiné la comptabilité

ii) **Look after** et **go through** (= examiner) sont des verbes composés. Ceux-ci sont souvent très idiomatiques, c'est-à-dire qu'on ne peut pas déduire leur sens du sens des différents éléments qui les composent, car ceux-ci peuvent rarement se traduire littéralement. Voici d'autres exemples :

go by (= suivre (des instructions))
pick on (= chercher querelle à, s'en prendre à)
get at (= attaquer ; graisser la patte à)

you can't do your own thing; you have to go by the book
tu ne peux pas faire ce que tu veux ; il faut agir selon les règles

the teacher's always picking on him
le professeur s'en prend toujours à lui

my mother is always getting at me
ma mère est toujours sur mon dos

I'm sure the jury have been got at
je suis sûr qu'on a graissé la patte au jury

iii) Certaines structures que l'on pourrait former avec un verbe + préposition introduisant un complément ne peuvent en aucun cas être formées avec les verbes composés. Par exemple, les interrogations avec les verbes composés admettent l'emploi des pronoms **who** et **what**, mais pas l'emploi des adverbes **where, when, how** :

they looked after the girl/who(m) did they look after?
ils se sont occupé de la petite fille/de qui se sont-ils occupé ?

they went through the accounts/what did they go through?
ils ont examiné la comptabilité/qu'est-ce qu'ils ont examiné ?

the police officer grappled with the thug/who(m) did he grapple with?
l'agent de police a lutté avec le voyou/avec qui a-t-il lutté ?

Mais les interrogations **where did they look?/where did they go?/how (ou where) did he grapple?** n'ont aucun sens. Par contre le verbe + préposition introduisant un complément admet souvent des interrogations introduites par un adverbe :

they went through Germany/where did they go?
ils sont passés par l'Allemagne/par où est-ce qu'ils sont passés ?

they worked with great care/how did they work?
ils ont travaillé avec beaucoup de soin/comment ont-ils travaillé ?

they danced after dinner/when did they dance?
ils ont dansé après le dîner/quand ont-ils dansé ?

iv) Un verbe composé étant considéré comme une seule unité, on peut souvent (mais pas toujours) l'employer dans une construction passive :

the child has been looked after very well indeed
on s'est vraiment très bien occupé de l'enfant

the accounts have been gone through
la comptabilité a été examinée

do you feel you're being got at?
est-ce que tu as l'impression qu'on est sur ton dos ?

On ne peut pas employer le passif avec un verbe + préposition introduisant un complément. On ne peut pas dire **the dinner was danced after** ou **great care has been worked with**.

b) *Les verbes composés séparables*

i) Une différence importante entre les verbes composés inséparables et les verbes composés séparables réside dans la possibilité qu'ont les verbes composés séparables d'admettre un complément d'objet direct avant la particule :

look up these words/look these words up
cherche ces mots (dans le dictionnaire)

turn down the television/turn the television down
baisse la télévision

have you switched on the computer?/have you switched the computer on?
est-ce que tu as mis l'ordinateur en marche ?

have you tried on any of their new line of shoes?/have you tried any of their new line of shoes on?
est-ce que tu as essayé des chaussures de leur nouvelle ligne ?

Et si le complément d'objet direct est un pronom, la particule **doit** être placée après celui-ci :

look them up/turn it down/switch it on
cherche-les/baisse-la/mets-le en marche

ii) Tandis que les verbes composés inséparables sont toujours transitifs (lorsqu'on les considère comme unités complètes), certains verbes composés séparables sont toujours transitifs et d'autres peuvent être transitifs ou intransitifs :

back up (= soutenir – seulement transitif) :
he always backs her up
il la soutient toujours

cool down (= faire refroidir – transitif) :
cool the rolls down in the fridge
fais refroidir les petits pains dans le frigidaire

cool down (= se refroidir – intransitif) :
let the rolls cool down
laisse les petits pains refroidir

iii) Avec les verbes composés séparables, la particule ne peut pas précéder un pronom relatif, alors que cela est la seule position possible avec les verbes composés inséparables. Nous pouvons ainsi dire :

this is a man on whom you can rely
c'est un homme sur lequel vous pouvez compter

parce que **rely on** est un verbe composé inséparable, tandis qu'on ne peut en aucun cas dire :

this is his wife up whom he has always backed

car **back up** est un verbe composé séparable.

iv) Comme de nombreux verbes composés inséparables (voir a) ii ci-dessus), de nombreux verbes composés séparables sont très idiomatiques :

square up (= régler – des dettes, etc.)
bring round (= faire reprendre connaissance à ; convertir à un point de vue)
set back (= coûter – de l'argent à quelqu'un) :

if you pay now, we can square up later
si tu payes maintenant, nous pourrons régler nos comptes plus tard

give him a brandy; that'll bring him round
donne-lui un cognac, ça lui fera reprendre connaissance

do you think anything will bring him round to our point of view?
est-ce que tu crois qu'on pourrait lui faire admettre notre point de vue ?

that car must have set you back at least £10,000
cette voiture doit vous avoir coûté au moins 10 000 £

c) *Les verbes composés seulement intransitifs*

Il y a aussi des verbes composés intransitifs (qui ne sont bien entendu jamais séparables) :

poor people often lose out
les pauvres sont souvent perdants

the entire species is on the verge of dying out
l'espèce entière est sur le point de disparaître

A la différence des verbes composés inséparables, ces verbes n'ont jamais de forme passive.

d) *Les verbes composés, transitifs, jamais séparables, à complémentation*

Ils sont composés de trois mots et non pas deux, par exemple :

come up with
trouver, concocter

Avec ces verbes, le complément d'objet ne peut jamais séparer le verbe et ses particules, c'est-à-dire que des phrases du type **have you come it up with?** sont impossibles. Le complément d'objet direct doit suivre la dernière particule.

we've come up with a great solution
nous avons trouvé une solution idéale

Les deux particules ne peuvent pas non plus précéder un pronom relatif. Ainsi on dira :

is there anything else (which) you can come up with?
est-ce que tu peux trouver quelque chose d'autre ?

Mais on ne peut PAS mettre les deux particules avant un pronom relatif comme dans la phrase (agrammaticale) : **is there anything else up with which you can come?**

Autres exemples de verbes composés, transitifs, jamais séparables, à complémentation (idiomatiques) :

make off with (voler)
make up to (essayer de se faire bien voir par)
live up to (se montrer à la hauteur de)
stand up for (prendre le parti de)
crack down on (sévir contre)

somebody made off with her suitcase
quelqu'un lui a volé sa valise

this is the teacher Fiona has been making up to throughout term, but her marks are no better
c'est le professeur dont Fiona a essayé de se faire bien voir tout le trimestre, mais ses notes n'en sont pas meilleures pour autant

it was difficult for him to live up to this reputation
il lui était difficile d'être à la hauteur de cette réputation

why didn't you stand up for me if you knew I was right?
pourquoi est-ce que tu n'as pas pris mon parti si tu savais que j'avais raison ?

every Christmas police crack down on drink-and-drive offenders
chaque année à Noël la police sévit contre ceux qui prennent le volant après avoir bu

21. LE TEMPS AU DISCOURS INDIRECT

Le discours indirect permet de rapporter les paroles de quelqu'un. La concordance des temps en anglais dans le discours indirect a les mêmes caractéristiques qu'en français :

Henry said/had said, 'I am unhappy' (direct)
Henry a dit/avait dit : "je suis malheureux"
Henry said/had said (that) he was unhappy (indirect)
Henry a dit/avait dit qu'il était malheureux

22. LISTE DES VERBES IRREGULIERS

Les américanismes sont indiqués par *. Les formes peu courantes, archaïques ou littéraires sont données entre parenthèses. Les traductions ci-dessous ne sont pas restrictives et ne donnent qu'un des sens de base.

infinitif		prétérit	participe passé
abide	(*supporter*)	**(abode)** [1]	**abided**
arise	(*surgir*)	**arose**	**arisen**
awake	(*s'éveiller*)	**awoke, awaked**	**awoken, (awaked)**
bear	(*porter*)	**bore**	**borne** [2]
beat	(*battre*)	**beat**	**beaten** [3]
become	(*devenir*)	**became**	**become**
befall	(*arriver*)	**befell**	**befallen**
beget	(*engendrer*)	**begot**	**begotten**
begin	(*commencer*)	**began**	**begun**
behold	(*apercevoir*)	**beheld**	**beheld**
bend	(*courber*)	**bent**	**bent** [4]
bereave	(*priver*)	**bereaved**	**bereft** [5]
beseech	(*implorer*)	**besought**	**besought**
bestride	(*chevaucher*)	**bestrode**	**bestridden**
bet	(*parier*)	**bet, betted**	**bet, betted**
bid	(*offrir*)	**bid**	**bid**
bid	(*commander*)	**bade**	**bidden**
bind	(*attacher*)	**bound**	**bound**
bite	(*mordre*)	**bit**	**bitten**
bleed	(*saigner*)	**bled**	**bled**
blow	(*souffler*)	**blew**	**blown**
break	(*casser*)	**broke**	**broken** [6]
breed	(*élever*)	**bred**	**bred**
bring	(*apporter*)	**brought**	**brought**
broadcast	(*diffuser*)	**broadcast**	**broadcast**
build	(*construire*)	**built**	**built**
burn	(*brûler*)	**burnt, burned**	**burnt, burned**
burst	(*éclater*)	**burst**	**burst**
buy	(*acheter*)	**bought**	**bought**
cast	(*jeter*)	**cast**	**cast**
catch	(*attraper*)	**caught**	**caught**
chide	(*gronder*)	**chid, chided**	**chid, (chidden), chided**
choose	(*choisir*)	**chose**	**chosen**
cleave	(*fendre*)	**clove, cleft,**	**cloven, cleft** [7]
cleave	(*adhérer*)	**cleaved, (clave)**	**cleaved**
cling	(*s'accrocher à*)	**clung**	**clung**
clothe	(*habiller*)	**clothed, (clad)**	**clothed, (clad)**
come	(*venir*)	**came**	**come**
cost	(*coûter*)	**cost**	**cost**
creep	(*ramper*)	**crept**	**crept**
crow	(*chanter*)	**crowed, (crew)**	**crowed**
cut	(*couper*)	**cut**	**cut**
dare	(*oser*)	**dared, (durst)**	**dared, (durst)**
deal	(*traiter*)	**dealt**	**dealt**
dig	(*fouiller*)	**dug**	**dug**
dive	(*plonger*)	**dived, dove***	**dived**
draw	(*dessiner, tirer*)	**drew**	**drawn**
dream	(*rêver*)	**dreamt, dreamed**	**dreamt, dreamed**
drink	(*boire*)	**drank**	**drunk** [8]
drive	(*conduire*)	**drove**	**driven**
dwell	(*demeurer*)	**dwelt, dwelled**	**dwelt, dwelled**
eat	(*manger*)	**ate**	**eaten**
fall	(*tomber*)	**fell**	**fallen**
feed	(*nourrir*)	**fed**	**fed**
feel	(*sentir*)	**felt**	**felt**
fight	(*battre*)	**fought**	**fought**
find	(*trouver*)	**found**	**found**
fit	(*aller à*)	**fit*, fitted**	**fit*, fitted**
flee	(*s'envoler*)	**fled**	**fled**
fling	(*lancer*)	**flung**	**flung**
fly	(*voler*)	**flew**	**flown**
forbear	(*s'abstenir*)	**forbore**	**forborne**
forbid	(*interdire*)	**forbad(e)**	**forbidden**
forget	(*oublier*)	**forgot**	**forgotten**
forgive	(*pardonner*)	**forgave**	**forgiven**
forsake	(*abandonner*)	**forsook**	**forsaken**
freeze	(*geler*)	**froze**	**frozen**
get	(*obtenir*)	**got**	**got, gotten*** [9]
gild	(*dorer*)	**gilt, gilded**	**gilt, gilded** [10]

gird	(*ceindre*)	**girt, girded**	**girt, girded** [10]
give	(*donner*)	**gave**	**given**
go	(*aller*)	**went**	**gone**
grind	(*grincer*)	**ground**	**ground**
grow	(*pousser*)	**grew**	**grown**
hang	(*pendre*)	**hung, hanged** [11]	**hung, hanged**[11]
hear	(*entendre*)	**heard**	**heard**
heave	(*lever*)	**hove, heaved** [12]	**hove, heaved**[12]
hew	(*tailler*)	**hewed**	**hewn, hewed**
hide	(*cacher*)	**hid**	**hidden**
hit	(*frapper*)	**hit**	**hit**
hold	(*tenir*)	**held**	**held**
hurt	(*blesser*)	**hurt**	**hurt**
keep	(*garder*)	**kept**	**kept**
kneel	(*s'agenouiller*)	**knelt, kneeled**	**knelt, kneeled**
knit	(*tricoter*)	**knit, knitted** [13]	**knit, knitted** [13]
know	(*savoir, connaître*)	**knew**	**known**
lay	(*coucher*)	**laid**	**laid**
lead	(*mener*)	**led**	**led**
lean	(*s'appuyer*)	**leant, leaned**	**leant, leaned**
leap	(*sauter*)	**leapt, leaped**	**leapt, leaped**
learn	(*apprendre*)	**learnt, learned**	**learnt, learned**
leave	(*laisser*)	**left**	**left**
lend	(*prêter*)	**lent**	**lent**
let	(*laisser*)	**let**	**let**
lie	(*coucher*)	**lay**	**lain**
light	(*allumer*)	**lit, lighted**	**lit, lighted** [14]
lose	(*perdre*)	**lost**	**lost**
make	(*faire*)	**made**	**made**
mean	(*signifier*)	**meant**	**meant**
meet	(*rencontrer*)	**met**	**met**
melt	(*fondre*)	**melted**	**melted, molten**[15]
mow	(*faucher*)	**mowed**	**mown, mowed**
pay	(*payer*)	**paid**	**paid**
plead	(*plaider*)	**pled*, pleaded**	**pled*, pleaded**[16]
put	(*poser*)	**put**	**put**
quit	(*quitter*)	**quit, (quitted)**	**quit, (quitted)**[17]
read	(*lire*)	**read**	**read**
rend	(*déchirer*)	**rent**	**rent**
rid	(*débarrasser*)	**rid, (ridded)**	**rid**
ride	(*monter à*)	**rode**	**ridden**
ring	(*sonner*)	**rang**	**rung**
rise	(*se lever*)	**rose**	**risen**
run	(*courir*)	**ran**	**run**
saw	(*scier*)	**sawed**	**sawn, sawed**
say	(*dire*)	**said**	**said**
see	(*voir*)	**saw**	**seen**
seek	(*chercher*)	**sought**	**sought**
sell	(*vendre*)	**sold**	**sold**
send	(*envoyer*)	**sent**	**sent**
set	(*mettre*)	**set**	**set**
sew	(*coudre*)	**sewed**	**sewn, sewed**
shake	(*secouer*)	**shook**	**shaken**
shear	(*tondre*)	**sheared**	**shorn, sheared**[18]
shed	(*perdre*)	**shed**	**shed**
shine	(*briller*)	**shone** [19]	**shone** [19]
shoe	(*chausser*)	**shod, shoed**	**shod, shoed** [20]
shoot	(*abattre, tirer*)	**shot**	**shot**
show	(*montrer*)	**showed**	**shown, showed**
shrink	(*rétrécir*)	**shrank, shrunk**	**shrunk, shrunken** [21]
shut	(*fermer*)	**shut**	**shut**
sing	(*chanter*)	**sang**	**sung**
sink	(*couler*)	**sank**	**sunk, sunken**[22]
sit	(*s'asseoir*)	**sat**	**sat**
slay	(*tuer*)	**slew**	**slain**
sleep	(*dormir*)	**slept**	**slept**
slide	(*glisser*)	**slid**	**slid**
sling	(*lancer*)	**slung**	**slung**
slink	(*s'en aller furtivement*)	**slunk**	**slunk**
slit	(*fendre*)	**slit**	**slit**
smell	(*sentir*)	**smelt, smelled**	**smelt, smelled**
smite	(*frapper*)	**smote**	**smitten** [23]
sneak	(*entrer, etc. à la dérobée*)	**snuck*, sneaked**	**snuck*, sneaked**

sow	(*semer*)	**sowed**	**sown, sowed**
speak	(*parler*)	**spoke**	**spoken**
speed	(*aller vite*)	**sped, speeded**	**sped, speeded**
spell	(*écrire*)	**spelt, spelled**	**spelt, spelled**
spend	(*dépenser*)	**spent**	**spent**
spill	(*renverser*)	**spilt, spilled**	**spilt, spilled**
spin	(*filer*)	**spun**	**spun**
spit	(*cracher*)	**spat, spit***	**spat, spit***
split	(*se briser*)	**split**	**split**
spoil	(*abîmer*)	**spoilt, spoiled**	**spoilt, spoiled**
spread	(*étendre*)	**spread**	**spread**
spring	(*bondir*)	**sprang**	**sprung**
stand	(*se tenir*)	**stood**	**stood**
steal	(*voler*)	**stole**	**stolen**
stick	(*enfoncer, coller*)	**stuck**	**stuck**
sting	(*piquer*)	**stung**	**stung**
stink	(*puer*)	**stank**	**stunk**
strew	(*répandre*)	**strewed**	**strewn, strewed**
stride	(*avancer à grands pas*)	**strode**	**stridden**
strike	(*frapper*)	**struck**	**struck, stricken** [24]
string	(*enfiler*)	**strung**	**strung**
strive	(*s'efforcer*)	**strove**	**striven**
swear	(*jurer*)	**swore**	**sworn**
sweat	(*suer*)	**sweat*, sweated**	**sweat*, sweated**
sweep	(*balayer*)	**swept**	**swept**
swell	(*gonfler*)	**swelled**	**swollen, swelled** [25]
swim	(*nager*)	**swam**	**swum**
swing	(*se balancer*)	**swung**	**swung**
take	(*prendre*)	**took**	**taken**
teach	(*enseigner*)	**taught**	**taught**
tear	(*déchirer*)	**tore**	**torn**
tell	(*dire*)	**told**	**told**
think	(*penser*)	**thought**	**thought**
thrive	(*fleurir*)	**thrived, (throve)**	**thrived, (thriven)**
throw	(*jeter*)	**threw**	**thrown**
thrust	(*pousser*)	**thrust**	**thrust**
tread	(*marcher*)	**trod**	**trodden**
understand	(*comprendre*)	**understood**	**understood**
undertake	(*s'engager*)	**undertook**	**undertaken**
wake	(*se réveiller*)	**woke, waked**	**woken, waked**
wear	(*porter*)	**wore**	**worn**
weave	(*tisser*)	**wove** [26]	**woven** [26]
weep	(*pleurer*)	**wept**	**wept**
wet	(*mouiller*)	**wet*, wetted** [27]	**wet*, wetted**[27]
win	(*gagner*)	**won**	**won**
wind	(*remonter*)	**wound**	**wound**
wring	(*tordre*)	**wrung**	**wrung**
write	(*écrire*)	**wrote**	**written**

(1) Régulier dans la construction **abide by** "se conformer à, suivre" : **they abided by the rules**.

(2) Mais **born** au passif = "né" ou comme un adjectif : **he was born in France/a born gentleman**.

(3) Remarquez la forme familière **this has me beat/you have me beat there** *cela me dépasse/tu m'as posé une colle* et **beat** dans le sens de "très fatigué, épuisé" : **I am (dead) beat**.

(4) Remarquez la phrase **on one's bended knees** *à genoux*.

(5) Mais **bereaved** dans le sens de "endeuillé" comme dans **the bereaved received no compensation** *la famille du disparu ne reçut aucune compensation*. Comparez : **he was bereft of speech** *il en perdit la parole*.

(6) Mais **broke** quand il s'agit d'un adjectif = "fauché" : **I'm broke**.

(7) **cleft** n'est employé qu'avec le sens de "coupé en deux". Remarquez **cleft palate** *palais fendu* et **(to be caught) in a cleft stick** *(être) dans une impasse*, mais **cloven foot/hoof** *sabot fendu*.

(8) Quand c'est un adjectif placé avant le nom, **drunken** "ivre, ivrogne" est parfois employé (**a lot of drunk(en) people** *beaucoup de gens ivres*) et il **doit** toujours être

employé devant les noms représentant des objets inanimés (**one of his usual drunken parties** *une de ses soirées habituelles où l'on boit*).

(9) Mais **have got to** se dit aussi en américain avec le sens de "devoir, être obligé de" : **a man has got to do what a man has got to do** *un homme doit faire ce qu'il doit faire.* Comparez avec : **she has gotten into a terrible mess** *elle s'est fourrée dans une sale situation.*

(10) Les formes du participe passé **gilt** et **girt** sont très couramment employées comme adjectif placé avant le nom : **gilt mirrors** *des miroirs dorés*, **a flower-girt grave** *une tombe entourée de fleurs* (mais toujours **gilded youth** *la jeunesse dorée*, dans lequel **gilded** signifie "riche et bienheureux").

(11) Régulier quand il a le sens de "mettre à mort par pendaison".

(12) **Hove** est employé dans le domaine nautique comme dans la phrase **heave into sight** : **just then Mary hove into sight** *et Mary pointa à l'horizon/apparut.*

(13) Irrégulier quand il a le sens de "unir" (**a close-knit family** *une famille unie*), mais régulier lorsqu' il a le sens de "fabriquer en laine" et quand il fait référence aux os – "se souder".

(14) Lorsque le participe passé est employé comme un adjectif devant un nom, **lighted** est souvent préféré à **lit** : **a lighted match** *une allumette allumée* (mais : **the match is lit, she has lit a match** *l'allumette est allumée, elle a allumé l'allumette*). Dans les noms composés, on emploie généralement **lit** : **well-lit streets** *des rues bien éclairées.* Au sens figuré (avec **up**) **lit** uniquement est employé au prétérit et au participe passé : **her face lit up when she saw me** *son visage s'illumina lorsqu'elle me vit.*

(15) On emploie **molten** uniquement comme un adjectif devant les noms, et seulement lorsqu'il signifie "fondu à une très haute température", par exemple : **molten lead** *du plomb fondu* (mais **melted butter** *du beurre fondu*).

(16) En anglais d'Ecosse et en américain, on emploie **pled** au passé et au participe passé.

(17) En américain, les formes régulières ne sont pas employées, et elles sont de plus en plus rares en anglais britannique.

(18) Le participe passé est normalement **shorn** devant un nom (**newly-shorn lambs** *des agneaux tout juste tondus*) et toujours dans la phrase **(to be) shorn of** *(être) privé de* : **shorn of his riches he was nothing** *privé de ses richesses, il n'était plus rien.*

(19) Mais régulier quand il a le sens de "cirer, astiquer" en américain.

(20) Quand c'est un adjectif, on n'emploie que **shod** : **a well-shod foot** *un pied bien chaussé.*

(21) **Shrunken** n'est employé que lorsqu'il est adjectif : **shrunken limbs/her face was shrunken** *des membres rabougris/son visage était ratatiné.*

(22) **Sunken** n'est employé que comme un adjectif : **sunken eyes** *des yeux creux.*

(23) Verbe archaïque dont le participe passé **smitten** s'emploie encore comme adjectif : **he's completely smitten with her** *il est complètement fou d'elle.*

(24) **Stricken** n'est utilisé que dans le sens figuré (**a stricken family/stricken with poverty** *une famille accablée/accablée par la pauvreté*). Il est très courant dans les noms composés (accablé par) : **poverty-stricken, fever-stricken, horror-stricken** (aussi **horror-struck**), **terror-stricken** (aussi **terror-struck**), mais on dit toujours **thunderstruck** *frappé par la surprise, abasourdi de surprise.*

C'est aussi un emploi américain **the remark was stricken from the record** *la remarque a été rayée du procès-verbal.*

(25) **Swollen** est plus courant que **swelled** comme verbe (**her face has swollen** *son visage a gonflé)* et comme adjectif (**her face is swollen/a swollen face**). **A swollen head** *une grosse tête*, pour quelqu'un qui a une haute opinion de soi-même, devient **a swelled head** en américain.

(26) Mais il est régulier lorsqu'il a le sens de "se faufiler" : **the motorbike weaved elegantly through the traffic** *la moto se faufila avec élégance dans la circulation.*

(27) Mais irrégulier aussi en anglais britannique lorsqu'il a le sens de "mouiller par de l'urine" : **he wet his bed again last night** *il a encore mouillé son lit la nuit dernière.*

23. LES AUXILIAIRES BE, HAVE, DO : LEURS FORMES

a) BE

Présent	*Prétérit*	*Participe passé*
1ère **I am**	1ère **I was**	**been**
2ème **you are**	2ème **you were**	
3ème **he/she/it is**	3ème **he was**	
1ère **we are**	1ère **we were**	
2ème **you are**	2ème **you were**	
3ème **they are**	3ème **they were**	

Contracté avec le mot précédant :

I'm = I am ; you're = you are ; he's/John's = he is/John is ; we're/you're/they're = we are/you are/they are

Contracté avec **not**

aren't I? (questions seulement) ; **am I not? ; you/we/they aren't ; he isn't ; I/he wasn't ; you/we/they weren't**

On a aussi : **I'm not ; you're not**, etc.

Pour le subjonctif, voir p A51-2.

b) HAVE

Présent	*Prétérit*	*Participe passé*
1ère **I have**	1ère **I had**	**had**
2ème **you have**	2ème **you had**	
3ème **he/she/it has**	3ème **he had**	
1ère **we have**	1ère **we had**	
2ème **you have**	2ème **you had**	
3ème **they have**	3ème **they had**	

Contracté avec le mot précédant :

I've/you've/we've/they've = I have, etc. **he's** = he has

I'd/you'd/he'd/we'd/they'd = I had, etc.

Vous noterez que **he's/she's** ne sont normalement pas contractés lorsqu'ils sont employés comme verbes en tant que tels et non comme auxiliaires au présent :

I've two cars	**he has two cars**
j'ai deux voitures	il a deux voitures

Contracté avec **not** :

haven't ; hasn't ; hadn't

c) DO

Présent	*Prétérit*	*Participe passé*
1ère **I do**	1ère **I did**	**done**
2ème **you do**	2ème **you did**	
3ème **he/she/it does**	3ème **he did**	
1ère **we do**	1ère **we did**	
2ème **you do**	2ème **you did**	
3ème **they do**	3ème **they did**	

Contracté avec **not** :

don't ; doesn't ; didn't

14. LES PREPOSITIONS

1. Les prépositions servent à exprimer des relations de temps, de lieu, de possession, etc. Elles sont normalement suivies d'un nom ou d'un pronom comme :

after – after the show	après le spectacle
on – on it	là-dessus
of – of London	de Londres

Cependant, dans certaines constructions les prépositions anglaises peuvent se placer en fin de proposition :

the people I came here with
les gens avec lesquels je suis venu

something I had never dreamed of
quelque chose dont je n'avais jamais rêvé

Voir aussi **Les Verbes Composés**, p A59, ainsi que **Les Pronoms Interrogatifs et Relatifs**, p A31, A32.

2. Voici une liste des prépositions les plus couramment employées. Etant donné que la plupart des prépositions ont toute une richesse de sens et d'emplois, seuls les usages les plus importants et ceux particulièrement intéressants ou susceptibles de poser des problèmes à ceux qui apprennent l'anglais, sont mentionnés ci-dessous.

★ **about** et **around**

i) "lieu" (dans les environs, en tous sens) :

Souvent il n'y a pas de différence entre **about** et **around**, bien qu'en anglais américain on préfère **around** :

they walked about/around town
ils se sont promenés dans la ville

he must be about/around somewhere
il doit être dans les parages

the dog was racing about/around in the garden
le chien courait en tous sens dans le jardin

ii) "autour de" :

he lives just (a)round the corner
tu tournes au coin et c'est là qu'il habite

she put the rope (a)round his chest
elle a mis la corde autour de sa poitrine

iii) "environ" :

I have about £1 on me
j'ai environ une livre sur moi

it'll cost you around £20
ça te coûtera environ 20 livres

iv) "au sujet de", "sur" (seulement **about**) :

what's the book about? – it's a story about nature
de quoi parle le livre ? – c'est une histoire sur la nature

on peut être plus technique, plus académique :

he gave a paper on Verdi and Shakespeare
il a donné une conférence sur Verdi et Shakespeare

a book on English grammar
un livre sur la grammaire anglaise

★ **above** (au-dessus de)

Comparez **above** avec **over**. Il y a en général peu de différence entre les deux :

he has a lovely mirror above/over the mantelpiece
il a un très joli miroir au-dessus de la cheminée

Mais **above** exprime normalement le fait d'être "situé au-dessus de" dans un sens purement physique :

the shirts had been placed in the wardrobe above the socks and underwear
les chemises avaient été placées dans l'armoire au-dessus des chaussettes et des sous-vêtements

mais :

he flung his coat over a chair
il a jeté son manteau sur une chaise

★ **across** (à travers)

Across et **over** ont souvent un sens très proche, cependant **across** a tendance à indiquer une dimension horizontale (sur la largeur de) :

he walked across the fields to the farm
il a traversé les champs jusqu'à la ferme

he laid out his suit across the bed
il a étendu son costume à travers son lit

★ **after** (après)

i) Dans un sens figuré, remarquez la différence entre **ask after** et **ask for** :

he asked after you
il m'a demandé de tes nouvelles

he asked for you
il a demandé à te parler

ii) dans un sens figuré impliquant un but :

they keep striving after the happiness which eludes them
ils recherchent le bonheur qui leur passe toujours à-côté

iii) Dans un sens temporel on pourrait comparer **after** et **since**. La différence entre les deux apparaît dans l'emploi des temps : prétérit (**after**) et present perfect (**since**). Comparez :

he wasn't well after his journey
il ne se sentait pas bien après son voyage

he hasn't been well since his journey
il ne se sent pas bien depuis son voyage

Voir aussi **to**

La même différence existe sans verbe dans la proposition. Ainsi il y a une grande différence entre :

Britain after the war
La Grande-Bretagne après la guerre

et

Britain since the war
La Grande-Bretagne depuis la guerre

★ **against** (contre)

i) Ceci implique normalement un obstacle :

they didn't fight against them, they fought with them
ils n'ont pas combattu contre eux, ils ont combattu avec eux

we're sailing against the current
nous naviguons à contre-courant

ii) Mais il peut impliquer un choc, comme dans :

he knocked his head against the wall
il s'est tapé la tête contre le mur

iii) pour dénoter une opposition par rapport à un fond :

she held the picture against the wall
elle a tenu l'image contre le mur

she was silhouetted against the snow
sa silhouette se découpait sur la neige

★ **among(st)** (parmi)

Alors que **between** (entre) implique deux éléments, **among(st)** implique une multitude :

he sat between John and Joan
il s'est assis entre John et Joan

he sat among(st) the flowers
il s'est assis parmi les fleurs

Remarquez que les "deux éléments" ne sont pas toujours mentionnés avec **between** (à la différence de l'exemple ci-dessus). Il signifie seulement qu'une division entre deux choses, deux personnes ou deux groupes est impliquée. Ainsi il est parfaitement correct de dire :

the road ran between the houses
la route passait entre les maisons

même s'il y en a 250. Ici on indique que la route sépare les maisons en deux groupes. Mais notez qu'on dirait :

the cats were running to and fro among the houses
les chats couraient en tous sens parmi les maisons

Ici on n'indique plus une séparation entre deux groupes de maisons. Bien sûr s'il n'y a que deux maisons, on dirait :

the cats were running to and fro between the houses

★ **at** (à)

Voir aussi **to**.

At ou **in** ? : **at** fait référence à un point précis (souvent sur une échelle réelle ou imaginaire). Ainsi on dirait :

the big hand stopped at six o'clock
la grande aiguille s'est arrêtée sur le six

et :

the train stops at Dundee, Edinburgh and York
le train s'arrête à Dundee, Edimbourg et York

Ces villes ne sont pas considérées comme villes dans la phrase ci-dessus, mais comme des étapes sur un itinéraire. On dirait :

he lives in Dundee
il vit à Dundee

Dans la phrase :

he is at Dundee
il est à Dundee

une fois de plus **Dundee** ne fait pas référence à la ville ; mais à une institution, comme l'université de Dundee, par exemple.

Cependant on peut employer **at** avec des noms de petites villes et de villages :

there's still a pier at Tighnabruaich
il y a toujours une jetée à Tighnabruaich

En revanche on ne dit pas :

he lives at Tighnabruaich

mais **in**.

Avec le verbe **arrive**, **at** est aussi employé pour marquer la un point précis :

they finally arrived at the foot of the hill
ils sont finalement arrivés au pied de la colline

sinon on emploie **in** :

when we arrived in London, we ...
lorsque nous sommes arrivés à Londres, nous ...

Dans un sens figuré, on emploie toujours **arrive at** :

have they arrived at any decision yet?
est-ce qu'ils sont déjà parvenus à une décision ?

at ou **by** ? :

i) pour exprimer un lieu, comparez :

(a) **he was sitting at the table**
il était assis à la table

(b) **he was sitting by the table**
il était assis près de la table

ii) pour exprimer le temps, comparez :

(a) **be there at six o'clock**
sois là à six heures

(b) **be there by six o'clock**
sois là avant six heures

At fait référence à un point dans le temps, tandis que **by** signifie "pas plus tard que".

★ **before** (devant, avant)

Il fait référence au temps et à l'espace :

be there before six o'clock
sois là avant six heures

he knelt before the Queen
il s'agenouilla devant la reine

i) Dans un sens spatial, il y a parfois une différence entre **before** et **in front of**. **In front of** est plus littéral en ce qui concerne la position. C'est le terme que l'on emploie le plus souvent en anglais courant :

he was standing in front of the judge in the queue
il se tenait devant le juge dans la file

tandis que **before** implique souvent une relation qui n'est pas purement locative :

he stood before the judge
il se tenait devant le juge

Remarquez aussi que dans les exemples ci-dessus **in front of** n'implique pas que les deux personnes sont face à face. **Before**, lui, implique cette idée.

ii) Dans le sens temporel de **before**, comparez son emploi avec des verbes à la forme négative et celui de **until**. **Before** signifie "plus tôt que" et **until** "jusqu'à (un certain temps)" :

(a) **you will not get the letter before Monday**
tu ne recevras pas la lettre avant lundi

(b) **you will not get the letter until Monday**
tu ne recevras pas la lettre avant lundi

Dans (a) la lettre arrivera lundi ou n'importe quel jour après lundi (mais pas avant), dans (b) la lettre arrivera lundi.

★ **below** (au-dessous de)

Below est le contraire de **above** (au-dessus de), et **under** (sous) est le contraire de **over**. Voir **above** ci-dessus. Exemples :

50 metres below the snow-line
à 50 mètres au-dessous de la limite des neiges éternelles

he was sitting under the bridge
il était assis sous le pont

below the bridge the water gets deeper
au-dessous du pont l'eau est plus profonde

his shoes were under the bed
ses chaussures étaient sous le lit

★ **beside** et **besides**

beside = à côté de :

sit beside me
assieds-toi à côté de moi

besides = en plus de, à part :

there were three guests there besides him and me
il y avait trois invités à part lui et moi

★ **between** (entre), voir **among** (parmi)

★ **but**

But employé comme préposition signifie "sauf", "excepté". On peut aussi employer **except** pour remplacer **but** dans pratiquement tous les cas, mais l'inverse n'est pas possible. Quand on emploie **but**, il est pratiquement toujours placé après des pronoms indéfinis ou interrogatifs, ou des adverbes comme **anywhere, where**, etc. :

nobody but/except you would think of that
personne à part toi ne penserait à ça

where else but/except in France would you ...?
où, sinon en France, est-ce qu'on pourrait ... ?

mais seul **except** est possible dans la phrase suivante :

you can all walk to the terminal except the old man here
vous pouvez tous marcher jusqu'au terminus sauf le vieil homme là-bas

★ **by**

Voir aussi **at** et **from**.

i) Il est utile de comparer **by** avec **on** dans son usage avec des mots faisant référence à des moyens de transport :

he goes by train
il prend le train

is there only one conductor on this train?
y-a-t-il un seul contrôleur dans ce train ?

By met l'accent sur le moyen de transport, et le nom qui suit n'a normalement pas d'article, sauf dans des cas comme :

I'll be coming on/by the three-thirty
j'arriverai par (le train/bus/l'avion) de trois heures trente

où l'on ne fait pas directement référence au moyen de transport.

On peut employer **in** à la place de **on** si l'idée d'intérieur domine :

it's often cold in British trains
il fait souvent froid dans les trains britanniques

Remarquez aussi **live by** et **live on**. **Live by** signifie "gagner sa vie d'une occupation", tandis que **live on** signifie "vivre avec un revenu de/de nourriture". L'emploi de **by** insiste sur le moyen :

he lives by acting in commercials
il gagne sa vie en jouant dans des pubs

he lives by his pen
il vit de sa plume

he lives on £100 a month
il vit avec 100 livres par mois

he lives on fruit
il se nourrit de fruits

Live by signifie aussi "vivre selon les règles de" :

it is difficult to live by such a set of doctrines
il est difficile de vivre en appliquant un tel ensemble de doctrines

ii) passif :

By s'emploie pour introduire le complément d'agent (celui par qui l'action est accomplie) dans des constructions passives :

his reaction surprised us
sa réaction nous a surpris

we were surprised by his reaction
nous étions surpris par sa réaction

★ **due to** (à cause de, grâce à)

Il a le même emploi que **owing to** (à cause de/en raison de) :

this was due to/owing to his alertness of mind
c'était grâce à sa vivacité d'esprit

Etant donné que **due** est un adjectif, certaines personnes soutiennent qu'il devrait se placer, comme un adjectif attribut, après une des formes du verbe **be** comme dans l'exemple ci-dessus, et qu'il est mal employé dans l'exemple ci-dessous. Cependant, il est de plus en plus courant d'employer **due to** dans des structures adverbiales dans lesquelles on le considère comme une locution prépositionnelle comme **because of, in front of**, etc. :

the train is late, due to an accident near Bristol
le train est en retard, à cause d'un accident près de Bristol

★ **during** (pendant), voir **for**

★ **except** (sauf), voir **but**

★ **for** (pour, pendant)

i) Lorsque **for** est employé comme préposition de temps, il est utile de la comparer avec **during** (pendant) et **in** (en). **For** insiste sur l'idée de durée (pendant combien de temps ?), tandis que **during** indique la période au cours de laquelle des actions se produisent (quand ?) :

for the first five months you'll be stationed at Crewe
pendant les cinq premiers mois, vous serez basés à Crewe

during the first five months you're likely to be moved
au cours des cinq premiers mois, vous serez vraisemblablement transférés

he let the cat out for the night
il a fait sortir le chat pour la nuit

he let the cat out during the night
il a fait sortir le chat pendant/dans la nuit

L'accent mis sur la durée par **for** est aussi parfois opposé à **in**, qui signifie "dans une période" :

I haven't seen her for five years
je ne l'ai pas vue depuis cinq ans

he didn't see her once in five years
il ne l'a pas vue une seule fois en cinq ans

Cependant, en anglais américain, on emploierait normalement **in** dans le premier exemple :

I haven't seen her in five years
je ne l'ai pas vue depuis cinq ans

et cet usage s'est étendu à l'anglais britannique.

Pour l'emploi de **for/since** avec des expressions de temps, voir p A48.

ii) Lorsque **for** est préposition de lieu, il est utile de la comparer avec **to** :

(a) **the flight for/to Dublin is at 3 o'clock**
le vol pour Dublin est à 3 heures

(b) **nothing went wrong on the flight to Dublin**
aucun incident ne s'est produit sur le vol pour Dublin

La différence entre les deux est que **to** implique l'arrivée à destination, tandis que **for** exprime uniquement le projet ou l'intention d'aller dans la direction de cette destination.

★ **from** (de (provenance))

i) Comme nous l'avons vu plus haut, (voir **by** ci-dessus), **by** insiste sur le moyen, et **from** indique la provenance, le point de départ. Comparez :

judging by experience, this is unlikely to happen
si l'on en juge par l'expérience, il y a peu de chances que cela se produise

judging from earlier experiences, he had now learnt not to be so easily led astray
par des expériences antérieures, il avait appris à ne pas se laisser entraîner aussi facilement

Bien sûr, il existe parfois peu ou pas de différence étant donné que la distinction entre le moyen et la provenance n'est pas pertinente :

judging by his clothes, he must be poor
si l'on en juge par ses vêtements, il doit être pauvre

judging from these figures, business is good
si l'on en juge par ces chiffres, les affaires se portent bien

L'idée de provenance évoquée par **from** apparaît aussi lorsqu'on l'oppose à **of, by** et **with** dans les exemples suivants :

the cat died from eating too much fish
le chat est mort pour avoir mangé trop de poisson

the cat died of cancer/by drowning
le chat est mort du cancer/en se noyant

the cat is trembling with fear
le chat tremble de peur

from what I have heard
d'après ce que j'ai entendu

ii) avec **different** :

On peut employer soit **from** ou **to** avec **different** :

that's different to/from mine
c'est différent du mien

that's different to/from what he said before
c'est différent de ce qu'il a dit auparavant

Mais **than**, bien qu'on l'entende souvent, n'est pas correct (**different** n'est pas un comparatif).

★ **in** et **into** (dans)

Pour **in**, voir aussi **at**, **by**, **for**.

En principe **in** signifie "dans un espace", tandis que **into** implique un mouvement d'un endroit à l'intérieur d'un autre :

he was sitting in the living room
il était assis dans la salle de séjour

he went into the living room
il est entré dans la salle de séjour

Pas de problème pour l'instant. Cependant, dans d'autres cas où l'action implique un mouvement d'un endroit à l'intérieur d'un autre (et où l'on pourrait s'attendre à trouver **into**), on emploie souvent **in** si l'accent est mis sur le **résultat** plutôt que sur le mouvement :

did you put sugar in my coffee?
est-ce que tu as mis du sucre dans mon café ?

Et réciproquement, on emploie parfois **into** lorsqu'il n'y a pas de verbe de mouvement, mais seulement si l'on implique le mouvement :

you've been in the bathroom for an hour
tu es dans la salle de bain depuis une heure

the kitchen is awful, have you been into the bathroom yet?
la cuisine est affreuse, est-ce que tu as été dans la salle de bain déjà ?

De même, dans un sens figuré :

he's into fast cars at the moment
il est branché voitures de sport en ce moment

this will give you an insight into how it works
cela vous donnera une idée sur la manière dont il fonctionne

★ **in front of** (devant), voir **before**

★ **of** (de), voir **about** et **from**

★ **on** (sur), voir **about**, **by** et **upon**

★ **opposite** (en face de)

Il est parfois accompagné de **to**, parfois pas :

the house opposite (to) ours is being pulled down
on est en train de démolir la maison en face de la nôtre

★ **outside** (dehors, en dehors de)

Il est souvent accompagné de **of** en américain, mais pas souvent en anglais britannique :

he reads a lot outside (of) his main subject area
il lit beaucoup en dehors de sa spécialité

★ **over** (par dessus), voir **above** et **across**

★ **owing to** (en raison de), voir **due to**

★ **since** (depuis), voir **after** p A64.

★ **till** (jusqu'à + complément de temps), voir **to**

★ **to** (jusqu'à, vers, à)

Voir aussi **for**, **from**.

Lorsqu'il est opposé à **until/till** (jusqu'à), **to** (jusqu'à) fait référence à un aboutissement dans le temps. **Until** et **till** font eux aussi référence à un aboutissement dans le temps, mais on insiste plus particulièrement sur l'activité exprimée dans la phrase :

he has one of those nine to five jobs
il a un des ces emplois de bureau routiniers

the shop is closed from 1 to 2 pm
le magasin ferme de 13 heures à 14 heures

he played his flute until 10 o'clock
il jouait de sa flûte jusqu'à 10 heures

last night I worked from eight till midnight
la nuit dernière j'ai travaillé de 8 heures jusqu'à minuit

Il n'y a pas de différence de sens entre **until** et **till**.

To dans un sens différent peut avoir des similarités avec **at** après certains verbes. Dans de tels cas, **to** indique tout simplement une direction vers un but, tandis que **at** a un sens plus fort, car il dénote un désir de rapport plus étroit de la part de celui qui fait l'action :

will we manage to get to the station in time?
est-ce qu'on va arriver à la gare à temps ?

those boxes on top of the wardrobe – I can't get at them!
ces boîtes sur l'armoire – je n'arrive pas à les attraper !

Remarquez l'expression **get at** dans un sens figuré :

why are you getting at me?
pourquoi est-ce que tu es toujours sur mon dos ?

what are you getting at?
où voulez-vous en venir ?

★ **toward(s)** (vers)

Voir aussi **against**.

Toward s'emploie normalement en anglais américain, **towards** en anglais britannique.

★ **under** (sous), voir **below**

★ **until** (jusqu'à + complément de temps), voir **before** et **to**

★ **upon** (sur)

Il existe peu de différences de sens entre **upon** et **on**, mais **upon** est bien plus livresque ou soutenu :

what are your views upon ...?
quelle est votre opinion sur ... ?

upon having, with great difficulty, reached Dover, he immediately set sail for France
après avoir, avec grande difficulté, atteint Douvres, il s'embarqua pour la France immédiatement

Mais on trouve aussi **upon** dans certaines expressions (assez désuètes) où **on** n'est pas possible :

upon my word!	par exemple !
upon my soul!	grand Dieu !

Upon ne peut remplacer **on** pour exprimer (a) une date, (b) un moyen (voir **by** ci-dessus), (c) un état, (d) "avec", "sur" :

(a) **can you come on Saturday?**
tu peux venir samedi ?

(b) **he lives on fruit; our heaters run on gas**
il vit de fruits ; nos radiateurs fonctionnent au gaz

(c) **he's on the phone; it's on TV; he's on edge**
il est au téléphone ; c'est à la télé ; il est à cran

(d) **have you got any money on you?**
tu as de l'argent sur toi ?

En cas de doute, **on** n'est jamais faux (à part dans les exceptions mentionnées ci-dessus).

★ **with** (avec) voir **from**

★ **without** (sans)

En anglais on emploie l'article :

without a/his hat	**without (any) butter**
sans chapeau	sans beurre

15. LES CONJONCTIONS

Les conjonctions sont des mots qui relient deux mots ou deux propositions. On distingue les conjonctions de "coordination" et les conjonctions de "subordination". Les conjonctions de coordination relient des mots ou des propositions qui ont une même fonction dans la proposition. Les conjonctions de subordination relient des propositions qui dépendent d'autres structures (normalement d'autres propositions). Voir plus loin **La Structure de la Phrase** p A72.

1. LES CONJONCTIONS DE COORDINATION

Elles peuvent être "simples" :

and	**but**	**or**	**nor**	**neither**
et	mais	ou	ni	ni

ou "corrélatives" :

both ... and	**either ... or**
à la fois ...	et soit ... soit
neither ...nor	
ni ... ni	

a) *Exemples de conjonctions de coordination simples* :

i) **you need butter and flour**
tu as besoin de beurre et de farine

she's old and fragile
elle est âgée et frêle

they ate and drank a great deal
ils ont beaucoup mangé et beaucoup bu

they finished their work and then they went out to dinner
ils ont terminé leur travail et puis ils sont sortis dîner

ii) **but** et **or** offrent les mêmes possibilités de combinaison que **and**, par exemple :

she's plain but rich
elle n'est pas très jolie mais elle est riche

trains to or from London have been delayed
les trains en partance et en provenance de Londres ont du retard

Remarquez aussi l'usage suivant :

we can but try
on ne peut qu'essayer

iii) **Nor** s'emploie devant le second élément (ou le troisième, etc.), après un **not** apparu plus tôt dans la phrase :

I don't eat sweets, nor chocolate, nor any kind of sugary thing
je ne mange pas de bonbons, ni de chocolat, ni aucunes sucreries

On peut aussi employer **or** dans cette même construction :

I don't eat sweets, or chocolate, or any kind of sugary thing

Nor s'emploie aussi pour relier des propositions. Il est parfois accompagné de **and** ou **but**. Remarquez l'inversion sujet-auxiliaire du verbe :

I don't like coffee, nor do I like tea
je n'aime pas le café et je n'aime pas le thé non plus

I don't like coffee, (and) nor does she
je n'aime pas le café, et elle non plus

I don't understand it, (but) nor do I need to
je ne comprend pas ça, mais ça n'est pas nécessaire

iv) **Neither** s'emploie seulement pour relier deux propositions :

I don't like coffee, neither does she
je n'aime pas le café, elle non plus

I don't understand it, (and/but) neither do I need to
je ne comprends pas, et/mais ça n'est pas nécessaire

v) Si **(n)either ... (n)or** relie deux noms, le verbe s'accorde en nombre avec le nom le plus proche du verbe :

either the record player or the speakers have to be changed
either the speakers or the record player has to be changed
il faut changer soit les enceintes, soit la platine

b) *Exemples de conjonctions de coordination corrélatives* :

you need both butter and flour
vous avez besoin de beurre et de farine

she's both old and fragile
elle est (à la fois) âgée et frêle

they both laughed and cried
ils ont à la fois ri et pleuré

you need either butter or margarine
tu as besoin soit de beurre, soit de margarine

she'll be either French or Italian
elle sera soit française, soit italienne

she was travelling either to or from Aberdeen
elle allait à Aberdeen ou bien elle en revenait

you need neither butter nor margarine
tu n'as besoin ni de beurre, ni de margarine

she's neither old nor fragile
elle n'est ni âgée, ni frêle

c) **or** recouvre quatre sens de base :

i) Un sens exclusif ou alternatif :

he lives in Liverpool or Manchester
il habite à Liverpool ou à Manchester

ii) Dans le même sens que **and** :

you could afford things like socks or handkerchiefs or ties
vous pourriez vous offrir des choses comme des chaussettes ou des mouchoirs ou des cravates

iii) Pour relier deux synonymes :

acquired immune deficiency syndrome, or Aids
le syndrome immuno déficitaire acquis, ou sida

iv) Lorsqu'il relie deux propositions dans le sens de "sinon" :

apologize to her or she'll never speak to you again
excusez-vous auprès d'elle, ou elle ne vous parlera plus jamais

2. LES CONJONCTIONS DE SUBORDINATION

Il existe un grand nombre de conjonctions de subordination. Certaines sont "simples", comme **because** (parce que) ou **so that** (si bien que) ; d'autres sont corrélatives (comparez avec 1 ci-dessus), comme **as ... as** (aussi ... que), **so ... that** (afin ... que), **more ... than** (plus ... que).

a) *Introduisant une proposition substantive* :

Les propositions substantives ont la même fonction que les (pro)noms et les groupes nominaux dans la phrase :

(a) **I told him that they had done it**
je lui ai dit qu'ils l'avaient fait

(b) **I told him the facts**
je lui ai dit les faits

Dans (a) une proposition substantive est complément d'objet direct de **told**, dans (b), c'est un groupe nominal.

Les conjonctions qui introduisent des propositions substantives sont **that** (que), **if** (si), **whether** (si + *choix*) et **how** (comment). **That** est parfois omis si la proposition subordonnée est le complément d'objet direct de la phrase, mais pas si elle en est le sujet :

he said (that) he wanted to see me (complément d'objet)
il a dit qu'il voulait me voir

that such people exist is unbelievable (sujet)
que de tels personnes existent est incroyable

he asked me if/whether I had any money (complément d'objet)
il m'a demandé si j'avais de l'argent (ou pas)

whether I have any money or not is none of your business (sujet)
que j'aie de l'argent ou non ne te regarde pas

he said how it was done (complément d'objet)
il a dit comment c'était fait

how it's done is immaterial (sujet)
la manière dont c'est fait est sans importance

That, **if**, **whether** et **how** employés comme ci-dessus ne doivent pas être confondus avec leur rôle lorsqu'ils introduisent un groupe adverbial (voir ci-dessous).

b) *Introduisant une proposition adverbiale*

i) Voir **Les Adverbes**, p A21. Il existe un grand nombre de conjonctions qui introduisent des propositions adverbiales ; parmi celles-ci on trouve beaucoup d'exemples de noms ou de verbes ayant fonction de conjonction, ce qui est le cas de **the minute** (à la minute où) et de **the way** (de la manière dont) dans :

he arrived the minute the clock struck twelve (= conjonction de temps, comparez avec **when**)
il est arrivé à la minute où la pendule sonnait midi

he didn't explain it the way you did (= conjonction de manière, comparez avec **how**)
il ne l'a pas expliqué de la manière dont tu l'as fait

ou **provided** (du moment que) et **considering**, comme dans :

provided you keep quiet, you can stay (= conjonction de condition, comparez avec **if**)
du moment que tu restes sage, tu peux rester

he's doing well considering he's been here for only a week (= conjonction de concession, comparez avec **although**)
il se débrouille bien si l'on considère qu'il n'est ici que depuis une semaine

Les conjonctions adverbiales principales :

ii) Conjonctions de temps : **after** (après que), **as** (alors que), **before** (avant que), **since** (depuis que), **until** (jusqu'à ce que), **when** (lorsque), **whenever** (chaque fois que), **while** (tandis que). L'idée de futur dans les subordonnées introduites par une de ces conjonctions est exprimée par un présent en anglais (voir p A49) :

he came back after the show had finished
il est revenu après que le spectacle fût/soit terminé

the phone rang as he was having a bath
le téléphone a sonné alors qu'il prenait son bain

before you sit down, you must see the bedroom
avant que tu ne t'asseyes, il faut que tu vois la chambre

they've been crying (ever) since their parents left
ils pleurent depuis que/le moment où leurs parents sont partis

he talked non-stop until it was time to go home
il a parlé sans s'arrêter jusqu'à ce qu'il fût/soit l'heure de partir

when he's ready we'll be able to get going at last
quand il sera prêt on pourra enfin se mettre en route

you don't have to go upstairs whenever the baby cries
tu n'es pas obligé de monter chaque fois que le bébé pleure

while I'm asleep, will you drive?
pendant que je dors, tu conduiras ?

iii) Conjonctions de lieu : **where** (où), **wherever** (où que) :

plant them where there is a lot of shade
plante-les là où il y a beaucoup d'ombre

wherever she goes, he follows
où qu'elle aille, il suit

iv) Conjonctions de manière, de comparaison ou d'intensité : **as** (comme), **as if** (comme si), **as though** (comme si), **how** (comment), **however** (cependant) :

he does it as he's always done it
il le fait comme il l'a toujours fait

he behaved as if/as though there was (were) something wrong
il s'est comporté comme si quelque chose ne se passait pas bien

you can pay how you want
tu peux payer comme tu veux

however hard you try, you won't manage
même si tu fais tout ce que tu peux, tu n'y arriveras pas

however exciting it may be, he won't be interested
si passionnant que ce soit, il ne sera pas intéressé

v) Conjonctions de cause : **as** (étant donné que), **because** (parce que), **only** (cependant, mais), **since** (puisque) :

as there was nothing but biscuits in the house, we went out to eat
puisqu'il n'y avait rien à part des petits gâteaux dans la maison, nous somme sortis manger

I love you because you are you
je t'aime parce que tu es telle que tu es

I would have done it really, only I didn't think there was time
vraiment je l'aurais fait, mais je ne pensais pas qu'on avait le temps

since you've been so kind to me, I want to give you a present
puisque tu as été tellement gentil pour moi, je veux te donner un cadeau

vi) Conjonctions de concession : **(al)though** (bien que), **even if** (même si), **even though** (bien que), **whether** (soit que) :

we let him come (al)though he was a nuisance
nous l'avons laissé venir bien qu'il nous ait apporté des ennuis

you can stay, even if/even though you haven't paid your rent
tu peux rester même si tu n'as pas payé ton loyer

I'm doing it whether you like it or not
je le fais que ça te plaise ou non

vii) Conjonctions de but : **in order to** (afin de), **lest** (de peur/crainte que/de), **so that** (afin que) :

they went to the stage door in order to get a glimpse of him
ils sont allés à la sortie des artistes afin de pouvoir l'apercevoir

I apologized lest she should be offended
je me suis excusé(e) de peur qu'elle ne fût/soit blessée

he did it so that she would be happy
il l'a fait afin qu'elle soit heureuse

Remarquez que **lest** a tendance à être employé dans un usage littéraire. Il est toujours possible d'employer **so that ... not** à la place :

I apologized so that she shouldn't be offended
je me suis excusé(e) afin qu'elle ne fût/soit pas blessée

viii) Conjonctions de conséquence : **so that** (si bien que) :

if you can arrange things so that we're all there at the same time
si tu peux tout organiser pour qu'on soit tous là en même temps

ix) Conjonctions de condition: **if** (si), **so/as long as** (tant que), **unless** (à moins que) :

only tell me if you want to
dis-le moi seulement si tu veux

so long as you promise to be careful
tant que tu promets d'être prudent

tell me, unless you don't want to
dis-moi, à moins que tu ne veuilles pas

c) **But** est une conjonction de subordination dans les sens suivants :

i) "sans que" (après **never** et **hardly**) :

it never rains but it pours (proverbe)
un malheur n'arrive jamais seul

hardly a day goes by but something happens
il ne se passe presque jamais un jour sans que quelque chose ne se produise

ii) employé avec **that** (après certains noms négatifs) :

there's no doubt but that he's responsible
il n'y a aucun doute qu'il est responsable

d) *Introduisant des propositions comparatives*

Les propositions subordonnées comparatives ne modifient pas d'autres propositions (comme le font les propositions adverbiales). Elles modifient des éléments de la proposition : groupes nominaux, groupes adverbiaux et adjectivaux.

Les conjonctions comparatives sont corrélatives (comparez avec **conjonctions de coordination**, p A68): **more ... than** (plus ... que), **less ... than** (moins ... que), et **as ... as** (autant ...que).

i) Modifiant un nom :

they killed more people than we can imagine
ils ont tué plus de gens que nous ne pouvons l'imaginer

they killed as many people as the other side (did)
ils ont tué autant de gens que les autres

ii) Modifiant un adjectif :

it was less comfortable than we'd thought
c'était moins confortable que nous n'avions pensé

it was as comfortable as we thought
c'était aussi confortable que nous le pensions

iii) Modifiant un adverbe :

you did it better than I could have done
tu l'as mieux fait que je n'aurais pu le faire

you did it as well as I could have done
tu l'as fait aussi bien que j'aurais pu le faire

Remarquez l'absence de négation dans les exemples anglais.

16. LES NOMBRES

1. Les nombres cardinaux et les nombres ordinaux

cardinaux		*ordinaux*	
1	**one**	1st	**first**
2	**two**	2nd	**second**
3	**three**	3rd	**third**
4	**four**	4th	**fourth**
5	**five**	5th	**fifth**
6	**six**	6th	**sixth**
7	**seven**	7th	**seventh**
8	**eight**	8th	**eighth**
9	**nine**	9th	**ninth**
10	**ten**	10th	**tenth**
11	**eleven**	11th	**eleventh**
12	**twelve**	12th	**twelfth**
13	**thirteen**	13th	**thirteenth**
14	**fourteen**	14th	**fourteenth**
15	**fifteen**	15th	**fifteenth**
16	**sixteen**	16th	**sixteenth**
17	**seventeen**	17th	**seventeenth**
18	**eighteen**	18th	**eighteenth**
19	**nineteen**	19th	**nineteenth**
20	**twenty**	20th	**twentieth**
21	**twenty-one**	21st	**twenty-first**
30	**thirty**	30th	**thirtieth**
40	**forty**	40th	**fortieth**
50	**fifty**	50th	**fiftieth**
60	**sixty**	60th	**sixtieth**
70	**seventy**	70th	**seventieth**
80	**eighty**	80th	**eightieth**
90	**ninety**	90th	**ninetieth**
100	**a/one hundred**	100th	**(one) hundredth**
101	**a/one hundred and one**	101st	**(one) hundred and first**
200	**two hundred**	200th	**two hundredth**
1,000	**a/one thousand**	1,000th	**(one) thousandth**
1,345	**a/one thousand three hundred and forty-five**	1,345th	**one thousand three hundred and forty-fifth**
1,000,000	**a/one million**		**millionth**
1,000,000,000 (9)	**a/one billion**		**billionth**
1,000,000,000,000 (10)	**a/one trillion**		**trillionth**

Remarquez qu'en anglais britannique, **a billion** était (et est encore parfois) 10^{12} (dix à la puissance douze) et **a trillion** 10^{18}. Les nombres donnés dans la liste sont des valeurs américaines, qui sont maintenant aussi employées en anglais britannique. 10^{9} (un milliard) était (et est encore parfois) appelé **a thousand millions** en anglais britannique.

Remarquez l'emploi de la virgule pour indiquer les milliers.

2. Les fractions

a) *Les fractions ordinaires* :

On écrit les fractions avec un nombre cardinal (ou parfois **a** à la place de **one**) + un nombre ordinal :

$^{1}/_{5}$ = **a/one fifth** un cinquième
$^{3}/_{8}$ = **three eighths** trois huitièmes
$3^{4}/_{9}$ = **three and four ninths** trois et quatre neuvièmes

$^{1}/_{2}$ = **a/one half**
$^{1}/_{4}$ = **a quarter**
$^{3}/_{4}$ = **three quarters**

Remarquez que 1 $^{1}/_{4}$ hours = **an/one hour and a quarter** ou **one and a quarter hours** (une heure et quart).

Remarquez que le **-s** est maintenu lorsque les fractions sont employées comme adjectifs :

they had a two-thirds majority
ils ont eu une majorité de deux tiers

L'emploi des fractions ordinaires est beaucoup plus courant en anglais qu'en français.

b) *Les nombres décimaux*

Alors que dans les autres pays européens on utilise une virgule pour les nombres décimaux, les anglophones se servent du point :

25.5 = twenty-five point five
vingt-cing virgule cinq

Les décimales sont énumérées une à une après le point :

25.552 = twenty-five point five five two
vingt-cinq virgule cinq cent cinquante-deux

3. Nought, zero, '0', nil

a) *Anglais britannique*

Nought et **zero** sont utilisés pour le chiffre 0. Dans les calculs, **nought** est habituel :

add another nought (ou zero) to that number
ajoute un autre zéro à ce chiffre

put down nought and carry one
je pose zéro et je retiens un

0.6 = nought point six
zéro virgule six

Pour un nombre sur une échelle, on préfère **zero** :

it's freezing – it's 10 below zero
il gèle – il fait moins 10

comme en anglais scientifique :

given zero conductivity
étant donné une conductivité de zéro

a country striving for zero inflation
un pays qui se bat pour atteindre une inflation nulle

Lorsqu'on prononce le chiffre comme la lettre "o" il s'agit normalement d'un numéro de téléphone.

Nil est toujours utilisé pour les points ou les buts en sports :

Arsenal won four nil (= 4-0)
ou :
Arsenal won by four goals to nil
Arsenal a gagné quatre buts à zéro

sauf au tennis, où l'on utilise 'love' :

Lendl leads forty-love
Lendl mène quarante zéro

(mot dérivé du français "l'œuf" à cause de sa ressemblance graphique)

Nil est aussi utilisé dans le sens de **nothing** (rien) (qui se dit aussi parfois **zero**) :

production was soon reduced to nil (ou **zero**)
la production fut rapidement réduite à zéro

b) *Anglais américain*

Zero est utilisé presque dans tous les cas :

how many zeros in a billion?
combien y a-t-il de zéros dans un milliard ?

my telephone number is 721002 (seven two one zero zero two)

Chicago Cubs zero (au basket)

Cependant, au tennis on utilise le mot **love**, voir **3. a)** ci-dessus.

4. Les dates

a) *Années*

1989 se dit :

nineteen eighty-nine

ou, plus rarement :

nineteen hundred and eighty-nine

1026 se dit :

ten twenty-six

Dans cet exemple, l'utilisation de **hundred** n'est pas habituel.

b) *Mois et jours*

On peut écrire la date de différentes manières :

12(th) May **May 12(th)**
the twelfth of May **May the twelfth**

En anglais américain parlé, il est plus courant d'omettre le mot **the** quand on fait commencer la date par le mois :

May 12 (dit : May twelfth/May twelve)

En anglais britannique, on écrit les dates en mettant le jour en premier, et en anglais américain, on met le mois en premier :

10/4/92 (= 10th April 1992, anglais britannique)
4/10/92 (= 10th April 1992, anglais américain)

5. Les numéros de téléphone

On lit les numéros de téléphone comme des chiffres séparés (voir aussi 3 ci-dessus) :

1567 = one five six seven
40032 = four double 'o' three two (anglais britannique)
four zero zero three two (anglais américain)

Mais à l'écrit, il est normal de les regrouper par groupes de chiffres pour faire apparaître les différents codes régionaux en opération :

041-221-5266

6. Les adresses

En Amérique du Nord les numéros à quatre chiffres se lisent :

3445 Sherbrooke Street
thirty-four forty-five Sherbrooke Street

7. Les opérations

Il existe plusieurs façons d'exprimer les opérations arithmétiques. Voici certaines des plus courantes :

$12 + 19 = 31$
twelve and/plus nineteen is/equals thirty-one

$19 - 7 = 12$
nineteen minus seven is/equals twelve

seven from nineteen is/leaves twelve

nineteen take away seven is/leaves twelve (emploi enfantin)

$2 \times 5 = 10$
twice five is ten
two fives are ten

$4 \times 5 = 20$
four times five is/equals twenty

four fives are twenty

$36 \times 41 = 1476$
thirty-six times forty-one is/equals one thousand four hundred and seventy-six

thirty-six multiplied by forty-one is/equals one thousand four hundred and seventy-six

$10 \div 2 = 5$
ten divided by two is/equals five

two into ten goes five(emploi plus familier)

8.

Pour **hundred, thousand, million (billion, trillion)** avec ou sans -**s**, voir **Les Noms**, p A8. Comparez aussi :

first they came in ones and twos, but soon in tens – at last in tens of thousands
ils sont d'abord arrivés par petits groupes, mais bientôt par dizaines – puis par dizaines de milliers

in the 1950s (= nineteen fifties)
dans les années cinquante

she's now in her eighties
elle est maintenant octogénaire (elle a entre 80 et 90 ans)

9. ***The former** et **the latter***

Au lieu d'employer **the first** on emploie **the former** si on fait référence à une personne/chose parmi deux qui viennent juste d'être évoquées ; et **the latter** (au lieu de **the last**) quand on fait référence à la dernière de deux personnes/choses :

trains and coaches are both common means of transport – the former are faster, the latter less expensive
le train et le car sont deux moyens de transport couramment utilisés – l'un est plus rapide, l'autre moins cher

De ces expressions, **the latter** est plus souvent utilisé, et il peut aussi faire référence à la dernière chose d'une énumération qui en comprend plus de deux :

Spain, Italy, Greece: of these countries the latter is still the most interesting as regards ...
l'Espagne, l'Italie, la Grèce : de tous ces pays, le dernier est le plus intéressant en ce qui concerne ...

Des noms peuvent suivre **the former/the latter** :

of the dog and the cat, the former animal makes a better pet in my opinion
du chien ou du chat, le premier des deux est le meilleur animal domestique, à mon avis

10. ***Once** et **twice***

Once est utilisé pour "une fois", **twice** pour "deux fois". **Thrice** (trois fois) est archaïque :

if I've told you once, I've told you a thousand times
je ne te l'ai pas dit une fois, je te l'ai dit mille fois

I've only seen her twice
je ne l'ai vue que deux fois

17. LA STRUCTURE DE LA PHRASE

L'ordre des éléments de la proposition, des mots

a) *Le sujet*

i) En général, le sujet précède l'auxiliaire et le verbe :

he may smoke
il peut fumer

L'inversion du sujet et du verbe a lieu dans les cas suivants (s'il y a plus d'un auxiliaire, seul le premier auxiliaire précède le sujet) :

ii) dans les questions :

may I? (when) can you come?
puis-je ? (quand) peux-tu venir ?

would you have liked to have the chance?
auriez-vous voulu avoir la possibilité ?

iii) dans les propositions conditionnelles, lorsque **if** est omis :

had I got there in time, she'd still be alive
si j'étais arrivé à temps, elle serait encore en vie

should that be true, I'd be most surprised
si c'était vrai, je serais vraiment surpris

iv) quand la phrase commence avec un mot qui a un sens négatif (comme **never**, **seldom**) :

never did I think this would happen
je n'aurais jamais pensé que cela allait se passer

I can't swim – nor/neither can I
je ne sais pas nager – moi non plus

little did I think this would happen
j'ai à peine pensé que cela pourrait arriver

hardly had he entered the room, when the ceiling caved in
à peine entrait-il dans la chambre, que les plafonds s'effondraient

seldom have I enjoyed a meal so much
j'ai rarement autant apprécié un repas

Mais **nevertheless, nonetheless** et **only**, qui font tous les trois référence à un affirmation précédente, sont suivi par les mots dans leur ordre normal :

I know he smokes, nevertheless/nonetheless he should be invited
je sais qu'il fume, mais on devrait quand même l'inviter

we'd like you to come, only we haven't got enough room
nous aimerions que vous veniez, mais nous n'avons pas assez de place

v) souvent quand une phrase commence avec un adverbe de degré :

so marvellously did he play, that it brought tears to the eyes of even a hardened critic like me
il a si bien joué qu'il est même parvenu à faire monter les larmes aux yeux d'un critique sans cœur comme moi

only too well do I remember those words
je m'en souviens trop bien, de ces paroles

vi) parfois lorsque la phrase commence avec un adverbe, si le verbe n'a pas un sens descriptif fort, et si le sujet a une certaine importance :

in that year came the message of doom that was to change their world
cette année-là arriva le message de ruine qui allait changer leur monde

on the stage stood a little dwarf
sur la scène se tenait un petit nain

out came a scream so horrible that it made my hair stand on end
on entendit tout à coup un cri si horrible que mes cheveux se dressèrent sur la tête

to his brave efforts do we owe our happiness (assez littéraire)
nous devons notre bonheur à son grand courage

pour donner un effet dramatique lorsqu'un adverbe est placé en position initiale :

a big black car pulled up and out jumped Margot
une grosse voiture noire arriva et Margot en sortit

vii) après **so** placé en position initiale (= aussi) :

I'm hungry – so am I
j'ai faim – moi aussi

viii) au discours direct :

Après le discours direct, le verbe d'expression précède parfois son sujet, surtout si c'est un nom (plus le nom a une signification forte dans la phrase, plus on aura tendance à inverser l'ordre des mots) :

'you're late again', said John/John said
"tu es encore une fois en retard", dit John

'you're late again !', boomed the furious sergeant (ou **the furious sergeant boomed**)
"tu es encore une fois en retard", hurla le sergent furieux

Mais l'ordre normal est obligatoire quand on utilise les temps composés :

'you're late again', John had said
"tu es encore une fois en retard", avait dit John

Si le sujet est un pronom, alors le sujet se met habituellement en première place :

'you're late again', he said
"tu es encore une fois en retard", dit-il

Quand le verbe précède le pronom, c'est fréquemment parce qu'une proposition relative suit ou parce qu'on veut donner un caractère de plaisanterie à la phrase :

'you're late again', said I, who had been waiting for at least five hours
"tu es encore une fois en retard", lui dis-je, car j'avais attendu au moins cinq heures

Les journalistes ont tendance à concentrer un grand nombre d'informations sur un sujet (**vivacious blonde Mary Lakes from Scarborough said : '...'** la blonde et enjouée Marie Lakes de Scarborough dit : " ..."). Vu qu'il est plutôt étrange en anglais de placer un mot à signification descriptive si faible comme **said** en dernière position dans la phrase, les journalistes changent souvent l'ordre de la phrase dans de tels cas :

said vivacious blonde Mary Lakes from Scarborough :
comme le dit la blonde et enjouée Mary Lakes de Scarborough ...

S'il y a un adverbe, l'inversion est moins courante, mais possible :

'you're back again', said John tentatively
"tu es de retour", dit John avec hésitation

Mais s'il y a un complément d'objet, après **ask** ou **tell** par exemple, on ne fait pas l'inversion :

'she is late again', John told the waiting guests
"elle est encore une fois en retard", dit John aux invités qui attendaient

b) *Le complément d'objet*

Le complément d'objet suit normalement le verbe, mais il est en position initiale dans les cas suivants :

i) dans les questions qui commencent par un pronom interrogatif qui est complément d'objet :

who(m) did you meet?
qui as-tu rencontré ?

ii) dans les propositions subordonnées interrogatives et relatives :

(please ask him) what he thinks
(demande-lui, s'il te plaît,) ce qu'il pense

(can we decide) which position we're adopting?
(pouvons-nous décider) quelle attitude nous prenons ?

(he brought back) what she'd given him
(il a ramené) ce qu'elle lui avait donné

iii) pour renforcer un objet, surtout quand l'objet est **that** :

that I couldn't put up with
cela, je ne pouvais pas l'accepter

that I don't know
ça, je ne sais pas

but his sort I don't like at all
son genre, je ne l'aime pas du tout

iv) si la phrase contient un complément d'objet direct et un complément d'objet indirect, le complément d'objet indirect précède le complément d'objet direct si un des deux (ou les deux) est un nom :

he gave her a kiss
il lui a donné un baiser

Mais si, au lieu du complément indirect, on a une locution prépositionnelle adverbiale, cette locution se place en dernière position :

he gave the old tramp a fiver

ou :

he gave a fiver to the old tramp
il a donné un billet de cinq livres au vieux mendiant

v) Quand les deux compléments sont tous les deux des pronoms, alors le complément d'objet indirect précède le complément d'objet direct :

could you please send her these in the mail tonight?
tu peux les lui envoyer par le courrier de ce soir ?

would you give me one?
tu veux bien m'en donner un ?

well, tell them that then
et bien, dis-le leur

he wouldn't sell me one
il ne voulait pas m'en vendre un

that secretary of yours, will you lend me her?
cette secrétaire que tu as, tu veux bien me la prêter ?

On fait une exception à cette règle dans l'emploi de **it** avec **give** ou **lend**, etc. pour lesquels il y a deux possibilités :

could you give it him when you see him?
could you give him it when you see him?
tu veux bien le lui donner quand tu le verras ?

Il est aussi possible de dire :

could you give it to him when you see him?

Si **to** est employé, alors l'ordre des mots est semblable à celui dans l'exemple ci-dessus :

he wouldn't sell one to me
il ne voulait pas m'en vendre un

18. NOTES CONCERNANT L'ORTHOGRAPHE

1. y en i

Un y placé après une consonne se change en **i** devant les terminaisons suivantes :

-able, **-ed**, **-er** (adjectifs ou noms)
-est, **-es** (noms et verbes)
-ly et **-ness**

ply : plies : pliable
cry : cried : cries : crier
happy : happier : happiest : happily : happiness

Exceptions :

shyly (timidement) et **slyly** (sournoisement) (on évite d'employer **slily** qui est rare). Par contre, **drily** est plus courant que **dryly** :

Les noms propres qui se terminent en **-y** prennent seulement **-s** :

there were two Henrys at the party
il y avait deux Henri à la soirée

Les composés en **-by** prennent **-s** :

standbys

De même **dyer** (teinturier) et parfois **flyer** (aviateur) (aussi **flier**).

Mais y précédé par une voyelle ne change pas et la terminaison des noms ou des verbes est **-s** au lieu de **-es** :

play : plays : playable : player
coy : coyer : coyest : coyly : coyness

Mais remarquez **lay : laid, pay : paid, say : said**, et **daily, gaily** (aussi **gayly**).

2. ie en y

Ce changement a lieu devant **-ing** :

die : dying, lie : lying

3. Chute de la voyelle finale -e

Normalement **-e** est omis si une syllabe qui commence par une voyelle est ajoutée :

love : loving : lovable
stone : stony

Mais il existe un certain nombre d'exceptions, comme **matey** (copain), **likeable** (aimable), **mileage** (distance parcourue en miles), **dyeing** (= teinture – à ne pas confondre avec **dying** = mourir), **hoeing** (binage), **swingeing** (= énorme, à ne pas confondre avec **swinging** = dans le vent).

Si le mot se termine en **-ce** ou en **-ge**, alors le **-e** est maintenu devant **-a** et **-o** :

irreplaceable, changeable, outrageous

Si la syllabe suivante commence avec une consonne, le **-e** est conservé habituellement :

love : lovely
bore : boredom

Mais encore, il existe des exceptions importantes, surtout :

due : duly, true : truly
whole : wholly, argue : argument

4. -our ou -or

Quand un suffixe est ajouté à certains des mots se terminant en **-our**, on fait tomber le **-u** :

humour : humorist
vigour : vigorous

Mais il y a une exception importante concernant cela pour le mot **colour** :

colour : colourful : colourlessness : colourist

Cela ne pose pas de problèmes pour les Américains qui ont définitivement laissé tomber le **-u** :

humor : humorist

5. Doublement des consonnes

Après une voyelle courte accentuée, on double la consonne finale lorsqu'elle est placée devant **-er**, **-est**, **-ed**, **-ing** :

fit : fitter : fittest : fitted : fitting
begin : beginner : beginning

Aussi après **-ur** ou **-er** :

occur : occurred : occurring
refer : referred referring

mais :

keep : keeper : keeping

ou :

cure : cured : curing

parce que la voyelle dans ce mot est longue

et :

vomit : vomited : vomiting

parce que le **-i** n'est pas accentué.

En anglais britannique **-l** est doublé même dans une syllabe non-accentuée :

revel : revelled : reveller : revelling
travel : travelled : traveller : travelling

Ce phénomène concernant le **-l** n'a pas lieu en anglais américain :

travel : traveled : traveler : traveling

Remarquez aussi :

kidnap : kidnapped : kidnapper (anglais britannique)

kidnap : kidnaped : kidnaper (anglais américain)

6. c en ck

Les mots qui se terminent en **-c** changent le **-c** en **-ck** avant **-ed**, **-er**, **-ing** :

frolic : frolicked : frolicking
picnic : picnicked : picnicker : picnicking

7. Variantes américaines

En plus des variantes américaines données en 4 et 5 ci-dessus, il faut noter les suivantes :

a) anglais britannique **-gue**, anglais américain **-g** :

catalogue : catalog

b) anglais britannique **-tre**, anglais américain **-ter** :

centre : center

c) anglais britannique **-nce**, anglais américain **-nse** :

defence : defense
offence : offense
pretence : pretense

d) Quelques mots différents. Le premier de chaque paire est en anglais britannique :

cheque : check, cigarette (aussi américain) **: cigaret**
pyjamas : pajamas
practise (pratiquer) **: practice** (le nom a **-ce** des deux côtés de l'Atlantique)
programme : program (mais en informatique aussi **program** en anglais britannique)
tyre : tire (pneu)

19. LES EXPRESSIONS DE TEMPS

A. L'HEURE

what's the time?, what time is it? quelle heure est-il ?

what time do you make it? quelle heure avez-vous ?

a) *les heures*

it's 12 noon (midday)/midnight	**it's one/two o'clock**
il est midi/minuit	il est une heure/deux heures
il est midi/minuit	

b) *les demi-heures*

it's half past midnight	**it's half past twelve (in the afternoon)**
il est minuit et demi(e)	il est midi et demi(e)

it's half past one, it's one thirty
it's half one *(familier)*
il est une heure et demie

c) *les quarts d'heure*

it's (a) quarter past two	**at (a) quarter to two**
il est deux heures et quart	à deux heures moins le quart

d) *les minutes*

it's twenty-three minutes past four, it's 4.23
il est 4 heures 23

it's twenty to five, it's 4.40
il est 5 heures moins 20

Remarquez qu'en anglais américain on peut aussi employer **after** au lieu de **past** et **of** au lieu de **to**.

e) ***a.m.*** *et* ***p.m.***

a.m.	**p.m.**
du matin	de l'après-midi/du soir
it is 7.10 p.m.	**it's ten to seven, it's 6.50**
il est 7 heures 10 du soir	il est sept heures moins dix

Les expressions du type "quinze heures", etc. (à la place de "trois heures", etc.) ne s'emploient pas dans l'anglais de tous les jours. On les rencontre cependant parfois dans les horaires et surtout dans le langage militaire (souvent suivis de **hours**) :

'o' five hundred hours	**fifteen hundred hours**
5 heures du matin	quinze heures

fifteen thirty hours
quinze heures trente

we took the sixteen-twenty to Brighton
nous avons pris le train de 16h20 pour Brighton

Remarquez les abréviations : **7.15** = 7h15.

B. LA DATE

1. Les mois, les jours et les saisons

a) *Les mois (**months**)*

January	janvier
February	février
March	mars
April	avril
May	mai
June	juin
July	juillet
August	août
September	septembre
October	octobre
November	novembre
December	décembre

b) *Les jours de la semaine (**the days of the week**)*

Monday	lundi
Tuesday	mardi
Wednesday	mercredi
Thursday	jeudi
Friday	vendredi
Saturday	samedi
Sunday	dimanche

c) *Les saisons (**the seasons**)*

spring (le printemps)	**summer** (l'été)
autumn (l'automne)	**winter** (l'hiver)

En anglais américain on dit aussi **fall** pour "l'automne". Pour l'emploi de l'article voir p. A7.

2. Les dates

a) On emploie les nombres ordinaux pour les dates (à la différence du français) :

the fourteenth of July	**the second of November**
le quatorze juillet	le deux novembre

I wrote to you on the third of March
je vous ai écrit le trois mars

Voir aussi **Les Nombres** p. A70.

C. EXPRESSIONS IDIOMATIQUES

at 5 o'clock	à cinq heures
about 11 o'clock	à onze heures environ
about midnight	vers minuit
(round) about 10 o'clock	vers (les) dix heures
it's past 6 o'clock	il est six heures passées
at exactly 4 o'clock	à quatre heures précises/pile
it has struck nine	il est neuf heures sonnées
on the stroke of three	sur le coup de trois heures
from 9 o'clock onwards	à partir de neuf heures
shortly/just before seven	peu avant sept heures
shortly/just after seven	peu après sept heures
sooner or later	tôt ou tard
at the earliest	au plus tôt
at the latest	au plus tard
it's late	il est tard
he is late	il est en retard
he gets up late	il se lève tard
he arrived late	il est arrivé en retard
the train is twenty minutes late	le train a vingt minutes de retard
my watch is six minutes slow	ma montre retarde de six minutes
my watch is six minutes fast	ma montre avance de six minutes
tonight	ce soir
tomorrow night	demain soir
yesterday evening	hier soir
last night	hier soir, cette nuit
tomorrow morning	demain matin
tomorrow week	demain en huit
the day after tomorrow	après-demain
the day before yesterday	avant-hier
the next day	le lendemain
the next morning	le lendemain matin
yesterday morning	hier matin
last week	la semaine dernière
next week	la semaine prochaine
on Monday	lundi
on Mondays	le lundi
every Saturday	tous les samedis
every Saturday evening/night	tous les samedis soirs
three weeks ago	il y a trois semaines
half an hour, a half-hour	une demi-heure
a quarter of an hour	un quart d'heure
three quarters of an hour	trois quarts d'heure
from time to time	de temps en temps
what's the date?	le combien sommes-nous ?
it's the third of April	c'est le trois avril
Friday the thirteenth of July	le vendredi treize juillet
in February	en/au mois de février
in 1992	en 1992

in the sixties/60s	dans les années soixante
in the seventeenth century	au dix-septième siècle
in the 17th C	au XVIIe
New Year's Day	le jour de l'An
to be thirteen years old	avoir treize ans
she's celebrating her twentieth birthday	elle fête ses vingt ans
a five-year plan	un plan quinquennal
a leap year	une année bissextile
a calendar year	une année civile
a light year	une année-lumière

Conçue et réalisée par
LEXUS
avec Gert Ronberg.

Guide pratique de conversation anglaise

Apologies

Apologising
The most common apology is
Sorry
I'm sorry
I'm so sorry
I'm terribly sorry
To say why, use:
Sorry/I'm sorry I'm late
Sorry/I'm sorry to (disturb you)
Sorry/I'm sorry about (damaging your car)
To apologise for a past action, use:
I'm afraid I (made a mistake)
I'm afraid I (forgot to post the letter)
I'm sorry that (my friend annoyed you)
I'm sorry for (making a noise last night)
To apologise about a continuing state, use:
I'm afraid (there's no more coffee)
Sorry, but I can't do it
No, I'm afraid not
To be very formal, use:
Please accept my apologies for (my friend's behaviour)
I must apologise for (seeming to be rude)

Giving reasons
To give a reason or excuse, use:
Sorry, I didn't (see you there)
Sorry to miss you, but I couldn't (get there in time)
To give a reason for a continuing state, use:
I'm afraid you can't, the (phone) isn't working
I'm afraid not, you see, I'm working very hard for my exams at the moment

Accepting apologies
To answer an apology, use:
That's all right/That's OK
It's nothing
It doesn't matter/It didn't matter
It's not important/It wasn't important
Never mind
Not at all
Don't worry about it
Think nothing of it

Dealing with receptionists

Contacting
To get a receptionist's attention, use:
Good morning/afternoon; Hello
Excuse me
Can you help me, please?
Can you help me?

Asking for service
To ask for people, use:
I'd like to speak to (Miss Jones), please
Where can I find (her)?
Who is the (office manager) here?
I have an appointment with (Dr Smith)
I have to meet (him) at (ten o'clock)
The receptionist may say:
Can you wait a moment?
Can you take a seat, please?
I'll ring (her)
I'll let (her) know you are here
If you have problems, you may want to use:
Is there someone else who can help me?
Who else is in that department?
Well, I'd like to see (her) superior/boss
May I use your telephone, please?
I'd like to leave a message
To ask for departments, use:
I'm looking for the (electronics) department
I want to see someone about (an order)?
Can you tell me where to go?
Who should I see over (payments)?
Where should I go for (radiology)?
The receptionist may say:
It's on the ground/first/second floor
Take the lift to the (third) floor
Go upstairs to the (first) floor
It's room (27)
It's through the doors; on the left/right

Explaining yourself
If the receptionist wants to know, use:
My name's (Smith)
I'm from (the travel office)
(Dr Jones) sent me
I have a (book) here for (him)

Apologies
(I'm) afraid (that) *je regrette que*
all right *cela ne fait rien*
annoy *ennuyer*
apologise *s'excuser*
behaviour *comportement*
(I) can't *(je)ne peux*
could *pourrais*
damage *abîmer*
disturb *déranger*
don't (worry) *ne vous faites pas de souci*
forget *oublier*
friend *ami*
It doesn't matter *peu importe*
Never mind *ne vous inquiétez pas*
mistake *erreur*
must *devoir*
rude *grossier*
see *voir*
seem *sembler*
so *ainsi*
sorry *pardon*
I'm sorry *je suis désolé*
state *état*
terribly *terriblement*
in time *à temps*
use *employer*
(it) isn't working *cela ne fonctionne pas*
worry *souci*
you *vous*

Dealing with receptionists
appointment *rendez-vous*
contact *contacter*
department *département*
(someone) else *quelqu'un d'autre*
Excuse me *excusez-moi*
help *aider*
(on the) left *(à) gauche*
let (someone) know *informer (quelqu'un)*
meet *rencontrer*
message *message*
(Good) morning *bonjour*
reception *réception*
receptionist *réceptioniste*
ring *téléphoner*
(Take a) seat *veuillez vous asseoir*
see *voir*
send *envoyer*
speak *parler*
superior *supérieur*
upstairs *en haut*
use *employer*
wait *attendre*
Wait a moment *attendre un moment*
where? *où?*
who? *qui?*

Making an appointment

Suggesting an appointment
To propose making an appointment, use:
Can I come and see you?
I'd like you to come and see me
Can you come and see me?
Let's meet

Talking about dates
To ask about dates, use:
What day would suit you?
To suggest a date, use:
What about (Thursday)?
I'd like to make it (soon)
I'm free on (Tuesdays)
(Next Friday) would suit me
To specify date, use:
On Monday/Tuesday/Wednesday
On the 25th of March/On March the 25th
Tomorrow; The day after tomorrow
Soon; In the next few days

Talking about time
To ask about time, use:
What time would suit you?
What time are you free?
To suggest a time, use:
What about (early afternoon)?
I'm free (in the afternoon)
I'd like to make it (about ten o'clock)
(Three-thirty) would suit me
To specify time, use:
In the morning/afternoon/evening
Before lunch/after lunch
At (about) eleven/eleven-thirty/twelve

Talking about place
To ask about place, use:
Where shall we meet?
Where would suit you?
To suggest a place, use:
What about (at my place)?
Let's make it (here)
To specify place, use:
At your/my office/home/hotel

Asking the way

Asking the way
To ask people for directions, use:
Excuse me
Where is (the police station)?
Could you direct me to (the station)?
How do I get to (the main street)?
Could you tell me the way to (the park)?
If you want special directions, use:
Which is the quickest way to (the Post Office)?
What's the best way to (the city centre)?
If you are in a car, you can also use:
What's the easiest way to (the coast road)?
Is there a lot of traffic (that way)?
Is there parking (in the centre)?
Asking about distances, use:
How far is it?
How long will it take (on foot/by car/by bus)?
Can I do it in (ten minutes)?
Should I take (a taxi)?

Giving directions
To tell people the way, use:
It's near the (church)
Go straight on/straight ahead
Turn left/right at the (second) street
Go towards (the park) and turn left
Cross/Go across the road
Go over/under the bridge
Go along the street
Go past the (Post Office)
To identify the place, use:
It's the (first) street
It's the (first) on the left/right
It's on the left/right hand side of the road
To tell people distances, use:
It's quite far
It's too far to walk
It's not very far/It's quite near here
It's about (two) kilometres
It's (ten minutes) on foot/walking
It's (three minutes) by car/driving
It's (an hour's) walk/drive
You should allow (an hour)
You should take (a taxi)

Making an appointment
after *après*
appointment *rendez-vous*
before *avant*
come *venir*
day *jour*
date *date*
early *tôt*
evening *soir*
few *quelques*
free *libre*
lunch *repas de midi*
make (an appointment) *prendre rendez-vous*
let's *je suggère*
meet *rencontrer*
next *prochain*
office *bureau*
place *endroit*
propose *proposer*
see *voir*
soon *bientôt*
suit *convenir*
suggest *suggérer*
time *temps*
What about? *que pensez-vous de ?*
Where? *où?*

Asking the way
across *à travers*
ask *demander*
best *meilleur*
Could you? *pourriez-vous?*
direct *direct*
drive *conduire*
easy *facile*
far *loin*
get (to somewhere) *arriver (quelque part)*
go *aller*
hour *heure*
How? *comment?*
(How) long? *combien de temps?*
minute *minute*
near *proche*
tell *dire*
park *parc*
past *au delà de*
police station *poste de police*
right *(à) droite*
station *gare*
straight (ahead) *tout droit*
street *rue*
take *prendre*
traffic *circulation*
turn *tourner*
walk *marcher*
way *direction*
Where? *où?*

Asking for professional help

Asking for a lawyer
With legal problems, use:
I want my lawyer
I want to see a lawyer
I want legal advice
I want to speak to a lawyer
To insist, use:
I'm not saying anything till I see a lawyer
I'm not doing anything until I've spoken to a lawyer
I insist on seeing a lawyer
When speaking to the lawyer, use:
I want legal help/advice
I'd like you to act for me
I'd like you to represent/advise me on (this)

Asking for a doctor
With medical problems, use:
I want a doctor
I want to see a doctor
I want medical advice
I want to speak to a doctor
To insist, use:
I'm not moving till I see a doctor
I'm not doing anything until I've spoken to a doctor
When speaking to the doctor, use:
I want a medical examination
I'd like you to examine/look at me
I'd like medical advice on (this)

Asking for a second opinion
To ask for further advice, use:
Is there someone else I can speak to?
I'd like someone else's opinion
I want a second opinion
I want an expert/a specialist on (this)
Who else can I speak to about this?

Asking for your consul
To ask for your consul's help, use:
I want to get in touch with my consulate
I need to contact the (Swiss) consul
I'd like to get in touch with my consul

Asking for toilet and washing

Asking for the lavatory
In a private house, use:
May I use your lavatory?
Where is the lavatory?
In a public place, use:
Where are the toilets?
For a man, use:
Where is the gents?
I need to use the gents
For a woman, use:
Where is the ladies?
I need to use the ladies
To be informal in America, use:
Where is the john?
I want to use the john
To be informal in Britain, use:
Where is the loo?
I want to use the loo

Asking for a bathroom
In a private house, use:
May I have a wash?
I'm rather dirty
I'm feeling a bit dirty
Could I use your bathroom?
I'd like to wash my hands
In a public place, use:
Is there a washroom/bathroom here?
Is there somewhere here I can clean up?
I want to wash my hands
In a hotel or guest house, you may need:
Where is the shower?
Where is the bathroom?

Washing clothes
To find out where to wash clothes, use:
Is there a launderette near here?
Where is the nearest launderette/laundromat?
I need to wash/dry clean some clothes
To get somone else to do the washing, use:
Is there a laundry here?
Is there a laundry service here?
I want to have some clothes washed
I want to have some clothes dry cleaned

Asking for professional help
act (for) *agir au nom de . . .*
advice *conseil*
advise *conseiller*
(not) anything *ne . . . rien*
consul *consul*
doctor *médecin*
(someone) else *quelqu'un d'autre*
examine *examiner*
examination *examen*
expert *expert*
insist *insister*
lawyer *homme de loi*
legal *légal*
look at *regarder*
medical *médical*
move *bouger*
opinion *opinion*
problems *problèmes*
represent *représenter*
second *second*
see *voir*
speak to *parler à*
specialist *spécialiste*
(in) touch (with) *en rapport avec*
until *jusqu'à*

Asking for toilet and washing
ask *demander*
bathroom *salle de bain*
clean *propre*
clothes *vêtements*
dirty *sale*
dry clean *nettoyer à sec*
feel *avoir la sensation de*
the gents *toilettes messieurs*
guest house *pension de famille*
here *ici*
john *toilettes*
the ladies *toilettes dames*
launderette/laundromat *laverie self-service*
laundry *blanchisserie*
lavatory *toilettes*
loo *toilettes*
May I? *puis-je?*
need *avoir besoin*
place *lieu*
private house *maison particulière*
public *public*
rather (dirty) *très (sale)*
shower *douche*
somewhere *quelque part*
toilet *toilettes*
use *employer*
wash *laver*
wash room *cabinet de toilette*

Handling baggage

Asking for the check-in
To find where to check in baggage, use:
Where's the check-in desk?
Where's the baggage check-in?
Where do I check in my baggage?
You may need to use:
It's heavy
Porter
Are there any porters here?
I need a porter
Where can I get a baggage trolley?
Are there any trolleys free?

Checking in baggage
To hand baggage in at the check-in, use:
I want to check in (these), please
There are (three) pieces
I'm taking (this) as hand baggage
I'm not checking (this) in
I'm taking (this) with me
Are they safe like that?
Do I have to pay any extra?

Baggage problems
You may need:
Where's the baggage office?
Who's in charge of lost baggage?
I checked in my baggage in (Paris) and it isn't here
My baggage hasn't been delivered
I was on the (Miami) flight
I can't find my baggage
My baggage is lost
It's damaged/broken
I've lost (some things) out of it

Identifying baggage
To identify your baggage, use:
It's a suitcase/a bag/a rucksack/a box
It's green/brown/yellow
It's about the same size as (that)
It's made of leather/plastic
It's got (leather straps)
It's got my name and address on it

Leaving luggage

Finding the facilities
To ask about left-luggage facilities, use:
Is there anywhere here I can leave my bags?
Is there a left-luggage place near here?
Can I leave my luggage anywhere here?
Where are the nearest left-luggage lockers?
I don't want to carry (this) round with me

At the left-luggage office
To speak to the employees, use:
Can I leave (these) here (until four o'clock)?
Will your office be open (after six o'clock)?
Do I pay now, or when I collect?
Please be careful with (the brown bag)

At the lockers
To ask someone for change, use:
Excuse me, have you got change for (a pound)?
Have you got any change for (this)?
To ask someone for help, use:
Do you know how to work these things?
Could you give me a hand with this?
If something goes wrong, use:
Excuse me, are you in charge of the left-luggage lockers?
My (case) is too big/It won't fit in
I put the money in/I put my luggage in
I can't open it/I can't make it work
I can't get my luggage out
I can't get my money back

At a hotel
To ask if you can leave bags somewhere, use:
Could I leave (my luggage) here (for an hour)?
Would it be possible for me to leave (these)?
Can I leave these here (until about six)?
Could you (please) look after (this) for me?
I'll pick it/them up (at six o'clock)
I'll be back (in a few hours)
To identify your baggage, use:
The (green) one is mine
Mine is (brown)
I left (two suitcases) here

Handling baggage
baggage *bagages*
box *boîte*
broken *brisé*
in charge *responsable*
check in *faire enregistrer*
damaged *endommagé*
deliver *délivrer*
desk *bureau*
extra *extra*
find *trouver*
flight *vol*
free *libre*
hand (baggage) *bagages à main*
heavy *lourd*
leather *cuir*
lost *perdu*
luggage *bagages*
office *bureau*
piece *pièce*
porter *porteur*
rucksack *sac à dos*
safe *en sécurité*
size *dimensions*
strap *courroie*
suitcase *valise*
take *prendre*
trolley *chariot*

Leaving luggage
after *après*
back *derrière*
bag *sac*
big *gros*
be careful *faites attention*
carry *porter*
case *valise*
change *monnaie*
in charge *responsable*
collect *retirer*
Could I? *pourrais-je?*
fit in *s'emboîter*
hand *main*
give someone a hand *donner un coup de main à qn*
leave *laisser/déposer*
left *déposés*
left luggage *bagages déposés*
locker *coffre*
open *ouvert*
out *hors de*
pay *payer*
pick up *retirer*
possible *possible*
put in *introduire*
until *jusqu'à*
to work something *organiser quelque chose*

Getting a car mended

Describing problems
To explain that something is wrong, use:
It isn't working
It's not going properly
It's broken down; It won't start
There's something wrong with the (ignition)

Giving a diagnosis
To say what you think is wrong, use:
I think it's the (fuel pump)
It may be (the electrical wiring)
The (dynamo) has gone wrong before
The battery is dead
The tyre's flat

Asking for an opinion
To find out if it's the right garage, use:
Do you handle (this make of car)?
Do you keep spares for (this make of car)?
Can you do anything with it?
Can you have a look at it?

Asking for directions
To ask for recommendations, use:
Is there a garage near here that can do it?
Is there a service station for (this make of car) near here?
Can you recommend a garage/mechanic nearby?
Do you know a garage/mechanic near here?

Asking for estimates
To ask how much and how long it will be, use:
When can you do it?
When will it be ready?
Can you give me an estimate?
How much do you think it will cost?
How long do you think it will take?
Can you give me an idea how much/how long?

Giving deadlines
To tell the garage when you need it, use:
Can you do it (immediately)?
I need the car (tomorrow)
I must have it (by the weekend)

Hiring a car

Asking directions
To find out where you can hire a car, use:
Can I hire a care here?
Is there a car-hire firm here?
With Americans, use the word **rent:**
Is there a car-rent firm here?
Where is the best place to hire/rent a car?
Where can I hire/rent a car cheaply here?

Stating preferences
To tell them what you want, use:
I want a medium/small/large car for (a week)
I want to hire/rent a car for (next Tuesday)
I want something cheap/comfortable
I need a four-seater
I want it (at nine o'clock tomorrow morning)
I need a car now/immediately
I need it for (the weekend)
I want to go to (Turin)
Can you deliver it?
Can I collect it?

Finding out terms
To ask about costs, use:
How much do you charge?
What is the tariff?
I'd like to see your table of charges
How much is a (four-door/five-door)?
Does the charge include mileage (kilometres)?
What do you charge per day/mile/kilometre?
Are there any extra charges?

Handling paperwork
To find out about the formalities, use:
I have (an international licence)
Is a (Swiss) driving licence all right?
Do you want proof of identity?
How much is the deposit?
Can I pay with (a Diners Club card)?
Do I need my passport?
What insurance is included?
I'd like a receipt, please
Where do I sign?
Do you want my signature?

Getting a car mended
battery *batterie*
breakdown *panne*
broken down *en panne*
car *voiture*
cost *coûter*
estimate *devis*
fuel pump *pompe à essence*
garage *garage*
(not) going *(ne pas) fonctionner*
handle *tenir*
ignition *allumage*
immediately *immédiatement*
keep *garder*
(have a) look *regarder*
make of (car) *marque (de voiture)*
mechanic *mécanicien*
properly *convenablement*
ready *prêt*
service *service*
service station *station-service*
spares *pièces de rechange*
start *démarrer*
tomorrow *demain*
tyre *pneu*
weekend *week-end*
wiring *fils électriques*
(not) working *(ne pas) fonctionner*
(something) wrong *quelque chose qui ne va pas*

Hiring a car
car *voiture*
charge *demander un prix*
cheap *bon marché*
collect *aller chercher*
cost *coût*
deliver *livrer*
deposit *dépôt*
extra *supplémentaires*
hire *louer*
identity *identité*
include *inclure*
insurance *assurance*
firm *compagnie*
large *grand*
licence *permis*
medium *moyen*
mileage *kilométrage*
per (day) *par (jour)*
receipt *reçu*
rent *louer*
(4) seater *(4) places*
sign *signer*
signature *signature*
table (of charges) *tarif*
tariff *tarif*
terms *conditions*

Calling emergency services

Stating urgency
To express that it is an emergency, use:
This is (very) urgent
It's an emergency
There's an emergency (here)
It's very serious
It looks very serious
We need help urgently
To specify what sort of emergency, use:
We need a police car/an ambulance immediately
Call the fire brigade/the hospital at once
Get a doctor/policeman straight away
We urgently need a rescue boat/an ambulance

Explaining the emergency
To state what sort of emergency it is, use:
There's been an accident
There's a fire/an accident
There's someone very ill/badly hurt
There are (two) people in the water
Someone's been badly hurt/injured
For a fire, ask for:
The fire brigade/The fire services
For a traffic accident or a crime, ask for:
The police
For a medical emergency, ask for:
An ambulance/The hospital
For a sailing emergency, ask for:
The coast guard/The life boat/
The rescue service

Telephoning emergency services
When you phone emergency, they ask:
What service do you want?
Fire, police or ambulance?
Where are you?/Where is it?
What's happened?
You reply:
Fire/Police/Ambulance
I'm at/It's at (the corner of South Street)
It's on the main road (to Bolton)
It's about two miles north of (Perth)
There's an accident/a fire
There are (several) people injured

Buying clothes

Getting attention
To speak to someone in the shop, use:
Excuse me
Can you help me, (please)?

Explaining
To explain what you want, use:
I'm looking for (something like this in green)
I'm looking for (a jacket)
I want to get (some trousers)
I'm looking for something (for about $40)

Discussing colour
To talk about colours, use:
Have you got another colour?
This is too dark/too light
I like/don't like (this colour)

Talking about price
To ask about price, use:
How much is it/are they?
Have you got anything cheaper/more expensive?
To comment on the price, use:
That's cheap/expensive; It's too expensive

Talking about size
To ask about size, use:
What size is this?
Will this fit me?
Have you got anything bigger/smaller?
Have you got this in a bigger/smaller size?
To comment on the size, use:
It is/They are too big/too small; too long/too short; too tight/too loose
It/They won't fit me

Asking about trying clothes on
To ask to try clothes on, use:
I'd like to try this on
Where can I change?
Can I try these on?
Is there a changing room here?
Where can I try these on?

Calling emergency services
accident *accident*
ambulance *ambulance*
boat *bateau*
coast guard *garde-côte*
doctor *médecin*
emergency *urgence*
fire *feu*
fire brigade *pompiers*
help *secours*
hospital *hôpital*
hurt *blesser*
ill *malade*
immediately *immédiatement*
injured *blessé*
life boat *bateau de sauvetage*
look *regarder*
need *besoin*
police *police*
policeman *agent de police*
rescue *sauver*
serious *grave*
straight away *tout droit*
traffic *circulation*
urgent *urgent*
water *eau*

Buying clothes
big *grand*
buy *acheter*
Can you help me *pouvez-vous m'aider?*
change *essayer*
cheap *bon marché*
colour *couleur*
dark *sombre*
Excuse me *excusez-moi*
expensive *cher*
fit *être à la taille de*
jacket *veste*
like *comme*
look for *chercher*
loose *lâche*
Please *s'il vous plaît*
price *prix*
shop *magasin*
short *court*
size *taille*
small *petit*
too (light) *trop (clair/léger)*
trousers *pantalon*
try on *essayer*
want *désirer*

Complaining about goods

Asking for someone
To ask for the right person, use:
I'd like to speak to (the manager)
I want to speak to the person in charge
I've got a complaint about (a shirt), and I'd like to speak to someone about it
On the telephone, use:
Give me the (manager) please
Could you put me through to (the manager)?
I've got a complaint about (a radio). Could you put me through to the right person?

Giving the background
To explain the background, use:
I bought (these goods) from you (last week)
You sent me (this) yesterday
I ordered (a camera) from your company
I've got/I haven't got a receipt
I've got/I haven't got the guarantee

Making a complaint
To express your complaint, use:
It doesn't work
It's broken/defective/faulty
It's not what I wanted/asked for/saw
It's the wrong size/shape/colour/model
I was told it would (be made of leather)
I was given/sent the wrong thing
I can't use it/wear it
It only lasted (two days)

Asking for action
To ask for something to be done, use:
I want my money back
I want it repaired/replaced (immediately)
Will you replace it?
I expect either a refund or a replacement

Talking about further action
To talk of further action, use:
I've returned it/I'm returning it
I'll be writing to (your boss) about this
I'm going to get in touch with (my solicitor)
I am sending you the bill

Complaining about service

Asking for the right person
To ask for the right person, use:
I'd like to speak to (the manager)
I want to speak to the person in charge of (the shipping department)
I've got a complaint about (delivery), and I'd like to speak to someone about it
On the telephone, use:
Could you put me through to (the manager)?
I've got a complaint about (a repair). Could you put me through to the right person?

Giving the background
To explain the background, use:
I was in your office/bank/shop/restaurant today
I left a car/pair of shoes/watch for repair
I wanted to take a taxi/bus/hire car
I left some film to be developed

Making a complaint
To express your complaint, use:
They said it would be (ready on Thursday) and (I'm still waiting)
I was told it would be (half an hour)
The food wasn't properly cooked
The repair wasn't properly done
The room wasn't properly cleaned
The service was slow/incompetent/very poor
The staff/people were rude/ignorant
Everybody was rude/unhelpful
I was insulted/kept waiting/overcharged

Asking for action
To ask for something to be done, use:
You will look into this, won't you?
I hope you will make sure that (this doesn't happen again)
I expect you to (give me 20% off)

Talking about further action
To talk of further action, use:
I'll be writing to (your boss) about this
I intend to get in touch with (the local government authority) about this

---

Complaining about goods
bill *facture*
broken *cassé*
buy *acheter*
in charge *responsable*
company *compagnie*
complain *réclamer*
complaint *réclamation*
faulty *défectueux/imparfait*
give *donner*
goods *marchandises*
guarantee *garantie*
last *dernier*
I'd like *je voudrais*
right *(celle-celui) qui convient*
manager *chef de rayon/directeur*
money *argent*
order *commande*
person *personne*
put through *mettre en rapport avec*
receipt *reçu*
refund *remboursement*
repair *réparation*
return *rendre/rapporter*
send *envoyer*
speak to *parler à*
want *vouloir*
wear *porter*

Complaining about service
bank *banque*
boss *chef*
delivery *livraison*
department *département*
expect *exiger*
happen *arriver*
insult *insulter*
intend *avoir l'intention de*
look into *s'occuper de*
(20%) off *réduction de (20%)*
office *bureau*
overcharge *surcharge*
properly *convenablement*
ready *prêt*
the right (person) *(la personne) concernée*
rude *impoli/grossier*
say *dire*
service *service*
shop *magasin*
shipping *expédition de marchandises*
slow *lent*
(make) sure *s'assurer*
tell *dire*
(get) in touch *se mettre en rapport avec*
wait *attendre*
yesterday *hier*

Addressing people correctly

Addressing people you know
Most British and American people use their first names in all informal situations:
John; Mary
To be more formal, check:
May I call you John?
Do you mind if I call you Mary?
To be formal, use titles and surnames:
Mr Smith; Mrs Jones; Miss Smith

Addressing strangers
There is no general word and most people use:
Excuse me
With a man, to be very formal, or to show that you are inferior, use:
Sir
To be informal or rude, use:
Hey you; Mister
To be formal to a woman, use:
Madam; Miss
To call a teenager, use:
Young man; Miss/Madam
To call a young child, use:
Son/Sonny; Little girl; Dear
To call a policeman, use:
Officer
To call a waiter or barman, use:
Waiter; Barman
To call a waitress or barmaid, use:
Miss; Waitress
With a few others, use the name of the job:
Nurse; Doctor; Postman; Guard

Writing letters
On the envelope, put both names, or use titles:
John Smith; Mary Jones
Mr John Smith; Miss Mary Jones
Mr J Smith; Miss M Jones
Starting the letter, to be formal, use:
Dear Mr Smith; Dear Miss Jones;
To be informal, use the first name:
Dear John; Dear Mary
To be very formal, use:
Dear Sir; Dear Madam

Being persistent

On the telephone
When someone is unavailable, you can use:
I'll wait/I'll hang on
When can I ring him back?
Well, please find him/please interrupt him
Will you please make sure (he) rings me back?
Where is he?
When will he be in?
Where can I find him?

In person
When you want to see someone and you are refused, use:
I'll wait
If you don't mind, I'll wait
I really must speak to (the manager)
I insist on speaking to (him)
I insist on seeing (him)
I am not leaving here until I see (him)
I'm not leaving until I've seen (him)

Giving the background
To give the background, use:
I've tried four times today
I've called/written several times
This is the (third) time I've tried to contact (him) this week
To explain, use:
It's about (money)
It really is important
We have to get this (payment) sorted out

Persuading people
To persuade people against their will, use:
It really is (important)
I really do think this is (what you should do)
I can convince you that (this is true)
Give me a chance to (explain it fully)
Let's start again
Let me put it another way
To be informal, use:
Come on/Go on
Don't be difficult
See it my way

Addressing people correctly
barman *barman*
dear *cher*
Dear Madam *Chère Madame*
Dear Sir *Cher Monsieur*
envelope *enveloppe*
Excuse me *Excusez-moi*
first name *prénom*
guard *garde*
little *petit*
Madam *Madame*
may I *puis-je*
mind *être importuné*
Do you mind? *Etes-vous importuné si?*
Miss *Mademoiselle Melle*
Mr *Monsieur Mr*
Mrs *Madame Mme*
Ms *Madame/Mademoiselle*
officer *officier*
nurse *infirmière*
postman *facteur*
rude *impoli*
Sir *Monsieur*
stranger *étranger*
son *fils*
surname *nom de famille*
title *titre*
waiter *serveur*
waitress *serveuse*
young (man) *jeune homme*

Being persistent
(give me a) chance *permettez-moi de*
convince *convaincre*
explain *expliquer*
find *trouver*
hang on *attendre (un instant)*
important *important*
insist *insister*
interrupt *interrompre*
leave *quitter*
money *argent*
must *devoir*
speak to *parler à*
persuade *persuader*
put (it like this) *présenter*
really *vraiment*
refuse *refuser*
ring back *rappeler*
see *voir*
sort out *démêler*
(make) sure *s'assurer*
(several) times *plusieurs fois*
try *essayer*
unavailable *indisponible*
wait *attendre*
write *écrire*

Describing something

Describing by size and shape
To describe by size, use:
It's/They're big/small
It's the size of a (football)
It's about 10 cm long and 5 cm wide
It's 20 m high
To ask about size, use:
How big is it?
How long/wide/high is it?
What sort of size is it?

Describing by appearance
To describe by shape, use:
It's round/circular
It's square
It's rectangular/oblong
It's sharp/pointed
It's banana-shaped/S-shaped/L-shaped
It looks like (an egg)
It has a shape like (a box)
To ask about shape, use:
Is it round or square?
What sort of shape is it?
To describe by texture, use:
It's rough/smooth
To describe by appearance, use:
It's green/blue/dark blue
It's striped/spotted
It has (a shiny surface)
To ask about appearance, use:
What colour is it?
What does it look like?
What's it like?

Describing by function
To describe what something does, use:
It's used for (opening bottles)
It (switches on the light)
You need it for (washing)
You use it to (keep the door open)
To ask about something's use, use:
What does it do?
What's it for?
What do you use it for?

Explaining

Asking for explanations
To ask someone to explain language, use:
What does (that) mean?
What's the meaning of (that word)?
Does that mean (yes) or (no)?
To be formal, use:
I'm afraid I don't understand
Could you explain (the first part) please?
If it becomes clear, use:
I see/I understand
Thank you, I see now
If it's still not clear, use:
I still don't see/understand
To be more formal, use:
I'm afraid I still don't understand/follow

Giving explanations
When people don't understand you, use:
I mean (this)
I'm trying to say (this)
In other words, (on Thursday)
What I mean is (this)
To check if people understand, use:
Do you understand?
Is that the right word?
Am I making myself clear?
To rephrase something, use a different order:
There's something wrong with my car
I mean, my car has got something wrong
I'll be out on Friday
In other words, on Friday I won't be here

Actions and processes
To explain an action or process, use:
We do it like this because (it's quicker)
That was because (we were late)
It's to (stop people parking here)
The reason for this is (money)
It's caused by (the hot weather)
To ask for explanations, use:
Why?
Why did he do that?
What's the reason for (this)?
Can you explain (this)?

Describing something
about (10 cm) *environ (10 cm)*
appearance *apparence*
big *grand*
circular *circulaire*
colour *couleur*
describe *décrire*
high *haut*
like (an egg) *comme (un oeuf)*
long *long*
oblong *oblong*
point *point*
rectangular *rectangulaire*
rough *rude*
round *rond*
shape *forme*
sharp *aigu*
shiny *brillant*
size *taille*
small *petit*
smooth *lisse*
sort of *sorte de*
square *carré*
stripe *rayure*
use *utiliser*
wide *large*

Explaining
action *action*
because *parce que*
cause *cause*
check *contrôler*
clear *clair*
different *différent*
explain *expliquer*
explanation *explication*
follow *suivre*
late *tard*
make (yourself) clear *expliquez-vous clairement*
mean *signifier*
money *argent*
order *ordre*
process *procédé*
quick *rapide*
reason *raison*
rephrase *exprimer autrement*
right *juste*
say *dire*
see *voir*
still *encore*
stop *arrêter*
try *essayer*
understand *comprendre*
Why? *pourquoi?*
word *mot*
in other words *en d'autres termes*

Introducing people

Making introductions
To introduce people to each other, use:
(John), this is (Mr Smith)
(Mr Smith), this is (my friend John Jones)
To be formal, use:
May I introduce (Mr Smith)?
I'd like to introduce you to (my friend)
To a group of people, being formal, use:
I have/take pleasure in introducing (Mr Jones)
It gives me great pleasure to introduce (him)
To be informal, use:
(John), (Mary)
Have you met?
Do you two know each other?
You haven't met, have you? (Mary, John)

Getting the name right
To get someone's name, use:
What was your name?
I didn't catch your name
Tell me your name so I can introduce you to (my friends)
To be formal, use:
I'm afraid I don't know your name
Could you tell me your name?
To be informal, use:
You are?
Who are you?
To check the name, use:
How do you spell that?
Can I check that your name is (Jones)?
What was your first/second name again?
Do you mind if I call you (by your first name)?
May I call you (John)?
To be informal, use:
It was (Mary), wasn't it?
You are (Mary), aren't you?

Giving information
To describe the people being introduced, use:
She/He comes from/lives in (Richmond)
She/He works at (the hotel)
She's/He's a friend of mine
She's/He's my (brother's boss)

Using greetings or farewells

Greetings
To greet someone, use:
Hello
Answer:
Hello
To be informal, use and answer:
Hi; Hi
To be more formal, from midnight till lunchtime, use and answer:
Good morning; Good morning
Morning; Morning
From lunch-time till late afternoon, use:
(Good) afternoon; (Good) afternoon
From late afternoon till midnight, use:
(Good) evening; (Good) evening
You can answer any of these with **'Hello'**
Hi; Hello
(Good) morning; Hello
To be very formal, at the first meeting only use and answer:
How do you do? How do you do?
Be careful! It is a greeting, not a question, and you must answer with a greeting
How do you do? How do you do?
How do you do? Hello

Polite phrases
After greeting someone, you can use:
How are you?
You can answer:
I'm fine/Fine/Very well, thanks/thank you
Fine. And you?/How are you?
To be informal, you can use:
How's life?/How are things?
And answer:
O.K./Fine
Not too bad, thanks, and you?

Saying goodbye
The most common to use and answer:
Goodbye; Goodbye
Bye; Bye
At night, when going to bed, use and answer:
(Good) night; (Good) night

Introducing people
(I'm) afraid *je suis désolé*
brother *frère*
boss *patron*
call *appeler*
catch *saisir*
come from *venir de*
each other *chacun d'eux*
first name *prénom*
friend *ami*
introduce *présenter*
introduction *présentation*
know *connaître*
(I'd) like *je voudrais*
live in (London) *habiter à (Londres)*
May I? *puis-je?*
meet *rencontrer*
Do you mind? *est-ce que cela vous ennuie?*
name *nom*
people *gens*
pleasure *plaisir*
second name *nom de famille*
spell *épeler*
tell *dire*
This is *c'est/voici*
work *travail*

Using greetings or farewells
afternoon *après-midi*
and *et*
answer *réponse*
(Not) bad *assez bien*
bed *lit*
common *commun*
good *bon*
Good (afternoon) *bon (après-midi)*
Goodbye *Au revoir*
evening *soirée*
fine *très bien*
greet *saluer*
How (are you)? *Comment allez-vous?*
How do you do? *Bonjour.*
(How's) life? *Comment ça va?*
I'm *je suis*
lunchtime *temps de midi*
morning *matin*
night *nuit*
not *pas*
polite *poli*
thanks/thank you *merci*
(How are) things? *Comment ça va?*
too *trop*
use *utiliser*
very *très*
well *bien*
you *tu/vous*

Making conversation

Talking to complete strangers
In a hotel, restaurant, etc., to be formal talk about the surroundings:
This is a nice/an interesting place, isn't it?
It's quite busy/quiet/comfortable, isn't it?
With British strangers, talk about the weather:
It's a nice/terrible day today, isn't it?
It's a bit colder/warmer/nicer today, isn't it?
To be informal, give some information about yourself, and ask for some back:
I've never been here before. Have you?
I'm from (Spain). Where are you from?
Complain about something:
The service is really bad, isn't it?
They keep these places far too hot, don't they?

Talking to partial strangers
In an office, or at a party, to be formal, ask questions:
Do you live/work near here?
Are you from (this part of the world)?
What do you do (for a living)?
Where do you live?
Talk about the surroundings:
This is a very quiet/pleasant/impressive place
It's nice here in (summer), isn't it?
To be informal, give some information about yourself, and ask for some back:
I don't know (this part of the world). Do you?
It's difficult to park here. Do you find that?

Personal information
To ask about someone, use:
Where do you live?
What do you do?/What's your job?
Where are you from?/Where do you come from?
Where do your family live/come from?
What sort of work/music/food/art do you like?
How do you find (living here)?
To talk about yourself, use:
I live in (Brussels)
I'm a (student); I work (in an office)
I'm from/I come from (Munich)
My family live in/come from (Berne)

Making your opinions clear

Like and dislike
To express strong liking, use:
I really like it
I love it
It's superb/great/terrific
I think it's great/he's great/she's great
To express strong dislike, use:
I hate it
I can't stand it
It's terrible/awful/disgusting
It think it's awful/he's awful/she's awful

Belief
To express strongly held opinions, use:
I firmly believe (that is true)
I strongly believe (it's true)
I really think so
I really do believe/think that
I am absolutely certain of (that)

Agreeing and disagreeing
To show strong agreement with opinions, use:
That's absolutely true
I completely agree
I couldn't agree more
To show agreement with suggestions, use:
That's a great idea
That's an excellent (thing to do)
To show strong disagreement with opinions, use:
I completely/strongly disagree
I think that's absolutely wrong
To be informal, or impolite, use:
That's rubbish
That's nonsense
To show disagreement with suggestions, use:
That's a terrible idea
That's a really bad (suggestion)
Certainly not

Showing you mean it
To show that you mean what you say, use:
I want you to understand this
I mean this
I want this to be perfectly clear

Making conversation
bad *mauvais*
busy *occupé*
cold *froid*
(Where do you) come from? *d'ou venez-vs?*
comfortable *confortable*
complete *complet*
difficult *difficile*
(What do you) do? *que faites-vous?*
family *famille*
(How do you) find? *que pensez-vs de?*
hot *chaud*
interesting *intéressant*
job *travail*
(Where do you) live? *où habitez-vs*
(for a) living *pour gagner sa vie*
nice *agréable/beau*
office *bureau*
partial *partiellement*
party *fête*
place *endroit*
quiet *tranquille*
service *service*
stranger *étranger*
terrible *terrible*
today *aujourd'hui*
warm *chaud*
weather *temps*
(this part of the) world *cette partie du monde*

Making your opinions clear
absolutely *absolument*
agree *être d'accord*
awful *affreux*
believe *croire*
certain *certain*
clear *clair*
complete *complet*
disagree *être en désaccord*
disgusting *dégoûtant*
dislike *détester*
excellent *excellent*
firm (opinion) *ferme (opinion)*
great *grand*
hate *haïr*
like *aimer*
love *aimer*
mean *signifier*
really *réellement*
(can't) stand *(ne pas pouvoir) supporter*
strong (belief) *forte (conviction)*
superb *superbe*
terrible *terrible*
terrific *formidable*
think *penser*
true *vrai*
wrong *faux*

Praising people

Congratulating
If someone has a baby, gets engaged, etc., use:
Congratulations!
If someone passes an exam, wins a prize, etc.:
Congratulations!
To be informal, use:
Great!
Well done!
If somebody does well at something, use:
Well done!

Praising
To praise an inferior or equal, use:
Well done!
That was very well done
That's very good
You did that very well
Your (meal) was excellent/very good/first class
The (food) is/was excellent
I was/am very pleased with (your work)
To praise a superior, use:
Well done!
I thought your (work was excellent)
I really admired/admire your (work)
To be very informal, use:
Super!
Great!
That's/That was super/great/fantastic
You were super/great/fantastic

Commiserating
When someone fails at something, use:
Bad luck!
Never mind!
If someone has had bad news, use:
I was sorry to hear about (your father)
That was bad luck about (your car)

Passing on praise
To praise a third person, use:
Please tell (her) I liked it very much
Tell (him) how good I thought (he was)
To be formal, use:
Give my compliments to (the cook)

Saying no

Refusing invitations
To refuse an invitation, to be polite, use:
Sorry, I can't
No, it's a pity, but I'll be (away then)
I'm afraid I can't make it (to your party)
To be more formal, use:
I'd love to, but I (have some work to do)
To be very formal, use:
I'd very much like to accept (your kind invitation) but I regret that (I cannot)
To be informal, use:
No, I can't
No, I'm working/I'm doing something else

Refusing offers
To refuse an offer, to be polite, use:
No thanks/No thank you
It's all right
No thanks, I don't need (help)
No, I don't want (any coffee), thanks
It's OK, thanks, I can (do it myself)
Thanks but there's no need to (help)
To be more formal, use:
That's very kind of you, but it's all right
Thank you for the offer, but I don't need (it)
To be very formal, in writing, use:
Thank you for your kind offer, but I regret we do not need (your services)
To be informal, use:
No
I don't want (any)

Resisting persuasion
To refuse to be persuaded, use:
No, really
Really, I don't want any
I really don't (want to go out)
I really can't (have another drink)
I'm not going to change my mind
You can't persuade me
You're not going to change my mind
Don't go on about it
I've made up my mind
I'm not (buying it), and that's that

Praising people
admire *admirer*
Bad luck *malchance*
commiserate *compatir*
compliment *compliment*
congratulate *féliciter*
Congratulations *félicitations*
engaged *fiancé*
fail (a test) *échouer (à une épreuve)*
fantastic *fantastique*
first class *première qualité*
good *bon*
inferior *inférieur*
like *aimer*
luck *chance*
mind *se soucier de*
Never mind *peu importe*
pass (an exam) *réussir (à un examen)*
pleased *satisfait*
sorry (to hear it) *désolé (d'apprendre cela)*
super *super*
superior *supérieur*
tell *dire*
think *penser*
very *très*
well *bien*
Well done *bien fait*
win (a prize) *gagner un prix*

Saying no
(I'm) afraid *je regrette*
(It's) all right *non, merci*
another (drink) *une autre (boisson)*
away *absent*
buy *acheter*
can't *ne pas pouvoir*
change (your mind) *changer (d'avis)*
go on (about) *ennuyer*
invitation *invitation*
kind *aimable*
(I'd) love to *j'aimerais*
(can't) make it *impossible*
make up (your mind) *se décider*
need *besoin*
No thanks *non, merci*
offer *offrir*
persuade *persuader*
pity *dommage*
really *vraiment*
refuse *refuser*
regret *regretter*
services *services*
sorry *désolé*
That's that *c'est comme çà*
want *désirer*

Saying you don't understand

Not hearing
When you don't hear something, use:
Sorry?
What was that?
What did you say?
I didn't hear that
I couldn't hear that
To ask people to repeat it, use:
Could you say that again?
Say that again
To be more formal, use:
I didn't catch that
Sorry, I missed that
Would you say that again?
To be informal, use:
What?

Not understanding
When you can't understand a phrase, use:
What does (that phrase) mean?
I don't understand (that)
I don't know (that word)
I understood (this), but not the bit after
Did you say (this) or (that)?
To be formal, use:
I'm afraid I don't understand (that)
Sorry, my English isn't very good
I missed/lost half of that
Could you spell that?
Could you write that down?
When people don't understand you, use:
Perhaps I used the wrong (word)
I'll try again

Asking them to be clear
When someone is difficult to understand, use:
Could you speak more slowly, please?
Slower, please
Slow down
I can't understand you
You're speaking too quickly for me
I don't understand
Can you translate that?
Do you speak any (other language)?

Telling people they're wrong

Putting people right
When someone is doing something wrong, use:
You're doing it wrong
You're going in the wrong direction
You've got it (upside down)
It's (the wrong way round)
You haven't (switched it on)
We should be going (north) not (south)
You should be (in there) not (in here)
Don't do it like that, do it like this
Let me show you
Let me show you how to do it
Shall I do it for you?

Interrupting
To stop someone who is getting it wrong, use:
Wait
Hold on/Hang on
Wait a minute/a moment/a bit
Just a minute/a moment
To be more formal and polite, use:
Excuse me
May I interrupt for a moment?
May I just say something?
Do you mind if I say something?

Correcting ideas
To tell someone he is wrong, use:
That's not right/That's wrong
That's the wrong (name/date/spelling)
I'm not/He's not/It's not (that)
There's a mistake there
There's something wrong here
You've made a mistake here
You've got it wrong
To be more formal and polite, use:
There seems to be a mistake/misunderstanding
Are you sure? Do you think (it's today)?
No, actually/in fact, it's (the opposite)
I'm fairly sure (it's Tuesday)
To tell someone he has the wrong ideas, use:
I disagree
No, that's not right/that's not true
No, it's not (dangerous), it's (quite safe)

Saying you don't understand
after *après*
again *de nouveau*
bit *le peu*
catch *saisir*
I couldn't *je ne pourrais pas*
Could you? *pourriez-vous?*
hear *entendre*
know *connaître*
language *langue*
lose *perdre*
miss *manquer*
other *autre*
phrase *phrase*
quick *vite*
repeat *répéter*
say *dire*
slow *lent*
slow down *ralentir*
sorry *pardon*
speak *parler*
spell *épeler*
translate *traduire*
try *essayer*
understand *comprendre*
use *utiliser*
What (was that)? *qu'est-ce (que c'était)?*
word *mot*
write *écrire*

Telling people they're wrong
correct *corriger*
dangerous *dangereux*
disagree *être en désaccord*
direction *direction*
hold on *un moment, S.V.P.*
idea *idée*
in fact *en fait*
interrupt *interrompre*
May I? *puis-je?*
minute *minute*
mistake *faute*
misunderstand *Se méprendre*
moment *moment*
the opposite *le contraire*
put right *rectifier*
right *juste*
safe *sûr/en sécurité*
say *dire*
Shall I? *ferais-je?*
should *devoir*
show *montrer*
sure *certain*
switch on *allumer*
true *vrai*
wrong *faux*
wrong way round *à l'envers*

Talking about the cost of living

Describing price changes
To talk about changes in prices, use:
The price has gone up
It went up (last month)
It went up sharply/gradually
The cost of (food) is rising
There was a rise in price
For changes downward, use:
In (summer) prices should go down
The cost of (this) went down (last year)
The price of (oil) may drop
We had a drop in (salary costs)
It was a sharp drop/a slight drop
They fell slightly/sharply
There was a fall in prices
For no change, use:
Prices stayed the same
The cost of living will stay level
Prices are at about the same level

Talking about living costs
To talk about the effects of costs, use:
(Houses) are very expensive/cheap
We can/can't afford (chocolate)
It's (not) hard/difficult
Some people find it difficult to cope
It's very hard for (people on a pension)
We're better off/worse off
To ask about other countries, use:
What's it like in (your country)?
How is it with you?

Talking about tax
To talk about taxes, use:
The government takes (30%) in tax
You have to pay income tax/sales tax/VAT
I pay (a third) in tax
(10%) of your salary goes for insurance
The taxes are high/low
There's good social security/insurance
You get a pension at (60)
To ask about taxes, use:
How much do you pay in (income tax)?
What are the taxes like?

Correcting people

Correcting facts
To tell someone he is factually wrong, use:
Actually my name's (this)
That's not right/That's wrong
That's the wrong (name/date/spelling)
I'm not/He's not/It's not (that)
There's a mistake there
There's something wrong here
You've made a mistake here
You've got it wrong
To be more formal and polite, use:
I'm afraid that's not right
There seems to be a mistake/misunderstanding
Are you sure? Do you think (he's French)?
No, actually
In fact, it's (Friday today)
I'm fairly sure (they're Swiss)

Correcting opinions
To tell someone he has the wrong ideas, use:
No, that's not right/that's not true
No, it's not (political), it's (economic)
No, you've got it wrong
You've got the wrong idea
To be more formal and polite, use:
Do you really think that?
I have a different impression
Really? I've always thought (she was pleasant)
I think you've misjudged (the situation)
I think you may have the wrong idea
I'm afraid you've got the wrong idea
To be very informal, use:
That's nonsense/That's rubbish

Answering correction
When you are corrected, use:
Really?
Sorry
Sorry, I thought (your name was Smith)
To be formal, use:
I was told (something different)
I was misinformed
I'm glad you put me right
Thanks for putting me right on (that)

Talking about the cost of living
afford *avoir les moyens*
change *changement*
cheap *bon marché*
cope *faire face*
cost *coût*
cost of living *coût de la vie*
drop *chuter*
expensive *cher*
fall *tomber*
go up *monter*
go down *baisser*
gradual *graduellement*
house *maison*
insurance *assurance*
level *niveau*
(well) off *aisé*
pay *payer*
pension *pension*
price *prix*
salary *salaire*
sharp *brusque*
slight *léger*
social security *sécurité sociale*
stay *rester*
tax *taxe*
VAT *TVA*

Correcting people
actually *en fait*
be afraid *avoir peur*
correct *corriger*
date *date*
different *autre/différent*
fact *fait*
in fact *en fait*
fairly sure *presque sûr*
glad *content*
idea *idée*
misinformed *mal renseigné*
misjudge *mal juger*
mistake *erreur*
misunderstanding *malentendu*
name *nom*
nonsense *absurdités*
pleasant *agréable*
really *vraiment*
right *vrai/juste*
rubbish *absurdités*
seem *sembler*
sorry *désolé*
spelling *orthographe*
sure *sûr*
thanks (for) *merci (de)*
think *penser*
wrong *faux*
be wrong *avoir tort*

Talking about personal documents

Asking what you need
To ask if documents are necessary, use:
What documents do I need?
Do I need any documents?
Are there any formalities?
Do I have to have (proof of identity)?
Do I need a (visa)?
Is my (driving licence) enough?
Will they accept a (banker's card)?

Describing personal documents, use:
To describe common personal documents, use:
It's my (driving licence/birth certificate)
It's a (Swiss passport)/an (identity card)
This is a (cheque book/credit card)
They're my papers
This is for (insurance)
You can't (get a job) without it
You must have (this)
To talk about their validity, use:
It's valid until (June)
It's all in order
This is out of date
They're all up to date
It expires in (June)

Organising documents
To apply for a document, use:
I need a form for (an exit visa)
I want to apply for (a work permit)
I must get a (tax form)
My (insurance) is going to run out (in July)
I have to renew it
I've lost my (credit card)
I want to renew my (visa)
I've got two passport photographs
This is a photocopy of my (birth certificate)
How many copies do I need?
I have/haven't put my signature on it
To ask for help, use:
Could you explain this form to me, please?
I don't understand this question
Can you help me fill in this form, please?
Could you help me with this?

Talking about learning English

Talking about yourself
To talk about your own English learning, use:
I want to learn English
I'm trying to learn English
I've been learning it for (three years)
I did (some) at school
I need it for my (work)
I'm going to stay with an (American) family
We have to learn English
It's useful/important/necessary

Talking about difficulties
To say what you find difficult or easy, use:
(Speaking) is easy/difficult
The (vocabulary) is (not) simple/easy
I (don't) find it very difficult to understand
There are too many (prepositions)

Talking about learning
To ask about ways of learning, use:
What is the best way to learn?
How can I improve my (vocabulary)?
How do you think I can learn it?
To give opinions or advice, use:
I think the best thing is to (read and listen)
You should try and (speak to English people)
You should practise

Talking about needs
To tell a teacher what you need, use:
I want to be more (fluent)
I want to work on my (pronunciation)
I'd like to get my (grammar) better
I want to improve my (reading)
My (reading) is all right, but not my (accent)
My (basic vocabulary) is weak

Talking about types of English
To talk about English phrases, use:
Is this good/correct English?
That's too formal/informal
That sounds polite/rude
Is that friendly/rude?
Can I use this to (a customer)?

Talking about personal documents
accept *accepter*
apply *demander*
bank card *carte bancaire*
birth certificate *certificat de naissance*
cheque book *carnet de chèques*
copy *copie*
credit card *carte de crédit*
document *document*
driving licence *permis de conduire*
enough *assez*
expire *expirer*
explain *expliquer*
form *formulaire*
formalities *formalités*
identity card *carte d'indentité*
insurance *assurance*
lose *perdre*
(It's) in order *(c'est) en règle*
need *besoin*
out of date *périmé*
papers *papiers*
proof (of identity) *preuve (d'identité)*
question *question*
renew *renouveler*
run out *être périmé*
up to date *à jour*
signature *signature*
tax *impôts/taxe*
valid *valide*

Talking about learning English
accent *accent*
advice *conseil*
basic *de base*
correct *correct*
customer *client*
fluent *fluide*
friendly *amical*
grammar *grammaire*
improve *améliorer*
informal *familier*
learn *apprendre*
(my) own *(mon) propre*
necessary *nécessairement*
phrase *phrase*
polite *poli*
pronunciation *prononciation*
read *lire*
school *école*
simple *simple*
stay *rester*
talk *parler*
teach *enseigner*
useful *utile*
vocabulary *vocabulaire*
weak *faible*

Eating with English speakers

Starting the meal
To say that the food is ready, use:
It's ready
Sit down/Shall we sit down?
(Dinner) is ready
There is no general phrase that English speakers use at the start of a meal:
Usually they say nothing at all
If you want to say something, use:
Bon appetit
This looks/smells good
I'm looking forward to this
Some Americans say
Enjoy
In the same way, there is no need to answer
With a drink, before the first drink, use:
Cheers
Good health
Answer:
Cheers

During the meal
You may want to use:
Pass the (salt), please?
Could you pass the (salt), please?
May I have the (salt), please?
Could I have some more (potato)?
It's very nice/delicious
It tastes very nice/delicious
What's the name of this dish?
If you are the host or hostess, use:
Would you like some more (potato)?
Is everything all right?
Would you prefer (tea) or (coffee)?

After the meal
If you are the guest, use:
Thank you for (lunch)
Thank you for (a delicious dinner)
That was very nice/delicious
I enjoyed that
If you are the host or hostess, use:
I hope you enjoyed it
I'm glad you liked it

Offering food and drinks

Offering food and drinks
To offer food or drink, use:
What would you like?
Can I get you anything?
Would you like a (coffee)?
Do you take it with (sugar)?
How about a (Scotch)?
Do you feel like (a drink)?
To be more formal, use:
Let me get you (something to drink)
To be informal, use:
Coffee? With sugar?
Scotch? Ice?
Help yourself
To accept the offer, use:
Yes please
Thanks/Thank you
That would be nice
To be informal, use:
Yes/Sure
Thanks
To refuse the offer, use:
No thanks/No thank you
I don't want (anything) at the moment
I don't feel like (a drink) just now

Recommending
To recommend a food or drink, use:
Do you know (this)?
This is a (speciality from here)
I like (this) very much
I can recommend (this wine)
To ask for a recommendation, use:
What do you suggest?
What do you recommend?

Asking about preferences
To ask a guest's preference, use:
Would you prefer (tea) or (coffee)?
Shall I get something else instead?
Do you mind it (without salt)?
To express preference, use:
Actually, I'd prefer to have (something cold)
Could I have it (with soda) please?

Eating with English speakers
Cheers *Santé*
Could you? *pourriez-vous?*
delicious *délicieux*
dinner *dîner*
dish *plat*
drink *boisson*
during *pendant*
enjoy *apprécier/prendre plaisir*
Good health *à votre santé*
have *avoir*
hope *espérer*
host/hostess *hôte/hôtesse*
look (good) *sembler (bon)*
look forward to *attendre impatiemment*
lunch *déjeuner (repas de midi)*
May I? *puis-je?*
meal *repas*
more *plus*
nice *bon*
pass (the salt) *passer (le sel)*
prefer *préférer*
ready *prêt*
sit down *s'asseoir*
smell (good) *sentir (bon)*
taste *goûter*

Offering food and drinks
anything *quelque chose*
Can I? *puis-je?*
coffee *café*
cold *froid*
feel like *avoir envie de*
food *nourriture*
get *aller chercher*
help yourself *servez-vous*
ice *glace*
instead *au lieu de*
know *connaître*
like *aimer*
Do you mind? *est-ce que cela vous ennuie?*
offer *offrir*
(I'd) prefer *je préférerais*
recommend *recommander*
salt *sel*
something (to drink) *quelque chose (à boire)*
speciality *spécialité*
sugar *sucre*
suggest *suggérer*
tea *thé*
want *vouloir*
wine *vin*
with (soda) *avec (soda)*
without *sans*
Would you like? *voudriez-vous?*
Yes please *oui, s'il vous plaît*

Ordering a meal

Getting ready to order
When going into a restaurant, use:
We'd like to eat
Could I have a table for (five)?
Could I have the menu/wine list, please?
I'd like to see the menu
To call the waiter or waitress, use:
Waiter/Miss
Excuse me

Ordering
To ask for recommendations, use:
Can you recommend the (fish)?
What do you recommend?
To ask about a dish on the menu, use:
What is this?
How is this made?
Is this (fish)?
To order, use:
I'll have the (soup)
I won't have a starter/an hors d'oeuvre
I'll just have a main course
I'll have the (steak) but no (chips) please
I don't want any dessert/anything else
(My friend) will have a (beer)

Paying
To ask for the bill, use:
The bill, please/Could I have the bill?
In American restaurants, use the word **check:**
The check, please/I'd like the check
To ask about costs, use:
Is service included?
Is tax/VAT included?
Does this include service and tax/VAT?
To question the charges, use:
What's this charge for?
Are you sure this is right?
There's a mistake in the bill/check
You've charged me for (two bottles of wine)
To ask about paying, use:
Do you accept (cheques)?
Do you take (bank cards)?
Can I pay with (my credit card)?

Talking about cooking

Describing a dish
To describe a dish, use:
It's (sweet/cold)
It's a (meat) dish
It's cooked in (a sauce)
It tastes very good/spicy/rich
To ask about a dish, use:
Is it (fried)?
How is it cooked?
What does it taste like?

Describing cooking processes
To say how something is prepared, use:
It's (not) very easy/simple
You need (about a kilo of chicken)
You cook it slowly, for about (forty) minutes
It takes (about an hour)
You put it in the oven/in the fridge
You fry it in a little oil or fat
After that, you add (pepper)
The recipe says (two glasses of wine)
To ask about the cooking process, use:
What's the recipe?
How do you make (this)?
How long do you (bake) it for?
Do you use (milk)?

Describing types of cooking
To identify a style of cookery, use:
It's (French/Italian)
It's a typical (Indian) dish
The recipe comes from (Mexico)
To ask about the type, use:
Where is this from?
Is this a (Spanish) dish?
To ask about tastes in cooking styles, use:
What do you think of (Indian) food?
Do you like (it)?
What's (Lebanese) food like?
What's a typical (Lebanese) dish?
To state your tastes, use:
I (don't) like (Japanese) food
I prefer (western) to (eastern) food
My favourite dish is (lasagne)

Ordering a meal
accept *accepter*
beer *bière*
bottle *bouteille*
bill/check *addition*
charge *compter*
chips *frites*
(main) course *plat principal*
credit card *carte de crédit*
dessert *dessert*
dish *plat*
eat *manger*
fish *poisson*
make *faire*
meal *repas*
menu *menu*
order *commander*
pay *payer*
recommend *recommander*
service *service*
soup *soupe*
starter *entrée*
steak *bifteck*
table *table*
take *prendre*
tax *taxe*
waiter/waitress *serveur/serveuse*
wine list *liste des vins*
VAT *TVA*

Talking about cooking
add *ajouter*
bake *faire cuire au four*
chicken *poulet*
cold *froid*
cook *faire cuire*
cookery *(l'art de la) cuisine*
describe *décrire*
dish *plat*
fat/oil *graisse/huile*
fridge *réfrigérateur*
fry *faire frire*
glass *verre*
meat *viande*
milk *lait*
oil *huile*
oven *four*
pepper *poivre*
recipe *recette*
rich (food) *(nourriture) riche*
sauce *sauce*
slow *lent*
sweet *sucré*
spice *épices*
take (an hour) *durer une heure*
taste *goûter*

Talking about diet

Asking about daily diet
To ask people about their normal diet, use:
Do you eat (eggs)?
What do you have for (breakfast)?
What's a normal (lunch) for you?
What do you normally do for (dinner)?
Do you eat a lot of (pasta)?

Describing normal diet
To describe normal diets, use:
We usually have (three meals a day)
We often have (eggs for breakfast)
I don't eat much (meat)
They eat a lot of (fruit)
They (don't) eat a lot in the (evening)

Asking about dieting
To ask someone about a special diet, use:
Are you on a diet?
Can you eat anything?
Do you eat anything?
Are you dieting?
What are you allowed to eat?

Talking about particular foods
To talk about particular foods, use:
Is there any (salt) in this?
I'm not allowed to have (salt)
Does this have (alcohol) in it?

Talking about dieting
To talk about a special diet, use:
I'm on a diet
The doctor's put me on a diet
I'm dieting
I'm trying to lose weight
I have to be careful of what I eat
It's a medical diet
I'm not allowed to (eat bread)
I can't (drink coffee)
British and American people talk of calories:
I have to keep to (600) calories a day
How many calories are you allowed a day?
How many calories are there in (this)?

Talking about health

Describing general health
To talk about your general health, use:
I'm (not) fit
I'm usually healthy
I have a (bad back)
My (heart) is (not) very strong
I have to take (pills)
I have to follow a diet/eat special food
I'm allergic to (penicillin)
I have a high/low blood pressure
I have a (stomach) condition/illness
I had (an accident last year)
I've (never) been in hospital

Describing symptoms
To talk about symptoms, use:
I'm not feeling well
I'm feeling (sick)
I've been feeling (tired)
I haven't been sleeping/eating well
I can't (sleep)
I have a headache/stomachache/earache
My (shoulder) hurts
I have a pain in my (back)
To suggest causes, use:
I think it's (flu)
It may be (from playing tennis)
I think it may be (something I ate)
It's probably (the weather)
To describe changes, use:
I'm feeling worse
It's getting worse
I'm feeling better
I'm/It's the same
The medicine/pills helped/didn't help

Asking about health
To ask someone about health problems, use:
How are you feeling (today)?
How is the (leg)?
Are you feeling any better/worse?
What did the doctor say?
Do you have any medicine/pills to take?
Have you had a (check-up)?

Talking about diet
alcohol *alcool*
allow *permettre*
bread *pain*
breakfast *petit déjeûner*
calorie *calorie*
careful *prudent*
coffee *café*
daily *quotidien*
diet *régime*
dieting *suivre un régime*
dinner *dîner*
doctor *médecin*
drink *boire*
eat *manger*
egg *oeuf*
fruit *fruits*
keep to *s'en tenir à*
lunch *déjeûner (repas de midi)*
meal *repas*
medical *médical*
normal *normal*
particular *particulier*
salt *sel*
sometimes *parfois*
special *spécial*
try *essayer*
usually *habituellement*
(lose) weight *(perdre) du poids*

Talking about health
(head) ache *mal de tête*
accident *accident*
allergic *allergique*
bad (back) *dos douloureux*
blood *sang*
check up *contrôle médical*
diet *régime*
doctor *médecin*
feel (well) *se sentir bien*
fit *en bonne forme*
flu *grippe*
general *général*
healthy *en bonne santé*
heart *coeur*
hospital *hôpital*
hurt *faire mal*
illness *maladie*
medicine *médicament*
pain *douleur*
pressure *pression*
sick *malade*
sleep *dormir*
stomach *estomac*
symptom *symptôme*
tired *fatigué*

Understanding a doctor

Doctors' questions
The doctor's first questions may be
What's wrong?
What's the matter?
What seems to be the matter/the problem?
For more specific questions, be ready for:
Where does it hurt?
Can you feel (anything here)?
Can you (touch your toes)?
Do you have any allergies?
Are you allergic to (anything)?
Are you taking any medicine/drugs?
Have you been treated for (this) before?
Have you seen a doctor about this before?
For more general questions, be ready for:
Have you been eating/sleeping properly?
When did you last visit your doctor?
Do you take much exercise?
How much do you drink/smoke a day/a week?
Have you been working hard?
Do you suffer from (indigestion/nerves)?
Do you get any (headaches/dizziness)?

In the consulting room
The doctor may say:
Take your coat/shirt off
Sit down
Take your clothes off
Lie down on that (couch)
Go behind that (screen)
Roll up your left/right sleeve
Breathe deeply
Breathe in; Breathe out
Open your mouth; Put your tongue out
Let me see your tongue/leg/eyes
Bend your (left arm)
Put your (hands on your hips)
To warn you of something, the doctor may say:
I'm going to (listen to your chest)
I'm going to (touch your shoulder)
I'm just going to (test your reflexes)
I want to (take your blood pressure)
Tell me if this hurts
This won't hurt; This may hurt a bit

Understanding medical orders

Talking about treatment
The doctor may say:
Stay in bed for a few days
Take it easy/Rest
Don't work too hard
Come back and see me (next Tuesday)
Come back if it doesn't get better
Come back when (you've finished the medicine)
You've been working too hard
You must (stop smoking)
Keep taking (the medicine)

Talking about medicines
When prescribing medicine, the doctor may say:
You can get this from the chemist/pharmacy
Take this to the chemist/pharmacy
The chemist will give you (a cream)
This will help your (headaches)
Take this/these (four) times a day
Take (5) millilitres in water
Take a (teaspoonful) after every meal
Don't (drive after taking this)
You mustn't (drink alcohol with these pills)
You must (finish the whole bottle)
Don't (take any aspirin)
Put it on/Rub it on (your knee)

Referring you to another doctor
The doctor may say:
I want you to see a specialist
I think you should have an X ray
I want you to have some tests done
I want you to go to the clinic/hospital
I'm making an appointment for you
Take this letter to (Doctor Smith)
I'm giving you a letter for the hospital
At the clinic
At the clinic or hospital, they may ask:
We're going to keep you here for observation
We want to do some tests/an X-ray
You've got a (virus)
There's nothing broken; It's nothing serious
You'll have to say here (for a few days)

Understanding a doctor
behind *derrière*
bend *plier*
breathe *respirer*
dizzy *étourdi*
doctor *médecin*
drug *médicament*
exercise *exercice*
feel *sentir*
hurt *faire mal*
indigestion *indigestion*
lie down *se coucher*
(What's the) matter? *qu'est-ce qui ne va pas?*
mouth *bouche*
nerves *nerfs*
roll up (your sleeve) *remonter (ses manches)*
seem *sembler*
smoke *fumer*
take (medicine) *prendre un médicament*
take off (your shirt) *enlever (sa chemise)*
test (your reflexes) *vérifier (les réflexes de qn)*
toe *orteil*
tongue *langue*
touch *toucher*
treat *traiter*
(What's) wrong *qu'est-ce qui ne va pas?*

Understanding medical orders
appointment *rendez-vous*
bed *lit*
bottle *bouteille*
broken *cassé*
chemist *pharmacien*
clinic *clinique*
come back *revenir*
cream *crème*
(a few) days *plusieurs jours*
(take it) easy *se ménager*
hospital *hôpital*
keep taking (the medicine) *continuer à prendre*
letter *lettre*
meal *repas*
observation *observation*
pharmacy *pharmacie*
pill *pillule*
prescribe *prescrire*
rest *se reposer*
rub *frictionner*
(nothing) serious *(rien de) grave*
specialist *spécialiste*
stay *rester*
take (it in water) *prendre (dans de l'eau)*
teaspoonful *cuillère à thé*
test *examen*
virus *virus*
X-ray *radiographie*

Talking about holidays

Holiday plans
To ask about holiday plans, use:
Are you taking/having a holiday (this year)?
To speak to Americans, use the word **vacation:**
Are you taking a vacation (this year)?
Are you going on holiday/vacation (this year)?
Have you made your holiday plans?
What are you doing for a holiday (this year)?
To describe holiday plans, use:
I'm/We're going on holiday/vacation (in August)
We'll/We won't be having a holiday this year
We have (four) weeks' holiday a year
I'm/We're taking a break in (winter)

Describing places
To ask about place, use:
Where are you going (this summer)?
Are you going away?
To describe place, use:
I'm/We're (not) going away
We're staying in a hotel/with friends
We're (not) going abroad/to a foreign country
I'm going to (Kenya)

Past holidays
To ask about past holidays, use:
Where did you go (for you holiday/vacation)?
What's it like?; What was it like?
What was the food/weather/hotel like?
To describe past holidays, use:
I/We went to (Switzerland)
I/We had/didn't have a good time
It was fun/a break/an experience
The weather was good/bad/hot/too hot
I enjoyed/disliked the food/scenery/weather

Public holidays
To talk about public holidays, use:
We have (eight) days off a year
There are (six) public holidays a year
(Tomorrow) is a public holiday
To ask about public holidays, use:
Is there a public holiday (today)?
What's it for?

Talking about home

Talking about location
To describe the location of your home, use:
It's in the city/the town/the country
I live in the suburbs/at the seaside
It's near (Houston)
For the more immediate location, use:
It's in a quiet area/a busy district
I live near a park/in a middle-class street
It's not very far from (the city centre)
It's near (the football stadium)
To ask about someone's home, use:
Where do you live?
What sort of area is it?
Is it near (Milan)?

Describing the type of home
To say what sort of home it is, use:
I/We have a flat/a house/a room
It's a (three-) room flat
To Americans, use the word **apartment:**
It's a three-room apartment
The flat/apartment is on the (third) floor
It's a flat/apartment with a (balcony)
We rent a house/own our house
It's got (three) bedrooms
It's got (three) floors
There's a (garden)
It has a (garage)
To ask about someone's home, use:
Do you live in a flat/apartment?
Do you rent it?
Have you bought it?
Is it your own?
How big is it?

Talking about the family
To describe who lives with you, use:
I have a husband/wife
We've got (two) children
We have a (son) and (two daughters)
I live with my parents
To ask about someone's family, use:
Do you live alone?
Do you have a family?

Talking about holidays
abroad *à l'étranger*
ask *demander*
(go) away *s'en aller*
(take a) break *être en vacances*
country *pays*
dislike *détester*
enjoy *apprécier*
food *nourriture*
foreign *étranger*
friend *ami*
fun *plaisir*
holiday *vacances*
(What's the hotel) like? *comment (est l'hôtel)?*
(a day) off *(un jour de) congé*
plan *projeter*
public *légal*
scenery *paysage*
stay *rester*
summer *été*
have (a good) time *se plaire*
today *aujourd'hui*
tomorrow *demain*
vacation *vacances*
weather *temps*
week *semaine*
winter *hiver*
year *année*

Talking about home
area *quartier*
busy *mouvementé*
buy *acheter*
centre *centre*
country *campagne*
daughter *fille*
district *district*
flat *appartement*
(third) floor *(troisième) étage*
garage *garage*
garden *jardin*
home *domicile*
house *maison*
husband *mari*
live *habiter/vivre*
own *posséder*
near *proche*
rent *louer*
(bed) room *chambre (à coucher)*
seaside *bord de mer*
son *fils*
street *rue*
suburbs *faubourgs*
town *ville*
wife *femme*

Booking a hotel

Specifying the hotel
Contacting the hotel, travel agent, etc., use:
I want something (cheap)
I want something with (two or three) stars
What sort of hotel is it?
How many stars has it got?
I want somewhere (near the station)
For cheaper places, use:
I want a pension/guest house
I'm looking for a bed and breakfast place

Booking rooms
To book the rooms, use:
A single room with bath, please
I'd like/I want a (single)
I'd like to book a (double room)
I want a (twin room)
I'd like a (family room with three beds)
Have you got (two adjoining rooms)?
For the extras, use:
I want a room with a (shower)
A room with a (balcony)
I'd like a (television)
To specify the dates, use:
I want a room for (one) night
For (three) nights
For (Thursday and Friday) nights
For the nights of the (3rd) to (10th) May
That's (eight) nights
I'll arrive on the (evening of the 15th)
and leave on the (morning of the 22nd)

Talking about the tariff
To specify the tariff, use:
I want (bed and breakfast/bed only)
I'd like (half board)
I want (lunch) included
I'll book it (full board)
To check, use:
What is the tariff?
How much is it (per person/per room)?
Does that include (breakfast)?
How much is it (half board/full board)?
Is that inclusive?

Booking an excursion

Stating your needs
To talk about places, use:
We want to go to (Greenwich)
I'd like to book a trip to (Rye)
We want to see (Sark)
To talk about dates, use:
We want to go on (Thursday)
I'd like to book it for (next Saturday)
Is there an excursion (in the next few days)?
When is your next excursion to (the beach)?
We want to go out somewhere (on Friday). Are there any good excursions we could take?
To talk about numbers, use:
There'll be (four) of us
It's for a party of (six)
We are (twelve adults and eight children)
I need space for (eight people)

Asking for recommendations
To find out about a trip, use:
Can you recommend it?
What's (the journey) like?
Is it interesting/worth seeing?
It is a long journey/a nice journey?
Is it suitable for (a family with children)?

Asking about cost
To find out about prices, use:
How much does it cost?
Does that price include (everything)?
How much would it be to (hire a taxi)?
What are your (group rates)?
Do you do (a reduced price for a party of 12)?
Do you have (special rates for large groups)?

Asking about details
To find out about time and place, use:
Where do we meet?
Where do we catch the (coach)?
When/What time should we be there?
When's the last time we should be (there)?
How long will the journey take?
When/What time will we get there?
When/What time will we get back?

Booking a hotel
adjoining *contigües*
arrive *arriver*
balcony *balcon*
bath *bain*
bed and breakfast *chambre et petit déjeûner*
(full) board *pension (complète)*
book (a room) *réserver (une chambre)*
cheap *bon marché*
date *date*
double *pour 2 personnes*
evening *soirée*
extra *extra*
family *famille*
guest house *pension de famille*
include *inclure*
lunch *déjeûner (repas de midi)*
leave *quitter*
morning *matinée*
night *nuit*
place *place*
shower *douche*
single *à un lit*
somewhere (near) *un endroit (proche)*
(What) sort of (hotel)? *(quelle) sorte d' (hôtel)?*
station *gare*
(three) stars *(trois) étoiles*
travel agent *agent de voyage*
twin *jumeau*

Booking an excursion
adult *adulte*
beach *plage*
book *livre*
catch (a coach) *monter dans un autocar*
children *enfants*
cost *coûter*
date *date*
excursion *excursion*
include *inclure*
journey *voyage*
meet *rencontrer*
next *prochain*
number *nombre*
party (of 5) *groupe (de 5)*
place *endroit*
price *prix*
rate *tarif*
reduce *réduire*
see *voir*
space *place*
suitable *convenable*
take *participer à*
trip *excursion*
want *vouloir*
worth (doing) *valoir (la peine)*

Understanding measurements

Dimensions
To ask about dimensions, use:
How (wide) is it?
To talk about dimensions, use:
It's (3 metres) long/wide/high
The room is (6 square metres/3 metres by 2)
British and American people use this system:
An inch = ca. 2.5 cm
A foot (twelve inches) = ca. 30 cm
A yard (three feet) = ca. 90 cm
A mile = ca. 1.4 km
He's nearly six foot three inches tall
To ask British or American people, use:
What's that in the metric system?
How many (kilometres) is that?

Weight
To ask about weight, use:
How heavy is he/she/that?
What does it/do you weigh?
To talk about weight, use:
It's (45) kilos
He's (76) kilos
It weighs a few grams
She weighs about (60) kilos
British and American people use this system:
An ounce = ca. 25 grams
A pound (16 ounces) = ca. 450 grams
Can I have three pounds of potatoes, please?
To ask British or American people, use:
What/How much is that in kilos?
What's that in the metric system?

Liquids
To ask about liquid measurements, use:
How much is that?
To talk about liquid, use:
It's (a litre)
British and American people use this system:
A pint = ca. 45 cl.
A gallon (eight pints) = ca. 3.5 l.
Add half a pint of milk
To ask British or American people, use:
What's that in (litres)?

Giving orders

Preparing people
To prepare people for instructions, use:
Listen
Watch/Look
I want you to (listen carefully)
I'm going to tell you (how to do this)

Giving orders
To give an order, use:
Send it to me at home, please
Ring me when you have finished
Give me my case, please
Please put it down here
To give reasons, use:
Turn left, or we'll go the wrong way
Put it down, or you'll break it
To give a negative order, use:
Don't ring me at home, please
Don't be silly
Please don't put it down here
To be more formal and polite, use:
Could you wake me at 7 o'clock, please?
Could you send it to me?
Could you give me my case, please?
Please could you not ring me at home?

Sequencing instructions
To tell people the sequence, use:
First, (switch on)
First of all, (check the name)
Then/Next, (put in the paper)
After that, (send it to me)
Before you do (that), do (this)
After you've done (that), do (this)

Ordering food and drink
To give an order for food or drink, use:
Two coffees, please
I'll have (a Scotch)
We'll both have (an orange juice)
Could I have (a sandwich), please?
Could we have (two coffees)?
I'd like (a hamburger)
Please, (send breakfast to my room)

Understanding measurements
about (60 miles) *environ (60 miles)*
big *grand*
(two) by (three) *(deux) sur (trois)*
dimension *dimension*
a few (grams) *quelques grammes*
half (a pint) *c. 3 dl.*
heavy *lourd*
high *haut*
liquid *liquide*
long *long*
How many? *combien?*
measure *mesurer*
measurement *mesures*
metric (system) *système métrique*
milk *lait*
How much? *combien?*
nearly *presque*
potato *pomme de terre*
room *salle/pièce/chambre*
square (metres) *mètres carrés*
tall *grand*
weigh *peser*
weight *poids*
What's that in (litres)? *quel est l'équivalent en*
wide *large*

Giving orders
after *après*
at home *à la maison*
before *avant*
careful *prudent*
case *mallette*
Could you? *Pourriez-vous?*
Don't (be silly) *ne (sois) pas (sot)*
first *d'abord/premièrement*
give *donner*
(I'm) going to (say) *je vais (dire)*
listen *écouter*
look *regarder*
or *ou*
next *après*
please *s'il vous plaît*
prepare *préparer*
put (it) down *poser*
ring (me) *téléphonez – (moi)*
send *envoyer*
sequence *séquence*
then *alors*
wake (me) *réveillez – (moi)*
watch *faites attention*
the wrong (way) *le faux (sens)*

Talking about children

Describing by age
To ask about a child's age, use:
How old is he/she?
To describe a child's age, use:
It's a baby
He's/She's about (six)
He's a schoolboy; She's a schoolgirl
They're schoolchildren
They're in their teens/They're teenagers
The eldest is (20) and the youngest is (5)

Talking about school
To ask about children and school, use:
Where does he/she go to school?
How does he/she like school?
How are they getting on at school?
To discuss children at school, use:
He/She goes to school (in the city)
They (don't) like/enjoy school very much
She gets on well at school
He's good at (mathematics)

Talking about hobbies
To ask about children's hobbies, use:
Does he have a hobby?
What does she like doing?
To describe a child's hobbies use:
He likes (drawing)
She's very keen on (modelling)
He's mad about (football)
She likes/loves (pop music)

Talking about the future
To ask about a child's future, use:
What's she going to do/be?
What's he going to be when he grows up?
Is he going to follow his father?
Are they going to go to university?
To describe children's future plans, use:
He'll leave school at (16)
(I think) he's going to be a (chemist)
She wants to be a (vet)
They're hoping to go to university
She's studying to be a (teacher)

Talking about men

Describing by appearance
To ask about a man, use:
What does he look like?
Is he (heavily built)?
What does he wear?
To describe a man to someone, use:
He's (medium height)
He's (thin)
He's the (older) one
He's the one with the (fair hair)
He's got (wavy hair)
He hasn't got much hair/He's bald
He's got a (brown) moustache/beard
He's wearing (a brown jacket)
He usually wears (a hat)
He's (not) good-looking/handsome

Describing by qualities
To ask about a man, use:
What is he like?
What sort of person is he?
To describe a man by qualities, use:
He's (friendly/pleasant)
He's usually (rather quiet)
He's (not) easy to get on with
He's good at (listening to people)
His main quality is his (honesty)

Describing by position
To ask about a man, use:
Is he married?
Does he have any children?
What's his job?
What does he do?
To describe a man by his position, use:
He (lives in our street)
He's (not) married
He's married to (a teacher)
He has (two) children
He doesn't have any children
He works for (the garage) as (a mechanic)
He's a (senior sales assistant)
He works under/over (me)
His job is (something political)

Talking about children
age *âge*
baby *bébé*
boy *garçon*
child/children *enfant/enfants*
drawing *dessin*
good at (mathematics) *doué en (mathématiques)*
eldest *le plus âgé*
enjoy *apprécier*
father *père*
follow *suivre*
get on (at school) *réussir (à l'école)*
girl *fille*
go to (university) *aller à (l'université)*
grow (up) *grandir*
hobby *violon d'Ingres*
hope *espérer*
keen on *enthousiasmé par*
leave (school) *quitter (l'école)*
like *aimer*
love *aimer*
mad about (football) *fou de (football)*
modelling *modelage, création de modèles*
school *école*
teenager *adolescence*
teens *adolescent*
university *université*
young *jeune*

Talking about men
bald *chauve*
beard *barbe*
child/children *enfant/enfants*
easy *facile*
fair *blond*
friendly *amical*
get on with (someone) *s'entendre avec (qn)*
good looking *beau*
hair *cheveu(x)*
handsome *beau*
hat *chapeau*
heavy (build) *de carrure large*
jacket *veston*
job *travail*
live *habiter*
look like *avoir l'air*
married *marié*
medium (height) *(de taille) moyenne*
old *vieux*
quiet *tranquille*
(What) sort of *(Quelle) sorte de*
street *rue*
thin *mince*
wavy *bouclé*
wear *porter (vêtements)*

Talking about women

Describing physically
To ask about a woman, use:
What does she look like?
Is she (grey-haired)?
What sort of clothes does she wear?
To describe a woman to someone, use:
She's (tall/slim)
She's the (younger) one
She's the one with (brown hair)
She's got (straight hair)
She's wearing (a green coat)
She usually wears (a hat)
She's (not) good-looking/pretty

Describing by qualities
To ask about a woman, use:
What's she like?
What sort of person is she?
To describe a woman by qualities, use:
She's (sociable)
She's a (calm) person
She's (not) easy to get on with
Her main quality is her (friendliness)

Describing by position
To ask about a woman, use:
Is she married?
Does she have any children?
What's her job?
What does she do?
To describe a woman by her position, use:
She's (not) married
She's married to (an engineer)
She has (two) children
She doesn't have any children
She works for (the bank) as (a cashier)
She's a (senior sales assistant)

Discussing feminism
To talk about the women's movement, use:
(I think) women are (not) oppressed
Women are well treated/badly treated
I agree/don't agree with the feminists' ideas
Women should/shouldn't have more power

Talking about the weather

Talking about the forecast
To ask about future weather, use:
What's the weather going to be like (tomorrow)?
Have you heard the weather forecast?
Do you know what it's going to be like?
What do you think it'll be like (on Sunday)?
To talk about future weather, use:
It's going to be (sunny) (tomorrow)
I think it's going to (rain)
It looks/feels as if it's going to (get warmer)
They say it'll be (windy) (tomorrow)
There may be (frost) later
It should (clear up) soon
I don't think it's going to (change)
There's a (high) pressure
There's (rain) coming in from (the west)

Talking about weather conditions
To ask about weather conditions, use:
What's the weather like (there) (in spring)?
What sort of temperature is it (in June)?
Do you get much (fog)?
Do I need (winter) clothes?
Is it (wet) (in autumn)?
To describe weather conditions, use:
It's generally (cold and wet)
It's (normally) mild now
It's very pleasant (at this time of year)
It's (not) often very (dry)
We rarely get (snow)
To ask about past weather conditions, use:
What was the weather like (on your holiday)?
How was the weather (last year)?
To describe past weather conditions, use:
It was very (hot) (last year)
We had a lot of (rain) (last month)
It's been very (cold) so far this year

Chatting about the weather
To make polite conversation, use:
It's very nice today, isn't it?
It's not very nice today, is it?
It's (warmer) than last week, isn't it?
It's not bad for the time of year, is it?

Talking about women
agree *être d'accord*
assistant *vendeuse*
brown *brun*
calm *calme*
cashier *caissière*
coat *manteau*
clothes *vêtements*
feminist *féministe*
green *vert*
grey (haired) *(aux cheveux) gris*
idea *idée*
movement *mouvement*
oppressed *oppressée*
person *personne*
power *pouvoir*
pretty *jolie*
quality *qualité*
sales *de vente*
senior *de degré supérieur*
slim *mince*
sociable *sociable*
straight *raide*
tall *grande*
(well) treated *(bien traitée)*
woman *femme*
work *travailler*
young *jeune*

Talking about the weather
autumn *automne*
clear (up) *se dégager*
cold *froid*
dry *sec*
fog *brouillard*
forecast *prévisions*
frost *gel*
hot *chaud*
(What's it) like? *Comment est-ce?*
mild *doux*
pleasant *plaisant*
(high) pressure *(haute) pression*
rain *pluie*
snow *neige*
spring *printemps*
sunny *ensoleillé*
temperature *température*
tomorrow *demain*
warm *chaud*
weather *temps*
west *ouest*
wet *humide*
wind *vent*
winter *hiver*
year *année*

Notifying a loss

Identifying the loss
To explain what is lost, use:
I've lost my (passport)
I can't find my (money)
I think I've lost my (driving licence)
I've lost a (new Canon camera)
To ask about a loss, use:
What have you lost?
What was it like?
What does it look like?
Can you describe it?

Describing when
To give a time, use:
I know I had it (this morning)
I must have lost it (last night)
I last saw it (yesterday morning)
To ask about time, use:
How long has it been lost?
When did you last see it?

Describing where
To give a place, use:
I lost it (on the beach)
I left it behind (on the train)
It was (in my room)
I may have left it (in the bank)
I must have lost it (at the theatre)
To ask about place, use:
Where did you last see it?
Where was it?

Leaving personal details
To leave personal details, use:
My name is
My address is
Here is my card
Here is my name and address
Please ring me at (this number) if you find it
Please write to (this address) if it's found
Can you return it to me at (this address)?
To ask about personal details, use:
What is your name and address?
Could I have your name and address?

Giving statements to the police

Stating the case
To report something, use:
I'd like to report (an accident/a robbery)
I want to report (a crime/an attack)
I'm reporting a (missing passport)
I've lost (my bag)
My (wife) has been robbed
My (car) has been stolen
There's been (an accident)
I've been (robbed)

Giving the circumstances
To explain the circumstances, use:
We were walking along the street
We were asleep
I was working/having dinner
I was shopping/going into the bank
It was at about (ten o'clock)
It was yesterday evening/last night
It was in the hotel/in the car park
This was on the beach/in the street
Two men took (my wife's handbag)
A man/A woman came up to me
Someone picked my pocket
They ran away; They drove off
I didn't see anyone
I didn't see/hear/notice anything

Describing
To describe the people involved, use:
He/She was about (25)
They were (quite young)
They were (tall)
She had a (light build)
He/She had (short dark hair)
They were driving a (Saab)
He was wearing a (zip-up jacket)
She had on (a brown coat)
They were dressed in (jeans and sweaters)
I didn't see his face very well
To describe objects, use:
It was a (blue Renault)
It's worth about ($400)
It has (my name on it)

Notifying a loss
address *adresse*
beach *plage*
card *carte*
describe *décrire*
driving licence *permis de conduire*
find *trouver*
the last (time) *la dernière (fois)*
leave (behind) *laisser/oublier*
(What's it) like? *comment est-ce?*
look like *avoir l'air*
lose *perdre*
lost *perdu*
money *argent*
(this) morning *(ce) matin*
name *nom*
notify *déclarer*
(phone) number *numéro de téléphone*
passport *passeport*
return *renvoyer/retourner*
ring *téléphoner*
room *chambre*
see *voir*
train *train*
write *écrire*
yesterday *hier*

Giving statements to the police
accident *accident*
asleep *endormi*
attack *attaqué*
bag *sac*
(light) build *fluette*
crime *crime*
dressed in (sweaters) *habillés en sweaters*
drive *conduire*
face *visage*
(short) hair *cheveux (courts)*
hear *entendre*
lose *perdre*
missing *manquant*
object *objet*
name *nom*
notice (something) *remarquer (qq chose)*
pick (my pocket) *voler (dans ma poche)*
report *rapporter*
rob *voler*
run away *s'enfuir*
see *voir*
steal *voler*
take *prendre/voler*
walk *marcher*
wear *porter (vêtements)*
work *travailler*
worth *valoir*
zip-up (jacket) *blouson*

Using the post office

Locating a post office
To ask for the post office, use:
Is there a post office near here?
Where is the (nearest) post office?
Where is the main/central post office?
To post a letter, use:
Where's the nearest post/mail box?

Talking about postage
To ask about rates, use:
How much is it for a letter to (Japan)?
What is the letter rate to (Europe)?
Is there a special rate for (cards)?
How much is this by airmail to (Canada)?
To get stamps, use:
Three to Europe, please
I'd like to send this (parcel post)
Could I have six stamps for (postcards)?
To ask about delivery, use:
When will this get to (Athens)?
How long does it take (by airmail)?
When should this reach (London)?

Postage problems
To talk about problems, use:
I posted a letter to (London) six days ago and it still hasn't arrived
This arrived damaged/torn
I've been expecting a package from (Denmark)
It was posted two weeks ago
Could you look into this?
Can you find out what's gone wrong?
Can you check for me?

Special services
To ask for the special services, use:
I want to send a telegram
What's the fastest/safest way of sending this?
I want to send this express to (Cairo)
I want this insured
I want this to go registered mail
I'd like proof of posting
I want to send it "recorded delivery"
Can I have a customs form, please?

Using the telephone

Calling someone
To speak when someone answers the phone, use:
Hello? Is that (the Midland Bank)?
When using American English, say:
Hello? Is this (the Midland Bank)?
To ask to speak to someone, use:
Can I speak to (the manager), please?
I'd like to speak to (Miss Grant)

Answering the phone
When answering the phone, use:
Hello
This is (6359)/(Smith Ltd)
If you want to know who is calling, use:
Who's speaking, please?
Who's calling?
If the caller asks for you, use:
Speaking
This is (me) speaking
If the caller wants someone else, use:
Hold on/Hang on
I'll call him/I'll get him
I'll put you through/I'll connect you
To end the conversation, use:
Goodbye

Problems
If you get the wrong number, use:
Sorry, wrong number
If someone rings you in error, use:
Wrong number/You've got the wrong number
This is (64589), you should dial again
If the person you want is out, use:
Can I leave a message?
I'll ring back later. When's a good time?
Can you ask (him) to call/ring me?
If the caller wants someone who is out, use:
Can I take a message?
Could you ring back (in half an hour)?
Shall I get (him) to ring you back?
If you have to speak to the operator, use:
I've been trying to get (6379)
It rings engaged all the time
I was cut off

Using the post office
airmail *courrier par avion*
arrive *arriver*
box *boîte*
card *carte*
central *central*
check *contrôler*
customs *douane*
damaged *endommagé*
delivery *livraison*
expect *attendre*
express *express*
form *formulaire*
insured *assuré*
letter *lettre*
mail *courrier*
main *principal*
package *paquet*
parcel *paquet*
post *poste*
postage *port*
post office *bureau de poste*
proof *preuve*
rate *taxe*
reach *atteindre*
recorded (delivery) *recommandé*
registered *enregistré*
stamp *timbre*

Using the telephone
again *de nouveau*
answer *répondre*
(ring) back *rappeler*
call *appeler*
connect *connecter*
conversation *conversation*
cut off *couper*
dial *composer*
engaged *engagé*
hang on *patienter*
hold on *patienter*
later *plus tard*
leave *laisser*
message *message*
operator *standardiste*
out *sorti*
put (you) through *(vous) mettre en communication*
ring *téléphoner*
speak *parler*
Speaking *lui-même*
Who's speaking? *Qui est à l'appareil?*
take (a message) *prendre un message*
(a good) time *(un bon) moment*
This is *c'est*
try *essayer*
wrong (number) *faux (numéro)*

Phone box instructions

Making a call
There are different types of public telephone in the English-speaking world:
Expect to see phrases like this:
First; Next; Then
First (lift the receiver)
Then (put in the money)
Before (dialling), insert the coins
When you hear (the tone), speak
The most common instructions are:
Lift the receiver
Put in money
Put in a minimum of (50c)
Insert (two 10p pieces)
Press in the coin
Wait for the dialling tone
Wait for the ringing tone
Listen for a high, continuous tone
Dial the number
Dial the area code
Dial the international code
Do not replace the receiver
Press the green button
Speak
Dial again
Put in more money when the light flashes
Put in another coin when you hear rapid pips
To continue a dialled call put in more money
To continue the call insert another coin
To ring (Directory Enquiries) dial (122)
To ring (International) dial (367)
To report a telephone out of order dial (137)

Telephone tones
The different noises you can hear when making a call have names like these:
a rapid broken tone/a series of high pips
a series of long high tones
a low broken tone
a continuous purring noise
the dialling tone
the ringing tone
the engaged tone
the unobtainable tone

Booking seats

Specifying the performance
Contacting the cinema, theatre, etc., use:
What's the programme (on Saturday)?
What's on (on Wednesday evening)?
I'm trying to get tickets for (Space Wars)
I want to see (Carmen) on (Thursday)
Is (Rigoletto) on on (Friday evening)?
What time is the performance (this evening)?
What time are your performances (tomorrow)?
What time is the show?

Booking seats
To book the seats, use:
I'd like two seats
I'd like to book two seats
Can I have two seats for tomorrow?
Have you got two good seats for this evening?
Have you got any seats left for this evening?
To specify time, use:
I'd like a seat for the (8 o'clock) show
I'd like two for the (7.30) performance
To specify where you want to sit, use:
In the stalls
In the balcony
Upstairs/Downstairs
At the front/Near the front
In the middle/Near the back
In the first row
In one of the back five rows
At the side/In the middle
To ask about the seats, use:
Is that a good seat?/Are those good seats?
What are they like?
Can you see/hear all right from there?

Asking about the show
To check, use:
When/What time should I/we be there?
Will you hold the tickets for me till (7.30)?
How long does it/the performance last?
What time does it end?
When does the performance end?
Is there an interval?
How many intervals are there?

Phone box instructions
before *avant*
(the green) button *le bouton (vert)*
(make a) call *(faire un) appel*
code *code*
coin *pièce de monnaie*
dial *composer*
flash *éclairer*
hear *entendre*
high *haut*
insert *insérer*
lift *soulever*
listen *écouter*
money *argent*
next *ensuite*
number *nombre*
out of order *en panne*
pip *signal*
press in *enfoncer*
public *public*
put in *enfoncer*
receiver *récepteur*
replace *replacer*
ring *téléphoner*
tone *son*
wait for *attendre*

Booking seats
back *à l'arrière*
balcony *balcon*
book *réserver*
downstairs *en bas*
end *fin*
(this) evening *(ce) soir*
front *à l'avant*
hear *entendre*
hold (the seats) *garder (les sièges)*
interval *entracte*
(How long does it) last? *(Cb de temps dure-t-il)?*
(any) left *(des) . . . libres*
middle *milieu*
What's on? *Qu'est-ce qu'on joue?*
performance *représentation*
(first) row *(première) rangée*
seat *siège*
see *voir*
should *devoir*
show *spectacle*
side *côté*
stalls *fauteuils*
ticket *ticket*
(What) time? *(à quelle) heure?*
tomorrow *demain*
upstairs *en haut*
When? *Quand?*

Buying a ticket

Finding the ticket office
To ask for the ticket office, use:
Where can I get a ticket?
Where do I buy a ticket?
Is there a ticket office (near here)?
For air travel, use:
Where can I get a plane ticket (to Beirut)?
Where's the nearest travel agency?
To describe where to buy tickets, use:
You can get your ticket (on the corner)
It's on the left/right
You get the ticket from the man (on the bus)

Asking about tickets
To ask about your ticket, use:
What sort of ticket do I need/should I get?
What do I need (to leave here today and return next Sunday)?
Should I get a (weekend return)?

Buying a ticket
To get tickets, use:
One, please
Two singles to Paris
London return
A return ticket to London, please
I'd like one seat on the two o'clock
Can I have a return ticket to Bristol, please?
To ask about price, use:
How much is it?
How much does it cost?
How much does a weekend return cost?
Is there a special price for (students)?
Is it cheaper (on Sundays)?
Can I pay by (cheque)?
To ask about the ticket, use:
Is this ticket all right for (the airport)?
Is this valid for (the return journey)?
Is this the right ticket for (this train)?
Does this take me (to Dover first class)?
For extras, use:
Can I book a (sleeper) here?
I'd like to (send my luggage ahead)
I want a (smoking) seat

Planning a journey

Asking about public transport
To find out about travel services, use:
What time is the (next train) to (London)?
Is there a plane to (Bonn) (tomorrow evening)?
What time are the (services) to (Boston)?
Is there a frequent service?
How often do (they) go?
How long does it take?
When does it arrive/get there?
What time/When does it leave?
Where does it leave from?
Does that go via (Ostend)?

Asking about road travel
To find out about roads, use:
What's the best road to (Boston)?
Which is the best route to (Milan)?
How long does it take to (York)?
How many miles/kilometres is it?
Is it a good road?
How much time should I allow?
How far is it to (York) by car/by road?
What's the road like to (Antwerp)?

Suggesting plans
To propose travel arrangements, use:
Let's take the morning plane
Let's drive up via (Leeds)
We can get a meal/stop on the way
We can stop over/break the journey in (Aix)
What about driving there via (Brussels)?
It'll be quicker (to go by train)
It would be more comfortable (by train)
It think the (coast road) is better
I think the best route is through (Belgium)
I think we should start (at about 9)
I don't want to (cross London)
I want to be there (before it gets dark)
If I leave at (7) I'll be there by (12)
If we catch the (3.30), we'll be in time
If we go via (Aachen) we can be there by (4)
To ask for suggestions, use:
What do you think?
What would you suggest?

Buying a ticket
all right *valide*
airport *aéroport*
air travel *voyage par avion*
book *réserver*
buy *acheter*
cheap *bon marché*
corner *coin*
cost *coûter*
first class *première classe*
get (a ticket) *aller chercher (un ticket)*
journey *voyage*
left *gauche*
luggage *bagages*
need *besoin*
pay *payer*
plane *avion*
price *prix*
return *retour*
right *droite*
seat *siège*
send (ahead) *envoyer (à l'avance)*
single *aller*
sleeper *couchette*
smoking *fumeur*
ticket office *guichet*
travel agent *agent de voyage*
valid *valide*
weekend *week-end*

Planning a journey
allow *prévoir*
arrive *arriver*
break (the journey) *interrompre*
car *voiture*
catch (a plane) *attraper (l'avion)*
cross (the city) *traverser (la ville)*
drive *conduire*
evening *soir*
get (there) *arriver (là)*
journey *voyage*
leave *quitter*
meal *repas*
morning *matin*
plane *avion*
public *public*
quick *rapide*
road *route*
service *service*
start *partir*
take (time) *prendre (du temps)*
train *train*
transport *transport*
travel *voyager*
(on the) way *(en) route*
via *via/par*

Using a bus

Finding where to catch a bus
To ask where you can catch a bus, use:
Is there a bus stop near here?
Where's the nearest bus stop?
Is this the right bus stop for the (32)?
Is this the right place for a bus to (town)?
To ask for the central terminus, use:
Could you direct me to the bus station?
Where's the central bus station?

Getting the right bus
To find out times, use:
Do you know when the next bus goes (to town)?
How often do these buses run?
When's the next bus for (the airport)?
To find out which is the right bus, use:
Which bus goes to (the park)?
Which bus do I take to get to (the college)?
What number bus should I catch for (the city)?
Is this the right bus for (the station)?
To tell someone about bus services, use:
There's a (42) which goes to (the city)
It goes from (this stop)
There's one every (ten minutes)
Take a (17) to the station
Change (there) onto the (university) bus
It takes about (half an hour)

On the bus
To check with the employees on the bus, use:
Is this the right bus for (the airport)?
Does this go to (the bus station)?
To buy a ticket, use:
The Central Park, please
I want to go to (the city)
How much is it?
What/How much is the fare?
Can I get a return ticket?
To ask about the journey, use:
Do I have to change?
How many stops is it?
How long does it take?
Could you tell me where to get off, please?
Which is my stop?

Using the underground

Finding where to catch the underground
To ask where to catch the underground, use:
Is there an underground station near here?
To ask Americans, use the word subway:
Is there a subway near here?
Where's the nearest underground/subway?
Can you tell me where there's an underground/a subway station near here?
Are there any underground stations round here?
Could you direct me to an underground station?

Getting the right train
To find out times, use:
Do you know when the next train goes (to town)?
How often do these trains run?
When's the next train for (the airport)?
To find out which is the right train, use:
Which line/train goes to (the park)?
Which line do I take to get to (the college)?
What number train do I catch for (the city)?
Is there a train that goes (to the airport)?
Is this the right line for (the station)?
To tell someone about the services, use:
Get a ticket from the (machine)
The (city) service goes from (platform 2)
You'll have to change at (Oxford Circus)
The trains run every (ten minutes)
You need the (C line)

At the station
To check with the employees, use:
Is this the right line for (the airport)?
Does this go to (the city centre)?
To buy a ticket, use:
The Central Park, please
I want to go to (the city)
How much is it?
What/How much is the fare?
Can I get a return ticket?
To ask about the journey, use:
Do I have to change?
How many stations/stops is it?
Which station should I get off, please?
Is mine the (last) stop?

Using a bus
airport *aéroport*
bus *bus*
bus station *gare des bus*
bus stop *arrêt de bus*
catch *attraper*
change *changer*
city *ville*
direct (me) *(me) diriger*
fare *prix du voyage*
get off *descendre*
go *aller*
How much? *Combien?*
nearest *le plus proche*
number *nombre*
park *parc*
return *retour*
run (every few minutes) *passer (toutes les . . . minutes)*
the right (stop) *le bon arrêt*
take (a bus) *prendre (un bus)*
take (half an hour) *prendre (une demi-heure)*
terminus *terminus/fin*
ticket *ticket/billet*
town *ville*
want *vouloir*
Which (bus)? *Quel (bus)?*

Using the underground
get on *monter*
get to (the park) *aller vers (le parc)*
have to *devoir*
How long? *Cb de temps?*
How much? *Combien?*
How often? *avec quelle fréquence?*
last (stop) *dernier (arrêt)*
line *ligne*
machine *machine*
near (here) *près d'ici*
need *besoin*
platform *quai*
return ticket *billet de retour*
round (here) *aux alentours*
(They) run (frequently) *(ils) circulent (fréquemment)*
service *service*
station *gare*
stop *arrêt*
subway *métro*
time *temps*
train *train*
underground *métro*
What (is the fare)? *Quel est le prix du voyage?*
When? *Quand?*
Where? *Où*

Talking about work

Talking about jobs
To describe your job, use:
I'm a (trainee)
I work for (a large company)
I do the (sales ledger)
I'm in the (accounts) section
I've been (there) for (six) years
To give your opinion of it, use:
I (don't) like my job
It's a good job/interesting/well paid
To ask about someone's job, use:
What do you do?
What's your job?
What do you do for a living?
Where do you work?
Who do you work for?
Is it interesting/hard work/well paid?

Talking about work routines
To describe the normal routines, use:
We start at (8.30) and finish at (4.30)
We normally work from (8) till (5)
We (don't) work on (Saturdays)
We have (forty minutes) for lunch
I do a lot of (travelling)
I spend a lot of time on (paper work)
We are busy (at the end of the month)
We get (four weeks) holiday a year

Talking about personnel
To talk about the people at work, use:
My boss is (the sales manager)
I work under (him)
There are (six) of us in my department
The others are mostly (women)
It's a (friendly) department/section
There are (600) people in all
The company has (600) employees

Unemployment
To talk about unemployment, use:
(He's) out of work/unemployed
There are (a thousand) unemployed people here
(She's) looking for a job

Talking about school work

Talking about the system
To describe the school or college, use:
It's a (technical school)
It specialises in (technical subjects)
There are (400) pupils/students
It's quite big/not very big
To describe the system, use:
There are (three terms) a year
You can leave school at (16)
You can start college at (17)
We start at (8.30) and go on till (1.30)
We have (Saturdays) off
We work a half day on (Wednesdays)
We go to lessons/lectures
We (don't) have to work very hard
We (don't) do a lot of sport
We have a lot of (homework)

Talking about exams
To talk about exams, use:
He's taking an exam in (June)
We're working for our exams
It's a (school leaving certificate)
It's for a (diploma)
The exams are hard/easy
Last year, I failed/passed
You need it (to get a good job)

Talking about subjects
To talk about school subjects, use:
We study (physics)
I find (maths) easy/difficult
She's (not) good at (languages)
We're (not) taught (art)
My favourite subject is/was (history)
I like/liked (chemistry)
We started a new subject this term/semester
We haven't the (facilities) for (sport)

Talking about teachers
To talk about the teachers, use:
(She's) (not) a good teacher/lecturer
(She) teaches (psychology)/lectures in (art)
(She's) (not) very strict

Talking about work
accounts *comptabilité*
boss *patron*
company *compagnie*
department *département*
employee *employé*
finish *terminer*
hard *dur*
holiday *vacances*
interesting *intéressant*
job *travail*
large *grand*
(for a) living *pour gagner sa vie*
lunch *déjeûner*
month *mois*
(well) paid *(bien) payé*
paper (work) *paperasserie*
people *gens*
sales (ledger) *(grand livre) de vente*
start *commencer*
trainee *stagiaire*
travel *voyager*
unemployed *chômeur*
week *semaine*
work *travail*

Talking about school work
art *art*
(school leaving) certificate *certificat (de fin d'études)*
(technical) college *collège (technique)*
facilities *facilités*
fail *échouer*
go on till (1 pm) *continuer jusqu'à (1 pm)*
a half (day) *un demi–(jour)*
history *histoire*
homework *devoir*
language *langue*
leave *quitter*
lecture *cours*
lecturer *chargé de cours*
lesson *leçon*
maths *maths*
(a day) off *(un jour) de congé*
pass (an exam) *réussir à (un examen)*
pupil *élève*
school *école*
specialise in (sport) *se spécialiser en (sport)*
start *commencer*
student *étudiant*
subject *sujet*
take (an exam) *passer (un examen)*
teach *enseigner*
teacher *enseignant*
term *trimestre*
work for (a diploma) *travailler pour (un diplôme)*

FRENCH-ENGLISH

A

A, a [ɑ] *nm* (the letter) A, a; *F* **il ne sait ni A ni B,** he can't read, he doesn't know his ABC; *Fig* he doesn't know A from B; **connaître un sujet de A (jusqu')à Z,** to know a subject from A to Z *or* thoroughly *or* inside out; **prouver qch par A plus B,** to prove sth in a logical *or* scientific fashion.

à [a] *prép* (*contracts with the article* **le** *into* **au**, *with the article* **les** *into* **aux**) **(a)** (*denoting direction*) **courir à qn,** to run (up) to s.o.; **revenir à la surface,** to come (up) to the surface again, to resurface; **aller à l'église/au cinéma,** to go to church/to the cinema; **monter à sa chambre,** to go up to one's room; **partir à la recherche de ses ancêtres,** to begin a search for one's ancestors; **de Paris à Lyon,** from Paris to Lyons; **se rendre au Japon/aux Antilles/à la Guadeloupe/à Terre-Neuve,** to travel to Japan/to the West Indies/to Guadeloupe/to Newfoundland; **au lit!,** off to bed!; **au feu!,** fire!; **au voleur!,** stop thief!; **courir à sa perte,** to head for disaster; **(de) vingt à trente personnes,** between twenty and thirty people;

(b) (*denoting position*) **au coin de la rue,** at the corner of the street, at the street corner; **vivre à Montpellier/à la campagne,** to live in Montpellier/in the country; **à l'horizon,** on the horizon; **à la page deux,** on page two; **à l'ombre,** in the shade; **au grenier,** in the attic; **à la maison,** at home; **au théâtre,** at the theatre; **au Canada,** in Canada; **aux États-Unis,** in the United States; **à la Jamaïque,** in Jamaica; **à Cuba,** in Cuba; **à Paris,** in Paris; **se tenir à la fenêtre,** to stand at the window; **à deux kilomètres d'ici,** two kilometres (away) from here; **avoir mal aux dents,** to have toothache; **à la télévision/à la radio,** on (the) television/on the radio; **le sourire aux lèvres,** with a smile on his *or* her *etc* lips; **un livre à la main,** with a book in one's hand; **au fond,** basically, fundamentally;

(c) (*denoting direction in time*) **du matin au soir,** from morning to *or* till night; **remettre une affaire à plus tard,** to put off *or* postpone something; **à jamais,** for ever; **à demain!,** see you tomorrow!; **de lundi à vendredi,** from Monday to Friday, *US* Monday thru Friday; **il sera là à 8 heures,** he'll be there at 8 o'clock; **au printemps,** in (the) spring; **le 2 au soir,** on the evening of the 2nd; **à Noël,** at Christmas; **au revoir,** goodbye (for now); **au premier mot,** at the first word; **à mon arrivée,** on my arrival; **à deux heures,** at two o'clock; **au vingtième siècle,** in the twentieth century; **à l'avenir,** in (the) future; **à l'aube,** at dawn;

(d) (*distribution*) **faire du 10 litres aux 100 (km),** to do 100 kilometres on 10 litres; **90 km à l'heure,** 90 km an *or* per hour; **payé au mois,** paid monthly *or* by the month; **vendre des oranges à la pièce,** to sell oranges separately *or* individually; **entrer deux à deux,** to come in two by two; **à toute heure du jour et de la nuit,** at all hours of the day and night; **se battre d'homme à homme,** to fight man to man; *Tennis* **quinze à,** fifteen all; **monter l'escalier quatre à quatre,** to go upstairs four (steps) at a time; **peu à peu,** little by little, gradually;

(e) (*introducing the indirect object of many verbs*) **attacher un cheval à un arbre,** to tie a horse to a tree; **attacher de l'importance à qch,** to attach importance to sth; **donner qch à qn,** to give sth to s.o., to give s.o. sth; **parler à qn,** to speak to s.o.; **penser à qn/qch,** to think of *or* about s.o./sth; **s'habituer à qch,** to become used to sth; **à quoi cela sert-il?,** what's that used for?; (*quel intérêt?*) what's the good of that?; **survivre à qn/qch,** to survive *or* outlive s.o./sth; **prendre qn à témoin,** to call s.o. to witness *or* as a witness; **s'opposer à qch,** to oppose sth; **résister à qn/qch,** to resist s.o./sth; **cacher/voler qch à qn,** to hide/steal sth from s.o.; **boire à (même) la bouteille,** to drink (straight) from the bottle; **faire faire qch à qn,** to make s.o. do sth, to get s.o. to do sth; **faire savoir qch à qn,** to tell s.o. about sth, to inform s.o. of sth; **laisser croire à qn que ...,** to let s.o. think *or* believe that ...;

(f) (*possession etc*) **ce livre est à Paul,** this book is Paul's, this is Paul's book, this book belongs to Paul; **un ami à moi,** a friend of mine; *F* **la soeur à Anne,** Anne's sister; **c'est à vous de décider,** it's for you *or* up to you to decide; **c'est à vous,** it's your turn; *Rad* **à vous,** over (to you); **la parole est à M. Dupont,** Mr Dupont will now speak; **une expression bien à Anne,** a typically Anne expression; **c'est aimable à vous d'être venu,** it's kind *or* good of you to have come;

(g) **tasse à thé,** teacup; **brosse à dents,** toothbrush; **moulin à vent,** windmill; **chambre à deux lits,** room with twin beds; **voiture à toit ouvrant,** car with a sun roof; **pompe à eau,** water pump; **enfant aux yeux bleus,** child with blue eyes, blue-eyed child; **homme à barbe noire,** man with a black beard; *Sp* **rugby à quinze/treize,** Rugby Union/League;

(h) (*manner*) **à pied,** on foot; **à la main,** by hand; **fait à la main,** handmade; **jouer un air au violon,** to play a tune on the violin; **arriver à l'improviste,** to arrive unexpectedly; **à toute allure,** at top speed; **à ce rythme, nous y sommes encore demain,** the way we're going *or* at this rate we'll still be at it tomorrow; **recevoir qn à bras ouverts,** to receive s.o. with open arms; **vendre des huîtres à la douzaine,** to sell oysters by the dozen; **cuisine à l'huile,** cooking with oil; **à la française,** in the French manner *or* way; **un repas à l'anglaise,** a typical(ly) English meal; *F* **encore une histoire à la Marie,** another one of Marie's typical stories; **manger à sa faim,** to eat one's fill; (*autant que possible*) to eat as much as one can; **faire qch à sa manière** *ou* **façon,** to do sth (in) one's own way; **nous l'avons fait à trois,** there were three of us doing it;

(i) **à mon avis,** in my opinion; **à ce qu'il dit,** according to him *or* to what he says, from what he says; **au reste,** moreover, besides; **à cette condition,** on this condition; **à la demande générale,** by popular request; **à ma grande surprise,** to my great surprise;

(j) **à quel prix vendez-vous cela?,** how much are you asking for that?; **un timbre à deux francs,** a two franc stamp; **à ce prix, on ne peut pas se plaindre,** at that price you can't complain;

(k) **indispensable à,** indispensable *or* essential to (*s.o.*); indispensable *or* essential for (*sth*); **parallèle à,** parallel to; **hostile à,** hostile to;

(l) (*introducing verb in infinitive*) **penser à faire qch,** to think of doing sth; **encourager qn à faire qch,** to encourage s.o. to do sth; **j'ai à écrire une lettre,** I have to write a letter; **il ne me reste qu'à vous remercier,** it only remains for me to thank you; **commencer à faire qch,** to begin to do sth, to start doing sth; **apprendre à lire,** to learn to read;

(m) (*destination*) for; **bon à jeter,** fit for the dustbin; **une machine à coudre,** a sewing machine; **j'ai une veste à nettoyer,** I have a jacket to be cleaned; (*c'est moi qui va le faire*) I have a jacket to clean; **j'ai une lettre à écrire,** I have a letter to write; **je voudrais quelque chose à boire,** I'd like something to drink; **maison à vendre,** house for sale;

(n) (*consequence*) **laid à faire peur,** frightfully ugly; **s'ennuyer à mourir,** to be bored to death; **c'est à se demander si elle sait de quoi elle parle,** you begin to wonder if she knows what she's talking about; **geler à pierre fendre,** to freeze hard; **un bruit à tout casser,** an ear-splitting noise;

(o) **je suis prêt à vous écouter,** I'm willing to listen to you; **habile à coudre,** good at sewing; **facile à comprendre,** easy to understand; **il est homme à se défendre,** he's the kind of man who will hit back; **elle est à plaindre,** she is *or* deserves to be pitied; **être le seul à faire qch,** to be the only one to do sth; **le troisième à arriver,** the third to arrive;

(p) **à partager les mêmes périls on apprend à se con-**

naître, by sharing the same dangers we learn to know each other; **à en juger par...,** judging by..., to judge by ...; **à les en croire,** according to them, if we are to believe them.

abaissant [abɛsɑ̃] *adj* degrading.

abaisse [abɛs] *nf Culin* thinly rolled pastry.

abaisse-langue [abɛslɑ̃g] *nm inv Méd* tongue depressor.

abaissement [abɛsmɑ̃] *nm* **(a)** lowering, pulling down (*of blind etc*); **(b)** fall; subsidence, sinking (*of ground, building*); fall, drop (*in temperature, prices*); reduction (*in prices*); **(c)** *Litt* abasement, humiliation.

abaisser [abese] **1** *vt* **(a)** to lower; to pull down (*a blind*); to let down (*drawbridge*); **(b)** to lower (*one's voice, prices*); to reduce (*prices, cost, pressure etc*); **(c)** *Litt* to humble, to abase; **(d)** *Math* **a. une perpendiculaire à une ligne,** to drop a perpendicular to a line; **a. le chiffre des dizaines,** (*dans une division*) to bring down the figure in the tens column; **(e)** *Culin* **a. une pâte,** to roll out pastry. **2 s'abaisser** *vpr* **(a)** to fall away, to dip, to slope down, to go down; **le terrain s'est abaissé,** the ground has subsided; **la fenêtre s'abaisse quand on appuie sur ce bouton,** the window slides down when you press this button; **(b)** (*chuter*) to drop, to fall; **la température s'abaisse,** the temperature is falling; **(c) s'a. jusqu'à faire qch,** (*consentir*) to stoop so low as to do sth; (*d'une personne orgueilleuse*) to condescend to do sth; **(d) s'a. devant Dieu,** to humble oneself before God.

abaisseur [abɛsœr] **1** *nm Anat* depressor. **2** *adj Él* (*transformateur*) step-down.

abandon [abɑ̃dɔ̃] *nm* **(a)** surrender (*of goods, rights etc*); renunciation (*of rights*); **faire l'a. de qch à qn,** to make over *or* relinquish *or* surrender sth to s.o.; **(b)** *Sp* retirement (*from race*); (*avant la course*) withdrawal; **(c)** *Jur* desertion, abandonment (*of children*); desertion, dereliction (*of duty*); **a. du domicile conjugal,** desertion; **(d)** (*état*) neglect; **finir sa vie dans l'a., délaissé des siens,** to end one's life alone, completely neglected by one's family; **à l'a.,** (completely) neglected; (*of children, garden*) running wild; *Nau* adrift, derelict; **(e)** (*détente*) lack of restraint; **parler avec un complet a.,** to speak quite freely *or* without restraint.

abandonné, -ée [abɑ̃dɔne] **1** *adj* (*personne*) abandoned, deserted; untidy (*appearance*); **navire a. en mer,** derelict; **maison abandonnée,** deserted house; *Com* **modèle a.,** discontinued line. **2** *n* **les abandonnés,** waifs and strays.

abandonner [abɑ̃dɔne] **1** *vt* **(a)** to desert, to abandon (*s.o.*); *Litt* to forsake; **a. un projet,** to abandon a project; **il a abandonné les études à quatorze ans,** he dropped out (of school) when he was 14; *Nau* **a. un homme,** to maroon a man; *Nau* **a. le bâtiment,** to abandon ship; *Av* **a. le bord** *ou* **un avion en vol,** to bale out; *Mil* **a. son poste,** to desert one's post;

(b) (*délaisser*) to abandon (*car*); to abandon, to desert (*village*); **mes forces m'abandonnent,** my strength is failing me; **abandonné par les médecins,** given up by the doctors; **a. la partie,** to throw in one's hand;

(c) (*renoncer à*) to surrender, to renounce, to give up (*sth*); **a. sa part d'héritage (à sa sœur),** to forgo one's share of an inheritance (in favour of one's sister); **a. ses prétentions,** to renounce *or* surrender one's claims;

(d) *Ordinat* to abort.

2 *vi Sp* to give up, to retire; *F* **c'est trop dur, j'abandonne,** it's too hard, I give up.

3 s'abandonner *vpr* **(a)** (*se laisser aller*) to let oneself go, *Fml* to be unconstrained;

(b) (*s'en remettre à*) **s'a. à son sort,** to resign oneself to one's fate; **s'a. au sommeil,** to abandon oneself to sleep;

(c) (*se confier*) to open up.

abaque [abak] *nm* **(a)** (*boulier*) abacus, counting frame; **(b)** *Math* chart, graph, table; *Spéc* plotter; **(c)** *Archit* abacus.

abasourdir [abazurdir] *vt* to deafen; *Fig* to astound, to bewilder, to stun; *Fig* **nous sommes restés abasourdis par la nouvelle,** we were flabbergasted *or* astounded *or* stunned by the news.

abasourdissant [abazurdisɑ̃] *adj* (*bruit*) deafening; *Fig* (*nouvelle*) stunning, astounding.

abasourdissement [abazurdismɑ̃] *nm* bewilderment, stupefaction.

abat [aba] *nm* **(a) abats,** offal, *Am* variety meat; (*de volaille*) giblets; **(b)** *Arch* slaughter; **pluie d'a.,** sudden shower.

abâtardi [abɑtardi] *adj* degenerate.

abâtardir [abɑtardir] **1** *vt* to cause (*a species*) to degenerate; to debase (*quality*). **2 s'abâtardir** *vpr* to degenerate, to deteriorate; (*of quality*) to become debased.

abâtardissement [abɑtardismɑ̃] *nm* degeneracy.

abat-jour [abaʒur] *nm inv* (*pour lampe*) lampshade; **mettre la main en a.-j.,** to shade one's eyes with one's hand.

abattage [abataʒ] *nm* **(a)** knocking down, pulling down (*of buildings*); felling, cutting down, clearing (*of trees etc*); *Min* cutting, working; *Min* **face d'a.,** working face; *Nau* **a. en carène,** careening; **avoir de l'a.,** to be full of energy *or* zest; *Fig* (*d'un acteur, d'un politicien etc*) to have charisma; **(b)** (*d'animal*) slaughtering, killing; **grand a. de gibier,** heavy bag of game; **(c)** *Com* **vente à l'a.,** sale at knock-down prices.

abattant [abatɑ̃] **1** *adj* **(a)** (*qui affaiblit*) **chaleur abattante,** energy-sapping heat; **(b) siège a.,** tip-up seat. **2** *nm* flap (*of counter, table, envelope*).

abattement [abatmɑ̃] *nm* **(a)** (*physique*) exhaustion, *Fml* prostration; **(b)** (*moral*) despondency, dejection, depression, low spirits; **(c)** *Fin* abatement; allowance (*against tax*).

abatteur, -euse [abatœr, -øz] *n* **(a) a. de besogne,** hard worker, *F* slogger; **(b)** feller (*of trees*); **(c)** slaughterer (*of animals*).

abattis [abati] *nm* **(a)** felling, clearing (*of trees*); **(b)** *Région* heap of felled trees; **a. de maisons,** heap of fallen houses; **(c)** *Culin pl* giblets; **(d)** *Arg pl* limbs, hands and feet; **si tu viens te battre avec moi, commence par numéroter tes a.!,** if you're going to pick a fight with me, you can say your prayers right now!

abattoir [abatwar] *nm* slaughterhouse, abattoir; **envoyer des hommes à l'a.,** to send men to the slaughter *or* to be slaughtered *or* butchered.

abattre [abatr] *v* (*conj like* **battre**) **1** *vt* **(a)** (*faire tomber*) to knock down, to throw down, to pull down; to overthrow (*régime*); **a. son rival,** to floor *or* fell *or* knock down one's opponent; *F* (*dans une course etc*) to flatten one's opponent; **a. une maison,** to pull *or* knock down a house; **a. de la besogne,** to get through a lot of work;

(b) to fell, to cut down, to clear (*trees*); **a. du minerai,** to break down *or* to stope ore;

(c) (*tuer*) to slaughter, to kill (*a person, a pig, an ox*); to destroy (*a cat, a dog*); *Arg* to bump (*s.o.*) off; **a. un avion,** to bring down *or* shoot down an aircraft; **c'est un homme à a.,** we have to bump him off;

(d) to lower; to dampen (*courage, enthusiasm*);

(e) to lay (*dust, wind*);

(f) (*of wind*) to blow down (*a tree*); to flatten (*corn*); *Nau* **a. navire en carène,** to careen a ship;

(g) *Fig* (*fatiguer*) (*de la chaleur*) to drain (*s.o.*) of energy; (*d'une maladie*) to lay (*s.o.*) low;

(h) (*démoraliser*) to dishearten, to depress; **ne vous laissez pas a.!,** bear up!;

(i) *Cartes* **a. ses cartes** *ou* **son jeu,** to lay one's cards on the table, to lay down one's hand; *Fig* to lay one's cards on the table;

(j) *Nau* to pay off; **a. à la côte,** to drift on shore.

2 s'abattre *vpr* **(a)** (*tomber*) to fall, to crash down, to collapse; **le pilier s'abattit,** the pillar came crashing down; **le Boeing s'est abattu 30 minutes après le décollage,** the Boeing crashed 30 minutes after take-off;

(b) s'a. sur qch, to pounce on sth; (*d'un oiseau*) to swoop down on(to) sth; **les journalistes s'abattent sur la vedette,** the journalists are swarming around the star; **les précipitations qui se sont abattues sur la région,** the torrential rain which has been falling on the region; **les injures n'ont pas cessé de s'a. sur l'orateur,** insults rained down constantly on the speaker;

(c) (*of fever, heat etc*) to abate, to subside; **le vent s'abat,** the wind is dropping.

abattu [abaty] **1** *adj* dejected, dispirited, low-spirited; **a. par la chaleur,** limp with the heat; **a. par l'échec,** depressed *or* demoralized by the failure; **visage a.,** drawn face. **2** *nm* **fusil à l'a.,** uncocked rifle.

abat-vent [abavɑ̃] *nm inv* **(a)** (*de fenêtre etc*) louvre boards; **(b)** (*de cheminée*) (chimney) cowl; **(c)** (*de jardin*) windbreak.

abbatial, -le, -aux [abasjal, -o] **1** *adj* **terres abbatiales,** abbey lands; **église abbatiale,** abbey (church). **2** *nf* **abbatiale,** abbey (church).

abbaye [abei] *nf* abbey.

abbé [abe] *nm* **(a)** (*supérieur d'une abbaye*) abbot; **(b)** (*general designation of and mode of address for a (Roman Catholic) priest*) **j'en parlerai à monsieur l'a.,** I shall mention it to the priest; **(Monsieur) l'a. Constantin,** Father Constantin.

abbesse [abɛs] *nf* abbess.

abc [abese] *nm inv* **(a)** (*livre pour apprendre à lire*) ABC, alphabet; (*livre scolaire*) primer; **(b)** *Fig* rudiments (*of a science*).

abcès [apsɛ] *nm* abscess; **a. à la gencive,** gumboil; *Fig* **crever** *ou* **vider l'a.,** to remove the cancer.

abdication [abdikɑsjɔ̃] *nf* abdication (*of monarch, authority*); renunciation, surrender (*of authority, rights*).

abdiquer [abdike] **1** *vt* to abdicate (*throne, authority*); to renounce, to surrender (*rights etc*). **2** *vi* to abdicate.

abdomen [abdɔmɛn] *nm Anat* abdomen.

abdominal, -aux [abdɔminal, -o] **1** *adj* abdominal. **2** *nm* **abdominaux,** abdominal *or* stomach muscles.

abducteur [abdyktœr] *Anat* **1** *adj* (*muscle*) abductor. **2** *nm* abductor muscle.

abécédaire [abesedɛr] **1** *adj Vieilli* alphabetical. **2** *nm* **(a)** ABC, alphabet book; **(b)** *Couture* sampler.

abeille [abɛj] *nf* (*insecte*) bee; **a. domestique,** hive bee, honey bee; **a. neutre** *ou* **ouvrière,** worker (bee); **a. mâle,** drone; **a. mère,** queen bee; **nid d'abeilles,** bees' nest, honeycomb; *Aut* **radiateur nid d'abeilles,** honeycomb radiator; *F* **elle ne cesse de travailler, c'est une vraie petite a.,** she never stops working, she's a real busy bee.

aberrant [abɛrɑ̃] *adj* **(a)** *Biol* aberrant; **(b)** (*absurde*) aberrant, illogical (*behaviour*); nonsensical (*remark*); **avoir une conduite aberrante,** to behave illogically.

aberration [abɛrɑsjɔ̃] *nf* (*of mind, conduct*) *& Astron Biol Math Opt* aberration; **a. de sphéricité,** spherical aberration; **a. chromosomique,** chromosome abnormality.

abêtir [abɛtir] **1** *vt* to make (*s.o.*) stupid; **la télévision finit par a. les enfants,** television deadens *or Fml* stultifies children's minds. **2** *vi* to grow *or* become stupid. **3 s'abêtir** *vpr* to grow *or* become stupid.

abhorrer [abɔre] *vt* to abhor, to loathe.

abîme [abim] *nm* **(a)** (*de l'océan*) abyss, chasm, depth(s); *Fig* gulf; *Géol* swallowhole; **les abîmes de l'océan,** the ocean depths; *Fig* **un a. d'incompréhension,** a gulf of incomprehension; *Fig* **le livre est un a. d'ennui,** this book is extremely boring *or* deadly dull; **un a. de science,** a person of immense learning; (*qui peut fournir beaucoup de renseignements*) a mine of information; *Litt* **les abîmes de l'histoire,** the earliest beginnings of history, the mists of time; **(b)** (*ruine*) (*financier*) ruin; (*moral*) despair; **il est au fond de l'a.,** he is in the depths of depression *or* despair.

abîmer [abime] **1** *vt* to spoil, to damage (*sth*); to injure (*s.o.*); **livre abîmé par la pluie,** book spoilt by the rain; **a. ses affaires,** to damage one's belongings; *F* **se faire a.,** to get beaten up *or* knocked about. **2 s'abîmer** *vpr* **(a)** *Litt* **s'a. dans les flots,** to sink; *Litt* to be engulfed *or* swallowed up by the sea; *Fig* **s'a. dans la douleur/dans ses pensées,** to be sunk in grief/lost in thought; **(b)** to get spoiled; (*d'un fruit*) to spoil, to go bad; **s'a. la santé,** to damage one's health; **tu t'abîmes les yeux,** you're ruining your eyes *or* eyesight.

abject [abʒɛkt] *adj Litt* abject (*poverty*); *Péj* mean, contemptible, despicable (*person, conduct*).

abjectement [abʒɛktəmɑ̃] *adv Litt* abjectly; *Péj* contemptibly, despicably.

abjection [abʒɛksjɔ̃] *nf Litt* abjectness, abjection; **se conduire avec a.,** to behave abjectly.

abjuration [abʒyrɑsjɔ̃] *nf* abjuration; renunciation (*on oath*); recantation (*of threat, heresy*).

abjurer [abʒyre] *vt* to abjure, to forswear; to renounce (*on oath*); to recant (*heresy*); to retract (*insult, confession*).

ablatif, -ive [ablatif, -iv] *Gram* **1** *adj* ablative. **2** *nm* ablative case; **à l'a.,** in the ablative; **a. absolu,** ablative absolute.

ablation [ablɑsjɔ̃] *nf* ablation; *Méd* **a. des amygdales,** removal of the tonsils, tonsillectomy.

ablette [ablɛt] *nf* (*poisson*) bleak.

ablution [ablysjɔ̃] *nf* washing; *Fml* ablution; *F* **faire ses ablutions,** to wash; *Hum* to perform one's ablutions.

abnégation [abnegɑsjɔ̃] *nf* abnegation, self-sacrifice.

aboi [abwa] *nm* (*used in*) **aux abois,** (*stag, enemy*) at bay; (*dans un état désespéré*) hard pressed, with one's back to *or* against the wall; **ils sont aux abois,** they are in desperate *or* dire straits.

aboiement [abwamɑ̃] *nm* bark, barking (*of dog*); bay, baying (*of hound*); *Fig Péj* **les aboiements de la presse,** the rantings of the press.

abolir [abɔlir] *vt* to abolish, to suppress; to cancel (*a debt etc*); **le téléphone abolit les distances,** the telephone brings people together *or* makes distances disappear.

abolissement [abɔlismɑ̃] *nm,* **abolition** [abɔlisjɔ̃] *nf* abolition, suppression; repeal, annulment (*of decree*); **l'a. de l'esclavage,** the abolition of slavery.

abolitionnisme [abɔlisjɔnism] *nm Hist* abolitionism.

abolitionniste [abɔlisjɔnist] *adj & n Hist* abolitionist.

abominable [abɔminabl] *adj* abominable, foul; heinous (*crime*); **une fin** *ou* **mort a.,** a horrible death; **l'a. homme des neiges,** the abominable snowman; *F* **temps a.,** abominable *or* filthy weather.

abominablement [abɔminabləmɑ̃] *adv* abominably.

abomination [abɔminɑsjɔ̃] *nf* **(a)** abomination, abhorrence; **avoir qch/qn en a.,** to loathe sth/s.o.; **(b)** (*chose atroce*) abomination; **ne l'écoute pas, elle ne dit que des abominations,** don't listen to her, she has a foul tongue; **ce café est une a.,** this coffee is abominable.

abominer [abɔmine] *vt* to abominate, to loathe.

abondamment [abɔ̃damɑ̃] *adv* abundantly, plentifully, copiously; **manger/boire a.,** to eat/drink in copious amounts; **se servir a. de pain/dans la caisse du magasin,** to help oneself to plenty of bread/from the till; **peu a.,** scantily.

abondance [abɔ̃dɑ̃s] *nf* **(a)** (*profusion*) abundance, plenty; **on trouve des pommes en a. sur le marché,** there is an abundant *or* a plentiful supply of apples on the market; **il y a une a. de fautes,** there are lots of mistakes, mistakes abound; **une a. de fruits,** an abundance of fruit; **corne d'a.,** cornucopia; **(b)** wealth (*of expression, details*); **vivre dans l'a.,** to live in affluence *or* plenty; **parler avec a.,** to speak volubly; *Litt* **parler d'a.,** to speak off the cuff, to speak extempore; **(c)** *Cartes* (*solo whist*) abundance.

abondant [abɔ̃dɑ̃] *adj* abundant, copious, plentiful; rich (*style, vocabulary*); luxuriant (*foliage*); copious, hearty (*meal*); profuse (*excuses, bleeding*); prolific (*author*); **une chevelure abondante,** long, flowing hair; **une récolte peu abondante,** a poor *or* scanty harvest; **elle m'a donné d'abondants conseils,** she gave me a great deal of advice.

abonder [abɔ̃de] *vi* **(a)** (*foisonner*) to be plentiful; to abound (**en,** in); **les bons vins abondent cet automne,** good wines are plentiful this autumn, there are plenty of good wines this autumn; **(b) rivière qui abonde de** *ou* **en poissons,** river that abounds in fish; **votre texte abonde en images,** your text abounds in imagery; **a. de biens,** to be blessed with riches; **(c) a. dans le sens de qn,** to be entirely of s.o.'s opinion, to agree entirely *or* thoroughly with s.o..

abonné, -ée [abɔne] **1** *n* subscriber (*to paper etc*); *Rail Th* season-ticket holder; *Admin* **abonnés du gaz/de l'électricité,** gas/electricity consumers. **2** *adj* (*à un journal*) subscribing; *Rail Th* holding a season ticket; **les membres abonnés au théâtre,** members holding a season ticket for the theatre; *Admin* **être a. au téléphone/gaz,** to be a telephone subscriber/gas consumer; *Fig* **j'ai l'habitude de ce genre d'ennui, j'y suis a.!,** I'm used to that kind of problem, it's the story of my life!

abonnement [abɔnmɑ̃] *nm* **(a)** subscription (*to paper etc*); **prendre un a. au Figaro,** to subscribe *or* take out a subscription to the Figaro; **(b)** *Admin* (telephone) rental; (water *etc*) rate; *Rail Th* **(carte d') a.,** season ticket; **prendre un a.,** to take out a season ticket.

abonner [abɔne] **1** *vt* to enrol (*s.o.*); to take out a subscription for (*s.o.*) (*to a magazine*); **je vais vous a. à cette revue,** I'll take out a subscription to that magazine for you. **2 s'abonner** *vpr* **(a) s'a. à une revue,** to take out a subscription to a magazine; **(b)** *Rail etc* to take out a season ticket; *Admin* **s'a. au téléphone,** to have the telephone installed.

abord [abɔr] **1** *nm* **(a)** access, approach (*to land*); **île d'un a. difficile,** island that is difficult to approach; **un auteur d'un a. difficile,** an author who is difficult to get to grips with *or* not very accessible;

(b) abords, approaches (**d'un endroit,** to a place); outskirts (*of a city*);

(c) (*façon d'accueillir*) approachability; **avoir l'a. facile/difficile,** to be approachable/not (very) approachable; **être d'un a. rude/chaleureux,** to have a rough/welcoming manner (with people).

2 *adv* **d'a., tout d'a.,** at first, to begin with; (*tout de suite*) straight away, at once; (*en premier point*) first, in the first place, first and foremost; **dès l'a.,** from the (very) first, from the outset; **à l'a., au premier a., de prime a.,** at first sight; (*au début, pour commencer*) to begin with; *F* **d'a., elle ne dit jamais merci;** for a start, she never says thank you; *Enf* **je ne t'écoute pas d'a.,** I'm not listening to you, so there!

abordable [abɔrdabl] *adj* **(a)** (*piste d'atterrissage etc*) easy to land on; (*lieu*) easy of access, accessible; **(b)** (*prix*) reasonable, affordable; **vos prix ne sont pas abordables,** your prices are not reasonable; (*pour moi personnellement*) your prices are beyond my means; **(c)** (*personne*) approachable; **peu a.,** aloof, standoffish; (*grincheux*) grumpy.

abordage [abɔrdaʒ] *nm Nau* **(a)** boarding (*as an act of war*); **monter** *ou* **sauter à l'a. (d'un navire),** to board a ship; **(b)** (*collision*) collision; **il y a eu un a. causé par le brouillard,** two ships collided in the fog; **(c)** (*pour attaquer*) boarding (*another boat*); (*pour s'amarrer*) coming alongside.

aborder [abɔrde] **1** *vi* to land, to make land; (*dans un port*) to berth; **a. à un port,** to reach a port. **2** *vt* **(a) a. qn,** to accost s.o.; **se faire a. dans la rue,** to be approached in the street; **(b) a. une question/une difficulté,** to tackle a question/difficulty; **(c)** to board, to grapple (*ship in a fight*); (*se mettre côte à côte*) to come alongside (*a ship*); **(d)** to collide with *or* run foul of *or* run down (*ship*).

aborigène [abɔriʒɛn] **1** *adj* native, indigenous (**de,** to); (*relatif aux peuplades australiennes*) Aboriginal. **2** *n* native (*of a country*); **les aborigènes d'Australie,** the (Australian) Aborigines.

abortif, -ive [abɔrtif, -iv] **1** *adj* **(a)** abortive; **(b)** *Méd* **pilule abortive,** abortion pill; *Jur* **manœuvres abortives,** (procuring of) abortion. **2** *nm Méd* abortifacient.

aboucher [abuʃe] **1** *vt* **(a)** (*faire rencontrer*) to put (*s.o.*) in touch *or* contact (*with s.o.*); **(b)** *Tech* **a. le tuyau au robinet,** to connect the pipe (up) to the tap. **2 s'aboucher** *vpr* **s'a. avec qn,** to get in touch with s.o., to contact s.o..

Aboukir [abukir] *nm* Ab(o)ukir; *Hist* **la bataille d'A.,** the battle of the Nile.

abouler [abule] *Arg* **1** *vt* to bring; (*donner*)to hand over; **aboule ça ici!,** bring it here!, hand it over! **2 s'abouler** *vpr* (*arriver*) to turn up, to show up; **s'a. en retard,** to turn up *or* show up late.

about [abu] *nm Tech* butt.

abouter [abute] *vt Tech* to join (*timbers etc*) end to end, to butt(-joint) (*timbers*).

aboutir [abutir] *vi* **(a) a. à** *ou* **dans** *ou* **en qch,** to end in sth, to result in sth; (*mener à*) to lead to sth; (*de différentes directions*) to converge on sth; **ce sentier aboutit à la grande route,** this path leads to the main road; **une pyramide aboutit en pointe,** a pyramid ends in a point; **n'a. à rien,** (*d'un projet*) to come to nothing, *F* to go up in smoke; **leur raisonnement aboutit à une évidence,** their reasoning leads to an obvious conclusion; **pour a. aux fins que nous poursuivons,** to attain the end (which) we have in view; **(b)** (*of plan etc*) to succeed; **ne pas a.,** to fail, to fall through; **faire a. qch,** to bring sth to a successful conclusion; **(c)** (*of abscess*) to come to a head.

aboutissants [abutisɑ̃] *nmpl* **connaître les tenants et les a. d'une affaire,** to know the ins and outs of an affair, to know all there is to know about an affair.

aboutissement [abutismɑ̃] *nm* result, outcome (*of effort etc*).

aboyer [abwaje] *vi* **(j'aboie, j'aboierai)** (*of dog*) to bark; (*of hound*) to bay; *Fig* **a. après qn,** to shout *or* yell at s.o..

aboyeur, -euse [abwajœr, -øz] **1** *adj* barking (*dog*). **2** *n F* tout, *US* barker. **3** *nm* (*oiseau*) sandpiper.

abracadabra [abrakadabra] *nm* abracadabra.

abracadabrant [abrakadabrɑ̃] *adj F* stupendous, amazing; cock-and-bull (*story*).

abraser [abraze] *vt Tech* to abrade.

abrasif, -ive [abrazif, -iv] *adj &.nm Tech* abrasive.

abrasion [abrazjɔ̃] *nf Tech* abrasion; *Géol* **a. de la roche par l'eau,** abrasion of the rock by the water.

abrégé [abreʒe] *nm* précis, summary; abridg(e)ment (*of novel*); abstract (*of thesis*); **a. d'histoire de France,** short history of France; **a. de philosophie,** a short guide to philosophy; **voici les faits en a.,** here are the facts in a few words *or* in brief; **en a.,** in abridged *or* abbreviated form.

abrégement [abrɛʒmɑ̃] *nm* **(a)** summarizing (*of speech etc*); shortening (*of syllable*); **a. d'un délai,** shortening of the amount of time allowed for sth; **(b)** (*texte*) summary, précis; abridg(e)ment (*of novel*); abbreviation (*of word*); **a. (d'un ouvrage),** abridged edition (of a work).

abréger [abreʒe] *v* **(j'abrège, n. abrégeons; j'abrégerai) 1** *vt* **(a)** to shorten, to cut short (*life, work etc*); **pour a. votre attente,** so as not to keep you waiting; **(b)** to abridge, to cut down (*article*); to abbreviate (*word*). **2** *vi* to be brief; **pour a.,** to be brief, to cut it short; *F* **allez, abrège!,** come on, get *or* come to the point!

abreuvage [abrœvaʒ] *nm,* **abreuvement** [abrœvmɑ̃] *nm* **(a)** watering (*of animals*); **(b)** priming (*of pump*); seasoning (*of casks*); drenching (*of meadow*).

abreuver [abrœve] **1** *vt* **(a)** to water (*horses, cattle etc*); to supply (*animals*) with (something to) drink; **(b)** to flood, to irrigate (*meadow etc*); to prime (*a pump*); to season (*casks*); **l'Égypte est abreuvée par le Nil,** Egypt is watered by the Nile; *Fig* **a. qn d'injures,** to shower *or* cover s.o. with insults, to heap insults on s.o.; **les téléspectateurs sont abreuvés de publicité,** the viewers are swamped *or* bombarded with advertising. **2 s'abreuver** *vpr* (*of horse*) to drink; *F* (*of person*) to swill it down.

abreuvoir [abrœvwar] *nm* **(a)** watering place (*in river etc*); **mener les chevaux à l'a.,** to water the horses; **(b)** (*baquet*) drinking trough.

abréviation [abrevjasjɔ̃] *nf* **(a)** shortening (*of term of imprisonment*); **(b)** abbreviation (*of word*).

abri [abri] *nm* shelter, cover; (*écran, paravent*) screen; (*pour les plantes*) (tent) cloche; **a. à outils/à vélos,** tool/bike shed; **a. public,** public shelter; **a. de sous-marins,** submarine pen; **a. souterrain,** air-raid shelter; **a. antinucléaire,** (nuclear) bunker; **a. bétonné,** bunker; **a. sous roche,** rock shelter; **prendre a.,** to take cover; **famille sans a.,** homeless family; **à l'a.,** sheltered, under shelter, under cover; **mettre qch à l'a.,** to shelter *or* screen sth; **se mettre à l'a.,** to take shelter; **à l'a. de qch,** sheltered *or* screened from sth; **se mettre à l'a. de la pluie,** to (take) shelter from the rain; **se mettre à l'a. de l'auvent,** to shelter in the doorway; **a. contre le vent,** windscreen; **à l'a. de toute suspicion,** free from (all) suspicion; *Fig* **personne n'est à l'a. d'une erreur,** anybody can make a mistake; **il sera toujours à l'a. du besoin,** he will always be protected from hardship, he will never experience hardship; *Nau* **à l'a. de la côte,** under the lee of the shore.

abribus [abribys] *nm* bus shelter.

abricot [abriko] **1** *nm* apricot. **2** *adj inv* apricot-coloured.

abricoté [abrikɔte] **1** *adj* apricot flavoured. **2** *nm* slice of crystallized *or* candied apricot.

abricotier [abrikɔtje] *nm* apricot tree.

abrier (s') [sabrije] *vpr Can* to cover oneself up (well).

abri-garage [abrigaraʒ] *nm* carport.

abriter [abrite] **1** *vt* **(a)** (*protéger*) to shelter, to screen, to shield, to protect; to shade (*one's eyes*); **a. ses yeux du soleil,** to shade one's eyes from the sun; **cet auvent nous abrite des regards indiscrets,** the awning shields us from prying eyes; **(b)** (*héberger*) to house; **cet hôtel peut a. cent personnes,** the hotel can accommodate a hundred people. **2 s'abriter** *vpr* to (take) shelter (*from the rain*) (**contre,** from); to take cover (*from gunfire*); **s'a. derrière qn,** to shelter behind s.o.; *Fig* **il s'abrite derrière le règlement,** he shelters *or* hides behind the rules.

abrivent [abrivɑ̃] *nm* windbreak.

abrogation [abrɔgasjɔ̃] *nf* abrogation, rescinding, repeal (*of law etc*).

abrogeable [abrɔʒabl] *adj* repealable.

abroger [abrɔʒe] *vt* **(j'abrogeai(s); n. abrogeons)** to abrogate, to rescind, to repeal (*law etc*).

abrupt [abrypt] **1** *adj* **(a)** sheer, steep (*rock, descent*); **(b)** *Fig* abrupt, blunt (*manner*); **répondre d'un ton a.,** to give an abrupt *or* short answer, to answer abruptly *or* shortly. **2** *nm* steep slope.

abruptement [abryptəmɑ̃] *adv* (*voir adj*) **(a)** steeply, abruptly; **(b)** *Fig* abruptly.

abruti, -ie [abryti] **1** *adj* **(a)** stupefied, dazed; exhausted (*by heat, work etc*); **a. par l'alcool,** stupefied *or* sodden with drink; **(b)** *F* stupid, idiotic, moronic; **avoir un air a.,** to look stupid *or* moronic. **2** *n F* idiot, fool.

abrutir [abrytir] **1** *vt* **(a)** (*fatiguer*) to exhaust (*s.o.*); **ce travail m'abrutit,** this work's exhausting me *or* wearing me out; **la chaleur m'abrutissait,** the heat was sapping my energy; **nous sommes abrutis de travail,** we are exhausted by work; **(b)** *Vieilli & Litt* to stupefy; **les buveurs, que l'alcool abrutit,** drinkers whose minds are (being) numbed *or* deadened by alcohol. **2 s'abrutir** *vpr* **(a)** (*se fatiguer*) to exhaust oneself; **s.'a. de travail/de discussions,** to work oneself to the point of exhaustion/to wear oneself out with discussion; **(b)** (*devenir stupide*) to become dazed *or* stupefied; **on s'abrutit à trop regarder la télévision,** too much television addles the brain.

abrutissant [abrytisɑ̃] *adj* **(a)** (*fatigant*) exhausting, wearing; (*bruit*) deafening; **travail a.,** exhausting work; (*pénible*) deadly dull work; **(b)** *Vieilli & Litt* degrading; mind-destroying (*banality*).

abrutissement [abrytismɑ̃] *nm* **(a)** (*abêtissement*) reducing (*of s.o.*) to a mindless state; **propagande qui cause l'a. des masses,** propaganda that stops people thinking for themselves; **(b)** *Vieilli* degradation.

abscisse [apsis] *nf* abscissa.

abscons, -onse [apskɔ̃, -ɔ̃s] *adj Péj* obscure, abstruse.

absence [apsɑ̃s] *nf* **(a)** (*de personne*) absence; **en** *ou* **pendant mon a.,** in *or* during my absence, when I am *or* was *etc* away; **en l'a. de ma secrétaire,** while *or* when my secretary is away; **en l'a. d'une secrétaire,** as *or* since I have no secretary; **remarquer l'a. de qn,** to miss s.o.; **nous avons regretté votre a.,** we were sorry that you weren't with us; *Fig* **nous regrettons tous les jours son a.,** (*of deceased*) we miss him every day; **briller par son a.,** to be conspicuous by one's absence; **a. de l'école,** non-attendance at *or* absence from school; **comment expliquez-vous toutes ces absences?,** how do you explain all these absences?; **faire des absences,** to play truant; *Mil etc* **a. illégale,** absence without leave;

(b) (*manque*) lack (*of furniture, principles, a father etc*); **a. de goût,** lack of taste, tastelessness; **a. d'imagination,** lack of imagination; **a. d'esprit,** absence of mind, absent-mindedness; **il a des absences,** he's apt to be absent-minded, he has *or* is prone to memory lapses; **dans un moment d'a.,** in a moment of absent-mindedness, in an absent-minded moment; (*de négligence, de manque d'attention*) without thinking;

(c) *Méd* **a. (épileptique),** epileptic vertigo.

absent, -ente [apsɑ̃, -ɑ̃t] **1** *adj* **(a)** absent, away; **il est a. de Paris en ce moment,** he isn't in Paris at the moment; **quand ma femme est absente je suis obligé de faire la cuisine,** I have to do the cooking when my wife's away; **a. sans permission,** absent without leave; **(b)** (*qui n'existe pas*) absent, missing; **une déclaration d'où tout humour était absent,** a statement totally lacking in humour; **chez cet animal les dents sont absentes,** this animal has no teeth; **(c)** (*distrait, rêveur*) vacant; **son esprit est a.,** his mind is far away, *F* he's miles away. **2** *n* (*à une réunion etc*) absentee; **les Français ont été les grands absents lors de la Coupe du Monde,** the French were the most notable absentees from the World Cup; **les absents ont toujours tort,** the absent are always in the wrong.

absentéisme [apsɑ̃teism] *nm* absenteeism.

absentéiste [apsɑ̃teist] **1** *adj* (regularly) absent; absentee (*landlord*). **2** *n* (regular) absentee.

absenter (s') [sapsɑ̃te] *vpr* to go away (*from home*); to stay *or* stop away (*from school*).

absidal, -aux [apsidal, -o] *adj* apsidal.

abside [apsid] *nf Archit* apse.

absidiole [apsidjɔl] *nf Archit* apsidal chapel.

absinthe [apsɛ̃t] *nf* **(a)** (*boisson*) absinthe; **(b)** (*plante*) wormwood.

absolu [apsɔly] **1** *adj* **(a)** absolute; **zéro a.,** absolute zero; *Gram* **ablatif a.,** ablative absolute; **poser une règle absolue,** to lay down a hard and fast rule; **refus a.,** flat refusal; **majorité absolue,** absolute majority; **(b)** (*total*) absolute; **pouvoir a.,** absolute power; **caractère a.,** autocratic nature; **liberté absolue,** absolute *or* total freedom; **(c)** peremptory (*tone, voice*). **2** *nm Phil* **l'a.,** the absolute; **juger qch dans l'a.,** to judge sth in the absolute *or* out of context.

absolument [apsɔlymɑ̃] *adv* **(a)** (*complètement*) entirely, quite (*unnecessary*); absolutely, utterly (*impossible*); **j'ai a. oublié,** I completely forgot; **a. rien,** nothing whatever; **(b)** (*strictement*) (*to speak*) peremptorily; **c'est a. défendu,** it is absolutely *or* strictly forbidden; **je le veux a.,** I insist on it; **nier a. qch,** to deny sth flatly; **(c)** (*sans faute*) simply, definitely, absolutely; **vous devez a. y aller!,** you simply MUST go!; **(d)** (*sans limite*) **régner a.,** to reign as an absolute monarch; **a. parlant,** speaking generally.

absolution [apsɔlysjɔ̃] *nf* **(a)** *Rel* absolution; **(b)** *Jur* discharge, acquittal.

absolutisme [apsɔlytism] *nm Pol* absolutism.

absorbant [apsɔrbɑ̃] *adj* **(a)** absorbent (*substance, properties*); **(b)** absorbing, engrossing (*book, task*).

absorber [apsɔrbe] **1** *vt* **(a)** (*of sponge etc*) to absorb, to soak up (*water etc*); *Ch* to occlude (*a gas*); **le noir absorbe la lumière,** black absorbs light; **(b)** to consume (*food etc*); to drink (*beer etc*); to take (*medicine*); *Écon Fig* **la multinationale va a. cette entreprise,** the multinational is going to take over *or F* swallow up the firm; **les travaux ont absorbé toutes mes économies,** the repairs have used up all my savings; **(c)** to absorb, to engross; to take up (*time*); **son travail l'absorbe,** he *or* she is completely wrapped up in his *or* her work; **cette pensée m'absorbe complètement,** I think about it constantly. **2 s'absorber** *vpr* to become absorbed *or* engrossed (**dans,** in); **être absorbé dans ses pensées,** to be lost in thought; **s'a. dans la lecture d'un livre,** to be absorbed *or* lost in a book.

absorption [apsɔrpsjɔ̃] *nf* absorption; **a. de médicaments,** (the) taking of medicines; *Fig Écon* **a. d'une petite société par une grosse,** the takeover of a small company by a large one.

absoudre [apsudr] *vt* (*prp* **absolvant**; *pp* **absous,** *f* **absoute**; *pr ind* **j'absous, il absout, n. absolvons, ils absolvent**; *pr sub* **j'absolve**; *p hist & p sub are lacking*; *fu* **j'absoudrai**) **(a) a. qn de qch,** to forgive s.o. sth; *Rel* **a. qn de ses péchés,** to grant s.o. remission of his sins, to forgive s.o. his sins; *Rel* **je vous absous,** I absolve you; **(b)** *Jur* to absolve (*s.o.*).

abstenir (s') [sapstənir] *vpr* (*conj like* **tenir**) to stand aside *or* aloof; *Pol* to abstain (from voting); **s'a. de qch,** to abstain from sth, to forgo sth; **s'a. de faire qch,** to refrain *or* abstain from doing sth; **s'a. de commentaires,** to refrain from comment; **s'a. de manger du chocolat/de boire de l'alcool,** to keep off chocolate/alcohol; **dans le doute abstiens-toi,** when in doubt, don't.

abstention [apstɑ̃sjɔ̃] *nf* abstention (**de,** from).

abstentionnisme [apstɑ̃sjɔnism] *nm Pol* abstention (*from voting etc*).

abstentionniste [apstɑ̃sjɔnist] *n Pol* abstainer, abstentionist; **le nombre des abstentionnistes,** the number of abstentions.

abstinence [apstinɑ̃s] *nf* abstinence; (*qualité d'une personne*) abstemiousness; *Rel* **jour d'a.,** day of abstinence; **faire a. le vendredi,** to abstain from eating meat on Fridays; **a. (sexuelle),** (sexual) abstinence.

abstinent, -ente [apstinɑ̃, -ɑ̃t] **1** *adj* abstemious. **2** *n* abstainer; (*qui ne boit pas d'alcool*) teetotaller; *Rel* person who practises abstinence.

abstraction [apstraksjɔ̃] *nf* **(a)** *Phil* abstraction; **un esprit capable d'a.,** a mind capable of abstract thought; **(b) faire a. de qch,** to disregard sth; **a. faite du style,** style apart; **(c)** (*idée abstraite*) abstract idea, abstraction; **se perdre dans des abstractions,** to lose oneself in abstractions.

abstraire [apstrɛr] *v* (*conj like* **traire**) **1** *vt* to separate, to isolate; to consider (*sth*) apart (*from sth*); *Phil* to abstract. **2 s'abstraire** *vpr* **s'a. dans** *ou* **en qch,** to become engrossed in sth.

abstrait [apstrɛ] **1** *adj* abstract (*idea, art etc*); abstruse, deep (*question*). **2** *nm* **(a)** (*abstraction*) abstract, abstraction; **dans l'a.,** in the abstract, in theory; **(b)** *Beaux-Arts* abstract art; (*artiste*) abstract artist; (*tableau*) abstract (painting).

abstraitement [apstrɛtmɑ̃] *adv* **(a)** (*en théorie*) in the abstract; **parler a.,** to talk in the abstract *or* in abstract terms; **(b)** (*distraitement*) abstractedly, absent-mindedly.

abstrus, -use [apstry, -yz] *adj* abstruse, recondite.

absurde [apsyrd] **1** *adj* absurd, preposterous, nonsensical; **votre conduite est totalement a.!,** your behaviour is totally preposterous; **votre pensée est totalement a.!,** what an absurd thought *or* nonsensical notion!; **elle est complètement a.,** she's completely ridiculous. **2** *nm* **l'a.,** absurdity; *Phil* the absurd; **réduire une théorie à l'a.,** to reduce a theory ad absurdum; *Phil* **démonstration par l'a.,** reductio ad absurdum; **l'a de la situation,** the absurdity of the situation, the absurd thing about the situation.

absurdement [apsyrdəmɑ̃] *adv* absurdly, preposterously.

absurdité [apsyrdite] *nf* **(a)** (*caractère absurde*) absurdity, preposterousness; **l'a. de l'existence,** the absurdity of existence; **(b)** (*chose absurde*) absurdity, piece of nonsense; **cette réaction est une a.,** this reaction is completely absurd; **dire des absurdités,** to talk nonsense.

abus [aby] *nm* **(a)** (*mauvais emploi*) abuse, misuse (**de,** of); (*excès*) overindulgence (**de,** in); **l'a. des médicaments,** the misuse of pharmaceutical drugs; **employer un terme par a.,** to misuse a term; **l'a. de boissons,** alcohol abuse; **faire a. de qch,** to indulge too freely in sth; **faire a. de son autorité,** to abuse one's authority; **(b)** *Jur* violation (*of rights*); **a. de confiance,** breach of trust; **a. d'autorité/de pouvoir,** abuse *or* misuse of (one's) authority/power; **(c)** (*pratique*) abuse, corrupt practice; **un écrivain connu pour ses a. de langage,** a writer known for murdering the language; **réformer un a.,** to remedy an abuse; **je ne supporte plus ses a.!,** I can't stand his *or* her outrageous behaviour any longer!; **faire quelques a.,** to overdo it, to overindulge; **c'est un a. (que) de croire que ...,** it is a mistake to suppose that ...; *F* **il y a de l'a.!,** that's going too far!

abuser [abyze] **1** *vi* **a. de qch,** to misuse sth; (*exploiter*) to take (unfair) advantage of sth; **vous abusez de vos forces,** you're overtaxing yourself; **a. du tabac,** to smoke too much; **il ne faut pas a. des bonnes choses,** good things should be enjoyed in moderation, enough is as good as a feast; **a. de l'amabilité de qn,** to impose on s.o. *or* on s.o.'s kindness; **a. de la confiance de qn,** to abuse s.o.'s confidence; **j'abuse de votre temps,** I am taking up too much of your time; **n'abusez point,** be moderate; **je ne voudrais pas a., j'ai peur d'a.,** I don't want to cause you any inconvenience; **c'est un peu fort, elle abuse!,** she's going a bit (too) far!; **vous abusez!,** that's a bit much!; **a. d'une femme,** to rape a woman.

2 *vt* to deceive; **il ne nous abusera pas par de belles paroles,** he will not deceive us with fine words.

3 **s'abuser** *vpr* to be mistaken; **je vous ai déjà rencontré, si je ne m'abuse,** I've met you before, if I'm not mistaken.

abusif, -ive [abyzif, -iv] *adj* **(a)** incorrect (*use of a word*); **il serait a. de l'affirmer,** it would be an exaggeration to say that; **(b)** (*excessif*) excessive; **emploi a. de la force,** excessive *or* unwarranted use of force; **mère abusive,** possessive mother.

abusivement [abyzivmɑ̃] *adv* incorrectly, wrongly; **employer un mot a.,** to use a word incorrectly *or* wrongly; **elle a profité a. de la situation,** she took unfair advantage of the situation.

abuter [abyte] **1** *vi Menuis* to abut, to butt. **2** *vt* **a. un camion à un quai,** to back a lorry against a platform.

abyssal, -aux [abisal, -o] *adj* abyssal (*fauna etc*); *Fig* unfathomable (*depths*); **la région abyssale,** the ocean deeps.

abysse [abis] *nm Géog* abyssal zone.

Abyssinie [abisini] *nf* Abyssinia.

abyssinien, -ienne [abisinjɛ̃, -jɛn] **1** *adj* Abyssinian. **2** *n* **A.,** Abyssinian.

A.C. [ase] *nf abrév* **appellation contrôlée.**

acabit [akabi] *nm Péj* nature (*of person*); (good, bad) quality (*of fruit etc*); **ils sont du même a.,** they're tarred with the same brush; **je me méfie des gens de cet a.,** I don't trust people like that.

acacia [akasja] *nm* (*arbre*) **a. vrai,** acacia; (*robinier*) **a. vulgaire, faux a.,** locust tree, false acacia.

académicien, -ienne [akademisjɛ̃, -jɛn] *n* academician, (*surtout*) member of the Académie française.

académie [akademi] *nf* **(a)** society (*of letters, science, art*); **l'A. française,** the French Academy; **(b)** (*école*) school, academy; **a. de musique,** music school, school of music; **a. de danse,** dancing school; **a. de dessin,** school of art, art school; **(c)** *Admin* educational district (*of France*); **(d)** academy (*of Plato etc*); **(e)** (*étude*) nude study.

académique [akademik] *adj* **(a)** academic; **les palmes académiques,** = insignia of decoration granted by the French Ministry of Education; *Admin* **inspection a.,** board of school inspectors; **séance a.,** sitting *or* meeting of an Academy; **occuper un fauteuil a.,** (*de l'Académie française*) to be a member of the French Academy; *Littér Péj* **style a.,** pedantic style; **débat a.,** academic discussion; **(b)** *Beaux-Arts* **figure a.,** nude.

académisme [akademism] *nm Beaux-Arts souvent Péj* academ(ic)ism.

Acadie [akadi] *nf Can Geog* = New Brunswick and Nova Scotia.

acadien, -ienne [akadjɛ̃, -jɛn] **1** *adj* Acadian. **2** *nm Ling* Acadian. **3** *n* **A.,** Acadian.

acajou [akaʒu] **1** *nm* **(a)** mahogany; **table en a.,** mahogany table; **(b) noix d'a.,** cashew nut; **a. à noix,** cashew nut tree. **2** *adj inv* reddish-brown, auburn.

acanthe [akɑ̃t] *nf Bot Archit* acanthus.

a capella [akapɛla] *adv Mus* a capella; **chanter a c.,** to sing a capella.

acariâtre [akarjɑtr] *adj* bad-tempered, cantankerous; **être d'humeur a.,** to be bad-tempered.

acarien [akarjɛ̃] *nm* (*insecte*) dust mite.

accablant [akɑblɑ̃] *adj* **(a)** overwhelming (*misfortune, proof*); **(b)** overpowering, oppressive (*heat*); **des responsabilités accablantes,** overwhelming responsibilities.

accablé [akɑble] *adj* overwhelmed (*with work etc*); overcome, weighed down (*with grief*); **a. de fatigue,** overwhelmed with fatigue; **a. par la chaleur,** overwhelmed *or* overcome by the heat.

accablement [akɑbləmɑ̃] *nm* dejection, despondency, depression; *Méd* prostration.

accabler [akɑble] *vt* to overpower, to overwhelm, to crush; **accablé de dettes,** burdened with debt; **être accablé de douleur,** to be grief-stricken; **il m'accable de travail,** he piles work on me; **il m'accable de questions;** he bombards me with questions; **son récit m'accable,** I am quite overcome by his *or* her story; **a. qn d'injures,** to heap abuse on s.o.; **elle nous accable de recommandations,** she heaps advice on us.

accalmie [akalmi] *nf* lull (*in the storm, in war*).

accaparant [akaparɑ̃] *adj* (*livre*) engrossing, absorbing; **leurs enfants sont très accaparants,** their children take up a lot of their time; **un emploi a.,** a demanding job.

accaparement [akaparmɑ̃] *nm* monopolizing; buying up (*of stocks*); cornering (*of goods*).

accaparer [akapare] *vt Péj* to buy up (*stocks*); to corner, to hoard (*goods*); to seize on (*sth*); **a. le marché de l'automobile,** to corner the automobile market; **a. la conversation,** to monopolize the conversation; **a. les meilleures places,** to secure *or* corner the best seats; **son travail l'accapare trop,** her work takes up too much of her time; **je ne voudrais pas vous a. toute la soirée,** I don't want to monopolize you for the whole evening.

accapareur, -euse [akaparœr, -øz] **1** *n* buyer-up (*of food etc*); (*société*) monopolist; *Péj* grabber. **2** *adj* possessive (*person*).

accastillage [akastijaʒ] *nm Nau* fittings (*of ship*).

accastiller [akastije] *vt Nau* to fit out (*a ship*).

accéder [aksede] *vi* **(j'accède, n. accédons; j'accéderai) (a)** (*atteindre*) to have access (**à,** to); **on accède à la porte par un escalier,** a flight of steps leads to the door; *Ordinat* **a à un programme,** to access a program; **(b)** (*accepter*) to comply, to agree; **a à une requête,** to comply with a request; **a. à une condition,** to agree *or* assent to a condition; **(c)** (*parvenir*) to accede **a. au trône,** to accede to the throne; **a à la propriété,** (*d'un appartement, d'une maison*) to be a first-time buyer.

accélérateur, -trice [akseleratœr, -tris] **1** *adj* accelerating. **2** *nm* accelerator; *Nucl* **a. de particules,** particule accelerator; **a. d'électrons,** betatron; *Aut* **appuyer sur l'a.,** to accelerate.

accélération [akselerasjɔ̃] *nf* acceleration; speeding up (*of work*); **a de la pesanteur,** gravitational acceleration; *Aut* **pédale d'a.,** accelerator (pedal).

accéléré [akselere] **1** *adj* quick, fast, rapid; accelerated (*motion*); **un cours a.,** a crash course. **2** *nm Cin* accelerated motion.

accélérer [akselere] *v* **(j'accélère, n. accélérons; j'accélérerai) 1** *vt* to accelerate, to speed up. **2** *vi* **dépêche-toi, accélère!,** hurry up, get a move on!; *Aut* **passe en seconde et accélère,** go into second and accelerate. **3 s'accélérer** *vpr* to accelerate, to speed up.

accent [aksɑ̃] *nm* **(a)** (*phonétique*) accent, stress; **a. d'intensité** *ou* **tonique,** tonic accent; **syllbe sans a.,** unstressed syllable; **(b)** *Gram* accent; **a. aigu/grave,** acute/grave accent; **e. a. circonflexe,** e circumflex; **(c)** (*prononciation*) accent; **parler le français avec un a. anglais,** to speak French with an English accent; **(d)** (*inflexion*) tone of voice; *Fig* **son récit a l'a. de la vérité,** his account rings true; *Ling* **a. de phrase,** sentence stress; *Fig* **mettre l'a. sur la présentation du produit,** to put the emphasis on *or* to emphasize the presentation of the product; **(e) les accents du désespoir,** the accents of despair; **il parlait avec des accents de rage/de terreur dans la voix,** his voice was angry/terror-stricken; **les accents de la Marseillaise,** the strains of the Marseillaise.

accentuation [aksɑ̃tɥasjɔ̃] *nf* **(a)** stressing (*of syllables etc*); **les règles de l'a. espagnole,** the stress rules in Spanish; **(b)** *Gram* accentuation, placing of the grammatical accents; **faire des fautes d'a.,** to put accents in the wrong place.

accentué [aksɑ̃tɥe] *adj* stressed, accented; *Fig* pronounced, marked; **les traits accentués par la fatigue,** features drawn with fatigue.

accentuer [aksɑ̃tɥe] **1** *vt* **(a)** to stress (*syllable etc*); **syllabe non accentuée,** unstressed syllable; **(b)** *Gram* to mark (*vowel*) with an accent; **(c)** *Fig* to emphasize, to accentuate; **traits fortement accentués,** pronounced *or* strongly marked features; **a. le chômage,** to increase *or* *add to unemployment.* **2 s'accentuer** *vpr* to become accentuated *or* more pronounced.

acceptabilité [aksɛptabilite] *nf* acceptability.

acceptable [aksɛptabl] *adj* **(a)** acceptable (**à,** to); **offre a.,** reasonable offer; **cadeau très a.,** very acceptable *or* welcome gift; **(b)** (*car, house, machine*) in fair condition; reasonably good (*performance*).

acceptablement [aksɛptabləmɑ̃] *adv* acceptably, in an acceptable manner.

acceptant, -ante [aksɛptɑ̃, -ɑ̃t] *adj & n Com Jur* acceptant.

acceptation [aksɛptasjɔ̃] *nf* acceptance.

accepter [aksɛpte] *vt* to accept; to take up (*a challenge*); to take on (*a bet*); to honour, to accept (*a bill*); **il n'accepte pas l'échec/la difficulté** he refuses to acknowledge failure/the difficulty; **elle n'arrive pas à a. le mariage de sa fille,** she can't come to terms with her daughter's marriage; **je n'accepte pas votre conduite,** I find you behaviour unacceptable; **je n'accepte pas cette théorie,** I don't agree with that theory; **a de faire qch,** to agree to do sth; (*invitation*) to accept an invitation to do sth; **elle n'accepte pas que son mari soit au chômage,** she can't *or* won't accept the fact that her husband is unemployed; **a. qn comme** *ou* **pour arbitre,** to accept s.o. as an arbitrator; **il a été accepté dans la famille,** he was accepted into the family; **acceptez-vous Jean-Guy Pierre pour époux?,** ≈ do you take this man, Jean-Guy Pierre, as your lawfully wedded husband?

accepteur [akseptœr] **(a)** *Com* acceptor, drawee (*of bill*); **(b)** *Ch Électron* acceptor.

acception [aksɛpsjɔ̃] *nf Fml* **(a)** meaning, sense, *Fml* acceptation (*of word etc*); **(b) sans a. de race/de sexe,** (*dans une offre d'emploi*) open to candidates of all races/of both sexes, race/sex immaterial.

accès [aksɛ] *nm* **(a)** (*approche*) access, approach; **les a. de la gare,** the station approaches, the approaches to the station; **le refuge est facile d'a.,** the shelter is easily accessible *or* easy to reach; **avoir a. à qch,** to have access to sth; **donner a. à qch,** to give access *or* to lead to sth; **avoir l'a.** *ou* **un a. facile à qch,** to have easy access to sth; **trouver a auprès de qn,** to be admitted to s.o.'s presence; **être d'a. facile/difficile,** (*d'une personne*) to be approachable/unapproachable; (*d'un auteur, d'un livre etc*) accessible/not very accessible; *Nau* **carte d'a à bord,** embarkation card; *Rail* **a. aux quais,** to the trains; *Ordinat* **code d'a,** access code; **à a. multiple,** multi-access; **temps d'a.,** access time;

(b) (*poussée*) fit, attack, outburst; **a. de fièvre,** attack *or* bout of fever; **des a. de toux,** Fits of coughing, coughing fits; **a. de faiblesse,** fainting fit; **a. d'enthousiasme,** burst *or* Fit of enthusiasm; **a. de colère/folie,** fit of anger/madness; **travailler par a.,** to work by *or* in fits and starts.

accessibilité [aksɛsibilite] *nf* accessibility.

accessible [aksɛsibl] *adj* **(a)** (*où l'on peut arriver*) accessible; **endroit a.,** accessible place, place that can be reached easily; **parc a. à tous,** park open to everybody; *Fig* **les prix sont très accessibles,** the prices are within everyone's reach, the prices are very affordable; **un livre tout à fait a.,** a wholly accessible book; **(b)** (*personne*) approachable; **elle est peu a.** (*en colère*) she's not very approachable; (*très occupée*) she's not very accessible; **a. à la pitié,** open to pity; **a. à la flatterie,** susceptible to flattery.

accession [aksɛsjɔ̃] *nf* **(a)** accession (*to power etc*); **l'a. à la propriété est rendue possible à tous,** home ownership is within everyone's reach; **a. au trône,** accession to the throne; *Fig* **l'a à l'indépendance du pays a eu lieu en 1968,** the country became independent *or* gained independence in 1968; **(b)** adherence, adhesion (*to a contract, to a party*).

accessit [aksɛsit] *nm* (*dans un examen*) honourable mention; **remporter un a. en musique,** to get an honourable mention in music.

accessoire [aksɛswar] **1** *adj* accessory; **jouer un rôle a.,** to play a subordinate role. **2** *nm* accessory, *Fml* appurtenance; *Th etc* **accessoires,** properties, *F* props; **magasin des accessoires,** property room; **chapeau et accessoires coordonnés,** hat and matching accessories.

accessoirement [aksɛswarmɑ̃] *adv* (*si besoin est*) if necessary, if need be; **je m'occupe a. de la comptabilité,** I look after the accounts in addition to my main duties.

accessoiriser [aksɛswarize] *vt* to accessorize (*clothing etc*).

accessoiriste [aksɛswarist] *n Th etc* props (man), property mistress.

accident [aksidɑ̃] *nm* **(a)** (*événement imprévisible*) accident; (*contretemps*) mishap; **je l'ai retrouvé par a.,** I found it by accident *or* accidentally; *Fig* **un a. de parcours,** a hitch; **cette conférence ne devait pas avoir lieu, c'est un a.,** the lecture is an addition t the (original) programme; **a. de chemin de fer,** railway accident; **accidents du travail,** industrial accidents; **a. d'avion** *ou* **d'aviation,** plane *or* air crash; **a mortel,** fataility; **être victime d'un a.,** to meet with an accident; **nous sommes arrivés sans a.,** we arrived safely *or* safe and sound; **(b)** *Mus* accidental; **(c) a. de terrain,** unevenness *or* irregularity of the ground.

accidenté, -ée [aksidɑ̃te] **1** *adj* **(a)** uneven, broken (*ground*); **(b)** *F* **voiture accidentée,** damaged car; **(c)** eventful (*life*). **2** *n* victim of an accident; **les accidentés,** the injured, the casualities; **accidentés de la route,** road accident victims.

accidentel, -elle [aksidɑ̃tɛl] *adj* **(a)** (*imprévu*) accidental; **une rencontre accidentelle,** a chance or an accidental meeting; **mort accidentelle,** (*par accident*) accidental death; **(b)** *Mus* **signes accidentels,** accidentals; (*armature constante*) key signature.

accidentellement [aksidɑ̃tɛlmɛ̃] *adv* accidentally; (*to die*) in *or* as a *or* the result of an accident.

accidenter [aksidɑ̃te] *vt* **(a)** to give variety to (*the landscape etc*); to vary (*one's style etc*); **(b)** *F* to damage (*a car*) in an accident.

acclamatif, -ive [aklamatif, -iv] *adj* acclamatory.

acclamation [aklamɑsjɔ̃] *nf* acclamation, cheering; **les acclamations de la foule,** the cheers *or* acclamations of the crowd; **discours salué d'acclamations,** speech greeted with cheers; **elle fut élue par a.,** she was elected by acclamation.

acclamer [aklame] *vt* to acclaim, to cheer (*s.o., a speech*); (*en tapant dans les mains*) to applaud; (*saluer*) to greet (*s.o., a speech*) with cheers; **a. qn empereur,** to acclaim s.o. emperor.

acclimatable [aklimatabl] *adj* acclimatizable, *US* acclimatable.

acclimatation [aklimatɑsjɔ̃] *nf* acclimatization; **jardin d'a.,** zoological gardens.

acclimatement [aklimatmɑ̃] *nm* acclimat(iz)ation.

acclimater [aklimate] **1** *vt* to acclimatize (**à,** to); *Fig* to introduce (*an idea*). **2 s'acclimater** *vpr* to become *or* get acclimatized.

accointance [akwɛ̃tɑ̃s] *nf Péj* **accointances,** dealings, relations; **avoir des accointances dans le milieu des affaires,** to have contacts in the business world.

accointer (s') [sakwɛ̃te] *vpr Péj Vieilli* **s'a. avec qn,** to take up with s.o..

accolade [akɔlad] *nf* **(a)** (*embrassade*) (formal) embrace; *Fig* **donner/recevoir l'a.,** to embrace/to be embraced; **(b)** accolade; *Fig* **recevoir l'a.,** ≈ to be knighted; **(c)** *Mus Typ* brace, bracket; **(d)** *Archit* **arc en a.,** ogee arch.

accolement [akɔlmɑ̃] *nm* joining, bracketing.

accoler [akɔle] **1** *vt* **(a)** (*joindre côte à côte*) to join side by side, to couple; *Typ* to brace, to bracket; **le nom de l'épouse est accolé à celui du mari,** the wife's surname is joined *or* added to that of the husband; **accolé aux murs,** built on the walls; **(b)** to tie up (*vine etc*). **2 s'accoler** *vpr* **(a)** (*of plants*) to intertwine, to cling; **(b)** *F* **s'a. avec une femme,** to take up with a woman.

accommodant [akɔmɔdɑ̃] *adj* good-natured, easy-going, easy to deal with, accommodating; **peu a.,** (*personne*) not easy to deal with; (*pas arrangeant*) difficult, not very accommodating; **a. en affaires,** easy to do business with.

accommodation [akɔmɔdɑsjɔ̃] *nf* **(a)** (*adaptation*) adapting; **a. d'une pièce aux usages d'un bureau,** adaptation *or* conversion of a room for office use; **(b)** *Physiol* accommodation (*of the eye*).

accommodement [akɔmɔdmɑ̃] *nm* compromise, arrangement; **en venir à un a.,** to come to a compromise *or* arrangement, to come to terms (**avec,** with); **politique d'a.,** give-and-take policy; *Com* **a. avec ses créanciers,** composition with one's creditors.

accommoder [akɔmɔde] **1** *vt* **(a)** (*satisfaire*) to suit (*s.o.*), to answer (*s.o.'s*) purpose; **difficile à a.,** difficult to please;

(b) *Culin* to cook, to prepare (*food*); **a. les restes,** to use up the leftovers; **a. une salade,** to dress a salad;

(c) a. qch à qch, to fit *or* adapt sth to sth; **a. une pièce à une usage particulier,** to adapt a room to *or* for a particular purpose; *Opt* **a. l'objectif sur l'infini,** to set *or* adjust the lens to infinity;

(d) *Arch* to make (*s.o.*) comfortable (*in an armchair etc*).

2 s'accommoder *vpr* **(a) s'a. à qch,** to adapt to sth; **il s'accommode à toutes les circonstances,** he's very adaptable; **je m'accommode à tout,** anything will do for me;

(b) s'a. de qch, to make the best of sth, to put up with sth; **il vous faudra vous a. de cette pièce pour dormir,** you'll have to make do with sleeping in this room;

(c) s'a. avec qn, to come to an agreement with s.o., (*par un compromis*) to compromise with s.o.; to compound with (*creditor*);

(d) *Arch* to make oneself comfortable, to settle down (*in armchair etc*).

accompagnateur, -trice [akɔ̃paɲatœr, -tris] *n* **(a)** *Mus* accompanist; **(b)** courier (*of tour*), tour guide.

accompagnement [akɔ̃paɲmɑ̃] *nm* **(a)** *Mus* accompaniment; **chanter sans a.,** to sing unaccompanied; **(b)** *Mil etc* close support; **tir d'a.,** supporting fire; *Av* **chasseur d'a.,** escort fighter; **(c)** *Culin* vegetables, rice (*served with meat*).

accompagner [akɔ̃paɲe] **1** *vt* **(a)** (*venir avec, aller avec*) to go *or* come with (*s.o.*); **est-ce que tu vas m'a.?,** are you coming with me?; **a. qn jusqu'à la gare,** to see s.o. to the station; **a. qn un bout de chemin,** to go part of the way with s.o.; *Culin* **a. une viande de pommes de terre,** to serve potatoes with meat; **(b)** to escort (*s.o.*); to act as courier *or* tour guide to (*a group of tourists*); **accompagné de sa** *ou* **son secrétaire,** accompanied by his *or* her secretary; **(c)** *Mus* **a. qn au piano,** to accompany s.o. on the piano; **(d)** (*ajouter à*) **il a accompagné ses mots d'un sourire,** he said it with a smile. **2 s'accompagner** *vpr* **(a)** *Mus* **elle s'accompagne elle-même,** she plays her own accompaniment; **(b)** *Culin* to be served (*with a vegetable etc*); **le porc s'accompagne bien de pommes de terre,** pork goes well with potatoes.

accompli [akɔ̃pli] *adj* accomplished (*musician, linguist, liar etc*); **fait accompli,** fait accompli, accomplished fact.

accomplir [akɔ̃plir] **1** *vt* **(a)** to accomplish, to achieve (*purpose etc*); to carry out (*task, order*); to fulfil (*wish, promise*); **(b)** to complete, to finish (*apprenticeship etc*); **il a quarante ans accomplis,** he's turned forty; **c'est une mauvaise action que tu as accomplie là,** it was very wrong of you to do that; **a. un geste,** to make a gesture. **2 s'accomplir** *vpr* to be realised, to come true; **notre souhait s'est accompli,** our wish came true; *Rel* **que la volonté du Seigneur s'accomplisse,** the Lord's will be done.

accomplissement [akɔ̃plismɑ̃] *nm* **(a)** accomplishment, performance, carrying out (*of task, duty*); fulfilment (*of wish*); **(b)** completion (*of apprenticeship*).

accord [akɔr] *nm* **(a)** (*traité*) agreement; (*non formel*) understanding; (*transaction commerciale*) bargain; settlement (*of a conflict*); **conclure un a.,** to enter into an agreement; **a. de principe,** agreement in principle; **arriver** *ou* **parvenir à un a.,** to come to an agreement, to reach (an) agreement; **un a. est intervenu d'après lequel ...,** an agreement has been reached by which ...;

(b) (*entente*) agreement (**sur,** on); **vivre en** *ou* **de bon a.,** to live in harmony; **l'a. parfait qui règne entre nous deux,** the perfect harmony between us; **être en a. avec la nature,** to be in harmony *or* at one with nature; **vivre en a. avec ses principes,** to live by one's principles; **d'a.,** in agreement, in accordance (**avec,** with); **mettre d'a. deux points de vue,** to reconcile two points of view; **se mettre d'a.** *ou* **tomber d'a. avec qn,** to come to an agreement with s.o.; **être d'a. avec qn,** to agree with s.o.; **les témoins ne sont pas d'a.,** the witnesses disagree *or* differ; **mes comptes sont d'a.,** my accounts balance; **tout est d'a.,** everything is settled *or* arranged; **c'est d'a., d'a.!,** agreed!, all right!, *F* O.K.!; **d'un commun a.,** by common consent, by mutual agreement;

(c) (*autorisation*) consent; **il a donné son a.,** he gave his consent;

(d) *Gram* agreement, concordance (**avec,** with); **l'a. de l'adjectif avec le nom,** the agreement of the adjective with the noun; **les règles d'a.,** the rules of agreement;

(e) *Mus* chord; **a. parfait,** common chord; **faux a.,** discord; **a. arpégé** *ou* **brisé** *ou* **figuré,** broken chord; **a. de sensible,** dominant seventh (chord);

(f) (*réglage*) *Mus* pitch; *Tech* tuning; *Mus* **être d'a.,** to be in tune; **mettre des instruments d'a.,** to tune instruments; **tenir l'a.,** (*of piano etc*) to keep in tune; *Rad* **a. précis,** fine tuning; *Rad* **a. silencieux,** aural null; *Électron* **a. d'antenne,** alignment input.

accordage [akɔrdaʒ] *nm*, **accordement** [akɔrdəmɑ̃] *nm* *Mus* tuning.

accordéon [akɔrdeɔ̃] *nm* accordion; **a. à touches,** piano accordion; **en a.,** (accordion-)pleated (*skirt*); *F* crumpled (up) (*mudguard etc*); *Fig* **voitures en a.,** pile-up; *Fig* **ça roule en a. jusqu'à l'aéroport,** it's stop and start all the way to the airport; *Fig* **ses bas sont en a.,** her stockings are coming down.

accordéoniste [akɔrdeɔnist] *n* accordionist, accordion player.

accorder [akɔrde] **1** *vt* **(a)** to reconcile (*enemies etc*);

(b) *Gram* **a. le verbe avec le sujet,** to make the verb agree with the subject;

(c) *Mus Rad* to tune (*piano, radio etc*); **a. les violons au ton du piano,** to tune the violins to the pitch of the piano; *Fig* **il faudrait a. vos violons,** (*of two or more people*) you'd better get your story straight;

(d) to grant (*favour etc*); **accorder des dommages-intérêts,** to award damages; **a. un escompte,** to allow a discount; **pouvez-vous m'a. quelques minutes?,** can you spare me a few minutes?; **je n'ai pas essayé très longtemps, je vous l'accorde,** I didn't try for very long, I grant you *or* I admit; **je t'accorde qu'il a tout pour plaire,** he's very attractive, I('ll) grant you that; **a. à qn de faire qch,** to give s.o. permission to do sth; **elle accorde la plus grande importance à ce travail,** she attaches the greatest importance to this job; **il n'accorde pas la moindre valeur à ce que je dis,** he doesn't attach the slightest value to anything I say; **on m'a accordé huit jours de congé,** I have been given a week's leave;

(e) (*harmoniser*) to match (up); **elle accorde ses rideaux à la couleur du canapé,** her curtains tone in with the colour of the couch.

2 s'accorder *vpr* **(a)** (*se mettre d'accord*) to agree, to come to an agreement (*about sth*) (**avec qn,** with s.o.); **s'a. sur le prix,** to agree on (the) price; **s'a. à** *ou* **pour faire qch,** to agree to do sth; **on s'accorde à penser que la maladie sera curable d'ici là,** there is a general belief *or* it is generally believed that the disease will be curable by then;

(b) (*s'entendre*) to get on (*well, badly*) (**avec qn,** with s.o.); **ils s'accordent mal ensemble,** they don't get on (at all) well; **ils s'accordent très bien,** they get on very well (together);

(c) (*aller avec, correspondre*) to correspond; (*de couleurs etc*) to harmonize; (*de chiffres*) to tally; (*de témoignages*) to square; (*d'un projet*) to fit in (**avec,** with); **cette action ne s'accorde pas avec son caractère,** this action is not in keeping *or* in line with his *or* her character; **cela ne s'accorde pas avec mes idées,** it doesn't fit in with my ideas; *Com* **faire a. les livres,** to agree the books; **il faut que la pratique s'accorde avec la théorie,** the practice should correspond to *or* with the theory; **cette ceinture s'accorde à toutes les tenues,** this belt goes with *or* can be worn with everything;

(d) *Gram* to agree; **le verbe s'accorde avec le sujet,** the verb agrees with the subject;

(e) (*se donner*) to allow *or* grant oneself; **s'a. dix minutes de repos,** to allow *or* give oneself ten minutes' rest.

accordeur [akɔrdœr] *nm* (piano) tuner.

accordoir [akɔrdwar] *nm* (piano) tuning key.

accostable [akɔstabl] *adj Nau* **plage a.,** = beach suitable for mooring.

accostage [akɔstaʒ] *nm* **(a)** *F* accosting (*of s.o.*); **(b)** *Nau* drawing alongside (*quay*); **(c)** *Astronaut* docking.

accoster [akɔste] **1** *vt* **(a)** to go *or* come up to, to accost (*s.o.*); (*pour agresser*) to accost (*s.o.*); **(b) a. un bateau le long du quai,** to moor *or* berth a boat alongside (the quay). **2** *vi Nau* to come on board (*ship*); (*d'un navire*) to berth, to dock; *Astronaut* to dock.

accotement [akɔtmɑ̃] *nm* **(a)** verge (*of road*); **a. non stabilisé,** soft verge, no hard shoulder; **(b)** *Rail* shoulder.

accoter [akɔte] **1** *vt* to lean (*sth against sth*); to shore up (*vessel, wall etc*); **accoté contre qch,** leaning against sth. **2 s'accoter** *vpr* to lean; **s'a. à** *ou* **contre un mur,** to lean against a wall.

accotoir [akɔtwar] *nm* armrest, elbow rest; (*pour la tête*) headrest.

accouchée [akuʃe] *nf* mother (*of newborn child*); *Méd* **salle des accouchées,** maternity ward.

accouchement [akuʃmɑ̃] *nm* childbirth; **a. prématuré** *ou* **avant terme,** premature delivery; **a. aux forceps,** forceps delivery; **a. naturel** *ou* **sans douleur,** natural childbirth; **elle a eu un a. difficile,** she had a difficult birth; **cours d'accouchement sans douleur,** natural childbirth classes; **ce médecin fait plusieurs accouchements par jour,** this doctor carries out *or* performs several deliveries a day.

accoucher [akuʃe] **1** *vi* **(a) a. d'un garçon,** to give birth to a boy; **elle accouchera dans un mois,** her baby's due in a month's time; **(b)** *F* **mais accouche(z) donc!,** come on, out with it! *or* spit it out!; **il a accouché de ce recueil de nouvelles,** he has laboured to bring forth this collection of short stories. **2** *vt* to deliver (*a mother in childbirth*).

accoucheur, -euse [akuʃœr, -øz] **1** *n* (*médecin*) obstetrician. **2** *nf* (*sage-femme*) **accoucheuse,** midwife.

accouder (s') [sakude] *vpr* to lean on one's elbow(s).

accoudoir [akudwar] *nm* **(a)** (*de fauteuil*) armrest, elbow rest; **(b)** *Archit* balustrade.

accouple [akupl] *nf* leash.

accouplement [akupləmɑ̃] *nm* **(a)** coupling, join(ing), link(ing); *Él* connecting; yoking (*of oxen*); *Tech* **a. à débrayage,** disengaging gear, clutch coupling; *Aut* **a. direct,** direct drive; *Av* **a. bendix,** bendix drive; **a. à glissement,** slip clutch; *Av* **a. à griffe(s),** dog clutch, coupling; *Mus* **pédale d'a.,** (*d'un orgue*) coupler (pedal); **(b)** (*d'animaux*) pairing, mating.

accoupler [akuple] **1** *vt* **(a)** (*unir par deux*) to couple, to join; to couple (up) (*parts*); *Él* to connect, to group (*batteries etc*); to yoke (*oxen*); **a. un moteur à une batterie,** to connect an engine up to a battery; **des idées accouplées à des images,** ideas linked to images; **(b)** to mate (*animals*). **2 s'accoupler** *vpr* to mate, to pair; (*avoir des relations sexuelles*) to copulate.

accourir [akurir] *vi* (*conj like* **courir**; *aux* **avoir** *or* **être**) to run (up), to rush up; **à mes cris, ils sont accourus,** they came running when they heard my cries; **ils ont accouru** *ou* **sont accourus à mon secours,** they ran *or* came running to help me.

accoutrement [akutrəmɑ̃] *nm souvent Péj* dress, garb; *F* get-up.

accoutrer [akutre] **1** *vt souvent Péj* to rig out (**de,** in); **accoutré d'une vieille capote,** rigged out in an old army greatcoat. **2 s'accoutrer** *vpr* to rig oneself out (**de,** in).

accoutumance [akutymɑ̃s] *nf* **(a)** (*adaptation*) familiarization (**à,** with); (*à la douleur etc*) inurement (**à,** to); **l'a. diminue le plaisir,** even pleasure palls; *Méd* **a. (à une drogue),** tolerance (to a drug); **l'effet d'a. des drogues dures,** the habit-forming effect of hard drugs; **(b)** *Litt* (*habitude*) habit, usage.

accoutumé [akutyme] **1** *adj* usual, habitual; **à l'heure accoutumée,** at the usual time. **2** *adv* **à l'accoutumée,** usually; **il est arrivé à huit heures comme à l'accoutumée,** he arrived at eight o'clock as usual.

accoutumer [akutyme] **1** *vt* **a. qn à qch,** to accustom s.o. to sth; **être accoutumé à qch,** to be accustomed *or* used to sth. **2 s'accoutumer** *vpr* **s'a. à,** to get *or* become used *or* accustomed to; **s'a. à la fatigue,** to become accustomed *or* used *or* hardened to fatigue; **je ne puis pas m'a. à le faire,** I can't get used to doing it.

accouvage [akuvaʒ] *nm* artificial incubation.

accréditation [akreditɑsjɔ̃] *nf* accreditation, accrediting (*of an ambassador, a journalist*).

accrédité, -ée [akredite] **1** *adj* of good standing, accredited; **notre représentant a.,** our authorized representative. **2** *n* agent; *Fin* holder of a letter of credit.

accréditer [akredite] **1** *vt* **(a)** to accredit (*an ambassador, a journalist*); *Fin* **a. un client,** to open an account for a client; **(b)** (*rendre plausible*) to substantiate, to give credence to; **cette rumeur est accréditée par ses dernières actions,** this rumour is substantiated *or* backed up by his latest actions. **2 s'accréditer** *vpr* (*of rumour etc*) to gain ground, to spread.

accréditif [akreditif] *nm* letter of credit.

accro [akro] *F* **1** *adj* (*à la drogue*) *&* *Fig* addicted (**à,** to), hooked (**à,** on). **2** *n* (*aux échecs etc*) addict.

accroc [akro] *nm* **(a)** tear, *Fml* rent (*in clothes etc*); **(b)** *Fig* hitch, difficulty, snag.

accrochage [akrɔʃaʒ] *nm* **(a)** hooking; *Aut* minor accident; *Nau* running foul; *Boxe* clinch; **(b)** *Rail* hitching on, coupling; **(c)** hanging (up) (*of picture etc*); **(d)** *El* synchronization, synchronizing; *Rad* picking up (*of a station*); **(e)** *Sp* recovery (*from a losing position*); **(f)** (*dispute*) altercation, squabble; *Mil* brush, skirmish.

accroche [akrɔʃ] *nf Vieilli* eye-catching advertisement; (*verbal*) striking (publicity) slogan.

accroche-casseroles [akrɔʃkasrɔl] *nm inv* saucepan rack.

accroche-coeur [akrɔʃkœr] *nm* kiss curl; (*pl accroche-coeurs*).

accrocher [akrɔʃe] **1** *vt* **(a)** to hook, to catch (*sth*); **a. un poisson,** to hook a fish; **titre qui accroche le lecteur,** striking *or* eye-catching title; **vitrine qui accroche le regard,** eye-catching display in a shop-window; **a. sa robe sur un clou,** to catch one's dress on a nail; *Aut* **il a accroché mon pare-choc,** he caught *or* hit my bumper; *F* **a. qn,** to buttonhole s.o.;

(b) *Rail* to hitch on, to couple (*carriage etc*);

(c) to grapple (*ship*);

(d) to hang (*sth*) up; *Constr* to hang (*door*); **a. son manteau,** to hang up one's coat; *Fig* **il faut avoir le cœur bien accroché,** you need a strong stomach *or* strong nerves; *Arg* **a. sa montre,** *Br* to put one's watch in hock, *Am* to pop one's watch;

(e) *Rad* **a. une station,** to tune in to a station.

2 *vi* to stick, to catch (*in s.o.'s clothes etc*); *Fig* **les négociations ont accroché,** there has been a hitch in the negotiations; **ça ne marche pas très bien entre eux, ça accroche souvent,** things aren't very good between them, they argue a lot; **ça n'a pas du tout accroché,** (*entre deux personnes*) they didn't get on *or* *F* click.

3 s'accrocher *vpr* **(a) s'a. à,** to cling to (*s.o., sth*); (*se coller à*) to fasten onto (*s.o., an idea*); **accroche-toi à la rampe,** hold on tight *or* hang on to the handrail; *Fig F* **accroche-toi, tu n'as pas tout entendu!,** brace yourself, you haven't heard everything yet!;

(b) (*se tenir*) **ça s'accroche au mur par un clou,** you fasten *or* attach it to the wall with a nail; *Fig* **elle s'accroche à lui, il est son seul espoir,** she's clinging to him as her only hope; **s'a. à des illusions,** to cling to illusions;

(c) (*tenir*) to stick at it, *F* to hang in there;

(d) *Boxe* to clinch; *Fig* **les deux voitures se sont accrochées,** the two cars clipped each other;

(e) *F* (*se disputer*) to have a row;

(f) tu peux te l'a.!, you can kiss goodbye to that!, you've had that!

accrocheur, -euse [akrɔʃœr, -øz] **1** *adj* **(a)** (*tenace*) tenacious, stubborn; **(b)** eye-catching (*title*). **2** *n* **c'est un a.,** he's a fighter.

accroire [akrwar] *vt* (*used only in*) **faire a. à qn que ...,** to make s.o. believe that ...; **elle veut nous en faire a.,** (*abuser de notre crédulité*) she's trying to fool us; (*se faire valoir*) she's trying to impress us.

accroissement [akrwasmɑ̃] *nm* **(a)** increase (**de,** in); **taux d'a.,** rate of increase; *Math* **a. d'une fonction,** increment of a function; **(b)** growth (*of plant etc*).

accroître [akrwatr] *v* (*prp* **accroissant**; *pp* **accru**; *pr ind* **j'accrois, il accroît, n. accroissons, ils accroissent**; *impf* **j'accroissais**; *p hist* **j'accrus**; *fu* **j'accroîtrai**) **1** *vt* to increase, to enlarge, to add to, to augment; to enhance (*reputation*). **2 s'accroître** *vpr* to increase, to grow.

accroupir (s') [sakrupir] *vpr* to squat (down), to crouch (down); **accroupi,** squatting, crouching.

accroupissement [akrupismɑ̃] *nm* crouching, squatting.

accru [akry] *nm Bot* sucker.

accu [aky] *nm Él F* battery; *Fig* **recharger ses accus,** to recharge one's batteries.

accueil [akœj] *nm* reception, welcome, greeting; **faire bon a. à qn,** to welcome s.o.; **a. hostile** *ou* **défavorable,** hostile reception; **discours/cérémonie d'a.,** welcoming speech/ceremony, speech/ceremony of welcome; *Com* **faire (bon) a. à une traite,** to honour a bill; **centre d'a.,** reception centre; **passez à l'a.,** go to the reception desk, go to reception.

accueillant [akœjɑ̃] hospitable, welcoming.

accueillir [akœjir] *vt* (*conj like* **cueillir**) to receive, to greet (*s.o., new idea*); **(bien) a. qn,** to welcome s.o.; **mal a. qn,** to give s.o. a bad reception; **cet hôtel peut a. jusqu'à 500 visiteurs,** the hotel can accommodate up to 500 visitors; **se faire a. par des volées de pierre,** to be greeted with *or* by volleys of stones; **le film a été mal accueilli par le public,** the film got a bad reception from the public; *Com* **a. une traite,** to meet *or* honour a bill.

acculer [akyle] **1** *vt* to drive (*s.o.*) back (**contre,** against); *Fig* to drive (*s.o.*) to the wall; to bring (*animal*) to bay *or* to a stand; *Fig* **être acculé aux aveux/à la ruine,** to be forced into a confession/into bankruptcy. **2** *vi Nau* **(a)** to pitch heavily astern; **(b)** to be down by the stern. **3 s'acculer** *vpr* **s'a. à** *ou* **contre qch,** to set one's back against sth; (*d'un animal*) to stand at bay.

accumulateur [akymylatœr] *nm Él* battery, accumulator.

accumulation [akymylɑsjɔ̃] *nf* **(a)** (*action*) accumulation; storage (*of energy*); hoarding (*of money*); **chauffage par a.,** storage heating; **chauffage à a. nocturne,** (night) storage heating; **(b)** (*stock*) accumulation; hoard (*of money, food*); collection (*of objects*).

accumuler [akymyle] **1** *vt* to accumulate, to amass, to gather (together); to hoard (*food, money*); (*entasser*) to heap up, to pile up; **a. les médailles,** to accumulate medals; **a. les preuves,** to gather evidence; **quand je suis fatigué, j'accumule les erreurs,** I make lots of mistakes when I'm tired. **2 s'accumuler** *vpr* to accumulate; *Fin* (*des intérêts*) to accrue.

accusateur, -trice [akyzatœr, -tris] **1** *adj* (*regard, doigt*) accusing, *Fml* accusatory; incriminating (*evidence*). **2** *n* accuser; impeacher, arraigner (*of public official*); *Hist* **a. public,** public prosecutor.

accusatif [akyzatif] *nm Gram* accusative (case), objective case; **mot à l'a.,** word in the accusative.

accusation [akyzɑsjɔ̃] *nf* **(a)** (*condamnation par qn*) accusation; **lancer** *ou* **porter une a. contre qn,** to bring an accusation against s.o.; **(b)** *Jur* **mettre qn en a.,** to commit s.o. for trial; **quels sont les chefs** *ou* **les sujets d'a.?,** what are the charges?; **(c)** *Pol* impeachment, arraignment; **faire une a. contre la politique extérieure actuelle,** to deliver an indictment against current foreign policy.

accusé, -ée [akyze] **1** *adj* prominent, pronounced, bold (*feature etc*); **rides très accusées,** very deep wrinkles. **2** *n* accused (*of crime*); (*in court*) defendant, prisoner at the bar. **3** *nm* **a. de réception,** acknowledgement (of receipt) (*of a letter*).

accuser [akyze] **1** *vt* **(a)** to accuse; **a. qn de (faire) qch,** to accuse s.o. of (doing) sth; *Fig* **a. le sort,** to blame fate; **(b) a. qch,** to own to sth, to profess sth; **elle accuse trente ans,** she admits to being thirty; (*elle en a l'air*) she looks (at least) thirty; *F* **j'accuse le coup, ça a été dur,** it was a terrible blow, and I'm still reeling from it; **(c)** (*faire ressortir*) to define, to show up, to accentuate; **esquisse qui accuse tous les muscles,** sketch that brings out every muscle; **paroles qui accusent une grande ignorance,** words that betray *or* show *or* reveal great ignorance; **(d) a. réception de qch,** to acknowledge (receipt of) sth; **(e)** (*rendre responsable*) to blame. **2 s'accuser** *vpr* **(a)** (*se rendre coupable*) to admit, to confess; **je m'accuse de vol/de vous avoir menti,** I admit to theft/to having lied to you; **(b)** (*se renforcer*) to become more pronounced *or* marked.

acerbe [aserb] *adj* sharp, harsh, acerbic; **réprimande a.,** sharp reprimand; **discussion a.,** ill-tempered discussion; **parler d'un ton a.,** to speak sharply.

acerbité [aserbite] *nf* sharpness, harshness, acerbity; **répondre avec a.,** to answer sharply.

acéré [asere] *adj* sharp (*blade etc*); *Fig* cutting, scathing (*remark*); **langue acérée,** sharp tongue.

acérer [asere] *vt* (**j'acère; j'acérerai**) (*rare*) to sharpen, to give a keen edge to (*sth*).

acétate [asetat] *nm Ch* acetate; **a. de cuivre,** copper acetate; *Tex* **a. de cellulose,** cellulose acetate.

acétique [asetik] *adj Ch* acetic; **odeur a.,** vinegary smell.

acétocellulose [asetoselyloz] *nf Ch* cellulose acetate.

acétone [aseton] *nf Ch* acetone.

acétylène [asetilen] *nm Ch* acetylene; **lampe à a.,** acetylene *Br* lamp *or Am* torch.

acétylsalicylique [asetilsalisilik] *adj Pharm* **acide a.,** acetylsalicylic acid.

A.C.F. [aseef] *nm* (*abrév* **Automobile Club de France**) = automobile association of France.

achalandage [aʃalɑ̃daʒ] *nm Jur Com* custom, customers, clientele.

achalandé [aʃalɑ̃de] *adj* **magasin bien a.,** well patronized shop; *F* well stocked shop.

achalander [aʃalɑ̃de] *vt F* to stock (*shop*).

achaler [aʃale] *vt Can* to annoy, to bother (*s.o.*).

achards [aʃar] *nmpl Culin* relish.

acharné [aʃarne] *adj* **(a)** (*enragé*) **meute acharnée à la poursuite,** pack in hot *or* eager pursuit; **hommes acharnés les uns contre les autres,** men fighting desperately against each other; **(b)** (*furieux*) **joueur a.,** inveterate gambler; **lutte acharnée,** desperate *or* bitter struggle; **concurrence acharnée,** cut-throat competition; **travail a.,** relentless work.

acharnement [aʃarnəmɑ̃] *nm* relentlessness; **a. au** *ou* **pour le travail,** passion for work; **avec a.,** relentlessly; **travailler avec a.,** to work relentlessly; **se battre avec a.,** to fight tooth and nail; *Pharm* **a. thérapeutique,** = use of intensive medication.

acharner [aʃarne] **1 s'acharner** *vpr* **s'a. après** *ou* **contre** *ou* **sur qn,** (*persécuter*) to be always after s.o.; (*en vouloir à qn*) to have one's knife into s.o.; **le malheur s'acharne après lui,** he is dogged by misfortune; **s'a. à** *ou* **sur qch,** to work desperately hard at sth, to slave (away) at sth; **il s'acharne à vous nuire,** he is set on harming you; **elle ne se décourage pas, elle s'acharne,** she doesn't let herself be discouraged, she just keeps at it *or F* keeps plugging away. **2** *vt Vieilli* **a. la meute après une bête,** to set the pack on (the track of) a quarry; **a. un chien,** to flesh *or* blood a hound.

achat [aʃa] *nm* **(a)** purchase, buying; **faire l'a. de qch,** to buy sth; **aller faire ses achats,** to go shopping; **pouvoir d'a.,** purchasing power; **prix d'a.,** purchase price; **centrale d'a.,** central purchasing office; *Can* **agent d'a.,** procurement officer; **(b)** (*ce qu'on a acheté*) purchase; **voilà mes achats,** look (at) what I've bought, this is what I've bought.

acheminement [aʃminmɑ̃] *nm* **(a)** (*progrès*) step, progress (**à, vers,** towards); **(b)** forwarding (*of goods, parcels*).

acheminer [aʃmine] **1** *vt* **(a)** (*conduire*) to set (*s.o.*) on his way (**sur, vers,** to(wards)); **(b)** to dispatch, to convey (*goods etc*) (**sur, vers,** to). **2 s'acheminer** *vpr* **s'a. vers la maison,** to set out for *or* to make one's way home; **s'a. vers le succès,** to be heading for success.

acheter [aʃte] *v* (**j'achète, n. achetons; j'achèterai**) **1** *vt* **(a) a. qch,** to buy sth, *Fml* to purchase sth; **a. en gros/en détail,** to buy wholesale/retail; **j'ai acheté ce livre 50 francs,** I bought this book for 50 francs; **a. qch (à) bon marché,** to buy sth cheap; *Fig* **vous l'achetez bien cher,** it's a high price to pay for it; **a. chat en poche,** to buy a pig in a poke; **a. qch à qn,** to buy sth from s.o.; **a. qch à** *ou* **pour qn,** to buy sth for s.o.; **je vais lui a. un livre,** I'm going to buy him *or* her a book; **(b)** *F* to bribe (*s.o.*), to buy (*s.o.*) off; **a. la complicité de qn,** to buy s.o.'s silence. **2 s'acheter** *vpr* **ça s'achète partout,** you can buy it *or* them everywhere; *Fig* **ces choses-là ne s'achètent pas,** such things cannot be bought *or* are not for sale.

acheteur, -euse [aʃtœr, -øz] *n* buyer, purchaser; *Jur* vendee; *Com* **elle est acheteuse pour Prisunic ®,** she is a buyer for Prisunic ®.

achevé [aʃve] *adj* accomplished (*horseman etc*); perfect (*piece of work*); *F* **sot a.,** utter *or* absolute fool; **menteur a.,** (*accompli*) consummate liar; (*sans honte*) out and out liar.

achèvement [aʃɛvmɑ̃] *nm* completion, finishing (*of work*); **travail en a.,** work in the process of completion; **date d'a.,** target date, completion date.

achever [aʃve] *v* (**j'achève, n. achevons; j'achèverai**) **1** *vt* **(a)** (*finir*) to end, to conclude (*a speech*); to finish (off), to complete (*piece of work etc*); **avant d'a. ma lettre,** before closing *or* finishing my letter; **a. ses jours** *ou* **sa vie,** to end one's days; *F* **achève!,** out with it!; **a. de faire qch,** to finish doing sth; **achève de boire ton café,** drink up *or* finish your coffee; **(b)** (*mettre à mort*) to finish off (*a person*); to put (*an animal*) out of its misery *or* out of pain; *F* **cette grosse perte l'a achevé,** this heavy loss was the end of him; *F* **ça m'a achevé,** that really finished me (off). **2 s'achever** *vpr* **(a)** (*finir*) to draw to a close, to end; **c'est ainsi que l'histoire s'achève,** that's how the story finishes *or* ends; **le jour s'acheva tristement,** the day closed *or* ended sadly *or* on a sad note; **(b)** (*of work*) to reach completion.

achigan [aʃigɑ̃] *nm* (*poisson*) *Can* (black) bass.

Achille [aʃil] *nm* Achilles.

achoper [aʃɔpe] *vi Can Fig* **a. sur qch,** to stumble over sth; **l'entente semble a. sur la présence d'observateurs étrangers,** the presence of foreign observers seems to be the stumbling block in the way of an agreement.

achoppement [aʃɔpmɑ̃] *nm Litt* obstacle, difficulty; **pierre d'a.,** stumbling block.

achopper [aʃɔpe] **1** *vi* **c'est là que ça achoppe,** that's the stumbling block. **2 s'achopper** *vpr Fig* to come to grief; to stumble (**à,** against).

achromatique [akrɔmatik] *adj* achromatic.

acide [asid] **1** *adj* acid(ic); (*au goût*) tart, sour; **une pomme a.,** a sour apple; *Fig* **une brunette a.,** a witty brunette; **milieu a.,** acidic environment. **2** *nm* (*drogue*) & *Ch* acid; **a. désoxyribonucléique,** deoxyribonucleic acid.

acidificateur [asidifikatœr] *nm* acidifier, acidifying agent.

acidification [asidifikasjɔ̃] *nf* acidification.

acidifier [asidifje] **1** *vt* to acidify. **2 s'acidifier** *vpr* to become acid, to turn sour.

acidité [asidite] *nf* acidity; (*d'une pomme etc*) sourness, tartness; *Fig* (*d'un commentaire*) wittiness; *Ch* **l'a. d'une solution,** the acidity of a solution; *Méd* **a. gastrique,** excess acid in the stomach, hyperacidity.

acidose [asidoz] *nf Méd* acidosis.

acidulé [asidyle] *adj* acidulous; **bonbons acidulés,** acid drops.

acier [asje] *nm* steel; **lame d'a.** *ou* **en a.,** steel blade; **a. trempé,** hardened *or* tempered steel; **a. inoxydable,** stainless steel; **a. au chrome/au nickel,** chrome/nickel steel; *Fig* **cœur d'a.,** heart of stone; **regard d'a.,** steely look.

aciérie [asjeri] *nf* steel works.

aciériste [asjerist] *nm* steel maker *or* manufacturer.

acmé [akme] *nf Litt* acme, peak; *Méd* crisis.

acné [akne] *nf* acne; **a. juvénile** *ou* **vulgaire,** teenage acne.

acolyte [akɔlit] *nm Péj* confederate, accomplice; *Rel* acolyte.

acompte [akɔ̃t] *nm* instalment, part(ial) payment, payment on account; **payer par acomptes,** to pay by *or* in instalments; **recevoir un a.,** to receive something on account; **a. de** *ou* **sur dividende,** interim dividend; *Fig* **ce sandwich, c'est un a. sur le repas,** this sandwich will keep the hunger pangs at bay.

aconit [akɔnit] *nm* (*plante*) aconite.

acoquiner (s') [sakɔkine] *vpr Péj* to team up, to fall in (**avec,** with).

Açores (les) [lezasɔr] *nfpl* the Azores.

à-côté [akote] *nm* **(a)** (*verbal*) aside; **(b)** (*point secondaire*)

les à-côtés d'une question, the side issues of a question; **les à-côtés de l'histoire,** sidelights on history; **(c)** *F* extra; **il a quelques à-côtés,** he makes a bit on the side.

à-coup [aku] *nm* jerk, jolt, jar, shock; *El* surge (of current); **il travaille par à-coups,** he works by *or* in fits and starts; *Aut* **le moteur a des à-coups,** the engine judders; **sans à-coups,** smoothly.

acousticien, -ienne [akustisjɛ̃, -jɛn] *n* acoustician.

acoustique [akustik] **1** *adj* acoustic(al); **cornet a.,** ear trumpet; **tuyau a.,** speaking tube; **voûte a.,** whispering gallery; **les phénomènes acoustiques,** acoustic phenomena. **2** *nf Phys* acoustics; **a. d'une salle,** acoustics of a hall.

acquéreur [akerœr] *nm* purchaser, buyer; *Jur* vendee; **notre voiture n'a pas trouvé a.,** we couldn't find a buyer for our car.

acquérir [akerir] *v* (*prp* **acquérant**; *pp* **acquis**; *pr ind* **j'acquiers, il acquiert, n. acquérons, ils acquièrent**; *pr sub* **j'acquière, n. acquérions**; *impf* **j'acquérais**; *p hist* **j'acquis**; *fu* **j'acquerrai**) **1** *vt* **(a)** (*obtenir*) to acquire, to obtain, to get, to win, to gain; to get into (*a habit*); **nous avons acquis la certitude de son innocence,** we have established beyond doubt that he *or* she is innocent; **l'expérience acquise au long d'une carrière,** the experience gained in the course of one's career; **a. de mauvaises habitudes,** to get into bad habits; *Prov* **un bien en acquiert un autre,** money attracts money;

(b) (*prendre*) to acquire;

(c) (*devenir propriétaire de*) to acquire; (*acheter*) to purchase, to buy; **a. une terre d'un voisin,** to purchase *or* buy land from a neighbour; **a. un bien par héritage,** to come into *or* to inherit some property.

2 s'acquérir *vpr* **(a)** (*se prendre*) **cette habitude s'acquiert facilement,** it's easy to get into the habit;

(b) (*s'attirer*) to win, to gain.

acquêt [akɛ] *nm Jur* acquisition; (*fortuit*) windfall; **communauté réduite aux acquêts,** = marriage settlement whereby only goods acquired since the marriage are deemed to be held in common.

acquiescement [akjɛsmɑ̃] *nm* acquiescence; *Jur* **a. licite/conditionnel,** lawful/conditional consent.

acquiescer [akjɛse] *vi* (**j'acquiesçai(s)**; **n. acquiesçons**) **a. à qch,** (*se résigner*) to acquiesce in sth; (*consentir*) to agree *or* assent to sth; **a. d'un signe de tête,** to agree with a nod of the head, to nod one's approval; **elle a acquiescé d'un sourire,** she gave a smile of agreement; *Jur* **a. à un acte,** to consent (fully) to an act.

acquis [aki] **1** *adj* acquired (*knowledge etc*); **fait a.,** established *or* accepted fact; **tenir pour a.,** to take for granted; **droits a.,** vested interests; **cela est a.,** that's been established; **ce droit lui est a.,** he *or* she has an established right in this respect; **je vous suis tout a.,** I entirely agree. **2** *nm* acquired knowledge; (*réussites*) attainments, achievements.

acquisitif, -ive [akizitif, -iv] *adj Jur* acquisitive.

acquisition [akizisjɔ̃] *nf* **(a)** (*fait*) acquisition; **faire l'a. de qch,** to acquire sth; (*acheter*) to purchase sth; **(b)** (*bien acquis*) acquisition; (*bien acheté*) purchase; **c'est ma dernière a.,** it's my latest acquisition; **acquisitions de l'esprit,** intellectual attainments.

acquit [aki] *nm* **(a)** *Com* receipt; **donner a. de qch,** to give a receipt for sth; **pour a.,** received (with thanks), paid; **(b)** clearance (*of ship*); **(c)** discharge, release (*from promise*); **par a. de conscience,** to ease one's conscience; **faire qch par manière d'a.,** to do sth as a matter of form; **(d)** *Jur* **sentence** *ou* **ordonnance d'a.,** order of acquittal.

acquit-à-caution [akiakosjɔ̃] *nm* bond note; (*pl acquits-à-caution*).

acquittement [akitmɑ̃] *nm* **(a)** discharge, payment (*of debt etc*); **(b)** *Jur* acquittal; **verdict d'a.,** verdict of not guilty.

acquitter [akite] **1** *vt* **(a) a. qn,** (*d'une obligation etc*) to release s.o. (*from an obligation etc*); **(b)** *Jur* **a. un accusé,** to acquit *or* discharge a defendant; **(c) a. une obligation,** to fulfil an obligation; **a. une dette,** to discharge a debt; **(d) a. une facture,** to receipt a bill. **2 s'acquitter** *vpr* **s'a. d'une obligation/d'un devoir,** to fulfil *or* carry out *or* discharge an obligation/a duty; **s'a. de son devoir,** to do one's duty; **comment pourrai-je m'a. envers vous?,** how can I repay you?

acre [akr] **1** *nf Hist* = acre. **2** *nm Can* acre.

âcre [ɑkr] *adj aussi Fig* bitter, tart (*taste, remark*); pungent (*smell*); **l'odeur â. de la fumée,** the acrid smell of smoke.

âcreté [ɑkrəte] *nf* bitterness (*of taste, remark*); pungency (*of smell*).

acrimonie [akrimɔni] *nf* (*bad temper*) acrimony; acrimoniousness, bitterness (*of speech, quarrel*).

acrimonieux, -euse [akrimɔnjø, -øz] *adj* acrimonious, bitter (*words, quarrel etc*).

acrobate [akrɔbat] **1** *n* acrobat; *Fig* **c'est un a.,** he can wriggle out of anything. **2** *nm* (*mammifère*) flying squirrel.

acrobatie [akrɔbasi] *nf* **(a)** (*art*) acrobatics; **tour d'a.** acrobatic feat; **faire des acrobaties,** to do *or* perform acrobatics; **a. aérienne,** stunt flying, aerobatics; **(b)** *Fig* (*virtuosité*) clever trick; **a. intellectuelle,** intellectual acrobatics; **il s'en sortira par une de ses acrobaties,** he'll wriggle out of it somehow.

acrobatique [akrɔbatik] *adj* acrobatic.

acronyme [akrɔnim] *nm Ling* acronym.

acropole [akrɔpɔl] *nf* acropolis.

acrostiche [akrɔstiʃ] *nm* acrostic.

acrylique [akrilik] **1** *adj Ch Tex* acrylic. **2** *nm Tex* acrylic; **pull en a.,** acrylic pullover.

acte [akt] *nm* **(a)** (*action*) action, act, deed; **moins de paroles! des actes!,** let's have less talk and more action!; **a. de courage,** act of bravery, brave action; **faire a. de bonne volonté,** to give proof of good will; **passer aux actes,** to take action; **faire a. de présence,** to put in an appearance; **faire a. de candidature à un emploi,** to submit an application *or* to apply for a job; **faire a. de souverain,** to exercise the royal prerogative; **a. de terrorisme,** act of terrorism; **a. de guerre,** act of war; **a. médical,** medical treatment; *Rel* **a. de foi/contrition,** act of faith/contrition;

(b) *Jur* = instrument (*establishing ownership*); deed, title; **a. de vente,** bill of sale; **a. authentique** *ou* **notarié, a. sur papier timbré,** deed executed and authenticated by a notary; **a. judiciaire,** writ; **a. d'accusation,** bill of indictment, charges; **dont a.,** duly noted *or* acknowledged;

(c) (*certificat*) record; **a. de naissance/de mariage/de décès,** birth/marriage/death certificate; **a. de dernière volonté,** last will and testament; **prendre a. de qch,** to record *or* note *or* take a note of *or* set down sth; *Fml* **nous prenons a. de votre candidature,** we acknowledge your application; **donner a. de qch,** to grant sth, to admit sth;

(d) actes, records (*of proceedings etc*); transactions (*of scientific body etc*); proceedings (*of conference*); *Bible* **les Actes des Apôtres,** the Acts of the Apostles;

(e) *Th* act; **dans le second a.,** in the second act.

acteur, -trice [aktœr, -tris] *n* **(a)** *Th Cin* actor; *f* actress; **se faire a.,** to go on the stage; **a. à transformations,** quick-change artist; **(b)** participant (*in an event*); (*in political theory*) actor.

actif, -ive [aktif, -iv] **1** *adj* **(a)** active (*supporter, participation, drug, Gram verb, voice*); potent (*drug etc*); **a. à défendre ses amis,** active in the defence of one's friends; *Econ* **population active,** labour force; *Mil* **armée active,** regular army; **service a.,** (active) service (*with an employer*); **citoyen a.,** person with the right to vote;

(b) active, brisk, sprightly, agile, alert (*person etc*); **sa grand-mère est très active pour son âge,** his grandmother is very sprightly for her age; **faire un commerce a.,** to do a brisk trade;

(c) *Com Jur* **dettes actives,** accounts receivable.

2 *nm* **(a)** *Com* assets; (*moyens financiers*) credit (account); **mettre qch à l'a. de qn,** to credit s.o. with sth; **il faut mettre sa patience à son a.,** you have to give him credit for patience; **avoir plusieurs prix à son a.,** to have several prizes to one's name *or* credit; **avoir plusieurs infractions à son a.,** to have several offences to one's name; **a. immobilisé,** capital assets;

(b) *Gram* **verbe à l'a.,** verb in the active voice.

3 *n* active person; **c'est un a.!,** he likes to do things, he's a doer.

action [aksjɔ̃] *nf* **(a)** (*acte*) action, act; **l'a. de marcher,** the act of walking; **une a. insensée,** a senseless act; **une bonne/mauvaise a.,** a good/bad deed; **a. d'éclat,** brilliant feat of arms;

(b) (*influence, effet*) action, effect (*of substance*); **a. sur qch,** action *or* effect on sth; **ce désherbant n'a aucune a. sur le liseron,** this weedkiller has no effect on bindweed; **a. sur qn,** influence over s.o.; **événements en dehors de notre a.,** events beyond our control; **sans a.,** ineffectual, ineffective; **a. de l'eau/du feu/etc,** effect of water/fire/*etc*; **par l'a. personnelle d'un membre du club,** through the personal intervention of a club member;

(c) (*activité*) action, motion, working, functioning (*of machine etc*); **entrer en a.,** (*of regulation etc*) to come into force *or* effect; **dans le feu de l'a.,** (*pendant la guerre*) in the heat of battle; *Fig* in the heat of the moment; *Pol* **recourir à l'a. directe,** to resort to direct action; **hors d'a.,** out of action; **développer son champ d'a.,** to expand one's sphere of activity *or* field of operations *or* the scope of one's activities; **homme d'a.,** man of action, action man; **passer à l'a.,** to take action, to act; **il faut que vous mettiez votre bon sens en a.,** you should use your common sense;

(d) action, gesture (*of orator etc*);

(e) (*intrigue*) action; plot (*of play, novel*); **scène qui retarde l'a.,** scene that delays the action; **un film d'a.,** action-packed movie; (*genre*) action movie; **l'a. se déroule à Prague,** the action is set in Prague;

(f) *Fin* share; (*document*) share certificate; **actions ordinaires,** *Br* ordinary share, *US* common stock; **actions privilégiées,** *Br* preference share, *US* preferred stock; **a. au porteur/nominative,** bearer stock/registered share; **compagnie par actions,** joint-stock company; **hausse/baisse des actions,** rise/fall in the value of shares; *Fig* **les actions du ministre montent/baissent,** the minister's stock is rising/falling;

(g) *Jur* action, lawsuit, trial; **intenter une a. à qn,** to bring an action against s.o.; to sue s.o. (*for money*); **a. en divorce,** divorce suit;

(h) *Mil* action, fight, engagement;

(i) *Suisse* **vente a.,** bargain offer.

actionnaire [aksjɔnɛr] *n Fin* shareholder.

actionnariat [aksjɔnarja] *nm* share ownership; **a. ouvrier,** workers owning shares in their company.

actionnement [aksjɔnmɑ̃] *nm* activation; **a. à distance,** remote-control operation.

actionner [aksjɔne] *vt* **(a)** (*mettre en marche*) to set (*sth*) in action *or* in motion; to operate, to drive, to run (*machine etc*); **actionné à la main,** hand operated; **a. les freins,** to apply *or* put on the brakes; *F* **a. qn,** to rouse *or* stir s.o. to action; **(b)** *Jur* to sue (*s.o.*), to bring an action against (*s.o.*); **a. qn en dommages-intérêts,** to sue s.o. for damages.

activation [aktivɑsjɔ̃] *nf* activation.

activé [aktive] *adj Ch* activated.

activement [aktivmɑ̃] *adv* actively, briskly, busily.

activer [aktive] **1** *vt* **(a)** (*presser*) to stimulate, to rouse; (*accélérer*) to speed up; **a. un ouvrage,** to press on with *or* to speed up a piece of work; *F* **activez!,** get a move on!; **(b)** *Ch Nucl etc* to activate. **2 s'activer** *vpr* to be busy, to bustle about; **s'a. (à qch),** to get on *or* press on (with sth).

activisme [aktivism(ə)] *nm Pol* activism.

activiste [aktivist] *adj & n Pol* activist.

activité [aktivite] *nf* activity; potency (*of drug etc*); **l'a. d'une ville,** the (amount of) activity in a city; **elle déploie une grande a. au travail,** she invests a lot of energy in her work; **maintenir l'a. de l'industrie,** to keep industry going; **une région reconnue pour son a.,** a region known for its industrial *or* cultural *etc* activity; **en a.,** in action, in operation, in progress; (*personne*) at work; **en pleine a.,** in full operation; **un moment de grande a.,** a very busy time; **marché sans a.,** dull market; **l'usine est en a.,** the factory is working *or* is in production; **a. solaire,** solar activity; **volcan en a.,** active volcano; **le temps d'a. d'un employé,** the length of (active) service of an employee; **être en a. (de service),** to be on active duty *or* on the active list; **je ne connais pas ses activités,** I know nothing about his activities; **le centre de jeunes propose les activités suivantes,** the following activities are available at the youth centre; *Scol etc* **activités dirigées,** projects.

actrice *voir* **ACTEUR**.

actuaire [aktɥɛr] *nm* actuary.

actualisation [aktɥalizɑsjɔ̃] *nf* **(a)** *Écon* discounting; **taux d'a.,** rate of discount; **(b)** *Phil* actualization.

actualiser [aktɥalize] **1** *vt* **(a)** (*un texte, une méthode de travail*) to update; **(b)** *Écon* to discount; **(c)** *Phil* to turn (*sth*) into a reality, to actualize (*sth*). **2 s'actualiser** *vpr* **(a)** (*se moderniser*) to become more up to date; **(b)** *Phil* to become a reality, to come into being.

actualité [aktɥalite] *nf* **(a)** question of the day *or* of the moment; **l'a. d'un problème,** the topicality of a problem; **l'a. politique française,** the current French political scene; **cette question est toujours d'a.,** this is still a topical question; **les actualités,** (*dans la presse*) current events; *TV* news; **(b)** *Phil* actuality, reality.

actuel, -elle [aktɥɛl] *adj* of the present day, existing, current; **le gouvernement a.,** the present government; **l'état a. du pays,** the present *or* current state of the country; **valeur actuelle,** present *or* current value; **à l'heure actuelle,** at the present time; **cette question est toujours actuelle,** this is still a topical question, the question is still relevant today.

actuellement [aktɥɛlmɑ̃] *adv* (just) now, at present, at the present time.

acuité [akɥite] *nf* acuteness, sharpness, keenness (*of pain etc*); sharpness (*of point*); **a. d'un son,** high pitch of a sound; **a. visuelle,** keenness of vision *or* eyesight.

acuponcteur, acupuncteur [akypɔ̃ktœr] *nm Méd* acupuncturist.

acuponcture, acupuncture [akypɔ̃ktyr] *nf Méd* acupuncture.

acutangle [akytɑ̃gl] *adj Math* acute-angled.

A.D.A.C. [adak] *nm* (*abrév* **avion à décollage et atterrissage courts**) STOL.

adage [adaʒ] *nm* adage, (common) saying; **selon l'a.,** as the saying goes.

adagio [adadʒjo] *adv & nm Mus* adagio.

Adam [adɑ̃] *nm* Adam; *F* **dans le costume d'A.,** in one's birthday suit.

adaptabilité [adaptabilite] *nf* adaptability (**to,** à).

adaptable [adaptabl] *adj* adaptable, flexible.

adaptateur, -trice [adaptatœr, -tris] **1** *nm* **(a)** *Él MecE Phot Ordinat* adapter; *Ordinat* **a. graphique amélioré,** enhanced graphics adapter, EGA; **(b)** *Rad* convertor. **2** *n* adapter (*of book for film etc*).

adaptation [adaptɑsjɔ̃] *nf* adaptation, adjustment, accommodation (**à,** to); *Rad* matching; **faculté d'a.,** adaptability; **a. d'une nouvelle au théâtre/pour la télévision,** adaptation of a short story for the stage/for television; **faire une nouvelle a. de 'Macbeth',** to do a new adaptation of 'Macbeth'.

adapter [adapte] **1** *vt* **(a) a. qch à qch,** to fit *or* adjust sth to sth; to adapt sth to sth, to make sth suitable for sth; **a. un règlement à un cas personnel,** to adapt a rule to (fit) individual circumstances; **est-ce vraiment adapté à la situation?,** is it really suitable for the situation?; **a. un tube à un autre,** to make one tube fit another; **a. son emploi du temps à un programme de travail,** to adapt *or* adjust one's timetable to fit in with a work schedule; **a. un roman à la scène,** to adapt a novel for the stage; **(b)** *Rad* to match. **2 s'adapter** *vpr* to adapt, to adjust; **la prise s'adapte à toutes les télévisions,** the plug fits all types of television; **s'a. aux conditions nouvelles,** to adapt (oneself) *or* adjust to new conditions; **il sait s'a.,** he's very adaptable *or* flexible.

A.D.A.V. [adav] *nm* (*abrév* **avion à décollage et atterrissage verticaux**) VTOL.

addenda [adɛ̃da] *nm inv* addendum (**à,** to).

additif, -ive [aditif, -iv] **1** *adj* additive. **2** *nm* **(a)** supplement, addition; **a. à un budget,** addition to a budget; **(b)** *Ch etc* additive; **sans additifs,** additive free.

addition [adisjɔ̃] *nf* **(a)** (*fait d'ajouter*) addition, adding (to); (*pour faire un total*) adding up; **faire l'a. des chiffres,** to add up *or F* tot up the figures; **l'a. d'un paragraphe à un texte,** the addition *or* adding of a paragraph to a text; **l'a. de thym améliorera le ragoût,** adding some thyme will improve the stew; **(b)** (*extension*) addition, extension; **faire une a. à une maison,** to build an extension to a house; **en a. à,** in addition to; **(c)** *Math* addition; **(d)** (*in restaurant etc*) bill, *Am* check; **(e)** *Typ* marginal note.

additionnel, -elle [adisjɔnɛl] *adj* additional, extra.

additionner [adisjɔne] **1** *vt* to add (up), *F* to tot up; **a. un alcool d'un peu d'eau,** to add a little water to a drink; **lait additionné d'eau,** watered down milk; **café additionné d'eau-de-vie,** coffee laced with spirits. **2** *vi* to add (up). **3 s'additionner** *vpr* to add up; **aux longues heures de travail s'additionnent celles passées daus le métro,** along with the long working hours, there are those spent on the underground.

additionneuse [adisjɔnøz] *nf* adding machine, adder.

adducteur, -trice [adyktœr, -tris] **1** *adj Anat etc* adducent; **canal a.,** feeder canal. **2** *nm* **(a)** *Anat* adductor; **(b)** *Constr* supply main.

adduction [adyksjɔ̃] *nf* **(a)** *Anat* adduction; **(b)** *Tech* admission, intake; *Constr* **a. d'eau,** canalization; **adductions d'eau,** water supply.

adénoïde [adenɔid] *adj Méd* **végétations adénoïdes,** adenoids.

adent [adɑ̃] *nm Menuis* dovetail.

adepte [adɛpt] *n* **(a)** (*partisan*) follower, adherent; **les adeptes de la marche à pied,** walking enthusiasts; **a. du cinéma,** film fan *or* buff; **a. des ordinateurs,** computer buff; **c'est une adepte du ski,** she loves skiing; **faire des adeptes,** to attract followers *or* a following; **(b)** (*rare*) (*personne initiée*) adept, initiate.

adéquat [adekwa] *adj* **(a)** appropriate (*person, place, expression, method*); **(b)** (*suffisant*) (*montant etc*) adequate.
adhérence [aderɑ̃s] *nf* adhesion, adherence; **a. des roues (à la route),** grip of the wheels (on the road).
adhérent, -ente [aderɑ̃, -ɑ̃t] **1** *adj* adherent (**à,** to); adhesive (*substance, properties*); **substance adhérente,** sticky substance. **2** *n* member; **a. d'un parti,** member of a party; (*partisan*) supporter of a party; **carte d'adhérent,** membership card.
adhérer [adere] *vi* (**j'adhère, n. adhérons; j'adhérerai**) **(a)** to adhere, to stick, to cling (**aux doigts**/*etc*, to the fingers/*etc*); **a. à la route,** (*of wheels*) to grip the road; **(b)** to adhere, to hold, to subscribe (*to opinion, ideal etc*); **(c)** (*s'inscrire*) **a. (à un parti),** to join (a party).
adhésif, -ive [adezif, -iv] **1** *adj* adhesive, sticky; **pansement a.,** sticking plaster; **papier a.,** sticky(-backed) paper. **2** *nm* adhesive.
adhésion [adezjɔ̃] *nf* **(a)** (*fait de coller*) adhesion, sticking; (*des pneus*) grip(ping), road-holding; **force d'a.,** adhesiveness; **(b)** (*accord*) agreement, approval; **donner son a. à un projet,** to support a plan; **(c)** (*inscription*) adhesion, adherence (**à,** to); membership (*of a party*); **le nombre des adhésions augmente,** the number of new members is increasing.
ad hoc [adɔk] *adj & adv* ad hoc.
adieu, *pl* **-eux** [adjø] **1** *int* **(a)** goodbye!; **dire a. à qn,** to say goodbye to s.o.; *Fig F* **dire a. à qch,** to kiss sth goodbye; **(b)** *Région* hello!, hi!; **allez a.!, à demain,** 'bye then, see you tomorrow. **2** *nm* farewell; **faire ses adieux,** to make one's farewells, to say one's goodbyes; **faire ses adieux à qn,** to say goodbye to s.o.; **baiser d'a.,** parting *or* farewell kiss.
adipeux, -euse [adipø, -øz] *adj* adipose, fatty (*tissue etc*); **un visage pâle et a.,** a pale, bloated face.
adiposité [adipozite] *nf* adiposity.
adjacent [adʒasɑ̃] *adj* adjacent, contiguous (**à,** to); adjoining (*room*); bordering (**à,** on); *Math* **angles adjacents,** adjacent angles.
adjectif, -ive [adʒɛktif, -iv] **1** *adj* adjectival (*phrase, expression etc*). **2** *nm* adjective; **a. attribut,** predicative adjective; **a. épithète,** attributive adjective.
adjectival, -aux [adʒɛktival, -o] *adj* adjectival.
adjoindre [adʒwɛ̃dr] *v* (*conj like* **joindre**) **1** *vt* **(a) a. qch à qch,** to unite *or* associate sth with sth; **a. un mode d'emploi à un appareil,** to include *or* enclose an instruction booklet with an appliance; **(b) a. qn à qn,** to give s.o. to s.o. as an assistant; **a. qn à un comité,** to add s.o. to a committee. **2 s'adjoindre** *vpr* to engage (*assistant*); **s'a. à d'autres,** to join (in) with others.
adjoint, -ointe [adʒwɛ̃, -wɛ̃t] **1** *adj* assistant, deputy; *Can* **Sous-ministre a.,** Assistant Deputy Minister. **2** *n* assistant; **a. au maire,** deputy mayor.
adjonction [adʒɔ̃ksjɔ̃] *nf* **(a)** (*fait d'ajouter*) adding, addition; **(b)** addition (*made to a text etc*); annexe (*of hospital*).
adjudant [adʒydɑ̃] *nm* **(a)** *Mil* warrant officer class II, *US* warrant officer (junior grade); **a.-chef,** warrant officer class I, *US* chief warrant officer; **(capitaine) a.-major,** adjutant, *US* executive officer; **(b)** (*oiseau*) adjutant bird.
adjudicataire [adʒydikatɛr] *n* successful tenderer (*for a contract*); highest bidder, purchaser (*at auction*).
adjudicateur, -trice [adʒydikatœr, -tris] *n* adjudicator; awarder (*of contract etc*).
adjudication [adʒydikɑsjɔ̃] *nf* adjudication, allocation; award (*of contract*); (*vente aux enchères*) selling *or* sale by auction; **mettre qch en a.,** (*marché administratif*) to invite tenders for sth; (*aux enchères*) to put sth up for (sale by) auction; **a. forcée,** compulsory sale.
adjuger [adʒyʒe] *v* (**j'adjugeai(s); n. adjugeons**) **1** *vt* **a. qch à qn,** to award *or* to allocate sth to s.o.; (*at auction*) to knock sth down to s.o.; **une fois! deux fois! adjugé!, vendu!,** going! going! gone! **2 s'adjuger** *vpr* **s'a. qch,** to appropriate sth, to take possession of sth; **elle s'est adjugée la plus belle part,** she took the biggest share for herself.
adjuration [adʒyrasjɔ̃] *nf* entreaty, plea.
adjurer [adʒyre] *vt* **a. qn de faire qch,** to adjure *or* entreat s.o. to do sth.
adjuvant [adʒyvɑ̃] *nm* **(a)** *Méd* adjuvant; **(b)** *Ch Tech* additive (**de,** to); *Pétr* dope; **(c)** *Fig* stimulus, spur; **son exemple lui a servi d'a.,** her example acted as a spur to him.
admettre [admɛtr] *vt* (*conj like* **mettre**) **(a)** (*accueillir*) to admit (*s.o.*), to let (*s.o.*) in; **les chiens ne sont pas admis,** (*sur la porte d'un magasin etc*) no dogs; **a. qn chez soi,** to let s.o. into one's house; **être admis à l'université,** to be accepted for university; **être admis à un examen,** to pass an examination;

(b) a. qn à faire qch, to authorize *or* allow *or* permit s.o. to do sth;

(c) a. qn à siéger, to admit s.o. as a (new) member; **être admis à se faire entendre,** to be permitted *or* allowed to speak; **a. qch,** to admit *or* admit of *or* permit *or* allow sth; **il n'admet pas mes explications,** he doesn't accept my explanations; **elle n'admet pas la discussion,** she won't allow *or* permit any discussion; **cette règle n'admet aucune exception,** the rule admits of no exceptions, there can be no exceptions to the rule; **l'usage admis,** the accepted custom; **non, cela je ne l'admets pas!,** no, I don't agree with that!; **cela je ne l'admettrai pas,** I won't allow it, I'm not having it;

(d) (*reconnaître*) to admit, to acknowledge; **il admet que c'est vrai,** he admits *or* acknowledges that it is true; **admettons que j'aie tort,** assuming *or* supposing (that) I'm wrong;

(e) *Jur* **a. un appel,** to grant leave to appeal;

(f) (*laisser entrer*) to admit (*steam, petrol*); **l'essence est admise dans le moteur par ce conduit,** the petrol enters the engine through this pipe.
administrateur, -trice [administratœr, -tris] *n* **(a)** administrator; **a. foncier,** land agent; (*qui vend maisons, appartements*) estate agent; **(b)** director (*of company, bank etc*); **(c)** (*de fondation*) trustee.
administratif, -ive [administratif, -iv] *adj* administrative.
administration [administrɑsjɔ̃] *nf* **(a)** administration, direction, management (*of business etc*); governing (*of country*); **conseil d'a.,** board of directors; **elle a confié l'a. de son affaire à des collaborateurs,** she entrusted the handling of her business to colleagues; **mauvaise a.,** mismanagement (*of company*);

(b) (*ensemble des directeurs*) board of directors; governing body (*of institution*); **l'a. est en délibération,** the board is meeting;

(c) (*service public*) government service; (*fonctionnaires*) authorities, officials; **entrer dans l'a.,** to become a civil servant; **l'a. des Eaux et Forêts,** *Br* ≈ the Forestry Commission; **a. publique, l'A.,** ≈ the Civil Service;

(d) administering, dispensing (*of justice, sacrament etc*); administering (*of medicine*); **l'a. des médicaments a lieu tous les matins,** medication is handed out every morning.
administré, -ée [administre] *n* citizen.
administrer [administre] *vt* **(a)** to administer, to manage (*business, estate*); to conduct (*business*); to govern (*country*); **(b)** to dispense (*justice*); *Rel* to administer (*sacraments*); **a. un remède à un malade,** to administer medication to a patient; **je vais lui a. une bonne correction,** I'm going to give him *or* her a good hiding; **(c)** *Jur* **a. des preuves,** to produce proofs.
admirable [admirabl] *adj* admirable, wonderful; **elle a été a. de courage/volonté,** she showed admirable courage/willpower; **quel temps a.!,** what glorious weather!
admirablement [admirabləmɑ̃] *adv* admirably, wonderfully, perfectly.
admirateur, -trice [admiratœr, -tris] **1** *adj* admiring. **2** *n* admirer; fan (*of pop star etc*).
admiratif, -ive [admiratif, -iv] *adj* admiring (*gesture etc*).
admiration [admirɑsjɔ̃] *nf* admiration; **avoir de l'a. pour qn,** to admire s.o., to be full of *or* filled with admiration for s.o.; **être en a. devant qch,** to be filled with admiration for sth; **il est en a. devant sa fille,** he is full of *or* filled with admiration for his daughter; **tu fais l'a. de plus d'un,** many people admire you.
admirer [admire] *vt* to admire; **admiré de tous,** admired by all.
admis, -ise [admi, -iz] **1** *adj* **(a)** (*reçu*) accepted; **être a. à un club,** to be admitted to a club; **être a. à un concours,** to pass a competitive examination; **(b)** (*autorisé à entrer*) admitted, allowed (in); **(c)** (*accepté*) allowed, acceptable. **2** *n Univ* successful candidate (*at an exam*).
admissibilité [admisibilite] *nf* admissibility; (*à un emploi*) eligibility; *Scol* **épreuves d'a. (à l'examen oral),** written examination.
admissible [admisibl] *adj* admissible, allowable (*excuse, proof, conduct*); *Jur* (*preuve*) admissible; **a. à un emploi,** eligible for a job; *Scol* **(candidats) admissibles,** candidates who have qualified for the oral examination.
admission [admisjɔ̃] *nf* **(a)** admission (**à, dans,** to); **a. à un club,** admission to a club; **cotisation d'a.,** entrance *or*

admission fee; **(b)** entry *(of goods)*; **a. en franchise,** duty-free entry; **(c)** *(entrée)* intake; **période d'a.,** induction stroke; **soupape d'a.,** inlet valve; **(d)** *Bourse* **a. à la cote,** admission to quotation; **(e)** *Univ* pass; **le nombre des admissions à un concours,** the number of passes *or* successful candidates at a competitive examination.
admixtion [admiksjɔ̃] *nf* admixture **(à,** with).
admonestation [admɔnɛstasjɔ̃] *nf* admonishing.
admonester [admɔnɛste] *vt* to admonish.
admonition [admɔnisjɔ̃] *nf* admonition.
A.D.N. [adeɛn] *nm (abrév* **acide désoxyribonucléique)** DNA.
ado [ado] *n F (adolescent)* teenager.
adobe [adɔb] *nm (brick, house)* adobe.
adolescence [adɔlesɑ̃s] *nf* adolescence, youth, teenage years, *F* teens.
adolescent, -ente [adɔlesɑ̃, -ɑ̃t] **1** *adj* adolescent, *F* teenage. **2** *n* adolescent, *F* teenager; *(jeune homme)* youth; *f* girl (in her teens).
adon [adɔ̃] *nm Can F* coincidence.
adonis [adɔnis] *nm* **(a)** *(bel homme)* Adonis; **(b)** *(insecte)* adonis.
Adonis [adɔnis] *nm Myth* Adonis.
adonner (s') [sadɔne] *vpr* **s'a. à qch,** to give oneself up to sth; **s'a. à l'étude,** to devote oneself to study; **s'a. à une profession,** to take up a profession; **s'a. à la boisson,** to take to drink.
adoptant, -ante [adɔptɑ̃, -ɑ̃t] *n* adoptive parent.
adopté, -ée [adɔpte] *adj & n* adopted (child).
adopter [adɔpte] *vt* **(a)** *(prendre sous sa tutelle)* to adopt *(a child)*; *Fig* **nous l'avons adopté comme un fils,** we treated him like a son; **a. qn pour ami,** to choose s.o. as a friend, to befriend s.o.; **(b)** *(choisir)* **a. un nom,** to adopt *or* assume a name; **a. une cause,** to adopt *or* take up *or* embrace a cause; **(c) a. un projet de loi/une résolution,** to adopt *or* pass *or* carry a bill/a resolution; **adopté à l'unanimité,** carried unanimously.
adoptif, -ive [adɔptif, -iv] *adj* adopted *(child, country)*; adoptive *(parent)*.
adoption [adɔpsjɔ̃] *nf* adoption *(of child, proposal, idea, fashion)*; *Parl* adoption, passage, carrying *(of bill)*; **mon pays d'a.,** my country of adoption, my adopted country.
adorable [adɔrabl] *adj* adorable, charming, delightful; **vous êtes a. dans cette robe,** you look charming in that dress.
adorablement [adɔrabləmɑ̃] *adv* adorably, delightfully.
adorateur, -trice [adɔratœr, -tris] *n* **(a)** *(d'une religion)* worshipper; **(b)** *(d'un chanteur)* ardent admirer, *F* fan; *(d'une femme)* admirer.
adoration [adɔrasjɔ̃] *nf* **(a)** adoration, worship *(of a god)*; **(b)** *(attachement très profond)* profound admiration **(de,** for); **aimer qn à l'a.,** to adore *or* worship s.o.; **être en a. devant son bébé,** to worship one's baby.
adorer [adɔre] *vt* **(a)** to adore, to worship *(a god)*; **(b)** to adore, to be passionately fond of *(s.o., sth)*; to idolize *(movie star, boyfriend etc)*; **j'adore monter à cheval,** I adore *or* love riding.
adossé [adose] *adj* **(a)** *(dos contre dos)* back to back; **(b) a. à qch,** *(personne)* with one's back against sth, leaning against sth; *(édifice etc)* backed on to sth.
adosser [adose] **1** *vt* **(a)** to place *(two things)* back to back; **(b) a. qch à** *ou* **contre qch,** to place *or* lean *or* rest sth (with its back) against sth; to put *(wardrobe, chair etc)* with its back against sth. **2 s'adosser** *vpr* **s'a. à** *ou* **contre qch,** to lean (up) against sth; **le village s'adosse à la colline,** the village is built against the hillside.
adouber [adube] *vt* **(a)** *Échecs* to adjust *(a piece)*; **(b)** *Arch* to dub *(a knight)*.
adoucir [adusir] **1** *vt* **(a)** to soften *(voice, water, fabric, skin)*; to tone down *(contrast, colour)*; to subdue *(light, one's voice)*; to sweeten *(drink, taste)*;
(b) *(tempérer)* to alleviate, to relieve, to ease *(pain, sorrow etc)*; to mitigate *(bad effects)*; to calm *(fears)*; to allay *(suspicions)*; **a. une situation tendue,** to ease *or* alleviate a tense situation; *Prov* **la musique adoucit les mœurs,** music hath charms to soothe the savage breast;
(c) to pacify, to mollify *(s.o.)*;
(d) to smooth *(metal, wood etc)*; to smooth off *(an angle)*; to (rough-)polish *(glass)*;
(e) *Métal* to temper; to soften *(cast iron)*.
2 s'adoucir *vpr* **(a)** *(of voice)* to grow softer, to soften, to mellow;
(b) *(of weather)* to grow milder;
(c) *(of pain)* to decrease;
(d) *(of character)* to mellow; **il s'est adouci avec l'âge,** he has mellowed with age; **ce cognac s'adoucit avec le temps,** this brandy mellows with age.
adoucissage [adusisaʒ] *nm* **(a)** *Métal* tempering; softening *(of cast iron)*; **(b)** *(de glace, de marbre)* polishing; **(c)** toning down *(of colours)*.
adoucissant [adusisɑ̃] **1** *adj* softening; **crème adoucissante pour les mains,** hand cream; **produit a. pour le linge,** fabric softener. **2** *nm (pour la peau)* skin cream; *(pour le linge)* fabric softener.
adoucissement [adusismɑ̃] *nm* **(a)** softening *(of voice etc)*; calming *(of temper)*; **(b)** alleviation *(of pain etc)*; **(c)** smoothing *(of surfaces, angles)*; **(d)** sweetening; *(de l'eau)* (water) softening; **(e)** *Métal* annealing.
adoucisseur [adusisœr] *nm* (water) softener.
ad(r). *abrév* **adresse**.
adrénaline [adrenalin] *nf Méd* adrenalin(e).
adresse [adrɛs] *nf* **(a)** address; **nom, profession et a.,** name, address and occupation; **nous avons échangé nos adresses,** we exchanged addresses; **carnet d'adresses,** address book; *Fig* **tu te trompes d'a.,** you've come to the wrong person; **il m'a donné une bonne a.,** *(of restaurant, good shop etc)* he recommended a restaurant *or* a shop *etc*; **inconnu à cette a.,** not known at this address; **une observation à votre a.,** a remark aimed at *or* meant for you; **à l'a. de,** for the benefit of; **a. télégraphique,** telegraph address; *Ordinat* **a. absolue,** absolute *or* specific address; *Ordinat* **a. de mémoire,** memory location; **(b)** (formal) address *(to an assembly)*; **(c)** *(habileté)* skill, dexterity; *(savoir faire)* tact, diplomacy; **tours d'a.,** tricks, sleight of hand; **dénué d'a.,** tactless, bungling; **il lui faudra une sacrée a. pour se tirer de cette situation,** he'll have to be damn clever to get out of this situation.
adresser [adrese] **1** *vt* **(a)** to address *(letter etc)*; **lettre mal adressée,** incorrectly addressed letter; **(b)** *(envoyer)* to send, to refer *(s.o.)* to *(s.o.)*; **on m'a adressé à vous,** I have been recommended to come and see you; I have been referred to you *(par un médecin etc)*; **le médecin m'a adressé à un spécialiste,** the doctor sent *or* referred me to a specialist; **(c)** to address, to aim *(remarks etc)*; **cette remarque a été adressée à Martin,** this remark was aimed at *or* meant for Martin; **a. un sourire à qn,** to smile at s.o. **2 s'adresser** *vpr* **(a) s'a. à qn,** to apply to s.o.; *(en parlant)* to speak to s.o.; **s.'a. ici,** apply within; *(pour des renseignements)* enquire within; **adressez-vous à l'agent,** ask the policeman; **(b) s'a. à l'imagination/au bon sens de qn,** to appeal to s.o.'s imagination/common sense; **le livre s'adresse aux enfants,** the book is aimed at children.
Adriatique [adriatik] **1** *adj* Adriatic. **2** *nf* **l'A.,** the Adriatic.
Adrien [adriɛ̃] *nm* Adrian; *Rom Hist* Hadrian.
adroit [adrwa] *adj* **(a)** *(habile)* dexterous, deft, skilful, handy; **être a. de ses mains,** to be clever *or* good with one's hands; **phrase adroite,** neatly turned phrase, neat turn of phrase; **(b)** shrewd, adroit *(answer, diplomat)*.
adroitement [adrwatmɑ̃] *adv* skilfully, cleverly *(made)*; *(to judge)* shrewdly; *(to finish)* neatly; **se défendre a.,** to defend oneself adroitly.
adr. tél. *abrév* **adresse télégraphique**.
adsorber [atsɔrbe] *vt Phys* to adsorb.
adsorption [atsɔrpsjɔ̃] *nf Phys* adsorption.
adulateur, -trice [adylatœr, -tris] *n Litt* adulator; *(flatteur)* sycophant.
adulation [adylasjɔ̃] *nf Arch* adulation, flattery **(de,** of); *Péj* sycophancy.
aduler [adyle] *vt* to idolize.
adulte [adylt] **1** *adj* adult, grown-up *(person)*; **l'âge a.,** adulthood; **plante/animal a.,** mature *or* fully-grown plant/animal; **ça n'est pas très a. cette réaction,** that is not a very mature way to react. **2** *n* adult, grown-up.
adultère[1] [adyltɛr] **1** *adj* adulterous. **2** *n* adulterer, *f* adulteress.
adultère[2] *nm* adultery; **commettre un a.,** to commit adultery.
adultérin, -ine [adylterɛ̃, -in] *n Jur* child conceived in adultery, adulterine.
ad valorem [advalɔrɛm] *adj & adv* **droits ad v.,** ad valorem duty.
advenir [advənir] *v impers (conj like* **venir**; *used only in the third person)* to occur, to happen; *Litt* to befall, to chance; **or, il advint que ...,** now it came to pass that ...; **quoi qu'il advienne, advienne que pourra,** come what may.
adventice [advɑ̃tis] *adj (imprévu)* adventitious; *(sans cause ou but précis)* casual.
adventif, -ive [advɑ̃tif, -iv] *adj Bot* adventitious *(root*

etc); *Géol* parasitic (*cone*).
adverbe [advɛrb] *nm* adverb; **a. de manière/de temps,** adverb of manner/time.
adverbial, -aux [advɛrbjal, -o] *adj* adverbial; **locution adverbiale,** adverbial phrase.
adversaire [advɛrsɛr] *n* adversary, opponent; (*dans un conflit, une guerre*) enemy.
adverse [advɛrs] *adj* (*hostile*) adverse, unfortunate, unfavourable; **fortune a.,** bad luck; **critique a.,** unfavourable criticism; *Jur* **la partie a.,** the opposing party, the other side.
adversité [advɛrsite] *nf Litt* **(a)** (*sort*) adversity, adverse circumstances; **(b)** (*malheur*) misfortune, trial.
ad vitam aeternam [advitametɛrnam] *adv F* from here to eternity, till kingdom come.
A.E.L.E. [aəɛlə] *nf* (*abrév* **Association européenne de libre-échange**) EFTA.
aérage [aeraʒ] *nm* **(a)** ventilation (*of room etc*); airing (*of room, clothes etc*); **(b)** aeration (*of water*).
aérateur [aeratœr] *nm* ventilator.
aération [aerasjɔ̃] *nf* = **AÉRAGE.**
aérer [aere] *v* (**j'aère, n. aérons; j'aérerai**) **1** *vt* **(a)** to ventilate (*mine*); to air (*room, linen*); **(b)** to aerate (*water*); **(c)** (*rendre moins dense*) to lighten (*un texte, un exposé etc*). **2 s'aérer** *vpr* to get some fresh air; **avoir besoin de s'a.,** to need some fresh air *or* a breath of fresh air.
aérien, -ienne [aerjɛ̃, -jɛn] *adj* **(a)** aerial (*plant, root*); atmospheric (*phenomenon etc*); *Mil* **les forces aériennes,** the air force; **défense aérienne,** air defence; **attaque aérienne,** air raid; *Av* **ligne aérienne,** airline; **poste aérienne,** air mail; **(b)** (light and) airy (*texture etc*); **marcher d'un pas a.,** to have a spring in one's step; **(c)** overhead (*cable etc*); elevated (*railway*).
aérium [aerjɔm] *nm* (open air) sanatorium.
aéro- [aerɔ] *préf* aero-.
aérobic [aerɔbik] *nm* aerobics; **professeur/cours d'a.,** aerobics teacher/class.
aérocâble [aerɔkɑbl] *nm* cableway.
aéro-club [aerɔklœb] *nm* flying club, aero club; (*pl aéro-clubs*).
aérodrome [aerɔdrom] *nm* aerodrome, airfield, *US* airdrome.
aérodynamique [aerɔdinamik] **1** *adj* aerodynamic; streamlined (*shape, car*). **2** *nf* aerodynamics.
aérodyne [aerɔdin] *nm* aerodyne.
aérofrein [aerɔfrɛ̃] *nm* air brake.
aérogare [aerɔgar] *nf* air terminal.
aéroglisseur [aerɔglisœr] *nm* hovercraft.
aérogramme [aerɔgram] *nm* air mail letter.
aérographe [aerɔgraf] *nf* airbrush.
aéromodélisme [aerɔmɔdelism] *nm* model aircraft making.
aéromoteur [aerɔmɔtœr] *nm* wind engine.
aéronaute [aerɔnot] *n* aeronaut.
aéronautique [aerɔnotik] **1** *adj* aeronautic(al). **2** *nf* aeronautics; **ingénieur d'a.,** aeronautical engineer.
aéronaval, -ale, -als [aerɔnaval] **1** *adj* air and sea (*forces etc*). **2** *nf* **l'Aéronavale,** ≈ *Br* the Fleet Air Arm, *US* the Naval Air Service.
aéronef [aerɔnɛf] *nm* aircraft; (*dirigeable*) airship.
aérophagie [aerɔfaʒi] *nf* **avoir** *ou* **faire de l'a.,** to suffer from flatulence.
aérophare [aerɔfar] *nm Av* air *or* aerial beacon.
aérophotographie [aerɔfɔgrafi] *nf* aerial photography.
aéroplane [aerɔplan] *nm Vieilli* aeroplane, *US* airplane.
aéroport [aerɔpɔr] *nm* airport.
aéroporté [aerɔpɔrte] *adj* airborne.
aéroportuaire [aerɔpɔrtɥɛr] *adj* (*équipement, installations etc*) airport.
aéropostal, -ale, -aux [aerɔpɔstal, -o] **1** *adj* airmail. **2** *nf Hist* **l'Aéropostale,** the (French) airmail service.
aéroroute [aerɔrut] *nf Av* air route, airway.
aérosol [aerɔsɔl] **1** *nm* aerosol. **2** *adj inv* aerosol; **bombe a.,** aerosol (can).
aérospatial, -aux [aerɔspasjal, -o] *adj* aerospace (*equipment etc*).
aérostat [aerɔsta] *nm* balloon, aerostat.
aérostatique [aerɔstatik] **1** *adj* aerostatic. **2** *nf* aerostatics.
aérostier [aerɔstje] *nm* balloonist.
Aérotrain ® [aerɔtrɛ̃] *nm* hovertrain.
aérotransporter [aerɔtrɑ̃spɔrte] *vt* to transport *or* carry by air, to fly (*goods, passengers*).
A.F. *abrév* **(a) allocations familiales; (b) Air France.**
affabilité [afabilite] *nf* graciousness, affability (**avec, envers,** to, towards).
affable [afabl] *adj* gracious, affable (**à, envers, avec,** to, towards, with).
affablement [afabləmɑ̃] *adv* graciously, affably.
affabulateur, -trice [afabylatœr, -tris] **1** *adj* **qu'est-ce que tu peux être a.,** you're too fond of telling tall stories. **2** *n* fibber, storyteller.
affabulation [afabylɑsjɔ̃] *nf* fabrication(s), distortion(s); **les résultats publiés ne sont qu'une a.,** the published results are pure invention.
affabuler [afabyle] *vi* to invent things, to make things up.
affadir [afadir] **1** *vt* **(a)** to make (*food etc*) insipid *or* tasteless; **(b)** to make (*sth*) dull *or* uninteresting. **2 s'affadir** *vpr* to become insipid.
affaiblir [afeblir] **1** *vt* **(a)** (*réduire*) to lessen, to reduce; **a. le courage de qn,** to dampen s.o.'s courage; *Phot* **a. un cliché,** to reduce (the contrasts of) a negative; **(b)** (*d'une maladie*) to weaken, *Fml* to enfeeble, to debilitate; **affaibli par la maladie,** weakened by illness. **2 s'affaiblir** *vpr* **(a)** (*devenir faible*) to grow *or* become weak(er) *or* feeble(r), to lose one's strength; (*of sound*) to become *or* grow fainter; **mes forces s'affaiblissaient,** my strength was failing; **la tempête s'affaiblit,** the storm is abating; **(b)** (*s'atténuer*) **le sens du mot s'affaiblit au XVIe,** the word took on a weaker meaning in the 16th century.
affaiblissement [afeblismɑ̃] *nm* **(a)** weakening; diminution (*of strength etc*); **(b)** (*faiblesse*) weakness; *Méd* debility.
affaire [afɛr] *nf* **(a)** business, concern; **ce n'est pas votre a.,** it's not *or* it's none of your business; **occupez-vous de vos affaires,** mind your own business; **ça c'est mon a.,** that's my business; (*je m'en occupe*) (you can) leave that to me; **mettre le nez dans les affaires de qn,** to stick one's nose into s.o.'s business; **ce n'est pas l'a. de tout le monde,** not everybody can do that; **c'est l'a. d'un médecin,** it's a case for a doctor; **a. d'argent,** money matter; **a. de cœur,** love affair; **a. d'honneur,** duel; **a. de conscience,** matter of conscience; **a. difficile,** difficult question *or* matter; **c'est (une) a. de goût,** it's a matter *or* question of taste; **ce n'est que l'a. d'un instant,** it won't take a minute; **ça, c'est une autre a.,** that's another question *or* another matter; **avoir a. à,** to deal with; **nous avons eu a. à un homme charmant,** we were dealt with by a charming man; **s'il continue à mentir, il aura a. à moi!** if he keeps on lying, he'll have me to contend with *or* to answer to!;
(b) (*compte*) **ça fait** *ou* **c'est juste mon a.,** that's just what I need *or* what I was looking for; **cela ne fera pas l'a.,** that won't do; **il fera votre a.,** he's just the man for you; **faire son a. à qn,** *F* to give s.o. what he deserves *or* what he's asking for *or* what was coming to him; *Arg* to do s.o. in, to bump s.o. off;
(c) (*ennui*) (difficult *or* serious) business; **c'est une sale a.,** it's a nasty business; **il cherche à étouffer l'a.,** he's trying to hush up the whole affair; **ce n'est pas une a.,** it's nothing serious; **ce n'est pas une petite a., c'est toute une a.,** it's quite a business; it's quite a proposition; **je n'en fais pas une a.,** I'm not making an issue of it; **en voilà une a.!,** here's a nice mess *or* a pretty kettle of fish!; (*ce n'était pas la peine*) it's a lot of fuss about nothing!; **la belle a.!,** is THAT all?, so what?; **se tirer d'a.,** to get out of a difficulty; **se faire une a. de qch,** to get all worked up about sth; *Pol* **l'a. de Suez,** the Suez Crisis; **l'a. est encore chaude,** (*toute la presse en parle*) it's still very much in the news; it's still hot news;
(d) (*transaction*) (business) transaction, deal; (*achat à bon marché*) bargain; **une bonne a.,** a good deal; **une mauvaise a.,** a bad bargain; **on fait des affaires dans ce magasin,** you get good bagains in this shop; **être dur en affaires,** to be a hard-headed businessman *or* woman; **ils font des affaires d'or,** they're coining it, they're making money hand over fist, they're raking it in; **faire des affaires avec qn,** to do business with s.o.; **il est sur une a. avec le Mozambique,** he's doing a deal with Mozambique; **chiffre d'affaires,** turnover; **homme d'affaires,** businessman; **femme d'affaires,** businesswoman; **voyage d'affaires,** business trip; **déjeuner d'affaires,** business *or* working lunch; **droit des affaires,** corporate law; **avocat d'affaires,** corporate lawyer;
(e) les affaires, business; **comment vont les affaires?,** how's business?; **parler affaires,** to talk business *or F* shop; **les affaires sont les affaires et on ne fait de cadeaux à personne,** business is business and nobody gets any favours *or* anything free; *Fig* **où en sont tes affaires?,** how's your love life?;

(f) (*entreprise*) firm, business; **une grosse a.,** a large firm;

(g) **affaires,** possessions, belongings, things; **ranger ses affaires,** to put one's things away, to tidy up one's things; **mettre de l'ordre dans ses affaires,** to put one's affairs *or* house in order; **mets tes petites affaires dans ce sac,** put your small things in this bag;

(h) *Pol* **les affaires de l'État,** affairs of State; **ce n'est pas une a. d'État,** it's of no great importance; **le Ministère des Affaires étrangères,** ≈ *Br* the Foreign (and Commonwealth) Office, *US* the State Department; *Can* **Ministère des Affaires Extérieures,** External Affairs Department;

(i) *Jur* case, lawsuit; **a. civile,** civil action; **qui plaide l'a.?,** who's defending (the case)?; *Hist* **l'a. Dreyfus,** the Dreyfus case *or* affair; **l'a. de la rue Coupe-Oreilles,** the Coupe-Oreilles Street incident; (*homicide*) the Coupe-Oreilles Street murder; **être sur une a.,** to be on a case.

affairé [afere] *adj* busy; **ils entraient et sortaient d'un air a.,** they were bustling in and out.

affairement [afɛrmɑ̃] *nm* bustle, bustling activity.

affairer (s') [safere] *vpr* to be busy, to busy oneself; **s'a. autour de qn,** to fuss (a)round s.o.; **s'a. à tout remettre en place,** to be busy tidying up.

affairiste [aferist] *n Péj* speculator, *F* get-rich-quick type; **ce n'est qu'un a.,** he thinks of nothing but making money *or* getting rich *or Am* making a fast buck.

affaissement [afɛsmɑ̃] *nm* (a) subsidence, sinking; collapse (*of floor, roof*); settling (*of foundation*); sagging (*of floor, beam*); (b) (*accablement*) depression, dejection, despondency; *Méd* prostration, collapse; **l'a. de l'enthousiasme,** the waning of enthusiasm; **l'a. du moral,** the collapse of morale.

affaisser (s') [safɛse] *vpr* (a) (*of thing*) to subside, to give way; (*of roof, floor*) to cave in, to collapse; (*of material*) to give, to yield; (*of beam etc*) to sag; (*of earth*) to settle; (b) (*tomber, s'écrouler*) to sink down *or* back (*in chair*); to collapse (*from exhaustion etc*); (c) *Fig Litt* (*décliner*) to decline, to sink; **il s'affaisse de jour en jour,** he is gradually declining *or* sinking.

affaler [afale] 1 *vt* to lower (*object*); *Nau* (*from below*) to haul down (*rope*); (*from above*) to pay down (*rope*); **affale!,** lower away!; **affalez la grande voile!,** lower the mainsail! 2 **s'affaler** *vpr* to collapse; **s'a. par terre,** to sink to the ground; **s'a. dans un fauteuil,** to sink *or F* flop into an armchair.

affamant [afamɑ̃] *adj* **régime a.,** starvation diet.

affamé, -ée [afame] 1 *adj* hungry, *F* starving, ravenous, famished; (*mourant de faim*) starving; **regarder qch d'un œil a.,** to look hungrily at sth. 2 *n* **les affamés,** the hungry, the starving.

affamer [afame] *vt* to starve (*s.o.*).

affectation [afɛktɑsjɔ̃] *nf* (a) *Péj* (*pose*) affectation, affectedness; (*simulacre*) pretence, affectation; **être sans a.,** to be without affectation, to be unaffected; **sans a.,** (*dire etc qch*) without affectation, unaffectedly; **avec une a. de générosité,** with a show of generosity; (b) (*fait de désigner*) assignment, allocation, allotment (*of sth*); *Fin* **a. de fonds,** appropriation of funds; **a. hypothécaire,** mortgage charge; (c) *Mil etc* assignment, posting; **avoir une** *ou* **être en a. spéciale,** ≈ to be in a reserved occupation.

affecté [afɛkte] *adj Péj* affected (*person, manner*).

affecter [afɛkte] 1 *vt* (a) (*désigner*) to assign (*sth*) (**à**, to); to earmark (*sth*), to allocate (*sth*), to set (*sth*) apart (**à**, for); **a. qn à un service,** to assign *or* appoint s.o. to a department;

(b) *Mil* to detail, to post, to draft (*soldier, detachment to a particular service*); *Nau* **être affecté à un navire,** to be posted to a ship;

(c) (*feindre*) to feign, to affect; **a. de faire qch,** to pretend to do sth; **a. la désinvolture la plus complète,** to feign *or* affect a totally casual attitude;

(d) (*toucher*) to affect, to move, to touch (*s.o.*); **vivement affecté de la nouvelle,** greatly moved by the news;

(e) (*agir sur*) to affect, to have an effect on (*career, health etc*); **la grève a affecté plusieurs usines,** the strike has affected *or* hit several factories; **les pluies qui affectent le nord de l'Europe,** the rain affecting *or* over northern Europe;

(f) to assume, to take on (*shape, colour etc*);

(g) *Vieilli* (*aimer*) to have a partiality for (*sth*); (*s'en servir beaucoup*) to make great use of (*sth*).

2 **s'affecter** *vpr* to be troubled *or* unsettled; **elle s'affecte de la moindre dispute,** she is upset by the slightest argument.

affectif, -ive [afɛktif, -iv] *adj* affective, emotional; emotive (*use of a word etc*); **sa vie affective,** his emotional life.

affection [afɛksjɔ̃] *nf* (a) (*attachement*) affection, fondness, attachment, liking (**pour,** for); **prendre qn en a.,** to become attached to *or* fond of s.o.; **terme d'a.,** term of affection; **avoir de l'a. pour qn,** to feel *or* have affection for s.o., to be fond of s.o.; **avec a.,** affectionately; (b) *Méd* disease, complaint, ailment.

affectionné [afɛksjɔne] *adj* affectionate, loving; **votre cousin(e) affectionné(e),** (*dans une lettre*) your affectionate cousin.

affectionner [afɛksjɔne] *vt* to be attached to, to be fond of (*friend, acquaintance etc*); to like (*dogs*); **affectionné de tous,** loved by all; **le genre de petits plats qu'il affectionne,** the type of food he likes *or* is fond of.

affectivité [afɛktivite] *nf* affectivity.

affectueusement [afɛktɥøzmɑ̃] *adv* affectionately; **a. à tous,** (*dans une lettre*) love to all.

affectueux, -euse [afɛktɥø, -øz] *adj* affectionate, loving.

afférent [aferɑ̃] *adj* (a) *Jur* **la part afférente à,** the portion accruing to; (b) **a. à,** relating to, pertaining to; (c) *Méd* afferent.

affermer [afɛrme] *vt* to lease, to rent (*farm etc*); to take (*land etc*) on lease.

affermir [afɛrmir] *vt* (a) to strengthen, to make firm (*foundations etc*); (b) to strengthen, to consolidate (*power, belief*); to improve (*health*); **a. qn dans sa position,** to strengthen *or* consolidate s.o. in his *or* her position. 2 **s'affermir** *vpr* to become stronger, to strengthen; (*of cement*) to harden; (*of jelly*) to set.

affermissement [afɛrmismɑ̃] *nm* strengthening; consolidation (*of power etc*); hardening (*of cement*); setting (*of jelly*).

affichage [afiʃaʒ] *nm* (a) billsticking, billposting; **tableau** *ou* **panneau d'a.,** notice board, *Am* bulletin board; (*dans aéroport, gare*) arrivals and departures (board); (b) flaunting (*of opinions etc*); (c) *Ordinat* display; **a. à cristaux liquides,** liquid crystal display; **horloge/montre à a. digital** *ou* **numérique,** digital clock/watch; (d) *Av* visual indicator.

affiche [afiʃ] *nf* poster, bill; (*de protestation*) placard; (*de publicité*) advertisement; **a. à la main,** handbill; **panneau à affiches,** (advertisement) hoarding, *Am* billboard; **a. électorale,** election poster; **des affiches publicitaires,** advertisements; **a. de théâtre,** playbill; **la pièce a tenu l'a.** *ou* **est restée à l'a. pendant deux ans,** the play ran for two years; **tenir longtemps l'a.,** to have a long run; **mettre à l'a.,** to bill; **quitter l'a.,** to close; **être en tête d'a.,** to head *or* be top of the bill.

afficher [afiʃe] 1 *vt* (a) to stick (up), to post (up) (*bills, notices*); **a. une vente,** to advertise a sale; **défense d'a.,** stick *or Am* post no bills; (b) (*montrer, étaler*) to parade, to show off, to flaunt, to make a display of (*sth*); *Ordinat* to display (*a message*) **a. son savoir,** to air *or* flaunt one's knowledge; **a. son ignorance,** to display *or* expose *or* betray one's ignorance; **a. sa pauvreté,** to plead poverty; **derrière cette nonchalance affichée,** behind this outwardly casual air; **a. son nouveau amant,** to flaunt *or* show off *or* parade one's latest lover; *Com* **a. un déficit/un excédent,** to show a deficit/a surplus. 2 **s'afficher** *vpr* to show off, to draw attention to oneself; **elle s'affiche avec un homme plus âgé qu'elle,** she's flaunting herself with an older man.

affichette [afiʃɛt] *nf* small poster *or* advertisement.

afficheur [afiʃœr] *nm* billsticker, billposter.

affichiste [afiʃist] *n* poster designer.

affidavit [afidavit] *nm Jur* affidavit.

affidé, -ée [afide] *n Péj* accomplice.

affilage [afilɑʒ] *nm* sharpening, whetting.

affilée (d') [dafile] *adv* **cinq heures d'a.,** five hours at a stretch *or* at a time *or* on end; **lire vingt chapitres d'a.,** to read twenty chapters in one go *or* straight off *or* at one sitting.

affiler [afile] *vt* to sharpen, to whet, to put an edge on (*blade etc*); *Fig* **avoir la langue bien affilée,** (*être méchant*) to have a wicked *or* nasty tongue.

affiliation [afiljɑsjɔ̃] *nf* affiliation; **l'a. d'un membre à un club,** a member's affiliation to a club.

affilié, -ée [afilje] 1 *adj* affiliated. 2 *n* affiliated member.

affilier [afilje] 1 *vt* to affiliate (**à**, to, with). 2 **s'affilier** *vpr* to join; (*of organization*) to affiliate; **s'a. à un parti,** to join a party.

affiloir [afilwar] *nm* oilstone; (*instrument*) knife sharpener,

steel.
affiloire [afilwar] *nf* oilstone.
affinage [afinaʒ] *nm Métal* refining; smelting (*of iron, steel*); maturing (*of wine, cheese*).
affinement [afinmɑ̃] *nm* refinement.
affiner [afine] **1** *vt* **(a)** (*purifier*) to improve, to refine, to make better; to refine (*iron, gold*); to ripen, to mature (*cheese etc*); **(b)** to sharpen (*the intelligence*); **ces livres lui ont affiné le jugement,** these books have sharpened his judgment. **2 s'affiner** *vpr* **(a)** (*d'une personne*) to become more refined; (*of features*) to become finer, to fine down; **elle s'est affinée en suivant un nouveau régime,** she has lost weight *or* slimmed down on her new diet; **(b)** (*of cheese etc*) to ripen, to mature.
affinité [afinite] *nf* **(a)** (*entre personnes*) affinity (**entre,** between); (*physique*) resemblance; (*de caractère*) similarity of character; **(b)** *Ch* attraction; **a. pour un corps,** affinity for a body.
affirmatif, -ive [afirmatif, -iv] **1** *adj* **(a)** affirmative, positive; **réponse affirmative,** affirmative answer, answer in the affirmative; **signe a.,** nod (of agreement); **(b)** assertive, positive (*person*); **il a été très a.,** he was very definite, he was quite certain in his mind. **2** *nf* **l'affirmative,** the affirmative; **dans l'affirmative,** if so, if the answer is yes, if you can *etc*; **répondre par l'affirmative,** to give an affirmative answer, to say *or* answer yes.
affirmation [afirmɑsjɔ̃] *nf* affirmation, assurance, assertion, statement; **a. trop générale,** sweeping statement; *Jur* **a. de créance,** proof of indebtedness; **a. sous serment,** affidavit; (*lors d'un procès etc*) statement on oath; **a. de soi,** self-assertion; **a. de la personnalité,** assertion of one's personality.
affirmativement [afirmativmɑ̃] *adv* in the affirmative.
affirmer [afirme] **1** *vt* **(a)** (*assurer*) to affirm (*statement, fact*); to insist, to state positively (that ...); **je n'affirmerais pas que ...,** I wouldn't swear to it that ...; **a. qch sous** *ou* **sur** *ou* **par serment,** to state sth on oath *or* on affidavit; **il affirme vous connaître,** he maintains that he knows you; **(b)** (*manifester, prouver*) to assert; **a. son autorité,** to assert one's authority, to make one's authority felt. **2 s'affirmer** *vpr* to assert oneself; (*d'un parent etc*) to assert one's authority; **beaucoup de vos observations se sont affirmées justes,** many of your observations have proved correct *or* have been confirmed.
affleurement [aflœrmɑ̃] *nm Géol* outcrop.
affleurer [aflœre] **1** *vt* to bring (*timbers etc*) to the same level; to make flush; **a. qch,** to be level *or* even *or* flush with sth. **2** *vi aussi Fig* to float *or* rise to the surface; *Géol* (*of lode*) to outcrop.
affliction [afliksjɔ̃] *nf* affliction, sorrow.
affligé, -ée [afliʒe] **1** *adj* **(a)** (*atteint*) afflicted, troubled (**de,** with); **a. de rhumatisme,** suffering from rheumatism; **(b)** (*peiné*) grieved, distressed. **2** *n* **les affligés,** the afflicted.
affligeant [afliʒɑ̃] *adj* distressing, painful (*news, sight*).
affliger [afliʒe] *v* (**j'affligeai(s)**; **n. affligeons**) **1** *vt* **(a)** (*atteindre*) to afflict (**de,** with); **(b)** (*peiner*) to pain, to distress, to grieve. **2 s'affliger** *vpr* to be grieved *or* distressed (**de qch,** about sth); **ne vous affligez pas ainsi,** don't take it so much to heart.
affluence [aflyɑ̃s] *nf* crowd (*of people*); **heures d'a.,** rush hours.
affluent [aflyɑ̃] *nm* tributary (*of river*).
affluer [aflye] *vi* (*of liquid*) to flow (**vers,** towards; **dans,** into); (*of blood*) to rush, to flow (**à,** to); **a. à** *ou* **dans un endroit,** to crowd *or* flock to a place.
afflux [afly] *nm Méd etc* rush (*of blood*); *Él* surge (*of current*); crowd (*of visitors*).
affolant [afɔlɑ̃] *adj* (*spectacle, nouvelle*) distressing, horrifying; *F* **c'est a.,** (*ce qu'elle a grandi etc*) it's frightening *or* incredible.
affolé [afɔle] *adj* **(a)** demented, frantic, panic-stricken; **il était a.,** he was scared out of his wits; **épouvante affolée,** wild *or* crazed terror; **(b)** *Tech* spinning, crazy (*compass needle*).
affolement [afɔlmɑ̃] *nm* **(a)** (*de personne*) panic, *F* flap; **voyons, pas d'a.,** come on, there's no need to panic; **(b)** perturbation, unsteadiness, spinning (*of magnetic needle*); **(c)** racing (*of engine, propeller etc*); disconnecting (*of pulley etc*).
affoler [afɔle] **1** *vt* **(a)** to madden (*s.o.*), to drive (*s.o.*) crazy *or* to distraction; to throw (*crowd*) into a panic; **(b)** to disturb, to perturb (*compass needle*); **(c)** to let (*machine*) race; to disconnect (*part of machine*). **2 s'affoler** *vpr* **(a)** (*paniquer*) to panic, to get in(to) a panic, *F* to lose one's head; **(b)** (*of compass needle*) to spin; **(c)** (*of machine*) to begin to race.
afforestation [afɔrɛstɑsjɔ̃] *nf* (re-)afforestation.
affouiller [afuje] *vt* (*of water*) to undermine, to erode, to wash away, to lay bare (*bank, foundation etc*).
affourager [afuraʒe] *vt* (**j'affourageais; n. affourageons**) to fodder (*cattle*).
affranchi, -ie [afrɑ̃ʃi] **1** *adj* (*esclave*) free(d), emancipated; *Fig* **un esprit a.,** an open mind; **un esprit a. des préjugés,** a mind free from prejudice. **2** *n* **(a)** (*esclave*) emancipated slave; **(b)** (*marginal*) free spirit.
affranchir [afrɑ̃ʃir] **1** *vt* **(a)** to free, to set free, to emancipate (*slave etc*); **a. qn/qch de qch,** to free *or* release s.o./sth from sth; **(b)** to pay the postage on (*sth*); (*tamponner*) to frank, to stamp (*letter*); **colis affranchi,** pre-paid parcel; **machine à a. (les lettres),** franking machine, franker, *US* postal meter; **(c)** *Cartes* to unblock (*suit*); **(d)** *F* (*renseigner*) **a. qn,** to put s.o. in the picture. **2 s'affranchir** *vpr* **s'a. du joug,** to cast off the yoke; **s'a. d'une habitude,** to break (oneself of) a habit; **s'a. d'idées préconçues,** to rid oneself of preconceived ideas.
affranchissement [afrɑ̃ʃismɑ̃] *nm* **(a)** emancipation, setting free (*of slave etc*); **(b)** (*de lettre*) prepayment; (*fait de tamponner*) stamping, franking; (*montant payé*) postage, carriage (*of letter, parcel etc*); **(c)** *Vieilli* release, deliverance, exemption (*from taxes, charges etc*).
affres [afr] *nfpl Litt* (*angoisse*) (spasm of) anguish; agonies, horrors (*of doubt etc*); **a. de la mort,** death throes; **a. de la faim,** pangs of hunger, hunger pangs; **découvrir toutes les a. du métier,** to discover the downside of the profession.
affrètement [afrɛtmɑ̃] *nm* chartering (*of ship*); **a. au voyage,** trip charter; **a. à temps,** time charter.
affréter [afrete] *vt* (**j'affrète, n. affrétons; j'affréterai**) to charter (*a ship, plane*); **a. un navire en travers,** to charter a ship by the bulk.
affréteur [afretœr] *nm Nau* **(a)** (*propriétaire*) freighter; **(b)** charterer, shipper.
affreusement [afrøzmɑ̃] *adv* (*en retard*) terribly, frightfully, *F* shockingly; (*blessé, torturé*) horribly; (*défiguré*) horribly, shockingly; **je suis a. coiffée,** my hair's a mess; **il parle a. mal,** his English *or* French *etc* is awful.
affreux, -euse [afrø, -øz] **1** *adj* **(a)** (*laid*) frightful, hideous, ghastly, atrocious; **un visage a.,** a horrible *or* hideous face; **il est a.,** he's terribly *or* horribly ugly; **un a. petit chapeau/chien,** a frightful *or* an ugly little hat/dog; **(b)** (*atroce*) frightful, horrible, dreadful, shocking (*news, poverty, crime etc*); **(c)** *F* (*détestable*) awful, dreadful; **mal de tête a.,** splitting headache; **qu'est-ce que ça a augmenté, c'est a.!,** it's dreadful *or* shocking how the price has gone up; **ce gamin est un a. jojo,** that child is a (frightful) little horror; **temps a.,** filthy *or* shocking weather. **2** *n* **(a)** *Mil F* white mercenary (*usu in Africa*); **(b)** *F* **c'est un a.,** he's a nasty piece of work.
affriander [afrijɑ̃de] *vt Litt* to entice, to allure.
affriolant [afrijɔlɑ̃] adj (*décolleté, vêtement*) alluring, tantalising; **ce travail n'a rien d'a.,** this work doesn't exactly fill me with enthusiasm.
affrioler [afrijɔle] *vt* to excite, to tempt.
affriquée [afrike] *nf Ling* affricate (consonant).
affront [afrɔ̃] *nm* affront, insult, *F* slap in the face; **faire** *ou* **infliger un a. à qn,** to slight s.o.; (*snober qn*) to snub s.o.; **doubler ses torts d'un a.,** to add insult to injury.
affrontement [afrɔ̃tmɑ̃] *nm* **(a)** facing, confronting, confrontation (*of enemy, danger etc*); **(b)** (*de deux choses*) joining edge to edge; *Chir* bringing into apposition.
affronter [afrɔ̃te] **1** *vt* **(a)** to face, to confront, to brave, to tackle (*s.o., sth*); **a. une épreuve avec courage,** to meet an ordeal bravely; **a. la colère de qn,** to brave the wrath of s.o.; **(b)** to join face to face *or* edge to edge; to bring together (*metal plates etc*); *Chir* to bring into apposition. **2 s'affronter** *vpr* (*d'ennemis etc*) to clash, to confront each other; *Sp* (*de deux équipes, joueurs etc*) to meet, to clash; **leurs personnalités s'affrontent constamment,** their personalities clash constantly; **deux thèses s'affrontent,** there are two conflicting theories.
affubler [afyble] *Péj* **1** *vt* **a. qn de qch,** to dress s.o. up *or* deck *or* rig s.o. out in sth. **2 s'affubler** *vpr* to rig *or* deck oneself out, to get oneself up (**de,** in).
affût [afy] *nm* **(a)** hiding place; hide (*for birdwatcher etc*); **chasse au cerf à l'a.,** deer stalking; **être** *ou* **se mettre à l'a. de,** to lie in wait for (*s.o.*); (*être vigilant*) to be on the watch *or* lookout for (*s.o., sth*); *Fig* **je suis à l'a. d'une paire de chandeliers,** I'm on the lookout for a pair of candlesticks; **il est toujours à l'a. du scandale,** he keeps

his ears open for scandal; **(b)** *Mil* carriage, mount(ing); stand, frame, rest, mounting (*of telescope etc*).

affûtage [afytaʒ] *nm* **(a)** sharpening, grinding (*of tool*); setting (*of saw*); **(b)** set of bench tools.

affûter [afyte] *vt* to grind, to sharpen, to whet (*tool*); to set (*saw*); *Courses de chevaux* **a. un cheval,** to bring a horse to the top of its form.

affûteur [afytœr] *nm* (tool)grinder, sharpener; setter (*of saws*).

affûteuse [afytøz] *nf* **(a)** sharpening machine (*for taps*); **(b)** grinding machine (*for tools*).

afghan, -ane [afgɑ̃, -an] **1** *adj* Afghan. **2** *n* **A.,** Afghan.

Afghanistan [afganistɑ̃] *nm* Afghanistan.

aficionado, -os [afisjɔnado, -os] *nm* aficionado.

afin [afɛ̃] *adv* **(a) a. de (faire qch),** (in order) to, so as to (do sth); **a. d'obtenir cette grâce,** in order to obtain this favour; **(b) a. que** + *sub*, so that, in order that; *Fml & Litt* that; **a. que les autres puissent le voir,** so that the others may see it.

AFNOR [afnɔr] *nf* (*abrév* **Association française de normalisation**) *Br* ≈ BSI; *US* ≈ ANSI.

a fortiori [afɔrsjɔri] *adv* a fortiori.

A.F.P. *abrév* **Agence France Presse.**

A.F.P.A. *abrév* **Association pour la formation professionnelle des adultes.**

africain, -aine [afrikɛ̃, -ɛn] **1** *adj* African. **2** *n* **A.,** African.

africanisation [afrikanizasjɔ̃] *nf Pol* Africanization.

africaniser [afrikanize] *vt* to Africanize.

africaniste [afrikanist] *n* student of African races and languages.

afrika(a)ns [afrikɑ̃] *nm Ling* Afrikaans.

Afrikander [afrikɑ̃dɛr] *n* Afrikaner.

Afrique [afrik] *nf* Africa; **l'A. du Nord,** North Africa.

afro [afro] *adj* Afro (*hairstyle*); **avoir une coiffure a.,** to have an Afro; **à l'a.,** Afro (style); **les cheveux à l'a.,** Afro hair.

afro-américain, -aine [afrɔamerikɛ̃, -ɛn] **1** *adj* Afro-American, Black American. **2** *n* **A.-A.,** Afro-American, Black American.

afro-asiatique [afrɔazjatik] **1** *adj* Afro-Asian. **2** *n* **A.-A.,** Afro-Asian.

afro-cubain, -aine [afrokybɛ̃, -ɛn] **1** *adj* Afro-Cuban. **2** *n* **A.-C.,** Afro-Cuban.

after-shave [aftœrʃɛv] **1** *nm* after-shave (lotion). **2** *adj* **lotion a.-s.,** after-shave (lotion).

A.G. *abrév* **assemblée générale.**

agaçant [agasɑ̃] *adj* annoying, irritating, aggravating.

agacement [agasmɑ̃] *nm* irritation, annoyance; **dire son a.,** to express one's annoyance *or* irritation.

agace-pissette [agaspisɛt] *nf Can Vulg* cock *or* prick teaser.

agacer [agase] *vt* **(j'agaçai(s), n. agaçons) (a)** to set (*teeth, nerves*) on edge; to grate on (*nerves, ears*); **(b)** (*énerver*) to annoy, to irritate, to aggravate (*s.o.*), to get on (*s.o.'s*) nerves; **a. un chien,** to tease a dog; **il m'agace avec ses questions,** he's getting on my nerves, asking all those questions.

agaceries [agasri] *nfpl* charms, wiles; **faire des a.,** to use one's charm(s) *or* wiles.

agape [agap] *nf Hum* **agapes,** feast, spread; **nous allons faire des agapes chez Jeannot,** we're going to have a real feast *or F* slap-up meal at Jeannot's.

agar-agar [agaragar] *nm* agar-agar.

agaric [agarik] *nm* (*champignon*) agaric.

agate [agat] *nf* **(a)** *Minér* agate; **a. noire** *ou* **d'Islande,** obsidian; **a. onyx,** sardonyx; **(b)** (*bille*) glass marble.

agave, agavé [agav, agave] *nm* (*plante*) agave; **a. d'Amérique,** American aloe, sisal hemp.

âge [ɑʒ] *nm* **(a)** (*d'une personne*) age; **quel â. avez-vous?,** how old are you?; **quand j'avais votre â.,** when I was your age; **à l'â. de six ans,** at the age of six; *Arg* **je ne t'ai pas demandé ton â.,** mind your own business; **quel â. lui donnez-vous?,** how old do you think he is *or* would you say he was?; **accuser** *ou* **faire son â.,** to look one's age; **dès son â. le plus tendre,** from his earliest years; **mourir à un grand â.** *ou* **à un â. avancé** *ou* **à un bel â.,** to die at a ripe old age; **faire plus jeune que son â.** to look younger than one really is, not to look one's age; **il n'a pas d'â., on ne peut pas dire quel â. il a,** it is difficult to tell how old he is; **être d'â. légal,** to be of age; **elle n'est pas encore d'â.,** she's still a minor, she's not of age yet; **j'ai passé l'â. de ce genre de choses,** I've grown out of that kind of thing; **ce n'est plus de mon â.,** I'm too old for that type of thing; **être en â. de se marier,** to be of an age to marry; **un whisky de 15 ans d'â.,** a 15 year-old whisky; **hors d'â.,** (*horse*) aged; **le bas â.,** infancy; **enfant en bas â.,** infant; **le premier â.,** childhood; (*tout premier*) infancy; **couches premier/deuxième â.,** nappies for children up to 12 months old/between 12 and 18 months; **le bel â.,** youth; **l'â. ingrat,** adolescence; **sans â.,** ageless; **avoir l'â. de raison,** to have reached the age of discretion; **l'â. d'homme,** manhood; **l'â. adulte,** adulthood; **être d'â. mûr** *ou* **entre deux âges** *ou* **d'un certain â.,** to be middle aged; **elle est bien pour son â.,** she's marvellous for her age; **un homme d'â.,** an old man; **le troisième â.,** retirement age; (*personnes*) the over sixties; **les gens du troisième â.,** the elderly, senior citizens, *Am* golden agers; **à l'â. que j'ai, à mon â.,** at my age, at my time of life; **mourir avant l'â.,** to die before one's time, to die young; *Psy* **l'â. mental,** mental age; **avoir un â. mental de six ans,** to have a mental age of six; *Fig* **être dans** *ou* **à la fleur de l'â.,** to be in the bloom *or* flower of youth; *Fig* **être dans la force de l'â.,** to be in one's prime *or* the prime of life;

(b) generation; **d'â. en â.,** from generation to generation;

(c) *Hist* age, period, epoch; *Archéol* **l'â. de (la) pierre,** the stone age; **l'â. de (la) pierre polie,** the neolithic age; **l'â. de** *ou* **du bronze,** the bronze age; **l'â. de** *ou* **du fer,** the iron age; *Hist* **le moyen â.,** the middle ages; **costumes du moyen â.,** medi(a)eval costumes; *Myth* **l'â. d'or,** the golden age; **l'â. d'or du cinéma muet,** the golden age of silent movies; **l'â. actuel,** the present time; **de son â.,** of one's time *or* period.

âgé [ɑʒe] *adj* **(a)** (*qui a tel âge*) old, aged; **â. de dix ans,** ten years old; **je suis plus/moins â. que vous,** I am older/younger than you; **(b)** (*vieux*) old, *Litt* aged ['eidʒid] ; **assez â.,** elderly; **les personnes âgées,** old *or* elderly people, senior citizens.

agence [aʒɑ̃s] *nf* **(a)** agency, bureau; **a. de renseignement(s),** information bureau; **a. de placement,** employment agency *or* bureau; **a. de presse,** press agency; **a. de tourisme** *ou* **de voyages,** travel agency, travel agent's; **(b)** (*de banque*) branch office.

agencement [aʒɑ̃smɑ̃] *nm* **(a)** arrangement; fitting (together) (*of parts of machine etc*); layout (*of house, radio set, gearbox etc*); **a. de l'intrigue,** (*d'un roman etc*) construction of the plot; **l'a. d'un spectacle,** the way a show is put together; **(b) agencements,** fixtures, fittings.

agencer [aʒɑ̃se] *vt* **(j'agençai(s), n. agençons)** to lay out, to design (*house etc*); to fit (together), to adjust (*parts of machine etc*); **local bien agencé,** well designed premises; **phrases mal agencées,** badly constructed sentences.

agenda [aʒɛ̃da] *nm* notebook; (*pour noter des rendez-vous*) diary; (*journal*) diary; **a. de poche/de bureau,** pocket/desk diary; **a. organisateur,** personal organizer, Filofax ®.

agenouiller (s') [saʒnuje] *vpr* to kneel (down).

agenouilloir [aʒnujwar] *nm* prie-Dieu; hassock (*in church*); bench (*for kneeling in church*).

agent [aʒɑ̃] *nm* **(a)** (*personne*) agent; *Com* **a. autorisé,** authorized representative; **a. de location/de publicité,** estate/advertising agent; **a. littéraire,** literary agent; **a. maritime,** shipping agent; **a. en douanes,** customs broker; **a. d'assurance(s),** insurance agent; **a. (de police),** police officer, police constable; **a. de circulation,** traffic policeman; **a. de change,** *Fin* stockbroker, exchange broker; *Com* mercantile broker; *Com* **a. de liaison,** contact; **a. de recouvrements,** debt collector; *Mil* **a. de liaison,** liaison officer; **a. de transmission,** runner, dispatch rider, messenger; **a. secret,** secret agent; **a. double,** double agent; **(b)** (*facteur*) agent, agency, medium; **a. chimique,** chemical agent; **a. monétaire,** circulating medium; **(c)** *Gram* agent.

aggiornamento [a(d)ʒjɔrnamento] *nm* adaptation to new circumstances; **le parti doit faire son a.,** the party has to move with the times.

agglomérant [aglɔmerɑ̃] **1** *adj* binding (*material*). **2** *nm* binding material, binder.

agglomérat [aglɔmera] *nm* agglomerate.

agglomération [aglɔmerasjɔ̃] *nf* **(a)** (*de ville*) agglomeration, built-up area; **les grandes agglomérations urbaines,** the great urban centres; **l'a. londonienne,** Greater London; **(b)** packing (*of snow etc*); (*of fuel etc*) caking.

aggloméré [aglɔmere] **1** *adj* conglomerate; **panneau de fibres agglomérées,** fibreboard. **2** *nm* **(a)** *Géol Constr* conglomerate; **(b)** (*briquette*) compressed fuel, briquette; **(c)** (*de bois*) fibreboard; **a. de liège,** agglomerated cork.

agglomérer [aglɔmere] *v* **(j'agglomère, n. agglomér-**

ons; **j'agglomérerai**) **1** *vt* to agglomerate. **2 s'agglomérer** *vpr* to agglomerate; (*d'un mélange, de substances différentes*) to cohere, to bind; (*of fuel etc*) to cake.
agglutinant [aglytinɑ̃] **1** *adj* **(a)** (*adhésif*) agglutinant, adhesive; **(b)** *Ling* agglutinative (*languages*). **2** *nm* bond (*of conglomerates*).
agglutination [aglytinɑsjɔ̃] *nf* **(a)** (*action*) agglutination, caking; binding (*d'un mélange, de substances différentes*); **(b)** clump (*of microbes*); *Ling* **phénomène d'a.**, agglutination.
agglutiner [aglytine] **1** *vt* to agglutinate; (*d'un mélange etc*) to bind. **2 s'agglutiner** *vpr* **(a)** (*de personnes*) to congregate, to gather; **(b)** *Méd* (*des bords d'une plaie*) to join, to unite.
aggravant [agravɑ̃] *adj Méd Jur etc* aggravating (*symptom, circumstance*).
aggravation [agravɑsjɔ̃] *nf* **(a)** aggravation (*of disease etc*); worsening (*of weather, conflict etc*); **(b)** augmentation (*of penalty*); increase (*in taxation*).
aggraver [agrave] **1** *vt* **(a)** to worsen, to aggravate (*disease, crime*); **pour a. les choses,** to make matters worse; **(b)** to increase, to augment (*penalty*); to increase (*difficulties, taxation*). **2 s'aggraver** *vpr* to worsen, to become worse, to deteriorate; **son état s'est aggravé,** his condition has deteriorated, he has taken a turn for the worse; **les choses s'aggravent,** things are getting worse.
agile [aʒil] *adj* agile, nimble; (*acrobate*) lithe; (*danseur*) light-footed; **esprit a.,** quick *or* agile mind; **elle est a. de ses doigts,** she's clever with her fingers; **il a la langue a.,** he's never at a loss for words *or* an answer.
agilement [aʒilmɑ̃] *adv* agilely, nimbly.
agilité [aʒilite] *nf* (*physical or mental*) agility; **a. d'un raisonnement,** agility of an argument.
agio [aʒjo] *nm Fin* premium; agio (*of exchange*); **les agios,** bank charges; interest payments (*of mortgage*).
agiotage [aʒjɔtaʒ] *nm Bourse* stock jobbing, agiotage; (*truquage*) rigging the market; (*en prenant des risques financiers*) gambling.
agioter [aʒjɔte] *vi Bourse* to speculate, to gamble.
agioteur, -euse [aʒjɔtœr, -øz] *n Bourse* speculator, gambler.
agir [aʒir] **1** *vi* **(a)** (*faire quelque chose*) to act; **a. de soi-même,** to act on one's own initiative; **maintenant agissons,** now let's get going *or* get down to it; **faire a. qn,** to get s.o. to act *or* to take action; **je vais a. en votre faveur (auprès du ministre),** I am going to intervene on your behalf (with the minister); **faire a. qch,** to set sth going *or* working, to put sth in motion; **a. en connaisseur,** to know what one is doing; **bien/mal a. envers qn,** to act *or* behave well/badly towards s.o.; **je n'aime pas sa manière d'a.,** I don't like the way he goes about things; **est-ce ainsi que vous agissez envers moi?,** is this how you treat me?;
(b) (*produire un effet*) to act, to operate, to take effect; **médicament qui agit vite,** quick-acting medicine, medicine that acts *or* takes effect quickly; **a. sur qch,** to act on sth; **a. sur qn,** to exercise an influence on s.o.; **a. sur les sentiments de qn,** to work on s.o.'s feelings; *Bourse* **a. sur le marché,** to rig the market;
(c) *Jur* **a. au nom de qn,** to act on behalf of s.o.; **a. civilement contre qn,** to sue s.o.
2 s'agir (de) *v impers* **(a)** (*il est question de*) **de quoi s'agit-il?,** what's the matter?, what's it all about?, *F* what's up?; **l'affaire dont il s'agit,** the matter in hand; **il ne s'agit pas d'argent,** it's not a question of money; **il s'agit de lui,** it concerns him, it is about him; **quand il s'agit d'aider, il est toujours occupé,** when it comes to helping, he always seems to be busy!; **il ne s'agit pas de cela,** that is not the question *or* not the point, that's neither here nor there; **s'agissant de ...,** as for ..., as far as ... is concerned;
(b) (*il faut*) it is a question of ...; **il ne s'agit que de les rendre heureux,** it is only a question of making them happy; **il s'agirait de savoir si ...,** the question is whether ...; **il s'agirait de se dépêcher,** we've got to hurry; (*c'est notre dernière chance*) it's a case of now or never.
âgisme [ɑʒism] *nm* ageism.
agissant [aʒisɑ̃] *adj* effective, efficacious.
agissements [aʒismɑ̃] *nmpl souvent Péj* dealings, manoeuvres, machinations.
agitateur, -trice [aʒitatœr, -tris] **1** *n* (*political*) agitator. **2** *nm* **(a)** *Ch* stirring rod, glass rod; **(b)** (*appareil*) stirring machine, agitator, mixer.
agitation [aʒitɑsjɔ̃] *nf* **(a)** roughness (*of the sea*); **(b)** (*inquiétude*) agitation; (*bougeotte*) restlessness, fidgetiness, fidgeting; (*excitation*) excitement; *Pol* ferment, agitation; *Psy* (state of) perturbation *or* disturbance; **l'a. de la ville,** the bustle of the city; **il l'a trouvée dans un état de grande a.,** he found her greatly excited; **cette nouvelle a provoqué l'a. des esprits,** the news greatly upset *or* worried people; **l'a. ouvrière,** (labour) unrest.
agité, -ée [aʒite] **1** *adj* **(a)** choppy, rough (*sea*); wild (*sky*); **(b)** *Méd* feverish, restless (*patient*); restless, sleepless (*night*); broken, fitful (*sleep*); **(c)** agitated, tumultuous (*crowd*); restless, excited, fidgety (*person*); perturbed, troubled (*mind*); unsettled (*times*); **vie agitée,** hectic life. **2** *n* restless *or* unsettled person; *Méd* **pavillon des agités,** security wing, wing for dangerous patients.
agiter [aʒite] **1** *vt* **(a)** to wave (*a handkerchief, a flag, one's arms*); to shake (*tree, bottle etc*); to flutter (*fan, wings*); to sway (*tree, branches*); to rouse (*sea*); to stir (*mixture*); to fan (*air*); **le chien agite sa queue,** the dog is wagging his tail; **le cheval agite la queue,** the horse is flicking its tail; **le vent agitait mes cheveux,** the wind was ruffling my hair; *Arg* **les a.,** to make oneself scarce, to scram; **a. avant de s'en servir,** shake before use;
(b) (*inquiéter*) to perturb, to trouble; to agitate, to excite (*patient*); **malade agité par la fièvre,** patient restless with fever; **elle est agitée par cette rencontre,** the meeting has upset her *or* has got her (all) worked up; **a. le peuple** *ou* **les masses,** to stir up the masses;
(c) to discuss, to debate (*a question*).
2 s'agiter *vpr* **(a)** to be agitated; (*s'affairer*) to bustle around; **s'a. dans l'eau,** to splash about in the water; **s'a. dans son sommeil,** to toss (about) *or* thrash around in one's sleep; **(b)** (*s'énerver*) to become agitated *or* excited, to get upset *or* worked up; (*of sea*) to get rough; **il ne faut pas que le malade s'agite,** care should be taken not to upset *or* excite the patient.
agit-prop [aʒitprɔp] *nf inv* (*abrév* **agitation-propagande**) agit-prop.
agneau, -eaux [aɲo] *nm* lamb; **(peau d')a.,** lambskin; **laine d'a.,** lamb's wool; *Fig* **c'est un a.,** he is as meek as a lamb; **doux comme un a.,** as gentle as a lamb; *Rel* **l'A. sans tache,** the Lamb (of God); *Culin* **côtelette d'a.,** lamb chop.
agnelage [aɲlaʒ] *nm* **(a)** (*mise à bas*) lambing; **(b)** (*saison*) lambing season.
agneler [aɲle] *vi* (**elle agnèle, elle agnèlera**) to lamb.
agnelet [aɲlɛ] *nm* lambkin, young lamb.
agneline [aɲlin] *nf* lamb's wool.
agnelle [aɲɛl] *nf* ewe lamb.
agnosticisme [agnɔstisism] *nm* agnosticism.
agnostique [agnɔstik] *adj & n* agnostic.
agonie [agɔni] *nf* death agony, death struggle, pangs of death; **être à l'a.,** to be at one's last gasp; **lente a.,** lingering death; *Fig* **l'a. d'un régime,** the death throes of a regime.
agonir [agɔnir] *vt* **a. qn d'injures/d'insultes,** to heap insults *or* abuse on s.o., to hurl insults *or* abuse at s.o..
agonisant, -ante [agɔnizɑ̃, -ɑ̃t] **1** *adj* dying, in the throes of death; **de sa voix agonisante,** with his dying breath; *Fig* **un règne a.,** a reign in its dying moments *or* death throes. **2** *n* dying person; **prières pour les agonisants,** prayers for the dying.
agoniser [agɔnize] *vi* to be dying *or* at the point of death; *Fig* (*of business*) to be on its last legs.
agoraphobe [agɔrafɔb] *adj Méd* agoraphobic.
agoraphobie [agɔrafɔbi] *nf Méd* agoraphobia; **souffrir d'a.,** to be agoraphobic.
agrafage [agrafaʒ] *nm* fastening; clipping together (*of sheets of paper*); clamping (*of object to workbench etc*); *Tech* dowelling.
agrafe [agraf] *nf* **(a)** hook, fastener; clasp (*of medal, of album*); buckle (*of strap*); staple (*for stapler*); *Chir etc* suture clip; **a. de diamants,** diamond clasp; **agrafes et portes (de couturière),** hooks and eyes; **(b)** *Constr* clamp, cleat, cramp iron; **(c)** hasp, catch (*of window etc*); **(d)** *Archit* keystone (*of arch*).
agrafer [agrafe] *vt* **(a)** (*accrocher*) to fasten, to clip together; (*avec une agrafeuse*) to staple; to hook up (*dress*); to buckle (*belt*); *F* **agrafe-moi ma robe!,** do me up!; **(b)** *Constr* to clamp, to cramp; **(c)** *F* (*de la police*) to nab (*s.o.*).
agrafeuse [agraføz] *nf* stapler.
agraire [agrɛr] *adj* agrarian; **mesures agraires,** land measures; *Jur* **loi a.,** land act.
agrammatical, -aux [agramatikal, -o] *adj Ling* ungrammatical.
agrandir [agrɑ̃dir] **1** *vt* **(a)** to make (*sth*) larger; to enlarge (*photograph etc*); to increase, to extend (*sth*); **a. qch en long/en large,** to lengthen/widen sth; **(b)** to make (*sth*)

appear larger, to magnify; **a. sa taille,** to make oneself look taller; **ce papier peint agrandit la pièce,** this wallpaper makes the room look larger; **(c)** (*développer*) to expand (*business*); **(d)** to uplift (*the mind etc*). **2 s'agrandir** *vpr* to grow larger; (*en quantité*) to become greater, to increase; (*prendre du volume*) to expand; **nous allons nous a.,** we are going to enlarge our premises; **elle veut s'a.,** (*dans son appartement*) she wants more space.

agrandissement [agrɑ̃dismɑ̃] *nm* **(a)** (*extension*) enlarging, extending; **a. en long/en large,** lengthening/widening; **(b)** extension (*of factory etc*); increase (*of holding etc*); **(c)** *Phot* enlargement.

agrandisseur [agrɑ̃disœr] *nm Phot* enlarger.

agrarien, -ienne [agrarjɛ̃, -jɛn] *adj & n Pol* agrarian.

agréable [agreabl] **1** *adj* pleasant, agreeable; pleasing (*appearance, arrangement*); prepossessing (*manner etc*); **un jeune homme très a.,** a very pleasant *or* nice young man; **se rendre a. à qn,** to be pleasant to s.o.; **a. au goût,** pleasant to the taste; **a. à voir,** pleasing to the eye; *F* (*woman*) easy on the eye; **peu a.,** disagreeable. **2** *nm* **joindre l'utile à l'a.,** to combine business with pleasure. **3** *n* **faire l'a.,** to make oneself pleasant (**auprès de,** to).

agréablement [agreabləmɑ̃] *adv* pleasantly, agreeably; **nous avons été a. surpris par ta décision,** we were pleasantly surprised by your decision.

agréé [agree] **1** *adj* approved (*sample etc*); *Can* **comptable a.,** chartered accountant. **2** *nm Jur* counsel (*before a tribunal de commerce*).

agréer [agree] **1** *vt* to accept, to recognize, to agree to (*sth*); **a. un contrat,** to approve an agreement; **veuillez a. l'assurance de mes salutations distinguées,** (*dans une lettre*) yours faithfully, yours truly. **2** *vi* to please; **si cela vous agrée,** if that suits you.

agreg [agrɛg] *nf Univ F* = **AGRÉGATION (a)**.

agrégat [agrega] *nm* aggregate.

agrégation [agregasjɔ̃] *nf* **(a)** *Univ* **(concours de) l'a.,** = competitive examination for posts on the teaching staff of lycées and universities; **(b)** aggregation, binding; **matière d'a.,** binding material (*for road etc*).

agrégé, -ée [agreʒe] *Univ* **1** *adj* who has passed the agrégation examination. **2** *n* graduate who has passed the agrégation examination.

agréger [agreʒe] **1** *vt* **(a)** (*rassembler*) **les cristaux agrégés dans la roche,** the crystals incorporated in the rock; **(b)** (*admettre*) to incorporate (*a company*); to admit (*an individual*). **2 s'agréger** *vpr* to combine, to merge.

agrément [agremɑ̃] *nm* **(a)** (*plaisir*) pleasure, amusement; **voyage d'a.,** pleasure trip; **livres d'a.,** light reading; **(b)** (*charme*) attractiveness, pleasantness, charm; **une ville sans a.,** an unattractive town; **(c) agréments,** amenities (*of place*); charm (*of person*); **(d)** *Mus* **notes d'a.,** grace notes; **(e)** (*accord*) approval, consent.

agrémenter [agremɑ̃te] *vt* to ornament; to trim (*dress etc*).

agrès [agrɛ] *nmpl* **(a)** *Nau* tackle; **(b)** *Sp* (gymnastics) apparatus.

agresser [agrese] *vt* to attack (without provocation); **se faire a.,** to be attacked; (*pour son argent*) *F* to be mugged; *F* **ne te sens pas agressé,** don't think you're being got at.

agresseur [agresœr] *nm* aggressor, assailant.

agressif, -ive [agresif, -iv] *adj* aggressive.

agression [agresjɔ̃] *nf* aggression; unprovoked assault (*on passer-by etc*); **être victime d'une a.,** to be assaulted *or* attacked; *F* to be mugged.

agressivement [agresivmɑ̃] *adv* aggressively.

agressivité [agresivite] *nf* aggressiveness.

agreste [agrɛst] *adj Litt* **(a)** rustic; rural (*site*); **(b)** uncouth (*person, manners*).

agricole [agrikɔl] *adj* agricultural (*produce, nation etc*); **comice(s) agricole(s),** agricultural show; **exploitation a.,** farming; (*ferme*) farm; **petite exploitation a.,** small farm, smallholding; **travail a.,** farmwork, farming; **ouvrier a.,** farm worker, farm hand; **la population a.,** the farming population.

agriculteur, -trice [agrikyltœr, -tris] *n* farmer; (*spécialiste*) agriculturist.

agriculture [agrikyltyr] *nf* agriculture, farming.

agriflamme [agriflam] *nm* flame gun.

agripper [agripe] **1** *vt* to clutch (at), to grip (*sth, s.o.*); (*saisir*) to seize (hold of) (*sth*). **2 s'agripper** *vpr* to cling; **il s'agrippait au bord de la fenêtre,** he was clinging to the window sill.

agro [agrɔ] *nm F abrév* **Institut national agronomique.**

agro-alimentaire [agrɔalimɑ̃tɛr] **1** *adj* (*industrie, secteur*) food. **2** *nm* agribusiness.

agrochimie [agrɔʃimi] *nf* agro-chemistry.

agronome [agrɔnɔm] *nm* agronomist, agricultural economist; **ingénieur a.,** agricultural engineer *or* scientist.

agronomie [agrɔnɔmi] *nf* agronomy; *Econ* agronomics.

agronomique [agrɔnɔmik] *adj* agronomic(al); **l'Institut national a.,** = (university level) college for students of agronomics.

agrume [agrym] *nm* citrus fruit.

agrumicole [agrymikɔl] *adj* citrus fruit-producing.

aguardiente [agwardjente, -jɑ̃t] *nf* aguerdiente, cheap Spanish brandy.

aguerrir [agerir] **1** *vt* to harden (*s.o.*) to war; to train (*troops*). **2 s'aguerrir** *vpr* **s'a. à** *ou* **contre qch,** to become hardened to sth; (*apprendre à accepter, se débrouiller*) to learn to take sth in one's stride; **ça va te permettre de t'a.,** (*d'aller en pension etc*) it will toughen you up a bit.

aguets [agɛ] *adv* **aux a.,** on the watch, on the lookout; **être** *ou* **se tenir aux a.,** to be on the watch *or* on the lookout; **avoir l'oreille aux a.,** to keep one's ears open.

aguichant [agiʃɑ̃] *adj* seductive, provocative.

aguicher [agiʃe] *vt* to excite, to arouse (*s.o.*); *F* to lead (*s.o.*) on.

aguicheur, -euse [agiʃœr, -øz] **1** *adj* seductive, provocative; **une fillette aguicheuse,** a coquettish little girl, a nymphet. **2** *nf* **aguicheuse,** provocative woman.

ah [ɑ] **1** *int* ah!; (*exprimant la surprise*) oh!; **ah, que c'est beau!,** isn't it beautiful!; **ah oui!,** well yes, of course!; *Iron* **ah ah, je savais bien que tu me cachais quelque chose,** aha! I knew that you were hiding something from me. **2** *nm inv* **pousser des oh et des ah,** to ooh and aah.

ahuri, -e [ayri] **1** *adj* (*regard*) astounded; (*personne*) stupefied, *F* flabbergasted; **avoir l'air a.,** to look astounded *or* stupefied. **2** *n* idiot, numbskull.

ahurir [ayrir] *vt* (*d'une remarque etc*) to astound, to stupefy (*s.o.*).

ahurissant [ayrisɑ̃] *adj* stupefying, astounding; *F* **il a un culot a.,** he's got one hell of a cheek.

ahurissement [ayrismɑ̃] *nm* stupefaction; **il ne revient pas de son a.,** he can't get over it.

aï [ai] *nm* (*mammifère*) three-toed sloth.

aide¹ [ɛd] *nf* help, assistance, aid; **venir en a. à qn, venir à l'a. de qn, donner a. à qn,** to help s.o., to come to s.o.'s assistance *or* aid; **recourir à l'a. d'un médecin,** to call in a doctor; **appeler à l'a.,** to call for help; **à l'a.!,** help!; **à l'a. de qch,** with the help *or* assistance of sth; **avec l'a. de qn,** with the help *or* assistance of s.o.; **faire qch sans a.,** to do sth without help *or* on one's own; **a. de l'État,** = national assistance; **a. sociale,** *Br* social security, *Am* welfare; **l'a. au retour,** financial and material help to returning immigrants; **a. publique au développement,** official development assistance.

aide² *n* assistant, helper; *Nau* mate; (*de géomètre*) chainman; **a. de cuisine,** assistant cook; **a. de camp,** aide-de-camp; **a. de laboratoire,** laboratory assistant; **a. ménagère,** home help; **a. maternelle** *ou* **familiale,** mother's help.

aidé [ede] *adj* **(a)** (*assisté*) **elle n'est pas très aidée,** she doesn't have much help (around the house); **(b)** *Admin* **contrat a.,** = employment contract whereby part of an employee's salary is paid by the state; **(c)** *Fig* **il n'est pas très a.,** he's not very smart, he's a bit of a dimwit.

aide-comptable [ɛdkɔ̃tabl] *nm* assistant accountant; (*pl aides-comptables*).

aide-mécanicien [ɛdmekanisjɛ̃] *nm* garage hand; (*pl aide-mécaniciens*).

aide-mémoire [ɛdmemwar] *nm inv* aide-memoire; *Scol* crib.

aider [ede] **1** *vt* to help, to assist, to aid (*s.o.*); **je me suis fait a. par un ami,** I got a friend to help me *or* to give me a hand; **a. qn à faire qch,** to help s.o. to do sth; **a. qn à monter/descendre/entrer/sortir,** to help s.o. up/down/in/out; **a. qn à mettre/ôter son pardessus,** to help s.o. on/off with his *or* her coat; **Dieu aidant,** with God's help; *Vieilli* **à qui se lève matin Dieu aide et prête la main,** the early bird catches the worm. **2** *vi* **a. à qch,** to contribute to(wards) sth; **elle n'aide jamais!,** she never helps (out), she never lends a hand. **3 s'aider** *vpr* **(a)** *Prov* **aide-toi et le ciel t'aidera,** God helps those who help themselves; **(b) s'a. de qch,** to make use of sth; **s'a. d'un dictionnaire,** to consult a dictionary; **il faut s'a. les uns les autres,** we must help one another.

aide-soignant, -ante [ɛdswaɲɑ̃, -ɑ̃t] *n* nursing auxiliary, auxiliary nurse; (*pl aides-soignant(e)s*).

aïe [aj] *int* (*indicating twinge of pain*) ow!, ouch!

AIEA [aiəa] *nf Nucl* (*abrév* **Agence internationale de l'énergie atomique**) IAEA.

aïeul, -eule [ajœl] *n* **(a)** (*ancêtre*) (*pl* **aïeux** [ajø]) ancestor; *F* **mes aïeux!,** goodness me!; **(b)** *Vieilli* (*pl* **aïeuls**) grandfather, *f* grandmother.

aigle [ɛgl] **1** *nm* **(a)** (*oiseau*) eagle; **a. royal** *ou* **fauve** *ou* **doré,** golden eagle; **grand a. des mers,** erne, sea eagle; **un regard** *ou* **des yeux d'a.,** keen *or* penetrating glance; **aux yeux d'a.,** eagle-eyed; **nez en bec d'a.,** hook *or* aquiline nose; **(b)** *Fig* genius, mastermind; **ce n'est pas un a.,** he's no genius; **(c)** (*lutrin*) lectern; **(d)** (*poisson*) **a. de mer,** eagle ray; **(e)** eagle; *Mil* **l'a. noir de Prusse,** the black eagle of Prussia; **(f)** (*skating*) **grand a.,** spread-eagle. **2** *nf* **(a)** *Hér* eagle; **a. de sable éployée,** eagle displayed sable; **double a., a. à deux têtes,** double-headed eagle; **(b)** *Mil* eagle, standard; **les aigles romaines,** the Roman eagles; **l'a. impériale (des armées napoléoniennes),** the imperial eagle.

aiglefin [ɛgləfɛ̃] *nm* (*poisson*) haddock.

aiglette [ɛglɛt] *nf Hér* eaglet.

aiglon, -onne [ɛglɔ̃, -ɔn] *n* (*oiseau*) eaglet, young eagle; *Hist* **L'A.,** Napoleon II.

aigre [ɛgr] **1** *adj* (*goût etc*) sour, sharp, acid, tart; *Fig* (*personne*) sour; (*éprouvant du ressentiment*) bitter; **lait a.,** sour milk; **des propos aigres,** cutting remarks; **son a.,** harsh *or* shrill sound. **2** *nm* **tourner à l'a.,** (*of food etc*) to turn sour; (*d'une discussion*) to turn nasty.

aigre-doux, -douce [ɛgrədu, -dus] *adj* sweet and sour (*sauce*); snide, *F* catty (*remark*).

aigrefin[1] [ɛgrəfɛ̃] *nm* (*poisson*) haddock.

aigrefin[2] *nm Péj* swindler; (financial) shark.

aigrelet, -ette [ɛgrəlɛ, -ɛt] *adj* (*vin*) (rather) sour; (*son, voix*) harsh, reedy.

aigrement [ɛgrəmɑ̃] *adv* acrimoniously, bitterly.

aigrette [ɛgrɛt] *nf* **(a)** aigrette (*of heron, of egret*); crest (*of peacock etc*); horn (*of owl*); tuft (*of hair, fur*); **(b)** (*panache*) aigrette, plume; **a. de diamants,** spray of diamonds; **(c)** *Bot* egret; tassel (*of maize*); **(d)** *El* aigrette, brush (*discharge*); **(e)** (*oiseau*) egret.

aigreur [ɛgrœr] *nf* **(a)** (*d'un goût*) sourness, tartness, acidity; sourness (*of temper*); acerbity, bitterness (*of remark*); **il en parle encore avec a.,** he's still very bitter about it; **(b)** *Métal* brittleness; **(c)** *Méd* **aigreurs (d'estomac),** acidity, excess acid in the stomach.

aigri [egri] *adj* embittered, soured.

aigrir [egrir] **1** *vt* to turn (*sth*) sour; to embitter (*person*). **2** *vi* to turn *or* grow sour; (*of milk*) to turn. **3 s'aigrir** *vpr* (*devenir acide*) to turn acid; **son caractère s'est aigri,** he has become embittered.

aigu, -uë [egy] *adj* **(a)** acute, sharp (*pain*); intense (*curiosity*); bitter (*conflict, jealousy*); penetrating (*look*); keen, sharp (*mind, sensation*); **elle a un sens a. du rôle de chacun,** she has a keen sense of what everybody's role should be; **(b)** sharp, pointed (*instrument*); *Math* **angle a.,** acute angle; **(c)** shrill, sharp, high-pitched (*sound*); **(d)** *Gram* **accent a.,** acute accent.

aigue-marine [ɛgmarin] *nf* aquamarine; (*pl* **aigues-marines**).

aiguillage [egɥijaʒ] *nm* **(a)** *Rail* switching *or* shifting of points; shunting (*of train*); **poste d'a.,** signal box; **(b)** (*appareil*) points, *US* switches; **a. à deux voies,** two-way switch; **(c)** *Fig* orientation; **faire une erreur d'a.,** to take the wrong turning *or* course.

aiguille [egɥij] *nf* **(a)** needle; **a. à coudre/repriser/tricoter,** sewing/darning/knitting needle; **travail à l'a.,** needlework; **a. à passer** *ou* **à lacet,** bodkin; *Méd* **a. hypodermique,** hypodermic needle; *Fig* **discuter sur la pointe d'une a.,** to split hairs; *Fig* **chercher une a. dans une botte de foin,** to look for a needle in a haystack; **de fil en a. nous en sommes venus à parler de notre enfance,** one thing led to another and we got talking about our childhood;

(b) *Ordinat* pin; **imprimante à aiguilles,** 24 pin printer;

(c) a. de glace, icicle; *Géol* **a. (rocheuse),** needle; spine (*of hill*); **a. de pin,** pine needle; **a. de mer,** (*poisson*) pipe fish; garfish; **a. à tracer,** scriber; **a. de graveur,** etching needle;

(d) *Rail* tongue rail, point rail, blade; **a. de raccordement,** points, *US* switches;

(e) needle, point (*of obelisk, peak etc*); (church) spire;

(f) needle (*of compass, speedometer etc*); hand (*of watch, clock*); **petite a.,** hour hand; **grande a.,** minute hand; **a. trotteuse,** second hand.

aiguillée [egɥije] *nf* (short) piece of thread.

aiguiller [egɥije] *vt Rail* to shunt, *US* to switch (*a train*); *Fig* **a. la police sur une fausse piste,** to put the police on a false scent; **on l'a aiguillé vers la profession de banquier,** he was steered into banking; **a. ses recherches vers un certain domaine,** to orient(ate) *or* direct one's research towards a particular field.

aiguilleur [egɥijœr] *nm Rail* pointsman, *US* switchman; *Av* **a. du ciel,** air traffic controller.

aiguillon [egɥijɔ̃] *nm* **(a)** (*pique-bœuf*) goad; *Fig* incentive, spur, stimulus; **(b)** *Bot* prickle, thorn; sting (*of wasp*).

aiguillonner [egɥijɔne] *vt* to goad (*oxen*); *Fig* (*de la jalousie, de l'ambition*) to spur (*s.o.*) on; (*d'une personne*) to urge (*s.o.*) on.

aiguisé [eg(ɥ)ize] *adj* sharp (*knife*); keen (*appetite*).

aiguiser [eg(ɥ)ize] *vt* **(a)** to sharpen, to put an edge on, to grind (*knife etc*); to set (*saw, razor*); to whet (*scythe*); to sharpen (*tool*) to a point; **(b)** *Fig* to arouse (*curiosity, envy*); to whet (*appetite*); to hone (*intelligence*).

aiguiseur, -euse [eg(ɥ)izœr, -øz] *n* grinder, sharpener (*of tools etc*).

aiguisoir [eg(ɥ)izwar] *nm* (*outil*) (knife) sharpener, steel; (*pierre à aiguiser*) whetstone.

aïkido [ajkido] *nm Sp* aikido; **faire de l'a.,** to do aikido.

ail [aj] *nm* (*pl* **ails,** *Vieilli* **aulx** [o]) **(a)** *Culin* garlic; **gousse d'a.,** clove of garlic; **un bulbe** *ou F* **une tête d'a.,** a head of garlic; **(b)** (*plante*) allium.

aile [ɛl] *nf* **(a)** (*d'oiseau, de papillon etc*) wing; (*de manchot*) flipper; **battre des ailes,** to beat its wings; **battre de l'a.,** (*d'un oiseau*) to flutter; (*d'une personne*) to be flustered *or* embarrassed; **l'entreprise bat de l'a.,** the firm is struggling (to survive) *or* is in a bad way; **avoir du plomb dans l'a., en avoir dans l'a.,** (*d'un oiseau*) to be winged; (*d'une personne*) to be hard hit; **la théorie a du plomb dans l'a.,** the theory doesn't stand up; *Fig* **la peur nous donnait des ailes,** fear lent us wings; *Fig* **voler de ses propres ailes,** to stand on one's own (two) feet; **vouloir voler avant d'avoir ses ailes,** to want to run before one can walk; *Culin* **a. de poulet,** chicken wing; *Fig F* **avoir un coup dans l'a.,** to have had a bit too much to drink; **prendre qn sous son a.,** to take s.o. under one's wing; *Fig* **travailler sous l'a. d'un grand professeur,** to be the protégé of an eminent professor;

(b) *Aut* wing, *Am* fender; wing (*of building, the stage*); wing, flank (*of army*), sail (*of windmill*); arm (*of semaphore*); blade (*of propeller, turbine*); helix (*of ear*); wing (*of nose*); flange (*of girder*);

(c) *Av* wing, aerofoil, *Am* airfoil; **a. courbe,** cambered wing; **a. en flèche,** swept-back wing; **a. à fente,** slotted wing; **a. en delta,** delta wing; **a. cantilever, a. en porte à faux,** cantilever wing;

(d) *Fb* wing; **les demi ailes,** the wing halves; *Rugby Fb* **jouer trois quarts a.,** to play wing three-quarters;

(e) a. delta *ou* **volante** *ou* **libre,** (*sport*) hang-gliding; (*objet*) hang-glider.

ailé [ele] *adj* **(a)** (*avec des ailes*) winged, feathered; *Spéc* alate; **(b) vis ailée,** butterfly screw, thumbscrew.

aileron [ɛlrɔ̃] *nm* **(a)** pinion (*of bird*); fin (*of shark etc*); **(b)** *Av* aileron, wing tip; **a. compensé,** balanced aileron; **(c)** *Av etc* fin; **a. stabilisateur,** stabilizer fin; **stabilisateur à a.,** fin stabilizer; **(d)** paddle board (*of water wheel*); **(e)** fin keel (*of submarine*).

ailette [ɛlɛt] *nf* **(a)** small wing (*of building etc*); **(b)** radiating plate, (cooling) flange, rib, fin, gill (*of radiator*); **tube à ailettes,** fanned *or* gilled tube; **(c)** lug, tenon (*of machine part*); stud (*of shell*); **vis à ailettes,** wing nut, thumbscrew; **(d)** vane (*of torpedo, fan, ventilator etc*); wing, fin (*of bomb, missile*); fin (*of aircraft*); blade (*of turbine*); **à ailettes,** (*wheel etc*) bladed; (*bomb, missile*) winged; **(e)** rib (*of aircraft*).

ailier [elje] *nm Fb* winger.

ailler [aje] *vt Culin* to flavour with garlic.

ailleurs [ajœr] *adv* **(a)** (*à un autre endroit*) elsewhere, somewhere else; **elle vient d'a.,** she's not from here, she's not from these parts; **on a dû passer par a.,** we had to come a different way; *Fig* **être a.,** to be miles away; **partout a.,** everywhere else; (*n'importe où*) anywhere else; **nulle part a.,** nowhere else; **vous mangerez ici comme nulle part a.,** you'll eat better here than you will anywhere else; *F* **va voir a. si j'y suis,** take a walk; **(b) d'a.,** besides, moreover; (*quoi qu'il en soit*) however; (*au fait*) come to that, for that matter; **(c) par a.,** in other respects; (*par qn d'autre etc*) from another source; (= **d'a.**) moreover.

ailloli [ajɔli] *nm Culin* garlic mayonnaise.

aimable [ɛmabl] *adj* **(a)** (*gentil*) kind, pleasant, agreeable; **vous êtes bien a., c'est très a. de votre part,** it's very kind of you *or* very good of you; **peu a.,** disagreeable; (*in thanks, victory etc*) ungracious; **(b)** (*que l'on peut aimer facilement*) lovable, attractive.

aimablement [ɛmabləmɑ̃] *adv* kindly, pleasantly.

aimant [ɛmɑ̃] *nm* magnet; **a. supraconducteur,** superconducting magnet.

aimant [ɛmɑ̃] *adj* (*parent etc*) loving.

aimantation [ɛmɑ̃tɑsjɔ̃] *nf* magnetization.

aimanter [ɛmɑ̃te] *vt* to magnetize.

aimer [ɛme] **1** *vt* **(a)** (*d'amour*) to love; **a. qn (d'amour),** to love s.o., to be in love with s.o.;

(b) (*apprécier, avoir de l'affection pour*) to like, to be fond of (*s.o., sth*); **a. qn d'amitié,** to be good friends with s.o.; **je n'aime guère Pierre,** I don't like Pierre very much, I don't care for Pierre very much; **je t'aime bien,** I like you a lot; **se faire a. de qn,** to win s.o.'s affection; **j'aime beaucoup la musique,** I'm very fond of music; **plante qui aime un sol calcaire,** plant that likes a chalky soil; **tu sais que nous n'aimons pas ce genre de choses,** you know we don't like that sort of thing; **a. (à) faire qch,** to like doing sth; **j'aurais aimé le voir,** I would like to have seen him; *Prov* **qui m'aime aime mon chien,** love me, love my dog; **je vais prendre un pot — qui m'aime me suive!,** I'm going for a drink — anyone want to join me?; **j'aime autant le cidre (que le vin),** I like cider just as much (as wine); **j'aime(rais) autant rester ici (que de ...),** I would just as soon stay here (as ...); **j'aime autant qu'il ne m'attende pas,** I would just as soon he didn't wait for me; **a. mieux,** to prefer; **j'aime** *ou* **j'aimerais mieux rester ici,** I would rather *or* sooner stay here; *F* **j'aime mieux pas,** I'd rather not.

2 s'aimer *vpr* **(a)** (*être fier de soi*) to think a lot of oneself; (*à une occasion particulière*) to be pleased with oneself;

(b) (*se plaire*) **je ne m'aime pas dans cette veste,** I don't like myself in this jacket;

(c) (*être attaché par amour*) to love each other, to be in love (with each other); **ils s'aiment,** they are in love (with each other); **ils se sont aimés toute la nuit,** they made love all night long.

aine [ɛn] *nf Anat* groin.

aîné, -ée [ɛne] **1** *adj* (*de deux personnes*) elder; (*de plus que deux personnes*) eldest; **mon frère a.,** my elder brother; (*plus de deux frères*) my eldest brother; **la branche aînée de la famille,** the elder *or* senior branch of the family; **a. de trois ans,** senior by three years. **2** *n* elder *or* eldest (child); **l'a. ne va pas encore à l'école,** the eldest doesn't go to school yet; **nos aînés,** our elders; **il est mon a.,** he is older than I (am).

aînesse [ɛnɛs] *nf* **droit d'a.,** law of primogeniture.

ainsi [ɛ̃si] **1** *adv* **(a)** (*de cette façon*) like this, like that, in this *or* that way; **c'est a. qu'il est devenu soldat,** and that is *or* was how he became a soldier; **s'il en est a.,** if that is the case, if (it is) so; **puisqu'il en est a. je n'ai plus rien à dire,** under the circumstances I have nothing more to say; **les choses étant a.,** if that's the way *or* how things are; **et a. de suite,** and so on, and so forth; **pour a. dire,** so to speak, as it were; **a. soit-il,** so be it; *Rel* amen; **(b)** (*par exemple*) for example, for instance; **il m'arrive des aventures, a., l'autre jour ...,** things happen to me, for instance, the other day ... . **2** *conj* **(a)** so; **a. vous ne venez pas?,** so you're not coming?; **(b)** as well as, and; **cette règle a. que la suivante me paraît** *ou* **paraissent inutile(s),** this rule, as well as *or* and the next, seems to me to be unnecessary.

aïoli [ajɔli] *nm Culin* garlic mayonnaise.

air [ɛr] *nm* **(a)** (*gaz*) air, atmosphere; **privé d'a., sans a.,** airless; **cela manque d'a. ici,** it's stuffy in here; **l'a. de la mer,** (the) sea air; **donner de l'a. à,** to ventilate, to air (*a room*); to give (*s.o.*) some (fresh) air; **à a. conditionné,** air conditioned; **a. comprimé/liquide,** compressed/liquid air; *Typ* **donner de l'a. à la composition,** to lead out *or* space out the type; **sortir prendre l'a.,** to go out for some fresh air; *Fig* **vivre de l'a. du temps,** to live on (next to) nothing *or* on air; **ne pas laisser à l'a.,** not to be exposed to the air; **allez, de l'a.!,** go on, clear off!; **au grand a., en plein a.,** in the fresh air, in the open air; **vie au grand a.,** open-air life; **vie de plein a.,** outdoor life; **concert en plein a.,** open-air concert; *Aut* **poste d'a.,** air line; **libre comme l'a.,** free as a bird;

(b) l'a., the air; **la conquête de l'a.,** the conquest of the air; **prendre l'a.,** (*of aircraft*) to take off; **la navette spatiale s'éleva dans les airs,** the space shuttle rose into the air; **tenir l'a.,** to keep flying; (*être en état de voler*) to be airworthy; **Ministère de l'A.,** = ministry responsible for air defence; **Armée de l'A.,** Air Force; **École de l'a.,** ≈ R.A.F. College, U.S.A.F. Academy; **hôtesse de l'a.,** air hostess; **en l'a.,** in the air; **regarder en l'a.,** to look up into the sky; *Fig* **être en l'a.,** to be in a state of confusion; **mettre tout en l'a.,** to throw everything into confusion, to turn everything upside down; *Fig* **ficher qch en l'a.,** to mess sth up; *Fig* **elle veut tout envoyer** *ou F* **foutre en l'a.,** she wants to throw it all up *or F* chuck *or* jack it all in; *Fig* **paroles en l'a.,** idle talk; **parler en l'a.,** to talk wildly *or* at random; **c'est une tête en l'a.,** he's got his head in the clouds;

(c) (*atmosphère*) **elle est passée prendre l'a. de l'atelier,** she looked in at the workshop to see how things were; *Fig* **changer d'a.,** to have a change of scene; **il y a quelque chose dans l'a.,** there's something in the air *or* wind, there's something brewing; **il y a de la dispute/de l'orage dans l'a.,** there's a dispute/storm brewing; **c'est dans l'a. du temps,** (*de se préoccuper de l'environnement etc*) it's the in thing;

(d) (*vent*) wind; **il fait de l'a.,** it's breezy; **courant d'a.,** draught; **il ne fait pas d'a.,** there's not a breath of air; **coup d'a.,** rush of air; **attraper un coup d'a.,** to catch a chill;

(e) (*allure*) appearance, look; **avoir bon** *ou* **grand a.,** (*d'une personne*) to look distinguished; (*d'une robe etc*) to be smart; (*être seyant*) to be becoming; **a. de famille,** family likeness; **un jeune homme, à l'a. très comme il faut,** a very respectable-looking young man; **avoir un faux a. de ...,** to have a vague *or* slight resemblance to ..., to look vaguely like ...; **il a un drôle d'a.,** he looks odd *or* funny; **cette fillette a un petit a. malin,** that little girl looks very mischievous; **la ville a un a. de fête,** the town is looking festive, the town has a festive look about it; *Péj* **elle, avec son a. de ne pas y toucher,** her with her innocent look;

(f) avoir l'a., to look, to seem; **avoir l'a. fatigué,** to look tired; *F* **avoir l'a. fin,** to look daft; **il a l'a. d'un étranger,** he looks as if he's a stranger; (*venant d'un autre pays*) he looks like a foreigner; **ils ont l'a. d'avoir peur,** they look as if they're afraid; **cela en a tout l'a.,** it looks like it; **n'avoir l'a. de rien,** (*d'une personne*) to seem *or* appear insignificant, to seem *or* appear of no importance; (*d'une maison etc*) to be unpretentious, to look nothing much (from the outside); (*d'un travail*) to look (deceptively) easy; **le temps a l'a. d'être à la pluie,** it looks like rain;

(g) airs, airs; **se donner des airs,** to give oneself *or* to put on airs, to (try to) look important; **ne prends pas tes grands airs!,** don't get on your high horse!;

(h) *Mus* tune, air, melody; **a. varié,** theme with variations; **un a. d'opéra,** an (operatic) aria;

(i) *Équitation* **les airs du manège,** the paces of a horse.

airain [ɛrɛ̃] *nm* (*cuivre et étain*) bronze; (*cuivre et zinc*) brass; *Litt* **avoir un cœur** *ou* **une âme d'a.,** to have a heart of stone; *Écon* **la loi d'a.,** (Lassalle's) iron law of wages.

air-air [ɛrɛr] *adj inv Mil* air-to-air; **missile a.-a.,** air-to-air missile.

airbus ® [ɛrbys] *nm Av* airbus ®.

aire [ɛr] *nf* **(a)** (*surface plane*) (plane) surface; (*plancher*) floor; roadway, floor (*of a bridge*); (*on motorway*) parking area, picnic area; **a. de services (principale),** service area; (*road sign*) services; *Av* **a. d'atterrissage,** landing area; *Av* **a. de manœuvre,** apron; *Av* **a. de stationnement,** tarmac; **a. de lavage,** *Aut* car wash, washing bay; *Av* washdown, *US* wash rack; *Astronaut* **a. de lancement,** launching site; **a. (d'une grange),** threshing floor; *Géol* **a. continentale,** continental shield; **(b)** area (*of field, triangle, building etc*); *Fig* **a. d'influence,** sphere of influence; *Géog* **a. de drainage,** drainage area, basin; **(c)** eyrie (*of eagle*); **(d)** *Nau* **les aires de vent,** the points of the compass.

airedale [ɛrdɛl] *nm* **a. terrier,** Airedale terrier.

airelle [ɛrɛl] *nf* (*plante*) **a. myrtille,** bilberry, blaeberry, *Am* blueberry, huckleberry; **a. coussinette,** cranberry.

air-sol [ɛrsɔl] *adj inv Mil* air-to-ground; **missile a.-s.,** air-to-ground missile.

aisance [ɛzɑ̃s] *nf* **(a)** ease; (*facilité*) freedom (*of movement etc*); **faire qch avec a.,** to do sth easily *or* with ease; **donner de l'a. à qch,** to ease sth; **parler** *ou* **s'exprimer avec a.,** to speak *or* express oneself with great ease *or* facility; *Jur* **a. de voirie,** easement; **jouir de l'a., être dans l'a.,** to be well off *or* comfortably off; **ils ont une belle a.,** they are very well off; **(b) fosse d'aisances,** cesspool; *Vieilli* **lieu** *ou* **cabinet d'aisances,** public convenience, lavatory.

aise [ɛz] **1** *nf* ease, comfort; **être à l'a.** *ou* **à son a.,** to be comfortable; (*avoir beaucoup de place*) to have (elbow) room; (*financièrement*) to be well off; **on tient à l'a. à six dans cette voiture,** this car holds six comfortably; *F* **à l'a.!,** ea-sy!, no problem!, it's a piece of cake *or Br* a doddle!; **ne pas être à son a., se sentir mal à l'a.,** to feel awkward, to feel uncomfortable, to feel ill at ease; (*physiquement*) to feel indisposed *or* off colour; **être (très) à l'a.,** to be relaxed; **je l'ai mis à l'a. en l'appelant Roger,** I put him at his ease by calling him Roger; *Iron* **elle peut en parler à son a.!,** it's easy (enough) *or* it's all right for her to talk!; **mettez-vous à votre a.,** make yourself comfortable; **il en prend à son a.,** he does as he likes; **faire qch à son a.,** to do sth at one's own convenience; **aimer ses aises,** to like one's comforts; **il prend ses aises,** he makes himself at home.

2 *adj Litt* **je suis bien a. de vous voir,** I am so pleased to see you; **nous serons tout aises de vous revoir,** we will be delighted to see you; **je suis bien** *ou* **tout a. de l'entendre parler ainsi,** I'm delighted to hear him talk this way.

aisé [eze] *adj* **(a)** easy, free (*manner*); comfortable (*clothes, situation*); (*financially*) comfortably off, well-to-do, well heeled; **morale aisée,** lax morals; **parler d'un ton a.,** to speak in a natural way; **(b)** easy (*task*).

aisément [ezemɑ̃] *adv* **(a)** comfortably, freely; **vivre a.,** to be comfortably off; **(b)** (*facilement*) easily, readily.

aisselle [ɛsɛl] *nf* **(a)** *Anat* armpit; **porter qch sous l'a.,** to carry sth under one's arm; **(b)** *Bot* axil(la).

A.I.T.A. [aitea] *nf* (*abrév* **Association internationale des transports aériens**) IATA.

Aix-la-Chapelle [ɛkslaʃapɛl] *nf* Aachen, Aix-la-Chapelle.

ajiste [aʒist] *n* (youth) hosteller.

ajointer [aʒwɛ̃te] *vt* to join up; to fit (*boards, pipes etc*) end to end.

ajonc [aʒɔ̃] *nm* (*plante*) furze, gorse.

ajour [aʒur] *nm* **(a)** opening, hole, orifice (*which lets the light through*); **(b)** (ornamental) perforation, openwork (*in carving etc*); *Couture* **ajours,** hemstitching.

ajouré [aʒure] *adj* perforated; openwork (*design*); *Menuis* **travail a.,** fretwork; *Couture* **travail a.,** drawn-thread work.

ajourer [aʒure] *vt* **(a)** to pierce an opening (*to let in light*); **a. une mansarde,** to make a window in an attic; **(b)** (*of ornamental work*) to perforate, to pierce; *Couture* to hemstitch.

ajournement [aʒurnəmɑ̃] *nm* **(a)** postponement (*of meeting*); (*après début de la séance*) adjournment; *Scol* referring (*of examinee*); *Mil* deferment (*of conscript*); **(b)** *Jur* writ of summons (to appear), subpoena.

ajourner [aʒurne] *vt* **(a)** to postpone, to put off, to defer (*meeting, decision, journey etc*); (*après début de la séance*) to adjourn; to delay (*plan*); *Pol* to table (*bill*); *Scol* to refer (*candidate*); *Mil* to grant deferment to (*conscript*); **(b)** *Jur* to subpoena (*s.o.*).

ajout [aʒu] *nm* addition, extension; *Av* **a. profilé,** fairing.

ajouté [aʒute] *nm* addition (*to manuscript, contract*).

ajouter [aʒute] **1** *vt* to add; **a. qch à qch,** to add sth to sth; **sans a. que ...,** not to mention the fact that ...; **a. aux embarras de qn,** to add to s.o.'s difficulties; **'venez aussi,' ajouta-t-il,** 'you come too,' he added; **nous devons a. que ...,** it should also be stated that ...; **a. foi à qch,** to believe sth. **2 s'ajouter** *vpr* to be added (**à**, to).

ajustable [aʒystabl] *adj* adjustable.

ajustage [aʒystaʒ] *nm* **(a)** fitting, trying on (*of dress etc*); **(b)** assembly (*of machine*); **atelier d'a.,** fitting shop; **a. mécanique,** machining; **(c)** fit; **a. serré,** tight fit; **a. lâche** *ou* **à jeu,** loose fit.

ajustement [aʒystəmɑ̃] *nm* **(a)** adjusting, adjustment (*of apparatus, prices etc*); (*fait de régler*) arrangement; settlement (*of quarrel etc*); **(b) ajustements,** fittings.

ajuster [aʒyste] **1** *vt* **(a)** to adjust (*apparatus, tool*); (*monter*) to set up (*machine*); to gauge (*a coin*); **tapis ajusté,** fitted carpet; **a. son fusil,** to aim one's gun; **feu bien ajusté,** well aimed fire; **a. qch à qch,** to fit *or* adjust *or* adapt sth to sth; *Couture* **a. un vêtement à qn,** to fit a garment on s.o.; **mi ajusté,** semi-fitting; **veste (bien) ajustée,** close- *or* tight-fitting jacket; **(b)** (*mettre au point*) to put (*sth*) right *or* straight; **a. une querelle,** to settle *or F* patch up a quarrel; **a. son chapeau devant le miroir,** to adjust one's hat in front of the mirror; *F* **comme vous voilà ajusté!,** what a sight you look! **2 s'ajuster** *vpr* (*de personne*) to straighten one's clothes, to tidy oneself up; **l'embout s'ajuste sur le tuyau,** the nozzle fits the pipe; **cette clef s'ajuste à chacune des serrures,** this key fits each of the locks.

ajusteur [aʒystœr] *nm* **a. sur métaux, a. mécanicien,** (metal) fitter, filer, bench hand; **a. de tubes (de chaudières),** tube setter.

alacrité [alakrite] *nf Litt* liveliness, alacrity.

Aladin [aladɛ̃] *nm* Aladdin.

Alain [alɛ̃] *nm* Allan, Alan.

alaire [alɛr] *adj Av* **charge a.,** wing load(ing); **surface a.,** wing area.

alaise [alɛz] *nf* drawsheet.

alambic [alɑ̃bik] *nm Ch Ind* still; **passer qch par** *ou* **à l'a.,** to distil sth.

alambiqué [alɑ̃bike] *adj* abstruse, overcomplicated (*text*); too subtle (*mind*).

alangui [alɑ̃gi] *adj* languid.

alanguir [alɑ̃gir] **1** *vt* to make languid; (*affaiblir*) to enfeeble; **la chaleur alanguit les ouvriers,** the heat is making the workers lethargic *or* listless. **2 s'alanguir** *vpr* to grow languid, to flag, to droop, to wilt.

alanguissement [alɑ̃gismɑ̃] *nm* languor.

alarmant [alarmɑ̃] *adj* alarming, frightening; **son état est a.,** his condition is giving serious cause for concern.

alarme [alarm] *nf* (*alerte*) alarm; *Av* warning signal; **donner/sonner l'a.,** to give/sound the alarm; *Rail* **tirer la sonnette d'a.,** to pull the communication cord; **porter l'a. dans un camp,** to raise the alarm; (*souvent non justifié*) to raise a scare; **prendre l'a.,** to take fright; **a. lumineuse,** warning light; *Fig* **à la prochaine a. il faudra vous amener à l'hôpital,** if there's another scare *or* alarm you'll have to be taken to hospital; *Fig* **une fausse a.,** a false alarm; **état d'a.,** state of alert.

alarmer [alarme] **1** *vt* to alarm, to frighten, to startle (*s.o.*); **la nouvelle ne nous a pas alarmés,** we were not alarmed at *or* by the news. **2 s'alarmer** *vpr* to take fright; **il s'alarme pour un rien,** the least thing frightens him; **il n'y a pas lieu de s'a.,** there is no cause for alarm *or* concern.

alarmiste [alarmist] **1** *adj* alarmist; **la presse a.,** the sensational press. **2** *n* alarmist.

Alaska [alaska] *nm* Alaska; **en A.,** in Alaska.

albanais, -aise [albanɛ, -ɛz] **1** *adj* Albanian. **2** *nm Ling* Albanian. **3** *n* **A.,** Albanian.

Albanie [albani] *nf* Albania.

albâtre [albɑtr] *nm* alabaster.

albatros [albatrɔs] *nm* (*oiseau*) albatross.

albigeois, -oise [albiʒwa, -waz] *npl Hist* **les A.,** the Albigenses, the Albigensians.

albinisme [albinism] *nm* albinism.

albinos [albinos] **1** *adj inv* albino; **un lapin a.,** an albino rabbit. **2** *n inv* albino.

Albion [albjɔ̃] *nf Hist* Albion, Britain; *Litt* **la perfide A.,** perfidious Albion.

album [albɔm] *nm Phot Mus etc* album.

albumen [albymɛn] *nm Biol* albumen.

albumine [albymin] *nf Ch* albumin.

alcali [alkali] *nm Ch* alkali.

alcalin, -ine [alkalɛ̃, -in] *adj Ch* alkaline.

alcaloïde [alkalɔid] *nm Ch* alkaloid.

alchimie [alʃimi] *nf* alchemy.

alchimiste [alʃimist] *nm* alchemist.

alcool [alkɔl] *nm* **(a)** alcohol; **a. absolu,** pure *or* absolute alcohol; **a. éthylique,** ethyl alcohol; **a. à brûler** *ou* **dénaturé,** methylated spirits; *Méd* **a. à 90°,** = surgical spirit, *US* rubbing alcohol; **lampe à a.,** spirit lamp, *US* alcohol lamp; **(b)** (*boisson*) alcohol; (*whisky, eau-de-vie etc*) spirits, hard liquor, *F* the hard stuff; **je ne bois jamais d'a.,** (*de liqueurs etc*) I never drink spirits; (*rien d'alcoolisé*) I don't drink (anything alcoholic); **a. blanc,** clear spirits (*par ex* kirsch); **a. de poire,** pear brandy; **vous prendrez bien un petit a.?,** would you like a liqueur *or* a brandy *etc*?

alcoolémie [alkɔlemi] *nf Méd* presence of alcohol in the blood; **taux d'a.,** level of alcohol in the blood.

alcoolique [alkɔlik] **1** *adj* alcoholic. **2** *n* alcoholic; **être un a.,** to be an alcoholic.

alcoolisation [alkɔlizɑsjɔ̃] *nf* alcoholization.

alcoolisé [alkɔlize] *adj* alcoholic (*drink*).

alcooliser [alkɔlize] **1** *vt* to fortify (*wine*). **2 s'alcooliser** *vpr* to drink too much.

alcoolisme [alkɔlism] *nm Méd* alcoholism.

alcoolo [alkɔlo] *n* alcoholic.

alcoomètre [alkɔmɛtr] *nm* alcohol(o)meter.

alcootest [alkɔtɛst] *nm* breathalyser test; **faire passer** *ou* **subir un a. à un conducteur,** to breathalyze *or* breath-test a motorist.

alcôve [alkov] *nf* alcove; **a. de dortoir,** cubicle; **secrets d'a.,** *F* pillow talk.

aldéhyde [aldeid] *nm Ch* aldehyde; **a. formique,**

formaldehyde.
aldin [aldɛ̃] *adj Typ* Aldine (*edition, type*).
ale [ɛl] *nf* (light) ale.
aléa [alea] *nm* risk, hazard, chance; **l'affaire présente trop d'aléas,** it's too risky a business; **les aléas de la vie,** the hazards of life.
aléatoire [aleatwar] *adj* random (*sampling*); problematical, chancy, uncertain (*result*); *Jur* aleatory (*contract etc*); *Math* **fonction/variable a.,** random function/variable; *Ordinat* **accès a.,** random access.
alémanique [alemanik] *adj Ling* **Suisse a.,** German-speaking Switzerland.
alêne [alɛn] *nf* awl; **a. plate,** bradawl.
alentour [alɑ̃tur] **1** *adv* around, round about; **les villages a.,** the surrounding *or* neighbouring villages; **le pays d'a.,** the surrounding *or* neighbouring countryside. **2** *nmpl* **alentours,** surroundings, vicinity; **aux alentours de la ville,** in the vicinity of the town; **il n'y avait personne aux alentours,** there was no-one around *or* in the vicinity; **il est arrivé aux alentours de midi,** he arrived (some time) around mid-day.
aléoute [aleut] **, aléoutien, -ienne** [aleusɛ̃, -jɛn] **1** *adj* Aleutian; **les (îles) Aléoutiennes,** the Aleutian Islands. **2** *n* **A.,** Aleut(ian).
alerte [alɛrt] **1** *nf* alarm; **donner/sonner l'a.,** to give/sound the alarm; **a. (aérienne),** air-raid warning; **en cas d'a.,** if the alarm sounds; **le système d'a. d'une maison,** the (burglar) alarm system of a house; **être en a.,** to be on the alert; *Mil* **fin d'a.,** all clear; *Av* **a. en piste,** scramble; **point d'a.,** danger point; **une chaude a.,** a narrow escape, a close shave; **a. à la bombe,** bomb scare. **2** *adj* **(a)** alert, quick; brisk (*walk*); **style a.,** lively style (*of writing*); **il est paralysé mais son esprit est très a.,** he's paralysed but his mind is (still) very alert; **(b)** *Arch* vigilant, watchful. **3** *int* look out!; *Arch* to arms!
alertement [alɛrtəmɑ̃] *adv* briskly.
alerter [alɛrte] *vt* to alert, to give the alarm to (*troops*); to alert, to warn (*the police etc*); **a. l'opinion publique,** to alert public opinion.
alésage [alezaʒ] *nm Métal* **(a)** (*opération*) boring (out); (*of cylinder*) reaming; **(b)** bore (*of rifle barrel*); bore (*of combustion engine*); internal diameter (*of cylinder etc*).
alèse [alɛz] *nf Méd* drawsheet.
aléser [aleze] *vt Métal* to bore (out); (*élargir*) to ream.
aléseuse [alezøz] *nf Métal* borer; (*pour élargir*) reamer.
alester [alɛste] **, alestir** [alɛstir] *vt Nau* **(a)** to lighten (*ship*); **(b)** to trim up, to tidy up (*rigging*).
alevin [alvɛ̃] *nm* alevin, fry.
alevinage [alvinaʒ] *nm* (*d'une rivière etc*) stocking with young fish.
aleviner [alvine] *vt* to stock (*a river*) with young fish.
alevinier [alvinje] *nm,* **alevinière** [alvinjɛr] *nf* breeding pond, nursery.
Alexandrie [alɛksɑ̃dri] *nf* Alexandria.
alexandrin, -ine [alɛksɑdrɛ̃, -in] **1** *adj* **(a)** *Littér* alexandrine; **poème en vers alexandrins,** poem in alexandrine verse *or* in alexandrines; **(b)** *Géog* Alexandrian; *Fig* **des discussions alexandrines,** convoluted discussions. **2** *nm Littér* alexandrine (verse).
alexie [alɛksi] *nf Méd* word blindness, alexia.
alezan, -ane [alzɑ̃, -an] **1** *adj* chestnut (*horse*). **2** *nm* **a. châtain,** chestnut sorrel; **a. roux,** red bay.
alèze [alɛz] *nf Méd* drawsheet.
alfa [alfa] *nm Bot* esparto (grass); **papier d'a.,** esparto paper; **tiré sur a.,** printed on esparto paper.
algarade [algarad] *nf* row, quarrel; **nous avons eu une a.,** we've had a row.
algèbre [alʒɛbr] *nf* algebra; **résoudre un problème par l'a.,** to solve a problem algebraically; *Fig* **c'est de l'a. pour moi,** it's all Greek to me.
algébrique [alʒebrik] *adj* algebraic.
Alger [alʒe] *nf* Algiers; *Hist* (the Department of) Alger.
Algérie [alʒeri] *nf* Algeria; **en A.,** in Algeria.
algérien, -ienne [alʒerjɛ̃, -jɛn] **1** *adj* Algerian. **2** *n* **A.,** Algerian.
algérois, -oise [alʒerwa, -waz] **1** *adj* of *or* from Algiers. **2** *n* **A.,** inhabitant *or* native of Algiers.
algie [alʒi] *nf* ache, pain.
algol [algɔl] *nm Ordinat* ALGOL.
algonkien, -ienne [algɔ̃kjɛ̃] *Géol* **1** *adj* Algonkian. **2** *nm* Algonkian.
Algonquin, -ine [algɔ̃kɛ̃, -in] **1** *adj* (*peuple*) Algonquin. **2** *nm Ling* Algonquian. **3** *n* Algonquin.
algorithme [algɔritm] *nm Math* algorithm.
algorithmique [algɔritmik] *adj Math* algorithmic.
algue [alg] *nf* **algues,** seaweed, *Spéc* algae.
alias [aljɑs] *adv* alias, otherwise known as ... .
alibi [alibi] *nm* alibi.
aliénable [aljenabl] *adj Jur* alienable, transferable.
aliénant [aljenɑ̃] *adj* alienating.
aliénation [aljenɑsjɔ̃] *nf* **(a)** (*de l'esprit*) alienation; **conditions d'a.** alienating conditions; *Psy* **a. mentale,** insanity; **(b)** *Jur* alienation, transfer (*of rights, property etc*).
aliéné, -ée [aljene] *Psy* **1** *adj* mad, insane. **2** *n* insane person; **les aliénés,** the insane; **hospice d'aliénés,** mental hospital; **a. interdit,** certified lunatic.
aliéner [aljene] *v* (**j'aliène, n. aliénerons**) **1** *vt* **(a)** to alienate, to estrange (*affections etc*); **ce commentaire vous a aliéné la sympathie de l'auditoire,** that comment lost you the audience's sympathy; **ces conditions de vie ne peuvent qu'a. les jeunes,** such living conditions can only alienate young people; **(b)** *Jur* to alienate, to transfer (*property, rights etc*); **a. sa liberté,** to give up one's freedom; **(c)** to derange, to unhinge (*the mind*). **2 s'aliéner** *vpr* to lose (*sth*); to alienate (oneself from) (*s.o.*); **s'a. la sympathie de l'électorat,** to lose the goodwill of the electorate; **s'a. un ami,** to alienate a friend; **s'a. l'amitié de qn,** to lose s.o.'s friendship.
aliéniste [aljenist] *n Méd* alienist.
alignement [aliɲmɑ̃] *nm* **(a)** alignment, aligning; *Mil* dressing (*of a line*); making up, balancing (*of accounts etc*); **se mettre à l'a.,** to fall into line, to line up; *Mil* **à droite a.!,** right dress!; **a. monétaire,** alignment of currencies; *Pol* **l'a. du parti sur la politique de l'URSS,** the party's alignment with the policy of the USSR; **(b)** alignment, line (*of wall etc*); **un a. de menhirs,** a line of menhirs; *Constr* **déborder** *ou* **dépasser l'a.,** to project beyond the building line; **maison frappée d'a.,** house scheduled for realignment; **(c)** *Rail* straight stretch (*of line*).
aligner [aliɲe] **1** *vt* **(a)** (*mettre en ligne*) to align, to line up, to put in a line; (*arranger*) to lay out; *Mil* to dress (a line); **a. un terrain,** to mark out a plot (of ground); *Typ* **a. des caractères,** to align *or* range type; *Pol* **a. sa politique sur celle des États voisins,** to fall into line with the policy of neighbouring states; **(b)** (*dire, faire à la suite*) to marshal (*arguments*); *F* **les a.,** to pay out, to cough up; **(c) a. un compte,** to balance an account. **2 s'aligner** *vpr* (*d'une politique, d'une action*) to be in line (*with sth*); (*d'un pays, d'une personne*) to fall into line; *Mil* to dress; *Arg* **tu peux toujours t'a.!,** just you try it!; *Pol* **la Hongrie s'alignait sur l'URSS,** Hungary used to follow the Soviet line.
aliment [alimɑ̃] *nm* **(a)** food; **a. pauvre/riche,** food that is low/high in nutritional value; **des aliments en conserve/surgelés,** tinned/frozen food; **a. périssable,** perishable food; *Physiol* **a. complet,** complete food; *Fig* **cette histoire a servi d'a. à la presse,** the press made a meal out of the story; **(b)** *Jur* **aliments,** alimony.
alimentaire [alimɑ̃tɛr] *adj* **(a)** nutritious (*food, plant etc*); **produits alimentaires,** food, foodstuffs; **conserves alimentaires,** tinned *or* canned food(s); **régime a.,** diet; *Jur* **pension** *ou* **provision a.,** alimony, maintenance; **payer** *ou* **verser une pension a.,** to pay alimony; **il est en retard dans le paiement de la pension a.,** he's late with his *or* the alimony; *Fig* **travail** *ou* **occupation a.,** job that pays the rent; *Admin Hist* **carte a.,** ration card; **surveiller son bol a.,** to watch what one eats; **mauvaises habitudes alimentaires,** bad eating habits; **(b)** *Physiol* **canal** *ou* **tube a.,** alimentary canal; **pompe a.,** feed pump.
alimentation [alimɑ̃tɑsjɔ̃] *nf* **(a)** food, nourishment; *Biol* nutrition; **avoir une a. équilibrée,** to have a balanced diet; **a. défectueuse,** malnutrition; **surveillez votre a.,** watch what you eat; **(b)** feeding (*of plants, animals etc*); supply (*of town, market etc*); **article d'a.,** foodstuff; *Com* **(magasin d') a.,** grocer's shop; **(rayon d') a.,** grocery department, food counter; **(c)** *Tech* feed(ing) (*of boiler etc*); feed mechanism (*of gun*); **pompe d'a.,** feed pump; **a. par pesanteur** *ou* **par gravité,** gravity feed; *Él* **bloc d'a.,** power supply; **câble** *ou* **fil d'a.,** feeder.
alimenter [alimɑ̃te] **1** *vt* **(a)** to feed, to nourish (*s.o.*); to supply (*market*) with food; **ruisseaux qui alimentent une rivière,** streams that feed a river; *Él* **a. une usine en courant,** to supply a factory with power; *Fig* **a. la curiosité de qn,** to feed s.o.'s curiosity; **a. la conversation par des anecdotes,** to keep the conversation going with anecdotes; **(b)** *Jur* **a. son épouse,** to provide maintenance *or* alimony for one's wife. **2 s'alimenter** *vpr* to eat; (*d'un malade*) to take (solid) food.
alinéa [alinea] *nm Typ* **(a)** (*renfoncement*) (indented) first line of paragraph; **en a.,** indented; **(b)** (*texte*) paragraph,

F para.

alité [alite] *adj* confined to (one's) bed, *F* laid up; (*infirme*) bedridden.

alitement [alitmɑ̃] *nm* confinement to bed; **trois jours d'a.,** three days in bed.

aliter [alite] **1** *vt* to confine (*s.o.*) to bed, to keep (*s.o.*) in bed. **2 s'aliter** *vpr* (*se mettre au lit*) to take to one's bed; (*rester au lit*) to stay in bed.

alizé [alize] *adj & nm* **les (vents) alizés,** the trade winds.

allaitant [alɛtɑ̃] *adj* suckling, nursing; **mère allaitante,** nursing mother.

allaitement [alɛtmɑ̃] *nm* feeding, nursing, suckling; **a. au biberon,** bottle-feeding; **a. mixte,** mixed feeding; **a. naturel,** breast-feeding; **durant l'a.,** during breast-feeding.

allaiter [alete] *vt* to breast-feed, to nurse (*child*); to suckle (*child or young*).

allant [alɑ̃] **1** *adj* (*personne*) active, mobile, busy, bustling, lively; (*personne âgée*) active, mobile, able to move *or* walk about. **2** *nm* initiative, drive, energy; **avoir de l'a., être plein d'a.,** to be full of go *or* (drive and) energy; **elle travaille avec a.,** she works energetically *or* with gusto.

alléchant [aleʃɑ̃] *adj* attractive, alluring, enticing, tempting (*offer, food*); appetizing (*smell etc*).

allécher [aleʃe] *vt* (**j'allèche, n. alléchons; j'allécherai**) to attract, to entice, to tempt, to allure; **j'étais alléché par cette proposition,** I was tempted by the proposal.

allée [ale] *nf* **(a)** (*dans un jardin*) path; (*entre deux immeubles*) passage, alley; (*dans une ville*) street, avenue; walk (*esp lined with trees*); **a. (cavalière),** bridle path; **l'a. mène à la maison,** (*grande*) the drive leads to the house; (*petite*) the path leads to the house; **a. des Acacias,** Acacia Avenue; **(b) allées et venues,** coming(s) and going(s), running about; **j'ai dû faire de nombreuses allées et venues pour obtenir ce visa,** I had to run all over the place to get this visa; **qu'est-ce que signifient ces allées et venues à cette heure tardive?,** what's the meaning of all these comings and goings at this time of night?

allégation [alegasjɔ̃] *nf* allegation.

allège [alɛʒ] *nf* **(a)** *Nau* lighter, hopper, barge; *Com* **frais d'a.,** lighterage; **franco a.,** free over side; **(b)** breast wall, basement (*of window*); balustrade, rail (*of window etc*).

allégeance¹ [aleʒɑ̃s] *nf* **(a)** (*nationalité*) nationality; **avoir la double a.,** to have dual nationality; **(b)** *Hist* **serment d'a.,** oath of allegiance.

allégeance² *nf Sp* handicapping (*of yachts*).

allégement [alɛʒmɑ̃] *nm* **(a)** alleviation, relief (*of pain, grief*); reduction (*of taxation*); **(b)** lightening (*of vessel*).

alléger [aleʒe] *vt* (**j'allège, n. allégeons; j'allégeai(s); j'allégerai**) **(a)** to reduce (*taxes*); to alleviate, to relieve, to soothe (*pain, grief*); to ease the strain on (*timbers etc*); **(b)** to lighten (*ships etc*); *Scol* **a. un programme scolaire,** to lighten a school syllabus; **a. qn de qch,** to relieve s.o. of (the weight of) sth; **(c)** *Tech* to reduce the volume of (*sth*); to plane down (*wood*); to file down, to fine down (*metal*).

allégorie [alegɔri] *nf* allegory; **par a.,** allegorically.

allégorique [alegɔrik] *adj* allegorical.

allégoriquement [alegɔrikmɑ̃] *adv* allegorically.

allègre [alɛgr] *adj* lively, jolly, cheerful; **musique a.,** lively music; **caractère a.,** cheerful disposition; **avoir le cœur a.,** to be light-hearted; **marcher d'un pas a.,** to walk briskly.

allégrement [alɛgrəmɑ̃] *adv* cheerfully; (*marcher*) briskly.

allégresse [alegrɛs] *nf* joy, cheerfulness, liveliness; **plein d'a.,** full of joy; **a. générale,** general rejoicing.

allegretto [alegrɛto] *adv & nm Mus* allegretto.

allegro [alegro] *adv & nm Mus* allegro.

alléguer [alege] *vt* (**j'allègue, n. alléguons; j'alléguerai**) **(a)** (*invoquer*) to allege, to plead; **a. l'ignorance,** to plead ignorance; **a. une excuse/raison,** to put forward *or* offer *or* give an excuse/reason; **a. comme raison que le temps manquait,** to give as one's reason lack of time; **il allégua que personne ne l'avait informé de ce projet,** he alleged that no-one had informed him of the plan; **(b)** to cite, to quote (*author, text etc*).

alléluia [aleluja] *int & nm Rel* alleluia, hallelujah.

Allemagne [almaɲ] *nf* Germany; **l'A. de l'ouest/de l'est,** West/East Germany; **l'ambassadeur d'A.,** the German ambassador; **l'union des deux Allemagnes,** the (re)unification of Germany, German unity.

allemand, -ande [almɑ̃, -ɑ̃d] **1** *adj* German; **la langue allemande,** the German language, German. **2** *nm Ling* German, the German language. **3** *n* **A.,** German; **A. de l'Est/de l'Ouest,** East/West German. **4** *nf Mus* **allemande,** allemande.

aller¹ [ale] **1** *vi* (*prp* **allant**; *pp* **allé**; *pr ind* **je vais** (*Arch & Dial* **je vas**), **tu vas, il va, n. allons, v. allez, ils vont**; *pr sub* **j'aille, n. allions, ils aillent**; *imp* **va (vas-y), allons, allez**; *impf* **j'allais**; *p hist* **j'allai**; *fu* **j'irai**; *the aux is* **être**) **(a)** (*se rendre*) to go; **a. à Paris,** to go to Paris; **navire allant à Bordeaux,** ship bound for Bordeaux; **on va sur Lyon,** we're going to *or* as far as Lyons; **a. chez qn,** to call on *or* visit s.o., to go and see s.o.; **qui va là?,** who goes there?; **ne faire qu'a. et venir,** to be always on the go *or* on the move; **je ne ferai qu'a. et revenir,** I shall come straight back; **a. où va toute chose,** to go the way of all things *or* of all flesh; **où allons-nous?,** where are we going?; *Fig* (*qu'est-ce qu'on va devenir?*) what are things coming to?; **je suis allé aux nouvelles,** I went to find out what was happening; **il va sur ses quarante ans,** he is getting on for forty, he is nearly forty (years old); **il ira loin,** he will go far *or* will distinguish himself; **vous allez trop loin,** you're going too far; **vous n'irez pas loin avec 50 francs,** 50 francs won't get you very far, you won't get very far on 50 francs; **soyez tranquille, cela n'ira pas plus loin,** don't worry, it won't go any further; **le pauvre vieux n'ira pas loin,** the poor old chap won't last long; **a. jusqu'au bout,** to see it through; (*avoir des rapports sexuels*) to go the whole way; **nous irons jusqu'au bout,** we shall carry on to the end; **décontractez-vous, laissez-vous a.,** relax, let yourself go; **reprends-toi, tu ne dois pas te laisser a.,** pull yourself together, you mustn't let yourself go; **se laisser a. à la tendresse/à de meilleurs sentiments,** to give way to tenderness/better feelings;

(b) (*se déplacer*) to go, to move; (*à pied*) to walk; **on va à la catastrophe,** we're heading for disaster; **on y va à pied,** we're walking there; **j'y suis allé très lentement,** I went very slowly; **a. en course/à la chasse/à la pêche/à cheval/en voiture/au galop/au trot,** *see these words*; **a. aux champignons,** to go mushroom-picking; *F* **a. aux courses,** to go shopping;

(c) *with adv* **a. bon train,** to go at a good pace; **a. grand train,** to race along;

(d) a. son (petit bonhomme de) chemin, to go one's way; *F* to chug along;

(e) (*mener*) to lead, to go; **chemin qui va à la gare,** road leading to the station; **tous les chemins vont à Rome,** all roads lead to Rome;

(f) (*être conçu pour*) **ces ciseaux vont bien pour couper les roses,** these scissors are good for cutting roses; **plat qui va au feu** *ou* **allant au feu** *ou* **au four,** fireproof *or* ovenproof dish;

(g) (*marcher*) to go (*well, badly*); **tout va bien,** everything is going well *or* is fine; **non, ça ne va pas du tout,** (*ce n'est pas ce que j'ai demandé*) no, that won't do at all; *F* **non mais ça va pas?!,** are you crazy?!, what's wrong with you?!; **ça ira!,** we'll manage!; **ça n'irait pas du tout,** that would never do; **ça va a. mal si tu me mens,** if you've been lying to me, there'll be trouble; **il y a quelque chose qui ne va pas,** there's something wrong; **je vous en offre cent francs, ça va?,** I'll give you 100 francs for it, O.K.?; **cela va sans dire** *ou* **de soi,** that goes without saying;

(h) (*of machine, clock etc*) to go, to work, to run; **la pendule va bien/mal,** the clock is/isn't working (properly); **quand le bâtiment va, tout va,** what's good for the construction industry is good for us all; **les affaires vont/ne vont pas,** business is good/slack; **faire a. un commerce,** to run a business; **tout va comme sur des roulettes,** everything is going like clockwork;

(i) (*of clothes etc*) **ce veston ne va pas bien,** this jacket doesn't fit well;

(j) (*tenir*) **c'est trop grand pour a. dans le panier,** it's too big to go *or* get into the basket;

(k) (*se porter*) **comment allez-vous?,** how are you?; **je vais bien,** *F* **ça va,** I'm well, I'm all right; **cela va mieux,** I'm better; **cela ne va pas,** I'm not feeling very well;

(l) a. à qn, (*of colours etc*) to suit s.o.; (*of clothes*) to fit s.o.; (*of climate, food*) to agree with s.o.; (*of plan etc*) to suit s.o.; **cela vous va comme un gant,** (*d'une robe etc*) it fits you like a glove; (*d'une situation etc*) it suits you down to the ground; **cette robe te va mal,** (*elle te grossit*) that dress doesn't suit you; **la chemise ne me va pas,** (*elle est trop petite*) the shirt doesn't fit me; **ça me va!,** agreed!, done!; **ça va!,** O.K.!; **ça te va bien de me conseiller,** you're a fine one to give me advice; **ça va comme ça,** it's all right as it is;

(m) (*of colours etc*) **a. avec qch,** to go well with sth, to match sth; **a. (bien) ensemble,** to go well together, to match; **chaussettes qui ne vont pas ensemble,** odd socks;

(n) (**aller** + *inf*) **a. voir qn,** to go and *or* to see s.o., to call on s.o.; **a. trouver qn,** to go and find s.o.; **a. se promener,** to go for a walk; **va donc le lui dire!,** go and tell him then!; *F* **allez vous promener!,** go (and) jump in the lake!; **n'allez pas vous imaginer que ...,** don't imagine that ..., don't go imagining that ..., don't get it into your head that ...; **allez donc savoir!,** how are you (supposed) to know?; *F* **allez vous faire voir!,** go to hell!;

(o) (*used as an auxiliary*) to be going, to be about (to do sth); **il va s'en occuper,** he is going to see about it, he'll deal with it; **il va venir,** he'll be coming; **elle allait tout avouer,** she was about to confess everything; **sa santé va (en) empirant,** his health is steadily deteriorating; **j'y vais,** (*ouvrir la porte*) I'll get it;

(p) (*avec y*) **j'y vais!, on y va!,** coming!; **est-ce comme ça que vous y allez?,** is that how you go about it *or* do it?; **allez-y doucement!,** easy *or* gently (does it)!; **y a. de tout son cœur,** to put one's heart and soul into it; **y a. carrément** *ou* **franchement,** to make no bones about it; **il n'y va pas par quatre chemins,** he doesn't mince matters *or* beat about the bush; **vas-y, dis-moi ce que tu as à dire!,** go on then, say what you've got to say!; **maintenant allons-y!,** now (let's get down) to it!; **allons-y!,** well, here goes!; **vas-y! allez-y!,** go!; (*travail etc*) get on with it!; (*questions*) fire away!; *F* **y a. de qch,** to lay *or* stake sth; **y a. de son reste,** to stake one's all; **y a. de sa personne,** to take a hand in it oneself; *F* to do one's bit; **il y est allé de son histoire/sa petite chanson/***etc*, he gave us his story/little song/*etc*;

(q) allons, dépêchez-vous!, come on, hurry up!; **allons donc!,** (*c'est vrai?*) well I never!; **allez, je vous écoute,** go ahead, I'm listening; **allez, c'est oublié,** don't worry, it's all forgotten; **ça va, ça va, on te pardonne,** OK, OK, you're forgiven; **allons bon!,** there now!; (*exprimant de l'irritation*) bother!; **mais va donc!,** get on with it!; **allons, sois un peu raisonnable!,** come on now, be reasonable!; **va pour une soirée au cinéma,** OK then, a night out at the cinema it is; **allez, allez, débarrasse la table,** come on *or* along (now), clear the table!; *F* **va donc, eh patate!,** if you don't like it, you can lump it!

2 s'en aller *vpr* (*pr ind* **je m'en vais**; *imp* **va-t'en, allons-nous-en, allez-vous-en, ne t'en va pas, ne nous en allons pas**; *perf* **je m'en suis allé(e), nous nous en sommes allé(e)s**) **(a)** (*partir*) to go away, to leave; **les voisins s'en vont,** the neighbours are moving; **s'en a. en vacances,** to go away on holiday; **elle s'en est allée** *ou* **s'est en allée assez satisfaite,** she went away quite satisfied; **allez-vous-en!,** go away!; **allons-nous-en!,** let's go!; **s'en aller en fumée,** to go up in smoke; **à demain, je m'en vais,** I'm off, see you tomorrow; **il faut que je m'en aille,** I must be going; **ses forces s'en allaient,** his strength was failing;

(b) (*mourir*) to pass away, to die; **le malade s'en va,** the patient is sinking (fast);

(c) votre lait s'en va, your milk is boiling over;

(d) les taches ne veulent pas s'en a., the stains won't come off *or* out;

(e) s'en a. faire qch, to go off and *or* to do sth; **je m'en vais lui dire ce que je pense,** I'm going to tell him exactly what I think; **va-t-en voir si il ne ment pas!,** how am I *or* how are we *etc* supposed to know if he's telling the truth or not!; **je m'en vais vous raconter ça,** I'll tell you all about it.

3 *v impers* **il va sans dire** *ou* **de soi que ...,** it stands to reason *or* it goes without saying that ...; **il en va de même pour lui/moi,** it's the same with him/me; **il va sans dire qu'elle a refusé,** it goes without saying that she refused, needless to say, she refused; **il y va de vingt francs,** it's a matter of twenty francs; **il y allait de sa vie,** it was a matter of life and death (for him), his life was at stake; **il y va de sa place,** his job is at stake; **il y va de votre santé,** your health is at risk, you're risking your health.

aller² *nm* going; outward journey (*of return journey*); **à l'a.,** on the way there; **je me suis arrêté en route à l'a.,** I stopped on my *or* the way (there); **cargaison d'a.,** outward cargo; **a.-retour, voyage d'a. et retour,** round trip, return journey, journey there and back; *Nau* voyage out and home; **billet a.-retour** *ou* **d'a. et retour,** return ticket; *F* **un a.,** a single ticket; *Sp* **match a.,** away match; **a.-retour du piston,** up and down stroke; *Nau* **police à l'a. et au retour,** round policy; *F* **si tu continues, tu vas recevoir un a. et retour dont tu te souviendras,** if you carry on you'll get a clip round the ear that you won't forget in a hurry.

allergène [alɛrʒɛn] *nm Méd* allergen.

allergie [alɛrʒi] *nf Méd* allergy.

allergique [alɛrʒik] *adj Méd Fig* allergic (**à,** to).

allergologiste [alɛrgɔlɔʒist] **, allergologue** [alɛrgɔlɔg] *n Méd* allergist.

aller-retour [alertur] *nm* return (ticket).

alliage [aljaʒ] *nm Métal* alloy; **sans a.,** pure, unalloyed; *Fig* **un a. d'idées fausses,** a mish-mash *or* hotchpotch of false ideas.

alliance [aljɑ̃s] *nf* **(a)** (*entente*) alliance; (*d'un couple*) marriage, union; **conclure une a.,** to enter into *or* conclude an alliance; **faire a. avec/contre qn,** to ally *or* team up with/against s.o., **entrer par a. dans une famille,** to marry into a family; **faire a. avec une autre famille,** to be joined to another family by marriage; **parent par a.,** relation by marriage; **traité d'a.,** treaty of alliance; **(b)** (*bague*) wedding ring; **(c)** (*combinaison*) combination (*of flavours etc*); **une a. de termes très réussie,** a very effective juxtaposition of terms.

allié, -ée [alje] **1** *adj* **(a)** allied (*nation etc*); **(b)** (*dans une famille*) related by marriage; **être bien a.,** to be well connected. **2** *n* ally; (*de famille*) relation by marriage; (*moins précis*) family connection; **il est d'accord avec nous, c'est un a.,** he agrees with us, he's on our side; *Hist* **les Alliés,** the Allies.

allier [alje] *v* (*impf & pr sub* **n. alliions, v. alliiez**) **1** *vt* **(a)** (*unir*) to ally, to unite; **intérêts communs qui allient deux pays,** common interests that unite two countries; **a. une famille à** *ou* **avec une autre,** to unite one family with another by marriage; **(b)** to alloy, to mix (*metals*); to harmonize, to blend, to match (*colours*); to combine (*qualities, words etc*) (**à,** with). **2 s'allier** *vpr* **(a)** (*s'unir*) to form an alliance, to become allies, to ally (**avec qn,** with s.o.); **s'a. à une famille,** to marry into a family; **(b)** (*of fluids*) to mix; (*of metals*) to alloy; (*of colours*) to harmonize, to blend; (*of tastes, qualities*) to combine.

alligator [aligatɔr] *nm* alligator.

allitératif, -ive [aliteratif, -iv] *adj* alliterative.

allitération [aliterasjɔ̃] *nf* alliteration; **a. en s,** alliteration of (the letter) s.

allô, allo [alo] *int Tél* hello!

allocataire [alɔkatɛr] *n* claimant, recipient (*of social security benefit etc*).

allocation [alɔkasjɔ̃] *nf* **(a)** allocation, granting (*of money, of land, supplies etc*); *Fin* allotment (*of shares etc*); *Jur* allocation, allowance (*of items in an account etc*); **(b)** (*prestation financière*) allowance, grant; **allocations familiales,** child benefit, family allowance(s), *US* dependents' allowances; *F* **elle touche les allocations,** she gets child benefit; **a. de maternité/(de) logement/(de) chômage,** maternity/housing/unemployment benefit.

allocution [alɔkysjɔ̃] *nf* **(a)** short speech, address; **(b)** *Rel Jur* charge (*by bishop, by judge to jury*).

allogène [alɔʒɛn] *adj* non-indigenous, non-native (*population etc*).

allonge [alɔ̃ʒ] *nf* **(a)** (extension) leaf (*of a table*); adaptor (*of retort, pipe etc*); lengthening tube; (*de machine*) coupling rod; **mettre une a. à qch,** to lengthen sth; **a. de tige,** extension rod; **a. de boucher,** meathook; **(b)** rider (*to a document*); **(c)** *Boxe* reach; **il a une bonne a.,** he has a long reach; **(d)** *Equitation* lunging rein, longe, lunge.

allongé, -ée [alɔ̃ʒe] **1** *adj* long; elongated (*shape, figure*); **avoir le visage allongé,** to have a long face; **les malades allongés,** recumbent patients; *Anat* **la moelle allongée,** the medulla oblongata; *Sp* **coup a.,** follow through. **2** *n Méd* recumbent patient.

allongement [alɔ̃ʒmɑ̃] *nm* **(a)** lengthening, extension (*of canal etc*); lengthening (*of dress*); elongation (*of metals etc*); strain; *Mil* lifting (*of fire*); **(b)** protraction, extension (*of time*); **a. de la journée de travail,** lengthening *or* extension of the working day; **a. de l'espérance de vie des femmes,** increase in women's life expectancy; **(c)** *Av* aspect ratio (*of wing*).

allonger [alɔ̃ʒe] *v* (**j'allongeai(s); n. allongeons**) **1** *vt* **(a)** (*rendre plus long*) to lengthen; to elongate (*shape, figure*); to let down (*garment*); to add a piece to (*sth*); *Mil* to lift (*fire*); **cette robe vous allonge,** this dress makes you look taller; *Culin* **a. la sauce,** to thin (down) the sauce; *Fig* to spin it out; *Sp* **a. l'allure,** to increase the pace;

(b) to stretch out (*one's arm*); to crane (*one's neck*); to extend, to draw out (*rope etc*); **a. le pas,** to quicken one's pace *or* step(s); *F* **a. qn,** to knock s.o. down, to floor s.o.; **a. un coup à qn,** to aim a blow at s.o.; *F* **je lui ai allongé une gifle dont il se souviendra,** I gave him a slap he'll remember for a long time; **a. l'argent,** to hand over *or* fork out the money;

(c) to protract, to prolong (*conversation etc*).

2 s'allonger *vpr* **(a)** (*of days etc*) to grow longer, to lengthen; (*of child*) to get taller, to grow; **(b)** (*se coucher*) to stretch oneself out, to lie down at full length; *F* **s'a. (par terre),** to fall flat on the ground, to come a cropper. **3** *vi* to extend; *Sp* **le peloton des coureurs allonge derrière,** the field is strung out behind; **les jours commencent à a.,** the days are starting to get longer.

allopathe [alɔpat] *Méd* **1** *adj* allopathic. **2** *n* allopath, allopathist.

allopathie [alɔpati] *nf Méd* allopathy.

allouer [alwe] *vt Admin* to grant (*salary etc*); to allocate, to apportion (*shares, rations etc*); **a. une dépense/un budget,** to allow *or* pass an item of expenditure/a budget; *Jur* **a. à qn une somme à titre de dommages-intérêts,** to award s.o. damages; **pendant le temps alloué,** (*faire qch*) within the allotted time, within the time allowed.

allumage [alymaʒ] *nm* lighting (*of lamp, fire*); switching on (*of electric light*); (*de moteur à combustion*) ignition; firing (*of mine*); **a. défectueux,** misfiring; **a. prématuré,** pre-ignition.

allumé, -ée [alyme] **1** *adj* **(a)** alight, burning; (*blast furnace*) in blast; **(b)** *F* (*ivre*) tiddly, lit up; **(c)** *F* (*dingue*) crazy, off one's head *or* rocker. **2** *n F* nutcase, nutter.

allume-cigare [alymsigar] *nm* cigar lighter; (*pl allume-cigares*).

allume-gaz [alymgaz] *nm inv* gas lighter (*for cooker*).

allumer [alyme] **1** *vt* **(a)** to light (*lamp, fire, pipe*); **veux-tu a. la lumière?,** will you switch on *or* put on the lights?; **a. un projecteur,** to switch on a searchlight; **a. une pompe,** to prime *or* fetch a pump; **(b)** *Fig* to inflame, to excite, to stir up, to arouse (*passions, people*); **a. l'imagination,** to fire the imagination; **elle allume les hommes,** she excites men, she turns men on; **se faire a.,** to get a ticking *or* telling off. **2 s'allumer** *vpr* to catch fire; (*of eyes*) to light up; **ça ne s'allume pas,** the light's not working; **s'a. prématurément,** (*of engine*) to backfire. **3** *vi* to switch on *or* put on *or* turn on the light(s).

allumette [alymɛt] *nf* **(a)** match; **a. de sûreté,** safety match; **pochette/boîte d'allumettes,** book/box of matches; **frotter une a.,** to strike a match; *F* **des jambes comme des allumettes,** matchstick legs; **(b)** *Culin* **a. au fromage,** cheese straw; **pommes allumettes,** game chips.

allumeur [alymœr] *nm* **(a)** (*appareil*) lighter, igniting device; (*de moteur*) distributor; **(b)** *Arch* lighter, igniter; **a. de réverbère,** lamplighter.

allumeuse [alymøz] *nf F* (*femme aguichante*) tease.

allure [alyr] *nf* **(a)** (*vitesse*) pace, speed; **marcher à (une) vive a.,** to walk at a brisk pace; **à toute a.,** at full *or* top speed; all out; *Sp* at full stretch; **pleine a.,** maximum speed; **a. économique de croisière,** cruising speed; **(b)** (*démarche*) walk, gait; (*manière de se tenir*) bearing; **allures d'un cheval,** paces of a horse; **(c)** working (*of furnace, engine etc*); **a. régulière,** smooth running; **a. de marche,** rating; **a. normale,** normal speed; **(d)** (*manière de se présenter*) manner; (*manière d'agir*) way(s) of doing things; (*de quelqu'un, des événements etc*) aspect, look (*of person, things, events*); **il prend** *ou* **se donne des allures de roi quand il est en visite,** he acts *or* behaves like royalty when he's visiting; **elle/la voiture a de l'a.,** she's/the car's got (real) style; **l'a. des affaires,** the way things are going; **prendre bonne a.,** to look promising, to look well.

allusif, -ive [alyzif, -iv] *adj* allusive; **sois moins a.,** talk straight!

allusion [alyzjɔ̃] *nf* allusion (**à,** to); *Péj* innuendo; **faire a. à qn/qch,** to refer to *or* to make an allusion to s.o./sth; **c'est à vous que s'adresse cette a.,** that's a dig at you, that's meant for you; **cette a. m'échappe,** I can't see what he's *etc* getting at.

allusivement [alyzivmɑ̃] *adv* allusively.

alluvial, -iaux [alyvjal, -jo] *adj Géol* alluvial.

alluvions [alyvjɔ̃] *nfpl Géol* alluvium.

almanach [almana] *nm* (*calendrier*) almanac; yearbook.

aloès [alɔɛs] *nm* (*plante*) aloe; *Pharm* **amer d'a.,** bitter aloes.

aloi [alwa] *nm* **(a)** standard, quality, kind (*of thing, people*); **de bon a.,** genuine; **un succès de bon a.,** a well-deserved *or* worthy success; **(b)** (*titre*) = proportion of precious metal in an alloy; **pièce de mauvais a.,** base coin, light coin; *Arch* degree of fineness (*of coin*); *Arch* **monnaie d'a.,** sterling money.

alopécie [alɔpesi] *nf Méd* alopecia.

alors [alɔr] **1** *adv* **(a)** (*à cette époque-là*) then, at that time, at the time; **que faisiez-vous a.?,** what were you doing then *or* at the time?; **jusqu'a.,** until then; **la vie d'a.,** life then *or* in those days; **le ministre d'a.,** the minister at the time, the then minister; **(b)** (*dans ce cas*) (well) then, in that case, in such a case; **a. vous viendrez?,** well then, you're coming?; **et (puis) a.?, a. quoi?,** and what then?; (*qu'est-ce que ça peut faire?*) so what?; *F* **non mais a.?, pour qui te prends-tu?,** just who do you think you are!; **(c)** (*donc*) therefore, so; **il n'était pas là, a. je suis revenu,** he wasn't there, so I came back. **2** *conj* **a. (même) que,** (at the very time) when, even when; (*bien que*) even though; **vous économisez, a. qu'il faudrait dépenser,** you're saving, when you should be spending; **a. même que je le pourrais,** even though I could.

alouette [alwɛt] *nf* **(a)** (*oiseau*) lark; **a. des champs,** skylark; **a. des bois,** woodlark; **a. de mer,** summer snipe, sea lark, dunlin; **(b)** *Culin* **a. sans tête,** veal olive.

alourdi [alurdi] *adj* heavy, dull; **a. de sommeil,** drowsy; **a. par le sommeil,** heavy with sleep; **style a. par trop de tournures compliquées,** style weighed down by too many complicated expressions; *Fin* **le marché est alourdi,** the market is dull.

alourdir [alurdir] **1** *vt* to make (*sth*) heavy; to weigh (*s.o., sth*) down; *Fig* to dull (*the senses*); to make (*phrase*) cumbersome *or* unwieldy. **2 s'alourdir** *vpr* to grow *or* become heavy.

alourdissant [alurdisɑ̃] *adj* oppressive (*heat, weather etc*).

alourdissement [alurdismɑ̃] *nm* (process of) growing heavy; growing heaviness (*of limbs etc*); dulling (*of the senses*); **sensation d'a.,** feeling of heaviness.

aloyau, -aux [alwajo] *nm Culin* sirloin (*of beef*); **bifteck d'a.,** T-bone (steak).

alpaga [alpaga] *nm Zool Tex* alpaca.

alpage [alpaʒ] *nm* (*pâturage*) alp, mountain pasture; (*droit*) right of pasture (*on mountain slopes*); (*saison*) = season spent by livestock in mountain pastures.

alpaguer [alpage] *vt F* to nab; **se faire a. par la police,** to get nabbed by the police.

alpe [alp] *nf* **(a)** *Région* (*pâturage*) alp, mountain pasture; **(b) Les Alpes,** the Alps; **les Alpes suisses,** the Swiss Alps; **cor des Alpes,** alpenhorn; **pavot des Alpes,** Alpine poppy; **les Alpes australiennes,** the Australian Alps; **les Alpes néo-zélandaises** *ou* **méridionales,** the Southern Alps.

alpestre [alpɛstr] *adj* alpine (*scenery, climate, resort, plant etc*) **plante a.,** alpine (plant).

alpha [alfa] *nm* **(a)** (*lettre de l'alphabet grec*) alpha; **l'a. et l'oméga,** Alpha and Omega, the beginning and the end; **(b)** alpha (*particle, rays, radiation*).

alphabet [alfabɛ] *nm* **(a)** alphabet; **apprendre son a. à un enfant,** to teach a child the alphabet; **(b)** *Scol* spelling book.

alphabetique [alfabetik] *adj* alphabetical; **par ordre a.,** in alphabetical order, alphabetically.

alphabétisation [alfabetizasjɔ̃] *nm* teaching (*of a population etc*) to read and write; **taux d'a.,** literacy rate.

alphabétiser [alfabetize] *vt* to teach (*s.o.*) to read and write.

alphanumérique [alfanymerik] *adj* alphanumeric.

alpin [alpɛ̃] *adj* alpine (*plant, troops*); **la chaîne alpine, le massif a.,** the Alps; **ski a.,** downhill skiing.

alpinisme [alpinism] *nm Sp* mountaineering, climbing; **faire de l'a.,** to go mountaineering *or* climbing.

alpiniste [alpinist] *n* mountaineer, climber.

Alsace [alzas] *nf* Alsace.

alsacien, -ienne [alzasjɛ̃, -jɛn] **1** *adj* from Alsace, Alsatian. **2** *nm Ling* Alsatian (dialect). **3** *n* **A.,** inhabitant of Alsace, Alsatian.

altérable [alterabl] *adj* liable to deterioration; **marchandise a.,** perishable goods.

altéragène [alteraʒɛn] *adj* (*substance*) harmful to the environment, noxious.

altérant [alterɑ̃] *adj* thirst-producing, thirst-making.

altération [alterasjɔ̃] *nf* **(a)** change (*for the worse*); impairing (*of health etc*); deterioration (*of food etc*); **a. de la voix,** breaking of the voice; **(b)** *Ordinat* corruption; **(c)** (*falsification*) debasing, debasement (*of coinage*); adulteration (*of food*); falsification (*of document*); garbling (*of text*); misrepresentation (*of facts*); **(d)** *Mus* sharp *or* flat sign, inflection; (*dans le courant du morceau*) accidental; **(e)** (*soif*) great thirst.

altercation [alterkasjɔ̃] *nf* altercation, dispute.

alter ego [alterego] *nm inv* alter ego.

altéré [altere] *adj* **(a)** faded (*colour*); drawn, haggard (*face*); **les faits sont altérés,** the facts have been distorted; **(b)** *Ordinat* corrupt; **(c)** (*assoiffé*) thirsty; **a. de**

sang, thirsting for blood, bloodthirsty.

altérer [altere] *v* (**j'altère, n. altérons; j'altérerai**) **1** *vt* **(a)** (*se détériorer*) to change (for the worse); to spoil, to taint, to corrupt (*meat, wine, character*); to adulterate (*wine, food*); to impair (*health*); **voix altérée par l'émotion,** voice faltering *or* husky with emotion; **(b)** *Ordinat* to corrupt; **(c)** (*fausser*) to tamper with (*sth*); to falsify (*document*); to garble (*text, story*); to debase (*coinage*); **a. la vérité,** to twist the truth; **(d)** *Mus* **a. une note,** to inflect a note; **(e)** to make (*s.o.*) thirsty. **2 s'altérer** *vpr* to deteriorate; (*of colours*) to fade.

alternance [altɛrnɑ̃s] *nf* **(a)** alternation (*of seasons, leaves etc*); **a. des cultures,** crop rotation; **en a.,** alternately; **(b)** *Pol* alternation (*of parties in government*); **(c)** *Él* alternation; **redresseur à deux alternances,** full-wave rectifier.

alternateur [altɛrnatœr] *nm* *Él* alternating-current generator, alternator.

alternatif, -ive [altɛrnatif, -iv] **1** *adj* **(a)** (*périodique*) alternative; **(b)** *Él* alternating (*current*); reciprocating (*engine, saw, motion*); **(c)** alternative (*plan, meaning etc*). **2** *nf* **alternative, (a)** (*succession*) alternation, succession; **des alternatives de lumière et d'obscurité,** alternation(s) of light and shade; **(b)** (*choix*) alternative, option, choice; **vous pouvez accepter ou refuser, c'est la seule a.,** take it or leave it, there's no other choice; **être dans une a.,** to have to choose one way or the other; **l'a. verte** *ou* **écologique,** the green alternative *or* option.

alternativement [altɛrnativmɑ̃] *adv* alternately, in turn.

alterne [altɛrn] *adj* alternate (*leaves, angles etc*).

alterner [altɛrne] **1** *vi* **(a)** (*succéder*) to alternate; **(b)** (*avec qn*) to take turns, to take it in turns (**pour,** to + *inf*); **ils alternent pour veiller,** they take it in turns to sit up; **a. à la surveillance,** to take (it in) turns to keep watch. **2** *vt* to rotate (*crops*).

altesse [altɛs] *nf* highness; **son A. impériale,** his *or* her Imperial Highness.

altier -ière [altje, -jɛr] *adj* haughty, proud, arrogant (*tone, bearing*).

altimètre [altimɛtr] *nm* altimeter, altitude indicator; *Av* **a. à contact,** altitude switch.

altiport [altipɔr] *nm* high altitude airport.

altiste [altist] *nm Mus* viola player.

altitraceur [altitrasœr] *nm* altitude recorder.

altitude [altityd] *nf* altitude; **à cent mètres d'a.,** at an altitude of 100 metres; **en a.,** at (a high) altitude; *Av* **prendre de l'a.,** to climb; **vol à haute a.,** altitude flight; **a. limite,** ceiling; *Méd* **cure d'a.,** high-altitude treatment; **mal d'a.,** altitude sickness; **ivresse d'a.,** altitude narcosis.

alto [alto] *nm Mus* **(a)** alto, counter-tenor (voice); **(b)** (*instrument à cordes*) viola, tenor violin; (*saxophone*) tenor saxophone (in E flat).

altocumulus [altɔkymylys] *nm inv Météo* altocumulus.

altostratus [altɔstratys] *nm inv Météo* altostratus.

altruisme [altrɥism] *nm* altruism.

altruiste [altrɥist] **1** *adj* altruistic. **2** *n* altruist.

altuglas ® [altyglas] *nm* = thick form of Perspex ®.

alumine [alymin] *nf Ch* alumina, aluminium oxide.

aluminium [alyminjɔm] *nm* aluminium, *Am* aluminum; **sulfate d'a.,** aluminium sulphate.

alun [alœ̃] *nm* alum; **pierre d'a.,** styptic pencil.

alunir [alynir] *vi* to land on the moon.

alunissage [alynisaʒ] *nm* moon landing.

alvéolaire [alveɔlɛr] *adj* cellular; honeycomb (*pattern*), alveolar (*nerve, vein, consonant*).

alvéole [alveɔl] *nm* **(a)** alveole, alveolus; cell (*of honeycomb etc*); pigeonhole (*of desk etc*); chamber (*of revolver*); **alvéoles pulmonaires,** alveoli of the lungs; **(b)** socket (*of tooth*); socket, seat(ing) (*of diamond*); **(c)** cavity, pit (*in stone etc*); *Él* **alvéoles d'un grillage,** interstices of an accumulator grid; **(d)** *Mil* gun pit.

alvéolé [alveɔle] *adj* honeycomb(ed); *Spéc* alveolate; **carton a.,** corrugated cardboard.

alysse [alis] *nf*, **alysson** [alisɔ̃] *nm* (*plante*) alyssum.

amabilité [amabilite] *nf* amiableness, amiability; (*bonté*) kindness; **auriez-vous l'a. de me dire ...?,** would you be good *or* kind enough to tell me ...?; **faites mes amabilités à ...,** give my kindest regards to ... .

amadou [amadu] *nm* tinder.

amadouement [amadumɑ̃] *nm* (*fait d'enjôler*) wheedling, coaxing; (*apaisement*) softening.

amadouer [amadwe] *vt* (*enjôler, gagner*) to coax, to wheedle, to persuade; (*apaiser*) to soften.

amagnétique [amaɲetik] *adj* non-magnetic.

amaigrir [amɛgrir] **1** *vt* **(a)** to emaciate; to thin down, to reduce (*column, beam etc*); **ce maquillage l'amaigrit,** that make-up makes her (face) look thinner; **(b)** *Agr* to impoverish (*soil*). **2 s'amaigrir** *vpr* to grow thin, to lose weight; **il s'est amaigri de dix kilos,** he has lost ten kilos.

amaigrissant [amɛgrisɑ̃] *adj* slimming (*diet*).

amaigrissement [amɛgrismɑ̃] *nm* **(a)** (*non volontaire*) wasting away, growing thin, emaciation; (*volontaire*) slimming; **cure d'a.,** slimming cure; **(b)** reducing (*in thickness*); thinning down (*of beam etc*).

amalgamation [amalgamɑsjɔ̃] *nf* amalgamation; *Fin* merger.

amalgame [amalgam] *nm* **(a)** *Ch* amalgam; **(b)** (*alliage*) mixture.

amalgamer [amalgame] **1** *vt* **(a)** to amalgamate (*gold, silver, Él zinc plates*); **(b)** to amalgamate (*banks, companies etc*); **il a tendance à a. les deux partis,** (*il ne voit pas la différence*) he tends to get confused between the two parties; (*il met tous les deux dans le même panier*) he tends to think of the two parties as one. **2 s'amalgamer** *vpr* to merge, to amalgamate.

amande [amɑ̃d] *nf* **(a)** (*fruit*) almond; **amandes amères/douces,** bitter/sweet almonds; **amandes pilées,** ground almonds; **pâte d'amandes,** almond paste; *Fig* **les yeux en a.,** almond(-shaped) eyes; **(b)** kernel (*of a drupe*).

amandier [amɑ̃dje] *nm* (*arbre*) almond tree.

amanite [amanit] *nf* (*champignon*) **a. phalloïde,** death cap; **a. tue-mouches,** fly agaric.

amant, -ante [amɑ̃, -ɑ̃t] *n* lover, *f* mistress; **a. de cœur,** lover.

amarante [amarɑ̃t] *nf* (*fleur*) amarant(h); **a. commune** *ou* **à fleurs en queue,** love lies bleeding.

amariner [amarine] **1** *vt Nau* **(a)** (*un navire ennemi*) to man; **(b)** (*un homme, un équipage*) to accustom to life at sea. **2 s'amariner** *vpr* to find *or* get one's sea legs.

amarrage [amaraʒ] *nm Nau* **(a)** mooring, fastening; stowing (*of equipment*); (*lieu*) berth, moorings; **droits d'a.,** berthing dues; **(b) faire un a. sur une corde,** to lash a rope.

amarre [amar] *nf* **(a)** (mooring) rope; (*d'avant*) painter; **navire sur ses amarres,** ship at her moorings; **rompre ses amarres,** (*of ship*) to break adrift, to break its moorings; **larguer les amarres,** to cast off; **(b)** (*câble*) cable, hawser; **a. de retenue,** guy.

amarrer [amare] *vt Nau etc* **(a)** to make fast, to moor (*ship etc*); **navire amarré à quai,** boat berthed *or* lying at the quay; **(b)** to belay (*a line*); to make (*a line*) fast; to secure (*gun*); *Constr* to brace (*wall etc*); **il a fallu a. les valises sur le toit,** the suitcases had to be secured to the roof; **(c)** to seize, to lash (*hawsers etc*).

amaryllis [amarilis] *nf* (*fleur*) amaryllis; **a. belle-dame,** belladonna lily.

amas [ama] *nm* **(a)** (*tas*) heap, pile, accumulation; **des a. de glace,** packs of ice; **(b)** store, hoard (*of money, provisions*); **un a. de livres,** a pile *or* stack of books; **(c)** *Astron* cluster; constellation; **(d)** (*de cristal*) colony; **(e)** *Min* lode.

amasser [amase] **1** *vt* **(a)** (*amonceler*) to amass, to heap up, to pile up; **(b)** (*de l'argent*) to hoard (up); **a. pour sa vieillesse,** to save up for one's old age; **(c)** (*rassembler*) to collect; to gather (*troops etc*) together. **2 s'amasser** *vpr* to build up, to pile up; **une foule s'amassait,** a crowd was gathering; **les preuves s'amassent contre vous,** the evidence is building up *or* piling up against you.

amateur [amatœr] *nm* **(a)** lover (*of sth*); **a. d'art,** art lover; **a. d'oiseaux,** bird fancier; **édition d'a.,** collector's *or* booklover's edition; **a. du cinéma,** film buff; **être a. de qch,** to be fond of *or* to have a taste for sth; **(b)** bidder (*at sale*); **est-ce qu'il y a des amateurs?,** any takers?; **(c)** (*non-professionnel*) amateur; **elle joue bien pour un a.,** she plays well for an amateur; *Sp* **championnat d'a.,** amateur championship; **faire qch en a.,** to do sth as a hobby, to dabble in sth; **travail d'a.,** work done by an amateur; *Péj* amateurish work.

amateurisme [amatœrism] *nm Sp etc* amateurism; *Péj* amateurishness, amateurism.

amazone [amazon] *nf* **(a)** *Myth* Amazon; **(b) l'A.,** the (river) Amazon; **(c)** horsewoman; **monter en a.,** to ride side-saddle; **(d)** (*jupe*) riding habit.

Amazonie [amazɔni] *nf* Amazonia.

ambages [ɑ̃baʒ] *nfpl* (*used only in*) **parler sans a.,** to speak plainly, not to beat about the bush.

ambassade [ɑ̃basad] *nf* **(a)** (*mission*) embassy; (*moins importante*) mission; **envoyer une a. extraordinaire,** to send a special mission; **être envoyé en a. auprès de qn,** to be sent on a mission to s.o.; **obtenir une a.,** to be appointed ambassador; **(b)** (*édifice*) embassy; (*personnel*) ambassador's staff, embassy; **l'a. de France/du Canada,** the French/Canadian embassy.

ambassadeur [ɑ̃basadœr] *nm* ambassador; (*représentant*) envoy; **a. extraordinaire,** ambassador extraordinary; **l'a. d'Angleterre,** the British ambassador; **a. auprès du roi** *ou* **de la reine d'Angleterre,** Ambassador to *or* at the Court of St James; *Fig* **l'a. de la poésie indienne,** the ambassador of Indian poetry; **vous êtes les ambassadeurs de votre pays,** you are ambassadors for your country.

ambassadorial, -iaux [ɑ̃basadɔrjal, -jo] *adj* ambassadorial.

ambassadrice [ɑ̃basadris] *nf* **(a)** (*diplomate*) (woman) ambassador; **(b)** (*femme de l'ambassadeur*) ambassador's wife; *Fig* ambassadress.

ambiance [ɑ̃bjɑ̃s] *nf* surroundings, environment, atmosphere, ambience; **une a. de travail,** a working atmosphere; **l'a. au travail,** the atmosphere at work; **régulateur d'a.,** thermostat; *Fin* **l'a. générale,** the prevailing tone; *F* **il y a de l'a. ici,** there's a cheerful *or* good atmosphere here.

ambiant [ɑ̃bjɑ̃] *adj* surrounding (*atmosphere etc*); **milieu a.,** environment; **température ambiante,** room temperature; *Tech* ambient temperature.

ambidextre [ɑ̃bidɛkstr] *adj* ambidextrous.

ambigu, -uë [ɑ̃bigy] *adj* ambiguous.

ambiguïté [ɑ̃bigɥite] *nf* ambiguity, ambiguousness; **répondre sans a.,** to give an unambiguous *or* unequivocal answer.

ambigument [ɑ̃bigymɑ̃] *adv* ambiguously.

ambitieusement [ɑ̃bisjøzmɑ̃] *adv* **(a)** ambitiously; **(b)** *Péj* pretentiously.

ambitieux, -ieuse [ɑ̃bisjø, -jøz] **1** *adj* **(a)** ambitious; **(b)** *Péj* **style a.,** pretentious style. **2** *n* ambitious person; *Péj* careerist.

ambition [ɑ̃bisjɔ̃] *nf* ambition (**de faire,** to do); **quelles sont vos ambitions?,** what are your ambitions?; **sans a.,** unambitious(ly); **mettre toute son a. à un travail,** to put everything one has into a piece of work, *F* to give it one's all; **avoir de l'a.,** to have ambition, to be ambitious.

ambitionner [ɑ̃bisjɔne] *vt* to set one's heart on (*sth, doing sth*).

ambivalence [ɑ̃bivalɑ̃s] *nf* ambivalence.

ambivalent [ɑ̃bivalɑ̃] *adj* ambivalent.

amble [ɑ̃bl] *nm Equitation* amble, pace; *US* single-foot; **a. rompu,** rack; **aller l'a.,** to amble.

ambler [ɑ̃ble] *vi* (*of horse etc*) to amble (along).

ambre [ɑ̃br] **1** *nm* **(a) a. gris,** ambergris; **pomme d'a.,** pomander; **(b) a. jaune,** (yellow) amber; **un collier en a.,** an amber necklace. **2** *adj inv* amber.

ambré [ɑ̃bre] *adj* **(a)** perfumed with amber(gris); **(b)** amber-coloured, *US* -colored; warm (*complexion, tint*); **un vin a.,** an amber-coloured wine.

ambroisie [ɑ̃brwazi] *nf* ambrosia; *Fig* **c'est de l'a.!,** it's like nectar!

ambulance [ɑ̃bylɑ̃s] *nf* ambulance.

ambulancier, -ière [ɑ̃bylɑ̃sje, -jɛr] *n* ambulance man, ambulance woman; (*conducteur, -trice*) ambulance driver.

ambulant [ɑ̃bylɑ̃] **1** *adj* strolling, itinerant, travelling, mobile; **épicier a.,** mobile grocer; **comédiens ambulants,** strolling players; **marchand a.,** itinerant dealer, hawker; **cirque a.,** travelling circus; *Méd* **érysipèle a.,** migrant erysipelas; *F* **c'est un cadavre a.,** he's a walking corpse, he looks like death warmed up; **c'est un dictionnaire a.,** he's a walking dictionary. **2** *nm Admin* itinerant collector (*of excise, taxes etc*).

ambulatoire [ɑ̃bylatwar] *adj* ambulatory; *Méd* **malade a.,** ambulatory patient, walking case; **(fièvre) typhoïde a.,** ambulant typhoid.

âme [ɑm] *nf* **(a)** *Rel Phil* soul; (*mort*) (departed) soul, spirit; (*principe et centre de la vie morale*) heart, feeling, soul, spirit; (*motif*) inspiration, soul, life; moving spirit (*of an undertaking*); **se donner corps et â. à qn.,** to give oneself body and soul to s.o.; **rendre l'â.,** to give up the ghost; **de toute mon â.,** with all my heart; **elle a l'â. d'une artiste,** she has the soul of an artist; **il est peintre dans l'â.,** he's a painter through and through *or* to the core; **il jouait de la flûte avec â.,** he played the flute with great feeling; **une déclaration sans â.,** an unfeeling *or* a soulless declaration; **Dieu ait son â.,** God rest his soul; **les âmes en peine,** the souls in Purgatory; **aller comme une â. en peine,** to wander around like a lost soul; **avoir l'â. chevillée au corps,** to have nine lives; **chercher la paix de l'â.,** to seek spiritual peace; **â. sœur,** kindred soul *or* spirit, soul mate; **en mon â. et conscience,** to the best of my knowledge and belief; **cet homme est d'une grandeur d'â. extraordinaire,** that man has an extraordinary nobility of spirit; **état d'â.,** state of mind, mood; **elle était l'â. de notre organisation,** she was the heart and soul of our organization;

(b) (*personne*) **une bonne â.,** a well-meaning person, a good soul; **ne pas rencontrer â. qui vive,** not to meet a (living) soul; **un hameau de 50 âmes,** a hamlet of some 50 inhabitants; *Iron* **il y a toujours de bonnes âmes pour conseiller quand c'est trop tard,** there are always plenty of people ready with helpful advice when it's too late!; **c'est une â. généreuse,** he's very giving; **je connais quelques hautes âmes,** I know a few high-minded people; **avoir charge d'âmes,** *Rel* to have the cure of souls; (*of children, passengers etc*) to have lives in one's care;

(c) bore (*of gun, pump*); core (*of statue, cable*); web (*of girder, beam*); centre rib (*of rail*); *Av* web (*of wing*); *Mus* sound post (*of violin*).

améliorable [ameljɔrabl] *adj* capable of being improved, improvable; **le système est a.,** the system could be improved.

améliorant [ameljɔrɑ̃] *adj Agr* **culture améliorante,** cover crop.

amélioration [ameljɔrasjɔ̃] *nf* **(a)** improvement, change for the better; **a. de santé,** improvement of *or* in (*s.o.'s*) health; **il y a de l'a.,** there's some improvement; **il y a de l'a. dans les affaires,** business is improving; **faire des améliorations dans qch,** to make improvements to sth; **travaux d'a.,** improvements; **(b)** *Jur* appreciation (*of property etc*).

améliorer [ameljɔre] **1** *vt* to improve (*a property, the soil, a translation etc*); **a. son état,** to improve one's situation. **2 s'améliorer** *vpr* to get better, to improve; **sa santé/le temps s'améliore,** his health/the weather is improving; **ça ne s'améliore pas,** it's not getting any better.

amen [amɛn] *nm inv* amen; *Fig F* **je ne vais pas lui dire a.,** I'm not going to give him my blessing.

aménagement [amenaʒmɑ̃] *nm* **(a)** arrangement, layout (*of house etc*); *Can* **a. paysager,** open-plan offices; **(b) aménagements,** fittings, fixtures, installations; *Nau Av* accommodation, berthing; **les nouveaux aménagements dans un quartier,** new developments in a district; *Nau* **les aménagements de l'équipage,** the mess decks; **(c)** equipping, arranging; fitting out (*of ship*); **a. d'une usine,** equipping *or* fitting out of a factory; **(d) a. urbain et rural,** town and country planning; **a. forestier,** forest management; *Econ Admin* **a. du territoire,** development, planning; **(e)** (*amendement*) adjustment; **un a. dans un contrat,** an adjustment to a contract; **(f)** harnessing (*of power*).

aménager [amenaʒe] *vt* **(j'aménageai(s); n. aménageons) (a)** to fit out (*house, ship etc*); **étable aménagée,** converted cowshed; **route aménagée,** made-up road; **a. une cuisine en salle à manger,** to convert a kitchen into a dining-room; **a. une douche dans une salle de gymnastique,** to install a shower in a gymnasium; **a. un emploi du temps,** to adjust a timetable; **(b)** to plan (*town*); to divide, to distribute (*supplies etc*); **a. une forêt,** to manage a forest; **(c)** to harness (*water power*).

amende [amɑ̃d] *nf* **(a)** fine, penalty; **être condamné à l'a.** *ou* **à une a.,** to be fined; *F* **mettre qn à l'a.,** to fine s.o.; **200F d'a.,** a 200 franc fine; **défense d'entrer sous peine d'a.,** trespassers will be prosecuted; **(b) faire a. honorable,** to make amends.

amendement [amɑ̃dmɑ̃] *nm* **(a)** improvement (*of the soil etc*); **(b)** (*engrais*) (soil) conditioner; **(c)** *Pol* amendment (*to a bill etc*).

amender [amɑ̃de] **1** *vt* **(a)** to make better; to improve (*soil etc*); **(b)** *Pol etc* to amend (*bill etc*). **2 s'amender** *vpr* to turn over a new leaf.

amène [amɛn] *adj* pleasing, agreeable; **peu a.,** unpleasant, disagreeable.

amenée [amne] *nf* **(a) tuyau** *ou* **conduite d'a.,** *Constr* branch pipe; (*d'eau*) supply pipe; *Él* lead; **(b)** (*d'air*) inlet, intake.

amener [amne] *v* **(j'amène, n. amenons; j'amènerai) 1** *vt* **(a)** to bring (*s.o.*); *Mil* to bring up (*reserves etc*); to lay on (*water, gas etc*); **amenez votre ami/chien avec vous,** bring your friend/dog (with you); **quel bon vent vous amène?,** what brings you here?; **les pipe-lines amènent le pétrole à la raffinerie,** the pipelines carry oil to the refinery; **et ceci nous amène à parler de la ponctualité,** which brings us to the question of punctuality; **a. qn à son opinion,** to bring s.o. round to one's point of view; **a. un sujet,** to bring up *or* raise a subject; **a. la conversation sur un sujet,** to bring the conversation round to a subject; *Culin*

a. l'eau à ébullition, bring the water to the boil; **a. une préparation à une certaine température,** to heat a mixture to a certain temperature; **a. qn à faire qch,** to get *or* induce s.o. to do sth; **un bon auteur sait a. le dénouement de son récit,** a good author knows how to bring his story to a conclusion; **a. une querelle,** to bring about *or* lead to a quarrel; **a. une mode,** to bring in a fashion;

(b) *Nau* to haul down (*signal*); to strike (*colours*); to lower (*boat, flag, sail*);

(c) (*tirer à soi*) to draw in, to bring in; **le pêcheur amène les filets,** the fisherman draws in the nets.

2 s'amener *vpr F* to turn up; **amène-toi ici!,** come (over) here!

aménité [amenite] *nf* **(a)** charm, graciousness (*of manners, greeting etc*); charm, grace (*of style*); **nous avons été traités sans a.,** we were treated ungraciously; **(b)** *Iron* **aménités,** insults, uncomplimentary remarks.

amenuisement [amənɥizmɑ̃] *nm* dwindling (*of hopes, resources*); diminishing (*of resources*).

amenuiser [amənɥize] **1** *vt* to reduce, to thin (down); to whittle down. **2 s'amenuiser** *vpr* (*d'une valeur*) to decline; (*de l'espoir, des chances*) to fade.

amer¹, -ère [amɛr] **1** *adj* (*goût, Fig souvenirs, personne*) bitter. **2** *nm* (*drink*) bitters.

amer² *nm Nau* seamark, landmark.

amèrement [amɛrmɑ̃] *adv* bitterly.

américain, -aine [amerikɛ̃, -ɛn] **1** *adj* American; **cuisine américaine,** = kitchen with a bar separating the cooking and eating areas; **idiotisme a.,** Americanism. **2** *n* **A.,** American. **3** *nm Ling* American (English). **4** *nf* **américaine (a) vivre à l'a.,** to live American-style; **(b)** *Culin* **homard à l'a.,** lobster américaine; **(c)** *Cyclisme* track relay (race).

américanisation [amerikanizɑsjɔ̃] *nf* Americanization.

américaniser [amerikanize] **1** *vt* to Americanize. **2 s'américaniser** *vpr* to become Americanized.

américanisme [amerikanism] *nm Ling* Americanism.

américaniste [amerikanist] *n* specialist in American studies.

amérindien, -ienne [amerɛ̃djɛ̃, -jɛn] **1** *adj* Amerindian, American Indian. **2** *n* **A.,** Amerind, Amerindian, American Indian.

Amérique [amerik] *nf* America; **l'A. du Nord/du Sud,** North/South America; **l'A. latine,** Latin America; **les Amériques,** the Americas.

Amerlo(t) [amɛrlo], **Amerloque** [amɛrlɔk] *n F* Yank.

amerrir [amerir] *vi* **(a)** *Av* to alight, to land (on the sea); **(b)** (*of space capsule*) to splash down.

amerrissage [amerisaʒ] *nm Av* alighting, landing (on the sea); splashdown (*of space capsule*); *Av* **a. forcé,** ditching.

amertume [amɛrtym] *nf* bitterness.

améthyste [ametist] *nf* amethyst.

ameublement [amœbləmɑ̃] *nm* **(a)** furnishing (*of house, office etc*); **(b)** (*meubles*) set *or* suite of furniture; **magasin d'a.,** furniture store; **tissu d'a.,** furnishing fabric.

ameublir [amœblir] *vt* **(a)** *Agr* to loosen, to break up, (*soil*); **(b)** *Jur* to convert (*realty*) into personalty; to bring (*one's realty*) into the communal estate.

ameublissement [amœblismɑ̃] *nm* **(a)** *Agr* loosening, breaking up (*of soil*); **(b)** *Jur* conversion (*of realty*) into personalty; inclusion (*of realty*) in the communal estate.

ameuter [amøte] **1** *vt* **(a)** to stir up (*the mob*); **(b)** to form (*hounds*) into a pack, to pack (*hounds*). **2 s'ameuter** *vpr* to form a mob.

ami, -e [ami] **1** *n* friend; **un de mes meilleurs amis,** one of my best friends; **a. intime,** close friend; **a. d'enfance,** childhood friend; **un a. de la maison,** a friend of the family; **en a.,** as a friend; **mon a.,** (*between friends*) my dear fellow; (*from wife to husband*) my dear; **mon amie,** my dear, my love; **être sans amis,** to be friendless, to have no friends; **faire a.-a.,** (*de deux personnes*) to decide to be pals; (*se réconcilier*) to make up (**avec,** with); **son a.,** her boyfriend; (*amant*) her lover; **sa petite amie,** his girl friend; (*sa maîtresse*) his mistress; **eh l'a.! viens donc m'aider!,** hey, you (over) there, come and give me a hand!; **un a. des arts,** a patron of art; **les amis de la nature/de bêtes,** nature/animal lovers; *Ling* **faux amis,** false friends, faux amis; *Spéc* deceptive cognates; *Géog* **les Îles des Amis,** the Friendly Islands, Tonga; **société des amis,** Society of Friends, Quakers.

2 *adj* friendly (**de,** to); favourable (*wind*); **un visage a.,** a friendly face; **peuple a.,** ally, friendly state.

amiable [amjabl] **1** *adj Jur* friendly, conciliatory, amicable; **partage a.,** amicable sharing arrangement; **a. compositeur,** arbitrator. **2** *adv* **à l'a.,** amicably; **différons à l'a.,** let us agree to differ; *Jur* **arranger une affaire à l'a.,** to settle a difference out of court; **s'arranger à l'a.,** to settle out of court; **divorce à l'a.,** no-fault divorce; **arrangement à l'a.,** amicable arrangement; **vente à l'a.,** private sale, sale by private contract.

amiablement [amjabləmɑ̃] *adv Jur* amicably, in a friendly manner; (*vendre*) privately.

amiante [amjɑ̃t] *nm Minér* asbestos; **carton d'a.,** asbestos board *or* sheet; **fibres d'a.,** asbestos fibres.

amibe [amib] *nf* amoeba, *US* ameba.

amibiase [amibjaz] *nf Méd* amoebiasis, *US* amebiasis.

amibien, -ienne [amibjɛ̃, -jɛn] *adj Méd* amœbic, *US* amebic; **dysenterie amibienne,** amœbic *or US* amebic dysentery.

amical, -ale, -aux [amikal, -o] **1** *adj* friendly (*advice, tone etc*); amicable (*relations*); **être a. avec qn,** to be friendly towards s.o.; **peu a.,** unfriendly; *Sp* **match a.,** friendly (match); **association amicale,** (professional) association. **2** *nf* **amicale,** (professional) association; *Br Scol* old-boys' *or* girls' *or* former pupils' association; *US Univ* alumni association; **l'amicale des anciens élèves d'une école d'ingénieurs;** the old boys' association of an engineering school; **l'amicale de St Germain,** *Sp* St Germain Amateurs; (*St Germain est une école*) St Germain Old Boys *or* Girls.

amicalement [amikalmɑ̃] *adv* in a friendly way, like a friend; **bien a. à vous,** (*dans une lettre*) yours (ever).

amide [amid] *nm Ch* amide.

amidon [amidɔ̃] *nm* starch.

amidonnage [amidɔnaʒ] *nm* starching.

amidonner [amidɔne] *vt* to starch.

amincir [amɛ̃sir] **1** *vt* to make (*sth*) thinner; to fine down, to thin down (*wood*); to machine down (*metal*); **cette robe t'amincit,** that dress makes you look thinner *or* slimmer. **2 s'amincir** *vpr* to get thinner; **la brume s'amincit,** the mist is clearing. **3** *vi* to get slimmer.

amincissant [amɛ̃sisɑ̃] *adj* (*dress*) slimming; *US* slenderizing; **régime a.,** (slimmer's *or* slimming) diet.

amincissement [amɛ̃sismɑ̃] *nm* (*de choses*) thinning down; (*du métal*) machining down; (*d'une personne*) growing thinner *or* slimmer; **a. rapide,** rapid loss of weight; **j'avais remarqué l'a. de son visage,** I had noticed how much thinner her face had got.

amine [amin] *nf Ch Pharm* **a. de réveil,** amphetamine.

aminé [amine] *adj Ch* **acide a.,** amino acid.

amiral, -aux [amiral, -o] **1** *nm* **(a)** *Mil* admiral, flag officer; **a. de la flotte,** admiral of the fleet; **(b)** (*coquillage*) admiral shell. **2** *adj* **vaisseau a.,** (*at sea*) flagship; (*in port*) guardship.

amirale [amiral] *nf* admiral's wife.

amirauté [amirote] *nf* **(a)** *Mil* Admiralty; **conseil d'a.,** ≈ *Br* Admiralty Board; *Jur* High Court of Admiralty; **(b) îles de l'A.,** the Admiralty Islands; **île de l'A.,** Admiralty Island (*British Columbia*).

amitié [amitje] *nf* **(a)** (*sentiment*) friendship; **éprouver de l'a. pour qn,** to have friendly feelings towards s.o.; **étroite a.,** close friendship; **concevoir de l'a. pour qn, prendre qn en a.,** to take a liking to s.o., to take to s.o.; **se lier d'a. avec qn,** to make friends with s.o., to become friendly with s.o.; **par a.,** out of friendship; **une très ancienne a.,** a long-standing friendship; *Pol* **l'a. qui existe entre nos deux pays,** the friendship between our two countries; **(b)** (*marque*) kindness, favour; **faites-moi l'a. de le lui dire,** do me the favour of telling him so; **mes amitiés à votre sœur,** my best wishes to your sister; **sincères amitiés de ...,** best wishes from ....

ammoniac, -iaque [amɔnjak] *Ch* **1** *adj* **gaz a.,** ammonia; **sel a.,** sal ammoniac. **2** *nm* ammonia.

ammoniaque [amɔnjak] *nf Ch* ammonia.

ammoniaqué [amɔnjake] *adj* ammoniated.

ammonite [amɔnit] *nf* (*fossile*) ammonite.

amnésie [amnezi] *nf Méd* amnesia; **souffrir d'a.,** to have amnesia.

amnésique [amnezik] *Méd* **1** *adj* amnesic; **être a.,** to have amnesia. **2** *n* amnesia case, amnesiac.

amniocentèse [amnisɛ̃tɛz] *nf Méd* amniocentesis; **se faire faire une a.,** to have amniocentesis.

amnistie [amnisti] *nf* amnesty; **accorder une a.,** to grant an amnesty.

amnistier [amnistje] *vt* (*pr sub & impf* **n. amnistiions, v. amnistiiez**) to amnesty, to pardon.

amocher [amɔʃe] *Arg* **1** *vt* to knock *or* bash (*s.o.*) about, to beat (*s.o.*) up; **la voiture est sérieusement amochée,** the car's been bashed up something rotten, the car's (in) one hell of a mess. **2 s'amocher** *vpr* to smash oneself up; **elle**

s'est bien amochée en tombant, she smashed herself up when she fell.

amoindrir [amwɛ̃drir] **1** *vt* to reduce, to decrease, to lessen, to diminish; (*affaiblir*) to weaken; (*déconsidérer*) to belittle (*s.o.*); to mitigate (*an evil*); **la fièvre amoindrit ses forces,** the fever is sapping his strength; **a. la puissance de qn,** to curtail s.o.'s power. **2 s'amoindrir** *vpr* to diminish, to grow less.

amoindrissement [amwɛ̃drismɑ̃] *nm* reduction, lessening, decrease, diminution.

amollir [amɔlir] **1** *vt* to soften (*substance, s.o.'s heart etc*); **pareille chaleur m'amollit,** heat like this makes me feel limp. **2 s'amollir** *vpr* to soften, to become soft; (*of courage etc*) to flag, to weaken.

amollissement [amɔlismɑ̃] *nm* softening; weakening, flagging (*of courage etc*); **pareille chaleur entraîne l'a. général,** heat like this makes everyone feel limp.

amonceler [amɔ̃sle] *v* (**j'amoncelle, n. amoncelons; j'amoncellerai**) **1** *vt* to pile up, to heap up; to accumulate, to amass; **a. des preuves,** to pile up *or* amass evidence; **il amoncelle sa fortune,** he's piling up a fortune. **2 s'amonceler** *vpr* to pile up, to accumulate.

amoncellement [amɔ̃sɛlmɑ̃] *nm* **(a)** (*action*) heaping (up), piling (up), accumulation; banking up (*of clouds*); **(b)** (*pile*) heap, pile; **a. de neige,** snowdrift.

amont [amɔ̃] **1** *nm* upper waters (*of river*); **en a., vers l'a.,** upstream, up river; **la Seine en a. de Paris,** the Seine above Paris; **vent d'a.,** off-shore wind; *Écon* **activités en a.,** upstream activities. **2** *adj inv* uphill; **ski a.,** uphill skiing.

amoral, -aux [amɔral, -o] *adj* amoral.

amoralité [amɔralite] *nf* amorality.

amorçage [amɔrsaʒ] *nm* **(a)** beginning, setting going (*of sth*); priming (*of pump, motor, cartridge etc*); building up (*of magnetic field*); *Méd* induction (*of sleep*); **(b)** baiting (*of hook, line*).

amorce [amɔrs] *nf* **(a)** beginning; initial section (*of road etc under construction*); **a. de négociations,** preliminary talks; **(b)** (*détonateur*) primer, fuse, detonator; (*d'une petite arme*) percussion cap, cartridge cap; *Él* fuse; priming (*of pump*); scarf (*of weld*); **(c)** *Pêche* bait; **(d)** *Cin* leader.

amorcer [amɔrse] *v* (**j'amorçai(s); n. amorçons**) **1** *vt* **(a)** to begin, to start (*building, road, attack, speech etc*); **a. des négociations,** to initiate negotiations; **(b)** *Ordinat* to boot (up); **a. de nouveau,** to reboot; **(c)** to prime, to fetch (*pump*); to cap (*shell*); *Él* to start, to excite (*dynamo*); to strike (*arc*); to scarf (*weld*); to fuse (*bomb*); **(d)** to bait (*line, trap etc*); **(e)** to entice, to decoy (*animal, person*). **2 s'amorcer** *vpr* to begin; **une baisse des cours s'amorce,** stocks and shares are showing a downward trend.

amorçoir [amɔrswar] *nm* **(a)** *Pêche* ground-baiting appliance; **(b)** (*vrille*) auger, twist bit, boring bit.

amorphe [amɔrf] *adj* **(a)** *Ch Minér Biol* amorphous; **(b)** (*sans énergie*) flabby, without personality; *F* spineless; **cette chaleur me rend totalement a.,** this heat is making me lethargic *or* listless.

amorti [amɔrti] **1** *adj* **(a)** *Phys* damped (*wave*); **(b) marteau a.,** cushioned hammer; **(c)** *Nau* **navire a.,** neaped ship. **2** *nm Tennis etc* drop shot.

amortir [amɔrtir] **1** *vt* **(a)** to deaden, to muffle (*sound*); to subdue (*light*); to dull (*pain*); to damp (*ardour*); to damp, to cool (*passion*); to tone down (*colour*); to break (*fall*); to absorb, to deaden (*shock*); to break the force of (*blow*);

(b) *Fin* to redeem, to pay off, to amortize (*debt*); **a. une voiture en la gardant longtemps,** to get one's money's worth out of a car by keeping it for a long time; **a. une maison,** to pay off the mortgage on a house; **la maison sera amortie dans 6 ans,** the mortgage on the house will have been paid off in 6 years' time;

(c) *Fin* to allow for depreciation; **l'équipement est amorti,** the capital cost of the equipment has been written off;

(d) *Phys* to damp down *or* out (*oscillations*);

(e) *Constr* to slack, to slake (lime).

2 *vpr* **s'amortir** to pay for itself; **cela s'amortira tout seul,** it will pay for itself.

amorti-sacrifice [amɔrtisakrifis] *nm Baseball* squeeze-bunt.

amortissable [amɔrtisabl] *adj Fin* redeemable.

amortissement [amɔrtismɑ̃] *nm* **(a)** *Fin* redemption, amortization, paying off, liquidation (*of debt*); **l'a. est plus rapide,** (*d'une voiture*) it pays for itself faster; **fonds** *ou* **caisse d'a.,** sinking fund; **(b)** (*perte de valeur*) depreciation; **provision pour a.,** depreciation allowance; **(c)** breaking (*of fall*); absorption (*of shock*); **a. du son,** sound-proofing (*of wall etc*).

amortisseur [amɔrtisœr] *nm* **(a)** *Aut etc* shock absorber, *US* snubber; **(b)** *MecE* **a. à moulinet,** air brake; **a. pneumatique,** air cushion; **(c)** *El* damper.

amour [amur] *nm* (*f in pl*) **(a)** (*entre personnes*) love; affection, passion; **l'a. d'une mère,** a mother's love; **l'a. du prochain,** love of one's neighbour; **avec a.,** lovingly; (*to treat, tend*) with loving care; **chagrin d'a.,** unhappy love affair; **a. platonique,** platonic love; **l'a. libre,** free love; **elle est folle d'a. pour lui,** she's madly in love with him; **a. intéressé,** cupboard love; **alors, c'est le grand a.?,** so, it's true love then?, *F* so, this is the big one then?; **chanson d'a.,** love song; **enfant de l'a.,** love child; **se marier par a.,** to marry for love; **mariage d'a.,** love match; **roman/film d'a.,** romantic novel/film; **histoire d'a.,** love story; *Fig* **c'est une véritable histoire d'a. qui me lie à cette ville,** I have a love affair with this city; **faire l'a.,** to make love (**avec,** with); **il n'y a point de laides amours,** beauty is in the eye of the beholder; **froides mains, chaudes amours,** cold hands, warm heart; **l'a. de Dieu,** the love of God; **pour l'a. du Ciel, tiens-toi bien!,** for heaven's sake, sit up straight!;

(b) amours, love affairs; **les premières amours,** first love, calf love; **à tes amours!,** (*en buvant*) your health!, cheers!; (*pour qn qui éternue*) bless you!; **où en sont tes amours?,** how's your love life?;

(c) (*personne*) **mon a.,** my love, my darling; **l'a. de sa famille,** the idol *or* darling of the family; **une de mes anciennes amours,** an old flame of mine; **les voitures sont ses seul(e)s amours,** cars are his sole passion;

(d) A., Cupid, Eros, the god of Love; **beau comme l'A.,** handsome as a Greek god; **quel a. d'enfant!,** what an adorable child!; **tu es un a.!,** you('re an) angel!; **sois un a.!,** be a dear, be an angel!; **tu serais un a. si tu voulais me chercher mes cigarettes,** be an angel and fetch my cigarettes; **un a. d'histoire,** a very sweet story;

(e) (*goût*) love (*of sth*); passion (*for sth*); **l'a. de la nature,** love of nature; **l'a. de la justice,** passion for justice.

amouracher (s') [samuraʃe] *vpr* to fall head over heels in love, to become infatuated (*with s.o.*).

amourette [amurɛt] *nf* **(a)** (*entre deux personnes*) love affair, passing fancy; **ce n'était qu'une a.,** it was only a passing fancy; **(b)** *Culin* **amourettes,** spinal marrow.

amoureusement [amurøzmɑ̃] *adv* (*avec tendresse*) lovingly; (*avec passion*) amorously.

amoureux, -euse [amurø, -øz] **1** *adj* **(a)** loving (*care, look, gesture*); **vie amoureuse,** love life; **être a. de qn,** to be in love with s.o.; **tomber a.,** to fall in love; **être a. de qch,** to be a lover of sth; **je suis a. de cette région,** I love that part of the country; **je suis a. de la nature,** I'm a nature-lover; **(b)** (*passionné*) amorous (*look, gesture*). **2** *n* suitor, lover; man *or* woman in love.

amour-propre [amurprɔpr] *nm* **(a)** (*dignité*) self-respect, (*legitimate*) pride; *Litt* amour-propre; **blesser l'a.-p. de qn,** to hurt *or* wound s.o.'s pride; **elle est blessée dans son a.-p.,** her pride is hurt; **(b)** (*vanité*) vanity, conceit; *Litt* amour-propre; **pétri d'a.-p.,** eaten up with conceit.

amovible [amɔvibl] *adj* **(a)** detachable; **siège a.,** sliding seat; **(b)** *Jur* **fonction a.,** = office that may be withdrawn from the holder (and given to another person); removable (*official*).

ampérage [ɑ̃peraʒ] *nm Él* amperage.

ampère [ɑ̃pɛr] *nm El* ampere.

ampèremètre [ɑ̃pɛrmɛtr] *nm Él* ammeter.

amphé [ɑ̃fe] *nf F* (*amphétamine*) speed.

amphétamine [ɑ̃fetamin] *nf* amphetamine.

amphi [ɑ̃fi] *nm F Univ* (*salle*) lecture room; *Univ* (*cours*) lecture; *Av Mil* briefing.

amphibie [ɑ̃fibi] **1** *adj Biol* amphibious (*plant, animal*); **appareil** *ou* **voiture a.,** amphibian; *Mil* **opération a.,** combined operation. **2** *nm* (*véhicule etc*) *& Biol* amphibian.

amphibiens [ɑ̃fibjɛ̃] *nmpl Zool* amphibians, Amphibia.

amphithéâtre [ɑ̃fiteɑtr] *nm* **(a)** *Univ* lecture room; **(b)** *Th* gallery, *F* the gods; **(c)** *Archit* amphitheatre; **en a.,** in tier, tier upon tier.

amphore [ɑ̃fɔr] *nf* jar; *Archéol* amphora.

ample [ɑ̃pl] *adj* **(a)** full (*dress, skirt etc*); **(b)** roomy, spacious (*shop, theatre etc*); **(c)** full (*account*); plentiful, ample (*supply*); **jusqu'à plus a. informé,** until fuller *or* more information is available; **le sujet est a.,** the subject is a wide one; **je vais vous donner de plus amples détails,** I will give you fuller *or* more details.

amplement [ɑ̃pləmɑ̃] *adv* amply, fully; **nous avons a. le temps,** we have plenty of time; **je vous ai a. servi,** I have given you plenty; **c'est a. suffisant,** it's more than enough.

ampleur [ɑ̃plœr] *nf* **(a)** width, fullness (*of garment*); copiousness (*of meal*); volume (*of voice*); extent (*of damages*); **(b)** (*importance*) scale, extent, size; **le mouvement politique prend de l'a.,** the (political) movement is growing in size *or* is taking on new dimensions; **devant l'a. du désastre,** in view of the extent *or* the scope of the disaster.

ampli [ɑ̃pli] *nm F* amplifier.

amplificateur, -trice [ɑ̃plifikatœr, -tris] **1** *adj Rad etc* amplifying; *Opt* magnifying. **2** *nm* amplifier.

amplification [ɑ̃plifikasjɔ̃] *nf* **(a)** amplification, development (*of a subject*); growth (*of political movement*); (*exagération*) exaggeration; **(b)** *Rad etc* amplification; *Opt* magnification.

amplifier [ɑ̃plifje] *v* (*impf & pr sub* **n. amplifiions, v. amplifiiez**) **1** *vt* **(a)** to amplify, to develop (*subject etc*); *Péj* to exaggerate; to embroider (*story*); to magnify (*danger*); **(b)** *Opt* to magnify; *Él* to amplify. **2 s'amplifier** *vpr* to grow (*in size, extent etc*); **le bruit s'amplifie,** the noise is growing *or* getting louder; **les revendications ouvrières s'amplifient,** the workers' demands are increasing, the workers are increasing their demands.

amplitude [ɑ̃plityd] *nf* **(a)** amplitude (*of oscillation*); *Rad* **modulation d'a.,** amplitude modulation; **(b)** (*variation*) range; **a. thermique,** range of temperature; **(c)** *Litt* amplitude, vastness (*of space etc*); magnitude, scale (*of disaster, catastrophe*).

ampoule [ɑ̃pul] *nf* **(a)** bulb (*of thermometer, electric light*); (electronic) tube; container (*of vacuum flask*); **une a. de 75 watt,** a 75 watt bulb; **a. de rechange,** refill; **(b)** blister (*on skin, metal etc*); **(c)** (*fiole*) phial.

ampoulé [ɑ̃pule] *adj Péj* inflated, bombastic (*speech*).

amputation [ɑ̃pytasjɔ̃] *nf* **(a)** amputation (*of limb etc*); **(b)** *Fig* curtailment, cutting down (*of book etc*); reduction (*of claim*); *F* **faire des amputations à un article,** to slash an article; **c'est une sérieuse a. à sa fortune,** it has cut into his fortune.

amputé, -ée [ɑ̃pyte] *n* amputee.

amputer [ɑ̃pyte] *vt* **(a)** to amputate (*a limb*); **il fut amputé du bras gauche,** his left arm was amputated; **(b)** *Fig* to cut down, to curtail (*article etc*); to cut, to reduce (*claim*) (**de,** by); **a. un capital,** to make inroads into s.o.'s capital.

amulette [amylɛt] *nf* amulet, charm.

amusant [amyzɑ̃] **1** *adj* amusing, entertaining, funny; **situation amusante,** amusing situation; **comme c'est a., je n'avais pas remarqué ...,** that's funny, I hadn't noticed ... . **2** *nm* **le plus a., c'est que ...,** the funniest *or* most amusing thing is that ...; **l'a. de l'histoire,** the amusing part of the story, what was funny *or* amusing about the story.

amuse-gueule [amyzgœl] *nm* cocktail snack.

amusement [amyzmɑ̃] *nm* amusement; **avoir besoin d'a.,** to need amusement *or* entertainment; **faire qch pour son a.,** to do sth for one's own amusement.

amuser [amyze] **1** *vt* to amuse, to entertain; *Fml Litt* to divert; **en attendant il faut a. la salle,** in the meantime we must keep the audience amused; **si tu penses que ça m'amuse!,** if you think I enjoy (doing) it!; **essaie de l'a. pendant que je prends la caisse,** try to distract him *or* his attention while I take the money; **il avait un regard amusé quand il nous a dit bonjour,** he looked amused *or* as if something was amusing him when he said hello to us.

2 s'amuser *vpr* (*se distraire*) to enjoy oneself, to have a good time; **je ne me suis jamais aussi bien amusé,** I've had the time of my life; **les enfants s'amusent dans le jardin,** the children are playing in the garden; **amusez-vous bien!,** enjoy yourselves!; **s'a. aux dépens de qn,** to amuse oneself at s.o.'s expense; **s'a. de qn,** to make fun of s.o.; **s'a. à faire qch,** to have fun doing sth; **faire qch pour s'a.,** to do sth for fun *or* for the fun of it; *F* **ne t'amuse pas à recommencer,** don't you dare do that again; **si tu crois que je vais m'a. à faire ça,** if you think I've nothing better to do than that; **si je dois m'a. à y aller à pied,** if I'm expected to walk there; **nous n'avons pas le temps de nous a. en chemin/à faire ça,** we can't afford to waste time on the way/doing that.

amusette [amyzɛt] *nf* **(a)** *Vieilli* pastime; diversion; **(b)** *Belg* frivolous person.

amuseur, -euse [amyzœr, -øz] *n* entertainer.

amygdale [ami(g)dal] *nf* tonsil; *Méd* **inflammation des amygdales,** tonsillitis; **se faire opérer des amygdales,** to have one's tonsils out.

amygdalectomie [ami(g)dalɛktɔmi] *nf Chir* tonsillectomy.

amygdalite [ami(g)dalit] *nf Méd* tonsillitis; **faire une a.,** to have tonsillitis.

an [ɑ̃] *nm* year; **l'an passé** *ou* **dernier,** last year; **l'an prochain,** next year; **deux fois par an,** twice a year; **tous les ans,** every year; **avoir dix ans,** to be ten (years old); **je gagne tant par an,** I earn so much a year; **ami de vingt ans,** friend of twenty years' standing; **bon an, mal an,** taking one year with another; **bon an, mal an, l'entreprise continue à produire des bénéfices,** year in, year out the firm continues to produce a profit; **je m'en moque comme de l'an 40,** I couldn't give a damn about it, I couldn't care less; **en l'an 2000,** in the year 2000; **le jour** *ou* **le premier de l'an, le nouvel an,** New Year's day.

anabaptisme [anabatism] *nm* Anabaptism.

anabaptiste [anabatist] *adj & n* Anabaptist.

anabolisant [anabɔlizɑ̃] **1** *nm Méd* anabolic steroid. **2** *adj* anabolic.

anacarde [anakard] *nm* cashew nut.

anacardier [anakardje] *nm* cashew tree.

anachorète [anakɔrɛt] *nm* recluse; *Rel* anchorite; **il mène une vie d'a.,** he lives the life of a recluse.

anachronique [anakrɔnik] *adj* anachronistic.

anachronisme [anakrɔnism] *nm* anachronism.

anaconda [anakɔ̃da] *nm* anaconda.

anagrammatique [anagramatik] *adj* anagrammatic(al).

anagramme [anagram] *nf* anagram.

A.N.A.H. [ana] *nf* (*abrév* **Agence nationale pour l'amélioration de l'habitat**) = housing department.

anal, -aux [anal, -o] *adj Anat Psy* anal.

analgésie [analʒezi] *nf Méd* analgesia.

analgésique [analʒezik] *adj & nm Pharm* analgesic.

anallergique [analɛrʒik] *adj* (*produit cosmétique*) hypoallergenic.

analogie [analɔʒi] *nf* analogy; **raisonner par a.,** to argue from analogy; **par a. avec,** by analogy with.

analogique [analɔʒik] *adj* analogical; *Électron* **calculatrice a.,** analog computer.

analogue [analɔg] **1** *adj* analogous (**à,** to, with); similar (**à,** to). **2** *nm* analogue, parallel; **ce mot anglais n'a pas d'a. en français,** this English word has no equivalent in French.

analphabète [analfabɛt] *adj & n* illiterate (person).

analphabétisme [analfabetism] *nm* illiteracy.

analysable [analizabl] *adj* analysable, *esp US* analyzable.

analyse [analiz] *nf* **(a)** (*étude*) analysis; **en dernière a.,** in the last *or* final analysis, when all is said and done, all things considered; **avoir l'esprit d'a.,** to have an analytical mind; **faire l'a. de qch,** to analyse sth; **roman/film d'a.,** psychological novel/film; *Écon* **a. économique,** economic analysis; *Ling* **a. grammaticale,** parsing; **a. logique,** analysis; **faire l'a. d'une phrase,** *Gram* to parse a sentence; (*logique*) to analyse a sentence; *Ordinat* **a. syntaxique,** parsing; *Ordinat* **a. factorielle/fonctionnelle,** factor/functional analysis; *Ch* **a. quantitative,** quantitative analysis; **a. volumétrique,** volumetric analysis; **a. qualitative,** qualitative analysis; *Méd* **laboratoire d'analyses,** pathology laboratory; **a. de sang/d'urine,** blood/urine test; *Math* **a. infinitésimale,** (*differential and integral*) calculus; **a. vectorielle,** vector analysis;

(b) *Psy* (psycho)analysis; **être en a.,** to be in analysis; **commencer/finir son a.,** to begin *or* go into analysis/to finish *or* come out of analysis;

(c) (*sommaire*) abstract, résumé, précis.

analyser [analize] **1** *vt* **(a)** to analyse, *esp US* to analyze (*facts etc*); *Méd* to test (*blood, urine etc*); *Ordinat* to parse; **a. une phrase,** *Gram* to parse a sentence; (*logique*) to analyse a sentence; **(b)** *Psy* to (psycho)analyse; **se faire a.,** to be (pycho)analysed. **2 s'analyser** *vpr* to analyse one's feelings; **elle s'a. trop,** she goes in for too much self-analysis.

analyseur [analizœr] *nm* analyser, *esp US* analyzer; *Ordinat* **a. syntaxique,** parser.

analyste [analist] *n Ordinat etc* analyst; *Psy* (psycho)analyst; *Ordinat* **a.-programmeur,** systems analyst; **être un bon a. de ses sentiments,** to be good at analysing one's feelings.

analytique [analitik] **1** *adj* analytic(al); **géométrie a.,** analytic geometry; **un esprit a.,** an analytical mind; *Psy* **suivre un traitement a.,** to be having psychoanalytical treatment. **2** *nf* analytics.

analytiquement [analitikmɑ̃] *adv* analytically.

anamorphose [anamɔrfoz] *nf* anamorphosis.

ananas [anana(s)] *nm* (*fruit*) pineapple; (*plante*) pineapple plant; **serre à a.,** pinery.

anaphore [anafɔr] *nf* anaphora.

anaphorique [anafɔrik] *adj* anaphoric.
anar [anar] *n F* = **ANARCHISTE**.
anarchie [anarʃi] *nf Pol & Fig* anarchy.
anarchique [anarʃik] *adj* anarchic(al) (*behaviour*); anarchistic (*philosophy, system*).
anarchiquement [anarʃikmɑ̃] *adv* anarchically, in an anarchic(al) manner; *Fig* chaotically, in a chaotic manner.
anarchisant [anarʃizɑ̃] *adj* with anarchist tendencies *or* leanings.
anarchisme [anarʃism] *nm* anarchism.
anarchiste [anarʃist] *Pol* **1** *adj* anarchist; *Fig* chaotic, disorderly; (*personne*) rebellious, non-conformist; **il refuse tout conseil, il est très a.,** he won't listen to advice, he just goes his own way *or* he's very much the rebel. **2** *n* anarchist; *Fig* rebel, non-conformist.
anastigmat [anastigma] **1** *adj* anastigmatic (*lens*). **2** *nm* anastigmat.
anastigmatique [anastigmatik] *adj* anastigmatic.
anathématiser [anatematize] *vt* to curse, *Fml* to anathematize.
anathème [anatɛm] *nm* anathema.
anatife [anatif] *nm* (*crustacé*) barnacle.
anatomie [anatɔmi] *nf* anatomy; *Méd* **a. pathologique,** morbid anatomy; *F* **une belle a.,** a great body; **pièce d'a.,** anatomical figure; **avoir une a. d'athlète,** to have the body of an athlete.
anatomique [anatɔmik] *adj* anatomical.
anatomiquement [anatɔmikmɑ̃] *adv* anatomically.
anatomiste [anatɔmist] *n* anatomist.
ancestral, -aux [ɑ̃sɛstral, -o] *adj* ancestral.
ancêtre [ɑ̃sɛtr] *nm* ancestor; *F* (*vieillard*) old man; **la maison de ses ancêtres,** his family home; (*château etc*) his ancestral home; **nos ancêtres les Gaulois,** our ancestors *or* forefathers the Gauls; **Bartok est l'a. de la musique contemporaine,** Bartok is the father of contemporary music.
anche [ɑ̃ʃ] *nf* **(a)** *Mus* reed, tongue (*of oboe, clarinet etc*); **jeu d'anches,** reed-stop (*of organ*); **(b)** spout (*of hopper*).
anchois [ɑ̃ʃwa] *nm* (*poisson*) anchovy; **a. de Norvège,** sprat; **beurre d'a./sauce aux a.,** anchovy paste/sauce; **filets d'a.,** anchovy fillets; *F* **serrés comme des a.,** packed like sardines.
ancien, -ienne [ɑ̃sjɛ̃, -jɛn] **1** *adj* **(a)** (*vieux*) ancient, old, antique; **monument a.,** ancient monument; **meubles anciens,** antique furniture;
(b) *Hist* ancient, old(en), early, bygone, past; **les peuples anciens,** people of antiquity; **le grec a.,** ancient *or* classical Greek; **dans l'a. temps,** in the old(en) days, in bygone days, in days gone by; **l'A. Testament,** the Old Testament; **c'est de l'histoire ancienne,** (*c'est oublié*) that's ancient history;
(c) (*révolu*) former, old, ex-(*teacher, pupil etc*); **a. président,** former *or* past president; **a. élève,** old pupil, old boy (*of a school*); *US Univ* alumnus; **je suis un de vos anciens élèves,** I'm a former pupil of yours; **anciens combattants,** ex-servicemen, *Am* veterans; **mon a. époux,** my ex-husband;
(d) senior (*captain, officer etc*); **je suis plus a. que vous dans la profession,** I've been in the profession longer than you; **il est votre a.,** he is senior to you.
2 *nm* **(a)** *Hist* **les anciens,** the ancients;
(b) *Rel Pol* elder; **les anciens du village,** the older inhabitants of the village; **les anciens de la tribu,** the elders of the tribe; **respecter les anciens,** to respect one's elders; *F* (*père*) **l'a.,** the old man;
(c) aimer l'a., (*meubles*) to like antique furniture *or* antiques; (*architecture*) to like old buildings;
(d) *Vieilli* (*de scouts*) patrol leader.
3 *n* (*par l'expérience*) **c'est une ancienne dans la maison,** she's been with the firm a long time, **il est mon a.,** he's been with the company *etc* longer than me; **les anciens de l'entreprise,** the company's long-time *or* long-serving employees.
ancienneté [ɑ̃sjɛnte] *nf* **(a)** age, antiquity (*of monument, race etc*); **de toute a.,** from time immemorial; **(b)** (*par l'expérience*) seniority, length of service; **a. de grade,** seniority in rank; **avoir 15 ans d'a. dans une entreprise,** to have 15 years' service with a firm; **avancer à l'a.,** to be promoted by seniority.
ancillaire [ɑ̃silɛr] *adj* ancillary.
ancolie [ɑ̃kɔli] *nf* (*fleur*) aquilegia, columbine.
ancrage [ɑ̃kraʒ] *nm* **(a)** *Nau* anchoring; (*attache*) anchorage; **(droits d')a.,** anchorage dues; **(b)** *Constr etc* (*action*) anchoring, anchorage, fixing; (*d'un mur*) bracing, staying; (*dispositif*) wall tie; **plaque/tige d'a.,** anchor plate/tie; *Fig* **l'a. de nouvelles idées,** the taking root of new ideas.
ancre [ɑ̃kr] *nf* **(a)** anchor; **a. de veille,** sheet anchor; **lever l'a.,** to weigh anchor; *Fig F* (*partir*) to get moving, to hit the road; **jeter l'a.,** to anchor; *Fig* to settle down; *Av* **a. de ballon,** balloon anchor, grapnel; **(b)** *Constr etc* anchor, cramp iron, tie (plate) (*of wall, furnace etc*); brace, stay (*of boiler*).
ancrer [ɑ̃kre] **1** *vt* **(a)** to anchor (*ship, balloon*); *Fig* **il faut lui a. cette idée dans la tête,** we *or* you *etc* have to get that into his head; **être ancré dans son comportement,** (*d'une caractéristique etc*) to be an integral part of one's behaviour; **(b)** *Constr* to brace, to tie, to stay, to anchor (*chimney, engine, boiler etc*). **2 s'ancrer** *vpr* to settle in, to get a firm footing; **elle a décidé de s'a. dans cette région,** she has decided to stay put in that region.
andalou, -ouse [ɑ̃dalu, -uz] **1** *adj* Andalusian. **2** *nm* **(a)** *Ling* Andalusian (dialect); **(b)** Andalusian horse. **3** *n* **A.,** Andalusian.
Andalousie [ɑ̃daluzi] *nf* Andalusia.
andante [ɑ̃dɑ̃t] *adv & nm Mus* andante.
andantino [ɑ̃dɑ̃tino] *adv & nm Mus* andantino.
Andes [ɑ̃d] *nfpl* **les A.,** the Andes; **la Cordillère des A.,** the Andean *or* the Great Cordillera.
andin [ɑ̃dɛ̃] *adj* Andean.
andorran, -ane [ɑ̃dɔrɑ̃, -an] **1** *adj* Andorran. **2** *n* **A.,** Andorran.
Andorre [ɑ̃dɔr] *n* Andorra; **le val/la principauté d'A.,** the Vale/Principality of Andorra.
andouille [ɑ̃duj] *nf* **(a)** *Culin* chitterlings (*made into sausages*); **(b)** *F* (*imbécile*) fool, twit; **faire l'a.,** to play the fool.
andouiller [ɑ̃duje] *nm* tine (*of antler*).
andouillette [ɑ̃dujɛt] *nf Culin* = (small) sausage (for frying) made of chitterlings.
André [ɑ̃dre] *nm* Andrew.
androgène [ɑ̃drɔʒɛn] **1** *adj* androgenic. **2** *nm* androgen, male hormone.
androgyne [ɑ̃drɔʒin] **1** *adj* androgynous. **2** *nm* androgyne.
Andromaque [ɑ̃drɔmak] *nf* Andromache.
Andromède [ɑ̃drɔmɛd] *nf* Andromeda.
andropause [ɑ̃drɔpoz] *nf* male menopause.
âne [ɑn] *nm* **(a)** donkey; *Litt & Vieilli* ass; **â. mâle,** jackass; **promenade à â.** *ou* **à dos d'â.,** donkey ride; *F* **têtu comme un â.,** as stubborn as a mule, pigheaded; *Prov* **on ne saurait faire boire un â. qui n'a pas soif,** you may lead a horse to water but you cannot make him drink; *Vieilli* **faute d'un point Martin perdit son â.,** for want of a nail the shoe was lost; **en dos d'â.,** ridged, razor-backed; **colline en dos d'â.,** hog's back; **pont en dos d'â.,** humpbacked bridge; **attention, dos d'â.,** (*sur panneau*) beware uneven road surface; **(b)** *F* fool, ass; (*ignare*) dunce, **bonnet d'â.,** dunce's cap.
anéantir [aneɑ̃tir] **1** *vt* to reduce to nothing; to annihilate, to destroy (*empire, town etc*); **a. les espérances de qn,** to dash s.o.'s hopes, to put an end to s.o.'s hopes; *Fig* **la nouvelle l'a anéantie,** she was staggered by the news; **je suis anéanti,** (*épuisé*) I am exhausted, *F* I'm dead beat. **2 s'anéantir** *vpr* **(a)** (*disparaître*) to come to nothing, to vanish, to melt into thin air; **(b)** *Rel* to humble *or* abase oneself (*before God*).
anéantissant [aneɑ̃tisɑ̃] *adj* exhausting (*work*); overwhelming (*misfortune*).
anéantissement [aneɑ̃tismɑ̃] *nm* **(a)** destruction, annihilation (*of hope, empire etc*); **l'a. de l'individu/de la personnalité,** the annihilation of the individual/the personality; **(b)** (state of) exhaustion.
anecdote [anɛkdɔt] *nf* anecdote.
anecdotique [anɛkdɔtik] *adj* anecdotal.
anémie [anemi] *nf Méd* anaemia, *US* anemia; **faire de l'a.,** to have anaemia; **a. pernicieuse,** pernicious anaemia; *Fig* **l'a. d'un secteur,** the enfeebled state of an industrial sector.
anémier [anemje] **1** *vt* to make (*s.o.*) anaemic *or US* anemic; *Fig* **la crise a anémié la sidérurgie,** the crisis has severely weakened the steel industry. **2 s'anémier** *vpr* to become anaemic *or US* anemic; *Fig* **un secteur qui s'anémie,** an industrial sector that is falling into decline.
anémique [anemik] *adj* **(a)** (*personne*) anaemic, *US* anemic; **(b)** *Fig* feeble, weak.
anémomètre [anemɔmɛtr] *nm* anemometer, wind gauge; **a. badin,** airspeed indicator.
anémone [anemɔn] *nf* anemone; **a. sylvie,** wood anemone; **a. de mer,** sea anemone.
ânerie [ɑnri] *nf F* **(a)** (*stupidité, bêtise*) stupidity; **il est d'une â.!,** what an idiot!; **quelle â.!,** (*ta décision etc*) how

idiotic!; **(b)** (*action, propos*) **faire des âneries,** to make an ass *or* a fool of oneself; **dire des âneries,** to talk tripe *or* rubbish.
anéroïde [anerɔid] *adj Météo* aneroid (*barometer*).
ânesse [ɑnɛs] *nf* she ass, jenny; **lait d'â.,** ass's milk.
anesthésiant [anɛstezjɑ̃] *adj & nm Méd* anaesthetic, *US* anesthetic.
anesthésie [anɛstezi] *nf Méd* anaesthesia, *US* anesthesia; **a. générale/locale,** general/local anaesthetic; **mettre un malade sous a.,** to anaesthetize a patient, to put a patient under anaesthetic; **elle est encore sous a.,** she's still under (the) anaesthetic.
anesthésier [anɛstezje] *vt Méd* to anaesthetize, *US* to anesthetise.
anesthésiologie [anɛsteziɔlɔʒi] *nf Méd Br* anaesthetics, *US* anesthesiology.
anesthésiologiste [anɛsteziɔlɔʒist] *n Méd* (*médecin*) *Br* anaesthetist, *US* anesthesiologist.
anesthésique [anɛstezik] *adj & nm Méd* anaesthetic, *US* anesthetic.
anesthésiste [anɛstezist] *n Méd* (*médecin*) *Br* anaesthetist, *US* anesthetologist; *US* (*infirmière*) anesthetist.
aneth [anɛt] *nm* (*plante*) fennel.
aneurine [anœrin] *nf* vitamin B.
anévrisme,-ysme [anevrism] *nm Méd* aneurism, aneurysm.
ange [ɑ̃ʒ] *nm* **(a)** *Rel* angel; **a. gardien,** guardian angel; **a. déchu,** fallen angel; *Beaux-Arts* **a. joufflu,** chubby little cherub; **être le bon a. de qn,** to be s.o.'s good angel; **être le mauvais a. de qn,** to be a bad influence on s.o.; **être aux anges,** to be in seventh heaven, to walk on air; *F* **rire aux anges,** to have an idiotic grin on one's face; *F* **faiseuse d'anges,** backstreet abortionist; *F* **un a. passe,** an angel passes (*said after awkward pause in conversation*); **oui mon a.,** yes (my) dear *or* darling; **beau comme un a.,** pretty as a picture; **sage comme un a.,** (as) good as gold; **une patience d'a.,** the patience of a saint; **une douceur d'a.,** angelic sweetness; *Natation* **saut de l'a.,** swallow dive, *US* swan dive; **son mari est un a.,** her husband is an absolute angel; **tu serais un a. si tu allais chercher mes cigarettes,** be an angel and fetch my cigarettes; *F* **sois un a.!,** be an angel!;

(b) (*poisson*) **a. (noir, de mer),** (black) angel fish; monkfish.
angélique [ɑ̃ʒelik] **1** *adj* angelic(al); *Rel* **la salutation a.,** the Hail Mary; **être d'une patience a.,** to have the patience of a saint. **2** *nf Culin* angelica.
angélisme [ɑ̃ʒelism] *nm* = tendency to see nothing but good in other people.
angelot [ɑ̃ʒlo] *nm* **(a)** little angel, cherub; **(b)** (*poisson*) monkfish, angel fish *or* ray *or* shark.
angélus [ɑ̃ʒelys] *nm Rel* angelus (bell).
angevin, -ine [ɑ̃ʒvɛ̃, -in] **1** *adj* Angevin, (of *or* from) Angers *or* Anjou. **2** *n* **A.,** Angevin, person from Angers *or* Anjou.
angine [ɑ̃ʒin] *nf Méd* tonsillitis; *Vieilli* quinsy; **a. de poitrine,** angina (pectoris).
anglais, -aise [ɑ̃glɛ, -ɛz] **1** *adj* English (*language etc*); (*incorrect au sens strict*) British (*army, goods etc*); *F* **filer à l'anglaise,** to take French leave, to slip away; *Culin* **pommes de terre à l'anglaise,** boiled potatoes. **2** *nm* English (language); **l'a. correct,** the King's *or* Queen's English. **3** *n* **A.,** Englishman, Englishwoman; (*incorrect au sens strict*) Briton; **les A.,** the English; (*incorrect au sens strict*) the British; *Can* **avoir la visite des A.,** to have one's period. **4** *fpl* **anglaises,** ringlets.
angle [ɑ̃gl] *nm* **(a)** corner, angle (*of wall, room etc*); **armoire d'a.,** corner cupboard; **boutique d'a.,** corner shop; **la maison qui fait l'a.,** the house on the corner; **l'a. de la rue,** the street corner; **à l'a. du chemin,** at the bend of the road; **l'a. de la table,** the corner of the table; **à l'a. des lèvres,** at the corner of his *or* her *etc* lips; *Fig* **arrondir les angles,** to soften one's approach; (*d'une réglementation etc*) to make more flexible;

(b) (*point de vue*) angle, point of view; **sous cet a.-là,** from that angle *or* point of view; **a. d'attaque,** line of attack, approach (*to a subject*); **sous l'a. de la régularité, il n'y a pas de critique à elle,** she can't be criticized as far as time keeping is concerned;

(c) *Géom* angle; **a. aigu/obtus,** acute/obtuse angle; **a. droit,** right angle; **les rues se coupent à angles droits,** the roads cross at right angles; **former un a. avec qch,** to be at right angles to sth; *Opt* **a. d'incidence/de réfraction,** angle of incidence/refraction; *Phot* **grand a.,** wide-angle lens; *Av* **a. critique,** stalling angle; **a. de cap,** track course; **a. mort,** dead angle; (*dans un rétroviseur etc*) blind spot; *Menuis etc* **abattre les angles de qch,** to chamfer sth; **soudure d'a.,** fillet weld; **roue d'a.,** bevel wheel, mitre wheel; **engrenage d'a.,** bevel gear; **fer d'a.,** angle iron; **a. oblique,** bevel rule, mitre square;

(d) edge (*of a tool*); **à angles vifs,** with sharp edges.
angledozer [ɑ̃glədɔzɛr] *nm* angledozer.
Angleterre [ɑ̃glətɛr] *nf* England; (*incorrect au sens strict*) Britain; **la bataille d'A.,** the Battle of Britain (*1940*); **point d'A.,** Brussels (bobbin) lace.
anglican, -ane [ɑ̃glikɑ̃, -an] *Rel* **1** *adj* Anglican; **l'Église anglicane,** the Church of England, the Anglican Church. **2** *n* Anglican.
anglicanisme [ɑ̃glikanism] *nm Rel* Anglicanism.
anglicisant,-ante [ɑ̃glisizɑ̃, -ɑ̃t] *n* student of English, English scholar.
angliciser [ɑ̃glisize] **1** *vt* to anglicize (*word etc*). **2 s'angliciser** *vpr* to become anglicized.
anglicisme [ɑ̃glisism] *nm Ling* Anglicism.
angliciste [ɑ̃glisist] *n* Anglicist.
anglo- [ɑ̃glɔ] *préf* Anglo-.
anglo-américain [ɑ̃glɔamerikɛ̃] **1** *adj* Anglo-American. **2** *nm Ling* American English. **3** *n* **A.-A.,** Anglo-American.
anglo-catholique [ɑ̃glɔkatɔlik] *Rel* **1** *adj* Anglo-Catholic. **2** *n* Anglo-Catholic.
anglo-irlandais, -aise [ɑ̃glɔirlɑ̃dɛ, -ɛz] **1** *adj* Anglo-Irish; **l'Accord a.-i.,** the Anglo-Irish Agreement. **2** *n* **A.-I.,** Anglo-Irishman, -woman.
anglomane [ɑ̃glɔman] *n* anglomaniac.
anglomanie [ɑ̃glɔmani] *nf* anglomania.
anglo-normand, -ande [ɑ̃glɔnɔrmɑ̃, -ɑ̃d] **1** *adj* **(a) les îles a.-normandes,** the Channel Islands; **(b)** *Hist* Anglo-Norman. **2** *nm Ling* Anglo-Norman.
anglophile [ɑ̃glɔfil] **1** *adj* anglophile, pro-English. **2** *n* anglophile.
anglophilie [ɑ̃glɔfili] *nf* anglophilia.
anglophobe [aglɔfɔb] **1** *adj* anglophobi(a)c. **2** *n* anglophobe.
anglophobie [ɑ̃glɔfɔbi] *nf* anglophobia.
anglophone [ɑ̃glɔfɔn] **1** *adj* English-speaking; *Can* anglophone. **2** *n* English-speaking person; *Can* Anglophone.
anglo-saxon, -onne [ɑ̃glɔsaksɔ̃, -ɔn] **1** *adj* Anglo-Saxon; **les pays a.-saxons,** the English-speaking countries. **2** *n Ling* Anglo-Saxon. **3** *n* **A.-S.,** English speaker; *Hist* Anglo-Saxon.
angoissant [ɑ̃gwasɑ̃] *adj* distressing (*news*); agonizing (*wait*); heart-rending (*sight*); tense, anxious (*moment*).
angoisse [ɑ̃gwas] *nf* anguish, distress; (*douleur*) agony; *Méd* **une crise d'a.,** an anxiety attack; **les angoisses de la mort,** the pangs of death; **vivre dans l'a. de la mort,** to live in fear (and dread) of dying; **considérer qch avec a.,** (*à l'avenir*) to dread sth; (*au passé*) to look back on sth with anguish; *F* **quelle a.!,** what a drag!
angoissé [ɑ̃gwase] **1** *adj* distressed, anxious; **j'étais a.,** my heart was in my mouth. **2** *n* person who suffers from anxiety; **c'est une grande angoissée,** she suffers a great deal from anxiety.
angoisser [ɑ̃gwase] **1** *vt* to fill (*s.o.*) with anxiety *or* distress *or* anguish; *F* **ça m'angoisse d'entrer dans un supermarché/d'être seul avec lui/***etc*, I can't face going into a supermarket/being alone with him/*etc*. **2** *vi F* to worry, to get worked up; **n'angoisse pas, ce n'est pas la peine,** don't worry (about it) *or* don't get worked up about it, it's not worth it. **3 s'angoisser** *vpr* to get anxious, *F* to get worked up; **elle s'angoisse pour un rien,** she gets worked up over nothing.
Angola [ɑ̃gɔla] *nm* Angola.
angolais, -aise [ɑ̃gɔlɛ, -ɛz] **, angolan, -ane** [ɑ̃gɔlɑ̃, -an] **1** *adj* Angolan. **2** *n* **A.,** Angolan.
Angora [ɑ̃gɔra] **1** *adj souvent inv* angora (*wool, sweater*); **poil de chèvre a.,** mohair. **2** *nm* **(a)** (*lapin*) angora rabbit; (*chat*) Persian cat; (*chèvre*) angora; **(b)** *Tex* angora (wool).
angstrœm, angström [ɑ̃gstrœm] *nm Phys* angström.
anguille [ɑ̃gij] *nf* (*poisson*) eel; **a. de mer,** conger eel; *Fig* **il y a a. sous roche,** there's something brewing *or* in the wind; (*qch de louche*) there's something fishy going on, I smell a rat; *F* **elle a filé comme une a.,** she ran off like greased lightning; **être souple comme une a.,** to be (as) flexible as rubber, to be made of rubber.
angulaire [ɑ̃gylɛr] **1** *adj* angular; *Constr* **pierre a.,** cornerstone. **2** *nm Phot* **grand a.,** wide-angle lens.
anguleux, -euse [ɑ̃gylø, -øz] *adj* angular, bony (*face, elbows etc*); rough, rugged (*outline etc*); *Fig* **caractère a.,** awkward disposition.
anicroche [anikrɔʃ] *nf* difficulty, hitch, snag; **se passer**

sans a., to go smoothly *or* without a hitch.

aniline [anilin] *nf Ch* aniline.

animal, -aux [animal, -o] **1** *nm* animal; **société protectrice des animaux,** society for the prevention of cruelty to animals; **a. domestique,** pet; **l'homme est un a. social,** man is a social animal;; *F* **quel a.!,** what a brute!, what a beast!; **il en a de la chance, cet a.-là!,** what a lucky beggar *or* brute!; **espèce d'a.!,** you bastard! **2** *adj* **(a)** animal (*kingdom, matter etc*); **chaleur animale,** animal warmth; **(b)** animal, brute (*instinct etc*); **avoir une confiance animale en qn,** to trust s.o. instinctively.

animalier [animalje] **1** *adj* animal (*painting etc*). **2** *nm* painter *or* sculptor of animals.

animalité [animalite] *nf* animality, animal nature; animal side (*of human beings*).

animant [animɑ̃] *adj* stimulating, exciting.

animateur, -trice [animatœr, -tris] **1** *adj* stimulating (*person*); life-giving (*power etc*). **2** *n* **(a)** stimulating person; life and soul (*of a party*); **(b)** *TV etc* presenter; (*d'émission de variétés*) compère, M.C., *US* emcee; quiz *or* question master; *Rad* presenter, radio personality; (*d'une émission de musique pop*) disc jockey, DJ, deejay; (*d'un débat*) moderator; **l'animatrice d'un centre de jeunes,** youth leader, organizer of a youth club; **(c)** *Cin* animator. **3** *nm* prime mover.

animation [animɑsjɔ̃] *nf* **(a)** (*vie*) animation, liveliness, vivacity; **l'a. des rues,** the bustle in the streets; **mettre de l'a. dans une soirée,** to liven up a party; **il parle avec beaucoup d'a.,** he speaks with great animation; **ville pleine d'a.,** town full of life; **a. du marché,** buoyancy of the market; **(b)** (*d'un groupe*) community activities; **(c)** *Cin* animation; **film d'a.,** animated film; **(d)** *Météo* **a. satellite,** satellite picture.

animé [anime] *adj* **(a)** animated, spirited, lively (*person, discussion etc*); (*agité*) heated (*discussion*); busy (*street*); **cheval a.,** fresh *or* frisky horse; *Fig* **marché a.,** brisk *or* buoyant market; **(b)** *Cin* **dessin a.,** cartoon.

animer [anime] **1** *vt* **(a)** (*stimuler*) to animate, to give life to (*s.o., sth*); **animé par un nouvel espoir,** buoyed up with new hope; **(b)** to move, to propel; to lead, to conduct (*discussion*); to lead, to mastermind (*enterprise*); to drive (*machine*); **animé d'un sentiment de jalousie,** prompted by feelings of jealousy; **animé de bonnes intentions,** motivated by good intentions; **(c)** to enliven (*conversation*); to stir up (*feelings*); *TV Rad* **a. une émission,** to present a programme. **2 s'animer** *vpr* to come to life; **la conversation s'animait,** the conversation was getting more lively *or* was warming up; **la ville s'anime avec le marché,** the town comes to life on market day; **la rue s'anime le soir,** the street wakes up at night; **son visage s'anima,** his face lit up; **les esprits s'animent, il va y avoir de la bagarre,** people are getting worked up, there's going to be trouble.

animosité [animozite] *nf* animosity, spite (**contre,** against); **avoir de l'a. contre** *ou* **pour qn,** to feel animosity toward s.o.; **garder de l'a. contre qn,** to nurse a grudge against s.o.; **agir par a.,** to act out of spite.

anion [anjɔ̃] *nm Phys* anion.

anis [ani(s)] *nm* (*plante*) anise; (*boisson*) **(sirop d')a.,** aniseed aperitif; *Culin* **(graine d')a.,** aniseed; **à l'a.,** aniseed-flavoured.

aniser [anize] *vt Culin* to flavour (*sth*) with aniseed.

anisette [anizɛt] *nf* anisette.

ankylose [ɑ̃kiloz] *nf* stiffness; *Méd* ankylosis.

ankyloser [ɑ̃kiloze] **1** *vt Méd* to ankylose; **être ankylosé,** to be stiff. **2 s'ankyloser** *vpr* to become *or* get stiff; *Fig* (*dans un métier etc*) to get into a rut.

annal, -aux [anal, -o] *adj Jur* valid for one year; **location annale,** yearly letting.

annales [anal] *nfpl* annals, (public) records; **les a. du crime,** the annals of crime; **les a. du bac,** = past examination papers (with annotations); *Fig* **ça restera dans les a.,** it will go down in (the annals of) history.

annamite [anamit] **1** *adj* Annamese, Annamite. **2** *nm Ling* Annamese. **3** *n* **A.,** person from Annam.

anneau, -eaux [ano] *nm* **(a)** (*cercle*) ring; *Bot* annulus; **a. de rideau,** curtain ring; **a. nuptial** *ou* **de mariage,** wedding ring; **a. épiscopal,** episcopal *or* bishop's ring; *Gym* **les anneaux,** the rings; **exercices aux anneaux,** ring exercises; **jeu des anneaux,** hoop-la; *Astron* **a. de Saturne,** ring of Saturn; **(b)** link (*of chain*); ringlet, curl (*of hair*); coil (*of serpent*); bow (*of key*); *F* **l'a. manquant,** the missing link; **(c)** *Tech* ring, collar; hoop (*of hub etc*); sling (*of rope*); **a. brisé,** key ring, split ring; **a. à fiche,** ring-bolt, eye-bolt; **(d)** *Nau* **a. de port,** = berth with facilities for hooking up to land-based power and water supplies.

année [ane] *nf* year; **a. solaire,** solar year; **a. civile,** calendar year; **a. bissextile,** leap year; **Bonne A.!,** Happy New Year!; **a. budgétaire/d'exercice fiscal,** financial/fiscal year; **a. scolaire,** school *or* academic year; **a. sabbatique,** sabbatical year, year's sabbatical; **une a. de vacances,** a year's holiday; **payer à l'a.,** to pay by the year; **a. après a.,** year after year; **d'a. en a.,** year by year; **une a. après l'autre,** year in year out; **nous nous connaissons depuis bien des années,** we've known each other for years; **il y a des années que je ne l'ai pas vue,** I haven't seen her for years; **les années 80,** the eighties, the 80s; **pendant les années de guerre/d'occupation,** during the war years/the years of occupation; **quelle est son a. de naissance?,** what year was he born?; **elle entre dans sa trentième a.,** she'll be 30 (on her) next birthday; *Univ* **entrer en troisième a. de médecine,** to go into one's third year of medicine; *Univ* **les classes de deuxième a.,** the second year students, *US* the sophomores.

année-lumière [anelymjɛr] *nf* light year; **à des années-lumière,** (*étoile etc*) light years away.

annelé [anle] *adj* ringed (*column, worm etc*).

annexe [anɛks] **1** *nf* **(a)** (*bâtiment*) annex(e); (*de ferme, château*) outbuilding; **(b)** rider (*to bill*); schedule (*to act*); supplement, appendix (*to book, report*); enclosure (*with letter*); **en a. à ma lettre,** enclosed with my letter; **(c)** *Rel* chapel of ease; **(d)** dependency (*of a state*); **(e)** *Nau* (*d'un bateau*) dinghy. **2** *adj* **établissement a.,** annex(e); **lettre a.,** covering letter; **industries annexes,** subsidiary industries; **revenus annexes,** supplementary income.

annexer [anɛkse] **1** *vt* **(a)** *Pol* to annex (territory); **(b)** to append, to attach (*document etc*); **pièces annexées (à une lettre),** enclosures; **(c)** *Ordinat* to append. **2 s'annexer** *vpr* **elle s'est annexé la meilleure place,** she grabbed the best seat for herself.

annexion [anɛksjɔ̃] *nf* annexation.

Annibal [anibal] *nm Antiq* Hannibal.

annihilant [aniilɑ̃] *adj* annihilating.

annihilation [aniilɑsjɔ̃] *nf* annihilation.

annihiler [aniile] *vt* **(a)** to annihilate, to destroy (*army etc*); **toute forme d'agressivité l'annihile,** he goes *or* falls to pieces when faced with any form of aggressive behaviour; **(b)** *Jur* to annul, to cancel.

anniversaire [anivɛrsɛr] **1** *adj* anniversary (*festival, ceremony*); **la date a.,** (*de la Libération etc*) the anniversary. **2** *nm* anniversary (*of victory, birth, death etc*); (wedding) anniversary; **le cinquantième a. de leur mariage,** their 50th wedding anniversary; **l'a. de ma naissance, mon a.,** my birthday; **mon vingtième a., l'a. de mes vingt ans,** my twentieth birthday; **bon a.!,** happy birthday!; **gâteau/carte/***etc* **d'a.,** birthday cake/card/*etc*.

annonce [anɔ̃s] *nf* **(a)** announcement; (*surtout par écrit*), notification, notice; *Cartes* declaration; bid; *Fig* sign, indication; *Rel* **faire l'a. d'un mariage,** to publish the banns; **faire une a.,** to make an announcement; **les annonces de la semaine,** the weekly notices; **le retour des hirondelles est l'a. du printemps,** it's a sign of spring when the swallows return; **(b)** (*de publicité etc*) advertisement; **passer une a. dans un journal/sur Minitel,** to put an ad(vert) in a newspaper/on Minitel; **petites annonces,** classified advertisements, small ads.

annoncer [anɔ̃se] *v* **(j'annonçai(s); n. annonçons) 1** *vt* **(a)** (*déclarer*) to announce, to give notice of, to give out (*sth*); **a. une mauvaise nouvelle à qn,** to break bad news to s.o.; **a. ses fiançailles en public,** to announce publicly one's engagement; *Fig* **a. la couleur,** to make one's intentions plain from the beginning;

(b) to advertise (*sale etc*);

(c) (*indiquer*) to promise, to foretell, to give promise of; **tout semble a. le succès,** everything points to success; **cela n'annonce rien de bon,** it looks unpromising, no *or* nothing good will come of that;

(d) to show (*s.o.*) in; (*à une occasion formelle*) to announce (*s.o.*);

(e) to give proof of (*sth*); to show (*sth*); **cela annonce de l'intelligence,** that shows intelligence; **le rire des enfants dans la cour annonce la fin des classes,** the sound of children laughing in the playground means that *or* is a sign that classes have finished.

2 s'annoncer *vpr* **cela s'annonce mal,** it looks unpromising, no *or* nothing good will come of that; **l'avènement de la démocratie s'annonce partout en Europe,** there are signs all over Europe of the advent of democracy.

annonceur [anɔ̃sœr] *nm* **(a)** (*de publicité*) advertiser; **(b)** *Rad TV* announcer.

annonciateur, -trice [anɔ̃sjatœr, -tris] **1** *nm Tél etc* indicator board, annunciator (board); **a. à volets,** drop indicator, drop annunciator; **a. de fin,** ring-off signal; *Él* **a. de couplage,** interlocking signal. **2** *adj* **signes annonciateurs du printemps/de la liberté,** signs that spring/freedom is on the way.
annonciation [anɔ̃sjasjɔ̃] *nf Rel* annunciation; **fête de l'A.,** Feast of the Annunciation, Lady Day.
annotateur, -trice [anɔtatœr, -tris] *n* annotator, commentator (*of text etc*).
annotation [anɔtasjɔ̃] *nf* **(a)** (*action*) annotating, making notes; **(b)** (*note*) annotation, note; **faire des annotations dans un texte,** to annotate a text.
annoter [anɔte] *vt* to annotate (*text*); to write notes in (*book*).
annuaire [anɥɛr] *nm* annual; (*d'un organisme international*) yearbook; **l'a. du téléphone** *ou* **téléphonique,** telephone directory, *F* the phone book; **je suis dans l'a.,** I'm in the book; **a. des marées,** tide table; **l'A. militaire,** the Army list; *US* the Army Register; **l'A. de la Marine,** the Navy List; **a. de l'université,** university calendar.
annuel, -elle [anɥɛl] *adj* annual, yearly; **plante annuelle,** annual; **rente annuelle,** annuity; **magistrature annuelle,** = judicial office held only for one year.
annuellement [anɥɛlmɑ̃] *adv* annually, yearly.
annuité [anɥite] *nf* **(a)** annual instalment (*in repayment of debt*); **(b)** (*rente*) annuity.
annulaire [anylɛr] **1** *adj* annular, ring-shaped. **2** *nm* ring finger, third finger.
annulation [anylasjɔ̃] *nf* cancelling, cancellation (*of contract, order, holidays etc*); *Jur etc* annulment (*of marriage*); quashing, setting aside (*of judgment*); abatement (*of writ*); voidance (*of contract*); setting aside (*of will*).
annuler [anyle] **1** *vt* **(a)** to cancel (*contract, order etc*); to call off (*a deal*); *Jur* to annul (*a marriage*); to render void, to repeal, to rescind (*law, judgment*); to set aside (*will*); **a. un ordre de grève,** to call off a strike; **(b)** *Banque* to cancel (*cheque etc*); **(c)** (*remplacer*) to supersede, to cancel; **ce catalogue annule les précédents,** this catalogue supersedes all previous issues; **(d)** *Fb* to disallow (*a goal*). **2 s'annuler** *vpr* to counterbalance each other, to cancel each other (out).
anoblir [anɔblir] *vt* to raise (*s.o.*) to the peerage.
anoblissement [anɔblismɑ̃] *nm* ennoblement (**de,** of).
anode [anɔd] *nf Él* anode, positive pole.
anodin [anɔdɛ̃] **1** *adj* harmless, innocuous; slight, minor (*injury*); mild (*infection*); **cette remarque n'était pas anodine,** this remark was not as innocent as it might seem; **une personne tout à fait anodine,** a totally insignificant person; *Méd* **remèdes anodins,** painkillers; *Fig* **moyen/remède a.,** ineffective method/remedy; **mensonge a.,** white lie. **2** *nm* palliative.
anodique [anɔdik] *adj Él* anodic, anodal; anode (*current*).
anomalie [anɔmali] *nf* **(a)** *Gram Astron* anomaly; **il y a une a. dans le fonctionnement de la machine,** the machine isn't working properly; **(b)** *Biol* anomaly; *Méd* disorder.
ânon [ɑnɔ̃] *nm* baby donkey.
ânonnement [ɑnɔnmɑ̃] *nm* mumbling.
ânonner [ɑnɔne] **1** *vt* to stumble *or* blunder through (*speech*). **2** *vi* to mumble.
anonymat [anɔnima] *nm* anonymity; **garder l'a.,** to remain anonymous.
anonyme [anɔnim] *adj* (*écrivain, lettre etc*) anonymous; (*décor, intérieur*) impersonal, anonymous; *Com* **société a. (par actions),** joint stock-company, limited (-liability) company.
anonymement [anɔnimmɑ̃] *adv* anonymously.
anorak [anɔrak] *nm* anorak.
anorexie [anɔrɛksi] *nf Méd* anorexia; **faire de l'a.,** to suffer from anorexia.
anorexique [anɔrɛksik] *adj & n Méd* anorexic.
anormal, -ale, -aux [anɔrmal, -o] **1** *adj* **(a)** (*irrégulier*) abnormal; **évolution anormale d'une maladie,** unexpected development of an illness; **enfants anormaux,** educationally subnormal children; **il est a. qu'à dix ans, un enfant ne sache lire,** it is not normal for a child of ten to be unable to read; **(b)** (*injuste*) unjust, unfair; **il est a. que** + *sub,* it is unfair that; **(c)** (*extraordinaire*) extraordinary; **l'a., c'est que ...,** the strange(st) *or* extraordinary thing is that ...; **il fait un temps a.,** it's abnormal weather, *F* the weather is all wrong for this time of year. **2** *n Méd Psy* mentally defective person; *F* **c'est un a.,** he's round the bend.
anormalement [anɔrmalmɑ̃] *adv* abnormally.
anormalité [anɔrmalite] *nf* abnormality.
ANPE [aɛnpeø] *n* (*abbr* **Agence nationale pour l'emploi**) *Br* ≈ Jobcentre; *Can* ≈ CEC; **être à l'ANPE,** to be registered with the Jobcentre.
anse [ɑ̃s] *nf* **(a)** handle (*of jug, basket*); shackle (*of padlock*); *Fig* **faire danser** *ou* **valser l'a. du panier,** (*d'un domestique etc*) to fiddle the books; *Archit* **voûte en a. de panier,** basket handle-arch; **(b)** loop, bight (*of rope etc*); *Anat* loop; **a. à vis,** screw eye(bolt); **(c)** *Géog* bight, cove.
antagonique [ɑ̃tagɔnik] *adj* antagonistic.
antagonisme [ɑ̃tagɔnism] *nm* (*de personne*) *& Physiol* antagonism.
antagoniste [ɑ̃tagɔnist] **1** *adj* antagonistic, opposed; **les partis antagonistes,** the opposing parties; **force a.,** antagonistic force; (*de contrôle*) controlling force, countercheck; *Anat* **muscles antagonistes,** antagonists; **couple a.,** opposing couple. **2** *n* antagonist, opponent.
antan [ɑ̃tɑ̃] *adv Arch & Litt* **d'a.,** of yesteryear; **où sont les neiges d'a.?,** where are the snows of yesteryear?
antarctique [ɑ̃tarktik] *Géog* **1** *adj* Antarctic; **cercle a.,** Antarctic circle. **2** *nm* **l'A.,** Antarctica, the Antarctic; **une expédition dans l'A.,** an Antarctic expedition.
anté- [ɑ̃te] *préf* ante-; pre-.
antécédent [ɑ̃tesedɑ̃] **1** *adj* antecedent, previous, anterior (**à,** to). **2** *nm* **(a)** *Ling Phil* antecedent; **(b) antécédents,** previous history, past record; *Fml & Litt* antecedents; **antécédents médicaux,** medical history; **il y a des antécédents cancéreux dans ma famille,** my family has a history of cancer; **avoir de bons/mauvais antécédents,** to have a good/bad record.
antéchrist [ɑ̃tekrist] *nm* antichrist.
antédiluvien, -ienne [ɑ̃tedilyvjɛ̃, -jɛn] *adj* antediluvian; *F* **ma télévision est antédiluvienne,** my television is an antique; **c'est une relation antédiluvienne,** I've known him for donkey's years.
antémémoire [ɑ̃tememwar] *nf Ordinat* cache (memory).
anténatal, -aux [ɑ̃tenatal, -o] *adj Méd* antenatal.
antenne [ɑ̃tɛn] *nf* **(a)** *Rad* aerial, antenna; (*d'un satellite, d'un robot*) antenna; **a. de télévision,** television aerial; **a. fermée** *ou* **en cadre,** loop aerial; **a. en V,** rabbit's ears; *Av* **a. pendante,** trailing aerial; *Fig* **passer à l'a.,** (*d'une émission*) to be broadcast *or* televised; (*d'une personne*) to be on television *or* radio; **rendre l'a.,** to go back, to return (*to the studio etc*); **je vous passe l'a., à vous l'a.!,** (I'll hand) over to you; **déclarer hors a. que ...,** to declare off the air that ...; **garder l'a.,** to stay on the air; **on est à l'a. dans cinq minutes,** we'll be on the air in five minutes; **(b)** antenna, feeler (*d'un insecte*); *Fig* **avoir des antennes,** to have a sixth sense, to be perceptive, to pick up on things; *Fig* **avoir ses antennes quelque part,** to have the feelers out, to have informers; **(c)** branch (*d'un tuyau*); *Rail* branch line (with sidings); **(d)** *Mil* **a. chirurgicale,** advanced surgical unit.
antépénultième [ɑ̃tepenyltjɛm] *adj & nf* antepenultimate, third (from) last.
antérieur, -eure [ɑ̃terjœr] *adj* **(a)** former (*period*); earlier (*date*); previous (*year*); prior (*engagement*); **cela est a. à ma naissance,** that was before I was born; **a. au mariage,** pre-marital; **dans une vie antérieure,** in a previous life *or* existence; *Gram* **futur a.,** future perfect; *Gram* **passé a.,** past anterior; **(b)** anterior (*muscle*); fore (*limb etc*); front (*wall, vowel etc*).
antérieurement [ɑ̃terjœrmɑ̃] *adv* previously, earlier; **son livre a paru a. au vôtre,** his book appeared before yours.
antériorité [ɑ̃terjɔrite] *nf* precedence; *Gram* anteriority.
anthère [ɑ̃tɛr] *nf Bot* anther.
anthologie [ɑ̃tɔlɔʒi] *nf* anthology.
anthologique [ɑ̃tɔlɔʒik] *adj* anthological.
anthracite [ɑ̃trasit] **1** *nm Minér* anthracite. **2** *adj inv* charcoal grey.
anthrax [ɑ̃traks] *nm Méd* carbuncle; **a. malin,** anthrax.
anthropoïde [ɑ̃trɔpɔid] **1** *adj* anthropoid. **2** *nm* anthropoid ape.
anthropologie [ɑ̃trɔpɔlɔʒi] *nf* anthropology.
anthropologique [ɑ̃trɔpɔlɔʒik] *adj* anthropological.
anthropologiste [ɑ̃trɔpɔlɔʒist], **anthropologue** [ɑ̃trɔpɔlɔg] *n* anthropologist.
anthropométrie [ɑ̃trɔpɔmetri] *nf* anthropometry.
anthropométrique [ɑ̃trɔpɔmetrik] *adj* anthropometric(al); *Admin* **service a.,** criminal anthropometry department; *Br* ≈ Criminal Records Office; **fiche a.,** = record containing fingerprints and details of height,

weight etc.
anthropomorphe [ɑ̃trɔpɔmɔrf] *adj* anthropomorphic.
anthropomorphisme [ɑ̃trɔpɔmɔrfism] *nm* anthropomorphism.
anthropophage [ɑ̃trɔpɔfaʒ] **1** *adj* cannibalistic, man-eating. **2** *n* cannibal.
anthropophagie [ɑ̃trɔpɔfaʒi] *nf* cannibalism.
anti¹ [ɑ̃ti] *préf* anti-.
anti² *préf* ante-.
antiaérien, -ienne [ɑ̃tiaerjɛ̃, -jɛn] *adj* anti-aircraft (*gun, defence*); **abri a.,** air-raid shelter.
anti-âge [ɑ̃tiɑʒ] *adj inv* anti-ageing (*treatment, cream*).
antialcoolique [ɑ̃tialkɔlik] *adj* temperance (*league etc*).
antialcoolisme [ɑ̃tialkɔlism] *nm* temperance, teetotalism.
antiallergique [ɑ̃tialɛrʒik] *adj* hypoallergenic.
antiatomique [ɑ̃tiatɔmik] *adj* antinuclear; **abri a.,** fall-out shelter; **manifestation a.,** ban-the-bomb *or* anti-nuclear demonstration.
antibiotique [ɑ̃tibjɔtik] *Pharm* **1** *adj* antibiotic; **un traitement a.,** a course of antibiotics. **2** *nm* antibiotic; **être sous antibiotiques,** to be on antibiotics.
antibrouillage [ɑ̃tibrujaʒ] *nm Rad etc* anti-jamming.
antibrouillard [ɑ̃tibrujar] *adj & nm Aut* **(phare) a.,** fog lamp.
antibruit [ɑ̃tibrɥi] *adj inv* soundproof (*wall*); **lutte a.,** noise abatement campaign.
antibuée [ɑ̃tibɥe] *adj & nm Aut* **(dispositif) a.,** demister.
anticalcaire [ɑ̃tikalkɛr] *nm* scale preventer, scale remover.
anticancéreux, -euse [ɑ̃tikɑ̃serø, -øz] *adj* **centre/sérum a.,** cancer hospital/serum.
anticasseurs [ɑ̃tikasœr] *adj inv Pol* **Loi a.,** = law banning violent behaviour during demonstrations.
anticathode [ɑ̃tikatɔd] *nf* anticathode.
antichambre [ɑ̃tiʃɑ̃br] *nf* waiting room, antechamber; **pilier d'a.,** hanger-on (*of minister etc*); **faire a.,** to hang around in the waiting room; *Fig* to wait patiently to see s.o.
antichar [ɑ̃tiʃar] *Mil* **1** *adj* anti-tank. **2** *nm* anti-tank device.
antichoc [ɑ̃tiʃɔk] *adj inv* shock-proof; *Méd* **traitement a.,** anti-shock treatment.
anticipatif, -ive [ɑ̃tisipatif, -iv] *adj* anticipatory, anticipative; **paiement a.,** prepayment.
anticipation [ɑ̃tisipasjɔ̃] *nf* anticipation; **payer par a.,** to pay in advance; **demander l'a. d'un paiement,** to ask for payment in advance; **littérature d'a.,** science fiction.
anticipé [ɑ̃tisipe] *adj* (*paiement*) advance; **prendre sa retraite anticipée,** to take early retirement.
anticiper [ɑ̃tisipe] **1** *vt* to anticipate (*a reaction, reply*); to forestall (*s.o.'s action*); **plaisir anticipé,** anticipated pleasure; **avec mes remerciements anticipés,** thanking you in anticipation; *Fin* **dividende anticipé,** advanced dividend; **remboursement anticipé,** redemption before due date. **2** *vi* to anticipate, to look *or* think ahead; *Sp etc* to anticipate one's opponent's moves; **n'anticipons pas,** let's not look *or* think too far ahead; **a. sur les événements,** to anticipate events; **je ne voudrais pas a. sur ce qui sera dit plus tard,** I don't wish to anticipate *or* pre-empt what will be said later; **a. sur ses revenus,** to spend one's income in advance.
anticlérical, -ale, -aux [ɑ̃tiklerikal, -o] *adj & n* anti-clerical.
anticléricalisme [ɑ̃tiklerikalism] *nm* anti-clericalism.
anticlimax [ɑ̃tiklimaks] *nm* anticlimax.
anticlinal, -aux [ɑ̃tiklinal, -o] *nm Géol* anticline.
anticoagulant [ɑ̃tikɔagylɑ̃] *adj & nm Pharm* anti-coagulant.
anticolonialisme [ɑ̃tikɔlɔnjalism] *nm* anti-colonialism.
anticommunisme [ɑ̃tikɔmynism] *nm Pol* anti-communism.
anticommuniste [ɑ̃tikɔmynist] *adj & n Pol* anti-communist.
anticonceptionnel,-elle [ɑ̃tikɔ̃sɛpsjɔnɛl] *adj* contraceptive (*pill*); birth-control (*measures etc*).
anticonformisme [ɑ̃tikɔ̃fɔrmism] *nm* non-conformism; **faire de l'a.,** to be a non-conformist.
anticonformiste [ɑ̃tikɔ̃fɔrmist] *adj & n* non-conformist.
anticonstitutionnel, -elle [ɑ̃tikɔ̃stitysjɔnɛl] *adj* anti-constitutional, unconstitutional.
anticonstitutionnellement [ɑ̃tikɔ̃stitysjɔnɛlmɑ̃] *adv* unconstitutionally.
anticorps [ɑ̃tikɔr] *nm* antibody.
anticyclique [ɑ̃tisiklik] *adj* anticyclic.
anticyclonal, -aux [ɑ̃tisiklɔnal, -o] *adj Météo* anticyclonic; **aire anticyclonale,** high-pressure area.
anticyclone [ɑ̃tisiklon] *Météo* **1** *nm* anticyclone. **2** *adj* **abri a.,** cyclone cellar.
anticyclonique [ɑ̃tisiklɔnik] *adj Météo* anticyclonic.
antidate [ɑ̃tidat] *nf* antedate.
antidater [ɑ̃tidate] *vt* to antedate (*contract etc*).
antidéflagrant [ɑ̃tideflagrɑ̃] *adj* explosion-proof; flame-proof.
antidémocratique [ɑ̃tidemɔkratik] *adj* antidemocratic, undemocratic.
antidépresseur [ɑ̃tidepresœr] *adj & nm* anti-depressant.
antidérapant [ɑ̃tiderapɑ̃] *Auto* **1** *adj* non-skid (*tyre*). **2** *nm* non-skid tyre.
antidétonant [ɑ̃tidetɔnɑ̃] *adj & nm* anti-knock.
antidiphtérique [ɑ̃tidifterik] *adj* **vaccin a.,** diphtheria vaccine.
antidopage [ɑ̃tidɔpaʒ] *nm*, **antidoping** [ɑ̃tidɔpiŋ] *nm Sp* **contrôle a.,** drug(s) test; **être positif au contrôle a.,** to fail a drugs test.
antidote [ɑ̃tidɔt] *nm Méd & Fig* antidote (**contre,** for).
anti-éblouissant [ɑ̃tiebluisɑ̃] *adj Aut* (*phares*) anti-dazzle.
antienne [ɑ̃tjɛn] *nf* antiphon; *Fig* **il dit cela à tout propos, c'est son a.,** he says that all the time, it's the same old tune.
antiesclavagisme [ɑ̃tiɛsklavaʒism] *nm Pol* anti-slavery movement, abolitionism.
antiesclavagiste [ɑ̃tiɛsklavaʒist] **1** *adj* anti-slavery, abolitionist. **2** *n* person opposed to slavery, abolitionist.
antifading [ɑ̃tifadiŋ] *nm inv* automatic volume control.
antifasciste [ɑ̃tifasist, -ʃist] *adj & n Pol* anti-fascist.
anti-g [ɑ̃tiʒe] *adj inv Av* **vêtement** *ou* **combinaison a.-g,** (anti) G suit.
antigang [ɑ̃tigɑ̃g] *adj* **brigade a.,** = police squad concerned with combating terrorism and organized crime.
antigaz [ɑ̃tigɑz] *adj* anti-gas.
antigel [ɑ̃tiʒɛl] *nm* antifreeze.
antigène [ɑ̃tiʒɛn] *nm Méd* antigen.
antigivreur, -euse [ɑ̃tiʒivrœr, -øz] **1** *adj Av* anti-icing; *Aut* de-icing. **2** *nm Av* anti-icer; *Aut* de-icer.
antiglisse [ɑ̃tiglis] *adj inv* **vêtements/tissu a.,** non-slip clothing/material.
antihéros [ɑ̃tiero] *nm* antihero.
antihistaminique [ɑ̃tiistaminik] *adj & nm Méd* anti-histamine.
antihygiénique [ɑ̃tiiʒjenik] *adj* unhygienic, insanitary.
anti-inflationniste [ɑ̃tiɛ̃flasjɔnist] *adj Écon* anti-inflation(ary).
antillais, -aise [ɑ̃tijɛ, -ɛz] **1** *adj* West-Indian. **2** *nm Ling* creole. **3** *n* **A.,** West-Indian.
Antilles [ɑ̃tij] *nfpl* **les A.,** the West Indies; **la Mer des A.,** the Caribbean (Sea).
antilog [ɑ̃tilɔg] *nm Math F* antilog.
antilogarithme [ɑ̃tilɔgaritm] *nm Math* antilogarithm.
antilope [ɑ̃tilɔp] *nf* antelope.
antimagnétique [ɑ̃timaɲetik] *adj* antimagnetic.
antimatière [ɑ̃timatjɛr] *nf* antimatter.
antimilitarisme [ɑ̃timilitarism] *nm* antimilitarism.
antimilitariste [ɑ̃timilitarist] *adj & n* antimilitarist.
antimissile [ɑ̃timisil] *adj* anti-missile; **missile a.,** anti-missile missile.
antimite(s) [ɑ̃timit] **1** *adj* mothproof (*clothing*); **bombe a.,** mothkiller. **2** *nm* **antimite,** mothkiller.
antimoine [ɑ̃timwan] *nm Ch* antimony.
antimonarchique [ɑ̃timɔnarʃik] *adj* antimonarchic(al).
antimonarchisme [ɑ̃timɔnarʃism] *nm* antimonarchism.
antimonarchiste [ɑ̃timɔnarʃist] *n* antimonarchist.
antinazi, -e [ɑ̃tinazi] *adj & n* anti-Nazi.
antinévralgique [ɑ̃tinevralʒik] *adj & nm Pharm* anti-neuralgic.
antinomie [ɑ̃tinɔmi] *nf* antinomy.
antinomique [ɑ̃tinɔmik] *adj* antinomic.
antinucléaire [ɑ̃tinykleɛr] *adj* anti-nuclear.
antipaludique [ɑ̃tipalydik] *Pharm* **1** *adj* antimalaria(l). **2** *nm* antimalarial (drug).
antipape [ɑ̃tipap] *nm Hist Rel* antipope.
antiparasitage [ɑ̃tiparazitaʒ] *nm Rad El* suppression.
antiparasitaire [ɑ̃tiparazitɛr] **1** *nm* pesticide. **2** *adj* pest-destroying.
antiparasite [ɑ̃tiparazit] **1** *nm* pesticide. **2** *adj & nm Rad Aut etc* **(dispositif) a.,** suppressor.
antiparlementaire [ɑ̃tiparləmɑ̃tɛr] *adj Pol* anti-parliamentary; unparliamentary (*language*).
antiparlementarisme [ɑ̃tiparləmɑ̃tarism] *nm* anti-parliamentarism.

antipathie [ɑ̃tipati] *nf* antipathy; **avoir de l'a. pour qn,** to have antipathy for *or* feel antipathy towards s.o.; **éprouver une grande a. pour qn,** to have great antipathy for *or* feel great antipathy towards s.o..
antipathique [ɑ̃tipatik] *adj* repugnant, antipathetic.
antipelliculaire [ɑ̃tipelikylɛr] *adj* **shampooing a.,** (anti-)dandruff shampoo.
antipersonnel [ɑ̃tipɛrsɔnɛl] *adj inv* antipersonnel.
antiphone [ɑ̃tifɔn] *nm Rel* antiphon.
antiphrase [ɑ̃tifraz] *nf Ling* antiphrasis.
antipodal, -aux [ɑ̃tipɔdal, -o] *adj* antipodean.
antipode [ɑ̃tipɔd] *nm Géog* antipodes; **la Nouvelle-Zélande est l'a. de la France,** New Zealand is on the other side of the world from France; **les antipodes,** the antipodes; **aux antipodes,** at the antipodes; *Fig* diametrically opposed, poles apart; *Fig* **son opinion est à l'a. de la mienne,** his opinion is diametrically opposed to mine *or* is poles apart from mine.
antipoétique [ɑ̃tipɔetik] *adj* unpoetic.
anti-poison [ɑ̃tipwazɔ̃] *nm Méd* antidote; **centre a.-p.** poison centre.
antipoliomyélite [ɑ̃tipɔljɔmjelit] *adj* **vaccination a.,** polio vaccination.
antipolitique [ɑ̃tipɔlitik] *adj* impolitic, ill-advised.
antipollution [ɑ̃tipɔlysjɔ̃] *adj inv* (*mesures*) anti-pollution.
antiprogressif, -ive [ɑ̃tiprɔgrɛsif, -iv] *adj* reactionary.
antiprotectionniste [ɑ̃tiprɔtɛksjɔnist] **1** *adj* free-trade (*policy*). **2** *n* antiprotectionist, free trader.
antipsychiatrie [ɑ̃tipsikjatri] *nf* anti-psychiatry.
antipyrétique [ɑ̃tipiretik] *adj* antipyretic.
antipyrine [ɑ̃tipirin] *nf* antipyrine.
antiquaille [ɑ̃tikaj] *nf Péj* (worthless old) junk.
antiquaire [ɑ̃tikɛr] *nm* antiquary, antiquarian; (*marchand*) antique dealer.
antique [ɑ̃tik] **1** *adj* old, ancient; antique (*furniture*); *Péj* old-fashioned, antiquated; **la Grèce a.,** ancient *or* classical Greece. **2** *nm* **(a)** (*objets anciens*) antiques; *Vieilli* work of art (*of classical antiquity*); **vendre/collectionner de l'a.,** to sell/collect antiques; **(b) l'a.,** the antique, classical antiquity; **(c)** *Typ* antique.
antiquité [ɑ̃tikite] *nf* **(a)** (*ancienneté*) antiquity, ancientness; **(b)** (*temps anciens*) ancient times, antiquity; **connu de toute a.,** known (about) since time immemorial; **(c)** *Hist* **l'a. grecque,** ancient Greek civilization; **(d) antiquités,** (*meubles etc anciens*) antiques; **les antiquités,** the works of classical antiquity; (*meubles etc anciens*) antiques; **magasin d'antiquités,** antique shop.
antirabique [ɑ̃tirabik] *adj Méd* (*piqûre*) anti-rabies.
antirachitique [ɑ̃tiraʃitik] *adj Méd* antirachitic.
antiracisme [ɑ̃tirasism] *nm* antiracialism, anti-racism.
antiraciste [ɑ̃tirasist] *adj & n* antiracist, antiracialist.
antiradar [ɑ̃tiradar] **1** *adj* anti-radar. **2** *nm* anti-radar device.
antireligieux, -euse [ɑ̃tirəliʒjø, -øz] *adj* antireligious.
antirépublicain, -aine [ɑ̃tirepyblikɛ̃, -ɛn] *adj & n* antirepublican.
antirévolutionnaire [ɑ̃tirevɔlysjɔnɛr] *adj & n* antirevolutionary.
antirides [ɑ̃tirid] *adj inv* anti-wrinkle (*cream*).
anti-roman [ɑ̃tirɔmɑ̃] *nm Littér* anti-novel; (*pl anti-romans*).
antirouille [ɑ̃tiruj] **1** *nm* rust preventive. **2** *adj inv* rust-proof, non-rusting (*metal*); rust-preventing (*substance, treatment*).
antiroulis [ɑ̃tiruli] *nm Nau Av* (gyro) stabilizer.
antiscorbutique [ɑ̃tiskɔrbytik] *adj & nm Pharm* antiscorbutic.
antiségrégationniste [ɑ̃tisegregasjɔnist] *adj & n* antisegregationist.
antisémite [ɑ̃tisemit] **1** *adj* anti-semitic. **2** *n* anti-semite.
antisémitique [ɑ̃tisemitik] *adj* anti-semitic.
antisémitisme [ɑ̃tisemitism] *nm* anti-semitism.
antisepsie [ɑ̃tisɛpsi] *nf Méd* antisepsis.
antiseptique [ɑ̃tisɛptik] *adj & nm Méd* antiseptic.
antisérum [ɑ̃tiserɔm] *nm Méd* antiserum.
antisocial, -aux [ɑ̃tisɔsjal, -o] *adj* antisocial.
anti-sous-marin [ɑ̃tisumarɛ̃] *adj* anti-submarine.
antisoviétique [ɑ̃tisɔvjetik] *adj* anti-Soviet.
antispasmodique [ɑ̃tispasmɔdik] *adj & nm Pharm* antispasmodic.
antisportif, -ive [ɑ̃tispɔrtif, -iv] *adj* (*opposé au sport*) anti-sport; (*contraire à l'esprit du sport*) unsportsmanlike, unsporting.
antistrophe [ɑ̃tistrɔf] *nf* antistrophe.
antisudoral, -aux [ɑ̃tisydɔral, -o] *adj & nm* antiperspirant.
antitabac [ɑ̃titaba] *adj inv* (*lutte, campagne*) anti-smoking.
antiterroriste [ɑ̃titerɔrist] *adj* anti-terrorist, anti-terrorism.
antitétanique [ɑ̃titetanik] *Méd* **1** *adj* antitetanus. **2** *nm* antitetanus serum.
antithèse [ɑ̃titɛz] *nf* antithesis; **je suis l'a. de ma sœur,** I'm the opposite of my sister.
antithétique [ɑ̃titetik] *adj* antithetic(al).
antitoxine [ɑ̃titɔksin] *nf Méd* antitoxin.
antitoxique [ɑ̃titɔksik] *adj Méd* antitoxic.
antitrust [ɑ̃titrœst] *adj inv Br* anti-monopoly, *surtout US* antitrust.
antituberculeux, -euse [ɑ̃titybɛrkylø, -øz] *adj Méd* antitubercular; **centre a.,** tuberculosis centre.
antitussif, -ive [ɑ̃titysif, -iv] *adj* **sirop a.,** cough mixture *or* syrup *or* medicine.
antivariolique [ɑ̃tivarjɔlik] *adj Méd* (*piqûre*) smallpox.
antivenimeux, -euse [ɑ̃tivənimø, -øz] *adj* anti-venomous.
antiviral, -aux [ɑ̃tiviral, -o] *adj Méd* antivirus.
antivirus [ɑ̃tivirys] *nm* antivirus.
antivivisection(n)iste [ɑ̃tiviviseksjɔnist] **1** *n* anti-vivisectionist. **2** *adj* antivivisection(ist); **société a.,** anti-vivisection society.
antivol [ɑ̃tivɔl] **1** *adj inv* anti-theft (*device*); thief-proof (*lock*); *Aut* **alarme a.,** car alarm. **2** *nm* lock (*esp for bicycle*).
Antoine [ɑ̃twan] *nm* Ant(h)ony.
antonyme [ɑ̃tɔnim] **1** *adj* antonymous. **2** *nm* antonym.
antre [ɑ̃tr] *nm* **(a)** (*caverne*) cave, cavern; den, lair, retreat (*of animal, brigand etc*); *Fig* **ce bar c'était un a. de voleurs,** that bar was a den of thieves; **(b)** *Anat* sinus.
anucléaire [anykleɛr] *adj Nucl* anuclear.
anurèse [anyrɛz] *nf Méd* anuresis.
anurie [anyri] *nf Méd* anuria.
anus [anys] *nm Anat* anus; *Chir* **a. artificiel,** colostomy.
Anvers [ɑ̃vɛr(s)] *nm* Antwerp.
anversois, -oise [ɑ̃vɛrswa, -waz] **1** *adj* of *or* from Antwerp. **2** *n* **A.,** native *or* inhabitant of Antwerp, person from Antwerp.
anxiété [ɑ̃ksjete] *nf* anxiety; **avec a.,** anxiously.
anxieusement [ɑ̃ksjøzmɑ̃] *adv* anxiously.
anxieux, -ieuse [ɑ̃ksjø, -jøz] **1** *adj* anxious, uneasy. **2** *n* worrier.
aorte [aɔrt] *nf Anat* aorta.
aortique [aɔrtik] *adj Anat* aortic, aortal.
août [u(t)] *nm* August; **en a., au mois d'a.,** in (the month of) August; **le premier/le sept a.,** (on) the first/the seventh of August, (on) August the first/the seventh, *US* (on) August first/seventh; **à la mi-a.,** in mid-August.
apache [apaʃ] *nm* **(a) A.,** Apache; **(b)** (*voyou*) tough, thug.
apaisant [apɛzɑ̃] *adj* appeasing (*gesture, words*); soothing (*news, effect etc*).
apaisement [apɛzmɑ̃] *nm* appeasement, appeasing (*of angry person, the gods*); calming (down) (*of angry or upset person*); alleviation (*of suffering*); (*paroles*) **donner des apaisements à qn,** to give (re)assurances to s.o.
apaiser [apeze] **1** *vt* to appease (*angry person, the gods*); to pacify (*s.o. who is angry*); to calm (*angry or anxious person*); to soothe (*pain*); to appease, to satisfy (*hunger*); to quench (*thirst*); to calm (*fears*). **2 s'apaiser** *vpr* (*of person*) to calm down; (*of wind*) to drop, to subside; (*of pain, of fears*) to subside; **la foule s'apaisait,** the crowd was calming down *or* becoming quieter.
apanage [apanaʒ] *nm* ap(p)anage; **les joies de la maternité c'est l'a. des femmes,** the joys of motherhood are one of the advantages *or* privileges of being a woman; **elle croit avoir l'a. de la sagesse,** she thinks she has a monopoly on wisdom.
aparté [aparte] *nm* **(a)** *Th* aside, stage whisper; **en a.,** aside, in a stage whisper; **(b)** private conversation.
apartheid [apartɛd] *nm* apartheid.
apathie [apati] *nf* apathy, listlessness; indifference.
apathique [apatik] *adj* apathetic, listless; (*peu soigné*) lackadaisical.
apatride [apatrid] *adj & n Jur* stateless (person).
apatridie [apatridi] *nf Jur* statelessness.
Apennins [apenɛ̃] *nmpl* Apennines.
apercevoir [apɛrsəvwar] *v* (*prp* **apercevant**; *pp* **aperçu**; *pr ind* **j'aperçois, n. apercevons, ils aperçoivent,** *pr sub* **j'aperçoive, n. apercevions,** *impf* **j'apercevais**; *p hist*

j'aperçus, *fu* **j'apercevrai**) **1** *vt* to perceive, to see; (*soudain, rapidement*) to catch sight of, to catch a glimpse of (*s.o., sth*); **je n'ai fait que l'a.**, I caught only a glimpse of him; **elle cherche à ne pas laisser a. sa fatigue**, she's trying not to let her tiredness show; **si on y pense bien, on aperçoit des difficultés**, as soon as you think about it, you start to see difficulties; **enfin nous avons aperçu un hôtel**, at last we saw a hotel.
2 s'apercevoir *vpr* to be noticeable; **cela ne s'aperçoit pas**, it isn't visible *or* noticeable *or* evident; (*d'une tache, d'une maladie etc*) it doesn't show; **s'a. de qch**, to realize *or* notice sth, to become aware *or* conscious of sth; **il s'est aperçu qu'il n'avait pas ses clés**, he realized that he hadn't got his keys with him; **sans s'en a.**, without being aware of it, without noticing it.

aperçu [apɛrsy] *nm* **(a)** (*coup d'œil*) glimpse; **a. sur la campagne**, glimpse of the countryside; **(b)** (*idée générale*) general idea, outline, summary; **par a.**, at a rough estimate; **ça te donnera un a. du travail à faire**, that'll give you an idea of the work to be done; **(c)** (*intuition*) insight (**sur**, into).

apériodique [aperjɔdik] *adj Él* aperiodic.

apéritif [aperitif] **1** *nm* aperitif, drink; **viens prendre l'a. chez moi demain soir**, come round and have a drink tomorrow evening. **2** *adj Litt* pre-prandial (*walk etc*).

apéro [apero] *nm F* = **APÉRITIF 1**.

aperture [apɛrtyr] *nf Ling* aperture.

apesanteur [apəzɑ̃tœr] *nf* weightlessness; **en état d'a.**, in weightless conditions.

à-peu-près [apøprɛ] *nm inv* approximation, rough estimate, guess; **calculer une somme par à-p.-p.**, to make a rough calculation.

apeuré [apœre, -øre] *adj* scared, frightened.

apeurer [apœre] *vt* to frighten, to scare.

apex [apɛks] *nm* apex.

aphasie [afazi] *nf Méd* aphasia.

aphasique [afazik] *Méd* **1** *adj* aphasiac. **2** *n* aphasic.

aphis [afis] *nm* aphis, greenfly.

aphone [afɔn] *adj Méd* voiceless; **elle était a. pour avoir trop crié**, she'd lost her voice through shouting too much, she was hoarse from shouting.

aphonie [afɔni] *nf Méd* loss of voice.

aphorisme [afɔrism] *nm* aphorism; *Péj* **s'exprimer par aphorismes**, to speak in platitudes.

aphrodisiaque [afrɔdizjak] *adj & nm Pharm* aphrodisiac.

aphte [aft(ə)] *nm Méd* mouth ulcer.

aphteux, -euse [aftø, -øz] *adj Méd Vét* **fièvre aphteuse**, foot-and-mouth disease.

à-pic [apik] *nm inv* cliff, bluff.

apicole [apikɔl] *adj* apiarian; **exploitation a.**, bee keeping.

apiculteur [apikyltœr] *nm* beekeeper, apiarist.

apiculture [apikyltyr] *nf* beekeeping, apiculture.

apitoiement [apitwamɑ̃] *nm* pity, compassion; **porté à l'a.**, compassionate; **pas d'a.!**, (*à mon égard*) don't commiserate (with me), don't be sympathetic.

apitoyant [apitwajɑ̃] *adj* pitiful; *Litt* piteous.

apitoyer [apitwaje] *v* (**j'apitoie, n. apitoyons; j'apitoierai**) **1** *vt* to move (*s.o.*) (to pity), to incite (*s.o.*) to pity. **2 s'apitoyer** *vpr* **s'a. sur qn**, to pity s.o., to feel pity for s.o.; **s'a. sur (le sort de) qn**, to commiserate with s.o.; **s'a. sur soi-même**, to feel sorry for oneself; **ça ne sert à rien de s'a. sur soi-même**, feeling sorry for yourself *or* himself *etc* won't help, self-pity won't help.

apivore [apivɔr] **1** *adj* bee-eating. **2** *n* bee-eating creature.

aplaner [aplane] *vt* to plane, to smooth (*wood*).

aplanir [aplanir] **1** *vt* to flatten, to smooth (*surface*); to plane (*wood*); to planish (*metal*); to level (*road etc*); to smooth out (*imperfections*); *Fig* to iron out (*difficulties*); *Fig* to settle (*dispute*). **2 s'aplanir** *vpr* (*of ground*) to become level; **les problèmes se sont aplanis d'eux(-)mêmes**, the problems have ironed *or* smoothed themselves out.

aplanissement [aplanismɑ̃] *nm* levelling (*of ground*); ironing out (*of difficulties*).

aplati [aplati] *adj* **(a)** flattened, flat; **(b)** oblate (*spheroid etc*).

aplatir [aplatir] **1** *vt* to make (*sth*) flat, to bring (*sth*) level; to flatten (*surface, seam*); to blunt (*angle*); *Métal* to clench (*rivet*); to hammer down (*rivet head*); to squash; **a. ses cheveux**, to plaster down one's hair; **a. les plis d'une jupe au fer à repasser**, to press the pleats in a skirt; **a. qch à coups de marteau**, to beat sth flat; *Fig F* **a. qn**, (*casser la figure à qn*) to flatten s.o.; **il l'a aplati d'un coup de poing**, he knocked him down *or* flattened him with one punch. **2 s'aplatir** *vpr* to become flat, to become flattened out; (*of balloon*) to collapse; (*of tyre*) to get flat; **s'a. par terre**, to lie down flat on the ground; *F* (*tomber*) to come a cropper; **s'a. contre un mur**, to flatten oneself against a wall; *Fig* **s'a. devant qn**, to grovel to s.o.

aplatissage [aplatisaʒ] *nm Tech* pressing; flattening (*of surface, seam*); hammering down (*of rivet*).

aplatissement [aplatismɑ̃] *nm* **(a)** flatness; **l'a. de la terre aux pôles**, the flattening of the earth at the poles; **(b)** *Fig* humiliation.

aplomb [aplɔ̃] *nm* **(a)** perpendicularity; **d'a.**, upright, vertical(ly), plumb; **bien d'a. sur ses pieds**, steady on one's feet; *F* **je ne suis pas d'a. aujourd'hui**, I'm out of sorts *or* off colour today; **voilà qui vous remettra d'a.**, that will revive you *or F* buck you up; **il me faut dix mille francs pour me remettre d'a.**, I need ten thousand francs to get straight; **hors d'a.**, out of plumb, out of true; *F* (*de personne*) wobbly, shaky; **à l'a. de qch**, straight above *or* below sth; *Tech* plumb with sth; **(b)** (*assurance*) (self-)assurance, coolness; **perdre son a.**, to lose one's self-assurance; *Péj* **avoir l'a. de dire/de faire qch**, to have the cheek *or* nerve to say/do sth; **il ne manque pas d'a.**, he's got a nerve *or* a cheek.

apnée [apne] *nf Méd* apnea.

apocalypse [apɔkalips] *nf* apocalypse, revelation; *Bible* **l'A.**, the Book of Revelation, the Apocalypse; **les quatre cavaliers de l'A.**, the four horsemen of the Apocalypse; *Fig* **vision d'a.**, apocalyptic vision; **un paysage d'a.**, a post-holocaust landscape.

apocalyptique [apɔkaliptik] *adj* apocalyptic(al); *Fig* **silence/paysage a.**, doom-laden silence/post-holocaust landscape.

apocryphe [apɔkrif] **1** *adj* apocryphal; *Péj* of doubtful authenticity. **2** *npl Bible* **les Apocryphes**, the Apocrypha.

apogée [apɔʒe] *nm Astron* apogee; **la lune est à son a.**, the moon is at its apogee; **à l'a. de sa gloire**, at the height of one's fame; **être à l'a. de sa carrière**, to be at the height *or* pinnacle of one's career.

apolitique [apɔlitik] *adj* apolitical.

apolitisme [apɔlitism] *nm* apolitical attitude.

apollon [apɔlɔ̃] *nm Fig* Adonis, Greek god.

Apollon [apɔlɔ̃] *nm Myth* Apollo; *Beaux-Arts* **A. du Belvédère**, Apollo Belvedere.

apologétique [apɔlɔʒetik] **1** *adj* apologetic, vindicatory. **2** *nf Rel* apologetics.

apologie [apɔlɔʒi] *nf* apologia (**de**, for); defence, vindication, (written) justification (**de**, of); **faire l'a. de qn/qch**, to vindicate *or* justify *or* defend s.o./sth.

apologiste [apɔlɔʒist] *n* apologist.

apoplectique [apɔplɛktik] *adj & n Méd* apoplectic.

apoplexie [apɔplɛksi] *nf Méd* apoplexy; **attaque d'a.**, apoplectic seizure, stroke.

apostasie [apɔstazi] *nf* apostasy; **faire acte d'a.**, *Rel* to apostatize, to become an apostate; *Fig* to renounce one's party *or* principles, to desert the cause.

apostasier [apɔstazje] *vi* (*pr sub & impf* **n. apostasiions, v. apostasiiez**) to apostatize, to become an apostate; *Fig* to renounce one's party *or* principles, to desert the cause.

apostat, -ate [apɔsta, -at] **1** *adj* apostate, renegade; **curé a.**, renegade priest. **2** *n* apostate; *Fig* **ce politicien est un a.**, that politician has renounced his principles.

a posteriori [apɔsterjɔri] *adv* a posteriori; **raisonner** *ou* **penser a p.**, to reason inductively, to use inductive reasoning; **méthode a p.**, a posteriori method.

apostolat [apɔstɔla] *nm Rel* apostolate; *Fig* **l'enseignement est un a.**, teaching is a vocation.

apostolique [apɔstɔlik] *adj* **(a)** apostolic (*times, Church etc*); **(b)** apostolic, papal; **vicaire a.**, vicar apostolic; **pères apostoliques**, apostolic fathers.

apostrophe[1] [apɔstrɔf] *nf* **(a)** *Ling Gram* apostrophe; **le vocatif est le cas de l'a.**, the vocative is the case of direct address; **(b)** (*interpellation*) reproach, reprimand; **les apostrophes des conducteurs énervés**, the rude remarks of angry motorists.

apostrophe[2] *nf Gram* apostrophe.

apostropher [apɔstrɔfe] **1** *vt* (*pour attirer l'attention*) to shout to (*s.o.*); (*être impoli*) to address (*s.o.*) rudely, to shout at (*s.o.*); (*insulter vivement*) to hurl abuse at (*s.o.*). **2 s'apostropher** *vpr* to shout at one another; **les supporters des équipes de foot s'apostrophent**, the football supporters hurl abuse at each other.

apothéose [apɔteoz] *nf* **(a)** apotheosis, deification; *Fig* (*consécration*) crowning moment, crowning glory; **cette promotion est l'a. de sa carrière**, this promotion is the crowning moment of his *or* her career; **l'a. du cinéma**

français, the supreme achievement *or* the crowning glory of French cinema; **(b)** *Th* grand finale.

apothicaire [apɔtikɛr] *nm Vieilli* apothecary; *Fig* **tenir des comptes d'a.,** to know where every penny goes.

apôtre [apotr] *nm* apostle; *Fig* **se faire l'a. du recyclage,** to become an advocate of recycling; **il fait toujours le bon a.,** he always puts on such a saintly air.

Appalaches [apalaʃ] *nmpl* **les (monts) Appalaches,** the Appalachian Mountains, the Appalachians.

appalachien, -ienne [apalaʃjɛ̃, -jɛn] *adj* Appalachian; **relief a.,** Appalachian relief.

apparaître [aparɛtr] *v* (*conj like* **paraître**; *the auxiliary is* **être**, *sometimes* **avoir**) **1** *vi* **(a)** (*devenir visible*) to appear, to become visible, to come into sight; **a. à travers le brouillard,** to loom out of the fog; **un spectre lui était apparu,** a ghost had appeared to him; **(b)** (*se révéler*) to become evident *or* apparent; **cette décision m'est apparue évidente,** it seemed the obvious decision; **(c)** (*sembler*) **le projet lui apparaissait impossible,** the plan seemed impossible to him; **il m'apparaît comme le seul capable d'y parvenir,** he seems to me to be the only person capable of doing it. **2** *vi impers* **il apparaît que vous avez été souvent absent,** it appears that you have frequently been absent; **selon les statistiques, il apparaîtrait que ...,** according to the statistics, it would appear that ... .

apparat [apara] *nm* pomp, show, display; **dîner d'a.,** banquet; **lettres d'a.,** illuminated letters.

apparatchik [aparatʃik] *nm Péj* apparatchik.

apparaux [aparo] *nmpl* **(a)** *Nau* tackle, gear; **les gros a.,** the purchase; **(b)** *Gym* apparatus.

appareil [aparɛj] *nm* **(a)** apparatus, equipment; *Ind* (*sing or pl*) plant; **appareils de laboratoire,** laboratory apparatus; **a. auxiliaire** *ou* **de secours,** stand-by equipment; **a. de pêche,** fishing tackle; *Min* **a. de forage,** drilling rig; **appareils ménagers,** household appliances; *Anat* **a. digestif,** digestive system; **a. respiratoire,** respiratory system; **a. à gaz,** gas appliance; *Rail* **a. de voie,** switch gear; **a. de prothèse,** prosthesis, artificial limb *etc*; **a. (dentaire),** brace; **a. à sous,** slot machine, fruit machine, one-armed bandit;

(b) *Tél* telephone; **Marcelline à l'a.,** Marcelline speaking *or* here; **qui est à l'a.?,** who's speaking?;

(c) *Av* aircraft, plane; **a. de chasse,** fighter; **a. d'école,** training aircraft, trainer;

(d) *Phot* **a. (photographique), a.-photo,** camera; **a. reflex,** reflex camera;

(e) (*administration etc*) bodies, authorities; **mettre en jeu l'a. de la justice,** to put the machinery of the law in motion; **l'a. du parti,** the party machine *or* apparatus;

(f) *Méd* dressing; (*pour fracture*) splint; plaster;

(g) *Constr* height (*of stones*); (*agencement*) bond; **assise de grand a.,** course of large stones;

(h) a. critique, critical apparatus;

(i) *Litt* display, magnifence, pomp; *Fig* **dans le plus simple a.,** in the nude.

appareillage [aparɛjaz] *nm* **(a)** installation, fitting (up), setting up (*of workshop etc*); **(b)** *Constr* bonding (*of stones, bricks*); **(c)** *Nau* getting under way, weighing (anchor), setting sail; **(d)** fittings, equipment, accessories; *Ind* plant; **a. électrique,** electrical equipment.

appareillement [aparɛjmɑ̃] *nm* **(a)** matching (*of colours etc*); **(b)** pairing, mating (*of animals for breeding*); pairing (*of oxen for the yoke*).

appareiller [apareje] **1** *vt* **(a)** to install, to fit up *or* out (*workshop etc*); **(b)** *Constr* to bond (*stones, bricks*); **(c)** to spread (*net*); **(d)** *Nau* **a. une voile,** to trim a sail; **(e)** (*assortir*) **a. une lampe,** to find a match for a lamp. **2** *vi Nau* to get under way.

appareilleur [aparɛjœr] *nm* **(a)** trimmer, fitter, dresser (*of stone etc*); **(b)** *Constr* foreman mason; **(c) a. à gaz,** gas fitter.

apparemment [aparamɑ̃] *adv* apparently.

apparence [aparɑ̃s] *nf* **(a)** (*aspect*) appearance, look; **donner une belle a. à sa maison en la repeignant,** to make one's house look nice by repainting it; **quelque a. de (la) vérité,** some semblance of truth; **un homme à l'a. négligée/soignée,** an untidy-looking *or* an unkempt (-looking) man/a tidy-looking *or* a neat(-looking) man; **selon toute a.,** to all appearances **contre toute a.,** against all expectations; **contre toute a.,** against all expectations;

(b) (*extérieur*) **sous de fausses apparences,** under false pretences; **sous une a. de douceur se cache une grande fermeté,** beneath a mild-mannered exterior there lies great strength of will; **il a l'air gentil, ce n'est qu'une fausse a.,** he seems nice, but it's only a façade; **il ne faut pas juger selon les apparences,** you shouldn't judge by *or* on appearance(s) (alone); **il ne faut pas s'arrêter à l'a.,** you should look beyond the façade; **en a.,** outwardly, on the surface; **plus difficile en a. qu'en réalité,** less difficult than it looks; **pour sauver les apparences,** for the sake of appearances; (*pour éviter une humiliation*) to save face;

(c) (*trace*) semblance, vestige; **elle n'a plus la moindre a. de respect pour lui,** she no longer has the slightest vestige of respect for him.

apparent [aparɑ̃] *adj* **(a)** (*visible*) visible, apparent; **peu a.,** hardly noticeable; **(b)** (*prétendu*) apparent, not real; **sans raison apparente,** for no apparent reason; **c'est la raison apparente, mais la vérité est autre,** that's the ostensible reason, but the truth is quite different; **mouvement a. du soleil,** apparent movement of the sun; **sous cette apparente bonté se cache un grand égoïsme,** beneath that kind exterior there lies great selfishness; **piété apparente,** outward piety; **(c)** *Jur* **héritier a.,** heir apparent.

apparenté [aparɑ̃te] *adj* related (*by marriage*); (*qui a des liens avec*) related, connected; *Jur* affinitive (**à, avec,** to); **bien a.,** well connected; *Pol* **candidat a. au Parti socialiste** *etc*, = candidate who, though not a member of the Socialist *etc* Party, can count on its support in an election; *Ch* **éléments apparentés,** related *or* affinitive elements.

apparentement [aparɑ̃təmɑ̃] *nm Pol* = practice of forming electoral alliances (under proportional representation).

apparenter (s') [saparɑ̃te] *vpr* **(a)** to marry (**à une famille,** into a family); **(b)** *Pol* to form an alliance (**à,** with); **(c)** *Fig* to have sth in common (**à,** with); **les deux tendances s'apparentent en de nombreux points,** the two trends have many things in common.

apparier [aparje] *v* (*impf & pr sub* **n. appariions, v. appariiez**) **1** *vt* **(a)** to couple, to pair, to mate (*birds for breeding*); **(b)** to match, to pair (*socks, horses etc*); to pair off (*opponents*). **2 s'apparier** *vpr* (*of birds*) to mate.

appariteur [aparitœr] *nm* mace bearer (*of university court, of corporation*).

apparition [aparisjɔ̃] *nf* **(a)** appearance, coming out, publication (*of book etc*); emergence (*of new state etc*); *Méd* **l'a. de la fièvre,** the outbreak of the fever; **l'a. des boutons/des symptômes,** the appearance of the spots/symptoms; **faire une courte a.,** to make a brief appearance; **la star a finalement fait son a. vers 18 heures,** the star finally appeared around six o'clock; **(b)** (*de fantôme*) apparition, ghost, spectre; vision (*of angels etc*); **voir des apparitions,** to have apparitions.

appartement [apartəmɑ̃] *nm* **(a)** flat, *Am* apartment; (*dans un hôtel etc*) suite, set of rooms; **a. de passage,** pied-à-terre; **a. de fonction,** company flat; **vivre en a.,** to live in a flat; **plantes d'a.,** indoor *or* house *or* pot plants; **(b)** (*in château etc*) **les grands appartements,** the state apartments.

appartenance [apartənɑ̃s] *nf* **(a)** (the fact of) belonging (*to sth*) *or* being part (*of sth*); *Math* membership (*of a set*); **a. à un parti,** membership of a party; **(b) appartenances,** appurtenances (*of house, castle*); *Equitation* (saddle) accessories.

appartenir [apartənir] *v* (*conj like* **tenir**) **1** *vi* **(a)** (*être la possession de*) to belong (**à,** to), to be owned (**à,** by); **cette maison lui appartient en propre,** this house is his own personal property;

(b) (*dépendre*) **pour des raisons qui t'appartiennent,** for your own private reasons; **cela n'appartient pas à mes fonctions,** this does not come within the scope of my duties;

(c) (*par famille etc*) to be part (*of sth*), to belong (*to sth*), to be a member (*of sth*); *Math* to be a member (*of a set*); **elle appartient à une famille très riche,** she comes from a very wealthy family.

2 s'appartenir *vpr* **je ne m'appartiens pas,** I'm not my own master; (*je n'ai pas de temps à moi*) I've no time to call my own.

3 *v impers* **à tous ceux qu'il appartient,** to all whom it may concern; **il appartient au comité de prendre la décision,** it is for the committee *or* up to the committee to decide, the decision lies with the committee; **il ne m'appartient pas de le critiquer,** it is not for me to criticize him; *Iron* **il vous appartient bien de me critiquer,** you're a fine one to criticize me.

appas [apɑ] *nmpl Litt* charms.

appât [apɑ] *nm* **(a)** (*de pêche*) bait; *Fig* lure (*of success*); **a. de fond,** ground bait; **mettre l'a. à la ligne,** to bait the line; **mordre à l'a.,** (*d'un poisson, Fig d'une personne*) to rise to the bait; **(b)** soft food (*for poultry*).

appâter [apɑte] *vt* **(a)** to lure (*birds, fishes etc*) with bait; *Fig* to entice (*person*); **a. qn par des promesses,** to entice s.o. with promises; **(b)** to feed (*poultry*) forcibly; to cram (*geese*); **(c)** to bait (*a hook etc*).

appauvrir [apovrir] **1** *vt* to impoverish; *Méd* **a. le sang,** to thin the blood; **a. la constitution de qn,** to weaken s.o.'s constitution. **2 s'appauvrir** *vpr* to grow poorer; (*of soil*) to lose its fertility; **la langue risque de s.'a.,** there is a risk that the language will become impoverished.

appauvrissement [apovrismɑ̃] *nm* impoverishment (*of country etc*); degeneration (*of race*); deterioration (*of health, stock*); thinning (*of blood*).

appel [apɛl] *nm* **(a)** appeal; calling in (*of specialist etc*); **faire a. à qn,** (*pour aider*) to appeal to s.o.; (*qui peut être utile*) to send for s.o.; (*qui est spécialiste, professionnel*) to call on s.o.'s services; **faire a. à la générosité de qn,** to appeal to s.o.'s generosity; **cette formation fait a. à des connaissances commerciales,** this training course calls for *or* requires some knowledge of business; **faire a. à tout son courage,** to summon up all one's courage; **il faut faire a. à tous vos souvenirs,** you have to search your memory; **l'a. à la révolte,** the call to revolt; **l'a. du Général de Gaulle,** General de Gaulle's appeal to the French nation; *Rad* **nous lançons un a. à tous les automobilistes sur la R.N.7,** we appeal to all motorists on the RN 7;

(b) *Jur* appeal (at law); **avis d'a.,** notice of appeal; **Cour d'a.,** Court of Appeal; **faire a. d'une décision,** to appeal (against) a decision; **juger en a. (d'une décision),** to hear an appeal (from a decision); **casser un jugement en a.,** to quash a sentence on appeal; **jugement sans a.,** final judgment; *Fig* **c'est ce que j'ai décidé, et c'est sans a.,** that's my decision and it's final *or F* that's that;

(c) (*impulsion*) call; **l'a. du printemps,** the call of spring; **l'a. du large,** the call of the wild; **l'a. de la mer,** sea fever; **l'a. de la conscience,** the voice of conscience;

(d) (*cri*) call, shout; **cri d'a.,** call for help; **entendre un a. au secours,** to hear a cry for help; **a. d'incendie,** fire alarm; **accourir à un a.,** to run in answer to s.o.'s call; *Fig* **il m'a fait un a. du regard pour que je lui vienne en aide,** his eyes pleaded with me to help; *Fig* **faire un a. du coude à qn,** to nudge s.o. (*in order to draw their attention to sth*); *Aut* **faire un a. de phares,** to flash one's headlights;

(e) *Fin* **faire un a. de fonds,** to call up capital; *Com* **faire un a. d'offres,** to invite bids *or* tenders;

(f) *Mil* **l'a. aux armes,** the call to arms; **devancer l'a.,** to join up before being enlisted; **a. de mobilisation,** mobilization order;

(g) *Télécom Tél* **touche d'a.,** call key; **signe d'a.,** ringing tone; *Rad* **indicatif d'a.,** call sign; **numéro d'a.,** (telephone) number; **a. téléphonique,** (tele)phone call; **il y a eu un a. pour vous,** there was a (telephone) call for you; **a. avec préavis,** person to person call;

(h) *Av* **a. particulier,** selective calling;

(i) (*pour vérifier*) roll call; **a. d'une classe,** calling up *or* call up of a class; **feuille d'a.,** roll; *Nau* muster roll; *Mil* **l'a. du soir,** tattoo; **manquant à l'a.,** missing;

(j) *Tech* **a. d'air,** intake of air; **vitesse d'a.,** inflow; **a. d'un aimant,** pull of a magnet; **le moteur part au premier a.,** the engine starts at the first touch of the switch;

(k) *Typ* **a. de note,** footnote reference, superior figure;

(l) *Sp* take-off; **quel est le pied d'a.?,** which is the take-off foot?; **un bon coup d'a. sur le tremplin,** a good kick off from the springboard;

(m) (*signal*) signal, call; **l'a. à la prière,** (Muslim) call to prayer;

(n) *Ordinat* call.

appelant, -ante [aplɑ̃, -ɑ̃t] *Jur* **1** *adj* appealing (*party etc*). **2** *n* appellant (against a judgement); **se porter a.,** to appeal.

appelé [aple] *nm Mil* conscript.

appeler [aple] *v* **(j'appelle, n. appelons, j'appellerai) 1** *vt* **(a)** to call to (*s.o., a dog*); to call, to hail (*taxi*); **a. au secours,** to call for help; **a. qn dans la rue,** to call to s.o. in the street; **a. qn de la main** *ou* **du geste,** to beckon (to) s.o.; **les noms sont appelés un à un,** the names are called out one by one; *Jur* **a. une cause,** to call (out) a case;

(b) *Tél* **a. qn (au téléphone),** to ring s.o. (up), *Am* to call s.o.; **a. Paris,** to dial Paris; **a. un taxi/un médecin,** to phone for a taxi/a doctor; **a. l'ascenseur,** to call the lift;

(c) (*convoquer*) to call in, to send for, to summon (*s.o.*); *Jur* to summon (*s.o.*) to attend; **a. les pompiers,** to call the fire brigade; **faire a. un médecin,** to call in *or* send for a doctor; **elle a été appelée auprès de son père mourant,** she was called to her dying father's bedside; *Mil* **a. une classe,** to call up a class; *Hum* **le devoir t'appelle,** duty calls; *Jur* **a. qn en justice,** to summon(s) s.o.; (*poursuivre qn*) to sue s.o.; **a. qn à témoin,** to call s.o. to witness; *Fin* **capital appelé,** called up capital;

(d) a. qn à, to appoint *or* assign s.o. to (*a post etc*); **être appelé à qch,** to be destined for sth; **cette technique est appelée à se développer partout dans le monde,** the technique is destined *or* set to spread throughout the world; **son courage l'appelle à ce genre d'action,** his courage inspires him to that kind of action;

(e) to call (*s.o.*) (by name); **nous l'avons appelé David,** we have called him David; **j'appelle cela une bêtise,** I call that *or* that's what I call a stupid mistake; **voilà ce que j'appelle un homme,** now that's what I call a man; **a. un chat un chat, a. les choses par leur nom,** to call a spade a spade; **tu l'appelles par son prénom?,** do you call him by his first name?; **vous appelez cela danser?,** (do) you call that dancing?;

(f) to appeal to (*s.o., sth*), to call on (*s.o., sth*); (*réclamer*) to call for (*sth*); to invite (*criticism*); **a. qn à faire qch,** to call on *or* invite s.o. to do sth; **je vous appelle tous à y réfléchir,** I invite you all to think about it; **sa sincérité appelle à une plus grande compréhension de votre part,** his sincerity calls for greater understanding on your part; **ce problème appelle une solution immédiate,** the problem calls for an immediate solution;

(g) (*entraîner*) to provoke, to arouse, to attract; *Prov* **un malheur en appelle un autre,** misfortunes never come singly; **la violence appelle la violence,** violence breeds *or* begets violence;

(h) *Ordinat* to call up (*file*).

2 *vi* **(a)** (*crier*) to call, to shout; **elle appelait à l'aide** *ou* **au secours,** she was calling *or* shouting for help; **si tu as un problème, tu appelles,** if you have a problem, just shout;

(b) en a. à qn, to appeal to s.o.; **j'en appelle à votre bon sens,** I appeal to your common sense; **j'en appelle à votre témoignage,** I call you to witness; **j'en appelle de votre décision,** I challenge your decision; *Jur* **a. d'un jugement,** to appeal against a sentence; **en a.,** to appeal.

3 s'appeler *vpr* to be called *or* named; **comment vous appelez-vous?,** what is your name?; **je m'appelle David,** my name is David; **nous nous appelons par nos prénoms,** we call each other by our first names, we're on first-name terms; **cela s'appelle un plaqueminier,** it's called a persimmon; *F* **voilà qui s'appelle pleuvoir!,** it's raining with a vengeance!; *Tél* **on s'appelle la semaine prochaine,** we'll call each other next week.

appellation [apɛlasjɔ̃] *nf* **(a)** name; (*de produit*) designation; *Fml* appellation; **a. injurieuse,** abusive term; **a. d'origine,** designation of origin; **a. contrôlée,** (*de vin*) guaranteed vintage; **vin sans a.,** non-vintage wine; **(b)** *Jur* appeal at law.

appendice [apɛ̃dis] *nm* **(a)** appendix, supplement (*of book*); **(b)** annex(e), appendage (*of building*); **(c)** *Anat* appendix; *Zool Bot* appendage; **se faire enlever l'a.,** to have one's appendix out; *Hum* **quel a. nasal!,** what a huge proboscis!; **(d)** neck (*of balloon*); tail (*of aircraft*).

appendicectomie [apɛ̃disɛktɔmi] *nf Méd* append(ic)ectomy.

appendicite [apɛ̃disit] *nf Méd* appendicitis; **a. chronique,** grumbling appendix; **se faire opérer de l'a.,** to have an operation for appendicitis, to have one's appendix out.

appentis [apɑ̃ti] *nm Constr* lean-to (building, roof); (*remise*) outhouse, shed.

appesantir [apəzɑ̃tir] **1** *vt* **(a)** to weigh (*sth, s.o.*) down; **yeux appesantis par le sommeil,** eyes heavy with sleep; **(b)** to bring (*sth*) down heavily. **2 s'appesantir** *vpr* to grow heavier; **son pas s'appesentit avec la fatigue,** his step grew slower *or* his tread grew heavier through fatigue; **s'a. sur un sujet,** to go on and on about a subject; **son autorité s'est appesantie sur nous,** the full weight of his authority come down on us; *F* **pas la peine de s'a., passons à autre chose,** there's no point going on about it, let's get on to something else.

appesantissement [apəzɑ̃tismɑ̃] *nm* slowing (down) (*of walk, research*); (growing) heaviness (*of steps*).

appétence [apetɑ̃s] *nf Litt* penchant, partiality; **une a. d'aventure,** a penchant for adventure.

appétissant [apetisɑ̃] *adj* (*nourriture*) appetizing, tempting; (*femme*) alluring.

appétit [apeti] *nm* **(a)** (*pour manger*) appetite; **couper l'a. à qn,** to spoil *or* take away s.o.'s appetite; **donner de l'a. à**

qn, to give s.o. an appetite; **mettre qn en a.,** to give s.o. an appetite; **demeurer** *ou* **rester sur son a.,** to eat sparingly, to curb one's appetite; *Fig* to remain unsatisfied; **manger de bon a.** *ou* **avec a.,** to eat heartily *or* with relish, *F* to tuck in; **avoir un a. de loup** *ou* **d'ogre,** to eat like a horse; **avoir un a. d'oiseau,** to have a small *or* poor appetite, to peck at one's food; **avoir bon a.,** to have a hearty appetite; **cette petite balade m'a donné de l'a.,** that little walk has given me an appetite; **bon a.!,** enjoy your meal!, bon appetit!; **je n'ai plus d'a.,** I'm off my food; *Prov* **l'a. vient en mangeant,** it's only once you start eating that you realize that you're hungry; *Fig* the more you get the more you want;

(b) desire, craving (**de,** for); **a. sexuel,** sexual desire; **a. du gain,** craving for money; **l'a. de la connaissance,** a thirst *or* hunger for knowledge.

applaudimètre [aplodimɛtr] *nm* clapometer.

applaudir [aplodir] **1** *vt* to applaud (*s.o., sth*); **se faire a. à tout casser,** to get tremendous applause, to bring the house down; *Fig* **je vous applaudis de tout cœur,** I congratulate you with all my heart. **2** *vi* to applaud, to clap; **a. à tout rompre,** to applaud *or* clap thunderously; *Fig* **nous applaudissons à la reprise des relations entre nos deux pays,** we welcome the resumption of relations between our two countries. **3 s'applaudir** *vpr* **s'a. (de qch),** to congratulate oneself, to pat oneself on the back (for having done sth).

applaudissement [aplodismɑ̃] *nm souvent pl* **(a)** applause, clapping; **un tonnerre d'applaudissements,** thunderous applause; **soulever des applaudissements,** to be applauded; **(b)** *Litt* approval.

applicable [aplikabl] *adj* **(a)** applicable; **cette règle est a. à tous les cas,** this rule applies to all cases; **a. à partir du premier janvier,** to take effect from the first of January; **mot a.,** appropriate *or* suitable word; **(b)** chargeable (*against sth*).

applicateur [aplikatœr] **1** *nm* (*device*) applicator. **2** *adj* **tampon a., pinceau a.,** applicator.

application [aplikɑsjɔ̃] *nf* **(a)** (*de peinture etc*) application, applying; **première a. de peinture,** first coat of paint; *Couture* **broderie d'a.,** appliqué (work); **bois d'a.,** veneer; **(b)** application (*of a rule*); **a. de la loi,** enforcement of the law; **mettre une théorie en a.,** to put a theory into practice; **entrer en a.,** to come into force; **faire l'a. de qch à qch,** to apply sth to sth; **a. d'un montant à un projet,** (the) use of a sum of money for a project; **en a. de ce décret,** in pursuance of this decree; *Ordinat* **logiciel d'a.,** application software; *Mil etc* **école d'a.,** school of instruction; **(c)** (*débouché*) application; use (*of raw material*); **(d)** application (to one's work), industriousness; **travailler avec a.,** to apply oneself to one's work, to work diligently.

applique [aplik] *nf* **(a)** (wall) bracket (*for lamp etc*); (*lampe*) sconce, bracket lamp; **lampe d'a.,** bracket lamp; **(b)** *Couture* appliquéd ornament.

appliqué [aplike] *adj* **(a)** hard working, painstaking (*person*); careful (*handwriting*); **(b)** applied (*sciences*); **informatique appliquée à la gestion,** computer technology applied to management.

appliquer [aplike] **1** *vt* **(a)** (*mettre*) to apply (*sth to sth*); **a. une couche de peinture sur qch,** to apply a coat of paint to sth; **a. une oreille au mur,** to put one's ear to the wall, to listen through the wall; **un coup bien appliqué,** a well-planted *or* well-aimed blow; **elle lui fit une bise bien appliquée,** she planted a kiss on his cheek;

(b) (*utiliser*) to apply; **a. une loi à un cas particulier,** to apply a law to a particular case; **a. (les dispositions de) la loi,** to apply the law; **a. un traitement à une maladie,** to apply a treatment to an illness; **a. une recette particulière,** to use a particular recipe; *Jur* **a. le maximum de la peine,** to impose the maximum penalty;

(c) (*concentrer*) to apply; **a. toute son attention à un problème,** to devote *or* apply all one's attention to a problem; **a. son esprit à ses études,** to apply one's mind to one's studies.

2 s'appliquer *vpr* **(a)** (*se concentrer*) to apply oneself, to take pains; **elle doit s'a. davantage,** she has to apply herself more; **s'a. à qch,** to apply oneself to sth, to take pains over sth; **elle s'applique à me contredire,** she is making a point of contradicting me; **il s'applique à apprendre le français,** he is making a serious effort to learn French;

(b) (*of law etc*) to apply (**à,** to); **à qui s'applique cette remarque?,** who is that remark intended for?; **le règlement s'applique pour tous,** the rule applies to everybody;

(c) (*se placer*) to be applied; **le cataplasme s'applique directement sur la peau,** the poultice should be applied directly (on) to the skin.

appoint [apwɛ̃] *nm* **(a)** *Com Fin* balance, odd money; **le public est tenu de faire l'a.,** no change given; **ressources d'a.,** additional (sources of) income; **chauffage/éclairage d'a.,** auxiliary heating/lighting; **siège d'a.,** extra chair; **un travail d'a.,** a second job; **ce travail à mi-temps lui fait un petit a.,** this part-time job brings him a little extra income; **(b)** (*contribution*) contribution; **apporter son a. à qch,** to contribute to sth, to take part in sth.

appointements [apwɛ̃tmɑ̃] *nmpl* salary; **toucher ses a.,** to draw one's salary.

appointer [apwɛ̃te] *vt* **(a)** (*payer*) to pay (a salary to) (*s.o.*); **être appointé à la semaine,** to be paid weekly *or* by the week; **(b)** to sharpen (*pencil etc*).

appontage [apɔ̃taʒ] *nm* landing on flight deck (*of aircraft carrier*); **officier d'a.,** landing officer; **crosse** *ou* **crochet d'a.,** arrester hook.

appontement [apɔ̃tmɑ̃] *nm Nau* (*wooden*) wharf, jetty, pier, quay; landing stage.

apponter [apɔ̃te] *vi* to land (*on deck of aircraft carrier*).

apport [apɔr] *nm* **(a)** (*action of bringing*) contribution, contributing; *Écon* inflow, influx; *Fin* **a. de capitaux,** contribution of capital; **capital d'a.,** initial capital; **actions d'a.,** founder's *or* promoter's shares; **l'a. du tourisme dans une région,** the financial contribution made by tourism to a region; **sans a. extérieur nous étions perdus,** without outside (financial) help we'd have been ruined; **l'a. de la civilisation grecque,** the contribution made by Greek civilisation; *Jur* **a. de pièces,** deposit(ing) of documents (*in a suit*); *Jur* **biens d'a.,** estate brought in by husband *or* wife on marriage; **a. en communauté,** = goods contributed by husband and wife to the joint estate; **terres d'a.,** earthworks; **a. d'argent frais,** injection of new money;

(b) (*thing brought*) *Fin* initial share (*in undertaking*); **un a. en nature,** a contribution in kind; *Jur* **a. dotal,** dowry, marriage portion; **les fruits donnent un a. de vitamines indispensable,** fruit provides essential vitamins; **l'a. en vitamines du foie,** the vitamins provided by liver, the vitamins present in liver; *Agr* **un gros a. de fumier,** a heavy dressing of manure; **a. de chaleur, a. calorifique,** heat supply *or* input;

(c) *Tech* coating, layer, deposit.

apporter [apɔrte] *vt* **(a)** to bring (**qch à qn,** sth to s.o.); **je t'ai apporté ce livre,** I've brought you this book; **(b) a. du soin à faire qch,** to do sth carefully; **a. des difficultés à qch,** to put difficulties in the way of sth; **(c)** (*donner*) **cette démonstration n'apporte aucune preuve supplémentaire,** this demonstration provides no additional proof; **cette expérience lui a beaucoup apporté,** the experience has been very beneficial for him; **qu'est-ce que ça peut t'a.?,** what good can that do you?; *Fin* **a. des capitaux,** to bring in capital; **(d)** to cause, to bring about (*changes etc*); **ce que l'avenir apportera,** what the future has in store.

apposer [apoze] *vt* to place, to put, *Fml* to affix; **a. une affiche sur un mur,** to stick a poster on a wall; *Jur* **a. les scellés,** to affix the seals (*to prevent unlawful entry*); *Jur* **a. sa signature à un acte,** to append one's signature to a deed; **a. une clause à un acte,** to insert a clause in *or* add a clause to an act.

apposition [apozisjɔ̃] *nf* **(a)** *Admin* affixing, appending (*of seal, signature etc*); **(b)** *Gram* apposition; **mot en a.,** word in apposition.

appréciable [apresjabl] *adj* (*évolution, changement etc*) appreciable, noticeable; **a. aux sens,** perceptible; **à une distance a.,** at an appreciable *or* considerable distance.

appréciateur, -trice [apresjatœr, -tris] *n* appreciator (**de,** of); *Com etc* appraiser, valuer; **a. du talent,** person who recognises talent, good judge of talent.

appréciatif, -ive [apresjatif, -iv] *adj* (*regard, silence*) appreciative; *Com* **devis a.,** estimate.

appréciation [apresjɑsjɔ̃] *nf* **(a)** (*évaluation*) valuation, estimating, estimation, estimate; judging (*of distance*); **faire l'a. des marchandises,** to value *or* to make a valuation of goods; *Jur* **l'a. du juge,** the judge's summing up; **(b)** judgement, opinion; appreciation (*of work of art, meal etc*); **les appréciations sont notées dans la marge,** the teacher's *etc* comments are in the margin; **je laisse cette tapisserie/ce problème à votre a.,** I'll leave you to form an opinion on this piece of tapestry/this problem; **(c)** (*en valeur*) appreciation, rise in value.

apprécier [apresje] *v* (*pr sub & impf* **n. appréciions, v. appréciiez**) **1** *vt* **(a)** (*évaluer*) to appraise; to estimate the value of, to value (*painting etc*); **tu ne l'apprécies pas à sa juste valeur,** you have no idea of his true worth; **(b)** to determine; (*approximativement*) to estimate (*temperature, distance, sound*); to judge (*distance*); to appreciate, to judge (*differences, distinctions*); **(c)** to appreciate (*meal, good thing*); **je n'apprécie pas ce genre de plaisanterie,** I don't appreciate *or* I don't much care for that kind of joke; **elle ne l'apprécie pas du tout,** she doesn't like him at all. **2** *vi F* **elle n'a pas apprécié,** she didn't appreciate that, she didn't much care for that. **3 s'apprécier** *vpr* to like each other.

appréhender [apreɑ̃de] *vt* **(a)** *Jur* **a. qn (au corps),** to seize *or* arrest *or* apprehend s.o.; **(b)** to dread, to fear (*sth*); **j'appréhende de rentrer** *ou* **le retour,** I'm dreading going back; **(c)** to grasp, to apprehend (*concept*).

appréhensif, -ive [apreɑ̃sif, -iv] *adj* apprehensive.

appréhension [apreɑ̃sjɔ̃] *nf* **(a)** (*crainte*) apprehension **(de,** of); **avoir de l'a.,** to be apprehensive; **(b)** (*d'une notion*) grasp.

apprendre [aprɑ̃dr] *v* (*conj like* **prendre**) **1** *vt* **(a)** to learn (*lesson, trade, language, method etc*);

(b) to learn, to hear (of), to get to know of (*piece of news etc*); **nous l'avons appris à la radio/aux informations,** we heard it on the radio/on the news; **j'ai appris que tu allais te marier,** I've heard that you're getting married; **je l'ai appris de bonne source,** I have it on good authority;

(c) a. qch à qn, to teach s.o. sth; **a. à qn à faire qch,** to teach *or* show s.o. how to do sth; **il m'a tout appris,** he taught me everything I know;

(d) (*informer*) **a. qch à qn,** to inform s.o. of sth, to tell s.o. sth; *F* **vous ne m'apprenez rien!,** you're telling me!, you're not tellimg me anything new!

2 *vi* to learn; **a. facilement,** to find learning easy; **a. (de qn) à faire qch,** to learn (from s.o.) how to do sth; **a. à lire/skier,** to learn to read/(how) to ski; *Prov* **on apprend à tout âge,** it is never too late *or* you're never too old to learn; *F* **je vous apprendrai à me parler de la sorte!,** I'll teach you to speak to me like that!; *F* **ça vous apprendra!,** serve(s) you right!, that'll teach you!; *F* **je vais lui a. à vivre,** I'm going to teach him a few manners.

3 s'apprendre *vpr* **ça s'apprend vite,** it's easy to learn, it can be learned quickly; **le chinois ne s'apprend pas facilement,** it isn't easy to learn Chinese.

apprenti, -ie [aprɑ̃ti] *n* apprentice; *Jur* articled clerk; **a. menuisier,** carpenter's apprentice; **a. conducteur,** learner (driver); **je ne suis qu'un a.,** I'm only a beginner *or* a novice; *Fig* **a. sorcier,** sorcerer's apprentice; **cesse donc de jouer les apprentis sorciers!,** stop meddling with things that you know nothing about!

apprentissage [aprɑ̃tisaʒ] *nm* apprenticeship; (*in liberal professions*) articles; **centre d'a.,** training school; **mettre qn en a. chez un patron,** to apprentice s.o. to an employer; **être en a. chez qn,** to be apprenticed *or* articled to s.o.; **faire l'a. de la vie,** to learn by experience.

apprêt [aprɛ] *nm* **(a)** (*opération*) dressing, finishing (*of fabrics, hides etc*); **(b)** (*substance*) (*de tissu etc*) finish, dress; (*de peinture*) primer, size; **(c)** (*manière etc*) affectation, affectedness.

apprêtage [aprɛtaʒ] *nm Tech* **(a)** (*of fabrics*) dressing, finishing; **(b)** (*of paint*) priming, sizing.

apprêté [aprete] *adj* **(a)** affected, stiff (*style, manner etc*); **(b) papier a.,** glossy paper.

apprêter [aprete] **1** *vt* **(a)** to prepare (*meal etc*); **a. un enfant,** to get a child ready, to dress a child; **les femmes apprêtent la mariée,** the women help the bride to dress *or* get ready; **(b)** to dress, to finish, to stiffen (*fabrics etc*); to finish (*leather*); **(c)** to prime (*surface*). **2 s'apprêter** *vpr* to get dressed; (*se donner un coup de peigne etc*) to tidy oneself (up); **s'a. à faire qch,** to be getting ready *or* preparing to do sth, to be on the point of doing sth.

apprivoisable [aprivwazabl(ə)] *adj* tameable.

apprivoisé [aprivwaze] *adj* tame (*animal etc*).

apprivoisement [aprivwazmɑ̃] *nm* taming, domestication.

apprivoiser [aprivwaze] **1** *vt* to tame (*animal*); to win over (*s.o.*); *Fig* **je veux a. cette peur,** I want to conquer this fear. **2 s'apprivoiser** *vpr* (*of animal*) to become domesticated *or* tame; (*d'une personne*) to become more sociable; **s'a. à une idée,** to get used *or* come round to an idea.

approbateur, -trice [aprɔbatœr, -tris] **, approbatif, -ive** [aprɔbatif, -iv] **1** *adj* (*geste, sourire etc*) approving; **regard a.,** look of approval. **2** *n Litt* approver.

approbation [aprɔbasjɔ̃] *nf* approval **(de qch,** of sth); certifying (*of accounts, of document*) **donner son a. à qch,** to give one's approval to sth, to approve sth; **le film a reçu l'a. du public,** the film was well received by the public; **a. tacite,** tacit approval; *Com* **pour a.,** for approval; **votre conduite est digne d'a.,** your behaviour is commendable; **cette étude mérite l'a. de tous,** this study merits general approval.

approchable [aprɔʃabl] *adj* approachable, accessible (*place, person*); **le refuge n'est pas a. en voiture,** the shelter is not accessible *or* cannot be reached by car; **elle n'est pas a. aujourd'hui,** (*elle est de mauvaise humeur*) she's not very approachable today.

approchant [aprɔʃɑ̃] *adj* approximating, similar **(de,** to); **offre approchante,** near offer; **je n'ai jamais rien vu d'a.,** I never saw anything like it *or* anything approaching it; **voilà ce qu'il a dit, ou quelque chose d'a.,** that is what he said, or something like it.

approche [aprɔʃ] *nf* **(a)** approach; **l'a. de l'hiver,** the approach of winter; **à son a.,** as he came up; **d'une a. difficile,** difficult of access; **à l'a. de la difficulté, elle abandonne,** she gives up whenever a difficulty arises; **un homme d'a. facile,** an approachable man; **aux approches de la trentaine,** as you *etc* near *or* approach thirty; **une nouvelle a. du problème,** a new approach to the problem; **travail d'a.,** manoeuvre, *US* manoeuver; **cette étude a nécessité un long travail d'a.,** the study required a great deal of preliminary work; *Av* **a. à vue,** visual approach; **chasse à l'a.,** deerstalking;

(b) les approches d'une ville, the approaches of a town; **aux approches du village,** on the outskirts of the village;

(c) *Typ* (*faute*) = extra space wrongly inserted between two letters; (*signe*) close-up sign *or* mark;

(d) *Zool* mating.

approché [aprɔʃe] *adj* approximate (*result*).

approcher [aprɔʃe] **1** *vt* to approach, to come near, to come close to (*s.o., sth*); **a. qch de qn/qch,** to bring *or* draw sth near (to) s.o./sth; **approchez votre chaise,** pull up your chair; **a. sa chaise de la lampe,** to move one's chair nearer the lamp; **ne m'approchez pas,** don't come near me; **elle approche les plus grands noms du spectacle,** she rubs shoulders with the biggest names in showbusiness; **a. des lions (dans un zoo) d'assez près,** to get quite close to the lions in a zoo; **on ne peut pas l'a.,** you can never see him; (*parce qu'il ne le veut pas*) you can't get near him, he's unapproachable.

2 *vi* **(a)** to approach, to draw near(er), to come nearer; **l'heure** *ou* **le moment approche,** it will soon be time; **la nuit approchait,** night was falling, it was beginning to get dark; **faites-le a.,** ask him to come closer; **a. de qn/qch,** to approach s.o./sth; **nous approchons de Paris,** we are approaching *or* getting near Paris; **a. du but,** to be nearing one's goal; **il approche de la trentaine,** he's nearing *or* approaching *or* getting on for thirty; **nous approchions alors doc 200 km/heure,** we were going at almost 200 km an hour;

(b) a. de qn/qch, to resemble s.o./sth; **ces vacances approchent du paradis,** this holiday is like heaven on earth; **il n'y a pas de pays qui en approche,** there is no country like it; **cela approche de la folie,** that borders on insanity;

(c) *Golf* to play an approach shot;

(d) *Zool* to mate.

3 s'approcher *vpr* to come *or* go closer *or* nearer, to draw near(er), to approach; **je me suis approché pour voir,** I went closer to have a look; **s'a. de qn/qch,** to come up to s.o./sth; **il faut t'a.!, viens!,** come on!, come closer!; **le navire s'approchait de la terre,** the ship was nearing land; **s'a. de la perfection,** to be almost perfect, to near perfection.

approfondi [aprɔfɔ̃di] *adj* elaborate, careful, extensive (*research*); **enquête approfondie,** detailed *or* in-depth enquiry *or* investigation; **connaissance approfondie,** thorough *or* in-depth knowledge.

approfondir [aprɔfɔ̃dir] **1** *vt* **(a)** to deepen, to excavate (*river bed etc*); *Litt* **cela approfondit ma tristesse,** it increases my sadness; **(b)** (*examiner*) to go deeply *or* thoroughly into (*a problem*); to study (*a subject*) thoroughly; **a. une affaire,** to get to the root of a matter; **sans a. la question** *ou* **le sujet,** without going into too much detail. **2 s'approfondir** *vpr* to become deeper, to deepen.

approfondissement [aprɔfɔ̃dismɑ̃] *nm* **(a)** deepening, excavating, excavation (*of canal etc*); **(b)** investigation, analysis (*of question*).

appropriation [aprɔprijasjɔ̃] *nf* **(a)** appropriation (*of property etc*); **a. de fonds,** embezzlement, misappropriation of funds; **(b)** *Arch & Belg* cleaning; tidying up.

approprié [aprɔprije] *adj* appropriate, adapted **(à,** to); appropriate, proper, suitable (*term, measure etc*).

approprier [aprɔprije] *v* (*pr sub & impf* **n. appropriions, v. appropriiez**) **1** *vt* **(a)** to arrange (*sth*) to fit (*sth*); to adapt (*sth to sth*); **a. son style à un public,** to adapt one's style to (suit) an audience; **(b)** *Arch & Belg* to clean; to tidy (*sth*). **2 s'approprier** *vpr* **(a) s'a. qch,** to appropriate sth; **(b)** (*s'adapter*) to be suitable *or* appropriate (*for sth*), to be in keeping (*with sth*), to suit (*sth*); **cette musique s'approprie à la situation,** this music is suitable for the occasion.

approuver [apruve] *vt* **(a) a. qch,** to approve of sth; **a. qch de la tête,** to nod approval; **a. qn de faire/d'avoir fait qch,** to commend s.o. for doing/having done sth; **(b)** to consent to, to agree to (*sth*); **nous vous approuvons dans votre choix,** we approve of your choice; **a. qch officiellement,** to agree formally to sth; *Com* **a. une facture,** to pass an invoice; **a. un contrat,** to ratify a contract; *Admin* **a. une nomination,** to confirm an appointment; **a. un appel,** to endorse an appeal; **lu et approuvé,** read and approved; **lessive approuvée par un grand nombre de fabriquants,** washing powder recommended by a large number of manufacturers; *Méd* **médicament approuvé,** approved drug *or* medicine.

approvisionné [aprɔvizjɔne] *adj* stocked, supplied (**de, en,** with); **bien a.,** well-stocked.

approvisionnement [aprɔvizjɔnmɑ̃] *nm* **(a)** provisioning, supplying (*of town, army*); catering (*for s.o.*); stocking (*of shop*); **l'a. de la ville en produits frais,** the supply(ing) of fresh produce to the town; **(b)** (*provision*) supply, stock, provisions; **faire un a. de qch,** to lay in a supply of sth.

approvisionner [aprɔvizjɔne] **1** *vt* to supply (**de,** with); to cater for (*s.o.*); to stock (*shop*); *Banque* **a. son compte,** to pay money into one's account; **a. une île en produits frais,** to supply an island with fresh produce. **2 s'approvisionner** *vpr* to lay in provisions; to get a stock *or* a supply (**en, de,** of); **s'a. chez (qn),** to get one's supplies from (s.o.); (*d'une ménagère etc*) to shop at (s.o.'s); **s'a. au marché,** to shop *or* to do one's shopping *or* to buy one's provisions at the market.

approximatif,-ive [aprɔksimatif, -iv] *adj* approximate, rough (*calculation, estimate*); *Math* approximation.

approximation [aprɔksimɑsjɔ̃] *nf* approximation, rough estimate; *Math* approximation.

approximativement [aprɔksimativmɑ̃] *adv* approximately, roughly; **dans une heure a.,** in an hour or so.

appt *abrév* **appartement.**

appui [apɥi] *nm* **(a)** (*support*) support, prop, stay, shore; *Archit* balustrade; **mur d'a.,** supporting *or* retaining wall; **barre d'a.,** handrail; **point d'a.,** fulcrum (*of lever*); *Mil* base (*of operations*); **à hauteur d'a.,** elbow high; **mettre un a. à un mur,** to shore up a wall; **prendre a. sur qch,** to be supported by *or* on sth; (*d'une personne*) to support oneself on sth; **prendre a. sur le pied gauche,** (*pour sauter*) to take off from the left foot; **a. de fenêtre,** window ledge, window sill; **a. de porte,** door sill; **a. d'escalier,** banisters;

(b) (*moral etc*) support, backing; **a. moral,** moral support; **prêter son a. à qn,** to support *or* lend support to s.o., to back s.o. up; **vous avez mon a.,** you have my support *or* backing; **être sans appui(s),** to be friendless; **avoir des appuis en haut lieu,** to have friends in high places; *Mil* **a. direct,** close *or US* direct support; **tir d'a.,** covering fire; **à l'a.,** in support (*of sth*); **à l'a. il me montra tes lettres,** to support *or* back up what he said he showed me the letters; **avec preuves à l'a.,** with supporting evidence; **à l'a. d'un témoignage,** in support of testimony.

appui-bras [apɥibra] *nm* armrest; (*pl appuis-bras*).

appuie- [apɥi] *compound nouns of which the first element is* **appui-** *have an alternative form* **appuie-**, *in which case they are invariable.*

appui-jambes [apɥiʒɑ̃b] *nm* leg rest; (*pl appuis-jambes*).

appui-queue [apɥikø] *nm Billard* (cue) rest, *F* jigger; (*pl appuis-queue*).

appui-tête [apɥitɛt] *nm* headrest; (*pl appuis-tête*).

appuyé [apɥije] *adj* laboured, *US* labored, heavy (*joke, irony*); **regard a.,** (fixed) stare.

appuyer [apɥije] *v* (**j'appuie, n. appuyons; j'appuierai**) **1** *vt* **(a)** to lean, to rest; **a. qch contre qch,** to lean *or* rest sth against sth; **a. sa tête contre la fenêtre,** to lean one's head against the window; **a. sa tête sur l'épaule de qn,** to rest one's head on s.o.'s shoulder; *Fig* **a. son opinion sur qch,** to base one's opinion on sth; **théorie appuyée sur des faits,** theory supported by facts;

(b) to press (*sth on sth*); **a. son pied sur la pédale de frein,** to put one's foot on the brake; **a. sur la valise pour la fermer,** to press down on the suitcase to close it; *Fig* **a. son regard sur qn,** to stare intently at s.o.; *Mus* **a. (sur) une note,** to dwell on a note;

(c) to support, to prop (up) (*joist, wall etc*); **a. une pétition,** to support a petition (**par,** by); **a. une proposition,** to second a proposal; **a. la demande de qn,** to support s.o.'s request.

2 *vi* **(a)** to bear (**sur,** on); **poutre qui appuie sur deux montants,** beam resting *or* bearing on two uprights;

(b) a. sur son stylo, to press on one's pen; **a. sur le bouton,** to press the button; *Aut F* **a. sur le champignon,** (*accélérer*) to step on it, to put one's foot down; **a. sur une syllabe,** to stress a syllable; **a. sur l'urgence d'un problème,** to stress the urgency of a problem; *Mil* **appuyez à droite/à gauche!,** on the right/left close!; **appuyez à droite à la sortie du village,** bear right as you leave the village.

3 s'appuyer *vpr* **(a) s'a. sur** *ou* **contre** *ou* **à qch,** to lean *or* rest on *or* against sth; **s'a. sur qn,** to lean on s.o.; *Fig* to rely *or* depend on s.o; **s'a. sur son expérience pour conseiller qn,** to draw on *or* to use one's experience to advise s.o.; **ses recherches s'appuient sur des découvertes récentes,** his research is based on recent discoveries;

(b) s'a. d'une autorité, to base oneself on an authority;

(c) *F* **s'a. une corvée,** to be lumbered with a chore; **c'est toujours moi qui m'appuie la vaisselle,** it's always me who gets lumbered with the dishes!; **s'a. un bon dîner/un gentil petit voyage,** to stand oneself *or* treat oneself to a good dinner/a nice little trip.

âpre [ɑpr] *adj* **(a)** (*aigre*) rough, harsh; **voix â.,** rasping voice; **goût â.,** tart taste; **vin â.,** rough wine; **(b)** bitter, biting, sharp (*frost, rebuke*); scathing (*irony*); **temps â.,** raw weather; **(c)** keen (*competition etc*); **homme â. (au gain),** grasping man.

ap(r).J.-C. (*abrév* **après Jésus-Christ**) AD.

âprement [ɑprəmɑ̃] *adv* bitterly, harshly, roughly.

après [aprɛ] **1** *prép* **(a)** (*order in time, space*) after; **il est arrivé a. moi,** he arrived after me; **a. tout,** after all; **fermé a. 20 heures,** closed from 8 o'clock (onwards); **a. bien des discussions, nous avons décidé de ...,** after a great deal of discussion, we decided to ...; **comprendre/réaliser a. coup,** to understand *or* realise too late *or* after the event; **jour a. jour,** day after day; **a. vous, monsieur/madame!,** after you!; **nous eûmes des huîtres et a. du saumon,** we had oysters followed by salmon; **et a. cela, madame?,** (*in shop*) anything else, madam?; **a. quoi,** after which; **je suis** *ou* **viens a. lui,** I am *or* come after him; **tourner à droite a. la poste,** turn right just past the post office; *F* **courir a. qn,** to run after s.o.; **jurer/maugréer a. qn,** to swear/grumble at s.o.; **il est toujours a. moi,** he's always nagging at me *or* getting at me; *F* **en avoir a. qn,** to have it in for s.o.; **les jeux passent a. le travail,** work comes before play;

(b) d'a., according to; **d'a. ce qu'elle a dit,** going by *or* according to what she said; **d'a. l'horloge il est trois heures,** according to the clock it's three; **d'a. elle, c'est d'accord,** as far as she's concerned it's OK, it's OK by her; **peint d'a. nature,** painted from nature; **paysage d'a. Turner,** landscape after Turner; **texte d'a. Cicéron,** text adapted from Cicero; **d'a. l'article 12,** under article 12; **d'a. vos instructions,** in accordance with your instructions;

(c) (*+ perf inf*) **a. avoir dîné,** after dinner.

2 *adv* afterwards, later; **parlez d'abord, je parlerai a.,** you speak first, I'll speak afterwards; **six semaines a.,** six weeks later; **les vacances, ça passe a.,** holidays are not a priority; **le jour (d')a.,** the next *or* following day, the day after; **la page d'a.,** the next *or* following page; **les chiens risquent de nous courir a.,** the dogs might run after us; **ces garçons qui te courent a.,** those boys who are (always) chasing (after) you; *F* **tout le monde leur court a.,** everybody runs after them; **et a.?,** what then?; *F* **eh bien, et puis a.?** well, what of it?, what about it?, so what?

3 *conj* **a. que,** after, when; **a. que je fus parti,** after I had gone; **a. que j'aurai fini,** when I have finished.

après- [aprɛ] *préf* post- ...; **la période de l'a.-soixante-huit,** the period after 1968, the post-1968 period; **le Moscou de l'a.-Gorbatchev,** Moscow in the post-Gorbachev era; **les jeunes de l'a.-sida,** the post-Aids generation.

après-demain [aprɛdmɛ̃] *adv* the day after tomorrow.

après-dîner [aprɛdine] *nm* evening; **discours d'a.-d.,** after-dinner speech; (*pl après-dîners*).

après-guerre [aprɛgɛr] *nm* post-war period, aftermath of war; (*pl après-guerres*).

après-midi [aprɛmidi] *nm or f inv* afternoon; **trois**

heures de l'a.-m., three in the afternoon, three p.m.
après-rasage [aprerazaʒ] **1** *adj inv* **lotion a.-r.**, aftershave (lotion). **2** *nm* aftershave (lotion).
après-ski [apreski] *nm inv* **des a.-s.**, snowboots; **station bien connue pour l'a.-s.**, resort well known for its après-ski activities.
après-vente [aprevɑ̃t] *adj inv Com* **service a.-v.**, aftersales service.
âpreté [ɑprəte] *nf* **(a)** roughness, harshness (*of wine, voice, winter etc*); tartness (*of fruit*); **(b)** asperity (*of tone etc*); sharpness, bitterness (*of cold, reproach*).
a priori [apriɔri] **1** *adv & adj* a priori; **raisonnement a p.**, a priori reasoning. **2** *nm* apriorism.
à-propos [aprɔpo] *nm* aptness, appropriateness, relevance (*of an expression etc*); **le don de (saisir) l'à-p.**, the knack of saying *or* doing the right thing; **répondre avec à-p.**, to give a suitable reply, to reply with a pertinent comment; **il fait des commentaires sans le moindre à-p.**, he makes comments that aren't the slightest bit relevant; **votre observation manque d'à-p.**, your remark is not to the point *or* is irrelevant; **son manque d'à-p. lui jouera des tours**, the fact that he's so slow on the uptake will backfire on him.
apte [apt] *adj* **(a) a. à faire qch/à qch**, fit *or* fitted *or* suited *or* qualified to do sth/for sth; **peu a. (à faire qch)**, unsuitable, ill-equipped (to do sth); **très a. à accomplir cette tâche**, very well suited *or* qualified to carry out this task; **a. à naviguer**, seaworthy; *Mil* **a. au service**, fit for military service; *Jur* **a. à hériter**, entitled to inherit; **(b)** apt, suitable (*example etc*); **peu a.**, unsuitable.
aptère [aptɛr] *adj* wingless; *Beaux-Arts* **victoire a.**, wingless victory.
aptéryx [apteriks] *nm* (*oiseau*) kiwi.
aptitude [aptityd] *nf* aptitude, fitness (**à, pour,** to); *Jur* capacity; **avoir une a. à (faire qch)**, to have the capacity (for doing sth); (*être doué*) to have a gift (for sth); **test d'a.**, aptitude test; **certificat d'a. professionnelle**, = vocational training certificate.
apurement [apyrmɑ̃] *nm* **(a)** auditing, agreeing (*of accounts*); **(b)** discharge (*of liability*).
apurer [apyre] *vt* **(a)** to audit, to pass, to agree (*accounts*); **(b)** to discharge (*liability*).
aquaculteur [akwakyltœr] *nm* fish farmer.
aquaculture [akwakyltyr] *nf* aquaculture; (*de poissons*) fish farming.
aquaplanage [akwaplanaʒ] *nm Aut* aquaplaning.
aquaplane [akwaplan] *nm Sp* aquaplaning; (*planche*) aquaplane.
aquaplaning [akwaplaniŋ] *nm Aut* = **AQUAPLANAGE**.
aquaplaniste [akwaplanist] *n Sp* aquaplaner.
aquarelle [akwarɛl] *nf Beaux-Arts* watercolour, *US* watercolor; **peindre à l'a.**, to paint in watercolours; **une a. de Matisse**, a watercolour by Matisse, a Matisse watercolour.
aquarelliste [akwarɛlist] *n* watercolourist, *US* watercolorist.
aquarium [akwarjɔm] *nm* aquarium; **a. d'eau de mer**, oceanarium.
aquatinte [akwatɛ̃t] *nf* aquatint.
aquatique [akwatik] *adj* **(a)** aquatic (*bird, plant, sport*); **(b)** marshy, watery (*land*).
aqueduc [ak(ə)dyk] *nm* **(a)** (*construction*) aqueduct; **(b)** *Anat* aqueduct, canal.
aqueux, -euse [akø, -øz] *adj* **(a)** watery (*drink*); waterlogged (*ground*); **(b)** *Anat Ch etc* aqueous, water; **humeur aqueuse**, aqueous humour.
à quia [akɥija] *adv Litt* **être à q.**, to be at a loss for words *or* a reply; **mettre qn à q.**, to render s.o. speechless, to nonplus s.o.
aquiculture [akwikyltyr] *nf* = **AQUACULTURE**.
aquifère [akɥifɛr] *adj Géol* **nappe a.**, aquifer.
aquilegia [akɥileʒja] *nf*, **aquilégie** [akɥileʒi] *nf* (*plante*) aquilegia, *F* columbine.
aquilin, -ine [akilɛ̃, -in] *adj* aquiline (*profile etc*); **nez a.**, aquiline *or* hook *or* Roman nose.
aquilon [akilɔ̃] *nm* north wind.
Aquin [akɛ̃] *nm* **Saint Thomas d'A.**, St Thomas Aquinas.
aquitain, -aine [akitɛ̃, -ɛn] **1** *adj* of *or* from Aquitaine. **2** *n* **A.**, native *or* inhabitant of Aquitaine, person from Aquitaine.
Aquitaine [akitɛn] *nf Hist* (province of) Aquitaine; **bassin d'A.**, Basin of Aquitaine.
A.R. (*abrév* **aller-retour**) return.
ara [ara] *nm* (*oiseau*) macaw.
arabe [arab] **1** *adj* **(a)** Arab (*horse, custom etc*); Arabian (*customs etc*); **(b)** *Ling etc* Arabic (*language, numerals etc*). **2** *nm Ling* Arabic. **3** *n* **A.**, Arab.
arabesque [arabɛsk] **1** *adj* arabesque, Arabian (*architecture etc*). **2** *nf* (*danse*) arabesque; **la fumée monte en arabesques**, the smoke curls up.
arabica [arabika] *nm* (*café*) arabica.
Arabie [arabi] *nf* Arabia; **A. séoudite** *ou* **saoudite**, Saudi Arabia; **le désert d'A.**, the Arabian desert.
arabique [arabik] *adj Com* **gomme a.**, gum arabic.
arabisant,-ante [arabizɑ̃, -ɑ̃t] *n* Arabic scholar, Arabist.
arabisation [arabizasjɔ̃] *nf* Arabization.
arabiser [arabize] *vt* to Arabize.
arable [arabl] *adj* arable (*land etc*).
arabophone [arabɔfɔn] **1** *adj* Arabic-speaking. **2** *n* Arabic speaker.
arachide [araʃid] *nf* (*plante*) peanut; *Br F* groundnut, monkey nut; **huile d'a.**, groundnut oil; **beurre d'a.**, peanut butter.
arachnéen, -enne [araknee̋, -ɛn] *adj* (*de l'araignée*) of spiders; *Litt* **légèreté arachnéenne**, gossamer lightness; **être d'une légèreté arachnéenne**, to be as light as thistledown.
arachnides [araknid] *nmpl Zool* Arachnida.
arachnoïde [araknɔid] *nf Anat* arachnoid (membrane).
araignée [areɲe] *nf* spider; **a. d'eau**, water spider; **toile d'a.**, cobweb, spider's web; *F* **avoir une a. au plafond**, to have a screw loose, to have bats in the belfry; *F* **a. de mer**, (*crustacé*) spider crab; (*poisson*) weever (fish).
araméen, -enne [arameɛ̃, -ɛn] *adj & nm Ling* Aramaic.
arase [araz] *nf Constr* **(pierres d')a., les arases**, levelling course (*of masonry*).
arasé [araze] *adj* flush; **armoire arasée**, built-in cupboard.
arasement [arazmɑ̃] *nm* **(a)** *Constr etc* levelling (*of wall*), making (*wall*) even *or* level *or* flush; **(b)** *Menuis* shoulder (*of tenon*); *Constr* levelling course (*of bricks or stones*).
araser [araze] *vt* **(a)** *Constr* to level (down) (*wall etc*), to make (*wall*) level *or* even; to make (*two stones etc*) flush; to plane (*plank*) even; **(b)** *Menuis* to saw off (*end*); to square (*plank*); to cut off, to strike off (*heads of piles*); to cut (*rails etc*) to length; **(c)** *Géol* to erode, to weather (*rock*).
aratoire [aratwar] *adj* agricultural (*implement*).
araucaria [arokarja] *nm* (*arbre*) araucaria, *F* monkey puzzle (tree).
arbalète [arbalɛt] *nf* crossbow.
arbalétrier [arbaletrije] *nm* **(a)** *Constr* principal rafter (*of roof etc*), **(b)** (*soldat*) crossbowman.
arbitrage [arbitraʒ] *nm* **(a)** *Sp* umpiring (*of tennis*); refereeing (*of football*); (*in industrial dispute*) arbitration; **conseil d'a.**, conciliation *or* arbitration board (*in industrial dispute*); *Sp* **erreur d'a.**, mistake by the referee *or* umpire; **(b)** *Banque etc* arbitrage; **a. de change**, arbitration of exchange; *Bourse* **a. en reports**, jobbing in contango(e)s.
arbitragiste [arbitraʒist] *nm Bourse* arbitrager.
arbitraire [arbitrɛr] **1** *adj* **(a)** arbitrary (*name, choice etc*); discretionary (*punishment etc*); **(b)** arbitrary, despotic, high-handed (*government, power, action etc*); arbitrary (*command*). **2** *nm* arbitrariness, arbitrary nature; **laisser qch à l'a. de qn**, to leave sth to s.o.'s discretion.
arbitrairement [arbitrɛrmɑ̃] *adv* arbitrarily.
arbitral, -aux [arbitral, -o] *adj Jur* arbitral; **tribunal a.**, court of arbitration; **solution arbitrale, règlement a.**, settlement by arbitration; **commission arbitrale**, board of referees.
arbitre [arbitr] *nm* **(a)** *Jur* arbitrator, referee, adjudicator; **a. rapporteur**, referee (*in commercial suit*); **(b)** *Sp* referee; *Tennis* umpire; **a. de touche**, *Fb* linesman; *Rugby* touch judge; **(c)** *Fig* arbiter (*of fashion etc*); **(d)** *Phil* **libre** *ou* **franc a.**, free will.
arbitrer [arbitre] *vt* **(a)** *Jur* to arbitrate; **(b)** *Sp* to referee (*football match*); to umpire (*tennis match*).
arboré [arbɔre] *adj* planted with trees.
arborer [arbɔre] *vt* to raise, to erect, to set up; to hoist (*flag*); *Nau* to step (*mast*); **a. l'étendard de la révolte**, to raise the standard of revolt; **a. une cravate rouge/une rose à la boutonnière**, to wear *or* sport a red tie/a rose in one's buttonhole; **elle arbore un sourire triomphant**, she is wearing a triumphant smile; **a. un air de mépris**, to affect an air of disdain.
arborescence [arbɔresɑ̃s] *nf Bot* arborescence.
arborescent [arbɔresɑ̃] *adj Bot* arborescent; **fougère arborescente**, tree fern.
arborétum [arbɔretɔm] *nm Bot* arboretum.
arboricole [arbɔrikɔl] *adj* **(a)** (*technique etc*) arboricultural; **(b)** tree-dwelling, arboreal (*animal*).
arboriculteur, -trice [arbɔrikyltœr, -tris] *n*

nurseryman, nurserywoman.

arboriculture [arbɔrikyltyr] *nf* arboriculture; **a. fruitière,** orcharding, fruit growing.

arborisation [arbɔrizɑsjɔ̃] *nf* dendritic marking (*of crystals*).

arborisé [arbɔrize] *adj Minér* dendritic.

arbouse [arbuz] *nf* arbutus-berry.

arbousier [arbuzje] *nm* (*arbre*) arbutus; **a. commun,** strawberry tree.

arbre [arbr] *nm* **(a)** (*végétal*) tree; **jeune a.,** sapling; **a. fruitier,** fruit tree; **des arbres d'agrément,** ornamental trees; **a. de plein vent,** standard; **a. en espalier,** espalier (tree); **a. vert,** evergreen (tree); **a. à feuille(s) caduque(s),** deciduous tree; **a. feuillu,** hardwood (tree); **a. résineux,** softwood (tree); **faire l'a. fourchu,** to walk on one's hands; (*sans bouger*) to do a handstand; *Prov* **se trouver entre l'a. et l'écorce,** to be between the devil and the deep blue sea; **les arbres cachent la forêt,** you can't see the wood for the trees; **dans son cas** *ou* **pour lui les arbres cachent la forêt,** he can't see the wood for the trees; **a. généalogique,** genealogical tree, family tree; **a. de Jessé,** tree of Jesse; **l'a. de la Croix,** the Rood; **a. de Noël,** Christmas tree; **a. de la liberté,** tree of liberty; **a. de Judée,** Judas tree; **a. à la gale, a. à la puce, a. à poison,** poison ivy; **a. à grives,** rowan, mountain ash; **a. aux lis** *ou* **aux tulipes,** tulip tree; **a. à caoutchouc,** rubber tree; **a. à pain,** bread(fruit) tree; **a. de paradis** *ou* **de vie,** thuya, tree of life, arbor vitae; **a. du voyageur,** traveller's tree; *Anat* **a. respiratoire,** respiratory system;
(b) shaft, spindle, axle; (*d'horloge etc*) arbor; **a. moteur** *ou* **de commande,** main shaft, driving shaft; **a. d'entraînement,** drive shaft; **a. fou,** loose shaft; **a. d'accouplement,** coupling shaft; **a. creux,** hollow spindle, tubular shaft; **a. à excentrique(s), a. excentré** *ou* **excentrique,** eccentric shaft; **a. coudé** *ou* **vilebrequin, a.-manivelle,** crankshaft; **a. de tour,** lathe spindle, mandrel; **a. à cardan** *ou* **de cardan(s),** cardan shaft; **a. à cames,** camshaft; **a. de transmission,** line shaft; *Aut* propeller shaft; *Aut* **a. arrière,** back axle shaft; **a. de culbuteur,** rocker shaft; *El* **a. d'induit,** armature shaft; **a. de l'hélice, a. porte-hélice,** propeller shaft.

arbrisseau, -eaux [arbriso] *nm* shrub; **plantation d'arbrisseaux,** shrubbery.

arbuste [arbyst] *nm* bush, (arborescent) shrub; **plantation d'arbustes,** shrubbery.

arc [ark] *nm* **(a)** (*arme*) bow; **tir à l'a.,** archery; **à la portée de l'a.,** within bowshot; **corde de l'a.,** bowstring; *Fig* **avoir plus d'une corde** *ou* **plusieurs cordes à son a.,** to have more than one string to one's bow; **ressort à a.,** bow spring; **scie à a.,** bow saw; **(b)** *Archit* arch; **a. en plein cintre, a. roman,** semicircular arch; **a. brisé** *ou* **aigu,** gothic arch; **a. en fer à cheval,** horseshoe arch; **a. de triomphe,** triumphal arch; **l'a. des sourcils/de l'aorte,** the arch of the eyebrows/of the aorta; **a. dentaire,** dental arch; **(c)** *Math* **a. de cercle,** arc of a circle; **assis en a. de cercle,** sitting in a semicircle; **a. denté,** toothed arc, segmental rack; *Él* **a. voltaïque,** voltaic arc; **a. électrique,** electric arc; **soudure en a.,** arc welding; **lampe à a.,** arc lamp.

arcade [arkad] *nf* **(a)** *Archit* archway; **a. feinte,** blind arch; **arcades,** arcade; **(b)** bridge (*of pair of spectacles*); arch (*of saddle etc*); *Anat* **a. dentaire/orbitaire,** dental/orbital arch; **a. sourcilière,** the arch of the eyebrows.

arcadé [arkade] *adj* arcaded (*court, walk etc*).

arcature [arkatyr] *nf Archit* arcature, blind arcade.

arc-boutant [arkbutɑ̃] *nm* (*pl arcs-boutants*) **(a)** *Archit* flying buttress; **(b)** *Constr* abutment pier.

arc-bouter [arkbute] **1** *vt* **(a)** to buttress (*a wall*), to support (*a wall*) with flying buttresses; **(b)** (*étayer*) to prop up, to shore up (*wall etc*). **2 s'arc-bouter** *vpr* **s'a.-b. contre un mur,** to support *or* brace oneself against a wall; to use a wall as support *or* to support oneself.

arc-doubleau [arkdublo] *nm Archit* transverse rib; (*pl arcs-doubleaux*).

arceau, -eaux [arso] *nm* **(a)** arch (*of vault*); **(b)** ring bow (*of padlock*); (croquet) hoop; *Méd* (bed)-cradle.

arc-en-ciel [arkɑ̃sjɛl] *nm* rainbow; (*pl arcs-en-ciel*).

archaïque [arkaik] *adj* archaic (*style etc*); antiquated (*appearance etc*).

archaïsme [arkaism] *nm* archaism.

archange [arkɑ̃ʒ] *nm* archangel.

arche[1] [arʃ] *nf* **(a)** *Rel* ark; **l'a. de Noé,** Noah's ark; **l'a. d'alliance, l'a. sainte,** the Ark of the Covenant; **(b) a. d'élevage,** coop.

arche[2] *nf* **(a)** arch (*of bridge etc*); *Géol* **a. naturelle,** natural arc; **(b)** (croquet) hoop.

archéologie [arkeɔlɔʒi] *nf* arch(a)eology.

archéologique [arkeɔlɔʒik] *adj* arch(a)eological.

archéologiquement [arkeɔlɔʒikmɑ̃] *adv* arch(a)eologically, from an arch(a)eological point of view.

archéologue [arkeɔlɔg] *n* arch(a)eologist.

archer [arʃe] *nm* archer, bowman.

archet [arʃɛ] *nm* **(a)** (*de violin etc*) bow; **scie à a.,** bow saw; **(b)** *Rail* pantograph.

archétype [arketip] **1** *adj* archetypal. **2** *nm* archetype, prototype.

archevêché [arʃəveʃe] *nm* **(a)** (*territoire*) archbishopric, archdiocese; **(b)** (*fonction*) archbishopric; **(c)** (*résidence*) archbishop's palace.

archevêque [arʃəvɛk] *nm* archbishop.

archiconnu [arʃikɔny] *adj F* very well known; **c'est a.,** everybody knows that.

archicube [arʃikyb] *nm Scol F* graduate of the École Normale Supérieure.

archidémon [arʃidemɔ̃] *nm* arch-fiend.

archidiacre [arʃidjakr] *nm Rel* archdeacon.

archidiocèse [arʃidiɔsɛz] *nm Rel* archdiocese, archbishopric.

archiduc [arʃidyk] *nm* archduke.

archiduchesse [arʃidyʃɛs] *nf* archduchess.

archiépiscopal,-aux [arʃiepiskɔpal, -o] *adj* archiepiscopal.

archiépiscopat [arʃiepiskɔpa] *nm* archiepiscopate, archiepiscopacy.

archifaux, -fausse [arʃifo, -fos] *adj F* dead wrong.

Archimède [arʃimɛd] *nm Hist* Archimedes; *Phys* **le principe d'A.,** Archimedes' principle; **vis d'A.,** *HydE* Archimedean screw; *Ind* spiral conveyor.

archimillionnaire [arʃimiljɔnɛr] *adj & n F* multi-millionaire.

archipel [arʃipɛl] *nm Géog* archipelago.

archisec, -sèche [arʃisɛk, -sɛʃ] *adj F* bone-dry.

archisecret, -ète [arʃisəkrɛ, -ɛt] *adj F* top secret, hush-hush.

architecte [arʃitɛkt] *nm* (*d'un immeuble, Fig d'une réforme*) architect; **a. paysagiste,** landscape gardener; **a. naval,** naval architect; **a. urbaniste,** town planner.

architectonique [arʃitɛktɔnik] **1** *adj* architectonic. **2** *nf* architectonics.

architectural, -aux [arʃitɛktyral, -o] *adj* architectural.

architecture [arʃitɛktyr] *nf* (*d'une ville, d'un ordinateur etc*) architecture; **a. navale,** naval architecture; *Fig* **l'a. du corps,** the way the body is designed, the structure of the body.

architrave [arʃitrav] *nf Archit* architrave.

archive [arʃiv] *nf Ordinat* archive.

archiver [arʃive] *vt* to archive.

archives [arʃiv] *nfpl* archives, records; **exemplaire des a.,** file copy; **les a. nationales,** ≈ the (Public) Record Office; *F* **ça restera dans les a.,** that'll go down in history, wonders will never cease!

archiviste [arʃivist] *n* archivist; (*fonction publique*) keeper of public records; *Com etc* clerk (in charge of records); filing clerk.

arçon [arsɔ̃] *nm* **(a)** (*de selle*) saddle bow; **vider les arçons,** to fall off one's horse; *Gym* **cheval d'arçons,** (vaulting) horse; **(b)** *Tex* (felter's) bow; frame (*of saw*); **foret** *ou* **drille à a.,** fiddle drill, bow drill.

arçonner [arsɔne] *vt Tex* to card *or* clean (*cotton, wool etc*) with a (felter's) bow.

arctique [arktik] **1** *adj* arctic; **cercle a.,** arctic circle. **2** *nm* **l'A.,** the Arctic.

ardemment [ardamɑ̃] *adv* (*aimer*) ardently, passionately; (*travailler*) zealously, eagerly.

Ardennes (les) [lezardɛn] *nfpl* the Ardennes; **la Bataille des A.,** the Battle of the Bulge.

ardent [ardɑ̃] *adj* **(a)** burning hot, scorching, blazing (*fire etc*); **soleil a.,** scorching sun; **cheveux d'un blond/roux a.,** strawberry *or* reddish blond/fiery red hair; **chapelle ardente,** mortuary chapel (*lit with candles*); **rouge a.,** fiery red; **(b)** (*passionné*) ardent, passionate, eager; **désir a.,** burning desire; **jeune homme a.,** a hot-blooded *or* passionate young man; **elle est ardente au travail,** she's a zealous worker; **ardente conviction,** deep-seated conviction; **j'en ai l'ardente conviction,** I am firmly convinced of it; **socialiste a.,** red-hot Socialist; **a. sportif,** keen sportsman; **(c)** (*vif*) keen (*attention*); lively (*imagination*); burning (*curiosity*); *F* keenly-fought (*struggle*); **être dans une colère ardente,** to be in a furious rage.

ardeur [ardœr] *nf* **(a)** heat (*of sun, fire etc*); **(b)** (*enthousiasme*) eagerness, ardour, *US* ardor, fervour, *US* fervor; **cheval plein d'a.,** high- spirited *or* high-mettled horse; **travailler avec a.,** to work zealously; **soutenir son opinion avec a.,** to argue one's case with passion *or* passionately; **modère tes ardeurs!,** calm down!, don't get excited!; **les ardeurs de la passion,** the heat of passion; **son a. à lire,** his passion for reading.

ardoise [ardwaz] **1** *nf* **(a)** *Minér* slate; **(feuille d')a.,** slate; **couvrir un toit en a.,** to slate a roof; **(b) a. (à écrire),** (writing) slate; *F* bill, cost; **crayon d'a.,** slate pencil; *F* **inscrire les consommations à l'a.,** to chalk up the drinks; to put the drinks on the slate, *Am* to put the drinks on one's tab; *F* **j'ai quelques ardoises a régler,** I've got a few bills to pay. **2** *adj* **(couleur) gris a.,** slate grey (colour).

ardoisé [ardwaze] *adj* slate-colour(ed), bluish-grey.

ardoiser [ardwaze] *vt* to slate (*roof*).

ardoisier, -ière [ardwazje, -jɛr] **1** *adj* slaty; **schiste a.,** slate clay, shale. **2** *nm* (*exploitant*) owner of a slate quarry; (*ouvrier*) slate worker, slate quarryman. **3** *nf* **ardoisière,** slate quarry.

ardt *abrév* **arrondissement**.

ardu [ardy] *adj* **(a)** steep, difficult (*path etc*); **(b)** arduous, difficult, hard (*task etc*); **travail a.,** uphill work.

are [ar] *nm Agr* are (= 100 square metres).

arec [arɛk] *nm* **(a)** areca palm (tree); **(b) (noix d')a.,** areca nut, betel nut.

areligieux, -ieuse [arəliʒjø, -øz] *adj* not religious.

aréna [arena] *nf Can* arena.

arène [arɛn] *nf* **(a)** (*d'amphithéâtre*) arena; (*de tauromachie*) bullring; *Fig* **descendre dans l'a.,** to take up the challenge, to enter the fray; *Fig* **l'a. politique,** the political arena; **les arènes d'Arles,** the amphitheatre of Arles; **(b)** *Arch & Litt* sand.

aréole [areɔl] *nf Anat Bot Méd* areola.

aréomètre [areɔmɛtr] *nm* hydrometer.

aréométrie [areɔmetri] *nf* hydrometry.

aréopage [areɔpaʒ] *nm Fig* learned gathering *or* assembly.

arête [arɛt] *nf* **(a)** (*de poisson*) (fish) bone; **poisson plein d'arêtes,** bony fish; **grande a.,** backbone (*of fish*); **dessin en a. de hareng** *ou Archit* **de poisson,** herringbone pattern; **(b)** bridge (*of the nose*); **(c)** *Constr etc* line; **a. d'un comble,** hip of a roof; **pierre d'a.,** quoin stone; **a. de voûte,** groin (*of an arch*); **(d)** *Av* **a. dorsale,** dorsal fin (*of fuselage*); **(e)** *Géog* arête, (serrate) ridge; **(f)** beard (*of ear, of barley etc*); **(g)** ridge, rib (*of sword blade, bayonet*).

arêtière [aretjɛr] *nf Constr* arris tile, hip tile.

argent [arʒɑ̃] *nm* **(a)** (*métal*) silver; **vaisselle d'a.,** (silver) plate; **a. en feuille,** silver foil, silver leaf; **bijoux en a.,** silver jewels; *Prov* **la parole est d'a., le silence est d'or,** speech is silver, silence is golden; *Sp* **gagner la médaille d'a.,** to win the silver (medal); *Fig* **cheveux d'a.,** silvery (-grey) hair; **reflets d'a. sur le lac,** silvery glints on the lake;
(b) *Fin* money; **avoir de l'a.,** to have (a lot of) money, to be well off; **a. de poche,** pocket money; **a. liquide,** ready money *or* cash, cash (in hand); **payer a. comptant,** to pay (in) cash; *F* **se faire un a. fou,** to make lots *or* loads of money; **les puissances de l'a.,** the rich and powerful; **l'a. lui fond entre les mains,** money just slips through his fingers; **elle le fait pour l'a.,** she does it for the money; **attendre une rentrée d'a.,** to be waiting for money to come in; *Fig* **jeter de l'a. par les fenêtres,** to throw money down the drain, to throw money away; **en avoir pour son a.,** to have *or* get one's money's worth, to get good value for one's money; *Fig* **prendre tout pour a. comptant,** to take everything at face value; **le temps, c'est de l'a.,** time is money.

argenté [arʒɑ̃te] *adj* **(a)** (*couleur*) silver(ed), silvery; **gris a.,** silver-grey; **reflet a.,** silvery glint, glint of silver; **renard a.,** silver fox; **(b)** (*plaqué, couvert*) silver-plated; **(c)** *F* rich, well-heeled; **touristes bien argentés,** tourists with well-lined pockets.

argenter [arʒɑ̃te] *vt* to silver(-plate); *Fig* **la lune argente le lac de ses reflets,** the moon gives the lake a silvery sheen.

argenterie [arʒɑ̃tri] *nf* (silver) plate, silverware.

argenteur [arʒɑ̃tœr] *nm* silverer, silver plater.

argentin[1], -ine [arʒɑ̃tɛ̃, -in] *adj* silver-toned (*voice*); silvery (*voice, laugh, waves*); tinkling (*bell*).

argentin[2], -ine 1 *adj* Argentinian, Argentine; **la République Argentine,** Argentina, the Argentine (Republic). **2** *n* **A.,** Argentinian, Argentine. **3** *nf* **l'Argentine,** Argentina, the Argentine (Republic).

argile [arʒil] *nf* clay; **a. à blocaux,** boulder clay; **a. schisteuse,** shale; **traitement par l'a.,** mud-pack treatment; **masque d'a.,** mud-pack; **a. cuite,** terracotta, earthenware; **une statue** *ou* **un colosse aux pieds d'a.,** an idol with feet of clay.

argileux, -euse [arʒilø, -øz] *adj* clayey.

argilifère [arʒilifɛr] *adj* clay-bearing.

argon [argɔ̃] *nm Ch* argon.

argonaute [argɔnot] *nm* **(a)** *Myth* Argonaut; **(b)** (*mollusque*) argonaut, paper nautilus.

argot [argo] *nm* slang; (*administratif, scientifique etc*) jargon; **l'a. (parisien),** Paris(ian) slang; **a. des voleurs,** thieves' cant; **a. du milieu,** underworld slang; **a. scolaire,** school slang.

argotique [argɔtik] *adj* slangy (*language*); **expression a.,** (*d'un milieu*) cant phrase; (*familier*) slang expression.

argotisme [argɔtism] *nm* slang expression.

arguer [argɥe] *v* **(j'argue** [ʒargy], **n. arguions** [nuzargyjɔ̃]) **1** *vt* **(a)** *Litt* to infer, to assert, to deduce; **que peut-il a. de ce fait?,** what can he deduce *or* infer from this fact?, what conclusion(s) can he draw from this fact?; **il argue qu'on ne l'avait pas prévenu,** his objection is that he was not informed; **(b)** *Jur* **a. une pièce de faux,** to assert a deed to be forged. **2** *vi* **a. de,** to argue that; **elle argua du manque d'informations fournies,** she argued that insufficient information had been provided.

argument [argymɑ̃] *nm* **(a)** (*démonstration*) argument; **par manière d'a.,** for argument's sake; **tirer a. de qch,** to argue from sth; **(b)** outline, summary, plot, argument (*of book etc*); synopsis (*of contents*); **(c)** *Math* argument.

argumentaire [argymɑ̃tɛr] *nm Com* **rédiger un a.,** to draw up a list of selling points.

argumentateur, -trice [argymɑ̃tatœr, -tris] *Péj* **1** *adj* argumentative. **2** *n* arguer.

argumentation [argymɑ̃tasjɔ̃] *nf* argument; **une a. serrée,** a series of closely argued points.

argumenter [argymɑ̃te] *vi* **(a)** to argue (**contre,** against); *F* to be argumentative; **on ne peut pas a. à partir de ce fait,** you can't base an argument on that fact; **(b) discours/démonstration bien argumenté(e),** well-argued speech/demonstration.

Argus [argys] *nm* **(a)** *Myth* Argus; **(b) l'A. (de l'Automobile),** ≈ Glass's Guide.

argutie [argysi] *nf* quibble, cavil.

aria [arja] *nf Mus* aria.

aride [arid] *adj* arid, dry, barren (*country, subject*); **une imagination a.,** a barren imagination.

aridité [aridite] *nf* aridity, aridness, barrenness; **l'a. d'un sujet,** the aridity of a topic.

arien, -ienne [arjɛ̃, -jɛn] **1** *adj* Aryan. **2** *n* **A.,** Aryan.

aristo [aristo] *n F* nob, toff.

aristocrate [aristɔkrat] *n* aristocrat.

aristocratie [aristɔkrasi] *nf* aristocracy.

aristocratique [aristɔkratik] *adj* aristocratic.

Aristote [aristɔt] *nm Phil* Aristotle; **la logique d'A.,** Aristotelian logic.

aristotélicien, -ienne [aristɔtelisjɛ̃, -jɛn] *adj & n Phil* Aristotelian.

arithméticien, -ienne [aritmetisjɛ̃, -jɛn] *n* arithmetician.

arithmétique [aritmetik] **1** *adj* arithmetical; *F* **c'est évident, c'est a.!,** it's obvious!, it stands to reason! **2** *nf* **(a)** arithmetic; **(b) une a.,** an arithmetic book.

arlequin [arləkɛ̃] *nm Th* Harlequin; **habillé en a.,** dressed in motley; **manteau d'a.,** proscenium arch.

arlequinade [arləkinad] *nf Th* harlequinade; *Fig* (piece of) buffoonery.

arlésien, -ienne [arlezjɛ̃, -jɛn] **1** *adj* Arlesian, of *or* from Arles. **2** *n* **A.,** person from Arles, native *or* inhabitant of Arles.

armada [armada] *nf Hist* armada; **l'Invincible A.,** the Invincible Armada.

armagnac [armaɲak] *nm* Armagnac.

armateur [armatœr] *nm Nau* fitter-out (*of ship, expedition*); (*propriétaire*) (ship)owner.

armature [armatyr] *nf* **(a)** reinforcement (*of concrete work*); truss (*of girder etc*); frame, brace, armature (*of window etc*); **soutien-gorge à a.,** underwired bra; **l'a. de nos principes moraux,** the underpinnings of our moral principles; **(b)** armouring, sheathing (*of electric cable*); **(c)** *Él* armature (*of magnet, small dynamo, magneto*); plate (*of condenser*); **a. de soupape/de pompe,** valve/pump gear; **(d)** *Mus* key signature.

arme [arm] *nf* **(a)** arm, weapon; (*en escrime*) sword; **salle d'armes,** armoury; (*d'escrime*) fencing school; **l'a. du**

crime, the murder weapon; **armes à feu,** firearms; **armes portatives,** small arms; **armes classiques** *ou* **traditionnelles** *ou* **conventionnelles,** conventional weapons; **a. non classique, a. non conventionnelle,** non-conventional weapon, advanced weapon; **combat à l'a. blanche,** knife fight; **a. nucléaire,** nuclear weapon; **a. de dissuasion,** deterrent; **porter une a. sur soi,** to carry a weapon; **prendre le pouvoir par les armes,** to take power by force; **nation en** *ou* **sous les armes,** nation in arms; **prendre les armes,** to take up arms, to rise up in arms (**contre,** against); *Mil* to parade under arms; **déposer les armes,** to lay down one's arms, to surrender; **porter les armes,** to be a soldier; *Mil* **aux armes!,** to arms!; guard turn out!; **le métier** *ou* **la carrière des armes,** the military profession, soldiering; **suspension d'armes,** cessation of hostilities; **frères d'armes,** brothers in arms; **place d'armes,** parade ground; **portez armes!,** shoulder arms!; **passer qn par les armes,** to have s.o. (court-martialled and) shot; **sans armes,** unarmed; *Fig* **passer l'a. à gauche,** to snuff it, to kick the bucket; (*dans un accident*) to cop it; **il fait ses premières armes,** he's earning his spurs; **fournir des armes à qn,** to provide s.o. with ammunition; **l'indépendance est une a. à double tranchant,** independence is a two-edged sword; *Fig* **la télévision est l'a. absolue des politiciens,** television is the politician's ultimate weapon; **à armes égales,** on equal terms; **avec armes et bagages,** (with) bag and baggage;

(b) arm (*as a branch of the army*); **douze mille hommes de toutes armes,** twelve thousand men of all arms *or* services;

(c) *Hér* **armes,** (coat of) arms.

armé [arme] **1** *adj* **(a)** armed; **troupe armée,** body of troops; **agression à main armée,** hold-up; **animal a. de piquants/d'une carapace,** animal with spines/a shell; **a. jusqu'aux dents,** armed to the teeth; **sortir a. de chez soi,** to go out carrying a weapon; *Fig* **être bien/mal a. pour partir dans la vie,** to be well/badly equipped to make one's way in the world; **mes enfants partiront armés dans le monde du travail,** my children will be well qualified to find a job; **(b)** (*renforcé*) fortified, strengthened; **poutre armée,** trussed beam; **béton a.,** reinforced concrete; **verre a.,** wired glass; **(c)** cocked; **pistolet à demi a.,** pistol at half cock. **2** *nm* **à l'a.,** (*d'un pistolet*) cocked.

armée [arme] *nf* **(a)** *Mil* army; **a. de métier,** professional army; **lever une a.,** to raise an army; **a. permanente,** standing army; **a. régulière** *ou* **active,** regular army; **l'a. de terre,** the army, the land forces; **l'a. de l'air,** the air force; **l'a. de mer,** the navy, the naval forces; **a. de secours,** relieving army; **les armées alliées,** the allied armies *or* forces; **être dans l'a.,** to be in the army; **la 8ème a.,** the 8th army; **le Dieu des armées,** the Lord of Hosts; **groupe d'a.,** army group; **(b)** *Hist* **la Grande A.,** the Grande Armée; **(c) l'A. du Salut,** the Salvation Army; **(d)** (*foule*) **quelle a. d'incapables!,** what a shower (of incompetents)!; **toute une a. de fonctionnaires,** a whole army of officials; **une a. d'insectes ravageurs,** an army of marauding insects.

armement [arməmɑ̃] *nm* **(a)** arming, equipping (*of army*); (*equipment*) armament, equipment; (*weapons*) **armements,** armaments, weaponry; **officier d'a.,** ordnance officer; **vente d'armements,** sale of arms; **la vente d'armements a diminué,** arms sales have decreased; **réduction des armements,** arms reduction; **course aux armements,** arms race;

(b) strengthening, bracing (*of girder etc*); sheathing (*of cable etc*);

(c) *Nau* commissioning, fitting out; (*equipment*) equipment, gear, stores; **mettre un navire en a.,** to put a ship in commission; **port d'a.,** port of registry;

(d) manning; crew (*of boat, gun etc*);

(e) *Com* merchant shipping;

(f) loading (*of gun*); arming (*of fuse*); setting (*of camera shutter etc*); cocking (*of loaded fire arm*); mounting, fitting up (*of machine etc*);

(g) mounting gear (*of machine*).

Arménie [armeni] *nf* Armenia.

arménien, -ienne [armenjɛ̃, -jɛn] **1** *adj* Armenian. **2** *nm Ling* Armenian. **3** *n* **A.,** Armenian.

armer [arme] **1** *vt* **(a)** (*munir d'armes*) to arm (*soldiers*) (**de,** with); **je sors toujours armé,** I always carry a weapon when I go out; **vol à main armée,** armed robbery; *Fig* **a. les enfants de patience,** to teach children patience; *Fig* **a. qn contre les difficultés de la vie,** to equip s.o. to deal with the difficulties of life; *Fig* **cette position l'arme de tous les pouvoirs,** this job puts him in a position of real power;

(b) to fortify (*a town*); to strengthen, to brace (*a girder*); to wind (*a dynamo*); to sheathe, to armour (*a cable*); **a. du béton,** to reinforce concrete;

(c) *Nau* to equip, to fit out, to commission (*ship*); to man (*boat etc*); to rig (*capstan*); **a. les avirons,** to ship the oars;

(d) to arm (*a fuse*); to set (*an apparatus*); to cock (*firearm*); to mount (*machine, battery of guns etc*); to fit up (*machine*); **a. son appareil photo,** to set one's camera;

(e) *Hist* **a. qn chevalier,** to knight s.o.;

(f) *Mus* **a. la clef,** to put the key signature (*to a piece of music*).

2 *vi* **(a)** *Mil* to arm, to prepare for war;

(b) *Nau* **le navire arme à Brest,** the ship is being commissioned at Brest; **a. sur un navire,** to serve on a vessel.

3 s'armer *vpr* to arm oneself; (*recourir à la lutte armée*) to take up arms; *Fig* **je me suis armé de mon livre préféré pour attendre,** I armed myself with my favourite book to read while I waited; **s'a. de courage/de patience,** to summon up (one's) courage/patience.

armistice [armistis] *nm* armistice; (*temporaire*) truce; **journée** *ou* **anniversaire de l'A.,** Armistice Day, Remembrance Day, *US* Veterans Day.

armoire [armwar] *nf* (*placard*) cupboard, *surtout Am* closet; (*pour les vêtements*) wardrobe, *surtout Am* closet; **a. à linge,** linen cupboard; **a. à provisions,** store cupboard; **a. à pharmacie,** medicine *or* first-aid cabinet; **a. frigorifique,** cold store; **a. de toilette,** bathroom cabinet; **a. à glace,** = large wardrobe with a mirror on the outside; *Fig Hum* **c'est une a. à glace,** he's built like a tank; **a. de cuisine,** kitchen cupboard.

armoiries [armwari] *nfpl Hér* (coat of) arms, armorial bearings.

armorial, -aux [armɔrjal, -o] *adj* armorial.

armoricain, -aine [armɔrikɛ̃, -ɛn] **1** *adj* Armorican; **massif a.,** Armorican massif. **2** *n Hist* **A.,** Armorican, ancient Breton.

Armorique [armɔrik] *nf* Armorica.

armoriste [armɔrist] *nm* heraldic artist.

armure [armyr] *nf* **(a)** (*cuirasse etc*) armour; defence (*of animals*); **a. complète,** suit of armour; **a. d'un navire de guerre,** armour (plating) of a warship; *Fig* **cette insolence est une a., elle s'en protège,** she uses insolence as a defence mechanism; **(b)** *Tex* weave, pattern, design; draught (*of warp*); cording and healds (*of loom*); **a. toile,** plain weave; **(c)** *El* pole piece (*of dynamo*); armouring; sheathing (*of cable*); **(d)** *Mus* key signature.

armurier [armyrje] *nm* **(a)** (*fabriquant etc*) arms manufacturer; (*de pistolets etc*) gunsmith; **(b)** *Mil etc* armourer.

A.R.N. [aɛrɛn] *nm* (*abrév* **acide ribonucléique**) RNA.

arnaque [arnak] *nf F* swindle, rip-off; **attention à l'a.!,** be careful you don't get ripped off!

arnaquer [arnake] *vt F* to cheat, to swindle, to rip off; **se faire a.,** to get ripped off.

arnaqueur, -euse [arnakœr, -øz] *n F* swindler, rip-off merchant.

arnica [arnika] *nf Pharm* arnica.

aromate [arɔmat] *nm* aromatic; spice.

aromathérapie [arɔmaterapi] *nf Méd* aromatherapy.

aromatique [arɔmatik] *adj* **(a)** aromatic; (*saveur*) spicy; **plantes aromatiques,** aromatic plants; **(b)** *Ch* **carbures aromatiques,** aromatics.

aromatisation [arɔmatizasjɔ̃] *nf Ch* aromatization.

aromatiser [arɔmatize] *vt* **(a)** to give aroma to (*sth*); *Culin* to flavour; **(b)** *Ch* to aromatize.

arome, arôme [arom] *nm* aroma; (*goût*) flavour.

aronde [arɔ̃d] *nf Menuis* **queue d'a.,** dovetail; **assembler qch en queue d'a.,** to dovetail sth.

arpège [arpɛʒ] *nm Mus* arpeggio.

arpéger [arpeʒe] *vt Mus* to play (*a chord*) as an arpeggio.

arpent [arpɑ̃] *nm Hist* arpent (*approx one acre*).

arpentage [arpɑ̃taʒ] *nm* surveying, land measuring; **faire l'a. d'un terrain,** to measure a piece of ground.

arpenter [arpɑ̃te] *vt* **(a)** to survey, to measure (*land*); **(b)** (*parcourir rapidement*) **a. le terrain,** to stride over the ground; **il arpentait le quai,** he was pacing up and down the platform.

arpenteur [arpɑ̃tœr] *nm* (land) surveyor.

arpion [arpjɔ̃] *nm Arg* (*pied*) hoof; (*orteil*) toe.

arqué [arke] *adj* arched, curved; cambered (*beam etc*); high-bridged (*nose*); bandy-legged (*horse*); **jambes arquées,** bow legs.

arquebuse [arkəbyz] *nf* (h)arquebus.
arquebusier [arkəbyzje] *nm (soldat)* (h)arquebusier.
arquer [arke] **1** *vt* to bend, to arch, to curve *(wood, iron etc)*; to camber *(surface)*; **a. le dos,** to bend *or* hump the back; *(of cat)* to arch its back. **2** *vi* **(a)** *(fléchir)* to bend, to sag, to buckle; **(b)** *F (marcher)* to walk; **je ne pouvais plus a.,** *(j'étais épuisé)* I couldn't walk another step, I couldn't put one foot in front of the other. **3 s'arquer** *vpr* to bend, to become bent *or* arched.
arrachage [araʃaʒ] *nm* pulling up, rooting up *(of plants etc)*; lifting *(of potatoes)*; pulling out, wrenching out, drawing, extraction *(of tooth, nail etc)*.
arraché [araʃe] **1** *adj Hér* erased. **2** *nm Sp (in weight-lifting)* snatch; *Fig* **obtenir un accord/gagner à l'a.,** to obtain a deal/to win with *or* after a terrific effort.
arrache-clou [araʃklu] *nm* nail drawer; *(pl arrache-clous)*.
arrachement [araʃmɑ̃] *nm* **(a)** *(d'un arbre etc)* rooting up *(of tree etc)*; **(b)** *(déchirure)* wrench; **l'a. du départ,** the wrench of leaving; **nous ne pouvons quitter Paris sans a.,** it will be a wrench leaving Paris; **(c)** *Constr* toothing; **(d)** *(en mécanique)* tearing, wrenching, stripping; **effort d'a.,** wrenching force; **(e)** *Méd etc* wrench.
arrache-pied (d') [daraʃpje] *adv* without interruption, relentlessly; **travailler d'a.-p.,** to work steadily; *(excessivement)* to slave away; **parler deux heures d'a.-p.,** to talk for two hours at a stretch *or* without stopping, to talk non-stop for two hours.
arracher [araʃe] **1** *vt* to pull (up, out, away); to draw *(nail)*; to root up, to uproot *(tree)*; to lift *(potatoes)*; to extract *(money from s.o.)*; to extract, to pull out *(tooth)*; to tear down, to pull down *(poster)*; to extract *(promise, secret)*; **a. qch de qch,** to pull sth off *or* from *or* out of sth; **nous sommes parvenus à lui a. cet aveu,** we managed to extract that confession from him; **a. qch à qn/des mains de qn,** to snatch sth from s.o./from s.o.'s hands; **se faire a. une dent,** to have a tooth extracted *or* pulled (out) *or* out; **a. qn de son foyer,** to drag *or* uproot s.o. from his home; **a. les yeux à qn,** to tear s.o.'s eyes out; *Fig* **j'avais envie de lui a. les yeux,** I wanted to strangle him; *Fig* **il faut a. son masque,** we *etc* must tear off his mask; **a. qn à la mort,** to snatch *or* rescue s.o. from the jaws of death; **a. qn au sommeil,** to rouse s.o. from (his) sleep; **la sonnerie du réveil m'a arraché du lit,** the alarm dragged me out of bed; **a. qn à son travail/à la télé,** to tear *or* drag s.o. away from his work/the TV; **a. le pain de la bouche à qn,** to snatch the bread from s.o.'s mouth; **cela m'arrache le cœur,** it breaks my heart; *Arg* **la tequila pure, ça arrache la gueule,** pure tequila will blow your head off.
2 *vi Can* **en a.,** to have difficulties.
3 s'arracher *vpr* **elle s'est arrachée la robe dans la grille,** she tore *or* ripped her dress on the railings; *Fig* **je n'y comprends rien, je m'arrache les cheveux!,** I don't understand it at all, I'm tearing my hair out!; **tu t'arraches les yeux à lire dans le noir!,** you'll ruin your eyesight reading in the dark!; *Fig* **tout le monde la demande, on se l'arrache,** she's very much in demand; they're even fighting over her; **on se l'arrache,** *(d'un livre etc)* copies are being snatched up; *Fig* **impossible de m'a. de ce pays,** I could never tear myself away from this country; *Fig F* **alors? on s'arrache?,** do you want to go?
arracheur, -euse [araʃœr, -øz] **1** *n* tearer (down); *(potato etc)* lifter; *Fig* **mentir comme un a. de dents,** to lie through one's teeth. **2** *nf Agr* **arracheuse,** grubbing plough, grubber; (potato) lifter; (beet) puller.
arrachoir [araʃwar] *nm Agr* (potato) lifter; (beet) puller.
arraisonnement [arɛzɔnmɑ̃] *nm Nau* boarding *(of ship)*; **a. de la patente (d'un navire),** examination of the bill of health, sanitary report.
arraisonner [arɛzɔne] *Nau* **1** *vt* **a. un navire,** to hail *or* speak a vessel; *(l'aborder)* to stop and examine a ship. **2** *vi* **a. avec les autorités du port,** to report to the port authorities.
arrangeant, -ante [arɑ̃ʒɑ̃, -ɑ̃t] *adj* accommodating, helpful.
arrangement [arɑ̃ʒmɑ̃] *nm* **(a)** *(fait d'arranger)* arranging, putting in order; *(manière d'être arrangé)* arrangement *(of furniture etc)*; **l'a. des fleurs dans un vase,** the arranging *or* arrangement of flowers in a vase; **l'a. de ses cheveux demande un soin constant,** his hairstyle demands constant attention; **l'a. des mots dans une phrase,** the word order *or* the order of the words in a sentence; *Mus* **a. pour violon,** arrangement for violin; **(b)** *(accord)* agreement, settlement; *(officieux)* understanding; **mal prendre ses arrangements,** to arrange *or* plan things badly; **sauf a. contraire,** unless otherwise agreed; **essayer de trouver un a. financier avec son banquier,** to try to come to (some kind of) arrangement with one's banker.
arranger [arɑ̃ʒe] *v* **(j'arrangeais, n. arrangeons) 1** *vt* **(a)** to arrange *(furniture etc)*; to put *(books, room)* in order; to tidy (up) *(room)*; to straighten *(one's tie etc)*; *Mus* to arrange *(song for violin etc)*; *F* **le voilà bien arrangé!,** he does look a mess!; **a. qn de la belle manière,** to tell s.o. off (in no uncertain terms); *F* **on vous a arrangé,** you've been had, you've been taken for a ride;
(b) to repair, to overhaul *(car, watch etc)*; to mend *(watch)*; **je vais t'a. ça,** I'll fix it for you;
(c) to arrange, to organize *(concert etc)*; **a. qch d'avance,** to arrange *or* plan sth in advance; **il arrange bien sa vie,** he's got his life well organized; **je vous ai arrangé un entretien avec lui,** I've arranged a meeting with him for you; **ne t'en fais pas, j'ai tout arrangé,** don't worry, I've made all the arrangements;
(d) to settle *(quarrel etc)*; **je vais essayer d'a. les choses,** I'll try to put things right; **cela n'arrangera rien,** that won't (be much) help; **cela n'arrange pas nos affaires,** that's no good (to us), that doesn't help (us);
(e) *(plaire, satisfaire)* to suit, to be convenient for *(s.o.)*; **faire qch pour a. qn,** to do sth to help s.o.; **on ne peut pas a. tout le monde,** you can't please everybody; **tu ne fais que ce qui t'arrange,** you only do what suits you; **ça t'arrange?,** does that suit you?
2 s'arranger *vpr* **(a)** *(s'organiser etc)* to manage; **si vous pouvez vous a. pour le voir,** if you can manage to see him *or* make the time to see him; **arrangez-vous pour être là,** you must make sure to be there; **s'a. d'un vieux lit,** to make do with an old bed; *F* **je ne sais pas comment tu t'arranges, mais tu es toujours en retard,** I don't know how you manage it, but you're always late; **il s'arrange de tout,** he's very adaptable;
(b) *(soi-même)* to tidy oneself up;
(c) s'a. avec qn, to come to an agreement *or* to terms with s.o.; **arrangez-vous,** settle it among yourselves; **on s'est arrangé à l'amiable,** we came to an amicable arrangement *or* agreement;
(d) *(s'améliorer)* to work out; **cela s'arrangera,** things will turn out all right; **cela s'arrangera tout seul,** that will sort itself out; **ça ne s'arrange pas!,** it's not getting any better!; **ça n'a pas l'air de s'a. entre eux,** things don't seem to have got any better between them;
(e) *F* **tu t'es fait mal? tu t'es bien arrangé!,** have you hurt yourself? look what a state *or* mess you're in!
arrangeur, -euse [arɑ̃ʒœr, -øz] *n Mus* arranger.
arrérages [areraʒ] *nmpl* **(a)** arrears *(of wages, rent etc)*; **(b)** *(intérêt)* back interest; **coupon d'a.,** interest *or* dividend warrant; **toucher ses a.,** to draw one's pension; to draw one's dividends.
arrestation [arɛstasjɔ̃] *nf* arrest; **mettre qn en a.,** to take s.o. into custody; **en état d'a.,** under arrest.
arrêt [arɛ] *nm* **(a)** stop; stoppage; stopping; **a. d'urgence,** emergency stop; **point d'a.,** stopping place *ou* point; *Mus* pause *(over a rest)*; **faire un a. au cours de son voyage,** to break one's journey, *Am* to stop over; **a. en cours de route,** break of journey, *Am* stopover; **trajet sans a.,** non-stop journey; **New York est un a. obligatoire,** New York is an absolute must; **il neige sans a. depuis mercredi,** it's been snowing non-stop *or* continuously since Wednesday; **dix minutes d'a.,** ten minutes' stop; *(pour café, repos etc)* ten minutes' break; **temps d'a.,** pause, halt; **chien d'a.,** setter, pointer; *Fig* **rester** *ou* **tomber en a. devant qn/qch,** to stop and stare at s.o./sth; **marquer un temps d'a.,** to pause, to halt, to mark time; **mettre a. à un chèque,** to stop a cheque; *Méd* **a. (de cœur),** heart failure; **a. (inopiné),** breakdown; *Rad TV* **a. d'émission,** break in transmission; **robinet d'a.,** stopcock; *Rail* **signal d'a.,** stop signal;
(b) *(bus etc)* stop; **a. facultatif,** request stop; **ne pas descendre avant l'a.,** do not get off before the bus *or* train *etc* has come to a complete stop;
(c) stop, catch *(of door etc)*; tumbler *(of a lock)*; **cran d'a.,** safety catch; **a. de pied,** toeclip;
(d) *Jur* judgement, adjudication *(prononcé par la cour d'assises, cour d'appel ou cour de cassation)* **prononcer** *ou* **rendre un a.,** to pronounce *or* deliver judgement; **a. par défaut,** judgement by default; **a. de défense,** stay of execution; **a. de mort,** death sentence; *Fig* **les arrêts de la Providence,** the decrees of Providence; **les arrêts de la mode,** the dictates of fashion;
(e) arrest; **ordre** *ou* **mandat d'a.,** warrant for the arrest *(of s.o.)*; **mettre un officier aux arrêts,** to put an officer

under arrest; **arrêts à la chambre, arrêts domestiques,** house arrest; **être en maison d'a.,** to be in prison, to be under *or* to be held in detention;

(f) seizure, impounding, attachment; **faire a. sur des marchandises,** to impound *or* seize goods;

(g) *Fb* tackle; *Rugby Fb* **a. de volée,** fair catch; **faire un a. de voleé,** to make a mark;

(h) *Nau* detention (*of ship*).

arrêt-court [arɛkur] *nm Can Baseball* shortstop.

arrêté [arete] **1** *adj* **(a)** (*of ideas etc*) fixed, decided; **homme aux opinions arrêtées,** dogmatic man, man with set ideas; (*décidé*) man with decided views; **c'est une chose arrêtée,** it's already been decided; **dessein a.,** settled design; **(b)** *Sp* **départ a.,** standing start. **2** *nm* **(a)** decision, order, decree; **a. ministériel,** departmental order (signed by a minister); **a. municipal,** by(e)-law; **a. d'exécution,** decree providing for the enforcement of a law; **(b)** *Com* **a. de compte(s),** settlement (of an account).

arrêter [arete] **1** *vt* **(a)** to stop (*s.o., sth*); to check (*attack*); to bring (*vehicle*) to a standstill; to hold up, to delay; to keep back; to detain (*person*); to stem (*flood, torrent etc*); **a. un cheval,** to pull up a horse; **rien ne l'arrêtera,** nothing will stop him, he will stop at nothing; **quel obstacle vous arrête?,** what's stopping you?; **a. le vent,** to break (the force of) the wind; *Aut* **a. le moteur,** to switch off the engine; **a. le paiement d'un chèque,** to stop (payment of) a cheque; **a. la croissance,** to arrest growth; **le brouillard/la neige a complètement arrêté toute circulation,** fog/snow has brought traffic to a (complete) standstill; *Fb* **a. un tir,** to save *or* stop a shot; **a. le gibier,** (*of dog*) to point game;

(b) (*fixer*) to fix, to fasten, to secure (*shutter, plank etc*); **a. l'attention,** to arrest attention; **je voudrais a. votre attention sur ce point,** I'd like to draw your attention to this point; **ce détail arrêta mon attention,** this detail caught my attention; *Couture* **a. un point,** to fasten off a stitch; *Tricot* **a. les mailles,** to cast off;

(c) to arrest, to seize (*criminal*); to seize (*contraband, books etc*); **l'assassin n'est pas encore arrêté,** the murderer is still at large;

(d) (*déterminer*) to decide sth; **a. un jour,** to fix *or* appoint a day; **la date n'a pas encore été arrêtée,** the date has not yet been decided on *or* fixed; **a. un prix,** to fix a price; **a. un programme/un projet,** to draw up a programme/plan; **il a été arrêté que la séance débuterait à 14 heures,** it has been decided that the meeting will begin at 2 o'clock;

(e) *Com* to make up, to close, to settle (*account*).

2 *vi* to stop, to halt; **dites au chauffeur d'a. devant l'hôtel de ville,** tell the driver to stop at the town hall *or* in front of the town hall; **elle n'arrête jamais de parler,** she never stops talking; **elle est toujours occupée à laver, elle n'arrête pas,** she's always washing something or other, she never stops; **arrête!, arrêtez!,** stop (it)!; that's enough!

3 s'arrêter *vpr* **(a)** (*s'immobiliser*) to stop, to come to a stop *or* a standstill; (*of moving body*) to come to rest; **s.'a. court,** to stop short; **ma montre s'est arrêtée,** my watch has stopped; **la voiture s'est arrêtée,** the car stopped *or* pulled up; (*en s'approchant*) the car drew up; **s'a. en route,** to break one's journey; **nous nous sommes arrêtés dans un village pittoresque,** we stopped in a picturesque village; **s'a. chez qn,** to call at s.o.'s house *etc*; **passer sans s'a.,** to pass without stopping;

(b) (*cesser*) to stop; **la pluie va s'a.,** the rain will stop *or* it will stop raining soon; **s'a. de faire qch,** to stop doing sth; **s'a. de fumer,** to give up smoking;

(c) (*faire attention à*) to fix one's attention (*on sth*); to dwell, to insist (*à qch,* on sth); **il ne faut pas s'a. aux apparences,** one should not pay too much attention to (outward) appearances.

arrhes [ar] *nfpl* deposit; **verser des a.,** to pay a deposit; **stipulation d'a.,** right to annul a sale by paying a fine.

arriération [arjerɑsjɔ̃] *nf Psy* retardation; backwardness (*of child etc*).

arrière [arjɛr] **1** *adv* **(a) en a.,** (*à une certaine distance*) behind; **rester en a.,** (*ne pas aller, sortir*) to remain *or* stay behind; (*en se promenant avec d'autres personnes*) to lag behind; *Nau* **avoir le vent en a.,** to have the wind astern; **en a. de qn/qch,** behind s.o./sth; **il est resté en a. de sa classe,** he stayed at the bottom of the class; **en a. de son siècle** *ou* **de son temps,** behind the times;

(b) (*en retard*) **locataire en a. pour ses loyers,** tenant in arrears with his *or* her rent;

(c) (*derrière*) backwards; **a.!,** (stand) back!; **cheveux en a.,** hair brushed *or* combed back, hair swept back; **revenir en a.,** to come back; **pencher la tête en a.,** to lean one's head back; **retourner en a.,** to go *or* turn back; *Fig* **il faut remonter loin en a. pour trouver une épidémie de ce genre,** you have to go back a long way (in, into history) to find such an epidemic; *Fig* **vous revenez en a., nous avons déjà parlé de ça,** you're going (back) over previous ground, we've already talked about *or* covered that; *Fig* **pas la peine de revenir en a., c'est oublié,** there's no point in looking back, it's all been forgotten; **regarder en a.,** to look back; *Nau* **en a. (à) toute (vitesse)!,** full speed astern!

2 *adj inv* back; **essieu a.,** back axle, rear axle; **faire marche a.,** to back; *Nau* to go astern; *Aut* to reverse; *Fig* to back down, to backtrack, to retract; *Aut* **feu a.,** rear light; **à moteur a.,** rear-engined; **siège** *ou* **banquette a.,** back seat (*of car*); **siège a. (de motocyclette),** pillion seat; *Couture* **point a.,** backstitch.

3 *nm* **(a)** back, back part, rear (*of house etc*); **assis à l'a. de la voiture,** sitting in the back of the car; *Aut* **un modèle tout à l'a.,** a rear-engined model; *Mil* **l'a.,** the rear; *Fig* **protéger ses arrières,** to protect one's rear, to leave oneself a way out;

(b) *Nau* stern (*of ship*); **vers l'a.,** aft, abaft; **sur l'a.,** astern; **aller à l'a.,** to go aft;

(c) *Fb* (full) back; *Rugby Fb* full back; *Fb* **a. gauche,** left back.

arriéré, -ée [arjere] **1** *adj* **(a)** late, behind(hand), in arrears; **paiement a.,** overdue *or* outstanding payment; **(b) être a.,** (*d'une personne*) to be behind the times; **idées arriérées,** old-fashioned ideas; *Écon* **pays arriérés,** underdeveloped *or* backward countries; **(c)** (*attardé*) backward (*child*). **2** *nm* arrears (*of account etc*); backlog (*of work, correspondence etc*); **a. du loyer,** rent arrears, arrears of rent; *Mil* **a. de solde,** back pay; **a. de permissions,** accumulated leave. **3** *n* backward *or* retarded person.

arrière-ban [arjɛrbɑ̃] *nm Fig* **tout le monde était là, le ban et l'a.-b. de ses connaissances,** they were all there, everybody and anybody he ever knew.

arrière-bassin [arjɛrbasɛ̃] *nm* inner dock; (*pl arrière-bassins*).

arrière-bouche [arjɛrbuʃ] *nf* back of the mouth; *Spéc* fauces; (*pl arrière-bouches*).

arrière-boutique [arjɛrbutik] *nf* back (premises) (*of a shop*); back shop, *US* back store; (*pl arrière-boutiques*).

arrière-cour [arjɛrkur] *nf* backyard; (*pl arrière-cours*).

arrière-cuisine [arjɛrkɥizin] *nf* scullery, back kitchen; (*pl arrière-cuisines*).

arrière-défense [arjɛrdefɑ̃s] *nf Fb* (the) back four (defence), the backs; (*pl arrière-défenses*).

arrière-fond [arjɛrfɔ̃] *nm* innermost depth(s); (*pl arrière-fonds*).

arrière-garde [arjɛrgard] *nf Mil* rearguard; *Nau* rear squadron; **c'est un professeur d'a.-g,** he's a teacher of the old guard; (*pl arrière-gardes*).

arrière-gorge [arjɛrgɔrʒ] *nf* back of the throat; **voix d'a.-g.,** throaty voice; (*pl arrière-gorges*).

arrière-goût [arjɛrgu] *nm* aftertaste, faint taste (**de,** of); (*pl arrière-goûts*).

arrière-grand-mère [arjɛrgrɑ̃mɛr] *nf* great-grandmother; (*pl arrière-grand-mères*).

arrière-grand-père [arjɛrgrɑ̃pɛr] *nm* great-grandfather; (*pl arrière-grands-pères*).

arrière-grands-parents [arjɛrgrɑ̃parɑ̃] *nmpl inv* great-grandparents.

arrière-main [arjɛrmɛ̃] *nm* **(a)** *Tennis etc* **(coup d')a.-m.,** backhand (stroke); **(b)** (hind)quarters (*of horse*); (*pl arrière-mains*).

arrière-neveu, -nièce [arjɛrnəvø, -njɛs] *n* grand-nephew, -niece; (*pl arrière-neveux, -nièces*).

arrière-pays [arjɛrpei] *nm inv* hinterland.

arrière-pensée [arjɛrpɑ̃se] *nf* ulterior motive; (*pl arrière-pensées*).

arrière-petit-fils, -petite-fille [arjɛpətifis, -pətitfij] *n* great-grandson, -grand-daughter; (*pl arrière-petits-fils, -petites-filles*).

arrière-petit-neveu, -petite-nièce [arjɛrpətinəvø, -pətitnjɛs] *n* great-grand-nephew, -niece; (*pl arrière-petits-neveux, -petites-nièces*).

arrière-petits-enfants [arjɛrpətizɑ̃fɑ̃] *nmpl* great-grandchildren.

arrière-plan [arjɛrplɑ̃] *nm* background; **à l'a.-p.,** in the background; (*derrière, en arrière*) at the back; *Th* upstage; *Fig* **ce projet est passé à l'a.-p.,** this plan has been shelved; *Fig* **se trouver relégué à l'a.-p.,** to be pushed into the background; *Th Fig* to be upstaged; (*pl arrière-plans*).

arrière-pont [arjɛrpɔ̃] *nm Nau* after deck; (*pl arrière-*

ponts).

arrière-port [arjɛrpɔr] *nm* inner harbour; (*pl arrière-ports*).

arriérer [arjere] *v* (**j'arrière, n. arriérons, j'arriérerai**) **1** *vt* to postpone, to delay, to defer (*payment etc*). **2 s'arriérer** *vpr* to fall into arrears.

arrière-saison [arjɛrsɛzɔ̃] *nf* (*pl arrière-saisons*) **(a)** late season, late autumn *or Am* fall; **(b)** *Agr* **les pêches sont chères dans l'a.-s.,** peaches are expensive at the end of the season.

arrière-salle [arjɛrsal] back room; (*pl arrière-salles*).

arrière-train [arjɛrtrɛ̃] *nm (of animal)* (hind)quarters; *F* (*of person*) rump, rear; (*pl arrière-trains*).

arrimage [arimaʒ] *nm Nau etc* **(a)** stowing, trimming (*of ship's cargo etc*); **bois d'a.,** dunnage; **(b)** (*stock*) stowage; **(c)** trim (*of ship*); **(d)** docking (*of spacecraft*).

arrimer [arime] **1** *vt* **(a)** *Nau etc* to stow (*cargo etc*); to trim (*ship*); **(b)** to secure *or* fasten (*gun for travelling etc*); **a. un chargement sur le toit d'une voiture,** to secure *or* fasten a load to the roof of a car. **2** *vi Astronaut* to dock.

arrimeur [arimœr] *nm Nau* **(a)** stower, trimmer; **(b)** (*docker*) stevedore.

arrivage [arivaʒ] *nm* arrival; consignment (*of goods*); **l'a. de vacanciers,** the influx *or* the (annual) descent of holidaymakers; *Fin* **a. de fonds de l'étranger,** accession of funds from abroad.

arrivant, -ante [arivɑ̃, -ɑ̃t] *n* arrival; **le dernier a.,** the last person to arrive; **les nouveaux arrivants,** the new arrivals, the newcomers.

arrivé, -ée [arive] **1** *adj* **être a. socialement,** to have made it in society. **2** *n* (*personne*) arrival; **un nouvel a.,** a newcomer, a new arrival.

arrivée [arive] *nf* **(a)** (*de personne etc*) arrival, coming; advent (*of new development, situation*); **on attend son a. pour la semaine prochaine,** he *or* she is expected to arrive next week; **à mon a.,** when I arrived; **gare d'a.,** station at which the train arrives; **arrivées,** arrivals; **tableau des arrivées,** arrivals board; **heures d'a.,** (*of mail*) times of delivery; **l'a. du printemps,** the coming *or* arrival *or* onset of spring; **(b)** inlet (*for steam etc*); intake, admission; *Tech* **a. (d'huile),** (oil) feed; **(c)** *Sp* (winning) post; finish; **ligne d'a.,** finishing line.

arriver [arive] *vi* (*aux* **être**) **(a)** to arrive, to come; **a. en voiture,** to come by car; **il est arrivé en courant,** he came running up; **il arrive de voyage,** he is just back from a journey; **a. chez soi,** to arrive home, to get back home; **a. à temps,** to be on *or* in time; **a. en retard,** to be late; **a. le premier,** to come *or* finish first; **a. dans les premiers,** to be among the first to finish; **le printemps est arrivé,** spring is here!, spring has arrived!; **l'avion devait a. à midi,** the plane was due at midday; **j'arrive!,** (I'm) coming!, I'll be with you in a moment!; **arrivez (vite)!,** hurry up!; **nous sommes presque arrivés,** we're almost there; **mangeons, ça la fera peut-être a.,** let's start eating, maybe that'll make her come;

(b) a. à un endroit, to reach *or* get to *or* arrive at a place; **a. par le train/le bateau,** to come by train/boat; **a. à bon port,** to arrive safely; **le paquet m'est arrivé trop tard,** the parcel reached me too late; **l'eau m'arrive aux chevilles,** the water comes up to my ankles; **ma fille m'arrive déjà à l'épaule,** my daughter comes up to my shoulder already; *Fig* **a. à la vérité,** to arrive at *or* get at the truth; *Fig* **a. au fait,** to come to the point;

(c) j'en étais arrivé là lorsque ..., I had got to that point when ...; **j'en arrive à me demander s'il n'est pas stupide,** I'm beginning to wonder whether he's stupid or something; *F* **si c'est pas malheureux d'en a. là!,** it's such a pity to be reduced to that!, what a pity it's come to that!; **en a. aux coups,** to come to blows;

(d) (*socialement*) to succeed; **c'est un homme qui arrivera,** he is a man who will succeed *or* get on *or* do well;

(e) (*parvenir*) to succeed; **a. à ses fins,** to succeed in one's aims *or* plans; **avec du courage on arrive à tout,** with courage one can achieve anything; **a. à faire qch,** to succeed in doing sth; **pour a. à le lui faire accepter, il faut être patient,** to get him to accept it, you'll *etc* just have to be patient; **je n'arrive pas à y croire,** I just can't believe it; **comment y a.?,** how can it be done?; **tu n'arriveras jamais à rien!,** you'll never amount to anything!, you'll never get anywhere in life!; *F* **tu y arrives?,** can you do *or* manage *or* get *or* make it?;

(f) (*se produire*) to happen, to occur; **cela arrive tous les jours,** it happens every day; *Prov* **un malheur n'arrive jamais seul,** misfortunes never come singly; **ça n'arrive qu'aux autres,** it's something that happens to other people; **cela ne nous arrivera jamais,** it will never happen to us; **cela n'arrive qu'à nous!,** just our luck!; **il lui est arrivé un accident,** he had an accident; **cela arrive à tout le monde,** it can happen to anyone; **quoi qu'il arrive,** whatever happens, whatever may happen, come what may; **devine ce qu'il m'arrive!?,** guess what!, guess what's happened (to me)!?; **il m'arrive souvent d'oublier,** I often forget, I'm apt to forget; **il pourrait a. qu'il se trompe,** he might have made a mistake, it could be that he's made a mistake; **s'il vous arrivait de la voir, dites-le-lui,** if you (should) happen to see her, tell her.

arrivisme [arivism] *nm Péj* unscrupulous ambition.

arriviste [arivist] *n Péj* (social) climber; careerist.

arrogance [arɔgɑ̃s] *nf* arrogance.

arrogant, -ante [arɔgɑ̃, -ɑ̃t] **1** *adj* arrogant, overbearing. **2** *n* arrogant person.

arroger (s') [sarɔʒe] *vpr* (**je m'arrogeai(s); n.n. arrogeons**) **s'a. un droit/un privilège,** to assume *or* claim a right/a privilege; **s'a. la meilleure chambre,** to take the best room as a matter of course.

arrondi [arɔ̃di] **1** *adj* **(a)** rounded, round; **visage a.,** round face; **chiffre a.,** round number; **(b)** well rounded (*sentence etc*). **2** *nm* **(a)** roundness, rounded form; round-off (*of edge etc*); *Av* fillet, fillet radius; **l'a. du visage,** the round shape *or* roundness of the face; **(b)** *Av* flare out; **atterrissage avec a.,** flared landing; **(c)** hemline (*of skirt*).

arrondir [arɔ̃dir] **1** *vt* **(a)** to round (*sth*) (off); to make (*sth*) round; **cette coupe de cheveux arrondit ton visage,** that haircut makes your face look round(er); **a. une jupe,** to level a skirt; **a. son bras,** to flex one's (arm) muscles; **les yeux arrondis par l'étonnement,** in wide-eyed astonishment;

(b) *Fig* **a. les angles,** to smooth down the rough edges, to smooth things over; *Ling* **a. une voyelle,** to round a vowel;

(c) *Fin etc* **a. sa fortune,** to get together a considerable capital; **a. ses fins de mois,** to supplement one's income; **vous pouvez a. à deux cent francs,** you can round it up to two hundred francs; **a. au franc supérieur,** to round up to the nearest franc; **a. son champ,** to add to *or* to round off one's land; *Math* **a. un résultat,** to correct a result (to the nearest whole number *or* to so many decimal places);

(d) *Nau* **a. un cap,** to round *or* double a cape;

(e) *Av* to flare out (*before touchdown*).

2 s'arrondir *vpr* to become rounded; to round out, to fill out; **pendant la grossesse, elle s'est arrondie,** she swelled up during her pregnancy; **sa fortune s'arrondit,** his fortune is growing.

arrondissement [arɔ̃dismɑ̃] *nm* **(a)** *Admin* arrondissement (*in Paris, Marseilles, Lyons*); ≈ (London) borough; (postal) district; major subdivision (*of département*); **(b)** rounding (off) (*of sentence, territory etc*); **(c)** roundness.

arrosage [arozaʒ] *nm* **(a)** watering; sprinkling, spraying (*of lawn etc*); wetting, moistening (*of dough etc*); *F* **un bon a.,** a good soaking; *Mil* heavy bombing *or* shelling; **a. des rues,** watering of the streets; **voiture d'a.,** water cart; **(b)** (*publicité*) bombardment; flood (*of advertising*); **l'a. continuel par les médias,** the constant media bombardment; **(c)** irrigation (*of a meadow*); **(d)** watering, diluting (*of wine etc*); **(e)** celebrating (*with drinks*).

arroser [aroze] *vt* **(a)** to water (*streets, plants*); to sprinkle, to spray (*lawn*); (*of advertising*) to bombard; *Culin* **a. un rôti,** to baste a joint; *Mil* **a. une ville,** to bomb *or* shell a town; **yeux arrosés de larmes,** eyes bathed in tears; *F* **j'ai été bien arrosé,** I got soaking wet; **bifteck arrosé d'une bouteille de bordeaux,** steak washed down with a bottle of claret; **café arrosé,** laced coffee; **(b) a. une prairie,** to irrigate a meadow; **rivière qui arrose une région,** river that waters a district; **la Seine arrose Paris,** the Seine flows through Paris; **(c)** to water down, to dilute (*wine, milk*); **(d)** *Fig F* **a. qn pour obtenir qch de lui,** to grease s.o.'s palm to get sth from him. **2 s'arroser** *vpr* **les cactus ça ne s'arrose pas,** cactuses don't need watering.

arroseur [arozœr] *nm* (*device*) sprinkle.

arroseuse [arozøz] *nf* (*de rue*) water(ing) cart, street sprinkler.

arrosoir [arozwar] *nm* watering can.

arr(t) *abrév* **arrondissement.**

arsenal, -aux [arsənal, -o] *nm* **(a)** *Mil* arsenal; **a. maritime** *ou* **de la marine,** naval dockyard; **(b) a. d'artillerie,** gun factory; **découverte d'un a. chez un particulier,** discovery of an arsenal of weapons in s.o.'s house; **(c)** *F* gear, paraphernalia; **il emporta son a. de drogues,** he took his whole stock of drugs with him.

arsenic [arsənik] *nm Ch* arsenic.

art [ar] *nm* **(a)** (*technique*) art, craft; **le Salon des Arts Ménagers,** ≈ the Ideal Home Exhibition; **les arts ménagers,** art of housekeeping, homecraft; **l'a. militaire** *ou* **de la guerre,** the art of war; **l'art poétique,** poetics; **l'a. culinaire,** the art of (good) cooking; **c'est un homme de l'a.,** he's a dab hand, he knows what he's doing;
(b) (*esthétique*) art; **l'a. pour l'a.,** art for art's sake; **a. égyptien/italien,** Egyptian/Italian art; **beaux-arts,** fine arts; **œuvre d'a.,** work of art; **ville d'a.,** city of artistic interest; **livre d'a.,** art book; **histoire de l'a.,** history of art; **a. déco,** art deco;
(c) arts plastiques/graphiques, plastic/graphic arts; **le septième/le huitième/le neuvième a.,** cinema/television/cartoons;
(d) l'a. de, the art of ...; **elle a l'a. de soirées réussies,** she's got a flair for organizing successful parties; *F* **il a l'a. de m'énerver,** he's got the *or* a knack of getting me annoyed; **les Français ont l'a. de vivre,** French people know how to live well *or* are fond of good living; **il a l'a. et la manière de parler aux femmes,** he has a way with women;
(e) (*adresse*) skill;
(f) *Scol Can* **maître ès arts,** master of arts;
(g) *Constr* **travaux** *ou* **ouvrages d'a.,** = (generic term for) bridges, tunnels, viaducts etc; constructive works.
artefact [artefakt] *nm Biol* artefact, artifact.
artère [artɛr] *nf* **(a)** *Anat* artery; **on a l'âge de ses artères,** you're as old as you feel; **(b)** *Fig* (*route etc*) main highway, thoroughfare.
artériel, -ielle [arterjɛl] *adj Physiol* arterial; **tension artérielle,** blood pressure.
artériosclérose [arterjɔskleroz] *nf Méd* arteriosclerosis.
artésien, -ienne [artezjɛ̃, -jɛn] *adj* Artesian (*well*).
arthrite [artrit] *nf Méd* arthritis; **a. sèche** *ou* **déformante,** rheumatoid arthritis.
arthritique [artritik] *Méd* **1** *adj* arthritic (*patient*). **2** *n* arthritic (patient), sufferer from arthritis.
arthro- [artrɔ] *préf* arthro-.
arthropode [artrɔpɔd] *nm* arthropod.
arthrose [artroz] *nf Méd* osteoarthritis.
Arthur [artyr] *nm* Arthur.
artichaut [artiʃo] *nm* (*légume*) globe artichoke; *Culin* **fonds d'artichauts,** artichoke hearts; *Fig* **c'est un cœur d'a.,** he *or* she flits from one affair to another.
article [artikl] *nm* **(a)** *Com* article, commodity; **articles,** goods, wares; **a. en réclame,** special offer; **nous ne suivons plus cet a.,** we don't stock that item any more; **articles de voyage,** travel goods; **articles de ménage,** household requisites; **articles de toilette,** toiletries; **a. pour hommes/femmes,** menswear/ladies' wear;
(b) item (*of bill etc*); **articles divers,** sundries;
(c) article (*in newspaper etc*); **a. de tête** *ou* **de fond,** editorial, leader, leading article; **un a. de dictionnaire,** a dictionary entry;
(d) article, clause (*of treaty etc*); **a. de foi,** article of faith;
(e) (*point critique*) critical point; **ce qu'il a dit à l'a. de la mort,** what he said just before he died; **être à l'a. de la mort,** to be at the point of death;
(f) *Bot Ent* joint;
(g) *Gram* **a. défini/indéfini,** definite/indefinite article.
articulaire [artikylɛr] *adj Anat* articular, articulatory; *Méd* **rhumatisme a.,** rheumatoid arthritis.
articulation [artikylasjɔ̃] *nf* **(a)** *Anat etc* joint; *Spéc* articulation; *Bot* node; **a. du doigt,** knuckle; **(b)** *Tech* connection, joint; **accouplement à a.,** jointed coupling; **a. à rotule,** ball-and-socket joint; **(c)** (*en parlant*) articulation, (manner of) speech; **(d) l'a. des idées d'un texte,** the structuring of ideas in a text; **(e)** *Jur* numeration (*of facts*).
articulé [artikyle] *adj* **(a)** articulate(d); jointed (*limb, coupling etc*); hinged; **poupée articulée,** doll with movable joints; *MecE* **courroie articulée,** chain belt, link belt; **(b)** *Ling* articulate (*speech*).
articuler [artikyle] **1** *vt* **(a)** (*assembler*) to articulate, to hinge, to link, to joint; **(b)** *Ling* to articulate; to pronounce distinctly; *Fig* (*dire*) **il n'a même pas pu a. son nom tant il était terrorisé,** he was so afraid he couldn't even say his own name; **(c)** *Jur* to enumerate, to set forth (*facts*); to state (*fact*) clearly *or* definitely. **2 s'articuler** *vpr* to be joined together; **la façon dont les os s'articulent,** the way the bones are joined together; **ces deux parties s'articulent assez bien,** the two parts of the text hang together well. **3** *vi* to articulate; **mal a.,** to mumble; **articule!,** speak clearly!, *Fml* articulate!
artifice [artifis] *nm* (*ruse*) artifice, contrivance, stratagem; **user de tous les artifices pour ...,** to resort to every trick (in the book) in order to ...; **les artifices de la toilette,** the little tricks women use to make themselves (look) beautiful; **feu d'a.,** fireworks; (*spectacle*) firework display; **pièce d'a.,** set piece.
artificialité [artifisjalite] *nf* artificiality.
artificiel, -ielle [artifsjɛl] *adj* artificial; imitation (*pearl etc*); false (*teeth etc*); **lumière/glace/fleur artificielle,** artificial light/ice/flowers; **jambe artificielle,** artificial leg; **colorant a.,** artificial colouring; **classification artificielle,** arbitrary classification; **rire a.,** forced laugh.
artificiellement [artifisjɛlmɑ̃] *adv* artificially.
artificier [artifisje] *nm* firework manufacturer; master of ceremonies (*at firework display*).
artificieusement [artifisjøzmɑ̃] *adv Litt* deceitfully, craftily.
artificieux, -ieuse [artifisjø, -jøz] *adj Litt* deceitful, wily.
artillerie [artijri] *nf* **(a)** artillery, ordnance; **a. de campagne,** field artillery; **a. légère/lourde,** light/heavy artillery; **a. navale,** naval artillery; **a. anti-chars,** *Belg* **a. anti-blindés,** anti-tank artillery; **a. anti-aérienne,** anti-aircraft artillery; **a. d'assaut,** assault artillery *or* guns; **tir d'a.,** artillery fire; *Aut* **roue type a.,** artillery type wheel; **(b)** (*collectif*) gunnery.
artilleur [artijœr] *nm* artilleryman, gunner.
artimon [artimɔ̃] *nm Nau* **(mât d')a.,** mizzenmast; **voile d'a.,** mizzen (sail); **a. de cape,** storm mizzen.
artisan, -ane [artizɑ̃, -an] *n* artisan, craftsman; *Fig* **il est l'a. de sa réussite,** he brought about his own success, he's the author *or* architect of his own success.
artisanal, -aux [artizanal, -o] *adj* **métier a.,** craft; **production artisanale,** small-scale production (by craftsmen); **magasin a.,** craft shop; **poterie artisanale,** handmade pottery.
artisanalement [artizanalmɑ̃] *adv* by artisans, by craftsmen.
artisanat [artizana] *nm* craftsmen (*as a class*); **l'a. indigène,** the native craftsmen; **encourager l'a.,** to encourage small-scale industry *or* the craft industries; **a. d'expression,** arts and crafts, handicrafts; **produits d'a. régional,** local handicrafts.
artiste [artist] **1** *n* **(a)** artist (*including musician etc*); **a. peintre,** painter; **(b)** *Th Mus* performer; *Th* actor, *f* actress; singer; dancer; (*en général*) entertainer; *Fml* artiste; **entrée des artistes,** stage door. **2** *adj* artistic (*temperament, style*); *Fig* **eh l'a.!, viens par là!,** hey, smarty pants, come over here!
artistement [artistəmɑ̃] *adv* artistically, tastefully.
artistique [artistik] *adj* artistic.
artistiquement [artistikmɑ̃] *adv* artistically.
arum [arɔm] *nm* (*fleur*) arum.
aryen, -enne [arjɛ̃, -ɛn] **1** *adj* Aryan. **2** *n* **A.,** Aryan.
as [ɑs] *nm* **(a)** *Cartes etc* ace; **amener deux as,** to throw two aces; **as de pique,** ace of spades; *F* rump (*of fowl*); *Culin* parson's nose; **être ficelé** *ou* **fichu comme l'as de pique,** to be dressed any old how; *Arg Fig* **être aux as** *ou* **plein aux as,** to be rolling (in it); **ma prime est passée à l'as,** my bonus never materialized; **les vacances sont passées à l'as,** that's the holidays out of the window; **(b)** (*dominoes*) one; **l'as blanc,** one blank; **(c)** *F* first-rater; (*aux jeux*) crack player, star; **au tennis c'est un as,** he's an ace at tennis; **as du volant,** crack (racing) driver; **quel as!,** what a brilliant driver *or* player *etc*!; **(d)** single-sculler (skiff).
a/s (*abrév* **aux soins de**) c/o.
A.S. *abrév* **assurances sociales.**
asbeste [azbɛst] *nm Minér* asbestos.
asbestose [azbɛstoz] *nf Méd* asbestosis.
ascendance [asɑ̃dɑ̃s] *nf* **(a)** *Astron* ascent; **(b)** (*de famille etc*) lineage; **l'une et l'autre famille avait une a. canadienne,** both families were of Canadian ancestry *or* descent; **a. maternelle,** forebears on his *or* her *etc* mother's side; **être d'a. noble,** to be of noble ancestry; **(c)** *Phys* **a. thermique,** thermal (current).
ascendant [asɑ̃dɑ̃] **1** *adj* ascending (*movement, current, scale, series*); upward (*motion etc*); *Av* **vol a.,** climbing flight; **course ascendante,** up stroke (*of piston*); **tuyau a.,** standpipe. **2** *nm* **(a)** *Astron etc* ascendant; **astre qui est à l'a.,** star in the ascendant; **(b)** (*influence*) ascendancy, influence; **avoir de l'a. sur qn,** to have the ascendancy over s.o., **elle subit l'a. de son mari,** she's dominated by her husband; **(c) ascendants,** ancestry; **(d)** *Astrol* rising sign; **Verseau a. Cancer,** Aquarius with Cancer as his rising sign *or* with Cancer in the ascendant.

ascenseur [asɑ̃sœr] *nm* lift, *Am* elevator; **a. de marchandises,** goods hoist; **a. à tous les étages,** lift to all floors; **a. à sas,** canal lift; **a. à saumon,** salmon ladder; *Fig* **renvoyer l'a.,** to reciprocate.

ascension [asɑ̃sjɔ̃] *nf* **(a)** ascent; rising (*of sap etc*); *Av* climb; **faire l'a. d'une montagne,** to climb a mountain; **une a. facile,** an easy climb; **l'a. du Mont Blanc,** the climbing *or* ascent of Mont Blanc; *Astron* **a. d'un astre,** ascension of a star; *Av* **angle d'a.,** climbing angle; **a. verticale,** *Av* vertical climb; *Astron* right ascension; *Rel* **fête** *ou* **jeudi de l'A.,** Ascension Day; **l'île de l'A.,** Ascension Island; **(b)** (*de personne*) progress, ascent; rise; **l'a. de Bonaparte,** the rise of Bonaparte.

ascensionnel, -elle [asɑ̃sjɔnɛl] *adj* upward (*motion*); *Av* **force ascensionnelle,** lifting power, lift; **vitesse ascensionnelle,** rate of climb, climbing speed; **mouvement a.,** up-stroke; *Sp* **parachutisme a.,** parascending.

ascensionner [asɑ̃sjɔne] *vi* to climb.

ascensionniste [asɑ̃sjɔnist] *n* climber, mountaineer.

ascèse [asɛz] *nf* asceticism.

ascète [asɛt] *n* ascetic.

ascétique [asetik] *adj* ascetic; **vie a.,** ascetic life.

ascétisme [asetism] *nm* asceticism.

ascorbique [askɔrbik] *adj* ascorbic (*acid*).

asdic [asdik] *nm Nau* (*abbr* **Allied Submarine Detection Investigation Committee**) asdic.

asepsie, aseptie [asɛpsi] *nf Méd* asepsis.

aseptique [asɛptik] *adj Méd* aseptic.

aseptisation [asɛptizasjɔ̃] *nf* (*d'une blessure, d'un pansement*) sterilization; (*d'une pièce*) disinfection.

aseptiser [asɛptize] *Méd vt* (*une blessure*) to sterilize; (*une pièce*) to disinfect; *Fig Péj* **un univers aseptisé,** a sanitized environment.

asexué [asɛksɥe] **, asexuel, -elle** [asɛksɥɛl] *adj Biol* asexual.

asiatique [azjatik] **1** *adj* Asian, Asiatic; **grippe a.,** Asian flu. **2** *n* **A.,** Asian, Asiatic.

Asie [azi] *nf* Asia; **l'A. Mineure,** Asia Minor.

asile [azil] *nm* **(a)** *Jur* sanctuary; **droit d'a.,** right of sanctuary; **a. politique/diplomatique,** political/diplomatic asylum; **demander l'a. politique,** to ask for political asylum; **(b)** (*abri*) shelter, refuge, retreat; **lieu d'a.,** (place of) refuge; **sans a.,** without refuge; *Arch* **a. des pauvres,** ≈ workhouse; **a. de nuit,** night shelter, *F* dosshouse; *F* **il faut le mettre à l'a.!,** he belongs in the loony bin *or US* at the funny farm!, he ought to be locked away!; **a. d'aliénés,** mental hospital, *Vieilli* lunatic asylum; **a. des marins,** sailors' home; *Litt* **a. de paix,** haven of peace; **le dernier a.,** the grave.

asinien, -ienne [azinjɛ̃, -jɛn] *adj* asinine.

asocial, -ale, -aux [asɔsjal, -o] *adj & n* asocial, maladjusted (person).

asparagus [asparagys] *nm* asparagus fern.

aspect [aspɛ] *nm* **(a)** (*vue*) sight, *Fml* aspect; **au premier a.,** at first sight *or* glance; **(b)** (*air*) aspect, appearance, look; **avoir un a. imposant,** to look imposing; **un démon qui pouvait prendre tous les aspects,** a demon who could take on any appearance; **(c)** (*angle*) angle, point of view; **considérer une affaire sous tous ses aspects,** to look at a problem from every angle *or* from all points of view; **je n'aime pas l'a. de l'affaire,** I don't like the look of the thing; **(d)** *Astrol* aspect, relative positions (*of stars*); **(e)** *Gram* aspect; **a. perfectif,** perfective.

asperge [aspɛrʒ] *nf* **(a)** (*plante*) asparagus; **a. plumeuse,** asparagus fern; **une botte d'asperges,** a bunch of asparagus; **pointe** *ou* **tête d'a.,** asparagus tip; **plant d'asperges,** asparagus bed; **(b)** *F* (*person*) beanpole.

asperger [aspɛrʒe] *vt* (**j'aspergeai(s), n. aspergeons**) to sprinkle (*linen etc*) with water; **a. qn d'eau bénite,** to sprinkle s.o. with holy water; **une voiture nous a aspergés d'eau,** a (passing) car sprayed us with water.

aspergès [aspɛrʒɛs] *nm Rel* **(a)** (*goupillon*) aspergillum, holy-water sprinkler; **(b)** (*rite*) Asperges.

aspérité [asperite] *nf* **(a)** unevenness, ruggedness, roughness (*of surface etc*); **(b)** asperity, harshness, sharpness (*of character, voice*).

asperme [aspɛrm] *adj Bot* seedless.

aspersion [aspɛrsjɔ̃] *nf* sprinkling; spraying (*of wound etc*); *Agr* drench.

aspersoir [aspɛrswar] *nm* **(a)** *Rel* aspergillum; **(b)** rose (*of watering can*).

asphaltage [asfaltaʒ] *nm Constr etc* asphalting.

asphalte [asfalt] *nm Minér* asphalt; **a. minéral,** pitch, bitumen; **route en a.,** asphalt road; *F* **arpenter l'a.,** to pace up and down the streets.

asphalter [asfalte] *vt* to asphalt (*road etc*).

asphérique [asferik] *adj Opt* aspheric(al).

asphodèle [asfɔdɛl] *nm* (*plante*) asphodel; **a. rameux,** branched lily, king's rod; **a. blanc,** king's spear.

asphyxiant [asfiksjɑ̃] **(a)** asphyxiating, suffocating; **gaz a.,** poison gas; **(b)** *Fig* stifling, suffocating (*atmosphere etc*).

asphyxie [asfiksi] *nf* asphyxia, asphyxiation, suffocation; *Min etc* gassing; *Fig* **a. économique,** economic strangulation.

asphyxié, -ée [asfiksje] **1** *adj* asphyxiated, suffocated (*person*); *Min etc* gassed; **mourir a.,** to die of asphyxiation. **2** *n* person who has been asphyxiated *or* who has (been) suffocated.

asphyxier [asfiksje] *v* (*pr sub & impf* **n. asphyxiions, v. asphyxiiez**) **1** *vt* to asphyxiate, to suffocate; *Min etc* to gas. **2 s'asphyxier** *vpr* (*accidentellement*) to be asphyxiated, to suffocate; (*au gaz*) to be gassed; (*exprès*) to suffocate oneself; (*au gaz*) to gas oneself.

aspic[1] [aspik] *nm* (*serpent*) asp.

aspic[2] *nm Culin* aspic.

aspidistra [aspidistra] *nm* (*plante*) aspidistra.

aspirant, -ante [aspirɑ̃, -ɑ̃t] **1** *adj* sucking; **pompe aspirante,** suction pump; **ventilateur a.,** suction fan; **course aspirante,** induction stroke, admission stroke. **2** *n* candidate. **3** *nm Nau* midshipman; *Mil* = officer cadet; *Nau* **a. pilote,** apprentice pilot.

aspirateur, -trice [aspiratœr, -tris] **1** *adj* aspiratory; suction (*device*). **2** *nm* (*pour la maison*) vacuum (cleaner), hoover ®; *Ch Ind Méd* (*gas, air*) exhauster; aspirator; **passer l'a. dans la maison,** to vacuum(-clean) *or* hoover ® the house; **passer une pièce/moquette à l'a.,** to vacuum(-clean) *or* hoover ® a room/rug; **un coup d'a.,** a quick once-over with the vacuum (cleaner) *or* hoover ®; **a. à céréales,** grain elevator; **a. de buées,** extractor fan.

aspiration [aspirasjɔ̃] *nf* **(a)** inhaling (of air into the lungs); *Spéc* inspiration; suction, sucking up (*of water into pump etc*); exhaustion; **ventilateur à a.,** exhaust fan; (*d'un moteur à combustion interne*) admission, induction; **clapet d'a.,** intake valve; **(b)** aspiration, yearning (**à, vers,** for, after); **aspirations à la scène,** ambitions to go on the stage; **(c)** *Ling* aspiration.

aspiré [aspire] *adj Ling* aspirate(d).

aspirée [aspire] *nf Ling* aspirate.

aspirer [aspire] **1** *vi* **(a)** (*inspirer*) to breath in, to inhale; **(b)** to aspire (**à,** to); **a. à la gloire/la célébrité,** to aspire to glory/fame; **a. à un poste,** to covet a post; **a. à faire qch,** to long to do sth; **elle aspire à devenir actrice,** she longs to become an actress. **2** *vt* **(a)** to inhale, to breathe (in) (*air, scent etc*); to sniff up (*powder etc*); **(b)** to suck up, to suck in, to draw (up) (*water etc*); **(c)** *Ling* to aspirate, to breathe (*a sound*); **l'h est aspiré en allemand,** the h is aspirated in German.

aspirine [aspirin] *nf Pharm* aspirin; **prenez deux aspirines,** take two aspirin(s).

assagir [asaʒir] **1** *vt* to make (*s.o.*) wiser; to sober (*s.o.*) (down); **le mariage l'a assagi,** marriage has made him settle down; **voilà qui l'assagira,** that will knock some sense into him; **la laque idéale pour a. les cheveux les plus rebelles,** the ideal lacquer to tame the most unmanageable hair. **2 s'assagir** *vpr* to settle down.

assagissement [asaʒismɑ̃] *nm* quietening (down), calming (down); (*d'esprits*) calming (down).

assaillant, -ante [asajɑ̃, -ɑ̃t] **1** *adj* attacking, assaulting. **2** *n* assailant, attacker, aggressor; (*assiégeant*) besieger; (*de l'avis opposé*) adversary.

assaillir [asajir] *vt* (*prp* **assaillant**, *pp* **assailli**, *pr ind* **j'assaille, n. assaillons, ils assaillent**, *impf* **j'assaillais**, *p hist* **j'assaillis**, *fu* **j'assaillirai**) to assault, to attack; **à mon retour j'ai été assailli de questions,** when I came back I was bombarded with questions; **de nombreuses difficultés l'assaillent,** he is beset by numerous difficulties.

assainir [asɛnir] **1** *vt* to make (*sth*) healthier; to cleanse, to purify (*atmosphere etc*); to sweeten (*soil etc*); to clean, to disinfect (*stable*); to drain (*marshes*); to improve the sanitation of (*town*); to stabilize (*currency, market etc*); **a. les finances/l'administration,** to reorganize finance/administration, *F* to put one's (*financial etc*) house in order; **a. une rivière,** to clean up a river. **2 s'assainir** *vpr* to become healthier; **la situation s'est assainie,** the situation has become healthier.

assainissant [asɛnisɑ̃] *adj* cleansing, purifying.

assainissement [asɛnismɑ̃] *nm* cleansing, purifying (*of atmosphere*); drainage (*of ground*); disinfecting (*of goods*); sweetening (*of soil etc*); improving of the sanitation (*of town*); *Fin* stabilization; **a. monétaire,** stabilization of the currency.

assaisonnement [asɛzɔnmɑ̃] *nm* **(a)** seasoning, flavouring (*of dish*); dressing (*of salad*); **(b)** (*aromate etc*) condiment, seasoning, flavouring; **(c)** *Fig* spice, zest, piquancy.

assaisonner [asɛzɔne] *vt* to season, to flavour (**de,** with); to dress (*salad*); *Fig F* **a. qn à grands reproches,** to give s.o. a real telling-off; **se faire a.,** to get a good telling-off.

assassin, -ine [asasɛ̃, -in] **1** *nm* murderer, *f* murderess; (*d'une personnalité politique etc*) assassin; **à l'a!,** murder!; **l'a. est Madame Duval,** the murderer is Mrs Duval. **2** *adj* **(a)** murderous (*horde etc*); **(b)** provocative, bewitching (*smile*).

assassinat [asasina] *nm* murder; (*d'une personnalité politique etc*) assassination; *Jur* premeditated murder, *US* murder in the first degree.

assassiner [asasine] *vt* to murder; to assassinate (*politician etc*); *F* to murder (*song etc*); **je ne vais pas vous a., c'est seulement 100 francs,** I'm not going to charge you the earth, it's only 100 francs.

assaut [aso] *nm* **(a)** (*attaque*) assault, attack, onslaught; *esp Mil* charge; **canon d'a.,** assault gun; **troupes d'a.,** storm troops; **a. à la baïonnette,** bayonet charge; **donner l'a. à,** to storm, to launch an attack on; *Fig* **partir à l'a. du Mont Blanc/d'une entreprise,** to set out to conquer Mont Blanc/to take over a firm; **les meilleures places ont été prises d'a.,** everybody made a rush for the best seats; **les assauts répétés d'une maladie,** the repeated attacks *or* onslaughts of a disease; **(b)** (*combat*) match, bout; **a. de lutte,** wrestling bout; **a. de boxe,** sparring match; **faire a. d'élégance/de zèle/de courtoisie/***etc*, to (try to) outdo each other in elegance/zeal/politeness/*etc*.

assèchement [asɛʃmɑ̃] *nm* drying (*of road*); draining, drainage (*of land, pond etc*); pumping dry (*of a mine*).

assécher [aseʃe] *v* (**j'assèche, n. asséchons; j'assècherai**) **1** *vt* to dry; to drain (*marsh etc*); to pump (*mine etc*) dry; to pump out (*mine*). **2** *vi* (*of land, stream etc*) to become dry, to dry up. **3 s'assécher** *vpr* to become dry, to dry up.

assemblage [asɑ̃blaʒ] *nm* **(a)** gathering (*of people*); collection, combination (*of objects*); blending (*of wines etc*); **a. de circonstances,** combination of circumstances; **(b)** assembling, assembly (*of parts of machine etc*); *Couture* sewing together; *Tricot* making up; gathering, collating, assembling (*of sheets*); **(c)** (*structure*) framework, support, structure; *Menuis etc* joint, jointing, joining, coupling, connection; **un a. de tiges métalliques,** an assembly *or* structure of metal shafts; **a. à queue d'aronde,** dovetail joint; **a. par vis/à rivets,** screw/rivet assembly; **a. à tenon et mortaise,** mortise-and-tenon joint; **(d)** *Ordinat* **langage d'a.,** assembly language; **programme d'a.,** assembler; **(e)** *El* connection; **a. en quantité,** parallel connection; **(f)** (*par soudure*) bond.

assemblée [asɑ̃ble] *nf* **(a)** (*réunion*) assembly; (*plus petite*) meeting; **se réunir en a.,** to assemble (for a meeting); **a. générale d'actionnaires,** general meeting of shareholders; **a. annuelle/extraordinaire,** annual/ extraordinary general meeting; **(b)** *Pol* **A. nationale,** National Assembly; *Br* ≈ House of Commons; *US* ≈ House of Representatives; **(c)** (*foule*) gathering; **une nombreuse a.,** a large gathering; **l'a. des fidèles,** the congregation.

assembler [asɑ̃ble] **1** *vt* **(a)** to assemble; to call (*people*) together; to convene (*committee etc*); to collect, to gather (together) (*ingredients, ideas, what one needs etc*); to blend (*wines etc*); *Nau* **a. l'équipage,** to muster the crew;

(b) to assemble, to fit together (*machine etc*); to collate (*documents*); to collate, to gather (*sheets*);

(c) *Menuis Tech etc* to join (up); to joint; to couple; **a. deux morceaux à plat,** to butt-joint two pieces; **a. deux pièces par soudure/collage,** to weld/glue two parts together;

(d) *Ordinat* to assemble (*program*); to link (*modules*);

(e) *El* to connect, to join up (*cells*).

2 s'assembler *vpr* to assemble, to meet, to gather; (*d'une foule*) to gather; **s'a. devant un spectacle insolite,** to gather in front of an unusual spectacle; **les membres s'assemblent deux fois par an,** the members meet twice a year; *Prov* **qui se ressemble s'assemble,** birds of a feather flock together.

assembleur, -euse [asɑ̃blœr, -øz] **1** *n* assembler; fitter (*of machines etc*). **2** *nf* **assembleuse,** (*machine*) gatherer. **3** *nm Ordinat* assembler.

asséner [asene] *vt* (**j'assène, n. assénons, j'assènerai**) to strike (*blow*); **coup bien asséné,** telling *or* well-planted blow; **a. une réplique,** to answer back like a shot; **la façon dont la propagande est assénée,** the way propaganda is thrust at you.

assentiment [asɑ̃timɑ̃] *nm* assent, consent, agreement; **avoir l'a. de tous,** to be supported unanimously; **sourire d'a.,** smile of consent.

asseoir [aswar] *v* (*prp* **asseyant;** *pp* **assis;** *pr ind* **j'assieds** [asje] , **il assied, n. asseyons, ils asseyent,** *or* **j'assois, il assoit, ils assoient;** *pr sub* **j'asseye, n. asseyions,** *or* **j'assoie;** *imp* **assieds, asseyons, asseyez;** *impf* **j'asseyais** *or* **j'assoyais;** *p hist* **j'assis;** *p sub* **j'assisse;** *fu* **j'assiérai, j'assoirai**) **1** *vt* **(a)** (*installer*) to seat, to sit, to set; **asseyez-le sur le gazon,** sit him down on the grass; **faire a. qn,** to ask s.o. to sit down *or* to take a seat;

(b) to place, to lay, to establish (*foundations etc*); **a. une pierre,** to bed a stone; **a. une statue sur un piédestal,** to stand a statue on a pedestal; **a. une tente/un camp,** to pitch a tent/(a) camp; *Av* **a. l'appareil,** to pancake; **a. son autorité/sa réputation,** to establish one's authority/ reputation; **a. une théorie sur des résultats scientifiques,** to base a theory on scientific results; **a. l'impôt sur le revenu,** to base taxation on income;

(c) a. une pension sur qn, to settle a pension on s.o.; **a. un impôt sur les tabacs,** to impose *or* lay *or* levy a tax on tobacco;

(d) *F* to amaze, to stagger; **ça m'assoit complètement de voir qu'il réussit aussi vite,** I'm staggered to see him succeeding so quickly.

2 s'asseoir *vpr* to sit (down); **s'a. par terre,** to sit on the ground; (*à l'intérieur*) to sit on the floor; **s'a. sur une chaise/dans une fauteuil,** to sit on a chair/in an armchair; **s'a. (sur son séant),** to sit up; *F* **s'a. sur qn,** to ignore s.o.; *F* **les ordres du patron, moi, je m'assois dessus,** I don't give a damn about the boss's orders!; **asseyez-vous,** (*à de nombreuses personnes*) sit down, be seated; (*à une ou deux personnes*) sit down, have *or* take a seat.

assermenté [asɛrmɑ̃te] *adj* sworn (in); (*witness etc*) on oath; **fonctionnaire a.,** sworn official; *Hist* **(prêtre) non a.,** non-juring (priest).

assermenter [asɛrmɑ̃te] *vt* to swear (*s.o.*) in, to administer the oath to (*s.o.*).

assertion [asɛrsjɔ̃] *nf* assertion.

asservi [asɛrvi] *adj* servo (*appliance*); **moteur a.,** servomotor.

asservir [asɛrvir] **1** *vt* **(a)** (*assujettir*) to enslave, to subjugate, to subdue; to reduce (*nation*) to slavery; **a. ses instincts,** to control one's instincts, to keep one's instincts under control; **être asservi à la mode,** to be a slave to fashion; **(b)** (*of actuating device etc*) to bring (*part*) under control. **2 s'asservir** *vpr* to submit.

asservissant [asɛrvisɑ̃] *adj* enslaving; **avoir un emploi a.,** to be tied down to one's job.

asservissement [asɛrvismɑ̃] *nm* **(a)** (*assujettissement*) (*d'un pays*) subjection (**à,** to); reduction to slavery; enslavement; (*envers qn plus fort*) subservience; **vivre dans l'a. des médias,** to believe everything the newspapers and television say; **(b)** control (*of mechanism*); servo control.

assesseur [asɛsœr] *nm* **(a)** *Jur* **(juge) a.,** assessor (*to magistrate etc*); **(b) être secondé par ses assesseurs,** to be supported by one's assistants.

assez [ase] *adv* **(a)** (*suffisamment*) enough; **vous travaillez bien a.,** you work quite enough; **elle parle a. bien l'anglais,** she speaks English quite *or* fairly well; **(c'est) a. parlé!,** (*agissons*) that's enough talking!; **j'ai dû attendre a. longtemps,** I had to wait quite a long time; **nous sommes a. de trois, plus serait trop,** three's enough, (any) more would be too many; **il est a. bête pour la croire!,** he's stupid enough to believe her; **il n'est pas a. bête pour dire oui,** he's not so stupid as to say yes; **être a. près pour voir,** to be near enough to see; **il n'avait pas a. pour vivre/pour acheter des cigarettes,** he hadn't enough to live on/enough (money) to buy cigarettes;

(b) (**a. de** + *n*) **il y a a. de temps que je l'attends,** I've been waiting for him long enough; **il y a a. de pain pour tous,** there's enough bread for everybody; **avez-vous a. d'argent?,** have you enough money?; **j'en ai a.!,** I've had enough (of it)!, I'm sick *or* tired of it!, I'm fed up!; **a. de promesses! des actes!,** enough (of) promises! let's see some action!; **en voilà a. sur ce sujet!,** that's enough about that!; **c'en est a.!,** that's enough of that!; **a. de larmes!,** stop crying!;

(c) *int* **a.!,** that's enough! stop!; **a.!, je ne veux plus t'entendre,** that's enough! I don't want to hear another sound out of you;

(d) (*plutôt*) rather, fairly, tolerably; **elle est a. jolie,** she's quite pretty; **je suis a. de votre avis,** I'm rather inclined to agree with you; **je suis a. content de ma carrière,** I'm quite *or* fairly happy with my career; **arriver a. tard,** to arrive rather *or* fairly late; **avoir a. de bon sens,** to have a fair amount *or* plenty of (common) sense; **il parle a. peu,** he doesn't talk much.

assidu [asidy] *adj* assiduous; industrious, hard-working, persevering (*employee, pupil etc*); constant (*care, attention*); regular, constant (*visitor*); **efforts assidus,** untiring efforts; **travailleur a.,** hard worker; **faire une cour assidue à qn,** to court s.o. assiduously; **présence assidue aux cours,** regular attendance at classes; **le médecin est a. auprès de ses malades,** the doctor takes good care of *or* is very attentive to his patients; **un amoureux a.,** a persistent suitor.

assiduité [asidɥite] *nf* (a) assiduity, perseverance; *Scol etc* regular attendance; **a. à (faire) qch,** assiduity in (doing) sth; **a. au travail,** devotion to work; (b) (*fréquence*) constant attention(s), constant care; **fréquenter qn avec a.,** to be a frequent visitor at s.o.'s house; **il la poursuit de ses assiduités depuis des années,** he's been forcing his attentions on her for years.

assidûment [asidymɑ̃] *adv* assiduously, unremittingly; **il y travaille a.,** he is hard at work on it.

assiégé, -ée [asjeʒe] **1** *adj* besieged. **2** *n* **les assiégés,** the besieged.

assiégeant, -ante [asjeʒɑ̃, -ɑ̃t] **1** *adj* besieging (*army etc*). **2** *n* besieger.

assiéger [asjeʒe] *vt* (**assiégeant, j'assiège, n. assiégeons, j'assiégerai**) to besiege, to lay siege to (*city, castle*); to surround, to crowd round (*person*); **les journalistes ont assiégé l'hôtel,** journalists besieged *or* laid siege to the hotel; **assiégé par l'inondation,** hemmed in by flood water; *Fig* **la ville est assiégée par les touristes,** the town is overrun with *or* by tourists; **a. qn de demandes,** to pester s.o. with requests.

assiette [asjɛt] *nf* (a) plate; **a. plate,** dinner plate; **a. creuse** *ou* **à soupe,** soup dish; **a. à dessert,** dessert plate; **manger dans une a.,** to eat off *or* from a plate; **elle mange le nez dans son a.,** she eats with her head right over her plate; *F* **a. au beurre,** cushy job; *Culin* **a. anglaise,** assorted cold meat(s), cold cuts;

(b) laying (down) (*of foundations*); bedding (*of stone*); pitching (*of camp*); laying out (*of railway line*); establishment (*of tax, of rates*); funding (*of annuity*);

(c) basis (*of a tax, of rules*); foundation, bottom, bed (*of a road*);

(d) seat (*on horse*); trim (*of boat*); situation, site (*of building etc*); disposition (*of camp*); lie (*of the land*); set (*of stone, beam etc*); *Av Nau* **angle d'a.,** trim angle; **avoir une bonne a.,** *Equitation* to have a good seat; *Nau* to be in good trim; *F* **ne pas être dans son a.,** to be out of sorts *or* off colour, not to be up to the mark; **a. des coupes,** felling plan; **prendre son a.,** (*of foundation, gun etc*) to set, to settle, to bed down.

assiettée [asjete] *nf* plate(ful); **une a. de potage,** a plate of soup.

assignable [asiɲabl] *adj* assignable (*limit*); (*cause, reason*) to which sth may be ascribed.

assignataire [asiɲatɛr] *adj* **banque a.,** warrant bank.

assignation [asiɲasjɔ̃] *nf* (a) *Fin* assignment, transfer (*of shares, of funds*) (**à,** to); (b) *Jur* (*action*) serving of a writ *or* summons *or* process; (*acte*) (writ of) summons, subpoena; **signifier** *ou* **faire** *ou* **donner** *ou* **envoyer une a. à,** to serve a writ on (*s.o.*), to issue a summons to (*s.o.*); to subpoena (*witness*); **a. à comparaître,** summons; **a. à résidence,** house arrest.

assigner [asiɲe] *vt* (a) to assign; to fix, to appoint (*time etc*); to fix, to arrange (*meeting*); to attribute, to ascribe (*cause*) (**à,** to); **a. une tâche à qn,** to assign *or* allot a job to s.o.; **être assigné d'un certain rôle,** to be assigned *or* allotted a certain role; **a. une somme à un paiement,** to earmark a sum for a payment, to allocate a sum to a payment; **a. une dépense sur le trésor public,** to charge an expense to public funds; (b) *Jur* to summon, to subpoena, to cite (*witness etc*); **a. qn en justice,** (*de la cour*) to issue a writ against s.o.; (*d'un demandeur*) to have a writ issued against s.o.; (*d'un huissier*) to serve a writ on s.o.; **a. qn à résidence,** to place s.o. under house arrest.

assimilable [asimilabl] *adj* easily assimilated (*knowledge, food*); **une maladie a. à une autre,** an illness comparable to another; **population très a.,** a population that assimilates easily.

assimilation [asimilasjɔ̃] *nf* (a) assimilation; **l'a. chlorophyllienne,** photosynthesis; *Ling* **a. de phonèmes,** assimilation of phonemes; **politique d'a.,** policy of assimilation; (b) *Mil Nau* correlation (*of ranks*).

assimilé [asimile] **1** *adj* (a) assimilated (*immigrants etc*); **le sucre et produits assimilés,** sugar and related products; (b) *Mil Nau* **être a. à ...,** to rank as *or* with, to be ranked as; **a. au grade de capitaine,** ranking *or* ranked as a captain. **2** *nm* **cadres et assimilés,** executives and acting executives; **officiers et assimilés,** officers and equivalent.

assimiler [asimile] **1** *vt* (a) to assimilate (*knowledge, immigrants etc*); (b) (*comparer*) to assimilate; to compare (**à,** to, with); **a. qch à,** to class sth as, to put sth in the same category as (*sth else*). **2 s'assimiler** *vpr* (*des aliments etc*) to be assimilated; (*d'immigrants etc*) to assimilate, to become assimilated; **ces minéraux s'assimilent facilement,** these minerals are easily assimilated; *Fig* **elle s'est assimilée la mentalité de ce milieu,** she now thinks the same way as the people she associates with.

assis [asi] *adj* sitting, seated; **nous étions a. auprès du feu,** we were sitting *or* seated round the fire; *F* **en rester a.,** to be flabbergasted; *Hér* **lion a.,** lion sejant; *Fig* **il a une situation bien assise,** he has a secure job; *Rail Th etc* **places assises,** seats; **il n'y a plus de places assises,** standing room only; **bien a. sur l'eau,** well trimmed (ship); *Jur* **magistrature assise,** the bench.

assise [asiz] *nf* (a) (*action*) seating, laying (*of foundation*); (b) seating, foundation; bed(plate) (*of engine etc*); *Géol* bed, stratum; **ajuster l'a. d'une soupape,** to seat a valve; (c) *Constr* course (*of masonry*); layer (*of cement*); (d) *Jur* **les assises,** the assizes; **cour d'assises,** Assize Court; **être envoyé devant la cour d'assises,** to be committed for trial; **avocat d'assises,** criminal lawyer; (e) **assises,** (*d'un congrès*) sittings; (*d'un syndicat*) conference; **tenir ses assises,** (*d'un parti*) to hold a conference; (*d'un club*) to hold a general meeting; (*d'un groupe d'amis*) to have a get-together; (f) *Hist* **les Assises de Jérusalem,** the Assizes of Jerusalem.

Assise [asiz] *nf* Assisi.

assistance [asistɑ̃s] *nf* (a) (*assemblée*) audience; *Sp* spectators; (*lors d'une manifestation etc*) onlookers; *Rel* congregation; (b) (*aide*) assistance, help, aid; **demander l'a. de qn,** to ask for s.o.'s assistance *or* help; **prêter son a.,** to lend (one's) assistance; **faire qch sans a.,** to do sth unaided *or* without help; **a. sociale,** welfare work; *Com* **a. maritime,** salvage; **a. judiciaire,** legal aid; **a. médicale/technique,** (*à un pays du Tiers Monde*) medical/technical aid *or* assistance; (c) **elle est à l'A. (publique) depuis l'âge de trois ans,** she's been in care since she was three; **les enfants de l'A. (publique),** children in care; (d) presence, attendance (*esp of magistrate or priest*).

assistant, -ante [asistɑ̃, -ɑ̃t] *n* (a) (*aide*) assistant; language assistant (*in school*); *Univ* demonstrator (*of practical work*); laboratory assistant; **l'a. du metteur en scène,** assistant producer; **maître a.,** ≈ senior lecturer, *US* assistant professor; **assistante sociale,** social worker, welfare worker *or* officer; (*in hospital*) medical social worker; (b) **assistants,** members of the audience; (*dans la rue*) bystanders, onlookers; *Sp* spectators; **quelques-uns d'entre vous, messieurs les assistants,** some of you gentlemen here.

assisté [asiste] *adj* (a) *Admin* (*person*) on social security; **enfants assistés,** children in care; (b) *Aut* **frein/direction assisté(e),** power brake/steering; (c) *Ordinat* **a. par ordinateur,** (*enseignement, fabrication etc*) computer-aided *or* -assisted.

assister [asiste] **1** *vi* **a. à qch,** to attend sth, to be (present) at sth, to take part in sth; **a. à une partie de football,** to go to (see) *or* attend a football match. **2** *vt* to help, to assist (*s.o.*); **tu devrais te faire a.,** you ought to get help, you ought to get s.o. to help you; **a. qn de ses conseils,** to give s.o. advice; **prêtre assisté de deux enfants de chœur,** priest attended by two altar boys.

associatif, -ive [asɔsjatif, -iv] *adj Math* **loi associative,** associative law; **mouvement a.,** voluntary sector; *Litt* **mémoire a.,** involuntary memory.

association [asɔsjasjɔ̃] *nf* (a) (*groupe, société*) society, association; *Com* partnership; **a. de parents d'élèves,** parent-teacher association; **a. syndicale,** trade union; **a. de secours,** friendly society; **a. à but non lucratif,** non-profit-making *or esp Am* not-for-profit organization; **a. de bienfaisance,** charity, charitable organization *or* institution; **a. sportive,** sports club; **A. internationale des transports aériens,** International Air Transport Association; (b) (*réunion*) association (*of words, ideas*); *El* connecting, grouping, coupling (*of cells*); **l'a. de ces deux**

aliments, the combination of these two foods; *Jur* **a. de malfaiteurs,** conspiracy.

associé, -ée [asɔsje] **1** *adj* associated; *esp Fin Bourse* joint; **porteurs** *ou* **souscripteurs associés,** joint holders (of stock); *Admin* **territoires associés,** associated territories. **2** *n* associate, honorary member (*of learned body etc*); *Com* partner; **a. principal,** senior partner; **a. commandité,** acting partner; **a. commanditaire,** sleeping partner.

associer [asɔsje] *v* (*pr sub & impf* **n. associions, v. associiez**) **1** *vt* **(a)** to associate, to unite, to join; *El* to connect, to join up (*cells etc*); **a. qn à qch,** to make s.o. a party to sth, to associate s.o. with sth; **j'ai toujours associé la neige à Noël,** I've always associated snow with Christmas; **a. des idées,** to associate ideas; **a. les travailleurs aux profits de leur entreprise,** to allow the workers to share in their firm's profits; **il a associé son frère à son expédition,** he brought his brother in on his expedition; **a. qn à sa maison** *ou* **à ses travaux,** to take s.o. into partnership;

(b) (*comparer*) to associate, to link.

2 s'associer *vpr* **(a) s'a. à qch,** to share *or* participate *or* join in sth; **s'a. à un voyage,** to come *or* go along on a trip; **je m'associe à votre douleur,** I share (in) your grief; **s'a. à un crime,** to be a party to a crime;

(b) s'a. à *ou* **avec qn,** to join forces with s.o. (*dans une lutte etc*); *Com etc* to enter into partnership with s.o.; **les deux pays se sont associés,** the two countries have joined forces;

(c) (*s'allier*) to combine; **les deux parfums s'associent merveilleusement bien,** these two fragrances combine *or* go wonderfully well together.

assoiffant [aswafɑ̃] *adj* thirsty (*work*).

assoiffé [aswafe] *adj* thirsty; **a. de sang,** bloodthirsty.

assoiffer [aswafe] *vt* to make thirsty.

assolement [asɔlmɑ̃] *nm Agr* rotation (*of crops*); **a. triennal,** three course system.

assombrir [asɔ̃brir] **1** *vt* to darken, to obscure; *Fig* to cast a gloom over (*s.o., sth*); **ciel assombri,** cloudy *or* overcast sky; **visage assombri,** gloomy face. **2 s'assombrir** *vpr* (*du ciel*) to become dark; (*du ciel, du visage*) to cloud over.

asombrissement [asɔ̃brismɑ̃] *nm* (*du ciel, de l'humeur*) darkening, clouding over; (*d'une pièce*) darkening.

assommant [asɔmɑ̃] *adj* **(a)** overwhelming (*heat, argument etc*); **(b)** *F* boring, tedious, deadly dull; **il est a., cet enfant-là!,** that child is a real pain!

assommer [asɔme] *vt* **(a) a. un bœuf,** to fell an ox; **a. qn,** (*tuer*) to brain s.o., to club s.o. to death; (*étourdir*) to knock (*s.o.*) senseless, to stun (*s.o.*); *Fig* **arrête ou je t'assomme!,** stop that or I'll knock your block off!; **la chaleur m'assomme,** I'm overwhelmed by the heat; **(b)** *F* to bore (*s.o.*) (to death); (*harceler*) to pester (*s.o.*).

assommeur, -euse [asɔmœr, -øz] *nm* slaughterer, slaughterman.

assommoir [asɔmwar] *nm* club, bludgeon; (*plus petit*) cosh, *US* blackjack; *Vieilli* pole-axe; (*bar*) low dive; *F* **porter un coup d'a. à qn,** to deal s.o. a knock-out blow.

assomption [asɔ̃psjɔ̃] *nf* **(a)** *Rel* **(fête de) l'A. (de la Vierge Marie),** (feast of) the Assumption (of the Blessed Virgin); **(b)** *Géog* **A.,** Asuncion; **(c)** (*hypothèse*) assumption.

assonance [asɔnɑ̃s] *nf Ling* assonance.

assorti [asɔrti] *adj* **(a)** (*en harmonie*) matched, matching; **bien a.,** well matched; **couple mal a.,** ill-matched *or* -assorted couple; **couleurs assorties,** colours that match; **pull avec jupe assortie,** jumper with matching skirt; **(b)** assorted, mixed (*sweets, nails etc*); **fromages assortis,** choice of cheeses; (*in restaurant*) cheese board *or* platter; **(c) bien a.,** well-stocked (*shop etc*).

assortiment [asɔrtimɑ̃] *nm* **(a)** (*ensemble*) assortment, variety, collection (*of goods etc*); set (*of tools*); **ample a. d'échantillons,** wide range of patterns; **a. de charcuterie,** assorted cold meats; **(b)** (*action*) matching; **a. parfait de couleurs,** perfect match(ing) of colours.

assortir [asɔrtir] *v* (**j'assortis, n. assortissons**) **1** *vt* **(a)** to match (*colours etc*); **a. son style à la matière,** to suit one's style to the subject; **a. les accessoires à sa robe,** to match one's accessories to *or* with one's dress; **a. des amis pour un repas,** to choose a good mix of friends for a meal; **nos mentalités sont bien/mal assorties,** we think/don't think the same way; **(b)** *Com* to restock. **2 s'assortir** *vpr* to match, to blend, to harmonize, to go well together; **la ceinture s'assortit à la robe,** the belt goes well with the dress; **le texte s'assortit d'illustrations,** the text is accompanied with *or* by illustrations.

assoupi [asupi] *adj* dozing, *Fml* somnolent; dormant (*volcano, passion*).

assoupir [asupir] **1** *vt* to make (*s.o.*) drowsy *or* sleepy, to send (*s.o.*) to sleep; to calm, to deaden, to dull (*pain, the senses*); **a. une dispute,** to calm a dispute. **2 s'assoupir** *vpr* to drop off to sleep, to doze off; (*of pain, grief*) to die down; (*of sound*) to die away.

assoupissant [asupisɑ̃] *adj* soporific.

assoupissement [asupismɑ̃] *nm* **(a)** (*somnolence*) drowsiness; somnolence; **(b)** *Fig* calming, lulling (*of pain etc*).

assouplir [asuplir] **1** *vt* to soften (*sth*); to make (*leather*) supple; *Fig* to ease, to relax (*regulations*); **cette lessive va a. votre linge,** this washing powder will make your clothes feel soft; **cela va finir par a. son caractère,** it'll eventually make him more flexible. **2 s'assouplir** *vpr* (*du cuir*) to become supple, to soften; **s'a. les muscles,** to limber up.

assouplissant [asuplisɑ̃] **1** *adj* **liquide a. (pour le linge),** (liquid) fabric softener. **2** *nm* fabric softener.

assouplissement [asuplismɑ̃] *nm* softening; suppling (*of leather*); easing (*of regulations*); **exercices d'a., assouplissements,** limbering-up exercises.

assouplisseur [asuplisœr] *nm* (fabric) softener.

assourdir [asurdir] **1** *vt* **(a)** to make (*s.o.*) deaf, to deafen; **(b)** to deaden, to muffle (*sound*); to muffle (*drum, bell, oars*); to mute (*violin*); *Constr* to soundproof; *Ling* to unvoice (*consonant*); **(c)** to soften, to subdue, to tone down (*light, colour*). **2 s'assourdir** *vpr Ling* to become unvoiced *or* voiceless.

assourdissant [asurdisɑ̃] *adj* deafening (*noise etc*).

assourdissement [asurdismɑ̃] *nm* (*de personne*) deafening; (*temporaire*) temporary deafness; deadening (*of sound*); muffling (*of drum, oars*); *Ling* unvoicing (*of consonant*); softening, subduing (*of light*).

assouvir [asuvir] **1** *vt* to appease, to satisfy, to assuage (*hunger, desire*); **a. sa soif,** to quench *or* slake one's thirst; **a. sa curiosité,** to satisfy one's curiosity. **2 s'assouvir** *vpr* (*faim*) to be satisfied *or* assuaged; (*passions*) to be assuaged.

assouvissement [asuvismɑ̃] *nm* satisfying, satisfaction (*of hunger etc*); quenching (*of thirst*); **un sentiment d'a.,** a feeling of satisfaction, a satisfied feeling.

assuétude [asyetyd] *nf Méd* addiction.

assujetti [asuʒeti] *adj* (*peuple*) subject, subjugated (**à,** to); **tous les citoyens sont assujettis à l'impôt,** all citizens are subject *or* liable to tax.

assujettir [asyʒetir] **1** *vt* **(a)** to subdue, to subjugate (*province etc*); **(b)** to subject, to make liable (**à,** to); **a. qn à faire qch,** to compel *or* oblige s.o. to do sth; **a. une population à des lois,** to subject a population to laws; **a. une population à l'impôt,** to make a population liable for tax; **(c)** to fix, to fasten (*sth*) (**à,** to); to make (*sth*) secure. **2 s'assujettir** *vpr* to submit (**à,** to).

assujettissant [asyʒetisɑ̃] *adj* exacting, demanding (*work*).

assujettissement [asyʒetismɑ̃] *nm* **(a)** (*action*) subjection, subjugation; **(b)** (*état*) subjection, subservience (*to s.o., sth*); **(c)** (*contrainte*) tie; **la grandeur a ses assujettissements,** greatness has its obligations.

assumer [asyme] **1** *vt* to assume, to take on, to take upon oneself (*right, responsibility etc*); **a. les frais,** to assume the costs; **a. un poste,** to hold a post; **a. la perte de qn de cher,** to come to terms with the loss of a loved one; **a. son service,** to take up one's duties. **2 s'assumer** *vpr* to take the responsibility for one's own actions.

assurable [asyrabl] *adj* assurable, insurable.

assurance [asyrɑ̃s] *nf* **(a)** (*confiance*) (self-)assurance, (self-)confidence; **parler avec a.,** to speak with confidence; **perdre son a.,** to lose one's self-assurance; **recevez l'a. de mes sentiments distingués,** (*dans une lettre*) yours faithfully; **vous pouvez l'acheter en toute a.,** you can buy it with complete confidence;

(b) (*garantie*) security, pledge; **elle vivait dans l'a. de la réussite,** she was assured of success; **je vous donne l'a. que tout sera fait d'ici demain,** I assure you *or* I guarantee (you) that everything will be done by tomorrow; **demander/recevoir des assurances,** to ask for/to receive assurances;

(c) *Com* insurance, assurance; **police d'a.,** insurance policy; **prime d'a.,** insurance premium; **compagnie** *ou* **société d'assurances,** insurance company; **a. sur la vie, a.-vie,** life insurance; **a. contre les accidents, a.-accident,** accident insurance; **a. contre l'incendie, a.-incendie,** fire insurance; **a. contre les accidents du travail,** employers' liability insurance; **a. automobile,** car insurance; **a. maritime,** marine insurance; **a. au tiers,** third-party insurance;

a. collective, group insurance; *Aut* **a. tous risques,** *Sui* **a. casco,** comprehensive insurance; **agent d'assurance(s),** insurance agent; **courtier d'assurance(s),** insurance broker; *F* **je vais écrire à mon a.,** I'll write to my insurance company;

(d) *Admin* **assurances sociales,** ≈ national insurance; **a. chômage,** (*payé par le patron et le salarié*) ≈ unemployment insurance; (*reçu par le chômeur*) ≈ unemployment benefit(s); **a. invalidité,** ≈ disability pension; **a. vieillesse,** ≈ retirement pension; **a. maternité,** ≈ maternity benefit(s); **a. maladie,** ≈ sickness benefit(s);

(e) (*sécurité*) making sure *or* safe; **(point d') a.,** (*d'alpiniste*) belay.

assuré, -ée [asyre] **1** *adj* firm, sure (*step, voice etc*); assured, confident (*air, person*); certain (*cure*); secure, safe (*retreat*); **voix mal assurée,** unsteady *or* quavering voice; **d'une main assurée,** with a sure hand; **il n'y a encore rien d'a.,** there is nothing fixed yet; **tenez pour a. qu'il vous écrira,** rest assured that he will write to you. **2** *n* policy holder, the insured; *Admin* **les assurés sociaux,** ≈ national insurance contributors, those who pay national insurance.

assurément [asyremɑ̃] *adv* assuredly, surely, undoubtedly, certainly; **il le fera a.,** he'll certainly do it, he's certain to do it; **a. non!,** certainly not!; **oui, a.!,** yes, of course!

assurer [asyre] **1** *vt* **(a)** to make (*sth*) firm *or* steady; (*attacher*) to fix, to secure, to fasten (*sth*); to steady (*ladder*); to prop up (*wall*); to make fast (*rope*); to belay (*climber*); **a. qn sec,** to give s.o. a tight rope;

(b) (*rendre sûr*) to ensure (*result*); **a. ses arrières,** *Mil* to protect one's rear; *Fig* to protect oneself against any eventuality; **a. un pays,** to make a country secure; **a. sa fortune,** to consolidate one's fortune;

(c) (*fournir*) to provide, to supply; **a. une rente à qn,** to settle an annuity on s.o.; **le courrier littéraire sera assuré par M. Leclerc,** the literary column will be in the hands of Mr Leclerc; **la France assure le rapatriement des touristes,** the French government is repatriating the tourists; **un service régulier est assuré entre Paris et Londres,** there is a regular service between Paris and London;

(d) (*garantir*) to ensure, to guarantee; **cette formation vous assure un avenir brillant,** this type of training will ensure *or* guarantee you a brilliant future; **ma retraite m'assure de quoi vivre,** my pension gives me enough to live on; **ce but assure la victoire des Allemands,** that goal assures the Germans of victory; **a. une créance,** to stand security for a debt;

(e) (*certifier*) **a. qch à qn, a. qn de qch,** to assure s.o. of sth; **il m'a assuré qu'il voulait bien le faire,** he assured me that he was willing to do it; **c'est bien vrai, je te l'assure** *ou F* **je t'assure,** it's quite true, I (can) assure you; **il vient de nous a. de sa participation,** he's just assured us that he will be taking part;

(f) (*par contrat*) **a. qn,** to insure s.o.; **se faire a. sur la vie,** to take out a life insurance (policy); **a. un immeuble contre l'incendie,** to insure a building against fire; **êtes-vous assuré?,** are you insured?

2 s'assurer *vpr* **(a)** (*s'affermir*) to settle oneself firmly; (*d'un alpiniste*) to belay oneself; **s'a. sur ses pieds,** to steady oneself on one's feet;

(b) s'a. de qch, to make sure *or* certain of sth; **je vais m'en a.,** I'll go and see; **assurez-vous que c'est encore possible,** make sure *or* check that it's still possible;

(c) to take out insurance, to insure oneself (**contre,** against); **s'a. au tiers/sur la vie,** to take out third-party/life insurance;

(d) (*se pourvoir*) **tu aurais dû t'a. de l'aide,** you should have got help; **les Allemands se sont assurés la victoire,** the Germans have ensured themselves of victory; **s'a. du transport**; to make sure one has transport.

assureur [asyrœr] *nm* insurer; underwriter.

Assyrie [asiri] *nf* Assyria.

assyrien, -ienne [asirjɛ̃, -jɛn] **1** *adj* Assyrian. **2** *nm Ling* (ancient) Assyrian. **3** *n* **A.,** Assyrian.

aster [astɛr] *nm* aster; **a. de Chine,** China aster; **a. œil-du-Christ,** Michaelmas daisy, *US* aster.

astérisque [asterisk] *nm Typ* asterisk.

astéroïde [asterɔid] *nm Astron* asteroid.

asthmatique [asmatik] *adj & n Méd* asthmatic.

asthme [asm] *nm Méd* asthma; **a. d'été** *ou* **des foins,** hay-fever; **être atteint d'a., avoir de l'a.,** to suffer from *or* to have asthma; **crise d'a.,** attack of asthma, asthma attack.

asticot [astiko] *nm* maggot; *F* (*type*) bloke, geezer.

asticoter [astikɔte] *vt F* to needle, to bug, to bait (*s.o.*).

astigmate [astigmat] *adj Méd* astigmatic.

astigmatisme [astigmatism] *nm Méd Opt* astigmatism.

astiquage [astikaʒ] *nm* polishing; tidying up.

astiquer [astike] *vt* (*la maison*) to clean; (*le parquet*) to polish; (*une casserole*) to scour.

astragale [astragal] *nm* **(a)** *Anat* ankle bone; **(b)** *Archit* astragal (*of column etc*).

astrakan [astrakɑ̃] *nm* astrakhan (fur); **manteau d'a.,** astrakhan coat.

astral, -aux [astral, -o] *adj* astral (*influence, body etc*); **esprits astraux,** astral spirits; **thème a.,** (astrological) star chart.

astre [astr] *nm* star, heavenly body; **contempler les astres,** to look at the stars, to stargaze; **consulter les astres,** to consult the stars; **beau comme un a.,** (as) handsome as a Greek god; **né sous un a. favorable,** born under a lucky star.

astreignant [astrɛɲɑ̃] *adj* exacting, demanding.

astreindre [astrɛ̃dr] *v* (*prp* **astreignant,** *pp* **astreint,** *pr ind* **j'astreins, il astreint, n. astreignons,** *impf* **j'astreignais,** *p hist* **j'astreignis,** *fu* **j'astreindrai**) **1** *vt* to compel, to oblige (*s.o.*) (**à faire qch,** to do sth); to tie (*s.o.*) down (**à un devoir,** to a duty); **astreint au service militaire,** liable to military service. **2 s'astreindre** *vpr* **s'a. à un régime sévère,** to keep to a strict diet; **s'a. à faire du sport,** to force oneself to do sport.

astreinte [astrɛ̃t] *nf* obligation; **les astreintes de la vie moderne,** the pressures of modern life.

astringence [astrɛ̃ʒɑ̃s] *nf Mil* astringency.

astringent [astrɛ̃ʒɑ̃] *adj & nm Méd* astringent.

astro- [astrɔ] *préf* astro-.

astrolab [astrɔlab] *nm* spacelab.

astrologie [astrɔlɔʒi] *nf* astrology.

astrologique [astrɔlɔʒik] *adj* astrologic(al).

astrologue [astrɔlɔg] *nm* astrologer.

astronaute [astrɔnot] *n* astronaut, space traveller.

astronauticien, -ienne [astrɔnotisjɛ̃, -jɛn] *n* research worker in astronautics.

astronautique [astrɔnotik] *nf* astronautics.

astronef [astrɔnɛf] *nm* spaceship.

astronome [astrɔnɔm] *nm* astronomer.

astronomie [astrɔnɔmi] *nf* astronomy.

astronomique [astrɔnɔmik] *adj Astron & Fig* astronomic(al); **heure a.,** sidereal time; *Fig F* **pratiquer des prix astronomiques,** (*d'un magasin*) to charge astronomical prices.

astronomiquement [astrɔnɔmikmɑ̃] *adv* astronomically.

astrophysicien, -ienne [astrɔfizisjɛ̃, -jɛn] *n* astrophysicist.

astrophysique [astrɔfizik] **1** *adj* astrophysical. **2** *nf* astrophysics.

astuce [astys] *nf* **(a)** (*finesse*) astuteness; *Péj* artfulness, wiliness, craftiness; **politicien plein d'a.,** crafty politician; **(b)** (*ficelle*) trick, wangle; **il doit y avoir une a.,** there must be a trick to it; **l'a., c'est de ne pas pointer en sortant,** the trick is not to clock off when you leave; **les astuces du métier,** the tricks of the trade; **(c)** (*plaisanterie*) witticism; pun; **je ne saisis pas l'a.** I don't see it *or* get it.

astucieusement [astysjøzmɑ̃] *adv* astutely.

astucieux, -ieuse [astysjø, -jøz] *adj* astute, clever (*person, behaviour*); *Péj* artful, wily, crafty, cunning, tricky (*person, behaviour*); **réponse astucieuse,** crafty *or* clever answer.

asymétrie [asimetri] *nf* asymmetry.

asymétrique [asimetrik] *adj* asymmetrical.

asymptomatique [asɛ̃ptɔmatik] *adj Méd* (*maladie*) asymptomatic; **porteur a.,** carrier without symptoms.

asynchrone [asɛ̃kron] *adj Ordinat* asynchronous.

atavique [atavik] *adj* atavistic; *Biol* **retour a.,** throwback.

atavisme [atavism] *nm* atavism; **faire qch par a.,** to do sth because it's in one's genes.

atchoum [atʃum] *int* (*sneeze*) atishoo!

atelier [atəlje] *nm* **(a)** (work)shop; (*dans une maison*) workroom; (*mansarde*) loft; **a. de réparations,** repair shop; *Tech* **a. de montage** *ou* **d'assemblage,** assembly shop; **a. d'ajustage,** fitting shop; **a. de constructions mécaniques,** machine shop; **a. de tissage,** weaving shed; **a. de constructions navales,** shipyard; **chef d'a.,** foreman; **il est devenu contremaître après cinq ans d'a.,** he became a foreman after five years on the factory floor; **camion a.,** repair van; **(b)** lodge (*of freemasons*); **(c)** studio (*of artist etc*); **(d)** staff (*of workshop etc*); (printer's) chapel.

atemporel, -elle [atɑ̃pɔrɛl] *adj* timeless.
atermoiement [atɛrmwamɑ̃] *nm* **(a)** *Com Jur* = arrangement with creditors for extension of time for payment; **a. d'une lettre de change,** renewal of a bill; **(b)** *F* **atermoiements,** delays, excuses; shillyshally(ing); **après mille atermoiements, elle dit oui,** after much shillyshallying, she said yes; **sans atermoiements,** without a moment's hesitation.
atermoyer [atɛrmwaje] *vi* to procrastinate.
athée [ate] **1** *adj* atheistic(al) (*person, argument*). **2** *n* atheist.
athéisme [ateism] *nm* atheism.
athénée [atene] *nm* **(a)** athenaeum; **(b)** *Belg Suisse* (state) secondary school.
Athènes [atɛn] *nf* Athens.
athénien, -ienne [atenjɛ̃, -jɛn] **1** *adj* Athenian. **2** *n* **A.,** Athenian.
athlète [atlɛt] *n* athlete; **avoir un corps d'a.,** to have the body of an athlete.
athlétique [atletik] **1** *adj* (*corps*) athletic. **2** *nf* athletics.
athlétiquement [atletikmɑ̃] *adv* athletically.
athlétisme [atletism] *nm* athletics, track and field; **épreuves d'a.,** athletic events, track and field events.
Atlantide [atlɑ̃tid] *nf* Atlantis.
atlantique [atlɑ̃tik] **1** *adj* **l'océan A.,** the Atlantic (Ocean). **2** *nm* **l'A.,** the Atlantic (Ocean); *Pol* **la Charte de l'A.,** the Atlantic Charter; **Organisation du Traité de l'A. Nord,** North Atlantic Treaty Organisation.
Atlas [atlas] *nm* **(a)** (*book of maps*) atlas; **(b)** *Myth Géog* Atlas; **(c)** *Anat* atlas.
atmosphère [atmɔsfɛr] *nf* **(a)** atmosphere; **humidité de l'a.,** atmospheric humidity; *Fig* **vivre dans l'a. de qn,** to breathe the same air as s.o.; **une a. de vacances,** a holiday atmosphere *or* feeling; *Fig* **avoir besoin de changer d'a.,** to need a change of atmosphere *or* scene(ry); **(b)** *Phys* (*pressure of* 760 *mm of mercury*) atmosphere.
atmosphérique [atmɔsferik] *adj* atmospheric; *Rad* **parasites atmosphériques,** atmospherics; **perturbations atmosphériques,** atmospheric disturbances.
atoca [atɔka] *nm Can* (*plante*) cranberry.
atoll [atɔl] *nm Géog* atoll.
atome [atom] *nm* particle, bit; *Phys* atom; **atomes de poussière,** specks of dust; *Fig* **avoir des atomes crochus avec qn,** to have a strong liking for s.o., to get on very well with s.o.; **nous n'avons aucun a. crochu,** we have nothing in common; **pas un a. de vérité,** not an atom *or* iota of truth.
atome-gramme [atomgram] *nm Phys* gram-atom; (*pl atomes-grammes*).
atomicité [atɔmisite] *nf Ch* atomicity.
atomique [atɔmik] *adj* atomic (*theory, weight etc*); **masse a.,** atomic mass; **nombre** *ou* **numéro a.,** atomic number; **sciences atomiques,** atomics; **bombe a.,** atom(ic) bomb; **guerre a.,** atomic war(fare); **énergie a.,** atomic energy; **sous-marin à propulseur** *ou* **propulsion a.,** nuclear(-powered *or* -propelled) submarine; **pile a.,** atomic reactor; **centre a.,** atomic research station; **usine a.,** atomic energy plant; **l'époque a.,** the nuclear *or* atomic age; **Commissariat à l'énergie a.,** ≈ Atomic Energy Authority, *US* Atomic Energy Commission.
atomisation [atɔmizasjɔ̃] *nf* atomization; *Pol Péj* **a. du pouvoir,** the dispersal of power.
atomisé, -ée [atɔmize] *n* person subjected to an atom bomb attack.
atomiser [atɔmize] *vt* **(a)** (*pulvériser*) to atomize; **a. de l'eau sur les fleurs,** to mist the flowers; **(b)** *F* to nuke; *Fig* to smash to smithereens.
atomiseur [atɔmizœr] *nm* atomizer, spray; **parfum en a.,** perfume in spray form.
atomisme [atɔmism] *nm Phil* the atomic theory.
atomiste [atɔmist] *nm* **(a)** (*savant etc*) nuclear *or* atomic physicist; **(b)** *Phil* atomist.
atomistique [atɔmistik] **1** *nf* nucleonics, nuclear engineering; atomics. **2** *adj* atomic; *Phil* **théorie a.,** atomistic theory.
atonal, -aux [atɔnal] *adj* (*musique*) atonal.
atone [atɔn] *adj* **(a)** dull, vacant, lacklustre (*look*); **un individu a.,** a lacklustre individual; **(b)** *Méd* atonic; **(c)** *Ling* unstressed, unaccented.
atonie [atɔni] *nf* **(a)** (*de personne*) lethargy, torpor, lack of vitality; **(b)** *Méd* poor physical condition; *Spéc* atony.
atours [atur] *nmpl* adornments, finery; **parée de ses plus beaux a.,** in all her finery.
atout [atu] *nm Cartes* trump; *Fig* asset, advantage; **a. maître,** master trump; **jouer a.,** to play a trump, to play trumps; **avoir tous les atouts dans son jeu,** to hold all the winning cards; *Fig* **ce candidat a des atouts,** this candidate has a lot going for him; **c'est un a. que de savoir l'anglais,** a knowledge of English is an asset.
atoxique [atɔksik] *adj Biol* non-poisonous.
âtre [ɑtr] *nm* **(a)** (*cheminée*) fireplace, hearth; **coin de l'â.,** chimney corner; **(b)** *Ind* hearth (*of forge etc*); (*du forgeron*) (blacksmith's) forge.
atroce [atrɔs] *adj* atrocious, heinous, abominable (*crime etc*); (*terrible*) dreadful, horrible; (*mauvais*) awful, ghastly; **douleur a.,** excruciating *or* agonizing pain; **j'avais une peur a. de le rencontrer,** I dreaded meeting him; **d'une laideur a.,** hideously ugly; **rhume a.,** shocking cold; **une odeur a.,** a foul *or* an awful *or* a horrible smell; **il fait un temps a.,** the weather is shocking *or* dreadful.
atrocement [atrɔsmɑ̃] *adv* (*cruellement*) atrociously, shockingly; (*horriblement*) dreadfully, awfully, horribly, terribly; **ça sentait a. mauvais,** it smelled awful *or* horrible; **il a fait a. froid,** it was dreadfully cold.
atrocité [atrɔsite] *nf* **(a)** (*cruauté*) atrociousness; (*d'un crime*) atrocity; **(b)** (*acte*) atrocious act, atrocity; **les atrocités commises pendant la guerre,** the atrocities committed during the war; *F* **on m'a raconté des atrocités sur votre compte,** I have been hearing dreadful things about you; *F* **ce tableau est une a.,** this picture is a real horror *or* an atrocity.
atrophie [atrɔfi] *nf Méd* atrophy (*of limb, liver*); **a. intellectuelle,** intellectual atrophy.
atrophié [atrɔfje] *adj* atrophied (*liver, intelligence*); wasted, withered (*arm*); emaciated (*person*).
atrophier [atrɔfje] **1** *vt* to atrophy (*limb, intelligence*). **2 s'atrophier** *vpr* (*of intelligence*) to atrophy; (*of person*) to waste away.
atropine [atrɔpin] *nf Ch* atropin(e).
attabler [atable] **1** *vt* to invite (*guests*) to sit down at the table. **2 s'attabler** *vpr* to sit down at the (dinner *etc*) table.
attachant [ataʃɑ̃] *adj* **(a)** interesting (*book*); fascinating (*spectacle*); **(b)** engaging, attractive (*personality*).
attache [ataʃ] *nf* **(a)** (*action*) fastening; (*avec de la ficelle etc*) tying up; *Couture* sewing on; *Constr etc* **point d'a.,** connection; **pièce d'a.,** fastening; **rivets d'a.,** jointing rivets; *Nau* **droit d'a.,** mooring right; **droits d'a.,** (*frais*) mooring dues, moorage; **port d'a.,** home port, port of registry; *Fig* home base; **borne d'a.,** *Nau* bollard; *Él* terminal;
(b) (*lien*) tie, fastener, fastening, attachment; head rope (*of horse*); lead, leash, chain (*of dog*); (*for holding down*) guy (rope); tether (*of donkey etc*); **chien d'a.,** guard dog; **mettre un chien à l'a.,** to put a dog on the lead; *Fig* **tenir qn comme un chien d'a.** *ou* **à l'a.,** to keep s.o. on a string; **nos attaches dans ce pays,** our close ties *or* links with this country; **sans attaches,** unattached, unconnected; **je n'avais plus aucune a. dans cette ville,** there was nothing to keep me in the town;
(c) rivet (*for mending china*); *Él* (wire) clamp; (*on clothing*) loop, tab; **a. de diamants,** diamond clasp; *Rail* **a. de rail,** rail fastening;
(d) *Anat* origin, attachment (*of muscle*); **a. de la main/du pied,** wrist/ankle joint; **avoir les attaches fines,** to have delicate wrists and ankles;
(e) *Constr etc* connection, bond, brace; binder (*of reinforced concrete beam*);
(f) *Bot* tendril.
attaché, -ée [ataʃe] **1** *adj* **(a)** fastened, tied up; chained up (*dog*); **yeux attachés au sol,** eyes fixed on the ground; **être a. à qn/qch,** to be attached *or* devoted to s.o./sth; **être très a. à une région/à ses responsabilités,** to be very attached to a region/very devoted to one's duties; **a. à une opinion,** wedded to an opinion; **rester a. à une opinion,** to cling to an opinion; **(b)** (*lié*) linked, attached; **les avantages attachés à une fonction,** the benefits of a post; **mon bonheur est a. au vôtre,** my happiness is bound up with yours; **(c) avoir des mains finement attachées,** to have delicate wrists; **(d)** (*dépendant*) attached; *Bourse* **coupon a.,** cum dividend. **2** *n* attaché; **a. militaire/commercial,** military/commercial attaché; **elle est attachée de presse,** she's a press attaché; **a. d'administration,** junior civil servant.
attaché-case [ataʃekɛz] *nm* attaché case.
attachement [ataʃmɑ̃] *nm* **(a)** (*pour qn*) attachment (**pour,** to); affection (**pour,** for); **a. à l'étude,** fondness for study; **(b)** (*relation*) liaison; **rompre un a.,** to break off a liaison; **(c)** *Constr* = daily statement of work carried out and expenses incurred.
attacher [ataʃe] **1** *vt* to attach, to fasten (**qch à qch,** sth to sth); (*avec ficelle, corde*) to tie (up); *F* to do up; **a. un**

cheval, to tie up *or* tether a horse; **a. qch avec une boucle,** to buckle sth; **a. qch avec des clous,** to nail sth (on, together); **a. qch avec une corde,** to rope sth (together); **a. qch avec des épingles,** to pin sth (on, together); **a. qch avec des rivets/avec des vis,** to rivet/screw sth (on, together); **a. un ruban à ses cheveux,** to tie a ribbon in one's hair; **a. un chien à sa laisse,** to put a dog on the lead; **a. une étiquette à un paquet,** to stick a label on a parcel; **il faut bien a. le paquet,** you should tie up the parcel securely; **a. un prisonnier au poteau,** to tie a prisoner to the stake; **attachez vos ceintures,** fasten your seat belts; **tu peux m'a. ma robe?,** can you fasten my dress?, *F* can you do up my dress?; **a. ses lacets** *ou* **chaussures,** to tie *or* fasten *or* do up one's shoelaces; **a. un certain sens à un acte,** to attribute a certain meaning to an act; **a. de l'importance à qch,** to attach importance to sth; **a. un nouveau secrétaire à une ambassade,** to attach a new secretary to an embassy; *Fig* **ce qui m'attache à lui,** what attaches me to him; *Fig* **tout ce qui nous attache à la vie,** everything that makes us cling to life.

2 *vi Culin F* **les pommes de terre ont attaché,** the potatoes have stuck to the pan; **casserole qui n'attache pas,** non-stick saucepan.

3 s'attacher *vpr* **(a)** (*d'une personne*) to attach oneself (**à,** to); (*d'une chose*) to cling, to stick (**à,** to); (*ne pas s'enlever*) to be attached *or* stuck (**à,** to); (*avec une agrafe etc*) to be fastened (**à,** to); (*avec ficelle, corde etc*) to be tied (**à,** on, to); **le lierre s'attache aux arbres,** ivy clings to trees; **collier qui s'attache avec une agrafe,** necklace that fastens with a clip; **la jupe s'attache par derrière,** the skirt fastens (up) *or F* does up at the back; **une certaine importance s'y attache,** some importance is attached to it; *Fig* **s'a. aux faits,** to stick to the facts; **s'a. à qn,** to become *or* grow fond of *or* attached to s.o., **s'a. à une région,** to become attached to a region; **je ne veux pas m'a.,** (*sentimentalement*) I don't want to tie myself down *or* get involved; *Fig* **elle sait s'a. ses élèves,** she knows how to gain her pupils' affection;

(b) s'a. à une tâche, to apply oneself to a job; **s'a. à qch,** to pay particular attention to sth; **s'a. à bien faire son travail,** to take particular care over one's work; **s'a. à l'honnêteté/l'éducation/***etc***,** to attach great importance to *or* to set great store by honesty/education/*etc*.

attaquable [atakabl] *adj* **(a)** *Mil* attackable, open to attack; **(b)** contestable (*fact, opinion etc*); open to attack (*codicil etc*).

attaquant, -ante [atakɑ̃, -ɑ̃t] **1** *adj* attacking. **2** *n* assailant, attacker.

attaque [atak] *nf* **(a)** *Mil etc* attack, assault, onslaught; hold-up (**do,** of) (*of a car, train etc*); **à l'a.!,** attack!, **a. concertée,** concerted attack; **reprise d'a.,** renewed attack; **corps d'a.,** attacking party; **passer à l'a.,** to take *or* go on the offensive; **repasser à l'a.,** to return to the attack; **monter une a.,** to mount an attack; **a. à main armée,** armed hold-up; **a. à la bombe,** bomb attack, bombing; *Av* **a. aérienne,** air raid *or* strike; *Av Nau* **bord d'a.,** leading edge (*of wing, propeller*); **angle d'a.,** leading angle; **son angle d'a. vis-à-vis d'un problème,** his approach to a problem; **a. de front,** direct *or* frontal attack; **subir une a.,** to be attacked; *Fig* **les attaques de la presse,** attacks by the press; *Fig* **diriger de violentes attaques contre qn,** to attack s.o. violently;

(b) *Sp* attack; (*à l'aviron*) beginning of a stroke; catch (*as the blade grips the water*); *Cartes* lead;

(c) d'a., vigorously; **se sentir d'a.,** to feel in good shape, *Am* to feel bright-eyed and bushy-tailed; **se sentir d'a. pour faire qch,** to feel up to *or* ready to do sth; **il y va d'a.,** he goes at it tooth and nail *or* hammer and tongs; **être d'a.,** (*en pleine forme*) to be on top form; **il est toujours d'a.,** he is still going strong;

(d) *Méd* attack (*of painful illness*); bout (*of fever, flu*); **a. d'épilepsie,** epileptic fit; **a. d'apoplexie,** (apoplectic) stroke; **a. de nerfs,** fit of hysterics; **une a. (cardiaque),** a heart attack;

(e) *MecE* **a. directe,** direct drive (*of motor*); **pignon d'a.,** driving pinion;

(f) *Mus* entry (*of instrument*); attack (*of note*); **chef d'a.,** first violin, leader (*of the orchestra*).

attaquer [atake] **1** *vt* **(a)** to attack (*s.o., enemy, stronghold etc*); to set upon, to assault (*s.o., enemy*); (*of acid*) to attack, to eat into, to corrode (*metal*); *Mil* **a. de front,** to make *or* to launch a frontal attack; **attaquez!,** engage!; *Hum* **être attaqué par les moustiques,** to be attacked by mosquitoes; **a. qn à coup de poings,** to lay into s.o.; *Fig* **a. les abus/les préjugés,** to attack abuses/prejudices; **a. qn sur un sujet,** to tackle s.o. on a subject; *Jur* **a. (la validité d')un testament,** to contest a will; **a. qn en justice,** to prosecute *or* sue s.o., to bring an action against s.o.; **a. la réputation/l'honneur de qn,** to attack s.o.'s reputation/honour; *Méd* **le poumon droit est attaqué,** the right lung is affected;

(b) to tackle, to get to work on (*meal, subject, piece of work etc*); **nous attaquons demain l'ascension du Mont Blanc,** tomorrow we('ll) attack *or* tackle Mont Blanc; **attaquons le repas avant que ça ne refroidisse,** let's tuck in *or* get stuck in before it gets cold;

(c) *Mus* to attack, *F* to strike up; **bien a. la note,** to hit the note well.

2 *vi* **(a)** to attack, to take the offensive; **qui a attaqué le premier?,** (*à deux enfants qui se battent*) who started it?;

(b) *Mus* **a. faux,** to hit the wrong note;

(c) *Cartes* **a. trèfle/de la reine,** to lead clubs/the queen;

(d) (*of acids etc*) to corrode.

3 s'attaquer *vpr* **s'a. à qn/qch,** to attack *or* make an attack on *or* tackle s.o./sth; **elle s'attaque à tout ce qu'on lui dit,** she takes issue with everything that's said to her; **s'a. à une difficulté/un problème,** to grapple with a difficulty/a problem.

attardé, -ée [atarde] **1** *adj* **(a)** belated (*traveller etc*); late; behindhand; **(b)** (*dans le temps*) behind the times; **idées** *ou* **conceptions attardées,** old-fashioned *or* outmoded ideas; **(c)** *Psy* (*dans sa scolarité*) backward (*child*). **2** *n* **(a)** *Psy* **a. (mental),** (mentally) retarded person; **(b)** (*dans une course etc*) **les attardés,** the laggards, the back markers, those that bring up the rear.

attarder [atarde] **1** *vt* to keep (*s.o.*) late, to delay (*s.o.*); **une crevaison nous a attardés,** we were delayed by a puncture; **je ne veux pas vous a.,** I don't want to hold you up *or* delay you *or* make you late. **2 s'attarder** *vpr* to linger, to loiter; (*en se promenant*) to lag behind, to dawdle; **s'a. en route,** to dawdle on the way; **ne nous attardons pas,** let's not linger; *F* let's not hang about; **nous nous sommes attardés chez nos amis,** we lingered at our friends' house; **elle s'est attardée au travail,** she stayed late at work; **s'a. pour regarder le paysage,** to linger in order to look at the scenery; **s'a. à qch,** to linger over sth; *Péj* to waste one's time on sth; **ne nous attardons pas sur ce point,** let's not dwell on this point.

atteindre [atɛ̃dr] *v* (*prp* **atteignant**; *pp* **atteint**; *pr ind* **j'atteins, il atteint, n. atteignons**; *impf* **j'atteignais**; *p hist* **j'atteignis**; *fu* **j'atteindrai**) **1** *vt* **(a)** (*parvenir à*) to reach; *Fml* to attain; **a. la ville,** to reach *or* to get to the town; **a. la plus haute étagère,** to reach the top shelf; **je ne peux pas l'a.,** I can't reach it; **a. qn,** to catch s.o. up; (*doubler*) to overtake s.o.; **a. l'ennemi,** to catch up with the enemy; **a. son but,** to attain *or* achieve one's end; **a. l'âge de soixante ans,** to reach the age of sixty; **le nombre des participants atteint le millier,** the number of participants is nearing the thousand mark; **très peu de montagnes atteignent 8 000 mètres,** very few mountains reach (a height of) 8,000 metres; **la pollution atteint la cote d'alerte,** pollution is reaching danger level; **a. un prix élevé,** to reach *or* fetch a high price;

(b) (*entrer en contact avec*) **comment puis-je vous a.?,** how can I reach you *or* get in touch with you?;

(c) (*toucher*) to hit, to reach; **a. le but,** to hit the target *or* the mark; **ne pas a. le but,** to fall short of the mark; **a. une couche pétrolifère,** to strike oil; **être atteint (d'un coup de feu) à la jambe,** to be wounded *or* shot in the leg; **être atteint d'une maladie,** to be struck down by a disease; (*of trees etc*) to be attacked by a disease; **le poumon est atteint,** the lung is affected; **un malade très atteint,** a seriously ill patient; *F* **il est complètement atteint,** he's completely cracked *or* potty; *Fig* **gravement atteint par une faillite,** heavily hit by a bankruptcy; **tu peux le lui dire, mais cela ne l'atteint pas,** you can tell him, but it doesn't have any effect; **elle est atteinte dans son amour-propre,** her pride has been wounded *or* hurt; **une perte que m'a profondément atteint,** a loss which affected me very badly.

2 *vi* **a. à qch,** to reach *or* attain sth (*with difficulty*); **a. à son but,** to achieve one's aim; **son travail atteint à la perfection,** his work is close to *or* is nearing perfection.

atteinte [atɛ̃t] *nf* **(a)** (*portée*) reach; **se mettre hors de l'a. de qn,** to get beyond *or* out of s.o.'s reach; **hors d'a.,** beyond reach, out of reach; *Fig* **sa réputation est hors d'a.,** his reputation is beyond attack *or* unassailable ; **se dérober** *ou* **se soustraire à l'a. de la loi,** to circumvent *or* get round *or F* dodge the law; (*s'échapper*) to get out of the clutches of the law; **(b)** (*attaque*) blow, stroke, attack; **légère a. au bras,** slight blow on the arm; **les premières atteintes d'une maladie,** the first attacks of an illness; **a. au crédit de qn,** blow to s.o.'s credit; **légère a. de goutte,** twinge *or* touch of gout; **porter a. à l'autorité de qn,** to undermine s.o.'s authority; **a. portée aux privilèges,** breach of privilege; **porter a. aux intérêts de qn,** to interfere with s.o.'s interests, to affect s.o.'s interests.

attelage [atlaʒ] *nm* **(a)** harnessing; yoking (*of oxen*); *Constr etc* attachment; (*de remorques etc*) tying, fastening; (*avec un crochet*) hooking on; *Rail* coupling; **l'a. d'engins spatiaux,** the docking of spacecraft; **(b)** (*animaux*) team; pair (*of horses*); yoke (*of oxen*); (*voiture*) carriage (and horses); **(c)** tie; (*crochet*) hook, fastening.

atteler [atle] *v* (**j'attelle, n. attelons; j'attellerai**) **1** *vt* **(a)** to harness (*horses etc*); to yoke (*oxen*); **toujours attelé à son travail,** always hard at work *or* at it; **(b) a. une voiture,** to attach horses to a carriage; **voiture attelée de quatre chevaux,** carriage drawn by four horses; *Sp* **course attelée,** trotting race; *Rail* **a. des wagons,** to couple (up) wagons. **2 s'atteler** *vpr* **s'a. à une tâche/un travail,** to buckle down *or* get down to a task/a job; **je m'y attelle tous les jours,** I force myself to do it every day.

attelle [atɛl] *nf Méd* splint.

attellement [atɛlmɑ̃] *nm* harnessing; yoking (*of oxen*).

attenant [atnɑ̃] *adj* contiguous (**à,** to), adjoining; bordering; **jardin a. au mien,** garden next to mine; **deux chemins attenants,** two intersecting paths.

attendre [atɑ̃dr] **1** *vt* to wait for (*s.o., sth*), *Fml Litt* to await (*s.o., sth*); **qu'attendez-vous?,** what are you waiting for?; **le déjeuner nous attend,** lunch is ready; **une surprise vous attend,** there's a surprise in store for you; **l'avenir nous attend,** the future lies before us; **j'attends midi pour lui téléphoner,** I'll wait until twelve o'clock before I telephone him; **aller a. qn à la gare,** to go to meet *or* to go and meet s.o. at the station; **a. la fin de l'histoire,** to wait for *or* until the end of the story; **il se fait a.,** he's keeping us waiting; **la réponse ne s'est pas fait attendre,** the reply wasn't long in coming; **tu t'es fait a.!,** and about time too!; **nous n'attendions que toi,** now you're here we can start *or* go *etc*; **on l'attend la semaine prochaine,** he is expected next week; **femme qui attend un bébé,** expectant mother; **elle attend un bébé,** she's expecting (a baby); **attendez voir,** just wait, wait and see; (*laissez-moi réfléchir*) let me see; **on ne t'attendait plus,** we'd given you up; **qu'attend-il de moi?,** what does he want *or* expect from me?; **elle n'attend que ça,** that's (just) what she wants *or* is waiting for; (*punition etc*) she's got it coming to her; **je n'attends qu'une chose, les vacances,** I (just) can't wait for the holidays to begin; **a. que qn fasse qch,** to wait for s.o. to do sth; **j'attendrai (jusqu'à ce) qu'il soit prêt,** I shall wait until he's ready; **a. qn au passage,** to lie in wait for s.o.; **a. son tour,** to wait one's turn.

2 *vi* **(a)** to wait; **perdre son temps à a.,** to waste one's time waiting; **le train n'attend pas,** the train won't wait; **j'attends de voir pour juger,** I'll wait and see before I pass judgment; **a. de faire qch,** to wait (until it is time) to do sth; **attendons jusqu'à demain,** let's wait until tomorrow; *F* **on ne va pas a. 107 ans,** we're not going to wait forever; **attendez (donc)!,** wait (a bit)!, just a moment *or* a minute!, hang *or* hold on!; **sans plus a.,** without further ado; *Prov* **tout vient à point à qui sait a.,** everything comes to him who waits; **il vaut mieux a. encore un peu,** it would be better to wait a bit longer; **a. une heure,** to wait (for) an hour; **il ne perd rien pour a.,** he's got it coming to him; **un plat qui n'attend pas,** a dish that won't wait, a dish you have to eat straight away;

(b) *F* **a. après qn/qch,** to wait for *or* to want s.o./sth; **portez-lui ce livre, il attend après,** take this book to him, he is waiting for it;

(c) en attendant, meanwhile, in the meantime; **en attendant son arrivée,** until he arrives, while waiting for him to arrive; **en attendant de vous voir,** until I see you.

3 s'attendre *vpr* **s'a. à qch,** to expect sth; **il faut s'a. à tout,** one must be prepared *or* ready for anything; **je m'y attendais,** I expected as much; **je m'attendais à ce que tu me le dises,** I was expecting you to tell me.

attendri [atɑ̃dri] *adj* **regard a.,** fond *or* compassionate look.

attendrir [atɑ̃drir] **1** *vt* **(a)** to soften (*s.o.'s heart*); to move, to touch (*s.o.*); **cela attendrirait un cœur de pierre,** it would melt a heart of stone; **(b)** to make (*meat*) tender, to tenderize (*meat*). **2 s'attendrir** *vpr* to be moved (to tears), to be touched; **s'a. sur qch,** to be moved (to tears) *or* touched by sth; **s'a. sur un bébé,** to gush over a baby; **s'a. sur soi-même** *ou* **sur son propre sort,** to feel sorry for oneself; **il s'attendrit facilement,** he is very emotional.

attendrissant [atɑ̃drisɑ̃] *adj* moving, touching, affecting; **sa crédulité est attendrissante,** his naivety is touching.

attendrissement [atɑ̃drismɑ̃] *nm* pity, emotion; **allons!, pas d'a.!,** come on, let's not get emotional; **a. sur soi-même,** self pity; **larmes d'a.,** tears of emotion.

attendrisseur [atɑ̃drisœr] *nm* (meat) tenderizer.

attendu [atɑ̃dy] **1** *adj* expected. **2** *prép* considering (*the circumstances*); owing to (*the events*); in consideration of (*his services*); **a. son attitude envers moi,** considering *or* in view of his attitude towards me. **3** *conj* **a. que** + *ind,* considering that, seeing that; *Jur* whereas.

attentat [atɑ̃ta] *nm* attack; **a. contre la vie de qn,** attempted murder, attempt on s.o.'s life, assassination attempt; **victime d'un a.,** victim of an attack; *Jur* **a. aux mœurs,** indecent behaviour, public indecency; **a. à pudeur,** indecent assault; **a. à la sûreté de l'État,** high treason; **a. à la liberté,** violation *or* infringement of liberty.

attentatoire [atɑ̃tatwar] *adj Jur* **action a. à l'autorité,** action that is a challenge to *or* in contempt of authority; **mesure a. à la liberté,** measure that constitutes an infringement of *or* attack on liberty.

attente [atɑ̃t] *nf* **(a)** (*fait d'attendre*) waiting; (*période*) wait; **être dans l'a. de qch,** to be waiting for sth; **une longue a.,** a long wait; **salle d'a.,** waiting room; **rester en a.,** to be held over; **liste d'a.,** waiting list; **file d'a.,** *Br* queue, *Am* line; *Ordinat* **liste de fichier à imprimer en a.,** print queue; *Mil* **combat d'a.,** delaying action; *Chir* **ligature d'a.,** temporary ligature; *Av* **circuit d'a.,** holding pattern, orbiting; **(b)** (*espoir*) expectation(s), anticipation; **contre toute a.,** contrary to all expectations; **remplir l'a. de qn, répondre à l'a. de qn,** to come up *or* live up to s.o.'s expectations; **être dans l'a. de qch,** to be waiting for sth; **dans l'a. de votre réponse,** (*dans une lettre*) awaiting your reply.

attenter [atɑ̃te] *vi* to make an attempt (**à,** on, against); **a. à la vie de qn,** to make an attempt on s.o.'s life; **a. à ses jours,** to attempt suicide; **a. à la liberté de qn,** to infringe upon s.o.'s liberty.

attentif, -ive [atɑ̃tif, -iv] *adj* **(a)** attentive (**à,** to); **il n'est pas a.,** he doesn't pay attention; **elle est très attentive avec ses employés,** she shows a lot of consideration towards her employees; **écouter d'un air a.,** to listen attentively; **être a. à qch,** to look after sth, to see to sth; **être a. à ses intérêts,** to look after one's (own) interests; **être a. à sa santé,** to look after oneself *or* one's health; **(b)** (*appliqué*) careful; **examen a.,** careful examination.

attention [atɑ̃sjɔ̃] *nf* **(a)** attention, care; **appliquer toute son a. à qch,** to give one's whole mind to sth, to devote one's whole attention to sth; **faute d'a.,** through not paying attention; **faire un effort d'a.,** to try to be more attentive, to try to concentrate; **écouter avec a.,** to listen attentively; *Com etc* **à l'a. de M. Martin,** for the attention of Mr Martin; **porter** *ou* **tourner** *ou* **diriger son a. vers** *ou* **sur qch,** to turn one's attention to sth; **attirer l'a.,** (*of object or fact*) to attract attention; **attirer l'a. de qn sur qch,** to draw s.o.'s attention to sth; **puis-je avoir votre a. s'il vous plaît,** (may I have) your attention please; **faire a. à sa santé,** to take care of one's health; **ne faire aucune a. à qch, ne pas prêter la moindre a. à qch,** to take no *or* to take not the slightest notice of sth; **(faites) a.!,** take care!, look out!, watch it!; *Scol* pay attention!; **a. à la peinture,** mind the paint; (*notice*) wet paint; **a. au départ!,** *Rail* ≈ stand clear of the doors!, mind the doors!; (*on bus*) ≈ hold tight!; **a. aux portes,** stand clear of the gates!; **a. au train,** beware of (the) trains; **a., verglas rapide,** caution, ice; **a. aux travaux,** road works ahead; **faites a. à** *ou* **de ne pas vous perdre,** be careful not to get lost; **faites a. (à ce) que personne ne sorte,** take care *or* be sure that no one leaves (the house); **faites a. qu'll n'a que dix ans,** remember *or* don't forget that he's only ten;

(b) (*amabilité*) attention(s), consideration; **être plein d'attention(s) envers qn,** to be full of attention *or* consideration for s.o.; **il a eu l'a. de m'avertir,** he was considerate enough to warn me.

attentionné [atɑ̃sjɔne] *adj* attentive; **être a. envers qn,** to be full of attention *or* consideration for s.o..

attentisme [atɑ̃tism] *nm* wait-and-see policy.

attentivement [atɑ̃tivmɑ̃] *adv* attentively, carefully; (*regarder*) closely.

atténuant [atenɥɑ̃] *adj Jur* mitigating, extenuating (*circumstances*).

atténuation [atenɥasjɔ̃] *nf* **(a)** attenuation, lessening, diminishing, reducing; dimming, subduing (*of light*); toning down (*of colour*); breaking (*of fall*); mitigation, reduction (*of punishment, sentence*); **(b)** *Phot* reduction (*of negative*); softening (*of contrasts*); **(c)** extenuation (*of crime*).

atténué [atenɥe] *adj* attenuated, diminished; *Jur* **responsabilité atténuée,** diminished responsibility.

atténuer [atenɥe] **1** *vt* **(a)** to attenuate, to lessen, to diminish, to reduce; to tone down (*colour*); to dim, to subdue (*light*); to mitigate (*punishment, consequences*); **a. une chute,** to break a fall; **(b)** *Phot* to reduce (*negative etc*); to soften, to tone down (*contrasts*); **(c)** to extenuate, to palliate (*offence*); to render (*crime etc*) less grave; **circonstances qui atténuent son action,** circumstances in extenuation of his action. **2 s'atténuer** *vpr* to lessen, to diminish; (*of light*) to fade.

atterrant [aterɑ̃] *adj* overwhelming; shattering, crushing (*news*); (*étonnant*) staggering, startling, astounding.

atterrer [atere] *vt* to stagger; **sa naïveté m'atterre,** I am staggered *or* appalled by his naivety; **ils se regardent atterrés,** they look at each other in consternation.

atterrir [aterir] *vi* **(a)** *Nau* to make *or* sight land, to make a landfall; (*of boat*) to ground, to run ashore; **(b)** *Av* to land; **a. sur la lune,** to land on the moon; **a. trop court,** to undershoot; **a. trop long,** to overshoot; **a. brutalement,** to crash (land); *F* **a. dans un bar/dans un fossé/à l'hôpital/***etc*, to land up *or* end up *or* finish up in a bar/a ditch/hospital/*etc*.

atterrissage [aterisaʒ] *nm* **(a)** *Av* landing, touchdown; **a. trop long,** overshoot; **a. trop court,** undershoot; **a. forcé,** forced landing; **a. à vue,** visual landing; **a. aux instruments,** instrument landing; **a. sans visibilité,** blind landing; **a. brutal,** crash landing; **a. en catastrophe,** emergency landing; **terrain d'a.,** (*ensemble des pistes*) runways; **pont d'a.,** landing deck (*of aircraft carrier*); *Astronaut* **a. en douceur,** soft landing; **(b)** *Nau* making (the) land, landfall; grounding, running ashore (*of ship*); **(c)** *Télécom* landing (*of marine cable*); **(d)** point of emergence of cable (from the sea).

atterrisseur [aterisœr] *nm Av* undercarriage, landing gear.

attestation [atɛstasjɔ̃] *nf* (*action*) attestation; (*certificat*) testimonial, certificate; **demander l'a. du professeur,** to ask for a reference from the teacher; **a. du médecin,** doctor's certificate; *Jur* **a. du titre,** warranty of title; **a. sous serment** *ou* **sur l'honneur,** affidavit.

attester [atɛste] *vt* **(a) a. qch,** to attest *or* certify sth, to bear testimony *or* to bear witness *or* to testify to sth; to vouch for (*s.o.'s reputation*); **a. que qch est vrai,** to attest *or* certify that sth is true; **c'est un fait attesté,** it is an established fact, it is beyond doubt; **sa réponse atteste sa mauvaise foi,** his reply bears witness to *or* demonstrates his bad faith; **(b)** (*prendre à témoin*) **a. qn (de qch),** to call s.o. to witness (to sth); **a. l'autorité de qn en faveur d'une affirmation,** to advance a statement on the authority of s.o.

attiédir [atjedir] **1** *vt* to make tepid *or* lukewarm; to cool (*hot water etc*); to warm, to take the chill off (*cold water*); *Fig* **a. les passions de qn,** to calm *or* cool s.o.'s passions. **2 s'attiédir** *vpr* (*de l'eau chaude*) to cool down, to become tepid *or* lukewarm; (*de l'eau froide*) to warm up; (*des passions*) to cool.

attifer [atife] **1** *vt F* to dress (*s.o.*) up, to get (*s.o.*) up, to deck (*s.o.*) out (**de,** in); **elle attife ses enfants sans soin,** she dresses her children any old how; **comme le voilà attifé,** what a sight he looks!; **2 s'attifer** *vpr* to dress oneself up *or* to get oneself up *or* to deck oneself out (**de,** in); **je ne m'attiferais pas comme ça!,** I wouldn't get myself up like that!

attiger [atiʒe] *vi* (**j'attigeais, n. attigeons**) *Arg Vieilli* (*exagérer*) to shoot a line; **tu attiges!,** come off it!

attique [atik] **1** *adj Antiq* Attic; Athenian. **2** *nm Archit* attic (*storey*).

attirail [atiraj] *nm* **(a)** apparatus, gear; set (*of tools etc*); (*de cuisine*) utensils; (*de jardin*) tools; **a. de pêche,** fishing tackle; **(b)** *F* paraphernalia.

attirance [atirɑ̃s] *nf* attraction (**vers,** to); lure, fascination (*of pleasure, place etc*); **éprouver de l'a. pour qn,** to be drawn *or* attracted to s.o..

attirant [atirɑ̃] *adj* attractive; drawing (*force etc*); alluring, engaging (*manners, smile*).

attirer [atire] **1** *vt* **(a)** (*of magnet, sun etc*) to attract, to draw; **quelque chose les attire,** something draws them together, there is some kind of attraction between them; **ce qui m'attire dans ce projet,** what attracts me *or* what I find attractive about this project; **je ne sais pas ce qui m'attire en** *ou* **chez elle,** I don't know what attracts me to her; **la Grèce, ça ne vous attire pas?,** doesn't Greece appeal to you?; **sa pièce attire un grand public,** his play is a great draw; **a. qn dans un coin,** to draw s.o. into a corner, to take s.o. into a corner; **a. qch à** *ou* **sur qn,** to bring sth on s.o.; **a. la colère de qn sur qn,** to bring down s.o.'s wrath on s.o.; **je voudrais a. votre attention sur ce point,** I'd like to draw your attention to this point; **cela risque de vous a. des ennuis/des ennemis,** that may cause you problems/make enemies for you;

(b) (*séduire*) to entice, to lure; **elle aime a. les hommes,** she likes to attract men, she likes being attractive to men; **a. qn dans un piège,** to lure s.o. into a trap; **a. qn par des promesses,** to entice s.o. with promises; **affiche qui attire les regards,** eye-catching poster; **a. l'imagination,** to appeal to the imagination.

2 s'attirer *vpr* to attract each other; **ils s'attirent,** they're attracted to each other; **s'a. l'attention publique,** to attract public attention; **s'a. des critiques/des éloges,** to come in for criticism/praise; **vous vous l'êtes attiré vous-même,** you have brought it (up)on yourself; **s'a. des sympathies/des ennemis,** to gain sympathy/to make enemies.

attisée [atize] *nf* armful of firewood; *Can* good fire, good blaze.

attiser [atize] *vt* **(a)** to stir (up), to poke (*fire*); *Ind etc* to stoke (*fire*); **(b)** *Fig* to fan (*fire, discontent*); **a. les haines,** to stir up hatred.

attitré [atitre] *adj* regular, appointed, recognized; accredited (*journalist*); **fournisseurs attitrés de sa Majesté,** purveyors by appointment to his *or* her Majesty; **mon marchand de légumes a.,** my usual *or* regular greengrocer; **mon fauteuil a.,** my chair, the chair I sit in.

attitrer [atitre] *vt* to appoint (*ambassador*).

attitude [atityd] *nf* **(a)** attitude, posture; **a. hostile/intransigeante,** hostile/uncompromising attitude (**envers, à l'égard de, pour, en face de,** towards); **quelle est votre a. vis à vis de ce problème?,** what is your stance *or* position on this problem?, how do you stand on this problem?; *Péj* **ce n'est qu'une a.,** it's only (an) affectation *or* pose; **(b)** (*conduite*) behaviour; **je n'aime pas son a.,** I don't like the way he behaves; **prendre une a. décontractée,** to adopt a casual air *or* manner.

attractif, -ive [atraktif, -iv] *adj* attractive, drawing (*power, force of magnet*); gravitational (*force*).

attraction [atraksjɔ̃] *nf* **(a)** attraction, pull (*of magnet etc*); *Phys* **a. universelle,** gravitation; **a. moléculaire,** molecular attraction; **(b)** attraction (*of place, person etc*); **l'a. de deux personnes,** the attraction between two people; **exercer une a. sur qn,** to attract s.o.; **leur a. a été immédiate,** they were drawn to each other immediately; **l'a. qui me porte vers cet endroit,** the attraction this place has for me; **(c)** number (*in cabaret*); *F* **il est la grosse a.,** he is the big attraction; **(d) attractions,** attractions; (*at fair*) sideshows; *Th* variety show; (*in restaurant*) cabaret show; **parc d'attractions,** amusement park; **les attractions passent à 21 heures,** the show starts at 9 o'clock.

attrait [atrɛ] *nm* **(a)** (*chose*) attraction, lure; (*état*) attractiveness; (*de la jeunesse etc*) charm; **l'a. de la mer,** the call of the sea; **l'a. de l'aventure,** the lure of adventure; **les attraits d'une carrière dans le commerce,** the attraction of a business career; **dépourvu d'a.,** unattractive, devoid of attraction; **(b)** (*penchant*) inclination; **se sentir de l'a. pour qn,** to feel drawn towards s.o., to feel a liking *or* a sympathy for s.o.; **(c) attraits,** (*d'une femme*) charms; **(d)** *Pêche* bait.

attrapade [atrapad] *nf*, **attrapage** [atrapaʒ] *nm F* **(a)** (*dispute*) quarrel, set-to; **(b)** (*critique*) ticking-off; **j'ai eu droit à un(e) bon(ne) a.,** I got a right telling-off.

attrape [atrap] *nf* **(a)** (*farce*) trick, hoax; **faire une a. à qn,** to play a trick *or* a practical joke on s.o.; (*tromper*) to take s.o. in; **c'est une a.,** there's a catch in it; **magasin de farces et attrapes,** joke shop; **(b)** *Arch* trap, gin snare (*for birds etc*).

attrape-couillon [atrapkujɔ̃] *nm F* gimmick; (*pl attrape-couillon(s)*).

attrape-mouche(s) [atrapmuʃ] *nm inv* **(a)** (*piège*) flypaper; **(b)** (*fleur*) Venus flytrap, Venus's-flytrap.

attrape-nigaud [atrapnigo] *nm* trick; (*pl attrape-nigaud(s)*).

attrape-poussières [atrappusjɛr] *nm inv F* white elephant.

attraper [atrape] **1** *vt* **(a)** (*capturer*) to catch (*s.o.*); to (en)trap, to (en)snare (*animal*); **a. qn,** (*tromper*) to trick *or* cheat s.o., to take s.o. in; **là, vous êtes bien attrapé,** you fell for it hook, line and sinker *or* good and proper;

(b) *(saisir)* to catch *(ball, thief etc)*; **les voleurs se sont fait a.,** the thieves were caught; **attention si je t'attrape!,** if I catch you there'll be trouble!; **a. un autobus/un train,** to catch a bus/a train; **vous avez bien attrapé la ressemblance,** you have caught the likeness; **en a. pour dix ans,** to get ten years' (imprisonment); *Aut etc* **a. une contravention,** to get a ticket; **a. un accent,** to pick up an accent; **je n'ai pu a. que quelques secondes/bribes de leur conversation,** I could only catch a few seconds/snatches of their conversation;

(c) to hit; **une pierre l'a attrapé au front,** a stone hit *or* caught him on the forehead;

(d) a. froid, to catch a chill; **a. un bon coup de soleil,** to get badly sunburned; **a. un rhume,** to catch (a) cold;

(e) *F* **a. qn à qch,** to catch s.o. doing sth; **et méfie-toi, si je t'y attrape encore une fois!,** don't let me catch you (at it) again!; **a. qn sur le fait,** to catch s.o. in the act *or* red-handed;

(f) *F (gronder)* **a. qn,** to scold s.o., to give s.o. a good talking to; **on va vous a.,** you'll catch it, you'll get it in the neck; **se faire a.,** to get hauled over the coals, to catch it.

2 s'attraper *vpr* **(a)** *(d'une maladie etc)* to be caught; **(b)** *(de personnes)* to scold each other.

attrape-touristes [atrapturist] *nm inv F* tourist trap.

attrayant [atrɛjɑ̃] *adj* attractive, engaging, alluring, enticing; **peu a.,** unattractive.

attribuable [atribɥabl] *adj* attributable, ascribable, **(à,** to); **erreur a. à ...,** error due to ....

attribuer [atribɥe] **1** *vt* **(a)** *(allouer)* to assign, to allot **(à,** to); to confer **(à,** (up)on); to award *(prize)*; **a. des rôles** *ou* **des fonctions,** to allocate duties **(à,** to); *Th* **a. un rôle à qn,** to cast s.o. for a part; **a. le rôle de Cyrano à qn,** to cast s.o. as Cyrano; **(b)** to attribute, to ascribe *(fact, book etc)* **(à,** to); to impute *(crime, mistake)* **(à,** to); to attach *(importance to sth)*; **ne m'attribue pas des motivations qui sont les tiennes,** don't attribute your motives to me; **a. un projet à qn,** to give s.o. the credit for a plan; **tableau attribué à Hogarth,** painting attributed to Hogarth. **2 s'attribuer** *vpr* **s'a. qch,** to claim *or* lay claim to sth; to take *(a duty)* upon oneself.

attribut [atriby] **1** *nm* attribute. **2** *adj Gram* attributive; **nom a.,** attributive noun.

attribution [atribysjɔ̃] *nm* assigning, attribution, attributing **(à,** to); allocation, allocating *(of duties)*; awarding *(of scholarships etc)*; *Th* casting *(of parts)*; **l'a. de cette œuvre à Maillol est inexacte,** this work is wrongly attributed to Maillol; *Gram* **complément d'a.,** indirect object; *Bourse* **actions d'a.,** bonus shares; **avis d'a.,** letter of allotment; **a. (d'essence/de sucre),** quota, ration (of petrol/sugar); **attributions,** prerogative, competence, powers; *(de fonction)* duties, functions, responsibilities; **cela entre dans ses attributions,** this comes within his competence *or* his province *or* is part of his duties.

attriqué [atrike] *adj Can* **mal a.,** badly dressed.

attristant [atristɑ̃] *adj* saddening, depressing *(news etc)*; **temps a.,** gloomy *or* depressing weather.

attristé [atriste] *adj* sad *(face)*; sorrowful *(look)*; **contempler qch d'un œil a.,** to gaze sadly at sth.

attrister [atriste] **1** *vt* to sadden, to grieve; **cette décision m'attriste,** I am saddened by this decision; **cela m'attriste de voir ...,** it makes me sad *or* I am saddened to see ... . **2 s'attrister** *vpr* to be sad, to grieve **(de qch,** about sth).

attroupement [atrupmɑ̃] *nm* crowd *(of demonstrators etc)*; *Jur* unlawful *or* riotous assembly; **la loi contre les attroupements,** ≈ the Riot Act; **un a. pacifique,** a peaceful assembly.

attrouper [atrupe] **1** *vt* to gather *(mob etc)* together. **2 s'attrouper** *vpr* to gather, to assemble; **les manifestants s'attroupaient,** the demonstrators were gathering.

atypique [atipik] *adj Méd etc* atypic(al).

au [o] *voir* **À.**

aubade [obad] *nf* dawn serenade.

aubaine [obɛn] *nf* **(a)** *(chance etc)* windfall, godsend; **profiter de l'a.,** to take advantage of one's good luck; **quelle a.!,** what a stroke of luck!; **(b)** *Can* bargain, good buy.

aube¹ [ob] *nf* **(a)** *(matin)* dawn; **à l'a. (du jour),** at dawn, at break of day, at daybreak; **partir dès l'a.,** to leave at dawn; **l'a. de la civilisation,** the dawn of civilization; **(b)** *Rel* alb.

aube² *nf* **(a)** *Nau* paddle, blade, float(board) *(of wheel)*; **roue à aubes,** paddle (wheel); **vapeur à roue à aubes,** paddleboat; **(b)** blade, vane *(of turbine)*; vane *(of fan)*.

aubépine [obepin] *nf (arbuste)* hawthorn, may (tree); **fleurs d'a.,** may (blossom).

aubère [obɛr] **1** *adj* red roan. **2** *nm* red roan horse.

auberge [obɛrʒ] *nf* inn; **tenir a.,** to keep an inn; *F* to keep open house; *Fig* **c'est un peu une a. espagnole,** what you get out of it depends on what you put in; **a. de jeunesse,** youth hostel; **il prend notre maison pour une a.,** he treats our house like a hotel; *F* **on n'est pas sorti de l'a.,** we're not out of the wood(s) yet.

aubergine [obɛrʒin] **1** *nf (plante)* aubergine, egg-plant; *Fig F (contractuelle)* (female) traffic warden. **2** *adj inv* aubergine-coloured.

aubergiste [obɛrʒist] *n* innkeeper.

aubette [obɛt] *nf surtout Belg* newspaper kiosk; *(abribus)* bus shelter.

aubriétie [obriesi] *nf (plante)* aubrietia.

auburn [obœrn] *adj inv* auburn.

aucun, -une [okœ̃, -yn] **1** *pron* **(a)** *(positif)* anyone, any; **il travaille plus qu'a.,** he works more than anyone (else);

(b) *(with implied negation)* **de tous vos soi-disant amis, a. interviendra-t-il?,** will any of your so-called friends intervene?;

(c) *(with negation expressed or understood, accompanied by* **ne** *or* **sans)** *(être humain)* no one, nobody; *(chose)* none, not any; **lequel des deux veux-tu? — a.,** which of the two do you want? – neither; **je ne me fie à a. d'entre eux,** I don't trust any of them; **a. d'autre que toi ne le fait aussi bien,** nobody does it as well as you do; **a. (des deux) ne viendra,** neither (of them) will come; **de tous ces élèves a. n'a répondu,** not one of these pupils answered;

(d) *Litt* **d'aucuns,** some people; **d'aucuns prétendent qu'il est encore en vie,** there are some who maintain that he is still alive.

2 *adj* **(a)** *(positif)* any; **un des plus beaux livres qui aient été écrits sur a. sujet,** one of the finest books written on any subject; **plus rapide qu'a. autre coureur,** faster than any other runner; **avez-vous aucune intention de le faire?,** have you any intention of doing it?;

(b) *(négatif)* **vendre qch sans a. bénéfice,** to make no profit on the sale of sth; **sans aucune exception,** without exception; **le fait n'a aucune importance,** the fact is of no importance; **il n'a a. mérite,** he is of no merit; **je n'ai aucune idée,** I don't have any idea, I have no idea; **oui, sans a. doute,** yes, without a doubt; **en aucune façon je ne l'aiderai,** I will not help him in any way (at all); **réparer qch sans a. mal,** to repair sth with no difficulty at all; **sans mentionner a. nom,** without mentioning any names; **il n'a jamais fait a. mal à personne,** he never did anyone any harm.

aucunement [okynmɑ̃] *adv (with negation expressed or understood)* in no way, not at all, by no means, not in the slightest, not in the least; **je n'en suis a. étonné,** I am not the slightest bit surprised; **je ne la connais a.,** I don't know her at all; **je ne m'attendais a. à ce qu'il vînt,** I never expected him to come.

audace [odas] *nf* **(a)** *(assurance)* audacity, audaciousness; boldness, daring; **il faut beaucoup d'a. pour le faire/réussir,** you need to be very bold *or* very daring to do it/to succeed; **(b)** *(aplomb)* audacity, impudence; **vous avez l'a. de me dire cela!,** you have the audacity *or* impudence *or* cheek *or* nerve to tell me that!; **ah! tu ne manques pas d'a.!,** you've got the cheek of the Devil!; **(c) une a.,** daring; **elle est jeune, elle a toutes les audaces,** she is young and daring; **une a. de style,** daring unconventionality of style.

audacieusement [odasjøzmɑ̃] *adv (voir adj)* **(a)** audaciously, boldly, daringly; **(b)** impudently.

audacieux, -euse [odasjø, -øz] *adj* **(a)** *(courageux)* audacious, bold, daring; **(b)** impudent; brazen *(lie etc)*.

au-deçà [odsa] *Arch* **1** *adv* on this side. **2** *prép* **au-d. de,** on this side of, without going as far as.

au-dedans [odədɑ̃] **1** *adv* inside. **2** *prép* **au-d. de,** inside, within.

au-dehors [odəɔr] **1** *adv* outside. **2** *prép* **au-d. de,** outside, beyond.

au-delà [odla] **1** *adv* beyond. **2** *nm* **l'au-d.,** the next world, the hereafter. **3** *prép* **au-d. de,** beyond, on the other side of; **n'allez pas au-d. de cent francs,** don't go above *or* beyond a hundred francs.

au-dessous [otsu] **1** *adv* **(a)** below, under (it); **sur la table et au-d.,** on the table and under it; **le château est en haut de la colline, le village est au-d.,** the castle is at the top of the hill, with the village down below;

(b) below, underneath; **les locataires au-d.,** the tenants below *or* downstairs; **les enfants âgés de sept ans et au-**

d., children of seven (years) and under; **on en trouve à 50 francs et même a.-d.,** you can get them for 50 francs or even less; **musique transposée deux tons au-d.,** music transposed two tones lower *or* two tones down.

2 *prép* **au-d. de (a)** below, under; **le village est au-d. du château,** the village lies at the foot of the castle; **cinquante kilomètres au-d. de Paris,** fifty kilometres below *or* down river from Paris; **au-d. du genou,** below the knee;

(b) below, underneath; **les locataires au-d. de nous,** the tenants (on the floor) below us; **quinze degrés au-d. de zéro,** fifteen degrees below zero; **au-d. de la moyenne/du pair,** below average/par; *Litt* **il est au-d. de lui de se plaindre,** it is beneath him to complain; **au-d. de cinq ans,** under five (years of age); **quantités au-d. de 30 kilos,** quantities of less than 30 kilos; **acheter qch au-d. de sa valeur,** to buy sth for less than it is worth; **son travail était au-d. de mon attente,** his work fell short of what I expected; **je suis au-d. de la tâche,** I'm not up to the job; **être au-d. de tout,** to be worse than useless.

au-dessus [otsy] **1** *adv* **(a)** above (it); **le village est en bas de la colline, le château au-d.,** the village is at the foot of the hill, with the castle (up) above (it);

(b) une terrasse avec une marquise au-d., a terrace with an awning over it *or* above; **la salle de bains est au-d.,** the bathroom is upstairs; **mille francs et au-d.,** a thousand francs and up(wards); **la qualité au-d.,** the next grade up; **tout ce qui est au-d. est bien meilleur,** everything up-market of this is a lot better; **musique transposée un ton au-d.,** music transposed a tone higher.

2 *prép* **au-d. de (a)** above; **le château est situé au-d. du village,** the castle stands above the village; **il a son nom au-d. de la porte,** his name is above *or* over the door; **les avions volaient au-d. de nos têtes,** the planes were flying overhead; **l'eau leur montait jusqu'au-d. des genoux,** the water came up above their knees; **deux degrés au-d. de zéro,** two degrees above zero; **au-d. de cinquante francs,** more than fifty francs; **cinquante kilomètres au-d. de Paris,** fifty kilometres above *or* up river from Paris; **au-d. de la moyenne,** above average; **au-d. de cinq ans,** over five (years of age);

(b) elle a une sagesse au-d. de son âge, she is wise beyond her years; **le colonel est au-d. du commandant,** a colonel is higher than a major; **la tâche est au-d. de leurs forces,** the job is too much for them *or* is beyond them; **vivre au-d. de ses moyens,** to live beyond one's means; **je suis au-d. de ça,** I'm above that, I wouldn't stoop to that; **être au-d. de sa classe,** to be ahead of one's class.

au-devant [odvɑ̃] (*used only in such phrases as* **aller** *ou* **courir** *ou* **se jeter** *ou* **se précipiter au-d.**) **1** *adv* **quand il y a du danger, je vais au-d.,** when there is danger ahead, I go to meet it; **quand je prévois une objection je vais au-d.,** when I anticipate an objection, I take steps in advance. **2** *prép* **aller/courir au-d. de qn,** to go/run to meet s.o.; **aller au-d. des désirs de qn,** to anticipate s.o.'s wishes; **aller au-d. d'un danger,** to anticipate a danger; **aller au-d. d'un complot,** to forestall a plot; **aller au-d. du danger/d'une défaite,** to court danger/failure.

audibilité [odibilite] *nf* audibility.

audible [odibl] *adj* audible.

audience [odjɑ̃s] *nf* **(a)** *Jur* hearing (by the court); sitting, session, court; **plaider en pleine a.** *ou* **en a. publique,** to plead in open court; **a. à huis clos,** hearing in camera; **tenir a.,** to hold a court *or* a sitting; **l'a. est reprise,** the case is resumed; **(b)** (*intérêt*) following; **ce cinéaste a trouvé a. auprès des jeunes,** this film-maker has gained a following among young people; **(c)** (*public*) audience; **(d)** audience, hearing; **recevoir qn sur lettre d'a.,** to interview s.o. by appointment; **tenir une a.,** (*of king*) to hold an audience; **donner une a. à qn,** to grant an audience.

audiencier[odjɑ̃sje] *nm Jur* **huissier a.,** court crier; usher.

audiofréquence [odjofrekɑ̃s] *nf* audiofrequency.

audiomètre [odjomɛtr] *nm* audiometer.

audionumérique [odjonymerik] *adj* digital audio; **disque a.,** compact disc.

audio-oral, -aux [odjɔɔral, -o] *adj* audio (*method, exercise*).

audioprothésiste [odjoprɔtezist] *n* hearing-aid specialist.

audio(-)visuel, -elle [odjɔvizɥɛl] **1** *adj* audiovisual. **2** *nm* audiovisual aids.

audit [odit] *nm* audit; **cabinet d'a.,** company of auditors; **être chargé de l'a. d'une société,** to audit a company; **a. social,** = management consultancy report.

auditer [odite] *vt* to audit (*a company*).

auditeur, -trice [oditœr, -tris] *n* **(a)** hearer, listener; **les auditeurs,** the audience; *Rad TV* **programme des auditeurs,** request programme; *Univ* **aller à la fac en a. libre,** to sit in on university lectures, *Am* to audit a course; **(b)** *Admin* **a. à la Cour des comptes,** = Commissioner of Audit; **(c)** (*chargé de l'audit*) auditor.

auditif, -ive [oditif, -iv] *adj* auditory (*nerve*); **prothèse** *ou* **aide auditive,** hearing aid; **mémoire auditive,** aural memory.

audition [odisjɔ̃] *nf* **(a)** audition (*of singer etc*); **avoir une a.,** to have an audition; **(b)** hearing (*of sounds*); audition; **juger d'un opéra à la première a.,** to judge an opera at the first hearing; **(c)** *Jur* **a. des témoins,** hearing *or* examination of the witnesses; **nouvelle a.,** rehearing; **(d) a. de piano,** (private) piano recital;

auditionner [odisjɔne] **1** *vt* to audition (*s.o.*). **2** *vi Th etc* to have an audition, to audition (**pour un rôle,** for a part).

auditoire [oditwar] *nm* **(a)** audience; *Rel* congregation; **(b)** *Jur* court; *Belg & Suisse* auditorium.

auditorium [oditɔrjɔm] *nm* auditorium; *Rad TV* (broadcasting, television) studio.

auge [oʒ] *nf* **(a)** (*pour animaux*) trough; **a. d'écurie,** manger; *F* **amène ton a.!,** (*assiette*) pass me your plate; **(b)** flume, channel (*for leading water to mill*); *HydE* = **AUGET (b)**; **(c)** (*d'un concasseur*) hopper.

auget [oʒɛ] *nm* **(a)** (small) trough; seed trough, water trough (*of a bird cage*); **(b)** bucket (*of water wheel*); **roue à augets,** bucket *or* overshot wheel.

augmentation [ɔgmɑ̃tasjɔ̃] *nf* **(a)** increase, growth; *Admin* increment; **a. de salaire,** rise *or* increase in wages, *Am* raise; **a. du capital,** increase in capital; **demander une a.,** to ask for a (pay-)rise *or Am* raise; **a. de prix,** increase in prices; **être en a.,** to be rising *or* on the increase; **(b)** *Mus* augmentation; **(c)** *Tricot* **faire une a.,** to make a stitch, to make one.

augmenter [ɔgmɑ̃te] **1** *vt* to increase, to enlarge; **a. ses terres,** to extend *or* add to one's estate; **a. la durée de cuisson,** to increase the cooking time; **édition augmentée,** enlarged edition; **a. une douleur,** to aggravate a pain; **cela risque d'a. sa colère,** that is liable to make him even more angry; **a. le prix de qch,** to raise *or* put up the price of sth; **a. qn,** to raise *or* increase s.o.'s salary *or* wages; *Mus* **en augmentant,** crescendo.

2 *vi* **(a)** to increase; **la criminalité augmente,** crime is increasing *or* on the increase; **empêcher les frais d'a.,** to keep expenses down; **tout augmente!,** everything's going up!; **le prix a augmenté de 10% par rapport à l'année dernière,** the price is up 10% on last year; **la douleur augmente,** the pain is worsening; **la chaleur augmente,** it is getting hotter; **la difficulté semble a. à mesure qu'on progresse,** it seems to get harder the more progress we make; **un conflit qui va en augmentant,** an escalating conflict;

(b) *Nau* **a. de toile,** to crowd on sail;

(c) *Tricot* to make a stitch, to make one; **a. de deux points au commencement du rang suivant,** increase two at the beginning of the next row.

3 s'augmenter *vpr* to increase; **notre société s'est augmentée d'une nouvelle part de capital/de trois nouveaux cadres/de filiales à l'étranger,** our firm has acquired new capital/three new managers/branches abroad.

augure¹ [ɔgyr] *nm Antiq* augur; **consulter les augures,** to consult the oracle; **le Collège des augures,** the College of Augurs.

augure² *nm* augury, omen; **tirer un bon/mauvais a. de qch,** to see a good/bad omen in sth; **de bon a.,** auspicious; **de mauvais a.,** ominous; **prendre les augures,** to take the auguries; *Fig* **oiseau de mauvais a.,** bird of ill omen.

augurer [ɔgyre] *vt* to augur, to forecast; **a. l'avenir,** to forecast *or* foresee the future; **a. bien/mal de qch,** to feel optimistic/pessimistic about sth; *Vieilli* to augur well/ill for sth; **que peut-on a. de cette rencontre?,** what is going to happen at this meeting?; **je n'augure rien de bon de tout cela,** I don't see any good coming of all this.

auguste [ɔgyst] *adj* august, majestic; **une a. assemblée,** an illustrious assembly.

Auguste [ɔgyst] *nm* **(a)** *Hist* Augustus; **le siècle d'A.,** the Augustan Age; **(b) l'a.,** the 'funny man' (*at circus*).

Augustin [ɔgystɛ̃] **1** *adj Rel* Augustinian. **2** *nm* **(a)** Augustine; **(b)** *Rel* Augustinian (friar); **les Augustins,** the Augustin friars.

augustinien, -ienne [ɔgystinjɛ̃, -jɛn] *adj Phil* Augustinian.

auj. *abrév* **aujourd'hui.**

aujourd'hui [oʒurdɥi] **1** *adv* today; **il arrive a.,** he is coming today; **quel jour sommes-nous a.?,** what day is it today?; **c'est a. le cinq/dimanche,** today is the fifth/is Sunday; **les jeunes gens d'a.,** (the) young people (of) today; **l'Europe d'a.,** modern- *or* present-day Europe, the Europe of today; **le journal d'a.,** today's paper; **ce sera tout pour a.,** that's all for today; **(d')a. en huit/en quinze,** today week/fortnight; **il y a a. huit jours,** a week ago today; **je ne l'ai pas vue a.,** I have not seen *or* set eyes on her today; **ce n'est pas d'a. que je la connais,** I have known her for a long time; *F* **c'est pour a. ou pour demain?,** (*je t'attends*) are you coming today *or* tomorrow? **2** *nm* **a. passé, on ne pourra plus y aller,** after today we shall no longer be able to go there.

aulne [on] *nm* (*arbre*) alder.

aulx *voir* **AIL.**

aumône [ɔmon] *nf* alms; **demander l'a.,** to beg; **faire l'a. à qn,** to give money to s.o.; **donner qch en a. à qn,** to give s.o. sth out of charity; **réduit à l'a.,** reduced to begging; *Fig* **faire l'a. d'un regard à qn,** to spare s.o. a glance; to condescend *or* deign to look at s.o..

aumônier [ɔmonje] *nm* chaplain; **aumônier militaire,** army chaplain.

aune[1] [on] *nm* (*arbre*) alder.

aune[2] *nf Arch* ell (1m.188); *Fig* **figure longue d'une a.,** face as long as a fiddle.

auparavant [oparavɑ̃] *adv* before(hand), previously; **a. il faut s'assurer de ...,** first we must make sure of ...; **l'année a.,** the preceding year, the year before; **comme a.,** as before; **mais a. nous devons parler,** but we must have a talk first *or* beforehand.

auprès [oprɛ] **1** *prép* **a. de (a)** close to, (close) by, beside, near; **tout a. de qn/qch,** close to *or* beside s.o./sth; **il a toujours une garde-malade a. de lui,** he always has a nurse with him *or* at hand; **ambassadeur a. du roi de Suède,** ambassador to the King of Sweden; **avocat a. du tribunal,** advocate attached to the tribunal; **(b)** (*indicating a relationship*) **agir a. de qn,** to use one's influence with s.o.; **être bien a. de qn,** to be in favour with s.o., to be in s.o.'s good books; **trouver grâce a. de qn,** to find favour in s.o.'s sight *or* eyes; **je sais que je passe pour un idiot a. d'eux,** I know that they take me for an idiot; **(c)** (*en comparaison de*) compared with, in comparison with. **2** *adv Litt* close *or* near to; **voilà l'église, la maison est tout a.,** there is the church, the house is close to it *or* nearby; **il n'y a rien à mettre a.,** there is nothing to be compared with it.

auquel [okɛl] *voir* **LEQUEL.**

aura [ɔra] *nf* aura; *Méd* **a. épileptique,** epileptic aura.

auréole [ɔreɔl] *nf* **(a)** halo (*of saint, moon*); corona (*of sun*); **il pare son épouse d'une a.,** he puts his wife on a pedestal; **entouré de l'a. de la gloire/réussite,** bathed in glory/flushed with success; *Com* **détachant qui ne laisse pas d'a.,** stain remover that leaves no ring; **(b)** *Phot* halation.

auréoler [ɔreɔle] **1** *vt* (*d'un peintre*) to surround with a halo; *Fig* to exalt, to glorify; **elle est auréolée de génie,** she positively radiates genius. **2 s'auréoler** *vpr* to be crowned (**de,** with).

auréomycine [ɔreɔmisin] *nf Méd* aureomycin.

auriculaire [ɔrikylɛr] **1** *adj* auricular (*confession etc*); **témoin a.,** auricular *or* ear witness; **le doigt a.,** the little finger; *Anat* **appendice a.,** auricular appendix; *Mil etc* **protecteur a.,** ear protector. **2** *nm* **l'a.,** the little finger.

auricule [ɔrikyl] *nf* **(a)** *Anat* auricle (*of the heart*); **a. de l'oreille,** lower lobe of the ear; **(b)** *Bot Zool* auricula, auricle; (*de mollusque*) auricula.

auriculothérapie [ɔrikylɔterapi] *nf Méd* aural acupuncture.

aurifère [ɔrifɛr] *adj* gold-bearing; **champ a.,** goldfield.

aurifier [ɔrifie] *vt* to put a gold filling in (*a tooth*).

Aurigny [ɔriɲi] *nm* Alderney; **vache d'A.,** Alderney cow.

auriol [ɔriɔl] *nm* (*oiseau*) oriole.

aurique [ɔrik] *adj Nau* **voile a.,** gaffsail; **gréement a.,** gaff rig; **à gréement a.,** gaff-rigged.

aurochs [ɔrɔks] *nm* aurochs, wild ox.

aurore [ɔrɔr] **1** *nf* **(a)** dawn, daybreak, break of day; **l'a. commence à paraître** *ou* **à poindre,** dawn is breaking; *Fig* **l'a. de la civilisation,** the dawn of civilization; **a. australe,** aurora australis; **a. boréale,** aurora borealis, northern lights; **a. polaire,** aurora polaris, polar light; **(b)** orange tip (*butterfly*). **2** *adj inv* (saffron, golden) yellow.

auscultation [ɔskyltɑsjɔ̃] *nf Méd* auscultation.

ausculter [ɔskylte] *vt Méd* to sound (*patient etc*).

auspices [ɔspis] *nmpl* (*présage*) auspice, omen; **mauvais a.,** ill *or* bad omen; **l'année commence sous d'heureux/de fâcheux a.,** the year begins auspiciously/inauspiciously; **sous les a. de qn,** under the auspices of s.o..

aussi [osi] **1** *adv* **(a)** (*in comparative sentences*) as; **pas a.,** not so, not as; **il est a. grand que son frère,** he is as tall as his brother; **tout a. au sud/à l'est que Paris,** as far south/east as Paris; **ma méthode est tout a. bonne que la vôtre,** my method is just *or* every bit as good as yours; **on pourrait a. bien rester là ce soir,** we might as well stay here this evening; **je le connais a. peu que son frère,** I don't know him any better than I know his brother;

(b) (*tellement*) so; **après avoir attendu a. longtemps,** after waiting so long *or* for such a long time; **je ne pensais pas que tu étais a. sensible,** I didn't think you were so sensitive; **une a. bonne affaire, ça ne se manque pas,** a deal as good as that shouldn't be passed up; **un homme a. travailleur que vous,** a man as hardworking as you; **je ne connais personne d'a. gentil,** I don't know anyone nicer; **avez-vous jamais entendu une symphonie a. bizarre?,** have you ever heard such a peculiar symphony?;

(c) (*également*) also, too; **c'est a. ce que je pense,** that's what I think too; **vous venez a.,** you are coming too; **elle fait du grec, et a. du latin,** she's doing Greek and Latin too; **je suis fatigué — toi a.?,** I'm tired — you too?; **gardez a. ceux-là,** keep those too *or* as well; **moi a.,** so am I, so can I, so do I, so shall I, so did I, so was I *etc*.; **et moi a. je suis peintre,** I'm a painter too *or* as well; **a. bien que,** as well as, (both)... and...; **le vieillard, a. bien que sa femme se frottaient les mains,** (both) the old man and his wife rubbed their hands;

(d) (*quelque*) however; **a. sincère qu'Anne soit,** however sincere Anne may be; **a. bizarre qu'il soit/semble** however odd *or* peculiar it may be/seem.

2 *conj* **(a)** therefore, consequently, so; **la vie est chère ici, a. nous devons** *ou* **devons-nous économiser,** the cost of living is high here, so we have to economize; **il ne regarde pas où il met les pieds, a. il tombe,** he doesn't watch where he's going so he falls; *F* **a., c'est ta faute,** after all, it's your fault;

(b) *Litt* **a. bien,** moreover, for that matter, in any case, besides, and as a matter of fact, though; **il faut patienter un peu, a. bien n'avez-vous que vingt ans,** you must be patient, after all, you are only twenty.

aussitôt [osito] **1** *adv* immediately, directly, at once; **a. dit, a. fait,** no sooner said than done; **a. l'argent reçu je vous paierai,** as soon as I get the money I will pay you; **a. après,** immediately after; **a. après son retour je suis parti,** as soon as *or* the minute he returned I left. **2** *conj* **a. que** + *ind*, as soon as; **il se repentit de ses paroles a. qu'il les eut prononcées,** he regretted his words as soon as he had said them.

austère [ɔstɛr] *adj* austere (*life*); strict (*fast*); severe (*style*); stern (*countenance*); plain, severe (*dress*).

austèrement [ɔstɛrmɑ̃] *adv* austerely.

austérité [ɔsterite] *nf* **(a)** austerity; **vivre dans l'a.,** to live in austerity; **la période d'a.,** the days of austerity; **mesures d'a.,** austerity measures; **(b) austérités,** asceticism, mortification of the flesh.

austral, -als *ou* **-aux** [ɔstral, -o] *adj* southern (*hemisphere etc*); **aurore australe,** southern lights.

Australasie [ɔstralazi] *nf* Australasia.

australasien, -ienne [ɔstralazjɛ̃, -jɛn] **1** *adj* Australasian. **2** *n* **A.,** Australasian.

Australie [ɔstrali] *nf* Australia; **l'A. méridionale,** South Australia; **l'A. occidentale,** Western Australia.

australien, -ienne [ɔstraljɛ̃, -jɛn] **1** *adj* Australian. **2** *n* **A.,** Australian.

austro-hongrois, -oise [ɔstroɔ̃grwa, -waz] *Hist* **1** *adj* Austro-Hungarian. **2** *n* **A.-H.,** Austro-Hungarian.

autant [otɑ̃] *adv* **(a)** (*intensité*) as much, so much; (*de choses individuelles*) as many, so many; **je ne le savais pas a. respecté,** I did not know he was so greatly respected; **travailles-tu toujours a.?,** (*qu'aujourd'hui*) do you always work this hard?; (*qu'avant*) are you working as hard as ever?; **a. en emporte le vent,** (*of promises etc*) it's all idle talk; **je consens, mais à charge d'a.,** I consent, but on condition that I do the same for you; **a. vous l'aimez, a. il vous hait,** he hates you as much as you love him; **tout a.,** quite as much, quite as many; **encore a., une fois a.,** as much again, as many again; **deux fois a.,** twice as much; **rendre à qn six fois a.,** to repay s.o. sixfold; *F* **cela vaut a.,** it's just as well; **cela t'augmente d'a.,** that will bring you in as much again; **j'aimerais a. aller au cinéma,** I would just as soon go to the cinema;

(b) ils ont a. dire accepté, they have practically accepted; **on a mis 10 heures, a. dire 12,** we took 10 hours, call it 12; **la bataille était a. dire perdue,** the battle was as good as lost; **a. le faire tout de suite,** better do it right away; **a. ne rien faire du tout,** we might as well do nothing at all; **le travail est fini ou a. vaut,** the work is as good as finished, the work is finished or as good as; **a. vaut rester ici,** we may as well stay here; **a. vaudrait dire que ...,** one might as well say that ...; **a. dire que c'était difficile/que je n'étais pas content,** as you can imagine, it was difficult/I wasn't happy;

(c) a. que, as much as; (*de choses individuelles*) as many as; as far as, as near as; **a. que possible,** as much as possible; **a. que de besoin,** as much as is necessary; **faites a. que vous pourrez,** do as much as you can; **(pour) a. que je sache,** as far as I know, to the best of my knowledge; **j'en sais a. que toi,** your guess is as good as mine, I know as much (about it) as you do; **c'est a. ta faute que la mienne,** it is as much your fault as mine, you're as much to blame as I am; **il est a. à craindre qu'elle,** he is as much to be feared as she is; *F* **a. ça qu'autre chose,** it's all the same to me; **a. qu'il est possible,** as far as it is possible; **a. que j'en puis(se) juger,** as far as I can judge; **pour a. qu'il est en mon pouvoir,** to the best of my ability;

(d) a. de, as much, so much; (*de choses individuelles*) as many, so many; **a. de filles que de garçons,** as many girls as boys; **ils ont a. de terrain/d'amis que vous,** they have as much land/as many friends as you; **on ne peut pas en dire a. de tout le monde,** you can't say as much for everybody; **essaie un peu d'en faire a.,** try to do the same; **peux-tu au moins en dire a.?,** can you say as much?; *Litt* **ce sont a. de (voleurs** *etc***),** they are nothing better than (a pack of thieves *etc*); **ce sera a. de moins à payer,** it will be so much the less to pay; **c'est a. de gagné,** that's so much gained *or* so much to the good;

(e) d'a., accordingly; **il faut se méfier avec l'ordinateur, d'a. que je ne suis pas un expert,** you have to watch what you're doing with the computer, especially since I'm no expert; **d'a. plus,** especially, particularly; **je suis trop fatigué pour y aller — d'a. plus!,** I'm too tired to go — all the more reason for doing so!; **d'a. plus/moins (que),** all the more/less (because); **j'en suis surpris, d'a. plus qu'au fond il est honnête,** I am all the more surprised because basically he is honest; **elle travaille d'a. mieux qu'elle se sait surveillée,** she works all the better for knowing that someone's keeping an eye on her; **cela vous sera d'a. plus facile que vous êtes jeune,** it will be all the easier for you since you are young;

(f) pour a., for all that; **elle ne s'en fait pas pour a.,** she doesn't worry for all that.

autarcie [otarsi] *nf Pol* autarky; **une communauté qui vit en a.,** a self-sufficient community.

autarcique [otarsik] *adj Pol* autarkic.

autel [otεl] *nm* altar; **maître a.,** high altar; **a. latéral,** side altar; **nappe d'a.,** altar cloth; **pierre d'a.,** altar stone, altar table; **tableau d'a.,** altarpiece; **conduire sa fille à l'a.,** to give one's daughter away (in marriage); **suivre qn à l'a.,** to marry s.o..

auteur [otœr] *nm* **(a)** author, writer (*of book*); composer (*of song*); painter (*of picture*); **femme a.,** woman writer; **droit d'a.,** copyright; **droits d'a.,** royalties; **un droit d'a. de 10%,** a royalty of 10%; *Fig* **citer ses auteurs,** to quote one's authorities; **(b)** author, maker, originator; founder (*of race*); perpetrator (*of crime*); promoter, sponsor (*of scheme*); *Jur* principal; **a. d'un accident,** party at fault in an accident; *Fig* **être l'a. de la ruine de qn,** to be the cause of s.o.'s downfall; **qui est l'a. de cette plaisanterie?,** whose idea was that joke?

authenticité [ɔ(o)tɑ̃tisite] *nf* authenticity, genuineness; **l'a. d'un événement,** the genuineness of an event; **mettre en doute l'a. d'une manifestation,** to question whether a demonstration is genuine.

authentification [ɔ(o)tɑ̃tifikɑsjɔ̃] *nf* authentication; **cachet d'a.,** approved stamp.

authentifier [ɔ(o)tɑ̃tifje] *vt* to authenticate.

authentique [ɔ(o)tɑ̃tik] *adj* authentic, genuine; **c'est un fait a.,** it's a positive fact; **bourgogne a.,** genuine burgundy; *Jur* **acte a.,** instrument drawn up by a solicitor; **copie a.,** certified copy; *Fin* **cours a.,** official quotation; *F* **je ne te mens pas!, c'est a.!, c'est ce qu'il a dit!,** I'm not lying to you, it's true! that's what he said!

authentiquement [ɔ(o)tɑ̃tikmɑ̃] *adv* authentically, genuinely.

authentiquer [ɔ(o)tɑ̃tike] *vt Vieilli* to authenticate, to certify, to legalize (*document etc*).

autisme [otism] *nm Psy* autism.

autiste [otist], **autistique** [otistik] *adj Psy* autistic.

auto [ɔto] **1** *nf F* (motor) car; **les autos tamponneuses,** dodgems, bumper cars; *Enf* **jouer avec des petites autos,** to play with toy cars. **2** *adj inv* **assurance a.,** car insurance; **budget a.,** car budget.

auto- [ɔtɔ] *préf* auto-, self-.

auto-accusation [ɔtɔakyzɑsjɔ̃] *nf* self-accusation.

auto-adhésif, -ive [ɔtɔadezif, -iv] *adj* self-adhesive; **bande auto-adhésive,** adhesive tape.

auto-allumage [ɔtɔalymaʒ] *nm* pre-ignition.

auto-amorçage [ɔtɔamɔrsaʒ] *nm* automatic priming (*of pump engine etc*).

autoberge [ɔtɔbεrʒ] *nf* = highway running along a river embankment.

autobiographie [ɔtɔbjɔgrafi] *nf* autobiography.

autobiographique [ɔtɔbjɔgrafik] *adj* autobiographic(al).

autobus [ɔtɔbys] *nm Aut* bus.

autocar [ɔtɔkar] *nm* **(a)** (motor) coach; **a. de luxe,** luxury coach; **(b)** (country) bus.

auto-censure [ɔtɔsɑ̃syr] *nf* self-censorship; **faire de l'a.-c.,** to practise self-censorship.

autochenille [ɔtɔʃnij] *nf* half-track vehicle.

autochrome [ɔtɔkrɔm] *adj* colour (*film*).

autochtone [ɔtɔktɔn] **1** *adj* aboriginal; *Can* native; *Géol* **terrain a.,** autochthonous rock. **2** *n* autochthon; *Can* native; **Conseil national des autochtones du Canada,** Native Council of Canada.

autocinétique [ɔtɔsinetik] *adj* autokinetic.

autoclave [ɔtɔklav] **1** *adj* hermetically-sealed, pressure-sealed. **2** *nm* **(a)** *Ch Ind* **(marmite) a.,** autoclave, digester; **(b)** *Méd* sterilizer; **(c)** *Culin Vieilli* pressure cooker.

autocollant [ɔtɔkɔlɑ̃] **1** *adj* self-adhesive. **2** *nm* sticker.

autoconduction [ɔtɔkɔ̃dyksjɔ̃] *nf Electron* mutual induction.

autoconsommation [ɔtɔkɔ̃sɔmɑsjɔ̃] *nf* subsistence farming; **économie d'a.,** subsistence economy.

autocopie [ɔtɔkɔpi] *nf* duplicating (*of documents*).

autocopier [ɔtɔkɔpje] *vt* (*pr sub & impf* **n. autocopiions, v. autocopiiez**) to duplicate.

auto-couchettes [ɔtɔkuʃεt] *adj inv* **train a.-c.,** ≈ motorail train.

autocrate [ɔtɔkrat] *n Pol* autocrat.

autocratie [ɔtɔkrasi] *nf Pol* autocracy.

autocratique [ɔtɔkratik] *adj* autocratic.

autocratiquement [ɔtɔkratikmɑ̃] *adv* autocratically.

autocritique [ɔtɔkritik] *nf* self-criticism.

autocuiseur [ɔtɔkɥizœr] *nm* pressure cooker.

autodafé [ɔtɔdafe] *nm Hist* auto-da-fé; **faire un a. de livres rares,** to burn rare books.

autodébrayage [ɔtɔdebrεjaʒ] *nm Aut* automatic clutch.

autodéfense [ɔtɔdefɑ̃s] *nf* self-defence.

autodestructeur, -trice [ɔtɔdεstryktœr, -tris] *adj* self-destructive.

auto-destruction [ɔtɔdεstryksjɔ̃] *nf* self-destruction.

autodétermination [ɔtɔdetεrminɑsjɔ̃] *nf Pol* self-determination.

autodidacte [ɔtɔdidakt] **1** *adj* self-taught, self-educated. **2** *n* autodidact.

autodrome [ɔtɔdrom] *nm* motor-racing track; (*pour les essais*) car-testing track.

auto-école [ɔtɔekɔl] *nf* school of motoring, driving school; (*pl auto-écoles*).

auto-érotique [ɔtɔerɔtik] *adj Psy* autoerotic.

auto-érotisme [ɔtɔerɔtism] *nm Psy* autoeroticism.

auto-fécondation [ɔtɔfekɔ̃dɑsjɔ̃] *nf Bot* self-pollination.

autofinancement [ɔtɔfinɑ̃smɑ̃] *nm Fin* self-financing, ploughing back of profits.

autofinancer (s') [sɔtɔfinɑ̃se] *vpr Fin* to be self-financing.

autofocus [ɔtɔfɔkys] *nm Phot* autofocus.

autogare [ɔtɔgar] *nf* coach *or* bus station.

autogène [ɔtɔʒεn] *adj* **(a) faire du training a.,** to learn how to relax; **(b) soudure a.,** autogenous weld.

autogenèse [ɔtɔʒənεz] *nf Biol* autogenesis.

autogéré [ɔtɔʒere] *adj* self-managed.

autogestion [ɔtɔʒεstjɔ̃] *nf* self-management.

autogestionnaire [ɔtɔʒεstjɔnεr] *adj* self-managing.

autogire [ɔtɔʒir] *nm Av* autogyro.

autograissage [ɔtɔgrεsaʒ] *nm MecE* self-lubrication.

autograisseur, -euse [ɔtɔgrεsœr, -øz] *adj* self-lubricating (*bearing etc*).

autographe [ɔtɔgraf] **1** *adj* autograph; handwritten (*letter etc*). **2** *nm* autograph.

autographier [ɔtɔgrafje] *vt* (*pr sub & impf* **n. autographiions, v. autographiiez**) to autograph.

autographique [ɔtɔgrafik] *adj* autographic.

autogreffe [ɔtɔgrɛf] *nf Chir* autograft.
autoguidage [ɔtɔgidaʒ] *nm* **(retour par) a.**, homing; **cellule d'a.**, homing eye.
autoguidé [ɔtɔgide] *adj* self-directional, homing (*missile*).
autogyre [ɔtɔʒir] *nm Av* autogyro.
auto-immune [ɔtoimyn] *adj Méd* autoimmune.
auto-immunisation [ɔtoimynizɑ̃sjɔ̃] *nf Méd* autoimmunization.
auto-induction [ɔtoɛ̃dyksjɔ̃] *nf Électron* self-induction.
auto-intoxication [ɔtoɛ̃tɔksikɑsjɔ̃] *nf* autointoxication, autotoxaemia.
autolubrifiant [ɔtɔlybrifjɑ̃] *adj* self-lubricating.
autolubrication [ɔtɔlybrifikɑsjɔ̃] *nf* self-lubrication.
auto-marché [ɔtɔmarʃe] *nm* car mart; (*pl auto-marchés*).
automate [ɔtɔmat] *nm* automaton, robot; **marcher comme un a.**, to walk like a zombie; **vivre comme un a.**, to live the life of an automaton.
automation [ɔtɔmɑsjɔ̃] *nf* automation.
automatique [ɔtɔmatik] **1** *adj* automatic (*action*); self-acting (*apparatus*); **'attention à la fermeture a. des portières'**, 'danger, automatically closing doors'; **à mise en marche a.**, self-starting; **réflexe a.**, automatic reflex; *Méd* involuntary reflex; **payer l'électricité par prélèvement a.**, to pay one's electricity bill by direct debit; *F* **votre dossier est envoyé à Paris, c'est a.**, your file has been sent to Paris, that's the usual procedure. **2** *nm* **(a)** (*téléphone*) automatic; **il faut passer par l'a.**, you have to go through the switchboard; **(b)** (*pistolet*) automatic. **3** *nf Tech* automatics; automation.
automatiquement [ɔtɔmatikmɑ̃] *adv* automatically; **votre nom est inséré a. dans le fichier**, your name is automatically entered in the file; *F* **si vous ne payez pas vos impôts, vous agissez a. contre la loi**, by not paying your tax you are automatically breaking the law.
automatisation [ɔtɔmatizɑsjɔ̃] *nf* automation.
automatiser [ɔtɔmatize] to automate.
automatisme [ɔtɔmatism] *nm* **(a)** *Physiol Méd* automatism; **(b)** *Tech* automatic working *or* functioning; **(c)** (*appareil etc*) automatic device.
automédication [ɔtɔmedikɑsjɔ̃] *nf* self-medication.
automitrailleuse [ɔtɔmitrajøz] *nf* armoured car.
automnal, -aux [ɔtɔ(m)nal, -o] *adj* autumnal.
automne [ɔtɔn] *nm* autumn, *Am* fall; **l'équinoxe d'a.**, the autumnal equinox; **en a., à l'à.**, in autumn; **une soirée d'a.**, an autumn evening; *Fig* **à l'a. de sa vie**, in the autumn of his *or* her life.
automobile [ɔtɔmɔbil] **1** *adj* **(a)** self-propelling; **voiture a.**, motor vehicle; **canot a.**, motor boat; **(b) club a.**, automobile club; **assurance a.**, car *or* motor insurance; **industrie a.**, automotive industry; **accessoires automobiles**, car accessories. **2** *nf* (motor) car, *Am* automobile; *Mil* **a. blindée**, armoured car; **salon de l'a.**, motor show; *Ind* **l'a. marche bien en France**, the car industry is doing well in France.
automobilisme [ɔtɔmɔbilism] *nm* motoring.
automobiliste [ɔtɔmɔbilist] *n* motorist.
automoteur, -trice [ɔtɔmɔtœr, -tris] **1** *adj* self-propelling (*vehicle*); self-acting (*valve etc*); **train a.**, multiple unit (Diesel) train. **2** *nf* **automotrice**, railcar. **3** *nm Nau* self-propelled barge.
automutilation [ɔtɔmytilɑsjɔ̃] *nf* self-mutilation.
autoneige [ɔtɔnɛʒ] *nf Can* snowmobile.
autonettoyant [ɔtɔnetwajɑ̃] *adj* **four a.**, self-cleaning oven.
autonome [ɔtɔnɔm] *adj* autonomous, self-governing; independent (*state etc*); self-contained (*apparatus*); *Ordinat* **calculateur a.**, stand-alone (computer).
autonomie [ɔtɔnɔmi] *nf* **(a)** *Pol* autonomy, self-government; **(b)** (*de personne*) self-sufficiency; **(c)** *Av* cruising radius, range; **l'avion a deux heures/800km d'a.**, the aircraft has a range of two hours/800km.
autonomiste [ɔtɔnɔmist] *n Pol* autonomist.
autoportant [ɔtɔpɔrtɑ̃], **autoporteur, -euse** [ɔtɔpɔrtœr, -øz] *adj Archit* self-supporting.
autoportrait [ɔtɔpɔrtrɛ] *nm* self portrait.
autopropulsé [ɔtɔprɔpylse] *adj* self-propelled.
autopropulsion [ɔtɔprɔpylsjɔ̃] *nf* driverless operation, self-propulsion.
autopsie [ɔtɔpsi] *nf* autopsy; **a. (cadavérique)**, post mortem (examination); *Fig* **faire l'a. d'une œuvre**, to take a work to pieces.
autopsier [ɔtɔpsje] *vt* to perform a post mortem (*examination*) on, *US* to autopsy.
autopunition [ɔtɔpynisjɔ̃] *nf Psy* self-punishment.
autoradio [ɔtɔradjo] *nm* car radio.
autorail [ɔtɔraj] *nm* railcar.
auto-régénérateur, -trice [ɔtɔreʒeneratœr, -tris] *adj Nucl* breeder (*reactor etc*).
autoréglage [ɔtɔreglaʒ] *nm Tech* self-regulation.
autorégulateur, -trice [ɔtɔregylatœr, -tris] **1** *adj* self-regulating. **2** *nm* self-acting regulator.
auto-relieur [ɔtɔrəljœr] *nm* spring-back binder; (*pl auto-relieurs*).
autorisation [ɔtɔrizɑsjɔ̃] *nf* **(a)** authorization, authority; **donner à qn une a. pour faire qch**, to authorize s.o. to do sth; **a. d'exporter**, export permit; **avoir l'a. de bâtir**, to have planning permission; **(b)** *Av* **a. de vol**, flight clearance; **(c)** (*document*) licence; **montrez-moi votre a.**, show me your permit.
autorisé [ɔtɔrize] *adj* **(a)** (*qualifié*) authorized, authoritative; **tenir qch d'une source autorisée**, to have sth from an authoritative source; **les milieux autorisés**, (the) official circles; **(b)** (*permis*) permitted, permissible, allowed; **tournure autorisée par l'usage**, turn of phrase enshrined in usage; **il se croit tout a.**, he thinks he can get away with anything; **(c)** approved (*stallion*).
autoriser [ɔtɔrize] **1** *vt* **(a) a. qn à faire qch**, to authorize *or* empower s.o. to do sth, to give s.o. authority to do sth; **je vous autorise à sortir de table**, you may leave the table; **(b)** (*justifier*) to justify, to authorize, to sanction (*an action*); **ces découvertes autorisent à penser que ...**, these discoveries entitle us to believe that ...; **rien ne nous autorise à le croire**, we have no reason to believe that; **(c)** to allow, to permit, to give permission (*to do sth*); **a. la pêche**, to allow fishing. **2 s'autoriser** *vpr* **s'a. de qn**, to act on the authority of s.o., to quote s.o. as a reason for doing sth; **s'a. de qch**, to act on the authority of sth.
autoritaire [ɔtɔritɛr] *adj* authoritative; *Péj* dictatorial, overbearing, *F* bossy; **régime a.**, authoritarian regime; **parler d'un ton a.**, to speak in an authoritative voice; **une femme a.**, an authoritarian woman.
autoritairement [ɔtɔritɛrmɑ̃] *adv* authoritatively; *Péj* in an overbearing manner.
autoritarisme [ɔtɔritarism] *nm* **(a)** *Pol* authoritarianism; **(b)** *F* bossiness.
autorité [ɔtɔrite] *nf* **(a)** (*domination*) authority; **exercer son a. sur qn**, to exercise authority over s.o.; **a. paternelle**, parental authority; **ce professeur n'a pas d'a. sur ses élèves**, this teacher can't keep order *or* has no control over his pupils; **être sous l'a. de qn**, to be under s.o.'s authority; **il veut tout emporter d'a.**, he wants his own way in everything, *F* he wants to run the whole show; **agir de pleine a.**, to act with full powers; **faire qch d'a.**, to do sth on one's own (responsibility) *or* off one's own bat, to take it upon oneself to do sth; **de sa propre a.**, on one's own authority; **territoire soumis à l'a. de ...**, area within the jurisdiction of ...; *Jur* **l'a. de la loi**, the force of the law;
(b) (*influence*) authority; **avoir de l'a. sur qn**, to have influence *or* authority over s.o.; **faire a. en qch**, to be an authority on sth; **ce livre fait a. dans le milieu**, this book is taken as the authority here; **ce scientifique a longtemps fait a.**, this scientist has long been an authority; *Jur* **cas d'espèce qui font a.**, leading cases; **parler avec a.**, to speak authoritatively *or* with authority; **sa parole a de l'a.**, his word carries weight;
(c) (*gouvernement*) **l'a.**, the authorities; **les représentants de l'a.**, the representatives of authority; **l'a. fiscale**, the (income) tax people; **les autorités**, the authorities, the powers that be;
(d) (*person*) **citer une a.**, to quote an authority; to quote chapter and verse; **c'est une a., elle est très écoutée**, she's an authority, people take a lot of notice of what she says.
autoroute [ɔtɔrut] *nf* motorway, *US* freeway, thruway, superhighway; **prendre l'a.**, to take the motorway; **a. à péage**, toll motorway, *US* turnpike (road).
autoroutier, -ière [ɔtɔrutje, -jɛr] *adj* **système a.**, motorway system *or* network.
autosatisfaction [ɔtɔsatisfaksjɔ̃] *nf* self-satisfaction.
auto-stop [ɔtɔstɔp] *nm* hitch-hiking, *F* hitching; **faire de l'a.**, to hitch-hike, *F* to hitch, to thumb a lift.
auto-stoppeur, -euse [ɔtɔstɔpœr, -øz] *n* hitch-hiker, *F* hitcher; (*pl auto-stoppeurs, -euses*).
autosuffisance [ɔtɔsyfizɑ̃s] *nf Écon* self-sufficiency.
autosuggestion [ɔtɔsygʒɛstjɔ̃] *nf* auto-suggestion.
autour¹ [otur] **1** *adv* round, around (it, them); **une vieille ville avec des murs tout a.**, an old walled town. **2** *prép* **a. de**, round, about; **nous nous sommes assis a. de la table**, we sat down round the table; **tourner a. d'un axe**, to

revolve about an axis; **enrouler qch a. de son cou,** to coil sth round one's neck; **ce qui se passe a. de nous,** what is going on around *or* round about us; *F* **il a a. de vingt ans,** he is (somewhere) about twenty, he's twentyish; **tourner a. de la question** *ou* **du pot,** to beat about the bush.

autour² *nm (oiseau)* **a. (des palombes),** goshawk.

autovaccin [ɔtɔvaksɛ̃] *nm Méd* autovaccine.

autre [otr] **1** *adj* **(a)** other, further; **tous les autres verbes que ceux en -er,** all verbs other than those in -er; **je ne pourrai pas y aller, entre autres raisons je suis à court d'argent,** I can't go, for one thing I'm short of money; **une a. semaine/un a. jour,** another week/another day; **une a. fois,** later; another time; **en voici un a. exemple,** here is another example (of it); **toute a. femme aurait agi de la même façon,** any other woman would have acted in the same way; **les choux et autres légumes,** cabbages and (all) other vegetables; **les choux et d'autres légumes,** cabbages and some other vegetables; **de l'a. côté du champ,** on the other side of the field; **l'a. monde,** the next world; **sans faire d'a. observation,** without making any further observation; **sans a. perte de temps,** without further loss of time; *F* **l'a. lundi,** Monday week;

(b) **vous autres hommes vous êtes seuls coupables,** it is you men who are alone to blame; **nous autres Anglais,** we English (people); **vous autres,** you others, all of you;

(c) *(second)* **il se croit un a. Napoléon,** he thinks he is a second *or* another Napoleon;

(d) *(différent)* other, different; **j'ai maintenant une a. maison,** I've a new *or* a different house now; *Prov* **autres temps autres mœurs,** other days other ways; **il est a. que je ne le pensais,** he is different from what I thought; **elle est devenue a.,** she has changed, she has become different; **cela a fait de lui un a. homme,** it made a new man of him; **une tout a. femme,** quite a different woman; **j'ai des idées autres,** I have different ideas, my ideas are different; **elle a de bien autres idées,** she has very different ideas; **être d'une a. opinion,** to think otherwise *or* differently;

(e) **a. chose,** something else; something different; **j'ai a. chose d'important à vous dire,** I have something else of importance to tell you; **avez-vous a. chose à faire?,** have you anything else to do?; **c'est a. chose que je n'avais d'abord pensé,** it is different from what I had first thought; *F* **a. chose, ma mère est partie hier,** not only that, but my mother left yesterday; **c'est tout a. chose!,** that's quite a different thing!; **une chose est de parler, a. chose est d'agir,** it's one thing to talk, it's another to act; **a. part,** somewhere else; **ils habitent maintenant a. part,** they now live somewhere else.

2 *pron* **(a)** **les défauts des autres,** the failings of others; **d'autres vous diront que ...,** others *or* other people will tell you that ...; **tous les autres sont là,** all the others are there; **encore un a.,** one more; another (one); **encore bien d'autres,** many more besides;

(b) **cela peut arriver d'un jour à l'a.,** it may happen any day; **je l'attends d'un moment à l'a.,** I expect him any moment; **je le vois de temps à a.,** I see him from time to time *or* now and again *or* now and then; **un jour ou l'a.,** one day or another, one of these days; **d'un bout à l'a.,** from one end to the other, from start to finish, from end to end;

(c) **la science est une chose, l'art en est une a.,** science is one thing, art is another; **il parle d'une façon et agit d'une a.,** he says one thing and does another;

(d) **l'un et l'a.,** both; **les uns et les autres,** *(tout le monde)* all (and sundry), one and all; *(deux groupes)* both parties; **il a parlé aux uns et aux autres,** he spoke to them all; **l'un et l'a. a été puni** *ou* **ont été punis,** both were punished; **il passe son temps chez l'un ou l'a.,** he spends his time with one friend or another;

(e) **l'un ou l'a.,** either; **ni l'un ni l'a.,** neither; **ni l'un ni l'a. ne sont venus,** neither of them came; **je ne les connais ni l'un ni l'a.,** I don't know either of them; **je n'ai vu ni les uns ni les autres,** I didn't see any of them;

(f) **l'un ..., l'a. ....,** one ..., the other ...; **l'un dit ceci, l'a. dit cela,** one says this and the other says that; **les uns ..., les autres ...,** some ..., others ...; some ..., some ...; **ils s'en allèrent, les uns par ci les autres par là,** they went off, some one way, some another; **sans prendre parti ni pour les uns ni pour les autres,** without taking either side; **l'un ne va pas sans l'a.,** you can't have one without the other, the two go hand in hand; **qui voit l'un voit l'a.,** there's no difference between them, you can't tell the two apart; **l'un vaut l'a.,** there's no difference between them, the one's just as good *or* as bad as the other;

(g) **l'un l'a.,** each other, one another; **on va s'aider l'un l'a.,** we'll help each other; **elles se moquent les unes des autres,** they make fun of each other; **vivre l'un pour l'a.,** to live for each other; **aller l'un à côté de l'a.,** to walk side by side; **ils dépendent l'un de l'a.,** they depend on each other; **l'un auprès de l'a., auprès l'un de l'a.,** near each other, near one another;

(h) **l'un dans l'a., il se fait mille francs,** one thing with another *or* on an average he earns a thousand francs; **une année dans l'a.,** taking one year with another;

(i) **c'est tout l'un ou tout l'a.,** there is no happy medium, it's either one thing or the other; **il faut choisir, c'est l'un ou l'a.,** you must choose one or the other;

(j) **d'a.,** else; **il n'y en a pas d'a.,** there's no other; **parler de choses et d'autres,** to talk of one thing and another; **personne d'a. ne le sait,** nobody else knows; **je ne demande rien d'a.,** I don't ask for anything more, I ask for nothing more; **que pouvait-il faire d'a.?,** what else could he do?; **que pouvaient-ils faire d'a. que de l'inviter?,** what could they do but invite him?; **qui d'a. que lui aurait pu le faire?,** who else (but him) could have done it?; **(dites cela) à d'autres!,** who do you think you're kidding?, get away!, tell that to the marines!; **quelqu'un d'a. le verra,** somebody else will see him; *F* **en voilà bien une a.!,** here we go again!; **j'en sais d'autres,** I can do better than that; **j'en ai vu bien d'autres,** I've been through worse than that;

(k) *(personne)* someone *or* somebody else; **adressez-vous à un a.,** ask someone else *or* somebody else; **je l'ai pris pour un a.,** I mistook him for someone else; **c'était un touriste comme un a.,** he was just an ordinary tourist; **c'est une raison comme une a.,** it's as good a reason as any; **c'est un homme pas comme les autres,** he is an exceptional man; *F* **comme dit l'a.,** as the saying goes, as they say; **il n'est pas plus bête qu'un a.,** he is no more stupid than anyone else; **nul a. ne l'a vu,** no one else *or* nobody else saw him; **elle sera heureuse avec un a.,** she will be happy with another; **tout a. le comprendrait,** anyone else would understand it; **il y avait des Écossais entre autres,** there were some Scots among others; *F* **je voudrais être riche, entre autres,** among other things, I would like to be rich.

autrefois [otrəfwa] *adv* formerly, in the past; *(à une époque particulière)* once; **il y avait a. un roi,** once upon a time there was a king; **c'était l'usage a.,** it was the custom in former times *or* in olden days; **d'a.,** of long ago; **sa vie d'a.,** his past life; **les hommes d'a.,** men of old *or* of olden times; **des chants d'a.,** old-time songs.

autrement [otrəmɑ̃] *adv* **(a)** *(différemment)* otherwise, differently; **il parle a. que vous,** he speaks differently from you; **faisons a.,** let's do *or* set about it (in) another way; **Alain, a. appelé Jojo,** Alain, otherwise known as Jojo; **le bouton d'or, a. appelé ...,** the buttercup, otherwise known as ..., the buttercup or ...; **a. dit,** in other words, put differently; **il ne put faire a. que d'obéir,** he had no alternative but to obey; **(b)** *(plus)* (far) more; **elle est a. intelligente,** she is far more intelligent, she is more intelligent by far; **c'est bien a. sérieux,** that is far more serious; **(c)** *(ou alors)* or (else); **venez demain, a. il sera trop tard,** come tomorrow, otherwise it will be too late; **(d)** **pas a.,** not particularly; **cela ne me surprend pas a.,** that does not surprise me particularly.

Autriche [otriʃ] *nf* Austria.

autrichien, -ienne [otriʃjɛ̃, -jɛn] **1** *adj* Austrian. **2** *n* **A.,** Austrian.

autruche [otryʃ] *nf (oiseau)* ostrich; **œuf d'a.,** ostrich egg; **chaussures/sac en a.,** ostrich-skin shoes/handbag; *F* **avoir un estomac d'a.,** to have a cast-iron stomach; *Fig* **pratiquer la politique de l'a.,** to bury one's head in the sand.

autrui [otrɥi] *pron indéf* others, other people; **convoiter le bien d'a.,** to covet one's neighbour's property; *Com* **pour le compte d'a.,** for account of a third party; **ne fais pas à a. ce que tu ne voudrais pas qu'on te fît,** do as you would be done by; **a. n'est pas toujours le meilleur conseiller,** other people don't always know best.

auvent [ovɑ̃] *nm* **(a)** porch roof; window roof; **(b)** canopy, awning *(of tent)*; **(c)** *Ind* hood *(over hearth etc)*; **(d)** *Constr* weatherboard; **un toit en a.,** a sloping roof; **s'abriter sous l'a.,** to shelter in the porch; **(e)** *Aut* **auvents de capot,** bonnet louvres.

auvergnat, -ate [ɔvɛrɲa, at] **1** *adj* of Auvergne. **2** *nm Ling* Auvergne dialect. **3** *n* **A.,** inhabitant of Auvergne.

aux [o] *voir* **À**.

auxiliaire [ɔksiljɛr, o-] **1** *adj* auxiliary *(verb, troops etc)*; **machine a.,** auxiliary engine; **bureau a.,** sub-office;

services auxiliaires de l'armée, non-combatant services; **maître a.,** supply teacher. **2** *n* (*aide*) auxiliary; helper, assistant; *Admin* temporary civil servant; **a. familiale,** ≈ mother's help; **a. de justice,** representative of the law; **a. médical,** medical auxiliary; **c'est un a. précieux,** he's a valuable helper. **3** *nm* **(a)** *Nau* auxiliary cruiser; **(b)** *Av Nau* **les auxiliaires,** the auxiliary engines; **(c)** *Mil* **auxiliaires,** auxiliaries; **(d)** *Gram* auxiliary verb; **(e) un mixer est un a. précieux,** a mixer is an invaluable piece of equipment.

auxquels [okɛl] *voir* **LEQUEL.**

av. *abrév* **avenue.**

avachi [avaʃi] *adj* **(a)** (*of boots etc*) out of shape (*through much use*); **(b)** flabby, sloppy (*figure*); **être a. dans un fauteuil,** to be slumped in an armchair; **(c) c'est un homme a.,** he has gone to seed.

avachir [avaʃir] **1** *vt* **(a)** to soften (*leather etc*); **(b)** to enervate, to make flabby; **la chaleur m'avachit,** the heat makes me feel quite limp. **2 s'avachir** *vpr* **(a)** (*du cuir*) to soften; **(b)** (*de personne*) to become flabby *or* sloppy; (*se laisser aller*) to let oneself go, to go to seed.

avachissement [avaʃismɑ̃] *nm* (*de cuir*) softening; (*de personne*) sloppiness.

aval¹, -als [aval] *nm Fin* endorsement (*on bill*); **donner son a. à un billet,** to endorse *or* back a bill; **donneur d'a.,** guarantor, backer (*of bill*); *Fig* **donner son a. à un projet,** to give a project one's backing *or* support.

aval² *nm* **(a)** downstream side; **les villages d'a.,** the villages downstream; **canal d'a.,** tail race (*of lock*); **porte d'a.,** tail gate, aft gate; **en a.,** downstream, down-river; *Rail* down the line; **en a. du village/du torrent,** downstream of the village/torrent; **le ski a.,** the downhill ski; **(b)** *Écon* **stade a.,** (*de la production*) downstream; **(c)** *Télécom* down side.

avalaison [avalɛzɔ̃] *nf* **(a)** spate, freshet; **(b)** heap of stones (*deposited by a torrent*); **(c)** downstream migration (*of fish*).

avalanche [avalɑ̃ʃ] *nf* avalanche; **a. de pierres,** avalanche of stones; **a. boueuse,** avalanche of mud; **couloir d'a.,** avalanche corridor; **a. électronique/ionique,** avalanche of electrons/ions; **a. d'injures,** shower of insults; **ce fut une a. de lettres,** letters came pouring in *or* arrived in shoals.

avalancheux, -euse [avalɑ̃ʃø, -øz] *adj* prone to avalanches; **couloir a.,** avalanche corridor.

avalé [avale] *adj* drooping (*shoulders etc*); flabby (*cheeks*); **lapin à oreilles avalées,** lop-eared rabbit; **chien à oreilles avalées,** dog with floppy *or* hanging ears.

avaler [avale] *vt* **(a)** (*absorber*) to swallow (down); **a. un noyau,** to swallow a plum *etc* stone; **a. son repas sans mâcher,** to swallow down one's meal without chewing it; **j'avale mon repas et j'arrive,** I'll just get my food down, then I'll be along; **a. son repas,** to bolt one's meal; **a. son vin à grandes gorgées** *ou* **d'un trait,** to gulp down one's wine; **j'ai avalé de travers,** it went down the wrong way; *Fig* **a. ses mots,** to swallow one's words; **a. la fumée,** to inhale; *Fig* **j'ai cru qu'elle allait m'a. tout cru,** I thought she was going to bite my head off; *F* **a. qn/qch des yeux,** to devour s.o. with one's eyes/to eye sth greedily; **je préfère a. ma salive et penser à autre chose,** I prefer to bite my tongue and think of something else; **on dirait qu'il a avalé son parapluie!,** he's as stiff as a poker!; **a. les kilomètres,** to eat up the miles; **il a avalé l'Étranger,** he couldn't put l'Étranger down;

(b) *Fig* **a. une couleuvre** *ou* **une insulte,** to pocket an insult; **celle-là est dure à a.,** that's a tall story, I can hardly swallow that; **a. le morceau** *ou* **la pilule,** to take one's medicine *or* one's punishment; **tu auras du mal à leur faire a. ça,** you'll have a job getting them to swallow that *or* making them believe that; **on peut lui faire a. n'importe quoi, il est tellement naïf,** he's so naive he'll swallow anything; *F* **tu as avalé ta langue?,** have you lost your tongue?, has the cat got your tongue?;

(c) *Arch* to lower (*cask into cellar etc*);

(d) a. une branche, to lop off a bough;

(e) *Min* **a. un puits,** to sink a shaft.

2 s'avaler *vpr* **cela s'avale facilement,** it goes down easily.

avale-tout [avaltu] *nm inv Arg* glutton.

avaleur [avalœr] *nm* **a. de sabres,** sword-swallower.

avaliser [avalize] *vt Com* to endorse, to back (*bill*); *Fig* **a. un projet,** to back a project.

avaliste [avalist] *nm Com* surety, backer.

à-valoir [avalwar] *nm inv* advance (*payment*).

avance [avɑ̃s] *nf* **(a)** (*marche*) advance, lead; **l'a. d'une armée/d'un mouvement de libéralisation,** the advance of an army/of liberalization; **mouvement d'a. et de recul,** backward and forward movement; **l'a. rapide de l'indice du coût de la vie,** the rapid rise *or* climb of the cost of living index; **a. et recul,** move and counter-move; *El* **a. d'une magnéto,** magneto lead; **mettre une cassette en a. rapide,** to fast-forward a cassette, to put a cassette on fast forward;

(b) (*anticipation*) lead; **avoir de l'a. sur qn,** to be ahead *or* in advance of s.o.; **garder son a. sur qn,** to maintain one's lead over s.o.; **prendre de l'a. sur un concurrent,** to draw away from a competitor; to steal a march on a competitor; to overtake a competitor; **l'a. des Français au niveau de la recherche,** the French lead in the sphere of research; **ma montre prend de l'a.,** my watch gains; **ma montre a dix minutes d'a.,** my watch is ten minutes fast; **(prendre un train) avec cinq minutes d'a.,** (to catch a train) with five minutes in hand *or* to spare; *F* **la belle a.!,** much good that will do you!; *Sp* **donner de l'a. à qn,** to give s.o. a (head) start; *Golf* **tant de trous d'a.,** so many holes up;

(c) *Tech* **mettre de l'a. à l'allumage,** to advance the ignition; **réduire l'a.,** to retard the ignition; **levier d'a.,** ignition lever; **a. à l'échappement,** exhaust lead;

(d) feed movement, travel (*of tool*); **mécanisme d'a.,** feed mechanism, feeding gear;

(e) (*partie saillante*) projection; **l'a. d'un toit,** the projecting part *or* eaves of a roof; **balcon qui forme a.,** balcony that juts out;

(f) a. (de fonds), advance, loan; *Fin* **par a., à titre d'a.,** by way of advance, as an advance; **faire une a. de mille francs à qn,** to advance s.o. a thousand francs; **faire les avances d'une entreprise,** to advance funds for an enterprise;

(g) faire des avances à qn, to make approaches *or* advances *or* overtures to s.o.; **faire des avances à une femme,** to make advances to a woman; **faire la moitié des avances,** to meet s.o. half way; **faire les premières avances,** to make the first move;

(h) d'a., à l'a., par a., in advance, beforehand; **jouir d'a. de qch,** to look forward to sth; **je m'en réjouis d'a.,** I'm looking forward to it greatly; **savourer un plaisir d'a.,** to anticipate a pleasure; **payer qn d'a.** *ou* **à l'a.,** to pay s.o. in advance; **payé d'a.,** prepaid; **payable à l'a.,** payable in advance; **je vous remercie d'a.,** thanking you in anticipation; **retenir** *ou* **louer une place huit jours à l'a.,** to book a seat a week in advance; **chose décidée à l'a.,** foregone conclusion; **et par a., merci,** thank you in advance *or* in anticipation;

(i) l'horloge est en a., the clock is fast; **partir en a.,** to go off in advance (of the party); **arriver en a.,** to arrive in advance *or* before the others; **je suis en a. d'une demi-heure,** I am half an hour early; **un enfant en a. sur son âge,** a child old beyond its years; *Scol* **il est en a. sur sa classe,** he is ahead of his class; **être en a. sur son temps,** to be ahead *or* in advance of one's time; **la moisson est en a. cette année,** the harvest is early this year.

avancé [avɑ̃se] *adj* **(a)** advanced; **position avancée,** advanced *or* forward position; *Rail* **signal a.,** distant signal;

(b) (*précoce*) forward; **les pommiers sont bien avancés cette année,** the apple trees are in advance this year; **c'est un esprit a.,** he's a progressive; **élève a.,** pupil ahead of his class; **opinions avancées,** advanced *or* progressive *or* left-wing ideas;

(c) (*dans le temps*) **à une heure avancée de la nuit,** late in the night, well on in the night; **à une heure peu avancée,** quite early on; *Can* **heure avancée,** daylight saving time; **l'été est bien a.,** summer is nearly over; **a. en âge,** elderly, getting on (in years); **à un âge a.,** late in life, at an advanced age;

(d) (*fruit*) overripe; **viande avancée,** high meat;

(e) (*presque à terme*) (far) advanced; **à un stade a. du projet,** at an advanced stage in the project; *F* **vous voilà bien a.!,** a lot of good that's done you!; **vous n'en êtes pas plus a.,** you're no further forward.

avancée [avɑ̃se] *nf* **(a)** (*saillie*) bulge, projection, protuberance; *Constr* **a. du toit,** eaves; **(b)** (*de la mer etc*) advance; **(c)** (*d'une ligne de pêche*) leader, trace; **(d)** (*marche*) advance; **l'a. de la devise américaine,** the rise of the dollar.

avancement [avɑ̃smɑ̃] *nm* **(a)** (*mouvement*) advancing, putting forward; **a. automatique,** automatic feed; *Ordinat* **a. ligne par ligne,** line feed; *Ordinat* **a. du papier,** form feed; **(b)** furtherance (*of plan*); **état d'a. des travaux,** progress report; **(c)** (*promotion*) promotion; **a. à l'ancienneté,** promotion by seniority; **avoir de l'a.,** to be promoted; **(d)** (*progrès*) advance(ment), progress; going ahead; **l'a. des sciences,** the progress of science; **(e)** *Jur* **a. d'hoirie,** =

part of inheritance given in advance.

avancer [avɑ̃se] *v* (**j'avançai(s)**; **n. avançons**) **1** *vt* **(a)** (*mettre en avant*) to advance, to put forward; to stretch out, to hold out (*one's hand etc*); **a. des chaises,** to pull forward chairs; *Échecs* **a. un pion,** to advance a pawn; *Min* **a. une galerie,** to drive a gallery; **a. la voiture jusqu'au portail,** to drive the car up to the door;

(b) *Fig* **a. une proposition,** to put forward *or* advance a proposal; **a. ses raisons,** to produce *or* set out *or* give one's reasons; **comment peut-il prouver ce qu'il avance?,** how can he prove his assertion?;

(c) to make (*sth*) earlier; to hurry (*sth*) on; **la réunion a été avancée du 14 au 7,** the meeting has been brought forward from the 14th to the 7th; **a. l'heure du dîner,** to put dinner forward; **a. une montre,** to put a watch forward *or* on; **a. son travail,** to push on with *or* get ahead with one's work; **a. une plante,** to bring on *or* force a plant;

(d) a. de l'argent à qn, to advance money to s.o., to lend s.o. money;

(e) *Fig* to promote, to forward, to further, to advance (*science, s.o.'s interests etc*); **a. qn,** to promote s.o.; **à quoi cela vous avancera-t-il?,** what good will that do you?, how much better (off) will you be for it?; *F* **cela ne va pas nous a. beaucoup,** it won't get us much further forward.

2 *vi* **(a)** (*progresser*) to advance; to move *or* go *or* step forward; (*of ship*) to make headway; **a. à grands pas,** to stride along; **a. à pas de loup** *ou* **à tâtons,** to creep along *or* feel *or* grope one's way; **a. d'un pas,** to take one step forward; **chaque année la mer avance un peu plus sur notre terrain,** each year the sea encroaches a little further on our land; **faire a. une chaise roulante,** to propel a wheelchair; **allez avance! on va être en retard,** come on, hurry up! we're going to be late; **avancez vers moi,** come towards me; **faire a. qn,** to bring s.o. forward; **faire a. les troupes,** to advance the troops, to move the troops forward; **faire a. des renforts,** to bring up reinforcements; **faire a. sa voiture jusqu'à la porte,** to drive one's car up to the door; **vous ne pouvez pas a., s'il vous plaît? je ne peux pas passer,** could you move please? I can't get past; **a. en âge,** to be getting on *or* to get on in years; **la nuit avance,** the night is getting on; **l'été avance,** summer is almost over;

(b) *Fig* to progress, to get on, to make headway; **le travail avance,** the work is coming along; **les choses n'avancent plus,** things are at a standstill; *F* **alors, ça avance?,** how is it coming along, then?; **cela ne nous avance guère,** that doesn't get us much further forward; **la lune avance,** the moon is waxing; *Prov* **plus on se hâte moins on avance,** more haste less speed;

(c) to advance, to be promoted (*in a service*); **a. en grade,** to rise in rank;

(d) (*dans le temps*) to be ahead of time; **l'horloge avance,** the clock is fast; **montre qui avance d'une minute par jour,** watch that gains a minute a day; **vous avancez de dix minutes,** your watch is ten minutes fast; **a. sur son époque,** to be ahead *or* in advance of one's time;

(e) (*of promontory, roof etc*) to jut out, to project, to protrude.

3 s'avancer *vpr* **(a)** (*aller devant*) to move forward, to advance; **s'a. vers qch,** to make one's way *or* to head towards sth; **s'a. d'un pas,** to take a *or* one step forward; **avance-toi si tu veux voir,** move forward if you want to see; **s'a. péniblement,** to drag oneself along; **elle en a profité pour s'a. dans son travail,** she made use of this to get ahead with her work;

(b) (*dans le temps*) **la nuit s'avance,** the night is getting on *or* is far advanced;

(c) *Fig* **il s'est trop avancé pour reculer,** he has gone too far to withdraw; **elle refuse de s'a. sur ce point,** she won't be drawn on this matter;

(d) (*of promontory etc*) to jut out; **une langue de terre s'avance dans la mer,** a strip of land runs out into the sea.

avanie [avani] *nf Litt* snub; **subir** *ou* **essuyer une a.,** to be snubbed.

avant [avɑ̃] **1** *prép* **(a)** before; **a. le temps,** too soon, prematurely; **venez a. midi,** come before twelve o'clock *or* midday; **a. J.-C.,** B.C.; **il sera ici a. une heure,** he will be here by one o'clock; (*dans moins d'une heure*) he will be here within an hour; **je le verrai a. quinze jours,** I shall see him within *or* in less than a fortnight; **pas a. lundi,** not before Monday; **elle est née a. toi,** she was born before you; **pas a. de nombreuses années,** not for many years to come; **la maison est a. la boucherie,** the house is before the butcher's; **il a terminé la course a. moi,** he finished the race before me; **l'article se place a. le nom,** the article is placed before the noun; **a. la ceinture noire, il y a la ceinture bleue,** the blue belt comes before the black belt; **les dames a. les messieurs,** ladies first; *Fig* **mettre la santé a. le reste,** to put one's health above all else; **pour lui la famille passe a. tout,** for him the family comes first; **(surtout et) a. tout,** first of all, above all; **a. toute chose,** in the first place; **a. tout, il faut que tu sois satisfait,** above all else, we want you to be satisfied;

(b) (**a. de** + *inf*) **je vous reverrai a. de partir,** I shall see you before I leave; **ne fais rien a. d'être tout à fait sûr,** do not do anything until you are quite certain;

(c) (**a. que** + *sub*) **je vous reverrai a. que vous (ne) partiez,** I shall see you again before you leave; **a. que vous ayez fini je serai parti,** by the time (that) you have finished I shall be gone; **il est parti a. que je (ne) le réalise,** before I realised it, he had gone; **ne partez pas a. qu'on vous le dise,** don't go until you are told;

(d) il est à quelques mètres en a. de nous, he's a few metres in front of us; *Litt* **il est bien en a. de son siècle,** he is well ahead of *or* in advance of his time;

(e) *Vieilli Jur* **a. faire droit/dire droit,** injunction/interim order.

2 *adv* **(a)** (= **auparavant**) **il était arrivé quelques mois a.,** he had arrived some months before *or* earlier; **réfléchis a., tu parleras après,** think first, speak later; **il l'a mentionné a. dans la préface,** he mentioned it before *or* earlier in the preface; **le jour d'a., tout était calme,** the day before, everything was quiet;

(b) (*dans l'espace*) **n'allez pas jusqu'à l'église, sa maison est a.,** do not go as far as the church, his house is before (you come to) it; **les dames passent a.,** ladies take precedence;

(c) (*loin*) far, deep; **pénétrer très a. dans les terres,** to penetrate far inland; **le harpon pénétra très a. dans les chairs,** the harpoon sank deep into the flesh; *Fig* **tu t'es engagé trop a.,** (*tu ne peux plus te désister*) you've got too involved, you're in too deep;

(d) (*tard*) far, late; **très a. dans la journée,** very late in the day;

(e) en a., in front, before, forward, ahead; **en a.!,** forward!; *Mil* **en a., (marche)!,** quick march!; **il est parti en a. pour reconnaître le chemin,** he set off ahead of us to spy out the route; **envoyer qn en a.,** to send s.o. ahead *or* on (in front); **aller en a.,** to push ahead, to press on; **se pencher en a.,** to lean forward(s); **regarder en a.,** to look ahead; **tomber en a.,** to fall forwards; **faire deux pas en a.,** to move forward two steps; *Fig* **mettre qn en a.,** to hide behind s.o.; **mettre le règlement/la loi en a.,** to quote the regulation/act; **mettre en a. un candidat,** to put a candidate forward; **mettre en a. une question,** to bring up a question; *Nau* **en a. (à) toute (vitesse),** full (steam) ahead.

3 *adj inv* fore, forward, front; **la partie a. du navire,** the fore part of the ship; **roue a.,** front wheel; *Aut* **à traction a.,** with front-wheel drive.

4 *nm* **(a)** *Nau* bow, head; eyes (*of a ship*); the steerage; *Aut etc* front; **les enfants ne peuvent pas s'asseoir à l'a.,** children may not sit in front; **tu seras mieux à l'a.,** you'll be better in the front; **les voitures à l'a.** *ou* **d'a. vont à Perpignan,** the front carriages go to Perpignan; **un modèle tout à l'a.,** a front-wheel drive model; **présenter l'a. à la lame,** to be head to sea; **le logement de l'équipage est à l'a.,** the crew's quarters are forward; **par tribord a.,** on the starboard bow; **l'a. de la voiture est complètement défoncé,** the front of the car is completely smashed in; **aborder un navire par l'a.,** to collide with a ship head on; **sur** *ou* **à l'a. du mât,** before the mast; **aller** *ou* **pousser** *ou* **marcher de l'a.,** to go *or* forge ahead; *Fig* **il ne faut pas stagner, cherche à aller de l'a.,** don't stagnate *or* get bogged down, try to get ahead; **a. partout!,** give way!; **retourner sur l'a.,** to come forward;

(b) front; nose (*of plane*); crank end (*of piston*); head end (*of locomotive piston*);

(c) *Fb etc* forward; **la ligne des avants,** the forward line; *Rugby* **a. de deuxième ligne,** second-row forward, lock (forward);

(d) *Mil* **l'a.,** the front; the forward area(s).

avantage [avɑ̃taʒ] *nm* **(a)** (*profit*) advantage; **a. pécuniaire,** monetary gain; **faire à qn tous les avantages possibles,** to give s.o. every possible advantage; **a. en nature,** perquisite; **il ne m'en revient aucun a.,** I'm not getting any advantage *or* benefit from it;

(b) (*atout*) **être à l'a. de qn,** to turn out to s.o.'s advantage; **posséder un ordinateur est un a. certain,**

owning a computer is a definite advantage; **cette position offre de nombreux avantages,** this position offers many advantages; **sa connaissance du français lui est un a. précieux,** his knowledge of French is a great asset to him; **tirer a. de qch,** to turn sth to advantage; **dans cette compétition, vous avez l'a.,** you are at *or* have an advantage in this competition; **prendre a. de qch,** to take advantage of sth; **la situation tourne à votre a.,** the situation is turning to your advantage; **s'habiller à son a.,** to dress to one's best advantage; **il est à son a. en uniforme,** he looks his best in uniform; **avoir l'a. du nombre/de l'âge,** to have the advantage of numbers/the benefit of age; **il a changé à son a.,** he has changed for the better; **avoir l'a. sur qn,** to have the advantage of *or* over s.o.; **remporter l'a. sur qn,** to get the better, best of s.o.; **cette solution a l'a. d'être rapide et efficace,** this solution has the advantage of being quick and effective; **trouver de l'a. à faire qch,** to find it an advantage *or* advantageous to do sth; **parler à l'a. de qn,** to speak in s.o.'s favour;

(c) *Jur* gift, donation; **à titre d'a.,** as a gift;

(d) *Sp Tennis* advantage; **donner l'a. à qn,** to give s.o. odds; **accorder** *ou* **concéder** *ou* **donner un a. à qn,** to give s.o. points; **il a l'a.,** the odds are in his favour; *Tennis* **a. service,** (*Leconte au service*) advantage Leconte; *Tennis* **a. dehors,** (*Leconte au service, Noah en face*) advantage Noah;

(e) il y a a. à + *inf*, it is best to, it is worth one's while to + *inf*; **il y aura a. à ce que vous soyez présent,** it will be a good thing *or* just as well if you are present; **tu aurais a. à être poli la prochaine fois,** you would do well to be polite next time;

(f) *Fml* **à quoi dois-je l'a. de votre venue?,** to what do I owe the honour of your visit?; **je n'ai pas l'a. de vous connaître,** I have not had the honour of making your acquaintance.

avantagé [avɑ̃taʒe] *adj* **être fort a. par rapport aux autres,** to enjoy many advantages over others; **a. par la nature,** well endowed; *Sp* **joueur a.,** player who has been given a start *or* been given odds.

avantager [avɑ̃taʒe] *vt* (**j'avantageai(s); n. avantageons**) **(a)** to favour (*s.o.*); to give (*s.o.*) an advantage; **être avantagé par la nature,** to be well endowed; **son bégaiement ne l'avantage pas,** his stammer doesn't help him; **(b)** (*physiquement*) **l'uniforme l'avantage,** he looks his best in uniform.

avantageur [avɑ̃taʒœr] *nm Sp* scratch player.

avantageusement [avɑ̃taʒøzmɑ̃] *adv* advantageously, to advantage; **parler de qn a.,** to speak favourably of s.o..

avantageux, -euse [avɑ̃taʒø, -øz] *adj* **(a)** (*intéressant*) advantageous, favourable; *Com* **prix a.,** reasonable price; **cet article est très a.,** this article is very good value; **(b)** (*de vêtements*) **robe avantageuse,** becoming dress; **portrait a.,** flattering portrait; **(c) poitrine avantageuse,** well-developed bust; **(d)** *Péj* conceited, vain; **prendre un ton a.,** to adopt a superior tone.

avant-aile [avɑ̃tɛl] *nm Rugby* wing-forward, flanker.

avant-bassin [avɑ̃basɛ̃] *nm Nau* outer basin, dock; (*pl avant-bassins*).

avant-bras [avɑ̃bra] *nm inv Anat* forearm.

avant-cale [avɑ̃kal] *nf Nau* fore hold; (*pl avant-cales*).

avant-centre [avɑ̃sɑ̃tr] *nm Fb* centre forward; (*pl avant-centres*).

avant-corps [avɑ̃kɔr] *nm inv Archit etc* projecting part (*of building*).

avant-cour [avɑ̃kur] *nf Archit* forecourt; (*pl avant-cours*).

avant-coureur [avɑ̃kurœr] (*pl avant-coureurs*) **1** *nm* forerunner; *Mil* scout; **2** *adj* premonitory (*symptom*); **choc a.-c. (de séisme),** preliminary tremor; **les signes avant-coureurs du changement,** the harbingers of change.

avant-dernier, -ière [avɑ̃dɛrnje, -jɛr] (*pl avant-derniers, -ières*) **1** *adj* last but one, penultimate; **l'avant-dernière fois,** the time before last; **2** *n* last but one, next to last.

avant-garde [avɑ̃gard] *nf* (*pl avant-gardes*) **(a)** *Mil* advance(d) guard; **détachement d'a.-g.,** advance(d) party; **(b) hommes d'a.-g.,** men in the van (*of reform etc*); pioneers; *Pol* **les éléments d'a.-g.,** the avant-garde; **livre d'a.-g.,** avant-garde book; **les découvertes de l'a.-g.,** the discoveries ot the avant-garde; **technique d'a.-g.,** avant-garde technique.

avant-gardisme [avɑ̃gardism] *nm* avant-gardism.

avant-gardiste [avɑ̃gardist] *adj & n* avant-gardist, avant-garde.

avant-goût [avɑ̃gu] *nm* foretaste; anticipation; first impression; **cela m'a donné un a.-g. de ce qu'allait être ma vie/mon travail,** it was a foretaste *or* gave me a taste of my life to come/of what my work would be like; (*pl avant-goûts*).

avant-guerre [avɑ̃gɛr] *n* pre-war period; (*pl avant-guerres*).

avant-hier [avɑ̃tjɛr] *adv* the day before yesterday; **a.-h au soir,** the night *or* evening before last.

avant-main [avɑ̃mɛ̃] *nm* (*pl avant-mains*) **(a)** forequarters, forehand (*of horse*); **(b)** *Anat* flat of the hand; **(c)** *Tennis* **coup d'a.-m.,** forehand stroke.

avant-plan [avɑ̃plɑ̃] *nm Beaux-Arts Phot etc* foreground; (*pl avant-plans*).

avant-pont [avɑ̃pɔ̃] *nm Nau* foredeck; (*pl avant-ponts*).

avant-port [avɑ̃pɔr] *nm Nau* outer harbour; (*pl avant-ports*).

avant-poste [avɑ̃pɔst] *nm Mil* outpost; **réseau d'a.-p.,** outpost screen *or* system; (*pl avant-postes*).

avant-première [avɑ̃prəmjɛr] *nf* (*pl avant-premières*) **(a)** private view, private viewing, preview (*of art exhibition etc*); *Th* dress rehearsal; **présenté en a.-p.,** previewed, given an advanced showing (*of film, play etc*); **(b)** *Journ* press preview; pre-performance write-up.

avant-propos [avɑ̃prɔpo] *nm inv* preface, foreword, avant-propos (*to book*); *Fig* **après quelques a.-p.,** after a few preliminary remarks; **en a.-p. à cette conférence,** before the lecture gets underway, as a prelude to this lecture.

avant-scène [avɑ̃sɛn] *nf Th* (*pl avant-scènes*) **(a)** *Antiq* proscenium, apron, forestage; **(b) (loge d') a.-s.,** stage box.

avant-spectacle [avɑ̃spɛktakl(ə)] *nm* pre-show performance; **en a.-s.,** as a curtain-raiser; (*pl avant-spectacles*).

avant-titre [avɑ̃titr] *nm* half-title (*of book*); (*pl avant-titres*).

avant-toit [avɑ̃twa] *nm* eaves (*of roof*); **comble avec a.-t.,** umbrella roof; (*pl avant-toits*).

avant-train [avɑ̃trɛ̃] *nm* (*pl avant-trains*) **(a)** *Aut* front-axle unit; **(b)** wheels (*of plough*); **(c)** *Mil* limber.

avant-veille [avɑ̃vɛj] *nf* two days before; **l'a.-v. de Noël,** two days before Christmas; (*pl avant-veilles*).

avare [avar] **1** *adj* **(a)** (*mesquin*) miserly, avaricious, tight; **(b) il n'est pas a. de son argent,** he's not mean with his money; **il n'est pas a. de ses conseils,** he's only too happy to offer advice. **2** *n* miser.

avarice [avaris] *nf* avarice, miserliness.

avaricieux, -ieuse [avarisjø, -jøz] **1** *adj* avaricious, miserly, stingy, niggardly, grasping. **2** *n* miser, skinflint; **un vieil a.,** an old miser.

avarie [avari] *nf* **(a)** damage (*to ship, engine etc*); **subir une a.,** to be damaged; to break down; **faire subir une a. à qch,** to damage sth; **(b) déclaration d'avaries,** (ship's) protest; **avaries matérielles de mer,** damage done by sea water; **(c) avaries-frais,** average; **règlement d'avaries,** adjustment of average; **répartiteur d'avaries,** average adjuster.

avarié [avarje] *adj* damaged, spoiled (*goods etc*).

avarier [avarje] *v* (*pr sub & impf* **n. avariions, v. avariiez**) **1** *vt* to damage (*goods etc*). **2 s'avarier** *vpr* to go off, to go bad, to rot (*of food etc*); to be damaged (*of non-edible goods*); **ces denrées se sont avariées,** these goods have deteriorated *or* perished *or* gone bad.

avatar [avatar] *nm* **(a)** avatar; (*transformation*) transformation, change, metamorphosis; **avatars,** ups and downs, vicissitudes (*of political life etc*); **(b)** (*mésaventure*) mishap, misadventure; **(c)** (*incarnation*) avatar, incarnation.

à vau-l'eau [avolo] *adv Fig* **voici mes projets partis à v.-l'e.,** there go all my plans, there are all my plans down the drain *or* up in smoke.

Ave [ave] *nm* **(a)** Ave; **L'A. Maria,** the Hail Mary; **(b) a.,** Ave Maria (*bead*).

avec [avɛk] **1** *prép* **(a)** (*accompaniment, collaboration*) with; **je vous ai vu a. lui,** I saw you with him; **déjeuner a. qn,** to lunch with s.o.; **je crois a. vous que ...,** like you, I believe that ...; **a. toi, c'est toujours pareil,** it's always the same with you, it's always the same old story with you; **le public est a. nous,** the public is behind us;

(b) (*indicating an adjunct or special feature*) **il est sorti a. son parapluie,** he has gone out with his umbrella; **chambre a. vue,** room with a view; **elle parle a. un léger accent anglais,** she speaks with a slight *or* faint English accent, she's got a slight English accent; **elle ressemble à sa sœur, a. des traits plus réguliers,** she is like her sister, but with more regular features; *Com* **et a. cela, madame?,** anything else, madam?;

(c) (*contemporaneity*) **il se lève a. le soleil,** he gets up at sunrise; **il est arrivé a. la nuit,** he arrived when it was getting dark *or* at nightfall *or* at dusk; **le paysage change a. les saisons,** the countryside changes with the seasons;

(d) (*suggesting cause*) **on n'y arrive plus a. cette vie chère,** it is becoming impossible to manage with the cost of living as high as it is; **a. ce soleil, rien ne pousse,** nothing will grow in this heat, it's so hot (that) nothing will grow;

(e) (*equivalent to* **malgré**) **a. tous ses défauts, je l'aime,** with *or* in spite of all his faults, I love him; **a. tout le respect que je vous dois,** with all due respect;

(f) (*manner*) **combattre a. courage,** to fight with courage *or* bravely; **parler a. réserve,** to speak with reserve, to speak guardedly, to watch what one is saying; **ce mot s'écrit a. un seul 't',** this word is written with (only) one 't';

(g) (*means, instrument*) **cela viendra a. le temps,** that will come in time; **a. l'aide de qn,** with s.o.'s help; **a. 200 francs, on s'en sort très bien,** you can buy *or* get quite a lot for *or* with 200 francs, you can get by *or* do perfectly well on *or* with 200 francs; **ouvrir une porte a. une clef,** to open a door with a key;

(h) (*association*) **un métal qui se combine a. un acide,** a metal which combines with an acid; **s'entendre bien/mal a. qn,** to get on well/badly with s.o.; **se marier a. qn,** to marry s.o., to get married to s.o.; **lier conversation a. qn,** to get *or* fall into conversation with s.o.;

(i) (*conformity*) **être d'accord a. qn,** to agree with s.o.; **s'harmoniser a. qch,** to harmonize *or* be in keeping with sth; **mot qui rime a. un autre,** word that rhymes with another;

(j) (*comparison*) **soutenir la comparaison a. qch,** to stand *or* bear comparison with sth;

(k) (*opposition equivalent to* **contre**) **lutter a. qch,** to struggle with sth; **se battre a. qn,** to fight s.o.;

(l) (*in expressing personal relationship*) **être bien/mal a. qn,** to be on good/bad terms with s.o.; **être sévère a. qn,** to be hard on s.o.; **être franc a. qn,** to be frank with s.o.;

(m) (*equivalent to* **en ce qui concerne**) **a. elle on ne sait jamais,** with her you never can tell; **c'est une idée qui ne me viendrait jamais a. vous,** it is an idea which would never occur to me as far as you are concerned;

(n) *F* **elle est grande et a. ça mince,** she is tall and, what's more, slim; **et a. ça, il n'est pas content,** and even so *or* now, he isn't happy; **ne dis pas a. ça qu'il n'a pas triché!,** don't say he didn't cheat!;

(o) d'a., from; **distinguer** *ou* **séparer le bon d'a. le mauvais,** to distinguish (the) good from (the) bad; **divorcer d'a. sa femme,** to divorce one's wife.

2 *adv* with it, with them; *F* **il a pris la caisse et s'est sauvé a.,** he ran off *or* scarpered with the takings.

aveline [avlin] *nf* (*fruit*) filbert, hazel nut, cob (nut).

avelinier [avlinje] *nm* (*arbre*) hazel.

aven [avɛn] *nm Géol* swallowhole.

avenant [avnɑ̃] **1** *adj* pleasing, prepossessing (*person, manners etc*); **mal a.,** uncouth (*manner etc*). **2** *nm* **(a) à l'a.,** in keeping, in conformity, correspondingly; **ils se sont conduits à l'a.,** they acted accordingly; **le bâtiment est beau et le jardin est à l'a.,** the building is beautiful and the garden is in keeping with it; **(b)** codicil (*to treaty*); **(c)** additional clause, endorsement (*to insurance policy*); **(d)** rider (*to verdict*).

avènement [avɛnmɑ̃] *nm* **(a)** advent (*of Christ etc*); coming (*of Messiah*); **depuis l'a. de l'automobile,** since the invention of the (motor) car; **(b)** (*accession*) advent, coming, arrival; **a. au trône,** accession to the throne.

avenir[1] [av(ə)nir] *nm* future; **qu'est-ce que l'a. nous réserve?,** what does the future hold for us?; what has the future in store for us?; **prédire l'a.,** to predict the future; **s'inquiéter de son a.,** to worry *or* be concerned about one's future; **jeune homme d'un grand** *ou* **de beaucoup d'a.,** young man of great promise; **c'est un homme d'a.,** he's a(n up-and-) coming man *or* a man with a future; *Sp* **un joueur d'a.,** a coming player; **une carrière d'a.,** a career with good prospects; **un avocat d'a.,** a lawyer with a great future (ahead of him), an up-and-coming lawyer; **situation sans a.,** job with no future *or* prospects, dead-end occupation; **assurer l'a. de qn,** to make provision for s.o.; **dans l'a.,** at some future date; **dans un a. très prochain,** in the very near *or* immediate future; **à l'a. je serai plus circonspect,** in future I shall be more cautious.

avenir[2] *nm inv Jur* writ of summons (*to opposing counsel*); **signifier un a. à la partie adverse,** to serve a writ on the other party.

Avent [avɑ̃] *nm Rel* Advent.

aventure [avɑ̃tyr] *nf* **(a)** (*affaire*) adventure; **homme d'aventures,** adventurous man, adventurer; **film d'aventures,** adventure film; **a. effrayante,** terrifying experience; **pour trouver des fruits en hiver, c'est tout une aventure,** it's quite a business *or F* a heck of a job, finding fruit in winter; **(b)** (*liaison*) intrigue, (love) affair; **(c) l'a.,** chance, luck, venture; **tenter l'a.,** to try one's luck; **vie d'a.,** life of adventure; **l'a. est au coin de la rue,** the unexpected is always round the corner; **à l'a.,** at random; **aller** *ou* **errer à l'a.,** to wander about aimlessly; **partir à l'a.,** to set off on an adventure; **vivre à l'a.,** to live in a happy-go-lucky fashion; **mettre tout à l'a.,** to leave everything to chance; *Litt* **par a., d'a.,** by chance; **(d) la bonne a.,** fortune-telling; **dire** *ou* **tirer la bonne a. (à qn),** to tell (s.o.'s) fortune; **diseuse de bonne a.,** fortune teller.

aventuré [avɑ̃tyre] *adj* risky, chancy.

aventurer [avɑ̃tyre] **1** *vt* to risk (*life etc*); to expose oneself (*to risks*); to take risks; **a. une grosse somme d'argent,** to risk *or* venture a large sum of money. **2 s'aventurer** *vpr* to venture (*into, onto*); **s'a. en pays inconnu,** to venture into an unknown country; *Fig* to venture into unknown territory; **je ne m'aventurerai pas à dire que ...,** I won't go so far as to say ... .

aventureusement [avɑ̃tyrøzmɑ̃] *adv* adventurously, venturesomely; in an adventurous manner.

aventureux, -euse [avɑ̃tyrø, -øz] **1** *adj* adventurous, venturesome; **homme a. au jeu,** reckless gambler; *Péj* **une explication aventureuse,** an unlikely *or* doubtful explanation; **projet a.,** hazardous *or* risky plan. **2** *n* **jeune a.,** a rash *or* venturesome young man.

aventurier, -ière [avɑ̃tyrje, -jɛr] *n* adventurer; **c'est un a.,** he lives by his wits.

aventurisme [avɑ̃tyrism] *nm Pol* adventurism.

avenue [avny] *nf* (*in town*) avenue; (*leading to house*) (carriage) drive(way); **les avenues du pouvoir,** the paths to power.

avéré [avere] *adj* authenticated, established (*fact etc*); (*fact*) beyond doubt; **crime a.,** patent and established crime; **ennemi a.,** avowed enemy; **voleur a.,** known thief; **marxistes avérés,** professed Marxists.

avérer [avere] *v* (**j'avère, n. avérons; j'avérerai**) **1** *vt Jur Vieilli* to aver (*fact*). **2 s'avérer** *vpr* to be proved correct; to be confirmed; **elle s'est avérée indispensable dans l'équipe,** she's proved *or* turned out to be an essential member of the team; **s'a. faux,** to be proved false; **il s'est avéré que ...,** it's turned out that ..., as it's turned out, ...

avers [avɛr] *nm* obverse (*of coin*).

averse [avɛrs] *nf* sudden shower, downpour; **essuyer une a.,** to be caught in a shower; *Fig* **célébrité née de la dernière a.,** person who has shot to fame overnight, person who has enjoyed a sudden rise to fame, an overnight sensation *or* celebrity; **une a. de félicitations,** a flood *or* stream of congratulations.

aversion [avɛrsjɔ̃] *nf* aversion (**pour,** to, for); dislike (**pour,** for, of); **avoir une** *ou* **de l'a. pour** *ou* **contre qn,** to have an aversion to *or* for s.o., to have a dislike for s.o., to find s.o. distasteful; **prendre qn en a.,** to take a dislike to s.o.

averti [averti] *adj* experienced (*observer etc*); **un homme a.,** an experienced man, an expert; **a. de qch,** aware *or* warned of sth; **se tenir pour a.,** to be on one's guard; to take the hint; **vous voilà a.!,** I give you fair warning!, don't say I haven't warned you!

avertin [avɛrtɛ̃] *nm Vét* staggers.

avertir [avɛrtir] *vt* **(a) a. qn de qch,** to warn *or* to notify *or* to advise *or* to inform s.o. of sth, to give s.o. notice *or* warning of sth; **a. qn du danger d'une situation,** to warn *or* tell s.o. of *or* about the danger(s) of a situaiton; **je l'en avais averti,** I had warned him of *or* against it; **je vous en avertis!,** I give you fair warning!; **(b)** *Aut* to signal (intention to turn).

avertissement [avɛrtismɑ̃] *nm* **(a)** (*avis préalable*) warning; **renvoyer qn sans a. préalable,** to discharge s.o. at a moment's notice; **lettre envoyée à titre d'a.,** letter sent as a reminder; (*avis*) warning letter; **(b)** (*réprimande*) reprimand; *Sp* warning, caution (*by the referee*); **(c)** (*signal*) danger signal *or* sign; warning signal; **a. de tempête,** gale warning; **(d) a. (au lecteur),** prefatory note, foreword (to book); **(e)** *Jur* **billet d'a.,** summons to appear before a magistrate; **(f)** *Admin* demand note.

avertisseur, -euse [avɛrtisœr, -øz] **1** *nm* **(a)** (*dispositif*) warning signal, alarm; *Tél* annunciator; *Aut* horn, hooter; *Ind* hooter; *Rail* signal; **a. d'incendie,** fire alarm; **avertisseurs sonores interdits après 22.00 heures,** no sounding of horns after 10 p.m.; **(b)** *Vieilli* warner; *Th* callboy. **2** *adj* **signal a.,** warning signal.

aveu, -eux [avø] *nm* **(a)** (*confession*) avowal, confession; *Jur* admission; **faire l'a. d'une erreur,** to own up *or* confess to a mistake; **passer aux aveux,** to make a confession; **faire des aveux complets,** to make a full confession; **de l'a. de tout le monde,** by common consent; **je dois vous faire un a., je n'y étais pas non plus,** I must confess *or* admit *or* I have to tell you, I wasn't there either; **arracher des aveux à un accusé,** to drag *or* wring *or* wrest a confession out of *or* from a defendant; **il est certain, de l'a. de tout le monde, que ...,** everyone agrees that ...; **(b)** *Jur* consent, authorization; **obtenir l'a. de qn pour faire qch,** to obtain s.o.'s consent to do sth; **(c)** *Hist* recognition between a vassal and his overlord; **homme sans a.,** vagabond, vagrant.

aveuglant [avœglɑ̃] *adj* blinding; dazzling; **une évidence/preuve aveuglante,** a glaringly *or* patently *or* blindingly obvious fact/proof.

aveugle [avœgl] **1** *adj* **(a)** (*atteint de cécité*) blind, sightless; **devenir a.,** to go blind; **a. d'un œil,** blind in one eye; **naître a.,** to be born blind, to be blind from birth; *Opt* **point a.,** blind spot; *F* **a. comme une taupe,** as blind as a bat;

(b) *Fig Archit* **fenêtre/arcade a.,** blind window/arch; **mur a.,** blind wall; *Tech* **écrou a.,** blind nut; **trou a.,** dead hole; **bout a. (d'un tuyau),** blind end;

(c) blind, unreasoning (*hatred*); implicit (*confidence etc*); **avoir une confiance a. en qn,** to trust s.o. implicitly *or* unreservedly; **obéissance a.,** blind *or* unquestioning obedience.

2 *n* a blind man; a blind woman; **les aveugles,** the blind; **aveugles de guerre,** blinded ex-servicemen; **suivre qn en a.,** to follow s.o. blindly *or* unreasoningly; *Vieilli* **aller à l'a.,** to grope one's way.

aveuglement [avœgləmɑ̃] *nm* **(a)** (*moral, mental*) blindness; **l'a. de la passion/de la colère,** the blindness of passion/of anger; **(b)** *Arch* blinding; **depuis son a.,** since his blindness.

aveuglément [avœglemɑ̃] *adv* blindly, blindfold; **obéir a.,** to obey blindly *or* without question.

aveugle-né, -née [avœglɔne] (*pl aveugles-né(e)s*) **1** *adj* (*man, woman*) blind from birth. **2** *n* congenitally blind person, person blind from birth.

aveugler [avœgle] **1** *vt* **(a)** (*rendre aveugle*) to blind (*s.o.*); **(b)** (*of light etc*) to dazzle, to blind; *Fig* **aveuglé par la colère,** blind with rage; **(c)** *Nau* **a. une voie d'eau,** to stop a leak; **(d)** (*boucher*) to plug, to stop (up), to block up, to fill in; **a. une fenêtre,** to wall up *or* block a window. **2 s'aveugler** *vpr Fig* to be blind, to shut one's eyes (*to sth*); **il ne faut pas t'a., ça ne sera pas facile,** don't delude yourself *or F* kid yourself, it won't be easy; **s'a. sur les défauts de qn,** to shut one's eyes *or* turn a blind eye to s.o.'s faults.

aveuglette (à l') [alavœglɛt] *adv* blindly; **aller à l'a.,** to feel *or* grope one's way; **avancer à l'a. vers qch,** to feel *or* grope one's way to(wards) sth; **choisir qch à l'a.,** to choose sth at random *or* in the dark *or* blindly; **lancer des coups à l'a.,** to hit out blindly; *Av* **voler à l'a.,** to fly blind.

aveulir [avølir] **1** *vt* to enervate; to sap (*s.o.'s*) energy; to deaden (*feelings etc*). **2 s'aveulir** *vpr* **il s'aveulit,** he's going to pieces.

aveulissement [avølismɑ̃] *nm* loss of will, enfeeblement, listlessness.

aviaire [avjɛr] *adj* **peste a.,** fowl plague, fowl pest.

aviateur, -trice [avjatœr, -tris] *n* aviator, airman, -woman; **mal des aviateurs,** altitude sickness.

aviation [avjasjɔ̃] *nf* air-force (*military*); air-fleet (*civil*); aviation; **a. civile/commerciale/militaire,** civil/commercial/military aviation; **compagnie d'a.,** airline; **champ** *ou* **terrain d'a.,** airfield; **base d'a.,** air base; **usine d'a.,** aircraft factory.

avicole [avikɔl] *adj* **élevage a.,** (*activité*) poultry farming; (*établissement*) poultry farm.

aviculteur [avikyltœr] *nm* poultry farmer, *US* poultryman.

aviculture [avikyltyr] *nf* **(a)** (*d'oiseaux*) aviculture; **(b)** (*de volailles*) poultry farming.

avide [avid] *adj* **(a)** (*passionné*) eager, avid, greedy; **a. de qch,** (*âpre*) greedy for sth; (*plein d'enthousiasme*) eager for sth; **espérances avides,** eager hopes; **a. de sang,** bloodthirsty; **a. de tout savoir,** eager for knowledge; **(b)** *Péj* greedy, covetous (**de,** of); grasping (*hands, nature*).

avidement [avidmɑ̃] *adv* greedily, hungrily; covetously; **écouter a.,** to listen eagerly *or* avidly.

avidité [avidite] *nf* avidity, greed(iness); voracity (*for food*); **manger avec a.,** to eat greedily; **écouter avec a.,** to listen eagerly *or* avidly.

avili [avili] *adj* degraded, debased, demeaned (*person*); debased (*coinage, currency*); depreciated (*goods*).

avilir [avilir] **1** *vt* **(a)** (*dégrader*) to degrade, to debase, to lower; **(b)** *Com* to depreciate, to lower, to bring down (*currency, prices etc*). **2 s'avilir** *vpr* **(a)** (*of person*) to lower *or* demean oneself; **(b)** (*of goods*) to depreciate, to come down (in value).

avilissant [avilisɑ̃] *adj* debasing, degrading.

avilissement [avilismɑ̃] *nm* **(a)** (*dégradation*) debasement, degradation; **(b)** depreciation; fall (*in price*).

aviné [avine] *adj* intoxicated, inebriated, in one's cups (*attrib*); **haleine avinée,** breath reeking of wine.

aviner [avine] *vt* to impregnate with wine (*cask*).

avion [avjɔ̃] *nm* aircraft, aeroplane, plane, *US* airplane; **j'ai fait une partie du trajet en a.,** I flew part of the way; **par a.,** (by) air mail; **voyager en a.,** to travel by plane *or* air, to fly; **prendre l'a. pour aller à Londres,** to get *or* take the plane to London, to fly to London; **a. commercial,** commercial aircraft; **a. de ligne,** airliner; **a. de transport,** transport aircraft; **accident d'a.,** plane crash; **détournement d'a.,** hijacking, hijack, skyjacking; **a. transbordeur,** air ferry; **a. de tourisme,** private aircraft; **a. bimoteur,** twin-engine aircraft; **a. de bombardement,** bomber; **a. de chasse,** fighter; **a. de pénétration,** intruder; **a. de reconnaissance,** reconnaissance aircraft; **a. ravitailleur,** tanker; **a. furtif,** stealth bomber; **a. d'attaque au sol,** ground attack aircraft; **a. à réaction,** jet aircraft; **a. à géométrie variable,** swing-wing aircraft; **a. à décollage et atterrissage courts/verticaux,** short/vertical take-off and landing aircraft.

avion-citerne [avjɔ̃sitɛrn] *nm Av* tanker (aircraft); (*pl avions-citernes*).

avion-école [avjɔ̃ekɔl] *nm* trainer, training aircraft; (*pl avions-écoles*).

avionique [avjɔnik] *nf Av* avionics.

avionneur [avjɔnœr] *nm* **(a)** (*concepteur*) airframe designer; **(b)** (*constructeur*) airframe manufacturer.

avion-taxi [avjɔ̃taksi] *nm* charter aircraft; air taxi, taxiplane; (*pl avions-taxis*).

aviron [avirɔ̃] *nm* **(a)** (*rame*) oar; *Can* (canoe) paddle; **a. de couple,** scull; **avirons de couple** *ou* **accouplés,** double-banked oars; **avirons de** *ou* **en pointe,** single-banked oars; **a. de galère,** sweep; **les avirons dans l'eau!,** hold water!; **engager son a.,** to catch a crab; **coup d'a.,** stroke; **(b)** *Sp* **l'a.,** rowing; **cercles d'a.,** rowing clubs; **faire de l'a.,** to row.

avironner [avirɔne] *vi Can* to paddle (*in canoe*).

avis [avi] *nm* **(a)** (*opinion*) opinion, judgment, decision; **a. d'expert,** expert advice *or* opinion; **exprimer** *ou* **émettre un a.,** to express a view *or* an opinion; **être du même a. que qn,** to be of the same opinion as s.o.; **ne pas être du même a. que qn,** to disagree with s.o.; **sauf meilleur a. je crois que ...,** with all due deference I think that ...; *Prov* **deux a. valent mieux qu'un,** two heads are better than one; **à** *ou* **selon mon a.,** in my opinion, I consider (that); **de l'a. de tous,** in the opinion *or* judgment of all; **je suis tout à fait de votre a.,** I entirely agree with you, *F* I'm with you; **j'ai changé d'a.,** I have changed my mind; **être d'a. de faire qch,** to be of a mind to do sth; **êtes-vous d'a. de rester ici?,** do you agree with *or* are you for staying here?;

(b) (*conseil*) advice, counsel; **a. paternel,** fatherly advice; **donner des a. à qn sur qch,** to advise s.o. on sth; **prendre** *ou* **demander l'a. de qn,** to ask s.o.'s advice; *F* **on ne t'a pas demandé ton a.!,** nobody asked you!, mind your own business!, keep your big nose out of it!, nobody asked your opinion!;

(c) (*avertissement*) notice, notification, announcement; **a. (au public),** public notice, notice (to the public); **donner a. de qch,** to give notice of sth; **donner a. à qn de qch,** to advise s.o. of sth; **a. par écrit,** notice in writing; **jusqu'à nouvel a.,** until further notice, until further orders, until you hear further; **à moins d'a. contraire,** unless I *or* you *etc* hear to the contrary; *Com* **note** *ou* **lettre d'a.,** advice note, notification of dispatch; **a. de livraison,** delivery note; **suivant a.,** as per advice; **a. de débit,** debit note, debit advice; *Bourse* **a. d'exécution,** contract note.

avisé [avize] *adj* sensible, wise, prudent, circumspect; intelligent, shrewd; **être trop a. pour faire qch,** to be too sensible *or* cautious *or* wary to do sth; **il est trop a. pour ...,** he knows better than to ...; **acheteur a.,** discriminating purchaser; **bien a.,** well-advised; **mesures mal avisées,** ill-advised *or* badly thought out measures.

aviser [avize] **1** *vt* **(a)** (*informer*) to inform, to notify, to advise; **a. qn de qch,** to inform *or* warn *or Com* advise s.o. of sth; **a. qn de faire qch,** to give s.o. notice to do sth; **a.**

qn que + *ind*, to warn s.o. that ...;
(b) *Arch & Litt* to perceive, to catch a glimpse of (*sth, s.o.*).
2 *vi* **a. à,** to decide what to do about (*situation etc*); to see about *or* to (*sth*); **vous ferez bien d'y a.,** you had better look into it; **a. à faire qch,** to see about doing sth; **a. à ce que qch se fasse,** to take steps to have sth done; **il est temps d'a.,** it is time to decide *or* to make up one's mind.
3 s'aviser *vpr* **(a) s'a. de qch,** to think of sth; **il ne s'avise de rien,** he never thinks of anything; **s'aviser que,** to notice, to become aware, to realize;
(b) s'a. de faire qch, to take it upon oneself to do sth; **ne vous en avisez pas!,** don't dare to do such a thing!, don't you dare!, you'd better not!

aviso [avizo] *nm* sloop; **a.-torpilleur,** torpedo gunboat; **a. d'escorte,** corvette; **canonnière-a.,** gunboat; *US Nau* **a. de croisière,** cruising cutter.

avitaminose [avitaminoz] *nf* vitamin deficiency, avitaminosis.

aviver [avive] **1** *vt* **(a)** to revive, to brighten (*colours etc*); to touch up (*colour, picture*); to irritate (*wound, sore*); to excite, stir up (*passion*); to fan, to revive, to stir up (*fire*); to sharpen (*appetite*); **a. d'anciennes rancunes,** to revive ancient grudges; **(b)** to burnish (*metalwork*); to polish (*marble*); **(c)** to clean up (*surfaces for soldering*); **(d)** to put a keen edge on, to whet (*tool etc*). **2 s'aviver** *vpr* to be stirred up, to be revived (*of memories, controversy etc*); to become brighter (*of colour*).

av.J.-C. (*abrév* **avant Jésus-Christ**) BC.

avocat[1], -ate [avɔka, -at] *n* **(a)** *Jur* barrister (-at-law), counsel; *Scot* advocate; **a. consultant,** counsel in chambers; **a. conseil,** consulting barrister; **a. général,** assistant public prosecutor (in a court of appeal); **plaider par a.,** to be represented by counsel; **elle est a.** *ou* **avocate,** she's a barrister; **être reçu a.,** to be called to the bar; **(b)** (*défenseur*) counsel for the defence, advocate; *Fig* **a. du diable,** devil's advocate.

avocat[2] *nm* (*fruit*) avocado (pear).

avocat-avoué [avɔkaavwe] *nm* ≈ attorney; (*pl avocats-avoués*).

avocatier [avɔkatje] *nm* (*arbre*) avocado (tree).

avocette [avɔsɛt] *nf* (*oiseau*) avocet.

avoine [avwan] *nf* oats; **a. commune,** common oats; **farine d'a.,** oatmeal; **flocons d'a.,** porridge oats; **bouillie d'a.,** (oatmeal) porridge; **galette d'a.,** oatcake; *Arch F* **semer sa folle a.,** to sow one's wild oats.

avoir[1] [avwar] *v* (*prp* **ayant**; *pp* **eu**; *pr ind* **j'ai, tu as, il a, n. avons, v. avez, ils ont**; *pr sub* **j'aie, tu aies, il ait, n. ayons, v. ayez, ils aient**; *imp* **aie, ayons, ayez**; *impf* **j'avais**; *p hist* **j'eus, tu eus, il eut, n. eûmes, v. eûtes, ils eurent**; *impf sub* **j'eusse**; *fu* **j'aurai**; **avoir** *is the auxiliary of all transitive and of many intransitive verbs*) **1** *vt* **(a)** (*posséder*) to have, to possess; **a. une maison/un appartement,** to have *or* own a house/flat *or* apartment; **a. beaucoup d'amis,** to have many friends; **il a deux voitures,** he has *or* runs two cars; **as-tu de quoi manger/vivre?,** have you (got) enough to eat/live on?; **a. du feu,** to have a light (*for cigarette etc*); **a. de la chance,** (*on a specific occasion*) to be in luck, to be lucky; (*long-term characteristic*) to be lucky; **a. le temps de réfléchir,** to have time to think; **il a des poulets,** he keeps chickens; **a. une opinion,** to hold an opinion; **qu'est-ce que vous avez là?,** what have you (got) there?; **a. des amis à dîner,** to have friends to dinner; **il a encore son père,** his father is still alive; **j'ai Bill pour ami/voisin,** Bill is a friend/neighbour of mine; **si je ne t'avais pas!,** (*in appreciation*) *& Iron* where would I be without you?; **en juin nous avons eu du beau temps,** in June we had fine weather; **Dieu ait son âme,** God rest his *or* her soul; **a. les mains pleines/les poches vides/les yeux ouverts,** to have one's hands full/one's pockets empty/one's eyes open; *Fig* **il a le bras long,** he is very influential; **a. qn/qch en horreur,** to loathe *or* detest *or* hate *or* have a horror of s.o./sth;
(b) (*mesure, âge*) **a. dix ans,** to be ten (years old); **mur qui a trois mètres de haut,** wall that is three metres high;
(c) *for the verbal phrases* **avoir affaire, faim, froid, pitié, raison,** *etc see under these words*;
(d) (*obtenir*) to get, to obtain (*sth*); **j'ai eu ce cheval (à) bon marché,** I got *or* bought this horse cheap; **j'ai bien eu mon train ce matin,** I caught my train all right this morning; **la propriété qu'il a eue de son père,** the property which he inherited from his father; **j'ai eu sa réponse ce matin,** I had *or* got his answer this morning; *Arg* **a. une femme,** to have *or* screw a woman;
(e) a. un enfant, to have *or* to give birth to a child;
(f) (*être muni de*) to have; **a. les yeux bleus,** to have blue eyes; **a. de grandes mains/de beaux yeux,** to have big *or* large hands/beautiful eyes; **a. du charme,** to be charming, to have charm, to be full of charm; **elle a un certain talent pour ...,** she has a certain talent *or* flair *or* knack *or* gift for ...;
(g) *F* to get the better of (*s.o.*), to con, to take in, to pull a fast one on (*s.o.*); **on l'a eu!,** he's been had!, he's been taken for a ride!;
(h) *Litt* (= **faire** *etc chiefly in p hist*) **il eut un mouvement brusque,** he made a sudden movement;
(i) (*souffrir de, sentir*) to have; **qu'avez-vous?, qu'est-ce que vous avez?,** what's the matter with you?; **a. de la peine/des soucis,** to be sad/to have troubles *or* worries, to be worried; **a. des remords/des scrupules,** to feel remorse/to have scruples *or* qualms *or* misgivings; **a. mal au cœur,** to feel sick; **a. de la fièvre,** to have *or* be running a temperature; **a. la rougeole,** to have measles; *F* **mais qu'est-ce qu'elle a, cette auto?,** what's wrong *or* the matter *or* up with this car?;
(j) nous en avons pour deux heures, it will take us two hours, we'll be two hours; **j'en ai assez,** I've had enough (of it), I'm tired *or* sick of it; I'm through (with it); **j'en ai eu pour 100 francs,** (*c'est le prix*) it cost me 100 francs; (*en quantité*) I had 100 francs' worth;
(k) en a. à *ou* **contre qn,** to have a grudge against s.o., to have it in for s.o.; **est-ce à moi que vous en avez?,** are you getting at me?;
(l) a. qch à faire, to have sth to do; **je n'ai rien à faire,** I have nothing to do; **j'ai à travailler,** I've work to do; **vous n'avez pas à vous inquiéter,** you have no need to worry; **je n'ai que faire de cela,** I don't need that.
2 *v impers* **il y a,** there is, there are; **(a)** (*pour énumérer etc*) **qu'est-ce qu'il peut y a. dans ce tiroir?,** I wonder what's in this drawer?; **combien y a-t-il de blessés?,** how many wounded are there?; **il n'y en a qu'un,** there is only one; **il n'y a qu'à demander,** you only have to ask, just ask; **il n'y en a que pour elle,** she gets all the attention; **un homme comme il y en a peu,** a man in a thousand; **il y en a qui disent que ...,** there are people who *or* some people say that ...; **il y en a un qui va être surpris,** someone is in for a surprise; **il n'y a pas de quoi,** please don't mention it, *US* you're welcome!; **qu'est-ce qu'il y a à voir?,** what is there to see?;
(b) (*se passer*) **il doit y a. quelque chose,** there must be something wrong; **qu'y a-t-il à présent?,** what now?; **qu'est-ce qu'il y a?,** what's the matter?; *F* what's up?; **il y a qu'on t'attendait hier,** we were expecting you yesterday, that's what's wrong *or* that's what's the matter;
(c) (*temps*) **il y a deux ans,** two years ago, **il y avait six mois que j'attendais,** I had been waiting for six months;
(d) (*distance*) **combien y a-t-il d'ici (à) Londres?,** how far is it (from here) to London?
3 *v aux* **j'ai fini,** I've finished; **attendez que nous ayons fini,** wait until we've finished; **je l'ai déjà vu,** I have already seen him, I have seen him before; **je l'ai vu/vue hier,** I saw him/her yesterday; **j'ai eu vingt ans hier,** I was twenty yesterday; **j'ai eu bientôt fini de m'habiller,** I (had) soon finished dressing; **quand il eut** *ou* **a eu fini de parler,** when he had finished speaking; **j'aurai bientôt fini,** I shall soon have finished.

avoir[2] *nm* property, possessions; **tout mon a.,** all I possess *or* have; *Com* **doit et a.,** debit and credit; **obtenir un a.,** to be given credit, to obtain credit, to get credit.

avoirdupois [avwardypwa] *nm* avoirdupois.

avoisinant [avwazinɑ̃] *adj* neighbouring, nearby; **il a cinquante ans ou un âge a.,** he's fifty or thereabout(s).

avoisiner [avwazine] *vt* **a. qch,** to be near *or* close to *or* adjacent to sth, to border on sth.

avortement [avɔrtəmɑ̃] *nm* **(a)** (*of woman*) **a. spontané,** miscarriage; **a. provoqué,** abortion; **(b)** (*of animal*) casting (*of young*); **(c)** *Fig* failure, miscarriage, falling through (*of plan etc*).

avorter [avɔrte] *vi* **(a)** (*d'une femme*) to miscarry, to abort; **faire a. qn,** to give s.o. an abortion; (*d'une injection etc*) to bring on a miscarriage; **(b)** (*of animals*) to cast (*young*); **(c)** *Bot* to develop imperfectly; to fail to ripen; to abort; **arbres avortés,** stunted trees; **(d)** *Fig* **projet qui a avorté,** plan that (has) miscarried *or* proved abortive *or* has gone wrong *or* come to nothing *or* fallen through.

avorteur, -euse [avɔrtœr, -øz] *n* abortionist.

avorton [avɔrtɔ̃] *nm* abortion; stunted plant *or* animal; puny *or* undersized child; *Péj* **(petit) a.,** little shrimp, squirt.

avouable [avwabl] *adj* avowable (*fact, motive*); **c'est un métier plus a.,** it's a more respectable trade.

avoué¹ [avwe] *nm Jur* ≈ solicitor, *US* attorney.
avoué² *adj* **(a)** acknowledged, admitted (*fact*); **(b)** confessed (*author of ...*); **(c)** ostensible (*purpose*).
avouer [avwe] **1** *vt* **(a)** to acknowledge, to recognize (*s.o., debt etc*); **(b)** (*reconnaître*) to acknowledge, to recognize, to admit; **a. qn pour frère,** to acknowledge s.o. as one's brother; **(c)** to confess, to admit, to own up to (*fault etc*); **elle avoue trente ans,** she admits to being thirty; **ceci me surprend, je l'avoue,** this surprises me, I confess *or* I must say; **a. avoir fait qch,** to confess *or* to own up to having done sth. **2** *vi* **(a)** to confess, to own up; **ils utilisent la torture pour faire a. leurs prisonniers,** they use torture to extract confessions from their prisoners; **(b)** to confess, to admit. **3 s'avouer** *vpr* to admit (to being + *adj*); **s'a. coupable,** to admit one's guilt; **s'a. vaincu,** to acknowledge oneself beaten, to acknowledge defeat.
avril [avril] *nm* April; **en a.,** in April; **au mois d'a.,** in the month of April; **pluie d'a.,** April showers; **le sept a.,** (on) the seventh of April, (on) April (the) seventh; **le premier a.,** the first of April; April Fools' Day; **poisson d'a.!,** April fool!
avunculaire [avɔ̃kylɛr] *adj* avuncular.
axe [aks] *nm* **(a)** *Géom* axis (*of plant, the earth, ellipse etc*); **grand/petit a.,** major/minor axis; *Constr* **a. d'une route/d'un pont,** centre line of a road/bridge; **a. de circulation,** major route; **les grands axes de la circulation,** trunk roads, major roads (*of road network*); main lines (*of rail network*); *Fig* **les grands axes de sa politique,** the main thrust of his policy; **conduire sur l'a. de la chaussée,** to drive on the crown of the road; *Math* **a. des x/des y,** x-axis/y-axis; **axes de coordonnées,** co-ordinate axes; *Tech* **axes principaux d'un corps,** principal axes of a body; **cristal à deux axes,** biaxial crystal;
(b) *MecE etc* axle, spindle, pin; **a. de pompe,** pump spindle; **a. d'une grue,** pin of a crane; **a. du piston,** (*d'un moteur*) gudgeon pin;
(c) *Hist* axis; **les Puissances de l'A.,** the Axis powers;
(d) *Mil* **a. de progression,** main direction of advance; **a. (principal) de ravitaillement,** main line of supply, main supply route;
(e) *Av* **a. de sustentation,** lift axis; **a. de descente,** glide path, line of descent; **a. balisé,** radio range course; **a. balisé d'atterrissage,** radio landing beam; **a. de référence,** datum line.
axer [akse] *vt* to centre; **être axé sur** *ou* **autour de,** to follow (*a tendency etc*), to centre on.
axial, -aux [aksjal, -o] *adj* axial (*line, plane*); **effort de compression axiale,** collapsible load; **plan a.,** *Géol* axial plane; **éclairage a.,** central overhead lighting (*of streets*).
axillaire [aksilɛr] *adj Anat Bot* axillary.
axiomatique [aksjɔmatik] *adj* axiomatic.
axiome [aksjom] *nm* axiom.
axis [aksis] *nm Anat* axis (second vertebra).
ayant [ɛjɑ̃] *nm* **(a)** *Jur* **a. cause,** (*beneficiary of will*) legal successor, successor in title, legatee, devisee; (*beneficiary of gift*) donee; (*beneficiary of transfer*) assignee; (*buyer*) vendee; (*nominated agent*) executor, trustee; (*pl ayants-cause*); **(b) a. droit,** = **ayant-cause**; eligible party, entitled beneficiary; (*pl ayants-droit*).
ayatollah [ajatɔla] *nm* ayatollah.
azalée [azale] *nf* (*plante*) azalea.
azimut [azimyt] *nm Astron etc* azimuth; *Nau etc* **prendre un a.,** to take a bearing; *F* **dans tous les azimuts,** everywhere, all over the place; **direction tous azimuts,** facing all ways, all directions; *Fig* **faire une campagne électorale tous azimuts pour récupérer la direction du parti,** to conduct an all-out electoral campaign for the leadership of the party.
azimutal, -aux [azimytal, -o] *adj* azimuth(al); **cercle a.,** azimuth circle; **compas a.,** azimuth compass.
azimuté [azimyte] *adj F* crazy, round the bend.
azotate [azɔtat] *nm Ch* nitrate; **a. de potasse,** nitre, saltpetre.
azote [azɔt] *nm Ch* nitrogen.
azoté [azɔte] *adj* nitrogenous; **engrais azotés,** nitrate fertilizers, nitrates.
azoter [azɔte] *vt* to nitrogenize.
azotique [azɔtik] *adj Ch* nitric.
azotite [azɔtit] *nm Ch* nitrite.
aztèque [aztɛk] **1** *adj* Aztec. **2** *n* **A.,** Aztec.
azur [azyr] *nm* **(a)** (*couleur*) azure, blue; **(b)** *Géog* **la Côte d'A.,** the French Riviera; **(c)** *Hér* **champ d'a.,** field azure; **(d) pierre d'a.,** lapis lazuli; **(e)** *Com* blue (*for laundry*).
azuré [azyre] *adj* **(a)** (sky-)blue, azure; **(b)** *Litt* tinged with blue.
azurer [azyre] *vt* **(a)** to blue (*linen etc*); **(b)** *Litt* to tinge with blue.
azyme [azim] **1** *adj* **pain a.,** unleavened bread, wafer. **2** *nm Jew Rel* **fête des azymes,** feast of unleavened bread, Passover.

B

B, b [be] *nm* **(a)** (the letter) B, b; **(b)** *Ch* (*symbole du bore*) B.
B.A. [bea] *nf* (*abrév* **bonne action**) good deed; **faire une/sa B.A.,** to do a good deed/one's good deed for the day.
B.A.-Ba [beaba] *nm F* ABC; **je ne connais que le B.A.-Ba de la comptabilité,** I only know the rudiments of accountancy; **c'est le B.A.-Ba de la physique quantique,** it's the kiddies' guide to quantum physics.
baba[1] [baba] *nm Culin* (rum) baba; *F* **elle l'a eu dans le b.,** she came unstuck.
baba[2] *adj inv F* dumbfounded, flabbergasted; **j'en suis resté b.,** I was absolutely flabbergasted; **j'en suis complètement b.,** I'm absolutely flabbergasted.
baba (cool) [baba(kul)] *n* hippie.
Babel [babɛl] *nf* Babel; **la tour de B.,** the Tower of Babel; *Fig* **c'est une vraie tour de B.,** it's a perfect Babel, it's pandemonium.
babeurre [babœr] *nm* buttermilk.
babil [babi(l)] *nm* prattling (*of child*); prattle (*of children*); twittering (*of birds*); babbling (*of a brook*).
babillage [babijaʒ] *nm* **(a)** = **BABIL**; **(b)** *Psy* lallation.
babillard, -arde [babijar, -ard] **1** *adj* garrulous, talkative; *Fig* **cours d'eau b.,** babbling brook. **2** *n* **(a)** (*personne*) chatterbox; **(b)** *Can* (*dans l'enseignement*) flannel board.
babillement [babijmɑ̃] *nm* = **BABIL**.
babiller [babije] *vi* (*of child*) to prattle, to chatter; (*of brook*) to babble; (*of bird*) to chirrup, to twitter.
babines [babin] *nfpl Zool* pendulous lips (*of monkey etc*); chops (*of ruminant*); *F* lips, chops (*of person*); **s'essuyer les b.,** to wipe one's lips *or* chops; **vous vous en lécherez les b.,** it will make you lick your lips *or* chops.
babiole [babjɔl] *nf* **(a)** (*bibelot*) curio, knick-knack, trinket; **(b)** (*incident*) trifling event, trifle.
bâbord [babɔr] *nm Nau* port (side); **la barre toute à b., b. toute!, b. la barre!,** hard a-port!; **la terre par b.!** land on the port side!; **aviron de b.,** stroke side-oar.
bâbordais [babɔrdɛ] *nm Nau* man of the port watch; **les b.,** the port watch.
babouche [babuʃ] *nf* Turkish slipper.
babouin [babwɛ̃] *nm* baboon.
baboune [babun] *nf Can F* **faire la b.,** to sulk.
baby [bebi] **1** *adj inv* **taille b.,** baby-size(d); **whisky b.,** small whisky. **2** *nm* small whisky.
baby-boom [bebibum] *nm* baby boom.
baby-foot [babifut] *nm* miniature *or* table football.
Babylone [babilɔn] *nf Antiq* Babylon.
Babylonie [babilɔni] *nf Antiq* Babylonia.
babylonien, -ienne [babilɔnjɛ̃, -jɛn] *Antiq* **1** *adj* Babylonian. **2** *n* **B.,** Babylonian.
baby-sitter [bebisitœr] *n* baby-sitter.
baby-sitting [bebisitiŋ] *nm F* **faire du b.-s.,** to baby-sit.
bac[1] [bak] *nm* **(a)** ferry (boat); **b. à piétons,** passenger ferry; **b. à voitures,** car ferry; **b. transbordeur,** train ferry; **passer qn dans un b.,** to ferry s.o. across; *Jur* **droit de b.,** ferry (right); **(b)** tank, vat; pot (*of electric cell*); box, container (*of accumulator*); box, container (*for food etc*); (miner's) truck, tub; tray (*of printer*); **b. à laver,** wash tub; **b. à douche,** shower cabinet *or* cubicle; **b. à glace,** ice tray (*in fridge*); *Belg* **b. à ordures,** dustbin; *Ordinat* **b. de feuilles,** paper tray; *Ordinat* **b. d'alimentation,** sheet feed.
bac[2] *nm F* = **BACCALAURÉAT**; **passer/préparer le b.,** to sit one's/study for one's baccalauréat.
baccalauréat [bakalɔrea] *nm* **(a) b. (de l'enseignement secondaire),** ≈ General Certificate of Education (A Level); (*in Scotland*) ≈ Scottish Higher Certificate of Education; (*in Eire*) ≈ School Leaving Certificate; **(b) b. en droit,** = degree granted when a student has passed his first two examinations for the Licence en Droit; **(c)** *Can Univ* bachelor's (degree); **b. ès arts/ès sciences,** Bachelor of Arts/Science.
baccara(t)[1] [bakara] *nm Cartes* baccarat.
baccarat[2] *nm* crystal (made at Baccarat).
bacchanale [bakanal] *nf* **(a)** (*orgie*) orgy; (*débauche*) drunken revel; (*danse*) noisy *or* uproarious dance; **(b)** *Antiq* **les bacchanales,** the bacchanalia.
bacchante [bakɑ̃t] *nf* **(a)** *Antiq* bacchante; **(b)** *F* **bacchantes,** moustache.
bâche [bɑʃ] *nf* **(a)** *Tech* (*réservoir*) tank, cistern; **b. d'alimentation,** feed tank; **(b)** (*serre*) forcing frame; **(c)** awning; (coarse canvas) cover (*for hayricks etc*); **b. goudronnée,** tarpaulin; **b. de campement,** ground sheet; **(d)** *Arg* (*casquette*) cap.
bachelier, -ière [baʃəlje, -jɛr] *n Scol* student who has passed the baccalauréat; *Jur* **b. en droit,** = student studying for a baccalauréat en droit.
bâcher [bɑʃe] *vt* to cover (*sth*) with a tarpaulin.
bachi-bouzouk [baʃibuzuk] *nm Hist* bashi-bazouk; *F* **espèce de b.-b.!,** you crackbrain!, you crackpot!
bachique [baʃik] *adj* bacchic; **scène b.,** bacchanalian scene; **chanson b.,** drinking song.
bachot[1] [baʃo] *nm Nau* wherry, punt.
bachot[2] *nm F* = **BACCALAURÉAT**; **boîte à b.,** crammer('s).
bachotage [baʃɔtaʒ] *nm Scol F* swotting, cramming; **faire du b.,** to do some swotting.
bachoter [baʃɔte] *Scol F vi* to swot, to cram.
bachoteur[1] [baʃɔtœr] *nm* wherryman.
bachoteur[2], -euse [baʃɔtœr, -øz] *n Scol F* student cramming *or* swotting up for an exam.
bacillaire [basilɛr] **1** *adj* bacillary. **2** *n* tubercular patient.
bacille [basil] *nm* **(a)** *Biol* bacillus; **(b)** (*insecte*) stick insect.
bacillose [basiloz] *nf Méd* bacillosis, bacillus infection; **b. pulmonaire,** pulmonary tuberculosis.
background [bakgrawnd] *nm* background.
bâclage [bɑklaʒ] *nm F* scamping, botching (up) (*of work*).
bâcle [bɑkl] *nf* bar (*of door*).
bâclé [bɑkle] *adj* slapdash (*work etc*); **un travail b.,** a botched (up) job.
bâcler [bɑkle] **1** *vt* **(a)** *F* to botch (up) (*work*); **(b)** *Arch* to bar, to bolt (*door etc*). **2** *vi* to do a botched job.
bacon [bekɔn] *nm Culin* bacon; **œufs au b.,** bacon and eggs.
bactéricide [bakterisid] **1** *adj* bactericidal. **2** *nm* bactericide.
bactérie [bakteri] *nf* bacterium, *pl* -ia.
bactérien, -ienne [bakterjɛ̃, -jɛn] *adj* bacterial.
bactériologie [bakterjɔlɔʒi] *nf* bacteriology.
bactériologique [bakterjɔlɔʒik] *adj* bacteriological; **guerre b.,** bacteriological *or* germ warfare.
bactériologiste [bakterjɔlɔʒist] **, bactériologue** [bakterjɔlɔg] *n* bacteriologist.
bactériophage [bakterjɔfaʒ] *nm* bacteriophage.
badaboum [badabum] *int F* **et b., il est tombé,** he fell down, bang, crash, wallop.
badaud, -aude [bado, -od] **1** *adj* gawping, *US* rubbernecking. **2** *n* stroller; (*curieux*) gawper.
badaudage [badodaʒ] *nm Vieilli* gawping.
badauder [badode] *vi Vieilli* to stroll about (idly); (*en regardant*) to gawp.
baderne [badɛrn] *nf F Péj* **une (vieille) b.,** an old fogey, an old fossil, an old stick-in-the-mud.
badge [badʒ] *nm* badge, *Am* button; (*pour scouts*) badge.
badigeon [badiʒɔ̃] *nm* (colour)wash, distemper (*for walls etc*); **b. à la chaux,** whitewash; *Méd* **faire un b. de teinture d'iode sur une blessure,** to paint a wound with tincture of iodine.
badigeonnage [badiʒɔnaʒ] *nm* **(a)** colourwashing, distempering; (*à la chaux*) whitewashing; **(b)** *Méd* painting (*with iodine etc*).
badigeonner [badiʒɔne] *vt* **(a) b. une surface de qch,** to

brush over a surface with sth; **b. un mur en blanc/en couleur,** to whitewash/to colourwash *or* distemper a wall; **(b)** *Méd* to paint **(d'iode, à l'iode,** with iodine).

badigeonneur [badiʒɔnœr] *nm* whitewasher; *F Péj* poor painter, dauber.

badin¹ [badɛ̃] *adj* playful.

badin² *nm Av* airspeed indicator.

badinage [badinaʒ] *nm* joking, banter.

badine [badin] *nf* cane, switch.

badiner [badine] *vi* to jest, to joke; **b. de tout,** to turn everything into a joke; **on ne badine pas avec l'amour,** one should never laugh at love; **il ne faut pas b. avec ce genre de choses,** these things are no laughing matter.

badinerie [badinri] *nf* joking, banter.

bad lands [badlɑ̃ds] *nfpl* badlands.

badminton [badmintɔn] *nm Sp* badminton.

bâdrant [bɑdrɑ̃] *adj Can* bothersome.

baffe [baf] *nf F* (*gifle*) slap, clip on the ear; **recevoir/donner une paire de baffes,** to get/give a couple of biffs.

Baffin [bafɛ̃] *nm* **la terre de B.,** Baffin Island.

baffle [bafl] *nm Électron* baffle.

bafouer [bafwe] *vt* to ridicule, to jeer at (*s.o.*); to flout (*regulations*).

bafouillage [bafujaʒ] *nm F* (*défaut de prononciation*) stammering, spluttering; (*propos incohérent*) nonsense; (*de moteur*) missing, misfiring.

bafouille [bafuj] *nf Arg* letter.

bafouiller [bafuje] *vi F* (*mal prononcer*) to splutter, to stammer; (*délirer*) to talk nonsense, to talk through one's hat; (*de moteur*) to miss, to misfire.

bâfrer [bɑfre] *Arg* **1** *vi* to stuff oneself, to guzzle. **2** *vt* to wolf (*one's food*).

bâfreur, -euse [bɑfrœr, -øz] *n Arg* glutton, greedy-guts.

bagage [bagaʒ] *nm* **(a)** (*équipement*) kit; **plier b.,** to pack up one's bags *or Mil* one's kit; **(b) bagages,** luggage, *Am* baggage; **bagages non accompagnés,** unaccompanied luggage, luggage in advance; **retrait des bagages,** baggage (re)claim; **bagages à main,** hand luggage; **fourgon à bagages,** luggage van, *Am* baggage car; **voyager avec peu de bagages,** to travel light; **faire ses bagages,** to pack (one's bags); **(c)** *Fig* (*connaissance*) knowledge; **avoir un bon b. en science éco,** to know a lot about economics; **son b. en mathématique est nul,** he doesn't know any maths.

bagagiste [bagaʒist] *nm* luggage *or* baggage handler.

bagarre [bagar] *nf* brawl, free-for-all; **il va y avoir de la b.,** there's going to be a fight; *Fig* **c'est la b. entre eux,** they're at daggers drawn.

bagarrer [bagare] *F* **1** *vi* to fight, to battle (**pour,** for); **aimer b.,** to like a fight; *Fig* **il faudra b. pour l'avoir,** you'll have to fight to get it. **2 se bagarrer** *vpr* to fight, to quarrel, to brawl.

bagarreur, -euse [bagarœr, -øz] *F* **1** *adj* quarrelsome, violent (*person, character*); *Fig* **elle est bagarreuse,** (*elle ne se laisse pas faire*) she's a fighter. **2** *n* brawler; *Fig* **c'est une bagarreuse,** she's a fighter.

bagatelle [bagatɛl] *nf* trifle, bagatelle; **se fâcher pour une b.,** to take offence at a (mere) trifle; **acheter qch pour une b.,** to buy sth for a song; **elle perd son temps à des bagatelles,** she's frittering away her time.

bagnard [baɲar] *nm* convict.

bagne [baɲ] *nm* **(a)** *Arch* convict prison; **b. flottant,** hulks; **(b) condamné à cinq ans de b.,** sentenced to five years' penal servitude; *Fig F* **quel b.!,** what a hole!; **cette chaleur, quel b.!,** what a hellish heat!

bagnole [baɲɔl] *nf Aut F* **(vieille) b.,** banger, jalopy; **c'est une belle b.,** she's a nice job; **ça, c'est de la b.!,** that's some motor!

bagou(t) [bagu] *nm F* glibness (of tongue); **avoir du b.,** to have the gift of the gab.

baguage [bagaʒ] *nm* ringing (*of birds, trees*).

bague [bag] *nf* **(a)** (*jewelled*) ring; **porter des bagues,** to wear rings; **b. en argent/en or,** silver/gold ring; **avoir la b. au doigt,** to be married; **passer à qn la b. au doigt,** to marry someone; **b. de fiançailles,** engagement ring; **(b)** ring-pull (*of can*); **b. d'un cigare,** cigar band; **(c)** *Tech* **b. d'assemblage,** collar, sleeve; thimble coupling, joint; **b. de serrage,** set collar *or* ring; clamping collar *or* ring; jubilee clip; **b. d'espacement,** sleeve; **b. à bride,** adapter; **b. de roulement,** ball race; bearing race; **b. (de garniture) de piston,** piston ring, packing ring; **b. d'appui,** washer; **(d)** (*d'oiseau*) ring.

baguenauder [bagnode] *F* **1** *vi* to mooch about. **2 se baguenauder** *vpr* to mooch about.

baguer¹ [bage] *vt* to ring (*bird, tree*); **cigare bagué d'or,** cigar with a gold band.

baguer² *vt Couture* to tack, to baste (*pleats etc*).

baguette [bagɛt] *nf* **(a)** (*tige*) rod, wand, stick; (*pain*) long thin loaf of French bread; **baguettes,** chopsticks; **manger avec des baguettes,** to eat with chopsticks; **b. magique,** magic wand; **baguettes de tambour,** drumsticks; *Fig* **avoir les cheveux raides comme des baguettes (de tambour),** to have hair that's as straight as a poker; **b. (de chef d'orchestre),** baton; *F* **commander** *ou* **mener** *ou* **faire marcher qn à la b.,** to rule s.o. with a rod of iron; **être sous la b. de qn,** to be under someone's thumb; **passer par les baguettes,** to run the gauntlet; **tu ne crois pas que tout va changer, comme ça, d'un coup de b.?,** surely you don't believe everything's going to change, just like that, as if by magic *or* as if by the wave of a magic wand?; **(b)** *Menuis etc* moulding, beading; **(c)** (*de bas etc*) seam.

baguier [bagje] *nm* ring case, ring stand.

bah [bɑ] *int* bah!, pooh!

Bahamas [baamas] *nfpl* **les (îles) B., l'archipel des B.,** the Bahamas.

Bahrain [barɛ̃] *nm* **les îles B.,** Bahrain, Bahrein.

bahut [bay] *nm* **(a)** (round-topped) chest; (*coffre*) sideboard; **(b)** *Arg* school; **(c)** *Arg* taxi.

bai [bɛ] *adj* bay (horse); **b. châtain,** chestnut bay.

baie¹ [bɛ] *nf Géog* bay; **une petite b. abritée,** a sheltered little cove; **la grande B. australienne,** the Great Australian Bight.

baie² *nf Archit* bay, opening; **b. vitrée,** picture window; **fenêtre en b.,** bay window.

baie³ *nf Bot* berry.

baignade [bɛɲad] *nf* **(a)** bathe, swim; **(b)** (*endroit*) bathing place.

baigner [beɲe] **1** *vt* (*mouiller*) to bathe; (*of sea*) to wash (*coast etc*); (*of river*) to water (*a district*); to bath, to give a bath to (*dog, baby etc*); *Fig* **baigné de soleil,** bathed in sunlight; **il était baigné de sueur,** he was dripping with sweat; **son visage est baigné de larmes,** his face is bathed in tears.

2 *vi* to soak, to steep (*in sth*); **les légumes baignent dans une sauce à la tomate,** the vegetables are floating in a tomato sauce; *F* **ça baigne dans l'huile!,** everything's going like clockwork!, everything's A-OK!; **il baignait dans son sang,** he was swimming in his own blood; **la ville baigne dans la brume,** the town is swathed in mist; *Fig* **cette histoire/maison baigne dans le mystère,** this story/house is shrouded in mystery.

3 se baigner *vpr* **(a)** (*se laver*) to have *or* take a bath, *Am* to bathe;

(b) (*nager*) to bathe, to have a swim; **on va se b.?,** shall we go for a swim?

baigneur, -euse [bɛɲœr, -øz] *n* **(a)** *Vieilli* bather; **(b)** small (naked) (*china, plastic*) doll.

baignoire [bɛɲwar] *nf* **(a)** (*dans la salle de bains*) bath, (bath)tub; **b. encastrée,** sunken bath; **b. sabot,** hip bath; **(b)** *Th* ground-floor box; **(c)** *Nau* upper part of submarine's conning tower.

bail, *pl* **baux** [baj, bo] *nm* lease; **b. commercial,** commercial lease; **b. à ferme,** farming lease; **l'expiration du b.,** the expiry of the lease; **prendre une maison à b.,** to take a lease on *or* to lease a house; **donner une maison à b.,** to lease a house; *F* **ça fait un b. que je ne l'ai pas vu,** I haven't seen him for ages.

baille [bɑj] *nf Nau* (*mauvais bateau*) tub, bucket, pail; *F* **la (grande) b.,** the sea, the drink; **tomber à la b.,** to fall into the drink.

bâillement [bɑjmɑ̃] *nm* **(a)** (*de personne*) yawn, yawning; **étouffer un b.,** to stifle a yawn; **(b)** gaping (*of seam etc*); **b. des rideaux,** gap between the curtains.

bâiller [bɑje] *vi* **(a)** to yawn; **b. de sommeil/d'ennui/de fatigue,** to yawn drowsily/with boredom/with tiredness; *Fig* **son histoire me fait b.,** his story is one big yawn; *F* **b. à se décrocher la mâchoire,** to yawn one's head off; **(b)** (*of seams etc*) to gape; (*of door*) to be *or* stand ajar.

bailleur, -eresse [bajœr, bajrɛs] *n* **(a)** *Jur* lessor; **(b) b. de fonds,** *Com* sleeping partner; financial backer.

bailli [baji] *nm Arch* bailiff, magistrate, judge.

bailliage [bajaʒ] *nm Arch* **(a)** (*district*) bailiwick; (*en France, en Suisse*) bailliage; **(b)** (*tribunal*) bailiff's court.

bâillon [bɑjɔ̃] *nm* gag; **mettre un b. à qn,** to gag s.o.; **mettre un b. à la presse,** to gag *or* muzzle the press.

bâillonner [bɑjɔne] *vt* to gag; **b. la presse,** to gag *or* muzzle the press.

bain [bɛ̃] *nm* **(a)** bath; (*baignoire*) bath(tub); **prendre un b.,** to have *or* take a bath, *Am* to bathe; **donner un b. à qn,**

to bath s.o.; **b. moussant,** bubble bath; **b. de pieds,** footbath; **b. de bouche,** mouthwash; **salle de bain(s),** bathroom; **peignoir** *ou* **sortie de b.,** bathrobe; **le b. est rempli/vidé,** the bath is full/empty; **fais-moi couler un b.,** run me a bath; **b. de vapeur/de boue,** steam/mud bath; **b. turc,** Turkish bath; *Fig F* **être dans le b.,** to be implicated in sth; (*être habitué*) to be in the know; *Fig* **ils sont dans le même b.,** they're in the same boat; **on peut les mettre dans le même b.,** they're tarred with the same brush; *Fig* **b. de jouvence,** rejuvenating experience; **ça m'a fait l'effet d'un b. de jouvence,** it rejuvenated me; **quel b. de foule!,** what a huge crowd!; **je déteste les bains de foule,** I hate crowds; **prendre un b. de foule,** (*d'une personne célèbre*) to go walkabout; (*d'un politicien*) to press the flesh; **bains de soleil,** sunbathing; **prendre un b. de soleil** *ou* **des bains de soleil,** to sunbathe; **b.-de-soleil,** (*corsage*) halter top, sun top; **petit b.,** (*à la piscine*) = paddling pool for small children; **grand b.,** (*à la piscine*) swimming pool; **bains publics,** public baths, *US* bath house;

(b) swim, bathe (*in sea etc*); **bains de mer,** sea bathing; *Vieilli* seaside resort; **b. en rivière,** river bathing; **b. en piscine,** bathing in a swimming pool; **maillot de b.,** swimming costume, swimsuit, *Am* bathing suit; **slip de b.,** bathing *or* swimming trunks;

(c) (*thermes*) baths, watering place, spa; **bains romains,** Roman baths;

(d) *Phot* **b. révélateur** *ou* **de développement,** developing bath; **b. de fixage** *ou* **fixateur,** fixing bath; *Tex* **le b. (servant à la teinture),** dye; **ce n'est pas le même b.,** it's not the same dye lot;

(e) (sheep) dip.

bain-marie [bɛ̃mari] *nm* bain-marie, double saucepan *or* boiler; **faire cuire qch au b.-m.,** to cook sth in a double boiler; (*pl bains-marie*).

baïonnette [bajɔnɛt] *nf* bayonet; **mettre/remettre la b.,** to fix/unfix bayonets; **charge à la b.,** bayonet charge; *Tech* **joint en b.,** bayonet joint; *Él* **douille à b.,** bayonet socket; *Él* **ampoule à b.,** bulb with a bayonet fitting.

baïram, beïram [bairam, beiram] *nm* Bairam.

baise [bɛz] *nf Vulg* screwing; **il ne pense qu'à ça, la b.,** all he ever thinks of is screwing.

baise-en-ville [bɛzɑ̃vil] *nm inv F* overnight bag; (*sac à main*) man's handbag.

baisemain [bɛzmɛ̃] *nm* hand kissing, kissing of hands; **faire le b. à qn,** to kiss s.o.'s hand.

baiser¹ [beze] **1** *vt* **(a)** to kiss; **b. une croix,** to kiss a cross; **b. qn au front,** to kiss s.o. on the forehead; **(b)** *Vulg* to fuck, to screw (*s.o.*); **(c)** *Arg* (*tromper*) to screw; **il m'a bien baisé,** he screwed me good and proper; **se faire b.,** to be screwed; **(d)** *Arg* (*comprendre*) **qu'est-ce qu'il dit? on n'y baise rien,** what's he saying? you can't make head nor tail of it. **2** *vi Vulg* **elle baise bien,** she's a good screw.

baiser² *nm* kiss; **gros baisers,** (*dans une lettre*) love and kisses; **b. de paix,** kiss of peace; **b. d'adieu,** parting kiss; **b. de Judas,** Judas kiss.

baiseur, -euse [bezœr, -øz] *n Vulg* **c'est un sacré b.,** he's a real stud.

baissant [besɑ̃] *adj* declining, diminishing; setting (*sun*); failing (*sight*).

baisse [bɛs] *nf* fall, drop; ebb (*of tide*); **être en b.,** to be dropping *or* falling; **température en b.,** falling temperature; **la b. de la natalité,** the fall *or* drop in the birthrate; **la b. du niveau scolaire,** the fall in educational standards; **b. des prix,** fall *or* drop in prices; *Bourse* **spéculations à la b.,** bear speculations; **jouer à la b.,** to bear; **actions en b.,** falling shares.

baisser [bese] **1** *vt* to lower (*a curtain, a blind*); to pull down (*blind etc*); to open (*car window*); *Aut* to dip (*headlights*); **b. une étagère d'un cran,** to lower a shelf by one notch; **b. la lampe,** to dim the light; (*d'un spot*) to point the light away; **le store est baissé,** the blind is down; **b. la radio/le chauffage,** to turn down the radio/the heating; **b. pavillon,** to lower the flag, to give in; **b. la tête** *ou* **le front,** to bend one's head; (*de honte etc*) to hang one's head; **b. brusquement la tête,** to duck; **donner tête baissée dans un piège,** to fall headlong into a trap; **b. les yeux,** to look down, to drop one's gaze; **yeux baissés,** downcast eyes; **sa remarque m'a fait b. les yeux de gêne,** his remark made me drop my gaze in embarrassment; **b. le nez,** to hang one's head in shame; *Fig* **il ne faut pas b. les bras, battez-vous!,** don't give in, fight!; **b. la voix,** to lower one's voice; **b. le ton,** (*après une dispute*) to climb down (a little); **je vous prie de b. le ton!,** please keep your voice down!; **b. le prix de qch,** to lower *or* reduce *or* cut the price of sth.

2 *vi* **(a)** to go *or* come down; (*of tide*) to ebb; (*of fire*) to burn low, to burn down; (*of sight, memory*) to fail; *Th* **les lumières baissent,** the lights are going down; **le baromètre baisse,** the barometer is falling; **la température baisse,** the temperature is dropping, *F* it's getting colder; **le jour baisse,** night is falling, it's getting dark;

(b) (*s'affaiblir*) to weaken; **le malade baisse,** the patient is sinking; **le moral baisse,** morale is sinking; **elle a baissé dans mon estime,** she's gone down in my estimation;

(c) (*of prices*) to fall, to come *or* go down; **la valeur de ces maisons a baissé,** these houses have gone down in value; **le niveau scolaire a beaucoup baissé,** educational standards have dropped a lot.

3 se baisser *vpr* to stoop, to bend down; **c'est en se baissant qu'il s'est cogné,** he banged himself as he bent down; *Fig* **il n'y a qu'à se b. pour les ramasser,** they're ten a penny.

baissier [besje] *nm Bourse* bear.

bajoues [baʒu] *nfpl* (*of pig etc*) cheeks, chaps, chops; *Péj* (*d'une personne*) flabby *or* pendulous cheeks.

bakchich [bakʃiʃ] *nm* baksheesh, tip.

bakélite [bakelit] *nf* bakelite; **téléphone en b.,** bakelite telephone.

baklava [baklava] *nm Culin* baklava, baclava.

bal, *pl* **bals** [bal] *nm* **(a)** (*fête*) ball, dance; **b. travesti,** fancy dress ball; **b. public,** public dance; **robe de b.,** ball gown, evening dress; **(b)** (*endroit*) ballroom, dance hall.

balade [balad] *nf F* walk, stroll; **faire une b.,** to go for a walk *or* stroll; (*en voiture*) to go for a run in the car; **une belle b.,** a lovely walk; (*en voiture*) a lovely run in the car.

balader [balade] *F* **1** *vt* to take (*s.o.*) out for a walk; (*avoir avec soi*) to drag (*sth*); **il balade toujours cette vieille valise avec lui,** he always drags that old suitcase around with him. **2 se balader** *vpr* to go for a walk; **se b. en montagne,** to walk in the mountains; **tu ne vas pas te b. en ville avec cette casquette?,** surely you're not going to go walk around town in that cap?; **ses affaires se baladent dans la maison,** his things are strewn all over the house.

baladeur, -euse [baladœr, -øz] **1** *adj* wandering, roving (*instinct*); *F* **avoir les mains baladeuses,** to have wandering hands; **train b.,** sliding gear. **2** *nf* **baladeuse (a)** trailer (*of car etc*); **(b)** portable lamp, inspection lamp. **3** *nm* personal stereo, Walkman ®.

baladin [baladɛ̃] *nm* wandering player *or* actor.

baladisque [baladisk] *nm* portable compact disc player, Discman ®.

balafre [balafr] *nf* **(a)** (*coupure*) cut, slash, gash; (*au sabre*) sabre cut; **(b)** (*cicatrice*) scar.

balafrer [balafre] *vt* to cut, to gash, to slash; **les agresseurs lui ont balafré le visage,** the attackers slashed his face; **visage balafré,** scarred face.

balai [balɛ] *nm* **(a)** broom; (long-handled) brush; **b. mécanique,** carpet sweeper; **manche à b.,** broomstick, brush handle; *Av* joystick; *F* (*personne*) beanpole; **passer le b.,** to sweep the floor; **donner un coup de b.,** to sweep (*a room*); *Fig* to make a clean sweep; *Fig* **il y a eu un coup de b.,** (*dans cette entreprise*) there's been a shake-out; **du b.!,** clear off!; **(b)** *F* last bus *or* underground train *etc* (*at night*); **(c)** *Él* brush; **(d)** *Aut* blade (*of windscreen wiper*).

balai-brosse [balɛbrɔs] *nm* long-handled scrubbing-brush.

balalaïka [balalaika] *nf Mus* balalaika.

balaise [balɛz] *adj & n* = **BALÈZE.**

balance [balɑ̃s] *nf* **(a)** (*appareil*) (pair of) scales; (*publique*) weighing machine; **b. à bascule,** weighbridge; **b. de cuisine,** kitchen scales; **b. (de salle de bains),** bathroom scales; **monter sur la b.,** to stand on the scales; *Astron Astrol* **la B.,** Libra, the Scales; **être du signe de la B.,** to be Libra *or* a Libran; **Jean-Pierre, c'est une B.,** Jean-Pierre is a Libran;

(b) *Fig* indecision; **être en b.,** to be undecided; **la victoire était** *ou* **restait en b.,** victory hung in the balance; **mettre qch en b.,** to weigh up the pros and cons of sth; **ce facteur pèse dans la b.,** this is an important factor; **cet argument est un poids dans la b.,** this argument weighs heavily; **faire pencher** *ou* **incliner** *ou* **emporter la b.,** to turn *or* tip the scales *or* balance; **votre qualification fera pencher la b. en votre faveur,** your qualification will tip the balance in your favour;

(c) *Com* **b. d'un compte,** balance *or* balancing of an account; **faire la b.,** to make up the balance (sheet); **la b. de l'actif et du passif,** the balance of assets and liabilities; **compte en b.,** account that balances; **b. du commerce** *ou* **commerciale,** trade balance, balance of trade; **la b. est en**

excédent, there is a trade surplus; **b. déficitaire,** trade deficit; **b. des paiements,** balance of payments; **b. des forces au pouvoir,** balance of power;
(d) *Pêche* shrimp net;
(e) *F (mouchard)* nark.
balancé [balɑ̃se] *adj* well-balanced (*sentence etc*); *F* **elle est bien balancée,** she's really shapely.
balancelle [balɑ̃sɛl] *nf* (*de jardin*) garden swing.
balancement [balɑ̃smɑ̃] *nm* **(a)** swing(ing), sway(ing), rocking (*of boat, trees etc*); **balancements,** (*dans la politique*) shilly-shallying; **(b)** balance (*of figures in picture etc*).
balancer [balɑ̃se] *v* **(je balançai(s); n. balançons) 1** *vt* **(a)** to balance (*weights etc*); *Com* **b. un compte,** to balance an account; **b. le pour et le contre,** to weigh up the pros and cons; **tout bien balancé, c'est d'accord,** all things considered, I agree;
(b) to swing (*one's arms etc*); to rock (*s.o. in a hammock etc*); to sway (*one's hips*); **b. un enfant sur ses genoux,** to rock a child on one's knees; **le vent balance les feuilles lentement,** the wind slowly shakes the leaves to and fro;
(c) *F* to throw, to chuck (*stones etc*); to fire (*s.o.*), to give (*s.o.*) the sack *or F* the push; to throw (*s.o., sth*) out; **elle a tout balancé,** (*en jetant*) she's thrown everything away; (*en abandonnant tout*) she's given it all up;
(d) *F (moucharder)* to grass; **il a balancé ses acolytes,** he shopped *or* grassed on his accomplices.
2 *vi Litt* to waver, to hesitate.
3 se balancer *vpr* **(a)** to swing; to sway, to rock; **se b. sur ses ancres,** (*of ship*) to ride at anchor; **se b. sur sa chaise,** to rock backwards and forwards on one's chair;
(b) (*sur une balançoire*) to play on a swing; (*sur une bascule*) to see-saw;
(c) *Arg* **je m'en balance!,** I don't care *or* give a damn!;
(d) *F* **il s'est balancé du 16ème étage,** he chucked himself off the 16th storey.
balancier [balɑ̃sje] *nm* **(a)** balancing pole (*of tightrope walker*); **(b)** (*in clock*) pendulum (bob); balance wheel (*of watch*); **(c)** handle (*of pump etc*).
balançoire [balɑ̃swar] *nf* (*bascule*) seesaw; (*suspendue*) (child's) swing; (*at fair*) swing-boat; **faire de la b.,** to be *or* go on the seesaw *or* the swing.
balayage [balɛjaʒ] *nm* **(a)** sweeping (*of room etc*); sweeping up (*of dirt etc*); **(b)** *Rad Électron TV* scan(ning), sweep; **fréquence de b.,** sweep frequency; **(c)** (*de cheveux*) streaks; **se faire faire** *ou* **demander un b.,** to have streaks put in one's hair, to have one's hair streaked.
balayer [baleje] *vt* **(je balaie, je balaye; je balaierai, je balayerai) (a)** to sweep (out) (*room etc*); to sweep up (*dirt etc*); **le vent a balayé les nuages,** the wind has swept the clouds away; **b. l'ennemi,** to drive away the enemy; *Fig* **b. devant sa porte,** to put one's (own) house in order; **les vacances ont balayé mes soucis,** the holidays have swept away my worries; **(b)** *Rad Électron TV* to scan, to sweep; **le radar balaie jusqu'à 100 km,** the radar has a sweep of 100 kilometres; **les projecteurs de la prison balaient les champs tout autour,** the prison searchlights sweep the fields all around.
balayette [balɛjɛt] *nf* (hearth, hand, toilet) brush.
balayeur, -euse [balɛjœr, -øz] **1** *n* (road) sweeper. **2** *nf* **balayeuse (a)** (*machine*) road sweeper; **(b)** *Can* vacuum cleaner.
balayures [balɛjyr] *nfpl* sweepings.
balbutiant [balbysjɑ̃] *adj* stuttering, stammering; **il répondit, tout b.,** he stammered an answer.
balbutiement [balbysimɑ̃] *nm* stuttering, stammering; (*dans sa barbe*) mumbling; **les balbutiements d'un jeune enfant,** the babbling of a child; *Fig* **l'informatique n'était alors qu'à ses balbutiements,** data processing was then only in its infancy.
balbutier [balbysje] *v* (*pr sub & impf* **n. balbutiions, v. balbutiiez) 1** *vi* to stammer; (*parler dans sa barbe*) to mutter; **parler en balbutiant,** to stammer. **2** *vt* (*des excuses*) to stammer; (*en parlant dans sa barbe*) to mumble (*qch*).
balcon [balkɔ̃] *nm* **(a)** *Archit* balcony; *F* **il y a du monde au b.,** she's well endowed; **(b)** *Th* circle; **nous étions placés au deuxième b.,** we were in the upper circle.
balconnet [balkɔnɛ] *nm* half-cup bra(ssière).
baldaquin [baldakɛ̃] *nm* baldachin, canopy (*of bed etc*); **lit à b.,** four-poster bed.
Bâle [bɑl] *nf* Basle, Basel.
Baléare [balear] *nfpl* **les Baléares,** the Balearic Islands.
baleine [balɛn] *nf* **(a)** whale; **b. à bosse,** humpbacked whale; **b. blanche,** white whale; **blanc de b.,** spermaceti; *Fig* **rire comme une b.,** to laugh like a drain; **(b)** (whale)bone (*of a corset etc*); rib (*of an umbrella*).
baleiné [balene] *adj* boned (*brassière*); stiffened (*collar*).
baleineau, -eaux [balɛno] *nm* whale calf.
baleinier, -ière [balenje, -jɛr] **1** *adj* whaling (*vessel, industry*). **2** *nf* **baleinière,** whaleboat; **b. de sauvetage,** lifeboat.
balénoptère [balenɔptɛr] *nm* (*mammifère*) rorqual; **b. à bec,** piked whale.
balèze [balɛz] *F* **1** *adj* hunky, brawny; **il est plutôt b., ce type,** that guy's really hunky; *Fig* **elle est vraiment b.,** (*intelligente*) she's so brainy! **2** *n Fig* **toi tu es une b., tu n'auras pas de mal,** a megastar like you won't have any difficulty with it.
balisage [balizaʒ] *nm* **(a)** (*signaux*) *Nau* buoys; *Av etc* beacons, markings, signs; **projecteur de b.,** direction beacon; **(b)** (*action*) *Nau* beaconing, buoying; *Av* (aerodrome) lighting; signalling, marking out (with beacons).
balise [baliz] *nf Nau* beacon; *Av* (approach) light, marker; (radio) beacon; *Nau* **b. flottante,** buoy; *Rad* **b. radar,** radar beacon.
baliser [balize] **1** *vt Nau* to beacon, to buoy, to mark out (*channel*); *Av* to equip (*airport*) with (approach) lights; to mark out (*route*) with beacons. **2** *vi* to have the jitters; **ne m'en parle pas, ça me fait b.,** don't talk to me about it, it gives me the jitters.
baliseur [balizœr] *nm* **(a) (bateau) b.,** ≈ Trinity House boat; **(b)** (*personne*) ≈ Trinity (House) buoy keeper.
balistique [balistik] **1** *adj* ballistic; **engin b.,** ballistic missile. **2** *nf* ballistics.
baliverne [balivɛrn] *nf* futile remark; **débiter des balivernes,** to talk twaddle *or* nonsense.
balkanique [balkanik] *adj* Balkan (*state etc*).
balkanisation [balkanizɑsjɔ̃] *nf Pol & Fig* Balkanisation.
ballade [balad] *nf* (*poème court*) ballade; (*poème long*) *& Mus* ballad.
ballant [balɑ̃] **1** *adj* swinging, dangling (*arms etc*); **assis les pieds ballants,** sitting with one's feet dangling. **2** *nm* **(a)** (*mouvement*) swing, rocking motion; roll, sway (*of vehicle etc*); **(b)** *Nau* slack (*in rope*).
ballast [balast] *nm* **(a)** *Constr etc* ballast, bottom (*of road, railway track*); **(b)** *Nau* ballast tank (*of submarine etc*).
ballastage [balastaʒ] *nm* **(a)** *Constr etc* ballasting (*of railway track etc*); **(b)** *Nau* (*en remplissant*) ballasting; (*en vidant*) unballasting.
ballaster [balaste] *vt* **(a)** *Constr etc* to ballast (*railway track etc*); **(b)** *Nau* (*remplir*) to ballast; (*vider*) to unballast.
balle¹ [bal] *nf* **(a)** ball; **b. de golf/de tennis,** golf/tennis ball; **jouer à la b.,** to play ball; **b. au mur,** *Br* ≈ fives; *Am* ≈ handball; **renvoyer/lancer la b.,** to return the ball/to serve; *Sp F* **c'est une belle b.!,** a lovely shot!; *Tennis* **faire des** *ou* **quelques balles,** to have a knock-up; **b. de filet,** net (ball); **b. de match/de set,** match point, set point; *Fig* **prendre** *ou* **saisir la b. au bond,** to jump at an opportunity *or* chance; *Fig* **se renvoyer la b.,** to pass the buck; **renvoyer la b. à qn,** *Fig* to answer someone back (*in argument*); *Fig* **la b. est dans votre camp,** the ball's in your court;
(b) (*d'arme*) bullet; **b. de fusil,** rifle bullet; **b. morte,** spent bullet; **b. perdue,** stray bullet; **b. plastique,** baton round, *F* plastic bullet; **b. traçante,** tracer bullet; *F* **recevoir douze balles dans la peau,** to go before the firing squad; **à l'épreuve des balles,** bullet-proof;
(c) *Vulg* **trou de b.,** arse-hole, asshole;
(d) enfant de la b., a child who follows in his father's footsteps.
balle² *nf* **(a)** *Com* bale (*of cotton etc*); **(b)** *Arg* (*visage*) mug, dial; **il a une drôle de b.,** he's an odd-looking chap; **quelle b.!,** what an ugly mug!
balle³ *nf* husk, chaff (*of wheat*); *Bot* glume (*of flower*); *Arg* **peau de b.,** nothing at all, damn all.
baller [bale] *vi* to hang (down), to be slack; **laisser b. ses bras,** to let one's arms dangle.
ballerine [balrin] *nf* **(a)** *Th* ballerina, ballet dancer; **(b)** (*chaussure*) ballerina shoe.
balles *nfpl F* francs; **je te le vends pour deux cents b.,** I'll sell it to you for two hundred francs; **t'as pas cent b.?,** (*said by tramp etc*) ≈ have you got any (spare) change?
ballet [balɛ] *nm Th* ballet; **maître de b.,** ballet master; **les ballets du Bolshoi,** the Bolshoi Ballet; *Fig Pol* **le b. de ministres,** the ministerial merry-go-round; **le b. diplomatique,** diplomatic to-ings and fro-ings.
ballon [balɔ̃] *nm* **(a)** (*aérostat*) balloon; **b. dirigeable,** airship, dirigible; **b. d'observation,** observation balloon; **b.**

gonflable *ou* **de baudruche,** balloon; **marchand de ballons,** balloon-seller; **b. de protection** *ou* **de barrage,** barrage balloon; **envoyer** *ou* **lancer un b. d'essai,** to send up a pilot balloon; *Fig* to put out feelers; **faire un voyage en b.,** to make a balloon journey; **monter en b.,** to go up in a balloon; *Méd* **b. d'oxygène,** oxygen bottle; **b. (d'alcootest),** (breathalyser) bag; **souffler dans le b.,** to blow into the bag;

(b) *Sp* ball; *Baseball* (*chandelle*) highball; **b. de football/de rugby,** football/rugby ball; **b. d'enfant,** child's ball; **b. ovale/rond,** rugby ball/football; (*sport*) rugby/football; **jouer au b.,** to play with a ball; **lancer le b. dans les buts;** to shoot at goal; **b. d'entraînement (pour boxeurs, à boxer),** punchball;

(c) (*de bande dessinée*) balloon;

(d) *Ch* balloon flask; *Ind* carboy; **(verre) b.,** brandy glass, balloon glass;

(e) *Nau* ball signal.

ballonné [balɔne] *adj* distended, swollen.

ballonnement [balɔnmɑ̃] *nm* distending (*of stomach etc*); **avoir des ballonnements,** to have wind.

ballonner [balɔne] *vt* to distend (*the stomach*); **manger ce genre de choses me ballonne,** eating that kind of thing gives me wind; **cette herbe risque de b. les bêtes,** this grass is liable to bloat the livestock.

ballon-panier [balɔ̃panje] *nm inv Can Sp* basketball.

ballon-sonde [balɔ̃sɔ̃d] *nm Météo* sounding balloon; (*pl ballons-sondes*).

ballot [balo] **1** *nm* **(a)** (*paquet*) bundle, package; **(b)** *F* nit(wit), clot; **quel b.!,** you wally!, what a wally! **2** *adj F* **t'es pas b.?,** are you mad?, are you daft?

ballotin [balɔtɛ̃] *nm* small box; **b. de chocolats,** small box of chocolates.

ballottage [balɔtaʒ] *nm Pol etc* failure to gain absolute majority; **scrutin de b.,** second ballot, *US* run-off election.

ballottement [balɔtmɑ̃] *nm* (*de train*) rolling motion; (*des passagers*) shaking, bouncing; (*de porte*) swinging to and fro; (*de navire*) tossing.

ballotter [balɔte] **1** *vt* to toss, to shake (about); **être ballotté par sentiments opposés,** to be pulled this way and that by contradictory feelings; **un enfant ballotté entre ses parents,** a tug-of-love child. **2** *vi* (*of door etc*) to swing to and fro; (*of ship*) to toss (on the water).

ballottine [balɔtin] *nf Culin* meat roll, galantine.

balloune [balun] *nf Can F* **être en b.,** to be pregnant.

ball-trap [baltrap] *nm* (clay pigeon) shooting, *Am* skeet shooting; (*pl ball-traps*).

bal(l)uchon [balyʃɔ̃] *nm F* bundle (*of clothes*); **faire son b.,** to pack up, to pack one's bags.

balnéaire [balneɛr] *adj* **station b.,** seaside resort.

balnéothérapie [balneɔterapi] *nf Méd* = form of therapy involving baths or bathing.

balourd, -ourde [balur, -urd] **1** *adj* awkward, clumsy, stupid (*person*); (*peu délicat*) loutish; (*lourd*) thick. **2** *n* lout; **un grand b.,** a great hulking fellow. **3** *nm MecE* unbalance.

balourdise [balurdiz] *nf* **(a)** (*manque de finesse*) awkwardness, clumsiness; (*lourdeur*) thickness; **(b)** (*gaffe*) stupid blunder, *F* clanger.

balsa [balza] *nm* balsa (wood).

balsamier [balzamje] *nm* (*arbre*) balsam tree.

balsamine [balzamin] *nf* (*plante*) balsam, *F* busy Lizzie.

balte [balt] *adj* Baltic; **les pays baltes,** the Baltic States.

balthazar [baltazar] *nm* (*de champagne*) Balthazar.

baltique [baltik] **1** *adj* **la mer B.,** the Baltic (Sea). **2** *nf* **la Baltique,** the Baltic (Sea).

balustrade [balystrad] *nf* **(a)** *Archit* balustrade; **(b)** (*clôture*) railing.

balustre [balystr] *nm Archit* baluster; **balustres,** banisters (*of stairs*).

balzacien, -ienne [balzasjɛ̃, -jɛn] *adj Littér* of *or* like Balzac; **style b.,** Balzac's style; **une description très balzacienne,** a description worthy of Balzac.

balzan [balzɑ̃] *adj* **cheval b.,** horse with white stockings.

balzane [balzan] *nf* white stocking (*of horse*).

bambin, -ine [bɑ̃bɛ̃, -in] *n F* tiny tot.

bamboche [bɑ̃bɔʃ] *nf F* spree, lark; **faire b.,** to live it up.

bambocher [bɑ̃bɔʃe] *vi F* to live it up.

bambocheur, -euse [bɑ̃bɔʃœr, -øz] *n F* reveller; **c'est un b.,** he likes living it up *or* going on the spree.

bambou [bɑ̃bu] *nm* (*plante*) bamboo (cane); *Culin* **pousses de b.,** bamboo shoots; *Fig F* **coup de b.,** sunstroke; *F* **il a le coup de b.,** he's mad *or* crackers *or* nuts; (*épuisé*) he's tired out *or* whacked; *Fig F* **c'est le coup de b.,** it's very pricy.

bamboula [bɑ̃bula] *nf F* spree, lark; **faire la b.,** to live it up.

ban [bɑ̃] *nm* **(a)** (proclamation of) banishment; **pratique mise au b.,** outlawed practice; **mettre qn au b.,** to banish s.o.; **être au b. de la société,** to be outlawed by society; **être en rupture de b.,** to be outside the law; **(b) bans,** banns (*of marriage*); **(c) le b. et l'arrière-b.,** *Hist* the ban and the arrière-ban; (*tout le monde*) the whole lot, all the world and his wife; **(d)** round of (rhythmical) applause; **un b. pour Monsieur le maire!,** = three cheers for the mayor!; **(e)** roll of drum (*before proclamation*); *Arch* (public) proclamation (*of event*).

banal [banal] **1** *adj* **(a)** (*pl* **banals**) commonplace, banal, ordinary, trite; **parler de choses banales,** to engage in small talk; **ça, c'est peu b.!,** that's unusual *or* a bit out of the ordinary!; **(b)** (*pl* **banaux**) *Hist* communal (*mill, bakehouse*). **2** *nm* **c'est d'un b.!,** it's as dull as can be, *F* it's dullsville!

banalement [banalmɑ̃] *adv* in a banal *or* commonplace manner, tritely.

banalisation [banalizɑsjɔ̃] *nf* **(a)** standardization; **la b. des transports aériens/des vacances** *etc*, the fact that air travel has/that holidays have become commonplace; **la b. des voitures de police,** the use of unmarked police cars; **(b)** *Rail* (*pour une voie à deux sens*) signalling for two-way working; **(c)** (*d'une locomotive*) use of engine by several crews.

banaliser [banalize] **1** *vt* **(a)** to make (*sth*) commonplace *or* ordinary; **b. les vacances,** to make holidays commonplace; **cette coupe de cheveux te banalise,** that haircut does nothing for you; **voiture banalisée,** unmarked police car; **(b)** *Rail* to signal (*track*) for two-way working; **b. une locomotive,** to have an engine manned by several crews. **2 se banaliser** *vpr* to become commonplace.

banalité [banalite] *nf* **(a)** (*caractère*) banality, triteness; **la banalité d'une remarque,** the triteness of a remark; **(b) banalités,** small talk; *Péj* clichés, platitudes; **un tissu** *ou* **ramassis de banalités,** a collection of platitudes.

banane [banan] *nf* **(a)** (*fruit*) banana; *Culin* **bananes flambées,** flambéed bananas; **(b)** *Mil F* (*médaille*) gong; **(c)** *Aut* overrider; **(d)** *Av F* (*hélicoptère*) chopper; **(e)** (*coiffure*) quiff; **porter la b.,** to have a quiff; **(f)** (*sac de skieur etc*) *Br* bum-bag, *Am* fanny pack.

bananier, -ière [bananje, -jɛr] **1** *nm* **(a)** (*arbre*) banana tree; **(b)** *Nau* banana boat. **2** *adj* **république bananière,** banana republic.

banc [bɑ̃] *nm* **(a)** (*siège*) bench, seat, form; **b. d'église,** pew; **b. d'œuvre,** churchwardens' pew; **b. à coulisses,** (*à l'aviron*) sliding seat; **b. d'école/de jardin,** school/garden bench; *Pol* **le b. des ministres,** = the front bench; *Jur* **b. des magistrats,** magistrates' bench; *Jur* **b. des prévenus** *ou* **des accusés,** dock; **b. des témoins,** witness box;

(b) *Tech* (work)bench; bed (*of lathe*); table (*of drilling machine*); **b. d'essai,** testing bench, test bed (*for engines*); *Fig* testing ground, test bed (*for sth new*);

(c) layer, bed (*of rock etc*); *Min* seam (*of coal*); **b. de sable,** sandbank; **b. de vase,** mudbank; **b. de glace,** ice floe, ice field; *Can* **b. de neige,** snowbank; **b. de roches,** reef; **b. d'huîtres,** oyster bed; *Géog* **b. continental,** continental shelf; **le Banc de Terre-Neuve,** the Banks (of Newfoundland); *Nau* **toucher au b.,** to run aground;

(d) shoal, school (*of fish*); **b. de harengs,** herring shoal.

bancable [bɑ̃kabl] *adj Fin* bankable, negotiable.

bancaire [bɑ̃kɛr] *adj* pertaining to banking; **opérations bancaires,** bank(ing) transactions; **chèque b.,** banker's draft, bank cheque; **compte b.,** bank account.

bancal, -als [bɑ̃kal] *adj* (*person*) who limps; wobbly, rickety (*furniture etc*); *Fig* **son raisonnement est b.,** his reasoning is shaky.

banco [bɑ̃ko] *nm Cartes* banco; **faire b.,** to go banco.

bandage [bɑ̃daʒ] *nm* **(a)** bandage; (*action*) bandaging, binding up (*of wound*); **b. herniaire,** truss; **(b)** (steel, rubber) tyre; hoop, band (*of wheel*); **(c)** tightening, winding (up) (*of spring*); stringing, bending (*of bow*).

bandagiste [bɑ̃daʒist] *n Méd* truss manufacturer *or* supplier.

bandant [bɑ̃dɑ̃] *adj Vulg* raunchy; *Fig* **une proposition bandante,** a turn-on.

bande[1] [bɑ̃d] *nf* **(a)** band, strip (*of cloth, paper, metal etc*); stretch, belt (*of land*); stripe (*on cloth, cup etc*); **b. molletière,** puttee; **par la b.,** in a roundabout way, indirectly; *Fig* **prendre qch/qn par la b.,** to get round sth/s.o.; **mettre un journal sous b.,** to put a wrapper round a newspaper; **b. de téléimprimeur,** ticker tape; **b. dessinée** *ou* **illustrée,** strip cartoon, comic strip; *Agr* **culture en**

bandes de niveau, strip contour farming; *Aut* **b. de stationnement,** layby; *Av* **b. d'envol,** airstrip, landing strip; **b. médiane,** (*on road*) white line;
(b) *Méd* (surgical) bandage;
(c) (*pellicule, film*) (reel of) (cine) film; **bandes vierges,** (film) stock; **tourner une b. d'essai,** to have a screen test; **faire tourner une b. d'essai à qn;** to give s.o. a screen test; **b. sonore,** sound track; **b. magnétique,** magnetic tape; **b. vidéo,** video tape;
(d) (steel) tyre (*of wheel*); **b. de roulement,** tread (*of tyre*);
(e) *Billard* cushion;
(f) *Opt* band (*of the spectrum*); *Rad* **b. de fréquences,** frequency band;
(g) (feeding) belt, strip (*of machine gun*);
(h) *Hér* bend;
(i) *Nau* side (*of ship*); (*inclinaison*) keel, list(ing); **donner de la b.,** to keel (over), to careen, to have a list.

bande² *nf* **(a)** (*de personnes*) band, party, troop; **b. de voleurs,** gang of thieves; **elle fait b. à part,** she goes her own way, she keeps herself to herself; **aller en b.,** to go about in a gang; **aller quelque part en b.,** to go somewhere as a group; **être de la b. de qn,** to belong to s.o.'s group; **toute la b.,** the whole gang, the whole lot of them; **b. d'imbéciles!,** you idiots!, you bunch of idiots!; **b. noire,** terrorist gang; **(b)** flight, flock (*of birds*); pack (*of wolves*); herd (*of buffaloes*); school, shoal (*of porpoises*); pride (*of lions*).

bandé [bɑ̃de] *adj* **(a)** bandaged; **les yeux bandés,** blindfold(ed); **main bandée,** bandaged hand; **(b)** *Hér* bendy.

bande-annonce [bɑ̃danɔ̃s] *nf Cin* trailer.

bandeau, -eaux [bɑ̃do] *nm* **(a)** (*pour les cheveux*) headband; **cheveux en bandeaux,** hair parted in the middle; **b. royal,** diadem; **(b)** (*sur les yeux*) blindfold; **mettre un b. à qn,** to blindfold s.o.; *Fig* **avoir un b. sur les yeux,** to be blind; **(c)** *Archit* string course.

bandelette [bɑ̃dlɛt] *nf* narrow band, strip (*of cloth*); **bandelettes,** bandages, wrappings (*of mummies*).

bander [bɑ̃de] **1** *vt* **(a)** to bandage, to bind (up) (*wound*); to put a bandage on (*s.o., sth*); **b. les yeux à** *ou* **de qn,** to blindfold s.o.; **(b)** to tighten, to stretch, to wind up (*spring etc*); **b. un arc,** to bend *or* to string a bow; **b. ses muscles,** to tense one's muscles. **2** *vi Vulg* to have an erection, to get a hard-on; *Fig* **faire b.,** (*plaire, intéresser*) to thrill, to excite; **le théâtre, ça la fait b.,** she gets a real buzz from the theatre.

banderille [bɑ̃drij] *nf* (*bullfighting*) banderilla.

banderole [bɑ̃drɔl] *nf* banderole, streamer.

bandit [bɑ̃di] *nm* (*voleur etc*) crook, swindler, rogue; *Vieilli* bandit, brigand, highwayman.

banditisme [bɑ̃ditism] *nm* violent crime; **recrudescence du b.,** crime wave.

bandoulière [bɑ̃duljɛr] *nf* **(a)** shoulder strap (*of bag etc*); **porter** *ou* **mettre qch en b.,** to carry *or* sling sth over *or* across one's shoulder; **le sac en b.,** with one's bag slung over one's shoulder; **(b)** *Mil* bandolier.

bang [bɑ̃g] *nm inv Av* (super)sonic boom.

banian [banjɑ̃] *nm* (*arbre*) banyan tree.

banjo [bɑ̃ʒo] *nm Mus* banjo.

banlieue [bɑ̃ljø] **1** *nf* suburbs, commuter belt; **la grande/petite b.,** outer/inner suburbs; **c'est une b. rouge,** it's a communist-voting suburb; **vivre en b.,** to live in the suburbs; *Rail* **ligne/gare de b.,** suburban line/station. **2** *nm Belg* stopping train.

banlieusard, -arde [bɑ̃ljøzar, -ard] *n F* commuter; **c'est un b.,** he lives in the suburbs.

banne [ban] *nf* **(a)** cart (*for coal etc*); **(b)** (*panier*) hamper, large basket; **(c)** awning, blind (*of shop etc*).

banneret [banrɛ] *nm Hist* banneret; **chevalier b.,** knight banneret.

banneton [bantɔ̃] *nm* **(a)** (*pour le pain*) basket (without handles); **(b)** (*pour la pêche*) corf.

banni, -ie [bani] **1** *adj* banished, outlawed. **2** *n* exile, outlaw.

bannière [banjɛr] *nf* banner; **il s'est rangé sous la b. des écologistes,** he's joined the ranks of the ecologists; **la b. étoilée,** the Star-Spangled Banner (of the U.S.A.); *Fig* **c'est la croix et la b. pour le faire manger,** it's a heck of a job getting him to eat.

bannir [banir] *vt* to banish, to exile, to outlaw; **bannissez les pensées négatives de votre esprit,** banish negative thoughts from your mind; **il a complètement banni la cigarette,** he has completely given up smoking.

bannissement [banismɑ̃] *nm* banishment.

banquable [bɑ̃kabl] *adj Fin* bankable, negotiable.

banque [bɑ̃k] *nf* **(a)** (*commerce*) banking; (*établissement*) bank; **opération de b.,** banking operation; **b. centrale,** central *or* issuing bank; **b. d'affaires,** merchant bank; **la B. Mondiale,** the World Bank; **b. d'émission,** bank of issue, issuing house; **b. notificatrice,** advising bank; **billet de b.,** banknote; **carnet** *ou* **livret de b.,** bankbook; **travailler dans la b.,** to be in banking; **avoir un compte en b. chez ...,** to bank with ...; **employé/directeur de b.,** bank clerk/manager; **b. privée/de l'État,** privately-owned/State bank; *Méd* **b. de** *ou* **du sang,** blood bank; **b. des yeux/du sperme,** eye/sperm bank; *Ordinat* **b. de données,** data bank; **(b)** *Cartes* bank; **tenir la b.,** to be (the) banker; **faire sauter la b.,** to break the bank.

banquer [bɑ̃ke] *vi F* to stump up, to cough up; **c'est toujours moi qui banque,** it's always me that has to cough up.

banqueroute [bɑ̃krut] *nf Jur* bankruptcy; **faire b.,** to go bankrupt.

banqueroutier, -ière [bɑ̃krutje, -jɛr] *n* bankrupt.

banquet [bɑ̃kɛ] *nm* banquet, feast; **salle de b.,** banqueting hall.

banquette [bɑ̃kɛt] *nf* **(a)** (*siège*) bench, seat, form; **b. de piano,** piano stool; *Aut* **la b. arrière,** the back seat; *Th* **jouer devant les banquettes,** to play to an empty house; **(b)** *Constr etc* bank (*of earth etc*); (foot)path (*of bridge, tunnel*); **b. de fenêtre,** windowledge; window seat.

banquier, -ière [bɑ̃kje, -jɛr] *n Fin Cartes* banker; *Fig* **crois-tu que je vais être ton b.?,** do you think I'm going to finance *or Am* bankroll you?

banquise [bɑ̃kiz] *nf* ice floe, ice pack.

bantam [bɑ̃tam] *nm* bantam.

bantou, -oue [bɑ̃tu] **1** *adj* Bantu. **2** *n* **B.,** Bantu.

baobab [baɔbab] *nm* (*arbre*) baobab (tree).

baptême [batɛm] *nm* **(a)** *Rel* baptism, christening; **conférer** *ou* **donner le b. à qn,** to baptize *or* to christen s.o.; **recevoir le b.,** to be baptised; **nom de b.,** Christian name, baptismal name; **(b)** blessing (*of a bell*); naming (*of a ship*); **b. de l'air,** first flight; *Mil* **b. du feu,** baptism of fire; *Nau* **b. de la ligne,** (ducking on) crossing the line.

baptiser [batize] *vt* **(a)** *Rel* to baptize, to christen (*s.o.*); (*surnommer*) to christen, to nickname; **on l'avait baptisé le 'Balafré',** they had nicknamed him 'Scarface'; **b. son vin/son lait,** to water down one's wine/milk; **(b)** *Rel* to bless (*bell etc*); to name (*ship*).

baptismal, -aux [batismal, -o] *adj* baptismal.

baptisme [batism(ə)] *nm* baptism.

baptistaire [batistɛr] *adj* **registre b.,** register of baptisms; **extrait b.,** certificate of baptism.

baptiste [batist] *adj & n Rel* Baptist.

baptistère [batistɛr] *nm Rel* baptist(e)ry.

baquet [bakɛ] *nm* **(a)** (*cuve*) tub, bucket; **(b)** *Aut* **(siège en) b.,** bucket seat.

bar¹ [bar] *nm* (*poisson*) bass; **b. commun,** sea perch.

bar² *nm* (public) bar; (*comptoir*) bar (*in kitchen*); **le b. du coin,** the bar *or* pub on the corner, the local; **b.-tabac,** = bar with tobacco licence; **prendre une consommation au b.,** to have a drink at the bar; **b. à vin,** wine bar.

bar³ *nm Météo* bar.

barachois [baraʃwa] *nm Can* sandbar (*in a river*).

baragouin [baragwɛ̃] *nm F* gibberish, jargon.

baragouinage [baragwinaʒ] *nm F* jabbering.

baragouiner [baragwine] *F* **1** *vt* to speak (*a language*) badly; **b. l'anglais,** to talk broken English. **2** *vi* to jabber (on); **qu'est-ce qu'il baragouine?,** what's he jabbering (on) about?

baragouineur, -euse [baragwinœr, -øz] *n F* jabberer.

baraka [baraka] *nf F* (good) luck; **avoir la b.,** to be lucky.

baraque [barak] *nf* **(a)** (*logement provisoire*) hut, shack, shed; **(b)** *F* hovel, hole (*of a place*); **quelle b.!,** what a dump!; **il n'y a rien à manger dans cette b.!,** there's nothing to eat in this joint!; **(c)** stall (*at fair etc*).

baraqué [barake] *adj F* hefty; **il est plutôt b.,** he's pretty hefty.

baraquement [barakmɑ̃] *nm* shacks; *Mil* hutted camp.

baraquer [barake] **1** *vt Arch* to lodge (*troops etc*) in huts. **2** *vi* (*of camel*) to kneel down.

baraterie [baratri] *nf Jur* barratry.

baratin [baratɛ̃] *nm F* chatter; (*d'un vendeur*) (sales) patter; (*pour draguer*) smooth talk; **quel b.!,** (*je n'y comprends rien*) what gibberish!; **faire du b.,** to spin a yarn, to shoot a line; **ce type me fait du b.,** this bloke's chatting me up.

baratiner [baratine] *F* **1** *vi* (*parler beaucoup*) to talk a lot, to chatter; (*parler sans sincérité*) to shoot a line, to spin a yarn; (*d'un vendeur*) to give one's patter *or* sales talk *or* spiel. **2** *vt* to sweet-talk; **b. un client,** to give a client one's patter *or* sales talk *or* spiel; **b. une fille,** to chat up a girl.

baratineur, -euse [baratinœr, -øz] *n F* (*bavard etc*) gasbag; (*dragueur*) smooth talker.

baratte [barat] *nf* churn.

baratter [barate] *vt* to churn (*milk*).

barbacane [barbakan] *nf* **(a)** (*ouvrage*) barbican, outwork; (*meurtrière*) loop(hole); **(b)** (*canalisation*) drainage channel.

Barbade [barbad] *nf* Barbados.

barbant [barbɑ̃] *adj F* boring.

barbaque [barbak] *nf F* meat.

barbare [barbar] **1** *adj* (*cruel, savage*) barbaric, barbarous; *F* **il écoute de la musique b.,** he's listening to that awful racket he calls music. **2** *n* barbarian.

barbaresque [barbarɛsk] *Vieilli* **1** *adj* Berber; **les États barbaresques,** the Barbary States. **2** *n* **B.,** Berber.

barbarie [barbari] *nf* **(a)** (*cruauté, action cruelle*) barbarity; **(b)** (*manque de civilisation*) barbarism.

Barbarie [barbari] *nf Vieilli* the Barbary States.

barbarisme [barbarism] *nm Gram* barbarism.

barbe[1] [barb] *nf* **(a)** beard; **sans b.,** clean-shaven; **se faire pousser la b.,** to grow a beard, to let one's beard grow; **faire la b. à qn,** to shave s.o.; **il avait une b. de huit jours,** he had a week's beard *or* growth; **brosse/savon à b.,** shaving brush/soap; **parler dans sa b.,** to mutter, to mumble; **femme à b.,** bearded lady; *Fig* **faire qch à la b. de qn,** to do sth right under one's nose; **rire dans sa b.,** to laugh up one's sleeve; *Culin* **b. à papa,** candy floss, *Am* cotton candy; *F* **quelle b.!,** what a drag!, what a bore!; **la b.!,** that'll do!, shut up!; **vieille b.,** old fogey;
(b) beard (*of goat, bird etc*); whiskers (*of cat*); barb(el), wattle (*of fish*); wattle (*of bird*); barb (*of feather, fish hook*); beard (*of wheat*);
(c) *Tech* bur(r) (*on casting etc*); **barbes,** deckle edge (*of paper*).

barbe[2] *nm* **(cheval) b.,** barb, Barbary horse.

barbeau[1], -eaux [barbo] *nm* **(a)** (*poisson*) **b. commun,** barbel; **b. de mer,** red mullet; **(b)** *Arg* pimp.

barbeau[2] **1** *nm* cornflower. **2** *adj inv* **(bleu) b.,** cornflower blue, light blue.

Barbe-Bleue [barbəblø] *nm* Bluebeard.

barbecue [barbəkju] *nm* barbecue.

barbelé [barbəle] **1** *adj* barbed (*arrow, hook*); **fil de fer b.,** barbed wire. **2** *nm* barbed wire; *Mil* **des barbelés,** barbed wire entanglement.

barber [barbe] *F* **1** *vt* to bore (*s.o.*) (to death). **2 se barber** *vpr* to be bored (stiff).

barbiche [barbiʃ] *nf* short (pointed) beard, goatee.

barbichette [barbiʃɛt] *nf F* goatee (beard).

barbier [barbje] *nm* **(a)** *Vieilli* barber; **(b)** *Can* (men's) hairdresser, *Am* barber; **salon de b.,** barber's, *Am* barbershop.

barbillon [barbijɔ̃] *nm* **(a)** wattle (*of cock, fish*); barbel (*of fish*); **barbillons,** barbels (*of horse, cattle*); **(b)** (*poisson*) barbel; **b. de mer,** red mullet.

barbital [barbital] *nm Pharm* barbitone, *Am* barbital.

barbiturique [barbityrik] *Pharm* **1** *adj* barbituric. **2** *nm* barbiturate.

barbiturisme [barbityrism] *nm Méd* barbiturate poisoning; (*dépendance*) barbiturism, addiction to barbiturates.

barbotage [barbɔtaʒ] *nm* paddling, splashing (about) (*in water*); *Ch* bubbling (*of gas through liquid*).

barboter [barbɔte] **1** *vi* to paddle, to splash (about) (*in water*); (*of gas*) to bubble (*through liquid*); **les enfants barbotent dans la piscine,** the children are splashing about in the swimming pool. **2** *vt Arg* to pinch, to nick (*sth*).

barboteur, -euse [barbɔtœr, -øz] **1** *n* **(a)** (*dans l'eau*) paddler; **(b)** *Arg* thief. **2** *nm Ch* bubbler, blower. **3** *nf* **barboteuse,** (child's) playsuit, rompers.

barbotière [barbɔtjɛr] *nf* duckpond.

barbotin [barbɔtɛ̃] *nm* sprocket wheel.

barbouillage [barbujaʒ] *nm* **(a)** (*action de peindre*) daubing, smearing; (*action d'écrire*) scrawling, scribbling; **(b)** (*mauvaise peinture*) bad picture, daub; (*griffonnage*) scrawl, scribble.

barbouiller [barbuje] *vt* **(a)** to daub, to smear (*with paint*); to smear, to dirty (*one's face*); to blot (*paper with ink*); **visage barbouillé de larmes/de chocolat,** tear-stained face/face smeared with chocolate; **(b)** (*griffonner*) to scribble, to scrawl; **b. un article,** to dash off an article; **(c)** *F* **ça me barbouille l'estomac** *ou* **le cœur,** it makes me feel sick, it turns my stomach; **avoir l'estomac barbouillé,** to feel queasy.

barbouilleur, -euse [barbujœr, -øz] *n* **(a)** (*de peinture*) dauber, so-called artist; **(b) b. (de papier),** scribbler, hack.

barbouze [barbuz] *nf F* **(a)** beard; **(b)** secret agent.

barbu, -ue [barby] **1** *adj* bearded. **2** *nm* bearded man. **3** *nf* **barbue,** (*poisson*) brill.

barcarolle [barkarɔl] *nf Mus* barcarol(l)e.

barcasse [barkas] *nf Nau* launch, boat.

Barcelone [barsəlɔn] *nf* Barcelona.

bard [bar] *nm* (wheelless) hand barrow.

barda [barda] *nm Mil etc Arg* kit, gear.

bardage [bardaʒ] *nm* **(a)** hand transport (*of heavy materials*); **(b)** boarding (*to protect a painting etc*); *Am* siding (*of building*).

bardane [bardan] *nf* (*plante*) burdock.

bardas [bardas] *nm Can* (*pagaille*) shambles; **être de b.,** (*déranger*) to be a nuisance.

barde[1] [bard] *nf* **(a)** *Culin* bard, bacon (*put over roast*); **(b)** bard (*protecting warhorse*).

barde[2] *nm* bard, poet.

bardeau, -eaux [bardo] *nm* **(a)** *Constr* shingle (board); **(b)** *Zool* hinny.

barder[1] [barde] *v impers F* **ça va b.!,** there's going to be trouble!; **c'est là que ça a commencé à b.,** and then the fun began!

barder[2] *vt* **(a)** *Culin* to bard (*fowl etc*); **(b)** *Hist* to bard; **chevalier bardé de fer,** steel-clad knight; **malle bardée d'étiquettes,** trunk stuck all over with labels; **il est bardé de diplômes,** he's got loads of qualifications.

bardot [bardo] *nm Zool* hinny.

barème [barɛm] *nm* **(a)** scale (*of marks, of salaries*); (printed) table, schedule (*of prices etc*), (price) list; **(b)** ready reckoner.

barge [barʒ] *nf* **(a)** *Nau* barge, lighter; **(b)** (*de foin*) (rectangular) haystack.

baril [bari(l)] *nm* barrel, keg, cask; *Pétr* barrel (42 gallons); **b. de lessive,** tub of washing powder.

barillet [barijɛ] *nm* **(a)** (*petit baril*) small barrel *or* keg *or* cask; **(b)** barrel piston chamber (*of pump*); cylinder (*of revolver*); **il n'y avait rien dans le b.,** the gun was empty; **b. (de ressort),** (*in clock*) spring box, spring drum.

barilleur [barijœr] *nm* cooper.

bariolage [barjɔlaʒ] *nm* variegation; (*de peinture*) painting *or* daubing with different colours; *Fig* medley, riot (*of colours*); *Péj* gaudy colour scheme.

bariolé [barjɔle] *adj* variegated; (*tissu*) multicoloured; *Péj* gaudy; **audience bariolée,** colourfully dressed audience.

barioler [barjɔle] *vt* to variegate; to paint, to daub (*sth*) in many *or Péj* gaudy colours.

bariolure [barjɔlyr] *nf* variegation; medley, splashes (*of colours*); *Péj* gaudy colour scheme.

barjo [barʒo] *F* **1** *n* fruit-cake, *Am* flake. **2** *adj* nutty, *Am* flakey.

barmaid [barmɛd] *nf* barmaid.

barman [barman] *nm* barman; (*pl barmen, barmans*).

barn [barn] *nm Nucl* barn (1024 cm^2).

barographe [barɔgraf] *nm Météo* barograph.

baromètre [barɔmɛtr] *nm Météo & Fig* barometer; **b. anéroïde,** aneroid barometer; **b. enregistreur,** recording barometer.

barométrique [barɔmetrik] *adj* barometric.

baron [barɔ̃] *nm* **(a)** (*seigneur*) baron; *Fig* **les (hauts) barons de la finance/de l'industrie,** financial/industrial tycoons; **(b)** *Arg* protector; **(c)** *Culin* **b. d'agneau,** baron of lamb.

baronnage [barɔnaʒ] *nm* **(a)** (*titre*) baronage; **(b)** (*domaine*) barony.

baronne [barɔn] *nf* baroness; **bonjour madame la b.,** good morning, Lady X; (*paroles d'un(e) domestique*) good morning, your ladyship *or* my lady.

baronnet [barɔnɛ] *nm Br* baronet.

baronnie [barɔni] *nf Arch* barony.

baroque [barɔk] **1** *adj* odd, strange, bizarre (*ideas etc*); *Archit Mus* baroque. **2** *nm* Baroque.

baroud [barud] *nm Mil F* fighting; **b. d'honneur,** last-ditch battle, last stand.

baroudeur [barudœr] *nm Mil F* (keen) fighter.

barouf(le) [baruf(l)] *nm F* noise, din, row, racket.

barque [bark] *nf Nau* **(a)** (*embarcation*) boat; **quelle b.!,** what an old tub!; **b. de pêcheur,** fishing boat, smack; **patron de b.,** skipper; *Fig* **bien mener** *ou* **bien conduire sa b.,** to manage one's affairs well, to play one's cards well; *Fig* **c'est elle qui mène la b.,** she's the boss; **(b) trois-mâts b.,** barque.

barquette [barkɛt] *nf* **(a)** (*gâteau*) (small) boat-shaped

pastry; **(b)** (*récipient*) small container (*for carry-out food etc*).
barracuda [barakyda] *nm* barracuda.
barrage [baraʒ] *nm* **(a)** (*fait de bloquer*) barring, blocking (off) (*of road etc*); blocking (*of harbour*); damming (*of valley*); closing, closure (*of street*); **faire b. à tout navire/camion étranger,** to deny entry to all foreign ships/lorries; **faire b. à toutes les nouvelles idées,** to block any new ideas; **(b)** (*fermeture*) barrier, obstruction; (harbour) boom; **b. routier** *ou* **de route,** roadblock; **b. de police,** police roadblock, cordon; **b. (de retenue),** barrage, dam; (*de petite taille*) weir; *Mil* **b. aérien,** anti-aircraft barrage; **(tir de) barrage,** barrage (fire).
barre [bar] *nf* **(a)** bar, rod, rail (*of metal, wood etc*); (wooden) batten; bar (*of chocolate*); *Sp* bar, barrier; (*de danse*) barre; *Nau* tiller (*of boat*); *Nau* helm (*of ship*); **b. de savon,** cake *or* bar of soap; *F* **c'est le coup de b.,** you've paid over the odds; *Fig F* **avoir un coup de b.,** to be shattered; **s'exercer à la b.,** to do exercises at the barre; **b. d'appui,** handrail; *Gym* **b. fixe,** horizontal bar; **barres parallèles,** parallel bars; *Aut* **b. de connexion,** crossbar, tie rod (*of steering gear*); *Aut* **b. de torsion,** torsion bar; **homme de b.,** man at the wheel, helmsman; **être à la b., prendre** *ou* **tenir la b.,** to be at the helm; *Fig* **à partir d'aujourd'hui je prends la b.,** as from today, I'm in charge; **avoir barre(s) sur qn,** to have an advantage over someone; **passer sous la b. de 2 000 francs,** to drop below the 2,000 franc mark; *Nau* **barres de hune,** crosstrees; *Jur* **b. d'un tribunal,** bar of a lawcourt; **b. des témoins,** ≈ witness box, *Am* witness stand; **paraître à la b.,** to appear before the court *or* at the bar;
(b) (sand)bar (*of river, harbour*); (*artificial*) (harbour) boom; **b. d'eau,** (tidal) bore; **b. de flot,** tidal wave; **b. de plage,** surf;
(c) bar (*of horse's mouth*);
(d) (*trait*) line, dash, stroke; *Hér* bend sinister; **b. d'un t,** cross(bar) of a t; *Mus* **b. de mesure,** bar (line); **double b.,** double bar;
(e) jeu de barres, prisoners' base.
barré [bare] *adj* **(a)** obstructed; **'route barrée',** road closed; **(b) chèque b.,** crossed cheque; **(c) dent barrée,** impacted tooth; **(d)** (*à l'aviron*) **un deux b.,** a coxed pair; **(e)** *F* **on est mal b.,** things don't look good; **(f)** *Hér* bendy sinister.
barreau, -eaux [baro] *nm* **(a)** small bar, rail; rung (*of ladder*); stretcher (*of chair*); **fenêtre garnie de barreaux,** barred window; **être derrière les barreaux,** to be behind (prison) bars; **(b)** *Jur* **le b.,** the bar; **être reçu** *ou* **admis au b.,** to be called to the bar; **rayer qn du b.,** to disbar s.o.
barrement [barmɑ̃] *nm* crossing (*of cheque*).
barrer [bare] **1** *vt* **(a)** to bar (*door etc*); *Can* to lock (*door, window etc*); to bar, to obstruct (*the way*); to dam (*stream*); to block, to close (*road*); **b. le passage** *ou* **la route à qn,** to block s.o.'s way; *Fig* to thwart s.o.; **(b)** to cross (*a t, a cheque*); **(c)** to cross out, to strike out (*word etc*); **je vais pouvoir b. ça de ma liste,** I can cross that off my list; **(d)** *Nau* to steer (*a boat*); (*à l'aviron*) to cox. **2 se barrer** *vpr F* to clear off, to beat it, to scram; **barre-toi!,** get lost!, push off!
barrette¹ [barɛt] *nf Rel* biretta.
barrette² *nf* **(a)** (*pour les cheveux*) (hair) slide, *Am* barrette; **(b)** (small) bar, rod, stick; *Aut* **b. (verticale),** overrider; **(c)** brooch, *Am* pin; **b. de médaille,** bar of medal; **(d)** (shoe) strap; **(e)** *Ind* damper (*of furnace*).
barreur [barœr] *nm* **(a)** *Nau* man at the helm, helmsman; **(b)** (*à l'aviron*) cox; **un deux sans b.,** a coxless pair.
barricade [barikad] *nf* **b. (de rue),** (street) barricade; *Fig* **de l'autre côté de la b.,** on the opposing side, on the other side of the fence.
barricader [barikade] **1** *vt* to barricade (*street, door etc*). **2 se barricader** *vpr* to barricade oneself in; **quand je ne veux pas les voir je me barricade chez moi,** when I don't want to see them I shut myself away in my room *or* at home; **se b. dans une chambre,** to barricade oneself in a room (**contre,** against); to shut *or* lock oneself up in one's room (*so as not to be disturbed*).
barrière [barjɛr] *nf* **(a)** barrier; fence (*around a field*); *Rail* (ticket collectors') gate, barrier; gate (*of level crossing*); **les barrières douanières/culturelles/sociales,** customs/cultural/social barriers; **le garde-b.,** the crossing-keeper; *Aut* **b. de dégel,** = barrier closing road to heavy traffic during a thaw; **b. à bascule,** drop-arm barrier; *Av* **b. anti-souffle,** blast wall; *Géog* **b. naturelle,** natural frontier; **la Grande B.,** the Great Barrier Reef; **ne pas savoir l'anglais est une b. très nette,** not knowing English is a distinct handicap; **(b)** *Hist* gate (*of town, castle etc*); (*péage*) toll gate, turnpike; **(c)** *Courses de chevaux etc* starting gate; **(d)** *Phys* **b. de potentiel,** potential barrier; **b. thermique,** thermal barrier, heat barrier.
barrique [barik] *nf* large barrel (*approx* 200 litres), cask, butt, hogshead; *F* **il est gros comme une b.,** he's as round as a barrel; *Fig F* **plein comme une b.,** (as) drunk as a lord.
barrir [barir] *vi* (*of elephant*) to trumpet.
barrissement [barismɑ̃] *nm*, **barrit** [bari] *nm* trumpeting (*of elephant*).
bartavelle [bartavɛl] *nf* **(perdrix) b.,** rock partridge.
barycentre [barisɑ̃tr] *nm Math* barycentre.
baryte [barit] *nf Ch Minér* baryta, barium oxide.
baryté [barite] *adj Méd* **bouillie barytée,** barium meal.
baryton [baritɔ̃] *Mus* **1** *adj* baritone (*voice*). **2** *nm* baritone.
baryum [barjɔm] *nm Ch Minér* barium.
barzoï [barzɔi] *nm* (*chien*) borzoi.
bas¹, basse [bɑ, bɑs] **1** *adj* **(a)** (*de peu de hauteur, d'altitude*) low; **maison basse de toit** *ou* **à toit b.,** house with a low roof; **b. sur pattes,** short-legged; *Boxe etc* **coup b.,** blow below the belt; **enfant en b. âge,** infant; **avoir la vue basse,** to be short-sighted; **voix basse,** low *or* deep voice; **parler à voix basse,** to whisper, to speak under one's breath; **une note basse,** a low note; **une clarinette basse,** a bass clarinet; **maintenir les prix b.,** to keep prices down *or* low; **prix les plus b.,** rock-bottom prices; **en ce b. monde,** here below; **au b. mot,** at the lowest estimate *or* valuation; **le soleil est b.,** the sun is low; *Météo* **plafond b.,** low ceiling (of clouds); **mer basse,** low water *or* tide; *Fig* **la tête basse,** with a hang-dog look; **le moral est très b.,** morale is very low; **terres** *ou* **régions basses,** lowlands; **le b. Rhin,** the lower Rhine; **la basse Normandie,** Lower Normandy; **la marée est basse,** the tide is out; **à marée basse,** at low tide; **le B.-Empire,** the Lower *or* Later *or* Byzantine Empire;
(b) (*dans hiérarchie*) low(er); **les basses classes,** the lower classes (*of society*); *Scol* the lower forms *or Am* grades; *Culin* **b. morceaux,** cheap cuts (*of meat*); **le b. clergé,** the lower clergy; *Pol* **la Chambre basse,** the Lower House; **la partie basse d'une ville, la basse ville,** the lower (part of a) town; **les bas quartiers,** the poor districts (*of a town*);
(c) (*dans le temps*) late; **le b. Moyen-Age,** the late Middle Ages; *Ling* **b. latin,** low Latin; **b. allemand,** low German;
(d) *Péj* mean, base, low; **motif b.,** base *or* contemptible motive; **terme/style b.,** vulgar expression/style; **c'est une basse vengeance,** that was a petty revenge.
2 *adv* **(a)** low (down); **être assis trop b.,** to be sitting too low down; **quelques marches plus b.,** a few steps further down, lower down; **dix lignes plus b.,** ten lines (further) down; **les hirondelles volent b.,** the swallows are flying low; **voir plus b.,** see below; *Fig* **mettre qn plus b. que terre,** to humiliate s.o.; *Bourse* **les cours sont tombés très b.,** shares are down; **la température est tombée b. pendant la nuit,** the temperature plummetted during the night; **comment a-t-elle pu tomber si b.?,** how could she fall so low?; **le malade est bien b.,** the patient is very low;
(b) chapeaux b.!, hats off!; **chapeau b.,** hat in hand; (*bravo*) I take my hat off to you; *F* **b. les mains** *ou* **les pattes!,** hands off!, keep your paws off!; **b. les pattes!,** (*to dog*) paws (down)!; *Nau* **mettre b. une voile,** to haul down a sail; **mettre pavillon b.,** *Nau* to lower *or* strike the colours; *F* to climb down;
(c) (*of animals*) **mettre b.,** to give birth to, to drop (young); (*of mare*) to foal; (*of sheep*) to lamb; (*of goat*) to kid; (*of bitch*) to pup, to whelp; (*of sow*) to farrow; **mettre b. avant terme,** to cast *or* slip its young;
(d) (*dans les sons*) low; **vous chantez trop b.,** you are singing in too low a key; (*doucement*) you are singing too softly; **parler (tout) b.,** to (speak in a) whisper; **tu pourrais mettre la télévision plus b.?,** could you turn down the television?; **parlez plus b., je vous prie,** please speak more quietly *or* lower your voice; **rire tout b.,** to chuckle to oneself; **entre haut et b.,** half aloud;
(e) (*en bas*) below; **tout le monde en b.!,** all hands below!; **la cuisine est en b.,** the kitchen is downstairs; **les gens d'en b.,** the people below *or* downstairs; **lever les bras de haut en b.,** to move one's arms up and down; **de haut en b.,** from top to bottom, from head to toe *or* foot; **il porte du neuf de haut en b.,** he's dressed from head to toe in new clothes *or F* things; **regarder qn de haut en b.,** to look s.o. up and down; **la tête en b.,** upside down;

tomber la tête en b., to fall head first; **en b. du village,** at the lower end of the village; **ce vase s'élargit par en b.,** this vase is wider at the bottom; **en** *ou* **au b. de,** at the foot of, at the bottom of; **en** *ou* **au b. de l'escalier,** downstairs;

(f) à b. la dictature!, down with dictatorship!; **à b. Martin!,** down with Martin!; **mettre** *ou* **jeter à b.,** to demolish, to pull down (*house*); to overthrow (*s.o., government*); **mettre b. les armes,** *Mil* to lay down one's arms; *Fig* to give up (*arguing*).

3 *nm* **(a)** lower part (*of sth*); foot (*of a hill*); **b. d'une échelle/d'une page,** foot *or* bottom of a ladder/page; **l'étage du b.,** the lower storey; **b. du dos,** small of the back; **le** *ou* **les b. du navire,** the ship's bottom; **b. américains,** turn-ups (*of trousers*), *Am* cuffs; *Typ* **b. de casse,** lower case;

(b) les hauts et les b., the ups and downs (*of life etc*); **avoir des hauts et des b.,** to have ups and downs *or* highs and lows.

bas² *nm* (*vêtement*) stocking; **b. à côtes,** ribbed stocking; *Vieilli* **b. diminué** *ou* **proportionné,** fully-fashioned stocking; **b. mousse,** stretch stocking; **b. 15 deniers,** 15 denier stocking; **b. de soie/de nylon,** silk/nylon stocking; **b. sans couture,** seamless stocking; **b. extensible,** stretch nylon; **b. filet** *ou* **résille,** fishnet *or* mesh stocking; **b. fin** *ou* **voile,** sheer stocking; **b. indémaillable,** run-resistant *or Br* ladder-proof stocking; **une paire de b.,** a pair of stockings; **b. de laine,** woollen stocking; *Fig* savings, nest egg; *Méd* **b. à varices** *ou* **élastique,** elastic *or* support stocking.

basalte [bazalt] *nm Géol* basalt.

basaltique [bazaltik] *adj Géol* basaltic.

basané [bazane] *adj* (*bronzé*) sunburnt, (sun)tanned; (*tanné*) weatherbeaten; (*naturellement*) swarthy.

basaner [bazane] *vt* to bronze, to tan (*face etc*).

bas-bleu [bablø] *nm Péj* bluestocking; (*pl bas-bleus*).

bas-côté [bakote] *nm* **(a)** shoulder, side (*of road etc*); **défense de stationner sur les b.-côtés,** no parking on the verge; **(b)** (side) aisle (*of church*).

basculant [baskylɑ̃] *adj* rocking, tilting; **wagon b.,** tip wagon; **pont b.,** drawbridge; **siège b.,** tip-up seat.

bascule [baskyl] *nf* **(a)** (*pièce mobile*) rocker; **mouvement de b.,** rocking motion; **(jeu de) b.,** seesaw(ing); **chaise/cheval à b.,** rocking chair/horse; *Fig* **politique de b.,** balancing act; **(b) (balance à) b.,** weighbridge; weighing machine; **b. automatique** *ou* **du pharmacien,** weighing machine; **b. romaine,** platform scales (*with steelyard*); **wagon à b.,** tip wagon; **(c)** *Électron* **(montage en) b.,** bistable trigger circuit, flip-flop circuit.

basculement [baskylmɑ̃] *nm* **(a)** (*de balançoire*) rocking, swinging; (*au jeu de bascule*) seesaw(ing); **(b)** (*renversement*) tipping (up), tilting (over); **(c)** (*chute*) toppling *or* falling over, overbalancing.

basculer [baskyle] **1** *vt* **(a)** (*culbuter*) to rock, to swing; (*au jeu de bascule*) to seesaw; **levier basculé par une came,** lever rocked by a cam; **(b)** (*renverser*) to tip (up), to tilt (over); **b. une charrette,** to tip a cart. **2** *vi* (*renverser*) to fall over, to overbalance; **tout a basculé,** the whole lot toppled over; **ce pays pourrait b. dans une économie de marché,** the country could shift to a market economy; *Fig* **nous étions heureux, et puis tout a basculé,** we were happy, then everything turned upside down.

basculeur [baskylœr] *nm* **(a)** (*de wagon etc*) tip(per), rocker; **(b)** *El* rocker switch.

base [bɑz] *nf* **(a)** lower part, foot, bottom, base (*of mountain etc*); foundation(s) (*of building*); *Anat Math* base (*of heart, triangle etc*); (*en arpentage*) base (line); base plate (*of machine*); **jeter** *ou* **poser les bases de qch,** to lay the foundation for sth; **b. de maquillage,** foundation cream, (makeup) base; **b. de vernis à ongles,** nail varnish base;

(b) *Mil etc* base (*of operations*); **b. de ravitaillement,** supply base; **b. aérienne/navale,** air/naval base; **b. de lancement (d'engins),** (missile) launching site;

(c) basis, foundation, grounds (*of suspicion etc*); **être à la b. de qch,** to be at the root *or* heart of sth; **argument qui pèche par la b.,** fundamentally unsound argument; **sans b.,** without foundation *or* basis; **vocabulaire/l'anglais de b.,** basic vocabulary/English; **les produits de b. pour la maison,** staple household goods, staples; **denrées de b.,** staple commodities, staples; **avoir des connaissances de b. en informatique,** to have an elementary *or* basic knowledge of information technology; **traitement de b.,** basic salary; **produits à b. d'amidon,** starch products; **boisson à b. de gin,** gin-based drink; *Ordinat* **b. de temps,** time base; *Ordinat* **b. de données,** data base; **mettre qch dans une b. de données,** to put sth in a data base, to data-base sth; **documents/données de b.,** source documents/data; *Pol etc* **la b.,** the rank and file, the grassroots (*of a trade union etc*); **militant de b.,** grassroots activist;

(d) *Math* base, radix (*of system of notation*); radix, root, basis (*of logarithm*); **calculer en b. 3,** to do calculations in base 3;

(e) *Ch* base;

(f) *Électron* base (electrode) (*of transistor*).

base-ball [bɛzbol] *nm Sp* baseball.

baseballeur [bɛzbolœr] *nm Sp* baseball player.

baser [baze] **1** *vt* to base, to ground, to found (*opinion etc*) (**sur,** on); **cette opinion n'est pas basée sur la réalité,** this opinion is not based on reality; **avions américains basés en Grande-Bretagne,** American aircraft based in Great Britain. **2 se baser** *vpr* **se b. sur qch,** to base one's argument on sth.

bas-fond [bafɔ̃] *nm* (*pl bas-fonds*) **(a)** (*creux*) low ground, hollow; *Fig* **les b.-fonds de la société,** the dregs of society; **les b.-fonds du journalisme,** the gutter press; **(b)** shallow, shoal (*in sea, river*).

Basic [bazik] *nm Ordinat* BASIC.

basilic¹ [bazilik] *nm* (*plante*) basil.

basilic² *nm* basilisk.

basilical, -aux [bazilikal, -o] *adj Archit* basilical.

basilique¹ [bazilik] *Anat* **1** *adj* basilic (*vein*). **2** *nf* basilic vein.

basilique² *nf Archit* basilica.

basin [bazɛ̃] *nm Tex* cotton damask.

basique [bɑzik] *adj* **(a)** *Ch Métal* basic (*salt, process etc*); **scorie b.,** basic slag; **(b)** basic (*facts etc*); *F* **des connaissances/produits basiques,** basic knowledge/products.

basket [baskɛt] *nf F* basketball; **une paire de baskets,** a pair of basketball boots; *Fig* **lâche-moi les baskets,** don't hassle me, get off my back.

basket-ball [baskɛtbol] *nm Sp* basketball.

basketteur, -euse [baskɛtœr, -øz] *n Sp* basketball player.

bas-mât [bamɑ] *nm Nau* lower mast; (*pl bas-mâts*).

basquais, -aise [baskɛ, -ɛz] **1** *adj* Basque. **2** *nf Culin* **poulet (à la) basquaise,** Basque chicken (*cooked with onion, tomato etc*).

basque¹ [bask] **1** *adj* Basque; **le Pays b.,** the Basque country. **2** *nm Ling* Basque. **3** *n* **B.,** Basque.

basque² *nf* skirt, tail (*of jacket etc*); *Fig* **être toujours pendu aux basques de qn,** to be always at s.o.'s heels.

bas-relief [barəljɛf] *nm Archit etc* bas relief, low relief; (*pl bas-reliefs*).

basse [bɑs] **1** *adj voir* **BAS¹**. **2** *nf* **(a)** *Mus* bass part; bass (*voice, singer*); **b. chiffrée** *ou* **continue** *ou* **figurée,** figured *or* thorough bass, basso continuo; **voix de b.,** bass voice; **b. chantante, b.-taille,** basso cantante, singing bass; **b. profonde, b.-contre, b. noble,** basso profundo; **une b. de la chorale,** a bass from the choir; **(b)** (*violoncelle*) 'cello; (*saxophone*) bass (saxophone); (*guitare*) bass (guitar); (*d'un instrument*) bass strings; *Arch* **b. de hautbois,** bassoon; **b. de viole,** bass viol; **(c)** *Nau* shoal, flat, sandbank.

basse-cour [baskur] *nf* (*pl basses-cours*) **(a)** (*cour*) farmyard; **(b)** (*volaille*) poultry, fowl.

basse-fosse [basfos] *nf* dungeon; **cul de b.-f.,** deepest dungeon, oubliette; (*pl basses-fosses*).

bassement [basmɑ̃] *adv* basely, meanly; **elle s'est b. vengée,** she took a petty revenge.

bassesse [basɛs] *nf* **(a)** baseness, lowness (*of birth, expression, action etc*); **la b. d'un hypocrite,** the baseness of a hyprocrite; **il n'ose pas le lui dire, c'est de la b.!,** he doesn't dare tell her, how low can you get?; **(b)** (*action*) low *or* mean *or* contemptible action; **homme prêt à toutes les bassesses,** man who would stoop to anything.

basset¹ [basɛ] *nm* (*chien*) basset (hound); **b. allemand,** dachshund.

basset² *nm Mus* **cor de b.,** tenor clarinet in F, basset horn.

basse-taille [bastaj] *nf Mus* basso cantante, singing bass; (*pl basses-tailles*).

bassin [basɛ̃] *nm* **(a)** (*récipient*) basin, bowl, pan; pan (*of scale*); *Méd* **b. (de lit),** bedpan;

(b) (*dans un jardin*) ornamental lake; (*plus petit*) pond, pool; (*de fontaine*) basin; (*réservoir*) reservoir, tank; **petit b.,** (*de la piscine*) = paddling pool for toddlers; **grand b.,** (*de la piscine*) swimming pool; **les bassins du Luxembourg,** the pools in the Luxembourg Gardens;

(c) dock, basin (*of port*); **b. de décantation,** settling tank; **b. filtrant,** filter bed; **b. à flot,** wet dock; **b. à marée,**

tidal dock, basin; **b. de radoub,** dry dock, graving dock; **entrer au b.,** to dock; **b. naturel/artificiel,** natural/artificial basin;
(d) *Géol* basin; (*dépression*) depression; **le b. parisien,** the Paris basin; **b. de réception,** catchment area; **le b. de la Tamise,** the Thames basin; **b. houiller,** coal basin; **b. minier,** mining area;
(e) *Anat* pelvis.

bassinant [basinɑ̃] *adj F* boring.

bassine [basin] *nf* pan, vat; **b. à confitures,** preserving pan; **b. à vaisselle,** washing-up bowl *or* basin; **une (pleine) b. de confiture,** a panful of jam.

bassiner [basine] *vt* **(a)** to bathe (*wound etc*); **(b)** *Arg* to bore, to annoy, to plague (*s.o.*); **(c)** *Arch* **b. un lit,** to warm a bed (with a warming pan).

bassinet [basinɛ] *nm* **(a)** *Anat* pelvis (*of the kidney*); **(b)** (*d'armure*) basinet, basnet.

bassinoire [basinwar] *nf* **(a)** (*instrument*) warming pan; **(b)** *Arg* bore, pain in the neck.

bassiste [bɑsist] *n Mus* **(a)** (double) bass player; **(b)** (*de tuba*) tuba player.

basson [bɑsɔ̃] *nm Mus* **(a)** (*instrument*) bassoon; **(b)** (*joueur*) bassoonist.

bassoniste [bɑsɔnist] *n* bassoonist.

bastide [bastid] *nf* **(a)** (*en Provence*) (small) country house, farm; **(b)** *Hist* (*en Provence*) fortified town; fortification.

bastille [bastij] *nf* fortress; *Hist* **la B.,** the Bastille; **la prise de la B.,** the storming of the Bastille.

bastingage [bastɛ̃gaʒ] *nm Nau* **(a)** (hand)rail; **accoudé aux bastingages,** leaning over the rails; **(b)** *Hist* bulwark, topside.

bastion [bastjɔ̃] *nm* bastion; *Fig* bastion, bulwark, stronghold (*of liberty etc*).

bastonnade [bastɔnad] *nf* **(a)** *F* (*dispute*) punch up; **(b)** *Arch* bastinado, beating (*with a stick*).

bastos [bastɔs] *nm Arg* bullet, slug.

bastringue [bastrɛ̃g] *nm F* **(a)** (*lieu*) (cheap) dance hall; (*orchestre*) (dance) band; (*bruit*) noise, din, racket; **(b)** (*affaires*) clobber, gear, paraphernalia; **prendre tout son b.,** to pack up all one's clobber.

bas-ventre [bɑvɑ̃tr] *nm Anat* lower abdomen; (*pl bas-ventres*).

bât [bɑ] *nm* pack(saddle); **cheval de b.,** packhorse; *Fig* **c'est là que le b. blesse,** that's where the shoe rubs *or* pinches.

bataclan [bataklɑ̃] *nm F* belongings, paraphernalia; **et tout le b.,** and all the rest of it, and so on; **vendez tout le b.!,** sell the whole lot!

bataille [bataj] *nf* **(a)** (*combat*) battle, fight; **b. terrestre/aérienne/navale,** land/air/naval battle; **b. perdue d'avance,** losing battle; **le fort de la b.,** the thick of the battle; **champ de b.,** battlefield; **cheval de b.,** warhorse; *Fig* hobby-horse; **livrer b. à,** to give battle to, to join battle with; *Fig* **c'est une b. constante,** it's a constant battle, it's an endless struggle; **la b. contre l'inflation,** the battle *or* fight against inflation; **en b.,** *Mil* in battle order *or* formation; *Arch* in battle array; **stationnement en b.,** angled parking; *Fig* **il portait son chapeau en b.,** his hat was all crooked; **cheveux en b.,** dishevelled hair; **(b)** *Cartes* beggar-my-neighbour.

batailler [bataje] *vi* to fight, to battle; **il est toujours prêt à b.,** he's always spoiling for a fight; *F* **j'ai dû b. pendant une heure pour ouvrir la porte,** I had to battle for an hour to open the door.

batailleur, -euse [batajœr, -øz] **1** *adj* quarrelsome, pugnacious, aggressive. **2** *n* fighter, battler.

bataillon [batajɔ̃] *nm Mil* battalion; *F* (*grand nombre*) crowd, swarm; **commandant de b.,** battalion commander; **b. d'Afrique,** French disciplinary battalion (formerly stationed in North Africa); *F* **elle a un b. de chatons,** she has a whole load of kittens.

bâtard, -arde [bɑtar, -ard] **1** *adj* illegitimate (*child*); bastard, hybrid, counterfeit (*product etc*); **chien b.,** mongrel; **écriture bâtarde,** bastard handwriting; *Typ* **format b.,** bastard size; **pain b.,** = large stick of French bread. **2** *nm* (*chien*) mongrel; (*pain*) = large stick of French bread. **3** *n* (*enfant*) bastard.

batardeau, -eaux [batardo] *nm* coffer(dam), caisson.

bâtardise [bɑtardiz] *nf* illegitimacy, bastardy; **la b. de cette solution,** this cobbled together solution.

bateau, -eaux [bato] **1** *nm* **(a)** boat; (merchant) vessel, craft; **b. à voiles,** sailing boat; **b. à vapeur,** steamboat, steamer; **b. à moteur,** motor boat, motor launch; **b. à rames,** rowing boat, *Am* rowboat; **b. de plaisance,** pleasure boat; **b. de pêche,** fishing boat, smack; **b. de sauvetage,** lifeboat; **b. de guerre,** warship, battleship; **faire du b. à voiles/à rames,** to go sailing/rowing; *Rail* **le train du b.,** the boat train; **je suis venu en** *ou* **par b.,** I came by boat; *F* **monter un b. à qn,** to have s.o. on, to pull s.o.'s leg; **encolure b.,** boat neck, scoop neck (*of dress etc*); **lit b.,** = type of bunk bed; **(b)** entrance (*to garage, drive etc, where pavement slopes down*). **2** *adj F* **sujet b.,** a subject that's been done to death, a hackneyed subject.

bateau-citerne [batositɛrn] *nm* tanker; (*pl bateaux-citernes*).

bateau-feu [batofø] *nm Nau* lightship, light vessel; (*pl bateaux-feux*).

bateau-lavoir [batolavwar] *nm Arch* wash-house (*on the Seine*); (*pl bateaux-lavoirs*).

bateau-mouche [batomuʃ] *nm* water bus; river boat (*in Paris etc*); (*pl bateaux-mouches*).

bateau-phare [batofar] *nm* lightship, light vessel; (*pl bateaux-phares*).

bateau-pompe [batopɔ̃p] *nm* fire boat; (*pl bateaux-pompes*).

batelage[1] [batlaʒ] *nm Nau* **(frais de) b.,** lighterage, waterage (charges).

batelage[2] *nm* (*art du jongleur*) juggling; (*acrobatique*) tumbling, acrobatics.

bateler [batle] *vi* **(je batelle, n. batelons, je batellerai)** (*du jongleur*) to juggle; (*de l'acrobate*) to tumble, to do trick acrobatics.

bateleur, -euse [batlœr, -øz] *n Arch* (*jongleur*) juggler; (*acrobate*) tumbler, acrobat.

batelier, -ière [batəlje, -jɛr] *n* boatman, boat woman; waterman; ferryman, -woman; **b. de chaland,** bargeman, bargee, lighterman.

batellerie [batɛlri] *nf* **(a)** inland water transport; **(b)** (*ensemble de bateaux*) small (*river, canal*) craft.

bat-flanc [baflɑ̃] *nm inv* **(a)** wooden partition (*in a dormitory*); **(b)** swinging bail (*of horse stall*).

bath [bat] *adj inv Arg* super, fantastic, stupendous; **t'es b.,** you're really great.

bathyal, -aux [batjal, -o] *adj* bathyal.

bathymètre [batimɛtr] *nm* bathometer, bathymeter.

bathymétrie [batimetri] *nf* bathymetry.

bathyscaphe [batiskaf] *nm* bathyscape, bathyscaph(e).

bathysphère [batisfɛr] *nf* bathysphere.

bâti [bɑti] *nm* **(a)** *Menuis* frame(work), structure, support, stand; **b. de fenêtre,** window frame; **b. moteur,** engine mounting; **(b)** *Couture* tacking, basting.

batifolage [batifɔlaʒ] *nm F* **(a)** (*jeu*) romping, larking *or* playing about *or* around; **(b)** (*flirt*) flirting.

batifoler [batifɔle] *vi F* to romp, to lark *or* play about *or* around.

batik [batik] *nm* batik; **une jupe en b.,** a batik skirt.

batillage [batijaʒ] *nm* wake (*of boat*).

bâtiment [bɑtimɑ̃] *nm* **(a) le b., l'industrie du b.,** (the) building (trade); **peintre en b.,** painter; **il est du b.,** he's in the same line of business; (*il s'y connaît*) he knows what he's doing; **(b)** (*construction*) building; **bâtiments de ferme,** farm buildings; **usine en trois corps de b.,** factory in three main buildings; **elle habite dans ces grands bâtiments,** she lives in one of those tower blocks; **(c)** *Nau* ship, vessel; **b. de guerre,** warship, battleship.

bâtiment-école [bɑtimɑ̃ekɔl] *nm Nau* training ship; (*pl bâtiments-écoles*).

bâtir [bɑtir] *vt* **(a)** (*construire*) to build, to construct; **b. une maison,** to build a house; **(se) faire b. une maison,** to have a house built; **terrain à b.,** building land *or* site; **b. une fortune,** to build up a fortune; **b. sur le sable,** to build on sand; **b. une théorie,** to develop a theory; **homme bien bâti,** well-built man; **un homme bâti comme moi,** a man of my build; **(b)** *Couture* to tack, to baste; **coton à b.,** tacking thread.

bâtisse [bɑtis] *nf* **(a)** (*partie en maçonnerie*) masonry, bricks and mortar; **(b)** (*bâtiment*) large building; **ce n'est qu'une grande b.,** it's a great (ugly) barracks of a place.

bâtisseur, -euse [bɑtisœr, -øz] *n* builder; *Fig* **un b. d'empires,** an empire-builder.

batiste [batist] *nf Tex* batiste, lawn, cambric.

bâton [bɑtɔ̃] *nm* **(a)** stick, staff, rod; **b. ferré,** iron-shod pole, alpenstock; **bâtons de ski,** ski sticks; **b. d'oranger,** orange stick; **b. de chaise,** rung *or* stretcher of a chair; *F* **vie de b. de chaise,** fast living; **b. d'une croix,** staff of a cross; **b. de pavillon,** flagstaff, flagpole; **b. de vieillesse,** support *or* prop of old age; *Can* **aller au b.,** to face the music; **donner des coups de b. à qn,** to beat s.o.; *F* **il faut le faire travailler à coup de b.,** he won't work unless he's pushed; *Fig* **mettre des bâtons dans les roues,** to throw a spanner in the works; **mettre des bâtons dans les roues à qn,** to put a spoke in s.o.'s wheel; *Can* **tenir le mauvais bout du b.,** to get the short end of the stick; **travailler à bâtons rompus,** to work by fits and starts; **conversation à bâtons rompus,** rambling conversation; **b. pastoral,** pastoral staff, crozier; **b. de maréchal,** field-marshal's baton; **b. (d'agent de police),** truncheon; **b. de chef d'orchestre,** conductor's baton; **b. de magicien,** conjurer's wand; **tour de b.,** conjuring trick; (*illégal*) illicit gains, pickings, perks;

(b) b. de rouge (à lèvres), lipstick; **b. de colle/de craie,** stick of glue/chalk;

(c) (*trait*) stroke (*of the pen etc*); **apprendre à un enfant à faire des bâtons,** to teach a child to write; *Typ* **capitale b.,** block letter.

bâtonner [bɑtɔne] *vt Vieilli* to beat, to cudgel, to cane.

bâtonnet [bɑtɔnɛ] *nm* **(a)** small stick; **b. de dynamite,** stick of dynamite; **b. (d'oranger),** orange stick; **(b)** *Biol* rod bacterium; *Anat* rodlike cell; **bâtonnets de la rétine,** retinal rods.

bâtonnier [bɑtɔnje] *nm* = leader of the barristers attached to a French lawcourt.

batraciens [batrasjɛ̃] *nmpl Zool* batrachians.

battage [bataʒ] *nm* **(a)** beating (*of carpet etc*); churning (*of butter*); threshing (*of corn*); **b. d'or,** gold beating; **b. des pieux,** pile driving; **(b)** *F* hype, blatant publicity (campaign); hype, promotion (*of a product, a person*); hard sell (technique); **il faudra faire beaucoup de b. pour vendre le livre,** it will take a lot of publicity to sell the book; **un grand b. publicitaire,** a major promotional campaign.

battant, -ante [batɑ̃, -ɑ̃t] **1** *adj* beating; **pluie battante,** driving *or* pelting rain, downpour; **porte battante,** (*qui claque*) banging door; (*automatique*) swing door; **le cœur b.,** with a pounding heart; **tambour b.,** with drums beating; *Fig* **mener qn tambour b.,** to treat s.o. high-handedly; **mener les choses tambour b.,** to hurry *or* hustle things along; **(tout) b. neuf,** brand new; **à onze heures b.** *ou* **battantes,** on the stroke of eleven.

2 *nm* **(a)** clapper, tongue (*of bell*); lift (*of latch*); *Nau* fly (*of flag*); slab (*of sail*); *Tex* batten, lathe, lay (*of loom*);

(b) leaf, flap (*of table, counter etc*); leaf (*of door, shutter*); door (*of cupboard etc*); **porte à deux battants,** double door, folding doors; **ouvrir les portes à deux battants,** to fling the gates wide open.

3 *n Sp etc* fighter, battler; **c'est une battante, elle va réussir,** she's a fighter, she'll succeed.

batte [bat] *nf* **(a)** (*action*) beating; **b. de l'or,** gold beating; **(b)** (*de tapis etc*) beater; (*maillet*) mallet; (*massue*) club; **(c)** *Cr* (cricket) bat.

battée [bate] *nf* jamb (*of door, window*).

battellement [batɛlmɑ̃] *nm Constr* eaves.

battement [batmɑ̃] *nm* **(a)** beat(ing) (*of drum*); stamp(ing), tap(ping) (*of feet*); clapping (*of hands*); flutter(ing) (*of wings, of eyelids*); flapping (*of sails*); banging (*of door*); rattling (*of shutters*); swing(ing) (*of pendulum*); tick-tock (*of clock*); high kick (*of dancer*); *Cartes* shuffling; *Phys* beating, pulsation (*of oscillations*); **b. de paupières,** blink(ing); **chaque b. de cœur,** every heartbeat; **avoir des battements de cœur,** to suffer from palpitations; *Fig* to be in a flutter;

(b) interval (*between two events etc*); **il y a quelques jours de b. avant d'attaquer le projet,** there are a few days clear before we get stuck into the project; **deux heures de b.,** two clear hours (before starting); **b. de cinq minutes entre les deux trains,** five minutes' wait between the two trains;

(c) shutter catch (*on window*).

batterie [batri] *nf* **(a)** *Mus* beat (*of drum*); roll (*on side-drum*); (*suite de notes*) quick succession of notes; broken chords; (*instruments*) percussion instruments, drums, drum kit; **tenir la b.,** to be on percussion *or* drums; **il joue de la b.,** he plays the drums; **à la b., Jean-Pierre!,** Jean-Pierre on drums;

(b) *Mil* (*number of guns*) battery; (*unit*) troop, *Am* battery; **b. antiaérienne/antichars,** anti-aircraft/antitank battery; **pièces en b.,** guns in firing position *or* in action; **en b.!,** action!; **b. d'instruction,** training battery;

(c) set, collection; battery (*for raising chicks*); **b. de chaudières/de fours à coke,** battery *or* range *or* bank of boilers/of coke ovens; **b. de projecteurs,** bank of spotlights; **b. de cuisine,** (set of) kitchen utensils; *F* one's whole set of medals, all one's gongs; **on lui a fait passer toute une b. de tests,** he was subjected to a whole battery of tests; **poulet de b.,** battery hen; **b. électrique,** electric battery; **b. de rechange,** refill (*for torch etc*).

batteur, -euse [batœr, -øz] **1** *nm* **(a)** *Mus* drummer (*in pop group etc*); *Cr* batsman; *Baseball* batter, striker; (*de chasse*) beater; **b. d'or,** gold beater; **b. en grange,** thresher; *F* **b. de pavé,** loafer, idler; **(b)** *Agr* beater drum (*of threshing machine*); *Culin* **b. électrique,** electric mixer; **b. à œufs,** egg beater *or* whisk; **(c) b. de coton,** cotton breaker *or* shaker. **2** *nf* **batteuse,** *Agr* threshing machine, thresher; *Métal* beater.

battoir [batwar] *nm* (*pour les tapis etc*) (carpet) beater; *Vieilli* (*pour le linge*) washerwoman's beetle; *F* (*grande main*) great paw *or* mitt.

battre [batr] *v* (*prp* **battant**, *pp* **battu**, *pr ind* **je bats** [ba], **tu bats, il bat, n. battons, ils battent**; *p hist* **je battis**, *fu* **je battrai**) **1** *vt* **(a)** to beat, to thrash, to flog; **b. qn à coups de poings/avec une canne,** to punch/cane s.o.; **b. qn comme plâtre,** to beat the living daylights out of s.o.; **il bat sa femme,** he is a wife-beater, he beats his wife; **b. un tapis,** to beat a carpet; **b. le tambour,** to beat the drum; **b. le fer (avec un marteau),** to hammer iron; **b. le fer à froid,** to cold-hammer iron; *Prov* **b. le fer pendant qu'il est chaud,** to strike while the iron is hot; **b. du blé,** to thresh wheat; **b. le beurre,** to churn butter; **battez-moi ces œufs,** beat (up) these eggs for me; **b. l'air en agitant les mains,** to saw the air; **la pluie bat les carreaux,** the rain is beating *or* lashing against the windowpanes; **la mer bat les rochers,** the sea breaks against the rocks; **île battue par les flots,** island washed by the waves; *Mil* **b. une position,** to fire on a position; **b. la mesure,** to beat time; **b. le réveil,** to beat *or* sound (the) reveille; **b. le rappel,** to call to arms; *Rel* **b. sa coulpe,** to beat one's breast (in penitence); **b. la campagne,** to scour *or* comb the countryside; *Méd* to be wandering; **b. un bois/les buissons,** to beat a wood/the bushes; *Nau* **b. un pavillon,** to fly a flag; **b. les cartes,** *Cartes* to shuffle the cards; **la nouvelle nous fit b. le cœur,** we were thrilled at the news;

(b) (*vaincre*) to beat, to defeat; **battre qn à plate(s) couture(s),** to beat *or F* lick s.o. hollow; **il va la b. facilement,** he'll easily beat her; *F* **je te bats, je gagne 1 500F de plus que toi,** I earn 1,500 francs more than you, that's one up for me!

2 *vi* **(a) le cœur lui battait,** his heart was beating; **porte qui bat,** banging door; **voile qui bat dans le vent,** sail flapping in the wind; **le vent faisait b. les volets,** the shutters were banging *or* rattling in the wind; **la montre bat,** the watch is ticking;

(b) b. des mains, to clap one's hands, to applaud; **b. du pied,** (*en cadence*) to tap (with) one's foot; **b. des paupières,** to blink.

3 se battre *vpr* to fight; **se b. avec** *ou* **contre qn,** (*physiquement*) to fight (with *or* against) s.o.; (*verbalement*) to argue *or* fight with s.o.; **se b. en duel,** to fight a duel; **il se bat avec ses devoirs,** he's struggling with his homework; **je m'en bats l'œil,** I couldn't care less, it doesn't matter to me; *F* **voyons, ne vous battez pas, il y en a pour tout le monde,** now don't quarrel *or* fight (over it), there's enough for everyone; **je me suis battu pour obtenir ce visa/avec ce tournevis,** I had a lot of trouble getting this visa/with that screwdriver; **il faut se b. pour réussir,** you've got to fight if you want to succeed.

battu [baty] *adj* beaten; **enfant/femme battu(e),** battered baby/wife; **avoir les yeux battus,** to have rings *or* circles round one's eyes; **un air** *ou* **regard de chien b.,** a hangdog look; **S.O.S. femmes battues,** ≈ battered wives' helpline; **armée battue,** defeated army; **ne pas se tenir pour b.,** to not admit defeat; **fer b.,** wrought iron; **or b.,** beaten gold; **chemin b.,** trodden path; *Tennis* **terrains en terre battue,** clay courts; **jouer sur la terre battue,** to play on clay; **suivre les sentiers battus** *ou* **le chemin b.,** to follow the beaten track; **œuf b. en neige,** stiffly beaten egg white; (*danse*) **pas b.,** pas battu.

battue [baty] *nf* battue, beat.

batture [batyr] *nf Can* sandbank.

bau, -aux [bo] *nm Nau* beam; **maître b.,** midship beam.

baud [bo] *nm Télécom Ordinat* baud; **à (une vitesse de) 1200 bauds,** at (a speed of) 1200 baud.

baudet [bodɛ] *nm* **(a)** (he-)ass, donkey; **(b)** *Menuis* (sawyer's) trestle, sawpit horse.

baudrier [bodrije] *nm* crossbelt, shoulder belt; *Sp* **b. d'escalade,** climbing harness; *Astron* **le B. d'Orion,** Orion's belt.

baudroie [bodrwa] *nf* (*poisson*) monkfish, anglerfish.

baudruche [bodryʃ] *nf* bladder; **ballon de b.,** balloon; *Fig Péj* front man.

bauge [boʒ] *nf* **(a)** lair, wallow (*of wild boar*); *F* **c'est une vraie b.,** it's a real pigsty; **(b)** *Constr* clay and straw mortar.

baume [bom] *nm* **(a)** balm, balsam; **b. de** *ou* **du Canada,** Canada balsam; *Pharm* **b. de benjoin,** friar's balsam; **(b)** *Litt* balm, consolation; **mettre du b. au cœur de qn,** to console s.o. **(c)** (*plante*) **b. sauvage** *ou* **des champs,** wild mint; **b. vert,** garden mint, spearmint.

baumier [bomje] *nm* (*arbre*) balsam (tree).

baux *voir* **BAIL, BAU.**

bauxite [boksit] *nf Minér* bauxite.

bavard, -arde [bavar, -ard] **1** *adj* **(a)** talkative, garrulous, *Am* gabby; **il est b. comme une pie,** he'd talk the hind leg off a donkey; **une analyse bavarde,** a wordy analysis; **(b)** (*indiscret*) indiscreet, gossiping. **2** *n* **(a)** (*parleur etc*) chatterbox; **(b)** (*personne indiscrète*) gossip, *F* blabbermouth.

bavardage [bavardaʒ] *nm* **(a)** (*action*) chattering, nattering; (*commérage*) gossiping; **un b. continuel,** a continuous chattering; **envoyé au coin pour b.,** sent into the corner for talking in class; **(b)** (*paroles*) chatter, natter; (*commérage*) gossip, tittle-tattle; **ce ne sont que des bavardages,** that is merely gossip.

bavarder [bavarde] *vi* **(a)** (*parloter etc*) to chatter, to natter; **(b)** (*commérer*) to gossip.

bavarois, -oise [bavarwa, -waz] **1** *adj* Bavarian. **2** *n* **B.,** Bavarian. **3** *nf Culin* **bavaroise,** Bavarian cream.

bavasser [bavase] *vi Can* to tell tales.

bave [bav] *nf* slaver, dribble; slobber (*of dog*); slime (*of snail*); froth, foam (*of horse, of mad dog*); spittle (*of toad*); *Fig* spiteful talk, mudslinging.

baver [bave] **1** *vi* to dribble, to slobber; (*d'un chien enragé*) to foam at the mouth; (*of pen*) to run; (*of ink*) to smudge; *F* **cela me fait b. de jalousie/de rage/d'admiration,** it makes me drool with *or* green with envy/makes me hopping mad/leaves me speechless with admiration; *F* **en b.,** to have a rough time of it; **elle m'en a fait b.!,** she gave me a rough time. **2** *vt F* **en b. des ronds de chapeaux,** to have eyes like saucers.

bavette [bavɛt] *nf* **(a)** (baby's) bib, feeder; bib (*of overalls etc*); **(b)** *Culin* **b. d'aloyau,** undercut of the sirloin; **dans la b. s'il vous plaît,** from the flank please.

baveux, -euse [bavø, -øz] **1** *adj* dribbling, slobbery (*mouth*); **omelette baveuse,** moist *or* runny omelette; *Typ* **lettres baveuses,** blurred *or* smeared letters. **2** *n Can* (*morveux*) pain, pest.

Bavière [bavjɛr] *nf* Bavaria.

bavocher [bavɔʃe] *vi* to blur, to smear; *Typ etc* to mackle.

bavochure [bavɔʃyr] *nf* blur, smear; *Typ* mackle.

bavoir [bavwar] *nm* (baby's) bib.

bavure [bavyr] *nf* **(a)** *Métal* burr, wire edge (*of casting etc*); barb (*of metal*); **(b)** smudge, smear; *Typ* mackle; (*erreur*) slip-up, mistake; **sans bavure(s),** (*used adjectively*) faultless; *Fig* impeccable; (*used adverbially*) faultlessly; *Fig* impeccably; **un coup sans b.,** (*cambriolage etc*) a perfect job; **les bavures de la police,** police misconduct.

bayer [baje] *vi* (**je baye, baie, n. bayons; je bayerai, baierai**) **b. aux corneilles,** to stand gaping.

bazar [bazar] *nm* **(a)** (*foule*) (oriental) bazaar; **(b)** (*magasin*) general shop, store; *F* untidy room *etc*; **de b.,** (of) poor quality, shoddy; **littérature de b.,** pulp literature; **quel b.!,** what a shambles!; **c'est un sacré b.,** it's a hell of a mess!; *F* **tout son b.,** all one's things *or* gear; **et tout le b.,** and all the rest of it, and the whole caboodle.

bazarder [bazarde] *vt F* to get rid of (*sth*); (*jeter*) to chuck out; (*vendre*) to flog, to sell off.

bazooka [bazuka] *nm Mil* bazooka.

B.C.B.G. [besebeʒe] *adj* (*abrév* **bon chic bon genre**) ≈ preppy.

B.C.G. [beseʒe] *nm Méd* B.C.G..

bd *abrév* **boulevard.**

B.D. [bede] *nf* (*abrév* **bande dessinée**) comic (strip); **lire des B.D.,** to read comics; **aimer la B.D.,** to like comics.

B. de F. *abrév* **Banque de France.**

bê [bɛ] *int* baa.

beagle [bigl] *nm* beagle.

béant [beɑ̃] *adj* (wide) open; gaping (*wound*); yawning (*chasm*); **regarder qch bouche béante,** to stare open-mouthed at sth; **les yeux béants,** wide-eyed.

béarnais, -aise [bearnɛ, -ɛz] **1** *adj* Béarn; (*person*) from the Béarn; *Culin* **sauce béarnaise,** béarnaise (sauce). **2** *nf Culin* **béarnaise,** béarnaise (sauce). **3** *n* **B.,** inhabitant of Béarn.

béat [bea] *adj Rel* blessed; (*plein de satisfaction*) self-satisfied, smug; **sourire b.,** self-satisfied smile.

béatement [beatmɑ̃] *adv* (*sourire*) smugly.

béatification [beatifikasjɔ̃] *nf* beatification, (*of martyr etc*).

béatifier [beatifje] *vt* (*pr sub & impf* **n. béatifiions, v. béatifiiez**) *Rel* to beatify (*s.o.*).

béatifique [beatifik] *adj Rel* beatific (*vision*).

béatitude [beatityd] *nf* **(a)** *Rel* beatitude; **les (huit) béatitudes,** the Beatitudes; **(b)** (*bonheur parfait*) bliss.

beatnik [bitnik] *adj & n* beatnik.

beau [bo], **bel** [bɛl], *f* **belle** [bɛl] (*the form* **bel** *is used before m sing nouns beginning with a vowel or a mute* **h**; *in the expression* **bel et bien**; *in* **Charles le Bel** *and* **Philippe le Bel**; *occ as in* **un bel et charmant enfant**) **1** *adj* **(a)** (*physiquement*) good-looking; (*femme, enfant*) beautiful; (*homme*) handsome; **un bel homme,** a handsome *or* good-looking man; **une belle femme,** a beautiful woman; **le b. sexe,** the fair sex; **ça n'est pas b. à voir,** that's not a pretty sight; **de beaux arbres,** beautiful *or* fine trees; *Hist* **Philippe le Bel,** Philip the Fair; **la mer est belle,** the sea is beautiful; (*calme*) the sea is calm; **nous avons eu (du) b. temps,** we had fine weather; **ami des beaux jours,** fairweather friend; **un (de ces) beau(x) jour(s),** one (of these) fine day(s); **et un b. jour, il est arrivé,** then one (fine) day, he arrived;

(b) (*moralement*) fine; **de beaux sentiments,** fine *or* noble feelings; **belle action,** fine deed; **une belle vie,** a full life; **trouver une belle mort,** to die a glorious death; *F* **avoir le b. rôle,** to be sitting pretty; **cela n'est pas b. de votre part,** that was unworthy of you; *F* **ce n'est pas b. de parler la bouche pleine,** it's not polite to speak with your mouth full; **il est b. joueur,** he's a good loser;

(c) (*excellent*) excellent, fine; **une belle page de littérature,** a fine piece of writing; **b. danseur,** excellent dancer; *Prov* **les beaux esprits se rencontrent,** great minds think alike; **c'est un b. parleur,** he's a good speaker; (*il est enjôleur*) he's got a smooth tongue, *F* he's got the gift of the gab; **un b. talent,** a promising *or* talented *or* gifted artist, writer *etc*; **20 ans! le bel âge!,** twenty — a great age to be!; **un bel âge,** a ripe old age; **belle santé,** good health; **belle occasion,** good *or* fine opportunity; **il a une belle situation,** he has an excellent job; **c'est une belle histoire,** it's a beautiful story; **nous avons vu un b. match,** we saw a fine match; **oh la belle balle!,** what a lovely shot!; **oh la belle bleue!,** (*à un feu d'artifice*) what a lovely blue (colour)!; **c'est trop b. pour être vrai,** it's too good to be true; **ce serait trop b.!,** that would be too much (to hope for)!; **le plus b. jour de ma vie,** the best day of my life; *Cartes* **avoir (un) b. jeu,** to have good cards *or* a good hand;

(d) (*élégant*) smart, spruce; **un b. monsieur,** a smartly dressed man; **le b. monde,** society, the fashionable set, the in crowd; **se faire b.,** to smarten oneself up, **vous voilà b.!,** you DO look smart!

(e) *Iron* **le bel avantage, ma foi!,** well, that's a great advantage!; **tout cela est fort b. mais ...,** that's all very fine *or* well but ...; **vous avez fait du b. travail!,** you HAVE done well!;

(f) (*intensive*) **au b. milieu de la rue,** right in the middle of the road; **il y a b. temps qu'il est parti,** he left a long time *or* ages ago; **une belle tranche de tarte,** a nice slice of tart; **une belle paie,** a good salary, good wages; **c'est une belle sole,** that's a lovely piece of sole; **belle fortune,** large *or* handsome *or* tidy fortune; **b. poulet,** good-sized *or* sizeable chicken; *Fig* **une belle femme,** a fine figure of a woman;

(g) (*mauvais*) fine; **une belle congestion pulmonaire,** a bad attack of pneumonia; **belle correction,** good thrashing; **b. tapage,** terrific din *or* racket; **un b. gâchis,** a fine mess; **son bras est dans un bel état,** his arm is in an awful state; **j'ai eu une belle peur,** I had an awful fright; *Arg* **un b. salaud,** a real *or* regular bastard;

(h) bel et bien, entirely, well and truly; **il est bel et bien venu,** he really did come; **vous voilà bel et bien grand-père!,** so you've actually become a grandfather!;

(i) tout b.!, steady (on)!, gently!;

(j) de plus belle, all the more, (even) more *or* worse than ever; **il recommença de plus belle,** he began again worse than ever;

(k) l'échapper belle, to have a narrow escape *or* a close shave;

(l) il ferait b. voir cela, that would be a fine thing to see;

(m) avoir b. faire qch, to do sth in vain; **j'avais b. chercher, je ne trouvais rien,** however hard I looked, I found nothing; **vous avez b. parler,** you can talk until you're blue in the face.

2 *n* **beau, belle (a) une belle,** a beauty, a beautiful woman; **la Belle et la Bête,** Beauty and the Beast; **la Belle au bois dormant,** the Sleeping Beauty; **allez ma belle, ça suffit,** now that's quite enough, my dear;

(b) un vieux b., an old roué; **faire le b.,** (*of dog*) to sit up and beg; *Arch* **un b.,** a dandy, a beau, *Am* a buck.

3 *nm* **(a) le b.,** the beautiful; **l'amour du b.,** love of beauty; **le b., le bien et le vrai,** beauty, goodness and truth;

(b) le b. de l'histoire c'est que ..., the best part of the story is that ...; **mais le plus b., c'est que ...,** but the best bit is ...; *F* **c'est du b.!,** that was very clever, wasn't it?;

(c) *Météo* fine weather; **le temps est au b. (fixe),** the weather is fine *or* is set fair; *Fig* **avoir l'humeur au b. fixe,** to be permanently in a good mood;

(d) (*choses belles*) beautiful things; **ne vouloir que du b.,** to want only *or* nothing but the best.

beaucoup [boku] *adv* (*une grande quantité*) much, a great deal, (a great) many, a lot; **il reste encore b. à faire,** there's still a lot to do; **b. de,** much, a great deal of, a lot of, (a great) many; **avoir b. d'argent,** to have plenty *or* a lot of money; **avec b. de soin,** very carefully; **avoir besoin de b. d'attention/d'eau,** to need a lot of attention/water; **j'en veux b., 20!,** I want a lot, 20!; **il n'en reste pas b.,** (*de la tarte etc*) there's not much left; (*des bonbons etc*) there aren't many left; **y a-t-il b. de champignons cette année? — oui, b./non, pas b.,** are there many mushrooms this year? — yes, there are/no, there aren't; **elle veut b.,** she wants a lot out of life; **c'est déjà b. s'il veut bien** *ou* **qu'il veuille bien vous parler,** it's (quite) something that he condescended to speak to you; **b. pensent que ...,** many people think that ...; **il y est pour b.,** he has had a great deal to do with it; **b. d'entre nous/d'entre vous,** many of us/you; **de b.,** much, by far; **c'est de b. le meilleur,** it's far and away the best, it's the best by a long chalk; **il s'en faut de b. que je sois riche,** I'm far from being rich; **elle vous aime b.,** she is very fond of you, she likes you a lot; **il parle b.,** he talks a lot; **il parle b. trop,** he talks far too much; **je me sens b. mieux,** I feel a lot better; **ambitieuse, elle l'est, et b.,** she's ambitious, very ambitious; **b. moins/plus vite,** a lot *or* much slower/faster; **il est b. plus âgé que sa femme,** he is much older than his wife; **ça te plaît? — pas b.,** do you like it? — not much; **j'y tiens b.,** it means a lot to me; **il a b. voyagé/lu,** he has travelled/read a great deal.

beauf [bof] **1** *nm F* **(a)** brother-in-law; **(b)** *Fig Péj* man who is set in his ways. **2** *adj Fig Péj* **il est très b.,** he's really set in his ways.

beau-fils [bofis] *nm* (*pl beaux-fils*) **(a)** (*gendre*) son-in-law; **(b)** (*après remariage*) stepson.

beau-frère [bofrɛr] *nm* brother-in-law; (*pl beaux-frères*).

beaujolais [boʒɔlɛ] *nm* Beaujolais.

beau-père [bopɛr] *nm* (*pl beaux-pères*) **(a)** (*père du conjoint*) father-in-law; **(b)** (*après remariage*) step- father.

beaupré [bopre] *nm Nau* bowsprit.

beauté [bote] *nf* **(a)** beauty; **être dans toute sa b.,** to be in the flower of one's beauty; **être en b.,** to be looking one's best; **une femme/vue de toute b.,** the loveliest woman/view; *F* **finir en b.,** to end with a flourish *or* in a blaze of glory; **grain de b.,** beauty spot, mole; **des bijoux de toute b.,** magnificent jewels; **institut de b.,** beauty parlour; **produits de b.,** beauty preparations, cosmetics; **la b. du diable,** youthful beauty; *F* **se (re)faire une b.,** to put one's make-up on; **(b)** *F* (*femme*) beauty, beautiful woman; **(c) les beautés artistiques de l'Italie,** the art treasures of Italy; **les beautés touristiques,** the sights.

beaux-arts [bozar] *nmpl* fine arts; **école des b.-a.,** *F* **les B.-A.,** art school (*of university standing*).

beaux-parents [boparɑ̃] *nmpl* parents-in-law, *F* in-laws.

bébé [bebe] *nm* **(a)** baby; **avoir un b.,** to have a baby; **attendre un b.,** to be expecting (a baby); *Fig* **c'est un vrai b., il ne sait rien faire seul,** he's just like a child, he can't do anything for himself; **faire le b.,** to behave childishly *or* like a baby; **(b)** *Com* (baby) doll; **(c)** *F* baby; **oui, mon b.,** yes, duck; **(d) b. gazelle/lapin,** baby gazelle/rabbit.

bébé-éprouvette [bebeepruvɛt] *nm* test-tube baby; (*pl bébés-éprouvette*).

bébelle [bebɛl] *nf Can* (*gadget*) gadget; (*bibelot*) ornament.

bébelleux, -euse [bebɛlø, -øz] *adj Can* gadget *or* ornament mad.

bébête [bebɛt] *adj F* silly, babyish; **rire b.,** giggle, titter.

bec [bɛk] *nm* **(a)** beak, bill (*of bird*); snout, beak (*of certain fishes etc*); **au b. long/court/jaune,** long-/short-/yellow-billed; **coup de b.,** peck; **donner un coup de b. à qn,** to peck s.o.; *F* to have a dig at s.o.; **l'oiseau se fait le b.,** the bird is sharpening its beak;

(b) *F* mouth; **claquer du b.,** to be starving; **fin b.,** gourmet; **être** *ou* **rester le b. dans l'eau,** to be stranded *or* left in the lurch *or* left high and dry; **il n'a pas ouvert le b. de la journée,** he hasn't said a word all day; **avoir la pipe au b.,** to have one's pipe in one's mouth; **ferme ton b.!,** shut up!; **clouer** *ou* **clore le b. à qn,** to shut s.o. up; **avoir bon b.,** to have the gift of the gab; **prise de b.,** quarrel, slanging match;

(c) nose (*of tool*); nozzle (*of tube*); lip (*of jug*); spout (*of coffee pot*); peak (*of bicycle saddle*); mouthpiece (*of clarinet*); *Av* **b. d'attaque,** leading edge (*of wing*); **b. de plume,** pen nib; **b. à gaz,** gas jet *or* burner; **b. Bunsen,** Bunsen burner; *Arg* **tomber sur un b. (de gaz),** to come a cropper;

(d) *Géog* (*nom de localité*) bill; **le B. de Portland,** Portland Bill.

bécane [bekan] *nf F* bike.

bécarre [bekar] *Mus* **1** *adj* natural (*sign*); **mi b.,** E natural. **2** *nm* natural.

bécasse [bekas] *nf* **(a)** (*oiseau*) **b. (des bois),** woodcock; **b. de mer,** oystercatcher; **(b)** *F* (*idiote*) stupid girl; **c'est une petite b.,** she's a little idiot.

bécasseau, -eaux [bekaso] *nm* (*échassier*) sandpiper; (*petit de la bécasse*) young woodcock.

bécassine [bekasin] *nf* **(a)** (*oiseau*) snipe; **(b)** *F* (*fille niaise*) naive girl.

bec-croisé [bɛkkrwaze] *nm* (*oiseau*) crossbill.

bec-de-cane [bɛkdəkan] *nm* (*pl becs-de-cane*) **(a)** catch (*in a lock*); **(b)** (*poignée*) (door) handle.

bec-de-lièvre [bɛkdəljɛvr] *nm Méd* harelip; (*pl becs-de-lièvre*).

becfigue [bɛkfig] *nm* (*oiseau*) (garden) warbler; (*fauvette*) blackcap; (*jaseur*) waxwing; (*pipi*) pipit.

bêchage [bɛʃaʒ] *nm* digging, turning over (*of earth*).

béchamel [beʃamɛl] *Culin* **1** *adj* **sauce b.,** béchamel sauce, white sauce. **2** *nf* béchamel sauce, white sauce.

bêche [bɛʃ] *nf* spade.

bêcher [bɛʃe] *vt* **(a)** to dig, to turn over (*earth*); **(b)** *F* to run (*s.o.*) down, to pull (*s.o.*) to pieces.

bêcheur, -euse [beʃœr, -øz] *n F* **(a)** (*critiqueur*) knocker; **(b)** (*snob*) stuck-up person.

bécot [beko] *nm F* kiss, peck.

bécoter [bekɔte] *vt F* to give (*s.o.*) a kiss *or* a peck.

becquée [beke] *nf* beakful, billful; *F* **encore une b.!,** (*to a child*) another little mouthful *or* bite!; **donner la b. à son bébé,** to feed one's baby.

becquerel [bɛk(ə)rɛl] *nm Nucl* becquerel, curie.

becquetance [bɛktɑ̃s] *nf Arg* grub.

becqueter [bɛkte] *vt* **(je becquète, n. becquetons; je becquèterai)** (*of bird*) to peck at (*sth*); *Arg* (*d'une personne*) to eat; **il n'y a rien à b.,** there's no grub.

bectance [bɛktɑ̃s] *nf Arg* grub.

becter [bɛkte] *vt* = **BECQUETER.**

bedaine [bədɛn] *nf F* (pot)belly, paunch; **il a une grosse b.,** he has a big pot belly *or* paunch; **avoir de la b.,** to be pot-bellied *or* paunchy.

bed and breakfast [bɛdɛ̃dbrɛkfast] *nm* bed and breakfast; **louer un b. and b.,** to stay in a bed and breakfast *or F* in a B and B.

bédane [bedan] *nm* mortise, (cold) chisel.

bédé [bede] *nf F* comic strip.

bedeau, -eaux [bədo] *nm Rel* verger.

bédéphile [bedefil] *n F* comic(s) fan.

bedon [bədɔ̃] *nm F* (pot)belly, paunch.

bedonnant [bədɔnɑ̃] *adj F* pot bellied.

bedonner [bədɔne] *vi F* to get *or* develop a paunch.

bédouin, -ouine [bedwɛ̃, -win] *n* bedouin.

bée [be] **1** *adj* **bouche b.,** agape; **rester bouche b. devant qch,** to stand gaping *or* open-mouthed in front of sth; **j'en suis resté bouche b.,** it staggered me, it left me open-mouthed in astonishment; **son culot me laisse bouche b.,** I am staggered by his cheek; **regarder qch bouche b.,** to gape at sth. **2** *nf* mill leat, *Am* flume.

béer [bee] *vi Litt* **(a) b. d'étonnement,** to stand open-mouthed in astonishment; **(b)** (*rêvasser*) to daydream.

beffroi [befrwa] *nm* **(a)** (*tour*) belfry; **(b)** (*cloche*) (alarm) bell (*hung in belfry*); **sonner le b.,** to sound the alarm.

bégaiement [begɛmɑ̃] *nm* **(a)** (*pathologique*) stammering, stuttering; **(b)** lispings (*of baby*); **(c)** *Fig* **bégaiements,** early attempts, tentative beginnings.

bégayant [begɛjɑ̃] *adj* (*involontairement*) stuttering, stammering; *Fig & Litt* hesitant, faltering.

bégayer [begeje] *v* (**je bégaye, bégaie, n. bégayons; je bégayerai, bégaierai**) **1** *vi* **(a)** (*pathologiquement*) to stutter, to stammer; **homme qui bégaie,** man with a stammer; **(b)** (*of babies*) to lisp. **2** *vt* **b. une excuse,** to stammer out an excuse.
bégayeur, -euse [begɛjœr, -øz] *adj* stuttering, stammering.
bégonia [begɔnja] *nm* (*plante*) begonia.
bègue [bɛg] **1** *adj* stuttering, stammering. **2** *n* stutterer, stammerer.
bégueule [begœl] **1** *adj* prudish; **ne sois pas b.,** don't be prudish, don't be a prude. **2** *nf* prude.
béguin [begɛ̃] *nm* **(a)** *F* **avoir le b. pour qn,** to have a crush on s.o.; *Arg* **c'est mon b.,** I've got a thing about him *or* her; **(b)** bonnet (*for baby etc*); hood (*of beguine nun*).
béguinage [beginaʒ] *nm Rel* beguine convent.
béguine [begin] *nf Rel* beguine (nun).
bégum [begɔm] *nf* begum.
behaviorisme [bia(e)vjɔrism] *nm Psy* behaviourism.
behavioriste [bia(e)vjɔrist] *Psy* **1** *adj* behaviourist(ic). **2** *n* behaviourist.
beige [bɛʒ] *adj & nm* beige.
beigne¹ [bɛɲ] *nf Arg* blow, slap, clout; **donner** *ou* **flanquer une b. à qn,** to give s.o. a clip on the ear.
beigne² *nm Région & Can* doughnut, *Am* donut.
beignet [bɛɲɛ] *nm* **(a)** fritter; **b. de** *ou* **aux pommes,** apple fritter; **b. de crevettes,** prawn cracker; (*in batter*) prawn fritter; **(b)** (*au sucre*) doughnut.
bel¹ [bɛl] *nm* bel.
bel² *voir* **BEAU**.
bélandre [belɑ̃dr] *nf* canal barge.
bêlant [bɛlɑ̃] *adj* (*troupeau etc*) bleating; *Fig* bleating, moaning; **un orateur b.,** a bleating speaker.
bel canto [bɛlkɑ̃to] *nm Mus* bel canto.
bêlement [bɛlmɑ̃] *nm* bleating; *Fig* **les bêlements des politiciens,** politicians' bleatings.
bélemnite [belɛmnit] *nf* (*fossile*) belemnite.
bêler [bele] *vi* to bleat; *Fig* **qu'est-ce que vous avez à b. comme ça?,** what on earth are you bellyaching *or* bleating about?
belette [bəlɛt] *nf* weasel.
belge [bɛlʒ] **1** *adj* Belgian; **histoire b.,** *Br* ≈ Irish joke; *Can* ≈ Newfie joke. **2** *n* **B.,** Belgian.
belgicisme [bɛlʒisism] *nm* Belgian word *or* expression.
Belgique [bɛlʒik] *nf* Belgium.
bélier [belje] *nm* **(a)** ram; **(b)** *Arch* battering ram; **(c)** *Constr* **b. (à pilotage),** pile driver, ram(mer); **b. mécanique,** bulldozer; **(d) b. hydraulique,** hydraulic ram; **(e)** *Astron Astrol* **le B.,** the Ram, Aries; **Marie est un B.,** Marie is an Aries.
bélière [beljɛr] *nf* **(a)** clapper ring (*of bell*); ring (*of watch etc*); **(b)** sheep bell (*of the bell-wether*).
belladone [beladɔn] *nf* (*plante*) belladonna, deadly nightshade.
bellâtre [belɑtr] *nm Péj* smoothie.
belle [bɛl] **1** *adj voir* **BEAU**. **2** *nf* **(a)** *Sp* deciding game *or* match; *Cartes* rubber game; **jouer** *ou* **faire la b.,** *Sp* to play the deciding game *or* match; *Cartes* to play the rubber game; **(b)** *Nau* waist (*of ship*); **en b.,** abeam; **(c)** *F* **se faire la b.,** to escape; to break out (*of prison*); **(d)** *F* **il en dit de belles,** he really comes out with them!; **j'en ai entendu de belles sur votre compte,** I've heard some nice things about you!; **vous en avez fait une b.!,** you've put your foot in it!
belle-dame [bɛldam] *nf* (*pl belles-dames*) **(a)** (*plante*) deadly nightshade; **(b)** (*insecte*) painted lady (butterfly).
belle-de-jour [bɛldəʒur] *nf* (*plante*) convolvulus, bindweed; (*pl belles-de-jour*).
belle-de-nuit [bɛldənɥi] *nf* (*pl belles-de-nuit*) **(a)** (*plante*) marvel of Peru, four o'clock; **(b)** *F* prostitute, lady of the night.
belle-doche [bɛldɔʃ] *nf F* mother-in-law; (*pl belles-doches*).
belle-famille [bɛlfamij] *nf* wife's family, husband's family, *F* in-laws; (*pl belles-familles*).
belle-fille [bɛlfij] *nf* (*pl belles-filles*) **(a)** (*épouse du fils*) daughter-in-law; **(b)** (*après remariage*) stepdaughter.
bellement [bɛlmɑ̃] *adv Arch* well and truly; **il est b. en prison,** he's well and truly in prison.
belle-mère [bɛlmɛr] *nf* (*pl belles-mères*) **(a)** (*mère du conjoint*) mother-in-law; **(b)** (*après remariage*) stepmother.
belle-sœur [bɛlsœr] *nf* sister-in-law; (*pl belles-sœurs*).
bellicisme [belisism] *nm* bellicosity, warmongering.
belligérance [beliʒerɑ̃s] *nf* belligerence.
belligérant, -ante [beliʒerɑ̃, -ɑ̃t] **1** *adj* belligerent. **2** *n* belligerent, combatant.
belliqueux, -euse [belikø, -øz] *adj* warlike, bellicose (*nation etc*); aggressive, quarrelsome (*person etc*); **humeur belliqueuse,** aggressive mood; **tenir des propos b.,** to speak aggressively.
belote [bəlɔt] *nf Cartes* belote; = pinochle; *F* **faire une b.,** to play belote.
belouga [beluga] *nm,* **beluga** [belyga] *nm* **(a)** (*mammifère*) beluga, white whale; **(b)** (*yacht*) cruising yacht.
belvédère [bɛlvedɛr] *nm* **(a)** (*construction*) belvedere, gazebo; **(b)** (*sur un site naturel*) viewpoint.
Belzébuth [bɛlzebyt] *nm Bible* Beelzebub.
bémol [bemɔl] *nm Mus* flat; **clarinette en si b.,** B-flat clarinet; *Fig* **mettre un b. à ses critiques,** to tone down one's criticism; *Fig F* **je te prie de mettre un b.,** please turn down the volume.
bémoliser [bemɔlize] *vt Mus* to flatten (*note*), to mark (*note*) with a flat, *Am* to flat (*note*).
ben [bɛ̃] *adv Arg* = **BIEN**; **b. oui!,** why, yes!; **b. voilà, euh ...,** yeah, well, er ... .
bénarde [benard] *nf* pin key lock, double-sided lock.
bénédicité [benedisite] *nm* grace (*before meal*); **dire le b.,** to say grace.
bénédictin, -ine [benediktɛ̃, -in] *Rel* **1** *adj* Benedictine (*monk, nun*); **un vrai b.,** a scholar; **un travail de b.,** a work of painstaking scholarship. **2** *n* Benedictine (monk, nun). **3** *nf* **bénédictine,** (*liqueur*) Benedictine.
bénédiction [benediksjɔ̃] *nf* blessing, benediction; consecration (*of church, colours*); **donner la b.,** (*of priest*) to give *or* pronounce the blessing; **il a donné sa b. au projet,** he gave the plan his blessing; **quelle b.!,** what a blessing!, what a godsend!; **il a dit oui, c'est une b.!,** it's a blessing he said yes!
bénef [benɛf] *nm Arg* profit; **petits bénefs,** perks; **faire 200 francs de b.,** to make 200 francs' profit.
bénéfice [benefis] *nm* **(a)** (*gain*) profit, gain; **réaliser de gros bénéfices,** to make large *or* handsome profits; **faites-vous du b.?,** do you make a profit?; **vendre qch à b.,** to sell sth at a profit; **participation aux bénéfices,** profit-sharing; **être intéressé aux bénéfices,** to share in the profits; **petits bénéfices,** perquisites, *F* perks; **(b)** (*avantage*) benefit; **avoir le b. de l'âge,** to have the benefit of age; **on peut lui accorder le b. du doute,** we can give him the benefit of the doubt; *Th Sp* **représentation/match à b.,** benefit performance/match; **concert donné au b. de la Croix-Rouge,** concert in aid of the Red Cross; **(c)** *Jur* **b. du doute,** benefit of the doubt; **(d)** *Rel* living, benefice.
bénéficiaire [benefisjɛr] **1** *adj Com* **solde b.,** profit balance; **compte b.,** account showing a credit balance; **marge b.,** profit margin. **2** *n* recipient, payee (*of cheque etc*); *Rel Jur etc* beneficiary.
bénéficier [benefisje] *vt* (*impf & pr sub* **n. bénéficiions, v. bénéficiiez**) to profit (**de,** by); to have the advantage (**de,** of); to gain (**de,** by, from); **faire b. qn de son expérience,** to give s.o. the benefit of one's experience; **cette carte d'abonnement vous fait b. d'une remise de 20%,** this season ticket entitles you to a 20 per cent reduction; *Jur* **il a bénéficié d'une ordonnance de non-lieu,** he was discharged; **bénéficiant d'une remise de dix pour cent,** subject to a discount of ten per cent.
bénéfique [benefik] *adj* favourable, beneficial (**à,** to); *Astrol* benefic, beneficent (*planet*); **ce séjour à la montagne vous sera b.,** this stay in the mountains will do you good.
Bénélux [benelyks] *nm* Benelux.
benêt [bənɛ] **1** *adj* silly, stupid. **2** *nm* simpleton.
bénévolat [benevɔla] *nm* voluntary service *or* work; **faire du b.,** to do voluntary service.
bénévole [benevɔl] **1** *adj* **(a)** unpaid (*service, work*); **aide b.,** voluntary help; **organisation b.,** voluntary organization; **infirmière b.,** voluntary nurse; **(b)** *Litt* benevolent, kindly, indulgent (*person*). **2** *n* volunteer.
bénévolement [benevɔlmɑ̃] *adv* **(a)** (*sans être payé*) voluntarily; **il travaille b.,** he does voluntary work; **(b)** *Litt* benevolently, kindly, out of kindness.
Bengale [bɛ̃gal] *nm* **(a)** Bengal; **(b) feu de B.,** Bengal light.
Bengali [bɛ̃gali] **1** *adj* Bengali, Bengalese. **2** *nm Ling* Bengali. **3** *n* Bengali.
bénignité [beniɲite] *nf* **(a)** mildness (*of climate, of a disease*); **(b)** *Litt* benignity, kindness.
bénin, -igne [benɛ̃, -iɲ] *adj* **(a)** slight, minor (*accident etc*); **tumeur bénigne,** benign *or* non-malignant tumour; **forme bénigne de (la) rougeole,** mild form of measles;

(b) *Litt* benign, kindly, indulgent (*person, criticism etc*).
béni-oui-oui [beniwiwi] *nm inv F* yes-man.
bénir [benir] *vt* **(a)** to bless (*s.o., a marriage etc*); to glorify, to render thanks to (God); **(que) Dieu vous bénisse!,** (may) (God) bless you!; **le ciel en soit béni!,** thank heaven(s)!; **je bénis tous les jours l'inventeur du lave-vaisselle,** every day I bless the person who invented the dish-washer; **(b)** to consecrate (*church, bread etc*).
bénit [beni] *adj* consecrated, blessed; **pain b.,** consecrated bread, holy bread; **eau bénite,** holy water.
bénitier [benitje] *nm* **(a)** *Rel* holy water basin *or* stoop *or* stoup; (*pour le baptême*) font; **(b)** (*mollusque*) giant clam.
benjamin, -ine [bɛ̃ʒamɛ̃, -in] *n* youngest child, benjamin; **le b. de la famille,** the youngest of the family.
benjoin [bɛ̃ʒwɛ̃] *nm Com* (gum) benzoin, benjamin.
benne [bɛn] *nf Min etc* skip, tub, bucket, truck; scoop (*of crane*); bucket (*of dredger*); (*de ski etc*) (cable) car; **(camion à) b. (basculante),** tip(per) wagon; (*camion*) dumper (*lorry, truck*).
Benoist, Benoît [bənwa] *nm* Benedict.
benoît [bənwa] *adj* smarmy.
benthique [bɛ̃tik] *adj* benthic (*fauna etc*).
benthos [bɛ̃tɔs] *nm* **(a)** benthos; **(b)** (*faune et flore*) benthic flora and fauna.
benzène [bɛ̃zɛn] *nm Ch* benzene.
benzine [bɛ̃zin] *nf* benzine.
benzol [bɛ̃zɔl] *nm Ch* benzol(e).
benzolisme [bɛ̃zɔlism] *nm Méd* benzole poisoning.
béotien, -ienne [beɔsjɛ̃, -jɛn] *adj Péj* philistine.
B.E.P. [beəpe] *nm Scol abrév* **brevet d'études professionnelles.**
B.E.P.C. [beəpese] *nm Scol abrév* **brevet d'études du premier cycle.**
béquille [bekij] *nf* **(a)** *Méd* crutch; **marcher avec des béquilles,** to walk on crutches; **(b)** prop; stand (*of motor cycle*); *Av* tail skid; *Nau* leg, shore, prop; tiller (*of rudder*); **(c)** catch (*in a lock*); (door) handle.
béquiller [bekije] **1** *vt Nau* to shore up, prop up (ship). **2** *vi F Arch* to walk on crutches.
ber [bɛr] *nm voir* **BER(S).**
berbère [bɛrbɛr] **1** *adj* Berber. **2** *nm Ling* Berber. **3** *n* **B.,** Berber.
bercail [bɛrkaj] *nm* fold (*of the Church etc*); **ramener au b. la brebis égarée,** to bring the lost sheep back to the fold; *F* **rentrer au b.,** to go (back) home; (*d'un mari etc qui a abandonné le foyer*) to return to the fold.
berçante [bɛrsɑ̃t] *nf Can* **(chaise) berçante,** rocking chair.
berce [bɛrs] *nf* **(a)** (*plante*) **b. commune,** hogweed; **(b)** *Belg Suisse* cradle.
berceau, -eaux [bɛrso] *nm* **(a)** (*de bébé*) cradle, cot, *Am* crib; **dès le b.,** from the cradle, from birth, from infancy; *Fig* **le b. d'un mouvement populaire,** the birthplace *or* cradle of a popular movement; *F* **il les prend au b.,** he's a baby *or* cradle snatcher; **(b)** *Typ etc* cradle, bed, support; *Mil* cradle (*of gun*); (*treillage*) arbo(u)r, bower; *Aut Av* **b. (du) moteur,** engine mounting; *Archit* **voûte en b.,** barrel vault.
bercelonnette [bɛrsəlɔnɛt] *nf* bassinet, (rocking) cradle.
bercement [bɛrsəmɑ̃] *nm* rocking, lulling.
bercer [bɛrse] *v* (**je berçai(s); n. berçons**) **1** *vt* **(a)** to rock (*a baby*); **bateau bercé par la houle,** boat rocked by the waves; *Fig* **j'ai été bercé là-dedans,** I took it in with my mother's milk; **(b)** to soothe (*grief, s.o.*); **b. qn de promesses,** to delude s.o. with promises. **2 se bercer** *vpr* **se b. d'une illusion/d'un espoir,** to cherish *or* indulge in an illusion/a hope.
berceur, -euse [bɛrsœr, -øz] **1** *adj* soothing, lulling. **2** *nf* **berceuse,** rocking chair; (*chanson*) lullaby, cradle song; *Mus* berceuse.
béret [berɛ] *nm* **b. (basque),** beret.
berge¹ [bɛrʒ] *nf* (steep) bank (*of river, railway track, road*); slope, side (*of valley*).
berge² *nf F* year; **un gosse de six berges,** a kid of six.
berger, -ère [bɛrʒe, -ɛr] **1** *n* shepherd, shepherdess; *Rel* shepherd, pastor; **chien de b.,** sheepdog; **l'étoile du b.,** the evening star. **2** *nm* **(chien) b. allemand,** Alsatian (dog), German shepherd. **3** *nf* **bergère,** wing chair.
bergerette [bɛrʒərɛt] *nf* (*oiseau*) wagtail.
bergerie [bɛrʒəri] *nf* **(a)** (*pour moutons etc*) sheepfold, sheep pen; **(b)** *Beaux-Arts Littér* pastoral (*poem, painting etc*).
bergeronnette [bɛrʒərɔnɛt] *nf* (*oiseau*) wagtail.
béribéri [beriberi] *nm Méd* beriberi; **avoir le b.,** to have beriberi.
berk [bɛrk] *int* yuk!
berkélium [bɛrkeljɔm] *nm Ch* berkelium.
berlander [bɛrlɑ̃de] *vi Can* to dawdle, to waste time *or* words.
Berlin [bɛrlɛ̃] *n* Berlin; **B.-Ouest/-Est,** West/East Berlin.
berline [bɛrlin] *nf Min* truck, tram; *Aut* (four-door) saloon, *Am* sedan; *Arch* berlin(e).
berlingot [bɛrlɛ̃go] *nm* **(a)** (*bonbon*) (boiled) sweet, humbug; **(b)** (pyramid-shaped) carton (*of milk*).
berlinois, -oise [bɛrlinwa, -waz] **1** *adj* of *or* from Berlin. **2** *n* **B.,** Berliner.
berlue [bɛrly] *nf* **avoir la b.,** to be seeing things; (*se faire des illusions*) to delude *or* deceive oneself.
berme [bɛrm] *nf* (*ouvrage*) berm; (foot)path, verge (*by canal, ditch, etc*).
bermuda(s) [bɛrmyda] *nm* Bermuda shorts; **porter un** *ou* **des bermuda(s),** to wear Bermuda shorts.
Bermudes [bɛrmyd] *nfpl* **les (îles) B.,** Bermuda.
bernache [bɛrnaʃ] *nf,* **bernacle** [bɛrnakl] *nf* **(a)** (*crustacé*) barnacle; **(b)** (*oiseau*) barnacle goose, brent goose.
bernardin, -ine [bɛrnardɛ̃, -in] *n* Bernardine, Cistercian (monk, nun).
bernard-l'(h)ermite [bɛrnarlɛrmit] *nm* (*crustacé*) hermit crab, soldier crab.
berne¹ [bɛrn] *nf Arch* tossing in a blanket.
berne² *nf* **(a)** *Nau* **pavillon en b.,** flag at half mast; **(b)** *Mil* **drapeau en b.,** flag furled and craped.
Berne [bɛrn] *n* Bern(e).
berner [bɛrne] *vt* **(a)** (*duper*) to fool, to hoax (*s.o.*); (*ridiculiser*) to ridicule (*s.o.*); **(b)** *Arch* to toss (*s.o.*) in a blanket.
bernicle [bɛrnikl] *nf,* **bernique¹** [bɛrnik] *nf* (*mollusque*) limpet.
bernique² *int F* no go!, nothing doing!
bernois, -oise [bɛrnwa, -waz] **1** *adj* Bernese. **2** *n* **B.,** Bernese.
ber(s) [bɛr] *nm* **(a)** (*charpente*) (launching) cradle; **(b)** *Can* (baby's) cradle, crib.
bertillonnage [bɛrtijɔnaʒ] *nm* Bertillon system (*of anthropometry*).
béryl [beril] *nm Minér* beryl.
béryllium [beriljɔm] *nm Ch* beryllium.
besace [bəzas] *nf Arch* (beggar's) bag; (pilgrim's) scrip.
besaiguë [bəzegy] *nf* **(a)** *Menuis* mortising axe; **(b)** (*marteau*) glazier's hammer.
besant [bəzɑ̃] *nm Archit Hér* bezant.
bésef [bezɛf] *adv Arg* = **BÉZEF.**
besicles [bezikl] *nfpl F* specs; *Arch* spectacles.
bésigue [bezig] *nm Cartes* bezique.
besogne [bəzɔɲ] *nf* (piece of) work, task, job; **se mettre à la b.,** to set to work; **rude b.,** hard job; **aller vite en b.,** to work *or* act quickly; *F* to cut corners; **abattre de la b.,** to get through a lot of work; **voilà de la belle b.!,** here's a pretty kettle of fish *or* a fine mess!; *Fig* **mâcher la b. à qn,** to do someone's work for them.
besogner [bəzɔɲe] *vi Péj* to work hard, to slave, to toil.
besogneux, -euse [bəzɔɲø, -øz] **1** *adj* poor, needy. **2** *n* poor *or* needy person.
besoin [bəzwɛ̃] *nm* **(a)** need, want, necessity, requirement; **pourvoir** *ou* **subvenir aux besoins de qn,** to provide for s.o.'s needs; **si le b. s'en faisait sentir,** if the necessity *or* need arose; **pour le b. de la cause,** for the sake of the cause; **cet enfant a de grands besoins,** this child is very demanding; **un b. de chaleur humaine,** a need for human warmth; *F* **faire ses (petits) besoins,** to relieve oneself, to spend a penny, to go to the loo; **au b.,** if necessary, if need(s) be, *F* at a pinch; **en cas de b.,** in an emergency; **avoir b. de qch/qn,** to need *or* require *or* want sth/s.o.; **j'ai b. de calme,** I need peace and quiet; **j'en ai b. pour lundi,** I need it for Monday; **j'ai grand b. de son aide,** I'm badly in need of *or* I really need his help; **il n'a pas b. de venir lundi,** he needn't come *or* there is no need for him to come on Monday; **(il n'y a, je n'ai) pas b. de dire qu'elle était là,** needless to say *or* it goes without saying that she was there; **elle a b. qu'on lui parle,** she needs someone to talk to; **vous aviez bien b. d'aller lui parler de cela!,** you WOULD go and tell him about that!; *Litt* **il n'est b. d'insister,** no need to insist; **s'il (en) est b., si b. (en) est,** if necessary, if need(s) be;
(b) (*misère*) poverty, indigence; **être dans le b.,** to be in need *or* straitened circumstances; **vieillards dans le b.,** needy *or* impoverished old people.
bessemer [bɛsmɛr] *nm Tech* **(convertisseur) b.,** Bessemer converter.

bestiaire [bɛstjɛr] *nm Littér* bestiary.
bestial, -aux [bɛstjal, -o] *adj* beastly, brutish; **un air b.,** a brutish look; **une souffrance bestiale,** brute suffering.
bestialité [bɛstjalite] *nf* brutishness; (*perversion*) bestiality.
bestiaux [bɛstjo] *nmpl* livestock, cattle; **cinquante b.,** fifty head of cattle.
bestiole [bɛstjɔl] *nf* (*bête*) small *or* tiny animal *or* creature; (*insecte*) insect, *Am* bug.
best-seller [bɛstsɛlœr] *nm* best-seller; (*pl best-sellers*).
bêta¹, -asse [bɛta, -ɑs] *F* **1** *adj* silly, stupid. **2** *n* idiot, nit(wit); **oh le gros b.!,** (*à un enfant*) silly billy!
bêta² [bɛta] *nm* **(a)** (*lettre de l'alphabet grec*) beta; **(b)** *Nucl* **particules/rayons b.,** beta particles/rays.
bêtabloquant [betablɔkɑ̃] *nm Pharm* beta-blocker.
bétail [betaj] *nm* livestock, cattle; **gros b.,** livestock (*including cattle, horses, asses, mules*); **menu** *ou* **petit b.,** smaller livestock; *Fig* **on était traité comme du b.,** we were treated like cattle.
bétaillère [betajɛr] *nf* (*pour bétail*) *& Fig* cattle truck.
bêtatron [bɛtatrɔ̃] *nm Nucl* betatron.
bête [bɛt] **1** *nf* **(a)** animal, beast; **b. à quatre pieds,** four-legged animal *or* beast; **b. à cornes,** horned animal *or* beast; **b. de trait,** draught animal; **les bêtes,** (*on farm*) the livestock; **donner aux bêtes,** to feed the animals; *F* **reprendre du poil de la b.,** (*reprendre le dessus*) to perk up, to pick up; **les bêtes féroces,** wild animals; **une b. sauvage,** a wild animal; **nos amies les bêtes,** our four-legged friends; *Fig* **c'est sa b. noire,** he's *or* it's *etc* his pet hate; **travailler comme une b.,** to work like a slave; *Fig Péj* **b. à concours,** *Br* swot, *Am* grind; **c'est une belle b., ce cheval,** that horse is a fine animal; *F* **tu as vu sa moto, c'est une belle b.!,** have you seen his motorbike?, it's a beauty!; **tu as vu son nouveau mec, c'est une belle b.!,** have you seen her new man?, he's absolutely gorgeous!; **elle m'a regardé comme une b. curieuse,** she looked at me as if I was from another planet;
(b) (*insecte*) insect, *Am* bug; **petites bêtes,** insects; (*nocives*) vermin; **b. à bon Dieu,** *Br* ladybird, *Am* ladybug; **il y a une b. dans ma pomme,** there's a maggot in my apple; *Fig* **chercher la petite b.,** to be over-critical, *F* to nit-pick;
(c) (*l'homme*) **la b. humaine,** the old Adam;
(d) (*idiot*) fool, idiot, nit(wit); **faire la b.,** to pretend to be stupid; (*sans le vouloir*) to act foolishly *or* stupidly.
2 *adj* stupid, silly, foolish; **que je suis b.!,** how silly *or* stupid of me!; **pas si b.!,** I'm *or* she's *etc* not such a fool (as all that)!, not likely!; **c'est vraiment b., j'ai oublié mes clés,** how stupid, I've forgotten my keys; **il n'est pas si b. qu'il en a l'air,** he's not as stupid *or* silly as he looks; **elle est b. comme un âne** *ou* **comme ses pieds,** she's a real idiot *or* fool; **mon Dieu qu'il est b.!,** God he's stupid!; **l'âge b.,** the difficult age; **b. et méchant,** stupid and nasty; **c'est b. comme chou,** it's as easy as pie *or* as anything; *Can* **rester tout b.,** (*décontenancé*) to be stupefied; **une mort b.,** a stupid *or* senseless death.
bétel [betɛl] *nm* (*plante*) betel.
bêtement [bɛtmɑ̃] *adv* stupidly, foolishly, idiotically; **mourir b.,** to die senselessly; **tout b.,** purely and simply.
Bethléem [betleɛm] *nm Bible* Bethlehem.
bêtifiant [betifjɑ̃] *adj* idiotic.
bêtifier [betifje] *v* (*pr sub & impf* **n. bêtifiions, v. bêtifiiez**) **1** *vt* to make (*s.o.*) stupid. **2** *vi* to talk nonsense; (*faire l'idiot*) to play the fool; **quand il parle à un enfant, il bêtifie,** he uses baby-talk to children.
bêtise [betiz] *nf* **(a)** (*imbécillité*) stupidity, silliness; **être d'une b. extrême,** to be exceedingly stupid;
(b) (*chose idiote*) nonsense, absurdity; **dire des bêtises,** to talk nonsense *or Br* rubbish; **quelle b.!,** what nonsense!, how ridiculous!; **se disputer pour des bêtises,** to argue over nothing; **perdre son temps à des bêtises,** to waste one's time on idiotic things; **dépenser tout son argent en bêtises,** to fritter away one's money;
(c) (*gaffe*) blunder, silly *or* stupid mistake; **faire des bêtises,** to play the fool; **faire une grande b.,** to do something extremely stupid *or* silly; **ça c'est une grosse b.,** that is *or* was very stupid; **une b.,** a stupid move; **il ne faudrait pas qu'elle fasse une b.,** we don't want her to do anything silly;
(d) *Can* **bêtises,** (*injures*) insults;
(e) bêtises de Cambrai, *Br* ≈ mint humbugs (*hard mint Br sweets or Am candies*).
béton [betɔ̃] *nm* **(a)** *Constr* concrete; **b. armé,** reinforced concrete; *Fig* **des muscles en b.,** rock-hard muscles; *F* **un alibi en b.,** a cast-iron alibi; **(b)** *Fb* **faire le b.,** to pack the defence; **(c)** *F* **laisse b.,** let it drop!, drop it!
bétonnage [betɔnaʒ] *nm* **(a)** *Constr* concreting; **(b)** *Fb* packing the defence.
bétonner [betɔne] *vt* **(a)** to build with concrete; (*couler du béton sur*) to concrete; **(b)** *Fb* to pack the defence.
bétonneuse [betɔnøz] *nf,* **bétonnière** [betɔnjɛr] *nf* concrete mixer, cement mixer.
bette [bɛt] *nf* (spinach) beet; **b. à carde (blanche), b. à côtes,** seakale beet, Swiss chard.
betterave [bɛtrav] *nf Br* beetroot, *Am* beet; **b. sucrière,** sugar beet; **b. fourragère,** mangel-wurzel, fodder beet.
betteravier, -ière [bɛtravje, -jɛr] **1** *adj* **l'industrie betteravière,** the beet industry. **2** *nm* sugar beet grower.
beuglante [bøglɑ̃t] *nf F* (*cri*) yell; **pousser une b.,** to shout one's head off.
beuglement [bøgləmɑ̃] *nm* (*of cattle*) lowing; (*of bull*) bellow(ing); *F* (*of person*) bawling; (*of radio etc*) blaring.
beugler [bøgle] **1** *vi* (*of cattle*) to low; (*of bull*) to bellow; *F* (*of person*) to bawl; (*of radio etc*) to blare; **pas la peine de b., je t'entends!,** no need to yell, I can hear you! **2** *vt F* **b. une chanson,** to bawl *or* bellow out a song.
beur [bœr] *nm* = North African born in France of immigrant parents.
beurre [bœr] *nm* butter; **b. salé/demi-sel,** salted/slightly salted butter; **b. fondu,** melted butter; **un paquet de b.,** a pack of butter; **une motte de b.,** a lump of butter; **b. de cacao,** cocoa butter; **b. de cacahouètes,** peanut butter; *Culin* **au b.,** with melted butter, cooked in butter; **crème au b.,** butter cream; **b. d'anchois,** anchovy butter; **au b. noir,** with black butter; *F* **avoir un œil au b. noir,** to have a black eye; **c'est entré comme dans du b.,** it went in very easily; *F* **cela compte pour du b.,** that doesn't count; *F* **il a fait son b.,** he's made his packet; **ça mettra du b. dans les épinards,** that will improve matters *or* ease the situation; **elle veut le b. et l'argent du b.,** she wants to have her cake and eat it.
beurrée [bœre] *nf Can* (*tartine*) slice of bread and butter.
beurre-frais [bœrfrɛ] *adj inv* buttercup-yellow.
beurrer [bœre] **1** *vt* to butter (*bread, a dish etc*); *F* **être complètement beurré,** to be plastered *or* sloshed. **2 se beurrer** *vpr Arg* to get plastered *or* sloshed.
beurrerie [bœrri] *nf* **(a)** (*laiterie*) dairy; **(b)** *Ind* the butter industry.
beurrier, -ière [bœrje, -jɛr] **1** *adj* **l'industrie beurrière,** the butter industry; **région beurrière,** butter-producing district. **2** *nm* butter dish.
beuverie [bøvri] *nf* drinking session, *Br F* booze-up.
bévatron [bevatrɔ̃] *nm Nucl* bevatron.
bévue [bevy] *nf* blunder, mistake, slip; **commettre une b.,** to blunder, to make a blunder.
bey [bɛ] *nm* bey.
Beyrouth [berut] *n* Beirut.
bézef [bezɛf] *adv F* **il n'y en a pas b.,** there's not much *or* a lot (of it); there's not many *or* a lot (of them).
bi [bi] *nm Can* **donner** *ou* **faire un bi,** to give a hand, *Br* to muck in (and help).
bi- [bi-] *préf* bi-; **bilatéral/bipartisan/***etc,* bilateral/bipartisan/*etc.*
biacide [biasid] *adj & nm Ch* diacid.
biais [bjɛ] **1** *adj Archit* oblique, sloping, slanting; **voûte biaise,** skew(ed) arch.
2 *nm* **(a)** skew (*of tool, of arch*); slant (*of wall*); **en b.,** on the slant, slantwise, at an angle, aslant, askew; *Couture* **tailler un tissu dans le b.,** to cut material on the bias;
(b) (*détour*) (indirect) manner, means (*of doing sth*); *Péj* expedient; **aborder de b. une personne/une question,** to approach a person/a question in a roundabout way *or* indirectly; **regarder qn de b.,** to look sideways *or* askance at s.o.;
(c) (*moyen*) way; **par quel b. envisager la chose?,** from what angle should we look at the issue?; **il faut considérer ce problème par deux b.,** we must look at the question from two angles; **il a pu dénicher cette maison par le b. de son voisin,** he found the house through his neighbour;
(d) *Couture* bias binding.
biaiser [bjeze] *vi* **(a)** (*obliquer*) to be on the slant; to edge off, to turn off *or* away (*towards sth*); **(b)** *Fig* to dodge the issue; **pour éviter cela, il va falloir b.,** we'll have to manoeuvre to avoid that.
biannuel, -elle [bianɥɛl] *adj* biannual.
biathlon [biatlɔ̃] *nm Sp* biathlon.
bibasique [bibazik] *adj Ch* dibasic.
bibelot [biblo] *nm* curio, knick-knack, trinket.
biberon [bibrɔ̃] *nm* (baby's feeding) bottle; **nourrir** *ou*

élever un enfant au b., to bottle-feed a child; **je ne les prends pas au b.,** I'm not a cradle snatcher.
biberonner [bibrɔne] *vi F* to booze, to tipple.
bibi [bibi] *nm* **(a)** *Arg* I, me, myself, yours truly, number one; **et ça, c'est pour b.,** that's for yours truly; **(b)** *F* (woman's) hat.
bibine [bibin] *nf F* tasteless drink; **c'est de la b. cette bière,** this beer is tasteless.
bibite [bibit] *nf Can Arg* bug, insect.
bible [bibl] *nf* bible; **la B.,** the Bible; **la b. du bricoleur,** the do-it-yourselfer's bible.
bibliobus [bibliɔbys] *nm* mobile library, *Am* bookmobile.
bibliographe [bibliɔgraf] *n* bibliographer.
bibliographie [bibliɔgrafi] *nf* bibliography.
bibliographique [bibliɔgrafik] *adj* bibliographic(al).
bibliomane [bibliɔman] *n* bibliomaniac, book lover *or* collector.
bibliomanie [bibliɔmani] *nf* bibliomania, book collecting.
bibliophile [bibliɔfil] *n* bibliophile.
bibliophilie [bibliɔfili] *nf* love of books, bibliophily.
bibliothécaire [bibliɔtekɛr] *n* librarian.
bibliothéconomie [bibliɔtekɔnɔmi] *nf* library science.
bibliothèque [bibliɔtɛk] *nf* **(a)** (*bâtiment, salle*) library; **b. de prêt,** lending library; **b. municipale,** municipal *or* public library; **(b)** (*meuble*) bookcase; **(c)** (*série*) *&* *Ordinat* library; **la b. verte/rose,** = series of books aimed at 7 to 15 year olds/at 5 to 7 year olds; *F* **c'est une b. ambulante** *ou* **vivante,** he's a walking encyclopaedia.
biblique [biblik] *adj* biblical.
bic ® [bik] **1** *adj* Bic ®; **stylo b.,** ballpoint pen, *Br* Biro ®; **pointe b.,** ballpoint. **2** *nm* ballpoint, *Br* Biro ®.
bicaméral, -aux [bikameral, -o] *adj Pol* bicameral (*system etc*).
bicaméralisme [bikameralism] *nm,* **bicamérisme** [bikamerism] *nm Pol* bicameral system.
bicarbonate [bikarbɔnat] *nm Ch* bicarbonate.
bicentenaire [bisɑ̃tnɛr] *nm* bicentenary, *Am* bicentennial.
bicéphale [bisefal] *adj & nm* bicephalous, two-headed (animal).
bicéphalisme [bisefalism] *nm Pol* dual system (of government).
biceps [bisɛps] *Anat* **1** *adj* biceps (*muscle*). **2** *nm* biceps; *F* **avoir du** *ou* **des b.,** to be muscular.
biche [biʃ] *nf* **(a)** (*mammifère*) hind, doe; **ventre de b.,** reddish-white; **table à pieds de b.,** table with cabriole legs; **aux yeux de b.,** doe-eyed; **(b)** *F* **ma b.,** my darling.
bicher [biʃe] *vi F* **(a)** (*aller bien*) **ça biche?,** how's things?; **ça biche, les affaires?,** how's business?; **(b)** (*se réjouir*) to be delighted, to be pleased as punch.
bichette [biʃɛt] *nf* **(a)** (*mammifère*) young *or* small hind; **(b)** *F* **ma b.,** my darling, my dear.
bichlorure [biklɔryr] *nm Ch* bichloride, dichloride.
bichon, -onne [biʃɔ̃, ɔn] *n* **(a)** lap-dog, toy dog; **(b)** *F* **mon b.,** my darling, my love, my dear.
bichonner [biʃɔne] **1** *vt* **(a)** (*préparer*) to make (*s.o.*) spruce *or* smart; **(b)** (*soigner*) to mollycoddle (*s.o.*). **2 se bichonner** *vpr* to spruce oneself up.
bichromate [bikrɔmat] *nm Ch* bichromate, dichromate.
bichromie [bikrɔmi] *nf* two-colour printing.
bicolore [bikɔlɔr] *adj* bicolour(ed), two-tone.
biconcave [bikɔ̃kav] *adj* biconcave.
biconvexe [bikɔ̃vɛks] *adj* biconvex.
bicoque [bikɔk] *nf* dilapidated house, *F* dump.
bicorne [bikɔrn] **1** *adj Biol Anat* bicorn(u)ate. **2** *nm* cocked hat.
bicot [biko] *nm* **(a)** (*biquet*) kid; **(b)** *F* (*terme injurieux*) wog.
bicross [bikrɔs] *nm Sp* cyclo-cross bicycle; **faire du b.,** to cyclo-cross, to go cyclo-crossing.
biculturalisme [bikyltyralism] *nm* biculturalism.
biculturel, -elle [bikyltyrel] *adj* bicultural.
bicuspide [bikyspid] *adj* bicuspid, bicuspidate.
bicyclette [bisiklɛt] *nf* bicycle; **aller à** *ou F* **en b.,** to ride a bicycle, to cycle; **faire de la b.,** to go cycling, to cycle.
bidasse [bidas] *nm Mil Arg* squaddie, *US* G.I..
bide [bid] *nm Arg* **(a)** belly; **c'est du b.,** it's a load of rubbish *or* codswallop; **(b) la pièce/le film a fait un b.,** the play's/film's a flop; **un b. complet,** a total flop.
bidet [bidɛ] *nm* **(a)** bidet (*de toilette*); **(b)** *Vieilli* pony, nag.
bidirectionnel, -elle [bidirɛksjɔnɛl] *adj Ordinat* bidirectional.
bidoche [bidɔʃ] *nf Arg* meat.
bidon [bidɔ̃] **1** *nm* can, tin, drum (*for oil etc*); *Mil etc* water bottle; *Arg* belly; **b. à lait,** milk churn; **se remplir le b.,** to stuff oneself; *Arg* **c'est du b.,** it's a load of rubbish *or* codswallop; *Arg* **c'est pas du b.,** it's the honest truth. **2** *adj Arg* fake, phoney.
bidonnant [bidɔnɑ̃] *adj Arg* hilarious, screamingly funny; **c'est b.,** it's a scream.
bidonner (se) [səbidɔne] *vpr Arg* to laugh one's head off.
bidonville [bidɔ̃vil] *nm* shantytown.
bidouiller [biduje] *vt* to patch (*sth*) up; *Ordinat* to patch (*program*).
bidule [bidyl] *nm Arg* thing, thingummy, whatsit.
bief [bjɛf] *nm* **(a)** (*portion du cours d'eau*) (canal) reach, level; **b. d'amont,** head bay; **b. d'aval** *ou* **de fuite,** tail bay, aft bay; **(b)** (*d'un moulin*) millcourse, millrace.
bielle [bjɛl] *nf Tech* (*sous tension*) (tie) rod; (*sous compression*) push rod, crank arm; *Aut* **b. d'accouplement,** track link; **tête de b.,** crank head; (*de moteur*) big end; **pied de b.,** crosshead; (*de moteur*) little end.
biellette [bjɛlɛt] *nf MecE* (*petite bielle*) small rod.
bien [bjɛ̃] **1** *adv* **(a)** (*convenablement*) well; **livre b. écrit,** well written book; **il parle b.,** he is a good speaker, he speaks well; **on y mange très b.,** you eat very well there; **aller** *ou* **se porter b.,** to be well *or* in good health; **tout va b.,** all's well, everything's O.K. *or* fine; *Iron* **voilà qui commence b.,** that's a fine start!; **vous arrivez joliment b.,** you've come just in the nick of time; **b.!,** good!; (*ça suffit*) that's enough!, that will do!; (*entendu*) all right!; **très b.!, fort b.!,** very good!, well done!; (*agreeing with speaker*) hear, hear!; **écoutez b. ceci,** now, listen carefully to this; **il faut b. les soigner** *ou* **les soigner b.,** they must be well looked after;
(b) (*moralement*) **vous avez b. fait,** you did the right thing; **se conduire b.,** to behave; **c'est b. fait (pour lui),** it serves him right; **voilà qui est b. dit,** well said!; **tu ferais b. de te méfier,** you would do well to beware;
(c) (*emphatic*) indeed, really, quite; **c'est b. cela,** that's right; **il y a b. deux ans que je ne l'ai vue,** it's at least *or* it must be two years since I (last) saw her; **je l'ai regardé b. en face,** I looked him full in the face; **être b. d'accord,** to be entirely in agreement; **b. à vous,** (*in letter*) yours; **je veux b. le croire,** I can quite believe it *or* him; **qu'est-ce que ça peut b. être?,** what ever *or* what on earth can it be?; **c'est b. lui,** it really is him; **c'est b. de lui,** it's just like him, that's typical of him; *F* **c'est b. à moi, ça?,** you're sure that's mine?; **est-ce b. le train pour Paris?,** is this the right train for Paris?; **je l'avais b. dit!,** didn't I say so?; **voulez-vous b. vous taire!,** DO shut up!; **il est b. entendu que ...,** it is quite understood that ...; **b. entendu,** of course; **je m'en doutais b.,** I thought as much; **il est b. venu, mais j'étais occupé,** he did come, but I was busy; **je ne veux pas que tu fasses cela — mais vous le faites b., vous!,** I don't want you to do that — YOU do it, don't you?; *Iron* **c'est b. le moment de parler comme ça!,** a fine time *or* what a time to talk like that!;
(d) (*très*) very; **b. malheureux,** very unhappy; **vous venez b. tard,** you're very late; **b. loin de,** far from; **c'est b. simple,** it's quite *or* very simple;
(e) (*beaucoup*) much, many, a great deal, a great many, a lot; **b. plus,** much *or* a lot more; **b. moins,** much *or* a lot less; **il a b. souffert,** he's suffered *or* been through a great deal; **j'ai eu b. de la peine** *ou* **du mal à la convaincre,** I had a great *or* a good deal of trouble in convincing her; **je l'ai vu b. des fois,** I have seen him many times; **b. d'autres,** many others, *F* lots more; **j'irais b. avec vous mais ...,** I'd love to go with you but ...; **j'y suis b. obligé,** I just *or* really have to;
(f) aussi b., in any case, after all, anyway; just as well, just as easily; **on fera aussi b. d'y aller par nous-mêmes,** we can just as well *or* equally well go there by ourselves;
(g) tant b. que mal, somehow (or other), after a fashion; **je m'en suis acquitté tant b. que mal,** I got through;
(h) b. que + *sub,* though, although; **je le respecte, b. qu'il ne me soit pas sympathique,** I respect him (even) though I don't like him;
(i) si b. que + *ind,* so that, and so, with the result that; **il ne reparut plus, si b. qu'on le crut mort,** he failed to come back, and so he was thought dead;
(j) ou b., or else, otherwise;
(k) *int* **eh b.!,** (oh) well!; **eh b. donc!,** well then!; **eh b. ça alors!,** well, I'm damned!, well, fancy that!
2 *adj inv* **(a)** (*satisfaisant*) right, proper; **c'est b.!,** good!, all right!; **comme c'est b. à vous d'être venu!,** how good of you to come!; **ce n'est pas b. de vous moquer de lui,** it's not kind of you to make fun of him;
(b) (*à l'aise*) comfortable; **êtes-vous b. dans ce**

fauteuil?, are you comfortable in that armchair?; **vous ne savez pas quand vous êtes b.**, you don't know when you're well off; **je ne me sens pas très b.**, I don't feel very well; **il est moins b.**, he's not as well (as he was); **être b. avec qn**, to be on good terms with s.o.;

(c) (*en apparence etc*) of good appearance *or* position *or* quality *etc*; **il est b. de sa personne**, he's a fine figure of a man; **tu es très b. dans cette robe**, that dress suits you perfectly.

3 *nm* **(a)** good; **le b. et le mal**, good and evil; right and wrong; **faire le b.**, to do good; **homme de b.**, good *or* upright man; **le b. public**, the public good; **c'est pour votre b.**, it's for your own good *or* for your benefit; **cela m'a fait beaucoup de b.**, it did me a lot of good; **grand b. vous fasse!**, much good may it do you!; **vouloir du b. à qn, vouloir le b. de qn**, to wish s.o. well; **une personne qui vous veut du b.**, a well-wisher; **tout le monde dit du b.** *ou* **parle en b. de lui**, everyone speaks well of him; **je trouve qu'il a changé en b.**, I think there's a change for the better in him, I think he's changed for the better; **mener une affaire à b.**, to bring a matter to a satisfactory conclusion;

(b) (*chose matérielle*) possession, property; *Jur* assets; (*argent*) wealth, fortune; **il a du b. (au soleil)**, he's well-to-do *or* wealthy *or* a landowner *or* a man of property; *Jur* **biens meubles** *ou* **mobiliers**, personal property, personal estate; **biens immobiliers**, real estate; **biens fonciers**, landed property; **biens dotaux**, dowry; **biens successoraux**, hereditaments; **biens vacants**, ownerless property; *Pol Écon* **biens de consommation**, consumer goods; **biens de production**, capital goods;

(c) *F* **en tout b. (et) tout honneur**, with the best of intentions.

bien-aimé, -ée [bjɛ̃neme] (*pl bien-aimé(e)s*) **1** *adj* beloved, darling; **mon chien/ami b.-a.**, my beloved dog/my very dear friend. **2** *n* beloved, darling; *Hist* **(Louis) le B.-A.**, Louis XV.

bien-être [bjɛ̃nɛtr] *nm* (*no pl*) (*physique*) well-being; (*matériel*) (material) well-being; welfare (*of population etc*); **sentiment de b.-ê.**, feeling of well-being.

bienfaisance [bjɛ̃fəzɑ̃s] *nf* (*générosité*) benevolence; (*charité*) charity; **bureau de b.**, welfare office; **organisation de b.**, charitable organization.

bienfaisant [bjɛ̃fəzɑ̃] *adj* **(a)** (*person*) charitable, kindly; **(b)** beneficial, salutary (*remedy etc*).

bienfait [bjɛ̃fɛ] *nm* **(a)** (*avantage*) benefit, kindness, service; **les bienfaits de la technique/du traitement**, the benefits of technology/of the treatment; **(b)** gift, blessing, boon; **un b. du ciel**, a godsend.

bienfaiteur, -trice [bjɛ̃fɛtœr, -tris] *n* benefactor, benefactress; **b. du peuple**, people's friend.

bien-fondé [bjɛ̃fɔ̃de] *nm* validity, merits (*of opinion, argument, claim*); *Jur* cogency.

bien-fonds [bjɛ̃fɔ̃] *nm* real estate, landed property; (*pl biens-fonds*).

bienheureux, -euse [bjɛ̃nœrø, -øz] **1** *adj* **(a)** (*heureux*) blissful, happy; **(b)** *Rel* blessed. **2** *n* blessed person; **dormir comme un b.**, to sleep the sleep of the just; *Rel* **les b.**, the blessed, the blest.

bien-jugé [bjɛ̃ʒyʒe] *nm* (*no pl*) *Jur* just and lawful decision *or* sentence *or* verdict.

biennal, -ale, -aux [bjenal, -o] **1** *adj* biennial, two-yearly; **contrat b.**, two-year contract; **exposition biennale**, biennial exhibition. **2** *nf* **biennale**, biennial festival *etc*.

bien-pensant, -ante [bjɛ̃pɑ̃sɑ̃, -ɑ̃t] **1** *adj* right-minded (*person*); *Péj* self-righteous (*person*). **2** *n Péj* prig.

bienséance [bjɛ̃seɑ̃s] *nf* propriety, decorum; **observer les bienséances**, to observe the proprieties.

bienséant [bjɛ̃seɑ̃] *adj* decorous, proper; **il est b. aux jeunes gens de respecter la vieillesse**, it is right and proper for young people to respect old age.

bientôt [bjɛ̃to] *adv* (very) soon, before long; **à b.!**, see you soon!, goodbye for now!; *Vieilli* **c'est b. dit!**, easier said than done!; **b. après**, soon after(wards), shortly (afterwards), not long after(wards).

bienveillance [bjɛ̃vɛjɑ̃s] *nf* benevolence, kindness (**envers, pour**, to); **par b.**, out of kindness.

bienveillant [bjɛ̃vɛjɑ̃] *adj* kind, kindly, benevolent (**envers, pour**, to); **examinateur b.**, lenient examiner.

bienvenu, -ue [bjɛ̃vny] **1** *adj* well-timed, opportune (*remark etc*). **2** *n* **soyez le b./la bienvenue!**, welcome!; **vous êtes toujours le b.**, you're always welcome, we're always pleased to see you.

bienvenue [bjɛ̃vny] **1** *nf* welcome; **souhaiter la b. à qn**, to welcome s.o.; **b. à nos amis de Russie**, welcome to our Russian friends. **2** *int Can* you're welcome!

bière¹ [bjɛr] *nf* beer; **b. blonde**, lager; *Br* light ale, pale ale; **b. brune**, brown ale; *Fig* **ce n'est pas de la petite b.**, it's no joke.

bière² *nf* coffin; **assister à la mise en b.**, to be present when the body is placed in the coffin.

biffe [bif] *nf Arg* infantry.

biffer [bife] *vt* to cross out, to strike out, to put a line through (*word etc*).

biffin [bifɛ̃] *nm* **(a)** *Arg* ragman, rag-and-bone man; **(b)** *F* infantryman.

biffure [bifyr] *nf* crossing out, striking out (*of word*); line (*through a word*).

bifide [bifid] *adj* bifid.

bifidus [bifidys] *nm Biol* live culture.

bifocal, -aux [bifɔkal, -o] *adj* bifocal (*lens etc*).

bifteck [biftɛk] *nm* (beef)steak; **b. de cheval**, horse(meat) steak; *F* **gagner son b.**, to earn a living.

bifurcation [bifyrkɑsjɔ̃] *nf* fork, branching (*of road, tree trunk etc*); change of direction, branching out (*in career etc*); **à droite à la b.**, take the right fork.

bifurquer [bifyrke] *vi* to fork, to divide, to branch off; **la route bifurque à Noyon**, the road forks at Noyon; **nous avons bifurqué vers** *ou* **sur la ville**, we turned off towards the town; **b. vers la politique**, to go *or* to branch out into politics.

bigame [bigam] **1** *adj* bigamous. **2** *n* bigamist.

bigamie [bigami] *nf* bigamy.

bigarade [bigarad] *nf* (*fruit*) bitter *or* Seville orange.

bigarré [bigare] *adj* variegated, multicoloured (*shirt etc*); motley, mixed (*crowd, group etc*).

bigarreau, -eaux [bigaro] *nm* (*fruit*) whiteheart (cherry).

bigarrer [bigare] *vt* to paint (*sth*) in a variety of colours.

bigarrure [bigaryr] *nf* medley, mixture, variegation (*of colours*); medley, variety, disparity (*of group etc*).

big(-)bang [bigbɑ̃g] *nm Astron* big bang.

bigle [bigl] *adj & n Vieilli & Hum* cross-eyed (person).

bigler [bigle] *F* **1** *vi* to squint, to have a squint, to be cross-eyed. **2** *vt* to squint at, to have a squint at (*sth*).

bigleux, -euse [biglø, -øz] **1** *adj F* cross-eyed (*person*); *Arg* short-sighted (*person*); **t'es b.?**, are you blind? **2** *n F* cross-eyed person.

bigophone [bigɔfɔn] *nm F* (*téléphone*) blower; **coup de b.**, ring, tinkle, buzz.

bigorne [bigɔrn] *nf* **(a)** (*enclume*) two-beaked anvil, two-horned anvil; **(b)** beak, horn (*of anvil*).

bigorneau, -eaux [bigɔrno] *nm* (*mollusque*) winkle.

bigorner [bigɔrne] **1** *vt Métal* to work (*sth*) on an anvil; *Arg* (*abîmer*) to bash, to smash (up). **2 se bigorner** *vpr Arg* to have a punch-up.

bigot, -ote [bigo, -ɔt] *Péj* **1** *adj* bigoted. **2** *n* (religious) bigot.

bigoterie [bigɔtri] *nf Péj* (religious) bigotry.

bigoudi [bigudi] *nm* roller; *Vieilli* (hair) curler; **se mettre en bigoudis**, to put one's hair in rollers; **se faire des bigoudis**, to curl one's hair.

bigre [bigr] *int F* gosh!, crikey!

bigrement [bigrəmɑ̃] *adv F* **vous avez b. raison!**, you're dead right!; **il fait b. froid**, it's awfully cold.

bigue [big] *nf* **(a)** *Tech* hoisting gin, sheers; **bigues**, sheerlegs; **(b)** *Nau* mast crane, jumbo derrick.

biguine [bigin] *nf Mus* beguine.

bihebdomadaire [biɛbdɔmadɛr] *adj* twice-weekly (*magazine etc*).

bijou, -oux [biʒu] *nm* jewel, gem; **bijoux**, jewellery; *Fig* **cette montre est un b. d'exactitude/de précision**, this watch is a marvel of accuracy/precision; **c'est un b.**, (*cette traduction etc*) it's a gem; *F* **mon b.!**, my precious!, my pet!

bijouterie [biʒutri] *nf* **(a)** jeweller's (shop); (*commerce, fabrication*) jeweller's trade *or* business; **(b)** jewellery, jewels; **(c)** (*art*) jewellery-making.

bijoutier, -ière [biʒutje, -jɛr] *n* jeweller.

bikini [bikini] *nm* bikini.

bilabial, -iale [bilabjal] *Ling* **1** *adj* bilabial. **2** *nf* **bilabiale**, bilabial.

bilan [bilɑ̃] *nm* **(a)** *Fin* (*état*) balance sheet; schedule (*of assets and liabilities*); **faire** *ou* **dresser un b.**, to draw up a balance sheet; **déposer son b.**, to file one's petition (in bankruptcy); **un dépôt de b.**, a petition in bankruptcy; **(b)** evaluation, results, consequences (*of a situation*); assessment (*of facts*); **faire le b. de la situation**, to take stock of the situation; **b. de santé**, complete (medical) check-up; **votre b. de santé est excellent**, your state of health is excellent, you are in excellent health; **faire le b. de santé de qn,** to give s.o. a (medical) check-up.

bilatéral, -aux [bilateral, -o] *adj* bilateral, two-sided (*paralysis, contract etc*); *Pol etc* bilateral (*talks etc*).

bilboquet [bilbɔkɛ] *nm* **(a)** (*jouet*) cup-and-ball; (*poussah*) tumbler; **(b)** *Typ* (piece of) job work.

bile [bil] *nf* **(a)** *Physiol* bile; **(b)** (*colère*) bad temper; **échauffer la b. de** *ou* **à qn,** to rouse s.o.'s anger; **il se fait de la b.,** he's fretting, he's worried sick.

biler (se) [səbile] *vpr F* to get worked up *or* all hot and bothered; (*être inquiet*) to be worried sick.

bileux, -euse [bilø, -øz] *adj F* easily upset; **elle n'est pas bileuse,** she doesn't let things worry her *or* get on top of her.

biliaire [biljɛr] *adj Anat* biliary (*vessels etc*); *Méd* **calcul b.,** biliary calculus, gallstone; **vésicule b.,** gall bladder; **cirrhose b.,** cirrhosis (of the liver).

bilieux, -ieuse [biljø, -jøz] *adj* **(a)** bilious (*temperament, complexion*); **(b)** (*colérique*) irritable, irascible (*person*); (*inquiet*) sick with worry.

bilingue [bilɛ̃g] *adj* (*personne, dictionnaire*) bilingual.

bilinguisme [bilɛ̃gɥism] *nm* bilingualism.

billard [bijar] *nm* **(a)** (*jeu*) (game of) billiards; **b. américain,** pool; **b. russe,** bar billiards; **b. électrique,** pinball, pin table; **(b)** (*table*) billiard table; *F* **monter** *ou* **passer sur le b.,** to have an operation; **(c)** (*salle*) billiard saloon; (*dans une maison*) billiard room.

bille[1] [bij] *nf* **(a)** (*pour le billard*) billiard ball; **(b)** *Arg* (*visage*) mug; **il a une bonne b.,** he looks pleasant enough; **quelle b., il ne comprend rien!,** what a mug, he just doesn't twig!; **il a une b. de billard,** he's as bald as a coot; **(c)** (*de verre*) marble, alley; **jouer aux billes,** to play marbles; *Fig* **reprendre ses billes,** to pull out; **elle touche sa b. en informatique,** she knows a thing or two about computers; **(d)** *Tech* ball; **roulement à billes,** ball bearing(s); **stylo (à) b.,** ballpoint (pen), biro ®; **flacon (à) b.,** roll-on (bottle).

bille[2] *nf* (saw)log, billet (*of timber*).

billet [bijɛ] *nm* **(a) b. (de banque),** (bank)note, *Am* bill; **la circulation des billets,** the circulation of banknotes; **un faux b.,** a forged banknote; **un b. de cent francs,** a hundred-franc note; **b. vert,** dollar, *esp Am F* greenback; *F* **je te fiche mon b. qu'il pleuvra!,** I bet my bottom dollar it'll rain!;

(b) *Com Fin* note, bill; **b. au porteur,** bill payable to bearer; **b. à ordre,** promissory note;

(c) (*pour voyager*) ticket; **b. simple, b. d'aller,** single *or Am* one-way ticket; **b. de retour** *ou* **d'aller (et) retour,** return *or Am* round trip ticket; **voyager sans b.,** to travel without a ticket; **prendre un b. pour Valence,** to buy a ticket for Valence; **b. d'avion,** air *or* plane ticket; **b. de quai,** platform ticket; **b. circulaire,** round trip ticket; **b. de cinéma,** cinema ticket; *Th etc* **b. de faveur,** complimentary ticket;

(d) *Litt* note, short letter; **b. doux,** love letter;

(e) *Vieilli* (*invitation*) notice, invitation; **b. de faire part,** card announcing a family event (*birth, marriage, death*);

(f) b. de naissance, birth certificate; **b. de santé,** certificate *or* bill of health;

(g) permit, permission; *Scol etc* **b. de sortie,** pass, exeat;

(h) *Mil* **b. de logement,** billet.

billette [bijɛt] *nf* **(a)** billet (*of firewood, of metal*); **(b)** *Archit* billet (moulding).

billetterie [bijɛtri] *nf* **(a)** (*opérations*) ticketing; (*lieu*) ticket office; **(b)** *Banque* (*distributeur de billets de banque*) cash dispenser.

billevesée [bijvəze] *nf* stupid idea, nonsense.

billion [biljɔ̃] *nm* **(a)** billion (10^{12}); *Am* trillion; **(b)** *Arch* milliard (10^{9}); *Am* billion.

billon [bijɔ̃] *nm* **(a)** *Agr* ridge of earth (*formed by two plough furrows*); **labourer en billons,** to rafter (*field*); **(b) (monnaie de) b.,** copper *or* nickel coinage.

billonnage [bijɔnaʒ] *nm Agr* ridging (*of field*).

billot [bijo] *nm* block (*of wood*); (butcher's) block; (*dans la cuisine*) butcher's block table; (*pour la décapitation*) executioner's block; **b. du cordonnier,** cobbler's last; **b. d'enclume,** anvil block *or* stock; **périr** *ou* **mourir sur le b.,** to be beheaded, to die on the block; *F* **j'en mettrais ma tête sur le b.,** I'd stake my life on it.

bilobé [bilɔbe] *adj Archit Biol* bilobate, bilobed.

bimane [biman] *adj & n Zool* bimanous, bimanal (animal).

bimbeloterie [bɛ̃blɔtri] *nf* **(a)** (*fabrication, commerce*) toy *or* fancy goods business *or* trade; **(b)** (*ensemble*) toys, fancy goods, knick-knacks, odds and ends.

bimbelotier [bɛ̃blɔtje] *nm* maker of *or* dealer in toys *or* fancy goods.

bimensuel, -elle [bimɑ̃sɥɛl] *adj* fortnightly, bimonthly, *Am* semimonthly.

bimensuellement [bimɑ̃sɥɛlmɑ̃] *adv* twice a month, every fortnight, *Am* semimonthly.

bimestre [bimɛstr] *nm Scol etc* term.

bimestriel, -elle [bimɛstriɛl] *adj* bimonthly, occurring every other month *or* every two months.

bimétallique [bimetalik] *adj* bimetallic.

bimillénaire [bimilenɛr] *adj* bimillenary.

bimoteur [bimɔtœr] *adj & nm* twin-engine(d) (aircraft).

binage [binaʒ] *nm Agr* second dressing *or* harrowing *or* hoeing.

binaire [binɛr] *adj Math etc* binary; **langage b.,** binary notation.

binard, binart [binar] *nm* (low) dray, lorry (*for carting stone*).

biner [bine] **1** *vt Agr* to hoe, to dig *or* harrow *or* dress (*ground*) for a second time. **2** *vi Rel* to celebrate mass twice in one day.

binette[1] [binɛt] *nf Agr* hoe.

binette[2] *nf Arg* face, mug.

bineuse [binøz] *nf Agr* cultivator, light plough.

bing [biŋ] *int* wham.

bingo [biŋgo] *nm* bingo; **jouer au b.,** to play bingo.

biniou [binju] *nm* **(a)** *Mus* Breton bagpipes; **(b)** *F* (*téléphone*) blower; **recevoir un coup de b.,** to get a call on the blower.

binoclard, -arde [binɔklar, -ard] *n F* someone who wears specs; **hé b.!,** hey four-eyes!

binocle [binɔkl] *nm* pince-nez.

binoculaire [binɔkylɛr] *adj* binocular (*vision etc*).

binôme [binom] *nm Math* binomial; **le b. de Newton,** the binomial theorem; **travailler en b.,** (*d'étudiants etc*) to work in twos.

binomial, -aux [binomjal, -o] *adj Math* binomial.

binot [bino] *nm Agr* = **BINEUSE**.

biochimie [bjɔʃimi] *nf* biochemistry.

biochimique [bjɔʃimik] *adj* biochemical; **demande b. en oxygène,** biochemical oxygen demand.

biochimiste [bjɔʃimist] *n* biochemist.

bioclimat [bjɔklima] *nm* bioclimate.

bioclimatique [bjɔklimatik] *adj* bioclimatic.

biodégradable [bjɔdegradabl] *adj* biodegradable.

bioéthique [bjɔetik] *nf Méd* **le débat sur la b.,** the bioethics debate.

biogenèse [bjɔʒənɛz] *nf Biol* biogenesis.

biographe [bjɔgraf] *n* biographer.

biographie [bjɔgrafi] *nf* biography.

biographique [bjɔgrafik] *adj* biographic(al).

bio-industrie [bjɔɛ̃dystri] *nf* biotechnology.

biologie [bjɔlɔʒi] *nf* biology.

biologique [bjɔlɔʒik] *adj* biologic(al); **horloge b.,** biological clock; **parents biologiques,** biological parents; **agriculture/jardinage b.,** organic farming/gardening; **aliments biologiques,** organic food.

biologiste [bjɔlɔʒist] *n* biologist.

biomasse [bjɔmas] *nf* biomass.

biomatériau [bjɔmaterjo] *nm* biomaterial.

biomédical, -aux [bjɔmedikal, -o] *adj* biomedical.

biométrie [bjɔmetri] *nf* biometrics.

bionique [bjɔnik] *nf* bionics.

biophysique [bjɔfizik] *nf* biophysics.

biopsie [bjɔpsi] *nf Chir* biopsy.

biorythme [bjɔritm] *nm* biorhythm.

biosphère [bjɔsfɛr] *nf* biosphere.

biosynthèse [bjɔsɛ̃tɛz] *nf* biosynthesis.

biotechnique [bjɔtɛknik] *nf*, **biotechnologie** [bjɔtɛknɔlɔʒi] *nf Pharm Ch* biotechnology.

biothérapie [bjɔterapi] *nf* = alternative medicine.

biotope [bjɔtɔp] *nm* biotope.

bioxyde [biɔksid] *nm Ch* dioxide.

bip [bip] **1** *int* beep. **2** *nm* beep; **après le b. sonore,** after the beep.

bipale [bipal] *adj* (*hélice*) twin-bladed.

biparti, -ie [biparti] **, bipartite** [bipartit] *adj* bipartite.

bipartisme [bipartism] *nm Pol* bipartite coalition.

bipède [bipɛd] **1** *adj* two-footed, two-legged, biped(al). **2** *nm* biped.

biphasé [bifɑze] *Él* **1** *adj* two-phase, diphase (*current*). **2** *nm* two-phase current, diphase current.

biplace [biplas] *adj & nm Aut Av* two-seater.

biplan [biplɑ̃] **1** *adj* **avion b.,** biplane. **2** *nm* two-seater.

bipolaire [bipɔlɛr] *adj El Phys etc* bipolar, two pole.

bipolarisation [bipɔlarizɑsjɔ̃] *nf Pol* = separation into

two blocs.
bipolarité [bipɔlarite] *nf* bipolarity.
biquadratique [bikwadratik] *Math* **1** *adj* biquadratic (*equation*). **2** *nf* biquadratic.
bique [bik] *nf F* **(a)** (*chèvre*) nanny goat; **peau de b.,** goatskin; **(b)** *Péj* (*woman*) old bag *or* hag *or* cow; **vieille b.,** old bag *or* hag; **quelle grande b.!,** what a beanpole!
biquet, -ette [bikɛ, -ɛt] *n* **(a)** (*petit de la chèvre*) kid; **(b)** *F* **mon b.,** my pet, my love.
biquotidien, -ienne [bikɔtidjɛ̃, -jɛn] *adj* occurring *or* published *etc* twice a day, twice-daily.
birbe [birb] *nm F* **vieux b.,** old man, old geezer.
biréacteur [bireaktœr] *nm* twin-jet (aircraft).
biréfringence [birefrɛ̃ʒɑ̃s] *nf Opt* double refraction, birefringence.
biréfringent [birefrɛ̃ʒɑ̃] *adj Opt* doubly-refractive, birefringent.
birman, -ane [birmɑ̃, -an] **1** *adj* Burmese. **2** *nm Ling* Burmese. **3** *n* **B.,** Burmese.
Birmanie [birmani] *nf* Burma.
biroute [birut] *nf* **(a)** *Mil Av F* (wind) sock, sleeve; **(b)** *Arg* (*pénis*) dick.
bis¹ [bi] *adj* greyish-brown, brownish-grey; **teint b.,** dark *or* swarthy complexion; **toile bise,** unbleached linen; **pain b.,** brown bread.
bis² [bis] *adv* **(a)** *Th etc* encore; *Mus* repeat; **(b)** (*in an address*) **10 b.,** 10A.
bisaïeul, -eule [bizajœl] *n Litt* great-grandfather, great-grandmother; (*pl bisaïeul(e)s*).
bisannuel, -elle [bizanɥɛl] *adj* biennial; **plante bisannuelle,** biennial (plant).
bisbille [bisbij] *nf F* petty quarrel, tiff, bickering; **être en b. avec qn,** not to see eye to eye with s.o.
Biscaye [biskaj] *n* Biscay; **le golfe de B.,** the Bay of Biscay.
biscornu [biskɔrny] *adj* **(a)** (*de forme*) mis-shapen, crooked; irregular, badly proportioned (*building etc*); **(b)** *F* bizarre, queer (*ideas*); illogical (*argument*); **quel esprit b.!, où va-t-il chercher cela?,** what a complicated mind he has!, wherever did he get that idea from?
biscoteaux [biskɔto] *nmpl F* biceps; **avoir des biscoteaux,** to have bulging biceps.
biscotte [biskɔt] *nf* rusk.
biscuit [biskɥi] *nm* **(a)** biscuit; (*salé*) cracker; **b. au chocolat,** chocolate biscuit; **b. à la cuiller,** sponge finger; **b. de Savoie,** sponge cake; **b. au fromage,** cheese biscuit; **biscuits salés,** savoury biscuits; *F* **b. de mer,** cuttlebone; **b. pour chien,** dog biscuit; **b. de fourrage,** cake (*of oats, peas etc*); **(b)** *Cér* unglazed porcelain, biscuitware, bisque.
biscuiterie [biskɥitri] *nf* **(a)** *Ind* biscuit factory; **(b)** *Com* biscuit trade.
bise¹ [biz] *nf* north wind.
bise² *nf F* kiss; **donner une b. à qn,** to kiss s.o.; **on se fait la b.,** = we're quite friendly.
biseau, -eaux [bizo] *nm* **(a)** *Menuis* chamfered *or* bevelled edge, chamfer, bevel; **taillé en b.,** bevel-edged, bevelled, chamfered; **(b)** (*d'horloge etc*) bezel; *Mus* lip (*of a recorder etc*); **(c)** (*outil*) bevel.
biseautage [bizotaʒ] *nm* **(a)** *Menuis* bevelling, chamfering; **(b)** marking (*of playing cards*).
biseauter [bizote] *vt* **(a)** *Menuis* to bevel, to chamfer; **(b)** to mark (*playing cards*).
biser¹ [bize] *vt Tex* to re-dye (*cloth*).
biser² *vi Agr* (*of grain*) to darken, to deteriorate.
biser³ *vt F* to kiss.
biset [bizɛ] *nm* (*oiseau*) rock pigeon.
bisexué [bisɛksɥe] *adj* bisexual; **animal b.,** hermaphrodite.
bisexuel, -elle [bisɛksɥɛl] *adj* bisexual; **personne bisexuelle,** bisexual.
bismuth [bismyt] *nm* bismuth.
bison [bizɔ̃] *nm Zool* bison, *Am* buffalo.
bisou [bizu] *nm F* kiss, smacker; **faire un b. à son papa,** to give Daddy a kiss.
bisque [bisk] *nf Culin* bisque.
bisquer [biske] *vi F* to be in a bad mood; **ça va le faire b.,** that'll send him off the deep end.
bissecteur, -trice [bisɛktœr, -tris] **1** *adj* bisecting (*line etc*). **2** *nf* **bissectrice,** bisector, bisecting line.
bissection [bisɛksjɔ̃] *nf Math* bisection.
bisser [bise] *vt* **(a)** to give an encore of, to repeat (*a song etc*); **(b)** to encore (*a song, performer etc*).
bissextile [bisɛkstil] *adj* **année b.,** leap year.
bissexué [bisɛksɥe] **, bissexuel, -elle** [bisɛksɥɛl] *adj* bisexual.
bistouri [bisturi] *nm Chir* bistoury, lancet.
bistournage [bisturnaʒ] *nm* castration (by twisting of the cord).
bistourner [bisturne] *vt* **(a)** (*courber*) to wring, to wrench; **(b)** (*castrer*) to castrate (by twisting the cord).
bistre [bistr] **1** *adj* bistre, blackish-brown; **teint b.,** swarthy complexion. **2** *nm* bistre.
bistré [bistre] *adj* brown, swarthy (*skin*).
bistrer [bistre] *vt* to darken, to tan (*complexion*).
bistro(t) [bistro] *nm F* = café.
bisulfate [bisylfat] *nm Ch* bisulphate.
bisulfite [bisylfit] *nm Ch* bisulphite.
bisulfure [bisylfyr] *nm Ch* disulphide, bisulphide.
bit [bit] *nm Ordinat* bit; **b. d'arrêt,** stop bit.
B.I.T. [beite] *nm* (*abrév* **bureau international du travail**) ILO.
bite [bit] *nf Vulg* cock, prick.
bitonal, -aux [bitɔnal] *adj Tel* **sonnerie bitonale,** two-tone ring.
bitos [bitɔs] *nm Arg* hat, titfer.
bitte¹ [bit] *nf Vulg* = **BITE**.
bitte² *nf Nau* bitt; bollard (*on ship*).
bitter [bitɛr] *nm* bitters.
bitture [bityr] *nf* **(a)** *Nau* range of cable; **(b)** *Arg* **prendre une b.,** to get canned *or Br* rat-arsed.
bitturer (se) [səbityre] *vpr Arg* to get canned *or Br* rat-arsed.
bitumage [bitymaʒ] *nm* **(a)** (*de route*) asphalting; **(b)** (*de papier etc*) tarring.
bitume [bitym] *nm Minér* **(a)** (*asphalte*) bitumen, asphalt; *F* **arpenter le b.,** to walk the streets; **(b)** (*goudron*) (mineral) pitch, tar.
bitum(in)er [bitym(in)e] *vt* **(a)** to asphalt (*road*), to cover (*road etc*) with bitumen; **(b)** (*goudronner*) to tar; **carton bitumé,** tarred felt.
bitum(in)eux, -euse [bitym(in)ø, -øz] *adj Minér* bituminous, asphaltic.
biture [bityr] *nf* = **BITTURE**.
biturer (se) [səbityre] *vpr Arg* = **BITTURER (SE)**.
biunivoque [biynivɔk] *adj Math* one-to-one.
bivalent [bivalɑ̃] *adj Ch etc* bivalent, divalent.
bivalve [bivalv] *adj & nm* bivalve.
bivouac [bivwak] *nm* bivouac; **faire un b.,** to bivouac; **feu de b.,** watchfire; **cet endroit sera un excellent b.,** this will be an excellent place to bivouac.
bivouaquer [bivwake] *vi* to bivouac.
bizarre [bizar] *adj* peculiar, eccentric, odd, strange, queer, bizarre; **b. ..., b. ..., comme c'est b. ...,** curiouser and curiouser. **2** *nm* **le b.,** the bizarre; **le b. de l'affaire, c'est que ...,** the funny thing is that ... .
bizarrement [bizarmɑ̃] *adv* peculiarly, strangely.
bizarrerie [bizarri] *nf* (*de situation, d'idée*) peculiarity, strangeness, oddness; (*de personne*) whimsicalness, eccentricity; **on lui pardonne ses bizarreries,** people forgive his oddities.
bizarroïde [bizarɔid] *adj F* weird; **ce type est b.,** that guy's a weirdo.
bizutage [bizytaʒ] *nm Univ F* ragging (*of freshmen*).
bizuter [bizyte] *vt Univ F* to rag (*a freshman*).
bizut(h) [bizy] *nm Univ F* freshman, fresher.
blabla(bla) [blabla(bla)] *nm F* claptrap, boloney; padding, waffle (*in a speech etc*); **et b. et ça discute,** chit-chat, chit-chat.
blackboulage [blakbulaʒ] *nm* blackballing; *F* failing (*of an exam candidate*).
blackbouler [blakbule] *vt* to blackball; *F* to fail (*candidate*); **se faire b. d'un bureau à l'autre,** to get shunted from one office to another.
black-out [blakaut] *nm* blackout; *Fig* **faire le b.-o. sur un scandale,** to hush up *or* cover up a scandal; **c'est le b.-o. total, on ne sait rien,** there's a complete black-out, we don't know a thing.
blafard [blafar] *adj* pallid, wan, pale (*moon, light etc*).
blague [blag] *nf* **(a)** (*plaisanterie*) joke, tall story; (*tour*) (practical) joke, trick, hoax; **tout ça c'est de la b.,** it's all bunkum *or* nonsense; **ne racontez pas de blagues,** you're having me on; **b. à part,** seriously, joking apart; **sans b.?,** really?, you're joking!, no kidding?; **il m'a fait une sale b.,** he played a dirty trick on me; **(b) b. (à tabac),** (tobacco) pouch; **(c)** *Vieilli* (*erreur*) mistake, blunder.
blaguer [blage] *F* **1** *vi* to talk through one's hat; **il aime bien b.,** he likes a joke; **tu blagues!,** you're joking *or* kidding *or* having me on! **2** *vt* to tease, to make fun of (*s.o., sth*).
blagueur, -euse [blagœr -øz] *F* **1** *n* joker, comedian. **2**

adj teasing, bantering, ironical (*remark*).

blair [blɛr] *nm Arg* conk, hooter.

blaireau, -eaux [blɛro] *nm* **(a)** (*mammifère*) badger; **(b)** (*pour se raser*) shaving brush; **(c)** *Beaux-Arts* (badger hair) brush.

blairer [blere] *vt Arg* **je ne peux pas le b.**, I can't stick him, I can't stand him at any price.

blâmable [blɑmabl] *adj* blameworthy, blamable.

blâme [blɑm] *nm* **(a)** (*reproche*) blame, disapproval; **rejeter le b. de qch sur qn,** to lay all the blame for sth on s.o.; **s'attirer le b. de ses parents,** to incur one's parents' disapproval; **(b)** *Admin* (*sanction*) reprimand; **donner un b. à qn,** to reprimand s.o.; **recevoir un b.,** to incur a reprimand *or* censure.

blâmer [blɑme] **1** *vt* **(a)** to blame (*s.o., an action*); to find fault with (*s.o.*); to censure (*government etc*); **b. qn de faire/d'avoir fait qch,** to blame s.o. for doing/having done sth; **(b)** *Admin* to reprimand. **2 se blâmer** *vpr* to blame oneself; **je ne peux que me b. d'avoir dit oui,** I can't forgive myself for having said yes.

blanc, blanche [blɑ̃, blɑ̃ʃ] **1** *adj* **(a)** white; **b. comme (la) neige,** white as snow, snow-white; **vieillard à cheveux blancs,** white-haired old man; **fromage b.**, cream cheese; **verre b.**, colourless glass; **vin b.**, white wine; **pain b.**, white bread; **chocolat b.**, white chocolate; **bruit b.**, white noise;

(b) (*de peau*) light-coloured, pale; **la race blanche,** the white race; **b. de peur,** white with fear; **b. de colère,** livid with anger; **b. comme un linge,** as white as a sheet; **elle a les mains blanches,** her hands are clean; **il a la peau blanche,** (*fragile*) he has a pale skin;

(c) *Litt* innocent, pure; **avoir les mains blanches,** to have clean hands, to be innocent;

(d) blank (*page etc*); plain, unlined (*paper*); **nuit blanche,** sleepless night; **examen b.**, mock examination; **mariage b.**, unconsummated marriage; **voix blanche,** toneless voice; **vers blancs,** blank verse; *Tennis* **jeu b.**, love game.

2 *nm* **(a)** (*couleur*) white; **robe d'un b. sale,** dingy white dress; **b. cassé,** off-white; **être habillé de b., être en b.**, to be dressed in white; **mariage en b.**, white wedding; **le b. est très à la mode,** white is very fashionable; **je vous l'écris noir sur b.**, I'm putting it in black and white;

(b) le b. des yeux, the whites of the eyes; **regarder qn dans le b. des yeux,** to look s.o. straight in the eye; **rougir jusqu'au b. des yeux,** to blush to the roots of one's hair;

(c) b. d'une cible, bull's eye of a target; **donner** *ou* **mettre dans le b.**, to hit the bull's eye;

(d) (*espace*) blank, gap, space; *Ordinat* blank; **laisser des blancs,** to leave blanks; **chèque en b.**, blank cheque;

(e) (*in dominoes*) **double b.**, double blank;

(f) saigner qn à b., to bleed s.o. white; **chauffer un métal à b.**, to bring a metal to a white heat; **chauffé à b.**, white-hot; *Fig* **cartouche à b.**, blank cartridge; **tirer à b.**, to fire a blank *or* blanks;

(g) (*d'aliment*) **b. de poulet,** breast of chicken, chicken breast, *Am* white meat; **tu veux le b. ou la cuisse?,** would you like breast or leg *or Am* white meat or dark?; **b. d'œuf,** white of egg, egg white;

(h) (*colorant*) **b. de billard,** billiard chalk; **b. de chaux,** whitewash; **b. de zinc,** zinc white, oxide of zinc; **b. de céruse** *ou* **d'argent** *ou* **de plomb,** white lead; **b. d'Espagne,** whiting, whitening;

(i) (*linge*) **(articles de) b.**, linen, *Am* white goods; **magasin de b.**, linen shop; **vente de b.**, sale of linen, white sale; *Com* **la grande quinzaine du b.**, the great fortnight-long white sale;

(j) (*vin*) white wine; **b. de b.**, = white wine made from white grapes;

(k) b. du rosier/de la vigne, rose/vine mildew.

3 *nf* **blanche (a)** *Billard* white (ball);

(b) *Mus* minim, *Am* half note.

4 *n* **B.**, white man, white woman.

blanc-bec [blɑ̃bɛk] *nm Péj* greenhorn, tenderfoot; (*adolescent*) callow youth; (*pl blancs-becs*).

blanchaille [blɑ̃ʃaj] *nf* **(a)** (*poisson*) small fry, bait; **(b)** *Culin* whitebait.

blanchâtre [blɑ̃ʃatr] *adj* whitish, off-white.

Blanche-Neige [blɑ̃ʃnɛʒ] *nf* Snow White.

blanchet [blɑ̃ʃɛ] *nm* (*tissu*) white woollen cloth; *Pharm* cloth filter, strainer; *Typ* (press) blanket.

blancheur [blɑ̃ʃœr] *nf* whiteness, paleness; *Fig* purity, innocence; **d'une b. de perle,** pearl-white; **sa peau est d'une telle b.!**, his skin is so white!

blanchiment [blɑ̃ʃimɑ̃] *nm* **(a)** whitening; whitewashing (*of wall etc*); **(b)** *Culin* blanching (*of vegetables*); **(c)** *Tex* bleaching.

blanchir [blɑ̃ʃir] **1** *vt* **(a)** to whiten, to make (*sth*) white; **b. (à la chaux),** to whitewash (*ceiling, wall etc*); *Typ* **b. la composition,** to space out the matter; **(b)** to wash, to launder; *Tex* to bleach; **donner du linge à b.**, to send clothes to the wash *or* the laundry; *Fig* **cette déclaration l'a blanchi complètement,** this statement has completely exonerated him; **b. de l'argent,** to launder money; **(c)** *Culin* to blanch (*vegetables*); *Ind* to refine (*sugar*); **(d)** *Can Sp* to shut (a team) out. **2** *vi* **(a)** (*devenir blanc*) to whiten, to turn white; **il commence à b.**, he's turning *or* going white; **(b)** (*pâlir*) to blanch, to turn pale. **3 se blanchir** *vpr* to clear oneself *or* one's name.

blanchissage [blɑ̃ʃisaʒ] *nm* **(a)** washing, laundering (*of linen etc*); **liste de b.**, laundry list; **(b)** *Ind* refining (*of sugar*); **(c)** *Can Sp* shutout.

blanchissant [blɑ̃ʃisɑ̃] *adj* **(a)** whitening, growing white; greying (*hair*); **agent b.**, whitener; **l'aube blanchissante,** the brightening dawn; **(b)** paling (*skin etc*).

blanchissement [blɑ̃ʃismɑ̃] *nm* **(a)** (*des cheveux*) whitening, turning *or* going grey *or* white; **(b)** (*de la peau*) blanching, turning pale; **(c)** (*de l'argent*) laundering.

blanchisserie [blɑ̃ʃisri] *nf* **(a)** *Com* laundry; **(b)** *Tex* bleachery.

blanchisseur, -euse [blɑ̃ʃisœr, -øz] *n* launderer, laundryman, *f* laundress; *Vieilli* washerwoman.

blanc-manger [blɑ̃mɑ̃ʒe] *nm Culin* = blancmange; (*pl blancs-mangers*).

blanc-seing [blɑ̃sɛ̃] *nm* signature to a blank document; **donner b.-s. à qn,** to give s.o. a free hand; (*pl blancs-seings*).

blanquette[1] [blɑ̃kɛt] *nf Culin* blanquette (*of veal*).

blanquette[2] *nf* **b. de Limoux,** = sparkling white wine from Limoux.

blasé, -ée [blɑze] **1** *adj* blasé, indifferent (*person*). **2** *n* blasé person.

blaser [blɑze] **1** *vt* to blunt, to cloy (*the palate etc*); to make (*s.o.*) blasé, indifferent. **2 se blaser** *vpr* to become blasé *or* indifferent (**de, sur qch,** to sth); **on se blase de ces plaisirs,** these pleasures pall.

blason [blazɔ̃] *nm Hér* **(a)** (*ensemble des signes*) coat of arms, armorial bearings, blazon; **(b)** (*connaissance, art*) heraldry, armory.

blasonner [blazɔne] *vt Hér* **b. un écu,** to blazon an escutcheon.

blasphémateur, -trice [blasfematœr, -tris] **1** *n* blasphemer. **2** *adj* blaspheming, blasphemous.

blasphématoire [blasfematwar] *adj* blasphemous.

blasphème [blasfɛm] *nm* blasphemy; **dire** *ou* **prononcer des blasphèmes,** to blaspheme.

blasphémer [blasfeme] *v* (**je blasphème, n. blasphémons; je blasphémerai**) **1** *vi* to blaspheme. **2** *vt Vieilli* to blaspheme; **b. le nom de Dieu,** to take the Lord's name in vain.

blastoderme [blastɔdɛrm] *nm Biol* blastoderm.

blastomère [blastɔmɛr] *nm Biol* blastomere.

blastomycose [blastɔmikoz] *nf Méd* blastomycosis.

blatérer [blatere] *vi* (**il blatère; il blatérera**) (*of camel*) to roar; (*of ram*) to bleat.

blatte [blat] *nf* (*insecte*) cockroach, black beetle.

blazer [blazœr] *nm* blazer.

bld *abrév* **boulevard.**

blé [ble] *nm* **(a)** (*céréale*) wheat, corn; **b. dur,** hard wheat, durum wheat; **b. tendre,** soft wheat; **champ de b.**, wheatfield; **grenier à b.**, granary; **halle aux blés,** corn exchange; **b. en herbe,** corn ripening; **un enfant blond comme les blés,** a child with corn-yellow hair; *Fig* **manger son b. en herbe,** to eat one's seed corn; **b. noir,** buckwheat; *Can* **b. d'Inde,** (Indian) corn; *Br* maize; **(b)** *F Fig* (*argent*) bread; **je n'ai plus de b.**, I've no bread left.

bled [blɛd] *nm* (*in North Africa*) inland country, interior; **dans le b.**, up country; *F* **dans mon b.**, in my part of the country; *F Péj* **en plein b.**, at the back of beyond, in the sticks; **un sale b.**, a godforsaken place, a dump.

blême [blɛm] *adj* **(a)** (*personne*) pallid, wan; **b. de peur,** pallid with fear; **un visage b. de fatigue,** a tired, wan face; **elle est devenue b. quand je le lui ai dit,** she went white *or* blanched when I told her; **(b)** *Fig* **lueur b.**, pale *or* wan light.

blêmir [blemir] *vi* **(a)** (*de personne*) to turn pale *or* livid, to blanch, to turn ghastly pale; **b. de rage,** to turn white with rage; **(b)** *Fig* to grow dim *or* faint *or* wan.

blêmissement [blemismɑ̃] *nm* turning pale, paleness.

blennorragie [blenɔraʒi] *nf Méd* gonorrhoea.

blennorragique [blenɔraʒik] *Méd* **1** *adj* gonorrhoeal. **2** *n* person suffering from gonorrhoea.
blépharite [blefarit] *nf Méd* blepharitis.
blèsement [blɛzmɑ̃] *nm* lisping, lisp.
bléser [bleze] *vi* (**je blèse, n. blésons; je bléserai**) to lisp.
blésité [blezite] *nf* lisping.
blessant [blɛsɑ̃] *adj* hurtful, cutting (*remark etc*).
blessé, -ée [blese] **1** *adj* (*par arme*) wounded; (*dans un accident*) injured, hurt; (*moralement*) hurt, upset; **b. au bras,** wounded in the arm; **b. à mort,** fatally injured; **être b. de qch,** to be hurt *or* offended at *or* by sth. **2** *n* wounded *or* injured person, casualty; **les blessés,** the wounded, the injured, the casualties; **les grands blessés,** the severely wounded *or* injured; **un mort et trois blessés,** one dead and three injured.
blesser [blese] **1** *vt* **(a)** (*par arme*) to wound; (*dans un accident*) to injure, to hurt; **la chute l'a grièvement blessée,** she was severely injured in the fall; **vous êtes blessé?,** are you hurt?; **ces souliers me blessent,** these shoes hurt *or* pinch me;
(b) (*moralement*) to offend, to hurt, to upset (*s.o.*); **b. la vue** *ou* **les yeux/l'oreille,** to offend the eye/to shock *or* grate on the ear; **b. qn au vif,** to cut s.o. to the quick; **b. l'amour-propre de qn,** to hurt *or* injure s.o.'s pride *or* self-esteem; **b. qn dans son orgueil,** to hurt s.o.'s pride; **cette suspicion de ta part me blesse,** I resent your suspiciousness.
2 se blesser *vpr* **(a)** (*physiquement*) to injure *or* wound *or* hurt *or* damage oneself (**avec,** with); **attention, tu vas te b.,** watch out, you'll hurt yourself; **il s'est blessé à la tête,** he's hurt his head;
(b) (*moralement*) to take offence (**de,** at); **il se blesse pour un rien,** he's very quick to take offence.
blessure [blesyr] *nf* (*par arme*) wound; (*dans un accident*) injury; **faire une b. à qn,** to wound s.o.; **panser une b.,** to dress a wound; **b. légère** *ou* **dans les chairs,** flesh wound; *Jur* **coups et blessures,** assault and battery; **une b. d'amour-propre,** a blow to one's pride *or* self-esteem.
blet, blette[1] [blɛ, blɛt] *adj* overripe (*fruit*).
blette[2] [blɛt] *nf* = **BETTE**.
blettir [bletir] *vi* (*of fruit*) to become overripe, to go soft.
blettissement [bletismɑ̃] *nm* (*d'un fruit*) overripeness.
bleu [blø] **1** *adj* blue; **enfant aux yeux bleus,** blue eyed-child; **le ciel est tout b.,** the sky is entirely blue; **conte b.,** fairytale, tall story; **b. de froid,** blue with cold; **colère bleue,** towering rage; **j'en suis resté b.,** I was flabbergasted; *Fig* **n'y voir que du bleu,** not to twig, not to catch on; **bifteck b.,** very rare steak; *Méd* **maladie bleue,** cyanosis; *Méd* **enfant b.,** blue baby.
2 *nm* **(a)** blue (colour); **b. clair,** light blue; **b. foncé,** dark blue; **b. ciel** *ou* **horizon,** sky blue; **b. de Prusse,** Prussian blue; **b. marine,** navy (blue); **b. roi,** royal blue; **b. d'outremer,** ultramarine (blue); **encre b.-noir,** blue-black ink; *Mil* **tirer dans le b.,** to fire at random; *Tex* **b. de teinturier,** blue, blueing; **passer du linge au b.,** to blue laundry;
(b) (*œdème*) bruise; **j'ai le bras couvert de bleus,** my arm's covered with bruises, my arm's black and blue;
(c) *F* (*novice*) novice, greenhorn, *Am* tenderfoot; *Mil* raw recruit, rookie;
(d) (*fromage*) blue cheese;
(e) *Culin* **poisson au b.,** fish au bleu;
(f) **bleu(s) (de chauffe, de travail),** overalls, dungarees, boiler suit; **il ne quittait pas ses bleus,** he would never change out of his overalls;
(g) *Tech* blueprint.
bleuâtre [bløɑtr] *adj* bluish.
bleuet [bløɛ] *nm* **(a)** (*plante*) cornflower; **(b)** *Can* blueberry.
bleuir [bløir] **1** *vt* to make (*sth*) blue. **2** *vi* to become *or* turn *or* go blue.
bleuissement [bløismɑ̃] *nm* making (*sth*) blue; becoming *or* turning *or* going blue; **le b. des lèvres montre combien ils ont froid,** their blue lips show how cold they are.
bleuté [bløte] *adj* bluish, blue-tinged (*light etc*); blue-tinted (*spectacles etc*).
bleuter [bløte] *vt* to give a blue tinge to (*glass, steel etc*).
blindage [blɛ̃daʒ] *nm* **(a)** *Constr Min* timbering, poling, sheeting (*of trench etc*); **(b)** *Mil etc* armour, (armour-)plate, (armour-)plating; **plaque de b.,** armour-plate; **(c)** *El* screen(ing) (*of valve*); shrouding (*of transformer etc*).
blindé [blɛ̃de] **1** *adj* **(a)** *Mil etc* armoured, armour-plated; **abri b.,** bombproof shelter; **train b.,** armoured train; **division blindée,** armoured division; **non b.,** soft-skinned (*vehicle*); **(b)** *F* **je suis b.,** (*ce n'est pas la première fois que ça m'arrive*) I'm hardened to it; **b. contre qch,** proof against sth, hardened *or* immune to sth; **(c)** *Arg* blind drunk; **(d)** *El* screened (*valve*); shrouded (*transformer*). **2** *nmpl Mil* **les blindés,** the armour.
blinder [blɛ̃de] **1** *vt* **(a)** *Constr Min* to sheet, to pole, to timber (*trench, mineshaft etc*); **(b)** *Mil* to armour (*plate*); to plate (*ship etc*); to make (*shelter*) bombproof; **(c)** *El* to screen, to shroud; **(d)** *F* to harden (*s.o.*), to make (*s.o.*) immune (**contre qch,** to sth). **2 se blinder** *vpr* to harden oneself, to develop an extra skin.
blinis [blinis] *nm Culin* blini.
blister [blistɛr] *nm* blister pack; **marchandise vendue sous b.,** goods sold in blister packs.
blizzard [blizar] *nm* blizzard.
bloc [blɔk] *nm* **(a)** block, lump (*of wood, stone etc*); *Sp* **b. de départ,** starting block; **taillé d'un seul b.,** cut from a solid block; **tout d'un b.,** in one go; **elle s'est retournée tout d'un b. et l'a giflé,** she turned round smartly and slapped him in the face; **coulé en b.,** cast in one piece; **acquérir des droits (de traduction** *etc*) **en b.,** to buy (the translation *etc*) rights outright; **visser** *ou* **serrer qch à b.,** to screw sth (up) as tightly as possible; **serrer les freins à b.,** to jam the brakes on hard; **hisser un signal à b.,** to hoist a signal close up; *F* **gonflé à b.,** full of beans, raring to go;
(b) block (*of houses*); **b. opératoire,** theatre block; **b. technique,** design department, technical services block (*of factory etc*); **il habite dans ce b.,** he lives in this block;
(c) *Pol etc* group, coalition, bloc; **faire b.,** to join forces, to unite, to combine, to form a bloc (**avec,** with; **contre,** against); **le b. occidental,** the Western bloc, the West; **le b. des gauches,** the left-wing bloc; **faire b. contre le fascisme,** to unite against fascism; **les deux partis font b.,** the two parties have formed a bloc; **faire b. avec un allié,** to unite *or* join forces with an ally;
(d) pad (*of paper*); **b. à dessin,** sketch pad; **b. de papier à lettre,** writing pad; **b. de bureau,** office pad, desk pad;
(e) unit; *Cin* **b. sonore,** sound unit;
(f) *Ordinat* block; **b. logique,** package; **quelle commande faut-il utiliser pour déplacer un b.?,** what's the command for moving a block?; **b. de touches,** keypad;
(g) *F* (*prison*) nick, clink; **être au b.,** to be in clink *or* the nick.
blocage [blɔkaʒ] *nm* **(a)** jamming, clamping, sticking (*of piece of machinery etc*); locking on, seizing (*of brakes*); jamming on (*of brakes*); *Écon* pegging; *Fin* freezing; *Sp* blocking (*of ball etc*); *Billard* jamming (*of the balls*); *Psy* block; **vis de b.,** locking screw; **b. des prix et des salaires,** wage and prices freeze; *Psy* **il a un b.,** he's got a (mental) block; **(b)** *Constr* rubble (stone); *Typ* turning (*of letters*).
blocaille [blɔkaj] *nf Constr* rubble (stone).
bloc-cuisine [blɔkkɥizin] *nm* kitchen unit; (*pl blocs-cuisines*).
bloc-cylindres [blɔksilɛ̃dr] *nm Aut* cylinder block, engine block; (*pl blocs-cylindres*).
bloc-diagramme [blɔkdjagram] *nm Géog* (block) diagram; (*pl blocs-diagrammes*).
bloc-évier [blɔkevje] *nm* sink unit; (*pl blocs-éviers*).
blockhaus [blɔkos] *nm* **(a)** (*construction*) blockhouse, pillbox; **(b)** *Nau* armoured tower; **b. de commandement,** conning tower.
bloc-moteur [blɔkmɔtœr] *nm Aut* engine block; (*pl blocs-moteurs*).
bloc-notes [blɔknɔt] *nm* writing pad; (reporter's, shorthand) notebook; *Ordinat* scratch pad; **mémoire b.-n.,** scratch pad memory; (*pl blocs-notes*).
bloc-système [blɔksistɛm] *nm Rail* block system (signalling).
blocus [blɔkys] *nm* blockade; **faire le b. d'un port,** to blockade a port; **lever/forcer le b.,** to raise/to run the blockade.
blond, -onde [blɔ̃, -ɔ̃d] **1** *adj* fair, blond (*hair, person*); fair-haired (*person*); **bière blonde,** lager; *Br* pale ale; **un demi de blonde,** = a half of lager; **(cigarette) blonde,** Virginia cigarette. **2** *n* fair(-haired) man *or* woman, blonde; *F* **il va voir sa blonde,** he's off to see his sweetheart *or* girl(friend); **une blonde décolorée,** a peroxide blonde. **3** *nm* **cheveux (d'un) b. doré,** golden hair; **b. ardent,** auburn; **b. vénitien,** strawberry blond, Titian red; **b. platine,** platinum blond; **b. cendré,** ash blond.
blondasse [blɔ̃das] *adj* insipidly fair, of a washed out blonde (*hair*).
blondeur [blɔ̃dœr] *nf* blondness, fairness.
blondin[1], -ine [blɔ̃dɛ̃, -in] *n* blond(e).

blondin² *nm Tech* cableway.

blondinet, -ette [blɔ̃dinɛ, -ɛt] *n* fair haired child.

blondir [blɔ̃dir] **1** *vi* (*of hair, person*) to go blond, to get fairer *or* lighter. **2** *vt* to make (*hair*) go lighter; **l'eau de mer blondit les cheveux,** sea water bleaches the hair; **il faut faire b. les oignons dans du beurre,** cook the onions in butter until they turn pale yellow. **3 se blondir** *vpr* **elle s'est blondi les cheveux,** she's bleached her hair.

bloquer [blɔke] **1** *vt* **(a)** to jam, to clamp (*piece of machinery etc*); to blockade (*port etc*); **b. les roues,** to lock the wheels; **b. les freins,** to jam the brakes on; **b. une porte,** to jam *or* wedge a door; **bloqué par la neige/le brouillard,** snowbound/fogbound; *F* **me voilà bloqué à l'hôpital,** here I am stuck in hospital; **(b)** *Constr* to block up *or* fill up (*wall*) with rubble; *Typ* **b. une lettre,** to turn a letter; **(c)** to stop (*cheque*); to block (*bank account*); to freeze (*prices, wages*); **(d)** to block, to obstruct (*road etc*); **b. le chemin à qn,** to block *or* be in *or* stand in s.o.'s way *or* path; *Sp* to block (*ball etc*); **(e)** *Belg F* to swot up, to mug up (*subject*); **(f)** *Psy* **être bloqué,** to have a psychological block. **2 se bloquer** *vpr* to jam, to stick, to lock, to get jammed *or* stuck.

blottir (se) [səblɔtir] *vpr* to curl up, to crouch; **village blotti au fond de la vallée,** village tucked away *or* nestling in the valley; **se b. dans son lit,** to curl up *or* snuggle up *or* down in bed; **se b. contre qn/dans les bras de qn,** to snuggle up to s.o./in s.o.'s arms; **blotti dans un coin,** huddled *or* huddling in a corner.

blousant [bluzɑ̃] *adj* loose-fitting; **forme ample et blousante,** ample, loose-fitting shape.

blouse [bluz] *nf* **(a)** (*d'écolier etc*) overall, smock; (surgeon's) gown; **(b)** *Vieilli* (*de femme*) (woman's) (over)blouse, smock.

blouser [bluze] **1** *vt F* to cheat, to trick, to con (*s.o.*), to take (*s.o.*) in. **2** *vi* (*of dress etc*) to blouse. **3 se blouser** *vpr F* to make a mistake *or* a blunder.

blouson [bluzɔ̃] *nm* (lumber)jacket; (*plus léger*) blouson; **b. en cuir,** leather jacket; **b. d'aviateur,** flying jacket; *F Vieilli* **b. noir,** = teddy boy.

blue-jean(s) [blu(d)ʒin(z)] *nm* jeans; (*pl blue-jeans*).

blues [bluz] *nm Mus* blues.

bluff [blœf] *nm* bluff; **faire du b.,** to bluff; **c'est un coup de b.,** it's all bluff, he's bluffing.

bluffer [blœfe] **1** *vt F* to bluff, to trick (*s.o.*), to have (*s.o.*) on; *Cartes* to bluff (*s.o.*). **2** *vi* to bluff; **il ne fait que b.,** he's only bluffing, he's just trying it on.

bluffeur, -euse [blœfœr, -øz] *n* bluffer.

blush [blœʃ] *nm* (*fard*) blusher.

B.N. [beɛn] *nf abrév* **Bibliothèque Nationale.**

B.N.P. [beɛnpe] *nf abrév* **Banque nationale de Paris.**

boa [bɔa] *nm* **(a)** (*serpent*) boa; **b. constricteur,** boa constrictor; **(b)** (*tour de cou*) boa.

boat people [botpipəl] *nmpl* boat people.

bob [bɔb] *nm F* bob(sleigh).

bobard [bɔbar] *nm F* tall story.

bobinage [bɔbinaʒ] *nm* **(a)** (*opération*) winding, reeling; **(b)** *Él* winding, coiling.

bobine [bɔbin] *nf* **(a)** reel (*of tape etc*); bobbin (*in sewing machine etc*); spool (*in typewriter, camera etc*); roll (*of film, paper etc*); **b. de fil,** reel *or* spool of cotton *or* of thread; **(b)** *Él* coil; **b. de dérivation,** shunt coil; **b. d'allumage,** ignition coil; **(c)** *Arg* (*visage*) mug.

bobiner [bɔbine] *vt* to wind, to reel (*cotton etc on bobbin*); to coil (*wire etc*).

bobineur, -euse [bɔbinœr, -øz] **1** *n Tex Él* winder. **2** *nf* **bobineuse,** winding machine, winder.

bobinier [bɔbinje] *nm Él* coil winder.

bobinoir [bɔbinwar] *nm Tex Él* winding machine, winder.

bobo [bobo] *nm Enf* (*douleur*) pain, sore, bump, bruise, cut; **j'ai b.,** it hurts; **ça fait b.?,** does it hurt?, is it sore?; **j'ai un b. au doigt,** I've hurt my finger; **se faire b.,** to hurt oneself.

bobonne [bɔbɔn] *nf Arg Péj* missis; *Vieilli* **(ma) b.,** (*to wife*) my dear, my love, my pet.

bobsleigh [bɔbslɛg)] *nm Sp* bobsleigh.

bocage [bɔkaʒ] *nm* **(a)** *Litt* copse; **(b)** *Géog* bocage.

bocager, -ère [bɔkaʒe, -ɛr] *adj* wooded.

bocal, -aux [bɔkal, -o] *nm* (wide-mouthed, short-necked) bottle, jar; **mettre des fruits en b.,** to bottle fruit; **b. à poissons rouges,** goldfish bowl.

bocard [bɔkar] *nm Métal* ore crusher, stamping mill.

bocardage [bɔkardaʒ] *nm Métal* crushing, stamping (*of ore*).

bocarder [bɔkarde] *vt Métal* to crush, to stamp (*ore*).

Boccace [bɔkas] *nm* Boccaccio.

boche [bɔʃ] *F Péj* **1** *adj* Boche, Kraut. **2** *n* **B.,** Boche, Kraut.

bock [bɔk] *nm* **(a)** (*verre*) beer glass; **(b)** (*contenu*) glass of beer (*approx* $\frac{1}{4}$ l. *or* $\frac{1}{2}$ pt).

bocson [bɔksɔ̃] *nm F* **quel b.!,** what a shambles!

body [bɔdi] *nm* (*sous-vêtement*) body stocking; (*avec bretelles*) teddy.

Boer [bur] *adj & n* Boer.

boët(t)e [bwɛt] *nf Pêche* bait.

bœuf, *pl* **bœufs** [bœf, bø] **1** *nm* **(a)** (*mammifère*) ox, bullock; **jeune b.,** steer; **bœufs à l'engrais,** beeves, *Am* beefs; **b. gras,** fatted ox, prize ox; **bœufs de boucherie,** beef cattle; **fort comme un b.,** as strong as an ox; **on n'est pas des bœufs,** I'm *or* we're not superhuman; **b. musqué,** musk ox; **b. à bosse,** zebu; **(b)** (*viande*) beef; *Culin* **b. (à la) mode,** stewed beef; **b. gros sel,** boiled beef; **b. bourguignon,** bœuf bourguignon. **2** *adj inv F* tremendous, amazing, great; **ça a fait un effet b.,** it had quite an impact; **c'est b.,** it's fantastic.

bof [bɔf] *int* I dunno.

bog(g)ie [bɔʒi] *nm Rail etc* bogie (truck), radial truck.

bogue [bɔg] *nf* **(a)** *Ordinat* bug; **dépourvu/plein de bogues,** bug-free/-ridden; **(b)** *Bot* chestnut bur, *Am* shuck.

bohème [bɔɛm] **1** *adj* bohemian; **un esprit b.,** an unconventional thinker; **être un peu/très b.,** to be a bit/very bohemian. **2** *n* bohemian; **mener une vie de b.,** to lead a bohemian *or* an unconventional *or* a free and easy life. **3** *nf* **la bohème,** bohemia, the artistic world.

Bohême [bɔɛm] *nf* Bohemia.

bohémien, -ienne [bɔemjɛ̃, -jɛn] **1** *adj* Bohemian. **2** *n* gipsy.

boire¹ [bwar] *nm* drink, drinking; **le b. et le manger,** food and drink, eating and drinking; *Fig* **tellement amoureuse qu'elle en a perdu le b. et le manger,** so in love that she can't eat or drink; *Can* **c'est l'heure de son b.,** (*tétée*) it's his feeding time.

boire² *v* (*prp* **buvant**; *pp* **bu, bue**; *pr ind* **je bois** [bwa], **il boit, n. buvons, ils boivent**; *pr sub* **je boive, n. buvions**; *impf* **je buvais**; *p hist* **je bus, n. bûmes**; *fu* **je boirai**) **1** *vt* **(a)** to drink (*sth*); **b. qch à petits coups,** to sip sth; **b. qch d'un (seul) trait** *ou* **d'un seul coup,** to drink sth at one gulp *or* straight off, to knock sth back; **b. à la santé de qn,** to drink somebody's health; **b. un verre jusqu'à la dernière goutte,** to drain a glass; *F* **b. un coup,** to have a drink; **tu viens b. un verre?,** are you coming for a drink?; *Fig* **b. les paroles de qn,** to drink in s.o.'s every word; *F* **b. la** *ou* **une tasse,** to get a mouthful (*when swimming*); *Fig* **ce n'est pas la mer à b.,** it's not all that hard (to do); *Fig Fin* **b. un bouillon,** to make a big loss, to come a cropper, *F* to take a bath; *Fig* **il boit du petit lait,** (*il est content*) he's (as) pleased as Punch;

(b) (*de l'alcool*) to drink (*alcohol*); **tu bois trop,** you drink too much; **il a (trop) bu, il a bu un coup (de trop),** he's had one too many;

(c) (*of plants, porous substances etc*) to soak up, to absorb (*moisture*).

2 *vi* (*of person, plant*) to drink; *Can* (*of baby*) to feed, to nurse; **b. à la bouteille,** to drink from the bottle; **b. à sa soif, b. jusqu'à plus soif,** to drink one's fill; **faire b. qn,** to give s.o. a drink *or* something to drink; **faire b. les chevaux,** to water the horses; *Fig* **il y a à b. et à manger,** it's got its pros and cons; **elle boit comme un trou,** she drinks like a fish; **il a commandé à boire,** (*pour lui*) he ordered a drink; (*pour deux, trois etc*) he ordered the drinks.

3 se boire *vpr* to be drunk; **ce vin se boit bien** *ou* **se laisse b.,** this wine is very drinkable *or* goes down well; **les vins sucrés se boivent au dessert,** sweet wines are drunk with dessert.

bois [bwa] *nm* **(a)** (*forêt*) wood; **petit b.,** spinney, grove, thicket; **Robin des B.,** Robin Hood; **le B. de Boulogne,** the Bois de Boulogne;

(b) (*arbre*) timber (trees); *surtout Can* **b. debout,** standing timber; **abattre** *ou* **couper le b.,** to cut down *or* fell timber; *F* **casser du b.,** (*of aircraft*) to crash-land;

(c) (*matériau*) wood, timber, lumber; **b. de chauffage, b. à brûler,** firewood; **petit b.,** kindling; **b. d'œuvre,** timber, lumber; **chantier de b.,** timber yard; **travail du b.,** woodwork; **train de b.,** float *or* raft of timber; **jambe de b.,** wooden leg; **meubles en b.,** wooden furniture; *Can* **maison en b. rond,** log house; **b. dur,** *Can* **b. franc,** hardwood; **b. tendre,** softwood; **b. de sapin, b. blanc,** deal, whitewood; **b. de rose,** rosewood; **b. de mai,** hawthorn; **b. des îles,** West Indian hardwood; *Fig* **elle n'est pas de b.,** she's not made of stone, she's got SOME feelings, she's only human; *Fig* **moi, je suis du b. dont on fait les flûtes,** I'm easy (either way); *Fig* **je leur ferai voir de quel b. je me chauffe,** I'll show them (what I'm made of); *F* **touchez du b.!,** touch wood!, *Am* knock on wood!; *Fig* **avoir la gueule de b.,** to be hung over, to have a hangover; *Fig* **la langue de b. des politiciens,** politicians' platitudes; *F* **chèque en b.,** rubber cheque, cheque that bounces;

(d) (*gravure*) woodcut;

(e) frame(work) (*of chair, racket etc*); *Tennis* **faire un b.,** to hit the ball off the wood *or* the frame; **b. de lit,** bedstead; **b. de fusil,** rifle stock; **b. de drapeau,** flagstaff;

(f) *Mus* **les b.,** the woodwind;

(g) **les bois,** antlers (*of deer*).

boisage [bwazaʒ] *nm* **(a)** timbering (*of shaft, gallery etc*); **(b)** (*ensemble des bois*) scaffold(ing), timber(ing), framing; frame(work).

boisé [bwaze] *adj* wooded, well-timbered (*country*); **pays b.,** woodland(s), wooded country.

boisement [bwazmɑ̃] *nm* (af)forestation (*of region*).

boiser [bwaze] *vt* **(a)** (*planter d'arbres*) to afforest, to plant with timber; **(b)** to timber, to prop (*mine*).

boiserie [bwazri] *nf Constr* woodwork, wainscot(ing), panelling.

boisseau, -eaux [bwaso] *nm* **(a)** *Arch & Can* bushel; *Fig* **mettre la lumière sous le b.,** to hide one's light under a bushel; **(b)** *Tech* drain tile; (*de cheminée*) chimney (flue) tile; (*de moteur*) throttle chamber.

boisselier [bwasəlje] *nm* (dry) cooper.

boisson [bwasɔ̃] *nf* **(a)** drink, beverage; **b. gazeuse,** fizzy drink; **b. fraîche,** cold drink; **boissons alcoolisées/non alcoolisées,** alcoholic/soft drinks; **(b)** (*alcool*) drink; **il s'est adonné à la b.,** he's taken to drink; **débit de boissons,** bar; **(c)** *Can* hard liquor, spirits.

boîte [bwat] *nf* **(a)** box; **b. en fer,** tin, can, canister; **b. de conserves,** can *or* tin of food; **b. de thon,** tin *or* can of tuna; **manger une b. de macédoine,** to eat a tin *or* can of mixed vegetables; **une b. de chocolats,** a box of chocolates; **b. à pain,** bread bin; **b. de secours,** first-aid box; *Aut* **b. à gants,** glove box *or* compartment; **mettre en b.,** to box (*goods*); to tin, to can (*sardines*); *Fig F* **mettre qn en b.,** to pull somebody's leg; **b. à** *ou* **aux lettres,** (*pour envoyer*) letterbox, pillarbox, postbox, *Am* mailbox; (*chez soi*) letterbox, *Am* mailbox; **b. postale 260,** Post Office Box 260; **b. à lettres électronique,** electronic mailbox; **b. d'allumettes,** box of matches; **b. à allumettes,** matchbox; **b. à outils,** toolbox; **b. à musique,** musical box, *Am* music box; **b. à violon,** violin case; **b. à malice** *ou* **à surprise,** jack-in-the-box; *Anat* **b. crânienne** *ou* **du crâne,** brainpan;

(b) *Tech* **b. d'une serrure,** case of a lock; **b. à feu,** firebox; **b. à vapeur,** steam chest; *Aut* **b. de vitesses,** gearbox; **b. de l'embrayage,** clutch casing; *Rail* **b. de l'essieu,** axle box; *El* **b. à fusible,** fuse box; *Av* **b. noire,** flight recorder, black box;

(c) *F* one's office *or* shop *or* school *etc*; **je travaille dans une b. d'informatique,** I work for a computer company; **sale b.,** rotten hole; **quelle b. affreuse!,** what a hole!, what a dump!;

(d) **b. (de nuit),** nightclub; **aller en b.,** to go out to a nightclub.

boiter [bwate] *vi* to limp, to walk with a limp; **b. d'un pied,** to be lame in one foot; **b. bas,** to limp badly; **homme qui boite,** lame man, man with a limp; *Fig* **sa démonstration boite,** his demonstration is shaky; **une explication qui boite,** a lame explanation.

boiterie [bwatri] *nf* lameness.

boiteux, -euse [bwatø, -øz] **1** *adj* lame, limping; *Fig* wobbly, rickety, shaky (*furniture*); lame (*argument, explanation*); **le facteur est b.,** the postman walks with *or* has a limp; **cheval b.,** lame horse; **vers b.,** limping verses. **2** *n* lame man *or* woman, cripple; **le b.,** the man with the limp.

boîtier [bwatje] *nm* case, casing, housing; **b. de montre,** watch case; **b. de chirurgien,** surgeon's instrument case.

boitiller [bwatije] *vi* to limp slightly, to have a slight limp.

boit-sans-soif [bwasɑ̃swaf] *nm Arg* tippler.

boitte [bwat] *nf Pêche* bait.

bol[1] [bɔl] *nm* **(a)** *Physiol* **b. alimentaire,** (alimentary) bolus; **(b)** *Pharm Vét* bolus, pellet.

bol[2] *nm* **(a)** (*pièce de vaisselle*) bowl, basin; **(b)** *Arg* luck; **manque de b.,** bad luck; **coup de b.,** stroke of luck; **pas de b.!,** we're *etc* out of luck!; **(c)** **en avoir ras le b.,** to be fed up, to be sick and tired (of it), to have had it up to here; **(d)** (*contenu*) bowl(ful); **avaler son b. de café,** to drink one's coffee; **on a pris un b. d'air frais** *ou* **pur,** we got a good breath of fresh air.

bolchevik [bɔlʃəvik] *adj & n* Bolshevik, Bolshevist.

bolchevisme [bɔlʃəvism] *nm Vieilli* Bolshevism.

bolcheviste [bɔlʃəvist] *adj & n* Bolshevik, Bolshevist.

bolduc [bɔldyk] *nm* (thin) coloured ribbon (*for tying up boxes of chocolates etc*).

bolée [bɔle] *nf* bowl(ful) (*of soup, cider etc*).

boléro [bɔlero] *nm* (*vêtement*) & *Mus* bolero.

bolet [bɔlɛ] *nm* (*champignon*) boletus.

bolide [bɔlid] *nm* (*voiture de course*) racing car; *Astron* meteor, fireball, bolide; **lancé comme un b. sur la route,** hurtling along the road.

bolivar [bolivar] *nm* (*monnaie*) bolivar.

Bolivie [bɔlivi] *nf* Bolivia.

bolivien, -ienne [bɔlivjɛ̃, -jɛn] **1** *adj* Bolivian. **2** *n* **B.,** Bolivian.

bollard [bɔlar] *nm Nau* bollard.

Bologne [bɔlɔɲ] *nf* Bologna.

bolonais, -aise [bɔlɔnɛ, -ɛz] **1** *adj* Bolognese; *Culin* **spaghetti bolonaise, spaghetti bolognese.** **2** *n* **B.,** Bolognese.

bombage [bɔ̃baʒ] *nm F* aerosol graffiti; **faire des bombages sur un mur,** to spray paint a wall with graffiti.

bombance [bɔ̃bɑ̃s] *nf F* feast(ing), carousing; **faire b.,** to go on a spree *or* a binge; (*manger*) to feast.

bombardement [bɔ̃bardəmɑ̃] *nm* **(a)** *Mil* bombardment, shelling, gunfire; pelting, showering (*with stones etc*); bombarding (*with questions etc*); **b. atomique d'Hiroshima,** the dropping of the atomic bomb on Hiroshima; **(b)** *Av* bombing; **b. aérien,** air raid; **avion de b.,** bomber; **(c)** *Phys* bombardment.

bombarder [bɔ̃barde] *vt* **(a)** *Mil* to bombard, to bomb, to shell; **maison bombardée,** bombed *or* shelled house; **b. qn de pierres,** to pelt s.o. with stones; **b. qn de questions,** to fire questions at s.o., to bombard s.o. with questions; **être bombardé de lettres,** to be bombarded *or* inundated with letters; **(b)** *Phys* to bombard (*with neutrons etc*); **(c)** *F* **on l'a bombardé ministre,** he's been made a minister out of the blue.

bombardier [bɔ̃bardje] *nm Mil* **(a)** *Av* (*aircraft*) bomber; (*aviateur*) bombardier; **(b)** *Arch* bombardier.

bombe [bɔ̃b] *nf* **(a)** bomb; **b. à fragmentation,** fragmentation *or* scatter bomb; **b. à retardement,** delayed-action bomb, time bomb; **b. incendiaire,** incendiary bomb; **b. lacrymogène,** tear gas bomb *or* grenade; **b. fumigène,** smoke bomb; **b. au plastic,** plastic bomb; **b. atomique, b. A,** atom(ic) bomb, A bomb; **b. à hydrogène, b. H,** hydrogen bomb, H bomb; **b. volante,** flying bomb; *F* doodlebug; **attaque** *ou* **attentat à la b.,** bomb attack; **lâcher** *ou* **larguer une b.,** to release *or* drop a bomb; *F* **entrer en** *ou* **comme une b.,** to come bursting in; *Fig* **cela a fait l'effet d'une b.,** it was a real bombshell; *Méd* **b. au cobalt,** cobalt bomb; *Culin* **b. glacée,** bombe glacée; *Géol* **b. volcanique,** volcanic bomb;

(b) *Com* aerosol; **b. à peinture,** paint spray; **une b. d'insecticide,** a fly spray;

(c) *Equitation* riding hat *or* cap;

(d) *F* (*fête*) party, do; **faire la b.,** to party.

bombé [bɔ̃be] *adj* convex, curved, rounded, bulging; **avoir le dos b.,** to be round-shouldered; **avoir le front b.,** to have a bulging forehead; **se tenir droit, la poitrine bombée,** to stand up straight with one's shoulders back; **chaussée bombée,** cambered road; **une cuiller bombée (de sucre),** a heaped *or* rounded spoonful (of sugar).

bombement [bɔ̃bmɑ̃] *nm* bulge, bulging, convexity; camber (*of road*).

bomber [bɔ̃be] **1** *vt* **(a)** to cause (*sth*) to bulge; to bend, to curve, to arch (*one's back etc*); to camber (*road*); **b. la poitrine,** to throw out one's chest; **b. le torse,** to swagger; **(b)** (*écrire à la bombe*) to spray; **b. des graffiti/des slogans,** to spray graffiti/slogans. **2** *vi* (*of wall etc*) to bulge (out).

bombonne [bɔ̃bɔn] *nf* = **BONBONNE**.

bôme [bom] *nf Nau* boom.

bon[1], bonne [bɔ̃, bɔn] **1** *adj* **(a)** good, upright, honest (*person etc*); **le b. M. Seguin,** good old Mr Seguin; **mon b. monsieur,** my dear sir; **défendre la bonne cause,** to fight the good fight; **bonne action,** good deed;

(b) good (*book, smell etc*); **bonne histoire,** good story; **bonne soirée,** pleasant evening; **j'aime un b. fauteuil,** I like a nice *or* comfortable armchair; **j'ai trouvé le rôti b.,** I enjoyed the roast; **la bonne société,** polite society; **c'est un b. job,** it's a good job; *F* **cela est b. à dire,** (it's) easier said than done;

(c) (*capable, apte*) clever, capable; good (*at one's work etc*); **un b. médecin/père,** a good doctor/father; **les bons élèves,** the bright pupils; **b. en anglais,** good at English;

(d) (*correct*) good, right, correct, proper, sound; **si j'ai**

bonne mémoire, if my memory serves me well; **c'est du b. travail,** it's good work; *Tex* **b. teint,** colourfast; **oui, c'est b.,** yes, that's right; **est-ce la bonne clé/réponse?,** is that the right key/answer?; **en b. état,** in good *or* working order; *Fig* **frapper à la bonne porte,** to come to the right person; **la bonne voie** *ou* **route,** the right path *or* track; **avoir une bonne vue,** to have good eyesight; **sa vue n'est plus très bonne,** he doesn't see too well any more; *Tennis* **la balle est bonne,** the ball is in;

(e) (*généreux*) good, kind(-hearted) (**pour, envers,** to); **c'est un b. garçon** *ou F* **type** *ou* **gars,** he's a good sort, he's all right; **elle est bonne pour sa mère,** she's very kind to her mother; **être b. public,** to be a good audience; **vous êtes bien b. de m'inviter,** it's very good *or* kind of you to invite me; *F* **c'est une bonne femme,** she's a good woman; *Iron F* **tu est b.!,** oh VERY funny!;

(f) (*intéressant*) good, profitable, advantageous (*investment etc*); **acheter qch à b. marché,** to buy sth cheap(ly); **c'est b. à savoir/à se rappeler,** it's worth knowing/remembering; **c'est toujours b. à avoir,** it's always worth having; **à quoi b.?,** what's the good of it?, what's the point?; **à quoi b. se plaindre?,** what's the use *or* the good *or* the point of complaining?; **c'est un b. conseil,** it's a good piece of advice; **quelle bonne idée!,** what a good idea!; **puis-je vous être b. à quelque chose?,** can I do anything for you?, can I be of any help (to you)?; **cet exercice est b. pour le dos,** this exercise is good for the back; **ce qui est b. pour les uns n'est pas toujours b. pour les autres,** what is good for some is not necessarily good for others;

(g) b. à *ou* **pour,** fit, suitable; **b. à manger,** good to eat; (*comestible*) fit *or* safe to eat; *Mil* **b. pour le service,** fit for duty; **c'est b. pour les nerfs,** it's good for your nerves; **il n'est b. qu'à cela,** that's all he's fit for; **elle n'est bonne à rien,** she's useless, she's good for nothing, she's no good at anything;

(h) (*souhaitable*) desirable; **si b. vous semble,** if you think it advisable; **il est b. que vous sachiez,** it's just as well that you should know; **trouver b. de faire qch,** to think *or* see fit *or* to think it advisable to do sth;

(i) good, favourable (*omen etc*); **souhaiter une** *ou* **la bonne année à qn,** to wish s.o. a happy New Year; **b. Noël,** Merry Christmas; **b. anniversaire!,** happy birthday!; **avoir la bonne vie,** to have it easy; **b. week-end!,** *Can* **bonne fin de semaine!,** have a good weekend!; **bonne chasse!,** good hunting!; **b. voyage!,** bon voyage!, have a good trip!; *Can* **bonne journée!,** have a good day!; **b. appétit!,** bon appetit!; (*surtout dans un restaurant*) enjoy your meal, *Am F* enjoy!; **bonne nuit,** good night; **bonnes vacances!;** have a good holiday, enjoy your holiday;

(j) good, sound, safe (*security, credit etc*); **il est b. pour 25 000 francs,** he is good for 25,000 francs; **billet b. pour trois mois,** ticket valid for three months; **son affaire est bonne!, son compte est b.!,** he's in for it!; **elle est bonne pour deux mois de prison,** she's going to get *or* she's looking at two months in prison; **tu est b. pour la contravention,** you're in for a fine; *F* **on est b!,** (*c'est raté*) we've had it!;

(k) (*intensif*) good, full, considerable; **un b. rhume,** a bad cold; **j'ai attendu deux bonnes heures,** I waited a full *or* a good two hours, I waited (for) two solid hours; **arriver b. premier,** to come in an easy first; **prendre une bonne moitié de qch,** to take a good half of sth; **donner bonne mesure,** to give good *or* full measure; **elle a reçu une bonne fessée,** she got a good spanking; **il faudrait qu'on ait une bonne discussion,** we must have a proper discussion *or* talk; **une bonne fois pour toutes,** once and for all;

(l) de b., *Litt* **tout de b.,** seriously, in earnest, really, truly; **est-ce pour de b.?,** are you serious?; **il pleut pour de b.,** it's raining in real earnest; **c'est b.!,** good!, enough said!;

(m) b.!, right!, good!, fine!; **b., je viendrai,** all right, I'll come; **il est malade, allons b.?,** he's ill, eh?; **ah b., je ne le savais pas,** oh, I didn't know; **b., b., d'accord,** all right, all right, *F* OK, OK.

2 *adv* **tenir b.,** to stand fast, to hold one's own; **tenez b.!,** hold tight!, hold on (tight)!; (*ne lâchez pas*) don't give up *or* in; **sentir b.,** to smell good; **il fait b. vivre,** it's good to be alive; **il ne fait pas b. se promener dans ce quartier,** it's not safe to walk in this district.

3 *n* **les bons,** the good, the righteous; *F* (*dans un film etc*) the goodies; **un b.** *ou* **une bonne à rien,** a good-for-nothing; **une histoire de bons et de méchants,** a goodies and baddies story.

4 *nm* **cela a du b.,** it has its good points, it has some advantages, there's some good in it; **il y a du b. à ne pas travailler,** there's something to be said for not working; **il y a du b. dans ce livre,** this book has some good parts; **le b. de l'histoire,** the best part of the story.

bon[2] *nm* **(a)** (*billet*) voucher, ticket, coupon; **b. de caisse,** cash voucher; *Com* **b. de livraison,** delivery note; **b. de commande,** purchase order; **b. de réduction,** money-off coupon *or* voucher; **b. d'achat,** gift voucher; **b. d'essence,** petrol coupon; **b. pour 200 francs d'achat,** voucher for 200 francs; **(b)** *Fin* bond, bill, draft; **b. au porteur,** bearer bond; **b. du Trésor,** treasury bond, exchequer bill; **b. d'exécution de contrôle,** performance bond; **(c)** I.O.U.; (*donné à un créancier*) note of hand; **(d)** *Typ* **b. à tirer,** final proof.

bonace [bɔnas] *nf* lull, calm (*before or after a storm*).

bonapartisme [bɔnapartism] *nm* Bonapartism.

bonapartiste [bɔnapartist] *adj & n* Bonapartist.

bonasse [bɔnas] *adj* weak(-willed), (too) easy-going.

bonbon [bɔ̃bɔ̃] *nm* **(a)** sweet, *Am* candy, *Austr* lolly; **bonbons anglais,** fruit drops, (boiled) fruit sweets; **bonbons acidulés,** acid drops; **(b)** *Belg* biscuit.

bonbonne [bɔ̃bɔn] *nf* **(a)** *Ind* carboy; **(b)** (*recipient*) demijohn; **b. en verre,** glass demijohn; **une b. de vin,** a demijohn of wine.

bonbonnière [bɔ̃bɔnjɛr] *nf* **(a)** (*pour les bonbons*) sweet box, bonbonnière, *Am* candy box; **(b)** *Fig* doll's house, bijou residence.

bond [bɔ̃] *nm* **(a)** (*saut*) bound, leap, jump, spring; **faire un b.,** to leap, to spring; **franchir qch d'un b.,** to clear sth at one bound; **se lever d'un b.,** to spring *or* to leap to one's feet; **les loyers ont fait un b.,** rents have shot up; **progresser par bonds,** to advance by leaps and bounds; **elle n'a fait qu'un b. jusqu'à la maison en feu,** she rushed over to the blazing house; **b. en avant,** breakthrough (*in technology etc*); **(b)** (*of ball etc*) bounce, rebound; **prendre la balle au b.,** to catch the ball on the bounce *or* the rebound; *Fig* to seize *or* jump at the opportunity; **faire faux b. à qn,** to leave s.o. in the lurch, to let s.o. down, to stand s.o. up.

bonde [bɔ̃d] *nf* **(a)** plug (*of sink, bath*); bung (*of cask*); sluice gate (*of pond*); **lâcher** *ou* **lever la b.,** to pull the plug out; *Fig* **lâcher la b. à sa colère,** to give vent to one's anger; **(b)** (*trou*) plughole (*of bath etc*); bunghole (*of cask*); drainage hole, outlet (*of pond etc*).

bondé [bɔ̃de] *adj* chock-full, crammed (*bus etc*); **des trains bondés de vacanciers,** trains chock-a-block *or* crammed with holiday makers; *Th* **salle bondée,** packed house.

bondieuserie [bɔ̃djøzri] *nf Péj* **(a)** (*bigoterie*) religiosity, bigotry; **(b)** (*objet*) devotional objects, religious knick-knacks.

bondir [bɔ̃dir] *vi* **(a)** (*sauter*) to leap (up), to spring (up), to jump (up); **b. sur qch,** to spring at *or* pounce on sth; **elle bondit sur moi et attrapa ma sacoche,** she pounced on me and grabbed my bag; *Fig* **il a bondi de colère,** he flew into a rage; **cela me fait b.,** it infuriates me, it makes me wild; **(b)** (*courir*) to rush (off), to dash (off); **(c)** (*gambader*) to gambol, to leap (about), to skip (about); **(d)** (*of ball etc*) to bounce.

bondissement [bɔ̃dismɑ̃] *nm* **(a)** (*saut*) bound(ing), leaping; **(b)** gambolling, frisking (*of lambs etc*).

bondon [bɔ̃dɔ̃] *nm* **(a)** (*bouchon*) bung; **(b)** (*ouverture*) bunghole; **(c)** (*fromage*) (cylindrical) cheese.

bon enfant [bɔnɑ̃fɑ̃] *adj inv* (*personne, atmosphère etc*) easy-going.

bonheur [bɔnœr] *nm* **(a)** (*chance*) good fortune, good luck, success; **j'ai eu le b. de la connaître,** I had the good fortune to know her; **porter b. à qn,** to bring s.o. (good) luck; **il ne connaît pas son b.,** he doesn't know how lucky he is; **quel b.!,** what a blessing!; **par b.,** luckily, fortunately, as luck would have it; **au petit b.,** haphazardly; **au petit b. la chance,** trusting to luck;

(b) (*bien-être*) happiness; **la recherche du b.,** the quest for happiness; **le b. de vivre,** the joy of living; **faire le b. de qn,** to make s.o. happy; **ces chocolats font mon b.,** I adore these chocolates; **l'argent ne fait pas le b.,** money can't buy you happiness; **il fait tout pour mon b.,** he does everything he can to make me happy; **j'ai eu le b. de voir ma fille naître,** I had the joy of seeing my daughter being born; **quel b. de voyager en avion,** what a pleasure *or* delight it is to travel by air;

(c) *Litt* (*réussite*) **texte écrit avec b.,** felicitous text; **le salé et le sucré s'allient avec b.,** savoury and sweet combine happily *or* are a happy combination.

bonheur-du-jour [bɔnœrdyjur] *nm* escritoire.
bonhomie [bɔnɔmi] *nf* simple good-heartedness, good nature, bonhomie; **avec b.**, goodnaturedly.
bonhomme [bɔnɔm] *nm F* (*homme, type*) fellow, chap, bloke, *Am* guy; **un vilain b.**, a nasty piece of work; **c'est un sacré b.**, he's a hell of a guy; **pourquoi pleures-tu, mon b.?**, (*à un petit garçon*) what are you crying for, sonny?; **il va son petit b. de chemin,** he's jogging quietly along; (*in car*) he's bumbling along; **dessiner des bonshommes,** to draw funny people *or* figures; **b. de** *ou* **en pain d'épice,** gingerbread man; **b. de neige,** snowman; (*pl bonshommes* [bɔ̃zɔm]).
boni [bɔni] *nm* bonus, profit; *Fin* surplus, balance in hand.
boniche [bɔniʃ] *nf Péj* young maid(servant); **je ne suis pas ta b., fais-le tout seul!,** I'm not your servant, do it yourself!
bonification [bɔnifikɑsjɔ̃] *nf* **(a)** improvement (*of land etc*); **(b)** *Com* allowance, bonus; **b. pour non sinistre,** no claims bonus; **(c)** *Sp* advantage.
bonifier [bɔnifje] *v* (*pr sub & impf* **n. bonifiions, v. bonifiiez**) **1** *vt* **(a)** to improve (*field, one's character etc*); **(b)** *Com* to make up, to make good (*shortage etc*); **(c)** to give (*s.o.*) a bonus. **2 se bonifier** *vpr* (*of wine etc*) to improve; **ses humeurs vont se b. avec le temps,** his nature will improve with time.
boniment [bɔnimɑ̃] *nm* **(a)** *Com* sales talk; **faire du b. à qn,** to try to coax s.o.; **faire du b. à qn pour qu'il fasse qch,** to try to coax *or* talk s.o. into doing sth; **(b)** *F* (*blague*) tall story; **tout ça c'est du b.**, that's all eyewash *or* claptrap.
bonimenter [bɔnimɑ̃te] *vi F* to hand out the sales talk.
bonite [bɔnit] *nf* (*poisson*) bonito.
bonjour [bɔ̃ʒur] *nm* good morning, good afternoon; *F* hello, *Am* hi!, *Fml* good day; (*quand on est présenté à qn*) how d'you do?; **dis b. à la dame,** (*à un enfant*) say hello to the lady; **(dis) b. à ta mère (de ma part),** (give) my regards *or* remember me to your mother, say hello to your mother for me; **c'est facile** *ou* **simple comme b.**, it's as easy as ABC; *F Iron* **b. les dégâts!,** wait for the mess!; **b. la soirée,** it's going to be a long evening!
bon marché [bɔ̃marʃe] *adj inv* cheap.
bonne [bɔn] *nf* **(a)** maid(servant); **b. à tout faire,** maid of all work; **b. d'enfants,** nursery nurse, nanny; **(b) en voilà une (bien) b.!,** that's a good one!; **il en a de bonnes!,** (*il croit que ça va marcher tout seul*) he must be joking!; **avoir qn à la b.**, (*d'un employeur, d'un professeur*) to have a soft spot for s.o.
Bonne-Espérance [bɔnɛsperɑ̃s] *n* **Cap de B.-E.,** Cape of Good Hope.
bonne-maman [bɔnmamɑ̃] *nf* grandmama; (*pl bonnes-mamans*).
bonnement [bɔnmɑ̃] *adv* **tout b.**, simply, plainly, frankly; **je lui ai dit tout b. que ...**, I just *or* simply told him that ... .
bonnet [bɔnɛ] *nm* **(a)** (*coiffure*) (brimless) cap, hat; (child's) bonnet; **b. de bain,** bathing cap, swimming cap; **b. de ski,** ski cap; **b. de douche,** shower cap; *Mil* **b. de police,** forage cap; **b. à poil,** bearskin, busby; *Fig* **prendre qch sous son b.**, to take it upon oneself to do sth, *F* to do sth off one's own bat; **opiner du b.**, to fall in with the majority; *Fig* **avoir la tête près du b.**, to have a short fuse; *Fig* **jeter son b. par dessus les moulins,** to throw caution to the winds; **c'est b. blanc et blanc b.**, it's six of one and half a dozen of the other; **b. de nuit,** nightcap; **être triste comme un b. de nuit,** to be as cheerful as the grave; **b. d'évêque,** bishop's mitre; *Culin F* parson's nose (*of fowl*); *Fig* **gros b.**, big shot, big noise, bigwig;
(b) cup (*of brassière*); **quelle profondeur de b.?,** what size cup?;
(c) *Zool* second stomach, honeycomb stomach, reticulum (*of ruminant*).
bonneterie [bɔnɛtri] *nf* **(a)** (*bas*) hosiery; **(b)** *Com* hosiery trade; (*magasin*) hosier's (shop).
bonnetier, -ière [bɔntje, -jɛr] *n* hosier.
bonniche [bɔniʃ] *nf Péj* young maid(servant).
bon-papa [bɔ̃papa] *nm* grandpapa; (*pl bons-papas*).
bonsaï [bɔnzai] *nm* (*arbre*) bonsai.
bonsoir [bɔ̃swar] *nm* good evening; (*quand on se quitte tard*) goodnight; **dire b.** *ou* **souhaiter le b. à qn,** to say good evening *or* goodnight to s.o.; *F* **tout est dit, b.!** there's nothing more to be said!, there's an end of it!, and that's that!
bonté [bɔ̃te] *nf* **(a)** (*qualité*) goodness, kindness, kindliness; **une femme d'une grande b.**, a very kind(ly) woman; **sourire plein de b.**, kindly *or* benevolent smile; **ayez la b. de me dire ...**, please tell me ...; *F* **b. divine** *ou* **du ciel!,** good heavens!; **auriez-vous la b. de ...?,** would you be so good as to ...?; **bontés,** kindnesses, kind actions; **je ne m'attendais pas à tant de bontés,** I didn't expect such kindness; **(b)** *Vieilli* goodness, good quality, excellence (*of things*).
bonus-malus [bɔnysmalys] *nm* = no-claims bonus system of car insurance.
bon vivant [bɔ̃vivɑ̃] **1** *adj* **il est b. v.,** he likes the good life. **2** *nm* **des bons vivants,** people who like the good life.
bonze [bɔ̃z] *nm* **(a)** *Rel* Buddhist priest *or* monk, bonze; **(b)** *Fig* (*personnage important*) *F* big shot; **(c)** *F* **vieux b.**, old fogey *or* dodderer.
bonzerie [bɔ̃zri] *nf* Buddhist monastery.
bonzesse [bɔ̃zɛs] *nf* Buddhist nun, bonze.
boogie-woogie [bugiwugi] *nm Am Mus* boogie-woogie.
bookmaker, *F* **book** [buk(mɛkœr)] *nm* bookmaker, *F* bookie.
booléen, -éenne [buleɛ̃, -eɛn] *adj Math Ordinat* Boolean.
boom [bum] *nm* **(a)** *Com Fin* boom; **(b)** *F* (young people's) party.
boomerang [bumrɑ̃g] *nm* boomerang; **l'effet b. du scandale,** the backlash of the scandal; *F* **son projet a fait b.**, his plan boomeranged *or* backfired.
booster [bustœr] *nm* (*amplificateur*) *& Astronaut* booster.
boots [buts] *nfpl* ankle boots.
boquer [bɔke] *vi Can* (*s'entêter*) to dig one's heels in.
borate [bɔrat] *nm Ch* borate.
borax [bɔraks] *nm Ch* borax.
borborygme [bɔrbɔrigm] *nm* (*usu pl*) rumbling(s), gurgling(s) (*in the stomach*); **borborygmes de la plomberie,** gurgling noises in the plumbing.
bord [bɔr] *nm* **(a)** *Nau* side (*of ship*); **jeter qch/tomber par-dessus b.**, to throw sth/to fall overboard; **moteur hors b.**, outboard motor; **b. au vent/sous le vent,** weather/lee side; **faux b.**, list; **le long du b.**, alongside; **être b. à quai,** to be alongside the quay; **les hommes du b.**, the ship's company, the crew; **être du même b.**, to be on the same side *or* of the same opinion; *Can* **se trouver du bon/mauvais b.**, to be on the right/wrong side; **journal de b.**, log, logbook; **à b. d'un navire/d'un avion,** on board *or* aboard a ship/an aircraft; **à b.**, on board (*ship*), aboard; **avoir qn à b.**, to have s.o. aboard; *Fig* **vous êtes le seul maître à b.**, you're the one in charge;
(b) (*bordée*) tack, leg; **courir** *ou* **tirer un b.**, to make a tack;
(c) edge (*of table etc*); border, hem (*of garment*); edge, verge (*of cliff etc*); brim (*of hat*); rim, brim (*of vase etc*); lip (*of cup, wound etc*); **un trait de khôl sur le b. de la paupière,** a line of kohl on the edge of the eyelid; **b. du trottoir,** kerb, *Am* curb; **remplir un verre jusqu'au** *ou* **à ras b.**, to fill a glass to the brim; **au b. de la route,** at *or* on the roadside, at *or* on the side of the road; *Can* **de l'autre b. de la rue,** on the other side of the street; **auberge au b.** *ou* **sur le b. de la route,** wayside *or* roadside inn; **hôtel au b. du lac,** lakeside hotel; **je l'ai trouvé au b. de la rivière,** I found it on the river bank; **aller au b. de la mer,** to go to the seaside; **maison au b. de la mer,** seaside house; **maison sur le b. de la mer,** house on the sea front *or* the (sea)shore; **le b. de mer est très construit,** there is a lot of development along the sea front; **b. à b.**, edge to edge; *Can* **de b. en b.**, from end to end; *Av* **b. d'attaque/de fuite,** leading/trailing edge (*of wing*); **chapeau à larges bords,** broad *or* wide-brimmed hat; **au b. du tombeau,** at death's door; **au b. des larmes,** on the verge of tears; **elle est au b. de la crise de nerfs,** she's on the brink of a nervous breakdown; **un peu voleur/bête/***etc* **sur les bords,** a bit light-fingered/stupid/*etc*.
bordage [bɔrdaʒ] *nm* **(a)** edging (*of dress etc*); **b. de pierres,** stone kerb *or Am* curb; **(b)** *Can* **bordages,** inshore ice; **(c)** *Nau* plank(ing), sheathing, plating (*of ship*).
bordé [bɔrde] **1** *adj* edged, fringed, bordered (**de,** with); **mouchoir b. de dentelle,** lace-edged handkerchief; **boulevard b. d'arbres,** tree-lined boulevard. **2** *nm* **(a)** edging, border (*of garment etc*); **(b)** *Nau* planking, planks, plating (*of ship*).
bordeaux [bɔrdo] **1** *nm* Bordeaux (wine); **b. rouge,** claret. **2** *adj inv* claret(-coloured), maroon.
bordée [bɔrde] *nf Nau* **(a)** broadside (*of guns, fire*); **lâcher une b.**, to let fly a broadside; *Fig* **b. de jurons** *ou* **d'injures,** torrent *or* hail of abuse; *Can* **b. (de neige),** heavy snowfall; **(b)** (*distance*) tack; **courir une b.**, to make a tack; **tirer des bordées,** to tack; *F* **tirer** *ou* **courir une b.**, to go on a binge *or* a pub crawl; **(c)** (*équipe*) watch; **b.**

de tribord/de bâbord, starboard/port watch.
bordel [bɔrdɛl] *nm* brothel; *Arg* **quel b.!,** what a mess!, what a shambles!; **tu en as fait un beau b.,** a fine mess you've made of this; **tout le b.,** the whole damn lot; **b.!,** bloody hell!
bordelais, -aise [bɔrdəlɛ, -ɛz] **1** *adj* (*native, inhabitant*) of Bordeaux. **2** *nm* **le B.,** the Bordeaux region. **3** *nf* **bordelaise** (*futaille*) = cask of about 225 litres; (*bouteille*) = bottle of about 4 litres. **4** *n* **B.,** inhabitant *or* native of Bordeaux.
bordélique [bɔrdelik] *adj F* (*pièce, bureau etc*) shambolic; **tu es très b.,** you're a real slob.
border [bɔrde] *vt* **(a)** to border; to edge, to fringe (*sth with sth*); **les peupliers qui bordent le chemin,** the poplars lining the road; *Nau* **navire qui borde la côte,** ship skirting the coast; **b. un lit,** to tuck in the bedclothes; **b. qn (dans son lit),** to tuck s.o. in *or* up; **(b)** *Nau* to plank, to plate (*a ship*); **(c)** to ship (*oars*); **(d)** *Nau* **b. une voile,** to haul the sheets taut.
bordereau, -eaux [bɔrdəro] *nm* statement; invoice, account (*of goods, cash etc*); (*dans un devis*) list, schedule; **b. de(s) prix,** price list; **b. d'expédition,** dispatch note; **b. de livraison,** delivery note; **b. d'achat,** contract note, purchase note; **b. de crédit,** credit note; **b. de versement,** paying-in slip; **b. de paie** *ou* **de salaire,** wage(s) slip, salary advice (note).
bordure [bɔrdyr] *nf* **(a)** border, rim; fringe, edging, edge (*of garment etc*); kerb, *Am* curb (*of pavement etc*); binding (*of hat etc*); welt (*of glove etc*); *Tricot* band; **papier à b. noire,** black-edged paper; **la banlieue se développe en b. de la ville,** suburbs grow up around the edge of the town; **hôtel en b. de mer,** seaside hotel; **(b)** frame, surround (*of mirror etc*).
bore [bɔr] *nm Ch* boron.
boréal, -aux [bɔreal, -o] *adj* boreal, north(ern).
borgne [bɔrɲ] **1** *adj* **(a)** one-eyed, blind in one eye; *MecE* **trou b.,** recessed hole; **(b)** *Fig* disreputable, shady (*house, street etc*); **café b.,** low dive. **2** *n* **un(e) b.,** one-eyed man *or* woman.
borique [bɔrik] *adj Ch* boric, boracic (*acid*).
boriqué [bɔrike] *adj Pharm* **pommade boriquée,** boracic ointment; **compresse en coton b.,** boracic lint compress.
bornage [bɔrnaʒ] *nm* demarcation, marking out (*of land boundaries*); **pierre de b.,** boundary stone.
borne [bɔrn] *nf* **(a)** (*limite*) boundary mark *or* stone *or* post; *F* kilometre; **b. kilométrique,** ≈ milestone; *Nau* **b. d'amarrage,** bollard (*on wharf*); **b. d'incendie,** hydrant; *Fig* **il était planté là comme une b..** he stood there as if he had taken root; *F* **il y a 200 bornes entre les deux villes,** the two towns are 200 kilometres apart; **bornes,** boundaries, limits, bounds, confines (*of kingdom, knowledge etc*); **dépasser toutes les bornes,** to go too far, *Am F* to be out of line; **sans bornes,** boundless, limitless, unlimited; **un bonheur sans bornes,** boundless happiness; **(b)** *El* terminal; **b. de mise à la terre** *ou* **de masse,** earth *or Am* ground terminal.
borné [bɔrne] *adj* limited, restricted (*intelligence etc*); narrow (*mind*); narrow-minded (*person*).
borne-fontaine [bɔrn(ə)fɔ̃tɛn] *nf* (*pl bornes-fontaines*) **(a)** (*fontaine*) public drinking fountain; **(b)** *Can* fire hydrant.
borner [bɔrne] **1** *vt* to mark out, to mark the boundary of (*field etc*); to form the boundary of (*country etc*); to limit, to restrict (*view, power etc*); to set limits *or* bounds to (*ambition, desires*); **b. une route,** to set up milestones along a road; **le chemin qui borne la forêt,** the path bordering the forest.

2 se borner *vpr* **(a)** (*se limiter*) to restrict *or* limit oneself, to exercise self-restraint; **je me borne au strict nécessaire,** I confine *or* limit myself to the absolute essentials; **se b. à faire qch,** to limit oneself to doing sth;

(b) (*of things*) to be confined, to be limited, to be restricted (**à qch,** to sth); **toute leur science se borne à cela,** this is the (full) extent of their knowledge; **voici à quoi se borne son raisonnement,** this is what his argument comes down to; **ses visites se bornent à quelques jours,** his visits are never any longer than a few days.
bortch [bɔrtʃ] *nm Culin* borsch(t), borshch.
bosnien, -ienne [bɔznjɛ̃, -jɛn] *Hist* **1** *adj* Bosnian. **2** *n* **B.,** Bosnian.
Bosnie [bɔzni] *nf Hist* Bosnia.
Bosphore (le) [ləbɔsfɔr] *nm* the Bosphorus.
bosquet [bɔskɛ] *nm* grove, thicket, copse.
boss [bɔs] *nm F* boss; *Fig* **c'est toi le b., après tout,** you're the boss *or* you're in charge, after all.
bossage [bɔsaʒ] *nm Archit* boss.
bossa-nova [bɔsanɔva] *nf Mus* bossa nova.
bosse [bɔs] *nf* **(a)** hump (*of hunchback, camel etc*); *F* **il a roulé sa b. partout,** he's knocked about *or* been about a bit; **(b)** bump, lump, swelling (*on the head etc*); unevenness, bump (*in the ground*); **se faire une b. en tombant,** to fall and get a bump; **la route est pleine de bosses,** the road is very bumpy; **sauter dans les bosses,** (*au ski*) to jump moguls; *Fig* **avoir la b. du commerce/des maths,** to have a good head for business/maths; **(c)** *Nau* painter (*of boat*).
bosselage [bɔslaʒ] *nm* embossing.
bosseler [bɔsle] *vt* (**je bosselle, n. bosselons; je bossellerai**) **(a)** (*travailler*) to emboss; **(b)** (*par accident*) to dent, to bash; **casserole toute bosselée,** battered saucepan.
bosselure [bɔslyr] *nf* **(a)** (*on silverware*) relief; **(b)** inequality, unevenness, bumpiness (*of surface*).
bosser [bɔse] *vi Arg* to slave, to slog.
bosseur, -euse [bɔsœr, -øz] *n Arg* hard worker, slogger.
bossoir [bɔswar] *nm Nau* **(a)** (*pour l'ancre*) cathead; (*de navire*) bow; **(b)** (*appareil de levage*) davit; **les bras de b.,** the davit guys.
bossu, -ue [bɔsy] **1** *adj* hunchbacked (*person*); humped (*animal*); **tu deviens b.,** you're getting a stoop. **2** *n* hunchback; *F* **rire comme un b.,** to laugh one's head off, to laugh like a hyena.
bossué [bɔsɥe] *adj* battered (*kettle etc*).
bossuer [bɔsɥe] *vt* = **BOSSELER (b)**.
boston [bɔstɔ̃] *nm* **(a)** *Cartes* boston; **(b)** (*danse*) boston; hesitation waltz.
Boston [bɔstɔn] *n* Boston.
bostonien, -ienne [bɔstɔnjɛ̃, -jɛn] **1** *adj* Bostonian. **2** *n* **B.,** Bostonian.
bot [bo] *adj* **pied b.,** clubfoot; (*personne*) clubfooted person; **main bote,** club hand.
botanique [bɔtanik] **1** *adj* botanical. **2** *nf* botany.
botaniste [bɔtanist] *n* botanist.
botte¹ [bɔt] *nf* bunch, bundle (*of carrots etc*); truss, bundle, sheaf (*of hay*); bale (*of hemp etc*).
botte² *nf* (high) boot; **une paire de bottes,** a pair of boots; **des bottes en cuir,** leather boots; **bottes à l'écuyère,** riding boots; **bottes de mer,** seaboots, jackboots; **bottes d'égoutier, bottes cuissardes,** waders; **bottes de** *ou* **en caoutchouc,** wellingtons, rubber boots, gumboots, *F* wellies; *Fig* **sous la b. de l'envahisseur,** under the heel of the invader; **la b. de l'Italie,** the boot of Italy; *F Vieilli* **à propos de bottes,** apropos of nothing at all, without rhyme or reason; *F* **en avoir plein les bottes,** to be fed up with sth; **cirer les bottes de qn,** to lick s.o.'s boots .
botte³ *nf Escrime* pass, thrust, lunge, hit; **porter une b.,** to lunge.
botte⁴ *nf Scol F* = students who leave the École Polytechnique with the highest marks.
botté [bɔte] *nm Can* (*in American football*) punt.
bottelage [bɔtlaʒ] *nm* trussing, tying up (*of hay*).
botteler [bɔtle] *vt* (**je bottelle, n. bottelons; je bottellerai**) to bundle, to tie up, to truss (*hay etc*).
botter [bɔte] **1** *vt* **(a)** to put (*s.o.'s*) boots *or* shoes on; (*fournir*) to supply (*s.o.*) with boots; **être bien botté,** to be well shod; **le Chat botté,** Puss in Boots; **(b)** *F* to boot, to kick (*a ball etc*); **il lui a botté les fesses,** he booted him *or* gave him a kick up the backside; **(c)** *F* (*plaire à*) **ça me botte,** I like that, I fancy that. **2** *vi Fb F* to kick the ball. **3 se botter** *vpr* to put one's boots on.
bottier [bɔtje] *nm* bootmaker, shoemaker.
bottillon [bɔtijɔ̃] *nm* (*de femme*) ankle boot.
bottin ® [bɔtɛ̃] *nm* telephone directory; **être dans le b.,** to be in the telephone directory.
bottine [bɔtin] *nf* ankle boot; (baby's) bootee.
boubou [bubu] *nm* bubu, boubou.
bouc [buk] *nm* (billy) goat; **(barbe de) b.,** goatee (beard); **b. émissaire,** scapegoat; *F* **puer comme un b., puer le b.,** to stink, to pong.
boucan [bukɑ̃] *nm Arg* hullabaloo, row, din, uproar; **un b. de tous les diables,** the devil of a row; **faire un sacré** *ou* **du b.,** to make *or* kick up a row *or* din.
boucane [bukan] *nf Can* smoke.
boucané [bukane] *adj* tanned, weatherbeaten, swarthy (*complexion*).
boucaner [bukane] *vt* to smoke, to cure (*meat, fish etc*); to tan (*s.o.'s skin*).
boucanier [bukanje] *nm* buccaneer, pirate.
bouchage [buʃaʒ] *nm* filling up *or* in, plugging, stopping (up) (*of gas pipe etc*); blocking (up), clogging (*of pipe etc*);

corking (*of bottle*); blocking up, walling up (*of passage etc*).

bouche [buʃ] *nf* **(a)** mouth; **avoir/parler la b. pleine,** to have/to talk with one's mouth full; **une pipe à la b.,** with a pipe in his mouth; **avoir bonne/mauvaise b.,** to have a pleasant/a nasty taste in one's mouth; **garder qch pour la bonne b.,** to save something until last *or* as a titbit; **cela fait venir l'eau à la b.,** it makes your mouth water; *Fig* **faire la fine b.,** to be awkward; **faire la petite b.,** to turn one's nose up; **faire la b. en cul de poule,** to purse one's lips; **dire qch la b. en cœur,** to say sth with a simper; **embrasser qn à pleine b.,** to kiss s.o. full on the lips *or* passionately, *F* to give s.o. a French kiss; **elle l'embrasse sur la b.,** she kisses him on the lips; **manger à pleine b.,** to eat greedily, to gobble one's food; **provisions de b.,** food; **dépenses de b.,** housekeeping expenses; **c'est une fine b.,** he's a gourmet; **avoir une douzaine de bouches à nourrir,** to have a dozen mouths to feed; **les bouches inutiles,** unproductive people; *Méd* **à prendre par la b.,** to be taken internally; **elle n'osait pas ouvrir la b.,** she didn't dare open her mouth; **je l'ai appris de sa propre b.,** I had it from his own lips; *Fig* **ôter** *ou* **enlever le pain de la b. de qn,** to take the bread from s.o.'s mouth; **son nom est dans toutes les bouches,** everyone's talking about him, his name is on everyone's lips; **elle n'a que ce mot à la b.,** that's all she ever says; **demeurer b. close,** to remain silent, to hold one's tongue; **b. cousue!,** not a word!, mum's the word!, don't breathe a word (of it)!; *Arg* **ta b.!,** shut up!, dry up!; *F* **il en avait la b. pleine** *ou* **plein la b.,** he was full of it, he couldn't talk of anything else; **de b. à oreille,** by word of mouth; (*officieusement*) off the record, unofficially;

(b) mouth (*of horse, fish etc*); **cheval sans b.** *ou* **fort en b.,** hard-mouthed horse; **cheval à la b. chatouilleuse,** tender-mouthed horse;

(c) mouth (*of river etc*); opening, aperture (*of crater, well etc*); muzzle (*of gun*); slot (*of money box etc*); **b. de métro,** underground *or Am* subway entrance; *Constr etc* **b. d'accès,** manhole (*of sewer*); **b. d'eau,** hydrant; **b. d'incendie,** fire hydrant, *Am* fireplug; **b. de chaleur,** hot air vent; **b. d'aération,** air vent; **b. d'égout,** gully hole.

bouché [buʃe] *adj* **(a)** blocked, choked (*pipe etc*); **nez b.,** blocked *or* stuffed-up nose; *Fig* **avoir l'esprit b., être b.,** to be dense *or* thick; **ce poste est b.,** this is a dead-end job; **être b. à l'émeri,** to be a complete moron; **temps b.,** cloudy *or* overcast weather; **(b) cidre b.,** bottled cider.

bouche-à-bouche [buʃabuʃ] *nm inv* mouth-to-mouth resuscitation, kiss of life; **pratiquer/faire le b.-à-b. à un blessé,** to give an injured person mouth-to-mouth resuscitation *or* the kiss of life.

bouchée [buʃe] *nf* **(a)** (*quantité*) mouthful; **juste une b. pour goûter,** just a mouthful to taste; *Fig* **acheter qch pour une b. de pain,** to buy sth for a song; **ne faire qu'une b. d'un mets,** to eat a dish quickly *or* greedily; *Fig* **ne faire qu'une b. de qn/de qch,** to make short work of s.o./sth; *Fig* **mettre les bouchées doubles,** to do a job in double quick time; **(b)** *Culin* small patty, pasty; **b. aux huîtres,** oyster patty; **b. à la reine,** chicken vol-au-vent; **b. (de chocolat),** chocolate.

boucher¹ [buʃe] **1** *vt* to fill up *or* in (*gap etc*); to block (up), to choke (up), to clog (*pipe etc*); to block (*view etc*); **b. un trou,** to plug *or* block up *or* stop (up) a hole; *Fig* **cela servira à b. un trou,** that will do as a stopgap, that will tide us over; **b. une bouteille,** to cork a bottle; **b. une fenêtre,** to block up *or* wall up a window; **b. le passage à qn,** to block *or* stand in s.o.'s way; *F* **il m'en a bouché un coin,** he shut me up, he took the wind out of my sails. **2 se boucher** *vpr* (*of pipe etc*) to get blocked (up) *or* choked (up) *or* clogged; **se b. le nez,** to hold one's nose; **se b. les oreilles,** to put one's fingers in one's ears; *Fig* to refuse to listen.

boucher² *nm* butcher; *Fig Péj* **c'est un vrai b.,** he's nothing but a butcher.

bouchère [buʃɛr] *nf* **(a)** (woman) butcher; **(b)** (*épouse du boucher*) butcher's wife.

boucherie [buʃri] *nf* butcher's (shop); (*trade*) butchery; *Fig* butchery, slaughter; **animaux de b.,** animals for slaughter; *Fig* **ce fut une vraie b.,** it was a real bloodbath.

bouche-trou [buʃtru] *nm F* substitute, stopgap, stand-in; **servir de b.-t.,** to act as a stopgap; (*pl bouche-trous*).

bouchon [buʃɔ̃] *nm* **(a)** cap, top (*of bottle*); stopper, plug, bung (*of cask*); **b. (de liège),** cork; **vin qui sent le b.,** corked wine; **b. de verre,** glass stopper; **b. à l'émeri,** ground(glass) stopper; *Aut* **b. de radiateur,** radiator cap; *MecE* **b. de vidange** *ou* **de trop plein,** drain(ing) plug *or* tap; **(b)** *Fig* (traffic) hold-up, traffic jam; **il y a un b. sur la Nationale 7,** there's a hold-up *or* traffic jam on the N7; **trois kilomètres de b.,** a three-kilometre tailback; **(c) b. d'air,** airlock (*in pipe*); **(d)** *Pêche* float, bob (*of line*); **(e)** wisp, handful (*of straw*); **(f)** *Arch* bush, sign (*of tavern*).

bouchonner [buʃɔne] **1** *vi F* to be jammed up; **ça bouchonne à partir d'Évreux,** from Évreux on it's traffic jams all the way. **2** *vt* **(a)** to rub down, to wisp down (*horse*); **(b)** to (molly)coddle, to cosset (*child*).

bouchot [buʃo] *nm* mussel bank *or* bed *or* farm.

bouclage [buklaʒ] *nm* **(a)** *F Mil etc* imprisonment, locking up; **(b)** surrounding, sealing off, cordoning off (*of area*); **(c)** *Ordinat* looping.

boucle [bukl] *nf* **(a)** buckle (*on belt, shoe etc*); **b. du harnais,** harness buckle; **(b)** loop, bow (*of ribbon, string etc*); *Nau* bight, eye (*of rope*); loop, sweep (*of river*); bend (*of river, road*); *Av Ordinat etc* loop; **faire une b. pour retourner à ...,** to loop back to ....; **b. à nœud coulant,** running loop; **décrire de nombreuses boucles,** (*of river*) to meander; **(c)** (*anneau*) ring; **b. de rideau,** curtain ring; **boucles d'oreilles,** earrings; **(d)** curl, ringlet, lock (*of hair*); **(e)** *Sp* lap.

bouclé [bukle] *adj* curly (*hair*); *Ordinat* **système b.,** looped system.

boucler [bukle] **1** *vt* **(a)** to buckle, to fasten (*belt etc*); *F* **boucle-la!, la boucle!,** belt up!, shut up!; *F* **b. une affaire,** to settle *or* clinch a matter; **b. les comptes,** to close the books; **b. sa valise,** to shut one's suitcase; (*se préparer à partir*) to get ready to leave; **(b)** to loop, to tie up, to knot (*ribbon, cord etc*); **b. la boucle,** *Av* to loop the loop; *Fig* to come full circle; **(c)** *F* to lock up, to imprison (*s.o.*), *F* to put (*s.o.*) inside; **(d)** to surround, to seal off, to cordon off (*an area*); **(e)** *Sp* to lap (*competitor*). **2** *vi* (*of hair*) to curl, to be curly; **la mer, ça me fait b.,** salt water makes my hair go curly; *F* **il n'y a plus qu'à b.,** we'll have to shut up shop *or* close down. **3 se boucler** *vpr F* **se la b.,** to belt up, to shut it, to shut up.

bouclette [buklɛt] **1** *nf* **(a)** (*petite boucle*) small buckle; **(b)** small curl (*of hair*). **2** *adj Tex* **laine b.,** bouclé wool.

bouclier [buklije] *nm* (*de guerre*) buckler, shield; *Constr* shield; (*de crustacé*) carapace; *Fig* **on s'attend à une levée de boucliers,** an outcry is expected; *Astronaut* **b. thermique,** heat shield; *Géol* **b. canadien,** Laurentian shield.

Bouddha [buda] *nm* Buddha; **acheter un bouddha de jade,** to buy a jade Buddha.

bouddhique [budik] *adj* Buddhist.

bouddhisme [budism] *nm* Buddhism.

bouddhiste [budist] **1** *adj & n* Buddhist.

bouder [bude] **1** *vi* to sulk. **2** *vt* **b. qn/qch,** not to have anything to do with s.o./sth; **tu me boudes?,** aren't you talking to me?; **il boude la peinture moderne,** he doesn't like modern art; **en été les Parisiens boudent les salles de cinéma,** Parisians don't go to the cinema in summer.

bouderie [budri] *nf* sulkiness; (fit of the) sulks; **la chaleur provoque la b. des visiteurs,** people stay away because of the heat.

boudeur, -euse [budœr, -øz] **1** *adj* sulky, sullen (*person*). **2** *n* sulky person. **3** *nf* **boudeuse,** courting couch.

boudin [budɛ̃] *nm* **(a)** *Culin* **b. (noir),** black pudding, *Am* blood sausage; **b. blanc,** white pudding; **clair comme du jus de b.,** as clear as mud; *F* **s'en aller en eau de b.,** (*of undertaking*) to go to pot *or* down the drain *or* the tubes; *F* **boudins,** fat *or* podgy fingers; **(b)** *Can F* **faire du b.,** to sulk; **(c)** *Belg* (*traversin*) bolster; **(d)** *Péj F* lump of a girl; **quel b.!,** what a fat lump!; **(e)** (*in hair*) corkscrew curl, ringlet; roll, twist (*of tobacco etc*); *Min etc* sausage (*of explosive*); flange (*on wheel etc*); *Nau* **b. gonflable,** (inflatable) fender.

boudiné [budine] *adj* **(a) b. dans un pantalon trop étroit,** bursting *or* bulging out of a tight pair of trousers; **(b)** podgy (*fingers etc*).

boudiner [budine] **1** *vt* **(a)** *Tex* to rove, to slub; **(b)** *Tech* to coil (*wire*); **(c)** *F* **cette robe me boudine,** this dress shows all my bulges. **2 se boudiner** *vpr* **se b. dans ses vêtements,** to squeeze into one's clothes.

boudoir [budwar] *nm* boudoir; (*biscuit*) ladyfinger.

boue [bu] *nf* **(a)** mud; **marcher dans la b.,** to walk in the mud; *F* **traîner qn dans la b.,** to drag s.o. through the mud; *F* **se vautrer dans la b.,** to wallow in mud; **couvrir qn de b.,** to throw *or* sling mud at s.o.; **(b)** (*pisé*) (building) clay; **(c)** (*vase*) sediment, mud, sludge; silt (*in river etc*); (*de l'océan*) ooze; **boues minérales,** mud baths; **bain de b.,** mud bath; **boues activées,** radioactive mud; (*épuration des eaux*) activated sludge; **la b. de l'encrier,** the sludge in the inkwell.

bouée [bwe] *nf Nau* buoy; **b. sonore,** sonobuoy; **b. à sifflet,** whistling buoy; **b. à cloche,** bell buoy; **b. d'amarrage** *ou* **de corps-mort,** mooring buoy; **b. lumineuse,** light buoy, floating light; **b. de sauvetage,** lifebuoy; **b. culotte,** breeches buoy; **elle se cramponne à cet espoir comme à une b.**, she is clinging to this hope like a lifeline.

boueur [buœr] *nm* dustman, refuse collector, *Am* garbage man, garbage collector.

boueux, -euse [buø, -øz] **1** *adj* muddy (*road, boots etc*); smudged, blurred (*writing, print etc*). **2** *nm* = **BOUEUR**.

bouffant [bufɑ̃] **1** *adj* puff(ed) (*sleeve*); full (*skirt*); baggy (*trousers*); **cheveux bouffants,** bouffant hair-do. **2** *nm* puff (*of sleeve*).

bouffarde [bufard] *nf F* (tobacco) pipe.

bouffe¹ [buf] *adj Mus* **opéra b.**, opera bouffe, comic opera.

bouffe² *nf F* **(a)** (*aliment*) grub, nosh; **acheter de la b.**, to buy grub; **(b)** (*repas*) eating; **venez, c'est l'heure de la b.**, grub up!

bouffée [bufe] *nf* **(a)** puff (*of smoke*); whiff (*of scent*); breath (*of air*); **tirer une b. de sa pipe,** to take a puff at one's pipe; **b. de chaleur,** blast of hot air; *Méd* hot flush; **(b)** (out)burst, gust, fit (*of eloquence, anger etc*); **travailler par bouffées,** to work by fits and starts.

bouffer [bufe] **1** *vi* **(a)** (*of dress etc*) to puff (out), to balloon (out); (*of bread*) to rise; **(b)** *F* to eat greedily, to gobble, to scoff, to guzzle; **j'ai bien bouffé,** that was a bloody good meal; **quand est-ce qu'on bouffe?**, when's grub up?; *Fig* **il ne va pas te b.**, he won't eat you. **2** *vt* **(a)** (*manger*) to eat (*sth*); **on n'a rien à b.**, there's no grub; **b. de l'essence,** (*of car*) to be heavy on petrol, *Am* to be a gas guzzler; **b. du kilomètre,** to eat up the miles; **avoir envie de b. du curé,** to be very anti-clerical; **(b)** to blow (*money*); **b. un million en six mois,** to run through a million in six months. **3 se bouffer** *vpr F* to be eaten; **ça se bouffe vite, ces petits biscuits,** these little biscuits go down quickly; *Fig* **elles se bouffent le nez constamment,** they're always bickering.

bouffetance [buftɑ̃s] *nf F* grub, nosh.

bouffeur, -euse [bufœr, øz] *n F* guzzler; **un gros b. de viande,** a great meat-eater; **un b. de curé,** an anti-clerical; **c'est un b. de kilomètre,** he likes driving for hours at a stretch, *Br* he likes doing long distances in a oner.

bouffi [bufi] **1** *adj* puffy, puffed (up), swollen (*eyes*); bloated (*face etc*); *Com* **hareng b.**, bloater; **b. d'orgueil,** puffed up with pride. **2** *nm* bloater.

bouffir [bufir] **1** *vt* to swell, to puff up. **2** *vi* (*of eyes, face*) to become swollen, to puff up; (*of face*) to become bloated *or* swollen, to swell.

bouffissure [bufisyr] *nf* **(a)** swelling, puffiness (*of eyes, face*); swelling (*of stomach*); **(b)** turgidity (*of style*).

bouffon, -onne [bufɔ̃, -ɔn] **1** *nm* buffoon, clown, fool; *Arch* jester; **quel b.!**, what a clown! **2** *adj* farcical, comical.

bouffonner [bufɔne] *vi* to play *or* act the buffoon *or* fool.

bouffonnerie [bufɔnri] *nf* buffoonery, clowning, antics; **faire des bouffonneries,** to play *or* act the buffoon *or* fool.

bougainvillée [bugɛ̃vile] *nf*, **bougainvillier** [bugɛ̃vilje] *nm* bougainvillea.

bouge [buʒ] *nm* **(a)** bulge (*of wall etc*); swell (*of wheel nave*); **(b)** *Péj* (*maison*) hovel, dump; (*bar etc*) low dive, sleazy bar; **la cuisine est un b.**, the kitchen is a real pigsty.

bougeoir [buʒwar] *nm* candlestick.

bougeotte [buʒɔt] *nf F* **avoir la b.**, to be fidgety, to have the fidgets; (*voyager sans cesse*) to be always on the move.

bouger [buʒe] *v* (**je bougeai(s)**; **n. bougeons**) **1** *vi* to move; **rester sans b.**, to stand *or* remain still; **ne bougez pas!**, don't move!, keep still!; **ne bouge pas de là,** don't move *or* budge!; *Phot* **ne bougeons plus!**, hold it!; **je ne bougerai pas de la terrasse,** I won't move from the terrace; *Fig* **vous verrez, ce chemisier ne bouge pas au lavage,** you'll find this blouse doesn't shrink or run in the wash; **les prix ne bougent pas,** prices are holding steady; **les ouvriers/étudiants bougent,** the workers/students are restless. **2** *vt F* to move, to shift; **il ne faut rien b.**, you mustn't move *or* shift anything; **elle n'a pas bougé le petit doigt,** she didn't lift a finger. **3 se bouger** *vpr F* to move; **il ne veut pas se b.**, he won't shift *or* budge.

bougie [buʒi] *nf* **(a)** candle; **à la b., aux bougies,** by candlelight; **ampoule de 100 bougies**, 100 watt bulb; *Aut* **b. (d'allumage),** spark(ing) plug; **(b)** *Arg* (*visage*) dial, mug.

bougnat [buɲa] *nm* coal-merchant.

bougnoule [buɲul] *n Arg* (*terme injurieux*) wog.

bougon, -onne [bugɔ̃, -ɔn] *F* **1** *n* grumbler, *Am* grouch. **2** *adj* grumpy, grouchy.

bougonnement [bugɔnmɑ̃] *nm F* grumbling, grousing.

bougonner [bugɔne] *vi F* to grumble, to grouse.

bougran [bugrɑ̃] *nm Tex* buckram.

bougre [bugr] *nm F* **(a)** *Vieilli* (*type*) chap, bloke; *Am* guy; **c'est un bon b.**, he's not a bad sort; **le pauvre b.**, the poor devil; **mauvais b.**, ugly customer; **(b) b. de temps,** filthy weather; **b. d'imbécile,** damn(ed) fool, bloody idiot; **(c) b.!**, blast!, damn it!; **b. que ça fait mal!**, that hurts like blazes!

bougrement [bugrəmɑ̃] *adv* damn(ed); **il fait b. chaud,** it's damn hot.

boui-boui [bwibwi] *nm F* dingy café, *Am* greasy spoon.

bouillabaisse [bujabɛs] *nf Culin* bouillabaisse, Provençal fish soup.

bouillant [bujɑ̃] *adj* **(a)** boiling; **de l'eau bouillante,** boiling water; **(b)** *Fig* fiery, hot-headed, impetuous; **b. de colère,** seething with anger; **b. d'impatience,** bursting with impatience.

bouille [buj] *nf* **(a)** *Arg* face, mug; **il a une bonne b.**, he looks a good sort; **(b)** (wooden) tub for collecting grapes.

bouilleur [bujœr] *nm* **(a)** (brandy) distiller; **b. de cru,** home distiller, still; **(b)** water space, room (*of boiler*).

bouilli [buji] *Culin* **1** *adj* boiled. **2** *nm* boiled meat; *Can* = beans, cabbage, potatoes, salt pork and ham cooked together for several hours.

bouillie [buji] *nf* **(a)** (*pour bébés etc*) gruel; **préparer la b. du bébé,** to prepare the baby's gruel; **mettre en b.**, to mash, to pulp; **légumes en b.**, watery *or* mushy vegetables; *Fig* **les malheureux voyageurs ont été réduits en b.**, the unfortunate passengers were crushed to a pulp; *F* **s'il me provoque je vais le mettre en b.**, if he provokes me I'll beat him to a pulp; **(b)** (*pour le papier*) pulp.

bouillir [bujir] *v* (*prp* **bouillant**; *pp* **bouilli**; *pr ind* **je bous** [bu], **tu bous, il bout, n. bouillons, v. bouillez, ils bouillent**; *pr sub* **je bouille, n. bouillions**; *imp* **bous, bouillons, bouillez**; *impf* **je bouillais**; *p hist* **je bouillis**; *p sub* **je bouillisse**; *fu* **je bouillirai**) **1** *vi* to boil; **commencer à b.**, to come to the boil; **cesser de b.**, to go off the boil; **faire b. qch,** to boil sth; **faire b. du linge,** to boil laundry; *F* **cela fera b. la marmite,** that will keep the pot boiling; *Fig* **b. de colère,** to seethe with anger; *Fig* **cela me fait b.**, that makes my blood boil. **2** *vt F* to boil (*milk etc*).

bouilloire [bujwar] *nf* kettle.

bouillon [bujɔ̃] *nm* **(a)** bubble (*given off by boiling liquid*); bleb, air bubble (*in glass*); blowhole (*in metal*); puff (*of material*); **bouillir à gros bouillons,** to boil fast; **le sang sortait à gros bouillons,** the blood was gushing out *or* welling out; **(b)** *Culin* (*meat, vegetable*) stock; **b. gras/maigre,** clear (meat) soup, bouillon/vegetable stock; **b. de légumes,** vegetable soup; **b. cube,** stock cube; **boire un b.**, to get a mouthful (*when swimming*); *F* to come to grief, to suffer a heavy loss, *Am* to take a bath (*in business*); **b. de culture,** culture medium; *Fig* breeding ground (*for discontent etc*); *Fig* **b. d'onze heures,** poisoned drink; **(c)** *Com* **bouillons,** returns, remainders, unsold copies (*of book, newspapers*).

bouillonnant [bujɔnɑ̃] *adj* bubbling, seething, foaming, frothing; *Fig* **b. de vie.**, bubbling over with life.

bouillonnement [bujɔnmɑ̃] *nm* bubbling, foaming, frothing; *Fig* **b. de la jeunesse,** effervescence *or* impetuousness of youth.

bouillonner [bujɔne] **1** *vi* **(a)** to bubble, to seethe, to foam, to froth up; *Fig* **toutes les idées qui bouillonnent dans sa tête,** all the ideas seething in his head; **b. de colère,** to boil *or* seethe with anger; **(b)** *Com* (*of newspaper, magazine*) to remain unsold. **2** *vt Couture* to gather (*material*) into puffs.

bouillotte [bujɔt] *nf* hot water bottle.

bouillotter [bujɔte] *vi* to boil gently, to simmer.

boul. *abrév* **boulevard**.

boulaie [bulɛ] *nf* birch plantation.

boulange [bulɑ̃ʒ] *nf F* bakery trade.

boulanger¹, -ère [bulɑ̃ʒe, -ɛr] *n* baker, *f* (woman) baker; (*épouse du boulanger*) baker's wife.

boulanger² *vt* (**je boulangeai(s)**; **n. boulangeons**) to knead (*the flour*).

boulangerie [bulɑ̃ʒri] *nf* **(a)** *Ind* bakery trade; **(b)** (*lieu de fabrication*) bakery; *Vieilli* bakehouse; (*magasin*) baker's (shop); **b.-pâtisserie,** baker's and confectioner's (shop).

boule [bul] *nf* **(a)** (*sphère*) ball, sphere, globe; *F* (*tête*) head, nut; **être rond comme une b.**, to be short and fat *or* podgy, *Am F* to be a butterball; **foudre en b.**, ball lightning; **arbre en b.**, bushy-topped tree; **b. de neige,** snowball; *Fig* **faire b. de neige,** to snowball; **se rouler** *ou*

se mettre en b., (*of hedgehog etc*) to curl (itself) up; *F* **se mettre en b.,** to get angry; *F* **elle me met en b.,** she gets my back up; *F* **j'ai les nerfs en b.,** my nerves are all on edge; **b. dans la gorge,** lump in one's throat; *F* **perdre la b.,** to go off one's head *or* round the bend; *F* **tu perds la b. ou quoi?,** are you off your head?; *Nau* **b. de signaux,** (red or black) ball; **b. de scrutin,** ballot (ball), voting ball; **b. d'amortissement** *ou* **de balustre,** banister knob;
(b) (*pour jouer*) bowl; (*croquet, hockey*) ball; **jouer aux boules,** to play bowls; **jeu de boules,** (game of) bowls; **lancer la b.,** to bowl; *Fig* **b. de billard,** bald head; **avoir une b. de billard,** to be as bald as a billiard ball *or* an egg; **la b.,** (the game of) boule; *F* **avoir les boules,** to be pissed off;
(c) (*de machine à écrire*) golf ball; **imprimante à b.,** golf ball printer.

bouleau, -eaux [bulo] *nm* (silver) birch (tree); (*bois*) birchwood.

boule-de-neige [buldənɛʒ] *nf* (*fleur*) guelder rose, snowball tree; (*pl boules-de-neige*).

bouledogue [buldɔg] *nm* bulldog.

bouler [bule] **1** *vi* to roll, to go rolling (along); *F* **envoyer b. qn,** to send s.o. packing. **2** *vt* **b. les cornes d'un taureau,** to pad a bull's horns.

boulet [bulɛ] *nm* **(a)** *Mil* **b. (de canon),** cannonball; *Fig* **tirer sur qn à boulet(s) rouge(s),** to go for s.o. hammer and tongs; **passer comme un b. (de canon),** to hurtle past *or* by; **(b)** (*de bagnard*) ball and chain; *Fig* **c'est un b. qu'il traînera toute sa vie,** it will be a millstone round his neck all his life; **(c)** (*de charbon*) *Com* (coal) nut; **(d)** fetlock joint, pastern joint (*of horse*).

boulette [bulɛt] *nf* **(a)** small ball, pellet (*of paper etc*); **(b)** *Culin* forcemeat ball, meatball; **b. (de pâte),** dumpling; **(c)** *Vét etc* (poison) ball, bolus; **(d)** *F* **faire une b.,** to drop a brick *or* a clanger, to put one's foot in it.

boulevard [bulvar] *nm* boulevard; **habiter sur les boulevards,** to be a boulevard dweller; **les boulevards extérieurs,** (*in Paris*) = the boulevards following the line of the old fortifications; *Th* **théâtre de b.,** variety show; *Th* **c'est du bon/mauvais b.,** it's good/poor light comedy.

boulevardier, -ière [bulvardje, -jɛr] *adj* facile (*humour*).

bouleversant [bulvɛrsɑ̃] *adj* distressing.

bouleversé [bulvɛrse] *adj* distressed, upset; **avoir l'esprit b.,** to be completely shattered *or* bowled over.

bouleversement [bulvɛrsəmɑ̃] *nm* overthrow, overturning, upsetting, upheaval (*of system etc*); disruption (*of plans, schedule etc*); distress, anxiety (*of s.o.*).

bouleverser [bulvɛrse] *vt* to upset, to overturn; to turn (*sth*) upside down; to throw (*sth*) into confusion; (*péniblement*) to unsettle, to upset, to distress (*s.o.*); (*avec surprise*) to overwhelm (*s.o.*); **ce changement de majorité a bouleversé la vie du pays,** this change of government threw the whole country into confusion; **la nouvelle l'a complètement bouleversé,** the news bowled him over.

boulier [bulje] *nm* **(a) b. (compteur),** abacus, counting frame; **(b)** (*de billard*) billiard scoring board.

boulimie [bulimi] *nf Méd* bulimia, morbid hunger; *Fig* **avoir une b. de connaître,** to have an unquenchable thirst for knowledge.

boulimique [bulimik] *adj & n Méd* bulimic.

bouline [bulin] *nf Nau* bowline; **naviguer à la b.,** to sail close-hauled *or* close to the wind; **nœud de b.,** bowline knot.

boulingrin [bulɛ̃grɛ̃] *nm* lawn, grass.

bouliste [bulist] *n* bowls player.

boulle [bul] *nm* boul(l)e, buhl; **cabinet de b.,** buhl *or* boul(l)e cabinet.

boulocher [bulɔʃe] *vi* (*d'un pull*) to pill.

boulodrome [bulɔdrom] *nm* bowling alley.

boulon [bulɔ̃] *nm* bolt; **b. à écrou,** screw bolt; **b. à œil,** eyebolt; **b. à oreilles,** wing bolt; **b. mécanique,** machine bolt; *Rail* **b. d'attelage,** coupling pin; *Fig* **le gouvernement doit à présent resserrer les boulons,** the government must now tighten its grip *or* the screws.

boulonnage [bulɔnaʒ] *nm* bolting (down).

boulonnais, -aise [bulɔnɛ, -ɛz] **1** *adj* (*native, inhabitant*) of Boulogne. **2** *n* **B.,** native *or* inhabitant of Boulogne.

boulonner [bulɔne] **1** *vt MecE etc* to bolt (down). **2** *vi F* to slog *or* slave (away).

boulonnerie [bulɔnri] *nf* **(a)** *Ind* nut-and-bolt works; *Com* nut-and-bolt trade; **(b) la b.,** nuts and bolts.

boulot[1], -otte [bulo, -ɔt] *adj & n F* dumpy, plump, tubby, chubby (person).

boulot[2] [bulo] *F* **1** *nm* work; **quel est son b.?,** what's his job?; **aller au b.,** to go to work; *Fig* **c'est toujours moi qui fais le sale b.,** it's always me that does the dirty work. **2** *adj inv* **être b. b.,** to take one's work very seriously.

boulotter [bulɔte] *F* **1** *vt* to eat; **il n'y a rien à b.,** there's no grub. **2** *vi* to tuck in.

boum [bum] **1** *int* bang! crash! boom!; *Enf* **bébé a fait b.,** baby's had a tumble. **2** *nm* **(a)** (*bruit*) bang, crash; **on a entendu un grand b.,** we heard a big bang; **(b)** *Com Fin* boom; **en plein b.,** in full spate *or* swing. **3** *nf* young people's party.

boumer [bume] *vi Arg* **ça boume!,** it's going fine!; **ça boume?,** how's things?

bouquet[1] [bukɛ] *nm* **(a)** (*gerbe*) bunch of flowers, bouquet; (*petit*) posy; cluster, clump (*of trees etc*); plume, tuft (*of feathers*); *Culin* **b. garni,** (bunch of) mixed herbs, bouquet garni; **(b)** bouquet (*of wine*); **(c)** crowning piece, finishing piece (*of firework display*); *F* **ça c'est le b.!,** that takes the biscuit!, that's the last straw!

bouquet[2] *nm* **(a)** (*lièvre*) hare; (*lapin mâle*) buck rabbit; **(b)** (*crevette*) prawn.

bouquetière [buktjɛr] *nf* flower seller.

bouquetin [buktɛ̃] *nm* ibex.

bouquin[1] [bukɛ̃] *nm* **(a)** *F* (*livre*) book; **(b)** old book.

bouquin[2] *nm* (*lièvre*) hare; (*lapin mâle*) buck rabbit.

bouquiner [bukine] *vi* **(a)** *F* (*lire*) to read; **(b)** (*fouiner*) to browse in bookshops; (*collectionner*) to hunt after *or* collect old books.

bouquiniste [bukinist] *n* second-hand bookseller.

bourbe [burb] *nf* mud, mire.

bourbeux, -euse [burbø, -øz] *adj* muddy, miry.

bourbier [burbje] *nm* slough, (quag)mire; *Fig* **se tirer d'un b.,** to get out of a scrape *or* a mess.

bourbillon [burbijɔ̃] *nm* core (*of boil, abscess etc*).

bourbon [burbɔ̃] *nm* (*whisky*) bourbon.

bourdaine [burdɛn] *nf* black alder.

bourde [burd] *nf F* **(a)** tall story; **raconter des bourdes à qn,** to have s.o. on; **(b)** (*faute*) blunder, bloomer, howler; **faire une b.,** to put one's foot in it, to drop a brick *or* a clanger.

bourdon[1] [burdɔ̃] *nm* pilgrim's staff.

bourdon[2] *nm* **(a)** *Mus* drone (*of bagpipes etc*); bourdon stop (*of organ*); (*note*) drone bass; **(b)** (*cloche*) great bell; **(c)** (*insecte*) bumblebee, humble bee; **faux b.,** drone; *Arg* **avoir le b.,** to be down (in the dumps).

bourdon[3] *nm Typ* omission.

bourdonnement [burdɔnmɑ̃] *nm* buzz(ing), hum(ming) (*of insects*); hum(ming) (*of engine*); murmur(ing), drone, droning (*of crowd, voices etc*); *Méd* buzzing in the ears; **avoir des bourdonnements d'oreilles,** to have a buzzing in one's ears.

bourdonner [burdɔne] *vi* (*of insects*) to buzz, to hum; (*of crowd etc*) to murmur; (*of voices*) to drone; (*of ears*) to buzz, to ring.

bourdonneur, -euse [burdɔnœr, -øz] **1** *adj* (*insecte etc*) humming. **2** *nm* (*oiseau*) hummingbird. **3** *nf* **bourdonneuse,** (*de ruche*) drone layer.

bourg [bur] *nm* **(a)** (*gros village*) small market town; **(b)** *Eng Hist* borough; **b. pourri,** rotten borough.

bourgade [burgad] *nf* straggling village, township.

bourgeois, -oise [burʒwa, -waz] **1** *adj* **(a)** middle-class (*person*); **la classe bourgeoise,** the middle class, the bourgeoisie; **quartier b.,** residential area; **cuisine bourgeoise,** simple *or* family *or* home cooking; **(b)** *Péj* middle-class, bourgeois, conventional; **tu es devenu bien b.!,** you've become quite middle-class!; **la sécurité bourgeoise,** the financial comfort of the middle-class. **2** *n* **(a)** middle class person; **les petits b.,** the lower middle class; **en b.,** in plain *or* civilian clothes; **(b)** *Péj* philistine, person with middle-class values; **c'est du dernier b.!,** it's horribly *or* hopelessly middle-class!; **chercher à épater le b.,** to try to shock the establishment; **(c)** (*roturier*) commoner; **(d)** *Arch* burgess, burgher, citizen. **3** *nf Arg* **la bourgeoise,** the wife, the missus, her indoors, the old lady.

bourgeoisement [burʒwazmɑ̃] *adv* in a middle-class way *or* style; **vivre b.,** to live comfortably *or* in a middle-class way; *Admin* **occuper b. un local,** to occupy premises for residential purposes.

bourgeoisie [burʒwazi] *nf* **(a)** the middle class(es); **la haute/petite b.,** the upper/lower middle class; **(b)** *Arch* burgesses, citizens, freemen (of a city); **droit de b.,** freedom of a city.

bourgeon [burʒɔ̃] *nm* **(a)** *Bot* bud; **(b)** *Vieilli F* spot, pimple; **(c)** *Anat* **b. gustatif,** gustatory *or* taste bud.

bourgeonnement [burʒɔnmɑ̃] *nm* **(a)** *Bot* budding;

(*saison*) budding time; **(b)** *Méd* granulation.

bourgeonner [burʒɔne] *vi* **(a)** *Bot* to bud, to shoot; **(b)** *F* (*avoir des boutons*) to come out in spots; **(c)** *Méd* (*of wound*) to granulate.

bourgmestre [burgmɛstr] *nm* burgomaster.

Bourgogne [burgɔɲ] **1** *nf Hist Géog* Burgundy. **2** *nm* **(vin de) b.,** burgundy (wine).

bourgot [burgo] *nm Can* moose caller.

bourguignon, -onne [burgiɲɔ̃, -ɔn] **1** *adj* Burgundian; *Culin* **bœuf b.,** bœuf bourguignon. **2** *nm Culin* bœuf bourguignon. **3** *n* **B.,** Burgundian.

bourguignotte [burgiɲɔt] *nf Vieilli* **(a)** burgonet (*helmet*); **(b)** *Mil F* steel helmet, tin hat.

bourlinguer [burlɛ̃ge] *vi* **(a)** *Nau* (*of ship*) to make heavy weather, to labour, to toil, to strain (*in a seaway*); **(b)** (*beaucoup naviguer*) to sail the seven seas; **il a bourlingué dans les mers de Chine,** he has sailed the China Seas; *F* **b. de par le monde,** to knock about the world; **tu as bien bourlingué en 3 ans,** you've got around quite a bit in three years.

bourlingueur, -euse [burlɛ̃gœr, -øz] *F* **1** *adj* adventurous. **2** *n* adventurer, rolling stone; **c'est un grand b.,** he's knocked about a bit.

bourrache [buraʃ] *nf* (*plante*) borage.

bourrade [burad] *nf* blow, push, shove; thump, slap (*on the back etc*); dig, poke, prod (*in the ribs*).

bourrage [buraʒ] *nm* **(a)** stuffing (*of chair etc*); cramming, packing tight (*of cupboard, bag etc*); filling (*of pipe with tobacco*); tamping (*of firearms, mines etc*); packing (*of stuffing-box*); *Scol* cramming; *F* **b. de crâne,** eyewash; *surtout Pol* propaganda; **(b)** (*material used*) stuffing, filling, packing.

bourrasque [burask] *nf* squall, gust of wind; (snow) flurry; *Fig* **une b. d'injures,** a flurry of insults.

bourratif, -ive [buratif, -iv] *adj F* stodgy, filling (*food*).

bourre[1] [bur] *nf* **(a)** flock, padding, wadding (*for stuffing chairs etc*); waste, fluff, linters (*of cotton etc*); *Bot* down, floss (*of buds*); *Tex etc* **b. de soie,** floss silk, silk waste; **(b)** wad (*of firearm*); **(c)** *Arg* **de première b.,** first-class, first-rate; **(d) (être) à la b.,** (to be running) late *or* behind time *or* behind schedule.

bourre[2] *nm Arg* (*policier*) cop.

bourré [bure] *adj* **(a)** stuffed, crammed (**de qch,** with sth, full of sth), full, packed tight, cram full; **le coffre est b.,** the boot is crammed full; **la tête bourrée de rêves,** with his head full of dreams; **être b. de complexes,** to be one big bundle *or* a mass of complexes; **(b)** *Arg* plastered, half-cut, sloshed; **être complètement b.,** to be legless.

bourreau, -eaux [buro] *nm* **(a)** (*tortionnaire*) executioner, hangman; **(b)** *Fig* tormentor, torturer; **être le b. de qn,** to torment *or* torture s.o.; **c'est un b. de travail,** he's a glutton for work *or* a workaholic; **un b. d'enfants,** child-beater; **b. des cœurs,** ladykiller.

bourrée [bure] *nf* **(a)** (*danse*) bourrée; **(b)** (*fagot*) faggot, bundle of firewood.

bourrèlement [burɛlmɑ̃] *nm Litt* anguish, (tormenting) pain; pangs (*of remorse etc*).

bourreler [burle] *vt* (**je bourrelle, n. bourrelons; je bourrellerai**) to torment, to torture (*s.o. mentally*); **bourrelé de remords,** stricken with remorse.

bourrelet [burlɛ] *nm* **(a) b. de graisse,** roll *or* fold of fat (*round the neck etc*); *F* spare tyre (*round the waist*); **(b)** (*contre les courants d'air*) draught excluder, weather strip(ping); **(c)** (*petit coussin*) pad, wad, cushion; **(d)** (*de roue*) rim, flange; (*de pneu*) bead.

bourrelier [burəlje] *nm* harness maker, saddler.

bourrellerie [burɛlri] *nf* harness maker's business *or* trade *or* shop, saddlery.

bourrer [bure] **1** *vt* **(a)** to stuff (*cushion etc*); to cram, to pack tight (*cupboard, bag etc*); to fill (*pipe with tobacco*); *F* **b. un élève de latin,** to cram a pupil with Latin; *F* **b. le crâne à qn,** to stuff *or* fill s.o.'s head with nonsense; **bourré à craquer,** full to bursting; **b. qn de coups,** to beat s.o. up; *F* **se faire b. la gueule,** to get one's face pushed in;

(b) (*with food*) to cram, to fill up; **ne le bourre pas de biscuits,** don't fill him up with biscuits;

(c) *Mil Min* to ram (*charge*) home; to stem, to tamp (*blast hole, mine*); to pack (*piston, stuffing box*).

2 *vi* **aliment qui bourre,** stodgy *or* filling food.

3 se bourrer *vpr* **(a)** (*de nourriture*) to stuff oneself, to fill oneself up (**de chocolat** *etc*, with chocolate *etc*);

(b) *F* (*d'alcool*) to get plastered *or* sloshed *or* half-cut; **se b. la gueule,** to get legless *or* rat-arsed;

(c) (*se dépêcher*) **bourre-toi!,** hurry up!, move it!

bourriche [buriʃ] *nf* basket, hamper (*for oysters, game etc*).

bourrichon [buriʃɔ̃] *nm F* **se monter le b.,** to get excited, to work oneself up into a state.

bourricot [buriko] *nm* (small) donkey.

bourrin [burɛ̃] *nm Arg* (*cheval*) nag.

bourrique [burik] *nf* **(a)** (*ânesse*) she ass; *F* (*imbécile*) dunce, duffer, ignoramus; (*personne têtue*) mule; **faire tourner qn en b.,** to drive s.o. crazy *or* round the bend; **b.! va!,** oh, you idiot *or* imbecile!; **têtu comme une b.,** stubborn as a mule; **(b)** *Arg* cop, pig.

bourriquet [burikɛ] *nm* **(a)** (*ânon*) ass's colt; **(b)** *Tech* windlass, winch.

bourru [bury] *adj* rough, rude, surly, churlish, gruff.

bourse [burs] *nf* **(a)** pouch, bag; (*porte-monnaie*) purse, *Am* coin-purse; **b. bien garnie,** well-lined purse; **la b. ou la vie!,** your money or your life!; **tenir les cordons de la b.,** to hold the purse strings; **sans b. délier,** without spending a penny; **faire b. à part,** to keep separate accounts; **faire b. commune,** to share expenses, to pool resources;

(b) *Anat* **bourses,** scrotum;

(c) *Scol* **b. (d'études),** grant, scholarship; **avoir une b. pour étudier à ...,** to win a scholarship to ...; **b. de voyage,** travelling scholarship;

(d) *Fin* **la B. (des valeurs),** the Stock Exchange; **en B.,** on the Stock Exchange; **valeur côtée en B.,** listed *or* quoted share; **jouer à la B.,** to speculate; **b. de commerce,** commodities exchange; **b. de l'emploi,** = employment exchange, job centre; **b. du travail,** (*réunion*) = meeting of local trade unions for the purpose of reaching agreement on how best to defend their interests and provide community services; (*endroit*) = local trade union centre.

boursicotage [bursikɔtaʒ] *nm Bourse* speculation (in a small way), dabbling.

boursicoter [bursikɔte] *vi Bourse* to speculate (in a small way), to dabble.

boursicoteur, -euse [bursikɔtœr, -øz], **boursicotier, -ière** [bursikɔtje, -jɛr] *n Bourse* small-time speculator.

boursier, -ière [bursje, -jɛr] **1** *adj* **opérations boursières,** Stock Exchange transactions. **2** *n* **(a)** *Scol* scholarship *or* grant holder; **(b)** *Bourse* speculator.

boursouflage [bursuflaʒ] *nm*, **boursouflement** [bursufləmɑ̃] *nm* puffing up, puffiness (*of flesh etc*); blistering (*of paint*); *Fig* turgidity (*of style*).

boursouflé [bursufle] *adj* swollen, puffy (*face, eyes*); bloated (*face*); blistered (*paint*); *Fig* turgid (*style*).

boursoufler [bursufle] **1** *vt* to swell, to puff up (*face*); to blister (*paint*). **2 se boursoufler** *vpr* (*of paint*) to blister.

boursouflure [bursuflyr] *nf* swelling, puffiness (*of face etc*); blister (*on paint*); *Fig* turgidity (*of style*).

bouscueil [buskœj] *nm Can* break-up (*of ice*), debacle.

bousculade [buskylad] *nf* scuffle, hustle, jostling; **une b. vers la porte,** a rush for the door; **être pris dans la b.,** to be caught up in the rush.

bousculer [buskyle] *vt* **(a)** (*faire tomber*) to knock over; **b. des objets,** to turn things upside down; *Fig* **cela va b. vos idées,** that'll liven up your ideas; **(b)** (*pousser*) to push; **b. qn,** to jostle s.o., to barge *or* bump *or* knock into s.o., to knock against s.o.; **(c)** (*presser*) to rush; **il ne faut pas la b.,** you mustn't push *or* rush her; **il est toujours bousculé,** he's always in a rush.

bouse [buz] *nf* dung; **b. de vache,** cow dung; **une b.,** a cowpat.

bousier [buzje] *nm* (*insecte*) dung beetle.

bousillage [buzijaʒ] *nm* **(a)** *F* (*d'un travail*) bungling, botching; (*d'une voiture*) wrecking, smashing (up); (*résultat*) bungle, botch(-up); **(b)** *Constr* cob, daub.

bousiller [buzije] *vt F* (*un travail*) to bungle, to botch (up); (*une voiture*) to wreck, to crash, to smash up; **b. qn,** to bump s.o. off, to do s.o. in.

bousilleur, -euse [buzijœr, -øz] *n F* botcher, bungler.

boussole [busɔl] *nf* compass; **b. de marine,** mariner's compass; **b. de poche,** pocket compass; *F* **perdre la b.,** to be all at sea.

boustifaille [bustifɑj] *nf Arg* grub, nosh.

bout [bu] *nm* **(a)** (*extrémité*) end; **assembler deux planches b. à b.,** to join two planks end to end *or* end on, to butt-joint two planks; **l'autre b.,** the other *or* the far end (*of the street etc*); **de b. en b.,** from beginning to end, from end to end; *Nau* from stem to stern; **je connais Paris de b. en b.,** I know Paris inside out; **d'un b. à l'autre,** from one end to the other, from beginning to end; **lire un livre d'un b. à l'autre,** to read a book from cover to cover *or* from start to finish; **d'un b. de la semaine/de l'année à l'autre,** week in week out/year in year out; *F* **il n'y a personne à l'autre b.,** (*au téléphone*) there's nobody on the other end; *Fig* **je n'en vois pas le b.,** I'm nowhere near the end of it; *Fig* **je n'arrive pas à joindre les deux bouts,** I can't make (both) ends meet; **au b. du compte,** after all, at the end of the day, when all's said and done; **au b. de la rue,** at the end *or* bottom *or* top of the street; **aller au b. du monde,** to go to the ends of the earth; *F* **c'est le b. du monde,** (*d'un lieu*) it's a godforsaken hole *or* a dump; (*d'un prix etc*) it's the outside limit; **au b. d'une heure/de quelques jours,** after an hour/a few days; **c'est ce qu'elle répète à tout b. de champ,** that's what she keeps saying at every opportunity; **nous ne sommes pas encore au b.,** we're not through yet, we're not out of the wood(s) yet; **il n'est pas au b. de ses peines,** his troubles aren't over yet; **jusqu'au b.,** to the (very) end; **aller jusqu'au b.,** to go the whole way *or* hog; (*d'un projet etc*) to go on to the bitter end, to see it through; (*avoir des rapports sexuels*) to go the whole way; **aller jusqu'au b. de ses idées,** to follow one's ideas to their logical conclusion; **il est au b. de sa carrière,** he's reached the top of the ladder; **être à b.,** to be exhausted *or F* all in; **pousser** *ou* **mettre qn à b.,** to exasperate s.o., *F* to drive s.o. round the bend; **à b. de patience,** at the end of one's patience *or* tether; **être à b. de ressources,** (*n'avoir plus rien à dire*) to have run out of ideas *or* suggestions; (*n'avoir plus d'argent*) to have run out of money *or* resources; **être au b. du rouleau,** (*n'en pouvoir plus*) to be at the end of one's tether; (*n'avoir plus d'argent*) to have run out of money; **venir à b. de la résistance de qn,** to break down s.o.'s resistance; **venir à b. d'une épidémie,** to stamp out an epidemic; **venir à b. de qch,** to succeed in doing sth; *Rel* **(messe du) b. de l'an,** mass, memorial service (*held on the anniversary of s.o.'s death*);

(b) (*pointe*) end, tip, end-piece; **b. du doigt/du nez/de la langue,** tip of the finger/nose/tongue; **avoir un mot sur le b. de la langue,** to have a word on the tip of one's tongue; **au b. de bras,** at arm's length; **b. de sein,** (*de femme*) nipple; (*d'animal*) teat; **b. de pied, b. renforcé,** toecap; **b. de pipe,** mouthpiece of a pipe; **ciseaux à bouts ronds,** round-ended scissors; **b. de l'archet (d'un violon),** point of the bow; **b. ferré, b. de canne,** ferrule (*of walking stick*); **b. d'un fusil,** muzzle of a gun; **à b. portant,** (at) point blank (range); *Mil* with open sights; **b. filtre,** filter tip (*of cigarette*); *El* **b. mort,** dead end (*of coil*); *Nau* **(bon) b.,** hauling end (*of rope*); **tenir le bon b.,** to have the best of it; *F* **elle est diplomate jusqu'au b. des ongles,** she's a diplomat to her finger-tips; **on ne sait jamais par quel b. le prendre,** you never know how to approach *or* tackle him; *Arg* **mettre les bouts,** to do a bunk;

(c) (*morceau*) bit, fragment, end; **b. de papier,** scrap of paper; **b. de ficelle,** piece of string; **b. de fromage,** piece of cheese; **b. de cigarette,** cigarette end *or* butt *or* stub; **un b. de jardin,** a bit of garden; **écrivez-moi un b. de lettre,** write me a note *or* a line or two; **en connaître un b.,** to know a thing or two about something; **un tout petit b. de femme,** a tiny little (slip of a) woman; **quel adorable b. de chou!,** what an adorable child!; **un b. de temps,** a little while; **un bon b. de temps,** quite a while; **nous avons fait un b. de chemin ensemble,** we went part of the way together; **nous avons fait un bon b. de chemin,** we've come *or* we went a good way; **c'est un bon b. de chemin,** it's a good step *or* way; *Cin TV* **b. d'essai,** screen test.

boutade [butad] *nf* **(a)** (*trait d'esprit*) sally, flash of wit; **(b)** (*caprice*) whim, caprice; **travailler par b.,** to work by fits and starts.

bout-dehors [budəɔr] *nm Nau* boom; **b.-d. de foc,** jib boom; (*pl bouts-dehors*).

boute-en-train [butɑ̃trɛ̃] *nm inv* exhilarating companion; the life and soul of the party; **c'est un b.-en-t.,** he's a real live wire; **c'est le b.-en-t. de la classe,** he's the bright spark of the class.

bouteille [butɛj] *nf* bottle; **un panier à bouteilles,** a bottle carrier; **nous allons boire une b.,** we'll have a bottle (of wine) together; **c'est une bonne b.,** it's a good drop of wine; **b. d'eau,** bottle(ful) of water; **b. isolante** *ou* **thermos,** vacuum flask; **mettre du vin en bouteilles,** to bottle wine; **mise en bouteilles,** bottling; *F* **aimer la b.,** to like one's drink, to be fond of the bottle; **avoir dix ans de b.,** (*d'un vin*) to be ten years old; *F* **prendre de la b.,** to be *or* get long in the tooth; **b. à gaz,** gas cylinder; **acheter une b. de gaz/butane,** to buy a cylinder of gas/butane; **b. d'oxygène,** oxygen cylinder; *El* **b. de Leyde,** Leyden jar, electric jar.

bouteillon [butɛjɔ̃] *nm Mil* dixie.

bouter [bute] *vt Arch* to push out; **b. l'ennemi hors de France,** to drive the enemy out of France.

bouteur [butœr] *nm Constr* bulldozer.

boutique [butik] *nf* shop, small *or* general store; (*de mode*) (fashion) boutique; **tenir b.,** to run a shop; **fermer b.,** to shut up shop, to close down; **parler b.,** to talk shop; *Fig* **être de la b.,** to be in the same business *or* game; **une b. de crèmerie,** tearoom; *F* **j'en ai assez de cette sale b.!,** I'm sick of this rotten dump!; *F* **il est temps que je change de b.,** it's time I had a change of job; **robe b.,** designer dress; **confection b.,** boutique-styled; **b. (en plein vent),** (market) stall.

boutiquier, -ière [butikje, -jɛr] *n* shopkeeper.

boutoir [butwar] *nm* snout (*of a boar*); *Fig* **coup de b.,** cutting *or* aggressive remark.

bouton [butɔ̃] *nm* **(a)** (*of flower*) bud; **b. de rose,** rosebud; **en b.,** budding, in bud; **(b)** (*on garment*) button; **b. à queue,** shank button; **b. de plastron de chemise,** stud; **b. de col,** collar stud; **boutons de manchette (jumelés),** cufflinks; **(c)** knob (*of door, radio etc*); handle (*of door, lid etc*); (push) button (*of machine etc*); button (*of foil*); button, tail pin (*of violin etc*); **b. (électrique),** switch; **b. de réglage (du volume),** volume control (knob); **tourner le b.,** to switch *or* turn (*the radio etc*) on *or* off; **appuyer sur le b.,** to press the button; **b. de sonnerie** *ou* **de sonnette** *ou* **d'appel,** bellpush; *Ordinat* **b. de clavier,** toggle key; **(d)** (*on face etc*) spot, pimple; (*caused by illness*) spot; **couvert de boutons,** spotty, pimply.

bouton-d'or [butɔ̃dɔr] *nm* (*plante*) buttercup; (*pl boutons-d'or*).

boutonnage [butɔnaʒ] *nm* buttoning (up); **b. devant/dans le dos,** front/back fastening.

boutonner [butɔne] **1** *vt* **(a)** to button (up) (*coat etc*); **(b)** *Escrime* to touch (*opponent*). **2 se boutonner** *vpr* to button up; **il a encore du mal à se b.,** he still has difficulty in doing up his buttons; **la robe se boutonne par derrière,** the dress buttons (up) at the back. **3** *vi* (*of dress etc*) **b. par derrière,** to button (up) at the back.

boutonneux, -euse [butɔnø, -øz] *adj* spotty, pimply (*face etc*).

boutonnière [butɔnjɛr] *nf* **(a)** (*de vêtement*) buttonhole; **faire une b.,** to make a buttonhole; **porter une fleur à la b.,** to wear a buttonhole *or US* a boutonniere; **(b)** *Chir* incision; **faire une b. à qn,** to pink s.o. (*with rapier*).

bouton-pression [butɔ̃prɛsjɔ̃] *nm* press stud, snap fastener, *Am* dome fastener, *F* popper; (*pl boutons-pression*).

bouturage [butyraʒ] *nm* propagation (*of plants*) by cuttings.

bouture [butyr] *nf* cutting; **faire des boutures,** to take cuttings.

bouturer [butyre] **1** *vi* (*of plants*) to make suckers. **2** *vt* to propagate by cuttings.

bouvet [buvɛ] *nm* grooving plane.

bouvier, -ière [buvje, -jɛr] *n* (*pour les bœufs*) cowherd, cowhand, cowgirl, cowman, herdsman, -woman; (*pour les troupeaux*) drover, cattleman; (*chien*) sheep dog.

bouvillon [buvijɔ̃] *nm* steer, young bullock.

bouvreuil [buvrœj] *nm* bullfinch.

bovidés [bɔvide] *nmpl Zool* Bovidae.

bovin [bɔvɛ̃] **1** *adj* bovine (*race, eyes etc*); **un air b.,** a bovine look. **2** *nmpl* **bovins,** bovines, cattle.

bovinés [bɔvine] *nmpl Zool* bovines, cattle.

bowling [bɔliŋ] *nm* **(a)** (*jeu*) (tenpin) bowling; **(b)** (*endroit*) (tenpin) bowling alley.

box¹ [bɔks] *nm* (*pl boxes*) **(a)** cubicle (*in dormitory*); *Jur* **b. des accusés,** dock; **(b)** *Aut* lock-up (garage); **(c)** horse box, loose box, stall (*in stable*).

box², box-calf [bɔks(kalf)] *nm* box calf.

boxe [bɔks] *nf* boxing; **faire de la b.,** to box; **match de b.,** boxing match; **b. anglaise,** boxing; **b. française,** kick boxing.

boxer¹ [bɔkse] *vi* to box, to spar.

boxer² [bɔksɛr] *nm* (*chien*) boxer (dog).

boxer³ [bɔksɛr] *nm* boxer shorts.

boxeur [bɔksœr] *nm* boxer.

box-office [bɔksɔfis] *nm* box office; **une pièce en tête du b.-o.,** a box-office hit.

boxon [bɔksɔ̃] *nm F* brothel; *Fig* **quel b.!,** what a mess!

boy [bɔj] *nm* (*native servant*) boy.

boyau, -aux [bwajo] *nm* **(a)** (*d'animal*) bowel, gut; **(corde de) b.,** (cat)gut; **une boisson à tordre les boyaux,** (*fort*) a drink that burns the throat; (*de mauvaise qualité*) rotgut; **(b)** (*tuyau*) hose(pipe); (*de vélo*) tubular tyre; **(c)** (*allée*) narrow alley(way); *Min* narrow gallery; *Mil* communication trench.

boycott(age) [bɔjkɔt(aʒ)] *nm* boycott(ing).

boycotter [bɔjkɔte] *vt* to boycott.

boycotteur, -euse [bɔjkɔtœr, -øz] *n* boycotter.

boyscout [bɔjskut] *nm Vieilli* Boy Scout; *Fig* **mentalité de b.-s.,** boy-scout mentality.

B.P. [bepe] *nf* (*abrév* **boîte postale**) PO box.

B.P.F. *Fin* (*abrév* **bon pour francs**) *Br* ≈ (*sur chèque*) PAY.

brabançon, -onne [brabɑ̃sɔ̃, -ɔn] **1** *adj* Brabantine. **2** *n* **B.,** Brabantine. **3** *nf* **la Brabançonne,** the Belgian national anthem.

Brabant [brabɑ̃] *nm* **(a)** *Géog* Brabant; **(b)** *Agr* **b.,** all-metal wheel plough; **charrue à double b.,** two-furrow plough.

bracelet [braslɛ] *nm* **(a)** bracelet, bangle; strap, bracelet, band (*of wristwatch*); **b. en argent/or,** silver/gold bracelet; **b. de force,** (leather) wrist-band, wristlet; **(b)** (*lien*) metal band *or* ring.

bracelet-montre [braslemɔ̃tr] *nm* wristwatch; (*pl bracelets-montres*).

brachial, -iaux [brakjal, -jo] *adj Anat* brachial (*artery etc*).

brachiopodes [brakjɔpɔd] *nmpl* (*mollusque*) brachiopod.

brachycéphale [brakisefal] *adj & n* brachycephalic (person).

braconnage [brakɔnaʒ] *nm* poaching.

braconner [brakɔne] *vi* to poach.

braconnier [brakɔnje] *nm* poacher.

bractée [brakte] *nf Bot* bract.

brader [brade] *vt* to sell off (*goods*); to sell (*sth*) dirt cheap *or* at a knockdown price.

braderie [bradri] *nf* (*foire*) (outdoor) jumble sale, rummage sale; (*liquidation*) clearance sale.

braguette [bragɛt] *nf* flies, fly (*of trousers*).

brahmane [braman] *nm* Brahmin.

brahmanisme [bramanism] *nm* Brahminism.

brahmine [bramin] *nf* Brahmani.

brai [brɛ] *nm* pitch, tar.

braillard, -arde [brɑjar, -ard] **1** *adj F* bawling, yelling, noisy (*crowd etc*); howling, squalling, bawling (*child*). **2** *n* bawler, loudmouth; **petit b.,** noisy brat.

braille [brɑj] *nm* Braille; **lire en b.,** to read Braille.

braillement [brɑjmɑ̃] *nm* bawling, yelling, squalling; **des braillements,** uproar; **pourquoi ces braillements?,** what's this uproar about?

brailler [brɑje] **1** *vi* to bawl, to shout, to yell; (*d'un enfant*) to squall, to howl, to bawl. **2** *vt* to bawl (out) (*a song*); to chant (*a slogan*).

brailleur, -euse [brɑjœr, -øz] *adj & n F* = **BRAILLARD**.

braiment [brɛmɑ̃] *nm* bray(ing) (*of donkey*).

brainstorming [brɛnstɔrmiŋ] *nm* brainstorming (session).

braintrust [brɛntrœst] *nm* think-tank, *US* brain(s) trust.

braire [brɛr] *vi* (*pr ind* **il brait, ils braient**; *fu* **il braira, ils brairont**; *cond* **il brairait, ils brairaient**) **(a)** (*of donkey*) to bray; **(b)** *F* = **BRAILLER**.

braise [brɛz] *nf* **(a)** (glowing) embers; (*charbon de bois*) (live) charcoal; **cuire la viande sur la b.,** to cook meat over the embers (of a fire); **des yeux de b.,** glowing *or* burning eyes; **être sur la b.,** to be on tenterhooks; **(b)** *Arg Vieilli* (*argent*) bread, dough.

braiser [breze] *vt Culin* to braise.

braisière [brezjɛr] *nf* braising pan.

bramement [brammɑ̃] *nm* (*hurlement*) howling, wailing; (*de cerf*) bell(ing), troat(ing).

bramer [brame] *vi* (*hurler*) to howl, to wail; (*de cerf*) to bell, to troat.

bran [brɑ̃] *nm* (*de son*) bran; **b. de scie,** sawdust.

brancard [brɑ̃kar] *nm* **(a)** shaft, pole (*of stretcher, cart etc*); **ruer dans les brancards,** (*of horse etc*) to kick when between the shafts; *Fig* to kick over the traces, to rebel; **(b)** (*civière*) stretcher.

brancardier, -ière [brɑ̃kardje, -jɛr] *n* stretcher bearer.

branchage [brɑ̃ʃaʒ] *nm* branches, boughs (*of trees*); **branchages,** cut *or* lopped (off) branches.

branche [brɑ̃ʃ] *nf* **(a)** branch, limb, bough (*of tree*); branch (*of nerve, river etc*); branch, division (*of industry etc*); **la maîtresse b.,** the main branch; **une b. morte,** a dead branch; **céleris en branches,** celery; **une b. de céléri,** a stick of celery; *Arg* **vieille b.,** old mate; *Fig* **avoir de la b.,** to look distinguished; *Fig* **être comme l'oiseau sur la b.,** to feel insecure; **notre b. de la famille,** our branch of the family; **la b. maternelle,** the mother's side, *Fml* the maternal line; **les branches de la physique,** the branches of physics; **c'est une b. très littéraire,** it is a very literary discipline; **branches des bois d'un cerf,** tines of a stag's antlers; **(b)** leg (*of compasses, dividers*); side (*of spectacle frame*); prong (*of pitchfork*); blade (*of propeller*); shank (*of key*); arm (*of horseshoe*); **les branches d'un chandelier,** the branches of a candelabra; **b. à coulisse,** telescopic leg (*of tripod*).

branché [brɑ̃ʃe] *adj F* trendy; **être b. sur qn/qch,** to be in (close) touch *or* contact with s.o./sth; **un magazine b.,** a trendy magazine; **c'est très b. d'avoir des lunettes,** wearing glasses is very trendy *or* is the in thing *or* is hip.

branchement [brɑ̃ʃmɑ̃] *nm* **(a)** plugging in, connecting (up), connection (*of electric appliance*); tap(ping) (*of telephone line, gas main etc*); branch(ing), junction (*of pipes, wires etc*); **(tube de) b.,** branch pipe; **(b)** *Rail* branch line; **b. de voie,** junction, points; **(c)** *Ordinat* branch, jump, (control) transfer.

brancher [brɑ̃ʃe] **1** *vt* **(a)** to plug in, to connect (up) (*electric appliance*); to plug in (*telephone*); *Tél* to put (*s.o.*) through, to connect; **b. une sonnerie sur le circuit de lumière,** to run a bell off the light circuit; *Fig* **b. qn sur un sujet,** to get s.o. onto *or* started on a subject; **il faut que je le branche sur cette affaire,** I must get him interested in this business; **(b)** *F* (*plaire à*) to give (*s.o.*) a buzz; **la peinture, ça te branche?,** are you into painting? **2** *vi* (*of bird*) to perch, to roost (*on a branch*). **3 se brancher** *vpr* (*of birds*) to perch, to roost; *Fig F* **se b. avec qn,** to get in touch with s.o.

branchette [brɑ̃ʃɛt] *nf* small branch, twig.

branchial, -iaux [brɑ̃ʃjal, -jo] *adj Zool* branchial.

branchie [brɑ̃ʃi] *nf Zool* branchia, gill (*of fish*).

branchu [brɑ̃ʃy] *adj* branchy, branching.

brandade [brɑ̃dad] *nf Culin* **b. (de morue),** = salt cod pounded with garlic, oil and cream.

brande [brɑ̃d] *nf* **(a)** (*bruyère*) heather; **(b)** (*terrain*) heath(land).

Brandebourg [brɑ̃dbur] *nm* **(a)** Brandenburg; **(b) b.,** frog (and loop); **à brandebourgs,** frogged.

brandir [brɑ̃dir] *vt* to brandish, to flourish (*weapon etc*); to wave (*sth to attract attention*).

brandon [brɑ̃dɔ̃] *nm* (fire)brand; torch (*of twisted straw*); *Fig* **c'est un b. de discorde,** (*personne*) he's a firebrand; (*sujet, affaire*) it's a bone of contention.

branlant [brɑ̃lɑ̃] *adj* shaky; loose (*tooth etc*); rickety (*chair, staircase*); ramshackle (*building*).

branle [brɑ̃l] *nm Fig* impulse, impetus; (*mouvement*) oscillation; **mettre une cloche en b.,** to set a bell swinging *or* ringing; **donner le b. à qch,** to give an impetus to sth, to get the ball rolling; **mettre qch en b.,** to set *or* to get sth going; **se mettre en b.,** to get going.

branle-bas [brɑ̃lbɑ] *nm inv* **(a)** *Nau etc* **faire le b.-b. de combat,** to clear the decks for action; **b.-b.!,** action stations!; **(b)** *Fig* bustle, commotion, confusion; **toute la ville était en b.-b. (de combat),** the whole town was in turmoil; **dans le b.-b. du départ,** in the commotion of setting off; **que signifie tout ce b.-b.?,** what's all the commotion about?; **il met toute la maison en b.-b.,** he's turning the whole house upside down.

branlement [brɑ̃lmɑ̃] *nm* shaking, nodding, wagging (*of one's head*).

branler [brɑ̃le] **1** *vt* **(a)** to shake, to nod, to wag (*one's head*); **(b)** *Vulg* to wank (*s.o.*) off. **2** *vi* to shake, to move, to rock, to be loose *or* shaky *or* rickety; **dent qui branle,** loose tooth; **b. dans le manche,** (*of tool*) to have a loose handle; *Arg Fig* **je ne sais pas ce qu'elle branle,** I don't know what the (bloody) hell she's up to. **3 se branler** *vpr Vulg* (*masturber*) to wank; *Fig* **franchement, je m'en branle,** to be honest, I couldn't give a fuck *or* a shit.

branleur, -euse [brɑ̃lœr, -øz] *n Vulg* (*bon-à-rien etc*) wanker.

braquage [brakaʒ] *nm* **(a)** turning (*of car wheels, aircraft controls*); **(angle de) b.,** steering lock (*of car*); **rayon** *ou* **cercle de b.,** turning circle; **b. (au) maximum,** full lock; **(b)** *Arg* hold-up; **faire un b.,** to do a hold-up.

braque [brak] **1** *nm* (*chien*) pointer. **2** *adj F* hare-brained, crazy, nutty, daft.

braquer [brake] **1** *vt* **(a)** (*diriger, tourner*) to point; **b. un fusil sur qn/qch,** to aim *or* point *or* level a gun at s.o./sth; **b. une lunette sur qn/qch,** to fix *or* train a telescope on s.o./sth; **il a toujours l'œil braqué sur nous,** he's got his eye (trained) on us all the time; **b. son attention sur qch,** to fix one's attention on sth; **(b)** *Aut* to manoeuvre, to turn (*car etc*); **(c)** (*monter*) to antagonize (*s.o.*); **b. qn contre qn/qch,** to turn s.o. against s.o./sth; **il est braqué contre le projet,** he's dead set against the plan; **(d)** *Arg* **b. une banque,** to hold up a bank. **2 se braquer** *vpr* to dig one's heels in. **3** *vi Aut* to turn the (steering) wheel; **braquez à**

gauche!, left hand down!; **b. au maximum**, to apply full lock; **voiture qui braque mal**, car with a poor lock.

braquet [brakɛ] *nm* gear ratio.

bras [bra] *nm* **(a)** *Anat* arm; **b. droit/gauche**, right/left arm; **allonger le b. vers qch**, to reach for sth; **offrir le b. à qn**, to offer s.o. one's arm; **avoir un panier au b.**, to have a basket on *or* over one's arm; **b. dessus b. dessous**, arm in arm; **les b. m'en tombent**, I'm astounded; **cela m'a coupé b. et jambes**, it bowled me over, it stunned me; **rester les b. croisés**, (*ne pas travailler*) to twiddle one's thumbs; (*être passif*) to stand idly by; *Fig* **avoir le b. long**, to have a lot of influence *or F* clout; **accueillir qn les b. ouverts**, to receive s.o. with open arms; **avoir qn/qch sur les b.**, to have s.o./sth on one's hands; *Fig* **elle a la responsabilité de l'affaire sur les b.**, she carries all the responsibility for the business *or* matter; **être le b. droit de qn**, to be s.o.'s right hand (man); **à b. (d'hommes)**, by hand; **voiture à b.**, handcart; **tenir qch à b. tendu(s)** *ou* **à bout de b.**, to hold sth at arm's length; **en b. de chemise**, in (one's) shirtsleeves; **il m'est tombé dessus à b. raccourcis**, he pitched into me; **une partie de b. de fer**, an arm-wrestling match; **projectile lancé à tour de b.**, stone *etc* thrown with all one's might; **faire un b. d'honneur**, ≈ to give the V-sign, to stick two fingers up; **faire un b. d'honneur à qn**, to give s.o. the finger; *Can* **b. téléguidé**, remote manipulator system, *F* Canadarm;
(b) (*homme*) hand, worker; **manquer de b.**, to be short-handed; **c'est un gros b.**, he's strong in the arm; **elle c'est la tête, et moi les b.**, she's the brains, I'm the brawn;
(c) arm(rest) (*of chair*); arm (*of lever, anchor*); jib (*of crane*); limb (*of cross*); handle (*of pump etc*); *Nau* brace (*of a yard*); **b. de manivelle**, crank arm; **b. de lecture**, pickup arm;
(d) *Géog* **b. de mer**, arm of the sea; **b. d'un fleuve**, arm of a river; **b. mort**, backwater;
(e) (*pouvoir*) arm; **le b. séculier**, the secular arm;
(f) (*de mollusque*) tentacle.

brasage [brɑzaʒ] *nm Métal* brazing.

braser [brɑze] *vt Métal* to braze.

brasero [brɑzero] *nm* brazier, charcoal pan.

brasier [brɑzje] *nm* glowing fire; (*incendie*) blaze, inferno; *Fig* hotbed (*of violence etc*); **la voiture n'était plus qu'un b.**, the car was reduced to a blazing mass.

brasiller [brazije] *vi* (*of sea*) to glitter, to sparkle.

bras-le-corps (à) [abralәkɔr] *adv* **saisir qn à b.-le-c.**, to seize s.o. round the waist; **prendre un problème à b.-le-c.**, to grapple with a problem.

brassage [brasaʒ] *nm* **(a)** brewing (*of beer*); **(b)** mixing, stirring, churning (up); *Aut* **b. des gaz**, mixture; *Fig* **le b. de peuples**, the mingling of races; **(c)** *Nau* bracing (*of yard*); *Av* swinging (*of propeller*).

brassard [brasar] *nm* armband; **b. de deuil/d'infirmier**, black armband/medic's armband.

brasse [bras] *nf* **(a)** *Natation* **b. (coulée)**, breast stroke; **nager la b.**, to swim breast stroke; **b. papillon**, butterfly stroke; **(b)** (*ancienne mesure*) fathom.

brassée [brase] *nf* armful.

brasser [brase] **1** *vt* **(a)** to brew (*beer etc*); **(b)** (*mélanger*) to mix, to stir, to churn (up); **b. la salade**, to toss the salad; *F* **b. des affaires**, to be doing good business; **b. les cartes**, to shuffle the cards; **b. de l'argent**, to handle large amounts of money; **(c)** *Nau* to brace (*yard*); *Av* to swing (*propeller*). **2** *vi F* **dans ce milieu, on brasse pas mal**, in these circles you get to meet lots of people.

brasserie [brasri] *nf* **(a)** (*fabrique*) brewery; (*industrie*) brewing, beer-making (industry); **(b)** (*restaurant*) restaurant (with bar).

brasseur, -euse [brasœr, -øz] *n* **(a)** brewer; **(b)** *Fig* **b. d'affaires**, big businessman, tycoon; **(c)** *Sp* breast-stroke swimmer; **une excellente brasseuse**, an excellent breast-stroker.

brassière [brasjɛr] *nf* **(a)** (child's sleeved) vest, *Am* undershirt; *Can* brassière, *F* bra; **b. de sauvetage**, life jacket, *Am* life vest; **(b) brassières**, shoulder straps, slings (*of bag etc*).

brasure [brɑzyr] *nf* **(a)** (*résultat*) braze, (brazed) seam, joint; **(b)** (*opération*) brazing, hard-soldering; **(c)** (*alliage*) hard solder.

bravache [bravaʃ] **1** *nm* blusterer, bully. **2** *adj* swaggering, blustering; **d'un air b.**, blusteringly.

bravade [bravad] *nf* bravado; **par b.**, out of bravado.

brave [brav] **1** *adj* **(a)** brave, courageous, bold; gallant (*man, deed etc*); **(b)** (*preceding the noun*) good, honest, worthy; **eh oui ma b. dame, c'est la vie**, well, my dear lady, that's life I suppose; **c'est un b. homme** *ou F* **type**, he's a good sort; **(c)** *Péj* (*naïf*) nice, soft; **il est bien b.**, (*il ne ferait pas de mal*) he's a softy. **2** *nm* **(a)** hero; **c'était un b.**, he was a gallant man; **(b) mon b.**, my good man; **(c)** *Péj* **faire le b.**, to bluster, to brag.

bravement [bravmɑ̃] *adv* (*voir adj*) bravely, courageously, boldly; gallantly.

braver [brave] *vt* **(a)** (*affronter*) to brave (*sth*), to face (*sth*) bravely; **toujours prêt à b. le danger**, always ready to face danger; **(b)** (*défier*) to defy, to dare (*s.o.*); **b. les lois/le règlement**, to flout the law/the rules.

bravo [bravo] **1** *int* bravo!, good!, well done!; (*dans un débat*) hear, hear!; **ah b.!**, (*tu as encore fait une sottise!*) oh, well done! **2** *nmpl* **des bravos**, applause, cheers.

bravoure [bravur] *nf* **(a)** (*courage*) bravery, gallantry; **(b)** bravura (*of performance etc*); *Mus* **chanter son air de b.**, to sing one's bravura passage; *Litt* **morceau de b.**, purple passage.

break[1] [brɛk] *nm Aut* estate (car), *Am* station wagon.

break[2] *nm* **(a)** *Mus* break; *Fig* **il nous faut un b.**, we need a break; **(b)** *Boxe* **b.!**, break!

breakfast [brɛkfœst] *nm* breakfast.

brebis [brәbi] *nf* **(a)** ewe; **lait/fromage de b.**, ewe's milk/ewe's-milk cheese; **(b)** *Rel* sheep; **les b.**, the flock; **b. égarée**, lost sheep; *Fig* **b. galeuse**, black sheep.

brèche [brɛʃ] *nf* breach, opening, gap, break (*in wall, hedge etc*); hole (*in ship's side*); notch (*in blade*); **faire une b. importante à son capital**, to make large inroads into one's capital; *Mil* **monter sur la b.**, to stand in the breach; *Fig* **être toujours sur la b.**, to be always on the go; **battre qn en b.**, to disparage s.o., to run s.o. down.

bréchet [breʃɛ] *nm Anat* breastbone, sternum.

bredouillage [brәdujaʒ] *nm*, **bredouillement** [brәdujmɑ̃] *nm* mumbling, spluttering.

bredouillant [brәdujɑ̃] *adj* mumbling.

bredouille [brәduj] *adj* **rentrer** *ou* **revenir b.**, to come back *or* home empty-handed.

bredouiller [brәduje] **1** *vi* to mumble, to splutter. **2** *vt* **b. une excuse/son nom**, to mumble an excuse/one's name.

bredouilleur, -euse [brәdujœr, -øz] **1** *adj* mumbling, spluttering. **2** *n* mumbler.

bref, brève [brɛf, brɛv] **1** *adj* brief, short; **soyez b.!**, be brief!, make it short!; **répondre d'un ton b.**, to give a curt answer, to answer curtly; *Ling* **voyelle brève**, short vowel. **2** *adv* briefly, in a word, in short; **raconter qch en b.**, to relate sth in a few words *or* briefly; **b., il accepte**, in short *or* to cut a long story short, he accepts; *F* **enfin b., elle n'est pas satisfaite**, well, in short, she isn't satisfied. **3** *nm* (Papal) brief.

bréhaigne [breɛɲ] *adj Vieilli* (*mare etc*) barren.

brelan [brәlɑ̃] *nm Cartes* three of a kind, pair royal; **b. d'as**, three aces.

breloque [brәlɔk] *nf* **(a)** charm (*on bracelet etc*); **bracelet à breloques**, charm bracelet; **(b)** *Mil* break-off; **battre la b.**, to sound the dismiss; to sound the all clear (*after air raid etc*); (*of watch*) to go erratically; *Fig* to wander (*in one's mind*); **mon cœur bat la b.**, (*bat vite*) my heart is racing; (*fonctionne mal*) my heart is playing me up; *F* **la télé bat la b.**, the telly's on the blink.

brème [brɛm] *nf* (*poisson*) bream.

Brême [brɛm] *nf* Bremen.

Brésil [brezil] *nm* Brazil.

brésilien, -ienne [breziljɛ̃, -jɛn] **1** *adj* Brazilian; **maillot/slip b.**, high-cut bathing costume/briefs. **2** *n* **B.**, Brazilian.

brésiller [brezije] *Tech & Litt* **1** *vt* to break (*sth*) into small pieces; (*broyer*) to crumble, to pulverize. **2** *vi* to crumble. **3 se brésiller** *vpr* to crumble.

Bretagne [brәtaɲ] *nf* Brittany; **Basse-B.**, Lower *or* Western Brittany.

bretelle [brәtɛl] *nf* **(a)** (*de soutien-gorge etc*) shoulder strap; **(paire de) bretelles**, (pair of) braces *or Am* suspenders; **(b)** (*lanière*) strap; **b. de fusil**, rifle sling; **l'arme à la b.**, with one's rifle slung over one's shoulder; **(c)** (*route*) access road; (motorway) spur, slip road, *Am* ramp (*to, from motorway*); *Rail* scissors crossover.

breton, -onne [brәtɔ̃, -ɔn] **1** *adj* Breton. **2** *nm Ling* Breton. **3** *n* **B.**, Breton.

bretonnant [brәtɔnɑ̃] *adj* of Lower Brittany; **Breton b.**, = Breton-speaking Breton who also preserves local traditions.

brett(el)er [brɛtle, brete] *vt* (**je brettelle** [brɛtɛl], **n. brettelons** [brɛtlɔ̃]; **je brettellerai**) to tool, to tooth (*stone etc*); to hatch, to chase (*jewellery*).

bretzel [brɛdzɛl] *nm* pretzel.

breuvage [brœvaʒ] *nm* **(a)** beverage, drink; **(b)** (*potion* *particulière*) draught, potion; **b. magique,** magic potion.

brève [brɛv] **1** *adj voir* **BREF. 2** *nf* **(a)** *Journ* small news item; **(b)** (*en poésie*) short syllable; *Ling* short vowel.

brevet [brəvɛ] *nm* **(a)** (*titre*) diploma, certificate; *Scol* **b. (des collèges),** *Arch* **b. d'études du premier cycle,** ≈ *Br* (G.C.E.) 'O' level; *Mil* **b. d'état-major,** = staff college certificate; *Nau* **passer son b. de capitaine,** to obtain one's master's certificate, *F* to get one's ticket; *Av* **b. de pilote,** pilot's licence, *Mil* wings; **b. d'apprentissage,** indentures, articles; *Jur* **b. de technicien,** = vocational training certificate (16 year olds); **b. de technicien supérieur,** = vocational training certificate (18 year olds); *Jur* **(acte en) b.,** contract delivered by notary in original; **(b) b. (d'invention),** (letters) patent; **prendre un b.,** to take out a patent; **(c)** *Fig* guarantee (*of peace, character etc*); **(d)** *Hist* (letters) patent, (royal) warrant.

brevetable [brəvtabl] *adj* patentable.

breveté [brəvte] *adj* **(a)** patented (*invention*); **inventeur b.,** inventor holding letters patent; **(b)** (*certifié*) certificated, qualified; **officier b. (d'état-major),** = officer who has passed staff college.

breveter [brəvte] *vt* **(je brevète, n. brevetons; je brevèterai)** to patent (*invention*); **faire b. une invention,** to take out a patent on an invention.

bréviaire [brevjɛr] *nm Rel* breviary.

brévité [brevite] *nf Ling* shortness (*of vowel etc*).

bribe [brib] *nf* **bribes,** scraps, fragments, bits, odds and ends (*d'une fortune*); **bribes de conversation,** snatches *or* scraps of conversation; **les bribes de sa fortune/du repas,** the remnants of his fortune/the leftovers of the meal; **apprendre qch par bribes,** to learn sth piecemeal *or* bit by bit.

bric [brik] *nm* (*used in*) **de b. et de broc,** from one source and another, haphazardly; **de b. ou de broc,** some way or other.

bric-à-brac [brikabrak] *nm inv* **(a)** odds and ends, bric-à-brac, jumble; **marchand de b.-à-b.,** second-hand dealer; **(b) (boutique de) b.-à-b.,** second-hand shop, *F* junk shop.

brick [brik] *nm* **(a)** *Nau* brig; **(b)** *Culin* **b. à l'œuf,** = egg enclosed in filo pastry and deep fried; **(c)** (*carton*) carton; **b. de lait/de jus d'orange/***etc*, a carton of milk/orange juice/ *etc*.

bricolage [brikɔlaʒ] *nm* pottering about, doing odd jobs; **grande surface de b.,** do-it-yourself centre; **un mordu du b.,** a do-it-yourself enthusiast; **les joies du b.,** the joys of do(ing)-it-yourself; *Fig* **ce n'est pas sérieux!, c'est du b.!,** that's not proper work!, it's a bodge-up!

bricole [brikɔl] *nf* **(a)** odd jobs, trifles, odds and ends; **une petite b.,** a little something; **s'occuper à des bricoles,** to potter about the house *or* the garden *or* the office *etc*, to do odd jobs; **(b)** breast strap (*for barrow etc*); breast harness (*of horse etc*).

bricoler [brikɔle] **1** *vt* **b. une affaire,** to arrange a piece of business (*often shady*); **elle a bricolé une table,** she's knocked together *or* knocked up a table; **il a bricolé le moteur,** he's tinkered with the engine. **2** *vi* to do odd jobs (about the house, garden *etc*).

bricoleur, -euse [brikɔlœr, -øz] *n* handyman, do-it-yourself enthusiast.

bride [brid] *nf* **(a)** (*du harnais*) bridle; **mettre la b. à un cheval,** to bridle *or* put the bridle on a horse; **lâcher la b. à un cheval/à qn,** to give free rein to a horse/to s.o., to give a horse/s.o. his head; **laisser à un cheval/à qn la b. sur le cou,** to give a horse his head/to give s.o. a free hand; **tenir un cheval en b.,** to curb *or* check a horse; *Fig* **tenir qn en b., tenir la b. haute à qn,** to keep a tight rein on s.o.; **aller à b. abattue** *ou* **à toute b.,** to ride at full speed, to ride full tilt, *F* to ride hell for leather; **partir à b. abattue,** to set off at top speed; **fureur sans b.,** unbridled fury; **(b)** *Couture* bar (*of buttonhole etc*); loop (*for button etc*); string (*of bonnet etc*); **(c)** *Tech* strap, tie; flange, collar (*of cylinder, pipe etc*); **b. de serrage,** clamp, cramp; **tuyau à brides,** flanged pipe.

bridé [bride] *adj* tied up, constricted; *Aut* **moteur b.,** governed engine; **yeux bridés,** slant(ing) eyes.

brider [bride] *vt* **(a)** to bridle (*horse*); to keep (*s.o., emotion etc*) in check; **b. ses passions,** to check *or* restrain *or* curb one's passions; **cette contrainte le bride,** it's a restraint on him; **(b)** to tie up, to fasten (up); *Culin* to truss (*fowl*); *Nau* to lash, to seize (*cable etc*); **ce pantalon me b.,** these trousers are too tight for me; **(c)** *Couture* to bind (*buttonhole*); **(d)** to flange, to clamp (*pipes*).

bridge [bridʒ] *nm* **(a)** *Cartes* bridge; **b. aux enchères,** auction bridge; **b. contrat,** contract bridge; **un tournoi/club de b.,** a bridge tournament/club; **faire un b.,** to have a game *or* hand of bridge; **(b)** (*prothèse dentaire*) bridge.

bridger [bridʒe] *vi* **(je bridgeai(s); n. bridgeons)** to play bridge.

bridgeur, -euse [bridʒœr, -øz] *n* bridge player.

bridon [bridɔ̃] *nm* snaffle (bridle).

brie [bri] *nm* Brie (cheese).

briefer [brife] *vt* to brief; **b. ses collègues sur une affaire,** to brief one's colleagues on a subject.

briefing [brifiŋ] *nm* briefing; **faire un b.,** to hold a briefing.

brièvement [briɛvmɑ̃] *adv* briefly, in short.

brièveté [briɛvte] *nf* shortness, brevity, briefness; **la b. de sa visite,** his brief visit.

brigade [brigad] *nf* **(a)** *Mil* brigade; *Av* **b. aérienne,** group, *US* wing; **(b)** squad, party, detachment (*of policemen etc*); gang, party (*of workmen etc*); **chef de b.,** foreman; *Hist* **brigades internationales,** International Brigades.

brigadier [brigadje] *nm* **(a)** *Mil* corporal; (*in artillery*) bombardier; **(b) b. (de police),** (police) sergeant; **(c)** foreman (*of gang of workmen etc*); **(d)** *Nau* bowman, bow oar(sman).

brigadier-chef [brigadjeʃɛf] *nm Mil* lance sergeant; (*pl brigadiers-chefs*).

brigand [brigɑ̃] *nm* (*pillard*) crook; (*personne malhonnête*) brigand, bandit; **le petit b.,** the little ruffian *or* scoundrel *or* rascal; **ce vendeur est un (vrai) b.,** that salesman is a real crook.

brigandage [brigɑ̃daʒ] *nm* brigandage, robbery, banditry; **des actes de b.,** (armed) robbery.

brigantin [brigɑ̃tɛ̃] *nm Nau Arch* brigantine.

brigantine [brigɑ̃tin] *nf Nau* spanker (sail).

brigue [brig] *nf Litt* intrigue.

briguer [brige] *vt* to solicit, to canvass for (*sth*); **b. un honneur/une amitié,** to solicit an honour/s.o.'s friendship; **b. des voix,** to canvass (for votes).

brillamment [brijamɑ̃] *adv* brilliantly.

brillance [brijɑ̃s] *nf* brilliance; *Opt* brilliancy; *TV* brightness (*of image etc*); *Mus* brightness of tone.

brillant [brijɑ̃] **1** *adj* brilliant (*career, pupil etc*); sparkling, glittering, bright (*light, gem, colour etc*); shiny, glossy (*hair etc*); sparkling (*conversation*); **b. orateur,** brilliant speaker; **spectacle b.,** splendid sight; **je ne suis pas b.,** I'm not too good, I'm not feeling too well *or* brilliant; **la situation n'est pas brillante,** the situation is far from brilliant. **2** *nm* **(a)** brilliancy, brilliance, brightness, lustre, sparkle, glitter (*of gem, metal etc*); glossiness (*of paper, material*); polish, shine (*on shoes etc*); **le b. de la conversation,** the sparkle of the conversation; **et vos cheveux retrouveront leur b. naturel,** and your hair will regain its natural shine; **b. à lèvres,** lip gloss; **(b)** (*diamant*) brilliant (diamond).

brillanter [brijɑ̃te] *vt* **(a)** to make (*sth*) shine *or* sparkle *or* glitter; to polish (*a metal surface*); *Tex* to gloss, to glaze (*thread*); **(b)** to cut (*diamond*) into a brilliant.

brillantine [brijɑ̃tin] *nf* brilliantine.

briller [brije] *vi* **(a)** (*of sun*) to shine; (*of steel*) to glisten, to glint, to gleam; (*of candle, water*) to glimmer; (*of stars*) to glitter, to sparkle, to twinkle; (*of moon, satin*) to shimmer; (*of headlights*) to glare; (*of embers*) to glow; *Prov* **tout ce qui brille n'est pas or,** all that glitters is not gold; **faire b. ses cuivres,** to shine up one's copperware; **des yeux qui brillent de colère/de joie/***etc*, eyes shining with anger/ happiness/*etc*; **(b)** *Fig* to shine, to do well, to be successful; **il brille en classe,** he shines in class; **b. dans la conversation,** to be a brilliant conversationalist; **b. par son absence,** to be conspicuous by one's absence; **elle ne brille pas par sa ponctualité,** she's not noted for her punctuality.

brimade [brimad] *nf* **(a)** (*tour*) rough joke (*played on freshmen, recruits, new boys*); **(b) brimades,** *Scol Mil* ragging, *US* hazing; (*plus grave*) persecution, bullying, victimization.

brimbalement [brɛ̃balmɑ̃] *nm* (*agitation*) swaying; wobbling (*of wheel*).

brimbaler [brɛ̃bale] *vt & vi F* = **BRINGUEBALER.**

brimborion [brɛ̃bɔrjɔ̃] *nm* bauble, knick-knack.

brimer [brime] *vt* to rag, *US* to haze (*recruit etc*); (*plus gravement*) to persecute, to bully, to victimize; **il se croyait brimé,** he felt he was being picked on *or* got at.

brin [brɛ̃] **1** *nm* **(a)** blade (*of grass etc*); sprig, twig (*of myrtle etc*); spray (*of mimosa*); wisp (*of straw*); shoot (*of tree*); **un beau b. de fille,** a fine strapping girl, a handsome girl; **(b)** *F* (*petite quantité*) bit, fragment; **pas un b. de pain,** not a scrap *or* a crumb of bread; **un b. d'air,** a breath of air; **avec un b. d'envie,** with a touch of envy; **un b. de toilette,** a lick and a promise, a quick wash (and brush up); **(c)** staple (*of wool, flax etc*); ply (*of wool*); strand (*of rope,* *wire etc*); **(d)** stick, rib (*of fan etc*); **gros b.**, butt (*of rod*); **brins d'une antenne,** wires of an aerial. **2** *adv* **il est un b. ennuyeux,** he's a bit of a bore.

brindezingue [brɛ̃dzɛ̃g] *adj F* mad, crazy, w(h)acky, scatty.

brindille [brɛ̃dij] *nf* twig, sprig; **brindilles,** brushwood.

bringue¹ [brɛ̃g] *nf Arg* **grande b.**, lanky *or* gangling girl.

bringue² *nf Arg* binge; **faire la b.**, to go on a binge.

bringuebaler [brɛ̃gbale] **, brinquebaler** [brɛ̃kbale] *F* **1** *vi* to sway; (*of wheel*) to wobble. **2** *vt* to carry *or* cart (*sth*) about.

brio [brijo] *nm Mus* **con b.**, con brio; **parler avec b.**, to talk brilliantly *or* with spirit.

brioche [brijɔʃ] *nf Culin* brioche; *F* **prendre de la b.**, to develop a paunch.

brioché [brijɔʃe] *adj* **pain b.** = milk bread *or* loaf.

brique [brik] **1** *nf* **(a)** (*de construction*) brick; **b. tubulaire** *ou* **creuse,** hollow brick; **maison de** *ou* **en briques,** brick (-built) house; *Arg* **bouffer des briques,** to live on air; **(b)** bar, cake (*of soap*); block, slab (*of concrete etc*); *Nau* **b. à pont,** holystone. **2** *adj inv* brick-red.

briquer [brike] *vt* (*nettoyer*) to scrub (*sth*) down; *Nau* to holystone (*deck*).

briquet¹ [brikɛ] *nm* (cigarette, cigar) lighter; *Arch* tinder box; **battre le b.**, to strike a light.

briquet² *nm* (*chien*) beagle.

briquetage [briktaʒ] *nm* (*maçonnerie*) brickwork; (*trompe-l'œil*) imitation brickwork.

briqueter [brikte] *vt* (**je briquette, n. briquetons; je briquetterai**) to brick (*sth*), to face (*sth*) with bricks; to face (*wall*) in imitation brickwork.

briqueterie [briktri] *nf* brickworks.

briqueteur [briktœr] *nm* bricklayer.

briquetier [briktje] *nm* brick manufacturer.

briquette [brikɛt] *nf* briquette.

bris [bri] *nm* **(a)** breaking (*of seals, glass etc*); **(b)** *Jur* wilful damage (*to property*); **b. de prison,** prison breakout; **b. de clôture,** breach of close.

brisant [brizɑ̃] **1** *adj* **explosif b.**, high explosive; **obus b.**, high-explosive shell. **2** *nm* **(a)** (*écueil*) reef, shoal; **brisants,** breakers; **(b)** = **BRISE-LAMES.**

brise [briz] *nf* breeze; *Nau* **forte b.**, stiff breeze.

brisé [brize] *adj* broken; **ligne brisée,** angled line; **être tout b.**, to be sore *or* aching all over; **b. de fatigue,** exhausted, tired out.

brise-bise [brizbiz] *nm inv* = small curtain in lower half of window.

brisées [brize] *nfpl* broken boughs (*to mark track of deer in wood*); track (*of deer etc*); *Fig* **suivre les b. de qn,** to follow in s.o.'s footsteps, to follow s.o.'s lead *or* example; *Fig* **aller** *ou* **courir sur les b. de qn,** to compete with s.o. on his home ground; *Fig* **revenir sur ses b.**, to retrace one's steps.

brise-fer [brizfɛr] *nm inv* destructive child.

brise-glace [brizglas] *nm inv* **(a)** (*ship*) ice breaker; **(b)** ice fender (*of a bridge pier*); ice beam (*of ship*).

brise-jet [brizʒɛ] *nm inv* tap nozzle.

brise-lames [brizlam] *nm inv* **(a)** (*digue*) breakwater, mole; **(b)** groyne (*across beach*).

brisement [brizmɑ̃] *nm Fig* **b. de cœur,** heartbreak.

brise-mottes [brizmɔt] *nm inv Agr* brake harrow.

briser [brize] **1** *vt* (*casser*) to break, to smash; to break up (*clods of earth, ship etc*); to pound (up), to crush (*ore etc*); to break (*treaty etc*); to crush, to break down (*opposition etc*); to exhaust (*s.o.*), to wear (*s.o.*) out; to break off (*conversation etc*); **b. une porte,** to break *or* burst open a door; **b. qch en éclats,** to smash sth to bits *or* to smithereens; **porter cette caisse m'a brisé les reins,** carrying that box has ricked my back; **brisé par la douleur,** crushed by grief; **cela me brise le cœur,** it breaks my heart. **2** *vi* **(a) b. avec qn,** to break with s.o.; **le mouvement de grève est brisé,** the strike has been broken; **(b)** (*of waves*) to break. **3 se briser** *vpr* (*of waves*) to break; (*of china, glass etc*) to break, to be smashed *or* shattered; **cela se brise comme du verre,** it's as brittle as glass; *Fig* **espoirs qui se brisent,** shattered hopes.

brise-tout [briztu] *n inv* clumsy person (who breaks everything); destructive child; **c'est un b.-t.**, he's like a bull in a china shop.

briseur, -euse [brizœr, -øz] *n* breaker; **b. de grève,** strike breaker, *F* scab.

brise-vent [brizvɑ̃] *nm inv* windbreak.

bristol [bristɔl] *nm* Bristol board; (*carte de visite*) visiting card.

brisure [brizyr] *nf* **(a)** break, crack; **(b)** break (*of hinge*); folding joint (*of shutter*); **(c)** *Hér* brisure.

britannique [britanik] **1** *adj* British; **les Îles Britanniques,** the British Isles. **2** *n* **B.**, Briton, British subject, *US* Britisher; **les Britanniques,** the British.

broc [bro] *nm* pitcher, (large) jug.

brocante [brɔkɑ̃t] *nf Com* dealing in antiques, bric-à-brac and secondhand goods; (*as shop sign*) Antiques.

brocanter [brɔkɑ̃te] **1** *vi* to deal in *or* sell antiques, bric-à-brac and secondhand goods. **2** *vt* to sell, to deal in (*antiques, bric-à-brac, secondhand goods*).

brocanteur, -euse [brɔkɑ̃tœr, -øz] *n* dealer in antiques, bric-à-brac and secondhand goods.

brocarder [brɔkarde] *vt* to gibe at (*s.o.*).

brocart [brɔkar] *nm Tex* brocade; **rideaux de b.**, brocade curtains.

brochage [brɔʃaʒ] *nm* **(a)** (*de livre*) stitching, sewing; **(b)** *Tex* brocading, figuring.

broche [brɔʃ] *nf* **(a)** *Culin* spit; **poulet à la b.**, chicken on the spit; **b. de boucher,** meat skewer; **(b)** (*bijou*) brooch; **(c)** *Tech* peg, pin; **b. de charnière,** hinge pin; **b. d'une serrure,** gudgeon of a lock; *El* **fiche à deux broches,** two-pin plug; **(d)** *Tex* spindle; **(e)** (*de dentiste*) broach; *Chir* pin.

broché [brɔʃe] **1** *adj* **(a)** *Tex* brocaded; **(b) livre b.**, paperback (book), paper-bound book. **2** *nm Tex* brocading (*de tissu*); (*tissu*) brocade.

brocher [brɔʃe] *vtr* **(a)** to stitch, to sew (*book*); **(b)** *Tex* to brocade, to figure (*material*); **tissu broché d'or,** gold brocade.

brochet [brɔʃɛ] *nm* (*poisson*) pike.

brochette [brɔʃɛt] *nf* **(a)** (*broche*) skewer; *Culin* kebab; **b. de poulet,** chicken kebab; **(b)** row (*of people etc*); **b. de décorations,** row of medals *or* decorations; *Iron* **vous faites une belle b.!**, what a line-up!

brocheur, -euse [brɔʃœr, -øz] **1** *n* **(a)** (*de livre*) stitcher, sewer; **(b)** *Tex* brocade weaver. **2** *nf* **brocheuse,** stitching machine; staple press, stapler. **3** *nm Tex* brocade loom.

brochure [brɔʃyr] *nf* **(a)** (*tract etc*) brochure, booklet, pamphlet; **(b)** stitching, sewing (*of books*); **(c)** *Tex* brocaded pattern.

brocoli [brɔkɔli] *nm* broccoli; **mange tes brocolis,** eat your broccoli.

brodequin [brɔdkɛ̃] *nm Hist* laced boot.

broder [brɔde] *vt* to embroider; *Fig* **b. une histoire,** to embroider *or* embellish a story; **tu brodes,** (*c'est inexact*) you're embroidering.

broderie [brɔdri] *nf* **(a)** (piece of) embroidery; **(b)** (*activité*) embroidering; **faire de la b.**, to embroider, to do embroidery; **b. anglaise,** broderie anglaise.

brodeur, -euse [brɔdœr, øz] **1** *n* embroiderer, *f* embroideress. **2** *nf* **brodeuse,** embroidering machine.

broiement [brwamɑ̃] *nm* = **BROYAGE.**

bromate [brɔmat] *nm Ch* bromate.

brome [brom] *nm Ch* bromine.

bromure [brɔmyr] *nm Ch* bromide.

bronche [brɔ̃ʃ] *nf Anat* bronchus, *pl* bronchi.

broncher [brɔ̃ʃe] *vi* **(a)** (*de cheval*) to stumble; **(b)** (*de qn*) to falter, to waver, to flinch; *F* to budge, to move; **sans b.**, without turning a hair; **le premier qui bronche aura des ennuis!**, (*qui bouge*) the first one to move will get it!; (*qui se plaint*) the first one to complain will be in trouble!

bronchiole [brɔ̃ʃjɔl] *nf Anat* bronchiole.

bronchique [brɔ̃ʃik] *adj Anat* bronchial.

bronchite [brɔ̃ʃit] *nf Méd* bronchitis; **faire** *ou* **avoir une b.**, to have bronchitis.

bronchitique [brɔ̃ʃitik] *adj & n Méd* bronchitic.

broncho-pneumonie [brɔ̃kɔpnømɔni] *nf Méd* bronchopneumonia; (*pl broncho-pneumonies*).

bronchoscopie [brɔ̃kɔskɔpi] *nf Méd* bronchoscopy.

brontosaure [brɔ̃tɔzɔr] *nm* brontosaurus.

bronzage [brɔ̃zaʒ] *nm* **(a)** (*de la peau*) tanning; (*hâle*) (sun)tan; **pour un b. rapide et sans danger,** for a quick, safe tan; **les adeptes du b. intégral,** people who go in for an all-over tan; **(b)** (*d'une statue etc*) bronzing; (*d'un canon*) browning, blueing (*of gun barrels etc*).

bronze [brɔ̃z] *nm* bronze; **un beau b.**, a fine bronze (statue); **b. à canon,** gunmetal; **c'est un cœur de b.**, he has a heart of stone.

bronzé [brɔ̃ze] *adj* **(a)** (sun)tanned, sunburnt, brown, bronze(d), *US* tan (*face etc*); **(b)** bronze(d) (*statue etc*).

bronzer [brɔ̃ze] **1** *vt* **(a)** to tan (*skin etc*); **(b)** to bronze (*statue etc*); to brown, to blue (*gun barrels etc*). **2** *vi* to (get a) tan, to go brown. **3 se bronzer** *vpr* to sunbathe; **elle se bronze au balcon,** she's sunbathing on the balcony.

bronzier [brɔ̃zje] *nm* maker of bronzes.

brook [bruk] *nm Sp* water jump.

broquette [brɔkɛt] *nf* (tin)tack.

brossage [brɔsaʒ] *nm* brushing.

brosse [brɔs] *nf* **(a)** brush; **b. à cheveux/à habits,** hairbrush/clothes brush; **b. à dents,** toothbrush; **b. métallique,** wire brush; **b. à tubes,** scaling brush; **donner un coup de b. à qch/qn,** to give sth a brush/to give s.o. a brush (down); **enlever la boue d'un coup de b.,** to brush off the mud; **cheveux en b.,** crew cut; **il porte la b. depuis l'âge de 11 ans,** he's had a crew cut ever since he was 11; *Can F* **partir sur une b.,** (*biture*) to go on a pub crawl *or Am* a bender; **passer la b. sur qch,** to paint sth out; **(b)** brush (*of fox*).

brosser [brɔse] **1** *vt* **(a)** to brush (*carpet, coat etc*); to scrub (*floor*); to brush down (*a horse*); *Belg* **b. un cours,** to cut a lecture; **(b)** (*peindre*) to paint (boldly); **b. les décors d'une pièce,** to paint the scenery for a play; **(c)** *Sp* to cut (*ball*). **2 se brosser** *vpr* to brush oneself down, to brush one's clothes; **se b. les dents,** to brush *or* clean one's teeth; *F* **tu peux te b.!,** you can whistle for it!

brosseur [brɔsœr] *nm* **(a)** *Tech* brusher, cleaner, polisher; **(b)** *Th* **b. de décors,** scene painter.

brossier [brɔsje] *nm* brushmaker; (*marchand*) dealer in brushes.

brou [bru] *nm* **(a)** husk, hull, *US* shuck (*of walnut, almond etc*); **(b) b. de noix,** walnut stain.

broue [bru] *nf Can Arg* froth; **faire** *ou* **péter de la b.,** to talk big, to show off.

brouet [bruɛ] *nm* (thin) gruel, broth, *Br* skilly.

brouette [bruɛt] *nf* **(a)** (*de jardin*) wheelbarrow; **(b)** *Arch* sedan chair (*on two wheels*).

brouettée [bruete] *nf* barrowful, barrowload.

brouetter [bruete] *vt* to carry *or* push (*sth*) in a wheelbarrow.

brouhaha [bruaa] *nm* brouhaha.

brouillage [brujaʒ] *nm Rad Électron etc* jamming, interference; *Électron Tél* scramble, scrambling; **zone de b.**, interference area, mush area; **b. sonore/visuel,** sound/visual interference.

brouillard [brujar] *nm* **(a)** fog; **il y a du b.,** it's foggy; **arrêté par le b., pris dans le b.,** fogbound; *Fig* **je suis dans le b.,** I can't make head nor tail of it; *TV* **b. de fond,** background mush; **(b)** *Com* day book, counter cash book; **(c)** *Phys* aerosol.

brouillasse [brujas] *nf* = **BRUINE**.

brouillasser [brujase] *v impers* = **BRUINER**.

brouille [bruj] *nf* quarrel, disagreement; **être en b. avec qn,** to be on bad terms with s.o.; **c'est une petite b. qui ne durera pas,** it's just a tiff, it won't last long.

brouillé [bruje] *adj* **(a)** (*mélangé*) jumbled, mixed, confused; (*photographie etc*) blurred; **œufs brouillés,** scrambled eggs; **teint b.,** blotchy complexion; **(b) être b. avec qn,** to be on bad terms with s.o.

brouiller [bruje] **1** *vt* **(a)** to mix up, to jumble; to throw (*sth*) into confusion; to muddle (*s.o.*); **b. des œufs,** to scramble eggs; **b. les cartes,** to shuffle the cards; *Fig* to spread confusion; **la pluie brouille les fenêtres,** the rain is blurring *or* misting (up) the windows; **b. les pistes,** to cover one's tracks; **cela risquerait de me b. les idées,** it might get me into a muddle;
(b) to cause a misunderstanding between (*people*);
(c) *Rad Électron* to jam (*a transmission*); *Tél Électron* to scramble.
2 se brouiller *vpr* **(a)** to become mixed *or* confused; **le temps se brouille,** the weather is breaking up; *Fig* things are looking black;
(b) (*of eyes*) to grow dim; *Fig* **yeux brouillés de larmes,** eyes blurred with tears;
(c) (*se disputer*) to quarrel, to fall out; *F* **elle s'est brouillée avec la physique,** she's taken a dislike to physics.

brouillerie [brujri] *nf F* tiff.

brouilleur [brujœr] **1** *adj Rad Électron* **émetteur b.,** jamming station; **signal b.,** jamming signal. **2** *nm Rad Électron* jammer, jamming transmitter; *Rad Électron Tél* **(circuit) b.,** scrambler.

brouillon, -onne [brujɔ̃, -ɔn] **1** *adj* muddleheaded; (*au travail*) disorganized, unmethodical; **esprit b.,** muddled mind; **travail b.,** unmethodical work. **2** *n* muddler. **3** *nm* (rough) draft, rough copy; *Scol* rough work; **(papier) b.,** scrap *or US* scratch paper; *Ordinat* **version b.,** draft version; **prendre des notes au b.,** to take rough notes; *Scol* **puis-je vous rendre le b.?,** can I give you my rough copy?, can I give it to you in draft (form)?; **(cahier de) b.,** rough (note)book; *Fig* **cette présentation n'est qu'un b.,** this is only a rough presentation.

broum [brum] *int* brum, brum!

broussaille [brusaj] *nf* (*souvent pl*) brushwood, undergrowth, scrub, bush(es); **cheveux en b.,** tousled *or* unkempt hair; **sourcils en b.,** shaggy eyebrows.

broussailleux, -euse [brusajø, -øz] *adj* covered with bushes *or* scrub (*country*); tousled, unkempt (*hair*); bushy (*eyebrows*); **terrain b.,** scrubland.

broussard [brusar] *nm* bushman.

brousse¹ [brus] *nf* **la b.,** the bush, *Austr* the outback; *F* the back of beyond; **feux de b.,** bush *or* brush fires.

brousse² *nf Région* = cream cheese made from goats' or ewes' milk.

broutage [brutaʒ] *nm*, **broutement** [brutmɑ̃] *nm* **(a)** (*par les bêtes*) browsing, grazing; **(b)** *MecE* jumping, judder(ing) (*of brake, tool*); grab(bing) (*of brake*).

brouter [brute] *vi* **(a)** (*des bêtes*) to browse, to graze; **(b)** (*of brake, tool*) to chatter, to jump, to judder; (*of brake*) to grab.

broutille [brutij] *nf* trifle, thing of no importance.

broyage [brwajaʒ] *nm* pulverizing (*of coal etc*); crushing, grinding (*of stone etc*); *Tex* braking (*of hemp*).

broyer [brwaje] *vt* **(je broie, n. broyons; je broierai)** to crush, to grind (*stone*); to pulverize (*coal*); *Tex* to brake (*hemp etc*); **b. des couleurs,** to grind colours; *Fig* **b. du noir,** to be down in the dumps; **la machine lui a broyé la main,** the machine crushed his hand; *Fig* **quand il te serre la main, il te la broie!,** he has a crushing handshake!

broyeur, -euse [brwajœr, -øz] **1** *adj* crushing, grinding (*mill etc*). **2** *n* (*person*) crusher, grinder; *Tex* hemp braker *or* dresser. **3** *nm Tech* crusher, grinder; (coal) pulverizer; **b. d'ordures,** waste *or Am* garbage disposal unit.

bru [bry] *nf Vieilli* daughter-in-law.

bruant [bryɑ̃] *nm* (*oiseau*) bunting; **b. jaune,** yellowhammer.

brucelles [brysɛl] *nfpl* tweezers.

brucellose [bryseloz] *nf Vét Méd* brucellosis.

bruche [bryʃ] *nm Ent* **b. des pois,** pea beetle, weevil.

brugnon [bryɲɔ̃] *nm* (*fruit*) nectarine.

brugnonier [bryɲɔnje] *nm* (*arbre*) nectarine (tree).

bruine [brɥin] *nf* drizzle, Scotch mist.

bruiner [brɥine] *v impers* to drizzle.

bruineux, -euse [brɥinø, -øz] *adj* drizzly.

bruire [brɥir] *vi* (*prp* **bruissant**; *pr ind* **il bruit, ils bruissent**; *impf* **il bruissait**) (*of leaves*) to rustle; (*of machinery*) to hum; (*of water, wind*) to murmur; (*of bees*) to buzz.

bruissement [brɥismɑ̃] *nm* rustling; hum(ming) (*of machinery*); murmur(ing) (*of brook*); buzzing (*of bees*).

bruit [brɥi] *nm* **(a)** noise, sound; (*vacarme*) noise; (*tapage, scandale*) noise, fuss; **lutte contre le b.,** noise abatement campaign; **b. de vaisselle,** clatter of dishes; **b. métallique,** clang; **b. de marteaux,** (sound of) hammering; **b. de pas,** (sound of) footsteps; **b. sourd,** thud, thump; **faire du b.,** to make a noise, to be noisy; **quel b.!,** what a row *or* din *or* racket!; **ne faites pas de b.!,** don't make a noise!; (*pas le moindre*) don't make a sound!; **b. de fond,** background noise; *Électron etc* **b. parasite,** parasitic noise; **cette histoire a fait du b. à l'époque,** the affair caused a scandal at the time; **beaucoup de b. pour rien,** much ado about nothing; **faire grand b. de qch,** to make a great to-do *or* a great fuss about sth; **sans b.,** noiselessly, silently, without any fuss, quietly;
(b) *Méd* (*heart, respiratory*) murmur;
(c) (*rumeur*) rumour; **le b. court que ...,** rumour has it that ...; **des bruits courent sur la démission du Premier Ministre,** there are rumours that the Prime Minister is going to resign.

bruitage [brɥitaʒ] *nm Th Cin TV* sound effects.

bruiter [brɥite] *vt Th Cin TV* to produce sound effects.

bruiteur [brɥitœr] *nm Th Cin TV* sound-effects man.

brûlage [brylaʒ] *nm* **(a)** burning (*of weeds, grass etc*); burning off (*of paint*); singeing (*of hair*); **(b)** scorching (*of clothes etc*); roasting (*of coffee*).

brûlant [brylɑ̃] *adj* (*très chaud*) burning, on fire; *Fig* fiery, passionate (*words etc*); **café b.,** boiling (hot) *or* scalding (hot) coffee; **il a les mains brûlantes,** his hands are burning hot; **désir b.,** burning desire; **soleil b.,** scorching *or* blazing sun; **question brûlante,** burning question.

brûlé [bryle] **1** *adj* burnt; *Culin* **crème brûlée,** caramel custard; **vin b.,** mulled wine; *F* **cerveau b., tête brûlée,** daredevil. **2** *nm* **(a) odeur de b.,** smell of burning; **goût de b.,** burnt taste; **avoir un goût de b.,** to taste burnt; **sentir le b.,** (*des avis*) to smack of heresy; (*être louche*) to look fishy; **(b)** *Can* burnt-out woodland area; **(c) crier comme un b.,** to scream like a madman.

brûle-parfum(s) [brylparfœ̃] *nm inv* incense burner.

brûle-pourpoint (à) [abrylpurpwɛ̃] *adv* point-blank; **dire qch à qn à b.-p.,** (*à son nez*) to tell s.o. sth point-blank *or* to his face; (*brusquement*) to spring sth on s.o.; *Arch* **tirer sur qn à b.-p.,** to fire at s.o. at close range.

brûler [bryle] **1** *vt* **(a)** to burn (*paper*); to burn (down) (*house etc*); to burn (up) (*rubbish etc*); to burn away (*metal*); to burn out (*s.o.'s eyes, electrical resistor etc*); to burn off (*paint*); to cauterize (*wound*); (*consumer*) to use, to burn (*fuel, electricity*); (*of acid*) to corrode; **elle fut brûlée vive,** (*par accident*) she was burnt to death; (*par supplice*) she was burnt at the stake; **b. la cervelle à qn,** to blow s.o.'s brains out; *Agr* **b. le terrain** *ou* **la brousse,** to burn the ground; **la chaudière brûle beaucoup de charbon,** the boiler burns *or* uses a lot of coal; **prendre une ville sans b. une cartouche,** to take a town without firing a shot;

(b) to burn (*toast*); to roast (*coffee*); to singe (*hair*); **le lait est brûlé,** the milk has caught; **tu vas b. ton gâteau,** you'll burn your cake; **l'argent lui brûle les mains,** money burns a hole in his pocket; **terre brûlée par le soleil,** sun-scorched earth; *F* **b. la route** *ou* **le pavé,** to scorch *or* tear along the road; **la gelée a brûlé les bourgeons,** the frost has nipped the buds; **la fumée me brûlait les yeux,** the smoke made my eyes smart;

(c) b. une gare, to run through a station without stopping; **b. un signal,** to overrun a signal; *Aut* **b. les feux** *ou* **un feu rouge,** to jump the lights, to go through a red light; **b. la politesse à qn,** to leave s.o. unceremoniously; (*passer devant*) to jump ahead of s.o. (*in queue*); *Sp* **b. un concurrent,** to race past a competitor, to leave a competitor standing;

(d) *F* **b. un espion,** to uncover a spy; **il est brûlé,** his cover's blown.

2 *vi* **(a)** to burn, to be on fire, to be alight; *Méd* to be feverish; (*of wound*) to smart; **b. lentement** *ou* **sans flamme,** to smoulder; **b. sec,** to burn like tinder; **laisser b. la lumière,** to leave the light on; **aïe, ça brûle!,** ow, that's hot!; *F* **on brûle ici,** it's baking in here; *F* **tu brûles,** you're getting hot; **b. de fièvre,** to be burning up (with fever);

(b) *Fig* **b. de curiosité,** to be consumed with curiosity; **b. d'indignation,** to seethe with indignation; **b. (du désir) de faire qch,** to be burning *or* dying to do sth; **les mains lui brûlent,** his hands are hot; *F* he is dying to be up and doing; *F* **les pieds lui brûlent,** he is itching to be off;

(c) (*of meat*) to burn; (*of milk*) to catch;

(d) *Vieilli* **b. pour qn,** to languish for s.o..

3 se brûler *vpr* (*par accident*) to burn oneself (**avec,** on); (*exprès*) to set fire to oneself; **se b. les doigts,** to burn one's fingers; **se b. la langue,** to burn *or* scald one's tongue.

brûleur [brylœr] *nm* **(a)** burner (*of gas cooker etc*); **b. à mazout,** oil-fired furnace; **(b) b. de café,** coffee roaster.

brûloir [brylwar] *nm* (*machine*) (coffee) burner, roaster.

brûlot [brylo] *nm* **(a)** *Fig* firebrand; **(b)** *Culin* burnt brandy (*cooked with sugar*); **(c)** *Can* gnat, midge; **(d)** *Arch* fire ship.

brûlure [brylyr] *nf* **(a)** (*blessure*) burn, scald; *Méd* **b. au premier/deuxième/troisième degré,** first/second/third-degree burn; **des traces de b. de cigarette sur un fauteuil,** cigarette burns on an armchair; **(b) (sensation de) b.,** burning, stinging, smarting (sensation); **b. d'estomac,** heartburn; **(c)** *Agr* frost nip; scorching (*by sun*); blight (*on corn*).

brume [brym] *nf* haze, mist (*surtout à la mer*); **b. de chaleur,** heat haze; *Fig* **la b. de ses explications,** his hazy explanations.

brumeux, -euse [brymø, -øz] *adj* foggy, misty, hazy; *Fig* obscure, vague, hazy (*ideas etc*).

brumisateur [brymizatœr] *nm* atomizer, spray.

brun, brune [brœ̃, bryn] **1** *adj* brown (*cloth, hair etc*); dark, dusky, swarthy (*skin, person*); brown, sunburnt, (sun)tanned, *Am* tan (*complexion*); **du tabac b.,** dark tobacco; **une bière brune,** a brown ale; **la robe brune d'un cheval,** a horse's brown coat; **elle est naturellement brune,** she is a natural brunette. **2** *n* **un b./une brune,** a dark(-haired) man/woman; **une belle brune,** a lovely brunette. **3** *nm* brown (colour); **b. foncé,** dark brown. **4** *nf* **(a) à la brune,** at dusk, at twilight; **(b) une brune,** a brown ale.

brunante [brynɑ̃t] *nf Can* dusk, twilight.

brunâtre [brynɑtr] *adj* brownish.

brunch [brœntʃ] *nm* brunch.

brunette [brynɛt] *nf* brunette.

brunir [brynir] **1** *vi* to become dark *or* (sun)tanned, to tan; to (go) brown. **2** *vt* to darken, to tan; to burnish (*gold etc*); to polish, to planish (*metal*).

brunissage [brynisaʒ] *nm* (*de l'or*) burnishing; (*d'autre métal*) polishing, planishing.

brunissement [brynismɑ̃] *nm* (*de la peau*) tanning; (*résultat*) (sun)tan.

brunisseur, -euse [brynisœr, -øz] *n Tech* burnisher.

brunissoir [bryniswar] *nm Tech* burnisher, polisher, polishing tool.

brunissure [brynisyr] *nf* **(a)** burnish, polish (*of metals*); **(b)** *Agr* (potato) blight, rot.

brushing [brœʃiŋ] *nm* blow-dry; **se faire un b.,** to blow-dry one's hair; **coupe et b.,** cut and blow-dry.

brusque [brysk] *adj* **(a)** abrupt, off-hand, curt, brusque (*person, manner*); **d'un ton b.,** in a curt *or* off-hand tone; **(b)** sudden, abrupt (*stop etc*); *Aut* **tournant b.,** sharp bend.

brusquement [bryskəmɑ̃] *adv* **(a)** (*soudainement*) suddenly, abruptly; **il a b. changé,** he suddenly changed; **la route plonge b.,** the road dips sharply; **(b)** *Vieilli* abruptly, brusquely, curtly.

brusquer [bryske] *vt* **(a) b. qn,** (*être impoli envers*) to be brusque *or* curt with s.o.; (*maltraiter*) to treat s.o. harshly; **(b) b. les choses,** to rush things; **attaque brusquée,** surprise attack; *F* **arrête de me b.,** stop rushing me.

brusquerie [bryskəri] *nf* abruptness, brusqueness.

brut [bryt] **1** *adj* **(a)** crude (*oil etc*); unrefined (*sugar*); rough, uncut (*diamond*); extra-dry (*champagne*); unpolished (*marble etc*); undressed (*timber, skin*); **toile brute,** unbleached cloth; **produit b.,** primary product; *Ordinat* **données brutes,** raw data; **matières brutes,** raw materials; **fonte brute,** pig iron; **or b.,** gold in nuggets; *Métal* **b. de fonte** *ou* **de coulée,** rough cast; **à l'état b.,** in the rough; **il nous a exposé le projet à l'état b.,** he gave us a general outline of the project; **faire de l'art b.,** to produce primitive art; **faits bruts,** bald *or* hard facts;

(b) *Com* gross (*profit, value, weight etc*); **salaire b.,** gross salary; **marge brute,** gross profit margin.

2 *nm* **(a)** crude (oil);

(b) (*champagne*) brut *or* extra dry champagne.

3 *adv* **le colis pèse b. 20 kilos,** the parcel weighs 20 kilos gross.

brutal, -aux [brytal, -o] *adj* (*violent*) brutal, savage; (*rude*) coarse, rough; **force brutale,** brute force; **coup b.,** brutal *or* savage blow; **les faits brutaux,** the hard *or* brutal facts; **vérité brutale,** plain *or* unvarnished truth; **être b. avec qn,** to treat s.o. roughly *or* harshly; **arrêt b.,** sudden *or* abrupt stop; **il peut être très b.,** he can be very rough; **frein/embrayage b.,** fierce brake/clutch; **avec sa manière brutale de dire les choses,** with his harsh way of saying things.

brutalement [brytalmɑ̃] *adv* (*violemment*) brutally, savagely; (*rudement*) harshly, roughly; (*sans ambages*) bluntly, plainly; (*soudainement*) abruptly, suddenly; **elle nous l'a annoncé b.,** she broke it to us bluntly; **la route tourne b.,** there is a sudden bend in the road, the road bends suddenly; **il a b. changé,** he has suddenly changed.

brutaliser [brytalize] *vt* to ill-treat, to maltreat (*one's wife, child*); to treat (*s.o.*) roughly *or* harshly, to bully (*s.o.*); *F* **il ne faut pas me b.,** (*laisse-moi réfléchir*) don't rush me.

brutalité [brytalite] *nf* **(a)** (*de personne*) (*violence*) brutality; (*grossièreté*) coarseness, roughness; **(b)** (*d'animal*) brutality, savagery, savage cruelty; **(c)** (*rapidité*) suddenness, abruptness; **(d)** (*acte violent*) brutal act.

brute [bryt] *nf* **(a)** (*personne violente*) brute, beast; (*personne grossière*) boor; **sale b.!,** filthy beast!; **frapper comme une b.,** to hit out brutally *or* violently; **(b)** *Litt* brute beast.

Bruxelles [brysɛl] *nf* Brussels.

bruyamment [brɥijamɑ̃] *adv* noisily, loudly; **rire b.,** to laugh boisterously.

bruyant [brɥijɑ̃] *adj* noisy; resounding (*success*); loud (*applause*); boisterous (*laughter*); **un quartier peu b.,** a quiet neighbourhood.

bruyère [bryjɛr] *nf* **(a)** (*plante*) heather, heath; (*terre*) heath(land), moor(land); **(b) racine de b.,** briar root; **pipe en** *ou* **de b.,** briar pipe.

bryone [brijɔn] *nf* (*plante*) bryony.

B.S.G.D.G. (*abrév* **breveté sans garantie du Gouvernement**) patent without Government warranty (of quality).

B.T. [bete] *nm abrév* **brevet de technicien.**

B.T.S. [beteɛs] *nm abrév* **brevet de technicien supérieur.**

buanderie [bɥɑ̃dri] *nf* laundry (room).

buandier, -ière [bɥɑ̃dje, -jɛr] *n* laundryman, laundress;

Vieilli washerwoman.

bubon [bybɔ̃] *nm Méd* bubo.

bubonique [bybɔnik] *adj Méd* bubonic (*plague*).

Bucarest [bykarɛst] *nf* Bucharest.

buccal, -aux [bykal, -o] *adj Anat* buccal (*cavity etc*); *Méd* **vaccin b.,** oral vaccine.

bucco-dentaire [bykodɑ̃tɛr] *adj* (*hygiène*) oral and dental.

bûche [byʃ] *nf* (*morceau de bois*) log; *F* blockhead, drip; *Culin etc* **b. de Noël,** Yule log; *F* **ramasser une b.,** to come a cropper; *F* **ne reste pas là comme une b.!,** don't just stand *or* sit there like a dummy!

bûcher[1] [byʃe] *nm* **(a)** (*pour le bois*) woodshed; **(b)** (*de supplice*) stake; **monter** *ou* **mourir sur le b.,** to be burnt at the stake; **(c)** (*funéraire*) (funeral) pyre.

bûcher[2] *Scol F vtr* **1** to work hard at, to slog away at (*sth*); to swot (*sth*) up. **2** *vi* to swot.

bûcheron [byʃrɔ̃] *nm* woodcutter, woodman, *surtout Am* lumberjack, logger.

bûchette [byʃɛt] *nf* stick, twig (*of dry wood*).

bûcheur, -euse [byʃœr, -øz] *F* **1** *n* hard worker, swot, slogger, *Am* grind. **2** *adj* hard-working (*student etc*).

bucolique [bykɔlik] *Littér* **1** *adj* bucolic, pastoral (*poem*). **2** *nf* pastoral poem, bucolic.

budget [bydʒɛ] *nm* budget; **b. de la marine/de la guerre,** navy/army estimates; **inscrire/porter qch au b.,** to budget for sth; **boucler le b.,** to balance the budget, to make both ends meet; **b. prévisionnel,** provisional budget.

budgétaire [bydʒetɛr] *adj* budgetary; fiscal, financial (*year*); financial (*period*); **les dépenses budgétaires,** budgetary expenditure; **comptabilité b.,** budgeting; **contrainte b.,** budget constraint; **déficit/excédent b.,** budget deficit/surplus.

budgétisation [bydʒetizɑsjɔ̃] *nf* budgeting, inclusion (*of item*) in budget.

budgétiser [bydʒetize] *vt* to include (*sth*) in the budget; to budget for (*sth*).

buée [bɥe] *nf* steam, vapour, condensation (*on window panes etc*); mist, moisture (*on mirror*).

buffet [byfɛ] *nm* **(a)** (*meuble*) sideboard; **b. de cuisine,** (kitchen) dresser; **(b) b. (d'orgue),** organ chest; **(c)** (*repas*) buffet (meal); **b. froid,** cold buffet; **b. de gare,** station buffet, refreshment room; **(d)** *F* (*ventre*) belly; **je n'ai rien dans le b. depuis hier soir,** I haven't had a bite to eat since yesterday evening.

buffetier, -ière [byftje, -jɛr] *n* manager, manageress (*of station buffet, refreshment room*).

buffle [byfl] *nm* buffalo; **cuir (de) b.,** buffalo hide.

bufflesse [byflɛs] *nf,* **bufflonne** [byflɔn] *nf* cow buffalo.

bugle[1] [bygl] *nm Mus* (key) bugle; flugelhorn.

bugle[2] *nf* (*plante*) bugle.

building [bildiŋ] *nm* large modern block (*of flats, offices*).

buire [bɥir] *nf* ewer, flagon.

buis [bɥi] *nm* (*arbre*) box (tree); (*bois*) box(wood).

buisson [bɥisɔ̃] *nm* thicket, spinney; **un b. de mûres,** a bramble thicket; *Bible* **b. ardent,** burning bush; (*chasse*) *& Fig* **trouver** *ou* **faire b. creux,** to draw a blank, to find the bird flown; *Culin* **b. d'écrevisses,** = crayfish served piled up on a dish.

buissonneux, -euse [bɥisɔnø, -øz] *adj* bushy (*country etc*).

buissonnier, -ière [bɥisɔnje, -jɛr] *adj* **(a) faire l'école buissonnière,** to play truant *or Am* hook(e)y; **(b)** *Arch* (*animal etc*) that lives in bushes.

bulbe [bylb] *nm* **(a)** *Bot* bulb, corm; **(b)** *Anat* bulb; **b. (rachidien),** medulla oblongata; **(c)** *Archit* rounded dome, cupola.

bulbeux, -euse [bylbø, -øz] *adj* bulbous.

bulgare [bylgar] **1** *adj* Bulgarian. **2** *nm Ling* Bulgarian. **3** *n* **B.,** Bulgarian.

Bulgarie [bylgari] *nf* Bulgaria.

bulldozer [buldozœr] *nm* bulldozer.

bulle [byl] **1** *nf* **(a)** bubble (*of air, water etc*); *Méd* blister, bleb; balloon (*in comic strips etc*); **b. de savon,** soap bubble; **faire des bulles,** to blow bubbles; *Fig* **coincer la b.,** to have a lazy time; **(b)** (*lettre du pape*) (papal) bull; **b. d'excommunication,** bull of excommunication. **2** *adj inv* **papier b.,** manila paper. **3** *nm* **du b.,** manila paper.

bulletin [byltɛ̃] *nm* **(a)** bulletin; report, summary (*of news etc*); *Am Univ* transcript (*of marks*); **b. météorologique,** weather report; *TV* **b. d'actualités,** news bulletin; *Scol* **b. trimestriel,** end-of-term report; *Méd* **b. de santé,** medical bulletin; *Journ* **le b. spécial,** special issue; **(b)** (*papier, certificat*) ticket, receipt, certificate; (*à remplir*) form; **b. de paie,** pay (advice) slip; *Com* **b. de commande,** order form; **b. (d'enregistrement) de bagages,** luggage ticket, luggage check; **b. de consigne,** cloakroom ticket; left-luggage ticket; **b. de vote,** ballot (paper); **b. blanc,** blank ballot; **b. (de vote) nul,** spoiled ballot.

bulleux, -euse [bylø, -øz] *adj Méd* covered with blisters; *Géol Méd* vesicular (*rock, fever*).

bull-terrier [bulterje] *nm* bull terrier.

bungalow [bœ̃galo] *nm* bungalow.

bunker [bunkɛr] *nm Mil* bunker.

buraliste [byralist] *n* (*de bureau de poste*) clerk; (*d'impôts*) receiver of taxes; (*de bureau de tabac*) tobacconist.

bure [byr] *nf Tex* frieze, rough homespun; frock (*of monk*).

bureau, -eaux [byro] *nm* **(a)** (*meuble*) desk, bureau; **le dessus du b.,** the desk top; **ordinateur de b.,** desk top computer; **b. à cylindre,** roll-top desk; **b. ministre,** kneehole desk; *Pol* **déposer un projet de loi sur le b.,** to table a bill;

(b) (*lieu*) office; (*à la maison*) study; **ceci fera d'excellents bureaux,** this will be very good office space; **je dois passer au b. à midi,** I have to drop by the office at midday; **b. d'études,** design *or* planning department *or* office; **fournitures de b.,** office supplies; **b. de poste,** post office; **b. central,** (*de poste*) main post office; *Tél* exchange; **b. de police,** police station; **b. de douane,** custom(s) house; **b. de location,** box office; **b. du théâtre,** (theatre) box office; **b. de placement,** employment agency *or* bureau; **b. de tabac,** tobacconist's (shop); *Can* **b. spécial de scrutin,** advance poll;

(c) (*personnel*) (office) staff; **un repas avec le b.,** a meal with the office;

(d) (*assemblée*) board, committee, executive; **élire le b.,** to elect the committee;

(e) department, division, bureau (*of the civil service etc*); **Deuxième B.,** Intelligence Branch *or* Service, *US* G2 (Division).

bureaucrate [byrokrat] *n Péj* bureaucrat.

bureaucratie [byrokrasi] *nf Péj* bureaucracy, officialdom, *F* red tape.

bureaucratique [byrokratik] *adj Péj* bureaucratic.

bureaucratisation [byrokratizɑsjɔ̃] *nf Péj* bureaucratization.

bureaucratiser [byrokratize] *vt Péj* to bureaucratize.

bureautique [byrotik] *nf* office automation.

burette [byrɛt] *nf* (*pour l'huile*) oilcan, oiler; *Ch* burette; *Rel* cruet; *F* **il me casse les burettes,** he gets on my tits.

burin [byrɛ̃] *nm* **(a)** (*de graveur*) graver, etcher's needle, burin; (*gravure*) engraving, print; **(b)** (*ciseau d'acier*) (cold) chisel.

burinage [byrinaʒ] *nm Tech* chiselling, chipping.

buriner [byrine] *vt* **(a)** to engrave (*copperplate etc*); **visage buriné,** (*par le temps*) seamed face; **(b)** *Tech* to chisel, to chip.

burineur [byrinœr] *nm Tech* chipper, trimmer, chiseller.

burlesque [byrlɛsk] *adj* **(a)** comical, ludicrous, ridiculous (*appearance etc*); **(b)** *Littér* burlesque (*poem etc*).

burlesquement [byrlɛskəmɑ̃] *adv* (*voir adj*) **(a)** comically, ludicrously, ridiculously; **(b)** in a burlesque manner.

burnous [byrnu(s)] *nm* burnous(e), cloak; *F* **faire suer le b.,** to use sweated labour.

bus [bys] *nm* **(a)** (*autobus*) bus; **(b)** *Ordinat* bus; **(c)** *Électron* bus (bar).

busard [byzar] *nm* (*oiseau*) harrier.

busc [bysk] *nm* **(a)** (*de métal*) (corset) steel; (*de baleine*) whalebone; **(b)** (*d'écluse*) locksill; **(c)** (*de fusil*) shoulder.

buse[1] [byz] *nf* **(a)** (*oiseau*) buzzard; **(b)** *F* (*idiot*) fool.

buse[2] *nf* channel, tube, pipe; nozzle (*of bellows etc*); *Métal* blast pipe; **b. d'injection,** injector (spray tip); *Aut* **b. de carburateur,** carburettor choke tube; *Min* **b. d'aérage,** air channel *or* pipe *or* shaft.

business [biznɛs] *nm F* **(a)** (*affaire*) business; **c'est un sacré b. que de le faire travailler,** it's a hell of a business *or* a to-do to get him to work; **(b)** (*truc*) thingummy, what's it.

businessman [biznɛsman] *nm* businessman; (*pl businessmen* [biznɛsmen] *ou businessmans*).

businesswoman [biznɛswumɑn] *nf* businesswoman; (*pl businesswomen* [biznɛswumen] *ou businesswomans*).

busqué [byske] *adj* hook(ed), aquiline, Roman (*nose*).

buste [byst] *nm* chest; bust (*of woman*); *Beaux-Arts* (*marble etc*) bust; **peindre (qn) en b.,** to paint a half-length portrait (of s.o.).

bustier [bystje] *nm* long-line (strapless) brassière; **robe de bal/maillot à b.,** strapless evening gown/bathing suit.

but [by(t)] *nm* **(a)** (*objectif*) object, end, aim, goal, purpose; **mesure ayant pour b. d'assurer ...,** measure intended to ensure ...; **un b. personnel,** a personal goal; **dans le b. de ...,** with the object *or* aim *or* intention of ...; **dans le b. de frauder,** with intent to defraud; **dans ce b.,** with this aim in view; **se fixer un b.,** to set oneself a goal *or* target; **je suis encore loin du b.,** I still have a long way to go; **poursuivre son b.,** to pursue one's goal *or* aim; **cette loi vise un double b.,** this law has a two-fold objective; **il touche au b.,** he has nearly reached his goal *or* achieved his aim; **aller droit au b.,** to go straight to the point; **errer sans b.,** to wander about aimlessly; **le b. d'une marche,** the destination of a walk; **le b. d'une recherche,** the aim *or* goal of a piece of research; **un coup au b.,** a direct hit; **(b)** *Fb etc* goal; **ligne de b.,** goal line; **entrée du b.,** goal mouth; **marquer un b.,** to score a goal; **tirer en plein dans le b.,** to shoot straight at goal; **gagner 3 buts à 1,** to win 3 - 1 *or* 3 goals to 1; **garder les buts,** to be in goal. **2** *adv* **(a) tirer de b. en blanc,** to fire direct *or* point-blank; **faire une offre de b. en blanc,** to make an offer on the spur of the moment; **(b) b. à b.,** even, without any advantage to either party.

butane [bytan] *nm Ch* butane; **gaz b.,** butane (gas).

butanier [bytanje] *nm Nau* (butane) tanker.

buté [byte] *adj* stubborn, obstinate; **visage b.,** fixed *or* set *or* determined expression.

butée [byte] *nf* **(a)** *Tech* thrust; **palier de b.,** thrust block *or* bearing; **b. (d'arrêt),** stop; **(b)** *Constr* abutment, buttress.

buter [byte] **1** *vi* **(a) b. contre qch,** to strike *or* knock against sth, to bump *or* bang into *or* against sth, to stumble over sth; **b. contre** *ou* **sur un problème,** to come up against a problem; **(b)** (*of beams etc*) to abut, to rest **(contre,** against). **2** *vt* **(a)** to prop up, to buttress, to shore up (*a wall*); **(b)** *Arg* to bump (*s.o.*) off. **3 se buter** *vpr* **(a) se b. à qn,** to come across *or* bump into s.o.; **se b. à un obstacle,** to come up against an obstacle; **(b) se b. à faire qch,** to be set on doing sth; **(c)** (*s'entêter*) to be(come) stubborn, to dig one's heels in.

buteur [bytœr] *nm Sp* (goal) scorer.

butin [bytɛ̃] *nm* booty; (*de pilleur*) spoils, plunder; (*de voleur*) loot; **le b. des recherches archéologiques,** the finds from the archaeological dig.

butiner [bytine] **1** *vi* (*of bees*) to gather pollen. **2** *vt* to gather, to collect (*information etc*).

butineur, -euse [bytinœr, -øz] *adj* pollen-gathering.

butoir [bytwar] *nm* stop, check; *Rail etc* buffer; **b. d'une porte,** door stop(per).

butor [bytɔr] *nm* **(a)** (*oiseau*) bittern; **(b)** *F* (*lourdaud*) lout, clod, oaf.

buttage [bytaʒ] *nm* earthing up (*of plants*).

butte [byt] *nf* **(a)** (*colline*) knoll, hillock, mound; *Géol* **b. témoin,** (flat-topped) outlier; **(b) b. (de tir),** butts; *Fig* **être en b. à qch,** to be a butt for sth.

butter [byte] *vt* **(a)** *Agr* to ridge (*ground*); to earth up (*plants*); **(b)** *Arg* to bump (*s.o.*) off.

buvable [byvabl] *adj* **(a)** (*potable*) drinkable, fit to drink; **c'est à peine b. tellement c'est mauvais,** it's so bad it's hardly drinkable; **(b)** *Méd* to be taken orally.

buvard [byvar] **1** *adj* **papier b.,** blotting paper. **2** *nm* blotter, blotting pad.

buvetier, -ière [byvtje, -jɛr] *n Vieilli* barkeeper, barman, barmaid.

buvette [byvɛt] *nf* **(a)** refreshment bar (*at railway station etc*); **(b)** pump room (*in spa*).

buveur, -euse [byvœr, -øz] *n* drinker; **c'est un grand** *ou* **gros b.,** he's a heavy drinker; **une buveuse de bière,** a beer-drinker.

B.V.P. [bevepe] *nm* (*abrév* **bureau de vérification de la publicité**) *Br* ≈ Advertising Standards Authority.

bye(-bye) [baj(baj)] *int* bye-bye.

by-pass [bajpɑs] *nm Chir Aut* bypass.

byronien, -ienne [birɔnjɛ̃, -jɛn] *adj* Byronic.

Byzance [bizɑ̃s] *n* Byzantium.

byzantin, -ine [bizɑ̃tɛ̃, -in] **1** *adj* Byzantine. **2** *n* **B.,** Byzantine.

C

C, c [se] *nm* **(a)** (the letter) C; **c. cédille,** c cedilla; **(b)** (*abrév* **Celsius**) C.

c' *voir* **CE**[1].

ça [sa] **1** *pron dém* **(a)** (*ceci, cela*) it, this, that; **donne-moi ça,** give it to me, give me that; **c'est dégoûtant ça,** that's disgusting; **une petite femme haute comme ça,** a little woman no taller than that *or* only so high; **je suis comme ça,** I'm like that; *F* **comme ça, vous déménagez?,** so you're moving, are you?; **allons, pas de ça!,** hey! none of that!; **ce n'est pas si facile que ça,** it isn't as easy as all that; **où ça?,** where('s that)?; **comment ça?,** how come?; **ça oui!,** yes indeed!, definitely!; **ça non!,** not on your life!; **pas de ça chez nous,** we don't want any of that here; **il ne manquait plus que ça,** that's all we *or* I *etc* needed; **ça existe aussi en bleu,** it comes in blue too; **ça dépend,** it *or* that depends; **ça va, ça vient,** it comes and goes; (*les touristes etc*) they come and go; **à part ça, tout va bien,** apart from that, everything's fine; **il y a un peu de ça, effectivement,** yes, there's an element of *or* a bit of that; **ça me fait de la peine de le voir malade,** it upsets me to see him ill; **elle n'était pas comme ça avant,** she wasn't like that before; **ça va?, — comme ça,** how are you? — so-so; **les soucis du travail, et tout ça,** work problems etcetera *or* and all that; **qui/quand/où ça?,** who/when/where's that?; **c'est qui/quoi ça?,** who's/what's that?; **ça alors!,** you don't say!, *F* well, I'm damned!; **ça alors, c'est incroyable!,** well I never! *or* blow me! that's incredible!; **ça y est!,** that's that!, that's it!; **c'est ça!,** that's it!, that's right!; **ah ça, non!,** no way!, no fear!, I'm not having (any of) that!; **comment ça, elle est partie?,** what do you mean 'she's gone'?;

(b) *Fig Péj* **ça bavarde là-bas dans le fond de la classe,** there's talking going on at the back of the classroom; **il faut voir ça pour le croire,** you have to see it to believe it; **regarde-moi ça!,** just look at that!; **écoute-moi ça!,** just listen to this!; **c'est ça les hommes!,** that's men for you!; **ça arrive en retard et ça veut qu'on l'attende,** he *etc* arrives late, and then expects me *etc* to wait for him *etc*;

(c) *F* (*le sexe*) it, the other; **il ne pense qu'à ça,** he's got a one-track mind, that's all he thinks about.

2 *nm Psy* **le ça,** the id.

çà [sa] **1** *adv* **çà et là,** this way and that, hither and thither; (*à certains endroits*) here and there. **2** *int* **ah çà!,** now then!

C.A. [sea] *nm* **(a)** *Él* (*abrév* **courant alternatif**) AC; **(b)** *Com* (*abrév* **chiffre d'affaires**) turnover.

cabale [kabal] *nf* **(a)** *Rel* cab(b)ala; **(b)** (*complot*) plot, scheme, cabal; **monter une c. contre qn,** to start a whispering campaign against s.o.; **(c)** (*ligue*) cabal, faction.

cabaliste [kabalist] *nm Rel* cab(b)alist.

cabalistique [kabalistik] *adj* cab(b)alistic; *Fig* **des formules cabalistiques,** arcane formulae.

caban [kabɑ̃] *nm Nau* (sailor's) peajacket, reefer.

cabane [kaban] *nf* **(a)** (*bicoque*) hut; *Péj* shack; (*of wood*) (log) cabin; shed (*for tools etc*); *Can* **c. à sucre,** saphouse; **(b) c. à lapins,** (rabbit) hutch; *Fig* **ils vivent dans des cabanes à lapins,** they live in rabbit hutches *or* shoeboxes; **(c)** *Arg* (*prison*) jail, clink, nick; **en c.,** in clink, in the nick.

cabanon [kabanɔ̃] *nm* **(a)** (*petite cabane*) hut, shed; **(b)** (*in Provence*) (country) cottage; **(c)** (*chalet de plage*) (beach) hut, cabin, chalet; **(d)** (*cellule*) padded cell; *F* **il est bon pour le c.,** he ought to be locked up.

cabaret [kabarɛ] *nm* **(a)** (*boîte*) night club, cabaret; **(b)** (*meuble*) liqueur stand; **(c)** *Arch* tavern, inn, public house.

cabaretier, -ière [kabartje, -jɛr] *n Arch* tavern keeper, innkeeper.

cabas [kabɑ] *nm* **(a)** (*panier*) shopping basket; (*en tissu*) shopping bag; **(b)** (*pour les fruits*) basket.

cabestan [kabɛstɑ̃] *nm Nau etc* capstan; **c. horizontal,** windlass; **c. à bras,** hand capstan; **grand c.,** main capstan; **virez au c.!,** heave!

cabillau(d) [kabijo] *nm* codfish, fresh cod.

cabillot [kabijo] *nm Nau* **c. d'amarrage,** toggle (pin); **c. de tournage,** belaying pin.

cabine [kabin] *nf* **(a)** cabin (*in ship, aircraft, spacecraft etc*); *Nau* **la c.,** the saloon; **c. de luxe,** stateroom; *Av* **c. de pilotage,** cockpit, flight deck; **(b) c. de bains,** beach hut; **c. de douche,** shower cubicle; **c. téléphonique,** (tele)phone box, *esp Am* call box; **c. d'essayage,** fitting room; *Rail* **c. d'aiguillage,** signal box; **(c)** cab, house (*of crane*); cab (*of locomotive, lorry*); cage, car (*of lift*).

cabinet [kabinɛ] *nm* **(a)** (*petite pièce*) small room; **c. de toilette,** = dressing room (with washbasin (and bidet)); *F* **les cabinets,** the lavatory, the loo, *Am* the john; **c. particulier,** (*au restaurant*) private dining room; **c. d'estampes,** print room (*in museum*); **(b)** (*lieu de consultation etc*) office; (*d'avocat*) chambers; (*de médecin*) (doctor's) consulting room *or* surgery, *Am* office; (*patients, clients etc*) practice; **c. d'experts-conseils,** consultancy (firm); **ce médecin a un gros c.,** this doctor has a large practice; **(c)** *Pol Vieilli* cabinet; **question de c.,** ministerial question; **c. (d'un ministre),** (minister's) departmental staff; **homme de c.,** adviser; **chef de c.,** = principal private secretary; **(d)** (*meuble*) cabinet.

câblage [kɑblaʒ] *nm* **(a)** *Él* connecting up, wiring; **(b)** *Tex Él* twisting, cabling (*of yarn, wires etc*); **(c)** cabling (*of message*).

câble [kɑbl] *nm* **(a)** *Él* cable, lead; *Télécom* cable; **poser un c.,** to lay a cable; **la télévision par c., le c.,** cable television; **c. à fibre optique,** optical fibre *or US* fiber cable; *Électron* **c. hertzien,** radio link; **(b)** cable; *Nau* **c. d'amarrage,** mooring cable; **c. de remorque,** towing line, tow(rope); **c. métallique,** wire cable; (*à brins*) stranded wire; *MecE* **c. de frein,** brake cable; **(c)** (*message*) cable, telegram; **envoyer un c. à qn,** to send s.o. a cable, to cable s.o..

câblé [kɑble] *adj* **(a)** *Él* **circuit c.,** cable (TV) network; **(b)** *F* (*à la mode*) hip, trendy.

câbler [kɑble] *vt* **(a)** to twist, to lay (*strands into cable*); **(b)** to cable (*message*).

câbleur, -euse [kɑblœr, -øz] *n Tech* cable-layer.

câblodistribution [kɑblɔdistribysjɔ̃] *nf* cable television, *Am Admin* community antenna television.

câblogramme [kɑblɔgram] *nm Arch* cablegram, cable.

cabochard, -arde [kabɔʃar, -ard] *adj & n* stubborn (person).

caboche [kabɔʃ] *nf* **(a)** (*tête*) *F* nut; **mets-le toi dans la c.!,** get that into your thick skull!; **avoir la c. dure,** (*être bête*) to be thick; (*être têtu*) to be as stubborn as a mule, to be pigheaded; **c'est une sale c.,** he's an obstinate swine; **(b)** (*clou*) heavy-headed nail; (*de cordonnerie*) hobnail; (*pour les meubles*) stud (nail).

cabochon [kabɔʃɔ̃] *nm* **(a)** (*pierre précieuse*) cabochon; **(b)** (*de carafe à liqueur*) (glass) stopper; **(c)** (*pour les meubles*) stud (nail).

cabosser [kabɔse] *vt* to dent (*metal, car etc*); to bash in (*hat*); **vieux chapeau cabossé,** battered old hat; **voiture cabossée,** car with a dent in it.

cabot [kabo] *F* **1** *adj* = **CABOTIN 1 (a)**. **2** *nm* **(a)** (*acteur*) = **CABOTIN 2 (a)**; **(b)** (*chien*) pooch, *Péj* mutt; **(c)** *Mil* corporal, corp.

cabotage [kabɔtaʒ] *nm Nau* coasting; coastal trade; **grand/petit c.,** offshore/inshore coastal traffic.

caboter [kabɔte] *vi Nau* to coast.

caboteur [kabɔtœr] *Nau* **1** *nm* coaster, coasting vessel. **2** *adj* coastal (*trade*).

cabotin, -ine [kabɔtɛ̃, -in] *F Péj* **1** *adj* **(a)** ham (*actor*); **(b)** histrionic (*person*); **il est c.,** he's a show-off. **2** *n* **(a)** (*mauvais acteur*) ham (actor), third-rate actor *or* actress; **(b)** (*vantard*) show-off.

cabotinage [kabɔtinaʒ] *nm F Péj* **(a)** *Th* third-rate *or* ham acting; **(b)** histrionics (*in politics etc*); (*vantardise*)

showing off.
cabotiner [kabɔtine] *vi F Péj* to play to the gallery, to show off.
caboulot [kabulo] *nm Arg* seedy pub, dive.
cabrage [kɑbraʒ] *nm (of horse)* rearing (up); *Av* pulling up (*of nose*).
cabré [kɑbre] *adj (horse)* rearing.
cabrer [kɑbre] **1** *vt* **(a)** to rear up (*horse*); **c. un avion,** to pull (the nose) up; **(b)** *Fig* **c. qn contre qn,** to turn *or* set s.o. against s.o.. **2** *vi Av* to pull (the nose) up. **3 se cabrer** *vpr* (*of horse etc*) to rear (up); *Fig* **se c. contre qch,** to jib at sth, to rise in protest against sth, to rebel against sth; **son orgueil se cabre,** his pride has been stung.
cabri [kabri] *nm* kid; *Fig* **sauter comme un c.,** to jump for joy.
cabriole [kabrijɔl] *nf* (*saut, bond*) leap, caper; (*danse*) cabriole; *Équitation* capriole, goat's leap; (*de gymnaste*) tumble, somersault; *Fig* subterfuge, way out; **faire des cabrioles,** to caper about, to cavort; **elle s'en est tirée par une c.,** she cleverly manoeuvred her way out of it.
cabrioler [kabrijɔle] *vi* to caper *or* cavort about, to cut capers.
cabriolet [kabrijɔlɛ] *nm* **(a)** *Aut* cabriolet, convertible; **(b)** *Arch* cab(riolet), gig.
caca [kaka] *nm Enf F* number two, big job, poo-poo; **as-tu fait c.?,** (*to child*) have you done your job *or* a jobbie?; **jette ça, c'est du c.,** throw that away, it's nasty *or* dirty; **c. d'oie,** yellowish green.
cacah(o)uète, cacahouette [kakawɛt] *nf* peanut, monkey nut; **beurre de c.,** peanut butter.
cacao [kakao] *nm Bot* cacao, cocoa bean; *Com* cocoa.
cacaoté [kakaɔte] *adj* cocoa-flavoured.
cacaotier [kakaɔtje] *nm Bot* cacao (tree).
cacaoui [kakawi] *nm Can* long-tailed duck, old squaw.
cacaoyer [kakaɔje] *nm Bot* cacao (tree).
cacatoès [kakatɔɛs] *nm* cockatoo.
cacatois [kakatwa] *nm Nau* royal (sail); **(mât de) c.,** royal mast; **c. de perruche,** mizzen royal.
cachalot [kaʃalo] *nm* cachalot, sperm whale.
cache [kaʃ] **1** *nf* hiding place, cache. **2** *nm* cover, guard; *Phot* mask (*for printing*).
caché [kaʃe] *adj* hidden.
cache-cache [kaʃkaʃ] *nm inv* hide-and-seek; **jouer à c.-c.,** to play (at) hide-and-seek.
cache-col [kaʃkɔl] *nm inv* scarf, muffler.
cachemire [kaʃmir] *nm Tex* (*laine*) cashmere.
Cachemire [kaʃmir] *nm* Kashmir.
cache-misère [kaʃmizɛr] *nm inv* coat, wrap (*hiding shabby appearance*).
cache-nez [kaʃne] *nm inv* scarf, muffler.
cache-pot [kaʃpo] *nm inv* flowerpot holder.
cacher [kaʃe] **1** *vt* to hide, to conceal (*s.o., sth*); to hide (*one's face etc*) from view; to cover up (*picture etc*); to hide, to conceal, to mask (*one's feelings etc*); **où a-t-il pu c. la clé?,** where could he have hidden the key?; **le mur nous cache la vue,** the wall blocks our view; **douleur cachée,** secret grief; **c. qch à qn,** to hide *or* conceal sth from s.o.; (*ne pas le dire*) to keep sth back from sth; **c. son jeu,** to keep one's cards hidden *or* close to one's chest; *Fig* **il a bien caché son jeu,** he kept his cards close to his chest; **il n'y a rien de caché dans cette affaire,** everything is open and above board in this transaction; **je ne vous cache pas que je suis déçu,** I won't hide it from you that I'm disappointed, I won't hide my disappointment from you; **c. son âge,** to keep one's age a secret; **pour ne rien te c.,** to be completely open with you; **il ne cache pas que ...,** he makes no secret of the fact that ... .
2 se cacher *vpr* to hide, to be hiding, to be hidden; (*d'un air suspect, maussade*) to skulk; **les voleurs se cachent,** the thieves are in hiding; **le soleil se cache,** the sun isn't shining, the sun is behind a cloud; **elle ne se cache pas pour dire qu'elle est communiste,** she doesn't hide the fact she's a communist; **se c. de qn,** to hide from s.o.; **sa timidité se cache derrière une certaine rudesse,** his shyness is hidden behind a bluff exterior; **je ne m'en cache pas,** I make no secret of it; **en se cachant,** secretly; *Péj* on the sly; **sans se c.,** openly.
cache-radiateur [kaʃradjatœr] *nm inv* radiator cover.
cache-sexe [kaʃsɛks] *nm inv* G-string.
cachet [kaʃɛ] *nm* **(a)** mark, stamp; stamp, seal (*on document*); *Hist* **lettre de c.,** = order under the King's private seal; **c. d'oblitération** *ou* **de la poste,** postmark; **c. d'un fabricant,** maker's trademark; **le c. du génie,** the stamp *or* hallmark of genius; **il a beaucoup de c.,** he has lots of style *or* a certain cachet; **manteau qui a du c.,** stylish coat; **(b)** fee (*of artiste, counsel, consultant etc*); **courir le c.,** to give private lessons (in pupils' homes); **(c)** *Pharm* tablet, pill; *Arch* cachet; **un c. d'aspirine,** an aspirin (tablet).
cachetage [kaʃtaʒ] *nm* sealing (*of letters etc*).
cache-tampon [kaʃtɑ̃pɔ̃] *nm inv* (game of) hunt-the-thimble *or* -slipper.
cacheter [kaʃte] *vt* (**je cachette, n. cachetons; je cachetterai**) to seal (up) (*letter, bottle etc*); **cire à c.,** sealing wax; **vin cacheté,** vintage wine.
cachette [kaʃɛt] *nf* (*pour chose ou personne*) hiding place; (*pour personne*) hideaway; **jouer à la c.,** to play hide-and-seek; **en c.,** secretly; (*d'amoureux*) on the quiet; *Péj* on the sly, in an underhand manner; **vendre en c.,** to sell under the counter; **boire en c.,** (*habituellement*) to be a secret drinker; **il boit en c. de sa famille,** he hides his drinking from his family.
cachot [kaʃo] *nm* **(a)** (*cellule*) prison, jail, *Br* gaol; **(b)** (*isolement*) solitary confinement; **être condamné au c.,** to be put *or* placed in solitary confinement.
cachotterie [kaʃɔtri] *nf* (affectation of) mystery; **faire des cachotteries,** to keep things secret.
cachottier, -ière [kaʃɔtje, -jɛr] **1** *adj* secretive, reticent (*person*). **2** *n* slyboots; **petit c.!,** you sly thing!
cachou [kaʃu] **1** *nm* **(a)** (*bonbon*) cachou; **(b)** (*teinture*) catechu. **2** *adj inv* reddy-brown.
cacique [kasik] *nm* (*chef*) cacique; *F* boss, big shot; **les caciques du parti,** the party bosses.
cacochyme [kakɔʃim] *adj Hum* doddery.
cacophonie [kakɔfɔni] *nf* cacophony.
cacophonique [kakɔfɔnik] *adj* cacophonous.
cactus [kaktys] *nm* cactus.
c.-à-d. (*abrév* **c'est-à-dire**) i.e..
cadastral, -aux [kadastral, -o] *adj* cadastral (*register, survey*).
cadastre [kadastr] *nm Admin* (*registre*) cadastre; **les employés du c.,** survey staff.
cadastrer [kadastre] *vt Admin* to register (*property*) in the cadastre.
cadavéreux, -euse [kadaverø, -øz] *adj* deathly pale; *Litt* cadaverous.
cadavérique [kadaverik] *adj* deathly pale; *Méd* cadaveric; **rigidité c.,** rigor mortis; **la rigidité c. s'est installée,** rigor mortis has set in.
cadavre [kadɑvr] *nm* **(a)** corpse, (dead) body, *US* cadaver; carcass (*of dead animal*); *F* **c'est un c. ambulant,** he's a walking corpse; (*très maigre*) he's a skeleton; **(b)** *Arg* empty (bottle).
caddie [kadi] *nm* **(a)** *Golf* caddie; **(b)** (*chariot*) trolley.
cadeau, -eaux [kado] *nm* present, gift; **c. d'anniversaire/de Noël,** birthday/Christmas present; **en c.,** as a present; **faire un c. à qn,** to give s.o. a present; **acheter un c. à** *ou* **pour qn,** to buy s.o. a present; **demander un emballage-c.,** to ask for sth to be gift-wrapped; **papier-c.,** gift-wrap(ping paper); **je n'en voudrais pas comme c.,** I wouldn't have it as a gift; **j'aimerais mieux en faire c.,** I'd rather give it away; *F* **il ne lui a pas fait de c.,** (*il ne l'a pas épargnée*) he didn't spare her; (*il n'a pas donné d'indication*) he didn't help her; *F* **ton frère, ce n'est pas un c.,** your brother's a real charmer!; **partir avec eux, ce n'était pas un c.,** going away with them was no picnic.
cadenas [kadna] *nm* padlock; **fermer la porte au c.,** to padlock the door.
cadenasser [kadnase] **1** *vt* to padlock (*door etc*). **2 se cadenasser** *vpr* to lock oneself away.
cadence [kadɑ̃s] *nf* **(a)** cadence, rhythm (*of verse, motion*); **en c.,** rhythmically, in time; **taper dans ses mains en c.,** to clap one's hands in time (to the music); **forcer la c.,** to force the pace; **à la c. de ...,** at the rate of ...; *Mil etc* **c. du tir,** rate of fire; **prendre la c.,** to get into step; **garder la c.,** to keep in step; **(b)** *Mus* cadence; cadenza (*in concerto*).
cadencé [kadɑ̃se] *adj* rhythmic(al); measured (*step etc*); **pas c., marche!,** quick march!; **marcher au pas c.,** to march *or* walk in step; (*rapidement*) to march *or* walk in quick time.
cadencer [kadɑ̃se] *vt* (**je cadençai(s); n. cadençons**) to give rhythm to (*one's style etc*); **c. son pas,** to get into step; (*garder la cadence*) to keep in step.
cadet, -ette [kadɛ, -ɛt] **1** *adj* **la sœur cadette,** (*de deux*) the younger sister; (*de plus de deux*) the youngest sister; **avoir trois frères cadets,** to have three younger brothers; **la branche cadette,** the younger branch. **2** *n* **(a)** (*de deux enfants*) the younger; (*de plus de deux enfants*) the youngest

child; (*de rang*) junior; **il est mon c. de deux ans,** he's two years younger than I am; *Fml* he's two years my junior; **c'est le c. de mes soucis,** that's the least of my worries; *Sp* **épreuve des cadets,** junior event; **(b)** *Golf* caddie; **(c)** *Hist* cadet.

Cadix [kadis] *nf* Cadiz.

cadmium [kadmjɔm] *nm Ch* cadmium.

cadogan [kadɔgɑ̃] *nm* = **CATOGAN.**

cadrage [kɑdraʒ] *nm Cin Phot etc* centring (*of image*).

cadran [kadrɑ̃] *nm* **(a)** (*of clock,barometer etc*) face, dial; (*of instrument, telephone etc*) dial; *Can* alarm-clock; **c. solaire,** sundial; **faire le tour du c.,** (*of hands of clock*) to go right round the clock; (*of person*) to sleep (right) round the clock; **(b)** *Nau* **c. de transmission d'ordres,** engine-room telegraph.

cadre [kɑdr] *nm* **(a)** frame (*of picture, door etc*); border (*of map etc*); setting (*of scene*); (*extent*) limits, bounds; (*structure*) framework; (*on form etc*) space, box; casing (*of ship's screw etc*); **une photo sous c.,** a framed photo; **c'est un c. splendide!,** it's a splendid setting!; **c. de vie,** environment; **vivre dans le c. familial,** to live in a family environment; **sortir du c. de ses fonctions,** to go beyond (the limits of) one's duties; **dans le c. de ce programme,** as part of this programme; **ne pas sortir du c. de la légalité,** to remain within the bounds of legality; **l'analyse régionale ne rentre pas dans le c. de cet article,** regional analysis is beyond the scope of this article; **ces produits n'entrent pas dans le c. de notre fabrication,** we do not manufacture these articles; **c. d'emballage,** packing case; **c. de déménagement,** container; *Rad* frame aerial, loop aerial;

(b) frame(work) (*of bicycle etc*); *Litt* outline, skeleton, plan (*of book etc*);

(c) *Ind Com* executive; **les cadres,** *Ind etc* managerial staff, management; *Mil etc* commissioned and non-commissioned officers; cadre, staff (*of skeleton unit etc*); books (*of company etc*); *Mil etc* **c. de réserve,** reserve list; **passer c.,** to become an executive, to be promoted to management; **une femme c.,** a female executive; **elle est c.,** she's an executive, she's in management; **c. supérieur,** senior executive; **c. moyen,** middle manager; **jeune c. dynamique,** dynamic young executive; **hors c.,** not on (the) strength; specially employed; **être mis hors c.,** to be seconded *or* detached; **rayé des cadres,** dismissed; *Mil* **le C. Noir,** = military riding school in Saumur.

cadrer [kadre] **1** *vi* to agree, to tally, to square, to fit in (**avec,** with); to conform (**avec,** to). **2** *vt* to centre (*a photograph*).

caduc, -uque [kadyk] *adj* **(a)** *Bot* deciduous (*leaf etc*); **(b)** *Jur* null and void (*legacy*); lapsed (*agreement*); statute-barred (*debt*).

caducée [kadyse] *nm* caduceus (*symbol of the pharmaceutical profession*).

caducité [kadusite] *nf* outmoded nature (*of a system etc*).

caecum [sekɔm] *nm Anat* caecum.

C.A.F. [seaɛf] **(a)** *Com* (*abrév* **coût, assurance, fret**) c.i.f.; **vente C.A.F.,** sale on c.i.f. basis; **(b)** *abrév* **Caisse d'allocations familiales.**

cafard, -arde [kafar, -ard] **1** *nm* (*insecte*) cockroach; *F* **avoir le c.,** to be fed up or down in the dumps; **avoir un coup de c.,** to be a bit down *or* fed up. **2** *n* **(a)** (*rapporteur*) sneak, creep; **(b)** *Arch* hypocrite. **3** *adj* **air c.,** hypocritical *or* sanctimonious air.

cafardage [kafardaʒ] *nm* sneaking, telling tales (out of school).

cafarder [kafarde] *vi* to tell tales (out of school), to sneak.

cafardeur, -euse [kafardœr, -øz] *n* = **CAFARD 2 (a).**

cafardeux, -euse [kafardø, -øz] *adj F* fed up, browned off, down in the dumps.

caf'conc' [kafkɔ̃s] *nm inv F abrév* **café concert.**

café [kafe] **1** *nm* **(a)** (*graine, boisson*) coffee; **c. vert/torréfié,** unroasted/roasted coffee; **grain de c.,** coffee bean; **c. en grains,** whole coffee, coffee beans; **c. moulu,** ground coffee; **c. en poudre** *ou* **instantané,** instant coffee; **c. noir,** *Suisse* **c. nature,** black coffee; **c. crème,** white coffee; **c. au lait,** white coffee (*esp for breakfast*); **c. turc,** Turkish coffee; **un c. (bien) serré,** a (very) strong coffee; **un c. léger,** a weak coffee; **deux cafés,** two coffees; **c. complet,** continental breakfast; **glace au c.,** coffee ice (cream); **c. liégeois,** = coffee ice-cream topped with whipped cream;

(b) café; (*bar*)bar, pub; **c. tabac,** = café with licence to sell tobacco; **garçon de c.,** waiter; (*derrière le bar*) barman;

(c) *Arch* coffee-house.

2 *adj inv* **c. (au lait),** coffee-coloured; *F* **leur fils est c. au lait,** their son is a half-caste.

café-concert [kafekɔ̃sɛr] *nm* cabaret (club).

caféier [kafeje] *nm* coffee tree.

caféine [kafein] *nf* caffeine; **sans c.,** decaffeinated, caffeine-free; **teneur en c.,** caffeine content.

cafetan [kaftɑ̃] *nm* kaftan, caftan.

cafétéria [kafeterja] *nf* cafeteria.

café-théâtre [kafeteɑtr] *nm* ≈ pub theatre.

cafetier, -ière [kaftje, -jɛr] **1** *n* café owner. **2** *nf* **cafetière (a)** (*récipient*) coffee pot; (*électrique*) coffee machine *or* maker; **cafetière automatique** *ou* **à pression,** percolator; **(b)** *F* (*tête*) bonce, nut.

cafouillage [kafujaʒ] *nm F* mess, muddle; missing, misfiring (*of car engine*).

cafouiller [kafuje] *vi F* to get into a mess *or* a muddle; (*of car engine*) to miss, to misfire; (*of TV set etc*) to be on the blink.

cafouilleur, -euse [kafujœr, -øz] *F* **1** *adj* muddle-headed (*person*). **2** *n* muddler.

cafouillis [kafuji] *nm F* shambles; **c'est un énorme c.,** it's a complete shambles; **le c. de ses explications,** his muddled explanations; **dans le c. de ses explications j'ai perdu ma concentration,** his explanations were so muddled I lost my concentration; **il y a beaucoup de c. dans la gestion de cette entreprise,** the management of this company is shambolic.

caftan [kaftɑ̃] *nm* kaftan, caftan.

cage [kaʒ] *nf* **(a)** cage; (hen) coop; (rabbit) hutch; cage (*of mine shaft*); shell, carcass (*of house*); *Fb* goal; **cage à oiseau/aux lions,** bird/lions' cage; **mettre un oiseau en c.,** to cage a bird; *F* **habiter une vraie c. à lapins,** to live in a poky little place *or* a rabbit hutch; *Fig* **être comme un animal en c.,** to be like a caged animal; **une c. dorée,** a gilded cage; **être dans les cages,** to be in goal; *Anat* **c. thoracique,** rib cage; **(b)** (*de montre etc*) (protective) cover; case, casing; **(c)** stair well; (lift) shaft; **(d)** *MecE* **c. à billes,** ball race; **(e)** *El* **c. de Faraday,** Faraday cage, electrostatic screen.

cageot [kaʒo] *nm* crate.

cagibi [kaʒibi] *nm F* **(a)** (*remise*) hut, shed; **(b)** (*débarras etc*) boxroom, lumber room; *Péj* poky little room.

cagne [kaɲ] *nf Scol F* = second-year arts class preparing to compete for entrance to the École normale supérieure.

cagneux, -euse [kaɲø, -øz] **1** *adj* knock-kneed (*person*); crooked (*legs*); knock (*knees*). **2** *n* **(a)** *Scol F* = student in the cagne; **(b)** knock-kneed person.

cagnotte [kaɲɔt] *nf* (*caisse commune*) kitty; (*de jeux*) pool, kitty, *surtout Am* pot; *F* (*économies*) nest egg.

cagot, -ote [kago, -ɔt] *Péj* **1** *n* (canting) hypocrite. **2** *adj* hypocritical, sanctimonious.

cagoule [kagul] *nf* **(a)** (monk's) cowl; **(b)** hood (*of penitent, robber*); **(c)** balaclava (helmet).

cahier [kaje] *nm* **(a)** notebook; *Scol* exercise book; **c. de brouillon,** rough (note)book; **c. de textes,** homework book; *Ind Com* **c. des charges,** specifications (*of a contract*); *Hist & Fig* (*des syndicats*) **c. de doléances,** list of grievances; **(b)** *Typ* signature; **(c)** (*revue*) periodical, review, journal.

cahin-caha [kaɛ̃kaa] *adv F* **aller c.-c.,** (*de la santé*) to be so-so; (*d'une personne*) to struggle *or* limp along; **les affaires vont c.-c.,** business is slow *or* slack; **la vie continue c.-c.,** life goes on (as it must).

cahot [kao] *nm* jolt, bump (*of vehicle*).

cahotage [kaɔtaʒ] *nm* = **CAHOTEMENT.**

cahotant [kaɔtɑ̃] *adj* **(a)** jolting, jolty (*car*); **(b)** rough, bumpy (*road*).

cahotement [kaɔtmɑ̃] *nm* (*mouvement*) jolting, shaking, bumping; (*heurt*) jolt, bump.

cahoter [kaɔte] *vt* to jolt, to shake; **vie cahotée,** life full of ups and downs; **des enfants cahotés par le divorce,** children shaken up by divorce.

cahoteux, -euse [kaɔtø, -øz] *adj* rough, bumpy (*road*).

cahute [kayt] *nf* hut, shanty, shack.

caïd [kaid] *nm* **(a)** (*in North Africa*) kaid; **(b)** *Arg* gang leader; **c'est le gros c. en maths,** he's our maths expert; *F* **jouer les caïds** *ou* **au c. dans la cour de récréation,** to be a playground bully; **il fait son c.,** he's acting all high and mighty.

caillage [kajaʒ] *nm* = **CAILLEMENT.**

caillasse [kajas] *nf* **(a)** *Géol* (gravelly) marl; **(b)** *F* (*cailloux etc*) road metal, loose stones, chippings; **marcher dans la c.,** to walk on scree *or* loose stones.

caille [kaj] *nf* quail; **gras comme une c.,** (as) plump as a partridge; **elle est chaude comme une c.,** she's as snug as a bug in a rug; *F* **ma c.,** my little dove.

caillé [kaje] *nm* curdled milk, curds.

caillebotis [kajbɔti] *nm* **(a)** *Nau etc* grating; **(b)** (*treillis, plancher*) duckboard(s).

caillebotte [kajbɔt] *nf* curds.

caillebotter [kajbɔte] *vt* to curdle, to clot (*milk*).

caillement [kajmɑ̃] *nm* clotting, curdling (*of milk*); clotting, coagulating, coagulation (*of blood*).

cailler [kaje] **1** *vt* to curdle (*milk*), to make (*milk*) turn; to coagulate, to congeal (*blood*). **2** *vi* **(a)** (*du lait*) to curdle; (*du sang*) to coagulate, to congeal; **faire c. du lait,** to curdle milk; **(b)** *Arg* **ça caille,** it's bloody freezing, it's real brass-monkey weather. **3 se cailler** *vpr Arg* **on se (les) caille,** it's bloody freezing.

caillette [kajɛt] *nf* fourth stomach, rennet stomach, abomasum (*of ruminants*).

caillot [kajo] *nm* clot (*of blood etc*).

caillou, -oux [kaju] *nm* **(a)** pebble, stone; **cailloux d'empierrement,** (loose) chippings, road metal; **avoir un c. dans sa chaussure,** to have a stone in one's shoe; *Fig* **avoir le cœur dur comme un c.,** to have a heart of stone; **(b)** (*grosse pierre*) boulder, rock; **(c)** (*bijou*) stone, rock; **(d)** *Arg* (*tête*) nut, bonce; **il n'a plus un poil sur le c.,** he's as bald as a coot.

cailloutage [kajutaʒ] *nm* road metal(ling); *surtout Rail* ballast(ing) (*of track*).

caillouter [kajute] *vt* to metal (*road*); *surtout Rail* to ballast (*track*).

caillouteux, -euse [kajutø, -øz] *adj* stony (*road etc*); pebbly, shingly (*beach*).

cailloutis [kajuti] *nm* broken stones, chippings, gravel; road metal.

caïman [kaimɑ̃] *nm* (*reptile*) cayman, caiman.

Caïn [kaɛ̃] *nm* Cain.

Caire (le) [(lə)kɛr] *nm* Cairo.

cairn [kɛrn] *nm* cairn.

cairote [kɛrɔt] **1** *adj* of *or* from Cairo. **2** *n* **C.,** Cairene, person from Cairo.

caisse [kɛs] *nf* **(a)** (packing) case; box, chest (*for tools etc*); chest (*for tea etc*); tub (*for plants*); tank, cistern (*for oil, water*); *Arg* (*poitrine*) chest; **c. à savon,** soapbox; **c. à claire-voie,** crate; **c. de melons,** crate of melons; **mettre des marchandises en c.,** to case goods; *Nau* **c. à eau douce,** freshwater tank; *Aut* **c. de l'embrayage,** clutch casing; *Arg* **il s'en va de la c.,** he's got a very bad chest;

(b) case (*of piano, clock*); body(work) (*of vehicle*); shell (*of pulley*);

(c) *Com Fin* (*coffre*) cash box; (*d'une caisse enregistreuse*) till; (*guichet*) pay desk, cash desk; (*dans un supermarché etc*) check-out; (*dans une banque etc*) cashier's office; **c. (enregistreuse),** cash register; **c. comptable,** cash register; **les caisses de l'État,** the coffers of the State; **payez à la c.,** pay at the (cash) desk *or* at the till; **tenir la c.,** to be in charge of the cash; (*dans un restaurant, un magasin etc*) to be the cashier; **passer à la c.,** to go to the cash desk; (*payer*) to pay; (*se faire payer*) to be paid; (*se faire licencier*) to be paid off;

(d) (*argent*) cash (in hand); (*recette*) takings; **livre de c.,** cashbook; **faire la** *ou* **sa c.,** to balance (up) one's cash; *F* to do the till, to cash up; **avoir tant d'argent en c.,** to have so much money in hand; **elle est partie avec la c.,** she made off with the cash;

(e) fund; **c. de défense,** fighting fund (*of an association etc*); *Pol* **c. noire,** bribery fund, slush fund, *Am* boodle, graft; **c. d'épargne,** savings bank; **c. d'allocations familiales/de retraite,** ≈ child benefit office/pension fund; *Can* **c. populaire,** credit union;

(f) *Mus* drum; **c. claire,** (high-pitched) side drum, snare drum; **grosse c.,** bass drum; *Fig* **battre la c.,** to run a big publicity campaign; *Anat* **c. du tympan,** middle ear;

(g) *Arg* (*voiture*) car, motor.

caissette [kɛsɛt] *nf* small case *or* box.

caissier, -ière [kɛsje, -jɛr] *n* (*dans un restaurant, un magasin etc*) cashier; *Banque* cashier, teller.

caisson [kɛsɔ̃] *nm* **(a)** box, case, chest; *Mil* wagon, caisson (*for ammunition etc*); *Arg* **se faire sauter le c.,** to blow one's brains out; **(b)** *Nau* locker, bin; **(c)** *Archit* **plafond à caissons,** panelled *or* coffered ceiling; **(d)** caisson (*for underwater work*); *Méd* **mal(adie) des caissons,** caisson disease, decompression sickness, *F* the bends; **c. à air comprimé,** decompression chamber.

cajoler [kaʒɔle] *vt* **(a)** to pet, to make a fuss of (*child etc*); **(b)** *Vieilli* to cajole, to coax, to wheedle.

cajolerie [kaʒɔlri] *nf* cajoling, coaxing, wheedling.

cajoleur, -euse [kaʒɔlœr, -øz] **1** *adj* cajoling, wheedling, coaxing. **2** *n* cajoler, wheedler, coaxer.

cajou [kaʒu] *nm* cashew (nut).

cake [kɛk] *nm* fruit cake; **mascara en c.,** block mascara.

cal, *pl* **cals** [kal] *nm Bot Méd* callus, callosity.

calabrais, -aise [kalabrɛ, -ɛz] **1** *adj* Calabrian. **2** *nm Ling* Calabrian dialect. **3** *n* **C.,** Calabrian.

Calabre [kalabr] *nf* Calabria.

calage [kalaʒ] *nm* **(a)** wedging, steadying (*of chair leg etc*); chocking (up) (*of wheel etc*); **(b)** (*fait d'appuyer etc*) propping (up); **(c)** wedging, keying (*of crank to shaft etc*); fixing (*of wheel on axle etc*); jamming, locking (*of valve etc*); **(d)** stalling (*of engine*); **(e)** (*réglage*) adjustment, setting; timing, tuning (*of valve, engine*).

calamar [kalamar] *nm* = **CALMAR**.

calamine [kalamin] *nf* **(a)** *Minér* calamine; **(b)** (*dépôt*) carbon (deposit).

calamistré [kalamistre] *adj* **cheveux calamistrés,** brilliantined hair.

calamité [kalamite] *nf* (*désastre*) calamity, disaster; (*malheur*) (great) misfortune; **quelle c.!,** what a disaster!; *F* **c'est une c. dans la cuisine,** he's a disaster in the kitchen.

calamiteux,-euse [kalamitø, -øz] *adj* disastrous, calamitous.

calandrage [kalɑ̃draʒ] *nm* (*paper-making*) & *Tex* calendering, hot-pressing, surfacing.

calandre [kalɑ̃dr] *nf* **(a)** (*paper-making*) & *Tex* calender, roller; **(b)** *Aut* radiator grille.

calandrer [kalɑ̃dre] *vt Tex etc* to calender, to roll, to press.

calandreur,-euse [kalɑ̃drœr, -øz] *n* (*pour les papiers*) & *Tex etc* calenderer.

calanque [kalɑ̃k] *nf* (*in the Mediterranean*) deep, narrow creek.

calcaire [kalkɛr] **1** *adj* chalky (*soil etc*); calcareous (*rock etc*); **terrain c.,** limestone region; *Ch* **sel c.,** calcium salt; **eau c.,** hard water. **2** *nm Minér* limestone; *F* fur (*in kettle*).

calcanéum [kalkaneɔm] *nm Anat* heel bone; *Spéc* calcaneum.

calcédoine [kalsedwan] *nf Minér* chalcedony.

calcification [kalsifikɑsjɔ̃] *nf Méd* calcification.

calcination [kalsinɑsjɔ̃] *nf* calcination.

calciner [kalsine] **1** *vt* (*brûler*) to char; *Ch Ind* to calcine; **rôti calciné,** joint burnt to a cinder; **désert calciné par le soleil,** sun-baked desert. **2 se calciner** *vpr* to burn *or* be burnt to a cinder.

calcium [kalsjɔm] *nm Ch* calcium.

calcul[1] [kalkyl] *nm* (*compte*) calculation, reckoning, computation; (*prévision*) calculation; **faire un c.,** to make a calculation, to do a sum; **faire ses calculs,** to do one's sums; **faire son c.,** to lay one's plans; **faux c., erreur de c.,** miscalculation, mistake in adding up; **problème de c.,** arithmetic problem; *Ordinat* **ordinateur de c. très rapide,** number cruncher; *Ordinat* **calculs très rapides,** number crunching; **agir par c.,** to act from selfish *or* ulterior motives; **selon nos calculs,** according to our calculations; **tout c. fait,** taking everything into account; *Scol* **le c.,** arithmetic, sums; **faible en c.,** bad at sums *or* arithmetic; **enseigner le c.,** to teach arithmetic; **apprendre le c.,** to learn (how) to count; **le c. mental,** mental arithmetic; *Math* **c. différentiel/intégral,** differential/integral calculus; **c. des probabilités,** theory of probability; **règle à calcul,** slide rule.

calcul[2] *nm Méd* calculus, stone (*in the bladder*); **avoir des calculs,** to have stones in the bladder; (*aux reins*) to have kidney stones; **c. rénal,** kidney stone.

calculable [kalkylabl] *adj* calculable, computable.

calculateur, -trice [kalkylatœr, -tris] **1** *n* (*personne*) **c'est un bon c.,** he's good at figures. **2** *nm* **(a)** *Ordinat* **c. (électronique),** (electronic) computer; **(b)** (*de poche*) (pocket) calculator. **3** *nf* **calculatrice,** adding machine, (large desk) calculator. **4** *adj* calculating, shrewd (*person, policy*).

calculé [kalkyle] *adj* calculated (*insult, risk*); premeditated (*malice*); deliberate (*insolence*); **une bonté calculée,** kindness motivated by self-interest.

calculer [kalkyle] **1** *vt* (*compter*) to calculate, to compute; to plan, to calculate (*behaviour etc*); to weigh (up) (*consequences*); **c. la surface du triangle/le prix de revient,** to calculate *or* work out the area of the triangle/the cost price; **c. qch de tête,** to work sth out in one's head; **c. un prix,** to work out a price; **tout bien calculé,** taking everything into account; **c. ses chances de réussite,** to calculate *or* to weigh up one's chances of success; **c. ses dépenses au plus juste,** to work out one's expenses to the nearest penny. **2** *vi* to calculate; *Péj* to count every penny; **c. vite et bien,** to be quick and accurate at figures; **machine à c.,** adding machine, desk calculator. **3 se**

calculer *vpr* **ça se calcule facilement à partir de la racine carrée,** it's easy to calculate *or* work out from the square root.

calculette [kalkylɛt] *nf* (pocket) calculator.

caldoche [kaldɔʃ] **1** *adj* = pertaining to the European community of New Caledonia. **2** *n* **C.**, = New Caledonian of European descent.

cale¹ [kal] *nf Nau* **(a)** hold (*of ship*); **eau de c.,** bilge water; **fond de c.,** bilge; **à fond de c.,** down in the hold; *F* **être à fond de c.,** to be on one's uppers, to be down and out; **c. à charbon,** bunker; **c. à eau,** water tank; **(b) c. de construction/de lancement,** (ship-building) stocks/ slip(way); **mettre un navire sur c.,** to lay down a ship; **(c)** (*bassin*) **c. sèche,** dry dock; **c. de radoub,** graving dock.

cale² *nf* **(a)** wedge, chock, block (*to steady furniture, stop wheel etc*); **mettre une voiture sur cales,** to put a car on blocks; *Av etc* **enlevez les cales!,** chocks away!; **(b)** (*support*) prop, strut; *MecE* key (*of shaft etc*).

calé [kale] *adj* **(a)** *F* difficult, complicated (*problem etc*); **être c. en qch,** to be well up in sth, to know all about sth; **elle est très calée en informatique,** she knows all there is to know about computers, she's a computer wizard; **ça c'est c.!,** that's cunning! that's clever!; **(b)** *Tech* **piston c.,** jammed piston; piston at one of the dead points; *Av* **hélice calée,** dead airscrew.

calebasse [kalbɑs] *nf* calabash, gourd; (*taillée dans le fruit*) water bottle.

calèche [kalɛʃ] *nf* (*voiture*) barouche.

caleçon [kalsɔ̃] *nm* boxer shorts; *Vieilli* **c. long,** long underpants, *F* long johns; *Vieilli* **c. de bain,** (swimming *or* bathing) trunks.

calédonien, -ienne [kaledɔnjɛ̃, -jɛn] **1** *adj* Caledonian. **2** *n* **C.**, Caledonian.

calembour [kalɑ̃bur] *nm* pun, play on words; **faire** *ou* **dire des calembours,** to make puns, to pun.

calendes [kalɑ̃d] *nfpl Antiq* calends, kalends; **renvoyer qn/qch aux c. grecques,** to put s.o./sth off indefinitely *or* to the Greek calends.

calendrier [kalɑ̃drije] *nm* **(a)** calendar; **bloc c.,** block calendar; **c. à effeuiller,** tear-off calendar; **c. perpétuel,** perpetual calendar; **(b)** timetable, programme, *esp Am* schedule (*of journey, work etc*).

cale-pied [kalpje] *nm inv* toe clip.

calepin [kalpɛ̃] *nm* notebook.

caler¹ [kale] **1** *vt* **(a)** to wedge, to steady (*chair leg etc*); to chock (up) (*wheel etc*); **c. une bouteille dans un casier,** to store a bottle in a rack; **c. un chargement,** to secure a load (firmly); **c. un malade sur des coussins,** to prop up a patient on cushions; **(b)** to wedge, to key (*crank to shaft etc*); to fix (*wheel on axle etc*); to jam, to lock (*valve etc*); **(c)** *Aut* to stall (*engine*); to adjust, to time, to tune (*valve, engine etc*). **2** *vi* (*of engine*) to stall. **3 se caler** *vpr* **(a)** to settle (oneself) comfortably (*in an armchair etc*); **(b)** *F* **se c. les joues, se les c.,** to stuff oneself, to have a good feed.

caler² *vi Nau* **navire qui cale vingt pieds,** ship that draws *or* whose draught is twenty feet (of water); **navire qui cale trop,** ship that is too deep in the water.

caler³ **1** *vt Nau* to house (*mast*); to strike (*sail*). **2** *vi* **(a)** *F* to give in, to give up; **(b)** *Can* to have a receding hairline.

caleter (se) [sәkalte] *vpr Arg* = **(SE) CALTER.**

calfat [kalfa] *nm Nau* ca(u)lker.

calfatage [kalfataʒ] *nm Nau* ca(u)lking.

calfater [kalfate] *vt Nau* to ca(u)lk.

calfeutrage [kalføtraʒ] *nm*, **calfeutrement** [kalføtrәmɑ̃] *nm* blocking up, stopping up, filling in (*of gaps*); draught-proofing (*of room etc*).

calfeutrer [kalføtre] **1** *vt* to block up, to stop (up), to fill (in) (*gaps*); **c. une pièce,** to make a room draught-proof. **2 se calfeutrer** *vpr* (*pour avoir chaud*) to make oneself snug; (*pour être seul*) to shut *or* lock oneself up (*in one's room etc*).

calibrage [kalibraʒ] *nm* **(a)** gauging, measuring (*of part*); calibration (*of thermometer etc*); *Com* grading (*of eggs etc*); **(b)** *Phot* trimming (*of print*); **(c)** *Typ* casting off (*of copy*).

calibre [kalibr] *nm* **(a)** calibre, bore (*of fire-arm, pipe etc*); size, diameter, calibre (*of bullet etc*); grade (*of eggs etc*); **fusil de c. 8 mm,** *Mil* 8-mm calibre rifle; *Sp* 8-mm gauge gun; **canon de gros c.,** heavy gun, large-bore gun; *Fig* **sa sœur est d'un autre c.,** his sister is of quite a different calibre, *F* his sister is in a different league; **il n'est pas de ce c.-là,** he's not a man of that calibre; **(b)** (*tool*) gauge, *US* gage; **c. d'épaisseur (à lames),** feeler gauge, set of feelers; **c. de profondeur,** depth gauge; **(c)** (*for reproduction*) template, pattern, mould, *US* mold; **(d)** (*for machine tool*) jig, former; **(e)** *Arg* (*gun*) shooter, *Am* rod, piece.

calibrer [kalibre] *vt* **(a)** to gauge, to measure; to calibrate (*thermometer etc*); *Com* to grade (*eggs etc*); **(b)** *Phot* to trim (*print*); **(c)** *Typ* to cast off (*copy*).

calibreur, -euse [kalibrœr, -øz] *n* calibrator.

calice¹ [kalis] **1** *nm Rel* chalice; *Fig* **boire le c. jusqu'à la lie,** to drain the cup to the dregs. **2** *int Can* hell!

calice² *nm* **(a)** *Bot* calyx; **(b)** *Anat* calix.

calicot [kaliko] *nm* **(a)** *Tex* calico, *Am* unbleached muslin; **(b)** streamer, banner (*bearing advertisement etc*); **(c)** *Vieilli* draper's assistant.

califat [kalifa] *nm* caliphate.

calife [kalif] *nm* caliph.

Californie [kalifɔrni] *nf* California.

californien,-ienne [kalifɔrnjɛ̃, -jɛn] **1** *adj* Californian. **2** *n* **C.**, Californian.

californium [kalifɔrnjɔm] *nm Ch* californium.

califourchon [kalifurʃɔ̃] **1** *adv* **à c.,** astride; **se mettre à c. sur qch,** to sit astride sth, to straddle sth; **monter à c. sur un cheval,** to ride a horse astride. **2** *nm Can* bottom, backside, behind.

câlin, -ine [kɑlɛ̃, -in] **1** *adj* coaxing, winning (*child, ways etc*); fond, affectionate (*look, tone etc*). **2** *n* wheedler, coaxer. **3** *nm* cuddle; **faire un c. à qn,** to give s.o. a cuddle.

câliner [kɑline] *vt* (*choyer*) to make a fuss of (*child etc*); (*caresser*) to caress, to fondle, to cuddle.

câlinerie [kɑlinri] *nf* **(a)** (*tendresse*) fondness, tenderness; **(b)** (*caresses etc*) caress, fondle; (*dans les bras*) cuddle; **faire des câlineries à qn,** to cuddle s.o..

calleux, -euse [kalø, -øz] *adj* callous, horny (*hand etc*).

call-girl [kɔlgœrl] *nf* call girl.

calligraphe [kaligraf] *n* calligrapher, calligraphist.

calligraphie [kaligrafi] *nf* calligraphy.

calligraphier [kaligrafje] *vt* (*pr sub & impf* **n. calligraphiions, v. calligraphiiez**) to write (*letter etc*) beautifully (and ornamentally); **nom calligraphié,** beautifully (hand)written name.

calligraphique [kaligrafik] *adj* calligraphic.

callosité [kalozite] *nf* callus, callosity.

calmant [kalmɑ̃] **1** *adj* calming, soothing (*words etc*); *Méd* (*pour les nerfs*) tranquillizing, sedative; (*pour la douleur*) painkilling. **2** *nm Méd* (*pour les nerfs*) tranquillizer, sedative; (*pour la douleur*) painkiller.

calmar [kalmar] *nm* squid.

calme [kalm] **1** *nm* calm, calmness; (*in difficult situation*) coolness, composure (*of person*); stillness (*of air, night etc*); peace (*of mind etc*); peace and quiet, quiet(ness), peacefulness (*of countryside*); **je cherche un peu de c.,** I'm looking for some peace and quiet; **je n'ai pas eu un moment de c. de toute la journée!,** I haven't had a minute's peace all day!; **connaître un moment de c. dans la douleur,** to have a moment of respite from one's suffering; **dans le c. de la nuit,** in the still of the night; **moment de c.,** lull; **du c.!,** keep cool *or* calm!; **perdre son c.,** to lose one's composure; **retrouver son c.,** to calm down; **garder son c.,** to keep one's composure, to keep calm *or* cool, *F* to keep one's cool; *Nau* **c. plat,** dead calm; **calmes équatoriaux,** doldrums.

2 *adj* calm, still, quiet (*air, night etc*); calm, unruffled, cool, composed (*person, manner*); calm, smooth, serene (*sea*); *Com* **marché c.,** flat *or* quiet *or* dull market; **nos affaires sont calmes en août,** business is quiet in August; **la Bourse a été c.,** the Stock Market has had a quiet day.

calmement [kalmәmɑ̃] *adv* calmly, quietly, coolly; **parler c.,** to speak calmly; **il faut considérer le problème c.,** the problem must be considered calmly *or* with calm.

calmer [kalme] **1** *vt* to calm (down), to quieten (down), *Am* to quiet down (*s.o.*); to calm, to allay, to still (*fears etc*); to calm, to soothe, to ease (*pain, conscience etc*); to quench (*thirst*); to appease (*hunger etc*); to damp, to cool (*ardour etc*); to calm, to pacify (*child, mob etc*); to abate (*fever etc*); **qu'il me parle comme ça! je vais le c.!,** how dare he speak to me like that! I'll soon shut him up *or* quieten him down!

2 se calmer *vpr* to become calm, to calm down, to cool down, to quieten down, *Am* to quiet down; (*of storm etc*) to abate, to die down, to blow over; (*of wind etc*) to drop, to subside; **elle ne pleure plus, elle se calme,** she's not crying any more, she's starting to calm down; **la douleur se calme,** the pain is easing *or* subsiding; **il faut vous c., les voisins vont se plaindre,** be quiet *or* calm down, the neighbours will complain; **calme-toi, ce n'est rien,** calm down, it's nothing to worry about.

calomel [kalɔmɛl] *nm Pharm* calomel.

calomniateur, -trice [kalɔmnjatœr, -tris] **1** *n* (*qui parle*) slanderer; (*qui écrit*) libeller; *Fml* calumniator. **2** *adj* (*paroles*) slanderous; (*écrits*) libellous.
calomnie [kalɔmni] *nf* calumny; (*parlée*) slander; (*écrite, publiée*) libel; **répandre des calomnies sur qn,** to cast aspersions on s.o.; **elle a été en butte à la c.,** she has been a victim of slander *or* libel, she has been slandered *or* libelled.
calomnier [kalɔmnje] *vt* to slander, to malign; (*dans la presse etc*) to libel; *Fml* to calumniate.
calomnieusement [kalɔmnjøzmɑ̃] *adv* slanderously; libellously.
calomnieux, -ieuse [kalɔmnjø, -jøz] *adj* (*paroles*) slanderous; (*écrits*) libellous.
caloporteur [kalɔpɔrtœr] **1** *adj* **fluide** *ou* **liquide c.,** coolant. **2** *nm* coolant.
calorie [kalɔri] *nf* calorie; **grande c.,** (large *or* great) calorie; **régime basses calories,** low-calorie diet; **l'avocat est riche en calories,** avocado is high in calories; **ration de calories,** calorie intake; **attention aux calories!,** watch the calories!
calorifère [kalɔrifɛr] **1** *adj* heat-conveying. **2** *nm* slow combustion stove; *Can* radiator.
calorifique [kalɔrifik] *adj Phys* calorific, thermal; **capacité c.,** heat capacity.
calorifuge [kalɔrifyʒ] **1** *adj* non-conducting; (heat-) insulating; heat-proof (*varnish etc*); **le bois est c.,** wood is a poor conductor of heat. **2** *nm* heat insulator *or* insulation; (*pour chaudière, tuyau*) lagging.
calorifugeage [kalɔrifyʒaʒ] *nm* heat insulation; (*de chaudière etc*) lagging.
calorifuger [kalɔrifyʒe] *vt* (**je calorifugeai(s); n. calorifugeons**) to insulate, to lag (*pipe etc*).
calorimètre [kalɔrimɛtr] *nm Phys* calorimeter.
calorimétrie [kalɔrimetri] *nf Phys* calorimetry.
calorimétrique [kalɔrimetrik] *adj Phys* calorimetric(al) (*unit etc*).
calorisation [kalɔrizasjɔ̃] *nf Tech* calorizing, calorization, aluminium plating.
calot¹ [kalo] *nm* **(a)** (*grosse bille*) (large) marble; **(b)** *Arg* (*œil*) peeper.
calot² *nm Mil* forage cap, *US* garrison cap.
calotin [kalɔtɛ̃] *nm F Péj* **(a)** (*prêtre*) priest; **(b)** (*bigot*) pious churchgoer.
calotte [kalɔt] *nf* **(a)** (*chapeau rond*) skullcap; *Rel* calotte; (*de chapeau*) crown (*of hat*); *Arg Péj* **la c.,** the priests, the clergy, the cloth; *Pol* the clerical party; **(b)** *Archit* calotte; *Math* **c. sphérique,** portion of a sphere; *Géol* **c. glaciaire,** ice cap, ice sheet; *Anat* **c. crânienne** *ou* **du crâne,** top part of the skull, skullcap; *Litt* **la c. des cieux,** the vault *or* canopy of heaven; **(c)** *F* (*gifle*) cuff, clout; **flanquer une c. à qn,** to give s.o. a clout, to box s.o.'s ears.
calotter [kalɔte] *vt F* to cuff, to clout (*s.o.*), to box (*s.o.'s*) ears.
calquage [kalkaʒ] *nm* tracing.
calque [kalk] *nm* **(a)** (*copie*) tracing, traced design; (*de poème, de portrait etc*) exact copy; **prendre un c. de qch,** to make a tracing of sth, to trace sth; *Fig* **elle est le c. de sa mère,** she's the dead spit *or* the spitting image of her mother; **(papier-)c.,** tracing paper; **(b)** *Ling* loan translation, calque.
calquer [kalke] *vt* (*reproduire*) to trace, to make a tracing of (*sth*); *Fig* to copy closely *or* exactly, to imitate; **dessin calqué,** tracing; **expression calquée sur l'anglais,** expression copied from *or* modelled on the English; **c. sa conduite sur celle de qn que l'on admire,** to model one's behaviour on that of s.o. one admires.
calquoir [kalkwar] *nm* tracing point, tracer.
calter (se) [səkalte] *vpr Arg* (*s'enfuir*) to make off, to hop it.
calumet [kalymɛ] *nm* calumet; (Red Indian's) pipe; *Fig* **fumer le c. de la paix avec qn,** to smoke the pipe of peace with s.o..
calva [kalva] *nm F abrév* **calvados.**
calvados [kalvados] *nm* apple brandy, calvados.
calvaire [kalvɛr] *nm* (*épreuve pénible*) agony; *Rel* calvary; (*croix*) calvary, wayside cross; *Rel* **Le C.,** (Mount) Calvary; **c'est un c. de devoir la supporter,** it's agonizing having to put up with her; **sa vie fut un long c.,** his life was one long ordeal.
calvinisme [kalvinism] *nm* Calvinism.
calviniste [kalvinist] **1** *adj* Calvinistic, Calvinist. **2** *n* Calvinist.
calvitie [kalvisi] *nf* baldness; **c. naissante,** incipient baldness.
calypso [kalipso] *nm* (*danse*) & *Mus* calypso.
camaïeu, -eux [kamajø] *nm* camaieu, monochrome (painting); (*gravure*) tint drawing.
camail [kamaj] *nm* **(a)** *Cathol* cape (*worn over the surplice*); **(b)** *Orn* neck feathers, hackles (*of fowl*).
camarade [kamarad] *n* friend, *F* mate; (*as term of address*) comrade, brother; **le c. Gorbatchev,** comrade Gorbachov; **c. d'école** *ou* **de collège,** school friend; **c. de classe** *ou* **de promotion,** classmate; **faire c.,** to put one's hands up, to surrender.
camaraderie [kamaradri] *nf* camaraderie, comradeship.
camard, -e [kamar, -ard] **1** *adj* (*nez*) flat; (*personne*) with a flat nose. **2** *nf F* **la camarde,** the (Grim) Reaper.
camarguais, -aise [kamargɛ, -ɛz] **1** *adj* of the Camargue. **2** *n* **C.,** native *or* inhabitant of the Camargue, person from the Camargue.
cambiste [kɑ̃bist] **1** *nm Fin* exchange broker, money changer. **2** *adj* **marché c.,** exchange market.
Cambodge [kɑ̃bɔdʒ] *nm Hist* Cambodia.
cambodgien, -ienne [kɑ̃bɔdʒjɛ̃, -jɛn] **1** *adj* Cambodian. **2** *n* **C.,** Cambodian.
cambouis [kɑ̃bwi] *nm* dirty oil, grease.
cambrage [kɑ̃braʒ] *nm* bending; arching (*of foot, back etc*); cambering, curving (*of wood etc*).
cambré [kɑ̃bre] *adj* bent; cambered, arched (*beam etc*); **pied très c.,** foot with a high instep; **taille cambrée,** arched *or* curved back; **jambes cambrées,** bow legs.
cambrement [kɑ̃brəmɑ̃] *nm* = **CAMBRAGE**.
cambrer [kɑ̃bre] **1** *vt* to bend; to arch (*one's foot etc*); to camber, to curve (*wood etc*); **c. la taille** *ou* **les reins,** to throw out one's chest; (*après s'être courbé*) to straighten one's back. **2 se cambrer** *vpr* to throw out one's chest; (*après s'être courbé*) to straighten one's back.
cambrien, -ienne [kɑ̃mbrijɛ̃, -jɛn] *adj & nm Géol* Cambrian.
cambriolage [kɑ̃brijɔlaʒ] *nm* housebreaking, burglary.
cambriole [kɑ̃brijɔl] *nf F* (*métier*) burglary, housebreaking; (*événement*) burglary, break-in.
cambrioler [kɑ̃brijɔle] *vt* to break into (*house*); to burgle, *Am* to burglarize (*a house*); **nous avons été cambriolés pendant les vacances,** we were burgled while we were on holiday, we had a burglary *or* break-in while we were on holiday.
cambrioleur, -euse [kɑ̃brijɔlœr, -øz] *n* housebreaker, burglar.
cambrique [kɑ̃brik] *nm Ling* Welsh; *Spéc* Cymric.
cambrous(s)e [kɑ̃bruz, -us] *nf F* country; **maison à la c.** *ou* **en pleine c.,** house in the middle of nowhere *or* (out) in the sticks *or* at the back of beyond.
cambrure [kɑ̃bryr] *nf* camber, curve (*of wood etc*); arch (*of foot, back*); **chaussures à forte c.,** shoes with a high instep; **c. des reins,** small of the back.
cambuse [kɑ̃byz] *nf* **(a)** *Nau* steward's room, storeroom; **(b)** canteen (*in shipyard*); **(c)** *Arg* hovel, dump.
cambusier [kɑ̃byzje] *nm* **(a)** (*à la cantine*) canteen keeper; **(b)** (*de stocks*) storekeeper.
came¹ [kam] *nf MecE* cam, lifter, wiper; **arbre à cames,** camshaft; **moteur avec arbre à cames en tête,** overhead camshaft engine.
came² *nf Arg* (*drogue*) dope, junk.
camé, -ée [kame] *n Arg* druggie, junkie.
camée [kame] *nm* cameo.
caméléon [kameleɔ̃] *nm* (*reptile*) & *Fig* chameleon.
camél(l)ia [kamelja] *nm* camellia.
camelot [kamlo] *nm* **(a)** *F* (*marchand dans la rue*) cheapjack, street hawker; **(b)** *Arch* (*vendeur de journaux*) newsvendor; *Hist* **les camelots du roi,** royalist group.
camelote [kamlɔt] *nf* **(a)** *F* (*pacotille*) cheap goods, trash, junk, rubbish; **maison de c.,** jerry-built house; **n'achète pas cette voiture, c'est de la c.!,** don't buy that car, it's an old junk heap!; **(b)** *Arg* (*toute marchandise*) stuff.
camembert [kamɑ̃bɛr] *nm* **(a)** camembert (cheese); **(b)** (*diagramme*) pie-chart.
camer (se) [səkame] *vpr Arg* to do drugs, to be on drugs.
caméra [kamera] *nf* film *or* cine camera, *Am* movie camera; *TV* camera.
cameraman [kameraman] *nm Cin* cameraman; (*pl cameramen*).
camérier [kamerje] *nm* chamberlain (*to Pope, cardinal*).
caméristé [kamerist] *nf Arch* maid of honour, lady-in-waiting.
Cameroun (le) [ləkamrun] *nm* **(a)** the Cameroon (Republic); **(b)** *Hist* the Cameroons.
camerounais, -aise [kamrunɛ, -ɛz] **1** *adj* Cameroonian. **2** *n* **C.,** Cameroonian.

caméscope [kameskɔp] *nm* camcorder.

camion [kamjɔ̃] *nm* **(a)** *Aut* lorry, *surtout Am* truck; **c. de déménagement,** removal van; **chauffeur de c.,** lorry *or Am* truck driver; **(b)** *(chariot)* dray, wag(g)on; **(c)** *(récipient)* (painter's) kettle.

camion-benne [kamjɔ̃bɛn] *nm* dump truck, dumper-truck; *(pl camions-bennes)*.

camion-citerne [kamjɔ̃sitɛrn] *nm* tanker (lorry), *Am* tank truck, tank trailer; *(pl camions-citernes)*.

camionnage [kamjɔnaʒ] *nm* haulage, cartage, *Am* truckage, trucking; **régler le c.,** to pay the haulage *or* transport costs.

camionner [kamjɔne] *vt* to transport *(goods)* by lorry, *Am* to truck *(goods)*.

camionnette [kamjɔnɛt] *nf* van, *Am* delivery truck.

camionneur [kamjɔnœr] *nm* **(a)** *(conducteur)* lorry driver, *Am* truck driver, trucker, teamster; *(de camionnette)* van driver; **(b)** *(transporteur)* haulier, haulage contractor, *Am* trucker.

camisole [kamizɔl] *nf* **(a) c. de force,** strait-jacket; **on lui a mis une c. de force,** he's in a strait-jacket; **(b)** *Can* vest, *Am* undershirt; **(c)** *Arch (chemise de nuit)* nightshirt; **(d)** camisole, sleeved vest, spencer.

camomille [kamɔmij] *nf* camomile; **tisane de c.,** camomile tea; **prendre une c.,** to have a cup of camomile tea.

camouflage [kamuflaʒ] *nm* camouflage; disguising, hiding *(of truth etc)*; **le c. d'une rentrée d'argent,** the concealment of a sum of money received; **le c. d'une faute,** the covering up of a mistake.

camoufler [kamufle] **1** *vt* to camouflage; to disguise, to hide *(truth etc)*; **c. un bouton,** to camouflage a spot. **2 se camoufler** *vpr* to camouflage oneself; *Fig* **faire qch en se camouflant,** to do sth secretly *or* in secret.

camouflet [kamuflɛ] *nm* **(a)** *Litt* affront, insult, snub; **(b)** *Mil* camouflet, stifler.

camp [kɑ̃] *nm* **(a)** *(campement)* camp; **établir un c.,** to pitch (a) camp; **lever le c.,** to strike camp; *Mil* **c. volant,** temporary camp; *Fig* **être en c. volant,** to be somewhere only temporarily; **lit de c.,** camp bed; **feux de c.,** camp-fires; **c. de vacances,** holiday camp; **partir faire un c.** *ou* **en c.,** to go camping; **c. de prisonniers,** prison camp; **c. de concentration/d'internement,** concentration/internment camp; **les camps de la mort,** the death camps; *F* **ficher le c.,** to clear off, to scram; *F* **fous-moi le c.!,** clear off!, beat it!; **(b)** *(parti)* party, faction, camp; **changer de c.,** to change sides; **le c. adverse,** the opposing camp *or* faction, the other side; **ils ne sont pas dans le même c.,** they're on different sides; **(c)** *(de jeux)* side; **tirer les camps,** to pick sides; **faire deux camps,** to form two teams.

campagnard, -arde [kɑ̃paɲar, -ard] **1** *adj* country *(gentleman, accent etc)*; rustic *(simplicity etc)*. **2** *n* countryman, countrywoman; *Péj* rustic.

campagne [kɑ̃paɲ] *nf* **(a)** country(side) *(as opposed to town)*; **à la c.,** in the country; **en pleine c.,** deep in the countryside; **vie de c.,** country life; **je n'aime pas la c.,** I don't like the country; *Fig* **son esprit bat la c.,** his mind is wandering; **en rase c.,** in (the) open country(side); **(maison de) c.,** small estate, little place in the country;

(b) *Mil* (the) field; **en c.,** in the field, on active service; **artillerie de c.,** field artillery; **la c. d'Égypte,** the Egyptian campaign; **tenue de c.,** field dress, combat kit; **entrer** *ou* **se mettre en c.,** to begin operations, to take the field; *Fig* to set to work;

(c) *Mil Pol etc* campaign; *Mil* **faire c.,** to campaign, to fight a campaign; **faire c.** *ou* **se mettre en c. pour qn/contre qch,** to campaign on s.o.'s behalf/against sth; **tous ses amis sont en c. pour lui trouver un emploi,** all his friends are busy trying to find him a job; **partir en c. contre le tabac,** to campaign against smoking, to launch an anti-smoking campaign; **c. publicitaire** *ou* **de publicité,** advertising campaign, publicity drive; **une c. de presse,** a press campaign; **c. électorale,** election campaign; **c. de calomnies,** smear campaign; **faire une c. pour** *ou* **en faveur de tel candidat,** to canvass *or* campaign for *or* on behalf of a candidate.

campagnol [kɑ̃paɲɔl] *nm* (field) vole.

campanile [kɑ̃panil] *nm Archit* campanile, bell tower.

campanule [kɑ̃panyl] *nf* campanula.

campé [kɑ̃pe] *adj* **bien c.,** well built *(person)*; **bien c. sur ses jambes,** standing firmly on his feet; **portrait bien c.,** well-sketched portrait; **récit bien c.,** well-constructed *or* well-told story.

campêche [kɑ̃pɛʃ] *nm* **(bois de) c.,** Campeachy wood, logwood.

campement [kɑ̃pmɑ̃] *nm* **(a)** camping; **(b)** *(installation)* encampment, camp; *(lieu)* camping ground *or* place; **établir un c.,** to camp, to pitch camp; **replier le c.,** to strike camp; **matériel de c.,** camping equipment.

camper [kɑ̃pe] **1** *vi* **(a)** *(faire du camping)* to go camping; to camp (out) *(in the garden etc)*; **(b)** *(établir un campement)* to (en)camp, to pitch camp; *Fig* to install oneself temporarily, to camp out *(in a hotel etc)*. **2** *vt* to encamp *(troops)*, to put *(troops)* under canvas; *(planter)* to place, to fix, to put, to construct *(story etc)*; **il a campé son chapeau sur sa tête,** he stuck *or* planted his hat on his head; **c. là qn,** to leave s.o. in the lurch; **écrivain qui campe bien ses personnages,** writer who is good at portraying characters; *Th* **c. un personnage,** to play a part effectively. **3 se camper** *vpr* to stand firmly, to plant one's feet firmly; **se c. devant qn,** to plant oneself in front of s.o..

campeur, -euse [kɑ̃pœr, -øz] *n* camper.

camphre [kɑ̃fr] *nm* camphor; **essence de c.,** camphor oil.

camphré [kɑ̃fre] *adj* camphorated *(oil etc)*.

camphrier [kɑ̃frije] *nm* camphor tree.

camping [kɑ̃piŋ] *nm* **(a)** *(activité)* camping; **faire du c.,** to go camping; **c. sauvage,** camping in the wild; **(b)** *(lieu)* camp(ing) site.

camping-car [kɑ̃piŋkar] *nm* camper, *Br* Dormobile ®; *(pl camping-cars)*.

camping-gaz [kɑ̃piŋgaz] *nm inv* Camping Gaz ®.

campos [kɑ̃po] *nm F* holiday; rest; **donner c. à qn,** to give s.o. a day *or* an afternoon off.

campus [kɑ̃pys] *nm* campus; **vivre sur le c.,** to live on campus.

camus [kamy] *adj* **(a)** flat- *or* snub- *or* pug-nosed *(person)*; pug-nosed *(dog etc)*; **(b)** flat, snub, pug *(nose)*.

Canada [kanada] *nm* Canada; **au C.,** in Canada.

Canadair ® [kanadɛr] *nm* water bomber.

canadianisme [kanadjanism] *nm Ling* Canadianism.

canadien, -ienne [kanadjɛ̃, -jɛn] **1** *adj* Canadian. **2** *n* **C.,** Canadian; **C. français(e),** French Canadian. **3** *nf* **canadienne,** *(veste)* sheepskin jacket, (fur-lined) lumber jacket; *(canoë)* Canadian canoe.

canaille [kanɑj] **1** *nf (crapule etc)* scoundrel, rogue, bad lot; **ne lui fais pas confiance, c'est une vraie c.,** don't trust him, he's a real bastard *or Am* son of a bitch; **petite c.!,** *(to child)* you little devil *or* rascal!; *Vieilli* **la c.,** the rabble, the riff-raff. **2** *adj* low, crooked *(action etc)*; vulgar, coarse *(song etc)*; **des paroles canailles,** dirty words.

canaillerie [kanɑjri] *nf* **(a)** low(-down) trick; **(b)** lowness, crookedness *(of action etc)*; vulgarity, coarseness *(of song etc)*.

canal, -aux [kanal, -o] *nm* **(a)** *Constr* canal; **c. d'irrigation,** irrigation canal; **c. maritime** *ou* **de navigation,** ship canal; **c. de dérivation,** diversion *or* bypass channel; **le C. de Suez,** the Suez Canal; **la Zone du C. (de Panama),** the Canal Zone;

(b) channel *(of river)*; **le C. de Mozambique,** the Mozambique Channel;

(c) *(conduite)* pipe, conduit, tube; *Anat Bot* canal, duct; **c. à air** *ou* **d'aérage,** air passage *or* duct; **c. d'amenée,** feeder, penstock; **c. de fuite,** waste pipe; **c. alimentaire,** alimentary canal; *Anat* **c. biliaire,** bile duct; **c. de graissage,** oil groove;

(d) *TV Can* channel;

(e) *Fig (moyen)* channel, medium, means; **par le c. de la poste,** through the post; *Écon* **c. de distribution,** distribution channel.

canalisable [kanalizabl] *adj* **eau c.,** water which can be channelled *or* canalized; *Fig* **une énergie difficilement c.,** energy which is difficult to channel *or* direct.

canalisation [kanalizasjɔ̃] *nf* **(a)** canalization *(of river etc)*; **(b)** *(conduites etc)* (system of) pipes, piping; conduit, mains ducting; (electric) conduit, cable, wiring; **(c)** pipeline *(for mineral oils etc)*.

canaliser [kanalize] *vt* **(a)** to canalize *(region, river etc)*; **(b)** to channel, to concentrate *(resources etc)*; **(c)** to direct *(traffic, crowd etc)*.

cananéen, -enne [kananeɛ̃, -ɛn] *Bible* **1** *adj* Canaanite. **2** *nm Ling* Canaanite. **3** *n* **C.,** Canaanite.

canapé [kanape] *nm* **(a)** sofa, couch, settee; **c. deux places,** two-seater sofa, *Am* loveseat; **c. trois places,** three-seater sofa; **c. convertible,** sofa bed; **(b)** *Culin* (cocktail) canapé.

canapé-lit [kanapeli] *nm* sofa bed, bed settee, studio couch; *(pl canapés-lits)*.

canaque [kanak] **1** *adj* kanak. **2** *n* **C.,** Kanak (= indigenous inhabitant of New Caledonia).

canard [kanar] *nm* **(a)** (*oiseau*) duck; (*mâle*) drake; **c. de Barbarie,** Muscovy duck; **c. sauvage,** wild duck, mallard; **c. siffleur,** wi(d)geon; **mare aux canards,** duck pond; **chasse aux canards,** duck shooting; *Culin* **c. à l'orange,** duck à l'orange; *F* **mon petit c.,** darling, ducky; *F* **marcher comme un c.,** to waddle; **(b)** *F* (*fausse nouvelle*) false report, hoax; **(c)** (*journal*) rag; **(d)** (*morceau de sucre*) = lump of sugar dipped in coffee or brandy etc; **(e)** *Mus* false note (*on reed instrument etc*); **(f)** *Can* kettle.
canardeau, -eaux [kanardo] *nm* duckling.
canarder [kanarde] **1** *vi* **(a)** (*of ship*) to pitch; **(b)** *Mus F* to play *or* sing a false note. **2** *vt F* to fire at (*s.o.*) from behind cover, to snipe at, to take pot shots at (*s.o.*); **se faire c. à coup de boules de neige,** to be pelted with snowballs; *Fig* **il s'est fait c. de questions,** he was bombarded with questions.
canardière [kanardjɛr] *nf* **(a)** (*mare*) duck pond; **(b)** (*lieu*) screen (*for duck shooting*); **(c)** (*fusil*) duck gun, punt gun.
canari [kanari] **1** *nm* canary. **2** *adj inv* **(jaune) c.,** canary yellow.
Canaries [kanari] *nfpl* **les (îles) C.,** the Canary Islands, the Canaries.
canasson [kanasɔ̃] *nm Arg* (*cheval*) nag.
canasta [kanasta] *nf Cartes* canasta; **jouer à la c.,** to play canasta.
cancale [kɑ̃kal] *nf* Cancale oyster.
cancan [kɑ̃kɑ̃] *nm F* **(a)** (*racontar, histoire*) (piece of) malicious gossip; **cancans,** tittle-tattle, gossip; **dire** *ou* **faire des cancans,** to gossip *or* talk (**sur,** about); **(b)** (*danse*) cancan (dance); **danser le c.,** to do the cancan.
cancaner [kɑ̃kane] *vi* **(a)** *F* to tittle-tattle, to gossip, to talk scandal (**sur,** about); **(b)** (*of duck*) to quack.
cancanier, -ière [kɑ̃kanje, -jɛr] *F* **1** *adj* fond of tittle-tattle, gossipy. **2** *n* gossip, scandalmonger, tattler.
cancer [kɑ̃sɛr] *nm* **(a)** *Méd* cancer; **c. du poumon/du sein,** lung/breast cancer; **c. de la peau,** skin cancer; **avoir un c.,** to have cancer; **avoir un c. à** *ou* **de l'estomac/***etc*, to have stomach/*etc* cancer; **mourir d'un c.,** to die of cancer; *Fig* **la pollution est un c. pour la campagne,** pollution is the scourge of the countryside; **(b)** *Astron* **le C.,** Cancer, the Crab; **du signe du C.,** Cancerian; **je suis C.,** I'm (a) Cancer; *Géog* **le Tropique du C.,** the Tropic of Cancer.
cancéreux, -euse [kɑ̃serø, -øz] **1** *adj* cancerous (*tumour etc*); **être c. en phase terminale,** to have terminal cancer, to be terminally ill with cancer. **2 les c.,** people with cancer, cancer victims.
cancériforme [kɑ̃serifɔrm] *adj Méd* cancriform, cancroid.
cancérigène [kɑ̃seriʒɛn] **, cancérogène** [kɑ̃serɔʒɛn] *adj* carcinogenic; **produit c.,** carcinogen.
cancérologie [kɑ̃serɔlɔʒi] *nf* cancerology.
cancérologue [kɑ̃serɔlɔg] *n* cancer specialist.
cancre [kɑ̃kr] *nm* **(a)** (*crustacé*) crab; **(b)** *F* dunce, duffer, dud.
cancrelat [kɑ̃krəla] *nm* cockroach.
cancroïde [kɑ̃krɔid] *nm Méd* cancroid (ulcer).
candélabre [kɑ̃delabr] *nm* **(a)** (*chandelier*) *F* candelabra, candelabrum, *pl* candelabra; **(b)** (*lampadaire*) street lamp post (with branched lamps).
candeur [kɑ̃dœr] *nf* ingenuousness, artlessness; **un regard plein de c.,** a look of naivety.
candi [kɑ̃di] *adj* candied; **fruits candis,** crystallized fruit; **sucre c.,** crystallized sugar, sugar crystals.
candidat, -ate [kɑ̃dida, -at] *n* candidate, applicant (**à une place,** for a place); (*at exam*) candidate; **se porter c. aux élections législatives,** to stand for Parliament.
candidature [kɑ̃didatyr] *nf* candidature, candidacy; **poser sa c. à un poste,** to apply for a post; **elle a retiré sa c.,** (*à un poste*) she withdrew her application.
candide [kɑ̃did] *adj* ingenuous, guileless, artless.
candidement [kɑ̃didmɑ̃] *adv* ingenuously, guilelessly, artlessly.
candir (se) [səkɑ̃dir] *vpr* (*of sugar*) to candy, to crystallize.
cane [kan] *nf* duck (*as opposed to drake*).
cané [kane] *adj F* dead-beat, whacked, bushed.
caner [kane] *vi Arg* (*avoir peur*) to have the jitters; (*se dégonfler*) to chicken out, *Br* to bottle out; (*mourir*) to snuff it, to kick the bucket.
caneton [kantɔ̃] *nm* (male) duckling.
canette[1] [kanɛt] *nf* (female) duckling.
canette[2] *nf* = **CANNETTE**.
canevas [kanvɑ] *nm* **(a)** *Tex* canvas; **broderie sur c.,** tapestry (work); **(b)** *Beaux-Arts Mus Littér* groundwork, sketch, outline (*of drawing, novel etc*).
caniche [kaniʃ] *nm* poodle.
caniculaire [kanikylɛr] *adj* sultry, scorching (*heat, day etc*); **les jours caniculaires,** the dog days.
canicule [kanikyl] *nf* heatwave; **quelle c.!,** what a scorcher!; **la c.,** the dog days; **pendant la c. du mois d'août,** during the August heatwave.
canif [kanif] *nm* penknife.
canin, -ine [kanɛ̃, -in] **1** *adj* canine; **exposition canine,** dog show. **2** *nf* **canine,** canine (tooth), eyetooth.
canisse [kanis] *nf* = **CANNISSE**.
caniveau, -eaux [kanivo] *nm* **(a)** (*le long des routes*) gutter; **(b)** *Él* (*pour câble*) trough, conduit.
cannabis [kanabis] *nm* cannabis.
cannage [kanaʒ] *nm* **(a)** caning; **(b)** (*résultat*) canework.
canne [kan] *nf* **(a)** (*tige*) cane; **c. à sucre,** sugar cane; **sucre de c.,** cane sugar; **(b)** (*pour s'appuyer*) walking stick, cane; **c. de marcheur,** thumb stick; **c. (à) épée,** swordstick; **(escrime à) la c.,** singlestick (play); **c. blanche,** white stick; *Fig* **les cannes blanches,** the blind; **(c) c. à pêche,** fishing rod; **(d)** (*travail du verre*) blowing iron, blowpipe; **(e)** *Can* (*de tomates etc*) can, tin; **(f)** *Arg* (*jambe*) leg, *Sl* pin; **avoir de belles cannes,** to have a nice pair of legs.
canné [kane] *adj* **chaise cannée,** cane(-seated) chair.
canneberge [kanbɛrʒ] *nf* cranberry; **sauce aux canneberges,** cranberry sauce.
cannelé [kanle] *adj* **(a)** (*colonne etc*) fluted; (*pneu*) grooved; (*ongle*) ridged; **(b)** (*plissé*) corrugated.
canneler [kanle] *vt* (**je cannelle, n. cannelons; je cannellerai**) (*une colonne*) to flute; (*un pneu*) to groove; (*un ongle*) to ridge.
cannelier [kanəlje] *nm* cinnamon tree.
cannelle[1] [kanɛl] *nf* cinnamon (bark); **bâton de c.,** cinnamon stick; **à la c.,** cinnamon(-flavoured).
cannelle[2] *nf* (*de tonneau*) spigot.
cannellonis [kanɛlɔni] *nmpl* cannelloni.
cannelure [kanlyr] *nf* **(a)** groove, channel, slot; *Archit* flute, fluting (*of column*); **(b)** (*de métal, carton*) corrugation; **(c)** *Bot etc* **cannelures,** striae; **(d)** *Géol* fault fissure.
canner [kane] *vt* to cane (*chair*).
cannette [kanɛt] *nf* **(a)** (*petite bouteille*) (beer) bottle; **c. de bière,** bottle of beer; **(b)** *Tex* cop, spool.
cannibale [kanibal] **1** *n* cannibal. **2** *adj* cannibalistic (*practices etc*); **tribu c.,** tribe of cannibals.
cannibalisme [kanibalism] *nm* cannibalism.
cannisse [kanis] *nf Région* split cane (*for making fences etc*).
canoë [kanɔe] *nm* canoe; **faire du c.,** to canoe, to go canoeing.
canoéisme [kanɔeism] *nm Sp* canoeing.
canoéiste [kanɔeist] *n* canoeist.
canon[1] [kanɔ̃] *nm* **(a)** *Mil etc* gun, cannon; **c. à âme lisse,** smooth-bore gun; **c. rayé,** rifled gun; **c. de 105 mm/de 280 mm,** 105 mm/280 mm gun; **c. antiaérien,** anti-aircraft gun; **c. antichar,** anti-tank gun; **c. de char,** tank gun; **c. de marine** *ou* **de bord,** naval gun; **c. de chasse,** bow chaser; **c. de retraite,** sternchaser; **poudre à c.,** gunpowder; *F* **chair à c.,** cannon fodder; **c. paragrêle,** cloud seeder; **le c.,** artillery, the guns; **le gros c.,** the heavy guns;
(b) barrel (*of rifle, watch, pen etc*); barrel, pipe (*of key, of lock*); spout (*of watering can*); body (*of syringe etc*); **fusil à deux canons,** double barrelled gun;
(c) *Arch* = wine measure equivalent to 0.058 l.; *Arg* **boire un c.,** to have a glass; *Arg* **je te paie un c.,** have one on me;
(d) *Vét* cannon (bone), shin, shank (*of horse*);
(e) (*X-rays*) *& TV* **c. à électrons,** electron gun.
canon[2] **1** *nm* **(a)** *Rel* canon, rule (*of an order, of the Mass etc*); **(b)** (*règle*) (general) formula, rule, canon; **(c)** *Mus* canon, round, catch; **c. à deux/trois voix,** canon for two/three voices; **reprendre un chant en c.,** to sing a round. **2** *adj* **(a) droit c.,** canon law; **(b)** *F* (*beau*) gorgeous(-looking).
cañon [kaɲɔ̃] *nm Géog* canyon, cañon.
canonial, -iaux [kanɔnjal, -jo] *adj Rel* **(a)** canonic(al) (*hours etc*); **(b)** of a canon (*chanoine*).
canonique [kanɔnik] *adj* canonical (*book etc*); **âge c.,** *Rel* canonical age (*for priest's housekeeper*); *F* respectable age; **ta bagnole a l'air d'avoir dépassé l'âge c.,** your car looks as if it's past it.
canonisation [kanɔnizasjɔ̃] *nf Rel* canonization.
canoniser [kanɔnize] *vt Rel* to canonize.
canon-mitrailleuse [kanɔ̃mitrajøz] *nm* pom-pom; (*pl canons-mitrailleuses*).

canonnade [kanɔnad] *nf* cannonade, gunfire.
canonner [kanɔne] *vt* to shell, to bombard, *Mil* to cannonade.
canonnier [kanɔnje] *nm Mil* gunner.
canonnière [kanɔnjɛr] *nf* **(a)** *Nau* gunboat; **(b)** (*ouverture*) loophole.
canot [kano] *nm Nau* **(a)** (*embarcation non pontée*) rowing boat, *Am* rowboat, dinghy; **grand c.,** longboat, pinnace; *Nau* **c. major,** officers' boat; **c. de sauvetage,** lifeboat; **petit c.,** jollyboat, gig; **c. pneumatique,** inflatable *or* rubber dinghy; **c. automobile,** motorboat, motor launch; **(b)** *Can* canoe.
canotage [kanɔtaʒ] *nm Nau* boating; (*à l'aviron*) rowing; (*à la voile*) (dinghy) sailing; *Can* canoeing; **faire du c.,** to canoe.
canoter [kanɔte] *vi Nau* to go (in for) boating; (*à l'aviron*) to go (in for) rowing; (*à la voile*) to go (in for) (dinghy) sailing; (*à l'aviron*) to row; (*à la voile*) to sail; *Can* to go (in for) canoeing, to canoe.
canoteur [kanɔtœr] *nm* boater; (*à l'aviron*) rower; *Can* canoeist.
canotier [kanɔtje] *nm* **(a)** (*rameur*) rower, oarsman; **(b)** (*chapeau*) straw hat, boater.
cantal [kɑ̃tal] *nm* Cantal (cheese).
cantaloup [kɑ̃talu] *nm* (*fruit*) cantaloup (melon).
cantate [kɑ̃tat] *nf Mus* cantata.
cantatrice [kɑ̃tatris] *nf* (professional) singer.
cantharide [kɑ̃tarid] *nf* (*insecte*) cantharis, Spanish fly.
cantilène [kɑ̃tilɛn] *nf Mus* cantilena.
cantilever [kɑ̃tilevœr] *adj Constr* cantilever; **pont c.,** cantilever bridge.
cantine [kɑ̃tin] *nf* **(a)** (*refectoire*) canteen; *Scol* dining hall; *esp Univ* refectory; *Scol* **déjeuner à la c.,** to have school lunch *or* dinner(s); **(b)** (*malle*) trunk; *Mil* (officer's) uniform case, tin trunk; *Mil* **c. médicale,** field medical chest.
cantinier, -ière [kɑ̃tinje, -jɛr] *n Mil Arch* canteen keeper *or* attendant.
cantique [kɑ̃tik] *nm Rel* canticle, hymn; **le c. des cantiques,** the Song of Songs *or* of Solomon.
canton [kɑ̃tɔ̃] *nm* **(a)** (*en France*) canton (= *administrative division of a department*); (*en Suisse*) canton; *Can* **les cantons de l'Est,** the Eastern Townships; **(b)** *Constr* section (*of road, railway etc*); **(c)** *Rail* block (*in block system*); *Arch* district, region.
cantonade [kɑ̃tɔnad] *nf* **(a) parler à la c.,** not to address anyone in particular; **elle l'a dit à la c.,** she's said it so that everyone could hear; **(b)** *Th* (the) wings; **parler à la c.,** to speak off.
cantonais, -aise [kɑtɔnɛ, -ɛz] **1** *adj* Cantonese. **2** *nm Ling* Cantonese. **3** *n* **C.,** person from Canton.
cantonal, -aux [kɑ̃tɔnal, -o] *adj* cantonal, district (*committee etc*); **les (élections) cantonales,** = elections to the council of a department.
cantonnement [kɑ̃tɔnmɑ̃] *nm* **(a)** *Mil* quartering, billeting (*of troops*); **(b)** section (*of forest etc*); stretch of river (*with fishing rights*); **(c)** *Mil* (*lieu*) quarters, billets, cantonment.
cantonner [kɑ̃tɔne] **1** *vt* to confine, to limit (**dans qch,** to sth); to isolate (*sick animals etc*); *Mil* to quarter, to billet (*troops*); **c. les jeunes employés à des tâches dérisoires,** to restrict junior employees to menial tasks. **2** *vi* (*of troops*) to be billeted *or* quartered. **3 se cantonner** *vpr* to lock oneself away (*in a room etc*); *Fig* (*se limiter*) to confine *or* limit oneself (**dans qch,** to sth); **se c. à une tâche,** to confine oneself to one task.
cantonnier [kɑ̃tɔnje] *nm* (*sur les routes*) roadman, roadmender; *Rail* line(s)man.
cantonnière [kɑ̃tɔnjɛr] *nf* (*de lit, de fenêtre*) valance.
Cantorbéry [kɑ̃tɔrberi] *n* Canterbury.
canular(d) [kanylar] *nm Scol F* (*histoire exagérée*) tall story; (*blague*) hoax, practical joke, *F* leg-pull; *Scol* rag.
canularesque [kanylarɛsk] *adj F* **une histoire c.,** a hoax, *F* a leg-pull.
canule [kanyl] *nf Méd* cannula; nozzle (*of syringe etc*).
canulé [kanyle] *adj* nozzle-shaped.
canuler [kanyle] *vt* **(a)** *Arg* (*ennuyer*) to get on (*s.o.'s*) wick; **(b)** *Scol F* to play a practical joke on (*s.o.*).
canyon [kanjɔn] *nm* = **CAÑON.**
C.A.O. [seao] *nf Ordinat* (*abrév* **conception assistée par ordinateur**) CAD.
caoua [kawa] *nm F* coffee.
caoutchouc [kautʃu] *nm* **(a)** (*substance*) rubber; **c. synthétique,** synthetic rubber; **c. mousse** ®, foam rubber, sponge rubber; **ballon en c.,** rubber ball; *Bourse* **caoutchoucs,** rubber shares, rubbers; **(b)** (*manteau*) raincoat, *Br* waterproof (coat), mackintosh; (*élastique*) rubber band, elastic band; **caoutchoucs,** (*souliers*) galoshes, rubber overshoes, *Am* rubbers.
caoutchoutage [kautʃutaʒ] *nm* treating with rubber, rubberizing.
caoutchouter [kautʃute] *vt* to treat (*sth*) with rubber, to rubberize (*sth*).
caoutchouteux, -euse [kautʃutø, -øz] *adj Péj* rubbery; **de la viande caoutchouteuse,** rubbery meat.
cap [kap] *nm* **(a)** *Géog* cape, headland, foreland; **le c. Horn,** Cape Horn; **le C.,** Capetown; *Hist* **la Colonie du c.,** Cape Colony; **passer** *ou* **franchir** *ou* **doubler un c.,** to round a cape; *Fig* to weather *or* overcome a difficulty; **quand on a franchi le c. de la quarantaine,** when you've turned forty; **notre usine va passer le c. des mille employés,** our factory will soon top the thousand-employee mark; **(b)** *Nau Av* (*direction*) course, heading, direction; **mettre le c. sur...,** to head for ..., to steer for..., **mettre le c. au large,** to stand out to sea; **c. au vent/au large,** head (on) to the wind/to sea; **changement de c.,** change of course; **c. de collision,** collision course; *Av* **conservateur de c.,** directional gyro; **le c. magnétique,** the magnetic heading; **(c) de pied en c.,** from head to foot *or* toe, from top to toe *or* bottom.
C.A.P. [seape] *nm* (*abrév* **Certificat d'aptitude professionnelle**) = vocational training certificate.
capable [kapabl] *adj* **(a)** capable; *Jur* entitled, qualified, competent (*to do sth*); **c. de qch,** capable of sth; **être c. de faire qch,** to be capable of doing sth; (*physiquement*) to be fit *or* able to do sth; **je n'en suis pas c.,** I can't do it; **il est c. de tout,** he's capable of anything; **c. du meilleur comme du pire,** capable of the best as well as the worst; **elle est bien c. d'avoir oublié les clefs!,** she's quite capable of forgetting the keys!; **cette maladie est c. de le tuer,** this illness might well kill him *or* may be enough to kill him; **(b)** capable, able, competent (*person*); **élève très c.,** very able pupil.
capacité [kapasite] *nf* **(a)** capacity (*of vase, accumulator etc*); *Él* **c. (électrostatique),** capacitance; *Méd* **c. vitale,** vital capacity; **(b)** capacity, ability, capability; (*aptitude*) talent; *Jur* capacity; **homme de grande** *ou* **de haute c.,** very capable man; **la c. de production d'une entreprise,** the production capacity of a firm; **je n'en ai pas les capacités,** I don't have the skills (to do it); **avoir les capacités pour faire qch,** to be qualified to do sth; **c. pour les affaires,** business ability; **de grandes capacités intellectuelles,** great intellectual capacity; *Jur* **certificat de c. en droit,** = certificate entitling holder to practise in some branches of the legal profession; *Jur* **avoir c. pour faire qch,** to be (legally) entitled *or* qualified to do sth; *Jur* **c. de jouissance,** legal right, legal entitlement; **c. légale,** legal capacity.
caparaçon [kaparasɔ̃] *nm Hist* caparison, trappings.
caparaçonner [kaparasɔne] *vt* to caparison (*horse*).
cape [kap] *nf* **(a)** (*vêtement*) cape; (*plus longue*) cloak; **roman de c. et d'épée,** historical romance; (*histoire d'espions*) cloak-and-dagger story; *Fig* **sous c.,** secretly, on the sly, on the quiet; *Fig* **rire sous c.,** to laugh up one's sleeve; **(b)** *Nau* **être** *ou* **se tenir à la c.,** to lie to, to be hove to; **(se) mettre à la c.,** to heave to.
capelage [kaplaʒ] *nm Nau* **(a)** rigging (*of mast*); **(b)** masthead (*under rigging*).
capeler [kaple] *vt* (**je capelle, n. capelons; je capellerai**) *Nau* to rig (*mast, spar etc*).
capeline [kaplin] *nf* (*chapeau*) sun hat, floppy hat; *Arch* riding hood.
C.A.P.E.S. [kapɛs] *nm Univ* (*abrév* **Certificat d'aptitude au professorat de l'enseignement secondaire**) = postgraduate teaching certificate.
capésien, -ienne [kapesjɛ̃, -jɛn] *n Scol F* ≈ graduate teacher.
Capharnaüm [kafarnaɔm] *nm* **(a)** *Bible* Capernaum; **(b)** *F* junk room, glory hole; **quel c.,** what a tip *or* pigsty!
capillaire [kapilɛr] **1** *adj* **(a)** capillary (*tube, attraction*); *Anat* **les vaisseaux capillaires,** the capillary blood vessels, the capillaries; **(b) lotion c.,** (*pour les cheveux*) hair lotion, hair tonic; **artiste c.,** hair stylist. **2** *nm* **(a)** *Bot* maidenhair; **(b)** *Anat* **les capillaires,** the capillaries.
capillarité [kapilarite] *nf Phys* capillarity, capillary action.
capilliculture [kapilikyltyr] *nf* hair care *or* treatment.
capilotade [kapilɔtad] *nf F* **mettre qn en c.,** to beat s.o. to a pulp, to beat s.o. black and blue, to make mincemeat of s.o.; **mettre qch en c.,** to smash sth to pieces *or*

smithereens.

capitaine [kapitɛn] *nm* **(a)** *Mil Nau* captain; *Nau F* skipper; **c. des gendarmes/pompiers,** ≈ police superintendent/fire chief; *Mil Av* **c. (d'aviation),** ≈ flight lieutenant; *US* ≈ (air) captain; *Nau* **c. de corvette,** lieutenant commander; **c. de frégate,** commander; **c. de vaisseau,** captain; **c. de la marine marchande,** captain, master (in the merchant navy); **c. de port,** harbour master; **c. au long cours,** master mariner; **(b)** chief, head, leader (*of band, gang etc*); captain, *F* skipper (*of football team etc*); *Mil* **un grand c.,** a great (military) leader; **les capitaines d'industrie,** the captains of industry.

capital, -ale, -aux [kapital, -o] **1** *adj* **(a)** *Jur* capital (*crime etc*); **la peine capitale,** capital punishment, the death penalty;

(b) (*essentiel*) fundamental, essential, chief, principal; **le point c.,** the essential *or* main point; **une décision capitale,** a major decision; **c'est c.,** it's essential; **son défaut c.,** his greatest fault; **d'une importance capitale,** of capital *or* paramount *or* the utmost importance; **les sept péchés capitaux,** the seven deadly sins;

(c) *Typ* **lettre capitale,** capital (letter).

2 *nm* **(a)** *Fin* capital, assets; **c. et intérêt,** principal and interest; **c. social,** registered capital; *Écon* **c. réel,** capital assets; **posséder un c.,** to have some capital; **les capitaux qui circulent,** the capital in circulation; **fuite des capitaux,** flight of capital; **association c.-travail,** profit-sharing scheme; *Fig* **le c. culturel d'un pays,** the cultural wealth of a country;

(b) capitalist class.

3 *nf* **capitale (a)** capital (city);

(b) *Typ* capital (letter); **(écrire en) capitales d'imprimerie,** (write in) block capitals.

capitalisable [kapitalizabl] *adj* capitalizable (*interest etc*).

capitalisation [kapitalizɑsjɔ̃] *nf* capitalization (*of interest etc*).

capitaliser [kapitalize] **1** *vt* to capitalize (*interest* etc). **2** *vi* to save.

capitalisme [kapitalism] *nm* capitalism.

capitaliste [kapitalist] **1** *adj* capitalist, capitalistic. **2** *n* capitalist.

capitation [kapitɑsjɔ̃] *nf Admin Arch* capitation, poll tax; *Arch* head money.

capiteux, -euse [kapitø, -øz] *adj* heady (*wine etc*); sensuous (*charm etc*); exciting, alluring (*woman*); **un parfum c.,** a heady fragrance.

Capitole (le) [ləkapitɔl] *nm* the Capitol (*of ancient Rome, Toulouse, Washington*).

capiton [kapitɔ̃] *nm* **(a)** (*rembourrage*) stuffing, padding; (*entre les piqûres*) cap, boss; **(b)** *Com* silk waste.

capitonnage [kapitɔnaʒ] *nm* **(a)** (*action*) upholstering, stuffing, padding; **(b)** (*matériel*) (upholstery) stuffing, padding.

capitonner [kapitɔne] *vt* to upholster, to stuff, to pad (*furniture*).

capitulaire [kapitylɛr] *adj* **salle c.,** chapter house.

capitulation [kapitylɑsjɔ̃] *nf* capitulation, surrender; **c. sans conditions,** unconditional surrender.

capituler [kapityle] *vi* to capitulate, to surrender; **forcer qn à c.,** to force s.o. to capitulate *or* give in.

capon, -onne [kapɔ̃, -ɔn] *F Vieilli* **1** *adj* cowardly, yellow. **2** *n* coward, funk.

caporal, -aux [kapɔral, -o] *nm* **(a)** *Mil* lance corporal; **c. d'ordinaire,** mess corporal; *Hist F* **le Petit C.,** = Napoleon; **(b)** caporal (*tobacco*).

caporal-chef [kapɔralʃɛf] *nm Mil* corporal; (*pl caporaux-chefs*).

caporaliser [kapɔralize] *vt* to militarize, to Prussianize.

caporalisme [kapɔralism] *nm* militarism; *Fig* authoritarianism.

capot¹ [kapo] *nm* **(a)** *Aut* bonnet, *Am* hood (*of car*); *Av* cowl(ing) (*of aircraft engine*); *Nau* tarpaulin; cover, hood, casing (*of arc lamp etc*); **(b)** *Nau* companion (hatch).

capot² *adj inv Cartes* **être c.,** not to take a single trick.

capotage [kapɔtaʒ] *nm* capsizing (*of boat*); *Aut Av* overturning.

capote [kapɔt] *nf* **(a)** *Aut* adjustable hood *or* top (*of convertible*); **baisser la c.,** to put the hood down; **(b)** *Mil* greatcoat, overcoat; **(c)** (*de dame*) (lady's) bonnet; **(d) c. anglaise,** French letter, rubber (johnny).

capoter¹ [kapɔte] *vt* (*garnir*) to put a hood on (*vehicle*); (*fermer*) to close the hood on (*vehicle*).

capoter² *vi* **(a)** *Nau* to capsize, to turn turtle; *Aut Av* to overturn; **(b)** *Can F* to talk drivel; **il est complètement capoté,** he's completely off his head.

cappucino [kaputʃinɔ] *nm* cappuccino.

câpre [kɑpr] *nf Bot Culin* caper.

caprice [kapris] *nm* caprice, whim, fancy; **avoir** *ou* **faire des caprices,** to throw tantrums, to be temperamental; **faire qch par c.,** to do sth on a sudden impulse *or* whim; **on lui passe tous ses caprices,** they indulge his every whim; **les caprices de la mode,** the vagaries of fashion; **avoir un c. pour qn,** to take a passing fancy to s.o..

capricieusement [kaprisjøzmɑ̃] *adv* capriciously.

capricieux, -ieuse [kaprisjø, -jøz] **1** *adj* capricious; temperamental (*person*); **moteur c.,** temperamental engine; **temps c.,** changeable weather; **être c.,** to throw tantrums, to be temperamental. **2** *n* capricious *or* temperamental person.

capricorne [kaprikɔrn] *nm* **(a)** *Astron* Capricorn, the Goat; *Astrol* **c'est un c.,** he's (a) Capricorn; **le Tropique du C.,** the Tropic of Capricorn; **(b)** (*insecte*) capricorn beetle.

câprier [kɑprije] *nm* caper bush *or* plant.

caprin, -ine [kaprɛ̃, -in] *adj* goat-like; *Spéc* caprine.

capsulage [kapsylaʒ] *nm* capping (*of bottles etc*).

capsule [kapsyl] *nf* **(a)** *Anat Bot Pharm* capsule; **(b)** (metallic) capsule, cap, (*of bottle*); **(c) c. (spatiale),** (space) capsule; **(d)** (*d'armes etc*) (firing) cap, primer; **c. (fulminante),** cap (*in toy gun*); **(e)** *Ch* **c. d'évaporation,** evaporating dish.

capsuler [kapsyle] *vt* to seal, to cap, to put a capsule on (*bottle*).

captage [kaptaʒ] *nm* **(a)** collecting, impounding (*of waters*); *Él* picking up (*of current*); **c. d'une émission,** picking up *or* reception of a broadcast; **(b)** (*lieu*) water catchment.

captateur,-trice [kaptatœr, -tris] *n Jur* inveigler; **c. de succession d'héritage,** legacy hunter.

captation [kaptɑsjɔ̃] *nf Jur* inveigling of an inheritance.

captatoire [kaptatwar] *adj Jur* inveigling, insidious (*means of obtaining an inheritance*).

capter [kapte] *vt* **(a)** to gain *or* capture (*s.o.'s attention*); **(b)** to collect, to pick up (*electric current etc*); to catch, to impound (*waters*); **(c)** *Rad Tél* to intercept, to pick up (*messages*); to tap (*a line*); **je n'arrive pas à c. France Inter** ®, I can't pick up *or* get France Inter ®.

capteur [kaptœr] *nm Phys* sensor; **c. solaire,** solar collector.

captieusement [kapsjøzmɑ̃] *adv* speciously.

captieux, -ieuse [kapsjø, -jøz] *adj* fallacious, specious (*argument etc*).

captif, -ive [kaptif, -iv] **1** *adj* **(a)** captive; **être c. du plaisir,** to be a slave to pleasure; **les citoyens captifs des ravisseurs,** the members of the public held captive by the kidnappers; **(b) ballon c.,** captive balloon. **2** *n* prisoner.

captivant [kaptivɑ̃] *adj* captivating (*person etc*); enthralling, gripping (*book, film etc*).

captiver [kaptive] *vt* to captivate, to enthral, to charm (*s.o.*); to capture (*s.o.'s attention*).

captivité [kaptivite] *nf* captivity; **être en c.,** to be in captivity.

capture [kaptyr] *nf* **(a)** capture, catching (*of thief etc*); capture, seizure (*of ship etc*); **(b)** (*proie*) capture, prize.

capturer [kaptyre] *vt* to capture, to catch (*thief etc*); to capture, to seize (*ship etc*); to catch (*whale etc*).

capuche [kapyʃ] *nf* hood; (*de poche et en plastique*) rainhood.

capuchon [kapyʃɔ̃] *nm* **(a)** hood (*on coat etc*); (monk's) cowl; (*pélerine*) hooded cloak *or* cape; *Biol* **à c.,** hooded (*seal etc*); **(b)** cap (*of pen, tyre valve*); cap, top, lid (*of tube of toothpaste etc*); (chimney) cowl.

capucin [kapysɛ̃] *nm* **(a)** Capuchin (friar); **(b)** *Zool* capuchin (monkey); *F* hare.

capucine [kapysin] *nf* **(a)** Capuchin (nun); **(b)** *Bot* nasturtium.

caque [kak] *nf* herring barrel; *Prov* **la c. sent toujours le hareng,** what's bred in the bone will come out in the flesh.

caquelon [kaklɔ̃] *nm* fondue dish.

caquet [kakɛ] *nm* **(a)** cackle, cackling (*of hens*); **(b)** *F* (noisy) chatter, cackle, gossip, tittle-tattle; **elle lui a rabattu** *ou* **rabaissé le c.,** she shut him up.

caquetage [kaktaʒ] *nm* **(a)** cackle, cackling (*of hens*); **(b)** *F* (noisy) chatter(ing), cackle, cackling, gossip(ing).

caquètement [kakɛtmɑ̃] *nm* **(a)** (*of hens*) cackling; **(b)** *F* cackling, prattling.

caqueter [kakte] *vi* (**je caquette, n. caquetons; je caquetterai**) **(a)** (*of hen*) to cackle; **(b)** *F* to gossip, to chatter, to cackle.

caqueteur, -euse [kaktœr, -øz] *n F* chatterer, tattler, gossip.

car¹ [kar] **1** *conj* for, because. **2** *nm inv* **les si et les c.,** the whys and wherefores.

car² *nm* bus, coach; **prendre le c.,** to take the bus *or* coach, to go by bus *or* coach; **c. de ramassage scolaire,** school bus; **c. de police,** police van; **c. de radio-reportage,** outside broadcasting van, mobile broadcasting unit.

carabe [karab] *nm* (*insecte*) ground beetle.

carabin [karabɛ̃] *nm F* medical student, medic.

carabine [karabin] *nf* rifle; **c. à air comprimé,** air gun; **tir à la c.,** rifle shooting.

carabiné [karabine] *adj* **vent c.,** strong *or* stiff gale; *F* **rhume c.,** heavy cold; **fièvre carabinée,** violent *or* raging fever.

carabinier [karabinje] *nm* **(a)** (*in Spain*) frontier guard; *Arch* carabineer; **(b)** (*in Italy*) police officer.

Carabosse [karabɔs] *nf* **la fée C.,** the wicked fairy (Carabossa).

caraco [karako] *nm* camisole.

caracole [karakɔl] *nf Équitation* caracole, half turn.

caracoler [karakɔle] *vi Équitation* to caracole, to prance about; *F* (*sautiller*) to gambol, to caper.

caractère [karaktɛr] *nm* **(a)** *Psy* character, nature, disposition; (*personnalité, détermination*) personality, character; **avoir (un) mauvais c.,** to be bad-tempered *or* ill-natured; **avoir (un) bon c.,** to be good-tempered *or* good-natured; *F* **quel fichu c.!,** what a bad-tempered so-and-so!; *F* **elle a un c. de cochon,** she's a bad-tempered so-and-so; **avoir du c.,** to have character; **manquer de c.,** to lack (strength of) character, to have no backbone *or* spirit, to be spineless; **cette maison a beaucoup de c.,** this house has a lot of character; **le c. français,** the French character;
(b) (*attribut*) characteristic, feature; **le c. particulier d'un projet,** the particular nature of a project; **l'affaire a pris un c. grave,** the matter has taken a serious turn; **publication de c. officiel,** publication of an official nature; **ce village a un c. rural,** this village has a rural character; *Biol* **c. héréditaire/acquis,** hereditary/acquired character; **maladie sans c. de gravité,** illness that is not in the least serious; **le c. sacré du chant,** the sacred character *or* nature of the song;
(c) (*signe*) character, letter; *Ordinat* character; *Math etc* symbol; *Typ* (metal) type; *Ordinat* **le choix** *ou* **la police de caractères d'une imprimante,** the character set of a printer; *Ordinat* **c. joker,** wildcard; **écrire en petits caractères,** to have small handwriting; **écrivez en caractères d'imprimerie,** write in block letters *or* in (block) capitals, please print; *Typ* **en petits/gros caractères,** in small/large type *or* print.

caractériel, -ielle [karakterjɛl] **1** *adj* of *or* pertaining to character; *Psy* **trouble c.,** psychopathic disorder; **enfant c.,** problem child. **2** *n Psy* psychoneurotic person; *F* problem child.

caractérisation [karakterizɑsjɔ̃] *nf* characterization.

caractérisé [karakterize] *adj* typical; **une rougeole caractérisée,** a typical *or* clear *or* unmistakable case of measles.

caractériser [karakterize] **1** *vt* to characterize, to be characteristic of, to distinguish (*sth*); **symptômes qui caractérisent une maladie,** characteristic symptoms of an illness; **la bonté qui la caractérise,** her characteristic kindness. **2 se caractériser** *vpr* to be characterized *or* distinguished (**par,** by).

caractéristique [karakteristik] **1** *adj* characteristic, distinctive, typical. **2** *nf* **caractéristique** (*particularité*) characteristic, feature; **caractéristiques,** specifications (*of car, aircraft etc*).

caractérologie [karakterɔlɔʒi] *nf* characterology.

carafe [karaf] *nf* **(a)** (*récipient*) (*pour le whisky etc*) (glass) decanter; (*pour le vin*) carafe; **(b)** *F* **rester en c.,** (*être oublié*) to be left in the lurch; **je suis resté en c. à Calais pendant huit heures,** I was stuck in Calais for eight hours; **une voiture restée en c. sur le bord de l'autoroute,** a broken-down car on the side of the motorway; **(c)** *F* (*tête*) nut, bonce; **il a reçu un bon coup sur la c.,** he took *or* got a good knock *or* blow on the bonce.

carafon [karafɔ̃] *nm* (*pour le whisky etc*) small decanter; (*pour le vin*) small carafe; *F* **mets-toi ça dans le c.,** get that into your head *or F* skull.

caraïbe [karaib] **1** *adj* Caribbean. **2** *nm Ling Arch* Carib. **3** *n* **C.,** Carib. **4** *npl* **la mer des Caraïbes,** the Caribbean (Sea).

carambolage [karɑ̃bɔlaʒ] *nm Billard* cannon, *Am* carom; *F* (multiple) pile-up (*of cars*).

caramboler [karɑ̃bɔle] **1** *vi Billard* to cannon, *Am* to carom. **2** *vt F* **c. une voiture,** to run into a car. **3 se caramboler** *vpr* **dix voitures se sont carambolées sur l'autoroute,** there has been a pile-up of ten cars on the motorway.

carambouillage [karɑ̃bujaʒ] *nm,* **carambouille** [karɑ̃buj] *nf F Vieilli* fraudulent conversion.

caramel [karamɛl] **1** *nm Culin* caramel, burnt sugar; **bonbons au c., des caramels,** caramels; **c. (dur) au beurre,** butterscotch, toffee. **2** *adj inv* caramel (coloured).

caramélisation [karamelizɑsjɔ̃] *nf Culin* caramelization.

caraméliser [karamelize] **1** *vt* **(a)** to caramelize (*sugar*); **(b)** (*mélanger avec du caramel*) to mix caramel with (*sth*); **(c)** to coat (*mould*) with caramel. **2** *vi* to caramelize, to turn to caramel. **3 se caraméliser** *vpr* (*of roast*) to brown (well); (*of sugar*) to caramelize.

carapace [karapas] *nf* carapace, shell (*of lobster etc*).

carapater(se) [səkarapate] *vpr Arg* to hop it, to scarper, to scram.

carat [kara] *nm* **(a)** carat; **or (à) dix-huit carats,** eighteen-carat gold; **(b) c. métrique,** carat (weight) (0,2 gr.).

Caravage(le) [ləkaravaʒ] *nm* Caravaggio.

caravanage [karavanaʒ] *nm* = **CARAVAN(N)ING.**

caravane [karavan] *nf* **(a)** (*du désert*) caravan, desert convoy; *F* conducted party, procession (*of tourists, schoolchildren etc*); **la c. qui suit les coureurs du Tour de France,** the caravan that follows in the wake of the Tour de France cyclists; **(b)** (*remorque*) caravan, *Am* (house) trailer, camper.

caravaneige [karavanɛʒ] *nm* **(a)** (*activité*) winter caravan(n)ing; **(b)** (*caravane*) caravan equipped for use in winter.

caravanier [karavanje] **1** *nm* **(a)** *Aut* caravan(n)er; **(b)** (*in desert*) caravaneer. **2** *adj* **chemin c.,** caravan route *or* track.

caravan(n)ing [karavaniŋ] *nm* **faire du c.,** to go caravan(n)ing.

caravansérail [karavɑ̃seraj] *nm* caravanserai; *Fig* **cette ville est un c.,** it's a very cosmopolitan city.

caravelle [karavɛl] *nf* **(a)** *Nau* car(a)vel; **(b)** *Av* Caravelle ® (air liner).

carbochimie [karbɔʃimi] *nf Ch* organic chemistry.

carbonate [karbɔnat] *nm Ch* carbonate; **c. de soude,** carbonate of soda, sodium carbonate; *Com* washing soda.

carbone [karbɔn] *nm Ch* carbon; **c. 14,** carbon 14, radiocarbon; **datation au c. 14,** radiocarbon dating; *Com* **(papier) c.,** carbon (paper).

carbonifère [karbɔnifɛr] **1** *adj Géol* Carboniferous. **2** *nm Géol* the Carboniferous.

carbonique [karbɔnik] *adj Ch* carbonic; **anhydride c., gaz c.,** carbon dioxide; **acide c.,** carbonic acid; **neige c.,** dry ice.

carbonisation [karbɔ̃nizɑsjɔ̃] *nf* carbonization.

carboniser [karbɔnize] *vt* to carbonize (*bones etc*); to char (*wood*); to burn (*meat etc*) to a cinder; **être carbonisé,** to be burnt to death.

carbon(n)ade [karbɔnad] *nf Culin* **bifteck à la c.,** charcoal-grilled steak.

carbonyle [karbɔnil] *nm Ch* carbonyl.

carborundum [karbɔrɔ̃dɔm] *nm Ch* carborundum.

carburant [karbyrɑ̃] **1** *nm* fuel; *Fig* **voilà cinquante francs, ça te servira de c. jusqu'à demain,** here's 50 F, that'll keep you going until tomorrow. **2** *adj* containing hydrocarbon; **mélange c.,** mixture (of petrol and air).

carburateur [karbyratœr] *nm Aut* carburettor, *US* carburetor.

carburation [karbyrɑsjɔ̃] *nf* **(a)** *Métal* carburization; **(b)** (*de l'essence etc*) carburation.

carbure [karbyr] *nm Ch* carbide; **c. de calcium,** calcium carbide.

carburé [karbyre] *adj* **(a)** *Métal* carburized; **(b)** carburetted (*air*).

carburéacteur [karbyreaktœr] *nm Tech* aviation fuel.

carburer [karbyre] **1** *vt Métal* to carburize. **2** *vi* **(a)** to vaporize; **le moteur carbure mal,** the mixture is wrong; **(b)** *F* to work, to go well; **ça carbure,** it's going fine *or* like a bomb; **ça ne carbure pas fort,** it's not going very well.

carcajou [karkaʒu] *nm* wolverine, *Am* carcajou.

carcan [karkɑ̃] *nm Fig* (*contrainte*) yoke, restraint; *Hist* iron collar; **le c. des horaires,** scheduling constraints.

carcasse [karkas] *nf* **(a)** (*pour la boucherie*) carcass, carcase; *F* body (*of living person*); *F* **promener sa c.,** to moon around; **(b)** frame(work) (*of umbrella etc*); shell, skeleton (*of house, ship etc*); carcass (*of ship, electric motor*); shape (*of hat etc*); casing (*of tyre*).

carcéral, -aux [karseral, -o] *adj* prison (*life*).
carcinogène [karsinɔʒɛn] *adj Méd* carcinogenic.
carcinologie [karsinɔlɔʒi] *nf Méd* oncology, study of cancer.
carcinome [karsinom] *nm Méd* carcinoma.
cardage [kardaʒ] *nm Tex* **(a)** carding, combing (*of wool etc*); **(b)** teaseling (*of cloth*).
cardan [kardɑ̃] *nm Aut* **c.** *ou* **joint de C.**, universal joint, Cardan joint.
carde [kard] *nf* **(a)** *Culin* chard; **(b)** *Tex* card, carding brush; teasel (*frame*).
carder [karde] *vt Tex* **(a)** to card (*wool etc*); **(b)** to teasel (*cloth*).
cardeur, -euse [kardœr, -øz] *Tex* **1** *n* carder, teaseler. **2** *nf* **cardeuse,** carding machine, carder.
cardiaque [kardjak] **1** *adj* cardiac (*nerves, murmur etc*); **crise c.,** heart attack; **être c.,** to have heart trouble *or* a weak heart. **2** *n* person with heart disease.
cardigan [kardigɑ̃] *nm* cardigan.
cardinal, -aux [kardinal, -o] **1** *adj* cardinal (*point, number, virtue*); chief (*altar etc*). **2** *nm* **(a)** *Cathol* cardinal; **(b)** cardinal (bird).
cardinalat [kardinala] *nm Cathol* cardinalship.
cardinalice [kardinalis] *adj Cathol* of a cardinal; **revêtir la pourpre c.,** to don the scarlet; **élever qn à la dignité c.,** to make s.o. a cardinal.
cardiogramme [kardjɔgram] *nm Méd* cardiogram.
cardiographe [kardjɔgraf] *nm Méd* cardiograph.
cardiographie [kardjɔgrafi] *nf Méd* cardiography.
cardiologie [kardjɔlɔʒi] *nf Méd* cardiology.
cardiologue [kardjɔlɔg] *n Méd* cardiologist, heart specialist; **chirurgien c.,** heart surgeon.
cardiorespiratoire [kardjɔrɛspiratwar] *adj Méd* cardiorespiratory.
cardio-vasculaire [kardjɔvaskylɛr] *adj Anat Méd* cardiovascular; *Méd* **accident c.-v.,** cardio-vascular accident, *F* stroke.
cardite [kardit] *nf Med* carditis.
cardon [kardɔ̃] *nm Bot* cardoon.
carême [karɛm] *nm* **(a)** (*période*) Lent; **(b)** (*jeûne*) (Lenten) fast(ing); **faire (son) c.,** to keep Lent, to fast; *Fig* **face de c.,** dismal face; **(c)** *Litt* (course of) Lenten sermons.
carême-prenant [karɛmprənɑ̃] *nm Arch* Shrovetide; (*pl carêmes-prenants*).
carénage [karenaʒ] *nm* **(a)** *Nau* careening, careenage (*of ship*); (*lieu*) careening beach, careenage; **(b)** *Av Aut* streamlining; fairing (*of the lines*).
carence [karɑ̃s] *nf* **(a)** *Méd* deficiency (**de,** in, of); **c. en vitamine E,** deficiency in vitamin E, vitamin E deficiency; **maladie de** *ou* **par c.,** deficiency disease; **c. affective,** emotional deprivation; **(b)** (*impuissance*) shirking of one's obligations; **la c. du père,** (*dans l'éducation de son enfant*) the father's non-participation; **(c)** *Jur* insolvency.
carencé [karɑ̃se] *adj Psy* emotionally deprived; **enfant c.,** emotionally deprived child.
carène [karɛn] *nf* **(a)** bottom, (underwater) hull (*of ship*); **abattre un navire en c.,** to careen a ship; **(b)** *Bot* carina, keel.
caréner [karene] *vt* **(je carène; je carénerai) (a)** *Nau* to careen (*ship*); **(b)** *Av Aut* to streamline.
carentiel, -ielle [karɑ̃sjɛl] *adj* **maladie carentielle,** deficiency disease.
caressant [karɛsɑ̃] *adj* tender (*look etc*); soft, gentle (*wind*); affectionate (*child etc*); **d'une voix caressante,** (*dire*) tenderly, affectionately; (*pour calmer*) soothingly.
caresse [karɛs] *nf* **(a)** (*d'affection*) caress; **faire des caresses à,** to caress (*s.o.*); to pat, to stroke, to make a fuss of (*dog*); *Fig* **la c. du soleil,** the sun's caress; **(b)** *Vieilli* (*flatterie*) flattery.
caresser [karese] *vt* **(a)** (*par affection*) to caress (*s.o.*); to pat, to make a fuss of (*animal*); **c. qn du regard,** to look affectionately at s.o.; **(b)** to cherish (*hope etc*); to toy with (*idea*); **c. un projet,** to nurture a project; **(c)** *Vieilli* to flatter (*s.o.*); **cette idée caresse son amour-propre,** the idea flatters his self-esteem.
car-ferry [karfɛri] *nm* car ferry.
cargaison [kargɛzɔ̃] *nf* cargo, freight; *F* load (*of passengers etc*); **c. de charbon/de marchandises,** cargo of coal/merchandise; **décharger la c.,** to unload the cargo; *Fig* **toute une c. d'histoires belges,** a whole load *or* repertoire of Belgian jokes; **j'avais préparé toute une c. d'excuses,** I had all sorts of excuses prepared.
cargo [kargo] *nm Nau* cargo boat, freighter; tramp (steamer); **c. mixte,** cargo and passenger vessel.
cargue [karg] *nf Nau* brail (*of sail*).
carguer [karge] *vt Nau* to take in, to clew (up), to brail (up) (*sail*).
cariant [karjɑ̃] *adj* **substance cariante,** substance that causes cavities *or* tooth decay.
cariatide [karjatid] *nf Archit* caryatid.
caribou [karibu] *nm Zool* caribou.
caricatural, -aux [karikatyral, -o] *adj* caricatural.
caricature [karikatyr] *nf* (*dessin etc*) caricature; **le film est un c. de la vie ouvrière,** the film is a caricature of working class life; *F* **quelle c. que cette femme!,** what a fright that woman is!
caricaturer [karikatyre] *vt* to caricature.
caricaturiste [karikatyrist] *n* caricaturist.
carie [kari] *nf* **(a)** *Méd* caries, decay (*of bone*); **c. dentaire,** dental caries, tooth decay; **(b)** blight (*of trees*); smut, bunt (*of cereals*).
carié [karje] *adj Méd* decayed, bad (*tooth*).
carier [karje] *Méd vtr* **1** to rot, to decay. **2 se carier** *vpr* to rot, to decay.
carillon [karijɔ̃] *nm* (*sonnerie*) chime(s), carillon; (*ensemble de cloches*) peal of bells; (*de porte*) (door) chime(s); *Mus* tubular bells, chimes; **(horloge à) c.,** chiming clock.
carillonnement [karijɔnmɑ̃] *nm* chiming, ringing (*of bells*).
carillonner [karijɔne] **1** *vi* (*faire sonner les cloches*) to ring the bells, to ring a peal; (*des cloches*) to chime; **c. à la porte,** to ring the (door) bell loudly. **2** *vt* to chime (*air*); to announce (*church festival*) with a full peal; *Fig* **c. la nouvelle,** to spread the news far and wide, to tell the news to all and sundry; **il carillonne la naissance de son enfant,** he's been telling everyone that he's a father; **fête carillonnée,** high festival.
carillonneur [karijɔnœr] *nm* bellringer.
cariste [karist] *n Tech* fork-lift truck driver.
caritatif, -ive [karitatif, iv] *adj* charitable; **association caritative,** charitable organization, charity.
carlin [karlɛ̃] *nm* (*chien*) pug.
carlingue [karlɛ̃g] *nf* **(a)** *Nau* ke(e)lson; **(b)** *Av* cabin.
carliste [karlist] *n Hist* Carlist.
carmagnole [karmaɲɔl] *nf Hist* **(a)** (*veste*) jacket (worn by Revolutionaries in 1793); **(b)** *Mus* (*ronde*) carmagnole.
carme [karm] *nm Rel* Carmelite (friar), White friar.
Carmel [karmɛl] *nm* **(a)** *Rel* **le C.,** the Carmelite order; **(b)** (*couvent*) Carmelite monastery *or* convent.
carmélite [karmelit] *nf Rel* Carmelite (nun).
carmin [karmɛ̃] **1** *adj inv* carmine, crimson. **2** *nm* carmine.
carminé [karmine] *adj* carmine-coloured, ruby.
carnage [karnaʒ] *nm* carnage, slaughter.
carnassier, -ière [karnasje, -jɛr] **1** *adj* carnivorous, flesh- eating (*animal*); *Zool* carnassial (*tooth*). **2** *nm* carnivore; **les carnassiers,** the Carnivora. **3** *nf* **carnassière (a)** *Zool* carnassial (tooth); **(b)** (*sac*) game bag.
carnation [karnɑsjɔ̃] *nf* **(a)** (*complexion*) complexion; **c. de blonde,** fair skin *or* complexion; **(b)** *Beaux-Arts* flesh tint, carnation.
carnaval, -als [karnaval] *nm* (*fête*) carnival; **Sa Majesté C.,** King Carnival; *F* **c'est un vrai c.,** he looks a real clown.
carnavalesque [karnavalɛsk] *adj* **tenue c.,** carnival costume; *Péj* **un accoutrement c.,** a ridiculous get-up.
carne [karn] *nf F* **(a)** (*viande*) tough meat; (*vieux cheval*) old nag; **(b)** *Arg* **quelle c.!,** what a pig *or* brute!; (*cette femme*) what a bitch *or* cow!
carné [karne] *adj* **(a)** (*rose*) flesh-coloured; **(b) régime c.,** meat diet.
carneau, -eaux [karno] *nm Tech* (boiler) flue.
carnet [karnɛ] *nm* notebook; **écrire qch dans son c.,** to write sth (down) in one's notebook; **c. d'adresses,** address book; *Com* **c. de commandes,** order book; *Scol* **c. (de notes),** = (school) report; *Vieilli* **c. de bal,** dance card; **c. à souche(s),** counterfoil book; **c. de chèques,** cheque book; **c. de timbres,** book of stamps; **c. (de tickets d'autobus** *etc*), book of tickets; *Aut etc* **c. de route** *ou* **de bord,** logbook.
•**carnier** [karnje] *nm* game bag.
carnivore [karnivɔr] *Zool* **1** *adj* carnivorous, flesh-eating (*animal*). **2** *nm* carnivore; **carnivores,** Carnivora.
carolingien, -ienne [karɔlɛ̃ʒjɛ̃, -jɛn] *Hist* **1** *adj* Carolingian, Carlovingian. **2** *n* **C.,** Carolingian, Carlovingian.
Caron [karɔ̃] *nm Myth* Charon.
caroncule [karɔ̃kyl] *nf Anat Bot Zool* caruncle; wattle (*of turkey*).
carotène [karɔtɛn] *nm* carotene.
carotide [karɔtid] *adj* carotid (*artery*).
carottage [karɔtaʒ] *nm* **(a)** *F* (*vol*) pinching, *Br* nicking;

(*escroquerie*) swindling, diddling; **(b)** *Min* taking (of) cores.
carotte [karɔt] **1** *nf* **(a)** (*plante*) carrot; *F* **la c. ou le bâton,** the carrot and the stick; *F* **Poil de c.,** Ginger; *F* **vos carottes sont cuites,** you've cooked your goose, you're done for; **(b)** *Min* core (sample); plug (*of tobacco*); *F* tobacconist's sign; **(c)** *F* **tirer une c. à qn,** to swindle *or* diddle s.o.; **(d)** *Tennis F* drop shot. **2** *adj inv* **cheveux (rouge) c.,** ginger *or F* carroty hair.
carotter [karɔte] *vt F* **(a)** (*voler*) to pinch, *Br* to nick (*sth*); (*faire de l'escroquerie*) to do, to swindle, to diddle (*s.o.*); **c. une permission/une signature,** to wangle leave/a signature; **(b)** *Min* to take a (core) sample of.
carotteur, -euse [karɔtœr, -øz] **, carottier, -ière** [karɔtje, -jɛr] *n F* (*voleur*) thief; (*escroc*) swindler.
carotteuse [karɔtøz] *nf Tech* core sampler.
caroube [karub] *nf Bot* carob (bean).
caroubier [karubje] *nm Bot* carob tree.
carpaccio [karpatʃio] *nm Culin* carpaccio.
Carpates [karpat] *nfpl* **les C.,** Carpathian Mountains, Carpathians.
carpe¹ [karp] *nm Anat* carpus, wrist.
carpe² *nf (poisson)* carp; *Natation* **saut de c.,** jack-knife (dive); **faire des sauts de c.,** to bounce around; **faire des yeux de c.,** to make sheep's eyes; **être muet comme une c.,** (*discret*) to be as silent as the grave; **tu étais muet comme une c. toute la soirée,** you didn't open your mouth all evening; **bâiller comme une c.,** to yawn one's head off.
carpeau, -eaux [karpo] *nm (poisson)* young carp.
carpette [karpɛt] *nf* rug, *Am* area rug; *F* **s'aplatir comme une c.,** to behave like a doormat; *Péj* **c'est une vraie c.,** he's a doormat.
carpiculture [karpikyltyr] *nf* carp farming.
carpien, -ienne [karpjɛ̃, -jɛn] *adj Anat* carpal (*bone etc*).
carquois [karkwa] *nm* quiver; *Litt* **il a vidé son c.,** he has shot his bolt.
Carrare [karar] *n* **(a)** Carrara; **(b) c.,** Carrara marble.
carre [kɑr] *nf* corner (*of book etc*); edge (*of skate, ski*); cross section (*of board etc*); **lâcher les carres,** to flatten *or* take the edge off the skis.
carré, -ée [kare] **1** *adj* **(a)** *Géom* square (*figure, garden etc*); square, broad (*shoulders*); *Math* **nombre c.,** square number; **dix mètres carrés,** ten square metres; **partie carrée,** foursome; *F* **tête carrée,** stubborn person;
(b) (*tranché*) plain, straightforward, blunt (*answer, person*); outspoken (*person*); **être c. en affaires,** to be honest in business.
2 *nm* square; *Math* square (*of a number*); *Can* (public) square; *Culin* loin (*of lamb etc*); *Math* **élever au c.,** to square; *Math* **le c. de 6** *ou* **six au c.,** 6 squared; **c. de papier,** slip of paper; **c. de soie,** silk square; **c. (d'un escalier),** landing; **c. de choux,** cabbage patch; *Nau* **c. (des officiers),** wardroom; *Mil* **former le c.,** to get into square formation; *Cartes* **c. de valets,** four jacks; **c. de l'Est,** = type of soft cheese.
3 *nf* **carrée (a)** *Mus Arch* breve;
(b) *F* (*chambre*) room, digs.
carreau, -eaux [karo] *nm* **(a)** (*motif*) small square; **tissu à carreaux,** check(ed) material; *Beaux-Arts* **mettre un croquis au c.,** to square up a sketch;
(b) (*de céramique etc*) (floor, wall) tile; (*dalle*) flag(stone);
(c) (*de fenêtre*) (window) pane; **laveur de carreaux,** window cleaner *or Am* washer; **regarder aux carreaux,** to look out of *or* in at the window; **un c. cassé,** a broken window;
(d) *F* **carreaux,** (*lunettes*) glasses, specs;
(e) (*sol*) floor; **laver le c.,** to wash the floor; **coucher qn sur le c.,** to lay s.o. out; **rester sur le c.,** (*être tué*) to be killed on the spot; (*être blessé*) to be critically injured; (*être éliminé*) to be out of the running; (*d'un boxeur*) to remain on the canvas; **le c. des Halles,** (*in Paris*) the (floor of the) market; *Min* **c. de mine,** pit head;
(f) *Cartes* diamond; *Fig* **se garder** *ou* **se tenir à c.,** to take every precaution.
carrefour [karfur] *nm* **(a)** (*de route*) crossroads; (*in town*) square, circus; **tête de c.,** T-junction; *Fig* **être à un c.,** to be at a crossroads; **un c. de nouvelles idées/de tendances,** a place for the exchange of new ideas/trends; **c. des transports/techniques,** (*ville, région*) transport(ation)/technology hub; **(b)** (*réunion*) forum, symposium.
carrelage [karlaʒ] *nm* **(a)** (*action*) tiling; **(b)** (*carreaux*) tiling, tiles; (*sol*) tile(d) floor; (*mur*) tiled wall; (*dalles*) flagstone pavement *or* floor(ing).
carreler [karle] *vt* (**je carrelle, n. carrelons; je carrellerai**) **(a)** (*mettre des carreaux*) to tile (*floor, walls*); (*mettre des dalles*) to lay (*floor*) with flags; to pave (*yard*); **(b)** (*tracer*) to draw squares on, to square (*sheet of paper etc*).
carrelet [karlɛ] *nm* **(a)** (*règle*) square ruler; **(b)** (*aiguille*) large needle; (*de cordonnerie*) sewing awl; **(c)** *Pêche* square dipping net; **(d)** (*poisson*) plaice.
carreleur [karlœr] *nm* tile layer, tiler; (*d'une cour*) paver.
carrément [karemɑ̃] *adv Géom* square(ly); **pièce coupée c.,** square-cut piece; *F* **il y est allé c.,** he made no bones about it, he didn't beat about the bush; **je lui ai dit c. ce que je pensais,** I told him straight (out) *or* in no uncertain terms what I thought.
carrer [kare] **1** *vt* to square (*plank, Math number etc*). **2 se carrer** *vpr* to settle (down) (**dans un fauteuil,** in an armchair).
carrier [karje] *nm* quarryman, quarrier; **(maître) c.,** quarry-owner.
carrière¹ [karjɛr] *nf* **(a)** (*professionnelle etc*) career; **suivre une c. dans le** *ou* **faire c. dans le commerce,** to be in business; **c. politique/des armes,** political/military career; **militaire de c.,** regular (soldier); **diplomate de c.,** professional *or* career diplomat; **elle est de la c.,** she is in the diplomatic service; **(b)** (*voie, chemin*) course (*of life*); *Arch* racecourse, arena; **être au bout de sa c.,** to be at the end of one's life; **la c. du succès,** the road to success; **(c) donner c. à un cheval,** to give free rein to a horse; *Fig* **donner (libre) c. à son imagination,** to give free rein *or* free play *or* full scope to one's imagination; **donner c. à ses sentiments** *ou* **à ses opinions, se donner c.,** to let oneself go.
carrière² *nf* (stone) quarry; **c. à ciel ouvert,** open quarry.
carriériste [karjerist] *adj & n Péj* careerist.
carriole [karjɔl] *nf* **(a)** (*petite charette*) light cart, carriole; **(b)** *Can* (horsedrawn) sled, sleigh.
carrossable [karɔsabl] *adj (chemin, route)* suitable for motor vehicles.
carrosse [karɔs] *nm* (horse-drawn) coach; **c. d'apparat,** state coach; *F* **rouler c.,** to live in great style; *Can* **c. de bébé,** pram, *Am* baby carriage.
carrosser [karɔse] *vt Aut* to fit the body to (*chassis*); *Arg* **elle est bien carrossée,** she's got curves in all the right places.
carrosserie [karɔsri] *nf Aut* **(a)** (*construction*) coachbuilding; **(b)** (*caisse*) body, coachwork (*of car etc*).
carrossier [karɔsje] *nm Aut* coachbuilder.
carroté [karɔte] *adj Can* (*chemise etc*) check(ed).
carrousel [karuzɛl] *nm* **(a)** (*d'une aérogare*) *& Équitation* carousel; **(b)** *Fig* **le c. des ministres,** the ministerial merry-go-round; **(c)** *Hist* (*parade*) tournament; (*lieu*) tiltyard.
carrure [kɑryr] *nf* **(a)** (*de personne, manteau*) width across the shoulders; **homme d'une belle c.,** well-built *or* burly man; **(b)** (*de mâchoire etc*) broadness, squareness; *Fig* **elle est d'une grande c.,** she's a very impressive woman; *Fig* **il est d'une autre c. que ses concurrents,** he is very much more impressive than his competitors; *Fig* **avoir la c. d'un cadre supérieur,** (*d'un employé*) to be senior management material.
carry [kari] *nm* = **CURRY.**
cartable [kartabl] *nm* school bag.
cartapuce [kartapys] *nf* smart card.
carte [kart] *nf* **(a)** (*géographique*) map; *surtout Nau* chart; **c. d'état-major,** = Ordnance Survey map; **c. météorologique,** meteorological *or* weather map *or* chart; **c. routière,** road map; **c. du ciel,** astronomical map *or* chart; **dresser la c. d'une région,** to map (out) an area;
(b) (*carton*) (piece of) card(board); **jeu de (52) cartes,** pack *or Am* deck of cards; **c. (à jouer),** (playing) card; **jouer aux cartes,** to play cards; **une partie de cartes,** a game of cards; **donner** *ou* **faire les cartes,** to deal (the cards); **château de cartes,** house of cards; *Fig* **jouer cartes sur table,** to put one's cards on the table; *Fig* **c'était la c. forcée,** it was Hobson's choice; *Fig* **voir le dessous des cartes,** to be in the know; *Fig* **brouiller les cartes,** to complicate matters, to confuse the issue; *Fig* **avoir plus d'une c. dans son jeu,** to have more than one string to one's bow; **c. (de visite),** (visiting, *Am* calling) card; **carte d'affaires,** business card; **laisser sa c. chez qn,** to leave one's card; **c. (postale),** (post)card; **c. de correspondance,** (plain) postcard; **c. de vœux,** greetings card; **c. d'anniversaire,** birthday *or* anniversary card; **c. d'entrée,** admission card; **c. d'abonnement,** (*pour la bibliothèque etc*) membership ticket; (*pour les transports, le théâtre etc*) season ticket; **c. de circulation,** (rail, bus *etc*)

pass; **avoir la c. du parti,** to be a card-carrying member of the party; *Av* **c. d'embarquement,** boarding pass; **c. d'identité,** identity card; **c. de séjour,** residence permit; **c. d'électeur,** voting card; **c. d'invitation,** (formal) invitation; **c. de lecteur,** library *or* reader's ticket; *Aut* **c. grise,** ≈ (vehicle) registration document; **c. de chemin de fer,** season ticket; **c. orange,** (*à Paris*) = combined monthly pass for the underground, bus and suburban train; *Admin* **c. de commerce,** trading licence; **c. d'alimentation,** ration book; **femme en c.,** registered prostitute; *Fig* **donner c. blanche à qn,** to give s.o. carte blanche *or* a free hand; **c. (de restaurant),** menu; **c. du jour,** menu for the day; **c. des vins,** wine list; **manger à la c.,** to eat à la carte;

(c) *Ordinat* card; **c. de circuits imprimés,** printed circuit board, *F* PCB; **c. d'extension,** expansion board; **c. fille,** daughterboard; **c. mère,** motherboard; **c. perforée** *ou* **mécanographique,** punch card;

(d) (*magnétique*) card; **c. bancaire,** cash card; **c. de crédit,** credit card; **c. Visa** ®/*etc*, Visa ®/*etc* card; **c. à puce** *ou* **à mémoire,** smart card; **c. de téléphone,** phonecard;

(e) *Com* card (*of buttons etc*); **c. d'échantillons,** sample card.

cartel¹ [kartɛl] *nm* (*d'horloge*) dial case; (*horloge*) (hanging) wall clock.

cartel² *nm* **(a)** *Écon* cartel, trust, combine; **c. de l'acier,** steel cartel; **c. de production,** production cartel; **(b)** *Pol* coalition.

carte-lettre [kart(ə)lɛtr] *nf* letter-card; (*pl cartes-lettres*).

cartellisation [kartelizasjɔ̃] *nf Écon* cartelization.

carter [kartɛr] *nm* case, casing, housing (*of gear etc*); cover (*of small machines etc*); *Aut* crankcase; **fond de c.,** sump.

carte-réponse [kartrepɔ̃s] *nf* reply card; (*pl cartes-réponses*).

carterie [kartəri] *nf Com* card shop; *Ind* greetings card industry.

cartésianisme [kartezjanism] *nm Phil* Cartesianism.

cartésien, -ienne [kartezjɛ̃, -jɛn] *adj & n Phil Math* Cartesian.

carte-vue [kartvy] *nf* picture postcard; (*pl cartes-vues*).

carthaginois, -oise [kartaʒinwa, -waz] *Hist* **1** *adj* Carthaginian. **2** *n* **C.,** Carthaginian.

cartilage [kartilaʒ] *nm Anat* cartilage; (*in meat*) gristle.

cartilagineux, -euse [kartilaʒinø, -øz] *adj Anat* cartilaginous; (*meat*) gristly.

cartographe [kartɔgraf] *n* cartographer.

cartographie [kartɔgrafi] *nf* cartography; **c. des gènes,** gene *or* genetic mapping.

cartographique [kartɔgrafik] *adj* cartographic(al).

cartomancie [kartɔmɑ̃si] *nf* fortune telling (by cards).

cartomancien,-ienne [kartɔmɑ̃sjɛ̃, -jɛn] *n* fortune teller (by cards).

carton [kartɔ̃] *nm* **(a)** (*feuille, support*) cardboard; (*plus mince*) pasteboard; **c. ondulé,** corrugated paper; **c. gris,** chipboard; **c. épais,** millboard; **c. bristol,** Bristol board; **poupée/masque de c.,** papier mâché doll/mask; *Fig* **caractère de c.-pâte,** (*factice*) cardboard character; *F* **maison de c.,** jerry-built house; **envoyer un c.,** to send an invitation; **(b)** (*boîte*) (cardboard) box, carton; (*dossier*) (cardboard) file; **des cartons de déménagement,** cardboard boxes for moving (house); **c. à chapeau(x),** hatbox; **c. à dessin,** portfolio; **(c)** *Beaux-Arts* cartoon, sketch; **(d) faire un c.,** (*au tir*) to fill a target; **faire un bon c.,** to make a good score; *Scol Fig F* **avoir un c.,** to get a bad mark; **(e)** *Géog* inset (map).

cartonnage [kartɔnaʒ] *nm* **(a)** (*objets en carton*) (cardboard) boxes, cases, packing; (*fabrication*) making of cardboard articles; cardboard trade; **(b)** (*reliure*) (binding in) paper boards; **c. pleine toile,** (binding in) cloth boards; **c. souple,** limp boards.

cartonner [kartɔne] *vt* to bind (*book*) in boards, to case (*book*); **livre cartonné,** hardback (book).

cartonnerie [kartɔnri] *nf* **(a)** *Ind* cardboard factory; **(b)** *Com* cardboard trade.

cartonneux, -euse [kartɔnø, -øz] *adj* like cardboard; **neige cartonneuse,** snow with a crust on top; **fromage c.,** cheese that tastes like cardboard.

cartonnier, -ière [kartɔnje, -jɛr] *nm* **(a)** *Ind Com* cardboard manufacturer; cardboard seller; **(b)** (*meuble*) filing cabinet.

carton-paille [kartɔ̃pɑj] *nm* strawboard; (*pl cartons-pailles*).

carton-pâte [kartɔ̃pɑt] *nm* pasteboard; **un décor de c.-p.,** cardboard scenery; (*pl cartons-pâtes*).

cartoon [kartun] *nm* cartoon.

cartopuciste [kartɔpysist] *n* (credit) card user; (phone)card user.

cartouche [kartuʃ] **1** *nm Archit etc* cartouche; (*pour titre*) title. **2** *nf* (*de fusil, d'explosif, de stylo*) cartridge; (*de machine à écrire*) *& Phot* cartridge, cassette; **cent cartouches,** a hundred rounds (*of ammunition*); **c. à blanc,** blank cartridge; **c. de chasse,** sporting cartridge; **c. de rechange,** (*de stylo*) refill; **une c. de cigarettes,** a carton of cigarettes.

cartoucherie [kartuʃri] *nf* (*fabrique*) cartridge *or* ammunition factory; (*dépôt*) cartridge *or* ammunition store.

cartouchière [kartuʃjɛr] *nf* (*sac*) cartridge pouch; (*ceinture*) cartridge belt.

carvi [karvi] *nm* (*plante*) caraway; **(graines de) c.,** caraway seeds.

caryatide [karjatid] *nf Archit* caryatid.

cas [kɑ] *nm* **(a)** (*situation*) case, circumstance, situation; (*événement*) occurrence; *Jur Méd* case; **c. limite,** borderline case; **c. imprévu,** unforeseen event; **c. général/particulier,** general/particular case; **c. urgent,** emergency *or* urgent case; **c. de vie ou de mort,** matter of life and death; **dans le premier c.,** in the first instance; **c'est bien le c. de le dire,** there's no mistake about it, you can say that again; **c'est le c. ou jamais de le faire;** now if ever *or* now or never is the time to do it; **en pareil c.,** in a similar situation, in similar circumstances; **c'est un c. d'espèce,** it depends upon the particular circumstances; **c. de divorce,** divorce case; (*raisons*) grounds for divorce; **c. de rougeole,** case of measles; **ce malade est un c. désespéré,** this patient is a hopeless case; *Fig* **c'est un c.!,** he is a case!; **c. de conscience,** matter of conscience;

(b) faire (grand) c. de qn/qch, to value s.o./sth (highly), to have a high opinion of s.o./sth, to set great store by s.o./sth; **faire peu de c. de qch,** to have a poor opinion of sth; **je ne fais pas grand c. de votre ami,** I don't think much of your friend; **ne faire aucun c. de qch,** to leave sth out of account, to take no notice of sth;

(c) *Gram* case; **au c. nominatif,** in the nominative (case);

(d) (*locutions*) **en** *ou* **dans ce c.,** in that case, if that is the case, if so, under those circumstances; **en aucun c.,** under no circumstances, on no account, not on any account; **en tout c., dans tous les c.,** in any case, in all events; **dans ce c.-là,** in that case; **dans tous les c. il est trop tard,** it's too late now anyway *or* anyhow; **le c. échéant,** should the occasion arise; **selon le c.,** as the case may be; **en c. de nécessité,** if need be, if necessary; **en c. de pluie,** in the event of rain; **en c. d'accident/d'urgence,** in case of (an) accident/(an) emergency; **au c. où** *ou* **dans le c. où il viendrait,** if he comes; **au c. où ce serait exact,** should it prove correct; *F* **je te le laisse au c. où,** I'll leave it for you just in case.

casanier, -ière [kazanje, -jɛr] **1** *adj* home-loving. **2** *n* homebody, *Péj* stay-at-home.

casaque [kazak] *nf* blouse, jacket (*of jockey*); *Fig* **tourner c.,** (*partir*) to flee, to turn tail; (*changer d'opinion*) to turn one's coat.

casbah [kazba] *nf* casbah, kasbah.

cascade [kaskad] *nf* **(a)** (*chute d'eau*) cascade, waterfall; **c. d'un glacier,** ice fall; *Fig* **cascades de rires,** peals of laughter; *Él* **montage en c.,** connection in series; **(b)** *Cin* stunt.

cascader [kaskade] *vi* **(a)** *Litt* to cascade; **(b)** *F Vieilli* (*faire la noce*) to live a wild life.

cascadeur, -euse [kaskadœr, -øz] **1** *adj F Vieilli* wild, loose, fast (*life etc*). **2** *n* **(a)** *Cin* stuntman, stuntwoman; (*de cirque*) acrobat; **(b)** *F Vieilli* (*noceur*) reveller.

cascher [kaʃɛr] = **KASCHER.**

case [kɑz] *nf* **(a)** (*hutte*) hut, cabin; **(b)** compartment, division (*of drawer etc*); pigeonhole (*of letter rack*); space, box (*on printed form*); square (*of crossword, chessboard*); **c. postale,** Post Office *or* P.O. box; *F* **il lui manque une c., il a une c. vide** *ou* **une c. en moins,** he's got a screw loose.

caséeux, -euse [kazeø, -øz] *adj* caseous.

caséine [kazein] *nf Ch* casein.

casemate [kazmat] *nf Mil* blockhouse, pillbox.

caser [kɑze] **1** *vt* **(a)** (*placer*) to put *or* stow (*sth*) away; **c. des papiers,** to file papers (away); **(b)** *F* (*loger*) to put (*s.o.*) up; **il est bien casé,** he's got a good place to live; **(c)** *F* (*établir dans une situation*) to find a job for (*s.o.*); **elle est bien casée,** she has got a good job; **(d)** *F* (*marier*) **elle a trois filles à c.,** she has three daughters to marry off. **2 se caser** *vpr F* (*se marier*) to (get married and) settle

down; (*trouver un emploi*) to find a job; (*trouver un logement*) to find somewhere to live.
caserne [kazɛrn] *nf Mil & F Péj* barracks; **quand j'étais à la c.,** when I was in the army; **plaisanteries de c.,** coarse jokes, barrackroom jokes; **c. de pompiers,** fire station.
casernement [kazɛrnəmɑ̃] *nm Mil* **(a)** barracking, quartering (*of troops*); **(b)** (*lieu*) barrack block.
caserner [kazɛrne] *vt Mil* to quarter (*troops*) in barracks, to barrack (*troops*).
casernier, -ière [kazɛrnje, -jɛr] *nm Mil* barrack warden.
cash [kaʃ] *adv F* cash; **payer c.,** to pay cash (down).
cash and carry [kaʃɛndkari] *Com* **1** *nm inv* cash-and-carry (store). **2** *adj inv* cash-and-carry (*sale etc*).
cash-flow [kaʃlo] *nm Com* cash flow.
casier [kɑzje] *nm* **(a)** (*pour le courrier*) (*meuble*) (set of) pigeonholes; (*compartiment*) pigeonhole; (*pour ses vêtements etc*) locker; **c. à bagages,** luggage locker; **(b) c. judiciaire,** police record; **son c. judiciaire est vierge,** he has a clean record; **(c) c. à bouteilles,** bottle *or* wine rack; **c. à disques,** record rack; **c. à musique,** music cabinet; **(d)** *Pêche* **c. (à homards),** lobster pot.
casino [kazino] *nm* casino.
casoar [kazɔar] *nm* **(a)** (*oiseau*) cassowary; **(b)** (*plumet*) plume (*worn by cadets of Saint-Cyr*).
Caspienne [kaspjɛn] **1** *adj* **la mer C.,** the Caspian Sea. **2** *nf* **la C.,** the Caspian Sea.
casque [kask] *nm* **(a)** helmet (*of soldier, fireman etc*); (crash) helmet (*of motorcyclist*); **le port du c. est obligatoire,** helmets must be worn; **c. colonial,** pith helmet, topee; **Casques blancs,** United Nations military observers; **les Casques bleus,** (*de l'ONU*) the Blue Berets; **(b)** *Rad etc* **c. (à écouteurs),** headphones, *Am* headset; **écouter un disque au c.,** to listen to a record on one's headphones ; **(c)** *Orn* casque; *Bot* helmet; **(d)** (*de salon de coiffure*) (hair) drier.
casqué [kaske] *adj* helmeted.
casquer [kaske] *vi Arg* (*payer*) to fork out, to shell out.
casquette [kaskɛt] *nf* (*chapeau*) cap; *Fig* **avoir plusieurs casquettes,** (*responsabilités*) to wear several hats.
cassable [kasabl] *adj* breakable.
cassage [kasaʒ] *nm* breaking; *F* **c. de gueule,** punch-up.
Cassandre [kasɑ̃dr] **1** *nf* Cassandra. **2** *n Fig* prophet of doom, Cassandra; **jouer les Cassandre,** to be a Cassandra, to prophesy doom and gloom.
cassant [kasɑ̃] *adj* **(a)** (*fragile*) brittle, fragile, breakable (*china, glass etc*); brittle (*wood, hair*); *Métal* short (*metal*); **c. comme du verre,** as brittle as glass; **(b)** *Fig* (*brusque*) abrupt, brusque (*person, tone etc*); **(c)** *Arg* (*fatigant*) **c'est pas trop c.,** it won't (exactly) break your back.
cassate [kasat] *nf Culin* (*glace*) cassata.
cassation [kasɑsjɔ̃] *nf* **(a)** *Jur* cassation, annulment (*of sentence, will etc*); **Cour de c.,** Supreme Court of Appeal; **se pourvoir en c.,** to take one's case to the Supreme Court of Appeal; **(b)** *Mil* reduction to the ranks.
casse[1] [cas] *nf Typ* (*boîte*) case; **bas/haut de c.,** lower-/upper-case letter.
casse[2] *nf* (*arbre*) cassia.
casse[3] *nf* (*action*) breaking, breakage, damage; (*ce qui est cassé*) things broken, breakages; **il va y avoir de la c.,** something will get broken; *F* (*des ennuis*) there'll be trouble; **est-ce qu'il y a eu de la c.?,** was anything broken?, were there any breakages?; **payer la c.,** to pay for the breakages *or* the damage; **vendre une voiture/un frigidaire/***etc* **à la c.,** to sell a car/fridge/*etc* for scrap; **envoyer une voiture à la c.,** to send a car to the scrapyard; **aller** *ou* **partir à la c.,** (*d'une voiture etc*) to go for scrap.
casse[4] *nm Arg* (*cambriolage*) burglary, break-in.
cassé [kase] *adj* broken (*object, leg etc*); bent, bowed (*old man etc*); cracked (*voice*); *F* (*ivre*) smashed; **blanc c.,** off-white.
casse-cou [kasku] *nm inv* **(a)** (*passage*) danger spot; **(b) crier c.-c. à qn,** to warn s.o. (*of a danger*); **(c)** (*personne*) daredevil, reckless individual.
casse-croûte [kaskrut] *nm inv* **(a)** (*repas*) snack, bite; **(b)** *Can* (*snack*) snack bar.
casse-cul [kasky] *F* **1** *adj inv* boring. **2** *n inv* (*personne*) pain (in the neck), bore.
casse-gueule [kasgœl] *F* **1** *nm inv* (*endroit*) danger *or* dangerous spot; (*entreprise*) risky *or Br* dodgy undertaking. **2** *adj inv* dangerous (*spot*); risky, *Br* dodgy (*undertaking*).
cassement [kasmɑ̃] *nm* **(a) c. de tête,** (*souci*) headache, worry; (*migraine*) splitting headache; **(b)** *Arg* (*cambriolage*) burglary, break-in.
casse-noisette(s) [kasnwazɛt] *nm inv* (pair of) nutcrackers, *Am* nutcracker.
casse-noix [kasnwɑ] *nm inv* **(a)** (pair of) nutcrackers, *Am* nutcracker; **(b)** (*oiseau*) nutcracker.
casse-pieds [kaspje] *F* **1** *adj inv* boring; **ce qu'il est c.-p.,** what a bore *or* pain in the neck (he is). **2** *n inv* (*personne*) bore, pain (in the neck).
casse-pierre(s) [kaspjɛr] *nm inv* stonebreaker's hammer; *Constr* (*machine*) stonebreaker, stone-crusher.
casse-pipes [kaspip] *nm inv Arg* war, front (line); **aller au c.-p.,** to go to war *or* to the front.
casser [kase] **1** *vt* **(a)** (*briser*) to break (*plate, chair, toy etc*); to break, to snap (*twigs, string*); to crack (*nuts*); to break, to fracture (*leg etc*); to break, to crush (*stones*); to break (*will, morale*); (*mettre hors d'usage*) to break (*appliance, watch etc*); **c. une grève,** (*l'interrompre*) to call off a strike; (*la gêner*) to break a strike; **c. les prix,** to slash prices; **c. du bois,** to chop wood; *Av* to crash on landing; *F* **c. la tête** *ou* **les oreilles à qn,** to deafen s.o.; *Fig* **c. du sucre sur le dos de qn,** to talk about s.o. behind their back; *F* **c. les pieds à qn,** to bore s.o. stiff *or* silly; *Vulg* **il nous casse les couilles, il nous les casse,** he gets on our tits; *F* **c. le cou** *ou* **la figure** *ou Arg* **la gueule à qn,** to smash *or* kick s.o.'s face in; *F* **c. sa pipe,** to kick the bucket, to pop one's clogs; *Arg* **c. le morceau,** (*avouer*) to spill the beans, to come clean; (*dénoncer*) to grass, to turn informer; *F* **ça ne casse rien, ça ne casse pas trois pattes à un canard,** it's not up to much, it's nothing to write home about, it's no great shakes; **cette nouvelle m'a cassé le moral,** the news depressed me; **un spectacle à tout c.,** a marvellous *or* fantastic *or* super show; **se faire applaudir à tout c.,** to bring the house down; **cela vaut 1 000 francs à tout c.,** it's worth 1,000 francs at the very most *or* at the outside;

(b) (*dégrader*) to break, to reduce (*officer*) to the ranks; to demote (*employee*);

(c) *Jur* to quash, to set aside (*verdict etc*); **c. un mariage,** to annul *or* dissolve a marriage.

2 *vi* to break; (*of twig, string*) to break, to snap; **l'assiette a cassé en tombant,** the plate fell and broke; **attention, ça casse!,** be careful, it's fragile!; **cela casse comme du verre,** it is as brittle as glass.

3 se casser *vpr* **(a)** to break; (*of twig, string*) to break, to snap; **elle s'est cassé la jambe,** she's broken her leg; *F* **se c. la figure,** (*tomber*) to fall flat on one's face, to come a cropper; (*rater, faire faillite*) to fail, to come a cropper; (*se blesser*) to smash oneself up; **se c. la tête,** to rack one's brains; *F Iron* **ne te casse pas la tête!,** don't strain yourself!, don't overdo it!; *Fig* **se c. le nez à la porte de qn,** to find nobody in *or* at home; *Fig* **il s'est cassé le nez,** he's failed *or* come a cropper; *F* **il ne s'est pas cassé pour m'aider,** he didn't overstrain himself *or Sl* bust a gut helping me; *F* **je me suis cassé à lui trouver cette adresse,** I really went out of my way *or Sl* bust a gut to find him that address;

(b) *Arg* (*partir*) to split, *Br* to push off; **on se casse?,** let's split *or* push off *or* blow.
casserole [kasrɔl] *nf* **(a)** (*de cuisine*) (sauce)pan; **veau à la** *ou* **en c.,** braised veal; *Arg* **passer à la c.,** (*subir des épreuves*) to go through a tough time; (*sexuellement*) to be screwed *or* laid; (*être tué*) to get bumped off; **(b)** *Arg* (*mauvais piano*) tinny piano; **(c)** *Cin Arg* projector.
casse-tête [kastɛt] *nm inv* **(a)** (*massue*) club; (*matraque*) truncheon, baton; **(b)** (*jeu*) puzzle, brainteaser; **c.-t. chinois,** Chinese puzzle; **(c)** (*problème*) headache.
cassette [kasɛt] *nf* **(a)** (*magnétique*) cassette; **écouter/passer une c.,** to listen to/to put on a cassette; **c. vidéo,** video (cassette); **enregistrer sur c.,** to record on to cassette; (*vidéo*) to make a video (recording) of; **(b)** (*de bijoux*) casket; *Arch* **c. du roi,** (*d'argent*) King's privy purse.
casseur, -euse [kasœr, -øz] **1** *n* **(a) c. de pierres,** stonebreaker; **(b)** *F* (*maladroit*) **c'est une grande casseuse,** she's always breaking things; **(c)** *F* (*bravache*) swaggerer; **(d)** (*manifestant*) destructive demonstrator; **(e)** (*ferrailleur*) scrap (metal) merchant, breaker; **dépôt de c.,** breaker's yard; **c. de voitures,** (car) breaker; **(f)** *Arg* (*cambrioleur*) burglar. **2** *adj* **il est c.,** he's always breaking things.
Cassin [kasɛ̃] *nm* **le mont C.,** Monte Cassino.
cassine [kasin] *nf F* (*baraque*) hovel, shack; *Arch* (*petite maison*) (country) cottage.
cassis[1] [kasis] *nm* **(a)** (*baie*) blackcurrant; **(b)** (*arbuste*) blackcurrant bush; **(c)** (*liqueur*) blackcurrant liqueur; **blanc c.,** kir.
cassis[2] [kɑsi(s)] *nm* (*creux en travers d'une route*) dip.
cassis[3] [kasis] *nm Arg* (*tête*) nut, block.
cassolette [kasɔlɛt] *nf* **(a)** (*pour parfums*) incense burner;

(b) *Culin* ramekin.

cassonade [kasɔnad] *nf* brown sugar.

cassoulet [kasulɛ] *nm Culin* cassoulet, = stew of beans, pork, goose etc (*made in Languedoc*).

cassure [kasyr] *nf* break; (*dans du plâtre etc*) crack; *Fig* (*dans une amitié etc*) break, rupture; *Géol* fault; (*de tissu*) fold mark, crease.

castagnette [kastaɲɛt] *nf* castanet; **jouer des castagnettes,** to play the castanets.

caste [kast] *nf* caste; **la c. des prêtres,** the priest caste; **esprit de c.,** class consciousness; **être hors c.,** to be an outcast.

castel [kastɛl] *nm* manor (house), mansion.

castillan, -ane [kastijɑ̃, -an] **1** *adj* Castilian. **2** *nm Ling* Castilian. **3** *n* **C.,** Castilian.

Castille [kastij] *nf* Castile.

casting [kastiŋ] *nm Cin Th* casting.

castor [kastɔr] *nm* **(a)** (*mammifère, fourrure*) beaver; **c. du Chili,** (*mammifère*) coypu; (*fourrure*) nutria; **c. du Canada,** (*mammifère*) muskrat; (*fourrure*) musquash (fur); **(b)** *Fig* **(mouvement des) castors,** = group of people building their own houses.

castrat [kastra] *nm* eunuch; *Mus* castrato.

castrateur, -trice [kastratœr] *adj Psy* castrating; *Fig* (*autoritaire*) repressive.

castration [kastrɑsjɔ̃] *nf* castration; gelding (*of stallion*); neutering (*of male cat, dog*); spaying (*of female cat, bitch*); *Psy* **complexe de c.,** castration complex.

castrer [kastre] *vt* to castrate; to geld (*stallion*); to neuter (*male cat, dog*); to spay (*female cat, bitch*).

castrisme [kastrism] *nm Pol* Castroism.

castriste [kastrist] *adj & n Pol* Castroist.

casuel, -elle [kazɥɛl] **1** *adj* **(a)** (*accidental*) fortuitous, accidental; **(b)** *Gram* **flexions casuelles,** case endings. **2** *nm (revenu variable)* perquisites; *Rel* surplice fees.

casuiste [kazɥist] *nm Rel & Fig Péj* casuist.

casuistique [kazɥistik] *nf Rel & Fig Péj* casuistry.

casus belli [kasysbɛli] *nm inv* casus belli.

catabolisme [katabɔlism] *nm Biol* catabolism.

cataclysmal, -aux [kataklismal, -o] *adj* cataclysmal.

cataclysme [kataklism] *nm Géol & Fig* cataclysm.

cataclysmique [kataklismik] *adj* cataclysmic, cataclysmal.

catacombes [katakɔ̃b] *nfpl* catacombs.

catadioptre [katadiɔptr] *nm (de véhicule etc)* reflector; (*sur la route*) cat's eye.

catafalque [katafalk] *nm* catafalque.

cataire [katɛr] *nf* catmint, catnip.

catalan, -ane [katalɑ̃, -an] **1** *adj* Catalan. **2** *nm Ling* Catalan. **3** *n* **C.,** Catalan.

catalepsie [katalɛpsi] *nf Méd* catalepsy; **tomber en c.,** to have a cataleptic fit.

cataleptique [katalɛptik] *adj & n Méd* cataleptic.

catalogage [latalɔgaz] *nm* cataloguing (*of goods etc*).

Catalogne [katalɔɲ] *nf* **(a)** Catalonia; **(b)** *Tex* rag rug.

catalogue [katalɔg] *nm* catalogue, *US* catalog, list; **c. méthodique,** subject catalogue; **faire le c. de,** to catalogue, to list.

cataloguer [katalɔge] *vt* to catalogue, to list; *Fig Péj* (*étiqueter*) to label (*s.o., sth*); **les média l'ont cataloguée parmi les révolutionnaires,** the media labelled her a revolutionary; **je l'ai catalogué tout de suite,** I sized him up immediately.

catalyse [kataliz] *nf Ch* catalysis.

catalyser [katalize] *vt Ch & Fig* to catalyse.

catalyseur [katalizœr] *nm Ch & Fig* catalyst.

catalytique [katalitik] *adj Ch* catalytic; *Aut* **pot c.,** catalytic converter.

catamaran [katamarɑ̃] *nm Nau* catamaran; *Av* floats (*of seaplane*).

cataphote ® [katafɔt] *nm* = **CATADIOPTRE**.

cataplasme [kataplasm] *nm Méd* poultice; **c. sinapisé,** mustard poultice *or* plaster; *F* **ce cake est un c. (sur l'estomac),** this fruitcake lies like lead on the stomach.

catapultage [katapyltaʒ] *nm* catapulting; *Av* catapult launch(ing); *Fig* (*dans un poste etc*) catapulting; *Av* **crochet de c.,** catapulting hook.

catapulte [katapylt] *nf Av Mil etc* catapult.

catapulter [katapylte] *vt* to catapult; *Fig* to catapult (*s.o.*) **(dans un poste/**etc, into a post/*etc*).

cataracte [katarakt] *nf* **(a)** (*d'eau*) cataract, falls; **des cataractes (de pluie),** torrents of rain; **(b)** *Méd* cataract; **se faire opérer de la c.,** to have a cataract operation.

catarrhal, -aux [kataral, -o] *adj Méd* catarrhal.

catarrhe [katar] *nm Méd* catarrh.

catarrheux, -euse [katarø, -øz] *Méd* **1** *adj* catarrhal (*person*). **2** *n* catarrhal person.

catastrophe [katastrɔf] *nf* catastrophe, disaster; **c. financière,** crash; **c'est la c.!,** the worst has happened!; *Av* **atterrir en c.,** to make a forced landing; **je suis passé au bureau en c.,** I went to the office in a mad rush *or* a panic; **cet enfant/votre devoir est une c.,** this child/your homework is a disaster; **c.!, il est déjà là!,** panic stations! he's already there!

catastrophé [katastrɔfe] *adj F* stunned; **il était c. de l'apprendre,** he was stunned to learn it.

catastropher [katastrɔfe] *vt F* to stun, to be a (great) blow to (*s.o.*).

catastrophique [katastrɔfik] *adj* (*événement, conséquence etc*) catastrophic, disastrous; *Fig* (*très mauvais*) disastrous, appalling.

catatonique [katatɔnik] *adj & n Méd* catatonic.

catch [katʃ] *nm Sp* (all-in) wrestling.

catcher [katʃe] *vi Sp* to wrestle.

catcheur, -euse [katʃœr, -øz] *n Sp* (all-in) wrestler.

catéchèse [kateʃɛz] *nf Rel* catechism.

catéchisation [kateʃizɑsjɔ̃] *nf Rel* catechization.

catéchiser [kateʃize] *vt Rel* to catechize; *Fig* (*endoctriner*) to indoctrinate; (*sermonner*) to preach at, to lecture.

catéchisme [kateʃism] *nm Rel* (*instruction, livre*) catechism; **aller au c.,** to go to catechism class; *Fig* **ce livre est son c.,** this book is his bible.

catéchiste [kateʃist] *n Rel* catechist.

catéchumène [katekymɛn] *n Rel* catechumen; *Fig* novice, tyro.

catégorie [kategɔri] *nf* category; (*d'hôtel, de personnel*) grade; (*de légumes, fruits*) category, grade, class; (*de boxeur*) class; **légumes de première c.,** grade one *or* class one *or* prime vegetables; **de dernière c.,** of poor quality.

catégoriel, -elle [kategɔrjɛl] *adj* **(a)** *Ind Pol* **revendications catégorielles,** differential claims; **(b)** *Ling* **symbole c.,** category symbol; **(c)** *Phil* categorical.

catégorique [kategɔrik] *adj* (*clair*) categoric(al) (*answer etc*); *Phil* categorical (*proposition etc*); **refus c.,** categoric *or* flat refusal; **elle a été c. sur ce point,** she was categorical *or* firm on this point.

catégoriquement [kategɔrikmɑ̃] *adv* categorically.

catégorisation [kategɔrizɑsjɔ̃] *nf* categorization; (*de personnel*) grading.

catégoriser [kategɔrize] *vt* to categorize; to grade (*staff*).

caténaire [katenɛr] **1** *adj* **(a)** *Rail* **suspension c.,** catenary; **(b)** **réaction c.,** chain reaction. **2** *nf Rail* catenary.

catgut [katgyt] *nm Chir* catgut.

cathare [katar] *Hist Rel* **1** *adj* Cathar(istic). **2** *n* **C.,** Cathar(ist).

catharsis [katarsis] *nf Psy Littér* catharsis.

cathartique [katartik] *adj Psy Littér* cathartic.

cathédrale [katedral] *nf* cathedral.

Catherine [katrin] *nf* Catherine, Katherine; **coiffer sainte C.,** (*of woman*) = to be still unmarried on one's twenty-fifth birthday.

catherinette [katrinɛt] *nf* = unmarried woman of 25 and over.

cathéter [katetɛr] *nm Méd* catheter.

cathétérisme [kateterism] *nm Méd* catheterization.

cathode [katɔd] *nf Él* cathode.

cathodique [katɔdik] *adj Él* cathodic; **rayons cathodiques,** cathode rays; **tube à rayons cathodiques, tube c.,** cathode-ray tube.

catholicisme [katɔlisism] *nm* (Roman) Catholicism.

catholicité [katɔlisite] *nf* **(a)** **la c.,** (*catholiques*) the (Roman) Catholic Church; **(b)** (*orthodoxie*) Catholicity.

catholique [katɔlik] **1** *adj* **(a)** *Rel* (Roman) Catholic; (*universel*) catholic, universal; **(b)** *F* **il/ce n'est pas (très) c.,** he/it is a bit fishy *or* doubtful *or* dubious. **2** *n* (Roman) Catholic.

cati [kati] *nm Tex* gloss, lustre.

catimini (en) [ɑ̃katimini] *adv F* stealthily, on the sly *or* quiet; **entrer/sortir en c.,** to steal *or* sneak in/out; **je suis allé l'acheter en c.,** I went to buy it on the quiet.

catin [katɛ̃] *nf Arg Vieilli* (*prostituée*) trollop, whore.

cation [katjɔ̃] *nm Él* cation.

catir [katir] *vt Tex* to gloss (*material*).

catissage [katisaʒ] *nm Tex* glossing.

catogan [katɔgɑ̃] *nm* hair ribbon.

Caton [katɔ̃] *nm* Cato.

catoptrique [katɔptrik] *Phys* **1** *adj* catoptric(al), reflecting. **2** *nf* catoptrics.

Caucase (le) [ləkokaz] *nm* the Caucasus.

caucasien, -ienne [kokazjɛ̃, -jɛn] **1** *adj* Caucasian. **2** *n* **C.**, Caucasian.
cauchemar [koʃmar] *nm* nightmare; **faire un c.**, to have a nightmare; *F* **il me donne des cauchemars**, I have nightmares about him; *Fig* **les réceptions officielles étaient son c.**, official receptions were a nightmare to *or* for him.
cauchemarder [koʃmarde] *vi* to have nightmares; *Fig* **cette idée me fait c.**, the idea gives me nightmares.
cauchemardesque [koʃmardɛsk], **cauchemardeux, -euse** [koʃmardø, -øz] *adj* nightmarish (*vision etc*); **sommeil cauchemardeux**, nightmare-filled sleep.
caudal, -aux [kodal, -o] *adj Zool* caudal.
cauri(s) [kori] *nm* cowrie (shell).
causal [kozal] *adj Gram Phil* causal.
causalité [kozalite] *nf Phil* causality.
causant [kozɑ̃] *adj F* chatty, talkative (*person*).
cause [koz] *nf* **(a)** (*origine*) cause; **c. réelle/apparente**, real/apparent cause; **c. de défiance**, cause *or* reason for distrust; *Phil* **c. première/seconde**, first/secondary cause; **être (la) c. de qch**, to be the cause of sth; **c'est elle qui en est c.**, it's her fault, she's to blame; **pour quelle c.?**, for what reason?, on what grounds?; **il s'est mis en colère, et pour c.**, he got angry, and for a very good reason; **absent pour c. de santé**, absent for health reasons *or* on medical grounds; **fermé pour cause de décès/d'inventaire**, closed owing to bereavement/for stocktaking; **à c. de**, because of, on account of, owing to; **c'est à c. de moi qu'il a manqué le train**, it was because of me (that) he missed the train, it was my fault he missed the train; **c'est à c. de toi!**, it's all because of you!, it's all your fault!;
(b) *Jur* case, (law)suit, action; **c. civile/criminelle**, civil/criminal action *or* case; **c. célèbre**, famous trial, cause célèbre; **gagner une c.**, to win a case; **avocat sans c.**, briefless barrister; **confier une c. à un avocat**, to brief a barrister; **affaire en c.**, case before the court; **entendre une c.**, to hear a case; *Fig* **la c. est entendue**, there's nothing more to add; **être en c.**, (*of person, interests etc*) to be involved; **votre probité n'est pas en c.**, your honesty is not in question *or* in doubt; **mettre en c. la probité de qn**, to question s.o.'s honesty; *Jur etc* **mettre qn en c.**, to summon *or* sue s.o.; (*impliquer*) to implicate s.o.; **mettre qn hors de c.**, to exonerate s.o.; **en tout état de c.**, at all events, in any case; **en connaissance de c.**, with full knowledge of the case *or* the facts;
(c) (*parti*) cause; **souffrir pour une c.**, to suffer in *or* for a cause; **c'est une c. perdue (d'avance)**, it's a lost cause; **faire c. commune avec qn**, to make common cause with s.o., to side with s.o..
causer[1] [koze] *vt* to cause, to be the cause of (*sth*); **c. un changement**, to bring about a change; **son départ nous a causé beaucoup de chagrin**, his departure distressed us greatly; **c. des ennuis à qn**, to cause s.o. problems, to give s.o. trouble.
causer[2] *vi* **(a)** (*parler*) to chat, to talk (**de**, about); **c. avec** *ou* **à qn**, to have a chat *or* a talk with s.o.; **c. de peinture/etc**, to talk about painting/*etc*; **causez toujours**, you can talk as much as you like (I'm not listening); **faire c. qn**, to make s.o. talk; **(b)** (*cancaner*) to talk, to gossip; **on commence à en c.**, people are beginning to talk *or* gossip (about it).
causerie [kozri] *nf* **(a)** (*discussion*) chat, talk; **(b)** (*conférence*) causerie, (informal) talk.
causette [kozɛt] *nf F* little chat; **faire la c.** *ou* **un brin de c. avec qn**, to have a little chat *or Br* a natter with s.o..
causeur, -euse [kozœr, -øz] **1** *n* (*personne*) chatterer. **2** *nf* **causeuse**, (*siège*) love seat. **3** *adj* chatty, talkative.
causse [kos] *nm Géog* = limestone plateau in central and southern France.
causticité [kostisite] *nf Ch* causticity; *Fig* causticity, caustic humour (*of person*); biting *or* caustic nature (*of remark etc*).
caustique [kostik] **1** *adj Ch* caustic; *Fig* caustic (*person, wit, humour*); biting, caustic, cutting (*remark etc*); **un esprit c.**, a caustic wit. **2** *nm Ch* caustic. **3** *nf Opt* caustic.
caustiquement [kostikmɑ̃] *adv Fig* caustically, bitingly, cuttingly.
cauteleux, -euse [kotlø, -øz] *adj Litt* wily, cunning.
cautère [kotɛr] *nm Méd* cautery; *F* **c'est un c. sur une jambe de bois**, it won't do any good whatever.
cautérisation [koterizasjɔ̃] *nf Méd* cauterization.
cautériser [koterize] *vt Méd* to cauterize (*wound etc*).
caution [kosjɔ̃] *nf* **(a)** (*gage*) *Com Fin* security, guarantee; *Jur* bail; *Fig* (*appui*) support, backing; *Jur* **donner** *ou* **fournir c. pour qn**, to go *or* stand bail for s.o., to bail s.o. out; *Jur* **mettre qn en liberté sous c.**, to release s.o. on bail; *Fig* **sujet à c.**, unreliable, unconfirmed (*news etc*); *Fig* **le gouvernement a donné sa c. au rachat**, the take-over has the government's support *or* backing; **(b)** (*personne*) surety, security, guaranty; **se porter c. pour qn**, *Jur* to go *or* stand bail for s.o.; *Com Fin* to stand surety *or* security for s.o..
cautionnement [kosjɔnmɑ̃] *nm* **(a)** (*contrat*) surety bond; **(b)** (*somme d'argent*) security, guarantee, guaranty; **c. électoral**, deposit.
cautionner [kosjɔne] *vt* **(a)** *Com Fin* to stand surety for, to act as guarantor for (*s.o.*); *Jur* to go *or* stand bail for (*s.o.*); to bail (*s.o.*) out; **(b)** *Fig* (*répondre de*) to answer for, to guarantee (*sth*); **(c)** *Fig* (*approuver*) to support, to back (*idea, action, government etc*).
cavalcade [kavalkad] *nf* **(a)** (*défilé*) cavalcade, procession; **(b)** *Fig* (*d'enfants etc*) swarm, unruly gang.
cavalcader [kavalkade] *vi* **(a)** (*of gangs of people etc*) to swarm (about); **(b)** *Arch* to ride (*in a cavalcade*).
cavale [kaval] *nf* **(a)** *Arg* (*évasion*) escape; **être en c.**, to be on the run; **(b)** *Litt* (*jument*) mare.
cavaler [kavale] *Arg* **1** *vi* to run (at full speed); (*fuir*) to run away, to scarper, to make tracks. **2** *vt* **c. qn**, to get on s.o.'s nerves, to plague *or* pester s.o..
cavalerie [kavalri] *nf* **(a)** *Mil* cavalry; **c. légère**, light cavalry, light horse; **c. motorisée**, motorized cavalry; **grosse c.**, armoured cavalry; **(b)** (*ensemble de chevaux*) stable.
cavaleur [kavalœr] *Arg* **1** *adj* womanizing. **2** *nm* skirt chaser, womanizer.
cavalier, -ière [kavalje, -jɛr] **1** *n* **(a)** (*à cheval*) rider; horseman, horsewoman; **habit de c.**, riding costume; *Bible* **les (Quatre) Cavaliers de l'Apocalypse**, the (four) Horsemen of the Apocalypse; **(b)** (*qui danse*) partner; *Fig* **faire c. seul**, to act alone, to go it alone. **2** *nm* **(a)** *Mil* trooper, cavalryman; *Échecs* knight; *Arch* (*gentilhomme*) gentleman; *Br Hist* **Cavaliers et Têtes rondes**, Cavaliers and Roundheads; **(b)** (*accompagnateur de dame*) escort; **(c)** *Ordinat* jumper; **(d)** *Tech* (*clou*) staple; (*curseur de balance*) rider; (*languette de fichier*) tab. **3** *adj* **(a)** **allée** *ou* **piste cavalière**, bridle path; **(b)** cavalier, offhand (*manner, person*).
cavalièrement [kavaljɛrmɑ̃] *adv* in a cavalier manner, off-handedly.
cave[1] [kav] *adj* **(a)** hollow, sunken (*cheeks, eyes*); **(b)** *Anat* **veine c.**, vena cava.
cave[2] *nf* **(a)** (*cellier, vins*) cellar; **c. à charbon**, coal cellar; **c. à vin**, wine cellar; **avoir une bonne c.**, to have *or* keep a good cellar; *Fig* **de la c. au grenier**, from top to bottom, thoroughly; **(b)** (*cabaret*) nightclub; **(c)** **c. à liqueurs**, (*meuble*) drinks cabinet.
cave[3] *nf Cartes* = stake.
cave[4] **1** *nm Arg* **(a)** outsider (*as opposed to a member of the underworld*); **(b)** (*dupe*) sucker, mug. **2** *adj* **ce qu'il est c.!**, what a sucker *or* mug (he is)!
caveau, -eaux [kavo] *nm* **(a)** (*petite cave*) small cellar; **(b)** (*cabaret*) nightclub; **(c)** (*funéraire*) burial vault.
caver[1] [kave] **1** *vt Arch & Litt* to hollow (out), to dig (out), to excavate. **2 se caver** *vpr* (*of eyes etc*) to become hollow *or* sunken.
caver[2] *Cartes* **1** *vt Arch* to put up (*a sum of money as a stake*). **2** *vi* to put up a stake. **3 se caver** *vpr* **se c. de deux cents francs**, to put up two hundred francs (*as a stake*).
caverne [kavɛrn] *nf* cave, cavern; *Anat* cavity (*in lungs etc*); **homme des cavernes**, caveman; **la c. d'Ali Baba**, Ali Baba's cave; *Fig* **c'est une véritable c. d'Ali Baba**, it's a real Aladdin's cave.
caverneux, -euse [kavɛrnø, -øz] *adj* **(a)** cavernous (*mountain, rock*); *Anat* cavernous (*tissue*); **(b)** cavernous, hollow, sepulchral (*voice, groan*).
cavet [kavɛ] *nm Archit* cavetto.
caviar [kavjar] *nm* **(a)** caviar; **c. rouge**, salmon roe; **(b)** *Fig* **passer au c.**, to censor (*newspaper article etc*).
caviardage [kavjardaʒ] *nm* censoring.
caviarder [kavjarde] *vt* to censor (*newspaper article etc*).
caviste [kavist] *nm* cellarman.
cavité [kavite] *nf* cavity, hollow; *Anat Méd* cavity; **c. articulaire**, socket (*of bone*); **c. buccale**, oral cavity.
Cayenne [kajɛn] *n* (*ville*) Cayenne; **poivre de C.**, cayenne (pepper).
c.c. [sese] *nm Él* (*abrév* **courant continu**) DC.
C.C. [sese] *nm Banque* (*abrév* **compte courant**) CA.
C.C.P. [sesepe] *nm* (*abrév* **compte courant postal, compte chèque postal**) = Giro account.

C.D. [sede] *nm abrév* **corps diplomatique.**

ce¹ [s(ə)] *pron dém* (**c'** *before parts of* **être** *beginning with a vowel*) **(a)** (*with adj or adv complement*) **c'est exact!,** that's right!; **ce doit être faux,** it's probably untrue; **c'est sur votre bureau,** it's on your desk; **le voilà, ce n'est pas trop tôt!,** there he is, and about time too!; **est-ce** [ɛs] **assez?,** is that enough?; **c'est facile,** it's easy; **c'est demain dimanche,** tomorrow is Sunday, it's Sunday tomorrow; **c'était inutile de sonner,** you need not have rung; **c'est assez qu'il veuille bien pardonner,** it is enough that he is willing to forgive; **c'est à vous de vous en occuper,** it's up to you to see to it;

(b) (*with noun or pron as complement; with a third person pl complement the verb should be in the plural but colloquial usage allows the singular*) **c'est moi/c'est nous/ce sont eux** *ou F* **c'est eux,** it's me/us/them, *Fml* it is I/we/they; **est-ce vous, Jean?,** is that you, John?; **c'est un bon soldat,** he's a good soldier; **ce ne sont pas mes chaussures,** they *or* these *or* those are not my shoes;

(c) si ce n'est, except; **personne si ce n'est vos parents,** no one except (possibly) your parents;

(d) ce ... ici, this; **ce n'est pas un hôtel ici!,** this is not a hotel!;

(e) ce ... là, that; those; **ce n'est pas là mon parapluie,** that is not my umbrella; **est-ce que ce sont là vos enfants?,** are those your children?;

(f) (*representing a subject which has been isolated in order to stress it*) **Paris, c'est bien loin!, c'est bien loin, Paris!,** it's a long way to Paris!, Paris is a long way away!; **le temps, c'est de l'argent,** time is money;

(g) (*used with* **que** *or* **qui** *to bring a word into prominence*) **c'est toi qui le dis!,** that's what you say!, says you!; **c'est moi qui lui ai écrit,** it was I *or F* me who wrote to him; **est-ce à moi que vous parlez?,** are you speaking to me?; *Litt* **c'est un bon petit garçon que Jean!,** what a fine little chap John is!; *Litt* **ce serait imprudence que d'y aller,** it would be unwise to go (there);

(h) (*used with* **que** *to introduce a statement*) **c'est que maman est malade,** you see *or* the point is mother's ill; **c'est qu'il fait froid!,** it's cold and no mistake!; **s'il chante, c'est qu'il est de bonne humeur,** when *or* if he sings it means *or* it's because he's in a good mood; **ce n'est pas qu'il n'y tienne pas,** it's not that he isn't keen on it, it isn't that he's not keen on it;

(i) (*used in* **est-ce-que** [ɛskə] *to introduce a question*) **est-ce que je peux entrer?,** may I come in?; **est-ce qu'il est là?,** is he there?;

(j) (*locutions*) **pour ce faire,** in order to do this, with this intention; **ce faisant,** in so doing; **ce disant,** saying which *or* this, so saying, with these words; **on l'a attaqué et ce** [sə] **en plein jour,** he was attacked, and in broad daylight (too); **sur ce ...,** thereupon ...; *Arch* **depuis ce ...,** since then ...; **tenez-vous beaucoup à ce qu'il vienne?,** are you very anxious for him to come? **pour ce qui est de la qualité et du prix,** with regard to *or* as regards quality and price; **pour ce qui est de cela,** for that matter; *Litt* **voilà, ce me semble, un avis excellent,** that, to my mind, is excellent advice;

(k) (*with a rel pron*) **ce qui, ce que,** what; **je sais ce qui est arrivé,** I know what has happened; **voilà ce que j'ai répondu,** this is what I answered; **je sais ce que c'est que la pauvreté,** I know what poverty is; **si vous saviez ce que c'est que de vivre seul,** if you knew what it means *or* what it's like to live alone; **voilà ce que c'est que de mentir,** that's what comes of telling lies; **c'est ce qu'il a dit,** that's what he said, so he said; **voici ce dont il s'agit,** this is the point, this is what it's all about; **ce qu'il y a de plus remarquable, c'est que ...,** what is most remarkable is that ...., the most remarkable thing about it is ...; **à ce qu'on dit,** by *or* according to *or* from what they say; **voici ce à quoi** [səakwa] **j'avais pensé,** this is what I had thought of;

(l) (*referring back to a clause*) **ce qui, ce que,** which; **il l'a quittée, ce qui est dommage,** he has left her, which is a pity; **il est déjà parti, ce que je ne savais pas,** he has already gone, which I didn't know;

(m) tout ce qui, tout ce que, everything, all (that); **voici tout ce que j'ai d'argent,** here's all the money I've got; **faites tout ce que vous voudrez,** do whatever you like;

(n) *F* **ce que ...!,** (*comme*) how...!; **(qu'est-)ce qu'elle a changé!,** how she has changed!; **ce que tu es grandi!,** how you've grown!, well, you HAVE grown!;

(o) (*with* **à** + *inf*) **c'est à mourir de rire,** it's absolutely hilarious; **c'est à se demander s'il n'est pas fou,** one may well wonder if he isn't mad; **c'est à voir,** that remains to be seen, we'll have to (wait and) see.

ce² (cet), cette, ces [sə (sɛt), sɛt, se *or* sɛ] *adj dém* (*the form* **cet** *is used before a n or adj beginning with a vowel or* **h** *mute*) **(a)** this, that, *pl* these, those; **un de ces jours,** one of these days; **il fera de l'orage cette nuit,** there will be a storm tonight; **j'ai mal dormi cette nuit,** I slept badly last night; **je l'ai vu/je le verrai ce matin/cet été,** I saw him/I'll see him this morning/this summer; **c'est une de ces personnes dont on ne peut pas se débarrasser,** he's one of those people *or* the sort of person you can't get rid of;

(b) the; **il a eu cette sensation que ...,** he had the feeling that ...; **rien de ce genre,** nothing of the kind; *F* **mais laissez-la donc, cette enfant!,** do leave that child alone!;

(c) ce dernier, the latter;

(d) ces, the; **que prendront ces messieurs?,** what will you take *or* have, gentlemen?; **ces dames sont au salon,** the ladies are in the drawing room;

(e) ce ... -ci, this; **ce... -là,** that; **prenez cette tasse-ci,** take this cup; **je n'oublierai jamais ce jour-là,** I shall never forget that day; **je la verrai ces jours-ci,** I'll see her in a day or two; **ces jours-ci, il fait chaud,** it's been warm lately *or* the(se) last couple of days;

(f) *F* **eh bien, et cette jambe?,** well, how's that leg of yours *or* how's the leg?; **cette question!,** what an absurd question!; **je lui ai écrit une de ces lettres!,** I wrote him such a letter!; **j'ai une de ces faims!,** I'm ravenous!; **elle a une de ces têtes!,** (*elle est fatiguée, malade*) she looks awful! ; (*elle est laide*) she's as ugly as sin!

C.E. [seə] *nm abrév* **Conseil de l'Europe.**

céans [seɑ̃] *adv* **(a) le maître de c.,** the master of the house; **(b)** *Arch* (here) within, in this house.

ceci [səsi] *pron dém inv* this (thing, fact *etc*); **écoutez bien c.,** (now) listen to this; **le cas offre c. de particulier que ...,** the case is peculiar in that ... .

cécité [sesite] *nf* blindness; **être frappé de c.,** to be struck blind; **c. verbale,** word blindness.

cédant, -ante [sedɑ̃, -ɑ̃t] *Com Jur* **1** *adj* granting, assigning (*party*). **2** *n* grantor, assignor.

céder [sede] *v* **(je cède; je céderai) 1** *vt* (*donner*) to give up, to part with (*sth*) (**à,** to); to give up, to surrender (*right*); *Jur* to transfer, to make over, to assign (**à,** to); to dispose of, to sell (*lease*); **c. sa place à qn,** to give up one's seat to s.o.; **c. le pas à qn,** to let s.o. go first, to give way to s.o.; **c. du terrain,** to give *or* lose ground; **maison à c.,** business for sale; **je vous le céderai pour cent francs,** I'll let you have it for a hundred francs; *Vieilli* **ne le c. en rien à qn,** to be s.o.'s equal, to be in no way inferior to s.o.; *Vieilli* **le c. à qn en qch,** to yield to s.o. in sth, to be inferior to s.o. in sth; *Vieilli* **pour l'intelligence elle ne (le) cède à personne,** in intelligence she's second to none.

2 *vi* (*se soumettre*) to yield, to give way (*under pressure*); to give in, to submit (**à,** to), *F* to knuckle under; (*s'écrouler*) to give way; **il a cédé à nos désirs,** he gave in to us; **c. devant les menaces,** to yield *or* give in to threats; **le gouvernement ne cédera pas aux intimidations,** the government will not yield *or* give in to intimidation; **le terrain m'a cédé sous le pied** *ou* **a cédé sous mes pieds,** the ground gave way beneath me; **le câble a cédé sous l'effort,** the rope gave way *or* parted under the strain; **c. sous le poids,** to give way *or* break beneath the weight; **c. au sommeil,** to succumb to sleep.

cédétiste [sedetist] *Pol* **1** *adj* of *or* relating to the CFDT (*French trade union*). **2** *n* member of the CFDT.

Cedex [sedɛks] *nm* (*abrév* **Courrier d'Entreprise à Distribution Exceptionnelle**) = special delivery service for business mail.

cédille [sedij] *nf Gram* cedilla.

cédrat [sedra] *nm* citron (tree); (*fruit*) citron; **confiture de cédrats,** citron marmalade.

cédratier [sedratje] *nm* citron (tree).

cèdre [sɛdr] *nm* cedar (*tree, wood*); **table en c.,** cedar table.

cédulaire [sedylɛr] *adj* pertaining to income tax schedules; **impôts cédulaires,** scheduled taxes.

cédule [sedyl] *nf* schedule (of taxes); **c. d'impôts,** tax bracket.

C.E.E. [seəə] *nf* (*abrév* **Communauté économique européenne**) EEC.

C.E.G. [seəʒe] *nm abrév* **collège d'enseignement général.**

cégep [seʒɛp] *nm Can* (*abrév* **collège d'enseignement**

général et professionnel) = general and vocational college; **elle va au c. l'an prochain,** she's going to CEGEP next year.
cégétiste [seʒetist] *Pol* **1** *n* member of the C.G.T. (*Confédération générale du travail*). **2** *adj* **délégué c.,** C.G.T. delegate.
ceindre [sɛ̃dr] *v* (*prp* **ceignant**; *pp* **ceint**; *pr ind* **je ceins, il ceint, n. ceignons**; *impf* **je ceignais**; *p hist* **je ceignis**; *fu* **je ceindrai**) *Litt* **1** *vt* **(a)** to gird; **c. une épée,** to gird on *or* buckle on a sword; **c. l'écharpe municipale,** to put on *or* assume one's sash of office; **c. la couronne,** (*du maire*) to put on *or* assume the crown; **(b) c. ses reins,** to gird up one's loins; **(c)** (*of a wreath etc*) to encircle (*s.o.'s head etc*); **tête ceinte d'une couronne de lauriers,** head wreathed with laurels; **(d) c. une ville de murailles,** to encircle *or* surround a town with walls. **2 se ceindre** *vpr* **se c. les reins,** to gird up one's loins.
ceinture [sɛ̃tyr] *nf* **(a)** belt; waistband (*of skirt, trousers*); waist, middle (*of body*); (*in wrestling*) waist lock; **porter une c.,** to wear a belt; **une c. de cuir,** a leather belt; **porter son écharpe en c.,** to tie one's scarf round one's waist; *Méd* **c. orthopédique,** surgical corset; **c. de chasteté,** chastity belt; **c. de sauvetage,** lifebelt; **c. de parachute,** parachute harness; *Aut Av* **c. de sécurité,** seat belt, safety belt; **c. marron/noire,** (*au judo*) brown/black belt; *F* **se serrer** *ou* **se mettre la c., faire c.,** to tighten one's belt; to go without (*sth*); **desserrer sa c. après un gros repas,** to loosen one's belt after a heavy meal; **c.! il n'en reste plus pour vous!,** you'll have to go without, there's nothing left!; **mais moi, c.!,** but I had to go without!; **coup au-dessous de la c.,** blow below the belt; *Anat* **c. pelvienne,** pelvic girdle; *Anat* **c. scapulaire,** pectoral *or* scapular arch *or* girdle;
(b) enclosure; circle (*of walls*); belt (*of hills*); **c. de verdure** *ou* **verte,** green belt;
(c) *Rail* **chemin de fer de c.,** circle line (*round a town*); **la grande/la petite C.,** (*à Paris*) the outer/inner circle railway;
(d) *Archit* cincture (*of column*).
ceinturer [sɛ̃tyre] *vt* **(a)** (*entourer*) to girdle, to surround; **ville ceinturée de murs,** walled town; **(b)** (*de lutteur*) to put a waist lock on (*s.o.*); *Rugby Fb* to tackle (*a player*).
ceinturon [sɛ̃tyrɔ̃] *nm Mil etc* belt, swordbelt.
cela [səla, sla] *pron dém* **(a)** that (*thing, fact etc*); **qu'est-ce que c'est que c.,** what's that?; **il y a deux ans de c.,** that was two years ago; **c'est pour c. que je viens,** that's what I've come for *or* why I've come; **sans c. je ne serais pas venu,** but for that *or* otherwise I wouldn't have come; **à c. près** *ou* **à part c., nous sommes d'accord,** we are agreed, with that one exception *or* except on that point; **s'il n'y a que c. de nouveau,** if that's all that's new;
(b) (**cela** *is the pron used as neut subject to all verbs other than* **être**, *and may be used with* **être** *as more emphatic than* **ce**) that, it; **c. ne vous regarde pas,** that's *or* it's none of your business, that's *or* it's no business of yours; **la voir si malheureuse, c. m'est pénible,** to see her *or* seeing her so unhappy is very painful to me;
(c) *F* **il m'a raconté qu'il était parti à la pêche, ceci c.,** he told me he'd been fishing etc etc; **il m'a dit ceci et c.,** he told me this, that and the other;
(d) (*idiomatic uses*) **ce n'est plus c.,** it's not what it was, it's not the same any more; **il n'y a que c. pour me tenir éveillé,** that's the only thing that will keep me awake; **ah, pour c., oui!,** yes, indeed!, yes, of course!; **et avec c., madame?,** (*dans un magasin*) anything else, madam?
céladon [seladɔ̃] *adj inv* celadon.
célébrant [selebrɑ̃] *Rel* **1** *adj* officiating. **2** *n* celebrant.
célébration [selebrasjɔ̃] *nf* celebration.
célèbre [selɛbr] *adj* famous, celebrated (**par,** for); **se rendre c. par un acte/une déclaration/***etc*, to become famous because of something one did/said/*etc*; **le cas si tristement c. de ...,** the notorious case of ... .
célébrer [selebre] *vt* (**je célèbre; je célébrerai**) **(a)** to celebrate (*a birthday, Rel mass etc*); to solemnize (*rite*); to observe, to keep (*feast*); **c. des funérailles,** to hold a funeral; **(b)** to extol (*s.o.*); **c. le courage de qn,** to praise *or* pay tribute to s.o.'s courage.
célébrité [selebrite] *nf* (*notoriété*) fame, celebrity; (*personne*) celebrity.
celer [səle] *vt* (**je cèle; je cèlerai**) *Arch & Litt* to conceal, to keep secret (**à,** from).
céleri [sɛlri] *nm* (*plante*) celery; **pied de c.,** head of celery; **morceau** *ou* **branche de c.,** stick of celery; *Culin* **c. rémoulade,** = celeriac in mayonnaise.
céleri-rave [sɛlrirav] *nm* celeriac; (*pl céléris-raves*).
célérité [selerite] *nf* speed, rapidity; **avec une étonnante c.,** with astonishing speed, at an astonishing rate.
célesta [selɛsta] *nm Mus* celesta, celeste.
céleste [selɛst] *adj* celestial, heavenly; *Fig* (*divin*) divine; *Litt* **la voûte c.,** the vault of heaven; **bleu c.,** sky blue, celeste; *Fig* **la colère c.,** divine wrath; *Arch* **le C. Empire,** the Celestial Empire.
célibat [seliba] *nm* single life; (*chasteté*) celibacy.
célibataire [selibatɛr] **1** *adj* (*non marié*) unmarried, single; (*chaste*) celibate; **mère c.,** unmarried mother. **2** *nm* bachelor; **un c. endurci,** a confirmed bachelor. **3** *nf* single woman; *Admin & Vieilli* spinster.
celle, celle-ci, celle-là *pron voir* **CELUI**.
cellérier, -ière [selerje, -jɛr] *n Rel* cellarer, *f* cellaress.
cellier [selje] *nm* storeroom (*for wine etc*).
cellophane ® [selɔfan] *nm* cellophane; **fromage sous c.,** cheese wrapped in cellophane.
cellulaire [selylɛr] *adj* **(a)** *Biol* cell(ular) (*tissue etc*); *Télécom* **téléphone c.,** cellular phone; **(b) convoi c.,** police convoy; **voiture c.,** police van, *F* Black Maria; **prison** *ou* **régime c.,** solitary confinement.
cellule [selyl] *nf* **(a)** cell (*of prison, honeycomb etc*); (*d'ermite*) cell; *Fig* (*section*) cell, section; *Fig* (*élément*) unit; *Mil* **dix jours de c.,** ten days in the cells *or F* the slammer; **les cellules du parti,** the party cells; *Fig* **la c. de la société,** the social unit; **(b)** *Biol* cell; **c. nerveuse,** nerve cell; **différenciation des cellules,** cell differentiation; **(c)** *Av* airframe; **(d) c. photoélectrique,** photoelectric cell, photocell; *TV* electric eye; **(e)** (*de tourne-disque etc*) cartridge.
cellulite [selylit] *nf Méd* cellulite; **avoir de la c.,** to have cellulite; **traitement anti-c.,** anti-cellulite treatment.
cellulitique [selylitik] *adj Méd* **tissu c.,** cellulite tissue.
celluloïd [selylɔid] *nm* celluloid.
cellulose [selyloz] *nf Ch Com* cellulose.
cellulosique [selylozik] *adj* cellulose (*varnish etc*).
celte [sɛlt] **1** *adj* Celtic. **2** *n* Celt.
celtique [sɛltik] **1** *adj* Celtic. **2** *nm Ling* Celtic.
celui, celle, *pl* **ceux, celles** [səlɥi, sɛl, sø, sɛl] *pron dém* **(a)** (*completed by an adj clause*) the one, *pl* those; **c. dont je t'ai parlé,** the one *or* the man I told you about; **celle à qui j'ai écrit,** the one *or* the woman I wrote to *or Fml* to whom I wrote; **c. qui était parti le dernier,** the one who started last;
(b) (*quiconque*) he, she, *pl* those; **c. qui mange peu dort bien,** he who eats little sleeps well;
(c) (*followed by* **de**) **mes livres et ceux de Jean,** my books and John's; **les hommes d'aujourd'hui et ceux d'autrefois,** the men of today and those of former times;
(d) tous ceux ayant la même idée, all those with the same idea; **toutes les maisons sont en bois sauf celles voisines de l'église,** all the houses are built of wood except those near the church;
(e) c.-ci, *pl* **ceux-ci,** (*en indiquant du doigt*) this (one), these; (*en se référant à qn ou qch précédemment cité*) the latter; **c.-là,** *pl* **ceux-là,** (*en indiquant du doigt*) that (one), those; (*en se référant à qn ou qch précédemment cité*) the former; **ceux-ci coûtent plus cher que ceux-là,** these cost more than those do; **ah, c.-là! quel idiot!,** oh him! that idiot!; **autre exemple, plus technique c.-là,** another example, a more technical one this time.
cément [semɑ̃] *nm* **(a)** *Anat* cement (*of tooth*); **(b)** *Métal* cement, cementation powder.
cémentation [semɑ̃tasjɔ̃] *nf Métal* cementation, case hardening.
cémenter [semɑ̃te] *vt Métal* to case-harden, to face-harden (*steel*); to cement (*armour-plate*).
cénacle [senakl] *nm* **(a)** (*côterie*) (literary) club, group, coterie; **(b)** *Antiq* cenacle; *surtout Bible* upper room (*of the Last Supper*).
cendre [sɑ̃dr] *nf* **(a)** ash(es), cinders; **laisser tomber de la c. (de cigarette) sur son pantalon,** to drop (cigarette) ash on one's trousers; **faire cuire des marrons sous la c.,** to roast chestnuts in the ashes; **mettre** *ou* **réduire une ville en cendres,** to reduce a town to ashes; *Rel* **le mercredi des Cendres,** Ash Wednesday; **visage couleur de c.,** ashen face; **(b) cendres,** (mortal) remains, ashes; *Litt* **les cendres du passé,** the embers of the past; **cendres volcaniques,** volcanic ash; *Tech* **cendres volantes,** fly ash.
cendré [sɑ̃dre] *adj* ash-grey, ashen, ashy; **blond c.,** ash blond.
cendrée [sɑ̃dre] *nf* **(a)** *Sp etc* (*piste*) cinder track, dirt track; (*matériel*) cinders; **(b)** (*chasse*) dust shot.
cendrer [sɑ̃dre] *vt* **(a)** to cinder (*path, track*); **(b)** to colour (*wall etc*) ash-grey.

cendreux, -euse [sɑ̃drø, -øz] *adj* **(a)** *(gris, terne)* ashy, ashen, ash-grey; **(b)** *(qui contient de la cendre)* full of ashes, ashy, gritty.
cendrier [sɑ̃drije] *nm* ashtray; ashpan *(of stove)*; ash pit *or* hole *(of furnace)*; ash box *(of locomotive)*.
Cendrillon [sɑ̃drijɔ̃] *nf* **(a)** Cinderella; **(b)** *Vieilli* **c.,** (household) drudge, slavey.
cène [sɛn] *nf* **(a)** *Bible Beaux-Arts* **La (Sainte) C.,** the Last Supper; **(b)** *Rel (in Protestant Church)* Holy Communion, Lord's Supper.
cenelle [sənɛl] *nf (baie)* haw.
cenellier [sənɛlje] *nm Can (arbuste)* hawthorn.
cénobite [senɔbit] *nm* c(o)enobite *(monk)*.
cénotaphe [senɔtaf] *nm* cenotaph.
cénozoïque [senɔzɔik] *Géol* **1** *adj* Cenozoic, Caenozoic. **2** *nm* the Cenozoic era.
cens [sɑ̃s] *nm* **(a)** *Admin* quota *(of taxes payable)*; *Hist (in feudal system)* (quit) rent; **c. électoral,** property qualification *(for the franchise)*; **(b)** *Antiq* census.
censé [sɑ̃se] *adj* supposed; **il est c. partir demain,** he is supposed *or* due *or* expected to leave tomorrow; **je ne suis pas c. le savoir,** *(ça dépasse ma compétence)* I can't be expected to know that; *(c'est confidentiel)* I'm not supposed to know about it; **nul n'est c. ignorer la loi,** ignorance of the law is no excuse.
censément [sɑ̃semɑ̃] *adv* supposedly; **il est c. le maître,** he's supposed to be the master.
censeur [sɑ̃sœr] *nm* **(a)** censor *(of the press etc)*; **(b)** *Scol* vice-principal, deputy headmaster *or* headmistress *(of lycée)*; **(c)** *(juge)* critic, faultfinder; **(d)** *Antiq* censor.
censitaire [sɑ̃sitɛr] *Hist* **1** *adj* **électeur c.,** elector qualified by property or by his assessment. **2** *nm* eligible voter.
censurable [sɑ̃syrabl] *adj* censurable, open to censure.
censure [sɑ̃syr] *nf* **(a)** censorship *(of the press etc)*; *Cin etc* (board of) censors; *Psy* (the) censor; **(b)** *Vieilli* censure, blame; **les censures de l'Église,** the censure of the Church; *Pol* **motion de c.,** vote of censure *or* no-confidence.
censurer [sɑ̃syre] **1** *vt* **(a)** to censor *(film, Psy one's emotions etc)*; *Cin* **c. une séquence,** to censor *or* cut a scene; **(b)** *(critiquer)* to censure, to find fault with *(s.o., sth)*. **2** *vi Psy* **il a tendance à c.,** he tends to censor his feelings.
cent[1] [sɑ̃] **1** *adj (takes a plural* **s** *when multiplied by a preceding numeral but not when followed by another numeral; does not vary when used as an ordinal)* (a, one) hundred; **c. élèves,** a hundred pupils; **deux cents hommes,** two hundred men; **deux c. cinquante hommes,** two hundred and fifty men; **page deux c.,** page two hundred; **l'an trois c.,** the year three hundred; **avoir c. ans,** to be a hundred (years old); **avoir c. deux ans,** to be a hundred and two; **cent un** [sɑ̃ œ̃] , one hundred and one; **je te l'ai dit c. fois,** (if I've told you once) I've told you a hundred times; **vous avez c. fois raison,** you're absolutely right; **le numéro trois c. gagne,** number three hundred is the winner, the winning number is three hundred; **habiter au c.,** to live at number a hundred; **c. fois mieux,** a hundred times better; *F* **je ne vais pas t'attendre (pendant) c. sept ans,** I'm not going to wait for you for ever; **faire les c. pas,** to pace up and down; *F* **faire les quatre cents coups,** to be up to all sorts of tricks; *F* **être aux c. coups,** to be desperate; *F* **je vous le donne en c.,** guess!
2 *nm* **(a)** *inv* a hundred; *F* **il y a c. à parier contre un que ...,** it's a hundred to one that ...; **sept pour c.,** seven per cent; *Ch* **solution à trente pour c.,** thirty per cent solution; **c. pour c.,** a hundred per cent;
(b) *var* hundred; *Com Vieilli* **un c. d'œufs,** a hundred eggs; *F* **elle gagne des mille et des cents,** she earns a packet; *Sp* **le c. mètres,** the hundred metres.
cent[2] [sɛn(t)] *nm surtout Can (coin)* cent.
centaine [sɑ̃tɛn] *nf* (about a) hundred; **une c. de francs,** about a hundred francs, a hundred francs or so; *Math* **la colonne/la chiffre des centaines,** the hundreds column/figure; **des centaines de livres,** hundreds of books; **quelques centaines de francs,** a few hundred francs; **atteindre la c.,** *(d'éléments, participants etc)* to be about a hundred; **les gens moururent par centaines/par centaines de mille,** people died in hundreds/in hundreds of thousands.
centaure [sɑ̃tɔr] *nm Myth* centaur.
centaurée [sɑ̃tɔre] *nf (plante)* centaury.
centenaire [sɑ̃tnɛr] **1** *adj* age-old; **ma grand'-mère est c.,** my grandmother is over a hundred; **plusieurs fois c.,** hundreds of years old; **toi, tu finiras c.!** you'll live to be a hundred!; **chêne c.,** ancient oak. **2** *n* centenarian. **3** *nm* centenary, *Am* centennial.
centenier [sɑ̃tənje] *nm Antiq* centurion.
centésimal, -aux [sɑ̃tezimal, -o] *adj* centesimal *(fraction, scale etc)*; *Méd* **dilution centésimale,** dilution to one part per hundred.
centiare [sɑ̃tjar] *nm* = one square metre or about 115 square yards.
centième [sɑ̃tjɛm] **1** *adj (anniversaire etc)* hundredth. **2** *n* hundredth. **3** *nm* hundredth (part). **4** *nf Th* hundredth performance.
centigrade [sɑ̃tigrad] *nm* centigrade.
centigramme [sɑ̃tigram] *nm* centigram(me).
centilitre [sɑ̃tilitr] *nm* centilitre, *US* centiliter.
centime [sɑ̃tim] *nm* centime; **ne pas avoir un c.,** to be hard up; *Admin* **centimes additionnels,** special surtax.
centimètre [sɑ̃timɛtr] *nm* **(a)** centimetre, *US* centimeter; **(b)** *(ruban)* tape measure.
centrage [sɑ̃traʒ] *nm* centring, *US* centering.
central, -ale, -aux [sɑ̃tral, -o] **1** *adj* central; middle *(point etc)*; *(principal)* central, principal, main, head *(office etc)*; **quartier c. de la ville,** town centre; **Amérique centrale,** Central America; **(prison) centrale,** = county gaol; **École centrale,** = (university level) State school of engineering; **chauffage c.,** central heating; **issue centrale,** central exit. **2** *nm* **(a) c. téléphonique,** telephone exchange; **(b)** *Tennis* **le c.,** the centre court. **3** *nf* **centrale (a)** *Él* **centrale (électrique),** power station; **centrale thermique/nucléaire,** thermal *or* coal-fired/nuclear power station; **centrale surgénératrice,** fast-breeder power station; **(b) centrale (syndicale),** trade union; **(c)** *Com* **centrale d'achat,** central purchasing department; **(d)** *Scol F* **Centrale,** = (university level) State school of engineering.
centralement [sɑ̃tralmɑ̃] *adv* centrally, in the centre.
centralien, -ienne [sɑ̃traljɛ̃, -jɛn] *n* student of the École centrale.
centralisateur, -trice [sɑ̃tralizatœr, -tris] *adj* centralizing *(force etc)*.
centralisation [sɑ̃tralizasjɔ̃] *nf* centralization, centralizing.
centraliser [sɑ̃tralize] *vt* to centralize.
centralisme [sɑ̃tralism] *nm Pol* centralism.
centraliste [sɑ̃tralist] *nm Pol* centralist.
centre [sɑ̃tr] *nm* **(a)** *(base) & Pol* centre, *US* center; *Fb etc (joueur, passe)* centre; **c. d'un cercle,** *(en géométrie)* centre of a circle; *(d'un cercle de gens)* middle of a circle; **il se croit le c. de l'univers,** he thinks (that) the world revolves round him; **le c. (de la) ville,** the town centre; *Com* **c. commercial,** shopping precinct, shopping centre; **c. d'intérêt,** centre of interest; **cette ville est un c. de rayonnement économique/culturel,** this town is an economic/cultural centre *or* powerhouse; **les grands centres urbains,** the great urban centres; **c. de recherche,** research centre; **c. d'art dramatique,** drama centre; *Rail* **c. de triage,** shunting *or* marshalling yard; *Pol* **le c. droit/gauche,** the centre right/left;
(b) *Tech* **c. d'un levier,** fulcrum of a lever; **c. de gravité,** centre of gravity; *Fig* **c. d'attraction,** centre of attraction, focus of attention; *Phys* **c. d'attraction** *ou* **de gravitation,** centre of attraction; *Météo* **c. de dépression,** storm centre;
(c) *Fig Litt (animateur)* driving force; **elle est le c. de notre groupe,** she's the driving force behind our group.
centrer [sɑ̃tre] *vt* to centre, *US* to center **(sur,** on); to adjust *(wheel, tool, lens etc)*; *Fb etc* to centre *(the ball)*; **roman centré sur un personnage,** novel centred *or* based on one character; **c. l'attention du lecteur sur qch,** to focus the reader's attention on sth; **c. un texte sur une page,** to centre a text on a page.
centreur [sɑ̃trœr] *nm Tech* centring *or US* centering tool.
centrifugation [sɑ̃trifygasjɔ̃] *nf* centrifugation, centrifuging.
centrifuge [sɑ̃trifyʒ] *adj* centrifugal *(force etc)*.
centrifuger [sɑ̃trifyʒe] *vt* to centrifuge *(liquid)*; to separate *(cream)*.
centrifugeur [sɑ̃trifyʒœr] *nm*, **centrifugeuse** [sɑ̃trifyʒøz] *nf* centrifuge; separator *(of cream)*.
centripète [sɑ̃tripɛt] *adj* centripetal *(force etc)*.
centrisme [sɑ̃trism] *nm Pol* centrism.
centriste [sɑ̃trist] *Pol* **1** *adj* (of the) centre. **2** *n* centrist; **les centristes,** the centre.
centuple [sɑ̃typl] **1** *adj* hundredfold; **mille est c. de dix,** a thousand is a hundred times (as much as) ten. **2** *nm* a hundred times.
centupler [sɑ̃typle] *vt & vi* to increase a hundred times *or* a hundredfold.

centurion [sɑ̃tyrjɔ̃] *nm Antiq* centurion.
cep [sɛp] *nm* **(a) c. de vigne** [sɛdviŋ, sɛpdəviŋ], vinestock, vine plant; **(b)** *Agr* sole (*of plough*).
cépage [sepaʒ] *nm* (variety of) vine.
cèpe [sɛp] *nm* (*champignon*) boletus, cepe.
cependant [s(ə)pɑ̃dɑ̃] **1** *conj* yet, still, nevertheless, however, though; **c., je l'aime,** I still love him, I love him nevertheless; **le Président Mitterrand, c., n'est pas d'accord,** President Mitterrand, however, does not agree; **vous le saviez depuis longtemps, c., vous ne m'avez pas averti,** you'd known about if for a long time but *or* and yet you didn't tell me. **2** *adv Arch* meanwhile, in the meantime; **c. que,** while, whilst.
céphalique [sefalik] *adj* cephalic.
céphalopode [sefalɔpɔd] *nm* cephalopod, *pl* cephalopoda.
céramique [seramik] **1** *adj* ceramic (*arts etc*); **industries céramiques,** pottery industry. **2** *nf* (*art*) ceramics, (art of) pottery; (*matière*) ceramic, pottery; (*objet*) ceramic, piece of pottery; **dalles en c.,** ceramic tiles; *Méd* **c. dentaire,** dental ceramics.
céramiste [seramist] *n* ceramist.
Cerbère [sɛrbɛr] *nm* **(a)** Cerberus; **(b) c.,** ill-tempered hall porter *or* janitor *etc*.
cerceau, -eaux [sɛrso] *nm* **(a)** (*cercle*) hoop; **c. de jupon,** crinoline hoop; **c. de baril,** barrel hoop; **faire courir un c.,** to trundle a hoop; **(b)** half hoop, round frame, bail (*of cart tilt*); cradle (*over bed*).
cerclage [sɛrklaʒ] *nm* hooping (*of barrels etc*); tyring (*of wheel*).
cercle [sɛrkl] *nm* **(a)** (*de personnes*) circle; (*d'amis etc*) circle, set; (*association*) club; *Math* circle; **former un c.,** to form *or* make a circle; **c. littéraire,** literary circle *or* society; **fonder un c.,** to set up *or* start a society *or* club; **c. militaire** *ou* **des officiers,** officers' club; **le rayon du c.,** the radius of the circle; **quart de c.,** quadrant; **les avions décrivaient des cercles au-dessus de nos têtes,** the planes were circling overhead; **entourer la bonne réponse d'un c.,** to ring *or* put a circle round the correct answer; **c. d'activités,** circle *or* sphere *or* range of activities; **le c. de ses occupations/responsabilités,** the range *or* scope of his work/responsibilities; **c. vicieux,** vicious circle; **se retrouver** *ou* **tomber dans un c. vicieux,** to be caught in a vicious circle; *Géog* **c. (polaire) arctique,** Arctic Circle; **(arc de) grand c.,** great circle; **élargir le c.,** to widen the circle; **le c. de la famille,** the family circle;
(b) (*objet circulaire*) (binding) hoop, ring; **c. d'une roue,** tyre of a wheel; **c. d'arpenteur,** protractor.
cerclé [sɛrkle] *adj* **lunettes cerclées d'écaille,** horn-rimmed spectacles; **yeux cerclés de bistre,** eyes with dark rings round them.
cercueil [sɛrkœj] *nm* coffin, *surtout US* casket; **c. de plomb,** lead casket.
céréale [sereal] *nf* cereal; **commerce des céréales,** corn *or* grain trade; **prendre des céréales au petit déjeuner,** to have cereal for breakfast.
céréalier, -ière [serealje, -jɛr] **1** *adj* cereal (*production etc*). **2** *n* cereal grower.
cérébelleux, -euse [serebɛlø, -øz] *adj Anat* cerebellar (*artery etc*).
cérébral, -ale, -aux [serebral, -o] **1** *adj* cerebral (*artery etc*); **hémorragie cérébrale,** brain haemorrhage; **travail c.,** (*intellectuel*) intellectual work; **surmenage c.,** mental exhaustion; **elle est trop cérébrale,** she's too cerebral. **2** *n* intellectual, thinker.
cérébro-cardiaque [serebrɔkardjak] *adj Méd* cerebro-cardiac (*neuropathy etc*); (*pl cérébro-cardiaques*).
cérébro-spinal [serebrɔspinal] *adj Anat Méd* cerebro-spinal; (*pl cérébro-spinaux*).
cérémonial, -als [seremɔnjal] **1** *adj Arch* ceremonial. **2** *nm* ceremonial; **c. de cour,** court etiquette; **selon le c.,** in accordance with protocol.
cérémonie [seremɔni] *nf* ceremony; **c'était une c. de mariage très réussie,** it was a very successful wedding; **faire une visite de c.,** to pay a ceremonial *or* formal call **(à, on)**; **tenue** *ou* **habit de c.,** dress suit; **maître de c.,** master of ceremonies; *Mil* **uniforme de c.,** (full) dress uniform; *Fig* **sans c.,** without ceremony; (*renvoyer etc qn*) unceremoniously; **faire des cérémonies,** to stand on ceremony; (*faire les choses en grand*) to make a fuss; **sans plus de c.,** without futher ado.
cérémonieusement [seremɔnjøzmɑ̃] *adv* ceremoniously, formally.
cérémonieux, -ieuse [seremɔnjø, -jøz] *adj* ceremonious, formal.
Cérès [serɛs] *nf* Ceres.
cerf [sɛr] *nm* stag, hart; *Culin* venison; **c. commun,** (red) deer.
cerfeuil [sɛrfœj] *nm Culin* chervil.
cerf-volant [sɛrvɔlɑ̃] *nm* (*pl cerfs-volants*) **(a)** kite; **faire voler un c.-v.,** to fly a kite; **(b)** (*insecte*) stag beetle.
cerisaie [s(ə)rizɛ] *nf* cherry orchard.
cerise [s(ə)riz] **1** *nf* (*fruit*) cherry; **clafoutis aux cerises,** cherries baked in batter. **2** *adj inv* cherry-red, cerise.
cerisier [s(ə)rizje] *nm* (*arbre*) cherry tree; (*bois*) cherrywood.
cérium [serjɔm] *nm Ch* cerium.
C.E.R.N. [sɛrn] *nm* (*abrév* **Conseil européen pour la recherche nucléaire**) = European nuclear research centre.
cerne [sɛrn] *nm* **(a)** circle (dark) shadow (*under eyes*); ring, circle (*round moon etc*); **avoir des cernes,** to have (dark) shadows *or* circles under one's eyes; **(b)** age ring (*of tree*).
cerné [sɛrne] *adj* **avoir les yeux cernés,** to have (dark) shadows *or* circles under one's eyes.
cerneau, -eaux [sɛrno] *nm* (*fruit*) green walnut.
cerner [sɛrne] *vt* **(a)** to encircle, to surround (*army etc*); to invest (*town*); to grasp, to determine (*argument etc*); **(b) rendez-vous, vous êtes cernés!,** give yourselves up, you're surrounded!; **une personne difficile à c.,** a difficult person to categorize; **(c)** to shell, to husk (*walnuts*); **(d)** (*entourer*) to ring; **c. la réponse exacte,** to put a circle round *or* circle the right answer.
céroplastique [serɔplastik] *nf* wax modelling.
certain, -aine [sɛrtɛ̃, -ɛn] **1** *adj* **(a)** certain, sure, unquestionable (*proof, news etc*); **il est c. qu'elle viendra,** it's certain *or* definite that she'll come, she'll definitely come; **tenir qch pour c.** *ou* **pour chose certaine,** to look on sth as a certainty; *F* **c'est sûr et c.,** it's absolutely certain; **il est c. de partir,** he's sure *or* certain to leave; **j'en suis c.,** I'm sure *or* certain of it; **moi, je n'en suis pas bien c.,** I'm not so sure myself, I'm not entirely convinced;
(b) (*avant le nom*) some, certain; **certaines gens affirment que ...,** some (people) maintain that ...; **après un c. temps,** after a certain time; **jusqu'à un c. point,** up to a point; **d'un c. âge,** middle-aged; **il faut un c. courage pour le faire,** you need a certain amount of courage to do it; **dans un c. sens,** in a sense, in a way; **on retrouve cette tradition dans certains pays,** this tradition can be found in a number of countries; *souvent Péj* **un c. M. Martin,** a certain Mr Martin.
2 *pron* **certains,** some (people); **certains pensent le contraire,** some people think the opposite *or* take the opposite view.
certainement [sɛrtɛnmɑ̃] *adv* certainly, undoubtedly; **il réussira c.,** he is sure to succeed; **vous l'avez c. lu,** I'm sure you've read it; **c.!** of course!, by all means!
certes [sɛrt] *adv* **(a) je n'irais c. pas jusqu'à penser que ...,** I really wouldn't go as far as that ...; **c., tout espoir n'est pas perdu ...,** we *or* I *etc* haven't given up hope of course, but ...; **(b)** *Vieilli* most certainly; **oui c.!,** yes indeed!
certificat [sɛrtifika] *nm* certificate; **c. de bonne vie et mœurs,** certificate of good character; **montrer ses certificats,** (*d'ouvrier etc*) to show one's references; *Méd* **c. médical,** medical certificate; **c. de chargement,** certificate of receipt; **c. de navigabilité,** *Nau* certificate of seaworthiness; *Av* certificate of airworthiness; **c. d'origine,** *Com* certificate of origin; pedigree (*of dog etc*); **c. de résidence,** certificate of residence; **c. de travail,** attestation of employment; **c. de garantie,** certificate of guarantee; *Fin* **c. provisoire,** share certificate, (provisional) scrip; **c. d'entrepôt,** warrant; *Scol Arch* **c. de licence** *ou* **d'études supérieures,** (*unité de valeur*) each of the four examinations for the licence; (*diplôme*) certificate so obtained; **c. d'aptitude professionnelle,** = vocational training certificate; **c. d'aptitude pédagogique à l'enseignement secondaire,** = postgraduate teaching certificate; *Arch* **c. d'études (primaires),** certificate given after an examination at the end of an elementary course of studies.
certificateur [sɛrtifikatœr] *nm Jur* certifier, guarantor.
certification [sɛrtifikasjɔ̃] *nf Jur Com* certification, authentication; **c. d'une signature,** witnessing of a signature.
certifié, -ée [sɛrtifje] *Scol* **1** *adj* **professeur c.,** = qualified (graduate) teacher. **2** *n* qualified teacher.
certifier [sɛrtifje] *vt* (*pr sub & impf* **n. certifiions, v. certifiiez**) to certify, to attest, to assure; **c. qch à qn,** to assure s.o. of sth; **c. une signature,** to witness *or* au-

thenticate a signature; *Jur* **copie certifiée,** attested *or* certified copy; **c. une caution,** to guarantee a surety; **je vous certifie qu'avec deux enfants on ne s'ennuie pas,** I can assure you that with two children you never get bored.
certitude [sɛrtityd] *nf* certainty, certitude; **j'en ai la c.,** I'm sure of it; **dire qch avec c.,** to speak with assurance.
cérumen [serymɛn] *nm Physiol* cerumen, earwax.
céruse [seryz] *nf* white lead; *Th etc* ceruse (*for making up*).
cerveau, -eaux [sɛrvo] *nm Anat* brain; (*esprit*) mind, intellect, brains; *F* (*personne*) brain; mastermind (*of a plan etc*); **c. antérieur,** forebrain; **c. moyen,** midbrain; **c. postérieur,** hindbrain; **avoir une tumeur au c.,** to have a brain tumour; **rhume de c.,** cold in the head, head cold; **vin qui monte au c.,** heady wine; *F* **se creuser le c.,** to rack one's brains; *F* **homme à c. étroit** *ou* **vide,** man of limited intelligence, emptyheaded man; *F* **avoir le c. dérangé** *ou* **fêlé,** to be mad *or* cracked *or* nuts; **c'est un c., elle pense à tout,** she's a genius, she thinks of everything; **c. brûlé,** hothead; **c. électronique,** electronic brain.
cervelas [sɛrvəla] *nm Culin* saveloy.
cervelet [sɛrvəlɛ] *nm Anat* cerebellum.
cervelle [sɛrvɛl] *nf Anat* brain (*as matter*); (*esprit*) mind, intellect, brains; **brûler** *ou* **faire sauter la c. à qn,** to blow s.o.'s brains out; *Culin* **c. de veau,** calves' brains; **se creuser la c.,** to rack one's brains; **vous me rompez la c.,** you're giving me a headache, you're getting on my nerves (with that noise); *F* **idée qui me trotte dans la c.,** idea running through my head; **sans c.,** brainless, dimwitted; **avoir une c. de moineau,** to be feather-brained *or* scatter-brained *or* empty-headed.
cervical, -aux [sɛrvikal, -o] *adj Anat* cervical.
cervidés [sɛrvide] *nmpl* deer family; *Spéc* Cervidae.
Cervin [sɛrvɛ̃] *nm* **le (Mont) C.,** the Matterhorn.
cervoise [sɛrvwaz] *nf Arch* barley beer.
ces *voir* **CE².**
C.E.S. [seəɛs] *nm Scol* (*abrév* **Collège d'Enseignement Secondaire**) *Br* ≈ secondary school, *Am* ≈ high school.
César [sezar] *nm* **Jules C.,** Julius Caesar.
césarien, -ienne [sezarjɛ̃, -jɛn] **1** *adj Hist* Caesarean, Caesarean. **2** *nf Méd* **césarienne,** Caesarean (section), *F* C section; **se faire faire une c.,** to have a Caesarean; **elle est née par c.,** she was born by Caesarean, she was a Caesarean.
césium [sezjɔm] *nm Ch* caesium.
cessant, -ante [sɛsɑ̃, -ɑ̃t] *adj* **toute(s) affaire(s)** *ou* **chose(s) cessante(s),** immediately.
cessation [sɛsasjɔ̃] *nf* cessation; **c. de paiements,** suspension of payments.
cesse [sɛs] *nf* **(a) sans c.,** unceasingly, constantly, incessantly, continually; **il est sans c. derrière moi,** he's constantly nagging me; **il a plu sans c. pendant les vacances,** it rained non-stop during the holidays; **il parle sans c.,** he never stops talking, he talks non-stop; **(b) il n'aura (pas) de c. qu'il n'ait réussi,** he won't stop *or* rest until he's succeeded.
cesser [sese] **1** *vi* to cease, to stop; **faire c. qch,** to put a stop to sth; **c. de faire qch,** to stop doing sth; **c. de fumer,** to give up *or* stop smoking; **la douleur va c.,** the pain will go away *or* stop; **il faudra que ça cesse,** this has to stop; **faire c. une rumeur,** to scotch a rumour; **il n'a pas cessé de nous observer,** he's been watching us all this time. **2** *vt* **c. le travail,** to stop *or* leave off work; **c. les affaires,** to give up business; **c. toutes relations avec qn,** to break off all relations with s.o.; **c. les paiements,** to stop *or* suspend *or* discontinue payment(s); *Mil* **cessez le feu!,** cease fire!
cessez-le-feu [seselfø] *nm inv* ceasefire.
cessible [sesibl] *adj Jur* transferable, assignable; (*pension etc*) negotiable.
cession [sɛsjɔ̃] *nf Jur* transfer, assignment; **faire c. de qch à qn,** to transfer *or* assign *or* surrender sth to s.o.; **acte de c.,** certificate *or* deed of transfer; **c.-bail,** lease back.
cessionnaire [sɛsjɔnɛr] *nm* **(a)** *Com* transferee, assignee; holder (*of bill*); *Jur* assignee, cessionary; **(b)** endorser (*of cheque*).
c'est-à-dire [setadir] *conj* that is (to say), i.e., in other words; **à la date exacte, c.-à-d. le 14 juillet,** on the exact date, i.e. the 14th of July; **un époux, c.-à-d. un compagnon,** a husband, that is to say, a companion; **un parent, c.-à-d. son oncle,** a relative, that is to say, his uncle; **vous l'avez prévenu? — c.-à-d. que non,** you let him know? – well, actually, I'm afraid I didn't; **c.-à-d. que je n'étais pas au courant,** (the thing is that) no-one told me; **j'ai raté mon train, c.-à-d. que je serai en retard,** I missed my train so I'll be late.
césure [sezyr] *nf* caesura.
cet *voir* **CE².**
C.E.T. [seəte] *nm Scol* (*abrév* **Collège d'Enseignement Technique**) ≈ technical college.
cétacé [setase] *adj & nm Zool* cetacean.
cette *voir* **CE².**
ceux *voir* **CELUI.**
cévenol, -ole [sevnɔl] **1** *adj* (*nature, inhabitant*) of the Cévennes (*region*). **2** *n* **C.,** an inhabitant of the Cévennes.
Ceylan [selɑ̃] *nm* Ceylon.
cf. [seɛf] cf.
CFC [seɛfse] *nmpl Ch* (*abrév* **chlorofluorocarbures**) CFCs.
C.F.D.T. [seɛfdete] *nf* (*abrév* **Confédération française démocratique du travail**) = French trade union.
C.G.C. [seʒese] *nf* (*abrév* **Confédération générale des cadres**) = French trade union of managerial staff.
C.G.T. [seʒete] *nf* (*abrév* **Confédération Générale du Travail**) = French trade union.
chabot [ʃabo] *nm* (*poisson*) (*de mer*) bullhead; (*d'eau douce*) chub, miller's thumb.
chacal, -als [ʃakal] *nm* jackal; *Fig Péj* (*homme d'affaires etc*) shark.
chacon(n)e [ʃakɔn] *nf Mus* chaconne.
chacun, -une [ʃakœ̃, -yn] *pron indéf* **(a)** (*chaque personne*) each (one), every one; **chacune d'elles a refusé,** each (one) *or* every one of them refused; **trois francs c.,** three francs each; **ils ont pris c. son** *ou* **leur chapeau,** each of them took their *or Fml* his hat, they each took their hat; **nous avons pris c. notre chapeau,** each of us took our *or Fml* his hat, we each took our hat; **ils sont partis c. de son côté** *ou* **c. de leur côté,** they (all) went their separate ways; **(b)** (*tout le monde*) everybody, everyone; **c. pour soi,** every man for himself; **c. ses goûts,** everyone to their own taste; **c. son tour,** each in turn; **c. son tour!,** wait your turn!; *F* **tout un c.,** all and sundry, every Tom, Dick and Harry.
chafouin, -ine [ʃafwɛ̃, -in] *adj* foxy-looking, sly-looking (*person*).
chagrin¹, -ine [ʃagrɛ̃, -in] **1** *adj Litt* morose, peevish; *Arch* sad, downcast. **2** *nm* (*peine*) grief, sorrow, affliction, trouble; *Arch* vexation, chagrin; **avoir du c.,** to be sorrowful, to grieve; **faire du c. à qn,** to grieve *or* distress s.o.; **usé par le c.,** careworn; **mourir de c.,** to die of a broken heart; **un c. d'amour,** an unhappy love affair; **elle a eu un gros c. de quitter ses amis,** she was brokenhearted at having to leave her friends.
chagrin² *nm* (*cuir*) shagreen.
chagrinant [ʃagrinɑ̃] *adj* distressing, sad; *Arch* annoying, vexing.
chagriner¹ [ʃagrine] **1** *vt* (*peiner*) to grieve, to distress, to afflict; *Arch* to vex, to annoy; **cela me chagrine lorsque je vois que ...,** it grieves me when I see that ...; **je ne voulais pas vous c. en vous le disant,** I didn't want to upset you by telling you. **2 se chagriner** *vpr* to grieve; to fret.
chagriner² *vt* to shagreen, to grain (*leather*); **papier chagriné,** pebbled *or* granulated paper.
chah [ʃa] *nm* shah.
chahut [ʃay] *nm F* noise, din; **faire du c.,** to make *or* kick up a din *or* a racket *or* a rumpus, to create an uproar; **les élèves ont fait un c. pour protester contre la décision,** the pupils kicked up a racket to show their disapproval of the decision.
chahuter [ʃayte] *F* **1** *vi* to make *or* kick up a din *or* a racket *or* a rumpus, to create an uproar. **2** *vt* to rag (*schoolmaster etc*); to boo (*play, speaker etc*); to heckle, to barrack (*speaker*); **les filles se sont fait c. par deux hommes éméchés,** two drunk men gave the girls a bit of a hard time.
chahuteur, -euse [ʃaytœr, -øz] *F* **1** *adj* rowdy, disorderly (*student etc*). **2** *n* rowdy; (*at political meeting*) heckler.
chai [ʃɛ] *nm* wine and spirits store(house).
chaînage [ʃɛnaʒ] *nm* **(a)** (*arpentage*) chaining, chain measuring; **(b)** *Constr* tying, clamping (*of walls*); (*armature*) tie irons, (series of) clamps, ties.
chaîne [ʃɛn] *nf* **(a)** chain (*of iron, gold etc*); *Nau* cable; **c. de montre,** watch chain; **c. de sûreté,** door chain, safety chain; **c. de bicyclette,** bicyle chain; **la c. saute facilement,** the chain keeps coming off; *Aut* **chaînes à neige,** snow chains; **mettre la c.,** to put the chain on; **mettre un chien à la c.,** to chain up a dog; *Fig* **briser sa c.** *ou* **ses chaînes,** to break free; **un prisonnier retenu par sa c.,** a prisoner tied to his chain; **faire la c.,** to form a chain (*in order to pass buckets etc*); *Ind* **c. de montage,** assembly

line; *Ind* **c. de fabrication,** production line; *Ind* **travail/travailleur à la c.,** assembly line *or* production line work/worker; **travailler à la c.,** to work on the assembly *or* production line; **c. d'arpenteur,** surveying chain, surveyor's chain; *Nau* **tour de c.,** foul cable; *Nau* **les chaînes,** the hawse; *Nau* **le navire a cassé sa c.,** the ship has parted her cable; *Nau* **c. de port,** harbour (chain) boom;

(b) (*série*) chain, succession, sequence, series; (*d'hôtels, magasins etc*) chain; (*par correspondance*) chain letter; **c. de montagnes,** range *or* chain of mountains; **c. de rochers,** line of rocks; **c. de chalands,** string of barges; **c. du commandement,** chain of command; **c. de combat,** firing line; **c. d'idées,** train of thought; **une grande c. de supermarchés,** a large supermarket chain; **réaction en c.,** chain reaction;

(c) *Constr* **c. de liaison,** stone pier (*in brickwork*); brick pier (*in rubble work*);

(d) *Ch Electron etc* chain; *Rad TV* network; station; *TV* channel; **c. (de haute-fidélité),** hi-fi; **changeons de c.,** let's change channel; **qu'est-ce qu'il y a sur les autres chaînes?,** what's on the other channels?;

(e) *Tex* warp.

chaîner [ʃɛne] *vt* **(a)** (*d'arpenteur*) to chain, to measure (*land*) with a chain; **(b)** *Constr* to chain, to tie (*walls etc*).

chaînette [ʃɛnɛt] *nf* **(a)** small chain; **c. antivol,** chain lock; **(b)** *Math* **(arc en) c.,** catenary (curve); **(c)** *Couture* **point de c.,** chain stitch.

chaînon [ʃɛnɔ̃] *nm* **(a)** link (*of chain*); *Fig* **le c. manquant,** the missing link; **(b)** *Géog* secondary chain (*of mountains*).

chair [ʃɛr] *nf* **(a)** flesh; flesh, pulp (*of peach, melon etc*); **c. vive,** raw flesh; **en c. et en os,** in the flesh, in person; **être (bien) en c.,** (*de poulet*) to be nice and plump; (*de personne*) to be plump *or F* tubby; **c. à canon,** cannon fodder; **c. (à saucisses),** sausagemeat; *Fig F* **je vais en faire de la c. à saucisses,** I'll make mincemeat of him; *Fig* **n'être ni c. ni poisson,** to be neither fish nor fowl (nor good red herring); **une odeur de c. fraîche,** a smell of fresh meat; *Fig* **il recherche de la c. fraîche,** he likes them young;

(b) skin, outer surface of flesh; *Beaux-Arts* **chairs,** flesh tints; **avoir la c. fraîche,** to have a rosy complexion; **c. de poule,** gooseflesh, goose pimples, *Am* goose bumps; **cela vous donne** *ou* **on en a la c. de poule,** it makes your flesh creep, it makes you shudder, *F* it gives you the creeps;

(c) *Rel* body; *Péj* flesh; **la résurrection de la c.,** the resurrection of the body; *Bible* **le Verbe s'est fait c.,** the Word was made flesh; **c. de sa c.,** his own flesh and blood; **souffrir dans sa c.,** to suffer in the flesh; **quand la c. se réveille,** when the flesh is aroused; **péché de c.,** sin of the flesh.

2 *adj inv* **(couleur) c.,** flesh-coloured.

chaire [ʃɛr] *nf* **(a)** (*dans une église*) pulpit; **monter en c.,** to go into the pulpit; **(b)** *Univ* chair, professorship; chair, desk rostrum (*of lecturer*); **elle a été nommée à la c. d'anglais,** she has been appointed to the chair of English; **être titulaire d'une c.,** to hold a chair; **(c)** chair, throne; **la c. de saint Pierre, la c. pontificale,** the Chair of St Peter, the Holy See; **c. d'un évêque,** bishop's throne.

chaise [ʃɛz] *nf* **(a)** (*siège*) chair, seat; **c. de paille/cannée,** straw-/cane-bottomed chair; **c. haute, c. d'enfant,** (baby's) high chair; **c. longue,** chaise longue; (*transatlantique*) deckchair; **faire de la c. longue,** to have a rest, to put one's feet up; **prenez donc une c.,** have *or* take a seat; **c. à bascule,** *Can* **c. berçante,** rocking chair; *Fig* **être assis entre deux chaises,** to be in an awkward position; **porter qn en c., faire la c. à qn,** to give s.o. a chair; **c. roulante,** wheelchair, *Vieilli* bath chair; **c. percée,** (night) commode; *Jur US* **c. électrique,** electric chair; **passer à la c. électrique,** to go to the chair;

(b) *Tech* support, bracket;

(c) *Constr* frame timberwork (*of windmill etc*); **c. de coussinet,** plummer block; *Rail* **c. de rail,** (rail) chair; *Arch* **c. d'hélice,** A bracket;

(d) c. à porteurs, sedan chair; **c. de poste,** post chaise;

(e) *Nau etc* rope sling; **nœud de c.,** bowline hitch.

chaisier, -ière [ʃezje, -jɛr] **1** *n* chairmaker. **2** *nf* **chaisière,** chair attendant (*in park, etc*).

chaland[1] [ʃalɑ̃] *nm Nau* barge, lighter; **transport par chalands,** lighterage.

chaland[2], -ande [ʃalɑ̃, -ɑ̃d] *n Arch* customer.

chalcédoine [kalsedwan] *nf Minér* chalcedony.

chaldaïque [kaldaik] **1** *adj* Chaldean. **2** *n* **C.,** Chaldean.

Chaldée [kalde] *nf Hist Géog* Chaldea.

chaldéen, -enne [kaldeɛ̃, -ɛn] **1** *adj* Chaldean. **2** *nm Ling* Chaldean. **3** *n* **C.,** Chaldean.

châle [ʃɑl] *nm* shawl.

chalet [ʃalɛ] *nm* **(a)** (*Swiss etc*) chalet; (*maison de campagne*) country cottage; **(b)** *Arch* **c. de nécessité,** public convenience.

chaleur [ʃalœr] *nf* **(a)** heat, warmth; *Fig* ardour, zeal; **il fait une grande c.,** it's very hot; **vague de c.,** heatwave; **c. étouffante,** sultry weather; **c. sèche/humide,** dry/humid heat; **craint la c.,** (*sur une étiquette*) store in a cool place; *Phys* **c. atomique d'un corps,** atomic heat of a body; **c. spécifique/latente,** specific/latent heat; *Méd* **éprouver des chaleurs, avoir des bouffées de c.,** (*d'une femme ménopausée*) to have hot flushes; **sensation de c.,** glow (*after cold bath etc*); (*brûlure*) burning sensation; *Méd* **coup de c.,** heatstroke; **les chaleurs,** the hot weather; **pendant les grandes chaleurs,** during the hot season; *Beaux-Arts* **c. de coloris,** warmth of colour; **dans la c. du combat,** in the heat of the battle; **rechercher la c. humaine,** to look for human warmth; **parler avec c.,** to speak warmly *or* enthusiastically;

(b) heat, rut (*of animals*); **en c.,** on heat, *surtout Am* in heat; *Vulg Fig* **elle est en c., celle-là!,** she's randy *or* on heat, that one!

chaleureusement [ʃalœrøzmɑ̃] *adv* warmly.

chaleureux, -euse [ʃalœrø, -øz] *adj* warm, cordial, hearty (*welcome etc*); glowing (*colour, terms*); enthusiastic (*applause etc*); **remercier qn en termes c.,** to thank s.o. warmly.

châlit [ʃali] *nm* bedstead.

challenge [ʃalɑ̃ʒ] *nm Sp* challenge match, tournament; *Fig* **ce sera un c. pour lui,** it will be a challenge for him.

challenger [ʃalɑ̃ʒɛr] *nm Sp etc* challenger.

chaloir [ʃalwar] *v impers Arch & Litt* (*used only in*) **peu me chaut, peu m'en chaut,** I don't give a fig, I care not.

chaloupe [ʃalup] *nf Nau* launch, longboat; rowing boat, *Am* rowboat; **c. à moteur,** motor launch; **c. de pêche,** fishing boat.

chaloupé [ʃalupe] *adj* swaying, swinging, rocking (*dance, walk*)

chalumeau, -eaux [ʃalymo] *nm* **(a)** (*paille*) (drinking) straw; **c. de roseau,** reed; **(b)** *Mus* pipe; **(c)** (*lampe*) blowlamp, blowtorch; **faire une soudure au c.,** to weld with a blowlamp; **c. oxyacétylénique,** oxyacetylene torch; **(d)** *Can* spout (*for collecting sap of maple tree*).

chalut [ʃaly] *nm Pêche* trawl; **pêcher au c.,** to trawl.

chalutage [ʃalytaʒ] *nm Pêche* trawling.

chalutier [ʃalytje] *nm* (*bateau*) trawler; (*homme d'équipage*) trawlerman.

chamade [ʃamad] *nf* **battre la c.,** to be in a panic; **mon cœur battait la c.,** my heart was thumping *or* beating wildly.

chamaille [ʃamaj] *nf F* squabble, row, quarrel.

chamailler (se) [səʃamaje] *vpr F* to bicker, to squabble, to quarrel.

chamaillerie [ʃamajri] *nf F* **(a)** (*fait de se disputer*) bickering, quarrelling, squabbling; **(b)** (*dispute*) squabble, row, quarrel.

chamailleur, -euse [ʃamajœr, -øz] *adj & n* quarrelsome (person).

chamarrer [ʃamare] *vt Litt* to bedeck, to adorn; *Tex* **des tissus chamarrés,** brightly-patterned fabrics.

chambard [ʃɑ̃bar] *nm F* (*désordre*) disorder, shambles; (*bouleversement*) upset, upheaval; (*bruit*) din, racket; **faire du c.,** to make *or* kick up a row *or* a shindy.

chambardement [ʃɑ̃bardəmɑ̃] *nm F* upset, upheaval; **cela a provoqué un grand c.,** it caused a tremendous upheaval.

chambarder [ʃɑ̃barde] *vt F* to upset, to ransack (*room etc*); (*révolutionner*) to turn (*a company*) upside down; **tout c.,** to turn everything upside down; **c. les plans de qn,** to upset s.o.'s applecart.

chambellan [ʃɑ̃belɑ̃] *nm* chamberlain.

chambouler [ʃɑ̃bule] *vt F* to ruin, to mess up (*plans etc*); **tout c.,** to turn everything topsy-turvey *or* upside down.

chambranle [ʃɑ̃brɑ̃l] *nm* frame casing (*of door, window*); (standing) window frame; mantelpiece.

chambre [ʃɑ̃br] *nf* **(a)** bedroom; **c. à coucher,** bedroom; **c. grand lit** *ou* **pour deux personnes,** double room; **c. à deux lits,** room with twin beds, twin-bedded room; **c. à un lit,** single room; **c. d'amis,** spare (bed)room, guest room; **c. d'enfants,** nursery; **c. meublée,** furnished room, bed-sittingroom, *F* bed-sit(ter); **faire c. à part,** to sleep in separate rooms; **faire sa c.,** to clean (out) *or* tidy (up) one's room; **c. forte,** safety vault, strong room; **c. des machines,** engine room; **c. de chauffe,** boiler room, *Nau*

stokehold; **c. à gaz,** gas chamber; **c. froide** *ou* **frigorifique,** cold (storage) room, cold store; *Nau* **c. des cartes,** charthouse, chart room; **travailler en c.,** to work at home; **ouvrier en c.,** homeworker; **stratège en c.,** armchair strategist; **musique de c.,** chamber music;
(b) *Admin Jur* chamber, house; division of a court of justice; **c. des métiers,** = guild chamber; **c. de commerce,** chamber of commerce; **c. des députés,** Chamber of Deputies; *Pol* **la C.,** the House, **siéger à la C.,** to sit in the House; **C. basse,** Lower House, Lower Chamber; **C. haute,** Upper House, Upper Chamber; *Fin* **c. de compensation,** clearing house;
(c) *Tech* chamber (*of gun, lock etc*); *Physiol* chamber (*of the eye*); *Aut etc* **c. à air,** inner tube (*of tyre*); **pneu sans c.,** tubeless tyre; *MecE* **c. de combustion** *ou* **d'explosion,** combustion chamber; *Phys* **c. à bulles,** bubble chamber; *Phot* **c. noire,** (*pièce*) darkroom.

chambrée [ʃɑ̃bre] *nf* **(a)** room(ful) (*of people sharing a room*); **(b)** *Mil* barrackroom.

chambrer [sɑ̃bre] *vt* **(a)** to confine, to lock up (*s.o.*); to keep (*s.o.*) locked up; **(b)** to bring (*wine*) to room temperature; **(c)** *F* **c. qn,** to pull s.o.'s leg.

chambrette [ʃɑ̃brɛt] *nf* little (bed)room.

chambrière [ʃɑ̃brijɛr] *nf* **(a)** *Arch* chambermaid; **(b)** (*fouet*) long whip, lunging whip; **(c)** (*de charrette*) (cart)prop.

chameau, -eaux [ʃamo] **1** *nm* **(a)** camel; **partir dans le désert en** *ou* **à dos de c.,** to set off into the desert by camel; **quel c.!,** (*d'un homme*) what a bastard!; (*d'une femme*) what a cow *or* bitch!; **(b)** *Nau* camel (*for raising ships*). **2** *adj F* **ce qu'il/elle est c.!,** what a bastard he is/ bitch she is!

chamelier [ʃaməlje] *nm* camel-driver, cameleer.

chamelle [ʃamɛl] *nf* she-camel.

chamois [ʃamwa] **1** *nm* chamois; **(peau de) c.,** wash-leather, chamois leather, shammy (leather). **2** *adj inv* buff(-coloured).

champ [ʃɑ̃] *nm* **(a)** field; **c. de blé,** field of wheat, wheatfield; **fleur des champs,** wild flower; **courir les champs,** to wander about the country; **aux champs,** in the fields; **prendre** *ou* **couper à travers champs,** to go *or* cut across country; **donner la clef des champs à qn,** to give s.o. his liberty; **prendre la clef des champs,** to decamp, to run off; **en plein(s) champ(s),** in the open (fields); **à tout bout de c.,** repeatedly, at every possible opportunity; **c. de foire,** fairground; **c. d'aviation,** airfield; **c. de courses,** racecourse, *Am* racetrack; **parier contre le c.,** to bet against the field; **c. de neige,** snowfield; **c. de glace,** icefield; *Mil* **c. de bataille** *ou* **d'honneur,** battlefield; **mort au c. d'honneur,** killed in action; **c. de manœuvres,** drill *or* exercise *or* parade ground; **c. de tir,** firing *or* shooting *or* rifle range; *Mil* practice ground; field of fire (*of gun*); **c. de mines,** minefield; *Arch* **c. clos,** lists; *Fig* battlefield; *Fig* **laisser le c. libre à qn,** to leave s.o. a clear field; *Fig* **le c. est libre,** the coast's clear;
(b) (*espace*) **prendre du c. (pour sauter/*etc*),** to give oneself (plenty of) room (to jump/*etc*); **donnez-moi du c.,** give me (some) elbow room;
(c) *Fig* (*domaine*) field; **ses lectures embrassent un c. très étendu,** his reading covers a very wide field *or* range of subjects; **élargir le c. de son activité,** to extend the scope of one's activities; **le c. de la connaissance,** the field of (human) knowledge; *Ling* **c. sémantique d'un mot,** the semantic field of a word;
(d) *Cin etc* shot, picture; *Opt* field (*of telescope etc*); **c. optique** *ou* **visuel** *ou* **de vision,** field of view *or* of vision; *Phot* **profondeur de c.,** depth of focus; **hors c.,** off camera; **être dans le c.,** to be in shot; **récit hors c.,** voice over;
(e) *Él Électron Rad Ordinat* field; **c. magnétique,** magnetic field;
(f) *Beaux-Arts* field, ground (*of picture*); *Hér* field (*of coat of arms*);
(g) *Chir* **c. opératoire,** operative field.

Champagne [ʃɑ̃paɲ] **1** *nf* **(a)** Champagne; **C. humide,** wet Champagne; **C. pouilleuse,** dry Champagne; **(b) fine c.,** liqueur brandy. **2** *nm* **(vin de) C.,** champagne.

champagnisation [ʃɑ̃paɲizasjɔ̃] *nf* champagnization.

champagniser [ʃɑ̃paɲize] *vt* to champagnize (*wine*).

champenois, -oise [ʃɑ̃pənwa, -waz] **1** *adj* **(a)** (*de la région*) of Champagne; **(b) méthode champenoise,** (natural) champagnization method, champagne method. **2** *n* **C.,** native *or* inhabitant of Champagne.

champêtre [ʃɑ̃pɛtr] *adj* rustic, rural; **vie c.,** country life; *Admin* **garde c.,** country *or* village policeman.

champignon [ʃɑ̃piɲɔ̃] *nm* **(a) c. (comestible),** mushroom; **c. vénéneux,** toadstool; **c. de couche** *ou* **de Paris,** cultivated mushroom, button mushroom; **blanc de c.,** mushroom spawn; *Fig* **pousser comme un c.,** to (spring up like a) mushroom; *Fig* **ville c.,** mushroom town, boom town; **c. atomique,** mushroom cloud; **(b)** *Méd* fungus, fungoid growth; **(c) c. de modiste,** milliner's hatstand; **(d)** cowl (*of chimney*); **(e)** *Rail* head (*of rail*); **(f)** *Aut F* accelerator (pedal); **appuyer sur le c.,** to put one's foot down, *Am* to step on the gas.

champignonnière [ʃɑ̃piɲɔnjɛr] *nf* mushroom bed.

champignonniste [ʃɑ̃piɲɔnist] *n* mushroom grower.

champion, -ionne [ʃɑ̃pjɔ̃, -jɔn] **1** *n Sp etc* **(a)** champion; **le c. du monde d'escrime,** the world fencing champion; **un c. de ski,** a ski champion; **(b)** champion, defender (*of a cause etc*); **se faire le c. de la protection des animaux,** to champion the protection of animals. **2** *adj F* great, champion; **c'est c.!,** it's first-rate!; **elle est championne, ta copine!,** your girlfriend is terrific *or* top notch!

championnat [ʃɑ̃pjɔna] *nm* championship; **c. du monde de course à pied,** world running championship.

chançard, -arde [ʃɑ̃sar, -ard] *F* **1** *adj* lucky (*man, woman*). **2** *n* lucky person; **quel c.!,** (he's a) lucky devil!

chance [ʃɑ̃s] *nf* **(a)** (*possibilité*) chance, likelihood; **vous avez toutes les chances d'être accusé, il y a toutes les chances (pour) que vous soyez accusé,** there is every chance *or* likelihood that you will be accused; **il a compris qu'il fallait mettre toutes les chances de son côté,** he realised he had to leave nothing to chance; **donner une c. à qn,** to give s.o. a chance; **il a peu de chances de réussir** *ou* **de succès,** he has little chance of succeeding, he's very unlikely to succeed; **elle a des chances égales d'être nommée,** she has an even *or* a fifty-fifty chance of being appointed; **il a des chances d'être choisi,** he stands a good chance of being chosen; **calculer** *ou* **évaluer ses chances de succès,** to work out one's chances of success; **il y a une c.,** it's just possible; **il y a une c. sur cent (pour) qu'elle le voie,** there's a chance in a hundred that she'll see him;
(b) (*sort*) (good) luck, fortune; **la c. lui sourit,** fortune smiles on him; **tenter la c.,** to try one's luck, to chance it; **la c. peut tourner à tout moment,** our *or* your *etc* luck could change at any time; **souhaiter bonne c. à qn,** to wish s.o. luck; **bonne c.!,** good luck!; **quelle c.!,** what a bit *or* stroke of luck!, what a blessing!; **avoir de la c.,** to be lucky *or* fortunate; **elle n'a pas eu de c.,** she was unlucky; **porter c. à qn,** to bring s.o. luck; **c'est bien ma c.!,** just my luck!; **pas de c.!,** hard luck!; **par c.,** luckily, fortunately, by a stroke of luck; **la c. est avec nous,** our luck's in.

chancelant [ʃɑ̃slɑ̃] *adj* staggering, wavering, unsteady; **pas chancelants,** staggering *or* tottering *or* unsteady footsteps; **une autorité chancelante,** shaky *or* wavering authority; **le pouvoir est c.,** the government is tottering *or* on the brink of collapse; **santé chancelante,** delicate *or* poor health; delicate constitution (*de nature*).

chanceler [ʃɑ̃sle] *vi* (**je chancelle, n. chancelons; je chancellerai**) to stagger, to totter, to wobble; to be unsteady (on one's legs); **avancer/reculer/entrer/sortir en chancelant,** to stagger *or* totter forward/back/in/out; **trône qui chancelle,** tottering throne; **c. dans sa résolution,** to waver *or* falter in one's resolution.

chancelier [ʃɑ̃səlje] *nm* chancellor; *Admin* **c. de l'université,** chancellor of the university; **Grand C.,** (*en Grande Bretagne*) Lord Chancellor; **C. de l'Échiquier,** Chancellor of the Exchequer.

chancelière [ʃɑ̃səljɛr] *nf* **(a)** (*épouse du chancelier*) chancellor's wife; **(b)** (*pour les pieds*) footmuff.

chancellerie [ʃɑ̃sɛlri] *nf* **(a)** chancellery; **(b)** chancery (*of an embassy*).

chanceux, -euse [ʃɑ̃sø, -øz] *adj* **(a)** lucky, fortunate; **vous voilà bien c.!,** you're lucky!, you're in luck!; *Can* **c.!,** (you) lucky devil!; **(b)** *Arch* hazardous, chancy.

chancir [ʃɑ̃sir] **1** *vi* to go mouldy. **2 se chancir** *vpr* to go mouldy.

chancre [ʃɑ̃kr] *nm Bot Méd Vét* canker; *Méd* **c. syphilitique** *ou* **mou,** soft chancre; *Arg* **manger comme un c.,** to eat like a horse, to make a pig of oneself; *Fig* **l'ambition est un c.,** ambition is a canker.

chandail [ʃɑ̃daj] *nm* jumper, sweater, pullover.

Chandeleur (la) [laʃɑ̃dlœr] *nf Rel* Candlemas.

chandelier [ʃɑ̃dəlje] *nm* candelabra.

chandelle [ʃɑ̃dɛl] *nf* **(a)** (*tallow*) candle; *Vieilli* (*cierge*) (church) candle, taper; **s'éclairer à la c.,** to use candlelight; **moucher une c.,** to snuff (out) a candle; **économies de bouts de c.,** cheeseparing; **faire des**

économies de bouts de c., to cheesepare; **travailler à la c.**, to work by candlelight; *Fig* **brûler la c. par les deux bouts,** to burn the candle at both ends; (*dépenser trop d'argent*) to be extravagant (with money); *Fig* **le jeu n'en vaut pas la c.**, the game is not worth the candle; *Fig* **tenir la c.**, *Br* to play gooseberry, *Am* to feel like a fifth wheel; (*se faire le complice*) to act as go-between in a love affair; *Fig* **en voir trente-six chandelles,** to see stars; *Fig* **je vous dois une fière c.**, I owe you more than I can repay; **(b)** *Arg* dewdrop, snot (*at the end of the nose*); **(c)** *Tennis Cr etc* lob; *Fb* high kick; *Rugby F* Garry Owen, up and under; *Gym* shoulder stand; **(d)** *Constr etc* stay, prop, shore, pillar, upright; **(e) c. romaine,** Roman candle; **monter en c.**, (*of aircraft*) to climb vertically, to rocket; *Av* **(montée en) c.**, vertical climb, chandelle.

chanfrein¹ [ʃɑ̃frɛ̃] *nm* nose, forehead (*of horse*).

chanfrein² *nm Archit* chamfered edge, chamfer, bevelled edge.

change [ʃɑ̃ʒ] *nm* **(a)** *Fin* exchange; **lettre de c.**, bill of exchange; **lettre de c. sur l'intérieur/l'extérieur,** inland/foreign bill; **bureau de c.**, foreign exchange office; **opérations de c.**, (foreign) exchange transactions; **cours du c.**, exchange rate, rate of exchange; **au c. du jour,** at the current rate of exchange; **agent de c.**, stockbroker; **contrôle des changes,** exchange control; **gagner** *ou* **ne pas perdre au c.**, to gain on *or* by the exchange, to lose nothing on the deal; **je n'y perdais pas au c.**, I came out (of it) ahead, I didn't lose by it; **(b) donner le c. aux chiens,** to put hounds on the wrong scent; *Fig* **donner le c. à qn,** to put s.o. on a false scent *or* trail; **(c)** (*couche-culotte*) disposable nappy *or Am* diaper.

changeable [ʃɑ̃ʒabl] *adj* changeable.

changeant [ʃɑ̃ʒɑ̃] *adj* changeable, variable; **caractère c.**, changeable *or* fickle disposition; **d'humeur changeante,** fitful; **temps c.**, unsettled weather; **taffetas c.**, shot silk.

changement [ʃɑ̃ʒmɑ̃] *nm* change (*of air, of residence, of condition etc*); *Scol* **c. (de section, de classe),** transfer; **il vous faudrait un c. d'air** *ou* **d'occupation,** you need a change; **'c. de propriétaire'**, 'under new management'; **c. de régime,** change of government; **c. de marée,** turn of the tide; **c. climatique** *ou* **du climat,** climate change; **c. de vent,** shift of wind; **c. en mal/en mieux,** change for the worse/the better; **il n'y a pas de c.**, (*dans son état*) there's (been) no change; **son c. est radical, ce n'est plus le même!**, he's changed completely, he isn't the same person any more!; **c. de vitesse,** (*action*) change of gear, gear change; (*levier*) gear lever; *Rail* **c. de voie,** points, turn-off; *Th* **c. à vue,** transformation scene.

changer [ʃɑ̃ʒe] *v* **(je changeai(s); n. changeons) 1** *vt* **(a)** (*remplacer*) *& Fin* to change, to exchange; **c. des meubles contre des tableaux,** to exchange furniture for pictures; **c. le personnel,** to change one's staff; **c. les draps,** to change the sheets; *Th* **c. le décor,** to shift *or* change the scenery; **c. un bébé,** to change a baby('s nappy, *Am* diaper); **c. un billet de banque,** to change a (bank)note; **c. des dollars contre des francs,** to change dollars into francs;

(b) (*modifier*) to change, to alter; (*divertir*) to be a change for; **c. sa manière de vivre,** to change one's way of life; **ça ne change rien à rien,** that doesn't change anything, it makes absolutely no difference; **c. sa façon de penser,** to change one's way of thinking; **il a bien fallu c. nos projets,** we had no choice but to change our plans; **les jeunes veulent tout c.**, the young want to change everything; **cette robe vous change,** that dress makes you look different; **cette expérience l'a beaucoup changée,** this experience has changed her a lot; **voilà qui change les choses du tout au tout,** that makes all the difference; **c. un livre de place,** to move a book; **c. un fonctionnaire de poste,** to transfer a civil servant; **c. l'ordre des mots,** to change the word order; **la campagne me changera,** the country will be a (good) change for me; **une promenade me changera les idées,** a walk will take my mind off things.

2 *vi* **(a)** to (undergo a) change, to alter; **cette région a beaucoup changé,** the region has changed *or* altered a great deal; **le temps va c.**, the weather's going to change; **il a changé en mal/en mieux,** he's changed for the worse/the better; *Iron* **pour c.**, (just) for a change; **tu n'as pas changé,** you haven't changed (a bit); *Rail etc* **où dois-je c.?**, where do I change?; **je dois c. à Bordeaux,** I have to change at Bordeaux;

(b) c. de, to change; **c. de secrétaire/de coiffeur/de médecin/***etc*, to change secretaries/hairdressers/doctors/*etc*; **c. de train,** to change trains; **c. de main,** to change hands, to use the other hand; *Fig* **c. de mains,** to change hands *or* ownership; **c. de place avec qn,** to change seats with s.o.; **c. de places,** to change places; **c. de maison,** to move (house); **la rue a changé de nom,** the name of the street has been changed, the street has changed its name; **le magasin a changé de propriétaire,** the shop is under new management; **c. de genre/de coiffure,** to change one's style/hairstyle; **c. de vêtements,** to change (one's clothes), to get changed; **c. de peau,** (*de serpent*) to change *or* shed *or* slough its skin; **c. d'avis/d'opinion,** to change one's mind/opinion; **c. d'attitude envers qn,** to change one's attitude towards s.o.; **c. de couleur,** to change colour; **elle changea de visage,** her expression changed *or* altered; **c. de sujet,** to change the subject; **c. de route,** to take another road; *Nau* to alter course; **c. de vitesse,** to change gear; **la rivière a changé de cours,** the river has shifted its course; **c. de ton,** to change one's tune.

3 se changer *vpr* to change (one's clothes).

changeur, -euse [ʃɑ̃ʒœr, -øz] **1** *n* (*personne*) money changer. **2** *nm* **(a)** *Rad* **c. de fréquence,** frequency changer; **(b) c. de disques,** record changer.

Changhai [ʃɑ̃gaj] *nm* Shanghai.

chanoine [ʃanwan] *nm Rel* canon; *F* **vie de c.** easy life.

chanson [ʃɑ̃sɔ̃] *nf* **(a)** *Mus* song; **c. à boire,** drinking song; **c. de route,** marching song; **c. de marins,** sea shanty; **c. réaliste,** cabaret song, music hall song; *F* **c'est toujours la même c.!**, it's always the same old story; *F* **voilà bien une autre c.!**, that's quite another story!; *F* **on connaît la c.!**, I've heard that one before!; *Arch* **chansons (que tout cela)!**, nonsense!; **(b)** *Littér* song, lay, verse chronicle; **la c. de Roland,** the Song of Roland; **c. de geste,** chanson de geste, epic poem.

chansonner [ʃɑ̃sɔne] *vt* to write satirical songs about (*s.o.*), to lampoon (*s.o.*) (in song).

chansonnette [ʃɑ̃sɔnɛt] *nf* little song, ditty.

chansonnier [ʃɑ̃sɔnje] *nm* **(a)** (*artiste*) = someone who sings in cabaret or in clubs; **(b)** (*recueil*) song book.

chant¹ [ʃɑ̃] *nm Mus* **(a)** singing, song; **leçon/maître de c.**, singing lesson/master; **apprendre le c.**, to take singing lessons; **le c. des oiseaux,** the song of the birds, birdsong; *Fig* **c'était son c. du cygne,** it was his swan song; **c. du grillon,** chirping of the cricket; **c. du coq,** crowing of the cock; **au c. du coq,** at cockcrow; **(b)** (*chanson*) song; (*mélodie*) melody, air; **c. de victoire,** song of victory; **c. de guerre,** battle song, war song; **c. de Noël,** Christmas carol; *Rel* **c. grégorien,** Gregorian chant; **c. funèbre,** dirge; **c. sacré,** hymn; **(c)** *Littér* song, lyric; (*d'un poème*) canto.

chant² *nm* edge, side; **pierres (posées) de c.** *ou* **sur c.**, stones set on edge *or* edgewise.

chantage [ʃɑ̃taʒ] *nm* blackmail; **c. sentimental,** emotional blackmail; **faire du c.**, to blackmail; **faire du c. au suicide,** to threaten (to commit) suicide.

chantant [ʃɑ̃tɑ̃] *adj* melodious, tuneful; musical (*verse etc*); **air c.**, catchy tune; **accent c.**, sing-song *or* lilting accent; **soirée chantante,** musical evening.

chanteau, -eaux [ʃɑ̃to] *nm Vieilli* hunk (*of bread*); *Tex* cutting (*of cloth*).

chantepleure [ʃɑ̃tplœr] *nf* **(a)** (*entonnoir*) wine funnel; *Ind* colander; **(b)** (*sorte d'arrosoir*) long-spouted watering can; **(c)** (*de tonneau*) tap; **(d)** (*de mur*) weephole; (*de gouttière*) spout.

chanter [ʃɑ̃te] **1** *vt* to sing (*song etc*); **c. qch sur l'air de ...**, to sing sth to the tune of ...; **c. victoire,** to exult, *F* to crow; **c. les louanges/le courage de qn,** to sing s.o.'s praises/to praise s.o.'s courage; *Rel* **c. la messe,** to sing mass; **c. Noël,** to celebrate Christmas in song; **pain à c.**, (unconsecrated) host, wafer; *Fig* **c. toujours la même chanson,** to be always harping on about the same thing; *F* **qu'est-ce que vous me chantez là?**, what are you talking about?; *F* **elle le chante sur tous les tons,** she says so at every possible opportunity.

2 *vi* (*of person, bird, kettle*) to sing; (*of cock*) to crow; (*of cricket*) to chirp; (*of butter*) to sizzle; **il chante en parlant,** he's got a sing-song accent; *F* **c'est comme si je chantais,** I'm wasting my breath; *Fig* **faire c. qn,** to blackmail s.o.; **je vais le faire c. sur un autre ton,** I'll make him change his tune; *F* **est-ce que cela vous chante?**, do you like the idea (of it)?, does that appeal to you?; **viens, si ça te chante,** come along, if you fancy the idea.

chanterelle¹ [ʃɑ̃trɛl] *nf* **(a)** decoy (bird); **(b)** *Mus* first *or* highest string (*of violin etc*); *F* **appuyer sur la c.**, to hammer a point home, to rub it in.

chanterelle² *nf* (*champignon*) chanterelle.

chanteur, -euse [ʃɑ̃tœr, -øz] **1** *n* singer, vocalist; **c. des rues,** street singer, busker; **c. de charme,** crooner; **maître**

c., (*qui fait du chantage*) blackmailer; *Mus Hist* mastersinger, meistersinger. **2** *adj* **oiseau c.**, songbird.

chantier [ʃɑ̃tje] *nm* **(a)** site; (*dépôt*) yard, depot; **c. (de construction),** building site; (*dépôt*) builder's yard; (*sur la route*) road works; **c. de bois,** timberyard, lumberyard; **chef de c.**, site foreman; **travailler au c.** *ou* **sur le c.**, to work on (the) site; **avoir une œuvre en c.** *ou* **sur le c.**, to have a piece of work in hand; *Fig* **il faudra mettre ce travail en c.** *ou* **sur le c. dès demain,** we must get started on this tomorrow; **'c.',** men at work, road works, road up; **fin de c.**, road clear; **c. interdit au public,** no admittance except on business; *Fig* **quel c.!,** what a mess!, what a shambles!; *Fig* **la chambre est un vrai c.** *ou* **est en c.**, the bedroom is a real tip; *Min* **c. d'exploitation,** working(s);
(b) *Nau* **c. naval** *ou* **de construction navale,** shipyard; **c. de l'État,** naval (dock)yard; **vaisseau sur le c.**, vessel on the slips;
(c) *Rail* **c. de voies de garage et de triage,** shunting yard;
(d) gantry, stand (*for barrels*).

chantonnement [ʃɑ̃tɔnmɑ̃] *nm* singing softly, crooning; (*fredonnement*) humming.

chantonner [ʃɑ̃tɔne] *vt & vi* to sing softly, to croon; (*fredonner*) to hum.

chantoung [ʃɑ̃tuŋ] *nm Tex* shantung.

chantourner [ʃɑ̃turne] *vt* to cut *or* saw (*sth*) round a curved outline, to jigsaw (*sth*); **scie à c.**, (*manuelle*) fretsaw; (*machine*) jigsaw, scroll saw.

chantre [ʃɑ̃tr] *nm* **(a)** *Rel* cantor; **grand c.**, precentor; **(b)** *Litt* (*poète*) poet; **les chantres des bois,** the woodland chorus.

chanvre [ʃɑ̃vr] *nm* hemp; **c. indien,** Indian hemp, hashish; **c. de la Nouvelle-Zélande,** New Zealand flax, flax lily; **cordage de** *ou* **en c.**, hemp(en) rope; *F* **cravate de c.**, hangman's noose; **c. du Bengale,** Bengal hemp; **c. de Manille,** Manila hemp.

chanvrier, -ière [ʃɑ̃vrije, -jɛr] **1** *adj* hemp (*industry etc*). **2** *n* hemp grower *or* worker.

chaos [kao] *nm* chaos; **tout est dans le c.**, everything is in a state of confusion, everything is chaotic.

chaotique [kaɔtik] *adj* chaotic, confused.

chapardage [ʃapardaʒ] *nm F* thieving, pinching, pilfering.

chaparder [ʃaparde] *vt F* to pinch, to pilfer.

chapardeur, -euse [ʃapardœr, -øz] *F* **1** *adj* thieving, pinching, pilfering. **2** *n* thief, pilferer.

chape [ʃap] *nf* **(a)** covering; *Aut etc* tread (*of tyre*); coping (*of bridge*); **(b)** *Rel* cope; *MecE* fork joint, yoke, clevis; shell (*of pulley*); **c. de cardan,** cardan fork; **chapes d'un moufle,** straps of a pulley block.

chapeau, -eaux [ʃapo] *nm* **(a)** (*coiffure*) hat; **c. mou,** felt hat, trilby, *Am* fedora; **c. de pluie,** rain hat; **c. de paille,** straw hat; **c. de soleil,** sun hat; **c. à cornes** *ou* **de gendarme,** cocked hat; **c. de cardinal,** cardinal hat; **le c. rouge,** the red hat; **c. melon,** bowler hat; **carton à c.**, hat-box; **ruban de c.**, hatband; **porter un c.**, to wear a hat; **mettre un c.**, to put on a hat; **saluer qn d'un coup de c.**, **donner un coup de c. à qn,** to raise one's hat to s.o.; *Can* **donner un coup de c.**, (*accepter les exigences de qn*) to give in; **tirer son c. à qn,** to take off one's hat to s.o.; **c.!,** bravo!, well done!, I take my hat off to you!; **chapeaux bas!,** hats off!; **c. bas,** hat in hand; **faire passer le c.**, to pass the hat round; *Arg* **il travaille du c.**, he's crazy *or* nutty; *Fig* **c'est vous qui portez le c. dans cette affaire,** you're carrying the can here;
(b) *Bot* pileus, cap (*of mushroom*); *Orn* cap (*of bird*);
(c) *Culin* piecrust; lid, top (*of vol-au-vent etc*); cap (*of fountain pen etc*); *Aut* **c. de roue,** hub cap; *F* **prendre un virage sur les chapeaux de roues,** to screech round a corner;
(d) *Typ Journ* introductory paragraph.

chapeauter [ʃapote] *vt* **(a) elle était bien chapeautée,** she was wearing a lovely hat; **(b)** *Fig* (*contrôler*) to be in charge (of), to head (up); **elle chapeaute les trois services,** she's in charge of the three departments.

chapelain [ʃaplɛ̃] *nm Rel* chaplain (attached to private chapel).

chapelet [ʃaplɛ] *nm* (*de prière*) rosary; **dire son c.**, to say the rosary; **défiler une dizaine de chapelets,** to say a decade (of the rosary); *F* **défiler son c.**, to have one's say, to speak one's mind; **c. d'invectives,** string of abuse; **c. de bombes,** stick of bombs; **c. de péniches/d'îles,** string of barges/islands; **c. d'oignons,** string *or* rope of onions; **réservoirs en c.**, reservoirs arranged in series; **pompe à c.**, **c. hydraulique,** chain pump.

chapelier, -ière [ʃapəlje, -jɛr] **1** *adj* hat(-making) (*trade etc*). **2** *n* hatter.

chapelle [ʃapɛl] *nf* **(a)** chapel (*in private house etc*); (side) chapel (*of church*); chapel of ease (*of parish*); **c. de la (Sainte) Vierge,** Lady Chapel; **c. ardente,** chapel of rest; **(b)** *surtout Rel* choir and/or orchestra; **maître de c.**, choir master; **(c)** *Rel* ornaments and plate (*for the celebration of mass*); **(d)** *Littér Beaux-Arts* clique, coterie; **(e)** *Constr* vault (*of baking oven*); **(f)** *Tech* **c. de pompe,** pump case; **soupapes en c.**, side valves.

chapellerie [ʃapɛlri] *nf* **(a)** *Com* hat trade; *Ind* hat industry; **(b)** (*magasin*) hatshop.

chapelure [ʃaplyr] *nf Culin* breadcrumbs.

chaperon [ʃaprɔ̃] *nm* **(a)** (*personne*) chaperon; **(b)** *Constr* coping (*of wall*); **(c)** (*de faucon*) hood; *Littér* **le Petit C. rouge,** Little Red Riding Hood; *Scol* (graduate's) hood; *Arch* hood; **(d)** (*couvercle etc*) protecting lid *or* cover.

chaperonner [ʃaprɔne] *vt* **(a)** to chaperon (*young woman*); **(b)** *Constr* to cope (*wall*); **(c)** to hood (*falcon etc*).

chapiteau, -eaux [ʃapito] *nm* **(a)** *Archit* capital (*of column*); cornice (*of wardrobe etc*); **(b)** head (*of still, rocket*); **(c)** big top (*of circus*).

chapitre [ʃapitr] *nm* **(a)** chapter (*of book*); head(ing), item (*of expenditure etc*); **nous traiterons demain ce c.**, we will deal with this subject *or* matter tomorrow; **elle est sévère sur le c. de la discipline,** she is strict as regards *or* in the matter of discipline; **en voilà assez sur ce c.**, that's enough about that, let's drop the subject; **(b)** *Rel* chapter (*of canons*); **salle du c.**, chapter house; *Fig* **avoir voix au c.**, to have a say in the matter.

chapitrer [ʃapitre] *vt F* to tell (*s.o.*) off, to tear (*s.o.*) off a strip; *Rel* to rebuke (*s.o.*) in chapter.

chaplinesque [ʃaplinɛsk] *adj* (*comique, personnage*) chaplinesque.

chapon [ʃapɔ̃] *nm Culin* capon.

chaptalisation [ʃaptalizasjɔ̃] *nf* chaptalization.

chaptaliser [ʃaptalize] *vt* to chaptalize (*wine*).

chaque [ʃak] **1** *adj* each, every; **c. chose à sa place,** everything in its place; **c. fois qu'il vient,** whenever *or* every time he comes; *F* **c. deux jours,** every other day. **2** *pron F* (= **chacun**) **ces livres coûtent 100 francs c.**, these books cost 100 francs each.

char [ʃar] *nm* **(a)** *Mil* **c. (de combat),** *Vieilli* **c. d'assaut,** tank; **les chars,** the armour; **régiment de chars,** armoured *or* tank regiment, *US* tank battalion; **(b)** (*de campagne*) waggon; *Can* car, *Am* automobile; *Antiq* chariot; **c. à bœufs,** ox cart; **c. funèbre,** hearse; *Arch* **c. à bancs,** (horse) charabanc; *F* **arrête ton c.**, stop exaggerating; **(c) c. (de carnaval),** float; *Litt* **le c. de l'État,** the Ship of State.

charabia [ʃarabja] *nm F* jargon, gibberish, gobbledegook.

charade [ʃarad] *nf* charade.

charançon [ʃarɑ̃sɔ̃] *nm* (*insecte*) weevil.

charançonné [ʃarɑ̃sɔne] *adj* weevil(l)ed, weevil(l)y.

charbon [ʃarbɔ̃] *nm* **(a)** (*combustible*) **c. (de terre),** coal; (*poussière*) coal dust; **marchand de c.**, coal merchant, coalman; **c. sans fumée,** smokeless fuel; *Fig* **aller au c.**, (*au travail*) to go to work; (*s'y mettre*) to muck in, to get stuck in; **avoir un c. dans l'œil,** to have a bit of grit in one's eye; **c. animal,** animal charcoal; **c. actif** *ou* **activé,** active *or* activated charcoal; **poisson grillé sur des charbons,** fish grilled on coals, barbecued fish; *Fig* **être sur des charbons ardents,** to be on tenterhooks; *Fig* **marcher sur des charbons ardents,** to be walking a tightrope; **c. (de bois),** charcoal; *Beaux-Arts* charcoal; *Ch* carbon;
(b) c. de cornue, gas carbon; *Él* **balai de c.**, carbon brush; *Méd* **prendre du** *ou* **des pastilles de c.**, to take charcoal tablets;
(c) *Agr* smut, black rust;
(d) *Méd Vét* anthrax.

charbonnage [ʃarbɔnaʒ] *nm* **(a)** (*exploitation*) coal mining; **(b) charbonnages,** collieries, coalfield; **les Charbonnages de France,** the (French) National Coal Board.

charbonner [ʃarbɔne] **1** *vt* **(a)** to blacken (*sth*) with charcoal; to scrawl (*words etc*) in charcoal; **(b)** *Beaux-Arts* to make a charcoal sketch of (*sth*). **2** *vi Nau* to coal ship, to bunker. **3 se charbonner** *vpr* **se c. le visage,** to black(en) one's face.

charbonneux, -euse [ʃarbɔnø, -øz] *adj* **(a)** (*de charbon*) coaly, carbonaceous; **dépôt c.**, sooty deposit, carbon deposit; **(b)** *Méd* anthracic, anthracoid, carbuncular; **mouches charbonneuses,** anthrax-carrying flies; **bactéridie charbonneuse,** anthrax bacillus.

charbonnier, -ière [ʃarbɔnje, -jɛr] **1** *adj* coal (mining) (*industry etc*); charcoal (*trade etc*); **navire c.,** collier, coaler. **2** *n* **(a)** *Com* (*marchand*) coal merchant; (*bougnat*) coalman; **(b)** *Nau* coaler, collier; charcoal burner; *Prov* **c. est maître dans sa maison** *ou* **chez soi,** an Englishman's home is his castle; **la foi du c.,** simple faith. **3** *nf* **charbonnière,** charcoal kiln.

charcuter [ʃarkyte] *F* **1** *vt* to hack up (*piece of meat*); to hack (*s.o.*) to pieces, to butcher (*s.o.*); **ce médecin est réputé pour c. ses malades,** this doctor has the reputation of being a butcher. **2 se charcuter** *vpr* **se c. le menton en se rasant,** to nick one's chin shaving.

charcuterie [ʃarkytri] *nf* **(a)** *Com* pork butcher's business *or* shop; ≈ delicatessen (shop); **(b)** *Ind* pork butchery; delicatessen trade; **(c)** (*viande de porc etc*) **assiette de c.,** plate of assorted delicatessen.

charcutier, -ière [ʃarkytje, -jɛr] *n* **(a)** (*commerçant, fabricant*) pork butcher; **(b)** *F Péj* (*chirurgien*) butcher.

chardon [ʃardɔ̃] *nm* **(a)** (*plante*) thistle; *Culin* **c. à la liqueur,** = coloured chocolate sweet with liqueur centre; **(b)** **chardons,** (clustered) spikes (*on iron railing etc*).

chardonneret [ʃardɔnrɛ] *nm* (*oiseau*) goldfinch.

charentais, -aise [ʃarɑ̃tɛ, -ɛz] **1** *adj* of Charente. **2** *n* **C.,** native *or* inhabitant of Charente.

charge [ʃarʒ] *nf* **(a)** (*poids*) load, burden; (*sur bateau, camion etc*) cargo; (*action*) loading (*of ship etc*); **bête de c.,** beast of burden; **cheval/mulet de c.,** packhorse/pack mule; **c. utile,** carrying capacity; **c. maximum (de rupture),** ultimate *or* breaking load; *Nau* **ligne de c.,** loadline; **prendre (un client) en c.,** (*de taxi*) to pick up (a fare); **prise en c.,** (*dans un taxi*) minimum fare;

(b) *Tech* load; *Él* charge (*of battery*); *Él* load (*of circuit etc*); *Él* **conducteur en c.,** live conductor; *Él* **mettre une batterie en c.,** to put a battery on charge; **c. de sécurité** *ou* **admissible,** safe load; **c. à vide,** empty weight; **facteur de c.,** load factor; **c. de rupture,** breaking *or* shearing stress; **c. d'explosif,** (*de fusil etc*) explosive charge; **c. creuse,** hollow(-shaped) charge; *HydE etc* **c. d'eau,** head of water;

(c) (*responsabilité*) charge, responsibility; **prendre qn/qch en c.,** to take charge of s.o./sth, to assume *or* take responsibility for s.o./sth; **cela est à votre c.,** that's part of your duty; **elle a la c. de réorganiser le service,** she's got the job of reorganizing the department; **enfants confiés à ma c.,** children entrusted to me *or* in my charge *or* in my care; *Rel* **avoir c. d'âmes,** to have a cure of souls; *Vieilli* **femme de c.,** housekeeper;

(d) **c. d'avoué,** solicitor's practice;

(e) (*obligation*) charge, expense; **les réparations sont à la c. du locataire,** the tenant is responsible for repairs; **être à la c. de qn,** to be dependent on s.o., to be supported by s.o.; **être à c. à qn,** to be a burden to s.o.; *F* **il est à c., vraiment!,** (*il est pénible*) he's a real pain (in the neck)!; **charges de famille,** dependents; **deux enfants à c.,** two dependent children; **loyer plus les charges,** rent plus service charge (and maintenance costs); **charges publiques,** public expenditure; **charges sociales,** national insurance contributions (*paid by employer*); **cahier des charges,** specifications; articles and conditions (*of sale etc*);

(f) **j'accepte, mais à c. de revanche,** I accept, but only on condition that you let me do the same for you some time; **à c. pour vous de payer,** on condition *or* provided that you pay;

(g) exaggeration (*of story*); *Th* overacting (*of part*); *Beaux-Arts Litt* caricature (*of character, portrait*);

(h) *Mil* charge; **sonner la c.,** to sound the charge; **c. de cavalerie,** cavalry charge; *Fig* **revenir** *ou* **retourner à la c.,** to try again;

(i) *Jur* charge, indictment; **les charges contre lui sont très lourdes,** the charges against him are very heavy; **quelles sont les charges contre elle?,** what's she being charged with?; **témoin à c.,** witness for the prosecution.

chargé, -ée [ʃarʒe] **1** *adj* **(a)** loaded, laden; **bateau fortement c.,** heavily laden ship; **train très c.,** crowded train; **j'étais chargé comme un bourricot!,** I was laden *or* loaded down, I felt like a beast of burden; *Fig* **avoir la conscience chargée,** to have a guilty conscience; **jour c.,** full *or* busy day; **regard c. de reconnaissance,** look full of gratitude; *Litt* **mourir c. d'ans,** to die at a ripe old age; **personnage c. d'honneur,** a person laden with honours; **le style est très c.,** the style is very ornate; **temps c.,** overcast weather; **avoir la langue chargée,** to have a coated tongue; **avoir l'estomac c.,** to have an overloaded stomach; **dés chargés,** loaded dice; *Mil* **obus c.,** live shell; **le revolver n'était pas c.,** the revolver wasn't loaded;

(b) **lettre chargée,** = registered letter (*value declared*);

(c) (*responsable*) responsible; **être c. de famille,** to have family responsibilities; **être c. d'une mission,** to be entrusted with a mission.

2 *nm* **c. d'affaires,** chargé d'affaires.

3 *n Univ* **c. de cours,** = (university) lecturer.

chargement [ʃarʒəmɑ̃] *nm* **(a)** loading (*of lorry, ship etc*); shipping (*of cargo*); **machine à laver à c. frontal,** front-loading washing machine; *Rail* **voie de c.,** goods siding; **(b)** *Mil* filling (*of cartridge, shell, bomb etc*); *Phot* loading (*of camera*); *Él* charging (*of battery*); **(c)** registration (*of letter*); **(d)** (*marchandise*) load, cargo, freight; **le c. est arrivé à bon port,** the cargo was brought safely to port *or* arrived intact; **c. bien arrimé,** well-stowed cargo; **(e)** (*paquet, lettre*) registered letter, parcel.

charger [ʃarʒe] *vt* (**je chargeai(s); n. chargeons**) **(a)** to load (*lorry, truck, ship etc*); **c. des marchandises,** to load *or Nau* to ship goods; **navire chargé de blé,** ship laden with wheat; *F* **c. un client,** (*d'un chauffeur de taxi*) to pick up a fare;

(b) **c. une lettre,** = to send valuables by post; (*l'affranchir*) to register a letter;

(c) to weigh (down); **toiture qui charge trop les murs,** roof that overloads the walls; **chargé de paquets,** weighed down with parcels;

(d) (*remplir*) to fill; **c. son récit d'anecdotes,** to pepper one's story with anecdotes; **table chargée de mets,** table laden with food; **mets qui chargent l'estomac,** food that lies heavy on the stomach; **c. sa mémoire de dates inutiles,** to clutter up one's mind with useless dates; **c. qn de reproches,** to heap reproaches on s.o.; **l'air est chargé du parfum des fleurs,** the air is heavy with the scent of flowers;

(e) to load (*gun, camera etc*); to fill (*pipe*); to put a refill into (*a pen*); *Él* to charge (*battery*); *Ordinat* to load (up);

(f) to entrust (*s.o. with (doing) sth*); to instruct (*s.o. to do sth*); **être chargé de l'entretien,** to be in charge of *or* responsible for maintenance;

(g) to turn (*a portrait*) into a caricature; to caricature (*s.o.*); to exaggerate, to embroider (*a story*); *Th* to overact (*a part*); **c. une description,** to overdo *or* exaggerate a description, *F* to lay it on thick;

(h) (*attaquer*) to charge;

(i) *Jur* to charge, to accuse, to indict (*s.o.*); **c. qn d'un crime,** to charge s.o. with a crime; **on le charge de tous les péchés,** he's charged with every sin in the book.

2 *vi* **(a)** *Ordinat* to load up;

(b) *Mil* to charge.

3 se charger *vpr* **(a)** (*s'alourdir*) to weigh oneself down;

(b) (*du temps*) to become overcast; **le temps** *ou* **ça se charge,** it's becoming overcast, it's clouding over;

(c) **se c. de (faire) qch,** to undertake (to do) sth; **je m'en chargerai,** I'll see to it, I'll take care of it.

chargeur [ʃarʒœr] *nm* **(a)** (*personne*) loader; *Nau* shipper; **(b)** (*d'arme*) magazine, (cartridge, loading) clip; *Phot* cassette; *Él* (battery) charger; **c. automatique,** self loader.

chargeuse [ʃarʒøz] *nf Tech* loader.

charia [ʃarja] *nf Rel* (*Islam*) sharia.

chariot [ʃarjo] *nm* **(a)** (*charrette*) wag(g)on, cart; (*pour diapositives*) cartridge; (*pour la manutention*) truck, trolley; *Cin* dolly; (*table roulante*) trolley; carriage (*of typewriter*); *Astron* **le Grand C.,** the Great Bear, Charles's Wain; *Am* the (Big) Dipper; **le petit C.,** the Little Bear; the Little Dipper; **c. d'enfant,** *Am* baby walker; **c. élévateur à fourche,** fork-lift truck; **c. à bagages,** luggage trolley; **le c. des desserts/à liqueurs,** the dessert/drinks trolley; **(b)** *Av* **c. d'atterrissage,** landing gear, undercarriage.

charismatique [karismatik] *adj* charismatic.

charisme [karism] *nm* charisma; **le c. d'un homme politique,** a politician's charisma; **avoir du c.,** to have charisma; **avoir un certain c.,** to have a certain charisma.

charitable [ʃaritabl] *adj* charitable, benevolent (**envers,** to, towards); **œuvre** *ou* **fondation c.,** charity; **vous êtes bien c.,** it's very kind of you; **conseil c.,** a friendly piece of advice.

charitablement [ʃaritabləmɑ̃] *adv* charitably, benevolently.

charité [ʃarite] *nf* **(a)** (*aimer*) charity, love; **faire qch par c.,** to do sth out of *or* for charity; *Prov* **c. bien ordonnée commence par soi-même,** charity begins at home; *Arch* **dame de c.,** district visitor; *Rel* **les Filles** *ou* **les Sœurs de la C.,** the Sisters of Charity; **(b)** (*don*) act of charity; **faire la c. à qn,** to give money *or* a donation to s.o.; **vivre de charités,** to live on charity; **demander la c.,** to ask for

charity.
charivari [ʃarivari] *nm* din, row, racket; **un c. de rires et de pas,** noisy laughter and footsteps.
charlatan [ʃarlatɑ̃] *nm* charlatan; **remède de c.,** quack remedy.
charlatanerie [ʃarlatanri] *nf* charlatanry; *F* **tout ça c'est de la c.,** that's all eyewash.
charlatanesque [ʃarlatanɛsk] *adj* quack (*remedy etc*).
charlatanisme [ʃarlatanism] *nm* charlatanism.
charleston [ʃarlɛstɔn] *nm* (*danse*) charleston.
Charlot [ʃarlo] *nm F* **(a)** Charley, Charlie; *Cin* Charlie Chaplin; **(b)** *F* **c.,** clown; **c'est un sacré c.,** he's a right clown.
charlotte [ʃarlɔt] *nf Culin* charlotte; **c. russe,** charlotte russe; **moule à c.,** charlotte mould.
charmant [ʃarmɑ̃] *adj* charming, delightful (*person, thing*); **une soirée charmante,** a delightful evening; **prince c.,** prince charming; *Fig* **attendre son prince c.,** to be waiting for prince charming *or* Mr Right to come along.
charme¹ [ʃarm] *nm* **(a)** (*attrait*) charm, attraction; **elle a beaucoup de c.,** she's absolutely charming; **cela donne du c. au paysage,** it lends charm *or* beauty to the landscape; **c'est ce qui en fait le c.,** that's what makes it so attractive, that's the charm of it; **elle n'est pas belle, mais elle a du c.,** she's not beautiful, but she is attractive; **cette proposition ne manque pas de c.,** the suggestion is not without a certain appeal; **faire du c.,** to turn on the charm; **charmes,** (physical) attractions, charms (*of a woman*); **chanteur de c.,** crooner; **(b)** (*magie*) charm, spell; **être sous le c.,** to be under the spell; **tenir ses auditeurs sous le c.,** to hold one's audience spellbound; **rompre le c.,** to break the spell; *Fig* **se porter comme un c.,** to be in the best of health, to be as fit as a fiddle.
charme² *nm* (*arbre*) hornbeam.
charmer [ʃarme] *vt* **(a)** (*plaire*) to charm, to delight, to enchant; **tableau qui charme les yeux,** picture that delights *or* charms the eye; **elle n'a pas eu de mal à c. son auditoire,** she had no difficulty (in) winning over her audience; **être charmé de faire qch,** to be delighted to do sth; **elle est charmée du cadeau,** she's delighted *or* enchanted with the gift; **j'ai été charmé de vous rencontrer,** it's been a pleasure to meet you; **(b)** to charm, to bewitch (*snake etc*); *Arch* to charm away (*cares etc*).
charmeur, -euse [ʃarmœr, -øz] **1** *adj* charming, appealing (*look etc*); **un sourire c.,** a charming *or* winning smile. **2** *n* **(a) c. de serpents,** snake charmer; **(b)** (*séducteur, -trice*) charmer.
charmille [ʃarmij] *nf* **(a)** (*allée*) hedge; **(b)** (*tonnelle*) bower, arbour.
charnel, -elle [ʃarnɛl] *adj* **(a)** carnal, fleshly (*desires etc*); **union charnelle,** the carnal act; **les liens charnels,** blood ties; **(b)** worldly (*goods etc*).
charnellement [ʃarnɛlmɑ̃] *adv Litt* carnally; **aimer qn c.,** to love s.o. carnally *or* sexually; **connaître qn c.,** to have carnal knowledge of s.o..
charnier [ʃarnje] *nm* (open) grave; *Arch & Litt* charnel (house).
charnière [ʃarnjɛr] *nf* (*de porte etc*) hinge; (*pour timbres*) stamp hinge; *Mil* (point of) junction (*of two armies etc*); *F* **nom à c.,** double-barrelled name; *Fig* **l'une des grandes charnières de l'histoire,** one of the great turning points of history; *Fig* **être à un moment c. de sa vie,** to be at a turning point in one's life; *Fig* **un domaine c. (entre deux disciplines),** an area (inter)linking two disciplines.
charnu [ʃarny] *adj* fleshy, plump; pulpy (*fruit*); **le poignet n'est pas une partie charnue du corps,** the wrist is not a fleshy part of the body; **des lèvres charnues,** fleshy lips.
charognard [ʃarɔɲar] *nm* **(a)** (*oiseau*) vulture; **(b)** *Arg* (*exploiteur*) shark, vulture.
charogne [ʃarɔɲ] *nf* **(a)** (*d'animal*) carrion, decaying carcass; **(b)** *Arg* (*salaud, crapule*) bastard; (*femme*) bitch.
charpente [ʃarpɑ̃t] *nf* frame(work), framing, skeleton (*of building etc*); frame (*of body*); skeleton (*of leaf*); framework, skeleton, structure (*of novel etc*); **bois de c.,** timber; **avoir la c. solide,** (*de personne*) to be solidly built; **avoir une c. fragile,** to be slightly built.
charpenté [ʃarpɑ̃te] *adj* built, constructed; **homme solidement c.,** well-built man; **pièce de théâtre bien charpentée,** well-constructed play.
charpenter [ʃarpɑ̃te] *vt* **(a)** to cut (*timber*) into shape; **(b)** to frame (up) (*roof etc*); to construct (*novel etc*); **c. un discours,** to construct *or* frame a speech.
charpenterie [ʃarpɑ̃tri] *nf* **(a)** (*métier*) carpentry; **faire de la c.,** to go in for carpentry; **(b)** (*atelier*) carpenter's (work)shop; (*chantier*) timberyard.
charpentier [ʃarpɑ̃tje] *nm* carpenter; **matelot c.,** ship's carpenter; **c. du bord,** shipwright.
charpie [ʃarpi] *nf* **(a) mettre qch en c.,** to tear sth to pieces *or* to shreds; **viande en c.,** meat cooked to shreds; **elle a déchiré son livre et en a fait de la c.,** she tore her book to shreds, she tore up her book and made confetti out of it; *F* **il vous mettra en c.,** he'll make mincemeat out of you; **(b)** *Arch* lint, shredded linen.
charretée [ʃarte] *nf* cartload, cartful.
charretier, -ière [ʃartje, -jɛr] **1** *nm* carter, carrier; *Fig* **parler/jurer comme un c.,** to speak like a fishwife/to swear like a trooper; **langage de c.,** coarse language. **2** *adj* **porte charretière,** carriage gate(way); **chemin c., voie charretière,** cart track.
charrette [ʃarɛt] *nf* cart; **c. anglaise,** dogcart, trap; **c. à bras,** handcart, barrow; *Hist* **c. (des condamnés),** tumbrel; *Suisse F* **c. de Paul!,** blinking Paul!
charriable [ʃarjabl] *adj* transportable.
charriage [ʃarjaʒ] *nm* **(a)** (*portage*) cartage, haulage, carriage; **(b)** *Géol* thrusting, overthrust.
charrier [ʃarje] *v* (*impf & pr sub* **n. charriions, v. charriiez**) **1** *vt* **(a)** (*transporter*) to cart, to carry, to transport; **(b)** (*entraîner*) to carry along, to wash down; **rivière qui charrie du sable,** river that carries *or* brings down sand; **nuages charriés par le vent,** wind-driven clouds; **(c)** *Arg* to poke fun at, to kid (*s.o.*); **se faire c. par ses amis,** to be kidded by one's friends. **2** *vi Arg* (*exagérer*) to shoot a line, to pile it on; **il charrie vraiment!,** he's really having you on!; *F* **(il ne) faut pas c.!,** come off it!
charroi [ʃarwa] *nm* cartage, haulage, carriage.
charron [ʃarɔ̃] *nm* cartwright (and ploughwright).
charroyer [ʃarwaje] *vt* (**je charroie; je charroierai**) to transport (*sth*) in a cart, to cart (*sth*).
charroyeur [ʃarwajœr] *nm* carter, carrier.
charrue [ʃary] *nf* **(a)** *Agr* plough, *US* plow; **mener** *ou* **pousser la c.,** to drive the plough; *F* **mettre la c. devant** *ou* **avant les bœufs,** to put the cart before the horse; **(b)** *Can* snowplough, *US* snowplow.
charte [ʃart] *nf* **(a)** (*convention*) charter; **compagnie à c.,** chartered company; *Eng Hist* **la Grande C.,** Magna Carta; *Pol Hist* **la C. de l'Atlantique,** the Atlantic Charter; **(b)** (*document ancien*) (ancient) deed, title; **l'École des chartes,** = the School of Palaeography and Librarianship (in Paris).
charte-partie [ʃartəparti] *nf Nau* charter party; (*pl chartes-parties*).
charter [tʃartœr] *nm* **(avion) c.,** charter, chartered aircraft; **vol c.,** charter flight; **voyager en c.,** to take a charter.
chartisme [ʃartism] *nm Eng Hist* chartism.
chartiste [ʃartist] *adj & n* **(a)** *Univ* (student) of the École des chartes; **(b)** *Eng Hist* chartist.
chartreuse [ʃartrøz] *nf* **(a)** (*couvent*) Carthusian monastery, charterhouse; **(b)** (*alcool*) Chartreuse; **c. jaune/verte,** yellow/green chartreuse.
chartreux, -euse [ʃartrø, -øz] *n Rel* Carthusian (monk, nun).
chartrier [ʃartrije] *nm* **(a)** (*gardien*) custodian of charters; **(b)** (*recueil*) collection of charters; **(c)** (*salle*) charter room.
Charybde [karibd] *nm* Charybdis; **tomber de C. en Scylla,** to fall out of the frying pan into the fire.
chas [ʃa] *nm* eye (*of needle*).
chasse [ʃas] *nf* **(a)** hunting; (*le tir*) (game) shooting; (*événement*) hunt, shoot; **c. à courre,** (stag, fox)hunt(ing); **c. au furet,** ferreting; **c. au lévrier,** coursing; **c. au renard,** foxhunt(ing); **c. aux perdrix,** partridge shoot(ing); **c. aux oiseaux,** fowling; **c. aux papillons,** catching butterflies; **c. au lapin,** rabbiting, rabbit shooting; **c. au daim (à l'affût),** deerstalking; **c. aux souris,** mousing; **c. à l'homme,** manhunt; **une c. à l'homme a été organisée à travers le pays,** a national manhunt has been launched; **c. sous marine,** underwater fishing; **aller à la c.,** to go hunting *or* shooting; **la c. est ouverte/fermée,** the shooting season has begun/ended; **c. fermée,** close season; **vivre de sa c.,** to live off one's catch; **la c. vient de passer,** the hunt has just gone by; **fusil de c.,** shotgun; **couteau/habit de c.,** hunting knife/coat; **faire bonne c.,** to have good sport, to make a good bag;
(b) (*réserve*) **c. gardée,** private game preserve; *Fig* **ah non, c. gardée!,** no poaching!, hands off!; **louer une c.,** to rent a shoot;
(c) (*poursuite*) chase; **donner la c. à qch/qn, prendre qch/qn en c.,** to chase *or* pursue *or* give chase to sth/s.o.; **faire la c. à qch,** to hunt sth down *or* out; **faire la c. aux abus,** to hunt *or* track down abuse(s); *F* **c. au mari,**

husband hunting; *F* **c. aux soldes,** bargain hunting; *F* **c. aux appartements,** flat hunting;

(d) *Mil Av* **la c.,** the fighter aircraft, the fighters; **pilote de c.,** fighter pilot;

(e) c. (d'eau), flushing system, flush; **tirer la c. (d'eau),** to flush the lavatory, to pull the chain;

(f) *MecE* play (*of wheels etc*); *Aut* trail (*of front wheels*); *Typ* overrun (*of page*).

châsse [ʃɑs] *nf* **(a)** *Rel* reliquary, shrine; **(b)** mounting, frame (*of spectacles*).

chassé [ʃase] *nm* (*danse*) chassé.

chasse-clou(s) [ʃasklu] *nm* nail punch, nail set; (*pl chasse-clous*).

chassé-croisé [ʃasekrwaze] *nm* (*pl chassés-croisés*) **(a)** rearrangement, reshuffling (*of staff etc*); **c.-c. de conseillers,** a reshuffling of advisers; **à cause d'un c.-c., je l'ai encore manqué,** I missed him again because of a mix-up; **(b)** (*danse*) set to partners.

chasse-marée [ʃasmare] *nm inv* **(a)** (*voiture*) fish cart; **(b)** (*bateau*) coasting lugger.

chasse-mouches [ʃasmuʃ] *nm inv* fly whisk, fly swat(ter).

chasse-neige [ʃasnɛʒ] *nm inv* **(a)** (*engin*) snowplough, *US* snowplow; **(b)** *Ski* stem, snowplough; **virage (en) c.-n.,** snowplough turn, stem turn.

chasse-pierres [ʃaspjɛr] *nm inv Rail* cowcatcher.

chasser [ʃase] **1** *vt* **(a)** to chase, to hunt; **c. le renard/la perdrix,** to go foxhunting/partridge shooting;

(b) to drive, to chase (*s.o.*) out *or* away, to turn (*s.o.*) out, to expel (*s.o.*); to dismiss (*employee*); *Bible* to cast out (*devils*); to dispel (*fog etc*); **c. qn du pays,** to drive *or* expel s.o. from the country; **je ne veux pas vous c. mais il est tard,** I'm not trying to get rid of you but it's getting late; **c. qn/qch de son esprit,** to dismiss s.o./sth from one's mind *or* thoughts; **c. une mouche (du revers de la main),** to brush away a fly; **le vent chassait la pluie contre les vitres,** the wind was driving the rain against the window panes; **c. une mauvaise odeur,** to get rid of a nasty smell.

2 *vi* **(a)** to hunt, to go hunting; (*tir*) to shoot, to go shooting; **c. au lion,** to hunt lions; **c. à courre,** to ride to hounds, to hunt, to go hunting; **c. au furet,** to ferret; *Fig* **c. sur les terres de qn,** to poach on s.o.'s preserves;

(b) (*venir*) to drive; **nuages qui chassent du nord,** clouds driving from the north;

(c) *Nau* (*of anchor*) to drag; *Aut* to skid; *Typ* (*of type*) to drive out; (*of matter*) to overrun; **navire qui chasse sur ses ancres,** ship dragging her anchors.

chasseresse [ʃasrɛs] *nf Litter* huntress; **Diane c.,** Diana the Huntress.

chasseur, -euse [ʃasœr, -øz] **1** *n* hunter, *f* huntress; (*surtout à courre*) huntsman; (*au tir*) (sportsman with) gun; **il est bon c.,** he's a good shot; **c. de têtes,** (*indigène, Fig recruteur*) headhunter; *Fig* **elle a été recrutée à l'aide d'un c. de têtes,** she was headhunted; **c. d'images,** keen photographer; (*professionnel*) news cameraman; **c. d'autographes,** autograph hunter; **c. de primes,** bounty hunter.

2 *nm* **(a)** (*dans un hôtel etc*) (*commissionaire*) commissionaire; (*messager*) page(boy), *Am* bellhop, bellboy;

(b) *Mil Av* fighter; **c. tout temps,** all-weather fighter; *Nau* **c. de sous-marins,** submarine chaser;

(c) *Mil* rifleman, light infantryman, chasseur; **les chasseurs (à pied),** the light infantry; **les chasseurs alpins,** the mountain light infantry; **chasseurs à cheval,** light cavalry; **c. à cheval,** light cavalryman; **c. de chars,** tank destroyer.

chasseur-bombardier [ʃasœrbɔ̃bardje] *nm* fighter-bomber; (*pl chasseurs-bombardiers*).

chassie [ʃasi] *nf* matter, gum (*in the eyes*).

chassieux, -euse [ʃasjø, -øz] *adj* gummy (*eyes*); bleary-eyed (*person*).

châssis [ʃɑsi] *nm* **(a)** (*charpente*) frame; stretcher of a canvas; **c. de porte/fenêtre,** door/window frame; **c. mobile,** sash; **c. dormant,** sash (frame); **c. à guillotine,** sash window; **(b)** (*de jardin*) (cold *or* forcing) frame; **culture sous c.,** forcing; **(c)** *Aut* chassis; *Rail* underframe (*of carriage*); *Aut* **faux c.,** sub-frame; *F* **elle a un beau c.,** she's got a great figure; **(d)** *Typ* chase.

chaste [ʃast] *adj* chaste, pure; **un baiser c.,** a chaste kiss.

chastement [ʃastəmɑ̃] *adv* chastely, purely.

chasteté [ʃastəte] *nf* chastity, purity.

chasuble [ʃazybl] *nf Rel* chasuble; **robe c.,** pinafore dress, *Am* jumper.

chat, chatte [ʃa, ʃat] **1** *n* cat; *m* tom(cat); *f* she cat, (*surtout de race*) queen; **c. siamois/persan,** Siamese/Persian cat; **c. de gouttière,** alley cat; **le C. botté,** Puss in Boots; **petit c.,** kitten; *F* **mon petit c., ma petite chatte,** my dear, my pet, my darling; *Fig* **il n'y avait pas un c. dans la rue,** there wasn't a soul in the street; **des langues de c.,** langues de chat, finger biscuits; **appeler un c. un c.,** to call a spade a spade; **acheter c. en poche,** to buy a pig in a poke; **avoir un c. dans la gorge,** to have a frog in one's throat; **faire une toilette de c.,** to give oneself a cat('s) lick *or* a lick and a promise; *Prov* **ne réveillez pas le c. qui dort,** let sleeping dogs lie; **à bon c. bon rat,** tit for tat; **c. échaudé craint l'eau froide,** once bitten twice shy; **le c. parti, les souris dansent,** when the cat's away the mice will play; **jouer au c. et à la souris avec qn,** to play cat and mouse with s.o.; **la nuit tous les chats sont gris,** all cats are grey in the dark.

2 *nm* **(a) c. à neuf queues,** cat(-o'-nine-tails);

(b) (*jeu*) tag, tig, he; (*celui qui cherche*) it; **jouer au c.,** to play tag *or* tig *or* he; **c. perché,** off-ground tag *or* tig *or* he.

3 *adj F* caressing, feline (*manner etc*).

châtaigne [ʃɑtɛɲ] *nf* **(a)** (*fruit*) (sweet) chestnut; **c. d'eau,** water chestnut; **(b)** *Arg* (*gifle*) biff, clout; **je vais lui flanquer une c.,** I'm going to clobber him.

châtaigneraie [ʃɑtɛɲrɛ] *nf* chestnut grove, chestnut plantation.

châtaignier [ʃɑtɛɲe] *nm* chestnut (*tree, wood*).

châtain [ʃɑtɛ̃] **1** *adj inv* (chestnut-)brown; **une femme châtain,** a brunette; **cheveux c. clair,** light brown hair. **2** *nm* chestnut brown.

château, -eaux [ʃɑto] *nm* **(a)** castle; (*manoir*) mansion, manor, hall; *Hist* (royal) palace; **c. fort,** (fortified) castle; *Fig* **c'est la vie de c.,** it's the life of Riley; *Fig* **elle mène une vie de c.,** she leads a life of luxury; *Fig* **c. de cartes,** house of cards; *Fig* **bâtir des châteaux en Espagne,** to build castles in Spain *or* the air; **le c. de Versailles,** the palace of Versailles; **(b)** (*exploitation vinicole*) château; **vin mis en bouteille au c.,** château-bottled wine; *Arg* **c. la-pompe,** (drinking) water, Adam's ale; **(c) c. d'eau,** water tower; *Rail* tank; **(d)** *Nau* **c. d'avant** *ou* **de proue,** forecastle, fo'c'sle; **c. d'arrière** *ou* **de poupe,** afterdeck.

chateaubriand, châteaubriant [ʃatobrijɑ̃] *nm Culin* chateaubriand, porterhouse steak.

châtelain [ʃɑtlɛ̃] *nm* **(a)** *Hist* lord (of the manor); **(b)** (*propriétaire d'un château*) owner *or* tenant of a château.

châtelaine [ʃɑtlɛn] *nf* **(a)** *Hist* lady (of the manor); **(b)** (*propriétaire*) (woman) owner *or* tenant of a château; (*épouse du propriétaire*) wife of owner *or* tenant of a château; **(c)** (*ceinture*) chatelaine (*for keys etc*).

châtelet [ʃɑtlɛ] *nm* small castle.

chat-huant [ʃaɥɑ̃] *nm* tawny owl, brown owl, wood owl; (*pl chats-huants*).

châtié [ʃɑtje] *adj* polished (*style, verse*); **en langage c.,** in refined language.

châtier [ʃɑtje] *vt* (*impf & pr sub* **n. châtiions, v. châtiiez**) *Litt* to punish, to chastise, to castigate (*child etc*); to polish (*style*); **c. son corps,** to mortify the flesh; **c. l'impudence de qn,** to punish s.o. for his impudence; *Prov* **qui aime bien châtie bien,** spare the rod and spoil the child.

chatière [ʃatjɛr] *nf* **(a)** (*pour chat*) cat door, cat flap; **(b)** (*pour aération*) ventilation hole; **(c)** (*passage étroit*) narrow underground passage.

châtiment [ʃɑtimɑ̃] *nm Litt* punishment, chastisement, castigation; **c. corporel,** corporal punishment; **il a reçu un c. sévère,** he was severely punished.

chatoiement [ʃatwamɑ̃] *nm* shimmer(ing), iridescence, sheen.

chaton[1] [ʃatɔ̃] *nm* **(a)** (*petit chat*) kitten; **(b)** *Bot* catkin.

chaton[2] *nm* **(a)** bezel, setting (*of stone*); **(b)** stone (*in its setting*).

chatonner [ʃatɔne] *vi* **(a)** (*de chatte*) to have kittens; **(b)** *Bot* to grow catkins.

chatouille [ʃatuj] *nf F* **faire des chatouilles à qn,** to tickle s.o.; **craindre les chatouilles,** to be ticklish.

chatouillement [ʃatujmɑ̃] *nm* tickling; **éprouver** *ou* **avoir un c. dans la gorge,** to have a tickle in one's throat.

chatouiller [ʃatuje] **1** *vt* to tickle; **arrête de c. ta sœur!,** stop tickling your sister!; *F* **c. les côtes à qn,** to give s.o. a thrashing; **vin qui chatouille le palais,** wine that pleases the palate; **c. la curiosité,** to excite *or* arouse curiosity; **c. l'amour-propre de qn,** to flatter s.o.'s vanity. **2** *vi* to tickle; **ah! ça chatouille,** oh! that tickles.

chatouilleux, -euse [ʃatujø, -øz] *adj* ticklish; *Fig*

sensitive, touchy; **elle est très chatouilleuse,** she's very ticklish; *Fig* **c. sur le point d'honneur,** touchy where honour is concerned, touchy on a point of honour.

chatouillis [ʃatuji] *nm F* gentle tickling, light tickling; **faire des c. à qn,** to tickle s.o. gently.

chatoyant [ʃatwajɑ̃] *adj* shimmering, glistening, iridescent; sparkling (*stone, imagination etc*); **soie chatoyante,** shot silk.

chatoyer [ʃatwaje] *vi* (**il chatoie; il chatoiera**) to shimmer, to glisten, to sparkle; **style qui chatoie,** sparkling *or* colourful style.

châtré [ʃɑtre] **1** *adj* castrated (*man*); **taureau/étalon c.,** steer, castrated bull/gelding, castrated stallion. **2** *nm* eunuch; *F* **voix de c.,** high-pitched *or* falsetto voice.

châtrer [ʃɑtre] *vt* **(a)** to castrate, to emasculate; to geld (*stallion*); to neuter (*cat*); **(b)** to bowdlerize, to expurgate (*literary work*).

chatte [ʃat] *nf* **(a)** *voir* **CHAT 1**; **(b)** *Vulg* (*vagin*) pussy.

chatteries [ʃatri] *nfpl* **(a)** (*tendresse etc*) wheedling ways, coaxing; **(b)** (*friandises*) delicacies, dainties.

chatterton [ʃatɛrtɔn] *nm El* (adhesive) insulating tape.

chat-tigre [ʃatigr] *nm* tiger cat; (*pl chats-tigres*).

chaud, chaude [ʃo, ʃod] **1** *adj* **(a)** warm; hot; **pendant la chaude saison,** during the warm weather; **soupe toute chaude,** steaming *or* piping hot soup; **prendre un repas c.,** to have a hot meal; **animal à sang c.,** warm-blooded animal; *Culin* **mettre dans un four c.,** cook in a hot oven; **pleurer à chaudes larmes,** to weep bitterly; **un enfant c. qui a de la fièvre,** a hot child running a temperature; **couverture chaude,** warm blanket; **le soleil est déjà c.,** the sun's already (quite) warm *or* hot; **elle n'est pas chaude pour le projet,** she's not keen on *or* not over-enthusiastic about the project; *Prov* **il faut battre le fer pendant qu'il est c.,** strike while the iron is hot, make hay while the sun shines; *Fig* **avoir la tête chaude,** to be hot-headed; **affaire chaude,** (*scandale*) scandal; **guerre chaude,** shooting war; **l'été va être chaud,** it'll be a hot summer; **un point c. du Proche-Orient,** a hot spot *or* (potential) flash point of the Middle East; **chaude dispute,** heated discussion; **nouvelle toute chaude,** (piece of) really hot news; **tout c. de ...,** straight from ..., hotfoot from ...; *Fig* **voix chaude,** sultry voice; *Beaux-Arts* **tons chauds,** warm tints;

(b) *Arg* **être c.,** to be hot stuff; **c'est un c. lapin,** he's a randy devil.

2 *adv* **j'aime manger c.,** I like my food hot; **il fait très c.,** it's hot, it's very warm; **cela ne me fait ni c. ni froid,** it makes no difference, it's all the same to me.

3 *nm* heat, warmth; **garder** *ou* **tenir qch au c.,** to keep sth hot; **tenir au c.,** (*on label*) to be kept in a warm place; **chez soi, au c.,** at home, in the warmth; **prendre un c. et froid,** to catch a chill; **marqué à c.,** branded; **avoir c.,** (*de personne*) to be *or* feel warm *or* hot; *F* **il a eu c.,** he was scared stiff, he had a narrow escape; **travailler un métal à c.,** to hot-work a metal; **être opéré à c.,** to have an emergency operation; **interroger les spectateurs à c.,** to sound out the audience on the spot; *Fig* **souffler le c. et le froid,** to blow hot and cold; to lay down the law.

chaude [ʃod] *nf* **(a)** *Métal* heat; **(b)** *Région* blaze, fire; **faire une c.,** to get a fire going; **se mettre devant la c.,** to sit in front of the fire.

chaudement [ʃodmɑ̃] *adv* warmly; **être vêtu c.,** to be warmly dressed; **approuver c.,** to approve heartily.

chaude-pisse [ʃodpis] *nf inv Arg* V.D., clap; **elle m'a passé la c.-p.,** she's given me a dose of clap.

chaud-froid [ʃofrwa] *nm Culin* **c.-f. de poulet/gibier,** = cold jellied chicken/game; (*pl chauds-froids*).

chaudière [ʃodjɛr] *nf* **(a)** (*de chauffage*) (central heating) boiler; **c. à vapeur,** steam boiler, steam generator; **(b)** *Arch* copper (*for washing etc*).

chaudron [ʃodrɔ̃] *nm* cauldron, *surtout US* caldron.

chaudronnerie [ʃodrɔnri] *nf* **(a)** *Ind* boiler-making; (*pour petits objets*) hollow-ware manufacture; **(b)** (*objets*) **grosse c.,** boilers and industrial hollow-ware; **petite c.,** domestic hollow-ware; **(c)** (*atelier*) boiler works; (*pour petits objets*) hollow-ware factory; (*magasin*) = hardware shop, *Br* ironmonger's.

chaudronnier, -ière [ʃodrɔnje, -jɛr] **1** *n* **(a)** (*fabricant*) boiler maker; (*de petits objets*) hollow-ware maker; **(b)** (*marchand*) = hardware merchant, *Br* ironmonger. **2** *adj* **industrie chaudronnière,** boiler-making; (*petite*) hollow-ware industry.

chauffage [ʃofaʒ] *nm* (*de pièce etc*) heating, warming (*of room etc*); (*de chaudière*) stoking, firing; (*appareil etc*) heating system, heating apparatus; *Aut* (car) heater; **bois de c.,** firewood; **appareil de c.,** heater; **le c. est difficile dans cette maison,** it's a difficult house to heat; **c. central,** central heating; **c. urbain,** district heating; **c. à l'électricité/au gaz/au mazout,** electric/gas/oil heating; **installer le c.,** to put central heating in; **le c. est détraqué,** the boiler *or* the heating is out of order.

chauffagiste [ʃofaʒist] *n Tech* heating engineer.

chauffant [ʃofɑ̃] *adj* heating, warming; **couverture chauffante,** electric blanket; **plaque chauffante,** hot plate.

chauffard [ʃofar] *nm F* **(a)** (*mauvais conducteur*) roadhog; **(b)** (*qui provoque un accident et ne s'arrête pas*) hit-and-run driver.

chauffe [ʃof] *nf* **(a)** (*chauffage*) heating; **(b)** *Tech* firing, stoking; **surface de c.,** heating surface; **chef de c.,** head stoker; *Nau* leading stoker; *Nau* **chambre de c.,** stokehold; **bleu de c.,** boiler suit; **(c)** *Métal* fire chamber (*of furnace*).

chauffe-assiettes [ʃofasjɛt] *nm inv* plate warmer, hot plate.

chauffe-bain [ʃofbɛ̃] *nm* water heater; (*pl chauffe-bains*).

chauffe-biberon [ʃofbibrɔ̃] *nm* bottle-warmer; (*pl chauffe-biberons*).

chauffe-eau [ʃofo] *nm inv* water heater; (*à réservoir*) immersion heater.

chauffe-pieds [ʃofpje] *nm inv* footwarmer.

chauffe-plats [ʃofpla] *nm inv* chafing dish, hot plate, plate warmer.

chauffer [ʃofe] **1** *vt* **(a)** to heat (up), to warm (up); **c. une maison au gaz,** to heat a house with gas, to have gas heating; **la chambre n'est pas chauffée,** there's no heating in the bedroom, the bedroom's not heated; **c. le fer à blanc/au rouge,** to make iron white-/red-hot; **chauffé à blanc/au rouge,** white-/red-hot; *Aut* **c. le moteur,** to warm up the engine; **c. une chaudière/une locomotive,** to fire/stoke (up) a boiler/an engine, to get up *or* raise steam (in a boiler/an engine);

(b) *F* to cram *or* coach (*s.o.*) for an examination; **il faut c. l'affaire,** we must strike while the iron is hot; **c. qn (à blanc),** to incite s.o., to get s.o. going;

(c) *Arg* (*voler*) to pinch, to nick.

2 *vi* **(a)** (*devenir chaud*) to get *or* become hot *or* warm; **l'eau chauffe,** the water is heating (up) *or* warming (up); **la soupe chauffe,** the soup's warming up, the soup's on; **mets la soupe à c.,** put the soup on (to heat); *F* **faire c. la colle,** to bring out the stretchers;

(b) *F* **ça chauffe, ça va c.,** things are getting hot *or* are beginning to hum;

(c) (*de roulement à billes etc*) to overheat, to run hot; **le moteur a tendance à c.,** the engine tends to overheat *or* get overheated.

3 se chauffer *vpr* to warm oneself (**au soleil,** in the sun); **se c. (les muscles),** to limber up, to warm up; **se c. au mazout,** to have oil-fired (central) heating; *Fig* **je vais lui montrer de quel bois je me chauffe!,** I'll show him what I'm made of!, I'll give him a good piece of my mind!

chaufferette [ʃofrɛt] *nf* **(a)** (*de table*) plate warmer, hot plate; **(b)** (*pour les pieds*) footwarmer.

chaufferie [ʃofri] *nf* boiler room; *Nau* stokehold.

chauffeur, -euse [ʃofœr, -øz] *n* **(a)** (*personnel*) driver; chauffeur; **c. de camion,** lorry driver; **elle est chauffeuse de taxi,** she's a taxi driver; **les chauffeurs du dimanche,** Sunday drivers; **(b)** stoker (*of steam engine etc*); **(c)** *TV* **c. de salle,** warm-up man.

chauffeuse [ʃoføz] *nf* low fireside chair.

chaufour [ʃofur] *nm* limekiln.

chaulage [ʃolaʒ] *nm* liming (*of ground etc*); whitewashing (*of walls etc*).

chauler [ʃole] *vt* to treat (*ground etc*) with lime; to whitewash (*walls etc*).

chaumage [ʃomaʒ] *nm Agr* cutting (*of stubble*).

chaume [ʃom] *nm* **(a)** (*paille*) thatch; **couvrir un toit de** *ou* **en c.,** to thatch a roof; **toit de c.,** thatched roof; **(b)** (*ce qui reste des céréales*) stubble; (*champ*) stubble field; **couper la c.,** to cut the stubble.

chaumer [ʃome] *vt Agr* to clear (*field*) of stubble.

chaumière [ʃomjɛr] *nf* thatched cottage.

chaussant [ʃosɑ̃] *adj* (*shoe*) that fits well; comfortable (*shoe*).

chausse [ʃos] *nf* **(a) des chausses, une paire de chausses,** breeches; *Fig* **courir après les chausses de qn,** to pester s.o.; **tirer ses chausses,** to take to one's heels; **(b)** (*sac*) straining bag (*for wine etc*).

chaussée [ʃose] *nf* **(a)** (*route*) roadway, *Am* pavement; **c. bombée,** cambered road; **c. défoncée** *ou* **déformée,** road in poor condition; **'c. déformée',** 'temporary road surface';

(b) (*digue*) dyke, embankment; (*dans un endroit marécageux*) causeway; **la C. des Géants,** the Giant's Causeway; **(c)** (*écueil*) reef, line of rocks.

chausse-pied [ʃospje] *nm* shoehorn; (*pl chausse-pieds*).

chausser [ʃose] *vt* **1 (a)** to put on one's (*shoes, boots etc*); **chaussé de pantoufles,** wearing (his) slippers; **c. les étriers,** to put one's feet into the stirrups; **c. ses lunettes,** to put one's spectacles on;

(b) (*mettre des chaussures à*) to put shoes on (*s.o.*); (*fournir en chaussures*) to supply *or* fit (*s.o.*) with footwear, to make footwear for (*s.o.*); **se faire c. chez Adrian,** to buy *or* get one's shoes at Adrian's;

(c) *Aut* to put tyres on (*car*);

(d) to earth up (*tree*).

2 *vi* to fit; **souliers qui chaussent bien,** shoes that fit well; **ce soulier chausse étroit,** this shoe comes in a narrow fitting; **combien chaussez-vous?,** what size do you take (in shoes)?; **elle chausse du 37,** she takes a (size) four.

3 se chausser *vpr* to put one's shoes on; **se c. avec aide,** to need help putting one's shoes on; **se c. tout seul,** (*d'un enfant*) to put one's shoes on all by oneself; **se c. chez Simone,** to buy one's shoes from Simone *or* at Simone's.

chaussette [ʃosɛt] *nf* sock; **une paire de chaussettes,** a pair of socks; **en chaussettes,** in one's socks, in one's stockinged feet; **c. de ski,** ski(ing) sock; *Mil etc* **c. russe,** footcloth; *Arg* **un vrai jus de c.,** watery coffee.

chausseur [ʃosœr] *nm* shoe manufacturer; **Arche est mon c. favori,** I like Arche's shoes best.

chausson [ʃosɔ̃] *nm* **(a)** (*pantoufle*) slipper; (*de danse etc*) ballet shoe; (*de bébé*) (baby's) bootee; **(b)** *Culin* **c. aux pommes,** apple turnover; **(c)** *Sp* kick boxing.

chaussure [ʃosyr] *nf* **(a)** shoe; **une paire de chaussures,** a pair of shoes; **chaussures de marche,** walking shoes; **c. à talon,** high-heeled shoe; **c. basse,** flat shoe; **c. montante,** ankle boot; **chaussures de ski,** ski boots; *F* **trouver c. à son pied,** to find the right woman *or* man; **(b)** *Ind* (boot and) shoe industry *or* trade; **(c)** footwear.

chauve [ʃov] **1** *adj* bald; *Fig* bare (*mountain etc*); **un homme c.,** a bald man; **ce traitement l'a rendue chauve,** the treatment made her bald; **à tête c.,** bald-headed; *F* **c. comme un genou** *ou* **comme un œuf** *ou* **comme une bille,** as bald as a coot. **2** *n* bald(-headed) person.

chauve-souris [ʃovsuri] *nf* bat; (*pl chauves-souris*).

chauvin, -ine [ʃovɛ̃, -in] *Péj* **1** *n* chauvinist, jingoist. **2** *adj* chauvinist(ic), jingoist(ic).

chauvinisme [ʃovinism] *nm Péj* chauvinism, jingoism.

chauviniste [ʃovinist] *adj & n Péj* = **CHAUVIN 1, 2.**

chaux [ʃo] *nf* lime; **c. vive,** quicklime; **c. éteinte,** slaked lime; **pierre à c.,** limestone; **lait** *ou* **blanc de c.,** whitewash; **blanchir un mur à la c.,** to whitewash a wall; **bâtir à c. et à sable** *ou* **à c. et à ciment,** to build firmly *or* solidly; *Fig* **être bâti à c. et à sable,** (*de personne*) to have an iron constitution.

chavirer [ʃavire] **1** *vi* **(a)** (*de bateau etc*) to capsize, to turn turtle, to overturn; *Fig* (*sombrer*) to collapse; **les plus grands empires chavirent,** even the greatest empires collapse *or* fall; **(b)** (*tourner*) to reel, to spin (round); **tout chavire autour de moi,** everything's spinning; **ses yeux chaviraient,** he was showing the whites of his eyes. **2** *vt* **(a)** to upset, to capsize, to overturn (*boat*); to cant (*boat for repairs*); **(b)** *F* (*retourner*) to upset (*s.o.*), to bowl (*s.o.*) over; **il en est tout chaviré,** it's knocked him for six.

chébran [ʃebrɑ̃] *adj inv F* (= **branché**) trendy.

chèche [ʃɛʃ] *nm* North African scarf.

chéchia [ʃeʃja] *nf* fez.

check-list [tʃɛklist] *nf Av etc F* checklist; (*pl check-lists*).

check-up [tʃɛkœp] *nm inv Méd* check-up; **faire un c.-up à qn,** to give s.o. a check-up.

chef [ʃɛf] *nm* **(a)** head (*of family etc*); chief, chieftain (*of tribe etc*); leader (*of political party etc*); principal, head (*of business*); *F* (*patron*) boss; foreman (*of jury*); founder (*of school of thought etc*); **c. (cuisinier** *ou* **de cuisine),** chef; **le plat du c.,** chef's special; **c. de famille,** householder; **c. d'état,** head of state; **c. de bande,** ringleader; **c. de musique,** bandmaster; **c. d'orchestre,** conductor; **les ordres du c.,** the boss's order; **c. de nage,** stroke (oar); **c. d'équipe,** *Sp* captain; *Ind* foreman, charge hand; *Admin* **c. de bureau,** chief clerk; **c. de service,** head of department, departmental manager; **c. infirmier,** *Br* charge nurse; **c. du personnel,** personnel manager, head of personnel; *Parl* **c. de cabinet,** =(minister's) principal private secretary; *Ind* **c. d'atelier** (shop) foreman; **ingénieur en c.,** chief engineer; **rédacteur en c.,** chief editor; **c. de rayon,** (*in shop*) head of department, department(al) manager; **les chefs d'industrie,** the captains of industry; *Rail* **c. de gare,** station manager; **c. de train,** guard, *Am* conductor; *Nau* **c. de quart,** officer of the watch; *Mil* **commandant en c.,** commander-in-chief; **c. de bataillon,** major; **c. de patrouille,** patrol leader; **il se débrouille comme un c.,** he's getting on *or* doing very well; **cette fille, c'est un c.!,** that girl's top-notch *or* first-rate;

(b) *Arch & Hum* head; *Litt* **il pense de son c.,** he thinks for himself; **faire qch de son (propre) c.,** to do sth on one's own authority *or* *F* off one's own bat; *Jur* **du c. de sa femme,** in one's wife's right;

(c) *Jur* **c. d'accusation,** count of an indictment, charge.

chef-d'œuvre [ʃɛdœvr] *nm* masterpiece, chef-d'œuvre; (*pl chefs-d'œuvre*).

chef-lieu [ʃɛfljø] *nm* chief town (*of department*); = county town, *Am* county seat; (*pl chefs-lieux*).

cheftaine [ʃɛftɛn] *nf* (*of Guides*) captain; (*of Brownies*) Brown owl; (*of Cubs*) cubmistress.

cheik(h) [ʃɛk] *nm* sheik(h).

chelem [ʃlɛm] *nm Cartes* slam; **grand c.,** grand slam; **petit c.,** little slam; **elle a fini par me faire c.,** I ended up not winning a trick against her; *Tennis* **Grand C.,** Grand Slam.

chemin [ʃ(ə)mɛ̃] *nm* **(a)** (*route*) way, road; (*voie*) road, path, track; **le plus court c. d'un point à un autre,** the shortest distance between two points; *F* **c. des écoliers,** roundabout way, longest way round; **demander son c.,** to ask one's way; **c'est sur mon c.,** it's on my way; **nous avons beaucoup de c. à faire,** we've a long way to go; **il y a dix minutes de c.,** it's ten minutes away (from here); **deux ou trois heures de c.,** two or three hours' travel; **faire la moitié du c.,** to meet s.o. half way; **aller (toujours) son c., aller son petit bonhomme de c.,** to jog along; **s'arrêter en c.,** to stop on the way; **c. faisant,** on the way; **faire un bout de c. avec qn,** to go part of the way with s.o.; **le c. de la gare,** the way to the station; **montrer le c.,** to lead *or* show the way; **être en bon c.,** to be getting on well; **leur affaire est en bon c.,** their business is off to a good start; **elle n'en prend pas le c.,** she's not going the right way about it; **nous sommes dans le bon c.,** we're on the right road *or* track; **le c. de la gloire/réussite,** the road to glory/success; **à moitié c., à mi-chemin,** half way; **se mettre en c. pour** *ou* **prendre le c. de la France,** to set out for France; **être dans** *ou* **sur le c. de qn,** to be *or* stand in s.o.'s way; **il n'a pas intérêt à se trouver sur mon c.,** he'd better keep out of my way; *Fig* **trouver son c. de Damas,** to see the light; **ne pas y aller par quatre chemins** *ou* **par trente-six chemins,** to go straight to the point; *Fig* **elle fera son c.,** she'll get on *or* make her way in the world; *Fig* **cette idée fait du c.,** the idea is gaining ground; **c. piéton(nier),** footpath; *Arch* **grand c.,** highway, high road; **voleur de grand c.,** highwayman; **c. de traverse,** side road; short cut; **c. vicinal,** by-road, minor road; **c. de terre,** dirt track; **c. creux,** sunken road; **c. de halage,** towpath; *F* **être toujours sur les chemins,** to be always on the go; **c. de ronde,** covered way; *MecE* **c. de roulement pour billes,** ball race;

(b) c. de fer, railway, *US* railroad; **aller** *ou* **voyager en** *ou* **par c. de fer,** to go *or* travel by rail *or* by train; **c. de fer omnibus/rapide,** local/express service; **accident de c. de fer,** rail(way) accident; **c. de fer français,** French railways; **Chemins de fer nationaux du Canada,** Canadian National Railways;

(c) c. de table, (table) runner; **c. d'escalier,** stair-carpet;

(d) *Nau* **faire du c.,** to make headway; **c. est,** easting.

chemineau, -eaux [ʃ(ə)mino] *nm* tramp, vagrant.

cheminée [ʃ(ə)mine] *nf* **(a)** fireplace; **(manteau de) c.,** mantelpiece, chimneypiece; **il y a une c. dans chaque pièce,** there's a fireplace in every room; **un feu dans la c.,** a fire in the grate; **pierre de la c.,** hearthstone; **c. prussienne,** stove; **c'est sur la c.,** it's on the mantelpiece; **c. en marbre,** marble mantelpiece; **(b)** (*conduit*) chimney (stack); **(conduit de) c.,** flue; **le Père Noël passe par la c.,** Father Christmas comes down the chimney; **c. d'usine,** factory chimney; **feu de c.,** chimney (on) fire; **col c.,** (*de pull etc*) cowl neck(line); (*de locomotive, bateau à vapeur*) funnel, smokestack; **(c)** (*de lampe à huile*) chimney; **c. d'aération,** air shaft, ventilating shaft; **(d)** *Géol* chimney; **c. volcanique,** vent (*of a volcano*).

cheminement [ʃ(ə)minmɑ̃] *nm* **(a)** (*progression*) tramping, walking, trudging (along); **le c. des touristes devant les toiles célèbres,** the filing past of the tourists in front of the famous paintings; **le c. des eaux,** the advance of the water; **(b)** *Mil* advancing (*to position, esp under* *cover*); **(c) c. de la pensée,** advance *or* progress *or* march of thought; (*processus*) thought processes; **(d)** (*de relevé*) plane table traversing.

cheminer [ʃ(ə)mine] *vi* **(a)** (*avancer*) to continue on one's way; **c. sous la pluie,** to trudge *or* plod along in the rain; **(b)** *Mil* to advance (*to position esp under cover*); *Fig* to gain ground; **(c)** (*faire une levée*) to traverse.

cheminot [ʃ(ə)mino] *nm* rail(way) worker *or* employee, railwayman, *US* railroader.

chemisage [ʃ(ə)mizaʒ] *nm* jacketing, casing (*of boiler, cylinder etc*); lining (*of gun, cylinder etc*).

chemise [ʃ(ə)miz] *nf* **(a)** shirt; **c. empesée,** starched shirt; **en bras** *ou* **en manches de c.,** in one's shirtsleeves; **c. de nuit,** nightshirt, (woman's) nightdress; **c. américaine,** (woman's) vest, *Am* undershirt; *Fig* **il change d'avis comme de c.,** he changes his mind as often as he changes his shirt; **se moquer de qch comme de sa première c.,** not to care a damn *or* two hoots about sth; *Hist* **Chemises rouges,** Red Shirts; **Chemises noires,** Blackshirts; **Chemises brunes,** Brownshirts; **c. de mailles,** shirt of mail; **(b)** folder, portfolio (*for papers*); **(c)** jacket(ing), casing, sheathing (*of boiler, cylinder etc*); lining (*of cylinder, furnace etc*); facing (*of wall*); **c. de vapeur,** steam jacket; **c. d'eau,** water jacket; **c. (de cylindre),** (cylinder) liner, sleeve (*of sleeve valve engine*).

chemiser [ʃ(ə)mize] *vt* to jacket, to case (*boiler, cylinder etc*); to line (*gun, cylinder etc*).

chemiserie [ʃ(ə)mizri] *nf Ind* shirt making; (*ensemble de vêtements*) shirts, underwear and ties; (*fabrique*) shirt factory; (*magasin*) shirt (and underwear) shop.

chemisette [ʃ(ə)mizɛt] *nf* (*pour hommes*) short-sleeved shirt.

chemisier [ʃ(ə)mizje] *nm* **(a)** (*fabricant*) shirt-maker; (*marchand*) men's outfitter; **(b)** (*corsage*) (woman's) (long-sleeved) shirt, blouse; **robe c.,** shirt-waister.

chênaie [ʃɛnɛ] *nf* oak grove, oak plantation.

chenal, -aux [ʃ(ə)nal, -o] *nm* **(a)** channel, fairway (*of river, harbour etc*); **au milieu du c.,** in mid channel; **(b)** (*courant d'eau*) millrace; **(c)** *Métal* **c. de coulée,** runner.

chenapan [ʃ(ə)napɑ̃] *nm Hum* rogue, scoundrel.

chêne [ʃɛn] *nm* (*arbre*) oak; **c. vert,** evergreen oak, holm oak, ilex; **table/***etc* **en c.,** oak table/*etc*; *Fig* **être fort comme un c.,** to be as strong as an ox.

chéneau, -eaux [ʃeno] *nm* gutter (*of roof*).

chêneau, -eaux [ʃɛno] *nm* oak sapling.

chêne-liège [ʃɛnljɛʒ] *nm* cork oak; (*pl chênes-lièges*).

chenet [ʃ(ə)nɛ] *nm* firedog, andiron.

chènevière [ʃɛnvjɛr] *nf* hemp field.

chènevis [ʃɛnvi] *nm* hempseed.

chenil [ʃ(ə)ni(l)] *nm* **(a)** (*pour chiens*) kennels; **(b)** *Suisse* (*désordre*) mess, shambles.

chenille [ʃ(ə)nij] *nf* **(a)** (*insecte*) caterpillar; band (*of caterpillar tractor*); **véhicule à chenilles,** tracked vehicle; **(b)** *Tex* chenille.

chenillé [ʃ(ə)nije] *adj* tracked (*vehicle*).

chenillette [ʃ(ə)nijɛt] *nf Mil* Bren gun carrier.

chenu [ʃ(ə)ny] *adj Litt* (*personne*) white-haired; snow-capped (*mountain*); **arbres chenus,** (ancient) trees that are dying back.

cheptel [ʃ(ə)tɛl, ʃɛptɛl] *nm* **(a)** livestock; **c. ovin d'une région,** sheep population of a region; **(b)** *Jur* **bail à c.,** lease of livestock; **c. (vif),** livestock leased; **c. mort,** farm equipment leased.

chèque [ʃɛk] *nm* cheque, *Am* check; **c. de 60 francs,** cheque for 60 francs; **carnet de chèques,** cheque book; **endosser un c.,** to endorse a cheque; **c. à ordre,** cheque to order; **c. au porteur,** bearer cheque; **c. barré,** crossed cheque; **c. ouvert,** open cheque; **c. en blanc,** blank cheque; **c. sans provision,** cheque without cover; *F* **c. en bois,** rubber cheque; **j'ai fait un c. sans provisions,** my cheque bounced; **c. certifié** *ou Can* **visé,** certified cheque; **c. postal,** post office cheque; **faire** *ou* **remplir un c.,** to write (out) *or* make out a cheque; **à qui dois-je adresser le c.?,** who should I make the cheque out to?; **payer qch par c.,** to pay for sth by cheque; **toucher un c.,** to cash a cheque; **encaisser un c.,** (*en espèces*) to cash a cheque; (*le mettre sur son compte*) to pay in a cheque; **c. de voyage,** traveller's cheque.

chèque-livre [ʃɛklivr] *nm* book token; (*pl chèques-livres*).

chèque-repas [ʃɛkrəpa] *nm,* **chèque-restaurant** [ʃɛkrɛstɔrɑ̃] *nm* luncheon voucher; (*pl chèques-repas, chèques-restaurant*).

chéquier [sekje] *nm* cheque *or Am* check book.

cher, chère [ʃɛr] **1** *adj* **(a)** (*aimé*) dear, beloved; **être c. à qn,** to be dear to s.o.; **tout ce qui m'est c.,** all that I hold dear; **ses espérances les plus chères,** his most cherished hopes; **bien chers frères,** dearly beloved brethren; **C. Monsieur,** (*dans une lettre*) Dear Mr X; (*officiel*) Dear Sir; **chers amis de la nature,** dear nature lovers;

(b) (*coûteux*) dear, expensive, costly; **c'est trop c. pour moi,** I can't afford it; **la vie est chère en ville,** it's expensive living in town, the cost of living is high in town(s); **ce marchand est trop c.,** this shopkeeper is too dear *or* expensive.

2 *adv* **payer qch c./trop c.,** to pay a high price/too much for sth; **c'est c. payer (sa liberté),** it's a high price to pay (for one's freedom); **il fait c. vivre à Paris,** it's expensive living in Paris, the cost of living is high in Paris; **vendre c. sa vie,** to sell one's life dearly; **il me le payera c.,** I'll make him pay for it; *F* **ça m'a coûté c. de ne pas écouter mon instinct,** not following my instinct cost me dear; **cela ne vaut pas c.,** it's not worth much; *F* **je l'ai eu pour pas c.,** I got it cheap.

3 *n* **mon c.,** my dear (fellow); **ma chère,** my dear (girl); **ah ma chère! quel plaisir de vous voir!,** (*avec préciosité*) how nice to see you, my dear!

chérant [ʃɛrɑ̃] *adj Can* pricey; **un plombier pas c.,** a plumber who doesn't charge too much, an inexpensive plumber.

chercher [ʃɛrʃe] **1** *vt* **(a)** (*essayer de trouver*) to search for, to look for, *Fml* to seek (*s.o., sth*); **je l'ai cherché partout,** I searched *or* looked for it high and low, I hunted for it everywhere; **c. un mot dans un dictionnaire,** to look up a word in a dictionary; **il cherchait des moyens de s'évader,** he looked around for means of escape; **c. un emploi,** to look for a job; **c. son chemin/une solution,** to try to find one's way/a solution; **c. ses mots,** to search for words; **je cherche son nom,** I'm trying to think of his name; *F* **où va-t-il donc c. tout cela?,** where on earth does he get that from?; **c. sa ruine,** to court one's own ruin; **partir c. du secours,** to go for help; **c. aventure,** to seek adventure; *F* **il l'a bien cherché,** he was asking for it;

(b) aller c. qn/qch, to (go and) fetch s.o./sth; **envoyer c. qn/qch,** to send for s.o./sth; **je suis allé le c. à la gare,** I went to meet him at the station; **viens me c. à 17 heures,** come for me at 5 pm;

(c) c. à faire qch, to try to do sth; **c. à se faire connaître,** to try to get oneself known, to try to make a name for oneself; **c. à se faire aimer,** to try to make oneself popular;

(d) *F* (*atteindre*) to come to, to amount to; **cela va c. dans les 10 000 francs,** it will cost about 10,000 francs;

(e) *F* (*provoquer*) to get at, to pick on; **tu me cherches?,** are you looking for a fight?; **si tu me cherches tu vas me trouver,** if you want a fight you'll get one.

2 *vi* to look, to search; **qui cherche trouve,** he who seeks finds; **il faut c. plus,** you'll have to look harder.

3 se chercher *vpr* to try to understand oneself.

chercheur, -euse [ʃɛrʃœr, -øz] **1** *adj* **(a) esprit c.,** enquiring mind; **(b) tête chercheuse,** (*d'un missile*) homing head. **2** *n* seeker, searcher; (*scientifique*) researcher, research worker; **c. d'or,** gold prospector. **3** *nm* **(a)** *Opt* finger (*of telescope*); **(b) c. de fuites,** gas leak detector.

chère [ʃɛr] *nf* fare, food; **faire maigre c.,** to eat frugally; **faire bonne c.,** to have a good meal, to eat well; **aimer la bonne c.,** to be fond of good living; **faire bonne c. à qn,** to make s.o. welcome.

chèrement [ʃɛrmɑ̃] *adv* **(a)** (*affectueusement*) dearly, lovingly; **penser c. à qn,** to think fondly of s.o.; **(b)** (*à haut prix*) dearly, at a high price; **vendre c. sa vie,** to sell one's life dearly.

chéri, -ie [ʃeri] **1** *adj* cherished, dear; **mes enfants chéris,** my dearest *or* beloved children; **c. des dieux,** beloved of the gods. **2** *n* darling; **mon c., ma chérie,** darling, dearest; **c'est le c. de tout le monde,** he's everybody's darling *or* favourite.

chérif [ʃerif] *nm* (Mohammedan) sherif.

chérir [ʃerir] *vt* to cherish (*s.o., one's freedom etc*).

chérot [ʃero] *adj m Arg* (*trop cher*) pricey.

cherry [ʃeri] *nm* cherry brandy.

cherté [ʃɛrte] *nf* dearness, expensiveness; **c. de la vie,** high cost of living.

chérubin [ʃerybɛ̃] *nm* (*ange*) *& F* cherub; **des chérubins,** cherubs, cherubim; *F* **potelé et blond comme un c.,** as chubby and blond as a cherub.

chester [ʃɛstɛr] *nm* Cheshire cheese.

chétif, -ive [ʃetif, -iv] *adj* **(a)** weak, puny, sickly (*person*); **arbuste c.,** stunted *or* puny shrub; **(b)** *Fig Litt* poor, miserable, wretched; **un repas fort c.,** a meagre *or* skimpy *or* scanty meal; **raison chétive,** paltry reason.

chétivement [ʃetivmɑ̃] *adv* (*voir adj*) **(a)** (*d'une façon malingre*) punily, weakly; **(b)** *Litt* (*médiocrement, mal etc*) poorly, miserably.

chevaine [ʃ(ə)vɛn] *nm* (*poisson*) chub.

cheval, -aux [ʃ(ə)val, -o] *nm* **(a)** horse; **c. d'attelage,** carriage horse; **c. de trait,** draught horse; **c. de carrosse,** coach horse; **voiture à deux chevaux,** carriage and pair; **c. de labour,** plough horse; **c. de selle,** saddle horse; **c. de manège,** school horse; **c. de chasse,** hunter; **c. de course,** racehorse; **c. de bât,** packhorse; **c. pur sang,** thoroughbred (horse); **c. de bataille,** warhorse, charger; *F* **c'est son c. de bataille,** that's his hobby-horse, he rides the subject to death; **homme de c.,** horse-lover, born horseman; **à c.,** on horseback; **gendarme à c.,** mounted policeman; **aller à c.,** to ride; **monter sur son c.,** to get on one's horse, to mount; **monter à c.,** (*faire de l'équitation*) to go in for riding; **tu sais monter à c.?,** can you ride?; **est-ce que tu montes à c.?,** do you ride?; **se tenir bien/mal à c.,** to have a good/poor seat, to sit a horse well/badly; **chute de c.,** fall off a horse; **culotte de c.,** jodhpurs; *Méd* **traitement contre la culotte de c.,** treatment for cellulitis; **être à c. sur qch,** to sit astride sth, to straddle sth; *Fig* **être à c. sur l'étiquette,** to be a stickler for etiquette; **être à c. sur deux siècles,** to straddle two centuries; **monter sur ses grands chevaux,** to get on one's high horse; *F* **c. de retour,** (*récidiviste*) old lag; *F* **c'est un c. à l'ouvrage,** he works like a Trojan; *F* **cette femme, c'est un vrai c.,** what a horsy-looking woman she is; *F* **remède de c.,** drastic remedy; *F* **fièvre de c.,** raging fever;

(b) c. marin, seahorse; **c. à bascule,** rocking horse; *Gym* **c. d'arçons,** (vaulting) horse; **c. de bois,** wooden horse; **chevaux de bois,** roundabout, merry-go-round; **petits chevaux,** = type of board game; *Myth & Fig* **c. de Troie,** Trojan Horse;

(c) petit c., donkey engine, auxiliary engine;

(d) *Tech Aut* (**cheval-vapeur**) horsepower; **c. fiscal,** horsepower (*as basis for calculating road tax*); **automobile de vingt chevaux,** *F* **une vingt chevaux,** twenty horsepower car.

chevaler [ʃ(ə)vale] *vt Constr* to shore up (*wall etc*).

chevaleresque [ʃ(ə)valrɛsk] *adj* chivalrous, knightly.

chevaleresquement [ʃ(ə)valrɛskəmɑ̃] *adv* chivalrously.

chevalerie [ʃ(ə)valri] *nf* **(a)** (*dignité*) knighthood; **(b)** *Hist* (*institution*) chivalry; **roman de c.,** tale of chivalry.

chevalet [ʃ(ə)valɛ] *nm* **(a)** (*support*) stand, support, trestle, frame; **c. de scieur,** sawbench, sawhorse; **c. de peintre,** easel; **(b)** *Mus* bridge (*of violin*); **(c)** *Arch* **c. (de torture),** rack.

chevalier [ʃ(ə)valje] *nm* **(a)** (*seigneur*) knight; **c. errant,** knight errant; **armer** *ou* **faire qn c.,** to knight s.o., to dub s.o.; **c. servant,** faithful admirer; **(b)** Chevalier (*of the Legion of Honour etc*); **(c) c. d'industrie,** adventurer, swindler, crook; **(d)** (*oiseau*) sandpiper.

chevalière [ʃ(ə)valjɛr] *nf* signet ring.

chevalin, -ine [ʃ(ə)valɛ̃, -in] *adj* equine; **boucherie chevaline,** horse-butcher's (shop); **figure chevaline,** horsy face.

cheval-vapeur [ʃ(ə)valvapœr] *nm* (French) horsepower (=32,549 foot-pounds per minute); (*pl chevaux-vapeur*).

chevauchant [ʃ(ə)voʃɑ̃] *adj* overlapping (*teeth, slates etc*).

chevauchée [ʃ(ə)voʃe] *nf* **(a)** (*course à cheval*) ride; **(b)** (*personnes*) cavalcade.

chevauchement [ʃ(ə)voʃmɑ̃] *nm* overlap(ping) (*of tiles, subjects etc*); crossing (*of wires etc*); (over)riding (*of fractured bone*); *Typ* falling *or* dropping out of place (*of type*); *Géol* (over)thrust (*of folds*); *Géol* **faille de c.,** overthrust fault.

chevaucher [ʃ(ə)voʃe] **1** *vi* **(a)** to overlap; (*of wires etc*) to cross; *Chir* (*of fractured bone*) to (over)ride; *Géol* to overthrust; *Typ* (*of type*) to fall *or* drop out of place; *Menuis* **joint chevauché,** lapped joint; **(b)** *Littér* to ride (a horse). **2** *vt* **(a)** to span (*gap etc*); **(b)** to straddle, to be astride (*wall etc*); *Littér* to ride (*horse etc*); **c. un balai,** (*d'une sorcière*) to ride a broomstick. **3 se chevaucher** *vpr* to overlap.

chevau-léger [ʃ(ə)voleʒe] *nm Hist* light horseman; **les chevau-légers,** the light horse, light cavalry.

chevêche [ʃəvɛʃ] *nf* (*oiseau*) (sparrow) owl.

chevelu, -ue [ʃəvly] **1** *adj* **(a)** (*personne*) long-haired; **(b)** *Péj* hairy; **(c) cuir c.,** scalp; *Astron* **comète chevelue,** bearded comet. **2** *n Péj* **un c.,** one of the long-haired brigade.

chevelure [ʃəvlyr] *nf* **(a)** (head of) hair; **avoir une belle c.,** to have beautiful hair *or* a beautiful head of hair; **c. emmêlée,** tangled hair; **(b)** *Astron* tail (*of comet*); *Bot* coma (*of seed*).

chevenne, chevesne [ʃ(ə)vɛn] *nm* (*poisson*) chub.

chevet [ʃ(ə)vɛ] *nm* **(a)** (*tête de lit*) bedhead; **lampe de c.,** bedside lamp; **table de c.,** bedside table, *Am* night table, nightstand; **j'en ai fait mon livre de c.,** I've made it my bedside reading *or* book; **rester au c. de qn,** to stay at s.o.'s bedside; **(b)** *Archit* apse (*of church*).

cheveu, -eux [ʃ(ə)vø] *nm* **(a)** (a single) hair; **arriver comme un c. sur la soupe,** to arrive at an awkward moment; *F* **il s'en faut d'un c. qu'il n'arrive,** it's touch and go whether he'll turn up; **être à un c. de la ruine,** to be within a hair's breadth of ruin; **il y a un c.,** there's a snag; **si on lui touche un c., vous êtes mort!,** if anybody lays a finger on him *or* touches a hair of his head, I'll kill you!;

(b) cheveux, hair; **avoir les cheveux longs/courts,** to have long/short hair, to wear one's hair long/short; **des cheveux raides/frisés,** straight/curly hair; **en cheveux,** without a hat (on), hatless, bare-headed; *Fig* **s'arracher les cheveux,** to tear one's hair (out); *Fig* **couper les cheveux en quatre,** to split hairs; *F* **elles se sont prises aux cheveux,** they had a regular set-to; **argument tiré par les cheveux,** far-fetched argument; **se faire des cheveux (blancs),** to worry oneself sick; *F* **avoir mal aux cheveux,** to have a hangover; **cheveux d'ange,** angel hair (*as Christmas decoration*); *Culin* = type of vermicelli.

chevillard [ʃ(ə)vijar] *nm* wholesale butcher.

cheville [ʃ(ə)vij] *nf* **(a)** (*pour accrocher*) peg, pin; **c. en bois,** peg, dowel; **c. en fer,** bolt; **c. ouvrière,** kingpin (*of vehicle*); *Fig* mainspring, kingpin (*of enterprise etc*); *Mus* **c. de violon,** peg of a violin; **vente à la c.,** wholesale butchery trade; *F* **être en c. avec qn,** to be in cahoots with s.o.; **(b)** (*pour boucher*) peg, plug; **(c)** *Anat* ankle; **jusqu'à la c.,** ankle deep; **se fouler la c.,** to sprain one's ankle; *Fig* **il ne vous arrive pas à la c.,** he can't hold a candle to you; **(d)** *Littér* padding (*in line of verse*).

cheviller [ʃ(ə)vije] *vt* to pin, to bolt, to peg (*sth*) (together); *Fig* **avoir l'âme chevillée au corps,** to be indestructible.

cheviotte [ʃəvjɔt] *nf Tex* **c. écossaise,** tweed.

chèvre [ʃɛvr] **1** *nf* **(a)** goat, *surtout* she goat, nanny goat; **fromage/lait de c.,** goat's cheese/milk; **barbe de c.,** goatee; *F* **ménager la c. et le chou,** to sit on the fence, to run with the hare and hunt with the hounds; *Fig* **il me rend c.!,** he drives me up the wall *or* round the bend; **(b)** *MecE Constr etc* gin, crab, derrick; **c. à haubans,** sheer legs; **(c)** (*chevalet*) (carpenter's) sawhorse, trestle. **2** *nm* goat('s) cheese.

chevreau, -eaux [ʃəvro] *nm* kid; **gants de c.,** kid gloves.

chèvrefeuille [ʃəvrəfœj] *nm* honeysuckle.

chevrette [ʃəvrɛt] *nf* **(a)** (*chevreau*) kid, young (she-) goat; **(b)** (*femelle du chevreuil*) (female) roe deer; **(c)** (*trépied*) tripod.

chevreuil [ʃəvrœj] *nm* roe deer; roebuck; *Can* deer; (*gibier*) venison; **peau de c.,** buckskin, deerskin; **quartier de c.,** haunch of venison.

chevrier, -ière [ʃɛvrije, -jɛr] **1** *n* goatherd, *f* goat girl. **2** *nm* (small green) kidney bean.

chevron [ʃəvrɔ̃] *nm* **(a)** *Constr* rafter (*of roof*); **(b)** *Mil etc* chevron, (service) stripe; *Hér* chevron; *Tex* **tissu à chevrons,** herringbone pattern(ed) material; *MecE* **engrenage à chevrons,** double helical gear(ing).

chevronné [ʃəvrɔne] *adj* **(a)** (*qui a de l'expérience*) experienced; **(b)** *Hér* chevronny.

chevrotain [ʃəvrɔtɛ̃] *nm* mouse deer, musk deer.

chevrotant [ʃəvrɔtɑ̃] *adj* quavering, tremulous (*voice*).

chevrotement [ʃəvrɔtmɑ̃] *nm* quaver(ing), tremulousness (*of voice*).

chevroter [ʃəvrɔte] *vi* **(a)** (*de chèvre*) to kid; **(b)** (*de personne*) to sing *or* speak in a quavering voice, to quaver; **sa voix chevrote,** his voice shakes *or* quavers.

chevrotine [ʃəvrɔtin] *nf* buckshot.

chewing-gum [ʃwiŋgɔm] *nm* chewing-gum; (*pl chewing-gums*).

chez [ʃe] **1** *prép* **(a)** (*dans la maison etc de*) **c. qn,** at s.o.'s house *or* home; **il n'est pas c. lui,** he's not at home *or* not in; **elle est rentrée** *ou* **allée c. elle,** she's gone home; **je l'ai reconduit c. lui,** I took him home; **je vais c. moi,** I'm going home; **je vais c. ma sœur/Nadine,** I'm going to my sister's (house)/Nadine's (house); **C. Paul,** Paul's (*restaurant, café etc*); **venez c. nous,** come to our house; **il demeure c. nous,** he lives with us; **vous vivez c. vos**

parents?, do you live with your parents?; **vous êtes ici c. vous, faites comme c. vous,** treat the place as your own, make yourself at home; *Iron* **eh bien, faites comme c. vous,** that's right, (you) just make yourself at home; **acheter qch c. l'épicier,** to buy sth at the grocer's; **il est allé c. le dentiste/le pédicure,** he's gone to the dentist('s)/ the chiropodist('s); **chacun c. soi,** everyone in their own home; **chez ...,** (*on letters*) care of ..., c/o ...; **c. nous,** in my *or* our country; **un bon vin bien de c. nous,** one of our good local wines; **c. nous c'est mieux,** it's better at home; **derrière c. moi,** behind my house; **il habite près de c. son ami,** he lives near his friend;

(b) with; **c'est devenu une habitude c. moi,** it's become a habit with me; **ce que j'admire c. cet homme c'est ...,** what I admire about the man is ...; **c. Molière,** in the works of Molière;

(c) (*au temps de*) during the time of; **c. les Vikings,** during the Viking period;

(d) (*parmi*) among; **cette expression est courante c. les jeunes,** the expression is current among young people; **c. les Américains,** among (the) Americans; **c. les animaux,** in the animal kingdom.

2 *nm inv* **son c.-soi,** one's home, one's house; **j'aime mon c.-moi,** I love my home.

chiader [ʃjade] *Arg* **1** *vi* to swot. **2** *vt* to swot (up) for (*an exam*).

chialer [ʃjale] *vi Arg* to snivel, to blubber; *Can* to whine, to moan.

chialeur, -euse [ʃjalœr, -øz] *n Arg* cry baby; *Can* whiner, moaner.

chiant [ʃjɑ̃] *adj Arg* bloody annoying *or* irritating; **qu'est-ce qu'elle est chiante, cette fille!,** that girl's a pain in the arse!

chianti [kjɑ̃ti] *nm* chianti.

chiard [ʃjar] *nm F* (*enfant*) brat, kid.

chiasse [ʃjas] *nf* **(a)** (*d'insecte*) fly speck, insect dirt; **(b)** *Arg* **avoir la c.,** (*la diarrhée*) to have the runs *or* the squitters; (*avoir peur*) to have the wind up, to be shit-scared.

chic [ʃik] **1** *nm* **(a)** (*savoir-faire*) skill, knack; **il a le c. pour (faire) cela,** he has a knack of doing that; **elle a le c. de me mettre au rage,** she's really got the knack of making me angry, she really knows how to make me angry;

(b) (*élégance*) smartness, stylishness; **il a du c.,** he has style; **femme/chapeau qui a du c.,** smart *or* stylish woman/hat;

(c) *Beaux-Arts* **dessiner de c.,** to draw without a model *or* from memory.

2 *adj inv* **(a)** (*élégant etc*) smart, stylish, chic; **restaurant c.,** fashionable *or* smart *or F* posh restaurant; **style c. et décontracté,** elegant but relaxed style; **elle est c.,** she's got style; **les gens c.,** the smart set;

(b) *F* **on a passé une c. soirée,** we had a really good evening; **c'est un c. type,** he's a good sort, *Am* he's a regular guy; **il a été très c. avec moi,** he's been very decent *or* nice to me; **c'est c. de ta part,** that's really good *or* decent of you.

3 *int F* **c. (alors)!,** fine!, great!

chicane [ʃikan] *nf* **(a)** (*querelle*) quibbling, wrangling; *Jur* chicanery, pettifoggery; **chercher c. à qn,** to try to pick a quarrel with s.o.; *Jur* **gens de c.,** pettifoggers; **(b)** *MecE* baffle(plate), deflector; **joints en c.,** staggered joints; **(c)** *Mil* zigzag trench; zigzag, chicane (*in road etc*).

chicaner [ʃikane] **1** *vi* to quibble (**sur,** over, about); *Jur* to chicane, to pettifog; **c. sur les frais,** to haggle *or* quibble over the expense. **2** *vt* **c. qn,** to wrangle with s.o. (**sur,** about); **c. qch,** to haggle over sth. **3 se chicaner** *vpr* to squabble (**avec,** with).

chicanerie [ʃikanri] *nf esp Jur* quibbling, chicanery.

chicaneur, -euse [ʃikanœr, -øz] **, chicanier, -ière** [ʃikanje, -jɛr] **1** *n* quibbler, haggler. **2** *adj* quibbling, haggling.

chiche[1] [ʃiʃ] *adj* (*repas, récolte etc*) scanty, poor; (*personne*) stingy, niggardly; **être c. de louanges,** to be sparing in one's praise; *F* **être c. de faire qch,** to dare to do sth; **c. (que tu ne le feras pas)!,** (I) bet you don't!; **c. (que je le fais)!,** bet you I will!; **c.!,** try it!, I dare you!

chiche[2] *adj* **pois c.,** chick pea.

chiche-kebab [ʃiʃkebab] *nm Culin* shish kebab.

chichement [ʃiʃmɑ̃] *adv* stingily, meanly.

chichi [ʃiʃi] *nm F* (*souvent pl*) **chichis,** affected manners; **pas tant de c.!,** not so much fuss!; **gens à chichi,** overpolite *or* gushing people; **faire des chichis,** (*se donner des airs*) to put on airs; (*compliquer les choses*) to make a fuss *or* a bother; **repas sans c.,** informal meal.

chichiteux, -euse [ʃiʃitø, -øz] *adj F* fussy.

chicorée [ʃikɔre] *nf* **(a)** (*plante*) **c. (frisée),** endive; **c. sauvage,** chicory; **(b) (poudre de) c.,** (ground) chicory; **boire de la c.,** to drink chicory (coffee).

chicot [ʃiko] *nm* stump (*of tree, tooth*).

chiée [ʃje] *nf Vulg* loads, masses; **avoir une c. de livres,** to have loads *or* masses of books; **elle a une c. de marmots,** she has a swarm of brats *or* kids.

chien, chienne [ʃjɛ̃, ʃjɛn] **1** *n* dog, *f* bitch; **jeune c.,** pup, puppy; **c. de berger,** sheepdog; **c. de garde,** guard dog, watchdog; **c. de race,** pedigree (dog); **c. bâtard,** mongrel; **c. de chasse,** gundog; **c. courant,** hound; **c. d'arrêt,** gundog; **c. couchant,** setter; *F* **faire le c. couchant auprès de qn,** to fawn on *or* crawl to s.o.; **c. de salon** *ou* **d'appartement** *ou* **de manchon,** lapdog; **c. d'aveugle,** guide dog, *Am* seeing-eye dog; **c. policier,** police dog; **c. méchant,** beware of the dog; *Natation* **nager à la c.,** to dog-paddle; *Journ F* **faire les chiens écrasés,** to be a hack reporter, to write fillers; *Fig* **ils vivent comme c. et chat,** they lead a cat-and-dog life; *Fig* **se regarder en chiens de faïence,** to stare rudely *or* glare at one another; **un c. regarde bien un évêque,** a cat may look at a king; **rompre les chiens,** to call off the hounds; *Fig* to change the subject (*of a conversation*); *F* **ce n'est pas fait pour les chiens,** it's there to be used; **garder à qn un c. de sa chienne,** to have it in for s.o., to have a grudge against s.o.; **entre c. et loup,** in the dusk *or* the twilight; *Can* **avec cette femme, mon c. est mort,** I don't have a chance with that woman any more; *Prov* **qui veut noyer son c. l'accuse de la rage,** give a dog a bad name (and hang him); **c. qui aboie ne mord pas,** his bark is worse than his bite; **il n'est pas bon à jeter aux chiens,** hanging is too good for him; **métier de c.,** drudgery; *F* **vie de c.,** dog's life; **quel temps de c.!, quel c. de temps!,** what awful *or* foul *or* filthy weather!; *Nau* **coup de c.,** squall; **elle le traite comme un c.,** she treats him like a dog; **mourir comme un c.,** to die forsaken *or* like a dog.

2 *nm* **(a)** *F* (*style*) **avoir du c.,** to have charm, to be attractive *or* fascinating;

(b) être coiffée à la c., to wear a fringe;

(c) *Tech* hammer (*of gun*); *F* **se coucher en c. de fusil,** to curl up in one's bed;

(d) (*poisson*) **c. de mer,** dogfish.

3 *adj* **être c.,** to be mean *or* stingy.

chien-chien [ʃjɛ̃ʃjɛ̃] *nm F* doggie; (*pl chiens-chiens*).

chiendent [ʃjɛ̃dɑ̃] *nm* **(a)** (*plante*) couch grass; *F* **voilà le c.!,** that's the snag *or* the trouble; **(b) brosse en** *ou* **de c.,** scrubbing brush.

chienlit [ʃjɑ̃li] *nf* **(a)** *F* (*pagaïe*) mess, shambles; **(b)** *Vieilli* (*carnaval*) masquerade; (*masque*) carnival mask.

chien-loup [ʃjɛ̃lu] *nm* wolfhound; (*pl chiens-loups*).

chiennerie [ʃjɛnri] *nf F* **(a)** (*avarice*) meanness, tightfistedness; **(b)** (*action malhonnête etc*) filthy trick.

chier [ʃje] *vi Vulg* to shit, to crap; **tu me fais c.,** you're a pain in the arse; **je me fais c. dans ce lycée,** this school pisses me off; **ça va c.,** there's going to be one hell of a row *or* stink!; **ça m'a bien fait c. de le voir,** it really pissed me off to see him; **il n'y a pas à c.!,** there are no two bloody *or Vulg* fucking ways about it!

chiffe [ʃif] *nf* **(a)** *F* **mou comme une c.,** like a wet rag; **c'est une c. (molle),** he's spineless, he's a drip *or* a weed; **(b)** *Arch* rag.

chiffon [ʃifɔ̃] *nm* **(a)** (*morceau de vieux tissu*) rag; **c. (à épousseter** *ou* **à poussière),** duster; **on pourra en faire des chiffons,** keep it for rags; **papier de c.,** rag paper; *F* **parler chiffons,** to talk (about) clothes; **(b) mettre ses vêtements en c.,** to leave one's clothes in a heap; **c. de papier,** scrap of paper.

chiffonnade [ʃifɔnad] *nf Culin* chiffonade.

chiffonnage [ʃifɔnaʒ] *nm* **(a)** (*de vêtement, de papier*) creasing, crumpling; (*de vêtement*) rumpling; **(b)** *Vieilli* slight annoyance.

chiffonné [ʃifɔne] *adj* **(a)** creased, crumpled, rumpled (*clothes*); creased (*paper etc*); **c'est tout c.,** it's all creased; **(b)** *Fig* tired(-looking), drawn (*face etc*); **minois c.,** nice *or* pleasing but irregular features.

chiffonner [ʃifɔne] **1** *vt* **(a)** to rumple, to crease (*dress etc*); to crumple (*pieces of paper etc*); **(b)** *F* (*ennuyer*) to worry, to bother; **quelque chose me chiffonne,** something's bothering me. **2** *vi* to do a bit of dressmaking. **3 se chiffonner** *vpr* (*of material etc*) to crease, to crumple.

chiffonnier, -ière [ʃifɔnje, -jɛr] **1** *n* ragman, rag-and-bone man; *Vieilli* rag picker; **se disputer comme des chiffonniers,** to go at it hammer and tongs. **2** *nm* (*meuble*) chiffonier.

chiffrable [ʃifrabl] *adj* calculable.

chiffrage [ʃifraʒ] *nm* **(a)** numbering (*of pages etc*); **(b)** working out, calculating (*of amount etc*); **(c)** ciphering, coding (*message*); **(d)** marking (*of linen etc*); **(e)** *Mus* figuring (*of bass*).

chiffre [ʃifr] *nm* **(a)** figure, number, numeral, digit; **chiffres arabes,** Arabic numerals; **nombre de trois chiffres,** three-figure number; **inflation à deux chiffres,** double digit inflation; **(b)** (*total*) amount, total; **le c. des réussites,** the success rate, the total number of successes; *Com* **c. d'affaires,** turnover; **(c)** (*code*) cipher, code; **écriture en c.,** cipher, writing in cipher; **officier du c.,** cipher officer; **(service du) c.,** coding *or* cipher department; **(d)** combination (*for lock of safe*); **(e)** (*monogramme*) monogram; **(f)** *Mus* figure.

chiffrement [ʃifrəmɑ̃] *nm* coding, ciphering (*of message etc*).

chiffrer [ʃifre] **1** *vt* **(a)** to number (*pages of book etc*); to page (*account book etc*); **(b)** to work out, to calculate (*amount etc*); **les dégâts ne sont pas encore totalement chiffrés,** the extent of the damage has not yet been fully assessed; **détails chiffrés,** figures (*of scheme etc*); **(c)** to write (*sth*) in code, to code, to encode (*sth*); **message chiffré,** coded message, message in code; **(d)** to mark (*linen etc*); **(e)** *Mus* to figure (*bass*). **2** *vi* to add up, to tally; **ça doit c.,** it must add up. **3 se chiffrer** *vpr* **se c. à,** to add up to, to amount to, to total; **à combien cela se chiffre-t-il?,** how much does it work out at *or* add up to *or* come to *or* amount to?

chiffreur, -euse [ʃifrœr, -øz] *n* cipher clerk.

chignole [ʃiɲɔl] *nf* hand drill; (*électrique*) electric drill.

chignon [ʃiɲɔ̃] *nm* chignon, bun; **se faire un c.,** to put one's hair in a bun; *Fig* **elles se sont crêpé le c.,** they had a fight *or* a set-to *or* a dust-up.

chihuahua [ʃiwawa] *nm* chihuahua.

chiite [ʃiit] *adj & n Rel* Shiite.

Chili [ʃili] *nm* Chile.

chili (con carne) [ʃili(kɔnkarne)] *nm Culin* chili (con carne).

chilien, -ienne [ʃiljɛ̃, -jɛn] **1** *adj* Chilean. **2** *n* **C.,** Chilean.

chimère [ʃimɛr] *nf* **(a)** (*monstre*) chim(a)era; **(b)** *Fig* (*rêve*) chim(a)era, dream; **le pays des chimères,** the land of fancy *or* imagination; **(c)** (*poisson*) chimaera, rabbit fish.

chimérique [ʃimerik] *adj* **(a)** (*rêveur*) visionary, fanciful (*mind*); **rêve c.,** pipe dream; **(b)** (*utopique*) chimerical; **projet c.,** unrealistic plan.

chimie [ʃimi] *nf* chemistry; **cours de c.,** chemistry course *or* class; **c. minérale,** inorganic chemistry; **c. organique,** organic chemistry; **c. nucléaire,** nuclear chemistry; **c. industrielle,** chemical engineering.

chimiothérapie [ʃimjɔterapi] *nf Méd* chemotherapy; **être en c.,** to be having *or* undergoing chemo(therapy).

chimique [ʃimik] *adj* chemical; **symbole c. d'un corps,** the chemical symbol of a body; **produit c.,** chemical; **société/raffinerie de produits chimiques,** chemical company/refinery; *Phys* **rayons chimiques,** actinic rays.

chimiquement [ʃimikmɑ̃] *adv* chemically.

chimiste [ʃimist] *n* (research) chemist; **ingénieur c.,** chemical engineer, industrial chemist.

chimpanzé [ʃɛ̃pɑ̃ze] *nm* chimpanzee, *F* chimp.

chinage [ʃinaʒ] *nm Tex* mottling.

chinchilla [ʃɛ̃ʃila] *nm* (*mammifère, fourrure*) chinchilla; **veste en c.,** chinchilla jacket.

chine [ʃin] **1** *nf* peddling; **vente à la c.,** peddling, hawking. **2** *n* (piece of) Chinese porcelain. **3** *nm* rice paper.

Chine [ʃin] *nf* China; **encre de C.,** Indian ink.

chiner¹ [ʃine] *vt Tex* to mottle (*fabric*); **tissu chiné,** mottled *or* chiné fabric.

chiner² **1** *vt* **(a)** (*faire les brocantes*) to hunt for (*antiques*); **(b)** F to make fun of (*s.o.*), to pull (*s.o.'s*) leg. **2** *vi* to go antique-hunting, to hunt for antiques.

chinetoque [ʃintɔk] *n Arg* (*terme injurieux*) Chink.

chineur, -euse [ʃinœr, -øz] *n* **(a)** (*brocanteur*) second-hand dealer; (*amateur*) antique-hunter; **(b)** *F* practical joker, ragger.

chinois, -oise [ʃinwa, -waz] **1** *adj* **(a)** (*de la Chine*) Chinese; **(b)** *F* (*compliqué*) involved, complicated, over-elaborate. **2** *nm* **(a)** *Ling* Chinese; *F* **c'est du c.,** it's all Greek to me; **(b)** (*orange*) = small green orange preserved in brandy; **(c)** *Culin* conical strainer. **3** *n* **C.,** Chinese (man), Chinese woman; **les C.,** the Chinese.

chinoiser [ʃinwaze] *vi* to quibble (**sur cent francs,** over *or* about a hundred francs).

chinoiserie [ʃinwazri] *nf* **(a)** (*objet*) chinoiserie, Chinese curio; **(b)** *F* (*complication*) unnecessary complication; **chinoiseries administratives,** red tape.

chinook [ʃinuk] *nm Météo* chinook.

chintz [ʃints] *nm Tex* chintz; **des rideaux en c.,** chintz curtains.

chiot [ʃjo] *nm* pup(py).

chiottes [ʃjɔt] *nfpl Arg* (*toilettes*) bog, *Am* john.

chipage [ʃipaʒ] *nm F* scrounging.

chiper [ʃipe] *vt F* **(a)** (*voler*) to pinch, to swipe, to knock off (*sth*); **(b)** (*attraper*) to catch (*cold*).

chipeur, -euse [ʃipœr, -øz] *F n* petty thief, filcher.

chipie [ʃipi] *nf* ill-natured woman; **vieille c.,** old cat; **cette petite fille est une vraie c.,** she's a real little madam.

chipolata [ʃipɔlata] *nf* chipolata (sausage).

chipotage [ʃipɔtaʒ] *nm* **(a)** (*fait de picorer*) nibbling, picking at one's food; **(b)** (*ergotage*) quibbling; (*marchandage*) haggling.

chipoter [ʃipɔte] **1** *vi* **(a)** (*picorer*) to nibble, to pick at *or* play with one's food; **(b)** (*ergoter*) to quibble (**sur,** over, about); (*marchander*) to haggle (**sur,** over, about). **2** *vt* **(a)** to play with, to pick at (*food*); **(b)** to haggle over (*price*).

chipoteur, -euse [ʃipɔtœr, -øz] **1** *adj* **(a)** (*avec la nourriture*) picky, fussy; **il est c.,** he nibbles *or* picks at his food; **(b)** (*ergoteur*) time-wasting, fiddling; **(c)** (*marchandeur*) haggling, quibbling. **2** *n* **(a)** (*avec la nourriture*) picky eater; **(b)** (*ergoteur*) time-waster, fiddler; **(c)** (*marchandeur*) haggler, quibbler.

chips [ʃips] *nfpl* **(pommes) c.,** (potato) crisps, *Am* chips.

chique¹ [ʃik] *nf* **(a)** quid (*of tobacco*); *Arg* **couper la c. à qn,** to cut s.o. short; **avaler sa c.,** (*mourir*) to snuff it, to die, to kick the bucket; **(b)** *Belg* sweet.

chique² *nf* (*insecte*) jigger.

chiqué [ʃike] *nm F* sham, pretence; **c'est du c.,** it's all bluff *or* a put-up job *or* a fake; **faire du c., faire qch au c.,** to sham, to put on an act.

chiquement [ʃikmɑ̃] *adv F* **(a)** (*avec élégance*) smartly, stylishly; **(b)** (*avec fair-play etc*) decently; **elle m'a c. invité,** she was good *or* kind *or* decent enough to invite me.

chiquenaude [ʃiknod] *nf* flick (of the finger); **donner une c. à qn,** to give s.o. a flick with one's finger; **d'une c.,** with a flick of the finger; *Fig* **il suffit d'une c. pour qu'elle dise oui,** she's on the verge *or* within an ace of saying yes.

chiquer [ʃike] **1** *vt* to chew (*tobacco*). **2** *vi* to chew tobacco.

chiqueur, -euse [ʃikœr, -øz] *n* tobacco chewer.

chirographie [kirɔgrafi] *nf,* **chiromancie** [kirɔmɑ̃si] *nf* palmistry, chiromancy.

chiromancien, -ienne [kirɔmɑ̃sjɛ̃, -jɛn] *n* chiromancer, palmist.

chiropracteur [kirɔpraktœr] *nm* chiropractor.

chiropractie [kirɔprakti] *nf* chiropractic.

chiropraticien, -ienne [kirɔpratisjɛ̃, -jɛn] *n* chiropractor.

chiropraxie [kirɔpraksi] *nf* chiropractic.

chiroptères [kirɔptɛr] *nmpl Spéc* Chiroptera.

chirurgical, -aux [ʃiryrʒikal, -o] *adj* surgical.

chirurgie [ʃiryrʒi] *nf* surgery; **c. plastique/esthétique/dentaire,** plastic/cosmetic/dental surgery; **il faut qu'on lui fasse de la c. plastique,** he has to have plastic surgery.

chirurgien [ʃiryrʒjɛ̃] *nm* surgeon; **c. esthétique,** plastic surgeon; **c. dentiste,** dental surgeon; **elle est c.,** she's a surgeon.

chistera [ʃistɛra] *nf* chistera, pelota racket.

chiure [ʃjyr] *nf* flyspeck, insect dirt.

ch.-l. *abrév* **chef-lieu.**

chlamydia [klamidja] *nf Méd* chlamydia; (*pl chlamydiae*).

chleuh [ʃlø] *adj & nm Hist Arg Péj* Jerry.

chloral [klɔral] *nm Ch* chloral; *Pharm* **c. hydraté, hydrate de c.,** chloral (hydrate); (*pl chlorals*).

chlorate [klɔrat] *nm Ch* chlorate.

chlore [klɔr] *nm Ch* chlorine.

chlorelle [klɔrɛl] *nf* (*plante*) chlorella.

chlorer [klɔre] *vt Ind* to chlorinate; **eau chlorée,** chlorinated water.

chlorhydrate [klɔridrat] *nm Ch* hydrochlorate.

chlorhydrique [klɔridrik] *adj Ch* hydrochloric (*acid*).

chlorique [klɔrik] *adj* chloric (*acid*).

chlorofluorocarboné [klɔrɔflyrɔkarbɔne] *adj Ch* **produits chlorofluorocarbonés,** chlorofluorocarbons, *F* CFCs.

chlorofluorocarbure [klɔrɔflyrɔkarbyr] *nm Ch* chlorofluorocarbon.

chloroforme [klɔrɔfɔrm] *nm* chloroform.

chloroformer [klɔrɔfɔrme] *vt* to chloroform.

chlorophylle [klɔrɔfil] *nf* chlorophyll.

chlorophyllien, -ienne [klɔrɔfiljɛ̃, -jɛn] *adj* chlorophyllous.

chlorure [klɔryr] *nm Ch* chloride; **c. de chaux,** chloride of lime, bleaching powder; **c. de calcium/sodium,** calcium/sodium chloride.

chlorurer [klɔryre] *vt* to chlorinate.

choc [ʃɔk] *nm* **(a)** shock, impact, bump, collision (*of two bodies*); **le c. des deux voitures,** the collision of the two cars; **c. violent,** violent collision; **résistant aux chocs,** shock-proof, shock-resistant; **c. sourd,** bump; **c. des verres,** clink of glasses; **c. des opinions,** clash *or* conflict of opinions; **troupes de c.,** shock troops; **soutenir le c. de l'ennemi,** to withstand the onslaught of the enemy, to bear the brunt of the enemy's attack;

(b) c. électrique, electric shock; **c. en retour,** *Él* return shock; *Fig* repercussion, reaction;

(c) shock (*to nervous system*); **c. opératoire,** post-operative shock; **ça a été un c. de l'apprendre,** it was a shock to hear about it; **être en état de c.,** to be in a state of shock;

(d) de c., dynamic, intense; **mesures de c.,** shock measures; **personnalité de c.,** a high-powered personality.

-choc [ʃɔk] *suff* drastic, shock; **images-/photos-c.,** images/photos that shock; *Com Fin* **prix-c.!,** drastic reductions!; **programme-c.,** crash programme.

chochotte [ʃɔʃɔt] *F Péj* **1** *nf* lah-di-dah woman; (*homme*) pouf, fairy; **petite c., va!,** you stuck-up so-and-so! **2** *adj* lah-di-dah, affected, mannered; **une discussion c.,** a simpering discussion.

chocolat [ʃɔkɔla] **1** *nm* chocolate; **c. à cuire,** cooking chocolate; **c. fondant,** fondant chocolate; **c. blanc/noir,** white/black chocolate; **c. à croquer,** plain chocolate; **c. au lait,** milk chocolate; **tablette de c.,** bar of chocolate; **éclair/gâteau/***etc* **au c.,** chocolate éclair/cake/*etc*. **2** *adj inv* chocolate-coloured; *F* **être c.,** to have been let down.

chocolaté [ʃɔkɔlate] *adj* (*boisson etc*) chocolate(-flavoured).

chocolaterie [ʃɔkɔlatri] *nf* (*fabrique*) chocolate factory; (*magasin*) chocolate shop.

chocolatier, -ière [ʃɔkɔlatje, -jɛr] **1** *adj* chocolate (*industry etc*). **2** *n* chocolate-maker *or* -seller. **3** *nf* **chocolatière,** chocolate pot.

chocottes [ʃɔkɔt] *nfpl Arg* (*dents*) ivories; **avoir les c.,** to have the jitters.

chœur [kœr] *nm* choir; *Archit* choir, chancel; (*de chanson*) chorus; *Antiq* (*grec*) chorus; **les chœurs,** (*d'un opéra, d'un spectacle*) the chorus; **elle est dans les chœurs,** she's in the chorus, she's a member of the chorus; **enfant de c.,** altar boy; (*qui chante*) choirboy; *F* **son air d'enfant de c.,** his angelic *or* choirboy look; **en c.,** together; **chanter en c.,** to sing in chorus; **s'informer en c.,** to enquire in chorus *or* unison; **tous en c.!,** all together!

choir [ʃwar] *vi* (*pp* **chu**; *pr ind* **je chois, il choit**; *p hist* **je chus**; *fu* **je choirai, je cherrai**; *the aux is* **être**) *Litt* **(a) se laisser c. (dans un fauteuil),** to drop, to flop, to sink (into an armchair); *F* **laisser c. qn/qch,** to drop s.o./sth; **(b)** *Arch* to fall.

choisi [ʃwazi] *adj* **(a)** (*sélectionné*) selected; **morceaux choisis de ...,** selected passages *or* extracts from ...; **(b)** (*élégant*) select, choice; polished (*language*); **parler en termes choisis,** to speak in carefully chosen terms, to choose one's words (carefully); **société choisie,** select company.

choisir [ʃwazir] **1** *vt* to choose, to select, to pick; **c. entre** *ou* **parmi plusieurs choses,** to choose from *or* between several things; **c. si l'on part,** to choose *or* decide whether one will leave; **c. ses fréquentations/lectures,** to choose *or* pick one's company/reading; **je l'ai choisi entre mille,** it was exactly what I was looking for. **2** *vi* to choose; **il faudra bien c.,** you'll *or* we'll *etc* have to choose *or* decide *or* make a choice; **c. de partir,** to choose *or* decide to leave.

choix [ʃwa] *nm* choice, selection; **l'embarras du c.,** the difficulty of choosing; **avoir** *ou* **n'avoir que l'embarras du c.,** to be spoiled for choice; **faites votre c.,** take your pick; **vous avez le c.,** you have a choice; **je vous laisse le c.,** you choose; **nous n'avons pas d'autre c. que de ...,** we have no option *or* choice but to ...; **viande ou poisson au c.,** (*sur le menu*) choice of meat or fish; **de premier c.,** (of the) best quality, first-class; **morceaux de viande de c.,** prime cuts; **un grand c. de sous-vêtements,** a large *or* wide selection *or* a wide range of underclothes; **c. de poésies,** a selection of poems; *Admin* **avancer au c.,** to be promoted by selection *or* on merit.

choléra [kɔlera] *nm Méd* cholera; **avoir le c.,** to have cholera.

cholérine [kɔlerin] *nf Méd* cholerine.

cholérique [kɔlerik] *Méd* **1** *adj* choleraic. **2** *n* cholera patient.

cholestérol [kɔlesterɔl] *Méd nm* cholesterol; **le taux de c.,** cholesterol level; *F* **j'ai du c.,** my cholesterol (level) is too high.

chômable [ʃomabl] *adj* (*jour*) non-working.

chômage [ʃomaʒ] *nm* unemployment; **le c. des femmes/des jeunes,** female/youth unemployment, unemployment among women/young people; **être au c.,** to be unemployed *or* out of work *or F* jobless; **allocation** *ou* **indemnité de c.,** unemployment benefit, *Br F* dole; **toucher le c.,** to claim unemployment benefit, to be on unemployment *or Br* on the dole; **s'inscrire au c.,** to sign on; **c. saisonnier,** seasonal unemployment; **c. partiel,** short-time (working); **être en c. partiel,** to be on short time; **c. technique,** lay-offs; **être en c. technique,** to have been laid off; **c. d'une usine,** closure of a factory.

chômer [ʃome] **1** *vt* to keep (*feast day*); **fête chômée,** public holiday. **2** *vi* **(a)** (*ne pas travailler*) (*d'une usine*) to be *or* lie idle; (*d'un employé*) to be unemployed *or* out of work; *Fig* to do nothing; **vous n'avez pas chômé!,** (*quel travail vous avez fait*) you've not been idle *or* twiddling your thumbs!; **l'an dernier je n'ai pas eu le temps de c.,** I didn't have a spare moment all last year; **laisser c. son argent,** to let one's money lie idle; **(b)** (*faire le pont*) to take time off; **c. entre Noël et le jour de l'An,** to take time off between Christmas and New Year.

chômeur, -euse [ʃomœr, -øz] *n* unemployed worker; **les chômeurs,** the unemployed.

chope [ʃɔp] *nf* (*récipient*) beer mug, pint pot, tankard; (*contenu*) mugful.

choper [ʃɔpe] *vt Arg* **(a)** (*voler*) to pinch, to nick; **(b)** (*arrêter, prendre*) to nab, to nick; **se faire c.,** to get nabbed *or* nicked; **(c)** (*attraper*) to catch (*cold*).

chopine [ʃɔpin] *nf* **(a)** *F* half-litre *or US* -liter bottle; **tu viens boire une c.?,** (are you) coming for a drink?; **(b)** *Can* (*mesure*) pint (0,568 l.).

choquant [ʃɔkɑ̃] *adj* (*attitude etc*) shocking; **un abus c.,** a gross *or* glaring abuse.

choquer [ʃɔke] **1** *vt* **(a)** to strike, to knock, to bump (*sth against sth*); **nous avons choqué nos verres,** we clinked *or* chinked glasses;

(b) (*contrarier, être désagréable à*) to shock, to offend; **nous avons été choqués par son manque d'égard,** we were shocked *or* appalled by his lack of consideration; **je suis tout à fait choqué par sa vulgarité,** I am deeply shocked by his coarseness; **être choqué de qch,** to be scandalized *or* shocked at *or* by sth; **sons qui choquent l'oreille,** sounds that grate on *or* offend the ear; **mot qui choque,** offensive *or* rude word; **de telles paroles choquent dans la bouche d'une jeune fille,** such language is shocking in the mouth of *or* coming from a young girl;

(c) to shock; **j'ai été choqué de le voir tellement changé,** I was shocked *or* it gave me a shock to see such a change in him; **la vue du sang l'a choqué,** the sight of blood has shaken him.

2 se choquer *vpr* to be shocked, to be scandalized, to take offence (**de,** at); **il n'y a pas de quoi se c.,** there's nothing to be shocked at.

choral, -ale, -als [kɔral] **1** *adj* choral; **chant c.,** choral singing; **société chorale,** choral society. **2** *nm* choral(e). **3** *nf* **chorale,** (*société*) choral society; (*chanteurs*) choir; **la c. de l'église,** the church choir.

chorée [kɔre] *nf Méd* chorea, *F* Saint Vitus's dance.

chorégraphe [kɔregraf] *n* choreographer.

chorégraphie [kɔregrafi] *nf* choreography; **faire la c. d'un spectacle,** to choreograph *or* do the choreography for a show.

chorégraphique [kɔregrafik] *adj* choreographic.

choria [ʃɔrja] *nf Rel* (*Islam*) sharia.

choriste [kɔrist] *n Mus* choir member; chorister (*in church*); chorus singer (*in opera*); chorus member (*of musical*); backup vocalist (*of singer*).

chorizo [tʃɔriso] *nm Culin* chorizo.

chorus [kɔrys] *nm* **(a) faire c.,** to chorus s.o.'s words; **(b)** (*jazz*) chorus; **reprendre un c.,** to take up the chorus.

chose [ʃoz] **1** *nf* **(a)** (*objet inanimé*) thing; **un tas de choses,** a pile *or* heap of things; **les êtres et les choses,** living creatures and objects *or* things; *Fig* **être la c. de qn,** to be s.o.'s creature;

(b) (*abstrait*) thing; **j'ai un tas de choses à faire,** I've loads *or* masses of things to do; **c'est de deux choses l'une,** it's up to you *or* him *etc*, the choice is yours *or* his *etc*; **chaque c. en son temps,** everything in its own time;

dites bien des choses de ma part à ..., remember me *or* give my regards to ...; **j'ai bien des choses à vous raconter,** I've a lot (of things) to tell you; **ce n'est pas c. aisée de ...,** it's no easy matter to ...; **réaliser cela est une c., l'admettre en est une autre,** being aware of it is one thing, admitting it is another; **la c. en question,** the case in point; **je vais vous expliquer la c.,** I'll explain it *or* the matter to you; **cela n'est plus la même c.,** that alters the case; **nous y sommes retournés, mais ce n'est plus la même c.,** we went back (there), but it wasn't the same; **je vois la c.,** I see how things stand, I understand; *F* **être porté sur la c.,** to be obsessed with sex, to have a one-track mind; **je vais te dire une bonne c.,** I'm going to *or* let me tell you something; **il a dit des choses sur moi?,** has he been saying things about me?; **elle dit de ces choses parfois!,** she says some awful things sometimes; **c. curieuse, personne n'en savait rien,** curiously enough, nobody knew anything about it; **avant toute c.,** first of all, above all; *Jur* **c. jugée,** res judicata;

(c) les choses, things; **dans l'état actuel des choses,** as things are *or* stand at the moment; **l'état des choses,** the state of things; **les choses de ce monde,** the things of this world; **par la force des choses,** by *or* through force of circumstance; **il fait bien les choses,** he does things in style; **il faut bien voir les choses en face** *ou* **telles qu'elles sont,** you have to face up to things, you have to face facts; **les choses étant ce qu'elles sont,** things being as *or* what they are; **ne pas faire les choses à demi,** not to do things by halves; **n'aie pas peur d'appeler les choses par leur nom,** don't be afraid to speak out *or* to call a spade a spade *or* to speak your mind.

2 *nm F* (*truc*) what's it, what's-its-name, thingummy; **passe-moi le c.,** pass me the what's-its-name *or* the what-d'you-call-it; **Monsieur/Madame C.,** Mr/Mrs what-d'ye-call-him/her, what's-his-name/what's-her-name, Mr/Mrs thingummy; **le petit C.,** little what's-his-name.

3 *adj inv F* **être** *ou* **se sentir/avoir l'air tout c.,** to feel/look funny *or* a bit peculiar.

chott [ʃɔt] *nm Géog* saline lake, chott.

chou, -oux [ʃu] **1** *nm* **(a)** (*plante*) cabbage; **c. pommé,** round cabbage; **c. frisé,** kale; **c. de Bruxelles,** Brussels sprout; **c. de Milan,** Savoy (cabbage); **c. rouge,** red cabbage; **c. marin,** sea kale; *F* **aller planter ses choux,** to go and live in *or* to retire to the country; **faire ses choux gras de qch,** (*s'enrichir*) to get rich on; **l'opposition a fait ses choux gras de la situation,** the opposition made capital out of the situation; **faire c. blanc,** to draw a blank; **mon petit c.,** darling, dear; **être dans les choux,** to be in a fix *or* a mess; **rentrer dans le c. à qn,** to attack *or* go for s.o.; *Fig* **feuille de c.,** (*journal*) rag; **(b)** (*ruban*) bow, rosette, chou (*of ribbon*); **(c)** *Culin* **c. à la crème,** cream bun; **pâte à choux,** choux pastry. **2** *adj inv F* pretty, lovely.

chouan [ʃuɑ̃] *nm Hist* chouan.

choucas [ʃuka] *nm* jackdaw.

chouchou, -oute [ʃuʃu, -ut] *n F* pet; *m* blue-eyed boy; **le c. du prof,** teacher's pet; **tu es sa chouchoute,** you're his favourite *or* pet.

chouchouter [ʃuʃute] *vt F* to pet, to coddle (*child*).

choucroute [ʃukrut] *nf Culin* sauerkraut; **c. garnie,** sauerkraut with meat.

chouette¹ [ʃwɛt] *nf* **(a)** (*oiseau*) **c. des clochers, c. effraie,** screech owl, barn owl; **c. des bois,** wood owl, brown owl; **c. hulotte,** tawny owl; **(b)** *F Péj* (*femme désagréable*) harpy, scold, shrew.

chouette² *F* **1** *adj* terrific, marvellous, great; **c'est c.!,** that's great *or* smashing; **un type vraiment c.,** a really great guy; *Iron* **tu as l'air c. avec ton chapeau,** you look something else in that hat. **2** *int* **c. (alors)!,** great!, fantastic!

chou-fleur [ʃuflœr] *nm* cauliflower; **oreille en c.-f.,** cauliflower ear; (*pl choux-fleurs*).

chou-navet [ʃunavɛ] *nm* swede, *Am* rutabaga; (*pl choux-navets*).

chou-palmiste [ʃupalmist] *nm Bot* palm cabbage; (*pl choux-palmistes*).

chou-rave [ʃurav] *nm* kohlrabi; (*pl choux-raves*).

chow-chow [ʃuʃu] *nm* chow (dog); (*pl chows-chows*).

choyer [ʃwaje] *vt* **(je choie; je choierai)** to pet, to coddle; **c. un espoir,** to cherish a hope.

chrême [krɛm] *nm Rel* chrism, holy oil.

chrétien, -ienne [kretjɛ̃, -jɛn] **1** *adj* Christian. **2** *n* Christian; **un bon c.,** a good Christian.

chrétiennement [kretjɛnmɑ̃] *adv* in a Christian manner, like a Christian.

chrétienté [kretjɛ̃te] *nf* Christendom.

Christ [krist] *nm* **(a) le C.** [ləkrist], Christ; **Jésus-C.** [ʒezykri], Jesus Christ; **(b) c.,** crucifix; **un c. d'ivoire/d'ébène,** an ivory/ebony crucifix.

christiania [kristjanja] *nm Ski* christiania, christie (turn).

christianisation [kristjanizɑsjɔ̃] *nf* christianization.

christianiser [kristjanize] *vt* to christianize.

christianisme [kristjanism] *nm* Christianity.

Christophe [kristɔf] *nm* Christopher.

chromage [kromaʒ] *nm* chromium plating.

chromate [krɔmat] *nm Ch* chromate.

chromatique [krɔmatik] *adj* **(a)** *Mus Opt etc* chromatic; **(b)** *Biol* chromosomal.

chromatiquement [krɔmatikmɑ̃] *adv Mus* chromatically.

chromatisme [krɔmatism] *nm Beaux-Arts Mus* chromatism, chromatic aberration.

chrome [krom] *nm* **(a)** (*sur auto etc*) chromium fitting; *Ch* chromium; *F* **faire (briller) les chromes,** to polish the chrome (*of cars, bicycles etc*); **(b)** *Com* chrome; **jaune de c.,** chrome yellow.

chromé [krome] *adj* **(a)** chromium-plated (metal); **(b) cuir c.,** chrome(-tanned) leather; **veau c.,** box calf; **acier c.,** chrome steel.

chromer [krome] *vt* **(a)** to chromium-plate (*metal*); **(b)** to chrome (*leather, steel*).

chromique [krɔmik] *adj Ch* chromic (*acid*).

chromo [krɔmo] *nm F* chromo(lithograph), colour print.

chromosome [krɔmozom] *nm Biol* chromosome.

chromosomique [krɔmozomik] *adj Biol* chromosomal; **maladie c.,** chromosomal *or* genetic illness.

chronicité [krɔnisite] *nf* chronicity (*of disease, unemployment etc*).

chronique¹ [krɔnik] *adj* chronic (*disease etc*); **mévente c.,** slump in sales.

chronique² *nf* **(a)** (*annale*) chronicle; **(b)** *Journ* (*financial etc*) news, report, column; **défrayer la c.,** to be the talk of the neighbourhood *or* town, to be the main topic of conversation.

chroniquement [krɔnikmɑ̃] *adv* chronically.

chroniqueur, -euse [krɔnikœr, -øz] *n* **(a)** *Journ* editor; **(b)** (*historien*) chronicler.

chrono [krɔnɔ] *nm F* stopwatch; **du 220 (km/h) (au) c.,** recorded speed of 220 (km/h); **son temps était de 4 minutes 6 secondes, c. en main,** his time by the clock was 4 minutes (and) 6 seconds.

chronographe [krɔnɔgraf] *nm Tech* chronograph.

chronologie [krɔnɔlɔʒi] *nf* chronology.

chronologique [krɔnɔlɔʒik] *adj* chronological.

chronologiquement [krɔnɔlɔʒikmɑ̃] *adv* chronologically.

chronométrage [krɔnɔmetraʒ] *nm* time-keeping; (*of race*) timing.

chronomètre [krɔnɔmɛtr] *nm* **(a)** (*pour le sport etc*) stopwatch; **(b)** (*montre de précision*) chronometer.

chronométrer [krɔnɔmetre] *vt* **(je chronomètre; je chronométrerai)** *Sp* to keep the time; to time (*race etc*).

chronométreur [krɔnɔmetrœr] *nm* **(a)** *Sp* timekeeper; **(b)** *Ind* time and motion (study) expert.

chronométrique [krɔnɔmetrik] *adj* chronometric(al).

chrysalide [krizalid] *nf Ent* chrysalis, pupa; *Fig* **sortir de sa c.,** to come out of one's shell.

chrysanthème [krizɑ̃tɛm] *nm* chrysanthemum.

chrysocale [krizɔkal] *nm Métal* pinchbeck.

chrysolithe [krizɔlit] *nf Minér* chrysolite, olivine.

C.H.U. [seaʃy] *nm inv* (*abrév* **centre hospitalo-universitaire**) ≈ teaching hospital.

chuchotement [ʃyʃɔtmɑ̃] *nm* whisper(ing).

chuchoter [ʃyʃɔte] **1** *vi* to whisper; **parler en chuchotant,** to speak in a whisper. **2** *vt* **c. qch à l'oreille de qn,** to whisper sth in s.o.'s ear.

chuchoterie [syʃɔtri] *nf* whisper(ing), whispered conversation.

chuchoteur, -euse [ʃyʃɔtœr, -øz] **1** *adj* whispering. **2** *n* whisperer.

chuintant, -ante [ʃɥɛtɑ̃, -ɑ̃t] *Ling* **1** *adj* **sons chuintants,** hushing sounds (*eg* ʃ, ʒ); **consonne chuintante,** palato-alveolar fricative. **2** *nf* **chuintante,** palato-alveolar fricative.

chuintement [ʃɥɛ̃tmɑ̃] *nm* **(a)** *Ling* pronunciation of s as sh; **(b)** (*sifflement*) hissing.

chuinter [ʃɥɛ̃te] *vi* **(a)** (*of owl*) to hoot; **(b)** *Ling* to pronounce s as sh; **(c)** (*of gas etc*) to hiss.

chut [ʃyt] *int* hush! sh!

chute [ʃyt] *nf* **(a)** fall; *Fig* fall, collapse (*of ministry etc*); drop, fall (*in pressure, temperature etc*); **faire une c. (de**

cheval/moto), to have a fall *or* a tumble *or* a spill, to fall off (one's horse/motorbike); **une c. de 10 mètres,** a 10 metre fall; **c. libre,** free fall; *Fig* **ses résultats scolaires descendent en c. libre,** his marks are plummeting *or* have taken a nose dive; **'c. de pierres',** 'danger!, falling stones'; *Th* **c. du rideau,** fall of the curtain; **c. de pluie/neige,** rain/snowfall; **c. du jour,** nightfall; *Litt* **c. des feuilles,** autumn, *Am* fall; **la c. des feuilles a eu lieu plus tôt que d'habitude cette année,** the trees lost their leaves sooner than usual this year; **c. des cheveux,** hair loss; **c. des prix,** fall *or* drop in prices; **la c. de l'homme,** the Fall; **il m'a entraîné dans sa c.,** he has dragged me down with him; *Th* **c. d'une pièce,** failure *or F* flop of a play; *Cartes* **avoir deux levées de c.,** to be two tricks down; *El* **c. de potentiel,** voltage drop;

(b) c. d'eau, waterfall; **les Chutes Victoria,** the Victoria Falls; **c. naturelle,** natural waterfall; **hauteur de c.,** fall, head (*of water*); drop (*of pile ram*);

(c) pitch (*of roof*); hang (*of dress*); cadence (*of voice etc*); **c. des reins,** small of the back;

(d) off-cut (*of wood*); snippets, trimmings (*of cloth etc*); scrap (*of metal*);

(e) *Ind Min* shoot.

chuter [ʃyte] *vi F* (*tomber*) to fall *or* tumble down; *Fig* to come a cropper; *Th* (*of play*) to be a failure, to flop; *Cartes* **c. de deux levées,** to be two tricks down.

Chypre [ʃipr] *nf* **(l'île de) C.,** Cyprus.

chypriote [ʃiprijɔt] **1** *adj* Cypriot. **2** *n* **C.,** Cypriot.

ci¹ [si] *adv* here; **ce livre-ci,** this book; **de-ci, de-là,** here and there, on all sides; **par-ci, par-là,** here and there; **ci-gît .../-gisent ...,** here lies .../lie ... .

ci² *pron dém inv F* **faire ci et ça,** to do this and that; **comme ci, comme ça,** so-so.

ciao [tʃao] *int F* ciao.

ci-après [siaprɛ] *adv* later, further on, below (*in the book etc*); *Jur* here(in)after.

cibiche [sibiʃ] *nf F* fag, ciggie, gasper.

cibiste [sibist] *n* user of citizen band radio, C.B. user.

cible [sibl] *nf* target, mark; (*publicité*) target; **servir de c. aux railleries de qn,** to be a butt *or* the target for s.o.'s jokes; **déterminer/atteindre la c.,** to define/to reach the target; **marché c.,** (*pour un produit*) target market.

ciblé [sible] *adj* (*campagne etc*) targeted (*sur*, at).

ciboire [sibwar] *nm Rel* pyx, ciborium.

ciboule [sibul] *nf Bot Culin* spring onion, *Am* scallion.

ciboulette [sibulɛt] *nf* (*plante*) *& Culin* chive(s).

ciboulot [sibulo] *nm Arg* (*tête*) noddle, nut.

cicatrice [sikatris] *nf* scar; *Fig* **cette séparation a laissé une c. profonde en lui,** the separation scarred him deeply *or* left a deep scar on him.

cicatriciel, -ielle [sikatrisjɛl] *adj* **tissu c.,** scar tissue.

cicatrisant [sikatrizɑ̃] **1** *adj* healing, *Spéc* cicatrizing (*lotion etc*). **2** *nm* healing lotion, healing cream.

cicatrisation [sikatrizasjɔ̃] *nf* healing, closing (up), *Spéc* cicatrization (*of wound etc*).

cicatriser [sikatrize] **1** *vt* to heal (*wound etc*). **2** *vi* (*of wound etc*) to heal (up), to scar over. **3 se cicatriser** *vpr* to heal up, to scar over; *Fig* to heal.

cicéro [sisero] *nm Typ* pica, twelve-point type.

Cicéron [siserɔ̃] *nm* Cicero.

cicérone [siserɔn] *nm Vieilli* guide, cicerone.

cicéronien, -ienne [siserɔnjɛ̃, -jɛn] *adj Litt* Ciceronian.

ci-contre [sikɔ̃tr] *adv* **(a)** (*en regard*) opposite; **porté ci-c.,** (*en comptabilité*) as per contra; **(b)** attached (*circular etc*).

ci-dessous [sitsu] *adv* hereunder, below, undermentioned.

ci-dessus [sitsy] *adv* above(-mentioned).

ci-devant [sidvɑ̃] **1** *adv* previously, formerly. **2** *n inv Fr Hist* ci-devant, aristocrat.

cidre [sidr] *nm* cider; **c. bouché,** champagne cider; **c. doux/brut,** sweet/dry cider.

cidrerie [sidrəri] *nf* **(a)** (*fabrique*) cider house; **(b)** (*fabrication*) cidermaking.

Cie (*abrév* **Compagnie**) Co.

ciel, ciels, cieux [sjɛl, sjø] *nm* **(a)** sky, heaven; **à c. ouvert,** in the open air, out of doors; **sous d'autres cieux,** beneath other skies, in other climes; **lever les bras au c.,** to raise one's arms to the sky *or* heavenwards; *F* **tomber du c.,** to be thunderstruck; *Fig* **ça ne va pas te tomber du c.,** it won't fall into your lap, you won't get it handed to you on a plate; *Fig* **remuer c. et terre,** to move heaven and earth (**pour faire qch,** to do sth); **être au septième c.,** to be in seventh heaven; *Fig* **élever qn aux cieux** *ou* **jusqu'au c.,** to laud s.o. to the skies; **être suspendu entre c. et terre,** to hang in mid-air; **(couleur) bleu (de) c.,** sky-blue; *Fig* **élever qn aux cieux** *ou* **jusqu'au c.,** to laud s.o. to the skies; **trouée de c. (bleu),** patch of (blue) sky; **les ciels de l'Italie,** the skies of Italy; *Beaux-Arts* **les ciels de Turner,** Turner's skies;

(b) (*paradis*) heaven; **notre Père qui es aux cieux,** our Father which art in Heaven; **le royaume des cieux,** the Kingdom of Heaven; **le c. m'en est témoin,** (as) Heaven is my witness; **(juste) c.!,** (good) heavens!, heavens above!; **aide-toi, le c. t'aidera,** God helps those who help themselves;

(c) (*pl* **ciels**) *Rel* baldachin, canopy; (*de lit*) canopy, tester; *Min* roof (*of quarry etc*); **carrière à c. ouvert,** open(cast) quarry.

cierge [sjɛrʒ] *nm* **(a)** *Rel* candle; **brûler un c. à un saint,** to burn a candle to a saint; **(b)** (*plante*) cereus.

cigale [sigal] *nf* **(a)** (*insecte*) cicada; **(b) c. de mer,** mantis-shrimp.

cigare [sigar] *nm* **(a)** (*à fumer*) cigar; **(b)** *Arg* (*tête*) nut, bonce; **avoir mal au c.,** to have a headache; **mets-toi ça dans le c.,** get that into your thick skull.

cigarette [sigarɛt] *nf* cigarette.

cigarillo [sigarijo] *nm* cigarillo.

cigogne [sigɔɲ] *nf* **(a)** (*oiseau*) stork; **(b)** (*levier*) crank lever.

ciguë [sigy] *nf* (*plante*) *Méd* hemlock.

ci-inclus [siɛ̃kly] **1** *adj* (*inv when it precedes the noun*) **la copie ci-incluse,** the enclosed copy. **2** *adv* **ci-i. copie de votre lettre,** enclosed is *or* herewith a copy of your letter.

ci-joint [siʒwɛ̃] **1** *adj* (*inv when it precedes the noun*) attached, enclosed herewith, hereto (annexed); **les pièces ci-jointes,** the enclosed *or* attached documents. **2** *adv* **vous trouverez ci-j. quittance,** please find receipt attached *or* enclosed.

cil [sil] *nm* **(a)** (eye)lash; **battre des cils,** to flutter one's eyelashes; **faire des battements de cils à qn,** to flutter one's eyelashes at s.o.; **faux cils,** false eyelashes; **(b)** *Biol* cilium, hair, filament.

cilice [silis] *nm* hair shirt.

cillement [sijmɑ̃] *nm* blinking.

ciller [sije] *vi* to blink; **personne n'ose c. devant lui,** no one dares move *or* bat an eyelid in his presence.

cimaise [simɛz] *nf Archit* ogee moulding; (*à hauteur d'appui*) dado.

cime [sim] *nf* **(a)** summit (*of hill etc*); top (*of tree, mast etc*); peak (*of mountain*); *Fig* **être à la c. de sa carrière/de la réussite,** to be at the height *or* peak of one's career/success; **(b)** *Bot* cyme.

ciment [simɑ̃] *nm* cement; **c. à prise rapide/lente,** quick-/slow-setting cement; **c. armé,** reinforced concrete.

cimentation [simɑ̃tasjɔ̃] *nf* cementing.

cimenter [simɑ̃te] *vt* to cement (*sth*), to render (*sth*) (with cement); *Fig* **c. une alliance/une amitié/une relation,** to cement *or* consolidate an alliance/a friendship/a relationship.

cimenterie [simɑ̃tri] *nf Ind* cement works.

cimeterre [simtɛr] *nm* scimitar.

cimetière [simtjɛr] *nm* cemetery, graveyard; (*d'église*) churchyard.

cimier¹ [simje] *nm* crest (*of helmet*).

cimier² *nm* haunch (*of venison*); rump (*of beef*).

cinabre [sinabr] *nm* cinnabar.

ciné [sine] *nm Br F* pictures, flicks, *Am* movies; **aller au c.,** to go to the pictures; **magazine de c.,** film *or* cinema magazine.

cinéaste [sineast] *n* film maker.

ciné-club [sineklœb] *nm* film club, cine-club; (*pl ciné-clubs*).

cinéma [sinema] *nm* **(a)** (*art*) cinema, movies, *Am* motion pictures; **l'invention du c.,** the invention of cinema *or* motion pictures; **faire du c.,** to be a film *or* movie actor; **acteur de c.,** film *or* movie actor; **c. muet/parlant,** silent/talking films, talkies; **c. en relief,** three dimensional *or* 3-D films; **industrie du c.,** film *or* movie industry, *Am* motion picture industry; **c. d'amateurs,** amateur film-making, home movies; *F* **c'est du c.,** it's all an act, it's all put on; **elle fait tout un c. pour ne pas y aller,** she's putting on an act so she doesn't have to go; **(b)** (*salle*) cinema, *Am* movie theater, *Br F* pictures; **c. permanent,** continuous performance; **ouvreuse de c.,** usherette.

cinémascope ® [sinemaskɔp] *nm* cinemascope.

cinémathèque [sinematɛk] *nf* film library.

cinématique [sinematik] **1** *adj* kinematic(al). **2** *nf* kinematics.

cinématographe [sinematɔgraf] *nm* cinematograph.

cinématographie [sinematɔgrafi] *nf* cinematography.

cinématographier [sinematɔgrafje] *vt* to film.

cinématographique [sinematɔgrafik] *adj* cinematogra-

phic; cinema, film (*production etc*).
cinémomètre [sinemɔmɛtr] *nm Tech* cinemometer, speedometer, speed gauge.
ciné-parc [sinepark] *nm Can* drive-in (*Br* cinema); (*pl cinés-parcs*).
cinéphile [sinefil] **1** *adj* film- *or* movie-loving; **public c.,** cinema-going public. **2** *n* film *or* movie enthusiast *or* buff.
cinéraire [sinerɛr] **1** *adj* cinerary (*urn etc*). **2** *nf* (*plante*) cineraria.
cinérama ® [sinerama] *nm* cinerama.
ciné-roman [sinerɔmɑ̃] *nm* = picture book of a film; *Vieilli* (film) serial; (*pl ciné-romans*).
cinétique [sinetik] **1** *adj* kinetic (*energy etc*). **2** *nf* kinetics.
cing(h)alais, -aise [sɛ̃galɛ, -ɛz] **1** *adj* Sin(g)halese. **2** *nm Ling* Sin(g)halese. **3** *n* **C.,** Sin(g)halese.
cinglant [sɛ̃glɑ̃] *adj* lashing (*rain etc*); cutting, biting (*wind etc*); bitter (*cold*); stinging, cutting, scathing (*remark*).
cinglé [sɛ̃gle] *adj F* cracked, potty; **il est complètement c.,** he's nuts *or* crackers.
cingler¹ [sɛ̃gle] *vi Nau Vieilli* **(a)** to sail (before the wind), to scud along; **(b)** (*aller dans une direction*) to steer a given course; **voilier qui cingle aux Canaries,** a yacht making *or* bound for the Canary Islands.
cingler² *vt* to lash, to cut (*horse etc*) with a whip; to lash out at (*s.o.*); **une branche m'a cinglé la figure,** a branch whipped (against) my face; **la grêle lui cinglait le visage,** the hail was stinging his face.
cinoche [sinɔʃ] *nm F* cinema, *Am* movie theatre *or US* theater; **aller au c.,** to go to the flicks *or* movies; **je me ferais bien un petit c. ce soir,** I quite fancy going to the pictures tonight.
cinoque [sinɔk] *Arg* **1** *adj* batty, crazy. **2** *n* nutcase, headbanger, loony.
cinq [sɛ̃k] **1** *adj inv* five; **c. (petits) garçons** [sɛ̃(pti)garsɔ̃] , five (little) boys; **c. hommes** [sɛ̃kɔm] , five men; **j'en ai c.** [sɛ̃k] , I've got five; **Henri C.,** Henry the Fifth; **le c. mars** [sɛ̃(k)mars] , March the fifth; **il était moins c.,** it was a near thing *or* a close shave; **attends c. minutes,** just give me a minute, *F* hang on a sec; **je lui ai répondu en c. lettres,** I told him where to go. **2** *nm inv* five; **le nombre c.,** the number five, 5; **faire une ligne de c.,** to make a row of fives; *Rad* **recevoir qn c. sur c.,** to receive s.o. loud and clear; *Fig* **faire qch en c. sec,** to do sth in five seconds flat; *Cartes* **un c. de pique,** a five of spades.
cinquantaine [sɛ̃kɑ̃tɛn] *nf* (about) fifty; **une c. de personnes,** about *or* some fifty people, fifty or so people; **approcher la c.,** to be getting on for fifty, **avoir passé la c.,** to be in one's fifties.
cinquante [sɛ̃kɑ̃t] **1** *adj inv* fifty; **billet de c. francs,** fifty-franc note; **page c.,** page fifty; **demeurer au numéro c.,** to live at number fifty; **les années c.,** the fifties. **2** *nm inv* fifty; **le numéro c.,** the number fifty, 50; **c. pour cent ont refusé,** fifty per cent refused.
cinquantenaire [sɛ̃kɑ̃tnɛr] **1** *nm* fiftieth anniversary. **2** *adj* fifty year(s) old.
cinquantième [sɛ̃kɑ̃tjɛm] **1** *adj* fiftieth. **2** *n* fiftieth; **être le c. dans un classement,** to be placed *or* come fiftieth in a classification *or* grading. **3** *nm* fiftieth (part).
cinquième [sɛ̃kjɛm] **1** *adj* fifth; **loger au c. étage,** to live on the fifth *or Am* sixth floor; **être la c. roue de la charrette** *ou* **du carosse,** to feel out of it, *Am* to feel like a fifth wheel. **2** *n* fifth; **elle est arrivée la c.,** she came (in) fifth, she came in in fifth place. **3** *nm* fifth (part). **4** *nf Scol* **(classe de) c.,** ≈ second form *or* year (of secondary school), *Am* seventh grade.
cinquièmement [sɛ̃kjɛmmɑ̃] *adv* fifthly, in (the) fifth place.
cintrage [sɛ̃traʒ] *nm* bend(ing) (*of pipes etc*).
cintre [sɛ̃tr] *nm* **(a)** (*pour les vêtements*) coathanger; **suspendre sa veste à un c.,** to put one's jacket on a (clothes) hanger; **(b)** (*courbure*) concave surface, curve; **(c)** *Archit* arch (*of tunnel etc*); soffit (*of arch*); **arc en plein c.,** semicircular arch; **(d)** *Th* **les cintres,** the flies.
cintré [sɛ̃tre] *adj* arched (*window etc*); bent, curved (*timber etc*); fitted (*jacket etc*); **taille cintrée,** nipped-in waist.
cintrer [sɛ̃tre] *vt* **(a)** to bend, to curve (*pipe, rail etc*); **(b)** to arch (*window*); **(c)** to take in (*jacket etc*) at the waist.
C.I.O. [seio] *nm* (*abrév* **Comité international olympique**) IOC.
cipaye [sipaj] *nm* sepoy; *Hist* **la révolte des cipayes,** the Indian Mutiny.
cirage [siraʒ] *nm* **(a)** waxing, polishing (*of floors etc*); **(b)** (*substance*) (wax, shoe) polish; **c. de couleur/incolore,** coloured/neutral polish; **c. pour cuir/parquet,** leather/floor polish; *F* **être dans le c.,** to be all at sea; *Av* to be flying blind.
circadien [sirkadjɛ̃] *adj Biol* **rythme c.,** circadian rhythm.
circoncire [sirkɔ̃sir] *vt* (*prp* **circoncisant**; *pp* **circoncis**; *pr ind* **je circoncis**; *pr sub* **je circoncise**; *p hist* **je circoncis**; *fu* **je circoncirai**) to circumcise.
circoncision [sirkɔ̃sizjɔ̃] *nf* circumcision.
circonférence [sirkɔ̃ferɑ̃s] *nf* **(a)** *Géom* circumference; circumference, girth (*of tree*); **(b)** perimeter, boundaries (*of town etc*); **avoir dix centimètres de c.,** to have a circumference of ten centimetres, to be ten centimetres in circumference.
circonflexe [sirkɔ̃flɛks] *adj* circumflex (*accent*).
circonlocution [sirkɔ̃lɔkysjɔ̃] *nf* circumlocution; **parler par circonlocutions,** to speak in circumlocutions *or* a roundabout way, *F* to beat about the bush.
circonscription [sirkɔ̃skripsjɔ̃] *nf* **(a)** *Admin etc* division, district, area; **c. électorale,** (*au niveau municipal*) ward; (*au niveau national*) constituency; **c. de remise gratuite,** radius of free delivery, free delivery area (*of telegrams etc*); **(b)** *Vieilli* circumscription, circumscribing.
circonscrire [sirkɔ̃skrir] *v* (*conj like* **écrire**) **1** *vt* to circumscribe, to draw a line round (*sth*); (*entourer*) to surround, to encircle (**par,** with, by); (*limiter*) to limit, to bound; **c. son sujet,** to define the scope of one's subject; **c. un incendie,** to bring a fire under control, to contain a fire. **2 se circonscrire** *vpr* to be bounded, to be limited; **tout le débat se circonscrit autour d'une seule idée,** the whole debate centres on *or* is centred around one idea.
circonspect [sirkɔ̃spɛ(kt)] *adj* circumspect, cautious, wary.
circonspection [sirkɔ̃spɛksjɔ̃] *nf* circumspection, caution, wariness; **avec c.,** circumspectly, warily, cautiously.
circonstance [sirkɔ̃stɑ̃s] *nf* **(a)** (*cas*) circumstance; **dans la c., il faut se montrer prudent,** given the circumstances *or* as things stand, we must go carefully; **en pareille c.,** under such circumstances, in such a case; **à la hauteur des circonstances,** equal to the occasion; **eu égard aux** *ou* **étant donné les circonstances,** all things considered, in *or* given the circumstances; **par un concours de circonstances,** by a combination of circumstances; **profiter de la c.,** to make the most of the opportunity, to profit from circumstances; **vers de c.,** occasional verse; **paroles de c.,** words suited to the occasion, appropriate *or* suitable words; **ce ne serait pas de c.,** it would not be appropriate;
(b) *Jur* **circonstances et dépendances,** appurtenances; **circonstances atténuantes,** extenuating circumstances.
circonstancié [sirkɔ̃stɑ̃sje] *adj* detailed (*account*).
circonstanciel, -ielle [sirkɔ̃stɑ̃sjɛl] *adj* **(a)** circumstantial; **des mesures rigoureusement circonstancielles,** measures dictated by exceptional circumstances; **déclaration/mesure circonstancielle,** declaration/measure dictated by the circumstances, **(b)** *Gram* **complément c. (de temps/de lieu/***etc***),** adverbial complement (of time/place/*etc*).
circonvenir [sirkɔ̃vnir] *vt* (*conj like* **venir**) to circumvent (*the law*); to thwart, to outwit (*s.o.*).
circonvolution [sirkɔ̃vɔlysjɔ̃] *nf Anat Archit* convolution; *Archit* circumvolution (*of volute etc*).
circuit [sirkɥi] *nm* **(a)** *Sp* round, lap; circuit (*for motor racing etc*); **c. (touristique),** (organized) trip, tour; *Écon* **circuits commerciaux,** commercial channels; **c. de distribution,** distribution channels *or* network; **refaire tout le c. à pied,** to go all the way back on foot; **prendre un nouveau c.,** to go a new way round;
(b) *Él* circuit; **mettre en c.,** to connect, to switch on; **couper le c.,** to switch off; **rétablir le c.,** to switch on (again); **mettre une lampe hors c.,** to disconnect a lamp; *Fig* **il est complètement hors c.,** he's completely out of touch; **c. ouvert/fermé,** open/closed circuit; **télévision à c. fermé,** closed circuit television; *Fig* **ils ont tendance à vivre en c. fermé,** they tend to lead their own separate existence *or* to live in a closed world; *Électron* **c. imprimé,** printed circuit; **c. intégré,** integrated circuit; *Fig* **ça fait longtemps que je ne suis plus dans le c.,** I've been out of it for ages, I'm hopelessly out of touch.
circulaire [sirkylɛr] **1** *adj* circular; **billet c.,** excursion ticket; **scie c.,** circular saw; *MecE* **mouvement c.,** rotary motion. **2** *nf* circular.
circulairement [sirkylɛrmɑ̃] *adv* in a circle.
circulant [sirkylɑ̃] *adj* circulating; *Fin* **billets/capitaux circulants,** notes/capital in circulation.

circulation [sirkylasjɔ̃] *nf* **(a)** (*d'autos, d'avions*) traffic; **c. aérienne,** air traffic; **c. à sens unique/à deux sens,** one-/two-way traffic; **c. interdite,** no thoroughfare; **arrêt de c.,** traffic block; **accident de la c.,** road accident; *Rail* **c. des trains,** running of trains; **la c. est très difficile,** the traffic is very heavy; **il y a beaucoup de c. sur les routes,** there's a lot of traffic on the roads; **(b)** circulation (*of air, blood, news etc*); **des troubles de la c.,** circulation problems; **mettre un livre en c.,** to put a book into circulation; **mettre un bruit en c.,** to spread *or* circulate a rumour; **mise en c. d'une nouvelle,** spreading of a piece of news; **(c)** *Fin* currency, circulation (*of banknotes etc*); **(d) libre c. des travailleurs/des citoyens,** free movement of workers/ of citizens.

circulatoire [sirkylatwar] *adj Anat* circulatory.

circuler [sirkyle] *vi* **(a)** (*of blood, air etc*) to circulate, to flow; **faire c. l'air,** to circulate the air; *Fin* **les capitaux qui circulent,** capital in circulation, circulating capital; **faire c. la bouteille,** to pass *or* hand the bottle round; **(b)** (*passer, avancer*) to circulate, to move about; **défense de c. sur l'herbe!,** please keep off the grass!; **circulez!,** move along!; **les autobus circulent jour et nuit,** the buses run day and night; **on a du mal à c. en ville,** it's not easy to drive in town; **des bruits circulent,** rumours are circulating *or* going about *or* round; **faire c. une nouvelle,** to spread a piece of news.

circumnavigation [sirkɔmnavigasjɔ̃] *nf* circumnavigation.

cire [sir] *nf* **(a)** wax; (*encaustique*) (wax) polish; **bouchon de c.,** (*dans l'oreille*) excessive wax (in the ear); **c. d'abeilles,** beeswax; **c. à cacheter,** sealing wax; **(b)** *Orn* cere (*of beak*).

ciré [sire] **1** *adj* waxed, polished; **parquet c.,** polished *or* waxed floor; **chaussures bien cirées,** well polished shoes; **toile cirée,** oilcloth. **2** *nm* (suit of) oilskins; (*pour la ville*) raincoat.

cirer [sire] *vt* to polish, to wax (*floors etc*); to wax (*thread etc*); **c. des chaussures,** to polish shoes; *F* **c. les bottes à qn,** to lick s.o.'s boots.

cireur, -euse [sirœr, -øz] **1** *n* **(a)** (*de chaussures*) shoeblack, *US* shoeshine boy; **(b)** (*de sols*) (floor) polisher. **2** *nf* **cireuse,** (*machine*) (electric) (floor) polisher.

cireux, -euse [sirø, -øz] *adj* waxy, wax-like, waxen; **teint c.,** waxen complexion.

cirque [sirk] *nm* **(a)** circus; **c. forain** *ou* **ambulant,** travelling circus; **aller au c.,** to go to the circus; **gens du c.,** circus people; **le c. Robin,** Robin's circus; *F* **quel c., ici!,** it's like a three-ring circus!; *Fig* **faire le c.,** to rampage around; **faire tout un c.,** to make a scene, to kick up a fuss; **(b)** *Géol* cirque, corrie, cwm.

cirr(h)e [sir] *nm* **(a)** *Bot* cirrus, tendril; **(b)** (*de poisson*) barbel; **(c)** *Zool* tentacle.

cirrhose [siroz] *nf Méd* cirrhosis; **c. du foie,** cirrhosis of the liver; **avoir une c. du foie,** to have cirrhosis (of the liver).

cirro-cumulus [sirɔkymylys] *nm inv Météo* cirrocumulus.

cirro-stratus [sirɔstratys] *nm inv Météo* cirrostratus.

cirrus [sirys] *nm inv Météo* cirrus, *F* mare's tail.

cisaille [sizaj] *nf* **(a)** parings, cuttings (*of metal*); **(b)** (*pour couper le papier*) guillotine, cutting press; **(c) cisailles,** shears; (*pour câble*) wirecutters; **c. à haies,** hedge clipper(s); **c. à bordures,** edging shears.

cisaillement [sizajmɑ̃] *nm* **(a)** cutting, shearing (*of metal*); clipping (*of coins*); pruning (*of branches*); shearing (off) (*of rivet*); **(b)** *Tech* (*contrainte*) shearing (stress), shear.

cisailler [sizaje] **1** *vt* **(a)** to cut, to shear (*metal*); to clip (*coins*); **(b)** to prune (*branches*). **2 se cisailler** *vpr* (*of metal*) to shear (off).

cisalpin [sizalpɛ̃] *adj Antiq* on the Roman side of the Alps, Cisalpine; *Hist* **République cisalpine,** Cisalpine Republic.

ciseau, -eaux [sizo] *nm* **(a)** chisel; **c. à froid,** cold chisel; **(b) ciseaux,** scissors; (*de jardin*) shears, clippers; **coup de ciseaux,** snip (of the scissors); *Couture* **ciseaux à denteler,** pinking shears; **(c)** *Sp* **c., saut en ciseaux,** scissors (jump).

ciselage [sizlaʒ] *nm* = **CISELLEMENT**.

ciseler [sizle] *vt* (**je cisèle; je cisélerai**) to chase, to engrave (*gold, silver*); to chisel, to carve (*wood*); to tool, to emboss (*leather*); to cut, to shear (*velvet*); *Fig* to polish up, to work on (*poem etc*); **visage délicatement ciselé,** finely chiselled features.

ciseleur [sizlœr] *nm* engraver; (*de bois*) carver.

cisellement [sizɛlmɑ̃] *nm* chiselling (*of wood*); chasing, engraving (*of gold, silver*); tooling, embossing (*of leather*); cutting, shearing (*of velvet*).

ciselure [sizlyr] *nf* chasing, engraving (*of gold, silver*); chiselling, carving (*of wood*); tooling, embossing (*of leather*).

cistercien, -ienne [sistɛrsjɛ̃, -jɛn] *Rel* **1** *adj* Cistercian; **architecture cistercienne,** Cistercian architecture. **2** *nm* Cistercian.

citadelle [sitadɛl] *nf* citadel, stronghold; *Fig* **une c. du protestantisme,** a Protestant stronghold, a stronghold of Protestantism.

citadin, -ine [sitadɛ̃, -in] **1** *n* townsman, townswoman. **2** *adj* (belonging to a) town *or* city.

citation [sitasjɔ̃] *nf* **(a)** (*extrait*) quotation, citation; **la référence de la c.,** the reference for the quotation, the quotation reference; **fin de c.,** end of quotation; (*dans une dictée*) close quotation marks; **(b)** *Jur* citation, (writ of) summons; **c. des témoins,** subpoena of witnesses; **notifier une c. à,** (*l'accusé*) to serve a summons on; (*témoin*) to subpoena; **(c)** *Mil* **c. (à l'ordre du jour),** ≈ mention in dispatches.

cité [site] *nf* **(a)** (*ville*) city, (large) town; **droit de c.,** freedom of the city; *Fig* **ce genre d'original n'a pas droit de c. dans notre entreprise,** there is no room for eccentrics like him in our company, our company doesn't take kindly to eccentrics like him; *Fig* **gagner droit de c.,** to be accepted; **(b)** (*groupe d'immeubles*) estate; **c. (ouvrière),** housing estate; **c. universitaire,** = students' hall(s) of residence.

Cîteaux [sito] *nm Rel* **l'ordre de C.,** the Cistercian Order.

cité-dortoir [sitedɔrtwar] *nf* dormitory town; (*pl cités-dortoirs*).

cité-ghetto [sitegɛto] *nf* ghetto housing estate; (*pl cités-ghettos*).

cité-jardin [siteʒardɛ̃] *nf* garden city; (*pl cités-jardins*).

citer [site] *vt* **(a)** to quote, to cite; **c. un auteur,** to cite *or* quote (from) an author; **c. qn en exemple,** to quote s.o. *or* hold s.o. up as an example; **c. les paroles de qn,** to quote s.o.'s words; **(b)** *Jur* to summon (*s.o. before the court*); to subpoena (*witness*); **(c)** *Mil* **c. qn (à l'ordre du jour),** ≈ to mention s.o. in dispatches.

citerne [sitɛrn] *nf* tank, cistern, reservoir.

cithare [sitar] *nf Mus* **(a)** zither; **(b)** *Antiq* cithara.

citoyen, -enne [sitwajɛ̃, -ɛn] *n* citizen; **droits de c.,** civic rights, citizenship; **c. d'honneur,** = freeman of a city; **elle se déclare citoyenne du monde,** she claims that she's a citizen of the world; *F* **c'est un drôle de c.!,** he's a queer customer!

citoyenneté [sitwajɛnte] *nf* citizenship; **la c. française,** French citizenship; **c. d'honneur d'une ville,** = freedom of a city.

citrate [sitrat] *nm Ch* citrate.

citrique [sitrik] *adj Ch* citric (*acid*).

citron [sitrɔ̃] **1** *nm* **(a)** (*fruit*) lemon; **gâteau au c.,** lemon cake; **c. pressé,** fresh lemon juice; **essence de c.,** lemon oil; **écorce de c.,** lemon peel; **(b)** (*generic term including*) lemon, lime, citron; **(c)** *Arg* (*tête*) nut. **2** *adj inv* lemon-yellow, lemon(-coloured); **jaune c.,** lemon-yellow.

citronnade [sitrɔnad] *nf* still lemonade, lemon squash.

citronné [sitrɔne] *adj* (*par l'odeur*) lemon-scented; (*par le goût*) lemon-flavoured.

citronnelle [sitrɔnɛl] *nf* **(a)** (*plante*) citronella; **(b)** (*liqueur*) lemon liqueur.

citronnier [sitrɔnje] *nm* (*arbre*) lemon tree; citrus (tree).

citrouille [sitruj] *nf* **(a)** (*plante*) pumpkin; **tarte à la c.,** pumpkin pie; **(b)** *Arg* (*tête*) nut.

cive [siv] *nf Bot Culin* chive(s).

civet [sivɛ] *nm Culin* stew (*of venison etc*); **c. de lièvre,** = jugged hare; **lapin/***etc* **en c.,** rabbit/*etc* stew.

civette[1] [sivɛt] *nf* **(a)** civet (cat); **(b)** *Com* civet (perfume).

civette[2] *nf Bot Culin* chive(s).

civière [sivjɛr] *nf* **(a)** (*brancard*) stretcher; **(b)** (*pour cerceuil*) bier.

civil, -ile [sivil] **1** *adj* **(a)** civil (*rights etc*); **guerre civile,** civil war; *Jur* **droit c.,** civil law; **liste civile,** civil list; *Jur* **se porter partie civile,** = to sue for damages someone being tried in a criminal court; **le tribunal c.,** civil court; **(b)** (*non ecclésiastique*) lay, secular; (*non militaire*) civilian; **mariage c.,** civil marriage; **dans la vie civile,** in private *or* civilian life; **(c)** *Arch Litt* polite, courteous. **2** *nm* **(a) un c.,** (*non ecclésiastique*) a layman; (*non militaire*) a civilian; **(b) dans le c.,** in private *or* civilian life; **en c.,** (*police*) in plain clothes; *Mil* in civilian clothes, in mufti, *F* in civvies; **(c)** *Jur* **poursuivre qn au c.,** to sue s.o. in the civil courts, to bring a civil action against s.o..

civilement [sivilmɑ̃] *adv* **(a)** *Jur* **se marier c.,** to be married at a registry office; **enterré c.,** buried without religious ceremony; *Jur* **poursuivre qn c.,** to bring a civil action against s.o.; **c. responsable,** liable for damages; **(b)** *Arch Litt* politely, courteously, civilly.
civilisable [sivilizabl] *adj* civilizable.
civilisateur, -trice [sivilizatœr, -tris] **1** *adj* civilizing. **2** *n* civilizer.
civilisation [sivilizɑsjɔ̃] *nf* civilization; **les bienfaits de la c.,** the benefits of civilization; **la c. pré-colombienne ,** the pre-Colombian civilization; **aire de c.,** area *or* zone of influence of a civilization.
civiliser [sivilize] **1** *vt* to civilize; *F* to make (*s.o.*) less uncouth *or* more refined. **2 se civiliser** *vpr* to become civilized *or F* more civilized.
civilité [sivilite] *nf* **(a) civilités,** civilities, compliments; **présenter ses civilités à qn,** to present one's compliments to s.o.; **(b)** *Litt Vieilli* civility, politeness, courtesy.
civique [sivik] *adj* civic (*duties etc*); civil (*rights*); **développer le sens c.,** to foster a sense of civic responsibility; *Scol* **instruction c.,** civics; *surtout Can* **bibliothèque c.,** municipal *or* public library.
civisme [sivism] *nm* good citizenship, public-spiritedness.
clabaudage [klabodaʒ] *nm* **(a)** (*aboiement*) yelping, baying; **(b)** *Fig* (spiteful) gossip, backbiting.
clabauder [klabode] *vi* **(a)** (*of dog*) to yelp, to bark a lot; **(b)** *Fig* **c. sur** *ou* **contre qn,** to say nasty things about s.o..
clabauderie [klabodri] *nf* = **CLABAUDAGE (b)** .
clabaudeur, -euse [klabodœr, -øz] **1** *adj* **(a)** (*chien*) yelping; (*limier*) baying; **(b)** *Fig* gossiping. **2** *n* **(a)** (*chien*) yapper; **(b)** *Fig* gossip, scandalmonger.
clac [klak] *int* crack!, slam!, snap!
clafoutis [klafuti] *nm Culin* **c. aux pommes/limousin,** apples/(black) cherries baked in batter.
claie [klɛ] *nf* **(a)** (*clôture*) fence; **(b) c. à fruits,** (wicker) fruit tray; **(c)** (*crible*) screen, riddle; *HydE* grid.
clair [klɛr] **1** *adj* **(a)** clear (*water etc*); **vitres claires,** transparent window panes; **teint c.,** clear complexion; **ciel c.,** clear *or* cloudless sky; **voix claire,** clear voice; *Mus* **caisse claire,** side *or* snare drum;

(b) clear, obvious, manifest, plain (*meaning etc*); **explication claire,** clear *or* lucid explanation; **ce n'est pas très c., précisez,** it's not very clear, be more precise; **il a été très c. là-dessus,** he was very clear about it; **il est c. qu'elle a tort,** she is obviously wrong; **voilà qui est c.!,** that's clear (enough)!; **c. comme le jour** *ou* **comme de l'eau de roche,** crystal clear, as clear as daylight *or* crystal; **c'est c. comme du jus de boudin,** it's as clear as mud; **sa conduite n'est pas claire,** his behaviour is suspicious *or F* fishy; **elle n'a pas l'esprit c.,** she's not very lucid; **avoir les idées claires,** to be clear in one's mind *or* in one's ideas; **c'est c. et net,** there are no two ways about it;

(c) bright, light (*room etc*); **il fait c.,** (*jour*) it's day(light); (*lumière*) there's plenty of light; **il ne fait pas c.,** there isn't much light here;

(d) light, pale (*colour*); **robe bleu c.,** pale blue dress;

(e) thin (*soup*); light, thin (*fabric*).

2 *adv* plainly, clearly; **il ne voit plus très c.,** he can't see too clearly *or* well; **parler c.,** to speak clearly; *Fig* **je commence à (y) voir c.,** I'm beginning to see *or* understand.

3 *nm* **(a)** (*lumière*) light; **c. de lune,** moonlight; **au c. de (la) lune,** in the moonlight; **les clairs d'une peinture,** the (high) lights in a painting;

(b) en c., in plain language; **message en c.,** message in clear;

(c) tirer du vin au c., to decant wine; **sabre au c.,** with drawn sword; *Fig* **tirer une affaire au c.,** to clear a matter up;

(d) il passe le plus c. de son temps à ..., he spends most *or* the best *or* the better part of his time in ... .

claire [klɛr] *nf* fattening pond (for oysters); **fines de c.,** = particularly fine variety of fattened oysters, with a green tinge caused by algae.
clairement [klɛrmɑ̃] *adv* clearly, plainly; **on le voit c. sur le tableau,** it's clearly visible on the board; **expliquer c. qch à qn,** to explain sth clearly to s.o.; **je te le dis c.,** I'm telling you quite plainly.
clairet, -ette [klɛrɛ, -ɛt] **1** *adj* **vin c.,** light-red wine; **voix clairette,** thin *or* high-pitched *or* reedy voice. **2** *nf* **clairette,** light sparkling wine. **3** *nm* light-red wine.
claire-voie [klɛrvwa] *nf* (*pl claires-voies*) **(a)** (*treillage*) open-work, lattice (-work); **porte à c.-v.,** (wicket) gate; **clôture à c.-v.,** fence, paling; **cloison à c.-v.,** grating; **caisse à c.-v.,** crate; **(b)** *Archit* clerestory; *Nau* skylight, deadlight.
clairière [klɛrjɛr] *nf* **(a)** (*dans forêt*) clearing, glade; **(b)** *Tex* thin place.
clair-obscur [klɛrɔpskyr] *nm* (*pl clairs-obscurs*) **(a)** *Beaux-Arts* chiaroscuro, light and shade; **(b)** (*lumière*) twilight.
clairon [klɛrɔ̃] *nm* **(a)** (*trompette*) bugle; **jouer du c.,** to play the bugle; **sonner le c.,** to sound the bugle; **(b)** (*joueur*) bugler; **(c)** clarion stop (*of organ*); upper register (*of clarinet*).
claironnant [klɛrɔnɑ̃] *adj* loud, brassy (*sound*); **voix claironnante,** loud and piercing voice.
claironner [klɛrɔne] **1** *vi* to sound the bugle; *Fig* (*crier*) to shout loudly. **2** *vt* **c. une nouvelle,** to trumpet a piece of news.
clairsemé [klɛrsəme] *adj* scattered, sparse (*population etc*); thinly sown (*corn*); thin (*hair*).
clairvoyance [klɛrvwajɑ̃s] *nf* perspicacity, clearsightedness, shrewdness, acumen.
clairvoyant [klɛrvwajɑ̃] *adj* perceptive, perspicacious, clear-sighted, shrewd; **esprit c.,** perceptive mind.
clam [klam] *nm* (*mollusque*) clam.
clamecer [klamse] *vi Arg* (*mourir*) to snuff it, to kick the bucket.
clamer [klame] *vt* to shout out, to proclaim; **c. son innocence,** to proclaim *or* protest one's innocence; **c. son mécontentement,** to proclaim one's displeasure.
clameur [klamœr] *nf* clamour, outcry; howling, roaring (*of wind etc*); **c. publique,** hue and cry.
clam(p)ser [klamse, klɑ̃pse] *vi Arg* (*mourir*) to kick it, to snuff it.
clan [klɑ̃] *nm* **(a)** (*tribu*) clan; **c. irlandais/écossais,** Irish/Scottish clan; **chef de c.,** head of the clan; **(b)** (*groupe*) set, clique.
clandestin, -ine [klɑ̃dɛstɛ̃, -in] **1** *adj* clandestine, secret; illicit (*betting etc*); **armée clandestine,** underground forces; **passager c.,** stowaway. **2** *n* (*voyageur*) stowaway; (*immigré*) illegal immigrant.
clandestinement [klɑ̃dɛstinmɑ̃] *adv* clandestinely, secretly; illicitly.
clandestinité [klɑ̃dɛstinite] *nf* clandestineness; **dans la c.,** in secret; **passer dans la c.,** to go underground.
clapet [klapɛ] *nm* **(a)** *Tech* valve; (*de moteur*) poppet valve, mushroom valve; **c. d'admission,** inlet valve; **c. d'échappement,** exhaust valve; **c. à charnière,** clack valve; **(b)** *Él* rectifier; **(c)** *Arg* (*bouche*) trap, *Br* gob; **ferme ton c.!,** shut your trap!; **il a un de ces clapets!,** he never stops (talking)!
clapier [klapje] *nm* **(a)** (*terriers*) rabbit warren; **(b)** (*case*) rabbit hutch; **(lapin de) c.,** tame rabbit; *F* **vivre dans un c. à lapin,** to live in a rabbit warren; **(c)** *Géol* (*dans les Alpes*) scree.
clapir [klapir] **1** *vi* (*of rabbit*) to squeal. **2 se clapir** *vpr* (*of rabbit*) to hide, to squat, to cower (in the burrow).
clapotage [klapɔtaʒ] *nm*, **clapotement** [klapɔtmɑ̃] *nm* lapping (*of waves*).
clapoter [klapɔte] *vi* (*of waves*) to lap; **mer qui clapote,** choppy sea.
clapoteux, -euse [klapɔtø, -øz] *adj* choppy (*sea*).
clapotis [klapɔti] *nm* lap(ping) (*of waves*).
clappement [klapmɑ̃] *nm* click(ing) (*of the tongue*).
clapper [klape] *vi* **c. de la langue,** to click (with) one's tongue.
claquage [klakaʒ] *nm* **(a)** strain, pulling (*of a muscle*); **se faire un c.,** to pull *or* strain a muscle; **(b)** *Él* (electric) breakdown; **c. thermique,** thermal breakdown.
claquant [klakɑ̃] *adj Arg* (*fatigant*) killing, knackering.
claque[1] [klak] *nf* **(a)** slap, smack (*on face etc*); **donner une c. à qn,** to give s.o. a slap *or* smack; **il mérite une bonne paire de claques,** he deserves a good slap; *F* **tête à claques,** unpleasant *or* nasty face; **(b)** *Arg* **il en a sa c.,** (*il est fatigué*) he's all in *or* dead beat; (*il en a assez*) he's fed up with it, he's had enough of it; **(c)** *Th* **la c.,** hired clappers, claque; **(d)** *Can* galoshes, *Am* rubbers.
claque[2] *adj & nm* **(chapeau) c.,** opera hat, crush hat.
claqué [klake] *adj F* fagged out, dog-tired.
claquement [klakmɑ̃] *nm* slam(ming), bang(ing) (*of a door*); chattering (*of teeth*); crack(ing) (*of whip*); flap(ping) (*of flag*); snap(ping) (*of fingers*); click(ing) (*of heels, tongue*); clatter(ing) (*of clogs etc*); (*in engine*) slapping of pistons.
claquemurer [klakmyre] **1** *vt* to shut, to coop (*s.o.*) up. **2 se claquemurer** *vpr* to shut oneself up; **se c. dans sa chambre,** to shut oneself up in one's room, to stay cooped

up in one's room.

claquer [klake] **1** *vi* **(a)** (*of door*) to slam, to bang; (*of flag*) to flap; (*of heels*) to click; (*of clogs etc*) to clatter; (*of piston etc*) to slap; **c. des mains,** to clap, to applaud; **elle claque des dents,** her teeth are chattering; **faire c. la porte en sortant,** to slam the door on the way out; *F* **c. du bec,** to be hungry *or* starving;

(b) *Arg* (*of person*) to kick the bucket, to snuff it; (*of business*) to go to pieces, to go bust; (*of machinery*) to give up, to go phut; (*of light bulb*) to go; **le moteur m'a claqué dans les mains,** the engine died on me.

2 *vt* **(a)** to slam, to bang (*door*); to crack (*whip*); to snap (*one's fingers*); to click (*one's heels*);

(b) to slap, to smack (*child etc*); *F* to tire *or* wear (*s.o.*) out; *F* to squander, to blow, to blue (*money*).

3 se claquer *vpr* **(a)** *F* (*se fatiguer*) to tire *or* wear oneself out;

(b) se c. un muscle/un ligament, to pull a muscle/to tear a ligament.

claquet [klakɛ] *nm* clapper (*of mill hopper*).

claquette [klakɛt] *nf* **(a)** *Cin* clapperboard; **(b) (danse à) claquettes,** tap dancing, tap dance; **faire des claquettes,** to do tap (dancing).

claquoir [klakwar] *nm* clapper; *Cin* clapperboard.

clarification [klarifikasjɔ̃] *nf* clarifying (*of liquid*); *Fig* (*information*) clarification, enlightenment; **demander des clarifications,** to ask for clarification.

clarifier [klarifje] **1** *vt* **(a)** to clarify (*wine etc*); **(b)** to clarify, to enlighten (*the mind*). **2 se clarifier** *vpr* to (become) clear.

clarine [klarin] *nf* cattle bell, cowbell.

clarinette [klarinɛt] *nf* clarinet.

clarinettiste [klarinɛtist] *n* clarinettist.

clarisse [klaris] *nf Rel* **(sœur) c.,** nun of the order of St Clare.

clarté [klarte] *nf* **(a)** clearness, clarity; limpidity (*of water etc*); transparency (*of glass etc*); lucidity, perspicuity (*of style etc*); **la c. de son teint,** the clearness of his complexion; **la c. de l'expression,** clarity of expression; **parler avec c.,** to speak clearly; **avoir de la c. d'esprit,** to be clear-minded; *Litt* **avoir des clartés sur un sujet,** to have some knowledge of a subject; **(b)** light, brightness (*of sun etc*); **à la c. de la lune,** by the light of the moon, by moonlight; **les premières clartés du soleil,** the first gleams of the sun.

classable [klasabl] *adj* classifiable.

classe [klas] *nf* **(a)** class, division, category; *Admin etc* rank, grade; **c. d'âge,** age group; *Av etc* **c. touriste,** tourist class; **billet de première/deuxième c.,** first-/second-class ticket; **les hautes classes,** the upper classes; **différence de c. sociale,** difference in *or* of social class; **la c. moyenne/ouvrière,** the middle/working class(es); **c. dirigeante/dominante,** ruling/dominant class; **société sans c.,** classless society;

(b) (*qualité*) class; **produits de première c.,** top quality goods; *F* **avoir de la c.,** to have class *or* style; **cette robe a beaucoup de c.,** that's a very classy *or* stylish dress, that dress has got a lot of class *or* style;

(c) *Scol* class, form, *Am* grade; **grandes classes, classes supérieures,** upper forms, senior school; **c. de sixième/première/terminale,** ≈ first year/lower sixth/ upper sixth; **la petite c.,** the junior school, the juniors; **il est dans quelle c.?,** which *or* what class is he in?;

(d) (*leçon*) class, lesson; **c. de français,** French class; **aller en c.,** to go to school; **être en c.,** to be in *or* at school; **partir en c. de neige,** = to go skiing with the school; **partir en c. verte,** = to spend time in the countryside with the school; **faire la c.,** to teach; **livre de c.,** schoolbook;

(e) (salle de) c., classroom, schoolroom; **en sortant de c.,** on coming out of school;

(f) *Mil* annual contingent (*of recruits*); **la c. 1965,** the 1965 class, the 1965 levy; **faire ses classes,** to undergo basic training;

(g) *Mil* (*rang*) **(soldat de) deuxième c.,** private; *Mil Av* aircraftman, *US* airman (basic); **(soldat de) première c.,** lance-corporal, *US* private first class; *Mil Av* leading *or* senior aircraftman, *US* airman first class.

classé [klase] *adj* **(a)** *Sp* ranked, graded; *Tennis* seeded; **(b)** (*information*) classified; **cette information est classée,** that information is classified.

classement [klasmɑ̃] *nm* **(a)** classification, classing (*of plants etc*); position, place (*in class, race etc*); *Scol* **c. trimestriel,** end of term results; *Scol* **ce trimestre je suis troisième au c.,** I'm third in the class this term; **donner le c.,** to give the results (*of a competition*); **avoir un bon/mauvais c.,** to be well/badly placed; **(b)** filing (*of documents*); sorting out, arranging (*of articles*); grading (*of ore etc*); *Rail* marshalling (*of trucks*).

classer [klase] **1** *vt* **(a)** to classify, to class; **monument classé,** scheduled *or* listed monument; **classés par pays,** classified according to country; *Courses de chevaux* **non classés,** also ran; *F* **je n'ai pas eu de mal à le c.,** it didn't take me long to size him up *or* to work out what sort of a person he was;

(b) to file (*documents*); to sort out, to arrange (*articles*); to grade (*ore etc*); *Rail* to marshal (*trucks*); **c. une affaire,** to consider a matter closed; **c'est une affaire classée,** the matter's closed.

2 se classer *vpr* to be classified, to rank; **ces faits se classent dans une autre catégorie,** these facts fall into another category; **elle se classe parmi les meilleurs de son année,** she's among the best in her year; *Sp etc* **se c. troisième,** to be placed *or* to come in third; *Tennis etc* **il n'a pas réussi à se c.,** he failed to get into the rankings.

classeur [klasœr] *nm* (*de bureau*) filing cabinet; (*pour la maison*) filing case; (*à feuilles mobiles*) (looseleaf) binder.

classicisme [klasisism] *nm* classicism.

classificateur, -trice [klasifikatœr, -tris] **1** *n* classifier. **2** *adj* classifying.

classification [klasifikasjɔ̃] *nf* classification.

classifier [klasifje] *vt* (*impf & pr sub* **n. classifiions, v. classifiiez**) to classify.

classique [klasik] **1** *adj* **(a)** *Scol* academic, for school use; **livres classiques,** school books; **langues classiques,** classical languages; **auteurs classiques,** classical authors;

(b) classical (*period, music etc*); classic (*beauty etc*); **études classiques,** classical studies;

(c) standard (*work etc*); classic (*example, joke etc*); **vêtement/tenu c.,** a classic(al) garment/outfit; **aimer le style c.,** to like the classic(al) style; **guerre c.,** conventional warfare; *F* **c'est le coup c.,** it's the same old story; **alors ça, c'est c.,** well that's just typical(, that is).

2 *nm* **(a)** (*auteur*) classical author;

(b) (*livre*) classic; **les classiques grecs/français,** the Greek/French classics; **relire ses classiques,** to reread the classics; **c'est un c. du genre,** it's a classic of its kind *or* of the genre;

(c) *Mus* classical music.

claudication [klodikasjɔ̃] *nf Méd & Litt* limp(ing).

claudiquer [klodike] *vi Litt* to limp.

clause [kloz] *nf Jur etc* clause; **c. additionnelle,** additional clause, rider; **c. pénale,** penalty clause; **c. de style,** formal clause.

claustra [klostra] *nm* stone railings.

claustral, -aux [klostral, -o] *adj* monastic, claustral.

claustration [klostrasjɔ̃] *nf* **(a)** cloistering (*in monastery etc*); **(b)** (*isolation*) (close) confinement.

claustrer [klostre] **1** *vt* **(a)** (*dans un monastère*) to cloister; **(b)** (*isoler*) to confine, to shut up. **2 se claustrer** *vpr* to shut oneself up.

claustrophobe [klostrɔfɔb] *adj Méd* claustrophobic.

claustrophobie [klostrɔfɔbi] *nf Méd* claustrophobia.

claveau, -eaux [klavo] *nm Constr Archit* archstone, voussoir; **c. droit,** keystone.

clavecin [klavsɛ̃] *nm Mus* harpsichord.

claveciniste [klavsinist] *n Mus* harpsichord player, harpsichordist.

clavetage [klavtaʒ] *nm MecE* keying, wedging, cottering (*of machine parts etc*).

claveter [klavte] *vt* (**je clavette; je clavetterai**) *MecE* to key, to wedge, to cotter.

clavette [klavɛt] *nf MecE* key (bolt), pin, cotter (pin).

clavicorde [klavikɔrd] *nm Mus* clavichord.

clavicule [klavikyl] *nf Anat* collarbone, clavicle.

clavier [klavje] *nm* **(a)** keyboard (*of piano, typewriter etc*); *Ordinat* **c. numérique,** numerical keypad; **(b)** range, compass (*of clarinet etc*); *Fig* **le c. des émotions amoureuses,** the range *or* gamut of love's emotions.

claviste [klavist] *n Typ* machine compositor; *Ordinat* keyboarder.

clayette [klɛjɛt] *nf* **(a)** wire tray *or* rack; (wire) shelf (*in fridge*); **(b)** crate (*for fruit etc*).

clayon [klɛjɔ̃] *nm* wicker tray (*for draining cheeses etc*); cake rack.

clé [kle] *nf* = **CLEF.**

clean [klin] *adj F* straight, clean-living; **elle a un look c.,** she has a clean-living *or* straight image *or* look.

clearing [kliriŋ] *nm Écon* clearing; **accord de c.,** clearing agreement.

clébard [klebar] *nm,* **clebs** [klɛps] *nm Arg* (*chien*) pooch, tyke, mutt.

clef [kle] *nf* **(a)** (*for door, to a code, mystery*) key; **c. de maison,** house key; latchkey; **fausse c.,** skeleton key; **trousseau de clefs,** bunch of keys; **fermer une porte à c.,** to lock a door; **donner un tour de c. à la porte,** to lock the door; **remise des clefs d'un appartement,** handing over the keys to a flat; **tenir qch sous c.,** to keep sth under lock and key; **on l'a mis sous c. depuis hier,** he's been under lock and key since yesterday; **la c. est sur la porte,** the key is in the lock; **louer une maison clefs en main,** to rent a house with immediate *or* vacant possession; **usine c. en main,** turnkey factory *or Am* plant; **mettre la c. sous la porte,** to do a moonlight flit; **les clefs de la ville,** the keys of the city; **Orléans, c. de la vallée de la Loire,** Orléans, gateway to the Loire Valley; **la philosophie, c. de la connaissance,** philosophy, the key to (all) knowledge; **position-c.,** key position; **industrie-c.,** key industry; **un secteur(-)c. de la recherche,** a key sector *or* area of research; **roman à c.,** = novel introducing real characters under fictitious names; **prendre la c. des champs,** (*d'un prisonnier etc*) to make a bid for freedom;

(b) *Mus* clef; (*armature*) key signature; **c. de sol/de fa,** treble/bass clef; **jouer avec des dièses à la c.,** to play in sharp keys; *Fig* **enquête avec récompense à la c.,** an investigation for the successful conclusion of which there is a reward;

(c) c. de voûte, keystone, crown (*of arch*); *Fig* **c'est la c. de voûte de notre entreprise,** he's the cornerstone of our firm;

(d) wrench, spanner; **c. anglaise,** adjustable spanner, monkey wrench; **c. à douille** *ou* **en** *ou* **à tube,** box spanner; **c. fermée,** ring spanner; **c. plate,** (open) end wrench;

(e) handle (*of tap*); plug (*of cock*); *Mus* peg (*of stringed instrument*); *Constr* **c. (de tuyau de poêle),** damper;

(f) *El* switch (key); *Tél* **c. d'appel,** call(ing) key, call button; *Télécom* **c. Morse,** Morse key;

(g) (*in wrestling*) lock.

clématite [klematit] *nf* clematis.

clémence [klemɑ̃s] *nf* **(a)** *Litt* clemency, mercy, leniency (**pour, envers,** to(wards)); **(b)** *Fig* mildness (*of the weather*).

clément [klemɑ̃] *adj* **(a)** *Litt* clement, merciful, lenient (**pour, envers,** to, towards); **(b)** *Fig* mild (*weather etc*).

clémentine [klemɑ̃tin] *nf (fruit)* clementine.

clenche [klɑ̃ʃ] *nf,* **clenchette** [klɑ̃ʃɛt] *nf* latch (*of door lock*).

Cléopâtre [kleɔpɑtr] *nf Antiq* Cleopatra.

cleptomane [klɛptɔman] *n* kleptomaniac.

cleptomanie [klɛptɔmani] *nf* kleptomania.

clerc [klɛr] *nm* **(a)** clerk (*in office*); **c. de notaire,** ≈ solicitor's clerk; **petit c.,** junior clerk; **(b)** *Rel* cleric; **(c)** *Arch* learned man, scholar; **(c) il n'est pas besoin d'être grand c. pour ...,** you don't have to be a genius in order to ... .

clergé [klɛrʒe] *nm* clergy.

clérical, -aux [klerikal, -o] *adj & nm Rel* clerical.

cléricalisme [klerikalism] *nm Rel* clericalism.

clic [klik] **1** *nm* click, clicking; **entendre un c.,** to hear a click *or* clicking sound. **2** *int* click.

clic-clac [kliklak] *nm* crack(ing) (*of whip etc*); clanking (*of machinery*); click-clack (*of heels*); clatter (*of clogs etc*).

clichage [kliʃaʒ] *nm Typ* **(a)** (*avec des planches stéréotypées*) stereotyping; **(b)** (*par électrolyse*) electrotyping.

cliché [kliʃe] *nm* **(a)** *Typ* stereotype; plate (*of type*); block (*of illustration*); **(b)** *Phot* negative; **(c)** (*résultat*) cliché.

clicher [kliʃe] *vt Typ* to stereotype; to take electros of (*pages of book etc*).

clicheur [kliʃœr] *nm Typ* stereotyper, electrotyper, blockmaker.

client, -ente [klijɑ̃, -ɑ̃t] *n* client, customer; (*doctor's*) patient; (*taxi driver's*) fare; (*hotel*) guest, patron; **ici, le c. est roi,** the customer is always right; **la France est un gros c. du Japon pour la robotique,** France is one of Japan's big customers for robotics; *F* **c'est un drôle de c.,** he's a queer customer; *Fig* **le c. à la médaille d'or,** the contender for the gold medal.

clientèle [klijɑ̃tɛl] *nf* **(a)** customers, clientèle (*of shop*); practice (*of barrister, doctor*); **(b)** custom; **obtenir la c. d'un consommateur/d'un pays,** to obtain a consumer's/country's custom *or* business; **accorder sa c. à,** to patronize.

clignement [kliɲmɑ̃] *nm* blink(ing), wink(ing), flicker of the eyelids; **regarder qn avec un c. d'yeux,** to blink at s.o.; **faire un c. d'œil,** to wink.

cligner [kliɲe] **1** *vt* **c. les yeux,** to screw up one's eyes; to blink. **2** *vi* **c. des yeux,** to screw up one's eyes; to blink; **c. de l'œil à qn,** to wink at s.o..

clignotant [kliɲɔtɑ̃] **1** *adj* blinking (*eyes*); twitching (*eyelid*); twinkling (*star*); flashing, winking (*light*); **signal c.,** *Nau* intermittent signal; *Aut* flashing light. **2** *nm* **(a)** *Aut* indicator, *US* flasher; **(b)** *Econ* (*signal*) warning light; **le c. de la hausse des prix/de la crise,** the warning light *or* signal that prices are rising/that recession is on the way.

clignotement [kliɲɔtmɑ̃] *nm* blinking (*of eyes*); twitching (*of eyelid*); twinkling (*of star*); flickering, flashing, winking (*of light*)

clignoter [kliɲɔte] *vi* **(a) c. des yeux,** to blink; **(b)** (*of eyelid*) to twitch; (*of star*) to twinkle; (*of light*) to flicker, to flash.

climat [klima] *nm* climate; *Fig* climate, atmosphere; **c. de détente,** climate *or* atmosphere of détente.

climatérique [klimaterik] *adj Med Arch etc* climacteric.

climatique [klimatik] *adj* climatic (*conditions etc*); **station c.,** health resort.

climatisation [klimatizɑsjɔ̃] *nf* air conditioning; **avoir la c. dans toutes les pièces,** to have air conditioning in every room.

climatiser [klimatize] *vt* to air-condition; **chambre climatisée,** air-conditioned bedroom.

climatiseur [klimatizœr] *nm* air conditioner.

climatologie [klimatɔlɔʒi] *nf* climatology.

climatologique [klimatɔlɔʒik] *adj* climatological.

clin [klɛ̃] *nm MecE* **joint à c.,** lap joint; *Nau* **bordé à clin(s),** clinker built.

clin d'œil [klɛ̃dœj] *nm* wink; **en un c. d'o.,** in the twinkling of an eye, in a flash.

clinicien [klinisjɛ̃] *adj & nm* **(médecin) c.,** clinician.

clinique [klinik] **1** *adj* clinical (*lecture etc*); **les signes cliniques d'une maladie,** the (clinical) symptoms of an illness. **2** *nf* **(a)** (*observation*) clinic; (*conférence*) clinical lecture; **(b)** (*privé*) clinic, nursing home; (*hôpital*) clinic, hospital.

cliniquement [klinikmɑ̃] *adv* clinically.

clinomètre [klinɔmɛtr] *nm* clinometer.

clinquant [klɛ̃kɑ̃] **1** *nm* **(a)** tinsel; **(bijoux de) c.,** imitation jewellery; **c. du style,** showiness of style; **(b)** *El etc* foil. **2** *adj* flashy, tawdry; **des colliers clinquants,** showy *or* flashy *or* tawdry necklaces; **une voiture c. neuf,** a brand *or* spanking new car.

clip [klip] *nm* **(a)** (*bijou*) clip; **(b)** (*film*) clip; **c. vidéo,** video clip.

clipper [klipœr] *nm* **(a)** *Av* transport aircraft; **(b)** *Nau* clipper.

clique [klik] *nf* **(a)** (*gang*) clique, gang, set; *F* **et toute la c.,** and the rest of the gang, and all the rest of them; **(b)** *Mil* (*drum and bugle*) band.

cliquer [klike] *vi Ordinat* to click on.

cliques [klik] *nfpl* **(a)** *F* **prendre ses c. et ses claques,** to pack up and leave, to pack one's bags and go; **(b)** *Arch* wooden shoes, pattens.

cliquet [klikɛ] *nm MecE etc* catch, pawl, ratchet.

cliqueter [klikte] *vi* (**il cliquette, il cliquettera**) (*de chaînes etc*) to rattle, to clank; (*de fleurets*) to click; (*de verre, pièces de monnaie*) to clink, to chink; (*de clés etc*) to jingle, to jangle; *Aut* to knock, to pink.

cliquetis [klikti] *nm* rattling, rattle, clank(ing) (*of chains etc*); clink(ing), chinking (*of glasses, coins*); jingling, jingle, jangling, jangle (*of keys etc*); clash (*of swords etc*); *Aut* knocking, pinking.

clisse [klis] *nf* wicker covering (*of bottle*); wicker tray (*for draining cheeses*).

clitoris [klitɔris] *nm Anat* clitoris.

clivage [klivaʒ] *nm* **(a)** gulf, rift (*in society*); **c. social,** social division; **c. idéologique,** ideological rift; **(b)** cleavage (*of rocks etc*); **(c)** cleaving (*of diamonds etc*).

cliver [klive] **1** *vt* to cleave, to split (*diamonds etc*). **2 se cliver** *vpr* (*of rock etc*) to cleave, to split.

cloaque [klɔak] *nm* **(a)** (*lieu malsain*) cesspool; **c. de vices,** sink of iniquity; **comment peut-il vivre dans ce c.?,** how can he live in that pigsty *or* midden?; **(b)** *Anat Zool* cloaca; **(c)** *Antiq* **le grand C.,** the Cloaca Maxima.

clochard, -arde [klɔʃar, -ard] *n F* tramp, *Am* hobo.

clochardisation [klɔʃardizɑsjɔ̃] *nf* destitution.

cloche [klɔʃ] **1** *nf* **(a)** bell; **sonner les cloches,** to ring the bells; *F* **sonner les cloches à qn,** to give s.o. a rocket *or* a good ticking off; **fleurs en c.,** bell-shaped flowers; *F* **déménager à la c. de bois,** to do a moonlight flit; *Fig* **voilà un autre son de c.,** that's quite a different version;

Nau **c. flottante,** bell buoy; **(b)** *Ch* bell jar; (*pour les semis*) cloche; (*pour le fromage etc*) dish cover; bell (*of gasometer*); **c. (de métal),** metal dish cover; **c. à plongeur,** diving bell; **(c) (chapeau) c.,** cloche (hat); **(d)** *F* **la c.,** vagrancy; **(e)** *Arg* **se taper la c.,** to have a good nosh, to stuff oneself; **(f)** *F* imbecile, idiot; **c'est une vraie c.,** he's a real imbecile *or* idiot. **2** *adj F* idiotic, stupid; **avoir l'air c.,** to look stupid.

cloche-pied (à) [aklɔʃpje] *adv* **sauter à c.-p.,** to hop (on one foot); **s'éloigner à c.-p.,** to hop away.

clocher¹ [klɔʃe] *nm* **(a)** belfry, bell tower, steeple; **course au c.,** point-to-point (race); **(b)** (*paroisse*) home town, native patch *or* heath; **disputes de c.,** petty local quarrels; **esprit de c.,** parochialism.

clocher² *vi* **(a)** *F* **il y a quelque chose qui cloche,** there's something wrong somewhere; **il y a quelque chose qui cloche dans son histoire,** there's something not right about his story; **(b)** *Arch* to limp, to hobble.

clocheton [klɔʃtɔ̃] *nm Archit* pinnacle (turret).

clochette [klɔʃɛt] *nf* **(a)** (*petite cloche*) small bell, handbell; **(b)** *Bot* (any) small bellflower.

clodo [klodo] *F* **1** *nm* tramp, down-and-out, *Am* hobo. **2** *adj* down-and-out; **avoir l'air c.,** to look like a down-and-out.

cloison [klwazɔ̃] *nf* **(a)** (*between rooms*) partition, division; **mur de c.,** dividing wall; **percer une c.,** to knock through a (dividing) wall; **coller l'oreille** *ou* **écouter à la c.,** to listen through the wall; **(b)** *Nau Av* bulkhead; **c. étanche,** *Nau* watertight bulkhead; *Av* pressure bulkhead; *Fig* watertight compartment; *Fig* **faire tomber les cloisons entre les classes,** to bring down class barriers; **(c)** *Aut* baffle plate (*of silencer*); **(d)** *Biol* septum.

cloisonnage [klwazɔnaʒ] *nm* partitioning.

cloisonné [klwazɔne] *adj* **(a)** partitioned off (*room*); *Fig* **tous ces services sont très cloisonnés,** all these departments are highly compartmentalized; **(b)** *Beaux-Arts* cloisonné (*enamel*); **(c)** *Biol* septate(d).

cloisonnement [klwazɔnmɑ̃] *nm* **(a)** partitioning (off) (*of room etc*); **le c. des services administratifs,** the compartmentalization of administrative services *or* departments; **(b)** *Biol* septation.

cloisonner [klwazɔne] *vt* to partition (off) (*room etc*); **c. la société,** to put up class barriers.

cloître [klwatr] *nm* **(a)** cloister(s) (*of monastery etc*); **(b)** monastery, convent; **vie de c.,** cloistered life.

cloîtrer [klwatre] **1** *vt* to cloister (*s.o.*); *Fig* to shut (*s.o.*) up *or* away; **nonne cloîtrée,** enclosed nun. **2 se cloîtrer** *vpr* (*de religieux*) to enter a convent *or* a monastery; *Fig* to shut oneself up *or* away, to live the life of a recluse.

clonage [klɔnaʒ] *nm Biol* cloning.

clone [klɔn] *nm Biol* clone.

cloner [klɔne] *vt Biol* to clone.

clope [klɔp] *nm Arg* fag, cig, *US* butt; **des clopes!,** nothing doing!, no way!

clopin-clopant [klɔpɛ̃klɔpɑ̃] *adv F* **aller c.-c.,** to limp along, to hobble about; *Fig* **commerce qui va c.-c.,** business that has its ups and downs *or* struggles along.

clopiner [klɔpine] *vi* to hobble, to limp.

clopinettes [klɔpinɛt] *nfpl F* sweet F.A., *esp Am* zilch; **tu auras que des c.,** you'll get damn all *or* sweet F.A.

cloporte [klɔpɔrt] *nm* (*insecte*) woodlouse, *Am* sowbug; *Fig Péj* **vivre comme un c.,** to live like a hermit; **c'est un vrai c.,** he's a real hermit, he's very antisocial.

cloque [klɔk] *nf* **(a)** blister (*on hand, paint etc*); lump, swelling (*from insect bite etc*); **(b)** *Agr* rust (*of wheat*); blight (*of tree*).

cloqué [klɔke] **1** *adj Agr* rusty (*wheat*); blighted, curled (*leaf*); *Tex* **tissu c.,** seersucker. **2** *nm Tex* seersucker.

cloquer [klɔke] *vi* (*of paint, skin etc*) to blister.

clore [klɔr] *v* (*pp* **clos**; *pr ind* **je clos, il clôt, ils closent;** *fu* **je clorai) 1** *vt* (= **fermer** *which has taken its place in most uses*) **(a)** to end (*discussion etc*); to conclude (*bargain*); to close (*account*); **c. les débats,** to close the meeting, to adjourn; **(b)** *Arch & Litt* to close, to shut (up); *Arch* to enclose (*park etc*). **2 se clore** *vpr* (*of meeting etc*) to (come to an) end.

clos, -ose [klo, -oz] **1** *adj* **(a)** (*fermé*) closed, shut; **volets c.,** closed shutters; **trouver porte close,** to find nobody in *or* (at) home; **à la nuit close,** after dark; *Jur* **à huis c.,** in camera; **réunion à huis c.,** closed session; **le sujet est c.,** the subject *or* matter is closed; **(b)** (*achevé*) finished, concluded; **la discussion est close,** the discussion is closed; **l'incident est c.,** the matter is closed. **2** *nm* enclosure; **c. (de vigne),** vineyard.

clôture [klotyr] *nf* **(a)** (*enceinte*) enclosure, fence, fencing, paling(s); *Can Sp* (*hockey sur glace*) rink; *Baseball* fence; **c. de fer,** iron railing; **c. métallique,** wire fence; **mur de c.,** enclosing wall; *Jur* **bris de c.,** breach of close; **(b)** closing, closure (*of offices etc*); conclusion, end (*of sitting etc*); closure (*of debate*); **prononcer la c. des débats,** to pronounce closure; *Bourse* **cours en c.,** closing price; **c. de la chasse,** close of season; **(c)** *Com* closing, winding up (*of account*); **(d)** *Rel* enclosure; **faire vœu de c.,** to take a vow of enclosure.

clôturer [klotyre] *vt* **(a)** to enclose, to shut in (*field etc*); **(b)** to close, to terminate, to end, to conclude (*session*); *Pol* **c. les débats,** to closure the debate; **(c)** *Com* to close, to wind up (*accounts etc*).

clou [klu] *nm* **(a)** nail; **c. étêté** *ou* **à tête perdue,** brad; **c. doré,** brass-headed nail, stud; **c. de tapissier,** (upholstery *or* carpet) tack; **c. cavalier,** staple; **c. à crochet,** hook; **souliers à gros clous,** hobnail(ed) boots; **attacher qch avec un c.,** to nail sth up *or* down; *F* **ça ne vaut pas un c.,** it's not worth a penny *or Am* a red cent; *F* **des clous!,** nothing doing!, no fear!, *esp Am* no way!; *F* **elle est maigre comme un c.,** she is as thin as a rake; *F* **mettre qch au c.,** to pawn sth;

(b) stud (*of pedestrian crossing*); **traverser dans les clous,** to cross at a pedestrian crossing *or Am* crosswalk;

(c) *F* star turn, chief attraction (*of show etc*); **ça a été le c. de la soirée,** it was the high point *or* highlight of the evening;

(d) *Mil Arg* (*prison*) cooler, slammer;

(e) *Méd* boil, carbuncle;

(f) *Culin* **c. de girofle,** clove;

(g) (vieux) c., (*voiture*) old banger, old crock; (*vélo*) old boneshaker.

clouage [kluaʒ] *nm* nailing.

clouer [klue] *vt* **(a)** to nail, to tack (*sth*); **c. une caisse,** to nail down a crate; *F* **c. le bec à qn,** to shut s.o. up; **(b)** *Fig* to pin (*sth, s.o.*) down; **c. qn au sol,** to pin s.o. down; **rester cloué sur place,** to stand stock-still, to be rooted to the spot; **être cloué à son lit,** to be bedridden; **(c)** *Échecs* to pin (*a piece*).

cloutage [klutaʒ] *nm* studding (*of shoe etc*).

clouté [klute] *adj* studded (*shoes etc*); **passage c.,** pedestrian crossing, *Am* crosswalk; **il s'est fait bouleversé alors qu'il était sur le passage c.,** he was knocked down on the crossing.

clouter [klute] *vt* to stud (*shoe etc*).

clovisse [klɔvis] *nf* (*mollusque*) clam.

clown [klun] *nm* clown, buffoon; *Fig* **ne fais pas le c.!,** stop acting the fool *or* goat!, stop clowning around!; **c'est un vrai c.,** he's a real comic *or* clown.

clownerie [klunri] *nf* clowning; *Fig* clowning around, playing the fool.

clownesque [klunɛsk] *adj* clownish.

club [klœb] *nm* **(a)** (*association*) (*political, sporting*) club; **c. sportif/de foot,** sports/football club; **(fauteuil) c.,** club chair; **(b)** (*de golf*) golf club.

cluse [klyz] *nf Géog* cluse, transverse valley.

clystère [klistɛr] *nm Méd Arch* clyster, enema.

cm. (*abrév* **centimètre**) cm.

C.N.R.S. [seɛnɛrɛs] *nm* (*abrév* **Centre national de la recherche scientifique**) *Br* ≈ SRC (Science Research Council); *Can* ≈ Science Council of Canada.

coaccusé, -ée [kɔakyze] *n Jur* co-defendant.

coach [kotʃ] *nm* **(a)** *Aut* two-door car; **(b)** (*entraîneur*) coach.

coacquéreur [kɔakerœr] *nm* joint purchaser.

coadjuteur, -trice [kɔadʒytœr, -tris] *n Rel* coadjutor.

coadministrateur, -trice [kɔadministratœr, -tris] *n* co-director; *Jur* co-trustee.

coagulable [kɔagylabl] *adj* coagulable.

coagulant [kɔagylɑ̃] *adj & nm* coagulant.

coagulateur, -trice [kɔagylatœr, -tris] *adj* coagulative.

coagulation [kɔagylasjɔ̃] *nf* coagulation, coagulating.

coaguler [kɔagyle] **1** *vt* to coagulate; to curdle (*milk*). **2** *vi* (*of blood etc*) to coagulate, to clot; (*of milk*) to curdle. **3 se coaguler** *vpr* (*of blood etc*) to coagulate, to congeal, to clot; (*of milk*) to curdle.

coalisé, -ée [kɔalize] **1** *adj* allied. **2** *n* **les coalisés,** the allies.

coaliser [kɔalize] **1** *vt* to unite, to combine (*powers etc*) in a coalition. **2 se coaliser** *vpr* to form a coalition, to unite; *Fig* **ils se sont tous coalisés contre moi,** they all ganged up on me *or* joined forces against me.

coalition [kɔalisjɔ̃] *nf* **(a)** (*alliance*) coalition, union, league; **ministère de c.,** coalition government; **(b)** *Fig Péj* (hostile) combination, conspiracy; **c'est une vraie c.!,** (*tout le monde est contre moi*) it's a real conspiracy!

coaltar [koltar] *nm* coal tar; *F* **être dans le c.,** to feel like a zombie, to be in a daze *or* stupor.

coassement [kɔasmɑ̃] *nm* croak(ing) (*of frog*).

coasser [kɔase] *vi* (*of frog*) to croak.

coassocié, -ée [kɔasɔsje] *n* copartner, joint partner.

coassurance [kɔasyrɑ̃s] *nf* mutual assurance.

coauteur [kootœr] *nm* **(a)** (*d'un livre etc*) joint author, co-author; **(b)** (*d'un crime*) partner in a crime.

coaxial, -aux [koaksjal, -jo] *adj* coaxial.

C.O.B. [seobe] *nf Bourse* (*abrév* **Commission des opérations de Bourse**) = Stock Exchange watchdog; *US* ≈ SEC.

cobalt [kɔbalt] *nm* cobalt; **bleu de c.,** cobalt blue; **bombe au c.,** cobalt bomb.

cobaye [kɔbaj] *nm* (*mammifère*) *& Fig* guinea pig; *Fig* **servir de c.,** to act as a guinea pig.

cobelligérant [kɔbeliʒerɑ̃] *adj & nm* cobelligerent.

Coblence [kɔblɑ̃s] *nf* Koblenz.

cobol [kɔbɔl] *nm Ordinat* COBOL.

cobra [kɔbra] *nm* cobra.

coca [kɔka] **1** *n Bot* coca. **2** *nf Pharm* coca.

coca (-cola) ® [kɔka(kɔla)] *nm* Coca-Cola ®, Coke ®; **prendre un c.,** to have a Coke ® *or* Coca-Cola ®.

cocagne [kɔkaɲ] *nf* **mât de c.,** greasy pole; **pays de c.,** land of milk and honey, land of plenty.

cocaïne [kɔkain] *nf Pharm* cocaine.

cocaïnomane [kɔkainɔman] *n* cocaine addict.

cocarde [kɔkard] *nf* rosette; *Hist* (*on hat*) cockade; *Av* roundel, fuselage marking; company crest (*on aircraft*); **la c. tricolore,** = tricolour cockade, worn on 14 July; *Fig* **changer de c.,** to change sides.

cocardier, -ière [kɔkardje, -jɛr] **1** *adj* fond of uniform(s) *or* all things military; (*chauviniste*) chauvinistic, jingoistic. **2** *n* chauvinist, jingoist.

cocasse [kɔkas] *adj F* comical, laughable.

cocasserie [kɔkasri] *nf F* comical nature, oddity.

coccinelle [kɔksinɛl] *nf* **(a)** (*insecte*) ladybird, *Spéc* coccinella; **(b)** *F* (Volkswagen ®) beetle.

coccyx [kɔksis] *nm Anat* coccyx.

coche[1] [kɔʃ] *nm* **(a)** *Arch* stagecoach; *Fig* **faire la mouche du c.,** to buzz around self-importantly; *F* **manquer le c.,** to miss the bus *or* boat; **(b)** *Arch* **c. (d'eau),** passenger barge.

coche[2] *nf* notch, nick; score (*on tally stick*); nock (*of arrow*).

cochenille [kɔʃnij] *nf* cochineal.

cocher[1] [kɔʃe] *nm* coachman, driver (*of horse-drawn vehicle*); *Arch* **c. de fiacre,** cabman, *F* cabby.

cocher[2] *vt* **(a)** (*faire une entaille*) to nick, to notch; to score (*tally*); **(b)** to tick (off), *Am* to check (*names etc*); **c. la case appropriée,** tick *or Am* check the appropriate box.

cochère [kɔʃɛr] *adj* **porte c.,** carriage gateway, main entrance.

cochet [kɔʃɛ] *nm* cockerel.

Cochinchine [kɔʃɛ̃ʃin] *nf Hist* Cochin-China.

cochon, -onne [kɔʃɔ̃, -ɔn] **1** *nm* **(a)** pig, hog, porker; **c. de lait,** suck(l)ing pig; **gardeur de cochons,** swineherd; **étable à cochons,** pigsty; *Fig* **copains comme cochons,** as thick as thieves; *F* **tu es sale comme un c.,** you're filthy; *Fig* **temps de c.,** rotten *or* stinking weather; *Fig F* **mon c.!,** you old rogue *or* devil!; **elle a une vraie tête de c.,** she's really pig-headed; **c'est une tête de c.,** he's a pig; *F* **un c. n'y retrouverait pas ses petits,** what a pigsty!; **c. d'Inde,** guinea pig; **c. d'Amérique,** peccary; **c. de mer,** porpoise;

(b) *Arg Péj* dirty pig, swine; **jouer un tour de c. à qn,** to play a dirty *or* rotten trick on s.o.; **c'est un c.,** (*il raconte des histoires immondes*) he's got a filthy mind.

2 *adj* indecent, dirty, smutty (*story etc*); dirty (*trick etc*); **film c.,** dirty *or* porn *or* blue film; **dix mille francs, c'est pas c.,** ten thousand francs? – that's not bad; **c. qui s'en dédit,** it's a deal.

cochonceté [kɔʃɔ̃ste] *nf F* (*propos*) filthy talk, foul language; (*vacherie*) dirty trick; **dire des cochoncetés,** to talk dirty.

cochonnaille [kɔʃɔnaj] *nf F* pork.

cochonner [kɔʃɔne] *vt F* to bungle, to botch, to muck up (*piece of work etc*).

cochonnerie [kɔʃɔnri] *nf Arg* **(a)** (*saleté*) filthiness; **faire des cochonneries,** (*des saletés*) to make a mess; **il fait des cochonneries avec la voisine,** he's up to no good with the woman next door; **dire des cochonneries,** to talk smut; **(b)** (*chose sans valeur*) trash, rubbish; (*nourriture*) pigswill; **(c)** (*tour*) dirty *or* lousy trick.

cochonnet [kɔʃɔnɛ] *nm* **(a)** (*petit cochon*) piglet; **(b)** (*at bowls*) jack.

cocker [kɔkœr] *nm* cocker spaniel.

cockney [kɔknɛ] **1** *adj* cockney; **accent c.,** Cockney accent. **2** *nm* Cockney; **parler c.,** to speak Cockney.

cockpit [kɔkpit] *nm Av etc* cockpit.

cocktail [kɔktɛl] *nm* (*boisson*) cocktail; (*soirée*) cocktail party; *F* (*mélange*) mixture; **cette réunion a fait un curieux c.,** there was a strange *or* curious mixture of types at the meeting; **c. Molotov,** Molotov cocktail.

coco[1] [koko] *nm* **(a)** (*plante*) **noix de c.,** coconut; **huile/beurre de c.,** coconut oil/butter; **(b)** *Arg* (*tête*) nut, bonce; (*estomac*) belly; **(c)** liquorice water.

coco[2] *nm* **(a)** *Enf* egg, eggie; **(b)** *F* (*type*) fellow, bloke; **drôle de c.,** odd bloke, strange guy; **attention, mon c.!,** careful chum *or* pal; **(c) mon petit c.,** my darling, my pet.

coco[3] *nf Arg* (*cocaïne*) snow, coke.

coco[4] *adj & n F* (*communiste*) commie, red.

cocon [kɔkɔ̃] *nm* cocoon (*of silkworm etc*); *Fig* **s'enfermer dans son c.,** to retire into one's shell; **il faut sortir de ton c.,** you must come out of your shell.

cocontractant, -ante [kɔkɔ̃traktɑ̃, -ɑ̃t] *n Jur* contracting partner.

cocooning [kɔkuniŋ] *nm* cocooning.

cocorico [kɔkɔriko] **1** *int* **(a)** three cheers for France!; **(b)** (*du coq*) cock-a-doodle-doo! **2** *nm* **(a)** (*cri*) = French victory cheer; (*victoire*) = French victory; **(b)** (*coq*) cock-a-doodle-do.

cocoter [kɔkɔte] *vi Arg* to stink; **ça cocote ici,** it stinks in here.

cocotier [kɔkɔtje] *nm* (*arbre*) coconut palm; *Fig F* **secouer le c.,** to get rid of the dead wood.

cocotte [kɔkɔt] *nf* **(a)** *Enf* hen, chicken, cluck-cluck; (*en papier*) = bird made out of folded paper; **(b)** *F* **ma c.,** darling; **(c)** (*prostituée*) tart; **(d)** *Culin* (large) stewpan; casserole (dish); **(e)** *F* **hue, c.!,** gee up!

cocotte-minute ® [kɔkɔtminyt] *nf* pressure cooker; (*pl cocottes-minute*).

cocu, -e [kɔky] *Arg* **1** *n* deceived husband *or* wife; (*homme*) cuckold; **faire c.(e) son mari/sa femme,** to cheat on one's husband/one's wife; **avoir une chance** *ou* **une veine de c.,** to have the devil's own luck. **2** *adj* deceived, cuckold(ed).

cocuage [kɔkɥaʒ] *nm Arg* cuckoldry.

cocufier [kɔkyfje] *vt Arg* to be unfaithful to, to cuckold.

coda [kɔda] *nf Mus* coda.

codage [kɔdaʒ] *nm Ordinat etc* coding.

code [kɔd] *nm* **(a)** (*symbole*) code, cypher; **écrire un message en c.,** to write a message in code, to write a coded message; **déchiffrer un c.,** to decipher *or* break *or* crack a code; **c. secret,** secret code; **c. postal,** postcode, postal code, *US* zip code; **c. à barres,** bar code; *Biol* **c. génétique,** genetic code;

(b) *Ordinat* code; **c. d'erreur,** error code; **c. héxadécimal,** hexa(decimal) code; **c. machine,** machine code; **codes,** codes, coding;

(c) *Jur* statute book; **c. civil,** Civil Code, ≈ Common Law; **c. pénal,** penal code; **c. de justice militaire,** military law; **c. de commerce,** commercial law; **c. maritime,** navigation laws; **se tenir dans les marges du c.,** to keep just within the law; **c. de la morale/de l'honneur,** moral code/code of honour; *Aut* **C. de la route,** Highway Code; *Aut* **se mettre en c.,** to dip one's headlights; *Aut* **phares c.,** dipped headlights.

codébiteur, -trice [kɔdebitœr, -tris] *n Jur* joint debtor.

codéine [kɔdein] *nf Ch* codeine.

codemandeur, -deresse [kɔdmɑ̃dœr, -drɛs] *n Jur* joint plaintiff.

coder [kɔde] *vt* to code (*message*).

codétenteur, -trice [kɔdetɑ̃tœr, -tris] *n Jur* joint holder.

codétenu, -ue [kɔdetny] *n* fellow prisoner.

codeur [kɔdœr] *nm Tech* coder.

codex [kɔdɛks] *nm* pharmacopoeia.

codicillaire [kɔdisilɛr] *adj Jur* codicillary.

codicille [kɔdisil] *nm Jur* codicil.

codification [kɔdifikasjɔ̃] *nf* codification, classification (*of laws etc*); *Ordinat* **c. binaire,** binary code.

codifier [kɔdifje] *vt* to codify (*laws etc*); (*mettre en système*) to systematize.

codirecteur, -trice [kɔdirɛktœr -tris] *n* joint manager *or* manageress; (*d'un P.D.G. etc*) co-director.

coédition [kɔedisjɔ̃] *nf* (*procédé*) joint publishing; (*livre*) joint publication.

coefficient [kɔefisjɑ̃] *nm* coefficient, factor; **c. de dilatation,** coefficient of expansion; **c. d'écrasement/d'élasticité,** modulus of compression/of elasticity; **c. de**

sécurité, safety factor; **on peut s'attendre à un c. d'erreur,** a certain margin of error is to be expected; **le c. d'augmentation,** the rate of increase.

cœliaque [seljak] *adj & n Méd* coeliac, *US* celiac.

cœlioscopie [seljɔskɔpi] *nf Méd* coelioscopy.

coéquation [kɔekwasjɔ̃] *nf Admin* proportional assessment.

coéquipier, -ière [kɔekipje, -jɛr] *n Sp etc* team mate.

coercible [kɔɛrsibl] *adj Phys* coercible (*gas etc*).

coercitif, -ive [kɔɛrsitif, -iv] *adj* coercive; **le pouvoir c. de son discours,** the persuasive power of his speech.

coercition [kɔɛrsisjɔ̃] *nf* coercion.

cœur [kœr] *nm* **(a)** heart; **maladie de c.,** heart disease; **greffe du c.,** heart transplant; **c. droit/gauche,** right/left side of the heart; **subir une opération à c. ouvert,** to have open-heart surgery; **tué d'une balle au c.,** killed by a bullet in the heart; **en c.,** heart-shaped; *Fig* **faire la bouche en c.,** to simper; *Fig* **joli comme un c.,** as pretty as a picture; **serrer** *ou* **presser qn contre** *ou* **sur son c.,** to hold *or* clasp s.o. to one's breast; *F* **faire le joli c.,** to put on airs (and graces);

(b) (*ventre*) **avoir mal au c.,** to feel sick; **ça fait mal au c. de voir tout cet argent gaspillé,** it makes you sick to see all that money wasted *or* go to waste; **cela soulève le c.,** it's nauseating *or* sickening; *F* **avoir le c. bien accroché,** to have a strong stomach;

(c) (*esprit*) soul, feelings, mind; **avoir** *ou* **garder qch sur le c.,** to have sth on one's mind; **dire ce qu'on a sur le c.,** to get it off one's chest; **en avoir le c. net,** to get to the bottom of it, to clear the matter up; *Fig* **ouvrir son c. à qn,** to open one's heart to s.o.; **parler à c. ouvert,** to speak freely, to have a heart to heart talk; **avoir la rage au c.,** to be raging *or* seething with anger; **au fond du c.,** in one's heart of hearts; **remercier qn de tout (son) c.** *ou* **du fond de son c.,** to thank s.o. wholeheartedly *or* from the bottom of one's heart; **je l'espère de tout mon c.,** I hope so from the bottom of my heart; **il me portait dans son c.,** he was very fond of me; *Euph* **je sais qu'elle ne me porte pas dans son c.,** I know she doesn't like me much *or* isn't very fond of me; **partir le c. léger,** to set off with a light heart; **de gaieté de c.,** with a light heart; **avoir le c. gros** *ou* **serré,** to be heavy-hearted *or* sad at heart; **avoir la mort dans le c.,** to be sick at heart; **prendre** *ou* **avoir à c. de faire qch,** to set one's heart on doing sth, to have one's heart set on doing sth; **la chose qui lui tient** *ou* **qu'il a** *ou* **prend à c. est de donner une éducation à sa fille,** he has his heart set on giving his daughter an education; **vous n'aurez pas le c. de faire cela,** you wouldn't have the heart to do that; **elle n'a le c. à rien,** she hasn't the heart for anything, she isn't interested in doing anything; **avoir le c. sur la main,** to be generous; **femme de c.,** warm- hearted woman; **je serai de c. avec vous,** I'll be with you in spirit; **si le c. vous en dit,** if you feel like it; **des gens selon mon c.,** people after my own heart; **une affaire de c.,** an affair of the heart; **le c. a ses raisons,** the heart has its reasons;

(d) par c., by heart *or* rote; **c'est du par c.,** it's been learnt (off) by heart *or* parrot-fashion; **apprendre/savoir qch par c.,** to learn/know sth by heart; **je la connais par c.,** I know her inside out;

(e) (*courage*) courage, spirit, pluck; **donner du c. à qn,** to give s.o. courage; *F* **avoir du c. au ventre,** to have plenty of guts; **faire contre mauvaise fortune bon c.,** to make the best of a bad job, to put a good face on it;

(f) (*énergie*) heart, will; **avoir** *ou* **mettre du c. à l'ouvrage,** to put one's heart into one's work; **je n'ai pas le c. à l'ouvrage aujourd'hui,** I haven't the heart for work today; **faire qch de bon c.** *ou* **de grand c.,** to do sth willingly *or* gladly; **faire qch de mauvais c.,** to do sth reluctantly *or* unwillingly; **rire de bon c.,** to laugh heartily; **y aller de bon c.,** to get down to it; **le c. n'y est pas,** his *or* my *etc* heart isn't in it;

(g) (*amour*) **donner son c. à qn,** to lose one's heart to s.o.; **aimer qn de tout son c.,** to love s.o. with all one's heart; *Prov* **loin des yeux, loin du c.,** out of sight, out of mind; **des histoires de c.,** affairs of the heart;

(h) (*bonté*) **c'est un** *ou* **il a bon c.,** he's kind-hearted, he's a kind-hearted soul; **avoir un c. d'or,** to have a heart of gold; **ne pas avoir de c.,** to be heartless;

(i) (*centre*) middle, core; *Fig* **le c. de la question,** the heart of the matter *or* question; **au c. de la ville,** in the centre of the town, in the heart of the city; **c. de palmier,** heart of palm; **c. d'un chou/d'un artichaut,** heart of a cabbage/an artichoke; *F* **avoir un c. d'artichaut,** to fall in love with every pretty girl *or* handsome boy one meets; **fromage fait à c.,** ripe cheese; **au c. de l'hiver/l'été,** in the depth of winter/the height of summer;

(j) *Cartes* heart(s); **dame de c.,** queen of hearts; **avez-vous du c.?,** have you any hearts?

coexistence [kɔɛgzistɑ̃s] *nf* coexistence (**avec,** with); *Pol* **c. pacifique,** peaceful coexistence.

coexister [kɔɛgziste] *vi* to coexist (**avec,** with).

coffrage [kɔfraʒ] *nm* **(a)** formwork, *Br* shuttering (*for concrete work*); **(b)** *Min etc* coffering, lining (*of shaft etc*).

coffre [kɔfr] *nm* **(a)** (*meuble*) chest; (*pour l'argent*) safe; (*qu'on peut louer à la banque*) safety deposit box; **c. en bois,** wooden chest; **c. à outils,** tool chest, toolbox; **c. à linge,** linen chest; **percer** *ou* **ouvrir un c.,** to break open *or* into a safe; **les coffres de l'État,** the coffers of State, the Treasury; **(b)** *Anat F* chest; **avoir du c.,** to have a sound chest, to have a lot of puff; **avoir le c. bon,** to be sound in wind and limb; **(c)** *Aut* boot, *Am* trunk (*of car*); **(d)** case (*of lock, piano etc*); **(e)** *Nau* **c. d'amarrage,** mooring buoy; *Nau* (*coque*) well deck.

coffre-fort [kɔfrəfɔr] *nm* safe; (*pl coffres-forts*).

coffrer [kɔfre] *vt F* **(a)** to put (*s.o.*) in prison *or* away; **faire c. qn,** to have *or* get s.o. put inside *or* behind bars; **(b)** *Min etc* to coffer, to line (*shaft etc*).

coffret [kɔfrɛ] *nm* small box, casket; **c. à bijoux,** jewel case; **c. à documents,** deed box.

cogérance [kɔʒerɑ̃s] *nf* co-management, joint management.

cogérant, -ante [kɔʒerɑ̃, -ɑ̃t] *n* joint manager, joint manageress.

cogérer [kɔʒere] *vt* to manage (*sth*) jointly.

cogestion [kɔʒɛstjɔ̃] *nf* joint management.

cogitation [kɔʒitasjɔ̃] *nf Iron & Vieilli* cogitation, reflection.

cogiter [kɔʒite] *vi Iron & Vieilli* to cogitate, to think.

cogito [kɔʒito] *nm Phil* cogito; **le c. de Descartes,** the cartesian cogito, Descartes' cogito.

cognac [kɔɲak] **1** *nm* cognac. **2** *adj inv* brandy (-coloured).

cognassier [kɔɲasje] *nm* quince (tree).

cogne [kɔɲ] *nm Arg* cop.

cognée [kɔɲe] *nf* axe, hatchet.

cognement [kɔɲmɑ̃] *nm* knocking (*of engine etc*); (*bruit*) thump(ing), banging.

cogner [kɔɲe] **1** *vt* to drive in, to hammer in (*nail etc*); (*heurter*) to knock, to bump; *Arg* to knock (*s.o.*) about; **c. qn en passant,** to bump into s.o. (in passing); **il cogne dur,** he's a hard hitter; **il cogne sa femme,** he beats his wife, he knocks his wife about; *F* **son mari lui cogne dessus chaque fois qu'il est ivre,** her husband knocks her about every time he gets drunk.

2 *vi* **(a)** to knock, to thump (**sur,** on); to bump, to bang (**contre,** against); **c. du poing sur la table,** to bang (one's fist) on the table; **c. à une porte,** to bang *or* hammer on a door;

(b) (*of engine etc*) to knock.

3 se cogner *vpr* **se c. à** *ou* **contre qch,** to knock against sth; *Fig* **se c. la tête contre les murs,** to bang one's head against a brick wall; **ils se cognent dessus chaque fois qu'ils boivent,** they bash each other about whenever they get drunk.

cogneur [kɔɲœr] *nm Boxe etc* hard hitter, bruiser.

cogniticien, -ienne [kɔgnitisjɛ̃, -jɛn] *n Ordinat* knowledge engineer.

cognitif, -ive [kɔgnitif, -iv] *adj Phil* cognitive; **thérapie cognitive,** cognitive therapy.

cognition [kɔgnisjɔ̃] *nf Phil* cognition.

cohabitation [kɔabitasjɔ̃] *nf* cohabitation; *Fr Pol* **sous le régime de la c.,** during the period of cohabitation.

cohabiter [kɔabite] *vi* to cohabit (**avec,** with).

cohérence [kɔerɑ̃s] *nf* (*of argument, speech*) coherence; (*of argument, behaviour*) consistency; **cette explication/ce raisonnement/il manque de c.,** that explanation/that line of argument/he is inconsistent; **parler sans c.,** to be incoherent.

cohérent [kɔerɑ̃] *adj* coherent, consistent (*argument*); consistent (*behaviour*); coherent (*in speech*).

cohéritier, -ière [kɔeritje, -jɛr] *n* coheir(ess), joint heir(ess).

cohésif, -ive [kɔezif, -iv] *adj* cohesive.

cohésion [kɔezjɔ̃] *nf* cohesion, cohesiveness.

cohorte [kɔɔrt] *nf* **(a)** *F* mob, band (*of people*); **(b)** *Hist* cohort.

cohue [kɔy] *nf* crowd, mob, throng.

coi, coite [kwa, kwat] *adj* **se tenir c.,** to keep quiet, to lie low; **en rester c.,** to be flabbergasted.

coiffage [kwafaʒ] *nm* **(a)** *(de cheveux)* hairdressing, doing *or* arranging of (one's, s.o.'s) hair; **(b)** *(pour recouvrir)* covering.
coiffe [kwaf] *nf* **(a)** headdress, cap *(surtout de costume régional)*; **(b)** *(doublure)* lining; **(c)** *(pour recouvrir)* cover; *Mil* breech cover; **c. de fusée,** fuse cap; *Nau etc* **c. blanche,** white cap cover; **(d)** *(du nouveau-né)* caul.
coiffé [kwafe] *adj* **(a) être c. d'un chapeau,** to be wearing a hat; **il est né c.,** he was born with a caul; *Fig* he was born with a silver spoon in his mouth; **(b) elle est bien coiffée ce soir,** her hair looks beautiful this evening; **je ne suis pas encore coiffée,** I haven't done my hair yet; **(c) être c. de qn,** to be infatuated with s.o. .
coiffer [kwafe] **1** *vt* **(a)** to cover *(the head)*; to cap *(bottle etc)*; **ce chapeau vous coiffe bien,** that hat suits you; **montagne coiffée de neige,** snow-capped mountain; *Fig* **c. Sainte-Catherine,** to be (left) on the shelf, to be 25 and still unmarried; **c. un chapeau,** to put on a hat; **(b) c. qn,** to do s.o.'s hair; **il coiffe bien,** he's a good hairdresser; **se faire c.,** to have one's hair done; **qui vous coiffe?,** who does your hair, who's your hairdresser?; **(c)** *Sp F* to overtake; *Sp etc* **se faire c. (au poteau),** to be pipped at the post; **(d)** *F* to control, to direct *(an organization etc)*; **c. un service,** to head a department. **2 se coiffer** *vpr* **(a) se c. d'une casquette,** to put on *or* wear a cap; **(b)** to do one's hair; **(c)** *F* **se c. de qn,** to become infatuated with s.o..
coiffeur, -euse [kwafœr, -øz] **1** *n* hairdresser, hair stylist; *(pour hommes)* barber. **2** *nf* **coiffeuse,** dressing table.
coiffure [kwafyr] *nf* **(a)** *(de cheveux)* hairstyle; **changer de c.,** to change one's hairstyle *or* hairdo; **(b)** *Com* hairdressing; **salon de c.,** hairdresser's, hairdressing salon; *(pour hommes)* barbershop, barber's; **(c)** *(chapeau etc)* headgear; *(de costume régional etc)* headdress.
coin [kwɛ̃] *nm* **(a)** *(angle)* corner; **maison du** *ou* **qui fait le c.,** corner house; **à tous les coins de rue,** on every street corner; **l'épicier du c.,** the grocer on the corner; *(du village etc)* the local *or* corner grocer; *F* **je ne voudrais pas le rencontrer au c. d'un bois,** I wouldn't like to meet him down a dark alley *or* on a dark night; **place de c.,** corner seat; **mettre un enfant au c.,** to put a child in the corner *(in disgrace)*; **regard en c.,** sidelong glance; **lancer un regard en c. à qn,** to look at s.o. sideways, to give s.o. a sidelong glance; **regarder qn du c. de l'œil,** to look at s.o. out of the corner of one's eye; **sourire en c.,** half smile; *Journ* **le c. du jardinier/de la femme,** gardener's/woman's page; **aux quatre coins du monde,** in the four corners of the earth; **elle a visité les quatre coins du monde,** she has travelled all over the world; **reliure avec coins,** binding with leather corners;
(b) *(endroit)* (retired) spot, nook; **un petit c. pas cher,** a cheap *or* inexpensive little place; **je ne suis pas du c.,** I'm not local, I'm not from round here, I don't live round here; *F* **le petit c.,** the smallest room (in the house), the loo; **coins et recoins,** nooks and crannies; **dans un c. de ma mémoire,** in a corner *or* the recesses of my memory, in the back of my mind; **il a dû se perdre dans un c.,** he must have got lost somewhere; **mon stylo est introuvable, il a dû tomber dans un c.,** I can't find my pen anywhere, it must have got lost somewhere; **chercher qch dans tous les coins,** to look everywhere *or* high and low for sth; *F* **connaître qch dans les coins,** to know sth inside out; **en boucher un c. à qn,** to flabbergast s.o.; **c. d'évier,** sink tidy; **c. du feu,** inglenook; **au c. du feu,** by the fireside;
(c) *(parcelle)* patch; **c. de légumes,** vegetable plot; **c. de ciel bleu,** patch of blue sky;
(d) *(cale)* wedge, key, quoin, chock; **en c.,** wedge-shaped; **tranchant du c.,** thin end of the wedge;
(e) *(pour frapper les monnaies)* stamp, die; *Fig* **marqué au c. du génie,** bearing the stamp *or* hallmark of genius.
coinçage [kwɛ̃saʒ] *nm,* **coincement** [kwɛ̃smɑ̃] *nm* wedging, jamming.
coincer [kwɛ̃se] *v* **(je coinçai(s); n. coinçons) 1** *vt* **(a)** to jam, to stick *(drawer etc)*; to wedge (up), to chock (up) *(rails etc)*; **ma bague est coincée à mon doigt,** my ring is stuck; **c'est coincé,** *(la porte, le tiroir)* it's jammed *or* stuck; **voiture coincée entre deux camions,** car jammed *or* stuck *or* caught between two lorries; **(b)** *(acculer)* to corner *(s.o.)*; **vous êtes coincé,** you're cornered; **il m'a coincé,** *(je n'ai pas su répondre)* he had me cornered; **(c)** *F (arrêter)* to run in; **il va finir par se faire c.,** he'll end up getting caught. **2 se coincer** *vpr* to jam, to stick; **se c. la tête dans des barreaux,** to get one's head stuck in railings; **se c. le doigt dans la porte,** to jam one's finger in the door.
coïncidence [kɔɛ̃sidɑ̃s] *nf* coincidence; **par une étrange c.,** by a strange coincidence.
coïncident [kɔɛ̃sidɑ̃] *adj* coincident, coinciding.
coïncider [kɔɛ̃side] *vi* to coincide (**avec,** with).
coin-coin [kwɛ̃kwɛ̃] **1** *nm inv (of ducks)* quack(ing). **2** *int* quack! quack!
coin-cuisine [kwɛ̃kɥizin] *nm* kitchen area; *(pl coins-cuisine(s))*.
coïnculpé, -ée [kɔɛ̃kylpe] *n* co-defendent, co-accused.
coing [kwɛ̃] *nm (fruit)* quince.
coin-repas [kwɛ̃r(ə)pɑ] *nm* dining area *or* recess; *(pl coins-repas)*.
coït [kɔit] *nm* coitus, coition.
coke [kɔk] *nm* coke.
cokéfaction [kɔkefaksjɔ̃] *nf* coking.
cokéfier [kɔkefje] *vt* to coke.
cokerie [kɔkri] *nf* coking plant.
col [kɔl] *nm* **(a)** collar *(of dress, shirt etc)*; **faux c.,** *(on shirt)* detachable collar; head *(of froth on glass of beer)*; **c. raide/mou,** stiff/soft collar; **c. cassé,** wing collar; **c. de fourrure/de dentelle,** fur/lace collar; **(pull à) c. roulé,** polo-neck (jumper); **c. Claudine,** Peter Pan collar; **c. châle,** shawl collar; **(b)** neck *(of bottle etc)*; *Anat* cervix *(of uterus etc)*; **(c)** *Géog* col; **(d)** *Arch & Litt* neck *(de personne)*; **homme au c. court,** short-necked man.
cola [kɔla] *nm (plante)* cola, kola.
col-blanc [kɔlblɑ̃] *nm F* white-collar worker; *(pl cols-blancs)*.
col-bleu [kɔlblø] *nm (pl cols-bleus) F* **(a)** *(marin)* sailor, bluejacket; **(b)** *(ouvrier)* blue-collar worker.
colchique [kɔlʃik] *nm (plante)* colchicum, meadow saffron, autumn crocus.
cold-cream [kɔldkrim] *nm* cold cream.
col-de-cygne [kɔldəsiɲ] *nm Tech* swan neck; *(pl cols-de-cygne)*.
colégataire [kɔlegatɛr] *n Jur* co-legatee, joint legatee.
coléoptère [kɔleɔptɛr] *nm* beetle; **les coléoptères,** the Coleoptera.
colère [kɔlɛr] **1** *nf* anger; *surtout Litt* wrath; **c. bleue** *ou* **noire,** towering rage; **être en c.,** to be angry; **se mettre en c.,** to get angry, to lose one's temper (**contre qn,** with, *Am* at s.o.); **mettre qn en c.,** to make s.o. angry, to anger s.o.; **avec c.,** angrily; **il avait des colères terribles,** he was subject to terrible fits of anger; **pas la peine de passer ta c. sur moi,** there's no point (in) taking your anger out *or* working your anger off on me; **piquer une c.,** to fly into a rage, to throw a tantrum; *Litt* **la c. de Dieu,** the wrath of God. **2** *adj* irate, angry *(voice)*; irascible *(person)*.
coléreux, -euse [kɔlerø, -øz] **, colérique** [kɔlerik] *adj* quick tempered *(person)*; irritable *(disposition)*.
colibacille [kɔlibasil] *nm* colon bacillus.
colibri [kɔlibri] *nm* humming bird.
colifichet [kɔlifiʃɛ] *nm* trinket, knick-knack; **colifichets,** rubbish, trash.
colimaçon [kɔlimasɔ̃] *nm* snail; **escalier en c.,** spiral staircase.
colin [kɔlɛ̃] *nm (poisson)* hake; coalfish, *Br* coley, saithe.
colin-maillard [kɔlɛ̃majar] *nm (jeu)* blindman's buff.
colique [kɔlik] **1** *adj Anat* colic *(artery etc)*. **2** *nf* severe stomach pains; *(surtout de bébé)* colic; **avoir la c.,** *(douleur)* to have stomach ache; *(diarrhée)* to have diarrhoea; *F* to have the wind up; *F* **cette idée suffit pour me donner la c.,** just the idea puts the wind up me; *F* **quelle c.!,** what a bore!, what a bind!
colis [kɔli] *nm* parcel, packet, package; **par c. postal,** by parcel post.
Colisée (le) [ləkɔlize] *nm* the Coliseum.
colistier [kɔlistje] *nm Pol etc* fellow candidate, *US* running mate.
colite [kɔlit] *nf Méd* colitis.
collabo [kɔlabo] *n F* = **COLLABORATEUR (b)**.
collaborateur, -trice [kɔlabɔratœr, -tris] *n* **(a)** *(associé)* fellow worker, associate, *Am* co-worker; **collaborateurs d'une revue,** contributors to a magazine; **(b)** *Pol Hist* collaborator, collaborationist.
collaboration [kɔlabɔrasjɔ̃] *nf* collaboration (**avec,** with).
collaborer [kɔlabɔre] *vi* **(a)** to collaborate (**avec,** with); **c. à un journal,** to contribute to a newspaper; **(b)** *Pol Hist* to collaborate.
collage [kɔlaʒ] *nm* **(a)** gluing, sticking *(of wood etc)*; pasting *(of paper etc)*; *Beaux-Arts* collage; **c. du papier (peint),** paper hanging; **(b)** *F (of unmarried couple)* living together; **(c)** *Tech* sizing; **(d)** fining, clarifying *(of wine)*.
collagène [kɔlaʒɛn] *nm* collagen; **crème de beauté au**

c., collagen(-based) cream.

collant [kɔlɑ̃] **1** *adj* **(a)** (*adhésif*) sticky; (*peinture, vernis*) tacky; **papier c.,** gummed paper; **(b)** (*qui moule*) tight- *or* close-fitting (*garment*); **(c)** *F* **qu'est-ce qu'il est c.!,** you just can't shake him off *or* get rid of him! **2** *nm* (pair of) tights.

collante [kɔlɑ̃t] *nf Scol F* = letter giving notice of the date and place of an examination.

collapsus [kɔlapsys] *nm Méd* collapse (*of patient*).

collatéral, -aux [kɔlateral, -o] **1** *adj* collateral; *Archit* **nef collatérale,** side aisle; *Jur* **parents collatéraux,** collaterals, relatives. **2** *nm* **(a)** *Archit* side aisle; **(b)** *Jur* **collatéraux,** collaterals, relatives.

collation [kɔlɑsjɔ̃] *nf* **(a)** granting, conferment (*of degree etc*); *Rel* advowson; **(b)** collation (*of documents etc*); **(c)** (*repas*) light meal, snack.

collationnement [kɔlasjɔnmɑ̃] *nm* collating, collation (*of documents etc*).

collationner [kɔlasjɔne] **1** *vt* to collate, to compare (*two written documents*). **2** *vi* to have a snack.

colle [kɔl] *nf* **(a)** paste, glue; (*pour papier peint*) size; **c. forte,** glue; **c. en tube/stick/pot,** a tube/stick/pot of glue; **c. à bois,** wood glue; **c. blanche,** paste; **c. de poisson,** fish glue, isinglass; **c. au caoutchouc,** rubber solution; **papier sans c.,** unsized paper; *F* **c'est un vrai pot de c.,** you just can't get rid of him, he sticks like a leech *or* like glue; **(b)** *Scol etc F* (*question difficile*) difficult *or* sticky question, poser; (*examen oral*) oral exam; (*punition*) detention; **(c)** *Arg* **vivre** *ou* **être à la c.,** to be shacked up together.

collecte [kɔlɛkt] *nf* **(a)** collection (*for the poor etc*); **faire une c.,** to make *or* take a collection; **(b)** *Rel* collect.

collecter [kɔlɛkte] *vt* to collect.

collecteur, -trice [kɔlɛktœr, -tris] **1** *n* collector; **c. d'impôts,** tax collector. **2** *nm Él* ring, commutator (*of dynamo etc*); *Rad* **c. d'ondes,** aerial; **c. d'échappement,** exhaust manifold. **3** *adj* **égout c.,** main sewer; *Él* **bague collectrice,** collector ring.

collectif, -ive [kɔlɛktif, -iv] **1** *adj* collective, joint (*action, report etc*); **ferme collective,** collective (farm); **contrat c.,** collective agreement; **l'inconscient c.,** the collective subconscious; **voyages collectifs,** group travel; **radiographie collective,** mass radiography; *Can Jur* **recours c.,** class action suit. **2** *nm* **(a)** *Gram* collective noun; **(b)** *Admin* block of flats; **(c)** *Fin* **c. budgétaire,** bill of supply; **(d)** (*groupe de collaborateurs*) team.

collection [kɔlɛksjɔ̃] *nf* **(a)** (*action*) collecting, gathering; **(b)** collection (*of butterflies etc*); file (*of newspapers*); series (*of books*); *Com* line (*of samples*); **présentation de c.,** fashion show; **la c. d'hiver,** the winter collection; **c. privée,** private collection; **j'en ai toute une c.,** I've got a whole collection *or* set of them; **quelle c. d'ignorants!,** what a bunch *or* crowd of ignoramuses!

collectionner [kɔlɛksjɔne] *vt* to collect (*stamps etc*).

collectionneur, -euse [kɔlɛksjɔnœr, -øz] *n* collector (*of stamps etc*).

collectivement [kɔlɛktivmɑ̃] *adv* collectively.

collectivisation [kɔlɛktivizɑsjɔ̃] *nf Écon* collectivization.

collectiviser [kɔlɛktivize] *vt Écon* to collectivize.

collectivisme [kɔlɛktivism] *nm Écon* collectivism.

collectiviste [kɔlɛktivist] *adj & n Écon* collectivist.

collectivité [kɔlɛktivite] *nf* **(a)** (*groupe*) community; **le sens de la c.,** community spirit; **vie en c.,** community life *or* living; *Admin* **c. locale,** local community; **collectivités nationales/professionnelles,** national/professional organizations; **(b)** (*propriété en commun*) common ownership.

collège [kɔlɛʒ] *nm* **(a)** *Scol* school; **c. d'enseignement secondaire** *ou Vieilli* **général,** ≈ secondary (modern) school, *Am* high school; **c. d'enseignement technique,** technical college; **c. libre,** private school; **le brevet des collèges,** ≈ school leaving certificate; **le C. de France,** College de France (= prestigious higher education institution); **(b) c. électoral,** electoral body *or* constituency, *surtout US* electoral college; **(c)** college; **le Sacré C.,** the College of Cardinals.

collégial, -iale, -iaux [kɔleʒjal, -jo] **1** *adj* collegial, collegiate. **2** *nf* **collégiale,** collegiate church.

collégialité [kɔleʒjalite] *nf* collegial structure (*of a society etc*).

collégien, -ienne [kɔleʒjɛ̃, -jɛn] *n* **(a)** schoolboy, schoolgirl; **(b)** *Iron* innocent; **c'est un c.,** he's an innocent.

collègue [kɔlɛg] *n* colleague, fellow worker, *surtout Am* coworker.

coller [kɔle] **1** *vt* **(a)** to paste, to stick, to glue (**à, sur,** to, on); **c. du papier peint sur un mur,** to paper a wall; **c. le timbre sur l'enveloppe,** to stick the stamp on the envelope; **la sueur avait collé ses cheveux,** her hair was matted with sweat; **c. son visage à** *ou* **contre la vitre,** to glue one's face to the window; *F* **on m'a collé cette tâche sans que j'aie dit oui,** I got stuck *or* lumbered *or* saddled with this job without agreeing (to do it); *F* **c. une gifle à qn,** to slap s.o. in the face;

(b) *F* to put; **collez ce vélo dans un coin,** stick that bike in a corner; **c. un élève,** (*le retenir*) to keep a pupil in; (*lui poser une question difficile*) to catch a pupil out (with a difficult question); **c. un candidat,** to fail a candidate;

(c) (*suivre*) to follow (about); **il me colle!,** he sticks to me like glue!;

(d) to size (*paper*);

(e) to clarify, to fine (*wine*).

2 *vi* to stick, to adhere, to cling (**à,** to); **robe qui colle au corps,** clinging dress; **il faut essayer de c. au style de l'auteur,** you must try to stick to the author's style; **ce travail/parfum/rôle te colle à la peau,** that work/perfume/role is just perfect for you *or* suits you down to the ground *or* is tailor-made for you; *F* **ça ne colle pas entre eux,** they don't hit it off; *F* **ça colle?,** how are things?, O.K.?; *F* **ça ne colle pas,** there's something wrong; **oui, ça colle,** yes, that makes sense *or Am* that figures.

3 se coller *vpr* **(a)** to stick, to adhere closely; **elle s'est collée contre lui,** she clung to him;

(b) *Arg* **se c. avec qn,** to live with s.o., *F* to shack up with s.o..

collerette [kɔlrɛt] *nf* **(a)** (*de vêtement*) ruff, collarette; **(b)** *Bot* annulus (*of mushroom*); **(c)** *MecE etc* flange (*of pipe, joint etc*).

collet [kɔlɛ] *nm* **(a)** collar (*of coat, dress etc*); **saisir qn au c.,** to collar s.o., to seize s.o. by the scruff of the neck; **la police lui mit la main au c.,** the police arrested him; **un c. monté,** a stiff-necked *or* strait-laced person; **elle est très c. monté,** she is very prim (and proper); **(b)** short cape (*of fur etc*); **(c)** neck (*of tooth, screw, violin etc*); shoulder (*of racket etc*); *Bot* neck, collar (*of mushroom etc*); *Culin* **c. de mouton,** neck *or* scrag of mutton; **(d)** *MecE etc* flange, collar, fillet (*of pipe etc*); **(e)** snare, noose (*for trapping small animals*); **prendre des lapins au c.,** to snare rabbits.

colleter [kɔlte] *v* (**je collette, n. colletons; je colletterai**) **1** *vt* to collar (*s.o.*), to seize (*s.o.*) by the collar. **2 se colleter** *vpr* to tussle; **se c. avec qn,** to tussle *or* grapple with s.o., to come to grips with s.o.; **se c. avec les difficultés,** to struggle *or* grapple with problems.

colleur, -euse [kɔlœr, -øz] **1** *n* **(a)** (*personne qui colle*) gluer, paster; **c. d'affiches,** billsticker; **(b)** sizer (*of paper etc*); **(c)** *Scol F* examiner. **2** *nf Cin* **colleuse,** film splicer, splicing unit.

collier [kɔlje] *nm* **(a)** (*bijou*) necklace, necklet; **c. de perles,** pearl necklace, string of pearls; **c. de fleurs,** necklace *or* garland of flowers;

(b) collar chain (*of order etc*); **c. de chien,** dog collar; **cheval de c.,** draught horse; **cheval franc du c.,** a willing *or* hard-working horse; *Fig* **elle a toujours été franche du c.,** she's always been very frank and open; *Fig* **donner un coup de c.,** to put one's back into it, to make a special effort; *Fig* **reprendre le c.,** to get back into harness; **c. de barbe,** narrow beard, fringe of beard;

(c) *MecE* collar, ring; *Tech* (*de renfort*) clip; **c. de serrage,** clamping ring, clamp; **c. de fixation,** bracket, clip; **c. de frein,** brake band; **c. de palier,** bearing collar;

(d) *Zool* collar, ring (*on birds etc*); **pigeon à** *ou* **au c.,** ringed *or* ring-necked pigeon;

(e) *Culin* neck (*of beef, mutton*).

collimateur [kɔlimatœr] *nm Astron* collimator, laying prism; *Opt* collimating lens; *Fig* **attention, je vous ai dans mon c.,** careful, I've got my eye on you.

colline [kɔlin] *nf* hill; **petite c.,** hillock.

collision [kɔlizjɔ̃] *nf* collision, impact; **entrer en c. avec qch,** to collide with *or* run into sth; *Fig* **c. des intérêts,** clash of interests; **c. nucléaire,** nuclear collision.

collocation [kɔlɔkɑsjɔ̃] *nf* **(a)** *Jur* (establishing the) order of priority of creditors (*in bankruptcy*); **(b)** *Ling* collocation.

collodion [kɔlɔdjɔ̃] *nm Ch etc* collodion.

colloïdal, -aux [kɔlɔidal, -o] *adj Ch etc* colloidal.

colloïde [kɔlɔid] *adj & nm Ch* colloid, gel.

colloque [kɔlɔk] *nm* **(a)** (*conférence*) seminar; **(b)** *F* conversation, confab; **avoir un c. avec qn,** to have a confab with s.o.; **être en c.,** to be having a confab.

collusion [kɔlyzjɔ̃] *nf Jur etc* collusion.

collusoire [kɔlyzwar] *adj Jur* collusive.

collutoire [kɔlytwar] *nm Pharm* mouth wash.

collyre [kɔlir] *nm Pharm* eyewash, eye lotion.

colmatage [kɔlmataʒ] *nm* **(a)** filling in (*of potholes in road*

etc); plugging (up) (*of hole etc*); *Mil* consolidation (*of position*); **(b)** *Agr* warping (*of land*).
colmater [kɔlmate] *vt* **(a)** to fill in (*potholes in road etc*); to plug (up) (*hole etc*); *Mil* to consolidate (*position*); **(b)** *Agr* to warp (*land*).
colo [kɔlo] *nf F abrév* **colonie de vacances.**
colocataire [kɔlɔkatɛr] *n* joint tenant, co-tenant.
Colomb [kɔlɔ̃] *nm* **Christophe C.,** Christopher Columbus.
colombage [kɔlɔ̃baʒ] *nm Constr* half-timbering; **maison en c.,** half-timbered house.
colombe [kɔlɔ̃b] *nf* (*oiseau*) *& Pol Fig* dove; **c. biset,** rock pigeon; *F* **ma c.,** my (little) dove.
Colombie [kɔlɔ̃bi] *nf* **(a)** Colombia; **(b) la C. britannique,** British Columbia.
colombien, -ienne [kɔlɔ̃bjɛ̃, -jɛn] **1** *adj* Colombian. **2** *n* **C.,** Colombian.
colombier [kɔlɔ̃bje] *nm* (*pigeonnier*) dovecot(e), pigeon loft.
colombophile [kɔlɔ̃bɔfil] **1** *adj* pigeon-fancying, pigeon-fancier's. **2** *n* pigeon fancier.
colombophilie [kɔlɔ̃bɔfili] *nf* pigeon fancying *or* breeding.
colon¹ [kɔlɔ̃] *nm* **(a)** (*pionnier*) colonist, settler; **(b)** (*enfant dans une colonie*) child at a holiday camp; **(c)** farmer, smallholder.
colon² *nm Mil Arg* colonel; **ben, mon c.!,** well, I'm damned!
côlon [kolɔ̃] *nm Anat* colon.
colonel [kɔlɔnɛl] *nm Mil* colonel; *Mil Av* group captain; *Mil* **oui mon c.,** yes Colonel.
colonelle [kɔlɔnɛl] *nf Mil* colonel's wife; *Mil Av* group captain's wife.
colonial, -iale, -iaux [kɔlɔnjal, -jo] **1** *adj* colonial. **2** *nm* (*habitant*) colonial; (*soldat*) soldier of the colonial troops. **3** *nf Hist Mil* **la coloniale,** the Colonial Army.
colonialisme [kɔlɔnjalism] *nm Pol* colonialism.
colonialiste [kɔlɔnjalist] *adj & n Pol* colonialist.
colonie [kɔlɔni] *nf* **(a)** (*lieu*) colony, settlement; **vivre aux colonies,** to live in the colonies; **administrations des colonies,** administration *or* government of the colonies, colonial administration; **c. de vacances,** children's holiday camp *or Am* vacation camp; **envoyer ses enfants en c.,** to send one's children to (holiday) camp; **la c. anglaise de Paris,** the English colony in Paris; **c. pénitentiaire,** penal settlement *or* colony; **(b)** colony (*of animals*).
colonisateur, -trice [kɔlɔnizatœr, -tris] **1** *adj* colonizing (*nation etc*). **2** *n* colonizer.
colonisation [kɔlɔnizɑsjɔ̃] *nf* colonization, settlement; *Fig* **la c. du centre-ville par les publicitaires,** the invasion of the town centre by advertising.
coloniser [kɔlɔnize] *vt* to colonize, to settle (*region*).
colonnade [kɔlɔnad] *nf Archit* colonnade.
colonne [kɔlɔn] *nf* **(a)** *Archit* column, pillar; **c. Morris,** = pillar used to advertise forthcoming events; **rangée de colonnes,** row of columns, line of pillars; *Fig* **c. de l'État,** a pillar of the state; **lit à colonnes,** four-poster bed; *Aut* **c. de direction,** steering column; *Anat* **c. vertébrale,** spinal column; **c. de mercure,** column of mercury; **c. d'eau,** waterspout; **c. de fumée,** column *or* plume of smoke; *Nau* **c. d'habitacle,** binnacle;
(b) c. montante, *Ind* rising main, riser (pipe); *El* service cable, service conductor, riser;
(c) *Mil* column; **c. par deux/trois/quatre,** column of twos/threes/fours; **c. de secours,** relief (column); **c. de véhicules en marche,** column of moving vehicles; *Nau* **en c.,** line ahead; *Pol* **cinquième c.,** fifth column;
(d) (*d'un dictionnaire, journal*) column; *Journ* **écrire une c.,** to write *or* have a column; *Journ* **cinq colonnes à la une,** a front-page five-column spread; *Math* **dans la c. des dizaines,** in the tens column; **des colonnes de chiffres/de noms,** columns of figures/names.
colonnette [kɔlɔnɛt] *nf Archit* little column, colonnette.
colophane [kɔlɔfan] *nf* rosin, colophony.
coloquinte [kɔlɔkɛ̃t] *nf* **(a)** (*plante*) colocynth, bitter apple; **(b)** *Arg* (*tête*) nut, bonce.
colorant [kɔlɔrɑ̃] **1** *adj* colouring, *US* coloring (*matter etc*). **2** *nm* **(a)** (*pour teindre*) colouring, dye; **(b)** (*alimentaire*) colouring (agent); **sirop garanti sans c.,** syrup guaranteed free from (artificial) colour(s).
coloration [kɔlɔrɑsjɔ̃] *nf* **(a)** (*fait de colorer*) colouring, *US* coloring, staining; **se faire faire une c.,** to have one's hair tinted; *Fig Litt* **la tristesse donnait une c. inhabituelle à sa voix,** sadness had altered his tone of voice; **(b)** colour(ing), *US* coloring (*of skin*).
coloré [kɔlɔre] *adj* coloured, *US* colored; **teint c.,** florid *or* ruddy complexion; *Fig* **style c.,** colourful style.
colorer [kɔlɔre] **1** *vt* to colour, *US* to color, to stain, to tinge, to tint; **c. qch en vert,** to colour sth green; *Fig* **c. un récit,** to lend colour to a tale; *Fig* **c. ses préjugés,** to disguise one's prejudices. **2 se colorer** *vpr* (*of fruit etc*) to colour; (*of face*) to colour, to become flushed; **sa voix s'est colorée de tendresse,** a note of tenderness crept into his voice.
coloriage [kɔlɔrjaʒ] *nm* (*action*) colouring, *US* coloring; **(b)** (*dessin*) coloured drawing; **album** *ou* **livre de c.,** colouring (in) book.
colorier [kɔlɔrje] *vt* (*impf & pr sub* **n. coloriions, v. coloriiez**) to colour, *US* to color (*map, drawing*).
coloris [kɔlɔri] *nm* shade; colour(ing), *US* color(ing) (*of painting, fruit etc*); **c. du style,** brilliance *or* richness of style; *Com* **carte de c.,** shade card; **disponible en quatre c.,** available in four shades *or* colours; (*combinaison de couleurs*) available in four colourways.
coloriste [kɔlɔrist] *n* **(a)** *Beaux-Arts* colourist, *US* colorist; **(b)** colourer, *US* colorer, painter (*of postcards, toys etc*); **(c)** (*coiffeur*) hairdresser specializing in tinting.
colossal, -aux [kɔlɔsal, -o] *adj* colossal, gigantic, huge.
colossalement [kɔlɔsalmɑ̃] *adv* colossally.
colosse [kɔlɔs] *nm* colossus, giant; *Fig* **c'est un c.!,** he's a giant (of a man)!
colostomie [kɔlɔstɔmi] *nf Chir* colostomy; **subir une c.,** to have a colostomy.
colportage [kɔlpɔrtaʒ] *nm* hawking, peddling (*of goods*); **c. de fausses nouvelles,** rumour mongering.
colporter [kɔlpɔrte] *vt* to hawk, to peddle (*goods*); to retail, to spread (*news*); to spread (*rumours*).
colporteur, -euse [kɔlpɔrtœr, -øz] *n* door-to-door salesman, hawker, pedlar; *Péj* **c. de nouvelles,** gossip monger.
colposcopie [kɔlpɔskɔpi] *nf Méd* colposcopy.
colt [kɔlt] *nm* Colt ®.
coltinage [kɔltinaʒ] *nm* porterage, carrying (*of heavy loads on one's back*).
coltiner [kɔltine] **1** *vt* to carry (*heavy loads*) on one's back. **2 se coltiner** *vpr F* **se c. qn/qch,** to get stuck *or* lumbered *or* landed with s.o./sth.
coltineur [kɔltinœr] *nm* porter (who carries heavy loads); **c. de charbon,** coal heaver.
columbarium [kɔlɔ̃barjɔm] *nm* columbarium.
col(-)vert [kɔlvɛr] *nm* (*oiseau*) mallard; (*pl cols-verts*).
colza [kɔlza] *nm* (*plante*) rape (seed), colza, coleseed; **huile de c.,** rapeseed oil, colza oil.
coma [kɔma] *nm Méd* coma; **être dans le c.,** to be in a coma; **il est dans un c. dépassé,** he's brain dead.
comateux, -euse [kɔmatø, -øz] *Méd* **1** *adj* comatose. **2** *n* **un c.,** a patient in a coma.
combat [kɔ̃ba] *nm* **(a)** *Mil* combat, fight, battle, engagement, action; **c. corps à corps,** hand-to-hand fight(ing); **c. aérien,** aerial combat, dog fight; **c. naval,** naval engagement *or* action; **c. terrestre,** land operation; **tenue de c.,** battle dress, *US* combat fatigues; **c. de rue,** street fight(ing); **engager le c.,** to go into action (**avec qn,** against s.o.); **mettre hors de c.,** to disable, to put out of action, to cripple; **hors de c.,** (*person*) hors de combat, disabled; (*equipment*) out of action; **(b)** (*dispute*) fight(ing), quarrel(ling); **c. de boxe,** boxing match; **c. de coqs,** cockfight; **(c)** *Fig* conflict, struggle; contest (*of wits etc*); **c. d'intérêts,** clash of interests; **c. contre la mort,** fight against death; **le c. contre l'inflation/le racisme,** the battle *or* fight against inflation/rac(ial)ism; **c'est un c. quotidien,** it's a daily struggle.
combatif, -ive [kɔ̃batif, -iv] **1** *adj* combative, pugnacious; **esprit c.,** fighting spirit. **2** *n* battler, fighter; **il n'a rien de c.,** he's no fighter.
combativité [kɔ̃bativite] *nf* combativeness, pugnacity.
combattant [kɔ̃batɑ̃] **1** *adj* fighting, combatant; *Mil* **unité combattante,** combatant *or* fighting unit. **2** *nm* **(a)** (*soldat*) combatant, fighter; *Mil* (*en service actif*) soldier on active service; (*qui combat*) soldier in a fighting unit; **anciens combattants,** ex-servicemen, *Am* veterans; **(b)** (*dans une dispute*) fighter, brawler; **(c)** (*coq*) game cock *or* fowl; **(d)** (*oiseau*) ruff.
combattre [kɔ̃batr] *v* (*conj like* **battre**) **1** *vt* to combat, to fight (against), to contend with, to battle with (*enemy, disease, temptation, opinion etc*). **2** *vi* to fight, to strive, to struggle; **c. pour/contre qn/qch,** to fight for/against s.o./sth.
combe [kɔ̃b] *nf Géog* coomb, anticlinal valley.
combien [kɔ̃bjɛ̃] **1** *adv* (*& conj when introducing a clause*) **(a)** how (much)!; **si tu savais c. je t'aime!,** if you knew

how much I love you!; **j'ai pu constater c. tu avais changé,** I could see (just) how much you'd changed, I could see how changed you were;

(b) (*en nombre*) how (many)!; **c. de gens!,** what a lot of people!; **c. de fois?,** how many times?, how often?; **c. sont-ils?,** how many of them are there?; **je ne sais pas c. il y en a,** I don't know how many of them there are; **c. de fois faudra-t-il le lui dire?,** how often *or* how many times will he have to be told?;

(c) (*en quantité*) how much?; **c. vous dois-je?,** how much do I owe you?; **(c'est) c.?,** *F* **ça fait c.?,** how much is it?, how much does that come to *or* make?; **depuis c. de temps est-il ici?,** how long has he been here?; **c. y a-t-il d'ici à Londres?,** how far is it (from here) to London?; **à c. sommes-nous de Paris?,** how far are we from Paris?; **c. vous a-t-il fallu pour venir?,** how long did it take you to come?; **c'est arrivé il y a je ne sais c. de temps,** it happened such a long time ago.

2 *nm inv F* **le c. sommes-nous?,** what's the date (today)?, what's today's date?; **il y a un car tous les c.?,** how often does the bus run?

combientième [kɔ̃bjɛ̃tjɛm] *F* **1** *adj* **tu as été reçu c. à l'examen?,** where did you come (in) in the exam? **2** *n* place; **elle est arrivée la c.?,** where did she come?, what was her place?, where was she placed?

combinaison [kɔ̃binɛzɔ̃] *nf* **(a)** combination, arrangement, grouping (*of letters, ideas etc*); (colour) scheme; *Math Ch* combination; **c. financière,** combine; **la c. gagnante,** (*au tiercé*) the winning combination (of numbers); **la c. du ministère,** the make-up *or* composition of the ministry; **une heureuse c. de couleurs,** a pleasing combination of colours; **(b)** (*solution*) plan, contrivance, scheme; **trouvez une c. pour en sortir!,** find a way of getting out of this!; **(c)** (*de travail*) boiler suit; *Av* one piece flying-suit; (*de femme*) full-length slip; **c. de plongée** *ou* **de planche à voile,** wetsuit; **(d)** combination (*of safe*); **je ne connais pas la c.,** I don't know the combination; **verrou à c.,** combination lock.

combinard, -arde [kɔ̃binar, -ard] *F* **1** *adj* scheming, devious; **il est c.,** he knows all the tricks. **2** *n* plotter, schemer.

combinateur [kɔ̃binatœr] *nm Él* controller; multiple-contact *ou* selector switch; *Rail* switchgroup.

combinatoire [kɔ̃binatwar] *adj* combinative; *Math* combinational.

combine [kɔ̃bin] *nf F* scheme, trick, fiddle; **il a une c. pour entrer sans payer,** he knows a way of getting in without paying; **c'est une bonne c.,** it's a good wheeze *or* scheme; **il faut le mettre dans la c.,** we'll have to bring him in on it *or* put him wise.

combiné [kɔ̃bine] **1** *adj* combined, joint (*action etc*). **2** *nm* **(a)** *Ch* compound; **(b)** (*de téléphone*) receiver; **(c)** (*hi-fi*) radiogram; (*électroménager*) blender, mixer and liquidiser; **(d)** *Ski* combined downhill and slalom competition; **(e)** (*sous-vêtement*) corselette.

combiner [kɔ̃bine] **1** *vt* **(a)** to combine, to unite (*forces etc*); to arrange, to group (*numbers, ideas etc*); *Ch* to combine; **(b)** *F* to contrive, to devise, to think out, to concoct (*plan etc*); **qu'est-ce que tu as combiné?,** what have you dreamed up?; **elle combine un sale coup,** she's plotting something nasty, she's planning a dirty trick. **2 se combiner** *vpr* to combine, to unite (**à, avec,** with).

comble [kɔ̃bl] **1** *nm* **(a)** (*maximum*) height, peak; *Fig* highest point; height (*of happiness, insolence*); depth (*of despair*); height, peak, summit (*of fame etc*); **le c. du ridicule serait de ...,** the height of absurdity would be to ..., to do ... would be the height of absurdity; **pour c. de malheur,** to cap *or* crown it all, **ça c'est le** *ou* **un c.!,** that's the limit *or* last straw!; **elle était au c. de la joie,** she was overjoyed *or* wild with joy *or* beside herself with joy;

(b) *Archit* roof (timbers), roofing; **c. à deux pans,** span roof; **c. brisé,** curb roof; **loger sous les combles,** to live in an attic; *Fig* **de fond en c.,** from top to bottom; **modifier une organisation de fond en c.,** to effect a major shake-up of an organisation, to make sweeping changes in an organisation.

2 *adj* full to bursting, overflowing; (*hall etc*) packed; (*measure etc*) heaped up, piled up; *Th* **salle c.,** house filled to capacity; *Th* **on a fait salle c.,** we had a full *or* capacity house.

comblé [kɔ̃ble] *adj* (*de personne*) happy, contented, satisfied; **il est c.,** he has everything he could wish for.

combler [kɔ̃ble] *vt* **(a)** to fill (up), to fill in (*well, ditch etc*); to make up, to make good (*a loss*); **c. une lacune,** to fill a gap; **c. une besoin,** to satisfy a need; **(b)** to overload, to overwhelm (*s.o., sth*); **c. les vœux de qn,** to fulfil s.o.'s desires; **vous me comblez,** you are too kind; **c. qn de cadeaux,** to shower s.o. with gifts.

comburant [kɔ̃byrɑ̃] **1** *adj Ch etc* combustive. **2** *nm* combustive agent; oxidant.

combustibilité [kɔbystibilite] *nf* combustibility.

combustible [kɔ̃bystibl] **1** *adj* combustible; **assemblage d'éléments combustibles,** fuel assembly. **2** *nm* fuel; propellant (*for rocket*); **refaire sa provision de c., se ré-approvisionner en c.,** to refuel; **c. nucléaire,** nuclear fuel; **c. liquide,** liquid fuel.

combustion [kɔ̃bystjɔ̃] *nf* combustion, burning; **poêle à c. lente,** slow combustion stove; **c. vive,** external combustion; **moteur à c. interne,** internal combustion engine.

Côme [kom] *nf* Como; **le lac de C.,** lake Como.

come-back [kɔmbak] *nm* (*d'une vedette*) come-back; **faire un c.-b.,** to make a come-back.

comédie [kɔmedi] *nf* **(a)** *Th* comedy; **c. de mœurs,** comedy of manners; **c. musicale,** musical (comedy); **la c. et la tragédie,** comedy and tragedy; *Fig* **c'est un vrai personnage de c.,** (*qu'on ne prend pas au sérieux*) the man's a buffoon; **jouer la c.,** to act in a play; *Fig* to put on an act; **allons! pas de c.!,** come on, stop acting!; **c'est toujours la même c.,** it's always the same, the same thing happens every time, it's the same old story; **(b)** *Arch* play.

comédien, -ienne [kɔmedjɛ̃, -jɛn] **1** *n* **(a)** (*acteur*) actor, *f* actress; **comédiens ambulants,** strolling players; **c'est plus un c. qu'un tragédien,** he's more of a comic actor than a tragic one; *F* **c'est une comédienne,** she is always putting on an act, she's a comedian; **(b)** (*child*) show-off. **2** *adj* theatrical; **il est très c.,** he's very theatrical *or* affected; **être plus c. que tragédien,** to be more of a comic than a tragic actor.

comédon [kɔmedɔ̃] *nm* blackhead.

comestible [kɔmɛstibl] **1** *adj* edible, eatable; **denrées comestibles,** comestibles, food. **2** *nmpl* **comestibles,** food.

comète [kɔmɛt] *nf* **(a)** *Astron* comet; (*feu d'artifice*) sky rocket; **l'année de la C.,** the Comet year (1811); **du vin de la c.,** excellent wine; *Fig* **tirer** *ou* **faire des plans sur la c.,** to build castles in Spain, to indulge in pipe-dreams; **(b)** (*tranchefile*) headband.

comice [kɔmis] *nm* **(a) c. agricole,** agricultural association; **comices agricoles,** agricultural show; **(b)** *Fr Hist* **comices,** electoral meeting.

comics [kɔmiks] *nmpl* comic strips, cartoon strips, *esp Am F* the funnies.

comique [kɔmik] **1** *adj* **(a)** comic (*actor, author, part etc*); **le genre c.,** comedy; **(b)** comic(al), funny, ludicrous (*story, face etc*). **2** *nm* **(a)** (*genre*) comedy; (*acteur*) comic actor; (*boute-en-train*) comic, comedian; **(b) le c. de l'histoire c'est que ...,** the funny part *or* the joke is that ... .

comiquement [kɔmikmɑ̃] *adv* comically.

comité [kɔmite] *nm* committee, board; **faire partie d'un c.,** to sit on a committee; **c. consultatif,** advisory board *or* commission; **c. d'enquête,** board of enquiry; *Ind* **c. d'entreprise,** joint production committee; **C. international olympique,** International Olympics Committee; *Th* **c. de lecture,** reading *or* selection committee; **c. secret,** secret session; **être en petit c.,** to be a select party *or* an informal gathering; **dîner en petit c.,** small (intimate) dinner party.

commandant, -ante [kɔmɑ̃dɑ̃, -ɑ̃t] **1** *adj* **(a)** (*qui dirige*) commanding, in command of; **(b)** (*autoritaire*) authoritarian, *F* bossy. **2** *nm* **(a)** (*officier*) commander, commanding officer (*of unit etc*); commandant (*of camp, base etc*); *Nau* captain (*of ship*) (*whatever his rank*); **c. en chef,** commander-in-chief; *Nau* executive officer, first lieutenant; *Av* **c. de bord,** captain; **(b)** (*rang*) *Mil* major; *Mil Av* squadron leader; **c. en chef des forces aériennes,** ≈ Marshal of the Royal Air Force. **3** *nf* **commandante,** wife of a commandant.

commande [kɔmɑ̃d] *nf* **(a)** *Com* order; **faire** *ou* **passer une c.,** to place *or* put in an order; **fait sur c.,** made to order; **on ne peut pas rire sur c.,** you can't laugh to order; **ouvrage écrit sur la c. de l'éditeur,** work commissioned by the publisher; **payable à la c.,** cash with order; **livrer une c.,** to deliver an order; *Fig* **sourire de c.,** forced smile;

(b) *MecE* control, operation; (*dispositif*) control; (*mécanisme*) drive, driving (gear); **bouton de c.,** control knob; **c. à distance,** remote control; **c. manuelle/à pied,** hand *or* manual/foot control; **c'est à c. manuelle,** it has manual controls, it is manually controlled; **levier de c.,** control *or* operating lever; *Av* control column; **prendre les commandes,** (*d'un avion etc*) to take over the controls; (*d'une société etc*) to take control; **avion à double c.,**

dual-control plane; *Él* **machine à c. électrique,** electrically driven machine; **à c. vocale,** voice-activated.

commandement [kɔmɑ̃dmɑ̃] *nm* **(a)** (*ordre*) command, order; *Mil Nau* order, (word of) command; *Jur* summons to pay before execution; *Rel* **les Dix Commandements,** the Ten Commandments; **(b)** (*pouvoir*) authority, command; **avoir/prendre le c.,** to be in/to take command; **avoir le c. sur ...,** to have authority over ...; *Mil Nau* **c. en chef,** command-in-chief; **c. suprême, haut c.,** higher command (*of British forces*); high command (*of French, German etc forces*).

commander [kɔmɑ̃de] **1** *vt* **(a)** to command; *Mil etc* to command, to order (*sth*); to be in charge *or* command of (*men*); **il commande deux cents hommes,** he has two hundred men under his command; **il n'aime pas qu'on le commande,** he doesn't like being ordered about;

(b) to order (*sth*); **c. qch à qn,** to give s.o. an order for sth, to order sth from s.o.; **c. des marchandises/un dîner,** to order goods/a dinner; **on peut c. le petit déjeuner par téléphone?,** can we order breakfast by phone?; **c. une peinture,** to commission a painting;

(c) (*exiger*) to demand, to command; **c. le respect/ l'attention,** to command respect/attention;

(d) (*dominer*) to command, to dominate; **le fort commande la vallée,** the fort commands *or* dominates the valley;

(e) *MecE* to control, to operate (*motion, valve etc*); to drive (*machine, shaft etc*); *Ordinat* to drive; *Ordinat* **commandé par menu,** menu-driven.

2 *vi* **c. à qn/qch,** to command *or* govern *or* control s.o./ sth; **je lui ai commandé de se taire,** I told *or* ordered him to be quiet; **c. à son impatience,** to control *or* curb one's impatience; **qui est-ce qui commande ici?,** who's in charge here?, who's giving the orders here?

3 se commander *vpr* **(a) ces choses-là ne se commandent pas,** (*sont incontrôlables*) these things are beyond our control; (*ne se font pas sur commande*) these things cannot be done to order; **il faut apprendre à vous c.,** you must learn to control yourself;

(b) (*donner accès à*) to give access to; **les pièces de cet appartement se commandent,** the rooms of this flat communicate with each other.

commanderie [kɔmɑ̃dri] *nf* commander's residence.

commandeur [kɔmɑ̃dœr] *nm* commander (*of the Légion d'Honneur*).

commanditaire [kɔmɑ̃ditɛr] *adj & nm Com* **(associé) c.,** = sleeping partner.

commandite [kɔmɑ̃dit] *nf Com* **(a) (société en) c.,** mixed liability company, limited partnership; **(b)** (*fonds*) interest of *or* capital invested by sleeping partner(s).

commandité [kɔmɑ̃dite] *adj & nm Com* **(associé) c.,** active partner.

commanditer [kɔmɑ̃dite] *vt Com* to subscribe capital to (*firm etc*) as sleeping partner; to finance (*enterprise etc*).

commando [kɔmɑ̃do] *nm Mil* commando (unit).

comme¹ [kɔm] *adv* **(a)** as; (*de la même manière*) like; **faites c. moi,** do as I do; **il a été vendu c. esclave,** he was sold as a slave; **se conduire c. un fou,** to behave like a madman; **tout c. un autre,** (just) like anyone else; **nous étions c. un seul homme,** we were as one man; **sortir tous les jours, été c. hiver,** to go out every day, summer and winter alike; **c. qui dirait,** as one might say; **c. dit l'autre,** as they say; *F* **c. ci c. ça,** so so; **(alors) c. ça vous venez de Paris?,** (and) so you come from Paris?; **rusé comme un (vieux) renard,** (as) sly *or* cunning as a fox; **doux c. un agneau,** (as) gentle as a lamb; **haut c. trois pommes,** knee-high to a grasshopper; **blanc c. neige,** snow-white, white as snow; *F* **drôle c. tout,** awfully *or* terribly funny; **c. par hasard,** as if by chance; **c. prévu,** as planned; *F* **c'est c. qui dirait une erreur,** you might say it is a mistake; **il a été puni c. de juste,** he's got his just desserts, he's been punished as he deserved; **quelque chose c. deux cents personnes,** something like two hundred people;

(b) c. (si), (**si** *is expressed only before a finite verb*) as if, as though; **il travaille c. s'il avait vingt ans,** he works as if he were twenty; **ils faisaient c. si rien ne s'était passé,** they acted as if *or* though nothing had happened; **c. si de rien n'était,** as if nothing had happened; **il leva la main c. pour me frapper,** he lifted his hand as if to strike me; *F* **c'est tout c.,** it amounts to the same thing;

(c) *F* **elle est anglaise, c. quoi elle ne comprend pas le français,** she's English, so she doesn't understand French; **elle a dit non, c. quoi elle était invitée ailleurs,** she said no because she'd been invited somewhere else;

(d) (*tel*) such as; **les bois durs c. le chêne et le noyer,** hard woods such as oak and walnut; **avoir qn c. ami,** to have s.o. as a friend;

(e) (*immediately before finite verbs*) as; **faites c. il vous plaira** *ou* **vous voulez,** do as you please; **insolent c. il est,** insolent as he is; **c'est arrivé à peu près c. je l'avais prédit,** it happened more or less as I predicted; **c. il faut,** proper(ly), comme il faut; *F* **il est très c. il faut,** he's well-brought up; he's very prim and proper; **tiens-toi c. il faut,** sit properly; (*tiens-toi droit*) don't slouch, sit up;

(f) (*pour*) as, in the way of; **qu'est-ce que vous avez c. légumes?,** what have you (got) in the way of vegetables?; **je l'ai eue comme professeur,** I had her as my *or* a teacher; **ce n'est pas mal c. film,** it's not bad as films go;

(g) *int* how!; **c. vous avez grandi!,** how you've grown!; **c. elle est bête!,** how stupid she is!; **c. je suis content de vous voir!,** how glad I am to see you!, *Am* am I glad to see you!;

(h) *F* (= **comment**) how; **il y est arrivé Dieu sait c.,** he managed it, God (only) knows how; **voilà c. elle est,** that's just like her, that's her way;

(i) j'ai c. une idée que ..., I have a sort of idea that ...; **elle a eu c. une hésitation avant de répondre,** she seemed to hesitate before answering; **il était c. pantelant,** he seemed to be gasping for breath.

comme² *conj* **(a)** (*puisque*) as, seeing that; **c. vous êtes mon ami je vous dirai tout,** since you're my friend I'll tell you everything; **(b)** (*alors que*) (just) as; **c. il allait frapper on l'arrêta,** (just) as he was about to strike he was arrested.

commémoratif, -ive [kɔmemɔratif, -iv] *adj* commemorative (**de,** of); memorial (*service etc*); **monument c.,** memorial.

commémoration [kɔmemɔrasjɔ̃] *nf* commemoration; **en c. d'un événement/d'une personne,** in commemoration of an event/a person.

commémorer [kɔmemɔre] *vt* to commemorate.

commençant, -ante [kɔmɑ̃sɑ̃, -ɑ̃t] **1** *adj* beginning, early. **2** *n* beginner; **manuel pour grands commençants,** handbook for adult beginners.

commencement [kɔmɑ̃smɑ̃] *nm* beginning, start; **commencements,** beginnings, initial stage(s); **au c.,** at the beginning *or* start *or* outset; **du c. jusqu'à la fin,** from beginning to end, from start to finish; **il faut un c. à tout,** you've got to start somewhere; **c. des travaux/de la rue,** beginning *or* start of the work(s)/street; *F* **c'est le c. de la fin,** (*quand quelqu'un tousse*) that sounds bad.

commencer [kɔmɑ̃se] *v* (**je commençai(s); n. commençons**) **1** *vt* to begin, to start (on), *Fml* to commence; **c. les hostilités** *ou* **la guerre,** to commence hostilities, to start a war; **c. un traitement,** to go on *or* start a course of treatment; **le mot qui commence la phrase,** the word which starts the sentence; **c. un élève en chimie,** to ground a pupil in chemistry.

2 *vi* to begin, to start; **c. à** *ou* **de faire qch,** to begin *or* start *or Fml* commence to do sth, to begin *or* start *or Fml* commence doing sth; **il commence à pleuvoir,** it's beginning *or* starting to rain; **la pluie vient de c.,** it's just started raining; **c. par faire qch,** to begin *or* start by doing sth; **commençons par votre frère/le commencement,** let's start *or* begin with your brother/at the beginning; **par où c.?,** (*il y a tellement de choses à dire*) where to start?, where should *or* shall I begin?; **nous allions c. sans vous,** (*eating etc*) we were going to start *or* begin without you; **commencez!,** fire away!; **je commence à en avoir assez!,** I've had just about enough!; *F* **ça commence à bien faire,** it's getting a bit too much, it's getting beyond a joke; **l'année commence le 1er janvier,** the year begins on January 1st; *Iron* **ça commence bien!,** that's a great start!; **pour c., je dois vous dire ...,** to begin *or* start with *or* first of all, I must tell you ... .

commensal, -aux [kɔmɑ̃sal, -o] *n* **(a)** (*hôte*) table companion; **(b)** *Biol* commensal.

commensurable [kɔmɑ̃syrabl] *adj* commensurable (**avec,** with, to).

comment [kɔmɑ̃] **1** *adv* **(a)** *interr* how; **c. allez vous?,** how are you?; **c. (dites-vous)?,** what did you say, I beg your pardon?; **c. faire?,** what can *or* should I *or* we *etc* do?; **c. s'appelle-t-il?,** what's his name?; **c. dit-on soleil en japonais?,** how do you say 'sun' in Japanese?; **c. est-il, ce garçon?,** what sort of young man is he?; **c. peut-il me dire des choses pareilles?,** how can he talk to me like that *or* say such things to me?; **c. se fait-il que vous soyez toujours en retard?,** how *or* why is it that you're always late?;

(b) (*affirmation*) the way (how), how; **elle me dira c.**

faire, she'll tell me how (to do it); **il faut voir c. elle lui parle,** you should see *or* hear the way she speaks to him; **faire qch n'importe c.,** to do sth in a slapdash manner *or F* anyhow *or* any old how;

(c) *int* what!, why!; **c.! vous n'êtes pas encore parti!,** what, haven't you gone yet!; **mais c. donc!,** why of course, by all means!; *F* **ça vous a plu? et c.!,** did you like it? and how! *or* you bet!

2 *nm inv* **les pourquoi et les c.,** the whys and wherefores.

commentaire [kɔmɑ̃tɛr] *nm* **(a)** (*remarque*) comment, remark; **un c. pertinent,** a pertinent observation; *F* **cela se passe de c.,** it speaks for itself, it's obvious; *F* **sans c.!,** no comment!; *F* **pas de c.!,** that's final!, I don't want any comments (from you)!; *Péj* **les commentaires vont bon train,** comment is rife; **(b)** *Rad TV* commentary; (*explication*) commentary, annotations (**sur,** on); *Scol* **c. de texte,** textual commentary.

commentateur,-trice [kɔmɑ̃tatœr, -tris] **1** *n Rad TV* (news) commentator. **2** *nm Littér* commentator, annotator.

commenter [kɔmɑ̃te] *vt* **(a)** to comment on, to annotate (*text etc*); *Rad TV* **c. une course,** to give the commentary on a race; **c. l'actualité** *ou* **les événements,** to comment on current events; **(b)** to comment on, to criticize (*s.o., sth*).

commérage [kɔmeraʒ] *nm F* piece of gossip; **commérages,** gossip(ing), tittle-tattle.

commerçant,-ante [kɔmɛrsɑ̃, -ɑ̃t] **1** *adj* commercial; business (*district*); **rue très commerçante,** busy shopping street; **un sourire c.,** a PR-type smile; **peu c.,** bad at business. **2** *n* shopkeeper; **c. en gros/en détail,** wholesaler/retailer; **les commerçants,** tradespeople.

commerce [kɔmɛrs] *nm* **(a)** commerce, trade, business; **c. en** *ou* **de gros/détail,** wholesale/retail trade; **c. intérieur/extérieur,** home/foreign trade; **ça se trouve dans le c.,** you can buy it in the shops; **maison de c.,** firm; **voyageur de c.,** commercial traveller, sales rep(resentative); **port de c.,** commercial port; **faire du c.,** to trade, to be in business; **livres de c.,** the books; **le c.,** (*activité*) trade; (*secteur*) the commercial world; **le petit c.,** small shopkeepers, small shops; **cela fait marcher le c.,** it's good for trade; **hors c.,** not for (general) sale; **c. des chevaux,** horse dealing; **(fonds de) c.,** business; **ouvrir un c.,** to open a business; **(b)** *Péj* (*trafic*) traffic, trade; **faire c. de son honneur/nom,** to trade on one's honour/name; **(c)** *Arch & Litt* intercourse, dealings; **avoir** *ou* **être en c. avec qn,** to be in touch *or* relationship with s.o., to have dealings with s.o.; **être d'un c. agréable,** to be easy to get on with *or* pleasant to deal with; **fuir le c. des hommes,** to flee the company of men.

commercer [kɔmɛrse] *vi* (**je commerçai(s); n. commerçons**) to trade, to deal (**avec,** with).

commercial, -iale, -iaux [kɔmɛrsjal, -jo] **1** *adj* commercial, trading, business (*relations*); *Péj* **film c.,** commercial film; **suivre une formation commerciale,** to take a business studies course. **2** *nf Aut* **commerciale,** (*voiture*) estate car, *Am* station wagon; (*camionnette*) small van. **3** *n* **c'est un c.,** he's in sales.

commercialement [kɔmɛrsjalmɑ̃] *adv* commercially.

commercialisable [kɔmɛrsjalizabl] *adj* marketable.

commercialisation [kɔmɛrsjalizasjɔ̃] *nf* marketing.

commercialiser [kɔmɛrsjalize] *vt* to commercialize (*art etc*); to market (*product*).

commère [kɔmɛr] *nf* gossip, busybody.

commettant [kɔmetɑ̃] *nm* **(a)** *Com Jur* principal (*to a deal*); **(b)** *Pol* **commettants,** constituents.

commettre [kɔmɛtr] *v* (*conj like* **mettre**) **1** *vt* **(a)** (*accomplir*) to commit (*crime, sin, injustice*); **c. une erreur,** to make a mistake; **(b)** *Jur* **c. qn à qch,** to appoint s.o. to sth, to put s.o. in charge of sth; **(c)** *Arch* (= **compromettre**) to expose; **c. sa réputation,** to risk one's reputation; **(d)** *Arch* **c. qch à qn,** to commit *or* entrust sth to s.o. *or* to s.o.'s keeping, to entrust s.o. with sth; **(e)** *Tech* to lay, to twist (*rope*). **2 se commettre** *vpr* to commit oneself; **il eut soin de ne pas se c.,** he was careful not to commit himself.

comminatoire [kɔminatwar] *adj* **(a)** *Jur* comminatory (*decree etc*); **(b)** threatening (*letter*).

commis [kɔmi] *nm* **(a)** (*employé*) clerk; (*dans un magasin*) shop assistant; **c. aux écritures,** book-keeper; **les grands c.,** the higher civil servants; **(b)** *Arch* **c. voyageur,** commercial traveller.

commisération [kɔmizerasjɔ̃] *nf* commiseration; **éprouver/avoir de la c.,** to feel *or* have sympathy; **témoigner de la c. à qn,** to show sympathy to s.o..

commis-greffier [kɔmigrefje] *nm* assistant to the clerk of court; (*pl commis-greffiers*).

commissaire [kɔmisɛr] *nm* **(a) c. (de police),** ≈ (police) superintendent; **c. principal,** ≈ chief superintendent; *Sp etc* steward; *Nau* **c. de la Marine,** supply and secretariat officer, *US* supply officer; *Nau* **c. du bord,** purser; *Fin* **c. aux comptes,** auditor; *Can* **c. d'école,** school commissioner; *Sp* **c. des courses,** race steward; **(b)** member of a commission, commissioner; **c. près du Conseil d'État,** government representative on the Council of State; **c. du gouvernment,** government representative; **c. parlementaire,** parliamentary commissioner.

commissaire-priseur [kɔmisɛrprizœr] *nm* auctioneer; (*pl commissaires-priseurs*).

commissariat [kɔmisarja] *nm* **(a) c. (de police),** police station; **(b)** (*fonction*) commissionership; **c. des comptes,** auditorship; *Nau* **c. du bord,** pursership; **(c) c. de la marine** *ou* **maritime,** supply and secretariat branch; **c. de l'air,** = air department (*of Ministry of Defence*).

commission [kɔmisjɔ̃] *nf* **(a)** (*course*) message, errand; (*achat*) shopping, purchase; **faire des commissions,** to run errands; **j'ai fait toutes mes commisssions,** I've done all my shopping; *Enf* **la petite/grosse c.,** number one/two;

(b) (*réunion*) committee, board; **c. d'enquête,** board *or* committee of inquiry; **c. parlementaire,** parliamentary commission; **c. paritaire,** joint commission (*with both sides equally represented*); **c. d'arbitrage,** arbitration committee; **renvoi d'un texte en c.,** referral of a bill to a committee; **C. des opérations de Bourse,** = Stock Exchange watchdog; *US* ≈ Securities and Exchange Commission;

(c) (*pourcentage*) *Com* commission, allowance; *Fin* brokerage; **c. de deux pour cent,** commission of two per cent; **3% de c.,** 3% commission;

(d) (*charge*) commission; *Jur etc* charge, warrant; **avoir la c. de faire qch,** to be commissioned *or* empowered to do sth; *Com* **maison de c.,** firm of commission agents, commission agency; **vente à c.,** sale on commission.

commissionnaire [kɔmisjɔnɛr] *nm* **(a)** messenger; (*in hotels, theatres*) commissionaire; **(b)** *Com* commission agent, broker; **c. exportateur/importateur,** export/import agent; **c. de transport** *ou* **de roulage,** forwarding agent, carrier; **c. en douane,** customs agent *or* broker.

commissionner [kɔmisjɔne] *vt* to commission; to appoint (*s.o.*) as buyer on commission.

commissure [kɔmisyr] *nf Anat Bot etc* commissure; corner (*of the lips etc*).

commode [kɔmɔd] **1** *adj* **(a)** (*pratique*) convenient, suitable, opportune (*moment etc*); handy (*tool etc*); convenient, comfortable (*house etc*); **c'est très c. pour ranger ses affaires,** it's very handy for storing things in; **(b)** (*facile*) easy; **ce que vous me demandez là n'est pas c.,** what you are asking me isn't very easy; *F* **c'est trop c.,** that's too easy; **(c)** accommodating, easy, easy-going, adaptable (*disposition etc*); **c. à vivre,** easy to live with; *F* **il n'est pas c.,** he's a tough *or* an awkward customer; **elle n'est pas c. ce matin,** she's not in the best of moods this morning. **2** *nf* chest of drawers.

commodément [kɔmɔdemɑ̃] *adv* (*assis*) comfortably; (*situé*) conveniently.

commodité [kɔmɔdite] *nf* **(a)** convenience; **pour plus de c.,** for convenience sake; **les commodités de la vie (moderne),** the comforts of (modern) life; **(b) commodités,** (*dans un musée etc*) toilets, *Am* rest rooms.

commodore [lɔmɔdɔr] *nm Mil* commodore.

commotion [kɔmosjɔ̃] *nf* **(a)** commotion, disturbance; **c. politique,** political upheaval; *Méd* **c. cérébrale,** concussion; **(b)** (*émotion*) shock, violent emotion.

commotionner [kɔmosjɔne] *vt* **(a)** *Méd* to cause a state of shock; **il a été fortement commotionné,** he was severely concussed, he had severe concussion; **(b)** (*choquer*) to shake, to shock; **cette nouvelle m'a commotionné,** this news has given me a terrible shock.

commuable [kɔmɥabl] *adj Jur* commutable (*sentence etc*).

commuer [kɔmɥe] *vt Jur* to commute (*penalty*) (**en,** to).

commun [kɔmœ̃] **1** *adj* **(a)** common (**à,** to); **jardin c. à deux maisons,** garden shared by two houses; **salle commune,** common room; (*in hospital*) ward; **maison commune,** town hall, municipal buildings; **avoir des intérêts communs,** to have interests in common, to have common interests; **faire cause commune avec qn,** to make common cause *or* join forces with s.o.; **amis communs,** mutual friends; **ceci est un travail c.,** this was a joint project; **il n'y a rien de c. entre eux,** they've (got) nothing in common; **c'est sans commune mesure,** there's no possible comparison; **vie commune,** community life; (*de couple*) conjugal life; **la vie commune n'est pas facile,** living together isn't easy; **d'un c. accord,** with one accord; *Math* **dénominateur c.,** common denominator; **en c.,** in common; **travailler en c.,** to work together *or* jointly; **rechercher le bien c.,** to seek the common good; **vivre en c.,** to live communally; **mettre l'argent/les ressources en c.,** to pool money/resources;

(b) common, universal, general (*custom, opinion etc*); common, usual, ordinary, everyday (*occurrence etc*); **le sens c.,** common sense; *Gram* **nom c.,** common noun; **lieu c.,** commonplace; **il est d'une force peu commune,** he's unusually strong;

(c) (*vulgaire*) common, vulgar; **terme c.,** common *or* vulgar expression.

2 *nm* **(a)** common run, generality (*of persons etc*); **le c. des mortels,** the ordinary *or* average man; **hors du c.,** out of the ordinary;

(b) les communs, outhouses, outbuildings.

communal, -ale, -aux [kɔmynal, -o] **1** *adj* **(a)** (*conjoint*) common, communal (*land, property*); **(b)** (*de la commune*) ≈ council (*property etc*); **école communale,** ≈ primary school. **2** *nmpl* **les communaux,** common land. **3** *nf* **communale,** ≈ primary school.

communard, -arde [kɔmynar, -ard] **1** *adj Hist* of the Commune. **2** *n* **(a)** *Hist* communard; **(b)** *Péj* (*communiste*) commie, red.

communautaire [kɔmynotɛr] *adj* communal; *Pol* (*aide, politique*) community; *surtout CE* Community; **centre c.,** community centre.

communauté [kɔmynote] *nf* **(a)** (*collectivité*) community; *Rel* community, order; **c. de travail,** working community; **c. urbaine,** urban community; **C. urbaine de Montréal,** Montreal Urban Community; **vivre en c.,** to live communally; **fonder une c.,** to found a community; **C. Économique Européenne,** European Economic Community; **c. de hippies,** hippie commune; **elle est partie vivre en c.,** she's gone off to live in a commune; **(b)** community (*of interests, ideas etc*); *Jur* joint estate (*of husband and wife*).

commune [kɔmyn] *nf* **(a)** *Admin Fr* (*smallest territorial division*) commune, *approx* ≈ parish, municipality; **(b)** *Hist Fr* free town; **(c) la Chambre des Communes, les Communes,** the (House of) Commons; **(d)** *Hist Fr* (*in 1789 and 1871*) **la C.,** the Commune.

communément [kɔmynemɑ̃] *adv* commonly.

communiant, -ante [kɔmynjɑ̃, -ɑ̃t] *n Rel* communicant; **premier c., première communiante,** person taking his *or* her first communion.

communicable [kɔmynikabl] *adj* communicable (*disease etc*); *Jur* transferable (*right*); (*file etc*) that can be made available.

communicant [kɔmynikɑ̃] *adj* communicating (*rooms etc*).

communicateur,-trice [kɔmynikatœr, -tris] *adj* connecting (*wire etc*).

communicatif,-ive [kɔmynikatif, -iv] *adj* **(a)** (*qui parle*) communicative, talkative; **peu c.,** uncommunicative; **(b)** infectious (*laughter etc*).

communication [kɔmynikasjɔ̃] *nf* **(a)** communication; **avoir des problèmes de c.,** to have problems *or* difficulties (in) communicating; **il n'a pas le don de la c.,** he's not very good at communicating; **c. d'idées,** interchange of ideas; **entrer** *ou* **se mettre en c. avec qn,** to get in touch with s.o.; **mettre deux personnes en c.,** to put two people in touch with each other; **communications de masse,** mass media; **études de c.,** media studies; **travailler dans la c.,** to work in the media; **voies de c.,** lines of communication, communication routes; **toutes les communications sont coupées,** all lines of communication are cut (off); *Tél* **c. téléphonique,** (telephone) call; **c. en P.C.V.,** reverse *or* transferred charge call, *Am* collect call; **mettez-moi en c. avec M. Martin,** put me through to Mr Martin; **je vous passe la c.,** I'll put you through; **vous avez la c.,** you're through; **la c. est mauvaise,** the line is bad; *Ordinat* **progiciel de c.,** communications *or F* comms package;

(b) (*message*) communication, message; **transmettre une c. à qn,** to pass on a message to s.o.; **portes de c.,** communicating doors; **faire une c. (à une société savante),** to read a paper (to a learned society); *Jur* **donner c. des pièces,** to communicate *or* give discovery of documents.

communier [kɔmynje] *vi* (*impf & pr sub* **n. communiions, v. communiiez**) *Rel* to receive Holy Communion.

communion [kɔmynjɔ̃] *nf* **(a)** (*communauté*) communion; **appartenir à la même c.,** to belong to the same persuasion *or* faith; **être en c. de sentiments avec qn,** to be in sympathy with s.o.; **être en c. avec la nature,** to commune with nature; **(b)** *Rel* (Holy) Communion; **la première c.,** first (Holy) Communion; **faire sa première c.,** to make one's first (Holy) Communion.

communiqué [kɔmynike] *nm* press release, official statement, communiqué.

communiquer [kɔmynike] **1** *vt* **(a)** to communicate, to impart, to convey (*information etc*); **c. qch à qn,** to bring sth to s.o.'s notice, to inform s.o. of sth; **c. qch par écrit à qn,** to communicate sth in writing to s.o.; **c. une maladie à qn,** to pass on *or* give an illness to s.o.; **c. ses impressions,** to pass on *or* communicate one's impressions;

(b) (*in library*) to issue (*a book*).

2 *vi* to be in communication; **avoir du mal à c. avec qn,** to find it hard *or* difficult to communicate with s.o.; **refus total de c.,** total unwillingness to communicate; **porte qui communique au** *ou* **avec le jardin,** door that leads into the garden; **toutes les chambres communiquent,** all the bedrooms communicate with one another; **canal qui fait c. deux rivières,** canal that connects two rivers.

3 se communiquer *vpr* **(a)** (*se transmettre*) to spread; **l'incendie s'est communiqué aux maisons voisines,** the fire has spread to the neighbouring houses;

(b) *Vieilli* to be communicative.

communisant, -ante [kɔmynizɑ̃, -ɑ̃t] **1** *adj* communist (*newspaper etc*). **2** *n* **c'est un c.,** he's a communist sympathizer, he's a fellow traveller.

communisme [kɔmynism] *nm* communism.

communiste [kɔmynist] **1** *n* communist; **être c.,** to be a communist. **2** *adj* communist; **la Chine c.,** communist China.

commutateur [kɔmytatœr] *nm Él* **(a)** commutator (*of dynamo etc*); **(b)** (*bouton*) switch; changeover *or* throw over switch; **c. sélecteur,** selector switch; *Ordinat* **c. de données,** data switch.

commutatif, -ive [kɔmytatif, -iv] *adj Jur Math* commutative.

commutation [kɔmytasjɔ̃] *nf* **(a)** *Jur* commutation (*of penalty*); **(b)** (*changement*) substitution, commutation; *Gram* replacement, substitution; **la c. de deux employés,** the swapping of duties *or* jobs of *or* by two employees; **(c)** *Él* changeover.

commutatrice [kɔmytatris] *nf Él* rotary converter, transformer.

commuter [kɔmyte] **1** *vt* **(a)** *Jur* to commute (*penalty*); **(b)** *Él* to commutate, to switch over, to change over (*current*); **c. les fonctions,** to swap duties. **2** *vi* **deux employés qui vont c.,** two employees who are going to swap jobs *or* duties; **faire c. deux éléments,** to commute two elements.

Comores [kɔmɔr] *nf Géog* **les îles C.,** the Comoro Islands.

compacité [kɔ̃pasite] *nf* compactness (*of soil etc*); density (*of metal*); denseness (*of crowd*).

compact [kɔ̃pakt] *adj* **(a)** (*de petit format*) compact; **voiture compacte,** small (compact) car, *Am* compact; **disque c.,** compact disc; **(b)** compact, close, dense (*mass, formation etc*); **majorité compacte,** large *or* solid majority; **poudre compacte,** pressed (face-)powder.

compact-disc [kɔ̃paktdisk] *nm* compact disc.

compagne [kɔ̃paɲ] *nf* **(a)** (*camarade*) (female) companion; **c'était ma c. d'école,** I was at school with her; **(b)** *Litt* partner (in life); wife; (*of animals*) mate.

compagnie [kɔ̃paɲi] *nf* **(a)** (*présence*) company, companionship; **n'avoir qu'un vieux chien pour toute c.,** to have only an old dog for company; **tenir c. à qn,** to keep s.o. company; **je vais vous fausser c.,** this is where I leave you; **dame de c.,** (lady's) companion; **être en c. d'amis proches,** to be in the company of close friends, to be with close friends; **rechercher la c. d'amis,** to seek the company of friends; **aller de c. avec ...,** to go (hand in hand) with ...; **ils ont voyagé de c.,** they travelled together;

(b) (*société*) company, party, society; **toute la c.,** everybody, all of them *or* us; **fréquenter la bonne/mauvaise c.,** to keep good/bad company; **une jeune fille de bonne c.,** a well-brought up girl;

(c) *Com Th etc* company; **c. de navigation,** shipping company; **compagnies républicaines de sécurité,** state security police (*in France*); **c. aérienne,** airline; **c. d'assurances,** insurance company *or* society; *Com* **la maison Thomas et C.,** (the firm of) Thomas and Company (*usu* and Co.); *Rel* **la C. de Jésus,** the Society of Jesus;

(d) *Mil* company; **c. de débarquement,** landing party; **(e)** covey (*of partridges*).

compagnon [kɔ̃paɲɔ̃] *nm* **(a)** (*camarade*) companion, comrade; *Ind* (workman's) mate; **cet enfant a besoin d'un c.,** the child needs a companion; **c. d'études,** fellow student; **c. de voyage,** travelling companion; **c'était mon c. de jeu,** I used to play with him; *Pol* **c. de route,** fellow traveller; **c. d'infortune/de misère,** companion in misfortune/in suffering; **(b)** (*ouvrier*) journeyman; **(c)** *F* (*plante*) **c. blanc/rouge,** white/red campion; **(d)** *Litt* companion, husband.

comparable [kɔ̃parabl] *adj* comparable (**à, avec qch/qn,** to, with sth/s.o.); **ce n'est pas c.,** there's no comparison.

comparablement [kɔ̃parabləmɑ̃] *adv* comparably; in comparison (**à,** with).

comparaison [kɔ̃parɛzɔ̃] *nf* **(a)** comparison; **soutenir la c.,** to bear *or* stand comparison; **tu peux faire la c. toi-même,** you can judge *or* see *or* make the comparison for yourself; **hors de toute c.,** beyond compare; **il est sans c. le plus grand,** he is by far the tallest; **en c. à lui tu ne sais pas grand chose,** compared with him, you don't know very much; **par c. au premier, ce film est excellent,** compared with the first film, this one's excellent; **c. n'est pas raison,** comparisons are odious; *Gram* **adverbe de c.,** adverb of comparison, comparative adverb; **les degrés de c.,** the degrees of comparison; **(b)** *Litt* simile.

comparaître [kɔ̃parɛtr] *vi* (*conj like* **paraître**) *Jur* **c. (en justice),** to appear before a court of justice; **c. en personne,** to appear in person; **c. par avoué,** to be represented by counsel; **c. comme témoin,** to appear as a witness; **être appelé à c.,** to be summoned to appear.

comparant, -ante [kɔ̃parɑ̃, -ɑ̃t] *Jur* **1** *adj* appearing (*before the court etc*). **2** *n* appearer.

comparatif, -ive [kɔ̃paratif, -iv] **1** *adj* comparative. **2** *nm Gram* **adjectif au c.,** comparative adjective; **c. d'infériorité,** comparative of lesser degree.

comparatiste [kɔ̃paratist] *n Ling* specialist in comparative linguistics; *Littér* specialist in comparative literature, comparativist.

comparativement [kɔ̃parativmɑ̃] *adv* comparatively; **il fait bien plus beau aujourd'hui, c. à hier,** it's much nicer today compared with yesterday.

comparé [kɔ̃pare] *adj* comparative (*anatomy, history etc*).

comparer [kɔ̃pare] **1** *vt* to compare (**à,** to; **avec,** with); **il compare les étoiles filantes à des cheveux,** he likens *or* compares shooting stars to strands of hair; **c. deux objets/textes,** to compare two objects/texts. **2 se comparer** *vpr* to be compared; **ça ne se compare pas,** there's no comparison.

comparse [kɔ̃pars] *n Cin* extra; *Th* supernumerary, *F* super; *Péj* associate, stooge; (*personne sans importance*) person playing a minor role in an undertaking; **rôle de c.,** walk-on part.

compartiment [kɔ̃partimɑ̃] *nm* compartment (*of railway carriage etc*); partition (*of box, drawer etc*); square (*of chessboard etc*); **c. de première classe,** first-class compartment.

compartimentage [kɔ̃partimɑ̃taʒ] *nm* partitioning; (*d'une administration etc*) compartmentalization.

compartimenter [kɔ̃partimɑ̃te] *vt* **(a)** (*diviser en espaces*) to partition, to divide into compartments; **(b)** (*d'administrations etc*) to compartmentalize.

comparution [kɔ̃parysjɔ̃] *nf Jur* appearance (*before the court*); **non-c.,** non-appearance, default.

compas [kɔ̃pa] *nm* **(a)** *Math* (pair of) compasses; **c. à pointes sèches,** dividers; **c. quart de cercle,** wing compasses; **c. de réduction,** reduction compasses; *F* **tout faire au c.,** to do everything with precision; **allonger le** *ou* **son c.,** to quicken one's pace; *Fig* **avoir le c. dans l'œil,** to have an accurate eye; *MecE etc* **c. d'épaisseur,** callipers; **(b)** *Nau etc* **c. (de mer),** (mariner's) compass; **c. de route,** steering compass; **c. gyroscopique,** gyrocompass.

compassé [kɔ̃pase] *adj* stiff, formal (*manner*).

compasser [kɔ̃pase] *vt* **(a)** to measure (*distances on map etc*) with compasses; *Nau* to prick (*chart*); **(b)** *Litt* to regulate, to control (*one's actions etc*).

compassion [kɔ̃pɑsjɔ̃] *nf* compassion, pity; **avec c.,** compassionately.

compatibilité [kɔ̃patibilite] *nf Ordinat etc* compatibility.

compatible [kɔ̃patibl] *adj Ordinat etc* compatible (**avec,** with); **ces deux fonctions ne sont pas compatibles,** these two functions are incompatible *or* not compatible.

compatir [kɔ̃patir] *vi* **c. au chagrin de qn,** to sympathize with *or* feel for s.o. in his grief.

compatissant [kɔ̃patisɑ̃] *adj* compassionate, sympathetic (**pour,** to, towards).

compatriote [kɔ̃patriɔt] *n* compatriot, fellow countryman *or* countrywoman.

compensateur, -trice [kɔ̃pɑ̃satœr, -tris] **1** *adj* compensating (*spring, magnet etc*); *Él* equalizing (*current*); balancing (*dynamo*); **indemnité compensatrice,** compensatory payment, compensation; **pendule c.,** compensation pendulum. **2** *nm* (pressure) equalizer; compensator, balancer (*of compass etc*); *Av* trimming tab, trimmer; (*d'horloge*) compensation pendulum.

compensation [kɔ̃pɑ̃sasjɔ̃] *nf* **(a)** compensation (*of loss*); **en c. de mes pertes,** to compensate for my losses; **il y a c.,** that makes up for it; **en c. vous avez droit à deux jours de vacances,** to compensate *or* to make up for it, you can have two days off; *Jur* **c. des dépens,** sharing of the costs; *Fin* **chambre de c.,** clearing house; **(b)** *Él etc* equalization, balancing (*of forces etc*); **loi de c.,** law of large numbers; **(c)** *Nau* adjustment (*of compass*); **(d) caisse de c.,** = equalization fund for payments such as child benefit, sickness benefit, pensions etc; **(e)** *Psy* compensation.

compensatoire [kɔ̃pɑ̃satwar] *adj* compensatory.

compenser [kɔ̃pɑ̃se] **1** *vt* **(a)** to compensate, to make up for (*sth*); to offset (*fault etc*); *Jur etc* to compensate, to balance, to set off (*debts*); **c. une perte,** to make good a loss; **talon compensé,** built-up heel; **son efficacité compense son mauvais caractère,** his efficiency makes up for his bad temper; **c. les dépens,** to divide out the costs; **(b)** *Nau* to adjust (*compass*). **2 se compenser** *vpr* to complement each other.

compère [kɔ̃pɛr] *nm* **(a)** accomplice, associate (*of conjuror etc*); **(b)** *F Vieilli* comrade, crony; **un bon c.,** a pleasant companion.

compère-loriot [kɔ̃pɛrlɔrjo] *nm* (*pl compères-loriots*) **(a)** (*oiseau*) golden oriole; **(b)** *Méd* stye (*on the eyelid*).

compétence [kɔ̃petɑ̃s] *nf* **(a)** (*capacité*) competence, ability, proficiency, skill (**pour faire qch,** to do sth); **avoir toutes les compétences requises pour faire qch,** to have all the necessary skills to do sth; **(b)** *Jur* competence, competency, jurisdiction, powers (*of court of justice etc*); **cela ne rentre pas dans** *ou* **cela n'est pas de sa c.,** that does not come within his province, that is outside his scope; **sortir de sa c.,** to exceed one's powers.

compétent [kɔ̃petɑ̃] *adj Jur etc* competent (*tribunal, authority etc*); **c. en matière de finance,** conversant with finance; **il est d'un âge c. pour signer,** he is of a suitable *or* proper age to sign; **je ne suis pas c. en la matière,** I am not competent to speak on the subject; **il est très c.,** he's very competent; *Com* **adressez-vous au service c.,** apply to the appropriate department *or* the department concerned.

compétiteur, -trice [kɔ̃petitœr, -tris] *n* competitor.

compétitif, -ive [kɔ̃petitif, -iv] *adj Com* competitive (*prices etc*).

compétition [kɔ̃petisjɔ̃] *nf* **(a)** (*rivalité*) competition, rivalry; **être en c. avec qn,** to be in competition with s.o., to compete with s.o.; **il y a toujours eu une petite c. entre eux,** there's always been a bit of rivalry *or* competition between them; **c. entre partis politiques,** political rivalry; **(b)** *Sp* contest, match; **c. sportive,** sporting event; **faire de la c.,** to go in for competitive sport; **du ski de c.,** competitive *or* competition skiing.

compétitivité [kɔ̃petitivite] *nf* competitiveness.

compilateur, -trice [kɔ̃pilatœr, -tris] **1** *nm Ordinat* compiler; **c. croisé,** cross-compiler. **2** *n* **(a)** compiler; **(b)** *Péj* plagiarist.

compilation [kɔ̃pilasjɔ̃] *nf* **(a)** *Ordinat* compilation; **(b)** (*enregistrement*) compilation; **(c)** (*de documents*) compiling, compilation; **(d)** *Péj* plagiarism.

compiler [kɔ̃pile] *vt* **(a)** *Ordinat* to compile; **(b)** (*réunir*) to compile; **(c)** *Péj* to plagiarize.

complainte [kɔ̃plɛ̃t] *nf* **(a)** *Arch* plaint, lamentation; **(b)** *Littér Mus* (plaintive) ballad, lay.

complaire [kɔ̃plɛr] *v* (*conj like* **plaire**) **1** *vi Litt* **c. à qn,** to please *or* humour *or* gratify s.o.. **2 se complaire** *vpr* to delight (in), to revel (in); **se c. dans qch/à faire qch,** to take *or* find pleasure *or* delight in sth/in doing sth; **se c. dans son idée,** to be satisfied with one's idea.

complaisamment [kɔ̃plɛzamɑ̃] *adv* **(a)** (*avec obligeance*) obligingly, willingly; **(b)** (*sourire*) complacently, smugly.

complaisance [kɔ̃plɛzɑ̃s] *nf* **(a)** (*bienveillance*) complaisance, obligingness; **faire qch par c.,** to do sth out of kindness; **faire qch par c. pour qn,** to do sth to oblige s.o.; **auriez-vous la c. de le faire?,** would you be so good *or* so kind as to do it?; *Com* **billet** *ou* **effet de c.,**

accommodation bill; **on a fini par lui délivrer un certificat de c.,** he was finally given *or* issued with a medical certificate (*to which he was not entitled*); **(b)** (*autosatisfaction*) complacence, complacency, (self-)satisfaction; **il s'écoute avec c.,** he likes the sound of his own voice; **ton plein de c.,** self-satisfied *or* smug tone; **sourire de c.,** smug smile; **sourire d'un air de c.,** to smile smugly, to give a smug smile.

complaisant [kɔ̃plɛzɑ̃] *adj* **(a)** (*bienveillant*) obliging, accommodating (**envers, pour,** towards); willing (*person, character etc*); **prêter une oreille complaisante à qn,** to lend a sympathetic *or* willing ear to s.o.; **mari c.,** complaisant *or* indulgent husband; **(b)** (*satisfait*) complacent, smug, self-satisfied (*smile etc*).

complément [kɔ̃plemɑ̃] *nm* rest, remainder; *Gram* complement; *Gram* extension (*of the subject, of the predicate*); *Biol Ch Math* complement; **faire le c. de qch,** to complement sth; **demander un c. d'information,** to ask for more *or* additional information; *Gram* **c. circonstanciel de temps,** adverbial phrase of time; *Gram* **c. (d'objet),** object (of verb); *Gram* **c. d'objet direct/indirect,** direct/indirect object.

complémentaire [kɔ̃plemɑ̃tɛr] *adj* complementary (*angle, colour etc*); **pour tout renseignement c., s'adresser à ...,** for further information apply to ....

complet, -ète [kɔ̃plɛ, -ɛt] **1** *adj* **(a)** complete, entire, whole (*outfit, works etc*); **rapport très c.,** very full *or* comprehensive report; **se faire une idée complète de la situation,** to get an overview *or* overall picture of the situation; **deux jours complets,** two full days; **examen c.,** full *or* thorough examination, **voyager dans le plus c. anonymat,** to travel completely incognito; **un c. abruti,** a complete moron; **c'est loin d'être c.,** it's a long way *or* far from being complete; **athlète c.,** all-round athlete; **échec c.,** complete *or* total *or* utter failure; **collection complète d'un auteur,** a full set of an author's works; **formation très complète,** thorough training; *F* **c'est c.!,** that's the last straw!, that's the limit!; **pain c.,** wholemeal bread; **café** *ou* **thé c.,** = continental breakfast; **elle a dû attendre deux jours complets,** she had to wait two full *or* whole days;

(b) full (*bus, Th house etc*); **'c.',** full (up); (*outside boarding house, motel etc*) no vacancies.

2 *nm* **(a) c. (-veston),** suit;

(b) au c., complete, full; **nous étions présents au grand c.,** we turned out in full force.

complètement [kɔ̃plɛtmɑ̃] *adv* completely, wholly, totally, fully; utterly (*ruined, lost, idiotic*); stark (*naked*); **finir c. un pot de crème,** to finish off a pot of cream.

compléter [kɔ̃plete] *v* (**je complète, n. complétons; je compléterai**) **1** *vt* to complete (*sth*), to make (*sth*) complete; **c. sa garde-robe/une collection,** to complete one's wardrobe/a collection; **c. sa formation,** to complete *or* round off one's training; **c. une somme,** to make up a sum (of money). **2 se compléter** *vpr* to be complementary; **les deux volumes se complètent,** the two volumes complement one another; **ils se complètent bien l'un l'autre,** they're well-matched, they complement each other.

complétif, -ive [kɔ̃pletif, -iv] *adj & n F Gram* **proposition complétive,** noun clause.

complexe [kɔ̃plɛks] **1** *adj* complex, complicated (*character, question etc*); *Gram* **sujet c.,** compound subject; *Math* **nombre c.,** compound number. **2** *nm* **(a)** complex; **le c. industriel de la vallée du Rhône,** the Rhone valley industrial complex; **c. commercial/sportif,** a shopping/sports centre *or* complex; **vivre dans un grand c.,** to live in a complex (of flats); **(b)** *Psy* **c. d'infériorité,** inferiority complex; *F* **ça me donne des complexes,** that *or* it gives me a complex *or* makes me feel inferior; *F* **elle va se faire un c.,** she'll get a complex; *F* **avoir des complexes,** to be hung up (**à cause de,** about).

complexé [kɔ̃plɛkse] *adj F* full of complexes, mixed up, hung up (**à cause de,** about).

complexer [kɔ̃plɛkse] *vt F* to give (*s.o.*) a complex.

complexifier [kɔ̃plɛksifje] **1** *vt* to make complex. **2 se complexifier** *vpr* to become (more) complex.

complexion [kɔ̃plɛksjɔ̃] *nf Litt* constitution, disposition, temperament.

complexité [kɔplɛksite] *nf* complexity.

complication [kɔ̃plikasjɔ̃] *nf* **(a)** (*ennui*) complication; **faire des complications,** to complicate the issue, to cause complications *or* problems; **il y a eu une c.,** there's been a complication; **(b)** (*de situation etc*) complexity, intricacy; **(c)** *Méd* **complications,** complication(s); **il y a eu des complications,** complications have set in.

complice [kɔ̃plis] **1** *adj* accessory (**de,** to); accomplice, abettor (**de,** of); **être c. d'une crime,** to be party to a crime; **c. en adultère,** co-respondent; **des regards complices,** knowing glances. **2** *n* accomplice; **les complices ont été arrêtés,** the accomplices have been arrested.

complicité [kɔ̃plisite] *nf* complicity; *Jur* aiding and abetting; *Jur* **agir de c. avec qn,** to act in collusion *or* complicity with s.o..

complies [kɔ̃pli] *nfpl Rel* compline.

compliment [kɔ̃plimɑ̃] *nm* **(a)** (*félicitation*) compliment; **compliments,** compliments, greetings; **mes compliments au chef,** my compliments to the chef; **faire des compliments à qn,** to pay s.o. compliments; **(je vous fais) mes compliments,** I congratulate you; *Iron* **mes compliments!,** congratulations!; **faites-lui mes compliments,** (please) give him my regards; **(b)** (*discours*) speech of congratulation.

complimenter [kɔ̃plimɑ̃te] *vt* to compliment (**de, sur,** on); to congratulate (**de, sur,** on); **il faut la c. pour son nouveau travail,** we must congratulate her on her new job.

complimenteur, -euse [kɔ̃plimɑ̃tœr, -øz] *Péj* **1** *adj* obsequious (*person*); **discours c.,** flattering speech. **2** *n* flatterer.

compliqué, -ée [kɔ̃plike] **1** *adj* complicated, elaborate, intricate (*mechanism etc*); involved (*style etc*); **je n'y arrive pas, c'est trop c.,** I can't do it, it's too difficult; *F* **mais c'est pas c.!,** it's simple!; **personne compliquée,** difficult person. **2** *n F* difficult individual.

compliquer [kɔ̃plike] **1** *vt* to complicate; **ça risque de c. les choses,** that may *or* might well complicate matters *or* make things tricky. **2 se compliquer** *vpr* to become involved, to become complicated; (*of plot*) to thicken; **il se complique l'existence,** he's making life difficult for himself; **la situation se complique,** the situation is getting complicated.

complot [kɔ̃plo] *nm* plot, conspiracy; **tramer un c.,** to hatch a plot; **chef de c.,** ringleader; **mettre qn dans le c.,** to let s.o. into the secret *or* plot.

comploter [kɔ̃plɔte] **1** *vi* to plot, to conspire (**contre,** against); **c. de faire qch,** to plot to do sth. **2** *vt* to plot; *F* **qu'est-ce que vous complotez là?,** what are you up to now? **3 se comploter** *vpr* **je me demande ce qui se complote par ici,** I wonder what's being hatched *or* plotted here.

comploteur [kɔ̃plɔtœr] *nm* plotter.

compo [kɔ̃po] *nf Scol F* test; (*plus important*) exam.

componction [kɔ̃pɔ̃ksjɔ̃] *nf* **(a)** *Rel* (*contrition*) compunction; **(b)** *Iron* **avec c.,** gravely, solemnly.

comportement [kɔ̃pɔrtəmɑ̃] *nm* behaviour, *US* behavior; **psychologie du c.,** behaviourism, *US* behaviorism; **type de c.,** behaviour pattern.

comportemental, -aux [kɔ̃pɔrtəmɑ̃ta, -o] *adj* behavioural, *US* behavioral.

comporter [kɔ̃pɔrte] **1** *vt* **(a)** to allow, to allow of, to admit of (*sth*); **règle qui comporte des exceptions,** rule that allows of exceptions; **(b)** (*comprendre*) to comprise, to include (*sth*); **objectif qui comporte quatre éléments,** lens that comprises *or* is made up of four elements; **les inconvénients que cela comporterait,** the difficulties this would involve *or* entail. **2 se comporter** *vpr* to behave, to act (**vis-à-vis de, envers,** towards); **se c. mal,** to misbehave; **se c. en** *ou* **comme un lâche,** to act *or* behave like a coward; **comment s'est-elle comportée devant la nouvelle?,** how did she react to the news?; **la voiture se comporte aussi bien sur neige que sur terrain sec,** the car handles equally well on snow or dry ground.

composant, -ante [kɔ̃pozɑ̃, -ɑ̃t] **1** *adj* component, constituent (*part*). **2** *nm* component, constituent. **3** *nf* **composante,** component (*of voltage, force, velocity etc*).

composé, -ée [kɔ̃poze] **1** *adj* **(a)** compound (*pendulum, interest, word, time etc*); *Ch* **corps c.,** compound; **résistance composée,** combined strength; *Gram* **temps c.,** compound tense; **(b)** *Bot* composite (*flower*); **(c)** composed (*attitude etc*). **2** *nm Ch Gram etc* compound. **3** *nfpl Bot* **composées,** Compositae.

composer [kɔ̃poze] **1** *vt* **(a)** to compose (*poem, symphony etc*); *Pharm* to make up (*prescription*); **(b)** *Typ* to set (*type*); *Tél* **c. un numéro,** to dial a number; **(c) les personnes qui composent notre famille,** the people who make up our family, all the members of our family; **(d) c. son visage,** to compose one's features. **2** *vi* **(a)** (*s'entendre*) to compromise, to come to terms (**avec,** with); **(b)** *Mus* to compose; *Scol* to sit an examination. **3 se composer** *vpr*

se c. (de), to be made up (of), to consist (of); **se c. un visage de circonstance,** to put on a suitable expression.

composite [kɔ̃pozit] *adj* composite, heterogeneous; **matériau c.,** composite (material); **un assemblage c.,** a varied *or* heterogeneous collection.

compositeur, -trice [kɔ̃pozitœr, -tris] *n* **(a)** *Mus* composer; **(b)** *Typ* compositor, typesetter.

composition [kɔ̃pozisjɔ̃] *nf* **(a)** composing, composition (*of sonata, poem etc*); construction (*of novel etc*); composition (*of water etc*); making up (*of prescription etc*); **(b)** *Typ* typesetting, composition; **(c)** composition, compound, mixture; **la c. d'un repas,** the composition of a meal; **la c. des équipes n'est pas encore connue,** the teams haven't been announced yet; **(d)** *Mus Litt etc* composition; **(e)** *Scol* essay; (*examen*) test; **(f)** (*arrangement*) arrangement, compromise; **entrer en c. avec qn,** to come to terms with s.o.; **(g) être de bonne c.,** to be good-natured.

compost [kɔ̃pɔst] *nm Agr* compost.

compostage [kɔ̃pɔstaʒ] *nm* (date) stamping, punching (*of ticket etc*).

composter¹ [kɔ̃pɔste] *vt Agr* to compost (*land*).

composter² *vt* to (date) stamp, to punch (*ticket etc*).

composteur [kɔ̃pɔstœr] *nm* **(a)** (*machine*) date stamp; punch; (automatic) ticket puncher; **(b)** *Typ* composing stick.

compote¹ [kɔ̃pɔt] *nf Culin* compote, stewed fruit; *F* **j'ai les jambes/la tête en c.,** my legs feel like jelly/my brain's gone to mush.

compote² *nf Scol F* test; (*plus important*) exam.

compotier [kɔ̃pɔtje] *nm* fruit dish.

compound [kɔ̃pund] *nm Tech* compound.

compréhensibilité [kɔ̃preɑ̃sibilite] *nf* comprehensibility.

compréhensible [kɔ̃preɑ̃sibl] *adj* comprehensible, understandable; **c'est tout à fait c. de sa part,** it's altogether understandable on his part.

compréhensif, -ive [kɔ̃preɑ̃sif, -iv] *adj* **(a)** (*vaste*) comprehensive; **(b)** (*personne*) understanding; **elle s'est montrée très compréhensive là-dessus,** she was very understanding about it.

compréhension [kɔ̃preɑ̃sjɔ̃] *nf* **(a)** comprehension, understanding; **la c. d'un terme,** (range of) meaning of a term; **pour la bonne c. du texte,** (in order) to fully understand the text; **(b)** (*bienveillance*) understanding; **il est plein de c.,** he is full of sympathy *or* understanding.

comprendre [kɔ̃prɑ̃dr] *v* (*conj like* **prendre**) **1** *vt* **(a)** (*par l'esprit*) to understand; **je ne comprends pas ce que vous voulez dire,** I don't understand what you mean, *F* I don't get you; **difficile à c.,** difficult *or* hard to understand; **c. une langue étrangère,** to understand a foreign language; **je n'arrive pas à c. cette phrase,** I can't make sense of this sentence; **c. la portée d'un acte,** to realise *or* understand the consequences of an action; **je ne comprends pas comment/pourquoi il a fait ça,** I don't understand *or* see how/why he did it; **ai-je bien compris que ...?,** am I to understand *or* do you mean to say that ...?; **vous m'avez mal compris,** you've misunderstood me; **on ne te comprend pas,** (*tu parles trop vite*) nobody understands you *or* can make out what you say; **je ne le comprends pas,** (*il est étrange*) I can't understand *or* fathom him out, I can't make him out; **il ne comprend rien de rien,** he hasn't a clue about anything; **tu peux lui expliquer, il comprend les choses,** you can explain to him, he understands about these things; **elle ne comprend pas la plaisanterie,** she can't take a joke; **elle n'a pas compris la plaisanterie,** she didn't get the joke; **elle comprend vite,** she's quick on the uptake, she catches on quick(ly); **tu comprends ce que je t'ai dit?,** did you understand *or* hear me *or* what I said?; **je n'y comprends rien,** I can't make head or tail of it; **c'est à n'y rien c.,** it's incomprehensible; **je lui ai fait c. que ...** + *ind*, I gave him to understand that ...; (*avec autorité*) I made it clear to him that ...; **comment c. ce tableau/ce poème/l'art?,** what is one to make of this picture/this poem/art?;

(b) (*inclure*) to comprise, to include; **service non compris,** service not included; **le prix comprend tous les frais d'hébergement,** the price is fully inclusive of accommodation; **jusqu'à et y compris le 31 décembre,** up to and including December 31st.

2 *vi* to understand; **ah! je comprends!,** oh! I see!; *Can F* **elle est belle, n'est-ce pas? — je comprends!,** she's lovely, isn't she? — you bet! *or* and how!; **tu comprends, on ne pouvait pas se le permettre,** you see, we just couldn't afford it; **elle finira par c.,** she'll understand eventually; **se faire c.,** to make oneself understood; **je comprends bien!,** I can well imagine it!

3 se comprendre *vpr* to understand each other, to get on well together; **ils ne se comprennent pas,** they don't get on (with one another); **se c. soi-même,** to know oneself.

comprenette [kɔ̃prənɛt] *nf F* **il a la c. un peu dure,** he's a bit slow on the uptake.

compresse [kɔ̃prɛs] *nf* compress.

compresseur [kɔ̃prɛsœr] **1** *nm MecE* compressor (*of air, gas, fluid*); (*de moteur*) supercharger. **2** *adj* compressing; *Constr* **rouleau c.,** road roller.

compressibilité [kɔ̃prɛsibilite] *nf* compressibility.

compressible [kɔ̃prɛsibl] *adj* **(a)** (*comprimable*) compressible; **(b)** reducible (*expenses, prison sentence etc*).

compressif, -ive [kɔ̃prɛsif, -iv] *adj* compressive (*bandage etc*).

compression [kɔ̃mprɛsjɔ̃] *nf* **(a)** compression (*of gas, steam etc*); **temps de c.,** compression stroke; **(b)** (*strength of materials*) compression, crushing; **(c)** (*réduction*) restriction, cutback; **c. des dépenses,** spending cuts; **c. de crédit,** credit squeeze; **c. du personnel,** reduction of staff; **mesure de c.,** cutback, reduction, retrenchment.

comprimable [kɔ̃primabl] *adj* compressible.

comprimé [kɔ̃prime] **1** *adj* compressed; **air c.,** compressed air; **outil à air c.,** pneumatic tool. **2** *nm Pharm* tablet; **un c. d'aspirine,** an aspirin.

comprimer [kɔ̃prime] *vt* **(a)** to compress (*gas, artery, Ordinat a file*); **c. la taille,** to squeeze the waist in; **(b)** to curb, to repress, to restrain (*one's feelings etc*); to repress, to hold back (*tears*).

compris [kɔ̃pri] *adj* **bien c.,** (thoroughly) understood; **mal c.,** misunderstood, misinterpreted; **alors, c'est c.?,** so, do you understand *or* have you understood?; **la leçon n'a pas été comprise,** the (point of) lesson wasn't understood.

compromettant [kɔ̃prɔmɛtɑ̃] *adj* compromising (*situation etc*).

compromettre [kɔ̃prɔmɛtr] *v* (*conj like* **mettre**) **1** *vt* **(a)** to compromise (*s.o., s.o.'s reputation etc*); **être compromis dans un crime,** to be implicated in a crime; **(b)** to endanger, to jeopardize (*life, safety etc*); **nos vacances sont compromises,** our holidays are at risk *or* threatened. **2** *vi* to accept arbitration, to compromise. **3 se compromettre** *vpr* to compromise oneself; (*s'engager*) to commit oneself.

compromis [kɔ̃prɔmi] *nm* **(a)** (*arrangement*) compromise, arrangement; **parvenir à un c.,** to reach a compromise, to come to an arrangement; **la robe est un c. entre l'élégance et la décontraction,** the dress is neither too elegant nor too casual; **(b)** *Jur* **mettre une affaire en c.,** to submit an affair for arbitration; **c. de vente,** provisional *or* preliminary sales agreement.

compromission [kɔ̃prɔmisjɔ̃] *nf souvent Péj* **(a)** compromising (*with one's conscience*); surrender (*of principle*); **(b)** (*résultat*) compromise.

comptabiliser [kɔ̃tabilize] *vt* to account for (*sth*), to enter (*sth*) in the accounts, to post (*sth*).

comptabilité [kɔ̃tabilite] *nf* **(a)** book-keeping, accountancy; **c. en partie simple/double,** single-/double-entry book-keeping; **livre de c.,** account book; **méthode de c.,** book-keeping *or* accounting method; **tenir la c. d'une maison,** to keep the books *or* the accounts of a firm; *Ind* **c. de temps (du personnel),** time keeping; **(b)** (*service*) accounts department.

comptable [kɔ̃tabl] **1** *adj* **(a)** *Com etc* book-keeping (*work etc*); **pièce c.,** voucher; **machine c.,** accounting machine; **(b)** (*responsable*) accountable, responsible; **être c. à qn de qch,** to be accountable to s.o. for sth. **2** *nm* accountant, book-keeper; *Can* **c. agréé,** chartered accountant; **expert c.,** chartered accountant; (*vérificateur*) auditor.

comptage [kɔtaʒ] *nm* counting (up), totalling; **c. des votes,** counting *or* telling votes.

comptant [kɔ̃tɑ̃] **1** *adj* **argent c.,** ready money, cash; *F* **prendre qch pour argent c.,** to take sth for gospel truth. **2** *adv* **payer c.,** to pay (in) cash. **3** *nm* cash; **payer** *ou* **acheter au c.,** to pay (in) cash.

compte [kɔ̃t] *nm* **(a)** *Fin* account; **tenir les comptes d'une maison,** to keep the accounts of a firm; **faire ses comptes,** to make up one's accounts, *F* to do one's accounts; **livre de comptes,** account book; **la Cour des Comptes,** = the Audit Office; **versement à c.,** payment on account; **régler son c.,** to settle one's account; *F* **régler son c. à qn,** to settle s.o.'s hash; **avoir un (petit) c. à régler avec qn,** to have a bone to pick with s.o.; **on réglera nos comptes plus tard,** we'll settle up later; **règlement de c.,** settling of accounts; *F* settling of scores *or* accounts; **donner** *ou* **régler son c. à un employé,** (*se mettre* *d'accord*) to settle up with an employee; (*le renvoyer*) to dismiss an employee; **avoir un c. chez qn,** to have an account with s.o.; **mettre un montant sur son c.,** to pay a sum into one's account; **c. en banque** *ou* **bancaire,** bank account; **c. courant, c. chèques,** current account, *Am* checking account; **c. courant postal, c. chèque postal,** = Giro account; **c. permanent,** = credit account, *Am* charge account; **c. (con)joint,** joint account; **être/se mettre** *ou* **s'installer à son c.,** to be/set up in business on one's own (account); **cela n'entre pas en ligne de c.,** that has nothing to do with the matter; **mettre un malheur sur le c. de qn,** to ascribe *or* attribute a misfortune to s.o., to blame s.o. for a misfortune; **apprendre qch sur le c. de qn,** to learn sth about s.o.; **faire qch pour le c. de qn,** to do sth on s.o.'s behalf; **pour mon c., j'aimerais mieux rester ici,** as far as I am concerned, I'd prefer to stay here;

(b) (*calcul*) reckoning, calculation; **faire le c. des dépenses,** to add up expenses; **le c. des morts,** the death toll *or* tally; **le c. y est,** it's the right amount *or* number; **ça ne fait pas le c.,** it doesn't come to the right amount; **c. rond,** round sum; **acheter qch à bon c.,** to buy sth cheap; **cela fait mon c.,** it's just the thing for me, that suits me; **il y trouve son c.,** he gets something out of it, there's something in it for him; **vous êtes loin du c.,** you're wide of the mark; *Fig* **au bout du c.,** after all, when all is said and done, at the end of the day; **en fin de c., tout c. fait,** all things considered, after all, taking everything into account; **à ce c.-là,** in that case; **tenir c. de qch,** to take sth into account *or* consideration; **ne tenir aucun c. de qn/qch,** to ignore *or* disregard s.o./sth; **c. tenu de son assiduité,** considering *or* bearing in mind *or* taking into account his regular attendance; **s'en tirer à bon c.,** to get off lightly; *F* **il a son c.,** (*il en a assez*) he's had enough; (*parce qu'il a bu*) he's had enough, he's had as much as he can carry; *F* **son c. est bon,** he's for it, he'll get what's coming to him;

(c) (*explication*) explanation, justification, account; **demander des comptes à qn,** to call s.o. to account; **elle ne doit de comptes à personne,** she is answerable to nobody; **rendre c. de qch,** to account for sth; **c. rendu,** report; (*littéraire*) (book) review; (*d'une réunion*) minutes; **faire le c. rendu,** (*pendant la réunion*) to take the minutes; (*à la réunion suivante*) to read the minutes; **se rendre c. de qch,** to realize sth, to understand sth; *F* **tu te rends c.!,** would you believe it!;

(d) *Boxe* count; **rester sur le plancher pour le c.,** to be counted out, to be out for the count.

compte à rebours [kɔ̃tar(ə)bur] *nm* countdown; **faire le c. à r.,** to count backwards; to count down (*for space launch*); **le c. à r. précédant Noël a commencé,** the countdown to Christmas has started.

compte-gouttes [kɔ̃tgut] *nm inv Pharm etc* dropper, pipette; **mesurer qch au c.-g.,** to dole sth out in driblets *or* sparingly; **il donne son argent au c.-g.,** he's very sparing with his money.

compter [kɔ̃te] **1** *vt* **(a)** to count (up), to reckon (up), to compute (*numbers etc*); **dix-neuf tous comptés,** nineteen in all *or* all told; **marcher à pas comptés,** to walk with measured tread; **ses jours sont comptés,** his days are numbered; **on ne les compte plus,** we've lost count of them, we can't keep track of them; **elle compte les jours,** she's counting the days; **il y a de cela vingt ans bien comptés,** a good twenty years have passed since then; **sans c. que ...,** not to mention that ..., besides the fact that ...; **il faut c. une heure pour faire cela,** we must allow *or* it will take an hour to do this;

(b) (*donner*) to give, to pay; **c. cent francs à qn,** to pay s.o. a hundred francs;

(c) (*inclure*) to include; **ils étaient vingt, sans c. le père et la mère,** there were twenty of them, not counting the father and mother; **je vous ai tous comptés?,** have I counted you all?; **je le compte parmi mes meilleurs amis,** I number *or* count *or* consider him among my best friends;

(d) (*prévoir*) to allow, to reckon; **j'ai compté deux cents grammes par personne,** I've allowed *or* reckoned on two hundred grammes per person; **elle compte rentrer à dix heures,** she expects *or* intends to be back by *or* at ten o'clock; **c'était sans c. les embouteillages,** that was without allowing for traffic jams *or* holdups.

2 *vi* **(a)** to count; **c. jusqu'à dix,** to count up to ten; **mal c.,** to miscount; **apprendre à c.,** to learn (how) to count; **je veux pouvoir vivre sans c.,** I want to be able to live without having to count the pennies; **il compte parmi les meilleurs,** he's one of the best, he ranks among the best; **à c. de ...,** (reckoning) from ...; *Admin* **à c. du 1er janvier,** to take effect on *or* with effect from January 1st;

(b) (*être important*) to count, to matter; **ce qui compte, c'est le travail,** work is what matters *or* counts; **ça ne compte pas,** that doesn't count *or* matter; **je ne joue pas, je ne compte pas,** I'm not playing, I don't count; *F* **elle compte pour du beurre,** she doesn't count, she counts for nothing;

(c) il faut c. avec le vent, you have to allow for the wind;

(d) tu peux c. sur lui, you can count *or* rely *or* depend on him; **j'y compte bien!,** I should hope so!;

(e) *Can Sp* to score.

compte-tours [kɔ̃ttur] *nm inv* revolution *or* *F* rev counter, tachometer.

compteur [kɔ̃tœr] *nm* meter; **c. d'électricité/à gaz/à eau,** electricity/gas/water meter; **le c. du taxi,** the taximeter, the taxi's meter; **le c. marquait 47 francs,** there was 47 francs on the meter; **relever le c.,** to read the meter; *Aut* **c. de vitesse,** speedometer; **remonter le compteur,** to wind the clock back; **c. kilométrique,** ≈ milometer, *surtout Am* odometer; *Nucl* **c. (de) Geiger,** Geiger counter.

comptine [kɔ̃tin] *nf* counting rhyme.

comptoir [kɔ̃twar] *nm* **(a)** *Com* counter; (*dans un bar*) bar; **garçon de c.,** barman, bartender; **prendre une consommation au c.,** to have a drink at the bar; **(b)** (*cartel*) (marketing) syndicate; **(c)** *Fin* bank; branch (*of bank*); **c. d'escompte,** discount house; **(d)** (*dans un pays éloigné*) trading post.

compulsation [kɔ̃pylsasjɔ̃] *nf* (*d'un ouvrage*) consultation.

compulser [kɔ̃pylse] *vt* to consult (*documents, books etc*).

compulsif, -ive [kɔ̃pylsif, -iv] *adj* compulsive (*drinker etc*); **conduite compulsive,** compulsive behaviour.

compulsion [kɔ̃pylsjɔ̃] *nf* compulsion.

computation [kɔ̃pytasjɔ̃] *nf* computation.

computer [kɔ̃pyte] *vt* to compute.

comte [kɔ̃t] *nm* count; (*en Grande Bretagne*) earl.

comté [kɔ̃te] *nm* **(a)** *Hist* earldom; **(b)** *Admin* county; **(c)** *Can Pol* riding; **(d)** (*fromage*) = type of Gruyère cheese.

comtesse [kɔ̃tɛs] *nf* countess.

con, conne [kɔ̃, kɔn] *Arg* **1** *adj* (*fem form rarely used*) bloody stupid, idiotic; **elle est trop c.!,** she's too stupid for words!; **c. comme la lune** *ou* **un balai,** (*personne*) daft as a brush, complete twerp, bloody idiot; **c. comme la lune,** (*film etc*) bloody stupid. **2** *n* bloody idiot, stupid bastard; **faire le c.,** to fool about; **pauvre c.!,** poor bastard *or* sod!; **t'es vraiment le roi des cons,** you really are an utter *or* a complete prat; **quel c. ce mec!,** what a bloody idiot that guy is!; **ce vélo à la c.!,** (this) damn useless bike. **3** *nm* *Vulg* (*sexe*) cunt, twat.

conard, -arde [kɔnar, -ard] *Arg* **1** *adj* bloody stupid. **2** *nm* silly bugger, damn fool.

conasse [kɔnas] *nf Arg* silly bitch, stupid cow.

concassage [kɔ̃kasaʒ] *nm* crushing, pounding, grinding.

concasser [kɔ̃kase] *vt* to break, to crush (*stone etc*); to grind (*pepper etc*) coarsely.

concasseur [kɔ̃kasœr] **1** *nm* crusher, crushing mill. **2** *adj* **rouleau c.,** crushing roller.

concave [kɔ̃kav] *adj* concave.

concavité [kɔ̃kavite] *nf* concavity; (*d'un objectif*) concave side; (*creux*) hollow, cavity.

concéder [kɔ̃sede] *vt* (**je concède, n. concédons; je concéderai**) **(a)** to concede, to grant, to allow (*privilege etc*); to grant (*land, concession*); **(b) c. qu'on a tort,** to admit that one is wrong; **(c)** *Sp* to concede; **c. un but,** to give away *or* concede a goal.

concentration [kɔ̃sɑ̃trasjɔ̃] *nf* **(a)** *Phys Ch* concentration, concentrating (*of heat etc*); *Nucl* concentration, focusing; **population à haute c.,** high-density *or* dense population; **zone à haute c. de population,** high-density area; **les grandes concentrations urbaines,** conurbations, large urban agglomerations; *Fig* **une grande c. d'oiseaux,** a large concentration *or* population of birds; **la c. des intellectuels dans la capitale,** the concentration of intellectuals in the capital; **camp de c.,** concentration camp; *Typ* **impression à haute c.,** high-density printing; **(b)** integration, merging (*of businesses*); **(c)** concentration (*of the mind*); **manquer de c.,** to lack concentration; **cela exige une très grande c.,** it demands great concentration.

concentrationnaire [kɔ̃sɑ̃trasjɔnɛr] **1** *adj* of a concentration camp. **2** *n* prisoner in a concentration camp, concentration camp inmate.

concentré [kɔ̃sɑ̃tre] **1** *adj* **(a)** concentrated; condensed (*milk*); **(b)** concentrating (*mind*); **caractère c.,** reserved character; **être très c.,** to be concentrating hard. **2** *nm* extract, concentrate; **c. de tomates,** tomato concentrate *or* purée.

concentrer [kɔ̃sɑ̃tre] **1** *vt* to concentrate (*heat, troops etc*); to focus (*sun's rays etc*); **c. son espoir sur une chose,** to concentrate *or* focus one's hopes on a thing. **2 se concentrer** *vpr* to concentrate, to gather one's thoughts; (**sur,** on); **taisez-vous, je me concentre,** be quiet, I'm trying to concentrate; **se c. sur un problème,** to concentrate on *or* think hard about a problem.

concentrique [kɔ̃sɑ̃trik] *adj Math etc* concentric.

concentriquement [kɔsɑ̃trikmɑ̃] *adv* concentrically.

concept [kɔ̃sɛpt] *nm* concept.

concepteur, -trice [kɔ̃sɛptœr, -tris] *n* ideas man, ideas woman; **c.-projecteur,** ideas man and project manager; **être c. dans une agence de publicité,** to work as an ideas man *or* on the creative side in an advertising agency.

conception [kɔ̃sɛpsjɔ̃] *nf* **(a)** (*d'un enfant, d'une idée*) conception; *Rel* **Immaculée C.,** the Immaculate Conception; **(b)** (*vue*) conception, idea; **une toute nouvelle c. des mathématiques,** a whole new way of looking at mathematics, a completely new approach to mathematics; **(c)** (*création*) design, creation; **c. assistée par ordinateur,** computer-aided *or* -assisted design.

conceptualisation [kɔ̃sɛptyalizasjɔ̃] *nf* conceptualization.

conceptualiser [kɔ̃sɛptyalize] *vt* to conceptualize.

concernant [kɔ̃sɛrnɑ̃] *prép* concerning, about, with regard to, regarding; **c. votre départ, voici quelques informations,** here's some information about your departure; **prière de vous rendre au bureau pour affaire vous c.,** please come to the office to discuss a matter which concerns *or* involves you; **les frais me c.,** the expenses for which I am liable.

concerner [kɔ̃sɛrne] *vt* to concern, to affect; **pour** *ou* **en ce qui concerne cette affaire,** with regard to this matter, as far as this matter is concerned; **en ce qui me concerne,** as far as I am concerned; **cela ne vous concerne en rien,** that's none of your business, it's no concern of yours; **est-ce que cela vous concerne?,** is it any business *or* concern of yours?; **ces problèmes vous concernent tous,** these problems concern *or* affect you all; **ne pas se sentir concerné,** not to feel concerned *or* affected.

concert [kɔ̃sɛr] *nm* **(a)** *Mus* concert; **aller à un c.,** to go to a concert; **billet pour un concert,** a concert *or Am F* symphony ticket; **salle de c.,** concert hall; *Fig* **ce fut un c. d'approbations,** there was a chorus of approval; **(b)** (*accord*) concert; entente (*between powers etc*); **agir de c. avec qn,** to act in cooperation with s.o., to take concerted action with s.o..

concertant [kɔ̃sɛrtɑ̃] *adj Mus* concerted (*composition*); concertante (*part*).

concertation [kɔ̃sɛrtɑsjɔ̃] *nf* co-ordination; **travailler en c.,** to work together; **la c. est de mise,** we must work together *or* co-operate.

concerté [kɔ̃sɛrte] *adj* concerted, united (*action*).

concerter [kɔ̃sɛrte] **1** *vt* to arrange *or* devise (*plan etc*) together. **2 se concerter** *vpr* to consult (each other); **se c. avec qn,** to act in concert with s.o.; **ils se concertèrent,** they put their heads together, they worked together; **ils se concertèrent sur le moyen d'agir,** they took counsel together as to how to act.

concertina [kɔ̃sɛrtina] *nm Mus* concertina.

concertiste [kɔ̃sɛrtist] *n* concert performer *or* artiste; soloist (*in a concerto*).

concerto [kɔ̃sɛrto] *nm Mus* concerto.

concessif, -ive [kɔ̃sɛsif, -iv] *adj* concessive.

concession [kɔ̃sɛsjɔ̃] *nf* **(a)** concession, granting (*of land etc*); yielding (*of point in dispute etc*); **faire des concessions,** to make concessions; **(b)** (*terre etc*) grant, concession; plot (*in cemetery*).

concessionnaire [kɔ̃sɛsjɔnɛr] **1** *adj* concessionary (*company etc*). **2** *n* concessionnaire, licence holder; *Com* agent, dealer; **votre c. Renault** ®, your Renault ® dealer.

concevable [kɔ̃svabl] *adj* conceivable.

concevoir [kɔ̃s(ə)vwar] *v* (*prp* **concevant**; *pp* **conçu**; *pr ind* **je conçois, n. concevons, ils conçoivent**; *impf* **je concevais**; *p hist* **je conçus**; *fu* **je concevrai**) **1** *vt* **(a)** to conceive (*child*); **(b)** to conceive, to imagine, to form, to devise (*idea, plan etc*); **c. de l'amitié pour qn,** to take a liking to s.o.; **la maison est très bien conçue,** the house is very well designed; **je ne conçois pas de ne jamais le revoir,** I don't imagine that I'll ever see him again; **ne pas pouvoir c. qch,** to find sth hard to believe *or* imagine *or* conceive of; **télégramme/lettre ainsi conçu(e),** telegram/letter worded as follows *or* that reads as follows. **2 se concevoir** *vpr* to conceive, to understand; **cela se conçoit facilement,** that is easily understood.

conchyliculture [kɔ̃ʃilikyltyr] *nf* shellfish-farming.

concierge [kɔ̃sjɛrʒ] *n* doorkeeper; caretaker (*of flats etc*), *Am* janitor, superintendent; *Scol* janitor; lodgekeeper (*of country estate*); *F* **c'est une vraie c.,** he's a terrible gossip.

conciergerie [kɔ̃sjɛrʒəri] *nf* **(a)** (*loge*) caretaker's lodge; **(b)** *Hist* **la C.,** the Conciergerie (prison); **(c)** *Can* block of flats.

concile [kɔ̃sil] *nm Rel* council, synod.

conciliable [kɔ̃siljabl] *adj* reconcilable (*qualities*).

conciliabule [kɔ̃siljabyl] *nm* **(a)** *F* confabulation, confab; **(b)** *Arch* secret meeting, secret assembly.

conciliaire [kɔ̃siljɛr] *adj* conciliar.

conciliant [kɔ̃siljɑ̃] *adj* conciliating, conciliatory (*reply etc*).

conciliateur, -trice [kɔ̃siljatœr, -tris] **1** *adj* conciliating. **2** *n* conciliator.

conciliation [kɔ̃siljɑsjɔ̃] *nf* conciliation, reconciliation; **comité de c.,** arbitration committee; **tentative de c.,** attempt at reconciliation.

conciliatoire [kɔ̃siljatwar] *adj* conciliatory (*measure etc*).

concilier [kɔ̃silje] *v* (*impf & pr sub* **n. conciliions, v. conciliiez**) **1** *vt* **(a)** to conciliate, to reconcile (*two parties etc*); **(b)** to win, to gain (*hearts, esteem etc*). **2 se concilier** *vpr* to agree (**avec,** with); **se c. qn** *ou* **la faveur de qn,** to gain s.o.'s goodwill.

concis [kɔ̃si] *adj* concise, terse.

concision [kɔ̃sizjɔ̃] *nf* concision, conciseness, terseness; **avec c.,** concisely.

concitoyen, -enne [kɔ̃sitwajɛ̃, -ɛn] *n* fellow citizen.

conclave [kɔ̃klav] *nm Rel* conclave.

concluant [kɔ̃klyɑ̃] *adj* conclusive, decisive (*experiment etc*); **peu c.,** inconclusive.

conclure [kɔ̃klyr] *v* (*prp* **concluant**; *pp* **conclu**; *pr ind* **je conclus, n. concluons, ils concluent**; *impf* **je concluais**; *p hist* **je conclus**; *fu* **je conclurai**) **1** *vt* **(a)** to conclude, to end, to finish (*a speech etc*), to bring (*a speech etc*) to an end *or* a conclusion; to arrive at (*an understanding*); **c. un traité,** to conclude a treaty; **c. un marché,** to drive *or* strike *or* clinch a bargain; **c'est une affaire conclue,** *Com* it's a bargain, it's a deal, *F* done!; (*on n'en parle plus*) that's settled;

(b) (*déduire*) to conclude, to decide; **nous avons conclu que ...,** we came to the conclusion *or* concluded that ...; **que pouvons-nous c. de tout cela?,** what conclusions can we draw from all this?

2 *vi* to come to a conclusion; **c. à qch,** to come to a conclusion about sth; **c. à une opération immédiate,** to decide that an immediate operation is necessary; **le jury a conclu au suicide,** the jury returned a verdict of suicide; **il faut savoir c.,** you've got to know when *or* how to stop *or* come to a close.

conclusion [kɔ̃klyzjɔ̃] *nf* **(a)** conclusion, close, end (*of speech, meeting etc*); **(b)** concluding, settlement (*of treaty, agreement etc*); **(c)** (*déduction*) inference; *Jur* finding, decision; *Jur* **conclusions,** pleas, submissions; **en c.,** in short, to sum up; **tirer une c. de qch/d'une expérience,** to draw a conclusion from sth/from an experience.

concocter [kɔ̃kɔkte] *vt* (*une histoire, une excuse*) to concoct; **il nous concocte des vacances originales,** he's cooking up some novel ideas for our holidays; **qu'est-ce que tu nous as concocté là?,** what's this you've concocted?, what kind of a concoction is this?

concombre [kɔ̃kɔ̃br] *nm* cucumber.

concomitance [kɔ̃kɔmitɑ̃s] *nf* concomitance.

concomitant [kɔ̃kɔmitɑ̃] *adj* concomitant, accompanying (*circumstance, symptoms etc*).

concordance [kɔ̃kɔrdɑ̃s] *nf* **(a)** concordance, agreement (*of evidence etc*); **(b)** *Gram* sequence (*of tenses*); **le respect de la c.,** observance of the sequence (of tenses); **(c)** (*index*) concordance.

concordant [kɔ̃kɔrdɑ̃] *adj* concordant, agreeing, in agreement.

concordat [kɔ̃kɔrda] *nm* **(a)** *Rel* concordat (*between pope and sovereign*); **(b)** *Com* (bankrupt's) certificate; composition.

concorde [kɔ̃kɔrd] *nf* concord, harmony.

concorder [kɔ̃kɔrde] *vi* (*of dates, evidence*) to agree, to tally (**avec,** with); **faire c. les efforts,** to synchronize *or* harmonize efforts.

concourant [kɔ̃kurɑ̃] *adj* concurrent, converging (*lines,* *circumstances etc*).

concourir [kɔ̃kurir] *vi* (*conj like* **courir**) **(a)** (*of lines etc*) to converge; **(b)** (*concorder*) to combine, to unite; **c. à (faire) qch,** to work towards (doing) sth; **les témoignages concourent à prouver que ...,** all evidence goes to prove that ...; **(c)** *Sp etc* to compete; **c. (avec qn) pour un prix,** to compete (with s.o.) for a prize.

concours [kɔ̃kur] *nm* **(a)** (*aide*) co-operation, assistance, help; **prêter son c. à qn,** to help *or* assist s.o.; **c. financier,** financial aid; *Th etc* **avec le c. de ...,** with the following cast ..., those taking part were ...; **avec l'aimable c. de Sophie,** assisted by Sophie;

(b) (*compétition*) competition; *Scol etc* competitive examination; *Sp* field events; (*exposition*) (competitive) show; **se présenter à un c.,** to enter a competition; *Scol etc* to sit a competitive examination; **recrutement par c.,** competitive entry; **c. interne/externe,** in-house *or* internal/open competition; *Scol* **c. général,** = competition between all the lycées at baccalauréat level; **c. d'entrée,** entrance examination; **c. agricole/hippique,** agricultural/horse show; **c. de beauté,** beauty contest; **un grand c. publicitaire,** an advertising *or* promotional competition;

(c) coincidence (*of events*); **par un c. de circonstances,** by a combination of circumstances;

(d) *Arch & Litt* concourse, gathering (*of people*).

concret, -ète [kɔ̃krɛ, -ɛt] **1** *adj* **(a)** concrete (*term etc*); **cas c.,** actual case, concrete example; **(b) musique concrète,** concrete music; **(c)** (*réel*) concrete, tangible, real; **je veux des résultats concrets,** I want concrete *or* tangible results. **2** *nm* (the) concrete (*as opposed to the abstract*).

concrètement [kɔkrɛtmɑ̃] *adv* in concrete terms, practically; **c. qu'est-ce que ça a changé?,** what has it changed in real terms?

concrétion [kɔ̃kresjɔ̃] *nf* **(a)** (*solidification*) coagulation; **(b)** (*corps*) concrete mass, concretion; *Méd* **concrétions calcaires,** chalk stones.

concrétiser [kɔ̃kretize] **1** *vt* to put (*idea, question*) in(to) concrete form. **2 se concrétiser** *vpr* to materialize, to take shape; **nos projets commencent à se c.,** our plans are beginning to take shape.

concubin, -ine [kɔ̃kybɛ̃, -in] *n* common law spouse.

concubinage [kɔ̃kybinaʒ] *nm* concubinage, cohabitation; **vivre** *ou* **être en c.,** to live together (as man and wife).

concupiscence [kɔ̃kypisɑ̃s] *nf* concupiscence.

concupiscent [kɔ̃kypisɑ̃] *adj* concupiscent.

concurremment [kɔ̃kyramɑ̃] *adv* **(a)** (*ensemble*) concurrently, jointly; **agir c. avec qn,** to act jointly *or* in conjunction with s.o.; **(b)** (*en concurrence*) competitively, in competition (**avec,** with).

concurrence [kɔ̃kyrɑ̃s] *nf* **(a)** (*compétition*) competition, rivalry; *Com* **faire c. à qn/qch,** to compete with s.o./sth; **la libre c.,** free *or* open competition; **faire jouer la c.,** to allow (the rules of) competition to operate; **prix défiant toute c.,** unbeatable price; **(b)** *Com etc* **jusqu'à c. de ...,** up to ..., not exceeding ..., to the amount of ...; **(c)** *Arch* concurrence, coincidence (*of events*).

concurrencer [kɔ̃kyrɑ̃se] *vt* (**je concurrençai(s); n. concurrençons**) to compete with (*s.o., sth*) (*in trade etc*).

concurrent, -ente [kɔ̃kyrɑ̃, -ɑ̃t] **1** *adj* **(a)** competitive, competing, rival (*industries etc*); **(b)** (*forces, actions etc*) co(-)operative. **2** *n Com* competitor; competitor (*for prize etc*); candidate (*for post etc*).

concurrentiel, -ielle [kɔ̃kyrɑ̃sjɛl] *adj Écon* rival, competitive (*companies, prices etc*).

concussion [kɔ̃kysjɔ̃] *nf* misappropriation (*of public funds*).

condamnable [kɔ̃danabl] *adj* reprehensible, blameworthy.

condamnation [kɔ̃danɑsjɔ̃] *nf* **(a)** *Jur* condemnation; conviction, judgment, sentence; **c. à la prison,** prison sentence; **c. à mort,** death sentence; **passer c. sur qch,** to admit that one is in the wrong (about sth); *Fig* **la c. d'un film par la critique,** slating *or* panning of a film by the critics; **(b)** (*reproche*) condemnation, reproof, blame, censure; **la c. de la société de consommation,** the condemnation of the consumer society.

condamné, -ée [kɔ̃dane] *n* convict, sentenced *or* condemned person.

condamner [kɔ̃dane] *vt* **(a)** *Jur* to condemn; to convict, to sentence, to pass judgment on (*criminal etc*); **c. qn. à trois mois de prison,** to sentence s.o. to three months' imprisonment; **c. qn à 10 000 francs d'amende,** to fine s.o. 10,000 francs; **tentative condamnée à l'insuccès,** attempt doomed to failure; **le médecin l'a condamné,** the doctor has given him up; **cela me condamne à l'attendre,** that forces me to wait for him; **être condamné à la solitude,** to be condemned to loneliness;

(b) (*interdire*) to forbid; **la loi condamne la bigamie,** bigamy is forbidden by law;

(c) (*fermer*) to lock, to bar, to block up; **c. une porte,** to block up *or* fill in a door; **c. sa porte,** to bar one's door to visitors;

(d) (*blâmer*) to blame, to censure, to reprove (*s.o.*); **c. un mot de son vocabulaire,** to remove *or* banish a word from one's vocabulary.

condensateur [kɔ̃dɑ̃satœr] *nm Él etc* condenser, capacitor; *Opt* condenser.

condensation [kɔ̃dɑ̃sɑsjɔ̃] *nf* condensation.

condensé [kɔ̃dɑ̃se] **1** *adj* condensed; **lait c.,** condensed milk; **texte c.,** digest. **2** *nm* résumé (of a literary work), digest.

condenser [kɔ̃dɑ̃se] **1** *vt* to condense (*gas, lecture etc*) (**en,** into); **c. un article,** to cut down an article. **2 se condenser** *vpr* to condense.

condenseur [kɔ̃dɑ̃sœr] *nm Phys Opt* condenser.

condescendance [kɔ̃dɛsɑ̃dɑ̃s] *nf* condescension; **parler avec c.,** to speak with condescension *or* condescendingly.

condescendant [kɔ̃dɛsɑ̃dɑ̃] *adj* condescending.

condescendre [kɔ̃dɛsɑ̃dr] *vi* to condescend (**à faire qch,** to do sth); **c. à une explication,** to condescend to give an explanation.

condiment [kɔ̃dimɑ̃] *nm Culin* condiment, seasoning.

condisciple [kɔ̃disipl] *nm* fellow student, schoolmate.

condition [kɔ̃disjɔ̃] *nf* **(a)** (*état*) condition, state; **en bonne c.,** in good condition; **être en c. de faire qch,** to be in a position to do sth; **cet athlète n'est pas en c. (pour courir),** this athlete is not fit (to run) *or* is not in condition (to race); **conditions,** conditions, circumstances; **voyager dans les meilleures conditions,** to travel under the most favourable conditions; **attendre que des conditions plus favorables se présentent,** to wait until conditions improve *or* are better; **les conditions de vie/travail,** living/working conditions; **dans ces conditions ...,** in these circumstances ...; in that case ...; **faire une escalade dans de mauvaises conditions (météorologiques),** to climb in bad (weather) conditions; **les conditions n'étaient pas réunies,** the conditions weren't quite right;

(b) (*stipulation*) condition, stipulation; **une c. essentielle/sine qua non,** an essential condition/a prerequisite *or* sine qua non; **c'est la c. de votre réussite,** that's what will determine your success; **conditions,** terms; **conditions d'une vente,** clauses governing a sale; **conditions de faveur,** preferential terms; **faire ses conditions,** to name one's (own) terms; **imposer une c.,** to lay down a condition *or* stipulation; **avez-vous posé vos conditions?,** did you state your terms *or* conditions?; **offre sans c.,** unconditional offer; **se rendre sans c.,** to surrender unconditionally; **sous c.,** conditionally; **acheter qch sous c.,** to buy sth on approval; **d'accord, mais à une c.,** O.K. but on one condition; **tu peux partir quand tu veux, à c. de me prévenir** *ou* **que tu me préviennes,** you can leave when you like provided (that) you let me know; **tu peux y aller à la c. d'être rentrée à dix heures,** you can go, provided *or* so long as *or* on condition that you're back by ten o'clock;

(c) mise en c. de produits frais, packaging of fresh produce;

(d) (*sort*) condition, destiny; **la c. humaine,** the human condition; *Jur* **la c. des étrangers,** foreigners' (legal) status; **il faut transformer la c. des ouvriers,** the workers' lot needs to be changed;

(e) (*classe sociale*) rank, station, status, position; **se marier avec qn de sa c.,** to marry s.o. of the same social status; *Arch* **personne de c.,** person of rank;

(f) *Arch* **être de** *ou* **en c. chez qn,** to be in service with s.o..

conditionné [kɔ̃disjɔne] *adj* **(a) à air c.,** air-conditioned; **chambre à air c.,** air-conditioned room; **il y a l'air c. dans toutes les pièces,** there's air-conditioning in every room; **(b)** *Com* **viande conditionnée,** pre-packaged meat; **(c)** *Phil Méd Psy* conditioned (*proposition, reflex*).

conditionnel, -elle [kɔ̃disjɔnɛl] **1** *adj* conditional; **promesse conditionnelle,** conditional promise. **2** *nm Gram* conditional (mood).

conditionnellement [kɔ̃disjɔnɛlmɑ̃] *adv* conditionally.

conditionnement [kɔ̃disjɔnmɑ̃] *nm* **(a)** conditioning (*of air, textiles etc*); **(b)** *Com* (*action*) packaging; (*emballage*) package; **(c)** *Psy* conditioning.

conditionner [kɔ̃disjɔne] *vt* **(a)** to condition (*air, textiles etc*); **(b)** (*être la condition de*) to govern; **la météo con-**

ditionne l'époque de la récolte, harvest time is determined by the weather conditions; **sa signature conditionne la validité du contrat,** his signature is required for the contract to be valid; **(c)** *Com* to package; **(d)** *Psy* to condition (*s.o.*).

conditionneur, -euse [kɔ̃disjɔnœr, -øz] **1** *nm* **c. d'air,** air conditioner. **2** *n Com* packager, packer.

condoléances [kɔ̃dɔleɑ̃s] *nfpl* condolences; **offrir** *ou* **présenter ses c.,** to offer one's condolences *or* sympathy; **toutes mes c.,** (please accept) my condolences *or* sincere sympathy.

condom [kɔ̃dɔm] *nm* condom.

condominium [kɔ̃dɔminjɔm] *nm Pol* condominium.

condor [kɔ̃dɔr] *nm* (*oiseau*) condor.

conductance [kɔ̃dyktɑ̃s] *nf Él* conductance.

conducteur,-trice [kɔ̃dyktœr, -tris] **1** *n Aut* driver; leader, guide (*of men etc*); **siège (du) c.,** driver's seat; **c. de bestiaux,** drover; **c. de camions,** lorry *or Am* truck driver; **c. d'une machine,** machine operator; **c. de travaux,** clerk of the works, (works) foreman. **2** *nm* **(a)** *Él Phys* conductor (*of heat, electricity etc*); **(b)** *Él* lead (wire), main. **3** *adj Phys Él* conducting, conductive.

conductibilité [kɔ̃dyktibilite] *nf Phys Él* conductivity.

conductible [kɔ̃dyktibl] *adj Phys Él* conductive.

conduction [kɔ̃dyksjɔ̃] *nf Phys etc* conduction.

conductivité [kɔ̃dyktivite] *nf Él* conductivity.

conduire [kɔ̃dɥir] *v* (*prp* **conduisant**; *pp* **conduit**; *pr ind* **je conduis, n. conduisons, ils conduisent**; *impf* **je conduisais**; *p hist* **je conduisis**; *fu* **je conduirai**) **1** *vt* **(a)** to conduct, to escort (*party etc*); to lead (*horse, blind man etc*); to guide (*child's first steps etc*); **j'ai dû le c. chez le dentiste de toute urgence,** I had to take him to the dentist urgently; **c. qn à la gare,** to take *or* drive s.o. to the station; **c. des amis dans la ville,** to show *or* take friends around town; **on nous a conduits dans cet endroit,** we were taken *or* driven to this place; **on la conduisit à sa chambre,** she was shown to her room; **cela va nous c. à la catastrophe/ruine,** it's going to lead us to catastrophe/ruin; **cette insolence va te c. au renvoi,** cheek like that will end up getting you the sack; **c. qn à faire qch,** to induce *or* prevail on s.o. to do sth;

(b) to drive (*horse, car etc*); to steer, to row (*boat*);

(c) to convey, to conduct (*water etc*); **corps qui conduit bien l'électricité,** good conductor of electricity;

(d) (*diriger*) to direct, to manage, to supervise, to run; **c. un orchestre,** to conduct an orchestra; **c. une affaire,** to manage a business.

2 *vi* **(a)** *Aut etc* to drive; **elle conduit bien,** she is a good driver;

(b) (*mener*) to lead; **quel est le chemin qui conduit à la gare?,** which is the way to the station?

3 se conduire *vpr* **(a)** (*se diriger*) **être d'âge à se c.,** to be old enough to take care of oneself;

(b) (*se comporter*) to behave; **se c. mal,** (*d'un enfant*) to behave badly, to misbehave; **se c. bien/mal avec qn,** to behave well/badly towards s.o..

conduit [kɔ̃dɥi] *nm Tech* conduit, duct, pipe, passage, channel; *Constr MecE* **c. d'aération,** air duct; **c. de ventilation,** ventilation shaft; *Nau* **c. de chaîne,** hawse hole *or* pipe; **c. de cordage,** fairlead; *Physiol* **c. auditif,** auditory meatus; **c. lacrymal,** tear duct.

conduite [kɔ̃dɥit] *nf* **(a)** conducting, leading, escorting (*of s.o.*); **elle est chargée de la c. d'une aveugle,** she is responsible for accompanying *or* escorting a blind girl *or* woman; *F* **faire un bout de c. à qn,** to go part of the way with s.o.;

(b) driving (*of cart, car etc*); navigation (*of boat, balloon*); **c. intérieure,** saloon (car), *Am* sedan; **c. à gauche/droite,** left-/right-hand drive; **leçons de c.,** driving lessons;

(c) direction, management, control (*of affairs etc*); command (*of army, fleet etc*); **être sous la c. de qn,** (*suivre des ordres*) to be under s.o.'s leadership; (*suivre des conseils*) to be under s.o.'s guidance; **c. des travaux,** supervision of works;

(d) (*comportement*) conduct, behaviour, *US* behavior; **c'est ma seule ligne de c.,** it's my guiding principle; **mauvaise c.,** misbehaviour; **adopter une c. différente,** to start to behave differently; **une c. d'échec,** defeatist behaviour; **un écart de c.,** misbehaviour, misconduct; **il n'a pas de c.,** he has no manners, he doesn't know how to behave; *Scol* **zéro de c.,** no marks for conduct;

(e) *Tech* pipe, conduit, duct; **conduites,** piping, tubing; **c. à air** *ou* **d'air,** air duct; **c. d'eau,** water pipe *or* main(s); **c. de gaz,** gas pipe *or* main(s); **c. souple,** hose, flexible pipe; **tuyau de c.,** conduit pipe; *HydE etc* **c. forcée,** (pressure) pipeline; **c. montante,** flow pipe, rising main.

cône [kon] *nm* **(a)** cone; **c. de pin,** pine cone; *Géol* **c. de déjection,** alluvial cone; *Astron* **c. d'ombre,** umbra (*of a planet etc*); *Nau* **c. de tempête,** storm cone; **c. de signalisation,** signal cone; **c. de chantier,** traffic cone; **(b)** (*shape*) taper; **en forme de c.,** cone-shaped, tapering.

confection [kɔ̃fɛksjɔ̃] *nf* **(a)** putting together, making (up) (*of garment etc*); preparing, preparation (*of meal*); **elle nous a offert des gâteaux de sa c.,** she offered us some of her home-made cakes; **(b)** (ready-to-wear) clothing industry; **robe de c.,** ready-made dress; **vêtements de c.,** off-the-peg clothes; **maison de c.,** (*pour femmes*) (ready-to-wear) dress shop; (*pour hommes*) tailor's, outfitter's; **travailler dans la c.,** to work in the clothing industry *or F* rag trade.

confectionner [kɔ̃fɛksjɔne] *vt* to make (up) (*dress*); to prepare (*dish etc*).

confectionneur, -euse [kɔ̃fɛksjɔnœr, -øz] *n* (*pour femmes*) dress-maker; (*surtout pour hommes*) tailor.

confédéral, -ale, -aux [kɔ̃federal, -o] *adj* confederation; **débat c.,** debate within the confederation.

confédération [kɔ̃federasjɔ̃] *nf* confederation, confederacy.

confédéré [kɔ̃federe] **1** *adj* confederate (*nations*); *Ind Pol* **syndicat non c.,** non-affiliated union. **2** *n Hist* **les Confédérés,** the Confederates.

confédérer [kɔ̃federe] *vt* (**je confédère, n. confédérons; je confédérai**) to confederate, to unite.

confer [kɔ̃fɛr] *vt* (*imperative form*) cf, compare.

conférence [kɔ̃ferɑ̃s] *nf* **(a)** (*assemblée*) conference, discussion; **tenir c.,** to hold a conference; **c. au sommet,** summit (conference); **c. de presse,** press conference; **(b)** *Univ etc* lecture; **maître de conférences,** lecturer; **salle de conférences,** lecture room.

conférencier,-ière [kɔ̃ferɑ̃sje, -jɛr] *n* lecturer, speaker; *Univ* lecturer; **c. invité,** guest speaker.

conférer [kɔ̃fere] *v* (**je confère, n. conférons; je conférerai**) **1** *vt* **(a)** to confer, to bestow, to grant, to award (*privileges etc*); **c. le grade de docteur à qn,** to confer a doctor's degree on s.o.; **par les pouvoirs qui me sont conférés,** by the authority vested in me; **(b)** to compare, to collate (*texts*). **2** *vi* to confer (**avec,** with); **nous avons conféré de l'affaire,** we talked the matter over.

confesse [kɔ̃fɛs] *nf* **aller/être à c.,** to go to/to be at confession.

confesser [kɔ̃fese] **1** *vt* **(a)** to confess; to plead guilty to (*sth*), to own (up) to (*sth*); **je confesse mon ignorance,** I admit *or* confess my ignorance; **il confesse qu'il s'est trompé,** he admits he was mistaken; **(b)** *Rel* to confess (one's sins); to declare one's belief in (*God etc*); to confess (*one's faith*); **(c)** (*of priest*) to confess (*penitent*); *Fig F* **on trouvera les moyens de le c.,** we'll find a way to make him talk. **2** *vi* **ce prêtre ne confesse pas,** this priest doesn't hear confessions. **3 se confesser** *vpr* to confess; *Rel* to confess (one's sins); *Rel* **se c. toutes les semaines,** to go to confession every week.

confesseur [kɔ̃fɛsœr] *nm* **(a)** *Rel & Fig* (father) confessor; **(b)** *Hist* confessor (*of one's religion, faith*).

confession [kɔ̃fɛsjɔ̃] *nf* **(a)** (*aveu*) confession, admission, avowal; **faire la c. de qch,** to confess *or* own up to sth; **je vais vous faire une c.,** I've got a confession to make to you; **(b)** *Rel* confession; *F* **on te donnerait le bon Dieu sans c.,** you look as though butter wouldn't melt in your mouth; **c. de foi,** confession of faith; **(c)** *Rel* (*par un prêtre*) hearing of confession; **(d)** (*croyance*) denomination, faith, religion; **des élèves de toutes confessions,** pupils of all denominations; **une école avec des élèves de toutes confessions,** a multi-denominational school.

confessional,-aux [kɔ̃fɛsjɔnal, -o] *nm Rel* confessional.

confessionnel,-elle [kɔ̃fɛsjɔnɛl] *adj* denominational (*matters, disputes*).

confetti [kɔ̃feti] *nm* confetti; *F* **tu peux en faire des confettis!,** you can chuck it out, you can throw it in the bin.

confiance [kɔ̃fjɑ̃s] *nf* **(a)** (*foi*) confidence, faith, trust; **avoir c. en** *ou* **faire c. à qn/qch,** to rely on s.o./sth, to trust s.o./sth, to put trust in s.o./sth; **il n'a pas c. dans les médecins,** he doesn't believe in doctors; **elle a une c. aveugle en toi,** she trusts you blindly *or* implicitly; **acheter qch de c.,** to buy sth on trust; **il me faut un homme de c.,** I need a man whom I can trust *or* rely on; **comment regagner sa c.?,** how can I *or* we *etc* win back *or* regain his confidence *or* trust?; **abuser de la c. de qn,** to abuse s.o.'s trust; **digne de c.,** trustworthy, reliable; **maison de c.,** reliable firm; **c'est un poste** *ou* **emploi de**

c., it's a position of trust; **avec c.,** (*avec espoir*) confidently; (*avec sincérité*) trustingly, trustfully; **je vous parle en toute c.,** I know I can trust you (with what I have to say); **tu sais que tu peux me faire c.,** you know you can trust me; **faites-moi c.,** trust me; *F* (*croyez-moi*) believe me; *Pol* **vote de c.,** vote of confidence; **un climat de c. économique,** a climate of economic confidence;

(b) (*assurance*) confidence, sense of security; **manquer de c. en soi,** to lack self-assurance *or* self-confidence.

confiant [kɔ̃fjɑ̃] *adj* **(a)** confiding, trusting, trustful (**dans,** in); **(b)** (*optimiste*) confident, sanguine (*disposition etc*); **(c)** self-confident, assured (*manner etc*).

confidence [kɔ̃fidɑ̃s] *nf* confidence; **faire une c. à qn,** to tell s.o. a secret; **faire c. de qch à qn,** to confide sth to s.o.; **mettre qn dans la c.,** to let s.o. into the secret; **dire qch en c.,** to say sth in confidence *or* confidentially.

confident,-ente [kɔ̃fidɑ̃, -ɑ̃t] *n* confidant, *f* confidante.

confidentiel,-ielle [kɔ̃fidɑ̃sjɛl] *adj* confidential; **à titre c.,** confidentially, in confidence, privately.

confidentiellement [kɔ̃fidɑ̃sjɛlmɑ̃] *adv* confidentially, in confidence.

confier [kɔ̃fje] *v* (*impf & pr sub* **n. confiions, v. confiiez**) **1** *vt* **(a)** (*laisser*) to trust, to entrust, to commit; **c. qch à (la garde de) qn,** to entrust s.o. with sth; **je leur ai confié les enfants,** I left the children with them; **c. une tâche à qn,** to entrust s.o. with a task; **(b)** (*dire*) to confide, to impart, to disclose; **c. qch à qn,** to tell s.o. sth in confidence. **2 se confier** *vpr* **(a)** (*s'en remettre*) to place one's trust (in); **se c. à qn/qch,** to put one's trust in s.o./sth; **(b) se c. à qn,** to confide in s.o..

configuration [kɔ̃figyrɑsjɔ̃] *nf* configuration, outline; form, shape (*of building*); lie (*of the land etc*); *Ordinat* configuration.

configurer [kɔ̃figyre] *vt Ordinat etc* to configure.

confiné [kɔ̃fine] *adj* **(a)** enclosed (*atmosphere etc*); stale (*air*); **(b)** (*enfermé*) cooped up, shut away, withdrawn; **vivre c. chez soi,** to shut oneself away.

confinement [kɔ̃finmɑ̃] *nm* confinement, confining.

confiner [kɔ̃fine] **1** *vi* **c. à** *ou* **avec un pays,** (*of country etc*) to border on *or* adjoin a country; *Fig* **courage qui confine à la témérité,** courage verging *or* bordering on foolhardiness. **2** *vt* to confine (*s.o.*), to shut (*s.o.*) up. **3 se confiner** *vpr* to confine oneself; **se c. chez soi,** to live a retired life, to shut oneself away.

confins [kɔ̃fɛ̃] *nmpl* confines, borders (*of country*); **aux c. de la science,** within the limits of science.

confire [kɔ̃fir] *vt* (*prp* **confisant**; *pp* **confit**; *pr ind* **je confis, n. confisons, ils confisent**; *impf* **je confisais**; *p hist* **je confis**; *fu* **je confirai**) to preserve (*fruit etc*); to candy (*peel etc*); **c. qch au sel/au vinaigre,** to salt sth down/to pickle sth.

confirmatif,-ive [kɔ̃firmatif, -iv] *adj* corroborative (*statement*); confirmative (*judgment*).

confirmation [kɔ̃firmɑsjɔ̃] *nf* **(a)** confirmation, corroboration (*of piece of news etc*); **c. d'un jugement,** confirmation of a sentence; **il m'en a donné c.,** he gave me confirmation of it; **c'est la c. de ce que je pensais,** it *or* that (just) confirms what I thought; **(b)** *Rel* (sacrament of) confirmation; **donner la c. à qn,** to confirm s.o..

confirmer [kɔ̃firme] **1** *vt* **(a)** to confirm (*news, judgment etc*); **c. un traité,** to ratify a treaty; **cela me confirme dans mon opinion,** that confirms *or* strengthens me in my opinion; **nous l'avons confirmé dans son choix,** we approved his choice; **elle n'a pas été confirmée dans ses fonctions,** she was not given the job (which she had been doing temporarily); **l'exception confirme la règle,** the exception proves the rule; **(b)** *Rel* to confirm (*s.o.*). **2 se confirmer** *vpr* to be confirmed (*of report, doubts etc*); **le bruit ne s'est pas confirmé,** the rumour proved false.

confiscation [kɔ̃fiskɑsjɔ̃] *nf* confiscation, seizure (*of property etc*).

confiserie [kɔ̃fizri] *nf* **(a)** preserving (*of fruit etc*) in sugar; **(b)** *Com* confectioner's shop, sweetshop, *Am* candy store; **(c)** (*bonbon*) confectionery, sweets, *Am* candy.

confiseur,-euse [kɔ̃fizœr, -øz] *n* = confectioner.

confisquer [kɔ̃fiske] *vt* to confiscate, to seize (*goods, property etc*); **le président veut c. le pouvoir,** the president wants to seize power.

confit [kɔ̃fi] **1** *adj* **fruits confits,** crystallized fruit; **avoir un air c.,** to look smarmy; **être c. en dévotion,** to be steeped in piety. **2** *nm Culin* conserve (*of goose etc*).

confiture [kɔ̃fityr] *nf Culin* jam; **c. d'oranges,** (orange) marmalade; *Fig* **ce serait donner de la c. aux cochons,** that would be throwing *or* casting pearls before swine, it would be wasted (on them)

confiturerie [kɔ̃fityrri] *nf* **(a)** *Ind* jam manufacture; **(b)** (*fabrique*) jam factory.

confiturier [kɔ̃tifyrje] *nm* jam maker, jam manufacturer.

conflagration [kɔ̃flagrɑsjɔ̃] *nf* cataclysm.

conflictuel, -elle [kɔfliktyɛl] *adj* (*témoignages, intérêts etc*) conflicting; **situation conflictuelle,** situation of conflict.

conflit [kɔ̃fli] *nm* conflict, struggle; clash, conflict (*of interests*); *Jur* conflict (*of authority, scope*); **c. (armé),** armed conflict, war; **être en c.,** to be at variance *or F* loggerheads (**avec,** with); (*of interests*) to clash, to conflict (**avec,** with); **arbitrage des conflits internationaux,** arbitration of international disputes; **entrer en c. avec qn,** to come into conflict with *or* clash with s.o.; **conflits sociaux,** industrial disputes; *Jur* **tribunal des conflits,** = jurisdictional court which decides whether a matter should be dealt with by a civil or other court.

confluence [kɔ̃flyɑ̃s] *nf* confluence.

confluent [kɔ̃flyɑ̃] *nm* confluence (*of rivers, veins etc*).

confluer [kɔ̃flye] *vi* to meet, to join, to unite; **l'Oise conflue avec la Seine,** the Oise flows into the Seine.

confondant [kɔ̃fɔ̃dɑ̃] *adj* (*qui met en confusion*) confusing; (*qui trouble*) confounding.

confondre [kɔ̃fɔ̃dr] **1** *vt* **(a)** (*réunir*) to merge, to mingle, to intermingle;

(b) (*se tromper*) to mistake, to confuse; **je les confonds toujours,** I always mistake one for the other, I always get them confused *or* mixed up; **c. des noms,** to confuse names;

(c) (*sidérer*) to astound, to stagger (*s.o.*); **son insolence me confond,** I'm astounded by his insolence;

(d) to confound (*criminal etc*); **c. un menteur,** to show up a liar.

2 *vi* to be mistaken; **tu dois c., ce n'est pas ça,** you must be mistaken, that's not it at all.

3 se confondre *vpr* **(a)** (*of colours etc*) to merge (into one another); to blend (**en,** into);

(b) (*of streams etc*) to merge, to flow into each other; (*of interests etc*) to merge, to be identical; **se c. en excuses/en remerciements,** to apologize profusely/to be profuse in one's thanks; **se c. en excuses/remerciements devant qn,** to apologise profusely to s.o./to thank s.o. profusely; **leurs voix se confondent au loin,** their voices merge *or* mingle in the distance.

confondu [kɔ̃fɔ̃dy] *adj* **(a)** (*décontenancé*) disconcerted, abashed; **je suis tout c. de votre bonté,** I am overwhelmed by your kindness; **(b)** (*sidéré*) dumbfounded, astounded (**de,** at); **en rester confondu,** to be (left) dumbfounded.

conformation [kɔ̃fɔrmɑsjɔ̃] *nf* conformation, structure (*of hills, parts of body etc*).

conforme [kɔ̃fɔrm] *adj* true, according (**à,** to); consistent (**à,** with); **copie c. à l'original,** exact copy; *Admin* **pour copie c.,** certified true copy; **il mène une vie c. à ses moyens,** he lives according to his means; **une pensée/une idée non c.,** an unorthodox thought, unorthodox thinking.

conformé [kɔ̃fɔrme] *adj* **bien c.,** well-formed (*child etc*); **mal c.,** misshapen (*limb etc*).

conformément [kɔ̃fɔrmemɑ̃] *adv* according (**à,** to); in conformity, in accordance, in compliance (**à,** with); **c. à la loi,** according to *or* in accordance with the law; **c. à vos ordres,** in accordance with your orders; **c. à ce qui a été prévu,** according to what was planned; **tout se passe c. aux plans,** everything's going according to plan.

conformer [kɔ̃fɔrme] **1** *vt* to model (**à,** on); **c. sa vie à certains principes,** to shape one's life according to certain principles. **2 se conformer** *vpr* to conform, to comply; **se c. à qch,** to conform to sth, to comply with *or* abide by sth; **se c. à la règle,** to conform to the rule; *Com* **se c. au modèle,** to keep (to) the pattern.

conformisme [kɔ̃fɔrmism] *nm* (*traditionalisme*) conformism, *Am* conformity; *Rel* conformity.

conformiste [kɔ̃fɔrmist] **1** *n* (*traditionaliste*) conformist, conventionalist; *Rel* conformist (*of Church of Eng*). **2** *adj* conformist.

conformité [kɔ̃fɔrmite] *nf* conformity, similarity; *Rel* conformity; **en c. avec,** in accordance with, according to; **en c. au règlement,** in accordance with the rule; **être en c. de goûts avec qn,** to have similar tastes to s.o..

confort [kɔ̃fɔr] *nm* comfort(s); **hôtel avec tout le c. moderne,** hotel with every modern convenience *or F* with all mod cons; **manquer de c.,** to be lacking in comfort, to be uncomfortable; **maison sans c.,** house with none of the comforts; **elle aime bien son petit c.,** she likes her creature comforts *or* little comforts.

confortable [kɔ̃fɔrtabl] *adj* comfortable, snug, cosy; (*financièrement*) comfortable, well off, comfortably off; *Fig* easy, comfortable; **fauteuil/maison c.,** comfortable armchair/house; **ces chaussures sont très confortables,** these shoes are very comfortable; **des appointements confortables,** a good salary; **une vie c.,** a comfortable life(-style); *Fig* **il est plus c. de penser que tout va bien,** it's easier *or* more comfortable to think that everything is going well.

confortablement [kɔ̃fɔrtabləmɑ̃] *adv* comfortably; **être c. rémunéré,** to be on a good salary, to be well-paid.

conforter [kɔfɔrte] *vt* to reinforce, to strengthen, to confirm; **cela me conforte dans mon opinion,** that reinforces *or* strengthens *or* confirms my opinion.

confraternel,-elle [kɔ̃fratɛrnɛl] *adj* fraternal, brotherly.

confraternité [kɔ̃fratɛrnite] *nf* brotherliness.

confrère [kɔ̃frɛr] *nm* colleague, confrère, fellow member (*of profession, society*).

confrérie [kɔ̃freri] *nf* (religious) brotherhood, sisterhood, confraternity.

confrontation [kɔ̃frɔ̃tasjɔ̃] *nf* **(a)** *Jur* confrontation, confronting (*of accused person with witness*); *Fig* clash, conflict; **la c. de deux idéaux/opinions,** the clash *or* conflict of two ideals/opinions; **(b)** comparison (**à, avec,** with); collation (*of texts*).

confronter [kɔ̃frɔ̃te] **1** *vt* **(a)** *Jur etc* to confront; to bring (*prisoner*) face to face (**avec, à,** with); **être confronté à un problème,** to be confronted with a problem; **(b)** to collate (*texts*); to compare (*materials etc*) (**avec, à,** with). **2 se confronter** *vpr* **se c. à un adversaire,** to confront *or* stand up to an opponent; **nous nous sommes confrontés,** we confronted each other (**au sujet de,** about).

confucianisme [kɔ̃fysjanism] *nm Hist Rel* Confucianism.

confus [kɔ̃fy] *adj* **(a)** (*mélangé*) confused, mixed, chaotic, jumbled (*heap etc*); indistinct (*noise*); dim, blurred (*vision*); obscure, ambiguous (*style etc*); **mélange c.,** jumble (**de,** of); **une affaire pour le moins confuse,** a confused *or* muddled business to say the least; **(b)** (*embarrassé*) embarrassed, abashed, ashamed; **je suis c.,** (*après un faux pas*) I'm so embarrassed, I don't know where to put myself; (*devant votre bonté*) I don't know what to say; **je suis c. de vous déranger,** I'm so sorry to disturb you.

confusément [kɔ̃fyzemɑ̃] *adv* confusedly, vaguely, indistinctly.

confusion [kɔ̃fyzjɔ̃] *nf* **(a)** (*mélange*) confusion, disorder, jumble, medley; **tout était en c.,** everything was in a mess *or* in disorder; **mettre la c. dans l'assemblée,** to throw the audience into confusion; **jeter la c. dans les esprits,** to confuse people; *Méd* **c. mentale,** mental aberration; **un moment de c.,** a moment of confusion, a moment's confusion; **(b)** (*erreur*) mistake, error, misunderstanding; **c. de dates/de noms,** confusion of *or* mistake in dates/names; **c'est une grossière c.,** a stupid *or* gross *or* crass error *or* mistake; **(c)** (*gêne*) confusion, embarrassment; **être rouge de c.,** to be covered in confusion, to blush with embarrassment; **(d)** *Jur* **avec c. des peines,** the sentences to run concurrently.

congé [kɔ̃ʒe] *nm* **(a)** leave (of absence); (*vacances*) holiday, *surtout Am* vacation; **en c.,** on leave; **c. de maladie,** sick leave; **c. de maternité,** maternity leave; **un après-midi de c.,** an afternoon off; *Ind* **c. payé,** paid holiday; *Admin* **c. annuel,** annual leave, *Am* vacation leave; **on a c. lundi,** Monday's a holiday; **prendre c. de qn,** to take (one's) leave of s.o.; **donner c. à qn,** to dismiss s.o.; **(b)** (*avis de renvoi*) (notice of) discharge, dismissal; **donner son c. à qn,** to give s.o. his notice; **demander son c.,** to hand in one's resignation, to give notice; **donner c. à un locataire,** to give a tenant notice to quit; **(c)** authorization, permit; release (*of wine from bond*); *Nau* **c. de navigation,** clearance certificate.

congédiable [kɔ̃ʒedjabl] *adj* due for discharge.

congédier [kɔ̃ʒedje] *vt* (*impf & pr sub* **n. congédiions, v. congédiiez**) **(a)** to dismiss (*servant etc*); **(b)** to dismiss (*caller*); *Mil Nau* to discharge (*men*); *Nau* to pay off (*crew*).

congelable [kɔ̃ʒlabl] *adj* suitable for (home) freezing; **aliment non c.,** foodstuff unsuitable for (home) freezing; (*sur l'emballage*) do not freeze.

congélateur [kɔ̃ʒelatœr] *nm* deep freeze, freezer (compartment).

congélation [kɔ̃ʒelasjɔ̃] *nf* (*d'aliments*) deep freezing; (*de l'eau etc*) freezing; (*de l'huile*) congealing; **point de c. de l'eau,** freezing point of water.

congeler [kɔ̃ʒle] *v* (**il congèle; il congèlera**) **1** *vt* to (deep) freeze (*food*); to freeze (*water etc*); **viande congelée,** frozen meat. **2 se congeler** *vpr* to freeze.

congénère [kɔ̃ʒenɛr] **1** *adj Biol* congeneric; *Anat* congenerous (*muscle*). **2** *nm Biol* congener; *F* **lui et ses congénères,** he and his like.

congénital,-aux [kɔ̃ʒenital, -o] *adj* congenital; *Méd* **malformation congénitale,** congenital deformity *or* malformation *or* abnormality; *F* **inconscience congénitale,** innate *or* congenital thoughtlessness; *F* **c'est un idiot c.,** he's a congenital idiot.

congère [kɔ̃ʒɛr] *nf* snowdrift.

congestif,-ive [kɔ̃ʒɛstif, -iv] *adj Méd* congestive (*disposition etc*).

congestion [kɔ̃ʒɛstjɔ̃] *nf Méd* congestion; **c. cérébrale,** stroke; **c. pulmonaire,** pneumonia.

congestionné [kɔ̃ʒɛstjɔne] *adj* flushed, red (*face*); congested (*roads*); **les routes sont très congestionnées,** the roads are very congested, there's a lot of congestion on the roads.

congestionner [kɔ̃ʒɛstjɔne] **1** *vt* **(a)** *Méd* to congest; to flush (*face*); **(b)** (*boucher*) to block, to congest; **les voitures congestionnent la rue,** the cars are blocking the street. **2 se congestionner** *vpr* to become congested.

conglomérat [kɔ̃glɔmera] *nm* **(a)** *Écon* conglomerate; **(b)** *Géol* conglomerate.

conglomération [kɔ̃glɔmerasjɔ̃] *nf* conglomeration.

conglomérer [kɔ̃glɔmere] *v* (**je conglomère, n. conglomérons; je conglomérerai**) **1** *vt* to conglomerate. **2 se conglomérer** *vpr* to conglomerate, to unite, to cluster together.

Congo [kɔ̃go] *nm* the Congo.

congolais,-aise [kɔ̃gɔlɛ, -ɛz] **1** *adj* of the Congo, Congolese. **2** *n* **C.,** Congolese. **3** *nm Culin* coconut cake.

congratulations [kɔ̃gratylasjɔ̃] *nfpl* congratulations; **mes c. pour ta réussite,** congratulations on your success.

congratuler [kɔ̃gratyle] **1** *vt* to congratulate (*s.o.*) (**pour,** on). **2 se congratuler** *vpr* to congratulate oneself, *F* to pat oneself on the back.

congre [kɔ̃gr] *nm* conger (eel).

congrégation [kɔ̃gregasjɔ̃] *nf* **(a)** *Rel* (*communauté*) community (= group of monasteries); congregation (*of Cardinals*); **(b)** *Fig* assembly.

congrès [kɔ̃grɛ] *nm* convention, congress; **C. des États-Unis,** United States Congress; **membre du C.,** congressman, congresswoman; **palais des congrès,** convention centre; **c. annuel,** (*d'un parti politique*) annual conference.

congressiste [kɔ̃grɛsist] *n* participant at a congress, *surtout Am* conventioneer; *Pol* conference delegate.

congru [kɔ̃gry] *adj* **(a) portion congrue,** (income providing a) bare living; *Rel* adequate emolument (*of priest*); **réduire qn à la portion congrue,** to put s.o. on short allowance; **(b)** *Math* congruent; **(c)** *Arch* sufficient, adequate.

congruence [kɔ̃gryɑ̃s] *nf Math* congruence.

conifère [kɔnifɛr] *nm Bot* conifer.

conique [kɔnik, ko-] *adj* **(a)** *Géom* cone-shaped, conical; **(b)** *Math* **section c.,** conic section; **(c)** *MecE etc* coned, taper(ing) (*shank, pin etc*); **engrenage c.,** bevel gearing.

conjectural,-aux [kɔ̃ʒɛktyral, -o] *adj* conjectural.

conjecture [kɔ̃ʒɛktyr] *nf* conjecture, surmise, guess; **se perdre en conjectures,** to get lost *or* lose oneself in conjecture(s); **ce n'est que pure c.,** that's sheer conjecture.

conjecturer [kɔ̃ʒɛktyre] **1** *vt* to conjecture, to surmise, to guess; **c. le développement du conflit,** to conjecture about *or* guess at the progress of the conflict. **2** *vi* to conjecture, to hypothesize, to wonder; **il conjecture sur ce qu'il ignore,** he makes guesses about things he knows nothing about.

conjoint [kɔ̃ʒwɛ̃] **1** *adj* **(a)** joint, united, conjoined; *Fin* **compte c.,** joint account; *Jur* **legs c.,** joint legacy; **légataires conjoints,** co-legatees; **(b)** *Jur* married. **2** *nm* spouse; **les conjoints,** husband and wife.

conjointement [kɔ̃ʒwɛ̃tmɑ̃] *adv* (con)jointly.

conjoncteur [kɔ̃ʒɔ̃ktœr] *nm Él* circuit closer; cut-in; **c.-disjoncteur,** make-and-break (switch).

conjonctif, -ive [kɔ̃ʒɔ̃ktif, -iv] *adj* conjunctive, connective (*tissue etc*); *Gram* **locution conjonctive,** conjunctive phrase; **proposition conjonctive,** conjunctive clause.

conjonction [kɔ̃ʒɔ̃ksjɔ̃] *nf* **(a)** (*réunion*) conjunction, union, connection; **(b)** *Gram* conjunction; **c. de subordination,** subordinating conjunction.

conjonctive [kɔ̃ʒɔ̃ktiv] *nf* conjunctiva (*of the eye*).

conjonctivite [kɔ̃ʒɔ̃ktivit] *nf Méd* conjunctivitis; **faire** *ou* **avoir de la c.,** to have conjunctivitis.
conjoncture [kɔ̃ʒɔ̃ktyr] *nf* conjuncture; (combination of) circumstances; **dans la c. actuelle,** at this (present) juncture, under the present circumstances; **c. favorable/défavorable,** favourable/unfavourable *or* adverse climate; *Pol Écon* **c. économique,** overall economic situation; **étude de c.,** study of the state of the economy.
conjoncturel, -elle [kɔ̃ʒɔ̃ktyrɛl] *adj* relating to the present economic climate; **crise conjoncturelle,** economic crisis.
conjoncturiste [kɔ̃ʒɔ̃ktyrist] *nm Écon* economic analyst.
conjugable [kɔ̃ʒygabl] *adj Gram* conjugable.
conjugaison [kɔ̃ʒygɛzɔ̃] *nf Gram Biol etc* conjugation (*of verb, of cells etc*); *Fig Litt* **grâce à la c. de leurs efforts,** thanks to their joint efforts.
conjugal,-aux [kɔ̃ʒygal, -o] *adj* (*devoirs*) conjugal; **vie conjugale,** married life; **le domicile c.,** home (*of married couple*); **bonheur c.,** wedded *or* married bliss; **le lit c.,** the marriage bed.
conjugalement [kɔ̃ʒygalmɑ̃] *adv* conjugally.
conjugué [kɔ̃ʒyge] *adj* joint, combined (*efforts etc*); *MecE* paired, twin; *Math Opt* conjugate; *Bot* **feuilles conjuguées,** conjugate leaves; **machines conjuguées,** paired engines.
conjuguer [kɔ̃ʒyge] **1** *vt* **(a)** *Gram* to conjugate; **(b)** (*unir*) to unite, to combine; **ils conjuguèrent leurs efforts,** they combined *or* united their efforts. **2 se conjuguer** *vpr Gram* to be conjugated.
conjuration [kɔ̃ʒyrɑsjɔ̃] *nf* **(a)** (*complot*) conspiracy, plot; **(b)** (*charme*) exorcism, conjuration.
conjuré,-ée [kɔ̃ʒyre] *n* conspirator.
conjurer [kɔ̃ʒyre] **1** *vt* **(a)** (*implorer*) **c. qn de faire qch,** to entreat *or* beg *or* beseech *or* implore s.o. to do sth; **je t'en conjure,** I beg *or* beseech you; **(b)** to avert, to ward off (*danger etc*); **(c)** to exorcise (*demon*); **(d)** *Arch* to plot, to conspire. **2 se conjurer** *vpr* to conspire (together) (**contre,** against).
connaissable [kɔnɛsabl] *adj* knowable.
connaissance [kɔnɛsɑ̃s] *nf* **(a)** (*savoir*) acquaintance, knowledge; **prendre c. de qch,** to make oneself acquainted with sth, to study *or* examine *or* enquire into sth; **avoir c. de qch,** to be aware of sth; **donner qch à la c. de qn,** to inform s.o. of sth, to make sth known to s.o.; **il n'a jamais, à ma c., été malade,** he has never, to my knowledge *or* as far as I know, had a day's illness; **en c. de cause,** with full knowledge of the facts, on good grounds;
(b) (*contact*) **faire c. avec qn, faire la c. de qn,** to make s.o.'s acquaintance, to meet s.o.; **quand je fis sa c.,** when I first knew him; **lier c. avec qn,** to strike up an acquaintance with s.o.; **une figure de c.,** a familiar face; **en pays de c.,** (*parmi des gens*) among familiar faces; *Fig* on familiar ground; **une personne de ma c.,** someone I know, an acquaintance;
(c) (*personne*) acquaintance; **c'est une de mes connaissances,** he is an acquaintance of mine; **je ne la connais pas, c'est une vague c.,** I don't (really) know her, she's just a nodding acquaintance; *F* **c'est une vieille c.,** I've known him for ages; *F Vieilli* **je l'ai rencontré avec sa c.,** I met him with his girl-friend;
(d) (*maîtrise*) knowledge, understanding; *Jur* cognizance; *Phil* cognition; **connaissances,** learning, attainments, acquirements; **avoir la c. de plusieurs langues,** to know several languages; **ma c. du russe,** my acquaintance with *or* knowledge of Russian; **sa c. du droit,** his knowledge of the law; **la c. de soi,** self-knowledge; **avoir de profondes connaissances en mathématiques,** to be very well versed in mathematics; **elle a des connaissances en maths,** she has some knowledge of maths; **l'acquisition des connaissances,** the acquisition of knowledge, the learning process; **avoir des connaissances sommaires sur qch,** to have a rudimentary knowledge of sth, to know the rudiments of sth;
(e) (*conscience*) consciousness; **perdre c.,** to lose consciousness, to faint; **avoir des pertes de c.,** to have blackouts *or* fainting fits; **reprendre c.,** to regain consciousness, *F* to come round; **sans c.,** unconscious; **il a toute sa c.,** he's quite *or* fully conscious.
connaissement [kɔnɛsmɑ̃] *nm Nau Com* bill of lading.
connaisseur,-euse [kɔnɛsœr, -øz] **1** *n* expert, connoisseur; **être bon c. en qch,** to be a good judge of *or* an authority on sth. **2** *adj* expert, knowledgeable; **je ne suis pas du tout c.,** I'm by no means an expert; **regarder qch d'un œil c.,** to look at sth with a critical *or* expert eye.
connaître [kɔnɛtr] *v* (*prp* **connaissant**; *pp* **connu**; *pr ind* **je connais, il connaît, n. connaissons**; *impf* **je connaissais**; *p hist* **je connus**; *fu* **je connaîtrai**) **1** *vt* **(a)** (*objet*) to know, to be acquainted with (*sth*); **c. les chemins,** to be familiar with the roads; **tu connais la route?,** do you know the way?; **je connais tous les détails,** I am aware of all the circumstances; **je ne connais pas les paroles de la chanson,** I don't know the words to *or* of the song; **je lui connaissais du talent,** I knew he had talent; **faire c. qch,** to bring sth to light, to make sth known; **il n'a jamais connu l'amour,** he has never experienced love; **elle n'a jamais connu la faim,** she's never known (what) hunger (means); **cette région connaît actuellement une famine,** that region is now experiencing a famine; **je ne connais pas Milan,** I don't know Milan; *F* **mais bien sûr, je ne connais que ça,** yes, yes it's on the tip of my tongue; **connaissez-vous la nouvelle?,** have you heard the news?; **sa bonté ne connaît pas de limites,** his goodness knows no bounds; **si tu te tais, ni vu ni connu,** if you keep quiet, no-one will be any the wiser; **elle ne connaît que son travail,** she knows nothing outside her work, she lives for her work; **il en connaît bien d'autres,** he has plenty more tricks up his sleeve; *F* **elle en connaît un rayon sur la question,** she knows quite a bit about the matter; **tu ne connais pas ta chance,** you don't know how lucky you are, you don't know your luck; *F* **je connais la musique,** I've heard it all before, it's always the same old story;
(b) (*personne*) to know, to be acquainted with (*s.o.*); **c. qn de nom/vue,** to know s.o. by name/sight; **c. qn de réputation,** to know s.o. by reputation, to have heard of s.o.; **c. son monde,** to know the people one has to deal with; **il est connu comme le loup blanc,** (just about) everybody knows *or* has heard of him; **il est connu ici,** he's well known around here; *F* **je le connais par cœur/comme ma poche,** I know him through and through/I can read him like a(n open) book; **c'est connu!,** I've heard that one before!; *F* **ça me connaît, le foot,** I know all there is to know about football; *F* **si tu fais ça, je ne te connais plus,** if you do that, I'll disown you;
(c) (*rencontrer*) to make the acquaintance of (*s.o.*), to come to know (*s.o.*); **se faire c.,** to introduce oneself (by name); (*par le public etc*) to become (well-)known; **je vous le ferai c.,** I'll introduce him to you;
(d) to know (*a language*); to be versed in (*science, art, language etc*); **c. à fond,** to be thoroughly conversant with (*sth*), to have a thorough knowledge of (*sth*); to have a thorough command of (*a language*); **elle connaît très bien le russe,** she has a good command of Russian; **je ne connais pas cette théorie,** I'm not familiar with that theory; **il n'y connaît rien,** he doesn't know anything about it;
(e) (*reconnaître*) to distinguish; **c. le bien du mal,** to know good from evil;
(f) *Bible* to know (*woman*).
2 *vi Jur* **c. de qch,** to take cognizance of sth.
3 se connaître *vpr* **(a) se c. (soi-même),** to know oneself;
(b) se c. en qch, to know all about *or* be a good judge of sth; *F* **il s'y connaît,** he's an expert;
(c) (*se rencontrer*) to meet; **ils se sont connus en 1970,** they met in 1970;
(d) il ne se connaît plus, he has lost control of himself; **il ne se connaît plus de joie,** he's beside himself with joy, he's walking on air.
connard, -arde [kɔnar, -ard] *adj & n* = **CONARD**.
connecter [kɔnɛkte] **1** *vt Él Électron* to connect; *Fig* **je vais vous c. avec lui,** I'll put you in touch with him. **2 se connecter** *vpr Él Électron* to be connected, to be in contact *or* connection; *Fig* **essayez de vous c. avec eux pour le voyage,** try to join up with them for the journey.
connecteur [kɔnɛktœr] *nm Él Électron* connector.
connerie [kɔnri] *nf Arg* (piece of) damned *or* bloody stupidity; **c'est une belle c.,** it's a load of (old) cobblers *or* crap *or* bloody nonsense *or* bollocks; **c'est de la c., ne le crois pas!,** bullshit *or* crap, don't believe it!; **tu as fait là une c. magistrale,** that was bloody stupid of you.
connétable [kɔnetabl] *nm Hist* High Constable.
connexe [kɔnɛks] *adj* connected, allied, related.
connexion [kɔnɛksjɔ̃] *nf* **(a)** connection (*of parts, ideas etc*); **à c. directe,** direct-acting; **(b)** connecting organ *or* part; *Él* lead, connection.
connivence [kɔnivɑ̃s] *nf* connivance, complicity; **agir** *ou* **être de c. avec qn,** to act in complicity *or* collusion with s.o., to connive with s.o..
connotation [kɔnɔtasjɔ̃] *nf* connotation.
connoter [kɔnɔte] *vt* to imply, to connote; *Ling* to connote.
connu [kɔny] **1** *adj* well known, famous; **un écrivain c.,** a

well known writer; **c'est (un fait) bien c.!**, that's a well-known fact!, everyone knows that!; **elle est bien connue, celle-là!**, everybody knows that joke, that's an old one! **2** *nm* **passer** *ou* **aller du c. à l'inconnu**, to go from the known to the unknown.

conque [kɔ̃k] *nf* **(a)** (*coquille*) conch, marine shell; **(b)** *Anat* external ear.

conquérant, -ante [kɔ̃kerɑ̃, -ɑ̃t] **1** *adj* conquering (*nation etc*); *F* **air c.**, swaggering air, swagger. **2** *n* conqueror; **Guillaume le C.**, William the Conqueror.

conquérir [kɔ̃kerir] *v* (*prp* **conquérant**; *pp* **conquis**; *pr ind* **je conquiers, n. conquérons, ils conquièrent**; *impf* **je conquérais**; *p hist* **je conquis**; *fu* **je conquerrai**) **1** *vt* to conquer, to subdue (*country, people*); to gain, to win (over), to make a conquest of (*s.o., sth*); **se battre pour c. un marché**, to fight (in order) to conquer *or* capture *or* win a market; **c. l'estime de qn**, to win *or* gain s.o.'s esteem. **2 se conquérir** *vpr* to be (hard) won *or* earned.

conquête [kɔ̃kɛt] *nf* **(a)** (act of) conquest; **faire la c. d'un pays**, to conquer a country; **faire la c. de qn**, to gain s.o.'s sympathy and respect, to make a conquest of s.o.; **vous avez fait sa c.**, you have won his heart; **(b)** acquisition, possession; (*territoire*) conquered territory; *F* **il nous a présenté sa dernière c.**, he introduced us to his latest conquest.

consacré [kɔ̃sakre] *adj* **(a)** consecrated, sacred (*vessel etc*); hallowed (*ground*); **(b)** sanctioned, established (*custom etc*).

consacrer [kɔ̃sakre] **1** *vt* **(a)** to consecrate (*altar, bread and wine etc*); **c. un évêque/un prêtre**, to consecrate a bishop/to ordain a priest; **(b)** to dedicate (*one's life to God etc*); to devote (*one's time, energy, to sth*); **c. sa vie à la lecture et à l'étude**, to devote one's life to reading and study; **combien de temps pouvez-vous me c.?**, how much time can you spare me?; **(c)** to sanctify, to hallow (*memory, place etc*); **(d)** (*entériner*) to establish, to sanction. **2 se consacrer** *vpr* to devote *or* dedicate oneself (to); **se c. à son travail/son foyer**, to devote oneself to one's work/home *or* family.

consanguin [kɔ̃sɑ̃gɛ̃] *adj* **(a) frère c./sœur consanguine**, half brother/sister (on father's side); **mariage c.**, marriage between blood relations, intermarriage; **(b)** inbred (*horse etc*).

consanguinité [kɔ̃sɑ̃gɥinite] *nf* **(a)** consanguinity (*through the father*); **(b)** (*de cheval etc*) inbreeding.

consciemment [kɔ̃sjamɑ̃] *adv* consciously, knowingly, wittingly.

conscience [kɔ̃sjɑ̃s] *nf* **(a)** *Physiol Psy* consciousness; *Phil* self-consciousness; **perdre c.**, to lose consciousness; **reprendre doucement c.**, to slowly regain consciousness *or* come round; **à 80 ans elle a encore toute sa c.**, at the age of 80 she is still very alert; **avoir c. de qch/d'avoir fait qch**, to be conscious *or* aware of sth/of having done sth; **c. de soi**, self-awareness; **avoir c. de ses capacités**, to be aware of one's abilities; **il finira par prendre c. de la gravité de la situation**, he'll eventually wake up to the seriousness of the situation; **prise de c.**, sudden awareness; **c'est la première fois que j'en ai pris c.**, it's the first time that it has come home to me; **la c. de classe**, class-consciousness; **la c. collective**, collective consciousness;

(b) (*morale*) conscience; **mauvaise c.**, guilty conscience; **c. large**, accommodating conscience; **écouter la voix de sa c.**, to listen to (the voice of) one's conscience; *F* **il a la c. élastique**, he is not over-scrupulous; **avoir qch sur la c.**, to have sth on one's conscience; **pour avoir la c. tranquille je vais vérifier que tout est bien fermé**, to set my mind at rest, I'll just make sure everything's locked up; **faire qch par acquit de c.**, to do sth for conscience's sake; **dire qch en c.**, to say sth in good faith; **manque de c.**, unscrupulousness; **ça m'est longtemps restée sur la c.**, it was on my conscience *or* preyed on my mind for a long time; **j'ai bonne c.**, my conscience is clear; **c'est un moyen pour se donner bonne c.**, it's a way of appeasing one's conscience; **liberté de c.**, freedom of conscience;

(c) (*dans son travail*) conscientiousness; **c. professionnelle**, professional integrity; **faire qch avec c.**, to do sth conscientiously.

consciencieusement [kɔ̃sjɑ̃sjøzmɑ̃] *adv* conscientiously.

consciencieux, -ieuse [kɔ̃sjɑ̃sjø, -jøz] *adj* conscientious (*person, work*).

conscient [kɔ̃sjɑ̃] *adj* **(a)** (*lucide etc*) conscious, (fully) aware (**de**, of; **que**, that); *Phil* self-conscious; **être c.**, sentient being; **c'est un choix tout à fait c.**, it's an entirely conscious choice; **être c. de ses devoirs**, to be aware of one's duties, to know where one's duty lies; **(b)** (*éveillé*) conscious, awake; **le malade n'est plus c.**, the patient is no longer conscious *or* has lost consciousness.

conscription [kɔ̃skripsjɔ̃] *nf Mil* conscription, *US* draft.

conscrit [kɔ̃skri] *nm* **(a)** *Mil* (*qui a l'âge d'être inscrit*) one liable to conscription; (*qui fait son service*) conscript, recruit, *US* draftee; **(b)** *Fig* novice, greenhorn, *F* sucker.

consécration [kɔ̃sekrasjɔ̃] *nf* **(a)** consecration (*of church, bishop etc*); ordination (*of priest*); **(b)** consecration (*of bread and wine*); **(c)** (*établissement*) establishing (*of custom, reputation*).

consécutif, -ive [kɔ̃sekytif, -iv] *adj* **(a)** (*qui se suivent*) consecutive; **pendant trois jours consécutifs**, for three days running; *Gram* **proposition consécutive**, consecutive clause; **(b) c. à**, following on; **fatigue consécutive à une longue marche**, fatigue resulting from a long walk.

consécutivement [kɔ̃sekytivmɑ̃] *adv* consecutively, in succession; **c. à cette invitation**, following (upon) this invitation.

conseil [kɔ̃sɛj] *nm* **(a)** (*recommandation*) (piece of) advice; **c'est un homme de bon c.**, he gives sound advice; **j'ai besoin de tes conseils** *ou* **ton conseil**, I need your advice; **c'est un bon c.**, that's a good piece of advice, that's good advice; **donner c. à qn**, to advise s.o.; **demander c. à qn**, to ask s.o.'s advice; **ne jamais suivre les conseils d'un jaloux**, never heed *or* listen to the advice of a jealous man; **elle m'a donné le c. de venir ici**, she advised me to come here; **les conseils de l'expérience**, the voice of experience; **pouvez-vous me donner quelques conseils?**, can you give me some hints *or* tips?; *Prov* **la nuit porte c.**, sleep on it;

(b) avocat-c., legal consultant; **ingénieur-c.**, consulting engineer; *Jur* **c. judiciaire**, = guardian, administrator, trustee (*of estate of mentally deficient young person*);

(c) (*réunion*) council, committee, board; **les membres du c.**, members of the board; **tenir c.**, to hold (a) council; **le c. des ministres**, the Cabinet; *Can* **c. exécutif**, council of ministers, Cabinet; **c. d'État**, Council of State; **c. municipal**, ≈ borough *etc* council; **c. général**, ≈ county council, regional council; *Com* **c. d'administration**, board of directors; *Fig* **tenir un c. de guerre**, to hold a council of war; *Mil* **passer en c. de guerre**, to be court-martialled; **c. de prud'hommes**, = industrial tribunal, industrial court of arbitration; *Scol etc* **c. de discipline**, disciplinary committee; **passer en c. de discipline**, to appear before the disciplinary committee; *Jur* **c. de famille**, family council; **C. de l'Europe**, Council of Europe; **C. de sécurité**, (*de l'O.N.U.*) Security Council;

(d) *Arch* (*of person*) counsellor, counsel;

(e) *Arch & Litt* (firm) resolution; **ne savoir quel c. prendre**, not to know what decision to make.

conseiller¹ [kɔ̃seje] *vt* to advise, to counsel; **c. qn**, to advise s.o., to give advice to s.o.; **c. qch à qn**, to recommend sth to s.o.; **c. un jeune dans ses sorties/lectures/fréquentations**, to advise a youngster as to where he should go/what he should read/the company he should keep; **je ne vous le conseille pas**, I wouldn't *or* shouldn't if I were you; **c. à qn de faire qch**, to advise *or* recommend s.o. to do sth; **l'expérience me conseille d'attendre**, experience tells *or* prompts me to wait; **nous avons été très mal conseillés**, we were very badly advised, we were given very bad advice.

conseiller², -ère [kɔ̃seje, -jɛr] *n* **(a)** (*conducteur*) counsellor, adviser; **la jalousie est mauvaise conseillère**, do not be guided by the voice of jealousy; **c. juridique/technique**, legal/technical adviser; **c. fiscal**, tax consultant; **c'est un très bon c.**, he gives very good advice; *Scol* **c. d'orientation**, careers adviser; **(b)** *Admin* **c. municipal**, town *or* borough councillor; **c. général**, ≈ county councillor; **(c)** *Jur* **c. à la cour (d'appel)**, appeal court judge.

conseilleur, -euse [kɔ̃sɛjœr, -øz] *n Péj* giver *or* dispenser of (unwanted) advice.

consensuel, -elle [kɔ̃sɑ̃sɥɛl] *adj* (*accord, décision*) reached by consensus.

consensus [kɔ̃sɛ̃sys] *nm* consensus (*of opinion*).

consentant [kɔ̃sɑ̃tɑ̃] *adj Jur* in agreement, agreeing; consenting (*party etc*); **elle est consentante**, she's willing.

consentement [kɔ̃sɑ̃tmɑ̃] *nm* consent, assent; **il lui faut le c. de ses parents**, he needs his parents' consent; **donner son c. à qch**, to assent *or* consent to sth.

consentir [kɔ̃sɑ̃tir] *v* (*conj like* **sentir**) **1** *vi* to consent, to agree; **c. à (faire) qch**, to consent *or* agree to (do) sth; **je consens (à ce) qu'il vienne**, I consent *or* agree to his coming; **il a fini par c.**, he finally agreed, *F* he came round in the end. **2** *vt* **(a) c. un prêt,** to grant a loan; **c. une remise à qn,** to allow s.o. a discount; **(b)** *(accepter)* to accept *(sth)*; **elle consent qu'on l'aide,** she agrees to being helped, she agrees to accept help.

conséquemment [kɔ̃sekamɑ̃] *adv* **(a) c. à,** as a result of, in consequence of; **(b)** *Arch & Litt* consequentially.

conséquence [kɔ̃sekɑ̃s] *nf* **(a)** *(résultat)* consequence, result; **il faut en subir les conséquences,** we *or* you *etc* must take the consequences; **tu traînes, tu traînes, c. on est encore en retard,** you keep dawdling and the result is *or* and as a result we're late again; **qu'est-ce que cela aura pour c.?,** what will be the effect *or* the result of it?; **cela ne tire pas à c.,** it's of no consequence; **cet événement eut plus d'une heureuse c.,** that event had several happy results; **en c.,** in consequence, consequently, as a result; **agir en c.,** to take appropriate action; **en c. de ...,** in consequence of ...; *(selon)* according to ...;

(b) *(conclusion)* inference; **tirer une c. de qch,** to draw an inference *or* a conclusion from sth;

(c) *(importance)* consequence, importance; **personne sans c.,** person of no importance *or* consequence.

conséquent, -ente [kɔ̃sekɑ̃, -ɑ̃t] **1** *adj* **(a)** consistent, rational *(mind, speech etc)*; **il n'est pas c. dans ses actions,** he's not consistent in his actions; **être c. avec soi-même,** to be consistent (in one's actions); **(b)** *Mus* **partie conséquente d'une fugue,** countersubject of a fugue; **(c)** *F* *(important)* important, of consequence; **homme/affaire conséquent(e),** important man/business; **(d) par c.,** consequently, accordingly, therefore. **2** *nm Gram Math* consequent. **3** *nf Mus* **conséquente,** consequent, answer.

conservateur,-trice [kɔ̃sɛrvatœr, -tris] **1** *n* **(a)** *(gardien)* keeper, warden; **c. de bibliothèque,** librarian; **c. d'un musée,** curator *or* keeper of a museum; **c. des hypothèques,** registrar of mortgages; **(b)** *Pol* conservative. **2** *nm* *(alimentaire)* preservative; **sans c.,** preservative- free, free of preservatives. **3** *adj* **(a)** *Pol* Conservative; **(b)** preserving, preservative *(process etc)*.

conservation [kɔ̃sɛrvasjɔ̃] *nf* **(a)** conserving, conservation, preserving, preservation *(of fruit, meat etc)*; **ils manquent de moyens de c.,** they have no means of keeping food fresh *or* of preserving food; **c. par le froid,** refrigeration; *(congélation)* freezing; **(b)** preservation, care *(of buildings, archives, health etc)*; *Biol* **instinct de c.,** instinct of self-preservation; **des bâtiments en bon état de c.,** well-preserved buildings; **(c)** retaining, keeping *(of rights, situation etc)*; **(d)** registration *(of mortgages)*; **c. des Eaux et Forêts,** *Br* ~ Forestry Commission; **(e)** (state of) preservation; **meubles d'une belle c.,** well-preserved *or* well-kept furniture.

conservatisme [kɔ̃sɛrvatism] *nm Pol etc* conservatism.

conservatoire [kɔ̃sɛrvatwar] **1** *adj Jur* conservatory *(act etc)*; **mesures conservatoires,** measures of conservation. **2** *nm* **(a)** *(musée)* repository, museum; **C. des arts et métiers,** museum and college of Arts and Crafts; **(b)** school, academy *(of music, of dramatic art)*, *Am* conservatory; **le C. (de Paris),** the Paris Conservatoire.

conserve [kɔ̃sɛrv] *nf* **(a)** *(alimentaire)* preserved *or* tinned *or* canned food; *(en bocal)* preserve; **boîte de c.,** tin, can; **conserves au vinaigre,** pickles; **bœuf de c.,** tinned beef, corned beef, *Am* canned beef; **petits pois en c.,** tinned peas; **mettre en c.,** to tin, to can; *F* **évitez de manger trop de conserves,** try not to eat too many tinned foods, *F* try not to live out of tins; *F* **je vais mettre cet argent en c.,** I'm going to hang on to this money; **(b)** *Nau* consort; **naviguer de c.,** to sail in company *or* together (**avec,** with).

conservé [kɔ̃sɛrve] *adj* **femme bien conservée,** well-preserved woman.

conserver [kɔ̃sɛrve] **1** *vt* **(a)** to preserve, to conserve *(fruit, meat etc)*; to preserve, to take care of *(building, furniture, clothes etc)*; **aliments conservés,** tinned *or* canned *or* bottled foods; **c. des tomates en bocaux,** to bottle tomatoes; **cette vie de plein air l'a bien conservé,** this outdoor life has kept him well-preserved; **(b)** to keep, to retain, to maintain *(rights, situation etc)*; **c. son sang-froid** *ou* **sa tête,** to remain cool, to keep one's head; **cette vieille citadelle a conservé sa dignité,** this old citadel has retained *or* maintained *or* preserved its dignity; **elle a réussi à c. ses cheveux malgré le traitement,** she has managed to keep *or* not to lose her hair in spite of the treatment; **c. l'allure,** to keep up *or* maintain the speed; *Mil* **c. une position,** to hold a position. **2 se conserver** *vpr* *(of goods etc)* to keep; **articles qui ne se conservent pas,** perishable goods.

conserverie [kɔ̃sɛrvəri] *nf* **(a)** *Ind* canning industry; **(b)** *(fabrique)* cannery, canning factory.

considérable [kɔ̃siderabl] *adj* considerable, large *(number, population)*; considerable, large, extensive *(property etc)*; considerable, significant *(change etc)*; **il lui reste un travail c. à faire,** he has still got a considerable *or* substantial amount of work to do; **un changement d'une importance c.,** a substantial *or* considerable change; **j'ai fait des dépenses considérables,** I have been *or* have gone to considerable expense.

considérablement [kɔ̃siderabləmɑ̃] *adv* considerably, significantly.

considérant [kɔ̃siderɑ̃] *nm Jur* preamble.

considération [kɔ̃siderasjɔ̃] *nf* **(a)** *(réflexion)* consideration, attention, thought; **sans c. de prix,** without considering *or* thinking about the price; **cette offre mérite toute notre c.,** this offer *or* bid deserves our full attention *or* consideration; **après c. de votre demande,** having considered *or* studied your application; **prendre en c.,** to take *(sth)* into consideration *or* account; to consider *(offer etc)*; **en c. de,** in consideration of, on account of;

(b) considérations, observations, reflexions, thoughts; **considérations sur l'histoire/sur la condition féminine,** reflexions on history/on the status of women *or* the female condition;

(c) *(motif)* reason, motive; **je ne peux pas entrer dans ces considérations,** I can't go into these considerations; **poussé par de nombreuses considérations,** driven *or* motivated by a variety of factors *or* considerations;

(d) *(estime)* regard, esteem, respect; **agir avec/sans c.,** to act considerately/inconsiderately; **n'avoir de c. pour personne,** to have no consideration for anyone, to be most inconsiderate; **tu as agi sans aucune c.,** that was most inconsiderate of you; **jouir d'une grande c.,** to be highly respected; **veuillez agréer, Monsieur, l'assurance de ma parfaite** *ou* **haute c.,** *(dans une lettre)* yours truly; **agréez l'assurance de ma c. distinguée,** yours faithfully *or* truly; **par c. pour,** out of consideration *or* regard for.

considéré [kɔ̃sidere] *adj* highly regarded *or* respected *(person)*.

considérer [kɔ̃sidere] *v* (**je considère, n. considérons; je considérerai**) **1** *vt* **(a)** to consider, to weigh up *(matter)*; **c. le pour et le contre,** to weigh up *or* consider the pros and cons; **tout bien considéré,** taking everything into consideration *or* account, all things considered, on the whole; **c'est à c.,** it must be borne in mind; *(à étudier)* it must be considered; **considérant que ...,** considering that ...;

(b) to contemplate, to gaze on, to look at *(sth)*;

(c) *(estimer)* to regard, to deem; **on la considère beaucoup,** she is highly thought of; **je considère votre lettre comme frivole,** I think your letter is flippant; **je le considère comme mon meilleur ami,** I regard *or* consider *or* look on him as my best friend; **je considère ce livre le meilleur de l'année,** I consider the book to be the best of the year; **je considère que tu aurais pu te renseigner auparavant,** I really think you could have found out beforehand.

2 se considérer *vpr* to consider *or* regard oneself; **se c. comme responsable,** to consider *or* hold oneself responsible.

consignataire [kɔ̃siɲatɛr] *nm* **(a)** *Jur* depositary; **(b)** *Com Nau* consignee.

consignation [kɔ̃siɲasjɔ̃] *nf* **(a)** deposit *(of money)*; **caisse des dépôts et consignations,** Deposit and Consignment Office; **(b)** *Com* consignment *(of goods)*; **marchandises en c.,** goods on consignment; **(c)** charging a deposit *(on container)*.

consigne [kɔ̃siɲ] *nf* **(a)** order(s), instructions *(to sentry etc)*; **il a pour c. de ne laisser passer personne,** his orders are to let nobody pass; **observer la c.,** to obey orders; **c'est la c.,** those are the orders; **(b)** *Mil* confinement *(to barracks etc)*; *Scol* detention; **deux heures de c.,** two hours detention; **(c)** *Rail* left-luggage office, *Am* checkroom; **c. automatique,** left-luggage lockers; **(d)** deposit *(on bottle etc)*.

consigner [kɔ̃siɲe] *vt* **(a)** to deposit *(money etc)*; **bouteille consignée,** returnable bottle; **emballage non consigné,** non-returnable packing; **(b)** *Com* to consign *(goods etc)* (**à,** to); **(c)** to register, to write down, to enter, to record, to put on record *(fact etc)*; **c. des impressions par écrit/sur un cahier,** to consign *or* commit one's thoughts to paper/in a notebook; **(d)** *Mil* to confine *(soldier)* to barracks; *Scol* to detain, to keep in *(pupil)*; **la salle est consignée,** the hall is closed; **c. sa porte à qn,** to bar one's door to s.o.; **(e)** *Rail* **c. ses bagages,** to put *or* deposit one's luggage in the left-luggage office *or Am* checkroom.

consistance [kɔ̃sistɑ̃s] *nf* **(a)** consistence, consistency (*of syrup, cream etc*); **prendre c.,** to thicken; *Fig* **ses projets semblent prendre (de la) c.,** his plans seem to be taking shape; **(b)** stability, firmness (*of mind, character*); **sans c.,** spineless; **(c)** *Fig* (*fondement*) credit; **bruit sans c.,** unfounded *or* groundless rumour.

consistant [kɔ̃sistɑ̃] *adj* firm, solid, stable (*substance*); thick (*paint etc*); **repas c.,** substantial meal; **méthode consistante,** coherent *or* consistent method; **information consistante,** reliable information.

consister [kɔ̃siste] *vi* to consist; **c. en qch,** to consist *or* be composed of sth; **le repas consiste en un sandwich et une pomme,** the meal consists of *or* comprises a sandwich and an apple; **en quoi consiste cette tâche?,** what does the job *or* task involve *or* entail?; **c. dans qch,** to consist in sth; **le bonheur consiste à rendre heureux les autres,** happiness consists *or* lies in making others happy.

consistoire [kɔ̃sistwar] *nm Rel* consistory.

consœur [kɔ̃sœr] *nf surtout Iron* fellow member, sister member, colleague.

consolable [kɔ̃sɔlabl] *adj* consolable.

consolant [kɔ̃sɔlɑ̃] *adj* consoling, comforting; **ce qui est c., c'est que ...,** the comforting thing (about it) is that ... .

consolateur, -trice [kɔ̃sɔlatœr, -tris] **1** *n Litt* consoler, comforter. **2** *adj* consoling, consolatory.

consolation [kɔ̃sɔlɑsjɔ̃] *nf* consolation, solace, comfort; **apporter la c. à qn,** to bring comfort to s.o., to comfort *or* console s.o.; **paroles de c.,** words of comfort, comforting *or* consoling words; **c'est ma seule c.,** it's my only consolation; **cette jeune fille est ma c.,** that young woman is my consolation.

console [kɔ̃sɔl] *nf* **(a)** *Ordinat* console; **(b)** (*meuble*) console (table), pier table; **(c)** *Archit* console, corbel, bracket; *Constr* **grue à console,** wall crane; **(d)** *Mus* console (*of organ*); neck (*of harp*).

consoler [kɔ̃sɔle] **1** *vt* to console, to solace, to comfort; **c. qn de sa peine,** to comfort *or* console s.o. in his grief; **le temps console,** time is a great healer; **si ça peut te c.,** if that's any comfort to you. **2 se consoler** *vpr* to console oneself, to find comfort *or* consolation; **se c. en pensant que ...,** to console oneself with the thought that ...; **se c. avec qn,** to console oneself with s.o.; **se c. d'une perte,** to get over a loss; **elle s'est vite consolée,** she soon got over it *or* consoled herself; **je ne pourrai jamais m'en c.,** I'll never get over it; **ça me console de voir que ça t'est déjà arrivé,** it consoles me *or* is a consolation that it's happened to you too.

consolidation [kɔ̃sɔlidɑsjɔ̃] *nf* **(a)** consolidation, strengthening, reinforcing (*of foundation, position, power etc*); **(b)** *Méd* healing (*of wound*); knitting (*of fracture*); **(c)** *Fin* funding (*of floating debt*).

consolidé [kɔ̃sɔlide] **1** *adj Fin* **dette consolidée,** funded debt; **fonds consolidés,** consolidated fund, consols. **2** *nmpl* **consolidés,** consols.

consolider [kɔ̃sɔlide] **1** *vt* **(a)** to consolidate, to strengthen, to reinforce (*foundations, position etc*); **(b)** *Méd* to heal (*wound*); to knit (*fracture*); **(c)** to fund (*debt*); to consolidate (*rates*). **2 se consolider** *vpr* **(a)** (*se renforcer*) to consolidate, to strengthen; **(b)** *Méd* to heal, to knit.

consommable [kɔ̃sɔmabl] *adj* consumable; (*solide*) edible; (*liquide*) drinkable.

consommateur, -trice [kɔ̃sɔmatœr, -tris] *n* consumer (*of products*); customer (*in restaurant, café*).

consommation [kɔ̃sɔmɑsjɔ̃] *nf* **(a)** accomplishment (*of work etc*); perpetration (*of crime*); consummation (*of marriage*); **jusqu'à la c. des siècles,** until the end of time; **(b)** use, consumption (*of electricity, petrol*); *Mil Nau* expenditure (*of stores, equipment etc*); **les biens de c.,** consumer goods; **faire une grande c. de papier,** to go through *or* use (up) a lot of paper; **société de c.,** consumer society; **coopérative de c.,** co(-)operative wholesale store, co(-)op; **crédit à la c.,** consumer credit; **(c)** drink (*in café*).

consommé [kɔ̃sɔme] **1** *adj* consummate (*skill etc*); accomplished (*writer etc*). **2** *nm Culin* clear soup, consommé.

consommer [kɔ̃sɔme] **1** *vt* **(a)** to accomplish, to achieve (*work etc*); to perpetrate (*crime*); to consummate (*marriage*); **(b)** to consume (*electricity etc*); to eat (*food*); **cette voiture consomme trop (d'essence),** this car is heavy on petrol *or Am* gas. **2** *vi* to use, to consume; **c. au bar,** to have a drink in *or* at the bar. **3 se consommer** *vpr* to be consumed *or* taken (*of food, drink etc*); **ce plat se consomme froid,** this dish is eaten cold.

consomption [kɔ̃sɔ̃psjɔ̃] *nf* **(a)** *Méd* wasting, decline; *Arch* consumption; **(b)** *Arch & Litt* consuming (*by fire*).

consonance [kɔ̃sɔnɑ̃s] *nf Mus Ling* consonance; **mots aux consonances harmonieuses/bizarres,** harmonious/queer sounding words.

consonant [kɔ̃sɔnɑ̃] *adj Mus Ling* consonant.

consonne [kɔ̃sɔn] *nf Ling* consonant; **c. occlusive/labiale,** plosive/labial (consonant).

consort [kɔ̃sɔr] **1** *adj* **prince c.,** prince consort. **2** *nm* **(a)** *Jur* **consorts,** jointly interested parties; **(b)** *Péj* **et consorts,** and company.

consortial, -aux [kɔ̃sɔrsjal, -o] *adj Com Fin* consortial.

consortium [kɔ̃sɔrsjɔm] *nm Com Fin* consortium, syndicate.

conspirateur, -trice [kɔ̃spiratœr, -tris] **1** *n* conspirator, conspirer. **2** *adj* conspiring, conspiratorial.

conspiration [kɔ̃spirɑsjɔ̃] *nf* conspiracy, plot; *F* **mais c'est une c.,** (*ils sont tous contre moi aujourd'hui*) it's a conspiracy.

conspirer [kɔ̃spire] *vi* **(a)** (*tramer*) to conspire, to plot (**contre,** against); **(b)** (*contribuer*) to conspire, to tend, to concur; **tout conspire à me mettre en retard,** everything's conspiring to make me late.

conspuer [kɔ̃spɥe] *vt* to boo, to shout down (*play, speaker etc*).

constamment [kɔ̃stamɑ̃] *adv* constantly, continually, continuously.

constance [kɔ̃stɑ̃s] *nf* **(a)** (*dans une tâche*) persistence, perseverance; (*en amour etc*) constancy; **manquer de c. en amour,** to be fickle; **il a de la c. à t'attendre depuis cinq ans,** he's been faithfully waiting for you for five years; **travailler avec c.,** to work steadily; **(b)** (*de la température etc*) constancy, invariability.

constant, -ante [kɔ̃stɑ̃, -ɑ̃t] **1** *adj* **(a)** constant (*heart, friendship etc*); firm, unshaken (*perseverance etc*); **(b)** established, patent (*fact etc*); **(c)** constant (*temperature*); continuous, uninterrupted (*traffic etc*); **à niveau c.,** at a constant level. **2** *nf Math Phys etc* **constante,** constant.

constat [kɔ̃sta] *nm* **(a)** *Jur* certified *or* official statement *or* report; **dresser un c. d'accident,** to write out an accident report; **c. à l'amiable,** unofficial account (of an incident); **c. d'huissier,** affidavit made by a process server; **(b)** (*fait*) established fact.

constatation [kɔ̃statɑsjɔ̃] *nf* **(a)** verification, establishment (*of fact etc*); noting, taking note; **procéder aux constatations d'usage,** to make the usual *or* routine investigations *or* inquiries; **(b)** (*fait*) observation; **constatations d'une enquête,** findings of an enquiry; **la première c. est la suivante,** the first point of note is the following.

constater [kɔ̃state] *vt* **(a)** to establish, to verify, to ascertain, to note (*fact etc*); **c. une erreur,** to discover *or* find a mistake; **vous pouvez c. vous-même qu'elle est partie,** you can see for yourself that she's gone; **(b)** (*reconnaître*) to state, to record (*sth*); **c. un décès,** to certify a death.

constellation [kɔ̃stelɑsjɔ̃] *nf* constellation; *Fig* **la c. des lumières de la ville,** the twinkling city lights.

consteller [kɔ̃stele] *vt* to constellate; **ciel constellé d'étoiles,** star-spangled sky; **robe constellée de pierreries,** dress studded *or* starred with jewels; **des taches de sang constellent sa chemise,** his shirt is spattered with blood.

consternant [kɔ̃stɛrnɑ̃] *adj* alarming, dismaying (*news*); **d'une bêtise consternante,** alarmingly stupid.

consternation [kɔ̃stɛrnɑsjɔ̃] *nf* consternation, dismay.

consterner [kɔ̃stɛrne] *vt* to dismay, to stagger (*s.o.*), to strike (*s.o.*) with consternation *or* dismay; **prendre un air consterné,** to look dumb-founded *or* stunned.

constipation [kɔ̃stipɑsjɔ̃] *nf Méd* constipation.

constipé, -ée [kɔ̃stipe] **1** *adj Méd* constipated; *F* (*air, manière etc*) embarrassed, ill at ease, stiff. **2** *n Méd* constipated *or Méd* costive person, constipation sufferer; *F* **quel c.!,** what a stuffed shirt!

constiper [kɔ̃stipe] *Méd* **1** *vt* to constipate. **2** *vi* to be constipated *or* costive; **nourriture qui constipe,** constipating food.

constituant, -ante [kɔ̃stitɥɑ̃, -ɑ̃t] **1** *adj* **(a)** component, constituent (*part, element*); **(b)** *Pol* **l'Assemblée constituante,** the Constituent Assembly (of 1789). **2** *nm* constituent part; **les constituants,** the members of the Constituent Assembly. **3** *nf* **la Constituante,** the Constituent Assembly (of 1789).

constitué [kɔ̃stitɥe] *adj* **(a)** constituted, organized (*authority etc*); **les corps constitués,** official bodies; **(b)** *Anat* constituted, formed; **enfant bien c.,** fine, healthy child.

constituer [kɔ̃stitɥe] **1** *vt* **(a)** (*former*) to constitute, to form, to frame, to make up; to constitute, to set up, to institute (*committee etc*); to incorporate (*an order, a society*); to form (*ministry etc*); **parties qui constituent le tout,** parts that constitute *or* (go to) make up the whole; **ce mobilier constitue tout mon bien,** this furniture represents all my worldly goods, this furniture is all I own; **cet acte constitue un outrage aux bonnes moeurs,** this action constitutes *or* represents an affront to public decency; **appartement constitué de six pièces,** six-roomed flat *or Am* apartment;

(b) *Jur etc* to constitute, to appoint; **c. qn son héritier,** to make s.o. one's heir; **c. une rente à qn,** to settle an annuity on s.o.

2 se constituer *vpr* **(a) se c. prisonnier,** to give oneself up (*to the police etc*); **se c. partie civile,** to bring an independent action to sue for damages;

(b) (*se réunir*) to unite; **ils se constituèrent en commission,** they resolved themselves into a committee.

constitutif, -ve [kɔ̃stitytif, -iv] *adj* **(a)** (*composant*) constituent, component; **les éléments constitutifs de l'air,** the constituent elements of air; **(b)** *Jur* constitutive, conferring a right; **titre c. (d'une propriété),** title deed.

constitution [kɔ̃stitysjɔ̃] *nf* **(a)** (*physique*) *& Pol* constitution; **avoir une bonne c.,** to have a sound constitution, to be fit; **loi conforme à la c.,** law complying with the constitution; **(b)** (*établissement*) constituting, appointing, establishing; **c. d'un comité,** forming of a committee; **c. de dot,** settlement of a dowry; *Jur* **c. de partie civile,** institution of civil action; **c. d'avoué,** briefing *or* instructions of lawyer; **(c)** composition (*of air, water*).

constitutionnaliser [kɔ̃stitysjɔnalize] *vt Jur* to constitutionalize.

constitutionnel, -elle [kɔ̃stitysjɔnɛl] *adj* constitutional.

constitutionnellement [kɔ̃stitysjɔnɛlmɑ̃] *adv* constitutionally.

constricteur [kɔ̃striktœr] **1** *adj* **(a) muscle c.,** constrictor muscle; **(b) boa c.,** boa constrictor. **2** *nm* constrictor (muscle).

constriction [kɔ̃striksjɔ̃] *nf* constriction (*of muscle, chest etc*).

constrictor [kɔ̃striktɔr] *adj & nm* **(boa) c.,** boa constrictor.

constructeur, -trice [kɔ̃stryktœr, -tris] *nm* constructor, builder; **c. mécanicien,** mechanical engineer; **c. (d') automobile(s),** car manufacturer; **c. d'ordinateurs,** computer manufacturer.

constructible [kɔ̃stryktibl] *adj* **terrain c.,** site approved for development.

constructif, -ive [kɔ̃stryktif, -iv] *adj* constructive.

construction [kɔ̃stryksjɔ̃] *nf* **(a)** (*d'un bâtiment*) construction, constructing, erecting, erection, building; construction (*of novel etc*); structure (*of sentence*); **matériaux de c.,** building materials; **c. navale,** shipbuilding; **maison en c.,** house under construction; **il y a plusieurs maisons en c. de l'autre côté de la rue,** several houses are being built on the other side of the street; **c. mécanique,** (mechanical) engineering; **jeu de c.,** construction set; **(b)** (*bâtiment*) structure, building; **un grand nombre de nouvelles constructions,** a large number of new buildings; **(c)** *Géom* figure, construction.

construire [kɔ̃strɥir] *v* (*prp* **construisant**; *pp* **construit**; *pr ind* **je construis, il construit, n. construisons**; *impf* **je construisais**; *p hist* **je construisis**; *fu* **je construirai**) **1** *vt* **(a)** to construct, to build (*a house*); to make, to lay out (*road etc*); **pendant qu'on construit la maison,** while the house is being built; **(b)** to assemble, to put together (*machine etc*); *Gram* **c. une phrase,** to construct a sentence; **c. une théorie,** to construct *or* put together a theory. **2 se construire** *vpr* to be constructed; **la région s'est beaucoup construite,** there has been a lot of building in the area, the area has become quite built-up; *Gram* **après que se construit avec l'indicatif,** après que takes the indicative.

consubstantiation [kɔ̃sypstɑ̃sjɑsjɔ̃] *nf Rel* consubstantiation, real presence.

consubstantiel, -ielle [kɔ̃sypstɑ̃sjɛl] *adj Rel* consubstantial, of one substance (**à, avec,** with).

consul [kɔ̃syl] *nm* consul; **le c. de France,** the French consul.

consulaire [kɔ̃sylɛr] *adj* consular.

consulat [kɔ̃syla] *nm* (*lieu*) consulate; (*charge*) consulship; *Fr Hist* **le C.,** the Consulate (1799).

consultable [kɔ̃syltabl] *adj* (*book etc*) available for consultation.

consultant, -ante [kɔ̃syltɑ̃, -ɑ̃t] **1** *adj* consulting; **médecin c.,** consultant. **2** *n* consultant; **agence de consultants,** consultancy.

consultatif, -ive [kɔ̃syltatif, -iv] *adj* consultative, advisory; **à titre c.,** in an advisory capacity; **assemblée consultative,** consultative assembly.

consultation [kɔ̃syltɑsjɔ̃] *nf* **(a)** (*conférence*) consultation, conference; **entrer en c. avec qn,** to consult *or* confer with s.o.; **(b)** (*avis professionnel*) *Méd* (medical) advice; *Jur* (legal) opinion; *Méd* visit to a doctor; *Méd* **cabinet de c.,** consulting room, surgery, *Am* (doctor's) office; *Méd* **heures de c.,** surgery hours; *Méd* **consultation externe,** outpatients department; *Jur* **cabinet de c.,** chambers; **(c)** (*de livre*) consulting, consultation; **encourager la c. des dictionnaires,** to encourage the use of dictionaries; **livre de c. facile,** book that is easy to consult *or* use.

consulter [kɔ̃sylte] **1** *vt* to consult, to ask the advice *or* opinion of (*s.o.*); to consult, to refer to (*sth*); **c. un médecin/un avocat,** to take medical/legal advice; **c. un dictionnaire,** to consult a dictionary; **c. les horaires de départ,** to check departure times; **ouvrage à c.,** reference work; **c. ses intérêts,** to look after one's own interests. **2** *vi* to hold a consultation (with a colleague); *Méd* to take surgery. **3 se consulter** *vpr* to confer; **nous tenons à nous c. avant de décider;** we are anxious to confer before coming to a decision; **ils se sont consultés,** they put their heads together; **se c. du regard,** to exchange glances, to look questioningly at one another.

consumer [kɔ̃syme] **1** *vt* **(a)** to consume, to wear away, to destroy; **consumé par le feu,** consumed by fire, burnt up; *Fig* **consumé par l'ambition,** consumed by *or* eaten up with ambition; **consumé par les soucis,** consumed *or* eaten up *or* gnawed by doubt; **(b)** *Litt* to waste, to spend (*fortune, energy*); **une activité qui consume beaucoup d'énergie,** an energy-consuming activity; **ils veulent c. leur vie,** they're intent on living (their life *or* lives) in the fast lane. **2 se consumer** *vpr* to waste away, to pine (away); **se c. en efforts inutiles,** to wear oneself out in useless efforts; **elle se consume d'inquiétude,** she's consumed *or* eaten up with worry *or* anxiety.

contact [kɔ̃takt] *nm* **(a)** (*relation*) contact, touch; **être/entrer en c. avec qn/qch,** to be in contact *or* come into contact with s.o./sth; **prendre c.** *ou* **se mettre en c. avec qn,** to get in touch with s.o., to contact s.o.; **avez-vous un point de c.?,** (where) can you be contacted?, where can I get hold of you?; **prise de c.,** preliminary contacts, first meeting; **au c. agréable,** pleasant to the touch; **le c. de deux surfaces/personnes,** contact between *or* of two surfaces/between two people; **au c. de l'eau,** on contact with water; **garder/perdre le c.,** to keep/lose touch; **il va changer au c. de ces jeunes travailleurs,** mixing with these young workers is going to change him; **lentille** *ou* **verre de c.,** contact lens;

(b) switch, contact; *El* connection, contact; **c. avec la terre,** contact to earth; **point de c.,** contact point; **les fils sont en c.,** the wires are in contact; *Aut* **clef de c.,** ignition key; **établir** *ou* **mettre le c.,** to make contact, to switch on; **couper le c.,** to break contact, to switch off; **fiche** *ou* **cheville de c.,** contact plug.

contacter [kɔ̃takte] *vt* to contact, to get in touch with.

contacteur [kɔ̃taktœr] *nm El* contactor.

contagieux, -ieuse [kɔ̃taʒjø, -jøz] **1** *adj* contagious, infectious, catching (*disease etc*); **rire c.,** infectious laugh; **tu y vas aussi?, c'est c.!,** you're going too?, it's contagious! **2** *n* **un c.,** a contagious patient *or* case.

contagion [kɔ̃taʒjɔ̃] *nf Méd etc* contagion; (*maladie*) infectious *or* contagious disease; **arrêter la c. d'un virus,** to stop a virus from spreading; **période de c.,** contagious stage; **la c. du rire,** the infectiousness of laughter.

container [kɔ̃tɛnɛr] *nm* container.

contaminateur, -trice [kɔ̃taminatœr, -tris] *adj & n Méd* carrier.

contamination [kɔ̃taminɑsjɔ̃] *nf* (*pollution*) contamination, pollution; *Méd* infection.

contaminer [kɔ̃tamine] *vt* (*polluer*) to contaminate, to pollute (*water etc*); *Méd* to infect; *Ordinat* **disque dur contaminé par un virus,** virus-infected hard disk.

conte [kɔ̃t] *nm* **(a)** (*histoire*) story, tale; **c. de fées,** fairy tale *or* story; **contes de bonnes femmes,** old wives' tales; **(b)** *Arch & Litt* (tall) story, yarn; **c. à dormir debout,** cock-and-bull story.

contemplateur, -trice [kɔ̃tɑ̃platœr, -tris] *n* contemplator.

contemplatif, -ive [kɔ̃tɑ̃platif, -iv] **1** *adj* contemplative. **2** *n* meditator; *Rel* contemplative.

contemplation [kɔ̃tɑ̃plasjɔ̃] *nf* **(a)** (*d'un tableau etc*) contemplate; **être en c. devant la mer,** to gaze (*in contemplation*) at the sea; **(b)** (*méditation*) contemplation, meditation; **plongé dans la c.,** lost in contemplation *or* meditation; **(c)** *Rel* contemplation.

contempler [kɔ̃tɑ̃ple] **1** *vt* to contemplate, to gaze at (*nature, picture etc*). **2 se contempler** *vpr* (*dans la glace*) to look at *or* contemplate oneself.

contemporain -aine [kɔ̃tɑ̃pɔrɛ̃, -ɛn] **1** *adj* **(a)** contemporary; present-day (*opinions etc*); **un écrivain c.,** a contemporary writer; **(b)** (*du même âge*) contemporaneous (**de,** with); **être c. de qn,** to be a contemporary of s.o.. **2** *n* contemporary; **ils sont contemporains,** they are contemporaries.

contenance [kɔ̃tnɑ̃s] *nf* **(a)** capacity, content (*of bottle etc*); **c. d'un navire,** burden of a vessel; **d'une c. de dix litres,** capable of holding ten litres, with a capacity of ten litres; **(b)** (*allure*) countenance, bearing; **avoir une c. modeste/fière,** to have a modest/proud demeanour *or* bearing; **faire bonne c.,** to put on a bold front; **perdre c.,** to lose one's composure; **faire qch pour se donner une c.,** to do sth to avoid losing face.

contenant [kɔ̃tnɑ̃] *nm,* **conteneur** [kɔ̃tnœr] *nm* container.

contenir [kɔ̃tnir] *v* (*conj like* **tenir**) **1** *vt* **(a)** (*renfermer*) to contain, to hold (*certain quantity, number*); **le théâtre contient mille places,** the theatre seats a thousand; **le dictionnaire contient plus de cinquante mille articles,** the dictionary contains *or* has fifty thousand entries; **la brochure contient tous les renseignements nécessaires,** the brochure contains all the neccessary details *or* information, everything you need to know is in the brochure; **lettre contenant chèque,** letter enclosing cheque; **(b)** to restrain, to keep *or* hold in check (*crowd, feelings etc*); to suppress (*anger*); to hold back (*tears*); **c. l'ennemi,** to contain the enemy, to keep the enemy in check. **2 se contenir** *vpr* to contain oneself, to control one's emotions; **apprendre à se c.,** to learn self-control, to learn to control one's emotions.

content [kɔ̃tɑ̃] **1** *adj* (*satisfait*) content, satisfied, pleased (**de,** with); (*ravi*) glad; **être c. de son sort,** to be content *or* satisfied with one's lot; **il est très c. ici,** he's very happy here; **elle a l'air c. de sa nouvelle voiture,** she seems pleased *or* happy with her new car; **je suis c. de vous,** I'm pleased with you; **je suis très c. de vous voir,** I am very pleased to see you; **un air trop c. de soi,** an overly self-satisfied *or* a smug manner; **non c. de mentir, il vole!,** not content with lying, he steals as well!; **votre père ne sera pas c.,** your father won't be (very) pleased *or* happy, your father won't like it; **je suis fort c. que vous soyez venu,** I'm so glad you've come. **2** *nm* **manger tout son c.,** to eat one's fill; **s'amuser tout son c.,** to enjoy oneself to one's heart's content.

contentement [kɔ̃tɑ̃tmɑ̃] *nm* (*état*) content(ment); (*satisfaction*) satisfaction (**de,** at, with); **c. de soi,** smugness, self-satisfaction.

contenter [kɔ̃tɑ̃te] **1** *vt* to content, to satisfy (*s.o.*); to satisfy, to gratify (*curiosity*); to gratify (*whim etc*); **un rien le contente,** the least thing makes him happy, he's very easily pleased; **on ne peut pas c. tout le monde,** you can't please everyone. **2 se contenter** *vpr* to be happy (**de,** with); **se c. de (faire) qch,** to be content *or* satisfied with (doing) sth; **je me contenterai de faire remarquer que ...,** I will merely point out that ...; **il se contente d'un repas par jour,** he has only *or* he is content with one meal a day; **pour toute réponse, elle se contenta d'un sourire,** by way of reply, she merely smiled.

contentieux, -ieuse [kɔ̃tɑ̃sjø, -jøz] **1** *adj* contentious (*matter*). **2** *nm Admin* contentious business, matters in dispute; *Jur* litigation; legal department (*of bank, administration etc*); **chef du c.,** (*company's etc*) solicitor.

contention¹ [kɔ̃tɑ̃sjɔ̃] *nf* **(a)** application, exertion (*of faculties*); **c. d'esprit,** intentness of mind; **(b)** *Arch* contention, dispute.

contention² *nf Méd* retention (*of fracture etc*) in place; *Psy* restraint, restraining (*by strait-jacket etc*).

contenu [kɔ̃tny] **1** *adj* restrained, suppressed (*passion, style etc*). **2** *nm* contents (*of parcel etc*); **le c. de sa lettre,** the content *or* tenor of his letter; *Ling* **le c. du mot,** the content *or* meaning of a word.

conter [kɔ̃te] *vt* to tell, to relate (*story etc*); *F* **allez c. ça ailleurs!** (go and) tell that to the marines!; **elle ne s'en laisse pas c.,** you can't fool her; *Hum* **c. fleurette à qn,** to whisper *or* murmur sweet nothings to s.o..

contestable [kɔ̃tɛstabl] *adj* contestable, debatable, questionable.

contestataire [kɔ̃tɛstatɛr] **1** *adj* anti-establishment; **j'ai eu un client c. aujourd'hui,** I had a cantankerous customer today. **2** *n* protester; **c'est une c.,** she's a rebel.

contestation [kɔ̃tɛstasjɔ̃] *nf* **(a)** (*controverse*) dispute; **être en c. avec qn,** to be at variance *or* issue with s.o.; **élever une c. sur qch,** to raise an objection to sth; **sans c. possible,** beyond all question, beyond dispute; **(b)** *Pol* protest.

conteste [kɔ̃tɛst] *adv* **sans c.,** indisputably, unquestionably, beyond question.

contester [kɔ̃tɛste] **1** *vt* to contest, to dispute, to challenge (*point, right etc*); **point contesté,** controversial point; **c. l'efficacité d'une méthode de travail,** to question *or* dispute the effectiveness of a method of working; **je lui conteste le droit,** I contest *or* question his right. **2** *vi* to take issue (**sur,** over); *Pol* to protest.

conteur, -euse [kɔ̃tœr, -øz] *n* **(a)** (*narrator*) narrator, storyteller; **(b)** (*écrivain*) story writer.

contexte [kɔ̃tɛkst] *nm* context; **le c. permet de mieux comprendre certain mots,** some words are more readily understood in context; **donner un c.,** to give a context, to put a word in(to) context; **c. historique,** historical background (*of an event*); **dans le c. de l'économie européenne,** within the context of the European economy.

contextuel, -elle [kɔ̃tɛkstyɛl] *adj Ling* contextual.

contexture [kɔ̃tɛkstyr] *nf* **(a)** (con)texture (*of bones, muscles etc*); **(b)** *Vieilli* structure, framework (*of story, poem*).

contigu, -uë [kɔ̃tigy] *adj* adjoining, adjacent, contiguous; **c. à** *ou* **avec qch,** next *or* adjacent *or* contiguous to sth; **idées contiguës,** analogous *or* related ideas.

contiguïté [kɔ̃tigɥite] *nf* adjacency, proximity (*of house etc*); *Fig* **la c. des idées/des vues,** closeness of ideas/opinions.

continence [kɔ̃tinɑs] *nf* continence.

continent¹ [kɔtinɑ̃] *adj* continent.

continent² *nm Géog* **(a)** (*étendue*) continent; **l'ancien/le nouveau c.,** the Old/the New World; **(b)** (*par rapport à l'île*) mainland.

continental, -aux [kɔ̃tinɑ̃tal, -o] **1** *adj* continental; **la France continentale,** mainland France. **2** *n* continental.

contingence [kɔ̃tɛ̃ʒɑ̃s] *nf Phil* contingency; **les contingences de la vie quotidienne,** everyday happenings; **ignorer les contingences,** to ignore the incidentals.

contingent [kɔ̃tɛ̃ʒɑ̃] **1** *adj Phil* contingent. **2** *nm* **(a)** *Mil* contingent; **le c. annuel d'une classe est de 250 000 hommes,** the annual intake *or* call-up *or US* draft totals 250,000 men; **(b)** (*quota*) quota; (*de marchandises*) contingent; (*part*) share, contribution.

contingentement [kɔ̃tɛ̃ʒɑ̃tmɑ̃] *nm Admin* quota system of distribution; apportioning of quotas; **le c. des importations,** import control (*by setting quotas*).

contingenter [kɔ̃tɛ̃ʒɑ̃te] *vt Admin* **(a)** to establish *or* set quotas for (*imports etc*); **(b)** to distribute (*films etc*) according to a quota.

continu [kɔ̃tiny] **1** *adj* continuous, unbroken (*line*); unceasing, incessant (*chatter*); sustained (*effort etc*); endless (*suffering*); **faire la journée continue,** to work all day (with only a short break for lunch); *Él* **courant c.,** direct current; *Ordinat* **papier c.,** continuous paper; *Ordinat* **texte c. sans alinéa,** running text. **2** *nm Phil Phys Math* continuum.

continuateur, -trice [kɔ̃tinɥatœr, -tris] *n* successor.

continuation [kɔ̃tinɥasjɔ̃] *nf* **(a)** continuation (*of work etc*); *F* **bonne c.!,** keep up the good work!, keep it up!; **(b)** duration, long spell, run (*of bad weather etc*).

continuel, -elle [kɔ̃tinɥɛl] *adj* continual, unceasing, ceaseless; **des plaintes continuelles,** constant *or* unending *or* perpetual complaints; **le c. devenir,** (*de l'individu*) continual evolution *or* development.

continuellement [kɔ̃tinɥɛlmɑ̃] *adv* continually.

continuer [kɔ̃tinɥe] **1** *vt* (*poursuivre*) to continue (with), to carry on (with), to go on with, to keep on with (*studies, efforts etc*); **c. sa route,** to continue on one's way. **2** *vi* **(a) c. à** *ou* **de faire qch,** to continue to do sth, to go on *or* carry on doing sth; **continuez!,** go on!, go ahead!, keep it up!, carry on!; **la guerre continue,** the war is still going on; **(b)** (*dans l'espace*) to extend; **jardin qui continue jusqu'à la rivière,** garden that extends to the river. **3 se continuer** *vpr* to continue, to be continued; **le chemin se continue et se perd dans un bois,** the path continues *or* carries on and disappears into *or* gets lost in a wood.

continuité [kɔ̃tinɥite] *nf* (*d'une action*) continuity; (*d'une tradition*) continuation; *Fig* **solution de c.,** (*pour un projet, une politique etc*) solution to ensure continuity; **assurer la**

c. d'une tradition, to perpetuate *or* carry on a tradition.
continûment [kɔ̃tinymɑ̃] *adv* continuously.
continuum [kɔ̃tinyɔm] *nm Math Phys etc* continuum; **c. espace-temps,** space-time continuum.
contondant [kɔ̃tɔ̃dɑ̃] *adj* **objet c.,** blunt object.
contorsion [kɔ̃tɔrsjɔ̃] *nf* contortion, twisting (*of face etc*); **il ne cesse de faire des contorsions,** he moves constantly when he speaks.
contorsionner (se) [səkɔ̃tɔrsjɔne] *vpr* to contort one's body *or* oneself, to writhe (about).
contorsionniste [kɔ̃tɔrsjɔnist] *n* contortionist.
contour [kɔ̃tur] *nm* **(a)** outline, contour; **(b)** (*in surveying*) contour (line).
contourné [kɔ̃turne] *adj* twisted, contorted, crooked (*limb, tree etc*); (over) elaborate (*furniture etc*); *Péj* **style c.,** tortuous style.
contournement [kɔ̃turnəmɑ̃] *nm* skirting (*of mountain etc*); *Rail* **(voie de) c.,** loop line.
contourner [kɔ̃turne] *vt* **(a)** to shape, to trace the outline of (*design, vase etc*); **(b)** to pass round, to skirt (round), to bypass (*hill, wood etc*); **c. la loi/une difficulté,** to get round *or* circumvent the law/a difficulty; **(c)** (*déformer*) to twist, to warp, to contort, to distort.
contraceptif, -ive [kɔ̃trasɛptif, -iv] *Méd* **1** *adj* contraceptive; **la pilule contraceptive,** the (contraceptive) pill. **2** *nm* contraceptive; **c. local/oral,** barrier/oral contraceptive.
contraception [kɔ̃trasɛpsjɔ̃] *nf* contraception; **méthode de c.,** method of contraception, contraceptive method; **changer de c.,** to change one's method of contraception; **les moyens de c.,** contraceptive methods *or* techniques.
contractant [kɔ̃traktɑ̃] *Jur* **1** *adj* contracting (*party*). **2** *nm* contracting party.
contracté [kɔ̃trakte] *adj* tense (*muscles etc*); *Gram* contracted; *Fig* **il était très contracté,** he was very tense.
contracter[1] [kɔ̃trakte] *vt* **(a)** to contract, to enter into (*alliance, marriage*); to incur, to contract (*debt*); **c. une assurance,** to take out an insurance policy; **(b)** to acquire (*habit*); to contract, to catch (*disease*).
contracter[2] **1** *vt* to contract, to draw together; to tense (*muscles*); **visage contracté par la douleur,** face drawn with pain. **2 se contracter** *vpr* (*of heart etc*) to contract; (*of muscle*) to tense up, to contract; *Ling* (*of word, article*) to contract, to be contracted (into).
contractile [kɔ̃traktil] *adj Physiol* contractile, contractible (*muscle etc*).
contraction [kɔ̃traksjɔ̃] *nf* contraction (*of body etc*); contraction, tensing (*of muscle*); *Ling* contraction; **sentir les premières contractions,** (*d'une femme qui va accoucher*) to feel the first contractions.
contractuel, -elle [kɔ̃traktɥɛl] **1** *adj* contractual (*obligation etc*); **agent c.,** = contractor working for the (local) council. **2** *n* = traffic warden.
contracture [kɔ̃traktyr] *nf Méd* spasm.
contradicteur [kɔ̃tradiktœr] *nm* contradictor.
contradiction [kɔ̃tradiksjɔ̃] *nf* **(a)** (*opposition*) contradiction; *Jur* opposition; **être en c. avec qn/les faits,** to be at variance with s.o./with the facts; **esprit de c.,** contrariness; **il ne supporte pas la c.,** he can't stand being contradicted; **(b)** (*inconséquence*) contradiction, inconsistency; **en c. avec qch,** inconsistent *or* incompatible with sth; **être en proie à des contradictions,** to be pulled both ways; *F* **cette théorie est un tissu de contradictions,** this theory is a tissue of contradictions *or* inconsistencies; **être en c. avec soi,** to contradict oneself.
contradictoire [kɔ̃tradiktwar] *adj* contradictory (**à,** to); inconsistent (**à,** with); contradictory, conflicting (*accounts etc*); *Jur* **jugement c.,** judgment after trial; **débat c.,** debate.
contradictoirement [kɔ̃tradiktwarmɑ̃] *adv Jur* after hearing both parties.
contraignant [kɔ̃trɛɲɑ̃] *adj* restricting, constraining.
contraindre [kɔ̃trɛ̃dr] *v* (*pp* **contraint**; *pr ind* **je contrains, n. contraignons, ils contraignent**; *impf* **je contraignais**; *p hist* **je contraignis**; *fu* **je contraindrai**) **1** *vt* **(a)** to restrain (*s.o., one's feelings*); **(b)** (*obliger*) to constrain, to compel, to force; **c. qn à** *ou* **de faire qch,** to constrain *or* force s.o. to do sth; **je fus contraint de me taire,** I was obliged *or* compelled to keep quiet; **cela va vous c. à revenir,** that will force you to come back (again); *Jur* **c. qn par voie de justice,** to bring an action against s.o.. **2 se contraindre** *vpr* **(a)** (*se retenir*) to restrain oneself; **(b) se c. à faire qch,** to force oneself to do sth, to make oneself do sth.
contraint [kɔ̃trɛ̃] *adj* constrained, cramped (*posture, style etc*); forced (*smile*); stiff (*manner*); **c. et forcé,** under duress.
contrainte [kɔ̃trɛ̃t] *nf* **(a)** restraint; **parler sans c.,** to speak freely; **(b)** (*obligation*) constraint, compulsion, coercion; **faire qch par c.,** to be forced to do sth; **agir sous la c.,** to act under pressure *or* duress; *Jur* **c. par corps,** imprisonment for debt; **c. sociale,** social pressure *or* constraint(s); **(c)** *Tech* **c. de cisaillement/de traction,** shearing/tensile stress *or* strain.
contraire [kɔ̃trɛr] **1** *adj* **(a)** opposite (*direction etc*); opposed, conflicting (*interest etc*); **en sens c.,** in the opposite direction; **sauf avis c.,** unless I *or* you *etc* hear to the contrary; **c. à la règle** *ou* **aux règlements,** against *or* contrary to the rules; **(b)** (*opposé*) adverse, opposed; **le sort lui est c.,** fate is against him; **vent c.,** adverse *or* contrary wind; **le climat lui est c.,** the climate does not agree with him. **2** *nm* opposite, contrary; **c'est le c.,** it's the other way round; **il ne vous dit pas le c.,** he's not denying it; **(bien) au c.,** on the contrary; **au c. de ses frères,** unlike his brothers; **au c. de ses parents, il est plutôt à gauche,** unlike *or* in contrast to his parents, he's a bit left-wing.
contrairement [kɔ̃trɛrmɑ̃] *adv* **c. à,** contrary to, in opposition to, unlike; **c. à son habitude, il sortit sans manteau,** contrary to his habit, he went out without a coat, he went out without a coat, which was unusual for him.
contralto [kɔtralto] *nm Mus* contralto; (*pl contraltos*).
contrariant [kɔ̃trarjɑ̃] *adj* (*personne, esprit*) perverse, contrary; (*ennuyeux*) tiresome, irritating; **comme c'est c.!,** how annoying!
contrarié [kɔ̃trarje] *adj* (*ennuyé*) annoyed, vexed; (*contrecarré*) thwarted.
contrarier [kɔ̃trarje] *vt* (*impf & pr sub* **n. contrariions, v. contrariiez**) **(a)** (*ennuyer*) to annoy, to bother; **il cherche à la c.,** he's trying to annoy her; **il y a quelque chose qui me contrarie,** something's annoying me; **(b)** (*contrecarrer*) to thwart, to oppose, to cross, to frustrate; **c. les desseins de qn,** to interfere with *or* thwart s.o.'s plans; **(c)** (*mélanger*) to disrupt, to mix up; **c. l'ordre d'une série,** to get a series out of sequence.
contrariété [kɔ̃trarjete] *nf* **(a)** (*agacement etc*) vexation, annoyance; **éprouver une vive c.,** to be very much annoyed; **(b)** clash(ing) (*of interests, tastes, colours etc*); **esprit de c.,** contrariness, perversity.
contrastant [kɔ̃trastɑ̃] *adj* contrasting (*colours etc*).
contraste [kɔ̃trast] *nm* contrast; **mettre une chose en c. avec une autre,** to contrast one thing with another; **être en c.** *ou* **faire c. avec,** to contrast with; **en c. avec le rouge,** in contrast to the red; **un effet de c.,** a contrasting effect; *TV* **le réglage des contrastes,** contrast control *or* adjustment; **le goût du c.,** a taste *or* liking for contrast(s); **le c. des idées,** the contrast(ing) of ideas.
contrasté [kɔ̃traste] *adj* contrasted, contrasting (*colours etc*).
contraster [kɔ̃traste] **1** *vi* **c. avec qch,** to contrast *or* stand in contrast with sth; **couleurs qui contrastent,** contrasting colours. **2** *vt* to put (*colours etc*) in contrast.
contrat [kɔ̃tra] *nm* contract, agreement; (*document*) deed; **rupture de c.,** breach of contract; **passer un c. avec qn,** to enter into *or* conclude an agreement with s.o.; **c. de mariage,** marriage settlement, *Am* premarital agreement; **c. d'assurance,** contract of insurance; **c. de vente,** bill of sale; *Aut* **c. de location,** rental agreement; *Cartes* **réaliser son c.,** to make one's contract; **c. de travail,** contract of employment, *US* labor contract; **c. social,** social contract; **c. collectif,** collective agreement.
contravention [kɔ̃travɑ̃sjɔ̃] *nf Jur* contravention, infringement (*of law etc*); (*de stationnement*) (parking) ticket; **être en c.,** to be contravening the law; **donner** *ou F* **flanquer une c. à qn,** to give s.o. a ticket, to book s.o.; **avoir une c. (sur son pare-brise),** to get a (parking) ticket (on one's windscreen).
contre [kɔ̃tr] **1** *prép* **(a)** (*opposition*) against; **nager c. le courant,** to swim against the current; **se battre c. qn,** to fight against *or* with s.o.; **se fâcher c. qn,** to get angry with s.o.; **c. toute attente,** contrary to all expectation(s); **c. son habitude,** contrary to his usual practice; **l'Angleterre c. l'Irlande,** England versus Ireland; **la loi c. l'avortement,** the anti-abortion law; **je n'ai rien c.,** I have nothing against it; **je n'ai rien c. lui,** I have nothing against him,
(b) (*protection*) from; **s'abriter c. la pluie,** to shelter from the rain; **sirop c. la toux,** cough mixture;
(c) (*échange*) (in exchange) for; **échanger une chose c. une autre,** to exchange one thing for another; **livraison c. remboursement,** cash on delivery;
(d) (*pour*) to; **parier à cinq c. un,** to bet five to one;

(e) *(près)* (close) to, by; **s'appuyer c. le mur,** to lean against the wall; **sa maison est tout c. la mienne,** his house adjoins mine;
(f) *(en dépit de)* in spite of; **faire c. mauvaise fortune bon cœur,** to put a good face on things; **c. toute apparence,** despite appearances (to the contrary).
2 *adv* against; **parler/voter pour et c.,** to speak/vote for and against; **la maison est tout c.,** the house is close by; **par c.,** on the other hand.
3 *nm* **(a) disputer le pour et le c.,** to argue the pros and cons; **il y a toujours du pour et du c.,** there are two sides to everything;
(b) *Boxe Escrime* counter;
(c) *Billard* kiss;
(d) *Cartes* double.

contre-accusation [kɔ̃trakyzɑsjɔ̃] *nf* counter-charge; (*pl contre-accusations*).

contre-alizé [kɔ̃tralize] *adj & nm Météo* countertrade, anti-trade (wind); (*pl contre-alizés*).

contre-allée [kɔ̃trale] *nf* side path *or* lane; (*pl contre-allées*).

contre-amiral [kɔ̃tramiral] *nm* rear-admiral; (*pl contre-amiraux*).

contre-appel [kɔ̃trapɛl] *nm Mil* check roll call, second call; (*pl contre-appels*).

contre-assurance [kɔ̃trasyrɑ̃s] *nf* reinsurance; (*pl contre-assurances*).

contre-attaque [kɔ̃tratak] *nf Mil* counter-attack; (*pl contre-attaques*).

contre-attaquer [kɔ̃tratake] *vi* to counter-attack.

contrebalancer [kɔ̃trəbalɑ̃se] *v* (**je contrebalançai(s); n. contrebalançons**) **1** *vt* to counterbalance, to counterpoise, to offset. **2 contrebalancer (s'en)** *vpr F* not to give a damn *or* toss; **il s'en contrebalance,** he couldn't care less.

contrebande [kɔ̃trəbɑ̃d] *nf* **(a)** *(activité)* contraband, smuggling; **faire la c.** to be a smuggler; **faire entrer des marchandises en c.,** to smuggle in goods; **(b)** *(marchandise)* contraband goods, smuggled goods.

contrebandier, -ière [kɔ̃trəbɑ̃dje, -jɛr] *n* smuggler.

contrebas (en) [ɑ̃kɔ̃trəbɑ] *adv* (lower) down, on a lower level, below; **le café est en c. de la rue,** the café is below street level.

contrebasse [kɔ̃trəbas] *nf Mus* *(instrument)* (double) bass; *(musicien)* (double) bass player.

contrebassiste [kɔ̃trəbasist] *nm Mus* (double) bass player.

contrebasson [kɔ̃trəbasɔ̃] *nm Mus* double bassoon, contrabassoon.

contrebatterie [kɔ̃trəbatri] *nf Mil* counterbattery.

contre-biais [kɔ̃trəbjɛ] *nm inv* diagonal cut against the twist (*of cloth*).

contre-bord (à) [akɔ̃trəbɔr] *adv Nau* **courir à c.-b.,** to sail on opposite tacks *or* on parallel and opposite courses.

contreboutant [kɔ̃trəbutɑ̃] *nm* **(a)** *Archit etc* buttress; **(b)** *Constr* shore.

contrebouter [kɔ̃trəbute] **, contrebuter** [kɔ̃trəbyte] *vt Constr etc* to buttress, to shore up.

contrecarrer [kɔ̃trəkɑre] *vt* to cross, to thwart, to oppose (*s.o., plans*).

contrechamp [kɔ̃trəʃɑ̃] *nm Cin* reverse shot.

contre-chant [kɔ̃trəʃɑ̃] *nm Mus* counterpoint; (*pl contre-chants*).

contrechâssis [kɔ̃trəʃɑsi] *nm inv* double (window) frame.

contrecœur[1] [kɔ̃trəkœr] *adv* **à c.,** unwillingly, reluctantly, grudgingly; **partir à c.,** to leave with regret *or* reluctantly.

contrecœur[2] *nm* **(a)** *Constr* backplate, fireback (*of fireplace*); **(b)** *Rail* guardrail, wingrail, checkrail (*at centre of crossover*).

contrecoup [kɔ̃trəku] *nm* recoil, rebound (*of bullet etc*); jar (*of blow etc*); after-effects, consequence (*of action, disaster*); **les contrecoups de la guerre,** the repercussions of war.

contre-courant [kɔ̃trəkurɑ̃] *nm Hyd* countercurrent; **nager à c.-c.,** to swim against the current *or* the stream; (*pl contre-courants*).

contredanse [kɔ̃trədɑ̃s] *nf* **(a)** quadrille (*dance, air*); **(b)** *F (amende)* (parking) ticket, fine.

contredire [kɔ̃trədir] *v* (*pr ind* **je contredis, n. contredisons, v. contredisez**; *other tenses like* **dire**) **1** *vt* **(a)** to contradict (*s.o.*); to deny, to refute; **(b)** to be inconsistent with, to be contrary to (*sth*); to belie (*expectations*); **les événements contredisent ses prédictions,** the events are at variance with his predictions. **2 se contredire** *vpr* to contradict oneself; **ces deux textes se contredisent,** these two texts do not agree; **tu ne cesses de te c.,** you keep (on) contradicting yourself.

contredit [kɔ̃trədi] *adv* **sans c.,** indisputably, unquestionably.

contrée [kɔ̃tre] *nf* (geographical) region.

contre-écrou [kɔ̃trekru] *nm MecE* lock nut; (*pl contre-écrous*).

contre-effet [kɔ̃trefɛ] *nm* contrary effect; (*pl contre-effets*).

contre-enquête [kɔ̃trɑ̃kɛt] *nf Jur* counter-enquiry; (*pl contre-enquêtes*).

contre-épreuve [kɔ̃treprœv] *nf* (*pl contre-épreuves*) **(a)** *(épreuve)* counterproof; **(b)** *Tech* check test.

contre-espionnage [kɔ̃trɛspjɔnaʒ] *nm* counter-espionage.

contre-essai [kɔ̃tresɛ] *nm* control experiment, check test; (*pl contre-essais*).

contre-exemple [kɔ̃trɛgzɑ̃pl] *nm* example to the contrary; (*pl contre-exemples*).

contre-expertise [kɔ̃trɛkspɛrtiz] *nf* countervaluation; (*pl contre-expertises*).

contrefaçon [kɔ̃trəfasɔ̃] *nf* **(a)** counterfeiting, fraudulently copying, imitating (*trademark etc*); **(b)** *(product)* counterfeit, forgery, fraudulent imitation; (*livre, disque, vidéo*) pirated edition.

contrefacteur [kɔ̃trəfaktœr] *nm* counterfeiter, forger (*of document*).

contrefaction [kɔ̃trəfaksjɔ̃] *nf* counterfeiting (*of coins etc*); forgery (*of banknotes etc*).

contrefaire [kɔ̃trəfɛr] *vt* (*conj like* **faire**) **(a)** *(calquer)* to imitate, to mimic (*s.o.*); to disguise (*one's voice, writing etc*); *Vieilli* to feign; **(b)** to counterfeit (*coin etc*); to forge (*signature, currency etc*); **(c)** to distort, to deform (*shape etc*); **(d)** to pirate (*book, video, audio-cassette etc*).

contrefait [kɔ̃trəfɛ] *adj* **(a)** counterfeit, forged (*money etc*); **(b)** deformed (*person*).

contre-feu [kɔ̃trəfø] *nm* (*pl contre-feux*) **(a)** (*dans cheminée*) fireback; **(b)** *(feu)* counterfire; *Am* backfire.

contre-fiche [kɔ̃trəfiʃ] *nf Constr* brace, strut; (*pl contre-fiches*).

contreficher (se) [səkɔ̃trəfiʃe] *vpr Arg* **je m'en fiche et m'en contrefiche,** I don't give a damn, I couldn't care less.

contre(-)fil [kɔ̃trəfil] *nm* opposite direction (*of water-course etc*); **travailler le bois à c.-f.,** to work wood against the grain; (*pl contre(-)fils*).

contre-filet [kɔ̃trəfilɛ] *nm Culin* sirloin; (*pl contre-filets*).

contrefort [kɔ̃trəfɔr] *nm* **(a)** *Archit* (close) buttress; **(b)** *Géog* spur (*of mountain*); **contreforts,** foothills; **(c)** stiffening (*of shoe*).

contre-haut (en) [ɑ̃kɔ̃trəo] *adv* higher up, on a higher level, above.

contre-indication [kɔ̃trɛ̃dikɑsjɔ̃] *nf Méd* contra-indication; (*pl contre-indications*).

contre-indiquer [kɔ̃trɛ̃dike] *vt Méd* to contra-indicate; **c'est contre-indiqué,** it's inadvisable *or* unwise.

contre-interrogatoire [kɔ̃trɛ̃tɛrɔgatwar] *nm Jur* cross-examination; (*pl contre-interrogatoires*).

contre-jour [kɔ̃trəʒur] *nm* (*pl contre-jours*) **(a)** *(éclairage)* (unfavourable) light from behind (*for picture etc*); **tableau pendu à c.-j.,** picture hung against the light; **photo prise à c.-j.,** photograph taken against the light; **assis à c.-j.,** sitting with one's back to the light; **(b)** *Beaux-Arts Cin Phot* backlight(ing); **un effet de c.-j.,** a backlit *or* contre-jour effect.

contre-lettre [kɔ̃trəlɛtr] *nm Jur* counter-letter, counter-deed; (*pl contre-lettres*).

contremaître, -tresse [kɔ̃trəmɛtr, -trɛs] *n* foreman, forewoman.

contremander [kɔ̃trəmɑ̃de] *vt* to countermand, to cancel, to revoke (*order, invitation etc*).

contre-manifestant, -ante [kɔ̃trəmanifɛstɑ̃, -ɑ̃t] *n Pol* counter demonstrator; (*pl contre-manifestant(e)s*).

contre-manifestation [kɔ̃trəmanifɛstɑsjɔ̃] *nf Pol* counter demonstration; (*pl contre-manifestations*).

contre-manifester [kɔ̃trəmanifɛste] *vi Pol* to counter-demonstrate, to hold a counter demonstration.

contremarche [kɔ̃trəmarʃ] *nf* **(a)** *Mil* countermarch; **(b)** *Constr* riser (*of stair*).

contremarque [kɔ̃trəmark] *nf* **(a)** countermark (*on coin, gold plate etc*); **(b)** *Th* passout ticket.

contremarquer [kɔtrəmarke] *vt* to countermark.

contre-mesure [kɔ̃trəmzyr] *nf* (*pl contre-mesures*) **(a)** countermeasure; *Mil* **c.-m. électronique,** electronic countermeasure, jamming (device); **(b)** *Mus* **jouer à c.-m.,** to play against the beat *or* out of time.

contre-offensive [kɔ̃trɔfɑ̃siv] *nf Mil* counter-offensive; (*pl contre-offensives*).

contre-ordre [kɔ̃trɔrdr] *nm* = **CONTRORDRE.**

contrepartie [kɔ̃trəparti] *nf* **(a)** opposite *or* opposing view (*in debate etc*); *Com Fin* other party, other side (*in transaction*); *Bourse* **faire la c.,** to operate against one's client; **(b)** (*compensation*) compensation; **en c.,** in return (**de,** for); **(c)** (*comptabilité*) counterpart (*of entry*); duplicate (*of register*); **en c.,** per contra; **(d)** *Mus* counterpart.

contre-pas [kɔ̃trəpɑ] *nm inv Mil* half-pace.

contre-passer [kɔ̃trəpase] *vt* **(a)** *Com Fin* to return, to endorse back (*bill to drawer*); **(b)** to reverse, to contra (*item, entry*).

contre(-)pente [kɔ̃trəpɑ̃t] *nf* reverse gradient, counterslope; (*pl contre(-)pentes*).

contre-performance [kɔ̃trəpɛrfɔrmɑ̃s] *nf Sp* substandard performance; (*pl contre-performances*).

contrepèterie [kɔ̃trəpetri] *nf* spoonerism.

contre-pied [kɔ̃trəpje] *nm* (*pl contre-pieds*) **(a)** (*inverse*) opposite; **prendre le c.-p.,** to take the opposite course *or* view (**de,** to); **il prend toujours le c.-p. de ce qu'on lui dit,** he always does the opposite of what he's told; **à c.-p. de,** contrary to; **(b)** *Sp* **prendre son adversaire à c.-p.,** to wrong-foot one's opponent; **prendre la balle à c.-p.,** to take the ball on the wrong foot; **(c)** (*à la chasse*) back scent.

contre(-)placage [kɔ̃trəplakaʒ] *nm* plywood construction; (*pl contre-plaquages*).

contre(-)plaqué [kɔ̃trəplake] *nm* plywood; (*pl contre-plaqués*).

contre-plongée [kɔ̃trəplɔ̃ʒe] *nf Cin* low angle shot; **vue en c.-p.,** low angle view; (*pl contre-plongées*).

contrepoids [kɔ̃trəpwɑ] *nm* **(a)** counterweight, counterbalance; *MecE* balance weight (*of clock, lift etc*); *Fig* **faire c. à qch,** to (counter)balance sth; **(b)** balancing pole (*of rope dancer*).

contre-poil (à) [akɔ̃trəpwal] *adv* the wrong way (*of the nap, of the hair*); *F* **prendre qn à c.-p.,** to rub s.o. up the wrong way.

contrepoint [kɔ̃trəpwɛ̃] *nm Mus & Fig* counterpoint.

contrepoison [kɔ̃trəpwazɔ̃] *nm* antidote.

contre-porte [kɔ̃trəpɔrt] *nf* storm door, *Am* screed door; (*pl contre-portes*).

contre-préparation [kɔ̃trəpreparasjɔ̃] *nf Mil* counter-preparation; (*pl contre-préparations*).

contre(-)projet [kɔ̃trəprɔʒɛ] *nm* counterplan; (*pl contre-projets*)

contre-proposition [kɔ̃trəprɔpozisjɔ̃] *nf* counter-proposal, counterproposition; (*pl contre-propositions*).

contre(-)publicité [kɔ̃trəpyblisite] *nf* adverse publicity, bad publicity; *Fig* **cet article fait de la c.-p. à son auteur,** this article is a poor advertisement for its author.

contrer [kɔ̃tre] *vt* **(a)** *F* (*repousser*) to thwart; **c. un argument,** to counter *or* refute an argument; **se faire c.,** to come a cropper; **(b)** *Boxe* to counter (*blow*); **(c)** *Cartes* to double.

contre-rail [kɔ̃trəraj] *nm Rail* guard rail, check rail; (*pl contre-rails*).

contre-réforme [kɔ̃trərefɔrm] *nf Hist Rel* Counter Reformation.

contre-révolution [kɔ̃trərevɔlysjɔ̃] *nf Pol* counter-revolution; (*pl contre-révolutions*).

contre-révolutionnaire [kɔ̃trərevɔlysjɔnɛr] *adj & n* counter-revolutionary; (*pl contre-révolutionnaires*).

contreseing [kɔ̃trəsɛ̃] *nm Jur* countersignature.

contresens [kɔ̃trəsɑ̃s] *nm* **(a)** misinterpretation (*of words etc*); mistranslation (*of passage etc*); **prendre les paroles de qn à c.,** to misunderstand what s.o. said; **faire un c.,** to mistranslate, to misinterpret; **faire un c. dans une traduction,** to make a mistake in a translation, to mistranslate; **ce résumé de l'histoire est un c.,** this summary of the story is a piece of nonsense; **(b)** wrong way (*of material*); **(c) à c.,** in the wrong way *or* direction; **voitures qui défilent à c.,** cars passing in opposite directions; **à c. de,** in the opposite direction to.

contresignataire [kɔ̃trəsiɲatɛr] *adj & n Jur* countersignatory.

contresigner [kɔ̃trəsiɲe] *vt* to countersign.

contretemps [kɔ̃trətɑ̃] *nm* **(a)** (*ennui*) mishap, hitch, contretemps; (*retard*) delay, inconvenience; **arriver à c.,** to arrive at the wrong moment; **(b)** *Mus* note played against the beat *or* on the unaccented portion of the beat; **jouer à c.,** to play out of time.

contre-terrorisme [kɔ̃trətɛrɔrism] *nm* counter-terrorism.

contre-terroriste [kɔ̃trətɛrɔrist] *adj & n* counter-terrorist; (*pl contre-terroristes*).

contre-tirer [kɔ̃trətire] *vt* to run off counter-proofs from, to take a counter-proof of.

contre-torpilleur [kɔ̃trətɔrpijœr] *nm Arch Nau* destroyer; (*pl contre-torpilleurs*).

contre-ut [kɔ̃tryt] *nm Mus* top C.

contre-valeur [kɔ̃trəvalœr] *nf Fin* exchange value; (*pl contre-valeurs*).

contrevenant, -ante [kɔ̃trəvnɑ̃, -ɑ̃t] **1** *adj* contravening, offending (*party etc*). **2** *n* offender; contravener, infringer (*of regulations*).

contrevenir [kɔ̃trəvnir] *vi* (*conj like* **venir**) **c. à,** to contravene, to infringe.

contrevent [kɔ̃trəvɑ̃] *nm* **(a)** (outside) shutter (*of window*); **(b)** *Constr* brace, strut.

contre(-)vérité [kɔ̃trəverite] *nf* (*pl contre(-)vérités*) **(a)** (*affirmation fausse*) untruth, falsehood; **(b)** ironical statement (*intended to convey the contrary*).

contre-visite [kɔ̃trəvizit] *nf* = for someone suspected of fraudulently claiming sickness benefit, visit to a specific doctor at Social Security's request; (*par médecin*) = house call made, at the request of an employer, by a doctor (approved by Social Security) to determine whether an employee is genuinely ill; (*pl contre-visites*).

contre-voie (à) [akɔ̃trəvwa] *adv Rail* **descendre à c.-v.,** to get out on the wrong side of the train.

contribuable [kɔ̃tribɥabl] *n* taxpayer; **c. à l'impôt foncier,** = ratepayer.

contribuer [kɔ̃tribɥe] *vi* to contribute; **c. à qch,** to contribute to(wards) something, to make a contribution to(wards) sth; **c. à faire qch,** to help do something; **nous y avons contribué pour une bonne part,** we made a handsome contribution to it; **cela contribue pour beaucoup à la rendre heureuse,** that goes a long way towards making her happy; **il a beaucoup contribué à ...,** he has played a great part in ..., he has been instrumental in ... .

contributif, -ive [kɔ̃tribytif, -iv] *adj* contributive, contributory.

contribution [kɔ̃tribysjɔ̃] *nf* **(a)** *Admin* (*à l'État*) tax; (*à la collectivité locale*) rate; **contributions indirectes,** indirect taxation; **c. foncière,** land tax; **(bureau des) contributions,** tax office, = Inland Revenue, *US* Internal Revenue; **lever** *ou* **percevoir une c.,** to collect *or* levy a tax; **(b)** (*part*) contribution, share; (*collaboration*) participation, contribution; contribution (*to learning*); **mettre qn à c.,** to call on s.o.'s services; **mettre qch à c.,** to make use of sth; **avec la c. de ...,** in collaboration with, with the collaboration *or* participation of ... .

contrister [kɔ̃triste] *vt Arch Litt* to sadden, to grieve.

contrit [kɔ̃tri] *adj* contrite, penitent.

contrition [kɔ̃trisjɔ̃] *nf Rel Litt* contrition, penitence.

contrôlable [kɔ̃trolabl] *adj* that can be checked *or* verified, verifiable.

contrôle [kɔ̃trol] *nm* **(a)** checking, verification (*of information, statements etc*); *Admin* inspection, supervision (*of services*); *Com* auditing, checking (*of accounts etc*); *Sp Aut* check, checkpoint; *Aut* control (point) (*in reliability run etc*); **c. d'identité,** identity check; **c. de police,** police check;

(b) (*surveillance*) authority; **exercer un c. sévère sur qn,** to keep s.o. under strict supervision, to maintain strict control over s.o.; **le c. des prix,** price control; *Ordinat* **touche c.,** control key; *Fin* **c. des changes,** exchange control; *Th etc* **c. des billets,** checking of tickets; **(bureau de) c.,** ticket office, booking office, *Am* reservation office; *Scol* **c. continu,** continuous assessment; **c. de soi-même,** self-control; **perdre tout c. de soi,** to lose all self-control; **c. des naissances,** birth control;

(c) *Tech* control, monitoring, testing, regulation (*of machine, craft etc*); *Av* **tour de c.,** control tower; **perdre le c. de la voiture,** to lose control of the car;

(d) (*marque*) hallmark; (*bureau*) assay office; **poinçon de c.,** hall-mark stamp;

(e) *Mil etc* roll, list, register; **c. de service,** duty roster; **rayer qn des contrôles de l'armée,** to remove s.o. from the army list.

contrôler [kɔ̃trole] **1** *vt* **(a)** to inspect, to supervise (*work etc*); to check, to audit (*accounts*); to check (*tickets*); to examine, to inspect (*passports*); to verify, to check (up) (*information, a fact etc*); **(b)** to control, to supervise (*operations etc*); **c. les naissances,** to control the birth-rate; **c. les prix,** to control *or* keep down prices; **l'armée contrôle toute cette région,** all of this region is under the control of the army, this whole region is controlled by the army; **(c)** (*maîtriser*) to control (*s.o.*); **c. ses émotions,** to control one's emotions; **(d)** to hallmark, to stamp (*gold, silver*). **2 se contrôler** *vpr* to control oneself.

contrôleur, -euse [kɔ̃trolœr, -øz] **1** *n* **(a)** controller (*of government department*); auditor (*of company accounts etc*); **c. aux liquidations,** controller in bankruptcy; **c. des contributions,** assessor *or* inspector of taxes; *Can* **Bureau du C. Général,** Office of the Controller General; **(b)** inspector, examiner, supervisor (*of work etc*); *Rail* ticket inspector; **(c)** *Av* **c. de la circulation aérienne,** air traffic controller. **2** *nm* regulator; *Rail* master controller; **c. d'atelier,** time recorder, time-clock; *Ordinat* **c. de disque,** disk controller.

contrordre [kɔ̃trɔrdr] *nm* counterorder, countermand; **il y a c.,** the orders have been changed; **sauf c.,** unless otherwise directed.

controuvé [kɔ̃truve] *adj* false, fabricated, concocted.

controversable [kɔ̃trɔvɛrsabl] *adj* controversial, debatable.

controverse [kɔ̃trɔvɛrs] *nf* controversy, debate; **cela prête encore à c.,** it is still a controversial topic *or* surrounded by controversy, it is still a matter of controversy *or* for debate; **hors de c.,** beyond dispute, indisputable.

controverser [kɔ̃trɔvɛrse] *vt* to discuss, to debate (*question etc*); **question controversée,** controversial *or* much debated question.

contumace¹ [kɔ̃tymas] *nf Jur* non-appearance (in court); **condamné par c.,** sentenced in absentia, sentenced in his absence.

contumace² [kɔ̃tymas] **, contumax** [kɔ̃tymaks] *adj Jur* contumacious, defaulting.

contus [kɔ̃ty] *adj* contused, bruised.

contusion [kɔ̃tyzjɔ̃] *nf* contusion, bruise.

contusionner [kɔ̃tyzjɔne] *vt* to contuse, to bruise.

conurbation [kɔnyrbasjɔ] *nf* conurbation.

convaincant [kɔ̃vɛ̃kɑ̃] *adj* convincing.

convaincre [kɔ̃vɛ̃kr] *vt* (*conj like* **vaincre**) **(a)** (*persuader*) to convince (**de,** of, **que,** that); **j'en suis convaincu,** I'm sure of it; **se laisser c.,** to let oneself be persuaded; **je l'ai finalement convaincu,** I finally convinced him; **(b)** to convict (*s.o.*), to prove (*s.o.*) guilty (**de,** of).

convaincu [kɔ̃vɛ̃ky] *adj* convinced; **parler d'un ton c.,** to speak with conviction.

convalescence [kɔ̃valɛsɑ̃s] *nf* **(a)** convalescence; **elle est en c.,** she's convalescing; **maison de c.,** convalescent home, nursing home; **(b)** *Mil etc* sick leave.

convalescent, -ente [kɔ̃valɛsɑ̃, -ɑ̃t] *adj & n* convalescent.

convecteur [kɔ̃vɛktœr] *nm* convector.

convection [kɔ̃vɛksjɔ̃] *nf Phys* convection.

convenable [kɔ̃vnabl] *adj* **(a)** (*approprié*) suitable, fitting, appropriate, proper; **juger c. de faire qch,** to think it proper *or* advisable to do sth; **(b)** (*décent*) decent, respectable, acceptable (*behaviour*); **peu c.,** unacceptable; **(c)** *F* adequate (*salary etc*).

convenablement [kɔ̃vnabləmɑ̃] *adv* **(a)** (*d'une façon appropriée*) suitably, fittingly, appropriately; **(b)** (*avec décence*) correctly, properly, decently; **(c)** *F* **on peut manger très c. à la cantine,** you can eat quite well in the canteen.

convenance [kɔ̃vnɑ̃s] *nf* **(a)** suitability, fitness, convenience, appropriateness, advisability; **pour des raisons de c. personnelle,** for personal reasons; **mariage de c.,** marriage of convenience; **trouver qch à sa c.,** to find sth suitable; **il le fera à sa c.,** he'll do it at his own convenience; **(b)** *Litt* conformity, agreement, affinity (*of tastes etc*); **(c) les convenances,** propriety, the proprieties, etiquette; **comportement contraire aux convenances,** unseemly conduct, improper behaviour.

convenir [kɔ̃vnir] *v* (*conj like* **venir**) **1** *vi* **(a)** (*conj with* **avoir**) to suit, to fit; **robe qui convient à la circonstance,** dress suitable for *or* befitting the occasion; **si cela vous convient,** if that suits you, if that is convenient (for you); **c'est exactement ce qui me convient,** it's just what I need;

(b) (*conj with* **avoir**, *and with* **être** *to denote a state of agreement*) to agree, to come to an agreement; **c. de qch,** (*être d'accord*) to agree on *or* about sth; (*reconnaître*) to acknowledge *or* admit sth; **j'ai eu tort, j'en conviens,** I was wrong, I admit; **ils sont convenus,** they are agreed; **il convient qu'il a eu tort,** he admits that he was wrong.

2 *v impers* **(a)** (*conj with* **avoir**) **il convient de ...,** it is fitting *or* advisable to ...; **ce qu'il convient de faire (c')est de ...,** the right thing to do is to ...; **il convient que vous y alliez,** you should *or* ought to go;

(b) (*conj with* **être** *and* **avoir**) **il fut convenu qu'ils le feraient venir,** it was agreed *or* arranged that they would send for him; **comme convenu,** as agreed.

convention [kɔ̃vɑ̃sjɔ̃] *nf* **(a)** (*accord*) agreement; *Jur* article, clause (*of deed etc*); **signer une c.,** to sign an agreement; **c. collective,** = collective (wage) agreement; *Pol* **c. internationale,** international convention; **cela n'est pas dans les conventions,** that's not done; **(b) les conventions (sociales),** the social conventions; **de c.,** conventional; *Péj* **amabilité de c.,** conventional *or* superficial courtesy; **(c)** *Pol* (extraordinary) assembly; *US* Convention; *Fr Hist* **La C. (nationale),** the (National) Convention (1792).

conventionné [kɔ̃vɑ̃sjɔne] *adj* **médecin c.,** ≈ National Health Service doctor; **médecin non c.,** ≈ private doctor.

conventionnel, -elle [kɔ̃vɑ̃sjɔnɛl] **1** *adj* **(a)** conventional (*value, symbol, Mil weapons*); *Ling* **langage c.,** conventional language; **(b)** contractual (*clause etc*); **(c)** *Péj* superficial; **affabilité conventionnelle,** conventional *or* superficial affability. **2** *nm Fr Hist* member of the National Convention.

conventionnellement [kɔ̃vɑ̃sjɔnɛlmɑ̃] *adv* conventionally; *Jur* by agreement.

conventuel, -elle [kɔ̃vɑ̃tɥɛl] *adj* conventual (*house, rule etc*); monastic (*life*); **bâtiment c.,** (*monastère*) monastery; (*couvent*) convent.

convenu [kɔ̃vny] *adj* **(a)** agreed; stipulated (*price etc*); appointed (*time*); **c'est une chose convenue,** that's generally agreed upon; **(b)** *Péj* conventional (*language etc*).

convergence [kɔ̃vɛrʒɑ̃s] *nf* convergence; *Fig* **c. des idées,** convergence of ideas, meeting of minds.

convergent [kɔ̃vɛrʒɑ̃] *adj* convergent, converging (*lines etc*).

converger [kɔ̃vɛrʒe] *vi* (**convergeant; ils convergeaient**) (*of roads, lines etc*) to converge; **leurs opinions convergent,** they are of like *or* one mind.

convers, -erse [kɔ̃vɛr, -ɛrs] **1** *adj* **(a) proposition converse,** converse proposition; **(b)** *Rel* lay (*brother, sister*). **2** *nf* **converse,** converse.

conversation [kɔ̃vɛrsasjɔ̃] *nf* conversation, talk; **lier** *ou* **entrer en** *ou* **engager une c. avec qn,** to enter *or* get into conversation with s.o.; **avoir une longue c. avec qn,** to have a long *or* lengthy conversation *or* chat with s.o.; **faire la c. à qn,** to chat with s.o.; **voilà qui a arrêté net la c.,** that stopped the conversation dead, that killed the conversation; **il a fait les frais de la c.,** he was the main subject of conversation; **langage/expressions de la c.,** colloquial language/expressions; **amener un sujet dans une c.,** to introduce a topic into a conversation; **c. téléphonique,** telephone call *or* conversation; **avoir de la c.,** to be a good conversationalist.

conversationnel, -elle [kɔ̃vɛrsasjɔnɛl] *adj Ordinat* **mode c.,** conversational *or* interactive mode.

converser [kɔ̃vɛrse] *vi* to converse, to talk (**avec,** with).

conversion [kɔ̃vɛrsjɔ̃] *nf* **(a)** (*changement*) conversion, change (**en,** into); *Ordinat Fin* conversion; *Math* **c. des fractions,** conversion of fractions; **(b)** *Ski* kick turn; *Mil etc* wheel(ing); **(c)** *Rel* conversion (*to a faith*).

converti, -e [kɔ̃vɛrti] **1** *adj* converted (*sinner etc*). **2** *n* convert.

convertibilité [kɔ̃vɛrtibilite] *nf Fin* convertibility.

convertible [kɔ̃vɛrtibl] **1** *adj* convertible (**en,** into); **rente c.,** convertible interest (paid by the State on banks securing a national debt); **canapé c.,** bed-settee, sofa bed; **2** *nm* **(a)** *Av* convertiplane; **(b)** (*canapé*) bed-settee, sofa bed.

convertir [kɔ̃vɛrtir] **1** *vt* **(a)** to convert (*sth into sth*); **c. un lingot en espèce,** to convert a gold ingot into cash; *Com Fin* **c. des rentes,** to convert stock; *Ordinat* **c. un système en numérique,** to digitize a system; **(b)** to convert (*s.o. to a faith, to a point of view etc*). **2 se convertir** *vpr* **(a)** to become converted (*to a faith etc*); **(b)** (*se transformer*) to change *or* turn into; **la neige s'était convertie en boue,** the snow had turned (in)to slush.

convertissement [kɔ̃vɛrtismɑ̃] *nm Bourse Fin* conversion (*of securities into money*).

convertisseur [kɔ̃vɛrtisœr] *nm* **(a)** *Métal* converter; **(b)** *Él Électron* converter; **c. à vapeur de mercure,** mercury-vapour rectifier; *Ordinat* **c. analogique numérique,** digitizer.

convexe [kɔ̃vɛks] *adj* convex.

convexité [kɔ̃vɛksite] *nf* convexity.

convict [kɔ̃vikt] *n Jur* convict.

conviction [kɔ̃viksjɔ̃] *nf* **(a)** (*certitude*) conviction; **avoir**

la c. que ..., to be convinced that ...; **une c. personnelle,** a personal conviction; **sans grande c.,** without much conviction; **(b)** *Jur* **pièce à c.,** object *etc* produced in evidence; exhibit (*in criminal case*).

convier [kɔ̃vje] *vt* (*impf & pr sub* **n. conviions, v. conviiez**) **(a)** (*inviter*) to invite; **c. qn à un mariage,** to invite s.o. to a wedding; **(b) c. qn à faire qch,** to urge s.o. to do sth.

convive [kɔ̃viv] *n* guest (*at table*).

convivial, -aux [kɔ̃vivjal, -o] *adj Ordinat* user-friendly.

convivialité [kɔ̃vivjalite] *nf Ordinat* user-friendliness.

convocation [kɔ̃vɔkasjɔ̃] *nf* calling together, convening (*of assembly etc*); *Jur* summons; **recevoir une c.,** to receive notice of a meeting; *Admin etc* to be asked to come for an interview; **répondre à une c.,** to appear for interview; **c. à l'examen,** notification of an examination.

convoi [kɔ̃vwa] *nm* **(a) c. (funèbre),** funeral procession, funeral cortège; **(b)** *Mil* **c. (de troupes),** convoy of troops; **c. administratif,** supply column; **c. de prisonniers,** convoy of prisoners; **(c)** (*de véhicules*) train, convoy; **c. automobile,** motorcade; *Rail* **c. de marchandises,** goods *or* freight train; **(d)** *Nau* (*qui escorte*) escorting vessel; (*qui est escorté*) merchant fleet under escort.

convoiement [kɔ̃vwamɑ̃] *nm* convoying, escorting.

convoiter [kɔ̃vwate] *vt* to covet (*position*); to lust after, *F* to hanker after (*woman, wealth*).

convoitise [kɔ̃vwatiz] *nf* covetousness; (*for person*) lust; **regarder qch avec c.,** to cast covetous glances *or* look covetously at sth.

convoler [kɔ̃vɔle] *vi* (*of widow, widower*) to remarry, to marry again; *F* **c. en justes noces,** to marry.

convoluté [kɔ̃vɔlyte] *adj Biol* convolute(d), whorled.

convoquer [kɔ̃vɔke] *vt* **(a)** to summon, to call together (*assembly*); to convene (*meeting*); **(b)** *Admin etc* to invite (*s.o.*) to an interview; **le directeur m'a convoqué dans son bureau,** the manager called me to his office.

convoyage [kɔ̃vwajaʒ] *nm* = **CONVOIEMENT**; *Nau* **faire un c. entre deux ports,** to escort (ships) between two ports.

convoyer [kɔ̃vwaje] *vt* (**je convoie, n. convoyons, ils convoient; je convoierai**) to convoy, to escort (*train, fleet etc*).

convoyeur [kɔ̃vwajœr] *nm* **(a)** *Mil* officer in charge of convoy; *Nau* convoying officer; (*navire*) convoy (ship), escort (ship); **(b)** *MecE Ind* conveyor; **(c) c. de fonds,** security guard.

convulser [kɔ̃vylse] **1** *vt* to convulse; **visage convulsé par la terreur,** face convulsed by *or* with terror. **2 se convulser** *vpr* to convulse, to contort; **sa figure se convulsa,** his face became contorted.

convulsif, -ive [kɔ̃vylsif, -iv] *adj* convulsive; **rire c.,** convulsive *or* uncontrollable laughter.

convulsion [kɔ̃vylsjɔ̃] *nf* convulsion; **convulsions cloniques,** clonic spasms; **se tordre dans des convulsions,** to writhe *or* double up in convulsions; **c. politique,** political upheaval.

convulsionner [kɔ̃vylsjɔne] *vt* to convulse.

convulsivement [kɔ̃vylsivmɑ̃] *adv* convulsively.

coobligé, -ée [kɔɔbliʒe] *n Jur* co-obligant, co-obligor.

cooccupant, -ante [kɔɔkypɑ̃, -ɑ̃t] *n* co-occupier.

cool [kul] *adj F* cool; **il n'est pas très c., ton père,** your father's a bit square *or* a bit of an old fogey; **c'est c., ça,** that's wicked; *Mus* **jazz c.,** hip *or* cool jazz.

coolie [kuli] *nm* (*porteur*) porter.

coopérateur, -trice [kɔɔperatœr, -tris] **1** *n* **(a)** (*collègue*) co-worker; **(b)** (*dans une coopérative*) member of co(-)operative. **2** *adj* **agent c.,** co(-)operating agent.

coopératif, -ive [kɔɔperatif, -iv] **1** *adj* co(-)operative (*society etc*). **2** *nf* **coopérative,** (*association*) co(-)operative; (*magasin*) co(-)operative store, *F* co(-)op; **c. de vente/production,** sales/production co(-)operative.

coopération [kɔɔperasjɔ̃] *nf* **(a)** (*appui*) co(-)operation; **(b)** = Voluntary Service Overseas; **partir en c. en Afrique,** to go off to do V.S.O. in Africa.

coopératisme [kɔɔperatism] *nm Écon* co(-)operation, the co(-)operative system.

coopérer [kɔɔpere] *vi* (**je coopère, n. coopérons; je coopérerai**) to co(-)operate, to work together; **c. au succès de qch,** to contribute to the success of sth.

cooptation [kɔɔptasjɔ̃] *nf* co-optation, co-option, co-opting.

coopter [kɔɔpte] *vt* to co-opt.

coordinateur, -trice [kɔɔrdinatœr, -tris] *adj & n* = **COORDONNATEUR**.

coordination [kɔɔrdinasjɔ̃] *nf* co(-)ordination; *Gram* **conjonction de c.,** co(-)ordinating conjunction.

coordonnateur, -trice [kɔɔrdɔnatœr, -tris] **1** *adj* co(-)ordinating. **2** *n* (*personne*) co(-)ordinator; *Av* air-traffic controller; **être le c. d'une entreprise,** to co-ordinate an operation.

coordonné, -ée [kɔɔrdɔne] **1** *adj* co(-)ordinated (*movement etc*); matching (*sheets and towels etc*); *Gram etc* co(-)ordinate (*clause etc*); **écharpe et gants coordonnés,** scarf and matching *or* co(-)ordinated gloves. **2** *nfpl* **coordonnées (a)** *Math Géog Astron* co(-)ordinates; **(b)** *F* **donnez-moi vos coordonnées,** give me your address and 'phone number; **(c)** (*accessoires*) co(-)ordinates.

coordonner [kɔɔrdɔne] *vt* to co(-)ordinate, to arrange (**à, avec,** with).

copain, -ine [kɔpɛ̃, -in] *F* **1** *n* pal, mate, *esp Am* buddy; **sa nouvelle copine d'école,** his new pal at school; **ma petite copine,** my girlfriend; **salut les copains!,** hi gang!; **les corvées, c'est toujours pour les petits copains,** we always get the rotten jobs. **2** *adj* pally; **ils sont très copains,** they're great pals *or surtout Am* buddies; **ils sont très c.-c.,** they're very pally *or* chummy *or* matey *or surtout Am* very buddy-buddy.

copartageant, -ante [kɔpartaʒɑ̃, -ɑ̃t] *n Jur* coparcener, coheir, coheiress.

coparticipant [kɔpartisipɑ̃] *nm Jur* copartner.

coparticipation [kɔpartisipasjɔ̃] *nf Jur* copartnership; **c. aux bénéfices,** profit sharing.

copeau, -eaux [kɔpo] *nm* shaving (*of wood*); chip, cutting (*of wood, metal*); **c. de tour,** turnings.

Copenhague [kɔpɛnag] *nf* Copenhagen.

copiage [kɔpjaʒ] *nm Scol* cribbing, copying.

copie [kɔpi] *nf* **(a)** (*reproduction*) copy, transcript; *Journ Typ* manuscript; copy; *Admin Jur* **pour c. conforme,** certified true copy; **c. certifiée conformée,** certified true copy; **c. au carbone,** carbon copy; *Ordinat F* **c. sur papier,** hard copy, print out; *Ordinat* **c. de secours,** backup; *Scol* fair copy (*of exercise etc*); (*d'examen*) (candidate's) paper; **c. simple/double,** single/double sheet of paper; **(b)** copy, reproduction (*of picture, statue etc*); imitation (*of novel, style etc*); **ce n'est qu'une pâle c. de l'original,** it's only a pale imitation of the original; *F* **la c. de son grand-père,** the spitting image *or* replica of his grandfather; **(c)** *Cin* (print) copy, print.

copier [kɔpje] *v* (*impf & pr sub* **n. copiions, v. copiiez**) **1** *vt* **(a)** to copy, to transcribe (*manuscript, music etc*); **c. qch au propre** *ou* **au net,** to make a fair copy of sth, to copy out sth (neatly); *Ordinat* **c. un document sur le disque dur,** to back up a document onto hard disk; **(b)** to copy, to reproduce (*statue, picture*); to imitate (*s.o., style etc*); *Scol* to copy, to crib; **elle me copie en tout,** she copies everything I do, she copies me in everything. **2** *vi Scol* to copy, to crib.

copieur, -ieuse [kɔpjœr, -øz] **1** *adj Scol etc* copying, cribbing. **2** *n Scol* copier, cribber. **3** *nm* copying machine, photocopier.

copieusement [kɔpjøzmɑ̃] *adv* copiously; **boire c.,** to drink deep.

copieux, -ieuse [kɔpjø, -jøz] *adj* copious; hearty, square (*meal*); generous (*portion*).

copilote [kɔpilɔt] *nm Av* copilot.

copinage [kɔpinaʒ] *nm F* pally *or* chummy relationship, palliness, chumminess; **dans ce milieu, ça ne marche que par c.,** around here it's who you know that matters, what counts around here is who you're friendly with.

copine [kɔpin] *nf F* friend; *voir* **COPAIN**.

copiner [kɔpine] *vi F* to chum up, to pal up, to be pally (**avec,** with).

copinerie [kɔpinri] *nf F* = **COPINAGE**.

copiste [kɔpist] *n* **(a)** (*clerc etc*) copyist, transcriber; **(b)** (*plagiaire*) copier, imitator.

coposséder [kɔposede] *vt* (*conj like* **posséder**) *Jur* to own (*sth*) jointly, to have joint ownership of (*sth*).

coppa [kɔpa] *nf Culin* coppa, Italian smoked pork sausage.

copra(h) [kɔpra] *nm* copra; **huile de c.,** coconut oil.

coprésidence [kɔprezidɑ̃s] *nf* co-chairmanship, co-presidency.

coprocesseur [kɔprɔsesœr] *nm Ordinat* co-processor; **c. arithmétique,** maths co-processor.

coproduction [kɔprɔdyksjɔ̃] *nf* coproduction, joint production.

coproduire [kɔprɔdɥir] *vt* to co produce.

copropriétaire [kɔprɔprijetɛr] *n Jur* co-owner, joint owner.

copropriété [kɔprɔprijete] *nf Jur* co-ownership, joint ownership.

copte [kɔpt] **1** *adj* Coptic. **2** *nm Ling* Coptic. **3** *n* **C.,** Copt.

copulation [kɔpylasjɔ̃] *nf* copulation.

copuler [kɔpyle] *vi* to copulate.

copyright [kɔpirajt] *nm* copyright.

coq¹ [kɔk] *nm* **(a)** *(oiseau)* cock, *Am* rooster; **jeune c.,** cockerel; **le c. gaulois,** the French cockerel; **au chant du c.,** at cockcrow; **combat de coqs,** cockfight(ing); **c. de combat,** fighting cock; *F* **rouge comme un c.,** red as a turkey cock; **jambes de c.,** wiry *or* spindly legs; **vivre comme un c. en pâte,** to be in clover; **le c. du village,** the cock of the walk; *Boxe* **poids c.,** bantam weight; *Culin* **c. au vin,** coq au vin; **(b)** *(oiseau mâle)* cock, male; **c. faisan,** cock pheasant; **c. de bruyère,** capercaillie, wood grouse; **c. de roche,** cock-of-the-rock; **(c)** *(girouette)* weathercock, vane.

coq² *nm Nau* **(maître-)c.,** (ship's) cook.

coq-à-l'âne [kɔkalɑn] *nm inv* sudden change of subject; **passer du c.-à-l'âne, faire des coq-à-l'âne,** to skip from one subject to another.

coquart [kɔkar] *nm F* black eye, shiner.

coque [kɔk] *nf* **(a)** shell *(of egg)*; shell, husk *(of nut, fruit)*; *(mollusc)* cockle; *Culin* **œuf à la c.,** (soft-)boiled egg; *Fig* **se renfermer dans sa c.,** to retire into one's shell; **(b)** *Nau* hull, bottom *(of ship)*; *Av* fuselage; body, shell *(of car)*; *Nau* **double c.,** double bottom; **(c)** loop *(of ribbon, hair etc)*.

coquelet [kɔklɛ] *nm Culin* cockerel.

coquelicot [kɔkliko] *nm Bot* red poppy.

coquelourde [kɔklurd] *nf Bot* pasque flower, dane flower, pulsatilla.

coqueluche [kɔklyʃ] *nf Méd* whooping cough; **avoir la c.,** to have whooping cough; *Fig* **être la c. des adolescents,** to be a teenage idol; **être la c. du bureau,** to be the darling of the office.

coquelucheux, -euse [kɔklyʃø, -øz] *adj Méd* **une toux coquelucheuse,** a whooping cough, a cough indicative of whooping cough.

coquerico [kɔkriko] *int* cock-a-doodle-doo.

coquet, -ette [kɔkɛ, -ɛt] **1** *adj* charming *(town)*; smart, stylish *(clothes etc)*; *Vieilli* coquettish, flirtatious *(woman, smile etc)*; **elle est coquette,** she likes pretty clothes, she's very clothes-conscious; *(qui aime séduire)* she likes to look attractive; **il est trop c.,** he's too conscious of his appearance; *F* **fortune assez coquette,** tidy fortune. **2** *nf Vieilli* **coquette,** flirt, coquette.

coquetier [kɔktje] *nm* egg cup; *F* **gagner le c.,** to hit the jackpot.

coquettement [kɔkɛtmɑ̃] *adv* smartly, stylishly, nattily *(dressed etc)*.

coquetterie [kɔkɛtri] *nf* **(a)** fastidiousness *(in dress)*; *Péj* affectation; *Vieilli (désir de plaire)* coquetry, flirtatiousness; **faire le fier par c.,** to give oneself airs and graces; **avoir de la c. pour sa tenue,** to be fastidious *or* particular about one's appearance; **(b)** smartness, stylishness *(of dress etc)*; **(c)** *F* **avoir une c. dans l'œil,** to have a cast in one's eye.

coquillage [kɔkijaʒ] *nm* **(a)** *(mollusque)* shellfish; **(b)** *(vide)* (empty) shell.

coquille [kɔkij] *nf* **(a)** shell *(of snail, oyster etc)*; *Fig* **il ne sort jamais de sa c.,** he never goes out, he always stays at home; *Fig* **rentrer dans sa c.,** to retire into one's shell; **(b) c. Saint-Jacques,** *(mollusque)* scallop; *(coquillage)* scallop shell; *(sur un meuble)* scallop; *Culin* = scallops (sometimes accompanied by other shellfish) in béchamel sauce, served on a scallop shell; **(c)** *(plat)* (scallop-shaped) dish; **(d)** shell *(of egg, nut etc)*; **c. de noix,** *(boat)* cockleshell; **peinture c. d'œuf,** off-white paint; **c. de beurre,** pat of butter (in the shape of a shell); **c. d'épée,** hand guard *or* shell of sword; **(e)** *Constr* soffit, underpart *(of spiral stair)*; **(f)** *Métal* chill, chill mould; *Boxe* box, shield; *Méd* spinal plaster; **(g)** *Typ* misprint, *F* literal.

coquillettes [kɔkijɛt] *nfpl Culin* pasta shells.

coquin, -ine [kɔkɛ̃, -in] **1** *n* **(a)** *(garnement)* rascal, scamp, rogue; **c. de sort!,** *(in Provence)* hang it!, damn it!; **petit c.!, petite coquine!,** you little rascal!; **(b)** rogue, rascal. **2** *nf Arch* **coquine,** loose woman, hussy. **3** *adj (sourire)* mischievous; *(sous-vêtement)* naughty; **un air c.,** a flirtatious *or* coquettish look; **des histoires coquines,** risqué stories.

coquinement [kɔkinmɑ̃] *adv* mischievously, roguishly.

coquinerie [kɔkinri] *nf* mischievousness, roguishness; *(tour)* mischievous *or* roguish trick, prank.

cor [kɔr] *nm* **(a)** horn; **cor (de chasse),** (hunting) horn; **sonner du c.,** to sound *or* blow the horn; *Fig* **réclamer qch à c. et à cri,** to clamour for sth; *Mus* **c. d'harmonie,** French horn; **c. à piston,** valve horn; **c. anglais,** English horn, cor anglais; **les cors,** the horns; **(b)** corn *(on toe, foot)*; **avoir un c. au pied,** to have a corn on one's foot; **(c)** tine *(of antler)*; **un cerf (de) dix cors,** a five pointer, a five pronger.

corail¹, -aux [kɔraj, -o] *nm (de mollusque, matière calcaire)* coral; **récif de c.,** coral reef; *Litt* **lèvres de c.,** coral lips.

corail² [kɔraj] *adj inv Rail* **train c.,** express (train).

corailleur, -euse [kɔrajœr, -øz] *n (pêcheur)* coral gatherer; *(artisan)* coral worker.

corallien, -ienne [kɔraljɛ̃, -jɛn] *adj* coralline; **récif c.,** coral reef.

Coran (le) [ləkɔrɑ̃] *nm* The Koran.

coranique [kɔranik] *adj* Koranic; **école c.,** Koranic school *(for teaching the Koran)*.

corbeau, -eaux [kɔrbo] *nm* **(a)** *(oiseau)* crow; **(grand) c.,** raven; **c. freux,** rook; **noir comme un c.,** raven *or* crow black; **(b)** *(auteur de lettres anonymes)* writer of poison-pen letters; **(c)** *Fig Péj (rapace)* rapacious person, shark; **(d)** *Archit* corbel, bracket.

corbeille [kɔrbɛj] *nf* **(a)** *(panier)* (open) basket *(without bow handle)*; **c. à pain,** breadbasket; **c. à papier,** waste(paper) basket; **corbeille à ouvrage,** workbasket; **c. de mariage,** wedding presents; **(b)** *(massif)* (round, oval) flower bed; **(c)** *Archit* corbel, bell, base *(of Corinthian capital)*; **(d)** *Bourse* stockbroker's central enclosure; *Th* dress circle; **(e)** *(plante)* **c. d'or,** rock alyssum; **c. d'argent,** sweet alyssum.

corbillard [kɔrbijar] *nm* hearse.

cordage [kɔrdaʒ] *nm* **(a)** stringing *(of racket etc)*; **(b)** *(corde)* rope; **c. en chanvre,** hemp rope; **cordages,** cordage, ropes; *Nau* gear, rigging; **le c.,** strings *(of racket etc)*.

corde [kɔrd] *nf* **(a)** rope, cord; **c. à linge,** clothes line; **danseur de c.,** tightrope dancer; **marcher** *ou* **danser** *ou* **être sur la c. raide,** to be (walking) on a tightrope; *Gym* **c. lisse,** climbing rope; **semelle en c.,** rope sole; **c. à nœuds,** knotted climbing rope; **c. à sauter,** skipping rope; **sauter à la c.,** to skip; *Fig* **trop tirer sur la c.,** to go too far, to push one's luck; *F* **il pleut des cordes,** it's raining cats and dogs;

(b) *(d'instrument)* string; **c. de boyau,** catgut; **c. de violon,** violin string; **instrument à cordes,** stringed instrument; **les cordes,** *(in orchestra)* the strings; **double c.,** double stopping; *Fig* **toucher la c. sensible de qn,** to touch upon s.o.'s favourite subject; *Fig* **avoir plus d'une c. à son arc,** to have more than one string to one's bow;

(c) *(de pendu)* halter, hangman's rope; *F* **se mettre la c. au cou,** to put one's head in the noose, to put a halter *or* rope round one's own neck; *Arg* to get spliced *or* hitched; *Fig* **parler de c. dans la maison d'un pendu,** to make a tactless remark, to raise a sore point; **dire cela, c'était comme parler de c. dans la maison d'un pendu,** that was very tactless;

(d) *Courses de chevaux* **la c.,** the rails; **tenir la c.,** to hug the rails, to be on the inside (lane); *Fig* to have the advantage; *Aut* **prendre un virage à la c.,** to cut a corner close, to hug the bend; *Boxe* **les cordes,** the ropes; **être dans les cordes,** to be in an unfavourable position, to be on the ropes;

(e) *Tex* thread; **drap usé jusqu'à** *ou* **qui laisse voir la c.,** threadbare cloth; *Fig* **plaisanterie/histoire usée jusqu'à la c.,** old joke/story;

(f) *Math* chord *(of segment, of arc)*;

(g) *Anat* **cordes vocales,** vocal cords; *Fig* **ce n'est pas dans mes cordes,** it's not in my line, it's not up my street, it's not my province;

(h) c. dorsale, spinal cord; **c. cervicale,** cervical nerve.

cordé [kɔrde] *adj Bot etc* cordate, heart-shaped.

cordeau, -eaux [kɔrdo] *nm* **(a)** *(petite corde)* line, string; **un c. de jardinier,** garden string line; *Fig* **tiré au c.,** perfectly straight, as straight as a die; **(b)** *Min Mil (mèche)* fuse, match; **c. Bickford,** Bickford fuse, safety fuse; **(c)** *Pêche* paternoster (line).

cordée [kɔrde] *nf* **(a)** *Com* **c. de bois,** cord of wood; **(b)** *(d'alpinistes)* rope, roped party; **premier de c.,** leader, first on the rope; **(c)** *Pêche* hook length.

cordelette [kɔrdəlɛt] *nf* small cord, string.

cordelier, -ière [kɔrdəlje, -jɛr] **1** *n* **(a)** *Rel* Franciscan friar, nun, *m* cordelier; **(b)** *Hist Fr* **le Club des Cordeliers,** = a left-wing club of the Revolutionary period. **2** *nf* **cordelière,** cord *(of dressing gown etc)*; *Archit* cable moulding.

corder [kɔrde] *vt* **(a)** to twist *(hemp etc)* into rope; **(b)** to cord *(trunk, bale etc)*; **(c)** to string *(racquet etc)*; **(d)** *Com* to measure *(wood)* by the cord.

corderie [kɔrd(ə)ri] *nf* **(a)** *Com* rope manufacture, rope trade; **(b)** *Ind* rope factory.

cordial, -iaux [kɔrdjal, -jo] **1** *adj* **(a)** cordial, hearty, warm (*welcome etc*); **(b)** *Pharm* stimulating (*medicine*). **2** *nm Pharm* cordial, tonic.

cordialement [kɔrdjalmɑ̃] *adv* cordially, heartily, warmly; **c. vôtre,** (*dans une lettre*) yours sincerely; **bien c.,** best wishes.

cordialité [kɔrdjalite] *nf* cordiality, heartiness.

cordier [kɔrdje] *nm* **(a)** *Ind* ropemaker; **(b)** *Mus* tailpiece (*of violin*).

cordillère [kɔrdijɛr] *nf Géog* cordillera.

cordite [kɔrdit] *nf* cordite.

cordon [kɔrdɔ̃] *nm* **(a)** cord, string; strand, twist (*of cable, rope*); ribbon, decoration (*of an order etc*); *Électron El* cord, flex; **corde à trois cordons,** three-stranded rope; **c. de soie,** silk cord; **c. de sonnette,** bellpull; *Vieilli* **c. de soulier,** shoelace; *Fig* **tenir les cordons de la bourse,** to hold the purse-strings; *Arch* **demander le c.,** to ask the concierge to open the door; *F* **c.-bleu,** cordon bleu (cook); **ma sœur est un c.-bleu,** my sister's a cordon bleu (cook); *Anat* **c. médullaire,** spinal cord; *Obst* **c. ombilical,** umbilical cord; *F* **il faut couper le c.,** you must get away from your mother's apron strings, you must branch out on your own;

(b) row, line (*of trees etc*); cordon (*of police, troops*); *Archit* string course, cordon (*in wall*); milled edge (*of coin etc*); **c. sanitaire,** sanitary cordon;

(c) *Géog* **c. littoral,** offshore bar.

cordonner [kɔrdɔne] *vt* to twist, to twine, to cord (*silk, hemp etc*).

cordonnerie [kɔrdɔnri] *nf* **(a)** (*métier*) shoemending; (*fabrication*) boot and shoe manufacture *or* trade, shoemaking; **(b)** shoemender's (shop), cobbler's (shop); *Com* shoemaker's.

cordonnet [kɔrdɔnɛ] *nm* braid, cord, twist.

cordonnier, -ière [kɔrdɔnje, -jɛr] *n* **(a)** (*réparateur*) cobbler, shoemender, shoe repairer; **(b)** (*fabricant*) shoemaker.

Cordoue [kɔrdu] *nf* Cordoba.

Corée [kɔre] *nf* Korea.

coréen, -enne [kɔreɛ̃, -ɛn] **1** *adj* Korean. **2** *n* **C.,** Korean.

coreligionnaire [kɔrəliʒjɔnɛr] *n* co-religionist.

Corfou [kɔrfu] *nf* Corfu.

coriace [kɔrjas] **1** *adj* **(a)** tough, leathery (*meat etc*); **(b)** hard, tough, hard-headed (*person*); **être c. en affaires,** to be hard-headed in business. **2** *n* hard-headed *or* tough businessman *or* businesswoman.

coriandre [kɔrjɑ̃dr] *nf Bot* coriander.

coricide [kɔrisid] *nm Pharm* corn cure, corn remover.

corindon [kɔrɛ̃dɔ̃] *nm Minér* corundum.

Corinthe [kɔrɛ̃t] *nf* Corinth; *Culin* **raisins de C.,** currants.

corinthien, -ienne [kɔrɛ̃tjɛ̃, -jɛn] **1** *adj* Corinthian. **2** *n* **C.,** Corinthian.

cormoran [kɔrmɔrɑ̃] *nm* (*oiseau*) cormorant.

cornac [kɔrnak] *nm* elephant keeper, mahout.

cornage [kɔrnaʒ] *nm* **(a)** *Vét* wheezing, roaring (*of horse*); **(b)** *Méd* wheezing, wheeze.

cornaline [kɔrnalin] *nf* cornelian.

cornard [kɔrnar] *nm Arg* cuckold.

corne [kɔrn] *nf* **(a)** (*d'animal*) horn; horn, feeler (*of snail*); horn, antenna (*of insect*); **bêtes à cornes,** horned animals; *F* **montrer les cornes,** to show fight; **donner un coup de c. à qn,** (*of bull*) to gore s.o.; (*of ram, goat*) to butt s.o.; **peigne de c.,** horn comb; **c. à chaussure,** shoehorn; *Fig* **avoir** *ou* **porter des cornes,** to be a cuckold; **faire (porter) des cornes à qn,** to cuckold s.o.; **prendre le taureau par les cornes** to take the bull by the horns; **faire les cornes à qn,** to jeer at s.o., to mock s.o.;

(b) (*cor*) (*hunting, shepherd's*) horn; *Nau* **c. de brume,** foghorn;

(c) *Nau* gaff (*of fore-and-aft sail*);

(d) tip (*of crescent etc*); horns, cusps (*of the moon*); dog-ear (*of page*); **chapeau à cornes,** cocked hat; **faire une c. à une carte de visite,** to turn down the corner of a visiting card;

(e) (*sur les pieds etc*) hard skin; **avoir de la c. au pied,** to have hard skin *or* calluses on one's foot; **cornes cutanées,** calluses;

(f) c. d'abondance, cornucopia, horn of plenty.

corné [kɔrne] *adj* **(a)** horny (*foot etc*); **(b) page cornée,** dog-eared page.

corned-beef [kɔrnbif] *nm* corned beef.

cornée [kɔrne] *nf Anat* cornea.

cornéen, -enne [kɔrneɛ̃, -ɛn] *adj Anat* corneal.

corneille [kɔrnɛj] *nf* crow, rook; **c. noire,** carrion crow; **c. mantelée,** hooded crow.

cornélien, -ienne [kɔrneljɛ̃, -jɛn] *adj Littér* Cornelian (*tragedy etc*).

cornemuse [kɔrnəmyz] *nf Mus* bagpipe(s); **joueur de c.,** (bag)piper; **c. écossaise/bretonne,** Scottish/Breton bagpipes.

cornemuseur [kɔrnəmyzœr] *nm* (bag)piper.

corner¹ [kɔrne] **1** *vt* **(a)** to blare out (*sth*); **c. les ordres à qn,** to bawl *or* yell out orders to s.o.; *F* **c. qch aux oreilles de qn,** to shout sth into s.o.'s ear; **(b)** to turn down the corner of (*page etc*). **2** *vi* **(a)** to sound a horn; *Aut* to sound one's horn, to hoot, to honk; **(b)** *F* to shout; **la télé nous cornait dans les oreilles,** the telly was blaring; **(c)** (*of ears*) to ring; **les oreilles lui cornent,** his ears are ringing; **(d)** (*of goat, ram*) to butt.

corner² [kɔrnɛr] *nm Fb* corner.

cornet [kɔrnɛ] *nm* **(a) c. acoustique,** ear trumpet; **c. à dés,** dice box; **c. de papier,** cornet, paper cone; **c. de glace,** ice cream cone *or* cornet; *Arg* **se mettre quelque chose dans le c.,** to have something to eat; **(b)** *Mus* **c. à pistons,** cornet; cornet stop (*of organ*); **(c)** *Arch* small horn; **(d)** *Anat* scroll bone, turbinate bone.

cornette [kɔrnɛt] **1** *nf* **(a)** (*salade*) scarole. **(b)** (nun's winged) coif, cornet; **(c)** *Mil Arch* pennant, standard (*of cavalry*). **2** *nm Arch* cornet, ensign (*of cavalry*).

cornettiste [kɔrnɛtist] *n Mus* cornetist, cornet player.

corn-flakes [kɔrnflɛks] *nmpl* cornflakes; **un bol de c.-f.,** a bowl of cornflakes.

corniaud [kɔrnjo] *nm* **(a)** mongrel (dog); **(b)** *F* idiot, twit.

corniche [kɔrniʃ] *nf* **(a)** *Archit* cornice; **(b)** ledge (*of rock*); cornice (*of ice, snow*); **(route en) c.,** corniche (road).

cornichon [kɔrniʃɔ̃] *nm* **(a)** gherkin; **(b)** *F* idiot, nitwit.

cornier, -ière [kɔrnje, -jɛr] **1** *adj* (at the) corner, angle; *Constr* **poteau c.,** corner *or* angle post. **2** *nf* **cornière (a)** *Constr* valley (*joining roofs*); **(b)** angle (iron, bar).

cornique [kɔrnik] **1** *adj* Cornish. **2** *nm Ling* Cornish.

corniste [kɔrnist] *nm Mus* horn player.

cornouaillais, -aise [kɔrnwajɛ, -ɛz] **1** *adj* of Cornouaille. **2** *nm Ling* Breton dialect (of Cornouaille). **3** *n* **C.,** inhabitant of Cornouaille (*in Brittany*).

Cornouaille [kɔrnwaj] *nf* Cornouaille (*in Brittany*).

Cornouailles [kɔrnwaj] *nf* Cornwall (*in England*).

cornouille [kɔrnuj] *nf Bot* dogberry, cornel berry.

cornouiller [kɔrnuje] *nm* **(a)** *Bot* corneltree; **(b)** *Com* dogwood.

cornu [kɔrny] *adj* horned (*animal*).

cornue [kɔrny] *nf* **(a)** *Ch* retort; **charbon de c.,** retort carbon; **(b)** *Métal* steel converter.

corollaire [kɔrɔlɛr] *nm* (*suite*) consequence, corollary; *Math* corollary.

corolle [kɔrɔl] *nf Bot* corolla.

coron [kɔrɔ̃] *nm* (*maison*) miner's cottage; (*village*) mining village.

coronaire [kɔrɔnɛr] *adj Anat* coronary.

corporatif, -ive [kɔrpɔratif, -iv] *adj* corporate, corporative.

corporation [kɔrpɔrasjɔ̃] *nf* (*ordre*) corporate body; *Hist* (trade)guild; **la c. des pharmaciens,** the guild of pharmacists, the pharmacists' guild.

corporatisme [kɔrpɔratism] *nm* corporatism.

corporel, -elle [kɔrpɔrɛl] *adj* corporeal (*being etc*); corporal (*punishment etc*); bodily (*needs etc*); tangible (*property*); **odeur corporelle,** body odour, *F* B.O..

corporellement [kɔrpɔrɛlmɑ̃] *adv* corporeally, corporally, bodily.

corps [kɔr] *nm* **(a)** body; **un c. robuste,** a strong *or* robust frame; **soigner son c.,** to look after one's body, to take care of oneself; **conserver un c. jeune,** to still have a youthful body; **elle a conservé un c. jeune,** she's well-preserved; **entrer dans l'eau à mi-c.,** to get into the water up to one's waist; **un petit c. et des grandes jambes,** a short body and long legs; **passer sur le c. de** *ou* **à qn,** to run over s.o.; *Fig* to trample s.o. underfoot; **il te passerait sur le c. pour obtenir ce qu'il veut,** he'd sell his grand-mother to get what he wants; *Fig* **je me demande ce qu'il a dans le c.,** I wonder what makes him tick; **prendre du c.,** to put on weight; **prendre c.,** to take shape; **il n'a rien dans le c.,** (*mangé*) he hasn't eaten anything; *Fig* he has no strength *or* energy; **ça va te tenir au c.,** (*tu n'auras plus faim*) that'll stick to your ribs; **gardes du c.,** bodyguards; *F* **c'est un drôle de c.,** he's a strange character *or Br* bod; **faire qch à son c. défendant,** to do something unwillingly; **pleurer toutes les larmes de son c.,** to cry one's heart out; **se jeter à c. perdu dans une passion,** to be utterly consumed by a passion; **se jeter à c. perdu dans un projet/son travail,** to throw oneself into a project/one's work; **se**

donner c. et âme à qn/à un travail, to give *or* devote oneself body and soul to s.o./to a task; *Jur* **séparation de c.,** legal *or* judicial separation; **ils ont fait une séparation de c.,** they are legally separated; **saisir qn à bras-le-c.,** to seize s.o. round the waist; **lutter c. à c.,** to fight hand to hand; *Fig* **affronter la réalité c. à c.,** to come to grips with reality;

(b) (*cadavre*) corpse, body, *Am* cadaver; **la levée du c. aura lieu à onze heures,** the coffin will leave the house at eleven o'clock; **deux c. ont été retrouvés,** two bodies have been recovered;

(c) *Ch Phys* body, substance, material; **c. simple,** element; **c. composé,** compound (body); *Nucl* **c. noir,** black body; *Méd Ch* **c. étranger,** foreign body; *Astron* **c. céleste,** celestial *or* heavenly body;

(d) (*consistance*) **étoffe qui a du/qui n'a pas de c.,** strong/flimsy material; **vin qui a du c.,** full-bodied wine;

(e) main part (*of sth*); body, bodice (*of dress*); body (*of coach, hub etc*); barrel (*of cylinder, pump etc*); shell (*of boiler etc*); **faire c. avec qch,** to be an integral part of sth; *Constr* **c. de bâtiment** *ou* **de logis,** main (part of a) building; *Nau* **perdu c. et biens,** lost with all hands; *Typ* **force de c.,** size of type body; **le c. d'une lettre,** the body of a letter;

(f) (*d'ancrage*) dolphin, moorings; **(bouée de) c. mort,** (anchor) buoy;

(g) *Jur* **c. du délit,** corpus delicti;

(h) (*groupe*) **le c. diplomatique,** the diplomatic corps; **le c. médical/enseignant,** the medical/teaching profession; **avoir l'esprit de c.,** to have team spirit; *Mil* **c. d'armée,** (army) corps; **c. de garde,** guardhouse, guardroom; **plaisanterie de c. de garde,** barrackroom joke; **c. de commerce,** trade association, guild body; **c. électoral,** electorate; **c. de la magistrature,** the magistrature; **c. de ballet,** corps de ballet;

(i) (*écrits*) corpus, collection of writing; **c. de preuves,** body of evidence; **c. de lois,** body of law(s).

corps-à-corps [kɔrakɔr] *nm* **un c.-à-c.,** a tussle, hand-to-hand fight(ing); *Boxe* a clinch.

corpulence [kɔrpylɑ̃s] *nf* stoutness, corpulence; **être d'une forte c.,** to be stoutly built *or* of stout build.

corpulent [kɔrpylɑ̃] *adj* stout, corpulent.

corpus [kɔrpys] *nm Jur Ling* corpus.

corpusculaire [kɔrpyskylɛr] *adj* corpuscular.

corpuscule [kɔrpyskyl] *nm* corpuscle.

corral [kɔral] *nm* corral, enclosure (*for cattle*).

correct [kɔrɛkt] *adj* correct (*language etc*); accurate (*copy etc*); *F* adequate, acceptable; *F* **il a dit oui? — c.!,** did he agree? — correct!, right!; **(très) c.,** (*personne*) conventional; **les occupants étaient corrects,** the occupying forces behaved correctly; **cela n'est pas c. de sa part,** that's not right of him; **elle a été correcte avec moi,** she behaved correctly towards me; **être c. en affaires,** to behave correctly *or* honestly in one's business dealings; *F* **repas c.,** a decent *or* perfectly acceptable meal.

correctement [kɔrɛktəmɑ̃] *adv* accurately; (*agir*) correctly, properly; accurately.

correcteur, -trice [kɔrɛktœr, -tris] **1** *n* corrector; *Scol* examiner, marker (*of papers*); *Typ* proofreader. **2** *nm Ordinat* checker; *Tech* corrector; *Ordinat* **c. d'orthographe** *ou* **orthographique,** spell-checker; **c. de tonalité,** tone control. **3** *adj* correcting, corrective (*lenses etc*).

correctif, -ive [kɔrɛktif, -iv] **1** *adj* corrective; *Méd* **gymnastique corrective,** remedial exercises. **2** *nm* **(a)** (*mise au point*) qualifying statement, rider; **(b)** (*contrepartie*) corrective, antidote; *Méd* corrective.

correction [kɔrɛksjɔ̃] *nf* **(a)** correction, correcting (*of exercise, fault etc*); *Typ* proofreading, correction (*of proofs*); **maison de c.,** reform school; *Scol* **la c. d'un exercice,** the marking *or* correcting of an exercise; **je crois, sauf c., qu'il vient demain,** unless I'm mistaken, he's coming tomorrow; **les corrections sont en rouge,** the corrections are in red; *Ordinat* **c. d'orthographe,** spelling check; **effectuer une c. d'orthographe,** to do *or* run a spelling check; *Av Nau etc* **c. de compas,** adjustment of the compass; **(b)** (*pour punir*) punishment, thrashing; **tu vas recevoir une bonne c.!,** you'll get a good hiding!; **(c)** correctness (*of dress, speech etc*); propriety (*of behaviour*); **j'apprécie la c. en affaires,** I appreciate honesty in business.

correctionnel, -elle [kɔrɛksjɔnɛl] **1** *adj Jur* **peine correctionnelle,** penalty of more than five days' (but less than five years') imprisonment; **tribunal de police correctionnelle,** court of summary jurisdiction. **2** *nf F* **correctionnelle,** criminal court.

corrélatif, -ive [kɔrelatif, -iv] *adj & nm* correlative.

corrélation [kɔrelɑsjɔ̃] *nf* correlation; **être en c. étroite,** to be closely connected *or* related.

corrélativement [kɔrelativmɑ̃] *adv* correlatively, correspondingly.

correspondance [kɔrɛspɔ̃dɑ̃s] *nf* **(a)** (*échange de lettres*) correspondence (*with s.o. by letter*); (*lettres*) letters, correspondence; **être en** *ou* **entretenir une c. avec qn,** to correspond *or* be in correspondence with s.o.; **enseignement par c.,** correspondence course; *Journ* **(petite) c.,** letters to the editor; **la c. commerciale,** commercial *or* business correspondence; *Scol* **carnet de c.,** school report (book); **ouvrir la c.,** to open *or* go through the mail; **publier la c. d'un auteur,** to publish an author's correspondence *or* (collected) letters;

(b) connection (*between trains*); *Av* connecting flight; *Can* (*ticket*) transfer; **assurer la c. avec ...,** (*of train, boat etc*) to connect with ...; **j'attend la c.,** I'm waiting for the connection;

(c) correspondence, agreement (*of tastes, between things etc*); conformity (*of ideas*).

correspondant, -ante [kɔrɛspɔ̃dɑ̃, -ɑ̃t] **1** *adj* corresponding (**à,** to, with); corresponding (*angle* etc); **membre c.,** corresponding member (*of institute etc*). **2** *n* **(a)** *Com Journ* correspondent; *Journ* **c. de guerre,** war correspondent *or* reporter; **c. permanent,** permanent *or* resident correspondent; **(b)** (*ami à qui l'on écrit*) pen friend *or* pal.

correspondre [kɔrɛspɔ̃dr] **1** *vi* **(a)** to tally, to agree, to square, to fit (**à,** with); to correspond (**à,** to, with); **cela ne correspond pas à votre promesse,** that wasn't what you promised; **la théorie ne correspond pas aux faits,** the theory does not square with the facts; **(b)** (*communiquer*) to communicate; **ces deux pièces correspondent,** these two rooms communicate with one another; **(c)** (*par lettres*) **c. avec qn,** to correspond with *or* write to s.o.; **ils ont cessé de c.,** they have stopped *or* are no longer writing (to each other). **2 se correspondre** *vpr* to match, to go together, to correspond; **ornements qui se correspondent,** ornaments that match; **leurs goûts se correspondent,** they have similar *or* the same tastes; **ils se correspondent parfaitement,** they are perfectly matched *or* suited.

corrida [kɔrida] *nf* **(a)** (*de taureaux*) bullfight, corrida; **(b)** (*à l'aéroport, aux magasins etc*) *F* carry-on, hassle; (*dispute*) ding-dong argument; **quelle c.!,** what a zoo, all hell broke loose!; **faire la c. dans sa chambre,** to kick up a shindig *or* racket in one's bedroom.

corridor [kɔridɔr] *nm* corridor, passage.

corrigé [kɔriʒe] *nm Scol* fair copy, correct version (*of exercise*); key (*to exercise*), *F* crib.

corriger [kɔriʒe] *v* **(je corrigeai(s); n. corrigeons) 1** *vt* **(a)** to correct, to mark (*exercise etc*); to rectify (*mistake etc*); *Typ* to proofread, to correct (*proofs*); *Journ* to sub-edit (*article*); *Nau* to adjust (*compass*); **c. le tir,** *Mil* to adjust one's aim; **c. qn d'une mauvaise habitude,** to cure *or* break s.o. of a bad habit; **(b)** (*pour punir*) to give (*s.o.*) a thrashing *or* a hiding. **2 se corriger** *vpr* to turn over a new leaf, to mend one's ways; **se c. de sa gourmandise,** to cure oneself of one's greed; **elle ne s'est donc pas corrigée!,** she hasn't mended her ways, then!

corrigible [kɔriʒibl] *adj* corrigible, rectifiable.

corroboration [kɔrɔbɔrɑsjɔ̃] *nf* corroboration.

corroborer [kɔrɔbɔre] *vt* to corroborate.

corrodant [kɔrɔdɑ̃] *adj & nm* corrosive.

corroder [kɔrɔde] *vt* to corrode (*metal*); to erode (*stone*); to eat away, to wear away (*metal, stone etc*).

corrompre [kɔrɔ̃pr] **1** *vt* to corrupt (*morals, person etc*); to spoil (*taste etc*); to debase (*language*); **c. la viande,** to taint meat. **2 se corrompre** *vpr* to become corrupt(ed); *Vieilli* (*of meat etc*) to become tainted.

corrompu [kɔrɔ̃py] *adj* corrupt (*person, morals*); tainted, putrid (*meat*); corrupt (*text*); *Ordinat* **disquette corrompue,** corrupt disk.

corrosif, -ive [kɔrozif, -iv] **1** *adj* corrosive; *Fig* **des propos corrosifs,** scathing *or* caustic remarks. **2** *nm* corrosive.

corrosion [kɔrozjɔ̃] *nf* **(a)** corrosion, corroding (*of metal etc*); **(b)** *Géol* corrosion, erosion (*of river banks etc*).

corroyage [kɔrwajaʒ] *nm* currying (*of leather*); welding (*of metal*).

corroyer [kɔrwaje] *vt* **(je corroie, n. corroyons; je corroierai)** to curry (*leather*); to trim, to rough-plane (*wood*); to weld (*metal*).

corroyeur [kɔrwajœr] *nm* currier.

corrupteur, -trice [kɔryptœr, -tris] **1** *n* corrupter (*of morals*); suborner, briber (*of witness etc*). **2** *adj* corrupt (ing) (*influence etc*).
corruptible [kɔryptibl] *adj* corruptible.
corruption [kɔrypsjɔ̃] *nf* corruption; bribery (*of witness*); decomposition (*of food etc*).
corsage [kɔrsaʒ] *nm* **(a)** (*chemisier*) blouse; **(b)** bodice, body (*of dress*).
corsaire [kɔrsɛr] **1** *nm Hist* (*navire*) corsair, privateer; (*homme*) corsair, privateer. **2** *adj* **pantalon c.,** pedal pushers.
corse[1] [kɔrs] **1** *adj* Corsican. **2** *nm Ling* Corsican. **3** *n* **C.,** Corsican.
Corse[2] *nf* Corsica.
corsé [kɔrse] *adj* full-bodied (*wine etc*); spicy (*sauce etc*); **histoire corsée,** risqué *or* spicy story; **affaire corsée,** sensational business.
corselet [kɔrsəlɛ] *nm Ent Mil etc* corselet.
corser [kɔrse] **1** *vt* to give body *or* volume *or* flavour to (*sth*); to enliven (*un récit*); **c. du vin,** to strengthen *or* fortify wine (*by adding spirits*); **c. l'action d'un drame,** to intensify the action of a drama. **2 se corser** *vpr* to intensify; **l'affaire se corse,** (*d'une enquête etc*) the plot thickens; (*dans la vie*) things are getting serious.
corset [kɔrsɛ] *nm* corset; **c. orthopédique** *ou* **médical,** (surgical) corset.
corseter [kɔrsəte] *vt* **(je corsète, n. corsetons; je corsèterai)** to corset; *Fig* to restrict, to constrain.
corsetier, -ière [kɔrsətje, -jɛr] *n* corset maker.
corso [kɔrso] *nm* **c. (fleuri),** procession of floral floats.
cortège [kɔrtɛʒ] *nm* **(a)** train, retinue, suite, cortège (*of sovereign etc*); **(b)** (*défilé*) procession; (funeral) cortège; **c. (nuptial),** bridal procession.
cortex [kɔrtɛks] *nm Anat Bot* cortex.
cortical, -aux [kɔrtikal] *adj Anat Bot* cortical.
cortisone [kɔrtizɔn] *nf Méd* cortisone.
corvée [kɔrve] *nf* **(a)** chore, drudgery; **quelle c.!,** what a drag *or* bind!; *Can* **faire une c.,** to pitch *or* muck in together (to get a job done); **(b)** *Mil etc* fatigue (duty); **c. de cuisine(s),** cookhouse fatigue, *US* kitchen police; **être de c.,** to be on fatigue; **la c. de ravitaillement,** supply duty; **(détachement de) c.,** fatigue party; **(c)** *Hist* corvée (*statutory forced labour*).
corvette [kɔrvɛt] *nf Nau* corvette.
coryphée [kɔrife] *nm* **(a)** ballerina (*in the corps de ballet*); **(b)** leader, chief (*of a sect, party*).
coryza [kɔriza] *nm Méd* head cold.
cosaque [kɔzak] *nm* cossack.
cosécante [kɔsekɑ̃t] *nf Math* cosecant.
cosignataire [kɔsiŋatɛr] *adj* co-signatory.
cosinus [kɔsinys] *nm Math* cosine.
cosmétique [kɔsmetik] **1** *adj* cosmetic. **2** *nm* hair oil, hair cream.
cosmétologue [kɔsmetɔlɔg] *n* cosmetics expert, beautician.
cosmique [kɔsmik] *adj* cosmic (*rays etc*).
cosmogonie [kɔsmɔgɔni] *nf* cosmogony.
cosmographie [kɔsmɔgrafi] *nf* cosmography.
cosmologie [kɔsmɔlɔʒi] *nf* cosmology.
cosmonaute [kɔsmɔnot] *n* cosmonaut.
cosmopolite [kɔsmɔpɔlit] *adj* cosmopolitan.
cosmopolitisme [kɔsmɔpɔlitism] *nm* cosmopolitanism.
cosmos [kɔsmɔs] *nm Phil* cosmos; *Astronaut* outer space.
cossard, -arde [kɔsar, -ard] *Arg* **1** *n* lazybones. **2** *adj* lazy, bone-idle.
cosse [kɔs] *nf* **(a)** pod, husk, hull (*of peas etc*); **(b)** *Nau* thimble, eyelet (*of rope*); **(c)** *Él* cable terminal (*of cable*); **(d)** *Arg* **avoir la c.,** to feel lazy.
cossin [kɔsɛ̃] *nm Can F* (*truc*) whatsit, thingamabob, thingamajig, thingummy.
cossu [kɔsy] *adj* wealthy, well-to-do, well-off (*person*); opulent (*house*).
costal, -aux [kɔstal, -o] *adj Anat* costal.
costard [kɔstar] *nm Arg* (man's) suit.
costaud, -aude [kɔsto, -od] **1** *adj* strong, sturdy. **2** *nm* strong man; *F* **tu peux avoir confiance, c'est du c.,** trust me, it's sturdily made.
costume [kɔstym] *nm* (*habit*) costume, dress; (*complet*) (man's) (three-piece) suit; **c. national,** national costume; **c. de cérémonie** *ou* **d'apparat,** ceremonial *or* formal dress; *F* **c. d'Adam, d'Ève,** birthday suit; *F* **en c. d'Adam,** in one's birthday suit, in the altogether; *Th* **répéter en c.,** to have a dress rehearsal.
costumé [kɔstyme] *adj* **bal c.,** fancy-dress ball, costume ball.
costumer [kɔstyme] **1** *vt* to dress (*s.o.*) (up). **2 se costumer** *vpr* to put on fancy dress, to dress up; **se c. en Turc,** to dress up as a Turk.
costumier, -ière [kɔstymje, -jɛr] *n* **(a)** *Com* costum(i)er, dealer in (fancy) costumes; **(b)** *Th* wardrobe keeper, wardrobe mistress.
cosy [kozi] **1** *nm* corner divan. **2** *F adj* cosy, comfy; **c'est très c.,** it's very cosy *or* comfy.
cotangente [kɔtɑ̃ʒɑ̃t] *nf Math* cotangent.
cotation [kɔtasjɔ̃] *nf Fin* quotation, quoting.
cote [kɔt] *nf* **(a)** *Bourse Com* quotation; **c. des prix,** share-list; *Com* list of prices; **c. d'une voiture d'occasion,** quoted value of a secondhand car; **actions inscrites à la c.,** listed shares; **marché hors c.,** unofficial *or Am* over-the counter market; **c. d'amour,** favouritism; *Pol* **pour faire monter sa c. de popularité,** to increase his popularity rating; *F* **avoir la c.,** to be popular (**auprès de,** with, by); *Courses de chevaux* **c. d'un cheval,** odds on (or against) a horse; **c. morale d'un film,** film rating;
(b) *Com Jur* (classification) mark, letter, figure, number (*of document etc*); (library) shelf mark, pressmark; *Nau* character, classification (*of ship*);
(c) *Scol* mark;
(d) quota, share, proportion (*of expense, taxes etc*); *Admin* assessment; **c. mobilière,** assessment on income; **c. mal taillée,** rough and ready settlement;
(e) (*taille*) (indication of) dimensions; **c. d'origine,** standard size;
(f) height; elevation (*above sea level*); altitude (*of a point in figures*); **c. d'alerte,** *HydE* critical level, flood level; *Fig* danger point; *Mil* **la c. 304,** hill 304.
côte [kot] *nf* **(a)** *Anat* rib; **côtes flottantes,** floating ribs; **c. à c.,** side by side; *F* **se tenir les côtes,** to split one's sides laughing; **on lui compterait les côtes,** he's nothing but skin and bone; *F* **avoir les côtes en long,** to be lazy *or* bone idle; *Culin* **c. de bœuf,** rib of beef; **c. de porc,** pork chop; **côtes découvertes,** spare ribs (of pork); **c. première,** loin chop;
(b) rib (*of melon*); midrib (*of leaf*); **tissu à côtes,** ribbed *or* corded material;
(c) hill, rise; slope (*of hill*); *Constr* gradient; **vitesse en c.,** speed uphill; *Aut* **démarrage en c.,** hill start; **ma voiture a du mal à monter les côtes,** my car has problems getting up hills; **à mi-côte,** halfway up *or* down the hill;
(d) *Géog* coast, coastline; **les côtes de (la) France,** the coast of France; **la c. (d'Azur),** the (French) Riviera; *Nau* **faire c.,** to beach, to run aground; *Nau* **jeter à la c.,** to drive ashore, to strand; *F* **être à la c.,** to be on one's beam ends *or* hard up.
côté [kote] *nm* **(a)** side (*of human body*); **couché sur le c.,** lying on one's side; **assis à mes côtés,** sitting by my side; **avoir un point de c.,** to have a stitch (in one's side);
(b) side (*of mountain, road, table etc*); **passer de l'autre c. de la rue,** to cross the street; **demeurer de l'autre c. de la rue,** to live on the other side of the street; **appartement c. jardin,** flat overlooking the garden; *Tennis* **service ou c.?,** side or service?; **la tour penche d'un c.,** the tower leans to one side *or* leans sideways; **les côtés d'un rectangle,** the sides of a rectangle; **les côtés de la médaille,** the (two) sides of the medal; **feuille de papier écrite des deux côtés,** a sheet of paper written on on both sides; *Nau* **présenter le c. à qch,** to be broadside on to sth; **navire sur le c.,** ship on her beam ends;
(c) (*aspect*) aspect; **le c. scientifique,** the scientific aspect; **le bon/le mauvais c. d'une affaire,** the good/bad side of a matter; **il a un c. méchant,** there's a mean streak in him; **on a tous ses mauvais côtés,** everyone has their bad side *or* points; **le vent vient du bon c.,** the wind is in the right quarter; **prendre les choses par le bon c.,** to look on the bright side of things;
(d) (*endroit*) side, direction, way; **de tous (les) côtés,** on all sides, from all quarters; **de c. et d'autre,** here and there; **se diriger du c. de Paris,** to go towards *or* in the direction of Paris; **il habitait du c. de la rivière,** he lived near the river; **on voit mieux de ce c.-là,** you can see better from that side, you can see better from over there; **venez de ce c.,** (*par ici*) come over here; (*à droite, gauche*) come this side; **de ce c.-ci/-là,** on this/that side; **ils s'en allèrent chacun de son c.,** they went their separate ways; **de quel c.?,** in which direction?, which way?; **se ranger du c. des plus forts,** to side with the strongest; **les parents du c. du père,** relations on the father's side; *Fig* **être né du c. gauche,** to be illegitimate; **d'un c. à l'autre,** from side to side; **d'un c. ..., d'un autre c. ...,** on the one

hand ...; **de mon c.,** for my part; *F* **de ce c. il n'y a rien à craindre,** there's nothing to worry about on that score;

(e) *F* (*question*) side, point, aspect; **c. vitesse, cette voiture est remarquable,** as far as speed is concerned *or* speedwise, this car is remarkable; **c. repos, ça aurait pu être mieux,** on the relaxation side *or* front, it could have been better, it could have been more restful;

(f) de c., sideways; on one side; **faire un saut de c.,** to leap aside, to jump sideways; **regard de c.,** sidelong glance; **mettre qch de c.,** to put sth aside *or* on one side; **mettre de l'argent de c.,** to put money by *or* aside, to save money; **laisser qn de c.,** to neglect s.o.;

(g) à c., to one side; (*près*) near; **la maison est tout à c.,** the house is quite near; **il habite à c.,** he lives next door; **tirer à c.,** to miss the mark; **le salon est à c. de la cuisine,** the drawing room is next to the kitchen; **il se tenait à c. de moi,** he stood at *or* by my side, he stood beside me; **à c. l'un de l'autre,** side by side; **vous êtes à c. de la question,** you're straying *or* have strayed from the point; **passer à c. d'une difficulté,** to avoid a difficulty; **mes ennuis sont petits à c. des vôtres,** my troubles are small compared with yours; **il n'est rien à c. de vous,** he's nothing compared to you.

coteau, -eaux [kɔto] *nm* (*versant*) slope, hillside; (*colline*) hillock, small hill.

côtelé [kotle] *adj Tex* **velours c.,** corduroy.

côtelette [kotlɛt, kɔ-] *nf Culin* cutlet; **c. d'agneau/de porc,** lamb/pork chop.

coter [kɔte] *vt* **(a)** *Com Bourse* to quote (*price etc*); **des actions cotées en bourse,** shares quoted on the Stock Exchange, listed *or* quoted shares; *F* **ma voiture est si vieille, elle n'est même pas cotée,** my car is so old it's not even listed (in the car buyer's guide); **très coté,** *Courses de chevaux* well backed, well *or* highly fancied; *Fig* highly considered; **(b)** *Scol* to mark (*exercise etc*); **(c)** *MecE etc* to mark the dimensions on (*drawing etc*); to put references on (*maps etc*); **point coté,** (*de relevé*) reference point, landmark; (*sur une carte*) spot height (*on map etc*); **(d)** *Com Jur* to classify, to number, to letter (*documents etc*); *Nau* to class (*ship*).

coterie [kɔtri] *nf Pol Péj* set, clique, coterie.

côtier, -ière [kotje, -jɛr] **1** *adj* coastal (*defence etc*); inshore (*fishery*); coastwise (*trade etc*); coast(ing) (*pilot etc*); **navigation côtière,** coasting; **fleuve c.,** short coastal river. **2** *nm Nau* coaster, coasting vessel.

cotillon [kɔtijɔ̃] *nm* **(a) cotillons,** party novelties *or* accessories; **(b)** *Arch* (*danse*) cotill(i)on; **accessoires de c.,** party novelties; **(c)** *Arch* petticoat; *F* **courir le c.,** to flirt with women.

cotisant, -ante [kɔtizɑ̃, -ɑ̃t] **1** *adj* paying (*member*) (**de,** to). **2** *n* subscriber (**de,** to).

cotisation [kɔtizasjɔ̃] *nf* **(a)** quota, share; contribution (*to common fund*); **c. de Sécurité Sociale,** ≈ National Insurance contribution; **(b)** subscription (*to club etc*).

cotiser [kɔtize] **1** *vi* **(a)** (*participer*) to contribute (**pour,** towards); **c. à un cadeau,** to contribute to a present, *F* to chip in for a present; **(b)** (*à un club*) to subscribe, to pay one's subscription. **2 se cotiser** *vpr* to club together (*in order to raise a sum of money*).

côtoiement [kotwamɑ̃] *nm* coming into contact with, encounter(s) with (*society, a situation etc*); **le c. des personnes célèbres lui monte à la tête,** rubbing shoulders *or* mixing with celebrities is going to *or* turning his head; **le c. quotidien de la mort,** the daily contact with death.

coton [kɔtɔ̃] **1** *nm* **(a)** cotton; **fil de c.,** sewing cotton; **c. retors,** cotton thread; **c. à broder,** embroidery thread; **c. à repriser,** darning thread *or* cotton; **chemise 100% c.,** pure *or* 100% cotton shirt; **(b)** *Arg* trouble, difficulty; *F* **filer un mauvais c.,** to be in a bad way (*in health, business*); **(c) c. (hydrophile),** cotton wool; *F* **j'ai les jambes en c.,** my legs feel like cotton wool *or* like jelly; **il a du c. dans les oreilles,** (*il n'entend pas*) he's deaf; (*il ne veut pas entendre*) he doesn't want to hear; *Fig* **élever un enfant dans du c.,** to (molly)coddle a child; **(d)** down (*on plants*); **(e) c. de verre,** glass wool. **2** *adj F* difficult; **ça, c'est plutôt c.!,** that's a bit tough *or* tricky!

cotonnade [kɔtɔnad] *nf* cotton fabric; **s'habiller de cotonnades,** to wear (clothes made of) cotton *or* cotton clothes.

cotonner (se) [səkɔtɔne] *vpr* **(a)** (*of material*) to become fluffy, to fluff up; **(b) fruit qui se cotonne,** fruit that becomes woolly.

cotonnerie [kɔtɔnri] *nf* cotton plantation.

cotonneux, -euse [kɔtɔnø, -øz] *adj* cottony; downy (*leaf, fruit etc*); woolly, fleecy (*clouds*); muffled (*sound*); thick (*fog*); **jambes cotonneuses,** legs like jelly; **style c.,** woolly style.

cotonnier, -ière [kɔtɔnje, -jɛr] **1** *adj* cotton (*industry, products etc*). **2** *n* cotton worker, spinner. **3** *nm* cotton plant.

coton-poudre [kɔtɔ̃pudr] *nm* guncotton, *US* nitrocotton; (*pl cotons-poudre*).

côtoyer [kotwaje] *vt* (**je côtoie, n. côtoyons; je côtoierai**) **(a)** to coast along, to keep close to, to hug (*shore etc*); to skirt (*forest etc*); **(b)** to border on (*river etc*); *Fig* **cela côtoie le ridicule,** it's verging on the ridiculous.

cotre [kɔtr] *nm Nau* cutter.

cottage [kɔtaʒ] *nm* (country) cottage.

cotte [kɔt] *nf* **(a)** *F* (*bleu*) (workmen's) overalls, dungarees; **(b)** *Mil* **c. d'armes,** tunic (*worn over armour*); **c. de mailles,** coat of mail; **(c)** *Arch* (*jupon*) short skirt, petticoat.

cotutelle [kɔtytɛl] *nf Jur* joint guardianship.

cotuteur, -trice [kɔtytœr, -tris] *n Jur* joint guardian.

cotylédon [kɔtiledɔ̃] *nm Anat Bot* cotyledon.

cou [ku] *nm* neck (*of animal, bottle etc*); **une chaîne en or autour du c.,** (with) a gold chain around his neck; **la peau du c.,** the scruff of the neck; **couper le c. à qn,** to behead s.o., to chop s.o.'s head off; **tendre le c.,** to offer oneself as a ready victim; **se jeter au c. de qn,** to throw one's arms round s.o.'s neck; **tordre le c. à une volaille,** to wring a bird's neck; *Fig* **je vais lui tordre le c.!,** I'll wring his neck (for him)!; *F* **endetté jusqu'au c.,** up to the eyes in debt; **prendre ses jambes à son c.,** to take to one's heels; **tu risques de te casser le c.,** watch *or* mind you don't break your neck.

couac [kwak] *nm Mus* squeak, goosenote (*on clarinet etc*); false note (*of voice*); **faire un c.,** to sing *or* play a false *or* discordant note.

couard [kwar] **1** *adj Litt & Région* cowardly. **2** *nm* coward.

couardise [kwardiz] *nf Vieilli* cowardice.

couchage [kuʃaʒ] *nm* **(a)** (*fait de se coucher*) lying in bed; **le c. des enfants,** putting the children to bed; **(b) (matériel de) c.,** bedding, bedclothes; **sac de c.,** sleeping bag; **(c)** *Arg* sleeping around, casual sex.

couchant [kuʃɑ̃] **1** *adj* **(a) soleil c.,** setting sun, sunset; **(b) chien c.,** setter; *Fig* **faire le chien c. auprès de qn,** to fawn on s.o.. **2** *nm* **(a)** (*de soleil*) (*moment*) setting sun; (*résultat*) sunset; **(b)** (*ouest*) west; **dans la direction du c.,** westward, in a westerly direction.

couche [kuʃ] *nf* **(a)** coat (*of paint etc*); layer (*of butter, dirt etc*); *Géol* bed, layer, stratum; **c. de houille,** coal bed *or* seam; **les couches de l'atmosphère,** the layers *or* strata of the atmosphere; **la c. d'ozone,** the ozone layer; **c. de fumier,** (*au jardin*) hotbed; **champignons de c.,** cultivated mushrooms; **couches sociales,** social strata, levels of society; **c. d'apprêt,** primer; **c. de fond,** undercoat; **c. de glace,** sheet of ice; **une c. de crème solaire,** a layer of suntan cream; **disposez les fruits et la crème en couches successives,** layer the fruit and cream; *Arg* **il a** *ou* **il en tient une c.!,** he's really thick!, what an idiot!;

(b) (*souvent pl*) **couches,** confinement, labour; **femme en couches,** woman in labour; **couches laborieuses** *ou* **pénibles,** difficult (child)birth; **fausse c.,** miscarriage; **faire une fausse c.,** to have a miscarriage;

(c) c. (de bébé), (baby's) nappy, *Am* diaper; **mettre une couche au bébé,** to put a nappy on the baby; **c.-culotte,** shaped nappy;

(d) *MecE* **arbre de c.,** engine shaft, main shaft, power shaft;

(e) *Litt* bed.

couché [kuʃe] *adj* **(a)** lying (down); (*au lit*) in bed; **(b)** (*incliné*) **écriture couchée,** slanting *or* sloping writing; **les blés couchés par le vent,** fields of corn flattened by the wind; **(c) papier c.,** art paper.

coucher[1] [kuʃe] *nm* **(a) l'heure du c.,** bedtime; **(b)** (*gîte*) accommodation; **cela va nous assurer le c.,** we'll be sure of a bed for the night; **le c. et la nourriture,** board and lodging; **(c)** (*du soleil*) setting; **au c. du soleil,** at sunset *or* sundown; **un superbe c. de soleil,** a magnificent sunset.

coucher[2] **1** *vt* **(a)** to put (*child etc*) to bed;

(b) (*offrir un lit à*) to put (*s.o.*) up, to provide (*s.o.*) with a bed; **je ne peux pas vous c.,** I can't put you up;

(c) to lay (*s.o., sth*) down; **la pluie a couché les blés,** the rain has flattened the wheat; **c. un navire,** to throw a vessel on her beam ends; **c. un fusil en joue,** to aim a gun; **c. qn en joue,** to take aim at s.o.; *Fig* **c. qn sur le carreau,** to floor s.o.;

(d) (*écrire*) to put down in writing, to inscribe; **c. qch par**

écrit *ou* **sur le papier,** to set *or* put sth down in writing; **c. qn sur son testament,** to mention s.o. in one's will.

2 *vi* **(a) c. à l'hôtel/chez des amis,** to sleep *or* spend the night at the hotel/with friends; **c. à la belle étoile/sous la tente,** to sleep in the open air *or* outside *or* under the stars/ in a tent *or* under canvas;

(b) *F* **c. avec qn,** to sleep with s.o.; *F* **elle ne couche pas,** she doesn't sleep around;

(c) (*to dog*) **(allez) couché!,** (lie) down!;

(d) *F* **avoir un nom à c. dehors,** to have an impossible name.

3 se coucher *vpr* **(a)** (*au lit*) **(aller) se c.,** to go to bed; **il est l'heure d'aller se c.,** it's bedtime; **je ne veux pas vous faire c. tard,** I don't want to keep you up; *F* **se c. comme les poules,** to go to bed early; *F* **va te c.!,** buzz off, clear off!, leave me alone!; *Prov* **comme on fait son lit on se couche,** as we make our bed, so must we lie in it;

(b) (*s'allonger*) to lie down; **se c. à plat ventre,** to lie on one's stomach; **ne te couche pas sur ton bureau! tiens-toi droit!,** don't slouch over your desk, sit up straight!;

(c) *Nau* (*of ship*) **se c. sur le flanc,** to heel over;

(d) (*of sun, stars*) to set, to go down.

coucherie [kuʃri] *nf Arg* screwing; **chez eux c'est la c. permanente,** they're always bonking *or* having it off; **la c. ce n'est pas mon genre,** I don't sleep around.

couchette [kuʃɛt] *nf* **(a)** *Nau* berth, bunk; *Rail* couchette; **(b)** (child's) cot, bed.

coucheur [kuʃœr] *nm F* **c'est un mauvais c.,** he's an awkward customer.

couci-couça [kusikusa] *adv F* so-so.

coucou [kuku] **1** *nm* **(a)** (*oiseau*) cuckoo; **(b) (pendule à) c.,** cuckoo clock; **(c)** (*plante*) cowslip; **(d)** *Av Arg* old crate, ancient kite. **2** *int* **c.! (me voilà),** peep-bo!, peek-a-boo!

coude [kud] *nm* **(a)** *Anat* elbow; **mettre les coudes sur la table,** to put one's elbows on the table; **coudes au corps,** elbows in; **c. à c.,** side by side, close together, shoulder to shoulder; **c. à c. fraternel,** friendly jostling; **coup de c.,** poke with the elbow; (*pour attirer l'attention*) nudge; **donner un coup de c. à qn,** to jog s.o.; (*pour attirer l'attention*) to nudge s.o., to give s.o. a nudge; **se serrer les coudes,** to help one another, to stick together; **jouer des coudes,** to elbow one's way (*through a crowd*); *Fig* to manœuvre (*to gain one's own ends*); *F* **lever le c.,** to lift *or* bend one's elbow, to booze; **huile de c.,** elbow grease; **mets-y de l'huile de c.,** put some elbow grease into it, use a bit of elbow grease; *Fig* **garder qch sous le c.,** to hold on to something (without doing anything about it); *Arg* **se fourrer le doigt dans l'œil jusqu'au c.,** to be completely wrong; **pull aux coudes usés,** pullover with holes in the elbows;

(b) (sharp) bend (*in road etc*); *MecE* bend, elbow (*of bar, pipe etc*); crank (*of shaft*); **arbre à deux coudes,** two-throw crankshaft.

coudé [kude] *adj* (*pipe etc*) bent, kneed, at an angle; (*shaft*) cranked.

coudée [kude] *nf* **(a) avoir ses coudées franches,** to have plenty of elbow room; *Fig* to have a free hand, to have free scope; **(b)** *Antiq* (*mesure*) cubit.

cou-de-pied [kudpje] *nm Anat* instep; (*pl cous-de-pied*).

couder [kude] *vt* to bend (*pipe etc*) at an angle; to crank (*shaft*).

coudoiement [kudwamɑ̃] *nm* contact, association.

coudoyer [kudwaje] *vt* (**je coudoie, n. coudoyons; je coudoierai**) to come into contact with (*s.o.*), to rub shoulders *or* hobnob with (*s.o.*); *Fig* **un texte où la vanité de l'auteur coudoie le ridicule,** a text in which the author's vanity borders on the ridiculous.

coudre [kudr] *vt* (*prp* **cousant**; *pp* **cousu**; *pr ind* **je couds, il coud, n. cousons, ils cousent**; *impf* **je cousais**; *p hist* **je cousis**; *fu* **je coudrai**) to sew, to stitch; **c. un bouton à une robe,** to sew *or* stitch a button on a dress; **c. une jupe,** to make *or* sew (up) a skirt; **machine à c.,** sewing machine; **c. une plaie,** to sew up a wound.

coudrier [kudrije] *nm* hazel (tree).

couenne [kwan] *nf* **(a)** rind (*of bacon*); *Arg* **quelle c.!,** what a twerp *or* idiot!; **(b)** *Méd* (diphtheric) membrane.

couette¹ [kwɛt] *nf* **(a)** (*dans housse*) duvet, continental quilt; **(b)** *Région* feather bed; **(c)** *MecE* bearing; **(d)** *Nau* **couettes courantes,** bilge ways.

couette² *nf F* lock (*of hair*); **elle était coiffée avec des couettes,** she wore her hair in bunches; **se faire des couettes,** to put *or* gather one's hair in bunches.

couffe [kuf] *nf*, **couffin** [kufɛ̃] *nm* frail, (straw) basket; (*pour bébé*) Moses basket.

coug(o)uar [kug(w)ar] *nm* cougar, puma, mountain lion.

couic [kwik] *int* eek!, cheep!, squeak!; *Arg* **faire c.,** to croak, to give one's last gasp.

couille [kuj] *nf Vulg* (*testicule*) ball, *Br* bollock; **une c. molle,** a drip; **avoir des couilles au cul,** to have balls *or* guts; **notre projet est parti en couilles,** our plan has gone down the tubes.

couillon [kujɔ̃] *nm Arg* idiot, fathead, cretin.

couillonner [kujɔne] *vt Arg* to swindle (*s.o.*); **je me suis fait c.,** I've been had *or* done *or* swindled.

couinement [kwinmɑ̃] *nm* squeak, squeal (*of animal*); **j'en ai marre de tes couinements,** I'm sick of your whining.

couiner [kwine] *vi* (*of animal*) to squeak; (*of rabbit*) to scream; (*of child*) to whine.

coulage [kulaʒ] *nm* **(a)** pouring, running; casting (*of metal*); pouring (*of molten metal, glass, soap etc*); **(b)** *F* (*gaspillage*) waste, wastage.

coulant [kulɑ̃] **1** *adj* running, flowing (*liquid*); runny (*jam etc*); smooth (*wine*); **nœud c.,** slip knot, running knot; (*autour du cou*) noose; **style c.,** easy *or* flowing style; *F* **personne coulante,** easy-going person; **il est très c.,** he's very easy to get on with *or* very easy-going. **2** *nm* **(a)** (*anneau etc*) sliding ring, sliding runner; **c. d'une ceinture,** loop of a belt; **(b)** runner (*of a plant*).

coule¹ [kul] *nf Arg* **être à la c.,** to know the tricks of the trade, to know the ropes, to know what's what.

coule² *nf* (monk's) cowl.

coulé [kule] **1** *adj* smooth (*movement*). **2** *nm* **(a)** *Mus* slur; **(b)** (*danse*) glide; **(c)** *Billard* follow-through.

coulée [kule] *nf* **(a)** running, flow(ing) (*of liquid*); **c. de lave,** lava flow; **(b)** *Métal* casting, tapping (*of molten metal*); **trou de c.,** tap(ping) hole, draw hole; **d'une seule c.,** in one movement, at one go; **(c)** *Natation* glide, push-off.

coulemelle [kulmɛl] *nf* parasol mushroom.

couler [kule] **1** *vt* **(a)** to run, to draw, to pour (*liquid*); to cast, to pour, to run (*molten metal*); to pour (*wax*); *Constr etc* to grout (*masonry*); to pour (*concrete*); **c. une pièce/ une statue,** to cast a piece/a statue; **c. une bielle/** *etc*, to burn out a connecting rod/*etc*;

(b) to sink (*a ship*); *Fig* **c. qn,** to discredit s.o., to ruin s.o., to bring s.o. down;

(c) (*glisser*) to slip, to glide; **c. un mot à l'oreille de qn,** to drop *or* whisper a word in s.o.'s ear; *Mus* **c. un passage,** to slur a passage;

(d) to pass, to spend (*time smoothly, pleasantly*); **c. une vie heureuse,** to lead *or* spend a happy life; *F* **se la c. douce,** to take life easily, to have a good time.

2 *vi* **(a)** (*of liquids, chocco, river etc*) to flow, to run; **faire c. l'eau,** to turn the water on; **faire c. un bain,** to run a bath; **la sueur coule sur son front,** sweat is trickling *or* running down his forehead; **ça coule de source,** it's obvious; (*par voie de conséquence*) it follows naturally; *Fig* **les années coulent,** the years slip by;

(b) (*of ship*) to sink;

(c) to slide, to slip; **une tuile coula du toit,** a tile fell off the roof;

(d) (*of barrel, fountain pen etc*) to leak; (*of nose*) to run; (*of verse*) to flow.

3 se couler *vpr* **(a)** to glide, to slip; **se c. entre les draps,** to slip into bed; **se c. dans la foule,** to slip *or* disappear into the crowd; **se c. le long du mur,** to hug the wall;

(b) *Fig* **tu risques de te c. à leurs yeux,** you risk discrediting yourself in their eyes.

couleur [kulœr] **1** *nf* **(a)** colour, *US* color; **la c. des yeux/ du ciel,** the colour of s.o.'s eyes/of the sky; **de quelle c. sont vos yeux?,** what colour are your eyes?; **de quelle c. est sa voiture?,** what colour car has he got?, what colour is his car?; **en quelle c. vas-tu repeindre la pièce?,** what colour are you going to paint the room?; **couleurs fondamentales,** primary colours; **couleurs primitives** *ou* **spectrales,** colours of the spectrum; **gens de c.,** coloured people, coloureds; **des gens hauts en c.,** picturesque *or* colourful individuals; **la c., les couleurs,** (*linge*) coloureds; **la lessive idéale pour vos couleurs,** the ideal soap-powder for your coloureds; **photographie/télévision (en) couleurs,** colour photography/television; *Pol* **la c. d'un journal,** the (political) colour *or* tone *or* complexion of a paper; *Fig* **c. locale,** local colour; **c'est très c. locale,** it's got plenty of local colour, it's really ethnic *or* quaint; **suivant la c. du temps,** according to the state of things; **sous c. de me rendre service,** under the pretext *or* guise of helping me *or* of doing me a service; **style/personnalité sans c.,** drab *or* colourless style/personality; **immédiatement, ça a pris une autre c.,** it immediately started to look different; *F* **il en a vu de toutes les couleurs,** he's been through the mill *or* a lot; **dépeindre qch sous des couleurs sombres,** to paint a dark picture of sth, to present a gloomy view of sth; *Culin* **prendre c.,** (*of joint*) to brown;

(b) (*de visage*) colour, complexion; **perdre/reprendre ses couleurs,** to become pale, to lose one's colour/to get back one's colour; **sans c.,** colourless, pale; *F* **quand il l'a su, il a changé de c.,** he went pale *or* changed colour *or* blanched when he found out; **tu as repris des couleurs,** you're getting some colour (back) in your cheeks; **tu as pris des couleurs,** you've got a touch of the sun; **tu as des couleurs aujourd'hui,** you're looking well today; **le vin lui avait donné des couleurs,** his face was flushed with wine;

(c) *Mil etc* **couleurs,** colours, flag; **envoyer** *ou* **hisser les couleurs,** to hoist the colours *or* the flag;

(d) *Sp Courses de chevaux* colours (*of club, stable*); **défendre les couleurs de son club,** to play for one's club;

(e) (*peinture*) colour, paint; **c. à l'eau/l'huile,** water colour/oil paint; **boîte de couleurs,** box of paints, paintbox; **des crayons de c.,** crayons, colouring pencils; *Com* **marchand de couleurs,** = ironmonger, *Am* hardware merchant;

(f) *Cartes* suit; **jouer dans la c.,** to follow suit; **annoncer la c.,** to call (*trumps*); *F* to have one's say, to state one's case; **je n'en ai pas encore vu la c.,** I've seen no sign of it yet.

2 *adj inv* **c. paille/chair,** straw/flesh coloured.

couleuvre [kulœvr] *nf* (*reptile*) *Can* worm; **c. (à collier),** grass snake; **c. lisse,** European smooth snake; **paresseux comme une c.,** bone-idle; **avaler des couleuvres,** to believe *or* swallow anything.

coulis¹ [kuli] *adj* **vent c.,** draught (*through crevice etc*).

coulis² *nm* **(a)** *Constr* grout(ing); **(b)** *Métal* molten metal; **(c)** *Culin* **c. de tomates/framboises,** tomato/raspberry sauce.

coulissant [kulisɑ̃] *adj* sliding (*door, panel etc*).

coulisse [kulis] *nf* **(a)** groove, slot, runner, slide; **fenêtre/porte à c.,** sliding window/door; **trombone à c.,** slide trombone; **regard en c.,** sidelong glance; **(b)** *Couture* hem (*through which to pass tape*); **(c)** *Th* runner, groove (*of scenery flat*); **les coulisses,** the wings, the slips; *Fig* **les coulisses de la politique,** behind the scenes in politics; the corridors of power; **rester dans les coulisses,** to stay in the background; **être dans les** *ou* **en coulisses,** to be standing *or* waiting in the wings; **(d)** *Bourse* outside market.

coulissé [kulise] *adj* grooved, slotted.

coulisseau, -eaux [kuliso] *nm* sliding block; slide (*of piece of machinery*); runner (*of drawer etc*).

coulisser [kulise] **1** *vi MecE etc* to slide. **2** *vt* **(a)** to provide (*sth*) with slides *or* runners; **(b)** *Couture* to run up (*hem*).

coulissier [kulisje] *nm Bourse* outside broker.

couloir [kulwar] *nm* **(a)** (*dans maison*) corridor, passage; (*d'un train*) corridor; *Pol* lobby; *Sp* (*athletics, swimming*) lane; *Tennis* tramlines; **propos** *ou* **bruits de c.,** confidential information; **(b)** *Ind etc* shoot, chute; *Cin* **c. du film,** film channel, track; **(c)** *Géog* channel, gully, gorge; **(d)** *Av* **c. aérien,** air corridor; **(e)** *Hist* **le c. de Dantzig,** the Polish Corridor.

coulpe [kulp] *nf* **battre sa c.,** to beat one's breast.

coup [ku] *nm* **(a)** (*choc*) knock, blow; rap, tap (*on door*); *Th* **les trois coups,** = the three knocks given just before the curtain rises; **donner de grands coups dans la porte,** to pound *or* bang at the door; **enfoncer un clou à coups de marteau,** to hammer a nail in; **se donner un c. contre qch,** to knock against sth; **c. de bec,** peck; **c. de bâton,** blow (with a stick); **c. sur les doigts,** rap over the knuckles; **il a reçu un c. de poing/de pied,** he was punched/kicked; **c. de couteau/de poignard,** stab (with knife/dagger); **coup d'épée,** thrust *or* lunge (with sword); **c. de hache,** blow *or* stroke (with an axe); *Fig* **ça m'a donné un c.!,** it gave me such a shock!; *F* **tenir le c.,** to hold out; **il faut que je tienne le c.,** I have to keep going *or* stick it out; **rendre c. pour c.,** to return blow for blow, to hit back, to strike back; *F* **faire les quatre cents coups,** to lead a reckless life; **faire d'une pierre deux coups, faire c. double,** to kill two birds with one stone; **c. bas,** hit below the belt; *F* **il m'a fait un c. bas,** he hit me below the belt, he played a lousy trick on me; *Jur* **coups et blessures,** assault and battery; **corps couvert de coups,** body covered with bruises; *F* **faire une traduction à coups de dictionnaire,** to do a translation with a dictionary; **je ne dis rien, je compte les coups,** I'm saying nothing, I'm keeping out of it; **c. de feu,** shot; **c. de fusil,** (gun)shot; **c. au but,** direct hit; **c. manqué,** miss; **fusil à deux coups,** double-barrelled gun; **il fut tué d'un c. de fusil,** he was shot (dead); **c. de grisou,** firedamp explosion; **c. de vent,** gust of wind; *Fig* **entrer dans une pièce en c. de vent,** to burst into a room; **partir en c. de vent,** to rush off; **je passe en c. de vent pour te dire ...,** I've just dropped in to tell you ...; **c. de tabac,** squall; **c. de froid,** *Météo* cold snap; *Méd* chill, cold; **c. de soleil,** sunburn; **c. d'aile,** stroke *or* flap of the wing; **c. de dents,** bite; **c. de queue,** flick of the tail; *F* **c. de gueule,** shout; **boire qch à petits coups,** to sip sth; *F* **un c. de rouge,** a glass of red wine; **allons boire un c.,** let's go and have a drink; **c. de crayon,** pencil stroke; **saluer qn d'un c. de chapeau,** to raise *or* tip one's hat to s.o.; **avoir un bon c. de fourchette,** to be a hearty eater; **passer un c. d'éponge sur la table,** to wipe over the table with a sponge, to give the table a wipe with a sponge; **donner un c. de frein,** to brake; **éviter un obstacle par un c. de volant,** to swerve to avoid an obstacle; **c. de cloche,** stroke of the bell; **l'horloge sonna trois coups,** the clock struck three; **sur le c. de midi,** on the stroke of twelve; **c. de filet,** cast; (*prise*) haul; **il va falloir en mettre un c.,** we're going to have to pull out (all) the stops; **c. de chance** *ou* *F* **de veine,** stroke of luck; **c. d'éclat,** distinguished action, glorious deed; **c. d'État,** coup (d'état); **c. de tonnerre,** (*sound*) clap *or* peal of thunder; **c. de sifflet,** blast of a whistle; **c. de sonnette,** ring of the bell; **c. de téléphone** *ou* *F* **de fil,** telephone call;

(b) *Golf* stroke; *Fb* kick; *Boxe* blow, punch; *Échecs etc* move; *Tennis* **c. droit,** forehand (stroke); **c. franc,** free kick; **c. d'envoi,** kickoff; **c. de tête,** header; *Boxe* **c. bas,** one below the belt; *Rugby* **c. tombé,** drop kick, drop; *Baseball* **c. sûr,** strike; *Cartes* **finir le c.,** to finish the hand;

(c) (*influence*) influence, power; **agir sous le c. de la peur,** to act through *or* out of fear; **j'ai répondu sous le c. de la colère,** I answered in a fit of anger; **il est sous le c. d'une forte émotion,** he's in a very emotional state; **tomber sous le c. de la loi,** to come within the provisions of the law; **être sous le c. d'une condamnation,** to have a current conviction;

(d) (*essai*) attempt; **c. d'essai,** trial shot *or* stroke; **à tous les coups l'on gagne,** you win every time; **tu as encore droit à un c.,** you've still got another go; **d'un seul c.,** at one go; **faire qch du premier c.,** to do sth at the first attempt *or* shot; **j'ai deviné du premier c.,** I guessed straight off; **marquer le c.,** to mark *or* celebrate the occasion; **accuser le c.,** to mark the occasion; *F* **ça vaut le c.,** it's worth while, it's worth trying; **ça ne vaut pas le c.,** it isn't worth it; **réussir un bon c.,** to make a hit; **c'est le c. classique,** it's the same old story; **c. de tête,** impulsive act; **faire qch sur un c. de tête,** to act impulsively; *Iron* **il a fait là un beau c.!,** he made a fine mess of it!;

(e) (*affaire*) thing, business, job; **il prépare un mauvais c.,** he's up to no good; **être sur un c.,** to be on to something good *or* a good thing *or* a winner; *F* **ça, c'est un sale c.!,** what a dirty trick!; **c'est encore un c. de ton ami,** it's another of your friend's tricks; *F* **il est dans le c.,** he knows what's going on; (*il en fait partie*) he's in on it; (*à la mode*) he's up to date; **il faut la mettre dans le c.,** we'll have to put her in the picture; (*l'impliquer*) we'll have to get *or* bring her in on it;

(f) **avoir le c. de main pour faire qch,** to have the knack of doing sth; **du (même) c.,** (*en même temps*) at the same time; (*donc*) as a result, and so; **il fut tué sur le c.,** he was killed outright; **sur le c., je n'ai pas compris,** at the time, I didn't understand; **pour le c.,** (*en conséquence*) as a result; (*cette fois*) this time; **après c.,** after the event; **tout à c., tout d'un c.,** suddenly, all of a sudden; **boire trois verres c. sur c.,** to drink three glasses one after the other *or* in a row; **encore un c.,** once again, once more; **à c. sûr,** definitely;

(g) *Arg* bang, screw; **tirer un c.,** to have a screw *or* shag; **un bon c.,** a good screw, a good lay.

coupable [kupabl] **1** *adj* guilty (*person*); **c. de vol,** guilty of theft; **s'avouer c.,** to admit one's guilt; **elle se sent c.,** she feels guilty (about it); *Jur* **plaider c.,** to plead guilty; **action c.,** culpable act; **faiblesse c.,** reprehensible weakness. **2** *n* culprit, guilty party; *F* **qui est le c.? qui a cassé le vase?,** own up, who broke the vase?

coupage [kupaʒ] *nm* **(a)** blending, mixing (*of wines*); **(b)** diluting (*of wine etc with water*).

coupant [kupɑ̃] *adj* cutting, sharp; **outils coupants,** edge tools, sharp(-edged) tools; **ton c.,** sharp tone.

coup-de-poing [kudpwɛ̃] *nm (pl coups-de-poing)* **(a)** **c.-de-p. (américain),** knuckle duster; *Fig* **opération c.-de-p.,** surprise *or* sudden raid; **une opération c.-de-p. contre l'alcool au volant,** a crackdown on drunk driving; **pu-**

blicité c.-de-p., advertising that pulls no punches, hard-hitting advertising; **(b)** (*silex taillé*) chellean pick, hand axe.

coupe¹ [kup] *nf* cup; (*contents*) cup(ful); *Sp* cup; **c. à champagne,** champagne glass; **c. à fruits,** fruit dish *or* bowl; **boire la c. jusqu'à la lie,** to drain the cup to the dregs; *Prov* **il y a loin de la c. aux lèvres,** there's many a slip 'twixt cup and lip; *Fb* **la C. du monde,** the World Cup; **jouer pour la c.,** to play for the cup.

coupe² *nf* **(a)** cutting (*of wheat etc*); cutting out (*of material*); felling (*of trees*); **c. de cheveux,** haircut; **une c. et un brushing,** a cut and blow-dry; **mettre un bois en c. réglée,** to make periodical cuttings in a wood; *F* **mettre qn en c. réglée,** to exploit s.o.; **c. sombre,** slight thinning (*of forest area*); drastic cut (*in personnel, spending*);
(b) length (*of material*); piece (*of wood*);
(c) cut (*of a garment*); **complet de bonne c.,** well-cut suit;
(d) *Archit* (*plan etc*) section; **c. longitudinale** *ou* **en long,** longitudinal section; **c. transversale** *ou* **en travers,** cross section, transverse section; **machine vue en c.,** section of a machine;
(e) *Cartes* cut, cutting; **être sous la c. de qn,** to lead after one's opponent has cut; *Fig* to be under s.o.'s thumb *or* power; **tenir qn sous sa c.,** to have s.o. under one's thumb *or* in one's power; **faire sauter la c.,** to make the pass, to slip the cut.

coupé [kupe] **1** *adj* **(a)** cut (up, out); **costume mal c.,** badly cut suit; **(b) vin c. d'eau,** wine and water; **(c)** *Tennis* **coup c.,** drive with a cut; **(d)** (*interrompu*) interrupted, cut (off), broken (off); **la route est coupée,** the road is cut off *or* blocked; **communication téléphonique coupée,** a broken *or* lost telephone connection; **(e) cheval c.,** gelding. **2** *nm* **(a)** coupé; *Am Aut* two-door sedan; **(b)** (*danse*) coupée.

coupe-cigare(s) [kupsigar] *nm* cigar cutter; (*pl coupe-cigares*).

coupe-circuit [kupsirkɥi] *nm inv Él* cutout, circuit breaker.

coupe-coupe [kupkup] *nm inv* machete.

coupée [kupe] *nf Nau* (*opening or port*) gangway; **échelle de c.,** accommodation ladder.

coupe-faim [kupfɛ̃] *nm inv Méd* appetite suppressant.

coupe-feu [kupfø] *nm inv* firebreak; **porte c.-f.,** fire-door.

coupe-file [kupfil] *nm inv* (*police etc*) pass.

coupe-frites [kupfrit] *nm inv* chip- *or Am* French fry-cutter *or* -slicer.

coupe-gorge [kupgɔrʒ] *nm inv* dangerous back alley *or* back street.

coupe-jarret [kupʒarɛ] *nm Vieilli* cut-throat, assassin; (*pl coupe-jarrets*).

coupe-légumes [kuplegym] *nm inv* vegetable-cutter *or* -slicer.

coupelle [kupɛl] *nf* **(a)** (*petite coupe*) small dish; **(b)** *Ch* cupel.

coupe-ongles [kupɔ̃gl] *nm inv* nail clippers.

coupe-papier [kuppapje] *nm inv* paper knife.

couper [kupe] **1** *vt* **(a)** to cut; **c. de la viande en morceaux,** to cut up meat; **c. un arbre,** to cut *or* chop down *or* fell a tree; **c. les cheveux à qn,** to cut *or* trim s.o.'s hair; **c. la tête à qn,** to cut off s.o.'s head; **c. bras et jambes à qn,** to stun s.o.; **c. l'herbe sous les pieds de qn,** to cut the ground from under s.o.'s feet, to pull the rug out from under s.o.'s feet; **c. dans le vif,** to cut to the quick; *Fig* to take extreme measures (*to settle sth*), to take strong *or* firm action; **c. le mal à la racine,** to strike at the root of an evil; **un brouillard/un silence à c. au couteau,** a fog/a silence you could cut with a knife; *Fig* **c. les cheveux en quatre,** to split hairs, to nitpick; **j'en donnerais ma tête à c.,** I'd stake my life on it, I'd bet my bottom dollar on it; **c. un vêtement,** to cut out a garment; *Golf etc* **c. une balle,** to cut *or* slice a ball;
(b) *Cartes* to cut; (*prendre avec l'atout*) to trump;
(c) (*traverser*) to cut, to cross, to intersect; **sentier qui coupe la route,** path that cuts across the road; **la rivière coupe le département en deux,** the river divides *or* cuts the département in two; *Aut* **c. la route à qn,** to cut in in front of s.o.; **c. la route d'un navire,** to cut across the bows of a ship;
(d) (*interrompre*) to cut off, to interrupt, to stop; **c. le chemin à qn,** to cut s.o. off, to bar s.o.'s way; **c. la retraite à qn,** to cut off s.o.'s retreat; **c. le souffle à qn,** to take s.o.'s breath away; (*d'un coup de poing*) to wind s.o.; **c. les vivres,** to cut off supplies; **c. les vivres à qn,** to stop s.o.'s allowance; **c. l'appétit à qn,** to spoil s.o.'s appetite, to take s.o.'s appetite away; **c. la parole à qn,** to interrupt s.o.; *Arg* **ça te la coupe!,** that shakes you!, that's floored you *or* taken the wind out of your sails!; *Arg* **c. le sifflet** *ou* **la chique à qn,** to shut s.o. up; *Tél* **c. la communication,** to ring off; **c. l'eau,** to turn off the water; *Él* **c. le courant,** to switch off the current; *Aut* **c. l'allumage** *ou* **le contact,** to cut off *or* switch off the ignition;
(e) c. du vin, (*en mélangeant*) to blend wine; (*avec de l'eau*) to water down *or* dilute wine;
(f) (*du vent*) to sting, to lash, to whip.
2 *vi* **(a)** *F* **c. à qch,** to avoid *or* get out of doing sth; **c. à une corvée,** to dodge *or* shirk an unpleasant job *or* chore; **il n'y coupera pas,** he won't get out of it;
(b) *Tél etc* **ne coupez pas!,** hold the line!; *Cin* **coupez!,** cut!; *F* **c. court à qn,** to cut s.o. short;
(c) (*trancher*) to cut, to slice; **le couteau coupe bien,** the knife cuts well; **attention, ça coupe!,** watch out *or* be careful, it's sharp!;
(d) *Cartes* to cut; **c'est à vous de c.,** it's your turn to cut;
(e) c. à travers champs, to cut across country; **c. par le plus court,** to take a short cut.
3 se couper *vpr* **(a)** to cut oneself; **il s'est coupé le** *ou* **au doigt,** he cut his finger; *Fig* **il se couperait en quatre pour elle,** he'd do anything for her;
(b) (*of roads etc*) to intersect;
(c) *F* (*se contredire*) to give oneself away;
(d) se c. de qn, to cut oneself off from s.o., to break with s.o., to sever links with s.o..

coupe-racines [kuprasin] *nm inv Agr* root-slicer *or* -cutter.

couperet [kuprɛ] *nm* **(a)** (*pour la viande*) (meat) chopper, cleaver; **(b)** blade, knife (*of the guillotine*).

couperose [kuproz] *nf* **(a)** blotchiness, blotches; *Méd* acne rosacea; **(b)** *Vieilli* **c. verte,** green vitriol, ferrous sulphate; **c. bleue,** blue vitriol, copper sulphate.

couperosé [kuproze] *adj* blotchy (*complexion*); *Méd* affected with acne rosacea.

coupeur, -euse [kupœr, -øz] *n* cutter (*of material, leather etc*); **c. de cheveux en quatre,** hair splitter, nit-picker; *Arch* **c. de bourses,** pickpocket.

coupe-vent [kupvɑ̃] *nm inv* **(a)** (*dispositif*) windbreak; **(b)** (*blouson*) windcheater, *Am* windbreaker.

couplage [kuplaʒ] *nm MecE* coupling, connecting (*of wheels etc*); coupling (*of railway engines*); *Él Électron* coupling.

couple [kupl] **1** *nm* **(a)** pair, couple; (*époux*) (married) couple; **c. bien assorti,** well-matched couple; **les invités sont tous venus en couples,** the guests all came in couples, the guests all came with (their) partners; **c. de pigeons,** pair of pigeons; **arrangés par couples,** arranged in pairs; **(b)** *Phys* couple; **c. moteur,** *MecE* **c. (de torsion),** torque; *Phys* **c. thermoélectrique,** thermocouple; **(c)** *Nau* frame, timber; **c. de construction,** bulkhead. **2** *nf* leash (*for hounds etc*).

couplé [kuple] *nm Courses de chevaux* accumulator; **c. placé,** each-way accumulator (bet).

coupler [kuple] *vt* **(a)** to couple, to attach (*things*) together; **c. deux bateaux,** to couple *or* attach (together) two boats; **(b)** to leash (*hounds*).

couplet [kuplɛ] *nm* verse (*of song*); **couplets,** song; *F* tirade, little piece.

coupleur [kuplœr] *nm Électron* coupler; *Ordinat* **c. acoustique,** acoustic coupler.

coupoir [kupwar] *nm* cutter.

coupole [kupɔl] *nf* **(a)** *Archit* cupola, dome; **être reçu sous la c.,** to be made a member of the Académie Française; **(b)** *Mil etc* (revolving) gun turret.

coupon [kupɔ̃] *nm* **(a)** *Com* remnant (*of material*); **(b)** *Fin* **c. d'action,** coupon; **c. attaché/détaché,** cum/ex dividend; **(c)** *Th* **c. de loge,** box ticket; *Rail* **c. d'aller/de retour,** outward/return half (*of ticket*); **carnet de 10 coupons,** book of 10 tickets.

coupon-réponse [kupɔ̃repɔ̃s] *nm* **c.-r. (international),** (international) reply coupon; (*pl coupons-réponse*).

coupure [kupyr] *nf* **(a)** cut, gash (*on finger etc*); (*fossé*) cut, drain, irrigation channel; **se faire une c.,** to cut oneself; **(b)** cutting, piece cut out; cut (*in play, book, film*); **c. de journal,** newspaper cutting *or* clipping; **(c)** *Él* **c. (de courant),** (power) cut; **il y aura une c. de 5 heures à 7 heures,** the gas *or* water *or* electricity will be cut off between 5 and 7 o'clock; **(d)** *Fig* gap, gulf; **la c. entre elle et sa famille,** the gulf *or* rift *or* gap between her and her family; **la c. entre ses espoirs et la réalité,** the gulf *or* chasm between his expectations and reality; **(e)** *Fin* (bank)note (*of small denomination*); **c. de 50 francs,** 50 franc note.

cour [kur] *nf* **(a)** court (*of sovereign*); **vivre à la c.,** to live at court; **gens de c.,** courtiers; **être bien/mal en c.,** to be in/out of favour; **elle a une c. de prétendants,** she has a retinue of suitors;

(b) (*à qn*) courting, courtship; **faire la c. à qn,** to curry favour with s.o.; **faire la c. à une jeune fille,** to court a girl;

(c) c. de justice, court of justice; **messieurs, la C.!,** ≈ all rise!; **c. martiale,** court martial; **passer devant la c. martiale,** to be court-martialled (**pour,** for); **Haute C.,** High Court (*for impeachment of president or ministers*); **la c. d'appel,** the court of appeal; **la C. suprême du Canada,** the Supreme Court of Canada; **c. internationale de justice,** International Court of Justice;

(d) *Archit* court, yard, courtyard; **c. de ferme,** farmyard; **c. d'honneur,** main courtyard; **c. de récréation** *ou* **d'école,** schoolyard, *Br* playground; **jouer dans la c.,** (*de l'école*) to play in the yard (*at school*); (*d'un groupe d'immeubles*) to play in the backyard *or* court; *Mil* **c. de quartier,** barrack square; *Th* **côté c.,** O.P. (side) (*opposite prompter*); **appartement 3 côté c.,** flat no 3 overlooking the yard.

courage [kuraʒ] *nm* courage, bravery, valour; **avoir du c.,** to have courage; **perdre c.,** to lose courage *or* heart; **prendre c.,** to take heart; **il lui a fallu un certain c. pour le faire,** it took a certain amount of courage for him to do it; **se sentir le c. de faire qch,** to feel up to doing sth; **prendre son c. à deux mains,** to pluck up courage; **être plein de c.,** to be full of energy; **(du) c.!,** cheer up!, buck up!; (*pour continuer*) keep it up!, keep going!; **avoir le c. de ses opinions,** to have the courage of one's convictions; **vous n'auriez pas le c. de les renvoyer!,** you wouldn't have the heart to dismiss them!; **se battre avec c.,** to fight bravely *or* courageously; **bon c.!,** good luck!, all the best!; *Iron* good luck, *Br* the best of British.

courageusement [kuraʒøzmɑ̃] *adv* (*bravement*) courageously, bravely; (*résolument*) zealously, with energy.

courageux, -euse [kuraʒø, -øz] *adj* **(a)** (*avec bravoure*) courageous, brave; **(b)** (*avec énergie*) energetic; **il n'est pas très c. pour l'étude,** he doesn't show much enthusiasm for his studies.

courailler [kuraje] *vi Can F* to chase after women.

courailleur [kurajœr] *nm Can F* womanizer.

couramment [kuramɑ̃] *adv* **(a)** (*facilement*) easily, readily; **parler c. une langue étrangère,** to speak a foreign language fluently; **(b)** (*généralement*) generally, usually; **ce mot s'emploie c.,** this word is in current use.

courant, -ante [kurɑ̃, -ɑ̃t] **1** *adj* running; flowing, running (*water etc*); current (*account etc*); **chien c.,** hound; *Typ* **titre c.,** running head(line); **chambre avec eau courante,** bedroom with running water; **dette courante,** floating debt; **le mois c.,** the present *or* current month; **le cinq c.,** the fifth inst., the 5th of this month; **fin c.,** at the end of this month; **vie courante,** everyday life; **mot d'usage c.,** word in current *or* general use, everyday word; **monnaie courante,** legal currency; *Fig* **c'est monnaie courante,** it's quite usual *or* widespread, it's common practice; **prix c.,** current price; (*liste*) price list; *Com* **marque courante,** standard make; **de taille courante,** of standard size.

2 *nm* **(a)** (*d'eau etc*) running water; (*dans une rivière etc*) current; (*ruisseau*) stream; **suivre/remonter le c.,** to go with/against the tide *or* current; **c. d'air,** draught; **c. sous-marin,** undercurrent, undertow; *Fig* **c. de population,** population movement; **le c. de l'opinion publique,** the trend of public opinion; **écrire au c. de la plume,** to write spontaneously *or* off the cuff;

(b) *Él* **c. (électrique),** electric current, power; **couper le c.,** to cut off the current, to break contact; **c. continu/alternatif,** direct/alternating current; **c. triphasé/biphasé,** triphase/biphase current; **c. de repos,** quiescent current;

(c) (*durée*) course; **dans le c. de l'année,** in the course of the year; **dans le c. de la semaine,** within the next week, some day this week; **c. des affaires,** course of events; **c. du marché,** current market prices;

(d) il est au c., he knows about it; **je n'étais pas au c.,** I didn't know; **mettre qn au c. d'une décision,** to tell *or* inform s.o. of a decision; **elle m'a mis au c.,** she told me all about it, she put me in the picture; **je me suis mis très vite au c.,** I got the hang of things very quickly; **le professeur est très au c. des nouvelles méthodes,** the teacher is very conversant *or* familiar with new methods.

3 *nf* **courante (a)** *Mus* (*danse*) courante;

(b) *Arg* **la courante,** (*diarrhée*) the runs *or* trots.

courbatu [kurbaty] *adj* (*personne*) stiff, aching (all over).

courbature [kurbatyr] *nf* stiffness, ache; **avoir une c.** *ou* **des courbatures,** to be aching *or* stiff all over.

courbaturer [kurbatyre] *vt* to tire *or* wear (*s.o.*) out; **je me sens tout courbaturé,** I'm stiff *or* aching all over.

courbe [kurb] **1** *adj* curved, curving. **2** *nf* curve; **la route fait une c.,** the road curves *or* bends (round); *Math* **c. plane,** plane curve; **c. de niveau,** contour (line); *Méd* **c. de température,** temperature graph; **c. des prix/des salaires,** prices/salary curve.

courber [kurbe] **1** *vt* to bend, to curve; **taille courbée par l'âge,** figure bowed *or* stooped *or* bent with age; **c. la tête,** to bow one's head; *Fig* **c. l'échine,** to submit; **c. qn sous son autorité,** to bend s.o. to one's will, to make s.o. submit to one's will. **2** *vi* to bend; **c. sous le poids,** to bend under the weight. **3 se courber** *vpr* to bow, to bend, to stoop; **se c. devant qn,** to bow to s.o.; *Fig* to submit to s.o.; **se c. en deux,** to bend double; *Fig* **elle ne se courba jamais devant l'autorité,** she never bowed (down) to authority.

courbette [kurbɛt] *nf* bow; *Équitation* curvet; **faire des courbettes à qn,** to bow and scrape to s.o..

courbure [kurbyr] *nf* curvature (*of line, surface etc*); bend, curve (*of piece of wood etc*); curve (*of the back*); camber (*of road etc*); sagging (*of beam etc*); **c. double** *ou* **en S,** S curve.

courette [kurɛt] *nf* small (court)yard.

coureur, -euse [kurœr, -øz] **1** *n* **(a)** runner; *Sp* runner, racer; **c. de fond/de demi-fond,** long-distance/middle distance runner; **c. de vitesse,** sprinter; **c. cycliste,** racing cyclist; **c. automobile,** racing driver; *Can Fig* **laisser la chance au c.,** to give s.o. a chance; **les coureurs,** (*oiseaux*) running birds; *Spéc* Ratitae, ratite birds; **(b)** (*marcheur*) wanderer, rover; (*habitué*) gadabout; *Can Hist* **c. de(s) bois,** trapper; **c'est un c. de bals/de cafés,** he's always at dances/in cafés; **c. (de filles),** womanizer; **c. de dot,** fortune-hunter. **2** *nf* **coureuse,** loose woman. **3** *adj* (*homme*) womanizing; (*femme*) manhunting; **elle est un peu coureuse,** she's a bit of a manhunter; **il est un peu c.,** he's a bit of a woman-chaser *or* womanizer.

courge [kurʒ] *nf* **(a)** (*plante*) gourd, marrow, *Am* squash; **(b)** *Arg* clot, berk, wally, prat.

courgette [kurʒɛt] *nf* (small) marrow, courgette, *Am* zucchini.

courir [kurir] *v* (*prp* **courant**; *pp* **couru**; *pr ind* **je cours, il court, n. courons, ils courent**; *pr sub* **je coure**; *p hist* **je courus**; *fu* **je courrai**; *the aux is* **avoir**) **1** *vi* **(a)** to run; (*de concurrents etc*) to race, to run (in a race); **monter/descendre la colline en courant,** to run up/down the hill; **arriver en courant,** to come running (up); **faire qch en courant,** to do sth in a hurry; **il nous fait toujours c.,** he's always rushing us; (*nous fait marcher*) he's always pulling our legs; **cet acteur fait c. tout Paris,** the whole of Paris is rushing to see this actor; **faire c. des chevaux,** to race *or* run horses; **cours acheter du pain,** run *or* nip out and get some bread; **c. après qn/qch,** to run after s.o./sth; **c. après les femmes,** to run *or* chase after the women; **cet homme me court après depuis plus de 5 ans,** that man's been (running) after me *or* chasing me for more than five years; **c. après la gloire,** to chase after glory; **j'ai couru le prévenir,** I ran to warn him; **je cours l'appeler,** I'll run and get him; **j'y cours,** I'll go at once; **c. à sa fin,** to draw to an end; *Sp* **elle court dans l'équipe de France,** she runs in the French team *or* is a member of the French running team; *F* **tu peux toujours c.!,** you can whistle for it!; *Arg* **c. sur le haricot à qn,** to get up s.o.'s nose *or* on s.o.'s nerves *or* wick, *Am* to bug s.o.;

(b) (*of ship*) to sail; **c. au large,** to stand out to sea; **c. à terre,** to stand in for the land; **c. devant le vent,** to run *or* scud before the wind; **c. de l'avant,** to forge ahead;

(c) (*se propager*) to be current; **le bruit court que ...,** rumour has it that ..., they say that ...; **faire c. un bruit,** to spread a rumour; **la mode qui court,** the present fashion;

(d) (*of blood, wine*) to flow; (*of water*) to rush, to run;

(e) le mois qui court, the current month; **par les temps qui courent,** nowadays, as things are at present; *Fin* **les intérêts qui courent,** the accruing interest; *F* **laisse c.!,** forget it!, drop it!

2 *vt* **(a)** to run after, to pursue, to chase (*sth*); **c. le cerf,** to hunt the stag, to go staghunting; *Fig* **c. deux lièvres à la fois,** to have two irons in the fire, to have a finger in more than one pie; **c. un risque,** to run a risk; **c. sa chance,** to try one's luck;

(b) c. une course, to run a race;

(c) c. le monde/la campagne, to roam the world/the countryside; **passer son après-midi à c. les magasins,** to spend one's afternoon shopping; **c. les théâtres,** to be an inveterate theatre goer; **c. les filles** *ou* **le jupon** *ou* **la prétentaine** *ou Can* **la galipote,** to run after girls, to womanize;

(d) *Nau* **c. un bord,** to make a tack, to tack.

3 se courir *vpr* to be decided, to be competed for (*of sporting event*); **la coupe se courra demain,** the cup will be competed for tomorrow; **dans l'épreuve qui se courait aujourd'hui à Auteuil,** in the race run at Auteuil today.

4 *v impers* **il court des bruits sur lui,** there are rumours going round about him.

courlieu [kurljø] *nm*, **courlis** [kurli] *nm Orn* **c. (cendré), (grand) c.,** curlew; **c. corlieu,** whimbrel.

couronne [kurɔn] *nf* **(a)** wreath, crown (*of flowers, laurel etc*); **c. funéraire,** (funeral) wreath; **enterrement sans fleurs ni couronnes,** simple burial (with neither flowers nor wreaths); **en c.,** in a ring *or* circle; **on a décidé de lui donner la c.,** it was decided to declare him the winner *or* champion, it was decided to crown him champion;

(b) (king's) crown; (*of nobleman*) (ducal) coronet; (*sovereignty*) the Crown; **la triple c.,** the (pope's) tiara; *Sp* the Triple Crown; **aspirer** *ou* **prétendre à la c.,** to lay claim to the throne;

(c) (*coin*) crown; (*reliure*) crown (size);

(d) (*anneau*) ring; loaf of bread (*in the shape of a ring*); *Bot Archit* corona; *Anat* crown (*of tooth*); *Astron* **c. solaire,** solar corona; *Méd* **se faire poser une c.,** to have *or* get a tooth crowned;

(e) *MecE* rim (*of pulley, wheel*); **c. dentée,** crown gear, crown wheel, ring gear (*of differential etc*); **c. d'embrayage,** clutch ring.

couronné [kurɔne] *adj* **(a)** wreathed (*with flowers etc*); **lauréat c.,** prizewinner; **roman c.,** prizewinning novel; **(b)** crowned (*sovereign*); **tête couronnée,** sovereign; **toutes les têtes couronnées de l'Europe y assistaient,** all the crowned heads of Europe were present; **(c)** *Bot* coronate(d); **(d)** *Vét* **cheval c.,** broken-kneed horse.

couronnement [kurɔnmɑ̃] *nm* **(a)** crowning, coronation (*of sovereign*); **(b)** capping (*of arch pier*); top, cap (*of building, column etc*); coping (*of wall etc*); ridge (*of roof*); **(c)** *Fig* climax, crowning achievement; **le c. de ma carrière,** the peak *or* pinnacle of my career; **(d)** scar (*on horse's knee*).

couronner [kurɔne] **1** *vt* **(a)** to crown (with a wreath); to award a prize to (*author, pupil etc*); **un diadème couronne sa tête,** a diadem crowns his head; **des pics couronnés de neige,** snow-capped peaks; *F* **et pour c. le tout ...,** to cap *or* crown it all ...; **mes efforts furent couronnés de succès,** my efforts were crowned with success; **(b)** (*sacrer*) to crown; **c. qn roi,** to crown s.o. king; **(c) c. une dent,** to crown a tooth; **(d) c. un cheval,** to let a horse down on its knees. **2 se couronner** *vpr* **se c. le genou,** to graze *or* skin one's knee.

courre [kur] *vi Arch* (= **courir**) *still used in* **chasse à c.,** hunt(ing).

courrier [kurje] *nm* **(a)** (*messager*) courier; messenger; **envoyer un document par c.,** to send a document by courier, to courier a document; **(b)** (*poste*) post, letters, *surtout Am* mail; **par retour du c.,** by return of post; **dépouiller son c.,** to open *or* go through one's mail; **faire son c.,** to write one's letters; **(c)** (*bateau*) mail boat; aircraft (flying a regular transport service); *Arch* (*voiture*) mail coach; *Mil Av* courier, liaison aircraft; **(d)** *Journ* (*title*) = Mail; **(e)** (*rubrique*) column; **c. des lecteurs,** letters to the Editor; **c. du cœur,** advice column, problem page, *F* agony column.

courriériste [kurjerist] *n Journ* columnist.

courroie [kurwa] *nf* strap; *MecE* belt; **c. de transmission,** driving belt; **c. de ventilateur,** fanbelt.

courroucé [kuruse] *adj surtout Litt* angry, incensed (*person*).

courroucer [kuruse] *v* **(je courrouçai(s), n. courrouçons)** *Litt* **1** *vt* to anger, to incense (*s.o.*). **2 se courroucer** *vpr* to become incensed.

courroux [kuru] *nm Litt* anger, wrath, ire.

cours [kur] *nm* **(a)** course (*of river*); course, path (*of sun, moon etc*); **descendre le c. de la Tamise,** to go down the Thames; **c. d'eau,** waterway; **le c. des siècles,** the course of the centuries; **suivre le c. de ses idées,** to follow one's train of thoughts; *Fig* **donner libre c. à son imagination/sa colère,** to give free rein to one's imagination/anger; **la maladie suit son c.,** the illness is running its course; **affaires en c.,** outstanding business; **travaux en c.,** work in progress *or* on hand; **année en c.,** current *or* present year; **en c. de route,** during the journey, on the way; **en c. de production,** in production; **au c. de la conversation,** in the course of the conversation;

(b) *Nau* **long c.,** foreign trade; **voyage au long c.,** ocean voyage; **capitaine au long c.,** captain of an ocean-going vessel;

(c) circulation, currency (*of money*); **c. légal,** legal tender; **c. forcé,** forced currency; **avoir c.,** to be legal tender; (*pour une pratique*) to be current, to be in current use; **donner c. à un bruit,** to spread a rumour;

(d) *Bourse etc* quotation, price; **c. du marché,** market prices *or* rates; **c. du change,** rate of exchange; **au c. (du jour),** at the current daily price; **quel est le c. du sucre?,** what is the quotation for sugar?;

(e) *Univ* lecture; *Scol* lesson; course (*of lectures etc*); **faire un c. d'histoire,** *Scol* to give a history lesson; *Univ* to lecture on history; **elle ne veut plus aller en c.,** she doesn't want to go to lectures any more; **c. par correspondance,** correspondence course; **il ne m'a pas rendu mes c.,** he hasn't given me my notes back; **prendre** *ou* **suivre un c.,** to take a class *or* course; **donner des c.,** to give classes, to teach; **c. particulier,** private lesson; **c. du soir,** evening *or* night class;

(f) (*livre*) text book, course; **c. élémentaire/moyen,** primary/intermediate course;

(g) (*avenue*) walk, avenue.

course [kurs] *nf* **(a)** (*allure*) run, running; **au pas de c.,** at a run; *Mil* at *or US* on the double; **prendre sa c.,** to set off (running); **arrêté en pleine c.,** stopped in full flight; (*de qn qui parle*) stopped in mid-stream;

(b) *Sp* race, racing; **c. de chevaux,** horse race; **les courses,** the races; **c. de plat,** flat race; **c. d'obstacles,** obstacle race; *Courses de chevaux* steeplechase; (*in athletics*) hurdle race; **c. de fond,** long-distance race; (*sport*) long-distance running; **c. de vitesse,** sprint; **champ** *ou* **terrain de courses,** racecourse; **voiture de c.,** racing car; **c. sur piste/route,** track/road racing; **c. de taureaux,** (*corrida*) bullfight; (*dans les rues*) bull-running; *F* **être dans la c.,** to be with it, to be in the know, to know what's what, to be in touch; **être encore dans la c.,** to be still in the running; **la c. à la Maison Blanche,** the race for the White House; **la c. aux armements,** the arms race; *Fig* **la c. au nucléaire,** the nuclear arms race;

(c) (*excursion*) excursion, outing, trip; (*en montagne*) climb; **payer (le prix de) la c.,** (*en taxi*) to pay the fare;

(d) (*pour affaires*) (business) errand; **faire une c.,** to run an errand; **garçon de courses,** errand boy; **faire des courses,** (*dans un magasin*) to go shopping; (*d'un coursier*) to run errands *or* messages;

(e) path, way, course (*of person, ship, planet etc*); course, flight (*of projectile*); *MecE etc* movement, travel (*of tool etc*); stroke (*of piston*); **je poursuivis ma c.,** I went on my way; *F* **être à bout de c.,** to be worn out *or* exhausted, to be done in; *MecE* **à bout de c.,** at full stroke; *MecE* **à mi-c.,** at half stroke;

(f) *Nau Arch* privateering.

courser [kurse] *vi F* to get a move on; **il a fallu c.,** we had to rush *or* go like the clappers.

coursier, -ière [kursje, -jɛr] **1** *n* messenger. **2** *nm* (*cheval*) steed.

coursive [kursiv] *nf Nau* alleyway, gangway.

court[1] [kur] **1** *adj* short; **avoir les jambes courtes** *ou* **être c. de jambes,** to have short legs, to be short in the legs; **avoir la vue courte,** to be shortsighted; *Fig* to lack forethought; **avoir l'intelligence c.,** to be of limited intelligence; **avoir la respiration** *ou* **le souffle court(e),** to be short-winded, to be short of breath; *Nau* **vague** *ou* **mer courte,** choppy sea; **le chemin le plus c.,** the quickest way; *F* **il m'a donné 100 francs, c'est un peu c.,** he gave me 100 francs, it's a bit mean; **c. intervalle,** short *or* brief interval; **à c. terme,** in the short term; **de courte durée,** short-lived; **un film très c.,** a very short *or* brief film; **avoir la mémoire courte,** to have a short memory, to be forgetful; **pour faire c.,** to cut a long story short; *Culin* **sauce courte,** thick sauce.

2 *adv* **(a)** short; **cheveux coupés c.,** short hair, (short-) cropped hair; *Fig* **s'arrêter c.,** to stop short *or* suddenly; **demeurer** *ou* **rester c.,** to be at a loss (*for ideas etc*); **tourner c.,** to turn sharply; **couper c. à qn/qch,** to cut s.o./sth short;

(b) tout c., simply, only, merely; **il m'a traité comme un chien, tout c.,** he just *or* simply treated me like a dog;

(c) prendre qn de c., (*en lui laissant peu de temps*) to give s.o. short notice; (*sans le prévenir*) to catch s.o. unawares;

(d) à c. (de), short of; **à c. d'argent,** short of money, hard up; **il n'est jamais à c. d'arguments/d'idées,** he's never at a loss for an argument *or* an answer/for ideas.

court² *nm* **c. (de tennis),** (tennis) court.

courtage [kurtaʒ] *nm Com* **(a)** (*profession*) broking, brokerage; **(b)** (*commission*) commission, brokerage.

courtaud, -aude [kurto, -od] *adj & n* **(a)** dock-tailed, crop-eared (animal); **(b)** dumpy, squat, stocky (person).

court-bouillon [kurbujɔ̃] *nm Culin* court-bouillon; (*pl courts-bouillons*).

court-circuit [kursirkɥi] *nm Él* short circuit; (*pl courts-circuits*).

court-circuitage [kursikɥitaʒ] *nm Él* short-circuiting.

court-circuiter [kursirkɥite] *vt Él* to short-circuit (*resistance etc*); *F* to short-circuit, to bypass (*sth*); **c.-c. la filière normale,** to bypass the usual channels *or* procedures.

court-courrier [kurkurje] *Av* (*pl courts-courriers*) **1** *adj* short-haul; **avion c.-c.,** short-haul plane. **2** *nm* short-haul plane.

courtepointe [kurtəpwɛ̃t] *nf* quilt, (quilted) bedspread.

courtier, -ière [kurtje, -jɛr] *n Com Fin* broker, agent; **c. d'assurances,** insurance broker; **c. maritime,** ship broker; **c. en immeubles,** estate agent, *Am* realtor; **c. en vins,** wine broker.

courtine [kurtin] *nf* (door) curtain.

courtisan [kurtizɑ̃] **1** *nm* courtier; *Péj* (*flatteur*) sycophant. **2** *adj* **manières courtisanes,** flattering *or* obsequious *or* toadying manners.

courtisane [kurtizan] *nf Hist Littér* courtesan.

courtiser [kurtize] *vt* **(a)** (*flatter*) to pay court to s.o.; *Péj* to fawn on (*s.o.*); **(b)** to court, to woo, to pay court to (*woman*).

court-jus [kurjy] *nm Arg* short circuit; **il y a eu un c.-j.,** there's been a short(-circuit); (*pl courts-jus*).

courtois, -oise [kurtwa, -waz] *adj* courteous (**envers, avec, pour,** to); **dire non d'un ton très c.,** to say no very courteously; *Littér* **la poésie courtoise,** court poetry.

courtoisement [kurtwazmɑ̃] *adv* courteously.

courtoisie [kurtwazi] *nf* **(a)** (*politesse*) courtesy, courteousness (**envers,** to, towards); **(b)** (*acte*) (act of) courtesy.

court-vêtu [kurvɛty] *adj* dressed in short clothes; (*woman*) short-skirted; **jeune fille c.-vêtue,** girl in *or* wearing a short skirt *or* dress.

couru [kury] *adj* **(a)** (*recherché*) sought after; **opéra très c.,** popular opera; **(b)** *F* **c'est c. (d'avance),** it's a cinch *or* a (dead) cert; **c'était c.,** it was bound to happen.

couscous [kuskus] *nm Culin* couscous.

couseuse [kuzøz] *nf* **(a)** sewer, seamstress; (*de reliure*) stitcher; **(b)** (*machine*) stitching machine.

cousin¹, -ine [kuzɛ̃, -in] *n* cousin; **c. germain,** first cousin; **cousins au second degré** *ou* **issus de germains,** second cousins; *F* **c. à la mode de Bretagne,** distant relation, sort of relation.

cousin² *nm* (*insecte*) = type of mosquito.

cousinage [kuzinaʒ] *nm Vieilli* **(a)** (*fait d'être cousin*) cousinship, cousinhood; **(b)** (*famille*) **tout le c.,** all the cousins.

coussin [kusɛ̃] *nm* **(a)** cushion; *Belg* pillow; pad(ding) (*of horse's collar etc*); **c. d'air,** air cushion; **(b)** *Baseball Arg* base.

coussinet [kusinɛ] *nm* **(a)** (*petit coussin*) small cushion, pad; **(b)** *MecE etc* bearing; **c. de tête de bielle,** big end bearing; *Rail* **c. de rail,** rail chair; **(c)** *Archit Constr* coussinet, cushion (*of Ionic column etc*).

cousu [kuzy] *adj* sewn; **c. à la main,** *F* **c. main,** hand-sewn; *Arg* **c'est du c. main,** it's first rate; **garder bouche cousue,** to keep one's mouth shut, to keep a secret; **bouche cousue!,** not a word!; **c. de fil blanc,** obvious, blatant, patent; **mensonge c. de fil blanc,** a blatant *or* obvious lie; **être (tout) c. d'or,** to be rolling in money.

coût [ku] *nm* cost; **le c. de la vie,** the cost of living; **le c. d'une erreur,** the price *or* consequences of a mistake.

coûtant [kutɑ̃] *adj* **à prix c.,** at cost price.

couteau, -eaux [kuto] *nm* **(a)** knife; **c. de cuisine,** kitchen knife; **c. à pain,** breadknife; **c. à fromage,** cheese-knife; **c. à découper,** carving knife; **c.-éplucheur** *ou* **à éplucher,** (potato) peeler; **c. à légumes,** vegetable knife; **c. de poche** *ou* **pliant,** pocket knife; **grand c. pliant,** clasp knife; **c. à cran d'arrêt,** flick knife, *Am* switch-blade (knife); **c. à palette** *ou* **de peintre,** palette knife; **c. à pierre,** chisel, stone-mason's knife; **c. de chasse,** hunting knife, *Am* bowie knife; **recevoir un coup de c.,** to be *or* get knifed; **planter un c. dans le ventre de qn,** to knife s.o. in the belly *or* stomach; **jouer du c.,** to use a knife *or* blade (for fighting); **ils sont à couteaux tirés,** they're at daggers drawn; **mettre le c. sous** *ou* **sur la gorge à qn,** to force s.o. (to do sth), to hold a pistol *or* gun to s.o.'s head; **(b)** *Phys* knife edge, fulcrum (*of balance beam*); **(c)** (*mollusque*) **(manche de) c.,** razor shell.

couteau-scie [kutosi] *nm* serrated knife; (*pl couteaux-scies*).

coutelas [kutlɑ] *nm* **(a)** (*épée*) cutlass; **(b)** (*de cuisine*) large (kitchen) knife.

coutelier, -ière [kutəlje, -jɛr] *n* cutler.

coutellerie [kutɛlri] *nf* **(a)** (*industry, wares*) cutlery; **c. chirurgicale,** surgical instruments; **(b)** *Com* cutlery shop; (*usine*) cutlery works.

coûter [kute] **1** *vi* to cost; **c. cher/peu,** to be expensive/inexpensive; **cela vous coûtera cher,** it'll cost you a lot; *Fig* you'll pay for this; **coûte que coûte,** at any cost, at any price, at all costs, whatever the cost; *F* **l'argent ne lui coûte guère,** money means nothing to him; **rien ne lui coûte,** (*parce qu'il peut tout faire*) nothing is an effort to him, everything comes easy to him; (*il est très énergique*) he spares no effort; **ça ne coûte rien d'essayer,** there's no harm in trying.

2 *v impers* **j'ai voulu l'aider, il m'en coûta,** I tried to help him, to my cost; **il m'en coûte de le dire,** it pains me to have to say this.

3 *vt* to cost; **ça ne coûte rien,** it's free; **cela coûte les yeux de la tête,** it costs an arm and a leg *or* the earth *or* a fortune; *F* **ça coûtera ce que ça coûtera!,** never mind the cost!, hang the expense!; *F* **ça m'a coûté la peau des fesses,** it cost me an arm and a leg, I had to pay through the nose for it; **cela lui a coûté la vie,** it cost him his life; **le succès lui a coûté sa vie tranquille,** success put an end to his quiet *or* peaceful life.

coûteusement [kutøzmɑ̃] *adv* expensively; **être c. logé,** to pay a lot for one's accommodation.

coûteux, -euse [kutø, -øz] *adj* costly, expensive, dear; **peu c.,** inexpensive.

coutil [kuti] *nm Tex* drill, twill; **c. pour matelas,** ticking.

coutre [kutr] *nm* coulter (*of plough*).

coutume [kutym] *nf* **(a)** (*tradition*) custom, habit; **respecter une c.,** to respect a custom *or* tradition; **avoir c. de faire qch,** to be in the habit of doing sth, to be accustomed to do sth; **plus aimable que de c.,** nicer *or* more amiable than usual; **comme de c.,** as usual; **je me suis levé plus tard que c.,** I got up later than usual; **une fois n'est pas c.,** it doesn't matter *or* it won't hurt for once, we're not making a habit of it; **(b)** *Jur* customary.

coutumier, -ière [kutymje, -jɛr] **1** *adj* **(a)** customary, usual; *Jur* **droit c.,** unwritten law, common law; **(b)** *Arch* in the habit of (doing sth); *souvent Péj* **il est c. du fait,** it's not the first time he's done that. **2** *nm Jur* customary.

couture [kutyr] **1** *nf* **(a)** (*activité*) sewing, needlework; **faire de la c.,** to sew; **elle est dans la c.,** she does dressmaking; **haute c.,** haute couture, high fashion; **maison de haute c.,** fashion house; **(b)** seam (*in dress etc*); **sans c.,** seamless; **c. rabattue/plate,** run and fell/flat seam; **c. anglaise,** French seam; **c. apparente,** over-stitching, topstitching; **faire une c. à grands points,** to tack *or* baste a seam; *Fig* **battre qn à plate(s) couture(s),** to beat s.o. hollow; **examiner qn/qch sur** *ou* **sous toutes les coutures,** to examine s.o./sth from every angle; *Nau* **c. à clin,** lapped seam. **2** *adj* **une veste c.,** a couture jacket.

couturé [kutyre] *adj* scarred (*face*).

couturier , -ière [kutyrje, -jɛr] **1** *n* dressmaker; (*de haute couture*) couturier. **2** *nf* **couturière (a)** (*ouvrière*) seamstress, needlewoman; **(b)** *Th* rehearsal preceding the final dress rehearsal. **3** *nm Anat* sartorius. **4** *adj Anat* sartorial; **muscle c.,** sartorius.

couvage [kuvaʒ] *nm* = **COUVAISON (b)**.

couvain [kuvɛ̃] *nm* **(a)** (*amas*) nest of insect eggs; **(b)** (*rayon*) brood comb.

couvaison [kuvɛzɔ̃] *nf* **(a)** brooding time, sitting time (*of bird*); **(b)** incubation, hatching (*of eggs*).

couvée [kuve] *nf* **(a)** clutch (*of eggs*); **(b)** brood (*of chicks, F of children*); **et apportez donc votre c.!,** and bring the kids with you!

couvent [kuvɑ̃] *nm* (*de femmes*) convent; (*hommes*) monastery; (*école*) convent school; **entrer au c.,** to go into a convent.

couventine [kuvɑ̃tin] *nf* (*religieuse*) nun conventual; (*pensionnaire*) convent schoolgirl.

couver [kuve] **1** *vt* (*of hen etc*) to sit on (*eggs*); to incubate, to hatch (out) (*eggs*); **c. des projets de vengeance,** to meditate schemes of vengeance; **c. un complot,** to hatch a plot; **je me demande ce qu'il couve,** I wonder what he's up to; **c. une maladie,** to be sickening for an illness; **c. qn des yeux,** (*avec affection*) to look fondly at s.o.; **il est couvé par sa mère,** his mother is over-protective. **2** *vi* to brood, to sit; (*of fire, passion*) to smoulder; (*of riot etc*) to be brewing; **poule qui veut c.,** broody hen; **la conspiration couvait depuis longtemps,** the conspiracy had been hatching for a long time.

couvercle [kuvɛrkl] *nm* lid, cover (*of box, pot, saucepan etc*); cap, top (*of jar etc*); *MecE* cover (*of piston*); **c. vissé,** screw cap.

couvert¹ [kuvɛr] *adj* **(a)** covered; **allée couverte,** covered walkway; **piscine couverte,** indoor swimming pool; **parler à mots couverts,** to speak in veiled terms; **ciel c.,** overcast sky; **(b)** (*avec un chapeau*) wearing a hat; **rester c.,** to keep one's hat on; **(c)** (*habillé*) dressed; **c. chaudement, bien c.,** warmly dressed, well wrapped up; **(d)** *Fig* (*protégé*) covered; **je suis c. par mon assurance,** I'm covered by my insurance, I'm insured; **avancer c. vers l'ennemi,** to advance on the enemy under cover.

couvert² *nm* **(a)** (*abri*) cover(ing), shelter; **le vivre et le c.,** board and lodging; **être à c.,** to be under cover; *Com* to be covered (*for a credit*); **se mettre à c.,** to take cover; **se mettre à c. de la pluie,** to shelter from the rain; **au c. de la nuit,** under cover of darkness; **mettre ses intérêts à c.,** to safeguard one's interests; **sous le c. de l'amitié,** under the cover *or* cloak *or* pretence of friendship; **il a agi sous le c. de ses chefs,** he acted with the authority of his superiors; **avancer à c. vers l'ennemi,** to advance on the enemy under cover;
(b) (*de cuisine*) knife, fork and spoon; (*collectif*) cutlery, *Am* flatware; **c. à poisson,** fish knife and fork;
(c) place setting (*at table*); **mettre le c.,** to lay *or* set the table; **mettre trois couverts,** to set *or* lay the table for three; **vous trouverez toujours votre c. mis,** you can come and have a meal with us anytime;
(d) (*in restaurant*) cover charge.

couverte [kuvɛrt] *nf Cér* glaze.

couverture [kuvɛrtyr] *nf* **(a)** (*en tissu, laine etc*) covering, cover; **c. de voyage,** (travelling) rug; **c. (de lit),** blanket; **c. chauffante,** electric blanket; *Fig* **amener** *ou* **tirer la c. à soi,** to take the lion's share; **c. d'un livre,** (dust) cover of a book; **sous c. d'amitié,** under the cover *or* cloak of friendship; **servir de c. à qn,** to cover up for s.o.; *Mil* **troupes de c.,** covering troops; *Av* **c. aérienne,** air cover; **(b)** *Constr* roofing; **c. en tuiles,** tiled roof; **(c)** *Agr* topping; **engrais en c.,** surface *or* top dressing; **(d)** *Com* cover; *Bourse* margin, cover; **(e) c. sociale,** social security cover; **(f)** *Journ* **la c. d'un événement par un journaliste,** coverage of an event by a journalist; **assurer la c. d'un événement,** to cover an event, to give coverage to an event.

couveuse [kuvøz] *nf* **(a)** sitting hen, brood hen, brooder; **c. artificielle,** incubator (*for eggs*); **(b)** incubator (*for infants*).

couvrant [kuvrɑ̃] *adj* **(a)** (*qui protège*) covering, giving cover; **(b)** (*paint etc*) that covers well.

couvre-chef [kuvrəʃɛf] *nm F & Hum* headdress, headgear, hat; (*pl couvre-chefs*).

couvre-feu [kuvrəfø] *nm inv Mil* curfew.

couvre-lit [kuvrəli] *nm* bedspread, coverlet; **c.-l. piqué,** (eiderdown) quilt, *Am* comforter; (*pl couvre-lits*).

couvre-livre [kuvrəlivr] *nm* (dust) jacket, book cover; (*pl couvre-livres*).

couvre-nuque [kuvrənyk] *nm* sun curtain (*of cap*); (*pl couvre-nuques*).

couvre-pied(s) [kuvrəpje] *nm* coverlet, bedspread, quilt; (*pl couvre-pieds*).

couvre-plat [kuvrəpla] *nm* dish cover; (*pl couvre-plats*).

couvreur [kuvrœr] *nm* roofer; **c. en tuiles/ardoises,** tiler/slater; **c. en chaume,** thatcher.

couvrir [kuvrir] *v* (*prp* **couvrant**; *pp* **couvert**; *pr ind* **je couvre, il couvre, n. couvrons**; *pr sub* **je couvre**; *impf* **je couvrais**; *p hist* **je couvris**; *fu* **je couvrirai**) **1** *vt* **(a)** to cover, to overlay, to screen (**de,** with); **c. une casserole,** to cover a saucepan; **il faut c. cet enfant,** the child needs to be well covered *or* wrapped up; **être couvert de poussière,** to be covered with *or* in dust; **mur couvert de lierre,** wall covered *or* overgrown with ivy, ivy-clad wall; **c. qn de cadeaux,** to shower s.o. with gifts; **c. qn de son corps,** to shield s.o. with one's body; **c. qn,** (*contre les risques, avec une arme*) to cover s.o.; **c. la retraite de l'armée,** to cover the army's retreat; **c. les risques,** to insure against risks; **le bruit de la cascade couvre les voix,** the noise of the waterfall drowns the sound of voices; **c. son jeu,** *Cartes* to hide one's hand; *Fig* to keep one's plans secret; *Cartes* **c. une carte,** to cover a card; **c. cinquante kilomètres en une heure,** to cover fifty kilometres in an hour; *Com* **le prix de vente couvre à peine les frais,** the selling price barely covers the cost; **c. un défaut/une faiblesse,** to hide a fault/weakness; **prière de nous c. par chèque,** kindly remit by cheque; **c. une enchère,** to make a higher bid;
(b) *Journ* **c. un événement,** to cover an event;
(c) *Constr* **c. un toit d'ardoises/de tuiles/de chaume,** to slate/to tile/to thatch a roof;
(d) (*of male animal*) to cover (*female*).
2 se couvrir *vpr* **(a)** (*pour sortir*) to put on warm clothes, to dress warmly; (*pour cacher sa nudité*) to cover oneself up; (*mettre son chapeau*) to put on one's hat; **se c. de gloire,** to cover oneself with *or* in glory;
(b) *Sp* to cover *or* protect oneself; *Escrime* to guard one's body; *Fig* (*se protéger*) to cover oneself; **se c. d'un alibi,** to provide oneself with an alibi;
(c) (*of weather*) to become overcast;
(d) les arbres se couvrent de feuilles, the trees are coming into leaf.

cover-girl [kɔvœrgœrl] *nf F* cover-girl; (*pl cover-girls*).

cow-boy [kaubɔj] *nm* cowboy; (*pl cow-boys*).

coxal, -aux [kɔksal, -o] *adj Anat* coxal; **os c.,** hip bone.

coxalgie [kɔksalʒi] *nf Méd* coxalgia.

coxarthrose [kɔksartroz] *nf Méd* arthritis of the hip.

coyote [kɔjɔt] *nm* coyote, prairie wolf.

C.Q.F.D. [sekyɛfde] (*abrév* **ce qu'il fallait démontrer**) Q.E.D..

crabe [krab] *nm* **(a)** (*crustacé*) crab; **marcher en c.,** to walk sideways *or* crabwise; *F* **c'est un panier de crabes,** they're always at each other's throats; **(b)** (*véhicule*) caterpillar tracked vehicle.

crac [krak] **1** *int* (*de bois*) crack, snap; (*de tissu*) rip; *F* **et c.! il est tombé par terre,** and bang! there he was on the floor. **2** *nm* (*de bois*) crack, snap; (*de tissu*) rip; **entendre un grand c.,** to hear a loud crack(ing noise).

crachat [kraʃa] *nm* **(a)** spittle, spit, *F* gob; *Méd* sputum; **(b)** *F* (*décoration*) gong.

craché [kraʃe] *adj F* **c'est sa mère tout crachée,** he's the spitting image of his mother; **c'est lui tout c.!,** that's him all over, that's just like him!

crachement [kraʃmɑ̃] *nm* spitting; crackling (*of loudspeaker*); **c. de sang,** spitting of blood; **c. d'étincelles,** shower of sparks; **c. de flammes,** burst of flames.

cracher [kraʃe] **1** *vi* to spit, *Fml* to expectorate; (*of pen*) to splutter; (*of loudspeaker*) to crackle; *F* **il ne crache pas sur le champagne,** he doesn't turn up his nose at champagne, he never says no to champagne. **2** *vt* to spit (out) (*saliva etc*); (*of chimney, volcano etc*) to belch out (*smoke etc*); **c. du sang,** to spit blood; **il va finir par c. ses poumons,** he's going to end up coughing his lungs up; **c. des injures,** to hurl abuse; *F* **j'ai dû c. mille francs,** I had to fork out *or* cough up a thousand francs; **crache-le par terre, on va trier,** spit it out.

cracheur, -euse [kraʃœr, -øz] *n* **c. de feu,** fire-eater.

crachin [kraʃɛ̃] *nm* (fine) drizzle; **il fait du c.,** it's drizzling.

crachiner [kraʃine] *vi* to drizzle.

crachoir [kraʃwar] *nm* spitoon, *Am* cuspidor; *F* **tenir le c.,** to monopolize the conversation; **tenir le c. à qn,** to listen to s.o. without getting a word in edgeways.

crachotement [kraʃɔtmɑ̃] *nm* sputtering, spluttering; *Rad* crackling.

crachoter [kraʃɔte] *vi* to keep on spitting; (*d'un feu, d'un moteur*) to sputter, to splutter; *Rad* to crackle.

crack [krak] *nm* **(a)** (*poulain*) crack horse, star horse; *F* genius, ace; **c'est un c. en anglais,** he's a genius at English; **(b)** (*drogue*) crack.

cracker [krakœr] *nm* (savoury) cracker.

cracking [krakiŋ] *nm Pétr* cracking (*of crude oil*).

Cracovie [krakɔvi] *nf* Cracow.

cracra [krakra] *adj inv Enf* dirty.

cradingue [kradɛ̃g] **, crado** [krado] *adj Arg* filthy, grotty.

craie [krɛ] *nf* chalk; **falaise de c.,** chalk cliff; **c. de tailleur,** tailor's chalk, French chalk; **bâton de c.,** stick of chalk; **inscrire qch à la c.,** to chalk sth up.

craindre [krɛ̃dr] *v* (*prp* **craignant**; *pp* **craint**; *pr ind* **je crains, il craint, n. craignons, ils craignent**; *pr sub* **je craigne**; *impf* **je craignais**; *p hist* **je craignis**; *fu* **je craindrai**) **1** *vt* to fear, to be afraid of (*s.o., sth*); **c. la mort,** to be afraid of death; **ne craignez rien!,** don't be alarmed *or* frightened!; **je crains de le laisser entrer,** I am afraid to let him in; **je crains qu'il (ne) soit parti,** I'm afraid he's left; **il est à c.** *ou* **il y a lieu de c. que... (ne)...,** it is to be feared that ...; **il n'y a pas à c. qu'il revienne,** there is no fear of his coming back; **elle craint de le revoir,** she's frightened of seeing him again; **c. pour qn,** to have fears for s.o.'s safety *or* future, to be anxious about s.o.; **ces plantes craignent le gel,** these plants can't stand the frost;

je crains le froid, I can't stand the cold; *Com* **craint l'humidité/le froid,** keep (in a) dry/warm (place).

2 *vi F* to be over the top; **ça craint,** it's too much, it's over the top; **du rose et du jaune, ça craint,** (*c'est ringard*) pink and yellow together are disgusting; **pour mon voyage, ça craint,** things aren't working out for my trip; **ça craint dans ce pays-là,** the situation in that country is something else; **il commence à c. ton copain,** your pal's too much *ou surtout Am* something else.

crainte [krɛ̃t] *nf* fear, dread; **avoir une c. respectueuse de qn,** to stand in awe of s.o.; **dans la c. de tomber,** for fear of falling; **de c. de se faire mal,** for fear of hurting oneself, lest one should hurt oneself; **de c. que ... (ne)** + *sub.*, lest; **il a parlé plus bas de c. qu'on ne l'entende,** he spoke more quietly for fear of being overheard; **sans c.,** fearless; (*agir*) fearlessly; **soyez sans c., n'ayez c.,** have no fear; **la c. du gendarme,** fear of retribution; **un sujet de c.,** a matter for worry, a worrying business; **avoir des craintes au sujet de qch,** to entertain fears *or* to be under some apprehension about sth.

craintif, -ive [krɛ̃tif, -iv] *adj* timid, timorous.

craintivement [krɛ̃tivmɑ̃] *adv* timidly, timorously.

cramer [krame] *F* **1** *vi* to burn, to be burnt; **tout a cramé,** everything went up in flames *or* smoke. **2** *vt* to burn; **elle a cramé le repas,** she burnt the meal. **3 se cramer** *vpr* to burn oneself; **se c. les doigts en fumant,** to burn one's fingers on a cigarette.

cramoisi [kramwazi] *adj* crimson; **devenir c.,** (*de honte, de timidité etc*) to flush crimson; (*de colère*) to get purple in the face.

crampe [krɑ̃p] *nf Méd* cramp; **avoir une c.,** to have *or* get cramp; **c. de l'écrivain,** writer's cramp; **c. du tennis,** tennis elbow; **c. d'estomac,** stomach cramp; *Arg* **tirer sa c.,** to get one's leg over.

crampon [krɑ̃pɔ̃] **1** *nm* **(a)** *Constr etc* cramp (iron), staple, clamp, holdfast; **(b) c. (à glace),** crampon; **(c)** stud (*for sole of boot*); spike (*for running shoe*); calk, cog (*of horse's shoe*); **(d)** *Bot* tendril; adventitious root; **(e)** *F* **quel c.!,** what a leech! **2** *adj inv F* clingy; (*bore*) persistent.

cramponnement [krɑ̃pɔnmɑ̃] *nm* clutching, clinging.

cramponner [krɑ̃pɔne] **1** *vt* **(a)** *Constr* to clamp, to cramp (*stones etc*) together; **(b)** *F* (*retenir*) to buttonhole; (*constamment*) to pester. **2 se cramponner** *vpr* to cling on, to hold on, to hang on; **se c. à qch/qn,** to hold on to *or* to hang on to *or* to cling (on) to *or* to clutch (at) sth/s.o.; **cramponne-toi!,** hold on!; **se c. à la vie,** to cling to life; **se c. à un espoir,** to clutch at a hope.

cran [krɑ̃] *nm* **(a)** (*entaille*) notch; catch, tooth (*of ratchet etc*); cog (*of wheel*); hole (*in belt, strap etc*); *Fig* (*degré*) rung, step; **c. de l'armé,** full cock notch; **c. de sûreté,** safety catch; **le c. de sûreté est enclenché,** the safety catch is on; *F* **être à c.,** to be on the point of losing one's temper; **lâcher une courroie d'un cran,** to let a strap out a hole; **resserrer sa ceinture d'un c.,** to take one's belt in a notch; *F* **avoir du c.,** to have guts; **avancer d'un c. dans la hiérarchie,** to go up a step *or* rung in the hierarchy; **(b)** (*coiffure*) crimp; **le c. revient à la mode,** crimping is coming back into fashion.

crâne [kran] **1** *nm Anat* skull, cranium; **fracture du c.,** fracture of the skull; **défoncer le c. à qn,** to brain s.o., to bash s.o.'s brains in; *F* **avoir mal au c.,** to have a headache *or* sore head; *F* **avoir le c. étroit,** to be thickheaded *or* thick-skulled; *F* **mets-toi ça dans le c.,** get that into your head *or* thick skull; **bourrer le c. à qn,** to fill s.o. up with stories; **bourrer le c. à des étudiants,** to stuff students with facts. **2** *adj Vieilli* swaggering, jaunty (*air*).

crânement [kranmɑ̃] *adv Vieilli* gallantly, bravely.

crâner [krane] *vi F* **(a)** (*fanfaronner*) to swagger, to show off; **(b)** (*être insolent*) to brazen it out.

crâneur, -euse [kranœr, -øz] *F* **1** *n* show-off. **2** *adj* swaggering, showy.

crânien, -ienne [kranjɛ̃, -jɛn] *adj Anat* cranial; **la boîte crânienne,** the skull.

craniologie [kranjɔlɔʒi] *nf* craniology.

cranter [krɑ̃te] *vt* to notch (*wheel etc*).

crapahuter [krapayte] *vi F* **(a)** (*d'un enfant etc*) to crawl about (all over the place); **(b)** *Mil* to trudge (*over difficult terrain*).

crapaud [krapo] **1** *nm* **(a)** toad; *F* (*gamin*) child, brat; *Arg* **c'est un vilain c.,** he's an ugly little squirt *or* toad; **(b) c. de mer,** angler(-fish), sea devil; **(c)** (*défaut*) blemish; (*fauteuil*) tub chair; **(d)** (*piano*) baby grand (piano). **2** *adj* **(a) fauteuil c.,** tub chair; **(b) piano c.,** baby grand (piano).

crapaudine [krapodin] *nf* **(a)** *Minér* toadstone; **(b)** *Culin* **poulet à la c.,** spatchcock (chicken); **(c)** *HydE* grating, strainer (*of inlet pipe of pond*); **(d)** *MecE* pivot bearing *or* box *or* hole; socket, gudgeon (*of door hinge etc*).

crapette [krapɛt] *nf Cartes* crapette, Russian bank.

crapule [krapyl] *nf* **(a)** (*canaille*) scoundrel, villain; **(b)** *Arch* debauchery, dissoluteness; **(c)** *Arch* (*collectif*) dissolute mob.

crapuleusement [krapyløzmɑ̃] *adv* dishonestly.

crapuleux, -euse [krapylø, -øz] *adj* **(a)** sordid, loathsome (*crime*); **(b)** *Arch* debauched, dissolute.

craquage [krakaʒ] *nm Tech* cracking (*of heavy oil*).

craquelé [krakle] **1** *adj* crackled; *Cér* craquelé. **2** *nm Cér* crackle (*ware, china, glass*).

craqueler [krakle] *v* (**je craquelle, n. craquelons; je craquellerai**) **1** *vt* to crack; *Cér* to crackle. **2 se craqueler** *vpr* to crack, to become cracked.

craquelure [kraklyr] *nf* crack; *Cér* crackle; *Beaux-Arts* craquelure.

craquement [krakmɑ̃] *nm* cracking (sound), crack, snap; crackling (*of dried leaves etc*); crunching (*of snow*); creaking (*of shoes etc*); **des craquements effrayants,** terrifying cracking *or* creaking noises.

craquer [krake] **1** *vi* **(a)** (*faire un bruit sec*) to crack, to make a cracking sound; (*of dried leaves etc*) to crackle; (*of hard snow*) to crunch; (*of shoes etc*) to creak, to squeak; **faire c. ses doigts,** to crack one's fingers; **(b)** (*se déchirer*) to rip, to tear, to burst; **les coutures ont craqué,** the seams have split; **plein à c.,** full to bursting (point); **(c)** (*échouer*) to fail, to go under; **son affaire craque,** his business is on the verge of collapse; **(d)** (*de personne*) to crack up; **j'étais sur le point de c.,** I was at breaking point, I was about to crack up; **j'ai fini par c.,** (*devant une tentation*) I finally cracked *or* gave in *or* succumbed. **2** *vt* **(a) c. une allumette,** to strike a match; **(b)** *Pétr* to crack (*oil*).

craqueter [krakte] *vi* (**il craquette; il craquettera**) to crackle; (*of cricket*) to chirp; (*of stork*) to clatter.

crash [kraʃ] *nm Av* crash landing.

crasse [kras] **1** *adj* gross, crass; **ignorance c.,** crass ignorance; **être d'une humeur c.,** to be in a foul mood. **2** *nf* **(a)** (*saleté*) (body) dirt, filth; **vivre dans la c.,** to live in squalor; *Méd* **c. sénile,** senile keratosis; **(b)** *Métal* dross, scum, slag; (*résidus*) hammer scale, forge scale; **(c)** *F* **faire une c. à qn,** to play a dirty trick *or* to do the dirty on s.o..

crasseux, -euse [krasø, -øz] *adj* dirty, filthy (*hands, linen etc*); squalid (*dwelling etc*).

crassier [krasje] *nm* slag heap, *Scot* bing.

cratère [kratɛr] *nm* **(a)** *Géog* crater (*of volcano*); **(b)** *Antiq* crater, (wine) bowl.

cravache [kravaʃ] *nf* riding whip, (hunting) crop; *Fig* **à la c.,** brutally.

cravacher [kravaʃe] **1** *vt* to flog (*horse*); to horsewhip (*person*). **2** *vi F* to slog, to work like mad (*to finish sth*).

cravate [kravat] *nf* **(a)** tie (*d'homme*); **c. blanche,** (*on invitation card*) white tie, tails; **c. noire,** (*on invitation*) black tie, dinner jacket, *US* tuxedo; **épingle de c.,** tiepin; *Mil* **c. d'un drapeau,** bow and tassels of colour stave; *F* **c. de chanvre,** hangman's rope; *F* **s'en jeter un derrière la c.,** to knock back a drink; **(b)** (*décoration*) insignia, ribbon; **(c)** (*lutte*) headlock; **(d)** *Nau* sling.

cravater [kravate] **1** *vt* **(a)** to put a tie on (*s.o.*); **(b)** (*attraper*) to grab s.o. round *or* by the neck; (*lutte*) to put in a headlock; **(c)** *Arg* to dupe (*s.o.*); **je me suis fait c.,** I got taken for a ride. **2 se cravater** *vpr* to put on one's tie.

crawl [krol] *nm Natation* crawl; **faire du c.,** to do the crawl.

crawler [krole] *vi Natation* to crawl; **dos crawlé,** back stroke *or* crawl.

crayeux, -euse [krɛjø, -øz] *adj* chalky; **d'un blanc c.,** chalky-white; **le teint c.,** chalky *or* chalk-white face.

crayon [krɛjɔ̃] *nm* **(a)** (*pour écrire*) pencil; **c. de plombagine** *ou F* **à mine de plomb,** lead pencil; **c. gras,** soft lead pencil; **écrit au c.,** written in pencil, pencilled; **c. de couleur,** coloured pencil, crayon; **c. feutre,** felt (tip) pen; **c. à bille,** ballpoint pen; **c. lithographique,** litho crayon, *US* grease pencil; **dessin au c.,** pencil drawing; **coup de c.,** pencil stroke; *Ordinat* **c. lumineux** *ou* **optique,** light pen; **(b)** (*dessin*) pencil drawing *or* sketch; **(c)** (*bâton*) stick; *Méd* pencil (*of caustic etc*); **c. de rouge à lèvres,** lipstick; **c. à lèvres,** lip pencil; **c. à sourcils,** eyebrow pencil; **c. noir,** eye pencil.

crayonnage [krɛjɔnaʒ] *nm* **(a)** (*action*) pencilling; (*traits*) pencil marks; **(b)** (*dessin*) pencil sketch.

crayonner [krɛjɔne] *vt* **(a)** (*dessiner*) to draw (*sth*) in pencil, to make a pencil sketch of (*sth*); **(b)** (*noter*) to pencil in, to make a pencil note of (*sth*); **(c)** *Fig* (*esquisser*) to draw (*outline of sth*); to outline, to describe (*character etc*).

créance [kreɑ̃s] *nf* **(a)** (*foi*) belief, credence, credit; **hors de c.,** unbelievable, incredible; **trouver c.,** to be believed, to be credible; **ajouter c. à qch,** to take sth seriously; **(b)** (*dette*) debt; *Jur* claim; **mauvaises créances,** bad debts; **c. exigible,** debt due; **créances gelées,** frozen credits; **c. hypothécaire,** debt secured by a mortgage; **(c)** *Arch* (*confiance*) trust; **lettres de c.,** letters of credence, credentials.

créancier, -ière [kreɑ̃sje, -jɛr] *n & adj* creditor.

créateur, -trice [kreatœr, -tris] **1** *adj* creative (*power, genius*); **une impulsion créatrice,** a creative impulse *or* urge; **industrie créatrice d'emploi,** job-creating industry. **2** *n* maker, inventor; *Th* creator (*of rôle*); *Rel* **le C.,** the Creator, God; **le c. exclusif d'un modèle,** the sole *or* exclusive designer of a model.

créatif, -ive [kreatif, -iv] **1** *adj* creative. **2** *n* designer.

création [kreasjɔ̃] *nf* **(a)** (*fait de créer*) creation, creating; founding, establishment (*of institution etc*); creation (*of work of art*); *Com* invention (*of new product*); *Th* first production (*of play*); **c. d'emplois,** job creation; **esprit de c.,** creativeness; **la c. (du monde),** the creation (of the world); **c. d'un rôle,** creation of a part; **c. de 10 000 emplois,** creation of 10,000 jobs; **je connais cette société depuis sa c.,** I have known this firm since it was founded;
(b) (*produit*) *Com* new product; **les merveilles de la c.,** the wonders of creation *or* of the universe; **il y avait tous les plus beaux hommes de la c. à cette soirée,** the handsomest men in creation were at the party; **une des plus belles créations humaines,** one of the finest works of man; **sa robe était une c. de chez Vénus et Cie,** her dress was a creation by Venus & Co; **la dernière c. d'un constructeur automobile,** a car manufacturer's latest model; **la dernière c. d'un metteur en scène,** a director's latest production.

créativité [kreativite] *nf* creativity.

créature [kreatyr] *nf* **(a)** (*être vivant*) creature; **c. humaine,** human being; **(b)** (*personne*) person, individual; *F* **une belle c.,** a beautiful woman; **une pauvre c.,** a poor *or* wretched creature; **(c)** *Péj* creature (*of minister etc*).

crécelle [kresɛl] *nf* (hand) rattle; **quelle c.!,** what a chatterbox!; **voix de c.,** rasping voice.

crèche [krɛʃ] *nf* **(a)** (*garderie*) day nursery, crèche; **mettre ses enfants à la c.,** to put one's children in the crèche; **(b)** *Arg* (*chambre*) pad; **(c)** (*de Noël*) crèche, crib.

crécher [kreʃe] *vi Arg* to live.

crédence [kredɑ̃s] *nf* credence (table), credenza.

crédibilité [kredibilite] *nf* credibility.

crédible [kredibl] *adj* credible.

crédit [kredi] *nm* **(a)** *Fin Com* credit; **c. bancaire,** bank credit; **c. en blanc** *ou* **à découvert,** blank *or* open credit; **c. d'impôt,** (*abattement*) tax rebate; (*report*) tax credit; **lettre de c.,** letter of credit; **carte de c.,** credit card; **vendre/acheter qch à c.,** to sell/buy sth on credit *or F* on tick; **faire c. à qn,** to give s.o. credit; *Fig* to trust s.o.; **ouvrir un c. chez qn,** to open a credit account *or F* an account with s.o.; **'la maison ne fait pas c.',** 'we do not give credit', 'please do not ask for credit(, as a refusal often offends)', 'no credit given'; **établissement** *ou* **société de c.,** loan society, credit establishment; **c. gratuit,** interest-free credit; **c. permanent,** revolving credit; **c. foncier,** = (government controlled) building society;
(b) *Litt* (*influence*) credit, repute, influence; **être en c. auprès de qn,** to have credit *or* influence with s.o.; **avoir du c. auprès de qn,** to enjoy s.o.'s confidence *or* trust; **il faut dire à son c. que ...,** to his credit it must be said that ...;
(c) credit(or) side (*of ledger, balance sheet*); **porter une somme au c. de qn,** to place a sum to s.o.'s credit, to credit s.o. with a sum;
(d) (*subvention*) allocation, sum voted by Parliament for supply; **voter des crédits,** to vote supplies;
(e) *Scol Can* credit, mark.

crédit-bail [kredibaj] *nm* leasing.

créditer [kredite] *vt* **(a)** *Fin* **c. qn du montant d'une somme,** to credit s.o. *or* s.o.'s account with a sum, to place *or* carry a sum to s.o.'s credit; **c. un compte,** to credit an account; **(b)** *Fig* **c. qn de qch,** to give s.o. credit for sth, to credit s.o. with sth.

créditeur, -trice [kreditœr, -tris] **1** *n* creditor. **2** *adj* having a credit; **compte c.,** account in credit; **solde c.,** credit balance.

credo [kredo] *nm inv* creed, *surtout* the Apostles' Creed, credo; **c. politique,** political creed *or* credo.

crédule [kredyl] *adj* credulous.

crédulité [kredylite] *nf* credulity, credulousness.

créer [kree] **1** *vt* (*des emplois etc*) to create; *Com* to create, to design; **c. une chaire,** to found *or* establish a chair; **c. une armée,** to form an army; **c. l'événement,** to be big news; **c. qch de toutes pièces,** to create sth out of nothing; **c. une entreprise,** to set up a business; **agence récemment créée,** recently established agency; **le pouvoir de c.,** the power of creation; **cette attitude va lui c. des problèmes,** that attitude is going to cause him problems *or* create problems for him, that attitude is going to get him into trouble; **c. des difficultés à qn,** to create *or* cause difficulties for s.o.; **c. un spectacle,** to produce a show (for the first time); *Th* **c. un rôle,** to create a part; **c. une pièce,** to produce a play (for the first time); **chemises créées par Dumaine,** shirts styled by Dumaine.
2 se créer *vpr* **se c. une clientèle,** to build up a clientele; **se c. des problèmes,** to create problems for oneself.

crémaillère [kremajɛr] *nf* **(a)** (*dans la cheminée*) pot hanger, trammel (hook); *F* **pendre la c.,** to give a house warming party; **(b)** *MecE etc* (toothed) rack; rack bar; *Rail* rack rail; **c. (et pignon),** rack and pinion; **engrenage à c.,** rack(-and-pinion) gearing; **chemin de fer à c.,** rack railway, cog railway.

crémant [kremɑ̃] *adj & nm* slightly sparkling (champagne).

crémation [kremasjɔ̃] *nf* cremation.

crématoire [krematwar] **1** *adj* crematory; **four c.,** crematorium. **2** *nm* crematorium.

crématorium [krematɔrjɔm] *nm* crematorium.

crème [krɛm] **1** *nf* **(a)** (*de cuisine*) cream; (*on boiled milk*) skin; **c. fouettée** *ou* **Chantilly,** whipped cream; **fromage à la c.,** cream cheese; **fraises à la c.,** strawberries and cream; **café c.,** white coffee; *F* **la c.,** (*personne*) the cream; **c'est la c. des hommes,** he's the best of men, he's one of the best; **c. anglaise,** (egg) custard; **c. pâtissière,** confectioner's custard; **c. brûlée,** crème brûlée; **c. au beurre,** butter cream; **c. (au) caramel,** caramel custard, cream caramel, crème caramel; **c. renversée,** crème caramel (turned out of its mould); **c. de marrons,** chestnut purée; **c. glacée,** *Can* **c. à la glace,** ice cream;
(b) c. pour chaussures, shoe cream *or* polish;
(c) c. de beauté, face cream; **c. hydratante,** moisturizing cream; **c. anti-rides,** anti-wrinkle cream; **c. écran,** barrier creeam; **c. à raser,** shaving cream;
(d) *Ch* **c. de tartre,** cream of tartar;
(e) c. de menthe/de cassis, peppermint/blackcurrant liqueur.
2 *nm F* **un grand c.,** a large (cup of) white coffee.
3 *adj inv* cream(-coloured).

crémer¹ [kreme] *vt* (**je crème, n. crémons; je crémerai**) to cremate.

crémer² *vi* (*of milk*) to cream.

crémerie [krɛmri] *nf* **(a)** *Com* creamery, dairy; **(b)** *Vieilli* small restaurant (serving light meals); *F* **changer de c.,** to move on, to go elsewhere.

crémeux, -euse [kremø, -øz] *adj* creamy.

crémier, -ière [kremje, -jɛr] *n* dairyman, dairywoman.

crémone [kremɔn] *nf* espagnolette.

Crémone [kremɔn] *nf* Cremona.

créneau, -eaux [kreno] *nm* **(a)** (*de rempart*) crenel, crenelle; loophole, slit (*in armoured turret, tank etc*); **(b)** gap, space; *Aut* **faire un c.,** to reverse into a parking space; **stationnement en c.,** parallel parking; **elle a raté son c.,** she's parked badly *or* made a mess of parking; **(c)** *Com* (market) niche, opening; **exploiter un nouveau c.,** to fill a new gap *or* niche in the market; **(d)** *Rad TV* slot; **c. horaire,** slot, time slot.

crénelage [krɛnlaʒ] *nm* **(a)** (*de rempart*) crenel(l)ation; cutting of loopholes (*in wall etc*); **(b)** toothing, milling (*of coin*).

crénelé [krɛnle] *adj* **(a)** crenel(l)ated (*wall etc*); loopholed; **(b)** *Bot* crenate(d), crenelled (*leaf etc*); **(c)** milled (*coin*).

créneler [krɛnle] *vt* (**je crénelle, n. crénelons; je crénellerai**) **(a)** (*faire des créneaux*) to crenel(l)ate, to crenel (*wall etc*); (*faire des meurtrières*) to cut loopholes in, to loophole (*wall etc*); **(b)** to notch, to tooth (*wheel etc*); to mill (*coin*).

crénelure [krɛnlyr] *nf* crenel(l)ation, indentation; *Bot* crenelling (*of leaf*).

créole [kreɔl] **1** *adj* Creole; **boucles d'oreilles créoles,** hoop earrings. **2** *n* **C.,** Creole. **3** *nfpl* **Créoles,** hoop earrings.

créosote [kreɔzɔt] *nf* creosote.

créosoter [kreɔzɔte] *vt* to creosote.

crêpage [krɛpaʒ] *nm* crimping (*of hair*); *F* **c. de chi-**

gnons, fight, dust-up (between women).

crêpe [krɛp] **1** *nf Culin* pancake; **faire sauter des crêpes,** to toss pancakes. **2** *nm* **(a)** *Tex* crêpe, crape; (*pour le deuil*) black mourning crêpe; **c. de Chine,** crêpe de Chine; **c. satin,** satin crêpe; **voile de c.,** mourning veil; **(b)** (*caoutchouc*) crêpe (rubber); **semelles (de) c.,** crêpe (-rubber) soles.

crêpelé [krɛple] *adj* (*hair*) frizzy.

crêper [krepe] **1** *vt* to backcomb (*hair*); to crimp (*material*). **2 se crêper** *F* **se c. (le chignon),** (*of women*) to fight, to tear each other's hair out, to have a ding-dong battle.

crêperie [krɛpri] *nf* pancake bar.

crépi [krepi] *adj & nm Constr* roughcast.

crépier, -ière [krepje, -jɛr] **1** *n Com* pancake seller. **2** *nf* **crépière,** pancake griddle.

crépine [krepin] *nf* **(a)** fringe (*on upholstered furniture*); **(b)** *Culin* caul; **(c)** strainer, rose, filter (*of pump etc*).

crépir [krepir] *vt Constr* to roughcast (*wall etc*).

crépissage [krepisaʒ] *nm Constr* roughcasting.

crépitation [krepitɑsjɔ̃] *nf* **(a)** crackling (*of fire, sparks etc*); **(b)** *Méd* **c. osseuse,** crepitation, crepitus; **c. pulmonaire,** crepitant rale, crepitations.

crépitement [krepitmɑ̃] *nm* crackling; (*of candle flame*) sputtering.

crépiter [krepite] *vi* (*of fire*) to crackle; (*of rain*) to patter; (*of candle flame, melted butter etc*) to sputter; **les applaudissements crépitèrent,** there was a ripple of applause.

crépon [krepɔ̃] *nm Tex* crepon; **papier c.,** crêpe paper.

crépu [krepy] *adj* woolly, frizzy, fuzzy (*hair*).

crépusculaire [krepyskylɛr] *adj* twilight; **lumière c.,** twilight, half light; **papillon c.,** moth; **oiseau c.,** night-bird.

crépuscule [krepyskyl] *nm* twilight; *Fig* decline; **c. du soir,** (evening) twilight, dusk.

crescendo [kreʃɛndo, -ʃẽdo] *Mus* **1** *adv* crescendo; **aller c.,** to grow louder and louder. **2** *nm inv* crescendo.

cresson [krɛsɔ̃] *nm Bot* cress; **c. de fontaine,** watercress.

cressonnière [krɛsɔnjɛr] *nf* watercress bed *or* pond.

Crésus [krezys] *nm Antiq* Croesus; **il est riche comme C.,** he's as rich as Croesus.

crésyl [krezil] *nm Ch* cresol, methyl phenol.

crétacé [kretase] *adj & nm Géol* cretaceous.

Crète [krɛt] *nf* Crete.

crête [krɛt] *nf* **(a)** comb, crest (*of bird*); horn (*of toad*); **c. de coq,** cockscomb; *F* **baisser la c.,** to look crestfallen; **(b)** crest, ridge (*of mountain*); crest (*of wave*); *Constr* crest, ridge (*of roof*); crest, top (*of parapet, wall*); *Anat* crest (*of bone*); crest (*of helmet*); *Géog* **(ligne de) c.,** watershed; **(c)** *Él* peak.

crête-de-coq [krɛtdəkɔk] *nf Bot* cockscomb; (*pl crêtes-de-coq*).

crétin, -ine [kretɛ̃, -in] **1** *n Méd* cretin; *F* (*idiot etc*) idiot, cretin; **quel c.!,** what a moron! **2** *adj F* idiotic, moronic; **vous êtes encore plus c. que lui,** you're even more of an idiot *or* a moron than he is.

crétinerie [kretinri] *nf* imbecility, stupidity.

crétinisant [kretinizɑ̃] *adj* mind-numbing.

crétiniser [kretinize] *vt* to turn into a moron *or* idiot.

crétinisme [kretinism] *nm Méd* cretinism; *F* stupidity, idiocy.

crétois, -oise [kretwa, -waz] **1** *adj* Cretan. **2** *n* **C.,** Cretan.

cretonne [krətɔn] *nf Tex* cretonne.

creusage [krøzaʒ] *nm,* **creusement** [krøzmɑ̃] *nm* digging (*of hole etc*); sinking (*of well etc*); cutting (*of canal*).

creuser [krøze] **1** *vt* **(a)** to excavate; to dig (out) (*trench etc*); to cut (*canal*); to examine (*a problem etc*); **c. un puits,** to bore *or* sink a well; **c. un chemin sous terre,** to burrow one's way underground; *Fig* **c. sa fosse** *ou* **sa tombe,** to dig one's own grave; **cela a creusé un abîme entre eux,** it has created a gulf between them; **c. une question,** to go thoroughly *or* deeply into a question;

(b) to hollow (out); to groove (*wood, metal etc*); to plough (*a furrow*); **c. la terre,** to dig; **front creusé de rides,** brow furrowed with wrinkles, deeply lined forehead; **la maladie lui avait creusé les joues,** illness had hollowed his cheeks; **travail qui creuse l'estomac,** work that gives you an appetite *or* that whets the appetite.

2 *vi* to dig; **c. dans le sable,** to dig *or* burrow in the sand; **c. très profond,** to dig down deep; *Fig* **plus on creuse, plus c'est intéressant,** the more (deeply) you go in to it, the more interesting it becomes, the deeper you go, the more interesting it gets.

3 se creuser *vpr* to grow hollow; **ses joues se creusent,** his cheeks are falling in; *Fig* **se c. la tête,** to rack *or* cudgel one's brains (**pour faire,** to do).

creuset [krøzɛ] *nm* **(a)** *Ch Ind* crucible, melting pot; *Fig* melting pot; **(b)** *Métal* crucible, well, hearth (*of blast furnace*).

creux, -euse [krø, -øz] **1** *adj* (*arbre, mur*) hollow; **yeux c.,** sunken *or* deep-set eyes; **joues creuses,** gaunt *or* hollow cheeks; **voix creuse,** deep voice; *Fig* **avoir l'estomac** *ou* **le ventre c.,** to be ravenous; **avoir la tête creuse,** to be empty-headed; *F* **avoir le nez c.,** to be shrewd *or* far-seeing; **chemin c.,** sunken road; **heures creuses,** off-peak hours; **période creuse,** slack season; **assiette creuse,** soup plate; *Péj* **paroles creuses,** empty *or* meaningless words; *Péj* **il est très c.,** (*sans personnalité*) he's a very shallow individual; **étude creuse,** pointless study; *Couture* **pli c.,** inverted pleat; *Fin* **marché c.,** sagging market; *Nau* **mer creuse,** rough sea.

2 *adv* **sonner c.,** to sound hollow; *Fig* to sound empty *or* false.

3 *nm* hollow (*of the hand, shoulder, in the ground etc*); hole (*in tree etc*); pit (*of the stomach*); trough (*of wave, curve*); belly (*of sail*); **succession de c. et de bosses,** succession *or* series of humps and hollows; **sonner le c.,** to sound hollow; **c. d'un rocher,** cavity of a rock; **le c. des reins,** the small of the back; **c. de l'aisselle,** armpit; *MecE* **c. d'une roue dentée,** clearance of a toothed wheel; *F* **avoir un c. dans l'estomac,** to be ravenous; **ce chanteur a du c.** *ou* **un bon c.,** this singer has a fine bass voice; **une période de c.,** a slack period.

crevaison [krəvɛzɔ̃] *nf* puncture (*in tyre*), *Am* flat.

crevant [krəvɑ̃] *adj* **(a)** *Arg* killing, exhausting, murderous (*work*); **(b)** hilarious, priceless, killing (*story etc*).

crevard, -arde [krəvar, -ard] *adj & n Arg* **(a)** dying (person); **(b)** hungry, starving (person).

crevasse [krəvas] *nf* crack (*in skin etc*); crack, fissure, crevice (*in wall etc*); fissure (*in ground*); crevasse (*in glacier*); **avoir des crevasses aux mains,** to have chapped hands.

crevasser [krəvase] **1** *vt* to crack (*sth*), to make cracks *or* fissures in (*sth*); to chap (*the hands*). **2 se crevasser** *vpr* to crack; (*of hands*) to chap, to get chapped.

crève [krɛv] *nf Arg* (*fort rhume*) stinking cold; **attraper la c.,** to catch a stinking cold.

crevé [krəve] **1** *adj* burst; punctured, *Am* flat (*tyre*); *F* (*mort*) dead; *F* (*fatigué*) worn out, fagged out, dead beat. **2** *nm* slash; **manches à crevés,** slashed sleeves.

crève-cœur [krɛvkœr] *nm inv* heartbreak, bitter disappointment; **c'est un vrai c.-c. de devoir te quitter,** it's heartbreaking having to leave you.

crève-la-faim [krɛvlafɛ̃] *nm inv F* down-and-out.

crever [krəve] *v* (**je crève, n. crevons; je crèverai**) **1** *vi* (*éclater*) to burst, to split; (*de bête, plante, Arg de personne*) to die, to snuff it; **mon pneu a** *ou F* **j'ai crevé,** I've got a puncture *or Am* a flat; **c. de jalousie/d'orgueil,** to be bursting with jealousy/pride; **c. de rire,** to split one's sides laughing; **mon géranium a fini par c.,** my geranium finally died (off); *F* **c. de faim,** (*mourir*) to starve to death; (*avoir faim*) to be starving *or* famished; **c. d'ennui,** to be bored to death; **il fait une chaleur à c.,** it's boiling; *F* **je crève de froid/de chaleur,** I'm freezing (to death)/I'm baking.

2 *vt* to burst (*balloon, bag etc*); to puncture (*tyre*); *Fig* **c. le cœur à qn,** to break s.o.'s heart; **c. un œil à qn,** to put out *or* gouge out s.o.'s eye; (*accidentally*) to blind s.o. in one eye; *F* **ça crève les yeux,** it stands out *or* sticks out a mile; *Cin Fig* **elle crève l'écran,** she fills the screen with her presence; *Fig* **les réservations/inscriptions crèvent le plafond,** the floor is giving way under the weight of reservations/registrations; **c. un cheval,** to ride *or* work a horse to death.

3 se crever *vpr* to knock oneself out, *F* to bust a gut (*with work*); **se c. au travail,** to work oneself to death; **se c. les yeux à lire,** to ruin one's eyes reading (too much); **se c. la santé à travailler sous la pluie,** to ruin one's health working in the rain.

crevette [krəvɛt] *nf* (*crustacé*) **c. grise,** shrimp; **c. (rose),** prawn; **faire la pêche à la c.,** to shrimp, to go shrimping; *F* **cette fille, c'est une vraie c.,** she's a real Twiggy.

crevettier [krəvɛtje] *nm* (*filet*) shrimping net; (*bateau*) shrimper, shrimp boat.

C.R.F. [seɛrɛf] *nf* (*abrév* **Croix-Rouge Française**) French Red Cross.

cri [kri] *nm* cry, shout, call; (*high pitched*) scream (*of person*); cry (*of animal*); chirp (*of cricket, bird*); squeak (*of mouse*); **c. du cœur,** cri de cœur; **j'ai entendu des cris dans la rue,** I heard shouting in the street; **je ne pouvais ignorer le c. de ma conscience,** I couldn't ignore the voice of conscience, my conscience was troubling me; **c. de guerre,** war cry; *Pol etc* slogan; **c. d'angoisse/d'horreur,** shriek *or* scream of anguish/horror; **pousser un c. aigu,** to scream, to shriek out; *F* **quand je lui ai dit ça, elle a poussé des cris,** she screamed when I told her; **jeter les hauts cris,** to make loud protests, to give vent to one's indignation; **appeler qn à grands cris,** to call loudly to *or* for s.o.; *F* **le dernier c.,** the latest fashion *or* style; **c'est le dernier c.,** it's all the rage, it's the latest thing; **la casquette est du dernier c.,** caps are the in thing now.

criailler [kri(j)ɑje] *vi* **(a)** (*of pheasant, guinea fowl*) to cry; (*of goose*) to honk; **(b)** (*appeler*) to cry out, to bawl, to shout; **(c)** (*se plaindre*) to whine, to complain, *F* to grouse, to whinge, to moan.

criailleries [krijɑjri] *nfpl* whining, complaining, *F* grousing, whinging, moaning.

criailleur, -euse [krijɑjœr, -øz] *F* **1** *adj* whining, complaining, *F* whinging, moaning. **2** *n* whiner, complainer, *F* grouser, moaner, whinger.

criant [kriɑ̃] *adj* glaring (*mistake*); striking (*contrast, proof*); **injustice criante,** flagrant *or* gross injustice; **c'est la preuve criante de sa mauvaise foi,** it's striking proof of his bad faith.

criard [kriar] *adj* **(a)** crying (*child etc*); *F* **femme criarde,** scolding *or* nagging woman; **(b)** (*aigu*) shrill; **voix criarde,** shrill *or* high-pitched *or* piercing voice; **dettes criardes,** pressing debts; *Péj* **couleur criarde,** loud *or* gaudy colour.

criblage [kriblaʒ] *nm* sifting, riddling (*of grain etc*); screening (*of coal, gravel etc*); grading (*of fruit*).

crible [kribl] *nm* sieve, riddle; *Min Constr* screen, jig, jigger; **c. à gravier/à sable,** gravel/sand screen; **passer qch au c.,** to pass sth through a sieve, to sift *or* sieve *or* screen sth; *Fig* to go through sth with a fine toothcomb.

criblé [krible] *adj* riddled (*with holes, bullets etc*); **la peau criblée de cicatrices,** skin covered in scars; (*d'acné, de vérole*) pock-marked skin; *Fig* **être c. de dettes,** to be up to one's eyes in debt.

cribler [krible] *vt* **(a)** to sift, to riddle, to sieve, to pass (*sth*) through a sieve; to screen (*gravel, coal*); to grade (*fruit*); **(b)** (*trouer*) to pierce (*sth*) with holes; **c. qn/qch de balles,** to riddle s.o./sth with bullets; *Fig* **c. qn de reproches,** to heap reproaches on s.o.; **c. qn de questions,** to bombard s.o. with questions.

cribleur, -euse [kriblœr, -øz] **1** *n* sifter, riddler, screener. **2** *nf* **cribleuse,** sifter, sifting machine.

cric¹ [krik] *nm* (lifting) jack; **c. hydraulique,** hydraulic jack; **c. à manivelle,** wheel crank; **c. à vis,** screw jack; **soulever (qch) au c.** *ou* **à l'aide d'un c.,** to jack (sth) up.

cric² [krik] *int* crack!, snap!; **c.-crac!,** rip!

cricket [krikɛt] *nm Sp* cricket.

cricoïde [krikɔid] *adj & nm Anat* cricoid (cartilage).

cri(-)cri [krikri] *nm inv* **(a)** (*bruit*) chirping (*of cricket*); **(b)** *F* (*insecte*) cricket.

criée [krije] *nf* **(vente à la) c.,** (sale by) auction.

crier [krije] *v* (*pr sub & p hist* **n. criions, v. criiez**) **1** *vi* **(a)** to cry, to call out, to shout; (*fort*) to scream, to shriek, to yell; **c. de douleur,** to cry out *or* scream *or* shriek with pain; **c. comme un sourd,** to shout one's head off; **on ne peut pas parler avec lui, il se met tout de suite à c.,** you can't talk to him, he just starts yelling *or* shouting; **enfant qui crie,** squalling child; **c. contre** *ou* **après qn,** to rail *or* cry out against s.o.; **ne criez pas!,** don't shout!; **c. au secours,** to shout for help; **c. au scandale,** to protest, to be up in arms; **c. au miracle,** to describe (*sth*) as a miracle; **je lui ai crié de se dépêcher,** I called out to him to hurry up;

(b) (*of mouse etc*) to squeak; (*of cricket*) to chirp; (*of birds*) to call;

(c) (*of door, axle etc*) to squeak, to creak;

(d) (*of colours*) to clash.

2 *vt* to shout (out), to yell (out); **c. un ordre,** to shout *or* yell (out) an order; **c. des injures à qn,** to shout abuse at s.o.; *Fig* **elle le crie sur tous les toits,** she's shouting it from the roof tops; **c. la vérité,** to proclaim the truth; **c. famine,** to cry famine; **c. misère,** to complain of hardship *or* distress; **c. vengeance,** to call *or* cry out for vengeance; **c. une vente,** to put (goods) up for auction; **c. des légumes,** to cry *or* hawk vegetables.

crieur,-euse [krijœr, -øz] *n* **(a)** (*dans la rue*) (street) hawker; **c. de journaux,** newspaper seller *or* vendor; *Hist* **c. public,** town crier; **(b)** *Th* call boy.

crime [krim] *nm* **(a)** crime, offence, *Jur* felony; **c. capital,** capital offence *or* crime; **c. d'État,** treason; **c. contre la sûreté de l'État,** breach of State security; **c. contre l'humanité,** crime against humanity; **commettre un c.,** to commit a crime; **c. d'incendie,** arson; **crimes de guerre,** war crimes; **le c. ne paie pas,** crime doesn't pay; *Fig* **c'est un c. que d'avoir démoli cette maison,** it's a crime *or* sin to have pulled down that house; **ce n'est pas un c.!,** it's not a crime!; **(b)** (*meurtre*) murder; **l'arme du c.,** the murder weapon.

Crimée [krime] *nf* **la C.,** the Crimea.

criminaliser [kriminalize] *vt* **(a)** *Jur* to refer (*a case*) to a criminal court; **(b)** (*rendre criminel*) to criminalize.

criminaliste [kriminalist] *n Jur* criminal jurist.

criminalité [kriminalite] *nf* **(a)** criminality, criminal nature (*of an act*); **(b)** (*collectif*) crime, delinquency; **taux de c.,** crime rate; **c. juvénile,** juvenile delinquency.

criminel, -elle [kriminɛl] **1** *adj* **(a)** guilty (*of crime*); *F* **ce serait c. de la jeter,** it would be criminal *or* a crime to throw it away; **(b)** *Jur* criminal (*law, attempt etc*). **2** *n* criminal; (*assassin*) murderer; **c. de guerre,** war criminal; *F* **voilà le c.,** there's the culprit. **3** *nm* **avocat au c.,** criminal lawyer; **poursuivre qn au c.,** to take criminal proceedings against s.o..

criminellement [kriminɛlmɑ̃] *adv* **(a)** criminally (*inclined etc*); **(b)** *Jur* before *or* in a court of law; **poursuivre qn c.,** to take criminal proceedings against s.o..

criminologie [kriminɔlɔʒi] *nf* criminology.

criminologiste [kriminɔlɔʒist] *n* criminologist.

crin [krɛ̃] *nm* hair (*of animal*), *surtout* horsehair; **le c.,** the mane and tail (*of horse*); **matelas de c.,** (horse)hair mattress; *Fig* **à tous crins,** diehard, fanatical; **révolutionnaire/conservateur à tous crins,** out and out *or* diehard *or* died-in-the wool revolutionary/Conservative; **être à c.,** to be in a bad mood.

crincrin [krɛ̃krɛ̃] *nm F* **(a)** (*mauvais violon*) squeaky violin, fiddle; **(b)** (*bruit*) squeaking, scraping (sound).

crinière [krinjɛr] *nf* **(a)** mane (*of horse, lion etc*); **c. d'un casque,** (horsehair) plume; **(b)** *F* (*of person*) abundant crop of (untidy) hair, mop, mane.

crinoline [krinɔlin] *nf Arch* crinoline; **robe à c.,** crinoline (dress).

crinquer [krɛ̃ke] *vt Can* to wind up; **c. un mécanisme,** to wind up a mechanism; *Fig* **il est crinqué,** he's hopping mad.

crique [krik] *nf* creek, cove, bay.

criquet [krikɛ] *nm* (*insecte*) locust; **c. pèlerin** *ou* **migrateur,** migratory locust.

crise [kriz] *nf* **(a)** (*marasme*) crisis; **c. ministérielle,** cabinet crisis; **c. économique,** economic crisis, slump; **c. du pouvoir,** leadership crisis; *Hist* **la c. de 1929,** the Great Depression (of 1929); **vivre une période de c.,** to be going through a rough patch; *F* **c'est la c., ils se sont disputés,** things are bad, they've had an argument; **c. du logement,** housing crisis *or* shortage;

(b) *Méd* attack, crisis (*in an illness*); **elle a été prise d'une c. d'appendicite,** she was struck down with appendicitis, she went down with appendicitis; **c. cardiaque,** heart attack; **avoir** *ou* **faire une c. cardiaque,** to have a heart attack; **c. d'épilepsie,** epileptic fit; **c. de foie,** bilious attack; **c. de nerfs,** attack of nerves, fit of hysterics; *F* **piquer une c.,** (*de nerfs*) to have hysterics; (*de colère*) to get in a rage; *F* **faire prendre une c. (de nerfs) à qn,** to send s.o. up the wall; **c. de conscience,** attack of conscience; *Rel* crisis of conscience.

crispant [krispɑ̃] *adj F* irritating, annoying; **c'est c., cette situation d'attente,** it's irritating having to wait like this.

crispation [krispɑsjɔ̃] *nf* nervous twitching, clenching (*of the hands*); wince (*of pain*); tensing (*of the face*); shrivelling up (*of leather etc*); **donner des crispations à qn,** to get on s.o.'s nerves; **provoquer les crispations de l'opinion,** to annoy *or* irritate the (general) public.

crispé [krispe] *adj* on edge, tense; nervous, strained (*smile etc*); **les deux mains crispées sur la serviette,** clutching the briefcase with both hands; **visage c.,** tense *or* strained face.

crisper [krispe] **1** *vt* **(a)** to clench (*fists etc*); to contract (*muscles etc*); to shrivel up (*leather etc*); **visage crispé par la souffrance,** face contorted *or* screwed up with pain; **le vent froid crispe la peau,** cold wind wrinkles the skin; **(b)** *F* (*irriter*) to irritate, to annoy; **cela me crispe,** it irritates me, it gets on my nerves. **2 se crisper** *vpr* to contract; **à cette nouvelle, son visage se crispa,** on hearing the news his features tensed; **ses mains se crispaient sur le volant,** his hands were clutching the wheel; *Fig* **elle se crispe quand elle est en ma**

compagnie, she tenses up *or* gets all edgy when she's with me.

crispin [krispɛ̃] *nm* gauntlet (*of glove*); **gants à c.,** gauntlets.

criss [kris] *nm* kris, creese.

crissement [krismɑ̃] *nm* grating, grinding (*of teeth*); squeaking (*of chalk on blackboard etc*); squealing, screeching (*of brakes*); crunching (*of gravel, snow*).

crisser [krise] *vi* to grate, to make a grating *or* grinding *or* rasping sound; (*of brakes*) to squeal, to screech; **c. des dents,** to grind one's teeth; **gravier/neige qui crisse sous les pas,** gravel/snow that crunches under one's feet.

cristal, -aux [kristal, -o] *nm* **(a)** *Minér* crystal; **c. de roche,** rock crystal; **(b)** crystal (glass); **cristaux,** crystal (ware); **boule de c.,** crystal ball; **regarder dans sa boule de c.,** to look in one's crystal ball, to crystal gaze; *Ordinat* **affichage à cristaux liquides,** liquid crystal display; **travail du c.,** glass cutting and engraving; *Fig* **voix de c.,** crystal-clear voice; **(c)** *Litt* (*eau*) pure water, ice; **(d)** *F* **cristaux (de soude),** washing soda; **(e)** *Électron* **oscillateur à c.,** crystal oscillator, quartz oscillator.

cristallerie [kristalri] *nf* (*verrerie*) crystal (glass) manufacture; (*fabrique*) (crystal) glassworks; (*collectif*) crystal (ware).

cristallier [kristalje] *nm* **(a)** (*artisan*) glass cutter and engraver; **(b)** (*chercheur de cristal*) crystal seeker, crystal hunter.

cristallin, -ine [kristalɛ̃, -in] **1** *adj* **(a)** crystalline (*rock etc*); crystal-clear (*water etc*); as clear as a bell (*sound*); **une voix cristalline,** a crystal-clear voice; **(b)** *Phys* **réseau c.,** crystal lattice. **2** *nm Anat* crystalline lens (*of the eye*).

cristallisation [kristalizasjɔ̃] *nf* crystallization, crystallizing; **la neige fait de belles cristallisations,** snow produces beautiful crystal formations *or* structures.

cristalliser [kristalize] **1** *vt* to crystallize; *Fig Litt* **cet événement accidentel a cristallisé ses impressions,** that chance occurrence crystallized his impressions. **2** *vi* to crystallize; *Fig Litt* **son idéal a cristallisé autour de ce souvenir,** his ideal took shape around that memory. **3 se cristalliser** *vpr* to crystallize; *Fig Litt* **son énergie s'est cristallisée dans ce projet,** his energy became focused on this project.

cristallographie [kristalɔgrafi] *nf* crystallography.

critère [kritɛr] *nm* criterion, *pl* criteria, test, measure; **son seul c. c'est l'avis de son père,** his father's opinion is his only criterion; *F* **ce n'est pas un c.,** (*on ne peut rien en conclure*) that's no criterion.

critérium [kriterjɔm] *nm* **(a)** *Courses de chevaux* **c. des deux ans,** = races to select the best two-year-old; **(b)** *Sp* (eliminating) heat.

critiquable [kritikabl] *adj* open to criticism.

critique¹ [kritik] *adj* (*crucial*) critical, decisive, crucial; **dans une situation c.,** in a critical situation, in a tight spot; in an emergency; **une période c.,** a critical period; **c'est c., sois prudent,** be careful, it's vital; *Phys* **point c.,** critical point; *Nucl & Fig* **masse c.,** critical mass; *Méd* **phase c.,** critical phase (*of an illness*); **c'est une phase c. dans les négociations,** it's a critical stage in negotiations; **l'âge c.,** the menopause; **le moment c.,** the crucial moment.

critique² **1** *adj* (*passing judgement*) critical; **examiner qch d'un œil c.,** to examine sth critically *or* with a critical eye; **ne sois pas aussi c.,** don't be so critical; **faire une analyse c.,** to produce a critique *or* a critical analysis; **esprit c.,** critical mind; **son attitude est trop c.,** his attitude is too critical, he's too critical in his attitude.

2 *nm* critic; **c. d'art,** art critic; **un c. de cinéma,** a film critic; **c. sévère,** harsh critic.

3 *nf* **(a)** (*jugement*) (art of) criticism; **c. des textes,** textual criticism; **c. dramatique,** dramatic criticism;

(b) (*examen*) critical article *or* paper; *Th Cin* review; **faire la c. d'une pièce,** to review a play; **sa pièce a eu quelques bonnes critiques,** his play got a few good reviews;

(c) (*condamnation*) censure; **exercer une sévère c. sur soi-même,** to be highly self-critical *or* a stern critic of oneself; **c. d'une politique/d'un régime,** criticism of a policy/a régime; **cela mérite une c. sévère,** that deserves a severe rebuke; **il ne supporte pas** *ou* **il n'accepte pas la c.,** he can't take criticism; **ce n'est pas une c., mais ...,** don't take this as a criticism, but ...; **formuler une** *ou* **des critique(s),** to express criticism, to make a criticism; **être l'objet des critiques du public,** to be a target for public criticism;

(d) la c., the critics; **la c. n'a pas aimé,** the critics didn't like it.

critiquer [kritike] *vt* **(a)** (*examiner, juger*) to assess (*sth*), to examine (*sth*) critically; **(b)** (*condamner*) to criticize, to censure, to find fault with (*s.o., sth*); **c. qn pour qch/pour ne pas avoir fait qch,** to criticize s.o. for sth/for not doing sth; **c. une attitude/une personne,** to criticize *or* find fault with an attitude/a person; **ce n'est pas pour te c., mais ...,** don't take this as a criticism, but ..., I don't mean to criticize (you), but ... .

critiqueur [kritikœr] *nm* captious *or* carping critic.

croassement [krɔasmɑ̃] *nm* caw(ing) (*of crow, rook*); croak(ing) (*of raven*).

croasser [krɔase] *vi* (*of crow, rook*) to caw; (*of raven*) to croak.

croate [krɔat] **1** *adj* Croatian. **2** *nm Ling* Croat(ian). **3** *n* **C.,** Croat(ian).

Croatie [krɔasi] *nf* Croatia.

croc [kro] *nm* **(a)** (*crochet*) hook; **c. de boucherie,** meat hook; **c. à pommes de terre,** potato hook, Canterbury hoe; **c. à fumier,** muck rake; **c. de marinier,** boathook; **(b)** fang (*of dog, wolf*); **montrer ses crocs,** to show one's teeth; **moustache en c.,** curled-up moustache; *Arg* **avoir les crocs,** to be famished, to be ravenous.

croc-en-jambe [krɔkɑ̃ʒɑ̃b] *nm* trip (*to bring down opponent*); *Fig* dirty trick; **faire un c.-en-j. à qn,** to trip s.o. up; *Fig* to pull a fast one on s.o.; (*pl crocs-en-jambe*).

croche [krɔʃ] *nf Mus* quaver, *Am* eighth note; **double c.,** semiquaver, *Am* sixteenth note; **triple/quadruple c.,** demisemiquaver/hemidemisemiquaver, *Am* thirty-second/sixty-fourth note.

croche-pied [krɔʃpje] *nm* = **CROC-EN-JAMBE**; (*pl croche-pieds*).

crocher [krɔʃe] **1** *vt* **(a)** *Nau* to hook (on to) (*sth*), to seize (*sth*) with a hook; *Région* **c. sa veste,** to hang up one's jacket; **(b)** (*tenir*) to grab hold of (*sth*). **2** *vi Nau* (*of anchor*) to grip, to bite, to hold.

crochet [krɔʃɛ] *nm* **(a)** hook; **clou à c.,** hook nail; **c. à vis,** screw hook; *Rail* **c. d'attelage,** coupling hook; **c. de boucherie,** meat hook; **c. à boutons,** buttonhook; **c. de bureau,** spike file; *Fig* **vivre aux crochets de qn,** to live off *or* sponge on s.o.; **(b)** (*pour l'ouvrage*) crochet hook; **(travail au) c.,** crochet work; **faire du c.,** to crochet; **faire qch au c.,** to crochet sth; **(c)** *MecE* **c. d'arrêt,** pawl, catch; **(d) c. de serrurier,** picklock; **(e)** (poison) fang (*of snake*); **(f)** *Typ* square bracket; **(g) faire un c.,** to make a detour; (*of road*) to take a sudden turn; (*of car*) to swerve (*to avoid sth*); **(h)** *Boxe* **c. du gauche/du droit,** left/right hook; **(i)** *Mus* hook (*of quaver*); **(j)** *Archit* crocket; **(k) c. radiophonique,** talent contest (*on radio*).

crochetable [krɔʃtabl] *adj* (*serrure*) that can be picked.

crochetage [krɔʃtaʒ] *nm* picking (*of a lock*).

crocheter [krɔʃte] *vt* (**je crochète, n. crochetons; je crochèterai**) **(a)** to pick (*lock*); **(b)** (*piquer*) to hook, to pick up with a hook.

crocheteur [krɔʃtœr] *nm* lockpicker, housebreaker.

crochu [krɔʃy] *adj* hooked (*wire, nose etc*); claw-like (*fingers, hands*); *F* **avoir les doigts** *ou* **les mains crochu(e)s,** to be mean *or* tight-fisted; *Hist Phil* **atomes crochus,** interlocking atoms; *F* **nous nous sommes senti des atomes crochus,** we hit it off (together); **ne pas avoir d'atomes crochus avec qn,** not to hit it off with s.o..

croco [krɔko] *nm F* crocodile (skin); *F* croc; **sac en c.,** crocodile(-skin) handbag.

crocodile [krɔkɔdil] *nm* **(a)** (*reptile*) crocodile; **larmes de c.,** crocodile tears; **sac à main en c.,** crocodile (-skin) handbag; **(b)** *Rail* alarm contact; contact ramp.

crocus [krɔkys] *nm* (*plante*) crocus.

croire [krwar] *v* (*prp* **croyant**; *pp* **cru**; *pr ind* **je crois, il croit, n. croyons, ils croient**; *impf* **je croyais**; *p hist* **je crus**; *fu* **je croirai**) **1** *vt* **(a)** to believe; **c. qch,** to believe sth; **ne pas croire qch,** not to believe sth, to disbelieve sth; **cela, je ne peux pas le c.,** I can't believe that, I find that hard to believe; **vous ne sauriez c. combien je suis content,** you can't think *or* imagine how glad I am; **j'aime à c. que ... +** *ind*, I hope *or* trust that ...; **il est à c. que ... +** *ind*, it is probable that ...; **tout porte à** *ou* **il faut c. que ...,** there is every indication that ..., it would seem that ...; **je ne crois pas que cela suffise,** I don't think that will be enough; **je crois que oui/non,** I believe *or* think so/not; **n'en croyez rien!,** don't believe (a word of) it!, *F* not a bit of it!; **à ce que je crois ...,** in my opinion ...; **croyez le ou non,** believe it or not; **c. qn riche,** to believe s.o. to be rich; **je vous croyais anglais,** I thought you were English; **on croirait qu'il dort,** you'd think he was asleep; **je ne suis pas celle que vous croyez,** I'm not that kind of girl; **j'ai**

cru bien faire, I believed *or* thought I was doing right *or* the right thing; **j'ai cru devoir le prévenir,** I thought I ought to warn him; **elle ne croyait pas si bien dire,** she didn't know how right she was; **je n'aurais pas cru cela de lui,** I wouldn't *or* would never have thought it of him; **c. qn,** to believe s.o., to take s.o.'s word for sth; **me croira qui voudra, mais ...,** believe me or not, but ...; *F* **je te** *ou* **vous crois!,** I should think so!; (*bien sûr*) of course!; **croyez-moi, ce n'était pas facile,** believe me, it wasn't easy;

(b) en c. qn, to take s.o.'s word for it; (*en suivant son conseil*); to take s.o.'s advice; **vous pouvez m'en c.,** (you can) take my word for it, you can take it from me; **s'il faut l'en c.** *ou* **à l'en c., ce n'est pas difficile,** according to him *or* going by what he says it's not difficult; **je ne pouvais en c. mes yeux/mes oreilles,** I couldn't believe my eyes/my ears.

2 *vi* **(a)** (*concevoir etc*) to believe (*in the existence of sth*); **c. aux fantômes,** to believe in ghosts; **c. à l'innocence de qn,** to believe in s.o.'s innocence; **personne ne croyait à la guerre,** nobody thought war would break out, nobody thought there would be a war; **le médecin crut à une rougeole,** the doctor thought it was measles; **franchement, je n'y crois pas,** quite frankly, I don't believe it; **c'est à ne pas y c.,** it's beyond belief, it's unbelievable; *F* **faut pas c.!,** don't you believe it!; **vous croyez?,** do you really think so?; **j'ai cru nécessaire de ...,** I thought it necessary to ...; **veuillez c.** *ou* **je vous prie de c. à l'expression de mes sentiments distingués,** = yours sincerely; **il ne croit plus au Père Noël,** he doesn't believe in Father Christmas any more;

(b) (*adhérer, avoir foi*) to believe (in), to trust (in), to have faith in; **je ne crois pas à ses promesses,** I have no faith in his promises; **c. en Dieu,** to believe in God; **il ne croit plus,** he has lost his faith (in God); **je ne peux pas c. sur commande, je dois comprendre,** you can't just ASK me to believe, I need to understand.

3 se croire *vpr* (*avec attribut*) to think oneself; **il se croit intelligent,** he thinks he's intelligent; **on se serait cru en octobre,** it felt like October; **il se croit tout permis,** he thinks he can do *or* get away with anything; *F* **qu'est-ce qu'il se croit?,** who does he think he is?; *F* **il se croit (beaucoup), il s'en croit,** he thinks a lot of himself, he thinks he's the bee's knees; **elle s'est toujours crue incapable de réussir,** she never thought she could succeed.

croisade [krwazad] *nf* **(a)** (*campagne*) crusade, campaign (*for, against sth*); **c. contre la drogue,** anti-drugs campaign *or* crusade; **(b)** *Hist* crusade; **partir en c.,** to go on a crusade.

croisé [krwaze] **1** *adj* **(a) feu c.,** crossfire; **mots croisés,** crossword; **rimes croisées,** alternate rhymes; **race croisée,** crossbreed; **(b)** double-breasted (*coat etc*); *Tex* twilled (*material*). **2** *nm* **(a)** *Hist* crusader; **(b)** *Tex* twill.

croisée [krwaze] *nf* **(a)** (*rencontre*) crossing; **c. de chemins,** crossroads; **être à la c. des chemins,** to stand at the crossroads *or* at the parting of the ways; **(b)** (*châssis*) casement; (*fenêtre*) casement window; **(c)** *Archit* **c. (du transept),** transept; **c. d'ogives,** intersecting ribs (*of a vault*).

croisement [krwazmɑ̃] *nm* **(a)** crossing, passing, meeting (*of traffic etc*); crossing (*of legs, arms*); **(b)** crossing, intersection (*of lines, roads etc*); **c. de routes** *ou* **de rues,** crossroads, junction; **c. dangereux,** dangerous crossroads; **(c)** crossing, crossbreeding (*of animals*); (*animal*) crossbreed, cross (**entre ... et ...,** between ... and ...); **faire des croisements de races,** to cross breeds; **c. consanguin,** interbreeding; (*of people*) interbreeding, intermarrying.

croiser [krwaze] **1** *vt* **(a)** to cross, to cut across, to intersect; **le pont croise l'autoroute,** the bridge goes over *or* crosses the motorway; **c. le fer avec qn,** to cross swords with s.o.; **c. les jambes,** to cross one's legs; **c. les bras,** to fold one's arms; *Fig* to refuse to work; **je croise les doigts pour que tu réussisses,** I've got my fingers crossed for you; **c. qn dans l'escalier,** to meet *or* pass s.o. on the stairs;

(b) to cross(breed), to interbreed (*animals, plants*).

2 *vi* **(a)** (*of garment*) to lap, to overlap, to fold over; **habit qui ne croise pas assez,** coat that does not have sufficient overlap;

(b) *Nau* to cruise.

3 se croiser *vpr* **(a)** to cross, to intersect; **ces deux chemins se croisent,** these two paths intersect; **se c. avec qn,** to meet and pass s.o.; **leurs regards se croisèrent,** their eyes met; **nos lettres se sont croisées,** our letters have crossed in the post;

(b) *Hist* to go on a crusade;

(c) (*s'accoupler*) to mate, to couple; **le cheval peut se c. avec l'âne,** the horse can be crossed with the donkey.

croiseur [krwazœr] *nm Nau* cruiser; **c. de bataille,** battle cruiser; **c. lourd/léger,** heavy/light cruiser.

croisière [krwazjɛr] *nf Nau etc* **(a)** cruising; **navire en c.,** cruising ship; **vitesse/altitude de c.,** cruising speed/altitude; **missile de c.,** cruise missile; *Fig* **adopter l'allure de c.,** to be ticking over normally; **atteindre le rythme de c.,** to reach cruising speed; *Fig* to be working at a comfortable rate *or* tempo; **(b)** (*voyage*) cruise; **faire une c.,** to go on *or* take a cruise; **être en c.,** to be on a cruise; **navire de c.,** cruise ship.

croisillon [krwazijɔ̃] *nm* crosspiece, crossbar (*of cross, window*); (cross)bar (*of chair etc*); *Archit* transept; **fenêtre à croisillons,** lattice window.

croissance [krwasɑ̃s] *nf* growth; **c. économique,** economic growth *or* development; **en pleine c.,** growing rapidly; **arrêté dans sa c.,** stunted; **enfant en pleine c.,** growing child; **la c. d'une banlieue,** the growth *or* spread of a suburb; **hormone de c.,** (human) growth hormone.

croissant¹ [krwasɑ̃] *adj* growing (*plant, tendency etc*); increasing (*wealth, anxiety etc*); rising (*heat etc*); **les jeunes diplômés arrivent en nombre c.,** there's an increasing number of young graduates (on the market).

croissant² *nm* **(a)** crescent (of moon); **le C. Rouge,** the Red Crescent (*Middle Eastern equivalent of the Red Cross*); **en c.,** crescent-shaped; **(b)** *Culin* croissant; **c. aux amandes,** almond croissant; **(c) c. à élaguer,** billhook, pruning hook.

croître [krwɑtr] *vi* (*prp* **croissant**; *pp* **crû**, *f* **crue**; *pr ind* **je crois, il croît, n. croissons, ils croissent**; *p hist* **je crûs**; *fu* **je croîtrai**; *pr sub* **je croisse**; *p sub* **je crûsse**) to grow, to increase (in size); (*of plants*) to grow; (*of moon*) to wax; (*of river*) to rise, to swell; (*of wind*) to rise; **c. en volume/nombre,** to increase in volume/number; **c. en beauté/sagesse,** to grow in beauty/wisdom; **les jours croissent,** the days are lengthening *or* getting *or* growing longer; **cela ne fait que c. et embellir,** it's getting better and better; *Iron* it's getting worse and worse; **la chaleur ne cesse de c.,** the heat is getting more and more intense; **c. dans l'estime de qn,** to rise in s.o.'s esteem; **là où croissent la vigne et l'olivier,** where the vine and olive(s) grow; *Prov* **mauvaise herbe croît toujours,** ill weeds grow apace.

croix [krwa] *nf* cross; **la sainte C.,** the Holy Cross; **mettre en c.,** to crucify; **le chemin de (la) C.,** the Way of the Cross, the via dolorosa; (*les quatorze arrêts*) the stations of the Cross; **faire un chemin de c.,** to do the stations of the cross; **le signe de (la) c.,** the sign of the cross; **faire le signe de c.,** to make the sign of the cross, to cross oneself; **porter une c. au cou,** to wear a crucifix; **chacun porte sa c.,** everyone has his cross to bear; **c. de bois c. de fer si je mens je vais en enfer,** ≈ cross my heart (and hope to die); **c'est la c. et la bannière,** it's the devil of a job; **la Croix-Rouge,** the Red Cross (organization); *Hist* **prendre la c.,** to go on a crusade; **la c. (de la Légion d'honneur),** the Cross of the Legion of Honour; *Mil* **la c. de guerre,** the Military Cross; **en (forme de) c.,** cross-shaped, in the shape of a cross; **mettre des bâtons en c.,** to lay sticks crosswise; **mettre les bras en c.,** to stretch one's arms out sideways; **marquer qch d'une c.,** to mark sth with a cross; **faire une c. en face d'un nom,** to tick off a name; **signer d'une c.,** to sign with a cross; *F* **faire une c. sur qch,** to give sth up for good; *Fig* **faire une c. sur la cheminée,** to mark sth in red letters; **c. de Saint-André,** St. Andrew's cross; **c. latine,** Latin cross; **c. grecque,** Greek cross; **c. de Malte,** Maltese cross; **c. gammée,** swastika; *Typ* **c. (mortuaire),** dagger; *Astron* **la C. du Sud,** the Southern Cross.

crooner [krunœr] *nm* (*chanteur*) crooner.

croquant¹ [krɔkɑ̃] *adj* crisp, crunchy (*biscuit, apple etc*).

croquant² *nm Péj* (country) bumpkin, yokel.

croque au sel (à la) [alakrɔkosɛl] *adv Culin* = raw and seasoned only with salt.

croque-madame [krɔkmadam] *nm inv Culin* = toasted cheese and ham sandwich topped with fried egg.

croque(-)mitaine [krɔkmitɛn] *nm* bogeyman; (*pl croque(-)mitaines*).

croque-monsieur [krɔkməsjø] *nm inv Culin* = toasted cheese and ham sandwich.

croque-mort [krɔkmɔr] *nm F* undertaker; **avoir une figure de c.-m.,** to have a long face; (*pl croque-morts*).

croquenot [krɔkno] *nm F* clodhopper.

croquer [krɔke] **1** *vi* (*of fruit, gravel etc*) to crunch (*between the teeth, underfoot*); **pomme qui croque,** crisp *or* crunchy apple; **la salade croque sous la dent,** lettuce is crisp *or* crunchy to eat; **c. dans une pomme,** to bite into an apple. **2** *vt* **(a)** to crunch, to munch; **chocolat à c.,** plain chocolate; *F* **il a croqué son sandwich en deux secondes,** he wolfed down his sandwich in two seconds flat; *Fig* **c. l'argent,** to squander one's money; **(b)** (*dessiner*) to sketch; *F* **elle est jolie** *ou* **mignonne à c.,** she's as pretty as a picture; **il est à c.,** (*d'un enfant mignon*) he looks good enough to eat; **(c)** *F* **c. le marmot,** to cool *or* kick one's heels.

croquet [krɔkɛ] *nm* **(a)** (*jeu*) croquet; **faire une partie de c.,** to play a game of croquet; **(b)** *Couture* braid; **(c)** *Culin* crisp almond biscuit.

croquette [krɔkɛt] *nf Culin* (*potato etc*) croquette; (*de chocolat*) chocolate drop.

croqueur, -euse [krɔkœr, -øz] *n F* **une croqueuse de diamants,** an expensive mistress, a gold digger; **croqueuse d'hommes,** man-eater.

croquignole [krɔkiɲɔl] *nf* = small crisp biscuit.

croquignolet, -ette [krɔkiɲɔlɛ, -ɛt] *adj F* sweet, pretty, *Am* cute; **histoire croquignolette,** amusing *or Am* cute story.

croquis [krɔki] *nm* sketch, rough drawing; **faire un c. de qch,** to make a (rough) sketch of sth, to sketch sth; *Math* **c. coté,** dimensional sketch.

crosne [kron] *nm* Chinese artichoke (*similar to Jerusalem artichoke*).

cross [krɔs] *nm F*, **cross-country** [krɔskuntri] *nm Sp* cross-country running *or* racing; (*événement*) cross-country run *or* race.

crosse [krɔs] *nf* **(a)** butt (*of rifle*); grip (*of pistol*); crosshead (*of piston*); scroll (*of violin etc*); *Bot* croisier (*of a fern*); *Anat* **c. de l'aorte,** arch of the aorta; *Culin* **c. de bœuf,** knuckle of beef; *F* **lever** *ou* **mettre la c. en l'air,** to surrender, to show the white flag, to lay down one's arms; **(b)** *Sp* (hockey) stick; (golf) club; *Can* (*lacrosse*) crosse; F **chercher des crosses à qn,** to pick a quarrel with s.o.; **(c)** (*bâton*) (bishop's) crook, crozier.

crotale [krɔtal] *nm* (*reptile*) rattlesnake, *Am F* rattler.

crotte [krɔt] *nf* **(a)** dung, droppings (*of horse, sheep etc*); *Arg* (*excrément*) shit; **des trottoirs couverts de crottes de chiens,** pavements covered in dog dirt *or* droppings *or Arg* shit; *F* **c'est de la c. (de bique),** it isn't worth anything, it's a load of rubbish *or* crap; *F* **elle ne se prend pas pour de la c. (de bique),** she thinks she's the cat's pyjamas *or* the bee's knees *or* the best thing since sliced bread; **une c. de chocolat,** a chocolate; *F* **ma petite c.,** my dear, (my) darling; *F* **c.!,** damn!; **(b)** *Vieilli* mud.

crotté [krɔte] *adj F* dirty, muddy, covered in mud.

crotter [krɔte] **1** *vt* to dirty, to soil, to cover in mud. **2** *vi F* (*of dog etc*) to do its business. **3 se crotter** *vpr* to get dirty, to get covered in *or* with mud.

crottin [krɔtɛ̃] *nm* **(a)** (*excrément*) (horse) dung; (sheep) droppings; **(b)** (*fromage*) small goat's-milk cheese.

croulant [krulɑ̃] **1** *adj* (*building*) crumbling, tumbledown, ramshackle; **empire c.,** tottering *or* ramshackle empire; *F* **un vieux monsieur c.,** a doddering old gent. **2** *nm Arg* old fogey, old buffer; **les croulants,** the crumblies; **un beau jour tu seras un vieux c.,** you'll be a crumbly *or* an old dodderer yourself one of these days.

crouler [krule] *vi* (*of building etc*) to crumble, to be on the point *or* verge of collapse; **il croule sous le travail depuis deux mois,** he's been staggering under his workload for the last two months; **faire c. un projet,** to ruin a plan; *Th* **faire c. la salle (sous les applaudissements),** to bring down the house.

croup [krup] *nm Méd* croup; **faux c.,** false croup; **avoir le c.,** to have croup.

croupade [krupad] *nf Équitation* croupade, curvet.

croupe [krup] *nf* **(a)** croup, crupper, rump, hindquarters (*of horse*); *F* (*de personne*) behind, rump, backside; **monter en c.,** to ride pillion; **(b)** brow, crest, top (*of hill*); *Archit* hip (*of roof*).

croupetons (à) [akruptɔ̃] *adv* squatting, crouching; **se tenir à c.,** to squat (down).

croupi [krupi] *adj* (*water*) stagnant, foul.

croupier [krupje] *nm* croupier (*in casino*).

croupière [krupjɛr] *nf* crupper; *Fig* **tailler des croupières à qn,** to put difficulties *or* obstacles in s.o.'s way, to spike s.o.'s guns.

croupion [krupjɔ̃] *nm* rump (*of bird*); *F* parson's nose, *US* pope's nose (*of cooked chicken etc*); *F* backside, behind (*of person*).

croupir [krupir] *vi* **(a)** (*of person*) to be sunk, to wallow (*in filth, vice, idleness etc*); **(b)** (*of water etc*) to stagnate, to grow foul.

croupissant [krupisɑ̃] *adj* stagnating; **eaux croupissantes,** stagnant water; *Fig* **esprit c.,** stagnating *or* vegetating mind.

croustade [krustad] *nf Culin* croustade.

croustillant [krustijɑ̃] *adj* **(a)** crisp (*biscuit, pie etc*); crusty (*loaf*); **(b)** *F* spicy (*story etc*).

croustiller [krustije] *vi* (*of food*) to crunch (*under the teeth*); **pain qui croustille,** crisp *or* crunchy bread.

croûte [krut] *nf* **(a)** crust (*of bread, pie etc*); rind (*of cheese*); **la c. terrestre,** the earth's crust; *Culin* **c. au fromage/à la tomate,** = toasted cheese/tomato sandwich; **pâté en c.,** = paté in a pastry case; *F* **casser la c.,** to eat; **casser une c.,** to have a snack, to have a bite to eat; *Arg* **à la c.!,** let's eat!, grub's up!; *F* **gagner sa c.,** to earn one's daily bread *or* one's bread and butter; **(b)** scab (*on wound etc*); **c. de rouille,** layer of rust; **(c)** *Méd* **croûtes de lait,** cradle cap; **(d)** (*de cuir*) undressed leather, hide; **(e)** *F* (*mauvaise peinture*) daub, badly painted picture; **(f)** *F* (*imbécile*) wally; **quelle c.!,** what a wally!; **une vieille c.,** an old fossil *or* buffer.

croûter [krute] *vi Arg* (*manger*) to nosh.

croûteux, -euse [krutø, -øz] *adj* scabby, covered with scabs.

croûton [krutɔ̃] *nm* **(a)** crust, crusty end (*of loaf*); **(b)** *Culin* croûton (*for soup*); **(c)** *Arg* **(vieux) c.,** old fossil, old stick-in-the-mud.

croyable [krwajabl] *adj* believable, credible; **une histoire à peine c.,** an unlikely story; **ce n'est pas c.,** it's unbelievable *or* incredible.

croyance [krwajɑ̃s] *nf* **(a)** (*fait de croire*) belief (**à,** in); **(b)** (*certitude*) belief, conviction; **c. en Dieu,** belief in God; **croyances religieuses,** religious beliefs; **c. politique,** political opinion.

croyant, -ante [krwajɑ̃, -ɑ̃t] **1** *adj* believing; **il n'est pas c.,** he does not believe, he's a non-believer. **2** *n* believer; **les croyants,** (*de l'Islam*) the Faithful.

C.R.S. [seerɛs] *nm* (*abrév* **Compagnie républicaine de sécurité**) ≈ State security police; **un C.,** a member of the State security police.

cru[1] [kry] **1** *adj* **(a)** raw, uncooked (*food*); raw (*silk, material etc*); crude (*ore*); untreated, raw (*leather*); crude, garish (*colour, light*); **de la viande crue,** raw meat; *Fig* **dans le jour c.,** in broad daylight; **réponse crue,** blunt answer; **eau crue,** hard water; **(b)** (*licencieux*) crude, coarse; **cette plaisanterie est un peu crue,** that's a rather coarse *or* crude joke. **2** *adv* **je vous le dis tout c.,** I'm not mincing my words; **j'ai envie de l'avaler tout c.,** I could eat *or* gobble him (all) up; (*j'étais en colère*) I could strangle him; **être chaussé à c.,** to wear one's shoes without any socks; **monter à c.,** to ride bareback; **construction à c.,** building without foundations. **3** *nm* **manger du c.,** to eat raw food.

cru[2] *nm* vineyard; **les meilleurs crus,** (*terroirs*) the best vineyards; (*vins*) the best wines; **un grand c.,** a vintage wine; **vin du c.,** local wine; **bouilleur de c.,** home distiller; *Fig* **une histoire de son (propre) c.,** a story of his own invention; **les gens du c.,** the locals.

cruauté [kryote] *nf* **(a)** (*dureté*) cruelty (**envers,** to); **faire preuve de c. mentale envers qn,** to show mental cruelty towards s.o.; **la c. d'une bête/de la vie,** the cruelty *or* ferocity of an animal/the cruelty *or* harshness of life; **(b)** (*acte*) (act of) cruelty.

cruche [kryʃ] *nf* **(a)** (*récipient*) (earthenware) jug, pitcher; (*contenu*) jugful; **(b)** *F* idiot, ass, twit; **être c.,** to be thick, to be an idiot, **il y en a qui sont plus cruches que d'autres,** some people are thicker than others.

cruchon [kryʃɔ̃] *nm* (*récipient*) small jug; (*contenu*) small jugful.

crucial, -iaux [krysjal, -jo] *adj* **(a)** crucial (*question, point*); **c'est c.,** it's crucial; **(b)** cross-shaped (*incision etc*).

crucifère [krysifɛr] *adj* cruciferous.

crucifiement [krysifimɑ̃] *nm* (*action*) crucifying, crucifixion; (*martyre*) crucifixion; **c. de la chair,** mortifying *or* mortification of the flesh.

crucifier [krysifje] *vt* (*pr sub & impf* **n. crucifiions, v. crucifiiez**) (*mettre en croix*) to crucify; (*torturer*) to torture; **c. la chair,** to mortify the flesh.

crucifix [krysifi] *nm inv* crucifix.

crucifixion [krysifiksjɔ̃] *nf* crucifixion.

cruciforme [krysifɔrm] *adj* cruciform.

cruciverbiste [krysivɛrbist] *n* crossword enthusiast *or* buff, crossword-puzzler.

crudité [krydite] *nf* **(a)** *Culin* **crudités,** raw vegetables; **(b)** crudity, crudeness (*of colours etc*); glare (*of light*); **(c)** coarseness (*of expression etc*).

crue [kry] *nf* (*d'une rivière etc*) rising, swelling; (*niveau

maximum) flood; **rivière en c.**, river in spate.
cruel, -elle [kryɛl] *adj* cruel (**envers, avec,** to); **un animal c.**, a ferocious animal; **une femme cruelle,** a cruel *or* hard-hearted woman; **ne sois pas si cruelle avec cet enfant,** don't be so hard on the child; **expérience cruelle,** bitter experience; **c'est une perte cruelle pour tous,** it's a cruel *or* bitter loss for everyone.
cruellement [kryɛlmɑ̃] *adv* cruelly, bitterly, grievously; **c. éprouvé,** sorely tried.
cruiser [kruzœr] *nm* (*petit yacht*) cruiser.
crûment [krymɑ̃] *adv* **(a)** (*durement*) crudely, roughly; **dire qch c.**, to say sth bluntly; **(b) éclairé c.**, garishly lit.
crustacé [krystase] *nm* **crustacés,** shellfish, crustaceans, *Spéc* Crustacea; **la crevette est un c.**, the prawn is a *or* prawns are shellfish; *Culin* **assiette de crustacés,** seafood platter.
cruzado [kruzado] *nm* crusado, cruzado.
cryobiologie [krjɔbiɔlɔʒi] *nf* cryobiology.
cryochirurgie [krjɔʃiryrʒi] *nf* cryosurgery.
cryoconservation [krjɔkɔ̃sɛrvɑsjɔ̃] *nf* cryoconservation.
cryogène [krijɔʒɛn] *adj* cryogenic; **mélange c.**, freezing mixture.
cryogénie [krijɔʒeni] *nf* cryogenics.
cryptage [kriptaʒ] *nm* encryption, encoding.
crypte [kript] *nf Archit Anat* crypt.
crypter [kripte] *vt* to encode.
cryptocommuniste [kriptɔkɔmynist] *adj & n* crypto-communist.
cryptogame [kriptɔgam] **1** *adj* cryptogamic. **2** *n* cryptogam.
cryptogénétique [kriptɔʒenetik] *adj* cryptogenetic.
cryptogramme [kriptɔgram] *nm* cryptogram, cipher (message).
cryptographie [kriptɔgrafi] *nf* cryptography, writing in cipher.
cryptographique [kriptɔgrafik] *adj* cryptographic.
cubage [kybaʒ] *nm* **(a)** (*action*) finding the cubic contents (*of pile of wood etc*); **(b)** (*volume*) cubage, cubic content *or* capacity, volume (*of reservoir etc*); air space (*of room etc*).
cubain, -aine [kybɛ̃, -ɛn] **1** *adj* Cuban. **2** *n* **C.**, Cuban.
cube [kyb] **1** *nm* **(a)** *Géom Math* cube; **le c. de 2 est 8,** the cube of 2 is 8; **élever (un nombre) au c.**, to cube (a number); **jeu de cubes,** building blocks, (wooden) bricks; **(b)** *Arg* student repeating a class for the second time. **2** *adj* (*mètre, centimètre etc*) cubic.
cuber [kybe] **1** *vt Math* to cube (*number etc*); (*évaluer*) to find the cubic content of (*sth*). **2** *vi* **(a)** (*contenir*) to have a cubic capacity of; **réservoir qui cube vingt litres,** tank with a cubic capacity of twenty litres; **(b)** *F* (*revenir cher*) to mount up, to work out expensive; **ça cube, ça finit par c.**, it mounts up.
cubi [kybi] *nm F* = **CUBITAINER.**
cubique [kybik] **1** *adj* cubic; *Math* **racine c.**, cube root. **2** *nf* cubic (curve).
cubisme [kybism] *nm Beaux-Arts* cubism.
cubiste [kybist] *adj & n Beaux-Arts* cubist.
cubitainer [kybitenɛr] *nm* = large cubic plastic container (*for bulk purchase of wine*).
cubital, -aux [kybital, -o] *adj Anat* ulnar.
cubitus [kybitys] *nm Anat* ulna.
cucu(l) [kyky] *adj F* **c. (la praline),** stupid, idiotic, goofy; **gentille, mais un peu c.**, nice enough, but a bit daft.
cucuterie [kykytri] *nf F* idiocy, stupidity.
cueillette [kœjɛt] *nf* (*action*) gathering, picking; (*fruits etc*) crop, harvest; **la c. des fraises,** strawberry picking.
cueilleur, -euse [kœjœr, -øz] *n* picker, gatherer (*of fruit etc*).
cueillir [kœjir] *vt* (*prp* **cueillant**; *pp* **cueilli**; *pr ind* **je cueille, il cueille, n. cueillons**; *impf* **je cueillais**; *p hist* **je cueillis**; *fu* **je cueillerai**) to gather, to pick, to pluck (*flowers, fruit etc*); **c. un baiser,** to steal *or* snatch a kiss; **c. des lauriers,** to win laurels; *F* **c. qn,** (*le chercher*) to meet *or* collect s.o., to pick s.o. up; (*l'arrêter*) to pick s.o. up, to nab s.o..
cueilloir [kœjwar] *nm* **(a)** (*outil*) fruit picker; **(b)** (*panier*) fruit basket.
cui-cui [kɥikɥi] *int & nm* cheeping, chirping, chirruping (*of birds*).
cuiller, cuillère [kɥijɛr] *nf* **(a)** spoon; (*contenu*) spoon(ful); **c. à dessert** *ou* **à entremets,** dessert spoon; **c. à soupe,** soup spoon; **c. à café,** coffee spoon; **petite c.**, teaspoon; **c. à pot,** ladle; *F* **il n'y va pas avec le dos de la c.**, he goes the whole hog, he doesn't go in for half measures; (*il est franc*) he doesn't pull his punches *or* mince his words; *F* **en deux coups de c. à pot,** in less than no time, in two shakes (of a lamb's tail); *F* **être à ramasser à la petite c.**, (*être blessé*) to be badly hurt *or* smashed up; (*être épuisé*) to be completely exhausted *or* all in; (*être déprimé*) to be down in the dumps; **on l'a ramassé à la petite c.**, he was scraped off the pavement; **avaler une c. de sirop,** to swallow a spoonful of medicine; **une c. pour papa, une c. pour maman,** (*à un enfant*) one (spoonful) for Daddy, one (spoonful) for Mummy; **deux cuillers de sucre,** two spoons of sugar;
(b) *Pêche* spoon (bait), trolling spoon; *Tech* spoon drill; safety catch (*of grenade*); **pêcher à la c.**, to troll, to spin (*for trout etc*); **mèche à c.**, spoon bit;
(c) *Constr* scoop, bucket (*of dredger*);
(d) *Arg* (*main*) paw, mitt.
cuillerée [kɥij(ə)re] *nf* spoonful; **une c. à soupe de sucre,** a tablespoonful of sugar; **une c. pour maman,** (*à un enfant*) one (spoonful) for Mummy.
cuilleron [kɥijrɔ̃] *nm* bowl (*of spoon*).
cuir [kɥir] *nm* **(a)** (*tanné*) leather; (*veste*) leather jacket; **c. vert** *ou* **brut,** rawhide; **c. en croûte,** undressed leather; **c. jaune,** tan leather; **c. verni,** patent leather; **c. bouilli,** cuir-bouilli; **pantalon en** *ou* **de c.**, leather trousers; **chaussures en c.**, leather shoes; **c. à rasoir,** razor strop; **cuirs de motocycliste,** motorcycle leathers; **(b)** hide (*of elephant etc, F of person*); *Vieilli* skin; **c. chevelu,** scalp; **tanner le c. à qn,** to give s.o. a good hiding, to tan s.o.'s hide; *F* **je ne tiens pas à ce qu'on m'enfonce une aiguille dans le c.!**, I don't fancy having a needle stuck in(to) me!; **(c)** *F* (*mauvaise prononciation*) incorrect liaison (*intrusive t or z*) (*par exemple* **cent idées** [sɑ̃zide], **moi aussi** [mwazosi]); **faire un c.**, to make an incorrect *or* false liaison.
cuirasse [kɥiras] *nf* **(a)** (*protection*) cuirass, breastplate; *Zool* cuirass; (*de poisson*) bony plate, carapace; *Fig* **trouver le défaut dans la c. de qn,** to find s.o.'s weak *or* vulnerable spot, to find a chink in s.o.'s armour; *Fig* **une c. de froideur,** a protective distant attitude; **(b)** armour (plating) (*of warship, tank*); **plaque de c.**, armour plate.
cuirassé [kɥirase] **1** *adj* (*armé*) armour-plated, armoured; *Nau* **croiseur c.**, armour-plated cruiser; *Fig* **être c. contre (les supplications/etc),** to be proof *or* hardened against (entreaties/*etc*). **2** *nm Mil Nau* armoured ship; **c. (de ligne),** battleship.
cuirassement [kɥirasmɑ̃] *nm* **(a)** armouring (*of ship etc*); **(b)** (*cuirasse*) armour-plating.
cuirasser [kɥirase] **1** *vt* **(a)** to armour(-plate) (*ship*); to enclose, to protect (*machine*); **(b)** to put a cuirass *or* breastplate on (*soldier*). **2 se cuirasser** *vpr* to put on one's cuirass *or* breastplate; *Fig* **se c. contre qch,** to steel *or* harden oneself against sth.
cuirassier [kɥirasje] *nm Mil* cuirassier.
cuire [kɥir] *v* (*prp* **cuisant**; *pp* **cuit**; *pr ind* **je cuis, il cuit, n. cuisons, ils cuisent**; *impf* **je cuisais**; *p hist* **je cuisis**; *fu* **je cuirai**) **1** *vt* **(a)** *Culin* to cook; **c. à l'eau,** to boil; **c. des légumes à la vapeur,** to steam vegetables; **c. la viande au grill,** to grill the meat; **c. au four,** to bake, to roast; **un four en terre cuit bien le pain,** bread bakes well in a clay oven; *Arg* **va te faire c. un œuf,** to hell with you; **elle peut aller se faire c. un œuf,** she can go to hell, to hell with her;
(b) to burn, to fire, to bake (*bricks, pottery etc*).
2 *vi* **(a)** (*of food*) to cook; **pommes à c.**, cooking apples; **chocolat à c.**, cooking *or* baking chocolate; **c. à petit feu** *ou* **à feu doux,** to cook slowly, to simmer; **le poulet a cuit trop longtemps,** the chicken is overcooked; *F* **être dur à c.**, to be stubborn; *F* **un dur à c.**, a tough nut, a tough customer; *F* **c. (dans son jus),** to be terribly hot; *F* **on cuit dans cette salle,** this room's like an oven;
(b) (*brûler*) to burn, to smart; **les yeux me cuisent,** my eyes are smarting.
3 se cuire *vpr* **se c. au soleil/sur la plage,** to roast in the sun/on the beach.
4 *v impers* **il vous en cuira,** you'll be sorry (for it), you'll regret it.
cuisant [kɥizɑ̃] *adj* smarting, burning (*pain etc*); biting (*cold*); caustic, biting, bitter (*remarks*); **déception cuisante,** bitter disappointment; **un échec c.**, a bitter setback *or* defeat.
cuiseur [kɥizœr] *nm* large cooking pot.
cuisine [kɥizin] *nf* **(a)** (*pièce*) kitchen; *Nau* (cook's) galley; **éléments de c.**, kitchen units; **articles** *ou* **ustensiles** *ou* **batterie de c.**, cooking utensils; *Mil* **c. roulante,** field kitchen; **recevoir ses amis à la c.**, to entertain one's friends in the kitchen; **latin de c.**, dog Latin; **(b)** (*préparation*) (art of) cooking, cookery, cuisine; **faire la c.**, to do the cooking; **il fait de la bonne c.**, he's a good cook; **c. au beurre/à l'huile,** cooking with butter/oil; **c. bourgeoise,** plain *or*

home cooking; **livre de c.,** cookery book, recipe book, *Am* cookbook; **(c)** *F* (*intrigue*) (dirty) tricks; **la c. parlementaire,** parliamentary intrigue; **(d)** (*table*) (cooked) food; **restaurant renommé pour sa c.,** restaurant famed for its food *or* cuisine; **la nouvelle c.,** nouvelle cuisine.

cuisiner [kɥizine] **1** *vi* to cook; **elle cuisine bien,** she's a good cook. **2** *vt* **(a)** to cook (*meat etc*); **plats cuisinés,** ready-cooked dishes, takeaway meals; **(b)** *F* **c. qn,** to interrogate *or* grill s.o..

cuisinette [kɥizinɛt] *nf* kitchenette.

cuisinier, -ière [kɥizinje, -jɛr] **1** *n* chef, cook. **2** *nf* **cuisinière,** cooker, stove; **c. électrique,** electric cooker *or* stove.

cuissage [kɥisaʒ] *nm Hist* **droit de c.,** droit de seigneur; *F* **son refus de se soumettre au droit de c. lui a fait perdre son emploi,** she lost her job because she refused to sleep with the boss.

cuissard [kɥisar] *nm* **(a)** (*pour cycliste*) racing shorts; **(b)** (*partie de l'armure*) *Arch* cuisse, thigh piece.

cuissardes [kɥisard] *nfpl* (*pour femme*) thigh boots; (*de pêche etc*) waders.

cuisse [kɥis] *nf Anat* thigh; *Culin* **c. de poulet,** chicken leg, *F* drumstick; **cuisses de grenouilles,** frogs' legs; **avoir la c. légère,** to sleep around, to be an easy lay; *F* **se croire sorti de la c. de Jupiter,** to think a lot of oneself.

cuisseau, -eaux [kɥiso] *nm Culin* leg (*of veal*).

cuissettes [kɥisɛt] *nfpl* = short shorts (*for athletes*).

cuisson [kɥisɔ̃] *nf* **(a)** (*d'aliments*) cooking; **temps de c.,** cooking time; **vérifier les temps de c.,** to check the cooking times; **le porc demande une longue c.,** pork has to be cooked for a long time; **plaque de c.,** hob; **(b)** burning, firing (*of bricks, porcelain etc*); **(c)** (*impression*) burning (sensation), smarting (pain).

cuissot [kɥiso] *nm Culin* haunch (*of venison*).

cuistance [kɥistɑ̃s] *nf Arg* cooking; (*nourriture*) grub, nosh.

cuistot [kɥisto] *nm F* cook.

cuistre [kɥistr] *Péj Litt* **1** *nm* (*conceited*) pedant. **2** *adj* pedantic.

cuistrerie [kɥistrəri] *nf Péj Litt* pedantry.

cuit [kɥi] *adj Culin* cooked; **bien c.,** well done; **c. à point,** done to a turn; **trop c.,** overdone, overcooked; **pas assez c.,** underdone, undercooked; **du vin c.,** liqueur wine; *Tech* cooked wine; **la salade est cuite, jette-la,** the lettuce is spoiled, throw it away; **terre cuite,** terracotta; *F* **être c.,** to be done for, to have had it; **je suis c.,** it's all up with me, I've had it, I'm done for; **c'est c.!,** that's it!, we've had it!; **le cinéma, c'est c. pour ce soir,** the cinema's out tonight; *F* **c'est du tout c.,** it's a cinch *or* a walkover *or* a doddle.

cuite [kɥit] *nf* **(a)** baking, firing (*of bricks etc*); **(b)** *F* **(se) prendre une (bonne) c.,** to get drunk *or* plastered.

cuiter (se) [səkɥite] *vpr Arg* to get drunk *or* tight *or* plastered.

cuivrage [kɥivraʒ] *nm Tech* coppering (*of metals etc*); copper plating.

cuivre [kɥivr] *nm* **(a)** (*métal*) **c. (rouge),** copper; **casserole en c.,** copper saucepan; **doublé en c.,** (*plaqué*) copper plated; (*par le fond*) copper bottomed; *Minér* **minerai de c.,** copper ore; **c. jaune,** brass; **les cuivres,** copper(ware); (*jaunes*) brasses; **faire (briller) les cuivres,** to polish the brassware, to do the brasses; **(b)** *Mus* **les cuivres,** the brass, the brass section; **(c)** (*planche*) copperplate.

cuivré [kɥivre] *adj* **(a)** (*hâlé*) copper coloured; **peau cuivrée, teint c.,** bronzed skin *or* complexion; **cheveux aux reflets cuivrés,** auburn hair; **(b)** resonant, ringing (*voice*); *Mus* **sons cuivrés,** brassy tones.

cuivrer [kɥivre] **1** *vt* **(a)** (*couvrir de cuivre*) to copper (*sth*), to coat *or* sheath (*sth*) with copper; **(b)** to bronze (*the skin, the complexion*). **2 se cuivrer** *vpr* to turn the colour of copper, to turn coppery.

cuivreux,-euse [kɥivrø, -øz] *adj Ch* cuprous (*oxide*).

cul [ky] **1** *nm* **(a)** *Arg* arse, *F* bum, *Am* fanny (*of person*); **un beau c.,** a great bum, a lovely arse; (*d'homme*) nice buns; *Vulg* **le trou du c.,** arsehole, *Am* asshole; **faux c.,** bustle; **c'est un faux c.,** he's two-faced; **renverser qn c. par-dessus tête,** to send s.o. flying *or* head over heels *or* arse over tip *or* elbow; *Fig* **il en est tombé** *ou* **resté sur le c.,** he was flabbergasted; **se taper le c. par terre,** to roar with laughter, to split one's sides laughing; **lécher le c. à qn,** to lick s.o.'s arse, *Am* to brown-nose s.o.; **des vacances? mon c.!,** holidays? my arse!; **avoir le feu au c.,** to go like greased lightning; **être porté sur le c.,** to be sex-mad; **un bouquin de c.,** a dirty book; **revue de c.,** porn magazine; **film de c.,** blue *or* porn movie; **être comme c. et chemise,** to be as thick as thieves; **ça vaut mieux qu'un coup de pied au c.,** it's better than a kick in the pants; **avoir qn dans le c.,** to hate s.o.'s guts; **en avoir plein le c. (de qch),** to be pissed off (with sth), to have had a bellyful (of sth); **ils l'ont dans le c.,** they've had it, that's really screwed them up, that's them buggered; *Mil Arg* **tirer au c.,** to swing the lead, to shirk; **c'est un tire-au-c.,** he's a shirker *or* skiver; *Can F* **n'avoir rien que le c. et les dents,** to be at rock-bottom; *Arg* **quel c.!,** what a bloody fool *or* prat *or* arsehole *or Am* asshole!;

(b) *Arg* (*chance*) luck; **avoir du c.,** to be lucky *or* jammy; **quel c.!,** you jammy devil!;

(c) haunches, rump (*of animal*); **tirer un oiseau au c. levé,** to shoot a bird on the rise;

(d) bottom (*of bag, bottle, barrel*); base (*of bottle*); **faire c. sec,** to down one's drink in one go; **c. sec!,** bottoms up!;

(e) *Nau* stern (*of ship*); **trop sur c.,** too much by the stern.

2 *adj* silly; **elle est un peu c.,** she's a bit of a twerp *or* twit *or Am* nerd.

culasse [kylas] *nf* **(a)** *Mil* breech (*of gun, rifle*); **c. mobile,** bolt (*of rifle*); **fusil se chargeant par la c.,** breech loader; **bloc de c.,** breech block; **(b)** culet (*of precious stone*); **(c)** (*of engine*) cylinder head; **joint de c.,** cylinder head gasket.

cul-blanc [kyblɑ̃] *nm* (*oiseau*) wheatear; (*pl culs-blancs*).

culbute [kylbyt] *nf* **(a)** (*cabriole*) somersault; **faire la c.,** to turn a somersault; **(b)** (*chute*) tumble, heavy fall; **faire une c.,** to fall head over heels; *F* **faire la c.,** (*of ministry*) to fall; (*business*) to go bust; *Com* **les revendeurs font la c.,** the dealers are making a killing *or* a huge profit.

culbuter [kylbyte] **1** *vi* **(a)** (*se renverser*) to topple over; (*de qn*) to fall head over heels; **la voiture a culbuté dans le fossé,** the car overturned in the ditch; **(b)** *F* (*of business*) to go bust; (*of ministry*) to fall, to collapse. **2** *vt* **(a)** (*renverser*) to knock (*s.o., sth*) down *or* over, to upset (*s.o., sth*); to overwhelm (*enemy*); to overthrow, to bring down (*ministry*); **(b)** *Arg* to lay (*a woman*).

culbuteur [kylbytœr] *nm* **(a)** (*jouet*) tumbler; **(b)** (*de moteur*) rocker arm; **(c)** *MecE* tripper device; (*de camion*) tipper.

cul-de-basse-fosse [kydbɑsfos] *nm* dungeon; (*pl culs-de-basse-fosse*).

cul-de-jatte [kydʒat] *nm* legless cripple; (*pl culs-de-jatte*).

cul-de-lampe [kydlɑ̃p] *nm* (*pl culs-de-lampe*) **(a)** *Archit* pendant, cul-de-lampe; **(b)** (*ornement*) bracket, corbel; **(c)** *Typ* tailpiece, cul-de-lampe.

cul-de-poule [kydpul] *nm Arg* **faire la bouche en c.-de-poule,** to pout, to purse one's lips.

cul-de-sac [kydsak] *nm* blind alley, cul-de-sac; *Rail* blind siding; **la rue se termine en c.-de-s.,** the street ends in a cul-de-sac; *Fig* **votre emploi est un c.-de-s.,** you've got a dead-end job; (*pl culs-de-sac*).

culée [kyle] *nf* **(a)** *Archit* pier (*of buttress*); *Constr* abutment (pier) (*of bridge*); **(b)** *Nau* sternway.

culer [kyle] *vi* **(a)** *Nau* to make *or* gather sternway; to drop astern; **nagez à c.!,** backwater!; **brasser à c.,** to brace aback; **(b)** (*of wind*) to veer astern.

culinaire [kylinɛr] *adj* culinary; **l'art c.,** the art of cooking, the culinary art.

culminant [kylminɑ̃] *adj Astron* culminant; **point c.,** culminating *or* highest point (*of range of mountains, of one's fortunes etc*); zenith (*of power etc*); height, peak (*of fame, glory*).

culminer [kylmine] *vi* to culminate, to reach its highest point, to reach its peak; **le Mont-Blanc culmine à 4 807 mètres,** Mont-Blanc is 4,807 metres at its highest point; *Fig* **sa carrière culmine,** it's the crowning point *or* pinnacle of his career.

culot [kylo] *nm* **(a)** *F* cheek, nerve, gall; bottom, base (*of lamp, bottle etc*); *Mil* base (*of cartridge case, shell etc*); head (*of cartridge*); *El* base (*of bulb*); (*in engine*) body of spark(ing) plug; *F* **tu ne manques pas de c.!, tu as du c.!,** you've got a nerve!; *F* **je n'aurais jamais eu le c. de le faire seul,** I'd never have had the nerve to do it by myself; **(b)** *Métal* slag, residue (*left in crucible*); dottle (*in tobacco pipe*).

culottage [kylɔtaʒ] *nm* colouring, seasoning (*of pipe*).

culotte [kylɔt] *nf* **(a)** (*vêtement d'homme*) **une c., une paire de culottes,** knee breeches; **c. courte/longue,** short/long trousers; **c. de cheval,** jodhpurs, riding breeches; **c. de golf,** plus fours; **c. de peau,** *Mil* buckskins; *Mil Péj* colonel Blimp; *F* **c'est la femme qui porte la c.,** it's the wife who wears the trousers; *Can* **avoir des culottes,** to have guts; *F* **user ses fonds de c. sur les bancs de l'école,** to idle away one's time at school; *F* **trembler** *ou*

Arg **faire dans sa c.,** to be scared stiff, to have the jitters, *Sl* to wet *or* pee oneself; **(b)** (*sous-vêtement*) (*woman's*) panties, knickers; (*child's*) pants; **(c)** *F* **prendre une c.,** to lose heavily, *Am* to take a bath (*at cards etc*); **(d)** *Culin* buttock, rump, aitch bone (*of beef*).

culotté [kylɔte] *adj* **(a)** (*pipe*) seasoned; (*leather*) mellowed; **(b)** *F* (*gonflé*) full of cheek *or* nerve, cheeky; **il est c. comme tout,** he's got a *or* one hell of a nerve.

culotter [kylɔte] **1** *vt* **(a)** to put (*s.o.'s*) trousers on; **(b)** to colour, to season (*a pipe*). **2 se culotter** *vpr* to put one's trousers on.

culpabilisation [kylpabilizasjɔ̃] *nf* *Psy* **(a)** (*action*) making feel guilty; **(b)** (*résultat*) (feeling of) guilt.

culpabiliser [kylpabilize] *Psy* **1** *vt* to make (*s.o.*) feel guilty. **2** *vi* to feel (very) guilty.

culpabilité [kylpabilite] *nf* guilt; *Jur* **nier sa c.,** to deny that one is guilty; *Jur* to plead not guilty; **sa c. dans cette affaire a été établie,** his guilt in the matter has been established; **sentiment de c.,** guilt complex.

culte [kylt] *nm* **(a)** (*culte*) worship; *Fig* **avoir le c. de l'argent,** to worship money; **le c. de la tradition,** the worship of tradition; **il ne faut pas en faire un c.,** we mustn't make a cult of it *or* him *etc*; **avoir un c. pour qn, rendre** *ou* **vouer un c. à qn,** to (hero) worship s.o.; **(b)** (*religion*) form of worship, cult, creed, religion; **liberté du c.,** freedom of worship; **changer de c.,** to change one's religion; **(b)** (*service protestant*) (church) service.

cul-terreux [kytɛrø] *nm* *F Péj* country bumpkin, yokel, *Am* rube, redneck; (*pl culs-terreux*).

cultivable [kyltivabl] *adj* suitable for cultivation.

cultivateur, -trice [kyltivatœr, -tris] **1** *n* farmer; **petits cultivateurs,** small farmers, smallholders. **2** *nm* cultivator. **3** *adj* agricultural, farming; **les peuples cultivateurs,** agricultural people, farming communities.

cultivé [kyltive] *adj* **(a)** cultivated (*land etc*); **(b)** cultured, cultivated (*person*); **être très/peu c.,** to be very/not very cultured; **gens cultivés,** cultured *or* educated people.

cultiver [kyltive] **1** *vt* **(a)** to cultivate, to farm, to till (*the soil etc*); **(b)** to cultivate, to raise, to grow (*cereals etc*); **c. son esprit,** to cultivate *or* improve one's mind; **c. un goût,** to cultivate *or* develop a taste; **il faut c. son jardin,** = concentrate on things close to home and don't try to change the world; **c. l'amitié de qn,** to cultivate s.o.'s friendship; **(c)** (*s'intéresser à*) to take an interest in (*sth*). **2 se cultiver** *vpr* to broaden *or* improve one's mind; **se c. en lisant,** to broaden one's mind by reading.

cultuel, -elle [kyltɥɛl] *adj* of *or* pertaining to worship; **édifice c.,** place of worship.

cultural, -aux [kyltyral, -o] *adj* farming (*methods*).

culture [kyltyr] *nf* **(a)** cultivation (*of the soil*); **la grande/la petite c.,** large-/small-scale farming; **c. sèche,** dry farming; **c. fruitière,** fruit farming; **cultures,** land under cultivation; **(b)** cultivation, cultivating (*of plants*); rearing, breeding (*of fish, oysters etc*); **(c)** *Biol* **c. (microbienne/de tissus),** culture (of bacteria/of tissue); **bouillon de c.,** culture medium; **(d)** (*intellectuelle*) culture, education; **c. scientifique,** scientific knowledge *or* background; **question de c. générale,** question of general knowledge; **avoir une solide c.,** to have a sound education; **c. physique,** physical training, *F* P.T.; *Admin* **maison de la c.,** = arts centre; **(e)** (*civilisation*) civilization; **la c. gréco-romaine,** Graeco-Roman culture *or* civilization; **c'est une autre c.,** it's a different culture *or* way of life.

culturel, -elle [kyltyrɛl] *adj* cultural, educational; **le milieu c. d'un individu,** an individual's cultural background; **relations culturelles,** cultural relations; **un voyage très c.,** a very educational *or* cultural trip; **attaché c.,** cultural attaché; **centre c.,** community arts centre; **choc c.,** culture shock; **subir un choc c.,** to suffer (from) culture shock.

culturisme [kyltyrism] *nm* body building, *F* pumping iron.

culturiste [kyltyrist] *n* body-builder.

cumin [kymɛ̃] *nm* cumin; **c. des prés,** caraway; **munster au c.,** Munster (cheese) with caraway seeds.

cumul [kymyl] *nm* **c. de fonctions,** plurality of offices, pluralism; **c. des traitements,** concurrent drawing of salary; *Jur* **c. des peines,** non-concurrence of sentences.

cumulable [kymylabl] *adj* **des fonctions cumulables,** offices which can be held concurrently; **des traitements cumulables,** salaries which can be drawn concurrently *or* simultaneously.

cumulard [kymylar] *nm* *F Péj* pluralist; holder of several (paid) jobs.

cumulatif, -ive [kymylatif, -iv] *adj* cumulative.

cumuler [kymyle] **1** *vt* **c. des fonctions,** to hold a plurality of offices *or* more than one office; **c. deux traitements,** to draw two (separate) salaries. **2** *vi* to hold two posts *or* offices concurrently; **il cumule,** he has more than one job, *F* he's a moonlighter.

cumulo-nimbus [kymylonɛ̃bys] *nm inv* *Météo* cumulonimbus.

cumulo-stratus [kymylostratys] *nm inv* *Météo* stratocumulus, cumulo-stratus.

cumulus [kymylys] *nm inv* *Météo* cumulus.

cunéiforme [kyneifɔrm] *adj* **(a)** *Anat* cuneiform (*bone*); **(b) écriture/caractère c.,** cuneiform writing/character.

cupide [kypid] *adj* *Litt Péj* greedy, grasping, money-grubbing.

cupidement [kypidmɑ̃] *adv* *Litt Péj* greedily.

cupidité [kypidite] *nf* *Litt Péj* cupidity, greed.

Cupidon [kypidɔ̃] *nm* *Myth* Cupid.

cuprifère [kyprifɛr] *adj* copper-bearing, cupriferous.

cuprique [kyprik] *adj* cupric.

cupule [kypyl] *nf* *Bot* cupule, cupula; cup (*of acorn*).

curable [kyrabl] *adj* curable (*disease etc*).

curaçao [kyraso] *nm* curaçao (liqueur).

curage [kyraʒ] *nm* clearing *or* cleaning out (*of drain, harbour etc*); flushing (*of drain*).

curare [kyrar] *nm* curare.

curatelle [kyratɛl] *nf* *Jur* trusteeship, guardianship.

curateur, -trice [kyratœr, -tris] *n* *Jur* trustee (*of succession etc*); guardian (*of minor, lunatic*).

curatif, -ive [kyratif, -iv] *adj* curative.

cure [kyr] *nf* **(a) n'avoir c. de qch,** not to care about sth, not to take any notice of sth; **(b)** (*fonction de curé*) office of a parish priest; (*paroisse*) parish; (*presbytère*) presbytery; **obtenir une c.,** to be appointed parish priest; **(c)** *Méd* (course of) treatment; **c. thermale,** hydrotherapy, course of treatment at a spa; **c. d'amaigrissement,** slimming cure, diet; **faire une c. de lait/de repos,** to go on a milk diet/rest cure; **elle a fait une c. à Vichy,** she took the waters at Vichy.

curé [kyre] *nm* *Cathol* parish priest; *F* (*any*) priest; **monsieur le c.,** Father; **il veut se faire c.,** he wants to become a priest *or* to enter the priesthood; *F* **bouffer** *ou* **manger du c.,** to be (violently) anti-clerical.

cure-dent(s) [kyrdɑ̃] *nm* toothpick; (*pl cure-dents*).

curée [kyre] *nf* parts of the stag given to the hounds; (*mise à mort*) kill.

cure-ongles [kyrɔ̃gl] *nm inv* nail cleaner.

cure-pipe [kyrpip] *nm* pipe cleaner; (*pl cure-pipes*).

curer [kyre] *vt* to pick (*one's teeth*); to clear *or* clean out (*drain, harbour etc*); to dredge (*river, pond etc*); to scrape (*pipe etc*) clean; **se c. les ongles/les oreilles,** to clean one's nails/to clean (out) one's ears.

cureter [kyrte] *vt* *Chir* to curette.

curet(t)age [kyr(ɛ)taʒ] *nm* *Chir* curetting, curettage.

curette [kyrɛt] *nf* *Tech* scraper; *Chir* curette.

curie¹ [kyri] *nf* *Antiq Cathol* curia.

curie² *nm* *Phys* curie.

curieusement [kyrjøzmɑ̃] *adv* (*étrangement*) curiously, strangely, oddly, peculiarly.

curieux, -ieuse [kyrjø, -jøz] **1** *adj* **(a)** (*intéressé*) curious, interested; inquiring, curious (*mind*); **être c. de tout/de la vie,** to be curious about *or* interested in everything/life; **elle est curieuse d'archéologie,** she is interested in archeology; **je serai c. de voir cela,** I'll be curious *or* interested to see it;

(b) (*indiscret*) curious, inquisitive; **elle est trop curieuse,** she's too nosey;

(c) (*étrange*) curious, odd, peculiar; **c'est c.,** that's odd *or* funny; **par une curieuse coïncidence,** by a strange coincidence; **chose assez curieuse,** curiously enough; **ne me regarde pas comme une bête curieuse,** don't look at me as if I were a strange animal.

2 *n* inquisitive person, *F* nos(e)y parker, busybody; **méfie-toi, c'est un c.,** watch out, he's nosey; **un attroupement de c.,** a crowd of onlookers *or* bystanders; **il était venu en c.,** he came just to have a look.

3 *nm* **le plus c. de l'affaire est que ...** (+ *ind*), the strangest part *or* thing about it is that ... .

curiosité [kyrjozite] *nf* **(a)** (*intellectuelle*) curiosity, interestedness, interest (**de,** for); **c. d'esprit,** inquisitiveness of mind; **développer sa c.,** to broaden one's mind; **satisfaire sa c.,** to satisfy one's curiosity; **regarder qn avec c.,** to look at s.o. curiously *or* enquiringly; **(b)** (*indiscretion*) curiosity, inquisitiveness, *F* nosiness; **par c.,** out of curiosity; **par simple c., dites-moi ...,** just out of curiosity, tell me ...; **(c)** (*monument*) interesting feature *or* sight; (*objet*) curio; **curiosités d'une ville,** sights of a town.

curiste [kyrist] *n* patient taking the waters (*at a spa*).

curling [kœrliŋ] *nm Sp* curling.

curriculum vitae [kyrikylɔmvite] *nm* curriculum vitae, c.v., *Am* resumé; **envoyer/établir son c.v.,** to send (off)/draw up one's c.v..

curry [kari] *nm Culin* curry; **poulet au c., c. de poulet,** curried chicken, chicken curry.

curseur [kyrsœr] *nm Ordinat* cursor; *Tech* cursor, slide, runner (*of mathematical instrument etc*); *Ordinat* **position/déplacement du c.,** cursor position/movement.

cursif, -ive [kyrsif, -iv] *adj* **(a)** cursive (*handwriting*); **(b)** (*rapide*) cursory.

cursus [kyrsys] *nm Univ* programme, *Am* program, course of study, curriculum; **établir son c.,** to fix *or* arrange one's course of study; **le c. médical,** the medical degree course.

curviligne [kyrviliɲ] *adj* curvilinear, rounded.

curvimètre [kyrvimɛtr] *nm* curvometer.

cuspide [kyspid] *nf Anat Bot* cusp.

custode [kystɔd] *nf* **(a)** *Rel* custodial (*for the host etc*); **(b)** rear side panel (*of car*).

cutané [kytane] *adj* cutaneous; **maladie cutanée,** skin disease.

cuti [kyti] *nf Méd F* skin test; **virer sa c.,** to have a positive reaction to a skin test; *Fig* to change one's sexual orientation.

cuticule [kytikyl] *nf Anat* cuticle, epidermis.

cutiréaction [kytireaksjɔ̃] *nf Méd* = **CUTI**.

cutter [kœtœr, kytɛr] *nm* Stanley knife ®.

cuvage [kyvaʒ] *nm,* **cuvaison** [kyvɛzɔ̃] *nf* fermenting *or* fermentation (*of wine, beer*) in vats.

cuve [kyv] *nf* (storage) tank, cistern; tub (*of washing machine*); vat, tun (*for fermenting wine etc*); **c. à lessive,** laundry vat; *Phot* **c. à laver/à développement,** washing/developing tank.

cuvée [kyve] *nf* **(a)** (*quantité*) vatful, tunful; **(b)** (*produit*) vintage; **vin de première c.,** wine of the first growth *or* vintage.

cuvelage [kyvlaʒ] *nm* lining, timbering, tubbing (*of mineshaft etc*); lining (*of borehole*); casing (*of well*).

cuveler [kyvle] *vt* (**je cuvelle, n. cuvelons; je cuvellerai**) to line, to timber, to tub (*mineshaft etc*); to line (*borehole*); to case, to consolidate (*well*).

cuver [kyve] **1** *vi* (*of wine, beer*) to ferment (*in the vats*). **2** *vt F* **c. son vin,** to sleep it off; **c. sa colère,** to simmer down.

cuvette [kyvɛt] *nf* **(a)** (wash)basin, (wash)bowl; **c. (de lavabo),** washbasin; **(b)** bowl, pan (*of W.C.*); cup, cistern (*of barometer*); bulb (*of thermometer*); cap (*of watch*); *Phot* (developing) dish; **(c)** (*dépression*) *Géog* basin, depression, *Br* punchbowl.

cyanose [sjanoz] *nf Méd* cyanosis.

cyanure [sjanyr] *nm Ch* cyanide.

cybernéticien, -ienne [sibɛrnetisjɛ̃, -jɛn] *n* cybernetician, cybernetics expert, cyberneticist.

cybernétique [sibɛrnetik] *nf* cybernetics.

cyclable [siklabl] *adj* **piste c.,** cycle track.

cyclamen [siklamɛn] *nm* cyclamen.

cycle [sikl] *nm* **(a)** cycle (*of events, poems etc*); series (*of lectures etc*); **c. solaire,** solar cycle; **c. économique,** economic cycle; **c. divisé en phases,** phased cycle; **c. menstruel,** menstrual cycle; *Scol* **premier/second c.,** first/second stage (*of secondary education*); **c. primaire/supérieur,** primary/higher education; **(b)** (*véhicule*) cycle; **magasin/fabricant de cycles,** cycle shop/manufacturer.

cyclique [siklik] *adj* cyclic(al).

cyclisme [siklism] *nm Sp* cycling.

cycliste [siklist] *Sp* **1** *n* cyclist. **2** *adj* cycle (*race etc*); **coureur c.,** racing cyclist.

cyclo-cross [siklɔkrɔs] *nm Sp* cyclo-cross.

cycloïdal, -aux [siklɔidal, -o] *adj Math* cycloidal (*curve etc*).

cycloïde [siklɔid] *nf Math* cycloid.

cyclomoteur [siklɔmɔtœr] *nm* moped.

cyclomotoriste [siklɔmɔtɔrist] *n* moped rider.

cyclonal, -aux [siklɔnal, -o] *adj Météo* cyclonic.

cyclone [siklon] *nm Météo* (*tempête*) cyclone; (*zone de basse pression*) cyclone, zone of low pressure, depression; (*vent très violent*) hurricane, typhoon; **œil du c.,** centre *or* eye of the cyclone; *Fig* **elle est entrée comme un c.,** she came in like a whirlwind.

cyclonique [siklɔnik] *adj Météo* cyclonic.

cyclope [siklɔp] *nm Myth* Cyclops; *Arg* **faire pleurer le cyclope,** to have a slash; *Fig* **travail de c.,** colossal undertaking, Herculean task.

cyclopéen,-enne [siklɔpeɛ̃, -ɛn] *adj* cyclopean, gigantic, colossal; **travail c.,** Herculean task.

cyclothymie [siklɔtimi] *nf Méd* manic-depression.

cyclothymique [siklɔtimik] *adj Méd* manic-depressive; **elle est c.,** she's a manic-depressive.

cyclotourisme [siklɔturism] *nm* bicycle touring.

cyclotron [siklɔtrɔ̃] *nm Nucl* cyclotron.

cygne [siɲ] *nm* swan; **jeune c.,** cygnet; **c. mâle,** cob; **c. femelle,** pen; **duvet de c.,** swansdown; **une robe d'une blancheur de c.,** a pure white dress; *Fig* **c'est son chant du c.,** it's his swansong; *Tech* **col de c.,** swan neck.

cylindrage [silɛ̃draʒ] *nm* **(a)** rolling (*of roads, steel etc*); **(b)** *Tex* calendering, mangling (*of cloth*); cylindrical turning (*of machine tool*); *Métal* **c. à froid,** cold rolling.

cylindre [silɛ̃dr] *nm* **(a)** *Math* cylinder; **c. de révolution,** cylinder of revolution; cylindrical solid of revolution; **(b)** cylinder (*of engine*); roller, roll (*of rolling mill, mangle, calender etc*); **moteur à quatre cylindres,** four-cylinder engine; **une quatre cylindres,** a four-cylinder (car); *Typ* **c. d'impression,** printing cylinder, drum; **c. compresseur,** road roller; **bureau à c.,** roll-top desk.

cylindrée [silɛ̃dre] *nf* (cubic) capacity (*of cylinder, engine*).

cylindrer [silɛ̃dre] *vt* **(a)** to roll (*road, lawn, metal etc*); to roll down (*surfacing of road etc*); **(b)** to roll (up) (*paper etc*); *Tex* to calender, to mangle (*cloth*).

cylindrique [silɛ̃drik] *adj* cylindrical.

cymbale [sɛ̃bal] *nf Mus* cymbal.

cymbalier [sɛ̃balje] *nm* cymbal player, cymbalist.

cyme [sim] *nf Bot* cyme.

cynique [sinik] **1** *adj* **(a)** cynical (*person, attitude etc*); **(b)** Cynic (*philosophy*). **2** *nm* **(a)** cynic; **(b)** *Phil* Cynic.

cyniquement [sinikmɑ̃] *adv* cynically.

cynisme [sinism] *nm* **(a)** cynicism; **(b)** *Phil* Cynicism.

cynocéphale [sinɔsefal] **1** *adj* dog-headed, *Spéc* cynocephalous. **2** *nm* dog-faced baboon, *Zool Spéc* cynocephalus.

cynodrome [sinɔdrom] *nm* greyhound (racing) track, dog track.

cynophile [sinɔfil] *n* dog lover.

cynor(r)odon [sinɔrɔdɔ̃] *nm* (*fruit*) rosehip; **confiture/tisane de c.,** rosehip jam/tea.

cyprès [siprɛ] *nm* cypress (tree).

cypriote [siprijɔt] **1** *adj* Cypriot. **2** *n* **C.,** Cypriot.

cyrillique [sirilik] *adj* Cyrillic (*alphabet etc*).

cystique [sistik] *adj Anat Méd* cystic (*duct, calculus etc*).

cystite [sistit] *nf Méd* cystitis.

cytise [sitiz] *nm* laburnum.

cytodiagnostic [sitɔdjagnɔstik] *nm Biol* cytodiagnosis, cytological diagnosis (*of smear test*).

cytogénétique [sitɔʒenetik] *nf Biol* cytogenetics.

cytologie [sitɔlɔʒi] *nf Biol* cytology.

cytologique [sitɔlɔʒik] *adj* cytological.

cytoplasme [sitɔplasm] *nm Biol* cytoplasm.

cytoplasmique [sitɔplasmik] *adj Biol* cytoplasmic.

czar [tsar] *nm* tsar, czar.

D

D, d [de] *nm* (the letter) D, d; *Fig* **le système D** (= **débrouillard**), resourcefulness; **c'est un champion du système D,** he's extremely resourceful.
D.A.B. [deabe] *nm Banque abrév* **distributeur automatique de billets.**
dac, d'ac [dak] *int F* O.K.
dacron ® [dakrɔ̃] *nm Tex* Terylene, *US* Dacron ®.
dactyle [daktil] *nm* dactyl.
dactylo [daktilo] **1** *n* typist. **2** *nf* typing; **il est bon à la d.,** he's good at typing, he's a good typist. **3** *nm Can* typewriter.
dactylo-facturière [daktilofaktyrjɛr] *nf* typist invoice clerk; (*pl dactylos-facturières*).
dactylographe [daktilɔgraf] **1** *n* typist. **2** *nm Can* typewriter.
dactylographie [daktilɔgrafi] *nf* typing.
dactylographier [daktilɔgrafje] *vt* to type.
dactylographique [daktilɔgrafik] *adj* typing (*material etc*).
dactylologie [daktilɔlɔʒi] *nf* dactylology.
dactyloscopie [daktilɔskɔpi] *nf* dactyloscopy.
dactyloscopique [daktilɔskɔpik] *adj* dactyloscopic; **examen d.,** examination of fingerprints.
dada [dada] **1** *nm* **(a)** *Enf* gee-gee; **aller à d.,** to play gee-gees; **(b)** *F* pet subject; **c'est son nouveau d.,** it's his latest hobby-horse; **enfourcher son d.,** to get on to one's pet subject; **(c)** *Beaux-Arts* **le d.,** Dadaism. **2** *adj Beaux-Arts* Dadaist; **le mouvement d.,** Dadaism.
dadais [dadɛ] *nm F* silly *or* awkward boy; **un grand d.,** a gawky great boy.
dadaïsme [dadaism] *nm Beaux Arts Littér* Dadaism.
dadaïste [dadaist] *n Beaux-Arts Littér* Dadaist.
dague [dag] *nf* (*sword*) dagger.
daguerréotype [dagereɔtip] *nm Phot* daguerreotype.
dahlia [dalja] *nm* dahlia.
daigner [deɲe] *vt* to deign, to condescend; **le roi a daigné lui parler,** the king condescended to speak to him; **elle n'a même pas daigné me voir,** she wouldn't even see me.
daim [dɛ̃] *nm* (fallow) deer; (*mâle*) buck; **(peau de) d.,** suede; **gants/veste/***etc* **en d.,** suede gloves/jacket/*etc*.
daine [dɛn] *nf* doe.
dais [dɛ] *nm* canopy; **recouvert d'un d.,** canopied; *Fig* **un d. de feuilles,** a canopy of leaves.
dal [dal] *nm Arg* (*rien*) zilch.
dallage [dalaʒ] *nm* **(a)** paving (*with flags etc*); **(b)** (*ensemble de pavés*) pavement, flagging, flagstones; **d. en céramique,** tiled floor.
dalle [dal] *nf* **(a)** *Constr* flag(stone), paving stone; slab (*of marble etc*); **d. de moquette/linoléum,** carpet/lino tile; **d. funéraire,** ledger; **(b)** *Arg* **je n'y vois que d.,** I can't see a bloody thing; **je n'ai compris que d.,** I didn't understand a bloody thing; **(c)** *Arg* **avoir la d.,** to be starving.
daller [dale] *vt* to pave (*with flagstones etc*); to flag (*pavement etc*); to tile (*floor*).
dalleur [dalœr] *nm* flag layer, pavio(u)r.
dalmatien [dalmasjɛ̃] *nm* Dalmatian.
dalmatique [dalmatik] *nf* dalmatic.
dalot [dalo] *nm Nau* scupper (hole).
daltonien, -ienne [daltɔnjɛ̃, -jɛn] **1** *adj* colour- *or US* color-blind (*person*). **2** *n* colour-blind man *or* woman.
daltonisme [daltɔnism] *nm* colour *or US* color blindness.
dam [dam] *nm Vieilli* **(a) au grand d. de qn,** to the great displeasure of s.o.; **(b)** *Rel* **peine du d.,** eternal damnation.
damage [damaʒ] *nm* ramming, tamping (*of earth*).
damas [damas] *nm Tex* damask; **nappe en d.,** damask tablecloth.
damasquinage [damaskinaʒ] *nm* damascening.
damasquiner [damaskine] *vt* to inlay, to damascene (*blade etc*).
damassé [damase] **1** *adj* **(a)** *Tex* damask; **nappe damassée,** damask tablecloth; **(b) acier d.,** damask steel. **2** *nm Tex* damask.
damasser [damase] *vt Tex Métal* to damask.
dame¹ [dam] *nf* **(a)** (*femme*) lady, *pl* ladies; (*épouse*) married woman; (*cavalière*) (gentleman's) partner; *Arch* (noble) lady; **la première d. l'URSS,** the wife of the President of the USSR, *US* the USSR's First Lady; *F* **elle fait la grande d.,** she puts on airs, she's all lah-di-dah; **dames,** (*on public convenience*) ladies; **que prendront ces dames?,** what will you take, ladies?; *F* **et pour vous, ma petite d.?** what can I get you, dear?; **d. nature,** mother nature; *Jur* **la d. Simon,** Mrs Simon; **d. d'honneur,** lady-in-waiting; *Vieilli* maid of honour; **d. de compagnie,** lady's companion; **les dames de France,** the royal princesses of France;
(b) (*pièce*) (*at draughts*) = king; *Échecs Cartes* queen; (*at backgammon*) piece; **jeu de dames,** = (game of) draughts, *Am* checkers; **aller à d.,** (*at draughts*) to make a king; *Échecs* to queen (a pawn);
(c) *Constr etc* (paving) beetle; (earth) rammer;
(d) d. de nage, rowlock, *Am* oarlock;
(e) *Bot* **d. d'onze heures,** star of Bethlehem.
dame² *int* **d. oui!,** well, yes!, why, yes!, rather!; **vous y allez? — d.!,** are you going? — what else can I do?
dame³ *nf Constr* dam (*across section of canal under construction*); *Métal* dam (stone) (*of furnace*).
dame-jeanne [damʒan] *nf* demijohn; (*pl dames-jeannes*).
damer [dame] *vt* **(a)** (*at draughts*) to crown (*a piece*); *F* **d. le pion à qn,** to outdo s.o.; **(b)** *Constr* to ram, to tamp (*earth*).
damier [damje] *nm* draughtboard, *Am* checkerboard; **tissu en d.,** checked material.
damnable [danabl] *adj Rel* deserving of damnation.
damnation [danasjɔ̃] *nf* damnation; *F* **enfer et d.!,** damn and blast!, hell and damnation!
damné, -ée [dane] **1** *adj* damned; **elle est damnée de lui,** she would sell her soul to the devil for him; **être l'âme damnée de qn,** to be a mere tool in s.o.'s hands. **2** *n* damned soul; **souffrir comme un d.,** to go through hell.
damner [dane] **1** *vt* to damn; *F* **faire d. qn,** to drive s.o. crazy. **2 se damner** *vpr* to incur damnation; **il s'est damné pour elle,** he would sell his soul to the devil for her.
Damoclès [damɔklɛs] *nm* **l'épée de D.,** the sword of Damocles.
dan [dɑ̃] *nm Sp* dan; **il est quatrième d.,** he is a fourth dan.
dancing [dɑ̃siŋ] *nm* dance hall.
dandinement [dɑ̃dinmɑ̃] *nm* rolling gait, waddle.
dandiner [dɑ̃dine] **1** *vt* to dandle (*baby*). **2 se dandiner** *vpr* to have a rolling gait, to waddle.
dandy [dɑ̃di] *nm* dandy; (*pl dandys*).
Danemark [danmark] *nm* Denmark.
danger [dɑ̃ʒe] *nm* danger, peril; (*cause de danger*) hazard; **à l'abri du d.,** out of danger; **courir un d.,** to be in danger; **il n'y a pas de d.,** it's quite safe; **mettre en d. la vie de qn,** to endanger s.o.'s life; **en d. de mort,** in mortal danger; **avec cette voiture, tu es un véritable d. public,** you're a proper public menace with that car; *Méd* **hors de d.,** out of danger, off the danger list; *F* **pas de d.!,** no fear!, not likely!; **il n'y a pas de d. qu'il revienne,** there's no danger of his coming back, he's unlikely to come back.
dangereusement [dɑ̃ʒrøzmɑ̃] *adv* dangerously; **il est d. blessé,** he is seriously injured; **vivre d.,** to live dangerously.
dangereux, -euse [dɑ̃ʒrø, -øz] *adj* dangerous (**pour,** to, for); *Mil* **zone dangereuse,** danger zone.
dangérosité [dɑ̃ʒerɔzite] *nf* dangerousness.
danois, -oise [danwa, -waz] **1** *adj* Danish. **2** *nm Ling* Danish. **3** *n* **(a) D.,** Dane; **(b) Grand D.,** (*chien*) Great Dane.
dans [dɑ̃] *prép* **(a)** (*à l'intérieur de*) in; **d. une boîte,** in(side) a box; **il est d. sa chambre,** he's in his room; **qu'est-ce que vous avez d. la main?,** what have you (got)

in your hand?; **il habite d. Paris même,** he lives (right) in Paris; **lire qch d. un journal,** to read sth in the newspaper; **d. un rayon de dix kilomètres,** within a radius of ten kilometres;

(b) (*avec mouvement*) into; **mettre qch d. une boîte,** to put sth in(to) a box; **il est entré d. leur chambre,** he went into their room; **tomber d. l'oubli,** to sink into oblivion;

(c) prendre qch d. qch, to take sth out of sth; **boire d. un verre,** to drink out of a glass; **copier qch d. un livre,** to copy sth out of *or* from a book; **découper un article d. le journal,** to cut an article out of the paper; *Culin* **un morceau d. la poitrine,** a cut off the breast;

(d) (*de temps*) in, within, during; **d. l'après-midi,** in *or* during the afternoon; **d. le temps,** long ago; **il l'a rencontrée d. le temps,** he met her a long time ago; **payer d. les dix jours,** to pay within ten days; **je serai prêt à partir d. cinq minutes,** I shall be ready to leave in five minutes;

(e) (*environ*) **il a d. les quarante ans,** he's about forty; **cela coûte d. les dix francs,** it costs about ten francs;

(f) être d. le commerce/le bâtiment/l'informatique, to be in trade/construction/computers;

(g) d. les circonstances, in *or* under the circumstances; **d. ce cas, faisons autrement,** in that case, let's do something else; **d. ce but,** with this aim in view; **d. l'espoir de,** in the hope of.

dansant [dɑ̃sɑ̃] *adj* **(a)** (*qui danse*) dancing; **pas d.,** springy step; **(b)** (*où l'on danse*) **thé d.,** tea dance; **donner une soirée dansante,** to give a dance; **(c)** lively (*tune*).

danse [dɑ̃s] *nf* dance, dancing; (*musique*) dance tune; **d. du ventre,** belly dance; **elle aime la d.,** she's fond of dancing; *Méd* **d. de Saint-Guy,** St Vitus's dance; **ouvrir la d.,** to open the ball; *F* **entrer en d.,** to join in (sth); *F* **donner une d. à qn,** to tell s.o. off.

danser [dɑ̃se] **1** *vi* **(a)** to dance; **faire d. qn,** to dance with s.o.; *F* to lead s.o. a dance; *Fig* **ne savoir sur quel pied d.,** to be all at sea; **le bouchon/le bateau danse sur l'eau,** the cork/the boat is bobbing up and down on the water; **(b)** (*of horse*) to prance. **2** *vt* to dance; **d. une valse,** to dance a waltz. **3 se danser** *vpr* (*d'une danse*) to be danced; **c'est un disque qui se danse,** it's a record you can dance to.

danseur, -euse [dɑ̃sœr, -øz] *n* **(a)** dancer, *surtout* ballet dancer, *f* ballerina; **danseuse de cabaret,** cabaret dancer; **d. de corde,** tightrope walker; **pédaler en danseuse,** to stand up on the pedals; **(b)** partner (*at dance*).

dantesque [dɑ̃tɛsk] *adj* Dantean, Dantesque; **vision d.,** Dantean *or* Dantesque vision; *F* **effort d.,** gigantic effort.

Danube [danyb] *nm* (the river) Danube.

danubien, -ienne [danybjɛ̃, -jɛn] *adj* Danubian.

dard [dar] *nm* **(a)** sting (*of insect*); forked tongue (*of snake*); tongue (*of flame*); **(b)** *Pêche* spear, harpoon.

darder [darde] *vt* **(a)** (*lancer*) to hurl (*pointed object*); *Fig* **il a dardé sur moi un regard chargé de haine,** he shot *or* flashed a glance of hatred at me; **(b)** to spear, to harpoon (*fish etc*).

dardillon [dardijɔ̃] *nm* **(a)** small dart; **(b)** barb (*of fish hook*).

dare-dare [dardar] *adv F* double-quick; **accourir d.-d.,** to come charging up.

darne [darn] *nf Culin* slice, steak (*of fish*).

darse [dars] *nf* harbour, wet dock (*in Mediterranean*).

dartre [dartr] *nf Méd* scurf.

dartreux, -euse [dartrø, -øz] *adj Méd* scabby.

darwinien, -ienne [darwinjɛ̃, jɛn] *adj* Darwinian.

darwinisme [darwinism] *nm* Darwinism.

darwiniste [darwinist] *adj & n* Darwinist, Darwinian.

datation [datasjɔ̃] *nf* dating.

date [dat] *nf* date; **mettre la d. à une lettre,** to date a letter; **sans d.,** undated (*letter etc*); **erreur de d.,** mistake in the date; **la lettre porte la d. du 5 mai,** the letter is dated (the) 5th May; **prendre d. pour qch,** to fix a date for sth; **faire d.,** (*of event*) to mark an epoch *or* era; **un événement qui a fait d.,** a momentous event; **être le premier en d.,** to come first; **amitié de fraîche/de vieille** *ou* **de longue d.,** recent/long-standing friendship; **je la connais de longue d.,** I have known her for a long time; **à cette d.,** at that time; **à cette d. j'étais déjà parti,** I'd already left by then; *Com* **en d. du 15 courant,** dated (the) 15th inst.; **à trente jours de d.,** thirty days after date; **d. limite,** deadline; **d. limite d'utilisation/de vente,** use-/sell-by date; *Fin* **emprunt à longue/à courte d.,** long-/short-dated loan.

dater [date] **1** *vt* to date (*letter etc*); **lettre datée du 20,** letter dated the 20th; **non daté,** undated. **2** *vi* to date (**de,** from); **à d. de ce jour,** from today; **à d. du 15,** on and after (the) 15th; **de quand date votre dernier repas?,** when did you last eat?; **événement qui date,** memorable event; **robe qui date,** old-fashioned dress; **cette mode commence à d.,** this fashion is becoming dated.

dateur [datœr] **1** *adj* date (*indicator etc*); **timbre d.,** date stamp. **2** *nm* date marker, date stamp.

datif [datif] *nm Gram* dative (case); **au d.,** in the dative.

datte [dat] *nf* date; **d. fourrée,** stuffed date.

dattier [datje] *nm* date palm, date tree.

daube [dob] *nf Culin* = meat, poultry etc braised in wine and stock with vegetables; **bœuf en d.,** braised beef.

dauber [dobe] *vt* **(a)** *Culin* to braise (*beef*); **(b)** *Arch & Litt* to make fun of (*s.o.*).

daubière [dobjɛr] *nf Culin* = earthenware pot for braising.

dauphin [dofɛ̃] *nm* **(a)** (*mammifère*) dolphin; **(b)** *Hist* Dauphin; *Fig* heir apparent (*to important position*); **(c)** shoe (*of drainpipe*).

dauphine [dofin] *nf Fr Hist* Dauphiness.

Dauphiné [dofine] *nm* Dauphiné.

dauphinois, -oise [dofinwa, -waz] **1** *adj* of *or* belonging to the Dauphiné; *Culin* **gratin d.,** = sliced potatoes baked with cream and browned on top. **2** *n* **D.,** inhabitant of the Dauphiné.

daurade [dorad] *nf* sea bream; **d. (royale),** gilthead (bream).

davantage [davɑ̃taʒ] *adv* more; **il m'en faut d.,** I need still more; **je n'en dis pas d.,** I shall say no more; **je ne l'interrogerai pas d.,** I won't question him any further; **vous êtes riche, mais il l'est d.,** you're rich, but he's richer; **nous ne resterons pas d.,** we won't stay any longer; **se baisser d.,** to stoop lower; **chaque jour d.,** more and more every day; **elle en a d. que lui,** she's got more than him *or* he (has).

davier [davje] *nm* **(a)** *Menuis* cramp; **(b)** *Nau* bow sheave; **(c)** (*de dentiste*) forceps.

dazibao [dazəbao] *nm* dazibao.

D.C.A. [desea] *nf Mil* (*abrév* **Défense contre avions**) AA.

D.D.A.S.S. [das] *nf Admin* (*abrév* **Direction départementale de l'action sanitaire et sociale**) = local social work department, one of whose tasks is to deal with children who have been abandoned or ill-treated.

D.D.T. [dedete] *nm Ch* (*abrév* **Dichloro-Diphényl-Trichloréthane**) DDT.

de [də] (*before vowels and h mute* **d'**; **de + le, les** *are contracted into* **du, des**) **1** *prép* **(a)** (*origin*) from; **il vient de Paris,** he comes from Paris; **apprendre qch de source sûre,** to hear sth from a reliable source; **l'idée est de vous,** the idea is yours *or* comes from you; **je l'ai oublié? c'est bien de moi,** did I forget it? that's just like me; **du matin au soir,** from morning till night; **de là à dire oui ...,** as for saying yes ...; **de vous à moi ...,** between ourselves ...; **calme de nature,** calm by nature; **de vingt à trente personnes,** between twenty and thirty people; **serrurier de père en fils,** locksmiths from father to son; **de jour en jour,** from day to day;

(b) (*time vaguely indicated*) **il est parti de nuit,** he left by night; **du temps de nos pères,** in our fathers' day;

(c) (*agent, means, instrument*) **accompagné de ses amis,** accompanied by his friends; **la statue est de Rodin,** the statue is by Rodin; **il est détesté de tout le monde,** everybody hates him; **apprécié de connaisseurs,** appreciated by connoisseurs; **j'ai fait cela de ma propre main,** it's all my own work;

(d) (*manner*) **il m'a regardé d'un air amusé,** he looked at me with an amused expression; **répondre d'une voix douce,** to answer in a gentle voice;

(e) (*cause*) **sauter de joie,** to leap for joy; **je tombe de fatigue,** I'm so tired, I'm ready to drop; **faire qch de soi-même,** to do sth of one's own accord;

(f) (*measure*) **âgé de seize ans,** sixteen years old; **ma montre retarde de dix minutes,** my watch is ten minutes slow; **il est plus grand que moi de la tête,** he's a head taller than I am; **une pièce de 20 centimes,** a 20-centime piece; **la terrasse a vingt mètres de long** *ou* **est longue de vingt mètres,** the terrace is twenty metres long; **un chèque de 100 francs,** a cheque for 100 francs;

(g) (*introducing complement of adj*) **digne d'éloges,** worthy of praise, praiseworthy; **altéré de sang,** thirsting for blood; **large de bassin,** wide-hipped;

(h) (*ownership*) **le livre de Pierre,** Peter's book; **le toit de la maison,** the roof of the house; **le meilleur élève de la classe,** the best pupil in the class; **les rues de Paris,** the streets of Paris; **la conférence de Berlin,** the Berlin conference; **la chambre du second,** the room on the second *or Am* third floor; **un hôtel de la rive gauche,** a hotel on the left bank; **scène de rivière hollandaise,** scene on a Dutch river;

(i) (*material*) **un pont de fer,** an iron bridge; **une robe de soie,** a silk dress;

(j) (*distinguishing mark*) **le chien de berger,** the sheepdog; **le chien du berger,** the shepherd's dog; **conflit de générations,** clash of generations; **le journal d'hier,** yesterday's paper; **à quatre heures de l'après-midi,** at four (o'clock) in the afternoon; **son devoir de père,** his duties as a father; **un don de voyance,** a gift of second sight; **la route de Paris,** the Paris road; **le professeur de français,** the French teacher; **une crème de beauté,** a beauty cream; **un conseil d'ami,** friendly advice;

(k) (*partitive*) **un verre de vin,** a glass of wine; **une livre de café,** a pound of coffee; **quelque chose de bon,** something good; **je n'ai pas de sœurs,** I haven't any sisters; **la moitié de ses économies,** half of his savings; **je ne l'ai pas vu de la soirée,** I haven't seen him all evening;

(l) (*forming compound prepositions*) **près de la maison,** near the house; **autour du jardin,** round the garden; **à partir de ce jour-là,** from that day (onward);

(m) (*connecting verb and object*) **nous approchons de Paris,** we're getting near *or* approaching Paris; **j'ai changé d'avis,** I've changed my mind; **manquer de courage,** to lack courage; **convenir d'une erreur,** to admit an error;

(n) (*serving as a link word introducing an infinitive*) **il est honteux de mentir,** it is shameful to lie; **le mieux était de rire,** it was best to laugh; **je crains d'être en retard,** I'm afraid of being late; **j'aime mieux attendre que de me faire mouiller,** I would rather wait than get wet;

(o) (*introducing an apposition or a predicative complement*) **la ville de Paris,** the city of Paris; **on l'a traité de lâche,** he was called a coward; **un drôle de type,** a funny chap; **il y eut trois hommes de tués,** three men were killed; **c'est un grand pas de fait,** that's a great step forward; *F* **la robe est d'un réussi!,** the dress is perfect!;

(p) *Litt* **la musique commença et les enfants de danser,** the music began, and the children started to dance.

2 *article partitif* (*used also as pl of* **un, une**) **n'avez-vous pas d'amis?,** haven't you got any friends?, don't you have any friends?; **sans faire de fautes,** without making any mistakes; **je ne veux pas qu'on lui mette de collier,** I won't have a collar put on him; **de grands artistes se trouvaient là,** there were some distinguished artists there; **elle ne mange plus de viande,** she no longer eats meat; **faire de la musique,** to make music; **c'est du Bach, n'est-ce pas?,** it's Bach, isn't it?; **je bois de l'eau,** (*toujours*) I drink water; (*maintenant*) I am drinking water; **donnez nous de vos nouvelles,** let's hear from you; **avez-vous du pain?,** have you any bread?; **donnez-moi de ce vin,** give me some of that wine; **donnez-moi du bon vin,** give me some good wine; **manger de tous les plats,** to have something of everything; *Iron* **elle en a des problèmes!,** she hasn't half got problems!; **mettre des heures à faire qch,** to spend hours over sth.

dé¹ [de] *nm* **(a)** (*pour jouer*) die, *plus souvent* dice, *pl* dice; **jeter les dés,** to throw the dice; **les dés sont pipés,** the dice are loaded; **coup de dé,** throw of the die *or* dice; **les dés sont jetés,** the die is cast; *Culin* **couper en dés,** to dice (*vegetables etc*); **(b)** *Archit* dado, die (*of pedestal etc*); **(c)** *MecE* bearing (bush), brass.

dé² *nm* **dé (à coudre),** thimble.

déambulation [deɑ̃bylasjɔ̃] *nf* strolling, walking around (*aimlessly*).

déambulateur [deɑ̃bylatœr] *nm* zimmer ®.

déambulatoire [deɑ̃bylatwar] *nm Archit* ambulatory.

déambuler [deɑ̃byle] *vi* to stroll (about), to walk up and down, to saunter.

débâcle [debɑkl] *nf* **(a)** debacle; downfall, collapse (*of business etc*); *Fin* crash; *Mil etc* debacle, rout; **d. de la santé,** breakdown in health; **(b)** break(ing) up (*of drift ice*).

débâcler [debɑkle] *vi* (*of ice*) to break up.

débâillonner [debɑjɔne] *vt Fig* to ungag, to unmuzzle (*the press*).

déballage [debalaʒ] *nm* **(a)** (*action*) unpacking; **(b) (vente au) d.,** pavement selling; **(c)** *F* (*aveu*) confession, outpouring.

déballer [debale] *vt* **(a)** to unpack (*goods, cases*); **(b)** *F* to disclose (*a secret etc*); to confess to (*the truth*).

débandade [debɑ̃dad] *nf* rout (*of army etc*); stampede (*of horses etc*); **à la d.,** in confusion, helter-skelter; **tout va à la d.,** everything's in a mess.

débander¹ [debɑ̃de] **1** *vt* **(a)** to relax (*sth under tension*); to unbend (*bow*); to unbrace (*drum*); to let down (*spring*); **(b)** (*enlever le bandage de*) to remove a bandage from, to unbandage, to unbind (*wound*). **2** *vi* to lose one's erection; *F* **travailler sans d.,** to work non-stop.

débander² **1** *vt* to disband (*troops, crew*). **2 se débander** *vpr* (*of crowd etc*) to disperse; *Mil etc* to scatter.

débaptiser [debatize] *vt* to change the name of, to rename (*person, street etc*).

débarbouillage [debarbujaʒ] *nm* face wash.

débarbouiller [debarbuje] **1** *vt* to wash (*s.o.'s*) face. **2 se débarbouiller** *vpr* to wash one's face.

débarbouillette [debarbujɛt] *nf Can* (face) flannel, face cloth, *Am* washrag.

débarcadère [debarkadɛr] *nm Nau* landing stage, wharf.

débardage [debardaʒ] *nm* unloading, unlading (*of timber etc*).

débarder [debarde] *vt* **(a)** *Nau* to unload, to discharge (*timber etc*); **(b)** to convey (*lumber, quarried stone*) to the railhead.

débardeur [debardœr] *nm* **(a)** (*tricot*) tank top; **(b)** (*personne*) docker, stevedore, *Am* longshoreman.

débarqué, -ée [debarke] **1** *adj* landed. **2** *n* newly-landed person. **3** *nm* **au d.,** immediately on landing *or* on disembarkation.

débarquement [debarkəmɑ̃] *nm* **(a)** unloading, discharge (*of cargo*); landing, disembarkation (*of passengers*); **carte de d.,** landing card; **quai de d.,** arrival platform; **(b)** *Mil* detraining; *Nau* disembarkation; *Mil Nau* landing; **troupes de d.,** landing force; **d. sur plage,** beach landing; *Hist* **le d. des alliés en Normandie,** the allied landings in Normandy; **(c)** *Nau* paying off, discharge (*of crew*).

débarquer [debarke] **1** *vt* **(a)** to unship, to unload, to discharge (*cargo*); to disembark, to land (*passengers*); to drop (*ship's pilot*); (*of bus*) to set down (*passengers*); **(b)** to pay off, to discharge (*crew*); *F* **d. qn,** to give s.o. the sack. **2** *vi* to land, to disembark (*from boat*); *surtout Can* to get off, to alight (*from train, bus*); *Mil* to detrain; *F* **elle a débarqué hier soir,** she turned up last night; *F* **tu débarques!,** where have you been?

débarras [debara] *nm* **(a) bon d.!,** good riddance!; **(b)** (*endroit*) boxroom, *F* glory hole.

débarrasser [debarase] **1** *vt* to clear (*table etc*); **d. qn de qch,** to relieve s.o. of sth; **d. qn de qn,** to take s.o. off s.o.'s hands; (*le tuer*) to get rid of s.o. for s.o.; *F* **d. le plancher,** to clear out. **2 se débarrasser** *vpr* **se d. de qch/qn,** to get rid of sth/s.o.; **se d. d'une situation difficile,** to extricate oneself from a difficult situation; **ils ont fini par se d. de ce témoin,** in the end they got rid of the witness.

débarrer [debare] *vt* to unbar (*door etc*).

débat [deba] *nm* **(a)** (*organisé*) debate; *Pol* **débats,** (parliamentary) debates, proceedings; **organiser un d.,** to organize a debate; **d. télévisé,** televised debate; **(b)** (*polémique*) dispute; **trancher un d.,** to settle a dispute; **être en d. sur une question,** to be at odds on a matter *or* question; **un d. intérieur,** an inner conflict *or* struggle.

débâtir [debatir] *vt* to remove the tacks from (*garment*).

débattement [debatmɑ̃] *nm Aut etc* clearance.

débattre [debatr] *v* (*conj like* **battre**) **1** *vt* (*discuter*) to debate, to discuss; **prix à d.,** price by arrangement; **d. les conditions d'un contrat,** to negotiate the conditions of a contract; **je n'ai pas débattu le prix,** I didn't haggle about the price. **2 se débattre** *vpr* to struggle; **se d. dans l'eau,** to flounder, to splash (about) in the water; **se d. comme un forcené,** to struggle like a madman; **se d. contre des agresseurs,** to defend oneself against attackers; **se d. contre une difficulté,** to struggle with a problem.

débauchage [deboʃaʒ] *nm* laying off (*of workmen*).

débauche [deboʃ] *nf* debauchery; **il vit dans la d.,** he lives a life of debauchery; **lieu de d.,** den of vice; *Jur* **excitation des mineurs à la d.,** incitement of minors to vice; *Fig* **se livrer à des débauches d'imagination,** to let one's imagination run riot; **le décor de cette pièce est une d. d'imagination,** the set is extremely imaginative.

débauché, -ée [deboʃe] **1** *adj* debauched, profligate. **2** *n* libertine, rake; *f* debauched woman.

débaucher [deboʃe] **1** *vt* (*au sens moral*) to lead (*s.o.*) astray; **d. un ouvrier,** to induce a worker to strike; (*du patron*) to make a worker redundant, to lay a worker off; **d. la jeunesse,** to corrupt the young; *F* **est-ce que je peux te d. et t'inviter au cinéma/restaurant/***etc***?,** can I tempt you with a film/dinner/*etc*?; *F* **c'est lui qui m'a débauché hier soir,** (*il m'a emmené au cinéma etc*) he led me astray last night. **2 se débaucher** *vpr* to become corrupted; *F* **arrête de travailler et débauche-toi un peu,** stop working for a minute and enjoy yourself.

débaucheur [deboʃœr] *nm* corrupter.
débecter [debɛkte] *vt Arg* to turn (*s.o.'s*) stomach, to sicken (*s.o.*); **ça me débecte,** it turns my stomach, it's sickening.
débet [debɛ] *nm Fin* balance due.
débile [debil] **1** *adj* **(a)** sickly (*child*); weak, feeble (*body*); poor (*health*); **avoir une volonté d.,** to be weak-willed; **(b)** *F* stupid, idiotic; **il est complètement d.,** he's a complete idiot. **2** *n* **un(e) d. (mental(e)),** a mental defective.
débilitant [debilitɑ̃] *adj* debilitating, weakening; *Fig* demoralizing; **remède d.,** debilitant; **des occupations débilitantes,** tiring occupations.
débilité [debilite] *nf* debility, weakness; **d. mentale,** mental deficiency.
débiliter [debilite] *vt* to debilitate, to weaken.
débinage [debinaʒ] *nm F* knocking, running down.
débine [debin] *nf F* poverty; **être dans la d.,** to be (stony) broke.
débiner [debine] *F* **1** *vt* to knock (*s.o.*), to run (*s.o.*) down. **2 se débiner** *vpr* to scram, to clear off.
débineur, -euse [debinœr, -øz] *n F* knocker.
débit¹ [debi] *nm* **(a) d. de tabac,** tocacconist's (shop); **d. de boissons,** bar, *F* ≈ pub; **(b)** (*écoulement*) (retail) sale; **marchandises de bon d.,** marketable *or* saleable goods; **(c)** cutting up (*of logs, meat etc*); **(d)** discharge, delivery (*of pump etc*); flow (*of river, tap etc*); rate (*of traffic flow*); *Ind* output; *El* power supplied; **(e)** delivery (*of orator*); **avoir le d. facile,** to have the gift of the gab, to have a glib tongue.
débit² *nm Com* debit; **porter 1 000 francs au d. de qn,** to debit s.o. with 1,000 francs.
débitable [debitabl] *adj* **(a)** (*bois etc*) that can be cut up; **(b)** (*compte*) that can be drawn on.
débitant, -ante [debitɑ̃, -ɑ̃t] *n* **(a) d. de tabac,** tobacconist; **(b)** *Vieilli* retailer.
débiter¹ [debite] *vt* **(a)** to sell (*goods*) retail; **(b)** to cut up, to convert (*timber*); to cut up (*meat*); **(c)** to discharge, to yield (*so many litres an hour etc*); *Ind* to produce; **les ascenseurs de la tour débitent 500 personnes par heure,** the lifts in the tower handle 500 people per hour; **cette usine débite 250 voitures par jour,** the output from this factory is 250 cars a day; **(d)** *Th* to recite (*one's part*); *F Péj* **d. une longue harangue,** to make a long speech; **d. des sottises,** to talk rubbish.
débiter² *vt Com* to debit; **d. une somme à qn, d. qn d'une somme,** to debit s.o. with an amount.
débiteur¹, -euse [debitœr, -øz] *n* **(a)** *Péj Vieilli* person who holds forth *or* talks rubbish; **d. de calomnies,** scandalmonger; **(b)** *MecE* feeding device; **(c)** shop assistant (*who takes customers to cash desk*).
débiteur², -trice [debitœr, -tris] **1** *n* debtor; *Fig* **je suis votre d. éternel,** I will be eternally indebted to you. **2** *adj* **(a) compte d.,** debit account; **(b)** *Cin* **bobine débitrice,** top spool, delivery spool.
débitmètre [debimɛtr] *nm Tech* flowmeter.
déblai [deblɛ] *nm Constr Rail etc* **(a)** excavation, cut(ting); **route en d.,** sunk road; **(b) déblais,** spoil earth.
déblaiement [deblɛmɑ̃] *nm* clearing (*of ground etc*).
déblatérer [deblatere] *v* (**je déblatère; je déblatérerai**) **1** *vt* **d. des sottises,** to talk nonsense; **d. des injures,** to fling abuse (**contre,** at). **2** *vi* **d. contre qn/qch,** to rail against s.o./sth.
déblayage [deblɛjaʒ] *nm* clearance; **le d. d'une chambre,** the clearing out of a room.
déblayer [debleje] *vt* (**je déblaye, je déblaie**) **(a)** to clear away, to remove (*spoil earth etc*); **d. la neige,** to shovel away the snow; **(b) d. un terrain,** to clear a piece of ground; *Fig* to clear the ground *or* the way (*for negotiations etc*).
déblocage [deblɔkaʒ] *nm* freeing, releasing; *Fin* unfreezing (*of prices etc*); *Psy* **le d. d'inhibitions/de complexes,** getting rid of inhibitions/complexes.
débloquer [deblɔke] **1** *vt* **(a)** (*libérer, mettre en marche*) to free, to release; *Fin* to unfreeze (*prices etc*); **(b)** to unjam (*machine*); **(c)** *Mil* to raise the blockade of (*town*). **2** *vi F* to be off one's rocker; **son grand-père est vieux, il commence à d.,** his grandfather is old and going gaga.
débobiner [debɔbine] *vt El* to unwind (*coil*).
déboguer [debɔge] *vt Ordinat* to debug.
débogueur [debɔgœr] *nm Ordinat* debugger.
déboire [debwar] *nm* disappointment; **essuyer bien des déboires,** to suffer many disappointments *or* setbacks.
déboisement [debwazmɑ̃] *nm* deforestation.
déboiser [debwaze] *vt* to deforest, to clear (*land*).
déboîtement [debwatmɑ̃] *nm* dislocation (*of limb etc*).
déboîter [debwate] **1** *vt* **(a)** to disconnect, to uncouple (*pipe etc*); **(b)** to dislocate (*joint*); **(c)** to remove (*watch etc*) from its case. **2** *vi* **(a)** *Mil* to break out of column; **(b)** *Aut* to filter. **3 se déboîter** *vpr* (*of ankle etc*) to become dislocated; **se d. l'épaule,** to put one's shoulder out; **se d. le genou,** to twist one's knee.
débonder [debɔ̃de] **1** *vt* to unbung (*cask*); to open the sluice gates of (*reservoir*); *Fig* **d. son cœur,** to pour out one's heart. **2** *vi* (*of liquid*) to gush out, to spill out.
débonnaire [debɔnɛr] *adj* goodnatured, easy-going.
débordant [debɔrdɑ̃] *adj* **(a)** (*expansif*) overflowing, brimming over (**de,** with); **d. de santé,** bursting with health; **avoir une imagination débordante,** to be brimful of imagination; **(b)** (*qui dépasse*) projecting, protruding; (*en se chevauchant*) overlapping.
débordé [debɔrde] *adj* **(a)** overflowing (*river etc*); **(b)** unable to keep pace, snowed under (*with work etc*); **elle est toujours débordée,** she's always snowed under; **(c) drap d.,** (*pour préparer le lit*) turned-back sheet; (*défait*) untucked sheet; **mon lit est d.,** my sheets have come untucked.
débordement [debɔrdəmɑ̃] *nm* **(a)** overflowing (*of river etc*); **d. d'injures,** outburst of abuse; **(b) débordements,** excesses, dissipation, dissolute living; **(c)** *Mil* outflanking (*of enemy*).
déborder [debɔrde] **1** *vi* (*du contenu d'un verre etc*) to overflow, to brim over, to run over; **verre plein à d.,** glass full to overflowing *or* to the brim; **la rivière a débordé,** the river has overflowed its banks; **elle déborde de vie,** she is bubbling over with *or* brimful of vitality; **d. d'imagination,** to be brimful of imagination; **c'est la goutte d'eau qui fait d. le vase,** it's the last straw; **son cœur déborde de reconnaissance,** his heart is brimming over with gratitude; **s'il continue à m'ennuyer, il va me faire d.,** if he keeps on annoying me, he'll make me boil over; **d. son adversaire,** (*dans une course*) to overtake one's competitor.
2 *vt* **(a)** (*dépasser*) to project, to jut out, to stick out, to protrude, to extend beyond (*sth*); to overlap (*sth*); *Mil* to outflank (*the enemy*); **cela déborde le cadre de notre débat/de mes responsabilités,** that goes beyond the ambit of our discussion/beyond my remit;
(b) d. les avirons, to unship the oars; **d. (les couvertures d')un lit,** to untuck a bed; *Nau* **d. une embarcation,** to shove off, to sheer off;
(c) (*enlever les bords de*) to remove the edging from (*sth*); **d. une tôle,** to trim the edges of an iron plate.
débotté [debɔte] *nm* **au d.,** immediately on arrival.
débotter [debɔte] **1** *vt* to take off (*s.o.'s*) boots. **2 se débotter** *vpr* to take off one's boots.
débouchage [debuʃaʒ] *nm* **(a)** unblocking (*of pipe*); uncorking (*of bottle*); **(b)** *Mil* setting (*of time fuse*).
débouché [debuʃe] *nm* **(a)** opening (*of passage etc*); entrance (*of valley*); exit (*from building etc*); inlet (*into pond*); **(b)** (*possibilité*) opening, opportunity; *Com* outlet; **quels débouchés y a-t-il pour lui?,** what (career) prospects has he (got)?; **cette formation n'offre aucun d.,** the training does not lead to any career openings.
déboucher¹ [debuʃe] **1** *vt* **(a)** to clear (*blocked pipe etc*); **(b)** to uncork (*bottle*); **(c)** *Mil* to set (*time fuse*). **2 se déboucher** *vpr* **il faut que tu te débouches les oreilles,** you'll have to listen more carefully.
déboucher² *vi* to emerge, to come out; **cette rue débouche sur la place,** this street runs into the square; **voilà sur quoi débouche la guerre,** that's what war leads to.
déboucheur [debuʃœr] *nm* drain clearer.
débouchoir [debuʃwar] *nm* **(a)** (*pour les sanitaires*) rubber plunger; **(b)** *Tech* clearing iron.
déboucler [debukle] *vt* **(a)** to unbuckle (*belt etc*); **(b)** to take the curl out of, to uncurl (*hair*).
déboulé [debule] *nm* **(a)** (*danse*) déboulé; **(b) tirer un lapin au d.,** to shoot a rabbit as it bolts from cover.
débouler [debule] **1** *vi* **(a)** (*tomber*) to fall head over heels; **(b)** (*of game*) to start, to bolt (from cover). **2** *vt* **d. l'escalier,** to roll downstairs.
déboulonnage [debulɔnaʒ] *nm*, **déboulonnement** [debulɔnmɑ̃] *nm* **(a)** *Tech* unriveting, unbolting; **(b)** *Fig* debunking.
déboulonner [debulɔne] *vt* **(a)** *Tech* to unrivet, to unbolt; **(b)** *Fig* to debunk (*s.o.*); (*de son poste*) to get rid of s.o., to kick s.o. out.
débourbage [deburbaʒ] *nm* clearing out (*of mud*).
débourber [deburbe] *vt* **(a)** to cleanse, to clear (*of mud*); to clean out (*cistern*); **d. le vin,** to draw off *or* decant wine; **(b)** to haul (*car etc*) out of the mud.
débourrage [deburaʒ] *nm* removal of stuffing (*from armchair, sofa etc*).

débourrer [debure] **1** *vt* to remove the stuffing from (*armchair, sofa etc*). **2** *vi* (*of armchair etc*) to lose its stuffing.

débours [debur] *nm* expenses; paying *or* laying out, disbursement (*of money*); **faire des d.,** to lay out money.

déboursement [debursəmɑ̃] *nm* paying out, disbursement.

débourser [deburse] *vt* to spend, to lay out (*money*); **sans rien d.,** without spending a penny; **je suis toujours à d.,** I'm always dipping my hand into my pocket.

déboussolant [debusɔlɑ̃] *adj* upsetting (*news*).

déboussoler [debusɔle] *vt F* to disorientate, *surtout Am* to disorient; **cette nouvelle l'a complètement déboussolé,** the news completely threw him.

debout [dəbu] **1** *adv* **(a)** (*chose*) upright, on end; (*personne*) standing; **mettre** *ou* **dresser qch d.,** to stand sth up *or* on end; **mettre les bouteilles d.,** to stand the bottles up(right); **tenir d.,** to be (standing) upright; **c'est si bas qu'on ne peut tenir d.,** it's so low that you can't stand up straight; **argument qui ne tient pas d.,** argument that won't hold water *or* won't stand up; **cette pratique tient encore d.,** the practice still persists; **se tenir d.,** to stand; **se tenir d. (sur ses pattes arrières),** (*de chien*) to stand on its hind legs; **elle est d. toute la journée,** she's on her feet all day; **se (re)mettre d.,** to stand up; **rester d.,** to remain standing; **places d. seulement,** standing room only; **conte à dormir d.,** silly *or* extravagant *or F* cock and bull story; **cent ans plus tard, la maison est encore d.,** the house is still standing a hundred years later; *Sp* **record encore d.,** unbeaten record; **son record est encore d.,** his record still stands *or* is still unbeaten; **être d.,** to be up; **tous les matins je suis d. à six heures,** I'm up *or* I get up at six o'clock every morning; **allons, d.!,** (*hors du lit*) come on, get up!; **il va mieux, il est déjà d.,** he's better, he's already up;
(b) *Nau* **d. à la mer** *ou* **à la lame/au vent,** head on to the sea/to the wind.
2 *adj m* **(a)** *Jur* **magistrature d.,** = public prosecutors; **(b)** *Nau* **vent d.,** head wind.

débouté [debute] *nm*, **déboutement** [debutmɑ̃] *nm Jur* nonsuit.

débouter [debute] *vt Jur* to dismiss (a *suit*); **d. qn (de sa demande, de sa plainte),** to nonsuit s.o.

déboutonner [debutɔne] **1** *vt* to unbutton; **rire à ventre déboutonné,** to split one's sides laughing. **2 se déboutonner** *vpr* (*pour se déshabiller*) to unbutton oneself; *Fig* (*se confier*) to get sth off one's chest.

débraillé [debraje] **1** *adj* untidy, slovenly (*person*); **tenue débraillée,** untidy *or* sloppy appearance; **manières débraillées,** bad manners. **2** *nm* untidiness, slovenliness.

débrailler (se) [sədebraje] *vpr F* to loosen one's clothing; *Fig* **l'atmosphère se débraille,** things are getting a bit too relaxed.

débrancher [debrɑ̃ʃe] *vt Él etc* to disconnect, to unplug (*iron etc*).

débrayage [debrɛjaʒ] *nm* **(a)** *Aut MecE* declutching, throwing out of gear; **(b)** *F* (*grève*) downing tools; (*à la fin de la journée*) downing tools, knocking off.

débrayer [debrɛje] *v* (**je débraye, je débraie**) **1** *vt MecE* to throw (*a part*) out of gear. **2** *vi* **(a)** *Aut* to release the clutch; **(b)** *F* (*se mettre en grève*) to down tools; (*à la fin de la journée*) to down tools, to knock off.

débridé [debride] *adj* unbridled (*tongue etc*).

débridement [debridmɑ̃] *nm* **(a)** unbridling (*of horse*); **(b)** *Chir* slitting up (*of adhesion etc*); lancing (*of boil*).

débrider [debride] **1** *vt* **(a)** to unbridle (*horse etc*); **(b)** *Chir* to incise, to slit up (*adhesion etc*); to lance (*boil, wound*); *Fig* **d. les yeux à qn,** to open s.o.'s eyes; **(c)** to unsling (*load*); **(d)** *Culin* to untruss (*fowl*). **2** *vi Fig* **travailler dix heures sans d.,** to work ten hours at a stretch.

débris [debri] *nmpl* remains, debris, fragments; *Fig* (*de mort*) remains; **d. de métal,** scrap (metal); **les d. d'une armée,** the remnants of an army; **les d. de sa fortune,** the remnants *or* remains of his fortune; *F* **ce n'est plus qu'un vieux d.,** he's just an old wreck.

débrocher [debrɔʃe] *vt* **(a)** to unstitch (*book*); **(b)** *Culin* to unspit.

débrouillard, -arde [debrujar, -ard] *F* **1** *adj* resourceful, smart. **2** *n* resourceful person.

débrouillardise [debrujardiz] *nf* resourcefulness; **faire preuve de d.,** to be resourceful.

débrouillement [debrujmɑ̃] *nm* unravelling, sorting out.

débrouiller [debruje] **1** *vt* **(a)** to unravel, to disentangle (*thread etc*); to sort out (*papers etc*); **d. une affaire,** to clear up *or* straighten out a situation; **d. une signature,** to make out *or* decipher a signature; **(b)** *F* **d. qn,** to wise s.o. up. **2 se débrouiller** *vpr* to extricate oneself (from difficulties), to manage; *F* **qu'il se débrouille!,** he'll have to sort it out for himself!; **débrouillez-vous!,** that's your lookout!; (*faites comme vous voulez*) you'll just have to manage; **elle s'est débrouillée pour rencontrer le directeur,** she worked it so that she got to meet the director; **je me débrouille,** (*ça ne va pas trop mal*) I'm managing, I'm coping; **je me débrouille en russe,** I can get by in Russian.

débroussailler [debrusaje] *vt* to clear (*ground*) of undergrowth; *Fig* **d. une question,** to clarify a matter.

débucher[1] [debyʃe] **1** *vi* (*of big game*) to break cover. **2** *vt* **(faire) d. un cerf,** to start a stag.

débucher[2], débuché *nm* breaking cover; (*on the horn*) gone away; **au débuché,** at the start.

débusquer [debyske] **1** *vt* **(a)** *Mil* to drive (*enemy*) out of ambush; to drive (*s.o.*) out (of refuge); **(b)** = **DÉBUCHER[1] 2**. **2** *vi* to come out of hiding; *Mil* to come out (of ambush).

début [deby] *nm* **(a)** (*commencement*) beginning, start, outset; **le d. de l'hiver/de la saison,** the beginning *or* start of winter/of the season; **au d.,** at the start *or* beginning; **dès le d.,** right at the start; from the outset (**de,** of); **je l'ai su dès le d.,** I knew from the outset *or* (right) from the start *or* the beginning; **je le savais depuis le d.,** I knew all along; **au d. des hostilités,** at the outbreak of hostilities; **appointements de d.,** starting salary; **être en d. de carrière,** to be at the start of one's career; **discours de d.,** maiden speech; **(b)** first appearance, debut (*of actor etc*); **faire son d.,** to make one's first appearance *or* one's début; **faire ses débuts (dans le monde),** to come out; **société/entreprise à ses débuts,** association/enterprise in its infancy; **(c)** (*de jeux*) first turn, first play; (*aux dés*) first throw.

débutant, -ante [debytɑ̃, -ɑ̃t] **1** *adj* novice; **cours pour les skieurs/***etc* **débutants,** skiing/*etc* classes for beginners; **si vous êtes skieur/***etc* **d.,** if you're learning (how) to ski/*etc*; **conducteur d.,** newly qualified driver. **2** *n* **(a)** beginner; **(b)** *Th* actor *etc* making his début. **3** *nf* **débutante,** debutante, *F* deb.

débuter [debyte] *vi* **(a)** (*commencer*) to begin, to start, to commence; **vous travaillerez ici pour d.,** you will work here to begin with; **(b)** (*de personne*) to make one's first appearance *or* one's début (*on stage etc*); **d. dans la vie,** to start a career; **faire d. une jeune fille dans le monde,** to bring a girl out; **(c)** (*pour un jeu*) to play first; (*dice*) to throw first.

déca [deka] *nm F* (*café*) decaf.

deçà [dəsa] **1** *adv Arch* on this side; **d. et delà,** here and there, on all sides; **jambe d., jambe delà,** astride. **2** *prép* **en d. de qch,** (on) this side of sth; **rester en d. de la vérité,** to be short of the truth.

décachetage [dekaʃtaʒ] *nm* unsealing, opening.

décacheter [dekaʃte] *vt* (*conj like* **cacheter**) to unseal, to break open (*letter etc*).

décade [dekad] *nf* **(a)** (*de dix jours*) period of ten days; (*period of ten years*) decade; **(b)** (*series of ten*) decade.

décadenasser [dekadnase] *vt* to unlock (*sth*), to take the padlock off (*sth*).

décadence [dekadɑ̃s] *nf* decadence; **être en d.,** to be decadent; **tomber en d.,** to fall into decay; (*d'une personne*) to start to decline.

décadent, -ente [dekadɑ̃, -ɑ̃t] **1** *adj* decadent. **2** *n Littér Beaux-Arts* Decadent.

décaèdre [dekaɛdr] *Math* **1** *adj* decahedral. **2** *nm* decahedron.

décaféiné [dekafeine] *nm* decaffeinated (coffee); **j'achète toujours du d.,** I always buy decaffeinated.

décaféiner [dekafeine] *vt* to decaffeinate; **un café décaféiné,** a (cup of) decaffeinated coffee.

décagonal, -aux [dekagɔnal, -o] *adj Math* decagonal.

décagone [dekagɔn] *nm Math* decagon.

décaissage [dekɛsaʒ] *nm* **(a)** unpacking (*of goods etc*); **(b)** planting out (*of plant, shrub*).

décaissement [dekɛsmɑ̃] *nm* **(a)** = **DÉCAISSAGE**; **(b)** *Com* outlay (*of cash*); **faire un d.,** to make an outlay.

décaisser [dekese] *vt* **(a)** to unpack, to uncase (*goods etc*); **(b)** to plant out (*plant, shrub*); **(c)** *Com* to pay out (*cash*).

décalage [dekalaʒ] *nm* **(a)** shifting the zero (*of instrument*); (*quantité etc*) (amount of) shift; **le d. d'un meuble,** the moving of a piece of furniture; **d. vers le haut,** upward movement; **d. à droite/gauche,** movement to the right/left; *Fig* **le d. entre la réalité et les espoirs,** the gap between reality and hopes; **d. d'opinions,** difference of opinions; **d. horaire,** time lag *or* difference; **d. de dates,** change of dates; **un d. de dates est prévu pour**

la réunion, the meeting has been rescheduled; **le d. de mon départ,** the postponement of my departure; **un d. du lancement de la fusée,** a change in the launch date; **(b)** (*action*) unwedging, unkeying; unscotching (*of wheel*).
décalaminage [dekalaminaʒ] *nm* (*de moteur*) decarbonizing, *F* decoking, decoke.
décalaminer [dekalamine] *vt* to decarbonize, *F* to decoke (*engine*).
décalcifiant [dekalsifjɑ̃] *adj Méd* decalcifying.
décalcification [dekalsifikɑsjɔ̃] *nf Méd* decalcification.
décalficier [dekalsifje] *Méd* **1** *vt* to decalcify. **2 se décalcifier** *vpr* to become decalcified.
décalcomanie [dekalkɔmani] *nf Cér etc* (*procédé*) decal(comania); (*résultat*) decal(comania), transfer; **faire de la d.,** to decal.
décaler [dekale] **1** *vt* **(a)** to move, to shift (*a piece of furniture*); to shift zero of (*instrument*); *Él* to displace, to shift (*the brushes etc*); **d. l'heure,** to alter the time, to change the time *or* the clock; **d. un meuble vers la droite,** to shift a piece of furniture to the right; **d. ses rendez-vous d'une heure,** (*les avancer*) to bring one's meetings forward by an hour; (*les reculer*) to put one's meeting back by an hour; **magnéto décalée,** magneto out of adjustment; **(b)** to set off (*part of machine etc*); to stagger (*rivets*); **(c)** *Tech* to unwedge, to unkey; to unscotch (*wheel*). **2 se décaler** *vpr* to move, to shift; **vous pourriez vous d. d'un rang/vers la gauche,** you could move up a row/move to the left.
décalitre [dekalitr] *nm* decalitre.
décalogue [dekalɔg] *nm Rel* (the) Decalogue.
décalotter [dekalɔte] *vt F* **d. une bouteille,** to open *or* crack a bottle.
décalquage [dekalkaʒ] *nm* (*de dessin*) tracing; (*par la chaleur etc*) transferring.
décalque [dekalk] *nm* **(a)** (*de dessin*) tracing; (*par la chaleur etc*) transferring; **papier à d.,** tracing paper; **(b)** (*dessin*) tracing; (*image*) transfer; *Fig* **un pauvre d. de mon travail,** a poor copy of my work.
décalquer [dekalke] *vt* to trace (*drawing*); (*par la chaleur*) to transfer (*design, coloured picture*).
décamètre [dekamɛtr] *nm* decametre, *US* decameter.
décamper [dekɑ̃pe] *vi F* to clear out *or* off; **décampez d'ici!,** get lost!
décan [dekɑ̃] *nm Astrol* decan.
décanat [dekana] *nm* deanship.
décaniller [dekanije] *vi* = **DÉCAMPER.**
décantation [dekɑ̃tɑsjɔ̃] *nf* decantation, decanting.
décanter [dekɑ̃te] **1** *vt* to decant (*wine*); *Fig* **il faut lui laisser le temps de d. ses projets,** you must leave him time to mull over his plans. **2 se décanter** *vpr* to settle; *Fig* **tous ces projets vont se d.,** all these plans will become clearer.
décapage [dekapaʒ] *nm* (*d'un meuble etc*) stripping.
décapant [dekapɑ̃] *nm* (*pour vernis, peinture*) remover, stripper.
décapeler [dekaple] *vt* (**je décapelle, n. décapelons; je décapellerai**) *Nau* to unrig (*yard*).
décaper [dekape] *vt* to strip, to remove (*paint, varnish*); to scour, to clean (*metal etc*); to pickle, to dip (*metal objects*); **d. une surface à peindre,** to strip a surface for painting.
décapeur [dekapœr] *nm* (*person*) pickler, dipper (*of metals*).
décapeuse [dekapøz] *nf Tech* scraper.
décapitation [dekapitɑsjɔ̃] *nf* decapitation, beheading.
décapiter [dekapite] *vt* to decapitate, to behead; (*un arbre*) to pollard; **d. un cours d'eau,** to capture the headwaters of a watercourse; *Fig* **d. un complot/une association,** to root out the ringleaders of a plot/the leaders of a society.
décapode [dekapɔd] *nm* (*crustacé*) decapod.
décapotable [dekapɔtabl] **1** *Aut adj* convertible; drop-head (*coupé*). **2** *nf* convertible.
décapoter [dekapɔte] *vt Aut* to lower the hood of (*car*).
décapsulage [dekapsylaʒ] *nm* opening.
décapsulation [dekapsylɑsjɔ̃] *nf Chir* decapsulation.
décapsuler [dekapsyle] *vt* to open, to take the top off (*a bottle*).
décapsuleur [dekapsylœr] *nm* bottle opener.
décapuchonner [dekapyʃɔne] *vt* to take the top off (*sth*).
décarburant [dekarbyrɑ̃] *Tech* **1** *adj* decarbonizing. **2** *nm* decarbonizer.
décarburer [dekarbyre] *vt Tech* to decarbonize, to decarburize (*steel, iron*).
décarcasser (se) [sədekarkase] *vpr F* to wear oneself out.
décarreler [dekarle] *vt* to remove the tiles from (*surface, room*).
décartellisation [dekartelizɑsjɔ̃] *nf Écon Hist* break-up of a cartel.
décasyllabe [dekasilab] **1** *adj* decasyllabic. **2** *nm* decasyllabic verse.
décasyllabique [dekasilabik] *adj* decasyllabic.
décathlon [dekatlɔ̃] *nm Sp* decathlon.
décathlonien, -ienne [dekatlɔnjɛ̃, -jɛn] *n Sp* decathlete.
décati [dekati] *adj* (*face*) wrinkled, that has lost its freshness; **vieillard d.,** decrepit old man.
décatir [dekatir] **1** *vt Tex* to take the gloss *or* finish off (*cloth*). **2 se décatir** *vpr* to lose one's freshness *or* one's beauty, to age.
décauser [dekoze] *vt Belg* to malign.
decauville [dəkovil] *nm* narrow-gauge railway.
décavé [dekave] *adj* **(a)** *F* (*personne riche*) ruined; (*aux cartes*) cleaned out; **(b)** (*face*) drawn, pinched.
décaver [dekave] *vt Cartes etc* **d. qn,** to clean s.o. out.
décédé, -ée [desede] *adj & n* deceased.
décéder [desede] *vi* (*conj like* **ceder**, *aux* **être**) *Admin* to die.
décelable [deslabl] *adj* detectable.
déceler [desle] *vt* (**je décèle; je décèlerai**) **(a)** (*découvrir*) to detect (*fraud etc*); **(b)** (*indiquer*) to point to, to indicate; **sa voix décelait la peur,** there was (a note of) fear in his voice; *Él* **d. des fuites,** to test for faults.
décélération [deselerɑsjɔ̃] *nf* deceleration.
décembre [desɑ̃br] *nm* December; **en d., au mois de d.,** in (the month of) December; **le 25 d.,** the 25th of December, December the 25th.
décemment [desamɑ̃] *adv* **(a)** (*convenablement*) properly; **se tenir d.,** to behave properly; (*être debout*) to stand properly; (*être assis*) to sit properly; **(b) elle parle anglais d.,** (*assez bien*) her English is reasonable *or* quite good; **(c)** (*raisonnablement*) reasonably; **d., je ne pouvais pas refuser,** I could not reasonably refuse.
décence [desɑ̃s] *nf* **(a)** (*bienséance*) propriety, decency, decorum; **se tenir avec d.,** to behave properly; (*être debout*) to stand properly; (*être assis*) to sit properly; **choquer la d.,** to offend against decency; **des mots/un comportement qui choque(nt) la d.,** offensive words/behaviour; **(b)** (*tact*) decency; **il aurait dû avoir la d. de s'excuser,** he ought to have had the decency to apologize; **(c)** (*réserve*) decency; **parler avec d.,** to speak in restrained terms.
décennal, -aux [desenal, -o] *adj* decennial.
décennie [deseni] *nf* decade.
décent [desɑ̃] *adj* **(a)** decent; modest (*attire etc*); **(b)** proper (*behaviour etc*); **peu d.,** indecent, unseemly; **(c)** (*correct*) reasonable; **lire d'une manière décente,** to read reasonably well.
décentralisateur, -trice [desɑ̃tralizatœr, -tris] **1** *adj* decentralizing. **2** *n Pol* advocate of decentralization.
décentralisation [desɑ̃tralizɑsjɔ̃] *nf* decentralization.
décentraliser [desɑ̃tralize] *vt* to decentralize.
décentration [desɑ̃trɑsjɔ̃] *nf*, **décentrement** [desɑ̃trəmɑ̃] *nm Opt Phot* decentring, throwing off centre.
décentré [desɑ̃tre] *adj* out of centre, out of true, off centre; *Fig* (*personne*) eccentric.
décentrer [desɑ̃tre] **1** *vt Opt MecE etc* to put (*sth*) out of *or* off centre, to decentre (*sth*). **2 se décentrer** *vpr* to come *or* move off centre.
déception [desɛpsjɔ̃] *nf* disappointment, *F* let-down; **éprouver une d.,** to be disappointed; **d. sentimentale,** unhappy love affair.
décérébré [deserebre] *adj Fig* lobotomized.
décérébrer [deserebre] *vt* to lobotomize.
décernement [desɛrnəmɑ̃] *nm* awarding (*of prize etc*).
décerner [desɛrne] *vt* **(a)** to award (*a prize etc*); **d. un honneur à qn,** to confer an honour on s.o.; **(b)** *Jur* **d. un mandat d'arrêt contre qn,** to issue a warrant for the arrest of s.o..
décès [desɛ] *nm surtout Admin* decease, (natural) death; *Jur* demise; **acte de d.,** death certificate; **fermé pour cause de d.,** closed on account of death.
décevant [des(ə)vɑ̃] *adj* **(a)** disappointing (*result etc*); **un livre très d.,** a very disappointing book; **(b)** (*mensonger*) deceptive; delusive (*appearance etc*).
décevoir [des(ə)vwar] *vt* (*conj like* **recevoir**) **(a)** to disappoint; **il m'a beaucoup déçu,** I was very disappointed in him; **ce voyage m'a profondément déçu,** I was very disappointed with the trip; **d. l'attente de qn,** to disappoint

s.o., not to live up to s.o.'s expectations; **(b)** *Arch* (*tromper*) to deceive, to delude.

déchaînement [deʃɛnmɑ̃] *nm* (*des éléments etc*) breaking loose; outburst (*of passion*); **d. de rage,** outburst of fury, fit of rage; **pourquoi a-t-il eu un tel d. contre moi?,** why did he fly into a rage with me like that?; **le d. de la tempête,** the breaking of the storm; **un d. de l'opinion,** a great wave of public opinion.

déchaîner [deʃene] **1** *vt* to unchain, to let loose (*dog etc*); **(b)** to unleash (*passions, anger etc*); *F* **les diables sont déchaînés,** all hell has broken loose; **d. l'hilarité,** to provoke laughter. **2 se déchaîner** *vpr* to break out; **la tempête s'est déchaînée,** the storm broke; **se d. contre qn,** to fly into a rage with s.o..

déchanter [deʃɑ̃te] *vi F* to change one's tune.

déchaper [deʃape] *vt Tech* to remove the cope from a mould.

décharge[deʃarʒ] *nf* **(a)** *El* discharge; **d. électrique,** electric shock; *Mil* discharge, volley (*of gunfire etc*); **(b)** *Fin* (tax) rebate; *Banque* letter of indemnity; *Jur* release, acquittal (*of accused person*); discharge (*from obligation*); **porter une somme en d.,** to mark a sum as paid; **d. de 50 pour cent,** composition of 50p in the pound; **(c)** (*sortie etc*) discharge, outlet; **tuyau de d.,** wastepipe; **d. (publique),** rubbish dump, tip; **d. interdite,** tipping prohibited; **décharges sauvages,** fly tipping, *Am* illegal dumping; **(d)** running (*of colour*); **(e)** *Typ* offset sheet; **(f)** *Jur* **témoin à d.,** witness for the defence; **(g)** *Archit* **arc de d.,** relieving arch.

déchargeoir [deʃarʒwar] *nm* wastepipe, overflow (pipe).

décharger [deʃarʒe] *v* (**je déchargeai(s); n. déchargeons**) **1** *vt* **(a)** to unload (*cart etc*); to unload, to unlade, to discharge (*ship*); to unship, to discharge (*cargo*); to tip, to dump (*gravel*); to unload, to discharge (*firearm*); to discharge (*accumulator*); *Fig* **d. sa conscience,** to ease one's mind (**de,** of); **d. sa conscience auprès de qn,** to (unburden) oneself to s.o.; **d. son cœur,** to unburden one's heart; **d. sa colère sur qn,** to vent one's anger on s.o.; **d. son fusil sur** *ou* **contre qn,** to let off *or* fire (off) one's gun at s.o.;

(b) (*soulager*) to relieve, to lighten, to ease (*horse, ship etc*) of part of its load; to take the strain off (*beam*); **d. qn d'une tâche/d'une responsabilité,** to relieve s.o. of a task/a responsibility; *Com* to receipt; **d. qn d'une accusation,** to acquit s.o. of a charge; **d. qn d'une dette,** to remit a debt; **failli déchargé/non déchargé,** discharged/undischarged bankrupt;

(c) to discharge, to empty (*reservoir etc*).

2 *vi Typ* **encre qui décharge,** ink that rubs off.

3 se décharger *vpr* **(a)** (*of gun*) to go off, (*of battery*) to run down, to discharge; (*of anger*) to vent itself (**sur,** on);

(b) se d. de qn/qch, to get rid of s.o./sth; **se d. d'un fardeau,** to put down *or* lay down a load; **se d. de qch sur qn,** to shift the responsibility for sth onto s.o.; **se d. d'une tâche sur qn,** to unload a task onto s.o.;

(c) le fleuve se décharge dans un lac, the river flows into a lake.

déchargeur [deʃarʒœr] *nm* **(a)** *El* (spark, lightning) arrester; **(b)** *Arch* stevedore, docker; (market) porter; **d. de charbon,** coalheaver.

décharné [deʃarne] *adj* **(a)** emaciated (*body, limbs etc*); emaciated, gaunt (*face*); bare (*tree*); bald (*style*); **(b)** fleshless (*bones etc*).

décharner [deʃarne] *vt* **(a)** to emaciate (*s.o.*); **(b)** to strip the flesh off (*bone*).

déchaumer [deʃome] *vt Agr* to plough (*stubble*).

déchaussé [deʃose] *adj* **(a)** (*sans chaussures*) barefoot(ed); **(b) avoir les dents déchaussées,** to have receding gums; **bâtisse aux murs déchaussés,** building with unsound foundations.

déchaussement [deʃosmɑ̃] *nm* **(a)** (*en enlevant les chaussures*) taking off of one's shoes; **(b)** (*de murs*) laying bare of foundations; (*de dents*) receding gums.

déchausser [deʃose] **1** *vt* **(a)** (*enlever les chaussures à*) to take off (*s.o.'s*) shoes; **(b)** to lay bare the roots of (*tree*); to bare, to expose (*tooth, foundations*). **2 se déchausser** *vpr* **(a)** (*enlever ses chaussures*) to take off one's shoes; **(b) ses dents se déchaussent,** he has receding gums.

dèche [dɛʃ] *nf F* **être dans la d.,** to be stony broke.

déchéance [deʃeɑ̃s] *nf* **(a)** (*dégradation, chute*) downfall; **sa d. a été causée par l'alcool,** drink was his downfall; **(b)** *Jur Fin* forfeiture (*of rights etc*); **action en d. de brevet,** action for forfeiture of patent; **d. de l'autorité paternelle,** loss of parental authority; **d. d'une police,** expiration of a policy.

déchet [deʃɛ] *nm* **(a) déchets,** waste, refuse; **des déchets de tissu,** scraps of fabric; **déchets radioactifs,** radioactive waste; **d. de métal,** scrap (metal); **déchets de viande,** scraps (of meat); **(b)** *Com* loss, decrease, diminution (*of weight, value*); **il y a du d.,** there is some wastage; **d. de route,** loss in transit; **(c)** (*de personne*) failure; **un d. de la société,** a social outcast.

déchetterie [deʃɛtri] *nf* dump, *Br* rubbish dump, tip.

déchevelé [deʃəvle] *adj* dishevelled.

déchiffonner [deʃifɔne] *vt* to smooth *or* iron out creases (*in material etc*).

déchiffrable [deʃifrabl] *adj* decipherable (*inscription*); decipherable, legible (*writing*); **code facilement d.,** code that is easy to crack *or* break.

déchiffrage [deʃifraʒ] *nm Mus* sight-reading.

déchiffrement [deʃifrəmɑ̃] *nm* deciphering.

déchiffrer [deʃifre] **1** *vt* **(a)** to decipher, to make out (*inscription etc*); to decode (*message*); to read, to interpret (*signals*); **d. les sentiments d'une personne,** to fathom s.o.'s feelings; **d. qn,** to make s.o. out; **je n'arrive pas à la d.,** I can't fathom *or* make her out; **d. un mystère,** to unravel a mystery; **(b)** to read, to play (*music*) at sight, to sight-read (*music*); **d. un morceau,** to sight-read a piece. **2** *vi Mus* to sight-read.

déchiffreur, -euse [deʃifrœr, -øz] *n* decipherer (*of inscription*); decoder (*of message*); code-breaker (of secret *message*); **d. de radar,** radar scanner.

déchiquetage [deʃiktaʒ] *nm* (*de papier*) shredding; (*de tissu*) slashing.

déchiqueté [deʃikte] *adj* **(a)** jagged (*edge*); jagged, ragged (*coastline*); **papier à bords déchiquetés,** deckle-edge paper; **(b)** (*object*) cut to bits *or* to shreds; **une couverture déchiquetée,** a tattered blanket.

déchiqueter [deʃikte] *vt* (**je déchiquette; je déchiquetterai**) to cut *or* slash *or* tear (*paper, flesh etc*) into strips *or* shreds; to hack (*chicken*); *Fig* to pull (*s.o.'s reputation*) to pieces.

déchiqueteuse [deʃiktøz] *nf* shredder.

déchiqueture [deʃiktyr] *nf* slash, long tear (*in cloth etc*).

déchirant [deʃirɑ̃] *adj* heartrending, harrowing; agonizing (*pain*); **des adieux déchirants,** heartrending farewells.

déchiré [deʃire] *adj* (*vêtement, couverture*) & *Fig* torn; **muscle d.,** torn muscle; **être d. entre deux personnes,** to be torn between two people; **la nation est déchirée,** the nation is torn.

déchirement [deʃirmɑ̃] *nm* tearing, *Fml* rending (*of material etc*); **d. d'un muscle,** tearing of a muscle; **d. de cœur,** heartbreak.

déchirer [deʃire] **1** *vt* to tear, *Fml* to rend (*garment etc*); to tear up (*paper etc*); to tear open (*envelope*); to tear apart (*a family, a country*); **d. qch en morceaux,** to tear sth to pieces *or* bits *or* shreds; *Fig* **sons qui déchirent l'oreille,** ear-splitting sounds; **un cri aigu déchire le silence,** a shrill scream pierced the silence; **cris qui déchiraient le cœur,** heartrending cries; **d. qn,** to slander s.o.; **la guerre qui déchire le pays,** the war which is tearing the country apart. **2 se déchirer** *vpr* (*of material*) to tear; **il s'est déchiré un muscle,** he's torn a muscle; **un couple qui se déchire,** a couple who are tearing each other apart; **mon cœur se déchira,** I was heartbroken.

déchirure [deʃiryr] *nf* (*dans tissu*) tear, rent, slit, rip; (*blessure*) laceration; **une d. musculaire,** a torn muscle.

déchloruré [deklɔryre] *adj Méd* (*diet*) salt-free.

déchoir [deʃwar] *vi* (*pp* **déchu**; *pr ind* **je déchois, n. déchoyons, ils déchoient**; *p hist* **je déchus**; *fu* **je déchoirai**; *aux* **être** *or* **avoir**) to fall (*from honour etc*); **ce quartier a déchu,** the area has gone down; **sa popularité déchoit,** his popularity is declining; **la maison déchoit de son prestige,** the firm is going down (in public estimation); **ce serait d.,** it would be demeaning; **il est déchu de ses droits,** he has forfeited his rights.

déchristianisation [dekristjanizasjɔ̃] *nf* dechristianization.

déchristianiser [dekristjanize] **1** *vt* to dechristianize, to turn (*s.o.*) from Christianity. **2 se déchristianiser** *vpr* to turn (away) from Christianity.

déchu [deʃy] *adj* fallen; **ange d.,** fallen angel; **roi d.,** dethroned king; **police déchue,** expired policy; **d. de la nationalité française,** deprived *or* stripped of French nationality.

déci [desi] *nm Suisse* = decilitre of white wine.

décibel [desibɛl] *nm Phys* decibel; **contrôler la puissance en décibels,** to monitor the decibel level.

décidé [deside] *adj* **(a)** settled (*matter etc*); **(b)** resolute, confident (*person, manner*); determined (*character*); **d'un ton d.,** decisively, resolutely; **être d. à faire qch,** to be determined *or* resolved to do sth, to be bent on doing sth; **être d. à ce que tout se passe bien,** to be determined that everything will go well; **elle y est bien décidée,** she's quite determined to do it, she's quite bent on doing it.

décidément [desidemɑ̃] *adv* **(a)** decidedly, positively, definitely; **d. je n'ai pas de chance!,** I really haven't any luck!; **d., elle est folle!,** she must be mad!; **(b)** *Arch* resolutely, firmly.

décider [deside] **1** *vt* **(a)** to decide, to settle (*question, dispute*); **voilà qui décide tout!,** that settles it!; **l'assemblée décida la guerre/la paix,** the assembly decided on war/peace;

(b) d. qn à faire qch, to persuade *or* induce s.o. to do sth;

(c) d. que + *ind*, to decide *or* settle that ...; **il fut décidé qu'on attendrait sa réponse,** it was decided to wait for his reply.

2 *vi* **(a)** (*prendre une décision*) to decide, to make *or* take a decision; **il faut que je décide,** I must decide, I must make a decision; **c'est moi qui décide,** (*tu n'as rien à dire*) I am the one who makes the decision *or* who decides; **je déciderai pour toi,** (*si tu n'arrives pas à te décider*) I'll decide for you; **d. en faveur de qn,** to decide *or Jur* to give a ruling in favour of s.o.; *Jur* **d. en faveur du plaignant,** to find for the plaintiff;

(b) d. de qch, to decide *or* determine sth; **événement qui a décidé de sa carrière,** event that determined his career;

(c) d. de + *inf*, to decide (after deliberation) to (*do sth*); **j'ai décidé de partir demain,** I've decided to leave tomorrow.

3 se décider *vpr* to make up one's mind, to come to a decision; **elle n'arrive pas à se d.,** she can't make up her mind; **allons décidez-vous,** come on, make up your mind; **se d. à qch** *ou* **à faire qch,** to make up one's mind (reluctantly) to do sth; **je ne puis pas me d. à le faire,** I cannot bring myself to do it; **se d. pour qn/qch,** to decide in favour of s.o./sth.

décideur, -euse [desidœr, -øz] *n Pol Écon etc* decision-maker.

décigramme [desigram] *nm* decigramme.

décilitre [desilitr] *nm* decilitre, *US* deciliter.

décimal, -aux [desimal, -o] *adj* decimal.

décimale [desimal] *nf* decimal.

décimalisation [desimalizɑsjɔ̃] *nf* decimalization.

décimaliser [desimalize] *vt* to decimalize.

décimation [desimɑsjɔ̃] *nf* decimation.

décime[1] [desim] *nm* **(a)** (*impôt*) 10% tax; **(b)** one tenth of a franc, ten centimes.

décime[2] *nf Rel Hist* tithe.

décimer [desime] *vt* to decimate.

décimètre [desimɛtr] *nm* decimetre, *US* decimeter.

décintrage [desɛ̃traʒ] *nm*, **décintrement** [desɛ̃trəmɑ̃] *nm Constr* centring (*of arch*).

décintrer [desɛ̃tre] *vt Constr* to remove the centring of (*arch*).

décisif, -ive [desizif, -iv] *adj* **(a)** decisive (*battle etc*); conclusive (*evidence*); **au moment d.,** at the critical *or* crucial moment; **(b)** decisive (*tone*).

décision [desizjɔ̃] *nf* **(a)** (*choix*) decision; *Jur* ruling, award; *Mil* (regimental) orders; **prendre/arriver à une d.,** to make *or* take/to come to *or* reach a decision (**quant à, au sujet de,** about); **elle a prit la d. de partir,** she decided to leave; **la d. ne m'appartient pas,** it's not up to me to decide, it's not my decision; **forcer une d.,** to bring matters to a head; **(b)** (*détermination*) resolution, determination; **affirmer qch avec d.,** to state sth decisively; **elle ne manque pas d'esprit de d.,** she does not lack decisiveness.

décisionnaire [desizjɔnɛr] *n* decision-maker.

décisivement [desizivmɑ̃] *adv* decisively.

déclamateur, -trice [deklamatœr, -tris] *n Péj* ranter, tub-thumper.

déclamation [deklamɑsjɔ̃] *nf* **(a)** (*éloquence*) oratory, (art of) declamation; **il a une mauvaise d.,** he is no orator; **(b)** *Péj* (*emphase*) ranting, spouting; **(c)** (*discours*) bombastic speech.

déclamatoire [deklamatwar] *adj Péj* declamatory, highflown (*style*); ranting, bombastic (*speech*).

déclamer [deklame] **1** *vt* **(a)** to declaim (*speech*); **(b)** *Péj* to rant. **2** *vi Litt* **d. contre qn,** to rail against s.o.

déclarable [deklarabl] *adj* liable to duty; **marchandise non d.,** duty-free goods; **revenu d.,** declarable income.

déclarant, -ante [deklarɑ̃, -ɑ̃t] *n Jur Admin* declarant.

déclaration [deklarɑsjɔ̃] *nf* declaration, proclamation, announcement; notification (*of birth, death etc*); **d. de guerre,** declaration of war; **d. de changement de domicile,** notification of change of address; **d. d'impôts,** tax return; **émettre une d.,** to issue a statement; **faire une d. à la police,** to make a statement to the police; **d. sous serment,** affidavit; **il n'a fait aucune d.,** he made no statement; **une d. télévisée,** a televised statement; **selon votre d. du ...,** according to your statement of the ...; **une d. de principe,** a statement *or* declaration of principle; **d. d'amour,** declaration of love; **d. en douane,** customs declaration.

déclaré [deklare] *adj* declared, avowed (*enemy, intention etc*); **un partisan d. de la peine de mort,** an avowed supporter of the death penalty.

déclarer [deklare] **1** *vt* to declare, to make known, to announce (*one's intentions, wishes etc*); to declare (*one's love*); **d. son incompétence,** to admit one's incompetence; *Cartes* **d. trèfle,** to declare *or* call clubs; **je déclare la séance levée,** I declare the meeting closed; **d. qn roi,** to declare s.o. king; **elle a déclaré qu'elle n'en avait jamais eu connaissance,** she declared that she had never known anything about it; **déclaré coupable,** found guilty; **déclaré coupable de vol,** convicted of theft; **d. la guerre à qn,** to declare war on s.o.; **avez-vous quelque chose à d.?,** have you anything to declare?; **d. ses revenus,** to declare one's income; **il ne déclare pas tout,** he does not declare everything.

2 se déclarer *vpr* **(a)** (*se prononcer*) to speak one's mind; **se d. pour/contre qch,** to declare oneself in favour of/against sth;

(b) (*faire une déclaration d'amour*) to declare one's love;

(c) (*of fire, disease*) to break out;

(d) (*se dire*) **se d. l'auteur du méfait,** to own up to the deed; **elle s'est déclarée satisfaite de l'accord passé,** she declared herself satisfied with the agreement that was reached.

déclassé, -ée [deklase] **1** *adj* **(a)** *Sp* relegated (*to lower division etc*); (*hotel*) downgraded; **(b)** *Rail Vieilli* reclassed; **(c)** *Péj* (*person*) déclassé. **2** *n Péj* person who has lost social position.

déclassement [deklasmɑ̃] *nm* change of class.

déclasser [deklase] *vt* **(a)** *Sp* to relegate; to downgrade (*a hotel*); **(b)** *Rail* to transfer (*passengers*) from one class to another; **(c)** to lower the social position (*of s.o.*); **(d)** *Mil* to declare (*weapon*) obsolete; *Nau* to strike (*warship*) off the list; **(e)** *Nau* to disrate (*seaman*); **(f)** (*déranger*) to put out of order; **qui a déclassé mes papiers?,** who put my papers out of order?

déclenchement [deklɑ̃ʃmɑ̃] *nm* **(a)** starting (up); setting (*of sth*) in motion; **le d. de la sonnerie,** the setting off of the alarm; *Fig* **le d. des protestations,** the triggering (off) of protests; **(b)** *MecE* releasing, disengaging (*of part*); *Phot* (shutter) release.

déclencher [deklɑ̃ʃe] *vt* **(a)** to set off (*mechanism*); to start (up) (*apparatus*), to set (*apparatus*) in motion; *Fig* to trigger (off) (*sth*); **d. les critiques,** to trigger criticism; *Mil* **d. une attaque,** to launch an attack; **(b)** *MecE* to release, to disconnect, to disengage (*part*).

déclencheur [deklɑ̃ʃœr] *nm Phot* shutter release.

déclic [deklik] *nm* **(a)** (*mécanisme*) pawl, catch; trigger; **chronomètre à d.,** stopwatch; **(b)** (*bruit*) click(ing sound).

déclin [deklɛ̃] *nm* decline, close (*of day*); wane, waning (*of moon*); fall (*of the year*); decline (*in talent*); **être en d.,** to be in decline, to decline; **le d. de la civilisation,** the decline of civilization; **le soleil est à** *ou* **sur son d.,** the sun is sinking *or* setting; *Fig* **au d. de sa vie,** in his declining years; **le d. d'un art,** the decline of an art form.

déclinable [deklinabl] *adj Gram* declinable.

déclinaison [deklinɛzɔ̃] *nf* **(a)** *Astron* declination (*of star*); **d. magnétique,** magnetic variation; **(b)** *Gram* declension; **deuxième d.,** second declension.

décliner [dekline] **1** *vi* **(a)** (*of compass*) to deviate (from the true line); **(b)** (*se dégrader*) (*of beauty, moon*) to wane; (*of talent, star*) to decline; (*of day*) to draw to a close; **une civilisation qui menace de d.,** a civilization threatened with decline. **2** *vt* **(a)** (*refuser*) to decline, to refuse (*offer etc*); to decline (*responsibility*); **d. une juridiction,** to refuse to acknowledge a jurisdiction; **(b)** *Gram* to decline (*noun etc*); **d. ses noms et prénoms,** to state *or* give one's full name. **3 se décliner** *vpr Gram* to be declined.

décliquer [deklike] *vt* to release (*pawl*); *Constr* **d. le mouton,** to release the monkey (*of pile driver*).

déclive [dekliv] **1** *adj* sloping, inclined. **2** *nf* slope; **en d.,** (*terrain, toit*) sloping.

déclivité [deklivite] *nf* slope, incline, gradient, *Fml* declivity; **angle de d.,** angle of gradient.

décloisonnement [deklwazɔnmɑ̃] *nm* (*de l'administration etc*) decompartmentalization.
décloisonner [deklwazɔne] *vt* to decompartmentalize.
déclouer [deklue] *vt* to take the nails out of (*packing case etc*).
décocher [dekɔʃe] *vt* to shoot, to let fly (*bolt from crossbow*); **d. un coup à qn,** to hit out at s.o.; **d. une remarque,** to fire a comment; **d. une œillade à qn,** to flash a glance *or* glance fleetingly at s.o..
décoction [dekɔksjɔ̃] *nf* decoction.
décodage [dekɔdaʒ] *nm* decoding; (*d'un code*) cracking.
décoder [dekɔde] *vt Ordinat etc* to decode; to decode (*message*); to crack (*code*).
décodeur [dekɔdœr] *nm TV Ordinat* decoder.
décoiffer [dekwafe] **1** *vt* **(a)** to remove (*s.o.'s*) hat; to uncap (*fuse*); **(b)** (*ébouriffer*) to tousle (*s.o.'s*) hair. **2 se décoiffrer** *vpr* to remove one's hat.
décoinçage [dekwɛ̃saʒ] *nm*, **décoincement** [dekwɛ̃smɑ̃] *nm* loosening; unwedging.
décoincer [dekwɛ̃se] *v* (**n. décoinçons; je décoinçai(s)**) **1** *vt* to loosen (*jammed part etc*); *F* to loosen (*s.o.*) up. **2 se décoincer** *vpr F* to get rid of one's hang-ups; **vers la fin elle s'est décoincée,** she loosened up a bit towards the end.
décolérer [dekɔlere] *vi* (**je décolère; je décolérerai**) to calm down; **il ne décolérait pas,** he was still fuming.
décollage [dekɔlaʒ] *nm* **(a)** (*de timbre etc*) unsticking, ungluing; **(b)** *Av* takeoff.
décollation [dekɔlɑsjɔ̃] *nm* decapitation, beheading.
décollé [dekɔle] *adj* **il a les oreilles décollées,** his ears stick out.
décollement [dekɔlmɑ̃] *nm* **(a)** (*de timbre etc*) unsticking, ungluing; **(b)** *Méd* **d. de la rétine,** detachment of the retina.
décoller [dekɔle] **1** *vt* **(a)** to remove (*stamp*); **d une enveloppe à la vapeur,** to steam open a letter; **(b)** to loosen, to disengage, to release (*part*). **2** *vi Av* to take off; *F* **il ne décolle pas d'ici,** he won't budge, he's staying put. **3 se décoller** *vpr* (*of envelope*) to come unstuck *or* undone; (*of part*) to work loose.
décolletage [dekɔltaʒ] *nm* **(a)** (*de robe*) lowering of neckline; **(b)** *Métal* screw cutting.
décolleté [dekɔlte] **1** *adj* **femme décolletée,** woman in a low- necked *or* low-cut dress; **robe décolletée,** low-necked dress; **tu ne trouves pas que c'est trop d.?,** you don't think it's too low?; **robe décolletée dans le dos,** dress cut low at the back. **2** *nm* neck opening, neckline; **d. carré,** square neck; **d. en pointe,** V neck; **en grand d.,** (*en robe de soirée*) in full evening dress; **avoir un beau d.,** to have a beautiful neck and shoulders; **il a jeté un œil dans mon d.,** he looked down the front of my dress; **décolletée jusqu'au nombril** *ou* **aux genoux,** showing everything she's got, showing a lot of cleavage.
décolleter [dekɔlte] *v* (**je décollète, je décollette** *are theoretical forms; the pronunciation is always* [dekɔlt]) **1** *vt* **(a)** to cut out the neck of (*dress*); **(b)** *Métal* to cut (*screw*); **tour à d.,** screw-cutting lathe. **2 se décolleter** *vpr* to wear a low-necked dress.
décolonisation [dekɔlɔnizɑsjɔ̃] *nf* decolonization.
décolorant [dekɔlɔrɑ̃] **1** *adj* bleaching. **2** *nm* bleaching agent, bleach.
décoloration [dekɔlɔrɑsjɔ̃] *nf* discolo(u)ration, fading (*of material*); (*chez le coiffeur*) bleaching (*of hair*); colourlessness (*of complexion, style*); **demander une d.,** to ask for one's hair to be bleached.
décolorer [dekɔlɔre] **1** *vt* to discolour, to fade, to take the colour out of (*sth*); to bleach (*hair*). **2 se décolorer** *vpr* to lose colour, to fade, to bleach; (*of person*) to grow *or* turn pale.
décombres [dekɔ̃br] *nmpl* ruins, debris (*of building*).
décommander [dekɔmɑ̃de] **1** *vt* to countermand (*order*); to cancel (*meeting, dinner*); to put off (*guest*); **d. une grève,** to call off a strike. **2 se décommander** *vpr* to cancel one's appointment; (*d'une invitation*) to cancel.
décomplexer [dekɔ̃plɛkse] *vt F* to rid (*s.o.*) of complexes, to cure (*s.o.'s*) hang-ups; **ça m'a décomplexé,** (*de voir que les autres n'étaient pas mieux lotis*) it made me feel better (about myself).
décomposable [dekɔ̃pozabl] *adj* (*texte*) that can be broken up, that can be divided into parts; (*composé*) that can be broken down.
décomposé [dekɔ̃poze] *adj* **(a)** (*meat, leaves*) decomposed, rotten; **(b) huile décomposée,** spent oil; **(c) visage d.,** face distorted by grief *or* terror; **il est arrivé, complètement d.,** he arrived quite distraught.
décomposer [dekɔ̃poze] **1** *vt* **(a)** *Phys Ch etc* to decompose; **d. la lumière,** to split light; **d. une fraction,** to split up a fraction; *Fig* **d. un pas de deux (en séquences),** to break down a pas de deux into separate sequences; **d. un problème,** to break down a problem; **(b)** to decompose, to rot, to decay (*organic matter*); **(c)** to contort, to distort (*features*); **le visage décomposé par la souffrance,** face drawn by suffering. **2 se décomposer** *vpr* **(a)** to decompose, to rot, to decay; **(b)** (*of face, features*) to become distorted (*with terror etc*).
décomposition [dekɔ̃pɔzisjɔ̃] *nf* **(a)** *Phys Ch etc* decomposition; **(b)** (*of meat, leaves*) decomposition, decay, rotting; *Fig* **la d. d'un empire,** the decay of an empire; **(c)** distortion (*of features*).
décompresser [dekɔ̃prese] **1** *vt Tech* to decompress. **2** *vi* to decompress; *Fig F* **avoir besoin de d.,** to need to unwind.
décompresseur [dekɔ̃presœr] *nm* decompressor.
décompression [dekɔ̃prɛsjɔ̃] *nf* decompression; **robinet de d.,** (*dans moteur*) compression tap; (*dans machine à vapeur*) petcock.
décomprimer [dekɔ̃prime] *vt* to decompress.
décompte [dekɔ̃t] *nm* **(a)** deduction (*from sum to be paid*); **j'ai fait le d. de ce que vous m'avez payé et de ce que vous me devez,** I've deducted what you've paid from what you owe me; *Fig* **trouver du d.,** to be disappointed (**à,** in); **(b)** *Admin Com* detailed account, breakdown.
décompter [dekɔ̃te] **1** *vt* to deduct (*sum from account*). **2** *vi* (*of clock*) to miscount (*on striking*).
déconcentration [dekɔ̃sɑ̃trɑsjɔ̃] *nf* devolution.
déconcentrer [dekɔ̃sɑ̃tre] **1** *vt* to devolve; **d. l'autorité gouvernementale,** to decentralize government; **d. une ville,** to decongest a city; **d. son attention,** to let one's attention lapse. **2 se déconcentrer** *vpr* to lose concentration.
déconcertant [dekɔ̃sɛrtɑ̃] *adj* disconcerting.
déconcerté [dekɔ̃sɛrte] *adj* disconcerted, taken aback.
déconcerter [dekɔ̃sɛrte] **1** *vt* **(a)** to disconcert (*s.o.*); **(b)** *Litt* to upset, to confound, to frustrate (*s.o.'s plans*). **2 se déconcerter** *vpr* to lose one's self-assurance; **sans se d.,** unabashed.
déconditionnement [dekɔ̃disjɔnmɑ̃] *nm Psy* aversion therapy.
déconditionner [dekɔ̃disjɔne] *vt Psy* to treat (*s.o.*) with aversion therapy; *Fig* **d. l'opinion publique,** to shake up public opinion.
déconfit [dekɔ̃fi] *adj* crestfallen, disheartened; **un air d.,** a crestfallen look.
déconfiture [dekɔ̃fityr] *nf* collapse, failure, downfall, ruin; bankruptcy (*of non-trader*); **tomber en d.,** to fail to meet one's liabilities.
décongélation [dekɔ̃ʒelɑsjɔ̃] *nf* defrosting, thawing (*of meat etc*).
décongeler [dekɔ̃ʒle] *vt* (**je décongèle; je décongèlerai**) to thaw, to defrost, to defreeze (*frozen meat etc*).
décongestif, -ive [dekɔ̃ʒɛstif, -iv] *adj & nm Méd* decongestant.
décongestionner [dekɔ̃ʒɛstjɔne] *vt* **(a)** *Méd* to relieve congestion in (*the lungs etc*); **(b)** *Fig* to clear (*street of traffic*).
déconnecter [dekɔnekte] *vt Él* to disconnect (*lead etc*).
déconner [dekɔne] *vi Arg* (*en parlant*) to talk a load of rubbish *or* drivel; (*en agissant*) to fool around; (*d'une machine*) to act up, to be on the blink; **tu déconnes!,** what on earth are you talking about?; **sans d., c'était super,** no fooling, it was great.
déconseiller [dekɔ̃seje] *vt* **d. qch à qn,** to advise s.o. against sth; **d. qn de faire qch,** to advise s.o. against doing sth; **un livre à d. pour les jeunes,** a book unsuitable for young people; **c'est fortement déconseillé,** it's extremely inadvisable.
déconsidération [dekɔ̃siderɑsjɔ̃] *nf* disrepute, discredit; **tomber en d.,** to fall into disrepute.
déconsidérer [dekɔ̃sidere] *v* (**je déconsidère; je déconsidérerai**) **1** *vt* to bring (*s.o., sth*) into disrepute. **2 se déconsidérer** *vpr* to fall into disrepute.
déconsigner [dekɔ̃siɲe] *vt* **(a)** *Rail* to take (*suitcase*) out of left-luggage office; **(b)** to return deposit on (*bottle etc*).
décontamination [dekɔ̃taminɑsjɔ̃] *nf* decontamination.
décontaminer [dekɔ̃tamine] *vt* to decontaminate.
décontenancé [dekɔ̃tnɑ̃se] *adj* confused, put out.
décontenancer [dekɔ̃tnɑ̃se] *v* (**je décontenançai(s); n. décontenançons**) **1** *vt* to embarrass, to confuse (*s.o.*). **2 se décontenancer** *vpr* to become embarrassed *or* confused.

décontracté [dekɔ̃trakte] *adj* relaxed; **une veste décontractée,** a casual jacket.
décontracter [dekɔ̃trakte] **1** *vt* to relax (*muscle, mind etc*). **2 se décontracter** *vpr* to relax.
décontraction [dekɔ̃traksjɔ̃] *nf* relaxation; **sa d. me sidère!,** I'm amazed at how laid back he is!
déconvenue [dekɔ̃vny] *nf* disappointment, mortification.
décor [dekɔr] *nm* **(a)** decoration (*of house etc*); **peintre en d.,** painter and decorator; **(b)** *Th Cin TV* set; setting (*of stage*); **décors,** scenery; **peintre de décors,** scene painter; *Fig* **il lui faut un changement de d.,** he needs a change (of scene); **(c)** (*atmosphère*) scene; **un d. de montagnes,** a background *or* backdrop of mountains; *Aut F* **rentrer dans le d.,** to drive off the road (*into tree etc*).
décorateur [dekɔratœr] *nm* **(a)** (*d'intérieur*) (interior) decorator; **(b)** *Th* stage designer; (*peintre*) scene painter.
décoratif, -ive [dekɔratif, -iv] *adj* decorative, ornamental; (*arbre*) ornamental; **arts décoratifs,** decorative arts; *Péj* **n'avoir qu'un rôle d.,** to have a purely decorative role.
décoration [dekɔrasjɔ̃] *nf* **(a)** (interior) decoration (*of house etc*); ornamentation, embellishment (*of church etc*); **(b)** (*médaille etc*) decoration, medal; ribbon, star (*of an order*); **porter une d. à la boutonnière,** to wear a decoration in one's buttonhole; **remise de décorations,** investiture.
décorativement [dekɔrativmɑ̃] *adv* decoratively.
décorer [dekɔre] *vt* **(a)** to decorate, to do up (*house etc*); **(b)** to decorate (*s.o.*).
décorner [dekɔrne] *vt* **(a)** to dehorn, to poll (*cattle etc*); *F* **un vent à d. les bœufs,** a howling gale; **(b)** (*redresser*) to smooth out.
décorticage [dekɔrtikaʒ] *nm* shelling (*of nuts*); husking (*of rice*).
décortication [dekɔrtikasjɔ̃] *nf* barking (*of timber*).
décortiquer [dekɔrtike] *vt* to shell (*nuts*); to husk (*rice*); to hull (*barley*); to bark (*timber*); *Fig* **d. un texte avant de le traduire,** to break down a text before translating it.
décorum [dekɔrɔm] *nm* decorum, propriety; **observer le d.,** to observe the proprieties; **faire qch pour le d.,** to do sth for the sake of decorum.
découcher [dekuʃe] *vi* (*ne pas coucher chez soi*) to sleep away from home; (*ne pas rentrer*) to stay out all night.
découdre [dekudr] *v* (*conj like* **coudre**) **1** *vt* **(a)** to unpick, to unstitch (*garment*); to rip (*seam*); **(b)** (*of horned animal*) to rip open, to gore (*dog etc*). **2** *vi* **en d.,** to fight; **être toujours prêt à en d.,** to be always ready for a fight. **3 se découdre** *vpr* to come unstitched.
découler [dekule] *vi* to ensue, to proceed, to follow (from); **il en découle que ...,** it follows that ... .
découpage [dekupaʒ] *nm* **(a)** cutting up (*of paper, cake etc*); carving (*of chicken etc*); **(b)** cutting out (*of patterns etc*); punching, stamping, cutting (*of sheet metal*); punching, pinking (*of leather etc*); **matrices pour d.,** cutting dies; **(c)** (*result*) cutout; **cahier de découpages,** scrap book; **un enfant occupé à ses découpages,** a child busy making paper shapes; **(d)** *Typ* cutting of the overlays; *Cin* (*scénario*) shooting script; *Pol* **d. électoral,** division into constituencies.
découpé [dekupe] *adj* **(a)** cut out; **bois d.,** fretwork; **des photos découpées,** cut-out photos; **(b)** *Bot* denticulate (*leaf etc*).
découper [dekupe] **1** *vt* **(a)** to cut up (*cake etc*); to carve (*chicken etc*); **couteau à d.,** carving knife; **(b)** to cut out (*design, paper*); to stamp (out), to punch, to cut (*metals*); to punch, to pink (*leather*); **d. un article dans un journal,** to cut an article out of a newspaper; **scie à d.,** fretsaw; **d. un texte en plusieurs parties,** to split a text into several parts; *Cin* **d. un scénario,** to make a shooting script. **2 se découper** *vpr* to stand out, to show up, to project (**sur,** on, against).
découpeur, -euse [dekupœr, -øz] **1** *n* (*personne*) carver; *Cin* cutter; **d. en cuir,** leather cutter. **2** *nf Tex etc* **découpeuse,** shearing *or* cutting *or* pinking machine.
découplé [dekuple] *adj* **bien d.,** well built, muscular (*person*).
découpler [dekuple] *vt* to slip, to uncouple (*hounds*); to uncouple (*horses, trucks*).
découpoir [dekupwar] *nm* **(a)** *Métal* cutter; (*ciseau*) shear; (*poinçon*) stamp; **(b)** *Couture* **d. à figures,** pinking shears.
découpure [dekupyr] *nf* **(a)** (*action*) cutting out; (*with punch*) punching, stamping (out); (*with shears*) pinking; (*ornamental*) fretwork; **(b)** (*result*) (*by punch etc*) stamping; (*from newspaper*) (newspaper) cutting; **(c)** indentation (*in coastline etc*); *Bot* denticulation (*in leaf*).
découragé [dekuraʒe] *adj* discouraged, disheartened, despondent, downcast.
décourageant [dekuraʒɑ̃] *adj* discouraging, dispiriting, disheartening, depressing; **une situation décourageante,** a disheartening situation; **vous êtes d.,** you're hopeless.
découragement [dekuraʒmɑ̃] *nm* discouragement; **tomber dans le d.,** to become disheartened *or* discouraged.
décourager [dekuraʒe] *v* (**je décourageai(s); n. décourageons**) **1** *vt* **(a)** to discourage, to dishearten; **cela ne m'a pas découragé,** that did not dishearten me; **se laisser d.,** to (let oneself) be discouraged *or* disheartened; **(b) d. qn de (faire) qch,** to discourage *or* deter s.o. from (doing) sth, to put s.o. off (doing) sth; **d. un projet,** to discourage a scheme; **un ton qui décourage tout humour,** a tone that discourages any attempt at humour. **2 se décourager** *vpr* to become discouraged *or* disheartened, to lose heart; **ne vous découragez pas!,** don't lose heart!, *F* cheer up!
découronner [dekurɔne] *vt* **(a)** to dethrone, to depose (*king etc*); *Fig* to debunk (*hero etc*); **(b)** (*volontairement*) to pollard (*tree*).
décours [dekur] *nm* **(a)** waning (*of the moon*); **lune à son d.,** moon on the wane; **(b)** abatement (*of fever*); decline (*of illness*).
décousu [dekuzy] **1** *adj* (*seam etc*) unstitched; disconnected, disjointed, incoherent (*words, ideas etc*); rambling, desultory (*remarks, conversation*); unmethodical (*work*). **2** *nm* (*of words, ideas etc*) disjointedness; (*of conversation*) desultoriness.
décousure [dekuzyr] *nf* **(a)** (*de vêtement*) rip in the seam; **(b)** gash, rip (*caused by horns, tusks*).
découvert [dekuvɛr] **1** *adj* uncovered; open (*country etc*); exposed, unprotected (*town etc*); **la tête découverte,** bareheaded; **à visage d.,** open, frankly; **coin de ciel d.,** bit of blue sky; *Tennis* **région découverte,** part of the court left uncovered (by player).
2 *nm* (*autorisé*) overdraft; **demander à bénéficier d'un d.,** to apply for an overdraft; **avoir un d. de 2 000 francs,** (*autorisé*) to have a 2,000 franc overdraft; (*non autorisé*) to be overdrawn by 2,000 francs; **votre compte est à d. de 2 000 francs,** your account is overdrawn by 2,000 francs.
3 *adv* **à d.,** uncovered, unprotected, open; **agir/parler à d.,** to act/speak openly; **mettre qch à d.,** to expose sth to view; **crédit à d.,** unsecured credit; **compte à d.,** overdrawn account; **mettre un compte à d.,** to overdraw an account; *St Exch* **vendre à d.,** to go a bear, to sell short.
découverte [dekuvɛrt] *nf* **(a)** discovery (*of land etc*); *Mil* scouting, reconnoitring; **aller** *ou* **partir à la d.,** to explore, to go exploring; **aller à la d. de qch,** to go in search of sth; **(b)** (scientific) discovery; discovery, exposure, detection (*of plot etc*).
découvreur, -euse [dekuvrœr, -øz] *n* discoverer.
découvrir [dekuvrir] *v* (*conj like* **couvrir**) **1** *vt* **(a)** to discover (*plot, virus, penicillin etc*); to detect (*error, criminal*); to bring (*crime etc*) to light; **il ne pouvait pas d. qui elle était,** he couldn't find out who she was; **d. des qualités insoupçonnées en** *ou* **chez qn,** to discover unsuspected qualities in s.o.; **le projecteur découvrit l'avion,** the searchlight picked out the aircraft;
(b) (*enlever ce qui couvre*) to uncover; to unveil (*statue*); to disclose (*secret*); to reveal (*plan*); **d. un pot,** to take the lid off a pot; **d. une maison,** to take the roof off a house; **un décolleté qui découvre les épaules,** a neck-line that leaves the shoulders bare; **d. ses dents,** to show one's teeth; **d. son cœur,** to open one's heart; *Échecs* **d. une pièce,** to uncover a piece;
(c) (*apercevoir*) to perceive, to discern; *Nau* to sight (*land*); **craindre d'être découvert,** to fear detection.
2 *vi* (*of reef*) to uncover (at low tide).
3 se découvrir *vpr* **(a)** (*enlever son chapeau*) to take off one's hat; (*se déshabiller*) to take off some of one's clothing; **se d. la tête,** to bare one's head;
(b) *Escrime Mil* to expose oneself;
(c) (*du ciel*) to clear;
(d) (*apparaître*) to come into sight; **les côtes se découvrent,** the coast comes into sight;
(e) (*se révéler*) to come to light; **la vérité se découvre toujours,** truth will out;
(f) (*se trouver*) to discover; **il s'est découvert une passion pour le jardinage,** he discovered (that) he had a passion for gardening; **se d. des parents éloignés,** to discover some distant relatives.
décrassage [dekrasaʒ] *nm,* **décrassement** [dekrasmɑ̃] *nm* cleaning, scouring.

décrasser [dekrase] **1** *vt* to clean, to cleanse, to scour; to remove the fouling from (*gun barrel*); **d. une chaudière,** to scale *or* clean a boiler; *Fig F* **d. qn,** to knock the rough edges off s.o.. **2 se décrasser** *vpr* (*se nettoyer*) to clean oneself up; (*en courant etc*) to clean out the system; *Fig F* (*devenir plus sophistiqué*) to lose one's rough edges.
décrêpage [dekrɛpaʒ] *nm* (*de cheveux*) straightening.
décrêper [dekrɛpe] *vt* (*les cheveux*) to straighten.
décrépir [dekrepir] *vt* to strip the plaster *or* roughcast off (*wall etc*).
décrépit [dekrepi] *adj* decrepit (*person, chair, house*); dilapidated (*chair, house*); tumbledown (*house*); broken-down (*horse*).
décrépitude [dekrepityd] *nf* decrepitude.
decrescendo [dekreʃɛndo] *Mus* **1** *adv* diminuendo, decrescendo; *Fig* **sa carrière va en d.,** his career's going down the tubes. **2** *nm* diminuendo, decrescendo.
décret [dekrɛ] *nm* decree, order; *Admin* **d. présidentiel,** = Order in Council; **c'est le d. de la mode,** fashion decrees it.
décréter [dekrete] *vt* (**je décrète; je décréterai**) to decree; to enact (*law*).
décret-loi [dekrɛlwa] *nm* = Order in Council; (*pl décrets-lois*).
décrier [dekrije] *vt* to disparage (*s.o., sth*), to run (*s.o., sth*) down.
décrire [dekrir] *vt* (*conj like* **écrire**) **(a)** (*représenter*) to describe, to depict (*s.o., sth*); **(b)** *Math etc* to describe, to draw (*curve, circle*); **la route décrit des courbes,** the road makes several bends.
décrispation [dekrispasjɔ̃] *nf Pol* détente; **climat de d.,** atmosphere of détente.
décrisper [dekrispe] **1** *vt* to relax (*s.o.*), to make (*s.o.*) less tense; **d. l'atmosphère,** to lighten the atmosphere, to make the atmosphere less tense; **d. la situation,** to ease the situation, to make the situation less tense; **la plaisanterie l'a décrispé,** the joke broke the ice. **2 se décrisper** *vpr* to relax, *F* to lighten up.
décrochage [dekrɔʃaʒ] *nm* disconnecting; (*d'un tableau*) unhooking; *Rad* **diffuser en d.,** to broadcast its own programmes; *Astron* **d. du vaisseau spatial,** undocking of the spacecraft.
décrochement [dekrɔʃmɑ̃] *nm Géol* thrust.
décrocher [dekrɔʃe] **1** *vt* to unhook, to take down (*coat from peg etc*); *Tél* to pick *or* lift up (*receiver*); to uncouple, to disconnect (*railway carriages etc*); to undo (*clasp etc*); to unsling (*hammock*); **d. les palmes** *ou* **la croix,** to receive a decoration; **d. le grand succès,** to make a big hit; **d. un bon poste,** to land a good job. **2** *vi Tél* to pick up the receiver; *Av* to stall; *Mil* to beat a retreat, to withdraw; *Fig* **elle a décroché,** (*elle n'écoute plus*) she's switched off; **si cet élève décroche, il est perdu,** if this pupil fails to keep up, he won't have a chance. **3 se décrocher** *vpr* to come unhooked; **la médaille s'est décrochée,** the medal has come unpinned; **se d. la mâchoire,** to dislocate one's jaw; *F* **bâiller à se d. la mâchoire,** to yawn one's head off.
décroisement [dekrwazmɑ̃] *nm* uncrossing.
décroiser [dekrwaze] *vt* to uncross (*one's legs etc*).
décroissance [dekrwasɑ̃s] *nf* decrease; diminution (*of population*); decline (*of strength*); abatement (*of fever*); **nos importations sont en d.,** our imports are decreasing.
décroissant [dekrwasɑ̃] *adj* decreasing; **par ordre d.,** in descending order.
décroissement [dekrwasmɑ̃] *nm* waning (*of moon*); shortening (*of days*).
décroît [dekrwa] *nm* last quarter (*of moon*); **la lune est sur son d.,** the moon is in its last quarter.
décroître [dekrwatr] *vi* (*prp* **décroissant**; *pp* **décru**; *pr ind* **il décroît, ils décroissent**; *p hist* **il décrut**; *fu* **il décroîtra**) to decrease, to decline, to diminish; **les jours commencent à d.,** the days are beginning to draw in *or* get shorter; **la lune décroît,** the moon is on the wane; **aller (en) décroissant,** to decrease, to grow gradually less.
décrottage [dekrɔtaʒ] *nm* cleaning (*of boots etc*).
décrotter [dekrɔte] *vt* to clean, to remove mud from (*boots etc*); (*les semelles*) to scrape; *F* to polish up (*s.o.'s manners*).
décrottoir [dekrɔtwar] *nm* shoe scraper; **tapis d.,** (wire) door mat.
décrue [dekry] *nf* **(a)** fall, drop in level (*of river etc*); **(b)** decrease, diminution, fall (*in numbers etc*).
décryptage [dekriptaʒ] *nm* deciphering.
décrypter [dekripte] *vt* to decipher (*code*).
déçu [desy] *adj* disappointed; *Fig Iron* **elle ne va pas être déçue du voyage,** she's got another think coming; *Fig Iron* **je ne suis pas d. du voyage!,** a fine state of affairs!
déculotter [dekylɔte] **1** *vt* to take (*s.o.'s*) trousers off; *F* to debag (*s.o.*). **2 se déculotter** *vpr* to take off *or* let down one's trousers; *F* to grovel.
déculpabilisation [dekylpabilizasjɔ̃] *nf* exculpation; **la d. de l'avortement,** removing the guilt surrounding abortion.
déculpabiliser [dekylpabilize] **1** *vt* to stop (*s.o.*) feeling guilty (**de qch,** about sth); **d. la contraception,** to take the guilt out of (using) contraception, to remove the aura of guilt surrounding contraception. **2 se déculpabiliser** *vpr* to get rid of one's guilt feelings, to stop feeling guilty.
déculturation [dekyltyrasjɔ̃] *nf* loss of culture.
décuple [dekypl] **1** *adj* tenfold (*amount*). **2** *nm* tenfold increase.
décuplement [dekypləmɑ̃] *nm* multiplication by ten.
décupler [dekyple] **1** *vt* to increase *or* multiply tenfold; **la peur décuplait mon allure,** fear quickened my pace until I was almost running. **2** *vi* to increase tenfold.
décuver [dekyve] *vt* to tun, to rack off (*wine*).
dédaignable [dedɛɲabl] *adj* worthy of disdain; **cette proposition/somme n'est pas d.,** this proposal is not to be despised/this is a not inconsiderable sum.
dédaigner [dedɛɲe] *vt* to disdain, to scorn; to turn up one's nose at (*offer etc*); **d. des injures/des conseils,** to disregard insults/advice; **d. qn,** to treat s.o. with disdain, to scorn s.o.; *Litt* **elle dédaigna de répondre,** she disdained to reply.
dédaigneusement [dedɛɲøzmɑ̃] *adv* disdainfully, scornfully.
dédaigneux, -euse [dedɛɲø, -øz] *adj* disdainful, contemptuous, scornful (**de,** of).
dédain [dedɛ̃] *nm* disdain, scorn (**de, pour,** for); disregard (**de qch,** of sth; **pour qn,** for s.o.); **avec d.,** disdainfully, scornfully; **témoigner du d. à qn,** to show contempt for s.o.; **avoir le d. de** *ou* **pour qch,** to have a contempt for sth; **considérer qn avec d.,** to look down on s.o.; **regarder qn/répondre avec d.,** to look at s.o./to answer with disdain *or* disdainfully.
dédale [dedal] *nm* labyrinth, maze (*of streets*); **perdu dans un d. de réflexions,** lost in the maze of one's thoughts.
Dédale [dedal] *nm Myth* Daedalus.
dedans [dədɑ̃] **1** *adv* inside; in (*it, them etc*); **la lettre est d.,** the letter is inside; *F* **mettre qn d.,** (*en prison*) to put s.o. inside; (*le tromper*) to take s.o. for a ride; **donner d.,** to fall into the trap; *F* **je vais lui rentrer d.,** I'll smash his face in; **une autre voiture nous est rentrée d., nous nous sommes fait rentrer d.,** another car smashed into us; **marcher les pieds en d.,** to be pigeon-toed; **de d.,** from within; **en d.,** (on the) inside, within; **il n'était pas si calme en d.,** inwardly, he was not so calm; **en d. de,** within; **y a-t-il quelqu'un là-d.?,** is anyone there?; **il y a du bon là-d.,** there's some good stuff in it.

2 *nm* inside, interior (*of house, box etc*); innermost heart (*of person*); **agir du d.,** to act from within (*a party etc*); **au d. et au dehors,** inside and out; **au-d.,** (on the) inside, within; **au(-)d. de,** inside, within; **elle le savait au(-)d. d'elle,** inwardly, she knew it.
dédicace [dedikas] *nf* **(a)** dedication (*of book etc*); **(b)** *Rel* dedication, consecration (*of building etc*).
dédicacer [dedikase] *vt* (**je dédicaçai(s); n. dédicaçons**) to write a dedication in (*book etc*); **d. sa dernier livre,** (*d'un auteur*) to sign copies of his latest book; **livre dédicacé par son auteur,** author's signed copy of a book.
dédicatoire [dedikatwar] *adj* dedicatory.
dédier [dedje] *vt* **(a)** to dedicate, to inscribe (*book etc*); **(b)** *Rel etc* to dedicate, to consecrate (*building etc*).
dédire (se) [sədedir] *vpr* (*conj like* **dire** *except pr ind* **v. v. dédisez**) **se d. de,** to retract, to withdraw (*a statement*); to withdraw (*an accusation*); **se d. d'une promesse,** to go back on one's word.
dédit [dedi] *nm* **(a)** retraction, withdrawal; **(b)** breaking (*of promise*); **(c)** forfeit, penalty (*for breaking contract etc*).
dédommagement [dedɔmaʒmɑ̃] *nm* **(a)** (*action*) indemnification, indemnifying (**de qn,** of s.o.); **(b)** (*compensation*) compensation, damages; **recevoir une somme en d. de qch,** to receive a sum as *or* in compensation for sth; **en d. de la peine que je vous ai causé,** to make up for the pain I caused you; **c'est un d. à** *ou* **pour votre patience,** it's in recognition of your patience.
dédommager [dedɔmaʒe] *v* (**je dédommageai(s); n. dédommageons**) **1** *vt* (*financially*) to indemnify, to compensate (*s.o.*); to make amends to (*s.o.*); **comment pourrai-je te d.?,** how can I ever repay you?; **d. qn de**

qch, to indemnify *or* compensate s.o. for sth; **d. qn d'une perte,** to make good a loss to s.o.; **se faire d. par qn,** to receive compensation from s.o.. **2 se dédommager** *vpr* **pour me d. des frais qu'il a causés,** to compensate me for *or* to make up for the expense he put me to; **pour me d. j'ai tenu à ce qu'il m'invite au restaurant,** I insisted he should take me out to dinner to make up for it; **se d. de ses pertes,** to recoup one's losses.

dédoré [dedɔre] *adj* tarnished, with the gilt rubbed off.

dédorer [dedɔre] *vt* to remove the gilt from (*sth*).

dédouanage [dedwanaʒ] *nm* clearance (*of goods*).

dédouanement [dedwanmɑ̃] *nm* clearance (*of goods*) through customs; *Fig* **le d. de la conscience,** the clearing of one's conscience.

dédouaner [dedwane] **1** *vt* to clear (*goods*), to take (*goods*) out of bond; **d. ses bagages,** to clear one's luggage through customs; *Fig* **d. un voleur,** to rehabilitate a thief. **2 se dédouaner** *vpr Fig* to redeem oneself.

dédoublage [dedublaʒ] *nm* **(a)** diluting (*of alcohol*); **(b)** removing lining (*of coat etc*).

dédoublement [dedubləmɑ̃] *nm* **(a)** opening out (*of folded cloth etc*); **(b)** *Psy* dividing *or* splitting into two; *Ch* double decomposition; **d. de la personnalité,** split personality; *Ch* double decomposition; *Rail* **d. d'un train,** running a relief train.

dédoubler [deduble] **1** *vt* **(a)** to open out (*folded cloth etc*); **d. les rangs,** to form single file; **(b)** (*partager*) to divide *or* cut *or* split (*sth*) into two; **(c) d. un train,** to run a relief train; **(d)** to remove the lining of (*garment*). **2 se dédoubler** *vpr* **(a)** to unfold (*a blanket*); **(b)** to divide, to split (*into two parts*); *Psy* to have a split personality; *F* **je ne peux pas me d.,** I can't be in two places at once.

dédramatisation [dedramatizɑsjɔ̃] *nf* making less alarming *or* dramatic.

dédramatiser [dedramatize] *vt* to make less alarming *or* dramatic.

déductible [dedyktibl(ə)] *adj* deductible.

déductif, -ive [dedyktif, -iv] *adj Phil* deductive (*reasoning*).

déduction [dedyksjɔ̃] *nf* **(a)** (*raisonnement*) deduction, inference; **(b)** *Com etc* deduction, allowance, abatement; **faire d. des sommes payées d'avance,** to deduct *or* allow for sums paid in advance; **d. forfaitaire,** (*dans les impôts*) standard allowance; **sous d. de 10%,** less 10%; **sans d.,** terms net cash.

déduire [dedɥir] *v* (*conj like* **conduire**) **1** *vt* **(a)** (*démontrer*) to deduce, to infer (*result*); **de là, on peut d. que ...,** from this it may be deduced that ...; **(b)** (*enlever*) to deduct; **d. 5%,** to take off or deduct 5%, to allow a deduction of 5%. **2 se déduire** *vpr* to be deduced; **la solution se déduit tout simplement,** the solution can be deduced *or* follows quite simply.

déesse [deɛs] *nf* goddess.

défaillance [defajɑ̃s] *nf* **(a)** (*faiblesse*) (moral, physical) lapse; **sans d.,** without flinching; **courage sans d.,** unflagging courage; **travailler sans d.,** to work tirelessly; **moment de d.,** weak moment; **d. de mémoire,** lapse of memory; **d. cardiaque,** heart failure; **la machine a eu une d.,** the machine developed a fault; **d. mécanique,** mechanical failure; **(b)** (*évanouissement*) fainting fit; **tomber en d., avoir une d.,** to faint; **(c)** *Jur* default(ing).

défaillant, -ante [defajɑ̃, -ɑ̃t] **1** *adj* **(a)** failing (*strength*); declining (*health*); weak (*heart*); **d. de fatigue,** exhausted; **(b)** (*qui s'évanouit*) faint; **(c)** *Jur* defaulting. **2** *n Jur* defaulter, absconder.

défaillir [defajir] *vi* (*prp* **défaillant**; *pp* **défailli**; *pr ind* **il défaille, n. défaillons**; *impf* **je défaillais**; *p hist* **je défaillis**; *fu parfois* **je défaillerai**) **(a)** (*décliner*) to become feeble, to lose strength; **sa mémoire/sa force commence à d.,** his memory/strength is beginning to fail; **à cette nouvelle son cœur défaillit,** his heart sank at the news; **(b)** (*faiblir*) to flinch; **j'accomplirai le travail sans d.,** I'll do the job without flinching; **(c)** (*s'évanouir*) to faint; **d. de faim,** to feel faint with hunger.

défaire [defɛr] *v* (*conj like* **faire**) **1** *vt* **(a)** to undo; to untie (*parcel, knot*); to unwrap (*parcel*); to unpack (*suitcase*); to unpick (*seam*); to undo, to unzip (*one's dress etc*); to strip (*bed*); **d. ses cheveux,** to let one's hair down; *Litt* **d. qn de qn/qch,** to rid s.o. of s.o./sth;

(b) to demolish (*wall etc*); to pull (*sth*) to pieces; to cancel, to annul (*treaty*); to break off (*alliance, marriage*);

(c) *Litt* (*battre*) to defeat, overthrow (*army etc*); to get the better of (*s.o.*).

2 se défaire *vpr* **(a)** (*of clothes, knot*) to come undone; (*of hair*) to come down; (*of things joined together*) to come apart;

(b) se d. de qn, to get rid of s.o.; (*le tuer*) to kill s.o., *F* to get rid of s.o., to bump s.o. off; **se d. de qch,** to get rid of *or* rid oneself of sth; **se d. de ses marchandises,** to sell off one's goods; **je ne veux pas m'en d.,** I don't want to part with it; **se d. d'une mauvaise habitude,** to get out of *or* break oneself of a bad habit.

défait [defɛ] *adj* **(a)** drawn, haggard (*features, face*); **la mine défaite,** with a haggard expression; **il est arrivé à l'hôpital, d.,** he arrived at the hospital in a state of near collapse; **(b)** dishevelled, disarranged (*hair, appearance*); **(c)** defeated, overthrown (*army etc*).

défaite [defɛt] *nf* defeat.

défaitisme [defɛtism] *nm* defeatism.

défaitiste [defɛtist] *adj & n* defeatist.

défalcation [defalkɑsjɔ̃] *nf* deduction, deducting; writing-off (*of bad debt*); **d. faite des frais,** after deduction of expenses.

défalquer [defalke] *vt* to deduct (*sum from total*); **d. ses frais,** to deduct one's expenses; **d. une mauvaise créance,** to write off a bad debt.

défatiguer [defatige] **1** *vt* to relax; **un bon bain chaud va vous d.,** a hot bath will relax you *or* help you (to) unwind. **2 se défatiguer** *vpr* to unwind.

défaufiler [defofile] *vt Couture* to remove the tacks from.

défausser[1] [defose] *vt* to straighten (*rod, blade etc*).

défausser[2] **(se)** [sədefose] *vpr Cartes* to discard; **se d. à cœur,** to discard one's hearts.

défaut [defo] *nm* **(a)** absence, (total) lack (*of sth*); *Jur* default; **d. de paiement,** failure to pay, non-payment; **le temps me fait d.,** I can't spare the time; **les provisions font d.,** there is a shortage of supplies, supplies are short; **un d. d'activité sportive,** a lack of sporting activity; **sa mémoire lui fait d.,** he can't remember; **la mémoire lui fait d.,** he has a bad memory; *Banque* **d. de provision,** no funds; **chèque marqué d. de provision,** ≈ refer to drawer; **à d. de qch,** for lack of sth; *Fig* **j'ai trouvé le d. de la cuirasse,** I've found the chink in his *etc* armour; *Jur* **faire d.,** to fail to appear, to default; *Jur* **jugement par d.,** judgment by default;

(b) (*imperfection*) (*d'une personne*) fault, shortcoming; (*d'un objet*) defect, flaw; (*d'une machine*) defect; **chacun a ses défauts,** everyone has his faults; **la curiosité est un vilain d.,** ≈ curiosity killed the cat; **c'est là son moindre d.,** that's the least of his faults; **les défauts d'une explication/d'une théorie,** the flaws in *or* shortcomings of an explanation/a theory; **d. de fabrication,** manufacturing fault; **avoir un d.,** (*d'une machine*) to be defective; **il y a un d. de fonctionnement,** it isn't working properly; **remarquer un d. sur un tissu,** to notice a flaw in a piece of fabric; **cette école n'a qu'un d.,** this school has only one drawback; **sans d.,** faultless, flawless; **d. de prononciation,** fault in pronunciation; **mettre les chiens en d.,** to throw the hounds off the scent; *Fig* **mettre qn en d.,** to throw s.o. off the scent, to put s.o. on the wrong track; **prendre qn en d.,** to catch s.o. out; **pécher par d.,** to sin by omission, to commit a sin of omission;

(c) *Ordinat* **lecteur/clavier/***etc* **par d.,** default drive/keyboard/*etc*.

défaveur [defavœr] *nf* disfavour, *US* disfavor, discredit; **tomber/être en d.,** to fall into/to be in disfavour (**auprès de,** with).

défavorable [defavɔrabl] *adj* unfavourable, *US* unfavorable (**à,** to); **les conditions (nous) sont défavorables,** conditions are against us.

défavorablement [defavɔrabləmɑ̃] *adv* unfavourably, *US* unfavorably.

défavorisé [defavɔrize] *adj* (*enfant, pays*) underprivileged; **candidat d.,** candidate at a disadvantage.

défavoriser [defavɔrize] *vt* to be unfair to (*s.o.*), to put (*s.o.*) at a disadvantage; **le climat du désert défavorise les soldats occidentaux,** Western soldiers are at a disadvantage in desert climates.

défécation [defekɑsjɔ̃] *nf* **(a)** *Physiol* defecation; **(b)** *Ch* defecation, clarification.

défectible [defɛktibl] *adj* fallible.

défectif, -ive [defɛktif, -iv] *adj* defective (*verb etc*).

défection [defɛksjɔ̃] *nf* defection from *or* desertion of a cause *or* a party *etc*; **je ne m'attendais pas à sa d.,** I did not expect him to defect; **en cas de d.,** if there are defections; **faire d.,** to desert, to defect, *F* to rat.

défectueusement [defɛktɥøzmɑ̃] *adv* defectively.

défectueux, -euse [defɛktɥø, -øz] *adj* defective, faulty, imperfect.

défectuosité [defɛktɥozite] *nf* **(a)** (*défaut*) defect, flaw;

(b) *(imperfection)* defectiveness.
défendable [defɑ̃dabl] *adj* defensible *(position etc)*.
défendeur, -eresse [defɑ̃dœr, -drɛs] *n Jur* defendant.
défendre [defɑ̃dr] **1** *vt* **(a)** to defend *(cause, prisoner etc)*; to defend, to champion *(opinion, cause)*; to defend, to maintain, to uphold *(opinion, right)*; to defend, to stand up for *(one's friends etc)* (**contre,** against); **il sait d. son opinion,** he can hold his own; **faire qch à son corps défendant,** to do sth reluctantly *or* grudgingly; **d. une théorie/une politique/une position,** to defend a theory/policy/position; **apprendre à d. ses idées,** to learn to stand up for *or* to defend one's ideas; *Jur* **qui est-ce qui la défend?,** who's defending her?; *Jur* **il la défend sur des accusations de corruption,** he's defending her on charges of corruption;
(b) *(protéger)* to protect, to shield, to guard (**contre,** against, from); *Mil* to defend; **l'isolant défend la pièce du froid,** the insulation shields the room from cold; *Mil* **pays bien/mal défendu,** well/poorly defended country;
(c) *(interdire)* to forbid, to prohibit; **fruit défendu,** forbidden fruit; **d. qch à qn,** to forbid s.o. sth; **la religion défend la consommation d'alcool,** the religion forbids the consumption of alcohol; **il défendit qu'on passât par là,** he forbade anyone to go that way.
2 *vi* **d. à qn de faire qch,** to forbid s.o. to do sth; **il est défendu de fumer,** smoking (is) prohibited, no smoking; **il m'est défendu de fumer,** I'm not allowed *or* I'm forbidden to smoke.
3 se défendre *vpr* **(a)** to defend oneself; **se d. avec une arme,** to defend oneself with a weapon; *F* **je me défends,** I'm holding my own, I'm getting along; **il se défend bien en affaires,** he's a good businessman; **se d. contre une critique,** to defend oneself against criticism; **cette attitude peut aussi se d.,** this attitude is also defensible; *Litt* **se d. d'avoir fait qch,** to deny having done sth;
(b) *(se protéger)* **se d. de** *ou* **contre qch,** to protect *or* shield oneself from *or* against sth; **se d. de la pluie,** to shelter from the rain; **se d. des tentations,** to steer clear of temptation;
(c) se d. de faire qch, to refrain from doing sth; **on ne peut se d. de l'aimer,** you can't help liking him;
(d) *(s'interdire) (the pron is the indirect object)* **se d. tout plaisir/toute gourmandise,** to deny oneself all pleasure/sweet things.
défense [defɑ̃s] *nf* **(a)** *(d'une politique etc) & Mil Jur* defence, *US* defense; **combattre pour la d. de son pays,** to fight in defence of one's country; **ligne de d.,** line of defence; **moyen de d.,** means of defence; **prendre la d. de qn,** to defend s.o.; **d. nationale,** national defence; **d. côtière/aérienne,** coastal/air defence; **d. contre avions,** anti-aircraft defence; **d. passive,** civil defence; **sans d.,** unprotected, defenceless; **être hors de d.,** to be unable to defend oneself; *Physiol* **la d. de l'organisme,** the organism's defence mechanisms; *Jur* **légitime d.,** self defence; **moyens de d.,** plea (of defendant); *Jur* **la parole est à la d.,** the defence may now speak; **les défenses de la cité,** the defences of the city; *Can* **Ministère de la D. nationale,** Department of National Defence; *Fig* **une loi qui sert de d. aux abus,** a law that protects the wrongdoer;
(b) tusk *(of elephant, wild boar etc)*;
(c) *(interdiction)* prohibition, interdiction; **d. d'entrer/de fumer,** no entry *or* admittance/smoking; *Vieilli* **faire d. à qn de faire qch,** to forbid s.o. to do sth.
défenseur [defɑ̃sœr] *nm* **(a)** protector, defender *(of child, town etc)*; supporter, upholder *(of a cause)*; **(b)** *Jur* counsel for the defence; **qui est son d.?,** who's defending him?
défensif, -ive [defɑ̃sif, -iv] **1** *adj* defensive. **2** *nf* **défensive,** defensive; **être** *ou* **se tenir sur la défensive,** to be on the defensive.
défensivement [defɑ̃sivmɑ̃] *adv* defensively.
déféquer [defeke] *v* (**je défèque, n. déféquons; je déféquerai**) **1** *vt Ch* to clarify, to clear *(sth)*. **2** *vi Physiol* to defecate.
déférence [deferɑ̃s] *nf* deference, respect, regard (**pour,** for); **par d. pour ...,** in *or* out of deference to ... .
déférent [deferɑ̃] **1** *adj* **(a)** deferential *(manner etc)*; **(b)** *Anat* deferent; **canal d.,** vas deferens. **2** *nm* mint mark.
déférer [defere] *v* (**je défère; je déférerai**) **1** *vt* **(a)** *Jur* to submit, to refer *(case to a court)*; **d. qn à la justice,** to hand over *or* give up s.o. to justice; **d. le serment à,** to administer the oath to *(s.o.)*; to swear *(witness)*; to swear in *(jury)*; **(b)** *Arch* to confer, to bestow *(honour)* (**à,** on). **2** *vi* **d. à qn,** to defer to s.o.; **d. aux ordres de qn,** to comply with s.o.'s orders; **d. à une demande,** to accede to a request.
déferlant, -ante [defɛrlɑ̃, -ɑ̃t] *Nau* **1** *adj* breaking *(wave)*; **vague déferlante,** breaker, beachcomber. **2** *nf* **déferlante,** breaker, beachcomber.
déferlement [defɛrləmɑ̃] *nm* breaking *(of waves)*; unfurling *(of sail, flag)*; **d. d'enthousiasme/de violence,** wave of enthusiasm/violence; **d. de colère,** fit of anger.
déferler [defɛrle] **1** *vt Nau* to unfurl, to shake out *(sail, flag)*; to break *(flag, signal)*; to set *(sail)*. **2** *vi (of waves)* to break; **la foule déferle dans la rue,** the crowd is surging down the street.
déferrage [defɛraʒ] *nm* removal of iron *(from sth)*; unshoeing *(of horse)*.
déferrer [defɛre] *vt* to remove the iron from *(sth)*; to unshoe *(horse)*.
défet [defɛ] *nm* waste *or* odd *or* spare sheet *(of paper)*.
défeuillaison [defœjɛzɔ̃] *nf* defoliation, fall of the leaves.
défeuiller [defœje] **1** *vt Litt* to strip the leaves off, to defoliate *(tree)*. **2 se défeuiller** *vpr (of tree)* to shed its leaves.
défi [defi] *nm* **(a)** challenge; **lancer** *ou* **jeter un d. à qn,** to challenge s.o.; **relever un d.,** to take up a challenge; **la jeunesse a besoin de d.,** young people need a challenge; **(b)** *(provocation)* defiance; **mettre qn au d. de faire qch,** to defy *or* dare s.o. to do sth; **avec un sourire de d.,** with a smile of defiance, with a defiant smile; **d'un air de d.,** defiantly; **son attitude est un d. à votre autorité,** his attitude challenges your authority.
défiance [defjɑ̃s] *nf* mistrust, distrust, suspicion, wariness; **inspirer** *ou* **éveiller la d.,** to arouse suspicion; **motion de d.,** motion of no confidence; **d. de soi-même,** diffidence, lack of self-confidence.
défiant [defjɑ̃] *adj* mistrustful, distrustful, cautious, wary.
défibrillation [defibrijasjɔ̃] *nf Méd* defibrillation.
déficeler [defisle] *v (conj like* **ficeler***)* **1** *vt* to untie, to undo *(parcel etc)*. **2 se déficeler** *vpr* to come untied *or* undone.
déficience [defisjɑ̃s] *nf* deficiency; **d. mentale,** mental deficiency; **d. (alimentaire),** malnutrition.
déficient [defisjɑ̃] *adj* deficient; **enfant d.,** mentally deficient child.
déficit [defisit] *nm* deficit, shortage *(in cash etc)*; **être en d.,** to show a deficit; **combler un d.,** to make good a deficit; **d. psychologique/mental,** psychological/mental deficiency; **d. budgétaire/commercial,** budget/trade deficit.
déficitaire [defisitɛr] *adj (account)* showing a debit balance; *(budget etc)* showing a deficit; **récolte d.,** short crop.
défier [defje] **1** *vt* **(a)** *(dans une lutte etc)* to challenge *(s.o.)*; **d. qn au combat/aux échecs,** to challenge s.o. to fight/to a game of chess; **(b)** to defy *(s.o., sth)*; **je vous défie de faire mieux,** I defy you to do better; **le spectacle défie toute description,** the sight defies *or* is beyond description; **(c)** to brave, to face *(danger, death)*. **2 se défier** *vpr* **se d. de qn/qch,** to mistrust *or* distrust s.o./sth; **se d. de soi-même,** to be diffident; **se d. de ses intuitions,** to mistrust *or* distrust one's intuition.
défiguration [defigyrasjɔ̃] *nf* disfigurement, disfiguration.
défigurement [defigyrmɑ̃] *nm* disfigurement; defacement *(of statue)*; distortion *(of truth)*.
défigurer [defigyre] *vt* to disfigure *(s.o., sth)*; to deface *(statue)*; to distort *(the truth)*; **d. le paysage,** to disfigure the countryside; **d. la pensée/les intentions de qn,** to misrepresent s.o.'s thoughts/intentions; **d. un texte,** *(d'un réviseur etc)* to ruin a text.
défilé [defile] *nm* **(a)** *(couloir)* defile; (mountain) pass; **(b)** *(file)* procession; *Mil etc* march past; *Av* **d. (aérien),** flypast; **d. de mode,** fashion parade; **un d. ininterrompu de touristes,** an endless stream of tourists.
défiler¹ [defile] **1** *vt* **(a)** to unstring, to unthread *(beads, necklace)*; **(b)** *Mil* to defilade *(fortress)*; to put *(company etc)* under cover. **2 se défiler** *vpr* **(a)** *(of beads etc)* to come unstrung; **(b)** *Mil* **se d. du feu de l'adversaire,** to take cover from the enemy's fire; **(c)** *F (se dérober)* to slip off on the quiet.
défiler² *vi* **(a)** *(passer en colonne)* to walk in procession; *Mil* to march past; **les manifestants défilent,** the demonstrators march past; **des centaines de voitures défilent vers la côte,** hundreds of cars are streaming towards the coast; **les images qui défilent devant nos yeux,** the pictures which pass before our eyes; **le paysage défile,** the countryside goes by; **faire d. une bande/une bobine de film,** to run a tape/reel of film; **(b)** *Mil* to defile; **d. en colonne par deux,** to file off in twos.

défini [defini] *adj* **(a)** (*précis*) clearly defined; **mot bien/mal d.,** well-/ill-defined word; **un travail bien d.,** a clearly defined piece of work; *Ordinat* **d. par l'utilisateur,** user-defined; *Ordinat* **pouvant être d. par l'utilisateur,** user-definable; **(b)** *Gram* definite (*article etc*); **passé d.,** past definite, preterite, past historic.
définir [definir] *vt* to define; **c'est difficile à d.,** it's difficult to define; **d. qn comme un bon à rien,** to stamp s.o. as a good-for-nothing.
définissable [definisabl] *adj* definable.
définitif, -ive [definitif, -iv] **1** *adj* definitive, final (*resolution, judgment etc*); **la biographie définitive de Proust,** the definitive biography of Proust; **une séparation définitive,** a permanent separation; **nommé à titre d.,** permanently appointed. **2** *adv* **en définitive,** finally, when all is said and done.
définition [definisjɔ̃] *nf* **(a)** (*de mot etc*) definition; **par d.,** by definition; **(b)** clue (*of crossword puzzle*); **(c)** *TV* **télévision à haute d.,** high definition television.
définitivement [definitivmɑ̃] *adv* definitely; **il est parti d.,** he's gone away for good.
déflagrateur [deflagratœr] *nm Él* spark gap.
déflagration [deflagrɑsjɔ̃] *nf* combustion.
déflagrer [deflagre] *vi* to combust.
déflation [deflɑsjɔ̃] *nf* **(a)** deflation (*of the currency*); **(b)** *Géog* wind erosion.
déflationniste [deflasjɔnist] *Écon* **1** *adj* deflationary. **2** *n* deflationist.
défléchir [defleʃir] *vt & vi* to deflect.
déflecteur [deflɛktœr] *nm Aut etc* deflector.
défleuraison [deflœrɛzɔ̃] *nf* falling of blossom.
défleurir [deflœrir] **1** *vi* (*of tree etc*) to lose its blossom. **2** *vt* to take the flowers off (*plant*).
défloraison [deflɔrɛzɔ̃] *nf* = **DÉFLEURAISON.**
défloration [deflɔrɑsjɔ̃] *nf* deflowering (*of virgin*).
déflorer [deflɔre] *vt* **(a)** *Fig* (*abîmer*) to take the freshness off, to spoil (*piece of news etc*); **(b)** to deflower (*virgin*).
défoliant [defɔljɑ̃] *nm Agr* defoliant.
défoliation [defɔljɑsjɔ̃] *nf* defoliation.
défonçage [defɔ̃saʒ] *nm* smashing in (*of box etc*); knocking down (*of wall*).
défonce [defɔ̃s] *nf F* (*par la drogue*) trip; **être en pleine d.,** to be on a trip.
défoncé [defɔ̃se] *adj* **(a)** (*éventré*) bashed in, battered; **(b)** **chemin d.,** rough *or* bumpy road; **(c)** *F* (*qui a pris de la drogue*) high, stoned.
défoncement [defɔ̃smɑ̃] *nm* = **DEFONÇAGE.**
défoncer [defɔ̃se] *v* (**je défonçai(s); n. défonçons**) **1** *vt* **(a)** to smash in, to bash in (*box, door etc*); to knock down (*wall etc*); to stave in (*cask, boat*); **(b)** to break up, to cut up (*road*). **2 se défoncer** *vpr F* **(a)** to get high (*on drugs*); **(b)** (*faire un grand effort*) to sweat blood; **(c)** (*passer du bon temps*) to have a whale of a time.
défonceuse [defɔ̃søz] *nf Agr* heavy plough, trenching plough.
déforestation [defɔrɛstɑsjɔ̃] *nf* deforestation.
déformant [defɔrmɑ̃] *adj* distorting.
déformation [defɔrmɑsjɔ̃] *nf* deformation; *Phot* distortion (*of image*); buckling (*of metal*); warping (*of wood*); **avoir une d.,** to be deformed; **être né avec une d.,** to be born deformed.
déformer [defɔrme] **1** *vt* to deform, to put (*sth*) out of shape; to warp (*metal*); to buckle (*wood*); *Phot* to distort (*image*); **chaussée déformée,** (*sur panneau*) uneven road surface; **d. les faits** *ou* **la réalité,** to distort *or* misrepresent the facts; **d. la pensée de l'auteur,** to misrepresent the author's thoughts; **il est déformé par son métier/l'habitude,** he is conditioned by his work/habits. **2 se déformer** *vpr* to get out of shape; (*de bois*) to warp; (*de métal*) to buckle.
défoulement [defulmɑ̃] *nm Psy F* letting off steam; *F* **séance de d.,** bitch session.
défouler [defule] **1** *vt Psy* to liberate. **2 se défouler** *vpr* to unwind, *F* to let off steam. **3** *vi F* **ça défoule,** (*de se mettre en colère*) it helps you to let off steam; (*de faire du sport*) it helps you unwind.
défourner [defurne] *vt* to draw (*pottery*) from the kiln; to draw (*bread*) from the oven.
défraîchi [defrɛʃi] *adj* (shop)soiled (*goods*); faded (*flowers, beauty*); **un Don Juan d.,** an ageing Don Juan.
défraîchir [defrɛʃir] **1** *vt* to take away the newness *or* freshness of (*sth*). **2 se défraîchir** *vpr* to lose one's *or* its freshness, to fade.
défrayer [defreje] *vt* (**je défraie, je défraye; je défraierai, je défrayerai**) **(a) d. qn,** to defray *or* pay s.o.'s expenses; **être défrayé de tout,** to have all expenses paid; **(b) d. la conversation,** (*la monopoliser*) to monopolize the conversation; (*en être le sujet*) to be the subject of conversation; **d. la chronique,** to be in the news.
défrichage [defriʃaʒ] *nm* clearing (*of land*).
défriche [defriʃ] *nf Agr* clearing, cleared patch (*in forest etc*).
défrichement [defriʃmɑ̃] *nm* clearing (*of land*).
défricher [defriʃe] *vt* to clear, to reclaim (*land for cultivation*); to bring (*land*) into cultivation; to break (*new ground*); *Fig* **d. un sujet/un nouveau domaine scientifique,** to do pioneer work in a subject/to pioneer a new field of science.
défricheur, -euse [defriʃœr, -øz] *n Agr* land clearer, settler; *Fig* pioneer (*in a subject*).
défriper [defripe] *vt* to smooth out (*crumpled garment*).
défriser [defrize] *vt* to uncurl, to straighten (*hair*); *F* **ça vous défrise?,** are you put out?
défroisser [defrwase] **1** *vt* to take the creases out of (*dress etc*). **2 se défroisser** *vpr* to lose its creases.
défroque [defrɔk] *nf* **(a)** effects (*of dead monk*); **(b)** *F* (*vieux habits*) cast-offs.
défroqué [defrɔke] *adj & nm* unfrocked (priest).
défroquer [defrɔke] **1** *vt* to unfrock (*priest*). **2** *vi* to leave the priesthood, to renounce one's order. **3 se défroquer** *vpr* to leave the priesthood.
défunt, -unte [defœ̃, -œ̃t] **1** *adj* defunct, deceased; **le roi d.,** the late king. **2** *n* deceased; **prier pour les défunts,** to pray for the dead.
dégagé [degaʒe] *adj* free and easy (*tone, manner*); free (*movements etc*); clear (*sky, road*); **allure dégagée,** swinging stride; **vue dégagée,** open view.
dégagement [degaʒmɑ̃] *nm* **(a)** redemption (*of pledge, mortgage*); taking out of pawn; **(b)** clearing (*of road, of the lungs etc*); disengagement, release (*of brake etc*); *Pol Mil* disengagement; *Fb* clearance; loosening, slackening (*of bolt etc*); *Escrime* disengaging (*of one's point*); **escalier de d.,** (*privé*) private staircase; (*de secours*) emergency stairs; **porte de d.,** (side) exit (*of cinema etc*); **(c)** escape, release (*of steam, gas etc*); emission, liberation (*of heat*); **tuyau de d.,** waste pipe; **(d)** open space, clearing (*in front of house etc*); clearance (*of car above the ground*); **voie de d.,** *Rail* siding; *Aut* slip road.
dégager [degaʒe] *v* (**je dégageai(s); n. dégageons**) **1** *vt* **(a)** to redeem (*pledge, mortgage*); to take (*sth*) out of pawn; **d. des titres,** to release (pledged) securities; **d. sa parole,** to take back one's word;

(b) (*libérer*) to disengage; to relieve the congestion in, to clear (*road, deck etc*); *MecE etc* to free (*a part*); to loosen, to slacken (*bolt*); to back off (*a tool*); *Escrime* to disengage (*the blade*); *Fb* to kick (*ball*) over the touchline, to clear (*ball*); *Pol* **d. une majorité,** to secure a (working) majority; **d. le frein,** to release the brake; **d. une ville,** to relieve a town; **d. les blessés des décombres,** to pull the injured clear of the wreckage; **d. qn d'une promesse,** to release s.o. from a promise; **d. sa responsabilité d'une affaire,** to disclaim responsibility in a matter; *Archit* **d. les vues,** to open vistas; **robe qui dégage les épaules/le cou,** dress that leaves the shoulders/the neck bare; **d. l'idée principale d'un texte,** to draw *or* derive the main idea from a text;

(c) to emit, to give off (*vapour, smell*); to emit, to give out (*heat*).

2 se dégager *vpr* **(a)** to free oneself, to get free; to get clear (**de,** of); (*de la surveillance*) to break loose, to break away (**de,** from); (*d'une situation difficile*) to extricate oneself (**de,** from); **d'un effort violent il s'est dégagé,** he wrenched himself free; **se d. d'une promesse,** to go back on a promise; **le ciel se dégage,** the sky is clearing; **mon nez commence à se d.,** my nose is starting to unblock;

(b) (*of gas, smell etc*) to be given off (**de,** by); to escape, to emanate (**de,** from); **il se dégage de l'oxygène,** oxygen is given off; *Fig* **le calme qui se dégage de sa présence,** the calm radiated by his presence; **le magnétisme qui se dégage d'elle,** the magnetism she radiates;

(c) (*ressortir*) to emerge, to come out; **la silhouette du navire s'est dégagée du brouillard,** the ship loomed up out of the fog; **la vérité se dégage peu à peu,** the truth is gradually coming out; **cette nécessité se dégage de l'étude de la situation,** this need becomes apparent after studying the situation.

3 *vi* **(a)** *F* to clear off; **dégagez, s'il vous plaît,** move along, please, clear the way please; **allez dégage!, je t'ai assez vu!,** go on, clear off!, I've seen enough of you;

(b) (*danse*) to stretch out one's foot in preparation for a step.

dégaine [degɛn] *nf F* (*allure*) awkward gait; (*apparence*) strange appearance.

dégainer [degene] *vt* to unsheathe, to draw (*sword*).

déganter (se) [sədegɑ̃te] *vpr* to take off one's gloves.

dégarni [degarni] *adj* (*frigidaire, placard etc*) empty; **arbre d.**, tree bare of leaves; **front d.**, receding hairline; **mon porte-feuille est d.**, I'm short of cash.

dégarnir [degarnir] **1** *vt* to empty (*fridge, cupboard etc*); to clear (*room etc*); to strip (*bed etc*); to draw (heavily) on (*bank account*); to withdraw troops from (*town etc*); to take the trimmings off (*a dress*); to unrig (*ship, capstan*); to thin out (*tree*). **2 se dégarnir** *vpr* (*of tree*) to lose its leaves; (*of head*) to go bald; (*of hall etc*) to empty; **il commence à se d.**, his hair is thinning, he's going bald; **les rayons se sont dégarnis en un rien de temps**, the shelves were emptied *or* stripped bare in next to no time.

dégât [degɑ] *nm* damage; **il y a eu du** *ou* **un sacré d.**, there was a lot of damage; **dégâts**, damage; **les gelées ont fait des dégâts dans les vignobles**, the frosts have caused havoc in the vineyards; **limiter les dégâts**, to limit the damage.

dégauchir [degoʃir] *vt* to surface, to rough plane (*board etc*); to straighten, to true (*piece of machinery etc*).

dégauchissage [degoʃisaʒ] *nm*, **dégauchissement** [degoʃismɑ̃] *nm* surfacing, rough planing (*of board*); straightening, truing up (*of piece of machinery*); trimming (*of stone*).

dégauchisseuse [degoʃisøz] *nf* surfacing machine, surfacer.

dégazage [degazaʒ] *nm Ch* **(a)** (*of water etc*) degassing; **(b)** (*of tanker*) cleaning out.

dégazer [degaze] *vt Ch* **(a)** to degas (*water etc*); **(b)** to clean out (*tanker*).

dégel [deʒɛl] *nm* **(a)** *Météo* thaw; **le temps est** *ou* **se met au d.**, it's beginning to thaw; **(b)** *Pol etc* thaw (in relations between two countries).

dégelée [deʒle] *nf* thrashing.

dégeler [deʒle] *v* (**il dégèle**; **il dégèlera**) **1** *vt* to thaw; *Fin* to unfreeze (*assets etc*); **d. un auditoire**, to warm up an audience; **d. qn**, to thaw s.o. (out); **d. les relations entre deux pays**, to bring about a thaw in relations between two countries. **2** *v impers* to thaw; **il dégèle**, it is thawing. **3 se dégeler** *vpr* to thaw (out); **dans quelques jours, elle se sera complètement dégelée**, she'll thaw out in a day or two; (*de quelqu'un qui arrive*) she'll settle in in a day *or* two.

dégénération [deʒenerasjɔ̃] *nf* degeneration, degeneracy.

dégénéré, -ée [deʒenere] **1** *adj* **(a)** degenerate; **(b)** *Psy* (*arriéré*) (mentally) defective. **2** *n Psy* mental defective.

dégénérer [deʒenere] *vi* (**je dégénère**; **je dégénérerai**) to degenerate (**de**, from; **en**, into); (*of quality*) to deteriorate; **son rhume a dégénéré en bronchite**, his cold developed into bronchitis.

dégénérescence [deʒenerɛsɑ̃s] *nf Méd* degeneration; *Fig* **la d. des mentalités**, the degeneration in the way people think.

dégénérescent [deʒenerɛsɑ̃] *adj Méd* degenerating, degenerative.

dégermer [deʒɛrme] *vt Agr* to degerm.

dégingandé [deʒɛ̃gɑ̃de] *adj F* (*personne*) gangling, lanky.

dégivrage [deʒivraʒ] *nm Av Aut* de-icing; (*de frigidaire*) defrosting.

dégivrer [deʒivre] *vt Av Aut* to de-ice; (*le frigidaire etc*) to defrost.

dégivreur [deʒivrœr] *nm Av Aut* de-icer; (*de frigidaire etc*) defroster.

déglacer [deglase] *v* (*conj like* **glacer**) **1** *vt* **(a)** to take the glaze off (*paper*); **(b)** to thaw, to melt the ice on (*pond etc*); to defrost (*refrigerator*); **(c)** *Culin* to deglaze (*frying pan etc*). **2** *vi Culin* to deglaze.

déglinguer [deglɛ̃ge] *vt F* to smash up, to bust up; **ma moto est toute déglinguée**, my motorbike is falling to pieces.

déglutir [deglytir] *vt Physiol* to swallow.

déglutition [deglytisjɔ̃] *nf Physiol* swallowing.

dégobiller [degɔbije] *Arg* **1** *vi* (*vomir*) to puke, *esp Am* to throw up. **2** *vt* to bring up (*one's food*); *Fig* **d. une leçon**, to regurgitate a lesson.

dégoiser [degwaze] **1** *vt F & Péj* to spout (*speech etc*); **qu'est-ce qu'il dégoise?**, what's he rattling on about? **2** *vi* to rattle on, to go on (and on).

dégommage [degomaʒ] *nm* **(a)** ungumming; **(b)** *F* sacking (*of s.o.*).

dégommer [degɔme] *vt* **(a)** to ungum, to unstick (*sth*); **(b)** *F* (*destituer*) to give (*s.o.*) the sack; (*vider*) to kick (*s.o.*) out; (*en gagnant*) to beat, to lick (*s.o.*) (at a game); **les militaires au pouvoir ont été dégommés**, the military has been ousted from power.

dégonflage [degɔ̃flaʒ] *nm*, **dégonfle** [degɔ̃fl] *nf F* backing *or* chickening out; **après son dégonflage**, after he chickened out.

dégonflé, -ée [degɔ̃fle] **1** *adj* **(a)** (*tyre etc*) flat, soft; **(b)** *F* chicken; **ce que tu peux être d.!**, you really are chicken! **2** *n F* coward, chicken, *US* yellowbelly.

dégonflement [degɔ̃fləmɑ̃] *nm* (*d'un pneu*) deflating, deflation.

dégonfler [degɔ̃fle] **1** *vt* **(a)** to deflate, to let the air out of (*tyre, balloon etc*); **(b)** to reduce, to bring down (*swelling*); **d. les prix**, to bring prices down; **(c)** *F* to debunk (*hero*); **d. la portée d'un événement**, to play down the importance of an event. **2 se dégonfler** *vpr* **(a)** (*of tyre, balloon etc*) to go flat; **(b)** (*of swelling*) to go down; **(c)** *F* to chicken out, to get cold feet. **3** *vi* (*of swelling*) to go down.

dégorgement [degɔrʒəmɑ̃] *nm* (*d'un égout, un évier*) unblocking, clearing; **le d. du vin**, = the process of removing sediment from wine prior to its final corking.

dégorger [degɔrʒe] *v* (**je dégorgeai(s)**; **n. dégorgeons**) **1** *vt* **(a)** to disgorge; **l'égout dégorge de l'eau sale**, the drain is discharging dirty water; **la rue a dégorgé un flot de gens**, a crowd of people surged from the street; **(b)** to free, to clear, to unstop (*passage, pipe*); **d. un évier bouché**, to clear a blocked sink, to unblock a sink; **(c)** to purify, to scour (*wool, leather*); **d. du vin**, = to remove sediment from wine prior to its final corking. **2** *vi* **(a)** (*of sewer, pond*) to flow out, to discharge (**dans**, into); (*of gutter, stream*) to overflow; **(b)** *Culin* **faire d. des concombres/etc**, to salt cucumbers/*etc* (*to make them release water*). **3 se dégorger** *vpr* (*d'une rivière, d'un égout*) to empty (**dans**, into).

dégot(t)er [degɔte] *vt F* to dig up; **où as-tu dégotté ce chapeau?**, wherever did you dig up that hat?

dégoulinade [degulinad] *nf* trickle, drip.

dégoulinement [degulinmɑ̃] *nm* trickling, dripping.

dégouliner [deguline] *vi* (*of water*) to trickle, drip; **la pluie me dégoulinait dans le cou**, the rain was trickling down my neck.

dégoupiller [degupije] *vt* to pull out the pin of (*grenade*).

dégourdi, -ie [degurdi] **1** *adj* bright, sharp, smart; **il n'est pas très d.**, he's not very bright, he's not really on the ball. **2** *n* **c'est un d./une dégourdie**, he's/she's pretty bright, he's/she's got what it takes.

dégourdir [degurdir] **1** *vt* to remove the stiffness *or* numbness from (*the limbs*); to revive (*by warmth, movement etc*); *Fig* **d. qn**, to sharpen s.o.'s wits; **Paris l'a dégourdi**, Paris has polished him up *or F* has taught him a thing *or* two; **d. de l'eau**, to take the chill off water. **2 se dégourdir** *vpr* (*en marchant*) to restore the circulation; *Fig* to grow smarter *or* more alert; **je vais me d. les jambes**, I'm going to stretch my legs a bit.

dégourdissement [degurdismɑ̃] *nm* removal of numbness.

dégoût [degu] *nm* **(a)** (*répulsion*) disgust, distaste, loathing; **il a un véritable d. pour le beurre**, he can't stand butter; **(b)** (*aversion*) dislike; **avoir du d. pour qch**, to dislike sth; **prendre qch en d.**, to take a dislike to sth; **le d. de la vie**, world-weariness; **le d. de soi**, self-loathing; **il a pris sa vie en d.**, he grew weary of the life he was leading; **cela fait partie de mes dégoûts**, that is one of my dislikes.

dégoûtant -ante [degutɑ̃, -ɑ̃t] **1** *adj* disgusting, revolting, loathsome, nauseating (*sight, smell etc*); **un homme d.**, a revolting man; **c'est d. de mentir/voler**, it's disgusting to lie/steal; **elle gagne encore!, c'est d.!**, she's won again!, it's disgusting! **2** *n* filthy character; **un vieux d.**, a dirty old man.

dégoûté, -ée [degute] **1** *adj* **(a)** (*écœuré*) disgusted (**de**, with); *F* sick (**de**, of); *F* **je suis d. de tes mensonges**, I'm sick of your lies; **d. de la vie**, weary of life; **je suis d. de la viande**, meat turns my stomach; **(b)** (*difficile*) fastidious, squeamish; *Iron* **vous n'êtes pas d.!**, you're not fussy! **2** *n* **faire le** *ou* **la dégoûté(e)**, to turn up one's nose (at sth).

dégoûter [degute] **1** *vt* to disgust; **cette vision m'a dégoûté à jamais du fromage**, this sight put me off cheese for good; **d. qn de qch**, to put s.o. off sth; **tout cela me dégoûte**, I'm sick of it all; **c'est à vous d. de l'Espagne/des hommes!**, it's enough to put you off Spain/men! **2 se dégoûter** *vpr* **se d. de qn/qch**, to take a dislike to s.o./sth; **il s'est dégoûté de Paris**, he got tired of (living in) Paris.

dégoutter [degute] *vi* **(a)** (*tomber*) to drip, to trickle, to fall drop by drop (**de,** from); **la pluie dégoutte de son chapeau,** the rain is dripping from his hat; **(b)** (*laisser tomber*) to be dripping (**de,** with); **un parapluie dégouttant d'eau,** a dripping wet umbrella.

dégradant [degradɑ̃] *adj* degrading.

dégradation¹ [degradɑsjɔ̃] *nf* **(a)** damage; defacement (*of monument etc*); **d. du matériel scolaire/de l'environnement,** damage to school equipment/the environment; **cette maison est dans un état de d. pitoyable,** this house is in a shocking state of repair; **(b)** (*détérioration*) deterioration; **la d. des relations,** the deterioration in relations; **d. du climat politique,** deterioration of the political climate; **(c)** (moral) degradation; **tomber dans la d.,** to lose all self-respect; **(d)** downgrading (*in rank etc*); **d. civique,** loss of civil rights; **(e)** *Phys* dissipation (*of energy*).

dégradation² *nf* shading off, graduation (*of colours, light*).

dégradé [degrade] *nm* (*of colours*) gradation; *Phot* graduated shading; **cheveux coupés en d.,** layered hair.

dégrader¹ [degrade] **1** *vt* **(a)** to deface, to damage (*monument*); **(b)** to degrade, to debase (*s.o.*); **des conditions de vie qui dégradent la personne,** degrading living conditions; **(c)** to downgrade (*s.o.*) (*in rank etc*); **(d)** *Phys* to degrade (*energy*). **2 se dégrader** *vpr* **(a)** (*s'abaisser*) to lower *or* demean oneself; **(b)** (*se détériorer*) to fall into disrepair; **les relations internationales se dégradent,** international relations are deteriorating; **(c)** *Phys* (*of energy*) to dissipate.

dégrader² *vt* to shade off, to graduate (*colours, light*); *Phot* to vignette; **écran de ciel dégradé,** gradual sky filter.

dégrafer [degrafe] **1** *vt* to unhook, to unfasten, to undo (*dress etc*); to unclasp (*bracelet*). **2 se dégrafer** *vpr* **(a)** (*of garment*) to come undone; **(b)** (*pour se déshabiller*) to undo one's dress.

dégraissage [degrɛsaʒ] *nm* **(a)** *Culin* skimming; *Fig* **d. d'une entreprise,** removing the fat from *or* downsizing a company; **(b)** (*nettoyage*) cleaning.

dégraisser [degrese] **1** *vt* **(a)** *Culin* to remove the fat from (*carcass of animal*); to skim the fat off (*soup etc*); *Fig* **d. une entreprise,** to cut the fat from a company, to downsize a company; **(b)** to dry clean (*clothes etc*); to scour (*wool*); **(c)** to bevel off, to trim (*piece of wood*). **2** *vi Fig* (*d'une entreprise*) to cut the fat, to downsize.

dégraisseur, -euse [degrɛsœr, -øz] **1** *n* dry cleaner (*of clothes etc*); scourer (*of wool*). **2** *nf* **dégraisseuse,** *Tex* scouring machine; (*tannerie*) grease extractor.

degré [dəgre] *nm* degree (*of circle, heat, relationship, musical scale*); step (*of stair, ladder*); proof (*of alcoholic drink*); **angle de 45 degrés,** 45-degree angle; **dix degrés au-dessous de zéro,** ten degrees below zero; **d. Fahrenheit/Celsius,** degree Fahrenheit/Centigrade *or* Celsius; **la température monte d'un d.,** the temperature rises by one degree; **cousins au second d.,** cousins once removed, second cousins; **d. de parenté,** degree of kinship; *Méd* **brûlure du troisième d.,** third degree burn; **les degrés de l'échelle sociale,** the rungs of the social ladder; **le plus haut/bas d. de la société,** the highest/lowest level of society; **atteindre le plus haut d. de la réussite,** to reach the high point of success; **elle est généreuse au plus haut d.,** she is generous in the extreme; **je veux bien aider, mais seulement jusqu'à un certain d.,** I would be pleased to help, but only up to a point; **par degré(s),** by degrees, gradually; *Math* **équation du second/du troisième d.,** quadratic/cubic equation; *Scol* **éducation du premier/second d.,** primary/secondary education; *Fig* **le d. zéro du cinéma/de la civilisation/***etc*, the beginnings of cinema/civilisation/*etc*; **quand l'homme était au d. zéro de la civilisation,** in the earliest stages of civilization.

dégréement [degremɑ̃] *nm Nau* unrigging (*of mast etc*).

dégréer [degree] *vt Nau* to unrig (*mast etc*); to dismantle, to take down (*crane*); to unsling (*hammock*).

dégressif, -ive [degrɛsif, -iv] *adj* **impôt d.,** degressive taxation.

dégrèvement [degrɛvmɑ̃] *nm* reduction, abatement (*of tax*).

dégrever [degrəve] *vt* (**je dégrève; je dégrèverai**) to reduce, to diminish (*tax*); to grant (*s.o.*) tax relief; to derate (*industry*); to reduce the assessment on (*building*); to disencumber (*estate*).

dégriffé [degrife] *adj* **manteau d.,** = coat which has lost its designer label and is sold at a reduced price.

dégringolade [degrɛ̃gɔlad] *nf F* **(a)** (*chute*) tumble, tumbling (*downstairs, downhill*); **(b)** *Fig* downfall (*of financier*); collapse (*of prices, firm etc*).

dégringoler [degrɛ̃gɔle] *F* **1** *vt* to tumble down; to come rushing down; **elle a dégringolé l'escalier,** she came tearing down the stairs. **2** *vi* to tumble; **tu risques de d. dans la pente!,** you're in danger of tumbling down the slope; *Fig* **maison (de commerce) qui dégringole,** firm that is losing business rapidly.

dégripper [degripe] *vt Tech* to unseize, to free (*mechanism*).

dégrisement [degrizmɑ̃] *nm* sobering up; *Fig* disillusionment.

dégriser [degrize] **1** *vt* to sober (*s.o.*) up; *Fig* to disillusion, to disenchant (*s.o.*). **2 se dégriser** *vpr* to sober up; *Fig* to become disillusioned (**au sujet de,** about).

dégrossir [degrosir] *vt* to give a rough *or* preliminary dressing to (*sth*); to rough down, to trim (*timber*); to roughhew (*stone*); to rough out (*design, piece of work etc*); *F* **d. qn,** to polish s.o. up, to lick s.o. into shape; **recrues mal dégrossies,** raw recruits.

dégrossissage [degrosisaʒ] *nm,* **dégrossissement** [degrosismɑ̃] *nm* roughing out *or* down; (*of timber*) trimming.

dégrouiller (se) [sədegruje] *vpr F* to get a move on, to buck up; **allez! dégrouille!,** come on, get a move on!

déguenillé, -ée [degənije] **1** *adj* ragged, tattered, in rags, in tatters. **2** *n* **un petit d.,** a little ragamuffin.

déguerpir [degɛrpir] *vi* to clear out *or* off; **d. au plus vite,** to bolt; **faire d. l'ennemi,** to scatter the enemy.

dégueu [degœ] *adj inv Arg* = **DÉGUEULASSE.**

dégueulasse [degœlas] **1** *adj Arg* rotten; (*sale*) filthy; **un repas d.,** a disgusting meal; **il fait un temps d.,** the weather is filthy; **j'ai passé un weekend d.,** I had a rotten weekend; **tu es d.,** (*d'avoir fait ça*) that was rotten of you; **c'est d. de lui mentir,** it's rotten to lie to him; **c'est pas d.,** it's not bad. **2** *n* **c'est un d.,** he's a rotten bastard.

dégueuler [degœle] *vi Arg* to spew, to puke; *Fig* **d. sur qn,** to say rotten things about s.o..

déguisé [degize] *adj* disguised; (*travesti*) dressed up; **être d.,** to be disguised *or* in disguise; **l'égoïsme d.,** disguised selfishness; *Culin* **fruits déguisés,** = prunes, dates etc stuffed with almond paste.

déguisement [degizmɑ̃] *nm* **(a)** disguise, get-up; (*pour bal masqué*) fancy dress, costume; **(b)** (*pour tromper*) dissimulation; **sans d.,** plainly, openly.

déguiser [degize] **1** *vt* **(a)** to disguise; **d. un enfant en clown,** to dress a child up as a clown; **(b)** to disguise, to conceal (*truth etc*); **parler sans rien d.,** to speak plainly *or* openly. **2 se déguiser** *vpr* (*pour ne pas être reconnu*) to disguise oneself; (*s'habiller*) to dress up; **je me sens déguisée dans cette robe,** I don't feel right in this dress, the dress isn't me.

dégurgiter [degyrʒite] *vt* to regurgitate; *Fig* **d. sa leçon,** to regurgitate one's lesson.

dégustateur, -trice [degystatœr, -tris] *n* wine taster.

dégustation [degystɑsjɔ̃] *nf* tasting, sampling; **d. de vin,** wine tasting; **ici, d. d'huîtres,** (*sur panneau*) oysters served here.

déguster [degyste] **1** *vt* **(a)** to taste, to sample (*wine etc*); **d. sa liqueur,** to sip one's liqueur; **(b)** (*savourer*) to eat *or* drink with relish; *Fig* to appreciate, to enjoy (*book etc*); **(c)** *Arg* **d. des coups,** to get a good hiding; **qu'est-ce qu'on a dégusté!,** we didn't half catch it! **2** *vi Arg* to suffer; **toute sa vie elle a dégusté,** she's had a hard life; **je te préviens, tu vas d.!,** you're going to catch it, I can tell you!; **faire d. qn,** to give s.o. a hard time.

déhaler [deale] *Nau* **1** *vt* to warp out, to haul out (*a ship*). **2 se déhaler** *vpr* to warp *or* haul itself out.

déhanché [deɑ̃ʃe] *adj* (*d'une personne*) who walks swaying the hips.

déhanchement [deɑ̃ʃmɑ̃] *nm* swaying of the hips; (*quand on est immobile*) standing with all one's weight on one foot; **faire des déhanchements,** to sway one's hips; *Méd* **je remarque un léger d.,** I notice a slight lopsidedness; **ce que je trouve le plus difficile à reproduire c'est le d. de la statue,** what I'm finding most difficult is drawing the curve of the statue's hip *or* reproducing the way the statue is standing with all its weight on one foot.

déhancher (se) [sədeɑ̃ʃe] *vpr* **(a)** to sway one's hips (*when walking*); **(b)** (*immobile*) to lean one's weight on one foot.

déharnachement [dearnaʃmɑ̃] *nm* unharnessing, unsaddling.

déharnacher [dearnaʃe] *vt* to unharness, to unsaddle (*horse*).

dehors [dəɔr] **1** *adv* out, outside; *Sp Cr* out; *Boxe* **compter qn d.**, to count s.o. out; **coucher d.**, to sleep out of doors *or* in the open; **dîner d.**, to dine out of doors *or* in the open; (*au restaurant*) to dine out; **histoire à coucher d.**, cock and bull story; **mettre qn d.**, to put *or* turn s.o. out; (*le renvoyer*) to dismiss s.o.; **j'ai des amis d.**, (*pas en prison*) I've got friends on the outside; *Nau* **toutes voiles d.**, with every sail set; **de d.**, from outside; **en d.**, (on the) outside, outwards; **tourner la jambe en d.**, (*en danse*) to turn one's leg out; **en d. de la maison,** outside the house; **c'est en d. de mes pouvoirs,** it is not within my competence; **rester en d. d'une dispute,** to keep out of an argument; **en d. du sujet,** beside the question; **cela s'est fait en d. de moi,** (*sans que je le sache*) it was done without my knowledge; (*sans que j'y participe*) I had no part in it; **au d.**, on the outside; **ne pas se pencher au d.!**, do not lean out of the window!; **mettre une embarcation au d.**, to get out a boat.

2 *nm* **(a)** outside, exterior (*of house etc*); **affaires du d.**, foreign affairs; **agir du d.**, to act from the outside;

(b) les dehors, (outward) appearance; **maison aux dehors imposants,** house with an imposing exterior; **sous des dehors aimables,** under a pleasant exterior;

(c) (*skating*) outside edge.

déhoussable [deusabl] *adj* (*canapé, siège*) with loose covers.

déification [deifikasjɔ̃] *nf* deification.

déifier [deifje] *vt* to deify, to make a god of (*s.o., sth*).

déisme [deism] *nm* deism.

déiste [deist] *adj & n* deist.

déité [deite] *nf* deity.

déjà [deʒa] *adv* **(a)** (*dès maintenant*) already; **il est d. trois heures,** it's already three o'clock; **tu as d. fini?,** have you finished already?; **elle a d. 20 ans!,** she's 20 already!; **d. en 1900,** as early as 1900; **(b)** before, previously; **je vous ai d. vu,** I've seen you before; **(c)** (*si tôt*) yet; **faut-il que vous partiez d.?,** need you go just yet?; **vous avez d. trop de travail,** you have too much work as it is; **(d)** (*pour renforcer*) **ce n'est d. pas si mal,** that's not bad at all; **qu'est-ce que vous faites d.?,** what did you say your job was?

déjanter [deʒɑ̃te] **1** *vt Aut* to remove (*tyre*) from rim. **2 se déjanter** *vpr* (*d'un pneu*) to come off the rim.

déjection [deʒɛksjɔ̃] *nf* **(a)** *Physiol* evacuation (*of bowels*); **déjections,** faeces; **(b)** *Géol* ejecta (*of volcano etc*).

déjeté [deʒte] *adj* crooked; **mur d.**, lopsided wall; **il est de plus en plus d.**, his posture is getting worse and worse; **colonne vertébrale déjetée,** deformed spinal column; *Fig* **d. à cause de son travail,** worn out by (his) work; **elle a la taille déjetée,** she has one shoulder higher than the other.

déjeter [deʒte] *v* (**il déjette; il déjettera**) **1** *vt* to make (*sth*) lopsided; to warp (*wood*); to buckle (*metal*). **2 se déjeter** *vpr* to grow lopsided; (*of wood*) to warp; (*of metal*) to buckle.

déjeuner[1] [deʒœne] *nm* **(a)** (*repas de midi*) lunch, *Fml* luncheon; **un d. d'affaires,** a business lunch; **petit d.**, breakfast; **d. sur l'herbe,** picnic (lunch); **(b)** (*tasse et soucoupe*) breakfast cup and saucer; *Fig* **ça a été un d. de soleil,** (*d'un tissu*) it soon faded; (*d'un sentiment, d'une résolution*) it soon faded, it didn't last long.

déjeuner[2] *vi* (*le matin*) to (have) breakfast; (*à midi*) to (have) lunch; **il est resté à d.**, he stayed for lunch.

déjouer [deʒwe] *vt* to thwart, to foil (*s.o.*); to frustrate (*plot*); **d. les plans de qn,** to spoil s.o.'s plans.

déjucher [deʒyʃe] *vi* (*of fowls*) to come off the roost.

déjuger (se) [sədeʒyʒe] *vpr* (*conj like* **juger**) to reverse one's judgment *or* decision *etc*.

de jure [deʒyre] *adv Jur* de jure.

delà [dəla] **1** *prép Arch Litt* beyond; **par d. les mers/monts,** beyond the seas/the mountains; **au d. de,** beyond; **n'allez pas au d. de 300 francs,** don't go above 300 francs; **elle est allé au d. de ses promesses,** she was better than her word. **2** *adv* **deçà (et) d.**, here and there; **au(-)d.**, beyond; **son savoir ne va pas au d.**, that's as much as *or* that's all he knows; **en d.**, further away. **3** *nm* **l'au-d.**, the next world, the hereafter.

délabré [delabre] *adj* dilapidated, shabby (*house, furniture*); **complètement d.**, ramshackle (*building*); **sa fortune est complètement délabrée,** his fortune is completely dissipated; **manteau d.**, shabby coat; **santé délabrée,** impaired health.

délabrement [delabrəmɑ̃] *nm* disrepair; **le d. de son entreprise,** the ruin of his company.

délabrer [delabre] **1** *vt* to dilapidate (*house*); to ruin (*health*). **2 se délabrer** *vpr* (*of house etc*) to fall into disrepair, to become dilapidated; **sa santé se délabre,** his health is deteriorating; **ses affaires se délabrent,** his business is going to rack and ruin.

délacer [delase] *v* (**je délaçai(s); n. délaçons**) **1** *vt* to unlace, to undo (*shoes etc*). **2 se délacer** *vpr* to come unlaced *or* undone.

délai [delɛ] *nm* **(a)** delay; **sans d.**, without delay, immediately; **(b)** time allowed (*for completion of a job etc*); **à court d.**, at short notice; **on vous accordera un d.**, we will give you more time; **dans le d. prescrit** *ou* **fixé,** within the required *or* allotted time; **il faut compter sur un d. de 10 jours,** you must allow ten days; **livrer dans les délais,** to deliver on time; **dans le plus bref d.**, as soon as possible; **d. de grâce,** period of grace; *Mil etc* **d. de route,** travelling time; *Com* **d. de paiement/congé,** term of payment/notice; **d. de livraison — un mois,** delivery within a month; **livrable dans un d. de trois jours,** can be delivered at three days' notice; **d. de préavis,** = **DÉLAI-CONGÉ**; *Ordinat* **d. d'attente,** wait time.

délai-congé [delɛkɔ̃ʒe] *nm Jur Com* term of notice (*to employee or employer*); (*pl délais-congés*).

délaissé [delese] *adj* forsaken; **épouse délaissée,** deserted wife; **enfant d.**, abandoned child; **une profession délaissée,** (*qui n'attire pas*) an unpopular profession.

délaissement [delɛsmɑ̃] *nm* **(a)** desertion, abandonment, neglect (*of wife, children etc*); (*solitude*) loneliness; **être dans un grand d.**, to be completely alone; **(b)** relinquishment, renunciation (*of right etc*); abandonment (*of ship to insurer*).

délaisser [delese] *vt* **(a)** (*abandonner*) to forsake, to desert, to abandon (*s.o.*); *Fig* **depuis qu'il est marié il délaisse ses amis,** since he got married he has dropped his friends; **la jeunesse délaisse cette profession,** young people are turning their backs on this profession; **(b)** *Jur* to relinquish, to forgo (*right, succession*); to abandon (*ship to insurer*).

délassant [delasɑ̃] *adj* refreshing, relaxing (*bath, rest etc*); light, entertaining (*reading*).

délassement [delasmɑ̃] *nm* rest, relaxation; **le sport est un d. pour elle,** sport is a relaxation for her; **avoir besoin de d.**, to need to relax.

délasser [delase] **1** *vt* to rest, to refresh (*s.o.*). **2 se délasser** *vpr* to (take some) rest, to relax.

délateur, -trice [delatœr, -tris] *n* informer, spy.

délation [delasjɔ̃] *nf* denouncement.

délavage [delavaʒ] *nm* washing out (*of colours etc*).

délavé [delave] *adj* **(a)** washed out (*colour etc*); **jean d.**, faded *or* stone-washed jeans; **(b) terre délavée,** sodden earth.

délaver [delave] *vt* **(a)** (*un tissu*) to fade; **(b)** (*la terre*) to soak (with water).

délayage [delɛjaʒ] *nm* thinning out (*of paint etc*); *Fig Péj* **cette copie n'est que du d.**, this copy is a mere rehash.

délayé [deleje] **1** *adj* **(a)** (*avec de l'eau*) thin, watery; **(b)** *Fig* wordy (*style*). **2** *nm* **c'est du d.**, it's mere verbosity.

délayer [deleje] *vt* (**je délaie, délaye; je délaierai, délayerai**) **(a)** to add water to (*powder etc*); to thin (*paint etc*) (**dans,** with); to water down (*liquid*); **d. de la farine dans du lait,** to mix flour with milk; **(b)** *Fig* **d. un discours/un texte/une théorie,** to spin out *or* pad out a speech/a text/a theory.

Delco ® [dɛlko] *nm Aut* distributor (*made by the Dayton Engineering Laboratories Company*).

déléatur [deleatyr] *nm inv Typ* delete (mark), dele.

délectable [delɛktabl] *adj* delicious, delightful.

délectation [delɛktasjɔ̃] *nf* delectation, delight.

délecter [delɛkte] **1** *vt Litt* to delight. **2 se délecter** *vpr* to enjoy oneself; **se d. à (faire) qch,** to take delight in (doing) sth.

délégant, -ante [delegɑ̃, -ɑ̃t] *n Jur* delegant.

délégataire [delegatɛr] *n Jur* delegatee.

délégateur, -trice [delegatœr, -tris] *n Jur* delegator.

délégation [delegasjɔ̃] *nf* **(a)** delegation (*of authority*); delegation, deputing (*of representatives*); assignment, transfer (*of debt*); **agir en vertu d'une** *ou* **par d.**, to act on the authority of s.o.; **d. de pouvoir,** delegation of authority; **(b)** (*groupe*) delegation, body of delegates; **envoyer une d. auprès d'un ministre,** to send a delegation to a minister.

délégatoire [delegatwar] *adj* delegatory (*power, authority*).

délégué, -ée [delege] **1** *adj* **membre d.**, delegate. **2** *n* **(a)** delegate (*at meeting etc*); representative; **d. du personnel,** (*syndiqué*) shop steward; (*non syndiqué*) staff representative; **d. syndical,** union representative; **(b)** deputy (professor *etc*).

déléguer [delege] *vt* (**je délègue; je déléguerai**) **(a)** (*désigner*) **d. qn pour faire qch,** to delegate s.o. to do sth; **(b)** (*transmettre*) to delegate; **d. son pouvoir,** to delegate *or* hand over one's powers; **d. une créance,** to assign a debt.

délestage [delɛstaʒ] *nm* **(a)** unballasting (*of ship etc*); **(b)** *Él* power cut.

délester [delɛste] **1** *vt* to unballast (*ship*); *Él* to cut off the power; to unload; **d. qn d'un fardeau,** to relieve s.o. of a burden; *F* **d. qn de son argent,** to steal s.o.'s money; **d. une route,** to close a road. **2 se délester** *vpr* (*of ship, balloon*) to jettison ballast; **se d. le cœur,** to unburden oneself.

délétère [deletɛr] *adj* deleterious; noxious, poisonous (*gas*); pernicious (*influence etc*).

délibérant [deliberɑ̃] *adj* deliberative (*assembly*).

délibératif, -ive [deliberatif, -iv] *adj* deliberative (*function*); **avoir voix délibérative,** to be entitled to speak and vote.

délibération [deliberasjɔ̃] *nf* **(a)** (*examen*) deliberation, debate, discussion; **pendant la d. du jury,** during the jury's deliberations, *F* while the jury was out; **la question est en d.,** the matter is under discussion *or* being deliberated; **(b)** (*réflexion*) consideration, reflection, cogitation; **après mûre d.,** after careful consideration; **(c)** (*décision*) resolution, decision, vote (*of an assembly*).

délibéré [delibere] **1** *adj* **(a)** (*résolu*) deliberate, determined, resolute (*tone, manner*); **(b)** (*intentionnel*) deliberate, intentional; **agir de propos d.,** to act deliberately *or* intentionally. **2** *nm Jur* consultation, private sitting (*of judges*).

délibérément [deliberemɑ̃] *adv* deliberately.

délibérer [delibere] *vi* **(a)** (*discuter*) to deliberate, to confer; **d. (avec qn) sur qch,** to discuss a matter (with s.o.); **le jury s'est retiré pour d.,** the jury retired to consider its verdict; **(b) d. de qch,** to deliberate sth; **elle délibérait de partir,** she was wondering whether to leave.

délicat, -ate [delika -at] **1** *adj* **(a)** sensitive, tender (*skin*); delicate, tender (*flower etc*); delicate, frail, weak (*health*); **(b)** delicate, gentle (*touch*); fine, refined, discerning, sensitive (*taste, person*); tactful (*behaviour*); **(c)** difficult, critical, ticklish (*problem etc*); tricky (*job*); delicate (*situation*); **(d)** scrupulous, particular, tender (*conscience*); **avoir une attention délicate,** to be thoughtful; **d. sur la nourriture,** fussy about food; **qu'est-ce qu'il est d.!,** isn't he fussy!; **peu d.,** not very scrupulous; **(e)** dainty (*dish etc*). **2** *n* fastidious person; **faire la délicate,** to put on airs (and graces).

délicatement [delikatmɑ̃] *adv* (*to touch*) delicately; (*to behave*) tactfully.

délicatesse [delikatɛs] *nf* **(a)** tenderness (*of skin etc*); frailty, fragility (*of object etc*); **(b)** delicacy, gentleness (*of touch*); refinement (*of taste*); scrupulousness (*of conduct*); tactfulness, thoughtfulness (*of behaviour*); **agir avec d.,** to behave tactfully; **(c)** delicacy, difficulty, awkwardness (*of situation etc*); **il est en d. avec la police/le gouvernement/***etc*, he has to watch his step with the police/the government/*etc*; **nous sommes en d.,** we've had words; **(d)** consideration (*for s.o.*); **elle avait des délicatesses pour moi,** she treated me very considerately; **(e)** fineness, softness (*of texture, colouring etc*).

délice [delis] *nm* delight, extreme pleasure; **cette tarte est un vrai d.,** this tart is delicious.

délices [delis] *nfpl* delight(s), pleasure(s); **faire les d. de qn,** to be the delight of s.o.; **faire ses d. de qch,** to delight in sth; **c'est un lieu de d.,** this place is heavenly.

délicieusement [delisjøzmɑ̃] *adv* deliciously; delightfully; **elle nous a reçus d.,** she entertained us delightfully, she was a delightful hostess.

délicieux, -euse [delisjø, -øz] *adj* delicious (*food*); delightful, charming (*person, dress etc*).

délictueux, -euse [deliktɥø, -ty-, -øz] *adj Jur* **(a)** punishable; **acte d.,** misdemeanour, offence; **(b)** felonious; malicious (*intent*).

délié [delje] **1** *adj* slender, fine; nimble, agile (*fingers*); **taille déliée,** slim figure; **avoir la langue déliée,** to be talkative, *F* to have the gift of the gab; **un esprit d.,** a sharp *or* astute mind. **2** *nm Typ etc* thin stroke.

délier [delje] **1** *vt* **(a)** (*libérer*) to untie, to undo; to loose (*fetters, prisoner*); **d. les mains à qn,** to untie s.o.'s hands; *Fig* **le vin lui a délié la langue,** the wine loosened his tongue; **(b) d. qn d'une promesse/d'une responsabilité,** to release s.o. from a promise/a responsibility. **2 se délier** *vpr* **(a)** (*se défaire*) to come undone *or* untied, to come loose; *Fig* **sa langue se déliait,** his tongue was beginning to wag; **(b) se d. d'un serment/d'une promesse,** to free oneself from an oath/a promise.

délimitation [delimitasjɔ̃] *nf* delimitation, demarcation; **poteau de d.,** boundary post.

délimiter [delimite] *vt* to delimit, to demarcate (*territory*); to define, to determine (*responsibility etc*).

délimiteur [delimitœr] *nm Ordinat* delimiter.

délinéament [delineamɑ̃] *nm* outline, shape, contour.

délinéer [delinee] *vt* to delineate, to outline.

délinquance [delɛ̃kɑ̃s] *nf* delinquency; **d. juvénile,** juvenile delinquency.

délinquant, -ante [delɛ̃kɑ̃, -ɑ̃t] **1** *adj Jur* delinquent; **jeunesse délinquante,** juvenile delinquents. **2** *n* delinquent; **d. juvénile,** juvenile delinquent; *Jur* **d. primaire,** first offender.

déliquescence [delikɛsɑ̃s] *nf* deliquescence; *Fig* **tomber en d.,** to fall into decay.

déliquescent [delikɛsɑ̃] *adj* deliquescent; *Fig Péj* **mœurs** *ou* **habitudes déliquiescentes,** decadent ways.

délirant [delirɑ̃] *adj* delirious, raving, lightheaded; **fièvre délirante,** delirious fever; **malade d.,** delirious patient; *F* **c'est d. de lui demander de tout payer!,** it's madness to ask him to pay for everything!; **joie délirante,** frenzied joy.

délire [delir] *nm* **(a)** *Méd* delirium; **avoir le d., être en d.,** to be delirious, to wander (in one's mind); **crise** *ou* **accès de d.,** attack of delirium; **(b)** (*frénesie*) frenzy; **foule en d.,** delirious *or* ecstatic crowd; *F* **cette soirée, c'est le d.!,** it's a wild party!

délirer [delire] *vi* (*d'un malade*) to be delirious *or* lightheaded, to wander (in one's mind); (*dire des bêtises*) to rave; **d. de joie,** to be delirious, to be mad with joy; **tu délires!,** (*qu'est-ce que tu racontes?*) you're raving!

délirium tremens [delirjɔmtremɛ̃s] *nm* delirium tremens, *F* DTs; **avoir le d. t.,** to have delirium tremens *or* *F* the DTs.

délit [deli] *nm Jur* misdemeanour, offence; **d. civil,** tort; **d. de presse,** violation of the press laws; **en flagrant d.,** red-handed, *Jur* in flagrante delicto; **prendre qn en flagrant d.,** to catch s.o. red-handed *or* in the act.

délivrance [delivrɑ̃s] *nf* **(a)** (*libération*) rescue, release; **la d. des otages,** the release *or* rescue of the hostages; **(b)** delivery, handing over (*of property, certificate*); issue (*of tickets*); **(c)** (*accouchement*) delivery; *Obst* delivery of the afterbirth; **la d. a été difficile,** it was a difficult delivery; **(d)** (*soulagement*) relief; **c'est fini!, quelle d.!,** it's over!, what a relief!

délivre [delivr] *nm Obst Vieilli* afterbirth.

délivrer [delivre] **1** *vt* **(a)** to rescue (*captive etc*); to release, to set free (*prisoner*); **d. qn de ses liens,** to free s.o. from his bonds; **(b)** to deliver, to hand over (*goods etc*); to deliver, to issue (*certificate, ticket*); **(c)** *Obst* **d. une femme,** (*du placenta etc*) to deliver a woman of the afterbirth; (*l'accoucher*) to deliver a woman of a child. **2 se délivrer** *vpr* **(a) se d. de qn/qch,** to get rid of s.o./sth; **se d. de ses soucis,** to shed one's worries; **(b)** (*être délivré*) to be issued; **le guichet où sont délivrés les tickets,** the counter where tickets are sold.

délogement [delɔʒmɑ̃] *nm* eviction (*of tenant*).

déloger [delɔʒe] *v* (*conj like* **loger**) **1** *vi* to leave (home); **délogez de là!,** get out of here! **2** *vt* to drive (*s.o.*) out; to evict (*tenant*); to dislodge (*the enemy*).

déloyal, -aux [delwajal, -o] *adj* disloyal, unfaithful (*friend etc*); dishonest, unfair (*practice*); **concurrence déloyale,** unfair competition; *Sp* **jeu d.,** foul play; **coup d.,** foul.

déloyalement [delwajalmɑ̃] *adv* disloyally, dishonestly.

déloyauté [delwajote] *nf* (*d'un ami*) disloyalty, treachery; (*d'un commerçant*) unfairness.

Delphes [dɛlf] *nfpl* Delphi.

delphien, -ienne [dɛlfjɛ̃, -jɛn] *adj* Delphic (*oracle*).

delta [dɛlta] *nm* (*lettre grecque*) *& Géog* delta; *Av* **aile (en) d.,** delta wing.

deltaplane [dɛltaplan] *nm Sp* hang-glider; **faire du d.,** to go hang-gliding.

deltoïde [dɛltɔid] *adj & nm Anat* deltoid (muscle).

déluge [delyʒ] *nm* deluge, flood; downpour (*of rain*); torrent (*of abuse*); **après moi le d.!,** when I'm gone I don't care what happens!; **cela remonte au d.,** it's as old as the hills.

déluré [delyre] *adj* sharp, knowing, smart; *Péj* **une fille un peu trop délurée,** a rather daring girl.

délustrer [delystre] *vt Tex* to remove the sheen *or* lustre from (*cloth*); to sponge, to steam (*cloth*).

démagnétisation [demaɲetizasjɔ̃] *nf* **(a)** *Phys* demagnetization; **(b)** *Nau* degaussing.

démagnétiser [demaɲetize] *vt* **(a)** *Phys* to demagnetize; **(b)** *Nau* to degauss.

démagogie [demagɔʒi] *nf* demagogy, demagoguery.

démagogique [demagɔʒik] *adj* demagogic.

démagogue [demagɔg] *nm* demagogue.

demaillage [demajaʒ] *nm* laddering.

démailler [demaje] **1** *vt* **(a)** to unshackle (*chain*); **(b)** to undo the meshes of (*net*); to unravel (*knitting*); **tes bas sont démaillés,** your stockings are laddered, *Am* you have runs in your stockings. **2 se démailler** *vpr* (*d'un collant*) to ladder, *Am* to run; **le filet se démaille,** the net is torn.

démailloter [demajɔte] *vt* **d. un bébé,** to take off a baby's nappy *or Am* diaper.

demain [dəmɛ̃] **1** *adv* tomorrow; **d. (au) soir,** tomorrow evening; **d. en huit,** a week tomorrow, *Vieilli* tomorrow week; **à d.!,** see you tomorrow!; **le journal de d.,** tomorrow's paper; **remettre un travail à d.,** to postpone *or* put off a job till tomorrow; **ce n'est pas pour d.,** *F* **c'est pas d. la veille,** that won't happen for a long time yet; **d. il fera jour,** tomorrow is another day; *Fig* **les parents de d.,** tomorrow's parents. **2** *nm* tomorrow; **tu as d. pour réfléchir,** you've got tomorrow to think about it; *Fig* **des demains peu heureux,** a not-too-rosy future.

démanché [demɑ̃ʃe] **1** *adj* (*tool etc*) without a handle; (*shoulder etc*) dislocated. **2** *nm Mus* shift.

démanchement [demɑ̃ʃmɑ̃] *nm* **(a)** removal of handle (*of tool etc*); **(b)** dislocation (*of shoulder etc*).

démancher [demɑ̃ʃe] **1** *vt* to remove the handle of (*tool etc*). **2** *vi Mus* to shift (*in playing the violin*). **3 se démancher** *vpr* **(a)** (*of tool etc*) to lose its handle; **(b)** (*se déboîter*) **se d. l'épaule/le dos/***etc*, to put one's shoulder/back/*etc* out; *F* **se d. pour obtenir qch,** to move heaven and earth to get sth.

demande [dəmɑ̃d] *nf* **(a)** (*requête*) request, application (**de,** for); *Com* demand; *Cartes* bid; **faire la d. de qch,** to ask for sth; **d. (en mariage),** proposal (of marriage), *Vieilli* offer of marriage; **faire sa d. (en mariage),** to propose; **faire qch sur la d. de qn,** to do sth at s.o.'s request; **à la d. générale,** by popular request; *Admin* **d. de remboursement de voyage,** travel claim; **il faut faire une d.,** you must fill in an application form; **faire une d. d'emploi,** to apply for a job; *Com* **l'offre et la d.,** supply and demand; *Com* **la d. est en hausse/en baisse,** demand is up/down; *Jur* **d. en divorce,** divorce petition; *Jur* **d. de dommages-intérêts,** claim for damages; **(b)** (*question*) question, inquiry, enquiry; **demandes et réponses,** questions and answers.

demander [dəmɑ̃de] **1** *vt* **(a)** (*réclamer*) to ask for (*sth*); to claim (*damages etc*); **d. du pain,** to ask for bread; **on nous a demandé nos passeports,** we were asked for our passports; **d. à qn son aide/sa protection/conseil,** to ask for s.o.'s help/protection/advice; **d. la permission,** to ask (for) permission; **puis-je vous d. une faveur** *ou* **un service?,** can I ask you a favour?; **je vous demande pardon,** I beg your pardon; **d. la main de qn,** to ask for s.o.'s hand (in marriage); **il a fini par la d. en mariage,** he eventually proposed (to her); **on vous demande,** you're wanted, somebody wants to see you; **combien demandez-vous de l'heure?,** how much do you charge an hour?; **d. qch à qn,** to ask s.o. for sth; **il ne demande que ça,** he'd be only too pleased; **je ne demande qu'une seule chose — qu'on me laisse tranquille,** all I ask is to be left alone; **je ne demande qu'une seule chose — qu'il fasse beau,** all I ask is for it to be fine; **il demande qu'on lui rende justice,** he asks for justice;

(b) (*rechercher, exiger*) to desire, to want, to need, to require; **on demande maçon,** builder wanted; **article très demandé,** article in great demand; **cela demande le plus grand soin,** it requires the greatest care; **la situation demande à être maniée avec tact,** the situation needs *or* calls for tactful handling; **cela demande à être bien réfléchi,** that calls for careful consideration; **le voyage demande trois heures,** the journey takes three hours;

(c) to demand; **d. à qn plus qu'il n'en peut faire,** (*attendre (de)*) to demand *or* expect from s.o. more than he can do; **c'est trop me d.,** it's too much to ask of me, it's asking too much; **il ne faut pas lui en d. trop,** you mustn't expect too much from him; **d. la lune,** to ask for the moon;

(d) (*s'enquérir de*) to ask, to enquire; **d. l'heure, d. quelle heure il est,** to ask the time; **je n'ai pas compris ce qu'il m'a demandé,** I didn't understand what he asked me; **d. son chemin à qn,** to ask s.o. the way; *F* **je ne t'ai rien demandé!,** I didn't ask for your advice *or* opinion!; **je ne t'ai pas demandé l'heure qu'il est,** mind your own business!; **je vous (le) demande, je vous demande un peu!,** I ask you!

2 *vi* **d. à qn de faire qch,** to ask s.o. to do sth; **d. à,** to ask (permission) to do sth; **je demande à parler,** may I *or* please let me speak; **d. à manger,** to ask for something to eat; **je ne demande qu'à rester ici,** I ask for nothing better than to stay here; *F* **il demande à ce qu'on lui rende son argent,** he's asking for his money back.

3 se demander *vpr* to ask oneself, to wonder; **c'est ce que je me demande,** that's what I'd like to know; **c'est à se d.** *ou* **on se demande s'il ne l'a pas fait exprès,** one wonders whether he didn't do it on purpose; **je me demande bien pourquoi/ce que/où ...,** I really can't think why/what/where ... .

demandeur[1], -eresse [dəmɑ̃dœr, -ərɛs] *n Jur* plaintiff; **d. en divorce,** petitioner; **d. en appel,** appellant.

demandeur[2], -euse [dəmɑ̃dœr, -øz] *n* **(a)** (*amateur*) petitioner, constant applicant for favours; **(b)** *Com* buyer; **(c)** *Tél* **d. (de la communication),** caller.

démangeaison [demɑ̃ʒɛzɔ̃] *nf* itching; **j'ai une d.,** I've got an itch, I'm itching; *F* **une d. de faire qch,** a longing *or* an itching to do sth.

démanger [demɑ̃ʒe] *vi* **(il démangea(it))** to itch; **l'épaule me démange,** my shoulder's itching; *Fig* **la main lui démangeait,** he was itching *or* dying for a fight; **ça me démange de lui dire ce que je pense,** I'm dying *or* itching to tell him what I think.

démantèlement [demɑ̃tɛlmɑ̃] *nm* demolition, demolishing; breaking up (*of organization*); bringing down (*of empire*).

démanteler [demɑ̃tle] *vt* **(je démantèle; je démantèlerai)** to demolish, to destroy (*fortifications etc*); to break up (*organization etc*); to bring down (*empire etc*).

démantibuler [demɑ̃tibyle] *F* **1** *vt* to break *or* smash up (*object*); **d. une machine,** to smash a machine to pieces. **2 se démantibuler** *vpr* to come to pieces, to break up.

démaquillage [demakijaʒ] *nm* removal of make-up; **crème pour le d.,** cleansing cream, make-up remover.

démaquillant [demakijɑ̃] **1** *adj* **lotion/crème démaquillante,** make-up removal *or* cleansing lotion/cream. **2** *nm* cleansing cream, make-up remover.

démaquiller [demakije] **1** *vt* to remove (*s.o.'s*) make-up. **2 se démaquiller** *vpr* to remove one's make-up.

démarcage [demarkaʒ] *nm* = **DÉMARQUAGE.**

démarcatif, -ive [demarkatif, -iv] *adj* demarcating (*line etc*).

démarcation [demarkasjɔ̃] *nf* demarcation; **ligne de d.,** dividing line, boundary line, demarcation line; **c'est sur ce problème que la d. entre les deux parties s'affirme,** it is on this problem that the dividing line between the two parties is most evident.

démarchage [demarʃaʒ] *nm Com* (*porte-à-porte*) door-to-door selling; (*prospection*) canvassing.

démarche [demarʃ] *nf* **(a)** (*allure*) gait, step, walk; **d. majestueuse,** majestic bearing; **reconnaître qn à sa d.,** to recognize s.o. by his walk; **elle avait une d. digne,** she moved with dignity; **(b)** (*requête*) step; **faire une d. auprès de qn,** to approach s.o.; **faire les démarches nécessaire pour s'inscrire,** to take the necessary steps to enrol; **faire les premières démarches,** to take the first steps; **d. collective,** joint representations; **(c)** *Fig* (*cheminement*) process; **d. de la pensée,** thought process.

démarcher [demarʃe] *vt Com* **(a)** (*faire du porte-à-porte*) to sell door-to-door; **(b)** (*prospecter*) to canvass for (*party*).

démarcheur, -euse [demarʃœr, -øz] *n Com* **(a)** (*représentant*) door-to-door salesman *or* saleswoman; **(b)** (*prospecteur*) canvasser.

démarquage [demarkaʒ] *nm* **(a)** removal of the (identification) mark(s) (*from linen, plate etc*); **(b)** (*plagiat*) plagiarism; **(c)** *Sp* breaking free from one's opponent.

démarque [demark] *nf Com* marking down (*of goods at sales*).

démarqué [demarke] *adj* **(a)** *Com* marked down; **(b)** *Sp* unmarked.

démarquer [demarke] **1** *vt* **(a)** to remove the identification mark(s) from (*linen, plate etc*); **(b)** *Com* to mark down (*goods*); **(c)** to plagiarize (*book*); **(d)** *Sp* to leave one's opponent unmarked. **2 se démarquer** *vpr Sp* to break free from one's opponent; *Fig* **un élève qui se démarque des autres,** a pupil who stands apart from the others.

démarrage [demaraʒ] *nm* **(a)** start, starting (*of engine etc*); moving off (*of car etc*); *Sp* (*sudden*) spurt; *Sp* **faire un d.,** to put on a spurt; *Ordinat* **d. à chaud/froid,** warm/cold start; *Aut* **d. en côte,** hill start; **d. d'une affaire/d'une campagne publicitaire,** start of a business/publicity campaign; **(b)** unmooring (*of ship*).

démarrer [demare] **1** *vt* **(a)** to start (*car etc*); **(b)** to unmoor, to cast off (*ship*). **2** *vi* **(a)** (*of train, car etc*) to start, to move off, to get away; (*of driver*) to drive away *or* off; *Sp* to put on a spurt; **son affaire commence à d.,** his business is beginning to take off; **(b)** (*of ship*) to cast off.

démarreur [demarœr] *nm Aut etc* starter (motor).

démasquer [demaske] **1** *vt* to unmask, to expose, to show up (*impostor*); *Fig* **d. ses batteries,** to show one's hand. **2 se démasquer** *vpr* to take off one's mask; *Fig* to drop the mask.

démâtage [dematɑʒ] *nm* dismasting.

démâter [demɑte] *vt* to dismast (*ship*).

démêlage [demɛlaʒ] *nm* disentangling.

démêlé [demele] *nm* contention; **avoir un d. avec un collègue,** to have an altercation with a colleague; **démêlés,** (unpleasant) dealings; **il a eu des démêlés avec la police,** he's been in trouble with the police.

démêler [demele] **1** *vt* to disentangle, to unravel (*string, silk etc*); to untangle, to comb out (*hair*); to tease (out) (*wool*); **d. un problème/un malentendu,** to sort out a problem/clear up a misunderstanding; **avoir qch à d. avec qn,** to have sth to clear up *or* sort out with s.o.; **on va d. ça ensemble,** we'll sort it out together. **2 se démêler** *vpr* to extricate oneself (from difficulty).

démêleur [demɛlœr] *nm* (*pour les cheveux*) cream rinse.

démêloir [demɛlwar] *nm* large-toothed comb.

démembrement [demɑ̃brəmɑ̃] *nm* breaking up, dismemberment (*of empire etc*); breaking up (*of ship*); **d. d'une propriété,** dividing up of an estate.

démembrer [demɑ̃bre] *vt* to dismember; to cut up, to joint (*chicken etc*); to divide up (*kingdom, estate*).

déménagement [demenaʒmɑ̃] *nm* moving (house); **c'est pour quand le d.?,** when are you *or* we *etc* moving?; **entreprise de d.,** removal firm; **camion de d.,** furniture *or* removal van; **frais de d.,** moving expenses *or* costs; *F* **votre d. est arrivé,** your furniture has arrived.

déménager [demenaʒe] *v* (**je déménageai(s); n. déménageons**) **1** *vt* to move; (*d'une entreprise*) to move, to relocate; **qui est-ce qui vous déménage?,** who's moving you?, which removal company are you using?; **d. ses meubles,** to move house. **2** *vi* **(a)** to move; **elle déménage à la fin du mois,** she's moving at the end of the month; **où déménage-t-il?,** where's he moving to?; *F* **d. à la cloche de bois,** to do a moonlight flit; *F* **il déménage!,** he's off his head!, he's round the bend!; *F* **allez! déménagez!,** scram! buzz off!; **(b)** *F* **de la moutarde qui déménage,** mustard that takes the top of your head off; **musique qui déménage,** powerful music.

déménageur [demenaʒœr] *nm* removal man, furniture remover *or Am* mover.

démence [demɑ̃s] *nf* (*folie*) insanity, madness; *Jur* lunacy; *Méd* dementia; **d. précoce,** *Méd* dementia praecox, *F* premature senility; *F* **c'est de la pure d.!,** it's insane!

démener (se) [sədemne] *vpr* (*conj like* **mener**) **(a)** (*s'agiter*) to thrash about, to throw oneself about, to struggle; **se d. comme un beau diable,** to break one's back (**pour faire qch,** to do *or* doing sth); **(b)** (*se dépenser*) to exert oneself, to make a great effort.

dément, -ente [demɑ̃, -ɑ̃t] **1** *adj* (*fou*) mad, insane (*person*); *Méd* demented (*person*); *F* **quel monde! c'est d.!,** what a crowd! it's unbelievable! **2** *n* mad *or* insane person; *Jur* lunatic; *Méd* demented person.

démenti [demɑ̃ti] *nm* **(a)** (flat) denial, contradiction; **donner** *ou* **opposer un d. formel à une accusation,** to deny an accusation; **ses actions donnent un d. à ses paroles,** his actions belie his words; **(b)** failure (*of efforts*); disappointment (*of expectations*).

démentiel, -elle [demɑ̃sjɛl] *adj* mad, insane; **accès d.,** fit of madness; *F* **à des prix démentiels,** at absurd prices.

démentir [demɑ̃tir] *v* (*conj like* **mentir**) **1** *vt* (*contredire*) to contradict, *Fml* to give the lie to (*s.o., sth*); (*nier*) to deny, to refute (*fact*); *Litt* **il a démenti nos espérances,** he has not come up to our expectations, he has disappointed us. **2 se démentir** *vpr* to contradict oneself; **politesse qui ne se dément jamais,** unfailing courtesy; **il a fait preuve d'une attention qui ne s'est jamais démentie,** he showed unfailing attention.

démerdard, -arde [demɛrdar, -ard] *Arg* **1** *adj* resourceful; **il n'est pas d.,** he's hopeless. **2** *n* resourceful person; **c'est un d.,** he knows a trick or two.

démerder (se) [sədemɛrde] *vpr Arg* to get out of a mess; **elle est assez grande pour se d. seule,** she's old enough to look after herself; **se d. pour obtenir qch,** to wangle sth; **apprendre à se d.,** to learn to look after oneself.

démerdeur, -euse [demɛrdœr, -øz] *adj & n* = **DÉMERDARD.**

démérite [demerit] *nm* **faire à qn un d. de qch,** to reproach s.o. for sth.

démériter [demerite] *vi* to act in a reprehensible manner; **d. auprès de qn,** to come down in s.o.'s estimation, to forfeit s.o.'s esteem.

démesure [deməzyr] *nf* disproportion, excessiveness.

démesuré [deməzyre] *adj* beyond measure, huge, enormous; inordinate (*pride*); excessive (*thirst*); unbounded (*ambition*).

démesurément [deməzyremɑ̃] *adv* enormously, inordinately.

démettre¹ [demɛtr] *v* (*conj like* **mettre**) **1** *vt* to dislocate (*joint*). **2 se démettre** *vpr* **se d. l'épaule,** to put one's shoulder out.

démettre² **1** *vt* **d. qn de ses fonctions,** to deprive s.o. of (his) office, to remove s.o. from office. **2 se démettre** *vpr* to resign, to retire; **se d. de ses fonctions,** to resign office, to resign from one's job.

démeubler [demœble] *vt* to remove the furniture from (*house etc*), to strip (*house etc*) of its furniture *or* fittings.

demeurant (au) [odəmœrɑ̃] *adv* **au d.,** after all, all the same, for all that.

demeure [dəmœr] *nf* **(a)** (place of) residence; **une belle d.,** a fine residence; **dernière d.,** last resting place; **(b)** *Arch* tarrying, delay; (*still used in such phrases as*) **sans plus longue d.,** without further delay; **il y a péril en la d.,** it is dangerous to delay; **(c)** *Jur* **mettre qn en d. de payer,** to give s.o. notice to pay; **mise en d.,** formal notice, summons; **(d) à d.,** fixed, permanent(ly); **meuble à d.,** fixture; **il est ici à d.,** he's here for good *or* to stay.

demeuré, -ée [dəmœre] **1** *adj* halfwitted, mentally retarded. **2** *n* halfwit.

demeurer [dəmœre] *vi* **(a)** (*conj with* **être**) to remain; to stay, to stop (in a place); **je demeure convaincu que ...,** I remain convinced that ...; **l'affaire n'en demeurera pas là,** the matter will not rest there; **demeurons-en là,** let's leave it at that; **ne pouvoir d. en place,** to be unable to keep still; **d. à l'état sauvage,** to remain in its *etc* wild state; **elle demeurait assise à nous écouter,** she sat listening to us; **d. en reste avec qn,** to remain under an obligation to s.o.; **(b)** (*conj with* **être**) (*être transmis*) to be left; **l'affaire lui est demeurée de sa famille,** he inherited the business from his family; **(c)** (*conj with* **avoir**) to live, to reside; **d. à la campagne,** to live in the country; **il demeure rue de Rivoli,** he lives in the rue de Rivoli.

demi, -ie [dəmi] **1** *adj* half; **deux heures et demie,** two and a half hours; (*heure*) half past two; **un d. congé,** a half-holiday; **une d. cuillère de sucre,** half a teaspoon of sugar; **d.-cuit,** half cooked. **2** *nm* **deux plus un d.,** two plus a half; **un d.,** (*beer*) = half a pint, a half; *Fb* **les demis,** the halfbacks; *Rugby* **d. de mêlée,** scrum half; **d. d'ouverture,** stand-off half; **à d.,** half; **à d. mort,** half dead; **faire les choses à d.,** to do things by halves; **à d. transparent,** semi-transparent. **3** *nf* **demie,** half hour; **il est la demie,** it's half past.

NOTE *in all the following compounds* **demi** *is inv and the second component takes the plural.*

demi-arbre [dəmiarbr] *nm Aut* halfshaft.

demiard [dəmjar] *nm Can* half pint.

demi-arrière [dəmiarjɛr] *nm Fb* halfback.

demi-bas [dəmiba] *nm* kneesock.

demi-botte [dəmibɔt] *nf* half boot.

demi-bouteille [dəmibutɛj] *nf* half bottle.

demi-cercle [dəmisɛrkl] *nm* semicircle, half circle; **en d.-c.,** semicircular.

demi-circulaire [dəmisirkylɛr] *adj* semicircular.

demi-clef [dəmikle] *nf Nau* half hitch.

demi-deuil [dəmidœj] *nm* half mourning.

demi-dieu [dəmidjø] *nm* demigod.

demi-douzaine [dəmiduzɛn] *nf* half dozen.

démieller [demjɛle] *vt* to remove the honey from (*honeycomb*).

demi-fin [dəmifɛ̃] **1** *adj* **(a)** (*petits pois, haricots etc*) medium; **(b)** (*or*) twelve carat. **2** *nm* twelve-carat gold; **bracelet en d.-f.,** twelve carat bracelet.

demi-finale [dəmifinal] *nf Sp* semifinal.

demi-finaliste [dəmifinalist] *n Sp* semifinalist.

demi-fond [dəmifɔ̃] *nm inv Sp* **(course de) d.-f.,** middle distance race.

demi-frère [dəmifrɛr] *nm* half brother.

demi-gros [dəmigro] *nm* **(commerce de) d.-g.,** cash and carry.

demi-grossiste [dəmigrosist] *n* wholesaler.

demi-heure [dəmiœr] *nf* **une d.-h.,** half an hour; **deux**

d.-heures, two half hours; **de d.-h. en d.-h., toutes les d.-heures,** every half hour.
demi-jour [dəmiʒur] *nm* half light; (*crépuscule*) twilight, dusk.
demi-journée [dəmiʒurne] *nf* half a day; (*de travail, de congé*) half day; **faire des d.-journées,** to work half days.
démilitarisation [demilitarizɑsjɔ̃] *nm* demilitarization.
démilitariser [demilitarize] *vt* to demilitarize.
demi-litre [dəmilitr] *nm* half litre *or US* liter.
demi-longueur [dəmilɔ̃gœr] *nf Sp* half a length, a half length.
demi-lune [dəmilyn] **1** *nf* half moon; (*fortification*) demi-lune. **2** *adj inv* semicircular.
demi-mal [dəmimal] *nm* **il n'y a que d.-m.,** it might have been worse.
demi-mesure [dəmiməzyr] *nf* **(a)** (*compromis*) half measure; **avec elle il n'y a jamais de d.-m.,** there's no half measures with her; **(b)** (*pour chaussures etc*) half-size.
demi-mondain, -aine [dəmimɔ̃dɛ̃, -ɛn] **1** *adj* belonging to the demi-monde. **2** *nf* **demi-mondaine,** demi-mondaine.
demi-monde [dəmimɔ̃d] *nm* demi-monde, fringes of society.
demi-mort [dəmimɔr] *adj* half-dead.
demi-mot (à) [ad(ə)mimo] *adv* **entendre (qn) à d.-m.,** to (know how to) take a hint; **il a compris à d.-m.,** he caught on at once (to what I meant).
déminage [deminaʒ] *nm* mine clearance; *Nau* minesweeping.
déminer [demine] *vt* to clear (*a field*) of mines.
déminéralisation [demineralizɑsjɔ̃] *nf Méd* demineralization.
déminéraliser [demineralize] *Méd* **1** *vt* to demineralize. **2 se déminéraliser** *vpr* to become demineralized.
démineur [deminœr] *nm* bomb disposal expert.
demi-pause [dəmipoz] *nf Mus* minim rest.
demi-pension [dəmipɑ̃sjɔ̃] *nf* half board; **sept jours en d.-p.,** seven days half board.
demi-pensionnaire [dəmipɑ̃sjɔnɛr] *n* half boarder; *Scol* day boarder.
demi-place [dəmiplas] *nf* half fare (*when travelling*); half price (*at theatre etc*).
demi-portion [dəmipɔrsjɔ̃] *nf F Péj* weed.
demi-produit [dəmiprɔdɥi] *nm Écon* semi-finished product.
demi-quart [dəmikar] *nm* **(a)** *Nau* half point (*of the compass*); **(b)** (*mesure*) = 2 ounces.
demi-queue [dəmikø] *adj & nm inv* baby grand (piano).
demi-reliure [dəmirəljyr] *nf* quarter binding; **d.-r. à (petits) coins,** half binding
démis [demi] *adj* (*épaule*) dislocated.
demi-saison [dəmisɛzɔ̃] *nf* between season, mid season; **vêtements de d.-s.,** spring *or* autumn clothes.
demi-sang [dəmisɑ̃] *nm inv* halfbred (horse).
demi-sel [dəmisɛl] **1** *adj inv* slightly salted (*butter etc*). **2** *nm* **(a)** (*fromage*) (slightly salted) cream cheese; **(b)** *F* small-time crook.
demi-sœur [dəmisœr] *nf* half sister.
demi-solde [dəmisɔld] **1** *nf Mil* half pay; **en d.-s.,** on half pay. **2** *nm inv* half-pay officer.
demi-sommeil [dəmisɔmɛj] *nm* drowsiness, somnolence.
demi-soupir [dəmisupir] *nm Mus* quaver rest.
démission [demisjɔ̃] *nf* **(a)** (*au travail*) resignation; **donner sa d.,** to tender *or* send in one's resignation, to resign; *Fig* to give up; **(b)** (*abandon*) renunciation; **la d. du père,** the father's abdication of his responsibilities.
démissionnaire [demisjɔnɛr] *adj* who has resigned (*his office etc*); resigning (*officer etc*); **père/mère d.,** father/mother who has abdicated his/her responsibilities.
démissionner [demisjɔne] **1** *vi* to resign (**de,** from); *F* **je démissionne!,** I give up! **2** *vt F Iron* to sack (*s.o.*).
demi-tarif [dəmitarif] *nm* half price; **billet (à) d.-t.,** half fare (ticket).
demi-tasse [dəmitas] *nf* **(a)** (*tasse*) small coffee cup, demitasse; **(b)** (*quantité*) half a cup, demitasse.
demi-teinte [dəmitɛ̃t] *nf Beaux-Arts Phot* halftone.
demi-ton [dəmitɔ̃] *nm Mus* semitone.
demi-tonneau [dəmitɔno] *nm Av* half roll.
demi-tour [dəmitur] *nm* half turn; *Mil* about turn; *Aut* U-turn; **un d.-t. de clé,** a half-turn of the key; **faire d.-t.,** to go back.
démiurge [demjyrʒ] *nm* demiurge.
demi-voix (à) [ad(ə)mivwa] *adv* in an undertone, under one's breath.
demi-volée [dəmivɔle] *nf Tennis* half volley.
démobilisation [demɔbilizɑsjɔ̃] *nf* demobilization, *F* demob (*of troops*).
démobiliser [demɔbilize] *vt* to demobilize, *F* to demob (*troops*).
démocrate [demɔkrat] **1** *adj* democratic. **2** *n* democrat.
démocrate-chrétien, -ienne [demɔkratkretjɛ̃,-jɛn] *adj & n Pol* Christian Democrat.
démocratie [demɔkrasi] *nf* democracy; *F* **on est en d., après tout!,** it's a free country!
démocratique [demɔkratik] *adj* democratic.
démocratiquement [demɔkratikmɑ̃] *adv* democratically.
démocratisation [demɔkratizɑsjɔ̃] *nf* democratization.
démocratiser [demɔkratize] **1** *vt* to democratize. **2 se démocratiser** *vpr* to become (more) democratic.
démodé [demɔde] *adj* (*vêtement, personne*) old-fashioned; (*vêtement*) out-of-fashion, out-of-date.
démoder (se) [sədemɔde] *vpr* (*of clothes etc*) to go out of fashion, to become old-fashioned.
démographe [demɔgraf] *n* demographer.
démographie [demɔgrafi] *nf* demography.
démographique [demɔgrafik] *adj* demographic; *Admin Pol Econ* **statistiques démographiques,** demographics; **poussée démographique,** population growth.
demoiselle [dəmwazɛl] *nf* **(a)** (*femme célibataire*) single *or* unmarried woman, *Vieilli & Admin* spinster; **d. d'honneur,** (*d'une souveraine*) lady-in-waiting, *Vieilli* maid of honour; (*d'une mariée*) bridesmaid; **d. de compagnie,** lady's companion; **les demoiselles Dupin,** the Misses Dupin; **(b)** (*jeune fille, employée*) young lady; **les demoiselles du téléphone,** the young ladies on the switchboard; **(c)** (*insecte*) dragonfly; **d. (de Numidie),** demoiselle (crane), Numidian crane; **(d)** *Tech* paving beetle.
démolir [demɔlir] *vt* **(a)** to demolish, to pull down (*house etc*); to break up (*ship*); to demolish, to wreck, to smash up (*car etc*); **(b)** to overthrow (*government, authority etc*); to demolish (*argument, theory etc*); to ruin (*reputation*); to slate (*author etc*); **d. un adversaire/un concurrent,** to demolish an opponent/a competitor; **la critique a démoli son premier roman/film/***etc*, the critics slated *or* demolished his first novel/film/*etc*; **(c)** *F* (*battre*) to beat (*s.o.*) up, to bash (*s.o.*) about; (*fatiguer*) to tire (*s.o.*); **je vais lui d. le portrait!,** I'll smash his face in!; **il s'est fait d.,** he got beaten up; **cette mauvaise grippe m'a démoli,** that bad bout of 'flu laid me out; **tout ce travail l'a démolie,** she's exhausted *or* shattered after all this work.
démolissage [demɔlisaʒ] *nm* severe criticism, *F* slating (*of author etc*).
démolisseur, -euse [demɔlisœr, -øz] *n* **(a)** (*de bâtiments*) demolition worker *or* contractor; (*de bateaux*) shipbreaker; **(b)** *Fig* demolisher, destroyer (*of argument etc*).
démolition [demɔlisjɔ̃] *nf* demolition, pulling down (*of structure*); **chantier de d.,** demolition yard.
démon [demɔ̃] *nm* **(a)** demon, devil, fiend; **le d.,** the Devil; **cette femme est un d.,** a wicked woman; **cet enfant est un petit d.,** that child is a little devil; **le d. de la jalousie,** the demon of jealousy; **le d. de midi,** midlife crisis; **(b)** (*génie, esprit etc*) (good, evil) genius; *Myth* daemon.
démonétisation [demɔnetizɑsjɔ̃] *nf* **(a)** demonetization, withdrawal from circulation (*of coinage*); **(b)** *Fig* discrediting (*of s.o.*).
démonétiser [demɔnetize] *vt* **(a)** *Fin* to demonetize; **(b)** *Fig* to discredit (*s.o.*).
démoniaque [demɔnjak] **1** *adj* demoniac(al), possessed of the devil. **2** *n* demoniac.
démonstrateur, -trice [demɔ̃stratœr, -tris] *n* demonstrator.
démonstratif, -ive [demɔ̃stratif, -iv] **1** *adj* **(a)** (*convaincant*) (logically) conclusive; **(b)** *Gram* demonstrative (*adjective etc*); **(c)** demonstrative, expansive (*person*); **peu d.,** undemonstrative. **2** *nm Gram* demonstrative.
démonstration [demɔ̃strɑsjɔ̃] *nf* **(a)** (*preuve*) demonstration, proof (*of theorem etc*); *Com* demonstration (*of article*); **d. par l'absurde,** reductio ad absurdum; **la meilleure d. se fait par l'expérience,** experience is the best teacher; *Boxe* **assaut de d.,** sparring match; *Mus* **cassette de d.,** demo (tape); **appareil de d.,** demonstration model; *Ordinat* **disquette de d.,** demo disk; **(b)** *Mil* show of force; **d. navale,** naval display; **faire de grandes démonstrations d'amitié,** to make a great show of friendship.
démontable [demɔ̃tabl] *adj* (*machine etc*) that can be dismantled; (*boat*) collapsible.
démontage [demɔ̃taʒ] *nm* dismantling, taking to pieces.
démonté [demɔ̃te] *adj* **(a)** (*rider*) thrown; *Fig*

(*déconcerté*) disconcerted, *F* thrown; **(b)** (*mechanism etc*) taken to pieces, dismantled; **(c)** stormy, raging (*sea*).
démonte-pneu [demɔ̃tpnø] *nm* tyre *or US* tire lever; (*pl démonte-pneus*).
démonter [demɔ̃te] **1** *vt* **(a)** to throw (off), to unseat (*rider*); **(b)** (*inquiéter*) to upset; **la nouvelle m'a démonté,** I was greatly upset *or* put out by the news; **se laisser d.,** to get upset *or* flustered, to be thrown; **(c)** to take down, to take to pieces, to take apart, to dismantle; to dismount (*gun*); to unhinge (*door*); to remove (*tyre*). **2 se démonter** *vpr* **(a)** (*of mechanism*) to come apart, to dismantle; **(b)** *F* **elle ne se démonte pas pour si peu,** she's not so easily put out *or* thrown.
démontrable [demɔ̃trabl] *adj* demonstrable, provable.
démontrer [demɔ̃tre] **1** *vt* to demonstrate; *F* **d. qch par A + B,** to conclusively prove sth. **2 se démontrer** *vpr* to be able to be proved, to be provable; **cela se démontre facilement,** that's easily proved.
démoralisant [demɔralizɑ̃] *adj* demoralizing.
démoralisateur, -trice [demɔralizatœr, -tris] *adj* demoralizing.
démoralisation [demɔralizasjɔ̃] *nf* demoralization.
démoraliser [demɔralize] **1** *vt* to demoralize, to dishearten. **2 se démoraliser** *vpr* to become demoralized, to lose heart.
démordre [demɔrdr] *vi* **ne pas d. de ses opinions,** to stand by *or* stick to one's opinions; **elle ne veut pas en d.,** she won't give up, she's sticking to her guns.
démotivé [demɔtive] *adj* (*sans motivation*) demotivated.
démotiver [demɔtive] *vt* to make (*s.o.*) lose motivation.
démotorisation [demɔtɔrizasjɔ̃] *nf* **la d. est de plus en plus répandue,** more and more people are giving up their cars.
démoulage [demulaʒ] *nm* removal (*of cast*) from mould *or US* mold; *Culin* turning out (*of jelly, cake*).
démouler [demule] *vt* to remove (*cast*) from the mould *or US* mold; *Culin* to turn out (*jelly, cake*).
démultiplicateur, -trice [demyltiplikatœr, -tris] *MecE* **1** *adj* reducing, reduction (*gear*). **2** *nm* reduction system; **d. de vitesse,** motor reduction unit.
démultiplication [demyltiplikasjɔ̃] *nf MecE* **(a)** (*of car, machine*) gearing down, (gear) reduction; **(b)** reduction ratio (*of gears*).
démultiplier [demyltiplije] *vt MecE* **(a)** to gear down (*car, machine*); **(b)** to reduce the gear ratio of.
démuni [demyni] *adj* **(a) les impôts les laissent totalement démunis,** the taxes leave them penniless; **d. d'argent,** without any money, penniless; **une soirée démunie d'intérêt,** an evening devoid of interest; **(b)** *Com* **être d. de qch,** to be out of sth, to be sold out of sth.
démunir [demynir] **1** *vt* to deprive (*s.o. of sth*). **2 se démunir** *vpr* to leave oneself short; **se d. de qch,** to part with sth.
démuseler [demyzle] *vt* (**je démuselle; je démusellerai**) to unmuzzle (*dog*); *Fig* **d. la presse,** to ungag the press.
démystifiant [demistifjɑ̃] *adj F* (*histoire, étude etc*) which debunks.
démystificateur, -trice [demistifikatœr, -tris] *F* **1** *adj* (*histoire, étude etc*) which debunks. **2** *n* debunker.
démystification [demistifikasjɔ̃] *nf F* debunking.
démystifier [demistifje] *vt* (*impf & pr sub* **n. démystifiions, v. démystifiiez**) *F* to demystify, to debunk.
dénantir [denɑ̃tir] *Jur* **1** *vt* to deprive (*creditor etc*) of pledges *or* of his securities. **2 se dénantir** *vpr* to part with one's securities.
dénatalité [denatalite] *nf* fall in the birthrate.
dénationalisation [denasjɔnalizasjɔ̃] *nf* denationalization.
dénationaliser [denasjɔnalize] **1** *vt* to denationalize. **2 se dénationaliser** *vpr* to lose one's nationality.
dénatter [denate] *vt* (*les cheveux*) to unplait.
dénaturalisation [denatyralizasjɔ̃] *nf* denaturalization.
dénaturaliser [denatyralize] *vt* to denaturalize (*person*).
dénaturant [denatyrɑ̃] *Ch* **1** *adj* denaturing. **2** *nm* denaturant, denaturing agent.
dénaturation [denatyrasjɔ̃] *nf* denaturation, changing the nature (*of sth*); **d. de l'alcool,** denaturing of alcohol.
dénaturé [denatyre] *adj* **(a)** (*transformé*) denatured; **(b)** (*dépravé*) negligent (*parents*); unnatural, perverted (*taste*).
dénaturer [denatyre] *vt* **(a)** to denature (*alcohol etc*); to misrepresent, to pervert, to distort (*words, actions*); **d. les faits,** to distort the facts; **(b)** (*dépraver*) to render (*sth*) unnatural; to pervert (*s.o.*).
dénazification [denazifikasjɔ̃] *nf* denazification.
dénazifier [denazifje] *vt* to denazify.
dénégateur, -trice [denegatœr, -tris] *n* denier.
dénégation [denegasjɔ̃] *nf* denial.
déneigement [deneʒmɑ̃] *nm* snow clearing.
déneiger [deneʒe] *vt* to clear (away) *or* remove snow from (*road etc*).
dengue [dɛ̃g] *nf Méd* dengue (fever).
déni [deni] *nm Jur* denial, refusal (*of sth which is due*); **d. de justice,** denial of justice.
déniaiser [denjeze] **1** *vt* **(a)** (*dégourdir*) to educate (*s.o.*) in the ways of the world; **(b)** *F* (*faire perdre son innocence à*) to take away s.o.'s innocence. **2 se déniaiser** *vpr* **(a)** (*se dégourdir*) to get smart; **(b)** *F* (*perdre son innocence*) to lose one's innocence.
dénichement [deniʃmɑ̃] *nm* **(a)** finding (*of sth*); **(b)** robbing (*of nest, eggs*).
dénicher [deniʃe] **1** *vt* **(a)** to find, to discover, to unearth (*s.o., sth*); **nous avons déniché une maison superbe,** we've found a beautiful house; **(b)** to take (*bird, eggs*) out of the nest; **(c)** to drive (*animal*) out of hiding. **2** *vi* (*of bird*) to leave the nest.
dénicheur, -euse [deniʃœr, -øz] *n* **(a)** *Fig* searcher; unearther (*of objects*); **d. de curiosités,** curio hunter; **(b)** (*d'oiseaux*) bird nester.
dénicotinisation [denikɔtinizasjɔ̃] *nf* denicotinization.
dénicotiniser [denikɔtinize] *vt* to reduce the amount of nicotine in (*tobacco*); **du tabac dénicotinisé,** low nicotine tobacco.
denier [dənje] *nm* **(a)** (*argent*) money, funds; **je l'ai payé de mes deniers,** I paid for it with my own money; **les deniers publics,** public money; *Cathol* **d. du culte,** church offering (*given privately to parish priest*); **(b)** *Hist* (*romaine*) denarius; *Arch Fr* denier; *Br* penny; *Arch* (*intérêt*) (rate of) interest; **le d. de la veuve,** the widow's mite; **d. à Dieu,** tip (*to concierge from new tenant*); **le d. de saint Pierre,** Peter's pence; **payer jusqu'au dernier d.,** to pay to the last farthing; **(c)** (*hosiery*) denier; **bas de 30 deniers,** 30 denier stockings.
dénier [denje] *vt* **(a)** to deny (*crime etc*); to disclaim (*responsibility*); **(b) d. qch à qn,** to refuse *or* deny s.o. sth; **d. à qn le droit de faire qch,** to deny s.o. the right to do sth.
dénigrant [denigrɑ̃] *adj* denigrating, disparaging.
dénigrement [denigrəmɑ̃] *nm* disparagement.
dénigrer [denigre] *vt* to disparage, to denigrate (*s.o., sth*), to run (*s.o., sth*) down.
dénigreur, -euse [denigrœr, -øz] *n* disparager.
dénivelé [denivle] **1** *adj* uneven, unlevel (*surface*). **2** *nm* = **DÉNIVELÉE.**
dénivelée [denivle] *nf* difference *or* variation in level *or* height.
déniveler [denivle] *vt* (*conj like* **niveler**) to make (*surface etc*) uneven.
dénivellation [denivɛlasjɔ̃] *nf*, **dénivellement** [denivɛlmɑ̃] *nm* **(a)** (*écart*) difference in level *or* height; **d. d'une route,** gradients *or* ups and downs of a road; **(b)** (*action*) making uneven; lowering *or* lifting of level.
dénombrable [denɔ̃brabl] *adj* countable.
dénombrement [denɔ̃brəmɑ̃] *nm* enumeration, counting; census (*of population*); *Méd* **d. des hématies,** blood count.
dénombrer [denɔ̃bre] *vt* to count, to enumerate; to take a census of (*population*).
dénominateur [denɔminatœr] *nm Math* denominator; **d. commun,** common denominator; **plus petit d. commun,** lowest common denominator.
dénominatif, -ive [denɔminatif, -iv] *adj & nm Ling* denominative.
dénomination [denɔminasjɔ̃] *nf* denomination, designation, name; *Pharm* **d. commune,** generic name.
dénommer [denɔme] *vt* to denominate, to name; *parfois Péj* **un dénommé Charles,** someone by the name of Charles.
dénoncer [denɔ̃se] *v* (**je dénonçai(s); n. dénonçons**) **1** *vt* **(a)** to denounce (*s.o.*), to inform against (*s.o.*); to denounce, to expose (*crime etc*); **d. un traité,** to denounce a treaty; **(b)** to indicate, to reveal; *Arch* to declare, to proclaim (*war etc*); **son attitude dénonce sa méfiance des autres,** his attitude betrays his mistrust of others. **2 se dénoncer** *vpr* to give oneself up.
dénonciateur, -trice [denɔ̃sjatœr, -tris] **1** *n* informer, denouncer; (*of crime*) exposer. **2** *adj* accusatory.
dénonciation [denɔ̃sjasjɔ̃] *nf* **(a)** notice of termination (*of treaty etc*); **(b)** denunciation; information (**de qn,** against s.o.).

dénotation [denɔtasjɔ̃] *nf* denotation.
dénoter [denɔte] *vt* to denote, to show, to indicate.
dénouement [denumɑ̃] *nm* result, outcome, conclusion (*of event*); solution (*of difficulty*); ending (*of plot, story*); *Th* dénouement.
dénouer [denwe] **1** *vt* to untie, to undo, to loose (*knot etc*); **d. ses cheveux,** to undo *or* let down one's hair; **d. une intrigue,** to clear up *or* unravel *or* resolve a plot. **2 se dénouer** *vpr* to come undone; (*of story etc*) to be resolved; **sa langue se dénoue,** he's finding his tongue.
dénoyauter [denwajote] *vt* to stone, *Am to* pit (*fruit*).
dénoyauteur [denwajotœr] *nm* (*machine*) stoner.
denrée [dɑ̃re] *nf* foodstuff, produce; (*pour le bétail*) feed; **denrées périssables,** perishable goods; **denrées de consommation courante,** staple foods, staples; **denrées alimentaires,** food products, foodstuffs; *Fig* **la patience est une d. rare,** patience is a rare commodity.
dense [dɑ̃s] *adj* **(a)** *Phys* dense; **(b)** dense, crowded; close (*formation of troops*); thick (*atmosphere*); concise, condensed (*style*); **une foule d.,** a dense crowd.
densité [dɑ̃site] *nf Phys* **(a)** density; **d. moyenne,** mean specific weight; **flacon à d.,** specific gravity flask; **(b)** density (*of population etc*); *Ordinat* **à double d.,** double-density; *Ordinat* **d. quadruple,** quad density.
dent [dɑ̃] *nf* **(a)** *Anat* tooth, *pl* teeth; **d. du fond/du devant,** back/front tooth; **d. de lait,** milk tooth, first tooth; **sans dents,** toothless; **percer** *ou* **faire ses dents,** (*d'un enfant*) to cut a tooth, to be teething; *Fig* **se faire les dents sur qn,** to take it out on s.o.; **mal** *ou* **rage de dents,** toothache; **coup de d.,** bite; *F* **avoir la d.,** to be hungry; **manger/rire à belles dents,** to eat hungrily *or* with relish/ to laugh heartily; **manger du bout des dents,** to pick at one's food; **rire du bout des dents,** to force a laugh; **avoir les dents longues,** (*être ambitieux*) *F* to be hungry; **avoir la d. dure,** to have a sharp tongue; **montrer les dents,** to show one's teeth; **serrer les dents,** to grit one's teeth; **ne pas desserer les dents,** not to open one's mouth; **avoir** *ou* **conserver** *ou* **garder une d. contre qn,** to have a grudge against s.o.; **n'avoir rien à se mettre sous la d.,** to not have a bite to eat; **ce bruit agace les dents,** that noise sets your teeth on edge; **parler entre ses dents,** to mumble, to mutter; **être sur les dents,** (*épuisé*) to be worn out; (*surmené*) to be overworked; **d. d'éléphant,** elephant's tusk;
(b) tooth (*of comb, saw*); cog (*of wheel*); prong (*of fork*); (jagged) peak (*of mountain*); **en dents de scie,** serrated, jagged; **roue à dents,** cogged wheel.
dentaire [dɑ̃tɛr] *adj Anat* dental (*pulp etc*); **plaque d.,** (dental) plaque; **hygiène d.,** dental hygiene; **l'art d.,** dentistry.
dental, -ale, -aux [dɑ̃tal, -o] *Ling* **1** *adj* dental (*consonant*). **2** *nf* **dentale,** dental consonant.
dent-de-lion [dɑ̃d(ə)ljɔ̃] *nf* dandelion; (*pl dents-de-lion*).
dent-de-loup [dɑ̃dlu] *nf Aut* ratchet tooth, catch; (*pl dents-de-loup*).
denté [dɑ̃te] *adj* cogged, toothed (*wheel*); dentate (*leaf*); **roue dentée,** cogwheel.
dentelé [dɑ̃tle] *adj* jagged, notched, indented; serrated (*leaf*); scalloped (*design*); perforated (*stamp*).
denteler [dɑ̃tle] *vt* (**je dentelle; je dentellerai**) to notch, to jag, to indent; to pink (out) (*leather*); to perforate (*postage stamp*).
dentelle [dɑ̃tɛl] *nf* **(a)** lace; **d. aux fuseaux,** pillow lace; **d. à l'aiguille** *ou* **au point,** point lace; **robe de d.,** lacy dress; **des dentelles de papier,** paper doilies; *Culin* **crêpe d.,** very thin pancake, crêpe; *Fig* **ne pas faire dans la d.,** (*y aller carrément*) not to mince one's words; (*manquer de finesse*) to lack polish; **ça n'est pas de la d.,** it's nothing fancy; **(b)** = wrought ironwork, sculpture etc that has the appearance of lace.
dentellerie [dɑ̃tɛlri] *nf* lacemaking.
dentellier, -ière [dɑ̃tɛlje, -jɛr] **1** *adj* lace (*industry etc*). **2** *n* lacemaker. **3** *nf* **dentellière,** lacemaking machine.
dentelure [dɑ̃tlyr] *nf* indentation; serration (*of leaf*); perforation (*at edge of postage stamp*); (jagged) mountain peaks.
dentier [dɑ̃tje] *nm* set of false teeth, dentures.
dentifrice [dɑ̃tifris] **1** *nm* toothpaste; *Vieilli* toothpowder. **2** *adj* **pâte d.,** toothpaste; **eau d.,** mouthwash; **poudre d.,** toothpowder.
dentine [dɑ̃tin] *nf Anat* dentine.
dentiste [dɑ̃tist] *n* dentist; **chirurgien d.,** dental surgeon.
dentition [dɑ̃tisjɔ̃] *nf* **(a)** (*croissance*) cutting of teeth, teething; **d. définitive** *ou* **permanente,** permanent teeth; **(b)** (*arrangement*) arrangement of the teeth, *Spéc* dentition.
denture [dɑ̃tyr] *nf* **(a)** (*arrangement*) set of (natural) teeth; **(b)** (*dentier*) set of false teeth, denture; **(c)** *MecE* teeth, cogs, gearing.
dénucléarisation [denyklearizasjɔ̃] *nf* denuclearization.
dénucléariser [denyklearize] *vt* to denuclearize.
dénudation [denydasjɔ̃] *nf Fml* stripping, laying bare, denudation.
dénudé [denyde] *adj* bare (*countryside*); stripped, bare (*tree etc*); bald (*head*); *Électron* bare (*wire*).
dénuder [denyde] **1** *vt* to strip, to lay bare, to denude; (*d'une robe*) to leave bare; **d. un arbre de son écorce,** to strip the bark off a tree. **2 se dénuder** *vpr* **(a)** (*perdre sa végétation*) to grow bare; **(b)** (*se mettre à nu*) to strip (naked).
dénué [denɥe] *adj* **d. de,** (*raison, intelligence, intérêt etc*) devoid of.
dénuement [denymɑ̃] *nm* destitution, penury, need; **être dans le d.,** to be destitute *or* poverty-stricken; **d. moral,** moral deprivation.
dénuer (se) [sədenɥe] *vpr Litt* to deprive oneself (**de,** of); **se d. de ses biens,** to part with all one's possessions.
dénutrition [denytrisjɔ̃] *nf Méd* malnutrition.
déodorant [deɔdɔrɑ̃] *adj & nm* deodorant.
déodoriser [deɔdɔrize] *vt* to deodorize.
déontologie [deɔ̃tɔlɔʒi] *nf* deontology; **code de d.,** code of (professional) ethics.
dépannage [depanaʒ] *nm* **(a)** (emergency) repairs (*to engine etc*); **service de d.,** breakdown service; **(b)** (*pour rendre service*) helping (*s.o.*) out.
dépanner [depane] *vt* **(a)** to repair, to do running repairs on (*broken-down engine, car etc*); **il m'a dépanné,** he got my car *or* T.V. *etc* going again; **(b)** (*aider*) to help (*s.o.*) out.
dépanneur [depanœr] *nm* **(a)** breakdown mechanic; (television) repairman; **(b)** *Can* corner shop, *Am* convenience store.
dépanneuse [depanøz] *nf Aut* breakdown van *or* lorry, *US* wrecker.
dépaquetage [depaktaʒ] *nm* unpacking (*of goods*).
dépaqueter [depakte] *vt* (*conj like* **paqueter**) to unpack (*goods etc*).
dépareillé [depareje] *adj* odd, incomplete, unpaired; **gant d.,** odd glove; *Com* **articles dépareillés,** oddments, job lot.
dépareiller [depareje] *vt* to remove one of a pair of, to spoil a pair of (*objects*).
déparer [depare] *vt* to spoil, to mar; **d. le paysage,** to be a blot on the landscape.
déparier [deparje] *vt* (*impf & pr sub* **n. dépariions, v. dépariiez**) = **DÉPAREILLER.**
départ [depar] *nm* departure (*of person, vehicle etc*); sailing (*of ship*); start (*of race etc*); **dès son d. j'ai rangé sa chambre,** as soon as he had gone I tidied his room; **le d. d'une association,** the foundation of an association; **le d. de la navette spatiale,** the launch of the space shuttle; **le d. du courrier,** the time the post leaves; **exiger le d. d'un employé,** to insist on the dismissal of an employee; **point de d.,** starting point; **prendre qch comme point de d.,** to take sth as one's starting point; **être sur le d.,** to be on the point of leaving; **produit de d.,** original material; **langue de d.,**(*d'une traduction*) source language; **qui a eu l'idée de d.?,** who had the original idea?; **signal de d.,** start signal; *Sp* **ligne de d.,** starting line; *Golf* **(tertre de) d.,** tee; *Rail* **quai du d.,** departure platform; **prix de d.,** (*at auction*) upset price; *Com* **prix d. usine,** prices ex works; **au d.,** at the outset; **excursions au d. de Chamonix,** trips (leaving) from Chamonix; *Sp* **d. arrêté,** standing start; *Sp* **d. lancé,** flying start; *Sp* **faux d.,** false start; *Sp* **donner le d.,** to start the race, *F* to give the off; *Sp & Fig* **prendre un bon/mauvais d.,** to get off to a good/bad start.
départager [departaʒe] *vt* (*conj like* **partager**) to decide between (*opinions etc*); *Litt* to separate; **d. les gagnants,** to decide the winners; **d. les votes,** to give the casting vote.
département [departəmɑ̃] *nm Admin* **(a)** (*ministère*) department, ministry; **le d. de l'intérieur,** the ministry of the Interior, *Br* ≈ the Home Office, *US* ≈ the Department of the Interior; **le d. de la peinture moderne,** (*dans un musée*) the modern art section; *F* **cela n'est pas dans mon d.,** that's not my department; **(b)** subdivision (*of France*) administered by a prefect, department.
départemental, -aux [departəmɑ̃tal, -o] **1** *adj* departmental. **2** *nf* **départementale,** secondary *or Br* B road.
départir [departir] *v* (*conj like* **partir,** *occ like* **finir**) **1** *vt* to distribute, to dispense, to deal out (*favours etc*). **2 se départir** *vpr* **se d. de qch,** to abandon *or* give up sth.
dépassé [depase] *adj* **(a) c'est d.,** (*de faire ça*) it's mediaeval; **(b) je suis d.,** (*je ne comprends plus rien*) it's

beyond me; **je suis d. (par les événements),** things are getting too much for me.

dépassement [depasmɑ̃] *nm* **(a)** surpassing (*of oneself*); exceeding (*one's credit etc*); **(b)** *Aut* overtaking; **d. interdit,** no overtaking.

dépasser [depase] **1** *vt* **(a)** to pass, to go beyond (*s.o., sth*); to overrun (*signal etc*); **nous avons dépassé la boulangerie,** we have passed the baker's; **d. le but,** to overshoot the mark; **il a dépassé la trentaine,** he has turned thirty, he is over thirty; **d. qn,** (*à la course etc*) to overtake *or* outrun *or* outstrip s.o.;

(b) d. qch en hauteur, to top sth; **d. qn de la tête,** to stand a head taller than s.o.; **cette maison dépasse l'alignement,** this house projects beyond the building line; **la beauté des lieux dépasse toute imagination,** the scene is beautiful beyond all imagination; **cela dépasse ma compétence,** it lies beyond *or* outside my area of responsibility; **d. les bornes,** (*aller trop loin*) to overstep the bounds *or* the mark, *Am* to be out of line; **cela dépasse mon entendement, cela me dépasse,** (*son comportement*) it is beyond me; (*discussion savante*) it is over my head; **être d. par les événements,** to be overtaken by events;

(c) (*excéder*) to exceed; **d. la limite de vitesse,** to exceed the speed limit; **d. son congé,** to exceed one's leave; **l'entretien ne dépassera pas un quart d'heure,** the interview won't take more than a quarter of an hour; **d. la durée autorisée de 20 minutes,** to take more than the 20 minutes allowed; **le prix ne doit pas d. dix francs,** the price must not exceed ten francs; **toutes ces voitures dépassent nos moyens,** all the cars are beyond our means; **ne pas d. la dose prescrite,** do not exceed the stated dose.

2 se dépasser *vpr* to surpass oneself.

3 *vi* **(a)** *Aut* **il est interdit de d. sur ce pont,** no overtaking on this bridge;

(b) (*être trop long*) **votre jupon dépasse,** your underskirt is showing; **son mouchoir dépasse de sa poche,** his handkerchief is sticking out of his pocket.

dépassionner [depasjɔne] *vt* to take the heat out of (*a debate*).

dépatouiller (se) [sədepatuje] *vpr F* to get out of a fix.

dépaver [depave] *vt* to take up the paving from (*yard, street*).

dépaysé [depeize] *adj* out of one's element; **je me sens d.,** I feel like a fish out of water, I don't feel at home.

dépaysement [depeizmɑ̃] *nm* disorientation (*of s.o.*).

dépayser [depeize] *vt* to remove (*s.o.*) from his usual surroundings *or* his element; (*désorienter*) to disorientate, *esp Am* to disorient (*s.o.*).

dépeçage [depəsaʒ] *nm* cutting up (*of a slaughtered or hunted animal*).

dépècement [depɛsmɑ̃] *nm* cutting up; *Fig* **le d. du pays fut complété par les barbares,** the barbarians completed the dismemberment of the country.

dépecer [depəse] *vt* (**je dépèce, n. dépeçons; je dépècerai**) **(a)** to dismember, to cut up (*carcass*); to carve, to cut up (*fowl*); to flense (*whale*); **le lion dépèce sa proie,** the lion tears its prey; **(b)** *Fig* to dismember (*territory*).

dépeceur, -euse [depəsœr, -øz] *n* cutter up (*of carcass etc*); **d. (de baleines),** flenser.

dépêche [depɛʃ] *nf* **(a)** (*lettre officielle*) (official) dispatch, message; **(b) d. (télégraphique),** telegram, *F* wire.

dépêcher [depeʃe] **1** *vt* **(a)** to dispatch (*sth*), to do (*sth*) quickly; **d. une besogne,** to dispatch *or* rush a job; **(b)** (*un courrier, un messager*) to dispatch. **2 se dépêcher** *vpr* to hurry, to be quick; **dépêchez-vous!,** hurry up!, get a move on!, buck up!, quick!; **se d. de faire qch,** to hurry to do sth; **dépêchez-vous de guérir,** get well soon; **se d. de rentrer,** to hurry home.

dépeigner [depeɲe] *vt* **d. qn,** to ruffle s.o.'s hair, to make s.o.'s hair untidy; **elle est toute dépeignée,** her hair's uncombed, she hasn't combed her hair.

dépeindre [depɛ̃dr] *vt* (*conj like* **peindre**) to depict, to picture, to describe (*s.o., sth*).

dépelotonner [deplɔtɔne] *vt* to unwind (*ball of wool etc*).

dépenaillé [depnaje] *adj* (*veste, pantalon etc*) ragged, tattered, torn; (*veste, vêtements, personne*) in rags, in tatters.

dépendance [depɑ̃dɑ̃s] *nf* **(a)** dependence (*of sth on sth*); **(b)** dependency (*of a country*); *Archit* **dépendances,** outbuildings; **(c)** (*asservissement*) dependence, *US* dependency; **l'abus de somnifères peut créer une d.,** excessive use of sleeping tablets can lead to dependence; **vivre dans la d. complète de qn,** to be completely dependent on s.o.; **être sous la d. de qn,** to be under s.o.'s domination *or* control.

dépendant [depɑ̃dɑ̃] *adj* dependent; **fonctions dépendantes l'une de l'autre,** functions dependent on each other, interdependent functions; **être d. de qn,** to be dependent on s.o.; **être d. de la drogue,** to be dependent on drugs.

dépendre¹ [depɑ̃dr] *vt* to take down (*hanging object*).

dépendre² *vi* **(a)** to depend; **d. de qn/qch,** to depend on s.o./sth; **tout dépend des circonstances,** everything depends on the circumstances; **ces événements ne dépendent pas de nous,** such events are not within our control; **cela ne dépend que de toi,** that depends on you alone; **il dépend de vous de le faire,** it lies *or* rests with you to do it; **cela dépend,** that depends; *F* **ça dépend s'il est marié,** it depends whether he's married;

(b) (*of land etc*) to be a dependency (**de,** of); to appertain to, to belong to (*the Crown*);

(c) (*être sous la domination de*) to be subordinate *or* subject (**de,** to); to be under (*s.o.'s*) domination; **il dépend financièrement de ses parents,** he is financially dependent on his parents; **je ne dépends pas de lui,** I don't take orders from him; **ne d. que de soi,** to be one's own boss; **un pays qui dépend d'un autre,** a country which is dependent (up)on another;

(d) (*of ship*) to hail (*from a port*).

dépens [depɑ̃] *nmpl* **(a) aux d. de,** at the expense of (*s.o., sth*); **s'amuser aux d. de ses études,** to enjoy oneself at the expense of one's studies; **il apprit à ses d. que ...,** he learnt to his cost that ...; **(b)** *Jur* costs; *Com* cost, expenses; **être condamné aux d.,** to be ordered to pay costs.

dépense [depɑ̃s] *nf* **(a)** expenditure, expense, outlay; **dépenses du ménage,** household expenses; **dépenses courantes,** current expenditures *or* expenses; **faire des dépenses,** to incur expenses; **faire qch au prix de dépenses énormes,** to do sth at enormous cost; **je n'aurais pas dû faire cette d.,** I shouldn't have spent that money; **pousser à d.,** to encourage people to spend; **c'est une grosse d.,** it's a lot of money; **faire trop de d.,** to spend too much (money); **se mettre en d.,** to incur expense; *F* to put oneself to a great deal of trouble; **on ne regardait pas à la d.,** there was no stinting, they didn't mind the cost, they spared no expense; **faire de folles dépenses,** to spend money extravagantly; **recettes et dépenses,** receipts and expenditure; **dépenses publiques,** public spending;

(b) *Tech* **d. d'essence,** petrol *or US* gas consumption; **d. à vide,** wasted energy; *Fig* **d. de temps/d'énergie,** expenditure of time/energy; **d. physique trop violente,** unduly severe physical exertion;

(c) (*d'une communauté etc*) bursary.

dépenser [depɑ̃se] **1** *vt* **(a)** to spend (*money*); **il dépense peu en livres,** he doesn't spend much on books; **je n'ai pas dépensé un sou,** I didn't spend a penny; **(b)** to use, to consume (*time, energy etc*); **la voiture dépense très peu d'essence,** the car uses *or* consumes very little petrol; **d. toute son énergie/ses forces (à qch),** to use up all one's energy/one's strength (in doing sth); **d. sa salive,** to talk a lot. **2** *vi* to spend (money); **d. sans compter,** to spend lavishly, to be free with one's money. **3 se dépenser** *vpr* to exert oneself; **se d. pour qn,** to spare no trouble on s.o.'s behalf; **se d. en démarches inutiles,** to waste one's energies in useless activities.

dépensier, -ière [depɑ̃sje, -jɛr] **1** *adj* extravagant. **2** *n* **(a)** (*personne prodigue*) spendthrift; **(b)** bursar (*of convent*).

déperdition [depɛrdisjɔ̃] *nf* waste, wastage, destruction (*of tissue etc*); loss (*of heat, energy*).

dépérir [deperir] *vi* (*of person*) to waste away; (*of health*) to decline; (*of flowers*) to wither; (*of tree*) to decay; (*of race*) to die out; (*of business*) to go downhill.

dépérissement [deperismɑ̃] *nm* (*of person*) wasting away; (*of flower*) withering; decay (*of tree*); dying out (*of race*); decline (*of business*).

dépersonnalisation [depɛrsɔnalizasjɔ̃] *nf* depersonalization.

dépersonnaliser [depɛrsɔnalize] **1** *vt* to depersonalize. **2 se dépersonnaliser** *vpr* to lose one's personality *or* character.

dépêtrer [depetre] *F* **1** *vtr* to extricate, to free (*s.o.*) (*from entanglement*); **d. qn d'une mauvaise affaire,** to get s.o. out of a scrape. **2 se dépêtrer** *vpr* to get out of a scrape; **se d. de qn,** to get rid of s.o., to shake s.o. off.

dépeuplé [depœple] *adj* (*pays, région*) depopulated; (*salle*) empty.

dépeuplement [depœpləmɑ̃] *nm* depopulation (*of coun-*

try etc); unstocking (*of pond*); thinning, clearing (*of forest*).
dépeupler [depœple] **1** *vt* to depopulate (*country etc*); to unstock (*pond*); to thin, to clear (*forest*). **2 se dépeupler** *vpr (d'un pays, d'une région)* to become depopulated.
déphasage [defazaʒ] *nm* **(a)** *Él* phase displacement; dephasing; difference in phase; **d. en avant,** (phase) lead; **d. en arrière,** lag; **(b)** *Fig* disorientation (*of s.o.*).
déphasé [defaze] *adj* **(a)** *Él* (*current*) out of phase; **d. en arrière,** lagging (*current*); **d. en avant,** leading (*current*); **(b)** *Fig* (*person*) (*désorienté*) disoriented; (*qui a perdu le contact*) out of touch.
déphaser [defaze] *vt* **(a)** *Él* to dephase (*current*); **(b)** *Fig* to disorientate *or esp Am* disorient (*s.o.*).
dépiauter [depjote] *vt F* to skin, to flay (*rabbit etc*); **d. un texte/un article,** to pull a text/an article to pieces.
dépigmentation [depigmɑ̃tasjɔ̃] *nf Méd* loss of pigmentation.
dépilation [depilasjɔ̃] *nf* **(a)** (*volontaire*) (superfluous) hair removal; **(b)** (*chute*) loss of hair.
dépilatoire [depilatwar] *adj* depilatory; **crème d.,** hair removing cream, depilatory.
dépiler [depile] *vt* **(a)** to remove (superfluous) hair from (*face etc*); **(b)** *Méd* to cause loss of hair; **(c)** to grain (*skin*).
dépiquage [depikaʒ] *nm Agr* treading out (*of corn*).
dépiquer¹ [depike] *vt* **(a)** *Agr* to tread out (*corn*); **(b)** to transplant (*shoots*).
dépiquer² *vt Couture* to unstitch, to unpick (*dress etc*).
dépistage [depistaʒ] *nm* tracking down, detection (*of criminal etc*); (early) detection, screening (*of disease, virus etc*).
dépister [depiste] *vt* **(a)** to track down (*game, criminal*); to detect (*a disease*); **d. un traquenard,** to spot a trap; **(b)** to put (*hounds*) off the scent; to throw (*s.o.*) off the scent; **il a dépisté la police,** he gave the police the slip.
dépit [depi] *nm* **(a)** (*ressentiment*) spite, resentment; **par d.,** out of spite; **pleurer de d.,** to cry with vexation; **concevoir du d. de qch,** to feel annoyed about sth; **(b) en d. de,** in spite of, in defiance of; **en d. du bon sens,** (*illogiquement*) contrary to common sense; (*très mal*) very badly; **en d. de ce que je sais,** in spite of what I know.
dépité [depite] *adj* annoyed; **être tout d.,** to be thoroughly annoyed.
dépiter [depite] **1** *vt* to annoy (*s.o.*), to cause (*s.o.*) annoyance; **je l'ai dit pour la d.,** I said it to annoy her. **2 se dépiter** *vpr* to take offence, to be annoyed.
déplacé [deplase] *adj* **(a)** out of (its) place; **avoir une vertèbre déplacée,** to have a slipped disc; **se sentir d.,** to feel out of place; **(b)** unwarranted, uncalled-for; **observation déplacée,** unwarranted *or* uncalled-for remark; **des scrupules déplacés,** unwarranted scruples; **(c)** *Pol* **personne déplacée,** displaced person.
déplacement [deplasmɑ̃] *nm* **(a)** moving, shifting (*of furniture etc*); transfer (*of official*); *Méd* **d. de vertèbre,** slipped disc; **(b)** change of location *or* site *or* position; *Mil* (*of troops*) change of station; **(c)** (*voyage*) travelling; moving, movement; journey; **être en d.,** to be on a (business) trip; **frais de d.,** travelling expenses; **moyen de d.,** means of transport; **(d) d. d'un navire,** displacement of a ship; **d. en charge,** displacement loaded, load displacement; **d. d'air,** air displacement.
déplacer [deplase] *v* (**je déplaçai(s); n. déplaçons**) **1** *vt* **(a)** to move, to shift (*an object*); to change the place of (*s.o., sth*); **meubles difficiles à d.,** furniture difficult to move; **d. un fonctionnaire/un service,** to transfer a civil servant/a department; *Fig* **d. la question** *ou* **le problème,** to shift the focus of a problem; **vous déplacez le problème,** you're missing the point;
(b) (*transporter*) to carry; **ce navire déplace dix mille tonneaux,** this ship has a displacement of ten thousand tons; **il ne peut rien d., il a mal au dos,** he can't carry anything, he has a bad back.
2 se déplacer *vpr* **(a)** (*changer de place*) to change one's place, to move (around); **interdit de se d.,** ≈ please remain seated; **avoir du mal à se d.,** to have difficulty in moving *or* getting around;
(b) (*voyager*) to move about, to travel; **son métier l'oblige à se d. souvent,** his work requires him to travel frequently;
(c) to get out of place, to shift; **le bateau se déplace lentement,** the boat moves slowly; **la façon dont les poissons se déplacent,** the way fish move; **se d. une vertèbre,** to slip a disc.
déplafonner [deplafɔne] *vt Admin* to remove the upper limit *or* the ceiling on (*prices*).
déplaire [deplɛr] *v* (*conj like* **plaire**) **1** *vi* **d. à qn,** (*irriter*) to displease *or* offend s.o.; (*ne pas plaire à*) to fail to please s.o., to be displeasing to s.o.; **odeur qui déplaît,** offensive *or* disagreeable smell; **tu lui déplais,** he dislikes you; **il me déplaît de le faire,** I don't like doing it; **cela ne me déplairait pas,** I wouldn't mind (it); **il a tout fait pour nous déplaire,** he has been utterly disagreeable; **cela m'a profondément déplu,** I was greatly *or* most displeased by that; *Iron* **n'en déplaise à la compagnie,** with all due respect to those present; **n'en déplaise à votre Altesse!,** may it please your Highness!; **ne vous en déplaise,** whether you like it or not. **2 se déplaire** *vpr* to be displeased *or* dissatisfied; **il se déplaît à Paris,** he doesn't like Paris.
déplaisant [deplɛzɑ̃] *adj* unpleasant, disagreeable.
déplaisir [deplezir] *nm* displeasure, annoyance; **à son grand d.,** to his great annoyance.
déplantage [deplɑ̃taʒ] *nm* digging up, lifting (*of plant*).
déplanter [deplɑ̃te] *vt* to take *or* dig up, to lift (*plant*).
déplantoir [deplɑ̃twar] *nm* hand fork.
déplâtrage [deplatraʒ] *nm* **(a)** stripping of plaster (*from wall etc*); **(b)** taking (*limb*) out of plaster.
déplâtrer [deplatre] *vt* **(a)** to strip plaster from (*wall etc*); **(b)** to take the plaster off (*limb*); **on la déplâtre demain,** she's having the plaster off tomorrow.
dépliage [deplijaʒ] *nm* unfolding, opening out.
dépliant [deplijɑ̃] **1** *adj* folding (*bed etc*). **2** *nm* (*album*) folding album; (*prospectus*) folder, brochure; (*feuille pliée*) fold-out page.
dépliement [deplimɑ̃] *nm* unfolding, opening out.
déplier [deplije] *v* (*pr sub & impf* **n. dépliions, v. dépliiez**) **1** *vt* to unfold, to open out, to spread out (*newspaper, handkerchief etc*); **d. sa marchandise,** to unpack *or* spread out one's wares. **2 se déplisser** *vpr* to unfold, to open out.
déplissage [deplisaʒ] *nm* taking the creases out (*of material etc*).
déplisser [deplise] **1** *vt* to take the creases out of, to smooth out (*material etc*). **2 se déplisser** *vpr* (*of material etc*) to lose its creases.
déploiement [deplwamɑ̃] *nm* **(a)** spreading out, unfolding (*of wings etc*); unfurling (*of flag*); deployment (*of troops, ships etc*); **(b)** display (*of force, of courage*); display, show (*of goods etc*); **un d. d'attention,** a display *or* show of attention.
déplombage [deplɔ̃baʒ] *nm* **(a)** removal of seal (*from electricity meter, parcel etc*); **(b)** removal of filling (*from tooth*).
déplomber [deplɔ̃be] *vt* **(a)** to remove the seal from (*electricity meter, parcel etc*); **(b)** to remove the filling from (*tooth*).
déplorable [deplɔrabl] *adj* deplorable, regrettable (*incident etc*); deplorable, disgraceful (*behaviour, results etc*).
déplorablement [deplɔrabləmɑ̃] *adv* deplorably, disgracefully.
déplorer [deplɔre] *vt* to deplore, to lament (*sth*), to regret (*sth*) deeply; **d. la mort/l'absence de qn,** to grieve over *or* to mourn s.o.'s death/to deplore s.o.'s absence.
déployer [deplwaje] *v* (**je déploie, n. déployons; je déploierai**) **1** *vt* **(a)** to unfold, to open out (*newspaper etc*); to unfurl (*flag*); to spread (*sails, wings*); to deploy (*troops*); **rire à gorge déployée,** to roar with laughter; **(b)** to display, show (*goods, patience etc*). **2 se déployer** *vpr* (*of sail, flag*) to unfurl; *Mil Nau* to deploy.
déplumé [deplyme] *adj* featherless; *F* (*chauve*) bald.
déplumer [deplyme] **1** *vt* to pluck (*chicken etc*). **2 se déplumer** *vpr* (*of bird*) to moult; *F* (*of person*) to go bald.
dépoitraillé [depwatraje] *adj F Péj* with one's shirt *etc* all undone (at the front).
dépolarisant [depɔlarizɑ̃] *Phys* **1** *adj* depolarizing. **2** *nm* depolarizer.
dépolarisation [depɔlarizasjɔ̃] *nf Phys* depolarization.
dépolariser [depɔlarize] *vt Phys* to depolarize.
dépoli [depɔli] *adj* frosted (*glass*).
dépolir [depɔlir] **1** *vt* to dull, to tarnish (*surface*); to frost (*glass*). **2 se dépolir** *vpr* to become dull, to tarnish.
dépolissage [depɔlisaʒ] *nm*, **dépolissement** [depɔlismɑ̃] *nm* dulling, tarnishing (*of surface*); frosting (*of glass*).
dépolitisation [depɔlitizɑ̃sjɔ̃] *nf* depoliticization.
dépolitiser [depɔlitize] *vt* to depoliticize.
dépolluer [depɔlye] *vt* (*une rivière etc*) to clean up.
dépollution [depɔlysjɔ̃] *nf* cleaning up.
déponent [depɔnɑ̃] *adj & nm Gram* deponent (verb).
dépopulation [depɔpylasjɔ̃] *nf* depopulation.
déportation [depɔrtasjɔ̃] *nf* **(a)** deportation (*of undesirable alien etc*); transportation (*of convict*); **(b)** internment (*in concentration camp*).

déporté, -ée [depɔrte] *n* **(a)** deportee; **(b)** internee, prisoner (*in concentration camp*).
déportement [depɔrtəmɑ̃] *nm* **(a) déportements,** excesses, dissolute life; **(b)** *Aut* skidding, swerving.
déporter¹ [depɔrte] *vt* **(a)** to deport (*undesirable alien*); to transport (*convict*); **(b)** to send (*prisoner*) to a concentration camp.
déporter² *vt* to carry off course; **voiture déportée par la violence du vent,** car blown off the road by the violence of the wind.
déposant, -ante [depozɑ̃, -ɑ̃t] *n* **(a)** depositor (*of money in bank etc*); **(b)** *Jur* deponent, witness.
dépose [depoz] *nf* lifting, taking up (*of carpet etc*); removal (*of engine etc*).
déposer¹ [depoze] *vt* to lift, to take up (*carpet etc*); **d. les rideaux,** to take down the curtains.
déposer² **1** *vt* **(a)** to lay *or* set *or* put (*sth*) down; (*of liquid*) to deposit (*sediment*); **ma voiture vous déposera à l'hôtel,** my car will drop you at the hotel; **puis-je vous d. quelque part?,** can I drop you somewhere?; **d. une lettre/un paquet chez qn,** to drop off a letter/a parcel at s.o.'s house; **défense de d. des ordures,** no dumping, *Br* no tipping; **d. les armes,** to lay down one's arms, to surrender;
(b) to deposit, to lodge (*sth*) in a safe place; *Com* to register (*a trademark*); **d. son argent à la banque,** to deposit one's money at the bank; *Com* **marque déposée,** registered trademark; *Jur* **d. une plainte contre qn,** to prefer a charge *or* lodge a complaint against s.o.; *Com* **d. son bilan,** to file one's petition (in bankruptcy); **d. un projet de loi,** to table *or* bring in a bill;
(c) to depose (*monarch etc*).
2 *vi* **(a)** *vi* **il faut laisser au liquide le temps de d.,** we must allow the liquid some time to settle;
(b) *Jur* **d. (en justice),** to give evidence **(contre,** against).
3 se déposer *vpr* (*of matter*) to settle, to form a deposit.
dépositaire [depoziter] *n* **(a)** depositary, trustee; possessor (*of secret etc*); **d. de valeurs,** holder of securities on trust; **(b)** *Com* sole agent (*for products*); **d. de journaux,** newsagent.
déposition [depozisjɔ̃] *nf* **(a)** *Jur* deposition, statement (made by witness); **recueillir une d.,** to take s.o.'s evidence; **(b)** deposing (*of monarch*); **(c)** *Beaux Arts* **D. de croix,** Deposition.
déposséder [depɔsede] *vt* (**je dépossède, n. dépossédons; je déposséderai**) to dispossess, to deprive (**de,** of); to oust (**de,** from); **d. qn de sa place/de sa charge,** to deprive s.o. of or oust s.o. from his seat/to remove s.o. from office, to deprive s.o. of his office.
dépossession [depɔsesjɔ̃] *nf* dispossession, deprivation.
dépôt [depo] *nm* **(a)** (*remise*) laying, depositing; (*chose confiée*) deposit; **d. d'une gerbe,** laying of a wreath; **banque de d.,** deposit bank; *Com* **d. d'une marque de fabrique,** registration of a trademark; *Jur* **d. légal,** registration of copyright; *Pol* **d. d'un projet de loi,** bringing in *or* tabling of a bill; **d. sacré,** sacred trust; **d. bancaire,** bank deposit; **compte de d.,** deposit account; **avoir** *ou* **détenir qch en d.,** to hold sth in trust; **marchandises en d.,** (*à la douane*) goods in bond; *Com* goods on sale *or* return;
(b) (*entrepôt*) depository, repository, store(house), depot; *Rail* engine shed; (*prison*) prison, jail; **d. de(s) marchandises,** goods depot; (*entrepôt*) warehouse; **d. de bois,** timber yard; **d. d'essence,** petrol storage depot; **d. de bouteilles** *ou* **de verre,** bottle bank; *Rail etc* **d. de(s) bagages,** left-luggage office; **il a passé la nuit au d.,** he spent the night in jail; *Jur* **mandat de d.,** committal, commitment (of prisoner); **d. d'ordures,** rubbish dump *or* *Br* tip;
(c) deposition, settling (*of precipitate, mud etc*); (*précipité*) deposit, sediment, silt (*of harbour etc*); fur (*in kettle*); scale (*in boiler*); **le d. d'un vin,** the sediment in a wine; **il y a du d.,** there is a sediment; *Géol* **d. calcaire/sédimentaire,** calcareous/sedimentary deposit.
dépotage [depɔtaʒ] *nm*, **dépotement** [depɔtmɑ̃] *nm* **(a)** decanting (*of liquid*); **(b)** repotting (*of plants*); planting out (*of seedlings*).
dépoter [depɔte] *vt* **(a)** to decant (*liquid*); **(b)** to repot (*plants*); to plant out (*seedlings*).
dépotoir [depɔtwar] *nm* **(a)** dump, *Br* rubbish tip; *Fig* **cette chambre est un vrai d.,** this room is a real tip *or* dump; **(b)** *Ind* sewage works.
dépouille [depuj] *nf* **(a)** skin, hide (*taken from animal*); slough (*of snake*); **d. (mortelle),** (mortal) remains; **(b) dépouilles,** spoils, booty (*of war*); effects, clothes (*of deceased person*); **(c)** *MecE* relief, clearance (*of drill, of machine tool*).
dépouillé [depuje] *adj* bald (*style etc*); bare (*tree*); **vin d.,** = wine that has lost its alcohol content; **d. de,** lacking in.
dépouillement [depujmɑ̃] *nm* **(a)** deprivation (*of s.o.*) of his belongings; **d. volontaire de ses biens,** relinquishment *or* renouncement of one's property; **(b)** (*examen*) **d. d'un rapport,** examination *or* analysis of a report; **d. des votes du scrutin,** counting of the votes (*at ballot, election*); **d. du courrier,** going through the mail.
dépouiller [depuje] **1** *vt* **(a)** (*priver*) to deprive, to strip; **d. qn de ses droits,** to deprive s.o. of his rights; **se faire d.,** (*dans une affaire*) to lose all one's money; **se faire d. par des voleurs,** to be robbed of all one's money; **d. un pays,** to plunder a country;
(b) (*examiner*) **d. un inventaire,** to examine *or* analyse an inventory; **d. le scrutin,** to count the votes; **d. le courrier,** to open *or* go through the mail;
(c) to skin (*rabbit etc*); *Litt* to cast off, to lay aside; **d. qn de ses habits,** to strip s.o.;
(d) *MecE* to back off, to give clearance to (*drill etc*).
2 se dépouiller *vpr* **(a)** (*of insect, snake*) to cast (off) its skin; (*of tree*) to shed its leaves; (*of wine*) to lose its strength;
(b) se d. de qch, to deprive *or* divest *or* rid oneself of sth; **se d. de ses vêtements,** to strip off one's clothes, *F* to strip; **un sentiment qui se dépouille de toute pitié,** a feeling devoid of all pity.
dépourvu [depurvy] *adj* **(a) d. de,** devoid of; **d. d'intelligence/d'intérêt/***etc*, devoid of intelligence/interest/*etc*; **pays d. d'arbres,** treeless country; **être d. (d'argent),** to be penniless; **(b) être pris au d.,** to be caught off one's guard.
dépoussiérage [depusjeraʒ] *nm Ind* vacuum cleaning, dust removal.
dépoussiérer [depusjere] *vt Ind* to vacuum clean, to remove the dust from (*sth*).
dépoussiéreur [depusjerœr] *nm Ind* dust remover, vacuum cleaner.
dépravant [depravɑ̃] *adj* depraving.
dépravation [depravasjɔ̃] *nf* (moral) depravity.
dépravé, -ée [deprave] **1** *adj* depraved. **2** *n* degenerate, depraved person.
dépraver [deprave] **1** *vt* to deprave. **2 se dépraver** *vpr* to become depraved.
dépréciateur, -trice [depresjatœr, -tris] *n* disparager, belittler (*of s.o.'s character etc*).
dépréciatif, -ive [depresjatif, -iv] *adj Ling* pejorative (*expression etc*); **mot d.,** derogatory word.
dépréciation [depresjasjɔ̃] *nf* **(a)** (*dévaluation*) depreciation, fall in value; **(b)** (*mauvaise évaluation*) underrating, undervaluing; (*dénigrement*) disparagement.
déprécier [depresje] *v* (*impf & pr sub* **n. dépréciions, v. dépréciiez**) **1** *vt* **(a)** to depreciate (*coinage etc*); **(b)** to underrate, to undervalue (*goods, merits*); **(c)** to disparage, to belittle (*s.o.*), *F* to run (*s.o., book*) down. **2 se déprécier** *vpr* **(a)** (*of values*) to depreciate, to fall; (*of goods*) to depreciate, to fall in value; **(b)** (*of person*) to belittle oneself.
déprédateur, -trice [depredatœr, -tris] **1** *n* **(a)** pillager; **(b)** *Fin* embezzler. **2** *adj* depredatory.
déprédation [depredasjɔ̃] *nf* **(a)** (*pillage*) depredation, pillaging; **(b)** *Fin* misappropriation (*of funds etc*), embezzlement.
déprendre (se) [sədeprɑ̃dr] *vpr* (*conj like* **prendre**) to detach oneself, to get free; **se d. d'une habitude/d'une personne,** to get out of a habit/to get clear *or* free of a person.
dépressif, -ive [depresif, -iv] *adj* depressive.
dépression [depresjɔ̃] *nf* **(a)** (*affaissement*) depression, hollow, dip (*in ground*); trough (*in ocean*); *Astron* dip (*of horizon*); *Mil* **angle de d.,** angle of depression (*of gun*); **(b)** (*chute*) fall (*in value*); **d. économique,** economic depression, slump; *Météo* **d. (barométrique),** (barometric) depression, low, trough; **(c)** *Psy* (mental) depression; **un moment de d.,** a moment of depression; **faire de la d.,** to be in a state of depression; *Méd* **d. nerveuse,** nervous breakdown.
dépressionnaire [depresjɔner] *adj Météo* **zone** *ou* **centre d.,** trough, area of low pressure; **système d.,** low-pressure system.
déprimant [deprimɑ̃] *adj* depressing.
déprime [deprim] *nf F* **la d.,** the blues.
déprimé [deprime] *adj* **(a)** (*person*) depressed; **(b)** depressed, low, flat, flattened (*surface etc*); **front d.,** low

forehead.

déprimer [deprime] **1** *vt* **(a)** to depress (*s.o.*); **(b)** to depress, to lower (*surface etc*). **2** *vi F* (*of person*) to be depressed.

déprogrammer [deprɔgrame] *vt* **(a)** *TV Rad etc* to take (*programme*) off the air; **d. un débat télévisé,** to cancel a televised debate; **(b)** *Ordinat* to remove (*sth*) from a program; *Fig* to deprogramme (*s.o.*).

dépuceler [depysle] *vt F* to deflower, to take the virginity of; **se faire d.,** to lose one's virginity, to have sex for the first time; **il aurait bien besoin de se faire d.,** he needs a good lay.

depuis [dəpɥi] **1** *prép* **(a)** (*of time*) since; for; **je ne suis pas sorti d. hier,** I have not been out since yesterday; **d. quand êtes-vous ici?,** how long have you been here?; **je suis ici d. trois jours,** I have been here for three days; **en vigueur d. le 1er avril,** in force since April the first; **d. ce temps-là, d. lors,** since then, since that time; **d. ce jour, tout a changé,** since that day, everything has changed; **je suis là d. le déjeuner,** I have been here (ever) since lunch; **d. quand est-il permis d'entrer sans frapper?,** since when can you come in without knocking?; **d. toujours,** right from the start, from the very beginning; **d. le matin jusqu'au soir,** from morning till night; **d. le temps que je te le dis,** (*tu devrais le savoir etc*) considering how often I've told you; **arrivé d. peu,** arrived a short while ago;

(b) (*of time, place etc*) from; **il ne m'a pas parlé d. Rouen,** he hasn't spoken to me since (we left) Rouen; **d. ma chambre, j'entends tout,** I can hear everything from my room; **un embouteillage d. La Rochelle,** a traffic jam all the way from La Rochelle; **téléphoner d. chez soi,** to ring from home; *Rad* **concert transmis d. Londres,** concert broadcast from London;

(c) (*of order, quantity*) **chemises d. 30F jusqu'à 150F,** shirts from 30 to 150 francs.

2 *adv* since (then), since that time; afterwards, later; **d. je comprends mieux son attitude,** since then *or* since that time I have understood his attitude better; **je l'ai connu d.,** I made his acquaintance later.

3 *conj* **d. que** + *ind*, since ...; **nous ne l'avons pas vu d. qu'il est marié,** we haven't seen him since he got married.

dépuratif, -ive [depyratif, -iv] *adj & nm Méd* depurative.

dépuration [depyrasjɔ̃] *nf* cleansing (*of blood*); purification (*of metal etc*).

dépurer [depyre] *vt* to cleanse, to clear (*the blood*); to purify (*metal, water*).

députation [depytasjɔ̃] *nf* **(a)** deputing, delegating (*of s.o.*); (*groupe*) deputation, delegation; **(b)** *Pol* membership (*of parliament*); **candidat à la d.,** parliamentary candidate; **se présenter à la d.,** to stand *or esp Am* run for parliament.

député [depyte] *nm* **(a)** (*représentant*) deputy, delegate; **(b)** *Pol* ≈ Member of Parliament (**de,** for); **La Chambre des députés,** the Chamber of Deputies; **elle a été élue d.** *ou* **députée,** ≈ she was elected a Member of Parliament; **d.-maire,** = MP and mayor.

députer [depyte] *vt* to appoint (*s.o.*) as deputy *or* delegate, to depute (*s.o.*) (**à, vers,** to).

déqualification [dekalifikasjɔ̃] *nf* being overqualified for one's job; **la d. (professionnelle) est de plus en plus fréquente,** more and more people are overqualified for their jobs *or* for the work they do.

der [dɛr] *n F* (= **dernier**) **la d. des d.,** the war to end all wars.

déraciné, -ée [derasine] **1** *adj* uprooted. **2** *n* exile, uprooted person.

déracinement [derasinmɑ̃] *nm* uprooting (*of stump, Fig of person*); eradication (*of fault*); **le d. d'une idée reçue,** the eradication of a preconceived idea.

déraciner [derasine] *vt* to uproot (*stump, Fig person*); to tear (*tree etc*) up by the roots; to eradicate (*fault, abuse*).

déraidir [deredir] **1** *vt* to unstiffen, to take the stiffness out of (*limb, material etc*); to soften (*s.o.'s character*). **2 se déraidir** *vpr* **(a)** (*of limb, material etc*) to lose its stiffness; **(b)** (*of person*) to unbend, to thaw.

déraillement [derajmɑ̃] *nm Rail* derailment.

dérailler [deraje] *vi* **(a)** (*of train, tram*) to become derailed, to leave the rails; (*of stylus*) to jump *or* leave the sound groove; **faire d. un train,** to derail a train; **(b)** *F* (*of machine etc*) to be on the blink; (*person*) to rave, to talk drivel.

dérailleur [derajœr] *nm Rail* derailer, derailing stop; (*de bicyclette*) derailleur (gears).

déraison [derɛzɔ̃] *nf Litt* unreasonableness, folly.

déraisonnable [derɛzɔnabl] *adj* unreasonable, irrational, senseless, foolish.

déraisonnablement [derɛzɔnabləmɑ̃] *adv* unreasonably.

déraisonner [derɛzɔne] *vi Litt* to talk nonsense.

dérangé [derɑ̃ʒe] *adj* (*mind*) deranged, unbalanced; (*stomach*) upset; *F* **tu es complètement d.!,** you're off your rocker!

dérangement [derɑ̃ʒmɑ̃] *nm* (*désordre*) disarrangement, disorder (*of books, furniture etc*); (*gêne*) disturbance, trouble; (*perturbation*) disturbed *or* unsettled state; *El* fault (*in line etc*); **causer du d.** *ou* **des dérangements à qn,** to put s.o. to trouble *or* bother; **je ne veux pas te causer de dérangements,** I don't want to put you to any trouble *or* bother; **excusez-moi pour le d.,** I'm sorry to disturb *or* trouble you; **d. d'esprit,** mental derangement; **d. de l'intestin,** upset stomach; *Tél* **la ligne est en d.,** the line is out of order.

déranger [derɑ̃ʒe] *v* (**je dérangeai(s); n. dérangeons**) **1** *vt* to disarrange (*papers, books etc*); (*perturber*) to put (*sth*) out of order; to upset (*s.o.*); (*gêner*) to disturb, to trouble; **je vous dérange?,** am I disturbing you?; *Iron* **je ne te dérange pas trop?,** am I in your way?; **excusez-moi de vous d.,** I'm sorry to disturb *or* trouble you; **si cela ne vous dérange pas,** if it's no trouble to you, if that's all right by you; *F Iron* **ça te dérangerait de me laisser tranquille?,** would you very much mind leaving me alone?; **d. l'esprit de qn,** to disturb s.o.'s mind; **quelque chose lui a dérangé l'estomac,** something has upset his stomach.

2 se déranger *vpr* to go to trouble; **merci de vous être dérangé,** thank you for putting yourself out *or* for the trouble you've gone to; **ne vous dérangez pas pour moi,** please don't put yourself out *or* go to any trouble on my account.

dérapage [derapaʒ] *nm* **(a)** *Aut etc* skid(ding); *Av* sideslip; *Ski* sideslip(ping); *Pol Fig* bad mistake; *Aut* **d. contrôlé,** controlled skid; *Fig* **d. du budget/de l'horaire,** slippage in the budget/timetable; *Fig* **le d. des prix,** spiralling prices; **le d. inflationniste,** the inflationary spiral; **(b)** *Nau* dragging (*of anchor*).

déraper [derape] *vi* **(a)** *Aut etc* to skid; *Av Ski* to sideslip; *Fig* (*des prix*) to be rising uncontrollably; *Fig* **le budget dérape,** there's some slippage in the budget; *Fig* **la mission a dérapé,** the mission went (badly) wrong *or* came unstuck; **les commentaires ont dérapé vers une critique sévère,** comment has turned into severe criticism; **(b)** *Nau* dragging (*of anchor*).

dératé [derate] *nm F* **courir comme un d.,** to run flat out.

dératisation [deratizasjɔ̃] *nf* extermination of rats.

dératiser [deratize] *vt* to clear of rats.

derby [dɛrbi] *nm* **(a)** *Courses de chevaux* **le d. d'Epsom,** the Derby; **(b)** *Fb* local derby.

derechef [dərəʃɛf] *adv Arch & Litt* a second time, yet again, once more.

déréglé [deregle] *adj* **(a)** (*machine, clock etc*) out of order; **(b)** upset (*stomach*); disordered (*mind*); irregular (*pulse*); **(c)** wild, dissolute (*life etc*); immoderate (*desires*); **une ambition déréglée,** unbounded ambition.

dérèglement [derɛgləmɑ̃] *nm* **(a)** malfunctioning (*of machine*); **(b)** disordered state (*of house, imagination etc*); unsettled state (*of weather*); irregularity (*of pulse*); **d. de l'esprit,** mental derangement; **(c)** dissoluteness (*of morals*).

dérégler [deregle] *v* (**je dérègle, n. déréglons; je déréglerai**) **1** *vt* **(a)** to disturb (*mechanism etc*), to put (*mechanism etc*) out of order; **(b)** to upset (*stomach*); to unsettle (*mind, habits*). **2 se dérégler** *vpr* **(a)** (*of clock etc*) to go wrong; **(b)** (*of stomach*) to be upset; (*of mind*) to become unsettled; **(c)** (*of morals*) to become dissolute.

dérider [deride] **1** *vt* to remove the lines *or* the wrinkles from (*brow*); *F* to cheer (*s.o.*) up, to brighten (*s.o.*) up; **c'est impossible de le d.,** it's impossible to get a smile out of him. **2 se dérider** *vpr* to brighten up, to cheer up.

dérision [derizjɔ̃] *nf* derision, mockery; **dire qch par d.,** to say sth derisively *or* in mockery; **geste de d.,** derisive gesture; **tourner qch en d.,** to deride sth; *Péj* **c'est une d.!,** it's ridiculous!

dérisoire [derizwar] *adj* derisory, ridiculous, laughable (*offer etc*); derisory, paltry (*salary etc*); **vendre qch à un prix d.,** to sell sth at an absurdly low price; **cette objection me paraît d.,** that seems an absurd objection to me.

dérisoirement [derizwarmɑ̃] *adv* laughably, pathetically; **il est payé d.,** he's paid a derisory *or* laughable *or* pathetic amount.

dérivatif, -ive [derivatif, -iv] **1** *adj Ling* derivative; derived (*word*). **2** *nm* relief, distraction (**à, de,** from); **c'est un d. à sa douleur,** it takes his mind off his grief; **le sport**

est un excellent d., sport is an excellent way of taking your mind off your worries.
dérivation [derivasjɔ̃] *nf* **(a)** *Aut* diversion; diversion, tapping (*of watercourse*); *Méd* derivation (*of blood etc from inflamed part*); *Él* shunt(ing), branching, tapping (*of current*); **canal de d.,** headrace, penstock; *Él* **monté en d.,** shunt connected; **(b)** *Ling* derivation (*of word*); *Math* derivation; **(c)** *Nau Av* drift.
dérive [deriv] *nf Nau* drift, leeway; *Av* drift; **angle de d.,** drift angle; **à la d., en d.,** adrift; **navire en d.,** drifting vessel; **(quille de) d.,** *Nau* drop keel, centre board; *Av* fin; *Fig* **tout va à la d.,** everything has been left to drift; **un mariage/une entreprise/***etc* **qui part à la d.,** a failing marriage/business/*etc*; *Géog* **d. des continents,** continental drift.
dérivé, -ée [derive] **1** *adj* **(a)** derived, secondary (*meaning etc*); *Math* derived (*function, curve*); *Ch* derived (*product*); **(b)** *El* **courant d.,** shunt current. **2** *nm Ling etc* derivative; *Ch Ind* derivative, by-product. **3** *nf Math* **dérivée,** derivative.
dériver¹ [derive] **1** *vt* **(a)** to divert *or* tap the course of (*running water*); *Él* to shunt, to branch (*current*); **(b)** *Ling Math* to derive. **2** *vi* **(a)** (*of stream*) to be diverted, to flow (**de,** from); **rien ne dérivera de cette discussion,** this discussion is pointless; **(b)** *Ling* to be derived (**de,** from).
dériver² *vt Tech* to unrivet.
dériver³ *vi* **(a)** *Nau Av* to drift; **d. à vau-l'eau,** to drift downstream; **(b)** *Fig* to drift away (*from subject etc*).
dériveur [derivœr] *nm Nau* **(a)** (*bateau*) sailing dinghy (*with centre board*); **(b)** (*voile*) storm sail.
dérivomètre [derivɔmɛtr] *nm Av* drift meter.
dermatite [dɛrmatit] *nf Méd* dermatitis.
dermato [dɛrmato] *n Méd F* (*abrév* **dermatologue**) dermatologist.
dermatologie [dɛrmatɔlɔʒi] *nf Méd* dermatology.
dermatologique [dɛrmatɔlɔʒik] *adj* dermatological.
dermatologiste [dɛrmatɔlɔʒist], **dermatologue** [dɛrmatɔlɔg] *n* dermatologist.
dermatose [dɛrmatoz] *nf Méd* dermatosis.
derme [dɛrm] *nm Anat* derm.
dermique [dɛrmik] *adj Anat* dermic, dermal.
dermite [dɛrmit] *nf Méd* = **DERMATITE.**
dernier, -ière [dɛrnje, -jɛr] **1** *adj* **(a)** (*ultime*) last, latest; **au d. moment,** at the last (moment); **faire un d. effort,** to make a final effort; **mettre la dernière main à qch,** to give *or* put the finishing *or* final touches to sth; **j'ai dépensé jusqu'à mon d. sou,** I've spent my last penny; **les derniers préparatifs,** the final preparations; **d. paiement,** final payment; **d. délai pour l'inscription,** deadline for registration; **je m'en souviendrai jusqu'à mon d. jour** *ou* **jusqu'à ma dernière heure,** I shall remember it to my dying day; **en d. recours,** as a last resort; **pour la dernière fois,** for the last time; **il veut toujours avoir le d. mot,** he must always have the last word;
(b) (*récent*) last; **au cours des dernières années,** over the past few years; **mardi d.,** last Tuesday; **la dernière fois il allait bien,** he was well last time I saw him; **le d. roman de cet auteur,** this author's latest novel; **dernières nouvelles,** latest news; **la dernière mode, le d. cri,** the latest fashion, the latest thing; *Bourse* **d. cours,** closing price; **le mois d.,** last month; **ces derniers temps,** lately;
(c) (*dans l'espace*) last; **la dernière maison du village,** the last house in the village; **le d. rang,** the last row;
(d) (*extrême*) utmost, highest; **de la dernière importance,** of the utmost *or* greatest importance; **au d. degré,** to the utmost *or* highest degree; **il me déplaît au d. point,** I dislike him intensely; **dans la dernière misère,** in utmost poverty;
(e) (*pire*) lowest, worst; **de d. ordre,** very inferior; **ça, c'est le d. de mes soucis,** that's the least of my worries; **être le d. élève de la classe,** to be last in *or* bottom of the class; **de la dernière catégorie,** in the last *or* lowest class.
2 *n* **(a)** (*dans classement*) last; *Sp* **il est arrivé le d.** *ou* **bon d.,** he came in last; **les six derniers,** the last six; **on la traite comme la dernière des dernières,** they treat her like dirt *or* the lowest of the low;
(b) (*dans chronologie*) last, latest; **c'est notre petit d.,** he's our youngest (child); **ce d. répondit ...,** (*dans conversation*) the latter answered ...; **le d. en date,** the most recent.
3 *adv* **en d.,** last (of all); **cela vient en d.,** that comes last.
dernièrement [dɛrnjɛrmɑ̃] *adv* lately, of late, recently.
dernier-né [dɛrnjene] *nm,* **dernière-née** [dɛrnjɛrne] *nf* last-born child, youngest child; (*pl derniers-nés, dernières-nées*).
dérobade [derɔbad] *nf* **(a)** evasion, avoidance (*of s.o., sth*); **(b)** swerve, jib (*of horse*).
dérobé [derɔbe] *adj* hidden, concealed, secret (*staircase, door etc*).
dérobée (à la) [aladerɔbe] *adv* stealthily, secretly, on the sly; **regarder qn à la d.,** to steal a glance at s.o.; **sortir à la d.,** to steal out.
dérober [derɔbe] **1** *vt* **(a)** (*voler*) to steal, to make away with (*sth*); **d. qch à qn,** to filch sth from s.o.; **d. un baiser,** to steal a kiss; **d. qn au danger,** to rescue *or* save s.o. from danger; **(b)** (*cacher*) to hide, to conceal; **d. qch à qn,** to hide sth from s.o.; **ce mur dérobe la vue,** the wall hides the view. **2 se dérober** *vpr* **(a)** (*s'échapper*) to escape, to steal away, to slip away (**à,** from); **se d. aux regards,** to escape observation, to avoid notice; **se d. à la curiosité,** to escape curiosity; **se d. à son devoir,** to evade *or* shirk one's duty; **je le lui ai demandé, mais il s'est dérobé,** I asked him, but he avoided the issue; **(b)** (*of horse*) to swerve (*at a jump*), to jib, to refuse; **(c)** (*manquer*) to give way (**sous,** under, beneath); **ses genoux se dérobèrent sous elle,** her knees gave way beneath her.
dérogation [derɔgasjɔ̃] *nf* derogation, impairment (**à une loi,** of a law); **faire d. à l'usage,** to depart from custom; **par** *ou* **en d. à cette règle,** this rule notwithstanding.
dérogatoire [derɔgatwar] *adj Jur* derogatory (*clause*).
déroger [derɔʒe] *vi* **(je dérogeai(s); n. dérogeons) d. à l'usage/à la loi,** to depart from custom/the law; **d. à un principe,** to waive a principle; *Hist* **d. à noblesse,** to lose rank; **d. à son rang,** to lower *or* demean oneself.
dérouillée [deruje] *nf Arg* belting, thrashing.
dérouiller [deruje] **1** *vt* **(a)** (*enlever la rouille à*) to take *or* rub the rust off (*sth*); **(b)** *Arg* (*battre*) to beat (*s.o.*) up. **2** *vi Arg* to catch it; **qu'est-ce qu'il a dérouillé!,** he really had a hard time! **3 se dérouiller** *vpr Fig* **se d. les jambes,** to stretch one's legs; *Fig* **se d. la mémoire,** to refresh one's memory.
déroulage [derulaʒ] *nm* unrolling; unwinding, uncoiling (*of cable etc*).
déroulement [derulmɑ̃] *nm* **(a)** unfolding, development, progress (*of plot, events*); **pendant tout le d. de la cérémonie,** throughout the ceremony; **(b)** (*de bobine etc*) unwinding.
dérouler [derule] **1** *vt* **(a)** to unroll (*blind etc*); to unwind, to uncoil (*cable etc*); **le serpent a déroulé ses anneaux,** the snake uncoiled itself;
(b) *Fig* (*passer en revue*) to review; **d. les événements marquants de l'année,** to review the major events of the year.
2 se dérouler *vpr* **(a)** (*of blind etc*) to come unrolled, to unroll; (*of cable etc*) to come unwound; (*of snake*) to uncoil;
(b) *Fig* to unfold, to develop; **le paysage se déroule devant nous,** the landscape unfolds *or* stretches out before us; **les événements qui se déroulent à Paris,** the events (that are) taking place in Paris; **la manifestation s'est déroulée dans le calme,** the demonstration went off peacefully *or* was peaceful; **son existence se déroule dans la plus grande monotonie,** he leads the most monotonous of existences.
dérouleur [derulœr] *nm Tech* tape drive.
déroutant [derutɑ̃] *adj* disconcerting.
déroute [derut] *nf* **(a)** (*débandade*) rout, disorderly retreat; **l'ennemi fut mis en d.,** the enemy was put to flight *or* was routed; **(b)** (*confusion*) **mettre qn en d.,** to disconcert s.o..
déroutement [derutmɑ̃] *nm Nau Av* rerouting, diversion.
dérouter [derute] **1** *vt* **(a)** (*confondre*) to confuse, to baffle; **la question a dérouté le candidat,** the question nonplussed the candidate; **(b)** (*tromper*) to lead astray; **d. la police,** to throw the police off the scent; **d. les soupçons,** to divert suspicion; **(c)** to divert, to reroute (*ship, aircraft etc*). **2 se dérouter** *vpr* to lose one's head, to become confused.
derrick [derik] *nm Pétr* derrick.
derrière [dɛrjɛr] **1** *prép* **(a)** (*au dos de*) behind, at the back of (*s.o., sth*), *US* the back of (*sth*); **il s'est caché d. le rideau,** he hid behind the curtain; **il faut toujours être d. elle,** you always have to keep an eye on her; **les uns d. les autres,** one behind the other; **ne vous inquiétez pas, je suis d. vous,** don't worry, I'll back you up; **d. des abords chaleureux,** (*se cache un hypocrite etc*) behind a cordial facade;
(b) de d., from behind; **sortir de d. un buisson,** to come out from behind a bush; **une bouteille de d. les fagots,** a very special bottle of wine; *F* **un repas de d. les fagots,** a

first-rate meal; **une idée de d. la tête,** an ulterior motive; **(c)** *Nau* astern of (*ship*); abaft (*the mast etc*).

2 *adv* **(a)** (*en arrière*) behind, at the back, in the rear; **laisser qn d.,** to leave s.o. behind; **enfiler un pull sens devant d.,** to put on a pullover back to front; **ça se ferme d.,** it fastens (up) at the back;

(b) par d., from behind; **attaquer qn par d.,** to attack s.o. from behind *or* from the rear; **cette robe s'attache par d.,** the dress does up at the back; **il a dû passer par d.,** he had to go round the back; *Fig* **elle le critique par d.,** she criticizes him behind his back;

(c) *Nau* astern; (*cabine*) aft.

3 *nm* **(a)** back, rear (*of building etc*); **le d. de la tête,** the back of the head; **ma chambre donne sur le d.,** my room looks out on the back; **porte de d.,** back door; **pattes de d.,** hind legs;

(b) (*postérieur*) behind, backside, bottom; (*of animal*) hindquarters; **tomber sur le d.,** to fall on one's behind; to sit down suddenly.

déruralisation [deryralizɑsjɔ̃] *nf* rural depopulation.

derviche [dɛrviʃ] *nm* dervish; **d. tourneur,** dancing *or* whirling dervish.

dès [dɛ] *prép* since, from, as early as, as long ago as (*a certain time*); **d. sa jeunesse,** from childhood; **d. l'abord,** from the outset, from the (very) first; **d. maintenant,** *Fml* **d. à présent,** from now on, *Fml* henceforth; **j'ai décidé de commencer le projet d. maintenant,** I've decided to start on the project now *or* immediately; **d. 1840,** as far back as 1840; **d. le matin,** first thing in the morning; **d. son arrivée,** the minute *or* the moment he arrived; **d. mon retour,** immediately on my return; **je te téléphonerai d. mon retour,** I'll call you as soon as *or* immediately I get back; **d. la porte il commença à crier,** he had no sooner reached the door than he began to shout; **d. que** + *ind*, as soon as; **d. lors,** (*dans le temps*) from that time on(wards), ever since (then); (*par conséquence*) consequently, therefore; **d. lors que vous refusez,** seeing that *or* since you refuse.

désabonnement [dezabɔnmɑ̃] *nm* cancellation (of subscription).

désabonner [dezabɔne] **1** *vt* **d. qn à une revue,** to cancel s.o.'s subscription to a magazine. **2 se désabonner** *vpr* to stop subscribing, to withdraw one's subscription (**à,** to).

désabusé, -ée [dezabyze] **1** *adj* disillusioned, disenchanted (*person etc*). **2** *n* **un d.,** a disappointed man.

désabusement [dezabyzmɑ̃] *nm* disillusionment.

désabuser [dezabyze] *vt Litt* to disillusion (*s.o.*), to open (*s.o.'s*) eyes; **c'est un esprit désabusé,** he's disillusioned.

désacclimater [dezaklimate] *vt* to remove (*s.o., sth*) from his *or* its normal climate.

désaccord [dezakɔr] *nm* (*désentente*) disagreement, dissension; clash (*of interests etc*); **être** *ou* **se trouver en d. avec qn sur qch,** to disagree *or* to be at odds with s.o. about sth; **sujet de d.,** bone of contention; **il y a d. entre ses paroles et sa conduite,** his words are inconsistent *or* not in keeping with his conduct; **vivre en d. avec son époque,** to be out of step with the age one lives in; **d. entre la théorie et les faits,** discrepancy between the theory and the facts.

désaccordé [dezakɔrde] *adj Mus* out of tune.

désaccorder [dezakɔrde] **1** *vt* **(a)** *Mus* to put (*instrument*) out of tune; **(b)** *Vieilli* to set (*people*) at variance. **2 se désaccorder** *vpr Mus* to go out of tune.

désaccoupler [dezakuple] *vt* **(a)** *Tech* to uncouple (*trucks etc*); *Él* to disconnect; **(b)** to slip, to uncouple (*hounds etc*).

désaccoutumance [dezakutymɑ̃s] *nf Litt* **d. de qch,** loss of the habit of *or* loss of familiarity with sth.

désaccoutumer [dezakutyme] **1** *vt* to disaccustom (*s.o. to sth*). **2 se désaccoutumer** *vpr* to lose the habit; **se d. de (faire) qch,** to get out of the habit of (doing) sth.

désacralisation [desakralizɑsjɔ̃] *nf* (*de la famille etc*) desanctification.

désacraliser [desakralize] *vt* (*la famille etc*) to desanctify.

désaffectation [dezafɛktɑsjɔ̃] *nf* putting (*of public building etc*) to another purpose; (*fermeture*) closing down (*of building*); deconsecration (*of church*).

désaffecter [dezafɛkte] *vt* to put (*public building etc*) to another purpose; (*fermer*) to close down (*building*); **église désaffectée,** deconsecrated church.

désaffection [dezafɛksjɔ̃] *nf* disaffection; **la d. d'une nation pour son président,** a nation's disaffection with its president.

désagrafer [dezagrafe] **1** *vt* to unfasten, to undo (*garment*). **2 se désagrafer** *vpr* to unfasten *or* undo one's dress *etc*.

désagréable [dezagreabl] *adj* disagreeable, unpleasant (**à,** to); **une remarque très d.,** a very unpleasant remark; *Euph* **ce n'est pas d.,** that's (a bit of) all right; **odeur d.,** unpleasant *or* nasty smell.

désagréablement [dezagreabləmɑ̃] *adv* disagreeably, unpleasantly.

désagrégation [dezagregɑsjɔ̃] *nf* disintegration, breaking up.

désagréger [dezagreʒe] *v* (**je désagrège, n. désagrégeons; je désagrégeai(s); je désagrégerai**) **1** *vt* to disintegrate, to break up. **2 se désagréger** *vpr* to disintegrate, to break up.

désagrément [dezagremɑ̃] *nm* trouble; **causer à qn du d.** *ou* **des désagréments,** (*des ennuis*) to cause unpleasantness for s.o., to get s.o. into trouble; **son attitude m'a crée bien du d.,** (*des ennuis*) his attitude got me into trouble; **son fils lui cause beaucoup de désagréments,** (*des soucis*) his son causes him a lot of worry; **les désagréments de la situation,** the unpleasantness of the situation; **les désagréments de ma situation,** the difficulties of my situation.

désaimanter [dezɛmɑ̃te] *vt* to demagnetize.

désaligné [dezaliɲe] *adj* out of alignment, out of line.

désaltérant [dezalterɑ̃] *adj* thirst-quenching.

désaltérer [dezaltere] *v* (**je désaltère, n. désaltérons; je désaltérerai**) **1** *vt* to quench (*s.o.'s*) thirst. **2** *vi* **le thé désaltère mieux qu'une boisson glacée,** tea is more thirst-quenching than an ice-cold drink. **3 se désaltérer** *vpr* to quench one's thirst.

désamorçage [dezamɔrsaʒ] *nm* unpriming (*of cartridge, fuse etc*); defusing (*of bomb, shell etc*); running down (*of dynamo*); *Fig* **le d. d'un conflit,** the defusing of a conflict.

désamorcer [dezamɔrse] *v* (**je désamorçai(s); n. désamorçons**) **1** *vt* to unprime (*cartridge, fuse, siphon etc*); to defuse (*bomb, shell etc*); to drain (*pump*); *Fig* (*neutraliser*) to render (*sth*) harmless, to take the sting out of (*sth*); **d. un conflit,** to defuse a conflict. **2 se désamorcer** *vpr* (*of pump etc*) to fail, to run dry; (*of dynamo*) to run down.

désapparier [dezaparje] *vt* to remove one of a pair, to spoil a pair (*of objects*); to separate (*pair of birds, animals*).

désappointement [dezapwɛ̃tmɑ̃] *nm Litt* disappointment.

désappointer [dezapwɛ̃te] *vt Litt* to disappoint.

désapprendre [dezaprɑ̃dr(ə)] *vt Litt* to forget.

désapprobateur, -trice [dezaprɔbatœr, -tris] *adj* disapproving; **regard d.,** disapproving look, look of disapproval.

désapprobation [dezaprɔbɑsjɔ̃] *nf* disapproval (**de,** of); **regard/murmure de d.,** disapproving look, look/murmur of disapproval.

désapprouver [dezapruve] *vt* to disapprove of, to object to (*s.o., sth*); **elle désapprouve mon projet,** she doesn't approve of my plan; **il désapprouve que je vienne,** he objects to my coming.

désarçonner [dezarsɔne] *vt* **(a)** (*of horse*) to unseat, to throw (*rider*); **(b)** *Fig* to floor (*s.o.*).

désargenté [dezarʒɑ̃te] *adj* **(a)** (*fourchette, cuiller etc*) tarnished; **(b)** *F* (*personne*) broke.

désarmant [dezarmɑ̃] *adj* disarming (*smile etc*).

désarmé [dezarme] *adj* (*qui n'a plus d'arme*) disarmed; (*ship*) laid up, out of commission; (*qui n'a jamais eu d'arme*) unarmed, defenceless; unloaded (*gun*).

désarmement [dezarməmɑ̃] *nm* **(a)** disarming (*of s.o.*); **(b)** *Mil Pol* disarmament; **d. progressif,** progressive disarmament; **d. multilatéral,** multilateral disarmament; **(c)** *Nau* laying up (*of ship*).

désarmer [dezarme] **1** *vt* **(a)** to disarm (*s.o., a country*); *Fig* **il montrait une franchise qui vous désarmait,** he was disarmingly frank; **(b)** *Mil* to unload (*gun*); to uncock (*rifle*); **(c)** *Nau* to lay up (*ship*). **2** *vi* **(a)** (*toucher*) to disarm; **(b)** (*cesser*) to relent; **haine qui ne désarme pas,** unrelenting hatred.

désarrimage [dezarimaʒ] *nm Nau etc* shifting (*of cargo*).

désarrimer [dezarime] *vt Nau etc* to unstow, to shift (*cargo*).

désarroi [dezarwa] *nm* disarray, confusion; **jeter qn dans le d.,** to throw s.o. into disarray; **il est en plein** *ou* **en grand d.,** he's in a state of utter disarray *or* confusion.

désarticulation [dezartikylɑsjɔ̃] *nf Méd* dislocation.

désarticuler [dezartikyle] **1** *vt Méd* to dislocate; *Fig* **d. une machine/un programme/***etc*, to dismantle a machine/a programme/*etc*. **2 se désarticuler** *vpr* to be double-jointed.

désassemblage [dezasɑ̃blaʒ] *nm* dismantling; disconnecting (*of joints etc*).

désassembler [dezasɑ̃ble] *vt* to dismantle (*sth*), to take (*sth*) apart; to disconnect (*joints etc*).

désassocier [dezasɔsje] *v* (*impf & pr sub* **n. désassociions, v. désassociiez**) **1** *vt* to disassociate, to dissociate (**de**, from). **2 se désassocier** *vpr* to disassociate *or* to dissociate oneself; **se d. de qn,** to disassociate oneself from s.o., to sever one's connection with s.o..

désassortir [dezasɔrtir] *vt* (*conj like* **assortir**) **(a)** to spoil, to break up (*set, collection etc*); **service de table désassorti,** dinner service made up of odd pieces; **(b)** to clear (*shop*) (of stock).

désastre [dezastr] *nm* disaster, calamity; **d. financier,** financial disaster, crash; **la soirée fut un vrai d.,** the party was a disaster.

désastreusement [dezastrøzmɑ̃] *adv* disastrously.

désastreux, -euse [dezastrø, -øz] *adj* disastrous; **un travail/conseil d.,** a dreadful *or* an appalling piece of work/a disastrous piece of advice.

désatellisation [desatelizasjɔ̃] *nf* **l'évolution des mentalités a contribué à la d. de la Tchécoslovaquie,** the fact that Czechoslovakia is no longer a satellite state is partly due to changes in thinking.

désatomisation [dezatɔmizasjɔ̃] *nf* nuclear disarmament.

désatomiser [dezatɔmize] *vt* to undertake the nuclear disarmament of (*a country*).

désavantage [dezavɑ̃taʒ] *nm* disadvantage, drawback; **avoir un d. sur qn,** to be at a disadvantage in comparison with s.o.; **cette solution a le d. d'être trop couteuse,** the drawback to *or* disadvantage of this solution is its expense; **c'est un d. de taille,** it's a sizeable drawback; **il vous a été présenté à son d.,** you saw him in a disadvantageous *or* an unfavourable light.

desavantagé [dezavɑ̃taʒe] *adj* at a disadvantage; (*surtout pays, enfant*) disadvantaged (**par**, by).

désavantager [dezavɑ̃taʒe] *vt* (**je désavantageai(s); n. désavantageons**) to put (*s.o.*) at a disadvantage; **être désavantagé par rapport à qn,** to be at a disadvantage by comparison with s.o.; **être d. par sa taille,** to be handicapped by one's size, to be at a disadvantage because of one's size.

désavantageusement [dezavɑ̃taʒøzmɑ̃] *adv* disadvantageously, unfavourably.

désavantageux, -euse [dezavɑ̃taʒø, -øz] *adj* disadvantageous, unfavourable (*position etc*).

désaveu [dezavø] *nm* **(a)** (*reniement*) disavowal, denial, disowning (*of sth*); *Jur* **d. de paternité,** repudiation of paternity; **(b)** (*condamnation*) disapproval; **encourir le d. de ses supérieurs,** to incur the disapproval of one's superiors.

désavouer [dezavwe] **1** *vt* **(a)** (*renier*) to disavow, to disown (*action, work etc*); to deny (*promise etc*); to retract (*opinion*); to disclaim, to deny (*paternity*); **d. un mandataire,** to disown an agent; **(b)** (*condamner*) to disapprove of (*s.o.'s behaviour, words, attitude etc*). **2 se désavouer** *vpr* to go back on one's word.

désaxé, -ée [dezakse] **1** *adj* **(a)** *MecE* eccentric (*cam etc*); **roue désaxée,** wheel out of true; **(b)** unbalanced (*mind*). **2** *n* unbalanced person.

désaxer [dezakse] *vt* **(a)** *MecE* to set over (*cylinder etc*); to put (*wheel*) out of true; **(b)** to unbalance (*mind*).

descellement [deselmɑ̃] *nm* **(a)** unsealing, breaking the seal (*of sth*); **(b)** loosening *or* pulling out of iron post (*from stone*).

desceller [desele] *vt* **(a)** to unseal, to break the seal of (*document etc*); **(b)** to loosen, to pull out (*iron post from stone*).

descendance [desɑ̃dɑ̃s] *nf* **(a)** (*origine*) descent, lineage; **(b)** (*postérité*) descendants.

descendant, -ante [desɑ̃dɑ̃, -ɑ̃t] **1** *adj* descending; downward (*motion*); *Br Rail* (*train, line*) down; **marée descendante,** falling tide; *Mil* **garde descendante,** guard being relieved; **ligne descendante,** (genealogical) line of descent; *Mus* **gamme descendante,** descending scale. **2** *n* descendant.

descendeur [desɑ̃dœr] *nm* **(a)** *Ski* downhill specialist *or* skier; **(b)** (*appareil*) descender.

descendre [desɑ̃dr] **1** *vi* (*the aux is* **être**, *occ* **avoir**) **(a)** to descend; (*en considérant le point d'arrivée*) to come down; (*en considérant le point de départ*) to go down; **d. d'un arbre,** to come down from a tree; **le fleuve descend vers la mer,** the river flows down to the sea; **le soleil descend sur l'horizon,** the sun is sinking below the horizon; **la nuit va d.,** it will soon be nightfall *or* dark; **d. en glissant/en courant/en boitant/***etc*, to slide/run/limp/*etc* down; *Av* **d. en vol plané/en parachute,** to glide/parachute down; **la marée descend,** the tide is falling *or* going out; **le baromètre descend,** the glass is falling; **d. (de Paris) en province,** to go to the provinces (from Paris); **d. en ville,** to go into town; *F* **mon dîner ne descend pas,** my dinner won't go down; **les prix devraient d. bientôt,** prices are expected to come down *or* fall soon; **sa voix ne descend pas plus bas,** his voice won't go any lower; **la police est descendue dans la boîte de nuit,** the police raided the nightclub;

(b) (*d'un escalier etc*) (*en considérant le point d'arrivée*) to come downstairs; (*en considérant le point de départ*) to go downstairs; **il n'est pas encore descendu,** he is not down yet; **faites-le d.,** (*en l'envoyant*) send him down; (*en l'appellant*) call him down; *Fig* **d. dans la rue,** to take to the streets;

(c) to alight (*from vehicle*); **d. de cheval,** to dismount; **c'est ici que je descends,** this is where I get off (*the bus etc*); **tout le monde descend!,** all change!; **d. à terre,** to go ashore, to land;

(d) *Fig* to lower oneself; *Péj* **d. jusqu'au mensonge,** to stoop to lying;

(e) (*loger*) to stay (**chez des amis**, with friends); **d. à l'hôtel,** to put up *or* stay at a hotel;

(f) (*étendre*) to extend downwards; (*of road, street*) to go downhill; **ses cheveux descendent jusqu'à la taille,** her hair comes down to her waist; **une robe qui descend jusqu'aux chevilles/genoux,** an ankle-/knee-length dress; **la colline descend jusqu'à la mer,** the hill slopes down to the sea; **la route descend en lacets,** the road winds down.

(g) *Fig* (*venir de*) to be descended (from); **ces gens-là descendent d'une ancienne famille,** these people are descended from an ancient family.

2 *vt* (*aux* **avoir**) **(a)** (*dévaler*) **d. les marches/la rue,** to go down the steps/the street; **d. la rivière,** to row *or* swim *or* float *etc* down the river; **d. un escalier quatre à quatre,** to race downstairs; *Mus* **d. la gamme,** to run down the scale;

(b) (*porter vers le bas*) (*en considérant le point de départ*) to take (*sth*) down; (*en considérant le point d'arrivée*) to bring (*sth*) down; **d. un tableau,** to take down a picture; **d. des sacs de la voiture,** to take the bags out of the car; *F* **elle n'a pas de mal à d. sa choucroute,** (*la manger*) she has no trouble at all in putting away her sauerkraut;

(c) *F* to shoot down, to kill (*partridge, man*); **d. un avion,** to bring down *or* shoot down an aircraft; **la police l'a descendu, il s'est fait d. par la police,** he was killed by the police; *Fig* **d. qn en flammes,** to shoot s.o. down in flames;

(d) *F* (*déposer*) to drop, to put down; **je vous descendrai à votre porte,** I'll drop you at your door.

descente [desɑ̃t] *nf* **(a)** (*action de descendre*) descent; *Ski* (*course*) downhill race; *Ski* **faire de la d.,** to do downhill (skiing); *Cyclisme* **être bon en d.,** to be good downhill *or* on the downhill sections; **c'était une d. difficile,** (*en alpinisme*) it was a difficult descent; **d. de cheval,** dismounting; *Av* **d. en vol plané,** glide; **mouvement de d.,** descending motion; (*d'un piston etc*) downstroke; **accueillir qn à la d. du train,** to meet s.o. off the train; **d. interdite,** (*on sign*) up only;

(b) (*incursion*) raid; **d. de police,** police raid; **faire une descente dans un pays,** to make an incursion into a country; *Jur* **d. sur les lieux,** visit to the scene (*of a crime etc*); *Fb* **d. des avants,** attack by the forwards;

(c) *Méd* (*d'un organe*) prolapse;

(d) (*d'un tableau etc*) taking down, letting down, lowering; *Beaux-Arts* **D. de croix,** Deposition;

(e) (*pente*) slope, incline; **une d. rapide,** a steep slope; **d. dangereuse,** dangerous hill; **d. de mine,** descending shaft; **ralentir dans la d.,** to slow down when going downhill;

(f) d. de lit, bedside rug;

(g) (*tuyau*) downpipe, rainwater pipe;

(h) *F* **avoir une bonne d.,** to have a good capacity (for drink).

descriptible [deskriptibl] *adj* describable.

descriptif, -ive [deskriptif, -iv] **1** *adj* descriptive. **2** *nm Constr* specification (*of work to be carried out*).

description [deskripsjɔ̃] *nf* description; **d. orale/écrite,** verbal/written description; **faire la d. de qn/qch,** to give a description of s.o./sth, to describe s.o./sth; **conforme à la d.,** as represented.

déséchouage [dezeʃwaʒ] *nm Nau* refloating (*of ship*).
déséchouer [dezeʃwe] *vt Nau* to refloat (*ship*).
désemballage [dezɑ̃balaʒ] *nm* unpacking (*of goods*).
désemballer [dezɑ̃bale] *vt* to unpack (*goods*).
désembobiner [dezɑ̃bɔbine] *vt* to unwind.
désembourber [dezɑ̃burbe] *vt* to extricate (*vehicle etc*) from the mud.
désembourgeoiser [desɑ̃burʒwaze] **1** *vt* to make (*s.o.*) become less conventional. **2 se désembourgeoiser** *vpr* to become less conventional *or* less bourgeois.
désembouteiller [dezɑ̃buteje] *vt* (*une route*) to unblock; (*une ligne téléphonique*) to unjam.
désembuer [dezɑ̃bɥe] *vt* to demist.
désemparé [dezɑ̃pare] *adj* **(a)** (*person*) distraught; **(b)** (*ship, aircraft*) disabled.
désemparer [dezɑ̃pare] **1** *vt Nau* to disable (*ship*). **2** *vi* **sans d.,** without stopping; **ils travaillent des heures sans d.,** they work for hours on end.
désemplir [dezɑ̃plir] **1** *vt* to empty (*bottle etc*) partially. **2** *vi* **son magasin ne désemplit pas,** his shop is always full (of customers). **3 se désemplir** *vpr* to empty.
désencadrer [dezɑ̃kadre] *vt* to take (*a picture*) out of its frame.
désenchaîner [dezɑ̃ʃene] *vt* to unchain.
désenchantement [dezɑ̃ʃɑ̃tmɑ̃] *nm* **(a)** (*décevoir*) disillusion; **(b)** *Vieilli* disenchantment.
désenchanter [dezɑ̃ʃɑ̃te] *vt* **(a)** (*décevoir*) to disillusion (*s.o.*); **sourire désenchanté,** wistful smile; **(b)** *Vieilli* to disenchant.
désenchanteur, -eresse [dezɑ̃ʃɑ̃tœr, -(ə)rɛs] *adj* **(a)** (*décevant*) disillusioning; **(b)** *Vieilli* disenchanting.
désenclaver [dezɑ̃klave] **1** *vt* to open up. **2 se désenclaver** *vpr* to open up.
désencombrement [dezɑ̃kɔ̃brəmɑ̃] *nm* clearing, freeing (*of passage etc*).
désencombrer [dezɑ̃kɔ̃bre] *vt* to clear, to free (*passage etc*).
désencrasser [dezɑ̃krase] *vt* to clean.
désencroûter [dezɑ̃krute] **1** *vt* to get (*s.o.*) out of a rut. **2 se désencroûter** *vpr* to get out of the *or* a rut.
désendetter (se) [sədezɑ̃dete] *vpr* to get out of debt.
désenfiler [dezɑ̃file] **1** *vt* to unthread (*needle*); to unstring (*beads etc*). **2 se désenfiler** *vpr* to come unthreaded; (*of beads*) to come unstrung.
désenflammer [dezɑ̃flame] *vt Méd* to reduce inflammation in (*wound etc*); *Fig* to quench (*s.o.'s passion*).
désenfler [dezɑ̃fle] **1** *vt* to reduce swelling of (*ankle etc*); to deflate (*tyre etc*). **2** *vi* to become less swollen; **ma joue/cheville/*etc* désenfle,** the swelling in my cheek/ankle/*etc* is going down, my cheek/ankle/*etc* is less swollen. **3 se désenfler** *vpr* = **2** *vi*.
désenflure [dezɑ̃flyr] *nf* reduction of swelling.
désengagement [dezɑ̃gaʒmɑ̃] *nm* disengagement.
désengager [dezɑ̃gaʒe] *v* **(je désengageai(s); n. désengageons) 1** *vt* to release (*s.o.*) from an obligation; **d. sa parole,** to obtain release from a promise. **2 se désengager** *vpr* to free oneself from an appointment; **je ne peux pas me d.,** I can't get out of it.
désengorgement [dezɑ̃gɔrʒəmɑ̃] *nm* unblocking (*of pipe etc*).
désengorger [dezɑ̃gɔrʒe] *vt* **(je désengorgeai(s); n. désengorgeons)** to unblock (*pipe etc*).
désengrenage [dezɑ̃grənaʒ] *nm* disengaging (*of toothed wheels etc*); throwing (*of machine etc*) out of gear.
désengrener [dezɑ̃grəne] *v* (*conj like* **engrener) 1** *vt* to disengage (*toothed wheels etc*); to throw (*machine*) out of gear. **2 se désengrener** *vpr* to get out of gear.
désenivrer [dezɑ̃nivre] **1** *vt* to sober (*s.o.*) up. **2** *vi* to sober up, to become sober; **il ne désenivre pas,** he's never sober.
désennuyer [dezɑ̃nɥije] *v* **(je désennuie, n. désennuyons; je désennuierai) 1** *vt* to amuse (*s.o.*); to relieve (*s.o.'s*) boredom. **2 se désennuyer** *vpr* to amuse oneself; to relieve one's boredom.
désenrayer [dezɑ̃reje] *vt* **(a)** to release (*brake, jammed part, mechanism*); **(b)** to unscotch (*wheel*).
désensabler [dezɑ̃sable] *vt* **(a)** to get (*ship*) off the sand; to dig (*car etc*) out of the sand; **(b)** to dredge (*channel etc*) of sand.
désensevelir [dezɑsəvlir] *vt* to disinter, to exhume (*corpse*); to dig up (*sth*).
désensibilisateur [desɑ̃sibilizatœr] *nm Phot* desensitizer.
désensibilisation [desɑ̃sibilizɑsjɔ̃] *nf Méd Phot* desensitization.
désensibiliser [desɑ̃sibilize] *vt Méd Phot* to desensitize; *Fig* **d. l'opinion,** to desensitize public opinion.
désensorceler [dezɑ̃sɔrsəle] *vt* **(je désensorcelle, n. désensorcelons; je désensorcellerai)** to free (*sth, s.o.*) from a magic spell.
désensorcellement [dezɑ̃sɔrsɛlmɑ̃] *nm* disenchantment.
désentortiller [dezɑ̃tɔrtije] *vt* to untwist (*thread etc*); to disentangle, to unravel (*wool etc*).
désentraver [dezɑ̃trave] *vt* to unshackle (*horse etc*).
désenvaser [dezɑ̃vaze] *vt* **(a)** to clean out (*sewer, harbour*); **(b)** to extract (*sth*) from the mud, to get (*sth*) out of the mud.
désépaissir [dezepesir] *vt* (*une sauce, les cheveux*) to thin.
déséquilibrant [dezekilibrɑ̃] *adj* (*effet*) unbalancing; **être d.,** to have an unbalancing effect (**pour,** on).
déséquilibre [dezekilibr] *nm Phys Psy etc* imbalance; *Psy* **d. émotif,** emotional maladjustment.
déséquilibré, -ée [dezekilibre] **1** *adj* unbalanced. **2** *n* unbalanced person.
déséquilibrer [dezekilibre] *vt* (*mentally, physically*) to unbalance (*s.o.*); to unbalance (*sth*), to throw (*sth*) out of balance; (*déconcerter*) to throw (*s.o.*) off balance.
désert [dezɛr] **1** *adj* deserted (*place*); uninhabited (*country, region*); deserted, lonely (*spot*); **le bar/le bureau/*etc* était d.,** the bar/office/*etc* was deserted; **une île déserte,** a desert island. **2** *nm* desert; **d. de sable,** sandy desert; **un d. de glace,** an icy waste; **prêcher dans le d.,** to preach to the wilderness; *Fig* **entamer sa traversée du d.,** to go into the wilderness.
déserter [dezɛrte] **1** *vt* to desert, to abandon; **d. son poste,** to desert one's post; **d. l'armée,** to desert (from the army); *Fig* **d. un idéal/une cause,** to abandon an ideal/to desert *or* abandon a cause. **2** *vi* to desert.
déserteur [dezɛrtœr] *nm* deserter.
désertification [dezɛrtifikɑsjɔ̃] *nf* desertification; *Fig* **la d. du Massif Central,** the desertion of the Massif Central.
désertion [dezɛrsjɔ̃, dɛ-] *nf* desertion (*from the army, from a party*).
désertique [dezɛrtik] *adj Géog* of the desert; **région d.,** desert region.
désertisation [dezɛrtizɑsjɔ̃] *nf* = **DÉSERTIFICATION.**
désescalade [dezɛskalad] *nf Pol Mil etc* de-escalation.
désespérance [dezɛsperɑ̃s] *nf Litt* loss of hope, despair.
désespérant [dezɛsperɑ̃] *adj* **(a) c'est d.,** it's enough to drive you to despair; **enfant d.,** child who drives one to despair; **cet enfant est d.,** that child will drive me to despair; **temps d.,** appalling weather; **(b)** *Littér* (*image, vision*) heartbreaking.
désespéré, -ée [dezɛspere] **1** *adj* (*sans espoir*) desperate; desperate, despairing (*look etc*); (*navré*) desperate, driven to despair; (*après décès, accident*) distressed; **être dans un état d.,** to be in a hopeless *or* desperate state; **prendre des mesures désespérées,** to take desperate measures; **2** *n* **(a)** desperate person; **agir en d.,** to act desperately; **(b)** (*suicidé*) suicide (victim).
désespérément [dezɛsperemɑ̃] *adv* (*avec désespoir*) despairingly, hopelessly; (*avec acharnement*) desperately; **j'essaie d. de le lui faire comprendre,** I am desperately trying to get him to understand it.
désespérer [dezɛspere] *v* **(je désespère, n. désespérons; je désespérai) 1** *vi* to despair, to lose hope; **il ne faut pas d.,** you *or* we *etc* mustn't despair; **je ne désespère pas d'y arriver un jour,** I still hope to get *or* I haven't given up hope of getting there one day; **d. de qn,** to despair of s.o. **2** *vt* to reduce *or* drive (*s.o.*) to despair. **3 se désespérer** *vpr* to be in despair, to give way to despair.
désespoir [dezɛspwar] *nm* **(a)** despair; **être au** *ou* **dans le d.,** to be in despair; **sombrer dans le d.,** to sink into despair; **enfant qui fait** *ou* **est le d. de sa famille,** child who is the despair of his family; **cette cuisine fait mon d.,** this kitchen will drive me to despair; **elle était au d. de ne pouvoir vous aider,** she was distressed that she wasn't able to help you; **réduire qn au d.,** to drive s.o. to desperation *or* to despair; **en d. de cause,** in desperation, when everything else fails; **(b)** (*plante*) **d. des peintres,** London pride.
désétatiser [dezetatize] *vt Écon Pol* to denationalize (*an industry*).
déshabiliter [dezabilite] *vt Jur* to disqualify.
déshabillage [dezabijaʒ] *nm* undressing.
déshabillé [dezabije] *nm* négligé(e); (*peignoir*) housecoat.
déshabiller [dezabije] **1** *vt* to undress (*s.o.*); **d. qn du regard,** to undress s.o. with one's eyes. **2 se déshabiller** *vpr*

to undress (oneself), to take off one's clothes, to strip; (*enlever son manteau etc*) to take off one's coat *etc*.
déshabituer [dezabitɥe] **1** *vt* **d. qn de (faire) qch,** to break s.o. of the habit of (doing) sth. **2 se déshabituer** *vpr* to lose *or* get out of the habit (**de,** of).
désherbage [dezɛrbaʒ] *nm* weeding.
désherbant [dezɛrbɑ̃] *nm* weedkiller.
désherber [dezɛrbe] *vt* to weed (*garden, field*).
déshérence [dezerɑ̃s] *nf Jur* default of heirs, escheat; **tomber en d.,** to escheat.
déshérité [dezerite] **1** *adj* (*sans héritage*) disinherited; (*démuni*) deprived. **2** *n* **les déshérités,** the underprivileged.
déshéritement [dezeritmɑ̃] *nm* disinheritance, disinheriting.
déshériter [dezerite] *vt* to disinherit (*s.o.*), to deprive (*s.o.*) of an inheritance; *Fig* **être déshérité par la nature,** (*d'un malade etc*) to be deprived of a normal life; (*d'une personne inintelligente*) to be not very bright; *Hum* (*d'une personne laide*) to be no oil painting.
déshonnête [dezɔnɛt] *adj Litt* improper, immodest, unseemly.
déshonnêtement [dezɔnɛtmɑ̃] *adv Litt* improperly, immodestly.
déshonnêteté [dezɔnɛt(ə)te] *nf Arch & Litt* impropriety, immodesty, unseemliness.
déshonneur [dezɔnœr] *nm* dishonour, *US* dishonor; **faire d. à qn,** to disgrace s.o..
déshonorant [dezɔnɔrɑ̃] *adj* (*conduite*) dishonourable, *US* dishonorable; (*comportement*) discreditable, disgraceful; **des paroles déshonorantes pour notre famille/la profession,** remarks that bring dishonour on *or* discredit the family/the profession.
déshonorer [dezɔnɔre] **1** *vt* **(a)** (*discréditer*) to dishonour, *US* to dishonor; to disgrace (*s.o.*), to bring dishonour *or* disgrace on (*s.o.*); **d. une jeune fille/une femme,** to seduce a girl/a woman; **(b)** *Fig* to maltreat, to disfigure, to spoil (*picture etc*). **2 se déshonorer** *vpr* to disgrace oneself, to lose one's honour.
déshuiler [dezɥile] *vt* to extract *or* separate *or* remove oil *or* grease from (*sth*).
déshumaniser [dezymanize] *vt* to dehumanize.
déshydratation [dezidratɑsjɔ̃] *nf* dehydration.
déshydrater [dezidrate] **1** *vt* to dehydrate; **je suis déshydraté,** I'm dehydrated; **noix de coco déshydratée,** desiccated coconut. **2 se déshydrater** *vpr* to become dehydrated; **on se déshydrate beaucoup en avion,** you get very dehydrated when you fly.
déshydrogénation [dezidrɔʒenɑsjɔ̃] *nf Ch* dehydrogenation.
déshydrogéner [dezidrɔʒene] *vt* (**je déshydrogène, n. déshydrogénons; je déshydrogènerai**) *Ch* to dehydrogenate.
déshypothéquer [dezipɔteke] *vt* (*conj like* **hypothéquer**) to disencumber (*estate*).
desideratum [dezideratɔm] *nm* desideratum, *pl* desiderata; (*pl desiderata*).
design [dizajn] **1** *nm* design. **2** *adj* designer; **intérieur très d.,** a designer interior.
désignation [deziɲɑsjɔ̃] *nf* **(a)** designation; description (*of goods etc*); **(b)** (*choix*) naming, appointment; **d. de qn pour un poste,** appointment *or* nomination of s.o. to a post.
désigner [deziɲe] **1** *vt* **(a)** to point out, to indicate; **est-ce que tu peux le d.?,** can you point him out?; **d. qch du doigt,** to point sth out, to point at sth; **il a pris le siège qu'on lui avait désigné,** he took the seat they indicated *or* pointed to; **d. qch à l'attention de qn,** to call *or* draw s.o.'s attention to sth; **je désigne à votre attention que ...,** I would call *or* draw your attention to the fact that ...; **d. qn par son nom,** to call s.o. *or* refer to s.o. by name;
(b) (*choisir*) to name, to appoint; **d. un jour,** to appoint *or* set *or* fix a day; **d. qn à** *ou* **pour un poste,** to appoint *or* nominate s.o. to a post; **il est tout désigné pour le faire,** he is just the man to do it, he is cut out for it; **sa compétence la désigne à cet emploi,** her ability makes her right for the job; **il a été désigné pour nous représenter,** he was chosen to represent us.
2 se désigner *vpr* **se d. volontaire,** to volunteer.
désillusion [dezilyzjɔ̃] *nf* disillusion.
désillusionnement [dezilyzjɔnmɑ̃] *nm* disillusionment.
désillusionner [dezilyzjɔne] *vt* to disillusion (*s.o.*).
désincarcérer [dezɛ̃karsere] *vt* to free (*s.o.*) (*from the wreckage of a car etc*).
désincarné [dezɛ̃karne] *adj* disembodied; *Iron* **il paraît toujours totalement d.,** his head is always in the clouds.
désincarner (se) [sədezɛ̃karne] *vpr* to become disembodied.
désincrustant [dezɛ̃krystɑ̃] **1** *adj* scaling (*substance*). **2** *nm* scale preventive.
désincrustation [dezɛ̃krystɑsjɔ̃] *nf* scaling (*of boiler etc*).
désincruster [dezɛ̃kryste] *vt* to scale (*boiler etc*); **un savon pour d. la peau,** a soap for removing ingrained dirt from the skin.
désinence [dezinɑ̃s] *nf Gram* (flexional) ending.
désinfectant [dezɛ̃fɛktɑ̃] *adj & nm* disinfectant.
désinfecter [dezɛ̃fɛkte] *vt* to disinfect.
désinfection [dezɛ̃fɛksjɔ̃] *nf* disinfection.
désinflation [dezɛ̃flɑsjɔ̃] *nf Écon* deflation.
désinformation [dezɛ̃fɔrmɑsjɔ̃] *nf* disinformation.
désinformer [dezɛ̃fɔrme] *vt* to disinform.
désintégration [dezɛ̃tegrɑsjɔ̃] *nf* disintegration, breaking up; weathering (*of rocks*); *Nucl* (nuclear) disintegration; *Nucl* splitting (*of the atom*); *Fig* **la d. de la famille/d'une société,** the disintegration of the family/of a society.
désintégrer [dezɛ̃tegre] *v* (**je désintègre, n. désintégrons; je désintégrerai**) **1** *vt* to disintegrate; to weather (*rocks*); *Nucl* to disintegrate (*matter*); *Nucl* to split (*the atom*); **d. un groupe,** to break up a group. **2 se désintégrer** *vpr* to disintegrate; (*of rocks*) to weather; *Nucl* (*of matter*) to disintegrate; (*of atom*) to split; *Fig* **un groupe d'amis qui se désintègre,** a group of friends which is breaking up.
désintéressé [dezɛ̃terese] *adj* disinterested, impartial (*opinion, advice etc*); disinterested, unselfish (*motive*); disinterested, selfless (*person*); **être d. dans une affaire,** to have no axe to grind in a matter.
désintéressement [dezɛ̃terɛsmɑ̃] *nm* disinterestedness, impartiality (*of opinion, advice*); disinterestedness, unselfishness (*of motive*); disinterestedness, selflessness (*of person*); buying out (*of partner etc*); paying off (*of creditor etc*).
désintéresser [dezɛ̃terese] **1** *vt* to buy out (*partner*); to pay off (*creditor*). **2 se désintéresser** *vpr* **se d. de qch/qn,** to take no further interest in sth/s.o..
désintérêt [dezɛ̃terɛ] *nm* disinterest.
désintoxication [dezɛ̃tɔksikɑsjɔ̃] *nf Méd* detoxification; **faire une cure de d.,** to undergo treatment for alcoholism *or* drug addiction.
désintoxiquer [dezɛ̃tɔksike] *Méd* **1** *vt* to treat (*s.o.*) for alcoholism *or* drug addiction; *Fig* **il ne fait que regarder la télévision, il faut le d.!,** all he does is watch television, we'll have to break him of the habit! **2 se désintoxiquer** *vpr* to come off alcohol *or* drugs; *Fig* **je cours tous les jours pour me d.,** I run every day to clean out my system; *Fig* **aller à la campagne pour se d.,** to go to the countryside to clean out one's system *or* to get the city air out of one's lungs.
désinviter [dezɛ̃vite] *vt* to cancel an invitation to (*s.o.*).
désinvolte [dezɛ̃vɔlt] *adj* airy, unembarrassed, unselfconscious (*manner*); easy, free (*movements*); *Péj* **d. à l'égard de qn,** casual *or* offhand with s.o..
désinvolture [dezɛ̃vɔltyr] *nf* (*naturel*) unselfconsciousness (*in manner etc*); ease (*of movement*); (*sans gêne*) free and easy manner; *Péj* offhand *or* airy manner; *Péj* **avec d.,** in an offhand *or* casual way.
désir [dezir] *nm* **(a)** desire; **avoir un d. de qch,** to have a desire for something; **d. de plaire,** desire to please; **d. ardent,** craving, longing; **ardent d. de réussir,** ardent desire to succeed; **selon le d. de son père,** in accordance with his father's wishes; **éprouver le d. de faire qch,** to want to do sth; **prendre ses désirs pour des réalités,** to indulge in wishful thinking; **tes désirs sont des ordres,** your wish is my command; **(b) d. (sexuel),** (sexual) desire.
désirable [dezirabl] *adj* desirable; **peu d.,** undesirable.
désirer [dezire] *vt* **(a)** (*souhaiter*) to want, to desire (*sth*); **d. ardemment qch,** to crave (*sth*), to yearn *or* long for sth; **d. qch de qn,** to want sth of *or* from s.o.; **je désire le voir,** I want *or* wish to see him; **je désire qu'il vienne,** I want him to come; **cela laisse à d.,** it leaves a lot to be desired; **elle se fait d.,** (*elle n'arrive pas*) she's keeping us waiting; **elle aime se faire d.,** (*ce n'est pas une femme facile*) she plays hard to get; **je n'avais plus rien à d.,** I had nothing left to wish for; **que désirez-vous?,** what would you like?; *F* **vous désirez?,** can I help you?; **(b)** to desire (*s.o.*) sexually; **je te désire,** I want you.
désireux, -euse [dezirø, øz] *adj* desirous (**de,** of); **d. de plaire,** anxious to please.
désistement [dezistəmɑ̃] *nm* **(a)** *Jur* waiver (*of claim*); withdrawal (*of suit*); **(b)** *Pol* withdrawal of one's candidature, standing down.

désister (se) [sədeziste] *vpr* **(a)** *Jur* **se d. d'une poursuite,** to withdraw an action; **se d. d'une demande,** to waive a claim; **(b)** to withdraw (one's candidature), to stand down.
désobéir [dezɔbeir] **1** *vi* **d. à qn/un ordre,** to disobey s.o./an order; **d. à une règle,** to break a rule. **2** *vt* **mes ordres ont été désobéis,** my orders were disobeyed.
désobéissance [dezɔbeisɑ̃s] *nf* disobedience (**à qn,** to s.o.; **à un ordre,** of an order); **d. à une règle,** disregard for *or* breaking of a rule.
désobéissant [dezɔbeisɑ̃] *adj* disobedient (**à,** to).
désobligeance [dezɔbliʒɑ̃s] *nf* disagreeableness, unkindness (**envers,** to).
désobligeant [dezɔbliʒɑ̃] *adj* disagreeable, unkind, ungracious, offensive (*person, manner, words etc*) (**envers,** to).
désobliger [dezɔbliʒe] *vt* (**je désobligeai(s); n. désobligeons**) to offend.
désobstruer [dezɔpstrye] *vt* to clear *or* to free (*sth*) of obstructions; to clear (*pipe etc*).
désodorisant [dezɔdɔrizɑ̃] *adj & nm* deodorant.
désodoriser [dezɔdɔrize] *vt* to deodorize.
désœuvré [dezœvre] **1** *adj* unoccupied, idle; **me trouvant d.,** finding myself with nothing to do, *F* being *or* finding myself at a loose end. **2** *n* **les désœuvrés,** people with nothing to do.
désœuvrement [dezœvrəmɑ̃] *nm* idleness; **par d.,** to kill time, for want of something to do.
désolant [dezɔlɑ̃] *adj* distressing, sad, disheartening (*news etc*); **ce temps est d.,** this weather is very depressing.
désolation [dezɔlasjɔ̃] *nf* **(a)** (*dévastation*) desolation, devastation, laying waste; **(b)** (*affliction*) grief, sorrow; **être plongé dans la d.,** to be grief-stricken.
désolé [dezɔle] *adj* **(a)** desolate, dreary (*region etc*); **(b)** (*navré*) very sorry, distressed; **je suis d. de vous avoir fait attendre,** I'm so *or* very sorry to have kept you waiting; **avoir/prendre un air d.,** to have/to take on a distressed look.
désoler [dezɔle] **1** *vt* **(a)** (*affliger*) to distress, to grieve (*s.o.*); **son échec à l'examen le désole,** he's very upset *or F* cut up about failing the exam; **(b)** *Vieilli & Litt* to devastate, to ravage, to lay waste (*country etc*). **2 se désoler** *vpr* to be distressed, to be upset.
désolidariser [desɔlidarize] **1** *vt* to split (*party etc*). **2 se désolidariser** *vpr* (*d'une personne*) to break away, to break ranks; **se d. de** *ou* **d'avec ses collègues,** to break with one's colleagues; **se d. d'une cause,** to withdraw one's support from a cause; **se d. d'un projet,** to withdraw from a project.
désopilant [dezɔpilɑ̃] *adj* screamingly funny, hilarious.
désordonné [dezɔrdɔne] *adj* untidy (*room etc*); (*personne*) (*qui n'est pas organisé*) disorganized; (*qui ne range pas*) untidy; *Litt* (*qui mène une vie dissolue*) disorganized, disorderly (*life etc*); uncoordinated (*movements*); reckless (*expenditure*).
désordre [dezɔrdr] *nm* **(a)** (*manque d'ordre*) disorder, confusion; (*dans une pièce etc*) untidiness; **quel d.!,** what a mess!; **être en d.,** (*d'une pièce etc*) to be untidy; **cheveux en d.,** tangled *or* untidy hair; *Fig* **mettre le d. dans les rangs,** to throw confusion in the ranks; **le d. qui règne à l'Assemblée Nationale ces jours-ci,** the present commotion in the National Assembly; **d. de la pensée,** confused thinking; *Méd* **d. nerveux,** nervous disorder; **(b) désordres,** disturbances, riots; **de graves désordres ont éclaté,** serious disturbances have broken out; **(c)** *Litt* (*licence*) disorderliness, licentiousness.
désorganisateur, -trice [dezɔrganizatœr, -tris] *adj* disorganizing.
désorganisation [dezɔrganizasjɔ̃] *nf* disorganization.
désorganiser [dezɔrganize] **1** *vt* to disorganize (*system etc*); to upset (*plans etc*). **2 se désorganiser** *vpr* to become disorganized.
désorientation [dezɔrjɑ̃tasjɔ̃] *nf* disorientation; (*déconcertation*) confusion, bewilderment.
désorienté [dezɔrjɑ̃te] *adj* (*confus*) puzzled, bewildered, at a loss; (*perdu*) lost; **être d.,** to be disoriented; **je suis tout d.,** I don't know where I am.
désorienter [dezɔrjɑ̃te] **1** *vt* **(a)** (*égarer*) to make (*s.o.*) lose his bearings, to disorient(ate) (*s.o.*); to throw (*compass, instrument*) out of adjustment; **(b)** (*déconcerter*) to disconcert, to bewilder (*s.o.*). **2 se désorienter** *vpr* **(a)** (*géographiquement*) to lose one's bearings; **(b)** (*devenir confus*) to become *or* get confused.
désormais [dezɔrmɛ] *adv* from now on(wards), in future, *Litt* henceforth.
désossé [dezɔse] *adj* (*viande, poisson*) boned; *Fig* (*personne*) supple; *Péj* (*style etc*) flabby, flaccid.
désossement [dezɔsmɑ̃] *nm* boning (*of meat etc*).
désosser [dezɔse] **1** *vt* to bone (*meat, fish*); *Fig* to dissect (*sentence, book*). **2 se désosser** *vpr* to contort oneself.
désoxydant [dezɔksidɑ̃] *Ch* **1** *adj* deoxidizing. **2** *nm* deoxidizer.
désoxyder [dezɔkside] *vt Ch Métal* to deoxidize.
desperado [desperado] *nm* desperado.
despote [despɔt] **1** *nm* despot; *F* **sa fille est un d.!,** her daughter is a regular tyrant! **2** *adj* **homme/femme d.,** despotic man/woman.
despotique [despɔtik] *adj* despotic (*power etc*).
despotiquement [despɔtikmɑ̃] *adv* despotically.
despotisme [despɔtism] *nm* despotism.
desquamation [deskwamasjɔ̃] *nf* exfoliation, peeling; *Méd* (*pathologique*) desquamation.
desquamer [deskwame] **1** *vt* to exfoliate. **2** *vi* to peel (off); *Méd* to desquamate.
desquels, desquelles [dekɛl] *voir* **LEQUEL.**
dessaisir [desezir] **1** *vt Jur* **d. un tribunal d'une affaire,** to remove a case from a court. **2 se dessaisir** *vpr* **se d. de qch,** to relinquish sth, to part with sth, to give sth up.
dessaisissement [desezismɑ̃] *nm* **(a)** *Jur* **d. d'un tribunal d'une affaire,** removal of case from a court; **(b) d. de qch,** relinquishment of sth.
dessalage [desalaʒ] *nm* soaking (*of fish, meat etc*) (to remove salt).
dessalaison [desalɛzɔ̃] *nf* **(a)** = **DESSALAGE; (b)** = **DESSALEMENT.**
dessalé [desale] *adj* **(a)** (*meat, fish etc*) freed of salt; **(b)** *F* wide awake, sharp (*person*).
dessalement [desalmɑ̃] *nm* desalination (*of sea water*).
dessaler [desale] **1** *vt* **(a)** to remove the salt from (*meat, fish*); to put (*meat, fish*) to soak; to desalinate (*sea water*); **(b)** *F* **d. qn,** to sharpen s.o.'s wits. **2** *vi Nau* to capsize. **3 se dessaler** *vpr* **(a)** (*devenir moins salé*) to become less salty; **(b)** *F* to learn a thing or two.
dessangler [desɑ̃gle] *vt* to ungirth, to take the girths off (*horse*).
dessaouler [desule] *vi & vt* = **DESSOÛLER.**
desséchant [deseʃɑ̃] *adj* (*vent*) drying.
desséché [deseʃe] *adj* (*étang, rivière*) dry; (*plante*) dry, withered; *Fig* (*personne*) (*maigre*) emaciated; (*insensible*) without feelings, without emotions; **il est d.,** he's dead inside, he's got no feelings left.
dessèchement [desɛʃmɑ̃] *nm* drying up (*of pond etc*); seasoning, drying (*of wood*); withering (*of plants*); *Fig* lack of feelings; *Fig* emaciation (*of body*).
dessécher [deseʃe] *v* (**je dessèche, n. desséchons; je dessécherai**) **1** *vt* **(a)** to dry up (*ground*); **(b)** to season (*wood*); to dry (*foodstuffs*); to desiccate (*coconut*); **(c)** (*du vent, de la chaleur etc*) to wither (*plant*); to dry (*skin*); to parch (*mouth*); (*de maladie etc*) to emaciate (*body*); *Fig* **d. le cœur de qn,** to harden s.o.'s heart. **2 se dessécher** *vpr* **(a)** to dry up, to become dry; (*of pond etc*) to go dry; **(b)** (*d'une plante*) to wither; *Fig* (*d'une personne*) to waste away; *Fig* (*devenir insensible*) to become insensitive.
dessein [desɛ̃] *nm* intention, purpose; **avoir le d. de faire qch,** to have the intention of doing sth; **former le d. de faire qch,** to plan to do sth; **dans ce d.,** with this intention, with this in mind; **à d.,** on purpose, purposely, intentionally; **c'est à d. que je n'ai pas répondu,** I deliberately didn't answer; **à d. de vous revoir,** in order to see you again.
desseller [desele] *vt* to unsaddle (*horse*).
desserrage [deseraʒ] *nm* loosening (*of screw, belt etc*); slackening (*of belt*).
desserre [desɛr] *nf F* forking out; **être dur à la d.,** to be tightfisted *or* stingy.
desserrement [desɛrmɑ̃] *nm* loosening, slackening.
desserrer [desere] **1** *vt* to loosen (*screw*); to loosen, to slacken (*belt, knot*); to unclench (*fist, teeth*); to release (*brake*); **d. son étreinte,** to relax one's hold; **je n'ai pas desserré les dents,** I didn't open my mouth, I didn't utter a word. **2 se desserrer** *vpr* to work loose; (*of grip etc*) to relax.
dessert [desɛr] *nm* dessert, *Br* pudding, sweet; **venez pour le d.,** come for dessert; **être privé de d.,** to go without dessert; **qu'est-ce qu'il y a comme** *ou* **au d.?,** what's for dessert?; **carte des desserts,** dessert menu.
desserte[1] [desɛrt] *nf* **(a)** (*service*) service; **d. d'un port par voie ferrée,** rail service to a port; **chemin de d.,** service road, *US* frontage road; **(b)** *Rel* duties of an officiating clergyman; care (*of parish*).
desserte[2] *nf* sideboard; **d. roulante,** (dinner) trolley.

dessertir [desɛrtir] *vt* to unset (*precious stone*).

desservant [desɛrvɑ̃] *nm Rel* priest in charge (*of parish etc*).

desservir¹ [desɛrvir] *vt* (*conj like* **servir**) **(a)** (*of railways etc*) to serve; (*of door*) to lead into (*room*); **ce train ne dessert pas toutes les gares,** this train does not stop at every station; **ville bien desservie,** town with efficient public transport; **(b)** *Rel* to minister to (*parish etc*).

desservir² *v* (*conj like* **servir**) **1** *vt* **(a)** to clear (*the table*); **(b)** (*nuire*) to do harm to; **desservir qn,** to do s.o. a disservice; **cela risque de vous d.,** that may be to your disadvantage; **cela desservirait mes intérêts,** it would be detrimental to my interests; **son perfectionnisme la dessert,** her perfectionism isn't doing her any good. **2** *vi* to clear away. **3 se desservir** *vpr* to do oneself a disservice; **il se dessert,** he's his own worst enemy.

dessiccation [desikɑsjɔ̃] *nf* dessication.

dessiller [desije] **1** *vt* (*les yeux*) to open; *Fig* **d. les yeux à** *ou* **de qn,** to open s.o.'s eyes (*to facts*). **2 se dessiller** *vpr* (*des yeux*) to open; *Fig* **ses yeux se dessillèrent,** his eyes were opened.

dessin [desɛ̃] *nm* **(a)** (*art*) (art of) drawing, sketching; (*croquis etc*) drawing, sketch; **être bon en d.,** to be good at drawing, to be a good drawer; **d. à la plume,** pen-and-ink sketch; *Cin* **dessin(s) animé(s),** cartoon; **d. humoristique,** cartoon; **d. à main levée,** freehand drawing; **un d. d'enfant,** a child's drawing; **les dessins de Degas,** Degas' drawings; **faire du d. publicitaire,** to be a commercial artist; *F* **faut-il que je te fasse un d.?,** do I have to draw a picture for you?;

(b) (*motif*) design, pattern; **tissu à d.,** patterned fabric; **d. de mode,** fashion design;

(c) *Tech* draft, drawing, plan (*of building, machine etc*); **(l'art du) d.,** draughtsmanship, *US* draftsmanship; **planche à d.,** drawing board; **d. industriel,** industrial drawing; **d. d'ensemble,** general assembly drawing; **d. de profil,** profile drawing;

(d) outline (*of face etc*); *Fig* **voici le d. du projet,** here is an outline of the project.

dessinateur, -trice [desinatœr, -tris] *n* **(a)** (*artiste*) sketcher, drawer; (*sans couleur*) black-and-white artist; (*de bandes dessinées*) cartoonist; **(b)** (*de papier peint etc*) designer; (*de mode*) fashion artist; **(c)** *Tech* draughtsman, *US* draftsman, -woman.

dessiner [desine] **1** *vt* **(a)** to draw, to sketch; **d. qch d'après nature,** to draw sth from nature; **d. à l'encre/à la craie,** to draw in ink/chalk; **(b)** to design (*wallpaper, material etc*); **(c)** *Fig* (*tracer*) to show, to outline (*sth*); **les montagnes dessinent leur courbe sur le ciel,** the line of the mountains stands out against the sky; **vêtement qui dessine bien la taille,** garment that shows off the figure; **visage bien dessiné,** finely chiselled face. **2 se dessiner** *vpr* to stand out, to be outlined; **les arbres se dessinent à l'horizon,** the trees stand out *or* are outlined on the horizon; **nos projets se dessinent,** our plans are taking shape.

dessouder [desude] *vt* to unsolder (*sth*); **le tuyau s'est déssoudé,** the pipe has come unsoldered.

dessoûler [desule] *F* **1** *vt* to sober (*s.o.*) up, to make (*s.o.*) sober. **2** *vi* to become sober, to sober up; **il ne dessoûle pas,** he's never sober.

dessous [dəsu] **1** *adv* under(neath), below, beneath; **passez (par) d.,** go underneath (it); **en d.,** underneath; **regarder qn en d.,** to look at s.o. furtively *or* stealthily; **rire en d.,** to laugh up one's sleeve; **agir en d.,** to act in an underhand way; **ci-d.,** below; **dans la note ci-d.,** in the note below; **là-d.,** under there; *Fig* **il y a quelque chose de bizarre là-d.,** there's something funny about it; **au-d.,** below; *Fig* **au-d., vous ne trouverez rien de solide,** you won't find anything decent for less; **il est bien au-d., il n'a pas ta valeur,** he's not nearly as good as you.

2 *nm* lower part, underside, bottom; **les gens du d.,** the people on the floor below (us), the downstairs neighbours; **d. d'une assiette,** bottom of a plate; **d. de bouteille,** coaster; *Fig* **verser un d. de table (à qn),** to pay (s.o.) a bribe; **avoir le d.,** to get the worst of it, to be defeated; **être dans le troisième** *ou* **trente-sixième d.,** to be in a very bad situation; **d. de robe,** slip, *Vieilli* petticoat; **les d.,** (ladies') underwear, *F* undies; *Fig* **les d. de la politique,** the shady side of politics.

3 *prép* **(a) de d. de,** from under(neath);

(b) par d., underneath; **passer par d. la table,** to go underneath the table;

(c) au d., under; **les cheveux au d. des épaules,** hair below *or* past the shoulders; **au d. de 500 francs on ne trouve rien,** you won't find anything under 500 francs; *Fig* **elle est bien au d. de toi,** she's not nearly as good as you; **il est au d. de sa tâche,** he's not up to the job; **tu es vraiment au d. de tout!,** you're beneath contempt!

dessous-de-bras [d(ə)sudbra] *nm inv* dress shield.

dessous-de-plat [d(ə)sudpla] *nm inv* table mat.

dessus [dəsy] **1** *adv* (up)on (it, them); **il a marché d.,** he trod on it; **j'ai failli lui tirer d.,** I nearly shot him; **mettre la main d.,** to lay hands on it *or* on them; **vous avez mis le doigt d.,** you've put your finger on it, you've hit the nail on the head; **marcher bras d. bras dessous,** to walk arm in arm; *Nau* **avoir le vent d.,** to be aback; **en d.,** at the top, on top, above; **mettre les meilleures pommes (en** *ou* **au) d.,** to put the best apples on top; **voir ci-d.,** see above; **là-d.,** up there; **il y a beaucoup à dire là-d.,** a lot could be said on that score; *F* **ne compte pas là-d.!,** don't count on it!; **et là-d. elle partit,** and with that, she left; **les voisins au-d.,** the neighbours above, the upstairs neighbours.

2 *nm* top (*of table etc*); **d. de plateau,** traycloth; *Th* **les d.,** the flies; *Fig* **le d. du panier,** the pick of the bunch; **avoir le d.,** to have the upper hand, to be on top; **(re)prendre le d.,** to get over (*illness*); to overcome one's feelings (*of sorrow etc*).

3 *prép* **(a) de d.,** from, off; **elle ne leva pas les yeux de d. son ouvrage,** she did not lift her eyes from *or* take her eyes off her work;

(b) au-d. de, above; **au-d. de 15 ans,** over 15, more than 15 (years old); **au-d. de Lyon,** north of Lyons; **nous volons au-d. de l'Alsace,** we are flying over Alsace; *Fig* **il est bien au-d. de toi,** he's much better than you are; **je suis au-d. de tout cela,** (*ça ne me touche pas*) I'm above all that;

(c) par-d, above, over; *F* **j'en ai par-d. la tête,** I've had it up to here.

dessus-de-lit [dəsydli] *nm inv* coverlet, bedspread.

déstabilisation [destabilizɑsjɔ̃] *nf* destabilization.

déstabiliser [destabilize] *vt* to destabilize.

déstalinisation [destalinizɑsjɔ̃] *nf Pol* destalinization.

destin [dɛstɛ̃] *nm* fate; **avoir un d. tragique,** to be ill-fated; **le d. d'une civilisation/d'un tableau,** the fate of a civilization/painting; **qui aurait pu prévoir son d.?,** who could have predicted his fate *or* what would become of him?; **le d. a voulu que ...,** fate decreed that ...; **le d. nous a réunis,** fate brought us together; **accepter son d.,** to accept one's fate *or* destiny; **se mettre dans les mains du d.,** to trust to fate.

destinataire [dɛstinatɛr] *n* addressee, recipient (*of letter etc*); consignee (*of goods*); payee (*of money order*).

destination [dɛstinɑsjɔ̃] *nf* **(a)** destination; **quelle est votre d.?,** where are you going to?; **trains/vols à d. de Paris,** trains/flights to Paris; **articles à d. de la province et de l'étranger,** goods for the provinces and for export; **arriver à d.,** to arrive at one's destination; **(b)** destination, intended purpose (*of building, sum of money etc*).

destinée [dɛstine] *nf* **(a)** (*vie*) destiny; **unir sa d. à celle de qn,** (*l'épouser*) to marry s.o.; *Litt* **destinées,** destinies, fortunes; **(b)** = **DESTIN**.

destiner [dɛstine] **1** *vt* **(a)** to intend; **d. qch à qn,** to intend *or* mean sth for s.o.; **le sort qui nous est destiné,** what fate holds in store for us; **la balle vous était destinée,** the bullet was meant for you; **cette remarque t'était personnellement destinée,** the remark was meant for *or* aimed at you; **ce paquet vous est destiné,** this parcel is meant for *or* addressed to you; **d. une somme d'argent à un achat,** to allot *or* assign a sum of money to a purchase; **il avait destiné son fils au barreau,** he had intended his son for the bar;

(b) (*vouer*) *Vieilli* to destine; **être destiné à mourir sur l'échafaud,** to be fated *or* doomed to die on the scaffold; **nous étions destinés à nous rencontrer,** we were destined *or* fated to meet.

2 se destiner *vpr* **se d. à qch,** to intend to take up sth (as a profession); **il se destine à la médecine,** he intends to be a doctor.

destituer [dɛstitɥe] *vt* to dismiss, to discharge (*s.o.*); to remove (*official*) from office; **d. un général de son commandement,** to relieve a general of his command.

destitution [dɛstitysjɔ̃] *nf* dismissal (*of official etc*).

destrier [dɛstrije] *nm Hist* charger, war horse.

destroyer [dɛstrɔjœr, dɛstrwaje] *nm Nau Mil* destroyer.

destructeur, -trice [dɛstryktœr, -tris] **1** *adj* destructive (*child, war etc*); destroying (*agent etc*). **2** *n* destroyer.

destructible [dɛstryktibl] *adj* destructible.

destructif, -ive [dɛstryktif, -iv] *adj* destructive.

destruction [dɛstryksjɔ̃] *nf* **(a)** destruction (*of evidence, papers etc*); extermination (*of rats etc*); **la d. d'une race,**

the extermination of a race; **(b)** *Mil* demolition (*by blasting etc*).

destructivité [dɛstryktivite] *nf* destructiveness.

destructuré [destryktyre] *adj* (*vêtement*) unstructured.

désuet, -uète [desɥɛ, -ɥɛt] *adj* obsolete (*word*); **théories désuètes,** obsolete *or* antiquated *or* out-of-date theories.

désuétude [desɥetyd] *nf* disuse; **tomber en d.,** to fall *or* pass into disuse; (*of right etc*) to lapse; (*of law*) to fall into abeyance; **mot tombé en d.,** obsolete word.

désuni [dezyni] *adj* divided, disunited (*people*); disconnected, divided (*parts etc*); uncoordinated (*manoeuvre*).

désunion [dezynjɔ̃] *nf* disunity (*of people etc*); dissension (*in family etc*).

désunir [dezynir] **1** *vt* to divide, to disunite (*people etc*); to disconnect (*parts etc*); **questions qu'on ne peut pas d.,** questions that cannot be treated separately (from each other), indissolubly linked questions. **2 se désunir** *vpr* (*of athlete*) to lose one's stride.

détachable [detaʃabl] *adj* detachable.

détachage [detaʃaʒ] *nm* removal of stains (*from clothes etc*).

détachant [detaʃɑ̃] **1** *adj* stain-removing. **2** *nm* stain remover.

détaché [detaʃe] **1** *adj* **(a)** loose, detached (*part*); untethered (*horse etc*); **pièces détachées,** spare parts; **(b)** (*délégué*) seconded (*to another department*); *surtout Mil* detached; **(c)** *Fig* detached (*manner etc*); **d. de ce monde,** detached from the world, unworldly. **2** *nm Mus* détaché, detached (bowing).

détachement [detaʃmɑ̃] *nm* **(a)** detaching, cutting off (*of sth*); **(b)** secondment, seconding (*of person*); **il est en d. à l'université de Cambridge,** he has been seconded to the University of Cambridge; **(c)** (*indifférence*) detachment (**de,** from); **d. de ce monde,** detachment from the world, unworldliness; **(d)** *Mil* detachment, draft (*of troops*), *US* detail; **d. de corvée,** fatigue party.

détacher¹ [detaʃe] **1** *vt* **(a)** (*défaire*) to detach (*sth*); to uncouple (*truck*); to untether (*horse*); **d. un rideau,** to take down *or* unhook a curtain; **d. une chaîne,** to undo a chain; **je ne peux pas en d. mes yeux,** I can't take my eyes off it; **d. un chèque du carnet,** to tear out a cheque; **d. les pétales d'une fleur,** to pick *or* pluck the petals off a flower;

(b) *Fig* **d. qn de qch,** to turn s.o. away from sth;

(c) to attach, to second; *surtout Mil* to detach; *Mil* **d. un officier auprès de qn,** to detach an officer to serve with s.o.; **fonctionnaire détaché à un autre service,** official temporarily attached *or* seconded to another department; **se faire d.,** to be seconded;

(d) (*découper*) **d. une figure dans un tableau,** to make a figure stand out in a picture; **d. les syllabes d'un mot,** to pronounce each syllable of a word separately; *Mus* **d. les notes,** to detach the notes.

2 se détacher *vpr* **(a)** (*of knot etc*) to come undone; (*of animal*) to slip its chain, to break loose; (*of handle*) to break off, to become detached; (*of button*) to come off; (*of parts*) to come apart; (*of paint*) to flake away *or* off; **l'écorce se détache,** the bark is peeling off the tree; *Fig* **se d. de sa famille/de qn,** to separate *or* break away from one's family/s.o.; (*se désintéresser*) to grow apart from one's family/s.o.;

(b) (*se séparer*) **un petit groupe de coureurs se détacha en avant,** a small group *or* bunch of runners pulled ahead (of the field) *or* broke away (from the field);

(c) se d. sur un fond/l'horizon, to stand out against a background/the horizon.

détacher² *vt* to remove stains *or* spots from (*clothing etc*).

détacheur, -euse [detaʃœr, -øz] **1** *adj* **flacon d.,** (bottle of) stain remover. **2** *nm* stain remover.

détail [detaj] *nm* **(a)** (*élément*) detail; **donner tous les détails,** to enter *or* go into all the details, to give full details *or* particulars; **elle n'a pas donné de détails,** she didn't go into detail, she didn't give any details; **raconter qch en d.** *ou* **dans les détails,** to give a detailed account of sth; **décrire qch en d.,** to describe sth in detail, to give a detailed description of sth; **demander plus de détails,** to ask for more details (**sur, à propos de,** about, of); **nous n'avons pas encore de détails,** (*sur le désastre etc*) there are no details as yet; **pour plus de détails,** for more details; **c'est un d.,** it's a detail, it's not important; **se perdre dans le d.,** to get bogged down in detail; **il y a quelques détails touchants,** there are a few touching details; **le d. d'un compte,** the items of an account; **le d. d'une facture,** the breakdown of an invoice;

(b) *Com* retail; **vendre au d.,** to sell (goods) retail; **magasin de vente au d.,** retail store; **marchand au d.,** retailer; **prix de d.,** retail price; **commerce de d.,** retailing; **être dans le commerce de d.,** to be in retailing;

(c) *Admin Mil etc* internal economy; **service de d.,** executive duties; **officier de détail,** quartermaster officer (= supply and pay officer).

détaillant, -ante [detajɑ̃,-ɑ̃t] *n Com* retailer.

détaillé [detaje] *adj* **(a)** detailed (*narrative, description etc*); **(b)** *Com* **état d. de compte,** detailed *or* itemized statement of account.

détailler [detaje] *vt* **(a)** *Com* to retail (*goods*), to sell (*goods*) retail; **(b)** to itemize (*account*); *Litt* (*énumérer*) to detail, to list (*reasons*); **(c) d. qn,** to scrutinize s.o., to look s.o. up and down.

détaler [detale] *vi F* (*d'une personne*) to bolt, to take (oneself) off; (*d'un cheval etc*) to bolt; **la souris détala vers son trou,** the mouse bolted for *or* scuttled off *or* scurried off to its hole.

détartrage [detartraʒ] *nm* descaling (*of boiler*); tartar removal, scaling (*of teeth*).

détartrant [detartrɑ̃] **1** *nm* (*for boiler*) scaler. **2** *adj* **dentifrice d.,** toothpaste for tartar removal.

détartrer [detartre] *vt* to (de)scale (*boiler*); (*d'un dentiste*) to scale (*teeth*); (*d'un dentiste, d'un dentifrice*) to remove the tartar from (*teeth*).

détartreur [detartrœr] *nm* scaler (*for boiler*).

détaxation [detaksɑsjɔ̃] *nf* removal of tax.

détaxe [detaks] *nf* tax refund *or* rebate.

détaxer [detakse] *vt* to take the tax off, to remove the tax on (*sth*); **marchandises détaxées,** duty-free goods.

détecter [detɛkte] *vt* to detect.

détecteur, -trice [detɛktœr, -tris] **1** *adj Tech* detecting, sensing; *Électron* **lampe détectrice,** detector valve. **2** *nm Tech* detector; *Électron* detector, sensor; **d. de fumée,** smoke detector *or* alarm; **d. de mines,** mine detector; *Électron* **d. d'ondes,** wave detector.

détection [detɛksjɔ̃] *nf* detection, location; **d. électromagnétique,** radio location; **d. sous-marine,** underwater detection; *Mil Nau* **d. des mines,** mine detection.

détective [detɛktiv] *nm* detective; **d. privé,** private detective, *F* private eye.

déteindre [detɛ̃dr] *v* (*conj like* **teindre**) **1** *vt* to take the colour out of (*sth*). **2** *vi* to fade, to lose colour; (*of colour*) to bleed; **d. au lavage,** to run in the wash; **le ruban a déteint sur ma robe,** the colour of the ribbon has come off on my dress; *Fig* **cela déteint sur eux,** it rubs off on them; *Fig* **j'espère que leur politesse déteindra sur elle,** I hope some of their politeness rubs off on her.

dételage [detlaʒ] *nm* **(a)** unharnessing, unhitching (*of horses*); **(b)** uncoupling (*of wag(g)ons*).

dételer [detle] *v* (**je dételle, n. dételons; je dételleral**) **1** *vt* **(a)** to unharness, to unhitch (*horse(s)*); to unyoke (*oxen*); **(b)** *Rail* to uncouple (*trucks etc*). **2** *vi F* to ease off, to stop working; **travailler dix heures sans d.,** to work for ten hours without letting up, to work non-stop for ten hours.

détendeur [detɑ̃dœr] *nm* pressure reducer, relief valve.

détendre [detɑ̃dr] **1** *vt* to slacken, to loosen (*sth that is taut*); to unbend (*bow*); **d. un ressort,** to release a spring; **d. la gachette,** (*d'une arme*) to squeeze the trigger; **d. l'atmosphère,** to relax the atmosphere; **d. des relations,** to make relations less strained; **d. les nerfs,** to steady the nerves; **d. un gaz,** to release the pressure (of a gas). **2 se détendre** *vpr* (*d'un tissu*) to stretch; (*d'un ressort*) to uncoil; (*de la vapeur*) to be reduced in pressure; (*se relaxer*) to relax; **se d. pendant une heure,** to relax for an hour; **son visage se détendit dans un sourire,** his face relaxed into a smile; **la situation se détend,** the situation is easing *or* becoming less tense.

détendu [detɑ̃dy] *adj* (*lâche*) slack; relaxed (*conversation etc*).

détenir [detnir] *vt* (*conj like* **tenir**) **(a)** to hold, to be in possession of (*sth*); **d. un objet volé,** to be in possession of a stolen object; **d. un secret/le pouvoir,** to have a secret/to hold power; **d. le record du monde,** to hold the world record; **(b)** to detain (*s.o.*), to keep (*s.o.*) prisoner.

détente [detɑ̃t] *nf* **(a)** loosening, slackening (*of sth that is taut*); relaxing (*of muscles*); easing (*of political situation etc*); *Pol* détente; *Sp* spring; **j'ai besoin de quelques instants de d.,** I need to relax for a moment, I need a moment's relaxation; *Sp* **sauteur qui travaille en d.,** jumper who uses his spring; **(b)** trigger (*of gun*); *F* **dur à la d.,** tightfisted, stingy (*person*); **(c)** expansion (*of steam, gases*); explosion *or* power stroke (*in engine*); **soupape de d.,** expansion valve.

détenteur, -trice [detɑ̃tœr, -tris] *n* holder (*of copyright,* *securities, challenge cup etc*); **d. de titres,** stockholder.

détention [detɑ̃sjɔ̃] *nf* **(a)** holding (*of securities etc*); possession (*of firearms etc*); **(b)** (*captivité*) detention, imprisonment (*of s.o.*); **d. préventive,** detention pending trial.

détenu, -ue [detny] *n* prisoner.

détergent [detɛrʒɑ̃] *adj & nm* detergent.

déterger [detɛrʒe] *vt Tech* to clean, to remove (*oil stains etc*).

détérioration [deterjɔrɑsjɔ̃] *nf* deterioration.

détériorer [deterjɔre] **1** *vt* to make (*sth*) worse. **2 se détériorer** *vpr* to deteriorate.

déterminable [determinabl] *adj* determinable.

déterminant [detɛrminɑ̃] **1** *adj* deciding (*factor, cause etc*). **2** *nm Ling* determiner; *Math* determinant.

déterminatif, -ive [detɛrminatif, -iv] *Ling Gram* **1** *adj* determinative, defining (*word etc*); **phrase déterminative,** defining clause. **2** *nm* determiner, determinative.

détermination [detɛrminɑsjɔ̃] *nf* **(a)** (*fermeté*) determination, resolution; **agir avec d.,** to act resolutely; **(b)** (*résolution*) resolve, determination; **(c)** (*d'une espèce, d'une date, d'une zone etc*) determination; (*du sang, d'une bactérie*) typing.

déterminé [detɛrmine] *adj* **(a)** determined, definite, well-defined (*area, purpose etc*); specific, particular (*aim*); **dans un sens d.,** in a given direction; **(b)** determined, resolute (*person, manner etc*); **être d. à faire qch,** to be determined to do sth.

déterminer [detɛrmine] **1** *vt* **(a)** (*définir*) to determine, to establish (*date, fact, name, value etc*); to determine (*species*); to type (*blood, bacteria*); **d. un lieu de rendez-vous,** to fix *or* decide on a meeting place; **(b)** (*causer*) to cause, to give rise to (*sth*); to determine (*one's actions*); **(c)** (*décider*) **d. qn à faire qch,** to induce *or* move *or* impel s.o. to do sth; **qu'est-ce qui vous a déterminé à partir?,** what made you (decide to) leave? **2 se déterminer** *vpr* to make up one's mind (**à faire qch,** to do sth).

déterminisme [determinism] *nm Phil* determinism.

déterministe [detɛrminist] *Phil* **1** *n* determinist. **2** *adj* determinist(ic).

déterré, -ée [detere] *n F* **il a un air** *ou* **une mine de d.,** he looks like death warmed up.

déterrer [detere] *vt* to dig up, to unearth (*buried treasure etc*); to uproot (*tree*); to exhume, to disinter (*corpse*); *Fig* to dig out (*old book etc*).

détersif, -ive [detɛrsif, -iv] *adj & nm* detergent.

détersion [detɛrsjɔ̃] *nf* (*nettoyage*) cleaning with a detergent; *Méd* cleansing (*of wound etc*).

détestable [detɛstabl] *adj* detestable, awful, hateful (*person etc*); very bad, execrable (*work etc*); foul, ghastly (*weather, mood*).

détestablement [detɛstabləmɑ̃] *adv* extremely badly; **chanter d.,** to sing appallingly (badly).

détester [detɛste] *vt* to detest, to hate; **je déteste être dérangé,** I hate to be *or* I hate *or* detest being disturbed; **elle ne déteste pas (de) courir,** she's quite fond of running; **il ne déteste pas les bonbons,** he rather likes sweets.

détonant [detɔnɑ̃] **1** *adj* explosive (*substance*); **explosif d.,** high explosive. **2** *nm* explosive.

détonateur [detɔnatœr] *nm* detonator; *Fig* **être le d. de qch,** to spark sth off.

détonation [detɔnɑsjɔ̃] *nf* (*explosion*) detonation; (*bruit*) explosion; (*bruit d'arme à feu*) report, bang.

détoner [detɔne] *vi* to detonate, to explode; **faire d.,** to detonate (*dynamite etc*).

détonnant [detɔnɑ̃] *adj* jarring; **elle était d'une bonne humeur détonnante,** her good mood clashed *or* was out of keeping with the general atmosphere.

détonner [detɔne] *vi* to be out of tune; (*de chanteur*) to sing out of tune, to sing flat *or* sharp; (*de pianiste etc*) to play out of tune; (*de couleurs*) to clash; **ses bijoux détonnent dans ce milieu,** her jewels are out of place *or* out of keeping in these surroundings; **il détonne dans cet entourage,** he looks out of place in that circle.

détordre [detɔrdr] **1** *vt* to untwist, to unravel (*yarn etc*); to unlay (*rope*). **2 se détordre** *vpr* (*of yarn etc*) to come untwisted, to untwist.

détortiller [detɔrtije] *vt* to untwist (*yarn etc*); to disentangle (*hair etc*).

détour [detur] *nm* **(a)** (*dans parcours*) detour; **faire un long d.,** to make a long detour; **d. obligatoire de 5 km,** (mandatory) 5 kilometre diversion; **(b)** *Fig* (*biais*) **user de détours pour arriver à un but,** to achieve one's end in a roundabout way; **répondre sans d.,** to give a plain *or* straightforward answer; **(c)** (*tracé*) turn, curve, bend (*in road, river*); **la route fait un brusque d.,** the road takes a sharp turn; **je l'ai aperçue au d. du chemin,** I saw her at the bend in the path.

détourné [deturne] *adj* indirect, roundabout (*road, route*); **chemin d.,** by-road; *Fig* **par des voies détournées,** indirectly, in a roundabout way.

détournement [deturnəmɑ̃] *nm* **(a)** diversion, diverting (*of river etc*); diversion, rerouting (*of traffic*); **d. d'avion,** hijacking; **(b)** embezzlement; misappropriation (*of funds*); **d. de pouvoir,** take-over (of power); *Jur* **d. de mineur,** (*enlèvement*) abduction of a minor; (*séduction*) seduction of a minor.

détourner [deturne] **1** *vt* **(a)** to divert (*traffic, river etc*); to turn (*one's head, eyes*) away; **d. l'attention de qn,** to divert *or* distract s.o.'s attention; **d. qn de sa route,** to take s.o. out of his way; **d. qn de la bonne voie,** to lead s.o. astray; **comment le d. de son travail?,** how can we *etc* get him away from his work?; **d. la conversation,** to change the subject; **d. les soupçons,** to avert suspicion; **d. la tête pour éviter qn,** to look the other way to avoid s.o.; **elle détourna les yeux,** she averted her gaze, she looked away; **d. un avion,** to hijack a plane; **(b)** to misappropriate, to embezzle (*funds*) (**à,** from). **2 se détourner** *vpr* to turn away *or* aside (**de,** from); *Fig* **se d. de ses études/amis,** to neglect one's studies/friends.

détoxication [detɔksikɑsjɔ̃] *nf* detoxication.

détoxiquer [detɔksike] *vt* to detoxicate.

détracter [detrakte] *vt Litt* to denigrate, to disparage.

détracteur, -trice [detraktœr, -tris] *n* detractor, disparager.

détraqué, -ée [detrake] **1** *adj* (*mechanism, digestion etc*) out of order; (*person*) deranged; **il a le cerveau d.,** his mind is unhinged; **avoir les nerfs détraqués,** to be a nervous wreck; **le temps est d.,** the weather is unsettled. **2** *n* **c'est un d.,** he's unbalanced.

détraquement [detrakmɑ̃] *nm* putting (*of mechanism etc*) out of order; breakdown (*of mechanism, health etc*).

détraquer [detrake] **1** *vt* to put (*apparatus*) out of order; to throw (*mechanism*) out of gear; *F* **cette déception lui a détraqué le cerveau,** the disappointment has unhinged his mind; **ça va te d. l'estomac,** that'll upset your stomach. **2 se détraquer** *vpr* (*of mechanism, health etc*) to break down; (*of stomach*) to be upset; (*of weather*) to become unsettled; **se d. l'estomac/les nerfs,** to ruin one's digestion/nerves.

détrempe¹ [detrɑ̃p] *nf* distemper; *Beaux-Arts* tempera.

détrempe² *nf* annealing, softening (*of steel*).

détremper¹ [detrɑ̃pe] *vt* to soak (*sth*); to slake (*lime*); **champ/terre/***etc* **détrempé(e),** sodden *or* waterlogged field/earth/*etc*.

détremper² *vt* to anneal, to soften (*steel*).

détresse [detrɛs] *nf* **(a)** (*angoisse*) grief, anguish, distress; **mère en d.,** grief-stricken mother; **(b)** (*dénuement*) financial straits *or* difficulties; **(c)** (*perdition*) danger; **navire en d.,** ship in distress; **voiture/avion en d.,** car/aircraft in difficulties; **signal de d.,** distress signal, SOS; *Aut* **feux de d.,** hazard warning lights.

détriment [detrimɑ̃] *nm* detriment; **au d. de qn/qch,** to the detriment of s.o./sth; **je l'ai appris à mon d.,** I found it out to my cost.

détritus [detritys] *nm* rubbish, refuse.

détroit [detrwa] *nm Géog* strait(s), sound; *Anat* strait (*of the pelvis*).

détromper [detrɔ̃pe] **1** *vt* to put (*s.o.*) right (**au sujet de,** about). **2 se détromper** *vpr* to realise that one was wrong; **détrompez-vous!,** open your eyes!

détrôner [detrone] *vt* **(a)** to dethrone (*monarch, Fig Sp champion*); **(b)** to supersede (*old method etc*).

détrousser [detruse] *vt Hum* to relieve (*s.o.*) of his valuables; *Arch* to rob (*s.o.*).

détrousseur [detrusœr] *nm Arch* highwayman, footpad.

détruire [detrɥir] *v* (*prp* **détruisant**; *pp* **détruit**; *pr ind* **je détruis, n. détruisons**; *impf* **je détruisais**; *p hist* **je détruisis**; *fu* **je détruirai**) **1** *vt* **(a)** (*anéantir*) to destroy, to ruin; **la pluie a détruit la moisson,** the rain has ruined the harvest; **le village a été complètement détruit,** the village has been completely destroyed; **d. les espérances de qn,** to destroy *or* dash s.o.'s hopes; **cela détruit son explication,** that ruins his explanation;

(b) (*démolir*) to demolish, to pull down, to raze (*building, town etc*); to overthrow (*empire etc*); to break up, to scrap (*ship etc*); to destroy, *F* to demolish, to write off (*car, aircraft etc*);

(c) (*tuer*) to kill; **l'épidémie va d. 200 000 personnes,** the epidemic is likely to kill 200,000 people.

2 se détruire *vpr* **(a)** (*pourrir*) to fall into decay, to rot; **(b)** (*se suicider*) to kill oneself; **(c)** (*anéantir*) to cancel (each other) out.

dette [dɛt] *nf Fin & Fig* debt; **faire des dettes,** to run into debt; **avoir des dettes,** to be in debt; **être perdu** *ou* **criblé de dettes,** to be up to one's ears in debt; **dettes actives,** (*en comptabilité*) accounts receivable, assets; **dettes passives,** (*en comptabilité*) accounts payable, liabilities; *Fin* **la d. publique** *ou* **de l'État,** the National Debt; **d. ex térieure,** foreign *or* floating debt; **d. à court terme** *ou* **flottante,** short-term *or* floating debt; **avoir une d. de reconnaissance envers qn,** to owe s.o. a debt of gratitude, to be under an obligation to s.o..

D.E.U.G. [døg] *nm* (*abrév* **Diplôme d'Études Universitaires Générales**) = degree.

deuil [dœj] *nm* **(a)** mourning; (*perte*) bereavement; (*procession*) funeral procession; **grand d.,** deep mourning; **porter le d., être en d.,** to be in mourning; **fermé pour cause de d.,** (*annonce*) closed owing to bereavement; **semaine de d.,** week of mourning; **conduire le d.,** to be chief mourner; *F* **faire son d. de qch,** to give sth up as *or* for lost; *F* **il avait toujours les ongles en d.,** his fingernails were always dirty.

deutérium [døterjɔm] *nm Ch* deuterium.

Deutéronome [døterɔnɔm] *nm Bible* Deuteronomy.

deux [dø, *before a vowel sound in the same wordgroup* døz] **1** *adj inv* **(a)** two; **d. enfants** [døzɑ̃fɑ̃], two children; **j'en ai d.** [dø], I have two (of them); **d. ou trois** [døzutrwɑ], two or three; **d. fois,** twice; **tous (les) d.,** both; **nous/vous/eux d.,** (*sujet, objet*) the two of *or* both of us/you/them; (*objet*) us/you/those two; (*sujet*) we/you/these two; **des d. côtés du fleuve,** on either side *or* on both sides of the river; **tous les d. jours,** every other day, every two days; **entre d. âges,** middle-aged; **vivre à d.,** to live together; **c'est à d. pas d'ici,** it is very close, it's only a short distance away; **j'ai d. mots à lui dire,** I've a bone to pick with him; **en d. temps, trois mouvements,** in two ticks, in next to no time; **les mathématiques/les ordinateurs/***etc* **et moi, ça fait d.,** I just don't get on with mathematics/computers/*etc*; **ma sœur et moi, ça fait d.,** my sister and I are two different people; **lui et moi, ça fait d.,** (*on ne s'entend pas*) he and I don't get on; *Vulg* **cette voiture de mes d.,** that fucking car;

(b) (*deuxième*) **Charles D.,** Charles the Second; **chapitre d.,** chapter two; *Sp etc* **il est arrivé d. ou troisième,** he came in second or third.

2 *nm inv* two; *Cartes* two, deuce; *Cartes* **le d. de cœur,** the two of hearts; **la table de d.,** the two times table; **d. fois d. font quatre,** two times two *or* twice two is four; *Fig* **c'est clair comme d. et d. font quatre,** it's as clear as daylight; **aujourd'hui nous sommes le d.,** today is the second, it's the second today; **casser qch en d.,** to break sth in two; **diviser** *ou* **couper une ligne en d.,** to bisect a line; **marcher par d.,** to walk in pairs; (*dans une procession*) to march two abreast *or Mil* in file; **entrer d. par d.,** to come in two by two *or* in twos; **à nous d.,** (*entre amis*) let's get on with it (together); (*à un adversaire*) let's fight it out; *Tennis* **à d.,** deuce; *F* **il fera ça en moins de d.,** he'll do it in two ticks *or* in no time at all; **pas de d.,** (*danse*) pas de deux; *Fig* **entre les d.,** average, OK; **jamais d. sans trois,** it never rains but it pours; *F* **je n'ai fait ni une ni d.,** I didn't think twice.

deux-deux (à) [adødø] *adj Mus* in two-two time.

deux-huit (à) [adøɥit] *adj Mus* in two-eight time.

deuxième [døzjɛm] **1** *adj* second; **appartement au d. étage,** second-floor flat, *Am* third-floor apartment; *Math* **équation du d. degré,** quadratic equation. **2** *n* second; **elle est née la d.,** she is the second child; **habiter au d.,** to live on the second *or Am* third floor.

deuxièmement [døzjɛmmɑ̃] *adv* secondly, in the second place.

deux-mâts [dømɑ] *nm* two-master.

deux-pièces [døpjɛs] *nm inv* **(a)** (*maillot de bain*) two-piece (swimsuit); (*ensemble, tailleur*) two-piece; **(b)** (*appartement*) two-roomed flat *or Am* apartment.

deux-points [døpwɛ̃] *nm Typ* colon.

deux-ponts [døpɔ̃] *nm inv* twodecked ship; double-decker (aircraft).

deux-quatre [døkatr] *nm inv Mus* two-four.

deux-roues [døru] *nm inv* two-wheeled vehicle.

deux-temps [døtɑ̃] *nm* **(a)** *Mus* two-two time; **(b)** (*moteur*) two stroke (engine); **(mélange) d.-t.,** two-stroke mixture.

deuzio [døzjo] *adv F* second(ly).

dévaler [devale] **1** *vi* to descend, to go down; (*of stream*) to rush down; **le jardin dévale jusqu'à la rivière,** the garden slopes down *or* extends down to the river. **2** *vt* **d. l'escalier,** to rush down the stairs; **d. la rue à toute vitesse,** to race down the street.

dévaliser [devalize] *vt* to rob (*s.o. of his money etc*); **d. une banque,** to rob a bank; **d. une maison,** to burgle a house; **d. le placard/le frigo/***etc*, to raid the pantry/the fridge/*etc*; *Fig* **j'ai dévalisé la boutique,** I bought up the shop.

dévalorisation [devalɔrizɑsjɔ̃] *nf* **(a)** (*action*) devaluation (*of currency*); (*result*) fall in value, depreciation; **(b)** *Fig* discrediting (*of s.o., a policy*).

dévaloriser [devalɔrize] **1** *vt* to devalue (*currency*); to mark down (*goods*). **2 se dévaloriser** *vpr* to depreciate.

dévaluation [devalɥɑsjɔ̃] *nf Écon* devaluation (*of currency*).

dévaluer [devalɥe] *vt* to devalue (*currency*).

devancement [dəvɑ̃smɑ̃] *nm Mil* **d. d'appel,** enlistment before call-up.

devancer [dəvɑ̃se] *vt* (**je devançai(s); n. devançons**) **(a)** (*dans le classement*) to come ahead of (*s.o., sth*); **(b)** (*distancer*) to leave (*s.o., the others*) behind; to outdistance, to outstrip (*s.o., the others*); (*prévenir*) to forestall; **je vous ai devancé,** I got here before you; (*j'ai anticipé*) I forestalled you; **j'ai devancé votre demande,** I anticipated your request; **d. les critiques,** to forestall *or* anticipate criticism; **d. les désirs de qn,** to anticipate s.o.'s wishes; **d. son époque,** to be ahead of one's time; *Mil* **d. l'appel,** to enlist before call-up; **d. une échéance,** to settle an account early.

devancier, -ière [dəvɑ̃sje, -jɛr] *n* predecessor.

devant [dəvɑ̃] **1** *prép* in front of (*s.o., sth*); **regardez d. vous,** look in front of you; **assis d. un verre de vin,** sitting over a glass of wine; **marchez tout droit d. vous,** walk straight ahead *or* on; **être courageux d. le danger,** to show courage in the face of danger; **éprouver de la gêne d. qn,** to feel ill at ease with s.o. *or* in s.o.'s presence; **égaux d. la loi,** equal in the eyes of the law; **sa position d. ce problème,** his position on the problem; **d. cet état de choses/votre silence,** in view of this state of affairs/your silence; **avoir du temps d. soi,** to have time to spare; **navire d. Calais,** ship off Calais; **aller au-de qn,** to meet s.o. on the way; **au d. du danger/des risques,** in the face of danger *or* risks.

2 *adv* in (the) front; **envoyer qn d.,** to send s.o. on (in front); **aller d.,** to go in front, to lead the way; **porter qch sens d. derrière,** to wear sth back to front; **arriver par d.,** to come in the front way; *Nau* **un navire d.!,** ship ahead!; *Nau* **être vent d.,** to be in stays, to be wind ahead; *Arch & Litt* **comme d.,** as before.

3 *nm* front (part); **d. (de chemise)** (shirt) front; *Tricot* **d. gauche/droit,** (*d'un gilet*) left/right front; **chambre sur le d.,** front room; **dents de d.,** front teeth; **pattes de d.,** (*d'un animal*) forelegs, front paws; **prendre les devants,** to go on ahead; *Fig* to make the first move; **gagner les devants,** to take the lead.

devanture [dəvɑ̃tyr] *nf* façade, front (*of building*); **d. de magasin,** shopfront, shop window.

dévastateur, -trice [devastatœr, -tris] *adj* devastating.

dévastation [devastɑsjɔ̃] *nf* devastation, destruction, havoc.

dévaster [devaste] *vt* to devastate, to lay waste, to ravage (*country etc*); **les cultures ont été dévastées par les pluies,** the crops have been destroyed *or* ruined by the rain.

déveine [devɛn] *nf F* (run of) bad luck; **être dans la d.,** to be down on one's luck; **quelle d.!,** (what) hard luck!

développé [devlɔpe] *nm* **(a)** *Sp* (*in weightlifting*) press; **(b)** (*ballet step*) developpé.

développement [devlɔpmɑ̃] *nm* **(a)** development, growth (*of the body*); development (*of muscles, flower, faculties etc*); **d. d'une affaire,** growth of a business; *Écon* **pays en voie de d.,** developing countries; **son d. en tant qu'actrice,** her development as an actress; **(b)** *Phot* developing, development; **(c)** spreading out, opening out (*of wings etc*); *Math* expansion, development (*of contracted expression etc*); **(d)** spread (*of branches of tree etc*); **(e) bicyclette avec un d. de 55 m. 25,** bicycle with a 66 inch gear *or* geared to 66 inches; **(f)** *Mus Beaux-Arts* development (*of theme*); *Fig* **se lancer dans de grands développements,** to go into detailed explanations *or* great detail.

développer [devlɔpe] **1** *vt* **(a)** to develop (*muscles, faculties, trade etc*); **d. ses dons naturels par l'étude,** to improve one's natural gifts by study; **d. un sujet/une idée/sa pensée,** to develop a subject/an idea/one's thinking;

(b) *Phot* to develop (*a negative*);

(c) to spread out, to open out (*wings etc*); to unroll (*map etc*); *Math* to expand, to develop (*contracted expression etc*);

(d) bicyclette qui développe ..., bicycle that has a gear of ..., that is geared to ... .

2 se développer *vpr* **(a)** (*of organs, country, flowers, the intelligence etc*) to develop; **l'enfant se développe rapidement,** the child is developing rapidly; **l'affaire ne va pas tarder à se d. et se transformer en scandale,** the affair will soon develop into a scandal;

(b) to spread out, to open out, to expand, to extend; **la plaine se développe à perte de vue,** the plain extends *or* stretches out as far as the eye can see.

devenir[1] [dəvnir] *nm* gradual change, development; **la langue est dans un perpétuel d.,** language is in a constant state of flux.

devenir[2] *vi* (*conj like* **venir**, *the aux is* **être**) to become; **elle est devenue très riche,** she became *or* got very rich; **il devint général,** he became a general; **que devenez-vous ces temps-ci?,** what are you doing these days?; **que vais-je d. sans toi?,** what will become of me without you?, what will I do without you?, where will I be without you?; **qu'est-il devenu?,** what has become of him?; **que devient votre cousin?,** how is your cousin getting on?; **il devient vraiment indiscret,** he's getting really indiscreet; **il était devenu homme,** he had grown into a man; **d. grand,** (*en taille*) to grow tall; (*en âge*) to grow up; **d. vieux,** to grow old, to get old; **c'est à d. fou!,** it's enough to drive you mad!

dévergondage [devɛrgɔ̃daʒ] *nm* **(a)** shamelessness; **(b)** extravagance (*of style, imagination*).

dévergondé, -ée [devɛrgɔ̃de] **1** *adj* **(a)** shameless; **(b)** extravagant (*style, imagination*). **2** *n* shameless person.

dévergonder (se) [sədevɛrgɔ̃de] *vpr* to become (quite) shameless.

dévernir [devɛrnir] *vt* to take the varnish *or* the polish off (*furniture etc*).

déverrouillage [deveruja ʒ] *nm* unbolting, unlocking (*of door etc*).

déverrouiller [deveruje] *vt* to unbolt, to unlock (*door etc*); to release the bolt of (*a gun*); *Ordinat* to lock off (*capitals*).

dévers [devɛr] *nm* **(a)** inclination, slope (*of wall etc*); banking (*of road at a bend*); *Rail* vertical slant, cant (*of outer rail at curve*); **(b)** warp, twist (*in timber etc*).

déversé [devɛrse] *adj* **(a)** (*incliné*) sloping, banked; **(b)** (*asymétrique*) lopsided; **(c)** (*voilé*) warped.

déversement[1] [devɛrsəmɑ̃] *nm* (*liquide*) discharge, overflow; (*action*) pouring out.

déversement[2] *nm* **(a)** (*d'un mur*) inclination, sloping; **(b)** (*voilement*) warping, warp.

déverser[1] [devɛrse] **1** *vt* to pour (*water*); to discharge (*overflow of canal etc*); to tip, to dump (*rubbish etc*); **le train les déversa sur le quai,** the train deposited them on the platform; *Fig* **d. le mépris sur qn,** to pour scorn on s.o.; **d. sa colère sur qn,** to take one's anger out on s.o.. **2 se déverser** *vpr* (*of river etc*) to empty, to flow (**dans,** into).

déverser[2] **1** *vt* **(a)** to slope (*wall etc*); to bank (*road*); to raise the outer rail of (*railway track*); **(b)** to warp (*timber*). **2** *vi* **(a)** (*of wall etc*) to incline, to lean; **(b)** (*of wood*) to warp.

déversoir [devɛrswar] *nm* **(a)** overflow (*of tank, basin etc*); *HydE* spillway (*of dam*); **(b)** *Fig* outlet (*for one's emotions, energies etc*); safety-valve (*for one's emotions*).

dévêtir [devetir] *v* (*conj like* **vêtir**) **1** *vt* to undress, to strip (*s.o.*). **2 se dévêtir** *vpr* (*complètement*) to undress, to strip, to take off one's clothes; (*partiellement*) to leave off some of one's clothing (*in warm weather*).

déviance [devjɑ̃s] *nf Psy* deviance.

déviant [devjɑ̃] *adj Psy* deviant.

déviation [devjasjɔ̃] *nf* deviation; variation (*of compass*); curvature (*of the spine*); displacement (*of uterus*); departure, deviation (*from proper conduct etc*); *Aut* **d.,** (*annonce*) detour, *Br* diversion; *Électron Él* **champ de d.,** deflecting field.

déviationnisme [devjasjɔnism] *nm Pol* deviationism.

déviationniste [devjasjɔnist] *adj & n Pol* deviationist.

dévidage [devidaʒ] *nm Tex etc* (*de bobine*) unwinding; (*pour faire une bobine*) reeling, spooling.

dévider [devide] *vt Tex etc* (*dérouler*) to unwind; (*faire une bobine*) to reel, to spool (*thread etc*); **d. son rosaire,** to reel off the rosary; *F* **il m'a dévidé son chapelet,** he reeled off his whole story to me.

dévideur, -euse [devidœr, -øz] *n Tex* reeler, wind(st)er.

dévidoir [devidwar] *nm Tex* reeling machine, reel, winder, spool; (*pour tuyaux*) hose reel; (*pour câbles*) drum.

dévié [devje] *adj* **route déviée,** diversion; **rayon de lumière d.,** refracted ray of light.

dévier [devje] *v* (*pr sub & impf* **n. déviions, v. déviiez**) **1** *vi* to deviate, to swerve, to diverge; (*of ball*) to veer (off course); *MecE* to run out of true; **faire d. une balle,** to deflect a bullet; **elle ne dévie jamais de ses principes,** she never deviates *or* never departs from her principles; *Nau Av* **d. de sa route,** (*par accident*) to be off course; (*volontairement*) to turn off course. **2** *vt* to turn (*blow etc*) aside; to deflect (*blow, ray etc*); **d. la circulation,** to divert the traffic.

devin, devineresse [dəvɛ̃, dəvinrɛs] *n* diviner; (*prophète*) soothsayer; *f* fortune teller; *F* **je ne suis pas d.,** I can't tell *or* predict the future.

devinable [dəvinabl] *adj* forseeable.

deviner [dəvine] *vt* to guess (*riddle, secret etc*); to predict (*the future*); to read (*s.o.'s character*); **d. la pensée de qn,** to read s.o.'s thoughts; **vous ne devinez pas?,** can't you guess?; **devine qui j'ai vu,** guess who I saw.

devinette [dəvinɛt] *nf* riddle, conundrum; (*jeu*) guessing game; **poser une d. à qn,** to ask s.o. a riddle.

dévirer [devire] *vt Nau* to veer (*the capstan*).

devis [dəvi] *nm* (*descriptif*) estimate; (*estimatif*) estimate, quotation; *Tech* specification; **ils m'ont fait un d. de 5 000 francs,** they quoted me 5,000 francs; **je voudrais qu'on me fasse un d.,** I'd like an estimate *or* quote (**pour,** for).

dévisager [devizaʒe] *vt* (**je dévisageai(s); n. dévisageons**) to stare *or* look hard at (*s.o.*).

devise [dəviz] *nf* **(a)** *Fin* currency; **devises étrangères,** foreign currency; **(b)** *Hér* device; (*de qn*) motto; **telle est ma d.,** that's my motto.

deviser [dəvize] *vi* to chat, to gossip.

dévissage [devisaʒ] *nm* **(a)** (*d'un écrou*) unscrewing; **(b)** (*en montagne*) fall.

dévisser [devise] **1** *vt* to unscrew (*bolt, nut etc*); *F* **d. son billard,** (*mourir*) to peg out. **2** *vi* (*of mountain climber*) to fall. **3 se dévisser** *vpr* to unscrew; (*par accident*) to come unscrewed.

dévitaliser [devitalize] *vt* to devitalize (*tooth*), *F* to kill the nerve of (*a tooth*).

dévoiement [devwamɑ̃] *nm* canting, tilting (*of flue etc*).

dévoilement [devwalmɑ̃] *nm Fig* disclosure (*of name, secret etc*).

dévoiler [devwale] **1** *vt* to unveil (*face, statue*); *Fig* to reveal, to disclose (*name, secret etc*); to unmask (*conspiracy*); to uncover (*fraud etc*). **2 se dévoiler** *vpr* (*of secret etc*) to come to light.

devoir[1] [dəvwar] *nm* **(a)** (*obligation*) duty; **manquer à son d.,** to fail in one's duty; **faire** *ou* **remplir son d. (envers qn/la patrie),** to do one's duty (by s.o./one's country); **se faire un d. de (faire qch),** to make a point of (doing sth); **se mettre en d. de faire qch,** to make it one's responsibility to do sth; **il est de mon d. de vous le dire,** it is my duty *or* my business to tell you; **je sais ce qui est de mon d.,** I know my duty, I know where my duty lies; **je l'ai fait par d.,** I did it from a sense of duty; **(b)** (*responsabilité*) obligation; **mes devoirs de citoyen/de père,** my duties *or* obligations as a citizen/as a father; **(c)** *Scol* exercise; **devoirs,** homework; **un d. de latin,** a Latin exercise; **(d) devoirs,** respects, duty; **rendre ses devoirs à qn,** to pay one's respects to s.o.; **rendre à qn les derniers devoirs,** to pay one's last respects to s.o..

devoir[2] *v* (*prp* **devant;** *pp* **dû,** *f* **due;** *pr ind* **je dois, n. devons, ils doivent;** *pr sub* **je doive, n. devions, ils doivent;** *impf* **je devais;** *p hist* **je dus;** *fu* **je devrai**) **1** *vt*

(a) (*obligation*) **je ne savais pas ce que je devais faire,** I didn't know what (I ought) to do; **il aurait dû m'avertir,** he should have warned me; **elle a cru d. refuser,** she thought it advisable to refuse; **tu dois honorer tes parents,** you should honour *or* it is your duty to honour your parents; **fais ce que dois, advienne que pourra,** do your duty come what may;

(b) (*commande*) **vous devez** *ou* **devrez vous trouver à votre poste à trois heures,** you must be at your post at three o'clock; **les commandes doivent être adressées à ...,** orders should be sent to ...;

(c) (*compulsion*) **tous les hommes doivent mourir,** all men must die; **enfin j'ai dû céder,** finally I had to yield *or* I was obliged to yield; **tu dois absolument lui en parler,** you really must talk to him about it;

(d) (*dans le futur*) **je dois partir demain,** I am to *or* have to leave tomorrow; **je devais la rencontrer à Paris,** I was to meet her in Paris; **le train doit arriver à midi,** the train is due (to arrive) at twelve o'clock; **dût-il m'en coûter la vie,** were I to die for it; **il ne devait plus les revoir,** he was (destined) never to see them again; **cela devait arriver!,** it was bound to *or* it had to happen!; **la pollution devrait s'accroître d'ici à la fin du siècle,** pollution is expected to increase by the end of the century; **(e)** *(opinion)* **vous devez avoir faim,** you must be hungry; **il a** *ou* **avait dû me prendre pour un autre,** he must have taken me for someone else; **il doit être trois heures,** it must be three o'clock; **il ne doit pas avoir plus de 40 ans,** he can't be more than 40; **(f)** *(être redevable de)* **d. qch à qn,** to owe s.o. sth; **il me doit mille francs,** he owes me a thousand francs; **d. du respect à son père,** to owe respect to one's father; **je lui dois d'être en vie, je lui dois la vie,** I owe my life to him; **je lui dois bien cela,** it's the least I can do for him; **sa réussite est due à ses parents,** it's thanks to his parents that he's so successful.

2 se devoir *vpr* **(a)** *(être obligé de se consacrer à)* **se d. à,** to have to devote oneself to *(s.o., sth)*; **je me dois à ma famille/mon travail,** I must devote myself to my family/my work; **je me dois de le faire,** it's my duty to do it; **(b) comme il se doit,** as is (only) right and proper.

dévoltage [devɔltaʒ] *nm* reduction of voltage.

dévolter [devɔlte] *vt El* to reduce the voltage of *(current)*.

dévolteur [devɔltœr] *nm El* reducing *or* stepdown transformer.

dévolu [devɔly] **1** *adj Jur (inheritance etc)* devolved; devolving **(à,** to, upon); **part dévolue à la ligne paternelle,** share that falls to the heirs on the father's side; **être d. à qn de faire qch,** to fall to s.o.'s lot to do sth. **2** *nm* **jeter son d. sur qch/qn,** to set one's heart on sth/s.o., to be determined to have sth/s.o.; *Hum Péj* to have designs on sth/s.o..

dévolution [devɔlysjɔ̃] *nf Jur* devolution; **d. d'un héritage à l'État,** escheat.

dévorant [devɔrɑ̃] *adj* **(a)** ravenous; **avoir une faim dévorante,** to be ravenous; **(b)** consuming *(fire etc)*; wasting *(disease)*; devouring *(passion)*.

dévorateur, -trice [devɔratœr, -tris] *adj* devouring, consuming.

dévorer [devɔre] *vt* to devour *(prey)*; *(of human beings)* to devour, to gobble up, to wolf *(food)*; **les flammes ont dévoré le bâtiment,** the flames devoured the building; **pour ne pas être dévoré par les moustiques,** so as not to be eaten alive by mosquitos; **l'ambition/la jalousie/***etc* **la dévore,** she is devoured by *or* eaten up with ambition/jealousy/*etc*; **d. un livre,** to devour a book; **d. qn des yeux,** to devour s.o. with one's eyes; **d. sa fortune,** to squander one's fortune; **il ne faut pas que cela dévore tout votre temps,** don't let it take up all your time; **l'angoisse le dévore,** he's sick with worry; **d. la route,** to tear along, to eat up the miles.

dévoreur, -euse [devɔrœr, -øz] *n* devourer; **d. de livres/de films,** avid reader, bookworm/avid cinema-goer; **d. de pellicule,** *Cin* avid *or* keen cinema-goer; *Phot* avid *or* keen photographer.

dévot, -ote [devo, -ɔt] **1** *adj* **(a)** *(fervent)* devout, religious, pious; **être d. à un saint,** to be a votary of a saint; **(b)** *Péj* sanctimonious *(person)*. **2** *n* **(a)** devout person; **(b)** *Péj* bigot; *Arch* **faux d.,** hypocrite.

dévotement [devɔtmɑ̃] *adv* devoutly.

dévotion [devosjɔ̃] *nf* **(a)** *(ferveur)* devoutness, piety; **faire ses dévotions,** to make one's devotions, to say one's prayers; *Péj* **être confit en d.,** to be sanctimonious; **fausse d.,** hypocrisy; **(b)** *(adoration)* devotion; **avoir une grande d. pour qn/qch,** to have a great devotion for *or* to be devoted *or* extremely attached to s.o./sth; **avoir une grande d. pour un acteur/écrivain,** to be a great admirer of an actor/a writer.

dévoué [devwe] *adj* devoted, staunch, loyal *(friend etc)*; **votre (tout) d.,** ≈ yours sincerely.

dévouement [devumɑ̃] *nm* **(a)** self-sacrifice, devotion to duty; dedication *(of scientist etc)*; **(b)** *(amour)* devotion, devotedness; **soigner qn avec d.,** to nurse *or* look after s.o. devotedly.

dévouer [devwe] **1** *vt* **(a) d. son temps/son énergie à une cause,** to devote one's time/energy to a cause; **(b)** *Arch* to dedicate, to consecrate *(s.o., sth)*. **2 se dévouer** *vpr* **(a)** *(se consacrer)* to sacrifice oneself; **se d. pour qn,** to sacrifice oneself for s.o.; **elle lui est toute dévouée,** she is entirely devoted to him; **il faut que quelqu'un se dévoue,** SOMEONE has to do it; **il est toujours prêt à se d.,** he is always ready to sacrifice himself; **(b)** *Vieilli* to devote oneself, to dedicate oneself; **se d. au secours des pauvres,** to devote oneself to the poor.

dévoyé, -ée [devwaje] **1** *adj* astray. **2** *n* delinquent; **un jeune d.,** a delinquent.

dévoyer [devwaje] *v* **(je dévoie, n. dévoyons; je dévoierai) 1** *vt Litt* to lead *(s.o.)* astray. **2 se dévoyer** *vpr* to go astray; to stray *(esp from path of duty)*.

déwatté [dewate] *adj El* wattless *(current)*.

dextérité [dɛksterite] *nf* dexterity, skill, skilfulness; **conduire ses affaires avec d.,** to manage one's business cleverly *or* skilfully.

dextrine [dɛkstrin] *nf Ch Ind* dextrin.

diabète [djabɛt] *nm Méd* diabetes; **d. sucré,** diabetes mellitus; **avoir du d.,** to have diabetes.

diabétique [djabetik] *Méd* **1** *adj* diabetic; **être d.,** to be (a) diabetic, to have diabetes. **2** *n* diabetic; **chocolat/confiture/***etc* **pour diabétiques,** diabetic chocolate/jam/*etc*.

diable [djɑbl] *nm* **(a)** devil; **le d.,** the devil, Satan, *F* Old Nick; **en d.,** extremely; *F* **faire le d. (à quatre),** to kick up a row; **tirer le d. par la queue,** to be hard up; **c'est bien le d. si ...,** it would be surprising if ...; *Can* **parler au d.,** to be psychic; **allez au d.!,** go to the devil!, go to hell!; **que le d. l'emporte!,** the devil take him!; **(que) le d. m'emporte si j'y comprends quelque chose!,** I'll be hanged *or* damned if I understand (it)!; **il demeure au d.,** he lives miles away; **au d. vauvert** *ou* **vert,** a long way (away), at the back of beyond; **c'est le d. pour lui faire entendre raison,** it's damned hard to make him see reason; **ce n'est pas le d.,** *(c'est facile)* it's not that difficult; *(ce n'est pas grave)* it's nothing to worry about; **où d. est-il allé?,** where the devil has he gone?; **d.!,** heavens!; **bruit de tous les diables,** the devil *or* a hell of a din; **à la d.,** anyhow; **c'est fait à la d.,** it's been done any old how; **pauvre d.!,** poor beggar!; **un drôle de petit d.,** a funny little chap; **un grand d.,** a big fellow; **c'est un bon d.,** he's not a bad type; **ce d. de parapluie,** that wretched umbrella; **un d. de temps, un temps du d.,** wretched *or* dreadful weather; **j'ai une faim du d.,** I'm ravenous; **il fait un froid/une chaleur du d.,** it's dreadfully cold/hot. **(b)** *(chariot)* (two-wheeled) trolley; *Rail* (railway porter's) barrow, luggage truck; *(jouet)* Jack in the box; **d. de mer,** *(poisson)* angler (fish), frog fish.

diablement [djɑbləmɑ̃] *adv F* devilish(ly) *(strong, good, funny etc)*; **il y a d. longtemps,** it's a hell of a long time ago; **il faisait d. froid,** it was hellish(ly) cold.

diablerie [djɑbləri] *nf* **(a)** *(espièglerie) F* devilry, devilment; **(b)** *Arch (sorcellerie)* devilry, sorcery; **(c)** *(intrigue)* machination, (evil) intrigue.

diablotin [djɑblɔtɛ̃] *nf* **(a)** *(petit diable)* little devil, imp; *(enfant coquin)* mischievous child, imp; **(b)** *(pétard)* (Christmas) cracker.

diabolique [djabɔlik] *adj* diabolic(al), fiendish; **possession d.,** demoniacal possession.

diaboliquement [djabɔlikmɑ̃] *adv* diabolically, fiendishly.

diabolo [djabɔlo] *nm* **(a)** *(jouet)* diabolo; **(b)** *(boisson)* lemonade (drink) with syrup; **d. menthe,** lemonade and mint (cordial).

diachronie [djakrɔni] *nf Ling* diachrony.

diachronique [djakrɔnik] *adj Ling* diachronic.

diaconesse [djakɔnɛs] *nf* deaconess.

diacre [djakr] *nm Rel* deacon.

diacritique [djakritik] *adj Ling* diacritic(al) *(mark, sign)*; **signe d.,** diacritic(al).

diadème [djadɛm] *nm* tiara.

diagnose [djagnoz] *nf* **(a)** *Méd* diagnostics; *(diagnostic)* diagnosis; **(b)** *Biol* diagnosis.

diagnostic [djagnɔstik] *nm Méd* diagnosis, *pl* diagnoses *(of disease)*; **porter un d.,** to make a diagnosis; **le d. de la maladie doit être porté le plus tôt possible,** the disease must be diagnosed as soon as possible; **quel est votre d.?,** what's your diagnosis?; *Fig* **le d. actuel de la situation,** the current diagnosis of the situation; *Ordinat* **programme de d.,** diagnostics program.

diagnostique [djagnɔstik] *adj Méd* diagnostic *(skill, sign etc)*.

diagnostiquer [djagnɔstike] *vt Méd & Fig* to diagnose; **la maladie a été diagnostiqué comme étant du diabète,** the illness has been diagnosed as diabetes.

diagnostiqueur [djagnɔstikœr] *nm Méd* diagnostician; **elle n'est pas bon d.,** she's not a good diagnostician, diagnosis is not her strong point.

diagonal, -ale, -aux [djagɔnal, -o] **1** *adj Math etc* diagonal. **2** *nf* **diagonale,** diagonal (line); **en diagonale,** di-

agonally.
diagonalement [djagɔnalmɑ̃] *adv* diagonally.
diagramme [djagram] *nm* diagram.
diagraphe [djagraf] *nm* diagraph.
dialectal, -aux [djalɛktal, -o] *adj Ling* dialectal.
dialecte [djalɛkt] *nm* dialect; **en d.**, in dialect.
dialecticien, -ienne [djalɛktisjɛ̃, -jɛn] *n* dialectician.
dialectique [djalɛktik] **1** *adj* dialectic(al) (*argument*). **2** *nf* dialectics.
dialectiquement [djalɛktikmɑ̃] *adv* dialectically.
dialogue [djalɔg] *nm* dialogue, *US* dialog; *Pol* dialogue, talks; *Ordinat* **mode de d.**, interactive mode; **c'est un d. de sourds,** it's a dialogue of the deaf.
dialoguer [djalɔge] **1** *vi* to hold a dialogue *or US* dialog, to converse; *Ordinat* **d. avec son ordinateur,** to interact with one's computer. **2** *vt Littér* to write (*literary work*) in dialogue *or US* dialog form.
dialoguiste [djalɔgist] *n Cin* screenwriter.
dialyse [djaliz] *nf Méd Ch* dialysis; *Méd* **il faut qu'on lui fasse une d. tous les mois,** he has to have dialysis once a month.
dialyser [djalize] *vt Ch* to dialyse.
dialyseur [djalizœr] *nm Méd* dialysis machine.
diam [djam] *nm F* (*diamant*) sparkler, rock.
diamant [djamɑ̃] *nm* diamond; **d. de première eau,** diamond of the first water; **d. brut,** rough diamond; **d. de vitrier,** glazier's diamond, diamond point.
diamantaire [djamɑ̃tɛr] **1** *adj* diamond-like, sparkling. **2** *nm* (*tailleur*) diamond cutter; (*vendeur*) diamond merchant.
diamanté [djamɑ̃te] *adj* set with diamonds.
diamanter [djamɑ̃te] *vt* **(a)** to set (*piece*) with diamonds; **(b)** to make (*sth*) shine like a diamond.
diamantifère [djamɑ̃tifɛr] *adj Géol etc* diamantiferous (*region etc*); diamond-yielding *or* -bearing (*gravel etc*).
diamétral, -aux [djametral, -o] *adj* diametric(al), diametral (*line etc*).
diamétralement [djametralmɑ̃] *adv* diametrically; **opinions d. opposées,** diametrically opposed views.
diamètre [djamɛtr] *nm Math etc* diameter; **la roue a 60 cm de d.**, the wheel is 60 cm in diameter *or* 60 cm across.
diane [djan] *nf Mil etc Arch & Litt* reveille; **battre** *ou* **sonner la d.**, to sound the reveille.
Diane [djan] *nf* Diana.
diantre [djɑ̃tr] *int Arch & Litt* (*euphemistic form of* **diable**) **que d. désirez-vous?**, what the devil do you want?; **d., c'est cher!**, it's devilish expensive!
diapason [djapazɔ̃] *nm Mus* **(a)** (*ton*) diapason, pitch; *Fig* **se mettre au d. de la compagnie,** to adapt oneself to the company, to fall in with the mood of the company; **(b)** (*appareil*) tuning fork; (*à vent*) pitch pipe; **(c)** (*registre*) compass, range (*of the voice*).
diaphane [djafan] *adj* diaphanous.
diaphragme [djafragm] *nm* **(a)** *Anat* diaphragm; **(b)** *Tech* diaphragm (*of telescope, electric cell etc*); *Phot* diaphragm stop (*of lens*); soundbox (*of speaker etc*); *Méd* (*contraceptive*) diaphragm, *F* (Dutch) cap; *Phot* **d. iris,** iris diaphragm.
diaphragmer [djafragme] *vt Phot* to stop down (*lens*).
diapo [djapo] *nf Phot F* slide, transparency.
diapositive [djapɔzitiv] *nf Phot* transparency, slide; **d. en couleurs,** colour slide.
diapré [djapre] *adj* variegated, mottled, speckled.
diaprer [djapre] *vt* to variegate, to mottle, to speckle.
diarrhée [djare] *nf Méd* diarrhoea; **avoir la d.**, to have diarrhoea.
diarrhéique [djareik] **1** *adj Méd* diarrhoeic, diarrhoeal. **2** *n* diarrhoeic subject.
diaspora [djaspɔra] *nf Rel Pol etc* diaspora.
diastase [djastɑz] *nf Ch* diastase.
diastasique [djastɑzik] *adj Ch* diastatic, diastasic.
diastole [djastɔl] *nf Physiol* diastole.
diathermie [djatɛrmi] *nf Méd* diathermy.
diathèse [djatɛz] *nf Méd* diathesis, predisposition (to disease).
diatomée [djatɔme] *nf* (*algue*) diatom.
diatomique [djatɔmik] *adj Ch* diatomic.
diatonique [djatɔnik] *adj Mus* diatonic (*scale, interval*).
diatoniquement [djatɔnikmɑ̃] *adv Mus* diatonically.
diatribe [djatrib] *nf* diatribe (**contre,** against).
dichotomie [dikɔtɔmi] *nf* dichotomy.
dichotomique [dikɔtɔmik] *adj* dichotomous; **test d.**, yes/no test, true/false test.
dichromatique [dikrɔmatik] *adj* dichromatic.
dico [diko] *nm F* dictionary.
dicotylédone [dikɔtiledɔn] *Bot* **1** *adj* dicotyledonous. **2** *nf* dicotyledon.
Dictaphone ® [diktafɔn] *nm* Dictaphone ®.
dictateur [diktatœr] *nm* dictator; **ton de d.**, dictatorial tone.
dictatorial, -iaux [diktatɔrjal, -jo] *adj* dictatorial.
dictatorialement [diktatɔrjalmɑ̃] *adv* dictatorially.
dictature [diktatyr] *nf* dictatorship.
dictée [dikte] *nf* dictation; *Scol* dictation (exercise); **d. musicale,** musical dictation; **prendre la d.**, (*d'une secrétaire*) to take dictation; **écrire qch sous la d. de qn,** to write sth at s.o.'s dictation; **agir sous la d. de son cœur,** to follow the dictates of one's heart.
dicter [dikte] *vt* to dictate (*letter etc*); **d. des conditions,** to dictate *or* lay down conditions; **votre conscience vous dictera votre devoir,** you must follow the dictates of your conscience; **d. sa volonté à qn,** to impose one's will on s.o.; **je ne veux pas qu'on me dicte ma conduite!**, I won't be dictated to!
diction [diksjɔ̃] *nf* diction; **professeur de d.**, elocution teacher.
dictionnaire [diksjɔnɛr] *nm* dictionary; **d. anglais-français,** English-French dictionary; **d. de poche,** pocket dictionary; **d. géographique,** gazetteer; **le d. d'un enfant de 10 ans,** the vocabulary of a 10 year-old child; *F* **c'est un d. ambulant,** he's a walking encyclopaedia; **elle parle comme un d.**, she talks as if she'd swallowed the dictionary.
dicton [diktɔ̃] *nm* (common) saying.
didacticiel [didaktisjɛl] *nm Ordinat* educational software.
didactique [didaktik] **1** *adj* **(a)** (*ouvrage, voyage*) educational; **(b)** (*mot etc*) technical. **2** *nf* didactics.
didactiquement [didaktikmɑ̃] *adv* educationally.
didactyle [didaktil] *adj Zool* didactyl(e).
dièdre [djɛdr] *Math* **1** *adj* dihedral (*angle*). **2** *nm* dihedron.
diélectrique [dielɛktrik] *El* **1** *adj* dielectric; insulating, non-conducting (*medium*). **2** *nm* dielectric.
diérèse [djerɛz] *nf Ling Chir* diaeresis.
dièse [djɛz] *Mus* **1** *nm* sharp; **double d.**, double sharp. **2** *adj* sharp; **fa d.**, F sharp.
diesel [djezɛl] *nm* diesel (engine).
diéséliste [djezelist] *n Tech* diesel fitter.
diéser [djeze] *vt* (**je dièse, n. diésons; je diéserai**) *Mus* to sharpen, *Am* to sharp (*note*).
diète¹ [djɛt] *nf* diet; (*jeûne*) fast; **d. lactée,** milk diet; **être à la d.**, (*régime*) to be on a diet; (*jeûne*) to be fasting; **mettre qn à la d.**, to put s.o. on a diet.
diète² *nf Hist Pol* diet.
diététicien, -ienne [djetetisjɛ̃, -jɛn] *n* dietitian, dietician.
diététique [djetetik] *Méd* **1** *adj* dietetic. **2** *nf* dietetics.
dieu, -ieux [djø] **1** *nm* **(a)** god; **les dieux d'Égypte,** the gods of Egypt; **grands dieux!**, heavens!; **faire de qch son d.**, to turn sth into a cult (object); **beau comme un d.**, like a Greek god;
(b) D., God; **la voix de D.**, the voice of God; **un homme de D.**, a holy man; **s'il plaît à D., si D. le veut,** please God, God willing; **D. merci!**, thank God!; **le bon D.**, God; **recevoir le bon D.**, to receive the Holy Sacrament; **on lui donnerait le bon D. sans confession,** he looks as though butter wouldn't melt in his mouth; **pour l'amour de D.**, for goodness' *or* God's sake; **devant D. et devant les hommes,** ≈ by Almighty God; **D. sait si j'ai travaillé,** heaven *or* God knows I've worked hard enough; **cela va D. sait comme,** God knows why, but things are alright.
2 *int* **(a)** (*admitted*) **mon D.!**, **grand D.!**, heavens (above)!; **mon D. oui!**, why *or* well, yes; **mon D. je veux bien!**, well, I don't mind!;
(b) (*profane*) **bon D.!**, **D. de D.!**, **bon D. de bon D.!**, **(sacré) nom de D.!**, for Christ's sake!, God almighty!, hell!
diffamant [difamɑ̃] *adj* (*paroles*) slanderous; (*écrits*) libellous.
diffamateur, -trice [difamatœr, -tris] *n* (*en paroles*) slanderer; (*par écrit*) libeller.
diffamation [difamɑsjɔ̃] *nf* defamation; (*paroles*) slander; (*écrits*) libel.
diffamatoire [difamatwar] *adj* defamatory; (*paroles*) slanderous; (*écrits*) libellous.
diffamer [difame] *vt* to defame; (*en paroles*) to slander; (*par écrit*) to libel.
différé [difere] *adj* deferred (*payment, call, annuity etc*); *El* **coupe-circuit à action différée,** time-lag cutout; *Phot* **obturateur à action différée,** delayed action shutter; *Rad TV* **émission en d.**, (pre-)recorded broadcast; *Ordinat* **traitement d.**, off-line processing.
différemment [diferamɑ̃] *adv* differently.

différence [diferɑ̃s] *nf* difference; **d. de goûts,** differences of taste; **la d. de A à B** *ou* **entre A et B,** the difference between A and B; **d. d'âges/d'opinions,** age difference/difference of opinions; **il n'y a pas de d. entre eux,** there's nothing to choose between them; **cela ne fait pas de d.,** it makes no difference *or* no odds; **c'est ça qui a fait la d.,** that's what made the difference; **quelle d. avec ...!,** what a difference from ...!; **faire la d. d'une chose avec une autre** *ou* **entre une chose et une autre,** to distinguish *or* discriminate between two things; **je vous dois la d.,** I'll owe you the difference; **à la d. de ...,** unlike ...; **à la d. que ...,** with this difference that ..., except that ... .

différenciateur, -trice [diferɑ̃sjatœr, -tris] *adj* differentiating.

différenciation [diferɑ̃sjɑsjɔ̃] *nf* differentiation.

différencier [diferɑ̃sje] *v* (*impf & pr sub* **n. différenciions**) **1** *vt* to differentiate (**de, d'avec,** from); *Math* to obtain the differential (coefficient) of (*equation etc*); **rien ne les différencie,** there's nothing to differentiate them. **2 se différencier** *vpr* **(a)** to be different (from each other), to differ; **(b)** to differentiate oneself (from s.o. *or* sth else).

différend [diferɑ̃] *nm* difference, dispute, disagreement (**entre,** between); **avoir un d. avec qn,** to disagree with s.o.; **régler un d.** to settle a difference *or* a dispute.

différent [diferɑ̃] *adj* different; **différents,** various; **différentes personnes l'ont vu,** different *or* various *or* a number of people saw him; **à différentes reprises,** at various times, off and on; **mœurs différentes des nôtres,** habits different from ours; **un avis d. du premier,** a different opinion from the first, an opinion that differs from the first; **ils habitent des maisons différentes,** they live in different houses; **une différente recette,** another *or* a different recipe; **je me suis adressé à une personne différente,** I approached a different *or* another person.

différentiation [diferɑ̃sjɑsjɔ̃] *nf Math* differentiation.

différentiel, -ielle [diferɑ̃sjɛl] **1** *adj* differential (*calculus, gear etc*); discriminating, discriminatory (*duty, tariff*). **2** *nm Aut etc* differential. **3** *nf Math* **différentielle,** differential.

différer [difere] *v* (**je diffère, n. différons; je différerai**) **1** *vt* to defer, to postpone (*judgment*); to defer, to put off (*payment*); **d. de faire qch,** to defer *or* put off doing sth. **2** *vi* to differ; **ils diffèrent entre eux par la taille,** they differ from one another in height; **ils diffèrent de race et de langue,** they are different in race and speech; **d. d'opinion,** to differ in opinion; **nous différons d'opinion,** our opinions differ.

difficile [difisil] **1** *adj* **(a)** difficult (*work, situation etc*); **ce raisonnement est d. à suivre,** this argument is difficult *or* hard to follow; **circonstances difficiles,** difficulties, trying circumstances; **les temps sont difficiles,** times are hard; **d'accès d.,** difficult to get to; **le plus d. est fait,** we've done the hardest part; **il m'est d. d'accepter,** it is difficult for me to accept, I can't very well accept; **(b)** difficult to get on with, hard to please (*person*); **enfant d.,** difficult *or* problem child; **elle est d. à vivre,** she is difficult to get on with; **il est d. sur la nourriture,** he's difficult *or* fussy about his food. **2** *n* **faire le d.,** to be hard to please; **ne faites pas le d.,** don't be difficult, stop fussing.

difficilement [difisilmɑ̃] *adv* with difficulty, not easily; **il apprend d.,** he is a slow learner.

difficulté [difikylte] *nf* difficulty; **la d. du problème,** the difficulty of the problem; **être en d.,** (*d'un nageur*) to be in difficulties *or* trouble; **il est en d.,** (*financièrement*) he's in trouble; **cela ne présente aucune d.,** there is no difficulty about it; **c'est sans d.,** it's easy; **aimer la d.,** to like to make things difficult for oneself; **faire** *ou* **élever des difficultés,** to create obstacles, to raise objections, to make difficulties; **avoir de la d. à faire qch,** to have difficulty in doing sth, to find it hard *or* difficult to do sth; **avoir des difficultés matérielles,** to be in financial difficulties; **créer des difficultés à qn,** to put difficulties in s.o.'s way; **cela ne fera pas de d., que je sache,** there won't be any difficulty as far as I know.

diffluence [diflyɑ̃s] *nf* diffluence.

diffluent [diflyɑ̃] *adj* diffluent (*tumour, stream*).

difforme [difɔrm] *adj* deformed, misshapen, twisted (*person, limb*); **troncs d'arbres difformes,** gnarled tree-trunks.

difformité [difɔrmite] *nf* deformity; malformation.

diffracter [difrakte] *vt Opt* to diffract.

diffraction [difraksjɔ̃] *nf Opt* diffraction.

diffus [dify, -yz] *adj* diffused (*light*); diffuse (*matter, inflammation etc*); vague (*thought etc*); **éclairs diffus,** sheet lightning; **style d.,** diffuse *or* prolix style; **écrivain d.,** verbose *or* prolix writer.

diffusément [difyzemɑ̃] *adv* diffusedly; (*penser*) vaguely; (*écrire*) diffusely; **la musique/la conversation/***etc* **nous parvenait d.,** we couldn't hear the music/the conversation/*etc* very clearly.

diffuser [difyze] **1** *vt* to diffuse, to spread (*light, heat etc*); **(b)** to broadcast (*programme etc*); to spread (*ideas, news*); to distribute, to circulate (*books, newspapers*). **2 se diffuser** *vpr* to spread.

diffuseur [difyzœr] *nm* **(a)** diffuser (*of light*); mixer, diffuser (*in engine*); **(b)** spreader (*of ideas, news etc*); distributor (*of books, newspapers*).

diffusion [difyzjɔ̃] *nf* **(a)** diffusion (*of light, heat etc*); **(b)** spreading (*of news etc*); broadcasting (*of programme*); distribution (*of books*).

digérer [diʒere] *v* (**je digère, n. digérons; je digérerai**) **1** *vt* **(a)** to digest (*food*); **je ne digère pas le porc,** pork does not agree with me; **(b)** *Fig* to digest, to think over, to assimilate (*what one reads, learns*); *F* (*accepter*) to swallow, to stomach, to put up with (*insult etc*); **vérités dures à d.,** unpalatable truths. **2** *vi* **je digère mal,** I have a bad digestion.

digest [daiʒɛst, diʒɛst] *nm Journ F* digest.

digeste [diʒɛst] *adj F* easily digestible.

digestibilité [diʒɛstibilite] *nf* digestibility.

digestible [diʒɛstibl] *adj* digestible.

digestif, -ive [diʒɛstif, -iv] **1** *adj* (*de la digestion*) digestive; (*substance*) which aids digestion; **le tube d.,** the digestive tract; **avoir des troubles digestifs,** to have digestive problems. **2** *nm* brandy, liqueur.

digestion [diʒɛstjɔ̃] *nf* digestion; **elle a une d. difficile,** she has digestive problems.

digit [diʒit] *nm Ordinat* **(a)** (*chiffre*) digit; **(b)** (*caractère*) character.

digital, -ale, -aux [diʒital, -o] **1** *adj* **(a)** *Ordinat* **code d.,** digital code; **affichage d.,** digital display; **horloge/montre à affichage d.,** digital watch/clock; **(b)** digital (*nerve etc*); **empreinte digitale,** fingerprint; **prendre les empreintes digitales de qn,** to take s.o.'s fingerprints, to fingerprint s.o.. **2** *nf Bot Méd* **digitale,** digitalis; *Bot* **digitale pourprée,** foxglove.

digitaline [diʒitalin] *nf Ch Pharm* digitalin.

digitaliser [diʒitalize] *vt Ordinat* to digitize.

digne [diɲ] *adj* **(a)** deserving, worthy (**de,** of); **cela est d. de récompense,** that deserves a reward; **il est d. qu'on le remercie,** he deserves thanks *or* to be thanked; **d. d'éloges,** praiseworthy; **d. de remarque,** noteworthy; **prouver qu'on est une mère d.,** to prove that one is a fit mother; **d. d'une mère,** motherly; **d. de ce nom,** worthy of the name; **il n'est pas d. de vivre,** he is not fit to live; **(b)** dignified (*air etc*); **(c) un d. homme,** a worthy man.

dignement [diɲmɑ̃] *adv* with dignity.

dignitaire [diɲitɛr] *nm* dignitary (*of the Church*).

dignité [diɲite] *nf* **(a)** (*grandeur*) dignity; **air/ton de d.,** dignified air/tone; **elle manque de d.,** she's undignified; **elle fit une entrée pleine de d.,** she came in with great dignity; **(b)** (*haute fonction*) high position, dignity; **être élevé à la d. de chancelier,** to be promoted *or* to rise to the dignity of chancellor; **installer qn dans une d.,** to install s.o. in an office.

digramme [digram] *nm Ling* digraph.

digraphie [digrafi] *nf Com* double-entry bookkeeping.

digression [digrɛsjɔ̃] *nf* digression, departure from the subject; **faire une d.,** to digress, to wander from the point.

digue [dig] *nf HydE* dyke, dam, causeway; embankment (*of waterway etc*); breakwater (*of stone*); sea wall (*against erosion*); barrier (*to passions etc*); **opposer une d. aux eaux/à la colère,** to stem the waters/a flood of anger.

diktat [diktat] *nm* diktat, dictate.

dilapidateur, -trice [dilapidatœr, -tris] **1** *adj* spendthrift, wasteful. **2** *n* (*de fortune*) spendthrift, squanderer; (*de fonds publics, de biens*) embezzler.

dilapidation [dilapidɑsjɔ̃] *nf* **(a)** wasting, squandering (*of fortune etc*); **(b)** embezzlement, misappropriation (*of funds*).

dilapider [dilapide] *vt* **(a)** to waste, to squander (*fortune etc*); **(b)** to misappropriate, to embezzle (*funds*).

dilatable [dilatabl] *adj* dilatable, expansible.

dilatant [dilatɑ̃] **1** *adj* dilating, dilative (*force etc*). **2** *nm Chir* dilator.

dilatateur, -trice [dilatatœr, -tris] **1** *adj* dilating, dilative. **2** *nm Chir* dilator.

dilatation [dilatɑsjɔ̃] *nf* dilation (*of pupils*); distension (*of stomach*); expansion (*of gas*); *Constr* **joint de d.,** expansion *or* dilatation joint.

dilater [dilate] **1** *vt* (*agrandir*) to dilate, to expand; to distend (*stomach*); *Fig* **d. le cœur,** to cheer *or* gladden the heart. **2 se dilater** *vpr* to dilate, to expand; (*of the stomach*) to become distended.

dilatoire [dilatwar] *adj Jur etc* dilatory; delaying (*tactics etc*); **faire des réponses dilatoires,** to stall for time.

dilemme [dilɛm] *nm* dilemma; **être dans un d.,** to be in a dilemma; **être dans un profond d.,** to be on the horns of a dilemma.

dilettante [dilɛtɑ̃t] *n* dilettante, amateur; **faire des sciences en d.,** to dabble in science.

dilettantisme [dilɛtɑ̃tism] *nm* dilettantism, amateurism.

diligemment [diliʒamɑ̃] *adv Arch & Litt* **(a)** (*avec soin*) diligently; **(b)** (*avec rapidité*) promptly, quickly.

diligence [diliʒɑ̃s] *nf* **(a)** *Litt* (*soin*) diligence, industry, application; **(b)** *Litt* (*rapidité*) haste, dispatch; **faire d.,** to hurry, to make haste; **(c)** (*véhicule*) (stage)coach; **(d)** *Jur* proceedings.

diligent [diliʒɑ̃] *adj Litt* **(a)** (*appliqué*) diligent, industrious; **soins diligents,** assiduous care; **(b)** (*rapide*) speedy, prompt.

diluer [dilɥe] *vt* to dilute (**de,** with); to water down (*drink etc*); to thin down (*paint*); to weaken (*power etc*).

dilution [dilysjɔ̃] *nf* dilution; thinning down (*of paint*) watering down (*of drink etc*).

diluvien, -ienne [dilyvjɛ̃, -jɛn] *adj* **(a)** diluvian (*fossils etc*); diluvial (*deposit, clay etc*); **(b)** *Fig* **pluie diluvienne,** torrential rain, downpour.

dimanche [dimɑ̃ʃ] *nm* Sunday; **d. des Rameaux/de Pâques,** Palm/Easter Sunday; **venez me voir d.,** come and see me on Sunday; **il vient le d.,** he comes on Sundays; **habits du d.,** (one's) Sunday clothes *or* best; *F* **chauffeur/peintre du d.,** weekend *or* Sunday driver/weekend painter.

dîme [dim] *nf Hist* tithe.

dimension [dimɑ̃sjɔ̃] *nf* (*grandeur*) dimension, size; **à deux/trois dimensions,** two-/three-dimensional; **prendre les dimensions de qch,** to take the measurements of sth; **la d. d'une gaffe,** the enormity of a blunder; *Fig* **prendre les dimensions d'une expédition,** to take on the dimensions of an expedition; *Fig* **prendre les dimensions de qn,** to size s.o. up; **taillé à la d.,** cut to size; **coupé dans sa grande/petite d.,** cut lengthways/crossways; **ce travail n'est pas à la d. de son talent,** this work is not equal to his talent.

diminué, -ée [diminɥe] **1** *adj* fully-fashioned (*clothes*); *Tricot* decreased (*row*); (*affaibli*) enfeebled, weakened; *Mus* diminished (*interval*); **colonne diminuée,** tapering column; **c'est un homme d.,** he is not the man he was. **2** *n* **d. physique,** physically handicapped person.

diminuer [diminɥe] **1** *vt* to lessen, to diminish; *Tricot* to decrease (*number of stitches*); to reduce, to bring down (*prices*); to lessen (*authority etc*); to taper (*column*); **d. les chances de succès,** to lessen *or* reduce the likelihood *or* chances of success; **d. sa consommation d'alcool,** to reduce *or* cut down one's alcohol consumption; **d. l'ardeur des foules,** to decrease the crowds' fervour; **cette maladie l'a considérablement diminuée,** the illness has weakened her considerably; **cela vous diminuerait aux yeux du public,** it would lower you in the eyes of the public; **d. le son,** to reduce the volume (of sound).

2 *vi* to diminish, to decrease, to lessen; (*of fever etc*) to abate; (*of profits*) to fall off, to decline; (*of prices*) to fall; (*of column*) to taper; **d. de vitesse,** to slow down, to reduce speed; **les jours diminuent,** the days are drawing in *or* are growing shorter; **ses forces ont diminué,** his strength has declined *or* is declining; *Nau* **d. de toile,** to shorten sail; *Nau* **d. de profondeur** *ou* **de fond,** (*of water*) to shoal.

3 se diminuer *vpr* to lower *or* demean oneself.

diminutif, -ive [diminytif, -iv] **1** *adj* diminutive; **suffixe d.,** diminutive suffix. **2** *nm* diminutive; **appeler qn par** *ou* **de son d.,** to call s.o. by his pet name *or* by his nickname; **'jupette' est le d. de 'jupe',** 'jupette' is the diminutive (form) of 'jupe'.

diminution [diminysjɔ̃] *nf* diminution, lessening; reduction, decrease, lowering (*of price etc*); abatement (*of fever etc*); cutting down (*of expenses*); slackening (*of speed*); tapering (*of column*); *Tricot* **commencer les diminutions,** to begin decreasing.

dimorphe [dimɔrf] *adj Biol* dimorphic, dimorphous.

dimorphisme [dimɔrfism] *nm Biol* dimorphism.

dinanderie [dinɑ̃dri] *nf* brassware; (*de cuisine*) brass kitchen utensils.

dinar [dinar] *nm* dinar.

dinde [dɛ̃d] *nf* **(a)** (*volaille*) turkey hen; *Culin* turkey; **(b)** *F* (*femme sotte*) stupid woman.

dindon [dɛ̃dɔ̃] *nm* turkey (cock); *Fig* **être le d. de la farce,** to be fooled *or* duped, to be made a fool of.

dindonneau, -eaux [dɛ̃dɔno] *nm* young turkey, turkey poult.

dîner¹ [dine] *nm* dinner; *Can Belg* lunch; **je donne un d. ce soir,** I'm having a dinner party tonight; **d.-débat/-concert,** dinner-debate/dinner-concert.

dîner² *vi* to dine, to have dinner; *Can Belg* to (have) lunch; **d. en ville,** to dine out; **à quelle heure dînez-vous?,** what time do you have dinner?; **avoir/inviter qn à d.,** to have/invite s.o. for *or* to dinner; *Can Belg* **elle est partie d.,** she's gone to lunch; *Prov* **qui dort dîne,** he who sleeps forgets his hunger.

dînette [dinɛt] *nf F* **(a)** (*repas*) dolls' tea party; (*service*) doll's teaset; **(b)** *Fig* informal meal (*between friends*).

dîneur, -euse [dinœr, -øz] *n* diner.

ding [diŋ] *int* ting-a-ling.

dingo¹ [dɛ̃go] *nm* dingo (*of Australia*).

dingo² *adj & n F* = **DINGUE**.

dingue [dɛ̃g] *F* **1** *adj* **(a)** (*fou*) crazy, nuts; **(b)** (*incroyable*) great, terrific. **2** *n* idiot, nutcase, loony.

dinguer [dɛ̃ge] *vi F* **s'en aller d.,** to go sprawling; **envoyer d. qch,** to fling sth away; **envoyer d. qn,** (*l'éconduire*) to send s.o. packing; (*le repousser*) to send s.o. sprawling (**contre,** against).

dinosaure [dinozɔr] *nm* dinosaur.

diocésain, -aine [djɔsezɛ̃, -ɛn] *adj & n Rel* diocesan.

diocèse [djɔsɛz] *nm Rel* diocese.

diode [djɔd] *nf Rad* diode; *Ordinat* **d. électroluminescente,** light-emitting diode; **d. en montage croisé,** cross-connected diode.

dionée [djɔne] *nf* (*plante*) Venus's-flytrap, Venus fly trap.

dionysiaque [djɔnizjak] **1** *adj* (*plante*) dionysiac; **culte d.,** dionysiac cult. **2** *nfpl* **les dionisiaques,** the Dionysia.

dioptrie [djɔptri] *nf Opt* dioptre, *US* diopter.

dioptrique [djɔptrik] **1** *adj* dioptric, refractive. **2** *nf* refraction, dioptrics.

diorama [djɔrama] *nm* diorama.

dioxine [diɔksin] *nf* dioxin.

dioxyde [diɔksid] *nm Ch* dioxide.

diphasé [difaze] *adj Él* two-phase (*system etc*).

diphtérie [difteri] *nf Méd* diphtheria; **avoir la d.,** to have diphtheria.

diphtérique [difterik] *adj Méd* diphther(it)ic, diphtherial.

diphtongue [diftɔ̃g] *nf Ling* diphthong.

diphtonguer [diftɔ̃ge] *vt Ling* to diphthongize.

diplégie [dipleʒi] *nf Méd* diplegia.

diplodocus [diplɔdɔkys] *nm* diplodocus.

diplomate [diplɔmat] **1** *nm* **(a)** diplomat; **un air d.,** a diplomatic appearance; **(b)** *Culin* ≈ trifle. **2** *adj* diplomatic.

diplomatie [diplɔmasi] *nf* **(a)** *Pol* diplomacy; **entrer dans la d.,** to enter the diplomatic service; **(b)** (*tact*) diplomacy; **user de d.,** to be diplomatic.

diplomatique [diplɔmatik] *adj* **(a)** diplomatic (*service, body etc*); **valise d.,** diplomatic bag, *F* the bag, *US* (diplomatic) pouch; **(b)** (*habile*) diplomatic, tactful; **ce n'était pas très d. de sa part,** that was not very diplomatic *or* tactful of him.

diplomatiquement [diplɔmatikmɑ̃] *adv* **(a)** *Pol* diplomatically; **(b)** (*habilement*) tactfully, discreetly.

diplôme [diplom] *nm* diploma (*of teacher, doctor etc*); *Univ* degree; **elle a ses diplômes,** *Univ* she has her degree, she is a graduate; (*elle est professionnelle*) she is qualified.

diplômé, -ée [diplome] **1** *adj Univ* = graduate; (*person*) holding a diploma; **architecte d.,** fully qualified architect. **2** *n* holder of a diploma; *Univ* = graduate.

diplopie [diplɔpi] *nf Méd* double vision.

dipode [dipɔd] *adj & n Zool* biped.

dipsomane [dipsɔman] **, dipsomaniaque** [dipsɔmanjak] *adj & n* dipsomaniac.

dipsomanie [dipsɔmani] *nf* dipsomania.

diptère¹ [diptɛr] *Ent* **1** *adj* dipterous, two-winged. **2** *nm* dipter(an); **les diptères,** the Diptera.

diptère² *adj Archit* dipteral (*temple*).

diptyque [diptik] *nm* diptych.

dire¹ [dir] *nm* statement, assertion; *Jur* allegation; **on ne peut pas se fier à leurs dires,** one cannot trust their statements *or* what they say; **au d. de l'expert,** according to expert opinion *or* the experts; **selon son d., à son d.,** according to him, by his own account.

dire² *vt* (*prp* **disant**; *pp* **dit**; *pr ind* **je dis, n. disons, vous dites, ils disent**; *impf* **je disais**; *p hist* **je dis**; *fu* **je dirai**) **1** *vt* **(a)** to say; **vous ne m'en avez jamais rien dit,** you never mentioned it *or* said a thing about it; **elle a dit 'amboule' au lieu d'ampoule',** she said 'amboule' instead of 'ampoule'; **envoyer d. à qn que ...,** to send word to s.o. that ...; **ce disant ..., ceci dit ...,** with these words ..., having said that ...; **d. du mal de qn,** to speak ill of s.o.; **qu'en dira-t-on?,** what will people say?; **je n'ai rien à d. contre lui,** I have no objection to him; (*à lui reprocher*) I have nothing to reproach him with; **alors, qu'est-ce qu'il t'a dit?,** well, what did he say to you?; **d. ce qu'on pense,** to say what one thinks, to speak one's mind; **un ami, que dis-je! un frère,** a friend, no, a brother!; **c'est justement ce que j'allais d.!,** that's just what I was about to say!; **d. bonjour à qn,** to say hello to s.o.; **d. bonsoir à qn,** to say goodnight to s.o., to wish s.o. goodnight; **comme dit l'autre, comme on dit,** as the saying goes, as they say; **comment dites-vous cela en français?,** how do you say that in French?, what is the French for that?; **d. que oui,** to say yes; **je vous dis que non,** I tell you, no; **là je ne dis pas non,** I wouldn't say no to that;

(b) (*pour informer*) to tell; **elle m'a dit que tu étais à Paris,** she told me you were in Paris; **c'est Sophie qui me l'a dit,** it was Sophie who told me; **d. un secret,** to tell a secret; **il faudra bien que tu le lui dises un jour,** you'll have to tell him some day; **quand je vous le disais!, je vous l'avais bien dit!,** I told you so!, didn't I say so?; **qui vous dit qu'il viendra?,** how do you know he will come?; **qui te l'a dit?,** (*comment le sais-tu?*) who told you?; **qui t'a dit ça?,** (*ce n'est pas vrai*) who told you that?; **puisque je vous le dis,** you can take it from me; **mais je vous dis qu'il ne viendra pas,** but I'm telling you he won't come; *F* **à qui le dites-vous?,** you're telling me!; **ne me dis rien — tu as gagné,** don't tell me *or* let me guess — you've won; **ne me dis pas que tu as gagné!,** don't tell me you've won!; **je me disais que tout était fini,** I thought it was all over; **que dites-vous de ce tableau?,** what do you think of this picture?; **alors, qu'est-ce que tu en dis?,** well, what do you think?; **à vrai d.,** to tell the truth; **pour tout d.,** in a word; **c'est tout d.,** I need say no more; **tout n'est pas dit,** we haven't heard the last of it; *F* **comme qui dirait ...,** ... as you might say; **à ce qu'elle dit,** according to her; **j'ai dit ce que j'avais à d.,** I've said what I had to say; *F* **vous l'avez dit!,** you('ve) said it!; **aussitôt dit, aussitôt fait,** no sooner said than done; **alors c'est dit, voilà qui est dit,** (well then) that's settled, that's decided; **on dirait qu'il va pleuvoir,** it looks like rain; **on dirait qu'il pleut,** it looks as if it is raining; **on dirait du Mozart,** it sounds like Mozart; **on dirait du gin,** it tastes like gin; **on aurait dit que ...,** it seemed as though ...; **dites donc, dis donc,** tell me now ...; (*à qn qui exagère*) look here, *Vieilli* I say; **et d. qu'elle n'a que vingt ans!,** and to think (that) she's only twenty!; **c'est beaucoup d.,** that's saying (quite) a lot, that's going rather far; *F* **je ne te dis que ça,** enough said; *Enf F* **on dirait qu'on serait des astronautes,** let's pretend we're astronauts;

(c) (*ordonner*) **d. à qn de faire qch.,** to tell s.o. to do sth; **faites ce qu'on vous dit,** do as you are told; **dites-lui d'entrer,** tell *or* ask him to come in; **dites qu'on le fasse entrer,** tell *or* ask them to show him in; **tenez-vous cela pour dit,** don't let me have to tell you again, that's my last word, that's it!;

(d) (*indiquer*) to show, to express; **horloge qui dit l'heure exacte,** clock that tells the right time; **cela en dit long sur son courage,** it speaks volumes for his courage; **ce nom ne me dit rien,** the name conveys *or* means nothing to me; **cela ne me disait rien de bon,** I didn't like the look of it;

(e) (*plaire à*) to suit (*s.o.*), to appeal to (*s.o.*); **cette musique ne me dit rien,** this music does not appeal to me, I don't care for this music; **ça te dit?,** what about it?, how about it?; **ça te dit de partir en vacances avec nous?,** how about coming on holiday with us?; **si cela te dit,** if you feel like it;

(f) **faire d. qch à qn,** (*en le forçant*) to make s.o. say *or* tell sth; (*en envoyant qn*) to send word of sth to s.o.; **je lui ai fait d. de venir,** I sent for him; **elle ne se le fit pas d. deux fois,** she didn't wait to be told twice; *F* **je ne vous le fais pas d.,** tell me something I don't know; **faire d. qch par qn,** to send word of sth through s.o.;

(g) **vouloir d.,** to mean; **je veux d. ...,** that is to say ..., I mean ...; **que voulez-vous d. par là?,** what do you mean by that?; **que veut d. ce mot?,** what does this word mean?;

(h) **qu'est-ce à d.?,** what does this mean?; **est-ce à d. qu'il ne viendra pas?,** does this mean he won't come?;

(i) **d. des vers** *ou* **de la poésie,** to recite poetry; **d. son chapelet,** to tell one's beads;

(j) (*with inf*) **vous m'avez dit adorer la musique,** you told me you loved music;

(k) (*faire passer pour*) **on le dit mort,** he is reported (to be) dead, he is said to be dead, they say he is dead; **on dit que c'est lui le coupable,** he is said to be the culprit; **Jacques, dit Jacko,** Jacques, also known as *or* alias *or F* aka Jacko; (*en le présentant*) Jacques, or Jacko to us.

2 *vi* **qui dit mieux?,** (*at auction sale*) any advance?; **dites toujours!,** go on!, say it!; *F* fire away!; **je ne sais comment d.,** I don't know how to put it; **pour ainsi d.,** so as to speak, as it were; **cela va sans d.,** that goes without saying; **il n'y a pas à d.,** there's no denying it, there's no doubt about it; **non mais, dis!,** do you mind, that's a bit thick!; **vous avez beau d.,** you can argue as much as you like.

3 se dire *vpr* **(a)** **comment ça se dit en français?,** how do you say that in French?; **ça se dit en français?,** can you say that in French?;

(b) (*être correct*) **cela ne se dit pas,** that isn't said; **cela ne se dit pas, des choses pareilles,** you don't say things like that;

(c) (*se croire*) **on se dirait en Suisse,** you might think you were in Switzerland.

direct [dirɛkt] **1** *adj* direct, straight; **descendre de qn en ligne directe,** to be a direct descendant of s.o.; **impôts directs,** direct taxes; **une personne directe,** a straightforward *or* direct person; *Gram* **complément d'objet d.,** direct object; *Rail* **train d.,** through train, fast train; *Av* **vol d.,** direct flight. **2** *nm* **(a)** *Rad* **émission en d.,** live broadcast; **(b)** *Boxe* **d. du droit,** straight right.

directement [dirɛktəmɑ̃] *adv* directly, straight; **elle est venu d. vers nous,** she came straight towards us; **se diriger d. au nord,** to go due north; **répondre d. à la question,** to give a direct *or* straight answer to the question; **expédier des marchandises d. à qn,** to send goods direct to s.o..

directeur, -trice [dirɛktœr, -tris] **1** *n* (*qui fait partie du conseil d'administration*) director; (*d'un magasin, un service*) manager; *Scol* headmaster, headmistress, *surtout Am* principal; (*de prison*) governor; (*d'orchestre*) conductor; (*de journal*) editor; (*d'une expédition etc*) leader; **d. gérant,** managing director; **(président) d. général,** general manager; **d. général,** *Com* chief executive officer; *CE* director general; *Admin* **d. général (d'un ministère),** permanent under-secretary; *Rel* **d. (de conscience),** spiritual adviser; *Univ* **d. de thèse,** thesis director. **2** *adj* directing, managing, controlling (*force etc*); guiding (*principle*); **roue directrice,** front wheel; **lignes directrices,** guidelines; **l'idée directrice d'un livre,** the central theme of a book.

directif, -ive [dirɛktif, -iv] *adj* directing, guiding (*rule etc*); *Péj* (*person*) managing; **c'est un chef très d.,** he's the kind of manager who takes all the decisions himself.

direction [dirɛksjɔ̃] *nf* **(a)** conduct (*of undertaking, war*); management, control (*of business, house etc*); leadership (*of party*); **elle a été promue à la d. du journal/du lycée,** she's been promoted to editor/headmistress; **orchestre (placé) sous la d. de Karajan,** orchestra conducted by Karajan; **projet mené sous la d. de Pr. Lacroix,** (*qui y a travaillé activement*) project carried out under the leadership of Prof. Lacroix; (*qui l'a supervisé*) project carried out under the supervision of Prof. Lacroix;

(b) (*personnes*) (*d'une administration*) management; **d. de l'enseignement,** (local) education authority; **une décision prise au niveau de la d.,** a management decision; **j'irai me plaindre à la d.,** I'll complain to the management;

(c) (*lieux*) offices (*of the board*); manager's office; head office (*of firm etc*);

(d) *Aut Nau* steering; *Aut* **d. assistée,** power steering; *Aut* **la d. est un peu raide,** the steering's a bit stiff;

(e) (*orientation*) direction; *Nau* bearing, course; **changer de d.,** to change direction; *surtout Nau* to alter course; **quelle d. ont-ils prise?,** which way did they go?; **ce train va en d. de Paris,** this train goes to Paris; **le courant de l'opinion prend une nouvelle d.,** opinion is taking a new turn.

directionnel, -elle [dirɛksjɔnɛl] *adj* directional (*aerial etc*).

directive [dirɛktiv] *nf* directive, order; *Pol* guideline.

directoire [dirɛktwar] *nm Hist Fr* **le D.,** the Directoire (1795); **chaise D.,** Directoire chair.

directorial[1], -aux [dirɛktɔrjal, -o] *adj Hist Fr* directorial (*constitution, government*).

directorial², -aux *adj* directorial, managerial.
dirigé [diriʒe] *adj* controlled, managed; **économie dirigée,** planned economy; *Scol* **activités dirigées,** extra-curricular activities; *Univ* **travaux dirigés,** classwork; (*au laboratoire*) lab work.
dirigeable [diriʒabl] **1** *adj* dirigible. **2** *nm Av* dirigible (balloon), airship.
dirigeant, -ante [diriʒɑ̃, ɑ̃t] **1** *adj* directing, guiding (*power, principle etc*); **classes dirigeantes,** ruling classes; *Pol* **le rôle d. du parti Communiste,** the leading role of the Communist Party. **2** *n* (*d'un parti etc*) leader; (*d'un pays*) leader, ruler.
diriger [diriʒe] *v* (**je dirigeai(s); n. dirigeons**) **1** *vt* **(a)** to direct, to control, to manage; to run (*business, school etc*); to conduct (*orchestra*); to edit (*newspaper*); to superintend, to conduct (*proceedings, election etc*); **d. la production,** to control production;
(b) to direct, to guide, to lead (*sth, s.o.*); to drive (*horse, car*); to steer, to navigate (*ship*); **d. un colis sur Paris,** to send a parcel off to Paris; **d. ses pas vers ...,** to go *or* move towards ...; **d. son attention sur qch,** to turn one's attention to sth; **d. ses accusations contre qn,** to level *or* aim accusations at s.o.;
(c) to aim, to level, to point (*rifle, gun, telescope*) (**sur,** at); **d. son regard vers** *ou* **sur qn/qch,** to look at s.o./sth.
2 se diriger *vpr* **se d. vers un endroit,** to make one's way towards a place, to make for *or* head for a place; **le navire se dirigea vers le port,** the ship steered *or* headed for the harbour; **se d. vers qn,** to go up to s.o..
dirigisme [diriʒism] *nm Écon* planned economy, dirigisme.
dirigiste [diriʒist] *Écon* **1** *adj* **système d.,** planned economy. **2** *n* advocate *or* exponent of planned economy.
discal, -aux [diskal, -o] *adj Méd* **hernie discale,** slipped disc.
discernable [disɛrnabl] *adj* discernible, visible.
discernement [disɛrnəmɑ̃] *nm* **(a)** (*distinction*) perception, distinguishing (by sight); discrimination (**de ... et de ...,** between ... and ...); **faire le d. de deux choses,** to distinguish *or* discriminate between two things; **(b)** (*jugement*) discernment, judgment; **agir sans d.,** to act without proper judgment; **âge de d.,** age of discretion.
discerner [disɛrne] *vt* **(a)** (*distinguer*) to discern, to distinguish (*sth*); **on discernait une maison dans le lointain,** we could (just) see *or* make out a house in the distance; **(b)** (*différencier*) to distinguish (*sth from sth*); to discriminate (*between sth and sth*); **d. le bien du mal,** to tell right from wrong; **(c)** (*sentir*) to detect, to discern; **d. de la tristesse dans la voix de qn,** to detect a note of sadness in s.o.'s voice.
disciple [disipl] *n* disciple, follower.
disciplinable [disiplinabl] *adj* that can be disciplined.
disciplinaire [disiplinɛr] *adj* disciplinary (*measure, punishment etc*).
discipline [disiplin] *nf* **(a)** (*règlement*) discipline; **garder la d.,** to maintain discipline *or* order; **il ne sait pas maintenir la d.,** he cannot keep discipline; **(b)** *Univ etc* (*matière*) discipline, branch of learning, subject; **(c)** (*fouet*) scourge.
discipliné [disipline] *adj* disciplined.
discipliner [disipline] **1** *vt* to discipline (*school*); to bring (*troops etc*) under control *or* under discipline; **d. ses cheveux avec de la laque,** to control one's hair with lacquer; *Fig* **d. ses instincts,** to curb one's instincts. **2 se discipliner** *vpr* to discipline oneself, to exercise self-control.
disc-jockey [diskʒɔkɛ] *nm* disc-jockey.
disco [disko] *adj & nm Mus* disco.
discobole [diskɔbɔl] *nm* **(a)** *Antiq* discobolus; **(b)** *Sp* discus thrower.
discographie [diskɔgrafi] *nf* set of records; **une d. de Beethoven,** a complete set of Beethoven's works (on record).
discoïde [diskɔid] **, discoïdal, -aux** [diskɔidal, -o] *adj* discoid(al), disc-shaped.
discontinu [diskɔ̃tiny] **1** *adj* discontinuous. **2** *nm* discontinuity.
discontinuer [diskɔ̃tinɥe] **1** *vi* to discontinue, to stop; **parler pendant des heures sans d.,** to talk for hours on end without a break. **2** *vt Arch & Litt* to discontinue, to stop (*sth*).
discontinuité [diskɔ̃tinɥite] *nf* discontinuity.
disconvenance [diskɔ̃vnɑ̃s] *nf Litt* **(a)** unsuitableness, unfitness (*of climate, occupation etc*); **(b)** disparity, dissimilarity (*between persons, objects*).
disconvenir [diskɔ̃vnir] *vi* (*conj like* **venir,** *the aux is* **avoir**) **d. de qch,** not to agree with sth; **je n'en disconviens pas,** I admit it, I don't deny it; **d. que** + *sub*, to deny that ... .
discophile [diskɔfil] *n* record enthusiast.
discordance [diskɔrdɑ̃s] *nf* **(a)** discordance, dissonance (*of sounds*); difference (*of opinions*); clash (*of personalities, colours*); **(b)** *Géol* unconformability (*of strata*).
discordant [diskɔrdɑ̃] *adj* **(a)** discordant, dissonant (*sound*); grating, jarring (*noise*); clashing (*colours*); conflicting (*evidence, opinions etc*); **(b)** *Géol* **stratifications discordantes,** uncomformable strata.
discorde [diskɔrd] *nf* discord, dissension, strife; **semer la d.,** to make trouble.
discothécaire [diskɔtekɛr] *n* record librarian.
discothèque [diskɔtɛk] *nf* **(a)** (*organisme*) record library; (*collection*) record collection *or* library; (*boîte de nuit*) discothèque, *F* disco; **(b)** (*meuble*) record cabinet.
discoureur, -euse [diskurœr, -øz] *n Péj* speechifier.
discourir [diskurir] *vi* (*conj like* **courir**) *souvent Péj* to discourse, to air one's opinions (**sur,** on).
discours [diskur] *nm* **(a)** (*allocution*) speech, oration; **prononcer** *ou* **faire un d.,** to make a speech; **tenir un d. à qn,** to address s.o. at length; *Pol* **d.-programme,** policy statement; **(b)** (*exposé*) discourse, dissertation, treatise; **(c)** (*langage*) diction, language; *Gram* **parties du d.,** parts of speech; **d. indirect/direct,** indirect/direct *or* reported speech; **(d)** (*parole*) talk; **ce sont des d. en l'air,** it's all (idle) talk.
discourtois [diskurtwa] *adj* discourteous.
discourtoisement [diskurtwazmɑ̃] *adv* discourteously.
discourtoisie [diskurtwazi] *nf Arch* discourtesy.
discrédit [diskredi] *nm* discredit, loss of credit; **être en d. auprès de qn,** to be in disfavour with s.o.; **jeter le d. sur qn,** (*d'un scandale etc*) to bring s.o. into disrepute.
discréditer [diskredite] **1** *vt* to disparage, to run down (*s.o.*); to discredit (*theory etc*); **d. l'autorité de qn,** to bring s.o.'s authority into disrepute. **2 se discréditer** *vpr* to become discredited (**auprès de qn,** in s.o.'s eyes), to lose credit (**auprès de qn,** with s.o.); to (bring) discredit (upon) oneself.
discret, -ète [diskrɛ, -ɛt] *adj* **(a)** discreet (*behaviour, conversation etc*); **elle est très discrète,** she's very discreet; **être trop d.,** to be too reticent; **sous pli d.,** under plain cover; **(b)** (*modeste*) quiet, unobtrusive, unassuming (*person*); sober, simple, plain (*clothes*); inconspicuous (*appearance etc*); modest (*request etc*); quiet, secluded (*place*); **une discrète touche de blue,** a discreet touch of blue; **(c)** *Math* discrete (*quantity*); *Phys* discontinuous (*function*).
discrètement [diskrɛtmɑ̃] *adv* **(a)** (*avec retenue*) discreetly, with discretion; **il lui a parlé d.,** he had a quiet word with him; **(b)** (*modestement*) quietly, unobtrusively, modestly, simply; **maquillé d.,** discreetly made up.
discrétion [diskresjɔ̃] *nf* **(a)** (*retenue*) discretion; **avoir de la d.,** to be discreet; **d. assurée,** discretion guaranteed; **la d. d'une intervention,** the discreetness of an intervention; **user de qch avec d.,** to use sth in moderation; **(b) être à la d. de qn,** to be in s.o.'s hands; **pain à d.,** unlimited bread, as much bread as one wants.
discrétionnaire [diskresjɔnɛr] *adj* discretionary (*powers etc*).
discriminant [diskriminɑ̃] **1** *adj* discriminating. **2** *nm Math* discriminant.
discrimination [diskriminɑsjɔ̃] *nf* discrimination; **ils étaient victimes de d.,** they were victims of discrimination, they were discriminated against; **d. raciale/sexuelle,** racial/sexual discrimination; **sans d. de race ni de sexe,** without discrimination on the grounds of race or sex.
discriminatoire [diskriminatwar] *adj* discriminatory, discriminating.
discriminer [diskrimine] *vt Litt* to discriminate, to distinguish.
disculper [diskylpe] **1** *vt* to exonerate (*s.o.*) (**de,** from); to clear (*s.o.*) (**d'un crime,** of a crime). **2 se discriminer** *vpr* to exonerate oneself (**de,** from), to clear oneself (**de,** of).
discursif, -ive [diskyrsif, -iv] *adj* discursive.
discussion [diskysjɔ̃] *nf* **(a)** discussion, debate; **avoir une d.,** to have a discussion (**sur, à propos de,** about); **la question en d.,** the question under discussion *or* under debate *or* at issue; **aborder la d. d'une question,** to take up a matter; **sans d. possible,** indisputably; **il s'exécuta sans d.,** he complied without arguing (the point); **pas de d., au travail!,** don't argue, get to work!; **entrer en d. avec qn,** to enter into discussion with s.o.; **(b)** *Jur* **d. de**

biens, enquiry into the assets of a debtor (*with a view to recovery of debt*).

discutable [diskytabl] *adj* debatable, questionable, arguable, doubtful (*point etc*).

discutailler [diskytaje] *vi F Péj* (*chicaner*) to quibble.

discuté [diskyte] *adj* disputed (*question*); much discussed (*book, subject*).

discuter [diskyte] **1** *vt* (*examiner*) to discuss, to debate; (*contester*) to question, to dispute; **d. un droit,** to dispute a right; **d. un problème,** to discuss a problem; **discutons la chose,** let's talk the matter over, let's talk it over; *F* **d. le coup** *ou* **le bout de gras,** to have a natter *or* a chat. **2** *vi* to debate; **d. avec qn sur qch,** to debate sth with s.o.; **d. de politique,** to discuss politics; **ne discutez pas,** no arguing, don't argue; **on ne peut pas d. avec toi,** it's impossible to have a discussion with you. **3 se discuter** *vpr* to be discussed *or* debated; **ça se discute,** (*ce n'est pas évident*) that's debatable.

discuteur, -euse [diskytœr, -øz] *n* arguer.

disert [dizɛr] *adj Litt* eloquent, fluent (*orator*).

disette [dizɛt] *nf* scarcity, *Fml* dearth; **d. d'eau,** drought; **vivre dans la d.,** to live in poverty.

diseur, -euse [dizœr, -øz] *n* **(a) d.** *ou* **diseuse de bonne aventure,** fortune teller; **(b)** (*qui déclame*) monologuist.

disgrâce [disgrɑs] *nf* disfavour, disgrace; **encourir la d. de qn,** to incur s.o.'s displeasure.

disgracié [disgrasje] *adj* out of favour, in disgrace.

disgracier [disgrasje] *vt* (*impf & pr sub* **n. disgraciions, v. disgraciiez**) to dismiss (*a government minister*).

disgracieux, -ieuse [disgrasjø, -jøz] *adj* **(a)** awkward, ungraceful (*person, movement, gesture*); **(b)** ungracious (*answer*); **(c)** (*laid*) ugly (*face etc*).

disjoindre [disʒwɛ̃dr] *v* (*conj like* **joindre**) **1** *vt* to disjoint, to separate, to disconnect, to take apart; *Jur* **d. deux causes,** to treat two cases separately. **2 se disjoindre** *vpr* to come apart, to separate.

disjoint [disʒwɛ̃] *adj* **(a)** disjoined, disjointed, disconnected (*parts etc*); **(b)** *Mus* disjunct (*motion*).

disjoncter [disʒɔ̃kte] *El* **1** *vt* to break (*circuit*). **2** *vi F* to trip.

disjoncteur [disʒɔ̃ktœr] *nm El* circuit breaker, cutout.

disjonctif, -ive [disʒɔ̃ktif, -iv] *adj* disjunctive.

disjonction [disʒɔ̃ksjɔ̃] *nf* disjunction, separation (*of parts of whole*); *Jur* severance (*of causes etc*).

dislocation [dislɔkasjɔ̃] *nf* dislocation (*of joint*); taking to pieces, dismantling (*of machine etc*); dismemberment (*of empire etc*); *Géol* fault; *Mil etc* dispersal, breaking up (*of troops etc*).

disloqué [dislɔke] *adj* dislocated (*shoulder, knee*); dismantled (*machine*); dismembered, broken up (*empire etc*).

disloquer [dislɔke] **1** *vt* to dislocate (*shoulder, knee*); to take (*machine*) to pieces, to dismantle (*machine*); to break up, to disperse (*troops*); to break up, to dismember (*state*). **2 se disloquer** *vpr* to break up, to fall to pieces; **son bras s'est disloqué,** he's dislocated his arm.

disparaître [disparɛtr] *vi* (*conj like* **paraître**) **(a)** to disappear, to vanish; (*d'une personne*) to go missing; **d. aux** *ou* **des regards,** to vanish out of sight, to disappear from view; **le soleil a disparu à l'horizon,** the sun sank below the horizon; **elle a disparu sans laisser de traces,** she's disappeared without trace; **tous ses amis ont disparu,** all his friends have died *or* are dead; **faire d. qn,** (*le tuer*) to get rid of s.o.; **faire d. une tache/une difficulté/***etc*, to get rid of *or* remove a stain/a difficulty/*etc*; **j'ai pris un cachet pour faire d. la douleur,** I took a pill to relieve *or* get rid of the pain; **cette mode disparaît,** this fashion is going out; **sa timidité disparaît peu à peu,** his shyness is wearing off; **(b)** (*être caché*) to be hidden; **la muraille disparaît sous le lierre,** the wall is hidden under the ivy.

disparate [disparat] *adj* (*différent*) dissimilar; (*qui ne s'accorde pas*) ill-matched, ill-assorted; **couleurs disparates,** clashing colours.

disparité [disparite] *nf* disparity (*of age etc*).

disparition [disparisjɔ̃] *nf* **(a)** (*départ*) disappearing, vanishing; **la d. du soleil sous l'horizon,** the sinking of the sun below the horizon; **(b)** (*absence*) disappearance; **remarquer la d. de qch,** to miss sth.

disparu, -ue [dispary] **1** *adj* **(a)** *Mil etc* missing (in action); **être porté d.,** to be reported missing; **marin d. en mer,** sailor lost at sea; **(b)** extinct, bygone (*race etc*); vanished (*world etc*). **2** *n* **(a)** (*défunt*) dead person, deceased; **nos chers disparus,** our dear departed; **(b)** *Mil* missing soldier (*believed dead*), *US* MIA (= missing in action).

dispatcher¹ [dispatʃœr, -ɛr] *nm* dispatcher.

dispatcher² [dispatʃe] *vt* to dispatch.

dispatching [dispatʃiŋ] *nm* dispatching.

dispendieusement [dispɑ̃djøzmɑ̃] *adv* expensively.

dispendieux, -ieuse [dispɑ̃djø, -jøz] *adj* expensive (*tastes, process etc*).

dispensaire [dispɑ̃sɛr] *nm* free clinic, free health centre.

dispensateur, -trice [dispɑ̃satœr, -tris] *n* dispenser (*of charity, justice etc*).

dispense [dispɑ̃s] *nf* **(a)** exemption (*from military service etc*); *Rel* dispensation; **d. d'âge,** waiving of age limit; **(b)** (*certificat*) certificate of exemption.

dispenser [dispɑ̃se] **1** *vt* **(a) d. qn de (faire) qch,** to exempt *or* excuse s.o. from (doing) sth; **dispensez-moi de ce voyage,** spare me this journey; **d. qn du service militaire,** to exempt s.o. from military service; **je vous dispense de vos commentaires,** you can keep your remarks to yourself; **(b)** to dispense, to distribute (*charity, favours etc*). **2 se dispenser** *vpr* **se d. de (faire) qch,** to excuse oneself from (doing) sth, to get out of (doing) sth; **on peut s'en d.,** we can do without it.

dispersal [dispɛrsal] *nm Av* apron.

dispersant [dispɛrsɑ̃] *nm Ch* dispersant, dispersal agent.

dispersé [dispɛrse] *adj* scattered (*leaves etc*); disorganized (*work etc*).

disperser [dispɛrse] **1** *vt* to disperse, to scatter, to break up (*crowd*); to disperse, to scatter, to spread (far and wide) (*leaves*); **d. une armée,** to rout an army; *Fig* **d. son attention sur plusieurs choses,** to divide one's attention among several things. **2 se disperser** *vpr* (*of clouds, crowd*) to disperse, to break up; (*of crowd*) to scatter; *Fig* **tu as tendance à trop te d.,** you tend to spread yourself too thin(ly).

dispersion [dispɛrsjɔ̃] *nf* **(a)** dispersion, dispersal (*of people*); dispersal, breaking up (*of crowd, clouds*); scattering (*of leaves etc*); rout (*of army*); *Fig* **la d. d'un esprit,** an unfocused mind; **(b)** *Opt* dispersion, decomposition (*of light*).

disponibilité [disponibilite] *nf* availability (*of s.o., seats, capital etc*); **avoir la d. de qch,** to have sth at one's disposal; *Mil* **la d.,** the reserve; **mettre qn en d.,** *Mil* to release s.o. temporarily from duty; *Ind* (*en chômage*) to lay s.o. off; *Fin* **disponibilités,** available funds, liquid assets.

disponible [disponibl] **1** *adj* available; at (*s.o's*) disposal; **places disponibles,** (*dans un train etc*) vacant *or* unoccupied seats; **êtes-vous d. ce soir?,** are you free tonight?; *Mil* **officier d.,** unattached officer, half-pay officer. **2** *nm* **(a)** *Com* **marché du d.,** spot market; **(b)** *Fin* **le d.,** liquid assets; **(c)** *Mil* member of the reserve.

dispos [dispo] *adj* fit, well, in good form, in good spirits, **frais et d.,** refreshed; **esprit d.,** fresh *or* alert mind.

disposé [dispoze] *adj* **(a)** (*personne*) disposed; **être bien/mal d.,** to be in a good/bad mood; **être bien d. pour** *ou* **envers qn,** to be well disposed towards s.o.; **être** *ou* **se sentir d. à faire qch,** to feel disposed *or* willing *or* in the mood to do sth; **je suis tout d. à pardonner,** I am fully prepared to forgive; **(b)** (*arrangé*) arranged, set out; **fleurs disposées avec goût,** tastefully arranged flowers.

disposer [dispoze] **1** *vt* **(a)** to set out, to arrange (*objects in order, in position*); to lay, to set (*table*);

(b) d. qn à (faire) qch, to dispose *or* incline s.o. to (do) sth.

2 *vi* **(a) d. de qn/qch,** to have s.o./sth at one's disposal; **disposez de moi,** I am at your service; **toutes les heures dont je puis d.,** every hour I can spare; **les renseignements dont je dispose,** the information at my disposal; **d. de capitaux importants,** to have a large capital in hand, to command a large capital; **vous pouvez en d.,** you may use it; **vous pouvez d.,** you may go; **d. de ses biens en faveur de qn,** to make over one's property to s.o.;

(b) (*décider*) to prescribe, to provide, to enjoin; **la loi ne dispose que pour l'avenir,** the law applies only to the future; *Prov* **l'homme propose, Dieu dispose,** man proposes, God disposes.

3 se disposer *vpr* **se d. à qch/à faire qch,** to get ready for sth/to do sth; **se d. à partir,** to get ready to leave.

dispositif [dispozitif] *nm* **(a)** *Tech* device, mechanism, appliance; **d. de commande/de manœuvre,** driving/controlling gear *or* mechanism; **d. de sûreté,** safety device; **(b)** *Mil* plan of action; disposition, deployment (*of troops in battle etc*); **d. d'attaque,** attack force; **d. de défense,** defence system; **(c)** *Jur* purview, enacting terms (*of statute etc*).

disposition [dispozisjɔ̃] *nf* **(a)** (*arrangement*) layout (*of house, garden etc*); **d. du terrain,** lie of the land;

(b) state (*of mind, body*); frame of mind; (*tendance*) predisposition; **dispositions,** natural ability, aptitude (*for sth*); **être en bonne d. pour faire qch,** to be disposed *or* inclined *or* in the mood to do sth; **être dans de bonnes dispositions à l'égard de qn,** to be favourably disposed towards s.o.; **avoir une d. au rhumatisme,** to have a tendency to rheumatism; **d. à pleurer souvent,** tendancy to weep often; **dispositions naturelles pour la musique,** natural bent for music; **cet enfant a des dispositions,** he is a (naturally) gifted child;

(c) dispositions, (*préparations*) arrangements; **prendre des dispositions pour faire qch,** to make the necessary arrangements *or* prepare for doing sth;

(d) dispositions, (*d'un testament, d'une loi*) provisions, conditions; (*d'une loi*) clauses; **les dispositions contenues dans l'article 34,** the provisions of article 34;

(e) (*disponibilité*) disposal; **avoir la libre d. de son bien,** to be free to dispose of one's property; **libre d. de soi-même,** self-determination; **avoir qch à sa d.,** to have sth at one's disposal; **fonds à ma d.,** funds at my disposal *or* under my control; **mettre qch à la d. de qn,** to place sth at s.o.'s disposal; **je suis à votre (entière) d.,** I am (entirely) at your service.

disproportion [disprɔpɔrsjɔ̃] *nf* disproportion, lack of proportion (**entre,** between).

disproportionné [disprɔpɔrsjɔne] *adj* disproportionate (**à, avec,** to); out of proportion (**à, avec,** with).

disputable [dispytabl] *adj* disputable, debatable.

dispute [dispyt] *nf* **(a)** (*querelle*) quarrel, *Fml* altercation; **chercher d. à qn,** to pick a quarrel with s.o.; **c'est un sujet de d. entre eux,** it is a bone of contention between them; **(b)** *Arch* debate, controversy, dispute; **sujet en d.,** subject under discussion.

disputer [dispyte] **1** *vt* **(a)** (*se battre pour*) **d. qch,** to dispute *or* contest sth; **d. le terrain,** to fight every inch of the way; **d. qch à qn,** to contend with s.o. for sth; **d. un match,** to play a match; **d. une course sur mille mètres,** to run a thousand metre race;

(b) *F* **d. qn,** to tick *or* tell s.o. off; **il s'est fait d. par son père,** he got told off by *or* he got a telling off from his father.

2 *vi* **(a)** (*discuter*) to quarrel, to argue (**avec,** with); **d. d'un sujet avec qn,** to quarrel *or* argue with s.o. about *or* over a subject;

(b) d. de zèle/d'élégance avec qn, to try to outdo s.o. in zeal/elegance.

3 se disputer *vpr* to quarrel, to wrangle, to argue (**pour,** over, about; **avec,** with); **deux chiens qui se disputent un os,** two dogs fighting over a bone; **ils se disputent à qui aura le plus gros morceau,** they are arguing about who should get the biggest piece; **le match se disputera à Wimbledon,** the match will be played *or* will take place at Wimbledon.

disquaire [diskɛr] *nm* record shop owner; **je vais chez le d.,** I'm going to the record shop; **en vente chez tous les disquaires,** on sale in all record shops.

disqualification [diskalifikasjɔ̃] *nf Sp* disqualification.

disqualifier [diskalifje] *vt* (*pr sub & impf* **n. disqualifiions, v. disqualifiiez**) **(a)** *Sp* to disqualify; **(b)** to discredit (*s.o.*).

disque [disk] *nm* **(a)** disc, *Am* disk; *Mus* record, disc; *Rail* disc signal; *Tech* **d. d'embrayage,** clutch plate *or* disc; *Tech* **frein à d.,** disc brake; *Mus* **d. microsillon** *ou* **(de) longue durée,** long-playing record, L.P.; *Mus* **d. compact,** compact disc; *F* **changer de d.,** to change the record *or* subject; **appareil photo à disques,** disc camera; *Anat* **d. intervertébral,** (intervertebral) disc; *Admin Aut* **d. de stationnement,** parking disc; **(b)** *Ordinat* disk; **d. magnétique,** magnetic disk; **d. dur,** hard disk; **d. de système,** system disk; **station de travail sans d.,** diskless workstation; **(c)** *Sp* discus; **lanceur de d.,** discus thrower; **arriver deuxième au lancer de d.,** to come in second in the discus.

disquette [diskɛt] *nf Ordinat* diskette, *F* floppy (disk).

disruptif, -ive [disryptif, -iv] *adj* disruptive (*force, electric discharge etc*).

dissection [disɛksjɔ̃] *nf* dissection (*of body, literary work etc*).

dissemblable [disɑ̃blabl] *adj* dissimilar, unlike; different (**de, à,** from, *US* than).

dissemblance [disɑ̃blɑ̃s] *nf* dissimilarity, difference (**entre,** between).

dissemblant [disɑ̃blɑ̃] *adj* dissimilar, different, unlike.

dissémination [diseminasjɔ̃] *nf* **(a)** scattering (*of seeds etc*); spreading (*of germs, troops etc*); **(b)** dissemination, spreading (*of ideas etc*).

disséminer [disemine] **1** *vt* **(a)** to scatter (*seeds etc*); to spread (*germs*); to deploy (*troops etc*); **(b)** to disseminate, to spread (*ideas etc*). **2 se disséminer** *vpr* to be spread.

dissension [disɑ̃sjɔ̃] *nf* dissension, discord.

dissentiment [disɑ̃timɑ̃] *nm* disagreement, dissent, difference of opinion.

disséquer [diseke] *vt* (**je dissèque; je disséquerai**) to dissect (*corpse, literary work etc*).

dissertation [disɛrtasjɔ̃] *nf* **(a)** *Vieilli* (*étude*) dissertation (**sur,** (up)on); **(b)** *Scol* **d. (française),** (French) essay.

disserter [disɛrte] *vi* **(a) d. sur un sujet,** to discourse on a subject; **(b)** *Péj* (*parler beaucoup*) to talk at length, *F* to hold forth.

dissidence [disidɑ̃s] *nf Rel etc* dissidence, dissent; **la d.,** dissidents.

dissident, -ente [disidɑ̃, -ɑ̃t] **1** *adj* dissident, dissenting (*sect, party etc*). **2** *n Pol* dissident; *Rel* dissenter, nonconformist.

dissimilation [disimilasjɔ̃] *nf Ling* dissimilation.

dissimilitude [disimilityd] *nf* dissimilitude, dissimilarity.

dissimulateur, -trice [disimylatœr, -tris] **1** *adj* dissembling. **2** *n* dissembler, deceiver.

dissimulation [disimylasjɔ̃] *nf* **(a)** (*hypocrisie*) dissembling, deceit; **agir avec d.,** to act in an underhand way; **(b)** concealment, covering up (*of the truth etc*); *Jur* **d. d'actif,** (fraudulent) concealment of assets.

dissimulé [disimyle] *adj* **(a)** (*caché*) hidden, secret; **(b)** (*hypocrite*) dissimulating, dissembling, secretive (*man, character*).

dissimuler [disimyle] **1** *vt* to hide, to conceal (*feelings etc*); to cover up (*fault*); **d. qch à qn,** to hide sth *or* keep sth (back) from s.o.; **le rideau dissimule le siège de WC,** the curtain screens off the lavatory; **d. ses revenus,** (*en ne les déclarant pas*) to conceal one's income; **il m'avait dissimulé qu'il voulait partir,** he hadn't told me he wanted to leave; **je ne (vous) dissimule pas qu'il en est ainsi,** I cannot hide the fact *or* I have to tell you that it is like this. **2 se dissimuler** *vpr* to hide; **parmi tant de qualités se dissimule un défaut,** a weakness lurks among so many qualities; **sa jalousie ne peut se d.,** he cannot hide his jealousy.

dissipateur, -trice [disipatœr, -tris] **1** *n* spendthrift, squanderer, waster. **2** *adj* prodigal; wasteful (*administration etc*).

dissipation [disipasjɔ̃] *nf* **(a)** squandering, wasting (*of money, time etc*); squandering (*of fortune*); dispersal (*of clouds etc*); dispelling (*of fears, suspicions*); **(b)** (*débauche*) dissipation, dissolute living; **(c)** inattention (*in school*).

dissipé [disipe] *adj* **(a)** (*débauché*) dissipated, dissolute; **mener une vie dissipée,** to lead a riotous life; **(b)** *Scol* inattentive (*pupil*).

dissiper [disipe] **1** *vt* **(a)** to squander, to waste (*fortune, time etc*); to ruin (*health etc*); to disperse, to scatter, to dispel (*clouds etc*); to clear up (*misunderstanding*); to dispel (*fears, suspicions*); **(b) d. qn,** to distract s.o.'s attention. **2 se dissiper** *vpr* **(a)** (*de visions, suspicions etc*) to vanish, to disappear; **le brouillard se dissipe,** the fog is lifting *or* clearing (away); **ses doutes se sont dissipés,** his doubts faded; **(b)** (*se laisser distraire*) to be inattentive, to misbehave (*in school etc*).

dissociable [disɔsjabl] *adj* dissociable, separable.

dissociation [disɔsjasjɔ̃] *nf* dissociation, separation; *Ch* decomposition, dissociation.

dissocier [disɔsje] *vt* **(a)** *Ch* to dissociate (*compound*); **(b)** to separate, to dissociate (*ideas etc*).

dissolu [disɔly] *adj* dissolute (*person, life*).

dissolubilité [disɔlybilite] *nf* dissolubility.

dissoluble [disɔlybl] *adj* **(a)** *Pol* dissoluble, dissolvable (*assembly etc*); **(b)** *Arch* soluble.

dissolution [disɔlysjɔ̃] *nf* **(a)** dissolution (*of parliament, marriage*); breaking up (*of meeting*); winding up (*of company*); **(b)** *Ch* dissolving (*of substance in liquid*); (*colle*) rubber solution; **(c)** disintegration, dissolution, decomposition (*of body etc*); **(d)** *Litt* (*débauche*) dissoluteness, licentiousness, profligacy.

dissolvant [disɔlvɑ̃] **1** *adj* **(a)** (*qui dissout*) solvent; **(b)** debilitating (*climate etc*); corrupt (*doctrine etc*). **2** *nm* solvent; **d. (pour ongles),** nail varnish remover.

dissonance [disɔnɑ̃s] *nf* **(a)** dissonance; clash (*of colours*); *Fig* **d. entre les principes et la pratique,** discrepancy between principles and practice; **(b)** *Mus* discord.

dissonant [disɔnɑ̃] *adj* dissonant, discordant; clashing (*colours*).

dissoudre [disudr] *v* (*prp* **dissolvant;** *pp* **dissous,** *f* **dissoute;** *pr ind* **je dissous, il dissout, n. dissolvons;** *impf* je dissolvais; *p hist & p sub are lacking*; *fu* **je dissoudrai**) **1** *vt* **(a)** to dissolve (*substance*) in a liquid; **(b)** to dissolve (*parliament, marriage*); to dissolve, to break (up) (*partnership*). **2 se dissoudre** *vpr* **(a)** to dissolve; **se d. dans l'eau,** (*of sugar etc*) to dissolve *or* melt in water; *Fig* **colère qui se dissout en larmes,** anger that dissolves into tears; **(b)** (*of assembly*) to break up.

dissuader [disɥade] *vt* **d. qn de (faire) qch,** to dissuade s.o. from (doing) sth, to talk s.o. out of (doing) sth; **d. qn de partir**; to persuade s.o. not to go away, to dissuade s.o. from leaving.

dissuasif, -ive [disɥazif, -iv] *adj* dissuasive.

dissuasion [disɥazjɔ̃] *nf* dissuasion (**de,** from); **d. nucléaire,** nuclear deterrent; *Mil Pol* **force de d.,** deterrent.

dissyllabe [disilab] **1** *adj* di(s)syllabic. **2** *nm* di(s)syllable.

dissyllabique [disilabik] *adj* di(s)syllabic.

dissymétrie [disimetri] *nf* asymmetry, dissymmetry.

dissymétrique [disimetrik] *adj* asymmetric(al), dissymmetrical, unsymmetrical.

distance [distɑ̃s] *nf* distance; **il y a une d. de 5 km entre ces deux points,** these two points are 5 km apart; **on ne voyait rien à cette d.,** you couldn't see anything from that distance; **suivre qn à d./à peu de d.,** to follow s.o. at a distance/at a short distance; **à quelle d. sommes-nous de la ville?,** how far are we from the town?; **à une courte d.,** within easy reach (**de,** of); **c'est à une grande d.,** it's a long way off (**de,** from); **une faible d.,** a short way *or* distance; *Mil etc* **à petite** *ou* **faible d.,** at short range; *Ordinat etc* **à d.,** remote; *MecE* **commande à d.,** remote control; **j'en juge mieux à d.,** I can judge better at *or* from a distance; **influencer qn à d.,** to influence s.o. at *or* from a distance; **tenir qn à d.,** to keep s.o. at a distance; **conserver** *ou* **garder ses distances, se tenir à d.,** to keep at a distance, to remain aloof; **d. de dix ans entre deux événements,** ten years' interval between two events; **d. entre générations,** generation gap; **de d. en d.,** at intervals; **prendre ses distances,** *Mil* to dress; *Gym* to space out; *Sp & Fig* **tenir la d.,** to go the distance, to stay *or* last the course; *Opt* **d. focale,** focal length; *Nau* **d. parcourue,** day's run.

distancement [distɑ̃smɑ̃] *nm Sp* disqualifying, disqualification (*of horse*).

distancer [distɑ̃se] *vt* (**je distançai(s)**; **n. distançons**) **(a)** *Sp etc* to outdistance, to outrun, to outstrip; **se laisser d.,** to drop away, to fall *or* lag behind; **le parti socialiste distance la droite de deux points,** (*dans les sondages*) the socialists are two points ahead of the conservatives; **ce périodique distance tous les autres par sa qualité,** this periodical surpasses all the others in quality; **(b)** to disqualify (*horse*).

distant [distɑ̃] *adj* **(a)** (*éloigné*) distant; **nos deux maisons sont distantes d'un kilomètre l'une de l'autre,** our two houses are a kilometre apart; **(b)** *Fig* (*froid*) distant, standoffish, aloof; **elle est très distante avec moi,** she's being very distant towards me.

distendre [distɑ̃dr] **1** *vt* **(a)** to distend (*stomach etc*); **(b)** to strain (*muscle etc*); to stretch (*rope etc*) to breaking point. **2 se distendre** *vpr* **(a)** (*se relâcher*) to become distended, to swell (out); **(b)** *Fig* (*d'un lien*) **notre relation se distend,** we're drifting apart.

distension [distɑ̃sjɔ̃] *nf* **(a)** distension (*of stomach etc*); straining (*of muscle etc*); **(b)** slackening, loosening (*of rope etc*).

distillateur [distilatœr] *nm* distiller.

distillation [distilasjɔ̃] *nf* (*of whisky*) & *Pétr* distillation, distilling; **d. fractionnée,** fractional distillation.

distiller [distile] **1** *vt* **(a)** to distil, *US* to distill (*spirits, petroleum etc*); *Litt* to refine (*one's thoughts*); **(b)** to distil, to exude, to secrete (*poison, moisture etc*); to exude (*anger etc*); **eau distillée,** distilled water. **2** *vi* to distil, to exude (**de,** from).

distillerie [distilri] *nf* (*lieu*) distillery; (*procédé*) distilling.

distinct [distɛ̃(kt)] *adj* **(a)** (*séparé*) distinct, separate (**de,** from); **(b)** (*voix, silhouette etc*) distinct, clear; (*voix*) audible.

distinctement [distɛ̃ktəmɑ̃] *adv* distinctly, clearly.

distinctif, -ive [distɛ̃ktif, -iv] *adj* distinctive, characteristic, distinguishing (*sign, feature etc*); **trait d.,** characteristic, peculiarity.

distinction [distɛ̃ksjɔ̃] *nf* **(a)** (*différence*) distinction; **faire une d. entre deux choses,** to make a distinction *or* to differentiate *or* distinguish between two things; **sans d.,** indiscriminately; **sans d. de race ou de couleur,** irrespective of race or colour; **d. sociale,** social *or* class distinction; **(b)** (*dignité*) distinction, honour, *US* honor; (*médaille etc*) decoration; **obtenir une d.,** to be awarded a medal; **(c)** (*éminence*) distinction, eminence; **un personnage de haute d.,** a highly distinguished person; **avoir de la d.,** to be distinguished.

distinctivement [distɛ̃ktivmɑ̃] *adv* distinctively.

distinguable [distɛ̃gabl] *adj* distinguishable.

distingué [distɛ̃ge] *adj* **(a)** (*person*) distinguished, eminent, noted (*writer, politician etc*); **(b)** refined (*taste, bearing etc*); smart (*costume etc*); **avoir un air d.,** to look distinguished; **(c) agréez mes sentiments distingués,** (*dans une lettre*) yours truly.

distinguer [distɛ̃ge] **1** *vt* **(a)** (*différencier*) to distinguish, to mark, to characterize; **sa mise soignée le distinguait de la foule,** his impeccable appearance made him stand out *or* set him apart from the crowd;

(b) (*pour honorer*) to honour, *US* to honor (*s.o.*); to single (*s.o.*) out (for distinction);

(c) (*faire la différence*) to distinguish (**entre deux choses,** between two things); **d. qch de qch** *ou* **d'avec qch,** to distinguish *or* tell sth from sth; **on peut à peine les d. l'un de l'autre,** you can hardly tell them apart;

(d) (*discerner*) to discern, to perceive; **je ne peux pas d. ses traits,** I cannot make out his features; **je l'ai distinguée dans la foule,** I spotted her in the crowd; **d. une nuance d'amertume dans la voix de qn,** to detect a trace of bitterness in s.o.'s voice.

2 se distinguer *vpr* **(a)** (*s'illustrer*) to distinguish oneself (**par ses talents,** by one's talents); (*dans une foule etc*) to be noticeable *or* conspicuous, to stand out; **chercher à se d.,** to seek to distinguish oneself;

(b) (*se différencier*) **se d. des autres,** to be distinguishable from others (**par,** by); **il se distingue de son frère par son grand nez,** you can tell him from his brother by his big nose;

(c) (*être perçu*) **au loin se distinguait la côte,** the coastline could be seen in the distance.

distinguo [distɛ̃go] *nm* = **DISTINCTION (a)**.

distique [distik] *nm* **(a)** (*French verse*) couplet; **(b)** *Antiq* distich.

distordre [distɔrdr] *vt* to distort (*features etc*).

distorsion [distɔrsjɔ̃] *nf* **(a)** distortion (*of face, optical image, electrical impulse etc*); *Rad* **d. de phase,** phase distortion; **(b)** imbalance (*between two factors*).

distraction [distraksjɔ̃] *nf* **(a)** (*inattention*) absentmindedness, lack of attention, abstraction; **par d.,** inadvertently, absentmindedly; **avoir des distractions,** to be absent-minded; **(b)** (*loisir*) amusement, distraction, recreation; **(c)** *Arch & Jur* division, severance (*of part from a whole etc*).

distraire [distrɛr] *v* (*conj like* **traire**) **1** *vt* **(a)** to distract, to divert (*s.o.'s attention etc*); **d. l'attention de qn,** to take s.o.'s attention *or* mind off sth; **d. qn de ses travaux,** to take s.o. from his work; **(b)** (*divertir*) to divert, to entertain, to amuse; **(c)** *Litt* to divert, to separate (*part from whole etc*). **2 se distraire** *vpr* to amuse oneself; **elle a besoin de se d.,** she needs to relax a bit *or* to enjoy herself.

distrait [distrɛ] *adj* absentminded; **air d.,** abstracted *or* distracted look; **vous êtes d.,** you're not paying attention; **d'une oreille distraite,** abstractedly, inattentively, with only half an ear; **élève d.,** inattentive pupil.

distraitement [distrɛtmɑ̃] *adv* absentmindedly, absently, abstractedly.

distrayant [distrɛjɑ̃] *adj* diverting, entertaining (*book, spectacle*).

distribanque [distribɑ̃k] *nf* cash dispenser.

distribuer [distribɥe] *vt* to distribute, to hand out, to give (*orders, prizes etc*); to issue, to share out (*provisions etc*); to deal (*cards*); (*of postman*) to deliver (*letters*); **d. les fleurs en plusieurs classes,** to classify flowers; *Th* **d. les rôles,** to assign *or* cast the parts (in a play), to cast a play; **d. un appartement,** to arrange (*the furniture etc in*) a flat; **d. son temps de la façon la plus logique,** to allocate *or* apportion one's time in the most logical fashion possible.

distributaire [distribytɛr] *n* recipient (*in distribution*); *Jur* distributee.

distributeur, -trice [distribytœr, -tris] **1** *n* distributor (*of prizes*); dispenser (*of favours etc*). **2** *nm* **(a)** *Cin* (film) distributor; **(b)** *Tech Aut* distributor; **d. d'essence,** petrol pump, *Am* gas(oline) pump; **d. automatique,** automatic vending machine, slot machine; **d. de billets,** ticket machine; **d. (automatique) de billets,** cash dispenser, cash point, *Am* bank machine; *El* **d. de courant,** distributor; **d. de vapeur,** steam distributor *or* regulator, steam valve; **d. d'engrais,** fertilizer spreader.

distributif, -ive [distribytif, -iv] *adj* distributive (*term, pronoun etc*).

distribution [distribysjɔ̃] *nf* distribution; allotment (*of duties etc*); issue (*of rations*); delivery (*of letters, goods*); arrangement (*of furniture etc*); layout (*of house, flat*); *Com Aut* distribution; **d. des plantes,** classification of plants; *Econ* **d. des richesses,** distribution of wealth; *Com* **réseau de d.,** distribution network; **droits de d.,** distribution rights; *Scol* **d. des prix,** prize giving, speech day; *Th* **d. des rôles,** (*action*) casting; (*liste*) cast; *Th Cin* **d. par ordre d'entrée en scène,** characters *or* cast in order of appearance; **d. des eaux,** water supply.

distributivement [distribytivmɑ̃] *adv* distributively.

district [distrik(t)] *nm* district, region.

dit [di] **1** *adj* **(a)** (*décidé*) settled, fixed; **prendre qch pour d.,** to take sth for granted; **à l'heure dite,** at the appointed time, at the time indicated; **(b)** (*appelé*) called; **la zone dite tempérée,** the temperate zone as it is called. **2** *nm Arch & Littér* traditional story (*usually in verse*); **le d. des trois larrons,** the story of the three thieves.

dithyrambe [ditirɑ̃b] *nm* (*panégyrique*) eulogy; *Littér* dithyramb; **se lancer dans un d. sur qch,** to go into raptures about sth.

dithyrambique [ditirɑ̃bik] *adj* eulogistic (*words etc*); *Littér* dithyrambic.

dito [dito] *adv* ditto.

diurétique [djyretik] *adj & nm Méd* diuretic.

diurne [djyrn] **1** *adj* diurnal (*motion of planet etc*). **2** *nmpl* **les diurnes,** butterflies.

diva [diva] *nf Mus* diva.

divagation [divagɑsjɔ̃] *nf* **(a)** digression (*in a speech etc*); **divagations d'un fou,** ravings *or* ramblings of a madman; **(b)** shifting (*of river*) from its course; *Jur* straying (*of cattle etc*).

divaguer [divage] *vi* **(a)** (*dans un discours*) to digress, to stray from the point; **malade qui divague,** patient whose mind is wandering *or* who rambles (in his speech); **vous divaguez!** you're raving!; **(b)** (*of river*) to shift its course; *Jur (of cattle etc)* to stray.

divan [divɑ̃] *nm* **(a)** (*meuble*) divan, couch; **d.-lit,** divan (bed); **(b)** *Hist* divan.

divergence [divɛrʒɑ̃s] *nf* divergence (*of lines, opinions, rays etc*); difference (*of opinions*).

divergent [divɛrʒɑ̃] *adj* divergent (*lines, opinions*); different (*opinions*).

diverger [divɛrʒe] *vi* (**il divergea(it); n. divergeons**) (*of lines, rays, opinions*) to diverge (**de,** from); **nos opinions divergent sur certains points,** our opinions differ on certain points.

divers [divɛr] *adj* **(a)** diverse, different, varied; **des opinions très diverses,** very varied opinions; **(frais) d.,** sundry expenses, sundries; *Journ* **faits d.,** news items; **un fait d.,** an incident; **(b)** (*always preceding the noun*) various; **diverses personnes l'ont vu,** various people saw him; **(c)** *Arch* changing, varying (*nature etc*).

diversement [divɛrsəmɑ̃] *adv* in various *or* different ways.

diversification [divɛrsifikɑsjɔ̃] *nf* diversification.

diversifier [divɛrsifje] *v* (*pr sub & impf* **n. diversifiions, v. diversifiiez**) **1** *vt* to diversify, to vary (*conversation, pursuits etc*); to variegate (*colours*). **2 se diversifier** *vpr* (*of matter, interests etc*) to change, to become different; (*of company*) to diversify.

diversion [divɛrsjɔ̃] *nf* **(a)** *Mil* diversion; **(b)** (*changement*) diversion, change, distraction; **faire d. à la tristesse de qn,** to cheer s.o. up.

diversité [divɛrsite] *nf* (*variété*) diversity, variety; (*différence*) difference.

divertir [divɛrtir] **1** *vt* **(a)** (*amuser*) to divert, to entertain, to amuse; **(b)** *Vieilli* to divert, to ward off (*blow etc*); to turn (*s.o.*) away (*from project etc*); to divert (*attention etc*); to misappropriate (*sum of money*). **2 se divertir** *vpr* to enjoy oneself.

divertissant [divɛrtisɑ̃] *adj* diverting, amusing, entertaining.

divertissement [divɛrtismɑ̃] *nm* **(a)** (*amusement*) diversion, entertainment, amusement; *Mus* divertimento; **(b) d. de fonds,** misappropriation of funds.

dividende [dividɑ̃d] *nm Math Fin* dividend.

divin [divɛ̃] **1** *adj* divine (*majesty, word etc*); sacred (*blood etc*); *F* heavenly, divine (*music, weather etc*); **le d. Enfant** [divinɑ̃fɑ̃], the Holy Child. **2** *nm* **le d.,** the divine.

divinateur, -trice [divinatœr, -tris] **1** *n Arch* diviner, soothsayer. **2** *adj* foreseeing, prophetic.

divination [divinɑsjɔ̃] *nf* **(a)** (*occultisme*) divination, soothsaying; **(b)** (*intuition*) intuition.

divinatoire [divinatwar] *adj* divinatory; **baguette d.,** divining rod, dowsing rod.

divinement [divinmɑ̃] *adv* divinely.

divinisation [divinizɑsjɔ̃] *nf* deification.

diviniser [divinize] *vt* to deify.

divinité [divinite] *nf* **(a)** (*nature de Dieu*) divinity, divine nature; godhead (*of Christ etc*); **(b)** (*dieu*) divinity, deity, god, *f* goddess.

diviser [divize] **1** *vt* **(a)** (*séparer*) to divide; **d. le travail,** to share (out) the work; **la semaine est divisée en jours,** the week is divided *or* split up into days; **d. une question en plusieurs points,** to break down a question into several points; *Math* **d. un nombre par un autre,** to divide one number by another; **(b)** (*délimiter*) to separate; to set (*people etc*) at variance; **les Pyrénées divisent la France d'avec l'Espagne,** the Pyrenees divide *or* separate France from Spain; **maison divisée contre elle-même,** house divided against itself; **d. pour régner,** divide and conquer. **2 se diviser** *vpr* to divide, to break up (**en,** into); **l'examen se divise en trois parties,** the examination is divided into three parts.

diviseur [divizœr] *nm* **(a)** *Math* divisor; **plus grand commun d.,** highest common factor; **nombre/fraction d.,** divisor number/fraction; **(b)** *Tech* divider; *Él* **d. de courant,** current divider.

divisibilité [divizibilite] *nf* divisibility.

divisible [divizibl] *adj* divisible.

division [divizjɔ̃] *nf* **(a)** division (**en,** into); dividing (*of whole into parts*); *Math* division; *Biol* **d. cellulaire,** cellular division; **d. du travail,** division of labour; **(b)** (*partie*) part, portion, section (*of whole*); (administrative) division, department, branch; *Scol* group, section; *Mil Nau* division; **les divisions d'un livre,** the sections of a book; *Mil* **d. blindée,** armoured division; **(c)** (*désaccord*) discord, dissension, disagreement; **(d)** *Typ* hyphen.

divisionnaire [divizjɔnɛr] **1** *adj Mil etc* divisional; *Admin* **commissaire d.** ≈ (police) superintendent. **2** *nm* (police) superintendent; *Mil* major general.

divorce [divɔrs] *nm Jur* divorce; **intenter une action en d.,** to take divorce proceedings (**contre qn,** against s.o.); **d. par consentement mutuel,** divorce by mutual consent; **d. à l'amiable,** no-fault divorce; **les enfants sont ceux qui pâtissent le plus du divorce,** divorce is hardest on the children; **demander le d.,** to ask for a divorce; *Jur* to sue for a divorce, to file a petition for divorce; *Fig* **le d. de la langue écrite avec la langue parlée,** the gulf between the written and the spoken language.

divorcé, -ée [divɔrse] **1** *adj* divorced. **2** *n* divorced man *or* woman, divorcee.

divorcer [divɔrse] *vi* (**je divorçai(s); n. divorçons**) **d. (d')avec qn,** to divorce s.o.; **il veut d.,** he wants a divorce; **ils ont divorcé l'année dernière,** they got divorced *or* they got a divorce last year.

divulgateur, -trice [divylgatœr, -tris] *n* (police) informer; discloser, betrayer (*of secrets*).

divulgation [divylgɑsjɔ̃] *nf* divulgence, disclosure (**de,** of).

divulguer [divylge] *vt* to divulge, to reveal, to disclose (*secret etc*).

dix [dis] **1** *adj inv* (*at the end of the word group* [dis]; *before n or adj beginning with a vowel sound* [diz]; *before n or adj beginning with a consonant* [di]) **(a) il est d. heures** [dizœr], it is ten o'clock; **j'en ai d.** [dis], I have ten; **(b)** (*ordinal uses etc*) **le d. mai** [lədimɛ], the tenth of May; **Charles D.,** Charles the Tenth; **le numéro d.,** number ten. **2** *nm inv* (*souvent* [dis]) **d. et demi** [disedmi], ten and a half; **j'habite au d.,** I live at Number 10; *Cartes* **le d. de trèfle,** the ten of clubs; *Scol* **devoir noté sur d.,** homework marked out of ten; **le X est le signe du d. romain,** X is ten in Roman numerals.

dix-huit [dizɥi(t)] **1** *adj inv* eighteen; **le d.-h. mai,** the eighteenth of May. **2** *nm inv* eighteen; **ça fait d.-h,** that makes eighteen.

dix-huitième [dizɥitjɛm] **1** *adj inv* eighteenth; **le d.-h. concurrent,** the eighteenth competitor. **2** *n* eighteenth.

dixième [dizjɛm] *adj & n* tenth.

dixièmement [dizjɛmmɑ̃] *adv* tenthly, in the tenth place.

dix-neuf [diznœf] **1** *adj inv* nineteen; **le d.-n. mai,** the nineteenth of May. **2** *nm inv* nineteen.

dix-neuvième [diznœvjɛm] *adj & n* nineteenth.

dix-sept [dis(s)ɛt] **1** *adj inv* seventeen; **le d.-s. mai,** the seventeenth of May. **2** *nm inv* seventeen.

dix-septième [dis(s)ɛtjɛm] *adj & n* seventeenth.

dizain [dizɛ̃] *nm Littér* ten-line stanza.

dizaine [dizɛn] *nf* about ten; *Math* ten; **une d. de personnes,** ten or so people, about ten people; **il y a une d. d'années,** about ten years ago, ten years ago or so; *Math* **compter par dizaines,** to count in tens.
djebel [dʒɛbɛl] *nm* (*in North Africa*) jebel, mountain.
djellaba [dʒɛlaba] *nf* djellaba.
djinn [dʒin] *nm* djin(n), jinn.
do [do] *nm Mus* **(a)** (the note) C; **(b)** (*in tonic sol-fa*) doh.
docile [dɔsil] *adj* docile, submissive, amenable (*child*); tractable (*animal etc*); manageable (*hair*).
docilement [dɔsilmɑ̃] *adv* submissively, obediently, with docility.
docilité [dɔsilite] *nf* docility.
dock [dɔk] *nm Nau* **(a)** (*bassin*) dock; **d. de carénage/flottant,** dry/floating dock; **(b)** (*cale de construction*) dock(s), dockyard; **(c)** *Com* warehouse.
docker [dɔkɛr] *nm* docker, *Am* longshoreman.
docte [dɔkt] **1** *adj Litt & (when it precedes noun) Iron* learned. **2** *nmpl* **les doctes,** scholars.
doctement [dɔktəmɑ̃] *adv Litt & Iron* in a learned manner, learnedly.
docteur [dɔktœr] *nm* **(a) d. (en médecine),** doctor (of medicine); **leur fille est d.,** their daughter is a doctor; **le d. Thomas,** Dr Thomas; **bonjour d.,** good morning doctor; **(b)** *Univ* **d. ès lettres,** = Doctor of Literature; **Mlle Laurent est d. ès sciences,** Miss Laurent is a doctor of science; **d. en droit,** doctor of law; **(c)** *Rel* **les docteurs de l'Église,** the Doctors of the Church.
doctoral, -aux [dɔktɔral, -o] *adj Péj* pompous (*manner*); bombastic (*tone*).
doctoralement [dɔktɔralmɑ̃] *adv Péj* pompously, bombastically.
doctorat [dɔktɔra] *nm Univ* doctorate; **d. d'État,** ≈ D.Litt., D.Sc. *etc*; **d. d'université,** ≈ Ph.D.
doctoresse [dɔktɔrɛs] *nf Vieilli* woman doctor.
doctrinaire [dɔktrinɛr] *adj* doctrinaire.
doctrinal, -aux [dɔktrinal, -o] *adj* doctrinal.
doctrine [dɔktrin] *nf* doctrine, tenet.
docudrame [dɔkydram] *nm TV* docudrama, faction, dramatized documentary.
document [dɔkymɑ̃] *nm* document; **nous avons des documents pour le prouver,** we have documents to prove it.
documentaire [dɔkymɑ̃tɛr] **1** *adj* documentary (*proof etc*); **à titre d.,** for (your) information; *Cin* **film d.,** documentary. **2** *nm Cin* documentary.
documentaliste [dɔkymɑ̃talist] *n* **(a)** (*d'archives etc*) documentalist, archivist; *Admin* keeper of records; **(b)** *TV etc* researcher.
documentariste [dɔkymɑ̃tarist] *n Cin* director of documentary films.
documentation [dɔkymɑ̃tasjɔ̃] *nf* (*action*) research; (*documents*) documentation; **je cherche de la d. sur ...,** I am looking for documentation on ... .
documenter [dɔkymɑ̃te] **1** *vt* to document (*matter*); to support (*statement etc*) with documentary evidence; **d. qn sur une question,** to brief s.o. on a question; **elle est bien documentée,** she is well informed on the subject; **son étude n'était pas solidement documentée,** his study was not well documented. **2 se documenter** *vpr* to gather documentation *or* information *or* material.
dodécaèdre [dɔdekaɛdr] *nm Math* dodecahedron.
dodécagone [dɔdekagɔn] *nm Math* dodecagon.
dodécaphonique [dɔdekafɔnik] *adj Mus* twelve-tone, dodecaphonic.
dodécaphonisme [dɔdekafɔnism] *nm Mus* twelve-tone system, dodecaphony.
dodelinement [dɔdlinmɑ̃] *nm* shaking (*of head, body*); (*parce qu'on a sommeil*) nodding (*of head*).
dodeliner [dɔdline] *vi* **d. de la tête/du corps,** to nod/shake.
dodo¹ [dodo] *nm Enf* (*sommeil*) sleep, bye-byes; (*lit*) bed; **faire d.,** to sleep; **aller à** *ou* **au d.,** to go to bed *or* to bye-byes.
dodo² *nm* (*oiseau*) dodo.
dodu [dɔdy] *adj F* plump.
doge [dɔʒ] *nm Hist* doge.
dogmatique [dɔgmatik] *adj* dogmatic.
dogmatiquement [dɔgmatikmɑ̃] *adv* dogmatically.
dogmatiser [dɔgmatize] *vi* to dogmatize; *Péj* to lay down the law.
dogmatisme [dɔgmatism] *nm* dogmatism.
dogme [dɔgm] *nm* dogma, tenet.
dogue [dɔg] *nm* mastiff; *Fig* **d'une humeur de d.,** like a bear with a sore head.
doigt [dwa] *nm* **(a)** finger; *Anat Zool* digit; **d. de pied,** toe; **mettre les doigts de pied en éventail,** to relax thoroughly, to do absolutely nothing; **le petit d.,** the little finger; *F* **mon petit d. me l'a dit,** a little bird told me; **lever le d.,** (*in class etc*) to put one's hand up; *Fig* **ne pas lever** *ou* **remuer le petit d.,** not to lift a finger; **compter sur ses doigts,** to count on one's fingers; **je peux compter mes amis sur les doigts de la main,** I can count my friends on the fingers of one hand; **porter une bague au d.,** to wear a ring on one's finger; **promener ses doigts sur qch,** to finger *or* feel sth; to run one's fingers over *or* along sth; **elle a des doigts de fée,** she's good with her hands; **se faire taper sur les doigts,** to be rapped over the knuckles; *Mus* **avoir un morceau dans les doigts,** to have mastered a piece; **savoir qch sur le bout des doigts,** to know sth inside out; **menacer qn du d.,** to shake *or* wag one's finger at s.o.; **elle lui fit signe du d. (de venir),** she beckoned to him (to come); **désigner** *ou* **montrer qn/qch du d.,** to point at s.o./sth; *Fig* **mettre le d. dans l'engrenage,** to get involved *or* mixed up in sth; **vous avez mis le d. dessus,** you've put your finger on it, you've hit the nail on the head; *F* **se mettre** *ou* **se fourrer le d. dans l'œil (jusqu'au coude),** to be completely wrong; **fourrer ses doigts partout,** (*d'un bébé etc*) to be into everything; *F* **mener qn au d. et à l'œil,** to keep a tight rein on s.o.; **se mordre les doigts,** to bite one's nails with impatience; **s'en mordre les doigts,** to regret it, to repent (of) it; *F* **ce gâteau, je m'en lèche les doigts!,** this cake is really delicious!; **ils sont ensemble comme les doigts de la main,** they are very close; *Péj* they are hand in glove; *F* **gagner les doigts dans le nez,** to win hands down;
(b) (*mesure*) finger's breadth; **la robe est trop courte d'un d.,** the dress is a fraction too short; **un d. de cognac,** a nip *or* drop *or* spot of brandy; **être à deux doigts de la mort,** to be within an an inch of death; **il s'en est fallu d'un d. pour que ça rate,** it was a hair's breadth away from failing; **il s'en est fallu d'un d. pour qu'elle signe,** she was a hair's breadth away from signing;
(c) (*finger-shaped object*) **doigts d'un gant,** fingers of a glove; *MecE etc* **d. d'encliquetage,** finger, pawl, click (*of ratchet-wheel etc*); **d. d'entraînement,** driving-plate pin, driver, catch pin (*of lathe*).
doigté [dwate] *nm* **(a)** *Mus* fingering (*of piece of music*); **exercises de d.,** five-finger exercises; **(b)** (*de dactylo etc*) touch; **(c)** *Fig* tact, diplomacy, judgment; **manquer de d.,** to be tactless.
doigter [dwate] *vt* **(a)** to finger (*piece of music*); **(b)** to mark (*music*) with the proper fingering.
doigtier [dwatje] *nm* fingerstall.
doit [dwa] *nm Com* debit, liability; **d. et avoir,** debit and credit; (*personnes*) debtor and creditor.
dol [dɔl] *nm Jur* fraud, wilful misrepresentation.
dolby ® [dɔlbi] *nm* Dolby ®.
doléances [dɔleɑ̃s] *nfpl* complaints; **conter ses d.,** to air one's grievances.
dolent [dɔlɑ̃] *adj* doleful, plaintive, complaining (*voice, person etc*).
doline [dɔlin] *nf Géol* doline, sinkhole.
dollar [dɔlar] *nm* dollar; **la zone d.,** the dollar area.
dolman [dɔlmɑ̃] *nm* dolman; short-skirted jacket (*of hussars etc*).
dolmen [dɔlmɛn] *nm* dolmen.
doloire [dɔlwar] *nf* (cooper's) adze, *US* adz; (mason's) larry.
dolomie [dɔlɔmi] *nf*, **dolomite** [dɔlɔmit] *nf Minér* dolomite; *Géog* **les Dolomites,** the Dolomites.
dolomitique [dɔlɔmitik] *adj Géol* dolomitic.
dolosif, -ive [dɔlɔzif, -iv] *adj Jur* fraudulent.
domaine [dɔmɛn] *nm* **(a)** (*terre*) domain; (real) estate, property; *Jur* demesne; **domaines de la Couronne,** Crown lands; **d. (de l'État),** State (administered) property; **d. public,** public property; **ouvrage tombé dans le d. public,** work the copyright of which has lapsed *or* run out, work out of copyright *or* in the public domain; **le d. forestier,** the national forests; **(b)** (*rayon*) **d. d'une science,** field *or* scope of a science; **cela n'entre pas dans le d. de mes connaissances,** that's not my field; **ce n'est pas de mon d.,** that is not my province *or* not my sphere; **le d. du possible,** the realm(s) of possibility.
domanial, -aux [dɔmanjal, -o] *adj* (*estates, forests etc*) national, (belonging to the) State.
dôme [dom] *nm* **(a)** *Archit* dome, cupola; **(b)** *Littér* vault, canopy (*of heaven, trees*); *Géog* dome; **(c)** *Tech* **d. de (prise de) vapeur,** steam dome.
domestication [dɔmɛstikasjɔ̃] *nf* domestication.

domesticité [dɔmɛstisite] *nf* **(a)** (*service*) domestic service; **(b)** (*personnel*) domestic staff, household; **(c)** (*of animal*) domesticity.

domestique [dɔmɛstik] **1** *adj* **(a)** domestic (*life etc*); household (*duties etc*); family, domestic (*quarrel etc*); **économie d.,** home economics; **animal d.,** (*chien, chat*) pet; **(b)** domestic (*service*). **2** *n* **(a)** servant; *f* maid; (*in formal speech*) *& Am* domestic.

domestiquer [dɔmɛstike] *vt* to domesticate (*animal*); to bring (*s.o.*) to a state of subjection, to subjugate (*s.o.*); to harness (*atomic energy etc*).

domicile [dɔmisil] *nm* (place of) residence, home; *Jur* domicile; **sans d. fixe,** of no fixed abode *or* address; **à d.,** at one's private house, at home; **élire d. au 3 rue Hoche,** to take up residence at no 3, Rue Hoche; **travailler à d.,** to work from home; **notre épicier livre à d.,** our grocer has a delivery service; **franco à d.,** carriage paid; *Jur* **d. conjugal,** marital *or* matrimonial home.

domiciliaire [dɔmisiljɛr] *adj* home (*visit etc*).

domiciliation [dɔmisiljasjɔ̃] *nf Com* domiciliation (*of bill of exchange*).

domicilié [dɔmisilje] *adj* resident, domiciled (**à,** at).

domicilier [dɔmisilje] *vt* (*pr sub & impf* **n. domiciliions, v. domiciliiez**) *Com* to domicile (*bill at bank etc*).

dominance [dɔminɑ̃s] *nf Biol* dominance.

dominant, -ante [dɔminɑ̃, -ɑ̃t] **1** *adj* **(a)** dominating, dominant, ruling (*power, passion etc*); **(b)** predominating, prevailing (*colour, opinion etc*); outstanding (*feature, idea etc*); *Biol* **caractère d.,** dominant (characteristic). **2** *nf* **dominante** **(a)** *Mus* dominant (note); **(b)** chief characteristic.

dominateur, -trice [dɔminatœr, -tris] **1** *n Litt* ruler. **2** *adj* **(a)** dominating, ruling (*power, country etc*); **(b)** *Péj* domineering, overbearing (*person, tone etc*).

domination [dɔminasjɔ̃] *nf* domination, rule, dominion; **d. morale,** moral influence; **d. de soi-même,** self control.

dominer [dɔmine] **1** *vi* to rule (**sur,** over); **couleur qui domine,** predominating colour; **les jeunes de moins de 15 ans dominent dans le club,** young people of under 15 years old are in the majority in this club; **aimer d.,** to like to wield power; **elle domine de très loin sur ses collègues,** she is far better than her colleagues.

2 *vt* to dominate; to master, to overcome (*shyness etc*); **l'ambition le domine,** he is dominated by ambition; **sa voix dominait toutes les autres,** his voice rose *or* was heard above all the others; **se laisser d. par un collègue autoritaire,** to be dominated by an authoritarian colleague; **d. une classe,** (*d'un professeur*) to control a class; *Sp* **d. la partie,** to dominate the game; **le château domine la vallée,** the castle dominates the valley; *Fig* **d. son sujet,** to master one's subject; **d. la situation,** to be master of the situation, to have the situation under control.

3 se dominer *vpr Fig* to to be self-controlled, to control one's feelings.

dominicain, -aine [dɔminikɛ̃, -ɛn] **1** *adj Rel* **(a)** dominican (*friar, nun*); **(b)** *Géog* Dominican; (*native, inhabitant*) of Santo Domingo; **la République Dominicaine,** the Dominican Republic, Santo Domingo. **2** *n* **(a)** *Rel* Dominican; **(b) D.,** Dominican.

dominical, -aux [dɔminikal, -o] *adj* **l'oraison dominicale,** the Lord's prayer; **repos d.,** Sunday rest.

dominion [dɔminjɔn] *nm Pol* Dominion.

domino [dɔmino] *nm* domino; **jouer aux dominos,** to play (at) dominoes.

dommage [dɔmaʒ] *nm* **(a)** (*préjudice*) damage, injury; **causer du d. à qn,** to do s.o. harm *or* an injury; **quel d.!,** what a pity!, what a shame!; **c'est (bien) d. qu'elle ne soit pas venue,** it's a (great) pity that she didn't come; **le plus d. c'est que tu ne l'aies jamais vu,** it's a great pity that you never saw him; **d. que tu n'aies pas le temps,** it's a pity you haven't the time; **(b) dommages,** damage (*to property etc*); **réparer les dommages,** to repair *or* make good the damage, to make up the losses; **les dommages causés par la grêle,** the damage caused by the hail; *Jur* **dommages et intérêts, dommages-intérêts,** damages; **dommages de guerre,** war damages.

dommageable [dɔmaʒabl] *adj* detrimental, injurious; *Jur* prejudicial; *Jur* **acte d.,** tort.

domotique [dɔmotik] *nf* home automation.

domptable [dɔ̃tabl] *adj* capable of being tamed *or* subdued, tamable.

domptage [dɔ̃(p)taʒ] *nm* taming (*of animals etc*).

dompter [dɔ̃(p)te] *vt* to tame, to train (*animal*); to break in (*horse*); to subdue, to overcome (*one's feelings etc*).

dompteur, -euse [dɔ̃t(p)œr, -øz] *n* tamer, trainer (*of animals*); **d. de chevaux,** horse breaker.

don [dɔ̃] *nm* **(a)** (*cadeau*) gift, present; (*à un musée, une œuvre*) donation; **d. de sang/sperme,** blood/sperm donation; **d. de M. Roland,** (*dans un musée*) gift of Mr Roland, donated by Mr Roland; **le d. de soi,** self-sacrifice; **un d. en nature/espèces,** a donation in kind/cash; **faire d. à qn de qch,** to make a present *or* a donation of sth to s.o.; **(b)** (*aptitude*) gift, natural quality, talent; **le d. des langues,** the gift for languages, a talent for languages; **avoir le d. de faire qch,** to have a talent *or* a genius for doing sth; *Iron* **elle a le d. de m'énerver,** she has a gift for annoying me; **(c)** (*action*) giving.

donataire [dɔnatɛr] *n Jur* donee.

donateur, -trice [dɔnatœr, -tris] *n* giver; *Jur* donor.

donation [dɔnasjɔ̃] *nf* donation, gift.

donc [dɔ̃k] **1** *conj* (*marque la conséquence*) therefore, accordingly, then, hence, consequently, so; **je pense, d. je suis,** I think, therefore I am; **j'en suis d. très satisfait,** so I'm very satisfied with it.

2 *adv* **(a)** (*emphatic*) **vous voilà d. de retour,** so you're back (again); **que voulez-vous d.?,** what(ever) do you want?; **mais taisez-vous d.!,** do be quiet!, *F* do shut up!; **allons d.!,** nonsense!, come on!, come now!; **comment d.?,** how do you mean?; **pensez d.!,** just think!; (*pas du tout*) that's what you think!, that'll be the day!; **tu as d. oublié?,** have you forgotten?; **où vas-tu d.** [dɔ̃]**?,** where are you going?; **cela vous plaît d.?,** you like it, then?; **dites d.!,** tell me now ...; (*à qn qui exagère*) look here!, *Vieilli* I say!;

(b) (*after interruption or digression*) **d. pour en revenir à notre sujet,** well, to come back to our subject; **je disais d. que ...,** I was saying, then, that ..., as I was saying ... .

dondon [dɔ̃dɔ̃] *nf F* fat woman; **grosse d.,** great lump of a girl *or* woman.

donjon [dɔ̃ʒɔ̃] *nm* **(a)** keep, donjon (*of castle*); **(b)** turret mast (*of warship*).

don Juan [dɔ̃ʒɥɑ̃] *nm* Don Juan.

donjuanesque [dɔ̃ʒɥanɛsk] *adj* Don Juan.

donnant [dɔnɑ̃] *adj* **(a) d.-d.,** give and take, tit for tat; **(b)** *Arch* generous, open handed.

donne [dɔn] *nf Cartes* deal; **à vous la d.!,** your deal!; **fausse d.,** misdeal.

donné [dɔne] *adj* **(a)** given; **propriété donnée en dot,** property given as a dowry; *F* **c'est d.,** it's dirt cheap, it's a gift; **(b)** (*défini*) given; **à un point d., à une distance donnée,** at a given *or* certain point *or* distance; **des quantités données,** given quantities; **(c) étant d. deux triangles,** given two triangles; **étant d. l'heure tardive,** in view *or* in consideration of the lateness of the hour; **étant d. qu'il est mineur,** since *or* as he is a minor.

donnée [dɔne] *nf* **(a)** given information (*of problem etc*); fundamental idea *or* subject (*of novel etc*); **(b) données,** data, particulars; *Ordinat* data; *Ordinat* **banque/base de données,** data bank/base; **le traitement des données,** data processing; **support de données,** data carrier; **commutateur de données,** data switch (*for printer sharing*).

donner [dɔne] **1** *vt* **(a)** to give; **d. un cadeau à qn,** to give a present to s.o., to give s.o. a present; **d. du sang,** to give blood; **il m'a donné 100 francs,** he gave me 100 francs; **d. un baiser/une caresse/une gifle/une fessée à qn,** to give s.o. a kiss/a caress/a slap in the face/a spanking; **d. des conseils,** to give advice; **d. un coup de peigne à ses cheveux,** to give one's hair a quick comb; **il faudrait d. une couche de peinture supplémentaire,** we'll have to put on an extra coat of paint; **donnez-moi ce livre s'il vous plaît,** give me that book, please; **il m'a donné son rhume,** he gave me his cold, I caught his cold; **je vous en donne dix francs,** I'll give you ten francs for it; **je vous le donne en mille,** you'll never guess; **d. un lit pour** *ou* **contre un vélo,** to give a bed in exchange for a bicycle; **elle donnerait tout au monde pour que ça se réalise,** she would give anything for that to come about; **je donnerais beaucoup pour le savoir,** I would give a lot to know (that); **je lui donne 40 francs de l'heure,** I pay him 40 francs an hour; **d. à boire à qn,** to give s.o. something to drink; **d. sa vie pour qn,** to give one's life for s.o.; **d. à qn qch à garder,** to entrust s.o. with sth, to give s.o. sth to look after; **d. ses chaussures à réparer,** to leave one's shoes to be repaired; **d. ses enfants à garder,** to leave one's children to be looked after; **d. à qn sa fille en mariage,** to give one's daughter to s.o. in marriage; **d. la main à qn,** to give s.o. one's hand; *Fig* **tu donnes ta langue au chat?,** do you give up *or* in?; **cela va vous d. de l'énergie,** that'll give you energy; **cette couleur donne de la lumière dans la**

pièce, that colour makes the room look lighter;

(b) (*produire*) to provide, to furnish; (*of crops*) to yield; **arbre qui donne des fruits,** tree that yields *or* bears fruit; **d. des preuves à qn,** to give s.o. proof, to provide *or* furnish s.o. with proof; **cela nous donne la preuve que ...,** that proves that ...; **d. du souci à qn,** to cause s.o. worry; **d. sujet** *ou* **matière à discussion,** to be a subject for discussion *or* debate; **cela donne l'idée que ...,** it conveys the idea that ...; **d. l'heure,** to tell the time; **les dictionnaires donnent souvent des traductions différentes,** dictionaries often give different translations; **d. une raison,** to give a reason; **d. un bon exemple,** to set a good example; *F* **ça n'a rien donné,** nothing came of it, it didn't work *or* turn out; **d. le la avec un diapason,** to give an A with a tuning fork; **le journal donne des nouvelles alarmantes sur la crise,** the newspaper gives alarming news of the crisis; **je me demande ce que cela va d.,** I wonder what will come of it *or* what the result of it will be;

(c) (*organiser*) to give; **d. un bal/un dîner/une conférence,** to give a ball/a dinner party/a lecture; **d. une pièce de théâtre,** to produce *or* perform a play; **qu'est-ce qu'on donne au cinéma aujourd'hui?,** what's on at the cinema today?;

(d) (*causer*) to give; **ça me donne envie de rire,** that makes me want to laugh; **d. faim/soif/sommeil/chaud à qn,** to make s.o. hungry/thirsty/sleepy/hot; **cette odeur me donne mal à la tête,** this smell is giving me a headache; *F* **ça m'a donné les boules,** that pissed me off;

(e) (*permettre*) **j'y reviendrais plus tard, si l'occasion m'en est donnée,** I'd go there again later if I got the chance; **il n'est pas donné à tout le monde d'être un écrivain,** not everybody can be a writer;

(f) (*attribuer*) to ascribe, to attribute (*sth to s.o.*); **on lui donne une grande fortune,** they say he has a large fortune; **je lui donne vingt ans,** I reckon he's about twenty; **d. tort/raison à qn,** to disagree/agree with s.o.;

(g) je lui ai donné à entendre que ..., I gave him to understand that ...; **cela me donne à croire que ...,** it leads me to believe that ...;

(h) *Arg* (*vendre*) to grass on (*s.o.*);

(i) d. les cartes, to deal (the cards).

2 *vi* **(a)** (*faire un don*) to give; **aimer d.,** to like to give; **d. aux pauvres,** to give to the poor; **si les blés donnent cette année,** if there is a good crop of wheat this year;

(b) la fenêtre donne sur la cour, the window looks onto the yard; **cette porte donne sur le jardin,** this door leads (out) into the garden;

(c) le soleil donne dans la pièce, the sun is shining into the room; **d. de la tête contre qch,** to knock *or* strike *or* bump one's head against sth; *F* **ne pas savoir où d. de la tête,** not to know which way to turn; **le navire a donné sur les rochers,** the ship ran onto *or* struck the rocks;

(d) (*tomber*) **d. dans le piège,** *F* **d. dans le panneau,** to fall into the trap; **il donne dans les préjugés,** he is very prejudiced;

(e) (*d'un tissu*) to give, to stretch; **le cordage a beaucoup donné,** the rope has stretched a good deal;

(f) *F* **s'ils se disputent, ça va d.,** if they argue there'll be trouble; *Cartes* **mal d.,** to misdeal;

(g) *Mil* **l'armée va d.,** the army's about to attack; **faire d. un bataillon,** to send a battalion into action.

3 se donner *vpr* **(a)** (*se consacrer*) to devote oneself; **se d. à une cause/son travail,** to devote oneself to a cause/one's work;

(b) (*prendre*) **se d. des airs,** to put on airs, to give oneself airs; **se d. un genre,** to make out you're something you're not; **c'est un genre qu'elle se donne,** it's just a front; **se d. en spectacle,** to make an exhibition of oneself; **se d. les chances de réussir,** to give oneself a chance of succeeding; **se d. le temps de réflechir,** to give oneself *or* take time to think; **s'en d. (à cœur joie),** to enjoy oneself (to the full), to have a good time;

(c) cela se donne, it can be had for the asking;

(d) *Cin Th* **Hamlet se donne ce soir,** they are playing Hamlet tonight;

(e) (*avoir*) **se d. du tourment,** to worry (oneself); **se d. du mal (pour faire qch),** to take (great) trouble (over sth); (*s'appliquer*) to work hard;

(f) (*of woman*) to give herself.

donneur, -euse [dɔnœr, -øz] *n* **(a)** giver, donor; *Méd* **d. de sang/sperme,** blood/sperm donor; *Com* **d. d'ordre,** principal; **d. d'avis** *ou* **de conseils,** busybody, know-all, *Am* wise guy; **(b)** *Cartes* dealer; **(c)** *Arg* (police) informer, squealer.

don-quichottisme [dɔ̃kiʃɔtism] *nm* quixotism.

dont [dɔ̃] *pron rel* **(a) la pièce d. elle sort,** the room she is coming out of; **la ville d. je viens,** the town I come from;

(b) (= **de qui, duquel, desquels** *etc*) from *or* by *or* with whom *or* which; **les aïeux d. je suis descendu,** my ancestors; **la femme d. il est amoureux,** the woman he is in love with; **la façon d. il me regardait,** the way he looked at me; **une fille d. on ne sait rien,** a girl we know nothing about;

(c) (*of, about, concerning*) whom, which; **le livre d. j'ai besoin,** the book (which, that) I want *or* need; **voici ce d. il s'agit,** this is what it's all about;

(d) (*complément de nom*) whose, of whom, of which; **la dame d. je connais le fils,** the lady whose son I know; **la dame d. le fils vous connaît,** the lady whose son knows you; **la chambre d. la porte est fermée,** the room with the closed door;

(e) quelques-uns étaient là, d. votre frère, there were a few people there, including your brother; **un rêve d. il ne me reste que cette image,** a dream of which I remember nothing but this image; **un film d. voici le résumé,** a film of which this is a summary.

donzelle [dɔ̃zɛl] *nf F Péj* woman who puts on airs.

dopage [dɔpaʒ] *nm* doping.

dopant [dɔpɑ̃] *nm Méd* dope.

dope [dɔp] *nf F* (*drogue*) dope.

doper [dɔpe] **1** *vt Sp etc* to dope. **2 se doper** *vpr* to take stimulants, to dope oneself.

doping [dɔpiŋ] *nm* doping.

dorade [dɔrad] *nf* (*poisson*) gilthead bream, sea bream.

doré [dɔre] **1** *adj* **(a)** (*recouvert d'or*) gilded, gilt; **d. sur tranche,** gilt-edged; **cheveux blond d.,** golden hair; **(b)** *Culin* glazed (*cake*); browned (*meat etc*). **2** *nm Can* (*poisson*) wall-eyed pike, yellow pike.

dorée [dɔre] *nf* (*poisson*) (John) Dory.

dorénavant [dɔrenavɑ̃] *adv* from now on, *Fml* henceforth.

dorer [dɔre] **1** *vt* **(a)** (*recouvrir d'or*) to gild; *Fig* **le soleil dorait les cimes,** the sun shed a golden light upon *or* cast a glow upon the hilltops; *Fig* **d. la pilule,** to sugar the pill; **d. à froid,** to stamp (*cover*) in blind; **(b)** *Culin* to glaze (*cake*); to brown (*meat, fish etc*). **2 se dorer** *vpr* to turn a golden colour; **elle se dore au soleil,** she's sunbathing, she's getting a suntan.

doreur, -euse [dɔrœr, -øz] *n* gilder.

dorien, -ienne [dɔrjɛ̃, -jɛn] **1** *adj Antiq* Dorian (*people*); Doric (*dialect*); *Mus* Dorian (*mode*). **2** *nm Ling* Doric.

dorique [dɔrik] *adj Archit* Doric.

dorlotement [dɔrlɔtmɑ̃] *nm* (*caresse*) fondling; (*d'un enfant, malade etc*) coddling.

dorloter [dɔlɔte] **1** *vt* (*caresser*) to fondle (*s.o.*); to coddle, to pamper (*un enfant, un malade*). **2 se dorloter** *vpr* to coddle *or* pamper oneself.

dormant [dɔrmɑ̃] **1** *adj* **(a)** still, stagnant (*water*); **(b)** fixed, immovable (*frame etc*); (*window etc*) that cannot be opened; **serrure dormante,** dead lock; **(c)** *Hér* dormant; **(d)** sleeping (*person*). **2** *nm* frame, casing (*of door, window*).

dormeur, -euse [dɔrmœr, -øz] **1** *adj* **poupée dormeuse,** sleeping doll. **2** *n* (*personne endormie*) sleeper; (*personne qui a envie de dormir*) sleepyhead; **un grand** *ou* **gros d.,** a heavy sleeper. **3** *nf* **dormeuse,** stud earring. **4** *nm* (*crustacé*) edible crab.

dormir [dɔrmir] *vi* (*prp* **dormant;** *pp* **dormi;** *pr ind* **je dors, n. dormons;** *impf* **je dormais;** *p hist* **je dormis) (a)** to sleep, to be asleep; **d. profondément** *ou* **d'un profond sommeil,** to be fast asleep; **bien/mal d.,** to sleep well/badly; **elle dort d'un sommeil léger,** she's a light sleeper; **d. du sommeil du juste,** to sleep the sleep of the just; **je n'ai pas dormi de la nuit,** I haven't slept a wink, I didn't sleep a wink (all night), I didn't sleep all night; **il n'en dort pas,** he can't (get to) sleep for thinking of it; **le café m'empêche de d.,** coffee keeps me awake; **d. trop longtemps,** to oversleep; **d. à poings fermés** *ou* **comme une souche** *ou* **comme un loir,** to sleep soundly *or* like a log; **d. comme un sabot** *ou* **une toupie,** to snore; **ne d. que d'un œil,** to sleep with one eye open; **vous pouvez d. sur les** *ou* **vos deux oreilles,** don't worry, rest assured; **avoir envie de d.,** to be *or* feel sleepy *or* drowsy; **il dort debout,** he's asleep on his feet, he can't keep his eyes open; **une histoire** *ou* **un conte à d. debout,** a tall *or* cock-and-bull story;

(b) *Fig* to remain inactive; to be *or* lie dormant; **il dort sur son travail,** he's slack at his work; **ses capitaux dorment,** his capital is lying idle; **eau qui dort,** stagnant *or* still water; *Prov* **il n'est pire eau que l'eau qui dort,** still waters run deep.

dormitif, -ive [dɔrmitif, -iv] *adj Méd* soporific.

dorsal, -ale, -aux [dɔrsal, -o] **1** *adj* dorsal; **région**

dorsale de la main, back of the hand; *Av* **parachute d.,** back-type parachute. **2** *nf* **dorsale (a)** *Ling* dorsal consonant; **(b)** *Géog* ridge (*of mountains*).

dortoir [dɔrtwar] *nm* dormitory; **ville-d., cité-d.,** dormitory town.

dorure [dɔryr] *nf* **(a)** (*couche d'or*) gilding; **d. à froid,** (*d'un livre*) blind tooling; **(b)** *Culin* glazing (*of cake*) (with egg yolk); **(c)** (*ornement doré*) gilt, gilding; **uniforme couvert de dorures,** gold-braided uniform.

doryphore [dɔrifɔr] *nm* Colorado beetle.

dos [do] *nm* **(a)** *Anat* back; **avoir le d. voûté,** to be round-shouldered; **voir qn de d.,** to have a back view of s.o., to see s.o.'s back; **dormir sur le d.,** to sleep on one's back; **partir sac au d.,** to set off with one's pack on one's back; **robe décolletée dans le d.,** low-backed dress; **elle porte ses cheveux dans le d.,** she wears her hair loose; *F* **ça fait froid dans le d.,** it's scary *or* creepy, it gives you the shivers; **ça me fait un frisson dans le d.,** it sends a shiver down my spine; **tourner le d. à qn,** to turn one's back on s.o.; (*quand on est debout, assis*) to stand *or* sit with one's back to s.o.; **dès qu'il a le d. tourné,** the moment *or* as soon as his back is turned; **faire qch derrière le d. de qn,** to do sth behind s.o.'s back; **avoir qn/qch sur le d.,** to be saddled with s.o./sth; **il me tombe toujours sur le d.,** he's always jumping down my throat; **faire le gros d.,** (*of cat*) to arch its back; **voyager à d. d'âne,** to ride *or* travel on a donkey; **se mettre tout le monde à d.,** to set everybody against you; **d. à d.,** back to back; **je n'ai rien à me mettre sur le d.,** I haven't a thing to wear; **il a bon d.,** he's got a broad back, he can take anything; *F* **j'en ai plein le d.,** I'm sick of it, I'm fed up with it; *F* **faire la bête à deux d.,** to have it off; *F* **faire la bête à deux d. avec qn,** to sleep with *or* have it off with s.o.;

(b) back (*of chair, page, knife etc*); bridge (*of the nose*); spine (*of book*); **scie à d.,** back saw; **signer au d. d'un chèque,** to endorse a cheque; **voir au d.,** (please) turn over, PTO.

dosage [dozaʒ] *nm* **(a)** *Ch etc* quantity determination, proportioning (*of ingredients*); **(b)** dosage (*of medicine*).

dose [doz] *nf* **(a)** *Ch etc* proportion, amount (*of constituent in compound*); **(b)** dose (*of medicine*); **d. mortelle,** lethal dose; **par petites doses,** in small quantities *or* doses; *Fig* **une légère d. d'ironie,** a tinge of irony; **forcer la d.,** to overdo it.

doser [doze] *vt* **(a)** *Ch etc* to determine the quantity of; to proportion (*constituent in compound*); **(b)** to measure out (*a dose of medicine*); *Fig* **il faut savoir d. l'ironie,** one must be able to include just the right amount of irony.

doseur [dozœr] *nm* measure; **verre d.,** *Culin* measuring jug; (*pour l'alcool*) measure.

dossard [dosar] *nm Sp* number (*worn by player, competitor*).

dossier [dosje] *nm* **(a)** back (*of seat etc*); **chaise à d. droit,** straight-backed chair; *Aut etc* **d. réglable,** adjustable back; **(b)** dossier, file; record (*of prisoner etc*); (*chemise*) folder, file; **d. scolaire,** school records; **verser une pièce au d.,** to file a document; **constituer un d. sur la pollution,** to build up a file on pollution; *Fig* **le d. de la couche d'ozone,** the matter of the ozone layer; *Fig* **le d. de la couche d'ozone est assez important,** the ozone layer is a fairly important matter; *Fig* **s'occuper du d. de l'environnement,** to be responsible for environmental matters.

dot [dɔt] *nf* **(a)** (*pour un mariage*) dowry, marriage settlement; **il l'a épousée pour sa d.,** he married her for her dowry; **coureur de d.,** fortune hunter; **(b)** (*pour une religieuse*) dowry.

dotal, -aux [dɔtal, -o] *adj* dotal (*property etc*); *Jur* **régime d.,** (marriage) settlement in trust.

dotation [dɔtasjɔ̃] *nf* endowment, foundation (*of hospital etc*); allowance (*made to royal family etc*); (*of department*) staffing; *Can Admin* **agent de d.,** staffing officer.

doter [dɔte] *vt* to endow (*hospital etc*); to dower (*bride*); **être doté de toutes les vertus,** to be endowed with every virtue; **d. une usine d'un matériel neuf,** to equip a factory with new plant; **la vie l'a dotée d'une intelligence remarquable,** life has bestowed unparalleled intelligence on her *or* has endowed her with unparalleled intelligence.

douaire [dwɛr] *nm* dower.

douairière [dwɛrjɛr] *adj & nf* dowager.

douane [dwan] *nf Admin* customs; **passer à la d.,** to go through customs; **passer qch (en fraude) à la d.,** to smuggle sth through customs; **formalités de d.,** customs clearance; **agent des douanes,** customs officer; **marchandises en d.,** bonded goods; **(bureau de) d.,** customs house; **(droits de) d.,** customs dues, (customs) duty; **franc de d.,** duty paid; **d. volante,** mobile customs and excise unit.

douanier, -ière [dwanje, -jɛr] **1** *adj* (of) customs; **tarif d.,** customs tariff; **union douanière,** customs union; **barrières douanières,** tariff barriers. **2** *nm* customs officer.

doublage [dublaʒ] *nm* **(a)** doubling (*of quantity etc*); doubling, folding in half (*of sheet of paper etc*); *Cin* dubbing; *Cin* **d. du film en anglais,** English dubbing of the film; **(b)** (process of) lining (*coat*); sheathing (*ship*).

double [dubl] **1** *adj* double, twofold (*measure, quantity etc*); **valise à d. fond,** suitcase with a false bottom; **mot à d. sens,** ambiguous word; **agent d.,** double agent; **jouer un d. jeu avec qn,** to play a double game with s.o.; **faire qch en d. exemplaire,** to do sth in duplicate; **coup d.,** right and left (*in shooting*); **mot qui fait d. emploi (avec un autre),** redundant word; **sa canne à pêche a une longueur d. de la mienne,** his fishing rod is twice the length of mine; **fermer une porte à d. tour,** to double-lock a door; **à d. effet,** dual *or* double action; **outil à d. usage,** dual-purpose tool; **comptabilité en partie d.,** double-entry book-keeping; **d. allumage,** (*d'un moteur*) dual ignition; **d. whisky,** double *or* large whisky; *Fig* **faire coup d.,** to kill two birds with one stone.

2 *adv* **voir d.,** to see double; **en d.,** in duplicate.

3 *nm* **(a)** (*quantité*) double; **j'ai le d. de votre âge,** I am twice your age; **ça m'a coûté le d.,** it cost me twice as much *or* double; **plier qch en d.,** to fold sth in two *or* in half; *Tennis* **d. messieurs/dames/mixte,** men's/ladies'/mixed doubles;

(b) (*exemplaire*) duplicate, copy; *Ordinat* back up; *Typ* carbon copy;

(c) (*personne*) double; **c'était ton d.!,** he was your double!

doublé [duble] **1** *adj* **(a)** doubled; **(b)** lined (*garment*); **(c)** *Cin* dubbed. **2** *nm* **(a) d. (or),** gold plate, rolled gold; (*bijouterie*) gold-plated jewellery; **d. argent,** silver plate; (*bijouterie*) silver-plated jewellery; **(b)** (*à la chasse*) *& Sp* (*deux réussites*) double.

doubleau, -eaux [dublo] *nm Constr* (ceiling) beam; *Archit* transverse rib.

double-blanc [dubləblɑ̃] *nm* (*at dominoes*) double blank; (*pl doubles-blancs*).

double-commande [dubləkɔmɑ̃d] *nf Av Aut* dual controls; (*pl doubles-commandes*).

double-corde [dubləkɔrd] *nf Mus* double-stopping (*on violin etc*); (*pl doubles-cordes*).

double-crème [dubləkrɛm] *nm* (type of) cream cheese; (*pl doubles-crèmes*).

double-décimètre [dublədesimɛtr] *nm* = ruler, foot rule; (*pl doubles-décimètres*).

doublement¹ [dubləmɑ̃] *adv* doubly.

doublement² *nm* doubling (*of number etc*); folding in two, doubling (*of piece of paper etc*).

doubler [duble] **1** *vt* to double (*the amount, size etc*); to line (*coat etc*); *Cin* to dub (*a film*); *Cin* to stand in for (*s.o.*); *F* to double-cross (*s.o.*); **d. sa fortune/la mise,** to double one's fortune/the stakes; **d. une feuille de papier,** to fold a sheet of paper in half *or* in two; *Scol* **d. une classe,** to repeat a year; *Th* **d. un rôle/un acteur,** to understudy a part/an actor; **d. le pas,** to quicken one's pace; **d. une voiture,** to overtake *or Am* pass a car; *Mus* **d. une partie,** to double a part; *Nau* **d. un cap,** to double *or* make *or* weather a cape.

2 *vi* **(a)** (*of population etc*) to double, to increase twofold; **(b)** *Aut* to overtake; **défense de d.,** no overtaking, *Am* no passing.

3 se doubler *vpr* **haine qui se double de mépris,** hatred coupled with contempt.

doublet [dublɛ] *nm Ling* (*pierre précieuse*) doublet.

doublon¹ [dublɔ̃] *nm Typ* double.

doublon² *nm Arch* doubloon.

doublure [dublyr] *nf* **(a)** lining (*of garment etc*); **(b)** *Th* understudy; *Cin* stand-in; (*cascadeur*) stunt man.

douce [dus] *nf* **(a)** *F* **ma d.,** my girlfriend; **allez, viens ma d.,** come on sweetheart; **(b) en d.,** discreetly, quietly, *F* on the Q.T..

douce-amère [dusamɛr] *nf* woody nightshade, bittersweet; (*pl douces-amères*).

douceâtre [dusɑtr] *adj* sweetish; sickly sweet (*taste*).

doucement [dusmɑ̃] *adv* (*délicatement*) gently; (*bas*) softly; (*en faisant attention*) gently, carefully, slowly; **allez-y d.!,** gently does it!, easy does it!; **les affaires vont d.,** business is so-so; *F* **(allez-y) d. avec le vin,** go easy on the wine; *Arg* **ça m'a fait d. rigoler,** I had a good laugh over it; **d. les basses!**, take it easy!

doucereux, -euse [dusrø, -øz] *adj* (a) sickly (sweet) (*taste etc*); (b) smooth, smooth-tongued (*person*); smooth, sugary (*voice, tone*).

doucet, -ette [dusɛ, -ɛt] **1** *adj Arch* meek, mild, demure (*person*). **2** *nf* (*plante*) **doucette,** corn salad, lamb's lettuce.

douceur [dusœr] *nf* (a) sweetness (*of honey, perfume etc*); (b) (*sucreries*) **douceurs,** sweets, sweet things; **aimer les douceurs,** to have a sweet tooth; (c) softness (*of sound, material etc*); mildness (*of climate*); (d) pleasantness; (*bien-être*) pleasant thing; **d. de vivre,** easy *or* gentle way of life; **les douceurs de l'amitié,** the comforts *or* pleasures of friendship; **dire des douceurs à une femme,** to say sweet nothings to a woman; (e) gentleness (*of character etc*); sweetness (*of smile*); **traiter qn avec d.,** to treat s.o. gently *or* with kindness; **employer la d. avec un enfant/un animal,** to be gentle with a child/an animal; **en d.,** gently; **la voiture a démarré en d.,** the car started smoothly; **allez-y en d.!,** gently does it!, easy does it!

douche [duʃ] *nf* (a) shower; (*installation*) shower (unit); **prendre une d.,** to take a shower; **les douches,** the shower room(s), the showers; **d. écossaise,** (alternately) hot and cold shower; *Fig* succession of good and bad news *or* experiences *etc*, ups and downs; *Fig* **il m'a administré une bonne d. écossaise,** it was the exact opposite of what he'd said earlier; (b) shower (*of rain etc*); *F* **administrer une d. à qn,** to give s.o. a telling-off; *Fig* **d. (froide),** terrible disappointment, let-down; (c) *Méd* douche.

doucher [duʃe] **1** *vt* (a) (*pour se laver*) to give (*s.o.*) a shower; (b) (*d'une averse*) to soak; **se faire d. par l'orage,** to get soaked in the storm; (c) (*réprimander*) to tell (*s.o.*) off; (*décevoir*) to disappoint (*s.o.*); **il s'est fait d.,** he got a telling-off; (d) *Méd* to douche. **2 se doucher** *vpr* to take a shower.

doué [dwe] *adj* gifted; **il n'est guère d. pour les langues,** he has no gift for languages, he's no linguist; **une petite fille douée,** a gifted *or* talented little girl.

douer [dwe] *vt* to endow (*s.o.*) (*with qualities, advantages*); **il est doué d'une bonne mémoire,** he has a good memory.

douille [duj] *nf* socket (*of tool etc*); lamp socket (*of electric light bulb*); case (*of cartridge etc*); *Culin* piping nozzle; **d. à (pas de) vis,** screw lamp holder.

douillet, -ette [dujɛ, -ɛt] **1** *adj* (a) (*coussin*) soft, downy; (*lit*) cosy; (b) (*trop délicat*) soft; **ne sois pas si d.!,** don't be such a baby! **2** *nf* **douillette,** (*de bébé*) quilted coat; (*de curé*) quilted overcoat.

douillettement [dujɛtmɑ̃] *adv* softly, delicately; (*tucked up*) cosily; **élever un enfant d.,** to coddle a child.

douleur [dulœr] *nf* (a) (*physique*) pain, ache; **d. aiguë,** sharp pain; **pousser un cri** *ou* **des cris de d.,** to cry out with pain; **se sentir des douleurs par tout le corps,** to ache all over; **sans d.,** painless (*childbirth, operation etc*); (b) (*morale*) sorrow, grief; **il a eu la d. de perdre sa mère,** he had the sorrow of losing his mother; **partager la d. de qn,** to share s.o.'s sorrow *or* grief, to feel for s.o..

douloureusement [dulurøzmɑ̃] *adv* (*voir adj*) (a) painfully; (b) sorrowfully.

douloureux, -euse [dulurø, -øz] **1** *adj* (a) painful; (*au contact*) sore, tender; **mon dos est d. aujourd'hui,** my back hurts *or* aches today, my back is hurting today; (b) sad, distressing, grievous (*loss, event etc*); pained, sorrowful (*look*); **des cris d.,** heart-rending *or* mournful cries. **2** *nf F* **la douloureuse,** the bill; **apportez-moi la douloureuse,** let's see what the damage is.

doute [dut] *nm* doubt, uncertainty, misgiving; **être dans le d.,** to be in doubt *or* to be doubtful (**au sujet de qch,** about sth); **avoir des doutes sur** *ou* **au sujet de qn/qch,** to have doubts *or* misgivings *or* suspicions about s.o./sth; **mettre qch en d.,** to question sth, to cast doubts on sth; **mettre en d. la parole de qn,** to challenge s.o.'s word; **c'est hors de d., il n'y a pas de d.,** it is beyond doubt *or* beyond (all) question; **laisser qn dans le d. est cruel,** it is cruel to leave s.o. in doubt *or* a state of uncertainty; **je ne lui ai laissé aucun d. quant à mes sentiments pour lui,** I left him in no doubt about my feelings for him; **cela ne fait plus aucun d.,** there is no longer any doubt about it; **avoir un d. (sur qch),** to have a misgiving (about sth); **nul d. qu'il (ne) soit mort,** there is no doubt that he is dead; **sans d.,** no doubt, probably; **sans aucun d.,** without (any) doubt; **vous ne me reconnaissez pas, sans d.,** I don't suppose you recognize me; **sans d. viendra-t-il, sans d. qu'il viendra,** I expect he'll come.

douter [dute] **1** *vi* to doubt; **d. du zèle de qn,** to doubt *or* question *or* have doubts about s.o.'s enthusiasm; **il était à n'en point d. courageux,** his courage was beyond all question; **j'en doute,** I doubt it, I have my doubts (about it); **j'en doute fort,** I doubt it very much; **je ne doute pas de la voir bientôt,** I have no doubt I shall see her before long; **elle doute de vous avoir rencontré,** she's not sure whether she's met you; **il ne doute de rien,** he is full of self-confidence.

2 *vt* **je doute qu'il soit assez fort,** I doubt whether he is strong enough; **je ne doute pas qu'il (ne) vous vienne en aide,** I am confident that he will help you.

3 se douter *vpr* to suspect; **se d. de qch,** to suspect sth; **je m'en doutais (bien),** I guessed *or* thought as much; **elle est surprise, je m'en doute,** she is surprised, I'm sure *or* I dare say; **il ne se doute de rien,** he doesn't suspect anything; **je ne me doutais pas qu'il fût là,** I had no idea that he was there; **je me doute bien que c'est un peu difficile,** I rather suspect *or* think it's going to be difficult.

douteur, -euse [dutœr, -øz] *n Litt* doubter.

douteusement [dutøzmɑ̃] *adv* doubtfully.

douteux, -euse [dutø, -øz] *adj* doubtful, uncertain, questionable; dubious (*honour, company*); **créance douteuse,** bad debt; **jour d.,** dubious *or* uncertain light; **des vêtements d.,** dubious clothes; **d'un blanc d.,** of a dubious white; **il est d. que** + *sub*, it is doubtful whether ...; **il n'est pas d. que ... (ne)** + *sub ou plus souvent* **que** + *ind*, there is no doubt that ... .

douve [duv] *nf* (a) *Agr* trench, ditch; *Courses de chevaux* water jump; **douves,** moat (*of castle*); (b) (*planche*) stave; (c) (*plante*) **grande d.,** spearwort; (d) *Vét* fluke(worm); **d. du foie,** liver fluke.

Douvres [duvr] *n* Dover.

doux, douce [du, dus] **1** *adj* (a) sweet; smooth, soft (*to the touch*); mild (*to the taste*); **eau douce,** fresh water; (*non calcaire*) soft water; **poisson d'eau douce,** freshwater fish; *F* **marin d'eau douce,** landlubber; **peau douce,** smooth *or* soft skin;

(b) pleasant, agreeable (*air, tone etc*); **d. souvenir,** pleasant memory; **mener une vie douce,** to lead a calm *or* peaceful life; *Arg* **se la couler douce,** to take it easy; **faire les yeux d. à qn,** to make sheep's eyes at s.o.; *Iron* **douce perspective!,** charming prospect!;

(c) gentle (*movement, voice*); soft, subdued (*light, colour, sound*); mellow (*light*); mild (*climate*); **un hiver très d.,** a very mild winter; **pente douce,** gentle slope; **chaleur douce,** moderate heat; *Culin* **faire cuire à feu d.,** to cook on a low heat *or* in a low oven; **fer d.,** soft iron; **lime douce,** smooth file; **tabac d.,** mild tobacco; **consonne douce,** soft consonant,

(d) mild, meek, gentle (*nature*); **être d. avec les enfants/les animaux,** to be kind to children/animals; **être d. avec les enfants,** (*d'un animal*) to be good *or* gentle with children; **il est très d. avec son petit garçon,** he's gentle with his little boy; **regard d.,** gentle *or* mild look; **d. comme un agneau,** as gentle as a lamb;

(e) *F* **c'est de la folie douce!,** it's sheer madness!

2 *adv F* **filer d.,** to give in; **là, tout d.,** steady, steady!

3 *nm* sweetness; **le d. de la mousse,** the softness of the moss; **préférer le sec au d.,** to prefer dry (wine) to sweet.

4 *n F* **c'est un d.,** he's a gentle creature.

douzain [duzɛ̃] *nm Littér* twelve-line poem.

douzaine [duzɛn] *nf* dozen; **trois douzaines d'œufs,** three dozen eggs; **une d. de personnes,** about a dozen people, a dozen or so people; **à la d.,** by the dozen; **il y en a à la d.,** there are dozens *or* lots of them.

douze [duz] **1** *adj inv* twelve; **le d. mai,** the twelfth of May; **Louis D.,** Louis the Twelfth; **d. heures,** twelve o'clock (noon). **2** *nm inv* twelve; **ça fait d.,** that makes twelve.

douzième [duzjɛm] *adj & n* twelfth.

douzièmement [duzjɛmmɑ̃] *adv* twelfthly, in the twelfth place.

doyen, -enne [dwajɛ̃, -ɛn] *n* (a) *Rel Scol* dean (*of chapter, of faculty*); doyen (*of diplomatic corps etc*); (b) (*personne la plus âgée*) senior; **elle est la doyenne de notre groupe,** she's the oldest in *or* the oldest member of our group; **d. d'âge,** oldest member (*of a club*).

doyenné [dwajɛne] **1** *nm Rel* (*dignité, résidence*) deanery. **2** *nf* comice (pear).

drachme [drakm] *nf* drachma.

draconien, -ienne [drakɔnjɛ̃, -jɛn] *adj* draconian, harsh, unduly severe (*regulations*); **régime d.,** very strict diet.

drag [drag] *nm Arch* (a) (*voiture*) drag; (b) drag(hunt).

dragage [dragaʒ] *nm* (a) dredging (*of river, harbour etc*); (b) dragging (*of river for body etc*); **d. des mines,** minesweeping.

dragée [draʒe] *nf* **(a)** (*confiserie*) sugar(ed) almond, dragée; *Pharm* sugar-coated pill; **tenir la d. haute à qn,** (*le faire attendre*) to keep s.o. waiting; (*le faire payer*) to make s.o. pay dearly (*for sth*); **(b)** (*petit plomb*) small shot.
dragéifier [draʒeifje] *vt Pharm* to coat (*pill*) with sugar, to sugar (*pill*); **comprimé dragéifié,** sugar-coated tablet.
drageon [draʒɔ̃] *nm* (*plante*) sucker.
dragon [dragɔ̃] *nm* **(a)** *Myth & Fig* dragon; *Fig* **c'est un d. de vertu,** she pretends to be such a paragon of virtue; **d. volant,** (*reptile*) flying lizard; **(b)** *Mil* dragoon; **dragons portés,** ≈ motorized cavalry.
dragonne [dragɔn] *nf* (*d'une épée, d'un sabre*) sword knot; (*de parapluie*) strap.
drague [drag] *nf* **(a)** *HydE* dredger; (*grappin*) drag, grappling hook; *Pêche* dredge, dragnet; **d. suceuse,** pump dredger; **d. à godets,** bucket dredger; **(b)** *Nau* drogue, sea anchor; **(c)** *F* chatting up men or women; **alors la d., ça marche?,** so, how's your love-life?; **il y a de la d. dans l'air,** someone's getting the come-on; **un champion** *ou* **professionnel de la d.,** an expert at chatting up women.
draguer [drage] **1** *vt* **(a)** to dredge (*river, harbour etc*); **(b)** to drag (*pond etc*); to sweep (*channel*); *Pêche* to dredge for (*oysters etc*); **(c)** to chat up, to try to pick up (*men, women*); **il m'a draguée,** he tried to pick me up. **2** *vi F* to chat up men or women; **ça drague sec** *ou* **dur ici,** there's a lot of chatting up going on here; **allons d. ce soir,** let's go cruising tonight.
dragueur, -euse [dragœr, -øz] **1** *nm* **(a)** *HydE* dredgerman; (*avec grapin*) dragman; **(b)** (*bateau*) dredger; **d. de mines,** minesweeper. **2** *n F* chat-up merchant; **c'est une sacrée dragueuse,** she's always chatting up the men.
drain [drɛ̃] *nm* **(a)** (*conduit*) drain(pipe); **(b)** *Chir* drainage tube.
drainage [drɛnaʒ] *nm* **(a)** drainage, draining (*of field, wound etc*); **(b)** drain (*of money, capital*).
drainer [drene] *vt* **(a)** to drain (*soil, abscess*); **(b)** to draw, to attract (*trade, capital, talent, workers etc*).
draisine [drɛzin] *nf Rail* track motor car, *US* gang car.
dramatique [dramatik] **1** *adj* dramatic (*art, situation etc*); **l'art d.,** drama; **école d'art d.,** drama school; **auteur d.,** playwright; **centre d.,** drama centre; *Fig* **je ne considère pas son départ comme d.,** I don't think his leaving is a tragedy. **2** *nf* film made for television.
dramatiquement [dramatikmɑ̃] *adv* dramatically.
dramatisation [dramatizasjɔ̃] *nf* dramatization.
dramatiser [dramatize] *vt* **(a)** to dramatize (*event etc*); **(b)** to dramatize *or* to adapt (*novel*) for the stage.
dramaturge [dramatyrʒ] *nm* dramatist, playwright.
dramaturgie [dramatyrʒi] *nf* dramatic art.
drame [dram] *nm* **(a)** drama (*as a literary genre*); *Arch* (*pièce*) play; **d. lyrique,** comic opera; **(b)** catastrophic event, drama, tragedy; **la scène a tourné au d.,** the scene took a tragic turn; **il ne faut pas en faire un d.,** there's no need to make a drama out of it *or* to dramatize it; *Journ* **d. dans un pavillon de banlieue,** drama in suburban home.
drap [dra] *nm* **(a)** *Tex* cloth; **d. fin,** broadcloth; **d. mortuaire,** pall; **d. d'or,** gold brocade; *Hist* **le camp du D. d'or,** the Field of the Cloth of Gold; **(b) d. (de lit),** sheet; **d. de dessous/dessus,** bottom/top sheet; *Fig* **être dans de beaux** *ou* **mauvais** *ou* **vilains draps,** to be in a fine mess *or* in a pickle *or* in a predicament; **(c)** *Belg* towel.
drapé [drape] **1** *adj* **(a)** (*couvert d'un drap*) covered with a sheet *or* a cloth; **(b)** (*à plis*) draped; **robe drapée sur les épaules,** dress draped at the shoulders. **2** *nm* drape (*of a garment*).
drapeau, -eaux [drapo] *nm* flag; *Mil* (regimental) colour; **d. blanc,** white flag; **arborer** *ou* **hisser un d.,** to hoist a flag; *Mil* **présentation du d.,** ≈ trooping the colour; *Fig* **être sous les drapeaux,** to serve in the (armed) forces; *Fig* **porter le d.,** to be the first to uphold an opinion; *Arg* **planter un d.,** to leave without paying (the bill); *Av* **mettre une hélice en d.,** to feather a propeller; *Rail* **le d. du chef de gare,** the station-master's flag; *Sp* **abaisser le d. à l'arrivée du premier concurrent,** to flag in the winner.
drapement [drapmɑ̃] *nm* draping (*of material*).
draper [drape] **1** *vt* **(a)** *Tex* to process (*wool*); **(b)** to drape (*cloth into folds etc*). **2 se draper** *vpr* to wrap oneself up, to drape oneself (**dans, de,** in); *Fig* **se d. dans sa dignité,** to stand on one's dignity.
draperie [drapri] *nf* **(a)** *Ind* cloth factory; *Com* drapery (trade); **(b)** *Beaux-Arts* drapery; **(c)** (*tenture*) curtains, *Am* drapes.
drap-housse [draus] *nm* fitted sheet; (*pl draps-housses*).
drapier, -ière [drapje, -jɛr] **1** *n* (*marchand*) draper; (*fabriquant*) cloth manufacturer. **2** *adj* **marchand d.,** cloth merchant.
drastique [drastik] **1** *adj* drastic (*remedy etc*). **2** *nm* drastic purgative.
drave [drav] *nf Can* drive (*of logs*).
draver [drave] *vt Can* to float, to drive (*logs*).
draveur [dravœr] *nm Can* driver, raftsman.
draw-back [drobak] *nm Com* drawback; (*pl draw-backs*).
drelin [drəlɛ̃] *int Vieilli* ting-a-ling, tinkle.
dressage [drɛsaʒ] *nm* **(a)** erection, raising (*of scaffolding etc*); pitching (*of tent*); **(b)** flattening, straightening (*of sth*); trimming, dressing (*of piece of wood etc*); straightening (*of rod, bar*); **(c)** training (*of animal*); *F* (severe) disciplining (*of child*); *Equitation* **d. (élémentaire),** breaking in (*of horse*); *Equitation* **d. (supérieur),** dressage.
dresser [drese] **1** *vt* **(a)** to erect, to put up, to raise (*mast, monument etc*); to put up (*ladder*); to set (*trap*); to pitch (*tent*); **d. la tête,** to hold up *or* lift one's head; (*pour regarder*) to look up; **d. les oreilles,** to prick up *or* cock one's ears;
(b) to prepare, to draw up (*plan, report, estimate etc*); to make out, to draw up (*list*); **d. un contrat,** to draw up a contract; **d. la table,** to lay the table;
(c) *Fig* **d. une personne contre une autre,** to set one person against another;
(d) to flatten, to straighten (*sth*); to trim, to dress, (*piece of wood*); to straighten out (*piece of wire*);
(e) to train (*animal*); to break in (*horse*); *Arch & Péj* to train, to drill (*a recruit*); *F* to discipline (*s.o.*) (severely); **ça le dressera!,** that'll teach him, that'll put him in his place!
2 se dresser *vpr* **(a)** (*se lever*) to stand up, to rise; (*sur une chaise, dans un lit*) to sit up; (*se tenir droit*) to hold oneself erect *or* straight; (*of horse*) to rear; (*of dog*) to stand up; **se d. sur la pointe des pieds,** to stand on tiptoe; **ses cheveux se dressaient (sur sa tête),** his hair stood on end; **les obstacles qui se dressent sur notre chemin,** the obstacles that stand *or* lie in our way; *Fig* **se d. contre qch,** to rise up (in protest) against sth, to revolt against sth;
(b) (*s'apprivoiser*) to be tamed; **les hérissons ne se dressent pas,** hedgehogs can't be tamed.
dresseur, -euse [drɛsœr, -øz] *n* trainer (*of animals*); **d. de chevaux,** horse breaker; **d. de fauves,** wild animal tamer.
dressing(-room) [drɛsiŋ(rum)] *nm* dressing room.
dressoir [drɛswar] *nm* dresser, sideboard.
dreyfusard, -arde [drɛfyzar, -ard] *n Hist* supporter *or* defender of Dreyfus.
dribble [dribl] *nm Fb etc* dribble.
dribbler [drible] *vt Fb etc* to dribble; **d. le ballon/un joueur,** to dribble the ball/round a player.
dribbleur [driblœr] *nm Fb etc* dribbler.
dribbling [dribliŋ] *nm Fb etc* dribbling.
drill[1] [drij] *nm* (*singe*) drill.
drill[2] [dril] *nm Mil etc* drill.
drille[1] [drij] *nm F* **un bon** *ou* **joyeux d.,** a good sort, a cheerful character.
drille[2] *nf Tech* hand drill.
driller [drije] *vt Tech* to drill, to bore.
dring [driŋ] *int* ting-a-ling.
drink [drink] *nm F* drink.
drisse [dris] *nf Nau* halyard.
drive [drajv] *nm Tennis Golf* drive.
drive-in [drajvin] *nm* drive-in; (*pl drive-ins*).
driver[1] [drajvœr, driv-] *nm* **(a)** *Sp* (*in trotting races*) driver; **(b)** *Golf* (*club*) driver.
driver[2] [drajve, dri-] **1** *vi Tennis Golf* to drive. **2** *vt* **(a)** *Tennis Golf* to drive (*ball*); **(b)** (*in trotting races*) to drive (*horse*).
drogman [drɔgmɑ̃] *nm Vieilli* dragoman.
drogue [drɔg] *nf* **(a)** (*stupéfiant*) narcotic, drug(s); **d. dure/douce,** hard/soft drug; **prendre de la d.,** to take *or* be on drugs; **trafic de d.,** drug trafficking; **l'argent de la d.,** drug money; *Fig* **la télévision est une d. pour beaucoup de gens,** many people are television addicts *or* are hooked on television; **(b)** (*produit chimique*) (any) chemical product (*found in food etc*); *Péj* something unpleasant to swallow; **ce café est une vraie d.,** this coffee tastes like medicine; **(c)** *Vieilli* pharmaceutical ingredient, drug; *Péj* nostrum, quack remedy.
drogué, -ée [drɔge] *n* drug addict; *Fig* **les drogués de l'information/de la cigarette,** information addicts/people hooked on cigarettes.
droguer [drɔge] **1** *vt* **(a)** to dose (*person*) (with medicine); to dope, *Arg* to nobble (*racehorse etc*); **(b)** to drug (*victim*). **2 se droguer** *vpr* **(a)** (*prendre des stupéfiants*) to take

drugs; **il se drogue,** he's a drug addict; **(b)** *Pharm* to be always taking drugs.

droguerie [drɔgri] *nf* (*magasin*) *Br* = ironmonger's (*selling paint, cleaning materials etc*), hardware store; *Com* = hardware trade.

droguet [drɔgɛ] *nm Tex* **(a)** (*étoffe*) = material of real or artificial silk with design made out of extra warp; **(b)** *Vieilli* drugget.

droguiste [drɔgist] *nm* = *Br* ironmonger (*dealing in paints, cleaning materials etc*), hardware dealer; **épicier d.,** grocer and general storekeeper.

droit[1], droite [drwa, drwat] **1** *adj* **(a)** (*raide*) straight, upright; plumb (*wall etc*); **tiens le pot bien d.,** hold the pot upright; **se tenir d.,** to hold oneself erect, to stand up straight; **col d.,** stand-up collar; **d. comme un i** *ou* **un piquet,** as straight *or* stiff as a poker; **porter une jupe droite,** to wear a straight skirt; *Math* **angle d.,** right angle; **section droite,** cross section;

(b) direct, straight (*road etc*); **coup d.,** *Escrime* straight thrust; *Tennis* forehand drive; **ligne droite,** straight line; **en ligne droite,** in a straight line, as the crow flies; **s'avancer en ligne droite vers qch,** to make a beeline for sth; *Nau* **mettre la barre droite,** to right the helm; *Nau* **d. la barre!,** helm amidships!;

(c) *Fig* straightforward, upright, honest (*person, conduct*); **un homme d.,** an upright man;

(d) right (*hand, side etc*); **être le bras d. de qn,** to be s.o.'s right-hand man.

2 *adv* (in a) straight (line), directly; **c'est d. devant vous** *ou* **tout d.,** it's straight ahead of you; *Fig* **marcher d.,** to toe the line; **aller d. au fait,** to go straight to the point; *Nau* **d. devant, d. debout,** right ahead.

3 *nf* **droite (a)** right (hand), right(-hand) side; **tourner à d.,** to turn (to the) right; **rouler à d.,** to drive on the right; **tenir** *ou* **garder la d.,** to keep to the right; *Aut F* **et votre d.!,** move over!; **j'entends dire à d. et à gauche** *ou* **de d. de gauche que ...,** I hear from all quarters *or* on all sides that ...; *Pol* **la D.,** the right (wing); (*in Britain*) the Conservatives; **candidat de d.,** right-wing candidate; *Nau* **à d. (la barre)!,** starboard!;

(b) straight line; **tracer une d. reliant A à B,** to draw a line connecting A and B.

droit[2] *nm* **(a)** right; **droits civils,** civil rights; **d. de passage,** right of way; **d. de cité,** freedom of a city; **d. d'aînesse,** birthright; **d. d'auteur,** copyright; **tous droits réservés,** all rights reserved; **faire valoir ses droits,** to assert one's rights; **droits acquis,** vested interests; **avoir d. à qch,** to have a right to sth, to be entitled to sth; **il a d. à mes excuses,** I owe him an apology; *F Iron* **il a eu d. aux inévitables recommandations,** he was treated to the inevitable good advice; **avoir le** *ou* **être en d. de faire qch,** to have a right to do sth, to be justified in doing sth, to be entitled to do sth; **je n'ai pas le d. de le faire,** I'm not allowed to do it; **tu n'as pas le d. de me reprocher cela,** you've no right to hold that against me; **Déclaration des droits de l'homme/l'enfant,** (*de l'ONU*) Declaration of Human Rights/the Rights of the Child; **Commission européenne des droits de l'homme,** European Commission of Human Rights; **Convention relative aux droits de l'enfant,** Convention on the Rights of the Child; **à bon d.,** (*d'une façon justifiée*) with good reason; (*selon la loi*) legitimately; **de d. et de fait,** de facto and de jure; **à qui de d.,** to whom it may concern; **s'adresser à qui de d.,** to apply to the proper quarter *or* to an authorized person; **être dans son d.,** to be within one's rights; **tu serais dans ton d. si tu lui demandais une compensation,** you'd be within your rights asking for compensation; **monarchie de d. devin,** kingship by divine right; **le d. du plus fort,** the law of the jungle; **de quel d. me critiques-tu?,** by what right do you criticize me?, what gives you the right to criticize me?, what right have you to criticize me?; **de quel d. êtes-vous entré?,** what right had you *or* what gave you the right to come in?; **faire d. à une demande,** to comply with *or* accede to a request; **les droits de l'amitié,** the claims of friendship;

(b) (*en argent*) charge, fee, due; **droits d'auteur,** royalties; **droits de port,** harbour dues; **d. de douane,** (customs) duty; **exempt de droits,** duty-free; *Admin* **d. de timbre,** stamp duty; **d. d'inscription,** registration fee;

(c) *Jur* law; **le d.,** the law; **d. écrit,** statute law; **d. coutumier** *ou* **commun,** common law; **d. pénal** *ou* **criminel,** criminal law; **d. des sociétés,** corporate law; **d. des obligations,** = law of contract; **d. aérien,** aviation law; **d. international,** international law; **responsable en d.,** legally responsible; **faire son d.,** to study *or* read law; **étudiant en d.,** law student;

(d) *Math* right angle.

droitement [drwatmɑ̃] *adv* uprightly, righteously, honestly, justly.

droitier, -ière [drwatje, -jɛr] **1** *adj* **(a)** right-handed; **(b)** *Pol F* right-wing. **2** *n* **(a)** right-handed person; **(b)** *Pol* right-winger.

droiture [drwatyr] *nf* rectitude, honesty.

drolatique [drɔlatik] *adj Litt* comic, humorous, droll.

drôle[1] [drol] *nm Arch* rascal, knave, scamp.

drôle[2] **1** *adj* (*amusant*) funny, amusing; (*étrange*) funny, odd, queer, strange; **je ne trouve pas ça très d.,** I don't think that's very funny; **je l'ai trouvé d.,** (*étrange*) he's behaving rather oddly *or* strangely; **c'est d. que je ne t'aie pas reconnu tout de suite,** it's funny *or* odd that I didn't recognise you immediately; *F* **se sentir tout d.,** to feel peculiar; *F* **vous êtes d.! qu'auriez-vous fait à ma place?,** you must be joking! what would you have done in my place?; **une d. d'odeur,** a funny *or* strange *or* peculiar smell; **quelle d. d'idée!,** what a funny *or* strange idea!; *F* **un d. de type,** a queer fish, an odd type; *F* **la d. de guerre,** the phoney war (*1939*); **il faut une d. de patience,** it needs a heck of a lot of patience. **2** *adv Arg* **ça m'a fait tout d. de te voir là,** it gave me an odd feeling to see you there.

drôlement [drolmɑ̃] *adv* **(a)** funnily, strangely, oddly; **(b)** *F* awfully; **il fait d. froid,** it's awfully cold; **les prix ont d. augmenté,** prices have gone up an awful lot; **je me suis d. amusé,** I had a great time *or* an awful lot of fun; **elle est d. bien,** (*sympa*) she's a great person; (*belle*) she's gorgeous.

drôlerie [drolri] *nf* (*caractère amusant*) funniness; (*parole, action*) joke; (*parole*) funny remark.

dromadaire [drɔmadɛr] *nm* dromedary.

drome [drɔm] *nf* **(a)** *Nau* spars *etc* lashed together, float, raft; (*équipement*) spare masts and yards, spare gear; **(b)** main beam (*of forge hammer*).

drop (goal) [drɔp(gol)] *nm Rugby Fb* drop goal.

droppage [drɔpaʒ] *nm Av* (parachute) drop; **zone de d.,** drop zone.

dropper [drɔpe] *vt* (*abandonner, déposer*) to drop.

drosophile [drɔzɔfil] *nf* fruit fly.

drosse [drɔs] *nf Nau* rudder chain.

drosser [drɔse] *vt Nau* (*of wind, current*) to drive (*ship*).

dru [dry] **1** *adj* thick, dense (*grass etc*); heavy (*rain*). **2** *adv* **tomber d.,** to fall thick and fast; **pousser d.,** (*of grass etc*) to grow thickly.

drugstore [drœgstɔr] *nm* drugstore.

druide, druidesse [drɥid, drɥidɛs] *n* druid, druidess.

druidique [drɥidik] *adj* druidic(al).

druidisme [drɥidism] *nm* druidism.

drummer [drœmœr] *nm Mus* drummer.

drupe [dryp] *n Bot* drupe.

dry [draj] **1** *adj inv* dry; **champagne d.,** dry champagne; **whisky d.,** neat *or* straight whisky. **2** *nm inv* dry martini.

dryade [drijad] *nf* **(a)** (*nymph*) dryad, wood nymph; **(b)** *Bot* dryas, mountain avens.

dû, due [dy] **1** *adj* **(a)** (*que l'on doit*) due, owing, owed; **en port dû,** carriage forward; **ce retard est d. à ...,** this delay is due to ...; **(b)** (*approprié*) due, proper; **en temps dû,** in due course; **contrat rédigé en bonne et due forme,** contract drawn up in due form, formal contract. **2** *nm* due; **à chacun son dû,** give the devil his due.

dualisme [dɥalism] *nm* dualism.

dualiste [dɥalist] **1** *adj* dualistic. **2** *n* dualist.

dualité [dɥalite] *nf* duality.

dubitatif, -ive [dybitatif, -iv] *adj* doubtful, dubious.

dubitativement [dybitativmɑ̃] *adv* doubtfully, dubiously.

duc [dyk] *nm* **(a)** duke; **(b)** (*oiseau*) horned owl; **grand d.,** eagle owl.

ducal, -aux [dykal, -o] *adj* ducal.

duché [dyʃe] *nm* duchy, dukedom.

duchesse [dyʃɛs] *nf* **(a)** duchess; *F Péj* **elle fait la d.,** she puts on airs; **(b)** (*fruit*) **(poire) d.,** duchess pear.

ductile [dyktil] *adj* ductile, tensile, malleable.

ductilité [dyktilite] *nf* ductility, malleability.

duègne [dɥɛɲ] *nf Arch* duenna, chaperon.

duel[1] [dɥɛl] *nm* duel; **se battre en d.,** to fight a duel; **provoquer qn en d.,** to challenge s.o. to a duel; **d. oratoire,** battle of words.

duel[2] *nm Gram* dual (number).

duelliste [dɥelist] *nm* duellist.

duettiste [dɥetist] *n Mus* duettist.

duffel-coat, duffle-coat [dœfœlkot] *nm* duffel coat, duffle coat; (*pl duffel-coats, duffle-coats*).

dum-dum [dumdum] *nf* dumdum bullet; (*pl dum-dums*).

dûment [dymɑ̃] *adv* duly, in due form.

dumping [dœmpiŋ] *nm Com* dumping; **faire du d.,** to dump; **être accusé de faire du d.,** to be accused of dumping.
dune [dyn] *nf* dune, sandhill.
dunette [dynɛt] *nf Nau* poop (deck).
Dunkerque [dœ̃kɛrk] *nf* Dunkirk.
duo [dɥo] *nm Mus* duet; *Th* duo; *F* **d. d'injures,** slanging match.
duodécimal, -aux [dɥɔdesimal, -o] *adj* duodecimal.
duodénal, -aux [dɥɔdenal, -o] *adj Anat* duodenal.
duodénite [dɥɔdenit] *nf Méd* duodenitis.
duodénum [dɥɔdenɔm] *nm Anat* duodenum.
dupe [dyp] **1** *nf* dupe, *F* sucker; **prendre qn pour d.,** to fool s.o., to take s.o. in; **c'est un marché de dupes,** I've *or* he's *etc* been had *or* taken in *or* swindled; **je ne suis pas d.,** I'm not fooled *or* taken in. **2** *adj* naive, gullible, easily deceived; **il me ment, mais je ne suis pas d.,** I'm well aware that he's lying to me.
duper [dype] **1** *vt* to dupe, to deceive, to fool (*s.o.*), to take (*s.o.*) in. **2 se duper** *vpr* to deceive oneself.
duperie [dypri] *nf* (*tromperie*) dupery, deception; (*naïveté*) gullibility, credulity.
dupeur, -euse [dypœr, -øz] *n* deceiver, trickster.
duplex [dyplɛks] **1** *adj inv* **(a)** duplex (*telegraphy etc*); **(b)** *TV Rad* link-up. **2** *nm inv* **(a)** *Rad TV* **(émission en) d.,** link-up; **(b)** maison(n)ette, *Am* duplex.
duplexer [dyplɛkse] *vt Télécom* to duplex.
duplicata [dyplikata] *nm inv* duplicate (copy).
duplicateur [dyplikatœr] *nm* duplicator, duplicating machine.
duplication [dyplikasjɔ̃] *nf* **(a)** *Math* duplication; *Biol* doubling; **(b)** *Télécom* duplexing.
duplicité [dyplisite] *nf* duplicity, double dealing.
dupliquer [dyplike] *vt Télécom* to duplex.
dur [dyr] **1** *adj* **(a)** hard (*substance*); tough (*meat*); **œuf d.,** hard-boiled egg; **pain d.,** stale bread; **être d. à cuire,** (*of food*) to take a lot of cooking; (*of person*) to be a tough nut; **eau dure,** hard water; **être d. à la peine,** to be a tireless worker; **être d. d'oreille,** to be hard of hearing; **avoir la tête dure,** to be obstinate *or* pig-headed; *F* **être d. à la détente,** to be slow on the uptake; (*têtu*) to be hard to convince; *Aut etc* **commande dure,** stiff control;
(b) hard, difficult (*work etc*); **c'est d. à croire,** it's hard *or* difficult to believe; **rendre la vie dure à qn,** to make s.o.'s life a misery; **avoir la vie dure,** to be resilient to physical pain; **la vie est dure,** it's a hard life; **enfant d.,** difficult *or* problem child;
(c) (*sévère, cruel*) hard, harsh, cruel, callous; **traits durs,** hard features; **avoir le cœur d.,** to be hard-hearted *or* callous; **être d. envers** *ou* **pour** *ou* **avec qn,** to be hard *or* rough on s.o., to be unkind to s.o.; **hiver d.,** hard *or* severe winter.
2 *adv* **travailler d.,** to work hard; **cogner d.,** to hit (out) hard.
3 *nm* **(a)** *Constr* **bâtiment en d.,** permanent building; **(b)** *Arg* train.
4 *n* **un d.,** *F* a tough guy, a hard nut; *Pol* a hard liner; *F* **un d./une dure à cuire,** a hard-boiled man/woman.
5 *nf* **coucher sur la dure,** (*sur le plancher*) to sleep on the bare floor; (*dehors*) to sleep rough; **il a été élevé à la dure,** he's had a hard upbringing, he was brought up in the school of hard knocks; *F* **en dire de dures à qn,** to tell s.o. where he gets off; *F* **elle en a vu de dures,** she's had a hard *or* tough time (of it).
durabilité [dyrabilite] *nf* durability.
durable [dyrabl] *adj* durable, lasting, long-lasting.
durablement [dyrabləmɑ̃] *adv* durably.
durant [dyrɑ̃] *prép* during; **d. toute sa vie, sa vie d.,** during his whole life, throughout his life; **parler des heures d.,** to talk for hours on end *or* for hours at a time; **d. quelques instants,** for a few moments.
durcir [dyrsir] **1** *vt* to harden, to make hard; *Fig* **d. la ligne du parti/son opinion,** to harden the party line/one's opinion. **2** *vi* to harden, to become hard; (*of cement etc*) to set, to harden. **3 se durcir** *vpr* to harden; **ses traits se sont durcis,** his features have hardened.
durcissement [dyrsismɑ̃] *nm* **(a)** hardening; setting (*of cement etc*); **(b)** stiffening (*of enemy resistance*); hardening (*of attitude*).
durée [dyre] *nf* **(a)** duration (*of reign, war etc*); *Mus* length, value (*of note*); **bonheur de courte/longue d.,** short-lived/lasting happiness; **d. d'un bail,** duration *or* term of a lease; **contrat à d. illimitée,** permanent contract; **quelle est la d. de votre congé?,** how long is your leave?, how long does your leave last?; **disque de longue d.,** long-playing record *or* disc, *F* L.P.; *Cin* **d. de projection,** running *or* projection time; **(b)** lasting quality, wear (*of material, building etc*); life (*of light bulb*).
durement [dyrmɑ̃] *adv* **(a)** (*avec vigueur*) hard, vigorously; **frapper d.,** to hit hard; **(b)** (*avec difficulté*) with difficulty; **d. éprouvé,** sorely tried; **(c)** (*sévèrement*) harshly, severely, unkindly; **on l'a élevée d.,** she had a harsh upbringing.
durer [dyre] *vi* **(a)** (*of things*) to last; **voilà trois ans que cela dure,** it's been going on for three years; **les vacances durent deux mois et demi,** the holidays last for two and a half months; **l'opération a duré 3 heures,** the operation lasted 3 hours; **votre congé dure combien de temps?,** how long is your leave?; *F* **ça va d. longtemps, cette plaisanterie?,** hasn't this gone on long enough?; **ça ne peut pas d.,** this can't go on; **cela ne durera pas,** it can't *or* won't last; *F* **ça durera ce que ça durera,** it won't *or* may not last long; **pierre dure plus que le bois,** stone lasts longer than wood; **ce costume a duré deux ans,** this suit has lasted two years; **tissu qui durera,** material which will wear well;
(b) (*of person*) to remain alive; *Arch* to live; *Région F* to hold out; **il ne peut pas d. en place,** he can't stay put *or* keep still.
dureté [dyrte] *nf* **(a)** hardness (*of substance, of water*); toughness (*of meat*); **d. d'oreille,** hardness of hearing; **(b)** harshness, callousness, unkindness (*of person*); severity (*of person, winter, climate*); hardness (*of features*); harshness (*of voice*); **d. de cœur,** hard-heartedness; **parler avec d.,** to speak harshly.
durillon [dyrijɔ̃] *nm* callus (*on hand, foot etc*); corn (*on foot*).
durit(e) ® [dyrit] *nf Aut Av etc* hose (connection).
duvet [dyve] *nm* **(a)** down (*on chin, young bird, peach etc*); **d. de l'eider/du cygne,** eiderdown/swan's down; **(b)** underfur (*of animal*); **(c)** (*sac de couchage*) sleeping bag; **(d)** *Suisse* duvet, continental quilt.
duveté [dyvte] *adj* downy.
duveter (se) [sədyvte] *vpr* to become downy.
duveteux, -euse [dyvtø, -øz] *adj* downy.
dyke [dik] *nm Géol* dyke.
dynamique [dinamik] **1** *adj* dynamic; *Av* **pression d.,** ram pressure; *F* **c'est un type d.,** he's lively *or* dynamic *or* go-ahead. **2** *nf* dynamics; **la d. de groupe,** group dynamics.
dynamiquement [dinamikmɑ̃] *adv* dynamically.
dynamisme [dinamism] *nm* dynamism; *F* (*vitalité*) dynamism, energy, vitality, drive.
dynamiste [dinamist] *n Phil* dynamist.
dynamitage [dinamitaʒ] *nm* dynamiting.
dynamite [dinamit] *nf* dynamite.
dynamiter [dinamite] *vt* to dynamite, to blow up (*building etc*).
dynamiteur, -euse [dinamitœr, -øz] *n* dynamiter.
dynamo [dinamo] *nf El* dynamo.
dynamographe [dinamɔgraf] *nm* dynamograph.
dynamomètre [dinamɔmɛtr] *nm* dynamometer.
dynamométrique [dinamɔmetrik] *adj* dynamometric(al).
dynaste [dinast] *nm* dynast.
dynastie [dinasti] *nf* dynasty.
dynastique [dinastik] *adj* dynastic.
dyne [din] *nf Phys* dyne.
dysenterie [disɑ̃tri] *nf Méd* dysentery.
dysentérique [disɑ̃terik] *adj Méd* dysenteric.
dyslexie [dislɛksi] *nf Méd* dyslexia.
dyslexique [dislɛksik] *adj* dyslexic.
dysménorrhée [dismenɔre] *nf Méd* dysmenorrhoea, *US* dysmenorrhea.
dyspepsie [dispɛpsi] *nf Méd* dyspepsia.
dyspepsique [dispɛpsik] **, dyspeptique** [dispɛptik] *adj & n Méd* dyspeptic.
dysphasie [disfazi] *nf Méd* dysphasia.
dystrophie [distrɔfi] *nf Méd* dystrophy; **d. musculaire progressive,** muscular dystrophy.
dytique [ditik] *nm* water beetle.

E

E,e [œ] *nm* (the letter) E, e.

EAO [œao] *nm Ordinat* (*abrév* **enseignement assisté par ordinateur**) CAL.

eau, *pl* **eaux** [o] *nf* **(a)** water; **e. dure,** hard water; **e. douce,** (*non salée*) fresh water; (*sans calcaire*) soft water; *F* **marin d'e. douce,** landlubber; **être comme l'e. et le feu,** to be as different as chalk and cheese; **laver le plancher à grande e.,** to swill down the floor; **de l'e. savonneuse,** soapy water; **e. de vaisselle, e. grasse,** washing-up water; **passer à l'e.,** to rinse; **e. potable,** drinking water; **e. non potable,** water unfit for drinking; *F* **compte là-dessus et buvez de l'e.!,** don't count on it!; **e. rougie,** wine and water; *Fig* **mettre de l'e. dans son vin,** to tone it down a bit; **whisky à l'e.,** whisky and water; **whisky sans e.,** neat whisky; **eaux thermales,** thermal springs, hot springs; **traitement des eaux usées,** waste water treatment; **e. minérale,** (natural) mineral water; **e. gazeuse/plate,** carbonated/still water; **ville d'eau(x),** spa; **prendre les eaux,** to take *or* drink the waters; **faire de l'e.,** (*of locomotive, ship*) to water, to take on water;
(b) e. de pluie, rainwater; **il tombe de l'e.,** it's raining; **le temps est à l'e.,** it's wet *or* rainy weather; **cours d'e.,** waterway; **jet d'e.,** fountain; **dimanche: grandes eaux à Versailles,** the fountains will play at Versailles on Sunday; *Fig F* **c'etait les grandes eaux de Versailles** (*il pleurait*) the waterworks started; **pièce d'e.,** (ornamental) lake; (*petit*) pool; **au bord de l'e.,** by the water's side *or* edge; **maison au bord de l'e.,** waterside house; **sur l'e.,** afloat; **revenir sur l'e.,** to surface; **tomber à l'e.,** to fall into the water; *Fig* (*of plan*) to fall through; **porter de l'e. à la rivière** *ou* **à la mer,** to bring *or* carry coals to Newcastle; **mortes eaux,** neap tides; **vives eaux,** spring tides; **hautes/basses eaux,** high/low water; **grandes eaux,** highwater; **eaux françaises/canadiennes/internationales/***etc*, French/Canadian/international/*etc* waters; **nager entre deux eaux,** to be floating beneath the surface; *Fig* (*ne pas s'engager*) to sit on the fence; **faire e.,** (*of ship*) to leak, to spring a leak; **chaussures qui prennent l'e.,** shoes that let in water *or* the wet; **être dans les eaux d'un navire,** to be in the wake of a ship; **mettre un navire à l'e.,** to launch a ship; **service des eaux,** water supply; **Société des Eaux,** ≈ Water Board; **e. de la ville,** main(s) water; **château d'e.,** water tower; **conduite d'e.,** water main(s); **faire mettre l'e. courante,** to have water laid on; **e. courante,** running water;
(c) juice (*of a melon etc*); **cela me fait venir l'e. à la bouche,** it makes my mouth water;
(d) être tout en e., to be dripping with perspiration;
(e) diamant de la première e., diamond of the first water;
(f) e. de Cologne, eau de Cologne; **e. de rose,** rose water; *Fig* **socialisme à l'e. de rose,** milk-and-water socialism; **e. de toilette,** toilet water; **e. oxygénée,** hydrogen peroxide; **e. de Javel,** bleach; *Nucl* **e. lourde,** heavy water.

eau-de-vie [odvi] *nf* (*plum etc*) brandy; (*pl eaux-de-vie*).

eau-forte [ofɔrt] *nf* (*pl eaux-fortes*) **(a)** *Ch* aqua fortis, nitric acid; **(b)** *Beaux-Arts* etching, etched engraving.

eaux-vannes [ovan] *nfpl* sewage (water).

ébahi [ebai] *adj* amazed, stupefied, flabbergasted, staggered, astounded, dumbfounded; **un regard é.,** a look of blank astonishment.

ébahir [ebair] **1** *vt* to amaze, to astound, to flabbergast (*s.o.*), to take (*s.o.'s*) breath away. **2 s'ébahir** *vpr* to gape, to stare; to be dumbfounded (**de,** at).

ébahissement [ebaismɑ̃] *nm* amazement, astonishment.

ébarbage [ebarbaʒ] *nm* trimming (*of sth*); clipping (*of hedge etc*); fettling (*of casting*).

ébarber [ebarbe] *vt* to trim, to remove rough edges from (*sth*); to clip (*hedge etc*); to fettle (*casting*).

ébarbeuse [ebarbøz] *nf Tech* trimming machine.

ébarboir [ebarbwar] *nm Tech* scraper, chipping chisel.

ébarbure [ebarbyr] *nf* burr, paring (*of metal etc*); trimming (*from paper*).

ébats [eba] *nmpl* playing (about).

ébattre (s') [sebatr] *vpr* (*conj like* **battre**) to frolic, to play (about); (*des agneaux*) to gambol.

ébaubi [ebobi] *adj F* flabbergasted.

ébauchage [ebɔʃaʒ] *nm* roughing out, sketching out (*of picture*); roughing out, outlining (*of novel etc*).

ébauche [eboʃ] *nf* rough sketch (*of picture*); outline, rough draft (*of novel etc*); draft (*of letter, translation*); **é. d'un sourire,** suspicion *or* ghost of a smile; **é. d'un espoir,** glimmer of hope.

ébaucher [eboʃe] *vt* to rough (*sth*) out; to sketch out, to outline (*picture, plan*); to rough-hew (*statue etc*); **é. un sourire,** to give a faint *or* wan smile.

ébauchoir [eboʃwar] *nm* (*sculptor's, mason's*) boaster; roughing-chisel; (*carpenter's*) paring chisel.

ébène [ebɛn] *nf* ebony; **(d'un noir) d'é.,** jet black.

ébénier [ebenje] *nm* (*arbre*) ebony tree; **faux é.,** laburnum.

ébéniste [ebenist] *nm* cabinet maker.

ébénisterie [ebenist(ə)ri] *nf* (*métier*) cabinet making; (*meuble etc*) cabinet work; cabinet (*for radio etc*).

éberlué [eberlɥe] *adj F* flabbergasted.

éblouir [ebluir] *vt* to dazzle; **ébloui par les phares d'une voiture,** dazzled by the headlights of a car; **il a préparé ce plat pour vous é.,** he prepared this dish to impress you.

éblouissant [ebluisɑ̃] *adj* dazzling, blinding; **d'une beauté éblouissante,** dazzlingly beautiful.

éblouissement [ebluismɑ̃] *nm* dazzling, dazzle, glare; *Fig* (*émerveillement*) amazement; **avoir des éblouissements,** to have fits of dizziness.

ébonite [ebɔnit] *nf* ebonite, vulcanite.

éborgnement [ebɔrɲəmɑ̃] *nm* (*action*) blinding in one eye; (*résultat*) blindness in one eye.

éborgner [ebɔrɲe] *vt* **(a) é. qn,** to blind s.o. in one eye, to put s.o.'s eye out; **j'ai failli m'é.,** I nearly put my eye out; **(b)** to disbud (*fruit tree*).

éboueur [ebuœr] *nm* dustman, *Am* garbage man.

ébouillanter [ebujɑ̃te] **1** *vt* to scald. **2 s'ébouillanter** *vpr* to scald oneself.

éboulement [ebulmɑ̃] *nm* **(a)** (*écroulement*) caving in, collapsing; **(b)** (*rocher*) landslide, landslip.

ébouler (s') [sebule] *vpr* to fall in, to collapse, to cave in; (*of cliff*) to slip.

éboulis [ebuli] *nm* mass of fallen earth; (*montagne*) scree.

ébourgeonnage [eburʒɔnaʒ] *nm,* **ébourgeonnement** [eburʒɔnmɑ̃] *nm* disbudding.

ébourgeonner [eburʒɔne] *vt* to disbud (*fruit tree*).

ébouriffant [eburifɑ̃] *adj F* breathtaking, startling.

ébouriffé [eburife] *adj* **(a)** (*cheveux etc*) dishevelled; **(b)** *Fig* amazed, startled.

ébouriffer [eburife] *vt* **(a)** to ruffle, to tousle (*s.o.'s hair*); **(b)** *F* to amaze (*s.o.*), to take (*s.o.'s*) breath away.

ébranchage [ebrɑ̃ʃaʒ] *nm,* **ébranchement** [ebrɑ̃ʃmɑ̃] *nm* stripping, lopping (*of tree*).

ébrancher [ebrɑ̃ʃe] *vt* to lop off *or* strip the branches from (*tree*).

ébranchoir [ebrɑ̃ʃwar] *nm* billhook.

ébranlement [ebrɑ̃l(ə)mɑ̃] *nm* **(a)** (*tremblement*) shaking, shock; **(b)** (*choc nerveux*) agitation, (nervous) shock; **é. de la raison,** unhinging of the mind; *Fig* **l'é. du régime/de la dictature,** the unsteadiness *or* shakiness of the regime/dictatorship.

ébranler [ebrɑ̃le] **1** *vt* **(a)** to shake, to rock (*building etc*); **é. une cloche,** to set a bell ringing; **(b)** *Fig* to shake, to disturb (*s.o.*); *Fig* **é. le régime/la dictature,** to shake the regime/dictatorship. **2 s'ébranler** *vpr* to shake, to totter; (*of train*) to start, to set *or* move off; (*of procession etc*) to move off.

ébrasement [ebrazmɑ̃] *nm Archit* **(a)** splaying; **(b)** splay (*of embrasure*).

ébraser [ebraze] *vt Archit* to splay (*embrasure*).

Èbre (l') [lɛbr] *nm* the (river) Ebro.

ébrécher [ebreʃe] *vt* (**j'ébrèche**; **j'ébrécherai**) to notch, to make a notch in (*sth*); to chip (*a plate*); to break (*a tooth*); *F* to damage (*reputation*); *F* to make a hole in (*one's capital*).

ébréchure [ebreʃyr] *nf* nick, notch (*in blade*); chip(ped place) (*in plate etc*).

ébriété [ebriete] *nf* (state of) drunkenness, intoxication, inebriation.

ébrouement [ebrumɑ̃] *nm* snorting, snort (*d'un cheval*); (*d'ailes*) flap(ping).

ébrouer (s') [sebrue] *vpr* **(a)** (*of horse etc*) to snort; **(b)** (*dans l'eau*) to splash about.

ébruitement [ebrɥitmɑ̃] *nm* spreading (*of rumour*).

ébruiter [ebrɥite] **1** *vt* to make (*sth*) known; to spread (*rumour*). **2 s'ébruiter** *vpr* (*of news etc*) to become known, to spread, *F* to get (a)round.

EBS [əbeɛs] *nf* (*abrév* **encéphalite bovine spongiforme**) BSE.

ébullition [ebylisjɔ̃] *nf* boiling point, boil; **entrer en é.**, to come to the boil; **amener à é.**, bring to the boil; **maintenir en é. pendant cinq minutes,** boil for five minutes; *Fig* **en é.**, in a state of agitation; *F* **être en é.**, to be boiling *or* seething with rage.

écaillage [ekajaʒ] *nm* **(a)** scaling (*of fish*); opening (*of oysters*); **(b)** flaking off, peeling off (*of paint*); scaling off, chipping (*of enamel*).

écaille [ekaj] *nf* **(a)** scale (*of fish etc*); **(b)** flake (*of paint*); chip (*of marble, enamel*); splinter (*of wood*); *Litt* **les écailles lui tombèrent des yeux,** the scales fell from his eyes; **(c)** shell (*of tortoise*); **lunettes à monture d'é.**, tortoiseshell-rimmed spectacles.

écaillement [ekajmɑ̃] *nm* (*d'un poisson*) scaling; (*de peinture*) peeling (off), flaking (off).

écailler¹ [ekaje] **1** *vt* **(a)** to scale (*fish*); to open (*oyster*); **(b)** to scale (*boiler*). **2 s'écailler** *vpr* (*of enamel*) to scale off; (*of paint*) to peel off, to flake (off), to chip.

écailler², -ère [ekaje, -ɛr] **1** *n* (*marchand*) oyster seller; (*dans un bar, un restaurant*) oyster opener. **2** *nf* **écaillère,** oyster knife.

écailleux, -euse [ekajø, -øz] *adj* scaly (*animal etc*); splintery (*wood*); flaky (*paint*).

écale [ekal] *nf* hull, husk (*of walnut*); shuck (*of chestnut*).

écaler [ekale] *vt* to hull, to husk (*walnuts*); to shuck (*chestnuts*).

écarlate [ekarlat] **1** *adj* scarlet; **devenir é.**, to blush, to turn scarlet. **2** *nf* scarlet.

écarquiller [ekarkije] *vt* **é. les yeux,** to open one's eyes wide, to stare, *F* to goggle.

écart¹ [ekar] *nm* **(a)** distance apart, gap; **é. d'opinions/de points de vue,** difference of opinions/points of view; **é. entre deux lectures,** difference *or* variation between readings (*of an apparatus*); **é. entre deux comptes,** discrepancy between two accounts; **réduire l'é. entre deux objets,** to reduce the gap between two objects; **é. de prix/de salaires,** price/wage differential; **é. entre le prix de vente et le coût,** margin between cost and selling price; *MecE* **é. admissible,** tolerance;

(b) separation, spreading out; straddling (*of the legs*); **faire le grand é.**, to do the splits;

(c) deviation; deflection (*of compass needle*); (*dans sa direction*) swerve, step(ping) aside; digression (*in speech etc*); **faire un é.**, to step aside; (*of horse*) to shy; **é. de l'imagination,** flight of the imagination; **écarts de conduite,** lapses of conduct; **écarts de jeunesse,** youthful indiscretions; **il ne fait pas d. écarts de régime,** he keeps *or F* sticks to his diet;

(d) *Vét* shoulder strain (*of horse*);

(e) à. l'é., aside, on one side, apart; **se tenir à l'é.**, to keep in the background; to keep oneself apart *or* aloof (*from the crowd etc*); **un terrain à l'é. de la ville,** a piece of land outside the town; **habiter à l'é.**, to live in a remote or lonely spot; **mettre à l'é. tout sentiment personnel,** to set aside *or* banish any personal feeling.

écart² *nm Cartes* **(a)** (*action*) discarding; **(b)** (*carte*) discard.

écarté¹ [ekarte] *adj* **(a)** isolated, lonely, remote (*house, spot*); *Cr* **balle écartée,** wide (ball); **(b)** (*distance*) (far) apart; widely spaced (*eyes*); **se tenir les pieds écartés,** to stand with one's feet apart.

écarté² *nm Cartes* (game of) écarté.

écartelé [ekartəle] *adj Hér* quartered, quarterly.

écarteler [ekartəle] *vt* (**j'écartèle**; **j'écartèlerai**) to quarter (*criminal, Hér* shield).

écartement [ekartəmɑ̃] *nm* **(a)** (*séparation*), separation, spreading out, spacing; *Tech* **pièce d'écartement,** spacer; **(b)** setting aside (*of obstacle*); **(c)** space, gap, clearance (*between bars etc*); *Rail* gauge (*of track*); *Aut* **é. des essieux,** wheelbase; **é. des roues,** track.

écarter¹ [ekarte] **1** *vt* **(a)** to separate, to part (*the fingers, branches etc*); to draw back, to open (*curtains*); to open (*one's arms*); to spread (*one's legs*); to square (*one's elbows*);

(b) to move *or* thrust (*s.o., sth*) aside; to divert (*suspicion etc*); **é. les obstacles de son chemin,** to brush aside the obstacles in one's path; **é. un coup/un danger,** to ward off *or* avert a blow/a danger; **é. une réclamation,** to turn down a claim.

2 s'écarter *vpr* **(a)** (*s'éloigner*) to move *or* draw *or* step *or* stand aside; **maison écartée du chemin,** house standing back from the road; **la foule s'écarte sur le passage des pompiers,** the crowd parts *or* draws aside to let the firemen through;

(b) (*se séparer*) to move apart, to diverge; (*of shot*) to spread;

(c) (*se dévier*) to deviate, to stray (**de,** from); **s'é. du sujet,** to digress, to deviate *or* wander (away) from the subject; **s'é. des règles,** to depart from the rules.

écarter² *vt Cartes* to discard.

ecchymose [ekimoz] *nf* bruise.

Écclésiaste (l') [leklezjast] *nm Bible* (the book of) Ecclesiastes.

ecclésiastique [eklezjastik] **1** *adj* ecclesiastical; clerical (*hat, dress*). **2** *nm* ecclesiastic, clergyman; **l'É.**, Ecclesiasticus.

écervelé, -ée [esɛrvəle] **1** *adj* harebrained, scatterbrained. **2** *n* scatterbrain.

échafaud [eʃafo] *nm* **(a)** scaffold; **monter sur** *ou* **à l'é.**, to go to the scaffold, to mount the scaffold; **(b)** *Vieilli* stand, platform.

échafaudage [eʃafodaʒ] *nm* **(a)** (*passerelles etc*) scaffolding; structure, fabric (*of argument*); pile (*of objects*); *Constr* **é. volant,** hanging stage, travelling cradle; **(b)** (*procédé*) erection of scaffolding; *Fig* building up (*of reputation etc*).

échafauder [eʃafode] **1** *vi* to erect (a) scaffolding. **2** *vt* to pile up (*objects*); to build up, to construct (*system, argument, plan*).

échalas [eʃala] *nm* cane, stake (*to support plant*); **jambes en é.**, long *or* spindly legs; *F* **grand é.**, beanpole.

échal(l)ier [eʃalje] *nm* **(a)** (*clôture*) barrier, hurdle (*closing gap*); **(b)** (*échelle*) stile.

échalote [eʃalɔt] *nf* (*plante*) shallot, *Can* scallion; *Can* **é. française,** shallot.

échancrer [eʃɑ̃kre] *vt* to make a V-shaped cut in (*neck of dress etc*); to indent, to notch (*plank etc*); **littoral échancré,** indented coastline.

échancrure [eʃɑ̃kryr] *nf* cut-out part, opening (*in garment, neckline*); notch, cut, nick (*in plank etc*); indentation (*in coastline etc*).

échange [eʃɑ̃ʒ] *nm* **(a)** exchange (*of prisoners, ideas, blows etc*); **faire un é. de qch pour** *ou* **contre qch,** to exchange sth for sth; **recevoir qch en é. (de qch),** to receive sth in exchange *or* in return (for sth); **est-il possible de faire l'é.?,** is it possible to exchange it?, can it be exchanged?; **échanges culturels,** cultural exchanges; **(b)** *Fin* exchange; (*commerce*) trade; **taux de l'é.**, rate of exchange; **le volume des échanges,** the volume of trade.

échangeable [eʃɑ̃ʒabl] *adj* exchangeable.

échanger [eʃɑ̃ʒe] *vt* (**j'échangeai(s)**; **n. échangeons**) to exchange; to barter, to trade (*sth*) (**contre,** for); **é. des idées,** to exchange ideas; **é. des impressions,** to compare impressions.

échangeur [eʃɑ̃ʒœr] *nm* **(a)** *Constr* (*on motorway*) (clover leaf) intersection; **(b)** *Phys* (heat) exchanger.

échangisme [eʃɑ̃ʒism] *nm* wife swapping.

échangiste [eʃɑ̃ʒist] *n Fin* exchanger.

échanson [eʃɑ̃sɔ̃] *nm Hist* cup-bearer.

échantillon [eʃɑ̃tijɔ̃] *nm* **(a)** sample, pattern (*of cloth*); sample, specimen (*of one's work*); population sample (*for opinion poll*); *Méd* specimen; **prendre** *ou* **prélever des échantillons de qch,** to sample sth; **livre d'échantillons,** pattern book; **conforme** *ou* **pareil à l'é.**, up to sample; **échantillons sans valeur,** samples of no (commercial) value; **(b)** *Vieilli* **brique/tuile d'é.**, standard brick/tile.

échantillonnage [eʃɑ̃tijɔnaʒ] *nm* **(a)** (*vérification*) testing, sampling; *Spéc* choice, selection (*of people etc for* *survey*); **(b)** *Com* making up of samples (*of wine etc*); making up of patterns (*of cloth etc*).

échantillonner [eʃɑ̃tijɔne] *vt* **(a)** to taste, to sample (*wine etc*); *Spéc* to sample (*the population*); **(b)** *Com* to prepare patterns *or* samples of (*sth*); **(c)** (*étalonner*) to make (*articles*) according to sample.

échantillonneur, -euse [eʃɑ̃tijɔnœr, -øz] *n Com Spéc* (*personne*) tester, sampler.

échappatoire [eʃapatwar] **1** *nf* **(a)** way out, loophole (*to escape from obligation*); **le sommeil est mon é.,** sleep is my escape mechanism; **(b)** *Aut* escape way. **2** *adj* **clause é.,** escape clause.

échappé [eʃape] *nm Sp Can* breakaway.

échappée [eʃape] *nf* **(a)** *Sp* breakaway (*in race*); *Sp* **être dans l'é.,** to be part of the breakaway group; **(b)** (*espace libre*) space, gap, interval; **é. de vue,** vista (**sur,** over); **é. de ciel,** patch of sky; **é. de soleil,** burst of sunshine; **é. de beau temps,** short spell of fine weather; *Fig* **faire qch par échappées,** to do sth by fits and starts; **(c)** turning space (*for vehicles*); **(d)** headroom (*of staircase*).

échappement [eʃapmɑ̃] *nm* **(a)** (*fuite*) escape, leakage (*of gas, water*); **(b)** exhaust, release (*of steam*); (*mouvement*) exhaust stroke; **(tuyau d')é.,** waste-steam pipe; *Aut* exhaust (pipe); *Aut* **pot d'é.,** silencer, *Am* muffler; **(soupape d')é. libre,** cut-out (*to silencer*); **gaz d'é.,** exhaust fumes; **clapet d'é.,** exhaust cut-out; **(c)** escapement (*of clock*); hopper (*of piano*); **montre à é.,** lever watch.

échapper [eʃape] **1** *vi* **(a)** (*aux* **être** *or* **avoir**) to escape; (*aux* **avoir**) to dodge (*sth*); **é. à qn/qch,** to escape s.o./sth; **le prisonnier nous a échappé,** the prisoner got away from us; **il n'y a pas moyen d'y é.,** there is no escaping *or* getting away from it; **ce fait a** *ou* **est échappé à mon attention, ce fait m'a échappé,** this fact escaped my attention *or* me; **pas un mot ne lui a échappé,** he didn't let anything slip; (*il écoutait attentivement*) he did not miss a single word; **la vérité lui échappe parfois,** he sometimes blurts out the truth; **son nom m'échappe,** his name escapes me, I can't remember his name; **é. à toute définition,** to defy definition; **é. à son destin,** to escape one's fate; **é. à un coup,** to dodge a blow; *F* **vous l'avez échappé belle,** you've had a narrow escape; **laisser é.,** to let (*s.o., sth*) escape; to set (*s.o.*) free; to let out (*air from balloon*); to let off (*steam*); to let fall (*a tear*); to let out (*secret, sigh, cry*); **laisser é. son stylo,** to let one's pen slip from one's fingers; **laisser é. l'occasion,** to let the opportunity slip;

(b) é. de, to escape from *or* out of; **é. de prison,** to (make one's) escape from prison; **é. d'une maladie/d'un naufrage,** to survive an illness/a shipwreck.

2 s'échapper *vpr* to escape, to break free *or* loose; **s'é. de prison,** to break (out of) prison; *F* **il faut que je m'échappe,** I must be off; **le gaz s'échappe,** the gas is leaking; **un cri s'échappa de ses lèvres,** a cry burst from his lips; **le sport me permet de m'é.,** (*de la routine*) sport gives me an outlet.

3 *vt Can* (*laisser échapper*) to drop.

écharde [eʃard] *nf* prickle, splinter, thorn (*under the skin*).

échardonner [eʃardɔne] *vt* **(a)** to clear (*ground*) of thistles; **(b)** to pick (*wool*).

échardonnet [eʃardɔnɛ] *nm Agr* thistle hook.

écharpe [eʃarp] *nf* (*de femme*) (lady's) scarf; (*de cérémonie*) official sash; (*au bras*) (arm) sling; **é. de fourrure,** fur stole; **porter le bras en é.,** to have one's arm in a sling; **en é.,** diagonally, crosswise; **se prendre en é.,** to collide at an angle, to hit sideways on; (*of trains*) to collide at the points; *Tech* **moise en é.,** diagonal brace.

écharper [eʃarpe] *vt* to slash, to gash, to hack (*one's finger etc*); to hack (up) (*meat*); to cut (*troops*) to pieces; **vous allez vous faire é.!,** you'll get torn to pieces!

échasse [eʃas] *nf* **(a)** stilt; **marcher** *ou* **être monté sur des échasses,** to be on stilts; *Fig* (*faire l'important*) to be pompous; *F* (*avoir de longues jambes*) to have long legs, to be long in the leg; **(b) é. d'échafaud,** scaffolding pole; **(c)** *Orn* stilt.

échassier [eʃasje] *nm Orn* wader.

échaudage [eʃodaʒ] *nm* scalding.

échaudé [eʃode] *adj* scalded; **blé é.,** wheat shrivelled by the sun.

échauder [eʃode] **1** *vt* to scald (*one's foot, a saucepan etc*); to scour (*wool*); *F* **se faire é. dans une affaire,** to get one's fingers burnt, to burn one's fingers. **2 s'échauder** *vpr* to scald oneself.

échauffant [eʃofɑ̃] *adj* (*aliment*) that causes constipation.

échauffé [eʃofe] *adj* overheated (*room*); hot (*bearings*); fermented (*hay*).

échauffement [eʃofmɑ̃] *nm* **(a)** heating (*of soil, bearings*); overheating (*of engine*); fermenting (*of hay*); chafing (*of rope*); **(b)** (*excitation*) (over)excitement; **(c)** (*constipation*) constipation; **(d)** (*d'athlète etc*) warm(ing)-up; **exercices d'é.,** warm-up *or* limbering-up exercises.

échauffer [eʃofe] **1** *vt* to overheat (*room, blood*); to cause fermentation in (*cereals, hay*); **frottement qui échauffe les roues,** friction that overheats the wheels; *F* **é. la bile** *ou* **les oreilles de qn,** to rub s.o. up the wrong way. **2 s'échauffer** *vpr* to become *or* get overheated; (*of athlete etc*) to warm *or* limber up; (*of bearings*) to run hot, to heat; (*of cereals etc*) to ferment; **ne vous échauffez pas,** don't get excited; **la dispute s'échauffait,** feelings were beginning to run high, the argument was beginning to heat up.

échauffourée [eʃofure] *nf* scuffle; clash (*between mobs*); *Mil* affray, skirmish.

échéance [eʃeɑ̃s] *nf* **(a)** date of payment; (*terme*) falling due, maturity (*of bill*); bill (falling due); **venir à é.,** to fall due; **payable à l'é.,** payable at maturity; **à trois mois d'é.,** at three months' date; **billet à longue/courte é.,** long-/short-dated bill; **politique à longue é.,** long-term policy; **é. à vue,** sight bill; **faire face à une é.,** to meet a bill; **(b)** expiry (*of tenancy etc*).

échéancier [eʃeɑ̃sje] *nm* **(a)** *Fin* bill book; **(b)** *Can* (*calendrier pour les travaux etc*) timetable, schedule.

échéant [eʃeɑ̃] *adj* **(a)** *Fin* falling due; **(b) le cas é.,** should the occasion arise, if necessary, if need be.

échec [eʃɛk] *nm* **(a)** failure; (*revers*) check, setback; (*at chess*) check; **reconnaître son é.,** to admit failure; **cela va se solder par un é.,** it will end in failure; **voué à l'é.,** bound to fail; **é. et mat,** checkmate; **faire é. au roi,** to check the king; *Fig* **tenir l'ennemi en é.,** to hold the enemy in check; **faire é. à,** to put a check on, to check (*activities etc*); **faire é. à qn/des projets,** to frustrate s.o./s.o.'s plans; **subir un é.,** to suffer a setback; **l'é. des discussions,** the failure *or* breakdown of the discussions; *Can* **mettre en é.,** (*au hockey*) to check; **(b) échecs,** chess; **une partie d'échecs,** a game of chess; **joueur d'échecs,** chess player.

échelle [eʃɛl] *nf* **(a)** ladder; **é. d'incendie** *ou* **de sauvetage,** fire escape; **é. brisée,** folding steps; **é. de corde,** rope ladder; **é. à coulisse,** extension *or* extending ladder; *Nau* **é. de commandement** *ou* **d'honneur,** companion ladder; **é. de revers,** Jacob's ladder; **faire la courte é. à qn,** to give s.o. a leg up *or Am* a boost; *F* **vous voulez me faire monter à l'é.,** you're having *or Am* putting me on, you're pulling my leg; **il faut** *ou* **il n'y a plus qu'à tirer l'é.,** there's no point in trying any further, we'd better give up;

(b) é. à poissons, fish ladder; salmon leap;

(c) *Gym* **é. suédoise,** rib stall;

(d) *Fig* **l'é. sociale,** the social ladder; **être en haut** *ou* **au sommet de l'é.,** to be at the top of the tree *or* the ladder; **é. des traitements,** salary scale; **é. mobile,** sliding scale (*of prices etc*); *Com Pol* escalator clause; **é. de Beaufort,** Beaufort scale;

(e) *Mus* scale;

(f) scale (*of map etc*); **carte à petite/grande é.,** small-/large-scale map; *Fig* **faire les choses sur une grande é.,** to do things on a large scale; **à l'é. mondiale/nationale,** on a world/national scale; **à l'é. de l'homme,** on a human scale; *Ordinat* **intégration à grande/petite é.,** large/small scale integration;

(g) scale (*of thermometer etc*); *Nau* **é. de tirant d'eau,** water marks, draft marks, *US* immersion scale; **é. de marée,** tide gauge;

(h) *Hist* **les échelles du Levant,** the (commercial) ports of the Levant.

échelon [eʃlɔ̃] *nm* **(a)** rung (*of ladder*); **(b)** (*degré*) step, grade, echelon (*of hierarchy, organization*); **monter par échelons,** to rise by degrees *or* by successive stages; **les échelons de l'administration,** the grades of the civil service; **le dernier/premier é.,** the bottom/top grade *or* step; **avancer/reculer d'un é.,** to go up/down a grade *or* step; **(c)** (*niveau*) level; **à l'é. ministériel,** at ministerial level; **à l'é. régional/national,** on a regional/national level; **à tous les échelons,** at all levels, at every level; **(d)** *Mil* **en é.,** in echelon, in stepped formation; *Av* **vol en é.,** stepped-up formation.

échelonnement [eʃlɔnmɑ̃] *nm* **(a)** *Mil* echelonment, echeloning (*of troops*); **(b)** spreading out (*of payments*); staggering (*of holidays*); **(c)** *El* staggering (*of brushes*).

échelonner [eʃlɔne] **1** *vt* **(a)** *Mil* to dispose (*troops*) in echelon *or* in depth; **(b)** to space out (*objects*); to place (*objects*) at intervals; to spread (out) (*payments*); **congés échelonnés,** staggered holidays; **(c)** *Él* to stagger (*brushes*). **2 s'échelonner** *vpr* (*of objects*) to be spaced out; **les paiements s'échelonnent sur deux ans,** the payments are spread (out) over two years.

écheniller [eʃnije] *vt* **(a)** to clear (*fruit trees etc*) of caterpillars; **(b)** *Fig* to clean up; to polish (*style etc*); to remove undesirable elements from (*society etc*).

écheveau, -eaux [eʃ(ə)vo] *nm* **(a)** hank, skein (*of yarn etc*); **(b)** *Fig* **é. de rues,** maze of streets; **l'é. d'une intrigue,** the intricacies *or* complexities of a plot; **un é. de mensonges/problèmes,** a tissue of lies/a host of problems.

échevelé [eʃəvle] *adj* **(a)** dishevelled (*hair, person*); tousled (*hair*); **(b)** *Fig* wild, disorderly (*dance etc*).

échevin [eʃvɛ̃] *nm* **(a)** *Arch* municipal magistrate; **(b)** *Belg* deputy mayor.

échidné [ekidne] *nm Zool* spiny anteater.

échinant [eʃinɑ̃] *adj Arg* back-breaking (*work*).

échine [eʃin] *nf* **(a)** *Anat* spine, backbone; *F* **crotté jusqu'à l'é.,** covered in mud from head to foot; **courber** *ou* **plier l'é.,** to kowtow, to toady (**devant qn,** to s.o.); *Fig* **avoir l'é. souple** *ou* **flexible,** to bow and scrape; **(b)** *Culin* loin (of pork).

échiner (s') [seʃine] *vpr* (*se fatiguer*) to exhaust oneself, to tire oneself out (**à faire qch,** doing sth); (*se donner du mal*) to go to great lengths, to make a great effort (**à faire qch,** to do sth).

échinoderme [ekinɔdɛrm] *nm Zool* echinoderm.

échiquier [eʃikje] *nm* **(a)** (*damier*) chessboard; **en é.,** in a chequered *or Am* checkered pattern; *Fig Pol* **l'é. mondial/européen,** the world/European stage *or* arena; **(b)** *Br Pol* **l'É.,** the Exchequer.

écho [eko] *nm* **(a)** echo; **faire é.,** to echo (back); *Fig* **se faire l'é. des opinions de qn,** to echo *or* repeat s.o.'s opinions; **je n'ai eu aucun é. de leur discussion,** I've heard nothing about their discussion; **ma proposition/mon offre est restée sans é.,** I had no comeback on my suggestion/offer, my suggestion/offer wasn't taken up; **trouver un é.,** to get a response; **(b)** *Ordinat* echo; *Électron* **éliminateur** *ou* **suppresseur d'é.,** echo suppressor; **échos parasites,** clutter; **(c)** *TV* ghost(ing); **(d)** *Journ* **échos,** news in brief; **é. mondains,** gossip column.

échographie [ekografi] *nf* (ultrasound) scan; **passer une é.,** to have a scan.

échoir [eʃwar] *vi* (*prp* **échéant**; *pp* **échu**; *pr ind* **il échoit, ils échoient**; *impf* **il échoyait**; *p hist* **il échut**; *fu* **il échoira**; *aux souvent* **être**) **(a) é. (en partage) à qn,** to fall to s.o.; **le devoir m'échut de lui apprendre la nouvelle,** it fell to me to break the news to him; **(b)** *Fin* (*of debt etc*) to fall due; (*of investment etc*) to mature; **billets échus,** bills (over)due; **intérêts échus,** outstanding interest, interest due; **intérêts à é.,** accruing interest; **(c)** (*of tenancy etc*) to expire.

échométrie [ekometri] *nf Phys* echometry, echo ranging.

échoppe¹ [eʃɔp] *nf Com* booth, covered stall, street stall; (*de cordonnier*) (cobbler's) small (work)shop.

échoppe² *nf Tech* graver, burin.

échopper [eʃɔpe] *vt* to grave, to gouge, to scoop.

écho-sondeur [ekosɔ̃dœr] *nm Nau* echo sounder, sonic depth finder; (*pl écho-sondeurs*).

échotier, -ière [ekɔtje, -jɛr] *n Journ* gossip columnist.

échouage [eʃwaʒ] *nm Nau* **(a)** (*dans bassin etc*) stranding, running aground, grounding; **(b)** (*sur la plage*) beaching.

échouement [eʃumɑ̃] *nm* = **ÉCHOUAGE**.

échouer [eʃwe] **1** *vi* **(a)** *Nau* to run aground, to be stranded, to ground; **navire échoué,** ship aground, stranded vessel *or* ship; **échoué à sec,** high and dry; *Fig* **elle a échoué dans un quartier déshérité/un pays hostile,** she ended up in a run-down district/a hostile country; **(b)** (*ne pas réussir*) (*of plan etc*) to fail, to come to nothing; (*of person*) to fail; **é. à un examen,** to fail an examination; **faire é. un projet,** to wreck a plan. **2** *vt Nau* to beach (*ship*), to run (*ship*) aground. **3 s'échouer** *vpr Nau* to run aground, to be driven ashore.

écimage [esimaʒ] *nm* topping, pollarding (*of tree*).

écimer [esime] *vt* to top, to pollard (*tree*).

éclaboussement [eklabusmɑ̃] *nm* splashing, spattering.

éclabousser [eklabuse] *vt* **(a)** (*avec un liquide*) to splash, to spatter (**de,** with); **(b)** *Fig* **é. qn,** (*salir*) to damage s.o's reputation, to sully s.o.'s (good) name; (*humilier*) to dazzle *or* overwhelm s.o. (**avec ses richesses/***etc*, with one's wealth/*etc*).

éclaboussure [eklabusyr] *nf* **(a)** splash, spatter (*of mud etc*); **(b)** *Fig* blemish, blot, smirch (*on reputation*).

éclair [eklɛr] *nm* **(a)** flash of lightning; **éclairs,** lightning; **éclairs en nappe,** sheet lightning; **é. arborescent** *ou* **en zigzag,** (flash of) forked lightning; **éclairs de chaleur,** heat lightning; **il fait des éclairs,** it's lightening; **rapide comme l'é.,** quick as lightning; *Fig* **en un é.,** quick as a flash; **la voiture passa comme un é.,** the car flashed by; **la pensée traversa mon esprit comme un é.,** the thought flashed through my mind; **visite é.,** lightning visit; **guerre é.,** blitzkrieg; **attaque é.,** lightning raid; **(b)** flash (*of gun etc*); **lancer des éclairs,** (*of diamond, eyes etc*) to flash; **é. de génie,** flash of genius; **é. de lucidité,** sudden insight; **(c)** *Culin* éclair.

éclairage [eklɛraʒ] *nm* **(a)** (*fait d'éclairer*) lighting, illumination; *Cin Th* lighting; **é. par projecteurs,** floodlighting; **é. des rues,** street lighting; **é. au gaz/à l'électricité,** gas/electric lighting; **é. direct/indirect,** direct/indirect lighting; *Aut* **é. intérieur automatique,** courtesy light; **heure d'é.,** lighting-up time; **(b)** *Fig* light; **sous cet é.,** (seen) in this light; **montrer qch dans un autre é.,** to show sth in a different light; **(c)** *Mil Nau* scouting.

éclairagiste [eklɛraʒist] *n Cin Th* lighting technician.

éclairant [eklɛrɑ̃] *adj* lighting, illuminating (*power etc*); **fusée éclairante,** flare; *Fig* **une explication éclairante,** an enlightening *or* illuminating explanation.

éclaircie [eklɛrsi] *nf* **(a)** break, opening, rift (*in clouds etc*); *Météo* bright interval; **(b)** clearing, glade (*in forest*).

éclaircir [eklɛrsir] **1** *vt* **(a)** to clear (*fog etc*);

(b) (*rendre plus clair*) to lighten (*colour etc*); **é. le teint,** to clear the complexion;

(c) *Fig* (*élucider*) to throw light on, to clear up (*mystery*); to clarify (*situation*);

(d) (*rendre moins épais*) to thin (*forest, sauce*); to thin out (*seedlings etc*).

2 s'éclaircir *vpr* **(a)** (*of the weather*) to clear (up), to become bright(er); (*of sky*) to clear; (*of complexion, voice*) to clear, to become clear(er); **s'é. la voix,** to clear one's throat; *Fig* **l'avenir semble s'é.,** the future seems to be getting brighter; **sa figure s'éclaircit,** his face brightened up *or* lit up;

(b) (*s'expliquer*) to make oneself clear;

(c) (*se dissiper*) to clear; (*of mystery, doubts*) to be cleared up; **la vérité s'éclaircit,** the truth is coming out;

(d) (*of hair*) to grow thin, to be thinning; (*of plants*) to thin (out); **enfin les arbres s'éclaircirent,** at length the trees thinned out.

éclaircissage [eklɛrsisaʒ] *nm* **(a)** polishing (*of glass*); **(b)** thinning out (*of plants*).

éclaircissement [eklɛrsismɑ̃] *nm* **(a)** (*élucidation*) enlightenment, elucidation; **(b)** (*explication*) explanatory statement; **demander des éclaircissements sur qch,** to ask for explanations about sth.

éclaire [eklɛr] *nf Région* (*plante*) celandine.

éclairé [eklere] *adj* enlightened, well-informed, educated (*person, mind, public*).

éclairement [eklɛrmɑ̃] *nm* illumination, lighting.

éclairer [eklere] **1** *vt* **(a)** to light, to illuminate (*room, window etc*); to light the way for (*s.o.*); **je suis nourri, logé et éclairé,** I get my board, lodging and lighting; **é. un angle sombre,** to light up a dark corner; **cafés éclairés au néon,** cafés with neon lights; **une pièce bien/mal éclairée,** a well-lit/badly lit room; *Fig* **un sourire éclairait son visage,** a smile lit up his *or* her face;

(b) (*expliquer*) to shed *or* throw light on (*a subject*);

(c) (*informer*) to enlighten (*s.o.*); **éclairez-moi sur ce sujet,** tell me what it's all about; *F* **si tu pouvais é. ma lanterne sur cette affaire,** if you could put me in the picture about this matter;

(d) *Cartes etc* **é. (le tapis),** to place *or* make one's bet;

(e) *Mil* **é. le terrain** *ou* **la marche,** to reconnoitre the ground, to scout.

2 *vi* **(a)** (*donner de la lumière*) **cette lampe éclaire bien/mal,** this lamp gives (a) good/poor light;

(b) *Arch & Région* **il éclaire,** it's lightening.

3 s'éclairer *vpr* **(a)** (*pour avoir de la lumière*) **il s'éclaire toujours au pétrole/gaz,** he still has *or* uses oil lamps/gaslight; **s'é. à la bougie/avec une lampe de poche,** (*pour montrer le chemin*) to light one's way with a candle/torch;

(b) (*devenir lumineux*) (*of town, street etc*) to light up; **sa figure s'est éclairée,** his face lit up *or* brightened;

(c) *Fig* (*devenir compréhensible*) (*of situation etc*) to become clear(er); **tout s'éclaire!,** things are *or* everything is becoming clear(er)!

éclaireur, -euse [eklɛrœr, -øz] **1** *nm* **(a)** *Mil* scout; *Fig*

partir en é., to go off for a scout around; **(b)** *Nau* scouting vessel, scout; *Av* **avion é.,** reconnaissance aircraft. **2** *n* (non-Catholic) (boy) scout, (girl) guide; **chef é.,** scoutmaster.

éclat [ekla] *nm* **(a)** (*fragment*) splinter, chip (*of wood, stone etc*); flake (*of mica*); **é. d'obus,** shell splinter; **voler en éclats,** to fly *or* burst into pieces; **briser qch en éclats,** to smash sth to pieces *or* to smithereens; **éclats de verre,** (*bris*) broken glass; (*projeté*) flying glass;

(b) (*bruit*) burst (*of noise, laughter etc*); **é. de colère,** outburst of anger; **de grands éclats de voix,** (*de colère*) voices raised in anger; (*bribes*) snatches of loud conversation; **é. de tonnerre,** thunderclap; **partir d'un grand é. de rire,** to burst out laughing; **rire aux éclats,** to roar with laughter;

(c) *Fig* (*scandale*) scandal, stir, fuss; **cette nouvelle fera (de l')é.,** this news will create a stir *or* a scandal; **sans é.,** quietly; without any fuss *or* scandal;

(d) flash (*of light*); **feu à éclats,** flashing light;

(e) glare (*of the sun*); glitter, lustre (*of diamond*); brilliance, vividness (*of colours*); **l'é. de ses yeux,** the sparkle in his *or* her eyes; **l'é. de la jeunesse,** the bloom *or* freshness of youth; **le soleil brille de son plus vif é.,** the sun is (shining) at its brightest *or* most brilliant; **sans é.,** dull, lustreless; lack-lustre (*eyes*);

(f) brilliance (*of style etc*); splendour, *US* splendor (*of ceremony, fame, period etc*); **action** *ou* **coup d'é.,** brilliant feat; **aimer l'é.,** to be fond of show *or* ostentation; **faux é.,** false glamour.

éclatant [eklatɑ̃] *adj* **(a)** loud, ringing (*sound, laughter*); piercing (*shriek*); **(b)** bright, dazzling, brilliant (*light, colour*); brilliant, dazzling (*success*); sparkling, glittering (*jewels*); **teint é.,** glowing *or* blooming complexion; **avoir des dons éclatants,** to be brilliantly gifted; **être dans une forme éclatante,** to be on brilliant *or* dazzling form; **d'une santé éclatante,** glowing *or* blooming with health; **mensonge é.,** blatant lie.

éclatement [eklatmɑ̃] *nm* bursting, explosion (*of boiler, shell, gun*); bursting, blow-out (*of tyre*); shattering (*of glass*); dispersal (*of convoy etc*); *El* **pont d'é.,** spark gap; **fréquence d'é.,** spark frequency; *Mil* **é. en surface,** surface burst; *Pol* **é. d'un parti,** splitting (up) of a party.

éclater [eklate] **1** *vt* **(a)** to split, to splinter (*branch, mast*); to burst (*tyre*);

(b) to divide, to split (*roots of plant for propagation*);

(c) to disperse (*cargo of crude oil*).

2 *vi* **(a)** (*of boiler, shell, gun*) to burst, to explode; (*of mine*) to blow up; (*of tyre*) to burst; (*of balloon*) to burst; (*of glass*) to shatter; (*of mast*) to split, to splinter; **faire é. qch,** to burst *or* explode *or* shatter *or* split sth; **faire é. un pétard,** to detonate a fog signal; *Fig* **le groupe a fini par é.,** the group finally split up;

(b) (*of war, fire, epidemic*) to break out; (*of storm*) to break; (*of anger*) to burst out; (*of dispute*) to break out; (*of scandal*) to break; **quand la guerre éclata,** at the outbreak of the war; **le tonnerre éclata,** there was a clap of thunder;

(c) é. de rire, to burst out laughing; **é. en applaudissements,** to burst into applause; **é. en larmes,** to burst into tears; **é. de colère,** to fly into a rage; *F* **si ça continue, je vais é.,** if this goes on, I'll explode;

(d) (*of jewels*) to sparkle, to glitter; *Fig* **l'indignation éclatait dans ses yeux,** his eyes were blazing with indignation;

(e) (*être manifeste*) to be obvious *or* evident, to stand out; **les préjugés de l'auteur éclatent à chaque page,** the author's prejudices stand out on every page.

3 s'éclater *vpr F* to have a wild *or* a really good time; **s'é. comme une bête,** to freak out.

éclateur [eklatœr] *nm El* discharger.

éclectique [eklɛktik] *adj & n* eclectic.

éclectisme [eklɛktism] *nm* eclecticism.

éclipse [eklips] *nf* eclipse (*of sun, moon*); **é. totale de la raison/mémoire,** total loss of reason/memory; *Nau* **feu à éclipses,** occulting *or* intermittent light; *Fig* **après une longue é.,** after a long absence; *Fig* **célébrité à éclipses,** celebrity who is in and out of the limelight.

éclipser [eklipse] **1** *vt* **(a)** *Fig* (*surpasser*) to eclipse, to outshine, to overshadow, *F* to put (*s.o.*) in the shade; to eclipse, to overshadow (*event, achievement etc*); **(b)** *Astron* to eclipse (*sun, moon*); to obscure (*beam of light*). **2 s'éclipser** *vpr* **(a)** *F* (*s'esquiver*) to make off, to make oneself scarce; **(b)** *Astron* to be eclipsed; (*être voilé*) to be obscured.

écliptique [ekliptik] *adj & nm Astron* ecliptic.

éclisse [eklis] *nf* **(a)** (*plaque de bois*) (wooden) wedge; **(b)** (*éclat*) piece of split wood; **(c)** *Méd* splint; **(d)** *Rail* fishplate; bond (*of live rail*).

éclisser [eklise] *vt* **(a)** *Méd* to put (*limb*) in splints, to splint; **(b)** *Rail* to fish (*rails*).

éclopé, -ée [eklɔpe] **1** *adj* lame, limping, (temporarily) crippled. **2** *nm Mil* temporarily disabled soldier. **3** *n Hum* lame *or* limping person.

éclore [eklɔr] *vi* (*pp* **éclos**; *pr ind* **il éclôt, ils éclosent**; *impf* **il éclosait**; *no p hist*; *fu* **il éclora**; *aux souvent* **être**, *parfois* **avoir**) **(a)** (*of eggs, chicks*) to hatch (out), to be hatched; **faire é. un œuf,** to hatch (out) an egg; **(b)** (*of flowers*) to open, to bloom; (*of buds*) to burst; *Fig* (*of talent*) to be born, to appear; **roses fraîches écloses,** fresh-blown roses; **le jour est près d'é.,** dawn is near; *Fig* **génie près d'é.,** budding genius; **faire é. un projet,** to realize a plan.

éclosion [eklozjɔ̃] *nf* **(a)** hatching (*of eggs, chicks*); **(b)** opening, blooming (*of flowers*); *Fig* birth (*of talent*).

écluse [eklyz] *nf* **(a)** (canal) lock; **droit d'é.,** lockage; **(porte d')é.,** lock gate, sluice (gate); **é. de moulin,** mill dam; *F* **lâcher** *ou* **ouvrir les écluses,** (*pleurer*) to turn on the waterworks; **(b)** tide gate (*of dock*).

écluser [eklyze] **1** *vt* **(a)** to equip (*canal*) with locks; **(b)** to pass (*barge*) through a lock; **(c)** *F* (*boire*) to knock back. **2** *vi F* **qu'est-ce qu'elle écluse!,** she doesn't half knock it back!

éclusier, -ière [eklyzje, -jɛr] *n* lock keeper.

éco- [ekɔ] *préf* eco-.

écœurant [ekœrɑ̃] **1** *adj* **(a)** (*dégoûtant*) nauseating, sickening; disgusting, loathsome (*person, food, conduct*); **(b)** *F* (*décourageant*) disheartening, discouraging, demoralizing (*work*); **c'est é., elle a encore une augmentation!,** it's sickening, she's got another rise!; *Can* **Steven est é. dans le rôle de Jake,** Steven is unreal in the role of Jake. **2** *nm Can* disgusting *or* loathsome man.

écœuranterie [ekœrɑ̃tri] *nf Can F* **(a)** filth; **(b)** (*coup bas*) dirty trick; **elle m'a fait une é.,** she played a dirty trick on me.

écœurement [ekœrmɑ̃] *nm* **(a)** (*physique*) nausea; **(b)** *Fig* (*dégoût*) disgust, loathing; **(c)** *Fig* (*découragement*) dejection, discouragement.

écœurer [ekœre] *vt* **(a)** (*physiquement*) to nauseate, to make (*s.o.*) feel sick; **(b)** *Fig* (*dégoûter*) to disgust, to make (*s.o.*) feel sick; (*révolter*) to disgust; *Can F* (*donner envie*) to make (*s.o.*) green with envy; **(c)** *Fig* (*décourager*) to dishearten, to discourage; *Can F* **elle est écœurée de son job,** she is sick of *or* fed up with her job.

écoinçon [ekwɛ̃sɔ̃] *nm Constr* corner piece *or* stone.

école [ekɔl] *nf* **(a)** school; **é. maternelle,** nursery school, kindergarten; **é. primaire,** primary school; **é. d'État,** state *or US* public school; **é. libre** *ou* **privée,** ≈ independent *or* private school; **maîtresse/maître d'é.,** (primary) schoolmistress/schoolmaster; **reprendre l'é.,** to go back to school; **aller à l'é. jusqu'à 16 ans,** to go to school until the age of 16; **faire l'é.,** to teach; *Fig Hum* **tu peux retourner à l'é.,** what did they teach you at school?; *Fig* **vous êtes à bonne é.,** you're in good hands; **les grandes écoles,** = colleges of university level specializing in professional training; **é. normale,** ≈ teacher training college; **École normale supérieure,** = university level college that prepares students for senior posts in teaching and other professions; **é. ménagère,** domestic training college; **le quartier des Écoles,** the Latin quarter (*in Paris*); *Mil* **É. (supérieure) de Guerre,** ≈ Staff College; **é. hôtelière,** catering school; **é. du soir,** night school, *Br* evening classes; **é. d'équitation,** riding school; *Fig* **à l'é. de la vie/misère,** in the school of life/poverty; **bateau-é.,** training ship; **auto-é.,** driving school;

(b) *Mil* (*exercice*) drill, training; **é du soldat,** recruit drill; **é. de tir,** rifle drill; *Nau* **é. de nœuds,** knotting and splicing; *Av* **appareil d'é.,** training aircraft;

(c) (*mouvement*) school (*of thought, art, literature*); **faire é.,** (*of theory, thinker etc*) to set a fashion, to win a following;

(d) *Hist* **l'É.,** the Schoolmen.

écolier, -ière [ekɔlje, -jɛr] *n* **(a)** (*du primaire*) (primary) schoolboy, schoolgirl; *Fig* **le chemin des écoliers,** the longest way round; **papier é.,** exercise paper; **(b)** (*débutant*) novice, beginner; **bévue d'é.,** childish mistake.

écolo [ekɔlo] *adj & n F* (= **écologiste**) green.

écologie [ekɔlɔʒi] *nf* ecology.

écologique [ekɔlɔʒik] *adj* ecological.

écologiste [ekɔlɔʒist] *n* ecologist.

écomusée [ekɔmyze] *nm* living museum (*showing man in his natural and social environment*).

éconduire [ekɔ̃dɥir] *vt* (*conj like* **conduire**) **(a)**

(*congédier*) to get rid of (*s.o.*) (politely); to show (*s.o.*) to the door; **(b)** (*refuser*) to reject (*suitor*); to refuse, to put off (*supplicant, claimant*).

économat [ekɔnɔma] *nm* **(a)** (*fonction*) stewardship, bursarship; **(b)** (*bureau*) steward's *or* bursar's office; **(c)** (*magasin*) staff (discount) store; *Com* (*coopérative*) multiple *or* chain store.

économe [ekɔnɔm] **1** *n* steward, bursar (*of college, institution etc*); *Bible* **l'é. infidèle,** the unjust steward. **2** *adj* economical, thrifty; **é. de paroles/de son temps/***etc*, sparing of words/of one's time/*etc*.

économétrie [ekɔnɔmetri] *nf* econometrics.

économie [ekɔnɔmi] *nf* **(a)** (*système*) economy; **é. politique,** political economy, economics; **é. dirigée,** planned economy; **é. humaine,** human economy; **é. sociale,** social economy; **é. de troc,** barter economy; **é. en expansion,** expanding economy; **(b)** (*gain*) economy, saving; (*vertu*) economy, thrift; **vivre avec é.,** to live economically *or* thriftily; **faire une é. de temps,** to save time; **faire l'é. de 500 francs,** to do without 500 francs; **faire une é. de vingt pour cent,** to save twenty per cent; **(c) économies,** savings; **faire des économies,** to save money; **faire des économies de chauffage,** to save money on heating; **faire des économies d'énergie,** to save energy; **prendre sur ses économies,** to break into *or* draw on one's savings; *F* **économies de bouts de chandelles,** cheeseparing (economy); **(d)** (*organisation*) arrangement, structure (*of literary work, law etc*).

économique [ekɔnɔmik] *adj* **(a)** *Écon* economic (*problem, doctrine etc*); **science économique,** economics; **(b)** (*bon marché, avantageux*) economical (*method, apparatus etc*); **vitesse é.,** economical speed (*of car etc*); **cycle é.,** (*de lave-vaisselle etc*) economy cycle; **bouteille/voiture é.,** economy bottle/car.

économiquement [ekɔnɔmikmɑ̃] *adv* (*à peu de frais*) & *Écon* economically; **les é. faibles,** those on low incomes.

économiser [ekɔnɔmize] **1** *vt* to economize, to save (*money, time*); to economize on, to save on (*electricity etc*); to conserve, to husband (*resources etc*); **é. l'énergie,** to save energy; **é. ses paroles,** to be sparing of one's words; **é. ses forces,** to conserve one's strength. **2** *vi* to economize, to save (**sur,** on).

économiseur [ekɔnɔmizœr] *nm Aut* fuel-saving device.

économiste [ekɔnɔmist] *n* economist.

écope [ekɔp] *nf Nau* bailer, scoop.

écoper [ekɔpe] **1** *vt* to bail (out) (*boat*); **é. l'eau d'une embarcation,** to bail out a boat. **2** *vi F* **(a) é. de cinq ans de prison,** to cop *or* get five years' prison; **(b)** (*être puni*) to get the blame, to catch *or* cop it.

écoperche [ekɔpɛrʃ] *nf* upright (pole), standard (*of scaffolding*).

écorçage [ekɔrsaʒ] *nm* barking (*of trees*); peeling (*of oranges*); husking (*of rice*).

écorce [ekɔrs] *nf* **(a)** *Bot* cortex; **(b)** bark (*of tree*); rind, peel (*of orange*); husk (*of rice*); **(c)** *Géog* **l'é. terrestre,** the earth's crust; **(d)** *Fig* (*apparence*) outward appearance.

écorcer [ekɔrse] *vt* **(j'écorçai(s); n. écorçons)** to bark (*tree*); to peel (*orange*); to husk (*rice*).

écorché, -ée [ekɔrʃe] **1** *nm* **(a)** *Beaux-Arts* anatomical model, écorché; **(b)** *Tech* sectional *or* cutaway view. **2** *n* **é. vif,** (*person*) tortured soul.

écorchement [ekɔrʃəmɑ̃] *nm* **(a)** flaying, skinning (*of animal*); **(b)** abrasion, grazing (*of the skin*); grazing, barking (*of shin*).

écorcher [ekɔrʃe] **1** *vt* **(a)** to flay (*large animal, criminal*); to skin (*rabbit, eel*); *F* **é. une langue/un nom/***etc*, to murder a language/name/*etc*; **é. les clients,** to fleece the customers; **(b)** (*érafler*) to graze, to chafe (*leg, the skin etc*); **(c)** to scrape, to scratch (*furniture*); to rasp (*throat*); **son qui écorche l'oreille,** sound that grates on the ear. **2 s'écorcher** *vpr* to graze oneself; **s'é. le tibia,** to graze *or* bark one's shin.

écorcheur, -euse [ekɔrʃœr, -øz] *n* **(a)** flayer, skinner; **(b)** *F* (*voleur*) fleecer, extortioner.

écorchure [ekɔrʃyr] *nf* graze, scratch.

écorner [ekɔrne] *vt* **(a)** to chip *or* damage the corner(s) of (*furniture, statue etc*); **é. (les pages d')un livre,** to dog-ear (the pages of) a book; **(b)** *Fig* **é. son capital/ses économies,** to break into one's capital/savings.

écornifler [ekɔrnifle] *vt F* to cadge, to scrounge (*meal, money*) **(à qn,** off s.o.).

écornifleur, -euse [ekɔrniflœr, -øz] *n F* sponger, cadger, scrounger.

écornure [ekɔrnyr] *nf* **(a)** (*fragment*) chip (*from a corner*); **(b)** (*brèche*) chipped corner.

écossais, -aise [ekɔsɛ, -ɛz] **1** *adj* Scottish (*scenery etc*); Scotch (*whisky, broth, pancake, mist*); Scottish, Scots (*person*); **tissu é.,** tartan, plaid. **2** *n* **É.,** Scot, Scotsman, Scotswoman. **3** *nm* **(a)** (*tissu*) tartan, plaid; **(b)** *Ling* Scots; (*langue celtique*) (Scots) Gaelic.

Écosse [ekɔs] *nf* Scotland; **la Haute É.,** the Highlands.

écosser [ekɔse] *vt* **(a)** to shell, to pod, to hull (*peas, beans*); **(b)** *Arg* (*dépenser*) to shell out.

écosystème [ekɔsistɛm] *nm Biol* ecosystem.

écot [eko] *nm* **payer son é.,** to pay one's share.

écoulé [ekule] *adj Com* of last month, ultimo, *F* ult.

écoulement [ekulmɑ̃] *nm* **(a)** (out)flow, flowing, discharge (*of liquid*); *Constr* run-off, drainage (*from roof etc*); **fossé d'é.,** drain; **(tube d')é.,** outlet tube; waste pipe (*of bath*); **trou d'é.,** plughole (*of a sink*); *Av* **é. (des filets) d'air,** air flow; **(b)** *Méd* discharge; **(c)** dispersal (*of a crowd*); **é. de la circulation,** flow of traffic; **(d)** *Com* sale, disposal (*of goods*); **marchandises d'é. facile,** goods that sell easily *or* fast, goods with a ready sale; **(e)** passage (*of time*).

écouler [ekule] **1** *vt* to sell (off), to dispose of, to move (*goods*); **é. de faux billets,** to issue *or Jur* utter forged notes. **2 s'écouler** *vpr* **(a)** (*of liquid etc*) to flow out, to run out (**de,** of); (*of crowd*) to disperse; **le public s'écoulait du théâtre,** the audience was pouring out of the theatre; **son argent s'écoule,** his money is dwindling away; **faire s'é. l'eau,** to run *or* drain off the water; **(b)** (*of goods*) to sell, to move; **(c)** (*of time*) to pass, to elapse.

écourter [ekurte] *vt* **(a)** to shorten (*dress, text, quotation etc*); to curtail, to cut short (*visit, speech*); to trim (*beard, moustache*); **(b)** to dock (*dog's tail, dog*); to crop (*dog's ears, dog*).

écoute[1] [ekut] *nf* **(a) être** *ou* **se tenir aux écoutes,** (*aux portes etc*) to eavesdrop; *Fig* to keep one's ears open; *Mil* **poste d'é.,** listening post; **(b)** *Tél Rad* listening-in; **é. de contrôle,** monitoring; **se mettre** *ou* **se porter à l'é., prendre l'é.,** to listen in; *Rad* **être à l'é.,** to be listening, to be tuned in (**de,** in); *Rad* **l'heure de grande é.,** peak listening time; *Rad* **ne quittez pas l'é.!, restez à l'é.!,** stay tuned (in)!, keep listening!; *Tél* **table d'é.,** tapping equipment; **(c) être toujours à l'é. des autres,** to be always willing to lend a sympathetic ear to others.

écoute[2] *nf Nau* sheet (*of sail*); **nœud d'é.,** sheet bend; **point d'é.,** clew.

écouter [ekute] **1** *vt* **(a)** to listen to (*s.o., sth*); **savoir é.,** to be a good listener; **se faire é.,** to get a hearing; **je vais te faire é. un morceau,** I'll play you some music; **é. qn jusqu'au bout,** to hear s.o. out; **é. à la porte** *ou* **aux portes,** to eavesdrop; **écoutez!,** listen!, look (here)!; **(b)** *Rad* to listen in to, to tune in to; **(c)** (*suivre*) to pay attention to (*s.o., advice*); **ne les écoutez pas!,** don't pay them any attention!; **é. sa conscience,** to listen to *or* be guided by one's conscience. **2 s'écouter** *vpr* to listen to oneself (*on radio etc*); **il s'écoute trop,** he coddles himself; **elle a tendance à s'é. parler,** she likes the sound of her own voice; **si je m'écoutais,** if I did what I wanted.

écouteur, -euse [ekutœr, -øz] **1** *n* **(a)** (*personne*) listener; **é. aux portes,** eavesdropper; **(b)** *Rad* (*personne*) listener. **2** *nm* **(a)** *Tél* receiver; **(b)** *Rad* **écouteurs,** earphones, headphones.

écoutille [ekutij] *nf Nau* hatchway.

écouvillon [ekuvijɔ̃] *nm* (baker's) oven mop; (bottle) brush; (gun) swab; *Méd* swab.

écouvillonnage [ekuvijɔnaʒ] *nm* mopping out, cleaning out (*of oven*); cleaning out (*of bottle*); swabbing out (*of gun*); *Méd* swabbing (*of cavity*).

écouvillonner [ekuvijɔne] *vt* to mop out, to clean out (*oven*); to clean out (*bottle*); to swab out (*gun*); *Méd* to swab (*cavity*).

écrabouillage [ekrabujaʒ] *nm*, **écrabouillement** [ekrabujmɑ̃] *nm F* crushing, squashing.

écrabouiller [ekrabuje] *vt F* to crush, to squash, to reduce (*s.o., sth*) to pulp.

écran [ekrɑ̃] *nm* **(a)** (*panneau*) screen; **é. de cheminée,** fire screen; **é. de fumée,** smoke screen; **é. protecteur** *ou* **de protection,** shield; *Cin* **é. de sûreté,** cut-off (*of projector*); **é. de ciel, é. filtre,** sky filter; **faire é. de son corps,** to make a shield with one's body (**à qn,** for s.o.); **(b) procédé à l'é. de soie,** silk-screen process; **(c)** *TV* screen; *Ordinat* **é. divisé,** split screen; *Ordinat* **é. tactile,** touch screen; *Cin Phot* **é. (de projection),** screen; **l'é.,** (*cinéma*) the cinema; **porter une pièce à l'é.,** to adapt a play for the screen; **la technique de l'é.,** film technique; **Bourvil crève l'é. dans ce film,** Bourvil gives a riveting performance in this film; **le petit é.**, the small screen, television; **le grand é.**, the big screen, cinema; **téléviseur à é. plat,** flat-screen television.

écrasant [ekrazɑ̃] *adj* crushing (*weight, defeat etc*); overwhelming (*proof, majority*); back-breaking (*work*); overpowering (*heat*).

écrasé [ekraze] *adj* **(a)** *Journ F* **rubrique des chiens écrasés,** small news items (*especially accidents*); **(b) nez é.**, flat nose.

écrasement [ekrazmɑ̃] *nm* crushing, squashing (*of fruit etc*); running over (*by car*); oppression (*of the people*); crushing defeat (*of army*); *Av* **é. (au sol),** crash.

écraser [ekraze] **1** *vt* **(a)** to crush, to squash (*fruit*); to crush (*limb*); to flatten out (*can etc*); to squash (*beetle*); to swat (*fly*); to stub out (*cigarette*); *Aut* to run over (*pedestrian etc*); *Aut* **se faire é.**, to get run over; **écrasé par une avalanche,** crushed by an avalanche; *Aut F* **é. l'accélérateur,** to step on the gas; **é. d'impôts,** to overburden with taxes; **écrasé de travail,** overwhelmed *or F* snowed under with work; *Fin F* **é. le marché,** to glut *or* flood the market; *Tennis* **é. la balle,** to kill *or* smash the ball; **coup écrasé,** smash;

(b) to dwarf (*building etc*);

(c) (*vaincre*) to crush, to rout (*opponent, troops etc*);

(d) *Arg* **en é.**, to sleep like a log.

2 *vi Arg* **écrase!,** shut up!

3 s'écraser *vpr* **s'é. sur le sol,** (*of person*) to crash to the ground; (*of aircraft*) to crash; **on s'écrase devant le cinéma,** there's a tremendous crush outside the cinema; **la neige s'écrase sous nos pieds,** the snow crunches under our feet; *F* **à sa place, je m'écraserais,** if I were him I'd keep my head down *or* keep a low profile; *Arg* **écrase-toi!,** (*tais-toi*) shut it!, button it!

écraseur, -euse [ekrazœr, -øz] *n Aut F* road hog.

écrémage [ekremaʒ] *nm* creaming, skimming (*of milk*).

écrémer [ekreme] *vt* **(j'écrème; j'écrémerai) (a)** to cream, to skim (*milk*); **lait écrémé,** skim(med) milk; **lait non écrémé,** full cream milk; **(b)** *Fig* to take the best *or* the cream of, to cream (off) (*a collection*).

écrémeuse [ekremøz] *nf* (cream) separator, creamer.

écrêter [ekrete] *vt* **(a)** to remove the comb of (*cock*); **(b)** to knock the heads off (*flowers etc*); **(c)** to lower the crest of (*hill*).

écrevisse [ekrəvis] *nf* (*crustacé*) (fresh-water) crayfish; *F* **rouge comme une é.**, as red as a lobster; *F* **marcher comme une é.**, to walk backwards.

écrier (s') [sekrije] *vpr* to cry (out), to exclaim.

écrin [ekrɛ̃] *nm* (jewel) case.

écrire [ekrir] *v* (*ppr* **écrivant**; *pp* **écrit**; *pr ind* **j'écris, n. écrivons, ils écrivent**; *p hist* **j'écrivis**; *fu* **j'écrirai**) **1** *vt* **(a)** to write; **é. qch à** *ou* **avec de l'encre,** to write sth in ink; **machine à é.**, typewriter; **é. une lettre à la machine,** to type a letter; **é. un mot à la hâte,** to scribble a note; **é. un mot à qn,** to drop s.o. a line; **é. à qn,** to write to s.o.; **je lui ai écrit de venir,** I have written asking him to come;

(b) (*noter*) to write (*sth*) down; *F* **il est écrit que je ne peux pas y aller,** I am fated not to get there; **c'est écrit,** it is *or* was bound to happen;

(c) *Littér Mus* to write (*book, song etc*); **é. ses mémoires,** to write one's memoirs;

(d) *Ordinat* **é. qch sur un disque,** to write sth to disk.

2 *vi* **il écrit bien,** he has good (hand)writing; he's a good writer (*of fiction etc*); **ce stylo écrit très bien,** this pen writes very well; **é. dans les journaux,** to write for the papers.

3 s'écrire *vpr* **(a)** (*s'orthographier*) to be written *or* spelt; **ce mot s'écrit avec un g.**, this word is written *or* spelt with a g;

(b) (*correspondre*) **ils s'écrivent,** they write to each other.

écrit [ekri] **1** *adj* written (*word, style, law*); **il n'y a rien d'é.**, there's nothing (down) in writing. **2** *nm* **(a) consigner** *ou* **coucher qch par é.**, to set sth down in writing; **convention par é.**, written agreement; **(b)** (*texte*) (written) document; **faire/signer un é.**, to draw up/to sign a document; **les écrits de Bossuet,** the writings *or* works of Bossuet; **(c)** *Scol* **échouer à l'é.**, to fail in the written examination.

écriteau, -eaux [ekrito] *nm* notice, placard; notice, bill, announcement (*posted up*).

écritoire [ekritwar] *nf* (*coffret*) writing case.

écriture [ekrityr] *nf* **(a)** (*système, caractères*) writing, script; **é. pictographique/cunéiforme,** pictographic/ cuneiform writing *or* script; **é. phonétique,** phonetic script; **é. arabe/grecque,** Arab/Greek writing *or* script;

(b) (*main*) (hand)writing; **é. à la machine,** typewriting, typing; **elle a une belle/mauvaise é.**, she has good/bad handwriting; **je ne peux pas lire son é.**, I can't read his (hand)writing;

(c) *Com* **écritures,** accounts; **tenir les écritures,** to keep the accounts; **employé aux écritures,** accounts *or* ledger clerk;

(d) (*en comptabilité*) entry, item; **écritures en partie double,** double entry;

(e) l'É. sainte, Holy Scripture, Holy Writ;

(f) *Littér* writing; **é. surréaliste,** surrealist writing.

écrivailler [ekrivaje] *vi F Péj* to be a hack (writer), to scribble.

écrivailleur, -euse [ekrivajœr, -øz] *n*, **écrivaillon, -onne** [ekrivajɔ̃, -ɔn] *n F Péj* hack (writer), scribbler.

écrivain [ekrivɛ̃] *nm* **(a)** author, writer; **femme é.**, (woman) writer, authoress; **(b) é. public,** (public) letter writer.

écrivasser [ekrivase] *vi F Péj* = **ÉCRIVAILLER**.

écrivassier, -ière [ekrivasje, -jɛr] *n F Péj* hack (writer), scribbler.

écrou¹ [ekru] *nm Jur* committal (to prison); **sous é.**, detained, in detention; **levée d'é.**, release, discharge (from prison).

écrou² *nm Tech* nut; **é. à ailettes** *ou* **à oreilles,** thumb *or* wing *or* butterfly nut; **é. crénelé** *ou* **à créneaux** *ou* **à encoches,** castellated nut.

écrouelles [ekruɛl] *nfpl Arch* scrofula, king's evil.

écrouer [ekrue] *vt Jur* to imprison, to commit to prison.

écrouir [ekruir] *vt Tech* **(a)** (*en frappant*) to hammer-harden, to cold-hammer; **(b)** (*en étirant*) to cold-draw; **(c)** (*en laminant*) to cold-roll.

écrouissage [ekruisaʒ] *nm* **(a)** (*en frappant*) hammer-hardening, cold-hammering; **(b)** (*en étirant*) cold drawing; **(c)** (*en laminant*) cold-rolling.

écroulement [ekrulmɑ̃] *nm* collapse, fall (*of building, bridge etc*); fall (*of earth, rock*); collapse (*of person*); ruin, downfall (*of hopes*); fall, collapse (*of empire*); **é. des crédits,** collapse of funds; **é. de la santé,** breakdown in health.

écrouler (s') [sekrule] *vpr* **(a)** (*of building, bridge etc*) to collapse, to fall, to give way; (*of hopes*) to crumble away; **empire près de s'é.**, empire on the verge of collapse; **(b) s'é. sur une chaise/***etc*, to drop *or* flop onto a chair/*etc*; **s'é. de fatigue,** to collapse *or* drop with exhaustion; **écroulé dans un fauteuil,** slumped in an armchair; *F* **écroulé de rire,** doubled up with laughter.

écroûter [ekrute] *vt* **(a)** to remove the crust from (*bread etc*); **(b)** *Agr* to scarify (*land*).

écru [ekry] *adj* (*of material*) unbleached, ecru, natural-coloured; **soie écrue,** raw silk; **toile écrue,** holland.

ectoderme [ɛktɔdɛrm] *nm Biol* ectoderm.

ectoplasme [ɛktɔplasm] *nm Biol* ectoplasm.

ectoplasmique [ɛktɔplasmik] *adj Biol* ectoplasm(at)ic.

ectropion [ɛktrɔpjɔ̃] *nm Méd* ectropion, ectropium; eversion (*of eyelid*).

écu [eky] *nm* **(a)** (*bouclier*) shield; **(b)** *Hér* escutcheon, coat of arms; **(c)** *Arch Fin* crown; *F* **avoir des écus,** to have pots of money; **(d)** (*monnaie européenne*) ECU; **(e)** (*plante*) **herbe aux écus,** moneywort, creeping jenny.

ECU [eky] *nm inv* (*abrév* **European Currency Unit**) ECU.

écubier [ekybje] *nm Nau* hawsehole.

écueil [ekœj] *nm Nau* reef, shelf; *Fig* (*danger*) pitfall; **donner sur les écueils,** (*of ship*) to strike the rocks; *Fig* **se heurter à un é.**, to hit a snag; **ce manque d'harmonie fut l'é. de l'entreprise,** this lack of harmony was the rock on which the company foundered.

écuelle [ekɥɛl] *nf* **(a)** (*assiette large*) bowl; **une é. de soupe,** a bowl(ful) of soup; **é. du chien/chat,** dog's/cat's bowl *or* dish; **(b)** (*plante*) *F* **é. d'eau,** marsh pennywort, water-cup.

éculé [ekyle] *adj* **(a)** down-at-heel (*shoe*); **(b)** well-worn (*trick, joke, argument etc*).

écumage [ekymaʒ] *nm* skimming, scumming (*of soup, jam, molten metal*).

écumant [ekymɑ̃] *adj* foaming, frothing (*sea, beer*).

écume [ekym] *nf* **(a)** froth, foam (*in mouth, on beer etc*); foam (*on sea*); **il avait de l'é. à la bouche,** he was foaming at the mouth; **cheval couvert d'é.**, foam-covered horse; *Ent* **é. printanière,** cuckoo spit; **(b)** scum (*on jam, soup, molten metal etc*); *Fig Péj* **é. de la société,** scum *or* dregs of society; **(c) é. (de mer),** (*magnésite*) meerschaum.

écumer [ekyme] **1** *vt* **(a)** to skim, to scum (*soup, jam, molten metal etc*); **(b)** (*piller*) to scour, to pillage (*country-side etc*); **é. les mers,** (*of pirates*) to scour the seas, to buccaneer. **2** *vi* **(a)** (*of wine, mouth etc*) to foam, to froth; (*of sea*) to foam; **cheval qui écume,** foaming horse; **é. (de rage),** to foam (with rage); **(b)** (*of jam, soup, molten metal etc*) to (form a) scum.

écumeur [ekymœr] *nm* **é. (de mer),** buccaneer, pirate; *Fig Péj* **é. littéraire,** plagiarist.

écumeux, -euse [ekymø, -øz] *adj* foaming (*sea, waves*); foamy, frothy (*beer etc*); scummy (*jam etc*).

écumoire [ekymwar] *nf* skimmer, skimming ladle, perforated ladle; **é. à friture,** slotted spoon; *Fig* **comme une é.,** (*troué*) riddled with holes.

écureuil [ekyrœj] *nm* squirrel; **é. volant,** flying squirrel.

écurie [ekyri] *nf* stable; **mettre les chevaux à** *ou* **dans l'é.,** to stable the horses; *F* **quelle é.!, c'est sale!,** what a pigsty! it's filthy!; **entrer comme dans une é.,** to barge in; **é. (de courses),** (racing) stable (*of horses, cars*).

écusson [ekysɔ̃] *nm* **(a)** *Hér* escutcheon, shield, coat of arms; **(b)** (*de serrure*) keyhole scutcheon, key-plate; (*emblème d'étoffe*) badge; **(c)** *Mil* tab, badge, (collar) patch; **(d)** (*greffe*) (shield) bud; **greffe en é.,** budding; **(e)** (*d'un insecte*) scutellum.

écussonnage [ekysɔnaʒ] *nm* (shield) budding (*of tree*).

écussonner [ekysɔne] *vt* to bud (*a tree*).

écussonnoir [ekysɔnwar] *nm* budding knife.

écuyer, -ère [ekɥije, -ɛr] **1** *nm* **(a)** (*instructeur*) riding master; **(b)** *Arch* (*gentilhomme*) squire, armour-bearer; (*servant la famille royale*) equerry; *Hist* **grand é.,** Master of the Horse. **2** *n* rider, horseman, horsewoman; **être bon é.,** to ride well, to be a good rider; **é. de cirque,** circus rider, equestrian, *f* equestrienne; **bottes à l'écuyère,** riding boots; **monter à l'écuyère,** (*of woman*) to ride astride.

eczéma [ɛgzema] *nm Méd* eczema; **avoir** *ou* **faire de l'é.,** to have eczema.

eczémateux, -euse [ɛgzematø, -øz] *adj Méd* eczematous.

edelweiss [edɛlvɛs, -vajs] *nf* (*plante*) edelweiss.

Éden (l') [ledɛn] *nm Bible* (the Garden of) Eden; *Fig* **un é.,** a paradise, a Garden of Eden.

édénique [edenik] *adj* Edenic.

édenté [edɑ̃te] **1** *adj* toothless (*person*); (*animal*) edentate. **2** *nmpl* **les édentés,** the Edentata, edentate animals.

édenter [edɑ̃te] *vt* to break the teeth of (*comb, saw, blade etc*).

EDF [ədeef, edeef] *nf* (*abrév* **Électricité de France**) (French) Electricity Board.

édicter [edikte] *vt* to enact, to decree (*law*); to decree, to prescribe (*penalty*).

édicule [edikyl] *nm F* (*urinoir*) public convenience.

édifiant [edifjɑ̃] *adj* edifying.

édification [edifikasjɔ̃] *nf* **(a)** erecting, erection, building (*of monument etc*); **(b)** building up (*of empire, fortune etc*); **(c)** (*instruction morale*) edification, moral improvement; **pour votre é.,** for your information.

édifice [edifis] *nm* **(a)** building, edifice; **édifices publics,** public buildings; *Fig* **apporter sa pierre à l'é.,** to make a contribution, to do one's bit; **(b)** *Fig* **tout l'é. social,** the whole fabric *or* structure of society.

édifier [edifje] *vt* **(a)** to erect, to build (*public building*); **(b)** (*créer*) to build up (*empire, fortune, system etc*); **(c)** (*of sermon etc*) to edify; *Iron* **alors je suis édifié,** well, now I know.

édile [edil] *nm* **(a)** (*in ancient Rome*) aedile; **(b)** (*magistrat officiel*) municipal official, town councillor.

Édimbourg [edɛ̃bur] *nm ou f* Edinburgh.

édit [edi] *nm Hist* edict.

éditer [edite] *vt* **(a)** (*publier*) to publish (*book etc*); to produce (*record*); **(b)** (*annoter*) to edit (*text*); **(c)** *Ordinat* to edit; **pouvant être édité,** editable.

éditeur, -trice [editœr, -tris] **1** *n* **(a)** (*d'une maison d'édition*) publisher; **(b)** (*commentateur*) editor (*of text*). **2** *nm Ordinat* (*of programme*) editor; **é. de texte,** text editor.

édition [edisjɔ̃] *nf* **(a)** (*activité, métier*) publishing; **maison d'é.,** publishing house *or* firm; **é. de disques,** record production; **travailler dans l'é.,** to work in publishing; **(b)** (*texte commenté*) edition; (*exemplaire*) edition, issue, impression; **é. scolaire,** school edition; **é. originale,** first edition; *Journ* **dernière é.,** final edition; **é. spéciale,** special edition; **(c)** (*action d'annoter*) editing; **(d)** *Ordinat* editing.

éditorial, -iaux [editɔrjal, -jo] *Journ* **1** *adj* editorial. **2** *nm* leading article, leader, editorial.

éditorialiste [editɔrjalist] *n Journ* leader writer.

Edmond [ɛdmɔ̃] *nm* Edmund.

Édouard [edwar] *nm* Edward.

édouardien, -ienne [edwardjɛ̃, -jɛn] *adj Hist* Edwardian.

édredon [edrədɔ̃] *nm* **é. (piqué** *ou* **américain),** eiderdown (quilt).

éduc(at)able [edykabl] *adj* teachable, educable (*child*).

éducateur, -trice [edykatœr, -tris] **1** *n* (*enseignant*) educator, instructor; (*spécialiste*) educationalist; **é. spécialisé,** special education worker. **2** *adj* educational (*book, method etc*); **le rôle é. des parents,** the educational role of parents.

éducatif, -ive [edykatif, -iv] *adj* educative, instructive (*experience etc*); educational (*film, toy, method etc*).

éducation [edykasjɔ̃] *nf* **(a)** (*enseignement etc*) education; **faire l'é. de qn,** to educate s.o.; **où as-tu fait ton é.?,** where were you educated?; **é. professionnelle,** vocational training; **l'é. politique de la jeunesse,** the political education of young people; **é. physique,** physical training *or* education; **(b)** (*par les parents etc*) upbringing; **sans é.,** ill-bred; **avoir de l'é.,** to be well-bred, to have good manners; **il manque d'é.,** he has no manners, he is ill-mannered *or* ill-bred; **(c)** *Fig* training (*of will, reflexes, mind etc*).

édulcorant [edylkɔrɑ̃] **1** *adj* sweetening. **2** *nm* sweetener; **é. de synthèse,** artificial sweetener.

édulcorer [edylkɔre] *vt* **(a)** to sweeten (*medicine, drink etc*); **boisson édulcorée,** sweetened drink; **(b)** *Fig* **é. une triste nouvelle,** to break a piece of bad news gently; **compte rendu édulcoré,** watered-down report.

éduquer [edyke] *vt* **(a)** (*donner enseignement à*) to educate (*child, the masses etc*); **(b)** (*élever*) to bring (*s.o.*) up (**à faire,** to do); **mal éduqué,** ill-bred; **(c)** *Fig* to train (*will, mind etc*).

effaçage [efasaʒ] *nm* **(a)** (*en gommant*) rubbing out, erasing; **(b)** (*en rayant*) crossing out.

effacé [efase] *adj* self-effacing, retiring (*person, manner*); small, insignificant (*role*); receding (*chin*).

effacement [efasmɑ̃] *nm* **(a)** (*par qn*) obliteration (*of word, stain etc*); (*par le temps etc*) wearing away (*of inscription*); fading (*of memories*); **(b)** self-effacement, retiring nature (*of person*).

effacer [efase] *v* (**j'effaçai(s); n. effaçons**) **1** *vt* **(a)** (*enlever*) to obliterate; **e. un mot,** (*en gommant*) to rub out *or* erase a word; (*en rayant*) to cross out a word; **e. le tableau,** to clean the blackboard; *Ordinat* **e. l'écran,** to clear the screen; *Ordinat* **e. un mot/une ligne,** to delete a word/a line; **e. une tache,** (*en lavant*) to wash out a stain; (*avec un chiffon*) to wipe out a stain; **e. des imperfections,** to smooth out imperfections; **sculptures effacées par le temps,** carvings worn away by time; *Fig* **e. un mauvais moment de ses souvenirs,** to erase an unhappy moment from one's memories; **le temps efface les douleurs,** time heals all wounds; **e. qch de sa mémoire,** to blot sth out of *or* erase sth from one's memory;

(b) (*éclipser*) to put (*s.o.*) in the shade;

(c) e. le corps, to stand sideways; **e. les épaules,** to throw back the shoulders;

(d) *Ordinat* (*détruire*) to erase, to delete, *F* to zap (*file, disk*).

2 s'effacer *vpr* **(a)** (*disparaître*) to become obliterated; (*of inscription etc*) to wear away; (*of memory*) to fade (away); **cela s'effacera à l'eau,** it will wash off; *Fig* **ton chagrin s'effacera,** you'll get over it;

(b) (*s'écarter*) to stand *or* move aside, to move to one side; *Fig* **depuis quelque temps il s'était effacé,** for some time he had kept in the background; **s'e. devant qn,** to give way to s.o., to submit to s.o.; **il a tendance à s'e. derrière elle,** he tends to hide behind her.

effaceur [efasœr] *nm* eraser; **e. d'encre,** (*stylo*) ink eraser; **e. total,** (*de magnétophone*) bulk eraser.

effarant [efarɑ̃] *adj* alarming; astounding (*price, stupidity etc*).

effarement [efarmɑ̃] *nm* alarm; **dans l'e.,** alarmed.

effarer [efare] *vt* to alarm, to scare, (*s.o.*); **son hypocrisie m'effare!,** his *or* her hypocrisy astounds me!; **je suis effaré par les prix!,** I'm astounded at the prices!

effarouchant [efaruʃɑ̃] *adj* frightening, startling.

effarouchement [efaruʃmɑ̃] *nm* (*action d'effrayer*) startling, frightening (away) (*of animal*).

effaroucher [efaruʃe] **1** *vt* **(a)** (*effrayer*) to startle, to scare away, to frighten away (*animal*); to scare, to alarm (*s.o.*); **(b)** (*choquer*) to shock (*s.o.*). **2 s'effaroucher** *vpr* **(a)** (*s'effrayer*) (*of animal*) to be startled *or* frightened away (**de,** by); to take fright (**de,** at); (*of person*) to be scared *or* alarmed (**de,** by); **(b)** (*s'offusquer*) to be shocked (**de,** by, at).

effectif, -ive [efɛktif, -iv] **1** *adj* **(a)** effective, efficacious (*treatment etc*); **(b)** effective, actual (*work, yield etc*); *Fin* active (*circulation*); real (*value*). **2** *nm* **(a)** (*nombre prévu d'hommes, de femmes*) strength, numbers (*of club, battalion etc*); *Nau* complement; **à e. réduit,** under *or* below strength; *Scol* **réduire l'e. des classes à 25,** to reduce the size of classes *or* reduce class numbers to 25; **l'e. est au complet,** we are at full strength *or* up to strength; **(b)** (*employés*) *& Mil* manpower; *Mil* **les effectifs,** the total strength; **crise d'effectifs,** shortage of manpower.

effectivement [efɛktivmɑ̃] *adv* **(a)** (*réellement*) actually, in reality, really; **(b)** (*en effet*) actually, in (actual) fact; **e.!,** quite (so)!, (yes) indeed!

effectuer [efɛktɥe] **1** *vt* to carry out, to bring into effect (*reform, measure etc*); to execute (*movement, operation*); to make, to effect (*payment*); to make (*journey*); to bring about (*reconciliation*); **e. une retraite,** to make good a retreat; *Math* **e. un calcul,** to make a calculation. **2 s'effectuer** *vpr* (*of reform etc*) to be carried out, to be brought into effect; (*of movement, operation*) to be executed; (*of payment, journey*) to be made; (*of reconciliation*) to be brought about.

efféminé [efemine] *adj* effeminate.

efféminer [efemine] *vt* to make effeminate; *Fig* to weaken.

effervescence [efɛrvɛsɑ̃s] *nf* **(a)** (*bouillonnement*) effervescence; **être en** *ou* **faire e.,** to effervesce; **(b)** *Fig* (*agitation*) agitation, turmoil; (*excitation*) excitement; **ville en e.,** town seething with excitement *or* in a turmoil (of excitement).

effervescent [efɛrvɛsɑ̃] *adj* **(a)** effervescent (*drink etc*); **comprimé e.,** effervescent tablet; **(b)** *Fig* excitable, exuberant (*disposition*); excited (*crowd*).

effet [efɛ] *nm* **(a)** (*résultat*) effect; **faire de l'e.,** to be effective; **avoir de l'e. sur le résultat,** to have an effect on *or* to affect the result; **produire l'e. voulu,** to produce the desired effect; **un rapport de cause à e.,** a cause and effect relationship; **ma remarque a eu son petit e.,** my remark caused a stir; **à cet e.,** for this purpose, with this end in view; **cela a eu pour e. de le mettre en colère,** it had the effect of making him angry; **à l'e. de,** for the purpose of, in order to; **sans e.,** ineffective, ineffectual; **mes conseils sont restés sans e.,** my advice had no effect *or* was ineffective; **cela a un e. nocif sur la santé/les jeunes,** it has a harmful effect on health/young people;

(b) (*fonctionnement*) action, operation, working; **mettre un projet à e.,** to put a plan into action *or* into effect; **prendre e.,** (*of law*) to come into *or* take effect, to become operative; **e. rétroactif d'une loi/d'un accord,** retroactive effect of a law/an argument;

(c) *Cr Tennis* spin, **balle qui a de l'e.,** ball that has spin; **donner de l'e. à sa balle,** to put spin on one's ball; *Billard* **e. de côté,** side (screw); **mettre trop d'e.,** to put on too much spin;

(d) *Tech* **e. utile,** efficiency; **e. réactif,** backlash; **à simple e.,** single-action, single-acting; **à double e.,** double-action, double-acting;

(e) *Électron* **e. Edison,** Edison effect; *Phys* **e. corona** *ou* **de couronne,** corona discharge; **e. photo-électrique,** photoelectric effect;

(f) en e., (*réellement*) actually, in (actual) fact; **oui, je m'en souviens, en e.,** yes, I do remember; **j'ai dû partir, en e. j'étais pressé,** I had to leave because I was in a hurry;

(g) (*impression*) impression; **voilà l'e. que cela m'a produit** *ou* **fait,** that is how it impressed *or* struck me; **cela fait mauvais e. de le faire attendre,** it looks bad to keep him waiting; *F* **ça m'a fait e. de la voir si pâle,** it gave me quite a turn to see her so pale; *F* **et c'est tout l'e. que ça te fait?,** is that all it means to you?; **faire de l'e.,** to make a show, to attract attention; **elle me fait l'e. d'une fille plutôt équilibrée,** she gives me the impression of being a fairly well-balanced girl; **sa réponse a fait l'e. d'une bombe,** his answer came as *or* was a bombshell; **cela fait bon e.,** it looks *or* sounds good; **manquer son e.,** to fail; (*of joke*) to misfire, to fall flat; **un e. de contraste,** contrasting effect; **phrases à e.,** words used for effect; **scène à e.,** striking *or* effective scene; **un orateur fait des effets de voix,** a speaker makes striking use of his voice; **des effets de jambes,** striking use of one's legs; *Beaux-Arts* **e. de lune,** moonlight effect; *Cin etc* **effets sonores,** sound effects; **e. d'optique,** visual effect;

(h) *Com* **e. de commerce,** bill of exchange; **e. à vue,** sight draft; **e. au porteur,** bearer security; **effets publics,** government stock *or* securities;

(i) effets, (*vêtements etc*) possessions, belongings; **faites vos effets,** pack up your things; **effets mobiliers,** personal effects; *Jur* goods and chattels.

effeuillage [efœjaʒ] *nm* **(a)** thinning out of leaves (*of fruit trees etc*); **(b)** *Hum F* striptease.

effeuillaison [efœjɛzɔ̃] *nf*, **effeuillement** [efœjmɑ̃] *nm* leaf fall.

effeuiller [efœje] **1** *vt* (*of person*) to thin out the leaves of (*fruit tree*); to pluck off the petals of (*flower*); (*of wind*) to blow off the leaves of (*tree*); **e. la marguerite,** to play 'he *or* she loves me, he *or* she loves me not'. **2 s'effeuiller** *vpr* (*of tree*) to lose *or* shed its leaves; (*of flower*) to shed its petals.

effeuilleuse [efœjøz] *nf F* stripper, striptease artist.

efficace [efikas] *adj* effective, efficacious, effectual (*action, remedy*); efficient (*machine*); efficient, capable (*person*); *El* effective (*value*); **prêter à qn un appui e.,** to give s.o. useful *or* helpful support.

efficacement [efikasmɑ̃] *adv* effectively, efficaciously, effectually; (*avec le minimum d'effort*) efficiently.

efficacité [efikasite] *nf* efficacy, effectiveness (*of remedy, prayer etc*); efficiency (*of machine etc*); **avoir le sens de l'e.,** to be efficient.

efficience [efisjɑ̃s] *nf* efficiency.

efficient [efisjɑ̃] *adj* **(a)** *Phil* efficient (*cause*); **(b)** *F* efficient (*person*).

effigie [efiʒi] *nf* **(a)** (*portrait*) effigy; **pendre qn en e.,** to hang s.o. in effigy; **(b)** (*sur une pièce etc*) effigy, head.

effilage [efilaʒ] *nm* fraying, ravelling out (*of material*).

effilé [efile] **1** *adj* **(a)** *Tex* frayed, fringed (*material*); **(b)** tapered, pointed (*tool*); tapering (*fingers*); slight (*figure*). **2** *nm Tex* fringe, fringed trimming.

effilement [efilmɑ̃] *nm* tapering.

effiler [efile] **1** *vt* **(a)** *Tex* to fray, to unravel, to ravel out; **(b)** (*amincir*) to taper, to make pointed; **e. les cheveux,** to taper hair. **2 s'effiler** *vpr* **(a)** (*of material*) to fray (out); **(b)** (*of face etc*) to taper, to come to a point.

effilochage [efilɔʃaʒ] *nm Tex* **(a)** (*en peignant*) teasing out; **(b)** (*en ouate, bourre*) fraying; **(c)** breaking, tearing (*of waste*); **drap de laine d'e.,** shoddy.

effiloche [efilɔʃ] *nf* **(a)** fringe (*of threads left loose*); **(b) effiloches,** (*soie*) floss silk.

effilocher [efilɔʃe] **1** *vt* **(a)** (*avec une peigne*) to ravel out, to tease out; **(b)** *Tex* to break, to tear (*wool, cotton waste*). **2 s'effilocher** *vpr* (*of material*) to fray.

efflanqué [eflɑ̃ke] *adj* lean, lean-flanked, raw-boned (*animal*); skinny, lanky (*person*).

effleurement [eflœrmɑ̃] *nm* **(a)** (*frôlement*) (light, gentle) touch; **(à touches) à e.,** (*calculatrice etc*) with finger-tip control; **(b)** skimming (*of the water*); **(c)** (*égratignure*) graze (*on skin*).

effleurer [eflœre] *vt* **(a)** (*frôler*) to touch lightly, to brush (against); *Fig* **e. un sujet,** to touch on a topic; **quelques soupçons l'avaient effleuré,** some misgivings had crossed his mind; **cette idée ne m'a jamais effleuré,** this idea never crossed *or* entered my mind; **(b)** to skim (*surface of water*); **(c)** (*égratigner*) to graze (*skin*).

efflorescence [eflɔrɛsɑ̃s] *nf Ch* **(a)** efflorescence; **(b)** *Méd* rash, eruption.

efflorescent [eflɔrɛsɑ̃] *adj Ch* efflorescent.

effluent [eflyɑ̃] **1** *adj* effluent. **2** *nm* (sewage) effluent (*no pl*); **e. radioactif,** radioactive waste.

effluve [eflyv] *nm* **(a)** (*émanation*) emanation; **des effluves riches,** rich fragrance; *Fig Litt* **les effluves de la mémoire/du passé,** the ghosts of one's memory/of the past; **(b)** *Él* brush discharge.

effondrement [efɔ̃drəmɑ̃] *nm* **(a)** collapse, fall (*of bridge etc*); falling in (*of roof, mine etc*); falling through (*of plan*); downfall, collapse (*of government, empire*); slump (*in prices*); **l'e. des marchés/du dollar,** the slump in the markets/of the dollar; **il est dans un état d'e. complet,** he is in a state of total collapse; **(b)** *Agr* subsoiling, trenching; **(c)** *Géol* subsidence.

effondrer [efɔ̃dre] **1** *vt* **(a)** *Agr* to subsoil, to trench (*the ground*); **(b)** (*briser*) to break in *or* down; to break open (*door*); to stave in (*barrel*). **2 s'effondrer** *vpr* (*of bridge etc*) to collapse, to fall; (*of roof, mine etc*) to fall in; (*of plan*) to fall through; (*of prices*) to slump; (*of person, government, empire*) to collapse; **toute son histoire s'effondre,** his whole story is collapsing *or* falling to pieces; **s'e. en larmes,** to break down and cry, to dissolve into tears; **s'e. dans un fauteuil,** to sink *or* flop into an armchair.

efforcer (s') [sefɔrse] *vpr* (**je m'efforçai(s); n. n. efforçons**) to strive, to endeavour, *US* to endeavor; **s'e. de faire qch,** to do one's utmost *or* do one's best *or* make every effort to do sth; **je m'y efforce,** I'm doing my best *or* utmost; **s'e. vers un but,** to strive towards a goal.

effort [efɔr] *nm* **(a)** effort; **faire un e. pour faire qch,** to make an effort to do sth; **elle a dû faire un violent e. pour se lever/s'en persuader,** she had to make a great effort to get up/convince herself; **faire un e. sur soi-même,** to exercise self-control; **cela va te demander un certain e.,** you'll need to exert yourself a bit; **faire tous ses efforts pour réussir,** to make every effort *or* do one's utmost to succeed; **e. de volonté,** effort of (the) will; **faire un e. d'adaptation,** to make an effort to adapt; **e. financier,** financial outlay; **sans e.,** effortlessly, without effort; **allons, encore un e.,** come on, try again *or* a bit more effort; **faire des efforts de mémoire,** to rack one's brains; **elle parle anglais sans e.,** she speaks English effortlessly; *F* **suivre la loi du moindre e.,** to take the line of least resistance; *Péj* **son travail sent l'e.,** his work reeks of effort;
(b) *MecE* strain, stress; **e. de tension,** tensile stress; **e. de torsion,** torque; **e. de rupture,** breaking strain; **e. de traction,** pull; **e. de cisaillement,** shearing stress;
(c) *Vieilli Méd* strain, rick; **se donner** *ou* **attraper un e.,** to rick one's back.

effraction [efraksjɔ̃] *nf Jur* breaking and entering; **entrer par e.,** to break in; **vol (de nuit) avec e.,** burglary; **à l'épreuve de l'e.,** burglar-proof.

effraie [efrɛ] *nf F* (*oiseau*) barn owl, screech owl.

effranger [efrɑ̃ʒe] *v* (**j'effrangeai(s); n. effrangeons**) **1** *vt* to fray (out) (*edges of material*). **2 s'effranger** *vpr* to fray (out), to become frayed.

effrayant [efrɛjɑ̃] *adj* **(a)** (*de peur*) terrifying, appalling; **(b)** *Fig* tremendous, frightful (*heat, appetite, price etc*).

effrayer [efreje] *v* (**j'effraie, j'effraye, n. effrayons; j'effraierai, j'effrayerai**) **1** *vt* **(a)** (*faire peur à*) to frighten, to scare; **(b)** (*inquiéter*) to alarm; **l'énormité de la besogne nous effraie,** the magnitude of the task appals *or* alarms us. **2 s'effrayer** *vpr* to get frightened, to take fright (**de,** at).

effréné [efrene] *adj* unbridled, unrestrained (*passion, curiosity etc*); frantic (*efforts*); wild, frantic (*rush, gallop etc*).

effritement [efritmɑ̃] *nm* crumbling (into dust), disintegration (*of plaster etc*); weathering (*of rock*); *Fig* erosion (*of authority, funds etc*).

effriter [efrite] **1** *vt* to cause (*sth*) to crumble *or* disintegrate; (*of the elements*) to weather (*rock*). **2 s'effriter** *vpr* (*of plaster work etc*) to crumble; (*of rock*) to weather; *Fig* (*of authority, majority, funds etc*) to be eroded.

effroi [efrwa, -ɑ] *nm Litt* terror, fear, dread; **silence qui inspire un e. religieux,** awe-inspiring silence.

effronté [efrɔ̃te] *adj* impudent, insolent, brazen (*person, manner etc*); cheeky (*child*); barefaced, brazen (*lie, liar*).

effrontément [efrɔ̃temɑ̃] *adv* impudently, insolently, brazenly; (*mentir*) brazenly, barefacedly.

effronterie [efrɔ̃tri] *nf* effrontery, insolence, impudence, cheek (*of person, manner etc*); brazenness (*of lie*); **payer d'e.,** to brazen it out.

effroyable [efrwajabl] *adj* **(a)** (*qui fait peur*) dreadful, appalling, horrifying; **visage e.,** hideous face; **(b)** *F* (*énorme*) tremendous (*expense, crowd, mistake etc*).

effroyablement [efrwajabləmɑ̃] *adv F* tremendously, terribly.

effusion [efyzjɔ̃] *nf* **(a) e. de sang,** bloodshed; **(b)** (*exubérance*) effusiveness; **avec e.,** effusively, gushingly; **une e. de tendresse,** an outpouring of affection.

égailler (s') [segaje] *vpr* to disperse, to scatter.

égal, -ale, -aux [egal, -o] **1** *adj* **(a)** (*équivalent*) equal (*share, weight etc*); **être é. à,** to be equal to, to equal; **à écartement é.,** equidistant; **toutes choses égales (d'ailleurs),** all (other) things being equal; **à travail é., salaire é.,** equal pay for equal work; **la partie n'est pas égale,** they are not evenly matched; **tu n'es plus é. à toi-même,** you're not half the person you used to be;
(b) (*constant*) even, regular (*breathing, sound etc*); steady (*pace, pulse*); level, even (*ground*); **homme d'humeur égale,** even-tempered man;
(c) cela m'est (bien) é., it's all the same to me; (*cela ne m'intéresse pas*) I don't care; **c'est é., elle aurait pu venir!,** all the same, she could have come!
2 *n* equal; **s'associer avec ses égaux,** to associate with one's equals; **elle est mon égale,** she is my equal; **traiter qn d'é. à é., traiter qn en é.,** to treat s.o. as an equal; **sans é.,** unequalled, matchless; **à l'é. de,** as much as; **il me chérit à l'é. d'un fils,** he loves me like a son.

également [egalmɑ̃] *adv* **(a)** (*de la même manière*) equally; **é. bon,** equally good; **servir tout le monde é.,** to give everyone an equal serving; **(b)** (*aussi*) also, as well, too; **j'en veux é.,** I want some too *or* as well.

égaler [egale] *vt* **(a)** (*rendre égal*) to make (*s.o., sth*) equal; **la douleur égale les hommes,** grief makes all men equal; **peut-on é. Mozart à Bach?,** can Mozart be considered the equal of Bach?; **(b)** (*être égal à*) to equal, to match up to (*person, score etc*) (**en,** in); **deux et deux égalent quatre,** two and two equal *or* make four; **é. un record,** to equal a record.

égalisateur, -trice [egalizatœr, -tris] *adj* equalizing, levelling (*system, effect etc*); *Sp* **but** *ou* **point é.,** equalizer.

égalisation [egalizɑsjɔ̃] *nf* **(a)** (*équilibrage*) equalization, equalizing; *Math* **é. à zéro,** equating to zero; *Sp* **(but** *ou* **point d')é.,** equalizer; **(b)** (*nivellement*) levelling, evening out (*of ground etc*).

égaliser [egalize] **1** *vt* **(a)** to equalize, to make equal (*wages, pressure etc*); to level, to even out (*ground*); **é. les cheveux de qn,** to trim s.o.'s hair; *Math* **é. une expression à zéro,** to equate an expression to zero; *Sp* **é. la marque,** to equalize, to draw level; **(b)** to level, to even out (*ground*). **2** *vi Sp* to equalize.

égaliseur [egalizœr] *nm Électron* equalizer; **é. graphique,** graphic equalizer.

égalitaire [egalitɛr] *adj & n* egalitarian.

égalitarisme [egalitarism] *nm* egalitarianism.

égalitariste [egalitarist] *adj & n* egalitarian.

égalité [egalite] *nf* **(a)** (*équivalence*) *& Pol* equality; **être sur un pied d'é. avec qn,** to be on an equal footing *or* on equal terms with s.o.; **à é. d'expérience,** when there is *or* in the case of equal experience; *Sp* **é. de points,** draw, tie; **à é.,** (*of teams*) level; (*of result*) drawn, tied; *Golf* all square; *Fig* **maintenant, nous sommes à é.,** now we're even; *Tennis* **é. (à 40),** deuce; *Sp* **course à é.,** dead heat, tie; *Courses de chevaux* **parier à é. sur un cheval,** to lay evens on a horse; **(b)** (*constance*) evenness, regularity (*of breathing, sound etc*); steadiness (*of pace, pulse*); evenness (*of ground*); equanimity (*of mind*).

égard [egar] *nm* **(a)** (*attention*) consideration; **avoir é. à qch,** to take sth into consideration *or* into account, to make allowance(s) *or* allow for sth; **eu é. aux circonstances,** in consideration of *or* due allowance being made for the circumstances; **sans é. à,** regardless of, irrespective of;
(b) à tous (les) égards, in all respects, in every respect; **à certains égards,** in some respects; **n'ayez aucune crainte à cet é.,** don't worry about that; **à l'é. de,** (*quant à*) with regard to, with respect to; (*en comparaison avec*) compared with; **être injuste à l'é. de qn,** to be unjust to(wards) s.o.;
(c) (*respect*) consideration, respect, regard; **faire qch par é. pour qn,** to do sth out of respect *or* consideration for s.o.; **être sans é. pour qn,** to have no consideration for s.o.; **avoir des égards pour qn,** to be considerate towards s.o., to show s.o. consideration.

égaré [egare] *adj* **(a)** lost (*traveller etc*); stray, lost (*sheep*); **balles égarées,** stray bullets; **village é.,** remote *or* out-of-the-way village; **(b)** (*fou*) distraught, distracted (*face, look*); wild (*eyes*).

égarement [egarmɑ̃] *nm* **(a) é. (d'esprit),** (mental) aberration; **(b)** deviation (*from virtue etc*); wildness (*of conduct*); **il est revenu de ses égarements,** he has seen the error of his ways.

égarer [egare] **1** *vt* **(a)** (*tromper*) to mislead, to misguide (*s.o.*); **les mauvais exemples l'ont égaré,** he has been led astray by bad examples; **(b)** (*perdre*) to mislay, to lose (*sth*); **(c)** *Fig* (*troubler*) **égaré par tant de malheurs,** distraught by so many misfortunes. **2 s'égarer** *vpr* **(a)** (*se perdre*) (*personne*) to lose one's way, to get lost; **colis qui s'est égaré,** parcel that has got lost *or* gone astray; **(b)** (*se dévier*) **s'é. loin du droit chemin,** to wander from the straight and narrow; **(c)** (*sortir hors du sujet*) to wander from the point; **son esprit s'égare,** his mind is wandering; **la discussion/le débat s'égare,** the discussion/debate is wandering *or* drifting from the point.

égayer [egeje] *v* (**j'égaie, j'égaye, n. égayons; j'égaierai, j'égayerai**) **1** *vt* to cheer up (*patient*); to amuse (*guests etc*); to enliven (*company, conversation*); to brighten (up) (*room, dress, s.o.'s life*). **2 s'égayer** *vpr* to have fun, to enjoy oneself; **s'é. aux dépens de qn,** to make fun of s.o.

Egée [eʒe] **1** *nm* Aegeus. **2** *adj* **la mer É.,** the Aegean (Sea).

égéen, -éenne [eʒeɛ̃, -eɛn] *adj* Aegean.

égide [eʒid] *nf* aegis, shield; *Fig* **sous l'é. de,** under the aegis *or* care of; **prendre qn sous son é.,** to take s.o. under one's wing.

églantier [eglɑ̃tje] *nm* wild rose *or* dog rose (bush).

églantine [eglɑ̃tin] *nf* (*fleur*) wild rose, dog rose.

églefin [egləfɛ̃] *nm* haddock.

église [egliz] *nf* **(a) l'É. (catholique romaine),** the (Roman) Catholic Church; **l'É. anglicane,** the Church of England, the Anglican Church; **l'É. et l'État,** Church and State; **gens d'É.,** churchmen; **entrer dans l'É.,** to go into the Church, to take holy orders; **(b)** (*bâtiment*) church; **l'é. Saint-Pierre,** St. Peter's (church); **aller à l'é.,** (*à l'office*) to go to church; **se marier à l'é.,** to get married in (a) church, to have a church wedding.

églogue [eglɔg] *nf Littér* eclogue.

ego [ego] *nm inv* ego.

égocentrique [egɔsɑ̃trik] **1** *adj* self-centred, egocentric. **2** *n* self-centred *or* egocentric person.

égocentrisme [egɔsɑ̃trism] *nm* egocentricity, self-centredness; *Psy* egocentrism.

égoïne [egɔin] *nf* **(scie) é.,** handsaw.

égoïsme [egɔism] *nm* egoism, selfishness; *Fig* **é. de classe,** clannishness.

égoïste [egɔist] **1** *n* egoist. **2** *adj* egoistic, selfish, self-centred.

égoïstement [egɔistəmɑ̃] *adv* egoistically, selfishly.

égorgement [egɔrʒəmɑ̃] *nm* cutting the throat (*of pig, hostage etc*).

égorger [egɔrʒe] *v* **(j'égorgeai(s); n. égorgeons) 1** *vt* **(a)** to cut the throat of (*animal, hostage*); **(b)** *Vieilli* (*ruiner*) to bleed (*s.o.*) white *or* dry. **2 s'égorger** *vpr F* to cut each other's throats.

égorgeur, -euse [egɔrʒœr, -øz] *n* (*assassin*) cut-throat.

égosiller (s') [segozije] *vpr* to bawl, to shout (oneself hoarse); (*chanter*) to sing away, *F* to sing one's head off; **mais je m'égosille à vous le dire!,** I've told you so till I'm blue in the face!

égotisme [egɔtism] *nm* egotism.

égotiste [egɔtist] **1** *n* egotist. **2** *adj* egotistic(al).

égout [egu] *nm* **(a)** (*gouttière*) gutter (*of roof*); **toit à deux égouts,** ridge roof; **(b)** (*canalisation souterraine*) sewer; **eaux d'é.,** sewage; **tuyau d'é.,** drainpipe; **é. collecteur,** main sewer; **jeter à l'é.,** to flush away; *Fig* to pour down the drain; **bouche d'é.,** manhole.

égoutier [egutje] *nm* sewerman.

égouttage [egutaʒ] *nm* drainage; draining (*of cheese, ground etc*).

égouttement [egutmɑ̃] *nm* **(a)** dripping (*of water etc*); **(b)** (*égouttage*) drainage, draining.

égoutter [egute] **1** *vt* to drain (*cheese, lettuce etc*). **2 s'égoutter** *vpr* (*of cheese, lettuce, washed dishes etc*) to drain. **3** *vi* to drain; **laisser é. la salade,** to drain the lettuce.

égouttoir [egutwar] *nm* **(a)** (*dans l'évier*) draining board; (*mobile*) drainer, draining rack; **(b)** (*passoire*) colander; **(panier) é.,** basket (*of deep fryer*).

égrappage [egrapaʒ] *nm* picking off (*of grapes etc from bunch*).

égrapper [egrape] *vt* to pick off (*grapes etc*) from the bunch.

égratigner [egratiɲe] *vt* **(a)** (*écorcher*) to scratch (*s.o., sth*); **(b)** *Fig* (*irriter*) to nettle, to have a dig at.

égratignure [egratiɲyr] *nf* **(a)** (*écorchure*) scratch; **je n'ai pas reçu une é.,** I escaped without a scratch; **(b)** *Fig* (*atteinte*) gibe, dig (*at s.o.*).

égrenage [egrənaʒ] *nm*, **égrènement** [egrɛnmɑ̃] *nm* shelling (*of peas etc*); picking off (*of* grapes); *Fig* **égrènement de lumières,** string of lights.

égrener [egrəne] *v* **(j'égrène, n. égrenons; j'égrènerai) 1** *vt* **(a)** to shell (*maize, peas etc*); to pick off (*grapes etc from the bunch*); to gin (*cotton*); **(b)** *Fig* **é. son chapelet,** to tell one's beads; **é. des sujets de conversation,** to try one subject of conversation after another. **2 s'égrener** *vpr* **(a)** (*of grapes, berries*) to fall *or* drop from the bunch; (*of wheat*) to seed; **(b)** *Fig* (*of procession etc*) to become strung out; **des lumières s'égrènent le long du quai,** a string of lights stretches along the quay.

égreneuse [egrənøz] *nf Agr* (*machine*) sheller; **é. de coton,** cotton gin.

égrillard [egrijar] *adj* ribald, bawdy (*person, manner etc*); risqué, spicy (*story etc*).

égrisage [egrizaʒ] *nm* grinding (*of glass, diamonds*).

égriser [egrize] *vt* to grind (*glass, diamonds etc*).

égrugeage [egryʒaʒ] *nm Tech* bruising (*of grain*); pounding (*of salt, sugar*).

égrugeoir [egryʒwar] *nm Tech* (*récipient*) mortar.

égruger [egryʒe] *vt* **(j'égrugeai(s); n. égrugeons)** *Tech* to bruise (*grain*); to pound (*salt, sugar*).

Égypte [eʒipt] *nf* Egypt.

égyptien, -ienne [eʒipsjɛ̃, -jɛn] **1** *adj* Egyptian. **2** *n* **É.,** Egyptian. **3** *nm Hist Ling* Egyptian. **4** *n Arch* (*bohémien*) gipsy. **5** *nf Typ* **égyptienne,** clarendon.

égyptologie [eʒiptɔlɔʒi] *nf* Egyptology.

égyptologue [eʒiptɔlɔg] *n* Egyptologist.

eh [e] *int* hey!; **eh bien!,** well!, now then!; **eh oui!,** that's right!; **eh! que voulez-vous que je fasse?,** why, what can I do?; **eh, là-bas!,** hello there!

éhonté [eɔ̃te] *adj* shameless, barefaced, brazen (*lie, liar etc*).

eider [ɛdɛr] *nm* (*oiseau*) eider (duck).

eidétique [ɛjdetik] *adj Psy* eidetic.

einsteinien, -ienne [ajnʃtɛnjɛ̃, -jɛn] *adj* of *or* typical of Einstein, Einsteinian.

einste(i)nium [ajnʃtɛnjɔm] *nm Ch* einsteinium.

éjaculation [eʒakylasjɔ̃] *nf Physiol* ejaculation; **é. précoce,** premature ejaculation.

éjaculer [eʒakyle] *vt Physiol* to ejaculate.

éjectable [eʒɛktabl] *adj Av* **siège é.,** ejector seat.

éjecter [eʒɛkte] *vt* **(a)** to eject (*fluid, cartridge, pilot etc*); **(b)** *F* (*expulser*) to throw (*s.o.*) out, to kick (*s.o.*) out; **elle risque de se faire é.,** she risks being thrown *or* kicked out.

éjecteur [eʒɛktœr] *nm* ejector (*of steam, water, cartridge etc*); outlet works (*of a reservoir*).

éjection [eʒɛksjɔ̃] *nf* **(a)** ejection (*of fluid, cartridge, pilot*); **éjections volcaniques,** ejecta; **(b)** *F* (*expulsion*) throwing out, kicking out (*of s.o.*).

élaboration [elabɔrasjɔ̃] *nf* working out, development (*of plan, idea*); drawing up (*of constitution etc*); *Biol* elaboration (*of bile, sap etc*).

élaborer [elabɔre] *vt* to work out, to develop (*plan, idea*); to draw up (*constitution etc*); *Biol* to elaborate (*bile, sap etc*).

élagage [elagaʒ] *nm* **(a)** pruning (*of tree*); **(b)** *Fig* pruning, cutting (down) (*of play etc*).

élaguer [elage] *vt* **(a)** to prune (*tree*); **(b)** *Fig* to prune, to cut (down) (*play etc*).

élagueur [elagœr] *nm* pruner.

élan¹ [elɑ̃] *nm* **(a)** *Sp etc* (*mouvement*) run-up; **d'un seul é.,** (*en sautant*) at one bound; (*en courant*) in one burst; *Sp* **prendre son é.,** to take a run(-up); **saut sans/avec é.,** standing/running jump; **(b)** (*vitesse*) momentum, impetus; **perdre son é.,** to lose momentum; **é. vital,** life force; **travailler avec é.,** to work enthusiastically *or* with a will; **impossible de les arrêter dans leur é.,** impossible to stop them once they've got going; **(c)** (*fougue*) fervour, *US* fervor; burst, outburst (*of feeling*); glow (*of enthusiasm*); **un é. créatif,** a creative outburst; **parler avec é.,** to speak with fervour; **avoir un é. (naturel) envers qn,** to feel (naturally) drawn to s.o.

élan² *nm* (Scandinavian) elk; **é. du Canada,** moose.

élancé [elɑ̃se] *adj* slim, slender (*figure, person, tree etc*); **aux formes élancées,** streamlined (*ship, car*).

élancement [elɑ̃smɑ̃] *nm* (*douleur*) shooting pain, twinge.

élancer [elɑ̃se] *v* **(j'élançai(s); n. élançons) 1** *vi* (*of finger etc*) to give (*s.o.*) shooting pains, to send shooting pains (*up the arm etc*), to give a twinge; **ma jambe m'élance,** I've got shooting pains *or* twinges in my leg. **2 s'élancer** *vpr* (*en courant*) to rush, to dash; *Sp* (*prendre son élan*) to take a run-up; **s'é. sur qn,** to rush *or* make a rush at s.o.; **le chat s'élança sur moi,** the cat flew at me; **s'é. à l'assaut,** to throw oneself into the fray; **s'é. vers le ciel,** to soar skywards. **3** *vt* **la cathédrale élance ses flèches vers le ciel,** the cathedral's spires soar skywards.

élargir [elarʒir] **1** *vt* **(a)** to widen, to broaden (*road etc*); to let out (*dress*); to stretch (*shoes*); to expand (*tube*); to enlarge (*hole*); **robe qui élargit les épaules,** dress which makes the shoulders look broader; **é. des règles,** to stretch rules; **(b)** *Fig* to enlarge, to extend, to add to (*estate, group, knowledge*); to broaden (*horizon, debate*); **(c)** *Jur* to release, to set (*prisoner*) free. **2** *vi F* **il a élargi,** he has broadened out. **3 s'élargir** *vpr* **(a)** (*of street etc*) to widen (out), to broaden (out); (*of shoes, dress etc*) to stretch; **(b)** *Fig* (*of ideas, group*) to grow, to extend; (*of horizon, debate*) to broaden.

élargissement [elarʒismɑ̃] *nm* **(a)** widening, broadening (*of road etc*); letting out (*of dress*); stretching (*of shoes*); **(b)** *Fig* expansion, extension (*of estate, group, knowledge*); **l'é. de la C.E.E.,** the enlargment *or* expansion of the EEC; **(c)** *Jur* release (*of prisoner*).

élasticité [elastisite] *nf* elasticity (*of body, etc*); springiness, spring (*of step*); *Fig* flexibility (*of person, principles etc*).

élastique [elastik] **1** *adj* **(a)** elastic (*body, material etc*); **gomme é.,** india rubber; **balle é.,** rubber ball; **la viande est é.,** the meat is rubbery; *Anat* **tissu é.,** elastic tissue;

d'un pas é., with a springy *or* buoyant step; **(b)** *Fig* flexible (*person, character, rule, principles etc*); *Péj* **conscience é.**, accommodating conscience. **2** *nm* **(a)** *Couture etc* elastic; **bretelles en é.**, elastic braces *or Am* suspenders; **(b)** (*de bureau*) elastic band, rubber band.

élastiqué [elastike] *adj* elasticated.

élastomère [elastɔmɛr] *nm Ch Ind* elastomer.

Elbe [ɛlb] **1** *nf* **(l'île d')E.**, (the island of) Elba. **2** *nm* (river) Elbe.

électeur, -trice [elɛktœr, -tris] *n* **(a)** *Pol* elector, voter; **mes électeurs,** my constituents; **avoir sa carte d'é.,** to have one's voting *or* polling card; **(b)** *Hist* **É.**, Elector; **Électrice,** Electress.

électif, -ive [elɛktif, -iv] *adj* elective.

élection [elɛksjɔ̃] *nf* **(a)** *Pol* election; **élections (législatives),** (parliamentary) election(s), general election; **élections municipales,** = local (council) elections; **é. partielle,** by-election; **jour des élections,** polling day; **annuler l'é. de qn,** to unseat s.o.; **se présenter aux élections,** to stand as a candidate (in the elections); **remporter les élections,** to win the election; **(b)** (*choix*) election, choice; **mon pays d'é.,** the country of my choice; *Jur* **faire é. de domicile,** to elect domicile; **(c)** *Rel* **peuple d'é.**, chosen people.

électoral, -aux [elɛktɔral, -o] *adj* electoral; **circonscription électorale,** constituency; **campagne électorale,** election *or* electoral campaign; **liste électorale,** electoral register *or* roll; **corps é.**, electorate; **comité é.**, election committee.

électorat [elɛktɔra] *nm* **(a)** *Pol* electorate; **consulter l'é.**, to go to the country; **l'é. communiste/féminin,** the communist/female vote; **(b)** (*droit de vote*) franchise; **(c)** *Hist* **É.**, electorate.

Électre [elɛktr] *nf* Electra.

électricien, -ienne [elɛktrisjɛ̃, -jɛn] *n* electrician; **ingénieur é.**, electrical engineer.

électricité [elɛktrisite] *nf* electricity; **allumer** *ou* **mettre l'é.**, to switch on the light; **éteindre** *ou* **couper l'é.**, to switch off the light; **panne d'é.**, power cut *or* failure; **faire poser** *ou* **installer l'é.**, to have electricity put in *or* installed; **é. statique/atmosphérique,** static (electricity)/atmospherics; *F* **il y a de l'é. dans l'air,** the atmosphere is electric.

électrification [elɛktrifikasjɔ̃] *nf* electrification.

électrifier [elɛktrifje] *vt* to electrify (*railway etc*); to bring electricity to, to electrify (*village etc*).

électrique [elɛktrik] *adj* **(a)** electric (*current, train etc*); **pile é.**, electric battery; **appareils électriques,** electric appliances; **(b)** electrical (*engineering etc*); **(c)** *Fig* (*tendu*) electric; **l'atmosphère est é.**, the atmosphere is electric; **ne lui en parle pas, ça la rend é.**, don't talk to her about it, it makes her bristle.

électriquement [eletrikmɑ̃] *adv* electrically.

électrisant [elɛktrizɑ̃] *adj Fig* electrifying.

électrisation [elɛktrizasjɔ̃] *nf* electrification (*of substance etc, Fig of audience etc*); **à é. positive,** positively charged, charged with positive electricity.

électriser [elɛktrize] *vt* to electrify (*substance etc*); *Fig* to elecrify, to thrill (*audience*); **fil électrisé,** live wire.

électro- [elɛktrɔ] *préf* electro-.

électro-acousticien, -ienne [elɛtrɔakustisjɛ̃, -jɛn] (*pl électro-acousticiens*) **1** *n* electroacoustics expert. **2** *adj* electroacoustic.

électro-aimant [elɛktrɔɛmɑ̃] *nm* electromagnet; (*pl électro-aimants*).

électrocardiogramme [elɛktrɔkardjɔgram] *nm Méd* electrocardiogram.

électrocardiographie [elɛktrɔkardjɔgrafi] *nf Méd* electrocardiography.

électrochimie [elɛktrɔʃimi] *nf* electrochemistry.

électrochimique [elɛktrɔʃimik] *adj* electrochemical.

électrochoc [elɛktrɔʃɔk] *nm Méd* electric shock treatment; **traitement par électrochocs,** electric shock treatment; **on lui a fait des électrochocs,** he was given electric shock treatment.

électrocoagulation [elɛktrɔkɔagylasjɔ̃] *nf Méd* electrocoagulation.

électrocuter [elɛktrɔkyte] *vt* to electrocute; **se faire é.**, to be electrocuted.

électrocution [elɛktrɔkysjɔ̃] *nf* electrocution.

électrode [elɛktrɔd] *nf* electrode.

électrodiagnostic [elɛktrɔdjagnɔstik] *nm* electrodiagnosis.

électrodynamique [elɛktrɔdinamik] **1** *adj* electrodynamic. **2** *nf* electrodynamics.

électro-encéphalogramme [elɛktrɔɑ̃sefalɔgram] *nm Méd* electroencephalogram; (*pl électro-encéphalogrammes*).

électro-encéphalographie [elɛktrɔɑ̃sefalɔgrafi] *nf Méd* electroencephalography.

électrogène [elɛktrɔʒɛn] *adj Él* **groupe é.**, generating unit.

électroluminescent [elɛktrɔlyminesɑ̃] *adj* light-emitting; **diode électroluminescente,** light-emitting diode.

électrolyse [elɛktrɔliz] *nf* electrolysis.

électrolyser [elɛktrɔlize] *vt* to electrolyse.

électrolyte [elɛktrɔlit] *nm Él* electrolyte.

électrolytique [elɛktrɔlitik] *adj* electrolytic.

électromagnétique [elɛktrɔmaɲetik] *adj* electromagnetic.

électromagnétisme [elɛktrɔmaɲetism] *nm* electromagnetism.

électromécanicien, -ienne [elɛktrɔmekanisjɛ̃, -jɛn] *n* electrical engineer.

électromécanique [elɛktrɔmekanik] **1** *adj* electromechanical. **2** *nf* electromechanics.

électroménager [elɛktrɔmenaʒe] **1** *adj* **appareils électroménagers,** (household) electric(al) appliances, *US* household electricals. **2** *nm* (household) electric(al) appliances, *US* household electricals.

électrométallurgie [elɛktrɔmetalyrʒi] *nf* electrometallurgy.

électromètre [elɛktrɔmɛtr] *nm* electrometer.

électromobile [elɛktrɔmɔbil] *adj* electrically driven *or* operated (*vehicle*).

électromoteur, -trice [elɛktrɔmɔtœr, -tris] **1** *adj* electromotive. **2** *nm* electromotor.

électron [elɛktrɔ̃] *nm Phys* electron.

électronicien, -ienne [elɛktrɔnisjɛ̃, -jɛn] *n* electronics specialist; **ingénieur é.**, electronics engineer.

électronique [elɛktrɔnik] **1** *adj* electronic; **faisceau/flux é.**, electron beam/flow; **microscope/télescope é.**, electron microscope/telescope. **2** *nf* electronics; **é. aérospatiale,** avionics.

électroniquement [elɛktrɔnikmɑ̃] *adv* electronically.

électronucléaire [elɛktrɔnykleɛr] **1** *adj* nuclear power (*industry etc*); **centrale é.**, nuclear power station. **2** *nm* nuclear power.

électronvolt [elɛktrɔ̃vɔlt] *nm* electronvolt.

électrophone [elɛktrɔfɔn] *nm* record player.

électroponcture [elɛktrɔpɔ̃ktyr] *nf Méd* electropuncture.

électropositif, -ive [elɛktrɔpɔzitif, -iv] *adj* electropositive.

électropuncture [elɛktrɔpɔ̃ktyr] *nf Méd* electropuncture.

électroscope [elɛktrɔskɔp] *nm* electroscope.

électrostatique [elɛktrɔstatik] **1** *adj* electrostatic. **2** *nf* electrostatics.

électrotechnique [elɛktrɔtɛknik] **1** *adj* electrotechnical. **2** *nf* electrotechnology, electrical engineering.

électrothérapie [elɛktrɔterapi] *nf Méd* (*pratique*) electrotherapy; (*étude*) electrotherapeutics.

électrum [elɛktrɔm] *nm Minér* electrum.

élégamment [elegamɑ̃] *adv* elegantly; (*agir*) courteously.

élégance [elegɑ̃s] *nf* elegance; courtesy (*of gesture, behaviour*); neatness (*of method etc*); **l'é. du chat siamois,** the elegance *or* grace of a Siamese cat; **femme qui a de l'é.**, (*naturelle*) elegant *or* graceful woman; (*vestimentaire*) well-dressed *or* smart woman; **savoir perdre avec é.**, to know how to lose gracefully; **elle a eu l'é. de ne pas protester,** she had the courtesy not to protest; **les élégances de la vie,** the refinements of life.

élégant, -ante [elegɑ̃] **1** *adj* elegant (*clothes, restaurant, style etc*); neat (*method, solution*); courteous (*gesture, behaviour*); **femme élégante,** (*naturellement*) elegant *or* graceful woman; (*par ses vêtements*) well-dressed *or* smart woman; **mensonge é.**, diplomatic lie. **2** *nm Arch* **un é.**, a man of fashion, a dandy. **3** *nf* **une élégante,** a well-dressed *or* fashionably dressed woman.

élégiaque [eleʒjak] *adj* elegiac.

élégie [eleʒi] *nf* elegy.

élément [elemɑ̃] *nm* **(a)** (*naturel*) element; **les quatre éléments,** the four elements; *Fig* **être dans son é.**, to be in one's element;

(b) *Ch* **les éléments qui forment un composé,** the elements of *or.* which make up a compound; *Phys* **é. radioactif,** radioactive element;

(c) (*constituent*) element, component, constituent (*of construction, problem etc*); ingredient (*of medicine*); **les élé-**

ments d'un ensemble, the elements *or* parts of a whole; **l'é. décisif,** the deciding factor; **les éléments indésirables de la population,** the undesirable elements of the population; **l'é. féminin,** the female element *or* contingent;

(d) *Tech* **é. chauffant,** heating unit *or* element; *Electron* **é. de calculateur** *ou* **de calculatrice** *ou* **électronique,** computer unit; **éléments préfabriqués,** prefabricated *or* ready-made units; **mobilier formé d'éléments,** unit furniture;

(e) *Él* cell (*of battery, accumulator*); **batterie de cinq éléments,** five-cell battery;

(f) éléments, (*rudiments*) elements, rudiments, first principles (*of science etc*); **bien connaître ses éléments,** to have a good grounding;

(g) éléments, (*données*) data;

(h) *Mil* **éléments,** units; **éléments blindés/motorisés,** armoured/motorized units.

élémentaire [elemɑ̃tɛr] *adj* **(a)** *Ch Phys* elementary (*chemical analysis, atomic particle etc*); **(b)** (*de base*) elementary (*knowledge, course, problem etc*); *Scol* **classes élémentaires,** junior school *or* classes; **(c)** (*minimal*) basic, rudimentary (*dwelling etc*); **c'est é.!,** (*évident*) it's elementary!, it's simple!; (*le minimum*) it's the least you could do!

éléphant [elefɑ̃] *nm* elephant; **é. mâle/femelle,** bull/cow elephant; **é. marin** *ou* **de mer,** elephant seal, sea elephant; **é d'Afrique/d'Asie,** African/Indian elephant.

éléphanteau, -eaux [elefɑ̃to] *nm* baby elephant, elephant calf.

éléphantesque [elefɑ̃tɛsk] *adj F* elephantine, gigantic, enormous.

éléphantiasis [elefɑ̃tjazis] *nf Méd* elephantiasis.

élevage [ɛlvaʒ] *nm* **(a)** breeding, rearing (*of cattle, horses, sheep etc*); **l'é.,** stock breeding; **é. intensif/en batterie,** intensive/battery farming; **é. des animaux à fourrure,** fur farming; **faire de l'é.,** to breed *or* rear (animals); **poulet d'é.,** battery-reared chicken; **(b)** (*ferme*) *Br* (stock) farm, *Am* ranch, *Austr* station.

élévateur, -trice [elevatœr, -tris] **1** *adj* **(a)** elevator (*muscle*); **(b) chariot é. à fourche,** fork-lift truck. **2** *nm* **(a)** (*appareil*) elevator, lift, hoist; **é. à bascule,** tip; **é. à augets** *ou* **à godets,** bucket elevator; **(b)** *Él* **é. de tension,** step-up transformer; **(c) é. (à fourche**), fork-lift truck.

élévation [elevasjɔ̃] *nf* **(a)** (*action d'élever*) raising (*of wall, load, temperature, water, voice, prices etc*); increasing (*of load, temperature, prices etc*); *Rel* elevation (*of the Host*); **(b)** (*action de dresser*) erection, setting up (*of statue etc*); **(c)** (*action de s'élever*) rise (*in temperature, price etc*); **é. du niveau des eaux,** rise in water level; **(d) é. du pouls,** quickening of the pulse; **(e) é. de style,** grandeur *or* loftiness of style; **é. des sentiments/du caractère,** nobility of sentiments/character; **(f)** *Archit* (*projection*) elevation; **(g)** (*tertre*) rise (in the ground), mound.

élévatoire [elevatwar] *adj* lifting, hoisting (*apparatus*).

élève [elɛv] **1** *n Scol* pupil, student; **l'é. d'un peintre,** the pupil of a painter; *Mil* **é. officier,** cadet; **é. pilote/***etc*, trainee *or* student pilot/*etc*. **2** *nf* **(a)** (*animal*) young stock animal; **(b)** (*plante*) seedling.

élevé [elve] *adj* **(a)** high (*mountain, price*); noble, elevated (*style, mind*); exalted, elevated (*position, rank*); **l'officier le plus é. en grade,** the senior *or* highest-ranking officer; **occuper un rang é.,** to rank high; **(b) pouls é.,** rapid pulse; **(c) bien é.,** well brought up, well-bred, well-mannered; **mal é.,** badly brought up, ill-bred, ill-mannered; *F* **c'est très mal é. de parler la bouche pleine,** it's very rude *or* very bad manners to speak with your mouth full; **c'est un mal é.,** what bad manners he has.

élever [elve] *v* **(j'élève, n. élevons; j'élèverai) 1** *vt* **(a)** (*faire monter*) to raise (*a wall, the temperature, water, one's voice, prices etc*); to increase (*a load, prices, the temperature etc*); to lift up, to raise (*load, person etc*); **é. un nombre au carré/au cube,** to square/cube a number; **é. un nombre à la puissance 4,** to raise a number to the power 4;

(b) (*porter à un rang supérieur*) to elevate (*s.o.*); **é. qn au rang de génie,** to elevate s.o. to the rank of genius;

(c) (*édifier*) to improve, to elevate (*the mind*);

(d) (*dresser*) to erect, to set up (*machine, statue etc*);

(e) (*lancer*) to raise (*objection, difficulties*);

(f) é. sur qch, to found (*a fortune*) on sth; to establish (*a doctrine*) on sth;

(g) (*éduquer*) to bring up, to raise (*child*); to rear, to breed (*cattle, horses etc*); to breed (*rabbits*); to keep (*bees, poultry*); to grow (*plants*); **bébé élevé au sein/au biberon,** breast-/bottle-fed baby.

2 s'élever *vpr* **(a)** (*avec mouvement*) to rise (up), to go up;

(b) (*sans mouvement*) to stand; **le château s'élève sur la colline,** the castle stands on the hill;

(c) (*of doubts, difficulties, objection*) to arise; **un cri s'éleva,** a shout went up; **le vent s'élève,** the wind is rising *or* getting up;

(d) *Fig* **s'é. contre qch/qn,** to protest *or* make a stand against sth/s.o.;

(e) (*se lever*) to raise oneself; **s'é. sur les pointes des pieds,** to stand on tiptoe; *Fig* **s'é. à force de travail,** to work one's way up; **s'é. socialement,** to climb up the social ladder; **s'é. au-dessus de ses préjugés,** to rise above one's prejudices;

(f) (*of temperature, prices etc*) to rise, to increase, to go up;

(g) s'é. à, (*atteindre*) to come to, to amount to; **le compte s'élève à mille francs,** the bill comes *or* amounts to a thousand francs.

éleveur, -euse [elvœr, -øz] **1** *n* (*de bétail*) stock breeder, cattle farmer; **é. de chevaux/chiens,** horse/dog breeder; **é. de moutons/poulets,** sheep/poultry farmer. **2** *nf* **éleveuse,** brooder (*for chicks*).

elfe [ɛlf] *nm* elf.

élider [elide] **1** *vt Ling* to elide (*vowel*). **2 s'élider** *vpr* to be elided, to elide.

Élie [eli] *nm* Elijah, Elias.

éligibilité [eliʒibilite] *nf Pol* eligibility.

éligible [eliʒibl] *adj Pol* eligible.

élimé [elime] *adj* worn, threadbare (*material, garment*).

élimer [elime] **1** *vt* (*of material, garment*) to wear thin. **2 s'élimer** *vpr* to wear thin.

élimination [eliminɑsjɔ̃] *nf* elimination; **en procédant par é.,** by a process of elimination; *Sp etc* **concours sur le principe d'é.,** knock-out competition; *Ind etc* **é. des déchets,** waste disposal; *Rad* **é. des parasites,** suppression of noise *or* interference.

éliminatoire [eliminatwar] **1** *adj* eliminatory (*examination etc*); disqualifying (*result*); *Sp* **épreuve é.,** qualifying *or* eliminating heat *or* round, qualifier. **2** *nf Sp* qualifying *or* eliminating heat *or* round, qualifier.

éliminer [elimine] **1** *vt* to eliminate (*candidate, suspect, problem etc*); to rule out, to exclude (*possibility, theory*); *Physiol* to get rid of, to eliminate (*body wastes*); *Sp* **être éliminé,** to be knocked out or eliminated (*in a tournament*); *Math* **é. une inconnue,** to eliminate an unknown quantity. **2** *vi Physiol* to get rid of *or* eliminate body wastes. **3 s'éliminer** *vpr* to cancel (each other) out.

élingue [elɛ̃g] *nf Nau* sling.

élinguer [elɛ̃ge] *vt Nau* to sling.

élire [elir] *vt* (*conj like* **lire**) **(a)** to elect, to choose (*candidate, representative etc*); **é. un député,** ≈ to elect *or* return *Br* a Member of Parliament *or US* a Representative; **é. qn président,** to elect s.o. president; (*en votant*) to vote s.o. in as president; **(b) é. domicile,** to take up residence (**à** in); *Jur* to elect domicile (**à**, in).

Élisabeth [elizabɛt] *nf* Elizabeth.

élisabéthain, -aine [elizabetɛ̃, -ɛn] **1** *adj* Elizabethan. **2** *n* **É.**, Elizabethan.

élision [elizjɔ̃] *nf Ling* elision.

élite [elit] *nf* élite, elite; **les élites,** the élite; **l'é. de ...,** the cream *or* élite of ...; **personnel d'é.,** select *or* hand-picked personnel; **régiment/tireur d'é.,** crack regiment/shot.

élitisme [elitism] *nm* elitism.

élitiste [elitist] *adj & n* elitist.

élixir [eliksir] *nm* elixir; **é. parégorique,** paregoric (elixir).

elle, *pl* **elles** [ɛl] *pron pers f* **(a)** (*subject*) (*of person*) she; (*of thing*) it; (*of baby, animal, nation, car*) it, she; **elles,** they; **e. chante,** she sings; **elles dansent,** they dance; **qu'e. est jolie, cette broche!,** how pretty that brooch is!; **(b) c'est e.,** it is her; **ce sont elles,** it is them; **je fais comme e.,** I do what SHE does; **ah!, e. est bien bonne, celle-là!,** that's a good one!; **(c)** (*object*) (*person*) her; (*thing*) it; (*baby, animal etc*) it, her; **elles,** them; **je suis content d'e./d'elles,** I am pleased with her/them; **e. ne pense qu'à e.,** she thinks only of herself; **dis-le-lui, à e.,** tell HER; **et e., tu l'oublies?,** and are you forgetting HER?; **ce n'est pas à moi, c'est à e.,** it's not mine, it's hers; **il aimait sa patrie et mourut pour e.,** he loved his country and died for it.

ellébore [ɛlebɔr] *nm* (*plante*) hellebore.

elle-même [ɛlmɛm] *pron pers* (*of person*) herself; (*of thing*) itself; (*of baby, animal, nation*) itself, herself; **elles-**

mêmes, themselves.
ellipse [elips] *nf* **(a)** *Gram* ellipsis; **(b)** *Géom* ellipse.
ellipsoïdal, -aux [elipsɔidal, -o] *adj Géom* ellipsoidal.
ellipsoïde [elipsɔid] *Géom* **1** *adj* ellipsoidal. **2** *nm* ellipsoid.
elliptique [eliptik] *adj Gram Géom* elliptic(al); **style e.,** elliptical style.
elliptiquement [eliptikmɑ̃] *adv Gram* elliptically.
élocution [elɔkysjɔ̃] *nf* (*diction*) elocution; (*débit*) delivery; **défaut d'é.,** speech impediment *or* defect.
éloge [elɔʒ] *nm* **(a)** (*discours*) eulogy; **é. funèbre,** eulogy, funeral oration; **(b)** (*louange*) praise; **faire l'é. de qn/qch,** to speak very highly of *or* in praise of s.o./sth; **faire son propre é.,** to sing one's own praises, *Br* to blow one's own trumpet; **digne d'éloges,** praiseworthy; **c'est tout à votre é.,** it's all to your credit.
élogieusement [elɔʒjøzmɑ̃] *adv* **parler é. de,** to speak very highly of.
élogieux, -ieuse [elɔʒjø, -jøz] *adj* eulogistic, laudatory (*speech etc*); **parler de qn/qch en termes é.,** to speak very highly of s.o./sth.
éloigné [elwaɲe] *adj* distant, remote (*place, past, future etc*); **la ville est très éloignée,** the town is a long way away *or* off; **la ville est éloignée de cinq kilomètres,** the town is five kilometres away; **ils sont éloignés d'un kilomètre,** they are one kilometre apart, there is a kilometre between them; **maison éloignée de la gare,** house a long way from the station; **une date plus éloignée,** a later date; **dans un avenir peu é.,** in the near *or* not-too-distant future; **parent é.,** distant relation; **un cousin é.,** a distant cousin; **rien n'est plus é. de ma pensée,** nothing is further from my thoughts; **se tenir é. de qch,** to hold (oneself) aloof from sth; *Fig* **je ne suis plus é. de croire que ...,** I'm coming round to believe that *or* to the belief that ... .
éloignement [elwaɲmɑ̃] *nm* **(a)** (*action*) removal, moving away (*of object, undesirable person etc*); postponement (*of departure etc*); deferment (*of payment etc*); **(b)** (*absence*) absence; **(c)** (*distance*) distance, remoteness (*in place, time*); **é. de sa femme,** alienation *or* estrangement from one's wife *Fig*; **voir qch avec é.,** to look at sth objectively; **vivre dans l'é. du monde,** to live apart *or* withdrawn from the world.
éloigner [elwaɲe] **1** *vt* **(a)** (*écarter dans l'espace*) to move away, to take away, to remove (*person, object*); **é. qch de qch,** to move sth away from sth; **é. qn du feu/de la voiture/***etc*, to move s.o. away from the fire/car/*etc*; **é. une crainte/une pensée/des soupçons,** to banish a fear/ dismiss a thought/avert suspicion; **é. qn de son travail,** to keep s.o. away from his work;
(b) (*dans le temps*) to postpone, to put off (*departure, date etc*); to defer (*payment*).
2 s'éloigner *vpr* **(a)** (*s'écarter dans l'espace*) (*personne*) to move *or* go away (**de**, from); (*objet*) to move away *or* off; **voudriez-vous vous é. un peu?,** would you please stand further away *or* back, would you please move back *or* away a little; **ne vous éloignez pas!,** don't go away!; **s'é. de la vérité,** to stray *or* wander from the truth; **l'orage s'éloigne,** the storm is passing; **s'é. de son devoir,** to neglect one's duty; **s'é. du sujet,** to wander from *or* off the subject;
(b) *Fig* **s'é. de tout le monde,** to distance oneself from everybody; **je sens bien que tu t'éloignes (de moi),** I feel you're growing away from me.
élongation [elɔ̃gasjɔ̃] *nf* **(a)** *Méd* pulled muscle; **se faire une é.,** to pull a muscle; **(b)** *Astron* elongation.
élonger [elɔ̃ʒe] *vt* **(j'élongeai(s); n. élongeons)** *Nau* to lay out, to run out (*cable*).
éloquemment [elɔkamɑ̃] *adv* eloquently.
éloquence [elɔkɑ̃s] *nf* **(a)** (*loquacité*) eloquence; *Fig* **l'é. d'un tableau/d'une expression du visage,** the eloquence of a painting/of a facial expression; **(b)** (*rhétorique*) oratory.
éloquent [elɔkɑ̃] *adj* eloquent (*person, speech, silence, gesture*); **ces chiffres sont éloquents,** these figures speak volumes *or* speak for themselves.
élu, -ue [ely] **1** *adj Pol* elected; **président é.,** president elect; *Bible* **le peuple é.,** the chosen people. **2** *n* **(a)** *Rel* **les élus,** the elect; **(b)** *Pol* (*député, conseiller*) elected representative; **les élus du peuple,** the people's representatives; **nouvel é.,** newly elected representative; **(c)** *Hum* **qui est l'heureuse élue?,** who's the lucky girl *or* lady?; **l'é. de son cœur,** her heart's desire.
élucidation [elysidɑsjɔ̃] *nf* elucidation.
élucider [elyside] *vt* to elucidate, to clear up, to clarify (*mystery etc*).
élucubrations [elykybrɑsjɔ̃] *nfpl* flights of fancy, wild imaginings.
éluder [elyde] *vt* to elude, to evade (*law, difficulty etc*); to evade, to dodge (*question, responsibility*).
élusif, -ive [elyzif, -iv] *adj* evasive (*answer, attitude*).
Élysée [elize] **1** *nm* **(a)** *Myth* **L'É.,** Elysium; **(b)** *Pol* **(le palais de) l'É.,** the Elysée palace (*the residence of the President of the French Republic*). **2** *adj* **les Champs Élysées,** *Myth* the Elysian Fields; (*à Paris*) the Champs Elysées.
élyséen, -enne [elizeɛ̃, -ɛn] *adj* **(a)** *Myth* Elysian; **(b)** *Pol* of the Élysée palace.
émaciation [emasjɑsjɔ̃] *nf* emaciation.
émacié [emasje] *adj* emaciated, wasted (*figure, face etc*).
émacier (s') [semasje] *vpr* to become emaciated, to waste away.
émail, -aux [emaj, -o] *nm* **(a)** (*substance*) enamel; *Cér* glaze; **en é.,** enamel(led) (*saucepan etc*); **(b)** *Hér* (*couleur*) tincture; **(c)** *Anat* enamel (*of the teeth*); **(d)** *Beaux-Arts etc* (*objet*) enamel; **émaux de niellure** *ou* **niellés,** niello enamels.
émaillage [emajaʒ] *nm* **(a)** enamelling (*of precious metals etc*); **(b)** *Cér* glazing.
émailler [emaje] *vt* **(a)** to enamel (*metal etc*); **émaillé au four,** stove-enamelled; **(b)** *Cér* to glaze (*porcelain*); **(c)** *Fig* (*of flowers, stars etc*) to fleck, to spangle (*fields, the sky etc*); **style émaillé de métaphores,** style studded with metaphors.
émailleur, -euse [emajœr, -øz] *n* enameller.
émaillure [emajyr] *nf* enamelling, enamel work.
émanation [emanɑsjɔ̃] *nf* emanation; **é. fétide,** foul smell; **é. du radium,** radium emanation, radon; *Fig* **cet ordre, é. de sa volonté ...,** this order, an expression *or* a product of his will ... .
émancipateur, -trice [emɑ̃sipatœr, -tris] **1** *adj* emancipatory. **2** *n* emancipator.
émancipation [emɑ̃sipɑsjɔ̃] *nf* emancipation; *Fig* liberation, freeing (*of spirit, thought etc*).
émancipé [emɑ̃sipe] *adj F* emancipated (*woman etc*).
émanciper [emɑ̃sipe] **1** *vt* to emancipate (*people, slave*); to emancipate, to liberate (*woman*); *Fig* to liberate, to free (*spirit, thought etc*). **2 s'émanciper** *vpr* to become emancipated; *Fig* to become liberated; *Hum* **elle s'est drôlement émancipée,** she's too emancipated by half.
émaner [emane] *vi* **é. de,** (*of fumes etc*) to emanate from; *Fig* (*of order, power*) to come from; (*of charm*) to emanate from.
émargement [emarʒəmɑ̃] *nm* **(a)** *Typ* trimming (*of pages*); **(b)** (*annotation*) marginal note; **(c)** (*initiales*) initialling (in the margin); **feuille d'é.,** pay sheet.
émarger [emarʒe] *v* **(j'émargeai(s); n. émargeons) 1** *vt* **(a)** *Typ* to cut down *or* trim the margins of (*sheets etc*); **(b)** (*annoter*) to make marginal notes in (*book etc*); **(c)** *Admin* to initial (*document, account etc*) (in the margin). **2** *vi* to draw one's salary; **il émarge aux fonds secrets,** he's paid out of the secret funds.
émasculation [emaskylɑsjɔ̃] *nf* **(a)** (*d'un individu mâle*) emasculation; **(b)** *Fig* (*affaiblissement*) emasculation, weakening.
émasculer [emaskyle] *vt* **(a)** (*castrer*) to emasculate; **(b)** (*affaiblir*) to emasculate, to weaken (*phrase, idea etc*).
embâcle [ɑ̃bakl] *nm* (*obstruction dans un cours d'eau*) blockage; (*par un bloc de glace*) ice block *or* jam.
emballage [ɑ̃balaʒ] *nm* **(a)** (*action*) packing; (*dans du papier*) wrapping (*of parcels, goods*); **papier d'e.,** packing *or* wrapping paper; **(b)** (*boîte etc*) packaging, packing (material); (*papier*) wrapping; **emballages vides,** (returned) empties; **e. perdu/consigné,** non-returnable/ returnable packaging; **(c)** *Cyclisme* (final) spurt.
emballé [ɑ̃bale] *adj F* (mad) keen, enthusiastic; **e. pour qch,** (mad) keen on sth.
emballement [ɑ̃balmɑ̃] *nm* **(a)** (*de moteur*) racing; **(b)** (*enthousiasme soudain*) burst of enthusiasm; (*colère*) surge of anger; **prompt aux emballements,** easily carried away; **(c)** *Bourse* boom.
emballer [ɑ̃bale] **1** *vt* **(a)** to pack; (*dans du papier*) to wrap (*parcel, goods*); *F* **e. qn dans un train,** to bundle s.o. into a train; *Arg* **e. qn,** (*arrêter*) to run s.o. in, to nick s.o.; **(b) e. le moteur,** to race the engine; **(c)** *F* (*enthousiasmer*) to excite, to thrill; **être emballé par qn/qch,** to be (mad) keen on s.o./sth. **2 s'emballer** *vpr* **(a)** (*of horse*) to bolt, to run away; **(b)** (*of engine*) to race; **(c)** *F* (*se laisser emporter*) (*par enthousiasme*) to get carried away, to get excited; (*par colère*) to get worked up (into a state); **ne vous emballez pas!,** keep your head!, keep cool!, don't get worked up!

emballeur, -euse [ɑ̃balœr, -øz] *n* packer.
embarbouiller [ɑ̃barbuje] **1** *vt* to muddle, to confuse (*s.o.*). **2 s'embarbouiller** *vpr* to get muddled up.
embarcadère [ɑ̃barkadɛr] *nm* landing stage, jetty.
embarcation [ɑ̃barkasjɔ̃] *nf* (small) boat, small craft; **e. à moteur,** motor boat, motor launch.
embardée [ɑ̃barde] *nf Nau* yaw; *Aut* swerve; **faire une e.,** (*of boat*) to yaw; (*of car*) to swerve.
embargo [ɑ̃bargo] *nm* embargo; **mettre/lever l'e. sur,** to put an embargo/raise *or* lift the embargo on.
embarquement [ɑ̃barkəmɑ̃] *nm* **(a)** (*action d'embarquer*) *Nau* embarkation (*of passengers*); shipping (*of goods*); *Rail Av Aut* boarding (*of passengers*); loading (*of goods*); *Rail Mil* entrainment (*of troops*); *Rail* **quai d'e.,** departure platform; (*de chargement*) loading platform; **(b)** (*action de s'embarquer*) *Nau* embarkation, boarding; *Rail Av Aut* boarding; **carte d'e.,** boarding card.
embarquer [ɑ̃barke] **1** *vt* **(a)** *Nau* to embark (*passengers*); to ship (*goods*); *Rail Av Aut* to take (*passengers*) on board; to load (*goods*); *Rail Mil* to entrain (*troops*); **e. qn dans un train,** to put s.o. on a train, to see s.o. onto a train; *Fig* **e. qn dans un procès,** to involve s.o. in a lawsuit; *Arg* **e. un voleur,** (*arrêter*) to run in a thief; *F* **ils ont embarqué l'argenterie,** they pinched the silver;
(b) *Nau* **e. de l'eau,** to take in *or* ship water;
(c) (*commencer*) to start on; **e. très mal un projet,** to make a bad start on a scheme; **une entreprise mal embarquée,** an undertaking that has got off to a bad start.
2 *vi* **(a)** *Nau* (*partir*) to embark (**pour,** for); **e. (sur un navire),** to go on board, to board (a ship); **e. (dans un train/un autobus),** to board *or* get on (a train/bus);
(b) *Nau* **le bateau embarque,** the boat is taking in water.
3 s'embarquer *vpr* **(a)** (*partir*) to embark (**pour,** for); **s'e. sur un navire,** to go on board *or* to board a ship; **s'e. en avion,** to board an aircraft;
(b) *Fig* **s'e. dans une entreprise/une discussion,** to embark on an undertaking/a discussion.
embarras [ɑ̃bara] *nm* **(a)** *Aut* **e. de voitures, e. de la circulation,** traffic hold-up; **(b)** *Méd* **e. gastrique,** upset stomach; **(c)** (*difficulté*) difficulty, trouble; **se trouver dans l'e.,** to be in (financial) difficulties; **tirer qn d'e.,** to help s.o. out of trouble *or* a difficulty; **je vous donne beaucoup d'e.,** I'm giving you a lot of trouble; **plonger qn dans l'e.,** put s.o. in an awkward position; **(d)** *F* (*complication*) **faire des** *ou* **de l'e.,** to make a fuss *or* a song and dance; **sans plus d'e.,** without more ado; **(e)** (*perplexité*) perplexity; **n'avoir que l'e. du choix,** to have far too much to choose from; **je suis dans l'e.,** I'm in a fix *or* quandary; **(f)** (*gêne*) confusion, embarrassment; **répondre avec e.,** to reply in confusion *or* with embarrassment.
embarrassant [ɑ̃barasɑ̃] *adj* **(a)** cumbersome (*parcel etc*); **(b)** perplexing, puzzling (*question*); **(c)** embarrassing, awkward (*situation*).
embarrassé [ɑ̃barase] *adj* **(a)** (*encombré*) hampered (*movements*); cluttered (*table etc*); involved (*style*); **avoir les mains embarrassées,** to have one's hands full; **être dans une situation (financière) embarrassée,** to be in (financial) difficulties; **prononciation embarrassée,** unclear *or* garbled pronunciation; **explications embarrassées,** involved *or* confused explanations; **(b)** *Méd* **avoir l'estomac e.,** to have an upset stomach; **(c)** (*gêné*) embarrassed (*person, smile, manner etc*); **(d)** (*perplexé*) perplexed, puzzled; **il n'est jamais e.,** he's never at a loss.
embarrasser [ɑ̃barase] **1** *vt* **(a)** (*encombrer*) to hamper (*s.o.*); to clutter up (*room etc*); **est-ce que ma valise vous embarrasse?,** is my case in your way?; **(b)** (*gêner*) to embarrass, to put in an awkward position; **(c)** (*rendre perplexe*) to perplex, to puzzle (*s.o.*). **2 s'embarrasser** *vpr* **(a)** (*s'encombrer*) to burden *or* hamper oneself (**de,** with); **(b)** (*s'inquiéter*) to trouble oneself, to be concerned (**de,** about); **(c)** (*s'embrouiller*) **s'e. dans,** to get tangled up in (*clothes, Fig lies etc*).
embauchage [ɑ̃boʃaʒ] *nm* taking on, hiring, engaging (*of workers etc*).
embauche [ɑ̃boʃ] *nf* **(a)** (*action*) = **EMBAUCHAGE**; **(b) chercher de l'e.,** to look for a job; **il n'y a pas d'e.,** there are no jobs *or* vacancies.
embaucher [ɑ̃boʃe] **1** *vt* to take on, to hire, to engage (*worker etc*). **2** *vi* to take on *or* hire *or* engage people. **3 s'embaucher** *vpr* to get taken on *or* hired (**comme,** as).
embaucheur, -euse [ɑ̃boʃœr, -øz] *n* hirer (*of workers etc*).
embauchoir [ɑ̃boʃwar] *nm* shoe tree; (*pour bottes*) boot tree.
embaumement [ɑ̃bommɑ̃] *nm* embalming (*of corpse*).
embaumer [ɑ̃bome] **1** *vt* **(a)** to embalm (*corpse*); **(b)** *Fig* (*parfumer*) to perfume, to scent; **air embaumé,** fragrant *or* balmy air; **(c)** *Fig* (*répandre une odeur de*) to be fragrant with; **l'église embaume l'encens,** the church is heavy with (the scent of) incense. **2** *vi* to be fragrant.
embaumeur [ɑ̃bomœr] *nm* embalmer (*of corpses*).
embéguiner (s') [sɑ̃begine] *vpr Vieilli* **s'e. de qn,** to become infatuated with s.o.
embellie [ɑ̃beli] *nf* (*éclaircie*) bright spell; *Nau* calm spell, lull; **courte e.,** bright interval.
embellir [ɑ̃belir] **1** *vt* **(a)** to make (more) attractive, to beautify (*room, park etc*); to make (*s.o.*) look (more) beautiful, to improve the looks of (*s.o.*); **(b)** *Fig* to improve on, to embellish (*story, truth etc*). **2** *vi* to grow more beautiful.
embellissement [ɑ̃bɛlismɑ̃] *nm* **(a)** (*fait de rendre plus beau*) beautifying (*of room, park etc*); **e. de qn,** improving s.o.'s looks; **(b)** *Fig* embellishment (*of story, truth etc*); **(c)** (*décoration*) embellishing touch.
emberlificoter [ɑ̃bɛrlifikɔte] **1** *vt F* **(a)** (*empêtrer*) to entangle, to tangle (*s.o.*) up; **(b)** (*duper*) to take (*s.o.*) in. **2 s'emberlificoter** *vpr* **s'e. dans,** to get tangled up in (*clothes, Fig lies etc*).
embêtant [ɑ̃bɛtɑ̃] *adj F* annoying (*person, problem etc*); awkward (*situation*); **c'est drôlement e.!,** it's really annoying!
embêtement [ɑ̃bɛtmɑ̃] *nm F* (*agacement*) annoyance; (*souci*) worry, trouble.
embêter [ɑ̃bete] *F* **1** *vt* (*agacer*) to annoy; (*ennuyer*) to bore; **ça m'embête d'y aller,** (*ça m'ennuie*) I can't be bothered going *or* to go; (*ça me gêne*) I wish I didn't have to go; **ça m'embête d'arriver en retard,** I hate being late. **2 s'embêter** *vpr* to be *or* get bored (stiff); *Iron* **je vois que tu ne t'embêtes pas!,** I see you don't do badly for yourself!
emblée (d') [dɑ̃ble] *adv* directly, right away, straight off; (*réussir*) at the first attempt.
emblématique [ɑ̃blematik] *adj* emblematic(al); *Fig* symbolic.
emblème [ɑ̃blɛm] *nm* (*insigne*) emblem, device; *Fig* (*symbole*) symbol.
embobiner [ɑ̃bɔbine] *vt F* (*duper*) to take (*s.o.*) in; **ne vous laissez pas e.,** don't let yourself be had *or* taken in.
emboîtable [ɑ̃bwatabl] *adj* stackable (*chair*); that fits into a nest (*box, table etc*).
emboîtage [ɑ̃bwataʒ] *nm* **(a)** (*action d'envelopper*) encasing; casing (*of book*); **(b)** (*étui*) slipcase (*of book*).
emboîtement [ɑ̃bwatmɑ̃] *nm* fitting (together); *Constr* jointing (*of pipes, timbers etc*).
emboîter [ɑ̃bwate] **1** *vt* **(a)** (*assembler*) to fit (*pieces etc*) together *or* into each other; to nest (*boxes, tables etc*); to stack (*chairs*); *Constr* to joint (*pipes, timbers etc*); **e. le pas à qn,** to follow close on s.o.'s heels; *Fig* to follow suit, to follow s.o.'s lead; **(b)** (*envelopper*) (*of box etc*) to encase; **e. un livre,** to case a book; **cette chaussure lui emboîte le pied,** this shoe encases *or* covers his foot. **2 s'emboîter** *vpr* (*of pieces etc*) to fit together *or* into each other; (*of boxes, tables etc*) to nest; (*of chairs*) to stack.
emboîture [ɑ̃bwatyr] *nf* (*manière*) fit (*of two things*).
embolie [ɑ̃bɔli] *nf Méd* embolism.
embonpoint [ɑ̃bɔ̃pwɛ̃] *nm* stoutness, corpulence; **avoir de l'e.,** to be stout *or* corpulent.
embouché [ɑ̃buʃe] *adj F* **mal e.,** foul-mouthed.
emboucher [ɑ̃buʃe] *vt* **(a)** to put (*trumpet etc*) to one's mouth; *F* **e. la trompette,** to trumpet the news; **(b) e. un cheval,** to put the bit in a horse's mouth.
embouchure [ɑ̃buʃyr] *nf* **(a)** mouthpiece (*of trumpet, blowpipe etc*); **(b)** opening, mouth (*of sack, vessel etc*); **(c)** mouth (*of river etc*).
embouquer [ɑ̃buke] *Nau* **1** *vt* **e. la passe,** to enter the channel. **2** *vi* to enter a *or* the channel.
embourber (s') [sɑ̃burbe] *vpr* **(a)** (*of car etc*) to get stuck (in the mud); **(b)** *Fig Péj* to flounder, to get bogged down (**dans des explications**/*etc*, in explanations/*etc*).
embourgeoisement [ɑ̃burʒwazmɑ̃] *nm* attainment of middle-class respectability (**de,** by).
embourgeoiser (s') [sɑ̃burʒwaze] *vpr* to become bourgeois *or* middle-class.
embourrer [ɑ̃bure] *vt* to stuff (*chair etc*).
embout [ɑ̃bu] *nm* ferrule, tip (*of umbrella, stick etc*); terminal (*of cable*); nozzle (*of hose*); connector (*of tie-rod, wire etc*).
embouteillage [ɑ̃butɛjaʒ] *nm* **(a)** *Aut* (traffic) hold-up, traffic jam; **l'heure de l'e. du métro,** the rush hour on the *Br* tube *or Am* subway; **(b)** *Nau* bottling up (*of fleet*).

embouteiller [ɑ̃buteje] *vt* **(a)** *Aut* to block (up), to jam (up) (*street etc*); **circulation embouteillée,** congested traffic; **route embouteillée,** road blocked with traffic; **(b)** *Nau* to bottle up (*fleet*).
emboutir [ɑ̃butir] **1** *vt* **(a)** *Métal* to stamp, to press, to swage (*metal*); **châssis en tôle emboutie,** pressed steel frame; **(b)** (*arrondir*) to emboss; **(c)** *F* (*déformer*) to bash (*sth*) in; *Aut* **e. un arbre,** to crash into a tree. **2 s'emboutir** *vpr Aut F* **s'e. sur** *ou* **contre un mur,** to crash into a wall.
emboutissage [ɑ̃butisaʒ] *nm* **(a)** *Métal* stamping, pressing, swaging (*of metals*); **(b)** (*fait d'arrondir*) embossing; **(c)** *F* (*of cars*) collision; **l'e. d'une voiture par un autobus,** the crashing of a bus into a car.
embranchement [ɑ̃brɑ̃ʃmɑ̃] *nm* **(a)** (*division*) branching (off) (*of tree, road, rail, pipe etc*); **(b)** (*croisement*) junction (*of road, rail, pipe etc*); (*bifurcation*) fork (*in road*); **(c)** (*route*) side road, branch (road); **(d)** *Rail* branch line; **(e)** branch (*of a science*); *Biol* sub-kingdom, phylum.
embrancher [ɑ̃brɑ̃ʃe] **1** *vt* to connect up, to join up (*road, pipe etc*) (**à,** to). **2 s'embrancher** *vpr* to join (up); **route qui s'embranche sur la grande route,** (*se relie*) road that forms a junction with the main road; (*se sépare*) road that branches off the main road.
embraquer [ɑ̃brake] *vt Nau* to haul taut, to tighten (*rope*).
embrasé [ɑ̃braze] *adj Litt* **(a)** blazing (*forest etc*); glowing (*coals etc*); **(b)** scorching, sweltering (*heat*).
embrasement [ɑ̃brazmɑ̃] *nm* **(a)** *Arch* (*incendie*) conflagration; **(b)** *Litt* **l'e. du couchant,** the blazing sunset.
embraser [ɑ̃braze] **1** *vt Litt* **(a)** to set (*house etc*) ablaze; **(b)** (*of sun*) to scorch (*ground*); **(c)** (*of sunset*) to set (*sky etc*) aglow; **(d)** *Fig* to fire, to inflame (*imagination, heart etc*). **2 s'embraser** *vpr* **(a)** (*prendre feu*) to blaze up; **(b)** (*rougeoyer*) to glow.
embrassade [ɑ̃brasad] *nf* embrace, hug.
embrasse [ɑ̃bras] *nf* (*de rideau*) tieback.
embrasser [ɑ̃brase] **1** *vt* **(a)** (*donner un baiser à*) to kiss; **je t'embrasse de tout mon cœur,** (*dans une lettre*) with fondest love; **e. qn sur la bouche/la joue,** to kiss s.o. on the mouth/cheek; **(b)** *Vieilli* (*étreindre*) to embrace, to hug (*s.o.*); **(c)** (*adopter*) to embrace (*cause, belief etc*); to take up (*career, cause etc*); to seize (*an opportunity*); **(d)** (*contenir*) to embrace, to take in (*subject etc*); **l'explication n'embrasse pas tous les faits,** the explanation does not cover all the facts. **2 s'embrasser** *vpr* to kiss (each other).
embrasure [ɑ̃brazyr] *nf* **(a)** *Constr* embrasure; **l'e. de la porte/fenêtre,** the door/window recess; **(b)** *Mil* (*dans un mur*) embrasure; *Nau* gun port.
embrayage [ɑ̃brɛjaʒ] *nm* **(a)** (*action*) *Tech* coupling, engaging (*of engine parts*); *Aut* letting in *or* engaging the clutch; **(b)** (*pièce*) *Aut* clutch; *Tech* coupling (gear); **pédale d'e.,** clutch pedal.
embrayer [ɑ̃breje] *v* (**j'embraie, j'embraye, n. embrayons; j'embraierai, j'embrayerai**) **1** *vt Tech* to couple, to engage (*engine parts*). **2** *vi* **(a)** *Aut* to let in *or* engage the clutch; **(b)** *F* **e. sur,** (*commencer à parler de*) to get going on (*subject etc*); (*avoir de l'influence sur*) to have influence over; **(c)** *Arg* (*reprendre le travail*) to go back to work.
embrigadement [ɑ̃brigadmɑ̃] *nm* recruitment (*of supporters etc*).
embrigader [ɑ̃brigade] *vt* to recruit (*supporter etc*) (**dans,** to).
embringuer [ɑ̃brɛ̃ge] *vt F* **e. qn dans qch,** to get s.o. mixed up in sth; **il ne veut pas se faire e.,** he doesn't want to get mixed up in it.
embrocation [ɑ̃brɔkasjɔ̃] *nf Méd* embrocation.
embrocher [ɑ̃brɔʃe] *vt* **(a)** *Culin* to put (*meat etc*) on a *or* the spit; **(b)** *F* **e. qn,** (*d'un coup d'épée*) to skewer s.o.
embrouillage [ɑ̃brujaʒ] *nm* = **EMBROUILLEMENT**.
embrouillamini [ɑ̃brujamini] *nm F* confusion, muddle.
embrouillé [ɑ̃bruje] *adj* **(a)** tangled (*skein etc*); **(b)** *Fig* muddled, mixed up (*papers etc*); confused, muddled (*situation, ideas etc*); complicated, involved (*style, business*).
embrouillement [ɑ̃brujmɑ̃] *nm* **(a)** (*action*) tangling, ravelling (*of threads etc*); muddling, mixing up (*of papers etc*); muddling, confusing (*of situation, ideas etc*); **(b)** (*état*) tangle (*of threads*); muddle, confusion (*of papers, ideas etc*).
embrouiller [ɑ̃bruje] **1** *vt* **(a)** to ravel, to tangle (*threads etc*); **(b)** *Fig* to muddle, to mix up (*papers etc*); to confuse, to muddle (*s.o., situation, ideas etc*); **e. la question,** to confuse *or* cloud the issue. **2 s'embrouiller** *vpr* **(a)** (*of threads etc*) to get tangled *or* into a tangle; **(b)** (*of papers etc*) to get muddled *or* mixed up; (*of person, situation, ideas etc*) to get muddled *or* confused; **ses affaires s'embrouillent,** his business is getting into a muddle.
embroussaillé [ɑ̃brusaje] *adj* covered with bushes *or* brushwood (*path etc*); **cheveux embroussaillés,** tousled hair.
embrumé [ɑ̃bryme] *adj* misty (*weather*); hazy (*horizon*); clouded (*countenance, mind*).
embrumer [ɑ̃bryme] **1** *vt* to cover (*landscape etc*) with mist *or* haze; *Fig* to cloud (*mind*); **craintes qui embrument l'avenir,** fears that darken the future. **2 s'embrumer** *vpr* to become misty *or* hazy; (*of sky*) to cloud over.
embruns [ɑ̃brœ̃] *nmpl* spray, spindrift.
embryologie [ɑ̃brijɔlɔʒi] *nf Biol* embryology.
embryologique [ɑ̃brijɔlɔʒik] *adj Biol* embryologic(al).
embryologiste [ɑ̃brijɔlɔʒist] *n Biol* embryologist.
embryon [ɑ̃brijɔ̃] *nm* embryo; *Fig* **œuvre encore en e.,** work still in embryo.
embryonnaire [ɑ̃brijɔnɛr] *adj Physiol* embryonic; *Fig* **œuvre à l'état e.,** work in an embryonic state; **sac e.,** embryo sac.
embryopathie [ɑ̃brijɔpati] *nf Méd* embryopathy.
embryotomie [ɑ̃brijɔtɔmi] *nf Obst* embryotomy.
embu [ɑ̃by] **1** *adj* flat, dull (*paint, painting*). **2** *nm* flatness, dullness (*of paint*).
embûches [ɑ̃byʃ] *nfpl* traps; **tendre** *ou* **dresser des e. à qn,** to set traps for s.o.; **sujet plein d'e.,** tricky subject.
embuer [ɑ̃bɥe] *vt* (*of steam etc*) to mist up, to cloud (*glass etc*); **yeux embués de larmes,** eyes dimmed *or* clouded with tears; **pare-brise embué,** misted(-up) windscreen.
embuscade [ɑ̃byskad] *nf* ambush; **dresser** *ou* **tendre une e. à qn,** to lay *or* set an ambush for s.o.; **attirer qn dans une e.,** to ambush *or* waylay s.o.; **se tenir en e.,** to lie in ambush *or* in wait; **tomber dans une e.,** to be ambushed *or* waylaid.
embusqué [ɑ̃byske] *nm* **(a)** *Mil* shirker, dodger; **(b)** *Rugby* **les embusqués,** the back row of forwards.
embusquer [ɑ̃byske] **1** *vt* **(a)** to place (*troops etc*) in ambush; **(b)** *Mil* (*planquer*) to find (*s.o.*) a safe posting (*in wartime*). **2 s'embusquer** *vpr* **(a)** (*se mettre dans une embuscade*) to lie in ambush; **(b)** *Mil* (*se planquer*) to shirk active service.
éméché [emeʃe] *adj F* slightly the worse for drink, tipsy.
émeraude [ɛmrod] **1** *nf* **(a)** *Minér* emerald; **(b)** (*couleur*) emerald green. **2** *adj inv* emerald green.
émergence [emɛrʒɑ̃s] *nf* emergence; **point d'é.,** source, point of emergence.
émergent [emɛrʒɑ̃] *adj* emergent.
émerger [emɛrʒe] *vi* (**j'émergeai(s); n. émergeons**) **(a)** to emerge (**de la mer/***etc*, from the sea/*etc*); **(b)** *Fig* (*of truth, fact etc*) to emerge, to come to light; (*of new writer etc*) to emerge.
émeri [ɛmri] *nm* emery; **papier (d')é.,** emery paper; **bouchon à l'é.,** (ground glass) stopper; **bouché à l'é.,** (*of flask*) stoppered; *F* (*of person*) as thick as two short planks.
émerillon [ɛmrijɔ̃] *nm* **(a)** (*oiseau*) merlin; **(b)** *Tech* swivel (hook).
émeriser [ɛmrize] *vt* to coat (*paper etc*) with emery.
émérite [emerit] *adj* **(a)** *Arch* emeritus (*professor*); **(b)** (*expérimenté*) skilled, experienced.
émersion [emɛrsjɔ̃] *nf Astron* emersion (*of moon*).
émerveillement [emɛrvɛjmɑ̃] *nm* **(a)** (*étonnement*) amazement; (*enchantement*) wonder; **(b)** (*chose*) amazing *or* wonderful thing; **c'était un é.,** it was amazing *or* wonderful.
émerveiller [emɛrveje] **1** *vt* (*étonner*) to amaze; (*enchanter*) to fill (*s.o.*) with wonder; **être émerveillé par,** to wonder *or* marvel at, to be filled with wonder by. **2 s'émerveiller** *vpr* **s'é. de** *ou* **devant,** (*s'étonner*) to be amazed at; (*s'enchanter*) to marvel at.
émétique [emetik] *adj & n* emetic.
émetteur, -trice [emetœr, -tris] **1** *adj* **(a)** *Fin* issuing (*bank etc*); **(b)** *Rad* **poste é.,** transmitter; **station émettrice,** transmitting *or* broadcasting station. **2** *n* issuer (*of banknotes, shares etc*). **3** *nm Rad* transmitter; *Phys* emitter (*of radiation, sound etc*).
émetteur-récepteur [emetœrresɛptœr] *nm Rad* transmitter-receiver, transceiver; **é.-r. (portatif),** walkie-talkie; (*pl émetteurs-récepteurs*).
émettre [emɛtr] *v* (*conj like* **mettre**) **1** *vt* **(a)** to emit (*sound, fluid etc*); to give, to utter (*sound, cry etc*); to give off (*fumes*); to give out (*heat, light*); **(b)** *Fig* to express (*opinion*); to raise, to put forward (*objection*); **(c)** *Rad TV* to send out, to transmit, to broadcast; **(d)** *Fin* to issue (*cheque etc*); to float (*loan*); to utter (*counterfeit money*). **2** *vi Rad TV* to transmit, to broadcast.

émeu, -eus [emø] *nm (oiseau)* emu.
émeute [emøt] *nf* riot, outbreak, disturbance; **faire é.,** to riot; **chef d'é.,** riot leader.
émeutier, -ière [emøtje, -jɛr] *n* **(a)** *(participant)* rioter; **(b)** *(chef)* riot leader.
émietter [emjete] **1** *vt* **(a)** to crumble (up) *(bread, biscuit, rock etc)*; **(b)** *Fig* to break up *(land, empire etc)*; to disperse *(fortune, power etc)*; to fritter away *(energy etc)*. **2 s'émietter** *vpr* **(a)** *(of bread etc)* to crumble; **(b)** *(of empire etc)* to break up; *(of fortune etc)* to disperse; *(of energy etc)* to be frittered away.
émigrant, -ante [emigrɑ̃, -ɑ̃t] **1** *adj* emigrating *(population etc)*; migratory *(birds)*. **2** *n* emigrant.
émigration [emigrɑsjɔ̃] *nf* **(a)** emigration *(of people)*; **pays à forte/faible é.,** country with high/low emigration; **é. des savants,** brain drain; **(b)** migration *(of birds, fish)*.
émigré, -ée [emigre] *n* (political) exile, émigré; **travailleurs émigrés,** migrant workers.
émigrer [emigre] *vi* **(a)** *(of person)* to emigrate; **(b)** *(of birds, fish)* to migrate.
émincé [emɛ̃se] *nm Culin (tranche)* thin slice *(of meat)*.
émincer [emɛ̃se] *vt* **(j'émincai(s); n. émincons)** to slice *(meat, vegetables etc)* thinly.
éminemment [eminamɑ̃] *adv (supérieurement)* eminently; *(extrêmement)* utterly.
éminence [eminɑ̃s] *nf* **(a)** *(géographique)* hill, *Litt* eminence; **(b)** *Anat* protuberance, eminence; ball *(of the thumb)*; **(c)** *Arch (excellence)* (moral, intellectual) superiority; eminence; **(d)** *Rel* **son É. le Cardinal,** his Eminence the Cardinal; **l'É. grise,** the power behind the throne, the éminence grise.
éminent [eminɑ̃] *adj* eminent, distinguished *(person, position etc)*; outstanding, distinguished *(service etc)*.
émir [emir] *nm* emir.
émirat [emira] *nm* emirate; **les Émirats arabes unis,** the United Arab Emirates.
émissaire [emisɛr] **1** *adj* **(a) bouc é.,** scapegoat; **(b)** *Anat* **veine é.,** emissary vein. **2** *nm* **(a)** *(envoyé)* emissary; **(b)** *Anat* emissary vein; **(c)** outlet, drainage channel *(of lake)*.
émission [emisjɔ̃] *nf* **(a)** emission *(of sound, fluid etc)*; utterance *(of sound, cry etc)*; giving out *(of heat, light)*; **tuyau d'é.,** discharge pipe; **(b)** *Rad TV (action)* transmission, sending out, broadcasting; **poste d'é.,** transmitter; **station d'é.,** transmitting *or* broadcasting station; **(c)** *Electron* **é. électronique,** electron emission; *Phys Nucl* **é. de particules,** particle emission; **(d)** *Fin* issue, issuing *(of banknotes etc)*; uttering *(of counterfeit money)*; **(e)** *TV Rad (ce qui est émis) Br* programme, *Am* program, broadcast; **é. en différé/en direct,** recorded/live broadcast; **une é. pour les enfants,** a children's programme *or* broadcast.
emmagasinage [ɑ̃magazinaʒ] *nm* storage, warehousing *(of goods)*; storing up, accumulation *(of electricity, heat)*.
emmagasiner [ɑ̃magazine] *vt* **(a)** to store, to warehouse *(goods)*; to house *(aircraft etc)*; *Fig* to store up *(memories, knowledge)*; **(b)** to store up, to accumulate *(electricity, heat)*.
emmailloter [ɑ̃majɔte] *vt* **(a)** to wrap (up), to swathe *(limb etc)*; **(b)** *Arch (langer)* to swaddle *(infant)*.
emmanchement [ɑ̃mɑ̃ʃmɑ̃] *nm* itting *or* fixing of a handle (**d'un outil/***etc*, (on)to a tool/*etc*).
emmancher [ɑ̃mɑ̃ʃe] **1** *vt* **(a)** to fit *or* fix a handle to; **(b)** to fit together, to joint *(pipes etc)*; **(c)** *Fig F* to start on, to set about *(scheme, job etc)*. **2 s'emmancher** *vpr F* **s'e. bien/mal,** to get off to a good/bad start.
emmanchure [ɑ̃mɑ̃ʃyr] *nf* armhole.
emmêlement [ɑ̃mɛlmɑ̃] *nm* **(a)** tangling *(of threads etc)*; *(état)* tangle; **(b)** mixing up, muddling *(of facts, story)*; *(état)* mix-up, muddle.
emmêler [ɑ̃mele] **1** *vt* **(a)** to tangle *(thread, hair etc)*; **(b)** to mix up, to muddle *(facts, story)*. **2 s'emmêler** *vpr* **(a)** *(of thread, hair etc)* to become tangled, to get into a tangle; **(b)** *(of facts, story)* to become mixed up *or* muddled, to get into a muddle.
emménagement [ɑ̃menaʒmɑ̃] *nm* **(a)** moving in *(to house)*; **(b)** moving in, installation *(of furniture etc)*; **(c) emménagements,** accommodation, appointments *(in ship, aircraft)*.
emménager [ɑ̃menaʒe] *v* **(j'emménageai(s)) 1** *vt* to move *(s.o.)* in *(to house)*; to move in, to install *(furniture etc)*. **2** *vi* to move in; **e. dans,** to move into.
emmener [ɑ̃mne] *vt* **(j'emmène, j'emmènerai) (a)** *(prendre avec soi)* to lead *or* take *(prisoner etc)* away; to take *(child etc)* (with one); **emmené en prison,** taken off to prison; **je vous emmène avec moi,** I'm taking you with me; **emmenez-le!,** take *or* lead him away!; **(b)** *(entraîner)* to lead *(troops, sports team etc)*; **(c)** *(transporter) (of boat, plane etc)* to take, to carry *(passengers etc)*.
emmenthal [emɛ̃tal] *nm (fromage)* Emment(h)al (cheese).
emmerdant [ɑ̃mɛrdɑ̃] *adj Arg (qui contrarie)* damned *or Br* bloody annoying; *(qui ennuie)* damned *or Br* bloody boring.
emmerdement [ɑ̃mɛrdəmɑ̃] *nm Arg* **un e.,** a damned *or Br* bloody nuisance; **emmerdements,** (damned) bother, trouble.
emmerder [ɑ̃mɛrde] **1** *vt Arg* **(a) e. qn,** *(contrarier)* to get up s.o.'s nose *or* on s.o.'s nerves; *(ennuyer)* to bore s.o. stiff *or* silly; **(b)** *(comme défi)* **je l'emmerde!,** he can go and get stuffed! **2 s'emmerder** *vpr Arg* to be *or* get bored stiff *or* silly; *Iron* **tu ne t'emmerdes pas!,** you're not doing badly for yourself!
emmerdes [ɑ̃mɛrd] *nfpl Arg* (damned) bother, trouble.
emmerdeur, -euse [ɑ̃mɛrdœr, -øz] *n Arg (qui contrarie)* damned *or Br* bloody nuisance, pain in the neck; *(qui ennuie)* damned *or Br* bloody bore.
emmitoufler [ɑ̃mitufle] **1** *vt* to muffle *(s.o.)* up (**dans, de,** in). **2 s'emmitoufler** *vpr* to get muffled up (**dans, de,** in).
emmurer [ɑ̃myre] *vt* to immure, to wall in *or* up *(victim)*; *(of rockfall)* to trap *(miners etc)*.
émoi [emwa] *nm (tumulte)* commotion, agitation; *(trouble)* emotion, agitation; *(plaisir)* excitement; *(anxiété)* anxiety; **être (tout) en é.,** *(troublé)* to be in a state of excitement, to be all in a flutter; **toute la ville était en é.,** the whole town was in a commotion; **au grand é. de sa mère,** to his mother's great anxiety; **non sans é.,** in some agitation.
émollient [emɔljɑ̃] *adj & nm* emollient, counter-irritant.
émoluments [emɔlymɑ̃] *nmpl* emoluments, remuneration.
émondage [emɔ̃daʒ] *nm* **(a)** pruning, trimming *(of tree)*; **(b)** cleaning *(of seed etc)*.
émonder [emɔ̃de] *vt* **(a)** to prune, to trim *(tree)*; *Fig* **é. un livre,** to cut down *or* prune a book; **(b)** to clean *(seed etc)*.
émondeur, -euse [emɔ̃dœr, -øz] *n* pruner.
émondoir [emɔ̃dwar] *nm* pruning hook.
émotif, -ive [emɔtif, -iv] **1** *adj* emotive *(words, subject etc)*; emotional *(person, reaction etc)*. **2** *n* emotional person.
émotion [emosjɔ̃] *nf* emotion; *F (inquiétude)* fright, shock; **vive é.,** strong emotion; *(exaltation)* excitement, thrill; **ressentir une vive é.,** to be greatly moved; *(exaltation)* to be thrilled; **parler avec é.,** to speak emotionally; *F* **j'ai eu une é.,** I've had a fright *or* shock.
émotionnable [emosjɔnabl] *adj F* emotional, excitable *(person)*.
émotionnel, -elle [emosjɔnɛl] *adj Psy* emotional *(reaction etc)*.
émotionner [emosjɔne] *vt F (exciter)* to excite *(s.o.)*; *(attendrir)* to upset *(s.o.)*.
émotivité [emɔtivite] *nf* emotionalism.
émou, -ous [emu] *nm (oiseau)* emu.
émoulu [emuly] *adj* **(a)** *Arch* sharpened, newly ground *(weapon)*; **(b)** *F* **jeune homme frais é. du collège/de son université,** young man fresh from school/university.
émoussé [emuse] *adj* blunt *(point, blade etc)*.
émousser [emuse] **1** *vt* **(a)** to blunt *(blade, point, pencil, angle etc)*; **(b)** to dull, to deaden, to blunt *(senses, passions etc)*; to take the edge off *(appetite)*. **2 s'émousser** *vpr* **(a)** *(of blade, point etc)* to get blunt; **(b)** *(of senses, passions etc)* to become blunted *or* dulled.
émoustillant [emustijɑ̃] *adj* exhilarating; *(sexuellement)* arousing, titillating.
émoustiller [emustije] *vt* to exhilarate; *(sexuellement)* to arouse, to titillate.
émouvant [emuvɑ̃] *adj (attendrissant)* moving, touching *(scene etc)*; *(passionnant)* stirring, thrilling *(incident etc)*.
émouvoir [emuvwar] *v (pp* **ému**; *otherwise conj like* **mouvoir) 1** *vt* **(a)** *(soulever)* to excite, to stir up, to rouse *(mob etc)*;

(b) *(affecter)* to move, to touch; *(inquiéter)* to upset; *(passionner)* to rouse, to stir; *(indigner)* to rouse; **é. qn (jusqu')aux larmes,** to move s.o. to tears; **cela ne m'émeut pas le moins du monde,** that doesn't upset *or* disturb me in the least; **être encore tout ému de la rencontre,** to be still very upset by the meeting; **facile à é.,** emotional, easily moved.

2 s'émouvoir *vpr* **(a)** *(s'enthousiasmer)* to get excited, to be roused; **le pays s'émeut,** the country is in a state of excitement;

(b) (*se troubler*) to be touched *or* moved; **ce qu'il me déclara sans s'é. le moins du monde,** which he announced to me with perfect composure; *F* **pas de quoi s'é.,** it's nothing to get worked up about.

empaillage [ɑ̃pajaʒ] *nm* **(a)** covering (*of plants*) with straw; **(b)** bottoming (*of chairs*) with straw; **(c)** stuffing (*of dead animals*).

empaillé, -ée [ɑ̃paje] **1** *adj* **(a)** stuffed (*bird, fox etc*); *F* **avoir l'air e.,** to be a bit lumpish; **(b)** *F* (*idiot*) doltish (*person*). **2** *n F* (*idiot*) dolt.

empailler [ɑ̃paje] *vt* **(a)** to cover (*plants*) with straw; **(b)** to bottom (*chair*) with straw; **(c)** to stuff (*dead animal*).

empailleur, -euse [ɑ̃pajœr, -øz] *n* **(a)** (*de chaises*) chair bottomer; **(b)** (*d'animaux*) taxidermist.

empalement [ɑ̃palmɑ̃] *nm* impalement (*of criminal etc*).

empaler [ɑ̃pale] **1** *vt* to impale. **2 s'empaler** *vpr* to impale oneself.

empanaché [ɑ̃panaʃe] *adj* plumed, decorated with plumes; **style e.,** pompous *or* flowery style.

empaquetage [ɑ̃paktaʒ] *nm* packing (up) (*of goods, present etc*).

empaqueter [ɑ̃pakte] *vt* **(j'empaquette; j'empaquetterai)** to pack up (*goods, present etc*).

empaqueteur, -euse [ɑ̃paktœr, -øz] *n* packer.

emparer (s') [sɑ̃pare] *vpr* **s'e. de,** to seize (*town, hostage, booty etc*); to grab (hold of), to seize (*phone, purse etc*); *Sp* to get hold of (*ball*); (*of doubt, obsession etc*) to take hold of (*s.o.*); **s'e. du pouvoir,** to seize power.

empâté [ɑ̃pɑte] *adj* coated, furry (*tongue*); thick (*voice*); fleshy, bloated (*face*).

empâtement [ɑ̃pɑtmɑ̃] *nm* **(a)** fattening out (*of person, body, face etc*); fattening (up), cramming (*of fowl*); thickening (*of voice*); **(b)** coating, furring up (*of tongue*); *Beaux-Arts* impasto.

empâter [ɑ̃pɑte] **1** *vt* **(a)** (*épaissir*) to fatten out (*person, body, face etc*); to fatten (up), to cram (*fowl*); to thicken (*voice*); **(b)** (*couvrir d'une pâte*) to coat, to fur up (*tongue*). **2 s'empâter** *vpr* **(a)** (*of person, body, face etc*) to fatten out; (*of voice*) to thicken; **(b)** (*of tongue*) to become coated, to fur up.

empathie [ɑ̃pati] *nf Psy* empathy.

empattement [ɑ̃patmɑ̃] *nm* **(a)** tenoning (*of timbers*); **(b)** footing (*of wall*); base plate (*of crane*); **(c)** wheelbase (*of car, engine*); **(d)** *Typ* serif.

empatter [ɑ̃pate] *vt* **(a)** to tenon (*timbers*); **(b)** to give footing to (*wall*).

empaumer [ɑ̃pome] *vt* **(a)** (*au jeu de paume*) to catch (*ball*) in the palm of the hand; (*frapper*) to strike (*ball*) with the palm of the hand; **(b)** *F* **se laisser** *ou* **se faire e.,** to be tricked *or* taken in; **(c)** (*of magician etc*) to palm (*card, coin etc*).

empêché [ɑ̃peʃe] *adj* **(a)** (*embarrassé*) embarrassed; **être e. de répondre,** to be at a loss for a reply; **(b)** (*of rope etc*) fouled; **(c)** *F* **être e. de sa personne,** to be awkward, not to know what to do with oneself; **(d)** (*retenu*) held up, detained.

empêchement [ɑ̃peʃmɑ̃] *nm* **(a)** (*contretemps*) obstacle, hindrance, impediment (**à**, to); **je n'ai pas pu venir car j'ai eu un e.,** I couldn't come as something turned up (at the last minute); **excusez-moi de mon retard, j'ai eu un e.,** I'm sorry I'm late, I got held up *or* detained; **sans e.,** without (let or) hindrance; **en cas d'e.,** should you be prevented from coming; **(b) e. de la langue,** impediment of speech; *Jur* **e. de mariage,** impediment to marriage.

empêcher [ɑ̃peʃe] **1** *vt* **(a) e. qn de faire qch,** to prevent *or* keep *or* stop s.o. from doing sth; **empêché, il a envoyé ses excuses,** unavoidably detained, he sent his apologies; **que rien ne vous en empêche!,** do it by all means!; **cette muraille empêche la vue,** this wall obstructs the view; **ce vent empêchera la pluie,** this wind will keep the rain off;

(b) (*ne pas permettre*) to prevent, to stop (*action, event etc*); to obstruct, to impede (*movement, progress etc*); **la pluie empêche que nous (ne) sortions,** the rain prevents *or* stops us from going out.

2 *v impers* **il n'empêche que cela nous a coûté cher,** all the same *or* nevertheless it has cost us dear; **cela n'empêche pas qu'il aurait pu s'excuser,** all the same *or* nevertheless, he could have apologized; **cela n'empêche qu'il soit sévère,** that doesn't prevent *or* stop him from being *or* his being strict; *F* **n'empêche,** all the same.

3 s'empêcher *vpr* (*souvent nég*) **s'e. de faire qch,** to stop oneself *or* prevent oneself *or* refrain from doing sth; **je ne pouvais m'e. de rire,** I couldn't help laughing, I had to laugh; **je ne peux pas m'en e.,** I can't help it, I can't stop myself.

empêcheur, -euse [ɑ̃peʃœr, -øz] *n F* **e. de danser en rond,** spoilsport, wet blanket.

empeigne [ɑ̃pɛɲ] *nf* upper, vamp (*of shoe*); *Arg* **gueule d'e.,** ugly mug.

empennage [ɑ̃pɛnaʒ] *nm* feathering, feathers (*of arrow*); fins, vanes (*of bomb*); fins (*of torpedo*); empennage, tail (*of aircraft*).

empenner [ɑ̃pene] *vt* to feather (*arrow*).

empereur [ɑ̃prœr] *nm* emperor.

empesage [ɑ̃pəzaʒ] *nm* starching (*of linen etc*).

empesé [ɑ̃pəze] *adj* **(a)** starched (*collar, shirt etc*); **(b)** *Fig* stiff, starchy, unbending (*manner*); stiff, affected (*style*).

empeser [ɑ̃pəze] *vt* **(j'empèse; j'empèserai)** to starch (*linen etc*).

empesté [ɑ̃pɛste] *adj* foul, pestilential (*air, odour etc*).

empester [ɑ̃pɛste] **1** *vt* to make (*room*) stink (**de**, of); **e. qn (avec sa fumée/***etc***),** to stink s.o. out (with one's smoke/*etc*); **e. l'alcool/le parfum/***etc*, to reek *or* stink of alcohol/perfume/*etc*; **air empesté par le tabac,** air reeking of tobacco. **2** *vi* to stink.

empêtrer [ɑ̃petre] **1** *vt* (*of net, ropes etc*) to entangle; **être empêtré de bagages,** to be hampered by luggage. **2 s'empêtrer** *vpr* to become entangled; **s'e. les pieds dans les broussailles,** to get one's feet caught in the undergrowth; *Fig* **s'e. dans une mauvaise affaire,** to get involved *or* mixed up in a bad business.

emphase [ɑ̃fɑz] *nf* bombast, grandiloquence, pomposity; **avec e.,** bombastically, grandiloquently, pompously.

emphatique [ɑ̃fatik] *adj* bombastic, pompous, grandiloquent (*style etc*).

emphatiquement [ɑ̃fatikmɑ̃] *adv* bombastically, grandiloquently, pompously.

emphysémateux, -euse [ɑ̃fizematø, -øz] *Méd* **1** *adj* emphysematous. **2** *n* emphysema sufferer.

emphysème [ɑ̃fizɛm] *nm Méd* emphysema.

empiècement [ɑ̃pjɛsmɑ̃] *nm* yoke (*of dress*).

empierrement [ɑ̃pjɛrmɑ̃] *nm* **(a)** metalling, macadamization (*of road*); *Rail* ballasting (*of track*); **(b)** (*couche de pierres etc*) macadam, (road) metal; *Rail* ballast.

empierrer [ɑ̃pjere] *vt* to metal, to macadamize (*road*); *Rail* to ballast (*track*).

empiètement [ɑ̃pjɛtmɑ̃] *nm* encroachment (**sur**, on); **e. sur les droits de qn,** infringement of s.o.'s rights.

empiéter [ɑ̃pjete] *vi* **(j'empiète; j'empiéterai) e. sur le terrain de qn,** to encroach (up)on s.o.'s land; **e. sur les droits de qn,** to infringe s.o.'s rights; **cela empiète sur notre temps,** that encroaches (up)on our time.

empiffrer (s') [sɑ̃pifre] *vpr Arg* to stuff *or* gorge oneself.

empilable [ɑ̃pilabl] *adj* stackable (*chair, box etc*).

empilage [ɑ̃pilaʒ] *nm*, **empilement** [ɑ̃pilmɑ̃] *nm* **(a)** (*action*) stacking, piling (up) (*of wood etc*); **(b)** (*pile*) pile, stack.

empiler [ɑ̃pile] **1** *vt* **(a)** to stack, to pile (up) (*books, wood etc*); **(b)** to cram (*passengers into vehicle etc*); **(c)** *F* (*rouler*) to cheat, to rook (*s.o.*). **2 s'empiler** *vpr* (*of books etc*) to pile up.

empire [ɑ̃pir] *nm* **(a)** (*domination*) authority, dominion; **e. des mers,** command of the sea; **sous l'e. d'un tyran,** under the rule *or Litt* sway of a tyrant; **(b)** (*contrôle*) influence, control; **avoir de l'e.** *ou* **exercer un e. sur qn,** to have influence *or* power over s.o.; **faire qch sous l'e. de la nécessité/de la boisson/de la colère,** to do sth under the pressure of necessity/under the influence of drink/in a fit of anger; **(c)** *Hist* empire; *Hist* **le Saint-E. romain (germanique),** the Holy Roman Empire; *Hist Fr* **le premier E., l'E.,** the First Empire; **style/meubles E.,** Empire style/furniture.

empirer [ɑ̃pire] **1** *vt* to worsen, to make worse, to aggravate (*situation, illness*); **pour e. les choses,** to make matters worse. **2** *vi* to worsen, to get *or* to grow worse, to deteriorate.

empirique [ɑ̃pirik] *adj* empiric(al).

empirisme [ɑ̃pirism] *nm* empiricism.

empiriste [ɑ̃pirist] *adj & n Phil* empiricist.

emplacement [ɑ̃plasmɑ̃] *nm* **(a)** site, location (*of tent, building etc*); *Mil* emplacement (*of gun*); position (*of troops on battlefield*); *Nau* **e. de chargement,** loading berth; **(b)** *Ordinat* slot; **e. pour carte d'extension,** expansion slot.

emplanture [ɑ̃plɑ̃tyr] *nf Nau* step (*of mast*); *Av* root, socket (*of wing*).

emplâtre [ɑ̃plɑtr] *nm* **(a)** *Pharm* (*pansement*) (sticking, adhesive) plaster; **e. contre** *ou* **pour les cors,** corn plaster; *F* **c'est mettre un e. sur une jambe de bois,** it's no earthly use; *F* **cette purée, quel e.!,** this mashed potato is really stodgy; **(b)** *F* spineless person; **c'est un e.,** he's got no backbone; **(c)** patch (*for repair of tyre*).

emplette [ɑ̃plɛt] *nf* **(a)** (*achat*) purchase; **aller faire ses emplettes,** to go shopping, to do one's shopping; **faire l'e. de qch,** to purchase sth; *Vieilli* **être de bonne e.,** to be worth buying, to be a bargain, to be a good buy; **(b) emplettes,** (*choses achetées*) purchases, shopping.

emplir [ɑ̃plir] **1** *vt* to fill; **la foule emplissait les rues,** the crowd filled the streets; **nouvelle qui m'emplit de joie,** news that fills me with delight. **2 s'emplir** *vpr* to fill (**de,** with).

emploi [ɑ̃plwa] *nm* **(a)** (*utilisation*) use (*of sth*); **mode d'e.,** directions *or* instructions for use; **je n'en aurais pas l'e.,** I wouldn't have any use for it; **e. du temps,** timetable, schedule; **elle a un e. du temps très chargé,** she has a very busy *or* full timetable *or* schedule; **mot qui fait double e.,** word that is redundant *or* superfluous; **faire un bon e. de qch,** to make good use of sth, to put sth to good use;

(b) (*situation*) job, post; (*travail*) employment, work; **agence nationale pour l'e.,** (French state) employment agency; ≈ *Br* Jobcentre ®; **être sans e.,** to be out of work *or* out of a job, to be unemployed *or F* jobless; **quel est son e.?,** what does he do (for a living)?; **e. public,** public office; *Journ* **demandes d'e.,** situations wanted; **offres d'e.,** situations vacant; **création d'emplois,** job creation; **sécurité de l'e.,** job security; **partage des emplois,** job-sharing; *Écon Pol* **plein e.,** full employment; **les sans e.,** the jobless;

(c) *Th* **tenir l'e. de père noble,** to play heavy father parts; *Fig* **il a tout à fait le physique de l'e.,** he looks the part completely.

employé, -ée [ɑ̃plwaje] *n* employee; **e. (de bureau),** office worker; **e. de magasin,** shop assistant *or Am* clerk; **e. à la vente,** salesman; **e. de banque,** bank clerk; **e. d'administration,** government employee, civil servant; **l'e. du gaz vient demain,** the gas man's coming tomorrow.

employer [ɑ̃plwaje] *v* (**j'emploie**; **j'emploierai**) **1** *vt* **(a)** (*utiliser*) to use (*tool, word, technique, force etc*); **e. toute son industrie à faire qch,** to devote all one energies to doing sth; **bien e. son temps,** to use one's time well, to make good use of one's time; **ne savoir à quoi e. son temps,** to have no idea what to do with one's time; **elle ne sait pas e. son argent,** she doesn't know how to spend *or* use her money; **e. son temps à nettoyer/étudier,** to spend one's time cleaning/studying; **vêtement qui emploie trois mètres d'étoffe,** garment that requires *or* uses three metres of material; **machine à écrire qui emploie de grands formats,** typewriter that takes large sizes;

(b) e. une somme en recette, to put *or* enter an amount in the receipts;

(c) (*faire travailler*) to employ (*workman, staff etc*); **e. qn comme secrétaire,** to employ s.o. as secretary; **e. qn à des corvées/des petits travaux,** to employ s.o. to do the chores/odd jobs.

2 s'employer *vpr* **(a) s'e. à faire qch,** to occupy oneself *or* spend one's time (in) doing sth;

(b) (*être utilisé*) to be used; **mot qui s'emploie au figuré,** word that is used in the figurative sense;

(c) *Vieilli* **s.'e. pour qn,** to exert oneself on s.o.'s behalf.

employeur, -euse [ɑ̃plwajœr, -øz] *n* employer.

emplumé [ɑ̃plyme] *adj* feathered.

empocher [ɑ̃pɔʃe] *vt* **(a)** (*toucher*) to pocket, to receive (*money, cheque etc*); **(b)** (*mettre dans sa poche*) to pocket; **(c)** *Fig* to swallow, to put up with (*an insult*).

empoignade [ɑ̃pwaɲad] *nf F* quarrel, row, set-to.

empoigne [ɑ̃pwaɲ] *nf F* **acheter qch à la foire d'e.,** to get sth dishonestly; **la vie n'est qu'une foire d'e.,** life's just a rat race *or* a free-for-all.

empoigner [ɑ̃pwaɲe] **1** *vt* **(a)** (*attraper*) to grasp, to seize, to grab (hold of) (*sth*); to seize, to grab (hold of), *F* to collar (*s.o.*); **(b)** to thrill, to grip, to take hold of (*reader, spectator etc*). **2 s'empoigner** *vpr* **ils se sont empoignés,** they quarrelled *or* had a set-to.

empois [ɑ̃pwa] *nm* (laundry) starch; *Tex* dressing.

empoisonnant [ɑ̃pwazɔnɑ̃] *adj F* (*irritant*) annoying, irritating; (*ennuyant*) boring.

empoisonnement [ɑ̃pwazɔnmɑ̃] *nm* **(a)** (*intoxication*) poisoning (*of s.o., food*); *Fig* **l'e. de la jeunesse par la drogue/les mauvaises lectures,** the poisoning of young people's lives by drugs/undesirable reading material; **(b)** *F* **quel e.!,** what a nuisance!, what a pest!

empoisonner [ɑ̃pwazɔne] **1** *vt* **(a)** (*intoxiquer*) to poison (*s.o., food*); **odeur qui empoisonne l'air,** smell that infects the air; *Fig* **e. la vie de qn,** to embitter *or* poison s.o.'s life; **(b)** *F* (*irriter*) to annoy, to irritate (*s.o.*); (*ennuyer*) to bore (*s.o.*). **2** *vi* (*of plant*) to be poisonous. **3 s'empoisonner** *vpr* **(a)** (*se tuer*) to poison oneself; *Fig* **s'e. l'existence,** to poison one's life; **(b)** (*s'ennuyer*) to get bored.

empoisonneur, -euse [ɑ̃pwazɔnœr, -øz] *n* **(a)** (*criminel*) poisoner; **(b)** *F* (*personne qui ennuie*) bore; (*personne qui irrite*) nuisance, pest.

empoissonner [ɑ̃pwasɔne] *vt* to stock (*pond etc*) with fish.

emporté, -ée [ɑ̃pɔrte] **1** *adj* irascible, quick-tempered, hot-headed (*person*). **2** *n* hot-head.

emportement [ɑ̃pɔrtəmɑ̃] *nm* **(a)** *Litt* (*élan*) burst, surge (*of enthusiasm, excitement etc*); **dans l'e. de la discussion,** in the heat of debate; **(b)** (*colère*) (fit of) anger; **répondre avec e.,** to reply angrily.

emporte-pièce [ɑ̃pɔrtəpjɛs] *nm inv Tech* punch; *Culin* pastry cutter; **découper qch à l'e.-p.,** to stamp sth out; *Fig* **style à l'e.-p.,** clear *or* incisive style; **mots à l'e.-p.,** biting *or* cutting words; **répondre à l'e.-p.,** to reply incisively *or* trenchantly.

emporter [ɑ̃pɔrte] **1** *vt* **(a)** (*partir et prendre avec soi*) to take (with one); (*enlever d'un lieu*) to take away (*object, prisoner etc*); **e. un blessé sur un brancard,** to carry off *or* take away a wounded man on a stretcher; **ils ont emporté de quoi manger,** they took some food with them; **plats à e.,** take-away food; *F* **il ne l'emportera pas au paradis,** I'll get my own back on him sooner or later; **(que) le diable l'emporte!,** to hell with him!;

(b) (*arracher*) to carry *or* sweep (*s.o., sth*) away; **le choléra l'emporta,** cholera carried him off; **le vent emporta son chapeau,** the wind blew off his hat; *F* **autant en emporte le vent,** it's all idle talk; *F* **cette moutarde vous emporte la bouche,** this mustard takes the roof off your mouth;

(c) (*conquérir*) to take (*fort etc*) (by assault); **e. la victoire/la journée,** to carry off *or* win the victory/to win *or* carry the day;

(d) (*of tool*) to cut out, to stamp out, to punch out (*piece*); *F* **e. le morceau,** to carry it off, to win out;

(e) (*emmener*) to carry *or* take away; **le train qui m'emporte vers le nord,** the train which is carrying *or* taking me northwards; *Fig* **se laisser e. par la colère,** to give way to *or* let oneself be carried away by anger;

(f) l'e. sur qn/qch, to get the better of s.o./sth; **l'équipe nantaise l'emporte par deux buts à zéro,** the Nantes team is winning *or* leading by two goals to nil; **le coureur hollandais l'emporte haut la main,** the Dutch runner is winning hands down; **considérations qui l'emportent sur toutes les autres,** considerations that override all others.

2 s'emporter *vpr* **(a)** to lose one's temper, to fly into a rage (**contre qn,** with s.o.);

(b) (*of horse*) to bolt.

empoté, -ée [ɑ̃pɔte] *F* **1** *adj* oafish, awkward, clumsy (*person*). **2** *n* (clumsy) oaf.

empoter [ɑ̃pɔte] *vt* to pot (*plants*).

empourprer [ɑ̃purpre] **1** *vt* to tinge (*sky etc*) with crimson. **2 s'empourprer** *vpr* (*of face*) to flush; (*of sky etc*) to turn crimson.

empoussiéré [ɑ̃pusjere] *adj* covered with dust, dusty.

empreindre [ɑ̃prɛ̃dr] *v* (*prp* **empreignant**; *pp* **empreint**; *pr ind* **j'empreins, il empreint, n. empreignons, ils empreignent**; *impf* **j'empreignais**; *p hist* **j'empreignis**; *fu* **j'empreindrai**) **1** *vt* to impress, to imprint, to stamp (*sth on wax, on the mind etc*); **visage empreint de mélancolie/de terreur,** face marked *or* stamped with sadness/full of terror. **2 s'empreindre** *vpr* (*of face, expression etc*) to be marked *or* stamped (**de,** with); **la jeunesse s'empreint de la mentalité de ses aînés,** young people are marked by *or* bear the stamp of their elders' mentality.

empreinte [ɑ̃prɛ̃t] *nf* **(a)** (*impression*) impression, (im)print; **e. en plâtre,** plaster cast; **e. des roues,** tyre tracks; **e. de pas,** footprint; **e. de doigt,** fingermark; **e. digitale,** fingerprint; **e. du génie,** stamp *or* mark of genius; **l'e. du passé/de l'éducation/***etc*, the mark *or* stamp of the past/of education/*etc*; **prendre l'e. de qch,** to take an impression of sth; **(b)** *Typ* mould, *US* mold (*from standing type*); **e. pour prothèse (dentaire),** denture impression.

empressé, -ée [ɑ̃prese] **1** *adj* eager, willing (*assistant etc*); attentive (*servant, doctor, admirer etc*), **des soins empressés,** assiduous attentions; **agréez mes salutations empressées,** (*dans une lettre*) yours faithfully; **il est e. à vous revoir,** he is eager to see you again. **2** *n Péj* **faire l'e. auprès de qn,** to dance attendance on s.o..

empressement [ɑ̃presmɑ̃] *nm* eagerness, willingness (*of assistant etc*) (**à faire qch,** to do sth); attentiveness (*of* *servant, doctor, admirer etc*); **faire qch avec e.,** to do sth readily *or* with alacrity; **mettre beaucoup d'e. à faire qch,** to show great eagerness in doing sth; **témoigner de l'e. auprès de qn,** to pay marked attention(s) to s.o..

empresser (s') [sɑ̃prese] *vpr* **(a)** (*se dépêcher*) to hurry; **s'e. de faire qch,** to hurry to do sth; **il s'empressa de répondre à ma lettre,** he lost no time in answering my letter; **(b) s'e. à faire qch,** to show eagerness *or* zeal in doing sth; **(c) s'e. auprès de qn,** to pay marked attention(s) to s.o.; **s'e. autour d'un accidenté de la route,** to rush to the assistance of the victim of a road accident.

emprise [ɑ̃priz] *nf* **(a)** *Jur* expropriation, acquisition (*of land etc for public purposes*); **(b)** (*domination*) ascendancy, hold; **avoir de l'e. sur qn,** to have ascendancy *or* a hold over s.o.; **sous l'e. de,** under the influence of.

emprisonnement [ɑ̃prizɔnmɑ̃] *nm* imprisonment; **e. cellulaire,** solitary confinement; **e. à perpétuité,** life imprisonment.

emprisonner [ɑ̃prizɔne] **1** *vt* **(a)** (*mettre en prison*) to imprison, to put (*s.o.*) in prison; **(b)** *Fig* (*enfermer*) to shut up; **col qui emprisonne le cou,** collar that is too tight. **2 s'emprisonner** *vpr* (*s'enfermer*) to shut oneself up.

emprunt [ɑ̃prœ̃] *nm* **(a)** (*action*) borrowing; **faire un e. à qn,** to borrow (money) from s.o.; **faire l'e. de qch,** to borrow sth; **offrir qch à qn à titre d'e.,** to offer sth to s.o. as a loan *or* on loan; **ce n'est pas à moi, c'est un e.,** it's not mine, it's borrowed; **nom d'e.,** assumed name; **route d'e.,** alternative road; **(b)** (*somme*) loan; **e. public,** public loan; **e. à court/long terme,** short-/long-term loan; **e. d'État,** government loan; **procéder à un nouvel e.,** to make a new loan issue; **(c)** *Ling* borrowing (**à l'anglais/***etc*, **from English/***etc*).

emprunté [ɑ̃prœ̃te] *adj* self-conscious, stiff, awkward (*manner, tone etc*).

emprunter [ɑ̃prœ̃te] *vt* to borrow (**à,** from); **e. un nom,** to assume a name; **le cortège emprunta la rue de Rivoli,** the procession took *or* went down the Rue de Rivoli.

emprunteur, -euse [ɑ̃prœ̃tœr, -øz] *n* borrower.

empuantir [ɑ̃pɥɑ̃tir] *vt* to infect (*the air*); to make (*place*) stink.

ému [emy] *adj* (*affecté*) moved, touched; (*inquiet*) upset; (*passionné, indigné*) roused; (*heureux*) excited; **voix émue,** voice filled with emotion; **se sentir un peu é.,** to feel a bit nervous; **garder un souvenir é. de qch,** to retain a touching memory of sth.

émulation [emylɑsjɔ̃] *nf* (*imitation*) emulation; (*concurrence*) competition, rivalry; *Ordinat* emulation.

émule [emyl] *n* (*imitateur*) emulator; (*concurrent*) rival.

émuler [emyle] *vt Ordinat* to emulate.

émulseur [emylsœr] *nm* (*appareil*) emulsifier.

émulsif, -ive [emylsif, -iv] *adj Pharm* emulsive; *Ch* emulsifying.

émulsifiable [emylsifjabl] *adj Ch* emulsifiable.

émulsifier [emylsifje] *vt* to emulsify.

émulsion [emylsjɔ̃] *nf* emulsion.

émulsionner [emylsjɔne] *vt* to emulsify.

en¹ [ɑ̃] *prép* **(a)** (*lieu*) in; (*vers*) to; (*sur*) on; **être/aller en ville,** to be in/to go (in)to town; **en province,** in the country, in the provinces; **il est parti en mer,** he's gone to sea; **venir en taxi/avion,** to come by taxi/by plane *or* air; **en tête/queue,** at the head/in the rear; **la suite en quatrième page,** continued on page four; **professeur en Sorbonne,** professor at the Sorbonne; **aller en France/Amérique,** to go to France/America; **être en Avignon/Arles,** to be in Avignon/Arles; **être en Saône-et-Loire,** to be in Saône-et-Loire; **en votre honneur,** in your honour; **regarder en l'air,** to look up at the sky; **s'épuiser en d'inutiles efforts,** to exhaust oneself in useless efforts; **le mariage aura lieu en l'église Saint-Jean,** the marriage will be celebrated *or* held at St. John's (Church);

(b) (*avec pron pers*) **il y a quelque chose en lui que j'admire,** there is something I admire about him; **un homme en qui** *ou* **en lequel j'ai confiance,** a man whom I trust; **ils créent le bonheur en eux,** they create happiness within themselves; **un sentiment qui existe en soi,** a feeling that exists in one;

(c) (*temps*) in; **en été/automne/hiver,** in (the) summer/autumn/winter; **né en 1905,** born in 1905; **en avril,** in April; **aujourd'hui en huit,** a week today, today week; **on peut y aller en cinq heures,** one can get there in five hours; **en l'an 1800,** in (the year) 1800; **en ce temps-là,** in those days, at that time;

(d) (*état*) in; **être en deuil/en loques/en tenue de sport,** to be in mourning/in rags/in sports clothes; **en l'absence du chef,** in the absence of the boss; **en présence de mon avocat,** in the presence of my lawyer; **arbres en fleur,** trees in blossom *or* flower; **être en guerre,** to be at war; **en vacances,** on holiday; **peindre qch en bleu,** to paint sth blue;

(e) (*composition*) made of; **montre en or,** gold watch; **c'est en or,** it's made of gold; **table en marbre,** marble table; **évier en inox,** stainless-steel sink; **pull en laine,** woollen sweater;

(f) (*manière*) **escalier en spirale,** spiral staircase; **chemin en pente,** sloping road; **faire cent à l'heure en palier,** to do 100 an hour on the level; **docteur en médecine,** doctor of medicine; **peintre en bâtiment,** house painter; **fort/faible en mathématiques,** good/bad at mathematics; **parler en français/anglais,** to speak in French/English;

(g) (*changement, division*) into; **changé en serpent,** changed into a serpent; **traduire une lettre en français,** to translate a letter into French; **briser qch en morceaux,** to break sth (in)to bits; **casser qch en deux,** to break sth in two; **pièce en trois actes,** play in three acts; **de mal en pis,** from bad to worse; **d'année en année,** from year to year, year by year;

(h) vendre en mètres/paquets/feuilles, to sell in metres/packets/sheets;

(i) (*comme*) **envoyer qch en cadeau,** to send sth as a present; **donner qch à qn en compensation,** to give s.o. sth by way of *or* as a compensation; **il mourut en brave,** he died a brave man *or* like the brave man that he was; **agir en honnête homme,** to act like an honest man; **prendre la chose en philosophe,** to take the thing philosophically;

(j) (*avec gérondif*) **il marchait en lisant son journal,** he walked along reading his paper; **il répondit en riant,** he answered with a laugh; **elle entra/sortit en dansant,** she danced into/out of the room; **on apprend en vieillissant,** we learn as we grow older; **en faisant cela vous l'offenserez,** by doing that you will offend him; **en arrivant à Paris,** on arriving in Paris; **en vous écrivant hier j'ai oublié de vous le dire,** when writing to you yesterday, I forgot to mention it; **en attendant,** while waiting, in the meantime; **tout en tricotant elle nous racontait des histoires,** as she knitted she told us stories; **s'enrhumer en marchant sous la pluie,** to catch a cold (through *or* from) walking in the rain.

en² *pron* **(a)** (*de cet endroit*) from there; **il en revient,** he's just come back from there; **où en étions-nous?,** (*livre, travail etc*) where were we?;

(b) (*de ce fait*) **si vous étiez riche, en seriez-vous plus heureux?,** if you were rich, would you be happier for it *or* any the happier?; **je n'en dors plus la nuit,** it keeps me awake at night, I can't sleep at night for thinking about it; **j'en ris encore,** I still laugh about it; **en tirer une conclusion,** to draw a conclusion from it;

(c) (*standing for a noun governed by* **de**) **j'aime mieux n'en pas parler** *ou* **ne pas en parler,** I would rather not speak about it; **combien en veut-il?,** how much does he want for it?; **qu'en pensez-vous?,** what do you think of *or* about it?; **les rues en sont pleines,** the streets are full of it *or* them; **il reçut une blessure et en mourut,** he received a wound and died of *or* from it; **il en devint amoureux,** he fell in love with her; **il faut en faire un film!,** they should make a film of it *or* turn it into a film!; **que vais-je en faire, de cette table?,** what am I going to do with this table?;

(d) (*of things, replacing the possessive*) **j'ai la valise mais je n'en ai pas la clef,** I have the suitcase but I haven't (got) the key (for it); **prends la boîte mais n'en perds pas le couvercle,** take the box, but don't lose the lid (to it);

(e) (*standing for a clause*) **il ne l'a pas fait, mais il en est capable,** he did not do it but he is (quite) capable of it;

(f) (*nombre, quantité*) **j'en ai un/trois/plusieurs,** I have one/three/several; **combien en voulez-vous?,** (*quantité*) how much do you want?; (*nombre*) how many do you want?; *F* **il en sait bien d'autres,** he knows lots of others, he has more where that came from; **elle en a déjà vu beaucoup pour son âge,** she has already seen a lot for her age; **j'en ai,** I have some; **je n'en ai pas,** I have none, I haven't any; **en avez-vous?,** have you any?; **parmi ses livres il y en a d'excellents,** among his books are some excellent ones;

(g) (*locutions*) **je n'en ai pas encore fini avec lui,** I haven't done *or* finished with him yet; **si le cœur vous en dit,** if you feel so inclined, if you feel like it; **en venir aux mains,** to come to blows; **j'en suis réduit là,** I've been reduced to that; **ne t'en fais pas!,** don't worry!; **il en va de même pour toi,** it's the same for you; **il en est ainsi,**

that's the way it is;
(h) *(after imperative)* **prenez-en,** take some; **prenez-en dix,** take ten (of them); **va-t'en,** go away.
EN [ən] *nf abrév* **École normale.**
ENA [ena] *nf abrév* **École nationale d'administration.**
enamouré [ɑ̃namure] *adj* amorous *(glance, smile etc)*; **être e. de qn,** to be enamoured of *or* in love with s.o..
enamourer (s') [sɑ̃namure] *vpr* to become enamoured **(de,** of), to fall in love **(de,** with).
énarque [enark] *n* = former student of the École nationale d'administration.
en-arrière [ɑ̃narjɛr] *nm inv (au patinage)* backward glide.
énarthrose [enartroz] *nf Anat* enarthrosis, ball-and-socket joint.
en-avant [ɑ̃navɑ̃] *nm inv* **(a)** *Fb* forward pass; *Rugby* knock-on; **(b)** *(au patinage)* forward glide.
en-but [ɑ̃by] *nm inv Rugby* in-goal.
encabaner (s') [sɑ̃kabane] *vpr Can* to shut oneself up *or* away.
encablure [ɑ̃kablyr] *nf Arch & Hum (mesure)* cable (length) *(approx 200 m)*.
encadré [ɑ̃kadre] *nm (dans un texte)* box.
encadrement [ɑ̃kadrəmɑ̃] *nm* **(a)** *(action)* framing *(of picture etc)*; **(b)** *Mil* officering *(of unit)*; *Admin Ind* management, supervision *(of staff etc)*; **(c)** *(cadre)* frame *(of picture, window etc)*; **dans l'e. de la porte,** in the doorway; **(d)** *(milieu)* setting *(of story etc)*; **(e)** *Mil* bracketing, straddling *(of target)*; **(f)** *(ceux qui encadrent) Mil* officers; *Admin Ind* management, managers.
encadrer [ɑ̃kadre] **1** *vt* **(a)** to frame *(picture etc)*; **jardin encadré de haies,** garden enclosed by hedges; *F* **il a encadré un arbre,** he wrapped his car round a tree; **(b) prévenu encadré par deux gendarmes,** *(accompagné)* accused man flanked by two policemen; **(c)** *Mil* to bracket, to straddle *(target)*; **(d)** *Mil* to officer *(unit)*; *Admin Ind* to manage, to supervise *(staff etc)*; **(e)** *F* **je ne peux pas l'e.,** I can't stand *or* abide him. **2 s'encadrer** *vpr* **s'e. dans la porte/fenêtre/***etc*, to be framed in the doorway/window/*etc*.
encadreur [ɑ̃kadrœr] *nm* picture framer.
encagement [ɑ̃kaʒmɑ̃] *nm* caging *(of bird etc)*.
encager [ɑ̃kaʒe] *vt* **(j'encageai(s); n. encageons)** to cage *(bird etc)*; **tenir qn encagé,** to keep s.o. caged up.
encagoulé [ɑ̃kagule] *adj* hooded *(robber etc)*.
encaissable [ɑ̃kɛsabl] *adj* cashable, *Br* encashable.
encaisse [ɑ̃kɛs] *nf Com* cash (in hand); **e. de 1 000 francs,** cash balance of 1,000 francs; **e. or et argent, e. métallique d'un pays,** gold and silver holding of a country; *Banque* **pas d'e.,** no funds.
encaissé [ɑ̃kɛse] *adj* deep *(valley)*, deeply embanked *(river)*; sunken, deep-cut *(road)*; **tournant e.,** blind corner.
encaissement [ɑ̃kɛsmɑ̃] *nm* **(a)** cashing, *Br* encashment *(of cheque)*; receipt, collection *(of money)*; collection *(of bill)*; **donner un chèque à l'e.,** to cash a cheque; **(b)** depth *(of valley)*; deep embankment *(of river)*; **dans l'e. de la route,** in the deep cutting made by the road.
encaisser [ɑ̃kese] **1** *vt* **(a)** to cash, *Br* to encash *(cheque)*; to receive, to collect *(money)*; to collect *(bill)*; **(b)** *F* **e. un coup,** *(of boxer etc)* to take a blow; **(c)** *F (supporter)* **je ne peux pas l'e.,** I can't stand him; **(d)** *(reserrer) (collines etc)* to hem in; *Tech* to embank *(river etc)*. **2 s'encaisser** *vpr (of river, road etc)* to be hemmed in. **3** *vi F* **il sait e.,** he can take punishment *or F* take it; **e. sans broncher,** to grin and bear it.
encaisseur [ɑ̃kɛsœr] *nm* collector *(of rent, debts etc)*.
encan [ɑ̃kɑ̃] *nm* **vendre qch à l'e.,** to sell sth by *or* at auction; **mettre qch à l'e.,** to put sth up for auction; *Fig* **la loi semble mettre la justice à l'e.,** the law seems to put a low price on justice.
encanailler (s') [sɑ̃kanaje] *vpr Hum* to get into *or* keep bad company.
encapuchonner [ɑ̃kapyʃɔne] **1** *vt* to put a hood on *(s.o., s.o.'s head)*; to hood, to cover *(machine etc)*; **moine/***etc* **encapuchonné,** hooded monk/*etc*. **2 s'encapuchonner** *vpr* to put on a *or* one's hood.
encart [ɑ̃kar] *nm* **(a)** *(attaché)* inset; **(b)** *(brochure etc)* (loose) insert.
encarter [ɑ̃karte] *vt* **(a)** to inset *(pages)*; **(b)** to insert *(leaflet in book)*; **(c)** to card *(pins, buttons etc)*.
encarteuse [ɑ̃kartøz] *nf* carding machine *(for pins, buttons etc)*.
en-cas [ɑ̃kɑ] *nm inv* snack (meal).
encastrable [ɑ̃kastrabl] *adj* that can be built in *or* fitted *(washing machine, cooker etc)*.
encastré [ɑ̃kastre] *adj* built-in, fitted *(washing machine, cooker etc)*; flush-fitting, set-in *(switch etc)*.
encastrement [ɑ̃kastrəmɑ̃] *nm* **(a)** *(action)* fitting, building in *(of washing machine, cooker etc)*; flush-fitting, setting in *(of switch etc)*; **(b)** *(espace prévu)* recess, housing; **(c)** *(boîtier)* frame, casing.
encastrer [ɑ̃kastre] **1** *vt* to build in, to fit *(washing machine, cooker etc)*; to flush fit, to set in *(switch etc)*; **e. dans,** to build *or* fit into; to set into. **2 s'encastrer** *vpr (of element etc)* to fit together; **s.e. dans, to fit into.**
encaustiquage [ɑ̃kɔ(o)stikaʒ] *nm* waxing, wax-polishing *(of floor, furniture etc)*.
encaustique [ɑ̃kɔ(o)stik] *nf* **(a)** *Beaux-Arts* encaustic (painting); **(b)** *(pour les meubles)* wax, polish.
encaustiquer [ɑ̃kɔ(o)stike] *vt* to wax, to polish *(floor, furniture etc)*.
encavement [ɑ̃kavmɑ̃] *nm* cellaring *(of wine)*.
encaver [ɑ̃kave] *vt* to cellar *(wine etc)*.
enceindre [ɑ̃sɛ̃dr] *vt (conj like* **ceindre)** to surround, to encompass **(de,** with).
enceinte¹ [ɑ̃sɛ̃t] *nf* **(a)** *(mur)* (surrounding) wall; *(palissade)* fence; **(b) parc qui a dix kilomètres d'e.,** park ten kilometres in circumference; **(c)** *(espace)* enclosure; *(d'église, de couvent etc)* precinct(s); *Courses de chevaux* ring; **dans l'e. du parc/***etc*, within *or* inside (the confines of) the park/*etc*; **(d) e. (acoustique),** loudspeaker.
enceinte² *adj* pregnant, *F* expecting, *Litt* with child; **femme e.,** pregnant woman, expectant mother; **e. de cinq mois,** five months pregnant.
encens [ɑ̃sɑ̃] *nm* incense; **e. mâle,** frankincense.
encensement [ɑ̃sɑ̃smɑ̃] *nm Rel* censing *(of the altar etc)*.
encenser [ɑ̃sɑ̃se] **1** *vt* **(a)** to cense *(altar etc)*; **(b)** to burn incense to *or* before *(idol)*; *Fig Péj* **e. qn,** to shower fulsome praise *or* flattery on s.o.. **2** *vi (of horse)* to toss its head up and down.
encenseur, -euse [ɑ̃sɑ̃sœr, -øz] *n* **(a)** *Rel* thurifer, censer bearer; **(b)** *Fig Péj* flatterer, sycophant.
encensoir [ɑ̃sɑ̃swar] *nm Rel* censer; *Fig Péj* **donner des coups d'e.,** to heap on the praise.
encéphale [ɑ̃sefal] *nm Anat* encephalon.
encéphalite [ɑ̃sefalit] *nf Méd* encephalitis; **e. léthargique,** sleeping sickness; *Vét* **e. bovine spongiforme,** bovine spongiform encephalopathy, BSE.
encéphalogramme [ɑ̃sefalɔgram] *nm Méd* (electro)encephalogram.
encéphalographie [ɑ̃sefalɔgrafi] *nf Méd* (electro)encephalography.
encéphalomyélite [ɑ̃sefalɔmjelit] *nf Méd* encephalomyelitis.
encéphalopathie [ɑ̃sefalɔpati] *nf* encephalopathy.
encerclement [ɑ̃sɛrkləmɑ̃] *nm* encircling, surrounding.
encercler [ɑ̃sɛrkle] *vt* to encircle, to surround *(enemy, demonstrators etc)*; to circle, to ring *(word etc)*.
enchaîné [ɑ̃ʃene] *nm Cin* dissolve, mix.
enchaînement [ɑ̃ʃɛnmɑ̃] *nm* **(a)** *(série)* chain, series, train *(of ideas, events etc)*; **(b)** *(liaison)* connection *(of ideas etc)*; **(c)** *Cin* mix, dissolve.
enchaîner [ɑ̃ʃene] **1** *vt* **(a)** to chain up *(dog etc)*; to put in chains, to chain up *(prisoner)*; *Fig* to curb, to tame *(the press)*; to curb *(passions)*; to rivet *(the attention)*; **(b)** *(lier)* to link (up), to connect *(ideas, facts, words etc)*; **e. à un poteau,** to chain (up) to a post; **e. la conversation,** to resume the conversation; *Cin* **fondu enchaîné,** mix, dissolve. **2 s'enchaîner** *vpr (of facts, episodes etc)* to be linked together; **on voit comme les choses s'enchaînent,** one can see how things hang *or* are linked together. **3** *vi* **(a)** *(reprendre la suite)* to go on, to carry on; **(b)** *Cin* to fade in *(to next scene)*.
enchanté [ɑ̃ʃɑ̃te] *adj* **(a)** *(magique etc)* enchanted *(person, object, place)*; **la Flûte enchantée,** the Magic Flute; **(b)** *(ravi)* enchanted, delighted; **être e. de qch,** to be enchanted by *or* delighted with sth; **e. (de faire votre connaissance),** pleased to meet you, how do you do?
enchantement [ɑ̃ʃɑ̃tmɑ̃] *nm* **(a)** *(magie)* enchantment, magic; *(effet)* (magic) spell; **comme par e.,** as if by magic; **(b)** *(ravissement)* enchantment, delight; *(merveille)* delight; **être dans l'e.,** to be enchanted *or* delighted **(de,** by).
enchanter [ɑ̃ʃɑ̃te] *vt* **(a)** *(ensorceler)* to enchant, to bewitch, to lay *(s.o., sth)* under a spell; **(b)** *(ravir, plaire)* to enchant, to delight; **cette idée ne l'enchante pas,** he is not taken with the idea.
enchanteur, -eresse [ɑ̃ʃɑ̃tœr, -rɛs] **1** *nm* **(a)** *(sorcier)* enchanter; **(b)** *Fig (charmeur)* charmer. **2** *nf* **enchanteresse,** enchantress. **3** *adj* bewitching, captivating *(smile)*; enchanting, delightful, charming *(speech, place etc)*.

enchâssement [ɑ̃ʃɑsmɑ̃] *nm* (*action*) setting, mounting (*of jewel*).

enchâsser [ɑ̃ʃɑse] **1** *vt* **(a)** *Rel* to enshrine (*relic*); **(b)** to set, to mount (*jewel*); **(c)** *Tech* to house (*axle*); **(d)** *Fig* to insert (**dans un texte**, in a text). **2 s'enchâsser** *vpr* to fit perfectly (**dans**, into).

enchâssure [ɑ̃ʃɑsyr] *nf* (*support*) setting, mount (*of jewel*); housing (*for axle*).

enchatonner [ɑ̃ʃatɔne] *vt* to set, to mount (*jewel in a bezel*).

enchausser [ɑ̃ʃose] *vt* to earth up; (*avec de la paille*) to straw up (*vegetables etc*).

enchère [ɑ̃ʃɛr] *nf* bid; **les enchères, l'e.**, the bidding; **faire** *ou* **porter une e.**, to make a bid; **vente aux enchères,** (sale by) auction; **couvrir une é.**, to make a higher bid, to bid higher; **pousser les enchères,** to raise the bidding; **vendre/acheter qch aux enchères,** to sell/buy sth at auction; **mettre qch aux enchères,** to put sth up for auction, to auction sth; **e. au rabais,** Dutch auction; *Cartes* **bridge aux enchères,** auction bridge.

enchérir [ɑ̃ʃerir] *vi* **(a)** (*dépasser*) to make a higher bid; **e. de dix francs,** to bid another ten francs; **e. sur qn,** to outbid s.o.; *Fig* to go one better than s.o.; **e. sur les idées de qn,** to improve on s.o.'s ideas; **(b)** *Vieilli* (*devenir plus cher*) to rise *or* go up in price.

enchérissement [ɑ̃ʃerismɑ̃] *nm Vieilli* rise, increase (*in price*).

enchérisseur, -euse [ɑ̃ʃerisœr, -øz] *n* bidder; **au dernier** *ou* **au plus offrant e.**, to the highest bidder.

enchevaucher [ɑ̃ʃ(ə)voʃe] *vt* to fix *or* lay (*tiles etc*) with an overlap.

enchevauchure [ɑ̃ʃ(ə)voʃyr] *nf* overlapping (*of tiles etc*).

enchevêtré [ɑ̃ʃ(ə)vetre] *adj* tangled (*skein*); confused, involved (*style*).

enchevêtrement [ɑ̃ʃ(ə)vɛtrəmɑ̃] *nm* **(a)** (*action*) tangling (up) (*of string, branches etc*); muddling (up), mixing up (*of objects, words, events etc*); confusing, muddling (*of situation*); **(b)** (*état*) tangle (*of string, branches*); confusion, muddle (*of objects etc*).

enchevêtrer [ɑ̃ʃ(ə)vetre] **1** *vt* to tangle (up) (*string, branches etc*); to muddle (up), to mix up (*objects, words, events etc*); to confuse, to muddle (*situation*). **2 s'enchevêtrer** *vpr* (*of string etc*) to get tangled *or* in a tangle; (*of objects etc*) to get muddled (up) *or* mixed up; (*of situation*) to get confused *or* muddled.

enchifrené [ɑ̃ʃifrəne] *adj* **il est e.**, his nose is blocked (with a cold).

enclave [ɑ̃klav] *nf* (*terrain*) *& Fig* enclave; **l'escalier fait e. dans la pièce,** the staircase leads directly from *or* into the room.

enclaver [ɑ̃klave] *vt* **(a)** to wedge in, to fit in (*timbers etc*); **(b)** to enclose, to make an enclave of (*territory*); **domaine qui enclave deux petites terres,** estate which encloses two small properties.

enclenchement [ɑ̃klɑ̃ʃmɑ̃] *nm Tech* engaging (*of gear, mechanism etc*); interlocking (*of parts*).

enclencher [ɑ̃klɑ̃ʃe] **1** *vt* to engage (*gear, mechanism etc*); to interlock (*parts*); *Fig* to set (*enterprise etc*) in motion. **2 s'enclencher** *vpr* (*of gear, mechanism etc*) to engage; (*of parts*) to interlock; *Fig* **s'e. bien/mal,** to get off to a good/bad start.

enclin [ɑ̃klɛ̃] *adj* inclined, disposed (**à qch**, to sth; **à faire qch**, to do sth); **e. aux accidents,** accident-prone.

encliquetage [ɑ̃kliktaʒ] *nm* (pawl-and-)ratchet mechanism; **doigt d'e.**, pawl.

encliqueter [ɑ̃klikte] *vt* (**j'encliquette**; **j'encliquetterai**) to cog, to ratchet (*wheel*); **roue encliquetée,** ratchet wheel, cog wheel.

enclitique [ɑ̃klitik] *nm Ling* enclitic.

enclore [ɑ̃klɔr] *vt* (*conj like* **clore**) to enclose; (*d'une palissade*) to fence in; (*d'un mur*) to wall in.

enclos [ɑ̃klo] *nm* **(a)** (*espace*) enclosure; (*pour chevaux*) paddock; **(b)** (*clôture*) enclosure; (*mur*) (enclosing) wall.

enclouage [ɑ̃kluaʒ] *nm* **(a)** *Arch* spiking (*of gun*); **(b)** *Chir* pinning (*of bone*).

enclouer [ɑ̃klue] *vt* **(a)** to prick (*horse*) (*in shoeing*); **(b)** *Arch* to spike (*gun*); **(c)** *Chir* to pin (*bone*).

enclume [ɑ̃klym] *nf* **(a)** anvil; **e. de cordonnier,** (shoemender's) last; *Fig* **être entre l'e. et le marteau,** to be between the devil and the deep (blue) sea; **(b)** *Anat* incus, anvil (*of inner ear*).

encoche [ɑ̃kɔʃ] *nf* notch, nick (*in stick etc*); nock (*of arrow*); notch (*for thumb index*); **livre avec encoches,** book with thumb index, thumb-indexed book; *El* **armature à encoches,** slotted armature.

encochement [ɑ̃kɔʃmɑ̃] *nm* notching, nicking.

encocher [ɑ̃kɔʃe] *vt* **(a)** to notch, to nick (*stick etc*); to thumb-index (*book*); **(b)** to nock (*arrow on bowstring*).

encodage [ɑ̃kɔdaʒ] *nm Ling Ordinat* encoding.

encoder [ɑ̃kɔde] *vt Ling Ordinat* to encode.

encodeur [ɑ̃kɔdœr] *nm Ordinat* encoder.

encoignure [ɑ̃kwaɲyr] *nf* **(a)** corner, angle (*of room, street*); **(b)** (*petit meuble*) corner cupboard.

encollage [ɑ̃kɔlaʒ] *nm* **(a)** (*action*) (*de colle*) pasting (*of paper*); (*d'apprêt*) sizing (*of paper, fabric, plaster etc*); **(b)** (*colle*) paste; (*apprêt*) size.

encoller [ɑ̃kɔle] *vt* (*de colle*) to paste (*paper*); to apply glue to (*wood etc*); (*d'apprêt*) to size (*paper, fabric, plaster etc*).

encolure [ɑ̃kɔlyr] *nf* **(a)** neck (*of camel, ostrich etc*); *Courses de chevaux* **gagner d'une** *ou* **par une e.**, to win by a neck; **(b)** *F* **homme de forte e.**, thickset *or* stocky man; **(c)** (*échancrure*) neck (opening) (*of garment*); **e. carrée,** square neck; **(d)** (*tour de cou*) neck size; **(e)** *Nau* crown (*of anchor*).

encombrant [ɑ̃kɔ̃brɑ̃] *adj* cumbersome, bulky (*furniture etc*); **colis encombrants,** bulky packages; *F* **c'est un personnage e.**, he's always in the way; *F* **un témoin e.**, unwanted witness.

encombre [ɑ̃kɔ̃br] *nm* **sans e.**, without mishap, without a hitch.

encombrement [ɑ̃kɔ̃brəmɑ̃] *nm* **(a)** (*état*) congestion (*of traffic etc*); *Aut* traffic jam, hold-up; overcrowding (*of streets, the air space*); **(b)** (*amas*) clutter, litter (*of objects*); **(c)** (*espace, volume*) (overall) dimensions (*of car, furniture etc*); **(d)** *Ordinat* footprint.

encombrer [ɑ̃kɔ̃bre] **1** *vt* to clutter (up) (*room*); to obstruct, to block (*passage, route etc*); to jam, to block (*phone lines*); **e. les rues,** to congest *or* overcrowd the streets; **table encombrée de papiers,** table littered with papers; **sentier encombré de ronces,** path overgrown with brambles; **e. le marché,** to glut *or* saturate the market; **e. une profession,** to overcrowd a profession. **2 s'encombrer** *vpr* **s.'e. de,** to load oneself down with (*parcels, equipment etc*); *Fig* to burden oneself *or* saddle oneself with (*obligations, children etc*).

encontre (à l') [alɑ̃kɔ̃tr] *adv* in opposition; **je n'ai rien à dire à l'e.**, I have nothing to say against it; **à l'e. de,** against, in opposition to, contrary to; **aller à l'e. de la loi,** to run counter to the law; **à l'e. d'elle, il ...,** unlike her, he ... .

encorbellement [ɑ̃kɔrbɛlmɑ̃] *nm Archit* corbelling (*of wall etc*); overhang (*of upper storey*); **fenêtre en e.**, oriel window; **trottoir en e.**, overhanging footway, cantilever footway (*of bridge*).

encorder (s') [sɑ̃kɔrde] *vpr* (*en alpinisme*) to rope up.

encore [ɑ̃kɔr] *adv* **(a)** (*toujours*) still; **je suis e. à chercher une explication,** I am still looking for an explanation; **tu es e. là?,** are you still there?; **je ne suis e. qu'étudiant,** I'm still only a student, I'm only a student as yet;

(b) **pas e.**, not yet; **un homme que je n'avais e. jamais vu,** a man I had never seen before;

(c) (*davantage*) more, again; **e. un mot,** (just) one word more; **en voulez-vous e.?,** would you like some more?; **e. du vin, s'il vous plaît!,** some more wine please!; **e. une tasse de café,** another *or* one more cup of coffee; **e. une histoire à mourir de rire,** another *or* one more hilarious story; **quoi e.?,** what else?; **pendant trois mois e., pendant e. trois mois,** for three months longer *or* more, for another three months; **réduire e. le prix,** to reduce the price still further *or* more; **c'est e. pire,** it's still *or* even worse, it's worse still; **e. une fois,** once more, once again; **voilà la pluie e.!,** here's the rain again!; **nous l'avons e. vu hier,** we saw him again yesterday; **e. autant,** as much again; **e. pis,** still *or* even worse; **e. vous!,** (what) you again?; **e. s'il vous plaît,** would you say that again please?; **comment s'appelle-t-il e.?,** what's his name again?;

(d) (*en plus*) moreover, furthermore; **non seulement stupide, mais e. têtu,** not only stupid, but also pigheaded;

(e) (*restrictive*) **hier e. je lui ai parlé,** I spoke to him only yesterday; **e. s'il était reconnaissant!,** if only he was at least grateful!; **il aura peut-être une chance là-bas, et e.!,** perhaps he'll have a chance over there, but only just *or* but not much of one!; **il vous donnera dix francs et e.!,** he will give you ten francs for it, if that!;

(f) (*with inversion of subject and verb*) **je n'ai qu'un ciseau, e. est-il émoussé,** I have only one chisel and even that is blunt; **e. vous aurait-il fallu me prévenir,** all the same *or* even so you should have let me know;

(g) e. (bien) que + *sub*, (al)though, even though; **e. qu'il ne me soit rien,** (al)though he is nothing to me; **temps agréable e. qu'un peu froid,** pleasant weather even though *or* (even) if rather cold;

(h) il a dit qu'il avait bien aimé — mais e.?, he said he liked it — but what EXACTLY did he say?

encorné [ɑ̃kɔrne] *adj* horned (*animal*).

encorner [ɑ̃kɔrne] *vt* (*of bull*) to gore (*s.o.*).

encornet [ɑ̃kɔrnɛ] *nm* (*mollusque*) squid.

encourageant [ɑ̃kuraʒɑ̃] *adj* encouraging (*person*); encouraging, cheering (*news, result, event etc*).

encouragement [ɑ̃kuraʒmɑ̃] *nm* encouragement; **prime** *ou* **récompense d'e.,** incentive; **e. à la vertu,** incentive to virtue; **recevoir peu d'encouragements à faire qch,** to receive little encouragement *or* little inducement to do sth.

encourager [ɑ̃kuraʒe] *vt* **(j'encourageai(s)) (a)** to encourage (*s.o.*); **e. qn à faire qch,** to encourage s.o. to do sth; **e. qn à bien faire,** to encourage s.o. to do the right thing; **(b)** to encourage, to foster, to promote (*the arts*); to promote (*scheme*); **la presse encourage l'utilisation de certaines drogues,** the press encourages the use of certain drugs; **l'oisiveté encourage les vices,** idleness encourages *or* promotes vice.

encourir [ɑ̃kurir] *vt* (*conj like* **courir**) to incur (*expense*); to bring (*punishment, reproaches*) upon oneself.

en(-)cours [ɑ̃kur] *nm inv Fin* bills outstanding (*and remitted by customer to bank*).

encrage [ɑ̃kraʒ] *nm Typ* inking (up).

encrassement [ɑ̃krasmɑ̃] *nm* dirtying (*of clothes, hands etc*); fouling (*of gun*); fouling, sooting (up) (*of spark plug*); clogging, choking (*of machine etc*).

encrasser [ɑ̃krase] **1** *vt* to dirty (*one's clothes, hands etc*); to foul (*gun*); to soot up (*spark plug*); to clog, to choke (*machine etc*). **2 s'encrasser** *vpr* to get dirty; to foul up; to soot up; to get clogged *or* choked.

encre [ɑ̃kr] *nf* **(a)** ink; **e. de Chine,** Indian ink; **e. d'impression,** printing ink; **e. sympathique,** invisible ink; **écrit à l'e.,** written in ink; **faire couler beaucoup d'e.,** to be much written about; **doigts couverts d'e.,** inky fingers, fingers covered in ink; *Fig* **nuit d'e.,** inky black night; *F* **c'est la bouteille à l'e.,** there's no making head or tail of it; **noir comme de l'e.,** inky black, black as ink; *Psy* **test de la tache d'e.,** inkblot test, Rorschach test; **(b)** *Zool* ink (*of cuttlefish*).

encrer [ɑ̃kre] *vt Typ* to ink (up).

encreur [ɑ̃krœr] *adj* **ruban e.,** (typewriter) ribbon; *Typ* **rouleau e.,** inker.

encrier [ɑ̃krije] *nm* inkpot, inkstand, inkwell; *Typ* ink trough.

encroûtant [ɑ̃krutɑ̃] *adj F* soul-destroying (*occupation etc*).

encroûté [ɑ̃krute] *adj F* (*routinier*) (stuck) in a rut, set in one's ways; **qu'est-ce que tu peux être e.!,** what a stick-in-the-mud you are!; **vieux bonhomme e.,** old fogey *or* stick-in-the-mud.

encroûtement [ɑ̃krutmɑ̃] *nm* **(a)** encrusting, crusting over (*of sth*); **(b)** *F* sinking into a rut; **se sentir menacé d'e.,** to feel as if one is sinking into *or* getting stuck in a rut.

encroûter [ɑ̃krute] **1** *vt* **(a)** to encrust, to crust over (*sth*); **(b)** *F* **ces habitudes ont fini par m'e.,** these habits finally made me set in my ways *or* got me stuck in a rut. **2 s'encroûter** *vpr* **(a)** (*of object*) to become encrusted *or* crusted over (**de,** with); **(b)** *F* (*of person*) to get into a *or* stuck in a rut, to get set in one's ways.

enculé [ɑ̃kyle] *nm Vulg* bugger, sod.

enculer [ɑ̃kyle] *vt Vulg* to bugger (*s.o.*); **va te faire e.!,** bugger off!, sod off!; *Fig* **il passe son temps à e. les mouches,** he's always farting around.

encuver [ɑ̃kyve] *vt* to vat (*hides, grapes*).

encyclique [ɑ̃siklik] *nf Rel* encyclical.

encyclopédie [ɑ̃siklɔpedi] *nf* encyclop(a)edia; *F* **e. vivante,** walking encyclop(a)edia.

encyclopédique [ɑ̃siklɔpedik] *adj* encyclop(a)edic.

encyclopédiste [ɑ̃siklɔpedist] *n* encyclop(a)edist.

endémie [ɑ̃demi] *nf* endemic (disease).

endémique [ɑ̃demik] *adj Méd & Fig* endemic (**à,** to).

endenté [ɑ̃dɑ̃te] *adj* **(a) mâchoires vigoureusement endentées,** jaws with strong rows of teeth; **(b)** indented (*line etc*).

endenter [ɑ̃dɑ̃te] *vt* **(a)** to tooth, to cog, to ratchet (*wheel etc*); **(b)** (*assembler*) to mesh (*wheels*); **(c)** to indent (*line etc*).

endetté [ɑ̃dete] *adj* in debt; **très e.,** deep(ly) *or* heavily in debt.

endettement [ɑ̃dɛtmɑ̃] *nm* **(a)** (*action*) running *or* getting into debt; **(b)** (*état*) debt; **ratio d'é.,** debt ratio.

endetter [ɑ̃dete] **1** *vt* to get (*s.o.*) into debt. **2 s'endetter** *vpr* to run *or* get into debt.

endeuiller [ɑ̃dœje] *vt* to plunge (*family, nation etc*) into mourning; to cast gloom over (*event*); **maison endeuillée,** house in mourning.

endèver [ɑ̃dɛve] *vt & vi Can F* **il m'endève, il me fait e.,** he infuriates me.

endiablé [ɑ̃djable] *adj* **(a)** reckless, devil-may-care (*courage etc*); wild, frenzied (*music, rhythm etc*); **(b)** devilish (*wind etc*).

endiguement [ɑ̃digmɑ̃] *nm* **(a)** (*action*) embanking, dyking (up) (*of river etc*); **(b)** (*digue*) embankment, dyke; **(c)** *Fig* checking.

endiguer [ɑ̃dige] *vt* **(a)** to embank, to dyke (up) (*river etc*); **(b)** *Fig* to check (*crowd, inflation, feelings etc*).

endimanché [ɑ̃dimɑ̃ʃe] *adj* all dressed up, in one's Sunday best.

endimancher (s') [sɑ̃dimɑ̃ʃe] *vpr* to put on one's best clothes *or* one's Sunday best, to get all dressed up.

endive [ɑ̃div] *nf* endive; (*chicorée*) chicory; *F* **pâle comme une e.,** as white *or* pale as a sheet.

endocarde [ɑ̃dɔkard] *nm Anat* endocardium.

endocardite [ɑ̃dɔkardit] *nf Méd* endocarditis.

endocarpe [ɑ̃dɔkarp] *nm Bot* endocarp.

endocrine [ɑ̃dɔkrin] *adj Physiol* endocrine (*gland*).

endocrinien, -ienne [ɑ̃dɔkrinjɛ̃, -jɛn] *adj Physiol* endocrine, endocrinal (*glands etc*).

endocrinologie [ɑ̃dɔkrinɔlɔʒi] *nf* endocrinology.

endoctrinement [ɑ̃dɔktrinmɑ̃] *nm* indoctrination.

endoctriner [ɑ̃dɔktrine] *vt* to indoctrinate, *F* to brainwash.

endoderme [ɑ̃dɔdɛrm] *nm Biol* endoderm.

endogame [ɑ̃dɔgam] **1** *adj* endogamous. **2** *n* endogamous person.

endogamie [ɑ̃dɔgami] *nf* endogamy.

endolori [ɑ̃dɔlɔri] *adj* painful, sore, tender (*arm etc*).

endolorir [ɑ̃dɔlɔrir] **1** *vt* to make (*arm etc*) painful *or* sore. **2 s'endolorir** *vpr* to become painful.

endolorissement [ɑ̃dɔlɔrismɑ̃] *nm* pain, soreness, tenderness.

endométrite [ɑ̃dɔmetrit] *nf Méd* endometritis.

endommagement [ɑ̃dɔmaʒmɑ̃] *nm* (*action*) damaging (**de,** of); (*résultat*) damage (**de,** to).

endommager [ɑ̃dɔmaʒe] *vt* **(j'endommageai(s))** to damage, to do damage to (*sth*).

endormant [ɑ̃dɔrmɑ̃] *adj* (*ennuyeux*) boring, wearisome (*speech, meeting etc*); boring, humdrum (*task*).

endormi, -ie [ɑ̃dɔrmi] **1** *adj* **(a)** asleep, sleeping (*person*); sleepy (*village*); **j'ai la jambe endormie,** my leg has gone to sleep *or* is numb; **(b)** *F* (*inerte, lent*) sluggish (*person*); **(c)** *Fig* dormant (*passion etc*). **2** *n* (*assoupi*) sleepyhead; (*inerte, lent*) sluggard.

endormir [ɑ̃dɔrmir] *v* (*conj like* **dormir**) **1** *vt* **(a)** (*of drug, hypnotist etc*) to put (*s.o.*) to sleep; (*of mother etc*) to send (*baby etc*) to sleep; **(b)** (*ennuyer*) to send (*s.o.*) to sleep; **(c)** (*apaiser*) to deaden (*pain*); **e. les soupçons,** to allay suspicion. **2 s'endormir** *vpr* **(a)** to fall asleep, to go to sleep, *F* to drop off (to sleep); **(b)** *Fig* (*of pain*) to die away; (*of suspicions*) to be allayed.

endormissement [ɑ̃dɔrmismɑ̃] *nm* falling asleep, *F* dropping off (to sleep).

endos [ɑ̃do] *nm* endorsement (*on cheque*).

endoscope [ɑ̃dɔskɔp] *nm Méd* endoscope.

endoscopie [ɑ̃dɔskɔpi] *nf Méd* endoscopy.

endosmose [ɑ̃dɔsmoz] *nf Phys* endosmosis.

endossable [ɑ̃dosabl] *adj* endorsable (*cheque*).

endossataire [ɑ̃dosatɛr] *n* endorsee.

endossement [ɑ̃dosmɑ̃] *nm* endorsement (*of cheque*); **e. en blanc,** blank endorsement.

endosser [ɑ̃dose] *vt* **(a)** to put on (*jacket etc*); **(b)** to assume, to shoulder (*a responsibility*); **(c)** to endorse (*cheque*); **(d)** (*en reliure*) to back (*book*).

endosseur, -euse [ɑ̃dosœr, -øz] *n* endorser (*of cheque*).

endothélium [ɑ̃dɔteljɔm] *nm Anat* endothelium.

endroit [ɑ̃drwa] *nm* **(a)** (*lieu*) place, spot; **c'est l'e. idéal pour un magasin,** it's the ideal place *or* spot for a shop; **rester au même e.,** to stay in the same place *or* spot; **par endroits,** here and there, in places; **en plusieurs/certains endroits,** in several/certain places; **j'ai perdu l'e.,** I've lost my place (*in the book etc*); **rire au bon e.,** to laugh in the right place; **le meilleur e. du film,** the best bit *or* part of the film; **ça me fait mal à cet e.,** it hurts me (just) here; *F*

le petit e., *Br* the loo, *Am* the john;

(b) prendre qn par son e. faible, to get on the soft side of s.o.;

(c) right side (*of material etc*); **à l'e.**, right way out *or* round *or* up; **tissu à deux endroits**, reversible material; *Tricot* **maille à l'e.**, plain stitch.

enduire [ɑ̃dɥir] *v* (*prp* **enduisant**; *pp* **enduit**; *pr ind* **j'enduis, il enduit**; *impf* **j'enduisais**; *p hist* **j'enduisis**; *fu* **j'enduirai**) **1** *vt* **e. de**, to coat *or* cover with (*paint, cement, paste etc*); to smear with (*cream, mud etc*). **2 s'enduire** *vpr* **s'e. de crème à bronzer**, to smear *or* rub *or* cover oneself with suntan cream.

enduit [ɑ̃dɥi] *nm* **(a)** coat, coating (*of tar, paint etc*); **(b)** *Constr* (*plâtre*) plastering, coat of plaster; **e. de ciment**, cement rendering; **(c)** *Cér* glaze, glazing.

endurable [ɑ̃dyrabl] *adj* endurable.

endurance [ɑ̃dyrɑ̃s] *nf* **(a)** (*physique*) endurance; stamina, staying power; **(b)** (*morale*) endurance, long-suffering; **(c)** *Aut etc* **épreuve/course d'e.**, endurance trial/run.

endurant [ɑ̃dyrɑ̃] *adj* **(a)** (*résistant*) resilient, tough; **(b)** *Vieilli* (*patient*) enduring, long-suffering.

endurci [ɑ̃dyrsi] *adj* **(a)** (*dur*) tough (*body, hands etc*); hard, callous (*heart, person*); **(b)** (*invétéré*) hardened (*sinner, criminal*); confirmed (*bachelor*); inveterate (*hatred*).

endurcir [ɑ̃dyrsir] **1** *vt* **(a)** (*cuirasser*) to harden (*s.o., s.o.'s heart*); **la vie va l'e.**, life will harden him; **(b)** (*rendre résistant*) to harden, to toughen (*s.o.*) (up); **être endurci à la fatigue**, to be inured *or* hardened to fatigue. **2 s'endurcir** *vpr* **(a)** (*devenir dur*) to harden, to become hard; **(b)** (*devenir résistant*) to become hardened.

endurcissement [ɑ̃dyrsismɑ̃] *nm* **(a)** (*action*) (*moral*) hardening (*of s.o., s.o.'s heart*); (*physique*) hardening, toughening (up) (*of s.o.*); **e. à la fatigue**, inuring to fatigue; **(b)** (*état*) (*moral*) hardness, callousness; (*physique*) hardness, toughness; **e. à la fatigue**, being inured to fatigue.

endurer [ɑ̃dyre] *vt* to endure, to bear (*hardship, ill-treatment etc*); **e. des railleries**, to put up with joking; **je n'endure pas que tu partes**, I can't bear your leaving; **il fait trop chaud pour e. un manteau**, it's too warm to need a coat *or* for a coat.

enduro [ɑ̃dyro] *nm Sp* enduro.

Énée [ene] *nm* Aeneas.

Énéide (l') [leneid] *nf Littér* the Aeneid.

énergéticien, -ienne [enɛrʒetisjɛ̃, -ɛn] *n* energetics specialist.

énergétique [enɛrʒetik] **1** *adj* **(a)** energizing, energy-giving (*medicine, food etc*); **dépense é.**, expenditure of energy; **(b)** *Écon* energy (*resources, needs etc*). **2** *nf* energetics.

énergie [enɛrʒi] *nf* **(a)** (*force*) energy; **apporter** *ou* **appliquer toute son é. à une tâche/à faire qch**, to devote *or* direct all one's energies to a task/to doing sth; **avec é.**, energetically; **elle a refusé avec é.**, she refused forcefully *or* vigorously; **l'é. d'un passage/d'un style**, the vigour of a passage/style; **sans é.**, listless(ly); **(b)** *Phys* **é. cinétique**, kinetic energy; **é. potentielle**, potential energy; **é. atomique**, atomic energy, nuclear power; **(c)** *Ind* energy, power; **faire des économies d'é.**, to save energy.

énergique [enɛrʒik] *adj* **(a)** energetic, dynamic (*person*); **un visage é.**, a strong face; **(b)** strong, drastic (*measures*); strong, forceful (*language*); emphatic (*gesture*); forceful (*kick, blow*); powerful (*medicine, remedy*).

énergiquement [enɛrʒikmɑ̃] *adv* energetically; **s'y mettre é.**, to put one's back into it; **refuser é.**, to refuse forcefully *or* vigorously.

énergisant [enɛrʒizɑ̃] **1** *adj* energizing, energy-giving (*food, medicine etc*). **2** *nm Méd* energizer, antidepressant.

énergumène [enɛrgymɛn] *n* **(a)** *F* (*fou etc*) fanatic, ranter; **(b)** *Vieilli* (*possédé*) energumen; **crier comme un é.**, to scream like one possessed.

énervant [enɛrvɑ̃] *adj* **(a)** irritating (*person, habit etc*); nerve-racking (*noise*); **(b)** *Vieilli* enervating (*climate*).

énervé [enɛrve] *adj* (*agacé*) irritated; (*excité*) on edge, agitated (*person*); nervous (*laughter*); **très é. à l'idée de ...**, all on edge at the idea of ... .

énervement [enɛrvəmɑ̃] *nm* (*agacement*) irritation; (*excitation*) edginess.

énerver [enɛrve] **1** *vt* **(a) é. qn**, (*agacer*) to get on s.o.'s nerves, to irritate s.o.; (*exciter*) to agitate s.o.; **(b)** *Vieilli* (*débiliter*) to enervate, to weaken. **2 s'énerver** *vpr* to get excited *or* agitated *or* (all) worked up; **s'é. pour un rien**, to get excited *or* agitated *or* (all) worked up about *or* over nothing.

enfaîteau, -eaux [ɑ̃fɛto] *nm Constr* ridge tile.

enfaîtement [ɑ̃fɛtmɑ̃] *nm Constr* ridge tiling, ridging.

enfaîter [ɑ̃fete] *vt Constr* to ridge (*roof*).

enfance [ɑ̃fɑ̃s] *nf* **(a)** (*jeunesse*) childhood; (*de garçon*) boyhood; (*de fille*) girlhood; **elle a eu une e. heureuse/difficile**, she had a happy/difficult childhood; **dans mon e.**, in my childhood; **souvenir/camarade d'e.**, childhood memory/friend; **première e.**, infancy; **l'e. de la civilisation**, the dawn *or* beginning of civilization; *F* **c'est l'e. de l'art**, it's (mere) child's play; **industrie encore dans son e.**, industry still in its infancy; **(b)** (*dégénérescence*) **retomber en e.**, to sink into one's second childhood *or* into one's dotage; **(c) l'e.**, (*enfants*) children.

enfant [ɑ̃fɑ̃] *n* **(a)** (*jeune*) child (*pl* children); *Jur* (*mineur*) infant; **e. en bas âge** *ou* **du premier âge**, infant; **éducation des enfants**, children's education; **les droits de l'e.**, children's rights; *Méd* **e. bleu**, blue baby; **c'est une belle e.**, she is a beautiful child; **e. naturel**, natural child; **e. unique**, only child; **e. trouvé**, foundling; **babil d'e.**, childish prattle; **e. de chœur**, *Rel* altar boy; *Fig* naive person; *Fig* **je ne suis plus un e. de chœur**, I wasn't born yesterday; *F* **ce n'est qu'un jeu d'e.**, it is child's play; *F* **il n'y a plus d'enfants**, you're a big boy *or* girl now; **elle me parle comme à un e.**, she talks to me as if I was a child; **e. terrible**, boisterous child; *Fig* enfant terrible; **se conduire en e., faire l'e.**, to behave childishly; **contes pour les enfants**, nursery tales;

(b) *F* (*terme d'affection*) **que t'arrive-t-il, mon e.?**, what's the matter my boy *or* my girl?; **allons-y, mes enfants!**, come on, boys and girls!;

(c) manière bon e., kindly *or* good-natured manner; **il est trop bon e. pour garder rancune**, he is too decent a fellow to bear a grudge;

(d) (*fils, fille*) child; **elle attend un e.**, she's expecting a child *or* baby; *F* **il va lui faire un e.**, he's going to get her pregnant; **être en mal d'e.**, (*d'une femme*) to be broody; *F* **c'est son e.**, (*création*) it's his baby *or* his brainchild; **couple sans e.**, childless couple; **mourir sans enfants**, to die childless *or Jur* without issue;

(e) (*descendant*) **les enfants d'Israël**, the children of Israel; **un enfant du peuple/de l'Église**, a child of the people/the Church; **un e. de Paris**, a native of Paris; **un e. de troupe**, an army child *or F* brat. **2** *adj* childlike; *Péj* childish; babyish (*smile etc*); **ne soyez pas si e.**, don't be so childish.

enfantement [ɑ̃fɑ̃tmɑ̃] *nm* childbirth; *Fig* giving birth (*to a literary work etc*).

enfanter [ɑ̃fɑ̃te] *vt* to bear, to give birth to (*child*); *Fig* to give birth to (*literary work etc*); **la discorde enfante le crime**, discord begets crime.

enfantillage [ɑ̃fɑ̃tijaʒ] *nm* **enfantillage(s)**, childishness; **ne fais pas d'enfantillages!**, don't be childish.

enfantin [ɑ̃fɑ̃tɛ̃] *adj* **(a)** childlike, childish (*voice, game etc*); *Péj* childish (*remark, action etc*); **littérature enfantine**, children's literature *or* books; **babil e.**, baby talk; **(b)** (*élémentaire*) elementary; **c'est e.**, it's just too easy, it's child's play; **c'est d'une simplicité enfantine**, it's childishly simple.

enfariné [ɑ̃farine] *adj* floured, covered with flour; *F* (*face, hair etc*) smothered in powder.

enfer [ɑ̃fɛr] *nm* **(a)** *Rel etc* **l'e.**, hell; **les enfers**, the underworld; *Myth* Hades; **l'E. de Dante**, Dante's Inferno; *Fig* **aller en e.**, to go to hell; **il fait de ma vie un e.**, he is making my life hell; **une vision d'e.**, a vision of hell; **aller un train d'e.**, to go at top speed *or F* hell for leather; **bruit d'e.**, hellish noise; *F* **une soirée/***etc* **d'e.**, (*génial*) a dream of a party/*etc*; **(b)** (*dans une bibliothèque*) = library department containing books not available to the public.

enfermer [ɑ̃fɛrme] **1** *vt* **(a)** to shut (*s.o., sth*) up; **e. qch/qn (à clef)**, to lock sth/s.o. up; **tenir qn enfermé**, to keep s.o. shut up *or* locked up; **e. qn dehors**, to shut *or* lock s.o. out; **j'ai été enfermé dans une pièce toute la journée**, I have been shut up *or* cooped up in a room all day; *F* **il est bon à e.**, he ought to be locked up; *Fig* **e. un mot dans une définition trop étroite/qn dans un rôle inadéquat**, to confine a word in an excessively narrow definition/s.o. in an inadequate role; **e. qn dans ses contradictions**, to trap s.o. in his own contradictions; **e. le savoir dans les bibliothèques**, to lock away *or* shut away knowledge in libraries; **enfermé dans ses pensées**, wrapped up in his thoughts; **vivre trop enfermé**, to stay at home too much;

(b) (*entourer*) to shut *or* hem in, to enclose, to surround;

Sp to hem *or* box in (*competitor*).

2 s'enfermer *vpr* to shut oneself up; (*à clef*) to lock oneself up; **s'e. dehors,** to lock oneself out; *Fig* **s'e. dans le silence/un rôle,** to retreat into silence/to confine oneself to a role.

enferrer (s') [sɑ̃fere] *vpr* to impale oneself (**sur,** on); *Fig* to get tangled up *or* bogged down (**dans une explication/ses mensonges/***etc*, in an explanation/one's lies/*etc*).

enfeu [ɑ̃fø] *nm Archit* recess (tomb).

enfichable [ɑ̃fiʃabl] *adj Él* that can be plugged in.

enficher [ɑ̃fiʃe] *vt El* to plug in.

enfieller [ɑ̃fjɛle] *vt* to embitter, to sour (*s.o.*).

enfiévré [ɑ̃fjevre] *adj* fevered (*brow*); feverish (*activity*).

enfièvrement [ɑ̃fjɛvrəmɑ̃] *nm* fever (of excitement).

enfiévrer [ɑ̃fjevre] *v* (**j'enfièvre; j'enfiévrai**) **1** *vt* **(a)** (*énerver*) to excite, to fire, to stir (*s.o., s.o.'s imagination etc*); **(b)** *Méd Vieilli* to give (*s.o.*) fever, to make (*s.o.*) feverish. **2 s'enfiévrer** *vpr* **(a)** (*se passionner*) to get excited *or* (all) worked up; **s'e. pour une cause,** to become passionate about a cause; **(b)** *Méd Vieilli* to grow feverish.

enfilade [ɑ̃filad] *nf* **(a)** succession, series (*of doors etc*); suite (*of rooms etc*); **maisons en e.,** row of houses; **(b)** *Mil* enfilade; **tir d'e.,** raking *or* enfilading fire.

enfiler [ɑ̃file] **1** *vt* **(a)** to thread (*needle*); to file (*papers on spike file*); to string (*beads*); to string (*words*) together; **(b)** to take, to go along (*a street etc*); **(c)** to slip on (*clothes*); to pull on (*trousers, stockings*); **blouse à e.,** slip-on blouse; **(d)** *Mil* to enfilade, to rake (*troops etc*). **2 s'enfiler** *vpr* **(a)** (*s'engager*) **s'e. dans un couloir/une rue/***etc*, to go off into a corridor/street/*etc*; **(b)** *F* (*consommer*) to down (*a drink*); **s'e. un bon dîner,** to have a slap-up meal; **(c)** *F* (*avoir à supporter*) to get stuck *or* landed with (*task*).

enfin [ɑ̃fɛ̃] *adv* **(a)** (*en dernier lieu*) finally, lastly; **e. et surtout,** last but not least;

(b) (*plutôt*) in fact, in a word, in short; **blonde, e. châtain clair,** blond, well, light brown; **e. d'une certaine façon, oui,** well, in some way, yes;

(c) (*finalement*) at last, finally, at length; **e. vous voilà!, vous voilà e.!,** here you are at last!; **j'y suis e. arrivée,** I finally made it, I made it at last;

(d) (*résignation*) that's that!; **e. c'est la vie,** well, that's life!; **mais e., s'il acceptait!,** but still, if he did accept!;

(e) e.! ce qui est fait est fait, anyhow *or* after all what is done is done; **e. quoi, tu n'as plus 10 ans!,** after all, you're not 10 any more!; **e. (bref) c'était la panique!,** in short *or* in a word, it was panic!; **e. je ne dis pas non, mais ...,** well, I'm not saying no, but ...; **mais e. je te l'avais déjà dit!,** but really, I'd already told you!; **c'est un homme, e.!, il a sa dignité!,** he's a man after all! he has his dignity!

enflammé [ɑ̃flame] *adj* **(a)** burning, blazing (*wood etc*); fiery (*sun, sunset*); **(b)** glowing (*cheeks*); **(c)** *Méd* inflamed (*wound, throat etc*); **(d)** *Fig* fiery (*speech, character etc*); **faire à une femme une déclaration enflammée,** to make a passionate declaration to a woman.

enflammer [ɑ̃flame] **1** *vt* **(a)** (*mettre en flammes*) to set (*sth*) on fire *or* ablaze; **e. une allumette,** to strike a match; **(b)** *Méd* to inflame (*wound, throat etc*); **(c)** *Fig* to excite, to fire, to stir up (*s.o., s.o.'s imagination*); **e. une dispute,** to stir up a quarrel; **la colère enflamme son regard,** his eyes are blazing with anger; **l'urgence de la situation enflamme ses talents d'orateur,** the urgency of the situation is arousing his talents as a speaker. **2 s'enflammer** *vpr* **(a)** (*prendre feu*) to catch fire, to burst into flames, to blaze up; **(b)** (*of wound, throat etc*) to become inflamed; **(c)** (*of person, imagination etc*) to be stirred up; **s'e. de colère,** to flare up (*in anger*).

enflé [ɑ̃fle] **1** *adj* swollen (*river, limb etc*); inflated (*price*); inflated, turgid, bombastic (*style*). **2** *nm F* **espèce d'e.!,** you idiot!

enfléchure [ɑ̃fleʃyr] *nf Nau* ratline.

enfler [ɑ̃fle] **1** *vt* **(a)** to swell, to cause (*limb, river etc*) to swell; to inflate (*price*); **e. les joues,** to puff out *or* blow out one's cheeks; **e. les voiles,** (*of wind*) to fill the sails; **e. la voix,** to raise one's voice; *Vieilli* **e. le nombre/la dépense,** to swell *or* add to the number/the expense; **(b)** *Fig* (*exagérer*) to exaggerate (*story, one's success etc*); **e. son style,** to inflate one's style. **2** *vi* (*of limb etc*) to swell. **3 s'enfler** *vpr* **(a)** (*of limb etc*) to swell; (*of voice*) to rise; **(b)** (*of river etc*) to swell, to rise; **(c)** (*of style*) to become inflated *or* turgid.

enflure [ɑ̃flyr] *nf* **(a)** swelling (*of cheek, limb etc*); **(b)** turgidity (*of style*); **(c)** *F* (*imbécile*) idiot.

enfoiré, -ée [ɑ̃fware] *n Vulg* bugger, bastard.

enfoncé [ɑ̃fɔ̃se] *adj* deep-set (*eyes*); sunken, deep (*cavity, ravine etc*); low-lying (*ground, village*).

enfoncement [ɑ̃fɔ̃smɑ̃] *nm* **(a)** (*action d'enfoncer*) driving in (*of pile, nail etc*); sticking in, pushing in (*of needle etc*); breaking open (*of door etc*); **(b)** (*action de s'enfoncer*) sinking (*of walls etc*); giving way (*of floor*); **(c)** (*creux*) hollow, depression (*in the ground*); alcove, recess (*in wall*); *Nau* bay, bight; **dans l'e. de la porte,** in the door recess *or* doorway.

enfoncer [ɑ̃fɔ̃se] *v* (**j'enfonçai(s)**) **1** *vt* **(a)** to drive in (*pile, nail etc*); to stick in, to push in (*needle, pin etc*); **e. un clou dans une planche,** to drive a nail into a plank; **e. un couteau dans,** to thrust *or* plunge *or* stick a knife into; **e. au marteau,** to hammer in; **e. la main dans sa poche,** to thrust one's hand into one's pocket; **e. son chapeau sur sa tête,** to jam *or* cram one's hat on one's head; **e. la clef dans la serrure,** to insert the key in the lock; **e. qn dans la misère,** to plunge s.o. into poverty; *F* **je ne peux pas lui e. cela dans la tête,** I can't get it into his head;

(b) (*défoncer*) to break open, to burst in (*door etc*); to stave in (*cask*); to smash (up) (*car*); **e. un carreau,** to break a window pane; **e. tous les obstacles,** to break through all obstacles; *Fig* **e. une porte ouverte,** to persist in stating the obvious;

(c) *F* (*battre*) to hammer, to get the better of (*s.o., team etc*).

2 *vi* to sink (*into mud, sea etc*); **le navire enfonçait,** the ship was sinking; **nous y avons enfoncé jusqu'aux genoux,** we sank into it up to our knees.

3 s'enfoncer *vpr* (*of nail, knife etc*) to sink *or* go in; (*of ship*) to sink; (*of floor*) to subside, to give way; (*of walls etc*) to sink; **la balle s'enfonça dans le mur,** the bullet embedded itself in the wall; **s'e. dans son fauteuil,** to sink into one's armchair; **s'e. dans l'ombre,** to disappear in *or* be swallowed up by the darkness; **s'e. dans une rue/dans un bois,** to turn into a street/to plunge into a wood; **s'e. dans l'étude/dans la rêverie,** to bury oneself in study/to sink into reverie; **s'e. dans le crime,** to sink deep(er) into crime; **s'e. dans son opinion,** to become entrenched in one's opinion.

enfonceur, -euse [ɑ̃fɔ̃sœr, -øz] *n* **c'est un e. de portes ouvertes,** he's got a gift for stating the obvious.

enfonçure [ɑ̃fɔ̃syr] *nf* depression, hollow.

enfouir [ɑ̃fwir] **1** *vt* to bury (*sth*) (**dans,** in; **sous,** beneath, under); *Agr* to plough in (*manure*); **les mains enfouies dans ses poches,** with his hands buried in his pockets. **2 s'enfouir** *vpr* to bury oneself *or* itself; **s'e. dans la campagne,** to bury oneself in the country.

enfouissement [ɑ̃fwismɑ̃] *nm* burying; *Agr* ploughing in (*of manure*).

enfourcher [ɑ̃furʃe] *vt* to get astride, to mount (*horse, bicycle*); *Fig* **e. son dada,** to get on one's hobbyhorse.

enfourchure [ɑ̃furʃyr] *nf Vieilli* fork (*of tree, legs*).

enfournage [ɑ̃furnaʒ] *nm*, **enfournement** [ɑ̃furnəmɑ̃] *nm* putting (*of bread etc*) in the oven; putting (*of pottery etc*) in the kiln.

enfourner [ɑ̃furne] *vt* to put (*bread etc*) in an oven; to put (*pottery, bricks etc*) in a kiln; *F* (*avaler*) to gobble (*sth*) up; **e. les passagers dans un autobus,** to pack *or* cram passengers into a bus.

enfourneur [ɑ̃furnœr] *nm* oven man; *Cér* kiln man.

enfreindre [ɑ̃frɛ̃dr] *vt* (*prp* **enfreignant**; *pp* **enfreint**; *pr ind* **j'enfreins, il enfreint, ils enfreignent**; *impf* **j'enfreignais**; *p hist* **j'enfreignis**; *fu* **j'enfreindrai**) to infringe, to break (*the law*); to contravene, to act contrary to (*rules, orders*); to break (*vow*); **e. les dispositions d'un traité,** to violate a treaty.

enfuir (s') [sɑ̃fɥir] *vpr* (*conj like* **fuir**) to run away, *Litt* to flee, to fly; (*of embezzler*) to abscond; (*of lovers*) to elope; **s'e. de prison,** to escape from prison; **à mesure que les jours s'enfuyaient,** as the days flew by; *Litt* **mon bonheur menace de s'e.,** my happiness is in danger of evaporating; **les côtes s'enfuient,** the coast recedes.

enfumé [ɑ̃fyme] *adj* **(a)** smoky (*room etc*); **(b)** smoke-blackened (*walls etc*).

enfumer [ɑ̃fyme] *vt* **(a)** to fill (*room etc*) with smoke; **(b)** to blacken (*walls etc*) with smoke; **(c)** to smoke out (*person, bees etc*).

enfûtage [ɑ̃fytaʒ] *nm* barrelling (*of wine*).

enfutailler [ɑ̃fytaje], **enfûter** [ɑ̃fyte] *vt* to barrel, to cask (*wine*).

engagé [ɑ̃gaʒe] **1** *adj* **(a)** *Archit* engaged (*column etc*); **(b) navire e.,** ship on her beam-ends; *Mil* **soldat e.,** volunteer; **(c)** *Littér Pol etc* committed (*literature, artist etc*). **2** *nm Mil* **e. (volontaire),** volunteer; *Courses de chevaux* **la liste des engagés,** the list of runners.

engageant [ɑ̃gaʒɑ̃] *adj* engaging, prepossessing (*manner etc*); winning, engaging (*smile*).

engagement [ɑ̃gaʒmɑ̃] *nm* **(a)** (*promesse etc*) promise, undertaking, commitment; **faire honneur à** *ou* **tenir** *ou* **respecter ses engagements,** to honour *or* meet *or* fulfil one's commitments; **contracter** *ou* **prendre un e.,** to enter into a contract; **elle a pris l'e. de le faire,** she undertook to do it; **sans e.,** without obligation (**de votre part,** on your part);

(b) *Fin* tying up, locking up (*of capital*); incurring (*of expenses*);

(c) (*mise en gage*) pawning, pledging (*of jewels etc*); mortgaging (*of estate*);

(d) (*embauche*) engagement, appointment (*of employee*); booking (*of pianist etc*); *Mil* (voluntary) enlistment; **se trouver sans e.,** to be out of work; *Th F* to be resting;

(e) *Sp* entering, entry (*for sporting event*);

(f) *Mil Nau* (*bataille*) engagement, action;

(g) (*coup d'envoi*) *Fb* kick-off; (*hockey*) bully-off; *Escrime* engagement;

(h) commitment (**à une cause/***etc*, to a cause/*etc*);

(i) *Physiol* **l'e. du foetus,** engagement of the foetus;

(j) (*encouragement*) encouragement; **c'est un e. à poursuivre votre effort,** it's an encouragement to continue your effort.

engager [ɑ̃gaʒe] *v* (**j'engageai(s)**) **1** *vt* **(a)** (*mettre en gage*) to pledge, to pawn (*jewellery etc*); to mortgage (*property*); **e. sa parole,** to pledge one's word; **cette lettre ne vous engage pas,** this letter does not bind *or* commit you;

(b) *Sp* to enter (*a horse*);

(c) (*embaucher*) to engage, to appoint (*employee*); to book (*pianist etc*); *Mil* to enlist (*recruit*);

(d) (*entraver*) to catch, to foul, to entangle (*rope etc*); to jam (*machinery*); **e. une ancre,** to foul an anchor; **e. un aviron,** to catch a crab; **e. un vaisseau,** to run a ship aground;

(e) (*entraîner*) to involve (**dans,** in); **la nation toute entière se voit engagée dans ce conflit,** the whole nation finds itself involved *or* caught up in this conflict; **cela n'engage que toi,** it involves only you; **e. qn dans une querelle,** to involve s.o. in *or* draw s.o. into a quarrel;

(f) *Fin* to lock up, to tie up (*money*); to incur (*expenses*); **e. sa fortune/des capitaux dans une affaire,** to lock up *or* tie up one's fortune/capital in a deal;

(g) *Tech* to engage (*machinery*), to put (*machinery*) into gear;

(h) e. le pied dans l'étrier, to put one's foot in the stirrup; **e. la clef dans la serrure,** to fit *or* insert the key in the lock; **e. un véhicule dans une allée,** to drive a vehicle into a lane;

(i) (*commencer*) to begin, to start, to open (*conversation, negotiations*); to set going (*enterprise etc*); *Jur* to institute (*proceedings*); **e. le combat,** to join battle, to engage; **e. des troupes,** to bring troops into action, to engage troops; **e. le jeu,** *Fb* to kick off; (*hockey*) to bully off; *Sp* **e. la partie,** to begin the match *or* game;

(j) (*encourager*) **e. qn à faire qch,** (*of person*) to encourage *or* urge *or* advise s.o. to do sth; (*of thing*) to encourage s.o. to do sth; **le beau temps nous engage à sortir,** the fine weather invites us to go out.

2 s'engager *vpr* **(a) s'e. à faire qch,** to undertake *or* commit oneself to do sth; **par ses écrits, l'écrivain s'engage,** the writer commits himself by what he writes; **s'e. par traité à faire qch,** to contract to do sth; **sans s'e. à rien,** without committing oneself to anything; **s'e. dans une aventure/un combat/une affaire,** to get involved in an adventure/a fight/a deal; **je suis trop engagé pour reculer,** I have gone too far to pull out;

(b) (*s'embaucher*) **s'e. chez qn,** to enter s.o.'s service; **s'e. comme cuisinier/***etc*, to get (oneself) a job as *or* get taken on as a cook/*etc*;

(c) *Mil* to enlist, to join up;

(d) *Sp* **s'e. pour une course,** to enter for a race;

(e) (*of rope, propeller etc*) to foul, to become fouled; (*of machine*) to jam;

(f) (*se loger*) to fit; **un tube s'engage dans l'ouverture,** a pipe fits into the opening;

(g) (*pénétrer*) **s'e. dans une rue/forêt,** to turn into a street/to enter a forest;

(h) (*of battle, conversation etc*) to begin.

engainer [ɑ̃gene] *vt* to sheathe (*dagger*).

engazonnement [ɑ̃gazɔnmɑ̃] *nm* **(a)** turfing (*of ground*); **(b)** (*fait de semer*) sowing with grass seed.

engazonner [ɑ̃gazɔne] *vt* **(a)** to turf (*ground*); **(b)** (*semer*) to sow with grass seed.

engeance [ɑ̃ʒɑ̃s] *nf F* **e. de scélérats,** bunch of scoundrels; **quelle e.!,** what a crew!

engelure [ɑ̃ʒlyr] *nf* chilblain.

engendrement [ɑ̃ʒɑ̃drəmɑ̃] *nm* **(a)** fathering, *Bible* begetting (of children); **(b)** generation (*of heat etc*); breeding (*of disease, poverty*).

engendrer [ɑ̃ʒɑ̃dre] *vt* **(a)** to father, *Bible* to beget (*child*); (*of stallion etc*) to sire; **(b)** *Fig* to engender, to give rise to (*strife*); to breed (*disease, poverty*); **(c)** to generate, to develop (*heat etc*).

engerbage [ɑ̃ʒɛrbaʒ] *nm Agr* sheaving.

engerber [ɑ̃ʒɛrbe] *vt Agr* to sheaf (*wheat etc*).

engin [ɑ̃ʒɛ̃] *nm* (*machine*) machine; (*outil*) device, contrivance; **engins de pêche,** fishing tackle; **e. de sauvetage,** life-saving apparatus; **passage d'engins,** heavy plant crossing; **engins de guerre,** engines of war; **e. de mort,** deadly weapon; **e. amphibie,** amphibious craft *or* vehicle; **e. téléguidé,** guided missile; **e. air-air,** air-to-air missile; **e. sol-sol,** ground-to-ground missile; **e. air-sol,** air-to-ground missile; **e. à moteur interne,** hot missile; **e. spatial,** spacecraft.

engineering [ɛnʒinəriŋ] *nm* engineering.

englober [ɑ̃glɔbe] *vt* **(a)** (*inclure*) to include (**dans,** in); **e. les innocents parmi les coupables,** to include the innocent with the guilty; **(b)** (*annexer*) to merge (**dans,** into); **ces États furent englobés dans l'Empire,** these states were merged into the Empire.

engloutir [ɑ̃glutir] **1** *vt* **(a)** (*avaler*) to gulp down (*drink*); to wolf down (food); **(b)** (*submerger*) to engulf, to swallow (*ship, village etc*) up; **(c)** (*dépenser*) to swallow up (*one's capital etc*); **e. une fortune dans une entreprise,** to sink a fortune in an undertaking. **2 s'engloutir** *vpr* (*of ship*) to sink.

engloutissement [ɑ̃glutismɑ̃] *nm* **(a)** gulping down (*of drink*); wolfing down (*of food*); **(b)** engulfing, swallowing up (*of village etc*); sinking (*of ship*); swallowing up (*of fortune etc*).

engluage [ɑ̃glyaʒ] *nm,* **engluement** [ɑ̃glymɑ̃] *nm* **(a)** liming (*of twigs, birds*); **(b)** (*enduit*) (bird)lime.

engluer [ɑ̃glye] **1** *vt* **(a)** to lime (*twigs, bird*); **(b)** *F* (*duper*) to catch (*s.o.*) out. **2 s'engluer** *vpr* (*of bird*) to get caught in lime; **s.'e. les doigts,** to get sticky fingers.

engoncer [ɑ̃gɔ̃se] *vt* (*of coat etc*) to make (*s.o.*) look hunched up; **être engoncé dans sa veste,** to be hunched up in one's jacket; *Fig* **être engoncé dans ses opinions,** to be entrenched in one's views.

engorgement [ɑ̃gɔrʒəmɑ̃] *nm* **(a)** (*action*) choking, blocking, clogging (*of passage, pipe etc*); **l'e. des marchés,** glutting of the markets; **(b)** (*bouchon*) obstruction, stoppage; *Méd* engorgement, congestion.

engorger [ɑ̃gɔrʒe] *v* (**j'engorgeai(s)**) **1** *vt* **(a)** to choke (up), to block, to clog (*passage, pipe etc*); **(b)** to glut (*market*); **(c)** *Méd* to engorge, congest (*organ*). **2 s'engorger** *vpr* **(a)** (*of pipe etc*) to become choked (up) *or* blocked (up) *or* clogged; **(b)** *Méd* (*of organ*) to become engorged *or* congested.

engouement [ɑ̃gumɑ̃] *nm* **(a)** (*admiration*) infatuation, craze (**pour qn/qch,** for s.o./sth); **(b)** *Méd* obstruction (*of hernia*).

engouer (s') [sɑ̃gwe] *vpr* **(a)** *Méd* (*of hernia*) to become obstructed; **(b) s'e. de qn/qch,** to become infatuated with *or* go crazy over s.o./sth.

engouffrement [ɑ̃gufrəmɑ̃] *nm* engulfment, engulfing, swallowing up (*of vessel by the sea etc*).

engouffrer [ɑ̃gufre] **1** *vt* to engulf, to swallow up (*ship etc*); **e. une fortune,** to swallow up a fortune; *F* **e. sa nourriture,** to devour *or* gulp down *or* wolf down one's food; **qu'est-ce que j'ai engouffré!,** I really wolfed *or* gulped it down! **2 s'engouffrer** *vpr* (*of ship etc*) to be engulfed *or* swallowed up; **il s'engouffra dans la gare,** he disappeared into the station; **le vent s'engouffra par la porte,** the wind swept in through the door.

engoulevent [ɑ̃gulvɑ̃] *nm* (*oiseau*) nightjar.

engourdi [ɑ̃gurdi] *adj* **(a)** numb (*limb, body etc*); **j'ai le pied e.,** my foot has gone to sleep *or* is numb; **(b)** *Fig* dull, sluggish (*mind*).

engourdir [ɑ̃gurdir] **1** *vt* **(a)** to numb (*limb, body etc*); **(b)** (*endormir*) to make (*s.o.*) drowsy; to dull (*mind, pain*). **2 s'engourdir** *vpr* **(a)** (*of limb etc*) to grow numb, to go to sleep; **(b)** *Fig* (*of the mind*) to become dull *or* sluggish; *F* **mon anglais s'est bien engourdi,** my English is stagnating; **(c)** (*of hibernating animal*) to become dormant.

engourdissement [ɑ̃gurdismɑ̃] *nm* **(a)** (*état*) numbness (*of limb etc*); dullness, sluggishness (*of mind*); torpor (*of *hibernating animal*); **(b)** (*action*) numbing (*of limb etc*); dulling (*of mind, pain*).

engrais [ɑ̃grɛ] *nm* **(a)** (*pour l'élevage*) **mettre des bœufs à l'e.,** to put cattle to fatten; **(b)** (*fumier*) fertilizer; **e. (animal),** manure; **e. chimiques,** chemical fertilizers; **e. verts,** green fertilizers.

engraissage [ɑ̃grɛsaʒ] *nm*, **engraissement** [ɑ̃grɛsmɑ̃] *nm* fattening (*of animals*).

engraisser [ɑ̃grese] **1** *vt* **(a)** to fatten (*animals*); **(b)** *Fig* to make (*s.o.*) fat; **(c)** to fertilize (*land*). **2** *vi* (*of person, animal*) to get fat. **3 s'engraisser** *vpr* (*s'enrichir*) to grow fat; **l'État s'engraisse sur le dos des travailleurs,** the State grows fat at the workers' expense.

engrangement [ɑ̃grɑ̃ʒmɑ̃] *nm* getting in, *Litt* garnering (*of cereals*).

engranger [ɑ̃grɑ̃ʒe] *vt* **(j'engrangeai(s); n. engrangeons)** to get in, *Litt* to garner (*cereals*).

engraver [ɑ̃grave] **1** *vt* **(a)** *Constr* to notch (*lead*); **(b)** to strand (*ship*). **2 s'engraver** *vpr* (*of boat*) to ground.

engrenage [ɑ̃grənaʒ] *nm* **(a)** *Tech* (*roues dentées*) gears; (*disposition du système*) gearing; **e. hélicoïdal,** helical gear, screw gear; **système** *ou* **jeu d'engrenages,** train *or* set of gear wheels; **(b)** *Fig* chain, mesh, web (*of events*); **être pris dans l'e.,** to get caught (up) in the system; **l'e. de la violence/de l'agressivité,** the spiral of violence/aggression; **mettre le doigt dans l'e.,** to get caught up in it.

engrènement [ɑ̃grɛnmɑ̃] *nm* **(a)** *Agr* (*of mill etc*) feeding with grain; **(b)** *Tech* engaging, meshing.

engrener [ɑ̃grəne] *v* **(j'engrène; j'engrènerai) 1** *vt* **(a)** *Agr* to feed grain into (*mill, threshing machine*); **(b)** *Tech* to engage, to mesh (*gear wheels*); **e. dans,** to engage into, to mesh with; *F* **e. une affaire,** to set a thing going. **2 s'engrener** *vpr Tech* to engage (**dans,** into), to mesh (**dans,** with); **roues qui s'engrènent,** wheels that engage into one another *or* that mesh with one another.

engrenure [ɑ̃grənyr] *nf* **(a)** *Tech* (*disposition de roues*) gearing; **(b)** *Chir* serrated suture.

engrosser [ɑ̃grose] *vt Arg* to make (*woman*) pregnant, *Br* to put (*woman*) in the club.

engueulade [ɑ̃gœlad] *nf F* (*réprimande*) bawling out; (*querelle*) row, *Br* slanging match; **passer une e. à qn,** to give s.o. a bawling out, to bawl s.o. out; **recevoir une e.,** to get a bawling out.

engueuler [ɑ̃gœle] *F* **1** *vt* **e. qn,** (*réprimander*) to give s.o. hell, to give s.o. a roasting; **se faire e.,** to be given a roasting; **e. qn comme du poisson pourri,** to call s.o. every name under the sun. **2 s'engueuler** *vpr* to have a row *or Br* slanging match.

enguirlander [ɑ̃girlɑ̃de] *vt* **(a)** (*décorer*) to garland (**de,** with); **(b)** *F* = **ENGUEULER 1.**

enhardir [ɑ̃ardir] **1** *vt* to embolden, to put courage into, to give courage to (*s.o.*). **2 s'enhardir** *vpr* to pluck up courage; **s.'e. (jusqu') à faire qch,** to pluck up the courage to do sth.

enharmonie [ɑ̃narmɔni] *nf Mus* enharmonic change.

enharnacher [ɑ̃arnaʃe] *vt* to harness (*horse*).

enherber [ɑ̃nɛrbe] *vt* to put (*land*) under grass.

énième [enjɛm] **1** *adj* nth; **pour la é. fois,** for the nth *or* umpteenth time. **2** *n* nth.

énigmatique [enigmatik] *adj* enigmatic.

énigmatiquement [enigmatikmɑ̃] *adv* enigmatically.

énigme [enigm] *nf* (*problème, mystère*) enigma, riddle; (*devinette*) riddle; **proposer une é. (à qn),** to ask (s.o.) a riddle; **trouver le mot de l'é.,** to find the answer to the riddle, to guess *or* solve the riddle; **parler par énigmes,** to speak in riddles; **ce garçon est une é. pour moi,** I can't make the boy out.

enivrant [ɑ̃nivrɑ̃] *adj* intoxicating, heady.

enivrement [ɑ̃nivrəmɑ̃] *nm* **(a)** (*par l'alcool*) intoxication, inebriation; **(b)** *Fig* exhilaration; **dans l'e. de,** intoxicated *or* exhilarated by.

enivrer [ɑ̃nivre] **1** *vt* **(a)** (*avec de l'alcool*) to intoxicate, to inebriate, to make (*s.o.*) drunk; **(b)** *Fig* (*exalter*) to intoxicate, to exhilarate; **enivré par le succès,** intoxicated *or* exhilarated by success. **2 s'enivrer** *vpr* **(a)** (*devenir ivre*) to become intoxicated *or* inebriated (**de,** with), to get drunk (**de,** on); **(b)** *Fig* **s'e. de mots,** to get drunk on words.

enjambée [ɑ̃ʒɑ̃be] *nf* stride; **marcher à grandes enjambées,** to stride along.

enjambement [ɑ̃ʒɑ̃bmɑ̃] *nm Littér* enjamb(e)ment.

enjamber [ɑ̃ʒɑ̃be] **1** *vt* to step over *or* across (*obstacle, ditch etc*); (*of bridge*) to span (*river etc*). **2** *vi* **(a) e. sur qch,** (*dépasser*) to jut *or* project over sth; (*empiéter*) to encroach on sth; **(b)** *Littér* to run on (*to the next line*).

enjaveler [ɑ̃ʒavle] *vt* **(j'enjavelle; j'enjavellerai)** *Agr* to lay (*wheat etc*) in swaths.

enjeu [ɑ̃ʒø] *nm* **(a)** (*au jeu*) stake; **(b)** *Mil Pol etc* stakes; **quel est l'e.?,** what is at stake?, what are the stakes?

enjoindre [ɑ̃ʒwɛ̃dr] *vt* (*conj like* **joindre**) *Litt* to enjoin; **e. à qn de faire qch,** to enjoin *or* call upon *or* charge s.o. to do sth.

enjôlement [ɑ̃ʒolmɑ̃] *nm* **(a)** (*action*) cajoling, wheedling, coaxing; **(b)** (*paroles etc*) cajolery, blandishment.

enjôler [ɑ̃ʒole] *vt* to cajole, to wheedle, to coax (*s.o.*).

enjôleur, -euse [ɑ̃ʒolœr, -øz] **1** *n* coaxer, cajoler, wheedler. **2** *adj* coaxing, cajoling, wheedling.

enjolivement [ɑ̃ʒɔlivmɑ̃] *nm* **(a)** beautifying, embellishing (*of room, dress etc*); **(b)** (*ornement*) embellishment, ornament; (*dans un récit*) embellishment.

enjoliver [ɑ̃ʒɔlive] **1** *vt* to beautify, to embellish (*room, dress etc*); to embellish, to embroider (*facts, story etc*). **2 s'enjoliver** *vpr* (*of legend etc*) to get embellished *or* embroidered.

enjoliveur, -euse [ɑ̃ʒɔlivœr, -øz] **1** *n* **c'est un e.,** he likes to embellish *or* embroider his stories. **2** *nm Aut* hub cap.

enjolivure [ɑ̃ʒɔlivyr] *nf* (*ornement*) *& Fig* embellishment.

enjoué [ɑ̃ʒwe] *adj* vivacious, lively, playful.

enjouement [ɑ̃ʒumɑ̃] *nm* vivaciousness, liveliness, playfulness.

enkystement [ɑ̃kistəmɑ̃] *nm Méd* encystation, encystment.

enkyster (s') [sɑ̃kiste] *vpr Méd* (*of tumour*) to become encysted.

enlacement [ɑ̃lasmɑ̃] *nm* **(a)** (*de rubans, branches*) intertwining, interlacing; **(b)** (*en entourant*) enlacing, entwining.

enlacer [ɑ̃lase] *v* **(j'enlaçais) 1** *vt* **(a)** to intertwine, to interlace (*ribbons, branches*); (*entourer*) to entwine, to enlace, to twine round (*sth*); to tie up (*papers*); **(b)** (*étreindre*) to clasp (*s.o.*) in one's arms, to hug, to embrace (*s.o.*). **2 s'enlacer** *vpr* **(a)** (*s'étreindre*) to hug, to embrace (each other); **amants enlacés,** lovers (clasped) in an embrace; **(b)** (*s'entrelacer*) to intertwine, to interlace.

enlaidir [ɑ̃ledir] **1** *vt* to make (*s.o.*) ugly, to disfigure (*s.o.*); to disfigure (*landscape, town etc*); **cette robe l'enlaidit,** that dress makes her look ugly *or* plain. **2** *vi* to grow ugly *or* plain. **3 s'enlaidir** *vpr* to make oneself look ugly *or* plain.

enlaidissement [ɑ̃ledismɑ̃] *nm* **(a)** (*par accident*) disfigurement; **(b)** (*naturel*) growing ugly *or* plain, loss of good looks.

enlevage [ɑ̃lvaʒ] *nm* (*dans une course d'aviron*) spurt.

enlevé [ɑ̃lve] *adj* lively, spirited (*performance, style etc*); executed in a lively *or* spirited fashion (*dance, sonata etc*).

enlèvement [ɑ̃lɛvmɑ̃] *nm* **(a)** removal, removing; (*of clothes, furniture, label, stain, paint etc*); collection (*of luggage, refuse*); **(b)** (*kidnapping*) kidnapping, abduction; *Jur* **e. de mineur,** abduction of a minor; *Hist* **l'e. des Sabines,** the rape of the Sabine women; **mariage par e.,** runaway match; **e. d'enfant,** baby-snatching; **(c)** *Mil* storming, carrying (*of position*).

enlever [ɑ̃lve] *v* **(j'enlève; j'enlèverai) 1** *vt* **(a)** to remove, to take off (*clothes*); to remove, to take away (*furniture etc*); to remove, to take off (*label, button, lid etc*); to take up (*carpet*); to take down (*curtains*); to peel off, to remove (*rind, paint etc*); **e. le couvert,** to clear away, to clear the table; *F* **il a fallu lui e. les végétations,** he had to have his adenoids removed *or* taken out; **e. une tache,** to remove *or* take out a stain; *Litt* **enlevé par la mer,** carried *or* washed away by the sea; **la mort l'enleva à vingt ans,** death carried him off at twenty; **e. qch à qn,** to take sth (away) from s.o.; **enlève-lui ces allumettes des mains,** take those matches off him; **une bombe lui a enlevé les jambes,** a bomb took *or* blew off his legs; **on m'a enlevé mon pardessus,** someone has made off with my overcoat; **il m'a enlevé mes cors,** he removed my corns; **cette erreur n'enlève rien à votre valeur,** this mistake takes nothing away from *or* in no way detracts from your merit;

(b) (*kidnapper*) to kidnap, to abduct; **se faire e.,** (*par son amant*) to elope;

(c) (*remporter*) *Mil* to carry, to storm (*position*); *Sp etc* to win (*race, victory, prize*);

(d) (*soulever*) to raise, to lift (up) (*weight, lid*); to send up (*balloon*); **le vent enlève la poussière,** the wind raises the dust; **e. son cheval,** to lift one's horse (*to a fence*); (*le faire partir*) to set one's horse at full gallop; *Fig* **la foule fut enlevée par ces paroles,** the crowd was carried away

by these words;
(e) e. un morceau (de musique), to play a piece of music in lively *or* spirited fashion.
2 s'enlever *vpr* **(a)** (*of paint, skin etc*) to come *or* peel off; (*of stain*) to come out;
(b) (*of goods*) to sell quickly, to be snapped up; **ça s'enlève comme des petits pains,** it's selling like hot cakes;
(c) (*of balloon etc*) to rise;
(d) (*d'un cheval*) to take off.

enlisement [ɑ̃lizmɑ̃] *nm* sinking (*into quicksand etc*).

enliser [ɑ̃lize] **1** *vt* to get (*car, wheel etc*) stuck (*in the mud, sand etc*). **2 s'enliser** *vpr* to sink, to be sucked down (*into bog etc*); (*of car etc*) to sink (*into mud, sand etc*); *Fig* **s'e. dans ses explications/ses habitudes,** to get bogged down in one's explanations/habits.

enluminer [ɑ̃lymine] *vt* **(a)** (*illustrer*) to illuminate (*manuscript, book etc*); **(b)** (*colorer*) to colour (*print, map etc*); **(c)** *Fig* **visage enluminé,** flushed *or* glowing face.

enlumineur, -euse [ɑ̃lyminœr, -øz] *n* illuminator.

enluminure [ɑ̃lyminyr] *nf* **(a)** (*action d'illustrer*) illumination, illuminating (*of manuscript etc*); **(b)** (*action de colorer*) colouring, *US* coloring (*of prints etc*); **(c)** *Fig* colour, *US* color (*of face*); **(d)** (*lettre, dessin*) illumination.

enneigé [ɑ̃neʒe] *adj* snow-covered (*mountain, field etc*); snowbound, snowed-up (*road, village etc*).

enneigement [ɑ̃nɛʒmɑ̃] *nm* (*action*) snowing up; (*état*) snow cover; **bulletin d'e.,** snow report.

ennemi, -ie [ɛnmi] **1** *n* enemy; **se faire un e. de qn,** to make an enemy of s.o.; **passer à l'e.,** to go over to the enemy; **e. public numéro un,** public enemy number one; **les ennemis de la liberté,** the enemies of freedom; **le mieux est l'e. du bien,** leave well alone; **je suis e. de la bouffonnerie,** I hate *or* won't have buffoonery. **2** *adj* **le camp e.,** the enemy('s) camp; **en pays e.,** in enemy country.

ennoblir [ɑ̃nɔblir] *vt* **(a)** to ennoble, to elevate (*mind etc*); **(b)** *Tex* to improve (the quality of) (*fabric etc*).

ennui [ɑ̃nɥi] *nm* **(a)** (*souci*) worry, anxiety; (*problème*) problem; **avoir des ennuis,** to be worried *or* anxious; to have problems; **avoir des ennuis de santé/d'argent/de voiture,** to have health/money/car problems; **petits ennuis,** petty annoyances; **créer** *ou* **susciter** *ou* **faire des ennuis à qn,** to make trouble for s.o.; **quel e.!,** what a nuisance *or* bother *or* bind!; **l'e., c'est que je ne lui ai rien expliqué,** the trouble is that I haven't explained anything to him; **(b)** (*lassitude*) boredom, *Litt* ennui; **être saisi d'e.,** to be bored stiff; **ils me font mourir d'e.,** they bore me to death.

ennuyé [ɑ̃nɥije] *adj* **(a)** (*contrarié*) annoyed, bothered (**de,** about); **(b)** (*las*) bored (**de,** with).

ennuyer [ɑ̃nɥije] *v* **(j'ennuie; j'ennuierai) 1** *vt* **(a)** (*contrarier*) to annoy, to bother; **cela vous ennuierait-il d'attendre?,** would you mind waiting?; **cela m'ennuie de ne pouvoir le lui expliquer,** it annoys me that I can't explain it to him; **(b)** (*agacer*) to annoy, to irritate; **qu'est-ce qu'elle m'ennuie avec ses chichis!,** I'm really getting tired of the fuss she makes!; **(c)** (*lasser*) to bore (*s.o.*); **il m'ennuie à mourir,** he bores me stiff. **2 s'ennuyer** *vpr* to be *or* get bored; **je m'ennuie à ne rien faire,** (*maintenant*) I'm bored *or F* fed up with doing nothing; (*en général*) I get bored if I have nothing to do; **s'e. de faire qch,** to get tired of doing sth.

ennuyeux, -euse [ɑ̃nɥijø, -øz] *adj* **(a)** (*contrariant*) annoying, irritating; **comme c'est e.!,** what a nuisance!; **(b)** (*lassant*) boring, tedious, dull; **mortellement e.,** deadly boring *or* dull.

énoncé [enɔ̃se] *nm* **(a)** statement (*of facts*); terms (*of problem, Jur sentence*); text, wording (*of contract, law etc*); wording (*of question*); **(b)** *Ling* utterance.

énoncer [enɔ̃se] *v* **(j'énonçai(s)) 1** *vt* to state (*opinion, fact, conditions etc*). **2 s'énoncer** *vpr* (*of person*) to express oneself; (*of opinion*) to be stated.

énonciation [enɔ̃sjasjɔ̃] *nf* stating, statement (*of fact etc*).

enorgueillir [ɑ̃nɔrgœjir] **1** *vt* to make (*s.o.*) proud. **2 s'enorgueillir** *vpr* **s'e. de qch/d'avoir fait qch,** to be proud of *or* pride oneself on sth/having done sth.

énorme [enɔrm] *adj* enormous, huge (*person, building, success, quantity etc*); **crime é.,** outrageous *or* monstrous crime; **perte é.,** grievous *or* tremendous loss; **majorité é.,** enormous *or* overwhelming majority; **mensonge é.,** whopping lie; *F* **mais c'est é!, c'est incroyable,** but that's outrageous!, it's unbelievable!

énormément [enɔrmemɑ̃] *adv* enormously, hugely, tremendously; **je le regrette é.,** I'm extremely *or F* awfully sorry; **elle a é. changé,** she has changed enormously *or* a great deal; **é. de bien/d'argent/***etc*, an enormous amount *or* a great deal of good/money/*etc*; **é. de gens/***etc*, a great many *or F* lots of people/*etc*.

énormité [enɔrmite] *nf* **(a)** enormity, outrageousness (*of demand, sin, crime etc*); **(b)** (*taille démesurée*) enormousness, hugeness (*of person, building*); **l'é. du gaspillage,** the huge *or* enormous amount wasted; **(c)** (*bévue*) (dreadful) blunder; **commettre une é.,** to put one's foot in it badly, to make a (dreadful) blunder; **ce traité est plein d'énormités,** this treaty is full of (written) mistakes *or F* howlers; **dire des énormités,** to say the most awful things.

enquérir (s') [sɑ̃kerir] *vpr* (*conj like* **acquérir**) to inquire, to make inquiries (**de,** about); **s'e. du prix,** to ask the price; **il s'est enquis de vous/de votre santé,** he inquired after *or* about you/your health.

enquête [ɑ̃kɛt] *nf Jur Parl etc* inquiry; (*policière*) investigation(s), inquiries; (*sondage*) survey, opinion poll; **l'inspecteur mène l'e.,** the inspector is leading the investigation(s) *or* inquiries; **ouvrir une e.,** to open an inquiry; *Jur* **e. administrative,** public inquiry; **e. scientifique,** scientific investigation; **e. sociologique,** sociological survey; **e. par sondage,** sample survey; **faire** *ou* **procéder à une e. sur qch,** *Jur etc* to hold *or* set up *or* conduct an inquiry into sth; (*police*) to carry out *or* set up an investigation into sth; **commission d'e.,** court of inquiry, *Br Parl* select committee; **elle a décidé de faire sa petite e.,** she decided to investigate.

enquêter [ɑ̃kete] *vi Jur* to hold an inquiry; (*police*) to make investigations; (*faire un sondage*) to conduct a survey (**sur,** into); **e. sur une affaire,** to inquire into a matter, to investigate a matter.

enquêteur, -euse [ɑ̃kɛtœr, -øz] **1** *adj Jur* **commissaire e.,** investigating commissioner. **2** *n* investigator; (*qui fait un sondage*) researcher; *Journ* interviewer.

enquêtrice [ɑ̃kɛtris] *nf* investigator; (*qui fait un sondage*) researcher; *Journ* interviewer.

enquiquinant [ɑ̃kikinɑ̃] *adj F* (*agaçant*) infuriating, irritating, aggravating; (*lassant*) boring.

enquiquiner [ɑ̃kikine] *vt F* (*agacer*) to infuriate, to irritate, to aggravate; (*lasser*) to bore (stiff).

enquiquineur, -euse [ɑ̃kikinœr, -øz] *n F* nuisance, pest; (*raseur*) (crashing) bore.

enraciné [ɑ̃rasine] *adj* deep-rooted, deep-seated (*habit, hatred etc*); **elle est enracinée dans cette région/ses habitudes,** she is firmly rooted in this region/her habits.

enracinement [ɑ̃rasinmɑ̃] *nm* **(a)** (*action d'enraciner*) digging in (*of sapling*); **(b)** (*action de s'enraciner*) taking root (*of tree, Fig idea etc*); putting down of roots (*of person*).

enraciner [ɑ̃rasine] **1** *vt* **(a)** to dig in, to root (*tree etc*); **(b)** *Fig* to establish, to implant (*principles etc*). **2 s'enraciner** *vpr* **(a)** (*of tree*) to take root; *Fig* (*of person*) to put down roots; **(b)** (*of feelings, habits, custom etc*) to take root, to become established *or* deeply rooted.

enragé, -ée [ɑ̃raʒe] **1** *adj* **(a)** mad (*dog etc*); **(b)** *F* rabid, out-and-out (*socialist etc*); keen (*angler etc*). **2** *n F* fanatic; **un e. de golf,** a golf fanatic *or* enthusiast, a keen golfer.

enrageant [ɑ̃raʒɑ̃] *adj* infuriating, maddening.

enrager [ɑ̃raʒe] *vi* **(j'enrageai(s); n. enrageons)** to be furious; **elle enrage de ne pas pouvoir le faire,** she's furious at not being able to do it; **faire e. qn,** to infuriate *or* madden s.o.; (*taquiner*) to tease s.o..

enrayage [ɑ̃rɛjaʒ] *nm* **(a)** (*blocage*) locking (*of wheel*); jamming (*of mechanism, gun etc*); **(b)** (*montage des rayons*) spoking (*of wheel*).

enrayer¹ [ɑ̃reje] *vt* **(j'enraye, j'enraie; j'enrayerai, j'enraierai)** *Agr* **e. un champ,** to plough the first furrow of a field.

enrayer² **1** *vt* **(a)** (*bloquer*) to lock, to jam (*firearm, machine etc*); *Fig* **e. une maladie/un fléau/***etc*, to arrest *or* check a disease/scourge/*etc*; **(b)** (*équiper de rayons*) to spoke (*wheel*). **2 s'enrayer** *vpr* **(a)** (*of firearm, machine etc*) to jam; **(b)** (*of epidemic*) to abate.

enrayure [ɑ̃rɛjyr] *nf* (*rayons*) spokes (*of wheel*).

enrégimenter [ɑ̃reʒimɑ̃te] *vt* **(a)** to enrol (*helper etc*) (*into party, organization etc*); **(b)** *Mil* to form into regiments.

enregistrable [ɑ̃r(ə)ʒistrabl] *adj* recordable (*music, broadcast etc*).

enregistrement [ɑ̃r(ə)ʒistrəmɑ̃] *nm* **(a)** (*action d'inscrire*) recording (*of facts etc*); *Jur* registration (*of birth, deed etc*); booking, entering (up) (*of an order*); registration (*of luggage*); **bureau d'e.,** registry office; (*à l'aéroport etc*) luggage office; **e. d'une compagnie,** incorporation of a company; *Admin* **droit d'e.,** stamp duty; **(b)** *Tech* (*action, disque etc*) recording; **e. vidéo,** video recording; **e. sur bande/cassette,** tape/cassette recording; **studio d'e.,** recording studio; *TV* **camion d'e. (du son),** sound van; **passer un e.,** to play a recording.

enregistrer [ɑ̃r(ə)ʒistre] **1** *vt* **(a)** (*inscrire*) to record (*facts etc*); *Jur* to register (*a birth, a deed etc*); to book, to enter up (*an order*); to register (*luggage*); **société enregistrée,** incorporated company; **(b)** *F* (*mémoriser*) to note, to memorize; **(c)** *Tech* to record (*music, broadcast etc*); **e. un disque,** to make a record; **e. sur bande,** to tape, to record on tape; **e. au magnétoscope,** to video, to record on video; **musique enregistrée,** recorded music; **(d)** *Ordinat* **programme enregistré,** stored programme. **2 s'enregistrer** *vpr* (*of cassette etc*) to record.

enregistreur, -euse [ɑ̃r(ə)ʒistrœr, -øz] **1** *adj* recording (*apparatus, device*); **caisse enregistreuse,** cash register. **2** *nm* (*appareil*) recorder; **e. de son** *ou* **sonore,** sound recorder; **e. à bande,** (strip) chart recorder; **e. à tambour,** drum recorder; *Av* **e. de vol,** flight recorder, *F* black box; **e. de pression,** pressure recorder; *Ind* **e. de temps,** time clock *or* recorder.

enrhumer [ɑ̃ryme] **1** *vt* to give (*s.o.*) a cold; **être enrhumé (du cerveau/de la poitrine),** to have a cold (in the head/chest). **2 s'enrhumer** *vpr* to catch (a) cold.

enrichi, -ie [ɑ̃riʃi] *Péj* **1** *adj* nouveau riche (*person*). **2** *n* nouveau riche, parvenu.

enrichir [ɑ̃riʃir] **1** *vt* **(a)** to enrich, to make (*s.o., country*) rich(er); **(b)** *Fig* to enrich (*art collection, mind etc*); **e. la langue française,** to enrich the French language; **(c)** *Phys* to enrich (*uranium etc*); **e. la terre,** to enrich the soil. **2 s'enrichir** *vpr* **(a)** (*of person, country*) to grow rich(er); **(b)** (*of language etc*) to grow *or* become richer (**de,** with; **en,** in); **s'e. par l'expérience,** to gain a wealth of experience.

enrichissant [ɑ̃riʃisɑ̃] *adj* enriching (*experience etc*).

enrichissement [ɑ̃riʃismɑ̃] *nm* **(a)** enriching, enrichment (*of mind, museum etc*); **e. personnel,** personal enrichment; **(b)** *Phys* enrichment (*of uranium etc*).

enrobage [ɑ̃rɔbaʒ] *nm*, **enrobement** [ɑ̃rɔbmɑ̃] *nm* (*action, enveloppe*) coating; **e. de sucre/chocolat,** a sugar/chocolate coating.

enrober [ɑ̃rɔbe] *vt* to coat (*sweet, pill etc*) (**de,** with); *Fig* **e. une nouvelle peu agréable dans un flot de paroles,** to wrap up a piece of unpleasant news in a mass of words.

enrôlé [ɑ̃role] *nm Mil* enlisted man.

enrôlement [ɑ̃rolmɑ̃] *nm* enrolment; *Mil* enlistment.

enrôler [ɑ̃role] **1** *vt* to enrol, to recruit (*members, workers*); *Mil* to enlist; *Hist* **e. de force,** to press-gang, to impress. **2 s'enrôler** *vpr* to enrol (oneself); *Mil* to enlist.

enroué [ɑ̃rwe] *adj* hoarse, husky (*person, voice*).

enrouement [ɑ̃rumɑ̃] *nm* hoarseness, huskiness.

enrouer [ɑ̃rwe] **1** *vt* to make (*voice, person*) hoarse *or* husky. **2 s'enrouer** *vpr* to get hoarse; **s'e. à force de crier,** to shout oneself hoarse.

enroulement [ɑ̃rulmɑ̃] *nm* **(a)** (*de tissu, tapis etc*) rolling up; (*de câble, ruban etc*) winding up; **(b)** *El* (*fil*) coil; **(c)** (*ornement*) scroll, volute.

enrouler [ɑ̃rule] **1** *vt* **(a)** (*rouler*) to roll up (*map, carpet etc*); to wind up (*cable, ribbon etc*); **(b)** (*envelopper*) to wrap up (**dans,** in). **2 s'enrouler** *vpr* (*of serpent etc*) to wind, to coil; (*of film, wire etc*) to wind; **s'e. dans une couverture/***etc*, to wrap oneself up in a blanket/*etc*.

enrubanner [ɑ̃rybane] *vt* to decorate with a ribbon *or* ribbons.

ENS [əenes] *nf abrév* **École normale supérieure.**

ensablement [ɑ̃sabləmɑ̃] *nm* **(a)** running aground, stranding (*of ship*); **(b)** silting up (*of harbour*); choking up (*of pipes*); **(c)** (*dépot*) sandbank, sand bar.

ensabler [ɑ̃sable] **1** *vt* **(a)** to strand, to run (*boat*) aground (*on the sand*); to get (*vehicle*) stuck in the sand; **(b)** (*of flood*) to cover (*land*) with sand; to silt up, to sand up (*harbour, river*). **2 s'ensabler** *vpr* **(a)** (*of ship, vehicle, fish*) to get stuck in the sand; **(b)** (*of harbour, river*) to silt up; (*of pipes*) to get choked up (with sand).

ensachage [ɑ̃saʃaʒ] *nm* bagging (*of sweets etc*); sacking (*of cereals etc*).

ensacher [ɑ̃saʃe] *vt to* put into bags, to bag (*sweets etc*); to put into sacks, to sack (*cereals etc*).

ensanglanter [ɑ̃sɑ̃glɑ̃te] *vt* to stain (*shirt, body etc*) with blood; **e. une nation,** to plunge a nation into a bloodbath; **mains ensanglantées,** bloodstained *or* bloody hands.

enseignant, -ante [ɑ̃sɛɲɑ̃, -ɑ̃t] **1** *adj* teaching; **corps e.,** teaching profession. **2** *n* teacher.

enseigne [ɑ̃sɛɲ] **1** *nf* **(a)** (*panonceau*) sign (*of shop, cinema etc*); **e. au néon,** neon sign; **à l'e. du Lion d'or,** at the (sign of the) Golden Lion; *F* **nous sommes tous logés à la même e.,** we are all in the same boat; *Prov* **à bon vin point d'e.,** good wine needs no bush; **(b) à telle e. que ...,** so much so that ...; **(c)** *Hist Mil* ensign. **2** *nm* **(a)** *Hist Mil* standard-bearer, ensign; **(b)** *Nau* **e. (de vaisseau),** *Br* sub-lieutenant; *US* ensign.

enseignement [ɑ̃sɛɲmɑ̃] *nm* **(a)** (*instruction*) teaching; **l'e. de l'anglais,** the teaching of English; **méthode d'e.,** teaching method; **il est dans l'e.,** he is a teacher, he teaches; **e. par correspondance,** correspondence course; **e. à distance/en groupe,** distance/group teaching; **e. assisté par ordinateur,** computer-aided *or* -assisted learning; **(b)** (*éducation, formation*) education; **e. des** *ou* **pour adultes,** adult education; **e. mixte,** coeducation; **e. du premier/second degré, e. primaire/secondaire,** primary/secondary education; **e. supérieur,** higher education; **(c)** (*leçon tirée de l'expérience*) lesson; **tirer un e. de qch,** to learn a lesson from sth.

enseigner [ɑ̃sɛɲe] **1** *vt* **(a)** (*apprendre*) to teach; **e. la grammaire à qn,** to teach s.o. grammar; **e. à qn à faire qch,** to teach s.o. (how) to do sth; **e. l'anglais,** to teach English; **l'expérience nous enseigne que ...,** experience teaches *or* shows us that ...; **(b)** (*instruire*) **e. les enfants,** to teach children; **(c)** *Vieilli* (*indiquer*) to show, to point out; **e. à qn son devoir,** to point out his duty to s.o.. **2** *vi* **il enseigne,** he's a teacher, he teaches.

ensemble [ɑ̃sɑ̃bl] **1** *adv* together; **vivre e.,** to live together; **ils se marièrent e.,** they married (each other); **être bien e.,** to be good friends; **ils vont mal e.,** they don't get on, *F* they don't hit it off; **choses qui vont e.,** things that belong *or* go together; **le tout e.,** the general effect; **vendre tous ses meubles e.,** to sell all one's furniture at once.

2 *nm* **(a)** (*totalité*) whole, entirety; **l'e. du travail est bon,** the work as a whole is good; **l'e. d'un tableau,** the general effect of a picture; **vue d'e.,** comprehensive *or* general view, overall picture; **idée d'e.,** broad *or* general idea (*of a subject*); **dans l'e.,** on the whole, taken all round, by and large; **les juges, pris dans leur e., étaient intègres,** the judges, taken as a body, were honest;

(b) (*unité*) cohesion, unity; **mouvement d'e.,** combined movement; **l'exécution manque d'e.,** the execution lacks cohesion *or* is ragged; **agir d'e.,** to act jointly *or* in concert *or* in unison; **avec e.,** all together, in unison, as one;

(c) (*groupe*) group (*of people*); set (*of objects, facts, conditions*); suite (*of furniture*); **e. vocal,** (small) choir; **e. de couleurs,** harmonious (group of) colours;

(d) (*vêtement*) ensemble, outfit;

(e) (*d'habitations*) block; **grand e.,** residential estate;

(f) *Math* set; **e. vide,** empty set.

ensemblier [ɑ̃sɑ̃blije] *nm* interior decorator; *Cin TV* assistant set designer.

ensemencement [ɑ̃s(ə)mɑ̃smɑ̃] *nm* **(a)** *Agr* sowing; **(b)** *Biol* seeding.

ensemencer [ɑ̃smɑ̃se] *vt* **(j'ensemençai(s)) (a)** *Agr* to sow (*field*); **(b)** *Biol* to seed (*culture medium*).

enserrer [ɑ̃sere] *vt* to encircle (*object, part of body*) tightly; **e. qn dans ses bras,** to clasp s.o. in one's arms, to embrace *or* hug s.o..

ensevelir [ɑ̃səvlir] **1** *vt* **(a)** *Litt* (*enterrer*) to bury, to entomb (*corpse*); *Fig* to hide away (*secret*); **(b)** (*mettre dans un linceul*) to shroud (*corpse*). **2 s'ensevelir** *vpr* to bury oneself (*in a book, in the country etc*); **enseveli dans la méditation,** lost *or* sunk *or* wrapped in thought; **enseveli sous la neige,** buried beneath the snow.

ensevelissement [ɑ̃səvlismɑ̃] *nm* (*de mort*) burial; (*dans un linceul*) shrouding; (*sous la neige, des décombres etc*) burying; *Fig* (*de secret*) hiding away.

ensilage [ɑ̃silaʒ] *nm* ensilage (*of crops*).

ensiler [ɑ̃sile] *vt* to ensile (*crops*).

ensoleillé [ɑ̃sɔleje] *adj* sunny (*resort, day etc*).

ensoleillement [ɑ̃sɔlɛjmɑ̃] *nm* **(a)** (*état*) sunniness; **(b)** (*période*) sunny period; **cinq journées d'e.,** five days of sun(shine).

ensoleiller [ɑ̃sɔleje] *vt* **(a)** to bathe (*room, wall etc*) in sunlight; **(b)** *Fig* to brighten (up), to light up (*s.o.'s life etc*).

ensommeillé [ɑ̃sɔmeje] *adj* sleepy, drowsy (*person*); sleepy (*eyes, face*).

ensorcelant [ɑ̃sɔrsəlɑ̃] *adj* bewitching (*smile etc*).

ensorcelé [ɑ̃sɔrsəle] *adj* bewitched, under a spell.

ensorceler [ɑ̃sɔrsəle] *vt* **(j'ensorcelle; j'ensorcellerai) (a)** (*envoûter*) to bewitch, to cast *or* put a spell (up)on (*s.o., sth*); **(b)** *Fig* to bewitch, to captivate (*s.o.*).

ensorceleur, -euse [ɑ̃sɔrsəlœr, -øz] **1** *adj* bewitching. **2** *nm* sorcerer; *Fig* charmer. **3** *nf* **ensorceleuse,** sorceress.

ensorcellement [ɑ̃sɔrsɛlmɑ̃] *nm* **(a)** (*action*) bewitching; (*état*) bewitchment; (*sorcellerie*) sorcery; **(b)** *Fig* (*charme*) charm, spell.

ensuite [ɑ̃sɥit] *adv* (*plus tard*) after(wards), later; (*puis*) then, next, after that; **et e.?,** what then?, what next?; *F* **e. de quoi** *ou* **de cela, il s'est mis en colère,** after which *or* after that he lost his temper; **les pompiers marchaient en tête, e. venait la musique,** the firemen led the procession, next came the band; **c'est très dangereux de faire cela, e. je te l'interdis,** it's very dangerous to do that, and anyway I forbid you to do it.

ensuivre (s') [sɑ̃sɥivr] *vpr* (*conj like* **suivre**) to follow, to ensue, to result; **jusqu'à ce que mort s'ensuive,** (*battre etc*) to death; **les résultats qui s'ensuivent,** the results which ensue *or* follow; **il s'ensuit qu'il est sans emploi,** the consequence is he's out of a job; **il ne s'ensuit pas que vous ayez raison,** it doesn't follow that you are right; *F* **et tout ce qui s'ensuit,** and all the rest of it, and all that goes with it.

entablement [ɑ̃tabləmɑ̃] *nm Archit* (*au-dessus d'une colonnade*) entablature; *Constr* (*support de toit*) coping.

entacher [ɑ̃taʃe] *vt* **(a)** to sully, to besmirch, to cast a slur on (*s.o.'s honour*); **religion entachée de superstition,** religion tainted with superstition; **(b)** *Jur* to vitiate (*contract etc*); **entaché de nullité,** voidable.

entaille [ɑ̃taj] *nf* **(a)** notch (*in piece of wood etc*); (*longue*) groove; **à entailles,** notched; **(b)** (*blessure*) gash, cut; (*petite*) nick, cut; **se faire une e. au menton,** to cut one's chin; *Fig* **une e. dans la confiance publique,** a blow to public confidence.

entailler [ɑ̃taje] **1** *vt* **(a)** to notch (*piece of wood etc*); (*d'une longue encoche*) to groove; **(b)** (*blesser*) to gash, to cut; (*superficiellement*) to nick, to cut. **2 s'entailler** *vpr* **s'e. le doigt,** to cut one's finger.

entame [ɑ̃tam] *nf* **(a)** first cut, outside slice (*of loaf, ham etc*); **(b)** *Cartes* opening (card) (*of a suit*).

entamer [ɑ̃tame] *vt* **(a)** to start on, to cut into (*loaf, ham etc*); to broach (*cask*); to start on, to open (*bottle, pot of jam etc*); to penetrate, to breach (*defence*); to cut into (*flesh*); **e. la peau,** to break the skin; **doutes qui entament la foi/les convictions de qn,** doubts that undermine *or* shake s.o.'s faith/convictions; **e. l'honneur de qn,** to damage s.o.'s honour; **e. son capital,** to break into one's capital; **(b)** (*commencer à entreprendre*) to begin, to commence, to start (on) (*conversation, work etc*); to initiate (*deal*); **e. des relations avec qn,** to enter into relations with s.o.; *Jur* **e. des poursuites contre qn,** to initiate *or* institute proceedings against s.o.; **e. un sujet,** to broach a subject; **(c)** *Cartes* **e. trèfle,** to open clubs.

entartrage [ɑ̃tartraʒ] *nm* furring, encrustation, scaling (*of boiler etc*).

entartrer [ɑ̃tartre] **1** *vt* to encrust, to fur, to scale (*boiler etc*). **2 s'entartrer** *vpr* (*of boiler*) to fur, to become furred.

entassement [ɑ̃tasmɑ̃] *nm* **(a)** (*action*) piling (up), heaping (up) (*of stones etc*); stacking (*of cases etc*); **(b)** crowding *or* packing together (*of passengers, cattle etc*).

entasser [ɑ̃tase] **1** *vt* **(a)** to pile (up), to heap (up) (*stones, books, clothes etc*); to stack (up) (*cases etc*); *Fig* to heap (up) (*insults*); to amass, to pile up (*money*); **(b)** (*serrer*) to pack *or* crowd *or* cram (*passengers, cattle etc*) together. **2 s'entasser** *vpr* **(a)** (*objects*) to pile up; **(b)** (*of persons*) to crowd *or* huddle together.

ente [ɑ̃t] *nf* **(a)** *Bot* (*greffe*) scion, graft; (*porte-greffe*) stock; **(b)** (*de pinceau*) handle.

entendement [ɑ̃tɑ̃dmɑ̃] *nm* understanding; **homme d'e.,** man of sense *or* of intelligence; **dépasser l'e.,** to be beyond all understanding.

entendeur [ɑ̃tɑ̃dœr] *nm* **à bon e. salut!,** a word to the wise (is enough).

entendre [ɑ̃tɑ̃dr] **1** *vt* **(a)** (*vouloir dire*) to mean; **qu'entendez-vous par là?,** what do you mean by that?;

(b) (*vouloir*) **e. faire qch,** to intend *or* mean *or* propose to do sth; **il n'y entend pas malice,** he means *or* intends no harm; **faites comme vous l'entendez,** do as you think best, do as you please; **j'entends que vous veniez,** I expect you to come; **je n'entends pas qu'on le vende,** I won't hear of it being sold;

(c) (*percevoir par l'ouïe*) to hear; **e. un concert/chanteur,** to listen to a concert/singer; **j'entendis un cri,** I heard a cry; **on l'entend à peine,** you can hardly hear him *or* it, he *or* it is scarcely audible; **je pouvais à peine me faire e.,** I could hardly make myself heard; **je l'entendis rire,** I heard him laugh *or* laughing; **tu n'as pas entendu quelque chose?,** didn't you hear anything?; **e. parler de qn/qch,** to hear of *or* about s.o./sth; **je ne veux plus e. parler de lui,** I don't want to hear him mentioned again; **e. dire que ...,** to hear (it said) that ...; **on entend dire que sa femme l'a quitté,** it is rumoured that his wife has left him; **je le sais par ce qu'on entend dire,** I know it by hearsay; **e. dire qch à qn,** to hear sth said to s.o.; **e. qn dire qch,** to hear s.o. say sth;

(d) (*écouter*) to hear, to listen to (*supplicant etc*); **on le congédia sans l'e.,** he was dismissed without a hearing; *Jur* **l'affaire sera entendue demain,** the case will be heard *or* comes up (for hearing) tomorrow; **à vous e., il a eu tort,** judging from what you say *or* according to you, he was in the wrong; **refuser d'e. une requête,** to turn a deaf ear to a request; **e. raison,** to listen to reason; **il n'a rien voulu e.,** he would not listen;

(e) (*comprendre*) to understand (*person, language, words etc*); **il ne l'entend pas ainsi,** he doesn't see it that way *or* like that; **donner à e. à qn que ...,** (*faire croire*) to lead s.o. to believe that ...; (*faire comprendre*) to give s.o. to understand that ...; **laisser e. qch,** to insinuate *or* imply sth; **il n'entend pas la plaisanterie,** he can't take a joke; **je n'y entends rien,** I don't know the first thing about it.

2 *vi* **(a)** (*par l'ouïe*) to hear; **il entend mal,** he is hard of hearing; **tu entends!,** (*menace*) do you hear me!;

(b) (*comprendre*) to understand.

3 s'entendre *vpr* **(a)** (*sympathiser*) to get on; (*se mettre d'accord*) to agree; **ils s'entendent bien,** they get on (well); **nous ne sommes pas faits pour nous e.,** we are not suited to each other; **entendons-nous!,** let's get things straight!; **s'e. directement avec qn,** to come to a direct understanding with s.o.; **s'e. pour commettre un crime,** to conspire to commit a crime; **ils s'entendent comme larrons en foire,** they are as thick as thieves;

(b) s'e. à, (*se connaître à*) to know (all) about, to understand (*horses, cars etc*); **s'e. aux affaires,** to be a good businessman *or* businesswoman; **s'e. mal à mentir,** to be a poor liar;

(c) (*être perçu par l'ouïe*) to be heard; **sa voix ne s'entend guère,** his voice is hardly audible *or* can hardly be heard; **on ne s'entend plus ici,** you can't hear yourself speak here;

(d) (*être compris*) to be understood; **cela s'entend,** of course, that goes without saying.

entendu, -ue [ɑ̃tɑ̃dy] **1** *adj* **(a)** (*au courant*) knowing (*look, smile*); **d'un air e.,** knowingly; **intérêt bien e.,** enlightened self-interest; **(b)** (*décidé*) **très bien, (c'est) e.,** fine, agreed *or* all right!; **c'est une affaire entendue,** that's agreed *or* settled; **et bien e., vous toucherez la moitié du bénéfice,** and of course, you'll get half the profit; **(c)** *Arch* (*compétent*) capable (*person*). **2** *n Vieilli* **faire l'e.,** to pretend to know all about it.

enténébrer [ɑ̃tenebre] *vt* (**il enténèbre; il enténébrera**) *Litt* to envelop *or* plunge in darkness *or* gloom.

entente [ɑ̃tɑ̃t] *nf* **(a)** (*entre personnes*) agreement, understanding (**entre,** between); **arriver à une e.,** to reach an agreement *or* understanding; **terrain d'e.,** common ground; **après e. avec les autorités,** after consultation with the authorities; **e. industrielle,** combine; **il faut vivre en bonne e. avec ses voisins,** one must live in harmony with one's neighbours; **la bonne/mauvaise e. qui règne dans la famille,** the good/bad feeling that prevails in the family; **(b)** (*intelligence*) understanding (**de,** of); (*compétence*) skill (**de,** in); **(c) mot à double e.,** word with a double meaning.

enter [ɑ̃te] *vt* to graft (*tree*).

entérinement [ɑ̃terinmɑ̃] *nm Jur* ratification, confirmation; *Fig* endorsement.

entériner [ɑ̃terine] *vt Jur* to ratify, to confirm; *Fig* (*approuver*) to endorse (*action, new word etc*).

entérique [ɑ̃terik] *adj Méd* enteric, intestinal.

entérite [ɑ̃terit] *nf Méd* enteritis.

enterrement [ɑ̃tɛrmɑ̃] *nm* **(a)** (*sous la terre*) burial, *Fml* interment; *Fig* **c'est l'e. de tous mes projets/espoirs,** that has killed off all my plans/hopes; **(b)** (*cérémonie*) funeral; *F* **figure** *ou* **tête d'e.,** long face; **(c)** (*cortège*) funeral procession.

enterrer [ɑ̃tere] **1** *vt* **(a)** (*enfouir*) to bury, to put (*sth*) in the earth; to plant (*bulbs*); **(b)** (*inhumer*) to bury, *Fml* to inter (*corpse*); *F* **il nous enterrera tous,** he will outlive us all; *Fig* **e. un projet,** to scrap a plan; **elle désire e. toute cette affaire,** she wants the whole thing buried and forgotten. **2 s'enterrer** *vpr Fig* **il s'est enterré au fond de la campagne,** he buried himself in the depths of the country.

entêtant [ɑ̃tɛtɑ̃] *adj* heady (*wine, perfume, music etc*).

en-tête [ɑ̃tɛt] *nm* (*pl* **en-têtes**) **(a)** heading (*of letter,* *document*); **en-t. de facture,** billhead; **papier à en-t.,** headed notepaper; **(b)** *Typ* headline (*of page etc*); *Ordinat* header.

entêté, -ée [ɑ̃tɛte] **1** *adj* obstinate, stubborn. **2** *n* obstinate *or* stubborn person.

entêtement [ɑ̃tɛtmɑ̃] *nm* obstinacy, stubbornness; **e. à faire qch,** persistence in doing sth.

entêter [ɑ̃tete] **1** *vt* **e. qn,** (*of wine, smell, music etc*) to go to s.o.'s head, to make s.o. giddy; **ces louanges l'entêtaient,** this praise went to *or* turned his head. **2 s'entêter** *vpr* **s'e. dans une opinion,** to persist in an opinion; **s'e. à faire qch,** to persist in doing sth.

enthousiasmant [ɑ̃tuzjasmɑ̃] *adj* exciting (*plan, idea etc*).

enthousiasme [ɑ̃tuzjasm] *nm* enthusiasm (**pour,** for); **avec e.,** enthusiastically, with enthusiasm; **faire qch sans e.,** to do sth half-heartedly *or* without enthusiasm.

enthousiasmer [ɑ̃tuzjasme] **1** *vt* to fire *or* fill (*s.o.*) with enthusiasm; **il est revenu enthousiasmé,** he came back full of *or* fired with enthusiasm. **2 s'enthousiasmer** *vpr* to be *or* become enthusiastic (**pour,** about).

enthousiaste [ɑ̃tuzjast] **1** *n* enthusiast. **2** *adj* enthusiastic.

entiché [ɑ̃tiʃe] *adj* infatuated (**de,** with), *F* crazy (**de,** about).

enticher (s') [sɑ̃tiʃe] *vpr* **s'e. de qn/qch,** to become infatuated with *or F* crazy about s.o./sth.

entier, -ière [ɑ̃tje, -jɛr] **1** *adj* **(a)** (*sans division, sans diminution*) entire, whole (*town, box, amount etc*); (*pas cassé, pas entamé*) intact, whole (*plate, cake etc*); full (*box, bottle etc*); **lait e.,** whole milk, *Br* full-cream milk; **la France entière,** the whole of France; **l'œuvre est tout entière à recommencer,** the whole work must be done again; **pendant des heures entières,** for hours on end; **conserver sa réputation entière,** to keep one's reputation intact; **le problème reste e.,** the problem is no nearer solution; **nombre e.,** integer, whole number; **cheval e.,** stallion; **payer place entière,** *Rail* to pay full fare; *Th* to pay full price;

(b) (*absolu*) complete, full (*authority, confidence etc*); **l'entière direction de qch,** the entire *or* sole management of sth; **se donner tout e. à son travail,** to devote oneself entirely to one's work; **elle est tout(e) entière à ce qu'elle fait,** she is engrossed in *or* intent on what she is doing; **jouir d'une entière liberté,** to enjoy complete freedom; **tout e. pour une ligne de conduite,** all in favour of a course of action;

(c) (*inébranlable*) unyielding, uncompromising (*person*).

2 *nm* **(a)** (*totalité*) entirety; **raconter une histoire dans son e.,** to relate a story in its entirety; **en e.,** wholly, entirely, totally; **nom en e.,** name in full, full name;

(b) *Math* (*nombre*) integer, whole number.

entièrement [ɑ̃tjɛrmɑ̃] *adv* entirely, wholly, completely; **il n'est pas e. mauvais,** he's not all bad.

entièreté [ɑ̃tjɛrte] *nf* entirety.

entité [ɑ̃tite] *nf* entity.

entoilage [ɑ̃twalaʒ] *nm* **(a)** (*action*) mounting (*of maps etc*) on canvas; *Couture* stiffening with canvas; **(b)** (*toile*) canvas mount.

entoiler [ɑ̃twale] *vt* to mount (*map etc*) on linen *or* canvas; **carte entoilée,** canvas-mounted map.

entôler [ɑ̃tole] *vt Arg* (*esp of prostitute*) to fleece, to rob (*client etc*).

entomologie [ɑ̃tɔmɔlɔʒi] *nf* entomology.

entomologique [ɑ̃tɔmɔlɔʒik] *adj* entomological.

entomologiste [ɑ̃tɔmɔlɔʒist] *n* entomologist.

entonner¹ [ɑ̃tɔne] *vt* to barrel, to cask (*wine etc*).

entonner² *vt* (*commencer à chanter*) to strike up, to start (*song*); (*chanter*) to sing; **e. les louanges de qn,** to sing s.o.'s praises.

entonnoir [ɑ̃tɔnwar] *nm* **(a)** (*ustensile*) funnel; **en (forme d') e.,** funnel-shaped; **(b)** (*cavité*) funnel; (*produit par une bombe etc*) crater.

entorse [ɑ̃tɔrs] *nf* **(a)** *Méd* sprain, wrench; **se faire une e. à la cheville/au poignet,** to sprain *or* twist *or* wrench one's ankle/wrist; **(b)** *Fig* **faire une e. à la loi/au règlement,** to bend *or* stretch the law/the rules; **faire une e. à la vérité,** to twist *or* distort the truth.

entortillé [ɑ̃tɔrtije] *adj Péj* convoluted, tortuous (*style, reply etc*).

entortillement [ɑ̃tɔrtijmɑ̃] *nm* **(a)** (*action*) twisting, wrapping (*of string, paper etc*); twisting, twining, coiling (*of snake, ivy etc*); **(b)** (*état*) entwinement.

entortiller [ɑ̃tɔrtije] **1** *vt* **(a)** (*envelopper*) to wrap (up) (*sweet etc*) (**dans,** in); (*enrouler*) to twist, to wrap (*string, paper etc*) (**autour de,** round); **(b)** (*circonvenir*) to get round (*s.o.*). **2 s'entortiller** *vpr* **(a)** (*of snake, ivy etc*) to twist, to twine, to coil (**autour de,** round); **(b)** (*s'empêtrer*) to get entangled (**dans,** in); *Fig* **elle s'entortillait dans des explications compliquées,** she tied herself in knots with complicated explanations.

entour [ɑ̃tur] *nm* **à l'e.,** (*alentour*) around, round about; **à l'e. de,** round (about) (*town etc*).

entourage [ɑ̃turaʒ] *nm* **(a)** (*bordure*) border (*of opening, flowerbed etc*); setting (*of jewel*); **miniature avec un e. de perles,** miniature set in pearls; **(b)** (*amis, relations*) circle (of friends, acquaintances); (*collègues*) associates; (*de ministre etc*) attendants; (*de souverain*) entourage, suite; **dans son proche e.,** in his close circle.

entourer [ɑ̃ture] **1** *vt* to surround (**de,** with); to encircle, to surround (*army*); **e. un champ d'une clôture,** to fence in a field; **il était très entouré,** he was the centre of attraction; **les gens qui vous entourent,** the people around *or* about you; **entouré de mystère,** wrapped *or* shrouded in mystery; **e. qn de soins/respect,** to lavish attention on s.o./to show respect to s.o.; **entouré de difficultés,** beset with difficulties. **2 s'entourer** *vpr* **s'e. d'amis/de belles choses/***etc*, to surround oneself with friends/fine things/*etc*.

entourloupette [ɑ̃turlupɛt] *nf F* dirty trick; **faire une e. à qn,** to play a dirty trick on s.o..

entournure [ɑ̃turnyr] *nf* (*de vêtement*) armhole; *F* **être gêné aux entournures,** (*mal à l'aise*) to feel awkward *or* ill at ease; (*financièrement*) to feel the pinch.

entracte [ɑ̃trakt] *nm* **(a)** (*intervalle*) *Th Cin Br* interval, *Am* intermission; *Fig* (*dans une activité*) break (**de, dans,** in); **à l'e.,** in the *Br* interval *or Am* intermission; **(b)** *Th* (*pièce*) entr'acte, interlude.

entraide [ɑ̃trɛd] *nf* mutual aid.

entraider (s') [sɑ̃trede] *vpr* to help one another.

entrailles [ɑ̃traj] *nfpl* **(a)** (*du corps*) entrails, intestines, bowels; *Fig* **les e. de la terre,** the bowels of the earth; **(b)** (*compassion*) compassion; **être sans e.,** to be heartless; **(c)** *Litt* (*de la mère*) womb.

entrain [ɑ̃trɛ̃] *nm* liveliness, spirit (*of party, music, conversation etc*); high spirits, spirit, liveliness (*of person*); **être plein d'e., avoir de l'e.,** (*of person*) to be full of life *or* of go; **musique pleine d'e.,** lively music; **manger avec e.,** to eat with gusto; **travailler avec e.,** to work with a will; **donner plus d'e. à la conversation,** to liven up the conversation; **ça manque d'e., tout ça,** that's all a bit half-hearted; **faire qch sans e.,** to do sth half-heartedly.

entraînant [ɑ̃trɛnɑ̃] *adj* lively (*tune, style etc*); stirring (*speech etc*).

entraînement [ɑ̃trɛnmɑ̃] *nm* **(a)** *Tech Ordinat* drive; **arbre d'e.,** drive shaft; **(b)** (*d'élève etc*) & *Sp* training; **suivre un e.,** to follow a training programme; **à l'e.,** in training; **partie d'e.,** practice game; **terrain d'e.,** training *or* practice ground; **(c)** (*de passions, d'habitudes*) force; **céder à des entraînements,** to get carried away; **dans l'e. de la discussion,** in the heat of the discussion.

entraîner [ɑ̃trene] **1** *vt* **(a)** (*of river etc*) to sweep along, to carry away; (*of locomotive etc*) to pull, to draw (along); **e. qn quelque part,** to drag *or* take s.o. off somewhere; **il m'a entraîné chez lui,** he took me along to his house; **il vous entraînera dans sa chute,** he will drag you down with him;

(b) *Tech* to drive (*part of machine etc*);

(c) (*exercer une influence sur*) **e. qn à faire qch,** to lead *or* induce s.o. to do sth; **être entraîné dans un piège,** to be lured *or* led into a trap; **cela nous entraînera dans des problèmes,** that will lead *or* get us into problems; **entraîné par l'éloquence de l'orateur,** carried away by the speaker's eloquence; **se faire e.,** to be *or* get led astray; **se laisser e.,** to allow oneself to be led astray; **se laisser e. à faire qch,** to be drawn into doing sth;

(d) (*causer*) to result in, to bring about (*accident, misfortune etc*); to entail, to involve (*problems, expense etc*); **cela entraînera un retard,** it will involve *or* lead to delay; **décision qui peut e. des inconvénients,** decision that may give rise to difficulties;

(e) (*former*) to train (*pupil etc*); *Sp* to coach, to train (*athlete, team*); to train (*racehorse etc*); to pace (*cyclist*); **e. qn à faire qch,** to train s.o. to do sth.

2 s'entraîner *vpr* (*élève etc*) to train oneself; *Sp* to train; **s'e. à faire qch,** to train oneself to do sth.

entraîneur [ɑ̃trɛnœr] *nm* **(a)** *Sp* (*d'athlète, d'équipe*) coach, trainer; (*de cheval etc*) trainer; (*de coureur, cycliste*) pacemaker, pacer; **(b)** (*chef*) **e. d'hommes,** leader of men.

entraîneuse [ɑ̃trɛnøz] *nf* hostess (*in nightclub etc*).

entrant [ɑ̃trɑ̃] **1** *adj* incoming, ingoing (*crowd etc*); newly appointed (*officials*); newly elected (*parliamentary re-

presentatives); **les élèves entrants,** the new pupils. **2** *n* **les entrants et les sortants,** those entering and those leaving.

entr'apercevoir [ɑ̃trapɛrsəvwar] *vt* (*conj like* **apercevoir**) to catch a fleeting glimpse of.

entrave [ɑ̃trav] *nf* **(a)** (*de cheval etc*) hobble; **entraves,** (*de forçat etc*) fetters, shackles; **(b)** *Fig* hindrance, impediment (**à**, to); **e. à la liberté,** interference with freedom.

entravé [ɑ̃trave] *adj* **jupe entravée,** hobble skirt.

entraver [ɑ̃trave] *vt* **(a)** to hobble (*horse etc*); to put (*convict etc*) in fetters *or* shackles; **(b)** *Fig* to hinder, to hamper, to impede (*action, career etc*); **e. la circulation,** to hold up *or* block the traffic; **(c)** *F* (*comprendre*) to get; **je n'y entrave rien,** I don't get it (at all).

entre [ɑ̃tr] *prép* **(a)** (*deux choses, personnes, dates etc*) between; **choisir e. deux choses,** to choose between two things; **distance de 10 kilomètres e. deux villes,** distance of 10 kilometres between two towns; **e. deux et trois (heures),** between two and three (o'clock); *Fig* **e. les deux,** (*ni l'un ni l'autre*) between the two; (*comme ci comme ça*) so-so; **être e. la vie et la mort,** to be between life and death;

(b) (*parmi*) among(st); **nous sommes e. amis,** we are among(st) friends; **e. ces murs,** within these walls; **nous dînerons e. nous,** we'll have dinner alone *or* by ourselves; **un homme dangereux e. tous,** a most dangerous man; **un homme qu'il admirait entre tous,** a man he admired above all others; **un jour e. mille,** a day in a thousand; **il y avait e. autres, un Dürer et un Rembrandt,** there were, among(st) other things *or* others, a Dürer and a Rembrandt; **ce jour e. tous,** this day of all days;

(c) tomber e. les mains de l'ennemi, to fall into the enemy's hands; **tenir qch e. les mains,** to hold sth in one's hands;

(d) d'e., (from) among; **plusieurs d'e. nous,** several of us;

(e) (*rapport réciproque*) among(st), between; **ils s'accordent e. eux,** they agree among(st) themselves; **qu'est-ce qu'il y a de semblable e. lui et moi?,** what similarities are there between him and me?; **mais qu'y a-t-il e. eux, exactement?,** but what's (going on) between them exactly?; **soit dit e. nous,** between ourselves;

(f) (*à travers*) through; **se faufiler e. les arbres,** to thread one's way through *or* between *or* among(st) the trees; **passer e. les mailles,** to slip through the net.

entrebâillement [ɑ̃trəbajmɑ̃] *nm* **l'e. de la porte/fenêtre,** the half-open door/window.

entrebâiller [ɑ̃trəbaje] *vt* to half-open (*door, window*); **la porte était entrebâillée,** the door was ajar.

entrebâilleur [ɑ̃trəbajœr] *nm* door chain.

entrechat [ɑ̃trəʃa] *nm* **(a)** (*saut de danse*) entrechat; **(b)** (*gambade*) leap; **faire des entrechats,** to prance (about), to cavort.

entrechoquer [ɑ̃trəʃɔke] **1** *vt* to knock together; **e. des verres,** to chink glasses. **2 s'entrechoquer** *vpr* to knock against one another; (*of glasses*) to chink; *Fig* (*of personalities, ideas etc*) to clash.

entrecôte [ɑ̃trəkot] *nf Culin* rib steak, entrecôte; **e. minute,** minute steak.

entrecoupé [ɑ̃trəkupe] *adj* interrupted, broken (*speech, sleep, journey etc*); interrupted (*performance, reading etc*); **d'une voix entrecoupée,** with a catch in one's voice.

entrecouper [ɑ̃trəkupe] *vt* to interrupt (*speech, journey, performance etc*) (**de**, with).

entrecroisement [ɑ̃trəkrwazmɑ̃] *nm* intersection, criss-cross (*of lines etc*); interlacing (*of threads etc*).

entrecroiser [ɑ̃trəkrwaze] **1** *vt* to intersect, to (criss)cross (*lines etc*); to interlace (*threads etc*). **2 s'entrecroiser** *vpr* (*of lines, roads etc*) to intersect, to (criss)cross; (*of threads etc*) to interlace.

entre-déchirer (s') [sɑ̃trədeʃire] *vpr* to tear each other to pieces.

entre-deux [ɑ̃trədø] *nm inv* **(a)** (*espace*) space (in) between; **la vérité est dans l'e.-d.,** the truth is between the two; **(b)** *Couture* (*bande*) insertion.

entre-deux-guerres [ɑ̃trədøgɛr] *nm inv* inter-war years (1918-1939).

entrée [ɑ̃tre] *nf* **(a)** (*action d'aller ou de venir*) entry, entrance; **e. (en scène) d'un acteur,** an actor's entrance (on the stage); **à leur e., tous se levèrent,** as they entered, everybody stood up; **faire son e.,** to make one's entrance; **faire son e. dans le monde,** (*of girl*) to come out (into society); **l'e. en gare du train,** the entry of the train into the station; **l'e. du Japon dans la politique mondiale,** the entry of Japan into world politics; *Scol* **e. en vacances,** break(ing) up; *Fig* **d'e. (de jeu),** from the outset, from the very beginning;

(b) (*accès*) admission, admittance (**dans un** *ou* **d'un lieu,** to a place); **avoir ses entrées dans un lieu,** to have the run of a place; **avoir ses entrées libres chez qn,** to have free access to s.o.; **e. interdite,** no admittance; **payer ses entrées,** to pay one's admission fee *or* entrance fee; **prendre une e. au musée/théâtre,** to get a museum/theatre ticket; **e. libre,** (*dans un musée*) admission *or* entrance free; (*dans une boutique*) no obligation to buy;

(c) (*action de devenir membre*) **e. dans l'armée/le club/le parti/***etc*, joining the army/club/party/*etc*; **e. dans l'enseignement/la finance/***etc*, going into *or* taking up teaching/finance/*etc*; **e. à l'université,** going to university;

(d) *Com* (*de marchandises importées*) importation; (*passage, porte etc*) entry; **droit d'e.,** import duty;

(e) way in, entrance (**de**, to); (*vestibule*) (entrance) hall;

(f) (*ouverture*) entrance, mouth (*of tunnel, harbour etc*); **e. de clef,** keyhole; **e. d'air,** air intake; *Rad* **e. de poste,** lead-in; *Fig* **à l'e. de l'hiver,** at the beginning of winter;

(g) *Ordinat* (*processus*) input, entry; (*information*) entry; **données d'e.,** input (data);

(h) *Culin* entrée; **qu'avez-vous en e.?,** what do you have as an entrée?;

(i) (*de dictionnaire, livre de comptes etc*) entry.

entrefaites [ɑ̃trəfɛt] *nfpl* **sur ces e.,** while this was going on, at that moment.

entrefilet [ɑ̃trəfilɛ] *nm Journ* paragraph, short item.

entregent [ɑ̃trəʒɑ̃] *nm* social sense, savoir-faire; **elle a de l'e.,** she knows how to get on with people.

entrejambe [ɑ̃trəʒɑ̃b] *nm Couture* crutch, crotch; **hauteur de l'e.,** inside leg measurement.

entrelacement [ɑ̃trəlasmɑ̃] *nm* interlacing (*of ribbons*); interweaving (*of threads*); intertwining (*of branches*).

entrelacer [ɑ̃trəlase] *v* (*conj like* **lacer**) **1** *vt* to interlace (*ribbons*); to interweave (*threads*); to intertwine (*branches*); **mains entrelacées,** hand in hand. **2 s'entrelacer** *vpr* to intertwine.

entrelacs [ɑ̃trəla] *nm* interlaced design, tracery.

entrelarder [ɑ̃trəlarde] *vt Culin* to lard (*meat*); *Fig* **e. un discours de citations,** to interlard a speech with quotations.

entremêlement [ɑ̃trəmɛlmɑ̃] *nm Arch* **(a)** (*action*) (inter)mingling; **(b)** (*résultat*) (inter)mixture.

entremêler [ɑ̃trəmele] **1** *vt* to (inter)mix, to (inter)mingle; **e. des couleurs,** to mix *or* blend colours; **ordres entremêlés de jurons,** orders interspersed with oaths. **2 s'entremêler** *vpr* to (inter)mix, to (inter)mingle.

entremets [ɑ̃trəmɛ] *nm Culin* **e. (sucré),** dessert, *Br* sweet.

entremetteur, -euse [ɑ̃trəmɛtœr, -øz] *n* **(a)** intermediary, mediator; **(b)** (*dans une liaison amoureuse*) go-between.

entremettre (s') [sɑ̃trəmɛtr] *vpr* (*conj like* **mettre**) (*dans une querelle*) to intervene, to mediate; (*dans une liaison amoureuse*) to act as go-between.

entremise [ɑ̃trəmiz] *nf* intervention, mediation; **par l'e. de qn,** through s.o.

entre-nœud [ɑ̃trənø] *nm Bot* internode; (*pl entre-nœuds*).

entrepont [ɑ̃trəpɔ̃] *nm Nau* 'tween decks; **passager d'e.,** steerage passenger.

entreposage [ɑ̃trəpozaʒ] *nm* storing; (*en douane*) bonding.

entreposer [ɑ̃trəpoze] *vt* to store; (*en douane*) to bond; *Fig* **puis-je e. mon sac chez vous pendant une heure?,** may I leave my bag with you for an hour?

entreposeur [ɑ̃trəpozœr] *nm* warehouse keeper, warehouseman.

entrepositaire [ɑ̃trəpozitɛr] *nm (en douane)* bonder.

entrepôt [ɑ̃trəpo] *nm* warehouse, store; **e. (de la douane),** bonded warehouse; **e. frigorifique,** cold store; **marchandises en e.,** goods in store; (*en douane*) goods in bond.

entreprenant [ɑ̃trəprənɑ̃] *adj* enterprising, go-ahead; (*auprès des femmes*) forward.

entreprendre [ɑ̃trəprɑ̃dr] *vt* (*conj like* **prendre**) **(a)** (*commencer*) to undertake (*task, study, journey etc*); **e. un commerce,** to start a business; **e. une étude,** to begin a study; **e. de faire qch,** to undertake to do sth; **(b) e. une femme,** to make advances to(wards) a woman; **(c) elle m'a entrepris sur son sujet favori,** she engaged me in conversation about *or* started talking to me about her favourite subject.

entrepreneur, -euse [ɑ̃trəprənœr, -øz] *n* **(a)** *Constr* contractor; **e. (en bâtiment),** building contractor; **e. de déménagements,** furniture remover *or Am* mover; **e. de transports,** carrier, forwarding agent; **e. de pompes funèbres,** undertaker, *Am* mortician; **(b)** (*patron*) entrepreneur.

entreprise [ɑ̃trəpriz] *nf* **(a)** (*action, initiative*) enterprise, undertaking, venture; *Écon* **la libre e.,** free enterprise; **l'e. privée,** private enterprise; **e. hardie,** bold enterprise; **(b)** (*firme*) company, firm, enterprise; **e. publique,** public corporation; **la petite/moyenne e.,** small/medium-sized companies *or* firms; **chef d'e.,** company head; **e. de transports,** carrying company, forwarding agency; **(c)** *Jur* contracting; **travail à l'e.,** contract work, work by *or* on contract; **mettre qch à l'e.,** to put sth out to contract; **(d) entreprises,** (*tentatives de séduction*) advances; **(e)** (*attaque*) assault (**contre,** on, against).

entrer [ɑ̃tre] **1** *vi* (*aux* **être**) **(a)** (*aller*) to go in, to enter; (*venir*) to come in, to enter; **e. dans une salle,** to enter *or* go into *or* come into a room; **entrez!,** come *or* go in!; **défense d'e.,** no admittance, private; **faire e. qn,** to show s.o. in; (*en l'appelant, l'annonçant*) to call s.o. in; **laisser e. qn,** to let s.o. in, to admit s.o.; **laisser e. qch,** to let sth in; **e. en passant,** to drop in, to look in (**chez qn,** on s.o.); **je n'ai fait qu'e. et sortir,** I just dropped in for a moment; **empêcher qn d'e.,** to keep s.o. out, to stop s.o. entering *or* getting in; **la clef n'entre pas dans la serrure,** the key won't go into the lock *or* doesn't fit; **faire e. qch dans qch,** to insert *or* put sth in sth; **une pareille idée ne lui est jamais entrée dans la tête,** such an idea never entered his head; *Th* **Hamlet entre (en scène),** enter Hamlet; **e. en courant/en dansant,** to run/dance in; **e. furtivement,** to steal in;

(b) e. dans l'armée/la police, to join the army/the police; **e. dans une carrière,** to take up a career; **e. dans la finance,** to go into *or* take up finance; **e. en religion,** to take (holy) orders; **e. en fonction,** to take up one's duties; *F* **la Roumanie entre en démocratie,** Romania is taking up democracy; *Mil* **e. en campagne,** to take the field; *Scol* **e. en vacances,** to break up (for holidays); *Ordinat* **e. en communication,** to log on *or* in;

(c) e. dans de longues explications, to go into long explanations;

(d) e. en colère, to get angry; **elle entre tout juste en convalescence,** she's just beginning to convalesce; **e. en ébullition,** to begin to boil, to come to the boil;

(e) (*s'engager*) **e. dans,** to join in (*dance, debate etc*); to share (*s.o.'s ideas, worries etc*); **je n'entrerai pas dans l'affaire,** I will have nothing to do with the matter; **cela ne peut pas e. en compte,** that cannot be taken into account *or* consideration; **cela entre dans ses projets,** that is part of his plans; **e. dans le jeu,** to enter into the spirit of the game; **e. dans une catégorie,** to fall into a category; **il est entré dans ma vie tout d'un coup,** he came into my life all of a sudden; **la maladie est entrée dans sa vie,** illness entered his life; **dans tout ceci l'imagination entre pour beaucoup,** in all this imagination plays a large part;

(f) *Aut* **e. dans,** (*heurter*) to go into, to run into (*tree, wall etc*).

2 *vt* (*aux* **avoir**) **(a)** (*introduire*) to bring in; (*vu de l'extérieur*) to take in; **e. des marchandises en fraude,** to smuggle in goods;

(b) (*enfoncer*) **elle a failli m'e. son parapluie dans l'œil,** she nearly poked me in the eye with her umbrella; **il m'a entré ses dents/ongles dans le cou,** he sank his teeth/nails into my neck;

(c) *Ordinat* to enter, to input (*data*).

entre-rail [ɑ̃trərɑj] *nm Rail* gauge (*of track*); (*pl entre-rails*).

entresol [ɑ̃trəsɔl] *nm* entresol, mezzanine (floor).

entre-temps [ɑ̃trətɑ̃] **1** *adv* meanwhile, in the meantime. **2** *nm inv Arch* **dans l'e.-t.,** in the meanwhile.

entretenir [ɑ̃trətnir] *v* (*conj like* **tenir**) **1** *vt* **(a)** (*soigner*) to maintain, to keep up (*house, garden, roads etc*); to maintain (*machine*); (*of supplier*) to service (*appliance*); **e. qch en bon état,** to keep sth in (good) repair; **j'entretiens la voiture moi-même,** I look after the car myself; **e. sa santé/sa beauté,** to look after *or* take care of one's health/beauty; **e. sa forme,** to keep fit; **e. son français,** to keep up one's French; **e. une correspondance avec qn,** to keep up a correspondence with s.o.; **e. l'espoir de qn,** to keep s.o.'s hopes alive; **e. qn dans l'ignorance,** to keep s.o. in ignorance; **e. qn dans l'erreur,** to allow s.o. to continue to labour under a misapprehension; **il faut e. l'idée que la paix va revenir,** we must keep alive the idea that peace will return; **e. le feu,** to keep the fire going;

(b) (*pourvoir à la subsistance de*) to maintain, to support, to keep (*family, mistress, fleet etc*);

(c) e. des soupçons/des craintes, to entertain *or* harbour suspicions/fears;

(d) (*parler à*) **e. qn de qch,** to converse *or* talk with s.o. about sth, to discuss sth with s.o..

2 s'entretenir *vpr* **(a) s'e. avec qn (de qch),** to converse *or* talk with s.o. (about sth), to discuss (sth) with s.o.;

(b) (*se maintenir en forme*) to keep fit;

(c) (*pourvoir à sa subsistance*) to support *or* keep oneself; **il ne gagne pas de quoi s'e.,** he does not earn enough to live on *or* to keep himself *or* to support himself.

entretenu [ɑ̃trətny] *adj* **(a) femme entretenue,** kept woman; **bien/mal e.,** well-kept/badly kept (*house, garden etc*); **(b)** *Rad* sustained (*oscillations*); undamped, continuous (*waves*).

entretien [ɑ̃trətjɛ̃] *nm* **(a)** (*soins*) upkeep, maintenance (*of house, garden, roads etc*); maintenance (*of machine*); (*par le fournisseur*) servicing, service (*of appliance*); **personnel d'e.,** maintenance staff; **manuel d'e.,** service manual; **produits d'e.,** (household) cleaning materials; **(b)** (*subsistance*) support, maintenance (*of family, army etc*); **(c)** (*conversation*) conversation, talk; (*audience*) interview; **j'ai eu un e. avec lui,** I had a talk *or* conversation with him; *F* **j'ai réussi à décrocher un e.,** (*pour une embauche*) I managed to get myself an interview; **avoir des entretiens avec le patronat,** to hold talks *or* discussions with the employers.

entretoile [ɑ̃trətwal] *nf Couture* (lace) insertion.

entretoise [ɑ̃trətwaz] *nf Constr Tech* brace, strut, stay.

entretoisement [ɑ̃trətwazmɑ̃] *nm Constr Tech* **(a)** (*action*) bracing, staying, strutting; **(b)** (*pièce*) = **ENTRETOISE**.

entretoiser [ɑ̃trətwaze] *vt Constr Tech* to brace, to stay, to strut.

entre-tuer (s') [sɑ̃trətɥe] *vpr* to kill one another.

entre-voie [ɑ̃trəvwa] *nf Rail* space between tracks (*pl entre-voies*).

entrevoir [ɑ̃trəvwar] *vt* (*conj like* **voir**) to catch sight *or* a glimpse of; (*indistinctement*) to make out; **je n'ai fait que l'e.,** I caught only a glimpse of him; **il entrevoyait la vérité,** he had an inkling of the truth; **j'entrevois des difficultés,** I foresee difficulties.

entrevue [ɑ̃trəvy] *nf* interview; (*entre hommes politiques, hommes d'affaires etc*) meeting; **avoir/fixer une e. avec qn,** to have/arrange an interview *or* a meeting with s.o..

entropie [ɑ̃trɔpi] *nf Phys* entropy.

entrouvert [ɑ̃truvɛr] *adj* half-open (*window, flower etc*); gaping, yawning (*chasm*); **laissez la porte entrouverte,** leave the door ajar; **la bouche entrouverte,** with one's mouth half-open.

entrouvrir [ɑ̃truvrir] *v* (*conj like* **ouvrir**) **1** *vt* to half-open (*door, eyes, mouth etc*). **2 s'entrouvrir** *vpr* to half-open; (*of chasm*) to open up, to gape, to yawn.

entuber [ɑ̃tybe] *vt F* (*duper*) to con, to have; **il s'est fait e.,** he was conned *or* had.

enturbanné [ɑ̃tyrbane] *adj* wearing a turban.

énucléation [enykleasjɔ̃] *nf Chir* enucleation.

énucléer [enyklee] *vt Chir* to enucleate (*tumour, eye*).

énumératif, -ive [enymeratif, -iv] *adj* enumerative.

énumération [enymerasjɔ̃] *nf* enumeration, listing.

énumérer [enymere] *vt* (**j'énumère, n. énumérons; j'énumérerai**) to enumerate, to list.

énurésie [enyrezi] *nf Méd* enuresis.

envahir [ɑ̃vair] *vt* to invade, to overrun (*country etc*); *Com* **e. le marché,** to flood the market; **envahi par les mauvaises herbes,** overgrown with weeds; **envahi par l'eau,** flooded; **quand le doute/le sommeil nous envahit,** when we are overcome with doubt/sleep; **la politique envahit tout,** politics gets into everything; *Fig F* **je ne voulais pas les e.,** (*déranger*) I didn't want to intrude (up)on them.

envahissant [ɑ̃vaisɑ̃] *adj* intrusive (*neighbours*); invasive (*plants*); *Fig* overwhelming (*desire, suspicion, smell etc*).

envahissement [ɑ̃vaismɑ̃] *nm* invasion.

envahisseur [ɑ̃vaisœr] *nm* invader.

envasement [ɑ̃vazmɑ̃] *nm* silting up (*of harbour etc*).

envaser [ɑ̃vaze] **1** *vt* to silt up (*harbour etc*); to run (*boat*) on the mud. **2 s'envaser** *vpr* **(a)** (*of harbour etc*) to silt up; **(b)** (*of boat, person*) to get stuck in the mud.

enveloppant [ɑ̃vlɔpɑ̃] *adj* **(a)** enveloping, enclosing; *Aut* **pare-chocs e.,** wrapround bumper; **(b)** *Fig* (*séduisant*) captivating (*person, words, manners etc*).

enveloppe [ɑ̃vlɔp] *nf* **(a)** wrapper, wrapping (*of parcel etc*); **(b)** (*pour lettre*) envelope; **envoyer qch sous e.,** to send sth under cover; **e. autocollante,** self-seal envelope; **e. à fenêtre,** window envelope; **e. matelassée,** padded envelope, Jiffy bag ®; **e. T.,** ≈ business reply envelope; *Philat* **e. premier jour,** first-day cover; *Litt Fig* **l'e. mortelle,** ≈ this mortal coil; *F* **recevoir une e.,** (*pot-de-vin*) to receive a bribe; *Fig* **l'e. de la recherche,** the research budget; *Fig* **un bon cœur sous une rude e.,** a rough diamond; **(c)** (*revêtement*) sheathing, casing, jacket (*of boiler*); *Aut* outer cover (*of tyre*); **e. calorifuge,** (insulating) lagging; **e. d'induit,** armature casing; **(d)** (*des graines etc*) hull.

enveloppé [ɑ̃vlɔpe] *adj F* **bien e.,** well-padded, plump (*person*).

enveloppement [ɑ̃vlɔpmɑ̃] *nm* **(a)** (*action*) wrapping (up) (*of parcel etc*); *Mil* **manœuvre d'e.,** pincer movement, envelopment; **(b)** *Méd* (*linges*) pack; **e. froid,** cold pack.

envelopper [ɑ̃vlɔpe] **1** *vt* **(a)** to wrap (up) (*goods, baby etc*); **e. un paquet,** to wrap up *or* do up a parcel; **enveloppé de bandages,** swathed in bandages; **enveloppé de mystère/brume,** shrouded in mystery/in mist; **(b)** (*entourer*) to surround, to encircle, to close in on (*s.o.*); **la nuit nous enveloppa,** darkness closed in on us; **(c)** *Fig Vieilli* **e. qn dans un désastre,** to involve s.o. in a disaster. **2 s'envelopper** *vpr* to wrap oneself up (**dans une couverture/***etc*, in a blanket/*etc*); **s'e. dans son silence,** to immure oneself in silence.

envenimé [ɑ̃vnime] *adj* poisoned, septic (*wound*); *Fig* **discussion envenimée,** acrimonious discussion.

envenimement [ɑ̃vnimmɑ̃] *nm* poisoning (*of wound*); *Fig* embittering (*of quarrel, discussion*); aggravation (*of situation*).

envenimer [ɑ̃vnime] **1** *vt* to poison, to make (*wound*) septic; *Fig* to envenom, to embitter (*quarrel, discussion*); to aggravate (*situation*). **2 s'envenimer** *vpr* (*of wound*) to fester, to turn septic; *Fig* (*of discussion, situation etc*) to grow acrimonious.

envergure [ɑ̃vɛrgyr] *nf* **(a)** wingspread, wingspan (*of bird, aircraft*); **(b)** *Fig* (*ampleur*) scope; **de grande e., d'e.,** far-reaching, wide-ranging (*reform, report, question*); large-scale (*operation, firm*); **esprit de grande e.,** wide-ranging mind; **(c) homme d'e.,** man of great ability.

envers[1] [ɑ̃vɛr] *nm* reverse, back (*of document, plate etc*); reverse (*of medal, coin*); **l'endroit et l'e. d'un tissu,** the right and the wrong side of a material; **tissu sans e. (ni endroit),** reversible material; **l'e. de la vie,** the seamy side of life; *Fig* **l'e. du décor,** the other side of the picture; **à l'e.,** (*du mauvais côté*) inside out; (*avec le haut en bas etc*) the wrong way up, upside down; (*dans le mauvais sens*) the wrong way round, back to front; (*en désordre*) upside down; **le monde à l'e.,** the world turned upside down; **il travaille? c'est le monde à l'e!,** he's working? wonders will never cease!; **j'ai la tête à l'e.,** my brain is in a whirl; *Tricot* **une maille à l'endroit, une maille à l'e.,** knit one, purl one.

envers[2] *prép* toward(s); **juste e. tous,** just to(wards) *or* with everyone; **leur devoir e. leur patrie,** their duty to(wards) their country; **e. et contre tous,** against the whole world.

envi (à l') [alɑ̃vi] *adv* **faire qch à l'e.,** to vie with one another in doing sth, to try to outdo each other doing sth.

enviable [ɑ̃vjabl] *adj* enviable.

envie [ɑ̃vi] *nf* **(a)** (*désir*) desire (**de qch,** for sth; **de faire,** to do); **avoir e. de qch/de faire qch,** to want sth/to do sth; **j'avais e. de dormir/boire/manger,** I felt sleepy/thirsty/hungry; **avoir bien e. de faire qch,** to want very much to do sth; **brûler d'e. de faire qch,** to long to do sth; *F* **ça m'a pris comme une e. de pisser,** it was a sudden urge; **donner à qn l'e. de faire qch,** to make s.o. want to do sth; **il a e. que je fasse cela,** he wants me to do that; *F* **ça va lui passer son e.,** it'll be just what he wants; **je vais lui ôter l'e. de s'amuser,** I'll stop his messing around; **regarder qch avec e.,** to look longingly at sth; **(b)** (*jalousie*) envy; **être dévoré d'e.,** to be consumed *or* green with envy; **faire e. à qn,** to make s.o. envious; **cette situation confortable, ça fait e.,** a good job like that makes people envious; **porter e. à qn,** to envy s.o.; **(c)** (*au doigt*) hangnail; **(d)** (*sur la peau*) birthmark.

envier [ɑ̃vje] *vt* (*impf & pr sub* **n. enviions**) to envy, to be envious of (*s.o., sth*); **e. qch à qn,** to envy s.o. sth; **je t'envie de ne jamais avoir faim!,** I envy your never being hungry!; **elle n'a rien à e. à personne,** she has no cause to be envious of anyone.

envieux, -ieuse [ɑ̃vjø, -jøz] **1** *adj* envious (**de,** of). **2** *n* envious person; **faire des e.,** to make people envious.

environ [ɑ̃virɔ̃] **1** *adv* (*à peu près*) about, around; **il a e. quarante ans,** he is about forty. **2** *nmpl* **environs,** surroundings, surrounding area (*of town etc*); **habiter aux** *ou* **dans les environs de Paris,** to live in the vicinity of *or* near Paris; **aux environs de Pâques/cinq heures,** around Easter/five o'clock; **aux environs de cent francs,** in the region *or* vicinity of a hundred francs, about *or* around a hundred francs.

environnant [ɑ̃virɔnɑ̃] *adj* surrounding (*country etc*).

environnement [ɑ̃virɔnmɑ̃] *nm* (*naturel, personnel*) environment; **protection de l'e.,** environmental protection, protection of the environment.

environnementaliste [ɑ̃virɔnmɑ̃talist] *n* environmentalist.

environner [ɑ̃virɔne] **1** *vt* to surround; **environné de,** surrounded by. **2 s'environner** *vpr* **s'e. d'intellectuels/***etc*, to surround oneself with intellectuals/*etc*.

envisageable [ɑ̃vizaʒabl] *adj* conceivable, imaginable; **ce n'est pas e.,** it's inconceivable *or* unimaginable.

envisager [ɑ̃vizaʒe] *vt* (**j'envisageai(s)**) (*considérer*) to consider (*issue, situation, remedy etc*); (*imaginer comme possible, projeter*) to envisage (*consequence, event etc*); **e. l'avenir,** to look to the future; **le cas que nous envisageons,** the case under consideration; **cas non envisagé,** unforeseen case; **comment envisagez-vous la question?,** what are your views on the matter?; **il n'envisageait pas de partir,** he wasn't thinking of leaving *or* considering leaving.

envoi [ɑ̃vwa] *nm* **(a)** (*action*) sending (*of representative, troops etc*); sending, dispatch(ing) (*of letter, parcel etc*); sending, remittance (*of money, funds*); sending, dispatch(ing), forwarding (*of goods*); **e. par mer,** shipment; **faire un e. tous les mois,** to send *or* dispatch goods every month; *Com* **lettre d'e.,** letter of advice; **faire un e. de fonds à qn,** to remit funds to s.o.; **(b)** *Fb* **coup d'e.,** kick off; **(c)** (*colis*) parcel; (*lettre*) letter; (*marchandises*) consignment (**de,** of); **e. de l'auteur,** presentation copy, with the compliments of the author; **(d)** *Littér* envoi (*of poem*).

envol [ɑ̃vɔl] *nm* **(a)** (*of birds*) taking flight, taking wing; **(b)** (*of aircraft*) takeoff; **piste d'e.,** (takeoff) runway; *Nau* **pont d'e.,** flight deck.

envolée [ɑ̃vɔle] *nf* **(a)** flight (*of birds*); *Av* takeoff; **(b)** *Fig* **e. d'éloquence,** flight of oratory; **l'e. du dollar,** the rapid rise in the dollar.

envoler (s') [sɑ̃vɔle] *vpr* **(a)** (*of bird*) to fly away, to fly off; **faire s'e. des oiseaux,** to put birds to flight; **(b)** (*of aircraft*) to take off; *Fig* **le franc français s'envole,** the French franc is rising rapidly; **(c)** (*emporté par le vent*) (*of hat etc*) to blow off; (*of papers etc*) to blow away; **le temps s'envole,** time flies; **(d)** *F* (*disparaître soudainement*) (*of person, handbag etc*) to vanish, to disappear.

envoûtant [ɑ̃vutɑ̃] *adj* (*fascinant*) bewitching.

envoûtement [ɑ̃vutmɑ̃] *nm* **(a)** (*maléfice*) bewitchment; **(b)** *Fig* (*fascination*) bewitchment, captivation; **cette région produit un e. sur moi,** this region has a bewitching *or* captivating effect on me.

envoûter [ɑ̃vute] *vt* (*en employant de la magie*) to bewitch (*s.o.*); *Fig* (*fasciner*) to bewitch, to captivate (*s.o.*).

envoûteur, -euse [ɑ̃vutœr, -øz] *n* worker of spells.

envoyé, -ée [ɑ̃vwaje] **1** *adj* **bien e.,** well-aimed (*Sp ball, F remark*); *F* **c'est e.!,** (*bien dit*) well said!; (*bien exécuté*) well done! **2** *n* (*messager*) messenger; (*de parti etc*) representative; (*du gouvernement*) envoy; *Journ* **e. spécial,** special correspondent.

envoyer [ɑ̃vwaje] *v* (**j'envoie, n. envoyons;** *fu* **j'enverrai**) **1** *vt* (*faire aller*) to send (*s.o.*); (*expédier*) to send, to dispatch (*letter, parcel etc*); to send, to remit (*money*); to send, to dispatch, to forward (*goods*); to send (*one's excuses, sympathy etc*); **e. qn à Paris,** to send s.o. to Paris; **e. une lettre à qn,** to send s.o. a letter; **je lui ai envoyé mes félicitations,** I sent him my congratulations; **envoyez-moi un petit mot,** drop me a line; **e. sa démission,** to send in *or* tender one's resignation; **elle lui a envoyé un regard noir/une gifle,** she gave him a black look/slap (in the face); **e. un baiser à qn,** to blow s.o. a kiss; **e. chercher qn,** to send for s.o.; **j'ai envoyé (qn) prendre de ses nouvelles,** I sent s.o. to ask after him; *F* **je ne le lui ai pas envoyé dire,** I told him straight *or* to his face; *F* **e. promener** *ou* **balader** *ou* **paître qn,** to send s.o. packing; *F* **j'en ai assez, je vais tout e. promener,** I've had enough, I'm going to chuck everything *or* throw in the towel; *Nau* **e. les couleurs/une vergue,** to hoist the colours/send up a yard.

2 *vi Nau* **envoyez!,** about ship!

3 s'envoyer *vpr* **ils s'envoient des cartes postales ré-**

gulièrement, they regularly send postcards to each other; *Arg* **s'e. un verre de vin,** to knock back a glass of wine; *F* **s'e. une corvée,** to get landed *or* stuck with a tedious job; *Vulg* **il ne pense qu'à s'e. en l'air,** all he thinks about is having it off *or* away; *Vulg* **s'e. une fille,** to have it off *or* away with a girl.

envoyeur, -euse [ɑ̃vwajœr, -øz] *n* sender; **retour à l'e.,** return to sender.

enzyme [ɑ̃zim] *n* enzyme; **produit de lavage aux enzymes,** cleaning product with biological action.

enzymologie [ɑ̃zimɔlɔʒi] *nf* enzymology.

éocène [eɔsɛn] *Géol* **1** *adj* Eocene (*period*). **2** *nm* Eocene.

éolien, -ienne [eɔljɛ̃, -jɛn] **1** *adj* **harpe éolienne,** aeolian harp; **érosion éolienne,** wind erosion; **énergie éolienne,** wind energy; **moteur é.,** wind engine. **2** *nf* **éolienne,** wind turbine.

épagneul, -eule [epaɲœl] *n* spaniel.

épais, -aisse [epɛ, -pɛs] **1** *adj* thick (*hair, finger, wall, slice, sauce etc*); dense, thick (*foliage, fog*); dense (*crowd*); thick, fat (*book*); deep, dark (*shadow, night*); deep (*silence*); bulky (*book*); **é. de deux mètres,** two metres thick; **fourré é.,** close thicket; **avoir la taille épaisse,** to be thickset; *F* **avoir l'esprit é.,** to be dense *or* thick; **avoir la langue épaisse,** to have a furred tongue; **peu é.,** thin. **2** *adv* **(a)** thick(ly); **semer é.,** to sow thick; **(b)** *F* (*beaucoup*) **il n'y en a pas é.,** it's not exactly thick on the ground. **3** *nm* **couper dans l'é.,** to cut into the thick part; **au plus é. de la foule/forêt,** in the heart of the crowd/forest.

épaisseur [epɛsœr] *nf* **(a)** (*de cheveux, mur, sauce etc*) thickness; (*de feuillage, brouillard*) density, thickness; (*de foule*) density; (*d'ombre, de nuit*) darkness; **le mur a deux pieds d'é.,** the wall is two feet thick; **courroie en trois épaisseurs,** three-ply belt; **une é. de neige,** a layer of snow; **le peu d'é. d'une planche,** the thinness of a board; **(b)** (*d'esprit*) dullness; **(c)** (*profondeur*) depth (*of person, character in novel, novel etc*).

épaissir [epesir] **1** *vt* to thicken (*sauce, paint etc*); to deepen (*shadow, mytery*). **2** *vi* (*of sauce etc*) to thicken, to get thick(er); (*of person*) to fill out. **3 s'épaissir** *vpr* (*of hair, fog, sauce etc*) to thicken, to get thick(er); (*of person*) to fill out; (*of shadow, mystery*) to deepen.

épaississant [epɛsisɑ̃] *nm* (*substance*) thickener.

épaississement [epɛsismɑ̃] *nm* thickening (*of fog, sauce etc*); filling out (*of person*).

épanchement [epɑ̃ʃmɑ̃] *nm* **(a)** *Arch & Litt* pouring out, discharge (*of liquid*); *Méd* **é. de synovie,** synovial extravasation; **(b)** *Fig* outpouring (*of thoughts, feelings*); *Litt* effusion; **en veine d'é.,** in an expansive mood.

épancher [epɑ̃ʃe] **1** *vt* **(a)** *Arch & Litt* to pour out, to discharge (*liquid*); *Fig* **é. sa bile,** to vent one's spleen; **(b)** *Fig* to pour out (*one's love, worries etc*); **é. son cœur,** to pour out one's heart, to unbosom oneself. **2 s'épancher** *vpr* **(a)** *Arch & Litt* (*of liquid*) to pour out; *Méd* (*of blood etc*) to extravasate; **(b)** *Fig* to pour out one's heart, to unbosom oneself.

épandage [epɑ̃daʒ] *nm* spreading (*of manure etc*); **champs d'é.,** sewage farm.

épandeur, -euse [epɑ̃dœr, -øz] *n* (*machine*) spreader (*of manure, asphalt etc*).

épandre [epɑ̃dr] **1** *vt* to spread, to scatter (*manure etc*). **2 s'épandre** *vpr Litt* to spread.

épanoui [epanwi] *adj* in full bloom, full-blown (*flower*); beaming (*face, smile*); **une jeune femme épanouie,** a young woman in full bloom.

épanouir [epanwir] **1** *vt* to open out (*flower, petals*); to spread (*sails, feathers*); **un large sourire lui épanouit le visage,** his face broadened into a grin. **2 s'épanouir** *vpr* **(a)** (*of flower*) to open out, to bloom, to blow; **(b)** (*of face*) to beam, to light up; (*of happy person*) to beam; **(c)** (*of young girl, personality, civilization etc*) to blossom.

épanouissement [epanwismɑ̃] *nm* **(a)** (*action*) opening out, blooming (*of flower*); lighting up (*of face*); blossoming (*of young girl, personality, civilization etc*); **(b)** (*plénitude*) (full) bloom; **elle atteint son e. physique et moral,** she is approaching her physical and mental peak.

épargnant, -ante [eparɲɑ̃, -ɑ̃t] **1** *adj* thrifty. **2** *n* saver, investor; **les petits épargnants,** small savers *or* investors.

épargne [eparɲ] *nf* **(a)** (*action, vertu*) saving, economy; *Fig* (*de temps, forces*) saving; **caisse d'é.,** savings bank; **plan d'é.-logement,** *Br* ≈ building society (savings) account, *Am* ≈ savings and loan association account; **(b)** (*sommes*) savings; **(c)** (*épargnants*) **la petite é.,** small savers *or* investors; **l'é. privée,** private investors.

épargner [eparɲe] *vt* **(a)** to save (up), to put by (*money, provisions*); to be sparing with (*butter, salt etc*); **é. ses forces,** to save one's strength; **(b)** to save (*energy, time*); **épargne-moi tes explications!,** spare me your explanations!; **é. à qn la peine de faire qch,** to save s.o. the trouble of doing sth; **(c)** to spare, to have mercy on (*prisoner etc*); **elle a toujours tenté d'é. ses enfants,** she has always tried to shield her children; **l'incendie a épargné notre village,** the fire spared our village.

éparpillement [eparpijmɑ̃] *nm* **(a)** (*action*) scattering (*of objects, hay etc*); scattering, dispersal (*of crowd, troops etc*); *Fig* dissipation (*of efforts, attention etc*); **(b)** (*état*) scattered state.

éparpiller [eparpije] **1** *vt* to scatter, to strew about (*objects, hay etc*); to scatter, to disperse (*crowd, troops etc*); *Fig* to dissipate (*efforts, attention etc*). **2 s'éparpiller** *vpr* (*of objects etc*) to scatter; (*of crowd, troops etc*) to scatter, to disperse; *Fig* (*of person*) to dissipate one's energies.

épars [epar] *adj* scattered (*houses, sheep etc*); sparse (*vegetation, population, information*); straggly (*hair*).

éparvin [eparvɛ̃] *nm Vét* spavin (*of horse*).

épatamment [epatamɑ̃] *adv F* splendidly, wonderfully.

épatant [epatɑ̃] *adj F* splendid, wonderful.

épate [epat] *nf F* swank, swagger; **faire de l'é.,** to show off, to swank; **on l'a fait à l'é.,** it was done to make an impression.

épaté [epate] *adj* **(a)** splay-footed (*table etc*); flat (*nose*); **(b)** *F* (*étonné*) dumbfounded, flabbergasted.

épatement [epatmɑ̃] *nm* **(a)** (*de nez*) flatness; **(b)** *F* (*étonnement*) astonishment, amazement.

épater [epate] *vt* **(a)** (*rendre plat*) to flatten out the base of (*sth*); **(b)** *F* (*étonner*) to astound, to amaze; **rien ne l'épate, il ne se laisse pas é.,** nothing surprises him, he isn't easily impressed.

épaulard [epolar] *nm* grampus, orc, killer whale.

épaule [epol] *nf* shoulder; **large d'épaules,** broad-shouldered; **hausser les épaules,** to shrug one's shoulders; *Culin* **é. d'agneau,** shoulder of lamb; **donner un coup d'é. à qn,** to give s.o. a push in the right direction; **regarder qn par-dessus l'é.,** to look down one's nose at s.o.; **charger un fardeau sur son é.,** to shoulder a burden; *Mil* **l'arme sur l'é.,** with rifle at the slope; **rouler les épaules,** (*en marchant*) to swagger.

épaulé-jeté [epoleʒ(ə)te] *nm* (*en haltérophilie*) clean-and-jerk; (*pl épaulés-jetés*).

épaulement [epolmɑ̃] *nm* **(a)** (*mur*) revetment (wall); **(b)** (*rempart*) breastwork; **(c)** shoulder (*of hill*).

épauler [epole] **1** *vt* **(a)** to bring (*gun*) to one's shoulder; **(b) é. qn,** (*aider*) to back s.o. up. **2** *vi* to take aim.

épaulette [epolɛt] *nf* **(a)** (*bretelle*) shoulder-strap (*of slip etc*); **(b)** *Mil* epaulette; **(c)** (*rembourrage*) shoulder pad.

épave [epav] *nf Nau* wreck; (*voiture*) wreck, write-off; *Fig* (*loque humaine*) (human) wreck; *Fig* **les épaves de la société,** the flotsam of society; **é. (de navire),** wreck; **épaves d'un naufrage,** wreckage; **épaves flottantes,** flotsam; **épaves rejetées,** jetsam.

épée [epe] *nf* sword; *Escrime* épée; **coup d'é.,** swordthrust; *Fig* **coup d'é. dans l'eau,** wasted effort; **Marc est une bonne é.,** Marc is a good swordsman.

épeiche [epɛʃ] *nf Orn* great spotted woodpecker.

épeichette [epɛʃɛt] *nf Orn* lesser spotted woodpecker.

épeler [eple] *v* (**j'épelle; j'épellerai**) **1** *vt* **(a)** to spell (*word, name etc*); **mot mal épelé,** misspelt word; **(b)** (*lire avec difficulté*) to spell out (*text*). **2** *vi* to spell.

épépiner [epepine] *vt* to remove the seeds *or* pips from (*grapes, tomatoes etc*); to stone (*raisins*); to core (*apples*).

éperdu [epɛrdy] *adj* distraught, frantic (*look*); violent (*love, need etc*); desperate (*resistance*); **é. de joie/douleur,** frantic with joy/grief.

éperdument [epɛrdymɑ̃] *adv* (*aimer*) madly, to distraction; (*travailler*) desperately, frantically; **é. amoureux,** head over heels in love, madly in love; *F* **je m'en fiche é.,** I couldn't care less, I don't give a damn.

éperlan [epɛrlɑ̃] *nm* (*poisson*) smelt, sparling.

éperon [eprɔ̃] *nm* **(a)** spur (*of horseman*); **donner de l'é. à son cheval, piquer de l'é.,** to spur (on) one's horse; **gagner ses éperons,** to win one's spurs; **(b)** spur (*of violet, mountain range, cock's leg*); **(c)** *Hist* ram (*of warship*); **(d)** cutwater (*of bridge*).

éperonner [eprɔne] *vt* **(a)** to spur (on), to put spurs to (*horse*); *Fig* **é. qn,** to spur *or* urge s.o. on; **(b)** *Hist* to ram (*enemy ship*); **(c)** to spur, to put spurs on (*boot etc*).

épervier [epɛrvje] *nm* **(a)** sparrowhawk; *Pol Fig* hawk; **(b)** *Pêche* castnet.

éphèbe [efɛb] *nm Iron* (*beau jeune homme*) Adonis, Apollo.

éphélide [efelid] *nf* freckle.

éphémère [efemɛr] **1** *adj* ephemeral, short-lived, passing, fleeting (*happiness etc*); **le chanteur n'a connu qu'un succès é.,** the singer enjoyed only a short-lived *or* brief success. **2** *nm Ent* ephemera, mayfly.

éphéméride [efemerid] *nf* **(a)** (*calendrier*) tear-off *or* block calendar; **(b)** *Astron* (*publication annuelle*) ephemeris; **éphémérides,** (*tables*) ephemerides.

Éphèse [efɛz] *n* Ephesus.

épi [epi] *nm* **(a)** ear (*of grain*); spike (*of flower*); **blés en é.,** wheat in the ear; **monter en é.,** (*of cereals*) to ear; *Culin* **é de maïs,** corn on the cob; **(b)** (*mèche de cheveux*) tuft of hair; **(c)** (*jetée*) spur, groyne; *Rail* spur (*of track*); *Archit* **é. de faîtage,** finial; *Aut* **stationnement en é.,** angle parking; *Constr* **appareil en é.,** herringbone work.

épicarpe [epikarp] *nm Bot* epicarp.

épice [epis] *nf* spice; **pain d'é.,** ≈ gingerbread.

épicé [epise] *adj* highly spiced, hot (*food, dish etc*); hot (*seasoning*); *F* **conte é.,** spicy story.

épicéa [episea] *nm* (*arbre*) spruce.

épicentre [episɑ̃tr] *nm* epicentre (*of earthquake*).

épicer [epise] *vt* (**j'épiçai(s)**) to spice (*food, dish etc*); *F* to add a bit of spice to (*story etc*).

épicerie [episri] *nf* **(a)** (*produits*) groceries; **être dans l'é.,** to be in the grocery business; **(b)** (*magasin*) grocer's (shop); **é. fine,** delicatessen; **(c)** *Can Fig* **liste d'é.,** shopping list (*of grievances etc*).

épicier, -ière [episje, -jɛr] *n* grocer; *Fig Péj* **c'est un é.,** (*il n'aime que l'argent*) he's a money-grubber; *Fig Péj* **d'é.,** common-or-garden (*ideas, novel etc*); cheap, ordinary (*ink, soap etc*); **mentalité d'é.,** small-town mentality.

épicurien, -ienne [epikyrjɛ̃, -jɛn] **1** *adj* epicurean; *Phil* Epicurean. **2** *n* epicure; *Phil* Epicurean.

épicurisme [epikyrism] *nm* **(a)** *Phil* Epicureanism; **(b)** (*recherche du plaisir*) epicur(ean)ism.

épidémie [epidemi] *nf Méd & Fig* epidemic; outbreak (*of suicides, burglaries etc*).

épidémiologie [epidemjɔlɔʒi] *nf* epidemiology.

épidémiologique [epidemijɔlɔʒik] *adj* epidemiological.

épidémique [epidemik] *adj Méd & Fig* epidemic.

épiderme [epidɛrm] *nm Anat Bot* epidermis, skin; *Fig* **avoir l'é. sensible** *ou* **délicat,** to be thin-skinned *or* touchy.

épidermique [epidɛrmik] *adj* epidermal, epidermic (*tissue etc*); *Fig* **une réaction é.,** a kneejerk reaction.

épidiascope [epidjaskɔp] *nm* epidiascope.

épier [epje] *vt* (*impf & pr sub* **n. épiions, v. épiiez**) **(a)** (*espionner*) to spy on, to keep a watch on (*s.o., s.o.'s activities etc*); **(b)** (*observer pour découvrir*) to watch out for (*sign, opportunity etc*); to watch for (*s.o.'s reaction*).

épierrer [epjere] *vt* to clear (*field*) of stones.

épigastre [epigastr] *nm Anat* epigastrium.

épigastrique [epigastrik] *adj Anat* epigastric.

épiglotte [epiglɔt] *nf Anat* epiglottis.

épigone [epigɔn] *nm Litt* (*successeur*) epigone.

épigramme [epigram] *nf* epigram.

épigraphe [epigraf] *nf* epigraph.

épigraphie [epigrafi] *nf* epigraphy.

épilation [epilɑsjɔ̃] *nf* removal of unwanted hair (**de,** from); plucking (*of eyebrows*).

épilatoire [epilatwar] **1** *adj* hair-removing, depilatory (*cream etc*). **2** *nm* depilatory.

épilepsie [epilɛpsi] *nf Méd* epilepsy.

épileptique [epilɛptik] *adj & n Méd* epileptic.

épiler [epile] *vt* to remove unwanted hair from; to pluck (*eyebrows*).

épilogue [epilɔg] *nm* epilogue; *Fig* **j'attends l'é. de cette histoire,** I'm waiting for the rest of the story.

épiloguer [epilɔge] **1** *vt Arch* to pass censure on (*s.o., sth*). **2** *vi* to go on (and on), to hold forth (**sur,** about).

épinard [epinar] *nm* (*plante*) spinach; *Culin* **épinards,** spinach; **épinards en branches,** leaf spinach; **un pull vert é.,** a spinach-green sweater.

épine [epin] *nf* **(a)** (*arbre*) thornbush; **é. blanche,** hawthorn; **é. noire,** blackthorn; **é. de rat,** butcher's broom; **(b)** (*piquant*) *Bot* thorn, prickle; *Zool* spine, prickle; *Fig* **la vie est hérissée d'épines,** life bristles with difficulties; **être** *ou* **marcher sur des épines,** (*anxieux, impatient*) to be on tenterhooks; *Fig* **une é. au pied,** a thorn in the flesh; **tirer à qn une é. du pied,** (*tirer d'embarras*) to get s.o. out of a mess; (*soulager*) to relieve s.o.'s mind; **(c)** *Anat* **é. dorsale,** backbone.

épinette [epinɛt] *nf* **(a)** *Can Bot* spruce; **(b)** *Mus* spinet; **(c)** (*cage*) hen coop.

épinettière [epinɛtjɛr] *nf Can* spruce grove.

épineux, -euse [epinø, -øz] **1** *adj* **(a)** thorny, prickly, spiky (*bush, stem*); spiny (*fish*); *Fig* thorny (*question, problem*); **être dans une situation épineuse,** to be in a ticklish situation; **(b)** *Anat* spinous (*process*). **2** *nm* thorn bush.

épinglage [epɛ̃glaʒ] *nm* pinning.

épingle [epɛ̃gl] *nf* pin; **é. de cravate,** tiepin; **e. de sûreté** *ou* **de nourrice,** safety pin; **é. à chapeau,** hatpin; **é. à cheveux,** hairpin; **virage en é. à cheveux,** hairpin bend; **é. à linge,** clothes peg *or Am* pin; **attacher qch avec des épingles,** to pin sth (up *or* down); *Fig* **tiré à quatre épingles,** immaculately turned out; *Fig* **tirer son é. du jeu,** to extricate oneself; *Fig* **coups d'é.,** pinpricks, petty annoyances; *Fig* **chercher une é. dans une botte de foin,** to look for a needle in a haystack; **monter qch en é.,** (*exagérer*) to make too much of sth.

épingler [epɛ̃gle] *vt* **(a)** (*attacher etc*) to pin, to fasten (*sth*) with a pin *or* pins (**à,** to; **sur,** on); **é. ses cheveux,** to pin up one's hair; **(b)** *F* (*arrêter*) to nab, to collar (*s.o.*).

épinière [epinjɛr] *adj Anat* **moelle é.,** spinal cord.

épinoche [epinɔʃ] *nf* stickleback.

Epiphanie [epifani] *nf Rel* Epiphany.

épiphénomène [epifenɔmɛn] *nm* epiphenomenon.

épiphyse [epifiz] *nf Anat* epiphysis.

épique [epik] *adj* epic; **poème é.,** epic (poem).

épiscopal, -aux [episkɔpal, -o] *adj Rel* episcopal.

épiscopat [episkɔpa] *nm* (*fonction, évêques*) episcopate.

épiscope [episkɔp] *nm* episcope.

épisode [epizɔd] *nm* episode; **feuilleton** *ou* **film à épisodes,** serial; *F* **la suite au prochain é.,** I'll let you know what happens; *Fig* **ce n'est qu'un é. malheureux,** it's just an unfortunate episode.

épisodique [epizɔdik] *adj* (*intermittent*) episodic; (*accessoire*) minor.

épisodiquement [epizɔdikmɑ̃] *adv* occasionally, now and again.

épisser [epise] *vt* to splice (*rope, cable*).

épissure [episyr] *nf* splice.

épistémologie [epistemɔlɔʒi] *nf* epistemology.

épistémologique [epistemɔlɔʒik] *adj* epistemological.

épistolaire [epistɔlɛr] *adj* epistolary.

épistolier, -ière [epistɔlje, -jɛr] *n* letter writer.

épitaphe [epitaf] *nf* epitaph.

épithélium [epiteljɔm] *nm Biol* epithelium.

épithète [epitɛt] *nf* epithet; *Gram* attribute.

épitoge [epitɔʒ] *nf* **(a)** *Univ* ≈ (graduate's) hood; **(b)** *Antiq* cloak.

épitomé [epitɔme] *nm* (*abrégé d'un ouvrage*) epitome.

épître [epitr] *nf* epistle; (*partie de la messe*) Epistle; **côté de l'é.,** Epistle side (*of altar*).

éploré, -ée [eplɔre] **1** *adj* tearful, weeping (*person*); tearful (*expression, voice*). **2** *n* tearful *or* weeping person.

épluchage [eplyʃaʒ] *nm* peeling (*of fruit, potatoes etc*); cleaning (*of salad*); peeling, shelling (*of shrimps*); shelling (*of nuts, peas*); *Fig* detailed examination (*of text, newspaper etc*).

épluche-légumes [eplyʃlegym] *nm inv* vegetable *or* potato peeler.

éplucher [eplyʃe] *vt* to peel (*fruit, potatoes etc*); to clean (*salad*); to peel, to shell (*shrimps*); to shell (*nuts, peas*); *Fig* to go through *or* examine (*text, newspaper, advertisements etc*) in detail.

épluchette [eplyʃɛt] *nf Can* **é. de blé d'Inde,** corn-husking party.

éplucheur, -euse [eplyʃœr, -øz] *n* (*instrument, personne*) peeler; **é. de pommes de terre,** potato peeler.

épluchure [eplyʃyr] *nf* (*pelure*) peeling.

épointage [epwɛ̃taʒ] *nm* (*en cassant*) breaking the point (*of pencil*); (*en usant*) blunting (*of needle, pencil, tool etc*).

épointé [epwɛ̃te] *adj* blunt (*needle, pencil, tool etc*).

épointer [epwɛ̃te] *vt* (*en cassant*) to break the point of (*pencil*); (*en usant*) to blunt (*needle, pencil, tool etc*).

éponge [epɔ̃ʒ] *nf* **(a)** (*naturelle*) sponge; **(b)** *Com* sponge; **é. métallique,** (pan) scourer, scouring pad; **donner un coup d'é. à qch,** to wipe sth with a sponge; **effacer une tache d'un coup d'é.,** to sponge out a stain; *Fig* **passons l'é. là-dessus,** let's forget it; *Boxe* **jeter l'é.,** to throw in the sponge *or* towel; *Fig* **l'industrie française jette l'é. pour la construction d'automobiles,** French industry is throwing in the sponge *or* towel as regards the building of cars; *Tex* **tissu é.,** (terry) towelling; **serviette é.,** terry towel; *F* **il boit comme une é.,** he drinks like a fish; **(c) é. végétale,** vegetable sponge, loofah.

épongeage [epɔ̃ʒaʒ] *nm* sponging up, mopping up (*of liquid*); sponging (down) (*of surface*).

éponger [epɔ̃ʒe] *v* (**j'épongeai(s), n. épongeons**) **1** *vt* **(a)**

to sponge up, to mop up (*liquid*); **(b)** to sponge (down), to mop (*surface*); to sponge down (*horse, car etc*); **(c)** *Fin* to absorb (*deficit etc*). **2 s'éponger** *vpr* **s'é. le front,** to mop one's brow.

épontille [epɔ̃tij] *nf Nau* shore, prop.

épontiller [epɔ̃tije] *vt Nau* to prop, to shore (up).

épopée [epɔpe] *nf Littér & Fig* epic.

époque [epɔk] *nf* **(a)** (*historique*) epoch, era, age; *Géol* age, period; **l'é. glaciaire,** the ice age; **la belle é.,** the Edwardian era; **quelle é. (nous vivons)!,** what times we live in!; **meubles d'é.,** period *or* (genuine) antique furniture; **à l'é., elle était très reconnue,** at the time she was highly regarded; **faire é.,** to mark an epoch; **découverte qui fait é.,** epoch-making discovery; **(b)** (*moment précis*) time, period; **à l'é. de sa naissance,** at the time of his birth; **à cette é. de l'année,** at this time of year.

épouillage [epujaʒ] *nm* delousing.

épouiller [epuje] *vt* to delouse.

époumoné [epumɔne] *adj* puffed, breathless.

époumoner (s') [sepumɔne] *vpr* to shout oneself hoarse.

épousailles [epuzɑj] *nfpl Arch* nuptials, wedding.

épouse [epuz] *nf* wife; *Admin & Hum* spouse.

épousée [epuze] *nf Vieilli* bride.

épouser [epuze] *vt* **(a)** to marry, *Vieilli* to wed (*s.o.*); **é. une grosse dot,** to marry (into) money; **(b)** *Fig* to espouse, to take up, to adopt (*cause, doctrine etc*); **les Français ont épousé le golf,** the French have taken to golf; **é. la forme de qch,** to take the exact shape of sth.

époussetage [epustaʒ] *nm* dusting (*of furniture etc*).

épousseter [epuste] *vt* (*conj like* **jeter**) to dust (*furniture etc*); to brush (the dust from) (*clothes etc*); to rub down (*horse*).

époustouflant [epustuflɑ̃] *adj F* amazing, startling.

époustoufler [epustufle] *vt F* to astound, to flabbergast.

épouvantable [epuvɑ̃tabl] *adj* dreadful, appalling.

épouvantablement [epuvɑ̃tabləmɑ̃] *adv* dreadfully, appallingly.

épouvantail [epuvɑ̃taj] *nm* **(a)** (*dans les jardins*) scarecrow; **(b)** (*personne terrifiante*) bogey; (*chose terrifiante*) bugbear, bogey; **(c)** (*personne laide ou bizarrement habillée*) fright.

épouvante [epuvɑ̃t] *nf* terror, fright; **jeter** *ou* **porter l'é. dans un pays,** to spread terror in a country; **saisi d'é.,** terror-stricken, frightened to death; **film d'é.,** horror film; **elle pense à cette rencontre avec é.,** she is thinking of this meeting with dread.

épouvanté [epuvɑ̃te] *adj* terror-stricken.

épouvanter [epuvɑ̃te] **1** *vt* to terrify, to scare (*s.o.*). **2 s'épouvanter** *vpr* to take fright.

époux [epu] *nm* husband; *Admin & Hum* spouse; **les é.,** the married couple, the husband and wife; **les é. Thomas,** Mr and Mrs Thomas.

éprendre (s') [seprɑ̃dr] *vpr* (*conj like* **prendre**) **s'é. de,** to fall in love with (*s.o.*); to become passionate about (*one's work, an idea etc*).

épreuve [eprœv] *nf* **(a)** (*essai*) test, trial; **é. d'un pont,** test(ing) of a bridge; **é. d'outrance,** resistance test; **faire l'é. de qch,** to test sth; **mettre qch/qn à l'é.,** to put sth/s.o. to the test; **à l'é. du feu/de l'eau,** fireproof/waterproof; **l'é.-vérité pour ...,** the critical test for ...; **mécanisme à toute é.,** foolproof mechanism; **bonté/courage/***etc* **à toute é.,** never-failing kindness/courage/*etc*;

(b) *Scol Univ* (*écrite*) (examination) paper; (*orale*) test;

(c) *Sp* event (*at athletic meeting*); **é. éliminatoire,** (preliminary) heat; **é. finale,** final; **épreuves sur terrain,** field events; **épreuves sur piste,** track events;

(d) *Hist* **l'é. du feu,** ordeal by fire;

(e) (*personnelle*) trial, ordeal; **passer par de rudes épreuves,** to go through a bad time;

(f) *Typ etc* proof; *Phot* print; **les épreuves d'un livre,** the proofs of a book; *Cin* **épreuves (de tournage),** rushes.

épris [epri] *adj* **(a) é. de qn,** in love with s.o.; **(b) é. de qch,** passionate about sth.

éprouvant [epruvɑ̃] *adj* (*pénible*) trying, tiring.

éprouvé [epruve] *adj* **(a)** (*testé*) proven, well-tried (*remedy*); proven (*expert, loyalty etc*); trusty, staunch (*ally*); tested (*materials*); **(b)** stricken (*family*); hard-hit (*district*); **troupes très éprouvées,** troops that have suffered greatly.

éprouver [epruve] *vt* **(a)** (*tester*) to test (*machine, materials, method etc*); to put (*person, courage etc*) to the test; **(b)** (*ressentir*) to feel, to experience (*sensation, pain etc*); **(c)** (*subir*) to sustain, to suffer (*a loss*); to meet with (*difficulties*).

éprouvette [epruvɛt] **1** *nf* test tube. **2** *adj* **bébé é.,** test-tube baby.

epsilon [ɛpsilɔn] *nm* (*lettre grecque*) epsilon.

épucer [epyse] *vt* (**j'épuçai(s)**; **n. épuçons**); to rid (*dog etc*) of fleas.

épuisant [epɥizɑ̃] *adj* exhausting.

épuisé [epɥize] *adj* **(a)** (*très fatigué*) exhausted, tired out, worn out; **(b)** worked-out (*soil, mine*); out of print (*book, edition*); out of stock (*goods*); **tous nos stocks sont épuisés,** all our stocks are exhausted; *El* **pile épuisée,** dead cell; *Phys Nucl* **uranium é.,** depleted *or* impoverished uranium.

épuisement [epɥizmɑ̃] *nm* **(a)** (*fatigue*) exhaustion; **(b)** exhaustion (*of provisions, ammunition, mine, soil, stock etc*); depletion (*of resources*); draining, emptying (*of tank*); *Phys Nucl* depletion, impoverishment (*of uranium*); *Com* **jusqu'à. é. des stocks,** while stocks last.

épuiser [epɥize] **1** *vt* **(a)** (*fatiguer*) to exhaust, to wear *or* tire (*s.o.*) out; **(b)** to use up, to exhaust (*provisions, ammunition etc*); to exhaust, to work out (*mine, soil*); to drain, to empty (*tank*); to exhaust (*stock*); to sell out (*goods*); **é. un sujet,** to exhaust a subject; **cette marche a épuisé toute mon énergie,** that walking has used up all my energy. **2 s'épuiser** *vpr* **(a)** (*se fatiguer*) to exhaust oneself, to tire *or* wear oneself out; **mais je m'épuise à vous le dire,** I've told you so until I'm blue in the face; **(b)** (*of spring etc*) to dry up, to run dry; (*of stock, money, provisions etc*) to run out, to give out.

épuisette [epɥizɛt] *nf* **(a)** *Pêche* landing net; **(b)** *Nau* (*pelle*) scoop, bailer.

épurateur [epyratœr] *nm Tech* purifier; **é. de gaz,** gas purifier, (gas) scrubber.

épuration [epyrɑsjɔ̃] *nf* purification (*of water*); purification, scrubbing (*of gas*); refining (*of oil, ore*); *Fig* refining (*of morals, language, style*); *Pol* purge, purging.

épure [epyr] *nf* working drawing; (*dessin fini*) finished plan (*of building, engine etc*).

épurer [epyre] *vt* to purify (*water*); to purify, to scrub (*gas*); to refine (*oil, ore*); *Fig* to refine (*morals, language, style*); *Pol* to purge (*party, staff etc*).

équanimité [ekwanimite] *nf Litt* equanimity.

équarrir [ekarir] *vt* **(a)** to square (*timber, stone*); **(b)** to quarter, to cut up (*animal*).

équarrissage [ekarisaʒ] *nm* **(a)** squaring (*of timber, stone*); **(b)** quartering, cutting up (*of animal carcasses*); **chantier d'é.,** knacker's yard.

équarrisseur [ekarisœr] *nm* knacker.

équarrissoir [ekariswar] *nm* **(a)** (*couteau*) knacker's knife; **(b)** (*abattoir*) knacker's yard; **(c)** *Tech* broach, reamer.

équateur [ekwatœr] *nm* equator; **sous l'é.,** at *or* on the equator; **é. magnétique,** magnetic equator; *Astron* **é. céleste,** celestial equator.

Équateur [ekwatœr] *nm* Ecuador.

équation [ekwɑsjɔ̃] *nf* equation; *Math* **é. du premier/du deuxième degré,** simple/quadratic equation.

équatorial, -iaux [ekwatɔrjal, -jo] **1** *adj* equatorial. **2** *nm Astron* equatorial (telescope).

équatorien, -ienne [ekwatɔrjɛ̃, -jɛn] **1** *adj* Ecuadorian. **2** *n* **É.,** Ecuadorian.

équerrage [ekɛraʒ] *nm Menuis* bevel, angle; **é. en gras/en maigre,** obtuse/acute angle.

équerre [ekɛr] *nf* **(a)** (*instrument*) **é. (à dessin),** set square; **é. à coulisse,** (sliding) calliper gauge; **fausse é.,** bevel square; **é. à onglet,** mitre square; **é. d'arpenteur,** cross-staff; **(b) en é.,** at right angles; **d'é.,** square, straight; **hors d'é.,** out of square, not straight; **couper qch à fausse é.,** to cut sth askew; **mettre qch d'é.,** to square sth; **(c)** (*pièce métallique*) corner plate.

équestre [ekɛstr] *adj* equestrian (*statue etc*); horseriding (*exercises etc*).

équeuter [ekøte] *vt* to remove the stalk(s) from, to tail (*fruit*).

équiangle [ekɥiɑ̃gl] *adj Géom* equiangular.

équidés [ekɥide] *nmpl Zool* Equidae.

équidistance [ekɥidistɑ̃s] *nf* equidistance.

équidistant [ekɥidistɑ̃] *adj* equidistant (**de,** from).

équilatéral, -aux [ekɥilateral, -o] *adj Géom* equilateral.

équilibrage [ekilibraʒ] *nm Aut* balancing (*of wheels*).

équilibrant [ekilibrɑ̃] *adj* balancing; **poids é.,** counterweight; *Psy* **c'est un facteur é. dans la vie d'un enfant,** it's a stabilizing factor in a child's life.

équilibration [ekilibrɑsjɔ̃] *nf Physiol* balancing.

équilibre [ekilibr] *nm* balance, equilibrium (*of body, object*); balance, harmony (*of elements in a composition*);

stability (*of aircraft*); (*mental*) (mental) balance; **cet acrobate fait de l'é.** *ou* **des tours d'é.**, this acrobat does balancing tricks; **il a un bon é.**, (*mental*) he's well balanced; **mettre qch en é.**, to balance sth; **budget en é.**, balanced budget; **tenir qch en é. sur son nez**, to balance sth on one's nose; **perdre l'é.**, (*physique*) to lose one's balance; (*mental*) to become unbalanced; **elle manque d'é.**, she is unbalanced; **faire perdre l'é. à qn**, to throw s.o. off (his, her) balance; **l'é. budgétaire**, balance in the budget; **é. européen**, balance of power in Europe; **l'é. des rapports/des forces**, (*entre deux pays*) the balance of relations/power; *Pol* **l'é. de la terreur**, the balance of terror.

équilibré [ekilibre] *adj* balanced; **esprit bien é.**, well-balanced mind; **mal é., non é.**, unbalanced.

équilibrer [ekilibre] **1** *vt* to balance (*load, budget, elements in a composition etc*); *Nau Av* to trim (*ship, aircraft*); **é. qch par un contrepoids**, to counterbalance sth; *Aut* **é. les roues**, to balance the wheels; **cette expérience de travail l'a équilibré**, this work experience has stabilized him. **2 s'équilibrer** *vpr* to balance each other (out); (*budget*) to balance.

équilibreur, -euse [ekilibrœr, -øz] **1** *adj* balancing (*action etc*). **2** *nm Av* stabilizer.

équilibriste [ekilibrist] *n* (*acrobate*) equilibrist; (*funambule*) tightrope walker.

équille [ekij] *nf* (*poisson*) launce, sand eel.

équin [ekɛ̃] *adj* equine; **pied é.**, club foot.

équinisme [ekinism] *nm Méd* (*difformité*) club foot.

équinoxe [ekinɔks] *nm* equinox; **é. de printemps/d'automne**, spring *or* autumn(al) equinox; **vent d'é.**, equinoctial gale.

équinoxial, -iaux [ekinɔksjal, -jo] *adj* equinoctial.

équipage [ekipaʒ] *nm* **(a)** (*de navire, d'avion, de camion, char*) crew; **maître d'é.**, boatswain; *Nau* **les hommes d'é.**, the crew; **(b)** *Mil* train, equipment; **(c)** (*suite*) equipage, retinue; **arriver en grand é.**, to arrive in state; **(d)** *Hist* (*voiture, chevaux etc*) equipage; **(e)** *Vieilli* (*tenue*) attire; **(f)** *Tech* equipment, gear; **é. de construction**, builder's equipment *or* gear.

équipe [ekip] *nf* **(a)** (*personnes qui travaillent ensemble*) team; (*d'ouvriers*) gang; *Mil* working party; *Rail* **é. de conduite** *ou* **de locomotive**, engine crew; **é. de jour/nuit**, day/night shift; **travailler par équipes**, to work in shifts; **homme d'é.**, navvy; **chef d'é.**, (gang) foreman; **é. de secours**, rescue team; **encourager le travail d'é.**, to encourage teamwork; **esprit d'é.**, team spirit; *F* **nous étions une é. de joyeux lurons**, we were a cheerful crew *or* crowd; *F* **en voilà une fine é!**, what a crew!; **(b)** *Sp* team; crew (*of rowing boat*); **é. de cricket**, cricket team *or* eleven; **sport d'é.**, team sport; **(c)** *Vieilli* (*flottille*) train of barges.

équipée [ekipe] *nf* (*frasque*) escapade, lark; (*promenade, voyage*) jaunt.

équipement [ekipmɑ̃] *nm* **(a)** (*action*) equipping, equipment, fitting out (**de**, with); **é. en hommes**, manning; **plan d'é. national**, national development plan; **(b)** (*matériel*) equipment; (*de soldat*) kit; (*de camping, ski etc*) gear, equipment; **e. de survie**, survival kit; **(c)** (*installations*) facilities; **équipements collectifs**, public facilities *or* amenities; **(d) é. électrique**, electrical fittings; **industrie de l'é. électrique**, electrical engineering industry.

équiper [ekipe] **1** *vt* to equip, to fit out (**de**, with); **é. un navire**, (*d'appareils etc*) to equip *or* fit out a ship; (*d'hommes*) to man a ship; **é. un atelier**, to fit out a workshop; *F* **comme vous voilà équipé!**, what a get-up! **2 s'équiper** *vpr* to equip oneself.

équipier, -ière [ekipje, -jɛr] *n Sp* team member; (*rameur*) crew member.

équitable [ekitabl] *adj* **(a)** equitable, fair, just (*dealing etc*); **(b)** impartial, fair-minded (*person*).

équitablement [ekitabləmɑ̃] *adv* equitably, fairly.

équitation [ekitɑsjɔ̃] *nf* (horse)riding, *Fml* equitation; **faire de l'é.**, to go riding; **école d'é.**, riding school.

équité [ekite] *nf* equity, equitableness, fairness.

équivalence [ekivalɑ̃s] *nf* equivalence; **ce diplôme donne droit à une é.**, this diploma will be recognized (as equivalent).

équivalent [ekivalɑ̃] **1** *adj* eqivalent (**à**, to). **2** *nm* equivalent; **sans é.**, without equal.

équivaloir [ekivalwar] *vi* (*conj like* **valoir**) to be equivalent *or* equal (in value) (**à**, to); **cela équivaut à un refus**, that amounts to a refusal.

équivoque [ekivɔk] **1** *adj* **(a)** (*ambigu*) equivocal, ambiguous (*words, facts, attitude etc*); **(b)** (*douteux*) questionable, doubtful, dubious (*conduct, honesty, past etc*). **2** *nf* **(a)** (*ambiguïté*) ambiguity; **sans é.**, unequivocal(ly); **user d'é.**, to quibble; **(b)** (*malentendu*) misunderstanding (**sur**, about).

érable [erabl] *nm* (*arbre, bois*) maple; **é. à sucre**, sugar maple; **sucre d'é.**, maple sugar.

érablière [erablijɛr] *nf Can* maple grove.

éradication [eradikasjɔ̃] *nf Méd* eradication.

érafler [erafle] **1** *vt* to scratch, to graze (*knee etc*); to scuff (*leather etc*). **2 s'érafler** *vpr* **s'é. les tibias**, to bark one's shins.

éraflure [eraflyr] *nf* scratch, graze; (*sur une surface, chaussure*) scuff (mark).

éraillé [eraje] *adj* **(a)** frayed (*material*); scratched (*surface*); fretted (*rope*); **(b) yeux éraillés**, bloodshot eyes; **(c)** hoarse (*voice*).

éraillement [erajmɑ̃] *nm* **(a)** fraying (*of material*); fretting (*of rope*); **(b)** scratching (*of surface*); **(c)** (*éraflure*) scratch; **(d)** hoarseness (*of voice*).

érailler [eraje] **1** *vt* **(a)** to fray (out) (*material*); to unravel (*hem etc*); to fret (*rope*); **(b)** to scratch (*the skin etc*); **(c)** to make (*voice*) hoarse. **2 s'érailler** *vpr* **(a)** (*of hem etc*) to unravel, to come unravelled; (*of material*) to fray; (*of rope*) to fret; **(b)** (*of voice*) to become hoarse.

éraillure [erajyr] *nf* (*marque*) scratch.

erbium [ɛrbjɔm] *nm Ch* erbium.

ère [ɛr] *nf* era; **en l'an 1150 de notre è.**, in 1150 A.D.; **avant notre è.**, B.C.; **è. de prospérité**, period of prosperity.

érecteur, -trice [erɛktœr, -tris] *adj Physiol* erector (*muscle etc*).

érectile [erɛktil] *adj* erectile (*tissue*).

érection [erɛksjɔ̃] *nf* **(a)** erection, setting up, raising (*of statue, mast etc*); **(b)** *Physiol* erection; **être en é.**, to have an erection.

éreintage [erɛ̃taʒ] *nm* = **ÉREINTEMENT (b)**.

éreintant [erɛ̃tɑ̃] *adj F* backbreaking, exhausting (*work etc*).

éreinté [erɛ̃te] *adj F* exhausted, whacked.

éreintement [erɛ̃tmɑ̃] *nm* **(a)** (*fatigue*) exhaustion, fatigue; **(b)** (*critique sévère*) savage criticism, *Br* slating.

éreinter [erɛ̃te] **1** *vt* **(a)** (*fatiguer*) to exhaust, to wear *or* tire out (*person, animal*); **(b)** (*critiquer*) to criticize savagely, *Br* to slate (*book, performance, author etc*). **2 s'éreinter** *vpr* to exhaust oneself, to wear *or* tire oneself out (**à faire**, doing).

éreinteur [erɛ̃tœr] *nm F* savage critic.

erg[1] [ɛrg] *nm Phys* (*unité*) erg.

erg[2] *nm Géog* erg (*of the Sahara*).

ergol [ɛrgɔl] *nm Astronaut* propellant.

ergonomie [ɛrgɔnɔmi] *nf* ergonomics.

ergonomique [ɛrgɔnɔmik] *adj* ergonomic.

ergot [ɛrgo] *nm* **(a)** spur (*of cock etc*); *F* **monter** *ou* **se dresser sur ses ergots**, (*se montrer menaçant*) to show one's teeth; **(b)** dewclaw (*of dog etc*); **(c)** *Agr Pharm* ergot; **(d)** *Tech* lug; **e. d'arrêt**, stop pin.

ergotage [ɛrgɔtaʒ] *nm* quibbling, cavilling.

ergoté [ɛrgɔte] *adj* **(a)** spurred (*bird*); dewclawed (*dog*); **(b)** *Agr* ergotted (*rye, wheat*).

ergoter [ɛrgɔte] *vi* to quibble, to cavil (**sur**, about).

ergoteur, -euse [ɛrgɔtœr, -øz] **1** *adj* cavilling, quibbling. **2** *n* quibbler, caviller.

ergothérapeute [ɛrgɔterapøt] *n* occupational therapist.

ergothérapie [ɛrgɔterapi] *nf* occupational therapy.

Érié [erje] *nm* **le Lac É.**, Lake Erie.

ériger [eriʒe] *v* (**j'érigeai(s)**) **1** *vt* **(a)** (*dresser*) to erect, to set up, to raise (*statue, temple, mast etc*); **(b)** (*créer*) to establish, to set up (*office, tribunal etc*); **(c)** *Fig* **é. qn/qch en**, to set s.o./sth up as, to elevate s.o./sth to the status of; **é. une église en cathédrale**, to raise a church to (the dignity of) a cathedral. **2 s'ériger** *vpr* **s'é. en spécialiste/***etc*, to set oneself up as a specialist/etc.

ermitage [ɛrmitaʒ] *nm* hermitage.

ermite [ɛrmit] *nm* hermit; **vivre en e.**, to live the life of a recluse.

éroder [erɔde] *vt* to erode, to wear away (*coast, rocks etc*); to corrode, to eat away (*metals etc*); *Fig* **é. les arguments de qn**, to slowly destroy s.o.'s arguments.

érogène [erɔʒɛn] *adj* erogenous (*zone etc*).

éros [erɔs] *nm* **(a)** *Psy* **l'é.**, Eros; **(b)** *Myth* **É.**, Eros.

érosif, -ive [erozif, -iv] *adj* erosive.

érosion [erozjɔ̃] *nf* erosion, wearing away; *Fig* erosion; **é. dentaire**, dental erosion; *Fig* **é. monétaire**, depreciation of money.

érotique [erɔtik] *adj* erotic.

érotiquement [erɔtikmɑ̃] *adv* erotically.
érotisation [erɔtizɑsjɔ̃] *nf* eroticization.
erotiser [erɔtize] *vt* to eroticize.
érotisme [erɔtism] *nm* (*caractère érotique*) eroticism; (*goût pour le plaisir sexuel*) erotism.
érotologue [erɔtɔlɔg] *n* sexologist.
errant [ɛrɑ̃] *adj* roving, wandering (*traveller, life etc*); **chevalier e.,** knight errant; **le Juif e.,** the Wandering Jew; **chien e.,** stray dog; **pensées errantes,** wandering thoughts.
errata [ɛrata] *nm inv Typ* errata; **feuille d'e.,** errata slip.
erratique [ɛratik] *adj* erratic (*pulse etc*).
erratum [ɛratɔm] *nm Typ* erratum, *pl* errata; (*pl errata*).
erre [ɛr] *nf* **(a)** *Nau* (*lancée*) way; **e. pour gouverner,** steerage way; **avoir de l'e.,** to have way on; **perdre de l'e.** *ou* **son e.,** to lose way; **(b) erres,** track, spoor, slot (*of stag etc*); **suivre les erres de qn,** to walk in s.o.'s footsteps.
errements [ɛrmɑ̃] *nmpl* erring *or* bad ways; **retomber dans** *ou* **revenir à ses anciens e.,** to fall back into one's bad old ways.
errer [ɛre] *vi* **(a)** (*d'un marcheur etc*) to roam, to rove, to wander (about); **e. par les rues,** to wander about *or* roam the streets; **laisser e. ses pensées,** to let one's thoughts wander *or* stray; **(b)** (*se tromper*) to be mistaken, to err.
erreur [ɛrœr] *nf* **(a)** (*faute, inexactitude*) error, mistake; **e. de plume,** slip of the pen; **e. de date,** mistake in the date; **e. de jugement,** error of judgment; **e. judiciaire,** miscarriage of justice; **e. de sens,** wrong meaning; **e. typographique,** misprint; *Ordinat* **message d'e.,** error message; *Ordinat* **corrections des erreurs,** error correction; **faire** *ou* **commettre une e.,** to make a mistake; **par e.,** by mistake; **sauf e.,** if I am not mistaken; *Com* **sauf e. ou omission,** errors and omissions excepted; **il y a e. sur la personne,** you've got the wrong person; **faire e.,** to be mistaken; *F* **c'est un malin, pas d'e.,** he's a smart one and no mistake; **e.!,** not so!;
(b) (*opinion fausse*) error; **être dans l'e.,** to be under a misapprehension, to be mistaken; **une e. courante,** a common mistake; **induire qn en e.,** to mislead s.o.;
(c) (*action regrettable ou blâmable*) error; **les erreurs de la jeunesse,** the errors of youth; **revenir de ses erreurs,** to turn over a new leaf.
erroné [ɛrɔne] *adj* erroneous (*statement etc*).
erronément [ɛrɔnemɑ̃] *adv* erroneously.
ersatz [ɛrzats] *nm inv* ersatz, substitute; **e. de café/littérature/***etc*, ersatz coffee/literature/*etc*.
erse¹ [ɛrs] *adj & nm Ling* Erse, Scots Gaelic.
erse² *nf Nau* grummet, grommet.
éructation [eryktɑsjɔ̃] *nf* belch(ing), eructation.
éructer [erykte] **1** *vi* to belch, to eruct(ate). **2** *vt Fig* **é. des injures,** to hurl abuse.
érudit, -ite [erydi, -it] **1** *adj* erudite, scholarly, learned. **2** *n* scholar.
érudition [erydisjɔ̃] *nf* erudition, learning, scholarship; **discourir avec é.,** to talk learnedly.
éruptif, -ive [eryptif, -iv] *adj* eruptive (*disease, rock etc*).
éruption [erypsjɔ̃] *nf* **(a)** eruption (*of volcano etc*); **faire** *ou* **entrer en é.,** to erupt; **(b) é. dentaire** *ou* **des dents,** cutting of teeth; **(c)** *Méd* eruption, rash; **(d)** *Fig* eruption, outburst (*of anger, joy etc*).
érysipèle [erizipɛl] *nm Méd* erysipelas.
érythème [eritɛm] *nm Méd* rash, *Spéc* erythema; **é. fessier,** *Br* nappy *or Am* diaper rash.
Érythrée [eritre] *nf* Eritrea.
ès [ɛs] *prép* (= **en les**) **docteur ès lettres** *ou* **sciences,** ≈ PhD, DPhil; **licencié(e) ès lettres/sciences,** ≈ Bachelor of Arts/Science, BA/BSc; *Admin Jur* **ès qualités,** ex officio.
esbroufe [ɛzbruf] *nf F* showing off, swagger; **faire de l'e.,** to show off, to swagger; **vol à l'e.,** pocket-picking (*by hustling one's victim*).
esbroufer [ɛzbrufe] *vt F* to impress, to overawe (*s.o.*).
esbroufeur, -euse [ɛzbrufœr, -øz] *n F* show-off.
escabeau, -eaux [ɛskabo] *nm* **(a)** (*tabouret*) (wooden) stool; **(b)** (*marchepied*) stepladder, *Br* (pair of) steps; **e. de bibliothèque,** library steps.
escadre [ɛskadr] *nf Nau* fleet, squadron; **l'e. de la Méditerranée,** the Mediterranean fleet; *Av* **e. aérienne,** wing; *Nau* **chef d'e.,** squadron commander; *Av* wing commander.
escadrille [ɛskadrij] *nf* **(a)** *Nau* flotilla; **(b)** *Av* (*unité*) flight.
escadron [ɛskadrɔ̃] *nm* **(a)** *Mil* squadron; **e. de chars,** armoured squadron; **chef d'escadron(s),** major; **(b)** *Av* squadron; **e. de chasse/bombardement,** fighter/bomber squadron; **(c)** *Fig* (*groupe*) troop, band.

escalade [ɛskalad] *nf* **(a)** scaling, climbing (*of wall, cliff etc*); *Sp* (rock)climbing; **faire de l'e.,** to go (rock)climbing; **(b)** climb; **(c)** escalation (*of war, prices, violence etc*); **les charges locatives n'ont pas cessé leur e.,** service charges are still escalating; **on a remarqué son e. verbale,** it was noted that he got more and more carried away as he spoke.
escalader [ɛskalade] *vt* to scale, to climb; *Hist Mil* to escalade (*fortress etc*).
escalator [ɛskalatɔr] *nm* esclator.
escale [ɛskal] *nf* **(a)** (*temps d'arrêt*) *Nau* call; *Av* stop(over); **faire e.,** *Nau* to put into port; *Av* to touch down; *Av* **escales prévues,** scheduled stops; **vol sans e.,** nonstop flight; **une e. de quatre heures,** a four-hour *Nau* call *or Av* stop(over); **(b)** (*lieu*) *Nau* port *or* place of call; *Av* stop(over).
escalier [ɛskalje] *nm* (*cage*) staircase; (*marches*) (flight of) stairs; **e. de service** *ou* **de dégagement,** backstairs; **e. de secours,** fire escape; *Nau* **e. des cabines,** companionway; **e. tournant** *ou* **en vis** *ou* **en colimaçon,** spiral staircase; **e. roulant** *ou* **mécanique,** *Can* **e. mobile,** escalator; **rencontrer qn dans l'e.,** to meet s.o. on the stairs; *Fig* **j'ai l'esprit de l'e.,** I always think of an answer when it's too late.
escalope [ɛskalɔp] *nf Culin* escalope.
escamotable [ɛskamɔtabl] *adj* concealable (*handle etc*); retractable (*aerial, Av undercarriage*); foldaway, collapsible (*piece of furniture*).
escamotage [ɛskamɔtaʒ] *nm* **(a)** (*par un illusionniste*) conjuring away, vanishing; **tour d'é.,** vanishing trick; **(b)** *Fig* skipping (*of task*); dodging (*of problem, issue*); **(c)** *Av* retraction (*of undercarriage*); **(d)** (*vol*) stealing, filching.
escamoter [ɛskamɔte] *vt* **(a)** (*of conjuror*) to conjure (*sth*) away, to make (*sth*) vanish; **(b)** *Fig* (*éviter*); to skip (*task*); to dodge (*problem, issue*); **(c)** *Av* to retract (*the undercarriage*); **(d)** (*voler*) to sneak off with; **on m'a escamoté ma montre,** someone's sneaked off with my watch.
escamoteur, -euse [ɛskamɔtœr,-øz] *n* **(a)** (*illusionniste*) conjuror; **(b)** (*voleur*) sneak thief.
escampette [ɛskɑ̃pɛt] *nf F* (*only in*) **prendre la poudre d'e.,** (*s'enfuir*) to make off, *Br* to do a bunk.
escapade [ɛskapad] *nf* (*excursion*) jaunt; (*fugue*) escapade; **faire une e.,** to run off *or* away.
escarbille [ɛskarbij] *nf* cinder.
escarboucle [ɛskarbukl] *nf* (*pierre précieuse*) carbuncle.
escargot [ɛskargo] *nm* snail; **allure d'e.,** snail's pace; *F* **il marche comme un e.,** he's walking at a snail's pace.
escargotière [ɛskargɔtjɛr] *nf* **(a)** (*parc*) snailery; **(b)** (*plat*) snail dish.
escarmouche [ɛskarmuʃ] *nf* skirmish.
escarmoucher [ɛskarmuʃe] *vi Vieilli* to skirmish.
escarpe¹ [ɛskarp] *nf* (*fortification*) (e)scarp.
escarpe² *nm Arch* (*bandit*) cutthroat.
escarpé [ɛskarpe] *adj* steep (*road, mountain*); steep, precipitous, abrupt (*slope*); sheer (*cliff*).
escarpement [ɛskarpəmɑ̃] *nm* (*versant*) steep slope; (*fortification*) *& Géog* escarpment; *Géog* **e. de faille,** fault scarp.
escarpin [ɛskarpɛ̃] *nm* pump, *Br* court shoe; (*pour danser*) pump.
escarpolette [ɛskarpɔlɛt] *nf Vieilli* (*balançoire*) swing.
escarre, eschare [ɛskar] *nf Méd* scab; (*dû aux draps etc*) bedsore.
Escaut (l') [lɛsko] *nm* the Scheldt.
eschatologie [ɛskatɔlɔʒi] *nf* eschatology.
Eschyle [eʃil] *nm* Aeschylus.
escient [ɛsjɑ̃] *nm* **à bon e.,** wisely, judiciously; **à mauvais e.,** unwisely.
esclaffer (s') [sɛsklafe] *vpr* to burst out laughing, to roar with laughter, to guffaw.
esclandre [ɛsklɑ̃dr] *nm* (*scandale, tapage*) (noisy) scene; **faire** *ou* **causer un e., faire de l'e.,** to make a scene.
esclavage [ɛsklavaʒ] *nm* slavery; **réduire qn en e.,** to enslave s.o., to reduce s.o. to slavery; *Fig* **l'e. du bureau,** the drudgery of the office; *F* **mais c'est de l'e.!,** (*exploitation*) but it's slave labour!
esclavagiste [ɛsklavaʒist] *Hist Am* **1** *n* proslaver. **2** *adj* **état e.,** slave state.
esclave [ɛsklav] **1** *n* slave; **marchand d'esclaves,** slave trader; **il fut vendu comme e.,** he was sold into slavery; **elle est l'e. de sa famille,** she is a slave to her family; **être l'e. de la mode/de son travail,** to be a slave to *or* the slave of fashion/one's work. **2** *adj* **être e. de ses habitudes/***etc*, to be a slave to *or* the slave of one's

habits/*etc*.

escogriffe [ɛskɔgrif] *nm* **(grand) e.,** (*homme grand*) beanpole.

escompte [ɛskɔ̃t] *nm* **(a)** *Com* discount; **accorder** *ou* **faire un e. sur les prix,** to allow a discount on the prices; **maison d'e.,** cut-price *or* discount store; **à e.,** at a discount; *Can* **50% d'e. sur toute la marchandise,** 50% discount on all goods; **(b)** *Fin* **e. (de banque),** discount; **e. officiel, taux d'e.,** discount rate; **prendre à l'e. un effet de commerce,** to discount a bill of exchange.

escompter [ɛskɔ̃te] *vt* **(a)** *Fin* to discount (*bill*); **(b)** (*s'attendre à*) to expect, to anticipate (**que,** that); **e. faire,** to expect to do, to anticipate doing; **le succès escompté,** the expected *or* anticipated success.

escorte [ɛskɔrt] *nf Mil Nau etc* escort; **faire e.** *ou* **servir d'e. à qn,** to escort s.o.; **sous (bonne) e.,** under escort, with an escort; **conduire un prisonnier sous (bonne) e.,** to escort a prisoner; *Nau* **sous l'e. d'une corvette,** convoyed *or* escorted by a corvette.

escorter [ɛskɔrte] *vt* to escort; *Nau* to convoy, to escort.

escorteur [ɛskɔrtœr] *nm Nau* escort (vessel).

escouade [ɛskwad] *nf* **(a)** squad, gang (*of workmen*); group (*of tourists, young people etc*); **(b)** *Hist Mil* squad.

escrime [ɛskrim] *nf Sp* fencing; **faire de l'e.,** to fence; **e. à la baïonnette,** bayonet drill.

escrimer (s') [sɛskrime] *vpr* to fight; *Fig* **s'e. des mâchoires,** to eat heartily; **s'e. des pieds et des mains,** to fight tooth and nail; **s'e. à faire qch,** to try very hard to do sth, to toil (away) at doing sth.

escrimeur, -euse [ɛskrimœr, -øz] *n Sp* fencer.

escroc [ɛskro] *nm* swindler, crook.

escroquer [ɛskrɔke] *vt* **e. qch à qn, e. qn de qch,** to swindle *or* to cheat *or* to trick s.o. out of sth.

escroquerie [ɛskrɔkri] *nf* (*action*) swindling; (*résultat*) swindle; *Jur* (*délit*) fraud; **mais c'est de l'e.!,** it's a swindle, *Br* it's daylight robbery!

escudo [ɛskydo] *nm* (*monnaie*) escudo.

eskimo, -os [ɛskimo] **1** *adj inv* Eskimo. **2** *nm Ling* Eskimo. **3** *n* **E.,** Eskimo.

Ésope [ezɔp] *nm* Aesop.

ésotérique [ezɔterik] *adj* esoteric.

ésotérisme [ezɔterism] *nm* esotericism.

espace [ɛspas] **1** *nm* **(a)** (*étendue, distance*) space; **laisser de l'e.,** to leave space *or* room; **e. aérien,** airspace; **espaces verts,** green spaces; **e. publicitaire,** advertising space; **un e. de dix mètres entre deux choses,** a distance *or* space of ten metres between two things; **laisser un e. entre deux mots,** to leave a space between two words; **l'e. parcouru,** the distance covered;

(b) (*durée*) **pendant le même e. de temps,** in the same space of time; **en l'e. d'une semaine,** within a week;

(c) *Mus* space;

(d) (*vide*) *& Astron* space; **regarder dans l'e.,** to stare into space; **e. lointain** *ou* **extra-atmosphérique,** outer space; **vol** *ou* **voyage dans l'e.,** space flight *or* travel;

(e) *Géom* space; **e. à trois/quatre dimensions,** three-/four-dimensional space;

(f) *Admin* **e. judiciaire européen,** common European legal framework; **e. social européen,** common European framework for labour laws.

2 *nf Typ* space; **e. fine/moyenne/forte,** hair/middle/thick space.

espacement [ɛspasmɑ̃] *nm* (*action*) spacing out; (*résultat*) spacing; (*distance*) space, distance; **barre d'e.,** (*de machine à écrire etc*) space bar.

espacer [ɛspase] *v* (**j'espaçai(s)**) **1** *vt* to space out (*objects, lines, payments, visits etc*); **e. des choses d'un mètre,** to space things out a metre apart; **il faut e. nos rencontres,** we must meet less often. **2 s'espacer** *vpr* **(a)** (*of visits, letters, cries etc*) to become less frequent; **(b) espacez-vous,** space yourselves out.

espace-temps [ɛspastɑ̃] *nm inv Math Phys* space-time (continuum).

espaceur [ɛspasœr] *nm* (*en génétique*) spacer.

espadon [ɛspadɔ̃] *nm* swordfish.

espadrille [ɛspadrij] *nf* espadrille, rope-soled sandal.

Espagne [ɛspaɲ] *nf* Spain.

espagnol, -ole [ɛspaɲɔl] **1** *adj* Spanish. **2** *nm Ling* Spanish. **3** *n* **E.,** Spaniard.

espagnolette [ɛspaɲɔlɛt] *nf* (window) fastener (*long vertical bar with pivoting central catch*).

espalier [ɛspalje] *nm* **(a) (arbre en) e.,** espalier; **(b)** (*mur*) wall (*for espaliers*).

espar [ɛspar] *nm Nau* spar.

espèce [ɛspɛs] *nf* **(a)** (*sorte*) kind, sort; **gens/livres/***etc* **de toute e.,** people/books/*etc* of all kinds *or* of every description; **il portait une e. d'uniforme brun,** he wore a kind *or* a sort of brown uniform; *F* **cette e. d'idiot,** that silly fool!; **e. d'idiot!,** you idiot!; **des gens de son e.,** people like him, people of his kind *or* sort; **(b)** *Jur etc* **dans chaque cas d'e.,** in each specific case; **loi applicable en l'e.,** law applicable to the case in point; *F* **mais je suis un cas d'e.,** but I'm a special case; **(c) espèces,** (*argent*) cash; *Hist* (*monnaie métallique*) coin; **payer en espèces,** to pay in cash; **espèces sonnantes et trébuchantes,** hard cash; **(d)** *Bot Zool* species; **l'e. humaine,** mankind; **(e)** *Rel* (Eucharistic) species.

espérance [ɛsperɑ̃s] *nf* hope; **vivre dans l'e.,** to live in hope; **dans l'e. de faire,** in the hope of doing; **dans l'e. que,** in the hope that; **fonder son e. sur qn/qch,** to found one's hopes on s.o./sth; **mettre ses espérances en qch,** to pin one's hopes on sth; **il a l'e. de finir à temps,** he has hopes of finishing on time; **l'affaire n'a pas répondu à nos espérances,** the business did not come up *or* live up to our expectations; *Hum* **avoir des espérances,** to have expectations (*of an inheritance*); **e. de vie,** life expectancy; **tu es toute mon e.,** you are my only hope.

espérantiste [ɛsperɑ̃tist] *Ling* **1** *n* Esperantist. **2** *adj* Esperanto (*society etc*).

espéranto [ɛsperɑ̃to] *nm Ling* Esperanto.

espérer [ɛspere] *v* (**j'espère; j'espérerai**) **1** *vt* to hope for (*sth*); (*s'attendre à*) to expect (*s.o., sth*); **j'espère vous revoir,** I hope I'll see you again; **j'espère qu'il viendra,** I hope he comes *or* will come; **je n'espère pas qu'il vienne,** I don't expect him to come; **je ne vous espérais plus,** I had given you up. **2** *vi* **(a) e. en Dieu,** to trust in God; **e. contre tout espérance,** to hope against hope; **(b) j'espère bien,** I hope so.

esperluète, esperluette [ɛspɛrlyɛt] *nf* ampersand.

espiègle [ɛspjɛgl] **1** *adj* mischievous (*child, reply etc*). **2** *n* (*enfant*) imp; **petit(e) e.,** little monkey.

espièglerie [ɛspjɛgləri] *nf* **(a)** (*caractère*) mischievousness; **par pure e.,** out of pure mischief; **(b)** (*tour*) prank.

espion, -ionne [ɛspjɔ̃, -jɔn] *n* (*de puissance étrangère*) spy, secret agent; (*de police*) *& Fig* spy; **e. double,** double agent; **avion-/satellite-e.,** spy plane/satellite.

espionnage [ɛspjɔnaʒ] *nm* espionage, spying; **faire de l'e.,** to spy; **réseau/roman d'e.,** spy network/novel; **l'e. industriel,** industrial espionage.

espionner [ɛspjɔne] **1** *vt* to spy on (*s.o., s.o.'s movements etc*). **2** *vi* to spy.

espionnite [ɛspjɔnit] *nf F Hum* spy fever.

esplanade [ɛsplanad] *nf* esplanade.

espoir [ɛspwar] *nm* hope; **avoir l'e. de faire qch,** to have hopes of *or* be hopeful of doing sth; **avoir de l'e.,** to have hope(s); **dans l'e. de vous revoir,** in the hope of seeing you again; **avoir bon e.,** to be full of hope; **mettre son e. en qch/qn,** to put one's hopes in *or* pin one's hopes on sth/s.o.; **nourrir l'e. de faire qch,** to live in hope of doing sth; **cas sans e.,** hopeless case; **vous êtes/ce plan est leur seul e.,** you are/this plan is their only hope.

esprit [ɛspri] *nm* **(a)** (*spirituel*) spirit; **le Saint-E., l'E. saint,** the Holy Ghost, the Holy Spirit; *Rel & Hum* **rendre l'e.,** to give up the ghost; **l'e. malin,** the Evil One;

(b) (*fantôme*) ghost, spirit (of the dead); **il revient des esprits dans cette maison,** this house is haunted; **e., es-tu là?,** (*dans une séance de spiritisme*) is there anybody there?;

(c) (*fée*) sprite; **e. follet,** elfish spirit, hobgoblin;

(d) (*de vie*) **esprits animaux,** animal spirits; **perdre/reprendre ses esprits,** (*connaissance*) to lose/regain consciousness;

(e) *Ch etc* (volatile) spirit; **e.-de-sel,** spirits of salt; **e. brut,** raw spirits; **e.-de-vin,** spirits of wine;

(f) (*intellectuel*) mind; **d'e. lent,** slow-witted; **d'e. vif,** quick-witted; **c'est une vue de l'e.,** that's theoretical *or* all theory; **avoir l'e. tranquille,** to be easy in one's mind; **perdre l'e.,** to go out of one's mind; **elle avait l'e. ailleurs,** her thoughts were elsewhere; **où aviez-vous l'e.?,** what were you thinking of?; **présence d'e.,** presence of mind; **ça m'est sorti de l'e.,** it slipped my mind, it went clean out of my head; **une pareille idée ne me serait jamais venue à l'e.,** such an idea would never have occurred to me *or* crossed my mind *or* entered my head; **dans mon e., ça ne veut pas dire la même chose,** to my mind that doesn't mean the same thing; **avoir l'e. de se taire,** to have the (good) sense to be silent;

(g) (*humour*) wit; **avoir de l'e.,** to be witty; **mots** *ou* **traits d'e.,** witticisms, witty remarks;

(h) (*attitude, qualité*) spirit; **e. de corps,** esprit de corps; **e. d'équipe,** team spirit; **e. de famille,** family feeling; **avoir bon e.,** to be good-natured; **je n'ai pas l'e. de sacrifice,** I'm not the sort to make sacrifices; **avoir l'e. d'analyse/scientifique/***etc*, to have an analytical/a scientific/*etc* (turn of) mind;

(i) (*sens*) spirit; **s'attacher à l'e. de la loi plutôt qu'à la lettre,** to go by the spirit of the law rather than the letter; **c'est dans cet e. qu'a été conçue cette organisation,** it is in this spirit that this organization was conceived;

(j) (*personne*) person; **les esprits sérieux,** serious-minded people; *Prov* **les grands esprits se rencontrent,** great minds think alike; **un e. fort,** a freethinker; **un e. dangereux,** a dangerous person *or* man *or* woman.

esquif [ɛskif] *nm* (*embarcation*) skiff.

esquille [ɛskij] *nf* splinter (of bone).

esquilleux, -euse [ɛskijø, -øz] *adj* comminuted (*fracture*); splintered (*bone*).

esquimau, -aude, -aux [ɛskimo, -od, -o] **1** *adj* (*occ inv in feminine*) Eskimo, *Can* Inuit, *Can Péj* Eskimo; **chien e.,** husky. **2** *n* **E.,** Eskimo, *Can* Inuit, *Can Péj* Eskimo. **3** *nm* **(a) esquimau** ®, (*glace*) *Br* ≈ choc-ice (*on a stick*), *Am* ≈ ice-cream bar, Eskimo Pie ®; **(b)** *Ling* Eskimo, *Can* Inuit, *Can Péj* Eskimo.

esquimautage [ɛskimotaʒ] *nm Sp* (canoe) roll.

esquintant [ɛskɛ̃tɑ̃] *adj F* exhausting, killing (*work, journey etc*).

esquinter [ɛskɛ̃te] *F* **1** *vt* **(a)** (*fatiguer*) to do in, to wear (*s.o.*) out; **(b)** (*abîmer*) to ruin (*watch, tool etc*); to bash up, *Br* to prang (*car etc*); to do in (*part of body*); **(c)** (*critiquer*) to slam, *Br* to slate (*author, film etc*). **2 s'esquinter** *vpr* **(a)** to do oneself in, to wear oneself out (**à faire,** doing); **(b) s'e. la santé/les yeux,** to ruin one's health/eyes (**à faire,** doing).

esquisse [ɛskis] *nf Beaux-Arts* (rough) sketch; *Fig* (*de projet, roman, d'époque historique etc*) sketch, outline; **l'e. d'un sourire,** the ghost *or* suggestion of a smile.

esquisser [ɛskise] *vt* to sketch (*portrait etc*); *Fig* to sketch, to outline (*plan, novel, historical period etc*); **e. un sourire,** to give a slight smile.

esquive [ɛskiv] *nf Sp etc* (*mouvement*) dodge; *Fig* (*de question, problème etc*) dodging, evasion; *Boxe etc* **e. de la tête,** dodge.

esquiver [ɛskive] **1** *vt* to avoid, to dodge, to evade (*blow, issue, duty, creditor etc*). **2** *vi Sp etc* to dodge; *Boxe etc* **e. de la tête,** to dodge. **3 s'esquiver** *vpr* to slip away *or* off, to make oneself scarce.

essai [esɛ] *nm* **(a)** (*épreuve*) test, trial (*of product, machine, car etc*); **e. d'usine,** shop trial, bench test; **e. de vitesse,** speed trial; **terrain d'e.,** testing ground; **en (cours d')e.,** undergoing trials *or* tests; **faire l'e. de qch,** to test sth, to try sth out; **mettre qn/qch à l'e.,** to put s.o./sth to the test; **prendre qch/qn à l'e.,** to take sth/s.o. on trial, to take s.o. on probation/sth on approval; **à titre d'e.,** experimentally, as an experiment; **vente à l'e.,** sale on approval; **commande d'e.,** trial order; **pilote d'e.,** test pilot; *Aut* **essais sur route, e. routier,** road test;

(b) *Métal* assay(ing) (*of gold, silver*); **fourneau d'e.,** assay furnace;

(c) (*tentative*) attempt, try; **faire un e.,** to make an attempt, to have a try; **au premier e.,** at the first attempt *or* try; **coup d'e.,** trial shot;

(d) *Littér* essay;

(e) *Rugby* try; **marquer un e.,** to score a try; **transformer un e. (en but),** to convert a try;

(f) *Cin* **bout d'e.,** screen test.

essaim [esɛ̃] *nm* swarm (*of bees, students etc*); bevy (*of girls*).

essaimage [esɛmaʒ] *nm* **(a)** swarming (*of bees*); *Fig* spreading (*of population*); **l'e. de notre entreprise,** the expansion of our firm's branch network; **l'e. de chercheurs dans les postes de direction,** the spreading of research workers into managerial positions; **(b)** (*époque*) swarming time.

essaimer [eseme] *vi* (*of bees*) to swarm; *Fig* (*of population*) to spread; (*of firm*) to expand.

essart [ɛsar] *nm Agr* freshly cleared ground.

essarter [esarte] *vt Agr* to grub, to clear (*ground*).

essayage [esɛjaʒ] *nm* trying on, fitting (*of clothes, shoes etc*); **cabine** *ou* **salon d'e.,** fitting room.

essayer [eseje] *v* (**j'essaie, j'essaye; n. essayons; j'essaierai, j'essayerai**) **1** *vt* **(a)** (*pour la première fois, avant d'acheter etc*) to try (out) (*new gadget, restaurant, hairdresser etc*); to try, to taste (*wine, dish etc*); to try on (*clothes, shoes etc*); (*utiliser*) to try (*remedy, politeness, one's strength etc*); *Tech* (*tester*) to test, to try out (*machine, product etc*); *Métal* to assay (*ore*); **(b) e. de,** to try, to taste (*wine, dish etc*); **(c) e. de faire qch,** to try *or* attempt to do sth; **n'essaie pas de me mentir,** don't try lying *or* to lie to me; **essayez de l'attraper,** try to *or* and catch it; **laissez-moi e.,** let me have a try. **2 s'essayer** *vpr* **s'e. à qch/à faire qch,** to try one's hand *or* one's skill at sth/at doing sth.

essayeur, -euse [esɛjœr, -øz] *n* **(a)** (*de vêtements*) fitter; **(b)** (*de machine, produit etc*) tester; (*d'or, d'argent*) assayer.

essayiste [esejist] *n* essayist.

esse [ɛs] *nf* **(a)** (*crochet*) S-hook; **(b)** (*cheville d'essieu*) linchpin; **(c)** (*de violin etc*) f-hole, sound hole.

essence [esɑ̃s] *nf* **(a)** *Aut Br* petrol, *Am* gas, gasoline; **e. ordinaire,** *Br* two-star petrol, *Am* regular gas; **e. sans plomb,** unleaded *Br* petrol *or Am* gas; **poste d'e.,** filling station, *Br* petrol *or Am* gas station; **(b)** (*extrait*) essence (*of plant, coffee, meat etc*); **e. de citron,** lemon oil; **e. de roses,** rose oil, attar of roses; **(c)** (*caractère fondamental*) *& Phil* essence; **l'e. de l'affaire/du livre,** the essence *or* gist of the matter/book; **par e.,** essentially; **(d)** (*espèce*) species (*of tree*); **essences résineuses,** resinous trees, conifers.

essentiel, -ielle [esɑ̃sjɛl] **1** *adj* **(a)** (*fondamental*) essential (*truth, character, oil etc*); *Anat* **les organes essentiels,** the vital organs; **(b)** (*nécessaire*) essential, necessary (**à, pour,** for); **(c)** (*très important*) essential. **2** *nm* **l'e.,** (*point*) the main point; (*quantité*) the main *or* greater part (**de,** of); **n'apportez que l'e.,** bring only the (bare) essentials *or* the basics; **l'e. est d'agir,** the main *or* important thing is to act.

essentiellement [esɑ̃sjɛlmɑ̃] *adv* **(a)** (*par nature*) essentially, fundamentally; **(b)** (*principalement*) essentially, mainly; (*avant tout*) above all.

esseulé [esœle] *adj* (*abandonné*) left alone; (*solitaire*) lonely (*person*).

essieu, -ieux [esjø] *nm* axle(tree) (*of wheel*); **e. moteur,** driving axle; **e. tournant,** live axle.

essor [esɔr] *nm* flight, soaring (*of bird*); *Fig* (rapid) growth, expansion (*of industry, economy, country etc*); **donner l'e. à un oiseau,** to release a bird; **donner libre e. à son génie,** to give full scope to one's genius; **prendre son e.,** (*se développer*) to take off; **prendre un grand e.,** to grow *or* expand very rapidly; **industrie en plein e.,** booming *or* fast-growing industry.

essorage [esɔraʒ] *nm* (*de linge*) spin-drying; (*à la main, avec une essoreuse à rouleaux*) wringing.

essorer [esɔre] *vt* to spin(-dry); (*à la main, avec une essoreuse à rouleaux*) to wring (*clothes*); to spin (*salad*).

essoreuse [esɔrøz] *nf* spin-dryer; **e. à rouleau,** wringer, mangle; **é. à salade,** salad spinner.

essoucher [esuʃe] *vt* to stub (*land*), to clear (*land*) of tree stumps.

essoufflé [esufle] *adj* out of breath, short of breath, winded.

essoufflement [esufləmɑ̃] *nm* shortness of breath, breathlessness.

essouffler [esufle] **1** *vt* to wind (*s.o., horse*), to make (*s.o., horse*) out of breath. **2 s'essouffler** *vpr* to get out of breath *or F* puff; *Fig* (*roman, personne créative, économie etc*) to run out of steam; *Fig* **s'é. à faire qch,** to struggle to do sth.

essuie-glace [esɥiglas] *nm Aut Br* windscreen wiper, *Am* windshield wiper; (*pl essuie-glaces*).

essuie-main(s) [esɥimɛ̃] *nm inv* hand towel; **e.-m. à rouleau,** roller towel.

essuie-meubles [esɥimœbl] *nm inv* duster.

essuie-pieds [esɥipje] *nm inv* doormat.

essuie-tout [esyitu] *nm inv* kitchen roll.

essuie-verres [esɥivɛr] *nm inv* glass cloth.

essuyage [esɥijaʒ] *nm* (*de vaisselle*) wiping, drying; (*de surface mouillée*) wiping (down); (*d'eau etc*) wiping up, mopping up; (*nettoyage*) wiping (clean); (*époussetage*) dusting.

essuyer [esɥije] *v* (**j'essuie; j'essuierai**) **1** *vt* **(a)** (*sécher*) to wipe, to dry (*plates etc*); to wipe (*surface*) (down); (*nettoyer*) to wipe (clean); (*épousseter*) to dust (*furniture etc*); (*éponger*) to wipe up, to mop up (*water etc*); to wipe away (*tears*); **e. la vaisselle,** to dry the dishes, to wipe; **(b)** (*subir*) to suffer, to endure, to be subjected to (*defeat, insults etc*); **e. un refus,** to meet with a refusal; **e. une perte,** to suffer a loss; **e. le feu de l'ennemi,** to come under enemy fire. **2 s'essuyer** *vpr* to wipe oneself, to dry oneself; **s'e. les pieds/la bouche/les yeux,** to wipe one's feet/mouth/eyes.

est[1] [ɛ] *voir* **ÊTRE**[2].

est[2] [ɛst] **1** *nm* east; **un vent d'e.**, an easterly wind; **le vent d'e.**, the east wind; **à l'e. de Suez**, (to the) east of Suez; **vers l'e.**, eastward, towards the east. **les pays de l'E.**, the countries of the Eastern bloc. **2** *adj inv* eastern (*coast, slope, regions etc*); easterly, eastward (*direction*).

establishment [ɛstabliʃmɛnt] *nm Pol* establishment.

estacade [ɛstakad] *nf Nau* (*pieux*) stockade; (*jetée*) pier (on piles).

estafette [ɛstafɛt] *nf* **(a)** *Hist* (*courrier*) courier; **(b)** *Mil* (*agent de liaison*) liaison officer.

estafilade [ɛstafilad] *nf* gash (*from razor, sword*).

estagnon [ɛstaɲɔ̃] *nm* (metal) container (*for oils etc*).

est-allemand [ɛstalmɑ̃] *adj* East German; (*pl est-allemand(e)s*).

estaminet [ɛstaminɛ] *nm* (small) café, bar (*esp in N France and Belgium*).

estampage [ɛstɑ̃paʒ] *nm* **(a)** *Tech* stamping (*of metal, coin, leather etc*); **(b)** *F* (*action d'escroquer*) swindling, fleecing; (*résultat*) swindle.

estampe [ɛstɑ̃p] *nf* **(a)** (*image*) print; **cabinet des estampes**, print room (*of library*); **(b)** (*outil*) stamp.

estamper [ɛstɑ̃pe] *vt* **(a)** *Tech* to stamp (*metal, coin, leather etc*); **(b)** *F* (*escroquer*) to swindle, to fleece (*s.o.*).

estampeur, -euse [ɛstɑ̃pœr, -øz] *n* **(a)** *Tech* (*personne, outil*) stamper; **(b)** *F* (*escroc*) swindler.

estampillage [ɛstɑ̃pijaʒ] *nm* stamping (*of document etc*); marking (*of goods*).

estampille [ɛstɑ̃pij] *nf* (*sur un document etc*) stamp; (*sur un produit*) mark.

estampiller [ɛstɑ̃pije] *vt* to stamp (*document etc*); to mark (*goods*).

este [ɛst] **1** *adj* Estonian. **2** *nm Ling* Estonian. **3** *n* **E.**, Estonian.

ester [ɛstɛr] *nm Ch* ester.

esthète [ɛstɛt] *n* aesthete, *US* esthete.

esthéticien, -ienne [ɛstetisjɛ̃, -jɛn] *n* **(a)** (*spécialiste des soins de beauté*) beautician, beauty specialist; **(b)** (*artiste, poète etc*) aesthetician, *US* esthetician.

esthétique [ɛstetik] **1** *adj* aesthetic, *US* esthetic; (*beau*) aesthetically *or US* esthetically pleasing; **chirurgie e.**, plastic surgery. **2** *nf* (*science*) aesthetics, *US* esthetics; (*beauté*) aesthetic *or US* esthetic quality.

esthétiquement [ɛstetikmɑ̃] *adv* aesthetically, *US* esthetically.

esthétisme [ɛstetism] *nm* aestheticism, *US* estheticism.

estimable [ɛstimabl] *adj* **(a)** (*honorable*) estimable (*person, quality*); **(b)** (*assez bon*) fairly good (*work, artist etc*).

estimatif, -ive [ɛstimatif, -iv] *adj* estimated (*cost etc*); **devis e.**, (preliminary) estimate (*of price*), quotation.

estimation [ɛstimɑsjɔ̃] *nf* **(a)** (*détermination de la valeur exacte*) estimation (*of value, price*); valuation, appraising (*of goods*); assessment (*of damage*); **faire une e.**, to give an estimation *or* a valuation *or* an assessment; **(b)** (*calcul approximatif*) estimation (*of distance, weight etc*); **(c)** (*valeur, quantité*) estimate.

estime [ɛstim] *nf* **(a)** (*approximation*) guesswork; *Nau* reckoning; **à l'e.**, by guesswork; *Nau* by dead reckoning; **navigation à l'e.**, dead reckoning; **(b)** (*respect*) esteem, regard; **témoigner de l'e. pour qn**, to show regard for s.o.; **tu as baissé dans mon e.**, you have gone down in my estimation; **tenir qn en grande/en médiocre e.**, to think highly/little of s.o.; **avoir un succès d'e.**, to be a critical (though not a popular) success.

estimer [ɛstime] **1** *vt* **(a)** (*déterminer la valeur exacte de*) to estimate (*price, value*); to value, to appraise (*goods*); to assess (*damage*); **e. la gloire à sa valeur**, to rate glory at its true value;

(b) (*calculer approximativement*) to estimate (*distance, weight etc*); *Nau* to reckon; **longitude estimée**, longitude by dead reckoning;

(c) (*considérer*) to consider; **j'estime qu'il est de mon devoir de parler**, I consider it my duty *or* that it is my duty to speak;

(d) (*respecter*) to have a high opinion of, to think highly of, to esteem (*s.o.*); to value, to have a high opinion of (*s.o.'s qualities, music etc*).

2 s'estimer *vpr* **(a)** **s'e. satisfait/heureux/***etc*, to consider oneself satisfied/lucky/*etc*;

(b) (*avoir bonne opinion de soi*) to have a high opinion of oneself, to think highly of oneself.

estivage [ɛstivaʒ] *nm Agr* summering (*of cattle etc*) on mountain pastures.

estival, -aux [ɛstival, -o] *adj* summer (*residence, resort, clothes, work etc*).

estivant, -ante [ɛstivɑ̃, -ɑ̃t] *n* (summer) *Br* holiday-maker, *Am* vacationer.

estiver [ɛstive] **1** *vt Agr* to summer (*cattle etc*) on mountain pastures. **2** *vi* (*of person*) to spend the summer, *Fml* to summer.

estoc [ɛstɔk] *nm* **frapper d'e. et de taille**, to cut and thrust.

estocade [ɛstɔkad] *nf* (*en tauromachie*) deathblow; **donner l'e. à**, to deal the deathblow to (*bull, Fig opponent*).

estomac [ɛstɔma] *nm* stomach; **avoir l'e. vide/plein**, to have an empty stomach/be full (up); **creux de l'e.**, pit of the stomach; **mal d'e.**, stomach ache; **avoir l'e. dans les talons**, to be ravenously hungry; *F* **avoir de l'e.**, (*courage*) to have plenty of guts; (*culot*) to have plenty of cheek.

estomaquer [ɛstɔmake] *vt F* to stagger, to astound, to flabbergast.

estompage [ɛstɔ̃paʒ] *nm Beaux-Arts* stumping, shading off.

estompe [ɛstɔ̃p] *nf Beaux-Arts* stump; **dessin à l'e.**, stump drawing.

estompé [ɛstɔ̃pe] *adj* indistinct, blurred (*outline, image, colours etc*); blurred, dim (*memories*).

estomper [ɛstɔ̃pe] **1** *vt Beaux-Arts* to stump, to shade off (*drawing*) with a stump; *Fig* to blur, to dim (*landscape, outline, memory etc*); to tone down (*contrast*). **2 s'estomper** *vpr* to become blurred.

Estonie [ɛstɔni] *nf* Estonia.

estonien, -ienne [ɛstɔnjɛ̃, jɛn] **1** *adj* Estonian. **2** *nm Ling* Estonian. **3** *n* **E.**, Estonian.

estoquer [ɛstɔke] *vt* (*d'un matador*) to kill (*the bull*).

estourbir [ɛsturbir] *vt F* **(a)** (*tuer*) to do (*s.o.*) in; **(b)** (*étonner*) to astound (*s.o.*), to knock (*s.o.*) flat.

estrade [ɛstrad] *nf* dais, rostrum, platform.

estragon [ɛstragɔ̃] *nm Bot Culin* tarragon.

estrapade [ɛstrapad] *nf Hist* (*supplice*) strappado (punishment); *Nau* dipping from the yard arm.

estrogène [ɛstrɔʒɛn] *nm Physiol* oestrogen, *US* estrogen.

estropié, -ée [ɛstrɔpje] **1** *adj* crippled, maimed; **être e. de la jambe**, to have a gammy leg. **2** *n* cripple.

estropier [ɛstrɔpje] *vt* (*impf & pr sub* **n. estropiions**) **(a)** to cripple, to maim (*s.o.*); **(b)** *Fig* to murder (*waltz, foreign language etc*); to mispronounce (*word*); to mutilate (*text*).

estuaire [ɛstɥɛr] *nm* estuary.

estudiantin [ɛstydjɑ̃tɛ̃] *adj* student (*life etc*).

esturgeon [ɛstyrʒɔ̃] *nm* (*poisson*) sturgeon.

et [e] **1** *conj* **(a)** and; **toi et moi**, you and me; **c'est un homme de grande énergie, et qui arrivera**, he is a man of great energy, who will succeed; **et son frère et sa sœur**, both his brother and his sister; **j'aime le café, et vous?**, I like coffee, do you?; **et les dix francs que je vous ai prêtés?**, and (what about) the ten francs I lent you?; **et le garçon de se sauver**, at this the boy ran off; **et elle de rire!**, and she burst out laughing!; **(b)** (*dans les nombres etc*) **vingt/trente/***etc* **et un**, twenty/thirty/*etc* -one; **soixante et onze**, seventy-one; **il est quatre heures et demie**, it's half past four. (*Note there is no liaison with* **et**, **j'ai écrit et écrit** [ʒeekrieekri]). **2** *nm* **(a)** **et commercial**, ampersand; **(b)** *Ordinat* **ET**, AND; **circuit ET**, AND gate.

étable [etabl] *nf* cowshed; **é. à cochons**, pigsty.

établi[1] [etabli] *nm* (work)bench.

établi[2] *adj* established (*government, reputation etc*); **l'Église établie**, the Established Church; **considérer qch comme chose établie**, to take sth for granted.

établir [etablir] **1** *vt* **(a)** (*créer*) to establish (*form of government, business, peace etc*); to set up (*statue, agency*); to put up (*building*); to construct (*dam, railway*); to settle, to fix (*place of residence*); to install (*machinery*); to set (*a sail*); to pitch (*a camp*); to quote, to fix (*price*); to institute, to create (*tax, tribunal etc*); to prescribe, to lay down (*rule*); to lay down (*principle*); **é. un record**, to set a record;

(b) (*démontrer*) to establish, to prove (*fact, s.o.'s innocence*); **é. une accusation**, to establish *or* substantiate a charge;

(c) (*dresser*) to draw up (*plan, proposal etc*); **é. un devis**, to draw up an estimate; **é. un compte/un bilan/un budget**, to draw up an account/a balance sheet/a budget; **é. une balance**, to strike a balance;

(d) (*faire valoir*) to establish (*authority, rights, reputation etc*);

(e) (*pourvoir d'une situation*) to set (*s.o.*) up (**dans**, in).

2 s'établir *vpr* **(a)** (*dans une ville, un pays etc*) to settle (**à, dans, en**, in);

(b) (*pour exercer un métier*) **s'é. épicier/***etc*, to set

(oneself) up as a grocer/*etc*; **elle s'est établie à son compte,** she set up (in) business on her own;
(c) (*se poser en*) **s'é. chef/juge/etc,** to set oneself up as a leader/judge/*etc*;
(d) (*of custom, idea, relations etc*) to become established.

établissement [etablismɑ̃] *nm* **(a)** establishment; setting up, putting up, fixing, installing (*of machinery etc*); setting (*of a sail*); establishing, building up (*of reputation, fortune etc*);
(b) establishment, proving (*of innocence, guilt*);
(c) working out (*of design etc*); drawing up, making up (*of accounts, schedule etc*);
(d) establishment, creating, forming (*of government etc*); laying down (*of rules*); founding (*of colony, industry*);
(e) establishment, settling (*of one's children etc*);
(f) establishment, setting up (*of a business*); **frais d'é., coût de premier é.,** initial outlay *or* expenditure, start-up costs;
(g) (*institution*) establishment, institution; **é. de charité,** charitable institution; **é. thermal,** hydropathic establishment; **é. hospitalier,** hospital; **é. scolaire,** school, educational establishment; **é. de crédit,** bank;
(h) *Hist* **établissements,** (*colonies*) settlements, colonies;
(i) *Com* business, firm; **les établissements Martin,** Martin & Co.; **é. principal,** main branch *or* office; **é. industriel,** factory.

étage [etaʒ] *nm* **(a)** (*de bâtiment*) floor, *Br* storey, *Am* story; **maison à un é.** *ou* **sans é.,** single-storeyed *or Am* single-storied house; **à deux étages,** two-storeyed; **au troisième é.,** *Br* on the third floor, *Am* on the fourth floor; **monter à l'é.,** to go upstairs; **dévaler les étages,** to race down the stairs;
(b) (*de construction, de terrain, d'armoire*) level; (*de jardin*) terrace; (*de gâteau*) tier; **gâteau à quatre étages,** four-tiered cake; *F* **menton à deux étages,** double chin;
(c) *Géol* stage, formation;
(d) *Tech* stage; **compression par étages,** compression by stages; **fusée à trois étages,** three-stage rocket;
(e) *Péj* **de bas é.,** mediocre, second-rate (*mind, story etc*);
(f) *Can Sp Fig* **le deuxième é.,** the (club) management.

étagement [etaʒmɑ̃] *nm* arrangement in tiers; terracing (*of vines on hillsides*).

étager [etaʒe] *v* **(j'étageai(s)) 1** *vt* **(a)** to arrange (*seats, books etc*) in tiers; **jardin étagé,** terraced garden; **vignes étagées,** vines arranged in terraces; **poulie étagée,** cone pulley; **(b)** to carry out (*operation, plan*) by stages; **compression étagée,** compression by stages, staged compression. **2 s'étager** *vpr* **(a)** (*of houses, vines etc*) to rise in tiers; **(b)** (*of operation, plan*) to be carried out in stages.

étagère [etaʒɛr] *nf* **(a)** (*meuble*) (set of) shelves; **(b)** (*planche*) shelf.

étai¹ [etɛ] *nm Nau* (*cordage*) stay; **voile d'é.,** staysail.

étai² *nm Constr etc* stay, prop, strut; **é. de mine,** pit prop.

étaiement [etɛmɑ̃] *nm Constr etc* staying, shoring, propping (up).

étain [etɛ̃] *nm* **(a)** (*métal*) tin; **é. battu, é. en feuilles,** thin sheet tin; **papier d'é.,** tinfoil, silver paper; **(b)** (*pour la vaisselle, les bijoux*) pewter; **vaisselle d'é.,** pewter (plate); **une très belle collection d'é.,** a very fine collection of pewter (pieces).

étal, -als [etal] *nm* **(a)** (*de boucher*) (butcher's) stall, meat stall; **(b)** (*au marché*) (market) stall.

étalage [etalaʒ] *nm* **(a)** *Com* display, show (*of goods*); (*vitrine*) (display) window; **é. de bouquiniste,** secondhand bookstall; **faire l'é.,** to set out one's goods; (*la vitrine*) to dress the window(s); **mettre qch à l'é.,** to display sth for sale; **article qui a fait l'é.,** shopsoiled *or Am* shopworn article; **(b)** *Fig* showing off, show, parade (*of wealth, knowledge etc*); **faire é. de ses bijoux/son savoir,** to show off *or* parade one's jewels *or* knowledge.

étalager [etalaʒe] *vt* **(j'étalageai(s))** *Com* to display (goods) for sale.

étalagiste [etalaʒist] *n* window dresser.

étale [etal] *Nau* **1** *adj* slack (*sea, tide*); steady (*breeze*). **2** *nm* **é. du flot,** slack water.

étalement [etalmɑ̃] *nm* **(a)** displaying (*of goods*); **(b)** spreading out (*of linen to dry, papers on table etc*); spreading (*of tablecloth, butter etc*); application (*of paint etc*); **(c)** staggering (*of holidays, payments etc*).

étaler [etale] **1** *vt* **(a)** *Com* to display (*goods*) for sale;
(b) (*étendre*) to spread out, to lay out (*linen to dry, papers etc*); to spread (*tablecloth, butter etc*); to apply (*paint, ointment*) (**sur,** to); *Cartes* to lay down (*one's cards*);
(c) to parade, to show off (*one's wealth, knowledge*);
(d) (*échelonner*) to stagger (*holidays, payments*) (**sur,** over);
(e) *Nau* to stem (*current, wind*).
2 s'étaler *vpr* **(a)** (*of village etc*) to spread out; **arbre à cime étalée,** large-crowned tree; **cette peinture s'étale mal,** this paint goes on badly;
(b) (*parader*) to flaunt oneself;
(c) (*se vautrer*) to stretch oneself out, to sprawl; **s'é. par terre,** (*tomber*) to fall flat on the ground;
(d) (*of holidays, payments etc*) to be spread (**sur,** over).

étalinguer [etalɛ̃ge] *vt Nau* to bend (*cable*) to the anchor.

étalon¹ [etalɔ̃] *nm* (*cheval*) stallion.

étalon² *nm* (*modèle de mesure*) standard; *Fig* (*modèle*) standard, yardstick; **mètre é.,** standard metre; *Econ* **l'é. (d')or,** the gold standard.

étalonnage [etalɔnaʒ] *nm,* **étalonnement** [etalɔnmɑ̃] *nm* **(a)** (*action de vérifier*) standardization (*of weight, measure*); gauging, testing (*of instrument*); **(b)** (*action de graduer*) calibration (*of thermometer etc*); **(c)** *Psy* standardization (*of test*).

étalonner [etalɔne] *vt* **(a)** (*vérifier*) to standardize (*weight, measure*); to gauge, to test (*instrument*); **(b)** (*graduer*) to calibrate (*thermometer, barometer etc*); **(c)** *Psy* to standardize (*test*).

étamage [etamaʒ] *nm* **(a)** tinning (*of copper etc*); tinplating (*of sheet iron*); **(b)** silvering (*of mirror*).

étambot [etɑ̃bo] *nm Nau* sternpost.

étamer [etame] *vt* **(a)** to tin (*copper etc*); to tinplate (*sheet iron*); **(b)** to silver (*mirror*).

étameur [etamœr] *nm* tinner, tinsmith; **é. ambulant,** tinker.

étamine¹ [etamin] *nf Tex* muslin; (*pour filtrer, cribler*) butter muslin, cheesecloth; **passer à l'é.,** to filter (*liquid*); to sift (*flour etc*); *Fig* to sift (*evidence etc*).

étamine² *nf Bot* stamen.

étampage [etɑ̃paʒ] *nm* punching (*of horseshoe*).

étampe [etɑ̃p] *nf* (*outil à percer*) punch.

étamper [etɑ̃pe] *vt* (*percer des trous dans*) to punch (*horseshoe*).

étanche [etɑ̃ʃ] **1** *adj* watertight (*boat, roof etc*); waterproof (*watch, boots etc*); **é. à l'eau/à l'air/à la poussière,** watertight/airtight/dustproof; **cloison é.,** *Nau* watertight bulkhead; *Fig* impenetrable barrier (*between departments etc*); *Av* **cabine é.,** pressure cabin. **2** *nf* **entretenir à é. d'eau,** to keep watertight.

étanchéité [etɑ̃ʃeite] *nf* watertightness (*of boat, roof etc*); waterproofness (*of watch, boots etc*); **é. à l'eau/à l'air,** watertightness/airtightness; **vérifier l'é.,** to check for leaks.

étancher [etɑ̃ʃe] *vt* **(a)** to check the flow of (*liquid*); to staunch (*blood*); to dry (*s.o.'s tears*); *Nau* **é. une voie d'eau,** to stop a leak; **(b)** to quench, to slake (*one's thirst*); **(c)** (*sécher*) to clear of water; **(d)** (*rendre étanche*) to make watertight.

étançon [etɑ̃sɔ̃] *nm Constr Nau* (*étai*) shore, stanchion.

étançonnement [etɑ̃sɔnmɑ̃] *nm* shoring up (*of wall, ship etc*).

étançonner [etɑ̃sɔne] *vt* to shore up (*wall, ship etc*).

étang [etɑ̃] *nm* pond, pool.

étant [etɑ̃] *voir* **ÊTRE²**.

étape [etap] *nf* **(a)** (*lieu*) stop(over), stopping place; **faire é.,** to stop; **nous avons fait é. à Bordeaux,** we stopped over(night) at Bordeaux; **brûler une é.,** *Rail etc* to fail to stop at a scheduled stop; *Fig* to press on; **brûler les étapes,** to get ahead of schedule; *Hist Mil* **zone des étapes,** area behind the lines; **(b)** (*distance à parcourir*) stage (*of journey, race etc*); **à** *ou* **par petites étapes,** by *or* in easy stages; **nous avons fait hier une é. de 500 kilomètres,** we covered *or* did 500 kilometres yesterday; **(c)** *Fig* (*phase*) stage (*of life, process etc*); **par étapes,** by *or* in stages; **d'é. en é.,** progressively, stage by stage.

état [eta] *nm* **(a)** (*condition*) state, condition; *Phys* state; **dans l'é. (actuel) des choses,** in the present circumstances *or* state of affairs; **en (bon) é.,** (*machine, car etc*) in good condition *or* (good) working order; (*house*) in good condition *or* repair; (*athlete*) in good condition *or* shape; **navire en bon é. (de navigabilité),** seaworthy ship; **en mauvais é., hors d'é.,** in need of repair, out of order; **mettre ses affaires en é.,** to put one's affairs in order; **remettre en é.,** to renovate, to rehabilitate (*house etc*); to overhaul, to recondition (*engine*); **laisser les choses en l'é.,** to leave things as they stand; **en é. de choc/d'ivresse,** in a state of shock/intoxication; **é. d'esprit,** state *or* frame of mind; **avoir des états d'âme,** to have doubts *or* uncertainties; **é. de guerre,** state of war; **le pays est en é. de guerre,** the country is at war *or* in a state of war; **c'est un é. de fait,** it's an undeniable *or* established fact; **être en é. de faire qch,** to be in a position to do sth; **cet é. de choses n'est pas définitif,** this state of affairs *or* this situation is not permanent; **n'être plus en é. de travailler,** to be not up to working any more; **hors d'é. de faire qch,** unable *or* not in a position to do sth; **hors d'é. de rendre aucun service,** totally unfit for use; *Hum* **elle s'est retrouvée dans un é. intéressant,** (*enceinte*) she found herself in the family way again; *F* **être dans tous ses états,** to be upset *or* in a real state;

(b) (*rapport*) statement, list (*of expenses, sales*); schedule, list (*of payments, goods*); **é. néant,** nil return; **é. des dépenses/de compte,** statement of expenses/account; *Jur* **é. de frais,** bill of costs; **é. des lieux,** inventory of fixtures (*in rented premises*); **le propriétaire est tenu de faire l'é. des lieux avec son locataire,** the landlord is obliged to agree an inventory of fixtures with the tenant; *Admin Mil* **é. de services,** record of service; **é. nominatif,** list of names, (nominal) roll; **rayer qn des états,** to strike s.o. off the rolls;

(c) faire é. de, (*s'appuyer sur*) to cite, to adduce; (*tenir compte de*) to take into account *or* into consideration; (*mentionner*) to mention; *Vieilli* (*compter sur*) to count *or* rely on; **faire grand é. de qn,** to think highly of s.o.;

(d) *Admin* **é. civil,** civil status; (*à la mairie*) register *or* *Br* registry office; **actes de l'é. civil,** = certificates of births, marriages and deaths; **informer l'é. civil d'un décès,** to register a death;

(e) (*profession*) profession (*of soldier, clergyman etc*); trade (*of shopkeeper etc*); **militaire/épicier de son é.,** soldier by profession/grocer by trade;

(f) *Hist* (*groupe social*) estate (of the realm); **le tiers é.,** the third estate, the commonalty; **les États généraux,** the States General;

(g) l'É., (*autorité centrale*) the state *or* State; **coup d'É.,** coup (d'état); **le budget de l'É.,** the state budget; **homme/femme d'É.,** statesman/stateswoman; **pour des raisons d'É.,** for reasons of state; **un É. dans l'É.,** a state within a state; **é. providence,** welfare state;

(h) (*nation*) state; **servir d'é. tampon,** to serve as a buffer state.

étatique [etatik] *adj Pol* (of the) state; **l'appareil é.,** the state machine.

étatisation [etatizasjɔ̃] *nf* (*action*) establishment of state control (**de,** over); (*doctrine*) state control.

étatisé [etatize] *adj* state-controlled, state-run.

étatiser [etatize] *vt* to bring (*firm etc*) under state control.

étatisme [etatism] *nm* state control.

étatiste [etatist] **1** *adj* **système/***etc* **é.,** system/*etc* of state control. **2** *n* partisan of state control.

état-major [etamaʒɔr] *nm* (*pl états-majors*) **(a)** *Mil etc* (*officiers*) (general) staff; **officier d'é.-m.,** staff officer; **carte d'é-m.,** *Br* ≈ Ordnance Survey map, *US* ≈ Geological Survey map; **(b)** (*lieu*) headquarters; **(c)** senior staff, management (*of firm, political party etc*).

États-Unis [etazyni] *nmpl* **les É.-U. (d'Amérique),** the United States (of America), *F* the States; **aller aux É.-U.,** to go to the United States; **habiter aux É.-U.,** to live in the United States; **venir des É.-U.,** to come from the United States.

étau, -aux [eto] *nm* **(a)** *Tech* vice; **é. d'établi,** bench vice; **(b)** *Fig* (*restrictions*) stranglehold.

étayage [etejaʒ] *nm Constr etc* staying, shoring, propping (up).

étayer [eteje] *v* (**j'étaie, j'étaye; j'étaierai, j'etayerai**) **1** *vt* **(a)** *Constr etc* to stay, to prop (up), to shore (up) (*wall etc*); **(b)** *Fig* to support, to back up (*statement etc*); **pour é. ses allégations,** in support of his allegations. **2 s'étayer** *vpr* **les déclarations s'étaient,** the statements support each other; **s'é. contre un choc,** to steady oneself against a shock; **il s'étaie sur ses amis,** he leans on his friends; **cette théorie s'étaie sur des découvertes récentes,** this theory is based *or* founded on recent discoveries.

etc. [ɛtsetera] *adv* etc.

et c(a)etera [ɛtsetera] *adv* etcetera.

été¹ [ete] *nm* summer; **en é.,** in (the) summer *or* summertime; **un jour d'é.,** a summer('s) day; **heure d'é.,** *Br* summer time, *Am* daylight (saving) time; **temps/vêtements/***etc* **d'é.,** summer weather/clothes/*etc*; **é. de la Saint-Martin, é. indien,** Indian summer.

été² *voir* **ÊTRE².**

éteignoir [etɛɲwar] *nm* **(a)** (candle) extinguisher; **en é.,** conical; **(b)** *F* (*personne*) killjoy, wet blanket.

éteindre [etɛ̃dr] *v* (*conj like* **teindre**) **1** *vt* **(a)** to extinguish, to put out (*fire, candle, cigarette etc*); to turn off (*the gas*); to switch off, to turn off (*electric light, radio, heater etc*); *F* to switch off (the lights) in (*room*);

(b) *Fig* (*mettre fin à*) to extinguish (*hope, enthusiasm*); to kill (*ambition, love*); to pay off, *Fml* to annul (*a debt*); to abolish (*a right*); to put an end to (*a quarrel*); **é. la soif,** to slake *or* quench one's thirst; **é. le feu de l'ennemi,** to silence the enemy's guns;

(c) *Tech* to slake, to slack (*lime*); to quench (*red-hot iron etc*);

(d) *Fig* (*affaiblir*) to fade, to soften (*colour*); to muffle, to smother, to deaden (*sound*); to appease, to allay (*passions*); to dim (*light, eyes etc*).

2 s'éteindre *vpr* **(a)** (*of fire, cigarette, lamp etc*) to go out;

(b) (*of colour etc*) to fade; (*of sound*) to die away, to subside; (*of passion*) to die down, to subside; **le jour s'éteint,** daylight is failing *or* fading;

(c) (*of person*) to pass away, to die; (*of race, family*) to become extinct, to die out.

3 *vi* **(a)** to switch off (the lights) (**dans,** in);

(b) laisser é. le feu, to let the fire go out.

éteint [etɛ̃] *adj* **(a) être é.,** (*of fire, cigarette, lamp etc*) to be out; (*of electricity, radio etc*) to be off; *Aut* **rouler tous feux éteints,** to drive without (any) lights; **(b)** extinct (*race, family, volcano*); **(c)** dull, faint (*colour, sound*); dull, lacklustre (*eyes*); faint, toneless, faraway (*voice*).

étendage [etɑ̃daʒ] *nm* **(a)** (*action*) hanging up (*of washing*); **(b)** (*cordes*) clotheslines.

étendard [etɑ̃dar] *nm* **(a)** *Mil* (*drapeau*) standard; **(b)** *Fig* (*symbole*) banner; **lever l'é. de la révolte,** to raise the flag of rebellion; **(c)** *Bot* vexillum, standard.

étendoir [etɑ̃dwar] *nm* **(a)** (*cordes*) clotheslines; **(b)** (*cour*) drying yard; (*salle*) drying room.

étendre [etɑ̃dr] **1** *vt* **(a)** to spread (out) (*map, tablecloth etc*); to hang up (*washing*); to spread (*butter, ointment etc*); to apply (*paint*) (**sur,** to); **é. qn,** (*sur un lit etc*) to stretch s.o. out; **é. le bras,** to stretch out *or* reach out (one's arm); **é. ses ailes,** (*of bird*) to spread its wings; **é. qn (par terre) d'un coup de poing,** to knock s.o. down, *F* to lay s.o. out; *Boxe etc* **se faire é.,** to be knocked out; *F* **se faire é. à un examen,** to fail an exam;

(b) (*développer*) to stretch (*sth*) out (*to more than original size*); *Fig* to extend, to widen (*influence, power, knowledge etc*); to extend (*limits*); **é. une peau,** to stretch a skin; **é. la pâte,** to roll out the dough; **é. les termes d'une loi,** to widen *or* broaden the terms of a law;

(c) (*diluer*) to dilute (*wine, milk etc*); **é. d'eau une boisson,** to water down a drink.

2 s'étendre *vpr* **(a)** (*s'allonger*) to stretch oneself out, to lie down (at) full length; *Fig* **s'é. sur un sujet,** to dwell *or* enlarge *or* expatiate (up)on a subject;

(b) (*aller*) to extend, to stretch; **la ligne s'étend depuis Ivry jusqu'à Charenton,** the line stretches *or* extends *or* runs from Ivry to Charenton; **aussi loin que le regard peut s'é.,** as far as the eye can see;

(c) (*of fire, epidemic etc*) to spread;

(d) (*se développer*) (*of fortune, business etc*) to expand, to grow larger; (*of influence, power*) to widen, to increase; (*of knowledge, vocabulary*) to widen, to broaden.

étendu, -ue [etɑ̃dy] **1** *adj* **(a)** wide, extensive (*plain, forest, Fig knowledge, vocabulary*); far-reaching, wide (*influence*); **(b)** outspread (*wings*); outstretched (*arms, legs*); **é. sur un divan,** stretched out *or* lying on a couch; **(c)** (*dilué*) diluted (**de,** with). **2** *nf* **étendue,** area, extent (*of field, region etc*); scale (*of calamity, mistake etc*); stretch, expanse (*of water, sand etc*); tract, expanse (*of land etc*); reach (*of the mind*); compass, range (*of a voice*); extent, scope (*of s.o.'s knowledge, vocabulary etc*); **l'é. de la vie,** the duration of life; **sur une grande é.,** over a wide area.

éternel, -elle [etɛrnɛl] **1** *adj* **(a)** eternal (*being, God etc*); **le père é.,** the Father Eternal; **(b)** eternal, everlasting, perpetual (*life, joy etc*); **les neiges éternelles,** the everlasting snow; **(c)** *Fig* eternal, endless (*regrets, discussion etc*); **un é. causeur,** an inveterate chatterer; **fumant son éternelle cigarette,** smoking the inevitable cigarette. **2** *nm* **l'É.,** (*Dieu*) the Eternal.

éternellement [etɛrnɛlmɑ̃] *adv* **(a)** (*durer*) eternally, for ever(more); (*attendre, rester etc*) for ever(more); **(b)** (*toujours*) constantly, endlessly.

éterniser [etɛrnize] **1** *vt* **(a) é. le nom/la mémoire de qn,** to immortalize s.o.'s name/memory; **si nous pouvions é. cette heure,** if only we could make this hour last for ever; **(b)** (*prolonger*) to drag out (*discussion, crisis, lawsuit* *etc*) interminably. **2 s'éterniser** *vpr (of discussion, crisis, lawsuit etc)* to drag on interminably; **s'é. chez qn,** to outstay one's welcome.

éternité [eternite] *nf* eternity; **de toute é.,** from time immemorial; **il y a une é.** *ou* **des éternités que je ne vous ai vu,** it's ages since I saw you.

éternuement [eternymɑ̃] *nm* sneeze.

éternuer [eternɥe] *vi* to sneeze.

êtes [ɛt] *voir* **ÊTRE²**.

étêtage [etetaʒ] *nm,* **étêtement** [etɛtmɑ̃] *nm* pollarding, topping (*of tree*).

étêter [etete] *vt* **(a)** to remove the head from (*fish, nail etc*); **(b)** to pollard, to top (*tree*).

éteule [etœl] *nf Agr* stubble.

éthane [etan] *nm Ch* ethane.

éther [etɛr] *nm* ether; *Litt (air, ciel)* ether.

éthéré [etere] *adj* ethereal (*region, Ch salt*).

éthéromane [eterɔman] *n* ether addict.

Éthiopie [etjɔpi] *nf* Ethiopia.

éthiopien, -ienne [etjɔpjɛ̃, -jɛn] **1** *adj* Ethiopian. **2** *n* **É.,** Ethiopian.

éthique [etik] **1** *adj* **(a)** ethical (*problem etc*); **(b) datif é.,** ethical dative. **2** *nf (science, règles de conduite)* ethics; **l'é. puritaine,** the Puritan ethic.

ethnie [ɛtni] *nf* ethnic group.

ethnique [ɛtnik] *adj* ethnic (*group etc*).

ethnocentrisme [ɛtnɔsɑ̃trism] *nm* ethnocentrism.

ethnocide [ɛtnɔsid] *nm* ethnocide.

ethnographe [ɛtnɔgraf] *n* ethnographer.

ethnographie [ɛtnɔgrafi] *nf* ethnography.

ethnographique [ɛtnɔgrafik] *adj* ethnographic(al).

ethnolinguistique [ɛtnɔlɛ̃gɥistik] *nf* ethnolinguistics.

ethnologie [ɛtnɔlɔʒi] *nf* ethnology.

ethnologique [ɛtnɔlɔʒik] *adj* ethnological.

ethnologue [ɛtnɔlɔg] *n* ethnologist.

éthyle [etil] *nm Ch* ethyl.

éthylène [etilɛn] *nm Ch* ethylene.

éthylique [etilik] **1** *adj Ch* ethylic; **alcool é.,** ethyl alcohol. **2** *n Méd* alcoholic.

éthylisme [etilism] *nm Méd* alcoholism.

étiage [etjaʒ] *nm (baisse d'eaux)* low water; *(niveau le plus bas)* lowest water level; **échelle d'é.,** water gauge.

Étienne [etjɛn] *nm* Stephen, Steven.

étincelage [etɛ̃slaʒ] *nm* **(a)** *Tech* **soudure par é.,** flash welding; **(b)** *Méd* electrotherapy.

étincelant [etɛ̃slɑ̃] *adj* sparkling, glittering, gleaming (*diamond, metal, lake etc*); twinkling, glittering (*star*); sparkling (*eyes, Fig wit, conversation, book etc*).

étinceler [etɛ̃sle] *vi* (**il étincelle; il étincelait; il étincellera**) *(of diamond, metal, lake etc)* to sparkle, to glitter, to gleam; *(of star)* to twinkle, to glitter; *(of eyes, Fig wit, conversation, book etc)* to sparkle; **ses yeux étincelaient de joie/de colère,** his eyes sparkled with joy/flashed with anger.

étincelle [etɛ̃sɛl] *nf* **(a)** spark (*of fire, ignition etc*); **lancer des étincelles,** to throw out sparks; *(of diamond, eyes)* to sparkle, to flash; *Fig* **elle a fait des étincelles dans cette discussion,** she was brilliant in that discussion; *Aut* **allumage par é.,** spark ignition; **(b)** *Fig* spark (*of life, genius*); glimmer (*of commonsense, courage*).

étincellement [etɛ̃sɛlmɑ̃] *nm* sparkle, glitter, gleam (*of diamond, metal, lake etc*); twinkle, glitter (*of star*); sparkle (*of eyes*).

étiolement [etjɔlmɑ̃] *nm* **(a)** wilting, withering (*of plant*); *Agr (intentionnel)* blanching, etiolation; **(b)** *Méd* etiolation; **(c)** *Fig* decline (*of mind, memory etc*).

étioler [etjɔle] **1** *vt* **(a)** to wilt, to wither (*plant*); *Agr (intentionnellement)* to blanch, to etiolate (*celery etc*); **(b) e. qn,** to make s.o. sickly; **(c) une intelligence étiolée,** an intellect in decline. **2 s'étioler** *vpr* **(a)** *(of plant)* to wilt, to wither; **(b)** *(of person)* to grow sickly, to decline; **(c)** *(of mind, memory etc)* to decline.

étiologie [etjɔlɔʒi] *nf Méd (étude, causes)* aetiology, *US* etiology.

étique [etik] *adj* emaciated, wasted.

étiquetage [etiktaʒ] *nm* **(a)** labelling; *(pour indiquer le prix)* labelling, ticketing; **(b)** *Fig* labelling (*of person*) (**comme,** as).

étiqueter [etikte] *vt* (**j'étiquète, j'étiquèterai**) **(a)** to label (*luggage, parcel etc*); *(pour indiquer le prix)* to label, to ticket (*goods*); **(b)** *Fig* to label, to classify (*politician, writer etc*) (**comme,** as).

étiqueteur, -euse [etiktœr, -øz] **1** *n (personne)* labeller. **2** *nf* **étiqueteuse,** *(machine)* labelling machine, labeller.

étiquette [etikɛt] *nf* **(a)** label (*of suitcase, parcel etc*); *(indiquant le prix)* (price) label, ticket; **é. à bagages,** luggage label; **é. à œillet,** tie-on label; **é. gommée,** gummed label; **é. de vitrine,** show card; **apposer une é. à un paquet,** to label *or* stick a label on a parcel; **(b)** *Fig (désignation)* label (*of politician, artist etc*); **(c)** *(protocole)* etiquette; **l'é. de la cour,** Court etiquette *or* ceremonial; **il est contraire à l'é. de s'asseoir,** it is bad form to sit down.

étirage [etiraʒ] *nm* drawing (out) (*of metal, glass etc*); **é. à chaud/froid,** hot/cold drawing; **é. du fil,** wire drawing; *Tex* **banc d'é.,** drawing frame.

étirer [etire] **1** *vt* to draw (out) (*metal, glass etc*); to draw (*wire, textiles*). **2 s'étirer** *vpr* **(a)** *(se détendre)* to stretch (*oneself, one's limbs*); **(b)** *(of fabric, garment)* to stretch.

étoffe [etɔf] *nf* **(a)** *Tex* material, fabric; **étoffes de soie/etc,** silk/etc fabrics; **(b)** *Fig* **l'é. dont sont faits les héros,** the stuff heroes are made of; **elle a de l'é.,** she has got what it takes; **il y a en lui l'é. d'un écrivain,** he has the makings of a writer.

étoffé [etɔfe] *adj* ample, full (*garment*); rich, full (*voice*); **homme bien é.,** stout *or* thickset man; **discours é.,** speech full of substance.

étoffer [etɔfe] **1** *vt Fig* **é. un discours/livre,** to give substance to *or* fill out a speech/book. **2 s'étoffer** *vpr (of person)* to fill out.

étoile [etwal] *nf* **(a)** *Astron* star; **é. filante,** shooting star; **à la clarté des étoiles,** in the starlight; **coucher** *ou* **dormir à la belle é.,** to sleep in the open; **né sous une bonne/mauvaise é.,** born under a lucky/an unlucky star; **(b)** *(ornement, objet etc)* star; **(c)** *Typ* asterisk, star; **les graviers ont fait des étoiles sur le pare-brise,** the gravel produced (star-shaped) cracks on the windscreen; **hôtel cinq étoiles,** five-star hotel; **c'est un deux étoiles,** it has a two-star rating; **(d)** *Aut Br* roundabout, *Am* traffic circle; **(e)** *Zool* **é. de mer,** starfish; **(f)** *Cin Th (vedette)* star; **une grande é. de la chanson,** a big singing star; **é. montante,** rising star.

étoilé [etwale] *adj* **(a)** starry, star-studded (*sky*); starry, starlit (*night*); **la Bannière étoilée,** the Star-Spangled Banner, the Stars and Stripes (*of the U.S.A.*); **(b)** star-shaped (*crack, object etc*).

étoiler [etwale] **1** *vt* **(a)** *(parsemer)* to stud (**de,** with); *(parsemer d'étoiles)* to stud with stars; **(b)** to make a (star-shaped) crack in (*glass etc*). **2 s'étoiler** *vpr (of sky)* to light up with stars.

étole [etɔl] *nf (fourrure) & Rel* stole.

étonnamment [etɔnamɑ̃] *adv* astonishingly, surprisingly.

étonnant [etɔnɑ̃] **1** *adj* **(a)** astonishing, surprising; **rien d'é. à cela,** that's not surprising, no wonder; **ce n'est pas é. qu'il soit malade,** it's not surprising *or* it's no wonder *or* not to be wondered at that he's ill; **comme c'est é., il m'avait dit le contraire,** how strange *or* odd, he had told me the opposite; *F* **vous êtes é.!,** you're the limit!; **(b)** *(remarquable)* amazing. **2** *nm* **l'é. est qu'il soit venu,** the surprising thing is that he came.

étonné [etɔne] *adj* astonished, surprised (**de qch,** at sth; **de voir/etc,** to see/etc).

étonnement [etɔnmɑ̃] *nm* astonishment, surprise, amazement; **frappé** *ou* **saisi d'é.,** taken aback; **à mon grand é.,** to my great surprise; **faire l'é. de tout le monde,** to be the talk of the town.

étonner [etɔne] **1** *vt* to astonish, to amaze, to surprise; **cela ne m'étonnerait pas,** it wouldn't surprise me, I shouldn't be surprised (at it); **ce qui m'étonne, c'est qu'il a menti,** what surprises me is that he lied; *F* **alors ça, ça m'étonnerait,** *(pas question)* well, don't count on it. **2 s'étonner** *vpr* to be astonished, to be surprised, to wonder (**de,** at); **je m'étonne de vous voir,** I'm surprised to see you; **je m'étonne qu'il ne voie pas le danger,** it amazes me *or* I'm surprised that he does not see the danger; **comment s'é. qu'il ait refusé?,** can you wonder that he refused?; **je ne m'étonne plus de rien,** nothing surprises me any more.

étouffant [etufɑ̃] *adj* stifling, suffocating (*air, heat, Fig atmosphere*); oppressive, sultry (*weather*).

étouffe-chrétien [etufkretjɛ̃] *nm inv F* stodge, stodgy food.

étouffée [etufe] *nf Culin* **cuire à l'é.,** to braise (*meat etc*).

étouffement [etufmɑ̃] *nm* **(a)** *(sensation)* feeling of breathlessness; **étouffements,** breathlessness; **(b)** *(asphyxie)* suffocation; **(c)** *Fig* smothering (*of fire*); stifling (*of opinion, creativity*); stamping out (*of epidemic*); hushing up (*of scandal*).

étouffer [etufe] **1** *vt* **(a)** *(avec un oreiller etc)* to suffocate, to smother (*s.o.*); *(en serrant)* to suffocate, to choke (*s.o.*); **la chaleur m'étouffe,** the heat is stifling (me); *Iron* **ce ne**

sont pas les scrupules qui l'étouffent, he's not being overscrupulous;
(b) *Fig* to stifle (*cry, passion, opinion, creativity*); to smother (*fire*); to stamp out (*epidemic*); to quell, to suppress (*revolt*); to damp, to muffle (*sound*); *Él* to quench (*spark*); **é. une affaire,** to hush up a matter; **é. un sanglot,** to choke back a sob;
(c) *Culin* to braise.
2 *vi* to suffocate; **é. de rire,** to choke with laughter; *Fig* **dans cette ville, j'étouffais,** I was suffocating in that town; **on étouffe ici,** it's stifling here.
3 s'étouffer *vpr* to suffocate; (*en mangeant*) to choke; **plantes qui s'étouffent,** plants that choke one another; **on s'étouffait pour entrer,** people crowded in.

étouffoir [etufwar] *nm* damper (*of piano*).

étoupe [etup] *nf* (*de chanvre*) tow; (*de vieux cordages*) oakum.

étouper [etupe] *vt* to stop up (*crevice*) with tow *or* oakum; to caulk (*boat*).

étoupille [etupij] *nf Min* fuse.

étourderie [eturdəri] *nf* **(a)** (*caractère*) thoughtlessness; **faute d'é.,** thoughtless mistake; **par é.,** inadvertently, in an unthinking moment; **(b)** (*action*) thoughtless action *or* mistake.

étourdi, -ie [eturdi] **1** *adj* (*irréfléchi*) thoughtless, careless (*person, action etc*); (*écervelé*) scatterbrained, harebrained (*person*). **2** *n* (*écervelé*) scatterbrain, harum-scarum. **3** *nf* **à l'étourdie,** thoughtlessly, heedlessly.

étourdiment [eturdimɑ̃] *adv* thoughtlessly, without thinking.

étourdir [eturdir] **1** *vt* **(a)** (*of blow, shock etc*) to stun, to daze (*s.o.*); *Fig* (*of wine, praise etc*) to make (*s.o.*) dizzy; **bruit qui étourdit les oreilles,** deafening noise; **(b)** (*calmer*) to ease, to deaden (*pain*); to allay (*grief, hunger*). **2 s'étourdir** *vpr* to try to forget; **s'é. dans la boisson,** to drown one's sorrows (in drink).

étourdissant [eturdisɑ̃] *adj* **(a)** deafening, ear-splitting (*noise*); **(b)** staggering, stunning, astounding (*news, success etc*).

étourdissement [eturdismɑ̃] *nm* (*vertige*) giddiness, dizziness; **avoir un é.,** to feel giddy *or* dizzy; **cela me donne des étourdissements,** it makes me feel giddy *or* dizzy, it makes my head swim.

étourneau, -eaux [eturno] *nm* **(a)** (*oiseau*) starling; **(b)** *F* (*personne*) scatterbrain.

étrange [etrɑ̃ʒ] *adj* strange, peculiar, odd; **chose é., il est revenu,** strange to say *or* strangely enough *or* oddly enough, he came back.

étrangement [etrɑ̃ʒmɑ̃] *adv* strangely, oddly, peculiarly; **cela ressemble é. à la rougeole,** it looks suspiciously like measles.

étranger, -ère [etrɑ̃ʒe, -ɛr] **1** *adj* **(a)** (*d'un autre pays*) foreign; **Ministère des affaires étrangères,** *Br* ≈ Foreign (and Commonwealth) Office, *US* ≈ State Department;
(b) (*inconnu*) strange, unfamiliar (**à,** to); **sa voix ne m'est pas étrangère,** his voice is not unfamiliar;
(c) (*différent*) foreign (**à,** to); *Méd & Fig* **corps é.,** foreign body; **cela est é. à la question,** that is beside the point *or* irrelevant; **elle est étrangère à cette firme/au projet,** she is not part of this firm/not involved in the plan; **la haine lui est étrangère,** he doesn't know what hatred is; **il est é. à la musique,** he has no knowledge of music.
2 *n* **(a)** (*d'un autre pays*) foreigner; *Admin* alien;
(b) stranger; **société fermée aux étrangers,** society not open to outsiders.
3 *nm* **l'é.,** (*pays étrangers*) foreign parts; **aller/vivre à l'é.,** to go/live abroad.

étrangeté [etrɑ̃ʒte] *nf* strangeness, oddness, peculiarity (*of conduct, dress etc*).

étranglé [etrɑ̃gle] *adj* constricted, narrow (*passage etc*); nipped-in (*waist*); choked, choking (*voice*); *Méd* strangulated (*hernia*).

étranglement [etrɑ̃gləmɑ̃] *nm* **(a)** strangling, strangulation (*of s.o.*); *Fig* strangling (*of freedom, the press*); **(b)** (*action de resserrer*) constriction, narrowing (*of waist, tube etc*); *Aut Tech* throttling; **soupape d'é.,** throttle valve; *Méd* **é. herniaire,** strangulated hernia; **(c)** (*partie resserrée*) narrow part; narrows (*of river*); bottleneck (*in road*).

étrangler [etrɑ̃gle] **1** *vt* **(a)** to strangle, to throttle (*s.o.*); *Fig* to strangle (*freedom, the press*); **sa cravate l'étrangle,** his tie is choking him; *Fig* **la colère l'étrangle,** he is choking with rage; **é. un complot au berceau,** to nip a plot in the bud; **(b)** (*resserrer*) to constrict (*waist, tube etc*); *Méd* to strangulate (*blood vessel*); *Tech* to throttle (*steam etc*); *Aut* **é. le moteur,** to throttle (down) the engine. **2 s'étrangler** *vpr* (*en mangeant*) to choke (**avec,** on); *Fig* **s'é. de colère,** to choke with rage. **3** *vi* **é. de soif,** to be parched (with thirst).

étrangleur, -euse [etrɑ̃glœr, -øz] **1** *n* (*personne*) strangler. **2** *nm Aut Tech* throttle.

étrave [etrav] *nf Nau* stem (*of ship*); **de l'é. à l'étambot,** from stem to stern; **lame d'é.,** bow wave.

être[1] [ɛtr] *nm* **(a)** (*existence*) **ceux qui vous ont donné l'ê.,** those who gave you life, those to whom you owe your being *or* existence; **(b)** (*âme*) being; **tout mon ê. se révolte à l'idée,** my whole being revolts at the idea; **(c)** (*personne*) being; **un ê. humain,** a human being; *Rel* **l'Ê. suprême,** (*Dieu*) the Supreme Being; *Iron* **pauvres petits êtres!,** poor little creatures!, poor little things!; **quel ê.!,** what a fellow!

être[2] *vi* (*prp* **étant**; *pp* **été**; *pr ind* **je suis, tu es, il est, n. sommes, v. êtes, ils sont**; *pr sub* **je sois, tu sois, il soit, n. soyons, v. soyez, ils soient**; *imp* **sois, soyons, soyez**; *impf* **j'étais**; *p hist* **je fus, tu fus, il fut, n. fûmes, v. fûtes, ils furent**; *p sub* **je fusse**; *fu* **je serai**) **(a)** (*exister*) to be; **je pense, donc je suis,** I think, therefore I am; **l'ancien projet n'est plus,** the old plan is a thing of the past; **elle n'est plus,** she is no more, she is dead; **cela étant,** that being the case; **cela n'est pas,** that is not so; **la plus belle voiture qui soit,** the finest car there is; **eh bien, soit!,** well, so be it!; **ainsi soit-il,** so be it; *Rel* amen; *Prov* **on ne peut pas ê. et avoir été,** you can't have your cake and eat it; **nous sommes le dix,** it's the tenth (today); **la vérité est entre ces extrêmes,** the truth lies between these extremes;
(b) (*copule*) to be; **c'est le chef de gare,** he's the stationmaster; **il est** *ou* **c'est un chef de gare,** he's a stationmaster; **soit AB la base d'un triangle,** let AB be the base of a triangle; **soit un triangle ABC,** given a triangle ABC; **l'homme est mortel,** man is mortal; **nous étions deux/plusieurs,** there were two/several of us;
(c) (+ *adv*) **elle est très mal/beaucoup mieux,** she is very ill/much better; **ê. bien avec qn,** to be on good terms with s.o.;
(d) (*locutions avec 'à' + nom*) **ê. au travail,** to be at work; **ê. à l'agonie,** to be dying; **vous n'êtes pas à ce que je dis,** you are not paying attention to what I say, you are not with me; **il est tout à son travail,** he is entirely engrossed in his work; **il est à Paris,** he is in Paris;
(e) (*locutions avec 'de' + nom*) **ce tableau est de Gauguin,** this picture is by Gauguin; **il est d'un bon caractère,** he's good-tempered; **il est de Londres,** he is from London; **il était du conseil municipal,** he belonged to the municipal council; **il n'est pas des nôtres,** he isn't one of us, he isn't with us; **il est de mes amis,** he's a friend of mine, he's one of my friends; **ê. de service,** to be on duty;
(f) (+ *à + inf*) **il est à travailler/à jouer,** he is at work/playing; **j'étais là à l'attendre,** I was there waiting for him; **la maison est à louer,** the house is to let;
(g) (*avec 'ce'*) **je sais ce qui est arrivé,** I know what happened; **est-ce vrai?,** is it true?; **serait-ce vrai?,** can it be *or* could it (possibly) be true?; **ne fût-ce que, ne serait-ce que,** if only; **vous venez, n'est-ce pas?,** you're coming, aren't you?; **vous ne venez pas, n'est-ce pas?,** you're not coming, are you?; **n'est-ce pas qu'il a de la chance?,** isn't he lucky?; **je le ferais (si ce) n'était que je vais partir,** I would do it if I weren't leaving; **n'était mon rhumatisme,** if it weren't *or* wasn't for my rheumatism;
(h) (*impers*) **il est midi,** it is twelve o'clock; **il est temps de partir,** it is time to go; *Litt* **il est de mon devoir de rester,** it is my duty to stay; **il n'est que de faire preuve d'initiative,** we *or* you *etc* need only show some initiative; **comme si de rien n'était,** as if nothing had happened; **soit dit sans offense,** if you don't mind my saying so; **il est un Dieu,** there is a God; **il était une fois une fée,** once upon a time there was a fairy; **un héros, s'il en fut (jamais),** a hero, if ever there was one;
(i) (*avec 'en' indéterminé*) **où en sommes-nous?,** how far have we got?, where are we?; **l'affaire en est là,** that is how things stand; **vous n'en êtes pas encore là!,** you haven't come to that yet!; **il n'en est pas à son coup d'essai,** this is not his first attempt; **je ne sais plus où j'en suis,** I don't know where I am *or* what I'm doing; **nous n'en sommes pas à le renvoyer,** we haven't reached the point of sacking him yet; **j'en suis pour mon argent,** I've spent my money to no purpose, I've thrown my money away; **j'en suis pour mille francs,** I am the poorer by a thousand francs; **j'en suis pour ce que j'ai dit,** I stick to

what I said; **il en est pour les changements,** he's all for change; **j'en suis!,** (*je veux y participer*) I'm game!, count me in!; **je n'en suis pas!,** (*je ne veux pas y participer*) count me out!; **c'en est trop!,** it's too much!, this is past bearing!; **c'en est assez!,** enough!; **il en est de l'homme comme de la nature,** it's the same with man as with nature; **puisqu'il en est ainsi,** since that is how things are; **il n'en est rien!,** nothing of the kind!;

(j) (*avec 'y' indéterminé*) **il y est pour quelque chose,** he's got something to do with it; **j'y suis pour un tiers,** I'm in for a third share; **ça y est!,** that's it!; **vous y êtes?,** (*vous comprenez?*) are you with me?; (*vous comprenez?, vous avez trouvé?*) have you got it?;

(k) (*appartenir*) **ê. à qn,** to belong to s.o.; **à qui sont ces livres?,** whose books are these?, who do these books belong to?; **ma vie est-elle à moi?,** is my life my own?; **je suis à vous dans un moment,** I'll be with you in a moment; **c'est à vous de jouer,** it's your turn to play; **c'est à vous de veiller sur l'enfant,** it's your job to look after the child;

(l) (*avec* **aller, rester, tomber** *etc aux temps composés*) **il est déjà arrivé,** he has already arrived; **il est arrivé hier,** he arrived yesterday; **elle est née en 1950,** she was born in 1950;

(m) (*avec vpr aux temps composés*) **nous nous sommes trompés,** we (have) made a mistake; **ils se sont aimés,** they loved each other *or* one another; **elle s'est fait mal,** she (has) hurt herself;

(n) (*pour indiquer le passif*) to be; **il fut puni par son père,** he was punished by his father; **il est aimé de tout le monde,** he is loved by everyone; **j'entends ê. obéi,** I mean to be obeyed;

(o) (= *aller aux temps composés et au passé simple*) **j'avais été à Paris,** I had been to Paris; **j'ai été voir Martin,** I've been *or* I went to see Martin; **on a été jusqu'à démissionner,** people have gone so far as to resign;

(p) (= *s'en aller au passé simple*) **il s'en fut ouvrir la porte,** he went off to open the door;

(q) quand il fut pour partir, just as he was about to leave.

étreindre [etrɛ̃dr] *vt* (*prp* **étreignant**; *pp* **étreint**; *pr ind* **j'étreins, il étreint, n. étreignons**; *impf* **j'étreignais**; *p hist* **j'étreignis**; *fu* **j'étreindrai**) to embrace, to hug, to clasp (*s.o.*) in one's arms; **é. qch (dans la main),** to grasp *or* grip *or* clutch sth; **é. la main de qn,** to wring s.o.'s hand; **spectacle qui vous étreint le cœur,** sight that wrings one's heart; **la peur l'étreignait,** fear gripped him; *Prov* **qui trop embrasse mal étreint,** grasp all, lose all.

étreinte [etrɛ̃t] *nf* **(a)** (*entre personnes*) embrace, hug; **(b)** (*dans la main*) grasp, grip; **(c)** *Fig* (*pression*) pressure; **sous l'é. de la misère,** in the grip of poverty.

étrenne [etrɛn] *nf* **(a)** (*cadeau*) **étrennes,** New Year's gift; **les étrennes du facteur/***etc*, ≈ the postman's/*etc* Christmas box; **(b)** (*premier usage*) first use; **avoir l'é. de qch,** to have the first use of sth.

étrenner [etrene] **1** *vt* to use for the first time, *F* to christen (*object*); to wear (*garment*) for the first time. **2** *vi Arg* **tu vas é.!,** (*être puni*) you're going to catch *or* get it!

êtres [ɛtr] *nmpl Vieilli* **connaître les ê. d'une maison,** to know one's way about a house.

étrésillon [etrezijɔ̃] *nm Constr* shore (*of trench*); strut, brace (*of wall*).

étrésillonner [etrezijɔne] *vt Constr* to shore (across) (*trench*); to strut, to brace (*wall*).

étrier [etrije] *nm* **(a)** *Equitation* stirrup; **à franc é.,** at full gallop; **vider les étriers,** to be thrown *or* unhorsed; *Fig* to be thrown *or* disconcerted; *Fig* **avoir le pied à l'é.,** to be on the point of leaving; (*être en bonne voie pour réussir*) to be off to a good start; **tenir l'é. à qn,** to help s.o. to mount; *Fig* to give s.o. a helping hand; **coup de l'é.,** stirrup cup; **(b)** *Méd* **é. (de soutien),** stirrup, leg rest; **é. (de traction, de réduction),** calliper; **(c)** *Anat* stirrup bone (*of ear*); **(d)** *Tech* stirrup (piece).

étrille [etrij] *nf* **(a)** (*brosse*) currycomb; **(b)** (*crustacé*) velvet swimming crab.

étriller [etrije] *vt* **(a)** to curry (*horse*); **(b)** *F* (*réprimander*) to give (*s.o.*) a dressing-down *or* telling-off; **(c)** *F* (*faire payer trop cher*) to fleece, to sting (*s.o.*).

étripage [etripaʒ] *nm* gutting (*of fish, hare*); drawing (*of chicken etc*); *F* (*tuerie*) slaughter.

étriper [etripe] **1** *vt* to gut (*fish, hare*); to draw (*chicken etc*); to disembowel (*horse etc*). **2 s'étriper** *vpr F* (*se battre*) to make mincemeat of each other.

étriqué [etrike] *adj* **(a)** skimpy, tight (*garment*); **(b)** *Fig* narrow, limited (*outlook, life*).

étriquer [etrike] *vt* **(a)** *Couture* to make (*garment*) too tight; **cette robe vous étrique,** that dress is too tight on you; **(b)** *Menuis* to thin (*plank etc*).

étriver [etrive] *Can* **1** *vt* to irritate, to annoy. **2** *vi* **faire é.,** to drive mad.

étrivière [etrivjɛr] *nf* stirrup leather.

étroit [etrwa] *adj* **(a)** narrow (*ribbon, path, shoulders etc*); narrow, confined, cramped (*space, room etc*); narrow (*limits*); *Fig* **la voie étroite,** the straight and narrow (way); **esprit é.,** narrow mind; **(b)** tight (*knot*); tight (-fitting) (*coat etc*); *Fig* close (*friendship, bond etc*); **alliance étroite,** close *or* intimate alliance; **je suis en rapport é. avec sa soeur,** his sister and I are close; **règlements étroits,** strict rules; **le sens é. d'un mot,** the strict meaning of a word; **(c) être à l'é.,** (*dans son logement etc*) to be cramped for room; (*financièrement*) to be in straitened circumstances.

étroitement [etrwatmɑ̃] *adv* **(a)** (*nouer, tenir*) tightly; *Fig* (*lier, collaborer*) closely; **ils sont é. liés d'amitié,** they are close friends; **(b)** (*observer une règle etc*) strictly; **surveiller qn é.,** to keep a close watch on s.o.

étroitesse [etrwatɛs] *nf* **(a)** narrowness (*of path, ribbon, shoulders etc*); **é. d'esprit,** narrow-mindedness; **l'é. de ce bureau,** the lack of space in this office; **(b)** *Fig* closeness (*of bond, friendship etc*).

étron [etrɔ̃] *nm* piece of excrement, *Vulg* turd.

étrusque [etrysk] **1** *adj* Etruscan. **2** *n* **É.,** Etruscan.

étude [etyd] *nf* **(a)** *Scol Univ etc* (*action*) study, studying (*of subject, text, author etc*); **programme d'études,** (*d'école*) curriculum; (*de matière*) syllabus; **faire des études de français/de droit,** to study French/law; **il a fait ses études à Eton/Oxford,** he was educated at Eton/he went to Oxford; **payer les études de qn,** to pay for s.o.'s education; **faire de bonnes études,** to do well at school; **faire son é. de qch, mettre son é. à qch,** to make sth one's study; *Péj* **cela sent l'é.,** it reeks of effort;

(b) *Scol* (*heure*) (private) study period; **(salle d')é.,** (private) study room;

(c) (*action de considérer*) study, investigation (*of question, plan etc*); *Constr* survey; **é. de cas,** case study; **bureau d'études,** research department; **é. d'un canal,** scheme *or* project for a canal; **moteur/voiture d'é.,** test engine/-car; **ingénieur d'études,** design engineer; **comité d'é.,** committee of enquiry; **voyage d'études,** study *or* field trip; **procéder à l'é. d'une question, mettre une question à l'é.,** to study *or* investigate *or* go into a question;

(d) (*texte, musique, peinture etc*) study; *Mus* **é. pour violon,** violin study; *Beaux-Arts* **é. de tête,** study of a head; **é. de bétail,** cattle piece;

(e) (*bureau*) office (*of solicitor, bailiff etc*);

(f) (*charge*) practice (*of lawyer*).

étudiant, -ante [etydjɑ̃, -ɑ̃t] **1** *n* student; **é. en médecine,** medical student; **é. de première/seconde année,** first/second-year student, *Am* freshman/sophomore. **2** *adj* student (*life, movement etc*).

étudié [etydje] *adj* **(a)** (*soigneusement préparé*) studied (*effect, speech etc*); **prix très étudiés,** cheapest possible prices; **(b)** *Péj* (*affecté*) studied, affected (*manners, politeness, gesture etc*); affected (*person*).

étudier [etydje] *v* (*impf & pr sub* **n. étudiions**) **1** *vt* **(a)** *Scol Univ etc* to study (*subject, text, author etc*); *Scol* to prepare (*lesson*); *Mus Th* to study (*instrument, role etc*); **é. une matière en vue d'un examen,** to read up a subject for an examination; **(b)** *Péj* (*affecter*) to study (*one's effect, appearance etc*); **(c)** (*considérer*) to study, to investigate, to look into (*question, plan, theory etc*); to make a study of (*case*); **(d)** (*observer*) to study (*society, person, face etc*). **2** *vi* to study. **3 s'étudier** *vpr* **(a)** (*se regarder, s'analyser*) to study oneself; **(b)** *Péj* (*manquer de naturel*) to be affected; **(c) s'é. à faire qch,** to take pains to do sth, to make a point of doing sth; **il s'étudiait à m'éviter,** he studiously avoided me.

étui [etɥi] *nm* case; **é. (de revolver),** holster; *Nau* **é. de voile,** sail cover; **é. de cartouche,** cartridge case; **é. à lunettes,** glasses case.

étuvage [etyvaʒ] *nm* (*séchage*) drying; (*stérilisation*) sterilization.

étuve [etyv] *nf* **(a)** steam room (*of baths*); **é. sèche,** hot-air steam cabinet; **é. humide,** steam *or* vapour bath; **(b)** *Ch Ind etc* (*pour sécher*) drying oven; (*pour stériliser*) sterilizer; **é. à incubation** *ou* **à cultures,** incubator; **(c)** *F* (*lieu où il fait trop chaud*) oven.

étuvé [etyve] *adj* **riz é.,** nonstick rice.

étuvée [etyve] *nf Culin* **à l'é.,** braised.

étuver [etyve] *vt* **(a)** (*sécher*) to dry (*fruit etc*); (*stériliser*) to sterilize (*contaminated clothing etc*); **(b)** *Culin* to braise.

étymologie [etimɔlɔʒi] *nf* (*science, origine*) etymology.

étymologique [etimɔlɔʒik] *adj* etymological.

étymologiquement [etimɔlɔʒikmɑ̃] *adv* etymologically.

étymologiste [etimɔlɔʒist] *n* etymologist.

eu [y] *voir* **AVOIR¹**.

eucalyptus [økaliptys] *nm* (*arbre*) eucalyptus; **essence d'e.**, eucalyptus oil.

Eucharistie (l') [løkaristi] *nf Rel* the Eucharist.

eucharistique [økaristik] *adj Rel* Eucharistic(al).

Euclide [øklid] *nm* Euclid.

euclidien, -ienne [øklidjɛ̃, -jɛn] *adj Math* Euclidean.

eudiomètre [ødjɔmɛtr] *nm Phys* eudiometer.

Eugène [øʒɛn] *nm* Eugene; (*pape*) Eugenius.

eugénique [øʒenik] *nf*, **eugénisme** [øʒenism] *nm* eugenics.

euh [ø] *int* er!

eunuque [ønyk] *nm* eunuch.

euphémique [øfemik] *adj* euphemistic.

euphémiquement [øfemikmɑ̃] *adv* euphemistically.

euphémisme [øfemism] *nm* euphemism.

euphonie [øfɔni] *nf* euphony.

euphonique [øfɔnik] *adj* euphonic, euphonious.

euphorbe [øfɔrb] *nf Bot* euphorbia.

euphorie [øfɔri] *nf* euphoria.

euphorique [øfɔrik] *adj* euphoric.

euphorisant [øfɔrizɑ̃] **1** *adj* exhilarating (*effect, atmosphere etc*); *Méd* euphoriant (*drug*). **2** *nm* euphoriant (drug).

Euphrate [øfrat] *nm* **l'E.**, the Euphrates.

eurafricain, -aine [ørafrikɛ̃, -ɛn] **1** *adj* Eurafrican. **2** *n* **E.**, Eurafrican.

Eurasie [ørazi] *nf* Eurasia.

eurasien, -ienne [ørazjɛ̃, -jɛn] **1** *adj* Eurasian. **2** *n* **E.**, Eurasian.

eurêka [øreka] *int* eureka!

eurent [yr] *voir* **AVOIR¹**.

Euripide [øripid] *nm* Euripides.

euro- [ørɔ] *préf* Euro-.

eurochèque [ørɔʃɛk] *nm* Eurocheque.

eurocommunisme [ørɔkɔmynism] *nm* Eurocommunism.

eurocrate [ørɔkrat] *n* Eurocrat.

eurodevise [ørɔdəviz] *nf Fin* Eurocurrency.

eurodollar [ørɔdɔlar] *nm Fin* Eurodollar.

euromarché [ørɔmarʃe] *nm Fin* Euromarket.

euromissile [ørɔmisil] *nm* Euromissile.

euromonnaie [ørɔmɔnɛ] *nf Fin* Eurocurrency.

Europe [ørɔp] *nf* Europe; **l'E. verte,** (European) Community agriculture *or* farming; **l'E. des douze,** the Europe of the Twelve; **en E.**, in Europe.

européanisation [ørɔpeanizasjɔ̃] *nf* Europeanization.

européaniser [ørɔpeanize] **1** *vt* to Europeanize. **2 s'européaniser** *vpr* to become Europeanized.

européen, -enne [ørɔpeɛ̃, -ɛn] **1** *adj* European; **le marché unique e.**, the single European market. **2** *n* **E.**, European.

europium [ørɔpjɔm] *nm Ch* europium.

eurostratégique [ørɔstrateʒik] *adj Mil* Eurostrategic.

Eurovision [ørɔvizjɔ̃] *nf* Eurovision.

Eurydice [øridis] *nf* Eurydice.

eurythmie [øritmi] *nf* eurhythmy.

eurythmique [øritmik] *adj* eurhythmic.

Eustache [østaʃ] *nm* Eustace; *Anat* **trompe d'E.**, Eustachian tube.

eut [y] *voir* **AVOIR¹**.

euthanasie [øtanazi] *nf* euthanasia.

eux [ø] *see* **LUI²**.

évacuateur, -trice [evakɥatœr, -tris] *adj* drainage (*pipe etc*).

évacuation [evakɥasjɔ̃] *nf* **(a)** evacuation, voiding, discharge (*of matter from the body*); draining (off) (*of water etc*); draining (*of abscess*); **course d'é.**, (*de moteur*) exhaust stroke; **(b)** evacuation (*of population*); *Mil* evacuation, withdrawal (*of troops, wounded*); *Mil* **hôpital d'é.**, clearing hospital; **(c)** evacuation (*of fortress, town etc*); evacuation, clearing (*of hall etc*); *Nau* abandoning (*of ship*).

évacué, -ée [evakɥe] *n* evacuee.

évacuer [evakɥe] *vt* **(a)** to evacuate, to discharge, to void (*matter from the body*); to exhaust (*steam*); to drain (off) (*water etc*); *Méd* to drain (*abscess*); **é. l'eau d'une chaudière,** to empty a boiler; **(b)** (*faire partir*) to evacuate, to withdraw (*troops*); to evacuate (*inhabitants*); **(c)** (*quitter*) to evacuate (*fortress, town etc*); **faire é. une salle/***etc*, to evacuate *or* clear a hall/*etc*; *Nau* **é. le bâtiment,** to abandon ship.

évadé, -ée [evade] **1** *adj* escaped, fugitive (*prisoner*). **2** *n* escaped prisoner, fugitive.

évader (s') [sevade] *vpr* (*de prison, la réalité etc*) to escape (**de**, from).

évaluateur, -trice [evalɥatœr, -tris] *n Can* valuer, appraiser.

évaluation [evalɥasjɔ̃] *nf* **(a)** (*action*) valuation, appraisal (*of property etc*); assessment (*of damages*); estimation (*of weight, number, risks etc*); **(b)** (*quantité, valeur*) valuation (*of property etc*); assessment (*of damages*); estimate (*of weight etc*).

évaluer [evalɥe] *vt* to value, to appraise (*property etc*); to assess (*damages*) (**à**, at); to estimate (*weight, number, risks etc*).

évanescent [evanesɑ̃] *adj* evanescent.

évangélique [evɑ̃ʒelik] *adj Rel* evangelical.

évangélisateur, -trice [evɑ̃ʒelizatœr, -tris] **1** *adj* evangelistic. **2** *n* evangelist.

évangélisation [evɑ̃ʒelizasjɔ̃] *nf* evangelization, evangelizing.

évangéliser [evɑ̃ʒelize] *vt* to evangelize.

évangélisme [evɑ̃ʒelism] *nm* evangelism.

évangéliste [evɑ̃ʒelist] *nm* evangelist; (*auteur de l'un des Évangiles*) Evangelist.

évangile [evɑ̃ʒil] *nm* **(a) l'É.**, the Gospel; **l'É. selon saint Jean,** the Gospel according to St. John; *Fig* **prendre qch pour parole d'é.**, to take sth for gospel (truth); *Fig* **ce n'est pas l'é.**, it's not Holy Writ; **(b) l'é.**, the gospel (for the day); **(c)** *Fig* (*livre important*) bible.

évanouir (s') [sevanwir] *vpr* **(a)** (*disparaître*) to vanish, to disappear; (*of memory, dream*) to fade (away); (*of sound*) to die away; *Rad* to fade; **(b)** (*perdre conscience*) to faint; **tomber évanoui,** to fall down in a faint; **on l'a trouvé évanoui,** he was found unconscious *or* in a (dead) faint.

évanouissement [evanwismɑ̃] *nm* **(a)** (*disparition*) vanishing, disappearance (*of ghost person etc*); fading (*of memory, dream*); dying away (*of sound*); *Rad* fading; **(b)** (*syncope*) faint(ing fit); **avoir un é.**, to faint.

évaporateur [evapɔratœr] *nm Ch Ind* evaporator.

évaporation [evapɔrasjɔ̃] *nf* evaporation.

évaporé, -ée [evapɔre] *Péj* **1** *adj* featherbrained (*person*). **2** *n* featherbrain.

évaporer [evapɔre] **1** *vt Arch* to evaporate (*liquid*); **faire é. un liquide,** to evaporate a liquid. **2 s'évaporer** *vpr* **(a)** (*of liquid, perfume etc*) to evaporate; **(b)** *F* (*disparaître*) to vanish (into thin air).

évasé [evɑze] *adj* wide-mouthed (*vase, pipe etc*); flared (*skirt etc*).

évasement [evɑzmɑ̃] *nm* wide mouth (*of vase, pipe etc*); flare (*of skirt etc*).

évaser [evɑze] **1** *vt* to widen (out) the opening of (*vase etc*); to open out (*pipe etc*); to widen (*opening*); *Couture* to flare (*skirt etc*). **2 s'évaser** *vpr* to widen, to open out; *Couture* to flare (out).

évasif, -ive [evazif, -iv] *adj* evasive.

évasion [evazjɔ̃] *nf* **(a)** escape (**de prison/***etc*, from prison/*etc*); **é. des capitaux,** flight *or* exodus of capital; **é. fiscale,** tax evasion; **(b)** *Fig* (*distraction*) escape; (*hors de la réalité*) escapism; **littérature d'é.**, escapist literature.

évasivement [evazivmɑ̃] *adv* evasively.

Ève [ɛv] *nf* Eve, Eva; *Bible* Eve; *F* **je ne le connais ni d'È. ni d'Adam,** I don't know him from Adam.

évêché [eveʃe] *nm* **(a)** (*région*) bishopric, see; **(b)** (*palais*) bishop's palace; **(c)** (*dignité*) bishopric.

éveil [evej] *nm* **(a)** (*action*) awakening (*of nature, curiosity, nation etc*); **être en é.**, (*of person*) to be on the alert; (*of mind*) to be alert; **(b)** (*alerte*) **donner l'é.**, to raise the alarm; **donner l'é. à qn**, to alert s.o.; to put s.o. on his guard.

éveillé [eveje] *adj* **(a)** awake; **rêve é.**, waking dream; **tenir qn é.**, to keep s.o. awake; **é. ou endormi,** waking or sleeping; **(b)** (*vif*) wide-awake, alert, bright (*person*); **garçon (à l'esprit) é.**, bright boy.

éveiller [eveje] **1** *vt* to awake(n) (*s.o.*); *Fig* to arouse, to awaken (*curiosity, suspicion etc*); to bring out, to develop (*intelligence, imagination etc*). **2 s'éveiller** *vpr* (*of person*) to awake(n); *Fig* (*of curiosity, suspicion etc*) to be aroused; (*of intelligence etc*) to show itself; *Litt* **elle s'éveille à l'amour,** she is awakening to love.

événement [evɛnmɑ̃] *nm* **(a)** event, occurrence; *Fig* (*livre, spectacle etc important*) event; **la suite des événements,** the course of events; **faire é.**, to cause a stir; **créer l'é.**, to make big news; **semaine pleine d'événements,**

eventful week; **en cas d'é.,** in case of emergency; **les événements (de mai),** the events of '68 (*student unrest etc*); *Hum* **quand il fait la vaisselle, c'est (tout) un é.,** when he does the dishes it's a cause for celebration *or* it's a red letter day; **(b) dans** *ou* **en l'é.,** as things turned out, in the event; **(c)** *Th* climax.

événementiel, -elle [evɛnmɑ̃sjɛl] *adj* factual (*information, history, television programme etc*).

évent [evɑ̃] *nm* **(a)** mustiness (*of food, wine, perfume*); flatness (*of beer*); **sentir l'é.,** to smell musty; **(b)** blowhole, spout (*of whale*); **(c)** *Tech* vent(hole).

éventail [evɑ̃taj] *nm* **(a)** fan; **en é.,** fan-shaped; *F Fig* **elle est restée les doigts de pied en é. toute la matinée,** she lazed around all morning; **voûte en é.,** fan vaulting; **(b)** (*choix*) range (*of goods for sale, salaries etc*).

éventaire [evɑ̃tɛr] *nm* **(a)** (*d'un marchand ambulant etc*) tray; **(b)** (*étal*) (street) stall.

éventé [evɑ̃te] *adj* musty (*food, wine perfume etc*); flat, stale (*beer*); *Fig* well-known (*secret*).

éventer [evɑ̃te] **1** *vt* **(a)** to air (*clothes, furniture etc*); to expose (*grain etc*) to the air; to ventilate (*mine*); **(b)** (*avec un éventail etc*) to fan (*s.o.*); **(c)** *Fig* (*pénétrer*) to find out, to discover (*secret, plot*); (*faire connaître*) to reveal, to divulge (*secret, plot*); **é. la mèche,** to discover *or* find out the secret; (*faire connaître*) to reveal *or* divulge the secret; **le secret est éventé,** the secret is out. **2 s'éventer** *vpr* **(a)** (*of food, wine, perfume*) to go musty; (*of beer*) to go flat *or* stale; **(b)** (*avec un éventail etc*) to fan oneself.

éventration [evɑ̃trasjɔ̃] *nf Méd* rupture, hernia.

éventrer [evɑ̃tre] *vt* to disembowel, to eviscerate (*person, animal*); to gut (*fish*); to draw (*poultry*); to rip *or* tear open (*parcel, envelope*); to break *or* smash open (*cask, box*); to burst open (*door*); to slit open (*sack, mattress*).

éventreur [evɑ̃trœr] *nm* disemboweller; **Jack l'É.,** Jack the Ripper.

éventualité [evɑ̃tɥalite] *nf* **(a)** (*circonstance*) possibility, contingency, eventuality; **parer à toute é.,** to provide for all eventualities *or* contingencies; **dans l'é. d'un changement de date,** in the event of a change of date; **(b)** (*possibilité*) possibility (*of war etc*).

éventuel, -elle [evɑ̃tɥɛl] *adj* possible, potential (*successor, profits, war etc*); **client é.,** potential *or* prospective customer; **rester é.,** to remain hypothetical.

éventuellement [evɑ̃tɥɛlmɑ̃] *adv* possibly, if necessary, should the occasion arise; **j'aurais é. besoin de votre concours,** I may need your help (later).

évêque [evɛk] **1** *nm Rel* bishop; *Prov* **un chien regarde bien un é.,** a cat may look at a king; **bonnet d'é.,** bishop's mitre; *F* parson's nose (*of fowl*). **2** *adj* **violet é.,** episcopal purple.

évertuer (s') [sevɛrtɥe] *vpr* to do one's utmost, to exert oneself; **s'é. à** *ou* **pour faire qch,** to do one's utmost *or* make every effort to do sth.

éviction [eviksjɔ̃] *nf* ousting, supplanting (*of rival, party leader etc*); eviction, dispossession (*of tenant*).

évidage [evidaʒ] *nm* hollowing out, scooping out (*of stone, wood etc*).

évidement [evidmɑ̃] *nm* **(a)** (*action*) hollowing out, scooping out (*of stone, wood etc*); *Chir* scraping out (*of bone*); **(b)** (*cavité*) hollow, cavity.

évidemment [evidamɑ̃] *adv* **(a)** (*bien sûr*) certainly, of course; **(b)** *Vieilli* (*incontestablement*) evidently, obviously, clearly.

évidence [evidɑ̃s] *nf* **(a)** obviousness, clearness (*of fact, truth etc*); **se rendre à l'é.,** to yield to *or* face the facts; **se refuser à l'é.,** to fly in the face of the facts; **de toute é., d'é. même,** clearly, obviously; **mais c'est une é.!,** but it's obvious *or* self-evident!; **(b) être en é.,** to be conspicuous *or* to the fore *or* in evidence; **mettre des marchandises en é.,** to display goods prominently; **se mettre en é.,** to put oneself to the fore.

évident [evidɑ̃] *adj* evident, obvious, clear, plain; **erreur évidente,** palpable *or* obvious *or* clear error; **il est é. qu'elle se trompe,** it is obvious *or* clear that she is mistaken; **il était d'une évidente mauvaise foi,** he was obviously *or* clearly insincere.

évider [evide] *vt* to hollow out, to scoop out (*stone, wood etc*); *Couture* to cut away, to slope out (*neck of dress*); *Chir* to scrape out (*bone*); **brique évidée,** airbrick.

évidoir [evidwar] *nm* (*outil*) gouge.

évier [evje] *nm* (*de cuisine*) sink.

évincer [evɛ̃se] *vt* (**j'évinçai(s)**) to oust, to supplant (*rival, party leader etc*); to evict, to dispossess (*tenant*).

éviscération [eviserasjɔ̃] *nf Chir* evisceration.

éviscérer [evisere] *vt* (**j'éviscère, n. éviscérons**) *Chir* to eviscerate.

évitable [evitabl] *adj* avoidable.

évitage [evitaʒ] *nm Nau* **(a)** (*mouvement*) swinging (*of ship*); **bassin d'é.,** turning basin; **(b)** (*espace*) room to swing, sea room.

évitement [evitmɑ̃] *nm* **(a)** avoidance (*of s.o., sth*); **faire une manœuvre d'é.,** to take evasive action; *Biol* **réaction d'é.,** avoiding reaction; **(b) voie** *ou* **gare d'é.,** siding; **ligne d'é.,** loop line; **(c) route d'é.,** bypass.

éviter [evite] **1** *vt* **(a)** (*ne pas heurter*) to avoid, to miss; (*ne pas subir*) to avoid, to steer clear of; (*ne pas rencontrer*) to avoid, to shun, to keep clear of (*s.o.*); to avoid (*gaze*); **é. l'alcool/le sucre/***etc*, to avoid *or* keep off alcohol/sugar/*etc*; **é. un coup,** to avoid *or* dodge a blow; **é. de la tête,** to duck; **é. de faire qch,** to avoid doing sth; **évite de recommencer,** don't start again; **é. la question,** to avoid *or* dodge the issue; **(b)** (*épargner*) **é. des ennuis/une corvée/***etc* **à qn,** to save *or* spare s.o. trouble/a chore/*etc*; **ça m'évitera d'avoir à le faire,** it will save me having to do it. **2** *vi Nau* **é. sur l'ancre,** to swing at anchor; **évité au vent,** riding the wind. **3 s'éviter** *vpr* **s'é. qch,** to avoid sth.

évocable [evɔkabl] *adj* evocable (*spirit, memory etc*); *Jur* **cause é.,** case that may be transferred to a higher court.

évocateur, -trice [evɔkatœr, -tris] *adj* evocative, suggestive (**de,** of).

évocation [evɔkasjɔ̃] *nf* **(a)** (*par la magie*) evocation, calling forth, conjuring up (*of spirit etc*); **(b)** (*de souvenir, passé etc*) evocation, conjuring up, recalling; **le pouvoir d'é. d'un lieu/d'un mot,** the evocative power of a place/word.

évolué [evɔlɥe] *adj* (highly) developed, advanced (*race, country, society*); mature, broadminded (*person*); advanced (*idea etc*); *Ordinat* high-level (*language*).

évoluer [evɔlɥe] *vi* **(a)** (*se déplacer*) (*of ship, troops etc*) *Br* to manœuvre, *US* to maneuver; (*of dancer etc*) to move around; *Fig* (*dans la haute société etc*) to move; **j'ignore dans quel milieu elle évolue maintenant,** I don't know what circles she moves in now; **(b)** (*se développer*) to evolve, to develop; (*of person*) to develop; (*of science*) to advance; (*of illness*) to take its course.

évolutif, -ive [evɔlytif, -iv] *adj* evolutionary; *Méd* progressive (*disease*); *Ski* **méthode évolutive, ski é.,** short-ski method; **salaire** *ou* **poste é.,** (*dans une annonce d'emploi*) salary under review.

évolution [evɔlysjɔ̃] *nf* **(a)** (*déplacement*) *Br* manœuvre, *Am* maneuver (*of ship, troops etc*); movement (*of dancer etc*); **(b)** (*développement*) evolution, development; development (*of person*); advance (*of science*); course (*of illness*); *Biol* evolution.

évolutionnisme [evɔlysjɔnism] *nm Biol* evolutionism.

évolutionniste [evɔlysjɔnist] *Biol* **1** *adj* evolutionist(ic). **2** *n* evolutionist.

évoquer [evɔke] *vt* **(a)** (*par la magie*) to evoke, to summon, to conjure up (*spirit etc*); **(b)** (*susciter*) to call to mind, to conjure up, to evoke (*memory, past etc*); (*faire penser à*) to be reminiscent of (*sth*); **qu'est-ce que cela vous évoque?,** what does that conjure up for you?; **(c)** (*effleurer*) to touch on, to mention; **nous n'avons fait qu'é. le sujet,** we've only touched on the subject.

ex [ɛks] *n F* (*mari, femme*) ex.

ex- [ɛks] *préf* ex-; **ex-femme/-champion,** ex-wife/-champion.

ex abrupto [ɛxsabrypto] *adv* impromptu.

exacerbation [ɛgzasɛrbasjɔ̃] *nf* exacerbation.

exacerber [ɛgzasɛrbe] **1** *vt* to exacerbate, to aggravate (*pain, irritation etc*). **2 s'exacerber** *vpr* to become acute.

exact [ɛgza(kt)] *adj* **(a)** (*précis*) exact, precise (*amount, number, calculation etc*); (*fidèle*) exact, accurate (*report, description, copy etc*); (*juste*) right, correct (*solution, word, reply etc*); **sciences exactes,** exact sciences; **l'heure/la date exacte,** the right *or* correct *or* exact time/date; **une montre exacte,** a precise *or* accurate watch; **e. à un millimètre près,** correct *or* accurate to within a millimetre; **c'est e.,** (*vrai*) it's quite true, it's a fact; **(b)** (*strict*) strict, rigorous (*diet, discipline etc*); **(c)** (*ponctuel*) punctual; **il est e. à payer son loyer,** he is punctual in paying his rent; **je n'ai pu être e. au rendez-vous,** I couldn't be on time for the appointment.

exactement [ɛgzaktəmɑ̃] *adv* (*précisément*) (*calculer, placer etc*) exactly, precisely; (*fidèlement*) (*rapporter, reproduire etc*) exactly, accurately; (*avec justesse*) (*répondre, raisonner etc*) rightly, correctly; **il est e. deux heures,** it is exactly *or* precisely two o'clock; **il avait e. l'air d'un spectre,** he looked exactly *or* just like a ghost; **un effet e. contraire,** a directly opposite effect.

exaction [ɛgzaksjɔ̃] *nf* **(a)** exaction (*of tax etc*); **(b)** (*vol*) extortion.
exactitude [ɛgzaktityd] *nf* **(a)** (*précision*) exactness, precision (*of amount, calculation etc*); (*fidélité*) exactness, accuracy (*of report, copy etc*); (*justesse*) rightness, correctness (*of solution, reply etc*); **calculer/mesurer avec e.,** to calculate/measure exactly *or* precisely; **(b)** (*ponctualité*) punctuality; **avec e.,** punctually.
ex æquo [ɛgzeko] **1** *adv Scol Sp etc* **être classés ex a.,** to tie, to be equally placed; **être troisième/***etc* **ex a.,** to tie for third/*etc* place, to be placed equal third/*etc*. **2** *n inv* **il y avait trois ex a. pour la premiere place,** three people tied for first place; **départager les ex a.,** to break the tie.
exagération [ɛgzaʒerɑsjɔ̃] *nf* exaggeration; **e. de la sensibilité,** hypersensitivity; **on peut dire sans e. que ...,** it is no exaggeration to say that ...; **se montrer ferme sans e.,** to be firm without overdoing it *or* going to extremes.
exagéré [ɛgzaʒere] *adj* exaggerated; **prix e.,** exorbitant price; **confiance exagérée,** overconfidence; **il n'est pas e. de dire que ...,** it is no exaggeration to say that ... .
exagérément [ɛgzaʒeremɑ̃] *adv* exaggeratedly; (*trop*) excessively.
exagérer [ɛgzaʒere] **1** *vt* to exaggerate, to overstate (*facts, truth, danger, s.o.'s qualities etc*); to exaggerate (*shape, proportions etc*); **il ne faut rien e.,** things should be kept in proportion, one shouldn't exaggerate. **2** *vi* (*parler*) to exaggerate; (*dépasser les bornes*) to go too far, to overstep the mark; *F* **il ne faut pas e.!,** let's not overdo it! **3 s'exagérer** *vpr* **s'e. qch,** to overestimate sth.
exaltant [ɛgzaltɑ̃] *adj* exciting, stirring (*speech, music etc*).
exaltation [ɛgzaltɑsjɔ̃] *nf* **(a)** *Rel* Exaltation (*of the Cross*); **(b)** (*action de louer*) exalting, extolling (*of virtue, person etc*); **(c)** (*excitation*) (great) excitement; *Méd* overexcitement; **e. mystique,** exaltation.
exalté, -ée [ɛgzalte] **1** *adj* wild, impassioned (*speech, feeling*); excited, wild (*imagination, mind*); fanatical, hotheaded (*person*). **2** *n Péj* fanatic, hothead.
exalter [ɛgzalte] **1** *vt* **(a)** (*exciter*) to stir, to fire (*imagination, mind*); to intensify (*resentment, pride etc*); to stir, to excite (*person*); **(b)** (*louer*) to exalt, to extol, to glorify (*s.o., s.o.'s qualities*). **2 s'exalter** *vpr* to grow excited.
examen [ɛgzamɛ̃] *nm* **(a)** (*observation, analyse*) examination (*of document, specimen, facts etc*); overhauling (*of a machine*); inspection (*of accounts*); *Méd* examination; **après un e. attentif de l'horizon,** after a careful scrutiny of the horizon; *Méd* **e. de la vue,** sight *or* eye test; **e. médical complet,** complete checkup; **faire un e. de sang,** to carry out *or* do a blood test; **cette assertion ne supporte pas l'e.,** this assertion will not bear examination; **la question à l'e.,** the matter under examination *or* consideration; **après e., e. fait,** (up)on examination; **e. de conscience,** examination of conscience; **(b)** *Scol Univ etc* exam, examination; **passer un e.,** to sit *or* take *or* go in for an exam; **être reçu/refusé à un e.,** to pass/fail an exam; **e. d'entrée,** entrance exam; **e. de passage,** *Br* end-of-year exam, *Am* final exam; **jury d'e.,** examining body, examiners; *Aut* **e. pour permis de conduire,** driving test.
examinateur, -trice [ɛgzaminatœr, -tris] *n* **(a)** (*d'examen*) examiner; **(b)** *Vieilli* (*observateur*) investigator.
examiner [ɛgzamine] **1** *vt* **(a)** (*étudier, analyser*) to examine (*document, specimen, facts etc*); to inspect, to go through (*accounts*); to overhaul (*machinery*); *Méd* to examine (*patient*); **se faire e. par un médecin,** to have oneself examined by a doctor; **e. l'horizon,** to scan *or* survey the horizon; *Fig* **elle m'a examiné de la tête aux pieds,** she eyed me from head to toe *or* up and down; **e. une question,** to look into *or* go into *or* consider a matter; **(b)** *Scol Univ etc* to examine; **e. qn en algèbre,** to examine s.o. in algebra. **2 s'examiner** *vpr* **(a)** (*dans une glace etc*) to examine oneself; **(b)** (*mentalement*) to examine one's conscience.
exanthème [ɛgzɑ̃tɛm] *nm Méd* exanthema.
exaspérant [ɛgzasperɑ̃] *adj* exasperating, irritating, aggravating.
exaspération [ɛgzasperɑsjɔ̃] *nf* **(a)** (*énervement*) exasperation, irritation, aggravation; **(b)** (*de douleur, sentiment*) aggravation.
exaspérer [ɛgzaspere] *v* **(j'exaspère; j'exaspérerai) 1** *vt* **(a)** to aggravate (*pain, feeling*); **(b)** (*énerver*) to exasperate, to irritate, to aggravate (*s.o.*). **2 s'exaspérer** *vpr* **(a)** (*of person*) to become exasperated *or* irritated; **(b)** (*of pain, feeling*) to become acute.
exaucement [ɛgzosmɑ̃] *nm* granting, fulfilment (*of wish, desire*).
exaucer [ɛgzose] *vt* **(j'exauçai(s); n. exauçons) (a)** to grant, to fulfil (*wish, desire*); **exauce ma prière!,** hear my prayer!; **(b) e. qn,** to grant *or* hear *or* answer s.o.'s prayer.
ex cathedra [ɛkskatedra] *adv Rel & Fig* ex cathedra.
excavateur, -trice [ɛkskavatœr, -tris] *n Constr* excavator, (mechanical) digger.
excavation [ɛkskavɑsjɔ̃] *nf* **(a)** (*trou*) excavation; (*creusée par une bombe*) crater; **(b)** (*action*) excavation, excavating.
excaver [ɛkskave] *vt* to excavate.
excédant [ɛksedɑ̃] *adj* exasperating, tiresome.
excédent [ɛksedɑ̃] *nm* excess, surplus; (*de budget, balance*) surplus; **somme en e.,** sum in excess; **budget en e.,** surplus budget; **vous garderez l'e.,** you will keep what is left over; **e. de poids,** excess weight; **e. de dépenses,** deficit; **e. de bagages,** excess luggage *or* baggage; **e. de blé,** wheat surplus; **la balance est en e.,** the balance shows a surplus *or* credit.
excédentaire [ɛksedɑ̃tɛr] *adj* excess, surplus (*production*); excess (*weight*); surplus (*budget*).
excéder [ɛksede] *vt* **(j'excède, n. excédons; j'excéderai) (a)** (*dépasser*) to exceed (*quantity, sum, period, Fig limit etc*); **le résultat a excédé mes espérances,** the result has surpassed *or* exceeded my expectations; **e. les moyens de qn,** to be beyond s.o.'s means; **e. ses pouvoirs,** to exceed *or* overstep one's powers; **(b)** (*irriter*) to exasperate (*s.o.*); **j'étais excédé,** I was exasperated, I had lost all patience; **(c)** *Vieilli* (*épuiser*) to tire *or* wear (*s.o.*) out; **excédé de fatigue,** worn out.
excellemment [ɛkselamɑ̃] *adv Litt* excellently.
excellence [ɛkselɑ̃s] *nf* **(a)** excellence; *Scol* **prix d'e.,** class prize (*for all-round standard*); **pianiste/***etc* **par e.,** pianist/*etc* par excellence; **aimer qch/s'intéresser à qch par e.,** to like sth/be interested in sth above all else; **(b)** (*titre*) **Son/Votre E.,** His *or* Her/Your Excellency.
excellent [ɛkselɑ̃] *adj* excellent, first-rate (**en qch,** at, in sth); **en excellente santé,** in the best of health, in excellent health.
exceller [ɛksele] *vi* to excel (**en qch,** at, in sth; **à faire qch,** in doing sth).
excentration [ɛksɑ̃trɑsjɔ̃] *nf Tech* off-centring.
excentrer [ɛksɑ̃tre] *vt Tech* to throw off centre.
excentricité [ɛksɑ̃trisite] *nf* **(a)** (*caractère, acte bizarre*) eccentricity; **(b)** (*de quartier etc*) remoteness; **(c)** (*de cercle, d'orbite etc*) eccentricity.
excentrique [ɛksɑ̃trik] **1** *adj* **(a)** (*bizarre*) eccentric, odd (*person, behaviour, idea etc*); **(b)** (*loin du centre*) remote (*suburb etc*); **(c)** *Math etc* eccentric (*circle, orbit etc*). **2** *n* (*personne*) eccentric. **3** *nm* (*mécanisme*) eccentric.
excentriquement [ɛksɑ̃trikmɑ̃] *adv* eccentrically.
excepté [ɛksepte] *prép* except, apart from; **tous les jours e. quand il pleut,** every day except *or* apart from *or* with the exception of when it rains; **la maison nous convient e. qu'elle manque de garage,** the house suits us except (for the fact) that there's no garage.
excepter [ɛksɛpte] *vt* to except, to exclude (*s.o., sth*) (**de,** from); **si l'on excepte une seule rue,** with the exception of *or* apart from one street; **les femmes exceptées,** except *or* apart from the women.
exception [ɛksɛpsjɔ̃] *nf* **(a)** exception (**à,** to); **faire une e. à une règle,** to make an exception to a rule; **faire e. à une règle,** to be an exception to a rule; **l'e. confirme la règle,** the exception proves the rule; **à quelques exceptions près,** with a few exceptions; **sans e.,** without exception; **par e.,** exceptionally; **tous, à l'e. du docteur** *ou* **e. faite du docteur,** all, except (for) *or* with the exception of the doctor; **(b)** *Jur* objection, plea (*by the defence*); **(c) mesures d'e.,** exceptional *or* extraordinary measures; **tribunal d'e.,** special court.
exceptionnel, -elle [ɛksɛpsjɔnɛl] *adj* **(a)** (*qui fait exception*) exceptional, special (*circumstances etc*); **congé e.,** special leave; **taille exceptionnelle,** outsize (*in clothes*); **(b)** (*remarquable*) exceptional, outstanding.
exceptionnellement [ɛksɛpsjɔnɛlmɑ̃] *adv* exceptionally; **e. tu peux partir maintenant,** just this once you can leave now.
excès [ɛksɛ] *nm* **(a)** (*excédent, démesure*) excess; **e. de l'offre sur la demande,** excess of supply over demand; **pécher par e. de zèle,** to be overzealous; *Tech* **clapet d'e. de pression,** relief valve; *Phot* **e. de pose,** overexposure; *Aut* **e. de vitesse,** speeding, exceeding the speed limit; **manger avec e.,** to eat too much, to overeat; **manger sans e.,** to eat moderately *or* in moderation; **réagir avec e.,** to overreact (**à qch,** to sth); **(jusqu')à l'e.,** to excess,

excessively; **se dépenser à l'e.,** to overexert oneself; **gentil/scrupuleux à l'e.,** kind/scrupulous to a fault, overkind/overscrupulous; **(b)** (*abus*) excess; **commettre des e.,** to overdo things, to go too far; **des e. (de table),** overeating; **évitez tout e.,** (*alimentaire*) avoid overeating; **des e. de conduite,** loose living; **des e. de langage,** immoderate language; **(c)** *Jur* **e. de pouvoir,** action ultra vires.

excessif, -ive [ɛksɛsif, -iv] *adj* excessive (*length, heat etc*); extreme (*opinion*); undue (*optimism etc*); exorbitant (*price*); immoderate (*eating, drinking. language*); inordinate (*pride*); **un travail e. l'a rendu malade,** he has become ill through overwork; **il est e.,** he goes to extremes.

excessivement [ɛksɛsivmɑ̃] *adv* **(a)** (*trop*) excessively; **manger e.,** to eat too much, to overeat; **(b)** (*extrêmement*) extremely.

exciper [ɛksipe] *vi Jur Litt* to put in a plea; **e. de sa bonne foi,** to plead one's good faith.

excipient [ɛksipjɑ̃] *nm Pharm* excipient.

exciser [ɛksize] *vt Chir* to excise, to cut out.

excision [ɛksizjɔ̃] *nf Chir* excision.

excitabilité [ɛksitabilite] *nf* excitability.

excitable [ɛksitabl] *adj* excitable.

excitant [ɛksitɑ̃] **1** *adj* exciting, stimulating (*news, music etc*); stimulating (*effect*); (*sexuellement*) sexy (*person*); sensual (*beauty*). **2** *nm* stimulant.

excitateur, -trice [ɛksitatœr, -tris] **1** *n* (*personne*) instigator (**de,** of). **2** *nm Él* discharger, (static) exciter. **3** *nf Él* **excitatrice,** (*dynamo*) exciter.

excitation [ɛksitɑsjɔ̃] *nf* **(a)** excitation (*of the senses etc*); **e. à la révolte,** incitement to rebellion; **(b)** (*état*) excitement; **e. (sexuelle),** (sexual) arousal, excitement; **(c)** *Él* excitation.

excité, -ée [ɛksite] *n* (*personne*) hothead.

exciter [ɛksite] **1** *vt* **(a)** to excite, to arouse, to stir up (*curiosity, jealousy etc*); to arouse (*pity*); to whet (*appetite*); to provoke (*laughter*); **e. la pitié de qn,** to move s.o. to pity; **(b)** (*encourager*) to urge (*s.o.*) on; **e. qn à la révolte** *ou* **à se révolter,** to incite s.o. to revolt; **e. qn contre qn,** to set s.o. against s.o.; **(c)** (*intellectuellement*) to excite, to thrill (*s.o.*); **(d)** (*sexuellement*) to arouse, to excite (*s.o.*); **(e)** *Physiol* to stimulate (*nerve, senses*); **(f)** *Él* to excite (*dynamo*). **2 s'exciter** *vpr* to get excited *or* worked up; (*sexuellement*) to get aroused *or* excited.

exclamatif, -ive [ɛksklamatif, -iv] *adj* exclamatory.

exclamation [ɛksklamɑsjɔ̃] *nf* exclamation; **point d'e.,** exclamation mark *or Am* point.

exclamer (s') [sɛksklame] *vpr* (*de joie, surprise, d'admiration*) to exclaim, to shout out; (*de douleur, colère*) to cry out, to shout out (**de,** in, with).

exclure [ɛksklyr] *v* (*prp* **excluant**; *pp* **exclu**; *pr ind* **j'exclus, n. excluons**; *impf* **j'excluais**; *p hist* **j'exclus**; *fu* **j'exclurai**) **1** *vt* **(a)** (*expulser*) (*de parti, d'école etc*) to expel (*s.o.*); (*de fonction publique*) to remove (*s.o.*); (*de salle, réunion*) to eject (*s.o.*) (**de,** from); **(b)** (*empêcher d'entrer*) to exclude (*s.o.*); **(c)** (*ne pas permettre ou admettre*) to exclude (*sth*) (**de,** from); **le mois d'août jusqu'au 31 exclu,** the month of August excluding the 31st; **(d)** (*ne pas considérer*) to rule out; **e. la possibilité d'un accord,** to rule out the possibility of an agreement; **il est exclu,** it's out of the question (**que,** that). **2 s'exclure** *vpr* (*of theories etc*) to be mutually exclusive, to be incompatible.

exclusif, -ive [ɛksklyzif, -iv] **1** *adj* **(a)** (*non partagé*) exclusive (*occupation, interest etc*); sole (*purpose, mission*); *Com* exclusive, sole (*right, agent etc*); exclusive (*article, model*); *Journ* exclusive (*report, interview etc*); **(b)** (*rigoureux*) (*dans ses opinions*) self-opinionated; (*dans ses goûts*) selective; **elle est très exclusive dans ses amitiés,** she is very selective in her choice of friends. **2** *nf* **exclusive,** (*mesure d'exclusion*) bar.

exclusion [ɛksklyzjɔ̃] *nf* **(a)** (*expulsion*) (*de parti, d'école etc*) expulsion; (*de fonction publique*) removal; (*de salle, réunion*) ejection (**de,** from); **(b) à l'e. de,** to the exclusion of; (*à l'exception de*) with the exception of.

exclusivement [ɛksklyzivmɑ̃] *adv* exclusively, solely; **parking e. réservé aux clients de l'hôtel,** parking reserved only for patrons of the hotel; **il aime e. l'opéra,** he only likes opera; **de lundi jusqu'à vendredi e.,** from Monday to Friday exclusive.

exclusivisme [ɛksklyzivism] *nm* exclusivism.

exclusiviste [ɛksklyzivist] *n* exclusivist.

exclusivité [ɛksklyzivite] *nf* **(a)** (*droit*) sole *or* exclusive rights (**de,** in); **film en e.,** exclusive film; *Journ* **article en e.,** exclusive, scoop; **(b)** *Com* (*article*) exclusive article; (*film*) exclusive film; *Journ* (*article*) exclusive, scoop.

excommunication [ɛkskɔmynikɑsjɔ̃] *nf* excommunication.

excommunier [ɛkskɔmynje] *vt* (*impf & pr sub* **n. excommuniions**) to excommunicate.

excrément [ɛkskremɑ̃] *nm* (*often pl*) *Litt* **excrément(s),** excrement.

excrémentiel, -elle [ɛkskremɑ̃sjɛl] *adj* excremental.

excréter [ɛkskrete] *vt* (**j'excrète; j'excréterai**) to excrete.

excréteur, -trice [ɛkskretœr, -tris] *adj* excretory.

excrétion [ɛkskresjɔ̃] *nf* **(a)** (*action*) excretion, excreting; **(b)** (*déchet*) excreted matter; **excrétions,** excreta.

excrétoire [ɛkskretwar] *adj* excretory.

excroissance [ɛkskrwasɑ̃s] *nf* excrescence.

excursion [ɛkskyrsjɔ̃] *nf* (*en car, voiture etc*) excursion, trip; (*de plusieurs jours*) tour; (*à pied*) hike, (long) walk; **faire une e.,** to go on an excursion *or* a trip *or* a tour *or* a hike *or* a walk; **e. scientifique,** scientific expedition.

excursionner [ɛkskyrsjɔne] *vi* (*en car, voiture etc*) to go on excursions *or* trips; (*pendant plusieurs jours*) to go touring; (*à pied*) to go hiking *or* walking.

excursionniste [ɛkskyrsjɔnist] *n* (*en car, voiture etc*) tourist, *Br* tripper; (*à pied*) hiker, walker.

excusable [ɛkskyzabl] *adj* excusable, pardonable.

excuse [ɛkskyz] *nf* **(a)** (*raison*) excuse; **trouver une e. à qch/pour faire qch,** to find an excuse for sth/for doing sth; **je prends mon travail comme e.,** I make my work the excuse; **erreur sans e.,** inexcusable *or* unpardonable error; **(b)** *Arg* **faites e.!,** sorry!; **(c) excuses,** apology; **faire** *ou* **présenter ses excuses à qn,** to make one's apologies *or* to apologize to s.o.; **il exige des excuses,** he demands an apology; **je vous dois des excuses,** I owe you an apology; **lettre d'excuses,** letter of apology.

excuser [ɛkskyze] **1** *vt* **(a)** (*défendre*) to make excuses for, to apologize for (*s.o., action*); **e. qn auprès de qn,** to apologize for s.o. to s.o.; **(b)** (*pardonner*) to excuse (*s.o., error*); **excusez-moi,** excuse me, pardon me; **e. qch à qn,** to excuse s.o. sth; **e. qn de faire qch,** to excuse s.o. for doing sth; (*en le dispensant*) to excuse s.o. from doing sth; **e. un juré,** to excuse a juror (from attendance); **l'ignorance n'excuse personne,** ignorance is no excuse. **2 s'excuser** *vpr* to apologize; **s'e. auprès de qn,** to apologize to s.o.; **s'e. de qch/de faire qch,** to apologize for sth/doing sth; **je m'excuse!,** sorry!, excuse me!; *Prov* **qui s'excuse s'accuse,** he who excuses himself accuses himself.

exécrable [ɛgzekrabl] *adj* execrable, abominable, atrocious.

exécrablement [ɛgzekrabləmɑ̃] *adv* execrably, abominably, atrociously.

exécration [ɛgzekrɑsjɔ̃] *nf* execration, detestation (*of crime etc*); **avoir qn en e.,** to loathe s.o..

exécrer [ɛgzekre] *vt* (**j'exècre; j'exécrerai**) to execrate, to loathe, to detest.

exécutable [ɛgzekytabl] *adj* practicable, feasible.

exécutant, -ante [ɛgzekytɑ̃, -ɑ̃t] *n* executant; *Mus* performer, executant.

exécuter [ɛgzekyte] **1** *vt* **(a)** to execute, to carry out (*work, plan*); to carry out, to act upon (*orders, decision*); to carry out, to fulfil (*promise*); to enforce, to give effect to (*decree, law etc*); to execute, to perform (*dance, piece of music*); **(b)** to produce (*painting, novel etc*); *Ordinat* to execute, to run (*program*); *Ordinat* to execute, to carry out (*command*); *Ordinat* **e. d'abord le sous-programme,** to run the subroutine first; **(c)** *Jur* to distrain upon (*debtor*); **(d)** *F* (*critiquer*) to savage (*work, author etc*); **(e)** (*mettre à mort*) to execute, to put (*criminal etc*) to death; *Sp F* (*battre*) to slaughter (*opponent*). **2 s'exécuter** *vpr* to comply; **il faudra bien vous e.,** you'll have to bring yourself to do it.

exécuteur, -trice [ɛgzekytœr, -tris] **1** *n* **(a)** *Jur* **e. testamentaire,** executor; **exécutrice testamentaire,** executrix; **(b)** *Arch* (*de plan, tâche*) executant. **2** *nm* (*bourreau*) **e. (des hautes œuvres),** executioner.

exécutif, -ive [ɛgzekytif, -iv] *Pol* **1** *adj* executive (*power etc*). **2** *nm* **l'e.,** the executive.

exécution [ɛgzekysjɔ̃] *nf* **(a)** execution, performance, carrying out (*of plan, work*); carrying out (*of orders, decision*); fulfilment (*of promise*); enforcement (*of law, decree etc*); performance, execution (*of dance, piece of music*); production (*of painting, novel etc*); **droit d'e.,** performing rights; **difficultés d'e. d'un morceau de musique,** difficulties in the performance *or* execution of a piece of music; **mettre un projet à e.,** to put a plan into execution *or* operation, to carry out a plan; **travaux en voie d'e.,** work in progress; **(b)** (*mise à mort*) **e. (capitale),** execution; **ordre d'e.,** death warrant; *Mil* **peloton d'e.,**

firing party; **(c)** *Jur* (*de débiteur*) distraint (**de,** upon).

exécutoire [ɛgzekytwar] *Jur* **1** *adj* **(a) jugement (de force) e.,** enforceable decision (*of the court*); **(b)** executory (*formula etc*). **2** *nm* writ of execution; **e. de dépens,** order to pay costs.

exégèse [ɛgzeʒɛz] *nf* exegesis.

exemplaire[1] [ɛgzɑ̃plɛr] *adj* exemplary (*behaviour etc*); **élève/employé/***etc* **e.,** model pupil/employee/*etc*.

exemplaire[2] *nm* **(a)** (*livre, gravure etc*) copy; **en deux/trois exemplaires,** in duplicate/triplicate; **édition tirée à dix mille exemplaires,** edition of ten thousand copies; **(b)** (*spécimen*) example (*of plant, animal etc*).

exemplairement [ɛgzɑ̃plɛrmɑ̃] *adv* exemplarily.

exemple [ɛgzɑ̃pl] *nm* **(a)** (*servant de modèle*) example, model; **donner l'e.,** to set an example (**à,** to); **suivre l'e. de qn, prendre e. sur qn,** to follow s.o.'s example; **prendre qn pour** *ou* **comme e.,** to take s.o. as one's model; **supposons à titre d'e. qu'il n'y a point de candidats,** let us suppose for argument's sake *or* for example that no one applies; **prêcher d'e.,** to practise what one preaches;

(b) (*leçon*) **faire un e. de qn,** to make an example of s.o.; **servir d'e. à qn,** to be a lesson *or* a warning to s.o.; **infliger une punition à qn pour l'e.,** to punish s.o. as an example *or* a warning to others;

(c) (*cas*) example, instance; (*mot, phrase*) example; **sans e.,** without parallel; **par e.,** for instance, for example; **un de ces jours, par e. dimanche,** one of these days, say *or* for example *or* for instance on Sunday; **par e.!,** (*étonnement*) who'd have thought it!; **ah non, par e.!,** I should think not!; **c'est utile, mais c'est cher, par e.,** it's useful but, mind you, it's expensive.

exemplification [ɛgzɑ̃plifikasjɔ̃] *nf* exemplification.

exemplifier [ɛgzɑ̃plifje] *vt* to exemplify.

exempt, -te [ɛgzɑ̃, -ɑ̃t] **1** *adj* **e. de,** exempt from (*military service, tax etc*); free from (*anxiety, disease etc*); **e. de soucis,** carefree; **e. de droits (de douane),** free of duty, duty-free; **e. de port,** carriage free. **2** *n* (*personne*) person who is exempt (**de,** from).

exempter [ɛgzɑ̃te] **1** *vt* (*d'impôt, de service militaire etc*) to exempt (*s.o.*) (**de,** from); (*d'anxiété, de risques etc*) to safeguard (*s.o.*) (**de,** against); **e. qn de faire qch,** to exempt *or* excuse s.o. from doing sth. **2 s'exempter** *vpr* **s'e. de qch/de faire qch,** to get out of sth/doing sth.

exemption [ɛgzɑ̃psjɔ̃] *nf* exemption (**de,** from); (*d'anxiété, de risques etc*) freedom (**de,** from); **liste d'exemptions,** (*de la douane*) free list.

exerçant [ɛgzɛrsɑ̃] *adj* practising (*doctor etc*).

exercé [ɛgzɛrse] *adj* experienced, practised, trained (*person*); trained (*eye, ear*); practised (*hand*).

exercer [ɛgzɛrse] *v* (**j'exerçai(s)**) **1** *vt* **(a)** (*former*) to exercise (*one's body, mind*); to train (*memory*); *Mil* to drill, to train (*soldiers*); **e. qn à qch/à faire qch,** to train s.o. in sth/to do sth;

(b) (*user de*) to exercise (*authority, charity, talent etc*); **e. son influence sur qn,** to exert *or* exercise one's influence on s.o., to bring one's influence to bear on s.o.; **e. une pression sur qch/qn,** to exert pressure on sth/s.o.; **e. ses droits,** to exercise one's rights;

(c) médecine qui exerce une action sur le foie, medicine that acts *or* has an action upon the liver;

(d) to practise (*profession*); to carry on (*business, trade*).

2 *vi* (*of doctor, lawyer etc*) to practise, to be in practice.

3 s'exercer *vpr* **(a)** (*of singer, sportsman etc*) to practise; **s'e. à qch/à faire qch,** to practise sth/doing sth;

(b) (*se manifester*) to make itself felt; **sa mauvaise foi s'exerce aussi contre ses proches,** his close relations also feel the effects of his dishonesty.

exercice [ɛgzɛrsis] *nm* **(a)** (*physique*) exercise; **prendre de l'e.,** to (take) exercise; **e. physique,** physical exercise; **(b)** *Mil* drill(ing), training; **être à l'e.,** to be on parade; **faire l'e.,** to drill; **(c)** *Sp Mus Scol etc* (*mouvement, tâche*) exercise; **exercices de grammaire,** grammar exercises; **faire** *ou* **jouer des exercices au piano,** to practise piano exercises; **(d)** exercise (*of power, privilege etc*); **(e)** practice (*of profession*); **dans l'e. de ses fonctions,** in the exercise *or* discharge of one's duties; **avocat/***etc* **en e.,** practising barrister/*etc*; **le président en e.,** the president in office; **(f)** *Rel* **l'e. du culte,** public worship; **(g)** (*en comptabilité*) financial year; **bilan en fin d'e.,** end-of-year balance sheet.

exerciseur [ɛgzɛrsizœr] *nm* (*appareil de gymnastique*) exerciser.

exergue [ɛgzɛrg] *nm* inscription, *Spéc* exergue (*of medal*); inscription (*of picture*); epigraph (*of text*); *Fig* **mettre une idée en e.,** to highlight *or* point up an idea.

exfoliation [ɛksfɔljasjɔ̃] *nf* exfoliation.

exfolier (s') [sɛksfɔlje] *vpr* to exfoliate, to scale off.

exhalaison [ɛgzalɛzɔ̃] *nf* (*odeur, vapeur*) exhalation; **exhalaisons,** fumes.

exhalation [ɛgzalasjɔ̃] *nf* (*action*) exhalation, exhaling.

exhaler [ɛgzale] **1** *vt* to exhale, to emit, to give off (*smell, vapour etc*); to breathe (*a sigh*); *Fig* to give vent to, to vent (*joy, anger etc*). **2 s'exhaler** *vpr* (*of smell, vapour etc*) to exhale, to be given off.

exhaussement [ɛgzosmɑ̃] *nm* increasing of the height (*of wall, building etc*).

exhausser [ɛgzose] *vt* to heighten, to increase the height of (*wall etc*); **e. une maison d'un étage,** to add a storey to a house.

exhausteur [ɛgzostœr] *nm Tech* suction pipe (*of vacuum-feed tank*).

exhaustif, -ive [ɛgzostif, -iv] *adj* exhaustive.

exhaustion [ɛgzostjɔ̃] *nf* (*en logique*) exhaustion.

exhaustivement [ɛgzostivmɑ̃] *adv* exhaustively.

exhaustivité [ɛgzostivite] *nf* exhaustiveness.

exhérédation [ɛgzeredasjɔ̃] *nf Jur* disinheritance.

exhéréder [ɛgzerede] *vt* (**j'exhérède; j'exhéréderai**) *Jur* to disinherit.

exhiber [ɛgzibe] **1** *vt* **(a)** to produce (*documents etc*); to present, to show (*passport, identity card etc*); **(b)** to exhibit, to show (*animals etc*); *Péj* to show off, to flaunt (*one's knowledge, clothes, wealth etc*). **2 s'exhiber** *vpr* to flaunt oneself.

exhibition [ɛgzibisjɔ̃] *nf* **(a)** *Jur* production (*of documents*); **(b)** (*présentation*) show (*of animals etc*); **(c)** *Péj* (*étalage*) flaunting, showing off (*of knowledge, wealth etc*); **pourquoi ces exhibitions?,** why are you flaunting yourself *or* is he flaunting himself *etc*?

exhibitionnisme [ɛgzibisjɔnism] *nm* exhibitionism.

exhibitionniste [ɛgzibisjɔnist] *n* exhibitionist.

exhortation [ɛgzɔrtasjɔ̃] *nf* exhortation (**à qch,** to sth; **à faire qch,** to do sth).

exhorter [ɛgzɔrte] *vt* to exhort, to urge (**à qch,** to sth; **à faire qch,** to do sth).

exhumation [ɛgzymasjɔ̃] *nf* **(a)** exhumation (*of body*); digging up, excavation (*of treasure, remains of town etc*); **(b)** *Fig* unearthing (*of old documents etc*); digging up (*of old grudges, memories etc*); exhumation (*of old law, custom etc*).

exhumer [ɛgzyme] *vt* **(a)** to exhume (*body*); to dig up, to excavate (*treasure, remains of town etc*); **(b)** *Fig* to unearth, to bring to light (*old documents etc*); to dig up (*old grudges, memories etc*); to exhume (*old law, custom etc*).

exigeant [ɛgziʒɑ̃] *adj* demanding, exacting (*person, job etc*); **être trop e.,** (*of person*) to expect too much, to be too demanding.

exigence [ɛgziʒɑ̃s] *nf* **(a)** (*caractère*) **elle est d'une e. insupportable,** she's intolerably demanding; **(b)** (*condition*) demand, requirement (*of customer etc*); **l'e.** *ou* **les exigences de l'étiquette,** the demands *or* requirements of etiquette; **selon l'e. du cas,** as may be required.

exiger [ɛgziʒe] *vt* (**j'exigeai(s)**) **(a)** (*demander en insistant*) to demand, to require, to insist on (*action, payment, silence etc*) (**de,** from); **e. qu'une chose soit faite,** to insist on a thing being done, to demand that a thing be done; **trop e. des forces de qn,** to overtax s.o.'s strength; **(b)** (*nécessiter*) to require, to necessitate, to call for (*care, action etc*); **prendre les mesures qu'exigent les circonstances,** to take the necessary measures.

exigible [ɛgziʒibl] *adj* payable (*debt, tax*).

exigu,-uë [ɛgzigy] *adj* cramped, tiny (*house, garden etc*); slender, meagre (*income, resources etc*).

exiguïté [ɛgziguite] *nf* crampedness, smallness (*of house etc*); slenderness, meagreness (*of income etc*).

exil [ɛgzil] *nm* (*expulsion*) exile; **envoyer qn en e.,** to send s.o. into exile, to exile s.o.; **vivre en e.,** to live in exile.

exilé, -ée [ɛgzile] *n* (*personne*) exile.

exiler [ɛgzile] **1** *vt* (*d'un pays*) to exile (**de,** from); (*d'une ville, de la cour etc*) to banish (**de,** from). **2 s'exiler** *vpr Pol* to go into (voluntary) exile; *Fig* **s'e. (du monde),** to cut oneself off *or* withdraw (from the world).

existant [ɛgzistɑ̃] **1** *adj* existing; **lois existantes,** existing laws, laws in force; *Zool* **espèce existante,** extant *or* existing species. **2** *nm Com* **e. en caisse/en magasin,** cash/stock in hand.

existence [ɛgzistɑ̃s] *nf* **(a)** *Phil* (*être*) existence, (state of) being; **(b)** (*vie*) existence, life; **changer d'e.,** to change one's (way of) life; **(c)** (*présence*) existence (**de,** of); **(d)** (*durée*) life (*of institution etc*); **(e)** *Com* **e. (en magasin),** stock (in hand).

existentialisme [ɛgzistɑ̃sjalism] *nm Phil* existentialism.
existentialiste [ɛgzistɑ̃sjalist] *adj & n Phil* existentialist.
existentiel, -elle [ɛgzistɑ̃sjɛl] *adj* existential.
exister [ɛgziste] *vi* **(a)** (*vivre, être réel, se trouver*) to exist; **la maison existe toujours,** the house still exists *or* is still standing; *Com* the firm still exists *or* is still in existence; **je n'arrive pas à croire qu'un autre monde puisse e.,** I just can't believe that there is another world *or* that another world exists; **rien n'existe pour lui que l'art,** nothing but art matters to him; **et l'amitié, cela existe, non?,** but friendship matters, doesn't it?; **(b)** *Zool* to be extant, to exist.
exit [ɛgzit] *adv F* **e. les solutions miracles,** out go miracle solutions.
ex-libris [ɛkslibris] *nm* (*vignette*) book plate, ex libris.
exocet [ɛgzɔsɛ(t)] *nm* **(a)** (*poisson*) flying fish; **(b) E.** ®, (*missile*) Exocet ®.
exocrine [ɛgzɔkrin] *adj Physiol* exocrine (*gland*).
exode [ɛgzɔd] *nm* **(a)** (*émigration*) exodus; **l'e. des cerveaux,** the brain drain; **e. rural,** rural depopulation; **(b)** *Bible* **l'E.,** (*livre*) Exodus; (*émigration des Hébreux*) the Exodus.
exogame [ɛgzɔgam] *adj* exogamous (*tribe etc*).
exogamie [ɛgzɔgami] *nf* exogamy.
exonération [ɛgzɔnerasjɔ̃] *nf* exemption; **e. d'impôts,** tax exemption.
exonérer [ɛgzɔnere] *vt* (**j'exonère, j'exonérerai**) to exempt (*s.o.*) (**d'un impôt**/*etc*, from a tax/*etc*); to exempt (*goods*) from import duty.
exophtalmie [ɛgzɔftalmi] *nf Méd* exophthalmus, exophthalmos.
exophtalmique [ɛgzɔftalmik] *adj Méd* exophthalmic (*goitre*).
exorbitant [ɛgzɔrbitɑ̃] *adj* exorbitant, outrageous (*price, demand etc*).
exorbité [ɛgzɔrbite] *adj* **ils regardaient, les yeux exorbités,** they were looking on, with their eyes bulging (out of their heads).
exorciser [ɛgzɔrsize] *vt* to exorcize (*demon, one possessed*); to cast out (*devil*); to lay (*ghost*).
exorciseur [ɛgzɔrsizœr] *nm* exorcizer.
exorcisme [ɛgzɔrsism] *nm* exorcism.
exorciste [ɛgzɔrsist] *n* exorcist.
exorde [ɛgzɔrd] *nm* exordium.
exosmose [ɛgzɔsmoz] *nf Phys* exosmosis.
exotique [ɛgzɔtik] *adj* exotic; **poisson e.,** tropical fish.
exotisme [ɛgzɔtism] *nm* exoticism.
expansé [ɛkspɑ̃se] *adj* expanded (*polystyrene*).
expansibilité [ɛkspɑ̃sibilite] *nf* expansibility (*of gas etc*).
expansible [ɛkspɑ̃sibl] *adj* expansible (*gas etc*).
expansif, -ive [ɛkspɑ̃sif, -iv] *adj* **(a)** (*exubérant*) expansive, effusive (*person*); **(b)** *Phys* expansive (*force etc*).
expansion [ɛkspɑ̃sjɔ̃] *nf* **(a)** *Phys* expansion (*of gases, universe etc*); **l'univers en e.,** the expanding universe; **(b)** (*développement*) expansion (*of town, industry etc*); spread (*of ideas, culture etc*); **e. coloniale,** colonial expansion; **taux d'e. économique,** economic growth rate; **(c)** (*exubérance*) expansiveness, effusiveness; **avec e.,** effusively; **(d)** *Ordinat* **carte d'e.,** expansion card.
expansionnisme [ɛkspɑ̃sjɔnism] *nm* expansionism.
expansionniste [ɛkspɑ̃sjɔnist] *adj & n* expansionist.
expansivité [ɛkspɑ̃sivite] *nf* expansiveness.
expatriation [ɛkspatrijasjɔ̃] *nf* expatriation; *Fin* **e. de capitaux,** investment of capital abroad.
expatrié, -ée [ɛkspatrije] *adj & n* expatriate, *F* expat.
expatrier [ɛkspatrije] *v* (*impf & pr sub* **n. expatriions**) **1** *vt* to expatriate (*s.o.*); to invest (*capital*) abroad. **2** **s'expatrier** *vpr* to settle abroad.
expectative [ɛkspɛktativ] *nf* (*attente*) expectation (**de,** of); **nous vivons dans l'e.,** we are living in hope *or* expectation; **rester dans l'e.,** to wait and see; **triste e.,** gloomy prospect.
expectorant [ɛkspɛktɔrɑ̃] *adj & nm Méd* expectorant.
expectoration [ɛkspɛktɔrasjɔ̃] *nf* (*action, crachat*) expectoration.
expectorer [ɛkspɛktɔre] *vt* to expectorate.
expédient [ɛkspedjɑ̃] **1** *adj* expedient; **il est e. de prendre les devants,** it is advisable to take the initiative. **2** *nm* expedient, makeshift; **vivre d'expédients,** to live by one's wits.
expédier [ɛkspedje] *vt* (*impf & pr sub* **n. expédiions**) **(a)** (*envoyer*) to dispatch, to send off (*letter, parcel goods*); **e. des marchandises par navire,** to ship goods; **e. un colis par chemin de fer,** to dispatch *or* send a parcel by rail; *F* **expédiez-le-moi!,** (*coupable etc*) send him along (to me)!; **(b)** (*se débarrasser de*) to get rid of, to dispose of (*s.o.*); **ce médecin est connu pour e. ses clients,** this doctor is known for getting through his patients quickly; **(c)** (*faire rapidement*) to deal promptly with, to dispatch (*task etc*); **e. son déjeuner,** to make short work of one's lunch; **(d) e. des marchandises en douane,** to clear goods; **(e)** *Jur* to draw up (*contract, deed etc*).
expéditeur, -trice [ɛkspeditœr, -tris] **1** *n* **(a)** sender (*of letter, parcel etc*); **e.** *ou* **expéditrice J. Martin,** from *or* sender J. Martin; **retour à l'e.,** return to sender; **(b)** *Com* consigner (*of goods*); (*par bateau*) shipper. **2** *adj* dispatching (*office etc*).
expéditif, -ive [ɛkspeditif, -iv] *adj* expeditious, speedy.
expédition [ɛkspedisjɔ̃] *nf* **(a)** (*envoi*) dispatch, sending (*of letter, parcel, goods*); **e. par mer,** shipping, shipment; **bulletin d'e.,** waybill; **(b)** (*marchandises*) consignment; **(c)** (*voyage, opération militaire*) expedition; **partir en e.,** to go (off) on an expedition; **(d)** (*de tache etc*) dispatch(ing); **(e)** **e. en douane,** (customs) clearance; **(f)** *Jur* (*de contrat etc*) (authentic) copy.
expéditionnaire [ɛkspedisjɔnɛr] **1** *adj Mil* **corps e.,** expeditionary force. **2** *n* shipping clerk; (*chargé de faire des copies*) copying clerk.
expérience [ɛksperjɑ̃s] *nf* **(a)** (*pratique*) experience; **avoir l'e. de qch,** to have experience of sth, to be experienced in sth; **faire l'e. de qch,** to experience sth; **connaître qch par e.,** to know sth from experience; **sans e.,** inexperienced (**de,** in); **(b)** (*essai*) experiment; **faire une e.,** to carry out *or* do an experiment (**sur,** on); **nous avons décidé de tenter l'e.,** we have decided to give it a try; **faire l'e. de la vie en communauté,** to try out communal living.
expérimental, -aux [ɛksperimɑ̃tal, -o] *adj* experimental; **les sciences expérimentales,** the experimental sciences.
expérimentalement [ɛksperimɑ̃talmɑ̃] *adv* experimentally.
expérimentateur, -trice [ɛksperimɑ̃tatœr, -tris] *n* experimenter; (*scientifique*) (scientific) research worker.
expérimentation [ɛksperimɑ̃tasjɔ̃] *nf* experimentation.
expérimenté [ɛksperimɑ̃te] *adj* experienced.
expérimenter [ɛksperimɑ̃te] **1** *vt* **(a)** (*tester*) to test, to try out (*remedy, model, vaccine etc*) (**sur,** on); **(b)** (*connaître par expérience*) to know (*sth*) from experience. **2** *vi* to experiment.
expert [ɛkspɛr] **1** *adj* expert, skilled (**en, dans,** in; **à faire qch,** in doing sth). **2** *nm* expert; (*d'assurance, d'objets d'art*) valuer, appraiser; *Nau* surveyor.
expert-comptable [ɛkspɛrkɔ̃tabl] *nm Br* ≈ chartered accountant, *Am* ≈ certified public accountant; (*pl experts-comptables*).
expertise [ɛkspɛrtiz] *nf* **(a)** (*évaluation*) (expert) valuation, appraisal (*of work of art etc*); (expert) assessment (*of damage*); *Jur* expert opinion; *Nau* **e. d'avarie,** damage survey; **(b)** (*rapport*) expert's report; **(c)** (*compétence*) expertise.
expertiser [ɛkspɛrtize] *vt* to value, to appraise (*work of art etc*); to assess (*damage*).
expiation [ɛkspjasjɔ̃] *nf* expiation (**de,** of), atonement (**de,** for).
expiatoire [ɛkspjatwar] *adj* expiatory.
expier [ɛkspje] *vt* (*impf & pr sub* **n. expiions**) to expiate, to atone for, to pay the penalty for (*sin, crime etc*).
expirant [ɛkspirɑ̃] *adj* dying (*person*); dying, guttering (*flame*); **voix expirante,** faint *or* barely audible voice.
expiration [ɛkspirasjɔ̃] *nf* **(a)** (*respiration*) breathing out, *Spéc* expiration; **(b)** (*de contrat, carte d'identité etc*) *Br* expiry, *Am* expiration; **venir à e.,** to expire, to run out.
expirer [ɛkspire] **1** *vt* to breathe out, *Spéc* to expire (*air*). **2** *vi* **(a)** (*mourir*) to die, *Fml* to expire; *Fig* (*of flame, sound, wave*) to die; **(b)** (*of contract, identity card etc*) to expire, to run out; **mon congé est expiré,** my leave is up *or* has expired; **(c)** (*respirer*) to breathe out, *Spéc* to expire.
explétif, -ive [ɛkspletif, -iv] *adj & nm Gram* expletive.
explicable [ɛksplikabl] *adj* explicable, explainable.
explicatif, -ive [ɛksplikatif, -iv] *adj* explanatory; **notice explicative,** *Littér* prefatory note; *Com* directions for use.
explication [ɛksplikasjɔ̃] *nf* explanation; **donner l'e. de qch,** to account for *or* explain sth; **je demande des explications!,** I want an explanation!; **avoir une e. avec qn,** (*discuter*) to talk things over with s.o.; (*se disputer*) to have it out with s.o.; *Scol Univ* **e. de textes,** literary appreciation.
explicite [ɛksplisit] *adj* explicit.
explicitement [ɛksplisitmɑ̃] *adv* explicitly.

expliciter [ɛksplisite] *vt* to clarify (*text, thoughts, clause of contract etc*).

expliquer [ɛksplike] **1** *vt* **(a)** (*communiquer*) to explain (*one's ideas, plans, reasons etc*) (**à qn,** to s.o.); **(b)** (*élucider*) to explain, to expound, to elucidate (*doctrine, theorem etc*); to explain (*mystery, meaning*); **(c)** (*indiquer la raison de*) to explain, to account for (*action, fact, attitude etc*). **2 s'expliquer** *vpr* (*communiquer ses idées etc, se justifier*) to explain oneself; **cela s'explique facilement,** that's easily understandable *or* explainable; **je m'explique,** this is what I mean; **je ne m'explique pas pourquoi,** I can't understand why; **s'e. avec qn,** (*discuter*) to talk things over with s.o.; (*se disputer*) to have it out with s.o.

exploit [ɛksplwa] *nm* **(a)** (*sportif, oratoire etc*) feat, achievement; (*militaire, amoureux*) exploit; **(b)** *Jur* **e. (d'huissier),** writ.

exploitable [ɛksplwatabl] *adj* farmable (*land*); workable (*mine, forest*); exploitable (*natural resources*); *Ordinat* **système dic.,** operating system; *Fig* exploitable (*situation, talent, Péj person*).

exploitant [ɛksplwatɑ̃] **1** *adj* **(a)** *Com* **société exploitante,** development company; **(b)** *Jur* **huissier e.,** writ server. **2** *nm* **(a)** (*d'entreprise, de mine*) operator; **e. (agricole),** farmer; **(b)** *Cin* exhibitor.

exploitation [ɛksplwatɑsjɔ̃] *nf* **(a)** (*action*) working (*of mine, forest etc*); running, operation (*of railway, farm etc*); farming (*of land*); exploitation (*of natural resources*); *Ordinat* **système d'e.,** operating system; *Fig* **société d'e.,** development company; *Péj* **c'est de l'e!,** it's exploitation!; **(b)** (*entreprise*) concern; **e. agricole,** farm; **e. forestière,** forestry development; **e. minière,** mine.

exploiter [ɛksplwate] **1** *vt* **(a)** *Com* to work (*mine, patent, forest etc*); to run, to operate (*railway, farm, newspaper etc*); to farm (*land*); to exploit (*natural resources*); to make the most of, to exploit (*situation, one's talent etc*); **e. un succès,** to exploit *or* make capital out of a success; **(b)** *Péj* (*abuser de*) to exploit, to take (unfair) advantage of (*s.o., s.o.'s ignorance etc*). **2** *vi Jur* to serve a writ.

exploiteur, -euse [ɛksplwatœr, -øz] *n* exploiter (*of labour, s.o.'s ignorance etc*).

explorateur, -trice [ɛksplɔratœr, -tris] **1** *n* (*personne*) explorer. **2** *nm* (*instrument*) *Méd* explorer; *Ordinat TV* scanner.

exploration [ɛksplɔrɑsjɔ̃] *nf* **(a)** exploration (*of country, house, Fig subject etc*); **voyage d'e.,** voyage of discovery; **(b)** *Ordinat TV* scanning; **(c)** *Méd* exploration, probing.

exploratoire [ɛksplɔratwar] *adj* exploratory (*discussions etc*).

explorer [ɛksplɔre] *vt* **(a)** to explore (*country, house, Fig subject, possibility etc*); **(b)** *Méd* to explore, to probe (*wound, cavity*); **(c)** *Ordinat TV* to scan.

exploser [ɛksploze] *vi* **(a)** (*of bomb, aircraft, boiler etc*) to explode, to blow up; (*of gas*) to explode; **faire e. une bombe,** to explode a bomb; **(b)** *Fig* (*se mettre en colère*) to explode, *F* to blow one's top; **sa colère explosa,** his anger burst out *or* exploded; **e. en injures,** to let loose a stream of abuse.

explosible [ɛksplozibl] *adj* explosive (*gas etc*).

explosif, -ive [ɛksplozif, -iv] **1** *adj* **(a)** explosive (*shell, force etc*); *Él* **distance explosive,** spark(ing) gap; **(b)** *Fig* explosive (*situation, question, temper etc*); **(c)** *Ling* plosive (*consonant*). **2** *nm* explosive; **e. à grande puissance,** high explosive; **e. propulsif,** propellant explosive.

explosion [ɛksplozjɔ̃] *nf* explosion; **e. atomique,** atomic explosion; **e. aérienne,** air burst; **faire e.,** to explode, to blow up; **moteur à e.,** internal combustion engine; **e. de fureur/rires,** (out)burst of fury/laughter; **e. des dépenses,** rocketing costs; **e. démographique,** population explosion; **e. nataliste,** baby boom; **e. technologique,** technological explosion.

expo [ɛkspo] *nf F* (= **exposition**) exhibition.

exponentiel, -ielle [ɛkspɔnɑ̃sjɛl] *adj Math* exponential.

exportable [ɛkspɔrtabl] *adj* exportable.

exportateur, -trice [ɛkspɔrtatœr, -tris] **1** *n* exporter. **2** *adj* exporting; **pays e. de vin,** wine-exporting country.

exportation [ɛkspɔrtɑsjɔ̃] *nf* (*action*) export(ation), exporting; (*produit*) export; *Ordinat* (*de fichier*) exporting; **articles d'e.,** exports; **faire l'e.,** to export; **exportations visibles/invisibles,** visible/invisible exports; **commerce d'e.,** export trade.

exporter [ɛkspɔrte] *vt Com Ordinat* to export (**vers,** to).

exposant, -ante [ɛkspozɑ̃, -ɑ̃t] **1** *n* **(a)** *Jur* petitioner, deponent; **(b)** (*artiste, firme etc*) exhibitor. **2** *nm* **(a)** *Math* exponent, (power) index; **(b)** *Typ* (*chiffre, lettre*) superscript, superior.

exposé [ɛkspoze] *nm* **(a)** statement, account, report (*of facts, situation etc*); **faire un e. des faits,** to give an account of the facts; **e. verbal (de mission),** briefing; **donner un e. d'un projet,** to sketch out a plan; **(b)** (*discours*) (short) talk; **faire un e.,** to give a (short) talk.

exposer [ɛkspoze] **1** *vt* **(a)** (*montrer*) to exhibit, to show, to display (*goods, works of art etc*); **objet exposé,** exhibit; **être exposé (sur un lit de parade),** to lie in state; **e. des marchandises en vente** *ou* **à la devanture,** to display goods for sale;

(b) (*expliquer*) to set out, to unfold, to expound (*plans, reasons, problem etc*); **je leur ai exposé ma situation,** I explained my situation to them;

(c) (*présenter*) to expose (**à la chaleur/lumière/***etc*, to heat/light/*etc*); to expose (*s.o.*), to lay (*s.o.*) open (**à la critique/un danger/***etc*, to criticism/danger/*etc*); *Hist* to expose (*newborn child*); **exposé à tous les vents,** exposed *or* open to the four winds; *Phot* **e. un film,** to expose a film; **maison exposée au nord,** house facing north;

(d) (*risquer*) to hazard, to risk (*one's life, honour etc*); **e. qn,** to put s.o. in danger;

2 s'exposer *vpr* to put oneself in danger; **s'e. à des critiques,** to lay oneself open *or* expose oneself to criticism; **il s'expose à des poursuites,** he is laying himself open to prosecution; **il s'expose à devenir ridicule,** he is in danger of becoming ridiculous.

exposition [ɛkspozisjɔ̃] *nf* **(a)** (*action de montrer*) display(ing), showing (*of goods, works of art, flowers etc*); exposition (*of Sacrament*); lying in state (*of body*); **salle d'e.,** exhibition room; *Can* showroom; **(b)** (*salon, foire*) exhibition, show; **e. interprofessionnelle,** trade exhibition *or* show; **e. universelle,** world fair; **(c)** (*au froid, danger etc*) exposure (**à,** to); **(d)** exposition (*of facts, reasons etc*); **(e)** *Littér Mus* exposition; **(f)** aspect, exposure (*of house*); **(g)** *Phot* exposure.

exprès¹, -esse [ɛksprɛs] **1** *adj* (*explicite*) express, distinct, explicit (*order, warning etc*); **volonté expresse,** express wish; **défense expresse de fumer,** smoking strictly prohibited. **2** *adj inv & nm Arch* **(lettre/paquet) e.,** special delivery *or Br* express letter/parcel; **par e.,** (by) special delivery, *Br* (by) express.

exprès² [ɛksprɛ] *adv* (*à dessein*) on purpose, intentionally, deliberately; (*spécialement*) specially; **outil façonné e.,** specially designed tool; **elle est sortie e. pour l'acheter,** she went out specially *or* expressly to buy it; **je ne l'ai pas fait e.,** I didn't mean to do it, I didn't do it on purpose *or* intentionally *or* deliberately; **il fait e. de vous contredire,** he makes a point of contradicting you; **c'est fait e.,** it's (quite) intentional *or* deliberate; **on dirait un fait e.,** of course it WOULD happen, you'd think it was done on purpose; *Iron* **par un fait e., il pleuvait,** as if on purpose, it rained.

express [ɛksprɛs] **1** *adj* **(a)** fast (*train*); **divorce e.,** quickie divorce; **(b)** espresso (*coffee*). **2** *nm* **(a)** (*train*) fast train; **(b)** (*café*) espresso (coffee).

expressément [ɛksprɛsemɑ̃] *adv* **(a)** expressly (*forbidden*); **(b)** (*spécialement*) expressly, specially.

expressif, -ive [ɛksprɛsif, -iv] *adj* expressive (*language, music, glance, face etc*); *Mus* **clavier e.,** swell (organ).

expression [ɛksprɛsjɔ̃] *nf* **(a)** expression (*of feeling, thought opinion, pain etc*); expression, look (*on face*); **au-delà de toute e.,** (*used adjectivally*) inexpressible; (*used adverbally*) inexpressibly; **recevez l'e. de mes sentiments distingués,** (*en fin de lettre*) yours faithfully; **l'e. de son visage ne changea pas,** his expression didn't change; **visage d'une e. triste,** face with a sad expression; **auteur d'e. anglaise,** author writing in English; **sans e.,** expressionless; *Mus* **jouer avec e.,** to play with expression *or* feeling; *Mus* **signe d'e.,** expression mark; **boîte d'e.,** swell box (*of organ*);

(b) (*locution*) expression, phrase; **e. familière,** colloquialism, colloquial expression;

(c) *Math* expression; **e. algébrique,** algebraic expression; **la famille, réduite à sa plus simple e.,** the family, reduced to its simplest expression;

(d) squeezing out (*of juice*).

expressionnisme [ɛksprɛsjɔnism] *nm Beaux-Arts* expressionism.

expressionniste [ɛksprɛsjɔnist] *adj & n Beaux-Arts* expressionist.

exprimable [ɛksprimabl] *adj* expressible.

exprimer [ɛksprime] **1** *vt* **(a)** to express (*feeling, thought, opinion, pain etc*) (**à qn,** to s.o.); (*of look, gesture etc*) to express, to show (*pain, pleasure etc*); **(b)** *Math* to express (*quantity, value etc*); **(c)** (*extraire en pressant*) to squeeze out (*juice*) (**de,** from). **2 s'exprimer** *vpr* (*en parlant, en*

agissant etc) to express oneself; **si l'on peut s'e. ainsi,** if one may put it this way *or* like this.
expropriation [ɛksprɔprijasjɔ̃] *nf Jur* expropriation (*of property, owner*).
exproprier [ɛksprɔprije] *vt* (*impf & pr sub* **n. expropriions**) *Jur* to expropriate (*property*).
expulser [ɛkspylse] *vt* **(a)** to deport, to expel (*alien*); to evict (*tenant*); to eject (*heckler etc*); to expel (*pupil, student, party member etc*) (**de,** from); *Sp* to send off (*player*); **(b)** *Physiol* to expel.
expulsif, -ive [ɛkspylsif, -iv] *adj Méd* expulsive.
expulsion [ɛkspylsjɔ̃] *nf* **(a)** deportation (*of alien*); eviction (*of tenant*); ejection (*of heckler etc*); expulsion (*of pupil, party member etc*); *Sp* sending off (*of player*); **(b)** *Physiol* expulsion.
expurgation [ɛkspyrgasjɔ̃] *nf* expurgation, bowdlerizing (*of book etc*).
expurgatoire [ɛkspyrgatwar] *adj Hist Cathol* **Index e.,** expurgatory Index.
expurger [ɛkspyrʒe] *vt* (**j'expurgeai(s)**) to expurgate, to bowdlerize (*book etc*).
exquis [ɛkski] *adj* exquisite (*beauty, manners, taste, food etc*); delightful (*person, smile, weather*).
exsangue [ɛksɑ̃g, ɛgzɑ̃g] *adj* anaemic, *US* anemic (*patient, organ, face etc*); *Fig* anaemic, bloodless (*work of art etc*).
exsudation [ɛksydasjɔ̃] *nf* exudation.
exsuder [ɛksyde] *vt & vi* to exude.
extase [ɛkstɑz] *nf* **(a)** *Rel Psy* ecstasy, trance; **(b)** (*admiration*) rapture, ecstasy; **être en e. devant qch,** to be enraptured by *or* in ecstasies *or* in raptures over sth.
extasié [ɛkstɑzje] *adj* ecstatic, enraptured (*person, look*).
extasier (s') [sɛkstɑzje] *vpr* (*impf & pr sub* **n. n. extasiions**) to be in *or* go into ecstasies *or* raptures (**sur,** about; **devant,** over).
extatique [ɛkstatik] *adj* ecstatic, enraptured (*person, look*); ecstatic (*state, vision*).
extenseur [ɛkstɑ̃sœr] **1** *adj Anat* extensor (*muscle*). **2** *nm* **(a)** *Gym* (chest) expander; **(b)** *Anat* extensor.
extensible [ɛkstɑ̃sibl] *adj* extensible; tensile (*substance*); expanding (*bracelet etc*); stretch(able) (*garment*); *Fig* flexible (*idea, definition etc*).
extensif, -ive [ɛkstɑ̃sif, -iv] *adj* **(a)** tensile (*force etc*); **(b)** *Agr* **culture extensive,** extensive farming; **(c) sens e.,** extended meaning (*of word*).
extension [ɛkstɑ̃sjɔ̃] *nf* **(a)** stretching, extension (*of muscle, arm, spring etc*); **(b)** *Fig* enlargement, expansion (*of territory, firm etc*); spread (*of a disease, language, fire etc*); *Ordinat* **carte d'e.,** expansion board; **donner de l'e. à une loi,** to extend a law; **prendre de l'e.,** (*of business etc*) to expand, to grow; (*of disease, fire*) to spread; **(c)** extended meaning (*of word*); **par e.,** by extension.
exténuant [ɛkstenɥɑ̃] *adj* exhausting (*work etc*).
exténuation [ɛkstenɥasjɔ̃] *nf* exhaustion (*of body, mind*).
exténuer [ɛkstenɥe] **1** *vt* to exhaust, to tire (*s.o.*) out; **être exténué (de fatigue),** to be tired out *or* worn out. **2 s'exténuer** *vpr* to tire oneself out (**à faire,** doing).
extérieur [ɛksterjœr] **1** *adj* **(a)** exterior, outer, external (*surface, part etc*); outside (*staircase, interests etc*); outer (*harbour, boulevards*); outward, external (*sign, appearance etc*); external (*factor, cause*); *Péj* superficial (*kindness, pity etc*); **le côté e. de qch,** the outer side *or* outside of sth; **le monde e.,** the outside world; **fonds extérieurs,** external financing; **sans aide extérieure,** without outside help, *F* under one's own steam;
(b) (*étranger*) external, foreign (*trade, policy etc*).
2 *nm* **(a)** exterior, outside (*of building, box etc*); **vu de l'e.,** seen from the outside; **à l'e.,** (*de bâtiment*) outside; (*de boîte etc*) on the outside; **à l'intérieur et à l'e.,** inside and out; *Sp* **match à l'e.,** away match; **à l'e. de la gare,** outside the station;
(b) l'e., (*pays étrangers*) foreign countries; **à l'e.,** abroad; **de l'e.,** from abroad;
(c) (*apparence*) (outward) appearance; **juger de l'e.,** to judge by (external) appearances; **avoir un e. imposant,** to have an imposing appearance, to look imposing;
(d) *Cin* location shot; **il tourne en e.,** he's on location.
extérieurement [ɛksterjœrmɑ̃] *adv* **(a)** (*dehors*) externally, on the outside; **(b)** (*en apparence*) on the surface, in appearance.
extériorisation [ɛksterjɔrizasjɔ̃] *nf* manifestation, display (*of feeling*); *Psy* exteriorization, externalization.
extérioriser [ɛksterjɔrize] **1** *vt* **(a)** *Psy* to exteriorize, to externalize; **(b)** to manifest, to display (*feeling*). **2 s'extérioriser** *vpr* (*of feeling*) to manifest itself; (*of person*) to express oneself.
exterminateur, -trice [ɛkstɛrminatœr, -tris] **1** *adj* exterminating (*angel etc*). **2** *n* exterminator, destroyer.
extermination [ɛkstɛrminasjɔ̃] *nf* extermination, destruction (*of race etc*); **camp d'e.,** extermination camp.
exterminer [ɛkstɛrmine] **1** *vt* to exterminate, to destroy, to wipe out (*race, army etc*). **2 s'exterminer** *vpr F* **s'e. à faire qch,** (*s'épuiser*) to kill oneself doing sth.
externat [ɛkstɛrna] *nm* **(a)** (*école*) day school; **(b)** (*élèves*) day pupils; **(c)** *Méd* non-resident (medical) studentship.
externe [ɛkstɛrn] **1** *adj* **(a)** external, outside, outer (*part, surface etc*); external (*cause*); **côté e.,** outside; **angle e.,** exterior angle; *Ordinat* **dispositif e.,** external device; *Pharm* **à usage e.,** for external use only; **(b) élève e.,** day pupil. **2** *n* **(a)** (*élève*) day pupil; **(b)** *Méd* non-resident (medical) student, *Am* extern.
exterritorial, -aux [ɛksteritɔrjal, -o] *adj* ex(tra)territorial.
exterritorialité [ɛksteritɔrjalite] *nf* ex(tra)territoriality.
extincteur, -trice [ɛkstɛ̃ktœr, -tris] **1** *adj* extinguishing (*material etc*). **2** *nm* **e. (d'incendie),** fire extinguisher; **e. automatique (d'incendie),** fire sprinkler.
extinction [ɛkstɛ̃ksjɔ̃] *nf* **(a)** extinguishing, putting out (*of fire etc*); *Mil* **e. des feux,** lights out; **(b)** *Jur* extinguishment (*of debt, right etc*); **(c)** dying out, extinction (*of race, species*); **espèce menacée d'e.,** endangered species; **(d) e. de voix,** loss of voice; **attraper une e. de voix,** to lose one's voice; **faire qch jusqu'à l'e. de ses forces,** to do sth to the point of exhaustion.
extirpateur [ɛkstirpatœr] *nm Agr* (*instrument*) weeder.
extirpation [ɛkstirpasjɔ̃] *nf* eradication; rooting out (*of plant, prejudice etc*); *Chir* extirpation (*of tumour etc*).
extirper [ɛkstirpe] *vt* to eradicate, to root out (*plant, Fig evil, prejudice etc*); *F* **e. qn de son lit,** to drag s.o. out of bed; *F* **e. de l'argent/un renseignement à qn,** to squeeze *or Br* winkle money/a piece of information out of s.o..
extorquer [ɛkstɔrke] *vt* to extort, to wring (*money, promise etc*) (**à qn,** from s.o.).
extorqueur, -euse [ɛkstɔrkœr, -øz] *n* extortioner.
extorsion [ɛkstɔrsjɔ̃] *nf* extortion.
extra [ɛkstra] **1** *nm inv* **(a)** (*chose extraordinaire*) something special; *Culin* (special) treat; **faire/s'offrir un e.,** to do/treat oneself to something special; **(b)** (*serviteur*) extra help *or* hand; **faire des e. chez qn,** to do occasional work for s.o.. **2** *adj inv* (*de qualité supérieure*) first-class, first-rate (*wine, meal, garment etc*); *F* (*remarquable*) fantastic, fabulous (*person, novel, holiday etc*).
extra- [ɛkstra] *préf* extra-.
extracteur [ɛkstraktœr] *nm* (*appareil, instrument*) extractor.
extractible [ɛkstraktibl] *adj* removable (*car radio etc*).
extractif, -ive [ɛkstraktif, -iv] *adj* extractive (*industry etc*).
extraction [ɛkstraksjɔ̃] *nf* **(a)** extraction (*of teeth*); extraction, mining (*of coal, ore*); quarrying (*of stone*); extraction (*of metal from ore, oil, gas etc*); *Chir* removal (*of bullet etc*); *Min* **machine d'e.,** winding gear; **(b)** *Math* extraction (*of root*); **(c)** *Fig* **de haute/basse e.,** of noble/humble extraction *or* birth.
extrader [ɛkstrade] *vt* to extradite; **e. qn vers la France,** to extradite s.o. to France.
extradition [ɛkstradisjɔ̃] *nf* extradition.
extrados [ɛkstrado] *nm* **(a)** *Archit* extrados (*of arch*); **(b)** *Av* upper surface (*of wing*).
extra-fin [ɛkstrafɛ̃] *adj* **(a)** (*petit, fin*) extra-fine (*peas, needle etc*); **(b)** *Com* (*de qualité supérieure*) superfine, top-quality (*chocolates etc*).
extra-fort [ɛkstrafɔr] **1** *adj* extra-strong. **2** *nm Couture* bias binding.
extra(-)galactique [ɛkstragalaktik] *adj Astron* extragalactic.
extraire [ɛkstrɛr] *v* (*conj like* **traire**) **1** *vt* to pull out, to draw out (*pin, nail etc*); to extract, to pull out (*tooth*); to extract, to mine (*coal, ore*); to quarry (*stone*); to extract (*metal from ore, oil, gas, juice etc*); to extract, to excerpt (*quotation, passage etc*); **e. des plants,** to lift seedlings; *Math* **e. une racine,** to extract a root; **on lui a extrait une balle du bras,** a bullet was removed from *or* taken out of his arm. **2 s'extraire** *vpr* **s'e. d'une position difficile,** to get out *or* wriggle out of an awkward position; **s'e. de sa voiture,** to wriggle out *or* squeeze out of one's car.
extrait [ɛkstrɛ] *nm* **(a)** (*produit*) extract, essence; **e. de viande,** meat extract; **e. de lavande,** lavender essence; **(b)** extract, excerpt (*from book, speech, author etc*); *Jur Fin* abstract (*of deed, account*); **e. de naissance,** birth

certificate.
extrajudiciaire [ɛkstraʒydisjɛr] *adj* extrajudicial.
extra-lucide [ɛkstralysid] *adj & nf* **(voyante) e.-l.**, clairvoyant; (*pl extra-lucides*).
extraordinaire [ɛkstraɔrdinɛr] *adj* **(a)** (*spécial*) extraordinary, special (*meeting, measures etc*); special (*messenger, mission*); **assemblée générale e.**, extraordinary general meeting; **ambassadeur e.**, ambassador extraordinary; **frais** *ou* **dépenses extraordinaires,** (*non prévues*) extras; (*uniques*) non-recurring expenditure; **(b)** (*étonnant*) extraordinary, astonishing (*news, event etc*); **cela n'a rien d'e.**, that's nothing out of the ordinary; **(c)** (*remarquable*) extraordinary, remarkable, outstanding (*person, beauty, success*); extraordinary (*heat, price*); **(d)** *F* (*très bon*) really good (*book, wine etc*); **(e) par e.**, by a *or* some remote chance.
extraordinairement [ɛkstraɔrdinɛrmɑ̃] *adv* extraordinarily.
extra-parlementaire [ɛkstraparləmɑ̃tɛr] *adj* extra-parliamentary.
extra-plat [ɛkstrapla] *adj* slimline (*watch, suitcase etc*).
extrapolation [ɛkstrapɔlɑsjɔ̃] *nf* extrapolation.
extrapoler [ɛkstrapɔle] *vt* to extrapolate (**à partir de,** from).
extra-scolaire [ɛkstraskɔlɛr] *adj* extra-curricular (*activities etc*).
extra-sec [ɛkstrasɛk] *adj* extra-dry, very dry (*wine*).
extra(-)sensoriel, -ielle [ɛkstrasɑ̃sɔrjɛl] *adj Psy* extrasensory (*perception etc*).
extrasyndical, -aux [ɛkstrasɛ̃dikal, -o] *adj* non-union.
extra(-)terrestre [ɛkstraterɛstr] *adj & n* extraterrestrial; (*pl extra(-)terrestres*).
extra-territorial, -aux [ɛkstrateritɔrjal, -o] *adj* extraterritorial.
extra-territorialité [ɛkstrateritɔrjalite] *nf* extraterritoriality.
extra-utérin [ɛkstrayterɛ̃] *adj Méd* **grossesse e.-utérine,** ectopic pregnancy.
extravagamment [ɛkstravagamɑ̃] *adv Litt & Vieilli* extravagantly.
extravagance [ɛkstravagɑ̃s] *nf* **(a)** extravagance (*of idea, behaviour, costume etc*); eccentricity (*of person*); exorbitance (*of price*); immoderateness (*of desire*); **(b)** (*action, remarque*) extravagant thing; **il a dit un tas d'extravagances,** he talked a lot of nonsense.
extravagant, -ante [ɛkstravagɑ̃, -ɑ̃t] **1** *adj* extravagant (*idea, plan, behaviour, costume etc*); eccentric (*person*); exorbitant (*price, demand*); immoderate (*desire*). **2** *n* eccentric (person).
extravaguer [ɛkstravage] *vi Vieilli* (*parler*) to rave, to talk nonsense; (*agir*) to act wildly *or* extravagantly.
extravasation [ɛkstravɑzɑsjɔ̃] *nf Physiol* extravasation (*of blood etc*).
extravaser (s') [sɛkstravɑze] *vpr Physiol* (*of blood etc*) to extravasate.
extraversion [ɛkstravɛrsjɔ̃] *nf Psy* extroversion.
extraverti, -ie [ɛkstravɛrti] *adj & n Psy* extrovert.
extrême [ɛkstrɛm] **1** *adj* **(a)** far, extreme, farthest (*point, limit etc*); extreme (*youth, old age*); **dans l'e. lointain,** in the far *or* extreme distance; *Pol* **e. droite/gauche,** far *or* extreme right/left; **(b)** (*intense*) extreme, intense (*cold, pleasure etc*); **(c)** (*excessif*) extreme, drastic, severe (*measure, solution*); extreme (*case, situation, opinion*); **elle est e. en tout,** she is extreme in everything; **être e. dans ses opinions,** to hold extreme opinions. **2** *nm* extreme; **les extrêmes,** the extremes (*of heat and cold, Math of a proportion*); **il passe d'un e. à l'autre,** he goes from one extreme to the other; **scrupuleux à l'e.,** scrupulous in the extreme *or* to a fault; **pousser les choses à l'e.,** to take *or* carry matters to extremes; *Prov* **les extrêmes se touchent,** extremes meet.
extrêmement [ɛkstrɛmmɑ̃] *adv* extremely, exceedingly.
extrême-onction [ɛkstrɛmɔ̃ksjɔ̃] *nf Rel* extreme unction.
Extrême-Orient (l') [lɛkstrɛmɔrjɑ̃] *nm* the Far East.
extrême-oriental, -ale, -aux [ɛkstrɛmɔrjɑ̃tal, -o] **1** *adj* Far Eastern. **2** *n* **E.-O.**, (Far Eastern) Oriental.
extrémisme [ɛkstremism] *nm* extremism.
extrémiste [ɛkstremist] *adj & n* extremist.
extrémité [ɛkstremite] *nf* **(a)** end (*of lake, road, leg, rope etc*); tip (*of finger, wing etc*); point (*of needle, sword etc*); **aux extrémités de la ligne,** at the ends of the line; **les extrémités de la terre,** the far *or* distant ends *or* corners of the earth; **les extrémités,** (*pieds et mains*) the extremities, the hands and feet; **(b)** (*excès*) **extrémité(s),** extremes; **pousser qch à l'e.,** to carry *or* take sth to extremes; **pousser qn à une e.** *ou* **à des extrémités,** to drive s.o. to extremes; **en venir à des extrémités,** to resort to extreme measures; (*à la violence*) to resort to violence; **(c)** (*situation désespérée*) extremity; **dans cette e.**, in this extremity; **réduit à l'e.**, in dire distress *or* straits; **être à la dernière** *ou* **à toute e.**, to be at the point of death, to be close to death.
extrinsèque [ɛkstrɛ̃sɛk] *adj* extrinsic; **valeur e.**, (*de monnaie*) face value.
extroverti, -ie [ɛkstrɔvɛrti] *adj & n Psy* extrovert, extravert.
extrusion [ɛkstryzjɔ̃] *nf Tech* extrusion.
exubérance [ɛgsyberɑ̃s] *nf* exuberance (*of person, vegetation, style etc*).
exubérant [ɛgzyberɑ̃] *adj* exuberant (*person, vegetation, joy, style etc*).
exultation [ɛgzyltɑsjɔ̃] *nf* exultation.
exulter [ɛgzylte] *vi* to exult, to rejoice (**de faire,** in doing).
exutoire [ɛgzytwar] *nm* outlet (**à sa colère/***etc*, for one's anger/*etc*).
ex-voto [ɛksvɔto] *nm inv Rel* ex-voto, votive offering.
eye-liner [ajlajnœr] *nm* eyeliner; (*pl eye-liners*).
Ézéchiel [eʒekjɛl] *nm* Ezekiel.

F

F, f [ɛf] *nm inv* (the letter) F, f; **un F2/3/***etc*, (*appartement*) a two-/three-/*etc* roomed flat *or Am* apartment.
f. (a) *abrév* **franc(s)**; **(b)** *abrév* **féminin**.
F. *abrév* **Fahrenheit**.
fa [fa] *nm inv Mus* (*note*) F; (*quand on chante la gamme*) fa; **clef de fa,** bass clef, F clef.
f. à b. [ɛfabe] *Com* (*abrév* **franco à bord**) f.o.b..
fable [fabl] *nf* **(a)** (*légende*) fable; **célèbre dans la f.,** famous in fable; **(b)** (*invention*) story; **c'est pure f.,** it's pure invention; **être la f. de toute la ville,** to be the laughing stock of the whole town.
fablier [fablije] *nm* book of fables.
fabricant, -ante [fabrikɑ̃, -ɑ̃t] *n* maker, manufacturer; **f. de chapeaux,** hat maker *or* manufacturer; **f. d'automobiles,** car maker *or* manufacturer; **gros/petit f.,** large/small manufacturer; **le plus grand f.,** the market leader.
fabricateur, -trice [fabrikatœr, -tris] *n* fabricator (*of lies etc*); **f. de fausse monnaie,** counterfeiter, forger; **f. d'un document,** forger of a document.
fabrication [fabrikasjɔ̃] *nf* **(a)** (*à la main*) making; *Ind* manufacture, manufacturing; **f. artisanale,** production by craftsmen; **f. industrielle,** industrial manufacture; **défaut de f.,** manufacturing defect; **f. en série,** mass production; *Péj* **la f. de romans,** the churning out of novels; **n'employer que la meilleure f.,** to employ only the best workmanship; **article de f. française,** article made in France; **(b)** fabrication (*of lies etc*); forging (*of document, counterfeit money*); **c'est de la f.,** it's pure fabrication; **(c)** *Typ* layout.
fabrique [fabrik] *nf* **(a)** (*fabrication*) manufacture; **prix de f.,** manufacturer's *or* factory price; **marque de f.,** trademark; **secret de f.,** trade secret; **(b)** (*établissement*) factory, works; **f. de papier,** paper mill; **valeur en f.,** cost price; **(c)** *Rel* **(conseil de) f.,** = (parochial) church council, vestry.
fabriquer [fabrike] *vt* **(a)** *Ind* to manufacture (*cloth, bicycles etc*); **f. des véhicules en série,** to mass-produce vehicles; **(b)** (*artisanalement*) to make (*sth*); **nous fabriquons nos produits à la main,** we make our products by hand; *Fig* **le coach qui a fabriqué le champion de ski,** the coach who created the ski champion; **(c)** (*pour tromper*) to fabricate, to make up (*lie etc*); **f. de la fausse monnaie,** to counterfeit *or* forge money; **histoire fabriquée de toutes pièces,** completely fabricated *or* made-up story; **(d)** *F* (*faire*) to do; **qu'est-ce qu'il fabrique?,** what's he up to?, what's he doing?
fabulateur, -trice [fabylatœr, -tris] **1** *adj* fantasizing; *Psy* confabulatory (*tendency etc*). **2** *n* fantasist.
fabulation [fabylasjɔ̃] *nf* fantasizing; *Psy* confabulation.
fabuler [fabyle] *vi* to fantasize; *Psy* to confabulate.
fabuleusement [fabyløzmɑ̃] *adv* fabulously.
fabuleux, -euse [fabylø, -øz] *adj* **(a)** fabulous, mythical (*beast*); mythical, legendary (*character, exploits etc*); **(b)** *Fig* (*incroyable*) fabulous, fantastic, incredible (*adventure, weather, sum of money etc*).
fabuliste [fabylist] *nm* fabulist.
fac [fak] *nf F* university; **quand j'étais à la f.** *ou* **en f.,** when I was a student *or* at university.
F.A.C. [ɛfase] *nm Admin abrév* **fonds d'aide et de coopération**.
façade [fasad] *nf* **(a)** (*de bâtiment*) façade, front; **hôtel en f. sur la place,** hotel facing the square; **(b)** (*apparence*) pretence, façade, show (**de,** of); **elle garde toujours une f. sérieuse,** she always maintains a serious appearance *or* exterior; **générosité/patriotisme/***etc* **de f.,** sham generosity/patriotism/*etc*; **(c)** *F* (*visage*) **se refaire la f.,** (*se maquiller*) to do *or* put on one's face; **démolir la f. à qn,** to smash s.o.'s face in.
face [fas] *nf* **(a)** (*visage*) face; **jeter la vérité/des accusations à la f. de qn,** to throw the truth/accusations in s.o.'s face; **les blessés de la f.,** those with facial injuries; **sauver la f.,** to save (one's) face; **perdre la f.,** to lose face; **tomber f. contre terre,** to fall flat on one's face; *Fig* **crier à la f. du monde,** to shout to the whole world;
(b) la f. des eaux/de la terre, the face of the waters/of the earth; *Fig* **la f. du monde,** the face of the world;
(c) flat (*of sword blade*); side (*of lens, gramophone record*); obverse (*of medal*); head (side) (*of coin*); **f.!,** (*en jouant à pile ou face*) heads!; **f. avant,** front; **f. arrière,** back; **polyèdre à douze faces,** twelve-sided polyhedron; *Ordinat* **à deux faces,** double-sided; **tissu (à) double f.,** reversible fabric; **ruban adhésif à double f.,** double-sided adhesive tape; **considérer qch sous toutes ses faces,** to consider sth from all sides *or* from every angle; **change le disque de f.!,** turn the record over!;
(d) faire f. à, to face, to be facing *or* opposite; *Fig* to meet (*liabilities, expenses, needs*); to face up to (*situation, difficulties*); **il faut bien faire f.,** one has to face up to things;
(e) portrait de f., full-face portrait; **vue de f.,** front view; **place de f.,** *Rail* seat facing the engine; *Th* front-facing seat; **les deux maisons se font f.,** the two houses face each other *or* are opposite each other; **se présenter de f.,** to be face on; **il l'a attaquée de f.,** he attacked her from the front; *Fig* he attacked her openly; **la maison (d')en f.,** the house opposite; **regarder qn (bien) en f.,** to look s.o. (full *or* straight) in the face; **il n'ose pas le lui dire en f.,** he dare not tell him to his face; **regarder les choses/la mort en f.,** to face facts/death; **en f. de,** opposite; **on est en f. d'un problème difficile,** we are faced with a difficult problem; **les maisons en f. de l'école** *ou F* **en f. l'école,** the houses opposite the school; **en f. du professeur, il change d'attitude,** in front of the teacher his attitude changes; **en f. l'un de l'autre, l'un en f. de l'autre,** opposite each other, facing each other;
(f) f. à, facing; **f. à cette situation, on n'avait pas le choix,** faced with that situation we had no choice; *Rail* **place f. à l'arrière,** seat with back to the engine; **f. à f.,** face to face (**avec,** with); **mettre deux témoins f. à f.,** to bring two witnesses face to face; **on s'est retrouvé f. à f.,** we found ourselves face to face.
face-à-face [fasafas] *nm inv TV etc* face-to-face encounter *or* debate.
face-à-main [fasamɛ̃] *nm* lorgnette; (*pl faces-à-main*).
facétie [fasesi] *nf* joke; **dire des facéties,** to crack jokes; **faire des facéties à qn,** to play jokes *or* pranks on s.o..
facétieux, -ieuse [fasesjø, -jøz] *adj* facetious.
facette [fasɛt] *nf* facet (*of diamond, insect's eye*); *Fig* facet (*of personality, problem etc*); **(taillé) à facettes,** (cut) in facets, facetted.
facetter [fasete] *vt* to facet (*diamond etc*).
fâché [faʃe] *adj* **(a)** (*mécontent*) angry, annoyed; **être f. contre qn,** to be angry *or* annoyed with s.o.; **être f. avec qn,** to have fallen out with s.o.; *F* **elle est fâchée avec les maths,** she can't get on with maths; **(b)** (*désolé*) sorry; **être f. de qch/pour qn,** to be sorry about sth/for s.o.; *Iron* **je ne suis pas f. que ça soit terminé,** I'm not exactly sorry *or* sad that it has finished.
fâcher [faʃe] **1** *vt* **(a)** (*rendre mécontent*) to anger, to annoy, to make (*s.o.*) angry; **(b)** (*affliger*) to grieve (*s.o.*). **2 se fâcher** *vpr* **(a)** (*se mettre en colère*) to get angry *or* annoyed, to lose one's temper; **attention! je vais me f.!,** be careful or I'll get angry!; **se f. contre qn,** to get annoyed *or* angry with s.o.; **(b)** (*se brouiller*) to fall out, to quarrel (**avec qn,** with s.o.).
fâcherie [faʃri] *nf* quarrel, disagreement.
fâcheusement [faʃøzmɑ̃] *adv* annoyingly.
fâcheux, -euse [faʃø, -øz] **1** *adj* annoying, unfortunate (*event, matter, complication, change etc*); awkward, unfortunate (*position, situation*); disturbing, distressing

(*news*); unfortunate (*example*); **c'est f.!**, what a nuisance!, how annoying! **2** *n* (*importun*) nuisance.

facho [faʃo] *adj & n F Péj* fascist.

facial, -iaux [fasjal, -jo] *adj* facial (*muscle, angle etc*); **massage f.**, facial *or* face massage.

faciès [fasjɛs] *nm* **(a)** (*aspect du visage*) features; *Méd etc* facies; **(b)** *Bot Géol* facies.

facile [fasil] **1** *adj* **(a)** easy (*work, problem, life etc*); **chose f. à faire,** thing easy to do *or* easily done; **c'est f. à dire, c'est plus f. à dire qu'à faire,** it's easier said than done; **avoir la vie f.**, to have an easy life; **c'est f. comme bonjour,** it's as easy as pie, it's child's play; **il lui est f. de le faire,** it's easy for him (to do it); **f. d'emploi,** easy to use; **d'une mise en place f.**, easily installed; **besognes faciles,** light *or* easy tasks;

(b) easy-going; **homme f. à vivre/en affaires/à travailler,** man easy to get along with/to deal with/to work with; **f. à émouvoir,** easily moved; **cet enfant est f.**, this child is no problem; *Péj Vieilli* **femme f.**, woman of easy virtue;

(c) (*superficiel*) facile (*joke, literature, style etc*); **je n'ai pas la parole f.**, words do not come easily to me; **il n'a pas l'argent f.!**, he's not forthcoming with his money!; **elle a les larmes faciles,** she is easily moved to tears.

2 *adv* (*au moins*) easily, at least; **on met trois jours f. pour traverser l'île,** it takes easily *or* at least three days to cross the island.

facilement [fasilmɑ̃] *adv* easily; **je mettrai f. deux jours pour le faire,** it'll take me easily *or* at least two days to do it.

facilité [fasilite] *nf* **(a)** easiness (*of task, problem etc*); (*en faisant qch*) ease; **avec f.**, easily, with ease; **c'est une solution de f.**, it's the easy solution *or* way out; **(b)** (*moyen, occasion*) **avoir la f. de faire qch,** to have the opportunity of doing sth; *Com* **facilités de paiement,** easy (payment) terms; *Banque* **facilités de crédit,** credit facilities; *Banque* **facilités de caisse,** overdraft facilities; **facilités de transport,** transport facilities; **(c)** (*aptitude*) aptitude, talent (**pour qch,** for sth); **écrire avec f.**, to write fluently *or* with ease; **f. à faire qch,** aptitude for doing sth; **f. de parole,** fluency; **(d)** (*complaisance*) readiness, willingness (**à faire,** to do).

faciliter [fasilite] *vt* to facilitate, to make (*sth*) easier; **f. qch à qn,** to make sth easier for s.o.; **cela ne va pas f. les choses,** it won't make things (any) easier.

façon [fasɔ̃] *nf* **(a)** (*manière de faire qch*) way, manner; **vivre à la f. des sauvages,** to live like savages; **il n'y a pas trente-six façons de le faire,** there are no two ways of doing it; **avoir une f. à soi de faire qch,** to have one's own way of doing sth; **je le ferai à ma f.**, I shall do it (in) my own way; **f. de parler,** manner of speaking; **ce n'est pas ma f. de faire,** (*mais je n'ai rien à dire*) it's not how I'd do things; **ils agissent tous de la même f.**, they all act alike *or* in the same way; **elle a une curieuse f. de voir les choses,** she has a strange way of looking at things; **de la bonne f.**, properly, nicely; **la f. dont l'anglais est enseigné,** the way (in which) English is taught;

(b) de cette f., (in) this way, thus; **venez avec nous, de cette f. cela ne vous coûtera rien,** come with us, that way it won't cost you anything; **d'une f. générale, on peut dire que ...**, generally speaking, one can say that ...; **de f. ou d'autre, d'une f. ou d'une autre,** one way or another, somehow or other; **de toute f. j'irai,** anyhow or in any case I shall go; **en aucune f.!**, not at all!, by no means!; **cela ne me dérange en aucune f.**, it doesn't disturb me in any way;

(c) de f. à, so as to; **parlez de f. à vous faire comprendre,** speak so that you can be understood; **elle parle de f. à ce que tout le monde l'entende,** she speaks so that *or* in such a way that everyone can hear her;

(d) de (telle) f. que, so that; **parlez de f. qu'on vous comprenne,** speak so as to be understood; **il pleuvait de telle f. que je fus obligé de rentrer,** it was raining so hard that I had to go home; **il pleuvait, de f. que je fus obligé de rentrer,** it was raining, (and) so I had to go home;

(e) façons, (*comportement*) manner, ways; **en voilà des façons!**, what a way to behave!;

(f) sans façon(s), (*of person*) unaffected, straightforward; (*of manners*) rough and ready; **traiter qn sans f.**, to treat s.o. in an offhand manner; **un repas sans f.**, an unpretentious *or* a simple meal; **non merci, sans f.**, no thanks, really (not); **sans plus de façons,** without further *or* any more ado; **faire des façons,** to stand on ceremony, to make a fuss;

(g) (*exécution*) making, fashioning; (*style*) style; **f. d'un manteau,** making (up) of a coat; (*coupe*) cut of a coat; **matière et f.**, material and labour; **compter cinquante francs de f.**, to charge fifty francs for labour; **on travaille à f.**, (*annonce*) customers' own materials made up; **poème de sa f.**, poem of his own composition; **robe qui a bonne f.**, well-cut dress; *Agr* **donner une f. à la terre,** to cultivate the soil; **cuir f. porc,** imitation pigskin.

faconde [fakɔ̃d] *nf* fluency (*of speech*), volubility; *Péj* garrulousness; **avoir de la f.**, to be fluent *or* voluble; *Péj* to be garrulous.

façonnage [fasɔnaʒ] *nm* **(a)** (*action de travailler*) working, shaping (*of wood etc*); turning (*of something on lathe*); fashioning (*of clay etc*); **(b)** (*fabrication*) (*à la main*) making, fashioning; *Couture* making (up); *Ind* manufacturing; **(c)** *Fig* moulding, *US* molding, shaping (*of person, history etc*).

façonné [fasɔne] *adj Tex* figured (*fabric*).

façonnement [fasɔnmɑ̃] *nm* = **FAÇONNAGE.**

façonner [fasɔne] *vt* **(a)** (*travailler*) to work, to shape (*wood, metal, stone etc*); to turn (*sth on lathe*); to fashion (*clay etc*); *Agr* **f. la terre,** to work the soil; **(b)** (*fabriquer*) (*à la main*) to make, to fashion; *Couture* to make (up); *Ind* to manufacture; **(c)** *Fig Br* to mould, *US* to mold, to shape (*person, character, history etc*).

façonneur, -euse [fasɔnœr, -øz] *n* (*qui fabrique qch*) maker; *Fig* **f. de l'histoire,** shaper of history.

façonnier, -ière [fasɔnje, -jɛr] *adj* affected, mannered (*person*).

fac-similé [faksimile] *nm* facsimile, exact copy; (*pl fac-similés*).

factage [faktaʒ] *nm* **(a)** carriage (and delivery) (*of goods*); **payer le f.**, to pay the carriage; **(b)** delivery (*of letters etc*).

facteur [faktœr] *nm* **(a)** (*de la poste*) *Br* postman, *Am* mailman; **(b)** (*élément*) factor; **le f. chance/humain/temps,** the chance/human/time factor; *Méd* **f. rhésus,** rhesus factor; **(c)** *Math* factor; **f. premier/commun,** prime/common factor; **mettre un nombre en facteurs,** to factorize a number; **(d)** *Mus* (*fabricant*) maker; **f. d'orgues,** organ builder; **f. de pianos,** piano maker.

factice [faktis] *adj* **(a)** false, artificial (*object*); *Com* (*en vitrine*) dummy (*box of chocolates etc*); **cuir/diamant f.**, imitation leather/diamond; **(b)** *Fig* false, feigned (*joy, pity etc*); forced (*smile*).

factieux, -ieuse [faksjø, -jøz] **1** *adj* factious, seditious. **2** *n* troublemaker.

faction [faksjɔ̃] *nf* **(a)** *Mil* sentry duty, guard; **être de** *ou* **en f.**, to be on guard *or* on sentry duty; **mettre qn en f.**, to put s.o. on guard; **(b)** (*groupe*) faction; **la Constituante était divisée en factions,** the Constituent Assembly was broken up into factions.

factionnaire [faksjɔnɛr] *nm* (*sentinelle*) sentry, guard; **poser/relever un f.**, to post/relieve a sentry *or* guard.

factitif, -ive [faktitif, -iv] *adj Gram* causative, factitive.

factorerie [faktɔrəri] *nf Arch* foreign (trading) post.

factoriel, -ielle [faktɔrjɛl] *adj & nf Math* factorial.

factoring [faktɔriŋ] *nm Com* factoring.

factotum [faktɔtɔm] *nm* factotum.

factrice [faktris] *nf* postwoman, *US* mailwoman.

factuel, -elle [faktɥɛl] *adj* factual.

facturation [faktyrɑsjɔ̃] *nf* invoicing, billing; **(service de) f.**, invoice department.

facture¹ [faktyr] *nf* **(a)** (*style*) composition (*of music, poem, painting etc*); style, technique (*of artist etc*); **pardessus f. soignée,** carefully tailored overcoat; **(b)** *Mus* (*fabrication*) making (*of pianos etc*); building (*of organs*).

facture² *nf Com* invoice, bill (of sale); **faire** *ou* **dresser** *ou* **établir une f.**, to make out an invoice; **f. d'électricité/de gaz,** electricity/gas bill; **selon** *ou* **suivant f.**, as per invoice; *Écon* **la f. pétrolière de la France,** France's oil bill.

facturer [faktyre] *vt* to invoice (*goods*); **le papier nous a été facturé cent francs,** we were invoiced a hundred francs for the paper.

facturier, -ière [faktyrje, -jɛr] **1** *nm* (*livre*) sales book. **2** *n* (*employé*) invoice clerk.

facultatif, -ive [fakyltatif, -iv] *adj* optional; **arrêt f.**, (*annonce*) request stop.

facultativement [fakyltativmɑ̃] *adv* optionally.

faculté [fakylte] *nf* **(a)** (*don, capacité*) faculty, ability, power; **facultés de l'esprit** *ou* **intellectuelles,** intellectual faculties; **jouir de toutes ses facultés,** to be in possession of all one's faculties; **elle n'a plus toutes ses facultés,** she no longer has all her faculties; **homme doué de grandes facultés,** man of great abilities;

(b) (*droit*) right; (*possibilité*) option; **avoir la f. de faire**

qch, to have the right to do sth; to have the option of doing sth; **f. de rachat,** buy-back option;

(c) facultés, (*ressources*) resources, means; **elle dépense au-dessus de ses facultés,** she spends beyond her means;

(d) *Univ* faculty (*of arts, law etc*); **professeur de f.,** = (university) professor; **la F.,** the Faculty of Medicine; (*les médecins*) the medical profession; *F* **la F. m'interdit de boire,** I'm forbidden to drink — doctor's orders; *F* **quand j'étais à la** *ou* **en f.,** when I was at university, when I was a student; *F* **entrer en f.,** to go to university.

fada [fada] *F* **1** *adj* (*fou*) screwy, crazy. **2** *n* crackpot.

fadaise [fadɛz] *nf* silly remark; (*chose insignifiante*) trifle; **débiter des fadaises,** to talk rot *or* nonsense *or* twaddle.

fadasse [fadas] *adj F* insipid, bland (*taste, drink, food etc*); pale, washed-out (*colour*); dreary, dull (*book, style etc*).

fade [fad] *adj* insipid, bland, tasteless, flavourless, *US* flavorless (*dish, drink etc*); insipid, bland (*taste*); tame (*joke*); banal, bland (*compliments*); drab, washed-out (*colour*); stale (*smell*); dull, dreary (*book, conversation, style etc*); insipid (*beauty*).

fadé [fade] *adj F* **être f.,** (*remarquable*) to beat them all, to take the cake *or* the biscuit.

fadement [fadmɑ̃] *adv* insipidly.

fadeur [fadœr] *nf* **(a)** insipidness, blandness (*of dish, drink, taste etc*); tameness (*of joke*); banality (*of compliments*); drabness (*of colour*); staleness (*of smell*); dullness, dreariness (*of book, style etc*); insipidness (*of beauty*); **(b) fadeurs,** (*compliments*) banal *or* bland compliments; **dire des fadeurs à qn,** to pay s.o. banal *or* bland compliments.

fading [fadiŋ] *nm Rad* fading.

fafiot [fafjo] *nm Arg* banknote.

fagot [fago] *nm* bundle of firewood; *Fig* **sentir le f.,** to savour of heresy; *Fig* **bouteille de vin de derrière les fagots,** bottle of wine from the hidden store *or* kept for special occasions; *Fig F* **un repas de derrière les fagots,** an extra-special meal; **une idée de derrière les fagots,** a remarkable idea.

fagotage [fagɔtaʒ] *nm* **(a)** tying up (*of wood etc*) in bundles; **(b)** *Péj* (*accoutrement*) ridiculous get-up *or* rig-out.

fagoter [fagɔte] **1** *vt* **(a)** to tie up (*wood etc*) in bundles; **(b)** *Péj* (*accoutrer*) to rig *or* deck out (*child etc*); **mal/bizarrement fagoté,** badly/oddly dressed. **2 se fagoter** *vpr Péj* to rig *or* deck oneself out.

faiblard [fɛblar] *adj F* (a bit) weak, weakish.

faible [fɛbl] **1** *adj* **(a)** (*physiquement*) weak, feeble (*person, limbs etc*); weak (*heart, eyes, constitution*); weak, unstable (*arch, branch etc*); *Fig* weak (*country, army etc*); **être f. des jambes/du cœur/***etc*, to have weak legs/a weak heart/*etc*; **avoir la vue f.,** to have weak *or* poor eyesight; **f. d'esprit,** feeble-minded, mentally deficient; **le sexe f.,** the weaker sex; **une f. femme,** a helpless woman;

(b) (*intellectuellement*) weak, poor (*person, idea, style, film etc*); low (*intelligence*); **élève f. en chimie,** pupil weak *or* poor in *or* at chemistry; **cote/point f.,** weak side/point; **et le terme est f.!,** and that's putting it mildly!;

(c) (*moralement*) weak, soft (*person*); weak (*character*); **être f. avec qn,** to be weak *or* soft with s.o.; **f. de caractère,** weak-willed;

(d) (*léger*) weak, thin (*coffee, wine etc*); faint, quiet (*sound, voice*); faint, slight (*smell*); faint, dim (*light*); light (*wind*); *Mus* **temps f.,** weak *or* unaccented beat; **boisson f. en alcool,** low-alcohol drink; **f. en calories,** low-calorie;

(e) (*petit*) small (*quantity, majority etc*); slight (*advantage, difference, reaction, chance, hope*); low (*price, income, rent etc*); poor (*harvest, return*); low, slow (*speed*); **à une f. hauteur/profondeur,** not very high up/deep down; **cela ne vous en donne qu'une f. idée,** that gives you only a vague idea of it; *Nau* **f. tirant d'eau,** shallow draught;

(f) *Gram* weak (*verb, conjugation*).

2 *n* (*personne sans force morale*) weakling, weak person; **les faibles,** the weak; **les faibles d'esprit,** the feeble-minded.

3 *nm* **(a)** (*défaut*) weak point, weakness; **le f. chez moi, c'est ...,** my weak point *or* weakness is ...;

(b) (*penchant*) weakness; **avoir un f. pour qch/qn,** to have a weakness for sth/a soft spot for s.o.; **prendre qn par son f.,** to take advantage of s.o.'s weakness.

faiblement [fɛbləmɑ̃] *adv* (*résister, insister etc*) weakly, feebly; (*éclairer*) faintly, dimly; (*parler, crier*) quietly, faintly; (*entendre*) faintly; **f. attiré/parfumé/***etc*, slightly attracted/flavoured/*etc*.

faiblesse [fɛblɛs] *nf* **(a)** (*physique*) weakness, feebleness (*of person, limbs etc*); weakness (*of heart, eyesight, constitution etc*); weakness, unstableness (*of arch, branch etc*); *Fig* weakness (*of government, army etc*); (*syncope*) (sudden) faintness; **f. d'esprit,** feeble-mindedness, mental deficiency; **je tombais de f.,** I was ready to drop (with exhaustion); *Vieilli* **tomber en f.,** to swoon, to faint;

(b) (*intellectuelle*) weakness, poorness (*of pupil, argument, style etc*); **f. d'intelligence,** low intelligence;

(c) (*morale*) weakness (**envers qn,** towards s.o.); **f. de caractère,** weakness of character; **la f. humaine,** human weakness *or* frailty; **la f. d'une mère,** a mother's indulgence; **il a eu la f. de se laisser exploiter,** he was weak enough to *or* so weak as to let himself be exploited;

(d) (*manque d'intensité*) faintness (*of sound, smell, light*); lightness (*of wind*);

(e) (*petitesse*) smallness (*of quantity, majority etc*); slightness (*of difference, reaction etc*); **la f. de leurs revenus,** their low income;

(f) (*défaut*) weakness, failing (*of person*); weakness (*of work of art etc*).

faiblir [fɛblir] *vi* to weaken, to grow weak(er); (*of sight, heart*) to fail; (*of wind*) to abate, to drop; (*of courage*) to fail, to flag; **le pont faiblit sous le convoi,** the bridge is weakening beneath the convoy; **le film faiblit vers la fin,** the film falls off *or* tails off towards the end; **si on lui parle avec conviction, il va f.,** if you speak to him with conviction, he will weaken.

faïence [fajɑ̃s] *nf* **(a)** (*matière*) earthenware; **f. fine,** china; **(b)** (*objet*) piece of earthenware; **faïences,** crockery, earthenware.

faïencerie [fajɑ̃sri] *nf* **(a)** (*articles*) crockery, earthenware; **(b)** (*fabrique*) pottery (works); **(c)** (*commerce*) pottery (trade).

faïencier, -ière [fajɑ̃sje, -jɛr] *n* (*fabricant*) crockery *or* earthenware maker; (*marchand*) crockery *or* earthenware dealer.

faignant [fɛɲɑ̃] *adj & n F* = **FAINÉANT.**

faille [faj] *nf* **(a)** *Géol* fault; **ligne de f.,** fault line; **(b)** *Fig* flaw (*in argument*); rift, breach (*in friendship*).

failli, -ie [faji] *adj & n Jur* bankrupt.

faillibilité [fajibilite] *nf* fallibility.

faillible [fajibl] *adj* fallible; **tout le monde est f.,** anybody can make a mistake.

faillir [fajir] *vi* (*prp* **faillant**; *pp* **failli**; *pr ind* **je faux, il faut, n. faillons**; *p hist* **je faillis**; *fu* **je faillirai**; *used mostly in inf, p hist and compound tenses*) **(a)** (*manquer*) **f. à son devoir,** to fail in *or* fall short of one's duty; **f. à une promesse,** to fail to keep a promise; **sans f.,** unfailingly; **la mémoire me faut,** my memory fails me; **(b) j'ai failli manquer le train,** I nearly *or* almost missed the train; **il faillit être écrasé,** he narrowly missed being run over; **j'ai bien failli me noyer,** I was very nearly drowned, I had a narrow escape from drowning.

faillite [fajit] *nf* **(a)** *Com* bankruptcy, insolvency; **être en (état) de f.,** to be bankrupt *or* insolvent; **f. simple,** bankruptcy; **faire f.,** to go bankrupt; **déclarer** *ou* **mettre qn en f.,** to adjudicate *or* adjudge s.o. bankrupt; **(b)** (*échec*) failure (*of project, hopes etc*).

faim [fɛ̃] *nf* hunger; **avoir f.,** to be *or* feel hungry; **avoir très f.** *ou F* **une grande f.,** to be *or* feel very hungry; **avoir un peu f.** *ou F* **une petite f.,** to be *or* feel a bit hungry; **avoir une f. de loup,** to be ravenous; **mourir de f.,** to die of starvation; (*avoir très faim*) to be starving; *F* **je crève de f.,** I'm starving; **manger à sa f.,** to eat one's fill; **rester sur sa f.,** to remain hungry; *Fig* to be left unsatisfied; *Fig* **avoir f. de gloire/d'absolus,** to hunger *or* thirst after glory/absolutes.

faîne [fɛn] *nf* beechnut; **faînes,** beech mast, beechnuts.

fainéant, -ante [feneɑ̃, -ɑ̃t] **1** *adj* idle, lazy. **2** *n* lazybones.

fainéanter [feneɑ̃te] *vi* to idle, to loaf (about).

fainéantise [feneɑ̃tiz] *nf* idleness, laziness.

faire[1] [fɛr] *nm* **(a)** doing; **il y a loin du dire au f.,** saying is one thing, doing another; **(b)** *Beaux-Arts Littér* technique.

faire[2] *v* (*prp* **faisant** [fəzɑ̃]; *pp* **fait** [fɛ]; *pr ind* **je fais, il fait, n. faisons** [fəzɔ̃], **v. faites** [fɛt], **ils font**; *pr sub* **je fasse**; *imp* **fais, faisons, faites**; *p hist* **je fis**; *fu* **je ferai**) **1** *vt* **(a)** (*façonner*) to make; **f. un gâteau/du cidre,** to make a cake/cider; **statue faite en** *ou* **de marbre,** statue sculpted in *or* made out of marble; **vêtements tout faits,** ready-made clothes; **expressions toutes faites,** ready-made *or* set phrases; **f. un poème/un tableau,** to write a poem/paint a picture; **f. un chèque de cent francs,** to make out *or* write a cheque for 100 francs; **je vais lui f. un chèque,** I'll make him out *or* write him a cheque; **f. la guerre,** to wage war; **f. un miracle,** to work *or* perform a miracle; **ferme où on fait de la betterave,** farm that grows beet;

(b) (*créer*) to make; **Dieu a fait l'homme à son image,** God made *or* created man in his own image; **ils ne veulent pas f. d'enfants,** they don't want to have (any) children; *F* **faire un enfant à qn,** to make *or* get s.o. pregnant; **les vieilles gens sont ainsi faits,** old people are like that; **comment est-il fait?,** what sort of man is he?; (*à quoi ressemble-t-il?*) what does he look like?; **il n'est pas fait pour cela,** he is not the man *or* not fitted *or* not cut out for that; **jambe bien faite,** shapely leg;

(c) f. un geste, to make a gesture; **f. de l'œil à qn,** to ogle s.o.;

(d) f. sa fortune, to make one's fortune;

(e) f. des provisions, to lay in provisions; **f. de l'eau/du charbon,** to take in water/coal; *F* **on m'a fait ma montre,** (*volé*) someone's pinched my watch;

(f) *Arg* **tu es fait, mon vieux!,** you've had it, chum!;

(g) (*activité*) to do; **qu'est-ce que vous faites?,** what are you doing?; **qu'est-ce qu'il y a à f.?,** what is there to do?; **il n'y a rien à f.,** (*pour résoudre le problème*) there is nothing to be done, there's no help for it; **je n'ai rien à f.,** (*je m'ennuie*) I've nothing to do; **je n'ai rien à f. avec eux,** I have nothing to do with them; **il n'a rien à f. ici,** he has no business here; **que f.?,** what is *or* was to be done?, what can *or* could he *or* we *etc* do?; **je ne sais que f.,** I don't know what to do; **qu'allez-vous f. de votre fils?,** what are you going to do with your son?; **qu'avez-vous fait de mon parapluie?,** what have you done with my umbrella?; **n'avoir que f. de qch,** to have no need *or* use for sth; **si f. se peut,** if it's possible; **c'est la dernière chose à f.,** it's the last thing that ought to be done; **je le regardais f.,** I watched him doing it; **est-ce que je peux ouvrir la fenêtre? — faites donc!,** may I open the window? — by all means *or* do!; **faites vite!,** look sharp!; **nous avons fort à f. pour joindre les deux bouts,** we are hard put to make ends meet; **homme à tout f.,** handyman; **grand bien vous fasse!,** much good may it do you!; **c'est bien fait!,** it serves you right!; **c'est toujours ça de fait,** that's a good job done; *F* **deux ans au chômage, faut le f.!,** unemployed for two years, it's not as easy as you think!; **voilà qui est fait,** that's done;

(h) (*dire*) to say; **'vous partez demain!' fit-il,** 'you leave tomorrow!' he said *or* exclaimed; **il fit un petit 'oh' de surprise,** he gave a little 'oh' of surprise;

(i) (*accomplir*) **f. son devoir,** to do one's duty; **f. la ronde,** to go one's rounds; *F* **f. ses besoins,** to relieve oneself; (*d'un chien, un chat*) to do its business;

(j) f. un métier, to practise a trade; **f. les cuirs/la laine,** to deal in leather/wool; **nous ne faisons que le gros,** we are wholesalers only; **quel article faites-vous?,** what's your line?;

(k) f. du sport/de la politique, to go in for sport/politics; **j'ai fait de l'anglais à l'école,** I did English at school; **il fait sa médecine/son droit,** he is reading *or* studying medicine/law; *F* **il veut f. médecin/pompier,** he wants to be a doctor/fireman;

(l) f. une maladie, to have an illness; **il doit f. une crise de foie,** he must have liver trouble; *F* **tu ne vas pas f. ta crise!,** you're not going to have one of your tantrums!; **f. son apprentissage,** to serve one's apprenticeship;

(m) (*déplacement*) **f. quelques pas dans le sentier,** to go *or* take a few steps along the path; **f. les magasins,** to go round *or* do the shops; **ce représentant fait la province,** this representative does *or* covers the provinces; **on a fait l'Inde l'année dernière,** we did India last year; **f. une promenade,** to go for a walk; *F* **f. du cent à l'heure,** to go *or* do a hundred kilometres an hour;

(n) (*causer*) to cause; **f. pitié/peur,** to arouse pity/fear; **cela me fait de la peine que tu partes,** it makes me sad *or* upsets me that you're going;

(o) (*mesure*) to amount to, to come to; **combien cela fait-il?, ça fait combien?,** how much does that come to?; **deux fois deux font quatre,** two twos are four, twice two is four; **je vous fais les deux cadres pour 200 francs,** I can let you have both frames for 200 francs; **ça fait trois jours qu'il est parti,** it's three days since he left; **ça fera bien 2 ans (que je ne l'ai pas revu),** it'll be a good two years (since I last saw him); **ce poulet fait trois kilos,** this chicken weighs three kilos; **combien faites-vous la livre de chocolat?,** how much do you charge for a pound of chocolate?;

(p) 'cheval' fait 'chevaux' au pluriel, 'cheval' becomes 'chevaux' in the plural;

(q) (*être, constituer*) to be; **f. l'admiration de tous,** to be the admiration of all; **cela fera mon affaire,** that will suit me; **quel taquin vous faites!,** what a tease you are!; *Prov* **l'habit ne fait pas le moine,** appearances are deceptive;

(r) (*importer*) to matter; **qu'est-ce que ça fait?,** what does it matter?, who cares?; **ça fait qu'on va le déranger encore une fois,** it means we'll have to disturb him again; **qu'est-ce que cela vous fait?,** what's that to you?; **si cela ne vous fait rien,** if you don't mind; **cela ne fait rien,** never mind, it doesn't matter; *F* **qu'est-ce que ça peut bien te f.?,** what has that got to do with you?; *F* **ça me fait que je dois encore t'attendre,** it means I have to wait for you again;

(s) (*replacing previous verb*) **pourquoi agir comme vous le faites?,** why do you act as you do?; **il m'a traité comme il aurait fait d'un** *ou* **pour un animal,** he treated me as he would an animal;

(t) (*former*) to form; **ce professeur fait de bons élèves,** this teacher turns out good pupils; **f. des chaussures à son pied,** to break in a pair of shoes;

(u) (*arranger*) to arrange; **f. la chambre,** to clean *or* do the room; **f. le ménage/la vaisselle,** to do the housework/the washing-up; **faire du rangement** *ou* **de l'ordre dans ses affaires,** to put one's things in order, to tidy up one's things; **f. sa valise,** to pack one's (suit)case; **f. ses ongles,** to do one's nails; *Cartes* **f. les cartes,** to deal (the cards); *Cartes* **à qui de f.?,** whose deal is it?;

(v) *F* **ça fait riche,** it looks expensive *or* stylish; *F* **ça fait jeune,** it makes you look young; **vases qui font bien sur la cheminée,** vases that look good on the mantelpiece; **il ne fait pas quarante ans,** he doesn't look forty;

(w) (*jouer le rôle de*) **il fait Hamlet,** he acts *or* plays Hamlet; **un des invités faisait le croupier,** one of the guests acted as croupier; **elle ne va pas f. la reine ici,** she isn't going to queen it here; **f. le pauvre,** to pretend to be poor; **il fait le mort,** he's pretending to be dead; **f. l'imbécile,** to play the fool; *F* **ne fais pas l'idiot!,** don't be stupid!;

(x) (*locutions avec 'en'*) **ne t'en fais pas,** don't worry; **il n'en fait qu'à sa tête,** he does what he likes; **n'en faites rien,** don't do any such thing; **c'en est fait de lui,** it's all up with him, he's done for;

(y) (*locutions avec 'y'*) **rien n'y fit,** nothing availed, it was all of no use; **que voulez-vous que j'y fasse?,** how can I help it?; **il sait y f.,** he knows what he's doing, he can fend for himself;

(z) *F* **la f. à qn,** to take s.o. in; **on ne me la fait pas!,** nothing doing!, I'm not going to be had!

2 *vi F* to relieve oneself; **un chien a fait sur le trottoir,** a dog has made a mess *or* done its business on the pavement.

3 *v impers* **(a) il fait beau (temps),** it is fine (weather); **il fait froid/chaud,** it's cold/hot; **il fait du soleil/de la neige,** it's sunny/snowing; **par le froid qu'il fait,** in this cold weather;

(b) il fait bon près de la cheminée, it's nice by the fireside; **il fait mauvais voyager par ces routes,** it is hard travelling on these roads; **il fait bon parler à ses amis,** it's nice *or* good to talk to one's friends.

4 *v aux* **(a)** (*avec 'que'*) **il ne fait que lire toute la journée,** he does nothing but read all day; **je n'ai fait que le toucher,** I only touched it; **je ne fais que d'arriver,** I have only just arrived; **vous n'aviez que f. de parler,** you had no business to speak; **c'est ce qui fait que je suis venu si vite,** that is why *or* this is how it happens that I came so quickly; **les événements qui font que les choses sont comme elles sont,** the events that make things what they are; **faites qu'il vienne demain,** see to it *or* make sure that he comes tomorrow;

(b) (*the noun or pron object is the subject of the inf*) **le soleil fait fondre la neige,** the sun makes the snow melt *or* melts the snow; **on le fit chanter,** he was made to sing; **il nous a fait venir,** he sent for us; **faites-le entrer,** show him in; **f. attendre qn,** to keep s.o. waiting;

(c) (*with vpr*) **faire asseoir qn,** to make s.o. sit down; **f. coucher un enfant,** to put a child to bed; **nous l'avons fait se cacher dans une armoire,** we made him hide in a cupboard; **je le fis s'arrêter,** I made him stop;

(d) (*the noun or pron is the object of the inf*) **f. bâtir une maison,** to have *or* get a house built; **f. f. deux exemplaires,** to have two copies made; **faites-le réparer,** get it mended;

(e) f. f. qch à qn, to get s.o. to do sth, to have s.o. do sth; **il fit lâcher prise à son adversaire,** he made his opponent let go, he got his opponent to let go; **faites-lui lire cette let-**

tre, get him to read *or* make him read this letter; **je lui ai fait observer qu'il se faisait tard,** I called his attention to the fact that it was getting late; **faites-lui comprendre qu'il n'est pas le bienvenu,** make him understand that he is not welcome; **je le ferai examiner par un médecin,** I shall have *or* get him examined by a doctor.

5 se faire *vpr* **(a)** (*devenir meilleur*) to develop, to mature; **ce fromage se fera,** this cheese will ripen; **son style se fait,** his style is forming;

(b) (*devenir*) to become; **se f. vieux,** to become *or* grow *or* get old; **se f. soldat,** to become a soldier;

(c) (*s'adapter*) **se f. à qch,** to get used *or* accustomed to sth; **se f. à la fatigue,** to become resistant *or* inured to fatigue; **tes chaussures vont finir par se faire,** your shoes will eventually get worn in; **permettre aux engrenages de se f.,** to run in the gears;

(d) se f. tant par mois, to make *or* earn so much a month; **se f. des amis,** to make friends; **ces choses-là ne se font pas,** these things are not done; **se f. une opinion/une idée sur qch,** to form an opinion/get some idea about sth;

(e) la mer/le vent se fait, the sea/the wind is getting up; **la nuit se fait,** night is falling;

(f) (*impers*) **il se fait tard,** it's getting late; **il se fit un long silence,** a long silence followed, there was a long silence; **comment se fait-il que vous soyez en retard?,** how is it that you're late?;

(g) (*s'accomplir*) **il est venu voir ce qui se faisait,** he came to see what was happening *or F* doing; **le miracle s'est fait tout seul,** the miracle came about *or* happened by itself; **le mariage ne se fera pas,** the marriage will not take place;

(h) (+ *inf*) **se f. photografier,** to have *or* get oneself photographed, to have one's photograph taken; **un bruit se fit entendre,** a noise was heard; **ne vous faites pas tant prier,** don't take so much asking; **il ne se le fit pas dire deux fois,** he didn't need to be told twice; **il s'est fait punir,** he's got himself punished; *Vulg* **il peut aller se f. foutre,** he can fuck off *or Br* get stuffed;

(i) *F* **(ne) t'en fais pas,** don't worry;

(j) il se fait plus pauvre qu'il ne l'est, he makes himself out to be poorer than he is;

(k) *Vulg* **il va se la f.,** (*sexuellement*) he's going to have *or* lay her; *Fig* **il faut se la f. quand elle est de mauvaise humeur,** she's a real pain (in the backside) when she's in a bad mood.

faire-part [fɛrpar] *nm inv* announcement (*of wedding, birth, death etc*); **le présent avis tiendra lieu de f.-p.,** friends please accept this intimation.

faire-valoir [fɛrvalwar] *nm inv* **(a)** *Agr* farming; **exploitation en f.-v. direct,** farm run by the owner; **(b)** (*personne*) foil (*to s.o.*); (*de comique*) stooge.

fair-play [fɛrplɛ] **1** *adj inv* **être f.-p.,** to play fair. **2** *nm inv* fair play.

faisabilité [fəzabilite] *nf* feasibility; **étude de f.,** feasibility study.

faisable [fəzabl] *adj* feasible, practicable.

faisan [fəzɑ̃] *nm* **(a) (coq) f.,** (cock) pheasant; **f. doré,** golden pheasant; **(b)** *Arg* (*escroc*) crook.

faisandage [fəzɑ̃daʒ] *nm Culin* hanging (*of game*).

faisandé [fəzɑ̃de] *adj* **(a)** *Culin* high, gamy (*meat*); **(b)** *F* (*corrompu*) decadent (*literature, person, society etc*).

faisandeau, -eaux [fəzɑ̃do] *nm* young pheasant.

faisander [fəzɑ̃de] *vt Culin* to hang (*game*).

faisanderie [fəzɑ̃dri] *nf* pheasantry, pheasant preserve.

faisane [fəzan] *nf* **(poule) f.,** hen pheasant.

faisceau, -eaux [fɛso] *nm* **(a)** (*rayons*) beam; **f. lumineux** *ou* **de lumière,** beam of light, *Spéc* pencil of rays; **f. laser,** laser beam; **f. de particules,** particle beam; **(b)** *Électron* **f. d'électrons** *ou* **électronique,** electron beam; **f. hertzien,** electromagnetic wave; *TV* **f. cathodique explorateur,** scanning electron beam; **f. radar,** radar beam; **(c)** bundle (*of sticks etc*); *Anat* fasciculus, fascicle (*of fibres*); cluster (*of electric bulbs*); *Rail* group (*of sidings*); *Fig* **un f. d'habitudes,** a body of customs; *Fig* **un f. de preuves,** a body of proof; *Antiq* **les faisceaux,** the fasces (*of lictor*); *Archit* **colonne en f.,** clustered column; *Mil* **former/rompre les faisceaux,** to pile/unpile arms.

faiseur, -euse [fəzœr, -øz] *n* **(a)** (*qui fabrique qch*) maker; **f. de dentelles,** lacemaker; **f. de ponts,** bridge builder; **costume du bon f.,** suit from a good tailor; **f. de miracles,** miracle worker; **f. de tours,** prestidigitator, conjurer; **f. d'embarras,** *Br* fusspot, *Am* fussbudget; **f. de projets,** schemer; **f. de mariages,** matchmaker; **faiseuse d'anges,** back-street abortionist; *Prov* **les grands diseurs ne sont pas les grands faiseurs,** the greatest talkers are the least doers; **(b)** *Péj* (*poseur*) pushy type.

fait[1] [fɛ] *adj* **(a)** (*mûr*) mature (*person*); ripe (*cheese*); **(b) avoir les ongles/yeux faits,** to have nail varnish *or Am* polish/eye shadow on.

fait[2] *nm* **(a)** (*acte*) act; **le f. de boire,** (the act of) drinking; **faits et dits,** sayings and doings; **faits et gestes,** doings, actions; **f. d'armes,** feat of arms; **cela est du f. d'un tel,** this is so-and-so's doing; **prendre qn sur le f.,** to catch s.o. in the act *or* red-handed; **se porter à des voies de f.,** to resort to force *or* to violence; **parler n'était pas son f.,** he was no talker, talking was not his line; **dire son f. à qn,** to talk straight to s.o., to give s.o. a piece of one's mind;

(b) (*réalité*) fact; **f. accompli,** fait accompli, accomplished fact; **les faits d'une cause,** the facts of a case; **prendre f. et cause pour qn,** to stand up for s.o.; **ceci est un f.,** this is a (matter of) fact; **roi de nom plutôt que de f.,** king in name rather than in fact; **possession de f.,** actual possession; **il est de f. que c'était un traître,** it is (a) fact that he was a traitor; **aller droit au f.,** to go straight to the point; **en venir au f.,** to come to the point; **être au f. de la question,** to know how things stand; **mettre qn au f.,** to acquaint s.o. *or* make s.o. acquainted with the facts; **mettre** *ou* **poser qch en f.,** to lay sth down as a fact; **au f.!,** get to the point!; **au f., que venez-vous faire ici?,** by the way, what have you come here for?; **en f., par le f., dans le f., de f.,** as a matter of fact, in point of fact, in actual fact, actually; **de f., cela est un refus,** that is in effect a refusal; **de ce f.,** for that reason, on that account; **du f.** *ou* **par le f. qu'il boite,** owing to the fact that *or* because he's lame; **par le seul f. d'y être,** by the mere fact of *or* simply by being there; **expert en f. de vins,** expert as regards wine *or* when it comes to wine; **qu'est-ce que vous avez en f. de rôti?,** what have you in the way of a joint?;

(c) (*événement*) occurrence, happening, event; **un f. nouveau s'est produit,** there was a new development; *Journ* **'faits divers',** 'news in brief'; **f. divers,** news item.

faîtage [fɛtaʒ] *nm Constr* **(a)** (*poutre*) rooftree; **(b)** (*couverture*) ridge tiling *or* sheathing.

faîte [fɛt] *nm* **(a)** *Constr* ridge (*of roof*); **(b)** *Géog* **ligne de f.,** watershed, crest line; **(c)** top (*of house, tree etc*); **le f. de la gloire,** the height *or* pinnacle of glory.

faîtière [fɛtjɛr] *adj & nf Constr* **(tuile) f.,** ridge tile; **(lucarne) f.,** skylight.

faitout *nm*, **fait-tout** *nm inv* [fɛtu] stewpot, casserole.

faix [fɛ] *nm* **(a)** (*poids*) burdon, load; **le f. des années,** the weight of years; **le f. des impôts,** the burden of taxation; **(b)** *Obst* fœtus and placenta.

fakir [fakir] *nm Rel Th* fakir.

falaise [falɛz] *nf* cliff.

falbalas [falbala] *nmpl Couture* furbelows, flounces.

fallacieusement [falasjøzmɑ̃] *adv* fallaciously; (*promettre*) misleadingly.

fallacieux, -ieuse [falasjø, -jøz] *adj* fallacious (*argument, reasoning etc*); fallacious, delusive (*hope*); misleading (*promise, appearance*).

falloir [falwar] *v* (*no prp; pp* **fallu**; *pr ind* **il faut**; *pr sub* **il faille**; *impf* **il fallait**; *p hist* **il fallut**; *fu* **il faudra**) **1** *vi impers déf* **(a)** (*par besoin*) **il lui faut un nouveau pardessus,** he needs a new overcoat; **avez-vous tout ce qu'il (vous) faut?,** have you got all you want *or* require *or* need?; **faut-il tout cela?,** is all that necessary?; **c'est juste ce qu'il (me) faut,** that's the very thing (I want), that's just the right thing; **nous en avons plus qu'il ne nous en faut,** we have more than enough *or* than we need; **il m'a fallu trois jours pour le faire,** it took me three days to do it; **elle fera ce qu'il faut,** she will do what is necessary *or* what needs to be done; **il a tout ce qu'il faut pour réussir,** he has everything he needs *or F* he's got what it takes to succeed; *F* **je lui ai tout donné, qu'est-ce qu'il lui faut de plus!,** I've given him everything, what more does he want!;

(b) comme il faut, properly; **se conduire comme il faut,** to behave properly *or* in a civilized manner *or* in the right way; **il/elle est très comme il faut,** he's very gentlemanly/she's very ladylike; **ce sont des gens très comme il faut,** they're very decent people; **votre toilette est tout à fait comme il faut,** your dress is just right;

(c) il faut partir, I *or* we *or* you *etc* must *or* have to go; **il faut dire qu'il s'est bien comporté,** it must be said *or* I am bound to say he behaved well; **il nous faut le voir, il faut que nous le voyions,** we must see him; **il lui faut se dépêcher,** he must hurry; **il faudra marcher plus vite,** we shall have to walk faster; **il fallait porter plainte,** you should have *or* ought to have made a complaint; **il fallait le dire!,** why didn't you say so?; **il n'aurait pas fallu attendre,** you shouldn't have *or* ought not to have waited; **comme il fallait s'y attendre,** as was (only) to be expected; **il faut qu'il ait été fâché pour dire cela,** he must have been angry to have said that; **c'est ce qu'il faudra voir!,** we must see about that!; **la police a arrêté l'homme qu'il ne fallait pas,** the police have arrested the wrong man; *Arg* **faut voir!,** you should see it!; **c'est simple, mais il fallait y penser,** it's simple once you've thought of it; **il a fallu qu'elle apprenne cet accident!,** she HAD to hear *or* she WOULD hear of that accident!; **encore faut-il que ce soit vrai,** even so it still must be true; **il ne faudrait pas que je les rencontre,** it would never do for me to meet them; **il ne faudrait pas qu'il le dise deux fois,** he'd better not say it again; **il ne faut pas y aller,** you must not go there;

(d) *(with le = noun clause)* **il viendra s'il le faut,** he will come if need be *or* if necessary *or* if he has to; **vous êtes revenu à pied? — il l'a** *ou* **il a bien fallu,** you walked back? — there was nothing else for it *or* I had no choice.

2 s'en falloir *vpr* **il s'en faut de deux francs,** it is two francs short; **je ne suis pas satisfait, il s'en faut de beaucoup** *ou* **tant s'en faut,** I am not satisfied, far from it *or* not by a long way; **il s'en faut de beaucoup que l'autobus (ne) soit plein,** the bus is far from being full, the bus is not full by a long way; **il s'en est fallu de peu** *ou* **peu s'en faut qu'il ne mourût,** he very nearly died, it was touch and go whether he died; **cinq livres ou peu s'en faut,** the best part of five pounds; **il s'en est fallu de rien qu'il (ne) fût écrasé,** he was within an ace *or* an inch *or* a hair's-breadth of being run over; **il s'en faut de peu qu'il accepte,** he is more than half inclined to accept; **vous êtes satisfait? — peu s'en faut!,** are you satisfied? — not a bit (of it)!

falot¹ [falo] *nm* **(a)** *(lanterne)* (hand) lantern; **(b)** *Mil* court martial.

falot², -ote [falo, -ɔt] *adj* *(terne)* dull, tame, drab *(person)*.

falsificateur, -trice [falsifikatœr, -tris] *n* forger *(of documents, signature, accounts)*; adulterator *(of food, wine etc)*.

falsification [falsifikasjɔ̃] *nf* falsification *(of documents, signature, accounts etc)*; adulteration *(of food, wine etc)*; *Fig* misrepresentation *(of s.o.'s thinking etc)*.

falsifier [falsifje] *vt* *(impf & pr sub* **n. falsifiions)** to falsify, to tamper with *(document, signature etc)*; to adulterate *(wine, food etc)*; **f. les comptes,** to falsify *or* doctor the accounts; **monnaie falsifiée,** spurious coin; **f. la pensée de l'auteur,** to misrepresent the author's thinking.

falzar [falzar] *nm Arg* trousers, *Am* pants.

famé [fame] *adj* **mal f.,** of ill repute.

famélique [famelik] *adj* half-starved, ill-fed.

fameusement [famøzmɑ̃] *adv F* *(très)* incredibly, really; **on s'est f. amusé,** we had a whale of a time.

fameux, -euse [famø, -øz] *adj* **(a)** *(ayant bonne réputation)* famous; *(ayant mauvaise réputation)* notorious **(par, pour,** for); *Iron* **le f. monsieur/livre dont tout le monde parle,** the (famous) gentleman/book that everyone is talking about; **le f. jour où tu es arrivé,** the great day when you arrived; **(b)** *F* *(très bon)* splendid, marvellous, tremendous; *(très mauvais)* terrible, awful; **vous commettez une fameuse erreur,** you're making a terrible *or* an awful *or* a (mighty) big mistake; **ce n'est pas f. ton boulot,** your job isn't up to much.

familial, -ale, -iaux [familjal, -jo] **1** *adj* family *(life, troubles etc)*; *Com* family-size *(packet, jar etc)*; **allocation familiale,** *Br* child benefit, *US* dependent's allowance; **maladie familiale,** hereditary disease. **2** *nf Aut* **familiale,** (family) estate car, *Am* station wagon.

familiariser [familjarize] **1** *vt* **f. qn avec qch,** to get s.o. used to sth, to familiarize s.o. with sth; **peu familiarisé avec,** unfamiliar *or* unacquainted with. **2 se familiariser** *vpr* **(a) se f. avec qch,** *(en le pratiquant)* to familiarize oneself with sth, to get to know sth; *(en s'y habituant)* to grow accustomed *or* used to sth; **se f. avec un lieu,** to get to know a place; **(b)** *(devenir amical)* to get friendly.

familiarité [familjarite] *nf* **(a)** *(intimité)* familiarity; **être d'une grande f. avec qn,** to be on terms of great familiarity with s.o.; **(b)** *(comportement amical)* informality, friendliness; **prendre trop de familiarités avec qn,** to be too familiar *or* to take liberties with s.o.

familier, -ière [familje, -jɛr] **1** *adj* **(a)** *(avec qn)* familiar; **être f. avec qn,** to be on familiar terms with s.o.; **prendre des airs trop familiers,** to be over-familiar; **expression familière,** colloquial *or* familiar expression, colloquialism; **le langage f.,** colloquial *or* familiar language; **animal f.,** pet;

(b) *(habituel)* **visage qui lui est f.,** face which is familiar *or* well-known to him; **ta voix ne lui est pas familière,** he doesn't know *or* recognize your voice; **mon cadre f.,** my usual surroundings; **cette question lui est familière,** he is familiar with the subject; **le mensonge lui est f.,** he is a habitual liar;

(c) *(de la maison)* domestic, of the family; **dieux familiers,** household gods.

2 *n* *(de café, club etc)* regular visitor **(de,** to), regular **(de,** of); **un des familiers de la maison,** a regular visitor to the house, an intimate friend of the household.

familièrement [familjɛrmɑ̃] *adv* familiarly; *(amicalement)* informally.

familistère [familistɛr] *nm* workers' co-operative association.

famille [famij] *nf* **(a)** *(mère, père, enfants)* family; *(ensemble des parents)* family, relatives, relations; **elle a une f. de six enfants,** she has a family of six; **il faut que je vous présente à ma f.,** *(parents)* I must introduce you to my parents; *(conjoint, enfants)* I must introduce you to my wife *or* husband and children; **réduction f. nombreuse,** family reduction *or* discount; **charges de famille,** dependants; **chef de f.,** head of the family; *Admin* householder, head of the household; **soutien de f.,** breadwinner; **fils de bonne f.,** young man of good social standing; **bijoux de f.,** family jewels; **avoir l'esprit de f.,** to have family feeling; **dîner en f.,** to dine at home with one's family; **avec eux je me sens en f.,** I feel quite at home with them; **cela tient** *ou* **vient de f.,** it runs in the family *or* in the blood; **la f. des Bourbons,** the house of Bourbon; **pension de f.,** (small) boarding house; **placement des enfants en f.,** placing of children in foster homes; *Jur* **prévenir la f.,** to inform the next of kin; *Cartes* **le jeu des sept familles,** happy families; *F* **on va se faire un repas des familles,** we'll make ourselves a nice little meal; *Fig* **ils appartiennent à la même f. politique/littéraire,** they belong to the same political/literary grouping;

(b) *Ling Bot Zool* family.

famine [famin] *nf* famine; **crier f.,** to complain of hard times; **salaire de f.,** starvation wages.

fan [fan] *nm F* *(admirateur)* fan.

fana [fana] *F* **1** *adj* *(enthousiaste)* dead keen **(de,** on). **2** *n* **f. du football/de la moto/***etc*, football/motorbike/*etc* fanatic *or* freak.

fanage [fanaʒ] *nm* tedding, tossing *(of hay)*.

fanal, -aux [fanal, -o] *nm* lantern; *Rail* *(de locomotive)* headlight; *Nau* *(sur les côtes)* beacon, lantern; *(sur un bateau)* (ship's) lantern.

fanatique [fanatik] **1** *adj* fanatic(al); **être f. de qn/qch,** to be keen *or* mad on s.o./sth. **2** *n* *(enthousiaste)* fanatic; *Pol Rel* fanatic, zealot; **f. du football/***etc*, football/*etc* fanatic; **fanatiques de Pavarotti,** Pavarotti fans.

fanatiquement [fanatikmɑ̃] *adv* fanatically.

fanatiser [fanatize] *vt* to make fanatical, to fanaticize *(crowd etc)*.

fanatisme [fanatism] *nm* *(enthousiasme)* fanaticism **(pour,** for); *Pol Rel* fanaticism, zealotry.

fanchon [fɑ̃ʃɔ̃] *nf* kerchief, headscarf.

fandango [fɑ̃dɑ̃go] *nm* fandango.

faner [fane] **1** *vt* **(a)** to ted, to toss *(hay)*; **(b)** to fade *(colour, cloth etc)*; to fade, to wither, to wilt *(flower, plant)*. **2 se faner** *vpr* *(of flower, plant)* to fade, to wither, to wilt; *(of colour, cloth, Fig beauty, health etc)* to fade.

faneur, -euse [fanœr, -øz] *Agr* **1** *n* *(ouvrier)* haymaker. **2** *nf* **faneuse,** *(machine)* tedder, tedding machine.

fanfare [fɑ̃far] *nf* **(a)** flourish, fanfare *(of trumpets etc)*; **sonner la f.,** to sound the fanfare; *Fig F* **réveil en f.,** sudden *or* rude awakening; **(b)** *(orchestre)* brass band; *Mil* military band.

fanfaron, -onne [fɑ̃farɔ̃, -ɔn] **1** *adj* boastful. **2** *n* braggart, boaster; **faire le f.,** to brag, to boast.

fanfaronnade [fɑ̃farɔnad] *nf* **(a)** *(caractère)* bragging, boasting; **(b) fanfaronnades,** *(actes, propos)* bragging, boasting.

fanfaronner [fɑ̃farɔne] *vi* to brag, to boast.

fanfreluche [fɑ̃frəlyʃ] *nf* trimming, *Péj* frill *(on dress, curtain etc)*.

fange [fɑ̃ʒ] *nf Litt* mud, mire; **élevé dans la f.,** brought up in the gutter; **par le scandale, elle a été traînée dans la f.,** in the scandal she *or* her name was dragged through the mud *or* mire.

fangeux, -euse [fɑ̃ʒø, -øz] *adj Litt* muddy, miry (*ground etc*).

fanion [fanjɔ̃] *nm* (*de club, bateau, corps d'armée etc*) pennant, pennon; *Ski* (*de balisage*) flag.

fanon [fanɔ̃] *nm* **(a)** (*de baleine*) whalebone, baleen; **(b)** dewlap (*of ox*); wattle (*of bird*); fetlock (*of horse*); **(c)** *Rel* lappet (*of mitre*).

fantaisie [fɑ̃tɛzi] *nf* **(a)** (*envie*) **il a eu** *ou* **il lui a pris la f. de se baigner,** he had a sudden notion to go swimming; **chacun s'amusait à sa f.,** everyone amused himself as the fancy took him *or* as he pleased; **articles (de) f.,** fancy goods; **pain (de) f.,** fancy bread (*not sold by weight*); **bijoux (de) f.,** novelty *or* fancy jewellery; **rayon de fantaisies,** fancy goods counter; **(b)** (*imagination*) imagination, fantasy; **sa vie manque de f.,** his life is very dull *or* unexciting; **de f.,** imaginary (*tale*); fanciful (*portrait*); **(c)** (*œuvre*) *Mus* fantasia; *Littér* fantasy.

fantaisiste [fɑ̃tɛzist] **1** *adj* capricious, eccentric (*person*); fanciful, far-fetched (*interpretation, news etc*). **2** *n* **(a)** (*original*) eccentric; **(b)** *Th* variety entertainer.

fantasmagorie [fɑ̃tasmagɔri] *nf* phantasmagoria.

fantasmagorique [fɑ̃tasmagɔrik] *adj* phantasmagoric(al).

fantasme [fɑ̃tasm] *nm* (*situation imaginée*) fantasy.

fantasmer [fɑ̃tasme] *vi* to fantasize (**sur**, about).

fantasque [fɑ̃task] *adj* whimsical (*person, manner etc*); odd, weird (*story, shape etc*).

fantassin [fɑ̃tasɛ̃] *nm* foot soldier, infantryman.

fantastique [fɑ̃tastik] **1** *adj* **(a)** (*imaginaire*) fantastic (*being, animal etc*); **(b)** (*surnaturel*) weird, eerie (*light, atmosphere etc*); **(c)** (*incroyable*) fantastic (*idea, story etc*); **(d)** (*formidable*) fantastic (*success, plan, amount etc*); **paysage d'une beauté f.,** fantastically beautiful scenery; **(e)** *Beaux-Arts Cin Littér* fantastic. **2** *nm* **le f.,** the fantastic; (*art*) fantasy art; (*littérature*) fantasy literature.

fantastiquement [fɑ̃tastikmɑ̃] *adv* fantastically; (*d'une manière surnaturelle*) weirdly, eerily.

fantoche [fɑ̃tɔʃ] **1** *nm* (*marionnette, Fig personne*) puppet. **2** *adj* **gouvernement f.,** puppet government.

fantomatique [fɑ̃tɔmatik] *adj* ghostly.

fantôme [fɑ̃tom] *nm* phantom, ghost, apparition; **train/vaisseau f.,** ghost train/ship; *Mus* **le Vaisseau F.,** the Flying Dutchman; *Fig* **ce n'est plus qu'un f.,** (*très maigre*) he's just a skeleton; *Pol* **gouvernement/cabinet f.,** shadow government/cabinet.

fanzine [fɑ̃zin] *nm* fanzine.

taon [tɑ̃] *nm* (*petit du cerf etc*) fawn, calf.

F.A.R. [ɛfaɛr] *nf Mil* (*abrév* **force d'action rapide**) = (French) strike force; *US* ≈ RDF.

farad [farad] *nm Él* (*unité*) farad.

faramineux, -euse [faraminø, -øz] *adj F* phenomenal, staggering (*price etc*).

farandole [farɑ̃dɔl] *nf* (*danse*) farandole.

faraud, -aude [faro, -od] *F Vieilli* **1** *adj* swanky, swaggering. **2** *n* swaggerer; **faire le f.,** to swank, to swagger.

farce [fars] **1** *nf* **(a)** *Culin* stuffing; **(b)** (*tour*) (practical) joke, prank; **faire des farces à qn,** to play tricks *or* (practical) jokes on s.o.; *Com* **farces et attrapes,** tricks and jokes; **(c)** *Th* farce; **la situation va tourner à la f.,** the situation is becoming farcical. **2** *adj F Vieilli* funny, comical.

farceur, -euse [farsœr, -øz] *n* **(a)** (*qui fait des tours*) practical joker; **(b)** (*blagueur*) wag, joker; **c'est un f. qui vous aura dit cela,** somebody's been pulling your leg.

farcir [farsir] **1** *vt* **(a)** *Culin* to stuff (*poultry, vegetable etc*); **(b)** *Fig* (*bourrer*) to cram (**de**, with); *F* **j'ai la tête farcie,** my head's fit to burst. **2 se farcir** *vpr* **(a) se f. la tête d'idées romantiques,** to fill one's head with romantic ideas; **(b)** *Arg Fig* to get landed *or* stuck *or Br* lumbered with (*work, washing-up etc*); **je ne l'aime pas moi non plus, il faut se le f.,** I don't like him either, he's impossible *or* really hard to get on with.

fard [far] *nm* makeup; **f. à joues,** blusher; **f. à paupières,** eye shadow; **la vérité sans f.,** the plain unvarnished truth; **parler sans f.,** to speak candidly *or* openly; *F* **piquer un f.,** to blush.

fardage [fardaʒ] *nm Com* camouflaging (*of inferior goods*).

fardeau, -eaux [fardo] *nm* burden, load; **le f. des impôts,** the burden of taxation; *Fig* **c'est un lourd f. qu'il traîne,** it's a millstone round his neck.

farder [farde] **1** *vt* **(a)** (*maquiller*) to make (*s.o., one's face*) up; **f. la vérité/les faits,** to gloss over the truth/facts; **(b)** *Com* to camouflage (*inferior goods*). **2 se farder** *vpr* to make up, to put on one's make-up; **se f. les yeux,** to put on eye shadow.

farfadet [farfadɛ] *nm* (hob)goblin, sprite.

farfelu, -ue [farfəly] *F* **1** *adj* weird, way-out (*person, idea etc*). **2** *n* weirdo.

farfouiller [farfuje] *vi F* to rummage.

faribole [faribɔl] *nf* (*propos*) piece of nonsense; **dire des fariboles,** to talk nonsense.

farinacé [farinase] *adj* farinaceous, floury.

farine [farin] *nf* **(a)** flour; **fleur de f.,** top quality flour; **folle f.,** flour dust, mill dust; **f. d'avoine,** oatmeal; **f. de maïs,** cornflour, *Am* cornstarch; **f. de moutarde,** mustard powder; *F* **ce sont gens de (la) même f.,** they are birds of a feather; *F* **rouler qn dans la f.,** to make a fool of s.o.; **(b)** *Tech* **f. de forage,** bore dust.

fariner [farine] *vt Culin* to dredge *or* coat (*sth*) with flour, to flour.

farineux, -euse [farinø, -øz] **1** *adj* **(a)** *Péj* (*au goût, au toucher etc*) floury; **(b)** (*contenant de la fécule*) starchy, *Spéc* farinaceous (*food*). **2** *nmpl* starchy food, *Spéc* farinaceous food.

farlouse [farluz] *nf Orn* meadow pipit.

farniente [farnjɛnte] *nm* (pleasurable) idleness.

farouche [faruʃ] *adj* **(a)** (*pas apprivoisé*) untamed (*animal, bird*); **leurs chats ne sont pas farouches,** their cats are quite tame; **(b)** (*timide*) shy, withdrawn (*person*); **(c)** (*acharné, violent*) fierce (*enemy, resistance, glance etc*); **volonté f.,** iron *or* unshakeable will; **(d)** (*peu civilisé*) wild, uncivilized (*people, land etc*).

farouchement [faruʃmɑ̃] *adv* fiercely.

fart [far(t)] *nm* (ski) wax.

fartage [fartaʒ] *nm* waxing (*of skis*).

farter [farte] *vt* to wax (*skis*).

fascicule [fasikyl] *nm* **(a)** instalment, part, section (*of publication*); **publier un livre par fascicules,** to publish a book in parts *or* instalments; **(b)** *Mil* **f. de mobilisation,** (reservist's) call-up instructions.

fasciculé [fasikyle] *adj Bot* fascicular, fasciculate.

fascinant [fasinɑ̃] *adj* fascinating (*person*); captivating, bewitching (*beauty, eyes, smile etc*).

fascinateur, -trice [fasinatœr, -tris] *adj Litt* captivating, bewitching.

fascination [fasinɑsjɔ̃] *nf* fascination.

fascine [fasin] *nf* faggot (*of brushwood*); *Constr* fascine.

fasciner[1] [fasine] *vt* **(a)** (*of snake*) to fascinate, to hypnotize (*prey*); **(b)** (*attirer l'attention de*) to fascinate (*s.o.*); (*charmer*) to captivate, to bewitch (*s.o.*); **cette volonté me fascine,** this wish has me in its grip; **elle se laisse f. par l'argent,** she lets herself be blinded *or* dazzled by money.

fasciner[2] *vt Constr* to line (*river bank etc*) with fascines; **route fascinée,** corduroy road.

fascisant [faʃizɑ̃] *adj Pol* with fascist tendencies.

fasciser [faʃize] *vt Pol* to make fascist.

fascisme [faʃism] *nm Pol* fascism.

fasciste [faʃist] *adj & n Pol* fascist.

faste[1] [fast] *nm* (*no pl*) ostentation, display, pomp; **mariage sans f.,** quiet wedding.

faste[2] *adj* **jour f.,** *Antiq* lawful day; (*jour favorable*) auspicious *or* lucky day; **c'est une période f.,** it's a period of (good) luck.

fast-food [fastfud] *nm* **(a)** (*restauration*) fast food; **(b)** (*lieu*) fast-food restaurant.

fastidieusement [fastidjøzmɑ̃] *adv* tiresomelessly, tediously.

fastidieux, -ieuse [fastidjø, -jøz] *adj* dull, tiresome, tedious; **besognes fastidieuses,** drudgery.

fastueusement [fastɥøzmɑ̃] *adv* ostentatiously.

fastueux, -euse [fastɥø, -øz] *adj* ostentatious, showy (*person, life*); sumptuous (*furnishings, dinner etc*).

fat [fa(t)] **1** *adj* conceited, self-satisfied (*person*). **2** *nm* conceited *or* self-satisfied person.

fatal, -als [fatal] *adj* **(a)** (*mortel, de la mort*) fatal (*accident, result etc*); **heure fatale,** fatal hour, hour of death; **coup f.,** deadly *or* mortal blow; **(b)** (*nuisible*) fatal (*beauty etc*); **f. à qn,** fatal *or* disastrous for s.o.; **erreur fatale,** fatal mistake; *Ordinat* fatal error; **femme fatale,** femme fatale; **(c)** (*inévitable*) fated, inevitable; **c'est f.,** it is bound to come, it's sure to happen.

fatalement [fatalmɑ̃] *adv* inevitably; **ils devaient f. se fâcher,** they were bound to fall out.

fatalisme [fatalism] *nm* fatalism.

fataliste [fatalist] **1** *n* fatalist. **2** *adj* fatalistic.

fatalité [fatalite] *nf* **(a)** (*destin*) fate; **poursuivi par la f.,** pursued by fate; **c'est la f.!,** it's just bad luck!; **c'est comme une f.!,** it is *or* was bound to happen!; **(b)**

(*malédiction*) mischance, misfortune; **(c)** (*inévitabilité*) inevitability (*of death etc*).

fatidique [fatidik] *adj* fateful.

fatigable [fatigabl] *adj* easily tired.

fatigant [fatigɑ̃] *adj* **(a)** (*épuisant*) tiring, exhausting; **c'est f. pour le cœur/les yeux,** it strains the heart/the eyes; **(b)** (*lassant*) tiresome, wearisome; **c'est f. de ne jamais réussir,** it's tiresome *or* wearisome never to be successful.

fatigue [fatig] *nf* **(a)** tiredness, weariness, fatigue (*of person, limbs etc*); **tomber** *ou* **être mort de f.,** to be tired out *or* exhausted; **ressentir une grande/légère f.,** to feel very/a bit tired *or* weary; **f. nerveuse,** nervous exhaustion; **f. intellectuelle,** mental strain; **f. oculaire,** eyestrain; **la f. des affaires,** the strain of business; **(b)** *Tech* fatigue (*of metal, part etc*); **(c)** (*effort pénible*) strain, effort; **épargner** *ou* **éviter à qn la f. de qch/de faire qch,** to save s.o. the strain *or* effort of sth/of doing sth.

fatigué [fatige] *adj* **(a)** (*épuisé*) tired (out), weary (*person, limbs etc*); tired (*features, look, voice etc*); strained (*eyes, heart*); tired, overworked (*brain*); **f. par le voyage,** travel-worn, travel-weary; **(b)** *Fig* **f. de qch/qn,** tired *or* weary of sth/s.o.; **f. de faire qch,** tired *or* weary of doing sth; **(c)** *Méd* (*dérangé*) upset (*stomach, liver etc*); **(d)** (*usé*) worn (out), shabby (*clothes, shoes etc*).

fatiguer [fatige] **1** *vt* **(a)** (*épuiser*) to tire (out), to make tired *or* weary; (*surmener*) to overwork; **f. le cœur,** to strain the heart/the eyes;

(b) (*soumettre à un long usage etc*) to strain (*machine, engine, joist etc*); to wear out (*clothes, shoes etc*); to exhaust, to impoverish (*field, soil*); **f. un livre,** to give a book a lot of hard wear;

(c) (*remuer*) to mix, to toss (*salad*); to turn over (*soil*);

(d) (*importuner*) to annoy, to irritate (*s.o.*); (*lasser*) to weary, to wear (*s.o.*) down.

2 *vi* (*of person*) to tire, to get tired (out); (*of ship, engine*) to labour; (*of joist etc*) to show strain.

3 se fatiguer *vpr* (*of person*) to tire, to get tired (out); (*en travaillant beaucoup*) to tire oneself out (**à faire qch,** doing sth); **se f. les yeux/le cœur,** to strain one's eyes/heart; *Iron* **il ne s'est pas (trop) fatigué,** he didn't exactly exert himself; **se f. de qch/qn,** to get tired *or* tire of sth/s.o.; **se f. de faire qch,** to get tired *or* tire of doing sth.

fatras [fatra] *nm* jumble, muddle, hotchpotch (*of ideas, papers etc*).

fatuité [fatɥite] *nf* self-conceit, self-satisfaction.

fauber(t) [fobɛr] *nm Nau* (deck) swab, mop.

faubourg [fobur] *nm* **(a)** (*quartier périphérique*) suburb; **accent des faubourgs,** (Parisian) working-class accent; **(b)** (*quartier de grande ville*) district.

faubourien, -ienne [foburjɛ̃, -jɛn] **1** *adj* (Parisian) working-class (*accent etc*). **2** *n* working-class Parisian.

fauchage [foʃaʒ] *nm* **(a)** reaping (*of wheat, wheatfield etc*); mowing, cutting (*of grass, meadow etc*); **(b)** *Mil* mowing down (*of troops*); (*procédé de tir*) sweeping of ground (with machine-gun fire).

fauchaison [foʃɛzɔ̃] *nf* **(a)** (*saison*) reaping time; (*où l'on fauche l'herbe*) mowing time; **(b)** (*action*) = **FAUCHAGE (a)**.

fauchard [foʃar] *nm Agr* double-edged slasher.

fauche [foʃ] *nf Arg* **(a)** (*vol*) pinching, thieving; **(b)** (*chose volée*) loot; **(c)** (*manque d'argent*) pennilessness.

fauché [foʃe] *adj F* **f. (comme les blés),** (*sans argent*) (flat) broke, *Br* stony-broke, *Am* stone-broke.

faucher [foʃe] **1** *vt* **(a)** to reap (*wheat, wheatfield etc*); to mow, to cut (*grass, meadow etc*); *F* **f. l'herbe sous les pieds de qn,** to cut the ground from under s.o.'s feet; **(b)** (abattre) to mow down (*pedestrian, troops etc*); **la voiture a fauché le poteau télégraphique,** the car brought down *or* flattened the telegraph pole; *Rugby Fb etc* **f. son homme,** to bring down one's man; **(c)** *F* (*voler*) to swipe, to pinch; **elle m'a fauché ma montre/mon mari,** she has swiped *or* pinched my watch/husband. **2** *vi* **(a)** *F* **ca fauche par ici,** things get nicked *or* nabbed round here; **(b)** *Mil etc* to sweep the ground (with machine-gun fire).

faucheur, -euse [foʃœr, -øz] **1** *n* (*personne*) reaper; (*qui fauche les herbes*) mower; **la Faucheuse,** (*La Mort*) the Grim Reaper. **2** *nm* (*insecte*) harvestman, *Am* daddy-longlegs. **3** *nf* **faucheuse,** (*machine*) reaper; (*pour herbes*) mower.

faucheux [foʃø] *nm* (*insecte*) harvestman, *Am* daddy-longlegs.

faucille [fosij] *nf* sickle, (reaping) hook; **la f. et le marteau,** (*emblème*) the hammer and sickle.

faucon [fokɔ̃] *nm* **(a)** (*oiseau*) falcon, hawk; **f. mâle,** tercel, tiercel; **f. pèlerin,** peregrine falcon; **chasser au f.,** to hawk; **chasse au f.,** hawking, falconry; **(b)** *Pol* hawk.

fauconneau, -eaux [fokɔno] *nm Orn* young falcon.

fauconnerie [fokɔnri] *nf* **(a)** (*lieu*) hawk house, falcon house; **(b)** (*chasse*) falconry, hawking.

fauconnier [fokɔnje] *nm* falconer.

faufil [fofil] *nm Couture* basting *or Br* tacking thread.

faufilage [fofilaʒ] *nm Couture* basting, *Br* tacking.

faufiler [fofile] **1** *vt Couture* to baste, *Br* to tack (*seam etc*). **2 se faufiler** *vpr* (*en zigzaguant*) to thread one's way (**dans, entre, parmi,** through); (*entrer*) to slip in, to sneak in; **il s'était faufilé avec les invités,** he had slipped in *or* sneaked in with the guests; **se f. entre les voitures,** to nip in and out of the traffic, to thread one's way through the traffic.

faufilure [fofilyr] *nf Couture* **(a)** (*couture*) basted *or Br* tacked seam; **(b)** (*action*) basting, *Br* tacking.

faune¹ [fon] *nm Myth* faun.

faune² *nf* (*animaux*) fauna, animal life (*of region etc*); *Fig Péj* **la f. des boîtes de nuit,** the night-club set.

faunesque [fonɛsk] *adj* faun-like.

faussaire [fosɛr] *n* forger.

fausse [fos] *adj voir* **FAUX¹**.

faussement [fosmɑ̃] *adv* falsely, erroneously; **un sourire f. aimable,** a deceptively pleasant smile.

fausser [fose] **1** *vt* **(a)** to distort (*meaning, reality, result, facts etc*); to skew (*information, figures*); to warp (*s.o.'s mind, judgment*); **(b)** to buckle, to twist, to bend (*key, lock, axle etc*); **(c) f. compagnie à qn,** to give s.o. the slip. **2 se fausser** *vpr* **(a)** (*of voice*) to become forced *or* strained; **(b)** (*of axle etc*) to buckle, to bend.

fausset¹ [fosɛ] *nm Mus* falsetto; **chanter en f.,** to sing falsetto; *Fig* **voix de f.,** high-pitched voice.

fausset² *nm* spigot, vent peg (*of barrel*); **trou de f.,** vent hole.

fausseté [foste] *nf* **(a)** falseness, falsity (*of statement, idea etc*); **(b)** falsehood, untruth; **(c)** (*de caractère*) duplicity; **f. de conduite,** double dealing.

faut [fo] *voir* **FALLOIR**.

faute [fot] *nf* **(a)** (*erreur*) mistake, error; (*responsabilité*) fault; **f. d'orthographe,** spelling mistake; **f. de jugement,** error of judgment; **f. de frappe,** typing error; **f. de français,** = grammatical mistake *or* error; **f. d'impression,** misprint; **f. d'étourderie,** careless *or* thoughtless mistake; **faire une f.,** to make a mistake *or* an error; **être en f.,** to be at fault; **trouver** *ou* **prendre qn en f.,** to catch s.o. in the act; *F* **ce n'est quand même pas ma f. s'il pleut!,** it's hardly my fault if it rains!, you can hardly blame me if it rains!; **il n'y a pas (de) f. de ma part, ce n'est pas (de) ma f.,** it's not my fault, I'm not to blame; **à qui la f.?,** whose fault is it?, who's to blame?; **c'est un peu (de) ma f.,** I'm partly to blame; **il a été tué par ma f.,** it's my fault he was killed; *F* **c'est la f. de personne,** it's nobody's fault, nobody's to blame;

(b) (*manque*) **faire f.,** to be lacking; **la main-d'œuvre nous fait f.,** we're short of labour; **votre jovialité nous a fait f.,** we missed your joviality; **ne se faire f. de rien,** to deny oneself nothing; **nous ne nous faisons jamais f. de lui écrire,** we never fail to write to him; **sans f.,** without fail; **f. de,** for want of, for lack of; **f. de réponse satisfaisante,** failing a satisfactory reply; **f. d'argent/de temps/***etc*, for lack *or* want of money/time/*etc*; **f. d'ordres précis,** in the absence of definite instructions; **f. de quoi,** failing which, otherwise; **f. d'essayer,** for want of trying; **f. de paiement,** non-payment;

(c) (*délit*) offence; (*mauvaise action*) misdemeanour; (*péché*) sin, transgression; (*mauvaise conduite*) misconduct; **f. professionnelle,** professional misconduct;

(d) *Fb etc* foul; *Tennis* fault; *Fb etc* **commettre une f. sur qn,** to foul s.o.; *Tennis* **double f.,** double fault; **f. de pied,** foot fault; **f. de main,** hand ball; **faire une f. de main,** to handle the ball.

fauter [fote] *vi F Vieilli* (*of woman*) to go astray.

fauteuil [fotœj] *nm* **(a)** armchair, easy chair; **f. à oreillettes,** wing chair; **f. à bascule,** rocking chair; **f. pliant,** folding chair; **f. de dentiste,** dentist's chair; **f. roulant,** wheelchair; *Th* **f. d'orchestre,** seat in the *Br* stalls *or Am* orchestra; *Th* **f. de (premier) balcon,** *Br* dress-circle seat, *Am* balcony seat; *Fig* **arriver dans un f.,** (*sans peine*) to win hands down, *Br* to walk it; **(b)** chair (*of meeting*); **occuper le f.,** to be in the chair; **(c) f. (d'académicien),** seat (in the French Academy).

fauteur [fotœr] *nm* **f. de troubles** *ou* **de désordre,** agitator, troublemaker; **f. de guerre,** warmonger.

fautif, -ive [fotif, -iv] **1** *adj* **(a)** (*incorrect*) faulty, incorrect; **monnaie fautive,** flawed currency; **calcul f.,**

miscalculation; **mémoire fautive,** defective memory; **(b)** (*coupable*) at fault, in the wrong; **enfant f.,** child who has been naughty. **2** *n* person at fault *or* in the wrong.
fautivement [fotivmɑ̃] *adv* faultily, incorrectly.
fauve [fov] **1** *adj* **(a)** (*couleur*) fawn, tawny; **(b) bête f.,** (*grand félin*) big cat; *Arch* (*cerf, daim*) deer; **(c) odeur f.,** musky smell; **(d)** *Beaux-Arts* Fauve, Fauvist. **2** *nm* **(a)** (*grand félin*) big cat; **chasse aux (grands) fauves,** big-game hunting; **sentir le f.,** to smell musky; **(b)** (*couleur*) fawn; **(c)** *Beaux-Arts* Fauve, Fauvist.
fauverie [fovri] *nf* big-cat house (*in zoo*).
fauvette [fovɛt] *nf Orn* warbler; **f. d'hiver** *ou* **des haies,** hedge sparrow, dunnock; **f. des roseaux,** reed warbler.
fauvisme [fovism] *nm Beaux-Arts* Fauvism.
faux[1], fausse [fo, fos] **1** *adj* **(a)** (*qui n'est pas vrai*) false, untrue; **fausse nouvelle,** false report; **f. témoin,** false witness; **fausse raison,** pretext; **f. témoignage,** perjury;
(b) (*qui n'est pas d'origine*) false (*hair, teeth, jewellery etc*); bogus (*doctor*); **fausse monnaie,** false *or* counterfeit coin(age); **f. besoins,** false needs; **fausse joie,** false joy; **fausse clef,** skeleton key; **fausse cartouche,** dummy cartridge; **f. plafond,** false ceiling; **fausse fenêtre,** blind window; *Ling* **f. ami,** false friend; **faire un f. sens,** to make a mistranslation; **f. chèque,** forged cheque; **un f. Monet,** a forged *or* fake Monet; **fausse déclaration,** misrepresentation; **f. nom,** false *or* assumed name; *Anat* **fausses côtes,** floating ribs; *Bot* **f. persil,** false parsley, fool's parsley; *Typ* **f. titre,** half *or* bastard title; **fausse sortie,** *Mil* feint sortie; *Th* sham exit;
(c) *Péj* (*hypocrite*) false, devious (*person*); **il est f. comme un jeton, c'est un f. jeton,** he's a hypocrite *or F* a phoney; **un f. frère,** a false friend;
(d) (*incorrect*) wrong; **fausse date,** wrong date; **raisonnement f.,** unsound reasoning; **présenter la conduite de qn sous un f. jour,** to misrepresent s.o.'s conduct; **situation fausse,** equivocal situation; **balance fausse,** inaccurate scales; **f. poids,** false weight; **faire un f. mouvement,** to make an awkward movement; **faire un f. pas,** (*en marchant*) to stumble; (*faire une gaffe*) to blunder, to make a faux pas; **faire fausse route,** to take the wrong road; *Fig* to be on the wrong tack *or* track; **f. calcul,** miscalculation; *Mus* **fausse note,** wrong note; *Fig* **il n'y a eu aucune fausse note,** there was no hitch, everything went smoothly.
2 *adv* **(a)** falsely, wrongly; **chanter f.,** to sing out of tune; **cela sonne f.,** that doesn't sound right; **rire qui sonne f.,** hollow laugh(ter);
(b) à f., wrongly; **poser le pied à f.,** to miss one's footing; **accuser qn à f.,** to wrongly accuse s.o.; **porter à f.,** to be out of true.
3 *nm* **(a) le f.,** the false, the untrue; **distinguer le vrai du f.,** to distinguish truth from falsehood;
(b) (*imitation*) imitation (*of work of art etc*); (*tableau*) forgery; **(bijouterie en) f.,** costume *or* imitation jewellery;
(c) (*contrefaçon*) forgery; *Jur* **usage de f.,** use of forgeries; **s'inscrire en f. contre qch,** to dispute the validity of sth.
faux[2] *nf* **(a)** *Agr* scythe; **(b)** *Anat* falx.
faux-bourdon [foburdɔ̃] *nm* (*pl faux-bourdons*) **(a)** *Mus* fauxbourdon; **(b)** *Ent* drone.
faux-filet [fofilɛ] *nm Culin* sirloin; (*pl faux-filets*).
faux-fuyant [fofɥijɑ̃] *nm* **(a)** (*prétexte*) subterfuge, evasion, dodge; **chercher des f.-fuyants,** to hedge, to prevaricate; **(b)** *Arch* (*sentier*) bypath.
faux-monnayeur [fomɔnɛjœr] *nm* forger, counterfeiter; (*pl faux-monnayeurs*).
faux-semblant [fosɑ̃blɑ̃] *nm* pretence, sham; (*pl faux-semblants*).
faveur [favœr] *nf* **(a)** (*aide, considération*) favour, *US* favor; **gagner** *ou* **obtenir la f. de qn,** to gain s.o.'s favour; **recevoir des marques de f. de qn,** to receive marks of favour from s.o.; **avoir la f. de qn,** to be in favour with s.o.; **être en (grande) f. auprès de qn,** to be in (high) favour with s.o.; **perdre la f. de qn,** to fall out of favour with s.o.; **prendre f.,** to come into vogue; **prix/traitement de f.,** preferential *or* special price/treatment; **jours de f.,** days of grace; **billet de f.,** complimentary ticket;
(b) (*bienfait*) favour, kindness; **faire une f. à qn,** to do s.o. a favour; **faites-moi la f. de venir dîner chez nous,** do me the favour of coming to have dinner with us; **elle lui accorde ses faveurs,** she encourages him;
(c) plaider en f. de qn, to plead on s.o.'s behalf *or* in s.o.'s favour; **on lui fit grâce en f. de sa jeunesse,** he was let off in consideration of his youth; **quête en f. de qn/qch,** collection in aid of s.o./sth;
(d) à la f. de qch, with the help of *or* by means of sth; **à la f. de la nuit,** under cover of darkness;
(e) (*ruban*) favour, ribbon.
favorable [favɔrabl] *adj* **(a)** (*bienveillant*) favourable, *US* favorable (*opinion etc*) (**à,** to); **il est f. à cette idée,** he is in favour of this idea; **mon impression lui fut f.,** he impressed me favourably *or US* favorably; **(b)** (*convenable*) favourable; auspicious (*situation, occasion, circumstances*); favourable (*position*); favourable, fair (*wind*); **le moment était f. pour lui parler,** it was a good moment to speak to him; **recevoir un accueil f.,** to be given a favourable reception; **peu f.,** unfavourable, *US* unfavorable.
favorablement [favɔrabləmɑ̃] *adv* favourably, *US* favorably.
favori, -ite [favɔri, -it] **1** *adj* favourite, *US* favorite (*person, object, racehorse etc*). **2** *n* (*personne*) favourite, *US* favorite. **3** *nf* **favorite,** (*maîtresse du roi*) favourite (mistress). **4** *nm Courses de chevaux* favourite, *US* favorite; **le grand f.,** the odds-on *or* clear favourite.
favoris [favɔri] *nmpl* (side) whiskers.
favoriser [favɔrize] *vt* **(a)** (*avantager*) to favour, *US* to favor (*s.o.*); **les événements l'ont/ne l'ont pas favorisé,** events were in his favour *or* on his side/not in his favour *or* against him; **favorisé par le talent,** blessed with talent; **(b)** (*encourager*) to encourage, to promote (*trade, the arts, crime, disease, growth etc*); **(c)** (*faciliter*) to assist, to further (*undertaking, escape etc*).
favorite [favɔrit] *adj & nf voir* **FAVORI.**
favoritisme [favɔritism] *nm* favouritism, *US* favoritism.
fax [faks] *nm* (*appareil*) fax (machine); (*message*) fax; **envoyer qch par f.,** to send sth by fax, to fax sth; **numéro de f.,** fax number.
faxer [fakse] *vt* to fax.
fayot [fajo] *nm Arg* **(a)** (*haricot sec*) haricot bean, kidney bean; **(b)** *Péj* crawler, creep; *Scol* swot.
fayoter [fajɔte] *vi Arg Péj* to crawl, to creep; *Scol* to swot.
F.B. [ɛfbe] *nm abrév* **franc belge.**
fco *adv Com abrév* **franco.**
f.c(t). (*abrév* **fin courant**) at the end of this month.
féal, -aux [feal, -o] *adj Arch* faithful, trusty (*vassal etc*).
fébrifuge [febrifyʒ] *adj & nm Méd* febrifuge.
fébrile [febril] *adj* feverish, febrile (*pulse, patient etc*); *Fig* feverish (*activity, conversation etc*).
fébrilement [febrilmɑ̃] *adv* feverishly.
fébrilité [febrilite] *nf* feverishness.
fécal, -aux [fekal, -o] *adj* faecal, *US* fecal; **matières fécales,** faeces, *US* feces.
fèces [fɛs] *nfpl* **(a)** faeces, *US* feces; **(b)** *Ch* sediment, precipitate.
fécond [fekɔ̃] *adj* fertile (*woman, animal, egg, mind*); fruitful (*earth etc*); fruitful, productive (*work, idea*); fertile, rich (*soil, imagination*); prolific, productive (*author etc*).
fécondabilité [fekɔ̃dabilite] *nf* **(a)** *Physiol* fertilizability; **(b)** *Écon* **taux de f.,** fertility rate.
fécondable [fekɔ̃dabl] *adj* fertilizable.
fécondateur, -trice [fekɔ̃datœr, -tris] *adj* fertilizing.
fécondation [fekɔ̃dasjɔ̃] *nf Biol* fertilization (*of egg, ovule*); impregnation (*of woman, female animal*); pollination (*of flower, plant*); **f. in vitro,** in vitro fertilization; **f. artificielle,** (*de femme*) artificial insemination; (*de fleur, plante*) artificial pollination.
féconder [fekɔ̃de] *vt Biol* to fertilize (*egg, ovule*); to impregnate (*woman, female animal*); to pollinate (*flower, plant*).
fécondité [fekɔ̃dite] *nf* **(a)** *Physiol* fertility, *Fml* fecundity; *Écon* **taux de f.,** reproduction rate; **(b)** *Fig* fertility (*of land, imagination etc*); fruitfulness, productiveness (*of idea*); productiveness (*of writer etc*).
fécule [fekyl] *nf* starch; *Culin* **f. de pommes de terre,** potato starch *or* flour.
féculent [fekylɑ̃] **1** *adj* starchy (*food*). **2** *nm* starchy food.
fédéral, -aux [federal, -o] **1** *adj* federal. **2** *nm Hist US* Federal.
fédéraliser [federalize] *vt* to federalize.
fédéralisme [federalism] *nm* federalism.
fédéraliste [federalist] *adj & n* federalist.
fédérateur, -trice [federatœr, -tris] **1** *adj* federative. **2** *n* unifier.
fédératif, -ive [federatif, -iv] *adj* federative.
fédération [federasjɔ̃] *nf* federation (*of states etc*); **f. de syndicats (ouvriers),** amalgamated (trade) unions; **f. sportive,** sports federation.
fédéré [federe] **1** *adj* federate (*states etc*). **2** *nm Hist* federate (*of 1871 etc*).

fédérer [federe] *v* **(je fédère; je fédérerai) 1** *vt* to federate, to federalize *(states etc)*. **2 se fédérer** *vpr* to federate.

fée [fe] **1** *nf* fairy; **conte de fées,** fairy tale *or* story; **pays des fées,** fairyland; **doigts de f.,** nimble fingers; **vieille f.,** old hag; **une f. du logis,** an ideal homemaker. **2** *adj* magic, enchanted.

feed-back [fidbak] *nm inv Électron Physiol etc* feedback.

feeder [fidœr] *nm* **(a)** *Él* feeder (cable); **(b)** *(de gaz)* (gas) pipeline.

feeling [filiŋ] *nm (sensibilité)* feeling; **avoir un bon f. pour qch,** to have a good feeling about sth; **faire qch au f.,** to do sth by feeling.

féerie [fe(e)ri] *nf* **(a)** *Th Cin* fantasy, extravaganza; **(b)** *(spectacle merveilleux)* enchanting vision; **paysage de f.,** enchanting scenery; **(c)** *Vieilli (pouvoir des fées)* (power of) enchantment; *(monde des fées)* fairyland.

féerique [fe(e)rik] *adj* **(a)** fairy, magic *(castle, world etc)*; **(b)** *Fig (d'une beauté irréelle)* fairylike, enchanting *(sight etc)*.

feignant, -ante [fɛɲɑ̃, -ɑ̃t] *Arg* **1** *adj* (bone) idle, lazy. **2** *n* loafer, idler.

feindre [fɛ̃dr] *v (prp* **feignant**; *pp* **feint**; *pr ind* **je feins, n. feignons**; *pr sub* **je feigne**; *impf* **je feignais**; *p hist* **je feignis**; *fu* **je feindrai) 1** *vt* to feign, to simulate, to sham *(illness, surprise etc)*; **f. de faire qch,** to pretend to do sth, to make a pretence of doing sth. **2** *vi* to dissemble; **inutile de f.,** it's no use pretending.

feint [fɛ̃] *adj* **(a)** *(simulé)* feigned, assumed, sham *(illness, joy etc)*; **(b)** *Archit* blind, dummy *(door, window)*.

feinte [fɛ̃t] *nf* **(a)** *(blague)* trick; **je lui ai fait une bonne f.,** I played a good trick on him; **(b)** *Boxe Escrime Mil* feint; *Fb Rugby etc* **faire une f. (de passe),** to (sell a) dummy; **(c)** *Vieilli (ruse)* sham, pretence; **sans f.,** frankly, without pretence; **c'était une f. pour le surprendre,** it was a dodge to catch him out.

feinter [fɛ̃te] **1** *vi Boxe Escrime* to feint, to make a feint; *Fb Rugby etc* to (sell a) dummy. **2** *vt F (duper)* take *(s.o.)* in.

feldspath [fɛldspat] *nm Minér* fel(d)spar.

fêlé, -ée [fele] **1** *adj* **(a)** cracked *(glass, voice etc)*; **(b)** *Fig F* **il a le cerveau f.** *ou* **la tête fêlée, il est f.,** he's a bit cracked *or* crazy; **tu est complètement f. de le lui avoir dit!,** you're absolutely crazy to have told him!; **f. de,** crazy *or* wild about. **2** *n F* **f. du jazz/des chocolats/***etc*, jazz/chocolate/*etc* freak.

fêler [fele] **1** *vt* to crack *(glass, china etc)*. **2 se fêler** *vpr (of glass etc)* to crack.

félicitations [felisitasjɔ̃] *nfpl* congratulations; **adresser des f.** *ou* **faire ses f. à qn,** to congratulate s.o. **(pour qch,** on sth); **(toutes mes) f.!,** (many) congratulations!; **il a eu les f. du jury,** he was congratulated by the jury, he received the jury's congratulations.

félicité [felisite] *nf* felicity, bliss(fulness), happiness.

féliciter [felisite] **1** *vt* to congratulate *(s.o.)*; **f. qn pour** *ou* **sur qch/d'avoir fait qch,** to congratulate s.o. on sth/on having done sth; *Iron* **je vous en félicite!,** well done!, how clever of you!; **je ne vous félicite pas!,** you'll get no thanks from me! **2 se féliciter** *vpr (être content)* to be pleased *or* satisfied **(de qch,** with sth); *(se louer)* to congratulate oneself **(de qch,** on sth; **d'avoir fait qch,** on having done sth); **félicitons-nous de ce que nous avons la vie sauve,** let us be thankful we came out alive.

félidés [felide] *nmpl Zool* **les f.,** the cat family, *Spéc* the Felidae.

félin, -ine [felɛ̃, -in] **1** *adj* feline *(race etc)*; *Fig* feline, cat-like *(grace etc)*. **2** *nm* feline; **les grands félins,** the big cats, the great felines.

fellah [fɛla] *nm* fellah, Arab peasant.

fellation [fɛlasjɔ̃] *nf* fellatio.

félon, -onne [felɔ̃, -ɔn] *Hist & Litt* **1** *adj* treacherous, disloyal. **2** *n* traitor.

félonie [felɔni] *nf Hist & Litt (déloyauté)* treachery, disloyalty; *(acte)* (act of) treachery.

felouque [fəluk] *nf (bateau)* felucca.

fêlure [felyr] *nf* crack *(in cup etc)*; **f. du crâne,** fracture of the skull; *Fig* **une f. dans notre amitié,** a rift between us.

femelle [fəmɛl] **1** *adj* **(a)** female *(sex etc)*; she-, female *(animal)*; cow *(elephant, whale etc)*; hen *(bird)*; **(b)** *Tech* female *(screw etc)*; *Él* **prise f.,** female socket; **(c)** *Bot* female, *Spéc* pistillate. **2** *nf (animal)* female; *Arg Péj (femme)* female.

féminin, -ine [feminɛ̃, -in] **1** *adj* feminine *(person, charm etc)*; female *(hormone, population)* women's *(team, band, magazine, fashion etc)*; **le sexe f.,** the female sex; **vêtements féminins,** women's clothes, clothes for women; **les conquêtes féminines d'un homme,** a man's female conquests. **2** *nm Gram* feminine (gender); **ce mot est du f.,** this word is feminine; **au f.,** in the feminine.

féminiser [feminize] **1** *vt* **(a)** *(donner le caractère féminin à)* to feminize, to make feminine; *(rendre efféminé)* to make effeminate; **f. une profession,** to make a profession largely female; **profession féminisée,** largely female profession; **(b)** *Biol* to feminize *(male animal)*; **(c)** *Gram* to make *(word)* feminine. **2 se féminiser** *vpr* **(a)** *(d'une femme)* to become more feminine; *(devenir efféminé)* to become effeminate; **la profession se féminise,** the profession is attracting more and more women; **(b)** *Biol (of male animal)* to feminize.

féminisme [feminism] *nm* feminism.

féministe [feminist] *adj & n* feminist.

féminité [feminite] *nf* femininity.

femme [fam] *nf* **(a)** *(personne)* woman, *pl* women; **les femmes, la f.,** *(le sexe féminin)* women, womankind; **l'émancipation de la f.,** the emancipation of women; **une f.-objet,** a sex object; **cherchez la f.,** there's a woman in the case; **elle est très f.,** she's very feminine; **la f. de ma vie,** the only woman for me; **f. auteur,** woman author, authoress; **f. ministre,** female minister; **f. metteur en scène,** woman *or* female director; **f.-cadre,** female executive; **f. d'État,** stateswoman; **f. médecin,** woman *or* lady doctor; **f. au foyer,** housewife; **parapluie de f.,** lady's umbrella; **elle n'est pas f. à se plaindre,** she's not the sort (of woman) to complain;

(b) *(épouse)* wife; **chercher f.,** to look for a wife; **il l'a prise pour f.,** he took her as his wife; *Jur* **la f. Dupont,** the wife of Dupont; **prendre f.,** to get married;

(c) *(domestique)* **f. de chambre,** housemaid; *(dans un hôtel)* chambermaid; **f. de charge,** housekeeper; **f. de ménage,** cleaning lady, domestic help;

(d) une bonne f., a simple *or* good-natured (old) woman; *F (femme)* a woman; **sa bonne f. de mère,** his old mother; *F* **ma bonne f.,** *(épouse)* my *or* the missus, my old woman;

(e) *Péj* **une vieille bonne f.,** a little old woman; **contes/remèdes de bonne f.,** old wives' tales/remedies.

femme-agent [famaʒɑ̃] *nf* policewoman; *(pl femmes-agents)*.

femmelette [famlɛt] *nf Péj (femme)* weak woman, weakling; *(homme)* weakling.

femme-soldat [famsɔlda] *nf* servicewoman; *(pl femmes-soldats)*.

fémoral, -aux [femɔral, -o] *adj Anat* femoral.

fémur [femyr] *nm Anat* femur, thighbone.

F.E.N. [fɛn] *nf abrév* **Féderation de l'Éducation Nationale.**

fenaison [fənɛzɔ̃] *nf* **(a)** *(action)* haymaking, hay harvest; **(b)** *(saison)* haymaking season.

fendage [fɑ̃daʒ] *nm Tech* splitting, cleaving *(of wood etc)*.

fendeur [fɑ̃dœr] *nm Tech* splitter *(of slates, wood etc)*.

fendillé [fɑ̃dije] *adj* cracked *(rock, wood, skin, paint etc)*; crazed *(glaze, china)*.

fendillement [fɑ̃dijmɑ̃] *nm* cracking *(of paint, wood, skin etc)*; crazing *(of glaze, china)*.

fendiller [fɑ̃dije] **1** *vt* to crack *(wood, rock, skin, paint etc)*; to craze *(glaze, china)*. **2 se fendiller** *vpr (of wood, skin, paint etc)* to crack; *(of china, glaze)* to craze.

fendre [fɑ̃dr] **1** *vt* to split, to cleave *(wood, slate, diamond etc)*; to crack, to fissure *(ground, wall, plaster etc)*; **f. le crâne/la lèvre à qn,** to split (open) s.o.'s skull/lip; **f. les eaux,** to plough through the waters; **f. l'air,** to cleave the air; *(of sound)* to rend the air; **f. la foule,** to force *or* elbow one's way through the crowd; **il gèle à pierre f.,** it's freezing hard, there's a hard frost; **c'était à f. l'âme** *ou* **le cœur,** it was heartbreaking *or* heartrending; **bruit à f. la tête** *ou* **à vous f. les oreilles,** ear-splitting noise. **2 se fendre** *vpr* **(a)** *(of wood etc)* to split, to crack; **se f. le crâne,** to split (open) one's skull; *F* **se f. la pipe** *ou* **la gueule** *ou* **la poire,** to laugh one's head off; **(b)** *Escrime* to lunge; **(c)** *Arg* **se f. de 200 francs,** to fork out 200 francs; **tu ne t'es pas fendu,** it didn't break you *or* the bank; *(pas fatigué)* you didn't bust a gut.

fendu [fɑ̃dy] *adj* split *(ring, pin)*; slit *(skirt etc)*; split *(skull, lip)*; cracked *(plate etc)*; cloven *(hoof)*; **né avec le palais f.,** born with a cleft palate; **bouche fendue jusqu'aux oreilles,** mouth that stretches from ear to ear; **yeux bien fendus,** large *or* wide-open eyes; **vis à tête fendue,** slotted screw.

fenestrage [f(ə)nɛstraʒ] *nm,* **fenêtrage** [fənɛtraʒ] *nm* windows, *Spéc* fenestration *(of building)*; *Ordinat*

windowing.
fenêtre [f(ə)nɛtr] *nf* **(a)** *Archit* window; **f. à guillotine,** sash window; **f. croisée** *ou* **à battants,** casement window; **f. à coulisse,** sliding window; **f. en saillie,** bay window; (*courbe*) bow window; *Rail* **siège côté f.,** window seat; **regarder par la f.,** to look out of the window; *Fig* **une f. sur le monde/l'actualité,** a window on the world/on current events; **(b)** blank, space (*in document*); **(c)** window (*in envelope*); **enveloppe à f.,** window envelope; **(d)** *Astronaut* **f. de lancement,** (launch) window; **(e)** *Ordinat* window.
fenêtrer [fənɛtre] *vt* to put windows in (*house etc*); to fenestrate (*bandage etc*).
fenil [fəni(l)] *nm* hayloft.
fennec [fenɛk] *nm Zool* fennec.
fenouil [fənuj] *nm Bot Culin* fennel.
fente [fɑ̃t] *nf* **(a)** (*fissure*) split, crack (*in wood etc*); crack (*in ground, wall etc*); **(b)** (*ouverture*) slot, slit (*of moneybox, letterbox etc*); slit, gap (*of shutter, wall etc*); slot, groove (*of screw head*); slit (*of skirt, sleeve, pocket*); vent (*of jacket*); **(c)** *Escrime* lunge.
féodal, -aux [feɔdal, -o] *adj* feudal.
féodalisme [feɔdalism] *nm* feudalism.
féodalité [feɔdalite] *nf Hist* feudality, feudal system.
fer [fɛr] *nm* **(a)** (*métal*) iron; **minerai de f.,** iron ore; **f. coulé** *ou* **de fonte,** cast iron; **f. en saumon** *ou* **en gueuse,** pig (iron); **f. forgé,** wrought iron; **fil de f.,** wire; *Fig* **corps/discipline de f.,** iron constitution/discipline; **homme de f.,** man of iron *or* steel; **dur comme (le) f.,** as hard as iron; **j'y crois dur comme f.,** I believe in it very firmly; **une santé de f.,** an iron constitution; **avoir une volonté** *ou* **une tête de f.,** to have an iron will *or* a will of iron;
(b) (*partie métallique*) head (*of axe, arrow*); blade (*of shovel*); tag (*of lace*); **f. de lance,** spearhead; *Fig* **le f. de lance du libéralisme,** the spearhead of liberalism; *Bot* **en f. de lance,** lanceolate; **f. de rabot,** plane iron;
(c) (*arme*) sword; **croiser** *ou* **engager le f. avec qn,** to cross swords with s.o.; **battre le f.,** to fence; **porter le feu et le f. dans un pays,** to put a country to fire and sword;
(d) (*instrument*) tool (*of bookbinder*); **f. (à repasser),** (*pour le linge*) iron; **f. électrique/à vapeur,** electric/steam iron; **donner un coup de f. à qch,** to press *or* iron sth; **f. à friser,** curling tongs *or* iron; *Obst* **fers,** forceps; **f. à souder,** soldering iron; **marquer au f. rouge,** to brand;
(e) *Golf* iron; **grand f.,** driving iron; **f. droit,** putter; **un f. 6,** a (number) 6 iron;
(f) fers, (*chaînes*) irons, chains, fetters; **être aux fers,** to be in irons *or* chains; **briser les fers à qn,** to set s.o. free;
(g) f. (à cheval), horseshoe; **en f. à cheval,** horseshoe (-shaped); **mettre un f. à un cheval,** to shoe a horse; **perdre un f.,** to cast a shoe; *F* **tomber les quatre fers en l'air,** (*of person*) to fall flat on one's back;
(h) *Méd* **(sels de) f.,** iron.
fer-blanc [fɛrblɑ̃] *nm* tin(plate); **boîte en f.-b.,** tin can; **articles en f.-b.,** tinware; (*pl fers-blancs*).
ferblanterie [fɛrblɑ̃tri] *nf* **(a)** (*industrie*) tinplate industry; (*commerce*) tinplate trade; **(b)** (*boutique*) hardware store, *Br* ironmonger's (shop); **(c)** (*articles en fer-blanc*) tinware; (*quincaillerie*) hardware, *Br* ironmongery.
ferblantier [fɛrblɑ̃tje] *nm* **(a)** (*ouvrier*) tinsmith; **(b)** (*marchand*) hardware dealer, *Br* ironmonger.
férié [ferje] *adj* **jour f.,** (public) holiday, *Br* bank holiday, *Am* legal holiday; **lundi prochain est f.,** next Monday is a (public) holiday.
férir [ferir] *vt* **sans coup f.,** without meeting any resistance *or* obstacle.
ferler [fɛrle] *vt* to furl (*sail*).
fermage [fɛrmaʒ] *nm* **(a)** (*mode d'exploitation*) (tenant) farming; **(b)** (*loyer*) (farm) rent.
fermail, -aux [fɛrmaj, -o] *nm* (ornamental) clasp.
ferme¹ [fɛrm] **1** *adj* **(a)** firm (*flesh, fruit, butter etc*); stiff (*dough*); firm, solid (*land*); *Culin* (*peu cuit*) tough; *Fig* firm (*person, action, decision etc*); firm, steady (*writing*); **poutre f.,** firm *or* rigid beam; **la terre f.,** dry land, terra firma; **fromage à pâte f.,** hard cheese; **le malade n'est pas encore f. sur ses jambes,** the patient is not yet steady on his legs; **il répondit d'une voix f.,** he replied in a firm *or* steady voice; **le marché reste très f.,** the market continues very steady; **il faut être f. avec elle,** you must be firm with her; **j'ai la f. intention de le lui dire,** I firmly intend telling him; **être f. dans ses desseins/sa décision,** to be firm *or* steadfast in one's intentions/decision; **attendre qn/qch de pied f.,** to be quite ready for s.o./sth;
(b) prendre un engagement f., to enter into a firm undertaking; **vente/offre f.,** firm *or* definite sale/offer.
2 *adv* (*frapper, pousser etc*) hard; (*parler etc*) firmly; (*travailler, boire*) hard; (*discuter*) keenly; **batailler f.,** to fight hard; **tenir f.,** (*of person*) to stand fast, to hold one's own (**contre,** against); (*of nail*) to hold fast; **f.!,** steady!; **j'y travaille f.,** I'm hard at it; **croire fort et f. aux esprits,** to be a firm believer in spirits; **vendre f.,** to make a firm sale.
ferme² *nf* **(a)** (*exploitation agricole*) farm; (*maison*) farmhouse; (*bâtiments*) farm buildings; **petite f.,** small farm, *Br* smallholding; **f. d'élevage,** cattle farm; **produits de f.,** farm produce; **(b) f. de santé,** health farm; **(c)** (*mode d'exloitation*) **bail à f.,** farming lease; **prendre une terre à f.,** to take a lease of *or* to lease a piece of land; **donner une terre à f.,** to farm out *or* lease out a piece of land; **(d)** *Hist Admin* farming (out) (*of taxes*); **(e)** *Constr* truss (*of roof, bridge*); **(f)** *Th* rigid flat.
fermé [fɛrme] *adj* **(a)** closed; (*shop, box, road etc*); fastened, done up (*garment*); landlocked (*sea*); **bout f.,** dead end (*of pipe etc*); **c'est f. à clé,** it's locked; **dormir à poings fermés,** to sleep soundly *or* like a log; **je pouvais y aller les yeux fermés,** I could go there blindfold *or* with my eyes closed *or* shut; **être f. à qch,** (*of person*) to have no feeling *or* no appreciation of sth; **il a l'esprit f. aux mathématiques,** mathematics is a closed book to him; *Ling* **voyelle fermée,** closed vowel; *Tech* **position fermée,** off position; **chasse fermée,** close season; **(b)** (*impénétrable*) impassive, irresponsive (*expression, face*); **(c)** (*sélect*) exclusive (*society, club*); **(d)** *El* closed (*circuit*).
fermement [fɛrməmɑ̃] *adv* firmly.
ferment [fɛrmɑ̃] *nm* ferment (*of wine etc, Fig of discontent etc*).
fermentation [fɛrmɑ̃tasjɔ̃] *nf* **(a)** fermentation (*of wine etc*); **(b)** *Fig* agitation, unrest, ferment.
fermenter [fɛrmɑ̃te] *vi* **(a)** (*of wine, beer*) to ferment, to work; (*of dough*) to rise; **(b)** *Fig* (*of mind, passions*) to be in a ferment.
fermer [fɛrme] **1** *vt* **(a)** to close, to shut (*door, window, box, umbrella, book etc*); to fasten, to do up (*garment*); **f. violemment la porte,** to slam *or* bang the door; **f. sa porte à qn,** to close one's door to s.o.; **f. la porte à clef/au verrou,** to lock/bolt the door; **f. les rideaux,** to draw *or* close the curtains; **f. le store,** to pull down the blind; **f. une maison,** to shut up a house; **f. boutique,** to shut up shop; **on ferme!,** closing time!; **f. une liste/un débat,** to close a list/a debate; **fermez la parenthèse,** close brackets; **f. la frontière,** to close the frontier; **f. une carrière à qn,** to close a career to s.o.; **f. un robinet/l'eau/le gaz,** to turn off a tap *or Am* a faucet/the water/the gas; **f. l'électricité/la radio,** to turn *or* switch off the light/the radio; *Él* **f. un circuit,** to close a circuit; *Fin* **f. un compte,** to close an account; *Rail* **f. la voie,** to block the line; **f. les yeux,** to close *or* shut one's eyes; **manger la bouche fermée,** to eat with one's mouth closed *or* shut; *F* **je n'ai pas pu f. l'œil de la nuit,** I couldn't sleep a wink all night; *Fig* **il faut f. les yeux sur ses erreurs,** one has to turn a blind eye *or* close *or* shut one's eyes to his mistakes; *Tricot* **f. cinq mailles,** to cast off five stitches; *Arg* **ferme ta gueule!, ferme-la!, la ferme!,** shut up!, shut it!, shut your trap!;
(b) f. la marche, to bring up the rear.
2 *vi* (*of door box, shop etc*) to close, to shut; (*of garment*) to fasten, to do up; **le couvercle ferme mal,** the lid doesn't shut *or* close properly; **on ferme le lundi,** we close *or* shut on Mondays, we are closed *or* shut on Mondays.
3 se fermer *vpr* (*of door, box, eyes etc*) to close, to shut; (*of garment*) to fasten, to do up; (*of wound*) to heal, to close up; **à cette demande son visage se ferma,** at this request his face froze.
fermeté [fɛrməte] *nf* **(a)** firmness (*of flesh, fruit, ground, writing etc*); stiffness (*of dough*); *Bourse* **f. des cours,** steadiness of prices; **(b)** (*résolution*) firmness; (*dans l'adversité*) steadfastness; **f. de l'esprit,** strength of mind; **agir avec f.,** to act firmly.
fermette [fɛrmɛt] *nf* (*petite ferme*) small farm; **(b)** (*maison de campagne*) (small) farmhouse.
fermeture [fɛrmətyr] *nf* **(a)** (*action*) closing, shutting (*of gates, door etc*); closing (*of road, frontier, list, debate*); **f. automatique des portières,** (*annonce*) doors close *or* shut automatically; **f. à clef,** locking; **f. des ateliers,** (*définitive*) closing down of the workshops; **heure de f.,** closing time (*of shop*); finishing time (*of factory, office*); **à l'heure de la f. des bureaux, la ville est encombrée,** when the offices come out the town is packed; **f. de la pêche/chasse,** close of the fishing/hunting season; **f. d'un compte,** closing of an account; *Él* **f. du circuit,** closing of the circuit; **(b) f. d'esprit,** narrow-mindedness; **(c)** (*dispositif*) fastener (*of garment, bag etc*); **f. éclair** ®, **f. à glissière,** zip (fastener), *Am* zipper; **f. à rouleau,** revolving shutter (*of shop*).

fermier, -ière [fɛrmje, -jɛr] **1** *nm* **(a)** *Agr* farmer; (*locataire*) (tenant) farmer; **(b)** *Hist Admin* **f. général,** farmer general. **2** *nf* **fermière,** (woman) farmer; (*épouse*) farmer's wife. **3** *adj* **beurre f.,** farm butter; **poulet f.,** farm *or* free-range chicken.
fermoir [fɛrmwar] *nm* (*agrafe*) clasp; (*bouton-pression*) (snap) fastener (*of bracelet, bag, book etc*).
féroce [ferɔs] *adj* ferocious, savage, fierce (*animal, person*); fierce, ferocious (*look, attack, criticism*); savage, cruel (*joy, mockery etc*); ravenous (*appetite*); raging, wild (*desire*); **bête f.,** wild animal *or* beast.
férocement [ferɔsmɑ̃] *adv* ferociously, savagely, fiercely.
férocité [ferɔsite] *nf* ferocity, ferociousness; **avec f.,** fiercely.
Féroé [ferɔe] *nm* **les îles F.,** the Faroe Islands, the Faroes.
ferrage [fɛraʒ] *nm* shoeing (*of horse*); rimming (in metal) (*of wheel*).
ferraillage [fɛrɑjaʒ] *nm Constr* (steel) framework (*of reinforced concrete building*).
ferraille [fɛrɑj] *nf* **(a)** (*métaux*) old iron, scrap (iron); **tas de f.,** scrap heap; *F* (*vieille auto*) heap of scrap; **mettre qch à la f.,** to put sth on the scrap heap; **faire un bruit de f.,** to rattle, to clank; **marchand de f.,** scrap merchant; **(b)** *F* (*petite monnaie*) coppers, small change.
ferraillement [fɛrɑjmɑ̃] *nm* **(a)** *Péj* (*combat à l'épée*) sword rattling; **(b)** (*bruit*) rattling, clanking (*of car etc*).
ferrailler [fɛrɑje] *vi* **(a)** *Péj* (*se battre à l'épée*) to clash swords, to slash about with swords; **(b)** (*faire un bruit de ferraille*) to clank, to rattle.
ferrailleur [fɛrɑjœr] *nm* **(a)** *Péj* (*bretteur*) sword rattler, swashbuckler; **(b)** (*revendeur*) scrap merchant.
ferrate [fɛrat] *nm Ch* ferrate.
ferré [fɛre] *adj* **(a)** metal-tipped (*stick etc*); hobnailed (*shoe*); metal-rimmed (*wheel*); shod (*horse*); tagged (*shoelace*); **cheval f. à glace,** roughshod horse; *Rail* **voie ferrée,** (*rails*) track; (*route*) railway *or Am* railroad (line); **par voie ferrée,** by rail; *Rail* **réseau f.,** railway *or Am* railroad system *or* network; **(b)** *F* (*calé*) **être f. sur,** to be well up in *or* on (*subject, chemistry etc*).
ferrer [fɛre] *vt* **(a)** to tip (*stick etc*) with metal; to nail (*shoe*); to rim (*wheel*) with metal; to shoe (*horse*); to tag (*shoelace*); **f. une porte,** to fit locks and hinges to a door; **(b)** *Pêche* to strike (*fish*).
ferret [fɛrɛ] *nm* tag (*of shoelace*).
ferreur [fɛrœr] *nm* **f. de chevaux,** farrier, shoeing smith.
ferreux, -euse [fɛrø, -øz] *adj Ch Minér* ferrous; **alliages f.,** iron alloys, ferro-alloys.
ferricyanure [fɛrisjanyr] *nm Ch* ferricyanide.
ferrique [fɛrik] *adj Ch* ferric (*salt etc*).
ferrite [fɛrit] *nf* ferrite; *Ordinat* **mémoire à f.,** ferrite core memory.
ferro- [fɛrɔ] *préf* ferro-.
ferrochrome [fɛrɔkrom] *nm Métal* ferrochrome, ferrochromium.
ferrocyanure [fɛrɔsjanyr] *nm Ch* ferrocyanide.
ferroélectricité [fɛrɔelɛktrisite] *nf* ferroelectricity.
ferroélectrique [fɛrɔelɛktrik] *adj* ferroelectric.
ferromagnétique [fɛrɔmaɲetik] *adj* ferromagnetic.
ferromagnétisme [fɛrɔmaɲetism] *nm* ferromagnetism.
ferronnerie [fɛrɔnri] *nf* **(a)** (*objets*) **f. (d'art),** (decorative) ironwork, wrought ironwork; **grille en f.,** wrought-iron gate; **(b)** (*métier*) ironwork; **(c)** (*atelier*) ironworks.
ferronnier, -ière [fɛrɔnje, -jɛr] *n* **(a)** (*artisan*) **f. (d'art),** worker in wrought iron; **(b)** (*commerçant*) ironware dealer.
ferrotypie [fɛrɔtipi] *nf Phot* ferrotype.
ferroviaire [fɛrɔvjɛr] *adj* railway, *Am* railroad (*network, company, traffic etc*); **transports ferroviaires,** rail transport; **les grandes lignes ferroviaires,** the main railway *or Am* railroad lines.
ferrugineux, -euse [fɛryʒinø, -øz] *adj* ferruginous; **source ferrugineuse,** chalybeate spring.
ferrure [fɛryr] *nf* **(a)** (*garniture*) (iron) fitting; **ferrures de porte,** door fittings; **ferrures en cuivre,** brass fittings; **(b)** shoeing (*of horse*).
ferry, *pl* **ferries** [fɛri] *nm* = **FERRY-BOAT**.
ferry-boat [fɛribot] *nm* (*pour voitures*) (car) ferry; (*pour trains*) (train) ferry; (*pl ferry-boats*).
fertile [fɛrtil] *adj* fertile (*soil, field etc*); *Fig* fertile, inventive (*mind, imagination*); inventive (*composer, writer etc*); **semaine f. en événements,** eventful week.
fertilisable [fɛrtilizabl] *adj* fertilizable.
fertilisant [fɛrtilizɑ̃] **1** *adj* fertilizing. **2** *nm* fertilizer.
fertilisation [fɛrtilizɑsjɔ̃] *nf* fertilization, fertilizing.
fertiliser [fɛrtilize] *vt* to fertilize (*soil etc*).
fertilité [fɛrtilite] *nf* fertility (*of soil, imagination etc*).
féru [fery] *adj* **f. de qn,** smitten with s.o.; **f. d'un sujet,** passionately interested in a subject; **être f. d'une idée,** to be set on an idea.
férule [feryl] *nf Hist Scol* ferule, = ruler (*for punishment on the hands*); *Fig* **être sous la f. de qn,** to be under s.o.'s sway *or* domination *or* rule.
fervent, -ente [fɛrvɑ̃, -ɑ̃t] **1** *adj* fervent, ardent, keen (*devotion, admirer, Christian etc*); ardent (*love*); fervent (*prayer*); enthusiastic (*approval*). **2** *n* devotee (**de,** of).
ferveur [fɛrvœr] *nf* fervour, *US* fervor; **avec f.,** (*prier*) fervently, earnestly; (*travailler*) with enthusiasm; (*aimer*) with devotion, ardently; (*écouter*) eagerly.
fesse [fɛs] *nf* **(a)** *Anat* buttock; **fesses,** buttocks, behind, bottom; *F* **donner à qn un coup de pied aux fesses,** to give s.o. a kick in the pants; *Arg* **poser ses fesses,** (*s'asseoir*) to park one's backside; *Arg* **attraper qn par la peau des fesses,** to grab hold of s.o. just in time; *Arg* **serrer les fesses,** (*avoir peur*) to have the wind up, to have the jitters; (*être courageux*) to sit tight; *Arg* **occupe-toi de tes fesses!,** mind your own damn business!; *Arg* **film/revue de fesses,** porn *or* dirty film/magazine; *Arg* **histoire de fesses,** dirty story; **(b)** (*de navire*) tuck.
fessée [fese] *nf* **(a)** (*coups*) spanking; **donner une f. à qn,** to give s.o. a spanking, to spank s.o.; **(b)** *Fig* (*défaite*) drubbing.
fesse-mathieu [fɛsmatjø] *nm Vieilli* skinflint, Scrooge; (*pl fesse-mathieux*).
fesser [fese] *vt* **f. qn,** to spank s.o., to smack s.o.'s bottom.
fessier, -ière [fesje, -jɛr] **1** *adj Anat* buttock, *Spéc* gluteal (*muscle etc*); **poche fessière,** hip pocket (*of trousers etc*). **2** *nm* **(a)** *Anat* gluteal muscle; **(b)** *F* (*fesses*) backside, behind.
festin [fɛstɛ̃] *nm* feast, banquet; **quel f.!,** what a feast!, what a spread!; **salle de f.,** banqueting hall; **faire (un) f.,** to feast, to banquet.
festival, -als [fɛstival] *nm* (musical) festival; **f. du film,** film festival.
festivalier, -ière [fɛstivalje, -jɛr] **1** *adj* festival. **2** *n* (*participant*) festival participant; (*visiteur*) festival-goer.
festivités [fɛstivite] *nfpl* festivites, celebrations.
feston [fɛstɔ̃] *nm* **(a)** festoon (*of flowers etc*); **(b)** *Couture* scallop; **à festons,** scalloped; **point de f.,** buttonhole stitch.
festonner [fɛstɔne] *vt* **(a)** (*de guirlandes etc*) to festoon; **(b)** *Couture* to scallop (*hem etc*).
festoyer [fɛstwaje] *vi* (**je festoie; je festoierai**) to feast, to carouse.
fêtard, -arde [fɛtar, -ard] *n F* reveller, roisterer.
fête [fɛt] *nf* **(a)** (*de village*) fete, fête, fair; (*de ville*) festival; **f. champêtre** *ou* **de village,** village fete *or* fair; **f. foraine,** fun fair; **f. de charité** *ou* **de bienfaisance,** charity fete *or* bazaar; **f. de la bière,** beer festival; **f. d'aviation** *ou* **aéronautique,** air display *or* show;
(b) (*soirée*) party; (*d'apparat*) entertainment; **donner une f.,** to give a party *or* an entertainment; **faire une f.,** to have a party; **une petite f.,** a party;
(c) (*gaiété*) **air de f.,** festive air; **le village était en f.,** the village was in a festive mood; **faire la f.,** to have a good time, to live it up; **faire f. à qn,** to welcome s.o. with open arms; **être de la f.,** to be one of the party; **se faire une f. de (faire) qch,** to look forward to (doing) sth; **il ne s'était jamais vu à pareille f.,** he had never had such a good time; *Iron* **il n'était pas à la f.,** he was having a bad time;
(d) (*du saint dont on porte le nom*) saint's *or* name day; **souhaiter une bonne f. à qn,** to wish s.o. a happy saint's day; *Iron* **ça va être ta f.!,** you're in for it!; **on va lui faire sa f.!,** he'll get what's coming to him!;
(e) (*célébration*) *Rel* feast, festival; (*civile*) holiday; **la f. des Morts,** All Soul's Day; **jour de f.,** *Rel* feast day; (*jour férié*) public holiday; **la f. nationale du 14 juillet,** Bastille Day; **la f. nationale de la victoire,** *Br* ≈ Armistice Day, *US* ≈ Veterans Day; **f. légale,** *Br* bank holiday, *Am* legal holiday; **les fêtes (de fin d'année),** the Christmas and New Year holidays; **c'est f. demain,** tomorrow is a holiday; *Fig* **ce n'est pas tous les jours f.,** Christmas comes but once a year; *F* **elle est de bonne humeur?, c'est la f.!,** she's in a good mood?, put the flags out!
Fête-Dieu [fɛtdjø] *nf Rel* Corpus Christi; (*pl Fêtes-Dieu*).
fêter [fete] *vt* **(a)** to celebrate (*victory, event, Christmas etc*); **f. la naissance de qn,** to celebrate s.o.'s birthday; **f. ses soixante ans,** to celebrate one's sixtieth birthday; **f. un saint,** to keep a saint's day; **(b)** (*accueillir chaleureusement*) to fete (*s.o.*); **dîner pour f. le nouveau membre,** dinner to welcome the new member.
fétiche [fetiʃ] *nm* (*objet de culte*) fetish; (*mascotte*)

mascot.

fétichiser [fetiʃize] *vt* to turn into a fetish.

fétichisme [fetiʃism] *nm* fetishism.

fétichiste [fetiʃist] **1** *adj* fetishistic. **2** *n* fetishist.

fétide [fetid] *adj* fetid, rank, stinking, foul.

fétidité [fetidite] *nf* fetidness.

fétu [fety] *nm* **f. (de paille),** (wisp of) straw; **être emporté comme un f.,** to be blown along like a straw in the wind.

fétuque [fetyk] *nf Bot* fescue (grass).

feu¹, *pl* **feux** [fø] **1** *nm* **(a)** *(élément, flammes, incendie)* fire; **le f. et l'eau,** fire and water; **craindre qch comme le f.,** to fear sth like the plague, to stand in dread of sth; *Fig* **jouer avec le f.,** to play with fire; **soleil de f.,** fiery sun; **faire f. des quatre pieds,** *(of horse)* to make the sparks fly; *(of person)* to go all out; **faire du f.,** to make a fire; **il fait f. de tout bois,** he makes the most of his opportunities, he turns everything to account; *F* **avoir le f. au derrière,** to be in a tearing hurry; **mettre (le) f. à qch,** to set fire to sth, to set sth on fire; **mettre une ville à f. et à sang,** to put a town to fire and sword; **enlever de la peinture au f.,** to burn off paint; **en f.,** on fire; **joues en f.,** burning cheeks; **visage en f.,** flushed face; **prendre f.,** to catch fire; *Fig* to fly into a rage; **f. de forêt,** forest fire; **il y a le f. à la grange!,** the barn is on fire!; **au f.!,** fire!; *Fig* **faire la part du f.,** to cut one's losses; *F* **il n'y a pas le f. au lac,** there's no particular hurry; **jeter f. et flamme (contre qn),** to rage (at s.o.); **est-ce que vous avez du f.?,** have you got a light?;

(b) *(passion)* ardour, *US* ardor, passion; *Arch* *(amour)* love; **tout f. tout flamme,** heart and soul; **parler avec f.,** to speak passionately; **dans le f. de la discussion,** in the heat of the debate;

(c) *(matières allumées)* fire; **f. nu,** open fire; **allumer/faire un f.,** to light/make a fire; **garniture de f.,** fire irons; **f. de joie,** bonfire; **f. de camp,** campfire; **feux d'artifice,** fireworks; **au coin du f.,** by the fire(side); *Fig* **leur amitié ne fera pas long f.,** their friendship won't last long;

(d) mettre une chaudière en f., to fire up a boiler;

(e) *(supplice)* **condamner qn au f.,** to condemn s.o. to be burnt at the stake; **j'en mettrais la main au f.,** I would swear to it; **épreuve du f.,** ordeal by fire; **mourir à petit f.,** to die by inches; **faire mourir qn à petit f.,** to kill s.o. by inches; *Fig* to keep s.o. on tenterhooks;

(f) *Culin* **faire cuire à f. doux** *ou* **à petit f.,** to cook gently *or* over a slow heat; *(au four)* to cook in a slow oven; **à grand f., à f. vif,** over a brisk heat; *(au four)* in a quick *or* hot oven; **ustensiles qui vont au f.,** fireproof utensils; **cuisinière à quatre feux,** four-burner cooker; **j'ai du lait sur le f.,** I have some milk on the stove; **coup de f.,** (slight) burning; *Fig* busiest time; *Fig* **être dans son coup de f.,** to be at one's busiest;

(g) *(maison)* **hameau de 50 feux,** hamlet of 50 houses; **n'avoir ni f. ni lieu,** to be homeless, to have neither hearth nor home;

(h) *Mil etc* *(tir)* fire; *(combat)* action; **arme à f.,** firearm; **bouche à f.,** piece of ordnance *or* artillery; **faire f. sur qn,** to fire *or* shoot at s.o.; **commencer** *ou* **déclencher** *ou* **ouvrir le f.,** to open fire; **f.!,** fire!; **sous le f.,** under fire; **faire long f.,** *(of pistol, Fig of plan etc)* to hang fire; **aller au f.,** to go into action; **coup de f.,** (gun)shot; **nous avons reçu des coups de f.,** we were fired on *or* shot at; **il n'a jamais vu le f.,** he has never heard a gun fired; **f. roulant,** running fire, drumfire; *Fig* **un f. roulant de questions,** a running fire of questions; *Fig* **être entre deux feux,** to be caught in the middle, to be between two fires;

(i) *Nau* *(lumière)* light; **feux (d'entrée) de port,** harbour lights; **droits de feux,** light dues; **f. à occultations** *ou* **à éclipses,** occulting light; **feux de route,** navigation lights; **feux de mouillage,** anchor lights *(of ship)*; **f. de tribord,** starboard light;

(j) *Av* *(lumière)* light; **feux de balisage,** boundary lights; **feux de piste,** runway lights; **feux de bord** *ou* **de navigation,** navigation lights;

(k) *Aut* *(de signalisation)* light; **f. rouge,** *(lumière)* red light; *(objet)* (traffic) lights; **f. orange/vert,** amber/green light; **feux (de signalisation),** (traffic) lights; **attendre au(x) feu(x),** to wait at the lights; *Fig* **donner le f. vert,** to give the green light *or* the go-ahead **(à,** to); *Fig* **mettre le f. rouge à un projet,** to veto a project; *Fig* **je lui a donné un f. orange,** I gave him a provisional go-ahead;

(l) *Aut* *(de véhicule)* light; **tous feux éteints,** without lights; **f. de brouillard,** fog lamp; **feux de croisement,** dipped headlights, *Am* low beam; **feux de détresse,** hazard (warning) lights; **feux de position,** sidelights; **feux de route,** main *or Am* high beam; **feux de stationnement,** parking lights;

(m) *Rail* **f. d'avant,** headlight *(of locomotive)*; **f. d'arrière,** tail light, rear light *(of train)*;

(n) feux d'un diamant, fire *or* sparkle of a diamond; **yeux pleins de f.,** flashing eyes; **n'y voir que du f.,** to make neither head nor tail of sth.

2 *adj inv* **rouge f.,** flame-coloured; **chien noir et f.,** black and tan dog.

feu² *adj* *(inv if preceding article or poss adj)* late; **la feue reine, f. la reine,** the late queen; **f. mon père,** my late father; **fils de feue Berthe Dupont,** son of the late Berthe Dupont, son of Berthe Dupont deceased.

feudataire [fødatɛr] *nm Hist* feudatory.

feuillage [fœjaʒ] *nm* leaves.

feuillaison [fœjɛzɔ̃] *nf* leafing, coming into leaf.

feuille [fœj] *nf* **(a)** leaf *(of plant, tree)*; **mettre** *ou* **prendre ses feuilles,** to (come into) leaf; **f. morte,** dead leaf; *Av* **descente en f. morte,** dead-leaf dive; **f. de vigne,** *(sur sculpture)* fig leaf; *Culin* vine leaf; **f. de chou,** cabbage leaf; *F Péj* *(journal)* rag; **oreilles en f. de chou,** cauliflower ears; *F* **il est dur de la f.,** he's hard of hearing;

(b) f. de métal, sheet of metal; **fer en feuilles,** sheet iron; **f. d'or,** gold leaf; **f. d'étain,** tinfoil; **f. de bois,** thin board;

(c) sheet *(of paper)*; **f. volante** *ou* **mobile,** loose sheet; **feuilles d'un livre,** leaves of a book; **f. de garde,** fly leaf *(of book)*; **bonnes feuilles (de publicité),** advance proofs;

(d) *(document)* sheet; **f. de paie,** payslip; **f. de présence,** attendance sheet *or* list; *Ind* time sheet; **f. d'impôt,** notice of (tax) assessment; **f. de température,** temperature chart; **f. de service,** (duty) roster; **f. de route,** *Com* waybill; *Mil* travel warrant; **f. de maladie,** = form given by doctor to patient for claiming reimbursement from Social Security;

(e) *(journal)* paper;

(f) *Ordinat* **f. de calcul,** spreadsheet.

feuillées [fœje] *nfpl Mil* latrines *(in camp)*.

feuille-morte [fœjmɔrt] *adj inv & nm inv* *(couleur)* russet.

feuiller [fœje] *vt Menuis* to rabbet, to groove *(board etc)*.

feuilleret [fœjrɛ] *nm Tech* rabbet plane, grooving plane.

feuillet [fœjɛ] *nm* **(a)** leaf *(of book)*; **(b)** thin sheet *(of wood etc)*; **(c)** *Zool* omasum, psalterium *(of ruminant's stomach)*.

feuilletage [fœjtaʒ] *nm Culin* **(a)** *(action)* rolling and folding *(of dough for flaky pastry)*; **(b)** *(aspect)* flakiness *(of pastry)*; **(c)** *(pâte)* flaky pastry.

feuilleté [fœjte] **1** *adj* foliated, laminated, lamellar *(rocks etc)*; laminated *(glass etc)*; **pare-brise (en verre) f.,** laminated windscreen *or Am* windshield; *Culin* **pâte feuilletée,** flaky pastry, *Br* puff pastry, *Am* puff paste. **2** *nm Culin* **un f.,** a pastry *(made from flaky pastry)*.

feuilleter [fœjte] *vt* **(je feuillette; je feuilletterai) (a)** *Culin* to roll and fold *(pastry)*; **(b) f. un livre,** to turn over the pages of a book; *(sommairement)* to leaf through *or* flip through a book; **livre bien feuilleté,** well-thumbed book.

feuilleton [fœjtɔ̃] *nm* **(a)** *Journ* *(chronique)* (regular) feature; **(b)** *Journ Rad TV* *(histoire)* serial; *(épisode)* instalment, episode; **publier un roman en feuilletons,** to serialize a novel.

feuilletoniste [fœjtɔnist] *n Journ* *(auteur de romans-feuilletons)* serial writer; *(chroniqueur)* feature writer.

feuillu [fœjy] **1** *adj* *(ayant beaucoup de feuilles)* leafy; *(à feuilles)* broad-leaved *(tree)*. **2** *nm* broad-leaved tree.

feuillure [fœjyr] *nf Menuis* rabbet, groove.

feulement [følmɑ̃] *nm* snarl, growl *(of tiger)*; growl *(of cat)*.

feuler [føle] *vi* *(of tiger)* to snarl, to growl; *(of cat)* to growl.

feutrage [føtraʒ] *nm* **(a)** *Tech* felting *(of hair, wool, fabric)*; **(b)** felting, covering *(of surface, object)* with felt; **(c)** matting, felting *(of woollen garment)*.

feutre [føtr] *nm* **(a)** *Tex* felt; **chaussons de f.,** felt slippers; **(b)** *(chapeau)* felt hat, fedora; **(c) (crayon) f.,** felt(-tip) pen, felt-tip; **stylo f.,** felt-tip (pen) (with fine nib).

feutré [føtre] *adj* **(a)** *(garni de feutre)* felt(-covered); **porte feutrée,** baize door; **(b)** muffled *(sound)*; **à pas feutrés,** with noiseless tread; **s'éloigner à pas feutrés,** to steal away, to slip quietly away; **(c)** *(après le lavage)* matted *(sweater etc)*.

feutrer [føtre] **1** *vt* **(a)** *Tech* to felt, to make *(hair, wool)* into felt; **(b)** *(garnir de feutre)* to cover with felt, to felt; **(c)** *Fig* to muffle *(sound etc)*. **2** *vi* *(of woollen garment)* to become matted, to felt. **3 se feutrer** *vpr* *(of woollen garment)* to become matted, to felt.

feutrine [føtrin] *nf* lightweight felt.

fève [fɛv] *nf* **(a)** (*plante, graine*) broad bean; **f. (des Rois),** (*fève, figurine etc*) charm (*put in Twelfth Night cake*); **(b)** *Can* (haricot) bean; **f. verte,** string bean; **f. jaune,** wax bean; **(c) f. de cacao,** cocoa bean.

février [fevrije] *nm* February; **en f., au mois de f.,** in (the month of) February; **le sept f.,** (on) the seventh of February, (on) February the seventh, *Am* (on) February seventh.

fez [fɛz] *nm* fez.

F.F. [ɛfɛf] *nm abrév* **franc(s) français.**

F.F.I. [ɛfɛfi] *nfpl Hist abrév* **Forces françaises de l'intérieur.**

F.F.L. [ɛfɛfɛl] *nfpl Hist abrév* **Forces françaises libres.**

fi [fi] *int* **(a)** *Vieilli & Hum* fie!, for shame!; **(b) faire fi de qch,** to despise *or* scorn sth.

fiabilité [fjabilite] *nf* reliability, dependability (*of machine, person etc*).

fiable [fjabl] *adj* reliable, dependable (*machine, person etc*).

fiacre [fjakr] *nm* (*voiture à cheval*) hackney (carriage, cab).

fiançailles [fjɑ̃saj] *nfpl* engagement; *Fig* **les f. de deux entreprises,** the planned merger of two companies.

fiancé, -ée [fjɑ̃se] **1** *adj* engaged (**à, avec qn,** to s.o.). **2** *nm* fiancé; **les fiancés,** (*couple*) the engaged couple. **3** *nf* **fiancée,** fiancée.

fiancer [fjɑ̃se] **1** *vt* to betroth (**à, avec qn,** to s.o.). **2 se fiancer** *vpr* to become *or* get engaged (**à, avec qn,** to s.o.).

fiasco [fjasko] *nm* fiasco; (*film, pièce de théâtre etc*) flop; **faire f.,** (*of plan*) to come to nothing; (*of film etc*) to be a flop, to flop.

fiasque [fjask] *nf* (Italian) flask.

fibranne [fibran] *nm Tex* staple fibre *or US* fiber.

fibre [fibr] *nf* **(a)** fibre, *US* fiber; **riche en fibres alimentaires,** rich in dietary fibre; **panneau de fibres agglomérées,** fibreboard, *US* fiberboard; **coton à fibres longues,** long-staple cotton; **la f. optique,** fibre optics; **fibres optiques,** optical fibres; **câble en fibres optiques,** fibre optic cable; **f. de verre,** glass fibre, fibreglass, *US* fiberglass; **(b)** *Fig* **avoir la f. sensible,** to be susceptible *or* impressionable; **faire jouer la f. paternelle/patriotique,** to play on paternal/patriotic feelings.

fibreux, -euse [fibrø, -øz] *adj* fibrous (*tissue etc*); stringy (*meat*); **panneau f.,** fibreboard, *US* fiberboard.

fibrille [fibrij] *nf Physiol Bot* fibril(la).

fibrine [fibrin] *nf Physiol* fibrin.

fibrineux, -euse [fibrinø, -øz] *adj Physiol* fibrinous.

fibrinogène [fibrinɔʒɛn] *nm Physiol* fibrinogen.

fibrome [fibrom] *nm Méd* fibroma, fibroid.

ficaire [fikɛr] *nf Bot* lesser celandine, pilewort.

ficelage [fislaʒ] *nm* **(a)** (*action*) tying up; **(b)** (*liens*) string(s).

ficelé [fisle] *adj* **(a)** (*lié*) tied up (*parcel, captive etc*); **(b)** *F* (*habillé*) got up.

ficeler [fisle] *vt* (**je ficelle; je ficellerai**) to tie up (*parcel etc*) (with string); to tie up (*captive etc*).

ficelle [fisɛl] *nf* **(a)** (*mince corde*) string, twine; **f. à fouet,** whipcord; **les ficelles de la marionnette,** the puppet's strings; **(b)** *Fig* **c'est lui qui tient** *ou* **tire les ficelles,** he's the one who pulls the strings; **connaître les ficelles,** (*du métier*) to know the ropes, to know the tricks of the trade; **(c)** (*pain*) long thin loaf.

fiche¹ [fiʃ] *nf* **(a)** *El* (*prise*) plug; (*broche*) pin; *Tél* (*de standard*) (patch) plug; **(b)** (*morceau de papier*) slip (of paper); (*formulaire*) form; (*dépliant*) leaflet; **f. scolaire,** school record (card); *Ind* **f. de contrôle,** checking form, *Br* docket; **f. dentaire,** dental chart; **f. médicale,** medical record (card); *Admin* **f. anthropométrique,** = (criminal) dossier; **f. d'état civil,** = record of civil status (*birth details and marital status*); *Ordinat* **f. d'état,** report form; **(c)** (*carte*) (index, record) card; **jeu de fiches,** card index; **mettre des informations en** *ou* **sur fiche(s),** to card-index data; **f. perforée,** perforated card; **(d)** (*cheville*) peg, pin (*of iron, wood etc*); **(e)** *Hist Cartes etc* (bone, ivory) counter, marker; *Fig* **f. de consolation,** crumb of comfort.

fiche² *vt & vpr F* = **FICHER².**

ficher¹ [fiʃe] **1** *vt* **(a)** (*enfoncer*) to drive in (*nail, stake etc*); to stick in (*pin*); **f. une épingle dans qch,** to stick a pin into sth; **(b)** (*mettre sur fiche*) to file (away), to put (*data, person*) on file. **2 se ficher** *vpr* to stick (**dans,** in).

ficher² *v* (*inf souvent* **fiche**; *pp* **fichu**) *F* **1** *vt* **(a)** (*mettre*) to stick, to shove, *Br* to bung; **f. par terre,** to chuck (*hat etc*) on the ground; *Fig* to bring down, to overthrow (*government*); to mess up, to put paid to (*plan*); **f. qn à la porte,** to chuck s.o. out; (*licencier*) to give s.o. the push, to fire s.o.; **f. qn dedans,** (*faire se tromper*) to land *or* drop s.o. in it; (*mettre en prison*) to put s.o. inside;

(b) (*faire*) to do; **il n'a rien fichu de la journée,** he's done damn all all day, *Br* he hasn't done a stroke (of work) all day;

(c) (*donner*) **f. une gifle à qn,** to give s.o. a slap in the face; **fiche-moi la paix!,** leave me alone!, clear off!; **je t'en fiche!,** no way!, you must be joking!; **ça la fiche mal,** (*fait mauvais effet*) it looks really bad (**de faire,** to do);

(d) f. le camp, (*s'enfuir*) to shove off, to clear off; **fiche-moi le camp!,** shove off!, clear off!; *F* **va te faire fiche!,** get the hell out of here!, get lost!

2 se ficher *vpr* **(a)** (*se mettre*) **se f. par terre,** (*tomber*) to go sprawling; (*se jeter*) to fling oneself to the ground; **se f. dedans,** (*se tromper*) to goof, to make a boo-boo;

(b) se f. de qn/qch, (*tourner en ridicule*) to make fun of s.o./sth; (*mépriser*) not to care *or* give a damn about s.o./sth; **vous vous fichez de moi!,** you're kidding (me)!, you're joking!; **ça, c'est se f. du monde!,** well, of all the nerve!, what a damned cheek!; **je m'en fiche (pas mal),** I don't care *or* give a damn, I couldn't care less.

fichet [fiʃɛ] *nm* peg (*used for backgammon*).

fichier [fiʃje] *nm* **(a)** (*ensemble de fiches*) card index; *Ordinat* file; **f. actif,** active file; **f. séquentiel,** batch *or* sequential file; **f. de travail,** working file; **volume du f.,** file size; **(b)** (*boîte*) card-index box; (*meuble*) card-index cabinet; **f. rotatif,** rotary (card) file.

fichiste [fiʃist] *n* filing clerk, card indexer.

fichtre [fiʃtr] *int F Vieilli* **(a)** (*étonnement*) golly!, good gracious!; **(b)** (*admiration*) my!, *Br* I say!; **(c)** (*contrariété*) blow!, blast!; **(d)** (*intensif*) **f. oui!,** I should say so!, rather!; **f. non!.** not likely!, no fear!

fichtrement [fiʃtrəmɑ̃] *adv F* (*extrêmement*) awfully, frightfully.

fichu¹ [fiʃy] *adj F* **(a)** (*maudit*) rotten, awful; **quel f. pays!,** what a godforsaken country!; **quel f. temps!,** what filthy weather!; **(b) il est f.,** (*perdu*) he's done for, it's all up with him, he's had it; **c'est f.!,** (*sans espoir*) (we can) forget it!; **ma robe est fichue,** my dress has had it; **(c)** (*habillé*) **être bien/mal f.,** to be well/badly turned out *or* dressed; **(d) être mal f.,** (*un peu malade*) to be off colour *or* out of sorts; **(e)** (*capable*) **elle serait fichue d'oublier le rendez-vous,** she'd be quite capable of forgetting the appointment.

fichu² *nm* headscarf; (*couvrant les épaules*) fichu, (small) shawl.

fictif, -ive [fiktif, -iv] **1** *adj* **(a)** (*imaginaire*) fictitious, imaginary (*person etc*); **(b)** (*faux*) false (*promise*); false, fictitious (*name etc*); sham (*fight*); **(c)** *Fin* **valeur fictive,** face value (*of notes*). **2** *nm* **le réel et le f.,** truth and fiction.

fiction [fiksjɔ̃] *nf* (*fait imaginé*) *& Littér* fiction; **f. légale,** legal fiction; **film de f.,** fictitional film; **livre de f.,** work of fiction; **la réalité dépasse la f.,** reality is stranger than fiction; **la politique-f.,** political pie in the sky.

fictivement [fiktivmɑ̃] *adv* fictitiously.

fidéicommis [fideikɔmi] *nm Jur* trust.

fidéicommissaire [fideikɔmisɛr] *nm Jur* trustee.

fidèle [fidɛl] **1** *adj* **(a)** (*loyal*) faithful, loyal (*friend, supporter etc*); faithful (*spouse, dog*); **lecteur f.,** regular *or* loyal reader (*of newspaper etc*); **client f.,** regular *or* loyal customer; **rester f. à une promesse,** to stand by *or* keep a promise; **être f. à ses engagements,** to stand by one's commitments; **rester f. à ses idées,** to remain true to one's ideas; **peu f.,** unreliable;

(b) (*exact*) faithful, accurate (*copy, translation, account etc*); **la traduction n'est pas f. au texte,** the translation is not faithful to the original; **mémoire f.,** reliable memory; **témoin f.,** accurate witness.

2 *n* (*partisan*) (loyal) supporter; *Com* regular *or* loyal customer; (*lecteur de journal etc*) regular *or* loyal reader; *TV* regular *or* loyal viewer; *Rel* **les fidèles,** the faithful; (*à l'église*) the congregation.

fidèlement [fidɛlmɑ̃] *adv* **(a)** (*servir etc*) faithfully, loyally; *Com* loyally; **(b)** (*traduire, reproduire etc*) accurately, faithfully.

fidéliser [fidelize] *vt* to win the loyalty of (*customers, readers, viewers etc*).

fidélité [fidelite] *nf* **(a)** (*loyauté*) faithfulness (*of friend, spouse, dog etc*); fidelity (*of spouse*); *Com* loyalty (*of customer, reader, viewer etc*); **serment de f.,** oath of allegiance; **f. conjugale,** marital fidelity; **f. à ses engagements,** standing by one's commitments; **(b)** (*exactitude*) faithfulness, accuracy (*of translation, copy etc*); reliability (*of memory*); **haute f.,** high fidelity, hi-fi.

Fidji [fidʒi] *adj* **les îles F.,** Fiji, the Fiji Islands.

fidjien, -ienne [fidʒjɛ̃, -jɛn] **1** *adj* Fijian. **2** *nm Ling* Fijian. **3** *n* **F.,** Fijian.
fiduciaire [fidysjɛr] **1** *adj* fiduciary (*loan, currency etc*); *Jur* **en dépôt f.,** in trust. **2** *nm Jur* fiduciary, trustee.
fiduciairement [fidysjɛrmɑ̃] *adv Jur* in trust.
fief [fjɛf] *nm* **(a)** *Hist* fief; **franc f.,** freehold; **(b)** *Fig* (*spécialité*) domain; **(c) f. électoral,** loyal constituency.
fieffé [fjefe] *adj* arrant (*liar*); rank (*impostor*); out-and-out (*scoundrel etc*).
fiel [fjɛl] *nm* **(a)** gall (*of ox, poultry etc*); **(b)** *Fig* (*venin*) bitterness, venom, malice; **épancher son f.,** to vent one's spleen.
fielleux, -euse [fjɛlø, -øz] *adj* rancorous, bitter.
fiente [fjɑ̃t] *nf* droppings (*of birds*).
fienter [fjɑ̃te] *vi* (*of bird*) to leave droppings.
fier[1], -ère [fjɛr] **1** *adj* **(a)** (*digne*) proud; **courage f.,** lofty courage; **être trop f. pour mendier,** to be too proud to beg; **être f. de ses enfants,** to be proud of one's children; **être f. de qch/d'avoir fait qch,** to be proud of sth/of having done sth; **(b)** (*hautain*) proud, haughty, **air f.,** lordly air; **il n'y a pas là de quoi être f.,** that's nothing to boast about; **f. comme Artaban,** as proud as a peacock; **(c)** (*sacré*) fine; **f. imbécile,** first-rate *or* real idiot; **tu m'as fait une fière peur,** a fine *or* rare fright you gave me. **2** *n* **faire le f.,** to show off.
fier[2] (se) [səfje] *vpr* (*impf & pr sub* **n. n. fiions**) **se f. à qn/qch,** (*avoir confiance en*) to trust (in) s.o./sth; (*compter sur*) to rely on *or* count on s.o./sth; **fiez-vous à moi,** (*action*) leave it to me; (*renseignement*) take my word for it; **ne pas se f. à ses yeux,** not to believe one's eyes; **je me fie à lui pour décider,** I am relying on *or* counting on him for a decision; **ne vous y fiez pas,** beware!; (*n'y croyez pas*) don't count on it.
fier-à-bras [fjɛrabra] *nm* swaggerer, braggart; (*pl fiers-à-bras*).
fièrement [fjɛrmɑ̃] *adv* **(a)** (*dignement*) proudly; **(b)** *Arch* (*d'une manière hautaine*) haughtily; **(c)** *F Vieilli* (*extrêmement*) famously.
fiérot, -ote [fjero, -ɔt] *F* **1** *adj* cocky (*person*). **2** *n* **faire le f.,** to swagger (around).
fierté [fjɛrte] *nf* **(a)** (*satisfaction*) pride; **tirer f. de qch,** to take pride in sth; **ma fille/maison est ma f.,** my daughter/house is my pride and joy; **(b)** (*arrogance*) pride, haughtiness; **(c)** (*amour-propre*) pride, self-respect.
fiesta [fjɛsta] *nf F* (*fête*) binge, fling; **faire une** *ou* **la f.,** to live it up, to have a good time; **c'est la f.!,** it's party time!
fièvre [fjɛvr] *nf* **(a)** *Méd* (*maladie*) fever; (*température*) temperature; **avoir une f. de cheval,** to have a raging fever; **avoir (de) la f.,** to be feverish, to have a (high) temperature; **elle a 40 de f.,** she has a temperature of 40 degrees; **f. typhoïde,** typhoid (fever); **f. paludéenne,** malaria; **(b)** (*excitation*) excitement, frenzy; **sans f.,** calmly; **dans la f. de la campagne électorale,** in the heat *or* excitement of the electoral campaign; **travailler avec f.,** to work feverishly; **(c)** (*désir*) passion (**de qch,** for sth); urge (**de faire qch,** to do sth).
fiévreusement [fjevrøzmɑ̃] *adv* feverishly, frantically.
fiévreux, -euse [fjevrø, -øz] *adj* **(a)** *Méd* feverish (*pulse, person etc*); **(b)** *Fig* feverish, frantic (*activity, preparations etc*); feverish (*imagination*); anxious (*wait*).
fifille [fifij] *nf F* little girl, daughter; **f. à son papa,** daddy's little girl.
fifre [fifr] *nm* **(a)** (*instrument*) fife; **(b)** (*joueur*) fife (player).
fifty-fifty [fiftififti] *adv* **faire f.-f.,** to go halves *or* fifty-fifty; **partager f.-f.,** to share fifty-fifty *or* half and half.
fig. (*abrév* **figure**) fig.
figer [fiʒe] *v* (**figeant, il figeait**) **1** *vt* to coagulate, to congeal (*blood*); to congeal (*oil, sauce etc*); **des cris qui vous figent le sang,** bloodcurdling cries; **ce spectacle lui a figé le sang,** this sight made his blood run cold; **figé sur place,** rooted to the spot; **locution figée,** set phrase; **style figé,** stilted style. **2 se figer** *vpr* (*of blood*) to coagulate, to congeal; (*of oil, sauce etc*) to congeal; *Fig* (*of look, features*) to freeze; *Fig* **son sang se figea,** his blood ran cold; **son sourire se figea quand il entendit la nouvelle,** his smile froze when he heard the news.
fignolage [fiɲɔlaʒ] *nm F* touching up (*of piece of work, drawing etc*).
fignoler [fiɲɔle] *F* **1** *vt* to put the finishing touches to, to touch up (*piece of work, drawing etc*). **2** *vi* to be meticulous.
fignoleur, -euse [fiɲɔlœr, -øz] **1** *adj* meticulous. **2** *n* perfectionist, meticulous worker.
figue [fig] *nf* **(a)** (*fruit*) fig; **mi-f., mi-raisin,** half one thing and half another; **un petit sourire mi-f., mi-raisin,** a half-hearted *or* wry *or* forced smile; **ton mi-f., mi-raisin,** tone (of voice) half in jest and half in earnest; **(b) f. de Barbarie,** prickly pear.
figuier [figje] *nm* fig (tree); **f. de Barbarie,** prickly pear (tree).
figurant, -ante [figyrɑ̃, -ɑ̃t] *n Th* walk-on, supernumerary, *F* super; *Cin* extra; **rôle de f.,** *Th* walk-on (part), bit part; *Cin* bit part; *Fig* **n'être qu'un f. dans qch,** to take no active part *or* be just an onlooker in sth.
figuratif, -ive [figyratif, -iv] **1** *adj* figurative (*plan etc*); figurative, representational (*art, artist etc*). **2** *n* figurative *or* representational artist.
figuration [figyrasjɔ̃] *nf* **(a)** (*représentation*) figuration, representation; **(b)** *Th* (*acteurs*) walk-on actors, *F* supers; (*rôle*) walk-on (part), bit part; **faire de la f.,** to do walk-on parts, to play bit parts; **(c)** *Cin* (*acteurs*) extras; (*rôle*) bit part; **faire de la f.,** to play bit parts.
figurativement [figyrativmɑ̃] *adv* figuratively.
figure [figyr] *nf* **(a)** (*visage*) face; **jeter qch à la f. de qn,** to throw sth in s.o.'s face; *F* **casser la f. à qn,** to smash s.o.'s face in; *F* **se casser la f.,** to fall flat on one's face; *Fig* (*échouer*) to come a cropper;
(b) (*mine*) face, *Fml* countenance; **faire bonne f. à qn,** to give s.o. a warm welcome; **faire une drôle de f.,** to pull a face, to give a funny look; **faire longue f.,** to pull a long face;
(c) (*représentation, image*) figure; **figures de cire,** waxworks, waxwork figures; **f. de proue,** figurehead (*of ship, Fig of political party etc*); *Cartes* **les figures,** the court cards, *Am* the face cards; **prendre f.,** to take shape; **les grandes figures de la Guerre,** the great figures of the War; **faire f. de richesse,** to give an impression of wealth; **elle fait f. d'intellectuelle dans ce milieu,** she gives the impression of *or* has the appearance of an intellectual amongst these people; **faire pauvre** *ou* **piètre f.,** to cut a sorry figure; **faire grande f. dans une entreprise,** to play an important role in a business;
(d) (*de danseur, patineur etc*) figure; **figures géométriques,** geometrical figures; **livre avec figures dans le texte,** book with figures *or* diagrams in the text;
(e) *Ling* figure; **f. de mots** *ou* **de rhétorique,** figure of speech.
figuré [figyre] **1** *adj* **(a)** diagrammatic (*plan etc*); figured (*material*); **(b)** *Ling* **sens f.,** figurative meaning. **2** *nm Ling* **au f.,** in the figurative sense, figuratively.
figurément [figyremɑ̃] *adv* figuratively.
figurer [figyre] **1** *vt* to represent; **une croix figure une église,** a cross stands for *or* represents *or* indicates a church; **la scène figure le camp des brigands,** the scene shows the brigands' camp. **2** *vi* **(a)** (*se trouver*) to appear, to figure; **je ne veux pas que mon nom figure dans l'affaire,** I don't want my name to appear *or* figure in the matter; **f. dans un catalogue,** to be listed *or* appear in a catalogue; **(b)** *Th* to have a walk-on (part); *Cin* to have a bit part. **3 se figurer** *vpr* to imagine (**que,** that); **se f. qch,** to imagine sth; **figurez-vous la situation,** imagine the situation, picture the situation (to yourself); **ne vous figurez pas que je sois satisfait,** do not imagine that I'm satisfied; **je suis à sec, figure-toi,** believe it or not, I'm broke.
figurine [figyrin] *nf* figurine, statuette.
fil [fil] *nm* **(a)** *Tex* (*brin*) thread, yarn; (*tissu*) linen; **f. de coton/nylon,** cotton/nylon yarn; **f. de lin,** linen yarn *or* thread; **des draps pur f.,** (pure) linen sheets; **f. d'emballage,** pack(ing) thread; **f. d'Écosse,** lisle thread; **bas de f.,** lisle stockings; **gants de f.,** cotton gloves; **laine trois/quatre fils,** three-/four-ply wool; **f. à coudre,** sewing thread, cotton; *Fig* **astuce cousue de f. blanc,** obvious *or* blatant trick; *Fig* **c'est cousu de f. blanc,** you can see right through it, it won't fool anybody; *Fig* **de f. en aiguille,** little by little, gradually, one thing leading to another; *Fig* **brouiller les fils,** to muddle things up; **démêler les fils d'une intrigue,** to unravel the threads of a plot; *Fig* **avoir un f. sur la langue,** to (have a) lisp; *Fig* **trouver le f. d'Ariane** *ou* **le f. conducteur,** to find the clue (to the mystery); **mince comme un f.,** thin as a rake *or* pole;
(b) strand (*of cable, rope etc*); **fils de marionnette,** puppet strings; **f. dentaire,** dental floss; *Fig* **c'est lui qui tient les fils,** he's the one who holds (all) the strings; *Fig* **être dans le droit f. de qch,** to be in line with sth; *Pêche* **donner du f. au poisson,** to give the fish some line; *Fig* **sa vie ne tenait qu'à un f.,** his life hung by a thread; *F* **avoir un f. à la patte,** (*être tenu par un engagement*) to be tied up;

(c) **f. d'araignée,** spider's thread; **fils de la vierge,** gossamer;

(d) **f. (métallique), f. de fer,** wire; **f. de fer barbelé,** barbed wire; *F* **il n'a pas inventé le f. à couper le beurre,** he'll never set the Thames on fire;

(e) *El* **f. (électrique),** (electric) wire; **f. (souple),** lead, cord, *Br* flex; **f. de masse** *ou* **de terre,** earth (wire), *Am* ground (wire); **f. téléphonique,** telephone wire; *Tél* **donner** *ou* **passer un coup de f. à qn,** to give s.o. a call, to call s.o. (up), *Br* to give s.o. a ring, *Br* to ring s.o. (up); **être au bout du f.,** to be on the line *or* phone; **je viens d'avoir Martin au bout du f.,** I've just had Martin on the line *or* phone; **télégraphie/téléphonie sans f.,** wireless telegraphy/telephony; **téléphone sans f.,** cordless telephone;

(f) grain (*of wood, meat*); **les haricots verts sont pleins de fils,** the green beans are stringy; **contre le f., à contre-f.,** against *or* across the grain; **couper de droit f.,** to cut (*wood*) along the grain; to cut (*cloth*) on the straight;

(g) *Fig* (*cours*) **au f. de l'eau** with the current, downstream; **se laisser aller au f. de l'eau,** to let oneself drift (with the current); **au f. des jours,** as the days go by, with the passing days; **le f. des événements,** the chain of events; **perdre/reprendre le f. de la conversation,** to lose/pick up the thread of the conversation; **suivre le f. des idées de qn,** to follow the thread of s.o.'s ideas;

(h) edge (*of knife, sword etc*); **donner le f. à un rasoir,** to put an edge on a razor; *Fig* **le président est sur le f. du rasoir,** the president is on a knife edge; *Litt* **passer des prisonniers au f. de l'épée,** to put prisoners to the sword.

filage [filaʒ] *nm* spinning (*of wool etc*).

filament [filamɑ̃] *nm* (a) fibre, *US* fiber (*of meat*); filament (*of electric lamp*); (b) *Biol* filament.

filamenteux, -euse [filamɑ̃tø, -øz] *adj* filamentous.

filandière [filɑ̃djɛr] *nf Tex Arch* (hand-)spinner.

filandreux, -euse [filɑ̃drø, -øz] *adj* (a) tough, stringy (*meat etc*); (b) *Fig Péj* involved, confused (*explanation, sentence etc*).

filant [filɑ̃] *adj* (a) (*qui coule*) fluid; (b) **étoile filante,** shooting star, falling star.

filasse [filas] 1 *nf* (*matière*) tow; **f. de chanvre,** hemp. 2 *adj inv* **cheveux (blond) f.,** tow-coloured hair; **aux cheveux (blond) f.,** towheaded.

filateur [filatœr] *nm* (spinning) mill owner.

filature [filatyr] *nf* (a) *Tex* (*action*) spinning; (b) (*fabrique*) spinning mill; **f. de coton,** cotton mill; (c) shadowing, tailing (*by detective etc*); **il a été pris en f.,** he was shadowed *or* tailed.

fil-de-fériste [fildəferist] *n* high-wire artiste; (*pl fil-de-féristes*).

file [fil] *nf* (a) line (*of people, cars etc*); **f. (d'attente),** queue, *Am* line; *Av* stacking; **se mettre** *ou* **se ranger en f.,** to line up; **prendre la f., se mettre à la f.,** to join the queue *or Am* line; **marcher à la f.** *ou* **en f.,** to walk in single file *or* one behind another; **à la** *ou* **en f. indienne,** in Indian *or* single file; **entrer/sortir en f.** *ou* **à la f.,** to file in/out; **cinq bières à la f.,** five beers in a row *or* in succession *or* one after another; **fumer des cigarettes à la f.,** to chain-smoke; **trois jours de f.,** three days in a row *or* in succession; *Aut* **stationner en double f.,** to double-park; *Mil* **par f. à droite/à gauche!,** right/left wheel!;

(b) *Aut* (*couloir*) lane; **ne changez pas de f.,** keep in lane; **rouler dans** *ou* **sur la f. de droite,** to drive in the right-hand lane.

filé [file] 1 *adj* (a) with a run, *Br* laddered (*stocking, tights*); (b) **verre f.,** spun glass. 2 *nm Tex Tech* thread; **f. d'or,** gold thread.

filer [file] 1 *vt* (a) to spin (*cotton, glass etc*);

(b) *Nau* to pay out, to run out (*cable*); to slip (*moorings*);

(c) to prolong, to spin out, to draw out (*story etc*); *Mus* to draw out, to sustain (*note*); to pour out (*oil*) in a trickle; **f. des jours heureux,** to spend *or* pass happy days; *F* **ils filent le parfait amour,** they are living love's dream; *Cartes* **f. les cartes,** to lay the cards down slowly;

(d) (*of detective etc*) to shadow, to tail (*suspect*);

(e) (*donner*) *F* **f. qch à qn,** to slip *or* give s.o. sth; **je lui ai filé ma voiture,** I gave him my car; **f. un coup de pied/une gifle à qn,** to give s.o. a kick/a slap;

(f) (*démailler*) to put a run in, *Br* to ladder (*stocking, tights*).

2 *vi* (a) (*passer*) **le temps file,** time flies; **laisser f. un câble,** to pay out a cable; **l'argent lui file entre les mains** *ou* **les doigts,** money runs through his hands *or* fingers like water; **train qui file à toute vitesse,** train rushing along at full speed; **les voitures filaient sur la route,** cars were speeding along the road; *Nau* **f. (à) vingt nœuds,** to proceed at twenty knots;

(b) *F* (*partir en vitesse*) to dash *or* rush off; **f. (en douce),** to slip away *or* off; **allez, filez!,** clear off!, scram!; **f. à l'anglaise,** to take French leave;

(c) *F* **f. doux,** (*se soumettre*) to knuckle under;

(d) (*of stocking, tights*) to run, *Br* to ladder; **j'ai un bas qui file,** I've got a run *or Br* ladder;

(e) **la lampe file,** the lamp is smoking;

(f) (*of oil etc*) to run; (*of wine*) to rope.

filet[1] [filɛ] *nm* (a) thin streak (*of light*); thin stream (*of air*); (thin) trickle, dribble (*of water etc*); thread, wisp (*of smoke*); **f. de voix,** thin *or* weak voice; *Culin* **ajoutez-y un f. de citron/vinaigre,** add a dash of lemon/vinegar; **f. d'une vis,** thread *or* worm of a screw; (b) *Anat* frenum, string (*of the tongue*); (c) *Bot* filament (*of stamen*); (d) (*de reliure*) *& Archit* filet; (e) *Typ* rule; (f) *Culin* fillet (*of fish, beef etc*); (g) (*de harnais*) snaffle.

filet[2] *nm* (a) net; (*au cirque*) (safety) net; **f. de pêche,** fishing net; **f. à papillons,** butterfly net; **être pris au f.,** to be caught in the net; *Fig* **faire tomber** *ou* **attirer qn dans ses filets,** to ensnare s.o.; **un beau coup de f. pour la police,** a good haul for the police; *Fig* **c'est du sans f.,** he is *or* they are *etc* out on a limb; **f. à provisions,** string *or* net bag; **f. pour cheveux,** hairnet; *Rail* **f. à bagages,** luggage rack; (b) *Tennis* net; **monter au f.,** to go up to the net; **jeu au f.,** net play; **balle de f.,** let (ball); **juge de f.,** net-cord judge; (c) *Fb etc* net.

filetage [filtaʒ] *nm Tech* (a) (*action*) threading, screw cutting; (b) (*filets*) thread, worm (*of screw*).

fileter [filte] *vt* (**je filète; je filèterai**) *Tech* (a) to wiredraw (*metal*); to draw (*wire*); (b) to thread, to screw (*bolt, rod etc*).

fileur, -euse [filœr, -øz] *n Tex* (a) (*de métier à tisser*) spinner; (b) (*avec la soie*) (silk) throwster.

filial, -ale, -aux [filjal, -o] 1 *adj* filial. 2 *nf Com* **filiale,** subsidiary (company).

filialement [filjalmɑ̃] *adv* filially.

filiation [filjɑsjɔ̃] *nf* (a) (*lien de parenté*) filiation; **en f. directe,** in direct line; (b) (*famille*) descendants; (c) *Fig* (*de mots, d'événements etc*) relationship (**de,** between).

filière [filjɛr] *nf* (a) *Admin* channels; **la f. administrative,** the (usual) official channels; **passer** *ou* **suivre la f.,** (*pour obtenir qch*) to go through the official channels; (*comme employé*) to work one's way up; **choisir la f. nucléaire,** to go down the nuclear road, to choose the nuclear path; *Scol* **suivre une f. scientifique/commerciale,** to study scientific/business subjects; (b) (*de trafiquants, terroristes etc*) network; **remonter la f.,** (*of police etc*) to go back along the network (to the person at the top); (c) *Tech* (*pour fileter une vis*) screw plate; (*pour étirer*) draw(ing) plate; **travailler un métal à la f.,** to draw a metal; (d) *Zool* spinneret (*of spider, silkworm*).

filiforme [filifɔrm] *adj* (a) *Zool* filiform, threadlike; (b) *F* (*très mince*) spindly (*person, legs etc*).

filigrane [filigran] *nm* (a) (*ouvrage d'orfèvrerie*) filigree; **broche en f.,** filigree brooch; (b) (*de papier, billet de banque etc*) watermark; *Fig* **lire en f.,** to read between the lines.

filigrané [filigrane] *adj* (a) filigreed (*brooch etc*); (b) watermarked (*paper etc*).

filin [filɛ̃] *nm* rope.

fille [fij] *nf* (a) (*descendante directe*) daughter; *Fig* **la superstition est (la) f. de l'ignorance,** superstition is the daughter of *or* is born of ignorance;

(b) (*enfant*) girl; **petite f.,** little girl; **jeune f.,** girl, young woman; **ma pauvre f.!,** my poor child *or* dear!; **nom de jeune f.,** maiden name; **école de filles,** girls' school;

(c) (*femme*) woman; **vieille f.,** old maid, spinster; **habitudes de vieille f.,** old-maidish habits; *Vieilli* **rester f.,** to remain single *or* unmarried;

(d) **f. d'honneur,** maid of honour (*at Court*);

(e) (*prostituée*) **f. (de joie), f. publique,** prostitute;

(f) *Rel* **les filles de Port-Royal,** the sisters *or* nuns of Port-Royal;

(g) (*employée*) **f. de service,** maidservant; **f. de cuisine,** kitchenmaid; **f. de salle,** (*dans un hôtel*) waitress; (*dans un hôpital*) ward orderly; **f. de comptoir,** barmaid.

fille-mère [fijmɛr] *nf Péj & Vieilli* unmarried mother; (*pl filles-mères*).

fillette [fijɛt] *nf* (a) (*petite fille*) little girl; (b) *Arg* (*bouteille*) half-bottle (*of wine*).

filleul, -eule [fijœl] 1 *nm* godson, godchild; **f. de guerre,** adopted godson, protégé (*during the war*). 2 *nf* **filleule,**

goddaughter, godchild.

film [film] *nm* **(a)** *Phot* film; **(b)** *Cin* (*pellicule*) film; (*œuvre*) film, picture, movie, *Am* motion picture; **le f.,** (*art*) film, cinema; **tourner un f.,** to make a film; **f. d'aventure/catastrophe,** adventure/disaster film; **f. noir,** film noir; **f. d'actualité,** newsreel, news film; **f. annonce,** trailer; **f. supplémentaire,** supporting film; **f. fixe (d'enseignement),** filmstrip; **(c)** *Fig* (*déroulement*) sequence (*of events, life etc*); **(d)** (*couche*) film; **f. dentaire,** (dental) plaque; **f. alimentaire,** clingfilm.

filmage [filmaʒ] *nm Cin* filming, shooting.

filmer [filme] **1** *vt* **(a)** *Tech* (*enduire*) to cover (*sth*) with a film; **(b)** *Cin* to film, to shoot (*scene*); to film (*novel etc*). **2** *vi Cin* to film.

filmique [filmik] *adj* cinematic.

filmographie [filmɔgrafi] *nf Cin* (*liste*) filmography.

filmologie [filmɔlɔʒi] *nf* film studies, study of the cinema.

filmothèque [filmɔtɛk] *nf* film library.

filon [filɔ̃] *nm* **(a)** *Min* vein, seam, lode (*of copper etc*); reef (*of gold*); **(b)** *Arg* (*situation lucrative*) cushy job; **il tient le f., il a déniché** *ou* **trouvé le (bon) f.,** he's struck it rich; **j'ai un bon f. pour avoir des vidéos gratuites,** I know where I can get free videos easily.

filou [filu] *nm* **(a)** (*voleur*) thief; **(b)** (*escroc*) rogue, swindler, crook.

filoutage [filutaʒ] *nm* **(a)** (*vol*) stealing; **(b)** (*escroquerie*) swindling, cheating.

filouter [filute] *vt* **(a) f. qch à qn,** to steal sth from s.o.; **(b) f. qn,** to swindle *or* cheat s.o.

filouterie [filutri] *nf* **(a)** (*action*) swindling, cheating; **(b)** (*manœuvre*) swindle, fraud.

fils [fis] *nm* son; **elle et ses deux f.,** she and her two boys *or* sons; *Péj* **f. à papa,** daddy's boy; **c'est bien le f. de son père,** he's a chip off the old block; **être le f. de ses œuvres,** to be a self-made man; **c'est le f. spirituel de René Char,** he's the spiritual son of René Char; **M. Duval f.,** Mr Duval junior; **le f. Duval,** young Duval; *Rel* **le F. de Dieu,** the Son of God.

filtrable [filtrabl] *adj Vieilli* filt(e)rable (*virus*).

filtrage [filtraʒ] *nm* **(a)** filtering (*of liquid, gas, sound etc*); **(b)** *Fig* (*contrôle*) screening (*of information, visitors etc*).

filtrant [filtrɑ̃] *adj* filtering (*agent etc*); **verre f.,** filter glass; **lunettes à verres filtrants,** glasses with filter lenses; *Vieilli* **virus f.,** filt(e)rable virus, filter passer.

filtration [filtrasjɔ̃] *nf* filtration, filtering.

filtre [filtr] *nm Tech Phot El etc* filter; **(bout) f.,** filter (tip) (*of cigarette*); **f. à café,** coffee filter; **(café) f.,** filter coffee; **papier f.,** filter paper; *Aut* **f. à air/huile,** air/oil filter; *Phot* **f. de couleur** *ou* **coloré,** colour filter; *Rad TV* **f. antiparasites,** interference filter *or* suppressor.

filtrer [filtre] **1** *vt* **(a)** to filter (*water, coffee, gas, sound, light etc*); **(b)** *Fig* (*contrôler*) to screen (*information, visitors etc*). **2** *vi* (*of liquid*) to filter, to percolate, to seep (**à travers,** through); **la lumière filtrait à travers** *ou* **par les branches,** the light filtered through the branches; **laisser f. une nouvelle,** to let a piece of news leak *or* filter out.

fin¹ [fɛ̃] *nf* **(a)** (*dernier moment*) end, conclusion (*of film, meeting, work etc*); expiration (*of contract etc*); end, fall (*of empire, régime etc*); end (*of hope, misfortunes etc*); (*mort*) end, death; *Cin* **'f.',** 'The End'; **le cinquième avant** *ou* **en commençant par la f.,** the fifth from the end, the last but four; **f. du jour,** close of day; **f. du mois,** end of the month; *Com* **f. de mois,** monthly statement; **assurer ses fins de mois,** to make sure one has enough money at the end of the month; **avoir des fins de mois difficiles,** to be always short of money at the end of the month; **payable f. prochain,** payable at the end of next month; **on se reverra f. mars** *ou* **à la f. de mars,** we'll meet again at the end of March; **en f. de soirée,** towards the end of the evening; **il est venu vers la f. de l'après-midi,** he came late in *or* towards the end of the afternoon; **l'année touche** *ou* **tire à sa f.,** the year is drawing to an end *or* a close; **en f. d'année,** at the end of the year; **jusqu'à la f. des temps** *ou* **des siècles,** till the end of time; **style f. de siècle,** fin de siècle *or* decadent style; **le vocabulaire est à la f. du livre,** the vocabulary is at the back of the book; **vis sans f.,** endless screw; **des activités sans f.,** never-ending *or* endless activities; **il parle sans f.,** he never stops talking, he talks endlessly; **f. prématurée,** untimely death *or* end; **il est sur sa f.,** he hasn't much longer to live; **la maison est sur ses fins,** the firm is on its last legs; **mettre f. à qch,** to put an end *or* a stop to sth; **mettre fin à sa vie** *ou* **ses jours,** to put an end to one's life; **mettre une entreprise à f.,** to bring an undertaking to an end, to complete an undertaking; **elle se marie pour faire une f.,** she's getting married in order to settle down; **prendre f., avoir une f.,** to come to an end; **mener une affaire à bonne f.,** to bring a matter to a successful conclusion, to deal successfully with a matter; **c'est la f.,** this is the end; (*d'une chose, personne*) this is the last of it *or* him *etc*; **la f. du monde,** the end of the world; **ce n'est pas la f. du monde après tout,** it's not the end of the world, after all; **c'est la f. de tout,** *F* **c'est la f. des haricots,** this is the last straw; **le mot de la f. a été dit par Georges,** George had the last *or* final word; **à la f. il répondit,** in the end *or* finally *or* at last he answered; *F* **tu es stupide à la f.,** you really are very stupid; **tu m'ennuies à la f.!,** you're really annoying me!; **à la f. du compte, en f. de compte,** (*après tout*) in the end, after all; (*tout bien considéré*) all things considered, taking everything into account; (*pour conclure*) finally, to conclude; *F* **à la f. des fins,** when all's said and done, at the end of the day;

(b) (*but*) end, aim, purpose; **la f. justifie les moyens,** the end justifies the means; **en venir** *ou* **arriver à ses fins,** to achieve one's aims *or* purpose, to get what one wants; **une f. en soi,** an end in itself; **à cette f. il faut avoir beaucoup de patience,** in order to attain *or* achieve this one must have a lot of patience; **à quelle f.?,** for what purpose?, with what end in view?; **à deux fins,** dual-purpose; **à toutes fins,** for all purposes, all-purpose; **à toutes fins utiles,** for whatever purpose it may serve; **aux fins de faire qch.,** with a view to doing sth; **à seule(s) fin(s) de l'aider,** for the sole purpose of helping him; **aller à ses fins,** to pursue one's point; *Jur* **aux fins de débauche,** for immoral purposes;

(c) *Jur* **renvoyer qn des fins de sa plainte,** to nonsuit s.o.; **renvoyé des fins de la plainte,** discharged, acquitted.

fin², fine [fɛ̃, fin] **1** *adj* **(a) dans le f. fond du hangar/du panier,** right at the back of the shed/at the very bottom of the basket; **au f. fond de la Sibérie,** in deepest Siberia; **au f. fond de moi,** in my heart of hearts;

(b) (*de première qualité*) fine, first-class; **vins fins,** choice wines; **or f.,** pure *or* fine gold; **linge f.,** fine linen; **un repas f.,** a choice *or* exquisite meal;

(c) (*habile*) fine, subtle, discriminating; **f. connaisseur de vins,** fine judge of wine; **f. tireur,** crack shot; **fine cuisinière,** gourmet cook; **fine ironie,** subtle irony; **avoir l'oreille fine,** to have sharp ears *or* an acute *or* a keen ear; **avoir le nez f.,** to have a keen sense of smell; **il est trop f. pour vous,** he's too quick for you; **elle n'est pas très fine, cette jeune femme,** that young woman isn't very quick on the uptake; **bien f. qui le prendra,** it would take a smart man to catch him; **plus f. que lui n'est pas bête,** he's no fool; *F* **une blague fine,** a subtle joke; *Iron* **qu'est-ce que c'est f.!,** oh, very funny!;

(d) fine (*rain, grains, needle*); fine, delicate (*features*); slender (*figure*); neat (*ankle etc*); **des souliers fins,** elegant shoes; **les fines nuances d'un raisonnement,** the subtle nuances of an argument;

(e) le f. mot de l'histoire, the truth of the matter.

2 *nm* **(a) savoir le fort et le f. d'une affaire,** to know the ins and outs of sth; **le f. de l'affaire,** the crux of the matter; **le f. du f.,** the ultimate, the ne plus ultra;

(b) jouer au (plus) f., to have a battle of wits;

(c) fineness (*of gold*);

(d) *Tex* fine linen.

3 *nf* **fine,** liqueur brandy; **une fine à l'eau,** = a brandy and soda.

4 *adv* **(a) tout était f. prêt,** everything was absolutely ready;

(b) (*finement*) finely; **café moulu f.,** finely ground coffee; **des crayons taillés f.,** sharp-pointed pencils.

final, -als [final] *adj* **(a)** final; last (*letter etc*); *Sp* **les épreuves finales,** the finals; **point f.,** full stop, *Am* period; *Fig* **mettre un point f. à une affaire,** to put a stop *or* an end to a matter; **va te coucher, point f.!,** bed time! and that's final!; **(b)** *Phil Gram* final (*cause, clause*).

finale [final] **1** *nf* **(a)** *Sp* final; **f. de coupe,** cup final; **aller/être en f.,** to get through to/to be in the finals; **(b)** *Mus* keynote, tonic; **(c)** end syllable (*of word*). **2** *nm Mus* finale (*of opera etc*).

finalement [finalmɑ̃] *adv* finally, at last, in the end.

finaliste [finalist] *adj & n Sp* finalist.

finalité [finalite] *nf* (*objectif*) aim, objective; *Phil* finality; *Biol* adaptation.

finance [finɑ̃s] *nf* **(a)** (*affaire*) finance; **monde de la f.,** financial world, world of finance; **la haute f.,** high finance; (*le milieu*) the financiers, the bankers; **être dans la f.,** to be in finance; **(b) finances,** finances; *F* **être mal dans ses finances,** to be hard up; **nos finances sont mal en point,**

our finances are in bad shape; **lois de finances,** financial laws; **ministre des Finances,** minister of Finance; *Br* ≈ Chancellor of the Exchequer; **le Ministère des Finances,** the Treasury; **(c)** *Arch* ready money; *F* **faire qch moyennant f.,** to do sth for a consideration *or* for cash.

financement [finɑ̃smɑ̃] *nm* financing, funding; (*surtout d'un mécène*) (financial) backing.

financer [finɑ̃se] *vt* (**je finançai(s); n. finançons**) to finance, to fund (*s.o., sth*); (*surtout d'un mécène*) to put up the money for (*sth*), to back (*s.o., sth*).

financier, -ière [finɑ̃sje, -jɛr] **1** *adj* financial; **avoir des embarras financiers,** to be in financial *or Fml* pecuniary difficulties; **crise financière,** financial crisis; **le marché f.,** the money market; *Culin* **sauce financière,** = white sauce containing small pieces of sweetbread, dumplings and mushrooms. **2** *nm* financier.

financièrement [finɑ̃sjɛrmɑ̃] *adv* financially.

finasser [finase] *vi* to resort to trickery.

finasserie [finasri] *nf* trick(s); **les finasseries du métier,** the tricks of the trade.

finasseur, -euse [finasœr, -øz] **, finassier, -ière** [finasje, -jɛr] *n Vieilli* trickster.

finaud, -aude [fino, -od] **1** *adj* wily, cunning (*peasant etc*). **2** *n* crafty type, wangler.

finauderie [finodri] *nf* trick(s).

finement [finmɑ̃] *adv* **(a)** (*délicatement*) finely, delicately, well (*executed etc*); **(b)** (*subtilement*) smartly, subtly, with finesse; **elle avait f. prévu ce coup-là,** she had shrewdly foreseen that that would happen.

finesse [finɛs] *nf* **(a)** fineness (*of material etc*); delicacy (*of execution*); **(b)** (*subtilité*) subtlety, shrewdness; **f. d'ouïe,** quickness *or* keenness *or* acuteness of hearing; **f. de l'odorat,** acuteness of smell; **f. de goût,** nicety *or* delicacy of taste; **f. d'esprit,** shrewdness; **discours plein de f.,** speech full of finesse; **parodie pleine de f.,** clever *or* subtle parody; **finesses d'un métier,** fine points *or* niceties of a craft; **il connaît toutes les finesses du métier,** he knows all the tricks of the trade; **(c)** fineness (*of dust etc*); slenderness, slimness (*of waist etc*); sharpness (*of point, optical image etc*); keenness (*of cutting edge*).

fini [fini] **1** *adj* **(a)** (*terminé*) finished, over, done with; **c'est f. (tout cela), tout est f.,** that's all over (and done with); **c'est f. entre nous,** it's all over between us; **c'est f. de rire,** nobody is laughing now; **c'est un homme f.,** he's finished, he's done for; **(b)** well finished (*piece of work*); accomplished (*actor*); *Péj* **un idiot·f.,** a complete idiot; **(c)** finite (*space, tense, number*). **2** *nm* **(a)** finish (*of manufactured article etc*); **(b) le f. et l'infini,** the finite and the infinite.

finir [finir] **1** *vt* to finish, to end (*task etc*); **f. un tableau/une sculpture,** to finish off a picture/sculpture; **tu as fini ton assiette?,** have you finished what's on your plate?

2 *vi* to end, to come to an end, to finish; **quand est-ce que ça finit?,** (*le film etc*) when does it finish?; **comment est-ce que ça a fini?,** (*le livre, le film etc*) how did it end?; **à quelle heure tu finis?,** (*le travail*) what time do you finish?; **f. en pointe,** to end *or* terminate in a point; **une histoire qui finit bien/mal,** a story with a happy/sad ending; **tout est bien qui finit bien,** all's well that ends well; **il finira mal,** he will come to a bad end; **l'histoire ne finit pas là,** that's not the end of the story; **tu vas f. par le faire pleurer,** you'll end up making him cry; **elle a fini dans un accident,** she died in an accident; **f. à l'hôpital/dans un fossé/***etc*, to finish *or* end up in hospital/a ditch/*etc*; **en f. avec qn/qch,** to be *or* have done with s.o./sth; **il faut en f. avec ces idées reçues,** we must break with *or* shake off these preconceived ideas; **je voudrais en f.,** I want to get it over (with); **cela n'en finit pas,** there's no end to it; **il n'en finit plus de se préparer dans la salle de bain,** he takes ages in the bathroom getting ready; **pour en f.,** to cut a long story short; **histoires à n'en plus f.,** never-ending *or* interminable stories; **c'était à n'en plus f.,** it was interminable, it seemed to go on for ever; **f. de faire qch,** to finish doing sth; **cette route n'en finit pas,** this road seems to go on (and on) for ever; **elle a des jambes à n'en plus f.,** she's very leggy; **f. par faire qch,** to end up doing sth; **elle finira par t'oublier,** she'll forget you eventually; **la justice finit par triompher,** justice triumphs in the end *or* in the long run *or* eventually; **tout finit toujours par arriver,** everything comes to those who wait.

finish [finiʃ] *nm Sp* (*fin*) finish; (*impulsion finale*) finish, final burst; **il a un bon f.,** he has a strong finish; *Fig* **on l'a eu au f.,** we got it in the end.

finissage [finisaʒ] *nm Ind* finishing (off).

finissant [finisɑ̃] *adj* ending, finishing; (*society*) in decline; **le jour f.,** dusk, twilight, *Scot & Littér* gloaming.

finisseur, -euse [finisœr, -øz] *n Ind Sp* finisher.

finition [finisjɔ̃] *nf* finishing; (*résultat*) finish; **les finitions,** the finishing touches; *Tricot* **je déteste faire les finitions,** I hate the sewing up.

finlandais, -aise [fɛ̃lɑ̃dɛ, -ɛz] **1** *adj* Finnish. **2** *n* **F.,** Finlander, Finn.

Finlande [fɛ̃lɑ̃d] *nf* Finland.

finnois [finwa] **1** *adj* Finnish. **2** *nm Ling* Finnish.

fiole [fjɔl] *nf* **(a)** (*flacon*) phial, flask; **(b)** *Arg* (*tête*) bonce, skull; **se payer la f. de qn,** to make a fool of s.o..

fiord [fjɔr] *nm Géog* fjord.

fioriture [fjɔrityr] *nf* flourish (*to handwriting etc*); embellishment (*of style*); *Mus* grace note(s); *Péj* **il y a trop de fioritures,** it's too flowery; **une lettre pleine de fioritures,** a flowery letter.

firmament [firmamɑ̃] *nm Litt* firmament, sky.

firme [firm] *nf* firm.

fisc [fisc] *nm Admin Br* ≈ the Inland Revenue, *US* ≈ Internal Revenue; *F* **les gens du f.,** the income tax people.

fiscal, -aux [fiskal, -o] *adj* fiscal; **dans un but f.,** for purposes of revenue; **l'administration fiscale,** the taxation authorities; **timbre f.,** (Inland) Revenue stamp; **fraude/évasion fiscale,** tax evasion/avoidance; **paradis f.,** tax haven; **abri f.,** tax shelter.

fiscalement [fiskalmɑ̃] *adv* for tax purposes.

fiscaliser [fiskalize] *vt* to tax.

fiscalité [fiskalite] *nf* fiscal system *or* policy.

fissible [fisibl] *adj Phys* fissionable, *esp Am* fissile.

fissile [fisil] *adj* **(a)** = **FISSIBLE**; **(b)** (*rock*) fissile, tending to split.

fission [fisjɔ̃] *nf Nucl* fission; **f. de l'atome,** atomic fission, splitting of the atom.

fissuration [fisyrɑsjɔ̃] *nf* cracking, fissuring.

fissure [fisyr] *nf* crack, fissure (*in rock etc*); *Fig* split (*between friends*); **les fissures du mur,** the cracks in the wall.

fissurer [fisyre] **1** *vt* to fissure, to split, to crack; *Fig* to split (up). **2 se fissurer** *vpr* to split.

fiston [fistɔ̃] *nm F* son, youngster; **allons (mon) f.!,** now then, young fellow *or* my lad *or* sonny!

fistule [fistyl] *nf Méd* fistula.

fistuleux, -euse [fistylø, -øz] *adj Méd* fistulous.

FIV [fiv] *nf Biol* (*abrév* **fécondation in vitro**) IVF.

fivète [fivɛt] *nf Biol* in vitro fertilization.

fixage [fiksaʒ] *nm* fixing (*of drawing etc*); *Phot* **bain de f.,** fixing bath.

fixateur, -trice [fiksatœr, -tris] **1** *nm* fixer (*of dyes etc*); *Phot* fixing solution *or* bath; *Biol* fixative; (*pour cheveux*) lacquer. **2** *adj* **bactéries fixatrices d'azote,** nitrogen-fixing bacteria.

fixatif [fiksatif] *nm* **(a)** fixative (*for drawings etc*); **(b)** (*pour cheveux*) lacquer.

fixation [fiksɑsjɔ̃] *nf* **(a)** fixing (*of date, price etc*); **(b)** fixing, attaching (*of shelf etc*); fixation (*of driftng sands, Ch of nitrogen*); **f. par bride** *ou* **par collier,** clamping; **vis de f.,** fixing screw, set screw; **patte de f.,** anchor(ing) clip; **(c)** *MecE* attachment, anchor; *Ski* (ski) binding; **(d)** *Psy* fixation (**à qn,** on s.o.); **faire une f. sur qch/qn,** to become fixated on sth/s.o., to have a fixation about sth/s.o..

fixe [fiks] **1** *adj* **(a)** (*immobile*) fixed, firm; **idée f.,** fixed idea; *Psy* obsession; *Litt* idée fixe; **regard f.,** intent gaze; **grue f.,** fixed *or* stationary crane; **essieu f.,** dead axle; *Mil* **f.!,** eyes front!; **(b)** (*arrêté*) fixed; **prix f.,** fixed *or* set price; **à prix f.,** at fixed prices; **frais fixes,** fixed costs; **traitement f.,** fixed salary; **résidence f.,** permanent residence; **sans domicile f.,** of no fixed abode; **prendre ses repas à heure f.,** to eat at fixed *or* set times; *Ordinat* **disque f.,** fixed disk; **beau (temps) f.,** set fair (weather); **arrêt f.,** compulsory stop. **2** *nm* fixed salary.

fixé [fikse] *adj* **(a)** set, fixed, stated (*time etc*); **(b) être f. sur qch,** to entertain no further doubts *or* have made up one's mind about sth; **ne pas être f.,** to have no fixed plans; **(c)** *Psy* suffering from a fixation; **être f. sur qn/qch,** to be fixated on s.o./sth.

fixe-chaussettes [fiks(ə)ʃosɛt] *nm inv* (sock) suspender(s), *Am* garter(s).

fixe-cravate [fiks(ə)kravat] *nm* tie clip, tie clasp; (*pl fixe-cravates*).

fixement [fiksəmɑ̃] *adv* fixedly; **regarder f. qch,** to stare at sth; (*scruter*) to look hard *or* intently at sth.

fixer [fikse] **1** *vt* **(a)** (*immobiliser*) to make (*sth*) firm *or* rigid *or* fast; **les vis qui fixent la serrure,** the screws that hold the lock; *Fig* **f. ses idées sur une feuille peut aider,** it may help to set one's ideas down on a sheet of paper; **f.**

qch dans sa mémoire, to fix sth in one's memory; **f. l'attention de qn,** to engage *or* hold *or* arrest s.o.'s attention; **f. les yeux sur qch/qn,** to fix one's eyes on sth/s.o., to gaze *or* stare at sth/s.o.; (*scruter*) to look hard *or* intently at sth/s.o.; **f. qn,** to stare at s.o.; **ça va le f.,** that will make him settle down;

(b) *Ch Phot* to fix;

(c) (*déterminer*) to fix, to set, to appoint (*time*); to fix, to set, to assess (*damages, taxes*); to fix, to lay down (*conditions, rules*); **à la date fixée,** on the set *or* appointed day; **f. un salaire,** to fix a salary;

(d) f. qn sur qch, to give s.o. definite information about sth; **je ne suis pas fixé,** I haven't made my mind up yet.

2 se fixer *vpr* **(a)** (*s'installer*) to settle down; **se f. dans un pays/à La Rochelle,** to settle in a country/in La Rochelle;

(b) (*s'arrêter*) to become fixed; **l'orthographe du mot se fixe au XVIII siècle,** the spelling of the word became fixed in the 18th century; **se f. à une opinion,** to stick to an opinion; **se f. un objectif,** to set oneself a target; **elle s'est fixée sur cette idée,** she's got the idea in her head (and nothing will shift it).

fixisme [fiksism] *nm Biol* creationism.

fixité [fiksite] *nf* fixity, steadiness (*of gaze*).

fjord [fjɔr] *nm Géog* fjord.

flac [flak] *nm & int* plop, slap; **faire f.,** to plop.

flaccidité [flaksidite] *nf* flaccidity, flabbiness, limpness.

flache [flaʃ] *nf* **(a)** (pot)hole (*in pavement, road*); **(b) f. (d'eau),** puddle.

flacon [flakɔ̃] *nm* small (stoppered) bottle; (*de laboratoire*) flask; **f. à parfum,** perfume bottle; **f. à liqueur,** liqueur decanter.

fla-fla [flafla] *nm F* ostentation, show; **faire du f.-f.,** to show off, to make a show.

flagada [flagada] *adj inv F* limp; (*legs*) like jelly; **se sentir tout f.,** to feel limp.

flagellation [flaʒelasjɔ̃] *nf* whipping, flogging; (*sur soi-même*) flagellation.

flagellé [flaʒele] *adj & nm Biol* flagellate.

flageller [flaʒele] **1** *vt* to flog, to whip. **2 se flageller** *vpr* to scourge oneself.

flageoler [flaʒɔle] *vi* (*of legs*) to shake, to tremble, to give way; **elle flageole sur ses jambes,** (*de peur*) she is shaking at the knees; (*de fatigue*) her knees are giving way, she's dead on her feet.

flageolet¹ [flaʒɔlɛ] *nm Mus* flageolet.

flageolet² *nm* haricot bean, flageolet.

flagorner [flagɔrne] *vt Péj* to suck up *or* toady to (*s.o.*).

flagornerie [flagɔrnəri] *nf Péj* toadyism.

flagorneur, -euse [flagɔrnœr, -øz] *n Péj* toady, creep.

flagrant [flagrɑ̃] *adj* flagrant (*injustice, lie etc*); **pris en f. délit,** caught in the act *or* red-handed; *F* **c'est f.!,** it's (glaringly) obvious!

flair [flɛr] *nm* **(a)** (*of dogs*) scent, (sense of) smell, nose; **(b)** (*of person*) intuition; **avoir du f.,** to have a gift for nosing things out.

flairer [flere] *vt* **(a)** (*of dog*) to scent, to smell (out), to nose out (*game*); *Fig* **f. le danger,** to scent *or* smell *or* suspect danger; **f. le monsonge,** to detect a lie; **(b)** (*sentir*) to smell, to sniff (at) (*sth*).

flamand, -ande [flamɑ̃, -ɑ̃d] **1** *adj* Flemish. **2** *nm Ling* Flemish. **3** *n* **F.,** Fleming.

flamant [flamɑ̃] *nm* flamingo; **f. rose,** pink flamingo.

flambage [flɑ̃baʒ] *nm* **(a)** singeing (*of hair, chicken etc*); sterilization (*of needle*); charring (*of stake etc*); **(b)** buckling, collapse (*of metal plate etc*).

flambant [flɑ̃bɑ̃] **1** *adv* **f. neuf,** brand new. **2** *adj* **(a)** blazing, flaming (*log, sun*); **(b) houille flambante,** bituminous *or* soft coal. **3** *nm* bituminous *or* soft coal.

flambard [flɑ̃bar] *nm F Vieilli* **faire le f.,** to show off.

flambé [flɑ̃be] *adj* **(a)** *Culin* flambé(ed); **(b)** *F* **il est f.,** he's done for, his goose is cooked.

flambeau, -eaux [flɑ̃bo] *nm* **(a)** (*torche*) torch; **descente/retraite aux flambeaux,** torch-lit descent/procession; **à la lueur des flambeaux, aux flambeaux,** by torchlight; *Fig* **le f. du progès,** the torch of progress; *Fig* **reprendre le f.,** to take up the torch; **(b)** (*candélabre*) candelabra.

flambée [flɑ̃be] *nf* **(a)** blaze, blazing fire; **il y a une f. dans la cheminée,** there is a good blaze in the hearth; **(b)** *Fig* outbreak (*of violence*); rocketing (*of prices*); outburst (*of anger*).

flambement [flɑ̃bmɑ̃] *nm* buckling, collapse (*of metal plate etc*).

flamber [flɑ̃be] **1** *vi* **(a)** to flame, to blaze, to be ablaze; **faire f. le feu,** to make the fire burn up, to stir the fire into a blaze; **f. comme une allumette,** to burn like matchwood; **(b)** (*of metal bar etc*) to buckle, to yield. **2** *vt* to singe (*hair, fowl etc*); to char (*stake etc*); *Culin* to flambé; **f. une aiguille,** to sterilize a needle (*in a flame*); *Fig* **elle a flambé l'argent du ménage au jeu,** she gambled away the housekeeping money.

flambeur [flɑ̃bœr] *nm Arg* big-time gambler.

flamboiement [flɑ̃bwamɑ̃] *nm* blazing, blaze.

flamboyant [flɑ̃bwajɑ̃] *adj* **(a)** flaming, blazing (*fire*); blazing (*eyes*); **(b)** *Archit* flamboyant; *Journ* **des titres flamboyants,** banner headlines.

flamboyer [flɑ̃bwaje] *vi* **(il flamboie)** (*of fire*) to blaze; (*of eyes*) **f. de colère,** to blaze *or* flash with anger.

flamingant, -ante [flamɛ̃gɑ̃, -ɑ̃t] **1** *adj* Flemish-speaking (*town, person*). **2** *n Pol* Flemish nationalist.

flamme [flam] *nf* **(a)** flame; **en flammes,** on fire, ablaze; **dévoré par les flammes,** consumed by flames; **jeter feu et f.,** to fly into a rage; **retour de f.,** back flash (*from gun*); *Tech* backfire, backfiring; **donner des retours de f.,** to backfire; **avoir des retours de f.,** (*of gas stove*) to flash back; **pointe de f.,** flashpoint (*of petrol*); **passer à la f.,** to singe; **(b)** *Litt* passion, love; **déclarer sa f. à une femme,** to declare one's love for a woman; **(c)** (*enthousiasme*) fire, enthusiasm; **discours plein de f.,** fiery speech; **(d)** *Mil etc* pennant, pennon, streamer; **(e)** (*sur lettre*) slogan (*accompanying postmark*).

flammèche [flamɛʃ] *nf* spark (*of fire*).

flan [flɑ̃] *nm* **(a)** *Culin* baked custard; **f. chimique** *ou* **en poudre,** custard powder; *Arg* **c'est du f.,** it's a lot of nonsense!; *Fig* **rester** *ou* **être comme deux ronds de f.,** to be flabbergasted; **(b)** blank (*of coin, gramophone record etc*); **(c)** *Typ* mould, *US* mold; **(d)** *Arg* **j'ai dit ça au f.,** I said it just for the sake of it.

flanc [flɑ̃] *nm* (*d'un animal*) side, flank; (*d'une personne*) side; (*d'un pneu*) wall; **route à f. de coteau,** road following the hillside; **être sur le f.,** (*malade*) to be laid up (*in bed*); (*épuisé*) to be quite worn out; **battre des flancs,** (*d'un cheval*) to heave, to pant; *Mil* **par le f. droit!,** by the right!; **attaquer de f.,** to attack on the flank; **le navire se présentait de f.,** the ship was broadside on (to us); **prêter le f. à la critique,** to lay oneself open to criticism; *F* **tirer au f.,** to shirk (a task), to skive.

flancher [flɑ̃ʃe] *vi F* **(a)** (*faiblir*) to flinch, to give in; **(b)** (*abandonner*) to quit; **ce n'est pas le moment de f.!,** don't give up now!; **(c)** (*d'une voiture etc*) to pack up *or* in.

flanchet [flɑ̃ʃɛ] *nm Culin* flank (*of beef*).

Flandre [flɑ̃dr] *nf* Flanders.

flandrin [flɑ̃drɛ̃] *nm F* **grand f.,** tall *or* lanky fellow.

flanelle [flanɛl] *nf* flannel; **f. (de) coton,** flannelette; **pantalon de f. gris,** grey flannels; *F* **il devrait mettre sa f.,** he ought to wear his jacket.

flâner [flɑne, flane] *vi* to stroll, to saunter; **perdre son temps à f.,** to idle away one's time.

flânerie [flɑnri, flanri] *nf* (*balade*) dawdling, strolling; (*oisiveté*) idling.

flâneur, -euse [flɑnœr, flanœr, -øz] **1** *n* **(a)** (*promeneur*) stroller, saunterer; **(b)** (*oisif*) loafer, idler. **2** *adj* **il est un peu f.,** he's a bit lazy *or* a bit of a loafer.

flanquer¹ [flɑ̃ke] *vt* to flank (*building etc, Mil a column, the enemy*); **flanqué de deux agents,** between *or* flanked by two policemen.

flanquer² **1** *vt F* to throw, to pitch, to chuck; **f. une gifle/un coup de pied à qn,** to give s.o. a slap/land s.o. a kick; **f. qn à la porte,** to throw s.o. out; (*licencier*) to fire *or* sack s.o.; **f. la trouille à qn,** to give s.o. the jitters. **2 se flanquer** *vpr* **se f. par terre,** to fall flat, to come a cropper.

flapi [flapi] *adj F* dead beat, fagged out.

flaque [flak] *nf* puddle.

flash, *pl* **flashes** [flaʃ] *nm* **(a)** *Phot* flash(light); **(b)** *Cin* shot, flash; **f. publicitaire,** brief advertisement; **(c)** *TV Rad* (news)flash.

flash-back [flaʃbak] *nm* flashback; **le film commence par un f.-b.,** the film begins with a flashback.

flasher [flaʃe] *vi F* **j'ai flashé sur cet appartement,** I (really) fell for the flat.

flasque¹ [flask] *adj* flaccid, flabby (*flesh*); limp (*style*); floppy (*hat*); **se sentir f.,** to feel limp.

flasque² *nf* flask.

flasque³ *nm Mil* cheek (*of gun carriage*); *Aut* hubcap, wheel disc.

flatter [flate] **1** *vt* **(a)** (*complimenter*) to flatter, to compliment; **f. qn sur son bel esprit,** to flatter s.o. on his wit; **être flatté de qch,** to feel flattered by sth; **je suis flatté de votre proposition,** I am flattered by your proposal; **cette coupe ne la flatte pas,** that style doesn't suit her; **peintre qui flatte ses modèles,** painter who flatters his sitters;

(b) (*plaire*) to delight, to please, to charm; **spectacle qui flatte les yeux,** sight that is pleasant to the eye; **f. les caprices de qn,** to humour *or* indulge s.o.'s fancies;

(c) (*en mentant*) to delude; **f. qn de l'espoir de qch,** to hold out false hopes of sth to s.o;

(d) to stroke, to caress (*an animal*); **f. un cheval,** to pat a horse.

2 se flatter *vpr* to flatter oneself, to delude oneself; **elle se flattait de réussir,** she flattered herself *or* felt sure that she would succeed; **il se flatte qu'on a** *ou* **ait besoin de lui,** he flatters himself that he is indispensable; **se f. de son habileté,** to congratulate oneself on one's cleverness; **se f. d'avoir fait qch,** to take the credit *or F* pat oneself on the back for having done sth; **à ta place, je ne m'en flatterais pas,** if I was in your place I wouldn't be proud of it.

flatterie [flatri] *nf* flattery.

flatteur, -euse [flatœr, -øz] **1** *adj* **(a)** pleasing, pleasant (*taste etc*); **(b)** flattering (*remark, portrait*); (*of person*) full of flattery; **peu f.,** unflattering; **il a fait un tableau f. de la situation,** he painted a rosy picture of the situation. **2** *n* flatterer.

flatteusement [flatøzmɑ̃] *adv* flatteringly.

flatulence [flatylɑ̃s] *nf Méd* flatulence; **avoir des flatulences,** to have wind.

flatulent [flatylɑ̃] *adj Méd* flatulent.

flatuosité [flatɥozite] *nf* wind; *Méd* flatus.

fléau, -aux [fleo] *nm* **(a)** (*calamité*) scourge, curse; *Fig* plague, pest, bane; *F* **c'est un vrai f.!,** he's a real pest!; **(b)** (*à céréales*) flail; **(c)** beam, arm (*of balance*).

fléchage [fleʃaʒ] *nm* arrowing (*of direction*).

flèche¹ [flɛʃ] *nf* **(a)** arrow; *Litt* shaft; **pistolet à flèches,** dart gun; **fer de f.,** arrowhead; **faire f. de tout bois,** to leave no stone unturned; **partir en** *ou* **comme une f.,** (*of person*) to shoot off; **monter en f.,** (*of aircraft etc*) to shoot (straight) up; (*of prices*) to shoot up *or* rocket; *Fig* **elle lui a décoché des flèches méchantes,** she let fly a few barbed remarks in his direction;

(b) (*de direction*) direction sign, arrow; **suivre les flèches,** to follow the arrows; *Aut Arch* **f. de direction,** trafficator;

(c) chevaux attelés en f., horses driven tandem; **cheval de f.,** leader;

(d) spire (*of church*);

(e) jib, boom (*of crane*);

(f) *Nau* pole (*of mast*); topsail (*of cutter*);

(g) *Archit* rise (*of arch*); *Av* camber (*of aerofoil*);

(h) sag, dip (*of cable etc*).

flèche² *nf* flitch (*of bacon*).

flécher [fleʃe] *vt* to arrow (*route, direction*); **itinéraire fléché,** arrowed *or* signposted route.

fléchette [fleʃɛt] *nf* dart.

fléchir [fleʃir] **1** *vt* **(a)** to bend, to flex (*arm etc*); **f. le genou devant qn,** to bend *or* bow the knee to s.o.; **(b)** (*émouvoir*) to move (*s.o.*) (*to pity, mercy etc*); **se laisser f.,** to let oneself be swayed *or* persuaded. **2** *vi* **(a)** to give way, to bend; (*of legs, troops etc*) to give way; (*of cable, beam*) to sag; **(b)** to diminish, to grow weaker; **les prix fléchissent,** prices are coming down; **le dollar fléchit,** the dollar is weakening; **son autorité fléchit,** his authority is weakening; **elle n'a pas fléchi,** she never budged.

fléchissement [fleʃismɑ̃] *nm* **(a)** bending (*of the knee etc*); yielding, bending (*of girder etc*); sagging (*of cable etc*); **(b)** falling, easing (*of prices*); weakening (*of currency*); *Bourse* **f. des cours,** fall in share prices.

fléchisseur [fleʃisœr] *adj & nm Anat* **(muscle) f.,** flexor.

flegmatique [flɛgmatik] *adj* phlegmatic, imperturbable, stolid.

flegmatiquement [flɛgmatikmɑ̃] *adv* phlegmatically, imperturbably, stolidly.

flegme [flɛgm] *nm* **(a)** (*imperturbabilité*) stolidness, imperturbability, coolness; **faire perdre son f. à qn,** (*le mettre en colère, le faire rire*) to make s.o. lose their cool; **(b)** *Méd* phlegm.

flémard, flemmard, -arde [flemar, -ard] *F* **1** *adj* idle, indolent, lazy. **2** *n* idler, slacker, loafer.

flemmarder [flemarde] *vi F* to loaf, to idle, to slack.

flemmardise [flemardiz] *nf F* idleness, laziness.

flemme [flɛm] *nf F* laziness, idleness, slacking; **j'ai la f. de le faire,** I can't be bothered with it *or* to do it; **j'ai la f., laisse-moi tranquille,** I can't be bothered, leave me alone.

flet [flɛ] *nm* flounder.

flétan [fletɑ̃] *nm* halibut.

flétrir¹ [fletrir] **1** *vt* to fade, to wilt; to make (*colours etc*) fade; to wither (up) (*plants*). **2 se flétrir** *vpr* (*of colours etc*) to fade; (*of plants*) to wither, to wilt; (*of skin*) to shrivel.

flétrir² *vt* **(a)** to brand (*criminal*); to stigmatize (*crime etc*); **(b)** to sully, to stain, to cast a slur on (*s.o.'s character*).

flétrissure¹ [fletrisyr] *nf* fading, withering.

flétrissure² *nf* stain, blemish (*on s.o.'s character*).

fleur [flœr] *nf* **(a)** flower; (*d'un arbre*) blossom, bloom; **arbre en fleur(s),** tree in blossom *or* in flower; **fleurs des champs,** wild flowers; **pot de fleurs,** flowerpot, plant pot; **fleurs en pot,** flowers in a pot; **ni fleurs, ni couronnes,** ≈ no flowers by request; **envoyer des fleurs à qn,** to send s.o. flowers; **f. artificielle/en papier,** artificial/paper flower; **tissu à fleurs,** flowered *or* flowery material; *Fig* **faire une f. à qn,** to do s.o. a favour; *Fig* **elle le couvre de fleurs,** she heaps praise (up)on him; **être f. bleue,** to be (naively) romantic; *F* **elle y est arrivée comme une f.,** she arrived without a hitch;

(b) *Fig Litt* **dans** *ou* **à la f. de l'âge,** in the prime of life; **dans la première f. de la jeunesse,** in the first flush *or* flower of youth; **la fine f. de la société,** the cream of society;

(c) flowers (*of antimony, wine etc*);

(d) à f. de, on the surface of, on a level with; **à f. d'eau,** at water level; **rocher à f. d'eau,** rock that is awash; **voler à f. d'eau,** to skim the water; *Tennis* **balle à f. de corde,** ball that just grazes *or* skims the net; **émotions à f. de peau,** skin-deep emotions; **avoir les nerfs à f. de peau,** to be on edge;

(e) hair side, grain side (*of skin*);

(f) f. de farine, top quality flour.

fleurage [flœraʒ] *nm* floral pattern (*on cloth, carpet*).

fleurdelisé [flœrdəlize] **1** *adj* lilied, decorated with fleurs-de-lis; *Hér* fleury. **2** *nm Can* (*drapeau du Québec*) flag of Quebec.

fleurer [flœre] *vi Litt* to smell, to be fragrant; **f. la violette,** to smell of violets; *Fig* **ça fleure l'intrigue,** there's plotting afoot.

fleuret [flœrɛ] *nm* **(a)** (*épée*) (fencing) foil; *Min* borer; **(b)** *Tex* floss silk.

fleurette [flœrɛt] *nf* **conter f. à qn,** to whisper sweet nothings to s.o..

fleuri [flœri] *adj* **(a)** (*en fleurs*) in bloom, in flower, in blossom; (*orné de fleurs*) decorated with flowers, flowered; **village f.,** ≈ village taking part in flower competition; **pot/vaisselle fleuri(e),** pot/tub of flowers; **avoir la boutonnière fleurie,** to have a flower in one's buttonhole; (*décoré*) to wear a decoration; **(b)** flowery (*path, style etc*); florid (*style, complexion*).

fleurir [flœrir] *v* (*prp* **fleurissant**, *Litt* **florissant**; *impf* **il fleurissait**, *Litt* **il florissait**) **1** *vi* **(a)** (*of plants*) to flower, to bloom, to blossom; (*of person*) to come out in spots *or* pimples; **(b)** (*of art, trade etc*) (*usu* **florissant**, **florissait**) to flourish, to prosper. **2** *vt* to decorate (*table*) with flowers; to put a flower in (*buttonhole*); to lay flowers on (*grave*).

fleuriste [flœrist] *n* **(a)** (*commerçant*) florist, flower seller; **(b)** (*horticulteur*) florist, flower grower; **(c)** (*de fleurs artificielles*) artificial flower maker.

fleuron [flœrɔ̃] *nm* **(a)** (*ornement*) flower-shaped ornament, fleuron; *Archit* finial; *Fig* **c'est encore un f. à sa couronne,** that's another feather in his cap; **c'est un nouveau f. à sa collection,** that's another precious item *or* jewel for his collection; *TV* **cette émission est le f. d'Antenne 2,** this programme is the flagship of Antenne 2; **(b)** *Bot* floret.

fleuve [flœv] **1** *nm* river (*as opposed to tributary*); **f. (côtier),** short coastal river; *Fig* **un f. de sang/larmes,** a river of blood/a flood of tears. **2** *adj* **roman-f.,** saga; **discours-f.,** lengthy speech.

flexibilité [flɛksibilite] *nf* flexibility; pliability (*of materials*); suppleness, litheness (*of body*); **f. des horaires,** flexitime.

flexible [flɛksibl] **1** *adj* **(a)** (*souple*) flexible, supple; (*matériaux*) pliable; **tuyau f.,** hosepipe; **(b)** (*adaptable*) adaptable (*mind*); accommodating (*disposition*); (*malléable*) pliable, pliant, **avoir des horaires flexibles,** to be on flexitime. **2** *nm* (*tuyau*) hosepipe; *Él* flexible lead, flex.

flexion [flɛksjɔ̃] *nf* **(a)** (*fléchissement*) flexion, bending, sagging; *Gym* **f. du corps,** trunk exercise; *MecE* **effort de f.,** bending stress; **(b)** buckling, collapse (*of rod etc*); **(c)** *Ling* inflexion (*of word*); **langue à flexions,** inflected language.

flexionnel, -elle [flɛksjɔnɛl] *adj Ling* inflected; **langue flexionnelle,** inflected language.

flibuste [flibyst] *nf Arch* (*piraterie*) buccaneering, freebooting, piracy; (*pirates*) pirates.
flibustier [flibystje] *nm* **(a)** *Arch* pirate, freebooter, buccaneer; **(b)** *F* (*escroc*) cheat, crook.
flic [flik] *nm F* (*policier*) cop, bobby; (*détective*) detective; **voilà les flics!**, it's the cops!
flic flac [flikflak] *nm* slap, smack; crack (*of whip*).
flingue [flɛ̃g] *nm F* (*arme*) shooter, rod.
flinguer [flɛ̃ge] *F* **1** *vt* to gun down (*s.o.*). **2 se flinguer** *vpr* to blow one's brains out; **il n'y a pas de quoi se f.**, it's not the end of the world.
flippant [flipɑ̃] *adj F* mind-blowing.
flipper¹ [flipɛr] *nm* (*appareil*) pinball (machine); (*jeu*) pinball; **jouer au f.**, to play (at) pinball.
flipper² [flipe] *vi F* **(a)** (*d'un drogué*) to be spaced out; **(b)** (*s'angoisser*) to freak out; **ça me fait f.**, that freaks me out; **elle flippe à cause de son travail**, her work is freaking her out.
flirt [flœrt] *nm* **(a)** (*amourette*) flirtation, flirting; **ce n'est qu'un f.**, I was *etc* only flirting; **(b)** *Vieilli* **mon f.**, my boyfriend *or* girlfriend; **un de mes anciens flirts**, an old flame of mine.
flirter [flœrte] *vi* to flirt; *F* **f. avec le danger**, to flirt with danger; *Fig* **il flirte avec la police/l'opposition**, he's in cahoots with the police/the opposition.
flirteur, -euse [flœrtœr, -øz] **1** *adj* flirtatious. **2** *n* flirt.
F.L.N. [ɛfɛlɛn] *nm Hist abrév* **Front de libération nationale**.
floc [flɔk] **1** *int* plop! **2** *nm* splash.
floche [flɔʃ] *adj* flossy; **soie f.**, floss silk.
flocon [flɔkɔ̃] *nm* **(a)** flake (*of snow, cereal*); **flocons d'avoine**, oat flakes; *Can* **flocons de maïs**, cornflakes; **purée en flocons**, instant mashed potato; **(b)** tuft, flock (*of wool, cotton*).
floconneux, -euse [flɔkɔnø, -øz] *adj* fleecy, fluffy.
flonflon [flɔ̃flɔ̃] *nm* (*usu pl*) **flonflons**, pom pom pom (*of big drum*).
flopée [flɔpe] *nf Arg* **une f., des flopées**, loads, masses (*of children, people*).
floraison [flɔrɛzɔ̃] *nf* flowering, blossoming.
floral, -aux [flɔral, -o] *adj* floral; **exposition florale**, flower show.
floralies [flɔrali] *nfpl* flower show.
flore [flɔr] *nf Bot* flora.
floréal [flɔreal] *nm Fr Hist* eighth month of the French Republican calendar (*April-May*).
Florence [flɔrɑ̃s] *nf* Florence.
florès [flɔrɛs] *nm* **faire f.**, to prosper; to shine (*in society*).
florifère [flɔrifɛr] *adj* floriferous, flower-bearing; **plante très f.**, prolific flowerer.
florilège [flɔrilɛʒ] *nm* anthology (*of verse*).
florin [flɔrɛ̃] *nm* florin.
florissant [flɔrisɑ̃] *adj* flourishing, prosperous (*business etc*); **d'une santé florissante**, in the best of health.
flot [flo] *nm* **(a)** (*vague*) wave; **(b)** (*marée*) flood (tide); **(c)** flood (*of tears*); torrent, stream (*of blood, abuse*); crowd (*of people*); stream (*of traffic*); **un f. de paroles**, a torrent *or* flood of words; **entrer à flots**, (*of people, sun*) to stream in; **f. de dentelle/rubans**, cascade of lace/ribbons; **couler à flots**, to pour out; **ce scandale va faire couler des flots d'encre**, a lot of ink will be spilt over this scandal; **(d) à f.**, (*of ship*) afloat; (*of person*) solvent; **mettre un navire à f.**, to launch a ship; **remettre un navire à f.**, to refloat a ship; **mon compte en banque est à f.**, my bank account is in the black *or* in credit; **remettre qn à f.**, to make s.o. solvent; **ce cours vous permettra de vous remettre à f. en russe**, this course will get you going in Russian again.
flottabilité [flɔtabilite] *nf* buoyancy; **caisson** *ou* **réservoir de f.**, buoyancy tank.
flottable [flɔtabl] *adj* **(a)** (*of river*) navigable, floatable (*for rafts of wood*); **(b)** (*of wood etc*) floatable, buoyant.
flottage [flɔtaʒ] *nm* floating *or* running (*of timber*) down a river; **bois de f.**, raft wood; **train de f.**, timber raft.
flottaison [flɔtɛzɔ̃] *nf* floating; *Nau* **(ligne de) f.**, waterline; **f. en charge**, load line; **f. lège**, light waterline.
flottant [flɔtɑ̃] *adj* **(a)** floating (*island, debt, engine etc*); *Ordinat* **virgule flottante**, floating point; **(b)** flowing, loose (*robe, hair*); **filet f.**, drift net; **(c)** (*électorat, opinion*) irresolute, undecided, wavering; **électeur f.**, floating voter.
flottard¹ [flɔtar] *nm F* naval cadet.
flottard² *adj F* watery; **sauce flottarde**, thin gravy.
flotte¹ [flɔt] *nf* **(a)** (*bateaux*) fleet; **f. de ligne** *ou* **de combat**, battle fleet; **f. de commerce**, merchant fleet; **être dans la f.**, to be in the navy; **f. aérienne**, air fleet; **(b)** *F* (*eau*) water, rain; **il tombe de la f.**, it's pouring with rain; **c'est de la f., ce café!**, this coffee's like water!
flotte² *nf* float (*of net etc*).
flottement [flɔtmɑ̃] *nm* wavering, swaying (*of line of troops etc*); flapping, fluttering (*of flag*); wobble (*of chain, wheel*); fluctuation (*of floating currency*); wavering, hesitation; **il y eut un moment de f.**, there was a moment's hesitation.
flotter [flɔte] **1** *vi* **(a)** (*sur l'eau*) to float; **(b)** (*au vent*) to float, to stream, to wave; (*des cheveux*) to stream; (*des vêtements*) to hang loosely; **(c)** (*hésiter*) to waver, to hesitate; (*des pensées*) to wander; (*de devises*) to fluctuate; **un sourire flottait sur ses lèvres**, a smile played on his lips; **(d)** *F* **il flotte**, it's raining; **(e) il flotte dans ses vêtements**, his clothes drown him. **2** *vt* **f. du bois**, to float timber (*down a stream*); **bois flotté**, driftwood.
flotteur [flɔtœr] *nm* **(a)** raftsman (*in charge of timber raft*); **(b)** float (*of fishing line, seaplane, carburettor etc*); **(c)** ball (*of ball tap etc*); **robinet à f.**, ballcock.
flottille [flɔtij] *nf* flotilla (*of ships*); squadron (*of aircraft*); **f. de pêche**, fishing fleet.
flou [flu] **1** *adj* blurred (*outline, painting*); blurred, fuzzy (*image*); muffled, indistinct (*sound*); hazy (*horizon*); hazy, vague (*idea*); soft, fluffy (*hair*); loose-fitting (*dress*). **2** *nm* blur, fuzziness (*of outline, image*); muffled nature (*of sound*); haziness (*of horizon*); haziness, vagueness (*of idea*); softness, fluffiness (*of hair*); looseness (*of dress*); **le f. revient à la mode**, loose-fitting dresses are back in fashion; *Phot* **f. artistique**, soft-focus effect.
flouer [flue] *vt F* to swindle (*s.o.*); **f. qn de qch**, to swindle s.o. (out) of sth.
flouse, flouze [fluz] *nm Arg* (*argent*) bread, dough, cash.
fluctuant [flyktɥɑ̃] *adj* fluctuating, varying; **un esprit f.**, a weathercock; **elle est fluctuante dans ses idées**, her ideas are liable to change.
fluctuation [flyktɥasjɔ̃] *nf* fluctuation.
fluctuer [flyktɥe] *vi* to fluctuate.
fluent [flyɑ̃] *adj* flowing; loose (*soil*); *Méd* **hémorroïdes fluentes**, bleeding piles.
fluer [flye] *vi* to flow; *Méd* (*of pus*) to run; (*of haemorrhoids*) to bleed.
fluet, -ette [flyɛ, -ɛt] *adj* thin, slender (*person etc*); thin, reedy (*voice*).
fluide [flyid] **1** *adj* fluid (*oil, situation*); flowing (*style*); **la circulation était f.**, the traffic kept moving. **2** *nm* **(a)** fluid; *Aut* **f. de frein**, brake fluid; **(b) avoir du f.**, (*d'un médium*) to have strange powers.
fluidité [flyidite] *nf* fluidity; **f. de la circulation**, steady flow of the traffic.
fluor [flyɔr] *nm Ch* fluorine; **dentifrice au f.**, fluoride toothpaste; *Minér* **spath f.**, fluorspar.
fluoration [flyɔrasjɔ̃] *nf* fluoridation (*of water supply etc*).
fluorescence [flyɔresɑ̃s] *nf* fluorescence; **éclairage par f.**, fluorescent *or* strip lighting.
fluorescent [flyɔresɑ̃] *adj* fluorescent; **éclairage f.**, fluorescent *or* strip lighting.
fluorine [flyɔrin] *nf Minér* fluorspar.
fluorure [flyɔryr] *nm Ch* fluoride.
flûte [flyt] **1** *nf* **(a)** (*instrument*) flute; **grande f.**, concert flute; **petite f.**, piccolo; **f. à bec**, recorder; **(b)** (*musicien*) flautist, flute, *esp US* flutist; **(c)** (*pain*) long thin loaf of French bread; **(d)** (*verre*) tall champagne glass, flute; **(e)** *F* (*jambes*) **flûtes**, (thin) legs; **jouer** *ou* **se tirer des flûtes**, to show a clean pair of heels. **2** *int F* damn!; **f. alors, il est déjà parti!**, blow it, he's gone already!
flûté [flyte] *adj* **voix flûtée**, flute-like *or* piping voice.
flûtiste [flytist] *n* flautist, flute player, *esp US* flutist.
fluvial, -iaux [flyvjal, -jo] *adj* river, fluvial; **police fluviale**, river police; **pêche fluviale**, river fishing, angling; **alluvions fluviales**, fluvial deposits; **port f.**, river port.
fluviatile [flyvjatil] *adj* **mollusques fluviatiles**, river *or* freshwater molluscs.
flux [fly] *nm* **(a)** flow, stream (*of words*); **(b)** flow, flood (*of the tide*); **le f. et le reflux**, the ebb and flow; *Pol F* the swing of the pendulum; **(c)** *Méd* flow, flux; **f. menstruel**, menstrual flow; **(d)** *Ch Métal* flux; **(e)** *Phys El* **f. magnétique**, magnetic flux; **f. lumineux**, luminous *or* light flux; **f. électronique**, electron flow *or* stream.
fluxion[flyksjɔ̃] *nf Méd* inflammation; **f. à la joue**, swollen cheek; **f. de la gencive**, gumboil; **f. de poitrine**,pneumonia.
F.M.I. [ɛfɛmi] *nm* (*abrév* **Fonds monétaire international**) IMF.
F.N. [ɛfɛn] *nm abrév* **Front National**.
F.N.I. [ɛfɛni] *nfpl Mil* (*abrév* **forces nucléaires intermédiaires**) INF.

F.O. [ɛfo] *nf abrév* **Force ouvrière.**
F.O.B. [ɛfɔbe] **, fob** [fɔb] *adj inv* FOB; **vente f.,** FOB sale.
foc [fɔk] *nm Nau* jib; **grand f.,** main *or* outer jib; **petit f.,** fore staysail; **bâton de f.,** jib boom.
focal, -aux [fɔkal, -o] *adj Math Opt* focal.
focalisation [fɔkalizɑsjɔ̃] *nf Opt Electron* focusing.
focaliser [fɔkalize] **1** *vt Opt Electron* to focus; *Fig* **f. son attention sur un point en particulier,** to focus one's attention on one particular point. **2 se focaliser** *vpr* to be focused; (*concentrer*) to concentrate.
foehn [føn] *nm* **(a)** (*vent*) foehn; **(b)** *Suisse* (*sèche-cheveux*) hair-dryer.
fœtal, -aux [fetal, -o] *adj* f(o)etal.
fœtus [fetys] *nm* f(o)etus.
fofolle [fɔfɔl] *adj & nf F* foolish, silly, daft (woman, dog).
foi [fwa] *nf* **(a) bonne f.,** good faith, honesty; **il est de bonne f.,** he is completely sincere; **mauvaise f.,** dishonesty, insincerity; **je le lui ai dit en toute bonne f.,** I told him that in good faith; **manquer de f. à qn,** to break faith with s.o.; **ma f., oui!,** yes indeed!; **c'est ma f. exact,** that is certainly right; **f. d'honnête homme,** on my word as a gentleman; **sur la f. de sa lettre,** on the strength of his letter;
(b) (*confiance*) belief, trust, confidence; **avoir f. en qn/qch,** to have faith *or* to believe in s.o./sth; **avoir f. en l'avenir,** to have confidence in the future; **ajouter** *ou* **attacher f. à une nouvelle,** to credit *or* to believe (in) a piece of news; **témoin de bonne/mauvaise f.,** truthful/dishonest witness; **témoin digne de f.,** trustworthy *or* reliable *or* credible witness; **texte qui fait f.,** authentic text; *Jur* **en f. de quoi,** in witness whereof; **ligne de f.,** *Opt* zero alignment; *Nau Av* lubber line;
(c) *Rel* (religious) faith, belief; **acte/article de f.,** act/article of faith; **profession de f.,** profession of faith; *Cathol* confirmation; *Pol* (*candidate's*) statement of policy; **répandre la f.,** to spread the Word; **la f. démocratique,** belief in democracy; **il n'a ni f. ni loi,** he fears neither God nor man.
foie [fwa] *nm* liver; **huile de f. de morue,** cod-liver oil; *Culin* **f. gras,** foie gras; *Fig* **se ronger** *ou* **se manger les foies,** to be very worried; *Arg* **avoir les foies,** to be scared out of one's wits.
foin [fwɛ̃] *nm* **(a)** (*fourrage*) hay; **faire les foins,** to make hay; **tas de f.,** haycock; **meule de f.,** haystack; **rhume des foins,** hay fever; *Arg* **faire du f.,** to make a fuss, to kick up a row; **(b)** choke (*of artichoke*).
foire [fwar] *nf* fair; **f. commerciale de Marseille,** Marseilles trade fair; **champ de f.,** fairground; *F* **c'est la f. ici,** it's bedlam in here; **faire la f.,** to celebrate, to go *or* be on a spree.
foirer [fware] *Vulg* **1** *vi* (*rater*) to balls up, to cock up; **la mission a complètement foiré,** the mission was a complete balls-up *or US* ballup *or* cockup; *Mil* **fusée qui foire,** shell that doesn't go off. **2** *vt* to make a balls-up *or* cockup of (*sth*).
foireux, -euse [fwarø, -øz] *adj Arg* **(a)** (*qui échoue*) failed; **c'est un film f.,** the film is a flop; **c'est un plan f.,** that plan's doomed to fail; **(b)** *F* (*lâche*) scared, chicken; **(c)** *Méd Vulg* suffering from the runs.
fois [fwa] *nf* **(a)** (*occasion*) time, occasion; **une f.,** once; *Belg* **venez une f. voir,** (= *donc*) just come and see; **une f. et une seule,** once and once only; **il y avait** *ou* **il était une f. un roi,** once upon a time there was a king; **deux f.,** twice; **par deux f.,** not (only) once but twice; **combien de f.?,** how many times?, how often?; **trois f. quatre font douze,** three times four is twelve; **trois f. plus grand,** three times as big; **c'est trois f. rien,** it's absolutely nothing; **encore une f.,** once more, once again; **y regarder à deux f. pour faire qch,** to think twice before doing sth; **une (bonne) f. (pour toutes),** once (and for all); **la première/la deuxième f.,** the first/second time; **c'est la première f. que j'en fais,** it's my first time, it's the first time I've done it; **une dernière f., arrête!,** for the last time, stop it!; **cette f.,** on this occasion, this time; **pour cette f.,** this once; **une autre f.,** another time, on another occasion; **d'autres f.,** at other times; **bien des f.,** many times, often; **deux f. par jour,** twice daily *or* a day; **il faut le boire en une f.,** you must drink it at one go; **toutes les f.** *ou* **chaque f. que j'y pense,** every time that *or* whenever I think about it; **pour une f. tu as raison,** you're right for once; **tu te souviens de la f. où tu étais arrivé en retard?,** do you remember the time when you arrived late?; **c'est la seule f. où j'ai regretté,** that's the only time I had regrets; **une f. que vous aurez des informations,** once *or* as soon as you have some information; **à la f.,** at (one and) the same time, at once; **à la f. utile et pas cher,** both useful and inexpensive; **pas tous à la f.!,** one at a time!; *Fig* **tu ne peux pas courir deux lièvres à la f.,** you can't do two things at once *or* at the same time;
(b) *F* **des f.,** sometimes, now and then; **vous n'auriez pas des f. un câble de remorque?,** you haven't by any chance got a towrope?; **des f. qu'il viendrait,** in case he should come; **non, mais des f.!,** that's a bit thick!
foison [fwazɔ̃] *nf Arch* abundance, plenty; **à f.,** plentifully, in abundance; **il y en a à f.,** there are plenty of them, they are abundant; **des pommes à f.,** apples in abundance, apples galore.
foisonnant [fwazɔnɑ̃] *adj* abundant, plentiful.
foisonnement [fwazɔnmɑ̃] *nf* **(a)** (*prolifération*) abundance; **(b)** (*multiplication*) multiplying; **(c)** swelling, expansion (*of lime etc*).
foisonner [fwazɔne] *vi* **(a)** to abound (**de, en,** in, with); to swarm, to teem (*with vermin*); **le gibier foisonne ici,** game is plentiful here; **(b)** (*of animals*) to multiply; **(c)** (*of lime etc*) to swell, to expand.
fol, folle [fɔl] *adj voir* **FOU.**
folâtre [fɔlɑtr] *adj* playful, lively (*child*); frisky (*lamb, foal etc*).
folâtrement [fɔlɑtrəmɑ̃] *adv* playfully.
folâtrer [fɔlɑtre] *vi* to romp, to frolic; (*of lamb*) to gambol, to frisk about.
folâtrerie [fɔlɑtrəri] *nf* **(a)** (*of lamb*) friskiness; (*of kitten*) playfulness; **(b)** (*blague etc*) frolic, romp.
folichon, -onne [fɔliʃɔ̃, -ɔn] *adj* playful, lighthearted; *F* **ce n'est pas f.,** it's not much fun.
folichonner [fɔliʃɔne] *vi Vieilli* to play *or* lark about.
folie [fɔli] *nf* **(a)** *Méd* madness, lunacy; **accès de f.,** fit of madness; **f. du suicide,** suicidal mania; **f. des grandeurs,** delusions of grandeur, megalomania; **être pris de f.,** to go mad; **avoir un grain de f.,** to be a bit touched; **aimer qn à la f.,** to be madly in love with s.o., to love s.o. to distraction; **aimer qch à la f.,** to be mad on *or* have a mania for sth; *F* **c'est de la f., tout ce monde!,** all these people – it's crazy!; **(b)** (*inconscience*) folly; **il a eu la f. de céder,** he was silly enough to give in; **dire des folies,** to talk wildly *or* extravagantly; **faire des folies,** to act irrationally; (*faire des achats extravagants*) to be extravagant; **(c)** *Archit* folly.
folio [fɔljo] *nm Typ etc* folio.
folioter [fɔljɔte] *vt* to folio; *Typ* to paginate.
folk [fɔlk] *adj & nm Mus* folk.
folklo [fɔlklo] *adj F* (*bizarre*) funny; **il est f.,** he's a funny guy *or* an oddball; **une soirée f.,** a funny *or* weird evening.
folklore [fɔlklɔr] *nm* **(a)** (*étude*) folklore; **(b)** (*traditions*) folk songs, country dancing, local traditions; *F* **c'est du f., ce n'est pas sérieux,** it's a bit daft, you can't take it seriously.
folklorique [fɔlklɔrik] *adj* traditional (*costume etc*); **danses folkloriques,** folk *or* country dancing; *F* **réunion f.,** odd meeting.
folkloriste [fɔlklɔrist] *n* folklorist, student of folklore.
folle [fɔl] *adj voir* **FOU.**
follement [fɔlmɑ̃] *adv* **(a)** (*avec excès*) madly, foolishly, rashly; **être f. amoureux,** to be madly in love; **(b)** (*au plus haut point*) madly, wildly, extravagantly; **s'amuser f.,** to have a wonderful time.
follet, -ette [fɔlɛ, -ɛt] *adj* **(a)** merry, lively; **esprit f.,** elfish spirit, sprite, (hob)goblin; **feu f.,** will-o'-the-wisp, Jack-o'-lantern; **c'est un vrai feu f.,** he's here today and gone tomorrow; **(b) poil f.,** down (*of bird, boy's face*); **cheveux follets,** stray lock(s).
follicule [fɔlikyl] *nm Bot Anat* follicle.
fomentateur, -trice [fɔmɑ̃tatœr, -tris] *n* agitator, troublemaker.
fomentation [fɔmɑ̃tɑsjɔ̃] *nf* fomentation.
fomenter [fɔmɑ̃te] *vt* to stir up, *Fml* to foment (*trouble*).
fonçage [fɔ̃saʒ] *nm* **(a)** bottoming, heading (*of cask*); **(b)** boring, sinking (*of well*).
foncé [fɔ̃se] *adj* (*couleur*) dark; **bleu f.,** dark blue.
foncer [fɔ̃se] *v* (**je fonçai(s); n. fonçons**) **1** *vt* **(a)** to deepen *or* darken the colour of (*sth*); **(b)** *Culin* to line (*mould*); **(c)** to bottom, to head (*a cask*); **(d)** to sink, to drive (in) (*pile*); to sink, to bore (*well*). **2** *vi* **(a) f. sur qn,** to rush at *or* swoop (down) on s.o.; (*of bull, footballer*) to charge s.o.; **(b)** *F* to speed along, to forge ahead; **(c)** to deepen, to darken (*in colour*).
fonceur, -euse [fɔ̃sœr, -øz] *F* **1** *n* go-ahead person. **2** *adj* go-ahead.
foncier, -ière [fɔ̃sje, -jɛr] **1** *adj* **(a)** of land; **propriété foncière,** landed property, real estate; **le propriétaire f.,**

the landowner; **rente foncière,** ground rent; **impôt f.,** land tax; **crédit f.,** land bank; **(b)** *Fig* (*fondamental*) deep-seated, fundamental (*common sense*). **2** *nm* land tax.

foncièrement [fɔ̃sjɛrmɑ̃] *adv* fundamentally, basically.

fonction [fɔ̃ksjɔ̃] *nf* **(a)** (*tâche*) function, office; **f. publique,** public office; **entrer en fonctions,** to take up one's duties; **être en f.,** to be in office; **faire f. de gérant,** to act as manager; **adjectif qui fait f. d'adverbe,** adjective that is used *or* functions as an adverb; **cela ne fait pas partie de mes fonctions,** that does not come within my remit; *Anat* **fonctions de l'estomac/du cœur,** functions of the stomach/heart; **(b)** *Math etc* function; **f. inverse,** inverse function; **(c) en f. de,** according to (*results etc*); **exprimer une quantité en f. d'une autre,** to express one quantity in terms of *or* as a function of another; **les prix varient en f. de la demande,** prices vary in accordance with *or* according to demand.

fonctionnaire [fɔ̃ksjɔnɛr] *n* official, *surtout* civil servant; **haut/petit f.,** high-/low-ranking official *or* civil servant; *Péj* **mentalité de f.,** bureaucratic mentality.

fonctionnalisme [fɔ̃ksjɔnalism] *nm* functionalism.

fonctionnaliste [fɔ̃ksjɔnalist] *adj* functionalist.

fonctionnariser [fɔ̃ksjɔnarize] *vt* to bring (*employees, profession*) into the civil service.

fonctionnarisme [fɔ̃ksjɔnarism] *nm Péj* officialdom, bureaucracy, *F* red tape.

fonctionnel, -elle [fɔ̃ksjɔnɛl] *adj* functional; **cette cuisine est très fonctionnelle,** this is a very functional kitchen.

fonctionnellement [fɔ̃ksjɔnɛlmɑ̃] *adv* functionally.

fonctionnement [fɔ̃ksjɔnmɑ̃] *nm* **(a)** functioning, working (*of government, plan etc*); **(b)** functioning, operation, running, working (*of a machine etc*); **entrer en f.,** to begin working; **en (bon) état de f.,** in (good) running *or* working order; **cycle de f.,** operating cycle.

fonctionner [fɔ̃ksjɔne] *vi* to function, to work; *Ordinat* to run; **les trains ne fonctionnent plus,** the trains are no longer running; **les freins n'ont pas fonctionné,** the brakes failed; **faire f. une machine,** to run *or* work a machine; *El* **f. sur courant continu,** to operate on direct current; **dans cette atmosphère mon cerveau ne peut pas f.,** my brain can't function in this atmosphere.

fond [fɔ̃] *nm* **(a)** bottom; crown (*of hat*); seat (*of chair, trousers*); bottom, head (*of cask*); heart (*of artichoke*); back (*of the throat*); **abîme sans f.,** bottomless chasm; **boîte à double f.,** box with a false bottom; **bateau à f. plat,** flat-bottomed boat; **f. de cale,** bilge; **f. de cylindre/chaudière,** cylinder/boiler head; **f. de bouteille,** dregs; **il n'en reste qu'un f.,** there's only a drop left; **f. de café,** coffee grounds; **faire ses fonds de tiroir,** to have a clear out; **râcler ses fonds de tiroir,** to scrape around (*for money*); **du f. du cœur,** from the bottom of one's heart; **tu connais le f. de ma pensée,** you know what my thoughts *or* feelings really are; *Fig* **au f., dans le f.,** fundamentally, basically, at bottom; **au f., c'est ce qu'il voulait,** (deep down) that's what he really wanted; **au f. il était très flatté,** in his heart of hearts he was extremely flattered; **aller au f. d'une affaire,** to get to the bottom *or* root of a matter; **à f.,** thoroughly; **enfoncer un clou à f.,** to hammer a nail home; **connaître un sujet à f.,** to have a thorough knowledge of a subject; **à f. (de train),** at top speed; *Fig* **elle est en train de toucher le f.,** she's reached the bottom *or* hit rock bottom;

(b) bottom, bed (*of the ocean*); **f. de sable,** sandy bottom; **prendre f.,** (*d'une ancre*) to bite, to grip; **envoyer un navire par le f.,** to send a ship to the bottom; **grands fonds,** ocean depths *or* deeps; **hauts/petits fonds,** shallows; **courant de f.,** undertow; **lame de f.,** ground swell; **trouver/prendre le f.,** to sound, to take soundings;

(c) foundation; **rebâtir une maison de f. en comble,** to rebuild a house from top to bottom; **être ruiné de f. en comble,** to be completely ruined; *Fig* **il a un bon f.,** he's good at heart *or* basically good; **f. de teint,** make-up foundation (cream); **f. de robe,** full-length slip; **faire f. sur qn/qch,** to rely *or* depend on s.o./sth; **le f. et la forme,** the form and the substance; **le f. de cette politique,** the essential features of this policy; **cheval qui a du f.,** horse with staying power; **course de (grand) f.,** long-distance race; *Ski* cross-country race; **coureur de f.,** long-distance runner; **ski de f.,** cross-country skiing, langlauf; **question de f.,** fundamental question; *Journ* **article de f.,** leading article, leader, editorial; *Mus* **jeu de f.,** pipe stop (*of organ*); **bruit de f.,** scratching (*of gramophone needle*); *Cin Rad* background noise; **f. sonore** *ou* **musical,** background music;

(d) background (*of picture*); far end (*of enclosed space*) **la salle du f.,** the room at the end (*of a corridor etc*), the far room; *F* **fonds de boutique,** oddments, old stock; **au (fin) f. du désert,** in the heart of the desert; *Th* **toile de f.,** backdrop, backcloth; *Fig* **avec la guerre en toile de f.,** against a backdrop of war; *Tennis* **ligne de f.,** baseline.

fondamental, -aux [fɔ̃damɑ̃tal, -o] *adj* fundamental, basic, underlying (*principle*); **pierre fondamentale,** foundation stone; **couleurs fondamentales,** primary colours; *Mus* **son f.,** root, generator (*of chord*); *Univ* **recherche fondamentale,** basic research.

fondamentalement [fɔ̃damɑ̃talmɑ̃] *adv* fundamentally, basically.

fondamentalisme [fɔ̃damɑ̃talism] *nm Rel* fundamentalism.

fondamentaliste [fɔ̃damɑ̃talist] *n* **(a)** (*scientifique*) scientist engaged in basic research; **(b)** *Rel* fundamentalist.

fondant [fɔ̃dɑ̃] **1** *adj* melting; **neige fondante,** melting *or* thawing snow; **poire fondante,** pear that melts in the mouth; **tons fondants,** blended shades (of colour). **2** *nm* (*bonbon*) fondant, bonbon; *Tech* flux.

fondateur, -trice [fɔ̃datœr, -tris] **1** *n* founder (*of city, business etc*). **2** *adj* **membre f.,** founder member.

fondation [fɔ̃dasjɔ̃] *nf* **(a)** founding, foundation (*of city, hospital etc*); **(b)** (*fonds*) endowment (fund), foundation; **(c)** (*établissement*) institution, foundation; **(d)** *Constr* **fondations,** foundations (*of house*).

fondé [fɔ̃de] **1** *adj* well-founded, reasonable, justified; **doutes (bien) fondés,** well-founded *or* well-grounded *or* (fully) justified suspicions; **mal f.,** groundless, unjustified (*suspicions*); **être f. à croire,** to have good reasons to believe; **qu'est-ce qu'il y a de f. dans ces bruits?,** what grounds are there for these reports? **2** *nm Jur* **f. de pouvoir,** agent (*holding power of attorney*).

fondement [fɔ̃dmɑ̃] *nm* **(a)** (*base*) foundation, base; **soupçons sans f.,** groundless *or* unfounded suspicions; **(b)** *F* (*derrière*) buttocks, bottom; **(c)** *Arch* =**FONDATION (d)**.

fonder [fɔ̃de] **1** *vt* to found (*city, business etc*); to start, to set up (*business, newspaper*); to float (*company*); **f. ses espérances sur qch,** to base *or* build one's hopes on sth; **document fondé sur des témoignages réels,** document based on authentic accounts. **2 se fonder** *vpr* **se f. sur qch,** to go by sth, to base one's opinion *or* decision *etc* on sth; **sur quoi se fonde-t-il pour le nier?,** what are his grounds for denying it?; **un espoir qui se fondait sur une information fausse,** a hope that was based *or* founded on misinformation.

fonderie [fɔ̃dri] *nf* **(a)** (*extraction*) smelting (*of ore*); (*fusion*) founding, casting (*of metals*); **(b)** (*d'extraction*) smelting works; (*de fusion*) foundry; **(c)** (*articles*) foundry.

fondeur[1] [fɔ̃dœr] *nm* (*maître de forges*) ironmaster; (*ouvrier*) (*d'extraction*) smelter; (*de fusion*) (metal) founder; **f. en cuivre,** brass founder; **f. en caractères, f. typographe,** type founder.

fondeur[2]**, -euse** [fɔdœr, -øz] *n Ski* cross-country skier.

fondre [fɔ̃dr] **1** *vt* **(a)** (*liquéfier*) to smelt (*ore*); to melt down (*metal*); to dissolve (*sugar etc*); to melt (*snow, wax etc*); **f. deux fils ensemble,** to fuse two wires together;

(b) to cast, to found (*bell, gun etc*);

(c) f. des teintes, to blend colours;

(d) *Com* to amalgamate (*companies*).

2 *vi* **(a)** to melt; (*of snow*) to melt, to thaw; (*of sugar etc*) to dissolve; **le beurre fond au soleil,** butter melts in the sun; *El* **faire f. un fusible,** to blow a fuse; *Fig* **mon cœur fondit de pitié,** my heart melted with pity; *Fig* **f. en larmes,** to dissolve in(to) tears; *Fig* **l'argent lui fond entre les doigts,** money runs through his fingers; **il fond à vue d'œil,** he's getting thinner every day;

(b) to pounce, to swoop down (**sur sa proie,** upon the prey).

3 se fondre *vpr* to mix, to merge; (*of companies*) to amalgamate; **se f. dans la brume,** to disappear into the mist; **se f. dans la foule,** to merge *or* blend into the crowd.

fondrière [fɔ̃drijɛr] *nf* pothole (*full of water*); *Can* **f. de mousse,** muskeg.

fonds [fɔ̃] *nm* **(a)** *Fin* funds; **fournir les f. d'une entreprise,** to supply the capital for an undertaking; **mise de f.,** paid-in capital; **mouvement de f.,** flow of capital; **rentrer dans ses f.,** to recoup one's losses; **appel de f.,** call upon shareholders; **mangez vos revenus, mais ne touchez pas au f.,** spend your income, but don't touch your capital; **placer son argent à f. perdus,** to purchase an annuity; **prêt à f. perdus,** loan without security; *Fig* **faire qch à f. perdus,** to do sth at a loss; **F. monétaire international,** International Monetary Fund; **f. commun,** pool;

être en f., to be in funds;

(b) *(entreprise)* **f. de commerce,** business (with goodwill); **f. de commerce à vendre,** business for sale (as a going concern);

(c) collections *(in museum)*; *Fig* **c'est un f. inestimable pour les chercheurs,** it is an invaluable resource for researchers;

(d) f. de terre, estate, (piece of) land;

(e) *Fin pl* **fonds,** stocks, securities; **f. d'État, f. publics,** Government stock(s);

fondu, -ue [fɔ̃dy] **1** *adj* melted *(butter etc)*; molten *(lead, lava)*; **neige fondue,** slush. **2** *nm* **(a)** blending *(of colours)*; **(b)** *Cin* dissolve; **ouverture en f.,** fade-in, fading in; **fermeture en f.,** fade-out, fading out; **faire un f. enchaîné,** to fade in-fade out. **3** *nf Culin* **fondue (savoyarde),** (cheese) fondue; **fondue bourguignonne,** fondue bourguignonne, beef fondue.

fongicide [fɔ̃ʒisid] **1** *adj* fungicidal. **2** *nm* fungicide.

fongueux, -euse [fɔ̃gø, -øz] *adj Méd* fungous.

fontaine [fɔ̃tɛn] *nf* **(a)** *(source)* spring *(of water)*; **f. de boue,** mud spring; **(b)** *(construite)* fountain; **(c)** *(petit réservoir)* cistern; **f. filtrante** *ou* **de ménage,** (household) filter.

fontainier [fɔ̃tenje] *nm* **(a)** water engineer; **(b)** *(qui cherche de l'eau)* well borer *or* sinker.

fontanelle [fɔ̃tanɛl] *nf Anat* fontanel(le).

fonte[1] [fɔ̃t] *nf* **(a)** melting, thawing *(of snow)*; melting down *(of gold, silver etc)*; smelting *(of ore)*; *Métal* casting, founding; **jeter du métal en f.,** to cast metal; **pièces de f.,** castings; **(fer de) f., f. de fer,** cast iron; **f. d'acier,** cast steel; **poêle en f.,** cast-iron stove; **(b)** *Typ* fount.

fonte[2] *nf* (saddle) holster.

fonts [fɔ̃] *nmpl* **f. (baptismaux),** (baptismal) font; **tenir un enfant sur les f.,** to be godfather *or* godmother to a child.

foot [fut] *nm F* football; **jouer au f.,** to play football.

football [futbol] *nm* football, *F* soccer.

footballer, footballeur, -euse [futbolœr, -øz] *n* footballer, football player.

footing [futiŋ] *nm* jogging; **faire son f.,** to (go) jog(ging).

for [fɔr] *nm* **le f. intérieur,** the conscience; **dans** *ou* **en son f. intérieur,** in one's heart of hearts.

forage [fɔraʒ] *nm* **(a)** *(action)* drilling, boring, sinking *(of well)*; **(b)** *(trou)* borehole, drill hole.

forain, -aine [fɔrɛ̃, -ɛn] **1** *adj* **(a)** *(itinérant)* itinerant; **spectacle f.,** travelling show *(at a fair)*; **acteur f.,** strolling player; **fête foraine,** funfair; **marchand f.,** stallkeeper *(at fair)*; **(b)** *Nau* **mouillage f.,** open berth. **2** *n* *(marchand etc)* stallholder.

forban [fɔrbɑ̃] *nm* pirate, buccaneer; *Fig* rogue, crook.

forçage [fɔrsaʒ] *nm* **(a)** forcing *(of plants)*; **(b)** = **FORCEMENT (a)**.

forçat [fɔrsa] *nm* *(prisonnier)* convict; *(galérien)* galley slave; *F* **mener une vie de f.,** to slave away.

force [fɔrs] **1** *nf* **(a)** strength; **f. d'âme,** strength (in adversity), fortitude; **dans la f. de l'âge,** in the prime of life; **être à bout de f.,** to be exhausted, to be on one's last legs; **travailler de toutes ses forces,** to work with all one's might, to work all out; **elle n'avait plus la f. de répondre,** she had no strength left to answer; **tour de f.,** feat of strength, tour de force; *(d'adresse)* feat of skill, tour de force; *Constr* **(jambe de) f.,** force piece, strut; **f. de résistance à la tension,** tensile strength; **ils sont de f. (égale),** they are equally matched *or* well matched; **joueur d'échecs/boxeur de première f.,** first-class chess-player/boxer; **je ne me sens pas de f. à faire cela,** I don't feel up to *or* equal to doing it;

(b) *(violence)* force, violence; **f. majeure,** circumstances outside one's control, force majeure; **faire appel à la f.,** to resort to force; **faire qch de vive f.,** to do sth by sheer force; **entrer** *ou* **pénétrer de f. dans une maison,** to force one's way into a house; **faire entrer qch de f. dans qch,** to force sth into sth; *Nau* **faire f. de voiles,** to crowd on (all) sail; **faire f. de rames,** to row *or* pull hard; **f. lui fut d'obéir,** he was obliged to obey, he had no option but to obey; **céder à la f.,** to yield *or* give in to force; *Prov* **la f. prime le droit, f. passe droit,** might is right; **de gré ou de f.,** willy-nilly; **de toute f. il nous faut y assister,** we absolutely must be present; **à toute f.,** in spite of all opposition; **il veut à toute f. entrer,** he is determined to get in;

(c) force *(of blow, the wind, an argument)*; **les forces de la nature,** the forces of nature; **c'est une f. de la nature,** he's a bundle of energy; **par la f. des choses,** through force of circumstances; **dans toute la f. du mot,** in every sense of the word;

(d) à f. de, by (dint of), by means of; **à f. de travailler,** by dint of hard work; **à f. de volonté,** by sheer force of will; **à f. de répéter,** by constant repetition; **il s'est enroué à f. de crier,** he shouted himself hoarse;

(e) *Phys* **f. motrice,** motive power; *Fig* driving force; **f. d'inertie,** inertia; **f. vive,** kinetic energy, momentum; *El* **f. (électrique),** (electric) power; **prise de f.,** power point;

(f) la f. armée, the military, the troops; **les forces armées,** the armed forces, the services; **f. tactique** *ou* **d'intervention,** task force; **la force publique, les forces de police** *ou* **de l'ordre,** the police (force), the forces of law and order; **nous étions là en force(s),** we turned out in (full) force; *Econ* **forces du marché,** market forces; **forces nucléaires intermédiaires,** intermediate-range nuclear forces.

2 *adj inv Arch & Litt* **f. gens,** a great number of *or* a lot of *or* (very) many people; **f. bière,** copious amounts of beer.

forcé [fɔrse] *adj* **(a)** forced; *Av* **atterrissage f.,** forced *or* emergency landing; *Jur* **travaux forcés,** hard labour; *F* **mariage f.,** shotgun wedding; **comparaison forcée,** forced comparison; **exemple f.,** far-fetched example; **(b)** *(affecté)* **rire f.,** forced *or* unnatural laugh; **sourire f.,** forced smile; **(c)** *F* **c'est f.!,** it's inevitable!

forcement [fɔrsəmɑ̃] *nm* **(a)** forcing (open); **f. de blocus,** blockade running; **(b) en raison de l'affluence, la S.N.C.F. a procédé à un f. du train,** due to the number of passengers, the SNCF has added more carriages to the train.

forcément [fɔrsemɑ̃] *adv* necessarily, inevitably.

forcené, -ée [fɔrsəne] **1** *adj* frantic, mad, frenzied. **2** *n* madman, madwoman, maniac; **crier comme un f.,** to scream like a madman.

forceps [fɔrsɛps] *nm Obst* forceps.

forcer [fɔrse] *v* **(je forçai(s)) 1** *vt* **(a)** *(obliger)* to force, to compel; **f. qn à faire qch,** to force *or* compel s.o. to do sth; **f. la main à qn,** to force s.o.'s hand; **f. le respect de qn,** to compel respect from s.o.; **être forcé de faire qch,** to be forced to do sth; **f. qn/qch,** to be violent with s.o./sth; **f. une femme,** to violate *or* rape a woman; *Mil* **f. un poste,** to take a post by storm *or* by force; **f. une serrure,** to force a lock; **f. la caisse,** to break into the till; **f. le destin,** to force the hand of destiny; **f. une porte,** to break open a door; **f. la porte de qn,** to force one's way in; **f. sa prison,** to break jail;

(b) to force *(voice, pace etc)*; to strain *(mast)*; to buckle *(plate)*; *F* **f. la note,** to overdo it; **f. le sens,** to strain the meaning; **f. un cheval,** to override a horse; **f. des fleurs,** to force flowers; **f. un cerf,** to run down a stag, to bring a stag to bay; **f. la dose d'un médicament,** to take *or* give too large a dose of a medicine.

2 *vi* **f. de voiles,** to crowd on sail; **f. sur les avirons,** to strain at the oars; **le vent force,** the wind is rising; *Cartes* **f. sur l'annonce de qn,** to overcall *or* overbid s.o.; **tu y arriveras sans f.,** you'll get there without straining yourself; **ne force pas!,** don't force it!; *F* **f. sur la bouteille,** to overdo the drinking.

3 se forcer *vpr* **(a)** *(s'obliger etc)* to overstrain oneself; **pourquoi te f.?, si ça ne te dit rien, ce n'est pas grave,** why force yourself? if you don't like it, it doesn't matter; **se f. à travailler,** to force oneself to work;

(b) se f. l'épaule, to wrench *or* strain one's shoulder.

forcing [fɔrsiŋ] *nm Sp* sustained pressure; *Fig F* **il a fallu faire du f. pour qu'il accepte,** we had to put a lot of pressure on him to get him to accept; **avoir qn au f.,** to pressurize s.o..

forcir [fɔrsir] *vi* **(a)** *(d'une personne)* *(devenir plus fort)* to fill out; *(devenir plus gros)* to put on weight; **(b)** *(des éléments)* **le vent/la tempête forcit,** the wind is picking up/the storm is getting stronger.

forer [fɔre] *vt* to drill, to bore *(rock)*; to drill, to bore, to sink *(a well)*.

forestier, -ière [fɔrɛstje, -jɛr] **1** *adj* forested *(area)*; **chemin f.,** forest road; **exploitation forestière,** forestry; **garde f.,** forester, (forest) ranger. **2** *nm* forester, *esp Am* lumberjack.

foret [fɔrɛ] *nm* **(a)** *(vrille)* drill; **(b) f. à bois,** gimlet; **f. de charpentier,** auger; **(c)** *(vilebrequin)* (brace) bit.

forêt [fɔrɛ] *nf* forest; **région couverte de forêts,** forested region; *Admin* **le service des Eaux et Forêts,** ≈ the Forestry Commission; *Fig* **une f. de mâts,** a forest of masts; *Prov* **les arbres vous cache la f.,** you can't see the wood for the trees; *Culin* **F. noire,** black forest gateau.

foreur [fɔrœr] *nm* borer, driller; *Pétr* **f. d'exploration,** oil prospector, *US F* wildcatter.

foreuse [fɔrøz] *nf* *(outil)* drill; *Min etc* rock drill; **f. à**

main, hand drill.

forfaire [fɔrfɛr] *vi (conj like* **faire**) *Arch & Litt* **f. à son devoir,** to fail in one's duty; **f. à l'honneur,** to forfeit one's honour *or US* honor; **f. à sa parole,** to break one's word.

forfait¹ [fɔrfɛ] *nm* heinous crime.

forfait² *nm* contract (*with all-in price*); **f.(-voyage),** package (deal); **travail à f.,** contract work; **prix à f.,** all-in price; **vente à f.,** outright sale; **f.-vacances,** holiday package; **f. de ski,** ski pass; **le f. comprend les frais de location et d'entretien du matériel,** the set price includes the cost of hire and maintenance of the equipment.

forfait³ *nm Courses de chevaux* fine, forfeit (*paid for scratching a horse*); **déclarer f. pour un cheval,** to scratch a horse; **déclarer f.,** (*d'un athlète, concurrent*) to scratch; *Fig* to throw in the towel; **l'équipe a déclaré f.,** the team withdrew.

forfaitaire [fɔrfɛtɛr] *adj* contractual; **marché f.,** fixed-price contract; **paiement f.,** lump sum; **prix f.,** all-in price; **voyage à prix f.,** package tour.

forfaiture [fɔrfɛtyr] *nf* (*abus de pouvoir*) abuse of authority; **f. au devoir/à l'honneur,** breach of duty/honour.

forfanterie [fɔrfɑ̃tri] *nf* bragging.

forge [fɔrʒ] *nf* forge; **pièce de f.,** forging; **f. (de maréchal-ferrant),** smithy; **mener un cheval à la f.,** to take a horse to the blacksmith's; **f. de serrurier,** locksmith's workshop; **maître de forges,** ironmaster.

forgeable [fɔrʒabl] *adj* forgeable (*metal*).

forgeage [fɔrʒaʒ] *nm* forging, smithing.

forger [fɔrʒe] *vt* (**je forgeai(s)**) **(a)** to forge (*metal*); **fer forgé,** wrought iron; *Prov* **c'est en forgeant qu'on devient forgeron,** practice makes perfect; **(b)** (*inventer*) to fabricate, to make up (*story, excuse*); to coin (*word*); to trump up (*charge*); to conjure up (*vision*); **histoire forgée de toutes pièces,** completely fabricated story.

forgeron [fɔrʒərɔ̃] *nm* (black)smith.

forgeur, -euse [fɔrʒœr, -øz] **1** *n* inventor, fabricator (*of news, lies*); coiner (*of words*). **2** *nm* (*forgeron*) (black)smith.

formage [fɔrmaʒ] *nm Tech* forming.

formaldéhyde [fɔrmaldeid] *nm* (*parfois f*) *Ch* formaldehyde.

formaliser [fɔrmalize] **1** *vt* to formalize; **logique formalisée,** formal logic. **2 se formaliser** *vpr* to take offence (**de,** at), to take exception (**de,** to).

formalisme [fɔrmalism] *nm* **(a)** formality; **f. administratif,** bureaucracy, *F* red tape; **(b)** *Beaux-Arts* formalism.

formaliste [fɔrmalist] **1** *adj* **(a)** bureaucratic; **(b)** *Beaux-Arts* formalist. **2** *n* **(a)** stickler for formalities; **(b)** *Beaux-Arts* formalist.

formalité [fɔrmalite] *nf* **(a)** (*procédure*) formality, formal procedure; **c'est une pure f.,** it's just a formality; **sans autre f.,** without further ado; **(b)** (*cérémonie*) ceremoniousness; **sans formalité(s),** without ceremony.

format [fɔrma] *nm* format (*of book*); size (*of paper, Phot of plate*); *Ordinat* format; **f. de poche,** pocket size; **f. de page,** page format; **appareil de petit f.,** miniature camera.

formater [fɔrmate] *vt Ordinat* to format.

formateur, -trice [fɔrmatœr, -tris] **1** *adj* formative; **expérience formatrice,** formative experience. **2** *n* trainer.

formation [fɔrmasjɔ̃] *nf* **(a)** (*constitution*) formation, forming, development (*of character*); **nation en voie de f.,** nation in the making; **mot de f. savante,** word of learned origin; **la f. du pluriel en anglais,** the formation of the plural in English; **(b)** (*éducation*) training; **avoir une excellente f.,** to have an excellent training; **f. continue** *ou* **permanente,** continuing education; **stage de f.,** training course; **la f. du goût/de la personnalité,** the development of taste/the personality; **f. sur le tas** *ou* **par la pratique,** on-the-job training; **(c)** make-up (*of train etc*); structure (*of rock etc*); **à sa f. le train avait 5 voitures,** when it started out the train had 5 carriages; *Mil* **f. serrée,** close formation; **(d)** *Mil* unit; *Mus* group; **f. sportive,** sports team; **f. politique,** political group.

forme [fɔrm] *nf* **(a)** form, shape; **formes,** lines (*of ship*); build (*of person*); curves (*of woman*); **les formes d'un tableau/paysage,** the lines of a picture/shapes of a landscape; **vêtement qui épouse les formes,** close-fitting garment; **en f. d'œuf,** egg-shaped; **yeux en f. de billes,** eyes like marbles; **sous la f. d'une nymphe,** in the form *or* shape of a nymph; **c'est une différente f. d'esprit,** it is a different way of thinking; **l'histoire racontée sous une nouvelle f.,** history told in a new way; **statistiques sous f. de tableau,** statistics in tabular form; **sous toutes ses formes,** in all its forms *or* guises; **sans f.,** shapeless; **la societé change de f.,** the shape of the company is changing; **prendre f.,** to take shape, to materialize;

(b) (*procédure*) form, method of procedure; **arrêt cassé pour vice de f.,** judgment quashed on a technical point; **renvoyer qn sans autre f. de procès,** to dismiss s.o. without ceremony; **avertir qn dans les formes,** to give s.o. formal *or* due warning; **faire qch dans les formes,** to do sth in the accepted way; **vérification de pure f.,** routine check; **pour la f.,** as a matter of form; **de pure f.,** purely formal;

(c) formes, manners, tact; **avoir des formes,** to be polite, to use tact; **il faut y mettre les formes,** it must be done tactfully;

(d) être en f., to be on form *or* in good form; **ne pas être en f., être en mauvaise f.,** to be in poor form; **équipe bien en f.,** team in very good form; **c'est bon pour la f.,** it's good for you, it'll do you good; *F* **alors, c'est la f.?,** how are you doing?; **la f., pas les formes,** fitness, not fatness;

(e) *Ind* former, forming block; mould, *US* mold (*for cheese etc*); (*de cordonnier*) last; (*pour élargir*) shoe tree; (*de chapelier*) block; **chapeau haut de f.,** top hat;

(f) *Nau* dock;

(g) *Typ* forme, *US* form.

formé [fɔrme] *adj* formed, full grown, fully developed; (*fruit*) set; **jeune fille formée,** fully developed girl; **un personnel bien f.,** well-trained staff.

formel, -elle [fɔrmɛl] *adj* **(a)** express (*order etc*); flat, categorical (*denial*); absolute (*veto*); **défense formelle,** strict prohibition; **(b)** (*de principe*) formal; **distinction formelle,** formal distinction; **attitude formelle,** formal attitude; **(c)** *Phil* formal (*cause*).

formellement [fɔrmɛlmɑ̃] *adv* **(a)** absolutely, strictly, expressly (*forbidden*); **promettre f.,** to promise faithfully; **(b)** formally; **c'est f. correct,** it is formally correct.

former [fɔrme] **1** *vt* **(a)** (*créer*) to form, to make; *Rail* to make up (*train*); **f. un projet,** to form *or* draw up a plan; **f. sa bibliothèque,** to build up a library; **f. un (nouveau) gouvernement,** to form a (new) government; **les murs forment un carré,** the walls form a square; **(b)** to school (*child*); to train (*pilot, horse etc*); to mould, *US* to mold (*character*); **f. son esprit/son goût,** to develop one's mind/taste; **cette université a formé des hommes remarquables,** this university has turned out some remarkable men; **(c) nous avons formé des vœux pour sa réussite,** we wished him every success. **2 se former** *vpr* to form, to develop; (*of plan*) to take shape; (*of fruit*) to set; **des cristaux se forment dans la roche,** crystals form in rock; **se f. aux affaires,** to acquire a business training.

formidable [fɔrmidabl] *adj* **(a)** (*extraordinaire*) tremendous; **des progrès formidables,** tremendous progress; **(b)** *F* (*bon*) tremendous, great, fantastic; *Iron* **tu es f.!,** you're incredible; **(c)** *Vieilli* fearsome, formidable.

formidablement [fɔrmidabləmɑ̃] *adv F* **(a)** (*énormément*) tremendously, fantastically; **(b)** *Arch* formidably.

formique [fɔrmik] *adj Ch* formic (*acid*).

formol [fɔrmɔl] *nm Ch* formalin, formol.

formulable [fɔrmylabl] *adj* **une opinion difficilement f.,** an opinion that is difficult to formulate.

formulaire [fɔrmylɛr] *nm* **(a)** (*imprimé*) (printed) form; **remplir un f.,** to fill in a form; **(b)** (*recueil*) formulary; (*de pharmaciens*) pharmacopoeia.

formulation [fɔrmylasjɔ̃] *nf* formulation, expressing (*of one's feelings etc*).

formule [fɔrmyl] *nf* **(a)** *Math Ch etc* formula; **(b)** (*paroles*) expression, (turn of) phrase; **f. magique,** magic formula; **f. finale** *ou* **de politesse,** formal ending (*of letter*); **trouver la f. juste,** to find the right phrase; **(c)** (*méthode*) method; **c'est la f. idéale pour les vacances en famille,** it's the ideal way to take a family holiday; **il doit bien y avoir une f. pour apprendre le chinois en deux mois/envoyer de l'argent à l'étranger,** there must be some way of learning Chinese in two months/of sending money abroad; **(d)** *Aut* **f. un/deux,** Formula One/Two; **(e)** *Admin* (printed) form; telegraph form.

formuler [fɔrmyle] *vt* to formulate (*doctrine*); to draw up (*document*); to express (*wish*); to formulate (*proposal*), to put (*proposal*) into words; to lodge (*complaint*); to lay down (*rule*); *Méd* to write out (*prescription*).

fornication [fɔrnikasjɔ̃] *nf* fornication.

forniquer [fɔrnike] *vi* to fornicate.

fors [fɔr] *prép Litt* except, save; **tout est perdu f. l'honneur,** all is lost save honour *or US* honor.

fort [fɔr] **1** *adj* **(a)** strong; **f. comme un Turc** *ou* **un bœuf,** as strong as an ox; **partisans de la manière forte,** believers in strong measures *or* violent action; **prêter main forte à qn,** to lend s.o. a hand, to give s.o. assistance; **je suis plus f. des bras que vous,** I have stronger arms than you; **trouver plus f. que soi,** to meet one's match; **un esprit f.,** a strong mind; **courage, il faut être f.,** cheer up! *or* take heart! you *or* we *etc* must be strong; **être f. de son expérience,** to derive strength from one's experience; **c'est une forte tête,** he's very independent-minded; **être f. en mathématiques/à tous les jeux,** to be good at mathematics/at games; **il est f. pour critiquer, mais quand il faut travailler ...,** he's good at criticizing, but when it comes to working ...;

(b) strong (*rope, drink etc*); high (*fever, wind*); intense (*heat*); heavy (*rain, soil*); loud (*voice*); **moutarde forte,** strong mustard; *Fig* **elle a fait (une) forte impression,** she made a good impression; **avoir une forte odeur,** to have a strong smell; **c'est plus f. que moi!,** I can't help it!; **j'avais une forte envie de rire/de lui casser la figure,** I was very tempted to laugh/to smash his face in; *F* **c'est trop f.!,** that's a bit thick!; **ce qu'il y a de plus f., c'est qu'on n'y peut rien,** the worst of it is that nothing can be done about it; **f. en gueule,** loud-mouthed;

(c) place/ville forte, fortress/fortified town;

(d) se faire f. de faire qch, to undertake to do sth; **elles se font f.** *ou* **fortes de le retrouver,** they undertake to find it; *Jur* **se porter f. pour qn,** to stand as security for s.o.;

(e) (*ample*) large, stout (*person*); thick, full (*lips*); heavy (*beard*); **elle est forte des hanches,** she's big round the hips, she's broad in the beam; **forte somme,** large sum of money; **forte différence,** great difference; **forte hausse des prix,** sharp *or* big rise in prices; **forte pente,** steep gradient; **armée forte de cinq mille hommes,** army five thousand strong; *Com* **prix f.,** full price.

2 *adv* **(a) crier f.,** to shout loudly; **frapper f.,** to strike *or* hit hard; **tirer f. la sonnette,** to pull the bell hard; **y aller f.,** to go over the top; **sentir f.,** to smell strong *or* high; **faire (très) f.,** to go for it;

(b) (*très*) very, extremely; **il a été f. mécontent,** he was extremely displeased *or* very annoyed;

(c) (*beaucoup*) **vous vous trompez f.,** you are greatly mistaken; **j'ai f. à faire,** I have a great deal to do.

3 *nm* **(a)** strong point; **le f. et le faible de l'affaire,** the strong and weak points of the matter; **le f. d'un bois,** the heart of a wood; **le f. de l'hiver,** the depth of winter; **au (plus) f. du combat,** in the thick of the fight; **au f. de l'été/de l'épidémie,** in the height of summer/at the height of the epidemic; **le plus f. c'est que je lui avais déjà dit,** the best of it is, I'd already told him; **la politesse n'est pas son f.,** politeness is not his strong point *or* his forte;

(b) (*personne*) strong man; **les forts des Halles,** the market porters; *Prov* **la raison du plus f. est toujours la meilleure,** might is right;

(c) (*citadelle*) fort, stronghold;

(d) *Péj* **f.-en-thème,** swot.

fortement [fɔrtəmɑ̃] *adv* hard, strongly; **tirer/pousser f. sur qch,** to pull/push hard at sth; **insister f. sur qch,** to insist firmly *or* strongly on sth; **f. épicé,** highly spiced; **f. irrité,** greatly *or* extremely irritated.

forteresse [fɔrtərɛs] *nf* fortress, stronghold.

fortiche [fɔrtiʃ] *F* **1** *adj* **(a)** (*malin*) smart; (*doué*) clever, smart; **(b)** (*robuste*) brawny. **2** *n* **(a)** (*personne maligne*) smart person, *F* smart aleck; (*personne douée*) smart *or* clever person; **(b)** (*personne robuste*) brawny person.

fortifiant [fɔrtifjɑ̃] **1** *adj* fortifying, strengthening. **2** *nm Méd* tonic.

fortification [fɔrtifikasjɔ̃] *nf* fortification, fortifying (*of town etc*); (*ouvrages*) defence work(s); **les fortifications,** the fortifications (*of a town*).

fortifier [fɔrtifje] *v* (*impf & pr sub* **n. fortifiions**) **1** *vt* **(a)** to fortify (*town etc*); to fortify, to strengthen (*wall, muscles, body*); **(b)** to confirm, to support (*suspicion etc*); **f. qn dans une résolution,** to support s.o. in a resolution. **2 se fortifier** *vpr* **(a)** (*devenir plus fort*) to become stronger; **(b)** *Mil* to raise a line of defences; (*en creusant des tranchées*) to entrench oneself, to dig oneself in.

fortifs (les) [lefɔrtif] *nfpl Arg Vieilli* the fortifications (*of Paris*).

fortin [fɔrtɛ̃] *nm* small fort.

Fortran [fɔrtrɑ̃] *nm Ordinat* FORTRAN; **programmer en F.,** to program in FORTRAN.

fortuit [fɔrtɥi] *adj* fortuitous, chance, casual (*encounter*); *Jur* **cas f.,** act of God.

fortuitement [fɔrtɥitmɑ̃] *adv* fortuitously, by chance, accidentally.

fortune [fɔrtyn] *nf* **(a)** (*chance*) fortune, chance, luck; **tenter la f.,** to try one's luck; **mauvaise f.,** misfortune; **revers de f.,** reversal, setback; **avoir la bonne/la mauvaise f. de rencontrer qn,** to have the good/bad luck to meet s.o.; **faire contre mauvaise f. bon cœur,** to make the best of a bad job; **s'attacher à la f. de qn,** to throw in one's lot with s.o.; **venez dîner à la f. du pot,** come and take pot luck; **installation de f.,** temporary *or* makeshift installation; **lit de f.,** makeshift bed; **réparations de f.,** emergency repairs; **disposez-vous de moyens de f.?,** have you anything you can make do with?; *Nau* **mât de f.,** jury mast; **(voile de) f.,** cross-jack (foresail); **f. de mer,** perils of the sea;

(b) (*richesse*) fortune, wealth; **faire f.,** to make one's fortune *or* a fortune; (*réussir*) to be successful; **avoir de la f.,** to be well off; **c'est une grosse f.,** he's a very wealthy man; **être l'artisan de sa f.,** to be a self-made man; **chercher** *ou* **tenter f.,** to seek one's fortune.

fortuné [fɔrtyne] *adj* **(a)** (*riche*) rich, well-off; **(b)** *Arch & Litt* fortunate, happy.

forum [fɔrɔm] *nm Antiq etc* forum; **f. sur l'éducation,** forum *or* symposium on education.

forure [fɔryr] *nf Tech* bore(hole).

fosse [fos] *nf* **(a)** (*creux*) pit, hole; (*d'océan*) trough; *Sp* (sand) pit; *Anat* fossa; *Min* pit; *Aut* **f. (de réparation),** inspection pit; **f. aux lions,** lions' den; **f. d'aisances,** cesspool; **f. septique,** septic tank; *Th* **f. d'orchestre,** orchestra pit; **(b)** (*tombe*) grave; **f. commune,** paupers' grave; *F* **avoir un pied dans la f.,** to have one foot in the grave.

fossé [fose] *nm* **(a)** (*tranchée*) ditch, trench; (*douve*) moat; *Géol* trough; **f. d'effondrement,** rift valley; **(b)** *Fig* rift (*between persons*); **le f. ne cesse de se creuser entre eux,** there is an ever-increasing gulf *or* rift between them.

fossette [fosɛt] *nf* dimple.

fossile [fosil] **1** *nm* fossil; *F* **un vieux f.,** an old fossil. **2** *adj* fossil, fossilized.

fossiliser [fosilize] **1** *vt* to fossilize. **2 se fossiliser** *vpr* to fossilize, to become fossilized; *Fig* **les mentalités se sont fossilisées,** attitudes have become fossilized.

fossoyeur [foswajœr] *nm* gravedigger.

fou [fu] **, fol, folle** [fɔl] (*the form* **fol** *is used in the masculine before a vowel or* **h** *mute*) **1** *adj* **(a)** mad, insane; **f. à lier,** raving mad, out of one's mind; **cette musique me rend fou,** that music is enough to drive me up the wall; **il y a de quoi devenir f.,** it's enough to drive you mad; **f. de joie/terreur,** beside oneself with joy/fear; **être f. de qn,** to be madly in love with s.o.; **f. de peinture,** mad about painting;

(b) (*extravagant*) foolish, silly; **illusions folles,** wild delusions; **les vierges folles,** the foolish virgins; **il n'est pas f.,** he's no fool; **il faudrait être f. pour dépenser plus,** you'd be mad to spend more; **des diamants? mais tu es f.!,** diamonds? you're crazy!; **un fol espoir,** a foolish *or* mad hope;

(c) (*énorme*) excessive, enormous; **succès f.,** tremendous *or* wild success; **mal de tête f.,** splitting headache; **il gagne un argent f.,** he makes pots of money, he rakes it in; **à une allure folle,** at breakneck speed; **il y avait un monde f.,** there was an enormous crowd; **un prix f.,** an exorbitant price; *F* **c'est f. ce que c'est grand!,** it's crazy how big it is!; **d'une gaieté folle,** wildly happy; **c'est f., New York!,** New York is fantastic!;

(d) (*incontrôlé*) loose (*lock of hair*); runaway (*truck*); crazy (*compass needle*); idle, free (*wheel*); loose (*pulley*); **f. rire,** uncontrollable laughter; **herbes folles,** rank weeds; *Bot* **folle avoine,** wild oats.

2 *n* **(a)** lunatic, madman, madwoman; **f. furieux,** raving lunatic, maniac; **c'est un f., méfie-toi,** he's a maniac, watch out; *F* **il travaille comme un f.,** he works like one possessed; **c'est une histoire de fous,** (*je n'y comprends rien*) I can't make head (n)or tail of it; *F* **maison de fous,** madhouse; **f. du volant,** reckless driver, *F* road hog; *Littér* **la folle du logis,** the imagination;

(b) (*bouffon etc*) (court) fool, jester; **faire le f.,** to play the fool; **plus on est de fous plus on rit,** the more the merrier.

3 *nm* **(a)** *Échecs* bishop;

(b) *Orn F* gannet.

fouace [fwas] *nf Culin* = **FOUGASSE.**

foucade [fukad] *nf Litt* caprice, passing whim.

foudre¹ [fudr] **1** *nf* lightning, thunderbolt; **maison frappée par la f.,** house struck by lightning; **coup de f.,** love at first sight; **ça a été le coup de f. avec cette maison,** I *etc* fell in love with this house at first sight. **2** *nmpl* **foudres,** (*colère*) wrath. **3** *nm* **un f. de guerre,** a great warrior; *Fig* **ce n'est pas un f. de guerre,** he's got no guts; **f. d'éloquence,** powerful orator.

foudre² *nm* (*tonneau*) tun, large cask.

foudroyant [fudrwajɑ̃] *adj* crushing (*attack, news*); withering (*look*); staggering (*success*); **progrès foudroyants,** lightning progress; **une mort foudroyante,** a sudden death.

foudroyer [fudrwaje] *vt* (**je foudroie; je foudroierai**) to strike (down) (*by lightning*); **arbre foudroyé,** tree struck by lightning; *Fig* **l'apoplexie l'a foudroyé,** he was struck down by apoplexy; **elle le foudroya d'un regard,** she gave him a withering look; **cette nouvelle m'a foudroyé,** I was thunderstruck by the news; **f. ses adversaires,** to crush one's opponents.

fouet [fwɛ] *nm* **(a)** whip; **donner le f. à qn,** to whip *or* flog s.o.; **coup de f.,** lash, stroke (*of whip*); *Fig* fillip, stimulus; **l'air de la mer lui a donné un coup de f.,** the sea air has perked him up *or* given him a lift; **donner un coup de f. à l'économie,** to stimulate *or* boost the economy; **faire claquer son f.,** to crack one's whip; *Mil* **coup de plein f.,** direct hit; **être frappé de plein f.,** (*d'une cible*) to receive a direct hit; **frapper la balle de plein f.,** to connect well with the ball; **il a reçu le ballon de plein f.,** the ball came straight at him; **collision de plein f.,** head-on collision; **(b)** (*de cuisine*) whisk; **(c)** tip (*of bird's wing, dog's tail*); *Nau* tail (*of pulley*).

fouettement [fwɛtmɑ̃] *nm* flapping (*of sail*); lashing (*of rope, rain etc*).

fouetter [fwete] **1** *vt* **(a)** to whip; to spank (*a child*); to beat, to whisk (*eggs*); to whip (*cream*); **la pluie fouette les vitres,** the rain is lashing against the panes; **il n'y a pas là de quoi f. un chat,** there's nothing to make such a fuss about; **avoir d'autres chats à f.,** to have other fish to fry; **(b)** *Fig* (*exciter*) to excite, to stimulate; **brise qui fouette le sang,** breeze that makes the blood tingle; **être fouetté par le désir,** to be spurred on *or* stimulated by desire. **2** *vi* **(a)** (*of moving part*) to lash, to whip; (*of cable*) to surge; (*of sail*) to flap; **la pluie fouette contre les vitres,** the rain is lashing against the panes; **(b)** *Arg* to be scared stiff; **(c)** *Arg* (*puer*) to stink, to pong.

foufou [fufu] *adj & nm F* foolish, silly, daft (person, dog).

fougasse [fugas] *nf Culin* flat bread (sometimes stuffed with anchovies, olives etc).

fougeraie [fuʒrɛ] *nf* patch of ferns.

fougère [fuʒɛr] *nf* fern; **f. aigle,** bracken; **f. arborescente,** tree fern.

fougue [fug] *nf* fire, spirit, passion, ardour, *US* ardor; **la f. de la jeunesse,** youthful high spirits; **cheval plein de f.,** spirited horse.

fougueusement [fugøzmɑ̃] *adv* ardently.

fougueux, -euse [fugø, -øz] *adj* fiery, ardent, (high-) spirited (*person*); spirited (*horse*); **tempérament f.,** fiery temperament.

fouille [fuj] *nf* **(a)** (*action de creuser*) excavation, digging, excavating; **(b)** (*fosse*) excavation, pit; **f. à ciel ouvert,** open pit; **(c)** *Archéol* **fouilles,** dig, excavations; **faire des fouilles,** to carry out excavations *or* a dig; **(d)** search(ing), frisking (*of suspect, traveller*).

fouillé [fuje] *adj* detailed, elaborate (*work*).

fouiller [fuje] **1** *vt* **(a)** to dig, to excavate; (*of rabbit etc*) to burrow into; (*of pig*) to root in (*the ground*); **(b)** to search (*house*); to ransack (*drawer*); to go through, to rummage in (*suitcase*); to scour, to comb (*woods*); **f. qn,** to search *or* frisk s.o.; **ses yeux fouillaient la salle,** he scanned the room; **f. un problème,** to go thoroughly into a problem. **2** *vi* **(a)** (*of rabbit etc*) to burrow; (*of pig*) to root; **(b) f. dans une armoire/dans sa poche,** to search *or* rummage in a cupboard/in one's pocket; **f. dans les librairies pour trouver un livre,** to rummage in bookshops for a book; **f. dans le passé,** to rake up the past. **3 se fouiller** *vpr* to go through *or* rummage in one's pockets; *Arg* **tu peux te f.!,** nothing doing!

fouilleur, -euse [fujœr, -øz] **1** *n* **(a)** *Archéol* excavator, digger; **(b)** (*à la douane*) officer who carries out body-searches; **(c)** (*fouineur*) rummager, searcher; **f. de brocantes/de bibliothèques,** an avid frequenter of second-hand shops/libraries. **2** *nf Agr* **fouilleuse,** subsoil plough.

fouillis [fuji] *nm* jumble, mess, muddle (*of papers etc*).

fouinard, -arde [fwinar, -ard] *F* **1** *adj* inquisitive, nosy. **2** *n* nosy parker.

fouine [fwin] *nf Zool* stone marten; *F* **à tête de f.,** weasel-faced, ferret-faced.

fouiner [fwine] *vi F* to ferret, to nose about; **f. dans les affaires d'autrui,** to poke one's nose into other people's business.

fouineur, -euse [fwinœr, -øz] *adj & n F* = **FOUINARD.**

fouir [fwir] *vt* to dig (underground); (*of rabbit etc*) to burrow.

fouisseur, -euse [fwisœr, -øz] **1** *adj* burrowing (*animal*). **2** *n* burrower.

foulage [fulaʒ] *nm* **(a)** pressing, crushing, treading (*of grapes*); **(b)** tanning (*of leather*); fulling (*of cloth*); **(c)** *Typ* impression.

foulant [fulɑ̃] *adj* pressing, crushing; **pompe foulante,** force pump; *Arg* **ce n'est pas bien f.,** it's not hard work.

foulard [fular] *nm* **(a)** (silk) scarf, headscarf; **(b)** *Tex* foulard.

foule [ful] *nf* **(a)** crowd (*of people*), *Litt* throng; host (*of ideas*); **psychologie des foules,** mob psychology; **mouvement de foule(s),** (near-)riot; **entrer en f.,** to crowd in, to come crowding in; **faire f. autour de qn,** to crowd round s.o., to mob s.o.; **fuir la f.,** to flee the crowds; **quelle f. dans les rues!,** how crowded the streets are!; **on en trouve en f.,** there are loads of them; **(b)** *Can* migration (*of caribou*).

foulée [fule] *nf* **(a)** tread (*of horse's hoof*); **(b) foulées,** stride; **parcourir les champs à longues foulées,** to stride over the fields; *Sp* **courir** *ou* **rester dans la f. d'un concurrent,** to follow close behind another competitor; **avoir une bonne f.,** to have a good stride; *Fig* **marcher dans la f. de qn,** to follow in s.o.'s footsteps; *Fig* **dans la f., j'ai aussi vérifié les comptes,** while I was at it, I checked the accounts; **(c) foulées,** tracks, spoor, track (*of game*).

fouler [fule] **1** *vt* **(a)** to trample (down), to tread down (*grass*); to tread, to press, to crush (*grapes*); **f. qch aux pieds,** to tread *or* trample sth underfoot; *Fig* **les droits de l'homme sont foulés aux pieds!,** human rights have been trampled underfoot!; **(b)** *Tex* to full (*cloth*); to tan (*leather*). **2 se fouler** *vpr* **(a) se f. la cheville,** to sprain *or* strain *or* twist one's ankle; **(b)** *F* **se f. (la rate),** to take a lot of trouble; **ne pas se f. (la rate),** to take things *or* it easy; **je vais le faire, mais sans me f.,** I'll do it, but I'm not going to strain myself.

fouleur, -euse [fulœr, -øz] *n* **(a)** (*de raisin*) (*personne*) winepresser; **(b)** *Tex* (*personne*) fuller (*of cloth*); tanner (*of leather*).

fouloir [fulwar] *nm* wine press.

foulon [fulɔ̃] *nm Tex* fuller (*of cloth*); **chardon à f.,** fuller's teasel; **terre à f.,** fuller's earth; **(moulin à) f.,** fulling mill.

foulonnier [fulɔnje] *nm* = **FOULEUR (b).**

foulque [fulk] *nf Orn* coot.

foulure [fulyr] *nf* sprain, wrench; **f. au genou,** sprained knee.

four [fur] *nm* **(a)** (*de cuisine*) oven; **f. à gaz,** gas oven; **f. électrique,** electric oven; **f. de boulanger,** baker's oven; **f. à micro-ondes,** microwave oven; **faire cuire au f.,** to bake (*bread*); to roast (*meat*); **noir comme dans un f.,** pitch black; **vaisselle allant au f.,** ovenware; (*à micro-ondes*) microwave-safe ware; **plat allant au f.,** ovenproof dish; (*à micro-ondes*) microwave-safe dish; *Culin* **petits fours,** petits fours; **(b)** *Ind* kiln; (*avec combustion du contenu*) furnace; **f. à chaux,** lime kiln; **f. à briques,** brick kiln; **f. à émaux,** enamelling kiln; **f. solaire,** solar furnace; **(c)** *Th F* failure, flop; **la pièce a fait un f.,** the play was a flop; **il a fait un f. avec son discours,** his speech was a flop.

fourbe [furb] **1** *adj* cheating, double-dealing, two-faced. **2** *n* cheat, rogue, double-dealer.

fourberie [furbəri] *nf* **(a)** (*hypocrisie*) deceit, cheating, double-dealing; **(b)** (*action*) underhand trick.

fourbi [furbi] *nm F* **(a)** (*attirail*) gear, clobber, tackle; (*de soldat*) (soldier's) kit; **tout le f.,** the whole (kit and) caboodle; *Fig* **quel f., je ne retrouve rien!,** what a muddle *or* mess, I can't find anything!; **(b)** (*truc*) thingummy, gadget.

fourbir [furbir] *vt* to polish up, to shine up, to furbish (*metal*); *Fig* **f. ses arguments,** to hone one's arguments.

fourbissage [furbisaʒ] *nm* rubbing up, polishing, furbishing (*of metal*).

fourbu [furby] *adj* exhausted, tired out, *F* dead tired, dead beat, fagged (out).

fourche [furʃ] *nf* **(a)** *Agr* fork; **f. à foin,** hayfork, pitchfork; **remuer le sol à la f.,** to fork the ground; **chariot (élévateur) à f.,** forklift (truck); **(b)** fork (*of bicycle, tree, road, river*); crotch, crutch (*of trousers*); **mes cheveux ont des fourches,** my hair has split ends; **en forme de f.,** forked; **(c)** *Hist* **les Fourches Caudines,** the Caudine Forks; *Fig* **faire passer qn sous les fourches caudines,** to put s.o. through the mill.

fourchée [furʃe] *nf* pitchforkful (*of hay*).

fourcher [furʃe] **1** *vi* **(a) la langue lui a fourché,** he made a slip of the tongue; **(b)** *Arch* to fork, to divide, to branch. **2**

vt to fork (*the ground*).
fourchet [furʃɛ] *nm Vét* foot rot.
fourchette [furʃɛt] *nf* **(a)** fork; **f. à poisson/à dessert,** fish/dessert fork; **f. en argent,** silver fork; *F* **il a un joli** *ou* **bon coup de f., c'est une bonne f.,** he's a hearty eater, he has a healthy *or* hearty appetite; **manger avec la f. du père Adam,** to eat with one's fingers; **(b)** *Mil* bracket; **prendre une cible en f.** *ou* **à la f.,** to bracket a target; **f. de salaire/de prix,** wage/price bracket; **(c)** *Cartes* tenace; **(d)** wishbone (*of fowl*); frog (*of horse's hoof*); **(e)** beam support (*of balance*); **(f)** *MecE* belt guide, shifter; **f. de débrayage,** clutch throw-out fork.
fourchon [furʃɔ̃] *nm* prong, tine (*of fork*).
fourchu [furʃy] *adj* forked; cleft (*stick, chin*); **pied f.,** cloven hoof; **avoir les cheveux fourchus,** to have split ends (in one's hair); **avoir la langue fourchue,** to speak with a forked tongue.
fourgon¹ [furgɔ̃] *nm* (*de cheminée*) poker; (*de four*) (fire) rake.
fourgon² *nm* **(a)** van; **f. automobile,** (motor) van; **f. mortuaire** *ou* **funéraire** *ou* **funèbre,** hearse; **f. bancaire,** bullion van; **f. de déménagement,** furniture *or* removal van; **f. de livraison,** delivery van; **(b)** *Rail* **f. à frein,** brake van; **f. de queue,** rear (brake) van, guard's van, *US* caboose; **f. à bagages,** luggage van, *US* baggage car.
fourgonner [furgɔne] **1** *vt* to poke, to rake (*the fire*). **2** *vi* to poke the fire; *F* **f. dans un tiroir,** to poke about *or* rummage about in a drawer.
fourgonnette [furgɔnɛt] *nf* light van.
fourmi [furmi] *nf* ant; *Fig* **c'est une vraie f.,** he's a busy bee, he's always beavering away (at something); **avoir des fourmis dans les jambes,** to have pins and needles in one's legs.
fourmilier [furmilje] *nm* anteater.
fourmilière [furmiljɛr] *nf* anthill, ant's nest; *Fig* **cette banlieue est une f. (humaine),** this suburb is bustling *or* teeming with life.
fourmi-lion [furmiljɔ̃] *nm Ent* ant-lion; (*pl fourmis-lions*).
fourmillement [furmijmɑ̃] *nm* **(a)** swarming (*of ants etc*); **un f. d'impressions,** a swarm of impressions; **(b)** (*dans les membres*) pins and needles.
fourmiller [furmije] *vi* to swarm, to teem; **les vers fourmillaient dans ce fromage,** the cheese was alive with maggots; *Fig* **ouvrage qui fourmille de fautes,** work full of *or* teeming with mistakes; **f. d'idées/d'envies,** to be bursting with ideas/desires.
fournaise [furnɛz] *nf* furnace; **cette chambre est une (vraie) f.,** this room's like an oven.
fourneau, -eaux [furno] *nm* **(a)** furnace (*of boiler etc*); **f. d'une pipe,** bowl of a pipe; **(b) f. de cuisine,** (kitchen) range; **f. à gaz,** gas stove *or* cooker; **c'est David qui est aux fourneaux ce soir,** David is the chef this evening; **(c)** *Métal* furnace; **haut f.,** blast furnace; **(d)** *Min* **f. de mine,** mine chamber, blast hole.
fournée [furne] *nf* batch (*of loaves etc*); *F* batch, contingent (*of tourists etc*).
fourni [furni] *adj* **(a)** well-stocked (*shop, library etc*); **(b)** thick (*hair etc*).
fournil [furni] *nm* bakehouse.
fourniment [furnimɑ̃] *nm F* gear, clobber.
fournir [furnir] **1** *vt* **(a)** (*approvisionner*) to supply; **f. qch à qn, f. qn en qch,** to supply s.o. with s.o.; **cet agriculteur nous fournit en légumes et en vin,** this farmer supplies us with vegetables and wine; **qui fournit la famille royale?,** who is the Royal Family's supplier?; **f. une maison en vin,** to supply a house with wine;
(b) (*produire*) to supply, to provide; to produce, to furnish (*documents etc*); **vignoble qui fournit un bon vin,** vineyard that yields *or* produces a good wine; **l'E.N.A. fournit de futurs hauts fonctionnaires,** the ENA produces *or* turns out the senior civil servants of the future; **f. un effort considérable,** to make a considerable effort; **f. des renseignements (à qn),** to give information to s.o., to furnish s.o. with information; **vous devez f. votre carte d'identité,** you must present *or* show your identity card; **pièces à f.,** required documents; *Cartes* **f. du trèfle,** to follow a club lead; *Sp* **f. un jeu remarquable,** to play an outstanding game.
2 *vi Vieilli* **f. aux dépenses,** to defray the expenses; **f. aux besoins de qn,** to supply s.o.'s wants.
3 se fournir *vpr* **(a) se f. en qch,** to provide oneself with sth, to get supplies of sth (**chez,** from); **ils se fournissent chez ce traiteur,** they get their supplies from this grocer;
(b) (*of beard etc*) to grow thick.
fournissement [furnismɑ̃] *nm Fin* contribution (*in shares*).
fournisseur, -euse [furnisœr, -øz] **1** *n Com* supplier; (*en produits comestibles*) supplier, caterer, purveyor; **le f. habituel de Madame Robin,** Madame Robin's usual shop *or* supplier; **f. de navires** *ou* **de la marine,** ships' chandler; **les fournisseurs,** suppliers, tradesmen. **2** *adj* **pays fournisseurs de la France,** the countries that supply France with goods.
fourniture [furnityr] *nf* **(a)** (*approvisionnement*) supplying, providing; **(b)** *Culin* seasoning (*of dish*); **(c) fournitures,** supplies, requisites; **façon et fournitures,** making and materials; **fournitures scolaires,** educational stationery; **fournitures de navires,** ships' chandlery; **fournitures de bureau,** office stationery.
fourrage [furaʒ] *nm* forage, fodder; **f. sec/vert,** hay/silage; **rentrer du f.,** to harvest forage.
fourrager¹ [furaʒe] *v* (**n. fourrageons; je fourrageai(s)**) **1** *vi* (*pour s'alimenter*) to forage; *F* (*fouiller*) to rummage, to forage. **2** *vt* **(a)** *F* to jumble up (*papers*); **(b)** *Arch* to pillage, to ravage (*country*).
fourrager², -ère [furaʒe, -ɛr] **1** *adj* **plantes fourragères,** fodder crops. **2** *nf* **fourragère (a)** (*champ*) field sown with fodder crop; **(b)** *Mil* shoulder braid.
fourrageur [furaʒœr] *nm Mil Arch* **charger en fourrageurs,** to charge in extended order.
fourré [fure] **1** *adj* **(a)** (fur-)lined (*coat, gloves etc*); thick, dense (*wood*); **chocolats fourrés à la crème,** chocolate creams; **bonbon f.,** sweet *or US* candy with a soft centre; **(b)** *Escrime* **coup f.,** exchanged hit, double hit; *Fig* **porter un coup f. à qn,** to deal s.o. a backhanded blow; **méfie-toi, c'est un coup f.,** look out, it's a trap; **faire un coup f. à qn,** to trick s.o.; *Vieilli* **paix fourrée,** hollow peace, mock peace. **2** *nm* thicket; (*à la chasse*) cover.
fourreau, -eaux [furo] **1** *nm* **(a)** sheath, scabbard (*of sword*); cover (*of umbrella*); (*robe*) sheath dress; **remettre l'épée au f.,** to sheathe one's sword; **(b)** *MecE* sleeve (*for shaft etc*); **soupapes à fourreaux,** sleeve valves. **2** *adj* **jupe/robe f.,** pencil skirt/sheath dress.
fourrer [fure] **1** *vt* **(a)** *F* (*mettre*) to stuff, to cram; **f. ses mains dans ses poches,** to stuff *or* bury one's hands in one's pockets; **je les avais fourrés dans le coin,** I had stuck them in the corner; **f. son nez partout,** to poke one's nose into everything; **f. qn au trou,** to chuck s.o. into jail, to run s.o. in;
(b) (*avec de la fourrure*) to cover *or* line with fur;
(c) *MecE* to pack (*joint*);
(d) f. un chocolat/une crêpe de liqueur, to fill a chocolate/pancake with liqueur; **f. une dinde de marrons,** to stuff a turkey with chestnuts.
2 se fourrer *vpr* to put oneself (*in a place*); **où est-il allé se f.?,** wherever has he hidden himself?; **se f. dans une sale affaire,** to get involved in a nasty business; *F* **il se fourre les doigts dans le nez,** (*d'un enfant*) he picks his nose; *Fig F* **si tu crois que je vais l'attendre, tu te fourres le doigt dans l'œil,** if you think I'm going to wait for him, you've another think coming.
fourre-tout [furtu] *nm inv* holdall (*for travelling*).
fourreur [furœr] *nm* furrier.
fourrier [furje] *nm Mil* quartermaster sergeant.
fourrière [furjɛr] *nf* (*animal, car*) pound; **mettre un chien/une voiture en f.,** to impound a dog/a car.
fourrure [furyr] *nf* **(a)** fur, skin; **manteau de f.,** fur coat; **f. de peau de mouton,** (fleecy) sheepskin; **elle avait mis sa f.,** she had put on her fur; **(b)** hair, coat (*of animal*); **(c)** packing (*of joint*); *Aut* **f. de frein,** brake lining.
fourvoyer [furvwaje] *v* (**je fourvoie; je fourvoierai**) **1** *vt* to mislead (*s.o.*), to lead (*s.o.*) astray. **2 se fourvoyer** *vpr* to lose one's way; **au retour, ils se sont fourvoyés,** on the way back they lost their way; *Fig* **tu te fourvoies, c'est faux,** you're on the wrong track, it's wrong.
foutaise [futɛz] *nf Vulg* bullshit; **c'est de la f.!,** that's a load of bullshit *or Br* of old cobblers!
foutoir [futwar] *nm Vulg* bloody shambles; **quel f. (dans cette chambre)!,** what a bloody shambles (this room is)!
foutre [futr] *v* (*pp* **foutu**; *pr ind* **je fous, n. foutons**) *Vulg* **1** *vt* **(a) f. qch par terre,** to chuck *or* fling sth on the ground; **je vais lui f. une bonne raclée,** I'll give him a good hiding; **elle m'a foutu la honte,** (*d'elle*) I was ashamed of her; (*de moi*) she made me ashamed of myself; **ça la fout mal,** that won't look too good; **ça a tout foutu en l'air,** that screwed *or Vulg* fucked everything up;
(b) il ne fout rien, he does damn all; **qu'est-ce que tu fous?,** what the hell are you doing?; **f. le camp,** to bugger off, to piss off; **qu'il aille se faire f.,** he can piss off *or Br* get stuffed; **fous-moi la paix!,** bugger off!, piss off!; **va te**

faire f.!, piss off!, fuck off!

2 se foutre *vpr* **se f. de qn/qch,** to take the mickey *or Br* the piss out of s.o./sth; **tu te fous du monde, ou quoi?,** who the hell do you think you are?; **elle se fout de tout/de ses études,** she doesn't give a damn about anything/her studies; **je m'en fous,** I don't give a damn *or* a shit; *Fig* **alors là, il se fout dedans!,** well, he's bloody wrong then!

foutriquet [futrikɛ] *nm Péj* little runt *or* squirt.

foutu [futy] *adj Vulg* **(a)** bloody awful; **(b)** (*condamné*) ruined, done for; **il est f.,** he's had it; **(c)** (*physiquement*) **je suis mal f.,** I feel bloody awful; **elle est plutôt bien foutue,** she's a damn good looker; **(d) elle n'est même pas foutue de le faire/de me le dire en face,** she hasn't the guts to do it/to say so to my face.

fox(-terrier) [fɔks(terje)] *nm* fox terrier.

fox-trot [fɔkstrɔt] *nm* foxtrot.

foyer [fwaje] *nm* **(a)** (*domicile*) hearth, home; **le f. familial,** the (family) home; **le f. conjugal,** the marital home; **rentrer dans ses foyers,** to come (back) home; **mère** *ou* **femme au f.,** housewife; **homme au f.,** househusband; **fonder un f.,** to start a family;

(b) source (*of heat, infection*); seat, centre (*of fire, learning, infection*); **f. d'intrigue,** hotbed of intrigue;

(c) (*âtre*) fire(place), hearth, grate; firebox (*of steam engine*); **f. de chaudière,** boiler furnace;

(d) f. d'étudiants, student residence; **elle a une chambre dans un f.,** she has a room in a student hostel;

(e) (*salle*) foyer; *Th* foyer; (*de lycée etc*) common room; **f. des artistes,** green room;

(f) focus (*of lens, curve etc*); **verres à double f.,** bifocal lenses, bifocals.

frac [frak] *nm* dress coat, tailcoat, *F* tails.

fracas [fraka] *nm* crash (*of broken glass, thunder*); din (*of thunder*); clash (*of arms*); **faire du f.,** to kick up a row *or* shindy; (*of event*) to create a sensation; **à grand f.,** ostentatiously; **elle a été renvoyée avec pertes et f.,** she was thrown out of her job.

fracassant [frakasɑ̃] *adj* (*bruit*) deafening; *Fig* **c'est une nouvelle fracassante,** it's a shattering *or* staggering piece of news; **succès f.,** resounding success.

fracasser [frakase] **1** *vt* to smash (*sth*) to pieces, to shatter (*sth*); **il aurait eu la tête fracassée,** he would have had his head smashed in. **2 se fracasser** *vpr* to crash, to smash; **tu vas te f. la tête!,** you'll smash your head (in)!

fraction [fraksjɔ̃] *nf* **(a)** *Math* fraction; **f. ordinaire,** vulgar fraction; **f. décimale,** decimal fraction; **f. périodique,** recurring decimal; **(b)** (*part*) part, portion, proportion; **ça a duré une f. de seconde,** it lasted a fraction of a *or* a split second; **(c)** *Rel* breaking (*of the bread*); **(d)** *Pol* splinter group.

fractionnaire [fraksjɔnɛr] *adj* fractional; **nombre f.,** improper fraction.

fractionnel, -elle [fraksjɔnɛl] *adj* divisive (*tactics*).

fractionnement [fraksjɔnmɑ̃] *nm* **(a)** dividing up, splitting up (*of estate, group*); **(b)** *Ch etc* fractional distillation; cracking (*of oil*).

fractionner [fraksjɔne] **1** *vt* **(a)** to divide into (*fractional*) parts; to split (up) (*shares*); *Math* to fractionize; **f. le paiement,** to pay in instalments; **(b)** *Ch etc* to fractionate (*distillation*); to crack (*mineral oils*). **2 se fractionner** *vpr* to split up, to divide (*people, items*) into groups; **le groupe se fractionne en deux,** the group splits in two.

fractionnisme [fraksjɔnism] *nm Pol* (*tactiques*) divisive *or* splinter tactics; (*caractère*) factionalism.

fracture [fraktyr] *nf* **(a)** breaking open, forcing (*of lock, door*); **(b)** *Méd Géol* fracture; *Méd* **réduire une f.,** to set a fracture; **f. du crâne,** fractured skull; **f. simple,** simple *or* closed fracture.

fracturer [fraktyre] **1** *vt* **(a)** to force, to break open (*lock, door*); to break open (*door, safe*); **(b)** to fracture (*bone*). **2 se fracturer** *vpr* to fracture, to break; **se f. le tibia,** to fracture one's tibia.

fragile [fraʒil] *adj* fragile, flimsy (*construction*); brittle (*glass*); frail, delicate (*person, health*); weak, delicate (*stomach*); weak, unstable (*authority*); precarious (*happiness*); **elle est f. de la gorge,** she has a delicate throat; **ne la brutalise pas, elle est encore f.,** (*psychologiquement*) don't treat her roughly, she's still (feeling) fragile.

fragilement [fraʒilmɑ̃] *adv* fragilely, weakly.

fragiliser [fraʒilize] *vt* to weaken, to make fragile.

fragilité [fraʒilite] *nf* fragility (*of construction*); brittleness (*of glass*); frailty, weakness, fragility (*of person*).

fragment [fragmɑ̃] *nm* fragment, chip (*of stone*); fragment, splinter (*of bone*); fragment, snatch (*of song*); extract (*from book*).

fragmentaire [fragmɑ̃tɛr] *adj* fragmentary.

fragmentairement [fragmɑ̃tɛrmɑ̃] *adv* incompletely, partially.

fragmentation [fragmɑ̃tasjɔ̃] *nf* fragmentation.

fragmenter [fragmɑ̃te] *vt* to fragment, to split up; **f. la publication d'un ouvrage,** to publish a work in parts.

frai [frɛ] *nm* **(a)** spawning (*of fish*); **(b)** (*œufs*) spawn; (*poisson*) fry; **(c)** abrasion, wear (*of coins*).

fraîche [frɛʃ] *adj voir* **FRAIS.**

fraîchement [frɛʃmɑ̃] *adv* **(a)** coolly; *F* **ça va f. ce matin,** it's cool this morning; **accueillir qn f.,** to give s.o. a cool welcome *or* reception; **(b)** (*récemment*) freshly, recently, newly.

fraîcheur [frɛʃœr] *nf* **(a)** (*température*) freshness, coolness; **dans la f. du soir,** in the cool of the evening; **une sensation de f.,** a feeling of freshness; **(b)** freshness (*of flowers, food, colours, ideas*); freshness, bloom (*of youth*); **elle a perdu sa f. d'esprit,** she has lost her freshness of mind; **la f. de ses remarques/d'un film,** the candour of his remarks/freshness of a film; **(c)** *Nau* catspaw, light air.

fraîchir [freʃir] *vi Météo* **(a)** (*devenir frais*) to freshen, to grow colder *or* cooler; **(b)** (*of wind*) to freshen.

frais[1], fraîche [frɛ, frɛʃ] **1** *adj* **(a)** fresh (*wind*); cool (*wind, dress, reception*); **il fait f.,** it's cool *or* fresh; **un accueil plutôt f.,** a rather cool welcome;

(b) (*récent*) new, recent; **œufs f.,** new-laid eggs; **fruits f.,** fresh fruit; **pain f.,** fresh bread; **les traces sont fraîches,** the tracks are fresh; **de fraîche date,** not long ago, recently; **encre encore fraîche,** ink still wet; *Litt* (*with adv force*) **roses toutes fraîches cueillies,** freshly gathered roses;

(c) teint f., fresh complexion; **cette robe n'est pas très fraîche, mais elle fera l'affaire,** this dress isn't very fresh, but it will do; **f. et dispos,** hale and hearty; *F* **me voilà f.!,** I'm in a (nice) mess *or* a pretty fix!;

(d) avoir de l'argent f., to have new money.

2 *nm* **prendre le f.,** to take some *or* a breath of (fresh) air; **à mettre au f.,** to be kept cool *or* in a cool place; **mettre le vin au f.,** to put the wine to cool; *F* **ils l'ont mis au f.,** they've locked him up *or* put him inside; **peint de f.,** freshly painted.

3 *nf* **à la fraîche,** in the cool (*of the day*).

frais[2] *nmpl* expenses, cost; **f. de déplacement,** travelling expenses; **faux f.,** incidental expenses; **note de f.,** expenses; **tous f. payés,** all expenses paid; **f. d'un procès,** costs of a lawsuit; **être condamné aux f.,** to be ordered to pay costs; **faire les f. de qch,** to bear the cost *or* the expense of sth; **rentrer dans** *ou* **couvrir** *ou* **faire ses f.,** to cover one's expenses; *Fig* **j'ai fait les f. de la plaisanterie,** the joke was at my expense; *Fig* **faire les f. de la conversation,** to keep the conversation going; (*at one's expense*) to be the subject of the conversation; **faire qch à ses f.,** to do sth at one's own expense; **à grands/à peu de f.,** at great/little cost; **se mettre en f.,** to go to expense, *F* to put oneself out (of pocket); **se mettre en f. de politesse,** to go out of one's way to be polite; **j'en suis pour mes f.,** I've had all my trouble for nothing; *Com* **f. généraux,** overhead expenses, overheads; **exempt de f., sans f.,** free of charge; (*on bill of exchange*) no expenses; **f. d'envoi,** carriage costs; **f. de scolarité,** school fees; **f. d'exploitation,** operating costs; **f. de pilotage,** pilotage; **f. de représentation,** expense account, entertainment allowance; *F* **aux f. de la princesse,** at the expense of the government *or* the firm *etc*; **j'ai mangé aux f. de la princesse, mon père a payé,** I got a free meal out of *or* from my father.

fraisage [frɛzaʒ] *nm* **(a)** *Métal* milling (*of surface*); countersinking (*of hole*); **(b)** (*par le dentiste*) drilling.

fraise[1] [frɛz] **1** *nf* strawberry; **f. des bois,** wild *or US* field strawberry; **tarte aux fraises,** strawberry tart; **confiture de fraises,** strawberry jam; **sirop de f.,** strawberry cordial; *Fig* **sucrer les fraises,** to have the shakes; *Arg* **un coup en pleine f.,** a punch in the kisser; **amène ta f.!,** come here!; **il est tout le temps à ramener sa f.,** he's always kicking up a row. **2** *adj inv* (*couleur*) **f. (écrasée),** (crushed) strawberry; **écharpe f.,** strawberry-pink scarf.

fraise[2] *nf* **(a)** *Culin* crow (*of calf, lamb*); **(b)** *Arch* ruff; **(c)** wattle (*of turkey*); **(d)** *MecE etc* milling cutter, mill; **f. (conique),** countersink; **(e)** (*de dentiste*) drill.

fraiser [freze] *vt* **(a)** to drill (*tooth*); **(b)** *MecE* to mill (*surface*); to countersink (*hole*).

fraiseraie [frɛzrɛ] *nf* strawberry field *or* bed.

fraiseuse [frɛzøz] *nf MecE* milling machine.

fraisier [frezje] *nm* strawberry plant.

fraisil [frezi(l)] *nm* coal cinders.
fraisure [frezyr] *nf* countersunk hole.
framboise [frɑ̃bwaz] **1** *nf* (*fruit*) raspberry; (*liqueur*) raspberry liqueur; **tarte aux framboises,** raspberry tart. **2** *adj inv* raspberry.
framboisé [frɑ̃bwaze] *adj* raspberry-flavoured.
framboisier [frɑ̃bwazje] *nm* raspberry bush *or* cane.
franc¹ [frɑ̃] *nm* franc; **f. suisse/belge,** Swiss/Belgian franc.
franc², franche [frɑ̃, frɑ̃ʃ] **1** *adj* **(a)** (*ouvert*) frank, open, candid; **situation franche,** clear *or* unequivocal position; **un regard f.,** an open look; **c'est net et f.,** it's all open and above board; **y aller de f. jeu,** to be quite straightforward about it; **jouer f. jeu (avec, contre qn),** to play a straightforward game (with s.o.); *Fig* to play fair and square (with s.o.);
(b) (*libre*) free; **f. de tout droit,** duty-free; **zone franche,** free zone; **port f.,** free port; *Fb* **coup f.,** free kick; *Mil* **corps f.,** commando (unit);
(c) pure (*colour, wine*); clean (*break*); downright, out-and-out (*scoundrel*); **c'est un f. Breton,** he's a true Breton; **vin f. de goût,** wine clean to the taste; **terre franche,** loam; *Péj* **c'est une franche plaisanterie,** it's an utter *or* absolute joke; **huit jours francs,** eight clear days.
2 *adv* **pour parler f.,** frankly *or* candidly speaking.
franc³, franque [frɑ̃, frɑ̃k] *Hist* **1** *adj* Frankish. **2** *n* Frank.
français, -aise [frɑ̃sɛ, -ɛz] **1** *adj* French; **impossible n'est pas f.,** = impossible? there's no such word; **c'est bien f. cette attitude,** that's a typically French attitude. **2** *nm Ling* French; **parler f.,** to speak French; (*correctement*) to speak properly; *F* **tu ne comprends pas le f.?,** ≈ don't you understand (plain) English?; **je vais te dire ce que ça signifie, en bon f.,** ≈ I'll tell you what that means in plain English. **3** *n* **F.,** Frenchman, Frenchwoman; **le F. moyen n'apprécie pas le théâtre,** the average Frenchman isn't keen on (the) theatre.
franc-bord [frɑ̃bɔr] *nm Nau* freeboard; **bordé à f.-b.,** carvel built; (*pl francs-bords*).
franc-bourgeois [frɑ̃burʒwa] *nm Hist* freeman; (*pl francs-bourgeois*).
France [frɑ̃s] *nf* France; **en F.,** in France; **les vins de F.,** French wines.
Francfort [frɑ̃kfɔr] *n* Frankfurt; **saucisse de F.,** frankfurter.
franchement [frɑ̃ʃmɑ̃] *adv* **(a)** (*ouvertement*) frankly, candidly, openly; **je vais te parler f.,** I'll be frank with you; **il me l'a dit f.,** he told me openly; **(b)** (*tout à fait, vraiment*) really, quite; **c'était f. stupide/mauvais,** it was sheer stupidity/really bad; **j'en suis f. dégoûté,** I'm absolutely sick of it; *F* **f., tu comprends ça, toi?,** honestly (now), do you understand that?
franchir [frɑ̃ʃir] *vt* **(a)** to clear, to get over (*obstacle, difficulty*); to jump (over), to clear (*ditch*); to shoot (*rapids*); to run past (*danger signal*); to exceed (*limit*); **(b)** to pass through (*doorway*); to cross (*river, frontier*); **f. le seuil,** to step over *or* to cross the threshold; **je l'ai senti dès que j'ai franchi le seuil,** I felt it as soon as I walked through the door; **f. le mur du son,** to break (through) the sound barrier; **il a franchi la quarantaine,** he has turned forty.
franchise [frɑ̃ʃiz] *nf* **(a)** (*exonération*) exemption; **faire entrer qch en f.,** to import sth duty free; **entrée en f.,** free import; **bagages en f.,** free allowance of luggage; **en f. (postale),** = O.H.M.S., official paid; **(b)** (*sincérité*) frankness, openness, candour; (*franc-parler*) plain speaking, outspokenness; **en toute f.,** quite frankly; **parler avec f.,** to speak frankly; **(c)** (*d'assurance*) (accidental damage) excess; **(d)** *Hist* **charte de f.,** charter (of freedom) (*of city*); **(e)** *Com* franchise.
franchisé, -ée [frɑ̃ʃize] **1** *n Com* franchisee. **2** *adj* **magasin f.,** franchise.
franchiser [frɑ̃ʃize] *vt* to franchise.
franchiseur, -euse [frɑ̃ʃizœr, -øz] *n Com* franchisor.
franchissable [frɑ̃ʃisabl] *adj* passable (*road*); negotiable (*mountain pass*); surmontable (*obstacle*).
franchissement [frɑ̃ʃismɑ̃] *nm* clearing (*of obstacle*); jumping (*of ditch etc*); crossing (*of river etc*).
franchouillard, -arde [frɑ̃ʃujar, -ard] *F Péj* **1** *adj* chauvinistically French. **2** *n* French chauvinist.
francisation [frɑ̃sizasjɔ̃] *nf* **(a)** gallicizing, *F* Frenchifying (*of foreign word etc*); **(b)** *Nau* registry as a French ship.
franciscain, -aine [frɑ̃siskɛ̃, -ɛn] *Rel* **1** *adj & nm* Franciscan. **2** *nf* **franciscaine,** (Poor) Clare.
franciser [frɑ̃size] *vt* **(a)** to gallicize, *F* to Frenchify (*foreign word etc*); **(b)** *Nau* to register (*ship*) as French.
francité [frɑ̃site] *nf* **Maison de la F.,** = French cultural centre.
franc-maçon [frɑ̃masɔ̃] *nm* freemason; (*pl francs-maçons*).
franc-maçonnerie [frɑ̃masɔnri] *nf* freemasonry.
franc-maçonnique [frɑ̃masɔnik] *adj* masonic.
franco [frɑ̃ko] *adv* **(a)** (carriage) free; **f. (de port),** postage paid; **livré f.,** delivery free (of charge), post(age) paid; **catalogue f. sur demande,** catalogue sent free on request; **f. (à) bord,** free on board, F.O.B.; **(b)** *F* readily, unhesitatingly; **vas-y f.!,** go ahead!, on you go!
franco-allemand [frɑ̃koalmɑ̃] *adj* Franco-German.
franco-américain [frɑ̃koamerikɛ̃] *adj* Franco-American.
franco-canadien, -ienne [frɑ̃kokanadjɛ̃, -jɛn] **1** *adj* French Canadian. **2** *nm Ling* Canadian French.
François [frɑ̃swa] *nm* Francis, Frank.
Françoise [frɑ̃swaz] *nf* Frances.
francophile [frɑ̃kɔfil] *adj & n* francophile.
francophilie [frɑ̃kɔfili] *nf* francophilia.
francophobe [frɑ̃kɔfɔb] *adj & n* francophobe.
francophobie [frɑ̃kɔfɔbi] *nf* francophobia.
francophone [frɑ̃kɔfɔn] *adj & n* French-speaking (person).
francophonie [frɑ̃kɔfɔni] *nf* French-speaking areas.
franc-parler [frɑ̃parle] *nm* plain speaking; **avoir son f.-p.,** to speak one's mind; (*plus fort*) to be outspoken.
franc-tireur [frɑ̃tirœr] *nm Mil* franc-tireur, irregular (soldier); *Fig* freelance; (*pl francs-tireurs*).
frange [frɑ̃ʒ] *nf* fringe (*of rug, hair etc*); *Fig* **il reste une f. importante de la population qui ne vote pas,** there is still a substantial minority of the population which does not vote.
franger [frɑ̃ʒe] *vt* (**je frangeai(s)**) to fringe, to border.
frangin [frɑ̃ʒɛ̃] *nm F* brother.
frangine [frɑ̃ʒin] *nf F* sister.
frangipane [frɑ̃ʒipan] *nf Culin* almond paste, frangipane.
frangipanier [frɑ̃ʒipanje] *nm Bot* frangipani (tree).
franglais [frɑ̃glɛ] *nm F* Franglais.
franquette [frɑ̃kɛt] *nf* **à la bonne f.,** simply, without ceremony; **on mangera à la bonne f.,** we will eat simply; **c'est à la bonne f. chez eux,** they don't stand on ceremony at home.
franquiste [frɑ̃kist] *Hist* **1** *adj* pro-Franco. **2** *n* supporter of Franco.
frappant [frapɑ̃] *adj* striking (*picture, likeness etc*).
frappe [frap] *nf* **(a)** *Typ* striking (*of the keys*); *Ordinat* keying; **erreur** *ou* **faute de f.,** typing error; **vitesse de f.,** typing speed; **(b)** striking, minting (*of coins*); **(c)** *Baseball* hit; *Boxe* punch; *Fb* strike, kick; **(d)** *Mil* **force de f.,** strike force; **(e)** *Arg* **petite f.!,** you little yob!
frappement [frapmɑ̃] *nm* (*action of*) striking; blow.
frapper [frape] **1** *vt* **(a)** to strike, to hit; **f. légèrement,** to tap; **f. un enfant,** to hit a child; **f. la table du poing,** to bang one's fist on the table; **f. qn avec la main,** to slap s.o.; **f. un coup,** to strike a blow; **être frappé à mort,** to be fatally *or* mortally wounded; **la balle l'a frappé en plein cœur,** the bullet went right through his heart; **f. des marchandises d'un droit,** to impose a duty on goods; **être frappé par une maladie,** to be struck down by a disease; **être frappé de mutisme,** to be struck dumb; **f. qn d'étonnement,** to strike s.o. with amazement; **cela a frappé son imagination,** that caught his imagination; **ce qui m'a frappé le plus c'était son sang-froid,** what struck *or* impressed me most was his coolness; *Th* **f. les trois coups,** to give the three knocks (*at the start of a play*); *Fig* **la police va devoir f. un grand coup contre les dealers,** the police will have to strike a determined blow against the drug-pushers;
(b) to strike (*medal, coin*); to mint (*coins*); to stamp, to emboss (*wallpaper*); to punch (out), to cut out (*paper pattern*); to block (*leather*); to type (*letter*);
(c) *Nau* to bend (*halyard*); to bend on (*signal*);
(d) (*refroidir*) to ice; to chill (*wine etc*); **f. le champagne,** to put the champagne on ice; **whisky frappé,** whisky on the rocks.
2 *vi* **(a)** to strike, to hit; **f. sur la table au poing,** to bang on the table; **f./f. doucement à la porte,** to knock/to tap on *or* at the door; **entrez sans f.,** come in without knocking; **on frappe,** there's a knock (at the door); *Fig* **vous frappez à la bonne/mauvaise porte,** you've come to the right/wrong place; **il va falloir f. à toutes les portes,** we will have to ask for help from all quarters; **le chômage frappe à nos portes,** unemployment is knocking at the door;
(b) f. des mains *ou* **dans ses mains,** to clap (one's

hands); **f. du pied,** to stamp (one's foot);

(c) *F* (*agir*) to strike; **le gang a encore frappé,** the gang has struck again; **la grippe va f. durement,** the flu will hit everyone hard.

3 se frapper *vpr* **(a) se f. contre qch,** to bang into sth; **se f. les cuisses,** to slap one's thigh(s);

(b) *F* to get oneself worked up, to get oneself into a flap *or* panic; **ne vous frappez pas,** don't panic, don't flap.

frappeur, -euse [frapœr, -øz] **1** *n Métal* striker; (*de papier peint*) stamper. **2** *adj* **esprit f.,** poltergeist.

frasque [frask] *nf* prank, escapade.

fraternel, -elle [fraternel] *adj* fraternal, brotherly; **geste f.,** friendly gesture.

fraternellement [fraternelmɑ̃] *adv* fraternally.

fraternisation [fraternizasjɔ̃] *nf* fraternization.

fraterniser [fraternize] *vi* to fraternize.

fraternité [fraternite] *nf* fraternity, brotherhood, fellowship; **on trouve une certaine f. d'esprit entre eux,** you can see a certain kinship of spirit between them.

fratricide [fratrisid] **1** *adj* fratricidal. **2** *nm* (*crime*) (crime of) fratricide. **3** *n* (*personne*) fratricide.

fraude [frod] *nf* fraud; (*à un examen*) cheating; **f. fiscale,** tax evasion; **en f.,** fraudulently, unlawfully; (*en cachette*) secretly; **f. à un concours,** cheating in a competition; **passer qch en f.,** to smuggle sth through the customs; **répression de la f.,** crack down on tax evasion; **f. électorale,** electoral fraud.

frauder [frode] **1** *vt* to defraud, to cheat, to swindle (*s.o.*); **f. la douane/le fisc,** to defraud the customs, to smuggle/to evade tax; **vin fraudé,** adulterated wine. **2** *vi* to cheat.

fraudeur, -euse [frodœr, -øz] *n* defrauder, cheat, swindler; (*trafiquant*) smuggler.

frauduleusement [frodyløzmɑ̃] *adv* fraudulently.

frauduleux, -euse [frodylø, -øz] *adj* fraudulent; **édition frauduleuse,** pirated edition.

frayer [freje] *v* (**je fraye** *ou* **fraie, n. frayons; je frayerai** *ou* **fraierai**) **1** *vt* **(a) f. un chemin,** to clear a path; *Fig* to blaze a trail; **le chemin frayé,** the beaten track; **f. la voie à qn,** to clear *or* pave the way for s.o.; **(b)** to scrape, to rub; to gall (*of horse*). **2** *vi* **(a)** (*of fish*) to spawn; **(b)** *Fig* **f. avec qn,** to associate with s.o.; **je ne fraye pas avec eux,** I don't mix with them. **3 se frayer** *vpr* **se f. un passage,** to clear a way (for oneself); **se f. un chemin à travers la foule,** to force *or* push *or* elbow one's way through the crowd.

frayeur [frejœr] *nf* fright (**de,** of); **tu m'as fait une de ces frayeurs!,** you really frightened me *or* gave me a fright!; **vous me donnez des frayeurs,** you're getting me worried.

fredaine [frədɛn] *nf* prank, escapade.

fredonnement [frədɔnmɑ̃] *nm* humming (*of tune*).

fredonner [frədɔne] *vt* to hum (*tune*).

free-jazz [fridjaz] *nm Mus* free jazz.

free-lance [frilɑ̃s] **1** *adj* freelance. **2** *nm* **travailler en f.-l.,** to (work) freelance. **3** *n inv* freelance, freelancer.

freezer [frizœr] *nm* freezing compartment.

frégate [fregat] *nf* **(a)** *Nau* frigate; **capitaine de f.,** commander; **(b)** *Orn* frigate bird.

frein [frɛ̃] *nm* **(a)** *Aut etc* brake; *Rail etc* **f. à vide,** vacuum brake; **f. à air (comprimé),** airbrake; *Aut* **f. à main,** *Can* **f. à bras,** handbrake; **f. à pédale** *ou* **au pied,** foot brake; **f. à disque,** disc brake; **f. à tambour,** drum brake; **f. moteur,** engine brake; **mettre le f.,** to apply *or* put on the brake(s), to brake; **il a fallu donner un coup de f. très rapide,** we had to brake very suddenly; *Fig* **donner un coup de f. à qn/une entreprise,** to pull s.o. up short/to put a brake on an undertaking; **un coup de f. à la création d'entreprises,** a check to reduce the number of new firms; **mettre un f. à la montée de la colère,** to stem the rising tide of anger;

(b) (*mors*) bit; **ronger son f.,** (*d'un cheval, Fig d'une personne*) to champ at the bit; **mettre un f. aux désirs de qn,** to curb *or* bridle s.o.'s desires; **curiosité sans f.,** unbridled curiosity;

(c) *Anat* fr(a)enum (*of the tongue*).

freinage [frenaʒ] *nm* **(a)** (*action*) braking; *Av* **parachute de f.,** brake parachute; *Fig* **f. de l'embauche,** slowing of recruitment; **(b)** (*système*) brake system, brakes.

freiner [frene, frɛne] **1** *vt* **(a)** to brake, to apply the brake(s) to (*vehicle*); **(b)** to curb (*inflation etc*); to check (*production*). **2** *vi* to brake, to apply the brake(s); **f. brusquement,** to jam *or* ram on the brake(s); *Fig* **ce sont les patrons qui freinent,** it's the bosses who are backpedalling. **3 se freiner** *vpr Fig* to keep oneself in check.

freinte [frɛ̃t] *nf Com* loss in volume *or* weight (*during transit, manufacture*).

frelatage [frəlataʒ] *nm* adulteration (*of wine, food etc*).

frelater [frəlate] *vt* to adulterate (*wine, food*); **une vie frelatée,** a corrupt life.

frêle [frɛl] *adj* frail, weak, fragile (*person*).

frelon [frəlɔ̃] *nm* hornet.

freluquet [frəlykɛ] *nm F* (young) whippersnapper.

frémir [fremir] *vi* **(a)** to vibrate, to quiver; (*of leaves*) to rustle; (*of wind*) to sigh; (*of hot water*) to simmer; **(b)** (*d'une personne*) to tremble, to shake, to quake, to shudder; **f. de crainte,** to shake *or* quiver with fear.

frémissant [fremisɑ̃] *adj* **regard f.,** a trembling gaze.

frémissement [fremismɑ̃] *nm* **(a)** rustle (*of leaves etc*); simmering (*of hot water*); sighing (*of wind*); **(b)** (*frisson*) shudder, tremor, quiver; **avec un f. de crainte,** quaking with fear; **f. de plaisir,** thrill of pleasure; **avec un f. dans la voix,** with a trembling voice; **des frémissements parcouraient son corps,** he was shaking all over.

frênaie [frɛnɛ] *nf* ash plantation.

french-cancan [frɛnʃkɑ̃kɑ̃] *nm* cancan.

frêne [frɛn] *nm* ash.

frénésie [frenezi] *nf* frenzy, agitation; **applaudir avec f.,** to applaud frantically; **travailler/parler avec f.,** to work/talk frenziedly.

frénétique [frenetik] *adj* frantic, frenetic, frenzied.

frénétiquement [frenetikmɑ̃] *adv* frantically, frenetically.

fréquemment [frekamɑ̃] *adv* frequently.

fréquence [frekɑ̃s] *nf* **(a)** (*occurrence*) frequency; **la f. d'un mot dans un texte,** the frequency of a word in a text; **la f. de ses voyages,** the frequency of his journeys; **f. du pouls,** pulse rate; **(b)** *Phys Rad etc* **basse/haute f.,** low/high frequency; **très haute f.,** very high frequency (V.H.F.); **bande de fréquences,** frequency band; **modulation de f.,** frequency modulation.

fréquent [frekɑ̃] *adj* frequent; **il est f. de voir des jeunes couples divorcer,** you frequently see young couples getting divorced.

fréquentable [frekɑ̃tabl] *adj* **il est f.,** he's pleasant enough to meet *or* to visit.

fréquentatif, -ive [frekɑ̃tatif, -iv] *adj Gram* frequentative.

fréquentation [frekɑ̃tasjɔ̃] *nf* **(a)** (*fait d'aller à*) frequenting; **f. des théâtres,** theatre-going; **f. assidue des conférences,** regular attendance at lectures; **la f. des cinémas a baissé,** cinema-going has decreased; **(b) fréquentations,** association (**de,** with); **mauvaises fréquentations,** bad company; **surveillez ses fréquentations,** keep a watch on the company he keeps.

fréquenté [frekɑ̃te] *adj* much visited, busy (*place*), busy (*road*); **hôtel bien f.,** hotel with a good clientele; **endroit mal f.,** place with a bad reputation.

fréquenter [frekɑ̃te] **1** *vt* **(a)** (*un endroit etc*) to frequent, to visit frequently; **(b) f. qn,** to associate with s.o., to see s.o. regularly; (*as girlfriend, boyfriend*) to go out with s.o.; **quels gens fréquente-t-il?,** what company does he keep?, who does he go around with? **2 se fréquenter** *vpr* to associate with each other, to see each other regularly; (*of boyfriend and girlfriend*) to go out with each other.

frère [frɛr] *nm* **(a)** brother; **f. de lait,** foster brother; **frères d'armes,** brothers-in-arms; **ils s'aiment comme des frères,** they love each other like brothers; **on va partager en frères,** we'll share it like brothers; *F* **f. trois-points,** freemason; *F* **tu es un f.,** you're a real friend; **faux f.,** false friend; **vieux f.,** old chap; **(b)** *Rel* friar; **f. lai,** lay brother; **mes très chers frères,** dearly beloved brethren.

frérot [frero] *nm F* (little) brother.

fresque [frɛsk] *nf* fresco; **peinture à f.,** painting in fresco; **ce roman est une f. historique,** this novel is a historical epic.

fresquiste [frɛskist] *adj & n* **(peintre) f.,** fresco painter.

fressure [fresyr] *nf* pluck (*of calf, sheep etc*); *Culin* (*lamb's, pig's*) fry.

fret [frɛ, frɛt] *nm* **(a)** (*prix*) (*de navire etc*) freight, freightage; **payer le f.,** to pay the freight; **(b)** (*louage*) chartering; **prendre un navire à f.,** to charter a ship; **avion de f.,** charter aircraft; **donner un navire à f.,** to freight (out) a ship; **(c)** (*cargaison*) cargo (*of ship, aircraft*); load (*of lorry*).

fréter [frete] *vt* (**je frète; je fréterai**) (*prendre, donner en location*) to freight (out), to charter (*ship*); to charter (*aircraft*); to hire (*car*).

fréteur [fretœr] *nm* shipowner.

frétillant [fretijɑ̃] *adj* (*poisson etc*) wriggling, wriggly; *Fig* (*personne*) lively.

frétillement [fretijmɑ̃] *nm* wriggling (*of fish etc*);

wagging (*of tail*); *Fig* fidgeting, quivering.

frétiller [fretije] *vi* (*of fish etc*) to wriggle; **le chien frétille de la queue,** the dog is wagging its tail; **l'enfant frétille d'impatience,** the child is fidgeting with impatience.

fretin [frətɛ̃] *nm Pêche & Fig* **(menu) f.,** small fry.

frettage [frɛtaʒ] *nm* binding, hooping.

frette¹ [frɛt] *nf* (binding) hoop, collar, ferrule; band (*of axle*); **f. de moyeu,** nave ring (*of wheel*).

frette² *nf Archit Hér* fret.

fretter [frete] *vt* to bind (with a ring), to band, to hoop.

freudien, -ienne [frødjɛ̃, -jɛn] *adj Psy* Freudian.

freudisme [frødism] *nm Psy* Freud(ian)ism.

freux [frø] *nm* rook; **colonie de f.,** rookery.

friabilité [frijabilite] *nf* friability, crumbliness.

friable [frijabl] *adj* friable, crumbly.

friand [frijɑ̃] **1** *adj* fond of delicacies; **être f. de sucreries,** to have a sweet tooth; *Fig* **f. de louanges,** fond of praise. **2** *nm Culin* (*feuilleté*) = sausage roll; (*gâteau*) small almond cake.

friandise [frijɑ̃diz] *nf* (*sucrée*) sweet; (*salée*) titbit.

Fribourg [fribur] *n* (*en Allemagne*) Freiburg; (*en Suisse*) Fribourg.

fric [frik] *nm Arg* (*argent*) dough, lolly; **j'ai plus de f.!,** I'm out of dough *or* lolly!, I'm skint!

fricassée [frikase] *nf Culin* fricassee; *Belg* bacon omelette; *Arg* **f. de museaux,** necking.

fricasser [frikase] *vt Culin* to fricassee.

fricatif, -ive [frikatif, -iv] *adj & nf Ling* fricative.

fric-frac [frikfrak] *nm Arg* burglary; (*pl fric-frac(s)*).

friche [friʃ] *nf* wasteland, fallow land; **f. industrielle,** industrial wasteland; **rester** *ou* **être en f.,** to lie fallow, to remain uncultivated; **elle laisse son talent/son génie en f.,** she's letting her talent/genius go to waste.

frichti [friʃti] *nm F* grub, nosh.

fricot [friko] *nm F* made-up dish, stew; **faire le f.,** to do the cooking.

fricotage [frikɔtaʒ] *nm F* fiddling, underhand dealing.

fricoter [frikɔte] **1** *vt F Culin* to stew, to cook; *Fig* (*manigancer*) to plot; **je me demande ce qu'il fricote,** I wonder what he's up to *or* what he's cooking up. **2** *vi* **(a)** to engage in small-scale, dishonest dealings, *F* to be on the fiddle; **(b)** (*avoir des relations sexuelles*) **ils fricotent ensemble,** they're sleeping together.

fricoteur, -euse [frikɔtœr, -øz] *n F* (*trafiquant*) dishonest dealer, fiddler; (*profiteur*) profiteer.

friction [friksjɔ̃] *nf* **(a)** rubbing, chafing (*of the limbs etc*); *Sp* rub down; (*du cuir chevelu*) scalp massage; **(b) embrayage à f.,** friction clutch; **réduire les frictions,** to reduce friction; *Ordinat* **entraînement par f.,** friction feed; **(c)** (*heurt*) disagreement; **cela reste un point de f.,** that remains a bone of contention.

frictionner [friksjɔne] **1** *vt* to rub, to chafe (*limb*); **f. qn,** to give s.o. a rub down; **f. la tête de qn,** to give s.o. a scalp massage. **2 se frictionner** *vpr* to rub oneself down.

Fridolin [fridɔlɛ̃] *nm Arg* (*terme injurieux*) Fritz, Jerry, Kraut.

frigidaire ® [friʒidɛr] *nm* refrigerator, fridge; *F* **mettre un projet au f.,** to put a plan into cold storage *or* on ice.

frigide [friʒid] *adj* frigid; *Litt* cold, icy.

frigidité [friʒidite] *nf* frigidity, frigidness.

frigo [frigo] *nm F* fridge, refrigerator; *F* **mettre un projet au f.,** to put a plan into cold storage *or* on ice.

frigorification [frigɔrifikasjɔ̃] *nf* refrigerating, chilling (*of meat*).

frigorifié [frigɔrifje] *adj* frozen; chilled (*meat etc*); *F* (*of person*) frozen stiff.

frigorifier [frigɔrifje] *vt* to refrigerate.

frigorifique [frigɔrifik] *adj* refrigerating, *US* frigorific; **appareil f.,** refrigerator; **mélange f.,** freezing mixture; **wagon f.,** refrigerator van; **entrepôt f.,** cold store.

frigoriste [frigɔrist] *nm* refrigerating engineer.

frileusement [friløzmɑ̃] *adv* with a shiver.

frileux, -euse [frilø, -øz] *adj* (*person*) chilly; **je suis très f.,** I feel the cold terribly.

frimaire [frimɛr] *nm Hist* third month of French Republican calendar (*21, 22 Nov - 21, 22 Dec*).

frimas [frimɑ] *nm Litt* (hoar)frost, rime.

frime [frim] *nf F* sham, pretence, make-believe; **tout ça, c'est de la f.,** that's a lot of nonsense; **il le fait pour la f.,** he does it for show.

frimer [frime] *vi F* to show off; **arrête de f.,** stop showing off.

frimeur, -euse [frimœr, -øz] *n* show-off.

frimousse [frimus] *nf F* sweet *or* pretty little face.

fringale [frɛ̃gal] *nf F* hunger; **avoir la f.,** to be ravenous *or* starving *or* famished; *Fig* **avoir une f. de voyage,** to have itchy feet.

fringant [frɛ̃gɑ̃] *adj* spirited, lively, frisky (*horse*); smart, dashing (*person*).

fringuer [frɛ̃ge] **1** *vt F* to dress (*s.o.*); **bien fringué,** well-dressed. **2** *vi Arch* to prance, to skip about. **3 se fringuer** *vpr* to get dressed (up); **il ne sait pas se f.,** he's got no dress sense.

fringues [frɛ̃g] *nfpl F* (*vêtements*) togs, gear.

friper [fripe] **1** *vt* to crumple, to crush, to crease (*dress etc*); **visage fripé,** worn *or* tired face. **2 se friper** *vpr* (*of garment*) to get crushed *or* crumpled.

friperie [fripri] *nf* (*magasin*) second-hand clothes shop; (*vêtements*) second-hand clothes.

fripes [frip] *nfpl* second-hand clothes.

fripier, -ière [fripje, -jɛr] *n* second-hand clothes dealer.

fripon, -onne [fripɔ̃, -ɔn] *F* **1** *n Vieilli* rogue, crook; *Fig* **petit f.!, petite friponne!,** you naughty little thing!, you little rascal! **2** *adj* mischievous, roguish (*smile etc*).

friponnerie [fripɔnri] *nf Vieilli* (*caractère*) roguery, knavery; (*action*) mischievous prank.

fripouille [fripuj] *nf* **(a)** *F* rogue, cad, rotter; **(b)** *Arch* rabble, riff-raff.

friqué [frike] *adj F* loaded, rolling in it.

friquet [frikɛ] *nm* tree sparrow.

frire [frir] *v* (*pp* **frit;** *pr ind* **je fris, tu fris, il frit;** *no pl; fu* **je frirai;** *for the vtr the parts wanting are supplied by* **faire f.**) **1** *vt* to fry; **je fris du poisson,** I'm frying fish. **2** *vi* to fry; **le poisson frit,** the fish is frying.

frisant [frizɑ̃] *adj* **lumière frisante,** oblique light.

frise [friz] *nf Archit* frieze; *Th* **frises,** borders, sky pieces.

Frise [friz] *nf* Friesland; *Mil* **chevaux de F.,** barbed wire.

frisé, -ée [frize] **1** *adj* curly; **salade frisée,** curly lettuce; **velours f.,** uncut velvet, terry; **elle est frisée comme un mouton,** she's got frizzy hair. **2** *nf* **frisée,** curly lettuce, endive. **3** *n F* **(a)** curly-haired child; **(b)** *Arg* (*terme injurieux*) (*non-Blanc*) nig-nog, spade.

friselis [frizli] *nm Litt* rustle (*of leaves*).

friser [frize] **1** *vi* (*of hair*) to curl. **2** *vt* **(a)** (*faire des boucles*) to curl, to wave; **f. (les cheveux de) qn,** to curl s.o.'s hair; **fer à f.,** curling tongs; **(b)** (*effleurer*) to touch, to skim; **f. un accident,** to have a narrow escape; **on a frisé la catastrophe,** we came within a hair's-breadth of disaster; **il frisait la soixantaine,** he was close on sixty.

frisette [frizɛt] *nf* ringlet, small curl.

frison¹ [frizɔ̃] *nm* curl (*of hair*); shaving (*of wood, paper etc*).

frison², -onne [frizɔ̃, -ɔn] **1** *adj* Friesian; **vache frisonne,** Friesian cow. **2** *nm Ling* Friesian. **3** *n* **F.,** Friesian.

frisotter [frizɔte] **1** *vt* **f. (les cheveux de) qn,** to crimp *or* frizz s.o.'s hair. **2** *vi* (*of hair*) to curl, to be frizzy.

frisquet, -ette [friskɛ, -ɛt] *adj F* chill(y); **il fait f.,** it is a bit chilly *or F* parky.

frisson [frisɔ̃] *nm* shiver, shudder (*from cold*); shudder, thrill (*of fear, pleasure*); **avoir des frissons,** to shiver, *F* to have the shivers; **j'en ai des frissons,** it makes me shudder; *Fig* **le f. de l'eau/des arbres,** the rippling of the water/quivering of the trees.

frissonnement [frisɔnmɑ̃] *nm* (*action*) shivering, shuddering, quivering; (*tremblement*) slight shiver *or* shudder *or* quiver.

frissonner [frisɔne] *vi* **(a)** to shiver, to shudder (*with cold, fear*); **f. de joie,** to be thrilled; **(b)** (*of foliage*) to quiver; (*of water*) to ripple.

frisure [frizyr] *nf* curling, curliness (*of the hair etc*); **frisures,** curly hair, curls.

frit, frite [fri, frit] **1** *adj* **(a)** fried; **pommes de terre frites,** *Br* chips, French fried potatoes, *Am* (French) fries; **(b)** *F* **il est f.,** he's had it. **2** *nf* **(a)** *Culin* **frites,** *Br* chips, *Am* (French) fries; **un steak frites, s'il vous plaît!,** steak and chips, please; **(b)** *F* **avoir la f.,** to be fit *or* in form; **ça va te donner la f.,** that'll perk you up.

friterie [fritri] *nf* chip stall.

friteuse [fritøz] *nf* deep fryer, *Br* chip pan; **f. électrique,** electric fryer.

fritillaire [fritilɛr] *nf Bot* fritillary.

friture [frityr] *nf* **(a)** (*action*) frying (*of food*); (*huile*) (deep) fat, oil (*for frying*); (*aliments*) fried food, *surtout* fried fish; **f. de poisson,** fried fish; **(b)** *Rad Tél* **(bruits de) f.,** crackling (noise), interference; **(c)** *Belg* chip stall.

Fritz [frits] *nm inv F* (*soldat allemand*) Jerry.

frivole [frivɔl] *adj* frivolous, shallow (*person*); futile (*occupation*); **des discussions/propos frivoles,** futile *or* trivial arguments/remarks.

frivolement [frivɔlmɑ̃] *adv* frivolously.
frivolité [frivɔlite] *nf* **(a)** frivolity, frivolousness, shallowness (*of mind*); (*futilité*) trifle; **cela fait partie des frivolités de la vie,** that's one of life's little pleasures; **(b)** *Couture* **frivolités,** (fancy) trimmings.
froc [frɔk] *nm* **(a)** (monk's) frock, gown; **prendre le f.,** to become a monk; **jeter le f. aux orties,** to unfrock oneself, to leave the priesthood; **(b)** *Arg* trousers.
froid [frwa] **1** *adj* **(a)** cold (*wind, weather, bath*); **la lumière froide de l'hiver,** the cold winter light; **le moteur est f.,** the engine is cold; **à table!, ça va être f.!,** dinner *etc* is ready, it's getting cold!; **repas f.,** cold meal; **buffet f.,** cold buffet; **viandes froides,** cold meat;
(b) *Fig* cold (*person*); cold, chilly (*manner*); cold, chilly, frigid (*reception*); stiff (*style*); **se montrer** *ou* **être f. avec** *ou* **envers qn,** to treat s.o. coldly *or* coolly; **garder la tête froide,** to keep cool (and collected); **cela me laisse f.,** it leaves me cold; **une colère froide,** controlled *or* suppressed anger; **la guerre froide,** the cold war; **tons froids,** cold tints.
2 *adv* **soluble à f.,** soluble when cold; *Aut* **démarrer à f.,** to start from cold; **parler à f. d'une catastrophe,** to speak calmly *or* unemotionally about a catastrophe; *Méd* **opérer à f.,** to perform non-emergency surgery.
3 *nm* **(a)** cold; **il fait f.,** it's cold; *F* **il fait un f. de canard** *ou* **de chien,** it's real brass-monkey weather; *Météo* **coup de f.,** cold snap; **prendre (un coup de) f.,** to catch a chill *or* a cold; **cela m'a fait** *ou* **donné f. (dans le dos),** it sent cold shivers down my spine; **avoir f.,** to be *or* feel cold; **avoir f. aux mains,** to have cold hands; *Fig* **elle n'a pas f. aux yeux,** she's very determined; (*elle a du culot*) she's got plenty of nerve; **battre f. à qn,** to cold-shoulder s.o.;
(b) l'industrie du f., (the) refrigerating (industry); **le f. industriel,** refrigeration;
(c) *Fig* coldness, coolness; **ils sont en f.,** there's a coolness between them; **je suis en f. avec lui,** there's a coolness between me and him.
froidement [frwadmɑ̃] *adv* **(a)** (*avec réserve*) coldly, coolly; **être f. accueilli,** to be given a cold welcome *or* cool reception; **il les a abattus f.,** he shot them in cold blood; **(b)** (*calmement*) calmly; **il faut étudier f. le problème,** we must consider the problem calmly.
froideur [frwadœr] *nf* **(a)** coldness, chilliness (*of manner*); **sa f. me met mal à l'aise,** his coldness makes me (feel) ill at ease; **la f. de son accueil,** the coldness of his welcome; **(b)** (*indifférence*) indifference; **contempler le spectacle avec f.,** to look coldly on; **(c)** (*manque de sensualité*) iciness.
froidure [frwadyr] *nf* cold.
froissant [frwasɑ̃] *adj* hurtful, wounding.
froissement [frwasmɑ̃] *nm* **(a)** (*action*) bruising (*of muscle etc*); rumpling, crumpling (*of paper, cloth etc*); **(b)** (*bruit*) rustle, rustling (*of paper, silk etc*); **(c)** *Vieilli & Fig* conflict, clash (*of interests*); **(d)** (*vexation*) giving *or* taking offence; **éviter tous froissements,** to avoid ruffling any feathers.
froisser [frwase] **1** *vt* **(a)** to bruise (*muscle etc*); to crease (*material*); to crumple (*paper, material*); **(b) f. qn,** to offend *or* give offence to s.o., to hurt *or* wound s.o.'s feelings. **2 se froisser** *vpr* **(a)** (*d'un tissu*) to crease, to crumple; **(b)** (*d'une personne*) to take offence *or* umbrage (**de,** at), to take exception (**de,** to).
frôlement [frolmɑ̃] *nm* (*contact*) slight rubbing *or* brushing (**contre,** against); (*bruit*) rustle (*of silk etc*).
frôler [frole] **1** *vt* to touch lightly, to brush, to graze; (*of bird etc*) to skim (*tree tops*); **il a frôlé la mort,** he came close to death *or* had a brush with death. **2 se frôler** *vpr* to touch one another lightly; **les deux voitures se sont frôlées,** the two cars brushed past each other.
fromage [frɔmaʒ] *nm* cheese; **f. bien fait,** ripe cheese; **f. blanc,** fromage blanc; **f. fondu,** processed cheese; **omelette/soufflé au f.,** cheese omelette/soufflé; *Fig F* **pas la peine d'en faire tout un f.,** it's not worth making a fuss about; *F* **un gentil petit f.,** a nice little earner; *Culin* **f. de tête,** brawn, *US* headcheese.
fromager, -ère [frɔmaʒe, -ɛr] **1** *adj* concerning cheese; **industrie fromagère,** cheese industry. **2** *n* (*commerçant*) cheesemonger; (*fabricant*) cheesemaker.
fromagerie [frɔmaʒri] *nf* (*lieu de fabrication*) cheese dairy; (*magasin*) cheese shop.
froment [frɔmɑ̃] *nm* wheat; **pain de f.,** wheaten bread.
fronce [frɔ̃s] *nf Couture* gather; **jupe à fronces,** gathered skirt.
froncement [frɔ̃smɑ̃] *nm* wrinkling, puckering; **f. de(s) sourcils,** frown, scowl.
froncer [frɔ̃se] *vt* (**je fronçai(s)**) **(a)** (*plisser*) to wrinkle, to pucker; **f. les sourcils,** to knit one's brows, to frown; **(b)** *Couture* to gather.
frondaison [frɔ̃dɛzɔ̃] *nf* (*apparition des feuilles*) foliation; (*feuillage*) foliage.
fronde¹ [frɔ̃d] *nf Bot* frond.
fronde² *nf* **(a)** (*arme*) sling; (*jouet*) (toy) catapult; **(b)** *Hist* **la F.,** the Fronde; *Fig* **esprit de f.,** spirit of revolt *or* rebellion.
fronder [frɔ̃de] **1** *vt Vieilli* (*critiquer*) to lampoon. **2** *vi* **(a)** *Hist* to belong to the Fronde; *Fig* to lampoon; **(b)** *Arch* to sling (*stone etc*).
frondeur, -euse [frɔ̃dœr, -øz] **1** *n* **(a)** *Hist* member of the Fronde; **(b)** (*rebelle*) rebel. **2** *adj* rebellious, anti-authority.
front [frɔ̃] *nm* **(a)** forehead, brow; **marcher le f. haut,** to walk with one's head (held) high; *Fig* **les victimes du tyran relèveront un jour le f.,** the tyrant's victims will one day get off their knees; **et vous avez le f. de me dire cela!,** you have the nerve to tell me that!;
(b) face, front (*of building etc*); brow (*of hill*); **f. de bataille,** battle front; **le f.,** the front (line); **nouvelles du f.,** news from the front; *Min* **f. de taille,** working face, coal face; *Météo* **f. chaud/froid,** warm/cold front; **f. de mer,** (sea)front; *Pol* **f. commun,** united *or* common front; **faire f. à qn/qch,** to face up to *or* stand up to s.o./sth; **faire f.,** to stand fast;
(c) de f., abreast; **mener plusieurs choses de f.,** to have several things on the go at once; *Mil* **marche de f.,** march in line; *Nau* **en ligne de f.,** line abreast;
(d) vue de f., front view; **attaque de f.,** frontal attack; **heurter qn/qch de f.,** to run head-on into s.o./sth.
frontal, -aux [frɔ̃tal, -o] **1** *adj* frontal, front; **os f.,** frontal bone; **chargement f.,** front loading; **lampe frontale,** (miner's) cap lamp. **2** *nm Anat* frontal bone.
frontalier, -ière [frɔ̃talje, -jɛr] **1** *adj* **régions frontalières,** frontier *or* border regions. **2** *n* inhabitant of a frontier zone; (*travailleur*) frontier worker.
fronteau, -eaux [frɔ̃to] *nm* **(a)** *Archit* small pediment; **(b)** *Rel* frontlet (*of nun etc*).
frontière [frɔ̃tjɛr] **1** *nf* frontier, border, boundary; **f. naturelle,** natural frontier; **f. linguistique,** linguistic boundary; **incident de f.,** border incident; *Fig* **faire reculer les frontières du savoir,** to roll back the frontiers of knowledge; **aux frontières de la vie et de la mort,** between life and death; **les frontières de la bienséance,** the limits of decency. **2** *adj* frontier (*town*); boundary (*stone*); **poste f.,** border *or* frontier post.
frontispice [frɔ̃tispis] *nm* frontispiece (*of book*).
fronton [frɔ̃tɔ̃] *nm Archit* fronton, pediment; (*pelote basque*) fronton.
frottage [frɔtaʒ] *nm* rubbing, chafing (*of limb etc*); polishing (*of floors etc*).
frottée [frɔte] *nf Vieilli* **(a)** (*volée*) beating, thrashing; **(b) f. (d'ail),** garlic bread.
frottement [frɔtmɑ̃] *nm* **(a)** (*friction*) rubbing, chafing; *Méd* **bruit de f.,** pleural rub; *Phot* **marques de f.,** stress marks; *Fig* **on a eu des frottements avec lui,** there has been some friction between us and him; **(b)** *MecE* friction; **f. de glissement,** sliding friction; **usure par f.,** abrasion.
frotter [frɔte] **1** *vt* to rub, to chafe (*limb*); to polish (*floor, copper*); **je vais te f. le dos pour te réchauffer,** I'll rub your back to warm you up; **f. une allumette,** to strike a match. **2** *vi* **la roue frotte (contre le frein),** the wheel is rubbing (against the brake); *Vieilli* **être frotté de latin,** to have a smattering of Latin. **3 se frotter** *vpr* **(a) se f. les mains,** to rub one's hands (together); **se f. les yeux,** to rub one's eyes; **se f. contre qch,** to rub against sth; **(b)** *Fig* **se f. à qn/qch,** to come up against s.o./sth; **ne vous y frottez pas!,** don't get involved!, don't meddle!; *Fig* **qui s'y frotte s'y pique,** = if you meddle, you'll get your fingers burnt.
frotteur, -euse [frɔtœr, -øz] **1** *n* (*personne*) floor polisher. **2** *nm* sliding contact; (collecting) shoe (*of electric train*).
frottis [frɔti] *nm* **(a)** *Beaux-Arts* scumble; **(b)** *Biol* smear (*for microscopic examination*); **f. vaginal,** cervical smear; **(c) prendre un f. d'une inscription,** to take a rubbing of an inscription.
frottoir [frɔtwar] *nm* (*ustensile*) rubber, polisher; (*brosse*) scrubbing brush; friction strip (*of matchbox*); brush (*of dynamo*).
frou-frou, froufrou [frufru] *nm* rustle, rustling (*of silk dress, leaves*); (*pl frou(-)frous*).
froufrouter [frufrute] *vi* (*of silk etc*) to rustle.
froussard, -arde [frusar, -ard] *F* **1** *adj* cowardly, chicken. **2** *n* coward, chicken.

frousse [frus] *nf F* fear, fright; **avoir la f.,** to be scared, to have the wind up; **ça m'a foutu la f.,** that put the wind up me.
fructidor [fryktidɔr] *nm Hist* twelfth month of the French Republican calendar (*August 18, 19 - September 17, 18*).
fructifère [fryktifɛr] *adj* fruitbearing.
fructification [fryktifikasjɔ̃] *nf* fruition, fructification (*of tree*); yield (*of investment*); *Fig* fruition (*of idea etc*).
fructifier [fryktifje] *vi* (*d'arbres*) to bear fruit; *Fig* **ses placements commencent à f.,** his investments are beginning to show *or* yield a profit; **il sait faire f. son argent,** he knows how to get a return on his money.
fructueusement [fryktɥøzmɑ̃] *adv* fruitfully, profitably.
fructueux, -euse [fryktɥø, -øz] *adj* fruitful, profitable.
frugal, -aux [frygal, -o] *adj* frugal (*person, meal*).
frugalement [frygalmɑ̃] *adv* frugally.
frugalité [frygalite] *nf* frugality.
frugivore [fryʒivɔr] **1** *adj* fruit-eating (*animal*). **2** *n* fruit-eater.
fruit[1] [frɥi] *nm* fruit; **producteur de fruits,** fruit grower; **fruits secs,** dried fruit; **f. vert,** unripe fruit; **le f. d'un mariage,** the offspring of a marriage; **le f. de plusieurs années de travail,** the fruit of several years' work; *F* **f. sec,** failure (*as a student etc*); **porter des fruits,** (*d'un arbre*) to bear fruit; *Fig* **porter ses fruits,** (*d'une action, un investissement etc*) to bear fruit; **étudier avec f.,** to study to good purpose; *Culin* **fruits de mer,** = seafood; *Rel* **le f. défendu,** the Forbidden Fruit.
fruit[2] *nm Constr* batter (*of wall, abutment etc*).
fruité [frɥite] *adj* fruity (*wine etc*).
fruiterie [frɥitri] *nf* (*magasin*) fruiterer's *or* greengrocer's shop; (*local*) storeroom for fruit.
fruiticulteur, -trice [frɥitikyltœr, -tris] *n* fruit grower.
fruitier, -ière [frɥitje, -jɛr] **1** *adj* **arbre f.,** fruit tree. **2** *n* fruiterer, greengrocer. **3** *nm* **(a)** (*local*) fruit store-room; (*étagère*) stand of fruit trays; **(b)** (*verger*) orchard.
fruitière [frɥitjɛr] *nf Suisse* cheese dairy.
frusques [frysk] *nfpl F* (*vêtements*) togs, clobber.
fruste [fryst] *adj* rough, unpolished (*style, person*); worn, defaced (*coin, statue*).
frustrant [frystrɑ̃] *adj* frustrating.
frustration [frystrasjɔ̃] *nf* **(a)** *Psy* frustration; **(b)** cheating, defrauding (*of legatee etc*).
frustré, -ée [frystre] *adj & n* frustrated (person).
frustrer [frystre] *vt* **(a)** *Psy* to frustrate; **(b)** (*priver*) to frustrate, to deprive, to thwart; **f. qn de qch,** to defraud s.o. of sth; **on m'a frustré de mes biens,** I have been cheated out of my property.
F.S. [ɛfɛs] *nm abrév* **franc suisse**.
fuchsia [fyʃja] **1** *nm Bot* fuchsia. **2** *adj inv* fuchsia, magenta.
fucus [fykys] *nm* (*algue*) fucus, sea wrack.
fuel(-oil) [fjul(ɔjl)] *nm* fuel oil.
fugace [fygas] *adj* fleeting, fugitive, transient; **impression f.,** fleeting impression.
fugacité [fygasite] *nf Litt* fleetingness, fugacity, transience.
fugitif, -ive [fyʒitif, -iv] **1** *adj* **(a)** (*personne*) fugitive, runaway; **(b)** (*fugace*) transitory, fleeting, ephemeral, short-lived, passing (*desire, emotion*); **ombre fugitive,** fleeting shadow. **2** *n* fugitive, runaway.
fugitivement [fyʒitivmɑ̃] *adv* fleetingly.
fugue [fyg] *nf* **(a)** *Mus Psy* fugue; **(b) faire une f.,** to run away from home.
fuguer [fyge] *vi F* to run away.
fugueur, -euse [fygœr, -øz] **1** *adj* runaway. **2** *n* runaway child.
fuir [fɥir] *v* (*prp* **fuyant**; *pp* **fui**; *pr ind* **je fuis, n. fuyons, ils fuient**) **1** *vi* **(a)** to flee, to run away (**devant,** from); **f. de son pays,** to flee one's country; **faire f.,** to put to flight; **le temps fuit,** time flies *or* is slipping by; **f. devant les responsabilités,** to shirk responsibilities; *Nau* **f. devant le vent,** to scud *or* run before the wind; **il a le regard qui fuit,** he has shifty eyes;
(b) (*of horizon, hairline*) to recede;
(c) (*of tap, cask etc*) to leak; (*of gas, water*) to leak, to run out, to escape.
2 *vt* **(a)** to shun, to avoid (*responsibility, friends*); to evade, to avoid (*issue*); **f. sa famille,** to shun one's family; *Litt* **f. le monde,** to flee society; **le sommeil me fuit,** I cannot sleep;
(b) to flee, to run away from; **f. son pays,** to flee one's country.
3 se fuir *vpr* **arrête de te f. et fais face à tes responsabilités!,** stop running away from yourself and face up to your responsibilities!
fuite [fɥit] *nf* **(a)** flight, running away (**devant,** from); **prendre la f.,** to take flight, to turn tail; **être en f.,** to be on the run; **mettre l'ennemi en f.,** to put the enemy to flight; *F* **la f. des cerveaux,** the brain drain; **renversé par une voiture qui a pris la f.,** run over by a hit-and-run driver; *Fig* **la f. en avant de la consommation,** the headlong rush of consumption; **(b)** leak (*of gas, information etc*); **(c)** evasion, avoidance (*of difficulties etc*); **(d) la f. du temps,** the passage of time; **(e)** *Beaux-Arts* **point de f.,** vanishing point.
fulgurant [fylgyrɑ̃] *adj* flashing (*like lightning*); *Méd* stabbing, searing (*pains*); **une découverte fulgurante,** a dazzling discovery; **une attaque fulgurante,** a lightning attack; **lancer un regard f. à qn,** to look daggers at s.o..
fulguration [fylgyrasjɔ̃] *nf* lightning; *Chir* fulguration.
fulgurer [fylgyre] *vi* to flash (*like lightning*).
fuligineux, -euse [fyliʒinø, -øz] *adj* smoky, sooty (*colour*); murky (*sky*).
fulmicoton [fylmikɔtɔ̃] *nm* gun cotton.
fulminant [fylminɑ̃] *adj* fulminating (*powder*); *Spéc* fulminant (*pain*); menacing (*tone*).
fulminer [fylmine] **1** *vt* to bellow (*accusations*). **2** *vi* **f. contre qn/qch,** to fulminate *or* inveigh against s.o./sth.
fumage[1] [fymaʒ] *nm,* **fumaison**[1] [fymɛzɔ̃] *nf* dunging, dressing, manuring (*of land*).
fumage[2] *nm,* **fumaison**[2] *nf* smoking, smoke-curing (*of fish, meat*).
fumant [fymɑ̃] *adj* **(a)** smoking; *F* **f. de colère,** fuming with anger; **(b)** steaming (*soup etc*); **(c)** *F* terrific, sensational.
fumé [fyme] *adj* **(a)** smoked, smoke-cured (*fish, meat etc*); **(b) verre f.,** smoked glass; **verres fumés,** dark glasses, sunglasses.
fume-cigare [fymsigar] *nm inv* cigar holder.
fume-cigarette [fymsigarɛt] *nm inv* cigarette holder.
fumée [fyme] **1** *nf* **(a)** smoke; **rideau de f.,** smokescreen; **noir de f.,** lampblack; **la f. (du tabac) vous gêne-t-elle?,** do you mind my smoking?; *Fig* **partir** *ou* **s'en aller en f.,** to come to nothing, to go up in smoke; *Prov* **il n'y a pas de f. sans feu,** there's no smoke without fire; **(b)** steam (*of soup etc*); fumes (*of charcoal*); vapours (*of alcohol*). **2** *adj inv* **gris f.,** smoke-grey, *US* -gray.
fumer[1] [fyme] *vt* to dung, to manure (*land*).
fumer[2] **1** *vi* **(a)** to smoke; **lampe qui fume,** smoking lamp; **tu fumes trop!,** you smoke too much!; **défense de f.,** (*annonce*) no smoking; **f. tranquillement,** to have a quiet smoke; **(b)** (*of soup etc*) to steam; **(c)** *F* to fume, to rage. **2** *vt* **(a)** to smoke(-cure) (*fish*); **(b)** to smoke (*a pipe, tobacco etc*).
fumerie [fymri] *nf* **f. d'opium,** opium den.
fumerolle [fymrɔl] *nf* smoke and gas (*from volcano*).
fumet [fymɛ] *nm* **(a)** aroma, (pleasant) smell (*of food cooking*); bouquet (*of wine*); **(b)** (*à la chasse*) scent.
fumeterre [fymtɛr] *nf Bot* fumitory.
fumeur, -euse [fymœr, -øz] *n* smoker; *Rail* **compartiment fumeurs/non fumeurs,** smoking/non-smoking compartment, *F* smoker/non-smoker.
fumeux, -euse [fymø, -øz] *adj* smoky, smoking (*lamp etc*); hazy (*sky, ideas*); **quel esprit f.!,** what a woolly mind!
fumier [fymje] *nm* **(a)** manure, dung; **fosse à f.,** slurry pit; **(b)** (*tas*) dunghill, manure heap; **(c)** *Vulg* **espèce de f.!,** you bastard!; **le f.!, il m'a menti!,** he lied to me, the bastard!
fumigation [fymigasjɔ̃] *nf* fumigation; *Méd* inhaling.
fumigène [fymiʒɛn] **1** *n* (*en horticulture*) *& Mil* smoke-producing device. **2** *adj Mil* **bombe f.,** smoke-bomb.
fumiger [fymiʒe] *vt* (**je fumigeai(s)**) to fumigate.
fumiste [fymist] **1** *nm* **(a)** *F* (*paresseux*) skiver, shirker; **(b)** heating engineer; **(c)** *Vieilli* practical joker. **2** *adj* (*paresseux*) skiving, shirking, idle.
fumisterie [fymistəri] *nf* **(a)** skiving, shirking; **(b)** heating engineering; **(c)** *F* practical joke, hoax; **c'est une vaste f.,** it's absolute poppycock.
fumivore [fymivɔr] *adj* smoke-absorbing.
fumoir [fymwar] *nm* smoking room (*of hotel etc*); smokehouse (*for meat, fish etc*).
fumure [fymyr] *nf* dunging, manuring (*of field*).
funambule [fynɑ̃byl] *n* tightrope walker, funambulist.
funambulesque [fynɑ̃bylɛsk] *adj* fantastic, grotesque (*story etc*).
funboard [fœnbɔrd] *nm* funboard.
funèbre [fynɛbr] *adj* **(a)** funeral (*ceremony etc*); **hymne** *ou* **chant f.,** dirge; **marche f.,** funeral *or* dead march; **(b)** (*lugubre*) funereal, dismal, gloomy.

funérailles [fyneraj] *nfpl* funeral (ceremony).
funéraire [fynerɛr] *adj* funeral (*expenses*); funerary (*urn*); **pierre f.**, tombstone; **drap f.**, pall.
funeste [fynɛst] *adj* **(a)** *Litt* deadly, fatal (*accident*); **(b)** fatal, disastrous, catastrophic (*mistake*); **influence f.**, disastrous influence; **(c)** *Arch* funereal, sombre, gloomy.
funiculaire [fynikylɛr] *adj & nm* funicular (railway).
funk [fœnk] *adj inv & nm Mus* funk.
funky [fœnki] *adj inv & nm Mus* funky (music).
fur [fyr] *nm* **au f. et à mesure des besoins,** as and when required; **payer qn au f. et à mesure de l'ouvrage,** to pay by instalments (as the work proceeds), *US* to make progress payments; **au f. et à mesure que tu en as besoin,** as and when you need it.
furax [fyraks] *adj F Hum* furious, livid.
furet [fyrɛ] *nm* **(a)** ferret; **chasse au f.**, ferreting; **chasser au f.**, to go ferreting; **jeu du f.**, ≈ hunt-the-slipper; **(b)** *F Péj* nosy parker.
furetage [fyrtaʒ] *nm* **(a)** ferreting (*for rabbits*); **(b)** searching, prying; (*dans l'armoire etc*) rummaging, ferreting (about).
fureter [fyrte] *vi* (**je furette; je furetterai**) **(a)** (*chasser*) to ferret, to go ferreting; **(b)** to pry, to nose around; **f. dans les armoires,** to ferret (about) *or* rummage in the cupboards.
fureteur, -euse [fyrtœr, -øz] **1** *n* **(a)** (*chasseur*) ferreter; **(b)** *F Péj* nosy parker. **2** *adj* prying, *F* nosy; **regard f.**, inquisitive look.
fureur [fyrœr] *nf* **(a)** (*colère*) fury, rage, wrath; **être en f.**, to be in a rage; **tu vas le mettre en f.**, you'll send him into a rage; **la f. des combats dans le Golfe,** the battle raging in the Gulf; **la f. des flots,** the fury of the waves; **(b)** (*passion*) fury, passion; **aimer qn/qch avec f.**, to be passionately fond of s.o./sth; **avoir la f. de bâtir,** to be mad on building; **chanson qui fait f.**, song that's all the rage.
furibard [fyribar] *adj F* furious.
furibond [fyribɔ̃] *adj* furious, full of fury; **elle lui a lancé un regard f.**, she glared at him.
furie [fyri] *nf* **(a)** (*passion*) fury, rage; **se battre avec f.**, to fight furiously; **applaudir avec f.**, to applaud frantically; **f. du jeu,** a passion for gambling; **en f.**, infuriated, enraged; **se mettre en f.**, to become furious, to fly into a rage; **(b)** *Myth* **les Furies,** the Furies; *Fig* **c'est une f.**, she's a shrew.
furieusement [fyrjøzmɑ̃] *adv* **(a)** furiously; **(b)** *Vieilli & Hum* (*très*) extremely, tremendously.
furieux, -ieuse [fyrjø, -jøz] **1** *adj* **(a)** furious, raging; **être f. contre qn,** to be furious with s.o.; **elle est furieuse qu'on ne l'ait pas prévenue,** she is furious that nobody told her; **rendre qn f.**, to enrage *or* infuriate s.o.; **tempête furieuse,** raging *or* howling storm; **il a un f. appétit,** he has a tremendous appetite; **(b)** (*forcené*) fanatic, mad; **c'est un fou f.**, he's a raving madman. **2** *n* **c'est un f.**, he's a raving madman.
furoncle [fyrɔ̃kl] *nm Méd* boil, furuncle.
furonculose [fyrɔ̃kyloz] *nf Méd* furunculosis.
furtif, -ive [fyrtif, -iv] *adj* furtive, stealthy.
furtivement [fyrtivmɑ̃] *adv* furtively, stealthily; **entrer/sortir f.**, to steal in/out.
fusain [fyzɛ̃] *nm* **(a)** (*arbre*) spindle tree; **(b)** *Beaux-Arts* charcoal (pencil); (*dessin*) charcoal sketch.
fusant [fyzɑ̃] *adj* fusing; **obus f.**, time shell.
fuseau, -eaux [fyzo] *nm* **(a)** *Tex* spindle; (*for lace*) bobbin; **f. de quenouille,** distaff; **en f.**, tapered, tapering; **jambes en f.**, spindly legs; **(b)** *Math* **f. sphérique,** spherical lune; **(c) f. horaire,** time zone; **(d)** *F* **fuseaux,** tapered trousers, *surtout* ski pants; **la mode du f.** *ou* **des fuseaux revient,** ski pants are coming back into fashion.
fusée [fyze] *nf* **(a)** (*projectile*) rocket; **lancer une f.**, to launch a rocket; **f. éclairante,** flare; **f. volante,** sky rocket; **f. à pétard,** maroon; **f. à un étage,** one-stage rocket; **f.-engin,** missile; **f. air-air,** air-to-air missile; *Astronaut* **f. interplanétaire,** space-rocket; **f. d'appoint,** booster; **f. sonde,** probe; **avion-f.**, rocket-propelled aircraft; *Nau* **f. porte-amarre,** life(-saving) rocket; **il est parti comme une f.**, he shot off *or* went off like a rocket; **(b)** fuse (*of bomb etc*); **f. percutante,** percussion fuse; **f. à temps,** time fuse; **(c)** spindle (*of shaft, axle*); barrel (*of capstan*); *Aut* stub axle; *Nau* **f. de vergue,** yard arm.
fuselage [fyzlaʒ] *nm Av* fuselage.
fuselé [fyzle] *adj* tapering (*column, fingers*); *Aut* streamlined.
fuseler [fyzle] *vt* (**je fuselle; je fusellerai**) to taper; *Aut* to streamline.
fuser [fyze] *vi* **(a)** (*of hot wax etc*) to spread, to run, to melt; *Fig* **des rires fusèrent de toutes parts,** laughter burst out all over; **(b)** *Ch* (*of salt*) to crackle; **(c)** (*of fuse*) to burn slowly.
fusibilité [fyzibilite] *nf* fusibility.
fusible [fyzibl] **1** *adj* fusible, easily melted. **2** *nm Él* fuse; (*fil métallique*) fuse wire; **f. de sûreté,** safety fuse, cut-out.
fusiforme [fyzifɔrm] *adj* spindle-shaped.
fusil [fyzi] *nm* **(a)** (*arme*) gun; **f. de chasse,** sporting gun, shotgun; **f. à deux coups,** double-barrelled gun; **f. à air comprimé,** air gun; **f. harpon,** harpoon gun; **f. rayé,** rifle; **f. automatique,** automatic gun *or* rifle; **f. à chargeur,** magazine rifle; *Fig* **changer son f. d'épaule,** to change (one's) tack; **coup de f.**, gunshot, rifle shot; *F* overcharging, fleecing (*in hotel etc*); **entendre un coup de f.**, to hear a shot; **c'est un de nos meilleurs fusils,** he's one of our best shots; **(b)** steel (*of tinder box*); (*pour aiguiser*) (sharpening) steel.
fusilier [fyzilje] *n* fusilier; **f. marin,** = marine.
fusillade [fyzijad] *nf* (*tir*) fusillade, rifle fire; (*mise à mort*) (execution by) shooting.
fusiller [fyzije] *vt* **(a)** to shoot; (*par un peloton d'exécution*) to shoot, to execute; *Fig* **f. qn d'un regard,** to look daggers at s.o.; **(b)** *F Vieilli* to mess up, to ruin (*car etc*).
fusil-mitrailleur [fyzimitrajœr] *nm* automatic rifle, light machine gun; (*pl fusils-mitrailleurs*).
fusion [fyzjɔ̃] *nf* **(a)** fusion, melting (*by heat*); *Métal* smelting; **point de f.**, melting point; **fer en f.**, molten iron; **(b)** *Nucl* fusion; **(c)** *Fig* coalescing (*of ideas etc*); **(d)** merger, merging (*of companies, political parties etc*); **fusions-rachats,** mergers and acquisitions; *Ordinat* **f. de fichiers,** file merge.
fusionnement [fyzjɔnmɑ̃] *nm Com* amalgamation, merging (*of companies*).
fusionner [fyzjɔne] **1** *vi* (*de sociétés, communes, partis politiques*) to amalgamate, to merge. **2** *vt* (*sociétés, communes, partis politiques*) to amalgamate, to merge; *Ordinat* to merge.
fustigation [fystigasjɔ̃] *nf Litt* thrashing, beating.
fustiger [fystiʒe] *vt* (**je fustigeai(s)**) *Arch* (*battre*) to thrash, to beat; *Fig Litt* (*critiquer*) to give (*s.o.*) a dressing down; *Fig* **f. l'attitude de qn,** to castigate s.o.'s attitude.
fût [fy] *nm* **(a)** stock (*of rifle etc*); handle (*of saw, racquet*); brace (*for bit*); **(b)** shaft (*of column, chimney*); stem (*of candelabra*); shank (*of rivet*); bole (*of tree*); (*baril*) cask, barrel, drum (*for oil*); **tirer de la bière du f.**, to draw beer from the wood.
futaie [fytɛ] *nf* wood, forest; **arbre de haute f.**, full-grown tree, timber tree.
futaille [fytaj] *nf* (*baril*) cask(s), barrel(s).
futaine [fytɛn] *nf Tex* fustian.
futé, -ée [fyte] **1** *adj* cunning, wily, crafty. **2** *n* **c'est un petit f.**, he's a sharp customer.
futile [fytil] *adj* futile, trivial, trifling (*argument*); frivolous (*person*); idle (*pretext*).
futilement [fytilmɑ̃] *adv* futilely.
futilité [fytilite] *nf* futility; **s'occuper à des futilités,** to fritter away one's time.
futur, -ure [fytyr] **1** *adj* future; **la vie future,** the life to come; **f. acheteur,** prospective buyer; **un f. artiste,** a future artist; *Hum* **mon f. emploi,** my next job. **2** *n Hum* **mon f., ma future,** my fiancé(e), my intended. **3** *nm* **(a)** future; **le f. m'inquiète,** I am worried about the future; **quel f. pour l'Europe?,** what will Europe's future be?; **(b)** *Gram* future (tense).
futurisme [fytyrism] *nm Beaux-Arts Archit* futurism; (*d'un projet etc*) **le f. de cet avion étonne tous les visiteurs,** all the visitors are stunned by how futuristic the plane is.
futuriste [fytyrist] *Beaux-Arts Archit* **1** *adj* futurist(ic). **2** *n* futurist.
fuyant [fɥijɑ̃] *adj* **(a)** receding (*line*); *Beaux-Arts* **lignes fuyantes,** perspective lines (*of picture*); **(b)** (*of person*) evasive; shifty (*eyes, person*).
fuyard, -arde [fɥijar, -ard] **1** *adj Arch* shy, timid. **2** *n* fugitive (soldier), runaway.

G

G,g [ʒe] *nm* (the letter) G, g; *Météo* **couche G,** G region (*of ionosphere*).
g. *abrév* **(a) gauche**; **(b) gramme(s)**.
gabardine [gabardin] *nf* **(a)** *Tex* gabardine; **(b)** (*imperméable*) (gabardine) raincoat.
gabare [gabar] *nf* **(a)** *Nau* sailing barge; (*pour charger, décharger un navire*) lighter; (*chaland*) transport vessel, store ship, scow; **(b)** *Pêche* dragnet.
gabaret [gabarɛ] *nm Pêche* (small) dragnet.
gabarit [gabari] *nm* **(a)** model (*of ship*); mould, *US* mold (*of ship's part*); *Constr* outline (*of building*); **(b)** *MecE etc* template, templet, former; **g. d'assemblage,** assembly jig, assembling gauge; **tour à g.,** copying lathe; **(c)** *Rail* clearance (*under bridge*); **g. de chargement,** loading gauge; **g. d'écartement (des voies),** rail *or* track gauge; **(d)** *F souvent Péj* **des gens de son g.,** people of his sort, people like him; **elles sont du même g.,** they come from the same mould.
gabbro [gabro] *nm Géol Beaux-Arts* gabbro.
gabegie [gabʒi] *nf* waste; (*désordre*) muddle, disorder.
gabelle [gabɛl] *nf Hist* salt tax, excise.
gabelou [gablu] *nm Péj* customs officer.
gabier [gabje] *nm Nau* topman; **g. breveté,** able(-bodied) seaman.
gable [gabl], **gâble** [gɑbl] *nm Archit* **(a)** gable; **(b)** (*charpente*) (triangular) window canopy.
Gabon (le) [ləgabɔ̃] *nm* Gabon.
gabonais, -aise [gabɔnɛ, -ɛz] **1** *adj* Gabonese. **2** *n* **G.,** Gabonese.
gâchage [gɑʃaʒ] *nm* **(a)** mixing (*of mortar etc*); **(b)** (*sabotage*) spoiling, bungling; (*de l'argent*) wasting.
gâche¹ [gɑʃ] *nf* **(a)** (*pour le plâtre*) trowel; **(b)** (*de pâtissier*) (cook's) spatula.
gâche² *nf* **(a)** (box) staple, keeper (*of lock*); (latch) catch (*of window*); striking box *or* plate; strike box (*of spring bolt*); **(b)** *MecE* notch (*for pawl*).
gâchée [gɑʃe] *nf Constr* batch (*of cement etc*).
gâcher [gɑʃe] *vt* **(a)** to spoil (*sheet of paper etc*); to bungle, to botch, to mess up (*job*); to waste, to squander (*fortune*); **il a gâché notre plaisir/la soirée,** he spoiled our pleasure/the evening; **g. le métier,** to undercut; **g. sa vie,** to waste one's life; **(b)** (*mélanger*) to mix, to wet, to temper; **g. du mortier,** to mix mortar; **g. la chaux,** to slack lime; **g. serré,** to temper (*clay etc*) hard.
gâchette [gɑʃɛt] *nf* **(a)** (*d'une arme*) trigger; *F* **avoir la g. facile,** to be trigger-happy; **(b)** spring catch (*of lock*); **(c)** *MecE* pawl; **(d)** *Electron* gate.
gâcheur,-euse [gɑʃœr, -øz] **1** *adj* bungling. **2** *n* bungler, botcher. **3** *nm* (mason's, carpenter's) mate.
gâchis [gɑʃi] *nm* **(a)** (*mortier*) wet mortar; **(b)** (*boue*) mud; **(c)** (*désordre*) mess, muddle; **quel g.!,** (*gaspillage*) what a waste!
gadarénien, -ienne [gadarenjɛ̃, -jɛn] *adj & n Bible* Gadarene.
gadelle [gadɛl] *nf Bot Can* redcurrant.
gadget [gadʒɛt] *nm F* gadget; **il n'y a pas de g. contre la pauvreté,** there is no miracle cure for poverty; **on qualifie cette décision de g.,** the decision has been described as a gimmick.
gadgétiser [gadʒetize] *vt F* to turn into a gimmick.
gadgétomanie [gadzetɔmani] *nf F* mania for gadgets.
gadin [gadɛ̃] *nm F* **prendre** *ou* **ramasser un g.,** to take a tumble.
gaditan,-ane [gaditɑ̃, -an] **1** *adj* of Cadiz. **2** *n* **G.,** native *or* inhabitant of Cadiz.
gadoue [gadu] *nf* (*engrais*) sewage sludge; (*boue etc*) mud, slush; *Arg* **je suis dans une belle g.,** I'm in a mess.
Gaël [gaɛl] *nm* Gael.
gaélique [gaelik] *adj & nm Ling* Gaelic.
gaffe [gaf] *nf* **(a)** *F* (*maladresse*) clanger, booboo; **faire une g.,** to put one's foot in it; **(b)** (*perche*) boathook; *Pêche* gaff; *Arg* **avaler sa g.,** to die, to kick the bucket; **(c)** *Arg* **faire g.,** to be on the lookout; **fais g.!,** look out!, watch it!; **(d)** *Arg* prison warder, screw.
gaffer [gafe] **1** *vt* to hook (*floating object etc*); *Pêche* to gaff (*salmon etc*). **2** *vi F* **(a)** (*commettre une bévue*) to put one's foot in it, to drop a brick *or* a clanger; **(b)** *Arg* (*regarder*) to look; **gaffe un peu!,** have a dekko!
gaffeur,-euse [gafœr, -øz] *n F* blunderer, blundering fool; **c'est un g.,** he's always putting his foot in it.
gag [gag] *nm Th Cin F* gag.
gaga [gaga] *F* **1** *n* old person, old dodderer. **2** *adj inv* gaga, doddering, senile.
gage [gaʒ] *nm* **(a)** *Com Jur* pledge, security; (*chez le prêteur sur gages*) pawned article; (*garantie*) surety; **laisser qch pour g.,** to leave sth as security *or* on deposit; **mettre qch en g.,** to pawn *or* pledge sth; **mise en g.,** pawning, pledging; **prêteur sur gages,** pawnbroker; **ma montre est en g.,** my watch is in pawn; **lettre de g.,** debenture bond; (*pour hypothèque*) mortgage bond; **rester en g.,** to remain as surety; **votre parole sera le meilleur des gages,** your word will be the best guarantee; **(b)** (*preuve*) token, sign; **g. d'amour,** love token; **(c)** (*aux jeux*) forfeit; **jouer aux gages,** to play at forfeits; **(d) gages,** wages, pay; **tueur à gages,** hired assassin; *Cin etc* **auteur à gages fixes,** staff writer.
gagé [gaʒe] *adj Jur* secured (*loan*); **meubles gagés,** furniture under distraint; **recettes non gagées,** unassigned *or* unpledged revenue.
gager [gaʒe] *vt* (**je gageai(s); n. gageons**) **(a)** *Litt* **je gagerais que ...,** I'd bet that ...; **(b)** to guarantee, to secure (*loan etc*).
gageure [gaʒyr] *nf* **(a)** (*action difficile*) difficult undertaking; **(b)** *Litt* wager; **(c)** *Can* (*pari*) bet, wager.
gagiste [gaʒist] *nm Jur* pledger, pawner.
gagnant, -ante [gaɲɑ̃, -ɑ̃t] **1** *adj* winning (*ticket etc*). **2** *n* winner; **partir g.,** (*à une course*) to start favourite; *Fig* to be a sure winner; **jouer g.,** to bet on a certainty.
gagne-pain [gaɲ(ə)pɛ̃] *nm inv* (means of) living, livelihood.
gagne-petit [gaɲ(ə)pəti] *nm inv* person earning a pittance *or* a low wage.
gagne-place [gaɲ(ə)plas] *nm F* spacesaver; (*pl gagne-places*).
gagner [gaɲe] **1** *vt* **(a)** *Fin* to earn; **g. de l'argent,** to earn money; **g. mille francs par mois,** to earn a thousand francs a month; **g. gros,** to make big money; (*d'une société*) to make large profits; **g. sa vie** *ou* **de quoi vivre,** to earn one's living; **ce que je gagne suffit à nos besoins,** I earn enough to keep us; *F* **il l'a bien gagné,** he's earned it; (*il l'a bien cherché*) it serves him (damn well) right;

(b) (*profiter*) to gain; to benefit, to profit (**à,** by); **g. du temps,** to save time; (*sur un délai serré*) to gain time; **chercher à g. du temps,** to play for time; **c'est autant de gagné, c'est toujours ça de gagné,** that's so much to the good; (*la décision a été prise*) at least that's settled; **nous ne gagnerons rien à attendre,** there is nothing to be gained by waiting;

(c) to win, to gain (*a victory*); *Mil* to take (*a town*); *Fig* **la partie n'est pas gagnée,** we haven't won yet; **si elle dit oui, c'est gagné,** if she says yes, it's OK;

(d) to win (*game, race*); **g. qn à une cause,** to win s.o. over to a cause; **g. qn à une idée,** to sell s.o. an idea; **g. la confiance de qn,** to win *or* gain s.o.'s confidence;

(e) to get, to catch (*disease etc*);

(f) to reach, to arrive at, to get to; **g. le haut,** to reach the top; *Nau* **g. le port,** to fetch into port;

(g) (*rattraper*) to gain on, to overtake; **g. un navire,** to gain on *or* overhaul a ship; **g. le devant,** to forge ahead, to take the lead; **la nuit nous gagna,** darkness overtook us; **le feu/l'épidémie/***etc* **gagne,** the fire/the epidemic/*etc* is spreading; **g. du terrain,** to gain ground; to reclaim land (*from the sea etc*); **la mer gagne du terrain,** the sea is encroaching on the land; **g. une marche sur qn,** to steal a march on s.o.; **la faim nous gagnait,** we were getting hungry; **gagné par le sommeil/les larmes,** overcome by sleep/with tears; *Nau* **le vent,** to make *or* fetch to windward; **g. le vent d'une pointe,** to weather a headland; **g. de l'avant,** to forge ahead;

(h) *Méd* to spread; **l'enflure a gagné la gorge,** the swelling has spread to the throat.

2 *vi* **(a)** (*être vainqueur*) to win; **g. dans un fauteuil,** to have a walkover; **g. haut la main,** to win in a canter, to win hands down;

(b) (*profiter*) to benefit; **tu gagnerais à partir,** it would be in your (best) interest to leave; **j'ai gagné au change,** I got the best of the bargain *or* deal; **et moi, qu'est-ce que j'y gagne?,** and what do I get out of it?, what's in this for me?, and where do I come in?;

(c) (*s'améliorer*) to increase, to improve, to gain; **le mécontentement gagne de force,** there is increasing discontent; **g. à être connu,** to improve on acquaintance;

(d) *Nau* **g. au vent,** to make *or* fetch to windward.

gagneur, -euse [gaɲœr, -øz] **1** *n* winner; **avoir un tempérament** *ou* **un caractère de g.,** to be a winner. **2** *nf Arg* **gagneuse,** prostitute, tart.

gai [ge] *adj* **(a)** cheerful, merry, lively (*person, song*); (*person*) in good spirits; cheerful, cheery (*voice*); bright, cheerful (*room, colour etc*); amusing (*talk, stories*); **g. comme un pinson,** happy as a lark *or* a sandboy; **avoir l'esprit g.,** to be of a cheerful disposition; *F* **être un peu g.,** to be tipsy *or* tight; **avoir le vin g.,** to be a happy drunk; *Iron* **ça va être g.!,** that WILL be nice!; **des couleurs gaies,** bright colours; **(b)** (*bolt, key etc*) free, easy; **hareng g.,** shotten herring.

gaiement [gemɑ̃] *adv* cheerfully, merrily, brightly, gaily.

gaieté [gete] *nf* cheerfulness, gaiety; **vous n'êtes pas d'une g. folle!,** you're getting me down!; **déborder de g.,** to be bubbling over with high spirits; **retrouver sa g.,** to recover one's spirits, to perk up, to buck up.

gaillard, -arde [gajar, -ard] **1** *adj* (*personne*) strong, well, vigorous; *Vieilli* merry, lively, cheery; risqué, off-colour, *US* off-color (*story, remark*); fresh (*wind*), cool (*weather*); **frais et g.,** hale and hearty; **il se sentait g.,** he felt in good form. **2** *n* (*homme*) hearty *or* vigorous type; **un grand et solide g.,** a great strapping young man; **une grande gaillarde,** a strapping young woman; *Arch* **un vert g.,** a rip. **3** *nm Nau* **g. d'avant,** forecastle; **g. d'arrière,** poop; **haut de g.,** deep-waisted. **4** *nf* **gaillarde (a)** (*danse*) galliard; **(b)** *Typ* eight-point type; brevier.

gaillardement [gajardəmɑ̃] *adv* **(a)** (*gaiement*) gaily, good-humouredly; **(b)** (*sans faiblir*) boldly, bravely, gallantly.

gaillardise [gajardiz] *nf* **conter des gaillardises,** to tell dirty *or* off-colour stories *or* jokes.

gaillette [gajɛt] *nf* cobbles (*of coal*).

gaîment [gemɑ̃] *adv* = **GAIEMENT.**

gain [gɛ̃] *nm* **(a)** winning (*of contest, war etc*); *Jur* **avoir** *ou* **obtenir g. de cause,** to win one's case; **donner g. de cause à qn,** to decide in favour of s.o.; **il y a chances égales de g. et de perte,** it's an even chance, there's a fifty-fifty chance;

(b) (*profit*) gain, profit; (*salaire*) earnings; (*au jeu*) winnings; **avoir l'amour du g.,** to be obsessed with making money; *Jur* **g. de la femme mariée,** wife's earned income; **g. fortuit,** capital gain; **les gains de la soirée,** the evening's winnings; **être en g.,** to be in pocket; **un g. de temps,** a saving of time; **g. retiré d'une lecture,** profit acquired from reading; **ce g. de renseignements nous a permis de trouver le coupable plus rapidement,** gaining this information allowed us to find the culprit more quickly;

(c) *El etc* gain; **g. en courant,** current gain; **g. en tension,** voltage magnification; *Electron* **g. d'étage,** stage gain; *Nucl* **g. de régénération,** breeding gain.

gainage [gɛnaʒ] *nm MecE Constr etc* casing, sheathing, sleeving; *Nucl* canning, casing, cladding (*of fuel etc*).

gaine [gɛn] *nf* **(a)** (*cache*) cover, case; casing, wrapping, jacket; **g. d'une momie,** mummy case; **g. en cuir,** leather case; **g. métallique,** metallic sheath *or* sleeve; **câble sous g.,** sheathed cable; **g. souple,** flexible sheath; *Nucl* **g. d'électrons/d'ions,** electron/ion sheath; **(b)** *Anat Bot* sheath; **(c)** (*sous-vêtement*) foundation (garment), corset, roll-on, girdle; **(d)** *Géol* gangue, matrix; **(e)** *Constr Min etc* (ventilation) shaft, passage, duct.

gaine-combinaison [gɛnkɔ̃binɛzɔ̃] *nf* corselet; (*pl gaines-combinaisons*).

gaine-culotte [gɛnkylɔt] *nf* pantie girdle; (*pl gaines-culottes*).

gainer [gene] *vt* to sheath, to cover, to case (*in leather etc*).

gal [gal] *nm Phys* gal.

Gal *n Mil* (*abrév* **Général**) Gen.

gala [gala] *nm* gala, fête; **en habit/toilette de g.,** in gala dress, in full dress; *Fig* in one's Sunday best; **dîner en grand g.,** to dine in state, to dine with great ceremony.

Galaad¹ [galaad] *nm* Gilead.

Galaad² *nm Littér* Galahad.

galactique [galaktik] *adj* galactic.

galamment [galamɑ̃] *adv* (*avec politesse*) politely, courteously; (*d'un homme*) gallantly, like a gentleman; *Litt* bravely, honourably, *US* honorably; **se tirer g. d'une affaire,** to come out of an affair with honour *or US* honor.

galandage [galɑ̃daʒ] *nm Constr* brick partition; half-timbered construction (*with brickwork in between the beams*).

galant¹ [galɑ̃] **1** *adj* (*homme*) attentive to women, gallant; *Arch* gay, elegant; **homme g.,** ladies' man; **vers galants,** love poems; **femme galante,** woman of loose morals; *Beaux-Arts Litt* **fête galante,** fête galante; *Hum* **être en galante compagnie,** to be in the company of the opposite sex; **intrigue galante,** love affair; **g. homme,** man of honour, gentleman; **se conduire en g. homme,** to behave like a gentleman; *Arch* **costume g.,** stylish *or* elegant costume. **2** *nm Vieilli & Litt* lover, gallant, ladies' man; (*flirt*) philanderer; **faire le g. auprès d'une dame,** to court *or* pay court to a lady; (*flirter*) to flirt with a lady.

Galant² *nm Littér* Wayland.

galanterie [galɑ̃tri] *nf* **(a)** (*envers les femmes*) politeness, attentiveness; **(b)** (*intrigue*) love affair, intrigue; **dire des galanteries,** to pay compliments.

galantine [galɑ̃tin] *nf Culin* galantine.

galate [galat] *adj & n Bible* Galatian.

Galatée [galate] *nf Myth* Galatea.

Galatie [galasi] *nf* Galatia.

galaxie [galaksi] *nf Astron* galaxy.

galbe [galb] *nm* **(a)** (*jambe etc*) curve (*of furniture, baluster etc*); curve(s), contour (*of the human figure*); sweep, outline, lines (*of car*); **(b)** *Archit* entasis (*of column*).

galbé [galbe] *adj* **(a)** (*jambe etc*) shapely, curved, well-proportioned; **(b)** *Archit* (*column*) with entasis.

galber [galbe] *vt* **(a)** to give curves to (*vase, chest of drawers etc*); *Tech* to curve, to bend (lightly) (*sheet metal*); **(b)** *Archit* to construct (*column*) with entasis.

galbord [galbɔr] *nm Nau* garboard (strake).

gale [gal] *nf* **(a)** *Méd* scabies; *F* scold, shrew (*of a woman*); **g. bédouine,** prickly heat; **arbre à la g.,** poison ivy, poison oak; *F* **être mauvais comme la g.,** to be a nasty piece of work; **(b)** *Vét* scab, mange; **(c)** *Bot* scurf, scale.

galé [gale] *nm Bot* sweet gale, bog myrtle.

galée [gale] *nf Typ* composing galley.

galéjade [galeʒad] *nf Région* tall story; **débiter** *ou* **dire des galéjades à qn,** to pull s.o.'s leg.

galéjer [galeʒe] *vi Région* to tell tall stories.

galène [galɛn] *nf Minér* galena, sulphide of lead.

galéopithèque [galeɔpitɛk] *nm Zool* flying lemur.

galère [galɛr] *nf* **(a)** galley, slave ship; *Arch* convict ship; **galères,** hulks; **vogue la g.!,** let things rip!; **mais que diable allait-il faire dans cette g.?,** but what the hell was he doing there?, whatever took him there?; *Nau* **avirons en g.!,** rest on your oars!; **condamné aux galères,** sentenced to penal servitude; *F* **c'est une vraie g.,** it's hell on earth; *F* **il est en retard?, quelle g.!,** he's late?, what a nuisance!; **(b)** *Zool* Portuguese man-of-war.

galérer [galere] *vi F* to be having a hard time.

galerie [galri] *nf* **(a)** gallery; *Archit* arcade, covered walk; *Can* porch; **g. de portraits,** portrait gallery; **g. d'art,** art gallery; **g. marchande,** shopping centre; **(b)** *Th etc* balcony, gallery; *Th* **première g.,** dress circle; **seconde g.,** upper circle; **troisième g.,** gallery, *F* the gods; **jouer pour la g.,** to play to the gallery; *Nau* **g. de poupe,** stern gallery, stern walk; **(c)** *Min* gallery, drift, level; **g. d'avancement,** heading; *Mil etc* **g. d'écoute,** listening gallery; *El* **g. des câbles,** cable tunnel; **(d)** *Aut* (*sur toit*) roof rack; **(e)** cornice, moulding, beading (*on furniture*); **(f)** run (*of mole*).

galérien [galerjɛ̃] *nm* galley slave; **travailler comme un g.,** to work like a galley slave; *F* **mener une vie de g.,** to lead a dog's life.

galet [galɛ] *nm* **(a)** pebble; **galets,** shingle; **galets de chaussée,** cobblestones; **civilisation du g. aménagé,** pebble culture; **plage de galets,** shingly *or* shingle beach; **(b)** *MecE* roller, runner, pulley, (rail)wheel; **g. de roulement,**

travelling *or* running wheel; **(c)** *Pêche* float (*of net*).

galetas [galtɑ] *nm* (*sous les toits*) garret, attic; *Péj* hovel.

galetouse [galtuz] *nf Arg* bowl, mess tin, dixie.

galette [galɛt] *nf Culin* buckwheat pancake; *Nau* (ship's) biscuit; *Arg* money, lolly; *Arg* **il a de la g.,** he's flush *or* loaded; **g. des Rois,** Twelfth Night cake; **g. aux pommes,** apple tart; *F* **plat comme une g.,** flat as a pancake.

galetteux, -euse [galɛtø, -øz] *adj Arg* rolling in it.

galeux, -euse [galø, -øz] *adj* mangy (*dog*); scurfy (*tree*); **plaie galeuse,** sore caused by scabies; **société galeuse,** rotten society; **murs galeux,** peeling *or* flaking walls.

galgal, -als [galgal] *nm Archéol* cairn, barrow.

galibot [galibo] *nm Min* pit boy.

Galice [galis] *nf* (*en Espagne*) Galicia.

Galicie [galisi] *nf* (*en Pologne*) Galicia.

galicien, -ienne [galisjɛ̃, -jɛn] **1** *adj* Galician (*of Spain or Poland*). **2** *n* **G.,** native *or* inhabitant of Galicia (*in Spain or Poland*).

Galien [galjɛ̃] *nm* Galen.

Galilée[1] [galile] *nf Bible* Galilee.

Galilée[2] *nm Hist* Galileo.

galiléen, -enne [galileɛ̃, -ɛn] *adj & n Bible* Galilean.

galimatias [galimatjɑ] *nm* gibberish.

galine [galin] *nf Sp* (*ice hockey*) puck.

galion [galjɔ̃] *nm Nau* galleon.

galipette [galipɛt] *nf F* somersault; **faire des galipettes,** (*d'un enfant*) to romp around.

galipot [galipo] *nm* **(a)** *Com* galipot, white resin; **(b)** *Can* **courir le g.,** to be a woman-chaser.

galle [gal] *nf Bot* gall(nut); **g. de chêne,** oak apple.

Galles [gal] *nf* **le pays de G.,** Wales; **la G. du Nord,** North Wales; **Prince de G.,** Prince of Wales; *Tex* Prince of Wales check.

gallican, -ane [galikɑ̃, -an] *adj & n Rel* Gallican.

gallicanisme [galikanism] *nm Rel* Gallicanism.

gallicisme [galisism] *nm* Gallicism.

gallinacé [galinase] *Orn* **1** *adj* gallinaceous. **2** *nmpl* **gallinacés,** Gallinaceae.

gallique[1] [galik] *adj Hist* Gallic, of Gaul.

gallique[2] *adj Ch* gallic (*acid*).

gallium [galjɔm] *nm Ch* gallium.

gallois, -oise [galwa, -waz] **1** *adj* Welsh. **2** *nm Ling* Welsh. **3** *n* **G.,** Welshman, Welshwoman; **les G.,** the Welsh.

gallomanie [galɔmani] *nf* gallomania.

gallon [galɔ̃] *nm* gallon.

gallo-romain [galɔrɔmɛ̃] *adj* Gallo-Roman; (*pl gallo-romain(e)s*).

gallup [galœp] *nm* Gallup poll.

galoche [galɔʃ] *nf* clog (*with leather upper*); *F* **menton en g.,** nutcracker chin; *Arg* **vieille g.,** old fogey.

galon [galɔ̃] *nm* **(a)** braid; **g. de finition,** upholstery binding; **(b)** *Mil* **galons,** (*N.C.O.'s*) stripes; (*officer's*) bands, gold braid; *Nau* (*officer's*) stripes; (*in Merchant Service*) bands; **priver qn de ses galons,** to reduce s.o. to the ranks; *F* **prendre du g.,** to be promoted; *Fig* to move up in the world; *F* **arroser ses galons,** to celebrate one's promotion.

galonné [galɔne] *nm Arg* (non-commissioned) officer.

galonner [galɔne] *vt* to (trim *or* ornament with) braid; **habit galonné d'or,** gold-laced coat.

galop [galo] *nm* gallop; **prendre le g.,** to break into a gallop; **au g. (allongé),** at a gallop; **grand g.,** full gallop; **g. de manège,** hand gallop; **petit g.,** canter; **partir au g.,** to gallop away; *Fig* **faire qch au g.,** to gallop *or* rush through sth, to skimp sth; **allez, au travail! et au g.!,** come on, to work!, and make it snappy!; *Fig* **ce séminaire ne constitue qu'un g. d'essai,** this seminar is just a trial run.

galopade [galɔpad] *nf Équitation* galloping, gallop, canter; *Fig* **son imagination prend la g.,** his imagination runs away with him; *Fig* **expédier son repas à la g.,** to bolt one's meal; **traverser la France à la g.,** to rush across France.

galopant [galɔpɑ̃] *adj* runaway; **démographie galopante,** rapid population growth; **inflation galopante,** galloping *or* runaway inflation.

galoper [galɔpe] **1** *vi* to gallop; *Fig* to gallop *or* rush around; **se mettre à g.,** to break into a gallop; **g. après qn/qch,** to run after s.o./sth. **2** *vt* to gallop (*horse*); *Fig* **g. les rues/la campagne,** to scour the streets/the countryside (*in search of sth*).

galopeur, -euse [galɔpœr, -øz] **1** *adj* galloping. **2** *n* (*horse*) galloper.

galopin [galɔpɛ̃] *nm* **(a)** *F* child, brat; **espèce de petit g.!,** little rascal!; **(b)** *MecE* idler, loose pulley; jockey wheel.

galure [galyr] *nm*, **galurin** [galyrɛ̃] *nm* (*chapeau*) titfer.

galvanique [galvanik] *adj* galvanic (*cell etc*); **plaqué g.,** electroplate; **dorure g.,** electrogilding.

galvanisation [galvanizasjɔ̃] *nf* (*métallisation*) galvanization, galvanizing; *Él* galvanism.

galvaniser [galvanize] *vt* **(a)** to give new life to (*undertaking etc*); to stimulate, to galvanize (*a crowd etc*); to galvanize (*corpse etc*); **(b)** *Métal* to galvanize; *Él* to (electro)plate; (*de zinc*) to zinc; **tôle galvanisée,** galvanized (sheet) iron.

galvanisme [galvanism] *nm Méd* galvanism.

galvano [galvano] *nm Typ F* electrotype plate, electro.

galvano- [galvano] *préf* galvano-.

galvanomètre [galvanɔmɛtr] *nm Él* galvanometer.

galvanoplastie [galvanɔplasti] *nf* galvanoplasty, electrodeposition; *Ind* electroplating; *Typ* electrotyping.

galvanoplastique [galvanɔplastik] *adj* galvanoplastic.

galvanoscope [galvanɔskɔp] *nm* galvanoscope; *Télécom* (linesman's) detector.

galvanotype [galvanɔtip] *nm Typ* electrotype.

galvanotypie [galvanɔtipi] *nf Typ* electrotyping.

galvauder [galvode] **1** *vt* to bring into disrepute; to prostitute (*one's talents*). **2 se galvauder** *vpr* to damage one's reputation.

gamba [gɔ̃ba] *nf* large prawn.

gambade [gɑ̃bad] *nf* leap, gambol; *Équitation* gambade; **gambades,** capers, antics; **faire des gambades,** to gambol, to leap *or* frisk about.

gambader [gɑ̃bade] *vi* to leap (about), to caper, to frisk (about), to gambol.

gamberge [gɑ̃bɛrʒ] *nf F* **une g.,** a think; **il va falloir une bonne g. pour s'en sortir,** we'll need to have a good think to get out of this one.

gamberger [gɑ̃bɛrʒe] *F* **1** *vi* to think deeply; **tu gamberges trop pour être heureux,** you spend too much time thinking to be happy. **2** *vt* to psych oneself up; **g. un match,** to psych oneself up for a match.

gambette[1] [gɑ̃bɛt] *nm* (*oiseau*) redshank.

gambette[2] *nf Arg* (*jambe*) pin; **jouer *ou* tricoter des gambettes,** to beat it, to leg it.

Gambie [gɑ̃bi] *nf* the Gambia.

gambiller [gɑ̃bije] *vi Arg* (*danser*) to jig about, to shake a leg.

gambit [gɑ̃bi] *nm Échecs* gambit; **(pion de) g.,** gambit pawn.

gamelle [gamɛl] *nf* **(a)** *Mil etc* (*de soldat*) dixie, dixy, mess tin; **manger à la g.,** to eat in the mess; *Arg* **ramasser une g.,** to come a cropper; **(b)** *Min* pan.

gamète [gamɛt] *nm Biol* gamete.

gamétocide [gametɔsid] *nm Méd* gametocide.

gamétocyte [gametɔsit] *nm Biol* gametocyte.

gamétogénèse [gametɔʒenɛz] *nf Biol* gametogenesis.

gamétophyte [gametɔfit] *nm Bot* gametophyte.

gamin, -ine [gamɛ̃, -in] **1** *n* (*enfant*) child; **une gamine de dix ans,** a girl of ten; **mon g.,** my boy, my son; **ce n'est qu'un grand g.,** (*d'un adulte*) he's just a big kid. **2** *adj* **(a)** (*espiègle*) lively, mischievous; **(b)** *Péj* **elle est encore gamine,** she's still just a child; **une réaction gamine,** a childish reaction.

gaminerie [gaminri] *nf* childish prank *or* trick; (*comportement*) childish behaviour; **il a passé l'âge de ces gamineries,** he's too old to behave in such a childish way.

gamma [gama] *nm* (*lettre*) & *Phot* gamma; *Nucl* **rayons g.,** gamma rays.

gammaglobuline [gamaglɔbylin] *nf Biol* gamma globulin.

gammamètre [gamamɛtr] *nm* gamma (radiation) meter.

gamme [gam] *nf* **(a)** range (*of colours etc*); **une vaste g. de produits,** a vast range of products; **toute la g. des sensations,** the whole gamut *or* range of sensations; *F* **toute la g.!,** the whole caboodle!; **produit bas/haut de g.,** bottom-of-the-range *or* down-market/top-of-the-range *or* up-market product; **(b)** *Mus* scale, gamut; **faire des gammes,** to do *or* practise scales; **changer de g.,** to alter one's tone, to change one's tune, to climb down.

gammée [game] *adj* **croix g.,** swastika.

gamopétale [gamɔpetal] *adj Bot* gamopetalous.

ganache [ganaʃ] *nf* **(a)** *Culin* = filling for cakes made from chocolate, butter and cream; **(b)** *F* (*imbécile*) fool, idiot; **vieille g.,** old fogey *or* buffer; **(c)** (*d'un cheval*) (lower) jaw, jowl.

Gand [gɑ̃] *nm* Ghent.

gang [gɑ̃g] *nm* gang (*of criminals etc*).

ganga [gɑ̃ga] *nm* pintailed (sand) grouse.

Gange (le) [ləgɑ̃ʒ] *nm* the (river) Ganges.
gangétique [gɑ̃ʒetik] *adj* Ganges (*delta etc*).
gangliforme [gɑ̃glifɔrm] *adj* gangliform.
ganglion [gɑ̃glijɔ̃] *nm* **(a)** *Anat* ganglion; **g. nerveux,** ganglion cell; **ganglions lymphatiques,** lymphatic glands, lymph glands; **j'ai des ganglions,** my glands are swollen, I have swollen glands; *Méd* **g. synovial,** ganglion; **(b)** *Vét* spavin.
ganglionnaire [gɑ̃glijɔnɛr] *adj Anat* ganglionic; **fièvre g.,** glandular fever.
gangrène [gɑ̃grɛn] *nf* **(a)** *Méd* gangrene; **avoir la g.,** to have gangrene; **g. gazeuse,** gas gangrene; **g. des os,** necrosis; **(b)** *Bot* canker; **(c)** *Fig* canker.
gangrené [gɑ̃grəne] *adj* **(a)** *Méd* gangrenous, gangrened; **(b)** *Fig* corrupt.
gangrener [gɑ̃grəne] *v* **(il gangrène; il gangrènera) 1** *vt* **(a)** *Méd* to gangrene; **(b)** *Fig* to corrupt. **2 se gangrener** *vpr* **(a)** *Méd* to become *or* go gangrenous; **(b)** *Fig* to become corrupt, to decay.
gangreneux, -euse [gɑ̃grənø, -øz] *adj* **(a)** *Méd* gangrenous, gangrened; **(b)** *Bot* cankerous.
gangster [gɑ̃gstɛr] *nm* gangster.
gangstérisme [gɑ̃gsterism] *nm* gangsterism.
gangue [gɑ̃g] *nf Minér* gang(ue), matrix (*of precious stone etc*).
gannet [ganɛ] *nm* gannet.
ganse [gɑ̃s] *nf* (*cordon*) braid, (plaited) cord, edging, piping (cord); **bordé de ganses,** piped; **g. de cheveux,** plait of hair.
gant [gɑ̃] *nm* **(a)** glove; (*armure*) gauntlet; **mettre ses gants,** to put on one's gloves; **gants en daim/tissu,** suède/fabric gloves; **gants fourrés,** lined gloves; **gants de caoutchouc,** rubber gloves; *Fig* **cela vous va comme un g.,** it fits you like a glove; *Fig* **il faut prendre des gants pour l'approcher,** you have to handle him with kid gloves (on); **jeter le g. à qn,** to throw down the gauntlet to s.o.; **relever le g.,** to take up the gauntlet, to accept the challenge; **souple comme un g.,** good-natured, easygoing; **gants de boxe,** boxing gloves; **g. de toilette,** ≈ facecloth, flannel, *Am* washcloth, washrag; **g. de crin,** friction glove; **(b)** *Bot* **g. de bergère** *ou* **(de) Notre-Dame,** (*digitale*) foxglove; (*ancolie*) columbine; **g. de Neptune,** glove sponge.
ganteló [gɑ̃tle] *adj* gauntleted; **la main gantelée,** the mailed fist.
gantelée [gɑ̃tle] *nf* foxglove.
gantelet [gɑ̃tlɛ] *nm* gauntlet.
ganter [gɑ̃te] **1** *vt* to glove; **être bien ganté,** to be well gloved. **2** *vi* **g. du sept,** to take a (size) seven in gloves. **3 se ganter** *vpr* to put on one's gloves.
ganterie [gɑ̃tri] *nf* **(a)** *Ind* glove-making, gloving; *Com* glove trade; **(b)** (*fabrique*) glove factory; (*magasin*) glove shop; (*rayon*) glove counter *or* department.
gantier, -ière [gɑ̃tje, -jɛr] *n* glover.
gantois, -oise [gɑ̃twa, -waz] **1** *adj* of Ghent. **2** *n* **G.,** native *or* inhabitant of Ghent.
garage [garaʒ] *nm* **(a)** (*de voiture*) garage; **g. à plusieurs étages,** multi-storey car park, *US* tiered parking lot; **g. de** *ou* **à bicyclettes,** bicycle *or* bike shed; **g. de canots,** boathouse, *US* boat shed; **g. d'autobus,** bus depot; **g. d'avions,** (aircraft) hangar; *Rail* **g. de machines,** engine shed; **j'ai mis la voiture au g.,** I've put the car into the garage; *Can* **vente de g.,** garage sale; **(b)** *Rail* shunting, side tracking; **voie de g.,** siding; *F* **mettre** *ou* **ranger qch sur une voie de g.,** to shelve sth; **mettre** *ou* **ranger qn sur une voie de g.,** to put s.o. on the sidelines, *Am* to sideline s.o.; **(c)** docking (*of boats*); dock, basin (*of canal, river*); **g. à sec,** dry basin; **(d)** passing place (*on narrow road*).
garagiste [garaʒist] *nm Aut* (*propriétaire*) garage owner; (*mécanicien*) garage mechanic; **j'emmène la voiture chez le g.,** I'm taking the car to the garage.
garance [garɑ̃s] *nf* **(a)** *Bot* madder(wort); *F* **petite g., g. de chien,** squinancy wort; **(b)** (*teinture*) madder (dye).
garant, -ante [garɑ̃, -ɑ̃t] **1** *n* guarantor; **se rendre** *ou* **se porter g. de qn,** to answer for s.o.; (*devant la justice*) to go bail for s.o.; (*à la banque*) to stand guarantor for s.o.; **je m'en porte g.,** I can vouch for it; **ça va marcher, j'en suis garante,** it will work, I give you my word; **elle vous en est garante,** she gives you her word for it; **prendre qn à g. de qch,** to call s.o. to witness sth; **être g. de ses faits,** to be answerable for one's actions. **2** *nm* guarantee.
garantie [garɑ̃ti] *nf* **(a)** (*précaution*) guarantee, safeguard (**contre,** against); *Jur* **g. parlementaire,** (*d'un député*) parliamentary privilege; **prendre des garanties contre les abus,** to insure against abuses;

(b) guarantee, pledge (*of execution of contract*); guaranty (*of payment*); **g. d'exécution,** contract bond; **fonds déposés** *ou* **détenus en g.,** funds lodged *or* held as security; **verser une somme en g.,** to leave *or* pay a deposit; **donner sa montre en g.,** to pledge one's watch; **donner une g. pour qn,** to stand security for s.o.; **g. accessoire,** collateral security;
(c) *Com* warranty, guarantee (*of quality etc*); **vendu avec g.,** sold with a guarantee; **la voiture est encore sous g.,** the car is still under guarantee; **sans g.,** unwarranted; **il va essayer, mais c'est sans g.,** he'll try, but there's no guarantee (that he'll succeed); **lettre de g. d'indemnité,** letter of indemnity;
(d) *Fin* underwriting; **syndicat de g.,** underwriters.
garantir [garɑ̃tir] **1** *vt* **(a)** to guarantee, to warrant; **g. une dette,** to guarantee a debt; **créance garantie,** secured debt; **pendule garantie (pour) deux ans,** clock guaranteed for two years; **g. un fait,** to vouch for a fact; **je vous garantis qu'il viendra,** I guarantee he'll come; **je peux te g. qu'il ne reviendra pas,** I can guarantee you he won't come back, he won't come back, I warrant you; **elle m'a garanti qu'elle serait à l'heure,** she guaranteed me she'd be on time;
(b) *Fin* to underwrite (*issue of shares etc*);
(c) (*protéger*) to shelter, to protect; **ces rideaux vont vous g. contre le froid,** these curtains will protect *or* shield you from the cold; **g. une maison contre l'incendie,** to secure *or* insure a house against fire;
(d) *Jur* **g. qn contre qch,** to indemnify s.o. from *or* against sth.
2 se garantir *vpr* **se g. contre le froid/le vent,** to protect oneself from the cold/the wind.
garce [gars] *nf* **(a)** *F Péj* (*salope*) bitch, slut, cow; **quelle g.!,** what a cow *or* bitch!; **cette g. de bagnole,** this bloody (awful) car; **(b)** *Vieilli* (*prostituée*) prostitute, tart.
garçon [garsɔ̃] *nm* **(a)** (*enfant mâle*) boy; **école de garçons,** boys' school; **petit g.,** small *or* little boy; **se sentir un petit g. à côté de qn,** to feel like a little boy *or* like a child beside s.o., to feel dwarfed by s.o.; **tu es un grand g.,** you're a big boy now; **c'est un g. manqué,** she's a tomboy;
(b) (*fils*) son; **il est venu avec ses deux garçons,** he came with his two sons *or* boys;
(c) (*jeune homme*) young man; **un g. d'une vingtaine d'années,** a boy *or* lad *or* youth of about twenty; **un bon** *ou* **brave g.,** a good lad; **un beau** *ou* **un joli g.,** a handsome young man; **il est assez beau g.,** he's quite a good-looking *or* handsome young man; **g. d'honneur,** best man; **un mauvais g.,** a bad lot;
(d) (*célibataire*) bachelor; *Vieilli* **il est encore g.,** he's still single *or* still a bachelor; **vieux g.,** old *or* confirmed bachelor; **appartement de g.,** bachelor flat *or* pad *or US* apartment;
(e) (*dans magasin etc*) assistant; **g. boucher,** butcher's boy; **g. coiffeur,** hairdresser's assistant; **g. de café** *ou* **de restaurant,** waiter; **g. de comptoir,** barman; **g.!,** (*in restaurant*) waiter!; **g. d'écurie,** groom; **g. d'étage,** (*in hotel*) bellboy; **g. d'ascenseur,** lift boy, liftman, *US* elevator operator; *Nau* **g. de cabine,** (cabin) steward; **g. de pont,** deck steward; **g. de salle,** auctioneer's messenger; **g. de bureau,** office boy, (office) messenger, *Arg* gofer; **g. de courses,** errand boy; **g. de recette,** bank messenger.
garçonne [garsɔn] *nf* **(a) être coiffé à la g.,** (*of woman*) to have an urchin cut; **(b)** *Vieilli* bachelor girl.
garçonnet [garsɔnɛ] *nm* (*petit garçon*) little boy; *Com* **taille g.,** small boys (size).
garçonnier, -ière [garsɔnje, -jɛr] *adj* **habitudes garçonnières,** (*d'une femme*) masculine *or* mannish habits.
garçonnière [garsɔnjɛr] *nf* bachelor flat *or* pad *or Am* apartment.
garde¹ [gard] *nf* **(a)** (*protection*) guardianship, care, protection, custody (*of a person*); care (*of thing*); **confier qch/qn à la g. de qn, confier la g. de qch/qn à qn,** to entrust s.o. with (the care of) sth/s.o.; **être sous bonne g.,** to be in safe custody *or* keeping; **avoir qch en g.,** to have charge of sth; **que Dieu nous ait en g.,** may God protect us; **je vous laisse les enfants en g.,** I'm leaving the children in your charge; *Jur* **g. à vue,** close watch; *Jur* **g. des enfants,** (*après un divorce*) custody of the children; **droit de g.,** (right of) custody;
(b) (*surveillance*) guarding, protection (*of frontier, machinery etc*); **soldat de g. à la porte,** soldier on guard at the door; **être de g.,** to be on guard *or Nau* on duty; **descendre de g.,** to come off guard *or* duty; **monter la g.,**

(*être en faction*) to mount guard; (*prendre son service*) to go on guard; **la police assurera la g. du tribunal,** the police will (mount) guard (on) the court, the court will be under police guard; **à la g.!,** guard turn out!; **assurer la g. de nuit,** to be on night call *or* duty; *Mil* **poste de g.,** guardroom; **chien de g.,** guard dog, watchdog; **sentinelle de g.,** duty sentry; **pharmacie de g.,** emergency *or* duty chemist;

(c) (*méfiance*) **mettre qn en g. contre qch/qn,** to put s.o. on his guard against sth/s.o., to warn s.o. against sth/ s.o.; **être** *ou* **se tenir sur ses gardes,** to be on one's guard, to look out; **prendre g. à qn/qch,** to beware of s.o./sth; **prenez g. aux orties!,** mind *or* watch the nettles!; **prenez g.!,** look out!, take care!;

(d) (*attention*) **prendre g. à qch/qn,** to attend to *or* be careful of sth/s.o.; **un fait auquel on n'a pas pris g.,** a fact that has been left out of consideration; **je n'y prendrais pas g.,** I should take no notice of it, I shouldn't take any notice of it; **faire qch sans y prendre g.,** to do sth without meaning to; **prendre g. que ...(ne)** + *sub*, to be careful *or* to take care that ... (*sth does not happen*); **prenez g. qu'il (ne) vous voie,** take care (that) he doesn't see you; **prendre g. à** *ou* **de ne pas faire qch,** to be careful not to do sth; **prenez g. à** *ou* **de ne pas vous perdre,** mind you don't get lost; *Vieilli* **prendre g. de faire qch,** to be careful not to do sth; **prenez g. de tomber,** mind you don't fall;

(e) (*groupe de soldats*) **le corps de g., la g.,** the guard; **g. montante,** new guard, relieving guard; **g. descendante,** old guard; **relever la g.,** to change the guard; **g. du drapeau,** colour party, colour *or US* color guard; **g. d'honneur,** guard of honour *or US* honor; **la g.,** the Guards; **la g. à cheval,** the Horseguards; **la g. à pied,** the Footguards; **la g. du corps,** the Lifeguards; **la G. républicaine,** = the Republican Guard (*of Paris*); **la G. mobile,** = security (state) police; *Hist* **la G. impériale,** (Napoleon's) Imperial Guard;

(f) *Boxe Escrime etc* (*position d'attente*) guard; **se mettre en g.,** to take one's guard, to square up; *Escrime* **en g.!,** en garde!;

(g) *Aut* **g. au sol,** ground clearance;

(h) *Tech* **gardes,** wards (*of lock*); (*partie d'une épée*) hilt; **(feuille** *ou* **page de) g.,** flyleaf;

(i) *Cartes* covering card, guard.

garde² **1** *nm* **(a)** keeper; *Hist Admin* **G. des Sceaux,** ≈ Lord Chancellor; *Hist* **G. des Archives,** ≈ Master of the Rolls; **(b)** (*personne qui surveille*) guard, watchman; *Mil* sentry; **g. de nuit,** night watchman; **g. champêtre,** rural policeman; **g. du corps,** bodyguard; **g. forestier,** forester, ranger, forest warden; **(c)** *Mil* guardsman; **gardes du corps,** lifeguards; **g. mobile,** mobile guard; = member of security police. **2** *nf* (*pour les malades*) nurse; (*pour les enfants*) nanny; **g. de nuit,** (*privately employed*) night nurse.

gardé [garde] *adj* guarded; *Cartes* **roi g.,** guarded king; **dame gardée,** guarded queen; **toute(s) proportion(s) gardée(s),** all things considered.

garde-à-vous [gardavu] *nm inv Mil* (position of) attention; **être** *ou* **se tenir au g.-à-v.,** to stand at *or* to attention; **au g.-à-v.,** at attention; **g.-à-v.!,** attention!

garde-barrière [gard(ə)barjɛr] *n* gatekeeper (*at level crossing*); (*pl gardes-barrière(s)*).

garde-boue [gard(ə)bu] *nm inv* mudguard (*of bicycle etc*).

garde-chasse [gard(ə)ʃas] *nm* gamekeeper; (*pl gardes-chasse(s)*).

garde-chiourme [gard(ə)ʃjurm] *nm Arch* warder (*of galley slaves*); *Fig* (*personne autoritaire et brutale*) martinet, tyrant, slavedriver; (*pl garde(s)-chiourme(s)*).

garde-corps [gard(ə)kɔr] *nm inv* (*mur*) parapet, balustrade; (*corde*) railing, side rail, guard rail, handrail (*of bridge etc*); *Nau* **g.-c. arrière,** stern rail.

garde-côte [gard(ə)kot] *nm* (*bateau*) coastguard vessel; coast-defence ship; *Vieilli* (*soldat*) coastguard (*pl garde-côte(s)*).

garde-feu [gard(ə)fø] *nm inv* fireguard.

garde-fou [gard(ə)fu] *nm* (*mur*) parapet, balustrade; (*en fer*) railing, handrail (*of bridge etc*); *Fig* safeguard; (*pl garde-fous*).

garde-frein [gard(ə)frɛ̃] *nm Rail* brakesman, *US* brakeman; (*pl gardes-frein(s)*).

garde-frontière [gard(ə)frɔ̃tjɛr] *nf* frontier guard; (*pl gardes-frontière(s)*).

garde-ligne [gard(ə)liɲ] *nm Rail* track watchman; (*pl gardes-ligne(s)*).

garde-magasin [gardmagazɛ̃] *nm* warehouseman; *Mil* quartermaster, barrack sergeant; (*pl gardes-magasin(s)*).

garde-malade [gard(ə)malad] *n* nurse; (*pl gardes-malade(s)*).

garde-manger [gardmɑ̃ʒe] *nm inv* meat safe.

garde-meuble [gard(ə)mœbl] *nm* furniture repository, warehouse; **mettre une table au g.-m.,** to put a table into storage *or* store; (*pl garde-meuble(s)*).

gardénal ® [gardenal] *nm Méd* ≈ Luminal ®.

gardénia [gardenja] *nm* gardenia.

garde-pêche¹ [gard(ə)pɛʃ] *nm* (*personne*) water bailiff, river keeper; (*pl gardes-pêche*).

garde-pêche² *nm inv* (*bateau*) fishery protection vessel.

garde-place [gard(ə)plas] *nm Rail* holder (*for reservation ticket*); **(ticket) g.-p.,** reservation ticket; (*pl garde-place(s)*).

garde-port [gard(ə)pɔr] *nm* wharfmaster (*on river*); (*pl gardes-port(s)*).

garder [garde] **1** *vt* **(a)** (*surveiller*) **g. la boutique,** to look after *or* mind the shop; **g. un troupeau,** to tend a flock; *F* **nous n'avons pas gardé les cochons ensemble!,** don't be so familiar!, don't take liberties!; **g. les enfants,** to mind the children; **elle garde des enfants pour se faire de l'argent de poche,** she does childminding to make a bit of pocket *or* extra money; **g. un prisonnier,** to guard *or* watch over *or* look after a prisoner; **g. qn à vue,** to keep a close watch on s.o.;

(b) (*protéger*) to guard, to protect, to keep watch over (*s.o., sth*); **g. qn d'un danger,** to protect s.o. from a danger; **que Dieu nous garde de la souffrance!,** may God protect *or* save *or* deliver us from suffering!;

(c) (*conserver*) to keep, to retain; **g. un vêtement,** to keep a garment; **donnez-moi votre veste — non merci, je la garde (sur moi),** give me your jacket — no thanks, I'll (just) keep it on; **g. qn à dîner,** to keep s.o. to dinner; **g. qn en otage,** to keep *or* hold s.o. as a hostage; **par cette chaleur il vaut mieux g. le lait au réfrigérateur,** it's better to keep the milk in the fridge in this heat; **g. une pièce intacte,** to keep a room as it was left *or* in its original state;

(d) (*continuer d'avoir*) to keep, to preserve; to put by, to keep (*a sum of money*); **g. les apparences,** to keep up appearances; **g. ses illusions/son innocence,** to keep one's illusions/innocence; **g. son sang-froid,** to keep cool (and collected); **g. rancune à qn,** to harbour *or US* harbor resentment against s.o.; **g. les yeux fermés,** to keep one's eyes closed; **g. le sourire,** to keep smiling; **g. son sérieux,** to keep a straight face; **g. la ligne,** to keep one's figure; **je garde un bon/mauvais souvenir de mon séjour en Italie,** I have (kept) a good/bad impression *or* memory of my stay in Italy;

(e) (*rester dans*) to remain in (*a place*); **g. la chambre,** to keep *or* stay in one's room; **être obligé de g. le lit,** to have to stay in bed, to be laid up;

(f) (*réserver*) to keep, to save; **garde-moi une place à côté de toi!,** save *or* keep me a place next to you!; **je vous ai gardé du café,** I've kept *or* saved you some coffee; *Fig* **g. une dent contre qn, g. un chien de sa chienne à qn,** to hold a grudge *or* have it in for s.o.; *Fig* **g. une poire pour la soif,** to keep sth in reserve, to keep sth for a rainy day; *Fig* **g. qch pour la bonne bouche,** to save the best till last *or* the end;

(g) (*respecter*) to observe, to respect; **g. les commandements,** to keep the commandments; **g. ses distances/son rang,** to keep one's distance/respect one's rank; **g. un secret,** to keep a secret; **garde ça pour toi,** (*je ne veux pas qu'on l'apprenne*) keep that to yourself.

2 se garder *vpr* **(a)** (*se méfier de*) **se g. de qn/qch,** to beware of s.o./sth;

(b) (*s'abstenir de*) **se g. de faire qch,** to take care not to do sth; **gardez-vous (bien) de le perdre,** mind you don't lose it!; **je m'en garderai bien!,** I shall do no such thing!, *F* no fear!;

(c) *Cartes* **se g. à trèfle,** to keep a guard in clubs;

(d) *F* (*conserver*) **tes réflexions, tu peux te les garder!,** you can keep your opinion(s) *or* thoughts *or* comments to yourself!;

(e) (*se conserver*) **viande qui ne se garde pas bien,** meat that does not keep well.

garderie [gard(ə)ri] *nf* **(a)** (*pour enfants en bas âge*) day nursery; (*dans magasin etc*) crèche; (*le soir, après l'école*) child-minding service; **(b)** (*forêt*) beat *or* domain of a ranger *or* keeper.

garde-rivière [gard(ə)rivjɛr] *nm* river policeman; (*pl gardes-rivière(s)*).

garde-robe [gard(ə)rɔb] *nf* (*meuble*) wardrobe; (*en-

semble des vêtements) wardrobe; **renouveler sa g.-r.,** to renew *or* replenish one's wardrobe; (*pl garde-robes*).

gardeur, -euse [gardœr, -øz] *n* keeper, tender; herdsman (*of animals*); **g. de cochons,** swineherd.

garde-voie [gard(ə)vwa] *nm Rail* track watchman; (*pl gardes-voie*).

gardian [gardjɑ̃] *nm* cowherd (*in the Camargue*).

gardien, -ienne [gardjɛ̃, -jɛn] **1** *n* guardian, keeper, watchman; (*concièrge*) caretaker, *US* janitor; (*museum, car park*) attendant; **g. de prison,** warder, *US* guard; **g. de nuit,** night watchman; **g. d'immeuble,** caretaker, concierge; **g. de la paix,** policeman; *Sp* **g. (de but),** goalkeeper; **g. des intérêts publics,** protector of the public interest; **se poser en g. de l'ordre,** to set oneself up as an upholder of public order. **2** *adj* **ange g.,** guardian angel; *Iron* bodyguard.

gardiennage [gardjɛnaʒ] *nm* guarding (*of bridges etc*); caretaking (*of building*); conservancy (*of port etc*); **société de g.,** security firm.

gardon [gardɔ̃] *nm* roach; *Fig* **frais comme un g.,** fresh as a daisy, *Am* bright-eyed and bushy-tailed.

gare[1] [gar] *nf* **(a)** (railway, *US* railroad) station; **g. (de voyageurs),** passenger station; **g. de marchandises,** goods *or* freight station *or* depot; **g. maritime,** harbour *or US* harbor station, maritime station; **(colis à prendre) en g.,** (parcel) to be (left till) called for; **g. de triage,** marshalling yard; **chef de g.,** stationmaster, station manager; **g. d'arrivée/de départ,** station of arrival/departure; **entrer *ou* arriver en g.,** (*d'un train*) to arrive in *or* come into the station; **café/hôtel de la g.,** station café/hotel; **(b) g. routière,** bus *or* coach station; **g. routière (de marchandises),** road haulage depot; **g. aérienne,** air terminal; **(c)** *Nau* **g. (fluviale),** (canal) wharf; basin, dock (*in river, canal*).

gare[2] *int* look out!, out of the way!, mind yourself!; **g. à toi/lui/*etc*,** woe betide you/him/*etc*, you've/he's/*etc* got it coming to you/him/*etc*; **g. à la casse!,** mind you don't break it!; **g. à la peinture!,** wet paint!; **sans crier g.,** without warning.

garenne [garɛn] *nf* **(a)** (rabbit) warren; **lapin de g.,** wild rabbit; **(b)** (*réserve*) (fishing) preserve.

garer [gare] **1** *vt* **(a)** (*une voiture*) to park; (*un bateau*) to dock; (*un train*) to shunt on to a siding; **(b)** (*mettre à l'abri*) to put (*car*) in the garage; to put (*aircraft*) into the hangar. **2 se garer** *vpr* **(a)** to park (*a car*); **la voiture s'est garée le long du trottoir,** the car parked *or* drew in beside the pavement; *F* **j'ai eu de la peine à me g.,** I've had trouble parking; **(b) se g. de qch,** to avoid *or* get out of the way of *or* steer clear of sth.

Gargantua [gargɑ̃tɥa] *nm F* glutton, guzzler.

gargantuesque [gargɑ̃tɥɛsk] *adj* gargantuan; **un appétit/un repas g.,** a gargantuan appetite/meal.

gargariser (se) [səgargarize] *vpr* to gargle; *F Péj* **se g. de formules pédantes,** to delight *or* revel in pedantic expressions.

gargarisme [gargarism] *nm* (*produit*) gargle; (*action de se gargariser*) gargling.

gargote [gargɔt] *nf Péj* (cheap) bad restaurant.

gargotier, -ière [gargɔtje, -jɛr] *n Péj* (*patron d'une gargote*) keeper of poor restaurant; (*mauvais cuisinier*) poor cook.

gargouille [garguj] *nf* **(a)** *Archit* gargoyle; **(b)** (water)spout (*of roof gutter, of pump*).

gargouillement [gargujmɑ̃] *nm* **(a)** (*eau*) gurgling, bubbling (*of water*); **(b)** rumbling (*of stomach*), *F* tummy rumbles.

gargouiller [garguje] *vi* **(a)** (*of water*) to gurgle, to bubble; **(b)** (*of the stomach*) to rumble; **(c) sol qui gargouille sous les pas,** squelchy *or* squishy ground.

gargouillis [garguji] *nm* = **GARGOUILLEMENT.**

garnement [garnəmɑ̃] *nm* (*child*) scamp, imp, rascal; **quel petit g., il a encore mangé tous les gâteaux!,** that little rascal *or* pest has gone and eaten all the cakes again!

garni [garni] **1** *adj* **(a) bien g.,** well-lined (*purse*); well-stocked (*shop*); well-appointed (*house*); **chevelure bien garnie,** thick head of hair; **panier g.,** food hamper, hamper of food; **(b)** *Culin* **plat g.,** meat with vegetables; **choucroute garnie,** sauerkraut with sausages; **(c)** *Vieilli* (*meublé*) furnished (*room*). **2** *nm Vieilli* (*meublé*) furnished room(s).

garnir [garnir] **1** *vt* **(a)** (*munir de ce qui protège, renforce etc*) to fit out, to furnish (**de,** with); **g. qch à l'intérieur,** to line sth; **garni de feutre,** felt-lined; **g. un mur de plaques de polystyrène,** to cover *or* line a wall with polystyrene tiles; **g. un fauteuil,** to stuff an armchair;

(b) (*embellir, compléter*) to trim (*dress, hat etc*); **une robe garnie de dentelle,** a dress trimmed with lace, a lace-trimmed dress; **la passementerie qui garnit cette veste est très colorée,** the braid trimming on that jacket is very colourful;

(c) *Culin* to garnish (*a dish*); **une entrecôte garnie de pommes frites et de salade,** a (rib) steak (served) with chips and salad;

(d) (*remplir*) **g. une étagère de disques,** to fill a shelf with records.

2 se garnir *vpr* **la salle se garnit,** the hall *or* the house is beginning to fill (up).

garnison [garnizɔ̃] *nf Mil* garrison; **mettre une g. dans une ville,** to garrison a town; **ville de g.,** garrison town; **être en g. *ou* tenir g. dans une ville,** to be garrisoned *or* in garrison *or* stationed in a town.

garnissage [garnisaʒ] *nm* **(a)** (*remplissage*) garnishing, furnishing; (*décoration*) trimming, facing (*of coat*); **(b)** *Tech* packing (*of piston*); lagging (*of boiler*); **(c)** (*matériau*) packing, stuffing; *Métal* lining (*of furnace*); **(d)** *Tex* napping, raising (*of cloth*).

garnisseur, -euse [garnisœr, -øz] *n* **(a)** garnisher, trimmer (*of hats, dresses etc*); **(b)** fitter (*of cases etc*); **(c)** (*of cloth*) *Tex* napper.

garniture [garnityr] *nf* **(a)** mountings (*of a rifle*); rigging (*of a ship*); (metal) furnishings (*of chest of drawers etc*); **g. de lit,** bedding; **garnitures d'une serrure,** wards of a lock; **g. d'une pompe à incendie,** hose of a fire engine; **g. intérieure d'une voiture,** upholstery of a car;

(b) (*ornement*) trimming, decoration (*of hat, dress etc*);

(c) (*ensemble de pièces pour consolider, protéger, orner*) (complete) set (*of buttons, ornaments etc*); **g. de feu *ou* de foyer,** fire irons; **g. de bureau,** desk *or* writing set; **g. de toilette,** toilet set; **g. de cheminée,** fireside *or* fireplace ornaments;

(d) *Culin* garnish(ing) (*of dish*); **pour la g., vous avez le choix entre des haricots verts ou des frites,** to go with it, you have a choice of green beans or chips;

(e) *Tech* packing (*of stuffing box*); stuffing (piece); (packing) ring (*of piston*);

(f) lagging (*of boiler*);

(g) *Aut etc* **g. de frein,** brake lining; (*of disc brake*) brake pad; **g. d'embrayage,** clutch lining;

(h) *Typ* furniture.

garrigue [garig] *nf Géog* garrigue.

garrocher [garɔʃe] *vt Can Arg* to throw (*stones etc*).

garrot[1] [garo] *nm* **(a)** *Méd* tourniquet; **appliquer un g.,** to put on a tourniquet; **(b)** *Tech* rack-stick, rack-pin; **g. d'une scie,** tongue of frame-saw; **(c)** *Arch* **(supplice du) g.,** gar(r)otting, gar(r)otte.

garrot[2] *nm Zool* withers (*of horse, cow etc*).

garrottage [garɔtaʒ] *nm* **g. d'une blessure,** putting a tourniquet on a wound.

garrotte [garɔt] *nf Arch* gar(r)otte, gar(r)otting.

garrotter [garɔte] *vt* to tie up, to pinion (*prisoner etc*); *Fig* **g. les opposants au régime,** to muzzle *or* silence the régime's opponents.

gars [gɑ] *nm F* boy, (young) man; **un petit g.,** a little boy; **un beau g.,** a fine *or* handsome young man; **un brave g.,** a good lad; **un drôle de g.,** an odd bloke; **d'où il sort ce gars-là,** and where was he brought up then?; **allons-y, les g.!,** come on, boys!; **bonjour, mon petit g.!,** (*à un enfant*) hullo young man!

Gascogne [gaskɔɲ] *nf* Gascony; **le Golfe de G.,** the Bay of Biscay.

gascon, -onne [gaskɔ̃, -ɔn] **1** *adj* Gascon. **2** *nm Ling* Gascon. **3** *n* **G.,** Gascon; **faire le G.,** to boast, to brag; **promesse de G.,** hollow *or* empty promise.

gasconnade [gaskɔnad] *nf* boasting, bragging.

gas(-)oil [gɑzɔjl] *nm* diesel oil, diesel fuel, *US* gas oil.

gaspard [gaspar] *nm Arg* rat.

gaspillage [gaspijaʒ] *nm* waste, wasting, squandering (*of money etc*); **pas de g.!,** don't be wasteful!; **quel g.!,** what a waste!

gaspiller [gaspije] *vt* to waste, to squander (*money*); **g. son temps,** to waste one's time; **g. sa vie,** to make a mess of one's life.

gaspilleur, -euse [gaspijœr, -øz] **1** *n* waster. **2** *adj* **il est très g.,** he's very wasteful.

gastéropode [gasterɔpɔd] *nm Zool* gast(e)ropod.

gastralgie [gastralʒi] *nf Méd* gastralgia, stomach pains.

gastralgique [gastralʒik] *adj Méd* gastralgic.

gastrectomie [gastrɛktɔmi] *nf Chir* gastrectomy.

gastrique [gastrik] *adj* gastric; **embarras g.,** stomach upset.

gastrite [gastrit] *nf Méd* gastritis.
gastro-entérite [gastrɔɑ̃terit] *nf Méd* gastroenteritis; (*pl gastro-entérites*).
gastro-entérologie [gastrɔɑ̃terɔlɔʒi] *nf Méd* gastroenterology.
gastro-entérologue [gastrɔɑ̃terɔlɔg] *n Méd* gastroenterologist; (*pl gastro-entérologues*).
gastronome [gastrɔnɔm] *nm* gastronome, gourmet.
gastronomie [gastrɔnɔmi] *nf* gastronomy.
gastronomique [gastrɔnɔmik] *adj* gastronomic(al).
gastropode [gastrɔpɔd] *nm Zool* gast(e)ropod.
gate [geit] *nf Electron* gate.
gâté [gɑte] *adj* **(a)** (*pourri*) damaged (*fruit etc*); **œufs gâtés,** rotten eggs; **viande gâtée,** meat that has gone off *or* is bad; **dents gâtées,** rotton *or* decayed teeth; **(b)** *Fig* **enfant g.,** (*à qui on cède tout*) spoilt or pampered child; (*chouchou*) pet, favourite, *US* favorite; **l'enfant g. de la famille,** the blue-eyed boy of the family.
gâteau, -eaux [gɑto] **1** *nm* **(a)** cake; (open) tart; (cold, sweet) pudding; **faire un g.,** to make *or* bake a cake; **gros g. à la crème,** gâteau; **g. sec,** (sweet) biscuit; **g. de riz,** ≈ rice pudding; **g. de semoule,** semolina pudding; **g. d'anniversaire,** birthday cake; *F* **c'est du g.,** it's a piece of cake; *F* **partager le g., avoir sa part du g.,** to share the profit *or* the loot, to have one's slice of the cake; **(b)** (*masse compacte, plate*) lump (*of any material*); disc (*of gun cotton etc*); **g. de miel,** (*dans une ruche*) honeycomb. **2** *adj inv F* **papa g.,** (*qui cède tout à ses enfants*) easy-going *or* over-indulgent daddy; (*qui gâte les enfants des autres*) friend of the family who spoils the children; *F* **marraine g.,** fairy godmother.
gâter [gɑte] **1** *vt* **(a)** to spoil, to damage; **la grêle gâte le blé,** hail damages wheat; **les mouches gâtent la viande,** flies infect meat; **g. un vêtement,** to spoil a garment; **ce qui ne gâte rien,** which won't do any harm, which is no bad thing; **il a tout gâté,** he's spoiled *or* made a hash of everything; **(b)** (*céder à tous les caprices de qn*) to pamper; **g. ses enfants,** to spoil *or* pamper *or* overindulge one's children; **à Noël, il a été très gâté,** he was really spoilt at Christmas. **2 se gâter** *vpr* to turn bad, to deteriorate; **le poisson se gâte facilement,** fish easily goes bad; **le temps se gâte,** the weather is breaking up, it's turning wet; **les affaires se gâtent,** things are going wrong *or* taking a turn for the worse.
gâterie [gɑtri] *nf* **(a)** (*petit cadeau*) treat, small present; **(b)** (*friandise*) treats, goodies (*for children*).
gâte-sauce [gatsos] *nm* kitchen boy; *Vieilli* bad cook.
gâteux, -euse [gɑtø, -øz] **1** *n* doddering old man *or* lady. **2** *adj* senile, gaga.
gâtisme [gɑtism] *nm* senility, senile decay.
GATT [gat] *nm Écon* (*abrév* **General Agreement on Tariffs and Trade**) GATT.
gauche [goʃ] **1** *adj* **(a)** (*maladroit*) awkward, clumsy (*person, manner*); clumsy, bungling (*attempt*); **son style est assez g.,** he's got a rather awkward style; **attraper un objet d'un geste g.,** to catch an object awkwardly *or* clumsily;
(b) (*par opposition à droit*) **main g.,** left hand; *Fig* **mariage de la main g.,** living together (*as man and wife*), common-law marriage; *Fig* **se lever du pied g.,** to get out of bed on the wrong side; **rive g.,** left bank (*of river*); *Equitation Aut* **côté g.,** near side;
(c) *Tech* (*déformé*) warped, crooked, out of true, skew (*surface etc*).
2 *nf* **(a)** (*côté*) **assis à ma g.,** seated on my left; **mon voisin de g.,** my left-hand neighbour; **le tiroir de g.,** the left-hand drawer; **à g.,** on the left(-hand side), to the left; **tournez à g.,** turn left; **la première rue à g.,** the first street on the left; **sur votre g., vous pouvez voir la tour Eiffel,** on your left (-hand side) you can see the Eiffel Tower; **à g. de la porte d'entrée,** on *or* to the left of the entrance; **en France, on double à g.,** in France, you overtake on the left; **lire de g. à droite,** to read from left to right; *F* **mettre de l'argent à g.,** to put money aside on the sly; *F* **passer l'arme à g.,** to kick the bucket; **vis/hélice à pas de g.,** left-handed screw/left-hand propeller; **jusqu'à la g.,** to the end, to the last, right up to the hilt; **ils nous ont eus jusqu'à la g.,** they cheated us left, right and centre;
(b) *Pol* **la G.,** the Left; **(politique) de g.,** left-wing (politics); **homme de g.,** man of the left; **l'extrême g.,** the far *or* extreme left; **être à g.,** to be on the left, to be left-wing; **voter à g.,** to vote on the left, to vote left-wing.
3 *nm Boxe etc* (*le poing gauche*) **feinter du g.,** to feint with the left; **un crochet du g.,** a left hook.
gauchement [goʃmɑ̃] *adv* awkwardly, clumsily.
gaucher, -ère [goʃe, -ɛr] **1** *adj* left-handed. **2** *n* left-hander.
gaucherie [goʃri] *nf* awkwardness, clumsiness, gaucherie.
gauchi [goʃi] *adj Tech* = **GAUCHE 1 (c)**.
gauchir [goʃir] **1** *vi* (*of wood etc*) to warp; (*of iron*) to buckle. **2** *vt* **(a)** (*déformer*) to camber (*sth*); **(b)** *Av* **g. l'aileron,** to bank; **(c)** *Fig* **g. une idée/un événement,** to misrepresent *or* distort an idea/event. **3 se gauchir** *vpr* (*of wood etc*) to warp; (*of iron*) to buckle.
gauchisant, -ante [goʃizɑ̃, -ɑ̃t] **1** *adj* **écrivain g.,** writer with left-wing tendencies. **2** *n* **c'est un g.,** he has left-wing tendencies, *F* he's a bit of a lefty.
gauchisme [goʃism] *nm Pol* leftism.
gauchissement [goʃismɑ̃] *nm* **(a)** warping, buckling; **(b)** *Av* banking.
gauchiste [goʃist] **1** *adj Pol* left-wing, leftist. **2** *n* left-winger, leftist, *F* lefty.
gaudriole [godrijɔl] *nf F Vieilli* **(a)** (*plaisanterie grivoise*) dirty *or* saucy story, broad joke; **(b) il/elle ne pense qu'à la g.,** he/she thinks of nothing but womanising/manhunting, he/she is interested in only one thing.
gaufrage [gofraʒ] *nm* embossing (*of leather etc*); goffering, fluting (*of linen*); crinkling, crumpling (*of paper*); blocking (*of cover*).
gaufre [gofr] *nf* **(a)** *Culin* waffle; **moule à gaufres,** waffle iron; **(b) g. de miel,** honeycomb.
gaufrer [gofre] *vt* to figure, to emboss (*leather, velvet etc*); to goffer, to flute (*linen*); to corrugate (*iron, paper*); to crinkle (*paper*); to block (*cover*).
gaufrette [gofrɛt] *nf Culin* wafer (biscuit).
gaufrier [gofrije] *nm Culin* waffle iron.
gaufrure [gofryr] *nf* (*on leather etc*) stamped design; (*on linen*) goffering.
gaule [gol] *nf* long thin pole *or* stick; *Pêche* fishing rod.
Gaule [gol] *nf Antiq* Gaul.
gauler [gole] *vt* to beat, to thrash (*fruit, walnut tree*).
gaullien, -ienne [goljɛ̃,-jɛn] *adj* de Gaulle-like.
gaullisme [golism] *nm Pol* Gaullism.
gaulliste [golist] *adj & n Pol* Gaullist.
gaulois, -oise [golwa, -waz] **1** *adj* Gallic, of Gaul; **esprit g.,** (broad) Gallic humour; **contes g.,** spicy stories. **2** *nm Ling* (the) Gallic (tongue). **3** *n* **les G.,** the Gauls. **4** *nf* **Gauloise** ®, Gauloise ® (*popular brand of cigarette*).
gauloiserie [golwazri] *nf* broad joke, spicy *or* saucy story.
gausser (se) [səgose] *vpr Litt* **se g. de qn,** to laugh at *or* make fun of *or* sneer at s.o..
Gautier [gotje] *nm* Walter.
gavage [gavaʒ] *nm* (*engraissement*) force-feeding, cramming (*of poultry*); *Méd* force-feeding.
gave [gav] *nm Géog* (mountain) torrent (*in the Pyrenees*).
gaver [gave] **1** *vt* **(a)** (*engraisser*) to cram (*poultry*); *Méd* to force-feed (*s.o.*); **(b)** to fill (*s.o.*) up, to stuff (*s.o.*) (*with food*). **2 se gaver** *vpr F* to gorge oneself.
gavotte [gavɔt] *nf Mus* gavotte.
gay [gɛ(e)] *adj & nm F* gay; **une boîte de nuit g.,** a gay night-club.
gaz [gɑz] *nm* **(a)** gas; **gisement de g.,** gas field; **g. des marais,** marsh gas; **g. rare,** rare gas; **g. carbonique,** carbon dioxide; **bouteille à g.** *ou* **tube de g. comprimé,** gas cylinder; **g. d'éclairage,** lighting gas, coal gas, town gas; **g. de ville,** town gas, mains gas; **faire la cuisine au g.,** to cook by gas; **cuisinière à g.,** gas cooker; **allumer/couper le g.,** to light/turn off the gas; **réchaud à g.,** gas ring; **usine à g.,** gasworks; **g. hilarant,** laughing gas; **g. asphyxiant** *ou* **toxique,** poison gas; **g. lacrymogène,** tear gas; **chambre à g.,** gas chamber; *F* **il y a de l'eau dans le g.,** there are *or* have been a few hiccups *or* hitches;
(b) *Aut* **g. d'échappement,** exhaust fumes; *F* **mettre les g.,** to open the throttle, to put one's foot down, *Am* to step on the gas; **à pleins g.,** with the throttle full open, flat out;
(c) *Méd* **avoir des g.,** to suffer from flatulence, to have wind; **lâcher un g.,** to break wind.
gazage [gazaʒ] *nm Mil* gassing.
gaze [gɑz] *nf* **(a)** gauze; **g. métallique,** wire gauze; *Méd* **g. oxygénée,** antiseptic *or* sterilized gauze; **(b)** *Vieilli* thin veil.
gazé, -ée [gaze] **1** *adj* gassed; **soldats gazés,** soldiers killed by (poison) gas. **2** *n* (*poison*) gas victim.
gazéification [gazeifikasjɔ̃] *nf Ch* gasification; (*des boissons*) carbonation.
gazéifier [gazeifje] *vt* (*pr sub & impf* **n. gazéifiions, v. gazéifiiez**) *Ch* to gasify; (*des boissons*) to carbonate.
gazelle [gazɛl] *nf* gazelle.
gazer [gaze] **1** *vt Mil* to gas (*troops*). **2** *vi F* (*aller vite*) to

go at top speed; **ça gaze!,** everything's O.K.!, we're doing fine!; **ça gaze?,** all right?, everything O.K.?

gazetier [gaztje] *nm Arch* journalist.

gazette [gazɛt] *nf Vieilli (journal)* gazette, news sheet; *F* **cette femme est la g. de l'immeuble,** that woman can tell you *or* knows everything that's happening in the building, that woman knows all the latest local gossip.

gazeux, -euse [gazø, -øz] *adj* **(a)** gaseous; **(b)** carbonated, fizzy (*water etc*); fizzy, sparkling (*drink*).

gazier, -ière [gazje, gazje, -jɛr] **1** *adj* **l'industrie gazière,** the gas industry. **2** *nm* (*dans une usine à gaz*) employee at gas works; (*chargé des installations dans les immeubles etc*) gas fitter, gasman; *Arg* **qui est ce g.-là?,** who's that guy over there?

gazinière [gazinjɛr] *nf* gas cooker.

gazoduc [gazɔdyk, gaz-] *nm* gas pipeline, gas main.

gazogène [gazɔʒɛn, gaz-] *nm* gas producer, gas generator; **gaz de g.,** producer gas.

gazole [gazɔl] *nm* = **GAS(-)OIL.**

gazoline [gazɔlin] *nf* gasolene, gasoline.

gazomètre [gazɔmɛtr] *nm* gasometer, gas holder.

gazon [gazɔ̃] *nm* **(a)** (*herbe*) grass, turf; **(b)** (*surface*) lawn; **défense de marcher sur le g.,** keep off the grass; **(c)** (*motte de terre*) turf, sod; **(d)** *Bot* **g. mousse,** mossy saxifrage.

gazonnage [gazɔnaʒ] *nm* turfing, planting with turf.

gazonné [gazɔne] *adj* grass-covered, turfed.

gazonnement [gazɔnmã] *nm* = **GAZONNAGE.**

gazonner [gazɔne] **1** *vt* to cover with turf, to turf. **2** *vi* (*of land*) to become covered with grass.

gazonneux, -euse [gazɔnø, -øz] *adj* turfy, covered with turf.

gazouillant [gazujã] *adj* (*d'un oiseau*) warbling, chirping, twittering; (*d'un bébé*) babbling, gurgling; (*d'un enfant*) prattle, prattling; **ruisseau g.,** babbling brook.

gazouillement [gazujmã] *nm* twittering, warbling, chirping (*of birds*); babbling, murmuring (*of running water*); prattle, prattling (*of children*).

gazouiller [gazuje] *vi* (*of bird*) to twitter, to warble, to chirp; (*of water*) to babble, to murmur; (*of child*) to prattle.

gazouilleur, -euse [gazujœr, -øz] *adj* warbling, twittering (*bird*); babbling (*stream*); prattling (*child*).

gazouillis [gazuji] *nm* = **GAZOUILLEMENT.**

G.B. [ʒebe] *nf* (*abrév* **Grande-Bretagne**) GB.

G.-C. [ʒese] *abrév* **grand-croix.**

GDF [ʒedeɛf] *nm abrév* **Gaz de France.**

geai [ʒɛ] *nm Orn* jay.

géant, -ante [ʒeã, -ãt] **1** *n* **(a)** *Myth* giant, *f* giantess; **(b)** (*personne anormalement grande*) giant; *Gym* **pas de g.,** giant stride; *Fig* **avancer à pas de g.,** to make giant strides forward, to make spectacular progress; **la Chaussée des Géants,** the Giant's Causeway; **(c)** (*personne exceptionnelle*) **les géants de l'art,** the great masters; **les géants du football,** the football stars *or* greats. **2** *adj* giant, gigantic; **arbre g.,** giant tree; *Com* **carton g.,** giant(-size) packet; *TV* **écran g.,** large screen.

gecko [ʒeko] *nm* gecko.

Gédéon [ʒedeɔ̃] *nm* Gideon.

géhenne [ʒeɛn] *nf Bible* Gehenna, Hell; *Fig Litt* **sa vie est une g.,** his life is a hell on earth.

geignant [ʒɛɲã] *adj* whimpering, whining, fretful.

geignard, -arde [ʒɛɲar, -ard] *F* **1** *adj* fretful, (given to) whining, grumbling; **une voix geignarde,** a whining *or* whinging voice. **2** *n* whiner.

geignement [ʒɛɲmã] *nm* (*action*) whining, whimpering; (*résultat*) whine, whimper.

geindre [ʒɛ̃dr] *vi* (*prp* **geignant**; *pp* **geint**; *pr ind* **je geins, il geint, n. geignons, ils geignent**; *impf* **je geignais**; *p hist* **je geignis**; *fu* **je geindrai**) **(a)** (*gémir*) to whine, to whimper; **g. de douleur,** to moan *or* groan with pain; **(b)** *F* (*se plaindre constamment*) to complain, to grumble; **arrête de g. comme ça!,** stop moaning *or* whining like that!

gel [ʒɛl] *nm* **(a)** (*congélation de l'eau*) frost, freezing; *Fig* **g. des négociations,** suspension of negotiations; **g. des subventions,** freezing of subsidies; **(b)** (*dans les produits cosmétiques*) (*pour les cheveux*) (hair) gel; **dentrifrice en g.,** gel toothpaste; **g. douche,** shower gel; **se mettre du g.,** to use *or* put gel on one's hair; **(c)** *Ch* gel.

gélatine [ʒelatin] *nf* gelatin(e); **g. détonante, g. explosive,** blasting gelatine, gum dynamite; *Culin* **feuille de g.,** sheet of gelatine.

gélatiné [ʒelatine] *adj* gelatinized.

gélatineux, -euse [ʒelatinø, -øz] *adj* gelatinous.

gélatinisant [ʒelatinizã] *nm Tech* plasticizer.

gelé [ʒ(ə)le] *adj* (*lac, rivière*) frozen; (*nez etc*) frostbitten; (*plante*) frost-nipped; *Fig* (*assistance*) cold, indifferent; *Fin* (*bloqué*) frozen (*assets etc*); *F* **je suis absolument g.,** I'm absolutely frozen; *F* **être g. jusqu'aux os,** to be chilled to the marrow *or* bone; **ils ont eu les pieds gelés,** they got frostbite in their feet.

gelée [ʒ(ə)le] *nf* **(a)** (*gel*) frost; **forte g.,** hard frost; **g. blanche,** hoar (frost), white frost; **temps à la g.,** frosty weather; **(b)** *Culin* jelly; **g. de veau/poulet,** veal/chicken jelly; **g. de cassis,** blackcurrant jelly; **g. royale,** (*des abeilles*) royal jelly.

geler [ʒ(ə)le] *v* (**je gèle, n. gelons; je gèlerai**) **1** *vt* **(a)** to freeze; **froid qui gèle les conduites d'eau,** cold that freezes the water pipes; **(b)** *Fin (bloquer)* to freeze (*credits, capital*). **2** *vi* (*d'un lac, d'une rivière*) to become frozen, to freeze; **l'étang a gelé d'un bout à l'autre,** the pond has *or* is completely frozen over; **plantes qui gèlent facilement,** plants easily damaged by frost; **on gèle dans cette salle,** this room is like an icehouse, it's freezing in here. **3** *v impers* **il gèle,** it is freezing; **il gèle dur** *ou* **à pierre fendre,** it's freezing hard; **il a gelé blanc cette nuit,** there was a white frost last night.

gélifier [ʒelifje] *Ch* **1** *vt* (*transformer en gel*) to gel. **2 se gélifier** *vpr* to gel.

gelinotte [ʒ(ə)linɔt] *nf* **g. (des bois),** hazel grouse; **g. des prairies,** prairie chicken.

gélose [ʒeloz] *nf Ch* agar-agar.

gélule [ʒelyl] *nf Pharm* capsule.

gelure [ʒ(ə)lyr] *nf* frostbite.

Gémeaux (les) [leʒemo] *nmpl Astron* Gemini; **être (du signe des) Gémeaux,** to be a Gemini.

gémellaire [ʒemelɛr] *adj* twin (*pregnancy etc*).

gémellité [ʒemelite] *nf* **taux de g.,** incidence of twin births.

gémination [ʒeminasjɔ̃] *nf Biol etc* gemination.

géminé [ʒemine] *adj* **(a)** *Biol* geminate, twin (*leaves etc*); *Ch* geminate; *Archit* **colonnes géminées,** twin columns; **(b)** *Ling* **consonnes/voyelles géminées,** doubled *or* geminate consonants/vowels.

gémir [ʒemir] *vi* **(a)** to groan, to moan; **g. de douleur,** to groan *or* moan with pain; **je gémissais de les voir (faire cela),** I could have wept to see them (doing that); **g. sous le joug de la tyrannie,** to groan under the yoke of tyranny; **le vent gémissait dans la cheminée,** the wind was moaning in the chimney; **(b)** (*d'une colombe, tourterelle*) to coo.

gémissant [ʒemisã] *adj* moaning; **voix gémissante,** wailing voice; **essieu g.,** creaking axle.

gémissement [ʒemismã] *nm* **(a)** groan(ing), moan(ing), **le g. du vent,** the moaning of the wind; **(b)** (*d'une colombe etc*) cooing.

gemmage [ʒemaʒ] *nm* tapping (*of trees for resin*).

gemme [ʒɛm] **1** *nf* **(a)** *Minér* gem, precious stone; **(b)** (*sève*) pine resin; **(c)** *Bot Arch* (leaf) bud. **2** *adj* **pierre g.,** gem stone; **sel g.,** rock salt.

gemmé [ʒeme] *adj Litt* gemmed, jewelled.

gemmer [ʒeme] **1** *vi* (*of trees*) to bud. **2** *vt* to tap (*trees for resin*).

gemmeur [ʒɛmœr] *nm* tapper.

gémonies [ʒemɔni] *nfpl Litt* **traîner** *ou* **vouer qn aux g.,** to hold s.o. up to public obloquy.

gênant [ʒɛnã] *adj* **(a)** (*embarrassant*) (*personne*) embarrassing; (*situation, silence*) embarrassing, awkward; **(b)** (*encombrant*) in the way; (*objet*) cumbersome; **votre fils n'est pas g.,** your son is no trouble; **les jupes longues sont gênantes,** long skirts are awkward *or* are a nuisance.

gencive [ʒãsiv] *nf* **(a)** *Anat* gum; **abcès à la g.,** abscess on the gum, gumboil; **(b)** *Arg* **gencives,** jaw(s); **un coup dans les gencives,** a punch on the jaw.

gendarme [ʒãdarm] *nm* **(a)** gendarme, member of the state police force, *Br* ≈ police constable; *F* (*woman*) martinet; **gendarmes à cheval,** ≈ mounted police; **gendarmes motocyclistes,** motorcycle police; **jouer aux gendarmes et aux voleurs,** (*of children*) to play (at) cops and robbers; *F* **faire le g.,** to boss people about; *F* **la peur du g.,** fear of being caught; **chapeau de g.,** = paper hat; **(b)** flaw (*in jewel*); **(c)** *Géol* rock pinnacle, gendarme; **(d)** *Culin F* (*hareng saur*) red herring; (*saucisson*) flat, dry sausage.

gendarmer (se) [səʒãdarme] *vpr* to be up in arms (*against s.o., a proposal etc*); **il n'y a pas de quoi se g.,** there's nothing to get worked up about.

gendarmerie [ʒãdarməri] *nf* **(a)** (*corps*) (*in France*) state police force; **la G. royale du Canada,** the Royal Canadian Mounted Police; **(b)** (*lieu*) barracks, headquarters (*of the* *gendarmes*).

gendre [ʒɑ̃dr] *nm* son-in-law.

gène [ʒɛn] *nm Biol* gene; **structure du g.,** gene structure; **banque/famille de gènes,** gene bank/family.

gêne [ʒɛn] *nf* **(a)** (*malaise*) embarrassment, constraint; **éprouver une certaine g. à parler en public,** to feel rather ill at ease *or* embarrassed when speaking in public; **ressentir de la g. en présence de qn,** to feel ill at ease *or* embarrassed *or* constrained in s.o.'s presence; **nous prions nos clients de bien vouloir excuser la g. occasionnée par les travaux,** we apologise to customers for the inconvenience caused by the work; *Prov* **où (il) y a de la g., (il n') y a pas de plaisir,** ≈ there's no need to stand on ceremony; **sentir de la g. dans la respiration,** to have difficulty (in) breathing; **vous ne me causerez aucune g.,** you won't inconvenience me in the least; **sans g.,** unconventional, free and easy; **il est sans g.!,** he's a cool customer!; **ça, c'est un peu sans g.!,** that's a bit much!;

(b) (*manque d'argent*) **être dans la g.,** to be in financial difficulties;

(c) *Arch* (*physical, moral*) torture.

gêné [ʒene] *adj* **(a)** (*embarrassé*) embarrassed, ill at ease; **il n'est jamais g.,** he's never embarrassed, he's got no inhibitions; **elle avait l'air g. d'arriver si tard,** she seemed embarrassed at arriving so late; **je serais trop g. de le lui dire,** I'm too embarrassed to tell him; **silence g.,** embarrassed *or* awkward *or* uneasy silence; **(b)** (*qui manque d'argent*) in financial difficulties.

généalogie [ʒenealɔʒi] *nf* **(a)** genealogy, pedigree, descent; pedigree (*of horse etc*); **(b)** (science of) genealogy.

généalogique [ʒenealɔʒik] *adj* genealogical; **arbre g.,** family tree, genealogical tree; **livre g.,** stud book (*of horses*); herd book (*of cattle*).

généalogiquement [ʒenealɔʒikmɑ̃] *adv* genealogically.

généalogiste [ʒenealɔʒist] *n* genealogist.

gêner [ʒene] **1** *vt* **(a)** (*perturber, empêcher*) to hinder, to obstruct; to be in (*s.o.'s*) way; to interfere with (*an activity*); **g. la circulation,** to hold up the traffic; **g. la vue,** to obstruct *or* block the view; **cette valise vous gêne-t-elle?,** is this bag in your way?; **j'ai été gêné par le manque de temps/place/***etc*, I was hindered by the lack of time/space *etc*; **cela vous gênerait-il que je revienne demain?,** would it disturb you *or* bother you *or* put you out if I come back tomorrow?; **le froid ne me gêne pas,** I don't mind the cold; **la fumée (de tabac) vous gêne-t-elle?,** do you mind my smoking?;

(b) (*serrer*) to constrict, to cramp; **mes souliers me gênent,** my shoes pinch *or* are too tight; **on est gêné ici,** it's cramped *or* too crowded here;

(c) (*mettre mal à l'aise*) to embarrass; **cela me gênerait de le rencontrer,** it would be awkward for me to meet him; **sa présence me gêne,** I feel awkward *or* embarrassed in his presence, his presence makes me feel ill at ease.

2 se gêner *vpr* (*par discrétion, timidité*) to put oneself under some restraint, to put oneself out; **je ne me suis pas gêné pour le lui dire,** I didn't hesitate to tell him so, I made no bones about telling him so; **il ne se gêne pas avec nous,** he doesn't stand on ceremony with us, he makes himself at home; **elle aurait tort de se g.,** she has no need to feel embarrassed; *Iron* **il ne se gêne pas!,** he's not backward in coming forward!; *Iron* **ne vous gênez pas!,** that's right! make yourself at home!; *Iron* **faut pas se g.!,** don't mind me!

général, -ale, -aux [ʒeneral, -o] **1** *adj* general; **assemblée/amnistie générale,** general assembly/amnesty; **appeler à une grève générale,** to call a general strike; *Th* **répétition générale,** dress rehearsal; **état g.,** general *or* overall condition; **médecine générale,** general medicine; **président directeur-g.,** chairman and managing director; **inspecteur g.,** inspector general; **quartier g.,** headquarters; *Fr Hist & Channel Islands* **états généraux,** states general; **officier g.,** *Mil etc* general officer; *Nau* flag officer; **le consentement g.,** common consent; **d'une façon générale,** generally speaking, broadly speaking; **en règle générale,** as a general rule, in general; **en g.,** in general, generally (speaking), as a rule; **la nature humaine en g.,** human nature in general; **en g., elle se couche tôt,** she goes to bed early as a rule.

2 *nm* **(a)** (*ce qui est universel*) the general; **passer du g. au particulier,** to go from the general to the particular;

(b) *Mil* general; **g. de brigade,** brigadier, *US* brigadier general; **g. de division,** major general; **g. de corps d'armée,** lieutenant general; **g. d'armée,** (army) general; *Mil Av* **g. de brigade aérienne,** air commodore, *US* brigadier general; **g. de division aérienne,** air vice-marshal, *US* major general; **g. de corps d'armée aérienne,** air marshal, *US* lieutenant general; **g. d'armée aérienne,** air chief marshal, *US* major general;

3 *nf* **générale (a)** *Th* dress rehearsal;

(b) (*alerte*) alarm call; **battre la générale,** to call to arms, to sound the alarm; *Nau* to beat to quarters;

(c) madame la générale, the general's wife.

généralement [ʒeneralmɑ̃] *adv* generally; **g. parlant,** generally speaking, on the whole, broadly speaking; **il y a g. une trentaine d'élèves par classe,** there are generally *or* usually about thirty pupils in a class; **une coutume très g. diffusée,** a very widespread custom.

généralisable [ʒeneralizabl(ə)] *adj* that can be generalized; **ça n'est pas g.,** (*ce que tu viens de dire*) you can't generalize like that, that's a bit sweeping.

généralisateur, -trice [ʒeneralizatœr, -tris] *adj* generalizing (*mind, method*).

généralisation [ʒeneralizasjɔ̃] *nf* **(a)** (*extension*) generalization; **craindre la g. d'un conflit,** to fear that a conflict will spread; *Méd* **g. d'un cancer,** spread of a cancer; **(b)** (*de propos*) generalization; **une g. hâtive,** a sweeping generalization.

généraliser [ʒeneralize] **1** *vt* to generalize; **g. une loi,** to extend a law; **il a tendance à tout g.,** he tends to generalize; *Méd* **un cancer généralisé,** a generalized cancer. **2** *vi* to generalise; **on ne peut pas g.,** you can't generalize. **3 se généraliser** *vpr* to become general; (*of custom etc*) to spread; **la crise économique s'est généralisée,** the economic crisis has spread.

généralissime [ʒeneralisim] *nm* generalissimo, commander-in-chief.

généraliste [ʒeneralist] **1** *n Méd* general practitioner, GP; **être g.,** to be a GP, to be in general practice. **2** *adj* **médecin g.,** general practitioner.

généralité [ʒeneralite] *nf* **(a)** (*majorité*) **dans la g. des cas,** in the majority of cases, in most cases; **(b)** (*notion générale*) generality; **s'en tenir à des généralités,** to confine oneself to generalities *or* to general remarks; **exposer quelques généralités dans un cours d'introduction,** to present some general ideas in an introductory course.

générateur, -trice [ʒeneratœr, -tris] **1** *adj* generating (*machine etc*); generative (*force, organ*); productive (**de,** of); **un colorant alimentaire g. de troubles gastriques,** a food colouring which causes gastric problems; *Fig* **une situation génératrice de conflits/d'idées,** a situation that generates conflict/ideas; *Él* **station** *ou* **usine génératrice,** generating station *or* plant; **chaudière génératrice,** steam boiler. **2** *nm* generator; **g. (de vapeur),** (steam) boiler, steam generator; *Él* **g. d'électricité,** electricity generator; *Électron* **g. d'impulsions,** pulse generator; **g. de signaux,** *Électron* signal(ling) generator; *TV* colour coder. **3** *nf* **génératrice,** generator, generating set; *Phys Nucl* **génératrice nucléaire,** nuclear power reactor.

génératif, -ive [ʒeneratif, -iv] *adj* generative.

génération [ʒenerasjɔ̃] *nf* **(a)** (*classe d'âge, degrés de filiation*) generation; **la g. actuelle,** the present generation; **la jeune g.,** the younger generation; **ils ne sont pas de la même g.,** they are not of the same generation; **la g. pub/Mittérrand/vidéo/***etc*, the advertising/Mittérrand/video/*etc* generation; **la nouvelle g. d'ordinateurs/de machines à laver/***etc*, the new generation of computers/washing machines/*etc*; **de g. en g.,** from generation to generation, through the generations; **les immigrés de la deuxième g.,** second-generation immigrants; **la g. de Noé,** the descendants of Noah;

(b) (*action de générer, produire*) (act of) generation, generating; production (*of steam etc*); formation (*of metals*); **la g. d'une idée,** the generation of an idea; *Biol* **g. spontanée,** spontaneous generation.

générer [ʒenere] *vt* (**je génère, n. générons; je générerai**) **(a)** (*faire naître*) to generate, to engender; **(b)** (*produire*) to generate, to produce (*electricity, steam etc*).

généreusement [ʒenerøzmɑ̃] *adv* generously; **il nous a servi g. à manger,** he gave us a generous meal.

généreux, -euse [ʒenerø, -øz] **1** *adj* (*charitable*) generous, open-handed; *Vieilli* (*noble*) noble, generous (*soul*); **il est très g. avec les enfants,** he is very generous towards children; **un don g.,** a generous gift; **cœur g.,** warm heart; **terre généreuse,** fertile soil; **vin g.,** generous wine, wine with a fine bouquet; **elle a des formes généreuses,** she is built on generous lines. **2** *n* generous person.

générique [ʒenerik] **1** *adj* generic (*drug, term etc*); **produit g.,** no-name product. **2** *nm Cin TV* credits; **son**

nom ne figure pas au g., his name does not appear in the credits.

génériquement [ʒenerikmɑ̃] *adv* generically.

générosité [ʒenerozite] *nf* (*libéralité*) generosity, open-handedness; **avec g.**, generously; **n'abuse pas de ma g.**, don't abuse my generosity; **générosités**, acts of generosity.

Gênes [ʒɛn] *nf* Genoa.

genèse [ʒənɛz] *nf* genesis, origin, birth; *Bible* **la G.**, (the Book of) Genesis.

genet [ʒ(ə)nɛ] *nm* jennet.

genêt [ʒ(ə)nɛ] *nm* broom.

généticien, -ienne [ʒenetisjɛ̃, -jɛn] *n* geneticist.

génétique [ʒenetik] **1** *adj* genetic; **code/empreinte/ manipulation g.**, genetic code/fingerprint/engineering; **fond g. commun**, gene pool. **2** *nf* genetics.

génétiquement [ʒenetikmɑ̃] *adv* genetically.

genette [ʒ(ə)nɛt] *nf* genet.

gêneur, -euse [ʒɛnœr, -øz] *n* nuisance.

Genève [ʒ(ə)nɛv] *nf* Geneva.

Geneviève [ʒənvjɛv] *nf* Genevieve.

genevois, -oise [ʒənvwa, -waz] **1** *adj* Genevan. **2** *n* **G.**, Genevan.

genévrier [ʒənevrije] *nm* juniper (tree).

génial, -aux [ʒenjal, -o] *adj* inspired, full of genius; *F* great (*idea, film, evening etc*); **œuvre géniale**, work of genius; *F* **un mec g.**, a great guy; *F* **tu es g.!**, (*tu as résolu le problème*) you're a genius!

génialement [ʒenjalmɑ̃] *adv* brilliantly, in a brilliant manner, with genius.

génialité [ʒenjalite] *nf* (quality of) genius; brilliancy (*of invention etc*).

génie¹ [ʒeni] *nm* **(a)** (*qualité, personne*) genius; **homme de g.**, man of genius; **une invention de g.**, an ingenious invention; **avoir un trait de g.**, to have a stroke of genius; **g. d'une langue**, essence *or* spirit of a language; **(b)** (*esprit*) (guardian) spirit; (presiding) genius; (*être mythique*) genie; **son mauvais g.**, his evil genius; **le petit g. de la forêt**, the forest sprite; **les génies des contes arabes**, the genies *or* the jinn of the Arabian Nights; **le g. de la Bastille**, the spirit of the Bastille.

génie² *nm Tech* engineering; **g. civil**, civil engineering; (*corps*) civil engineers; **g. atomique**, atomic *or* nuclear engineering; (*corps*) atomic *or* nuclear engineers; **g. maritime**, marine *or* naval architecture; (*corps*) marine *or* naval architects; *Mil* **le (Corps du) G.**, = the Royal Engineers, the Engineers; *US* the Corps of Engineers, the Engineer Corps; **g. aéroporté**, airborne engineers; **g. de l'air**, aviation engineers; *Mil* **officier du g.**, engineer officer; *Mil* **soldat du g.**, engineer, *Br* sapper; *Méd* **g. génétique**, genetic engineering.

genièvre [ʒənjɛvr] *nm* **(a)** (*fruit*) juniper berry; (*arbre*) juniper (tree); *Pharm* **essence de g.**, juniper oil; **(b)** (*alcool*) gin.

génique [ʒenik] *adj Méd* **thérapie g.**, gene therapy.

génisse [ʒenis] *nf* heifer.

génital, -aux [ʒenital, -o] *adj* genital; **les organes génitaux**, the genitals; **appareil g.**, genitalia.

géniteur, -trice [ʒenitœr, -tris] **1** *nm Zool* sire. **2** *n Hum* father, mother; **nos géniteurs**, our parents.

génitif [ʒenitif] *nm Gram* genitive (case); **au g.**, in the genitive.

génito-urinaire [ʒenitɔyrinɛr] *adj Anat* genito-urinary.

génocide [ʒenɔsid] *nm* genocide.

génois, -oise [ʒenwa, -waz] *adj & n* Genoese.

génoise [ʒenwaz] *nf* sponge cake.

genou, -oux [ʒ(ə)nu] *nm* **(a)** *Anat* knee; **sa robe lui arrivait au dessus du g./au g.**, her dress came down to just above the knee/to her knees; **enfoncé jusqu'aux genoux dans la boue**, knee-deep in mud; **avoir les genoux en dedans**, to be knock-kneed; **se mettre à genoux**, to kneel (down), to go down on bended knee; **à genoux**, kneeling, on one's knees; *Fig F* **être à genoux devant qn**, to worship s.o.; **demander qch à genoux**, to ask for sth on one's knees *or* on bended knee; *Fig* **être sur les genoux**, to be worn *or* tired out; **ce projet m'a mis sur les genoux**, this project has worn me out; **tenir un enfant sur ses genoux**, to hold a child on one's knees *or* in one's lap; **sur les genoux des dieux**, in the lap of the gods; **faire du g. à qn**, to play kneesie with s.o.; *F* **ronds de genoux**, knee patches (*in trousers*);

(b) *MecE* **joint à g.**, ball-and-socket joint; toggle joint.

genouillère [ʒ(ə)nujɛr] *nf* **(a)** (*protection du genou*) kneepad, knee guard; *Méd* knee bandage; **(b)** *MecE* **articulation à g.**, toggle joint.

genre [ʒɑ̃r] *nm* **(a)** (*sorte*) kind, sort, type; **quel g. de vie mène-t-il?**, what kind *or* sort of (a) life does he lead?; **toutes les tentatives de ce g. ont échoué**, all such attempts have failed; **c'est plus dans son g.**, that's more in his line; **dans son g., c'est un artiste**, he is an artist in his way; **très bon dans son g.**, very good of its kind; **décorations en tout** *ou* **tous genre(s)**, decorations of all kinds; **c'est dans le g. de ...**, (it's) like ...; **un peu dans le g. de ...**, rather like ...; **une actrice unique en son g.**, an actress (who is) unique of her kind; **ce n'est pas mon g.**, it's not my style; **coucher à droite et à gauche ce n'est pas mon g.**, I'm not into sleeping around, sleeping around's not my thing; **ce n'est pas son g.**, that's not like him; **vin blanc g. sauternes**, white wine of the Sauterne type; **étui g. maroquin**, case in imitation morocco;

(b) *Beaux-Arts Littér* genre; **le roman policier est un g. littéraire très populaire**, the detective novel is a very popular literary genre; **le g. comique**, comedy; **le g. tragique**, tragedy; **peinture de g.**, genre painting; **tableau de g.**, subject picture;

(c) (*race*) family, race, kind; *Bot Zool etc* genus, *pl* genera; **le g. humain**, the human race, humanity, mankind;

(d) (*goût*) manners, fashion, taste; **c'est bon/mauvais g.**, it is good/bad form *or* in good/bad taste; *Péj* **bon chic, bon g.**, ≈ preppy;

(e) *Gram* gender; **s'accorder en g. et en nombre**, to agree in gender and number.

gens [ʒɑ̃] *nmpl* (*was originally feminine and most adjectives preceding* **g.** *still take the feminine form; the word group is nevertheless felt to be masculine*; **ces bonnes g. sont venus me trouver, heureux les petites g. éloignés des grandeurs!, quels sont ces g.?, quels** *or* **quelles sont ces bonnes g.?**; **tout** *varies according to whether the adjective has a distinct feminine ending or not* **toutes ces bonnes g.**, *but* **tous ces pauvres g.**; *the compounds in* **(b)** *below never have a feminine adjective*; **de bons petits jeunes g.; les malheureux g. de lettres**)

(a) (*individus*) people; **il y avait peu de g. dans la salle**, there were not many people in the hall; *Th* there was a poor house; **des braves g.**, good people; **petites g.**, humble people; **des g. sans histoires**, nice, ordinary people; **beaucoup de g.** *ou* **bien des g. l'ont vu**, lots of *or* many people have seen it; *F* **un tas de g. pense que ...**, loads of people think that ...; **qui sont ces g.-là?**, who are these people?; **il y a des g. qui ...**, there are people who ..., some people ...;

(b) (*individus de même profession, état etc*) **les g. du pays**, the locals; **jeunes g.**, (*garçons et filles*) young people, adolescents; (*jeunes hommes*) young men; **g. du monde**, society people; **g. d'Église**, clergy; **g. de lettres**, men of letters; **g. de théâtre**, the acting profession;

(c) (*nation*) nations, peoples; **le droit des g.**, the law of nations;

(d) *Vieilli* servants, domestics; (*de roi etc*) retinue.

gent [ʒɑ̃] *nf Arch & Hum* tribe, race; **la g. moutonnière**, sheep; **la g. masculine**, the male sex.

gentiane [ʒɑ̃sjan] *nf* **(a)** *Bot* gentian; **(b)** (*liqueur*) gentian bitters.

gentil¹, -ille [ʒɑ̃ti, -ij] *adj* nice; **un g. petit village**, a nice *or* pretty little village; **tu es bien g. de m'aider**, it's very nice *or* kind *or* good of you to help me; **elle a été très gentille pour** *ou* **avec moi**, she was very nice *or* kind to me; **c'est g. de votre part de m'écrire**, it is very kind *or* good of you to write to me; **dire un mot g. à qn**, to say a kind word to s.o.; **sois gentil(le)**, (*à un enfant*) be a good boy *or* girl; (*à un adulte*) be an angel, be a dear; **une gentille somme**, a nice little sum.

gentil² *nm Hist Rel* Gentile.

gentilhomme [ʒɑ̃tijɔm] *nm* gentleman; *Hist* **g. de la Chambre du Roi**, gentleman of the Privy Chamber; (*pl gentilshommes* [ʒɑ̃tizɔm]).

gentilhommière [ʒɑ̃tijɔmjɛr] *nf* **(a)** country seat, manor house; **(b)** (*en Belgique*) boarding house for men.

gentilité [ʒɑ̃tilite] *nf Hist Rel* the gentiles.

gentillesse [ʒɑ̃tijɛs] *nf* (*bonté*) kindness; **elle a fait cela par g.**, she did that out of kindness; **auriez-vous la g. de ...**, would you be so kind as to ...; **dire des gentillesses à qn**, to say nice *or* kind things to s.o..

gentillet, -ette [ʒɑ̃tijɛ, -ɛt] *adj* rather *or* quite nice; **romans gentillets**, pleasant light reading.

gentiment [ʒɑ̃timɑ̃] *adv* pleasantly; **elle m'a g. tenu compagnie**, she was kind enough to keep me company; *Iron* **vous voilà g. arrangé!**, that's a nice mess you're in!

gentleman [dʒɛntləman] *nm* gentleman, *pl* gentlemen; *Courses de chevaux* amateur jockey; (*pl gentlemen*).

gentleman-farmer [dʒɛntləmanfarmœr] *nm* gentleman farmer; (*pl gentlemen-farmers*).
génuflexion [ʒenyflɛksjɔ̃] *nf* genuflexion; **faire une g.,** to genuflect.
géo [ʒeo] *nf Scol F* geography.
géocentrique [ʒeosɑ̃trik] *adj Astron* geocentric.
géocentrisme [ʒeosɑ̃trism] *nm* geocentrism.
géochimie [ʒeoʃimi] *nf* geochemistry.
géodésie [ʒeɔdezi] *nf* geodesy, geodetics.
géodésique [ʒeɔdezik] geodesic, geodetic; **point g.,** triangulation point.
géodynamique [ʒeɔdinamik] **1** *adj* geodynamic. **2** *nf* geodynamics.
géographe [ʒeɔgraf] **1** *n* geographer. **2** *adj* **ingénieur g.,** surveyor.
géographie [ʒeɔgrafi] *nf* **(a)** geography; **g. économique,** economic geography; **g. humaine,** human geography; **(b)** (*livre*) geography (text)book.
géographique [ʒeɔgrafik] *adj* geographic(al); **carte g.,** map; **dictionnaire g.,** gazetteer; **Institut G. National,** *Br* ≈ Royal Geographical Institute.
géographiquement [ʒeɔgrafikmɑ̃] *adv* geographically.
geôle [ʒol] *nf Arch & Litt* gaol, prison.
geôlier, -ière [ʒolje, -jɛr] *n Arch & Litt* gaoler.
géologie [ʒeɔlɔʒi] *nf* geology.
géologique [ʒeɔlɔʒik] *adj* geological.
géologiquement [ʒeɔlɔʒikmɑ̃] *adv* geologically.
géologue [ʒeɔlɔg] *n* geologist.
géomagnétique [ʒeɔmaɲetik] *adj* geomagnetic.
géomagnétisme [ʒeɔmaɲetism] *nm* geomagnetism.
géomancie [ʒeɔmɑ̃si] *nf* geomancy.
géométral, -aux [ʒeɔmetral, -o] **1** *adj* flat (*projection, elevation*) (*as opposed to perspective view*). **2** *nm* flat projection.
géomètre [ʒeɔmɛtr] *nm* **(a)** geometer, geometrician; **(arpenteur) g.,** (land) surveyor; **(b)** *Ent* geometer (moth).
géométrie [ʒeɔmetri] *nf* geometry; **g. plane,** plane geometry; **g. analytique,** analytical *or* co-ordinate geometry; **g. dans l'espace** *ou* **à trois dimensions,** solid *or* three-dimensional geometry; *Aut* **g. de la direction,** steering geometry; *Phys Nucl* **g. du réseau (du réacteur),** lattice design, lattice pitch (of reactor); *Av* **avion à g. fixe/variable,** fixed-/variable-geometry aircraft.
géométrique [ʒeɔmetrik] *adj* geometric(al); **progression g.,** geometrical progression; **figures/formes/motifs géométriques,** geometric(al) figures/shapes/patterns; **esprit g.,** orderly mind.
géométriquement [ʒeɔmetrikmɑ̃] *adv* geometrically.
géomorphologie [ʒeɔmɔrfɔlɔʒi] *nf* geomorphology.
géophone [ʒeɔfɔn] *nm* geophone, sound detector.
géophysique [ʒeɔfizik] **1** *adj* geophysical. **2** *nf* geophysics.
géophyte [ʒeɔfit] *nm Bot* geophyte.
géopolitique [ʒeɔpɔlitik] *nf* geopolitics.
Georges [ʒɔrʒ] *nm* **(a)** George; **(b)** *Av F* George (*automatic pilot*).
Georgette [ʒɔrʒɛt] *nf* Georgina; *Tex* **crêpe g.,** georgette.
Géorgie [ʒeɔrʒi] *nf* Georgia; **G. du Sud,** South Georgia (*Tierra del Fuego*).
géorgien, -ienne [ʒeɔrʒjɛ̃, -jɛn] **1** *adj* Georgian. **2** *n* **G.,** Georgian.
Géorgiques (les) [leʒeɔrʒik] *nfpl Littér* the Georgics (*of Virgil*).
géostationnaire [ʒeostasjɔnɛr] *adj Astronaut* **satellite g.,** geostationary satellite.
géosynclinal, -aux [ʒeɔsɛ̃klinal, -o] *Géol nm* geosyncline.
géothermie [ʒeɔtɛrmi] *nf* geothermics.
géothermique [ʒeɔtɛrmik] *adj* (*énergie etc*) geothermal.
gérance [ʒerɑ̃s] *nf* (*action*) management, direction (*of business etc*); (*fonction*) managership, administratorship; **mettre un commerce/***etc* **en g.,** to appoint a manager for a business/*etc*; **une g. de cinq ans,** a five-year managership.
géranium [ʒeranjɔm] *nm* (*sauvage*) geranium, crane's bill; (*ornemental*) pelargonium, *F* geranium.
gérant, -ante [ʒerɑ̃, -ɑ̃t] *n* manager, manageress; *Journ* **g. d'un journal,** managing editor of a newspaper.
Gérard [ʒerar] *nm* Gerald, Gerard.
gerbable [ʒɛrbabl] *adj* (*paniers etc*) stacking, stackable.
gerbage [ʒɛrbaʒ] *nm* **(a)** (*des céréales*) binding, sheaving; **(b)** (*action d'empiler*) stacking, piling (*of casks, bales*).
gerbe [ʒɛrb] *nf* **(a)** sheaf (*of corn*); **mettre le blé en gerbes,** to sheave *or* sheaf the wheat; **g. de fleurs,** sheaf *or* spray of flowers; **g. d'étincelles,** shower of sparks; **g. d'eau,** spray *or* shower of water, splash; **(b)** *Mil* cone of fire.
gerber [ʒɛrbe] *vt* **(a)** (*mettre en gerbes*) to bind, to sheave, to sheaf (*corn etc*); **(b)** *Tech* (*empiler*) to stack (*barrels, crates, shells*); **(c)** *Vulg* (*vomir*) to throw up, *Am* to upchuck.
gerbeuse [ʒɛrbøz] *nf* stacker, stacking machine (*for barrels etc*).
gerbier [ʒɛrbje] *nm* stack (*of corn*).
gerbille [ʒɛrbij] *nf* gerbil.
gerboise [ʒɛrbwaz] *nf* jerboa.
gerce [ʒɛrs] *nf* **(a)** (*fente*) crack, fissure (*in wood*); **(b)** *Ent* clothes moth.
gercé [ʒɛrse] *adj* cracked, cleft; chapped (*hands, lips*).
gercer [ʒɛrse] *v* **(il gerçait; il gerça) 1** *vt* to chap (*hands etc*); to crack (*wood, soil*). **2** *vi* (*des lèvres, mains*) to become chapped. **3 se gercer** *vpr* (*des lèvres, mains*) to become chapped.
gerçure [ʒɛrsyr] *nf* chap (*in skin*); crack, cleft, fissure (*in ground*); *Tech* shake, flaw (*in wood*); hair crack, hairline (*in metal*); **avoir des gerçures aux mains/lèvres,** to have chapped hands/lips.
gérer [ʒere] *v* **(je gère, n. gérons; je gérerai) 1** *vt* to manage, to run (*newspaper, hotel etc*); to manage, to administer (*estate etc*); **mal g. ses finances,** to mismanage one's finances. **2 se gérer** *vpr Jur* **se g. créancier,** to come forward as creditor.
gerfaut [ʒɛrfo] *nm* gyrfalcon, gerfalcon.
gériatre [ʒerjatr] *nmf Méd* geriatrician.
gériatrie [ʒerjatri] *nf Méd* geriatrics.
gériatrique [ʒerjatrik] *adj Méd (hôpital etc)* geriatric.
germain[1], -aine [ʒɛrmɛ̃, -ɛn] *Hist* **1** *adj* Germanic, Teutonic. **2** *n* **G.,** German, Teuton.
germain[2] *adj Jur* **frère g.,** full brother; **sœur germaine,** full sister; **cousin g.,** first cousin; **cousins issus de germains,** (*dont les parents sont germains*) second cousins.
germandrée [ʒɛrmɑ̃dre] *nf Bot* germander.
germanique [ʒɛrmanik] **1** *adj* **(a)** (*relatif aux Germains*) Germanic, Teutonic; *Hist* **l'Empire g.,** the German(ic) Empire; **(b)** (*relatif aux Allemands et à l'Allemagne*) German. **2** *nm Ling* Germanic.
germanisant, -ante [ʒɛrmanizɑ̃, -ɑ̃t] *n* Germanophile; *Univ* student of German.
germanisation [ʒɛrmanizasjɔ̃] *nf* Germanization.
germaniser [ʒɛrmanize] *vt* to Germanize.
germanisme [ʒɛrmanism] *nm* Germanism.
germaniste [ʒɛrmanist] *n Ling* Germanist, student of German.
germanium [ʒɛrmanjɔm] *nm Ch* germanium.
germanophile [ʒɛrmanɔfil] *adj & n* Germanophile.
germanophobe [ʒɛrmanɔfɔb] **1** *adj* Germanophobic. **2** *n* Germanophobe.
germanophobie [ʒɛrmanɔfɔbi] *nf* Germanophobia.
germanophone [ʒɛrmanɔfɔn] *adj & n* German-speaking (person).
germe [ʒɛrm] *nm* **(a)** (*embryon, plantule etc*) *Biol* germ; eye (*of potato*); **germes de soja,** bean sprouts; **(b)** (*virus etc*) germ; **germes pathogènes,** pathogenic bacteria; *Fig* **les germes d'une révolution/de la corruption,** the seeds of a revolution/of corruption.
germer [ʒɛrme] *vi* (*of plant*) to germinate; (*of potatoes*) to sprout; *Fig* (*of idea etc*) to germinate.
germicide [ʒɛrmisid] **1** *nm* germicide. **2** *adj* germicidal.
germinal, -aux [ʒɛrminal, -o] **1** *adj Biol* germinal. **2** *nm Hist* = the seventh month of the French Republican calendar (*March-April*).
germinateur, -trice [ʒɛrminatœr, -tris] *adj* germinative.
germinatif, -ive [ʒɛrminatif, -iv] *adj Biol* germinative, germinal; **plasma g.,** germ plasm.
germination [ʒɛrminasjɔ̃] *nf Biol* germination.
germoir [ʒɛrmwar] *nm* **(a)** (*pour les plantes*) seed bed; **(b)** (*d'une brasserie*) malt house, malting.
gérondif [ʒerɔ̃dif] *nm Gram* **(a)** (*en français*) gerund; **(b)** (*cas latin*) gerundive; **au g.,** in the gerund(ive).
gérontocratie [ʒerɔ̃tɔkrasi] *nf Pol* gerontocracy.
gérontologie [ʒerɔ̃tɔlɔʒi] *nf Méd* gerontology.
gérontologue [ʒerɔ̃tɔlɔg] *n Méd* gerontologist.
gésier [ʒezje] *nm Orn* gizzard; *Arg* (*estomac*) guts.
gésir [ʒezir] *vi déf* (*used only in the following forms: prp* **gisant**; *pr ind* **il gît, n. gisons, vous gisez, ils gisent**; *impf* **je gisais** *etc*) *Litt* **(a)** to lie; **il gisait dans son sang,** he was lying *or* weltering in his blood; **ci-gît/-gisent ...,** (*on gravestone*) here lies/lie ...; **des papiers froissés gisaient çà et là,** crumpled papers were lying all over the place; *Fig*

c'est là que gît le lièvre, that's the point, there's the rub.

gesse [ʒɛs] *nf Bot* vetch, everlasting pea; **g. odorante,** sweet pea.

gestapo [gɛstapo] *nf Hist* Gestapo.

gestation [ʒɛstɑsjɔ̃] *nf Physiol* (period of) gestation; *Fig* **projet en g.,** plan in embryo.

geste[1] [ʒɛst] *nm* **(a)** (*mouvement*) gesture, motion, movement; **faire un g.,** to make a gesture; **d'un g., il nous a fait entrer,** he waved us in *or* showed us in with a flourish; **d'un g. de la main,** with a wave of the hand; **sans faire un g.,** without moving; **faire un g. de la main,** (*pour dire au revoir*) to give a wave of the hand; **la précision de ses gestes,** the neatness of his gestures; **écarter qn d'un g.,** to wave s.o. aside; **g. de résignation,** shrug of resignation; **joindre le g. à la parole,** to suit the action to the word; **(b)** (*action*) gesture; **un beau g.,** a handsome *or* fine gesture; **un g. de générosité,** a generous gesture; **faire un g.,** to make a gesture; **faire un g. pour les sans-abri,** to do something for the homeless, to do something to help the homeless; **avoir le g. large,** to be open-handed.

geste[2] *nf* **(a)** *Litt* **(chanson de) g.,** chanson de geste (*mediaeval verse chronicle of heroic exploits*); **(b)** (*conduite*) **rendre compte de ses faits et gestes,** to give an account of oneself; (*surtout à la police*) to give an account of one's movements.

gesticulation [ʒɛstikylɑsjɔ̃] *nf* gesticulating, gesticulation.

gesticuler [ʒɛstikyle] *vi* to gesticulate.

gestion [ʒɛstjɔ̃] *nf Fin* management (*of business, works etc*); conduct (*of affairs*); **g. administrative,** administration; **mauvaise g.,** bad management, mismanagement; *Ind* **g. de la production/de stock,** production/stock control; *Ordinat* **g. de fichiers,** file management.

gestionnaire [ʒɛstjɔnɛr] **1** *adj* administrative; **compte g.,** management account. **2** *n* administrator; (*d'un service*) manager.

gestuel, -elle [ʒɛstɥɛl] **1** *adj* (of the) body. **2** *nf* **gestuelle,** body language.

Gethsémani [ʒɛtsemani] *n Bible* Gethsemane.

geyser [ʒɛzɛr] *nm* geyser.

Ghana [gana] *nm* Ghana.

ghaneen, -eenne [ganeɛ, -eɛn] *adj* Ghanaian.

ghetto [gɛto] *nm* ghetto.

gibbeux, -euse [ʒibø, -øz] *adj* gibbous.

gibbon [ʒibɔ̃] *nm* gibbon (ape).

gibbosité [ʒibozite] *nf* hump.

gibecière [ʒibsjɛr] *nf* game bag *or* pouch.

giberne [ʒibɛrn] *nf Arch* cartridge pouch; *Prov* **tout soldat a un bâton de maréchal dans sa g.,** every soldier carries a marshal's baton in his knapsack.

gibet [ʒibɛ] *nm* gibbet, gallows.

gibier [ʒibje] *nm* game; **gros/menu g.,** big/small game; **g. à poil,** game animals; **g. à plumes,** game birds; **g. d'eau,** waterfowl; **manger du g.,** to eat game; *Fig* **g. de potence,** gallows bird, jailbird.

giboulée [ʒibule] *nf* sudden shower; **giboulées de mars,** ≈ April showers.

giboyeux, -euse [ʒibwajø, -øz] *adj* abounding in *or* well stocked with game.

gibus [ʒibys] *nm* crush hat, opera hat.

giclée [ʒikle] *nf* spurt, squirt (*of water, blood*).

giclement [ʒikləmɑ̃] *nm* splashing up, squelching (*of mud etc*); spurting (*of blood etc*).

gicler [ʒikle] *vi* (*of blood, water etc*) to spurt (up, out); (*of water*) to squirt (out); (*of mud etc*) to splash up.

gicleur [ʒiklœr] *nm Aut* jet; **g. (d'incendie),** (fire) sprinkler; *Aut* **g. de ralenti,** idling jet.

gifle [ʒifl] *nf* slap in the face, box on the ear; *Fig* slap in the face; **donner** *ou F* **flanquer une g. à qn,** to slap s.o.'s face; **prendre** *ou* **recevoir une g.,** to get a slap in the face *or* a box on the ear.

gifler [ʒifle] *vt* to slap *or* smack (*s.o.'s*) face, to box (*s.o.'s*) ears; **visage giflé par le vent,** face lashed by the wind; *Fig* **mots qui giflent,** stinging words.

gigahertz [ʒigaɛrts] *nm Phys* gigahertz.

gigantesque [ʒigɑ̃tɛsk] *adj* gigantic; **d'une taille g.,** gigantic, of a gigantic size.

gigantesquement [ʒigɑ̃tɛskəmɑ̃] *adv* gigantically.

gigantisme [ʒigɑ̃tism] *nm Méd* gi(g)antism; **le g. des villes,** the gigantic size of the cities.

gigaoctet [gigaɔktɛ] *nm Ordinat* gigabyte.

gigogne [ʒigɔɲ] *adj* **table g.,** nest of tables; **lit g.,** trundle *or* truckle bed; **poupée g.,** nest of (Russian) dolls; *Mil* **fusée g.,** multistage rocket.

Gigogne [ʒigɔɲ] *nf* **la mère G.,** ≈ the Old Woman who lived in a shoe; **une mère G.,** = the mother of a large and ever-increasing family.

gigolo [ʒigɔlo] *nm F* gigolo.

gigot [ʒigo] *nm* **(a)** *Culin* leg of lamb; **manche g.,** leg-of-mutton sleeve; **(b)** (*d'un cheval*) hind leg; *F Hum* (*d'une personne*) leg, thigh.

gigoter [ʒigɔte] *vi* **(a)** *F* (*se trémousser*) to wriggle, to fidget; **(b)** (*of dying animal*) to give a convulsive jerk.

gigue[1] [ʒig] *nf* (*danse*) jig.

gigue[2] *nf* **(a)** *Culin* haunch (*of venison*); **(b)** *F* **gigues,** (*jambes*) stumps, pins; **(c)** *F* **une grande g.,** (*fille grande et maigre*) a beanpole.

gilde [gild] *nf Hist* g(u)ild.

gilet [ʒilɛ] *nm* (*sans manches*) waistcoat, *Am* vest; (*veste en laine*) cardigan; *Fig F* **pleurer dans le g. de qn,** to cry on s.o.'s shoulder; **g. de sauvetage,** life jacket; **g. d'armes,** fencing jacket.

Gilles [ʒil] *nm* Giles.

gin [dʒin] *nm* gin.

gindre [ʒɛ̃dr] *nm* baker's assistant.

gingembre [ʒɛ̃ʒɑ̃br] *nm* ginger; **racine de g.,** root ginger, fresh ginger; **biscuits au g.,** ginger biscuits.

gingival, -aux [ʒɛ̃ʒival, -o] *adj Anat* gingival.

gingivite [ʒɛ̃ʒivit] *nf Méd* gingivitis; **g. expulsive,** pyorrhoea, *US* pyorrhea.

ginseng [ʒɛsɑ̃] *nm Bot etc* ginseng.

girafe [ʒiraf] *nf* **(a)** giraffe; *Fig* (*personne*) giraffe, beanpole; *F* **peigner la g.,** to waste one's time; (*ne rien faire*) to do damn all; *Fig* **avoir un cou de g.,** to have a long neck; **(b)** *Cin Arg* (*de micro*) boom.

girafeau, -eaux [ʒirafo] *nm*, **girafon** [ʒirafɔ̃] *nm* baby giraffe.

girandole [ʒirɑ̃dɔl] *nf* **(a)** (*chandelier*) chandelier; (*feux d'artifice*) girandole; **(b)** (*grappe*) cluster (*of blooms*); girandole (*of jewels*).

girasol [ʒirasɔl] *nm Minér* fire opal, girasol.

giration [ʒirɑsjɔ̃] *nf* gyration; *Nau* **cercle de g.,** turning circle (*of ship*).

giratoire [ʒiratwar] *adj* gyratory (*movement etc*); **sens g.,** roundabout, *Am* traffic circle.

giravion [ʒiravjɔ̃] *nm Av* rotary wing aircraft, rotorcraft.

girelle [ʒirɛl] *nf* revolving table (*of potter's wheel*).

girl [gœrl] *nf* chorus girl, showgirl.

girofle [ʒirɔfl] *nm Bot* clove; **un clou de g.,** a clove; **huile de g.,** oil of cloves.

giroflée [ʒirɔfle] *nf Bot* stock; **g. jaune** *ou* **des murailles,** wallflower; *Fig F* **une g. (à cinq feuilles),** a slap in the face.

giroflier [ʒirɔflije] *nm Bot* clove tree.

girolle [ʒirɔl] *nf* chanterelle (mushroom).

giron [ʒirɔ̃] *nm* **(a)** (*partie du corps*) lap; **tenir un enfant dans son g.,** to hold a child in one's lap; *Fig* **garder un enfant dans son g.,** to wrap a child in cotton wool, to mollycoddle a child; **se réfugier dans le g. de sa famille,** to take refuge in the bosom of one's family; **le g. de l'Église,** the bosom of the Church; **(b)** *Constr* tread (board) (*of step*).

girond [ʒirɔ̃] *adj Arg* (*souvent au sujet d'une femme*) easy on the eye.

Gironde [ʒirɔ̃d] *nf* the (river) Gironde.

girondin [ʒirɔ̃dɛ̃] **1** *adj* **(a)** *Hist* Girondin; **(b) le vignoble g.,** the vineyards of the Gironde. **2** *n* **G.,** Girondin.

girouette [ʒirwɛt] *nf* weathercock, (weather)vane; *Fig* (*personne*) weathercock.

gisant [ʒizɑ̃] **1** *adj Litt* (*personne*) lying (*helpless or dead*); *Nau* **navire g.,** stranded vessel. **2** *nm Beaux-Arts* recumbent figure (*on tomb*).

gisement [ʒizmɑ̃] *nm* **(a)** deposit; *Min* lode, vein; **g. pétrolifère,** oilfield; **gisements houillers,** coal deposits; *Archéol* **g. préhistorique,** prehistoric site; **(b)** *Av Nau etc* bearing; **g. à la boussole,** compass bearing; *Vieilli* **connaître le g. de la côte,** to know the lie of the coast.

gitan, -ane [ʒitɑ̃, -an] **1** *adj* gipsy; **la culture gitane,** gipsy *or* Romany culture. **2** *n* (Spanish) gipsy. **3** *nf* **Gitane** ®, Gitane ® (*popular brand of cigarette*).

gîte[1] [ʒit] *nm* **(a)** resting place, lodging; lair (*of deer*); form, seat (*of hare*); **ne pas avoir de g.,** to be homeless; **revenir au g.,** to return to one's old home; **offrir le g. et le couvert à qn,** to offer s.o. board and lodging; **g. rural,** = self-catering holiday accommodation; **trouver un lièvre au g.,** to find a hare sitting; **(b)** *Min* stratum, bed, deposit (*of ore etc*); **gîtes houillers,** coal deposits; **(c)** *Culin* **g. à la noix,** silverside.

gîte[2] *nf Nau* list(ing); **avoir** *ou* **prendre de la g.,** (*of ship*) to have *or* take a list, to list, to heel (over); **donner de la g.**

sur tribord, to list to starboard.
gîter [ʒite] *vi* **(a)** *Nau* to list, to heel; **(b)** *Vieilli* to lodge, to live; (*of animal*) to find shelter, to bed; (*of bird*) to perch.
givrage [ʒivraʒ] *nm Av etc* icing.
givre [ʒivr] *nm* **(a)** *Météo* hoar frost, rime; **(b)** frost (*forming in refrigerator etc*).
givré [ʒivre] *adj* **(a)** (*couvert de givre*) frosty, covered with hoar frost; *Av* iced up; **(b)** *Culin* **orange givrée,** = orange sorbet served in an orange skin; **un verre givré avec du sucre,** a glass frosted with sugar; **(c)** *F* (*fou*) nuts, batty; **il est complètement g.,** he's completely off his rocker.
givrer [ʒivre] **1** *vt Météo* to cover with hoar frost. **2** *vi Av* to ice up. **3 se givrer** *vpr Av* to ice up.
givreux, -euse [ʒivrø, -øz] *adj* (*diamonds etc*) with icy flecks.
givrure [ʒivryr] *nf* icy fleck (*in diamond etc*).
glabre [glɑbr] *adj Biol* glabrous, smooth; **visage g.,** (*rasé*) clean-shaven face; (*imberbe*) hairless face.
glaçage [glasaʒ] *nm* **(a)** *Culin* icing, *Am* frosting (*of cake etc*); glazing (*of pastry etc*); **(b)** *Tech* glazing, glossing; surfacing (*of paper*).
glaçant [glasɑ̃] *adj Fig* chilling, frigid (*manner, reception*); *Vieilli* freezing (cold); icy (*coldness, wind*).
glace [glas] *nf* **(a)** (*eau à l'état solide*) ice; **patiner sur la g.,** to skate on the ice; **cube de g.,** ice cube; *Can* **sur g.,** (*drink*) on the rocks; **vous voulez de la g.?,** do you want ice (in it); **avec g. ou sans g.?,** with or without ice?; **un pain de g.,** a block of ice; **glaces de fond,** bottom ice, anchor ice; **g. flottante,** floating ice, drift ice; **navire retenu** *ou* **pris par les glaces,** icebound ship; *Fig* **rester de g.,** to remain impassive; *Fig* **un accueil de g.,** a frigid *or* icy reception; *Fig* **rompre la g.,** to break the ice;
(b) (*vitre*) glass; *Aut etc* window; (*miroir*) mirror; **g. (de vitrine),** plate glass; **se regarder dans la g.,** to look at oneself in the mirror; *Fig* **ne plus pouvoir se regarder dans une g.,** not to be able to look oneself in the face; **g. sans tain,** two-way mirror; **g. à main,** hand mirror; **Galerie des Glaces,** (*à Versailles*) Hall of Mirrors;
(c) (*crème congelée*) ice cream; **g. à la vanille/à la fraise,** vanilla/strawberry ice (cream); **un cornet de g.,** a(n ice-cream) cone *or Br* cornet; **marchand de glaces,** ice-cream man;
(d) *Culin* glaze (*on pastry etc*); icing, *Am* frosting (*on cake etc*);
(e) (*défaut*) flaw (*in diamond*).
glacé [glase] *adj* **(a)** (*congelé*) frozen (*river etc*); (*très froid*) freezing, icy; (*avec des glaçons*) iced (*coffee etc*); **j'ai les pieds glacés,** my feet are freezing *or* frozen, my feet are (as) cold as ice; **g. jusqu'aux os,** chilled to the bone; *Fig* **politesse glacée,** frosty *or* icy politeness; **regard g.,** cold stare; **(b)** (*lustré*) glazed, glossy (*paper etc*); **gants glacés,** glacé kid gloves; **soie glacée,** watered silk; **fil g.,** glazed thread; *Phot* **épreuve glacée,** glossy print; *Culin* **cerises glacées,** glacé cherries.
glacer [glase] *v* **(je glaça(i)s; n. glaçons) 1** *vt* **(a)** (*congeler*) to freeze; (*refroidir*) to chill; **cela me glace le sang,** it makes my blood run cold; *Fig* (*décourager par sa froideur*) to turn (*s.o.*) cold; **g. d'effroi/de terreur,** to paralyse *or* freeze (*s.o.*) with fear/terror; **(b)** *Culin* to ice, *Am* to frost (*cake etc*); (*recouvrir d'une surface lisse*) to glaze (*thread, pastry etc*); **(c)** (*lustrer*) to surface (*paper*). **2 se glacer** *vpr* (*of water etc*) to freeze (over); **son sang se glaça,** his blood ran cold.
glacerie [glasri] *nf* (*fabrique*) glass works; *Com* glass trade.
glaceur [glasœr] *nm* glazer (*of material etc*).
glaceux, -euse [glasø, -øz] *adj* flawed (*diamond etc*).
glaciaire [glasjɛr] **1** *adj Géol* glacial; glaciated (*valley etc*); **période g.,** ice age. **2** *nm* ice age.
glacial, -als *or* **-aux** [glasjal, -o] *adj* (*pl rarely used*) frigid, icy (*temperature*); frigid (*air*); *Fig* (*tone, manner, politeness etc*) glacial, icy; **vent g.,** icy *or* cutting *or* bitter wind; **zone glaciale,** arctic region.
glacialement [glasjalmɑ̃] *adv* glacially, icily, frigidly.
glaciation [glasjɑsjɔ̃] *nf* glaciation.
glacier¹ [glasje] *nm Géol* glacier.
glacier² *nm* **(a)** (*fabricant*) ice-cream manufacturer; (*vendeur*) ice-cream seller *or* man; **pâtissier-g., g.-confiseur,** confectioner (*who also sells ice cream*).
glacière [glasjɛr] *nf* **(a)** (*de pique-nique*) cool bag *or* box, *Austr F* Esky ®; **(b)** *F* (*de frigidaire*) freezer compartment; **cette chambre est une vraie g.!,** this room's like an ice box *or* ice house!; **(c)** *Arch* ice cave.
glacis [glasi] *nm* **(a)** *Mil Géol* glacis; **(b)** *Constr* ramp; **(c)** *Beaux-Arts* scumble, glaze.
glaçon [glasɔ̃] *nm* **(a)** (*pour rafraîchir une boisson*) ice cube; **whisky avec glaçons,** whisky on the rocks; *F* **c'est un g.!,** he's a cold fish!; **(b)** (*pendant*) icicle; **(c) glacons,** drift ice, broken ice (*on river*).
glaçure [glasyr] *nf Cér etc* glaze.
gladiateur [gladjatœr] *nm* gladiator; **combat de gladiateurs,** gladiatorial combat.
glaïeul [glajœl] *nm* gladiolus, *pl* gladioli; **g. des marais,** (sword) flag.
glaire [glɛr] *nf* **(a)** (*d'œuf*) white (of egg); **(b)** *Méd* mucus, phlegm.
glaireux, -euse [glɛrø, -øz] *adj* glaireous, glairy.
glaise [glɛz] *nf* **(terre) g.,** clay, loam.
glaiser [glɛze] *vt* **(a)** (*amender avec de la glaise*) to clay (*soil*), to dress (*soil*) with clay; **(b)** (*enduire de glaise*) to line (*sth*) with clay.
glaiseux, -euse [glɛzø, -øz] *adj* clayey, loamy.
glaisière [glɛzjɛr] *nf* clay pit.
glaive [glɛv] *nm Arch & Litt* sword, blade; *Fig Litt* **le g. de la justice,** the sword of justice.
glanage [glanaʒ] *nm* gleaning.
gland [glɑ̃] *nm* **(a)** (*passementerie*) tassel (*of curtain etc*); acorn (*of sword knot*); **(b)** *Bot* acorn; **glands,** (*pour les cochons*) mast; **(c)** *Anat* glans.
glande [glɑ̃d] *nf Anat Bot* gland; **glandes sexuelles,** genitalia; *Vulg* **ça me fout les glandes,** it gets on my tits.
glander [glɑ̃de] *vi F* to hang *or* mooch *or* moon about *or* around.
glandeur, -euse [glɑ̃dœr, -øz] *n F* moocher; **c'est un vrai g.,** he just hangs *or* mooches *or* moons about *or* around.
glandouiller [glɑ̃duje] *vi F* to hang *or* mooch *or* moon about *or* around.
glandulaire [glɑ̃dylɛr]**, glanduleux, -euse** [glɑ̃dylø, -øz] *adj* glandular; **infection glanduleuse,** glandular infection.
glane [glan] *nf Agr* **(a)** (*action*) gleaning; **glanes,** gleanings; **(b)** (*d'oignons*) string, rope.
glaner [glane] *vt Agr* to glean; *Fig* **g. des renseignements,** to glean information.
glaneur, -euse [glanœr, -øz] *n Agr* gleaner.
glanure [glanyr] *nf Agr* gleaning(s).
glapir [glapir] *vi* to yelp, to yap; (*of fox*) to bark.
glapissant [glapisɑ̃] *adj* yapping, yelping (*dog*); **voix glapissante,** shrill voice.
glapissement [glapismɑ̃] *nm* yapping, yelping (*of puppies*); barking (*of foxes*).
glas [glɑ] *nm* knell; salvo of guns (*at military or State funeral*); **sonner le g.,** to toll the knell *or* the passing bell; **sonner le g. de ...,** to sound *or* ring the knell of ....
glasnost [glasnɔst] *nf* glasnost.
glaucome [glokom] *nm Méd* glaucoma.
glauque [glok] *adj* **(a)** (*couleur*) blue-green, glaucous; **(b)** *F* (*ambience etc*) heavy.
glèbe [glɛb] *nf* **(a)** *Arch (motte de terre)* clod (*of earth*), sod; **(b)** *Arch & Litt* (*sol cultivé*) soil, land (*under cultivation*), glebe.
glène¹ [glɛn] *nf Anat* glene, socket.
glène² *nf Pêche* creel.
glissade [glisad] *nf* sliding; (*danse*) glissade, glissando; **faire une g.,** to slide; *Av* **g. sur l'aile,** side slip; *Av* **g. sur la queue,** tail slide.
glissage [glisaʒ] *nm* sliding down (*of cut timber in the mountains*).
glissant [glisɑ̃] *adj* **(a)** slippery (*eel, pavement etc*); *Fig* **terrain g.,** delicate *or* touchy subject; **(b)** *MecE* **joint g.,** sliding joint, slip joint.
glissé [glise] *adj & nm (danse)* **(pas) g.,** glissade, glide.
glissement [glismɑ̃] *nm* slip; (*action*) sliding, slipping; *Av* sideslipping; *Électron* **g. de fréquence,** frequency variation; *Géol* **g. de terrain,** landslide; (*moins important*) landslip; *Ling* **g. de sens,** shift in meaning; *Pol* **g. à gauche** *ou* **vers la gauche,** swing to the left.
glisser [glise] **1** *vi* **(a)** (*par accident*) to slip; (*of wheel*) to skid; **le couteau lui a glissé des mains,** the knife slipped from his hands; **son pied a glissé,** his foot slipped; *Fig* **g. entre les mains** *ou* **les doigts de qn,** to slip through s.o.'s fingers; *Av* **g. sur l'aile,** to sideslip;
(b) (*volontairement*) to slide (*on ice etc*); **faire g.,** to slide (*part of machine etc*); **se laisser g. le long d'une corde,** to slide down a rope;
(c) (*avancer comme en glissant*) to glide (*over the water etc*); *Fig* **un sourire ironique glissa sur ses lèvres,** he gave a brief ironic smile;
(d) g. sur, to touch lightly on (*subject*); **l'épée lui glissa sur les côtes,** the sword glanced off his ribs; *Fig* **mes re-**

proches ont glissé sur lui comme l'eau sur les plumes d'un canard, I took him to task but it was like water off a duck's back; **glissons (là-dessus),** let's not dwell on that;

(e) (*avoir une surface glissante*) to be slippery; **fais attention, ça glisse ce matin,** watch out, it's slippery this morning.

2 *vt* (*introduire, passer etc*) **g. une lettre sous la porte,** to slip a letter under the door; **g. qch dans la poche de qn,** to slip sth into s.o.'s pocket; **elle me glissa un papier,** she slipped me a piece of paper; **g. un mot à l'oreille de qn,** to drop a word in s.o.'s ear.

3 se glisser *vpr* to slip, to creep, to steal (**dans,** into); **il s'est glissé discrètement dans la salle de conférence,** he slipped discreetly into the lecture theatre; **se g. dans son lit,** to slip *or* creep into bed.

glisseur, -euse [glisœr, -øz] *nm* (*d'une machine*) slide block; *Av* glider; *Math* sliding vector.

glissière [glisjɛr] *nf* **(a)** (*coulisse*) groove, slide; **fermeture à g.,** zip (fastener); **porte à glissières,** sliding door; **à g.,** skid-mounted; **banc à glissières,** (*en aviron*) sliding seat. **(b)** (*d'une machine*) (slipper) guide, slipper, slide bar, guide rod; *Mil* recoil slide; **(c) g. (de sécurité),** (*alongside road*) crash barrier; **(d)** *Ind* shoot (*for coal etc*).

glissoir [gliswar] *nm* **(a)** (*d'une machine*) slide, sliding block; **(b)** (*pour le bois*) timber slide *or* shoot.

glissoire [gliswar] *nf* slide (*on ice or snow*).

global, -aux [glɔbal, -o] *adj* total, inclusive, global (*sum etc*); lump (*payment*).

globalement [glɔbalmɑ̃] *adv* in the aggregate, globally.

globe [glɔb] *nm* **(a)** (*sphère*) globe, sphere; **(b)** (*terre*) globe; orb (*of regalia*); **la surface du g.,** the surface of the globe; **une partie inhabitée du g.,** an uninhibited part of the globe; **faire le tour du g.,** to go round the world; **le g. du soleil,** the orb of the sun; **(c)** (*en verre*) glass cover *or* shade (*of clock etc*); **g. électrique,** electric light globe; **statuette sous g.,** statuette under glass; **c'est à conserver sous g.,** it ought to be in a glass case; **(d)** *Anat* **g. oculaire,** eyeball; **(e)** *Météo* **g. de feu,** fireball, globe lightning.

globe-trotter [glɔbtrɔtœr] *nm* globetrotter; (*pl globe-trotters*).

globine [glɔbin] *nf Biol* globin.

globulaire [glɔbylɛr] *adj* globular; *Méd* **numération g.,** blood count.

globule [glɔbyl] *nm* globule (*of air, water*); drop (*of water*); *Physiol* (blood) corpuscle, blood cell; *Pharm* globule, small pill.

globuleux, -euse [glɔbylø, -øz] *adj* globular; **yeux g.,** protruding eyes.

glockenspiel [glɔkɛnʃpil] *nm Mus* glockenspiel.

gloire [glwar] *nf* **(a)** glory; **se couvrir de g.,** to cover oneself in glory; **elle a eu son heure de g.,** she has had her hour of glory; **il est mort en pleine g.,** he died at the height of his fame; **se faire** *ou* **tirer g. de qch,** to glory in sth, to pride oneself on sth; **mettre sa g. à** *ou* **en qch,** to boast of *or* glory in sth; **travailler pour la g.,** to work for the glory (of it) *or* for nothing;

(b) (*personne célèbre*) celebrity; **une g. oubliée,** a forgotten celebrity;

(c) (*splendeur*) **la g. de Dieu,** the glory of God; **la famille royale dans toute sa g.,** the royal family in all its splendour;

(d) (*manifestation de respect*) glory, praise; **rendre g. à Dieu/qn,** to glorify God/s.o.; **g. à Dieu!,** glory (be) to God; **g. aux soldats morts pour la France!,** glory to the soldiers who died for France!;

(e) *Beaux-Arts* halo.

gloria [glɔrja] *nm* **(a)** *Rel* Gloria; **(b)** *F Vieilli* coffee served with spirits.

glorieusement [glɔrjøzmɑ̃] *adv* gloriously.

glorieux, -euse [glɔrjø, -øz] **1** *adj* **(a)** glorious; **une bataille glorieuse,** a glorious battle; **ce n'est pas très g.,** that's nothing to be proud of; **porter un nom g.,** to have a glorious *or* celebrated name; **il est promis à un avenir g.,** he has a glorious future ahead of him; **un soldat g.,** a renowned soldier; **(b)** *Arch & Litt* proud; **g. de qch,** vain *or* conceited about sth. **2** *nmpl* **les g.,** the saints in glory.

glorification [glɔrifikasjɔ̃] *nf* glorification.

glorifier [glɔrifje] *v* (*impf & pr sub* **n. glorifiions, v. glorifiiez**) **1** *vt* to praise, to glorify; *Rel* **que ton nom soit glorifié!,** hallowed be thy name. **2 se glorifier** *vpr* to boast; **se g. de (faire) qch,** to glory in (doing) sth, to boast of (doing) sth.

gloriole [glɔrjɔl] *nf F* **pour la g.,** for the sake of kudos; **faire de la g.,** to talk big; **c'est une attitude de g.,** he's just showing off.

glose [gloz] *nf* (*explication*) gloss, commentary; **g. marginale,** marginal note; **dire la vérité sans g.,** to speak the plain *or* unvarnished truth.

gloser [gloze] **1** *vt* (*expliquer*) to gloss, to expound (*text*). **2** *vi* to comment (**sur,** on); *Péj* to gossip (**sur,** about); *Vieilli* **g. sur qch,** to find fault with *or* carp at sth.

glossaire [glɔsɛr] *nm* **(a)** (*pour termes spécifiques*) glossary; **(b)** (*d'une langue*) vocabulary.

glossine [glɔsin] *nf* tsetse fly.

glottal, -aux [glɔtal, -o] *adj Ling Anat* glottal.

glotte [glɔt] *nf Anat* glottis; *Ling* **coup de g.,** glottal stop.

glouglou [gluglu] *nm* **(a)** (*bruit d'un liquide*) glug-glug, gurgle, bubbling; **faire g.,** to gurgle; **(b)** (*cri*) gobble (*of turkey*).

glouglouter [gluglute] *vi* (*of turkey*) to gobble.

gloussement [glusmɑ̃] *nm* clucking, cluck (*of hen*); gobbling, gobble (*of turkey*); *F* chuckling, chuckle, chortle (*of person*).

glousser [gluse] *vi* (*of hen*) to cluck; (*of turkey*) to gobble; *F* (*of person*) to chuckle, to chortle.

glouteron [glutrɔ̃] *nm* burdock, burr.

glouton, -onne [glutɔ̃, -ɔn] **1** *adj* greedy, gluttonous. **2** *n* glutton; **c'est un petit g.,** he's a regular little pig. **3** *nm Zool* glutton, wolverine.

gloutonnement [glutɔnmɑ̃] *adv* gluttonously, greedily, *F* like a pig.

gloutonnerie [glutɔnri] *nf* gluttony.

gloxinie [glɔksini] *nf* gloxinia.

glu [gly] *nf* bird lime; (*colle*) glue, gum; **prendre des oiseaux à la g.,** to lime birds; *Fig* **être pris à la g.,** to be caught in a trap; *Fig* **il a de la g. aux mains,** money sticks to his fingers; *Fig F* **c'est une vraie g.,** he sticks like a limpet, you can't shake him off.

gluant [glyɑ̃] *adj* sticky, gummy, gluey.

gluau, -aux [glyo] *nm* lime twig, snare.

glucide [glysid] *nm Biol Ch* glucide; **riche en g.,** high *or* rich in glucides.

glucose [glykoz] *nm* glucose; **g. sanguin,** blood sugar.

glucosé [glykoze] *adj* containing glucose; **une solution glucosée,** a glucose solution.

glume [glym] *nf* chaff; *Bot* glume.

gluten [glytɛn] *nm* gluten; **sans g.,** gluten-free.

glutineux, -euse [glytinø, -øz] *adj* glutinous.

glycémie [glisemi] *nf Méd* glycaemia.

glycérine [gliserin] *nf Ch* glycerin(e), glycerol.

glycériner [gliserine] *vt* to rub *or* treat (*sth*) with glycerin(e).

glycérol [gliserɔl] *nm Ch* glycerol, glycerin(e).

glycine¹ [glisin] *nf* wisteria, wistaria.

glycine² *nf Biol Ch* glycine.

glycogène [glikɔʒɛn] *nm Ch* glycogen.

glycol [glikɔl] *nm Ch* glycol.

glyphe [glif] *nm Archit* glyph, groove, channel.

glyptique [gliptik] *nf* glyptics.

gnangnan [ɲɑ̃ɲɑ̃] *F* **1** *adj inv* flabby, spineless, wet. **2** *n* spineless person, wet.

gnaule [ɲol] *nf Arg* brandy, spirits, rotgut.

gneiss [gnɛs] *nm Géol* gneiss.

gniole, gnole, gnôle [ɲol] *nf Arg* brandy, spirits, rotgut.

gnocchi [ɲɔki] *nmpl Culin* gnocchi.

gnognote, gnognotte [ɲɔɲɔt] *nf F* **c'est de la g.,** it's a load of rubbish.

gnome [gnom] *nm* gnome.

gnomique [gnomik] *adj* gnomic (*poetry etc*).

gnon [ɲɔ̃] *nm Arg* (*coup de poing*) biff; **se prendre un g.,** to get biffed.

gnose [gnoz] *nf,* **gnosie** [gnozi] *nf* **(a)** *Hist Rel* gnosticism; **(b)** *Vieilli* gnosis.

gnosticisme [gnɔstisism] *nm Hist Rel* gnosticism.

gnostique [gnɔstik] *adj & n Rel* gnostic.

gnou [gnu] *nm* gnu, wildebeest.

go (tout de) [go] *adv F* **tout de go,** without ceremony, all of a sudden; **répondre tout de go,** to answer straight off.

G.O. [ʒeo] *nfpl Rad* (*abrév* **grandes ondes**) L.W..

goal [gol] *nm Fb etc* goalkeeper, *F* goalie.

gobelet [gɔblɛ] *nm* goblet, cup; beaker; **(verre) g.,** tumbler; *Culin* **g. gradué,** measuring jug; **joueur de gobelets,** thimblerigger; **tour de g.,** conjuring trick (*with glasses*).

gobeleterie [gɔblɛtri] *nf* hollow glass trade.

gobeletier [gɔblətje] *nm* manufacturer of *or* dealer in glassware.

gobe-mouches [gɔbmuʃ] *nm inv* **(a)** *Orn* flycatcher; **(b)** *Bot* **dionée g.-m.,** Venus's fly trap, Venus flytrap; **(c)** *F*

(*personne*) simpleton, dope.
gober [gɔbe] **1** *vt* to gulp down (*food*); **g. l'appât** *ou* **le morceau** *ou* **la mouche,** to swallow *or* rise to the bait; *F* **g. des mouches,** to stand gaping; *Fig* **il gobe tout ce qu'on lui dit,** he believes everything he's told, he'll swallow anything. **2 se gober** *vpr F* to think a lot of *or* to fancy oneself.
goberger (se) [səgɔbɛrʒe] *vpr* (**je me gobergeai(s); n.n. gobergeons**) *F* to do oneself well *or* proud.
gobeur, -euse [gɔbœr, -øz] *n* gulper, swallower; *Fig F* **c'est un g.,** he's very gullible, he'll swallow anything.
gobie [gɔbi] *nm* (common sand) goby.
godailler [gɔdaje] *vi* = **GODER.**
godasse [gɔdas] *nf Arg* shoe; (*qui n'est pas élégante*) clodhopper.
Godefroi [gɔdfrwa] *nm* Godfrey.
godelureau, -eaux [gɔdlyro] *nm Péj* dandy, *Am* dude.
goder [gɔde] *vi* (*of cloth*) to pucker, to ruck (up); **g. aux genoux,** (*of trousers*) to bag at the knees.
godet [gɔdɛ] *nm* **(a)** bowl; **g. à couleur,** saucer for mixing water colours; **g. à huile,** waste oil cup (*of machine*); **g. d'une pipe,** bowl of a pipe; *Arg* **viens boire un g.,** come and have a drink; **(b)** (*noria*) scoop; bucket (*of dredger, excavator, waterwheel*); *MecE etc* socket (*for foot of machine etc*); *Min* skip; **roue à godets,** overshot wheel; **(c)** *Couture* (*ondulation*) flare; (*lé*) gore; **à godets,** flared; (*à lés*) gored.
godiche [gɔdiʃ] **, godichon, -onne** [gɔdiʃɔ̃, -ɔn] *F* **1** *adj* (*stupide*) stupid, silly; (*empoté*) awkward, clumsy, hamfisted. **2** *nf* **quelle godiche, cette fille!,** what a lump (of a girl)!
godille [gɔdij] *nf* **(a)** *Nau* stern oar, scull; **aller à la g.,** to (single-)scull; **(b)** *Ski* wedel; **faire de la g.,** to wedel.
godiller [gɔdije] *vi* **(a)** *Nau* to (single-)scull; **(b)** *Ski* to wedel.
godilleur [gɔdijœr] *nm Nau* sculler.
godillot [gɔdijo] *nm* (military) boot; *F* shapeless old shoe.
godron [gɔdrɔ̃] *nm* **(a)** *Archit* gadroon; **(b)** (*orfèvrerie*) boss beading; *Couture Vieilli* pleat, goffer; **godrons,** fluting.
godronnage [gɔdrɔnaʒ] *nm Couture* goffering, fluting.
godronner [gɔdrɔne] *vt Couture* to goffer, to flute.
goéland [gɔelɑ̃] *nm* (sea)gull.
goélette [gɔelɛt] *nf Nau* (*navire*) schooner; **(voile) g.,** trysail.
goémon [gɔemɔ̃] *nm* (*algues*) wrack.
goglu [gɔgly] *nm Can* (*oiseau*) bobolink.
gogo¹ (à) [agogo] *adv F* (*livres etc*) galore; **avoir de l'argent à g.,** to have money galore *or* to burn.
gogo² *nm F* sucker.
goguenard [gɔgnar] *adj* mocking; (*sarcastique*) sarcastic.
goguenardise [gɔgnardiz] *nf* sarcasm, sarcastic remarks.
goguenot [gɔgno] *nm Arg* (*pot de chambre*) po, jerry; **goguenots,** (*toilettes*) bog, *Am* john.
goguette [gɔgɛt] *nf F* **être en g.,** to be (a bit) tight *or* merry.
goï, *pl* **goïm** [gɔj, gɔim] *nm Rel juive* goy, *pl* goyim.
goinfre [gwɛ̃fr] *F* **1** *nm* greedyguts, pig. **2** *adj* greedy, piggy.
goinfrer (se) [səgwɛ̃fre] *vpr F* to guzzle, to gorge (oneself).
goinfrerie [gwɛ̃frəri] *nf* gluttony, guzzling.
goitre [gwatr] *nm Méd* goitre, *US* goiter.
goitreux, -euse [gwatrø, -øz] **1** *adj* goitrous (*neck, swelling, person*). **2** *n* goitrous person.
golden [gɔldɛn] *nf inv* golden delicious (apple).
golem [gɔlɛm] *nm* (*folklore juif*) golem.
golf [gɔlf] *nm Sp* golf; **g. miniature,** miniature golf; **(terrain de) g.,** golf course, links; **jouer au g.,** to play golf; **pantalon de g.,** plus fours.
golfe [gɔlf] *nm* gulf, bay; **le Courant du G.,** the Gulf Stream; **le G.,** the Gulf.
golfeur, -euse [gɔlfœr, -øz] *n* golfer.
gomina ® [gɔmina] *nf* solid brilliantine, hair cream.
gominer (se) [səgɔmine] *vpr* to plaster down one's hair (*with brilliantine etc*).
gommage [gɔmaʒ] *nm* **(a)** (*action*) gumming; **(b)** *Tech* sticking, gumming (*of valves, pistons*); **(c)** (*pour effacer ou atténuer des ombres etc*) toning down, smoothing out; **(d)** (*produit de beauté*) face scrub; **se faire un g.,** to give oneself a face scrub.
gommant [gɔmɑ̃] *adj* cleansing; **crème gommante,** face scrub.
gomme [gɔm] *nf* **(a)** gum; **g. arabique,** gum arabic; **g. laque,** shellac; **g. à mâcher,** chewing gum; **boule de g.,** (*chewing gum*) gum; **(b)** (*pour effacer*) rubber, *Am* eraser; **g. à encre,** ink eraser; *F* **histoire à la g.,** pointless story; **individu à la g.,** useless individual; **(c)** *F* **mettre (toute) la g.,** to get a move on, to go all out; *Aut* to put one's foot down.
gomme-gutte [gɔmgyt] *nf* gamboge; (*pl gommes-guttes*).
gomme-laque [gɔmlak] *nf* shellac, lac; (*pl gommes-laques*).
gommer [gɔme] *vt* **(a)** (*enduire de gomme*) to gum; **(b)** (*effacer*) to erase, to rub out; *Fig* **g. une partie de son passé,** to erase part of one's past; **(c) g. les cellules mortes de la peau,** to remove dead skin; **(d)** *Tech* to stick, to jam; **piston gommé,** gummed piston.
gomme-résine [gɔmrezin] *nf* gum resin; (*pl gommes-résines*).
gommette [gɔmɛt] *nf* coloured sticker.
gommeux, -euse [gɔmø, -øz] **1** *adj* gummy, sticky; **plante gommeuse,** gum-yielding plant. **2** *nm F Vieilli* dandy, fop, *Am* dude.
gommier [gɔmje] *nm* gum tree.
gonade [gɔnad] *nf Biol* gonad.
gond [gɔ̃] *nm* hinge (*of door*); **mettre une porte sur ses gonds,** to hang a door; *F* **sortir de ses gonds,** to lose one's temper, to fly off the handle.
gondolage [gɔ̃dɔlaʒ] *nm* warping (*of wood*); curling (*of paper*); buckling (*of sheet iron etc*).
gondolant [gɔ̃dɔlɑ̃] *adj F* side-splitting, uproariously funny (*story etc*).
gondole [gɔ̃dɔl] *nf* **(a)** (*barque*) gondola; **(b)** (*présentoir*) island, gondola.
gondolement [gɔ̃dɔlmɑ̃] *nm* = **GONDOLAGE.**
gondoler [gɔ̃dɔle] **1** *vi* (*of wood*) to warp; (*of paper*) to curl; (*of sheet iron*) to buckle; (*of car bumper etc*) to crumple up. **2 se gondoler** *vpr* **(a)** =**1** *vi*; **(b)** *F* to split one's sides laughing.
gondolier, -ière [gɔ̃dɔlje, -jɛr] *n* gondolier.
gonfalon [gɔ̃falɔ̃] *nm*, **gonfanon** [gɔ̃fanɔ̃] *nm Arch* gonfalon (*banner, streamer*).
gonflage [gɔ̃flaʒ] *nm Aut etc* inflation; **vérifier le g. (des pneus),** to check the tyre *or Am* tire pressure.
gonflé [gɔ̃fle] *adj* **(a)** (*boursouflé*) swollen, puffy (*eyes*); bloated (*face*); (*estomac*) bloated, swollen; *Fig* **g. d'orgueil,** puffed up with pride; **avoir le cœur g. de chagrin,** to be heart-broken; **(b)** (*sail*) full; **(c)** *F* **tu es g.,** (*culotté*) you've got a nerve; **g. à bloc,** keyed up; (*en pleine forme physique*) full of beans; (*sûr de soi*) sure of oneself; *Aut F* **moteur g.,** hotted-up *or* souped-up engine; **(d)** (*exagéré*) **prix gonflés,** exaggerated prices.
gonflement [gɔ̃fləmɑ̃] *nm* inflating, inflation (*of tyres, balloon*); swelling (*of stomach*).
gonfler [gɔ̃fle] **1** *vt* **(a)** to blow up, to pump up, to inflate (*tyre*); to puff out, to blow out, to bulge (*one's cheeks*); **g. un ballon/un matelas pneumatique,** to inflate *or* blow up a balloon/an airbed; **le vent gonfle les voiles,** the wind fills the sails; **(b)** (*faire augmenter de volume*) to swell; **torrent gonflé par les pluies,** torrent swollen by the rains; **(c)** *Fig* (*grossir*) to swell; **g. les chiffres d'un sondage,** to inflate the figures from a poll; **g. un événement,** to hype up an event; **(d)** *Aut F* to hot up, to soup up (*an engine*). **2** *vi* to become inflated; to swell; **le bois a gonflé,** the wood has swollen; **laisser de la pâte g.,** to let dough rise. **3 se gonfler** *vpr* = **2** *vi*; **les poumons se gonflent,** the lungs fill; *Fig* **se g. d'orgueil,** to be swollen up with pride.
gonfleur [gɔ̃flœr] *nm* (air) pump.
gong [gɔ̃(g)] *nm* **(a)** *Mus* gong; **(b)** *Boxe* bell; *Fig* **sauvé par le g.,** saved by the bell.
gonio [gɔnjo] *nm Nau Av F* direction finder, radiogoniometer.
goniomètre [gɔnjɔmɛtr] *nm Rad etc* goniometer, position finder, direction finder; *Mil* dial sight.
goniométrie [gɔnjɔmetri] *nf* goniometry, position finding, direction finding.
gonocoque [gɔnɔkɔk] *nm Méd* gonococcus.
gonze [gɔ̃z] *nm Arg* (*homme*) bloke, type, guy.
gonzesse [gɔ̃zɛs] *nf Arg* (*femme*) bird, *Am* broad; **il est venu avec sa g.,** he came along with his bird.
gordien [gɔrdjɛ̃] *adj Fig* **trancher le nœud g.,** to cut the Gordian knot.
goret [gɔrɛ] *nm* piglet; *F* dirty little child, pig; **manger comme un g.,** to eat like a pig.
gorge [gɔrʒ] *nf* **(a)** (*cou*) throat; **couper la g. à qn,** to cut s.o.'s throat; **le chien lui a sauté à la g.,** the dog leapt at his throat; *Fig* **avoir le couteau sous la g.,** to have a gun at one's head; **je le tiens à la g.,** I've got him by the throat, I've got a stranglehold on him; **avoir mal à la g., avoir un mal de g.,** to have a sore throat; **avoir un serrement de**

g., to gulp; **avoir la gorge serrée,** to have a lump in one's throat; **crier à pleine g.,** to shout at the top of one's voice; **avaler qch à pleine g.,** to gulp sth down; **rire à g. déployée,** to roar with laughter; **faire des gorges chaudes de qch,** to laugh sth to scorn; **prendre à la g.,** to catch in the throat; *Fig* **rendre g.,** to make restitution;

(b) (*poitrine*) bosom, bust (*of woman*); **g. d'un pigeon,** pigeon's breast;

(c) *Géog* gorge;

(d) *Tech* groove; *Archit* quirk, gorge; furrow (*of screw*); neck (*of gun, cartridge case*); tumbler (*of lock*); *Archit* **moulure à g.,** grooved moulding.

gorgé [gɔrʒe] *adj* gorged, replete; **une éponge gorgée d'eau,** a sponge full of water; **sol g. d'eau,** sodden soil; *Biol* **des cellules gorgées de sang,** cells engorged with blood.

gorge-de-pigeon [gɔrʒdəpiʒɔ̃] *adj inv* dove-coloured.

gorgée [gɔrʒe] *nf* mouthful (*of wine etc*); **petite g.,** sip; **avaler qch d'une g.,** to swallow sth in one (gulp).

gorger [gɔrʒe] *v* (**je gorgeai(s); n. gorgeons**) **1** *vt* (*élevage*) to cram (*geese*). **2 se gorger** *vpr* to stuff *or* gorge oneself.

Gorgone [gɔrgɔn] *nf Myth* Gorgon.

gorille [gɔrij] *nm* **(a)** (*mammifère*) gorilla; **(b)** *Fig* gorilla, bodyguard.

gosier [gozje] *nm* (*pharynx*) gullet; (*arrière-gorge*) windpipe; **s'éclaircir le g.,** to clear one's throat; **avoir une arête dans le g.,** to have a fishbone stuck in one's throat; *F* **avoir le g. sec.,** to be dry *or* thirsty; **rire à plein g.,** to laugh loudly *or* heartily; *F* **avoir le g. serré (d'émotion),** to have a lump in one's throat.

gosse [gɔs] *n* **(a)** (*enfant*) *F* youngster, kid, nipper; **c'est encore une g.,** she's just a kid; **elle est venue avec ses deux gosses,** she came along with her two kids; **(b)** *F* (*jeune homme, jeune fille*) **c'est une belle g.,** she's a smashing girl; **il est plutôt beau g.,** he's quite good-looking; **(c)** *Can Arg* **gosses,** balls.

gosser [gɔse] *vt Can F* to whittle.

Goth [gɔt] *n Hist* Goth.

gothique [gɔtik] **1** *adj* Gothic. **2** *nm Archit Ling* Gothic. **3** *nf Typ* black letter.

gotique [gɔtik] *nm Ling* Gothic.

gouache [gwaʃ] *nf Beaux-Arts* gouache; **peindre à la g.,** to paint in gouache.

gouailler [gwaje] *vi Vieilli* to joke.

gouailleur, -euse [gwajœr, -øz] *Vieilli* **1** *adj* joking, mocking, bantering (*tone*). **2** *n* joker.

goualante [gwalɑ̃t] *nf F Vieilli* popular song.

gouape [gwap] *nf Arg* lout.

gouda [guda] *nm Culin* Gouda.

goudron [gudrɔ̃] *nm* tar; **g. de gaz** *ou* **de houille,** coal tar; **g. de bois,** wood tar; **g. minéral,** asphalt, bitumen.

goudronnage [gudrɔnaʒ] *nm* tarring.

goudronner [gudrɔne] *vt* to tar; *Nau* to pay; **route goudronnée,** tarred road; **toile goudronnée,** tarpaulin; **papier goudronné,** tar-lined paper.

goudronneur [gudrɔnœr] *nm* tar sprayer *or* spreader.

goudronneuse [gudrɔnøz] *nf* (*machine*) tar sprayer; (*pour l'asphalte*) asphalt spreader.

goudronneux, -euse [gudrɔnø, -øz] *adj* tarry; gummy (*oil*).

gouffre [gufr] *nm* gulf, pit, abyss; (*tourbillon*) whirlpool, vortex; *Géol* swallow hole; **g. béant,** yawning gulf *or* chasm; **g. sous-marin,** oceanic abyss; *Fig* **le g. de l'oubli/du désespoir,** the depths of oblivion/despair; *Fig* **être au bord du g.,** to be on the edge of the abyss; *Fig* **cette voiture est un g.,** this car is just a bottomless pit; *Fig* **c'est un g. (cet homme-là)!,** money just slips through his fingers!

gouge [guʒ] *nf Tech* gouge, hollow chisel.

gouine [gwin] *nf Arg* lesbian.

goujat [guʒa] *nm* boor, lout, churl.

goujaterie [guʒatri] *nf* boorishness, churlishness.

goujon[1] [guʒɔ̃] *nm* gudgeon.

goujon[2] *nm Constr* gudgeon, joggle (*in stonework*); *Menuis* tenon, joggle (*on foot of post etc*); *MecE* bolt; *Menuis* **g. perdu, g. prisonnier,** dowel (pin); *MecE* **g. de jonction,** assembling pin, bolt; **g. de charnière,** pin *or* pintle of a hinge; **g. d'arbre,** gudgeon of a shaft.

goujonner [guʒɔne] *vt Menuis* to dowel; *Constr* to joggle; *MecE* to pin, to bolt.

goulache, goulasch [gulaʃ] *nf Culin* (Hungarian) goulash.

goulag [gulag] *nm* Gulag.

goulée [gule] *nf F* big mouthful, gulp.

goulet [gulɛ] *nm* **(a)** *Géog* (*défilé*) gully; **(b)** *Nau* (*chenal*) gut, bottleneck, narrows (*of harbour*); **le G. de Brest,** the Brest Channel.

goulot [gulo] *nm* neck (*of bottle*); **boire au g.,** to drink (straight) from the bottle; *Aut etc* **g. d'étranglement,** bottleneck.

goulotte [gulɔt] *nf Tech* shoot, chute; spout (*of coal hopper etc*).

goulu, -ue [guly] **1** *adj* **(a)** (*glouton*) greedy, gluttonous; **(b) pois g.,** sugar pea. **2** *n* glutton.

goulûment [gulymɑ̃] *adv* greedily, voraciously.

goupil [gupi] *nm Arch* fox; *Littér* Reynard the Fox.

goupille [gupij] *nf Tech* pin; **g. fendue,** split pin, cotter; **g. d'arrêt,** stop bolt.

goupiller [gupije] **1** *vt* **(a)** *Tech* to pin, to key; to cotter (*bolt*); **(b)** *F* (*arranger*) to contrive, to wangle (*sth*); **bien/mal goupillé,** well/badly organized. **2 se goupiller** *vpr* **ça s'est bien goupillé,** it worked out well.

goupillon [gupijɔ̃] *nm* **(a)** *Rel* aspergillum, sprinkler (*for holy water*); **(b)** brush (*for gum, bottle etc*).

gourbi [gurbi] *nm* **(a)** hut, shack; **(b)** *F* hovel.

gourd [gur] *adj* numb(ed) (with cold); **avoir les doigts gourds,** to have numb fingers.

gourde [gurd] **1** *nf* **(a)** *Bot* gourd; **(b)** (*récipient pour boissons*) water bottle; (*coloquinte*) gourd, calabash; **(c)** *F* (*fille, femme stupide*) idiot, dimwit, dope. **2** *adj F* stupid, dimwitted.

gourdin [gurdɛ̃] *nm* club, cudgel, bludgeon.

gourer (se) [səgure] *vpr Arg* to boob, to make a boob *or* bloomer; **se g. de route,** to lose one's way.

gourmand, -ande [gurmɑ̃, -ɑ̃d] **1** *adj* **être g.,** to be greedy; *Fig* **être g. de qch,** to be greedy for sth; **herbes gourmandes,** parasitical weeds; **pois g.,** sugar pea, mangetout, *Am* snowpea. **2** *n* (*personne*) greedy person. **3** *nm* (*branche parasite*) sucker.

gourmander [gurmɑ̃de] *vt* **(a)** *Litt* to rebuke, to chide; **(b)** *Arch* to saw at (*horse's mouth*).

gourmandise [gurmɑ̃diz] *nf* **(a)** greediness, gluttony; **manger avec g.,** to eat greedily; **(b) gourmandises,** goodies.

gourme [gurm] *nf* **(a)** *Méd* impetigo; **(b)** *Vét* strangles; **(c)** *Fig Vieilli* **jeter sa g.,** to sow one's wild oats.

gourmé [gurme] *adj Litt Péj* stiff, starched, affected.

gourmet [gurmɛ] *nm* gourmet; **un fin g.,** a discerning gourmet.

gourmette [gurmɛt] *nf* **(a)** (*d'une montre*) curb watch chain; (*bracelet*) chain (bracelet); **(b)** (*pour les chevaux*) curb (chain).

gourou [guru] *nm Hindu Rel* guru.

gousse [gus] *nf* pod, shell, husk (*of peas etc*); **g. d'ail,** clove of garlic.

gousset [gusɛ] *nm* **(a)** pocket; **il a le g. bien garni,** his pockets are well-lined; **montre de g.,** fob watch; **(b)** *MecE etc* (shoulder) bracket, stay plate, gusset (plate).

goût [gu] *nm* **(a)** (*sens*) (sense of) taste; **avoir le g. fin,** to have a fine palate; *F* **faire passer le g. du pain à qn,** (*le tuer*) to get rid of s.o.; (*le faire changer d'avis*) to put the wind up s.o.;

(b) (*saveur*) taste, flavour, *US* flavor; bouquet (*of wine*); **g. amer/épicé/***etc*, bitter/spicy/*etc* taste; **g. de terroir,** native tang; **cela a le g. de ...,** it tastes like ...; **donner du g. à un mets,** to give a dish flavour; **manquer de g., ne pas avoir de g.,** (*d'un plat*) to have no taste; **sans g.,** tasteless(ly);

(c) (*préférence*) *Culin* **ajouter du sucre et du citron selon son g.,** add sugar and lemon to taste; **chacun ses goûts, des goûts et des couleurs on ne discute pas, tous les goûts sont dans la nature,** everyone to his (own) taste, there's no accounting for taste; **affaire de g.,** matter of taste;

(d) (*prédilection, convenance*) taste, liking; **avoir des goûts de luxe,** to have expensive tastes; **il a des goûts bizarres,** he has strange tastes; **une maison à mon g.,** a house to my taste *or* liking; **le g. des affaires,** a taste *or* liking for business; **g. passager,** passing fancy; **avoir du g. pour** *ou* **le g. de qch,** to have a taste *or* liking for sth; **elle n'est pas à mon g.,** I don't care for her; **faire qch par g.,** to do sth from inclination; **je n'habite pas ici par g.,** I don't live here from choice; **prendre g. à qch,** to acquire a taste *or* develop a liking for sth; **avec le temps elle y a** *ou* **en a pris g.,** it grew on her, she developed a liking for it; **elle n'a plus (de) g. à rien,** she no longer wants to do anything; **reprendre g. à la vie,** to regain one's zest for living, to find life worth living again;

(e) (*discernement, jugement*) taste; **g. parfait,** perfect taste; **il a du g.,** he has (good) taste; **remarque d'un g. douteux,** remark in doubtful taste; **une plaisanterie de mauvais g.,** a joke in bad taste; **une robe de mauvais g.,** a tasteless dress; **décoration de bon g.,** tasteful decoration; **elle s'habille avec g.,** she has (a) good dress sense *or* a flair for clothes;

(f) *Litt* style, manner; **peint dans le g. de Watteau,** painted in the Watteau manner; **quelque chose dans ce g.-là,** something of that sort *or* style.

goûter¹ [gute] *nm* snack; (*à quatre heures*) (afternoon) tea; **c'est l'heure du g.,** it's time for tea; **elle est invitée pour le g.** *ou* **à un g.,** she has been invited to tea; **il a mis son g. dans son cartable,** he put his snack in his satchel.

goûter² 1 *vt* **(a)** (*savourer*) to taste (*food*); (*tester*) to taste, to try, to sample (*food, drink*); **(b)** *Fig* (*aimer, apprécier*) to enjoy, to appreciate, to relish; **g. la musique,** to enjoy music; **g. le silence de la nuit,** to relish the silence of night. **2** *vi* **(a) g. à quatre heures,** to have tea *or* a snack at four o'clock; **(b) g. de qch,** to taste sth for the first time; *Fig* **elle a goûté de tous les petits boulots,** she's had a go at all sorts of jobs; **g. à qch,** to taste sth, to take a little of sth; **goûtez donc à ce vin!,** just try this wine!

goûteur, -euse [gutœr, -øz] *n* taster.

goutte [gut] **1** *nf* **(a)** drop (*of liquid*); **g. à g.,** drop by drop; **tomber g. à g.,** (*of liquid*) to drip; *Fig* **c'est la g. d'eau qui fait déborder le vase,** it's the last straw (that breaks the camel's back); **se ressembler comme deux gouttes d'eau,** to be like two peas in a pod; **c'est une g. d'eau dans la mer,** it's a drop in the ocean; **il suait à grosses gouttes,** the sweat was pouring off him; **il n'y a pas eu une g. de pluie depuis trois mois,** there hasn't been a drop of rain for three months; **il tombait quelques gouttes,** it was spitting with rain; *F* **avoir la g. au nez,** to have a runny *or* dripping nose; **g. d'eau,** drop of water, drip; (*bijouterie*) teardrop;

(b) (*petite quantité*) small quantity, sip; **g. de cognac,** dash of brandy (*in sauce*); **boire une goutte de cognac après le repas,** to have a drop *or* nip of brandy after one's meal; **encore une g. de café?,** a drop more coffee?; *F* **boire la g.,** to have a nip;

(c) *Pharm* **gouttes,** drops; **prendre des gouttes,** to take drops; **gouttes pour le nez,** nasal drops;

(d) *Méd* gout; **avoir la g.,** to suffer from gout, to be gouty.

2 *adv Arch & Hum* **ne ... g.,** not at all; **je n'entends g. à ce que vous dites,** I don't understand a word of what you're saying; **je n'y vois g.,** I can't see a thing.

goutte-à-goutte [gutagut] *nm inv Méd* drip; **g.-à.-g. intraveineux,** intravenous (drip); **on lui fait un g.-à-g.,** he's on an intravenous.

gouttelette [gutlɛt] *nf* droplet, tiny drop.

goutter [gute] *vi* (*d'un robinet*) to drip.

goutteux, -euse [gutø, øz] *adj & n Méd* gouty (*person*).

gouttière [gutjɛr] *nf* **(a)** *Constr* (*le long du toit*) gutter, guttering; **chat de g.,** alley cat; **(b)** (*le long du mur*) spout, rain pipe; **(c)** *Anat* groove (*of bone*); **(d)** *Méd* cradle, (cradle-like) splint.

gouvernable [guvɛrnabl] *adj* governable, manageable; **peu g.,** unmanageable.

gouvernail [guvɛrnaj] *nm Nau* rudder, helm; **roue du g.,** (steering) wheel; **tenir le g.,** to be at the wheel *or* at the helm, to steer; *Fig* **tenir le g. de l'État/d'une affaire/***etc*, to be at the helm of the state/a business/*etc*; **g. de plongée,** horizontal rudder (*of submarine*); **g. de profondeur,** diving rudder, plane, hydroplane; *Av* **g. de direction,** rudder; **g. de profondeur,** elevator.

gouvernant, -ante [guvɛrnɑ̃, -ɑ̃t] **1** *adj* governing, ruling; (*party*) in power. **2** *n* **les gouvernants,** the party in power; (*pouvoir exécutif*) the executive.

gouvernante [guvɛrnɑ̃t] *nf* (*qui garde les enfants*) governess.

gouverne [guvɛrn] *nf* **(a)** *Nau* steering; *Fig* **pour votre g.,** for your guidance; **(b)** *Av* **gouvernes,** control surfaces; **g. de direction,** rudder; **g. de profondeur,** elevator; **g. compensée,** balanced surface.

gouvernement [guvɛrnəmɑ̃] *nm* **(a)** *Pol* (the) government; **le g. français/britannique,** the French/British government; **le chef du g.,** the head of government; **former un nouveau g.,** to form a new government; **g. monarchique/républicain/parlementaire,** monarchic(al)/republican/parliamentary government; **(b)** government, management, direction, administration (*of household, business, state etc*); (*charge*) governorship; *Mil* command.

gouvernemental, -aux [guvɛrnəmɑ̃tal, -o] *adj* governmental; **politique gouvernementale,** government(al) policy; **le parti g.,** the government party; **un journal g.,** a government newspaper.

gouverner [guvɛrne] **1** *vt* **(a)** (*diriger*) to govern (*a country*); (*dominer*) to govern, to rule, to control, to direct; **Dieu gouverne l'univers,** God is the ruler of the universe; **g. ses passions,** to control *or* govern one's passions; *Tech* **mouvement gouverné par une pendule,** movement regulated *or* governed *or* controlled by a pendulum;

(b) *Nau* to steer, to handle (*ship*); **faire g.,** to con; **g. sur un port,** to steer *or* stand *or* head for a port, to bear in with a port; **g. à la lame,** to steer by the sea; **gouvernez droit!,** steady!;

(c) *Gram* **verbe qui gouverne l'accusatif,** verb that governs *or* takes the accusative;

(d) *Vieilli* to manage, to administer; **bien g. ses ressources,** to husband one's resources.

2 *vi* **(a)** to govern; **un parti qui gouverne depuis des années,** a party which has been in government *or* power for years;

(b) *Nau* **navire qui ne gouverne plus,** ship that no longer answers to her helm.

3 se gouverner *vpr* to govern oneself, to be self-governing; **droit des peuples à se g. eux-mêmes,** right of peoples to self-government.

gouverneur [guvɛrnœr] *nm* governor (*of province, bank etc, US of State*); *Mil* commanding officer (*of fortified position*); *Can* **G. Général,** Governor-General; *Can* **Lieutenant-G.,** Lieutenant Governor.

goy, goyim [gɔj, gɔim] *nm Jewish Rel* goy, *pl* goyim.

goyave [gɔjav] *nf* guava.

goyavier [gɔjavje] *nm Bot* guava (tree).

G.Q.G. [ʒekyʒe] *nm Mil* (*abrév* **grand quartier général**) GHQ.

gr. *nm(pl)* (*abrév* **gramme(s)**) gr.

Graal (le) [ləgral] *nm Litt* the (Holy) Grail; **la quête du G.,** the quest for the (Holy) Grail.

grabat [graba] *nm* pallet, litter (*of straw, rags etc*); **mourir sur un g.,** to die in abject poverty.

grabataire [grabatɛr] *adj & n* bedridden (person).

grabuge [grabyʒ] *nm F* quarrel, row, rumpus; **il y aura du g.,** there'll be ructions; **faire du g.,** to have a stinking row.

grâce¹ [grɑs] *nf* **(a)** (*charme*) grace, gracefulness, charm; **avoir de la g.,** to be graceful; **avec g.,** gracefully; **se déplacer avec g.,** to move gracefully; **il fait des grâces devant le miroir,** he's preening himself in front of the mirror; **de bonne g.,** willingly, readily; **de mauvaise g.,** unwillingly, ungraciously; **il serait de mauvaise g. de refuser,** it would be ungracious to refuse; **il aurait mauvaise g. à nous laisser ici,** (*après ce que nous avons fait pour lui*) it would be ungracious of him to leave us here;

(b) (*bienveillance, faveur*) favour, *US* favor; **obtenir/accorder une g.,** to obtain/to grant a favour; **faites-moi la g. d'oublier cette histoire,** do me the kindness of forgetting this matter; **trouver g. devant qn** *ou* **auprès de qn** *ou* **aux yeux de qn,** to find favour in s.o.'s eyes; **se mettre dans** *ou* **entrer dans** *ou* **obtenir les bonnes grâces de qn,** to obtain the good graces of s.o., *F* to get into s.o.'s good books; **de g.!,** please!, for pity's sake!; **faire une g. à qn,** to do s.o. a favour *or* a kindness; **les grâces de Dieu,** God's blessings; **demander une g. à qn,** to ask a favour of s.o.; **c'est trop de grâces que vous me faites!,** you really are too kind!; *Com* **jours** *ou* **terme de g.,** days of grace; *Rel* **en état de g.,** in a state of grace; *Fig* **être en état de g. auprès de qn,** to be in someone's good books; **l'an de g. 1802,** the year of grace 1802; **coup de g.,** finishing stroke, quietus, coup de grâce; **donner le coup de g. à un animal,** to put an animal out of its pain;

(c) g. à, (*avec l'aide de*) thanks to, owing to; **g. à votre aide,** thanks to your help; **g. à Dieu,** with God's help, by God's grace;

(d) (*remerciements*) thanks; **rendre g. à Dieu,** to give thanks to God; **(rendons) g. à Dieu!,** thanks be to God; **action de grâce(s),** thanksgiving; *Can* **Jour de l'action de g.,** Thanksgiving Day;

(e) *Jur* free pardon; **lettre(s) de g.,** reprieve; **je vous fais g. cette fois-ci,** I'll let you off this time; **demander** *ou* **crier g.,** to cry for mercy; **g.!,** mercy!; **droit de g.,** right of reprieve; **accorder sa g. à qn,** to pardon *or* reprieve s.o.; **je vous fais g. du reste,** I'll spare you the rest; (*ne m'en dites ou n'en faites pas plus*) you needn't do *or* say any more;

(f) (*titre honorifique*) **sa G. le duc,** His grace the Duke.

Grâce [grɑs] *nf Myth* **les trois Grâces,** the three Graces.

gracier [grasje] *vt* (*impf & pr sub* **n. graciions, v.**

graciiez) to pardon, to reprieve.
gracieusement [grasjøzmɑ̃] *adv* **(a)** (*avec grâce*) gracefully, becomingly; **se déplacer g.**, to move gracefully; **(b)** (*aimablement*) graciously, kindly; **(c)** (*gratuitement*) without payment, free of charge.
gracieuseté [grasjøzte] *nf* graciousness, affability, kindness; **faire une g. à qn,** to do s.o. a kindness *or* a favour *or US* favor.
gracieux, -euse [grasjø, -øz] *adj* **(a)** (*qui a de la grâce, du charme*) graceful, pleasing (*figure, style etc*); **(b)** (*aimable*) gracious (*manner etc*); **sourire g.**, charming smile; **(c)** (*gratuit*) free (of charge); **à titre g.**, as a favour *or US* favor, gratis, free of charge; **exemplaire envoyé à titre g.**, complimentary *or* presentation copy; **(d)** (*pour exprimer le respect*) **notre g. souverain,** our gracious Sovereign.
gracile [grasil] *adj* slender (*person, stalk etc*); slim (*person*).
gracilité [grasilite] *nf* slenderness, slimness.
Gracques (les) [legrak] *nmpl Antiq* the Gracchi.
gradation [gradɑsjɔ̃] *nf* gradation; **avec une g. lente,** by slow degrees; **par g.,** gradually.
grade [grad] *nm* **(a)** *Mil etc* rank; **g. honorifique,** honorary rank; **g. (à titre) définitif,** permanent rank; **g. honoraire,** brevet rank; **avoir le g. de caporal/sergent/***etc*, to have the rank of corporal/sergeant/*etc*; **monter en g.,** to be promoted; *F* **en prendre pour son g.,** to be told off *or* hauled over the coals; **(b)** *Univ* (university) degree; **être admis au g. de docteur ès lettres,** ≈ to obtain one's D. Litt; **(c)** *Math* grade; **(d)** *Tech* grade (*of engine oil*).
gradé [grade] *nm* **(a)** *Mil etc* non-commissioned officer, N.C.O.; **tous les gradés,** all ranks (*commissioned and non-commissioned*); **(b)** *Nau* **les gradés,** the petty officers.
grader [gradœr] *nm Constr* grader.
gradient [gradjɑ̃] *nm* gradient.
gradin [gradɛ̃] *nm* **(a)** tier of seats; *Sp* **être assis dans les gradins,** *Br Fb* to be seated on the terraces; *Am Baseball* to be sitting in the bleachers; **(b)** *Tech* **poulie à gradins,** cone pulley, stepped pulley; *Él* **disposer les balais en gradins,** to stagger the brushes (*of a dynamo*).
graduation [gradɥɑsjɔ̃] *nf* **(a)** graduating (*of scale*); (*résultat*) graduation; **(b)** (*ensemble des divisions*) scale.
gradué [gradɥe] *adj* **(a)** (*qui porte une graduation*) graduated; **verre g.,** measuring glass; **(b)** (*progressif*) graded, progressive (*exercises etc*).
graduel, -elle [gradɥɛl] *adj* gradual.
graduellement [gradɥɛlmɑ̃] *adv* gradually.
graduer [gradɥe] *vt* **(a)** to graduate, to calibrate (*thermometer etc*); **(b)** to grade (*studies etc*).
graffiti [grafiti] *nmpl* graffiti.
graillé [graje] *adj Can* (*pour faire qch*) well-equipped; *F* (*bien monté*) well-hung.
grailler [grɑje] *vi* **(a)** to speak huskily; (*d'une corneille*) to caw; **(b)** *Arg* (*manger*) to nosh.
graillon [grɑjɔ̃] *nm* **sentir le g.,** to smell of burnt fat; **avoir un goût de g.,** to taste greasy.
graillonner [grɑjɔne] *vi* to speak huskily.
grain¹ [grɛ] *nm* **(a)** (*graine, fruit de petite taille*) grain; **g. de blé,** grain of wheat; **g. d'orge,** barleycorn; *Menuis* barleycorn; **g. de moutarde/grenade,** mustard/pomegranate seed; **g. de café,** coffee bean; **g. de poivre,** peppercorn; **poivre en grains,** peppercorns; **g. de raisin,** grape; *Fig* **mettre son g. de sel dans une conversation,** to put one's oar in, *Am* to put in one's ten cents' worth; *Prov* **le bon g. finit toujours par lever,** quality will tell in the end;
(b) (*céréales*) cereals, grain, corn; hard food (*for poultry*); **entrepôt de g.,** granary; **alcool de g.,** grain alcohol; **poulet de g.,** corn-fed chicken;
(c) (*petite chose*) grain (*of sand, powder*); speck (*of dust*); *Méd* sty(e); **g. de beauté,** beauty spot, mole; **g. de chapelet,** rosary bead; *Fig* **g. de coquetterie/jalousie,** touch *or* hint of coquetry/jealousy; **une g. de folie,** a touch of madness; **pas un g. de bon sens,** not a grain *or* not an ounce of common sense;
(d) *Fig F* **il a un g.,** he's not quite right in the head, he's not all there;
(e) *Tex* grain, texture (*of substance*); rough side (*of skin etc*); **côté g. du cuir,** grain side of leather; **contre le g.,** against the grain; **à gros grains,** coarse-grained; **à grains fins/serrés,** fine-/close-grained; **cassure à grains,** granular fracture; **ruban gros g.,** petersham;
(f) *Pharm* pellet; **g. de plomb,** (*balle*) pellet; *Él* **grains platinés,** platinum points;
(g) *Phot* grain;
(h) *Arch & Can* grain (= 0.0647 g).
grain² *nm Nau* squall, gust of wind; **essuyer un g.,** to meet with a squall; **veiller au g.,** to look out for squalls; *Fig* to keep a weather eye open (for trouble).
graine [grɛn] *nf Bot etc* seed; **g. de lin,** linseed; **g. de moutarde,** mustard seed; **g. d'anis,** aniseed; **monter en g.,** (*of plant*) to run *or* bolt to seed; *Fig* (*of woman*) to be (left) on the shelf; *F* **en prendre de la g.,** to profit from s.o.'s example; **c'est une mauvaise g.,** he's a bad lot; *Péj* **g. de voyou/voleur!,** you little lout/thief!
grainer [grɛne] *vt* to granulate (*gunpowder*); to shred (*wax*); to grain (*salt*).
graineterie [grɛntri] *nf Com* seed trade; (*boutique*) seed shop.
grainetier, -ière [grɛntje, -jɛr] *n* corn chandler.
grainier, -ière [grɛnje, -jɛr] *n* (*personne*) seedsman, seed merchant.
graissage [grɛsaʒ] *nm Tech* greasing, oiling, lubrication; **g. par gravité,** gravity-feed lubrication; **g. sous pression,** pressure greasing; **huile de g.,** lubricating oil; **circuit de g.,** lubrication system.
graisse [grɛs] *nf* **(a)** grease, fat; **g. animale/végétale,** animal/vegetable fat; **g. de rognon,** suet; **g. de rôti,** dripping; **g. de porc,** lard; **g. de baleine,** blubber; **g. minérale,** crude paraffin, mineral jelly; **g. pour essieux,** axle grease; **g. pour engrenages,** gear lubricant; **pistolet** *ou* **pompe** *ou* **injecteur à g.,** grease gun; **(b)** *Typ* thickness of type; **(c)** (*altération*) **tourner à la g.,** (*d'un vin*) to become ropy.
graisser [grese] **1** *vt* (*enduire de gras*) to grease, to oil, to lubricate; to oil, to dubbin (*boots*); (*par accident*) to get grease on (*one's clothes*), to make (*one's clothes*) greasy; **g. la patte à qn,** to bribe s.o., to grease s.o.'s palm. **2** *vi* **(a)** (*of wine*) to become ropy; **(b) onguent qui ne graisse pas,** non-greasy ointment.
graisseur, -euse [grɛsœr, -øz] *MecE* **1** *adj* **godet g.,** grease box; **pistolet g.,** grease gun. **2** *n* (*ouvrier*) greaser, oiler. **3** *nm* (*appareil*) greaser, lubricator.
graisseux, -euse [grɛsø, -øz] *adj* **(a)** greasy, oily, fatty, adipose (*tissue*); **(b)** (*altéré*) ropy (*wine*).
graminacées [graminase] *nfpl Bot* Graminaceae.
graminé [gramine] *Bot* **1** *adj* graminaceous. **2** *nfpl* **graminées,** Graminaceae.
grammaire [gramɛr] *nf* **(a)** grammar; **faute/règle de g.,** grammatical error/rule; **(b)** (*livre*) grammar (book).
grammairien, -ienne [gramɛrjɛ̃, -jɛn] *n* grammarian.
grammatical, -aux [gramatikal, -o] *adj* grammatical.
grammaticalement [gramatikalmɑ̃] *adv* grammatically.
gramme [gram] *nm Phys* gram(me) (= 0,0353 oz); *Fig F* **il n'a pas un g. de fantaisie,** he hasn't an ounce of imagination.
gramme-force [gramfɔrs] *nm Phys* gram weight; (*pl grammes-force*).
gramme-poids [grampwa] *nm Phys* gram weight; (*pl grammes-poids*).
gramophone [gramɔfɔn] *nm Arch* gramophone.
grand, grande [grɑ̃, grɑ̃d] **1** *adj* **(a)** (*de taille*) big, large; **grande ville/maison,** large *or* big town/house; **grands pieds,** big feet; **grands bras/grandes jambes,** long arms/legs; **grande distance,** great distance; **plus g. que nature,** larger than life; **un g. lit,** a big *or* large bed; (*à deux personnes*) a double bed; **faire des grands pas,** to take large strides; *Fig* **marcher à grands pas vers la gloire/la sagesse,** to stride towards glory/wisdom; **avancer à grands pas,** (*en progressant*) to make great strides; *Opt* **objectif g. angle,** wide angle lens; **les grandes vacances,** the summer holidays; *Univ* the long vacation; **un g. A,** a capital A; **le G. Montréal,** Greater Montreal; **une grande société,** a big *or* large company; **les grandes sociétés pétrolières,** the big *or* major oil companies; **g. changement,** big *or* major change;
(b) (*de taille élevée*) tall; **homme g.,** tall man; **un g. homme blond,** a tall fair man; **un g. palmier,** a tall palm tree; **cet enfant est très g. pour son âge,** that child is very tall for his age; **pas plus g. que ça,** only so high; **grande échelle,** tall *or* long ladder;
(c) (*principal*) chief, main; **la grande rue,** the high street, *Am* the main street; **grandes marées,** spring tides; **la grande messe,** high mass; **le g. salon,** the main drawing room; **g. ressort,** mainspring; *Nau* **le g. mât,** the mainmast; *Rad* **grandes ondes,** long wave; *Mil* **g. quartier général,** general headquarters;
(d) le g. public, the general public, the public at large;
(e) (*qui n'est plus enfant*) **quand tu seras g.,** when you're big *or* grown up, when you're old enough; **elle n'est**

pas assez grande pour comprendre, she's not old enough to understand; **je suis assez g. pour me débrouiller tout seul,** I'm big *or* old enough to fend for myself; **les grandes personnes,** the grown-ups; *Scol* **les grandes classes,** the upper forms; **un g. garçon,** a big boy; **son g. frère,** his big brother;

(f) (*en quantité, intense*) **g. bruit,** loud noise; **g. froid,** severe cold; **g. désordre,** great disorder; **g. buveur,** big *or* heavy *or* hard drinker; **grandes pluies,** heavy rains; **g. vent,** high wind; **les grands départs,** the holiday rush; **laver à grande eau,** to wash down (*floor, yard etc*); *Fig* **les grandes eaux (de Versailles),** the fountains of Versailles; **vivre au g. air,** to live in the open air; **étaler sa vie privée au g. jour,** to reveal one's private life to the public gaze;

(g) (*pour insister*) **une grande heure,** a full *or* good hour; **il fait g. jour,** it's broad daylight; **il est g. temps de partir,** it's high time we left; **avec le plus g. plaisir,** with the greatest pleasure; **ils sont grands amis,** they are great friends; **yeux grands ouverts,** wide open eyes;

(h) (*important, puissant*) great; **une grande découverte,** a great discovery; **un g. nombre,** a large number; **dans le plus g. détail,** in the greatest *or* fullest detail; **en grande partie,** largely, to a great extent; **un g. jour,** a great day; **grandes dates de l'histoire,** great dates in history; **un g. regret,** a great regret; **grande douleur,** great suffering; **un g. amour,** a great love; **les grands blessés,** the seriously wounded; **les grands brûlés,** seriously burned people; **les grandes écoles,** = specialist institutes of higher education; **au g. complet,** all together; **un acteur sans g. talent,** an undistinguished actor; **grands vins,** great *or* vintage wines; **un g. cru de bordeaux,** a great Bordeaux vintage; **un g. savant/écrivain,** a great scientist *or* scholar/writer; **une grande dame,** a great lady, a grand lady; **les grands hommes,** great men; **le g. monde,** (high) society; **un g. seigneur,** a nobleman; **la grande bourgeoisie,** the upper middle class; **se donner des grands airs,** to give oneself airs; **les grandes puissances,** the great *or* major powers;

(i) (*fastueux, ambitieux*) **un g. projet,** a great *or* grand plan; **un g. mariage,** a big wedding;

(j) (*dans un titre, un grade*) **g. officier de la légion d'honneur,** Grand Officer of the Legion of Honour.

2 *adv* **faire g.,** to do things in a big way *or* on a large *or* grand scale; **voir g.,** to have big ideas; **ouvrir la fenêtre tout grand,** to open the window wide; **en g.,** (*largement*) on a large scale; (*dans une dimension importante*) full size; **faire les choses en g.,** to do things in a big way *or* on a large *or* grand scale; **statue en g.,** life-size statue; **reproduction en g.,** enlarged copy; **ouvrir toutes les fenêtres en g.,** to open all the windows wide; **il n'y avait pas g. monde,** there weren't many people there; **il n'y a pas g. vent,** there's not much wind.

3 *n* (*personne de grande taille, adulte*) **grands et petits,** (*en taille*) big and small; (*en âge*) old and young, grown-ups and children; *Scol* **les grands,** the senior boys; **mon g./ma grande,** my boy/girl; *Scol* **la cour des grands,** the older children's playground; *Fig* **jouer dans la cour des grands,** to be like the big boys.

4 *nm* (*homme, état puissant*) **g. (d'Espagne),** grandee; **les grands de la terre,** the great of the earth *or* of this world; **les grands,** great men; **Alexandre le G.,** Alexander the Great; *Pol* **les Grands,** the Great Powers; **les Quatre Grands,** the Big Four; **les grands du pétrole,** the oil majors.

grand-angulaire [grɑ̃tɑ̃gylɛr] *adj & nm Opt* wide-angle (lens *etc*); (*pl grand(es)-angulaires*).

grand-chose [grɑ̃ʃoz] *n inv* (*souvent employé avec* **pas**) **(a)** (*peu de choses*) **elle ne fait pas g.-c.,** she doesn't do much; **il ne sera** *ou* **ne fera jamais g.-c.,** he'll never amount to much; **cela ne fait pas g.-c.,** it's of no great importance, it doesn't matter much; **cela ne vaut pas g.-c.,** it's not worth much; **(b)** *F* (*personne*) **un pas g.-c.,** a dead loss, a wet.

grand-croix [grɑ̃krwa] **1** *nf inv* Grand Cross (*of the Legion of Honour*). **2** *nm* Knight Grand Cross; (*pl grands-croix*).

grand-duc [grɑ̃dyk] *nm* (*pl grands-ducs*) **(a)** (*noble*) grand duke; *F* **faire la tournée des grands-ducs,** to go out on the town, to go round the night clubs; **(b)** (*oiseau*) great horned owl, eagle owl.

grand-ducal, -aux [grɑ̃dykal, -o] *adj* grand-ducal.

grand-duché [grɑ̃dyʃe] *nm* grand duchy; (*pl grands-duchés*).

Grande-Bretagne [grɑ̃dbrətaɲ] *nf* Great Britain.

grande-duchesse [grɑ̃ddyʃɛs] *nf* grand duchess; (*pl grandes-duchesses*).

grandelet, -ette [grɑ̃dlɛ, -ɛt] *adj F* tallish.

grandement [grɑ̃dmɑ̃] *adv* **(a)** (*noblement*) grandly, nobly; **(b) faire les choses g.,** (*généreusement*) to do things lavishly *or* on a grand scale; **(c)** (*largement*) greatly, largely; **se tromper g.,** to be greatly mistaken; **avoir g. raison,** to be completely *or* absolutely right; **avoir g. le temps,** to have ample time; **il est g. temps de ...,** it is high time to ...; **avoir g. de quoi vivre,** to have plenty to live on.

grand ensemble [grɑ̃tɑ̃sɑ̃bl(ə)] *nm* housing scheme *or* estate; **vivre dans un g. e.,** to live on a housing estate.

grandeur [grɑ̃dœr] *nf* **(a)** (*taille*) size; height (*of tree*); bulk (*of parcel*); **échelle de grandeurs,** scale of sizes; **g. nature,** full-size(d), life-size(d); **une poupée de la g. d'un enfant de deux ans,** a doll the size of *or* as big as a two-year-old child; **deux vases de la même g.,** two vases of the same size; **nous sommes de la même g.,** we are the same height *or* size; *Fig* **regarder qn du haut de sa g.,** to look down on s.o.;

(b) (*importance, ampleur*) importance; magnitude (*of offence*); grandeur (*of conception*); *Math* magnitude; **la g. d'un amour,** the greatness of a love; *Astron* **étoile de première g.,** star of the first magnitude;

(c) (*importance dans la société*) **se donner des airs de g.,** to give oneself airs; **avoir la folie des grandeurs,** to have delusions of grandeur;

(d) (*gloire*) grandeur, majesty, splendour, *US* splendor; **g. et décadence d'un empire,** rise and fall of an empire; **la g. de Rome,** the grandeur *or* greatness of Rome;

(e) (*dignité, noblesse*) nobility (*of character etc*);

(f) (*titre honorifique*) **sa G.,** his Highness; **sa G. l'archevêque,** his Grace the Archbishop; **votre G.,** your Lordship; (*à un roi, une reine*) your Highness; (*à un duc, une duchesse, un archevêque*) your Grace.

grandiloquence [grɑ̃dilɔkɑ̃s] *nf* grandiloquence.

grandiloquent [grɑ̃dilɔkɑ̃] *adj* grandiloquent.

grandiose [grɑ̃djoz] *adj* grand, imposing, grandiose; imposing, awe-inspiring (*spectacle*).

grandir [grɑ̃dir] **1** *vi* (*en taille*) to grow (tall); (*en âge*) to grow up; **elle a grandi,** she has grown, she is taller; **il a grandi l'année dernière,** he shot up last year; **un arbre qui grandit vite,** a tree which grows quickly, a fast-growing tree; **en grandissant,** as one grows up, as one grows older; *Fig* **g. en sagesse,** to grow in wisdom; **son influence grandit,** his influence is increasing *or* growing. **2** *vt* (*faire paraître plus grand*) to make (*sth*) greater, to increase (*sth*); **ses talons la grandissent,** her heels make her look taller; *Fig* **ses malheurs l'ont grandi,** he is all the greater for his misfortunes; *Fig* **cela ne la grandit pas à mes yeux,** that does not improve her standing in my eyes. **3 se grandir** *vpr* **se g. en se haussant sur la pointe des pieds,** to make oneself taller by standing on tiptoe.

grandissant [grɑ̃disɑ̃] *adj* growing, increasing; **tempête grandissante,** rising storm; **une peur grandissante,** a growing fear.

grandissement [grɑ̃dismɑ̃] *nm* **(a)** *Opt* magnification; **(b)** *Vieilli* growth, increase.

grand(-)livre [grɑ̃livr] *nm Com* ledger; (*pl grands(-)livres*).

grand-maman [grɑ̃mamɑ̃] *nf F* grandma, granny, nan; (*pl grand(s)-mamans*).

grand-mère [grɑ̃mɛr] *nf* grandmother; *F* (*vieille femme*) old woman; (*pl grand(s)-mères*).

grand-messe [grɑ̃mɛs] *nf Rel* high mass; (*pl grand(s)-messes*).

grand-oncle [grɑ̃tɔ̃kl] *nm* great-uncle; (*pl grands-oncles*).

grand-papa [grɑ̃papa] *nm F* grandpa, grandad; (*pl grands-papas*).

grand-peine (à) [agrɑ̃pɛn] *adv* with great difficulty.

grand-père [grɑ̃pɛr] *nm* grandfather; *F* (*vieil homme*) grandad, old man; (*pl grands-pères*).

grand-prêtre [grɑ̃prɛtr] *nm* high priest; (*pl grands-prêtres*).

grand-route [grɑ̃rut] *nf* highway, main road; (*pl grand-routes*).

grand-rue [grɑ̃ry] *nf* high street, main street; (*pl grand-rues*).

grands-parents [grɑ̃parɑ̃] *nmpl* grandparents.

grand-tante [grɑ̃tɑ̃t] *nf* great aunt; (*pl grand(s)-tantes*).

grand-vergue [grɑ̃vɛrg] *nf Nau* mainyard; (*pl grand(s)-vergues*).

grand-voile [grɑ̃vwal] *nf Nau* mainsail; (*pl grand(s)-voiles*).

grange [grɑ̃ʒ] *nf* barn.

grangée [grɑ̃ʒe] *nf Agr* barnful.
granit(e) [granit] *nm* granite; *Fig* **cœur de g.,** heart of stone.
granité, -ée [granite] **1** *adj* granite-like; **une assiette granitée noir sur blanc,** a black and white speckled plate. **2** *nm Tex* pebble weave. **3** *nf* **granitée** *Culin* (*glace*) = water ice.
graniteux, -euse [granitø, -øz] , **granitique** [granitik] *adj* granite.
granivore [granivɔr] **1** *adj* granivorous. **2** *n* granivore.
granulaire [granylɛr] *adj* granular.
granulation [granylɑsjɔ̃] *nf Tech* granulation.
granule [granyl] *nm* granule.
granulé [granyle] **1** *adj* granulated. **2** *nm Pharm etc* pellet, granule.
granuler [granyle] *vt* to granulate.
granuleux, -euse [granylø, -øz] *adj* granular, granulous; *Biol* **cellule granuleuse,** granule cell.
grape(-)fruit [grɛpfrut] *nm* grapefruit.
graphe [graf] *nm* graph.
graphie [grafi] *nf Ling* graph.
graphique [grafik] **1** *adj* graphic (*sign, method etc*); **arts graphiques,** graphic arts; *Ordinat* **palette g.,** graphics palette. **2** *nm* diagram; (*sur un axe*) graph. **3** *nf* graphics, graphic arts.
graphiquement [grafikmɑ̃] *adv* graphically.
graphisme [grafism] *nm* **(a)** hand(writing); **(b)** *Beaux-Arts* **le g. élégant de Degas,** Degas's elegant style of drawing *or* handling of line; *Ordinat* **graphismes,** graphics.
graphitage [grafitaʒ] *nm Tech* graphitizing, graphitization.
graphite [grafit] *nm* graphite.
graphité [grafite] *adj* **huile graphitée,** graphite oil.
graphiteux, -euse [grafitø,-øz] , **graphitique** [grafitik] *adj* graphitic.
graphologie [grafɔlɔʒi] *nf* graphology.
graphologique [grafɔlɔʒik] *adj* graphological.
graphologue [grafɔlɔg] *n* graphologist.
grappe [grap] *nf* **(a)** cluster, bunch (*of grapes etc*); *Fig* cluster, group (*of people*); **g. d'oignons,** string of onions; **(b)** *Bot* raceme.
grappillage [grapijaʒ] *nm* **(a)** *Fig* (*d'argent*) making something on the side; (*petits vols*) pilfering; **(b)** (*de raisin*) gleaning.
grappiller [grapije] **1** *vt* **(a)** *Fig* (*recueillir au hasard*) to pick up; **g. des renseignements,** to glean information; **(b)** *Fig* (*faire des profits*) to make something on the side; (*piquer, voler*) to pilfer. **2** *vi* to glean (*in vineyard*).
grappin [grapɛ̃] *nm* **(a)** *Nau etc* grapnel, grappling (iron); *Fig* **mettre le g. sur qch/qn,** to hook *or* lay hands on *or* get hold of sth/s.o.; **(b)** (*benne*) grab (*of dredger*); clutch (*of crane*).
gras, grasse [grɑ, grɑs] **1** *adj* **(a)** fat (*meat*); fatty (*tissues*); rich (*food etc*); **matières grasses,** fats; *Ch* **acide g.,** fatty acid; **mardi g.,** Shrove Tuesday; **fromage g.,** full cream cheese;
(b) fat, stout (*person*); fatted, fat (*animal*); plump (*chicken*); **g. comme un porc,** as fat as a pig; *Arg* **être g. du bide,** to be flabby; *Fig* **tuer le veau g.,** to kill the fatted calf; **plante grasse,** succulent (plant);
(c) (*maculé de graisse*) greasy, oily (*rag, hair etc*); **eaux grasses,** swill, swillings;
(d) (*épais*) heavy, clayey (*soil*); **crayon g.,** stick of greasepaint; *Typ* **caractères g.,** heavy *or* bold(-faced) type; **crème grasse,** cream for dry skin; **boue grasse,** thick *or* slimy mud; **vin g.,** ropy wine; **toux grasse,** loose *or* phlegmy cough; **voix grasse,** oily voice;
(e) *Fig* **offrir une grasse récompense,** to offer a handsome reward; **faire la grasse matinée,** to have a lie in; *Arg* **il n'y en a pas g.,** there's not much of it;
(f) (*graveleux*) dirty, smutty (*story etc*).
2 *adv* **(a) faire g., manger g.,** to eat meat (*esp on a fast day*);
(b) rire g., to give a belly laugh.
3 *nm* **(a)** (*personne*) **les g. et les maigres,** fat and thin people;
(b) *Anat* **le g. de la jambe,** the calf of the leg;
(c) g. de jambon, ham fat.
gras-double [gradubl] *nm Culin* tripe.
grassement [grɑsmɑ̃] *adv* **(a)** (*confortablement*) **vivre g.,** to live off the fat of the land; **(b)** (*d'une façon peu élégante*) **rire g.,** to give a belly laugh; **(c)** (*largement*) **récompenser qn g.,** to reward s.o. handsomely *or* generously.
grasseyement [grasɛjmɑ̃] *nm* exaggeration of one's r's.
grasseyer [graseje] *vi* to exaggerate one's r's.
grassouillet, -ette [grɑsujɛ, -ɛt] *adj* plump (*person*); chubby (*child*).
grateron [gratrɔ̃] *nm Bot* goose-grass, cleavers.
graticuler [gratikyle] *vt* to divide (*drawing etc*) into squares.
gratification [gratifikɑsjɔ̃] *nf* **(a)** bonus; **g. du jour de l'an,** ≈ Christmas bonus; **(b)** *Psy* gratification.
gratifier [gratifje] *vt* (*impf & pr sub* **n. gratifiions, v. gratifiiez**) **(a)** to present (**qn de qch,** s.o. with sth); **il a été gratifié d'une grosse récompense,** he was presented with a large reward; *Iron* **être gratifié d'une amende,** to be landed with a fine; **(b)** *Psy* to gratify (*s.o.*).
gratin [gratɛ̃] *nm* **(a)** *Culin* (*chapelure*) (seasoned) breadcrumbs; (*fromage*) cheese topping; **au g.,** (cooked) with (breadcrumbs and) grated cheese; **chou-fleur au g.,** = cauliflower cheese; **un g. dauphinois,** = sliced potatoes baked with cream and browned on top; **(b)** *Fig F* **le g.,** (*le beau monde*) the upper crust.
gratiné, -ée [gratine] **1** *adj Culin* sprinkled with (breadcrumbs and) cheese, au gratin; *Fig* **une addition gratinée,** (*excessive*) an enormous bill; **c'est g.!,** that's a bit much!; **une histoire gratinée,** a smutty story. **2** *nf Culin* **gratinée,** (onion) soup au gratin.
gratiner [gratine] **1** *vt* to cook (*sth*) au gratin. **2** *vi* **un plat qui gratine au four,** a dish browning in the oven.
gratis [gratis] **1** *adv* gratis, for nothing, free of charge. **2** *adj* free (*ticket etc*).
gratitude [gratityd] *nf* gratitude.
grattage [grataʒ] *nm* **(a)** (*d'un mur*) scraping; *Chir* scraping (*of a bone*); **(b)** *Tex* teaseling, napping, raising.
gratte [grat] *nf* **(a)** *F* (*profits illicites*) pickings, rake-off, profits on the side; **faire de la g.,** to get a rake-off, to make a bit on the side; **(b)** *F* (*guitare*) guitar; **jouer de la g.,** to play the guitar; **(c)** *Can* (snow) plough.
gratte-ciel [gratsjɛl] *nm inv* skyscraper, high-rise building.
gratte-dos [gratdo] *nm inv* backscratcher.
grattement [gratmɑ̃] *nm* scratching.
gratte-papier [gratpapje] *nm inv Péj* pen-pusher.
gratte-pieds [gratpje] *nm inv* (metal) doormat.
gratter [grate] **1** *vt* **(a)** (*avec les ongles*) to scratch; (*avec qch de dur*) to scrape; (*effacer*) to scratch out (*a word etc*); **g. (la terre) du pied,** (*of horse*) to paw the ground; **g. le dos de qn,** to scratch s.o.'s back; *F* **ça me gratte terriblement,** it makes me itch like mad; **poil à g.,** itching powder; **vin qui gratte le gosier,** wine that rasps the throat; *Fig* **g. les fonds de tiroir,** to scrape the bottom of the barrel; **c'est une affaire où il n'y a pas grand-chose à g.,** you can't make much out of that;
(b) *F* (*dépasser*) to overtake, to pass (*a competitor, another car*);
(c) *Tex* to teasel, to raise, to nap; **laine grattée,** brushed wool.
2 *vi* **(a) pull qui gratte,** scratchy pullover; **g. à la porte,** to scratch at the door;
(b) (*jouer en amateur*) **g. du violon/de la guitare,** to scrape on the fiddle/to strum away on the guitar;
(c) (*ne pas glisser*) **plume qui gratte,** scratchy nib.
3 se gratter *vpr* **(a)** (*avec les ongles*) to scratch oneself; **se g. jusqu'au sang,** to scratch oneself raw; **se g. la tête/l'oreille,** to scratch one's head/ear;
(b) *Arg* **tu peux toujours te g.!,** you can whistle for it!, nothing doing!
gratteron [gratrɔ̃] *nm Bot* goose grass, cleavers.
gratteur, -euse [gratœr, -øz] *n* scratcher.
grattoir [gratwar] *nm* scraper; *Typ* slice; **g. de bureau,** erasing knife, scraper eraser.
gratuit [gratɥi] *adj* free (of charge); *Fig* gratuitous (*insult etc*); **à titre g.,** gratis, free of charge; *Fig* **un acte g.,** a gratuitous act.
gratuité [gratɥite] *nf* exemption from payment; *Fig* gratuitous nature (*of insult etc*); **la g. de l'enseignement,** free education.
gratuitement [gratɥitmɑ̃] *adv* for nothing, free of charge; *Fig* (*sans motif*) gratuitously, without provocation.
gravats [grava] *nmpl* **(a)** (*après criblage du plâtre*) screenings (*of plaster*); **(b)** (*après démolition*) rubbish, rubble.
grave [grav] **1** *adj* **(a)** (*digne, solennel*) grave, serious (*face*); grave, solemn (*tone*); sober (*expression*); (*très important*) important, weighty (*business*); (*qui a des conséquences fâcheuses*) severe, serious (*wound*); **elle ne s'absente de son travail que pour raison g.,** she never stays away from work except in serious circumstances; **commettre une g. erreur,** to make a serious mistake;

subir une g. opération, to undergo a serious operation; **accident qui a fait un mort et deux blessés graves,** accident in which one person died and two were seriously injured; **hélas!, il y avait plus g.,** alas! there was worse to come;

(b) *Mus etc* low(-pitched), deep (*note, voice*); **sons graves,** bass tones;

(c) *Gram* **accent g.,** grave accent;

(d) *Arch* heavy; *Phys* **corps g.,** heavy body.

2 *nm Mus* low(-pitched) *or* deep note, bass.

gravé [grave] *adj* **pierre gravée,** engraved stone; **image gravée,** graven image.

gravelé [gravle] *adj Tech* **cendre gravelée,** pearl ash.

graveleux, -euse [gravlø, -øz] *adj* **(a)** gravelly (*soil*); **(b)** smutty, rude (*story, song*).

gravelle [gravɛl] *nf Méd Arch* gravel.

gravelure [gravlyr] *nf* smutty talk *or* story.

gravement [gravmɑ̃] *adv* **(a)** (*avec dignité*) gravely, solemnly, soberly; **(b)** (*d'une manière importante, dangereuse*) seriously (*ill*); **il s'est g. trompé,** he was seriously *or* greatly mistaken.

graver [grave] *vt* to cut, to engrave, to carve (*material, design*); *Mus* **g. un disque,** to make *or* cut a record; **g. à l'eau-forte,** to etch; **gravé par le feu,** burnt in; *Fig* **cela reste gravé dans ma mémoire,** it is engraved on my memory.

graveur [gravœr] **1** *nm* engraver; carver (*on stone etc*); **g. à l'eau-forte,** etcher; **g. sur bois,** wood engraver. **2** *adj* **bain g.,** etching bath.

gravide [gravid] *adj Méd* (*enceinte*) gravid.

gravier [gravje] *nm* gravel; **terrain de g.,** gravelly soil; **couvrir un chemin de g.,** to gravel a path.

gravillon [gravijɔ̃] *nm* fine gravel, grit; **gravillons,** (*annonce*) loose chippings *or Am* gravel.

gravillonnage [gravijɔnaʒ] *nm* (*de chemin*) (fine-) gravelling; (*de route*) gritting.

gravillonner [gravijɔne] *vt* to (fine-)gravel (*path etc*); to grit (*a road*).

gravillonneuse [gravijɔnøz] *nf* (*machine*) gravel spreader; (*pour le verglas etc*) grit spreader, gritter.

gravimétrie [gravimetri] *nf Phys* gravimetry.

gravimétrique [gravimetrik] *adj Phys* gravimetric.

gravir [gravir] *vt* to climb (*mountain, stairs*); to climb, to mount (*ladder*); *Fig* **g. les échelons,** to climb the ladder, to rise through the ranks.

gravitation [gravitasjɔ̃] *nf Phys* gravitation.

gravitationnel [gravitasjɔnɛl] *adj Phys* gravitational; **force gravitationnelle,** force of gravity.

gravité [gravite] *nf* **(a)** *Phys* gravity; **g. spécifique,** specific gravity; **centre de g.,** centre of gravity; **alimentation par g.,** gravity feed; **(b)** (*réserve, sérieux*) gravity, seriousness; soberness (*of bearing*); **(c)** (*danger*) severity, seriousness (*of illness*); seriousness (*of operation*); **blessure sans g.,** slight wound; **(d)** (*importance*) gravity, seriousness (*of a problem*).

graviter [gravite] *vi* **(a)** to revolve (**autour de,** round); **g. autour de la terre,** to orbit the earth; *Fig* **g. autour de qn,** to hover around s.o.; **(b)** *Vieilli* to gravitate (**vers,** towards).

gravois [gravwa] *nmpl Vieilli* = **GRAVATS**.

gravure [gravyr] *nf* **(a)** (*action*) engraving; **g. sur bois,** woodcutting, wood engraving; **g. en taille-douce,** copperplate engraving; **g. en creux,** intaglio engraving; **g. à l'eau-forte,** etching; **(b)** (*ouvrage*) engraving, etching; **g. en taille-douce, g. sur cuivre,** copperplate (engraving); **g. sur bois,** woodcut, wood engraving; **g. en couleurs,** colour print; **g. hors texte,** full-page plate; **g. avant la lettre,** proof before letters; **g. de mode,** fashion plate; *Fig* **cette fille est une g. de mode,** that girl's a real fashion plate; **(c)** *Mus* making, cutting (*of record*).

grayé [greje] *adj Can* (*pour faire qch*) well-equipped; *F* (*bien monté*) well-hung.

gré [gre] *nm* **(a)** (*goût*) liking, taste; **à mon g., selon mon g.,** to my liking, to my taste; (*à mon avis*) in my opinion; **je m'habille à mon g.,** I dress to please myself; **trouver qch à son g.,** to find sth to one's liking; **une chambre à mon g.,** a room that I like *or* that suits me;

(b) (*volonté*) will, pleasure; **se marier contre le g. de son père,** to get married against one's father's wishes; **bail renouvelable au g. du locataire,** lease renewable at the option of the tenant; **de mon propre g., de mon plein g.,** of my own free will, of my own accord; **de bon g.,** willingly, gladly; **de mauvais g.,** reluctantly; **elle va et vient à son (bon) g.,** she comes and goes as she pleases; **bon g. mal g.,** whether we like it or not, willy-nilly; **de g. ou de force,** willy-nilly, by fair means or foul; **au g. des flots,** at the mercy of the waves; **de g. à g.,** by (mutual) agreement; *Fig* **au g. des événements/circonstances,** as events/circumstances allow;

(c) (*gratitude*) **savoir (bon) g. à qn de (faire) qch,** to be grateful to s.o. for (doing) sth; **savoir mauvais g. à qn de qch,** to be annoyed with s.o. about sth.

grèbe [grɛb] *nm* grebe.

grébiche [grebiʃ] *nf*, **grébige** [grebiʒ] *nf Typ* file number (*of manuscript etc*).

grec, grecque [grɛk] **1** *adj* Greek; **les orateurs grecs,** the Greek orators; **tragédie grecque,** Greek tragedy; **profil g.,** Grecian profile; **Église grecque,** Greek Orthodox church. **2** *nm Ling* Greek; **g. ancien/moderne,** Ancient/ Modern Greek. **3** *n* **G.,** Greek. **4** *nf* **grecque (a)** *Culin* **à la g.,** stewed with oil and herbs; **(b)** *Archit Beaux-Arts* Greek key pattern, Greek border; **(c) coiffure à la grecque,** hair done in the Grecian style.

Grèce [grɛs] *nf* Greece.

gréciser [gresize] *vt* to Hellenize; **g. une phrase,** to give a Greek turn to a phrase.

gréco-latin, -ine [grekɔlatɛ̃, -in] *adj Ling* Gr(a)eco-Latin; (*pl gréco-latin(e)s*).

gréco-romain, -aine [grekɔrɔmɛ̃, -ɛn] *adj* Gr(a)eco-Roman; (*pl gréco-romain(e)s*).

gredin, -ine [grədɛ̃, -in] *n* (*voleur*) rogue, scoundrel; *F* (*vaurien*) rascal, wretch; *F* **petit g.!,** you little horror!

gredinerie [grədinri] *nf Vieilli* mean *or* underhand behaviour *or* action.

gréement [gremɑ̃] *nm Nau* **(a)** (*ensemble des voiles*) rigging; (*équipement*) gear; **(b)** (*disposition des mâts et des voiles*) rig (*of ship*); **g. Marconi,** Bermuda rig.

gréer [gree] *vt Nau* to rig (*mast, vessel etc*); to sling (*hammock, nets*); **gréé en carré,** square-rigged; **g. une vergue,** to send up a yard.

gréeur [greœr] *nm Nau* rigger.

greffage [grɛfaʒ] *nm Chir Bot* grafting.

greffe¹ [grɛf] *nf* **(a)** *Chir* graft (*of skin, tissue etc*); *Chir* transplant (*of organ*); *Bot* graft, slip; *Chir* **g. cutanée,** skin graft; *Chir* **g. du cœur/du rein,** heart/kidney transplant; *Chir* **g. épidermique,** skin grafting; **(b)** (*action*) *Bot* **g. par œil détaché,** budding; *Bot* **g. en écusson,** shield grafting *or* budding.

greffe² *nm* **(a)** *Jur* office of the clerk of the court; **(b)** *Fin* registry (*of joint stock company*).

greffé [grɛfe] *n Méd* **g. cardiaque** *ou* **du cœur,** heart transplant patient.

greffer [grefe] *vt Chir Bot* to graft (*skin, tissue, cutting*); *Chir* to transplant (*an organ*).

greffeur [grefœr] *nm Bot* grafter, budder.

greffier [grefje] *nm* **(a)** *Jur* clerk (of the court); **(b)** *Admin Fin* registrar.

greffoir [grɛfwar] *nm* grafting knife.

greffon [grɛfɔ̃] *nm Chir* (*of tissue, skin*) graft; (*of organ*) transplant; *Bot* graft, slip.

grégaire [gregɛr] *adj* gregarious; **l'instinct g.,** the herd instinct.

grégarisme [gregarism] *nm* gregariousness.

grège [grɛʒ] *adj* **(a)** (*brut*) raw (*silk*); **(b)** (*couleur*) whiteish-beige.

grégeois [greʒwa] *adj Arch* (= **grec**) **feu g.,** Greek fire.

Grégoire [gregwar] *nm* Gregory.

grégorien, -ienne [gregɔrjɛ̃, -jɛn] *adj* Gregorian (*chant etc*).

grêle¹ [grɛl] *adj* slender, thin (*leg, stalk etc*); thin, high-pitched (*voice*); *Anat* **intestin g.,** small intestine.

grêle² *nf* hail; **orage accompagné de g.,** hailstorm; *Fig* **g. de coups/balles,** hail *or* shower of blows/bullets.

grêlé [grele] *adj* pockmarked (*skin*).

grêler [grele] **1** *v impers* **il grêle,** it's hailing. **2** *vt* to damage *or* destroy (*crops etc*) by hail.

grelin [grəlɛ̃] *nm Nau* hawser, rope.

grêlon [grɛlɔ̃] *nm* hailstone.

grelot [grəlo] *nm* (small) bell; (*de traîneau*) sleigh bell; *Fig* **attacher le g.,** to bell the cat; *Arg* **avoir les grelots,** (*avoir peur*) to have the wind up.

grelottement [grəlɔtmɑ̃] *nm* **(a)** (*tremblement*) shivering; **(b)** (*tintement*) tinkling, jingling.

grelotter [grəlɔte] *vi* **(a)** (*trembler*) to tremble, to shake, to shiver (*with cold, fear etc*); **(b)** (*tinter*) to jingle, to tinkle.

grenade [grənad] *nf* **(a)** (*projectile*) *Mil* grenade; **g. à main,** hand grenade; **g. fumigène,** smoke grenade; *Nau* **g. sous-marine,** depth charge; **(b)** (*fruit*) pomegranate.

Grenade [grənad] *nf* **(a)** Granada (*Spain*); **(b)** Grenada (*Windward Islands*).

grenadier¹ [grənadje] *nm* pomegranate (tree).

grenadier[2] *nm Mil* grenadier; *Fig* tall and masculine woman; **boire comme un g.,** to drink like a fish.
grenadière [grənadjɛr] *nf Mil* band (*of rifle*).
grenadine [grənadin] *nf* **(a)** *Culin* grenadine (= pomegranate juice); **(b)** *Tex* grenadine.
grenaillage [grənɑjaʒ] *nm Tech* shot blasting.
grenaille [grənɑj] *nf* **(a)** (*grains*) shot; **g. de plomb,** lead shot; **(b)** (*pour la volaille*) refuse grain, tailings; **(c)** *Belg* **grenailles errantes,** (*sur panneau*) loose chippings *or Am* gravel.
grenailler [grənɑje] *vt* to granulate (*metal etc*).
grenaison [grənɛzɔ̃] *nf* seeding (*of cereals etc*).
grenat [grəna] **1** *nm* garnet. **2** *adj inv* garnet-red.
grené [grəne] **1** *adj* stippled. **2** *nm* stipple.
greneler [grənle] *vt* (**je grenelle, n. grenelons; je grenellerai**) to grain (*paper, leather*).
grener [grəne] *v* (**je grène, n. grenons; je grènerai**) **1** *vi* (*of cereals etc*) to seed. **2** *vt* **(a)** (*réduire en grains*) to granulate (*gunpowder*); to shred (*wax*); to grain (*salt*); **(b)** (*donner un aspect grené à*) to grain (*paper, leather*).
grènetis [grɛnti] *nm* milled edge (*of coin*).
greneur [grənœr] *nm Tech* grainer, stippler.
grenier [grənje] *nm* **(a)** (*pour grain, fourrage*) granary, storehouse; **g. à foin/blé,** hayloft/cornloft; *Fig* **l'Égypte était le g. du monde ancien,** Egypt was the granary of the ancient world; **(b)** (*sous les combles*) attic, garret; **chercher qch de la cave au g.,** to hunt high and low for sth; **(c)** *Nau* dunnage.
grenouillage [grənujaʒ] *nm F Péj* shady dealing, wangling.
grenouille [grənuj] *nf* **(a)** frog; **g. bœuf** *ou* **mugissante,** bullfrog; *Fig* **g. de bénitier,** = bigoted female churchgoer; **(b)** *F* (*tirelire*) ≈ piggy bank; **manger la g.,** to make off with the cash.
grenouillère [granujɛr] *nf* **(a)** (*marécage*) frog-pond; **(b)** (*pour bébé*) all-in-one; (*pyjama*) sleepsuit.
grenu [grəny] **1** *adj* **(a)** (*wheat etc*) grainy, full of grain; **(b)** grained (*leather etc*); coarse-grained, crystalline (*salt*). **2** *nm* granularity (*of marble etc*).
grenure [grənyr] *nf* **(a)** *Beaux-Arts* stippling, stipple; **(b)** (*du cuir*) grain(ing).
grès [grɛ] *nm* **(a)** *Géol* sandstone; **g. rouge,** red sandstone; **g. bigarré,** Bunter *or* new red sandstone; **g. à bâtir** *ou* **de construction,** freestone, brownstone; **g. à meule,** millstone grit; **g. à pavés,** paving stone; **(b)** (*céramique*) **poterie de g., g. cérame,** stoneware; **cruche en g.,** stone jug.
gréseux, -euse [grezø, -øz] *adj* gritty, sandy; **roches gréseuses,** sandstones.
grésil [grezi(l)] *nm* hail.
grésillement [grezijmɑ̃] *nm* crackling (*of fire*); sputtering (*of flame*); sizzling (*of frying pan*).
grésiller[1] [grezije] *v impers* to sleet, to hail.
grésiller[2] *vi* (*of fire*) to crackle; (*of flame*) to sputter; (*of frying pan*) to sizzle.
gressin [grɛsɛ̃] *nm Culin* bread stick.
grève [grɛv] *nf* **(a)** (*arrêt du travail*) strike, walkout; **se mettre en g.,** to go *or* come out on strike, to strike, to take strike action *or* industrial action; **être en g., faire g.,** to be on strike; **g. d'avertissement** *ou* **g. symbolique,** token strike; **g. générale,** general strike; **g. perlée,** go-slow (strike), *Am* slowdown; **g. sauvage,** wildcat strike; **g. de solidarité,** sympathy strike; **g. surprise,** lightning strike; **g. sur le tas,** sit-down strike; **g. tournante,** rotating strike; **g. du zèle,** work(ing) to rule; **g. de la faim,** hunger strike; **piquet de g.,** (strike) picket; **droit de g.,** right to strike; **lancer un ordre de g.,** to issue a strike order; **g. de train/métro/***etc*, train/underground/*etc* strike; **briseur de g.,** strike breaker;

(b) (*le long de la mer*) (sea)shore, (sandy) beach; (*d'un fleuve*) (sandy) bank, *Litt* strand; **les grèves de la Loire,** the sandbanks of the Loire; *Hist* **la (place de) G.,** the Strand (*open space on the banks of the Seine where dissatisfied workmen used to assemble*).
grever [grəve] *vt* (**je grève, n. grevons; je grèverai**) **(a)** (*alourdir*) to burden, to encumber (*estate*); **grevé d'impôts,** saddled with tax; **ce week-end aux sports d'hiver a grevé notre budget,** this winter sports weekend has put a strain on our budget; **(b)** *Jur* to entail (*estate*); to mortgage (*property*).
gréviste [grevist] **1** *n* striker; **g. de la faim,** hunger striker. **2** *adj* **mouvement g.,** strike movement.
gribouillage [gribujaʒ] *nm* (*écriture*) scrawl, scribble; (*dessin*) doodle.
gribouille [gribuj] *nm* simpleton, nitwit, clot.
gribouiller [gribuje] *vi & vtr* (*écrire*) to scribble, to scrawl; (*dessiner*) to doodle.
gribouilleur, -euse [gribujœr, -øz] *n* scribbler, scrawler.
gribouillis [gribuji] *nm* = **GRIBOUILLAGE**.
grief [grijɛf] *nm* grievance, ground for complaint; **faire g. à qn de qch,** to harbour resentment against s.o. on account of sth, to hold sth against s.o..
grièvement [grijɛvmɑ̃] *adv* seriously, severely, badly (*wounded*).
griffade [grifad] *nf* scratch (*of the claw*).
griffe [grif] *nf* **(a)** claw (*of tiger etc*); talon (*of hawk*); **faire ses griffes,** (*of cat*) to sharpen its claws; *Fig* to cut one's teeth; **coup de g.,** scratch; **donner un coup de g. à qn,** to claw *or* scratch s.o.; *Fig* to have a dig at s.o.; *Fig* **montrer les griffes,** to show one's claws; *Fig* **arracher qn des griffes de qn,** to snatch s.o. out of s.o.'s clutches; *Fig* **tomber sous la g. de qn,** to fall into s.o.'s clutches;

(b) *MecE etc* claw, clip, clamp; (*outil*) dog; (*sur un bijou*) claw; **accouplement/embrayage à griffes,** claw coupling/clutch; **griffes de monteur,** climbing irons;

(c) *Bot* tendril (*of vine*); crown (*of asparagus*);

(d) (*empreinte*) stamped signature; (*ce qui sert à faire cette empreinte*) (signature) stamp; (*on clothes*) label; *Fig* **on reconnaît la g. de Zola dans ce roman,** the novel bears Zola's stamp; **on reconnaît la g. de Saint-Laurent,** you can recognize the Saint-Laurent style.
griffer [grife] *vt* **(a)** (*d'un chat etc*) to scratch, to claw; **(b)** (*signer*) to stamp (*circular etc*) with a signature.
griffon [grifɔ̃] *nm* **(a)** *Myth* griffon, gryphon, griffin; **(b)** (*chien*) griffon (terrier); **(c)** (*oiseau*) griffon (vulture).
griffonnage [grifɔnaʒ] *nm* (*écriture*) scrawl, scribble; (*dessin*) doodle.
griffonnement [grifɔnmɑ̃] *nm Beaux-Arts* wax *or* clay model.
griffonner [grifɔne] *vt* (*écrire*) to scrawl, to scribble (*letter etc*); (*dessiner*) to doodle.
griffu [grify] *adj* **patte griffue,** clawed foot; **main griffue,** claw-like hand.
griffure [grifyr] *nf* scratch.
grigner [griɲe] *vi Tex* (*of felt*) to pucker, to crinkle up.
grignotage [griɲɔtaʒ] *nm Fig* wearing down *or* away (*of resistance etc*).
grignotement [griɲɔtmɑ̃] *nm* nibbling.
grignoter [griɲɔte] **1** *vt* to nibble (at) (*sth*); to pick at (*food*); *Fig* **g. son capital,** to eat into one's capital; *Fig* **il trouve toujours à g. qch,** (*financièrement*) he always manages to make a bit on the side. **2** *vi* to nibble.
grignoteur, -euse [griɲɔtœr, -øz] **1** *n* nibbler. **2** *nf* **grignoteuse** *Tech* nibbling machine.
grigou [grigu] *nm F* miser, skinflint.
gri-gri [grigri] *nm* amulet; (*porte-bonheur*) charm.
gril [gri(l)] *nm* **(a)** (*de cuisine*) grill (pan), *Am* broiler; **faire cuire qch sur le g.,** to grill sth; *Fig F* **être sur le g.,** to be on tenterhooks; **(b)** *Tech* grating (*protecting sluice gate*); *Rail Nau* gridiron; *Th* **le g.,** the upper flies; **(c)** *Anat* **g. costal,** rib cage.
grillade [grijad] *nf Culin* grilled *or Am* broiled meat *or* steak, *US* broil; *Can* grilled *or Am* broiled chop *or* cutlet; (*assortiment*) mixed grill; **on va faire des grillades,** we're having a barbecue.
grillage[1] [grijaʒ] *nm* **(a)** roasting (*of nuts, coffee etc*); **(b)** *Métal* calcining, roasting (*of ores*); **(c)** *Tex* singeing.
grillage[2] *nm* **(a)** (metal) grating, grill(e); **g. en fil de fer,** wire netting; **poser un g. électrifié,** to put up an electrified fence; **(b)** *El* grid, frame (*of accumulator plate*).
grillager [grijaʒe] *vt* (**je grillageai(s); n. grillageons**) **(a)** (*garnir d'un grillage*) to fit a grill(e) to (*window etc*); **fenêtre grillagée,** window covered with wire mesh; **verre grillagé,** wired glass; **(b)** (*entourer d'un grillage*) to surround (*court etc*) with wire netting.
grille [grij] *nf* **(a)** (*à l'entrée d'un parc, jardin etc*) (entrance) gate (*to grounds etc*); (*clôture basse*) railings (*round monument etc*); **séparé de la rue par une g.,** railed off from the road;

(b) (*pour l'écoulement*) grating, grate (*of sink, drain etc*);

(c) (*à mailles fines*) screen, netting; grill(e) (*of convent parlour*);

(d) *Aut* **g. de radiateur,** radiator grille;

(e) *El* grid (*of accumulator, electron tube*); **courant de g.,** grid current;

(f) (*tableau quadrillé*) grid (*of crossword*); **g. des salaires, g. indiciaire,** salary structure; **g. d'avancement,** career structure; *Rad TV* **g. des programmes,** programme schedule; **g. d'horaires,** timetable, schedule.
grille-pain [grijpɛ̃] *nm inv* toaster.

griller¹ [grije] **1** *vt* **(a)** (*rôtir, passer au gril*) to grill, *Am* to broil (*meat*); to toast (*bread*); to roast (*coffee, chestnuts*);
(b) *Métal* to roast, to calcine (*ore*);
(c) *Tex* to singe;
(d) (*brûler*) to scorch, to burn; *Él F* to burn out (*bulb etc*); **végétation grillée par le soleil,** vegetation scorched by the sun; *F* **g. une cigarette,** (*fumer*) to smoke *or* have a cigarette; *Arg* **il est grillé,** (*dévoilé*) his game's up; (*rayé*) he's had it; *Sp* **g. un concurrent,** (*le dépasser*) to leave a competitor standing; *Aut F* **g. un feu rouge,** to jump the lights; *F* **g. une station,** (*of bus, train*) to go past a stop (without stopping); **g. les étapes,** (*dans sa carrière*) to shoot up the ladder; (*ne pas tourner autour du pot*) not to beat about the bush.
2 *vi* **(a)** *Culin* (*of meat*) to grill; (*of bread*) to toast; (*of chestnuts*) to roast; *Fig* **g. d'impatience,** to be burning with impatience; *Fig* **g. d'envie de faire qch,** to be bursting *or* itching to do sth;
(b) *El* (*sauter*) to burn out.
3 se griller *vpr* **se g. au soleil,** to roast in the sun; *F* **se g. auprès de qn,** to blot one's copybook with s.o..

griller² *vt* to cover (*window etc*) with wire mesh.

grilloir [grijwar] *nm* grill.

grillon [grijɔ̃] *nm* cricket.

grill-room [grilrum] *nm* grill (room); (*pl grill-rooms*).

grimaçant [grimasɑ̃] *adj* grimacing.

grimace [grimas] *nf* grimace, wry face; **faire la g.,** to make *or* pull a face, to grimace; **faire une g. de douleur,** to wince; *Prov* **on n'apprend pas à un vieux singe à faire des grimaces,** ≈ don't teach your grandmother how to suck eggs; **faire des grimaces,** (*être maniéré*) to put on airs.

grimacer [grimase] *v* (**je grimaçai(s); n. grimaçons**) **1** *vi* to grimace, to make *or* pull a face. **2** *vt* **g. un sourire,** to force a smile, to give a wry smile.

grimacier, -ière [grimasje, -jɛr] **1** *adj* grimacing; *Vieilli* (*maniéré*) affected. **2** *n Vieilli* affected person.

grimage [grimaʒ] *nm Th* (*action*) making up; (*résultat*) make-up.

grimer [grime] **1** *vt Th* to make up (*an actor, one's face*). **2 se grimer** *vpr Th* (*d'un acteur*) to make up.

grimoire [grimwar] *nm* **(a)** (*de sorcier*) wizard's book of spells; **(b)** (*ouvrage confus et illisible*) gibberish, mumbo-jumbo.

grimpant [grɛ̃pɑ̃] **1** *adj* climbing, trailing, creeping (*plant*); climbing (*animal*); **rose grimpante,** climbing rose, climber; **plante grimpante,** creeper, climbing plant, *Am* vine. **2** *nm Arg* (*pantalon*) trousers, *Am* pants.

grimpée [grɛ̃pe] *nf* (stiff) climb.

grimper [grɛ̃pe] **1** *vi* **(a)** (*monter*) to climb (up), to clamber (up); (*faire de l'escalade*) to rock-climb; **il a** *ou* **est grimpé sur la muraille,** he climbed (up) the wall; *Fig* **g. au pouvoir,** to climb to power; **(b)** (*of plants*) to climb, to trail; **(c)** *Fig* (*des prix etc*) to climb. **2** *vt F* to climb (*a mountain*); **g. l'escalier,** to go up the stairs.

grimpette [grɛ̃pɛt] *nf* (*chemin*) steep path.

grimpeur, -euse [grɛ̃pœr, -øz] **1** *adj* climbing, *Spéc* scansorial (*bird*). **2** *nm* climber; (*en cyclisme*) hill climber; (*de rocher*) rock-climber; **c'est un bon/mauvais g.,** (*ce cycliste*) he's good/bad on hills.

grinçant [grɛ̃sɑ̃] *adj* **(a)** (*qui grince*) creaking; **(b)** (*caustique*) caustic (*remark*); **elle a un humour g.,** she has a caustic wit.

grincement [grɛ̃smɑ̃] *nm* creaking (*of door, wheels etc*); **g. de dents,** grinding *or* gnashing of teeth.

grincer [grɛ̃se] *vi* (**je grinçai(s); n. grinçons**) (*of door, wheels etc*) to creak; (*of bat*) to squeak; **g. des dents,** to grind *or* gnash one's teeth; **cela fait g. des dents,** it sets your teeth on edge; **porte qui grince sur ses gonds,** creaking door.

grincheux, -euse [grɛ̃ʃø, -øz] **1** *adj* grumpy, bad-tempered. **2** *n* grumpy *or* bad-tempered person.

gringalet [grɛ̃galɛ] **1** *nm* (little) shrimp (*of a man, boy*). **2** *adj m* puny.

griotte [grijɔt] *nf* **(a)** *Bot* morello (cherry); **chocolats aux griottes,** cherry liqueur chocolates; **(b)** *Minér* griotte (marble).

grippage [gripaʒ] *nm*, **grippement** [gripmɑ̃] *nm Tech* seizing, jamming, binding (*of bearing, piston etc*).

grippal, -aux [gripal, -o] *adj Méd* flu; **soulage les états grippaux,** relieves flu symptoms; **virus g.,** flu virus.

grippe [grip] *nf* **(a)** *Méd* influenza, *F* flu; **g. gastro-intestinale,** gastric flu; **se faire vacciner contre la g.,** to be vaccinated against influenza; **attraper la g.,** to catch flu; **(b)** *Arch* (*aversion*) dislike, aversion; **prendre qn en g.,** to take a dislike to s.o..

grippé [gripe] *adj* **(a) être g.,** to be sickening for *or* coming down with (the) flu; **(b)** *Tech* seized-(up) (*engine etc*); **(c)** *Méd* pinched, drawn (*face*).

gripper [gripe] **1** *vt MecE* to seize up, to jam (*mechanism*). **2** *vi* **(a)** (*of material*) to crinkle (up), to wrinkle, to pucker; **(b)** (*of bearings*) to seize (up), to bind, to jam. **3 se gripper** *vpr* = **2** *vi* **(b)**.

grippe-sou [gripsu] *nm* miser, skinflint; **c'est un vieux g.-s.!,** he's an old skinflint *or* Scrooge!; (*pl grippe-sou(s)*).

gris [gri] **1** *adj* **(a)** (*couleur*) grey, *US* gray; (*brumeux*) grey, cloudy, dull, overcast (*weather*); **g. de poussière,** grey with dust; **papier g.,** (coarse) brown paper; **g. souris,** soft grey; **g. perle,** pearl grey; **g. (de) fer/g. acier,** iron/steel grey; **g. ardoise,** slate grey; **g.-bleu,** blue-grey; **g.-vert,** greenish-grey; **g. anthracite,** charcoal grey; **g. fumé,** smoke grey; **g. argent,** silver grey; **g. pommelé,** (*horse*) dapple-grey; **robe g. clair,** light grey dress; **aux cheveux g.,** grey-haired; *Fig* **ça m'a fait des cheveux gris,** it gave me a few grey hairs; *Anat* **substance grise,** grey matter; *F* **faire fonctionner sa matière grise,** to get one's grey matter working; **vin g.,** rosé wine; **faire grise mine,** to look anything but pleased; **faire grise mine à qn,** to give s.o. a poor welcome *or* the cold shoulder; **pensées grises,** sombre *or US* somber thoughts;
(b) (*ivre*) tipsy.
2 *nm* **(a)** grey (colour); **s'habiller en g.,** to dress in *or* wear grey;
(b) (*cheval*) grey horse;
(c) (*tabac gris*) = shag.

grisaille [grizaj] *nf* **(a)** *Fig* (*caractère morne*) dinginess, greyness; **vivre dans la g. des villes industrielles,** to live in the dreariness of industrial cities; **(b)** *Beaux-Arts* grisaille; **peindre en g.,** to paint in grisaille.

grisailler [grizaje] **1** *vt Beaux-Arts* to paint (*sth*) in grisaille. **2** *vi* to turn *or* become grey.

grisant [grizɑ̃] *adj Fig* intoxicating, exhilarating, heady; **un succès g.,** intoxicating *or* exhilarating *or* heady success; **une atmosphère grisante,** a heady atmosphere; **à une vitesse grisante,** at (an) exhilarating speed.

grisâtre [grizɑtr] *adj* greyish, *US* grayish.

grisbi [grizbi] *nm Arg* (*argent*) dough, lolly.

griser [grize] **1** *vt* **(a)** to paint *or* tint with grey *or US* gray; **(b)** (*enivrer*) to make (*s.o.*) drunk *or* tipsy; *Fig* **grisé par le succès,** intoxicated by *or* with success. **2 se griser** *vpr* **se g. d'air pur,** to get drunk on fresh air.

griserie [grizri] *nf* **(a)** (*ivresse*) tipsiness; **(b)** *Fig* (*enivrement*) intoxication, exhilaration, excitement.

grisette [grizɛt] *nf Arch* = young dressmaker *or* milliner (*of easy virtue*).

gris-gris [grigri] *nm* amulet; (*porte-bonheur*) lucky charm.

grisonnant [grizɔnɑ̃] *adj* (*cheveux*) greying, *US* graying, touched with grey *or US* gray; **avoir les tempes grisonnantes,** to be greying at the temples; **un cinquantenaire g.,** a greying fifty-year-old.

grisonner [grizɔne] *vi* to grow *or* go grey *or US* gray; **elle grisonne,** she's going grey.

grisou [grizu] *nm Min* firedamp; **coup de g.,** firedamp explosion.

grive [griv] *nf* (*oiseau*) thrush; **soûl comme une g.,** drunk as a lord; *Prov* **faute de grives on mange des merles,** beggars can't be choosers, half a loaf is better than no bread.

grivelé [grivle] *adj Arch* speckled (*plumage*).

grivèlerie [grivɛlri] *nf Jur* = (offence consisting of) ordering a meal in a restaurant without having the money to pay for it.

grivois, -oise [grivwa, -waz] *adj* risqué, bawdy (*story, song, joke*).

grivoiserie [grivwazri] *nf* (*plaisanterie*) risqué *or* bawdy joke; (*histoire*) risqué *or* bawdy story; (*acte*) rude gesture.

grizzli, grizzly [grizli] *nm* grizzly (bear).

Groenland [grɔɛnlɑ̃(d)] *nm* Greenland; **au G.,** in Greenland.

groenlandais, -aise [grɔɛnlɑ̃dɛ, -ɛz] **1** *adj* from Greenland. **2** *nm Ling* Greenlandic. **3** *n* **G.,** Greenlander.

grog [grɔg] *nm* grog, toddy.

groggy [grɔgi] *adj inv Boxe etc F* groggy.

grognard, -arde [grɔɲar, -ard] **1** *adj Vieilli* grumbling. **2** *nm Hist* = soldier of Napoleon's Old Guard. **3** *n Vieilli* grumbler.

grognement [grɔɲmɑ̃] *nm* **(a)** grunt(ing) (*of pig etc*); growl(ing) (*of dog etc*); **pousser des grognements,** (*d'un cochon*) to grunt; **(b)** (*of person*) grumbling, grousing, moaning; **pousser un g.,** to growl.

grogner [grɔɲe] **1** *vi* **(a)** (*of pig etc*) to grunt; (*of dog etc*) to growl; **(b)** (*of person*) to grumble, to grouse, to moan; **g. contre qn,** (*d'une personne*) to grumble *or* complain about s.o.. **2** *vt* **g. un refus,** to growl out a refusal.

grogneur, -euse [grɔɲœr, -øz] *adj* grumbling, grousing; **figure grogneuse,** sulky *or* disagreeable face.

grognon [grɔɲɔ̃] **1** *n* grumbler, grouser, moaner. **2** *adj* (*f* **grognon** *or* **grognonne**) grumbling, peevish; **c'est une femme g.** *ou* **grognonne,** she's always moaning.

grognonner [grɔɲɔne] *vi* (*of person*) to grouse, to grumble, to moan.

groin [grwɛ̃] *nm* snout (*of pig etc*); *Fig Péj* ugly face.

grole, grolle [grɔl] *nf Arg* (*chaussure*) shoe.

grommeler [grɔmle] *v* (**je grommelle, n. grommelons; je grommellerai**) **1** *vi* to grumble. **2** *vt* **g. un juron,** to mutter an oath.

grommellement [grɔmɛlmɑ̃] *nm* grumbling; rumbling (*of thunder etc*).

grondement [grɔ̃dmɑ̃] *nm* **(a)** growl(ing), snarl(ing) (*of dog etc*); **(b)** rumble, rumbling (*of thunder*); roar(ing) (*of mountain torrent, engine etc*); booming (*of waves, guns etc*).

gronder [grɔ̃de] **1** *vi* **(a)** (*d'un chien*) to growl, to snarl; **(b)** (*du tonnerre*) to rumble; (*des fusils*) to boom; (*des vagues*) to roar; **la révolte gronde,** there are rumblings of rebellion. **2** *vt* (*réprimander*) to scold (*s.o.*), to tell (*s.o.*) off; **g. un enfant,** to scold a child; **attention, tu vas te faire g.!,** watch out, or you'll get into trouble!; **g. qn d'avoir fait qch,** to scold s.o. *or* tell s.o. off for having done sth.

gronderie [grɔ̃dri] *nf* scolding.

grondeur, -euse [grɔ̃dœr, -øz] *adj* **(a)** grumbling, scolding, nagging (*voice etc*); **(b)** rumbling (*storm etc*).

grondin [grɔ̃dɛ̃] *nm* (*poisson*) gurnard, gurnet.

groom [grum] *nm* **(a)** (*in hotel*) page, bellboy, *Am* bellhop; **(b)** *Equitation Arch* groom.

gros, grosse [gro, gros] **1** *adj* **(a)** big, large; **g. morceau,** big *or* large piece, lump; **grosse corde,** thick *or* stout rope; **g. pullover,** thick *or* heavy *or* chunky sweater; **g. bout,** thick end (*of stick etc*); **g. moteur,** high-powered engine; **g. doigt du pied,** big toe; **grosses lèvres,** thick lips; **g. souliers,** strong *or* stout shoes; **grosses chaussettes,** thick *or* heavy socks; **avoir un g. ventre,** (*être bien en chair*) to have a paunch; (*être enceinte*) to be expecting; **avoir une grosse tête,** to have a large head; *Fig* **avoir la grosse tête,** to be big- *or* swollen-headed; **une orange grosse comme le poing,** an orange the size of your fist; *Fig* **un mensonge g. comme une maison,** a whopping lie, a whopper of a lie; *Fig* **faire les g. yeux,** to glare, to glower; **yeux g. de larmes,** eyes swollen with tears; **avoir le cœur g.,** to have a heavy heart; *Fig* **elle a un cœur g. comme ça,** she's so big-hearted; *Péj* **g. nigaud** *ou* **bêta!,** you great twit!; **écrire qch en g. caractères,** to write sth in big letters; **g. gibier,** big game; **grosse cavalerie,** heavy cavalry; **g. mangeur,** big *or* hearty eater; **g. appétit,** big *or* hearty appetite; **g. rhume,** heavy cold; **grosse fièvre,** high fever; **un g. kilo,** a good kilo; **avoir un g. chagrin,** to be very upset; **une grosse récolte,** a bumper harvest; *Nau* **grosse mer,** heavy *or* high sea; **g. temps,** stormy *or* bad weather; **grosse averse/pluie,** heavy shower/rain; **g. vent,** high wind;

(b) (*corpulent*) big, fat, stout; **un g. bébé,** a big *or* fat baby; **un g. bonhomme,** a fat gentleman;

(c) (*pas fin*) **grosse toile,** coarse linen; **g. sel,** cooking salt; **g. rouge,** plonk; **grosse voix,** gruff voice; **faire la grosse besogne,** to do the heavy work;

(d) (*grossier*) **un peu g.,** not very subtle, a bit too obvious; **c'est un peu g.!,** that's a bit much!; **g. rire,** coarse laugh; **g. mot,** swear word; **grosse indélicatesse,** gross impropriety;

(e) (*important*) **grosse somme,** large sum (of money); **ce n'est pas une grosse affaire,** (*entreprise*) it's not a big company; (*préoccupation*) it's no big deal; **la plus grosse partie de nos affaires,** the bulk of our business; **grosse faute,** gross *or* serious mistake; **g. propriétaire,** big landowner; **grosse héritière,** wealthy heiress; *F* **les g. bonnets,** *F* **les grosses légumes,** the bigwigs, the top brass, the brass hats.

2 *adv* (*beaucoup*) **gagner g.,** to earn a great deal, to make big money; **il y a g. à parier qu'il ne viendra pas,** a hundred to one he won't come!; **il risque g.,** (*en investissant son argent dans cette affaire*) he's taking a big risk; *Cartes etc* **jouer g.,** to play for high stakes.

3 *n* (*personne corpulente*) large *or* fat person; *F* (*personne riche*) rich person; **eh bien, mon g.!,** well, old man! *or* old chap!; (*à un enfant*) well, my boy!, well, son!; **se faire manger par les g.,** to be gobbled up by the big boys.

4 *nm* **(a)** (*partie la plus importante*) bulk; **le g. de la cargaison,** the bulk of the cargo; **le g. de l'armée,** the main body *or* bulk of the army; **le g. du peuple,** the mass *or* bulk of the people; **le g. d'une mission,** the main part of a mission; **le plus g. est fait,** the biggest part of the job is done; **g. de l'été/l'hiver,** height of summer/depth of winter; **g. d'un mât,** thick end of a mast;

(b) *Com* wholesale (trade); **marchand de g.,** wholesaler; **vente de g.,** wholesale; **commerce de g.,** the wholesale business; **boucher de g.,** wholesale butcher;

(c) **écrire en g.,** to write in large letters; **raconter ce qui s'est passé en g.,** to tell roughly what happened; **il y avait en g. quinze personnes,** there were about fifteen people there; **acheter en g.,** to buy wholesale; (*en grosse quantité*) to buy in bulk; **vendre en g.,** to sell wholesale.

gros-bec [grobɛk] *nm* hawfinch, grosbeak; (*pl gros-becs*).

groseille [grozɛj] *nf* **g. (rouge),** redcurrant; **g. (blanche),** white currant; **gelée de groseille(s),** redcurrant jelly; **g. à maquereau,** gooseberry.

groseillier [grozeje] *nm* (red)currant bush; **g. à maquereau,** gooseberry bush.

gros-grain [grogrɛ̃] *nm Tex* grosgrain; (*pl gros-grains*).

Gros-jean [groʒɑ̃] *nm Prov* **être G.-j. comme devant,** to be disillusioned, to come down to earth again.

grosse [gros] *nf* **(a)** *Com* gross, twelve dozen; **(b)** *Jur* engrossed document, engrossment; **(c)** *Arch* roundhand (writing).

grossesse [grosɛs] *nf* pregnancy; **g. gémellaire,** twin pregnancy; **g. extra-utérine,** ectopic pregnancy; **g. nerveuse,** false pregnancy; **interruption volontaire de g.,** abortion; **robe de g.,** maternity dress; **pendant sa g.,** during her pregnancy, while *or* when she was pregnant.

grosseur [grosœr] *nf* **(a)** (*taille, volume*) size, bulk, volume; thickness (*of lips etc*); **un objet de la g. d'un œuf,** an object the size of an egg; **(b)** *Méd* growth, tumour, *US* tumor.

grossier, -ière [grosje, -jɛr] *adj* **(a)** (*impoli*) rude, unmannerly (**envers,** to); vulgar, coarse, gross, ill-mannered; **air g.,** uncouth appearance; **un g. personnage,** an uncouth individual; **il a été on ne peut plus g.,** he was extremely rude; **langage g.,** coarse *or* crude language; **plaisanterie grossière,** crude joke; **(b)** (*commun, rudimentaire*) coarse, rough (*food, cloth etc*); crude (*method etc*); unrefined, coarse (*tastes, features etc*); **esprit g.,** ignorant person, Philistine; **(c)** (*de taille*) **stupidité grossière,** crass stupidity; **ignorance grossière,** gross *or* crass ignorance; **faute grossière,** blunder; **une ruse grossière,** a very obvious trick.

grossièrement [grosjɛrmɑ̃] *adv* **(a)** (*imparfaitement*) coarsely, roughly, crudely; **table g. façonnée,** roughly made table; **(b)** (*approximativement*) roughly; **calculer g. un prix/le nombre de personnes/***etc*, to roughly calculate a price/the number of people/*etc*; **(c)** (*de façon importante*) **se tromper g.,** to be grossly mistaken; **(d)** (*de façon impolie*) crudely, coarsely; **répondre g.,** to answer rudely.

grossièreté [grosjɛrte] *nf* **(a)** (*caractère rudimentaire*) coarseness, roughness (*of object*); **(b)** (*vulgarité*) vulgarity, coarseness (*of manner etc*); **(c)** (*parole grossière*) **dire des grossièretés à qn,** to say crude *or* coarse things to s.o., to be offensive to s.o..

grossir [grosir] **1** *vt* to enlarge, to increase; **torrent grossi par les pluies,** torrent swollen by the rain; **ce pantalon le grossit,** those trousers make him look fatter; **objet grossi trois fois,** object magnified three times; **g. sa voix,** to raise one's voice; *Fig* **g. les faits/une affaire/***etc*, to exaggerate the facts/a matter/*etc*. **2** *vi* to increase, to grow bigger *or* larger; **il grossit chaque jour,** he's getting fatter *or* putting on more weight every day; **le vent/la mer grossit,** the wind/the sea is rising.

grossissant [grosisɑ̃] *adj* **(a)** (*qui devient plus gros*) growing, swelling (*crowd etc*); **(b)** (*qui rend plus gros*) enlarging (*lens etc*); **verre g.,** magnifying glass.

grossissement [grosismɑ̃] *nm* **(a)** (*augmentation de taille*) increase in size, swelling; **(b)** (*action de rendre plus gros*) magnifying, enlargement (*of object through lens etc*); **(c)** (*capacité d'un instrument d'optique*) magnification, magnifying power (*of lens etc*).

grossiste [grosist] *n* wholesaler.

grosso modo [grosomɔdo] *adv* roughly (*speaking*); **raconter l'affaire g. m.,** to give a general account of the matter; **il y avait g. m. cinquante personnes,** there were roughly fifty people.

grossoyer [groswaje] *vt* (**je grossoie, n. grossoyons; je**

grossoierai) *Jur* to engross (*document*).
grotesque [grɔtɛsk] **1** *adj* grotesque, ludicrous (*person etc*); *Beaux-Arts* grotesque (*figure*). **2** *nm* freak, figure of fun; *Beaux-Arts* grotesque figure; **cet homme est d'un g.!**, the man's ridiculous!
grotesquement [grɔtɛskəmɑ̃] *adv* grotesquely, ridiculously, absurdly.
grotte [grɔt] *nf* grotto, (underground) cave; **g. naturelle/préhistorique**, natural/prehistoric cave.
grouillant [grujɑ̃] *adj* crawling, alive, seething (**de**, with); **rue grouillante de monde**, street swarming with people; **foule grouillante**, teeming crowd.
grouillement [grujmɑ̃] *nm* swarming, crawling; **g. de piétons**, swarming mass of pedestrians.
grouiller [gruje] **1** *vi* to crawl, to swarm, be alive (**de**, with); *Vieilli* to move; **fromage qui grouille de vers**, cheese crawling *or* alive with maggots; **la foule grouillait dans la rue**, the street was teeming *or* swarming with people. **2 se grouiller** *vpr Arg* to get a move on; **grouille(-toi)!**, get cracking!, get a move on!
grouillot [grujo] *nm Bourse* messenger (boy).
group [grup] *nm Banque* sealed bag of cash.
groupage [grupaʒ] *nm Com* collecting, bulking (*of parcels*).
groupe [grup] *nm* **(a)** group (*of people, things*); party (*of people*); group, clump (*of trees etc*); battery (*of lights*); group, cluster (*of stars etc*); bank (*of machines, instruments etc*); unit, block (*of mechanical elements*); **marcher en g.**, to walk in a group; **en groupes de trois**, in groups of three; **ils arrivaient par groupes de deux ou trois**, they arrived in twos and threes; **travailler en g.**, to work as a team; **g. de travail**, working party; **g. d'étude**, study group; **g. ethnique**, ethnic group; *Pol* **g. de pression**, pressure group; *Pol* **g. parlementaire**, parliamentary group; *Fin* **g. financier**, financial consortium; *Pol Écon* **le G. des 7**, the Group of Seven; *Méd* **g. sanguin**, blood group; **quel est votre g. sanguin?**, what's your blood group?, what blood group are you?; **faire partie d'un g. de rock**, to be in a rock group *or* band; **g. de(s) cylindres**, (*d'un moteur*) cylinder block; **g. mobile**, (*transports*) mobile unit; *Él* **g. électrogène**, generating set; *Phys Nucl* **g. de séparation (des isotopes)**, (isotope) separation unit; *Rail* **g. de changements de voie**, set of points; **(b)** *Mil* **g. de combat**, squad; **demi-g.**, section, *US* half squad; **g. d'artillerie**, battery, *US* battalion; **g. d'intervention**, mobile force, task force; **g. d'aviation**, squadron (*of transport aircraft*).
groupement [grupmɑ̃] *nm* **(a)** (*action*) grouping; *Ind Com* pooling (*of interests etc*); **g. des enfants d'après l'âge**, classification of children by age groups; **(b)** (*association*) group; **g. de consommateurs**, consumer('s) group; **(c)** *Mil* group, formation; **g. tactique**, task force; **g. d'infanterie**, brigade group, *US* battle group.
grouper [grupe] **1** *vt* to group, to arrange (in groups); *Com* to bulk (*parcels*); *Él* to connect up, to group, to couple (*cells etc*); **g. des moyens**, to pool resources. **2 se grouper** *vpr* to form a group; **se g. autour du feu**, to gather round the fire; **se g. autour d'un chef**, to gather *or* rally round a leader.
groupie [grupi] *nf F* groupie.
groupuscule [grupyskyl] *nm Pol Péj* small group; **des groupuscules néo-nazis**, small neo-Nazi groups.
gruau [gryo] *nm* **(a) (farine de) g.**, (finest) wheat flour; **pain de g.**, fine wheaten bread; **(b) g. (d'avoine)**, groats.
grue [gry] *nf* **(a)** (*oiseau*) crane; *Arg* tart; *F* **faire le pied de g. (en attendant qn)**, to hang about, to kick *or* cool one's heels (waiting for s.o.); **cou de g.**, long scraggy neck; **(b)** *MecE etc* crane; **g. à volée** *ou* **à flèche**, jib crane; **g. à pivot**, revolving crane; **g. à flotteur**, pontoon crane; *Rail* **g. d'alimentation**, (water) crane; *Cin* **g. de prise de vue**, camera crane.
gruger [gryʒe] *vt* (**je grugeai(s)**; **n. grugeons**) **(a)** to swindle, to exploit (*s.o.*); **(b)** *Can* **g. l'avance de qn**, (*dans un sondage etc*) to nibble away at s.o.'s lead.
grume [grym] *nf* **(a)** (*écorce*) bark; **bois en g.**, rough timber, undressed timber; **(b)** (*bûche*) log.
grumeau, -eaux [grymo] *nm* **(a)** lump (*in sauce etc*); **pâte à crêpes pleine de grumeaux**, lumpy pancake mixture; **(b)** (*grain*) (finely divided) curd (*of milk, soap etc*); **grumeaux de sel**, specks of salt, salty deposit.
grumeler (se) [səgrymle] *vpr* (**il se grumelle**; **il se grumellera**) **(a)** (*of sauce etc*) to go lumpy; **(b)** (*of milk*) to clot, to curdle.
grumeleux, -euse [grymlø, -øz] *adj* **(a)** lumpy (*sauce etc*); **(b)** curdled (*milk*); **(c)** (*d'aspect granuleux*) gritty (*pear*).
grutier [grytje] *nm* crane driver *or* operator.
gruyère [gryjɛr] *nm* Gruyère (cheese); **crème de g.**, processed cheese.
Guadeloupe [gwadlup] *nf* Guadeloupe.
guano [gwano] *nm* guano.
Guatemala [gwatemala] *nm* Guatemala.
guatémaltèque [gwatemaltɛk] **1** *adj* Guatemalan. **2** *n* **G.**, Guatemalan.
gué [ge] *nm* ford; **passer une rivière à g.**, to ford a river, to wade through a river.
guéable [geabl] *adj* fordable (*river*).
guède [gɛd] *nf Bot* woad, pastel.
guéer [gee] *vt* to ford (*stream*).
guelfe [gɛlf] *nm Hist* Guelph.
guelte [gɛlt] *nf Com* commission, percentage (*on sales*).
guenille [gənij] *nf* **(a)** tattered garment, old rag; **en guenilles**, in rags (and tatters); **(b)** (*chose sans intérêt*) worthless object.
guenon [gənɔ̃] *nf* **(a)** female monkey; **(b)** *F* (*femme*) ugly woman, fright.
guépard [gepar] *nm* cheetah.
guêpe [gɛp] *nf* **(a)** wasp; **nid de guêpes**, wasps' nest; **piqûre de g.**, wasp sting; *Fig* **taille de g.**, wasp waist; **(b)** (*femme rusée*) artful *or* crafty woman; *F* **pas folle, la g.!**, she's nobody's fool!
guêpier [gepje] *nm* **(a)** wasps' nest; *Fig* **se fourrer** *ou* **tomber dans un g.**, to stir up a hornets' nest; **(b)** (*oiseau*) bee eater.
guêpière [gepjɛr] *nf* (*gaine*) wasp-waisted corset.
guère [gɛr] *adv* (*always with neg expressed or understood*) hardly (any), not much, not many, only a little, only a few; **je ne l'aime g.**, I don't care much for him; **la voyez-vous? — guère!**, do you see her? — hardly ever!; **cet appel n'a eu g. de succès**, the appeal met with very little success; **il n'a g. d'argent**, he hasn't much money, he has hardly *or* scarcely any money; **vous n'en avez g. non plus**, you haven't much either; **il ne tardera g. à venir**, he'll not be long in coming; **il n'y a g. qu'elle qui soit au courant**, she's about the only one (who's) in the picture; **il ne mange g. que du pain**, he eats hardly anything but bread; **cela ne se dit plus g.**, hardly anybody says that now; **je n'y tiens plus g.**, I'm not as keen (on it) as I used to be; **il n'en reste plus g.**, there's hardly any left; **il n'y a g. plus de six ans**, it's barely more than six years ago; **il ne s'en faut (de) g.**, it's not far short; **sans g. avoir d'amis, il était respecté**, although he had very few friends, he was respected.
guéret [gerɛ] *nm* fallow land.
guéri [geri] *adj* cured; (*rétabli*) better, recovered; *Fig* **être g. d'une peur/d'un préjugé/***etc*, to be cured of a fear/a prejudice *etc*.
guéridon [geridɔ̃] *nm* pedestal table.
guérilla [gerija] *nf* **(a)** (*guerre*) guer(r)illa warfare; **(b)** *Vieilli* (*groupe*) band *or* troop of guer(r)illas.
guérillero [gerijero] *nm* guer(r)illa.
guérir [gerir] **1** *vt* to cure (*s.o., an illness*); to heal (*wound*); *Fig* **g. qn d'une habitude**, to cure *or* break s.o. of a habit. **2** *vi* (*of person*) to get better, to be cured, to recover; (*of wound etc*) to heal; (*of flu etc*) to be better; **il n'en guérira pas**, he won't get over it; *Fig* **un chagrin qui ne guérit pas**, an incurable grief. **3 se guérir** *vpr* to get better, to be cured; *Fig* **se g. de ses préjugés**, to overcome one's prejudices, to cure oneself of one's prejudices.
guérison [gerizɔ̃] *nf* **(a)** (*rétablissement*) recovery; **en voie de g.**, on the way *or* road to recovery; **(b)** (*action de guérir*) cure (*of disease*); healing (*of wound*); *Fig* **la g. d'une peine**, the healing of a sorrow.
guérissable [gerisabl] *adj* curable; (*wound etc*) that can be healed.
guérisseur, -euse [gerisœr, -øz] *n* healer; (*d'une tribu*) medicine man; *Péj* (*rebouteur*) quack (doctor).
guérite [gerit] *nf* **(a)** *Mil* sentry box; **(b)** (*petit abri*) cabin, shelter (*for watchman etc*).
guerre [gɛr] *nf* **(a)** (*conflit armé*) war, warfare; **g. classique**, conventional warfare; **g. terrestre**, land warfare; **g. aérienne**, air warfare; **g. atomique**, atomic warfare; **g. planétaire**, global war; **g. totale**, total war(fare); **g. éclair**, lightning war, blitzkrieg, *F* blitz; **g. d'embuscade**, bush warfare, guerilla warfare; **g. de rues**, street fighting; **g. de positions**, static warfare; **g. de tranchées**, trench warfare; **g. civile**, civil war; **g. d'usure**, war of attrition; **guerres de religion**, wars of religion; **g. sainte**, holy war; **la g. a éclaté entre ...**, war has broken out between ...; **déclarer la g. à un pays**, to declare war on a country; **pays en g.**, country at war; **être sur le pied de**

g., to be on a war footing; **se mettre en g.**, to go to war; **en temps de g.**, in wartime; **état de g.**, state of war; **crime/criminel de g.**, war crime/criminal; **ruse de g.**, tactics; **blessés de g.**, war wounded; **nom de g.**, nom de guerre; *Fig* pseudonym; **on entre dans une logique de g.**, war is the only logical outcome; **faire la g. à** *ou* **contre un pays,** to wage *or* make war on *or* against a country; **faire la g. avec qn,** (*aux côtés de qn*) to be in the war with s.o., to serve with s.o.; (*sous les ordres de qn*) to serve under s.o.; *Arch* **le Ministère de la G.**, *F* **la G.**, the War Department, the War Office; *Hist* **la g. de Trente ans,** the Thirty Years War; **la guerre de 70,** the Franco-Prussian War; *Eng* **la g. des deux roses,** the Wars of the Roses; **la Grande G.**, the Great War; **la première/la deuxième g. mondiale,** the first/the second world war, World War I/II; **la drôle de g.**, the phoney war (1939);

(b) *Fig* **g. idéologique,** ideological war; **g. froide,** cold war; **g. des nerfs,** war of nerves; **partir en g. contre la drogue/l'injustice/***etc*, to declare war on drugs/injustice/*etc*; **elle fait la g. à son fils pour qu'il ne fume pas,** she's fighting a running battle with her son about smoking; **faire la g. aux inégalités,** to wage war on inequality; **entre Jean et lui, c'est la petite g.**, Jean and he are always trying to score off each other; **être en g. ouverte avec** *ou* **contre qn,** to be openly at war with s.o.; *Com* **g. des prix,** price war; **de g. lasse j'y consentis,** I gave in for the sake of peace and quiet; **il est sur le pied de g. depuis 8 heures ce matin,** he's been on the go since 8 o'clock this morning; **à la g. comme à la g.**, we'll *or* you'll *etc* have to do the best we *or* you *etc* can, we'll *or* you'll *etc* have to make the best of what we've *or* you've *etc* got; (*tous les moyens sont justifiés*) if that's the way he *etc* wants it (that's the way he'll get it); **c'est de bonne g.**, it's fair enough, all's fair in love and war.

guerrier, -ière [gɛrje, -jɛr] **1** *adj* warlike, martial; **danse guerrière,** war dance. **2** *nm* warrior.

guerroyer [gɛrwaje] *vi* (**je guerroie, n. guerroyons; je guerroierai**) to war, to wage war (**contre,** against); *Fig* **g. contre l'inégalité,** to struggle against *or* wage war on inequality.

guet [gɛ] *nm* **(a)** (*action*) watch(ing), lookout; *Mil etc* **poste de g.**, lookout post; **faire le g.**, to be on watch; **chien de bon g.**, good watchdog; **(b)** *Arch* **le g.**, the watch.

guet-apens [gɛtapɑ̃] *nm* (*pl guets-apens*) **(a)** (*piège*) ambush, trap; *Fig* snare, trap; *Mil* ambuscade; **attirer qn dans un g.-a.**, to ambush s.o.; **tomber dans un g.-a.**, to fall into an ambush *or* a trap, to be ambushed; **(b)** *Jur* **de g.-a.**, with premeditation.

guêtre [gɛtr] *nf* gaiter; **demi-guêtres,** spats.

guetter [gete] *vt* to watch for (*an opportunity*); **le guépard guettait sa proie,** the cheetah was lying in wait for its prey; **g. l'arrivée/la sortie/le passage de qn,** to watch out for s.o. arriving/leaving/going past; **la mort la guette,** she's at death's door.

guetteur [gɛtœr] *nm Mil Nau* lookout (man); **poste de guetteurs,** lookout post.

gueulante [gœlɑ̃t] *nf Arg* uproar, din; **elle a poussé une g.**, (*parce qu'on était en retard etc*) she raised the roof, she kicked up a stink.

gueulard[1], -arde [gœlar, -ard] **1** *adj* **(a)** *Arg* (*qui crie*) loudmouthed; **(b)** *F* (*gourmand*) greedy. **2** *n* **(a)** *Arg* (*personne qui crie*) loudmouth; **(b)** *F* (*gourmand*) greedy guts; **3** *nm Nau* loudhailer.

gueulard[2] *nm Métal* mouth (*of furnace*).

gueule [gœl] *nf* **(a)** mouth (*of animal, fish*); **se jeter dans la g. du loup,** to put one's head in the lion's mouth;

(b) *Arg (bouche)* mouth; **c'est un fort en g.**, he's got far too much to say for himself; **jeter des injures à pleine g.**, to bawl out abuse; **coups de g.**, slanging match; **(ferme) ta g.!**, shut up!, belt up!; **s'en mettre plein la g.**, to stuff oneself; **avoir la g. de bois,** to have a hangover; **une fine g.**, a gourmet;

(c) *Arg* (*visage*) mug; **avoir la g. enfarinée,** to look all innocent; **avoir une sale g.**, (*être moche*) to have an ugly mug; (*avoir mauvaise mine*) to look rotten; (*être déprimé*) to look down in the mouth; **il a été arrêté pour délit de sale g.**, he was arrested because they didn't like the look of his face; **avoir une bonne g.**, to look a good sort; **faire la g.**, to sulk, to look sulky; **faire une g. d'enterrement,** to look thoroughly depressed; **casser la g. à qn,** to bash s.o.'s face in; **se casser la g.**, to fall flat on one's face, to come a cropper; **g. noire,** coal-miner; *Mil Hist* **les gueules cassées,** = soldiers with serious facial injuries;

(d) *F (allure)* **avoir de la g.**, to have an air about one; **ce tableau a de la g.**, that's some picture; **ce chapeau a une drôle de g.**, that's a queer sort of hat;

(e) (*ouverture*) mouth (*of sack, well, tunnel etc*); muzzle (*of gun*); **g. bée,** open sluice, (cylindrical) opening.

gueule-de-loup [gœldəlu] *nf (pl gueules-de-loup)* **(a)** *Bot* snap-dragon; **(b)** *Constr* (chimney) cowl, chimney jack; **(c)** (*de machine*) (exhaust) muffler.

gueulement [gœlmɑ̃] *nm F* (*cri*) yell; **il a poussé un g. de souffrance,** he let out a yell of pain.

gueuler [gœle] *Arg* **1** *vi* to bawl; **faire g. la radio,** to turn the radio on full blast. **2** *vt* to bawl out (*song, orders etc*).

gueules [gœl] *nm Hér* gules.

gueuleton [gœltɔ̃] *nm F* spread, blowout; **faire un bon petit g. entre amis,** to have a good blowout with some friends.

gueuletonner [gœltɔne] *vi F* to have a good blowout.

gueuse [gøz] *nf* **g. (de fonte), fer en g.**, pig (iron).

gueuserie [gøzri] *nf* **(a)** *Arch & Litt* (*condition*) beggary; **(b)** *Vieilli* (*action*) foul deed.

gueux, gueuse [gø, gøz] *n* **(a)** *F* **courir la gueuse,** to chase women; (*de façon générale*) to be a woman-chaser; **(b)** *Arch & Litt* (*mendiant*) beggar, tramp; **(c)** *Vieilli* (*fripon*) rascal, rogue.

gueuze, gueuse [gøz] *nf (bière)* = type of Belgian beer.

gui[1] [gi] *nm Bot* mistletoe; **boules de g.**, clumps of mistletoe.

gui[2] *nm Nau* **(a)** (*espar*) boom; **(b)** (*corde*) guy(rope).

guibol(l)e [gibɔl] *nf Arg* (*jambe*) pin; **jouer des guibolles,** to stir one's stumps.

guibre [gibr] *nf Nau & Arch* cutwater.

guiches [giʃ] *nfpl* kiss curls.

guichet [giʃɛ] *nm* **(a)** *Banque etc* position, *Am* wicket; *Rail etc* booking office; *Th* box office (window); **g. fermé,** (*annonce*) position closed; **concert à guichets fermés,** sold-out concert; *Can Banque* **g. automatique,** bank machine, *Br* cash dispenser; **(b)** spy hole, grille, grating (*in door*); (service) hatch (*in restaurant etc*); wicket (gate) (*of prison etc*); **(c)** *Cr* wicket; **gardien de g.**, wicket keeper.

guichetier [giʃtje] *nm* clerk, assistant; (*qui prend des réservations*) booking clerk; *Th* box- office assistant.

guidage [gidaʒ] *nm* **(a)** *Electron etc* (*d'un avion etc*) guidance; **tête de g.**, homing head; *Av* **g. par radio-maillage** *ou* **par radio-mailles,** grid guidance; **(b)** *MecE* guiding (*of moving part*); centring, *US* centering (*on boring lathe*); **(c)** guides, guide rails, bars (*of pile-driver monkey etc*).

guide [gid] **1** *nm* **(a)** guide; **g. de haute montagne,** mountain guide; *Fig* **en tout sa sœur était son g.**, his sister was his guide in everything; **la loyauté a toujours été son g.**, loyalty has always guided him; **(b)** (*manuel*) guide (book); **g. de tourisme/des rues de Londres,** tourist/London street guide; **(c)** *Tech* **g. de courroie,** belt guide; *Electron* **g. d'ondes,** wave guide. **2** *nf* **(a)** *Équitation* rein; *Fig* **mener la vie à grandes guides,** to live in lavish style; **(b)** (*fille faisant du scoutisme*) (girl)guide, *Am* girl scout; **g. aînée,** ranger.

guide-âne [gidɑn] *nm Vieilli* (elementary) handbook of instructions; (*pl guide-âne(s)*).

guide-courroie [gidkurwa] *nm* strap guide, belt guide; (*pl guide-courroie(s)*).

guider [gide] *vt* to guide, to lead (*s.o.*); to drive (*car, horse*); to steer (*boat*); *Tech* **guidé par radio,** radio-controlled; **g. un enfant dans le choix d'une carrière,** to guide *or* advise a child in the choice of a career; **se laisser g. par son intuition,** to be guided by one's intuition.

guidon [gidɔ̃] *nm* **(a)** (*de vélo*) handlebar; *Fig F* **moustaches en g. de bicyclette,** handlebar moustache; **(b)** *Mil* (*étendard*) guidon, pennant; *Nau* (*pavillon*) burgee; **(c)** (*viseur*) foresight, bead (*of gun, rifle*).

guignard, -arde [giɲar, -ard] **1** *n F Vieilli* (*malchanceux*) unlucky person, Jonah. **2** *nm* (*oiseau*) **pluvier g.**, dotterel.

guigne[1] [giɲ] *nf Bot* heart cherry; *F* **se soucier de qch/qn comme d'une g.**, not to give *or* care a damn *or* a fig about sth/s.o..

guigne[2] *nf F* bad luck; **porter la g. à qn,** to bring s.o. bad luck; **avoir la g.**, to be out of luck.

guigner [giɲe] *vt* to give a surreptitious *or* sidelong glance at (*sth, s.o.*); *Fig* (*avoir des vues sur*) to covet, to look enviously at (*sth*); *Cartes* **g. le jeu du voisin,** to look at one's opponent's hand.

guignol [giɲɔl] *nm* **(a)** (*personnage*) ≈ Punch; (*spectacle*) ≈ Punch and Judy show; **aller au g.**, ≈ to go to see the Punch and Judy show; *F* **faire le g.**, to play *or* act the fool; **(b)** *Av etc* kingpost (*of aircraft*); **g. d'aileron,** aileron lever.

guignolet [giɲɔlɛ] *nm* cherry brandy.

guignon [giɲɔ̃] *nm F Vieilli* bad luck.

guilde [gild] *nf* **(a)** *(club)* *(record, book etc)* club; **(b)** *Hist* g(u)ild; **g. de commerçants,** merchant guild.

guillaume [gijom] *nm* rabbet(ing) plane; rabbet; **g. à onglet,** mitre plane, *US* miter plane.

Guillaume [gijom] *nm* William; **G. le Conquérant,** William the Conqueror.

guilledou [gijdu] *nm F* **courir le g.,** to chase after women; *(d'une façon générale)* to be a woman- chaser.

guillemets [gijmɛ] *nmpl* inverted commas, quotation marks, *F* quotes; **mot entre g.,** word in *or* between inverted commas; **ouvrez/fermez les g.,** *(when dictating)* quote/unquote, open/close quotation marks; **c'est un artiste entre guillemets,** he's an artist, between inverted commas *or* quote unquote.

guillemot [gijmo] *nm (oiseau)* guillemot.

guilleret, -ette [gijrɛ, -ɛt] *adj* **(a)** *(gai)* lively, gay, brisk *(person, tune)*; **(b)** *(léger)* broad, risqué *(joke)*.

guillotine [gijɔtin] *nf* guillotine; **fenêtre à g.,** sash window; **cisailles à g.,** guillotine shears; **aller à la g.,** to go to the guillotine.

guillotiner [gijɔtine] *vt* to guillotine.

guimauve [gimov] *nf Bot* marshmallow; *Culin* **(pâte de) g.,** marshmallow; *Bot* **g. rose,** hollyhock; *Fig Péj* **sentimentalité de** *ou* **à la g.,** mushy sentimentality.

guimbarde [gɛ̃bard] *nf* **(a)** *Mus* Jew's harp; **(b)** *F (vieille voiture)* old, banger *or* jalopy; **(c)** *(outil)* router plane, grooving plane.

guimpe [gɛ̃p] *nf* **(a)** *(de religieuse)* (nun's) wimple; **(b)** *(chemisette)* chemisette.

guincher [gɛ̃ʃe] *vi Arg* to dance.

guindage [gɛ̃daʒ] *nm* hoisting.

guindé [gɛ̃de] *adj* stiff, *F* starchy *(person)*; stiff, strained *(atmosphere)*; affected *(language etc)*; stilted, stiff *(style)*; **être mal à l'aise dans une réception guindée,** to feel ill at ease at a posh reception.

guindeau, -eaux [gɛ̃do] *nm Nau* windlass.

guinder [gɛ̃de] **1** *vt Tech* to hoist, to windlass; *Nau* to send up, to sway up *(mast)*. **2 se guinder** *vpr (d'une personne, d'un style, d'une ambiance)* to become stiff; *(d'un style)* to become stilted; *(d'une ambiance)* to become strained.

guinée [gine] *nf Arch (monnaie)* guinea.

Guinée [gine] *nf* Guinea.

guinéen, -enne [gineɛ̃, -ɛn] **1** *adj* Guinean. **2** *n* **G.,** Guinean.

guingois [gɛ̃gwa] *adv* **de g.,** askew, lopsided; **tout va de g.,** everything's going wrong.

guinguette [gɛ̃gɛt] *nf* (suburban) café *(with music and dancing, often in the open)*.

guipage [gipaʒ] *nm Tech* taping, wrapping, lapping; *El* sleeve, sheath.

guiper [gipe] *vt Tech* to tape, to wrap, to lap; *El etc* **g. un fil,** to cover a wire.

guipure [gipyr] *nf* point lace, pillow lace.

guirlande [girlɑ̃d] *nf* garland *(of flowers etc)*; **g. de perles,** string of pearls; **g. lumineuse,** *(pour sapin de Noël)* string of lights.

guise [giz] *nf* manner, way, fashion; **faire qch à sa g.,** to do sth in one's own way; **faire** *ou* **agir à sa g.,** to have one's (own) way, to do as one pleases; **en g. de,** *(comme)* by way of; *(à la place de)* instead of; **des caisses en g. de chaises,** boxes used as chairs.

guitare [gitar] *nf Mus* guitar; **g. électrique,** electric guitar; **g. hawaïenne,** Hawaiian guitar.

guitariste [gitarist] *n* guitarist, guitar player.

guitoune [gitun] *nf* **(a)** *F (tente)* tent; **(b)** *Mil Arg* dugout, shelter.

guppy [gypi] *nm (poisson)* guppy.

gustatif, -ive [gystatif, -iv] *adj* gustative, gustatory; **papilles gustatives,** taste buds.

gustation [gystɑsjɔ̃] *nf* tasting.

gutta-percha [gytapɛrka] *nf* gutta-percha.

guttural, -ale, -aux [gytyral, -o] **1** *adj* guttural *(sound)*; throaty *(voice)*; *Anat* **artère gutturale,** carotid artery. **2** *nf Ling* **gutturale,** guttural.

guyanais, -aise [gɥijanɛ, -ɛz] **1** *adj* Guianese, Guyanese. **2** *n* **G.,** Guianese, Guyanese.

Guyane [gɥijan] Guyana; **G. française,** French Guiana; *Hist* **G. britannique,** British Guiana.

gym [ʒim] *nf F* gym; **faire de la g.,** to do gym; **un cours de g.,** a gym class.

gymkhana [ʒimkana] *nm* gymkhana.

gymnase [ʒimnaz] *nm* gymnasium.

gymnaste [ʒimnast] *n* gymnast.

gymnastique [ʒimnastik] **1** *adj* gymnastic; **partir au pas g.,** to set off briskly. **2** *nf* gymnastics; **g. rythmique,** eurhythmics; *Méd* **g. passive,** passive movements; **g. corrective,** remedial gymnastics; **g. respiratoire,** breathing exercises; **g. matinale,** morning exercises, *F* daily dozen; *Fig* **g. d'esprit,** mental gymnastics.

gymnote [ʒimnɔt] *nm* electric eel.

gynécée [ʒinese] *nm Antiq Bot* gynaeceum.

gynécologie [ʒinekɔlɔʒi] *nf* gyn(a)ecology.

gynécologique [ʒinekɔlɔʒik] *adj (examen)* gyn(a)-ecological.

gynécologiste [ʒinekɔlɔʒist]**, gynécologue** [ʒinekɔlɔg] *n* gyn(a)ecologist.

gypaète [ʒipaɛt] *nm* bearded vulture, lammergeyer.

gypse [ʒips] *nm* **(a)** *Minér* gypsum, plasterstone; **(b)** *Com* plaster of Paris.

gypseux, -euse [ʒipsø, -øz] *adj Minér* gypseous.

gypsophile [ʒipsɔfil] *nf Bot* gypsophila.

gyrocompas [ʒirɔkɔ̃pɑ] *nm Nau* gyrocompass.

gyromètre [ʒirɔmɛtr] *nm Av* gyrometer.

gyrophare [ʒirɔfar] *nm (de voiture de police)* flashing light.

gyropilote [ʒirɔpilɔt] *nm Av* gyropilot, automatic pilot.

gyroscope [ʒirɔskɔp] *nm* gyroscope; *Av* **g. directionnel,** directional gyroscope.

gyroscopique [ʒirɔskɔpik] *adj* gyroscopic; **compas g.,** gyrocompass.

gyrostabilisateur [ʒirɔstabilizatœr] *nm* gyro-stabilizer.

gyrostat [ʒirɔsta] *nm* gyrostat.

gyrostatique [ʒirɔstatik] *adj* gyrostatic.

H

H *Words beginning with an aspirate* **h** *are shown by an asterisk.*

H, h [aʃ] **1** *nm* (the letter) H, h; **h muet,** mute h; **h aspiré,** aspirate h; *Mil etc* **l'heure H,** zero hour; **bombe H,** H bomb. **2** *nm F* (*haschisch*) **trois grammes de H,** three grams of hash.

***ha** [ɑ] *int* ah!; (*laughter*) **ha, ha!,** ha!, ha!

habile [abil] *adj* **(a)** clever, skilful, able, capable; (*rusé*) cunning; **elle n'est pas h. de ses mains,** she's not good with her hands; **mains habiles,** skilled hands; **façonner qch d'une main h.,** to make sth skilfully; **h. à faire qch,** clever at doing sth; **ce n'était pas très h. de ta part,** that wasn't very clever *or* bright of you; **(b)** *Jur* **h. à succéder,** able *or* competent to inherit.

habilement [abilmɑ̃] *adv* cleverly, skilfully; cunningly.

habileté [abilte] *nf* **(a)** (*adresse*) ability, skill, skilfulness; **(b)** (*intelligence*) cleverness; **(c)** *Jur* = **HABILITÉ.**

habilitation [abilitasjɔ̃] *nf Jur* **h. de qn à faire qch,** enabling (of) s.o. to do sth.

habilité [abilite] *nf Jur* ability, title; **avoir h. à hériter,** to be entitled to succeed.

habiliter [abilite] *vt Jur* **h. qn à faire qch,** to enable *or* entitle s.o. to do sth.

habillage [abijaʒ] *nm* **(a)** dressing (*of child etc*); **(b)** (*préparation*) preparing, preparation; *Culin* dressing; drawing and trussing (*of poultry*); cleaning (*of fish*); trimming (*of meat*); **(c)** pruning, trimming (*of trees*); **(d)** assembly, putting together (*of watch etc*); **(e)** *Tech* (*of boiler etc*) lagging; **(f)** *Com* packaging (*of goods*); **(g)** *Aut* **h. intérieur,** trim.

habillé [abije] *adj* **(a)** dressed; **h. en femme/cosmonaute,** dressed up as a woman/spaceman; **h. de bleu/d'un complet** dressed in blue/in a suit; **h. chaudement,** warmly clad *or* dressed; **s'endormir tout h.,** to go to sleep with one's clothes on; **(b)** (*élégant*) smart; **soirée habillée,** reception, formal occasion; **c'est trop h. pour la soirée,** it is too dressy for the party; **cette robe fait h.,** this dress is very smart.

habillement [abijmɑ̃] *nm* **(a)** (*action*) clothing, dressing; **(b)** (*vêtement*) clothes, dress.

habiller [abije] **1** *vt* **(a)** (*de vêtements*) to dress; **h. un enfant en soldat,** to dress a child up as a soldier; *F* **h. qn,** to speak ill of *or* slate *or* slag s.o.;

(b) (*préparer*) to prepare; *Culin* to dress (*meat, fowl*); to draw and truss (*poultry*); to clean (*fish*); to trim (*meat*);

(c) to prune, to trim (*tree*);

(d) to put *or* piece (*watch etc*) together; to assemble (*parts*); *Typ* **h. une gravure,** to run type round a block;

(e) (*fournir en vêtements*) to clothe; to provide (*s.o.*) with clothes; **elle se fait h. par Lacroix,** she has clothes made for her by Lacroix; **ma mère nous habillait,** my mother made all our clothes;

(f) to cover (up), to wrap up; to lag (*boiler etc*); *Com* to label, to package (*goods*); **h. une pièce,** to decorate a room; **tableau de bord habillé de cuir,** leather-padded dash(board); **h. des meubles de housses,** to put loose covers on furniture;

(g) (*aller*) to suit; **un rien t'habille,** you look good in anything; **ce tissu l'habille bien/mal,** this material suits/does not suit him *or* flatters/does not flatter him.

2 s'habiller *vpr* **(a)** to dress (oneself); to get dressed; (*of priest etc*) to robe; **s'h. en femme,** to dress up as a woman; **elle ne sait pas s'h.,** she has no dress sense; **comment vous habillez-vous pour la soirée?,** what are you wearing to the party?; **s'h. long/court/jeune,** to wear long/short/young clothes;

(b) s'h. sur mesure, to have one's clothes made to measure; **elle s'habille chez Dior,** she buys her clothes from Dior; **s'h. de neuf,** to put on one's new clothes;

(c) to dress (*for dinner etc*); **faut-il s'h.?,** do we have to get dressed up?

habilleur, -euse [abijœr, -øz] *n Th* dresser.

habit [abi] *nm* **(a)** dress, costume; **habits,** clothes; **mettre ses habits,** to put on one's clothes; **je n'ai plus d'habits mettables,** I've nothing to wear; **marchand d'habits,** (*fripier*) dealer in second-hand clothes; **h. du dimanche,** Sunday best; **h. de travail,** working clothes; **h. de cour,** court dress; **en h. ecclésiastique,** in clerical attire *or* garb; **h. de cheval,** riding habit *or* clothes; **(b)** *Fig* **h. vert,** member of the Académie française; **(c) h. (de soirée),** evening dress, tails; **être en h.,** to be in evening dress *or* in tails; **l'h. est de rigueur,** formal *or* evening dress must be worn; **(d)** (*monk's, nun's*) habit; (*monk's*) frock; **prendre l'h.,** to become a monk *or* priest; *Prov* **l'h. ne fait pas le moine,** appearances can be deceptive.

habitabilité [abitabilite] *nf* **(a)** (*d'une maison*) habitability, fitness for habitation; **(b)** (*capacité*) capacity.

habitable [abitabl] *adj* (in)habitable, fit for habitation; **ce n'est pas un pays h.,** this country is uninhabitable.

habitacle [abitakl] *Av* cockpit; *Nau* binnacle; *Aut* passenger compartment.

habitant, -ante [abitɑ̃, -ɑ̃t] **1** *n* **(a)** inhabitant, resident (*of town*); occupier, occupant (*of house*); **ville de 10 000 habitants,** town of 10,000 inhabitants; **nombre d'habitants au kilomètre carré,** number of inhabitants per square kilometre; **loger chez l'h.,** *Mil* to be billeted with the locals; (*en voyage*) to rent a room in s.o.'s house; **(b)** *Litt* **les habitants des bois,** the inhabitants *or* creatures of the woods; **(c)** *Can* small-scale farmer, *Can* habitant [abitɑ̃]. **2** *adj Can Péj* **il est un peu h.,** he's a bit of a country bumpkin.

habitat [abita] *nm* **(a)** habitat (*of animal, plant*); **(b)** accommodation (*of people*); **h. rural/urbain,** rural/urban housing; **h. nomade/sédentaire,** nomadic/sedentary settlement; **dans cette région l'h. est groupé/dispersé,** in this area the houses are grouped/scattered.

habitation [abitasjɔ̃] *nf* **(a)** habitation; **impropre à l'h.,** unsuitable *or* unfit for human habitation; **locaux à usage d'h.,** premises for residential use; **(b)** (*lieu*) dwelling (place), residence, abode; **h. à loyer modéré,** *Br* ≈ council flat; **groupe d'h.,** (*lotissement*) housing estate.

habiter [abite] **1** *vt* to live in (*a house, a place*); **elle habite une petite maison à la campagne,** she lives in a little house in the country; **h. Paris/la banlieue,** to live in Paris/in the suburbs; **cette pièce n'a jamais été habitée,** this room has never been lived in; **Vénus est-elle habitée?,** is there life on Venus?; **vaisseau spatial habité,** manned spacecraft; *Fig* **la certitude qui m'habite,** my personal conviction. **2** *vi* to live (**à,** in, at); **h. à Paris/la campagne,** to live in Paris/in the country; **j'habite au 3, place des Cardeurs,** I live at number 3, place des Cardeurs; **h. en Italie/chez son frère,** to live in Italy/at one's brother's; **elle habite avec son frère/cet homme,** she lives with her brother/this man.

habitude [abityd] *nf* **(a)** habit, custom, practice, use; **bonne/mauvaise h.,** good/bad habit; **faire qch par h.,** to do sth from *or* out of habit, to do sth from force of habit; **prendre l'h. de faire qch,** to get into the habit of doing sth; **se faire une h. d'arriver en retard,** to have a habit of being late; **avoir l'h.** *ou* **avoir pour h. de faire qch,** to be in the habit of doing sth; **ça ne la gênera pas, elle a l'h.,** that won't bother her *or* she won't mind, she's used to it; **je n'ai pas l'h. de mentir,** I'm not in the habit of lying; **prendre de mauvaises habitudes,** to get into bad habits; **c'est une question d'h.,** it's a question of habit; **avoir une longue h. du travail en commun,** to have long experience of working together; **ce n'est pas une h. chez moi, ce n'est pas dans mes habitudes,** I don't make a habit of it; **à** *ou* **selon** *ou* **suivant son h.,** as is *or* was his custom *or* wont; **se défaire d'une h., perdre une h.,** to get out of a habit; **faire perdre une h. à qn,** to break s.o. of a habit; **d'h.,** usually, ordinarily, normally; **meilleur que d'h.,**

better than usual; **comme d'h.,** as usual; **plus tôt que d'h.,** earlier than usual;
(b) *(manuelle)* knack; **je n'en ai plus l'h.,** I'm out of practice;
(c) habitudes, ways, customs; **les habitudes du pays,** the customs of the country.
habitué, -ée [abitɥe] *n (d'une maison)* frequent *or* regular visitor; *(d'un restaurant, d'un magasin)* regular customer, regular.
habituel, -elle [abitɥɛl] *adj* usual, customary, regular; **cette attitude ne lui est pas habituelle,** this is not his usual attitude, he doesn't usually take this attitude; *F* **c'est le coup h.,** it's the same old story, it's par for the course.
habituellement [abitɥɛlmɑ̃] *adv* habitually, usually, regularly.
habituer [abitɥe] **1** *vt* to accustom, *Fml* to habituate; **h. qn à qch,** to accustom s.o. *or* get s.o. used to sth; **maintenant j'y suis habitué,** I'm used to it now; **elle est habituée à rester seule,** she's used to being alone; **h. qn à faire qch,** to get s.o. into the habit of *or* used to doing sth; **h. des enfants à la politesse,** to get children into the habit of being polite; **h. qn à la fatigue,** to inure s.o. to fatigue. **2 s'habituer** *vpr* to get used, to get *or* grow accustomed (**à,** to); **je n'arrive pas à m'y h.,** I just can't get used to it; **s'h. à une idée,** to get used to an idea.
***hâblerie** [ɑbləri] *nf* **(a)** *(attitude)* bragging, boasting; **(b)** *(propos)* boast.
***hâbleur, -euse** [ɑblœr, -øz] **1** *adj* bragging, boasting. **2** *n* boaster, braggart.
***Habsbourg** [apsbur] *nm Hist* **la maison de H.,** the House of Hapsburg.
***hachage** [aʃaʒ] *nm* chopping (up), mincing *(of meat etc)*; cutting *(of chaff etc)*.
***hache** [aʃ] *nf* axe, *surtout Am* ax; **h. à main,** hatchet; **fait** *ou* **taillé à coups de h.,** rough-hewn, hacked out; *Arch* **h. d'armes,** battleaxe; **h. de guerre,** tomahawk; *Fig* **enterrer la h. de guerre,** to bury the hatchet; **porter la h. dans les dépenses publiques,** to axe *or* cut public spending; **il est mort sous la h.,** he was beheaded.
***haché** [aʃe] **1** *adj* **(a)** minced, chopped; **bifteck h.,** minced beef, mince, *Am* ground beef; **(b)** staccato, jerky *(style etc)*; **(c)** (cross)hatched *(drawing)*; hachured *(map)*. **2** *nm Culin* minced meat, *surtout* minced beef, mince, *Am* ground beef.
***hache-légumes** [aʃlegym] *nm inv Culin* vegetable cutter, chopper.
***hachement** [aʃmɑ̃] *nm* = **HACHAGE**.
***hache-paille** [aʃpaj] *nm inv Agr* chaffcutter.
***hacher** [aʃe] *vt* **(a)** to chop (up); to mince, *Am* to grind *(meat etc)*; **h. menu,** to mince finely, to chop up small; *Fig* **h. qn menu comme chair à pâté,** to make mincemeat of s.o.; *Fig* **se faire h.,** to be cut to pieces; *Fig* **elle est prête à se faire h. pour lui,** she'd do anything for him; *Fig* **plutôt me faire h. (menu) que de dire oui,** I'd rather die than say yes; **(b)** = **HACHURER**.
***hachette** [aʃɛt] *nf* hatchet.
***hache-viande** [aʃvjɑ̃d] *nm inv Culin* mincing machine; mincer.
***hachis** [aʃi] *nm Culin* minced *or Am* ground meat, forcemeat, mince; **h. de veau,** minced veal; **h. Parmentier,** ≈ cottage pie, shepherd's pie; **h. d'herbes,** chopped herbs.
***hachisch** [aʃiʃ] *nm* hashish.
***hachoir** [aʃwar] *nm Culin* **(a)** *(couteau)* chopping knife, chopper; **(b)** *(planche)* chopping board; **(c)** *(électrique)* mincing machine, mincer.
***hachure** [aʃyr] *nf* (cross)hatching; *(on map)* hachures; **carte en hachures,** hachured map.
***hachurer** [aʃyre] *vt* to (cross)hatch; to hachure *(a map)*.
***haddock** [adɔk] *nm Culin* smoked haddock.
Hadrien [adrjɛ̃] *nm* Hadrian.
***Haendel** [ɛndɛl] *nm* Handel.
***hagard** [agar] *adj* haggard, wild(-looking) *(appearance etc)*; drawn *(face)*.
hagiographe [aʒjɔgraf] *n* hagiographer.
hagiographie [aʒjɔgrafi] *nf* hagiography.
hagiographique [aʒjɔgrafik] *adj* hagiographic(al).
***haie** [ɛ] *nf* **(a)** *(clôture)* hedge(row); **h. vive,** quickset hedge; **(b)** *Sp* hurdle; *Equitation* fence; *Sp* **course de haies,** *(short-distance)* hurdle race, *F* the hurdles; **400 mètres haies,** 400 metre hurdles; **(c)** line, row *(of trees etc)*; **faire** *ou* **former la h.,** to line up; **h. d'honneur,** guard of honour *or US* of honor.
***haillon** [ɑjɔ̃] *nm* rag *(of clothing)*; **être en haillons,** to be in rags and tatters.
***haine** [ɛn] *nf* hatred (**de, pour, contre,** of, for), detestation, hate; **avoir la h. de qch/qn, avoir de la h. pour qch/qn,** to hate *or* detest sth/s.o.; **prendre qch/qn en h.,** to take a strong aversion to sth/s.o.; **en h.** *ou* **par h. de qch,** out of hatred of *or* for sth.
***haineusement** [ɛnøzmɑ̃] *adv* with (bitter) hatred.
***haineux, -euse** [ɛnø, -øz] *adj* full of hatred *or* hate; **regard h.,** a look full of hate; **d'un ton h.,** with hate in his *or* her *etc* voice; **une femme haineuse,** a hateful woman.
***haïr** [air] *v* (**je hais** [ɛ], **tu hais, il hait, n. haïssons,** *etc; imp* **hais**; *otherwise regular*) **1** *vt* to hate, to detest, to loathe; **h. qn d'avoir fait qch,** to hate s.o. for doing *or* having done sth; *Can F* **h. qn à s'en confesser,** to hate s.o.'s guts. **2 se haïr** *vpr (soi-même)* to hate oneself; *(de deux personnes)* to hate each other; **je me hais de lui avoir menti,** I feel really bad about lying to him, I can't forgive myself for lying to him.
***haire** [ɛr] *nf* **(a)** *(chemise)* hairshirt; **(b)** *Tex* haircloth.
***haïssable** [aisabl] *adj* hateful, detestable.
***Haïti** [aiti] *n* Haiti.
***haïtien, -ienne** [aisjɛ̃, -jɛn] **1** *adj* Haitian. **2** *n* **H.,** Haitian.
***halage** [alaʒ] *nm* **(a)** *(d'un navire)* warping, hauling; **(b)** *(remorquage)* towing; **chemin/corde de h.,** towpath/towing line.
***hâle** [ɑl] *nm* (sun)tan, sunburn.
***hâlé** [ɑle] *adj* (sun)tanned, sunburnt.
haleine [alɛn] *nf* breath; **avoir l'h. fraîche,** to have fresh breath; **avoir mauvaise h., avoir l'h. forte,** to have bad breath; **à son h. j'ai compris qu'il avait bu,** I could tell from his breath that he'd been drinking; **retenir son h.,** to hold one's breath; **(tout) d'une h.,** all in one breath, in the same breath; *Fig* at one go; **avoir l'h. courte,** to be short-winded *or* short of breath; **reprendre h.,** to get *or* catch one's breath, to get one's breath back; **perdre h.,** to get out of breath, to lose one's breath; **courir à perdre h.,** to run until one is out of breath; **discuter à perdre h.,** to argue nonstop *or F* hammer and tongs; **hors d'h.,** out of breath, breathless; **travail de longue h.,** long and exacting task; **tenir qn en h.,** to hold s.o.'s attention, to keep s.o. in suspense.
***haler** [ale] **1** *vt* **(a)** to warp *(ship)*; **(b)** to tow *(barge etc)*; **(c) h. une embarcation au sec,** to haul up a boat (on the beach); **(d)** *Nau* to pull, to haul in, to heave *(rope etc)*; **(e)** *Nau* **h. le vent,** to sail closer to the wind. **2** *vi Nau* **h. sur une manœuvre,** to haul *or* pull on a rope, to heave at a rope.
***hâler** [ɑle] *vt (of sun etc)* to tan, to burn, to brown.
***haletant** [altɑ̃] *adj* panting, breathless, out of breath; gasping *(for breath)*; **respiration haletante,** panting, gasping; *Fig* **elle est haletante d'impatience,** she's burning with impatience, she can't wait.
***halètement** [alɛtmɑ̃] *nm* panting; gasping (for breath); puffing (and blowing).
***haleter** [alte] *vi* (**je halète; je halèterai**) to pant; to gasp (for breath); to puff (and blow); *Fig* **le cinéaste fait h. son public,** the film-maker keeps his audience on the edge of their seats.
***haleur, -euse** [alœr, -øz] *n* hauler, tower *(of boats)*.
***half-track** [aftrak] *nm Mil* half-track.
***hall** [ol] *nm* entrance hall; *(hotel)* foyer; **h. de gare,** station concourse.
***hallage** [alaʒ] *nm Com* market dues.
hallali [alali] *nm* mort; **assister à l'h.,** to be in at the death *or* finish *or* kill.
***halle** [al] *nf* (covered) market; *(grande salle)* hall; **h. aux poissons,** fish market; **h. au blé,** corn exchange; **les Halles (centrales),** the Halles *(the central market in Paris)*.
***hallebarde** [albard] *nf Arch* halberd, halbert; bill; *F* **il pleut** *ou* **tombe des hallebardes,** it's raining cats and dogs.
***hallebardier** [albardje] *nm Arch* halberdier.
***hallier** [alje] *nm* **(a)** thicket, copse, brake; **(b) halliers,** brushwood.
Halloween [alɔwin] *nf* Halloween.
hallucinant [alysinɑ̃] *adj* hallucinating *(drug etc)*; haunting *(thought)*; striking *(likeness etc)*.
hallucination [alysinasjɔ̃] *nf* hallucination, delusion; **avoir des hallucinations,** *(d'un malade, d'un ivrogne)* to have hallucinations; *Fig (se tromper)* to imagine *or* see things; **une h. collective,** a collective *or* mass hallucination.
hallucinatoire [alysinatwar] *adj* hallucinatory.
halluciné, -ée [alysine] *adj & n* hallucinated, *F* mad,

loony (person).
halluciner [alysine] *vt* to hallucinate.
hallucinogène [alysinɔʒɛn] *Pharm* **1** *nm* hallucinogen. **2** *adj* hallucinogenic.
***halo** [alo] *nm* **(a)** *Météo etc* halo; **(b)** *Opt* blurring; **(c)** *Phot* halation; **un h. de gloire,** a cloud of glory; **s'entourer d'un h. de mystère,** to shroud oneself in mystery.
halogène [alɔʒɛn] **1** *adj* halogenous. **2** *nm* halogen; **lampe à h.,** halogen lamp.
***halte** [alt] *nf* **(a)** *(arrêt)* stop, halt; **faire h.,** to (make a) halt, to (come to a) stop; **h.(-là)!,** stop! halt!; *Fig* **h.-là, je ne suis pas d'accord!,** hold on *or* not so fast, I don't agree!; **h. à l'armement!,** stop the arms build-up!; **dire h. à l'inflation,** to put a stop *or* an end to inflation; **(b)** stopping place, resting place; *Rail* halt.
***halte-garderie** [altgardəri] *nf* crèche.
haltère [altɛr] *nm* dumb-bell; barbell; **faire des haltères,** to do weightlifting *or* weight training.
haltérophile [alterɔfil] *n* weightlifter.
haltérophilie [alterɔfili] *nf* weightlifting; **elle fait de l'h.,** she does weight lifting *or* weight training.
***hamac** [amak] *nm* hammock; **accrocher/décrocher un h.,** to sling/unsling a hammock.
hamadryade [amadrijad] *nf Myth* hamadryad, dryad, wood nymph.
hamamélis [amamelis] *nm Bot* witch hazel, hamamelis.
***Hambourg** [ɑ̃bur] *nm* Hamburg.
***hambourgeois, -oise** [ɑ̃burʒwa, -waz] **1** *adj (native, inhabitant)* of Hamburg. **2** *n* **H.,** Hamburger.
***hamburger** [ɑ̃burgœr] *nm Culin* hamburger.
***hameau, -eaux** [amo] *nm* hamlet.
hameçon [amsɔ̃] *nm* (fish-)hook; **h. sans œillet,** blind hook; *Fig* **mordre à l'h.,** to swallow *or* rise to the bait.
hameçonner [amsɔne] *vt* **(a)** to hook *(fish)*; **(b)** to put hooks on *(fishing line)*.
***hammam** [amam] *nm* Turkish baths.
***hammerless** [amɛrlɛs] *nm* hammerless sporting gun.
***hampe¹** [ɑ̃p] *nf* **(a)** staff, pole *(of flag etc)*; stave, shaft *(of spear etc)*; shank *(of fish-hook)*; *Typ* **la h. du p,** the stem of the p; **(b)** *Bot* scape, stem; **h. (florale),** spike.
***hampe²** *nf Culin* thin flank *(of beef)*; breast *(of venison)*.
***hamster** [amstɛr] *nm Zool* hamster.
***han** [ɑ̃] *int (sound of breath accompanying violent effort)* oof!; **pousser un h. à chaque coup,** to give a grunt at every stroke.
***hanap** [anap] *nm Arch* goblet, tankard.
***hanche** [ɑ̃ʃ] *nf* **(a)** *Anat* hip; **les poings sur les hanches,** (with his) hands on (his) hips, (with) arms akimbo; **rouler les hanches,** to swing one's hips; **être large des hanches,** to have broad hips, *F* to be broad in the beam; **tour de hanches,** hip measurement; **(b)** haunch *(of horse)*; **hanches,** hindquarters; **(c)** *Nau* quarter *(of ship)*; **par la h.,** on the quarter.
***hand-ball** [ɑ̃dbal] *nm Sp* handball.
***handballeur, -euse** [ɑ̃dbalœr, -øz] *n Sp* handball player.
***handicap** [ɑ̃dikap] *nm* handicap; *Fig* **j'ai un h. à l'examen,** I'm at a disadvantage in the exam; *Fig* **ne pas avoir d'ordinateur est un sérieux h.,** being without a computer is a serious handicap; *Fig* **la Pologne part avec un h.,** Poland is handicapped from the outset.
***handicapé, -ée** [ɑ̃dikape] *adj & n* handicapped (person); **h. physique/mentale,** physically/mentally handicapped; **les handicapés,** the handicapped, the disabled; **les handicapés mentaux,** the mentally handicapped.
***handicaper** [ɑ̃dikape] *vt* to handicap.
***handicapeur** [ɑ̃dikapœr] *nm Courses de chevaux* handicapper.
***handisport** [adispɔr] *adj Sp* **tennis h.,** tennis for the disabled; **jeux handisports,** games for the handicapped.
***hangar** [ɑ̃gar] *nm* **(a)** shed, shelter; *(pour les trains, bus etc)* depot; **h. à bateaux,** boathouse; **(b)** *Av* hangar.
***hanneton** [antɔ̃] *nm* cockchafer, maybug; *Am* June beetle *or* bug; *F* **un froid qui n'est pas piqué des hannetons,** intense cold; *F* **une dispute/un examen pas piqué(e) des hannetons,** a stinker of an argument/exam.
***Hanovre** [anɔvr] *nm* Hanover.
***hanovrien, -enne** [anɔvrijɛ̃, -ɛn] *Hist* **1** *adj* Hanoverian. **2** *n* **H.,** Hanoverian.
***hanse** [ɑ̃s] *nf Hist* Hanse, Hansa; **la H.,** the Hanseatic league.
***hanséatique** [ɑ̃seatik] *adj Hist* Hanseatic.
***hanté** [ɑ̃te] *adj* haunted; **maison hantée,** haunted house.
***hanter** [ɑ̃te] *vt (of ghost)* to haunt *(house etc)*; *Fig* **il hante les boîtes,** he's never out of the night clubs; **cette idée le hante,** he is obsessed *or* haunted by the idea; **ce souvenir me hante,** the memory haunts me.
***hantise** [ɑ̃tiz] *nf* haunting memory *or* thought; **j'ai la h. de ce genre de réunion,** I dread this kind of meeting; **j'avais la h. d'aller à cette réunion,** I was dreading (going to) the meeting.
***happe** [ap] *nf* **(a)** *Menuis Constr etc* cramp *or* clamp iron; **(b)** *(anneau)* staple; **anneau à h.,** ring and staple.
***happement** [apmɑ̃] *nm* snapping (up), snatching, seizing.
***happening** [apniŋ] *nm* happening; **un h. politique,** a political happening *or* event.
***happer** [ape] *vt (of birds etc)* to snap up, to snatch, to seize, to catch *(insects etc)*; **la voiture a été happée par un train,** the car was hit by a train; *Fig* **h. qn,** to catch *or* buttonhole s.o..
happy [api] *nf Cin etc* **h. end,** happy ending; **j'aime les h. ends,** I love happy endings.
***haquenée** [akne] *nf Arch* palfrey.
hara-kiri [arakiri] *nm* hara-kiri; **(se) faire h.-k.,** to commit hara-kiri.
***harangue** [arɑ̃g] *nf* harangue; **nous avons eu droit à une de ses harangues,** we were treated to one of his harangues *or* lectures.
***haranguer** [arɑ̃ge] *vt* to harangue, to lecture.
***haras** [ara] *nm* stud farm.
***harassant** [arasɑ̃] *adj* exhausting.
***harassé** [arase] *adj* worn out, exhausted; **h. de travail,** overwhelmed with work.
***harassement** [arasmɑ̃] *nm* fatigue, exhaustion.
***harasser** [arase] *vt* to tire out, to exhaust.
***harcelant** [arsəlɑ̃] *adj* harassing.
***harcèlement** [arsɛlmɑ̃] *nm* harassing, harassment; **h. de la police,** police harassment; **dénoncer le h. sexuel,** to speak out against sexual harassment; **subir le h. sexuel de son patron,** to be sexually harassed by one's boss; **subir un h. sexuel,** to be sexually harassed.
***harceler** [arsəle] *vt* **(je harcèle; je harcèlerai)** to harass *(s.o.)*; to bait *(an animal)*; **h. qn de questions,** to badger *or* pester *or* plague s.o. with questions; **h. qn pour obtenir qch,** to pester s.o. for sth; **elle est harcelée de soucis,** she's plagued by worries.
***harceleur, -euse** [arsəlœr, -øz] *n* pesterer, tormentor.
***harde¹** [ard] *nf* herd, bevy *(of deer)*.
***harde²** *nf* leash *(for hounds)*.
***hardes** [ard] *nfpl* worn *or* old clothes.
***hardi** [ardi] **1** *adj (audacieux)* bold, daring; *(téméraire)* rash; *(osé)* impudent, brazen; **écriture hardie,** bold hand(writing); **faire un commentaire h.,** to make a bold comment; **jugement h.,** rash judgement; **mensonge h.,** barefaced lie; **un décolleté h.,** a daring neckline; **une interprétation hardie,** a bold interpretation. **2** *int* go on!, go to it!; **h. les gars!,** come on lads!
***hardiesse** [ardjɛs] *nf (audace)* boldness, daring; *(effronterie)* nerve, impudence, effrontery; *(originalité)* boldness; **avoir la h. de faire qch,** to be so bold as to do sth; **il a eu la h. de m'écrire,** he had the audacity *or* the cheek to write to me; **remarque la h. du style de ce peintre,** note the boldness of this painter's style; **hardiesses,** liberties; **se permettre des hardiesses envers qn,** to take liberties with s.o..
***hardiment** [ardimɑ̃] *adv (avec audace)* boldly, audaciously, daringly; *(avec effronterie)* impudently; *(à la légère)* rashly; **vous avez agi bien h.,** you acted very rashly.
***hard-top** [ard'tɔp] *nm Aut* hard top; *(pl hard-tops)*.
***hardware** [ardwɛr] *nm Ordinat* hardware.
***harem** [arɛm] *nm* harem.
***hareng** [arɑ̃] *nm* herring; **h. (salé et) fumé,** kipper; **h. saur,** red *or* smoked herring; **h. bouffi,** bloater; *F* **être sec comme un h.,** to be as skinny *or* thin as a rake; *F* **on était serré comme des harengs dans le bus,** we were packed together like sardines in the bus.
***harengère** [arɑ̃ʒɛr] *nf Péj* fishwife.
***harenguier** [arɑ̃gje] *nm* herring boat.
***hargne** [arɲ] *nf* bad temper, surly disposition.
***hargneusement** [arɲøzmɑ̃] *adv* bad-temperedly.
***hargneux, -euse** [arɲø, -øz] *adj* bad-tempered, cantankerous *(person)*; nagging *(woman)*; snarling, vicious *(dog)*; **ton h.,** bad-tempered tone; **des remarques hargneuses,** vicious remarks.
***haricot** [ariko] *nm* **(a)** bean; **h. blanc,** haricot bean, *US* bush bean; **h. rouge,** (red) kidney bean; **h. beurre,** butter bean; **haricots en grains,** dried beans; **h. vert,** French *or*

Am string bean; **h. d'Espagne,** scarlet runner; **h. mange-tout,** mange-tout; **h. à rames,** runner bean; *Arg* **des haricots!,** not a sausage *or* bean!; *Arg* **la fin des haricots,** the bloody limit; *Arg* **courir sur le h. à qn,** to get on s.o.'s wick; **(b)** *Culin* **h. de mouton,** ≈ Irish stew.

***haridelle** [aridɛl] *nf* old horse.

***harissa** [arisa] *nf Culin* harissa.

***harki** [arki] *nm Mil* harki (*Algerian soldier who fought on French side during War of Independence, and his descendants*).

***harle** [arl] *nm Orn* merganser.

harmonica [armɔnika] *nm Mus* harmonica, mouth organ; **jouer de l'h.,** to play the mouth organ.

harmonie [armɔni] *nf* **(a)** *Mus* harmony; **table d'h.,** sounding board (*of piano*); **(b)** (*accord*) harmony; **être en h. avec qch,** to be in keeping *or* in harmony *or* in accordance with sth; to fit in with sth; **l'h. qui règne dans cette famille est remarquable,** the harmony which reigns within this family is remarkable, this family gets on remarkably well together; **vivre en h.,** to live in harmony *or* harmoniously; **(c)** (*de l'orchestre*) wind secton.

harmonieusement [armɔnjøzmɑ̃] *adv* harmoniously.

harmonieux, -euse [armɔnjø, -øz] *adj* harmonious, melodious, tuneful (*sound*); harmonious (*arrangement etc*); **couleurs harmonieuses,** harmonious colours.

harmonique [armɔnik] *adj & nm Mus* harmonic.

harmoniquement [armɔnikmɑ̃] *adv* harmonically.

harmonisation [armɔnizɑsjɔ̃] *nf* harmonization, harmonizing; *Ling* **h. vocalique,** vowel harmony.

harmoniser [armɔnize] **1** *vt* **(a)** *Mus* to harmonize (*melody etc*); **(b)** (*mettre en accord*) to harmonize (*ideas*); to match (*colours*). **2 s'harmoniser** *vpr* to be in keeping *or* in harmony, to harmonize, to agree (**avec,** with); **s'h. avec qch,** (*of colours*) to match *or* go well with sth.

harmonium [armɔnjɔm] *nm* harmonium.

***harnaché** [arnaʃe] *adj* (*d'un cheval*) harnassed; *F* **il part à la pêche tout h.,** he goes off fishing all kitted out; **curieusement h.,** wearing the strangest gear.

***harnachement** [arnaʃmɑ̃] *nm* **(a)** (*action*) harnessing; **(b)** (*harnais*) harness, trappings; (*selles etc*) saddlery; *F* (*vêtements*) (absurd) rig-out.

***harnacher** [arnaʃe] **1** *vt* to harness (*horse etc*); *F* **h. qn,** to dress s.o. up, to rig s.o. out. **2 se harnacher** *vpr* to rig oneself out.

***harnais** [arnɛ] *nm* **(a)** (*sellerie*) harness; **reprendre le h.,** to get back into harness, to go back to work again; **(b)** *Arch* (*armure*) armour, equipment; **(c)** *MecE* **h. d'engrenage,** train of gear wheels, gearing.

***harnois** [arnwa] *nm* **(a)** *Arch* = **HARNAIS (b)**; *Fig* **blanchi sous le h.,** grown grey in service.

***haro** [aro] *int & nm* **(clameur de) h.,** outcry, hue and cry; **crier h.,** to raise a hue and cry (**sur,** about).

harpagon [arpagɔ̃] *nm* miser, skinflint, scrooge.

***harpe** [arp] *nf Mus* harp; **jouer** *ou* **pincer de la h.,** to play the harp; **h. éolienne,** Aeolian harp.

***harpie** [arpi] *nf* **(a)** *Myth* harpy; *Fig* harpy, shrew; **(b)** *Orn* harpy eagle.

***harpiste** [arpist] *n Mus* harpist.

***harpon** [arpɔ̃] *nm Pêche* harpoon; **pêche** *ou* **chasse (sous-marine) au h.,** (underwater) spear fishing.

***harponnage** [arpɔnaʒ] *nm*, ***harponnement** [arpɔnmɑ̃] *nm* harpooning.

***harponner** [arpɔne] *vt* **(a)** *Pêche* to harpoon; **(b)** *Arg* (*de la police*) to arrest, to collar (*s.o.*); (*happer*) to stop, to corner (*s.o.*).

***harponneur** [arpɔnœr] *nm Pêche* harpooner.

***hasard** [azar] *nm* **(a)** chance, luck, accident; **coup de h.,** stroke of luck, fluke; **par un coup de h.,** by a mere chance; **jeu de h.,** game of chance; **un heureux h. a fait que ... +** *sub,* I *or* we *etc* had the good fortune to ...; **ne rien laisser au h.,** to leave nothing to chance; **le h. fit que** + *ind,* **le h. voulut que** + *ind or sub,* (as) luck would have it; **le h. fait bien les choses,** what a stroke of luck; **au h.,** haphazardly, at random; **choix fait au h.,** random choice; **au h. de ses voyages,** in the course of his travels, as he travelled from one place to another; **par h.,** by accident, by chance; **par pur h.,** quite by chance, entirely by accident; **si par h. vous le voyez,** if you (should) happen to see him; **sauriez-vous son adresse par h.?,** do you happen to know his address?; **et comme par h., il est tombé malade,** and as if by chance, he fell ill; **à tout h.,** on the off chance, just in case; **à tout h. je vais lui demander,** I'll ask him just in case *or* on the off chance;

(b) (*danger*) risk, danger, hazard; **les hasards de la guerre,** the hazards of war.

***hasardé** [azarde] *adj* hazardous, risky, foolhardy (*undertaking etc*); rash (*words etc*).

***hasarder** [azarde] **1** *vt* to risk, to venture, to hazard (*one's life etc*); **h. une opinion,** to venture an opinion; **h. 500 francs,** to gamble 500 francs. **2 se hasarder** *vpr* to take risks; **se h. à faire qch,** to venture to do sth; **se h. dans la jungle,** to venture (out) into the jungle.

***hasardeux, -euse** [azardø, -øz] *adj* hazardous, perilous, risky, rash.

***hasch** [aʃ] *nm F* (*drogue*) hash, pot.

***haschisch** [aʃiʃ] *nm* hashish; **fumer du h.,** to smoke hashish.

***hase** [ɑz] *nf Zool* doe (*of hare, wild rabbit*).

hassidisme [asidism] *nm Rel* Chassidism, Hassidism.

hast [ast] *nm Arch* shaft; **arme d'h.,** shafted weapon.

***hâte** [ɑt] *nf* haste, hurry; **avoir h. de faire qch,** to be in a hurry to do sth; (*avoir envie*) to be eager *or* to long to do sth; **mettre trop de h. à faire qch,** to be in too great *or* too much of a hurry to do sth; **il n'a qu'une h. — que tout soit fini,** all he wants is to get it over with; **à la h.,** in a hurry, in haste, hastily, hurriedly; **travail fait à la h.,** slapdash work; **déjeuner à la h.,** to hurry over one's lunch, *F* to bolt one's lunch; **en h.,** hastily, in haste, hurriedly; **en toute h.,** with all possible speed, posthaste; **sans h.,** without haste, in a leisurely way.

***hâter** [ɑte] **1** *vt* to hasten, to hurry (*sth*) on; to force (*fruit etc*); **h. le pas,** to quicken one's pace *or* step; **h. le mouvement,** to hurry things up *or* along. **2 se hâter** *vpr* to hurry, to hasten; **se h. de faire qch,** to hurry to do sth, to lose no time in doing sth; *Prov* **hâtez-vous lentement,** more haste, less speed.

***hâtif, -ive** [ɑtif, -iv] *adj* **(a)** forward, early (*spring, fruit etc*); **(b)** hasty, hurried, ill-considered, premature (*measure, decision etc*).

***hâtivement** [ɑtivmɑ̃] *adv* hastily, in a hurry, hurriedly.

***hauban** [obɑ̃] *nm Nau* (*cordes*) shrouds, rigging; (*corde, câble*) guy, stays.

***haubaner** [obane] *vt Nau* to guy, to stay, to brace.

***haubert** [obɛr] *nm Arch Mil* coat of mail.

***hausse** [os] *nf* **(a)** rise, increase (*in prices*); **baromètre en h.,** rising barometer; **la h. soudaine de la température,** the sudden rise *or* increase in temperature; *F* **les affaires sont en h.,** things are looking up; *Com Fin* **marché à la h.,** rising market; **h. de 4%,** 4% rise; **les maisons sont en h.,** house prices are going up; **les blés ont subi une h. considérable,** wheat has gone up considerably (in price); **h. à la pompe,** rise in the price of petrol; *Bourse* **jouer à la h.,** to speculate on a rising market, to bull the market; *Bourse* **spéculateur à la h.,** bull; **(b)** *Tech* prop, block, stand; *HydE* flush board, shutter; **(c)** *Mil* (back)sight, sighting gear (*of rifle*).

***haussement** [osmɑ̃] *nm* **h. d'épaules,** shrug(ging) (of the shoulders).

***hausser** [ose] **1** *vt* to raise, to lift, to make higher; to heighten (*wall*); to put up (*prices*); **h. la voix,** to raise one's voice; **h. les épaules,** to shrug (one's shoulders). **2** *vi Nau* (*of land, lighthouse*) to rise (over the horizon). **3 se hausser** *vpr* to raise oneself (up); **se h. jusqu'au poste de P.-D.G.,** to climb to the position of Chairman, to rise to be Chairman; **se h. sur la pointe des pieds,** to stand on tiptoe; **se h. jusqu'à qn,** to raise oneself to s.o.'s level.

***haussier** [osje] *nm Bourse F* bull.

***haut, haute** [o, ot] **1** *adj* **(a)** high; high, tall (*grass etc*); high, lofty (*building etc*); high (*cliff*); **femme de haute taille,** tall woman; **mur h. de six mètres,** wall six metres high; **h. comme trois pommes,** knee high to a grasshopper; **pièce haute de plafond,** room with a high ceiling; **des talons hauts,** high heels; **hautes terres,** highlands, uplands; **hautes eaux,** high water; **haute mer,** open sea, high seas; **à mer haute,** at high water, at high tide;

(b) (*éminent*) exalted, important, great; **de la plus haute importance,** of the greatest *or* utmost importance; **de h. rang,** of high rank, high ranking; **h. fonctionnaire,** high-ranking official; **hauts faits,** deeds of valour *or US* valor; *Fig* **en h. lieu,** in high places; *F* **un h. lieu touristique,** a tourist Mecca; **haute finance,** high finance; **haute cuisine/couture/***etc,* haute cuisine/couture/*etc*; **h. comique,** high comedy; **les hautes cartes,** the high cards, the picture cards;

(c) (*levé*) raised; **marcher la tête haute,** to hold one's head high; **elle va partout la tête haute,** she walks around with her head held high; **avoir/garder la main haute sur ses affaires,** to be in/to retain control of one's affairs; **voix haute,** loud voice; (*aiguë*) high(-pitched) voice; **lire à**

haute voix, to read aloud; **pousser de hauts cris,** to shout out loud; **elle n'a jamais une parole plus haute que l'autre,** she never raises her voice;

(d) mécanisme de haute précision, precision device; **haute trahison,** high treason; *Fig* **personnage h. en couleur,** colourful character; **avoir une haute idée de soi-même,** to have a high opinion of oneself; **haute pression,** high pressure; **mécanisme de** *ou* **à haute sécurité,** high security device; *Rad* **haute fréquence,** high frequency;

(e) (*supérieur*) upper, higher; **les hauts étages,** the upper storeys; **les hautes branches,** the upper branches, the top branches; **le plus h. étage,** the top floor; **la plus haute branche,** the topmost *or* uppermost branch; **les hautes classes,** the upper classes (*of society*); the higher *or* upper forms (*of school*); **les hautes mathématiques,** higher mathematics; **le h. allemand,** High German; *Géog* **le h. Canada,** Upper Canada; **le H.-Rhin,** (*département*) the Haut-Rhin; **le h. Rhin,** (*fleuve*) the upper Rhine; **la Haute Volta,** the Upper Volta; **les Hautes Terres (de l'Écosse),** the Highlands (of Scotland); *Nau* **les hautes voiles,** the upper sails;

(f) (*ancien*) **la haute antiquité,** remote antiquity; **le h. Moyen Âge,** the Early Middle Ages.

2 *adv* **(a)** high (up), above, up; **h. les mains!,** hands up!; **h. les cœurs,** cheer up!; *Rail* **h. le pied,** (*of engine*) running light; **parler h.,** to speak loudly; **parlez plus h.!,** speak up!; **une voix h. perchée,** a high-pitched voice; **parler** *ou* **penser tout h.,** to talk *or* think aloud *or* out loud; **dire tout h. ce que tout le monde pense tout bas,** to say out loud what everyone else is thinking; **parler h. et clair,** to speak one's mind; **femme h. placée,** woman in a high position; **viser h.,** to aim *or* set one's sights high; **il l'estime très h.,** he thinks very highly of him; **il la place très h. dans son estime,** he has a very high opinion of her, he holds her in very high regard *or* esteem; *Nau* **l'ancre est h.,** the anchor is up; **gagner h. la main,** to win hands down;

(b) (*en arrière*) back; **remonter plus h. (dans le temps),** to go further back; **comme il est dit plus h.,** as indicated above *or* earlier.

3 *nm* **(a)** height; **le mur a six mètres de h.,** the wall is six metres *or US* meters high; *Fig* **regarder qn du h. de sa grandeur,** to look down one's nose at s.o.; **tomber de (son) h.,** to fall flat on the ground *or* headlong; (*être surpris ou déçu*) to be very much taken aback, to be floored;

(b) (*sommet*) top, upper part; (*instruction on packing cases*) this side up; **h. de la table,** head of the table; **le h. de la robe est en dentelle,** the top of the dress is made of lace; **du h. de l'escalier,** from the top of the stairs; **les hauts et les bas,** the ups and downs (of life *etc*); **h. de l'eau,** high water; **les hauts (d'un navire),** the topsides (of a ship); *Typ* **h. de casse,** upper case, *F* caps; **l'étage du h.,** the top floor; **le monsieur du h.,** the gentleman upstairs; **du h. de la falaise,** from *or* off the top of the cliff; **arriver en h. de la côte,** to reach the top of the hill; *Fig* **le h. du panier,** the top of the heap, the pick of the bunch; **gloire à Dieu au plus h. des cieux,** Glory to God in the Highest; **de** *ou* **du h. en bas,** downwards, from top to bottom; **regarder qn de h. en bas,** to look s.o. up and down; **regarder qn de h.,** to look down on s.o.; **traiter qn de h.,** to patronize s.o.; **prendre les choses de h.,** to be very aloof; **en h.,** above, at the top; *Nau* aloft; (*étage supérieur*) upstairs; **lancer qch en h.,** to throw something up in *or* up into *or* into the air; **en h. du placard,** at the top of the cupboard; **tout en h.,** at the very top, right at the top; *Nau* **en h. tout le monde!,** all hands on deck!; **en h. de l'échelle,** at the top of the ladder; **d'en h.,** from above, from on high; (*étage inférieur*) from upstairs; *Fig* **la décision vient d'en h.,** the decision comes from the top.

4 *nf F* **haute,** upper crust; **un gars de la h.,** a toff.

***hautain** [otɛ̃] *adj* haughty, lofty.

***hautainement** [otɛnmɑ̃] *adv* haughtily, loftily.

***hautbois** [obwa] *nm Mus* oboe.

***hautboïste** [oboist] *n Mus* oboe player, oboist.

***haut-de-chausse(s)** [odʃos] *nm Arch* breeches, trunk hose; (*pl hauts-de-chausse(s)*).

***haut-de-forme** [odfɔrm] *nm* top hat; (*pl hauts-de-forme*).

***haute-contre** [otkɔ̃tr] *Mus* (*pl hautes-contre*) **1** *nf* counter tenor (*voice*). **2** *adj & nm* counter tenor.

***haute-fidélité** [otfidelite] *adj* hi-fi; **chaîne h.-f.,** hi-fi.

***hautement** [otmɑ̃] *adv* (*à un haut degré*) highly; *Vieilli* (*ouvertement*) openly.

***hauteur** [otœr] *nf* **(a)** height, elevation; altitude (*of star, triangle etc*); *Mus* pitch (*of note*); loftiness (*of ideas etc*); **prendre de la h.,** (*of aircraft etc*) to climb, to gain height; **pour résoudre ce problème, il convient de prendre de la h.,** in order to solve this problem, we must rise above it; *Fig Litt* **la h. de vues d'un fonctionnaire supérieur,** the loftiness *or* lofty attitude of a senior civil servant; **à h. d'appui,** at elbow height; **le peu de h. du plafond,** the lowness of the ceiling; **h. libre** *ou* **de passage,** headroom (*of bridge etc*); **la h. sous plafond,** ceiling height; **le pont manque de h. pour laisser passer les camions,** there isn't enough clearance for lorries under the bridge; **tomber de (toute) sa h.,** to fall flat on one's face *or* headlong; **à la h. de qch,** abreast of *or* level with sth; **arriver à la h. de qn/qch,** to draw level with s.o./sth; **à la h. de l'œil,** at eye level; **être** *ou* **se montrer à la h. d'une tâche,** to be *or* to prove equal to a task, *F* to be up to a job; *F* **être à la h.,** to be up to scratch *or* up to it; *Nau* **à la h. du cap Horn,** off *or* abreast of Cape Horn; *Couture* **h. du dos,** = length of back; *Sp* **saut en h.,** high jump; *Bourse* **M. Martin, actionnaire de Perrier ® à h. de 5%,** Mr Martin, a shareholder in Perrier ® with *or* holding 5% of the shares; *Archit* **h. sous clef,** rise (*of arch*);

(b) *Péj* haughtiness, arrogance; **de toute sa h.,** scornfully, disdainfully; **avec h.,** haughtily, arrogantly;

(c) height; hill(top); **une cabane sur la h.,** a cabin on the hilltop.

***haut-fond** [ofɔ̃] *nm* shoal, shallow (*in sea, river*); (*pl hauts-fonds*).

***haut(-)fourneau** [ofurno] *nm Métal* blast furnace; (*pl hauts(-)fourneaux*).

***haut-le-cœur** [olkœr] *nm inv* heave (*of stomach*); **avoir un** *ou* **des h.-le-c.,** to retch, to heave; **j'ai eu un h.-le-c. de dégoût,** my bile rose in disgust.

***haut-le-corps** [olkɔr] *nm inv* (sudden) start, jump; **faire un h.-le-c.,** (*d'un cheval*) to start; **avoir un h.-le-c.,** (*d'une personne*) to give a start, to jump.

***haut-mal** [omal] *nm inv Méd Arch* epilepsy, falling sickness.

***haut-parleur** [oparlœr] *nm Rad* (loud-)speaker; (*pl haut-parleurs*).

***haut-relief** [orəljɛf] *nm Beaux-Arts* high relief, alto-relievo; (*pl hauts-reliefs*).

***hauturier, -ière** [otyrje, -jɛr] *adj Nau* of the high seas; **navigation hauturière,** ocean navigation; **pilote h.,** deep-sea pilot.

***havage** [avaʒ] *nm Min* (under)cut(ting).

***havanais, -aise** [avanɛ, -ɛz] **1** *adj* of *or* from Havana. **2** *n* **H.,** a native *or* inhabitant of Havana.

***Havane** [avan] **1** *nf* Havana. **2** *nm* **h.,** Havana (cigar). **3** *adj inv* **cuir h.,** (light) brown *or* tan leather.

***hâve** [ɑv] *adj* haggard, emaciated, gaunt (*face*); sunken (*cheeks*); pale (*skin*).

***haveuse** [avøz] *nf Min* (*machine*) coalcutter.

***havrais, -aise** [ɑvrɛ, -ɛz] **1** *adj* (*native, inhabitant*) of Le Havre. **2** *n* **H.,** native *or* inhabitant of Le Havre.

***havre** [ɑvr] *nm Litt* haven, port; harbour, *US* harbor; **un h. de paix,** a haven of peace.

***havresac** [avrəsak] *nm* haversack; *Mil Arch* knapsack, pack.

Hawaï [awai] *n* Hawaii; **les îles H.,** the Hawaiian Islands.

hawaïen, -ïenne [awajɛ̃, -jɛn] **1** *adj* Hawaiian. **2** *n* **H.,** Hawaiian.

***Haye (la)** [laɛ] *nf* the Hague.

***hayon** [ajɔ̃] *nm* rear door, back door (*of vehicle*); hatchback (*of car*); tailboard (*of cart*).

***hé** [e] *int* (*to call attention*) hey (there)!; (*to reinforce*) **hé! hé!,** well, well!; **hé oui!,** yes indeed!

***heaume** [om] *nm* helm(et).

heavy [ɛvi] *nm Mus* **h. metal,** heavy metal; **écouter du h. metal,** to listen to heavy metal.

hebdomadaire [ɛbdɔmadɛr] *adj & nm* weekly.

hebdomadairement [ɛbdɔmadɛrmɑ̃] *adv* weekly, once a week.

hébergement [ebɛrʒ(ə)mɑ̃] *nm* accommodation; lodging, sheltering; taking in.

héberger [ebɛrʒe] *vt* **(j'hébergeai(s); n. hébergeons)** to accommodate, to lodge (*paying guest*); to put (*friend*) up; to take (*homeless person, refugee*) in; to harbour, *US* to harbor (*fugitive*).

hébété [ebete] *adj* dazed, vacant, bewildered (*expression etc*); **h. de douleur,** numb with grief.

hébétement [ebetmɑ̃] *nm* stupefaction, bewilderment.

hébéter [ebete] *vt* **(j'hébète; j'hébéterai)** to dull, to stupefy (*the senses etc*); to daze.

hébétude [ebetyd] *nf Méd* hebetude; *Litt* stupor.

hébraïque [ebraik] *adj* Hebraic, Hebrew.
hébraïsant, -ante [ebraizɑ̃, -ɑ̃t] *n* (*érudit, étudiant*) Hebraist.
hébraïser [ebraize] *vt* to hebraize.
hébraïsme [ebraism] *nm* Hebraism.
hébraïste [ebraist] *n* Hebraist, Hebrew scholar.
hébreu, -eux [ebrø] **1** *adj* (**hébraïque** *is used for the feminine*) Hebrew. **2** *nm Ling* Hebrew; *F* **c'est de l'h. pour moi,** it's double Dutch *or* all Greek to me. **3** *n* **H.,** Hebrew.
Hébrides (les) [lezebrid] *nfpl* the Hebrides.
H.E.C. [aʃəse] *nf* (*abrév* **Hautes Études Commerciales**) (*à Paris, à Montréal*) = prestigious business school; **faire H.E.C.,** to study at the HEC.
hécatombe [ekatɔ̃b] *nf* hecatomb, slaughter, massacre; *Fig F* **ça a été une h. cette année au bac!,** the results for the bac were disastrous this year!
hectare [ɛktar] *nm* hectare (= 2.47 acres).
hectique [ɛktik] *adj Méd* hectic (*fever*).
hecto [ɛkto] *nm* (*hectogramme*) hectogram(me); (*hectolitre*) hectolitre, *US* hectoliter.
hectogramme [ɛktɔgram] *nm* hectogram(me).
hectolitre [ɛktɔlitr] *nm* hectolitre, *US* hectoliter.
hectomètre [ɛktɔmɛtr] *nm* hectometre, *US* hectometer.
hectométrique [ɛktɔmetrik] *adj* hectometric.
hectopascal, -als [ɛktɔpaskal] *nm Météo* hectopascal.
hectowatt [ɛktɔwat] *nm Él* hectowatt.
hédonisme [edɔnism] *nm* hedonism.
hédoniste [edɔnist] **1** *n* hedonist. **2** *adj* hedonist(ic).
hégélianisme [egeljanism] *nm Phil* Hegelianism.
hégélien, -ienne [egeljɛ̃, -jɛn] *adj & n Phil* Hegelian.
hégémonie [eʒemɔni] *nf* hegemony.
hégire [eʒir] *nf Rel* Hegira.
***hein** [ɛ̃] *int F* eh?, what?; **il fait beau aujourd'hui, h.?,** fine *or* nice day, isn't it?; **et qu'est-ce que tu lui diras, h.?,** so, what are you going to tell him now, eh?; **h. qu'il fait bien la cuisine!,** he does cook well, doesn't he?; **arrêtez, h.,** hey, stop.
***hélas** [elɑs] *int* alas!; **mais h., c'était trop tard,** but sadly *or Fml* alas it was too late; **h., trois fois h.!,** alas and alack!
Hélène [elɛn] *nf* Helen, Helena; **H. de Troie,** Helen of Troy.
***héler** [ele] *vt* (**je hèle, je hélerai**) to hail, to call (*s.o., a taxi*); *Nau* to hail, to speak (*a ship*).
hélianthe [eljɑ̃t] *nm Bot* helianthus, sunflower.
hélianthine [heljɑ̃tin] *nf Ch* helianthin(e), methyl orange.
héliaque [eljak] *adj Astron* heliac(al).
hélice [elis] *nf* **(a)** *Math Archit* helix; **escalier en h.,** spiral staircase; **(b)** *Nau Av* propeller; *Nau* screw.
hélicoïdal, -aux [elikɔidal, -o] *adj* helicoid(al), helical; **mèche hélicoïdale,** twist drill.
hélicoïde [elikɔid] *adj & nm Math* helicoid.
hélicon [elikɔ̃] *nm Mus* helicon.
hélicoptère [elikɔptɛr] *nm Av* helicopter; *Mil* **h. de combat,** helicopter gunship.
héligare [eligar] *nf* heliport.
héliocentrique [eljɔsɑ̃trik] *adj Astron* heliocentric.
héliographe [eljɔgraf] *nm* heliograph.
héliographie [eljɔgrafi] *nf* heliography.
héliograveur [eljɔgravœr] *nm* photogravure worker.
héliogravure [eljɔgravyr] *nf* photogravure.
héliomarin [eljɔmarɛ̃] *adj Méd* **cure héliomarine,** = course of treatment based on sun and sea air; **centre h.,** = seaside convalescent home where heliotherapy is used.
héliothérapie [eljɔterapi] *nf Méd* heliotherapy; **h. artificielle,** sunray treatment.
héliotrope [eljɔtrɔp] *nm Bot* heliotrope, turnsole.
héliport [elipɔr] *nm* heliport.
héliportage [elipɔrtaʒ] *nm* transporting by helicopter.
héliporté [elipɔrte] *adj* transported by helicopter.
hélisurface [elisyrfas] *nf Nau Pétr* helideck; (*sur un immeuble*) helipad.
hélitreuiller [elitrœje] *vt* to winch into a helicopter.
hélium [eljɔm] *nm Ch* helium.
hélix [eliks] *nm Anat* helix (of the ear).
hellébore [elebɔr] *nm Bot* hellebore.
hellène [elɛn] **1** *adj* Greek; *Hist* Hellenic. **2** *n* **H.,** Hellene.
hellénique [elenik] *adj* Greek; *Hist* Hellenic; **la politique h. à l'égard de la communauté Européenne,** Greek policy towards the European Community.
hellénisant, -ante [elenizɑ̃, -ɑ̃t] **1** *adj* Hellenistic. **2** *n* Hellenist.
hellénisation [elenizɑsjɔ̃] *nf* Hellenization.
helléniser [elenize] *vt* to Hellenize.
hellénisme [elenism] *nm* Hellenism.
helléniste [elenist] *n* Hellenist.
hellénistique [elenistik] *adj Hist* Hellenic.
***hello** [ɛllo] *int F* hello.
helvète [ɛlvɛt] *adj & n Hist* Helvetian; *Hum* = Swiss.
Helvétie [ɛlvesi] *nf Hist* Helvetia.
helvétique [ɛlvetik] *adj* Helvetic, Swiss; **le gouvernement h.,** the Swiss government; **la Confédération h.,** the Swiss Federal Republic.
helvétisme [ɛlvetism] *nm Ling* Swiss French expression.
***hem** [ɛm] *int* (*pour attirer l'attention, se rader la gorge*) ahem!; (*question*) eh?, what?; (*exprimant le doute etc*) h'm!
hématie [emati] *nf Physiol* red blood corpuscle.
hématite [ematit] *nf Minér* h(a)ematite.
hématologie [ematɔlɔʒi] *nf Méd* h(a)ematology.
hématologiste [ematɔlɔʒist], **hématologue** [ematɔlɔg] *n Méd* h(a)ematologist.
hématome [ematom] *nm Méd* h(a)ematoma.
hémicycle [emisikl] *nm Archit* hemicycle; **en h.,** semicircular (*vault etc*); *Pol* **les députés présents dans l'h.,** (*à l'Assemblée nationale*) the MPs present in the chamber.
hémione [emjɔn] *nm Zool* hemione, dziggetai.
hémiplégie [emipleʒi] *nf Méd* hemiplegia.
hémiplégique [emipleʒik] *adj & n Méd* hemiplegic.
hémiptère [emiptɛr] **1** *adj* hemipterous, hemipteral. **2** *nm* hemipter.
hémisphère [emisfɛr] *nm* hemisphere; **l'h. nord/sud,** the northern/southern hemisphere.
hémisphérique [emisferik] *adj* hemispheric(al).
hémistiche [emistiʃ] *nm* hemistich.
hémoculture [emɔkyltyr] *nf* h(a)emoculture, blood culture.
hémoglobine [emɔglɔbin] *nf* h(a)emoglobin.
hémophile [emɔfil] *Méd* **1** *adj* h(a)emophilic. **2** *n* h(a)emophiliac.
hémophilie [emɔfili] *nf Méd* h(a)emophilia.
hémoptysie [emɔptizi] *nf Méd* h(a)emoptysis, spitting of blood (*from lungs*).
hémorragie [emɔraʒi] *nf Méd* h(a)emorrhage, bleeding; **h. interne,** internal bleeding; *Fig* **il faut arrêter cette h. humaine,** we must stop this squandering of human life; *Fig* **l'h. des réserves d'or,** the heavy drain on the gold reserve.
hémorragique [emɔraʒik] *adj Méd* h(a)emorrhagic.
hémorroïdaire [emɔrɔidɛr] *adj & n Méd* **(personne) h.,** person suffering from h(a)emorrhoids.
hémorroïdal, -aux [emɔrɔidal, -o] *adj Méd* h(a)emorrhoidal.
hémorroïdes [emɔrɔid] *nfpl Méd* h(a)emorrhoids, piles.
hémostatique [emɔstatik] *Méd* **1** *adj* h(a)emostatic. **2** *nm* h(a)emostat(ic).
hendécagone [ɛ̃dekagɔn] *nm* hendecagon.
hendécasyllabe [ɛ̃dekasilab] **1** *adj* hendecasyllabic. **2** *nm* hendecasyllable.
***henné** [ɛne] *nm Bot* henna; **se faire un h.,** to henna one's hair, to give one's hair a henna rinse.
***hennir** [ɛnir] *vi* to whinny, to neigh.
***hennissement** [ɛnismɑ̃] *nm* (*action*) whinnying, neighing; (*cri*) whinny, neigh.
Henri [ɑ̃ri] *nm* Henry.
Henriette [ɑ̃rjɛt] *nf* Henrietta.
henry [ɑ̃ri] *nm Él* henry; (*pl henrys*).
***hep** [ɛp] *int* hey (there)!
héparine [eparin] *nf Pharm* heparin.
hépatique [epatik] **1** *adj* hepatic. **2** *n* person suffering from a liver complaint. **3** *nf Bot* hepatic, liverwort.
hépatisme [epatism] *nm Méd* liver ailments (*in general*).
hépatite [epatit] *nf Méd* hepatitis.
hépatologie [epatɔlɔʒi] *nf Méd* hepatology.
heptacorde [ɛptakɔrd] *Mus* **1** *adj* seven-stringed. **2** *nm* heptachord (instrument, scale).
heptaèdre [ɛptaɛdr] *nm* heptahedron.
heptagonal, -aux [ɛptagɔnal, -o] *adj* heptagonal.
heptagone [ɛptagɔn] *nm* heptagon.
heptamètre [ɛptamɛtr] *nm* heptameter.
heptarchie [ɛptarʃi] *nf Hist* heptarchy.
heptasyllabe [ɛptasilab] *adj* heptasyllabic.
Heptateuque (l') [lɛptatøk] *nm Bible* the Heptateuch.
héraldique [eraldik] **1** *adj* heraldic. **2** *nf* heraldry.
héraldiste [eraldist] *n* heraldist.
***héraut** [ero] *nm* **(a)** *Hist* **h. (d'armes),** herald; **(b)** *Litt* herald, harbinger (*of spring etc*).
herbacé [ɛrbase] *adj Bot* herbaceous.
herbage [ɛrbaʒ] *nm* (*prairie*) pasture; (*herbe*) grass, pasture.
herbagement [ɛrbaʒmɑ̃] *nm Agr* putting (*of animals*) out

to grass.
herbager[1] [ɛrbaʒe] *vt Agr* **(j'herbageai(s); n. herbageons)** to put (*animals*) out to grass.
herbager[2], **-ère** [-ɛr] *n Agr* grazier.
herbe [ɛrb] *nf* **(a)** (*de gazon etc*) grass; **brin d'h.,** blade of grass; **touffe d'h.,** tuft of grass; **faire de l'h.,** to cut grass (*for rabbit etc*); *Fig* **couper l'h. sous les pieds de qn,** to cut the ground from under s.o.'s feet; **déjeuner sur l'h.,** to picnic, to have a picnic (lunch); *Golf* **être dans l'h. longue,** to be in the rough;
(b) (*plante*) herb; *Arg* (*drogue*) grass; *Culin* **fines herbes,** mixed herbs; **herbes marines,** seeweed; **mauvaise h.,** weed; *Fig* **le garçon a grandi comme une mauvaise h.,** the boy has shot up *or* really sprouted;
(c) *Bot* (*common names*) **h. aux chats,** catmint, *Am* catnip; **h. au cœur** *ou* **aux poumons,** lungwort; **h. à éternuer,** sneezewort; **h. sacrée** *ou* **à tous les maux,** wild vervain; **h. aux écus,** moneywort; **h. aux puces,** fleawort; *Can* **h. à la puce,** poison ivy;
(d) en h., green, unripe (*corn etc*); budding (*poet etc*); *Fig* **manger son blé en h.,** to spend one's money before one gets it; **pour le pianiste en h.,** for the budding pianist.
herbeux, -euse [ɛrbø, -øz] *adj* grassy.
herbicide [ɛrbisid] *nm* weedkiller.
herbier [ɛrbje] *nm* (*collection*) herbarium.
herbivore [ɛrbivɔr] *Zool* **1** *adj* herbivorous. **2** *nm* herbivore.
herborisation [ɛrbɔrizasjɔ̃] *nf* botanizing, gathering of plants.
herboriser [ɛrbɔrize] *vi* to botanize, to gather plants.
herboriste [ɛrbɔrist] *n* herbalist.
herboristerie [ɛrbɔristəri] *nf* (*boutique*) herbalist's (shop); *Com* herb trade.
herbu [ɛrby] *adj* grassy.
***hercher** [ɛrʃe] *vi Min* to haul (*coal, ore*).
Herculanum [ɛrkylanɔm] *nm* Herculaneum.
Hercule [ɛrkyl] *nm* Hercules; **travail d'H.,** Herculean task; **il est bâti en h.,** he's built like a tank; **h. de foire,** (professional) strong man.
herculéen, -enne [ɛrkyleɛ̃] *adj* Herculean.
hercynien, -ienne [ɛrsinjɛ̃, ɛn] *adj Géol* Hercynian.
***hère** [ɛr] *nm* **pauvre h.,** poor creature, poor blighter, poor devil.
héréditaire [ereditɛr] *adj* hereditary; (*disease*) that runs in the family.
héréditairement [ereditɛrmɑ̃] *adv* hereditarily.
hérédité [eredite] *nf* **(a)** *Biol* heredity; **avoir une h. chargée** *ou* **une lourde h.,** to come from a family with a history of mental *or* physical illness; **h. de la couronne,** royal succession by birth; **(b)** *Jur* (*droit*) right of inheritance.
hérésie [erezi] *nf* heresy; *Fig* **c'est une h.!,** it's *or* that's sacrilege!
hérétique [eretik] **1** *adj* heretical. **2** *n* heretic.
***hérissé** [erise] *adj* **(a)** (*garni*) bristling **(de,** with); **planche hérissée de pointes,** spiky plank, plank covered in spikes; **(b)** (standing) on end, spiky (*hair*); bristly (*moustache, person*); prickly (*stem, fruit*).
***hérissement** [erismɑ̃] *nm* bristling.
***hérisser** [erise] **1** *vt* **(a)** (*d'un animal*) to bristle (up); **h. ses plumes,** (*of bird*) to ruffle up *or* put up its feathers; **(b)** to make (*sth*) bristle; to cover *or* surround (*sth*) with spikes; to make (*hair*) stand on end; *Fig* **l'épreuve était hérissée de pièges,** the test was full of pitfalls, the test had one pitfall after another; *Fig* **il a été hérissé par cette remarque,** the remark got his back up *or* made him bristle; *Fig* **h. sa conversation de citations,** to lard *or* pepper one's conversation with quotes. **2 se hérisser** *vpr* to bristle (up); (*of hair*) to stand on end; *Fig* (*of person*) to get one's back up, to bristle.
***hérisson** [erisɔ̃] *nm* **(a)** hedgehog; *Fig* bristly person; **h. de mer,** sea urchin; (*poisson*) porcupine fish; **(b)** (*pour bouteilles*) bottlebrush; **(c)** (*de cheminée*) (sweep's) flue brush; *Agr* toothed cylinder, toothed roller.
héritage [eritaʒ] *nm* inheritance, heritage; **part d'h.,** portion; **faire** *ou* **recueillir un h.,** to receive a legacy; (*argent*) to come into money; **il l'a eu par h.,** he inherited it, it was handed down to him; *Fig* **h. de honte,** legacy of shame; **h. spirituel,** spiritual inheritance.
hériter [erite] **1** *vi* **h. d'une fortune,** to inherit *or* succeed to *or* come into a fortune; **j'ai hérité de ce service de table,** this table linen was handed down to me; *Fig F* **il a hérité de dix jours de prison,** he got *or* landed ten days in prison. **2** *vt* **h. une fortune de son grand-père,** to inherit a fortune from one's grandfather; *Fig* **h. une tradition,** to inherit a tradition.
héritier, -ière [eritje, -jɛr] *n* heir, *f* heiress; **h. de qch/qn,** heir to sth/s.o.; **h. présomptif,** *Jur* next of kin; (*du trône*) heir apparent; **h. légitime** *ou* **naturel,** heir-at-law, rightful heir; **lui donnera-t-elle un h.?,** will she give him an heir?
hermaphrodisme [ɛrmafrɔdism] *nm Biol* hermaphroditism.
hermaphrodite [ɛrmafrɔdit] **1** *nm Biol* hermaphrodite. **2** *adj* hermaphrodite, hermaphroditic.
Hermaphrodite [ɛrmafrɔdit] *nm Myth* Hermaphroditus.
herméneutique [ɛrmenøtik] **1** *adj* hermeneutic. **2** *nf* hermeneutics.
hermès [ɛrmɛs] *nm* **(buste en) h.,** bust where the shoulders, chest and arms have been cut away at an angle.
Hermès [ɛrmɛs] *nm Myth* Hermes.
hermétique [ɛrmetik] *adj* **(a)** hermetic (*philosophy, alchemy*); *Fig* abstruse, obscure (*text etc*); **un poète h.,** an abstruse poet; **(b)** tight (closed), hermetically sealed, hermetic (*seal*); **joint h.,** airtight *or* watertight joint.
hermétiquement [ɛrmetikmɑ̃] *adj* hermetically (*sealed etc*), tight(-shut), close(-shut).
hermétisme [ɛrmetism] *nm Littér* hermetism; abstruseness, obscurity (*of text etc*).
hermine [ɛrmin] *nf Zool* stoat, ermine; *Com* ermine (*fur*).
herminette [ɛrminɛt] *nf* adze.
***herniaire** [ɛrnjɛr] **1** *adj* hernial (*tumour etc*); **bandage h.,** truss. **2** *nf Bot* rupture wort.
***hernie** [ɛrni] *nf Méd* hernia, rupture; *Aut* bulge, swelling (*in tyre*); **h. étranglée,** strangulated hernia; **h. discale,** slipped disc.
***hernié** [ɛrnje] *adj Méd* herniated (*intestine etc*).
Hérode [erɔd] *nm* Herod.
Hérodote [erɔdɔt] *nm* Herodotus.
héroï-comique [erɔikɔmik] *adj* mock-heroic; (*pl héroï-comiques*).
héroïne[1] [erɔin] *nf* heroine.
héroïne[2] *nf Ch* heroin.
héroïnomane [erɔinɔman] *n* heroin addict.
héroïnomanie [erɔinɔmani] *nf* heroin addiction.
héroïque [erɔik] *adj* heroic.
héroïquement [erɔikmɑ̃] *adv* heroically.
héroïsme [erɔism] *nm* heroism.
***héron** [erɔ̃] *nm* heron.
***héros** [ero] *nm* hero; **mourir en h.,** to die like a hero *or* a hero's death; **le h. national,** the national hero; **le h. du jour,** the hero of the day *or* hour.
herpès [ɛrpɛs] *nm Méd* herpes; (*buccal*) cold sore.
herpétique [ɛrpetik] *adj Méd* herpetic.
herpétologie [ɛrpetɔlɔʒi] *nf* herpetology.
***hersage** [ɛrsaʒ] *nm Agr* harrowing.
***herscher** [ɛrʃe] *vi* = ***HERCHER**.
***herse** [ɛrs] *nf Agr* harrow; *Arch* portcullis.
***herser** [ɛrse] *vt Agr* to harrow.
***herseur** [ɛrsœr] *nm Agr* harrower.
***herseuse** [ɛrsøz] *nf Agr* harrow.
hertz [ɛrts] *nm Él* hertz.
hertzien, -ienne [ɛrtsjɛ̃, -jɛn] *adj Él* hertzian; *Rad* **réseau h.,** radio relay system.
hésitant, -ante [ezitɑ̃, -ɑ̃t] **1** *adj* hesitant, wavering, undecided (*character etc*); faltering (*voice, footsteps etc*). **2** *n* **il faut convaincre les hésitants,** we must convince the waverers.
hésitation [ezitɑsjɔ̃] *nf* hesitation, hesitancy, wavering; **parler avec h.,** to speak hesitatingly; **après bien des hésitations,** after much hesitation; **sans h.,** unhesitatingly, without hesitation.
hésiter [ezite] *vi* **(a)** to hesitate, to waver; **h. sur qch/entre deux choses,** to hesitate over sth/between two things; **h. sur ce qu'on fera,** to hesitate as to what one will do; **h. à faire qch,** to hesitate to do sth; **il n'hésita pas une seconde à se jeter à l'eau,** without a moment's hesitation, he jumped into the water; *Fig* without a moment's hesitation he took the plunge; **il n'y a pas à h.,** there's no room *or* time for hesitation; **je ne sais pas, j'hésite,** I don't know, I can't make up my mind *or* I'm undecided; **(b)** to hesitate, to falter (*in speaking*); **h. devant l'obstacle,** (*d'un cheval*) to refuse a fence.
hétéro [etero] *F* **1** *adj* heterosexual; **couple h.,** heterosexual couple. **2** *n* heterosexual.
hétéroclite [eterɔklit] *adj* (*collection*) heterogeneous, ill-assorted; (*bizarre*) unusual, strange, odd, eccentric; **mélange h.,** odd assortment.
hétérodoxe [eterɔdɔks] *adj* heterodox.
hétérodoxie [eterɔdɔksi] *nf* heterodoxy.

hétérodyne [eterɔdin] *adj & nf Rad* heterodyne (receiver).
hétérogène [eterɔʒɛn] *adj* (*différent*) heterogeneous; incongruous (*collection etc*); mixed (*society*).
hétérogénéité [eterɔʒeneite] *nf* heterogeneousness, heterogeneity.
hétéroplastie [eteroplasti] *nf Chir* heteroplasty.
hétérosexualité [eterɔsɛksɥalite] *nf* heterosexuality.
hétérosexuel, -elle [eterɔsɛksɥɛl] *adj & n* heterosexual.
***hêtraie** [ɛtrɛ] *nf* beech grove *or* plantation.
***hêtre** [ɛtr] *nm* beech (*tree, wood*); **h. rouge** *ou* **pourpre,** copper beech.
***heu** [ø] *int* (*doubt*) h'm!; (*in hesitating speech*) ... er... .
heur [œr] *nm Iron & Litt* **je n'ai pas l'h. de la connaître,** I have not the pleasure of her acquaintance; **je n'ai pas eu l'h. de lui plaire,** I did not have the good fortune to win his favour.
heure [œr] *nf* **(a)** (*soixante minutes*) hour; *Scol* **h. de cours,** period; **j'ai attendu une bonne h.,** I waited a full *or* good *or* solid hour; **cent kilomètres à l'h.,** a hundred kilometres *or US* kilometers an hour; **être payé à l'h.,** to be paid by the hour; **toucher 30 francs l'h.** *ou* **de l'h.,** to get 30 francs an hour; **semaine de 40 heures,** 40-hour week; **heures supplémentaires,** overtime; **faire des heures supplémentaires,** to do overtime; *Fig* **la situation peut s'inverser à toute h.,** the situation can *or* could change at any time; **cette mode a eu son h.,** this fashion has had its day; **un partisan de la première h./de la dernière h.,** a supporter from the word 'go'/at the very last minute; **j'attends mon h.,** I'm biding my time;
(b) (*dans la journée*) **à toutes heures du jour,** at all hours of the day; **à toute h.,** at any time, at all hours of the day, round the clock; **repas chauds à toute h.,** hot meals 24 hours a day; **un médecin de garde peut être appelé à toute h. du jour ou de la nuit,** a doctor is on call round the clock *or* at all times; **tout à l'h.,** (*dans le passé*) just now, a few minutes ago; (*dans le futur*) soon, presently, in a few minutes; **à tout à l'h.!,** (*dans un futur proche*) so long!, see you soon *or* later!; **de bonne h.,** early, in good time; (*dans l'histoire*) at an early period; **il est de trop bonne h. pour rentrer,** it's too early to go home; **de meilleure h.,** earlier; **heures d'affluence** *ou* **de pointe,** rush hour, peak period; **heures creuses,** off-peak hours, slack period; **d'h. en h.,** hour by hour/hourly; *Journ* **nouvelles de dernière h.,** latest news, stop-press (news); **l'h. de Greenwich,** Greenwich mean time; **h. astronomique,** sidereal time; **h. légale,** official *or* standard time; **h. d'été,** *Can* **h. avancée,** *Br* Summer Time, *Am* daylight (-saving) time; **quelle h. est-il?,** what time is it?, what's the time?; **quelle h. avez-vous?,** what time do you make it?; **il est deux heures,** it's two o'clock; **cinq heures moins dix,** ten (minutes) to five; **dix-huit heures,** eighteen hundred (hours); **vingt heures quarante,** twenty forty; **le train de neuf heures,** the nine o'clock train; **où serai-je demain à cette h.-ci?,** where will I be this time tomorrow?; **à une h. avancée (de la journée),** late in the day; **à cinq heures juste(s)** *ou* **sonnant(es)** *ou* **tapant(es),** (right, exactly) on the stroke of five, at five on the dot, at five o'clock sharp; **mettre sa montre à l'h.,** to set one's watch (right); **ma montre n'est pas à l'h.,** my watch is wrong; **les trains partent à l'h.,** the trains leave on the hour; (*sans retard*) the trains leave on time; *Rel* **livre d'heures,** Book of Hours;
(c) *Fig* **le parti communiste est à l'h. de la Russie,** the Communist party is under Russian influence; **vivre à l'h. espagnole,** to adopt a Spanish lifestyle, to go Spanish; **les Britanniques vont devoir se mettre à l'h. européenne,** the British are going to have to come into line with the rest of Europe; **mettre l'administration à l'h. de l'informatique,** to bring (the) administration into the computer age;
(d) (*moment précis*) **l'h. du dîner,** dinner time; **l'h. d'aller se coucher,** bedtime; **son h. est venue,** his time has come; **à l'h. dite,** at the appointed *or* agreed time; **être à l'h.,** to be punctual *or* on time; **arriver à l'h. exacte,** to arrive dead on time; **arriver/avoir fini avant l'h.,** to arrive/have finished ahead of time; **il est** *ou* **c'est l'h.,** the hour has come, it's time, time (is) up;
(e) (*moment présent*) **pour l'h.,** for the present, for the time being; **l'h. est grave,** these are difficult times, things are looking bad; **la question de l'h.,** the question of the moment, the current question; **à l'h. qu'il est,** by this time, by now; (*maintenant*) nowadays, now, currently; *surtout Am* presently; **faire qch sur l'h.,** to do sth at once *or* right away; **je vais le faire dès cette h.,** I'll do it at once;
(f) *Fig* **à ses heures, il était charmant,** when he liked *or* when he felt like it *or* when he was in the mood, he could be charming;
(g) à la bonne h.!, well done!, good (for you)!, all right!, fine!
heureusement [œrøzmɑ̃] *adv* **(a)** (*par bonheur*) luckily, fortunately; **h. que j'étais là,** it's a good thing I was there, fortunately I was there; **(b)** (*avec succès*) successfully; *Fig* **commencer h.,** to begin auspiciously, to get off to a good start; **h. exprimé,** well expressed.
heureux, -euse [œrø, -øz] **1** *adj* **(a)** happy; **h. comme un poisson dans l'eau,** as happy as a sandboy; **vivre h.,** to live happily; **heureuse ignorance,** blissful ignorance; **je suis très h. de ce cadeau,** I'm very happy *or* pleased with *or* about this gift; **je suis très h. de vous faire savoir que ...,** I'm very happy *or* pleased to inform you that ...; **nous serions h. que vous acceptiez,** we should be glad if you would accept; **époque heureuse,** happy times; **heureuse année!,** Happy New Year!;
(b) (*favorable*) successful; felicitous, happy, apt (*phrase etc*); **h. mariage,** joyful wedding (ceremony); **mariage h.,** happy marriage; **un h. mariage de couleurs,** a happy blend of colours; **l'issue heureuse des négociations,** the successful outcome of the negotiations; *Fig* **début h.,** auspicious beginning; **le résultat n'est pas très h.,** it wasn't very successful, it didn't work out;
(c) (*favorisé*) fortunate, favoured; **h. au jeu/en amour,** lucky at cards/in love; **il peut s'estimer h.,** he can think *or* consider himself lucky; *Bible* **h. sont les pauvres en esprit,** blessed are the poor in spirit;
(d) (*chanceux*) lucky, fortunate; **c'est fort h. pour vous,** that's very lucky for you; **c'est h. que vous soyez libre,** it's a good thing *or* a good job that you're free; *F* **encore h. qu'il ait gardé le ticket de caisse!,** it's just as well that he held on to the receipt!; **par un h. hasard,** by a happy coincidence.
2 *n* **vous avez fait un h.,** you have made one man very happy.
heuristique [œristik] **1** *adj* heuristic. **2** *nf* heuristics.
***heurt** [œr] *nm* clash (*of interests, colours etc*); collision (*of vehicles etc*); **tout s'est fait sans h.,** everything went smoothly *or* without a hitch.
***heurté** [œrte] *adj* abrupt, halting (*style*); *Beaux-Arts* contrasting (*colours*).
***heurter** [œrte] **1** *vt* **(a)** to knock (against), to run into, to bump into (*s.o., sth*); to collide with (*s.o.*); *Nau* to hit, to strike (*a rock*); **h. qch de la tête,** to knock *or* bump one's head against sth;
(b) to shock, to offend (*s.o.'s feelings etc*); **h. toutes les idées reçues,** to go against *or* run counter to all conventions.
2 *vi* **h. à la porte,** to knock at *or* on the door; **sa tête a heurté contre le pare-brise,** he hit his head against the windscreen, his head struck the windscreen.
3 se heurter *vpr* **(a)** (*se cogner*) to collide (with each other); **se h. à** *ou* **contre qn/qch,** to run (slap) into *or* collide with *or* bang into *or* bump into s.o./sth; **se h. la tête à** *ou* **contre qch,** to knock *or* bump one's head against sth; *Fig* **se h. à l'indifférence générale,** to come up against the apathy of the public; **se h. à une difficulté,** to come up against a difficulty;
(b) (*de couleur, intérêt etc*) to clash; *Fig* **au cours de la réunion ils se sont heurtés violemment,** during the last meeting they clashed violently.
***heurtoir** [œrtwar] *nm* (*de porte*) (door) knocker; (*amortisseur*) catch, stop; *Rail* buffer.
hévéa [evea] *nm Bot* hevea.
hexacorde [ɛgzakɔrd] *nm Mus* hexachord.
hexadécimal, -aux [ɛgzadesimal] *adj Ordinat* hexadecimal, *F* hex.
hexaèdre [ɛgzaɛdr] **1** *adj* hexahedral. **2** *nm* hexahedron.
hexagonal, -aux [ɛgzagɔnal, -o] *adj* hexagonal; *Fig* French; **l'économie ne peut plus être structurée sur le modèle h.,** the structure of the economy can no longer be based on the French model.
hexagone [ɛgzagɔn] *nm* hexagon; **l'H. (français),** France.
hexamètre [ɛgzamɛtr] **1** *adj* hexametric(al). **2** *nm* hexameter.
hiatal, -aux [jatal, -o] *adj Méd* hiatal; **hernie hiatale,** hiatus hernia.
hiatus [jatys] *nm* (*when aspirated* **le hiatus**, *when silent* **l'hiatus**) gap, break (*in narrative etc*); *Ling Anat* hiatus; **le h. entre la production et les besoins,** the gap between production and needs.
hibernal, -aux [ibɛrnal, -o] *adj* hibernal (*germination, sommeil etc*).

hibernant [ibɛrnɑ̃] *adj* hibernating (*animal*).
hibernation [ibɛrnasjɔ̃] *nf* hibernation; *Fig* **être dans un état d'h. intellectuelle,** to have switched off intellectually; **la gauche sort de son h.,** the left is coming in from the cold; **mettre un dossier en h.,** to shelve a document; **h. artificielle,** cryogenic suspension.
hiberner [ibɛrne] *vi* to hibernate.
hibiscus [ibiskys] *nm Bot* hibiscus.
***hibou, -oux** [ibu] *nm* owl; **jeune h.,** owlet; **des yeux de h.,** eyes like saucers; *Péj* **quel h.!,** he is a real recluse!
***hic** [ik] *nm F* **voilà le h.!,** that's the snag *or* the trouble!, there's the rub!; **le h., c'est que ...,** the trouble *or* snag is that ... .
***hickory** [ikɔri] *nm Bot* hickory.
***hideur** [idœr] *nf* (*qualité*) hideousness.
***hideusement** [idøzmɑ̃] *adv* hideously.
***hideux, -euse** [idø, -øz] *adj* hideous; **h. à voir,** hideous-looking; **un crime h.,** a heinous crime.
hier [jɛr] **1** *adv* yesterday; **h. (au) matin,** yesterday morning; **h. (au) soir,** yesterday evening, last night; **on s'en souvient comme si c'était h.,** I *or* we can remember it as if it were (only) yesterday; **le journal d'h.,** yesterday's paper; *Fig* **cela ne date pas d'h.,** that's nothing new, it's not the first time; *F* **je ne suis pas né d'h.,** I wasn't born yesterday. **2** *nm* **tu avais tout h.** *ou* **toute la journée d'h. pour te décider,** you had all (day) yesterday to make up your mind.
***hiérarchie** [jerarʃi] *nf* hierarchy.
***hiérarchique** [jerarʃik] *adj* hierarchical; **il est mon supérieur h.,** he is senior (in rank) to me; **par (la) voie h.,** through (the) official channels.
***hiérarchiquement** [jerarʃikmɑ̃] *adv* hierarchically.
***hiérarchiser** [jerarʃize] *vt* (*organiser*) to form into a hierarchy; (*régler*) to manage (*state etc*) on the hierarchical system.
hiératique [jeratik] *adj* hieratic.
***hiéroglyphe** [jerɔglif] *nm* hieroglyph(ic).
***hiéroglyphique** [jerɔglifik] *adj* hieroglyphic(al).
***hi-fi** [ifi] *adj & nf Rad etc F* hi-fi, high-fidelity; **chaîne hi-fi,** hi-fi.
***hi-han** [iɑ̃] *int & nm* (donkey's) hee-haw; (*pl hi-hans*).
hi hi [ii] *int* (*sound of tittering*) tehee!, tee-hee!
hilarant [ilarɑ̃] *adj* hilarious; *Ch* **gaz h.,** laughing gas.
hilare [ilar] *adj* (*visage*) beaming.
hilarité [ilarite] *nf* hilarity, mirth.
***hile** [il] *nm Anat Bot* hilum.
himalayen, -enne [imalajɛ̃, -ɛn] *adj* Himalayan; *Fig* **les sommets himalayens de la bêtise,** the (absolute) height of stupidity.
***hindi** [indi] *nm Ling* Hindi.
hindou, -oue [ɛ̃du] **1** *adj* Hindu. **2** *n* **H.,** Hindu.
hindouisme [ɛ̃duism] *nm* Hinduism.
hindouiste [ɛ̃duist] *adj & n* Hindu.
Hindoustan [ɛ̃dustɑ̃] *nm Géog* Hindustan.
hindoustani [ɛ̃dustani] *nm Ling* Hindustani.
hinterland [interlɑ̃d] *nm* hinterland.
***hippie** [ipi] *adj & n* hippie.
hippique [ipik] *adj* relating to horses, equine; **concours h.,** horse show.
hippisme [ipism] *nm* horse racing *or* riding.
hippocampe [ipɔkɑ̃p] *nm Myth* hippocampus; (*poisson*) sea horse.
Hippocrate [ipɔkrat] *nm Antiq* Hippocrates; **le serment d'H.,** the Hippocratic oath.
hippocratique [ipɔkratik] *adj* Hippocratic.
hippodrome [ipɔdrom] *nm* racecourse; *Antiq* hippodrome, circus.
hippomobile [ipɔmɔbil] *adj* horse-drawn.
hippophagie [ipɔfaʒi] *nf* hippophagy.
hippopotame [ipɔpɔtam] *nm* hippopotamus, *F* hippo.
hippopotamesque [ipɔpɔtamɛsk] *adj F Hum* hippopotamus-like, of a hippopotamus; **une lourdeur/grâce h.,** the weight/grace of a hippo.
hippotechnie [ipɔtɛkni] *nf* (technique of) horse breeding and training.
***hippy** [ipi] *adj & n* hippie.
hirondelle [irɔ̃dɛl] *nf* **(a)** (*oiseau*) swallow; **h. de fenêtre,** house martin; **h. de rivage,** sand martin; *Prov* **une h. ne fait pas le printemps,** = one swallow doesn't make a summer; *Culin* **nid d'h.,** bird's nest; **(b)** *F Vieilli* cycle cop.
hirsute [irsyt] *adj* hirsute, hairy, shaggy.
hispanique [ispanik] *adj* Hispanic, Spanish.
hispanisant [ispanizɑ̃] *n* Hispani(ci)st; student of *or* expert on Spanish.
hispanisme [ispanism] *nm Ling* Hispanicism.
hispano-américain, -aine [ispanɔamerikɛ̃, -ɛn] (*pl hispano-américain(e)s*) **1** *adj* Hispano-American, Spanish-American. **2** *n* **H.-A.,** Hispano-American, *F* Hispanic.
hispano-arabe [ispanɔarab], **hispano-moresque** [ispanɔmɔrɛsk] *adj* Hispano-Moorish, Hispano-Moresque; (*pl hispano-arabes, -moresques*).
hispanophone [ispanɔfɔn] *adj* Spanish-speaking.
hispide [ispid] *adj Bot* hispid; hairy.
***hisser** [ise] **1** *vt* to hoist (up), to pull up; *Nau* to trice (up) (*sail*); to hoist in (*boat*); to run up (*signal*); **hissez!,** hoist away!; *Nau* up sails!; **oh! hisse!,** (yo-)heave-ho! **2 se hisser** *vpr* **se h. jusqu'à la fenêtre,** to pull *or* hoist oneself up to the window; **se h. sur la pointe des pieds,** to stand on tiptoe.
histoire [istwar] *nf* **(a)** history; **h. du moyen âge/naturelle,** medi(a)eval/natural history; **h. de l'art,** history of art; **l'h. des sciences,** history of science; **livre d'h.,** history book; **l'H. sainte,** Biblical history; **la petite h.,** sidelights on history; **l'h. de (la) France,** the history of France, French history; **l'h. de notre pays,** the history of our country; *Fig* **tout cela, c'est de l'h. ancienne,** that's all ancient history *or* dead and buried;
(b) (*livre*) history book; **j'ai acheté une h. d'Allemagne,** I've bought a history of Germany;
(c) (*récit*) story, tale; *F* (*mensonge*) lie, fib, story; **h. de marin,** sailor's yarn; **livre d'histoires,** story book; **h. de fous,** shaggy dog story; *F* **c'est toujours la même h.,** it's (always) the same old story; **tout ça, ce sont des histoires,** that's all nonsense *or* rubbish; **le plus beau de l'h., c'est que ...,** the best part of the story is that ...; *F* **il est sorti, h. de prendre un peu l'air,** he went out merely *or* just to get a breath of fresh air; **ce que j'en dis, c'est h. de parler,** you can take or leave what I've said; **c'est toute une h.,** (*à raconter*) it's a long story; (*pour faire qch*) it's no end of a job;
(d) *F* **faire des histoires** *ou* **un tas d'histoires,** to make a fuss *or* a to-do; **en voilà une h. pour pas grand-chose,** what a fuss about nothing; **faire des histoires à qn,** to make trouble for s.o.; *F* **en voilà une h.!,** what a fuss!, what a song and dance!; (*c'est incroyable*) that's quite a story; **il faut éviter d'avoir des histoires,** you *or* we *etc* must keep out of trouble; *F* **pas d'histoires!,** no fuss!; **quelle h.!,** that's quite a story!
histologie [istɔlɔʒi] *nf* histology.
histologique [istɔlɔʒik] *adj* histological.
historié [istɔrje] *adj* historiated (*initials etc*); illuminated (*Bible etc*).
historien, -ienne [istɔrjɛ̃, -jɛn] *n* historian.
historiette [istɔrjɛt] *nf* anecdote, short story.
historiographe [istɔrjɔgraf] *nm* historiographer, chronicler.
historiographie [istɔrjɔgrafi] *nf* historiography.
historique [istɔrik] **1** *adj* historic(al); *Gram* **présent h.,** historic present; **être classé monument h.,** (*of building*) to be listed *or* classified as an ancient monument *or* as a place of historic interest; **c'est un événement h. dans la famille,** it's a historic event *or* red letter day for the family. **2** *nm* historical record *or* account; **faire l'h. des événements,** to give a chronological account of events.
historiquement [istɔrikmɑ̃] *adv* historically.
histrion [istrijɔ̃] *nm Th Arch* histrion, play actor; *Litt Péj* second-rate actor.
hitlérien, -ienne [itlerjɛ̃, -jɛn] **1** *adj* Hitlerite; **le gouvernement h.,** the Hitler government. **2** *n* Hitlerite.
hitlérisme [itlerism] *nm* Hitlerism.
***hit-parade** [itparad] *nm* charts, hit parade; **chanteur n° 1 au h.-p.,** number 1 in the charts *or* hit parade.
***hittite** [itit] *Antiq* **1** *adj* Hittite. **2** *n* **H.,** Hittite.
hiver [ivɛr] *nm* winter; **en h.,** in winter; **temps d'h.,** wintry weather; **vêtements/sports d'h.,** winter clothes/sports; **jardin d'h.,** winter garden; *F* **le bonhomme H.,** Jack Frost; *Fig* **h. nucléaire,** nuclear winter.
hivernage [ivɛrnaʒ] *nm* **(a)** wintering (*of cattle, ships, polar expedition etc*); **(b)** (*endroit*) winter quarters, *Nau* winter harbour; **(c)** (*fourrage*) winter fodder).
hivernal, -aux [ivɛrnal, -o] *adj* winter (*cold etc*); wintry (*weather*).
hivernant, -ante [ivɛrnɑ̃, -ɑ̃t] *n* winter visitor *or* tourist (*in holiday resort etc*).
hiverner [ivɛrne] **1** *vi* to winter; (*of ship*) to lie up (for the winter). **2** *vt* to winter (*cattle*).
H.L.M. [aʃɛlɛm] *n* (*abrév* **habitation à loyer modéré**) ≈ *Br* council flat; **vivre dans un(e) H.L.M.,** to live in a council flat.
***ho** [o] *int* (*call*) hey!; (*surprise*) oh!

***hobby** [ɔbi] *nm* hobby.
***hobereau, -eaux** [ɔbro] *nm Fig souvent Péj* (country) squire; *Orn* hobby.
***hochement** [ɔʃmɑ̃] *nm* **h. de tête,** (*négatif*) shake of the head; (*affirmatif*) nod (of the head); (*of person, horse*) toss of the head.
***hochepot** [ɔʃpo] *nm Culin* meat and vegetable stew; hotchpotch.
***hocher** [ɔʃe] *vt* **h. la tête,** to toss one's head; (*pour dire non*) to shake one's head; (*pour dire oui*) to nod (one's head); (*of horse*) to toss its head.
***hochet** [ɔʃɛ] *nm* (*d'enfant*) (child's) rattle; *Fig* bauble, toy.
***hockey** [ɔkɛ] *nm Sp* (*jeu*) hockey, *Can* ice hockey; *Can* (*crosse*) (ice) hockey stick; **h. sur gazon/glace,** (field) hockey/ice hockey, *Am* hockey; **partie de h.**, hockey game *or* match.
***hockeyeur, -euse** [ɔkɛjœr, -øz] *n* (ice) hockey player.
hoirie [wari] *nf Jur* **avance** *ou* **avancement d'h.**, advancement.
***holà** [ɔla] **1** *int* (*pour appeler*) stop!, hold on!, enough!, whoa! **2** *nm* **mettre le h. à qch,** (*stop*) to check *or* put a stop to sth.
***holding** [ɔldiŋ] *nm or f Fin* holding company.
***hold-up** [ɔldœp] *nm inv F* hold-up, *surtout Am* stick-up.
***hollandais, -aise** [ɔlɑ̃dɛ, -ɛz] **1** *adj* Dutch. **2** *nm Ling* Dutch. **3** *n* **H.**, Dutchman, Dutchwoman; **les H.**, the Dutch.
***hollande** [ɔlɑ̃d] **1** *nm* (*fromage*) Dutch cheese. **2** *nf Tex* holland.
***Hollande** [ɔlɑ̃d] *nf* Holland.
hollywoodien, -ienne [ɔliwudjɛ̃, -ɛn] *adj* (of) Hollywood, Hollywood-style.
holmium [ɔlmjɔm] *nm Ch* holmium.
holocauste [ɔlɔkost] *nm* **(a)** (*sacrifice*) sacrifice; (*des juifs*) holocaust; (*avec immolation*) burnt offering; **(b)** (*victime*) sacrifice.
hologramme [ɔlɔgram] *nm* hologram.
holographe [ɔlɔgraf] *nf* = **OLOGRAPHE.**
holographie [ɔlɔgrafi] *nf* holography.
holothurie [ɔlɔtyri] *nf Zool* holothurian, sea slug, sea cucumber.
***homard** [ɔmar] *nm* lobster; *F* **rouge comme un h.**, (*with embarrassment*) as red as a beetroot; (*with sunburn*) as red as a lobster.
hombre [ɔ̃br] *nm Cartes Arch* (game of) ombre.
***home** [om] *nm* home.
homélie [ɔmeli] *nf* homily.
homéopathe [ɔmeɔpat] *Méd* **1** *adj* hom(o)eopathic. **2** *n* hom(o)eopath.
homéopathie [ɔmeɔpati] *nf* hom(o)eopathy.
homéopathique [ɔmeɔpatik] *adj* hom(o)eopathic.
Homère [ɔmɛr] *nm Littér* Homer.
homérique [ɔmerik] *adj* Homeric.
homicide [ɔmisid] **1** *adj Arch & Litt* homicidal; murderous (*weapon*). **2** *n Litt* (*personne*) homicide, murderer, *f* murderess. **3** *nm Jur* (*crime*) homicide; **h. volontaire,** wilful homicide, murder; **h. excusable,** justifiable homicide; **h. par imprudence, h. involontaire,** manslaughter (*through negligence*); **h. sans préméditation,** culpable homicide.
hommage [ɔmaʒ] *nm* **(a)** homage; **rendre h. à qn,** to pay homage *or* (a) tribute to s.o.; **(b) hommages,** respects, compliments; **présenter ses hommages à une dame,** to pay one's respects to a lady; **(c)** tribute, token (*of respect, esteem*); **faire h. de qch à qn,** to offer sth to s.o. as a token of (one's) esteem; **h. de l'éditeur,** complimentary copy, presentation copy; **h. de l'auteur,** with the author's compliments.
hommasse [ɔmas] *adj Péj* (*of woman*) masculine, mannish; **elle a des manières hommasses,** she acts like a man.
homme [ɔm] *nm* **(a)** man, *pl* men; **soyez un h.!,** be a man!; **h. fait,** grown man; **jeune h.,** young man; **je ne suis plus un jeune h.,** I'm no youngster (anymore); **merci jeune h.,** thank you, young man; *Com* **rayon hommes,** men's department, menswear; **parler à qn d'h. à h.,** to speak to s.o. man to man; **un bel h.,** a handsome man; *F* **mon h.,** my man *or* husband; **h. à femmes,** ladykiller;
(b) (*individu*) (*pl* **hommes** *or* **gens**) man, *pl* men; **il n'est pas** *ou* **ce n'est pas mon h.,** he's not the man for me; **trouver son h.,** to meet one's match; **h. à tout faire,** odd-job man; *surtout Am* handyman; **il n'est pas h. à souffrir un affront,** he's not a man to stand being insulted; **h. d'État,** statesman; **h. de mer,** seafaring man; **h. de journée** *ou* **de peine,** (day) labourer; *Mil* **les officiers et les hommes,** the officers and (the) men; *Nau* **les hommes (d'équipage),** the crew, the ship's company; **l'abominable h. des neiges,** the abominable snowman;
(c) man, mankind; *Prov* **l'h. propose, Dieu dispose,** man proposes, God disposes; **tous les hommes,** all men, all mankind; **de mémoire d'h.,** within living memory; **les droits de l'h.**, human rights.
homme-grenouille [ɔmgrənuj] *nm* frogman; (*pl hommes-grenouilles*).
homme-orchestre [ɔmɔrkɛstr] *nm* one-man band; (*pl hommes-orchestres*).
homme-sandwich [ɔmsɑ̃dwitʃ] *nm* sandwich man; (*pl hommes-sandwich(e)s*).
homo [ɔmo] *adj & n* gay.
homocentrique [ɔmɔsɑ̃trik] *adj Math* homocentric.
homogène [ɔmɔʒɛn] *adj* homogeneous.
homogénéisation [ɔmɔʒeneizasjɔ̃] *nf* homogenization.
homogénéiser [ɔmɔʒeneize] *vt* to homogenize; **lait homogénéisé,** homogenized milk.
homogénéité [ɔmɔʒeneite] *nf* homogeneousness, homogeneity.
homographe [ɔmɔgraf] **1** *nm* homograph. **2** *adj* homographic.
homologation [ɔmɔlɔgasjɔ̃] *nf Jur* confirmation (*of deed etc*); probate (*of will*); official approval; *Sp* ratification (*of record etc*).
homologie [ɔmɔlɔʒi] *nf* homology.
homologue [ɔmɔlɔg] *Biol etc* **1** *adj* homologous. **2** *nm* homologue. **3** *n* counterpart, opposite number; **le Ministre des Finances français a rencontré son h. italien,** the French Minister of Finance met his Italian counterpart.
homologuer [ɔmɔlɔge] *vt Jur* to confirm, to endorse (*deed etc*); *Jur* to prove (*will*); to ratify (*decision*); *Sp* to ratify (*record*); *Admin* **prix homologués,** authorized charges; *Sp* **record homologué,** official record.
homoncule [ɔmɔ̃kyl] *nm* = **HOMUNCULE.**
homonyme [ɔmɔnim] *Ling* **1** *adj* homonymous. **2** *nm* (*mot*) homonym; (*personne*) namesake.
homonymie [ɔmɔnimi] *nf Ling* homonymy.
homophone [ɔmɔfɔn] **1** *adj Ling Mus* homophonous, homophonic. **2** *nm Ling* homophone.
homophonie [ɔmɔfɔni] *nf* homophony.
homosexualité [ɔmɔsɛksɥalite] *nf* homosexuality.
homosexuel, -elle [ɔmɔsɛksɥɛl] *adj & n* homosexual.
homuncule [ɔmɔ̃kyl] *nm Arch* homunculus; *Fig Péj* manikin, dwarf.
***hondurien, -ienne** [ɔ̃dyrjɛ̃, -jɛn] **1** *adj* Honduran. **2** *n* **H.**, Honduran.
***hongre** [ɔ̃gr] **1** *adj* gelded, castrated (*horse*). **2** *nm* gelding.
***hongrer** [ɔ̃gre] *vt Vét* to geld, to castrate.
***Hongrie** [ɔ̃gri] *nf* Hungary.
***hongrois, -oise** [ɔ̃grwa, -waz] **1** *adj* Hungarian. **2** *nm Ling* Hungarian. **3** *n* **H.**, Hungarian.
honnête [ɔnɛt] *adj* **(a)** (*intègre*) honest, honourable, *US* honorable (*person etc*); **homme h., h. homme,** honest man, man of honour *or US* honor; **peu h.**, dishonourable; **moyens honnêtes,** fair means; **(b)** (*décent*) decent, seemly, becoming (*behaviour etc*); **attitude peu h.**, unseemly *or* unbecoming attitude; **(c)** (*acceptable*) reasonable, moderate, fair (*price etc*); **un repas h. sans plus,** a reasonable *or* an OK meal, but nothing more *or* nothing to write home about; **(d)** *Arch* courteous, polite, well-bred; **h. homme,** gentleman.
honnêtement [ɔnɛtmɑ̃] *adv* **(a)** (*avec intégrité*) honestly, honourably, *US* honorably; **(b)** (*raisonnablement*) reasonably, fairly; **(c)** *Vieilli* courteously, politely.
honnêteté [ɔnɛtte] *nf* **(a)** (*intégrité*) honesty, integrity; **(b)** (*décence*) decency, propriety, decorum; **(c)** (*dans les rapports*) fairness, fair dealing; **(d)** *Arch* courtesy, politeness.
honneur [ɔnœr] *nm* **(a)** honour, *US* honor; **homme d'h.**, man of honour, honourable *or US* honorable man; **mettre un point d'h. à faire qch,** to make it a point of honour to do sth; **déclarer sur l'h. que ...,** to state on one's honour that ...; **(ma) parole d'h.!,** (on) my word of honour!; **se faire un h. de qch/de faire qch,** to be proud of sth/to do sth; **en tout bien tout h.,** (fair and) above-board; **affaire d'h.**, affair of honour; duel; **dette d'h.**, debt of honour;
(b) (*hommage*) **réception en l'h. de qn,** reception in honour of s.o. *or* in s.o.'s honour; **assis à la place d'h.,** in the seat of honour; **cour d'h.**, main quadrangle, main courtyard; **table d'h.**, ≈ high *or* top table (*at university*); **escalier d'h.**, main *or* grand staircase; *Mil etc* **garde d'h.**, guard of honour; **hôte d'h.**, guest of honour; **président**

d'h., honorary president; **faire h. à qn,** to do honour to *or* to honour s.o.; **faire h. au dîner,** to do justice to the dinner; **à qui ai-je l'h. (de parler)?,** to whom have I the honour *or* the pleasure of speaking?; **j'ai l'h. de vous faire savoir que ...,** I beg to inform you that ...; *F* **en quel h. vous voit-on ici?,** to what do I *or* we *etc* owe the honour (of your visit)?; (*avec irritation*) what right have you to be here?; **à vous l'h.,** after you; **jouer pour l'h.,** to play for love; **le cricket est à l'h. en Angleterre,** cricket holds a place of honour *or* pride of place in England; *Golf* **avoir l'h.,** to have the honour;

(c) (*crédit*) credit; **faire h. à/être l'h. de son pays,** to do credit/to be an honour *or* a credit to one's country; **son attitude lui fait h.,** his attitude is a credit to him; **on doit dire à leur h. que ...,** it must be said to their credit that ...; **il en est sorti à son h.,** he came out of it with flying colours; **son refus est tout à son h.,** it speaks well for him *or* it is greatly to his credit that he did not accept; **avec h.,** creditably; **h. à lui!,** all honour to him!;

(d) (*marques d'estime*) **rendre les derniers honneurs** *ou* **les honneurs suprêmes à qn,** to pay the last tribute to s.o.; **faire (à qn) les honneurs de la maison,** to do (s.o.) the honours of the house; *Mil* **rendre les honneurs à qn,** to present arms to s.o., to give *or* pay (military) honours to s.o.; **avec tous les honneurs de la guerre,** with all the honours of war;

(e) faire h. à sa signature, to honour one's signature; *Com* **faire h. à une traite,** to honour *or* meet a bill;

(f) *Cartes* **les honneurs,** honours; **quatre d'honneurs,** four by honours; **honneurs partagés,** honours even.

***honnir** [ɔnir] *vt* to disgrace, to dishonour, *US* to dishonor; **honni soit qui mal y pense,** evil be to him who evil thinks; **honni de tous,** spurned by all.

honorabilité [ɔnɔrabilite] *nf* honourableness, *US* honorableness; (*d'une famille, une profession etc*) respectability; **porter attente à l'h. de qn/qch,** to bring dishonour on s.o./sth; **l'h. de ses intentions ne fait aucun doute,** his intentions are completely honourable.

honorable [ɔnɔrabl] *adj* **(a)** honourable, *US* honorable; **sentiments honorables,** honourable feelings; **vieillesse h.,** respected old age; **(b)** respectable, reputable (*family, profession etc*); **(c)** creditable (*performance, results etc*).

honorablement [ɔnɔrabləmɑ̃] *adv* **(a)** honourably, *US* honorably, with honour, *US* with honor; **famille h. connue,** family of good reputation; **(b) s'acquitter h. de qch,** to acquit oneself creditably in sth.

honoraire [ɔnɔrɛr] **1** *adj* honorary (*duty, member etc*); **professeur h.,** emeritus professor. **2** *nmpl* **honoraires,** fee(s) (*of professional man*); honorarium; (*lawyer's*) retainer.

honorariat [ɔnɔrarja] *nm* honorary membership.

honoré, -ée [ɔnɔre] **1** *adj* honoured, *US* honored; **mon h. confrère,** my respected colleague. **2** *nf* **votre honorée du ...,** (*dans une lettre*) yours of the ... .

honorer [ɔnɔre] **1** *vt* **(a)** to honour, *US* to honor (*s.o.*); to respect (*s.o.'s good qualities etc*); **(b)** (*gratifier*) to do honour to (*s.o.*); **h. qn de sa confiance,** to honour s.o. with one's confidence; **h. une cérémonie de sa présence,** to grace a ceremony with one's presence; **(c)** *Com* to honour, to meet (*bill*); *Com Jur* **refuser d'h. (un contrat),** to repudiate (a contract); **(d)** (*valoir de l'estime à*) to be an honour to, to do credit to, to be a credit to (*s.o., sth*). **2 s'honorer** *vpr* to gain distinction; **s'h. de qch/d'avoir fait qch,** to be proud of sth/of having done sth; **notre ville s'honore de ses peintres,** our town is proud of its painters *or* takes pride in its painters.

honorifique [ɔnɔrifik] *adj* honorary (*title, rank etc*); **président à titre h.,** honorary president.

***honte** [ɔ̃t] *nf* **(a)** (sense of) shame; **avoir perdu toute h.** *ou* **tout sentiment de h., avoir toute h. bue,** to have lost *or* be dead to all sense of shame, to have no (sense of) shame; **h. à vous!,** shame (on you)!; **sans h.,** shameless(ly); **avoir h.,** to be ashamed (of oneself); **avoir h. de faire qch, avoir** *ou* **éprouver de la h. à faire qch,** to be *or* feel ashamed to do sth *or* of doing something; **avoir h. pour qn,** to be ashamed of s.o.; **faire h. à qn,** to make s.o. ashamed, to put s.o. to shame; **couvrir qn de h.,** to bring shame *or* disgrace (up)on s.o.; **fausse** *ou* **mauvaise h.,** self-consciousness, bashfulness;

(b) (cause of) shame, disgrace, dishonour, *US* dishonor; **faire** *ou* **être la h. de qn,** to be a disgrace to s.o.; **quelle h.!,** *F* **oh là là, la h.!,** what a disgrace!; **c'est une h.,** it's a disgrace.

***honteusement** [ɔ̃tøzmɑ̃] *adv* shamefully, disgracefully, ignominiously; **ce travail est h. mal payé,** the pay for this work is a disgrace.

***honteux, -euse** [ɔ̃tø, øz] *adj* **(a)** ashamed; **être h. d'avoir fait qch,** to be ashamed of having done sth; **(b)** (*après une erreur*) bashful, shamefaced, sheepish; **(c)** *Péj* shameful, disgraceful, ignominious (*conduct etc*); **c'est h.!,** it's a disgrace!

***hooligan** [uligan] *nm* hooligan.

***hooliganisme** [uliganism] *nm* hooliganism.

***hop** [ɔp, *occ* hɔp] *int* **allez h.!,** (*saute!*) jump!; (*pars!*) off you go!; **h.-là!,** oops (-a-daisy)!

hôpital, -aux [ɔpital, -o] *nm* hospital; *Nau* **navire h.,** hospital ship; **h. psychiatrique,** psychiatric hospital; **h. militaire,** military hospital; **être emmené à l'hôpital,** to be taken to hospital *or Am* the hospital.

***hoquet** [ɔkɛ] *nm* **(a)** *Physiol* hiccup, hiccough; **avoir le h.,** to have (the) hiccups; **(b)** gasp (*of surprise, terror etc*); **avoir un h. de surprise,** to catch one's breath, to gasp in amazement.

***hoqueter** [ɔkte] *vi* (**je hoquette, n. hoquetons; je hoquetterai**) to hiccup, to hiccough, to have (the) hiccups.

horaire [ɔrɛr] **1** *adj* **(a)** (*qui correspond à une heure*) hourly; **salaire h.,** hourly rate *or* wage; *Ind* **débit h.,** hourly output, output per hour; **(b)** horary; **fuseau h.,** time zone. **2** *nm* timetable, schedule; **avoir un h. chargé,** to have a full timetable.

***horde** [ɔrd] *nf* horde.

***horion** [ɔrjɔ̃] *nm* blow, punch.

horizon [ɔrizɔ̃] *nm* horizon, skyline; **la ligne d'h.,** the horizon; **à l'h.,** on the horizon, on the skyline; **le soleil descend sur l'h.,** the sun goes down beneath the horizon; *Fig* **l'h. 2000,** the year 2000; **tour d'h.,** overview, survey; **faire un tour d'h. politique,** to test political opinion; **ouvrir des horizons nouveaux,** to open up new horizons *or* vistas.

horizontal, -ale, -aux [ɔrizɔ̃tal, -o] **1** *adj* horizontal. **2** *nf* **horizontale (a)** horizontal; **le livre est posé à l'horizontale,** the book is lying flat; **(b)** (*droite*) horizontal line.

horizontalement [ɔrizɔ̃talmɑ̃] *adv* horizontally; (*in crosswords*) across.

horizontalité [ɔrizɔ̃talite] *nf* horizontality.

horloge [ɔrlɔʒ] *nf* clock; **h. normande** *ou* **de parquet,** grandfather clock; **l'h. parlante,** the speaking clock; **h. à quartz,** quartz crystal clock; *Ordinat* **h. en temps réel,** real-time clock; **il est deux heures à l'h.,** it's two by the clock; **j'ai attendu une bonne heure d'h.,** I waited a full *or* solid hour by the clock; **l'h. physiologique,** biological clock.

horloger, -ère [ɔrlɔʒe, -ɛr] **1** *adj* **l'industrie horlogère,** the clock and watchmaking industry. **2** *n* clock and watchmaker.

horlogerie [ɔrlɔʒri] *nf* (*fabrication*) clock and watchmaking; (*magasin*) clockmaker's, watchmaker's (shop); **l'h.,** clocks and watches; **mouvement d'h.,** clockwork.

***hormis** [ɔrmi] **1** *prép Litt* (*no liaison*, **h. elle** [ɔrmi elle]) except, but, save; **personne h. vous,** no one but you, no one besides yourself. **2** *conj Litt* **h. que,** except *or* save that.

hormonal, -aux [ɔrmɔnal, -o] *adj Méd* hormonal; **insuffisance hormonale,** hormone deficiency.

hormone [ɔrmɔn] *nf* hormone.

***hornblende** [ɔrnblɛ̃d] *nf Minér* hornblende.

horodaté [ɔrɔdate] *adj* pay and display; **stationnement h.,** pay and display parking; **ticket h.,** pay and display sticker.

horodateur [ɔrɔdatœr] *nm* pay and display machine.

horoscope [ɔrɔskɔp] *nm* horoscope; **tirer l'h. de qn,** to cast s.o.'s horoscope; **consulter son h.,** to read *or* consult one's horoscope.

horreur [ɔrœr] *nf* **(a)** (*effroi*) horror; **à ma grande h.,** to my unspeakable horror; **frappé** *ou* **glacé d'h.,** horror-stricken, horror-struck;

(b) (*répugnance*) horror, repugnance, disgust, abhorrence; **faire h. à qn,** to horrify s.o., to fill s.o. with horror, to be repulsive to s.o.; **avoir qn/qch en h., avoir h. de qn/qch,** to have a horror of s.o./sth, to hate *or* detest *or* abhor *or* loathe s.o./sth;

(c) (*chose horrible*) (cause, object of) horror; **tu la trouves belle?, c'est une h.!,** you think she's beautiful? she's a sight!; **quelle h.!,** how awful!, how revolting!, how horrid!;

(d) les horreurs de la guerre, the horrors of war; **commettre des horreurs,** to commit atrocities; **dire des horreurs de qn,** to say horrid *or* horrible *or* dreadful things about s.o.;

(e) *F* **le lycée, c'est l'h.!,** school is the pits!

horrible [ɔribl] *adj (effrayant)* horrible, dreadful, horrid; *(répugnant)* ghastly, gruesome; **spectacle h.,** ghastly *or* gruesome *or* hideous sight; **une soif h.,** a terrible thirst; **il est h. sans sa moustache,** he looks awful without his moustache.

horriblement [ɔribləmɑ̃] *adv* horribly, awfully, dreadfully; **c'est h. cher,** it's awfully *or* dreadfully expensive.

horrifiant [ɔrifjɑ̃] *adj* horrifying, shocking, appalling.

horrifier [ɔrifje] *vt* to horrify; **être horrifié de qch,** to be horrified at sth.

horrifique [ɔrifik] *adj F Hum* horrific, hair-raising.

horripilant [ɔripilɑ̃] *adj* exasperating, maddening.

horripilation [ɔripilɑsjɔ̃] *nf* exasperation.

horripiler [ɔripile] *vt* to exasperate.

***hors** [ɔr] *prép (liaison with* **r**, **h. elle** [ɔrɛl]) **(a) h. de,** out of, outside; **h. d'usage,** out of action *or* service *or* use; **c'est arrivé h. d'ici/de l'eau,** it happened outside/out of the water; **tomber h. du lit,** to fall out of bed; **h. de la ville,** outside the town; **dîner h. de chez soi,** to dine out; **h. d'ici!,** get out (of here)!; **h. d'haleine,** out of breath; **h. de combat,** *(of gun, ship etc)* out of action; *(of man)* disabled; **être h. d'affaire,** to have got through one's difficulties; *(of sick person)* to be out of danger; **h. de portée,** out of *or* beyond reach; **un talent h. série,** an exceptional talent, a talent (that is) out of the ordinary; **h. de là,** apart from that, otherwise; **être h. de soi,** to be beside oneself *(with rage etc)*; **c'est h. de prix,** the price is prohibitive, it's too expensive; *Archit* **h. d'œuvre,** out of alignment, projecting;

(b) *Fb* **h. jeu,** *(of player)* offside; **skier h. piste,** to ski off piste; **longueur h. tout,** overall length; **h. taxe,** exclusive of tax, tax free; duty-free; **mettre qn/qch h. la loi,** to outlaw s.o./sth;

(c) *Litt* except, save, but; **tous h. un seul,** all but one.

***hors-bord** [ɔrbɔr] *nm inv* motor boat *or* speedboat *(with outboard motor)*; **moteur h.-b.,** outboard motor.

***hors-concours** [ɔrkɔ̃kur] **1** *adv* not competing, out of competition; **être (mis) h.-c.,** to be disqualified. **2** *adj inv* ineligible to compete; *Fig* above competition, unrivalled, outstanding. **3** *nm inv* = person or exhibit ineligible for competition (because of superiority).

***hors-d'œuvre** [ɔrdœvr] *nm inv* **(a)** *Culin* hors d'œuvre, starter; **(b)** *Archit* annexe, outwork.

***hors-jeu** [ɔrʒø] **1** *nm inv Sp* offside. **2** *adj inv* **joueur h.-j.,** offside player, player in an offside position.

***hors-la-loi** [ɔrlalwa] *nm inv* outlaw.

***hors-piste** [ɔrpist] *nm inv Ski* off piste; **faire du h.-p.,** to go ski-ing off piste.

***hors-texte** [ɔrtɛkst] *nm inv* (inset) plate.

hortensia [ɔrtɑ̃sja] *nf Bot* hydrangea.

horticole [ɔrtikɔl] *adj* horticultural; **exposition h.,** flower show.

horticulteur [ɔrtikyltœr] *nm* horticulturist.

horticulture [ɔrtikyltyr] *nf* horticulture.

hosanna [ozana] **1** *int* hosanna! **2** *nm* (act of crying) hosanna.

hospice [ɔspis] *nm* **(a)** *(maison)* hospice *(on the Saint-Bernard etc)*; **(b)** *(foyer)* (old people's *or* children's) home; **mourir à l'h.,** to die in the poorhouse; **(c)** *(hôpital)* hospice.

hospitalier[1], -ière [ɔspitalje, -jɛr] *adj* hospitable.

hospitalier[2], -ière 1 *adj* **(a)** pertaining to hospitals; **personnel h.,** hospital staff; **(b)** *Rel* **religieux h.,** hospitaller; **sœur hospitalière,** Sister of Charity. **2** *n Rel* Hospitaller.

hospitalisation [ɔspitalizɑsjɔ̃] *nf (admission, séjour)* hospitalization; **h. à domicile,** being nursed at home.

hospitalisé, -ée [ɔspitalize] *n* (in-)patient *(in hospital)*.

hospitaliser [ɔspitalize] *vt* to hospitalize *(s.o.)*, to admit *(s.o.)* to a nursing home *or* hospital.

hospitalité [ɔspitalite] *nf* hospitality; **demander l'h. à qn,** to ask s.o. for hospitality; **offrir l'h. à qn,** to offer s.o. hospitality.

hostellerie [ɔstɛlri] *nf* (fashionable) country inn.

hostie [ɔsti] *nf Rel* (eucharistic) host.

hostile [ɔstil] *adj* hostile; unfriendly *(action)*; **être h. à qn/qch,** to be hostile *or* opposed *or* adverse to s.o./sth; **tenir des propos hostiles à qn,** to make hostile *or* unfriendly remarks to s.o..

hostilement [ɔstilmɑ̃] *adv* hostilely, in a hostile manner.

hostilité [ɔstilite] *nf* **(a)** hostility **(contre, envers,** to(wards)); **acte d'h.,** act of war; **(b) hostilités,** hostilities.

hosto [ɔsto] *nm F (abrév* **hôpital***)* hospital; **aller à l'h.,** to go to hospital.

***hot-dog** [ɔtdɔg] *nm* hot dog; *(pl hot-dogs)*.

hôte, hôtesse [ot, otɛs] *n* **(a)** host, *f* hostess; *Vieilli* landlord, *f* landlady *(of tavern etc)*; **dîner à la table d'h.,** to have a table d'hôte dinner, to have the set menu; **(b)** *(invité) (f* **hôte***)* guest, visitor; **h. payant,** paying guest; **(c)** *Litt (habitant)* dweller; **les hôtes des bois,** creatures of the woods.

hôtel [otɛl] *nm* **(a)** hotel; **descendre à l'h.,** to put up at a hotel; **une chambre d'h.,** a hotel room; **h. deux/trois étoiles,** two/three star hotel; **h. de passe,** (hotel used as a) brothel; **h. meublé,** residential hotel *(providing lodging but not board)*; **on n'est pas à l'h. ici!,** this isn't a hotel, you know!; **rat** *ou* **souris d'h.,** hotel thief; **(b) h. (particulier),** mansion, town house; **(c)** *Admin* public building; **h. de ville,** town hall; **l'H. de la Monnaie,** ≈ the Royal Mint; **h. des ventes,** auction rooms *or* salerooms.

hôtel-Dieu [otɛldjø] *nm* hospital; *(pl hôtels-Dieu)*.

hôtelier, -ière [otəlje, -jɛr] **1** *n* (small) hotel keeper. **2** *adj* **l'industrie hôtelière,** the hotel trade.

hôtellerie [otɛlri] *nf* **(a)** *(hôtel)* inn; hostelry; **(b)** *Ind* **l'h.,** the hotel trade; **crise de l'h.,** crisis in the hotel trade; **(c)** guest quarters *(of convent)*.

hôtesse [otɛs] *nf voir* **HÔTE**; *Av* **h. de l'air,** air hostess; **h. d'accueil,** receptionist *(in large organization)*.

***hotte** [ɔt] *nf* **(a)** basket *(carried on the back)*; (bricklayer's) hod; **la h. du Père Noël,** Father Christmas' *or* Santa's sack; **(b)** hood *(in forge, laboratory, over cooker)*.

***hottentot, -ote** [ɔtɑ̃to, -t] **1** *adj* Hottentot. **2** *n* **H.,** Hottentot.

***hou** [u] *int* boo!; **h.! la vilaine!,** tut-tut, you naughty girl!

***houblon** [ublɔ̃] *nm Bot* hop.

***houblonnier, -ière** [ublɔnje, -jɛr] **1** *adj* **région houblonnière,** hop(-growing) district. **2** *nm* hop grower. **3** *nf* **houblonnière,** hop field.

***houe** [u] *nf* hoe.

***houille** [uj] *nf* coal; **mine de h.,** coalmine, colliery; **h. blanche,** hydroelectric power; **h. bleue,** wave power.

***houiller, -ère** [uje, -ɛr] **1** *adj* carboniferous, coal-bearing; **dépôt** *ou* **bassin h.,** coal bed *or* basin; **production houillère,** coal output. **2** *nf* **houillère,** coalmine, colliery.

***houle** [ul] *nf* swell, surge *(of sea)*; **grosse h.,** heavy swell.

***houlette** [ulɛt] *nf* **(a)** *(de berger)* (shepherd's) crook; *(crosse)* (bishop's) crosier; *Fig* **sous la h. de notre guide,** under the leadership of our guide; **(b)** *(petite bêche)* trowel, spud.

***houleux, -euse** [ulø, -øz] *adj* swelling, surging *(sea)*; *Fig* surging, tumultuous *(crowds)*; **réunion houleuse,** stormy meeting.

***houp** [up, *occ* hup] *int* = **HOP**.

***houppe** [up] *nf* tuft *(of feathers, hair etc)*; crest *(of feathers)*; **h. à poudrer,** powder puff.

***houppelande** [uplɑ̃d] *nf* greatcoat; cloak.

***houpper** [upe] *vt* to tuft; to comb *(wool)*.

***houppette** [upɛt] *nf* small tuft *(of feathers etc)*; *(à poudre)* powder puff.

***hourdage** [urdaʒ] *nm Constr* roughcasting.

***hourder** [urde] *vt Constr* to roughcast.

***houri** [uri] *nf Rel* houri.

***hourra** [ura] **1** *int* hurrah!; **hip, hip, hip, h.!,** hip, hip, hooray! **2** *nm* hurrah; **pousser trois hourras,** to give three cheers.

***hourvari** [urvari] *nm Litt* uproar, tumult.

***houspiller** [uspije] *vt (réprimander)* to chide *(s.o.)*, to tell *(s.o.)* off.

***housse** [us] *nf* **(a)** *(meubles)* cover; *(contre la poussière)* dust sheet; *(dans une voiture)* seat cover; **h. à vêtements,** protective bag *(for clothing)*; **(b)** *(pour cheval)* trappings.

***houx** [u] *nm* holly.

hovercraft [ɔvɛrkraft] *nm* hovercraft.

***huard, huart** [ɥar] *nm* **(a)** osprey, *Am* fish hawk; **(b)** *Can* black-throated diver.

***hublot** [yblo] *nm* porthole *(in ship)*; window *(in aircraft, washing machine)*; *Fig F* **elle portait des hublots,** she was wearing thick glasses *or F* milk bottle glasses.

***huche** [yʃ] *nf (pétrin)* kneading trough; *(coffre)* bin; **h. à pain,** bread bin.

***hue** [y, hy] *int (to horse)* gee up!; **l'un tire à h. et l'autre à dia,** they're pulling in different directions.

***huée** [ɥe] *nf (usu pl)* **huées,** booing, jeering; **quitter la scène sous les huées,** to be booed off the stage.

***huer** [ɥe] **1** *vt* to boo *(actor etc)*; to barrack *(speaker etc)*. **2** *vi (of owl)* to hoot.

***huguenot, -ote** [ygno, -ɔt] *Hist* **1** *adj* Huguenot. **2** *n* **H.,** Huguenot.

***Hugues** [yg] *nm* Hugh.
hui [ɥi] *adv Arch* today; *Jur* **ce jour d'h.,** this day.
huilage [ɥilaʒ] *nm* oiling, lubrication.
huile [ɥil] *nf* oil; **frit à l'h.,** fried in oil; **tache d'h.,** oil stain; **mauvais exemple qui fait tache d'h.,** bad example that's spreading; **jeter** *ou* **verser de l'h. sur le feu,** to add fuel to the fire; *F* **h. de bras** *ou* **de coude,** elbow grease; *Arg* **les huiles,** the big shots, the top brass; *Beaux-Arts* **peinture à l'h.,** oil painting; **portrait à l'h.,** portrait in oils; **une de ses huiles,** one of his oil paintings; **h. comestible** *ou* **de table,** edible oil, salad oil; **h. végétale,** vegetable oil; **h. d'olive,** olive oil; **h. de tournesol,** sunflower (seed) oil; **h. minérale,** mineral oil; **h. de paraffine,** paraffin oil; **h. de graissage,** lubricating oil; **h. de machine,** engine oil; **moteur à h. lourde,** heavy-oil engine; **h. de lin,** linseed oil; **h. solaire,** suntan oil; **h. de foie de morue,** cod liver oil; **h. essentielle,** essential oil; **h. de ricin,** castor oil.
huiler [ɥile] *vt* to oil, to lubricate.
huilerie [ɥilri] *nf Ind* oil works; *Com* oil trade; **il s'est enrichi dans l'h.,** he made his money in the oil business.
huileux, -euse [ɥilø, -øz] *adj* oily, greasy.
huilier [ɥilje] *nm* **(a)** *(de table)* oil and vinegar cruet; **(b)** *Ind* oil manufacturer.
huis [ɥi] *nm Arch* door; **entretien à h. clos,** conversation behind closed doors; *Jur* **entendre une cause à h. clos,** to hear a case in camera; **ordonner le h. clos,** to order a case to be heard in camera.
huisserie [ɥisri] *nf Constr (d'une porte, d'une fenêtre)* frame.
huissier [ɥisje] *nm* **(a)** *Jur* process server; ≈ sheriff's officer, bailiff; **h. audiencier,** court usher; **(b)** *(portier)* usher.
***huit** [ɥit] **1** *adj inv (as cardinal adj before a noun or adj beginning with a consonant sound* [ɥi] *)* eight; **h. (petits) garçons** [ɥi(pti)garsɔ̃] , eight (little) boys; **h.** [ɥit] **hommes,** eight men; **j'en ai h.** [ɥit] , I have eight (of them); **le h. mai** [ɥimɛ] , the eighth of May, May the eighth; **h. jours,** a week; **aujourd'hui en h.,** a week today, today week; **donner ses h. jours à qn,** to give s.o. a week's notice. **2** *nm inv* figure of eight.
***huitain** [ɥitɛ̃] *nm Littér* octet.
***huitaine** [ɥitɛn] *nf* **(a)** (about) eight; **(b)** *(une semaine)* week; **dans une h. (de jours),** in a week or so; **affaire remise à h.,** case adjourned for a week.
***huitante** [ɥitɑ̃t] *num adj inv Suisse* eighty.
***huitantième** [ɥitɑ̃tjɛm] *num adj & n Suisse* eightieth.
***huitième** [ɥitjɛm] **1** *adj & n* eighth. **2** *nm* eighth (part); *Sp* **être en h. de finale,** to be in the last sixteen. **3** *nf Sch* **(classe de) h.,** ≈ third form of junior school; *US* ≈ eighth grade.
***huitièmement** [ɥitjɛmmɑ̃] *adv* eighthly, in eighth place.
huître [ɥitr] *nf* **(a)** oyster; **h. perlière,** pearl oyster; **(b)** *F* fool, mug.
***huit-reflets** [ɥir(ə)flɛ] *nm inv* top hat.
huîtrier, -ère [ɥitrije, -ɛr] **1** *adj* **industrie huîtrière,** oyster farming. **2** *nm Orn* oyster catcher. **3** *nf* **huîtrière,** oyster bed.
***hulotte** [ylɔt] *nf* tawny owl.
***hululement** [ylylmɑ̃] *nm* hoot(ing) *(of owls)*.
***hululer** [ylyle] *vi (of owl)* to hoot.
***hum** [œm, hœm] *int* hem! h'm!
humain [ymɛ̃] **1** *adj* **(a)** human; **le genre h., les êtres humains,** human beings, humans; mankind; **sciences humaines,** social sciences; *Mus* **voix humaine,** *(of organ)* vox humana; **ressources humaines,** human resources; **(b)** *(compréhensif)* humane. **2** *nm* human (being).
humainement [ymɛnmɑ̃] *adv* **(a)** humanly; **(b)** *(avec bonté)* humanely.
humanisation [ymanizasjɔ̃] *nf* humanization, humanizing.
humaniser [ymanize] **1** *vt* **(a)** to humanize, to make human; **(b)** *(rendre plus charitable)* to make *(s.o.)* more humane. **2 s'humaniser** *vpr* **(a)** to become more human; **(b)** *(devenir plus charitable)* to become more humane.
humanisme [ymanism] *nm* **(a)** *Litt Phil* humanism; **(b)** humanitarianism; **(c)** *(bonté)* humanity.
humaniste [ymanist] **1** *n* humanist. **2** *adj* humanist(ic).
humanitaire [ymanitɛr] *adj* humanitarian; **œuvre h.,** humanitarian work; *(institution)* humanitarian organization; **aide h.,** humanitarian aid.
humanitarisme [ymanitarism] *nm* humanitarianism.
humanité [ymanite] *nf* **(a)** *(genre humain)* humanity, mankind; **(b)** *(of Christ)* human nature; **(c)** *(bonté)* humanity, humaneness; **(d) humanités,** humanities, classics.
humanoïde [ymanɔid] *nm* humanoid.
humble [œbl] *adj* humble, lowly; **à mon h. avis,** in my humble opinion.
humblement [œbləmɑ̃] *adv* humbly.
humectage [ymɛktaʒ] *nm* dampening, moistening.
humecter [ymɛkte] **1** *vt* to dampen, to moisten. **2 s'humecter** *vpr* **s'h. les lèvres,** to moisten one's lips; *F* **s'h. le gosier,** to wet one's whistle.
***humer** [yme] *vt* **(a)** *(sentir, aspirer)* to inhale, to sniff; **h. l'air frais,** to inhale *or* breathe in the fresh air; **h. le parfum d'une fleur,** to smell a flower; **(b)** to suck in *or* up *(liquid)*.
huméral, -aux [ymeral, -o] *adj Anat* humeral.
humérus [ymerys] *nm Anat* humerus.
humeur [ymœr] *nf* **(a)** *(disposition)* humour, *US* humor, mood, spirits; **être de bonne h.,** to be in a good mood *or* in good spirits; **un livre/film plein de bonne h.,** a good-humoured book/film; **être de mauvaise h.,** to be in a bad mood; **passer sa mauvaise h. sur qn/qch,** to take one's bad mood out on s.o.; **de méchante h.,** in a (bad) temper, grumpy, cross; **être d'une h. massacrante** *ou F* **de chien,** to be in a foul mood *or* temper; **être d'une h. noire,** *(déprimé)* to feel depressed; *(mécontent)* to be in a (bad) temper; **être** *ou* **se sentir d'h. à refuser,** to be in the mood to refuse;
(b) *(caractère)* temper, temperament; **avoir l'h. vive,** to be quick-tempered; **il y a incompatibilité d'h. entre nous,** we are temperamentally unsuited; **homme d'h. égale,** even-tempered man;
(c) *Litt* ill humour, bad mood; **mouvement d'h.,** outburst of temper; **montrer de l'h.,** to show (ill) temper; **avec h.,** testily, irritably; **je redoute ses sautes d'h.,** I dread his changes of mood; **épancher son h. sur qn,** to vent one's spleen on s.o.;
(d) *Méd Arch* humour; *Anat* **h. aqueuse/vitrée,** aqueous/vitreous humour *(of the eye)*.
humide [ymid] *adj* damp, moist, humid; **draps humides,** damp sheets; **couloir sombre et h.,** dark, dank passage; **temps h. et chaud,** muggy *or* close weather; **temps h. et froid,** raw weather; **les yeux humides (de larmes),** eyes moist with tears; **elle me lançait des regards humides,** she looked at me with moist eyes.
humidificateur [ymidifikatœr] *nm* humidor *(in a spinning mill)*; humidifier.
humidification [ymidifikasjɔ̃] *nf* humidification; dampening, moistening.
humidifier [ymidifje] *vt* to humidify; to dampen, moisten.
humidité [ymidite] *nf* humidity, damp(ness), moisture, moistness, wet(ness); **craint l'h.,** *(on packet)* store in a dry place; **taches d'h.,** damp patches, mildew; **teneur en h.,** moisture content; **il y a de l'h. dans l'air,** it's going to *or* it feels like rain.
humiliant [ymiljɑ̃] *adj* humiliating, mortifying.
humiliation [ymiljasjɔ̃] *nf* humiliation, mortification, affront.
humilier [ymilje] **1** *vt (abaisser)* to humiliate; *Vieilli & Rel (rendre humble)* to humble. **2 s'humilier** *vpr (s'abaisser)* to humiliate oneself; *(devenir humble)* to humble oneself; **je ne veux pas m'h. devant eux,** I'm not going to go grovelling to them; **s'h. jusqu'à faire qch,** to stoop to doing sth.
humilité [ymilite] *nf* humility, humbleness.
humoral, -aux [ymɔral, -o] *adj Méd Arch* humoral.
humoriste [ymɔrist] **1** *adj* humorous *(writer etc)*. **2** *n* humorist.
humoristique [ymɔristik] *adj* humorous, humoristic *(talker, writer etc)*; **dessin h.,** cartoon.
humour [ymur] *nm* humour, *US* humor; **faire preuve d'h.,** to keep smiling, *F* to grin and bear it; **avoir (le sens) de l'h.,** to have a (good) sense of humour; **h. noir,** sick humour, black humour; **h. anglais,** English (sense of) humour.
humus [ymys] *nm* humus.
***Hun** [œ̃] *nm Hist* Hun.
***hune** [yn] *nf Nau* top; **h. de vigie,** crow's nest; **h. de direction de tir,** fire control top.
***hunier** [ynje] *nm Nau* topsail.
***huppe¹** [yp] *nf Orn* hoopoe.
***huppe²** *nf* tuft, crest *(of bird)*.
***huppé** [ype] *adj* tufted, crested *(bird)*; *F* high-class; **les classes huppées,** the upper classes; **une famille huppée,** a high-class family.
***hure** [yr] *nf* **(a)** head *(of boar etc)*; jowl *(of salmon)*; **(b)** *Culin* brawn, *Am* headcheese.
***hurlement** [yrləmɑ̃] *nm* howl(ing) *(of wolf, dog)*;

yell(ing), roar(ing), scream(ing) (*of person*); **pousser un h.**, to give a howl.
***hurler** [yrle] **1** *vi* (*of dog, wolf*) to howl; (*of wind, storm*) to roar; (*of person*) to howl, to roar, to yell; **h. de douleur,** to howl *or* scream (out) with pain; **h. à la lune,** to bay at the moon; **il faut h. avec les loups,** when in Rome, do as the Romans do; **couleurs qui hurlent,** colours that clash (with one another). **2** *vt* to roar out, to bawl out (*song, speech etc*).
***hurleur, -euse** [yrlœr, -øz] **1** *adj* howling, yelling. **2** *n* howler, yeller. **3** *nm* howler (monkey).
hurluberlu [yrlybɛrly] *nm* eccentric (person); **cet h. de Michel a encore fait des siennes,** what a scatterbrain Michel is, he's gone and done it again.
***hussard** [ysar] *nm Mil* hussar.
***hussarde** [ysard] *nf* **à la h.,** roughly, cavalierly.
***hussite** [ysit] *nm Hist Rel* Hussite.
***hutte** [yt] *nf* hut, shed, shanty.
hyacinthe [jasɛ̃t] *nf* **(a)** *Arch* (*fleur*) hyacinth; **(b)** (*pierre*) hyacinth, jacinth.
hyalin [jalɛ̃] *adj Minér* hyaline, glassy; **quartz h.,** rock crystal.
hyaloïde [jalɔid] *adj Anat etc* hyaloid.
hybridation [ibridɑsjɔ̃] *nf Biol* hybridization; cross-breeding.
hybride [ibrid] *adj & nm Biol Ling* hybrid.
hybrider [ibride] *vt Biol* to hybridize, to cross(-breed).
hybridité [ibridite] *nf Biol* hybridity, hybridism.
hydracide [idrasid] *nm Ch* hydracid.
hydratant [idratɑ̃] **1** *adj* moisturizing (*cream*). **2** *nm* moisturizer.
hydratation [idratɑsjɔ̃] *nf Ch* hydration.
hydrate [idrat] *nm Ch* hydrate; **h. de potasse,** caustic potash; **h. de carbone,** carbohydrate.
hydrater [idrate] *Ch* **1** *vt* to hydrate. **2 s'hydrater** *vpr* to hydrate, to become hydrated.
hydraulicien [idrolisjɛ̃] *nm* hydraulic engineer.
hydraulique [idrolik] **1** *adj* hydraulic; **roue h.,** waterwheel. **2** *nf* hydraulics, hydraulic engineering.
hydravion [idravjɔ̃] *nm* seaplane.
hydre [idr] *nf* hydra.
hydrique [idrik] *adj* hydrous.
hydrocarbure [idrɔkarbyr] *nm Ch* hydrocarbon.
hydrocéphale [idrɔsefal] *adj & n Méd* hydrocephalic *or* hydrocephalous (patient).
hydrocortisone [idrɔkɔrtizɔn] *nf* hydrocortisone.
hydrodynamique [idrɔdinamik] **1** *adj* hydrodynamic. **2** *nf* hydrodynamics.
hydro-électricité [idrɔelɛktrisite] *nf* hydroelectricity.
hydro-électrique [idrɔelɛktrik] *adj* hydroelectric; **centrale/énergie h.,** hydroelectric power station/power.
hydrofoil [idrɔfɔil] *nm Nau* hydrofoil.
hydrofuge [idrɔfyʒ] *adj* (*of cloth, material*) waterproof.
hydrofuger [idrɔfyʒe] *vt* **(j'hydrofugeai(s); n. hydrofugeons)** to waterproof (*cloth, material*).
hydrogénation [idrɔʒenɑsjɔ̃] *nf* hydrogenation.
hydrogène [idrɔʒɛn] *nm Ch* hydrogen; **h. lourd,** heavy hydrogen.
hydrogéné [idrɔʒene] *adj* hydrogenated.
hydrogéner [idrɔʒene] *vt* to hydrogenate.
hydroglisseur [idrɔglisœr] *nm* jetfoil.
hydrographe [idrɔgraf] *adj & nm* **(ingénieur) h.,** hydrographer.
hydrographie [idrɔgrafi] *nf* hydrography.
hydrographique [idrɔgrafik] *adj* hydrographic(al).
hydrologie [idrɔlɔʒi] *nf* hydrology.
hydrologique [idrɔlɔʒik] *adj* hydrological.
hydrologiste [idrɔlɔʒist] **, hydrologue** [idrɔlɔg] *n* hydrologist.
hydrolyse [idrɔliz] *nf Ch* hydrolysis.
hydrolyser [idrɔlize] *vt Ch* to hydrolize, to hydrolyse.
hydromel [idrɔmɛl] *nm* mead.
hydromètre [idrɔmɛtr] **1** *nm* hydrometer; (*d'océan*) depth gauge. **2** *nf Ent* water spider.
hydrométrie [idrɔmetri] *nf Phys* hydrometry.
hydrométrique [idrɔmetrik] *adj* hydrometric(al).
hydrophile [idrɔfil] *adj* absorbent (*cotton wool etc*).
hydrophobe [idrɔfɔb] *adj & n Ch* hydrophobic; *Méd* hydrophobic (patient).
hydrophobie [idrɔfɔbi] *nf Méd* hydrophobia.
hydropique [idrɔpik] *adj & n Méd* dropsical (patient).
hydropisie [idrɔpizi] *nf Méd* dropsy.
hydroponique [idrɔpɔnik] *adj* hydroponic.
hydroquinone [idrɔkinɔn] *nf Ch Phot* hydroquinone.
hydrosol [idrɔsɔl] *nm Ch* hydrosol.
hydrosoluble [idrɔsɔlybl] *adj* water-soluble.
hydrosphère [idrɔsfɛr] *nf* hydrosphere.
hydrostatique [idrɔstatik] **1** *adj* hydrostatic. **2** *nf* hydrostatics.
hydrothérapie [idrɔterapi] *nf Méd* (*traitement*) hydrotherapy, water cure; (*science*) hydrotherapeutics.
hydrothérapique [idrɔterapik] *adj* hydrotherapeutic.
hydrothermal, -aux [idrɔtermal, -o] *adj* hydrothermal.
hydroxyde [idrɔksid] *nm Ch* hydroxide.
hydrure [idryr] *nm Ch* hydride.
hyène [jɛn] *nf* (*when aspirated* **la hyène**, *when silent* **l'hyène**) hyena.
hygiaphone [iʒjafɔn] *nm* grill (*for speaking through in booking office, station etc*).
hygiène [iʒjɛn] *nf* hygiene; **h. publique,** public health; **mauvaise h. alimentaire,** malnutrition; **vous devriez surveiller votre h. alimentaire,** you should watch your diet *or* what you eat.
hygiénique [iʒjenik] *adj* **(a)** (*sanitaire*) hygienic, sanitary; **cuisine peu h.,** unhygienic cooking (methods); **papier h.,** toilet paper; **serviette h.,** sanitary towel, *US* sanitary napkin; **(b)** (*bon pour la santé*) healthy; **une promenade h.,** a healthy walk.
hygiéniquement [iʒjenikmɑ̃] *adv* (*voir adj*) **(a)** hygienically; **(b)** healthily.
hygiéniste [iʒjenist] *n* hygienist.
hygrométrie [igrɔmetri] *nf Phys* hygrometry.
hygroscope [igrɔskɔp] *nm Phys* hygroscope.
hygroscopique [igrɔskɔpik] *adj Phys* hygroscopic(al).
hymen [imɛn] *nm* **(a)** *Litt* marriage; **(b)** *Anat* hymen.
hyménée [imene] *nm Litt* marriage.
hyménoptère [imenɔptɛr] *Ent* **1** *adj* hymenopterous. **2** *nmpl* **hyménoptères,** Hymenoptera.
hymne [imn] **1** *nm* song (*of praise*); **h. national,** national anthem. **2** *n Rel* hymn.
hyoïde [jɔid] *adj & nm Anat* hyoid (bone).
hyperacidité [iperasidite] *nf Méd* hyperacidity.
hyperbole [ipɛrbɔl] *nf Littér* hyperbole, exaggeration; *Math* hyperbola.
hyperbolique [ipɛrbɔlik] *adj Littér Math* hyperbolic(al).
hyperboliquement [ipɛrbɔlikmɑ̃] *adv Littér* hyperbolically.
hyperboloïde [ipɛrbɔlɔid] *Math* **1** *adj* hyperboloidal. **2** *nm* hyperboloid.
hyperboréen, -enne [ipɛrbɔreɛ̃, -ɛn] *adj* hyperborean.
hypercritique [ipɛrkritik] *adj* hypercritical, overcritical.
hyperfréquence [ipɛrfrekɑ̃s] *nf Rad* ultra high frequency, very high frequency.
hyperglycémie [ipɛrglisemi] *nf Méd* hyperglyc(a)emia.
hypermarché [ipɛrmarʃe] *nm* hypermarket.
hypermétrope [ipɛrmetrɔp] *adj Méd* hypermetropic.
hypermétropie [ipɛrmetrɔpi] *nf Méd* hypermetropia.
hypernerveux, -euse [ipɛrnɛrvø, -øz] *adj & n* highly strung (person).
hypersensibilité [ipɛrsɑ̃sibilite] *nf* hypersensitivity, oversensitiveness.
hypersensible [ipɛrsɑ̃sibl] *adj* hypersensitive, oversensitive.
hypertendu [ipɛrtɑ̃dy] *adj & n Méd* hypertensive (patient); (person) suffering from high blood pressure.
hypertensif, -ive [ipɛrtɑ̃sif, -iv] *adj & n Méd* hypertensive.
hypertension [ipɛrtɑ̃sjɔ̃] *nf Méd* hypertension, high blood pressure.
hypertrophie [ipɛrtrɔfi] *nf Méd* hypertrophy; **h. des amygdales,** enlarged tonsils; *Fig* **l'h. urbaine,** urban sprawl; **elle souffre d'h. du moi,** she's got a swollen ego.
hypertrophier [ipɛrtrɔfje] *Méd* **1** *vt* to hypertrophy; **amygdales hypertrophiées,** enlarged tonsils. **2 s'hypertrophier** *vpr* to hypertrophy, to become too large.
hypertrophique [ipɛrtrɔfik] *adj Méd* hypertrophic.
hypervitaminose [ipɛrvitaminoz] *nf Méd* hypervitaminosis.
hypnose [ipnoz] *nf* hypnosis; (hypnotic) trance.
hypnotique [ipnɔtik] *adj & n* hypnotic.
hypnotiser [ipnɔtize] *vt* to hypnotize.
hypnotiseur [ipnɔtizœr] *nm* hypnotist.
hypnotisme [ipnɔtism] *nm* hypnotism.
hypoallergénique [ipɔalɛrʒenik] *adj* hypoallergenic.
hypocalorique [ipɔkalɔrik] *adj* **régime h.,** low-calorie diet.
hypocentre [ipɔsɑ̃tr] *nm Géol* hypocentre, focus.
hypocondre [ipɔkɔ̃dr] **1** *nm Anat* hypochondrium. **2** *n* hypochondriac.
hypocondriaque [ipɔkɔ̃drijak] **1** *adj* hypochondriac(al).

2 *n* hypochondriac.
hypocondrie [ipɔkɔ̃dri] *nf* hypochondria.
hypocras [ipɔkras] *nm Arch* hippocras.
hypocrisie [ipɔkrizi] *nf* hypocrisy.
hypocrite [ipɔkrit] **1** *adj* hypocritical. **2** *n* hypocrite.
hypocritement [ipɔkritmɑ̃] *adv* hypocritically.
hypodermique [ipɔdɛrmik] *adj* hypodermic.
hypogastrique [ipɔgastrik] *adj Anat* hypogastric; *Méd* **ceinture h.**, abdominal belt.
hypogée [ipɔʒe] *nm Archéol* hypogeum.
hypoglycémie [ipɔglisemi] *nf Méd* hypoglyc(a)emia.
hypophosphite [ipɔfɔsfit] *nm Ch* hypophosphite.
hypophyse [ipɔfiz] *nf Anat* hypophysis; pituitary gland.
hypostase [ipɔstaz] *nf* hypostasis.
hypostatique [ipɔstatik] *adj Phil Rel* hypostatic.
hypostyle [ipɔstil] *adj Archit* hypostyle, pillared.
hypotendu, -ue [ipɔtɑ̃dy] *adj & n Méd* hypotensive (patient); (person) suffering from low blood pressure.
hypotenseur [ipɔtɑ̃sœr] *nm Méd* hypotensive.
hypotension [ipɔtɑ̃sjɔ̃] *nf Méd* hypotension; low blood pressure.
hypoténuse [ipɔtenyz] *nf* hypotenuse.
hypothécable [ipɔtekabl] *adj* mortgageable.
hypothécaire [ipɔtekɛr] *adj* **prêt h.**, mortgage (loan); **contrat h.**, mortgage deed; **créancier h.**, mortgagee; **débiteur h.**, mortgager.
hypothécairement [ipɔtekɛrmɑ̃] *adv Jur* by *or* on mortgage.
hypothèque [ipɔtɛk] *nf* mortgage; **franc** *ou* **libre d'hypothèques**, unmortgaged; **prendre une h.**, to take out a mortgage; **prêt sur h.**, mortgage loan; **purger une h.**, to pay off *or* clear off *or* redeem a mortgage.
hypothéquer [ipɔteke] *vt* (**j'hypothèque**; **j'hypothéquerai**) **(a)** to mortgage (*estate etc*); **(b)** to secure (*debt*) by mortgage.
hypothermie [ipɔtɛrmi] *nf Méd* hypothermia; **mourir d'h.**, to die of hypothermia.
hypothèse [ipɔtɛz] *nf* hypothesis; **selon cette h.**, on this assumption.
hypothétique [ipɔtetik] *adj* hypothetic(al).
hypothétiquement [ipɔtetikmɑ̃] *adv* hypothetically.
hypothyroïdie [ipɔtirɔidi] *nf Méd* hypothyroidism, thyroid deficiency.
hypovitaminose [ipɔvitaminoz] *nf Méd* hypovitaminosis, vitamin deficiency.
hypsomètre [ipsɔmɛtr] *nm* hypsometer.
hypsométrie [ipsɔmetri] *nf* hypsometry.
hypsométrique [ipsɔmetrik] *adj* hypsometric(al); **courbe h.**, contour line; **carte h.**, contour map.
hysope [izɔp] *nf Bot* hyssop.
hystérectomie [isterɛktɔmi] *nf Chir* hysterectomy.
hystérie [isteri] *nf Méd* hysteria; **h. collective**, mass hysteria; *F* **avec lui, c'est toujours de l'h.**, he is always (getting) hysterical.
hystérique [isterik] *Méd* **1** *adj* hysterical. **2** *n* hysterical person, hysteric.
hystérotomie [isterɔtɔmi] *nf Chir* hysterotomy; **h. abdominale**, caesarean, *US* cesarean (section).

I

I, i [i] *nm* **(a)** (the letter) I, i; *Fig* **droit comme un i,** bolt upright; **mettre les points sur les i,** to dot the i's, to speak plainly *or* unambiguously; **(b) i grec,** (the letter) Y, y.
iambe [jɑ̃b] *nm* **(a)** (*pied*) iamb, iambus; **(b)** (*vers*) iambic; **(c) iambes,** satirical poem.
iambique [jɑ̃bik] *adj* iambic (*line, verse*).
ibère [ibɛr] **1** *adj* Iberian. **2** *n* **I.,** Iberian.
Ibérie [iberi] *nf Arch* Iberia.
ibérien, -ienne [iberjɛ̃, -jɛn] **1** *adj* Iberian. **2** *n* **I.,** Iberian.
ibérique [iberik] *adj* Iberian; **la péninsule i.,** the Iberian peninsula.
ibidem, ibid., ib. [ibidɛm] *adv* ibid., ib.
ibis [ibis] *nm* (*oiseau*) ibis.
Icare [ikar] *nm* Icarus.
iceberg [ajsbɛrg, isbɛrg] *nm* iceberg.
icelui [isəlɥi], **icelle** [isɛl], **iceux** [isø], **icelles** [isɛl] *pron dém & adj Arch & Jur ou Hum* = **CELUI(-CI), CELLE(-CI), CEUX(-CI), CELLES(-CI).**
ichneumon [iknømɔ̃] *nm* **(a)** *Arch* (*mangouste*) ichneumon, Pharaoh's rat; **(b)** (*insecte*) ichneumon (fly).
ichtyocolle [iktjɔkɔl] *nf* fish glue, isinglass.
ichtyologie [iktjɔlɔʒi] *nf* ichthyology.
ichtyologique [iktjɔlɔʒik] *adj* ichthyologic(al).
ichtyologiste [iktjɔlɔʒist] *n* ichthyologist.
ichtyophage [iktjɔfaʒ] **1** *adj* fish-eating, ichthyophagous. **2** *n* ichthyophagist.
ichtyosaure [iktjɔsɔr] *nm* ichthyosaurus.
ici [isi] *adv* **(a)** (*à cet endroit-ci*) here; **i. et là,** here and there; **les gens d'i.,** the people (who live) here, the locals; **je ne suis pas d'i.,** I'm a stranger here, I'm not from here; *F* **ah oui, je vois cela d'i.!,** yes, I can see it from here; **i.-bas,** here below, on earth; **il y a vingt kilomètres d'i. à Paris,** it's twenty kilometres from here to Paris; **c'est à dix minutes d'i.,** it's ten minutes away; **par i.,** in here, out here, over here; **il habite par i.** *ou* **près d'i.,** he lives near here *or* around here; **passez par i.,** (come) this way, please; **c'est i.,** this is the place; **le car vient jusqu'i.,** the bus comes as far as here *or* as far as this; *Fig* **j'utilise i. ses propres paroles,** and here I'm using his own words; *Tél* **i. Thomas,** (it's) Thomas speaking, Thomas here; *Rad* **i. Radio Luxembourg,** this is Radio Luxembourg;
(b) (*dans le temps*) **jusqu'i.,** until now, up to now; **d'i.,** from today, from now on; **d'i. lundi,** between now and Monday, by Monday; **d'i. là,** by that time, by then; **d'i. peu,** before long; **d'i. à ce que vous ayez fini, je serai parti,** by the time you've finished, I'll have gone.
icône [ikon] *nf Rel* icon, ikon; *Ordinat* icon.
iconoclasme [ikɔnɔklasm] *nm* iconoclasm.
iconoclaste [ikɔnɔklast] **1** *adj* iconoclastic. **2** *nm* iconoclast.
iconographe [ikɔnɔgraf] *n* iconographer.
iconographie [ikɔnɔgrafi] *nf* iconography.
iconographique [ikɔnɔgrafik] *adj* iconographic(al).
iconoscope [ikɔnɔskɔp] *nm TV* iconoscope.
ictère [iktɛr] *nm Méd* icterus, jaundice; **i. du nouveau-né,** neonatal jaundice.
ictérique [ikterik] *Méd* **1** *adj* **(a)** jaundiced (*person, eyes etc*); **(b)** icteric(al) (*disorder*). **2** *n* person suffering from jaundice.
ictus [iktys] *nm* **(a)** *Littér* ictus, stress; **(b)** *Méd* (apoplectic) stroke; (epileptic) fit.
idéal, -als *ou* **-aux** [ideal, -o] **1** *adj* ideal. **2** *nm* ideal; **avoir des idéaux,** to have ideals; **l'i. du beau,** the ideal of beauty; **l'i., c'est de pouvoir t'exprimer,** the ideal thing is for you to be able to express yourself; **l'i. serait que tu y ailles tout seul,** ideally, you should go alone.
idéalement [idealmɑ̃] *adv* ideally.
idéalisation [idealizasjɔ̃] *nf* idealization, idealizing.
idéaliser [idealize] *vt* to idealize.
idéalisme [idealism] *nm* idealism.
idéaliste [idealist] **1** *adj* idealistic. **2** *n* idealist.
idée [ide] *nf* **(a)** (*conception*) idea, *F* notion; **juste pour vous donner une i. de la situation,** just to give you an idea of the situation; **je n'en ai pas la moindre i.,** I haven't the least *or* faintest idea, I haven't a clue; **l'i. qu'il a du travail,** his idea of work; **on n'a pas i. de cela,** you can't imagine it; **quelle i.!,** what an idea!, what a thought!, the very idea!; **i. de génie, i. lumineuse,** brilliant idea, brainwave; **bonne i.!,** good idea!; **qu'est ce-qui vous a donné l'i. de venir?,** what gave you the idea *or* made you think of coming?; **où a-t-elle pu prendre cette i.?,** where did she get that idea from?; **ce livre me donne des idées de voyage,** the book gives me some ideas for holidays; **avoir une i. derrière la tête,** to have an idea at the back of one's mind; **j'ai (comme une) i. qu'il va venir ce soir,** I've an idea he'll come tonight; **l'i. ne te viendrait pas qu'elle a peut-être ses problèmes?,** doesn't it occur to you that she has problems too?; **donner des idées à qn,** to put ideas into s.o.'s head, to give s.o. ideas; **avoir des idées noires,** to be worried *or* depressed;
(b) (*par l'imagination*) imagination; **essayez de vous faire une i. de notre situation,** try to imagine our position; **voir qch en i.,** to see sth in the mind's eye; **se faire des idées,** to imagine things; **i. fixe,** obsession, idée fixe;
(c) (*opinion*) view, opinion; **avoir une haute i. de qn/qch,** to have a high opinion of s.o./sth; **avoir des idées arrêtées sur qch,** to have set ideas *or* very decided views on sth; **agir à son i.,** to act according to one's own ideas; **on a tous une i. différente sur la question,** we all have a different opinion on the matter; **changer d'i.,** to change one's mind; **avoir des idées larges/étroites,** to be broad-/narrow-minded;
(d) (*caprice*) whim, fancy; **comme l'i. m'en prend,** just as the fancy takes me; **c'était juste une i. en l'air,** it was just an idea;
(e) (*esprit*) mind; **j'ai dans l'i. que ...,** I have an idea that ...; **il me vient à l'i. que ...,** it occurs to me that ...; **je ne peux pas lui ôter cela de l'i.,** I can't get it out of his mind *or* head; **cela m'est sorti de l'i.,** it's gone right out *or* clean out of my mind *or* head; **il me revient à l'i. que ...,** now I remember that ...;
(f) i.-..., ... -idea; **des idées-vacances,** holiday ideas; **ce livret contient des idées-repas,** the booklet offers ideas for meals; **une i.-rangement astucieuse,** a clever storage idea.
idem [idɛm] *adv* idem, ditto.
identifiable [idɑ̃tifjabl] *adj* identifiable.
identificateur [idɑ̃tifikatœr] *nm Ordinat* identifier.
identification [idɑ̃tifikasjɔ̃] *nf* identification; *Méd* **i. des types (de bactéries/de virus),** typing (of bacteria/viruses); *Ordinat* **i. de l'utilisateur,** user identification.
identifier [idɑ̃tifje] **1** *vt* (*confondre*) to identify (**avec, à,** with); (*reconnaître*) to identify (*s.o.*); **i. des empreintes digitales,** to identify fingerprints. **2 s'identifier** *vpr* to identify (oneself), to become identified (**avec, à,** with).
identique [idɑ̃tik] **1** *adj* identical; **à l'i.,** identical. **2** *adv* **à l'i.,** identically.
identiquement [idɑ̃tikmɑ̃] *adv* identically.
identité [idɑ̃tite] *nf* identity; **bracelet d'i.,** identity bracelet; **établir l'i. d'un enfant perdu,** to determine the identity of a lost child; *Admin* **carte d'i.,** identity card; **pièces d'i.,** identification papers; **avez-vous une pièce d'i.?,** do you have some identification *or esp Am F* I.D.?; **l'I. judiciaire,** *Br* ≈ the Criminal Records Office.
idéogramme [ideɔgram] *nm Ling* ideogram, ideograph.
idéographie [ideɔgrafi] *nf Ling* ideography.
idéographique [ideɔgrafik] *adj* ideographic(al).
idéologie [ideɔlɔʒi] *nf* ideology.
idéologique [ideɔlɔʒik] *adj* ideological.
idéologue [ideɔlɔg] *n* ideologist, ideologue.

idiomatique [idjɔmatik] *adj Ling* idiomatic; **expression i.,** idiom, idiomatic expression.
idiome [idjom] *nm Ling* idiom.
idiosyncrasie [idjɔsɛ̃krazi] *nf* idiosyncrasy.
idiot, -ote [idjo, -ɔt] **1** *adj* idiotic, absurd; senseless (*joke etc*); *Méd* idiot (*child etc*); **si tu es assez i. pour le croire,** if you're stupid enough to believe it; **ce serait i. de ne pas le faire,** it would be idiotic not to. **2** *n* idiot, fool, *F* clot, dope; *Méd* idiot, imbecile; *F* **l'i. du village,** the village idiot; **faire l'i.,** to act *or* play the fool; **elle me prend pour un i.,** she takes me for an idiot.
idiotement [idjɔtmɑ̃] *adv* idiotically, stupidly.
idiotie [idjɔsi] *nf* **(a)** (*bêtise*) stupidity, idiocy; (*chose, parole idiote*) idiotic *or* stupid thing; **ne dites pas d'idioties!,** don't talk rubbish *or* nonsense!; **faire une i.,** to do something stupid *or* idiotic; *Cin Th* **ne va pas voir cette i.!,** don't go and see that rubbish!; **(b)** *Méd* idiocy, imbecility, mental deficiency.
idiotisme [idjɔtism] *nm* idiom, idiomatic expression.
idoine [idwan] *adj Arch & Jur* fit, able; *Jur* **apte et i. à tester,** fit and competent to make a will.
idolâtre [idɔlɑtr] **1** *adj* idolatrous. **2** *n* idolater, *f* idolatress.
idolâtrer [idɔlɑtre] *vt* to be passionately fond of (*s.o., sth*); to idolize (*s.o.*).
idolâtrie [idɔlɑtri] *nf* idolatry.
idolâtrique [idɔlɑtrik] *adj* idolatrous.
idole [idɔl] *nf* idol, image; **faire une i. de qn,** to idolize s.o.; **faire son i. de l'argent,** to make a god of money; **c'est l'i. des jeunes,** he's a teenage idol.
I.D.S. [ideɛs] *nf Mil* (*abrév* **initiative de défense stratégique**) SDI.
idylle [idil] *nf* (*aventure*) romance; *Littér* idyll.
idyllique [idilik] *adj* idyllic.
if [if] *nm* **(a)** (*arbre*) yew (tree); **(b)** draining rack (*for bottles*).
igame [igam] *nm* (*abrév* **inspecteur général de l'Administration en mission extraordinaire**) = administrator in charge of the prefects of a large district.
I.G.F. [iʒeɛf] *nm inv* (*abrév* **impôt sur les grandes fortunes**) wealth tax.
igloo, iglou [iglu] *nm* igloo.
Ignace [iɲas] *nm* Ignatius.
igname [iɲam] *nf* (*plante*) yam.
ignare [iɲar] **1** *adj* ignorant. **2** *n* ignoramus.
igné [igne] *adj Géol* igneous (*rock etc*).
ignifugation [ignifygɑsjɔ̃] *nf* fireproofing.
ignifuge [ignifyʒ] **1** *adj* non-(in)flammable, fireproof; (*qui retarde l'embrasement*) fire-resistant, flame retardant. **2** *nm* fireproof material.
ignifugé [ignifyʒe] *adj* fireproofed (*material*).
ignifugeant [ignifyʒɑ̃] *adj* = **IGNIFUGE 1.**
ignifuger [ignifyʒe] *vt* (**j'ignifugeai(s); n. ignifugeons**) to fireproof.
ignoble [iɲɔbl] *adj* **(a)** ignoble, base (*person, conduct*); vile, disgraceful, unspeakable (*conduct etc*); **(b)** wretched, filthy (*dwelling etc*).
ignoblement [iɲɔbləmɑ̃] *adv* ignobly, basely, disgracefully.
ignominie [iɲɔmini] *nf* ignominy, shame, disgrace; **s'abaisser aux pires ignominies,** to stoop to the lowest kinds of behaviour.
ignominieusement [iɲɔminjøzmɑ̃] *adv* ignominiously.
ignominieux, -ieuse [iɲɔminjø, -jøz] *adj* ignominious, shameful, disgraceful.
ignorance [iɲɔrɑ̃s] *nf* **(a)** ignorance; **par i.,** through *or* out of ignorance; **tenir qn dans l'i. de qch,** to keep s.o. in ignorance of sth *or* in the dark about sth; **il est d'une i. crasse,** he is incredibly ignorant; **les siècles d'i.,** the dark ages; *Jur* **prétendre cause d'i.,** to plead ignorance; **(b) ignorances,** errors, mistakes.
ignorant, -ante [iɲɔrɑ̃, -ɑ̃t] **1** *adj* **(a)** (*inculte*) ignorant; **être i. en latin,** not to know (any) Latin; **(b)** (*non informé*) ignorant, unaware (**de,** of). **2** *n* ignoramus.
ignoré [iɲɔre] *adj* unknown; (*négligé*) ignored; **vivre i.,** to live in obscurity; **i. de** *ou* **par ses contemporains,** unknown to his contemporaries; (*négligé*) ignored by his contemporaries.
ignorer [iɲɔre] **1** *vt* **(a)** (*ne pas savoir*) not to know (about) (*sth*), to be ignorant *or* unaware of (*sth*); **il ignore tout de ...,** he knows nothing whatever about...; **nul n'est censé i. la loi,** ignorance of the law is no excuse; **je n'ignore pas les difficultés,** I am not unaware of the difficulties; **elle ignore qui je suis,** she doesn't know who I am; **ne pas i. qch,** to be well aware of sth; **(b)** to ignore (*s.o.*); **(c) i. que** + *sub or* + *ind,* not to know that, to be unaware that; **personne n'ignore que ...,** everybody knows that ...; **j'ignorais si vous viendriez,** I didn't know whether you would come; **un fusil qu'il ignorait être chargé,** a gun which he did not know to be loaded. **2 s'ignorer** *vpr* not to know oneself; **charme qui s'ignore,** unconscious charm; **c'est un artiste qui s'ignore,** he is unaware of his artistic talents.
iguane [igwan] *nm* (*reptile*) iguana.
il, ils [il] *pron pers* **(a)** (*person*) he, they; (*thing*) it, they; (*ship*) she, they; **sont-ils arrivés?,** have they come?; **ton père a-t-il ouvert la bouteille?,** has your father opened the bottle?; **ils veulent nous faire payer plus d'impôts,** they want us to pay more taxes; **(b)** (*impersonal*) it, there; **il est/il doit être six heures,** it is/it must be six o'clock; **il est facile de s'en assurer,** it's easy to make sure; **il est vrai que j'étais là,** it's true that I was there; **il était une fois une fée,** once upon a time there was a fairy; **il pleut/neige,** it's raining/snowing; **il faut partir,** it's time to go, we must go; **il y a quelqu'un à la porte,** there's someone at the door.
île [il] *nf* island; **habiter dans une î.,** to live on an island; **î. coralienne,** coral island; **î. déserte,** desert island; **l'Î. de Man,** the Isle of Man; **les îles Anglo-Normandes,** the Channel Islands; *Culin* **î. flottante,** floating islands; **les Îles,** the (French) West Indies.
iléon [ileɔ̃] *nm Anat* ileum.
Iliade (l') [liljad] *nf* the Iliad.
iliaque [iljak] *adj Anat* iliac; **os i.,** hip bone.
illégal, -aux [ilegal, -o] *adj* illegal, unlawful.
illégalement [ilegalmɑ̃] *adv* illegally, unlawfully.
illégalité [ilegalite] *nf* (*d'une action*) illegality, unlawfulness; **commettre une i.,** to break the law.
illégitime [ileʒitim] *adj* illegitimate (*child etc*); unlawful (*marriage etc*); unwarranted (*claim etc*).
illégitimement [ileʒitim(ə)mɑ̃] *adv* illegitimately, unlawfully.
illégitimité [ileʒitimite] *nf* illegitimacy (*of child*); unlawfulness (*of marriage*); unwarranted nature (*of claim*).
illettré, -ée [iletre] **1** *adj* illiterate. **2** *n* illiterate (person).
illettrisme [iletrism] *nm* illiteracy.
illicite [ilisit] *adj* illicit, unlawful; *Sp* **coup i.,** foul.
illicitement [ilisitmɑ̃] *adv* illicitly, unlawfully.
illico [iliko] *adv F* at once, there and then, pronto.
illimité [ilimite] *adj* unlimited, limitless, boundless, unbounded; **congé i.,** indefinite leave.
illisibilité [ilizibilite] *nf* illegibility.
illisible [ilizibl] *adj* **(a)** illegible, unreadable (*writing etc*); **(b)** *Fig* unreadable (*book etc*).
illisiblement [ilizibləmɑ̃] *adv* illegibly.
illogique [ilɔʒik] *adj* illogical.
illogiquement [ilɔʒikmɑ̃] *adv* illogically.
illogisme [ilɔʒism] *nm* illogicality, illogicalness.
illumination [ilyminɑsjɔ̃] *nf* **(a)** lighting (*of room etc*); **i. (par projecteurs),** floodlighting; **(b) illuminations,** lights, illuminations; **(c)** (*inspiration*) enlightenment; **j'ai eu une i.,** I've had an inspiration *or* a brilliant idea.
illuminé, -ée [ilymine] **1** *adj* (*édifice*) illuminated, floodlit. **2** *n F* visionary; *Péj* fanatic; (*eccentrique*) crank.
illuminer [ilymine] **1** *vt* **(a)** to illuminate, to light up (*for festivity*); **(b)** *Rel Phil* to enlighten. **2 s'illuminer** *vpr* to light up (**de,** with).
illusion [ilyzjɔ̃] *nf* illusion; **se nourrir d'illusions,** to cherish illusions; **elle l'a entretenu dans cette i.,** she did not shatter his illusion; **se bercer d'illusions, se faire des illusions,** to delude oneself, to live in a fool's paradise; **faire i.,** to deceive oneself, to be *or* to labour under a delusion; **cela n'a pas fait i.,** no-one was taken in; **cet éclairage fait i. de lumière naturelle,** the lighting gives the impression of natural light; *Phys* **i. d'optique,** optical illusion.
illusionner [ilyzjɔne] **1** *vt* to delude (*s.o.*). **2 s'illusionner** *vpr* to labour under a delusion, to delude oneself, to deceive oneself.
illusionnisme [ilyzjɔnism] *nm* conjuring.
illusionniste [ilyzjɔnist] *n* illusionist, conjurer.
illusoire [ilyzwar] *adj* illusory, illusive.
illusoirement [ilyzwarmɑ̃] *adv* illusively, illusorily.
illustrateur [ilystratœr] *nm* illustrator (*of books etc*).
illustration [ilystrɑsjɔ̃] *nf* **(a)** (*action*) illustration, illustrating; **(b)** (*dessin*) illustration, picture; **i. en couleur,** coloured illustration; **l'i. du livre,** the illustrations in the book; **texte et illustrations de ...,** text and illustrations by ... .
illustre [ilystr] *adj* illustrious, famous, renowned; *Hum* **un i. inconnu,** = someone nobody's ever heard of.
illustré [ilystre] **1** *adj* illustrated; **abondamment i.,** fully

illustrated. **2** *nm* illustrated magazine.

illustrer [ilystre] **1** *vt* **(a)** to illustrate (*book etc*); **(b)** *Arch & Litt* to make illustrious. **2** *vpr* **s'illustrer** (*d'une personne*) to distinguish oneself (**par**, by); (*du courage etc*) to be shown *or* illustrated.

ilôt [ilo] *nm* (*petite île*) islet, small island; (*groupe d'immeubles*) cluster of buildings; *Fig* **i. de verdure,** island of greenery; *Fig* **i. de résistance,** pocket of resistance.

ilote [ilɔt] *n Hist* helot.

image [imaʒ] *nf* **(a)** image; reflection (*in water etc*); *Cin* frame; *TV* picture; *Opt* **i. réelle,** real image; **i. virtuelle,** virtual image; *Cin TV* **à 25 images par seconde,** at 25 frames per second;

(b) *Fig* image; **l'i. de son père,** the image of his father; **Dieu créa l'homme à son i.,** God created man in his own image; **ils sont l'i. du bonheur/de la réussite/***etc*, they are the picture of happiness/success/*etc*;

(c) (*dessin*) picture; **livre d'images,** picture book; **récit en images,** pictorial record; **images pieuses,** holy pictures; *Scol* **voici une i.,** ≈ here's a gold star; *Fig* **sage comme une i.,** good as gold;

(d) (*représentation*) (mental) picture, idea, impression; **i. visuelle forte,** strong visual impression; **garder l'i. d'une personne en mémoire,** to keep an image of s.o. in one's memory; **la première image qui vient à l'esprit,** the first image that comes to mind; **expression qui évoque une i.,** evocative expression; **i. de marque,** brand image (*of product*); (public) image (*of politician etc*);

(e) *Litt* image; **images,** imagery.

imagé [imaʒe] *adj* vivid, full of imagery (*style etc*).

imager [imaʒe] *vt* **(j'imageai(s); n. imageons)** *Litt* to colour, *US* to color (*style, speech*).

imagerie [imaʒri] *nf* **(a)** *Littér* imagery; **(b)** *Com* colour *or US* color print trade; (*usine*) colour *or US* color print works; **(c)** *Méd* **i. par résonance magnétique,** magnetic resonance imaging.

imagier [imaʒje] *nm* **(a)** painter; *Arch* image maker; (*sculpteur*) sculptor, carver; **(b)** (*dessinateur*) drawer of pictures; **(c)** (*imprimeur*) colour *or US* color print maker; **(d)** *Com* colour *or US* color print seller.

imaginable [imaʒinabl] *adj* imaginable, conceivable; **cela n'était pas i. il y a quelques années,** it was inconceivable a few years ago; **toutes les solutions possibles et imaginables,** every conceivable solution.

imaginaire [imaʒinɛr] *adj* imaginary, make-believe; *Math* imaginary (*quantity*); **personnage i.,** imaginary person; *Hum* **malade i.,** hypochondriac.

imaginatif, -ive [imaʒinatif, -iv] **1** *adj* imaginative. **2** *n* person with imagination.

imagination [imaʒinasjɔ̃] *nf* **(a)** (*faculté*) imagination; **voir qch en i.,** to see sth in one's mind's eye *or* in one's imagination; **avoir de l'i.,** to have imagination, to be imaginative; **tu manques d'i.!,** you have no imagination!; **vivre qch en i.,** to experience sth in one's imagination; **(b)** (*rêve*) fancy, invention; **de pure i.,** baseless, unfounded.

imaginer [imaʒine] **1** *vt* **(a)** (*inventer*) to imagine, to conceive, to invent, to devise; **i. une méthode,** to devise *or* think up a method; **i. un dispositif,** to think up a device; **bien imaginé,** well thought out;

(b) (*concevoir*) to imagine, to picture; **imaginez un peu mon étonnement,** just imagine my surprise; **tu l'imagines avec des enfants!,** just think of him *or* her with children!; **je n'imaginais pas que cela était faisable,** I didn't think it could be done; **tout ce qu'on peut i. de plus beau,** the finest thing imaginable; **que vas-tu i. là?,** how can you think such a thing?; **nous avions imaginé de ne rien vous dire,** we had planned not to tell you anything; **vous plaisantez, j'imagine,** you must be joking!; **i. que ...,** to imagine that ... .

2 s'imaginer *vpr* **(a)** (*croire à tort*) to delude oneself (with the thought) (that ...), to imagine (that ...), to think (that ...); **elle s'imagine que tout le monde l'admire,** she thinks everyone admires her; **elle s'est imaginé que ...,** she got it into her head that ...; **il s'imagine tout savoir,** he thinks he knows everything;

(b) (*se figurer*) to imagine, to picture; **comme on peut se l'i.,** as you can (well) imagine;

(c) (*se voir*) to picture *or* see oneself; **je m'imagine sur la scène/à quarante ans,** I can (just) picture *or* see myself on the stage/at forty.

imago [imago] *n* imago.

imam [imam] *nm*, **iman** [imɑ̃] *nm Islam Rel* imam.

imbattable [ɛ̃batabl] *adj* invincible, unbeatable (*champion*); unbeatable (*prices etc*); *Sp* unbreakable (*record*).

imbécile [ɛ̃besil] **1** *adj* imbecile, imbecilic, idiotic; *Méd* imbecile. **2** *n* idiot, fool, imbecile; *Méd* imbecile; **le premier i. venu vous dira cela,** any fool will tell you that; **un i. heureux,** a (contented) sheep; **faire l'i.,** to play *or* act the fool.

imbécilement [ɛ̃besilmɑ̃] *adv* idiotically, foolishly.

imbécillité [ɛ̃besilite] *nf* **(a)** (*stupidité*) imbecility, idiocy; *Méd* imbecility, feebleness of mind; **l'i. de ton comportement,** your imbecile *or* imbecilic behaviour; **(b)** (*parole, chose stupide*) idiotic thing; **dire des imbécillités,** to talk nonsense *or* rubbish.

imberbe [ɛ̃bɛrb] *adj* beardless.

imbiber [ɛ̃bibe] **1** *vt* **i. qch (de qch),** to soak *or* steep sth (in sth); to saturate *or* moisten *or* impregnate sth (with sth); **imbibé d'eau,** waterlogged, saturated (with water); **chiffon imbibé d'huile,** oil-soaked rag. **2 s'imbiber** *vpr* **(a)** to absorb; to become saturated (**de**, with); **(b)** *F* **s'i. d'alcool,** to drink too much, to drink like a fish.

imbibé [ɛ̃bibe] *adj F* drunk, tipsy.

imbrication [ɛ̃brikasjɔ̃] *nf* overlap(ping) (*of tiles, scales etc*).

imbriquer [ɛ̃brike] **1** *vt* to overlap. **2 s'imbriquer** *vpr* to overlap, to fit in.

imbroglio [ɛ̃brɔljo] *nm* imbroglio.

imbrûlable [ɛ̃brylabl] *adj* fireproof.

imbu [ɛ̃by] *adj* **i. de,** full of, steeped in (*prejudice etc*); **i. de sa personne,** full of one's own importance; **elle est vraiment imbue d'elle-même,** she's really full of herself.

imbuvable [ɛ̃byvabl] *adj* undrinkable; *Fig* (*personne*) insufferable.

imitable [imitabl] *adj* imitable.

imitateur, -trice [imitatœr, -tris] **1** *n* imitator; *Th* impersonator. **2** *adj* imitative, imitating.

imitatif, -ive [imitatif, -iv] *adj* imitative.

imitation [imitasjɔ̃] *nf* **(a)** (*action*) imitation, imitating, copying; **à l'i. de qn/qch,** in imitation of s.o./sth; **(b)** (*de personne etc*) imitation, mimicking, mimicry; *Th* impersonation; **elle fait d'excellentes imitations,** she does great imitations, she is an excellent mimic; **(c)** forgery, forging (*of signature etc*); counterfeiting (*of money*); **(d)** (*copie*) copy; **bijoux en i.,** imitation *or* costume jewellery; **i. d'un meuble d'époque,** reproduction; *Péj* fake antique; **manteau (en) i. loutre,** imitation sealskin coat; **(e)** (*parodie*) forgery, counterfeit; *Péj* **une pâle i.,** a pale imitation.

imiter [imite] *vt* **(a)** (*copier*) to imitate, to copy; **il leva son verre et tout le monde l'imita,** he raised his glass and everyone followed suit *or* did the same; **i. un chant d'oiseau,** to imitate bird song; **(b)** to mimic (*s.o.*), *F* to take (*s.o.*) off; *Th* to impersonate (*s.o.*); **(c)** to forge (*signature*); to counterfeit (*money*); **matière qui imite le cuir/le bois/***etc*, material that simulates leather/wood/*etc*.

immaculé [imakyle] *adj* immaculate; **une réputation immaculée,** a spotless reputation; *Rel* **l'Immaculée Conception,** the Immaculate Conception.

immanence [imanɑ̃s] *nf* immanence.

immanent [imanɑ̃] *adj* immanent; **justice immanente,** divine retribution.

immangeable [ɛ̃mɑ̃ʒabl] *adj* uneatable, inedible.

immanquable [ɛ̃mɑ̃kabl] *adj* **(a)** (*cible etc*) that cannot be missed; **(b)** certain, inevitable (*event etc*).

immanquablement [ɛ̃mɑ̃kabləmɑ̃] *adv* inevitably, without fail, for certain.

immatérialité [imaterjalite] *nf* immateriality.

immatériel, -ielle [imaterjɛl] *adj* **(a)** (*spirituel*) immaterial, unsubstantial; **(b)** intangible (*assets etc*); **d'une pâleur presque immatérielle,** of an almost ethereal pallor.

immatriculation [imatrikylasjɔ̃] *nf* **(a)** registering, registration (*of deed, car etc*); *Aut* **plaque d'i.,** number plate, *Am* license plate; **numéro d'i.,** registration number; **(b)** registration, enrolment (*of student etc*).

immatriculer [imatrikyle] *vt* to register (*document, car, student etc*); **voiture immatriculée SPF 342 T/dans le Var,** car with the registration number SPF 342 T/with a Var number *or Am* license plate.

immature [imatyr] *adj* immature.

immaturité [imatyrite] *nf* immaturity.

immédiat [imedja] **1** *adj* **(a)** immediate; direct (*cause, successor etc*); *Ch* **analyse immédiate,** proximate analysis; **(b)** close (*proximity*); **être en contact i. avec le feu,** to be in direct contact with the fire; **(c)** (*dans le temps*) immediate, without delay; **changement i.,** instant change; **(mécanisme) à action immédiate,** quick-acting (mechanism); **résultat i.,** immediate result. **2** *nm* **dans l'i.,** in the immediate future, for the time being.

immédiatement [imedjatmɑ̃] *adv* immediately.
immédiateté [imedjat(ə)te] *nf Phil* immediacy.
immémorial, -iaux [imemɔrjal, -jo] *adj Litt* immemorial; **de temps i.,** from *or* since time immemorial, from time out of mind.
immense [imɑ̃s] *adj* immense, vast, huge.
immensément [imɑ̃semɑ̃] *adv* immensely, vastly, hugely.
immensité [imɑ̃site] *nf* vastness, immenseness, hugeness.
immensurable [imɑ̃syrabl] *adj* immeasurable.
immergé [imɛrʒe] *adj* submerged; **plante immergée,** aquatic plant.
immerger [imɛrʒe] *v* (**j'immergeai(s); n. immergeons**) **1** *vtr* to immerse, to plunge, to submerge; to lay (*cable*) underwater; to get rid of *or* dispose of (*waste*) in the sea, to dump (*waste*) at sea; to bury (*s.o.*) at sea. **2 s'immerger** *vpr* (*of submarine*) to submerge, to dive.
immérité [imerite] *adj* unmerited, undeserved.
immersion [imɛrsjɔ̃] *nf* **(a)** immersion; laying (*of cable*) underwater; disposal (*of waste*) in the *or* at sea; **(b)** submergence, submersion (*of submarine*); **(c)** (*funérailles*) burial *or* funeral at sea.
immettable [ɛ̃mɛtabl] *adj* unwearable.
immeuble [imœbl] **1** *adj Jur* real, fixed; **biens immeubles,** real estate. **2** *nm* **(a)** *Jur* real estate, landed property; **(b)** (*tour*) building, block; (*de bureaux*) office block; (*d'appartements*) block of flats, *Am* apartment block; **i. de 10 étages,** 10-storey building; **i. de rapport,** rental property; **i. locatif,** rental building.
immigrant, -ante [imigrɑ̃, -ɑ̃t] **1** *adj* immigrant. **2** *n* immigrant; *Can* **i. reçu,** landed immigrant.
immigration [imigrɑsjɔ̃] *nf* immigration; **agent du service de l'i.,** immigration officer.
immigré, -ée [imigre] **1** *adj* immigrant. **2** *n* immigré.
immigrer [imigre] *vi* to immigrate; **i. en Europe/aux États-Unis,** to immigrate to Europe/the United States.
imminence [iminɑ̃s] *nf* imminence.
imminent [iminɑ̃] *adj* imminent, impending.
immiscer (s') [simise] *vpr* (**je m'immisçai(s); n. n. immisçons**) to interfere, to meddle (**dans,** in, with).
immixtion [imikstjɔ̃] *nf* interference, meddling.
immobile [imɔbil] *adj* **(a)** motionless, still, immobile; fixed, set (*face etc*); **rester complètement i.,** to stand stock-still; **(b)** *Fig* (*principe etc*) immovable, firm, steadfast.
immobilier, -ière [imɔbilje, -jɛr] *Jur* **1** *adj* real; **biens immobiliers,** real estate, *esp Am* realty; **vente immobilière,** sale of property; **société immobilière,** *Br* ≈ building society; **agence immobilière,** estate agency, *Am* real estate office; **agent i.,** estate agent, *Am* real estate agent, realtor. **2** *nm* real estate, *Am* realty.
immobilisation [imɔbilizɑsjɔ̃] *nf* **(a)** (*fait de ne plus bouger*) immobilization, immobilizing; standstill; **l'i. du malade est essentielle,** it is essential to immobilize the patient; **attendre l'i. totale du train,** wait until the train comes to a complete stop; **(b)** *Jur* conversion into real estate; **(c)** *Com* locking up, tying up, immobilization (*of capital*); **(d) immobilisations,** fixed assets, capital assets.
immobiliser [imɔbilize] **1** *vt* **(a)** (*rendre immobile*) to immobilize, to bring to a standstill; **i. un blessé,** to immobilize s.o. who has been injured; **(b)** to immobilize (*sth*), to fix (*sth*) in position; **(c)** *Jur* to convert into realty; **(d)** *Com* to lock up, to tie up, to immobilize (*capital*). **2 s'immobiliser** *vpr* (*d'un véhicule*) to come to a stop *or* a standstill; (*of moving body*) to come to rest.
immobilisme [imɔbilism] *nm* opposition to progress, ultra-conservatism.
immobiliste [imɔbilist] **1** *adj* opposed to progress. **2** *n* ultra-conservative.
immobilité [imɔbilite] *nf* immobility, motionlessness; **être condamné à l'i. pour une semaine,** (*d'un malade, d'une jambe cassée*) to be kept immobile for a week.
immodération [imɔderɑsjɔ̃] *nf* immoderation, immoderateness.
immodéré [imɔdere] *adj* immoderate, excessive, inordinate.
immodérément [imɔderemɑ̃] *adv* immoderately, excessively, inordinately.
immodeste [imɔdɛst] *adj Vieilli* immodest.
immodestement [imɔdɛstəmɑ̃] *adv Vieilli* immodestly, shamelessly.
immodestie [imɔdɛsti] *nf Vieilli* immodesty.
immolateur [imɔlatœr] *nm Arch & Litt* immolator, sacrificer.
immolation [imɔlɑsjɔ̃] *nf Litt* immolation, sacrifice.
immoler [imɔle] **1** *vt* to immolate, to sacrifice. **2 s'immoler** *vpr* to immolate oneself.
immonde [imɔ̃d] *adj* **(a)** (*sale*) foul, filthy, vile; **(b)** (*ignoble*) foul; **(c)** *Rel* unclean.
immondices [imɔ̃dis] *nfpl* refuse, rubbish.
immoral, -aux [imɔral, -o] *adj* immoral.
immoralement [imɔralmɑ̃] *adv* immorally.
immoralisme [imɔralism] *nm Phil* immoralism.
immoraliste [imɔralist] *Phil* **1** *adj* immoralist. **2** *n* immoralist.
immoralité [imɔralite] *nf* immorality.
immortaliser [imɔrtalize] **1** *vt* to immortalize. **2 s'immortaliser** *vpr* to gain immortality, to win everlasting fame.
immortalité [imɔrtalite] *nf* immortality.
immortel, -elle [imɔrtɛl] **1** *adj* immortal (*life etc*); everlasting, undying (*fame etc*). **2** *n* immortal; *Fig* (*membre de l'Académie française*) member of the Académie Française. **3** *nf* (*plante*) **immortelle,** everlasting (flower), immortelle.
immotivé [imɔtive] *adj* unmotivated, groundless.
immuabilité [imɥabilite] *nf* immutability.
immuable [imɥabl] *adj* immutable, unalterable, fixed, unchanging.
immuablement [imɥabləmɑ̃] *adv* immutably, unalterably.
immunisation [imynizɑsjɔ̃] *nf Méd etc* immunization.
immuniser [imynize] *vt Méd* to immunize; **être immunisé contre qch,** *Méd* to be immunized against sth; *Fig* to be immune to *or* from sth.
immunitaire [imynitɛr] *adj Méd* **système i.,** immune system.
immunité [imynite] *nf* immunity; **i. parlementaire,** parliamentary privilege *or* immunity; **i. diplomatique,** diplomatic immunity.
immunodéficitaire [imynɔdefisitɛr] *adj Méd* immunodeficient.
immunologie [imynɔlɔʒi] *nf* immunology.
immutabilité [imytabilite] *nf* immutability.
impact [ɛ̃pakt] *nm* impact, shock; **point d'i.,** point of impact; **l'intervention du ministre a eu un certain i.,** the Minister's intervention had something of an impact.
impair [ɛ̃pɛr] **1 adj** odd, uneven (*number etc*); *Rail* **voie impaire,** down line; **jour i.,** odd day; *Ordinat* **parité impaire,** uneven parity. **2** *nm* blunder, *F* bloomer; **commettre un i.,** to blunder, *F* to drop a brick, to put one's foot in it.
impalpable [ɛ̃palpabl] *adj* impalpable, intangible.
imparable [ɛ̃parabl] *adj* unstoppable (*shot etc*).
impardonnable [ɛ̃pardɔnabl] *adj* unpardonable, unforgivable; **il serait i. de ne pas les aider,** it would be a crime not to help them.
imparfait [ɛ̃parfɛ] **1** *adj* **(a)** *Litt* unfinished, uncompleted (*book etc*); **avoir une connaissance imparfaite de qch,** to have an imperfect knowledge of sth; **(b)** (*qui a des défauts*) imperfect, defective. **2** *nm Gram* imperfect (tense).
imparfaitement [ɛ̃parfɛtmɑ̃] *adv* imperfectly.
impartial, -iaux [ɛ̃parsjal, -jo] *adj* impartial, unbias(s)ed.
impartialement [ɛ̃parsjalmɑ̃] *adv* impartially.
impartialité [ɛ̃parsjalite] *nf* impartiality.
impartir [ɛ̃partir] *vt Jur & Litt* to grant (*right, favour*); to assign (*task*) (**à,** to); to bestow (*gift*) (**à,** on); **délai imparti,** time limit.
impasse [ɛ̃pas] *nf* **(a)** (*cul-de-sac*) dead end, cul-de-sac, blind alley; (*sur panneau*) no through road; **(b)** *Fig* impasse, deadlock; **se trouver dans une i.,** to find oneself in a dilemma *or F* in a fix; **il faut sortir de l'i.,** the deadlock has to be broken; **les négociations sont dans l'i.,** the talks are deadlocked; **aboutir à une i.,** to come to a deadlock; **(c)** *Fin* **i. budgétaire,** budget deficit; **(d)** *Cartes* **faire une i.,** to finesse; *Fig Scol* **faire une i. sur un sujet,** to give a subject a miss when revising for an exam.
impassibilité [ɛ̃pasibilite] *nf* impassiveness, impassivity.
impassible [ɛ̃pasibl] *adj* impassive.
impassiblement [ɛ̃pasibləmɑ̃] *adv* impassively.
impatiemment [ɛ̃pasjamɑ̃] *adv* impatiently.
impatience [ɛ̃pasjɑ̃s] *nf* **(a)** (*énervement*) impatience; (*enthousiasme*) eagerness; **avec i.,** impatiently; **montrer des signes d'i.,** to show signs of impatience; **elle brûle d'i. de te le dire,** she's dying to tell you; **avoir une grande i.** *ou* **être dans l'i. de faire qch,** to be most impatient to do sth; **(b)** *Litt* intolerance (**de,** of); **(c)** *Litt* **impatiences,** fits of impatience.
impatient, -ente [ɛ̃pasjɑ̃, -ɑ̃t] **1** *adj* **(a)** impatient; **d'un air i.,** impatiently; **être i. de faire qch,** to be impatient *or* eager *or* anxious to do sth; **être i. avec qn,** to be impatient

with s.o.; **(b)** *Litt* intolerant (**de,** of). **2** *nf* (*plante*) **impatiente,** impatiens, busy Lizzie.
impatientant [ɛ̃pasjɑ̃tɑ̃] *adj* annoying, provoking.
impatienter [ɛ̃pasjɑ̃te] **1** *vt* to annoy, to provoke (*s.o.*); **tes questions m'impatientent,** I'm getting impatient with your questions. **2 s'impatienter** *vpr* to lose patience, to get impatient (**de,** at; **contre,** with).
impayable [ɛ̃pɛjabl] *adj* **(a)** *F* priceless (*joke etc*); **elle est i.!,** she's priceless!; **(b)** *Arch* inestimable, invaluable, priceless.
impayé, -ée [ɛ̃peje] **1** *adj* unpaid (*debt etc*); outstanding (*payment*). **2** *nm* outstanding payment; **j'ai un tas d'impayés,** I've got a stack of unpaid bills.
impec [ɛ̃pɛk] *adj F* = **IMPECCABLE**.
impeccable [ɛ̃pɛkabl] *adj* impeccable; **d'une propreté i.,** impeccably clean.
impeccablement [ɛ̃pɛkabləmɑ̃] *adv* impeccably.
impécunieux, -euse [ɛ̃pekynjø, -øz] *adj Litt* impecunious.
impédance [ɛ̃pedɑ̃s] *nf Él* impedance.
impedimenta [ɛ̃pedimɛ̃ta] *nmpl* impedimenta.
impénétrabilité [ɛ̃penetrabilite] *nf* **(a)** (*densité*) (*d'une forêt*) impenetrability; (*à l'eau*) imperviousness; **(b)** (*mystère*) inscrutability.
impénétrable [ɛ̃penetrabl] *adj* **(a)** impenetrable (*forest etc*); **i. à l'eau,** impervious to water; **(b)** inscrutable (*face*); unfathomable (*mystery etc*); close (*secret*); **prendre un air i.,** to adopt an inscrutable air.
impénitence [ɛ̃penitɑ̃s] *nf* impenitence.
impénitent [ɛ̃penitɑ̃] *adj* impenitent, unrepentant.
impensable [ɛ̃pɑ̃sabl] *adj* unthinkable.
imper [ɛ̃pɛr] *nm F* (= **imperméable**) mac.
impératif, -ive [ɛ̃peratif, -iv] **1** *adj* imperious, imperative, peremptory (*tone etc*); *Jur* mandatory (*law*). **2** *nm* **(a)** (*exigence*) requirement; **un diplôme est un i.,** a diploma is essential; **savoir nager est un i.,** it is essential to be able to swim; **les impératifs de la mode,** the dictates of fashion; **(b)** *Gram* imperative (mood).
impérativement [ɛ̃perativmɑ̃] *adv* imperatively; **il faut i. que je la voie,** it is imperative that I see her.
impératrice [ɛ̃peratris] *nf* empress.
imperceptibilité [ɛ̃pɛrsɛptibilite] *nf* imperceptibility.
imperceptible [ɛ̃pɛrsɛptibl] *adj* imperceptible; **elle fit un sourire i.,** she gave a barely perceptible smile.
imperceptiblement [ɛ̃pɛrsɛptibləmɑ̃] *adv* imperceptibly.
imperdable [ɛ̃pɛrdabl] *adj* **le match est i.,** the match can't be lost; **le match est i. pour la France,** France can't lose.
imperfectible [ɛ̃pɛrfɛktibl] *adj* imperfectible.
imperfectif, -ive [ɛ̃pɛrfɛktif, -iv] *adj Gram* imperfective.
imperfection [ɛ̃pɛrfɛksjɔ̃] *nf* **(a)** (*état imparfait*) imperfection; (*état bâclé*) incompletion, incompleteness; **(b)** (*présence de défauts*) defectiveness; **(c)** (*défaut*) defect, fault, flaw, blemish; (*d'une personne*) shortcoming.
impérial, -aux [ɛ̃perjal, -o] **1** *adj* imperial; **prendre un air i.,** to adopt an imperial air. **2** *nf* **impériale (a)** top (deck) (*of bus etc*); **autobus à i.,** doubledecker (bus); **(b)** (*barbe*) imperial; tuft (*under lower lip*) (as worn by Napoleon III).
impérialement [ɛ̃perjalmɑ̃] *adv* imperially.
impérialisme [ɛ̃perjalism] *nm* imperialism.
impérialiste [ɛ̃perjalist] **1** *adj* imperialist(ic). **2** *n* imperialist.
impérieusement [ɛ̃perjøzmɑ̃] *adv* **(a)** (*avec dédain*) imperiously, haughtily; **(b)** (*de façon pressante*) urgently; **il a i. besoin de manger,** he is urgently in need of something to eat.
impérieux, -euse [ɛ̃perjø, -øz] *adj* **(a)** (*dédaigneux*) imperious, domineering; **(b)** urgent, pressing (*necessity etc*).
impérissable [ɛ̃perisabl] *adj* imperishable; (*amour*) undying.
imperméabilisation [ɛ̃pɛrmeabilizasjɔ̃] *nf* (water-) proofing.
imperméabiliser [ɛ̃pɛrmeabilize] *vt* to (water)proof.
imperméabilité [ɛ̃pɛrmeabilite] *nf* impermeability; *Fig* imperviousness (**à,** to).
imperméable [ɛ̃pɛrmeabl] **1** *adj* impermeable; *Fig* impervious (**à,** to); **i. à l'eau,** waterproof; **i. à la poussière,** dustproof; *Fig* **être i. à la critique,** to be impervious to criticism. **2** *nm* raincoat, mackintosh.
impersonnalité [ɛ̃pɛrsɔnalite] *nf* impersonality.
impersonnel, -elle [ɛ̃pɛrsɔnɛl] *adj* impersonal.
impersonnellement [ɛ̃pɛrsɔnɛlmɑ̃] *adv* impersonally.
impertinemment [ɛ̃pɛrtinamɑ̃] *adv* impertinently.
impertinence [ɛ̃pɛrtinɑ̃s] *nf* impertinence, rudeness; **dire des impertinences à qn,** to speak impertinently to s.o.; **répondre avec i.,** to answer impertinently.
impertinent, -ente [ɛ̃pɛrtinɑ̃, -ɑ̃t] **1** *adj* impertinent, rude (*person*). **2** *n* impertinent *or* rude person.
imperturbabilité [ɛ̃pɛrtyrbabilite] *nf* imperturbability.
imperturbable [ɛ̃pɛrtyrbabl] *adj* imperturbable, unruffled.
imperturbablement [ɛ̃pɛrtyrbabləmɑ̃] *adv* imperturbably.
impétigo [ɛ̃petigo] *nm Méd* impetigo.
impétueusement [ɛ̃petɥøzmɑ̃] *adv Litt* impetuously.
impétueux, -euse [ɛ̃petɥø, -øz] *adj* **(a)** (*fougueux*) impetuous, hotheaded, impulsive; **(b)** *Litt* rushing, raging (*torrent etc*).
impétuosité [ɛ̃petɥozite] *nf* impetuosity, impulsiveness.
impie [ɛ̃pi] **1** *adj* impious. **2** *n* impious person.
impiété [ɛ̃pjete] *nf* **(a)** impiety, godlessness, ungodliness (*of person*); impiousness (*of wish etc*); **(b)** (*blasphème*) blasphemy.
impitoyable [ɛ̃pitwajabl] *adj* (*tyran*) pitiless, ruthless, merciless (**à, envers, pour,** towards); (*journaliste, critique*) ruthless, merciless.
impitoyablement [ɛ̃pitwajabləmɑ̃] *adv* pitilessly, ruthlessly, mercilessly.
implacabilité [ɛ̃plakabilite] *nf* implacability.
implacable [ɛ̃plakabl] *adj* implacable, relentless, unrelenting (**à, pour, à l'égard de,** towards); **logique i.,** implacable logic.
implacablement [ɛ̃plakabləmɑ̃] *adv* implacably.
implant [ɛ̃plɑ̃] *nm Méd* implant.
implantation [ɛ̃plɑ̃tasjɔ̃] *nf* introduction, establishment (*of system, fashion, custom*); setting up (*of industry etc*); *Méd* implantation; **l'i. des réfugiés s'est faite rapidement,** refugees rapidly established themselves; *Méd* **on lui a fait une i. de cheveux,** he's had a hair implant.
implanter [ɛ̃plɑ̃te] **1** *vt* to introduce, to establish (*system etc*); to implant (*idea etc*); to set up (*factory etc*). **2 s'implanter** *vpr* (*d'un usage etc*) to be established *or* set up; (*d'une société*) to locate, to set up.
implication [ɛ̃plikasjɔ̃] *nf* **(a)** *Jur* implication (**dans,** in); **(b)** (*engagement*) involvement, entanglement.
implicite [ɛ̃plisit] *adj* implicit; *Ordinat* **option i.,** default option.
implicitement [ɛ̃plisitmɑ̃] *adv* implicitly; *Ordinat* by default; **le lecteur c est utilisé i.,** drive c is the default; **le lecteur utilisé i. est ...,** the default drive is ... .
impliquer [ɛ̃plike] *vt* **(a)** (*compromettre*) to implicate, to involve; **véhicule impliqué (dans un accident),** vehicle involved (in an accident); **(b) i. que ...,** to imply that ... .
implorant [ɛ̃plɔrɑ̃] *adj* imploring; **d'un ton i.,** imploringly.
imploration [ɛ̃plɔrasjɔ̃] *nf* entreaty.
implorer [ɛ̃plɔre] *vt* to implore, to beseech, to entreat (**de faire qch,** to do sth).
imploser [ɛ̃ploze] *vi* to implode.
implosion [ɛ̃plozjɔ̃] *nf* implosion.
impolarisable [ɛ̃pɔlarizabl] *adj Él* impolarizable.
impoli [ɛ̃pɔli] *adj* impolite, uncivil, rude, discourteous.
impoliment [ɛ̃pɔlimɑ̃] *adv* impolitely, uncivilly, rudely, discourteously.
impolitesse [ɛ̃pɔlitɛs] *nf* **(a)** (*caractère impoli*) impoliteness, rudeness, lack of manners; **(b)** (*acte*) act of rudeness; **dire des impolitesses,** to be impolite, to say impolite things.
impolitique [ɛ̃pɔlitik] *adj* impolitic, ill-advised.
impondérabilité [ɛ̃pɔ̃derabilite] *nf* imponderability.
impondérable [ɛ̃pɔ̃derabl] **1** *adj* imponderable. **2** *nmpl* **impondérables,** imponderables.
impopulaire [ɛ̃pɔpylɛr] *adj* unpopular.
impopularité [ɛ̃pɔpylarite] *nf* unpopularity.
importable¹ [ɛ̃pɔrtabl] *adj* importable (*goods etc*).
importable² *adj* unwearable (*dress etc*).
importance [ɛ̃pɔrtɑ̃s] *nf* **(a)** importance; **affaire d'i.,** important matter; **l'affaire est d'i.,** the matter is of some importance; **de peu d'i.,** of little importance, of no great significance; **sans i.,** unimportant; **c'est sans i.,** it's not important; **événement de la première** *ou* **de haute i.,** event of outstanding importance, all-important event; **avoir de l'i.,** to be important; **cela n'a pas d'i.,** it's of no importance *or Fml* of no consequence; **cela n'a aucune i.,** it doesn't matter one bit; **le mouvement prend de l'i.,** the movement is gaining ground; **prendre de l'i.,** (*d'une société etc*) to expand; **attacher de l'i. à qch,** to attach importance to sth; **tu attaches** *ou* **tu donnes trop d'i. à cela,** you

attach too much importance to it; **et alors? quelle i.?,** so what?;

(b) size (*of town etc*); extent (*of damage etc*); magnitude (*of sum, project*); **i. d'une blessure,** seriousness of a wound; **on ne connaît pas encore l'i. de ses blessures,** the extent of his injuries is not yet known;

(c) (*autorité*) social importance, position, standing.

important, -ante [ɛ̃pɔrtɑ̃, -ɑ̃t] **1** *adj* **(a)** important, significant; **peu i.,** unimportant, immaterial; **rien d'i.,** nothing important, nothing of significance; **ce n'est pas très i.,** it's not very important; **il est i. que ...,** it is important that ...; **personnage i.,** important *or* influential person; **c'est quelqu'un d'i.,** he is important; **(b)** large, major (*town, company etc*); considerable (*sum of money etc*); **la recette a atteint un chiffre i.,** the takings reached a high *or* a considerable figure; **un retard i.,** a considerable delay; **(c)** self-important (*person*). **2** *n* busybody; *Péj* **faire l'i.,** to act big, to put on airs. **3** *nm* **l'i.,** the important thing, the main point; **l'i., c'est que tu sois satisfait,** the important thing is for you to be satisfied.

importateur, -trice [ɛ̃pɔrtatœr, -tris] **1** *n* importer. **2** *adj* importing (*firm etc*).

importation [ɛ̃pɔrtɑsjɔ̃] *nf* **(a)** importation, import, importing (*of goods*); **articles d'i.,** imports; **licence d'i.,** import licence; **l'i. de la cuisine japonaise,** the introduction of Japanese cooking; **(b)** (*produit*) import.

importer[1] [ɛ̃pɔrte] *vt* **(a)** to import (*goods*); to introduce (*custom etc*) (into a country); **(b)** *Ordinat* to import.

importer[2] *v* (*used only in the third person participles and inf*) **1** *vi* (*compter*) to be of importance *or* of consequence, to matter, to signify; **les choses qui importent,** (the) things that matter; **ton opinion m'importe beaucoup,** your opinion is very important to me; **les vacances lui importent peu,** holidays don't matter much to him; **que m'importe la vie!,** what is life to me!

2 *v impers* **(a) il importe que** + *sub,* it is important that ...; **il importe qu'elle soit consciente de ses responsabilités,** it is important that she should be *or Am* she be aware of her responsibilities; **ce qui importe c'est que tu viennes,** the important thing is for you to come; **peu importe que ...,** it doesn't matter much whether ...; **peu m'importe,** I don't mind, it's all the same to me; **peu importe le prix,** the price isn't important; **qu'importe?,** what does it matter?; **qu'importe qu'il vienne ou non?,** what does it matter whether he comes or not?; **que m'importe?,** what do I care?;

(b) faire qch n'importe comment/où/quand, to do sth no matter how/where/when, to do sth anyhow/anywhere/(at) any time; *Péj* **tu l'as fait n'importe comment,** you did it any old how; *Péj* **tu arrives n'importe quand et tu t'attends à ce que je sois là,** you arrive no matter when and expect to find me here; **n'importe,** never mind; **le vert ou le bleu? — n'importe,** the blue or the green? — it doesn't matter, either; **n'importe quelle autre personne,** anybody else; **venez n'importe quel jour,** come any day; **donnez-moi n'importe lequel,** give me any of them *or* whichever you like; **n'importe comment, c'est trop tard,** anyway, it's too late;

(c) n'importe qui, anyone, anybody; no matter who; **n'importe qui réagirait de la même manière,** anyone would have the same reaction; **coucher avec n'importe qui,** to sleep around; **je ne suis pas n'importe qui, je suis ta femme,** I'm not just anybody, I'm your wife; *F* **ce n'est pas n'importe qui,** he isn't just anybody; **n'importe quoi,** anything; no matter what; *Péj* **il dit n'importe quoi!,** he's talking nonsense.

import-export [ɛ̃pɔrɛkspɔr] *nf Com* import-export (business).

importun, -une [ɛ̃pɔrtœ̃, -yn] **1** *adj* importunate; obtrusive, troublesome, tiresome (*person*); unwelcome (*visitor*); ill-timed (*arrival*); **je crains de vous être i.,** I'm afraid I'm disturbing you. **2** *n* (*personne*) nuisance; **s'introduire en i. dans les conversations,** to intrude on other people's conversations.

importunément [ɛ̃pɔrtynemɑ̃] *adv* importunately.

importuner [ɛ̃pɔrtyne] *vt* **(a)** (*ennuyer*) to importune (*s.o.*), *F* to bother, to pester, to badger (*s.o.*); **ses questions m'importunent au plus haut point,** I find his questions extremely annoying; **(b)** (*déranger*) to disturb, to trouble, to inconvenience (*s.o.*); **j'espère que je ne vous importune pas,** I hope I'm not disturbing you.

importunité [ɛ̃pɔrtynite] *nf* importunity.

imposable [ɛ̃pozabl] *adj* **(a)** taxable (*person, income*); **(b)** rateable, assessable (*property*).

imposant [ɛ̃pozɑ̃] *adj* imposing (*figure, ceremony*); commanding, stately, dignified (*person*); **d'une stature imposante,** of imposing stature; **une imposante majorité,** an impressive majority.

imposé, -ée [ɛ̃poze] **1** *adj Com* **prix i.,** fixed price. **2** *n* taxpayer.

imposer [ɛ̃poze] **1** *vt* **(a)** to impose, to prescribe; to set (*task*); **i. des conditions,** to impose *or* dictate conditions; **i. une règle,** to lay down *or* enforce a rule; **i. silence à qn,** to impose silence on s.o.; **i. sa manière de voir,** to carry one's point, to force one's opinions on s.o.; **i. du respect à qn,** to inspire s.o. with respect; **i. le respect,** to command *or* compel respect;

(b) *Admin* **i. des droits sur qch,** to impose *or* put a tax on sth, to tax sth; **être lourdement imposé,** to be heavily taxed; **i. qn,** to tax s.o.; **i. qch,** to make sth taxable; **i. un immeuble,** to levy a rate on *or* to assess a building;

(c) to give, to assign (*name*);

(d) *Typ* to impose (*sheet*);

(e) *Rel* to lay on (*hands*).

2 *vi* **en i.,** to inspire respect *or* awe; **en i. à qn,** to impress s.o.

3 s'imposer *vpr* **(a)** (*faire reconnaître sa valeur*) to assert oneself; (*d'un sportif*) to win; **s'i. à l'attention,** to command attention; **la conviction s'imposa à mon esprit que ...,** the conviction forced itself upon me that ...; **elle s'est imposée par sa compétence,** she got where she is through ability; **il s'est imposé sans difficulté,** he found it easy to assert himself;

(b) s'i. à qn, (*déranger*) to foist *or* thrust *or* force oneself upon s.o.; (*importuner*) to impose on s.o.; **je ne voulais pas m'i.,** I didn't want to impose;

(c) (*être nécessaire*) to be indispensable; **la discrétion s'impose,** discretion is imperative *or* essential; **prendre les mesures qui s'imposent,** to take the necessary steps; **une visite au Louvre s'impose,** you *or* we *etc* must visit the Louvre, *F* a visit to the Louvre is a must;

(d) (*se contraindre*) **s'i. un labeur,** to set oneself *or* to undertake a task; **s'i. de faire qch,** to make it a duty *or* a rule to do sth.

imposition [ɛ̃pozisjɔ̃] *nf* **(a)** imposing, laying down (*of conditions*); setting, prescribing (*of task*); **(b)** imposition (of tax), taxation; **(c)** *Typ* imposing, imposition; **(d)** assessment (*of property*); **(e)** *Rel* laying on of hands.

impossibilité [ɛ̃pɔsibilite] *nf* impossibility; **être** *ou* **se trouver dans l'i. matérielle de faire qch,** to find it impossible to do sth; (*malgré ses prévisions*) to be unavoidably prevented from doing sth; **accomplir des impossibilités,** to do the impossible.

impossible [ɛ̃pɔsibl] **1** *adj* **(a)** impossible; **cela m'est i.,** it's not possible for me, I can't; **il m'est i. de le faire,** I can't (possibly) do it; **il m'est i. de ne pas croire que ...,** I can't help believing that ...; **c'est i. à faire,** it can't be done; **il est i. qu'il revienne avant lundi,** he can't possibly be back before Monday; **c'est matériellement i.,** it's (physically) impossible; **la résolution du problème est i.,** it is impossible to solve the problem, the problem can't be solved; **i. n'est pas français,** ≈ there's no such word as can't; **vous lui rendez la vie i.,** you're making life impossible for him, you're making his life a misery; **tu est i.!,** you're impossible!;

(b) *F* extravagant, absurd; ridiculous (*hat etc*); **il a fallu nous lever à une heure i.,** we had to get up at an unearthly hour; **encore une de tes histoires impossibles!,** another one of your incredible stories!

2 *nm* **(a) l'i.,** the impossible; **tenter l'i.,** to attempt the impossibe; **il a fait l'i. pour nous secourir,** he did his utmost *or* did everything possible to help us; *Prov* **à l'i. nul n'est tenu,** one can't do the impossible;

(b) si par i. il est encore vivant, if, by some remote chance *or* some miracle, he is still alive.

imposte [ɛ̃pɔst] *nf Archit* **(a)** impost (*of bearing arch*), springer; **(b)** (*fenêtre*) fanlight, *US* transom (window).

imposteur [ɛ̃pɔstœr] *nm* impostor.

imposture [ɛ̃pɔstyr] *nf* imposture.

impôt [ɛ̃po] *nm* **(a)** tax; **i. foncier,** land tax; **impôts locaux,** *Br* rates, *US* local tax; **i. sur le revenu,** income tax; **i. retenu à la source,** tax deducted at source; *Br* ≈ pay as you earn, PAYE, *Am* ≈ pay as you go; **i. sur les plus-values,** capital gains tax; **payer mille francs d'impôts,** to pay a thousand francs in tax(es); **déclaration d'impôts,** income tax form *or* statement *or* return; **faire sa déclaration d'impôts,** to fill out one's income tax form, *F* to do one's taxes; **frapper qch d'un i.,** to tax sth, to put a tax on sth; **i. sur les grandes fortunes** *ou* **sur la fortune,** wealth tax; **(b)** (*taxes*) taxes, taxation.

impotence [ɛpɔtɑ̃s] *nf* disability; (*causée par la vieillesse*) infirmity.
impotent, -ente [ɛpɔtɑ̃, -ɑ̃t] **1** *adj* disabled, crippled; **être i. de la jambe gauche,** to have lost the use of the left leg; (*boiter*) to be lame in the left leg. **2** *n* disabled person, cripple; **les impotents,** the disabled.
impraticabilité [ɛ̃pratikabilite] *nf* impracticability.
impraticable [ɛ̃pratikabl] *adj* **(a)** (*irréalisable*) impracticable, unfeasible, unworkable, impractical (*plan*); **(b)** (*où l'on ne peut pas passer*) impassable; **chemin i. aux** *ou* **pour les automobiles,** road unfit for motor vehicles; **(c)** *Sp* (*ground*) unplayable, unfit for play.
imprécation [ɛ̃prekɑsjɔ̃] *nf* curse, *Fml* imprecation.
imprécatoire [ɛ̃prekatwar] *adj* imprecatory.
imprécis [ɛ̃presi] *adj* **(a)** (*vague*) vague, imprecise, indefinite; **(b)** inaccurate (*fire*).
imprécision [ɛ̃presizjɔ̃] *nf* **(a)** (*caractère vague*) imprecision; looseness (*of terminology etc*); vagueness (*of statement etc*); **(b)** inaccuracy (*of fire*).
imprégnation [ɛ̃preɲɑsjɔ̃] *nf* impregnation, permeation.
imprégné [ɛ̃preɲe] *adj* impregnated; **un regard i. de tristesse,** a look full of sadness.
imprégner [ɛ̃preɲe] *v* (**j'imprègne; j'imprégnerai**) **1** *vt* to impregnate, to permeate (**de,** with); *Fig* **imprégné de préjugés,** (*personne, livre, film etc*) full of prejudice; **être imprégné d'une atmosphère,** (*d'un livre, d'un film*) to be full of atmosphere. **2 s'imprégner** *vpr* to become impregnated *or* permeated (**de,** with); **s'i. d'eau,** to be saturated *or* soaked with water; *Fig* **s'i. d'un auteur,** to immerse oneself in an author; **s'i. d'anglais,** to immerse oneself in English.
imprenable [ɛ̃prənabl] *adj* impregnable; **vue i.,** (*from house*) view that cannot be obstructed.
impréparation [ɛ̃preparɑsjɔ̃] *nf* unpreparedness.
impresario [ɛ̃presarjo] *nm* impresario; business manager (*for filmstar etc*).
imprescriptibilité [ɛ̃preskriptibilite] *nf Jur* imprescriptibility, indefeasibility (*of a right etc*).
imprescriptible [ɛ̃preskriptibl] *adj Jur* imprescriptible, indefeasible (*right etc*).
impression [ɛ̃presjɔ̃] *nf* **(a)** (*reproduction*) *Typ Tex* printing; **livre à l'i.,** book in (the) *or* at press; **faute d'i.,** misprint; **troisième i. d'un livre,** third impression *or* printing of a book; **i. en couleurs,** colour *or US* color printing; *Phot* **double i.,** double exposure; *Ordinat* **i. rapide,** draft;
(b) (*sensation*) (mental) impression; **il nous a fait** *ou* **il nous a donné l'i. que ...,** he gave us the impression that ...; **faire i.,** to make an impression; **j'ai l'i. de l'avoir déjà vue** *ou* **que je l'ai déjà vue,** I've an idea *or* a feeling that I've seen her before; **ça fait une drôle d'i. de s'entendre parler,** it's a funny feeling, hearing yourself speak; **j'ai l'impression qu'elle est assez timide,** I have the impression that *or* my impression of her is that she's rather shy; **il ne m'a pas fait une grande i.,** he did not make a good impression on me; **l'i. que j'ai d'elle n'est pas excellente,** I do not have an excellent opinion of her;
(c) (*image*) print; **i. en couleurs,** colour print;
(d) (*première couche*) primer, undercoat;
(e) (*motif*) **tissu à impressions,** printed *or* patterned material;
(f) *Vieilli* impression, imprint (*on wax, ground etc*); **i. de pas,** footprint.
impressionnabilité [ɛ̃presjɔnabilite] *nf* **(a)** (*sensibilité*) impressionability; **(b)** *Phot* sensitivity.
impressionnable [ɛ̃presjɔnabl] *adj* **(a)** (*sensible*) impressionable; **(b)** *Phot* sensitive (*plate etc*).
impressionnant [ɛ̃presjɔnɑ̃] *adj* impressive; sensational (*news*); spectacular (*effect*).
impressionner [ɛ̃presjɔne] *vt* **(a)** (*frapper, bouleverser*) to impress, to affect, to move, to make an impression (up)on (*s.o.*); (*d'une mauvaise nouvelle*) to upset; **il ne faut pas se laisser i.,** (*par ses grands airs*) don't let yourself be overawed; **vision** *ou* **vue qui impressionne,** impressive sight; **(b)** *Opt* to act on (*the retina*); *Phot* to produce an image on (*sensitized paper etc*); to expose (*film*).
impressionnisme [ɛ̃presjɔnism] *nm Beaux-Arts* impressionism.
impressionniste [ɛ̃presjɔnist] *Beaux-Arts* **1** *adj* impressionist(ic). **2** *n* impressionist.
imprévisibilité [ɛ̃previzibilite] *nf* unpredictability.
imprévisible [ɛ̃previzibl] *adj* unforeseeable, unpredictable.
imprévoyance [ɛ̃prevwajɑ̃s] *nf* lack of foresight, improvidence.
imprévoyant [ɛ̃prevwajɑ̃] *adj* lacking in foresight, improvident.
imprévu [ɛ̃prevy] **1** *adj* unforeseen, unexpected. **2** *nm* **(a)** (*caractère*) unexpected character (*of event*); **elle aime l'i.,** she likes the unexpected; **(b)** (*incident*) unexpected *or* unforeseen event; **sauf i., à moins d'i.,** barring accidents, unless something unforeseen happens; **en cas d'i.,** in (case of) an emergency.
imprimable [ɛ̃primabl] *adj* printable.
imprimante [ɛ̃primɑ̃t] *nf Ordinat* printer; **i. par points** *ou* **matricielle,** dot matrix (printer); **i. à impact,** impact printer; **i. page par page,** page printer; **i. laser,** laser printer; **i. à jet d'encre,** ink-jet (printer).
imprimatur [ɛ̃primatyr] *nm inv* imprimatur.
imprimé [ɛ̃prime] **1** *adj* printed. **2** *nm* **(a)** (*document etc*) printed paper, book; **remplir un i.,** to fill in a form; **imprimés,** printed matter; **département/catalogue des imprimés,** (*in library*) department/catalogue of printed books; **(b)** *Ordinat* **i. ligne par ligne,** line printout; **carte de circuits imprimés,** printed circuit board; **(c)** *Tex* print; **un i. à fleurs/à motifs géométriques,** a flower/geometric print.
imprimer [ɛ̃prime] *vt* **(a)** (*marquer*) to (im)print, to impress, to stamp (*sth on sth*); *Tex* to print (*material*); *Fig* **un moment imprimé dans mon cœur/ma mémoire,** a moment engraved on my heart/in my memory; **indienne imprimée,** printed cotton, cotton print; *Électron* **circuit imprimé,** printed circuit; **(b)** *Typ* to print; to publish (*book*); *Ordinat* to print (off); **presse à i.,** printing press; **il aime à se voir imprimé,** he likes to see himself in print; **(c)** to communicate (*direction etc*); **i. le mouvement à un corps,** to impart *or* transmit motion to a body.
imprimerie [ɛ̃primri] *nf* **(a)** (*technique*) (art of) printing; **caractères d'i.,** block capitals; **(b)** (*atelier, usine*) printing house, printing works, (printing) press, printery.
imprimeur [ɛ̃primœr] *nm* **(a)** (*propriétaire*) (master) printer; (*ouvrier*) (working) printer; **i.-libraire,** printer and bookseller; **i.-éditeur,** printer and publisher; **(b)** *Tex* **i. d'indiennes,** calico printer.
improbabilité [ɛ̃prɔbabilite] *nf* improbability.
improbable [ɛ̃prɔbabl] *adj* improbable, unlikely.
improbité [ɛ̃prɔbite] *nf Litt* dishonesty, lack of integrity.
improductif, -ive [ɛ̃prɔdyktif, -iv] *adj* unproductive.
improductivité [ɛ̃prɔdyktivite] *nf* unproductiveness.
impromptu [ɛ̃prɔ̃pty] **1** *adv* without preparation, impromptu. **2** *adj* unpremeditated (*departure etc*); impromptu (*meal etc*); impromptu, extempore, off the cuff (*speech etc*). **3** *nm Th Mus* impromptu.
imprononçable [ɛ̃prɔnɔ̃sabl] *adj* unpronounceable.
impropre [ɛ̃prɔpr] *adj* **(a)** inappropriate, incorrect (*term*); **(b) i. à (faire) qch,** unfit *or* unsuitable for sth, unfit to do sth; **i. à la consommation,** unfit for human consumption.
improprement [ɛ̃prɔprəmɑ̃] *adv* improperly, incorrectly.
impropriété [ɛ̃prɔprijete] *nf* impropriety; inappropriateness, incorrectness (*of word*).
improuvable [ɛ̃pruvabl] *adj* unprovable.
improvisateur, -trice [ɛ̃prɔvizatœr, -tris] *n Mus etc* improviser.
improvisation [ɛ̃prɔvizɑsjɔ̃] *nf Mus etc* improvisation; **i. sur un thème,** improvisation on a theme; **faire une i.,** to improvise.
improvisé [ɛ̃prɔvize] *adj* improvised, extempore, off the cuff (*speech etc*); impromptu (*dance*); *Sp* scratch (*team*); **organiser une fête avec des moyens improvisés,** to organize an impromptu celebration.
improviser [ɛ̃prɔvize] **1** *vt* to improvise; **i. un discours,** to make an impromptu *or* extempore speech, to speak off the cuff, *F* to ad-lib; **on dut m'i. infirmière pour la circonstance,** they appointed me nurse for the occasion. **2** *vi* to improvise; **i. à l'orgue,** to improvise on the organ. **3 s'improviser** *vpr* **l'organisation, ça ne s'improvise pas,** organisation isn't something you can improvise.
improviste (à l') [alɛ̃prɔvist] *adv* unexpectedly, unawares, without any warning; **prendre qn à l'i.,** to take s.o. unawares *or* by surprise; **visite à l'i.,** surprise visit.
imprudemment [ɛ̃prydamɑ̃] *adv* imprudently, rashly, recklessly, unwisely.
imprudence [ɛ̃prydɑ̃s] *nf* imprudence, foolhardiness, rashness, recklessness; **commettre une i.,** to act rashly *or* imprudently; **j'ai peur qu'il fasse une i.,** I'm afraid he may do something rash; *Jur* **homicide par i.,** manslaughter (by negligence).
imprudent, -ente [ɛ̃prydɑ̃, -ɑ̃t] **1** *adj* imprudent, foolhardy, rash, reckless, unwise. **2** *n* imprudent *or* rash *or* reckless person.

impubère [ɛ̃pybɛr] **1** *adj* impubescent; **2** *n Jur* impubescent minor.
impubliable [ɛ̃pyblijabl] *adj* unpublishable.
impudemment [ɛ̃pydamɑ̃] *adv* impudently; (*avec cynisme*) brazenly, shamelessly.
impudence [ɛ̃pydɑ̃s] *nf* **(a)** impudence; (*effronterie*) effrontery; (*cynisme*) shamelessness; **quelle i.!,** what impudence!; **(b)** (*action, parole*) impudent action *or* remark.
impudent [ɛ̃pydɑ̃] *adj* impudent, insolent; (*cynique*) shameless, brazen.
impudeur [ɛ̃pydœr] *nf* shamelessness, immodesty.
impudicité [ɛ̃pydisite] *nf* shamelessness; (*obscénité*) lewdness.
impudique [ɛ̃pydik] *adj* shameless; (*obscène*) lewd.
impudiquement [ɛ̃pydikmɑ̃] *adv* shamelessly; (*d'une manière obscène*) lewdly.
impuissance [ɛ̃pɥisɑ̃s] *nf* **(a)** (*incapacité*) impotence, powerlessness, helplessness; **i. à faire qch,** powerlessness *or* inability to do sth; **je suis dans l'i. de le sauver,** it is beyond my power to save him; **(b)** *Méd* impotence (*of man*).
impuissant [ɛ̃pɥisɑ̃] **1** *adj* **(a)** (*incapable*) impotent, powerless, helpless; **i. à faire qch,** powerless *or* unable to do sth; **(b)** unavailing, ineffective (*effort etc*); **(c)** *Méd* impotent (*man*). **2** *nm Méd* impotent man.
impulsif, -ive [ɛ̃pylsif, -iv] *adj* impulsive.
impulsion [ɛ̃pylsjɔ̃] *nf* **(a)** (*influence*) impulse; **sous l'i. du moment,** on the spur of the moment; **(b)** (*élan*) impulse, impetus, boost; **donner de l'i. au commerce,** to give a boost to trade; **les affaires ont reçu une nouvelle i.,** business has received fresh impetus *or* shows renewed activity; **(c)** *Tech* impulse; **force d'i.,** impulsive force; *El* **i. de courant,** current impulse; **radar à impulsions,** pulse radar.
impulsivité [ɛ̃pylsivite] *nf* impulsiveness.
impunément [ɛ̃pynemɑ̃] *adv* with impunity.
impuni [ɛ̃pyni] *adj* unpunished.
impunité [ɛ̃pynite] *nf* impunity; **agir en toute i.,** to act with impunity.
impur [ɛ̃pyr] *adj* (*eau etc*) impure, foul, tainted; (*personne*) (morally) impure; *Rel* unclean (*flesh etc*).
impurement [ɛ̃pyrmɑ̃] *adv* impurely.
impureté [ɛ̃pyrte] *nf* **(a)** impurity, foulness (*of water etc*); (*d'une personne*) (moral) impurity; *Rel* uncleanness; **(b) impuretés,** impurities (*in water etc*).
imputabilité [ɛ̃pytabilite] *nf* imputability.
imputable [ɛ̃pytabl] *adj* **(a)** imputable, ascribable, attributable (**à,** to); **erreur i. à la distraction,** mistake caused by absent-mindedness; **(b)** *Fin* **frais imputables sur un compte,** expenses chargeable to an account.
imputation [ɛ̃pytɑsjɔ̃] *nf* **(a)** (*accusation*) imputation, charge; **imputations calomnieuses,** slanderous charges; **(b)** *Com* charge, charging (*of expenses etc*); **i. d'une somme sur une quantité,** deduction of a sum from a quota.
imputer [ɛ̃pyte] *vt* **(a)** to ascribe, to attribute (*crime etc*) (**à,** to); **ils l'ont imputé à son ignorance,** they attributed it to *or* put it down to his ignorance; **(b)** *Com* **i. qch sur qch,** to charge sth to sth; **i. des frais sur un compte,** to charge expenses to an account.
imputrescible [ɛ̃pytresibl] *adj* incorruptible; (*polypropylène etc*) indestructible.
in [in] *adj inv F* in; **être in,** to be in; **les gens in,** the in crowd.
inabordable [inabɔrdabl] *adj* (*endroit*) unapproachable, inaccessible; (*personne*) unapproachable; (*prix*) prohibitive.
inabrogeable [inabrɔʒabl] *adj* unrepealable.
inaccentué [inaksɑ̃tɥe] *adj* **(a)** unaccented (*vowel*); **(b)** unstressed (*syllable etc*).
inacceptable [inakseptabl] *adj* unacceptable, objectionable.
inaccessibilité [inaksesibilite] *nf* inaccessibility.
inaccessible [inaksesibl] *adj* **(a)** (*inabordable*) inaccessible; **dans une région i.,** in an out-of-the-way place, *F* at the back of beyond; **se fixer un objectif i.,** to set oneself an unattainable goal; **i. au grand public,** (*livre*) not accessible to the general public; **elle est i.,** (*très occupée*) she can't be disturbed; (*elle voyage*) she can't be reached; **(b) i. à la pitié,** incapable of pity; **i. à la flatterie,** proof against *or* impervious to flattery.
inaccompli [inakɔ̃pli] *adj* unaccomplished, unfulfilled.
inaccordable [inakɔrdabl] *adj* **(a)** irreconcilable (*facts*); **(b)** inadmissible (*request etc*).
inaccoutumé [inakutyme] *adj* **(a)** (*inhabitué*) unaccustomed, unused (**à,** to); **(b)** (*inhabituel*) unusual; **une agitation inaccoutumée,** (*dans les rues etc*) unusual activity.
inachevé [inaʃve] *adj* unfinished, uncompleted.
inachèvement [inaʃɛvmɑ̃] *nm* incompletion.
inactif, -ive [inaktif, -iv] *adj* (*personne*) inactive, idle; **la population inactive,** the non-working population, *Br* the unwaged; *Com* **marché i.,** dull market.
inaction [inaksjɔ̃] *nf* inaction, idleness.
inactivité [inaktivite] *nf* inactivity; *Com* dullness (*of market*); **période d'i.,** period of inactivity; *Com* dead period; **en i.,** *Admin* (temporarily) unemployed; *Mil* not on the active list.
inadaptation [inadaptɑsjɔ̃] *nf* maladjustment.
inadapté, -ée [inadapte] **1** *adj* maladjusted (*person*); **il est i.,** he's a (social) misfit; **il est i. pour cet emploi,** he's not suited to the job; **vie inadaptée à ses besoins,** life unsuited to one's needs. **2** *n* maladjusted person; **les inadaptés,** the maladjusted, the social misfits.
inadéquat [inadekwa] *adj* inadequate.
inadéquation [inadekwɑsjɔ̃] *nf* unsuitability.
inadmissibilité [inadmisibilite] *nf* inadmissibility.
inadmissible [inadmisibl] *adj* inadmissible (*request etc*); **votre proposition est i.,** your proposal is out of the question.
inadvertance (par) [parinadvertɑ̃s] *adv* inadvertently, by mistake.
inaliénabilité [inaljenabilite] *nf Jur* inalienability, indefeasibility (*of right*).
inaliénable [inaljenabl] *adj Jur* inalienable, indefeasible (*right*).
inalliable [inaljabl] *adj Métal* that cannot be alloyed, nonalloyable.
inaltérabilité [inalterabilite] *nf* **(a)** resistance to deterioration, permanence (*of material*); fastness (*of colour*); **l'i. à l'air de ce métal le rend idéal,** this metal is ideal because it is not affected by air; **(b)** unalterableness (*of planetary motion etc*); **(c)** unfailingness (*of good humour etc*); **l'i. de votre bonté,** your unfailing kindness.
inaltérable [inalterabl] *adj* **(a)** that does not deteriorate, permanent; fast (*colour*); **i. à l'air/l'eau,** unaffected by air/water; **(b)** unalterable (*course of the stars etc*); **(c)** unfailing, unvarying (*good humour etc*).
inaltéré [inaltere] *adj* unspoilt, unimpaired; unweathered (*stone etc*).
inamical, -aux [inamikal, -o] *adj* unfriendly.
inamovibilité [inamɔvibilite] *nf Admin* fixity of tenure; irremovability (*of judge etc*).
inamovible [inamɔvibl] *adj* irremovable; *Jur* holding appointment for life; (*post*) held for life, *Univ* tenured; *F* **il est vraiment i.,** he's a permanent fixture.
inanimé [inanime] *adj* **(a)** (*matière etc*) inanimate, lifeless; **(b)** (*ayant perdu conscience*) senseless, unconscious; **tomber i.,** to fall down unconscious, to faint.
inanité [inanite] *nf* inanity; futility (*of effort*).
inanition [inanisjɔ̃] *nf* starvation; **mourir d'i.,** to die of starvation, to starve to death.
inapaisable [inapezabl] *adj* inappeasable (*hunger etc*); unquenchable (*thirst*); (*grief*) that nothing can assuage.
inapaisé [inapeze] *adj* unappeased (*hunger etc*); unquenched (*thirst*); unassuaged (*grief etc*).
inaperçu [inapersy] *adj* unseen, unobserved, unnoticed; **passer i.,** to escape notice, to pass unnoticed; *Euph* **cet événement ne passa pas i.,** the event did not go unnoticed.
inappétence [inapetɑ̃s] *nf Méd* lack of appetite.
inapplicable [inaplikabl] *adj* inapplicable.
inapplication [inaplikɑsjɔ̃] *nf* **(a)** (*d'une personne*) lack of application; **(b) i. d'une loi,** failure to put a law into effect.
inappliqué, -ée [inaplike] *adj* **(a)** (*personne*) lacking in application, careless; **(b)** unapplied (*method etc*); (*loi*) in abeyance.
inappréciable [inapresjabl] *adj* **(a)** inappreciable (*quantity etc*); imperceptible (*difference etc*); **(b)** *Fig* (*sans prix*) inestimable, invaluable, priceless; **un conseil i.,** invaluable advice.
inapprécié [inapresje] *adj* unappreciated.
inapprivoisable [inaprivwazabl] *adj* untamable.
inapte [inapt] **1** *adj* **(a)** (*incapable*) unfit, unfitted (**à,** for); (*à un emploi*) unsuited (**à,** to); **i. à faire qch,** incapable of doing sth; **(b)** *Mil* unfit (*for military service*). **2** *nmpl surtout Mil* **les inaptes,** the unfit; (*blessés*) the incapacitated.
inaptitude [inaptityd] *nf* inaptitude; unfitness (**à,** for); incapacity (*for work, military service etc*).
inarticulé [inartikyle] *adj* **(a)** inarticulate (*sound etc*); **(b)** not jointed; *Zool* inarticulate(d).

inassimilable [inasimilabl] *adj* unassimilable.
inassouvi [inasuvi] *adj* unsatiated, unappeased, unsatisfied (*hunger etc*); unslaked, unquenched (*thirst etc*); unfulfilled (*desire*).
inassouvissable [inasuvisabl] *adj* insatiable.
inattaquable [inatakabl] *adj* unassailable (*position etc*); unquestionable (*right etc*); unimpeachable (*evidence etc*); *Ch etc* **i. par les acides,** acid-proof, acid-resisting.
inattendu [inatɑ̃dy] *adj* unexpected, unforeseen.
inattentif, -ive [inatɑ̃tif, -iv] *adj* inattentive (**à,** to); (*négligent*) unobservant, heedless (**à,** of).
inattention [inatɑ̃sjɔ̃] *nf* carelessness; inattention (**à,** to); negligence, unobservance (**à,** of); **faute d'i.,** slip; *Péj* careless mistake; **se tromper par i.,** to make a careless mistake.
inaudible [inodibl] *adj* inaudible.
inaugural, -aux [inogyral, -o] *adj* inaugural; **voyage i.,** maiden voyage.
inauguration [inogyrasjɔ̃] *nf* inauguration; (official) opening (*of factory etc*); unveiling (*of statue*); **discours d'i.,** inaugural speech.
inaugurer [inogyre] *vt* to inaugurate (*building etc*); to unveil (*statue etc*); to open (*fête etc*); to usher in (*epoch*).
inauthenticité [inotɑ̃tisite] *nf* unauthentic nature.
inauthentique [inotɑ̃tik] *adj* unauthentic.
inavouable [inavwabl] *adj* shameful.
inavoué [inavwe] *adj* unacknowledged; (*délit etc*) unconfessed.
Inca [ɛ̃ka] **1** *adj inv* Inca. **2** *n* Inca.
incalculable [ɛ̃kalkylabl] *adj* incalculable; **nombre i. de ...,** countless number of ... .
incandescence [ɛ̃kɑ̃desɑ̃s] *nf* incandescence; *Él* **lampe à i.,** incandescent lamp.
incandescent [ɛ̃kɑ̃desɑ̃] *adj* incandescent; *Fig* glowing (*imagination*).
incantation [ɛ̃kɑ̃tasjɔ̃] *nf* incantation.
incantatoire [ɛ̃kɑ̃tatwar] *adj* magical, spell-binding; incantatory.
incapable [ɛ̃kapabl] **1** *adj* **(a)** incapable, incompetent (*person*); **(b) i. de faire qch,** incapable of doing sth; (*parce qu'incompétent*) unable to do sth; (*par impossibilité physique*) unfit to do sth; **i. d'amour,** incapable of love. **2** *n* **c'est un i.,** he's useless *or* no use.
incapacité [ɛ̃kapasite] *nf* **(a)** incompetence (*of person*); **i. de faire qch,** incapability of doing sth, incapacity to do sth; inability to do sth; **(b)** (*invalidité*) disability; *Admin* **i. permanente,** permanent disablement; **i. de travail,** industrial disablement; **(c)** *Jur* **i. légale d'exercice des mineurs,** disability *or* incapacity of a minor.
incarcération [ɛ̃karserasjɔ̃] *nf* incarceration, imprisonment.
incarcérer [ɛ̃karsere] *vt* (**j'incarcère; j'incarcérerai**) to incarcerate, to imprison.
incarnat [ɛ̃karna] **1** *adj* rosy pink, flesh-coloured. **2** *nm* rosy tint (*of dawn*); rosiness (*of complexion*).
incarnation [ɛ̃karnasjɔ̃] *nf* (*de personne*) incarnation; *Fig* incarnation, embodiment (*of vice etc*).
incarné [ɛ̃karne] *adj* **(a)** *Rel* incarnate; *Fig* **la vertu incarnée,** virtue incarnate *or* personified; **(b)** *Méd* ingrowing (*nail*).
incarner [ɛ̃karne] **1** *vt* **(a)** to incarnate, to embody, to personify; **(b)** *Th etc* to play the part of (*person*). **2 s'incarner** *vpr* **(a)** *Rel etc* to become incarnate; **(b)** *Méd* (*of nail*) to become ingrown.
incartade [ɛ̃kartad] *nf* **(a)** (*mauvaise conduite*) prank; indiscretion; **(b)** *Équitation* sudden swerve (*of horse*).
incassable [ɛ̃kasabl] *adj* unbreakable.
incendiaire [ɛ̃sɑ̃djɛr] **1** *adj* incendiary (*bomb*); *Fig* inflammatory (*speech*). **2** *n* (*personne*) incendiary, arsonist, fire raiser; *Psy* pyromaniac.
incendie [ɛ̃sɑ̃di] *nm* (outbreak of) fire, *Fml* conflagration; **i. de forêt,** forest fire; **échelle d'i.,** fire escape; **pompe à i.,** fire engine; **i. volontaire,** arson; **provoquer un i.,** to start a fire; *Jur* to commit arson; *Litt* **l'i. du soleil couchant,** the blaze of the setting sun.
incendié, -ée [ɛ̃sɑ̃dje] **1** *adj* (*en feu*) on fire, burning; (*en ruine*) burnt down. **2** *n* victim of a fire.
incendier [ɛ̃sɑ̃dje] *vt* to set (*sth*) on fire, to set fire to (*sth*); (*détruire*) to burn (*sth*) down; *Litt* to set (*sky etc*) ablaze; *Fig* to fire (*imagination*); *Arg* to tell (*s.o.*) off, to tear (*s.o.*) off a strip; **se faire i.,** to get a telling off.
incertain [ɛ̃sɛrtɛ̃] *adj* uncertain, doubtful; dubious (*result etc*); unsettled (*weather*); unreliable (*memory*); **couleur incertaine,** vague colour; **d'un âge i.,** of uncertain age; **à une date incertaine,** at a date to be decided; **i. de qch,** (*d'une personne*) uncertain *or* unsure of *or* about sth; (*qui n'a pas encore pris de décision*) undecided about sth.
incertitude [ɛ̃sɛrtityd] *nf* **(a)** uncertainty, doubt; dubiousness (*of result etc*); **(b)** indecision, perplexity (*of mind*); **être dans l'i.,** to be in a state of uncertainty (**quant à,** about).
incessamment [ɛ̃sesamɑ̃] *adv* **(a)** immediately, without delay, at once; **elle arrivera i.,** she'll be arriving (at) any moment; **(b)** *Arch* unceasingly, incessantly.
incessant [ɛ̃sesɑ̃] *adj* unceasing, incessant, ceaseless.
incessibilité [ɛ̃sesibilite] *nf Jur* inalienability.
incessible [ɛ̃sesibl] *adj* (*d'un billet etc*) non-transferable, not negotiable; *Jur* inalienable (*right*).
inceste [ɛ̃sɛst] *nm* incest.
incestueux [ɛ̃sɛstɥø] *adj* incestuous (*person*); **relation incestueuse,** incestuous relationship; **enfant i.,** child of an incestuous relationship.
inchangé [ɛ̃ʃɑ̃ʒe] *adj* unchanged (*price etc*).
inchangeable [ɛ̃ʃɑ̃ʒabl] *adj* unchangeable.
inchantable [ɛ̃ʃɑ̃tabl] *adj* unsingable.
inchauffable [ɛ̃ʃofabl] *adj* (*pièce etc*) which cannot be heated.
inchavirable [ɛ̃ʃavirabl] *adj* uncapsizable, self-righting (*boat*).
incidemment [ɛ̃sidamɑ̃] *adv* incidentally.
incidence [ɛ̃sidɑ̃s] *nf* **(a)** *Méd* incidence (*of disease*); **(b)** (*influence*) influence; (*répercussion*) repercussion; (*impact*) effect, impact; **quelle i. aura la démission du ministre sur la situation?,** how will the Minister's resignation affect the situation?; **(c)** *Tech* incidence; *Opt* **angle d'i.,** angle of incidence.
incident [ɛ̃sidɑ̃] **1** *adj* **(a)** incidental (*question etc*); **(b)** *Opt* incident (*ray*). **2** *nm* **(a)** (*événement*) incident, occurrence, happening; **(b)** *Jur* point of law; **(c)** (*problème*) difficulty, hitch; (*accident*) mishap; **i. technique,** technical hitch; **i. diplomatique,** diplomatic incident.
incinérateur [ɛ̃sineratœr] *nm* incinerator.
incinération [ɛ̃sinerasjɔ̃] *nf* incineration; (*d'une personne*) cremation.
incinérer [ɛ̃sinere] *vt* (**j'incinère; j'incinérerai**) to incinerate, to burn to ashes; (*une personne*) to cremate.
incirconcis [ɛ̃sirkɔ̃si] *adj* uncircumcised.
incise [ɛ̃siz] *nf Gram* interpolated clause, incidental clause.
inciser [ɛ̃size] *vt* to incise, to cut (*sth*), to make an incision in (*sth*); to lance (*boil*); to tap (*tree*) (for resin).
incisif, -ive [ɛ̃sizif, -iv] **1** *adj* **(a)** incisive, sharp, cutting (*remark etc*); (*personne*) incisive; **(b) dent incisive,** incisor tooth. **2** *nf* **incisive,** incisor tooth.
incision [ɛ̃sizjɔ̃] *nf* **(a)** (*action*) incision, cutting; tapping (*of tree*) (for resin); lancing (*of boil*); **(b)** (*coupure*) incision, cut; **faire une i.,** to make an incision (**dans qch,** in sth).
incitateur, -trice [ɛ̃sitatœr, -tris] *n* inciter (**à,** to).
incitation [ɛ̃sitasjɔ̃] *nf* incitement (**à,** to).
inciter [ɛ̃site] *vt* to incite, to urge (on); **i. qn à faire qch,** to incite *or* prompt s.o. to do sth; **cette réponse m'incite à la prudence,** the answer inclines me to be cautious; **son attitude n'incite pas à l'aider,** his attitude does not incline you to help him.
incivil [ɛ̃sivil] *adj* uncivil, rude.
incivilement [ɛ̃sivilmɑ̃] *adj* uncivilly, rudely.
incivilisable [ɛ̃sivilizabl] *adj* which cannot be civilized.
incivilité [ɛ̃sivilite] *nf* **(a)** (*manque de politesse*) incivility, rudeness; **(b)** (*remarque, action impolie*) rude remark *or* action.
incivique [ɛ̃sivik] *adj Vieilli* with no sense of civic duty.
inclassable [ɛ̃klasabl] *adj* unclass(ifi)able.
inclémence [ɛ̃klemɑ̃s] *nf* inclemency.
inclément [ɛ̃klemɑ̃] *adj* (*temps*) inclement.
inclinable [ɛ̃klinabl] *adj* (*dossier de siège*) reclining.
inclinaison [ɛ̃klinɛzɔ̃] *nf* **(a)** (*action*) tilting, canting; **(b)** incline, gradient, slope (*of hill etc*); inclination (*of line etc*); pitch, slant, cant (*of roof etc*); tilt (*of head, hat etc*); heel, list (*of ship*); rake (*of mast*); dip (*of magnetic needle*); angle (*of trajectory*); **comble à forte/faible i.,** high-/low-pitched roof; **i. magnétique,** (magnetic) declination, magnetic variation; **degré d'i. d'une courbe,** steepness of a curve.
inclination [ɛ̃klinasjɔ̃] *nf* **(a)** *Fig* inclination, tendency, propensity, bent; **avoir de l'i. à faire qch,** to be inclined to do sth; **suivre ses inclinations,** to follow one's inclinations; **montrer de l'i. pour la musique/le français/*etc*,** to show an inclination for music/French/*etc*; **avoir de l'i. pour qch,** to like *or* have a liking for sth; *Vieilli* **mariage d'i.,** love match; **(b)** bending, bow(ing) (*of body*); nod (*of head*).

incliné [ɛ̃kline] *adj* **(a)** (*penché*) sloping, tilting, tilted; **la tête inclinée,** with bowed head; **plan i.,** inclined plane; **(b)** *Fig* **i. à (faire) qch,** inclined *or* disposed to (do) sth.
incliner [ɛ̃kline] **1** *vt* **(a)** (*pencher*) to incline; to slant, to slope, to cant; to tip up, to tilt (*plank etc*); to bend, to bow, to incline (*the head etc*); **i. la tête,** to nod (one's head);
(b) *Fig* **i. qn à faire qch,** to predispose *or* influence s.o. in favour of doing sth; **i. qn à la prudence,** to predispose s.o. to caution.
2 *vi* **(a)** (*of wall etc*) to lean, to slope; (*of ship*) to list;
(b) *Fig* **i. à la pitié,** to incline *or* be disposed to pity; **i. vers** *ou* **à la modération,** to be disposed to moderation; **i. à faire qch,** to be *or* feel inclined to do sth.
3 s'incliner *vpr* **(a)** to slant, to slope; (*of ship*) to heel (over); (*of aircraft*) to bank;
(b) (*se pencher*) to bend over *or* down; to bow (down) (**devant,** before); **s'i. devant les arguments de qn,** to bow *or* yield to s.o.'s arguments; **s'i. devant qn,** to yield to s.o.; **j'ai dû m'i.,** I had to give in; **s'i. devant son adversaire,** to yield to one's opponent, to admit defeat.
inclure [ɛ̃klyr] *vt* (*conj like* **conclure** *except pp* **inclus,** *but little used except in pp*) **(a)** to enclose (*document in letter etc*); **(b)** *Jur* to insert (*clause in contract etc*).
inclus [ɛ̃kly] *adj* **(a)** enclosed (*in letter etc*); (*service*) included; **jusqu'à la page 5 incluse,** up to and including page 5; **(b) dent incluse,** impacted tooth.
inclusif, -ive [ɛ̃klyzif, -iv] *adj* inclusive.
inclusion [ɛ̃klyzjɔ̃] *nf* inclusion, insertion; *Math* inclusion; enclosing (*of document in letter etc*).
inclusivement [ɛ̃klyzivmɑ̃] *adv* inclusively; **du vendredi au mardi i.,** from Friday to Tuesday inclusive, *Am* Friday through Tuesday.
incoercible [ɛ̃kɔɛrsibl] *adj* **(a)** *Phys etc* incoercible; **(b)** *Litt* uncontrollable (*cough*); irrepressible (*laughter*).
incognito [ɛ̃kɔɲito] **1** *adv* incognito. **2** *nm* **garder l'i.,** to remain incognito; **rechercher l'i.,** to seek anonymity.
incohérence [ɛ̃kɔerɑ̃s] *nf* incoherence, incoherency; disjointedness (*of speech etc*); inconsistency (*in story etc*); **le discours était un tissu d'incohérences,** the speech was totally incoherent.
incohérent [ɛ̃kɔerɑ̃] *adj* incoherent; (*histoire, attitude*) inconsistent; **tenir des propos incohérents,** to speak incoherently.
incollable [ɛ̃kɔlabl] *adj F* who cannot be caught out *or* stumped *or* floored; **elle est i. sur la question,** you can't catch her out on the subject.
incolore [ɛ̃kɔlɔr] *adj* colourless, *US* colorless.
incomber [ɛ̃kɔ̃be] *vi* (*used only in third person*) **i. à qn,** to be incumbent on s.o.; **les devoirs qui lui incombent,** the duties which fall on him; **la responsabilité incombe à l'auteur,** the responsibility lies *or* rests with the author, it is the author's responsibility; **il m'incombe de pourvoir à leurs besoins,** it is my duty to provide for their needs; **il incombe au gouvernement d'indemniser les sinistrés,** the onus lies on the government to compensate the victims.
incombustibilité [ɛ̃kɔ̃bystibilite] *nf* incombustibility.
incombustible [ɛ̃kɔ̃bystibl] *adj* incombustible, non-(in)flammable, fireproof.
incommensurable [ɛ̃kɔmɑ̃syrabl] *adj* **(a)** (*immense*) immeasurable, huge; **(b)** *Math* incommensurate; incommensurable (**avec,** with); **racine i.,** irrational root.
incommensurablement [ɛ̃kɔmɑ̃syrabləmɑ̃] *adv* **(a)** (*immensément*) immeasurably; **(b)** *Math etc* incommensurably.
incommodant [ɛ̃kɔmɔdɑ̃] *adj* unpleasant, disagreeable, annoying.
incommode [ɛ̃kɔmɔd] *adj* inconvenient (*time*); uncomfortable (*chair etc*); clumsy, awkward (*tool etc*); difficult (*person*); **un arrangement i.,** an inconvenient arrangement.
incommodé [ɛ̃kɔmɔde] *adj* **(a)** (*gêné*) ill at ease; **être i. par la chaleur,** to feel the heat; **(b)** *Vieilli* unwell, off colour.
incommodément [ɛ̃kɔmɔdemɑ̃] *adv* uncomfortably, awkwardly.
incommoder [ɛ̃kɔmɔde] *vt* **(a)** (*gêner*) to inconvenience, to disturb (*s.o.*); **la fumée ne vous incommode pas?,** you don't mind my smoking?; **(b)** (*d'aliment etc*) to disagree with (*s.o.*), to upset (*s.o.*).
incommodité [ɛ̃kɔmɔdite] *nf* (*d'une situation*) discomfort, awkwardness; (*d'un arrangement, d'un appartement*) inconvenience.
incommunicabilité [ɛ̃kɔmynikabilite] *nf Litt* (*d'un secret*) strict confidentiality.
incommunicable [ɛ̃kɔmynikabl] *adj* incommunicable.
incommutable [ɛ̃kɔmytabl] *adj Jur* non-transferable (*property*); indefeasible (*right*).
incomparable [ɛ̃kɔ̃parabl] *adj* incomparable, unrivalled, matchless; **ce n'est pas la même chose, c'est i.,** the two (things) can't be compared.
incomparablement [ɛ̃kɔ̃parabləmɑ̃] *adv* incomparably, beyond compare.
incompatibilité [ɛ̃kɔ̃patibilite] *nf* incompatibility (*of duties etc*); **i. d'humeur,** incompatibility of temperament; *Méd* **i. de groupes sanguins,** incompatibility of blood groups.
incompatible [ɛ̃kɔ̃patibl] *adj* incompatible, inconsistent, at variance (**avec,** with); **fonctions incompatibles,** incompatible duties; *Méd* **groupes sanguins incompatibles,** incompatible blood groups.
incompétence [ɛ̃kɔ̃petɑ̃s] *nf* **(a)** *Jur* incompetence, incompetency (*of person, tribunal*); **(b)** (*ignorance*) **reconnaître son incompétence,** to acknowledge one's ignorance *or* one's shortcomings; **son i. dans ce domaine,** his lack of knowledge in this area.
incompétent [ɛ̃kɔ̃petɑ̃] *adj* **(a)** (*incapable*) incompetent, inefficient; *Jur* not qualified, unqualified (*to try case*); **(b)** (*ignorant*) **i. en qch,** ignorant about sth.
incomplet, -ète [ɛ̃kɔ̃plɛ, -ɛt] *adj* incomplete.
incomplètement [ɛ̃kɔ̃plɛtmɑ̃] *adv* incompletely.
incomplétude [ɛ̃kɔ̃pletyd] *nf Psy* (sense of) inadequacy, non-fulfilment.
incompréhensibilité [ɛ̃kɔ̃preɑ̃sibilite] *nf Litt* incomprehensibility.
incompréhensible [ɛ̃kɔ̃preɑ̃sibl] *adj* incomprehensible; **c'est i., je les avais posées là!,** I don't understand it, I put them right there!
incompréhensif, -ive [ɛ̃kɔ̃preɑ̃sif, -iv] *adj* uncomprehending; obtuse (*mind etc*); **père i.,** unsympathetic father.
incompréhension [ɛ̃kɔ̃preɑ̃sjɔ̃] *nf* incomprehension.
incompris, -ise [ɛ̃kɔ̃pri, -iz] **1** *adj* misunderstood. **2** *n* **faire l'i.,** to act as if one was misunderstood; **il fut le grand i. du XIXe siècle,** he was one of the most unappreciated artists of the 19th century.
inconcevable [ɛ̃kɔ̃s(ə)vabl] *adj* inconceivable, unthinkable, unimaginable; **elle a eu une chance i.,** she had incredible luck.
inconcevablement [ɛ̃kɔ̃s(ə)vabləmɑ̃] *adv* inconceivably.
inconciliabilité [ɛ̃kɔ̃siljabilite] *nf* irreconcilability, incompatibility (*of theories etc*).
inconciliable [ɛ̃kɔ̃siljabl] *adj* irreconcilable, incompatible (**avec,** with).
inconditionnalité [ɛ̃kɔ̃disjɔnalite] *nf Pol* unwavering support.
inconditionné [ɛ̃kɔ̃disjɔne] *adj* unconditional; unconditioned.
inconditionnel, -elle [ɛ̃kɔ̃disjɔnɛl] **1** *adj* unconditional; unquestioning (*obedience*); absolute (*liability etc*); *Pol etc* unwavering (*supporter*). **2** *n* **un i. de la pêche,** a fishing fanatic.
inconditionnellement [ɛ̃kɔ̃disjɔnɛlmɑ̃] *adv* unconditionally; (*obéir*) unquestioningly.
inconduite [ɛ̃kɔ̃dɥit] *nf* loose living; *Jur* misconduct.
inconfort [ɛ̃kɔ̃fɔr] *nm* discomfort.
inconfortable [ɛ̃kɔ̃fɔrtabl] *adj* uncomfortable; *Fig* **sa situation est extrêmement i.,** he *or* she is in an extremely uncomfortable situation.
inconfortablement [ɛ̃kɔ̃fɔrtabləmɑ̃] *adv* uncomfortably.
incongru [ɛ̃kɔ̃gry] *adj* incongruous, out of place; inappropriate, improper, unseemly (*question etc*).
incongruité [ɛ̃kɔ̃grɥite] *nf* **(a)** (*absurdité*) incongruity, absurdity; impropriety (*of behaviour*); **(b)** (*remarque, action*) incongruity, inappropriate *or* improper remark *or* action.
incongrûment [ɛ̃kɔ̃grymɑ̃] *adv* (*rare*) **(a)** (*absurdement*) incongruously; **(b)** (*impoliment*) improperly.
inconnaissable [ɛ̃kɔnɛsabl] *adj & nm* unknowable.
inconnu, -ue [ɛ̃kɔny] **1** *adj* unknown (**de, à,** to); **il m'était i.,** I didn't know him; **il était i. de tout le monde,** nobody knew him; **visages inconnus,** strange faces; **c'est un problème qui lui est totalement i.,** the problem is totally foreign to him; **i. à cette adresse,** not known at this address; *F* **Durand? i. au bataillon!,** Durand? — never heard of him! **2** *n* (*étranger*) stranger; (*personne sans importance*) (mere) nobody; **une belle inconnue,** a beautiful stranger. **3** *nm* **l'i.,** the unknown; **faire un saut dans l'i.,** to take a leap in the dark. **4** *nf Math etc* **inconnue,** unknown (quantity).

inconsciemment [ɛ̃kɔ̃sjamɑ̃] *adv* unconsciously, unknowingly, unwittingly; **il a signé un peu i.**, he signed without thinking too much.

inconscience [ɛ̃kɔ̃sjɑ̃s] *nf* **(a)** (*physique*) unconsciousness; **sombrer** *ou* **tomber dans l'i.**, to become unconscious; **(b)** (*manque de jugement*) unawareness, obliviousness (*of sth*); **faire preuve d'i.**, to be thoughtless; **c'était de l'i. pure**, it was sheer thoughtlessness.

inconscient, -ente [ɛ̃kɔ̃sjɑ̃, -ɑ̃t] **1** *adj* unconscious (*act*); automatic (*movement etc*); **i. de ce qui se passe autour de lui**, oblivious *or* unaware of what is going on around him; **tu es i.!**, you're irresponsible! **2** *n* irresponsible person. **3** *nm Psy* **l'i.**, the unconscious, the subconscious.

inconséquemment [ɛ̃kɔ̃sekamɑ̃] *adv* inconsistently, inconsequently, inconsequentially.

inconséquence [ɛ̃kɔ̃sekɑ̃s] *nf* inconsistency, inconsequence.

inconséquent [ɛ̃kɔ̃sekɑ̃] *adj* inconsistent, inconsequent(ial) (*argument, person*); rambling (*speech*); irresponsible, rash (*words*).

inconsidéré [ɛ̃kɔ̃sidere] *adj* **(a)** (*imprudent*) unconsidered, ill-considered, rash (*act*); **(b)** *Vieilli* inconsiderate (*person*).

inconsidérément [ɛ̃kɔ̃sideremɑ̃] *adv* inconsiderately, thoughtlessly, rashly.

inconsistance [ɛ̃kɔ̃sistɑ̃s] *nf* **(a)** unsubstantiality; softness (*of mud*); looseness (*of soil*); weakness (*of nature*); **(b)** inconsistency (*of person, act*).

inconsistant [ɛ̃kɔ̃sistɑ̃] *adj* **(a)** unsubstantial; soft (*mud*); loose (*soil*); weak (*nature*); **(b)** inconsistent (*conduct, person*).

inconsolable [ɛ̃kɔ̃sɔlabl] *adj* inconsolable (*person, grief, sadness*); disconsolate (*person*).

inconsolé [ɛ̃kɔ̃sɔle] *adj* unconsoled.

inconsommable [ɛ̃kɔ̃sɔmabl] *adj* unfit for consumption.

inconstance [ɛ̃kɔ̃stɑ̃s] *nf* **(a)** (*d'une personne*) inconstancy, inconsistency; fickleness (*of person, love*); **(b)** *Litt* changeableness (*of thing*).

inconstant [ɛ̃kɔ̃stɑ̃] *adj* **(a)** inconstant, inconsistent; fickle (*person, love*); **(b)** *Litt* (*thing*) changeable.

inconstatable [ɛ̃kɔ̃statabl] *adj* unascertainable, unverifiable.

inconstitutionnalité [ɛ̃kɔ̃stitysjɔnalite] *nf Jur* unconstitutionality.

inconstitutionnel, -elle [ɛ̃kɔ̃stitysjɔnɛl] *adj Jur* unconstitutional.

inconstitutionnellement [ɛ̃kɔ̃stitysjɔnɛlmɑ̃] *adv Jur* unconstitutionally.

inconstructible [ɛ̃kɔ̃stryktibl] *adj* (*area*) that cannot be developed.

incontestabilité [ɛ̃kɔ̃tɛstabilite] *nf Jur* incontestability.

incontestable [ɛ̃kɔ̃tɛstabl] *adj* incontestable, undeniable, indisputable, beyond all doubt; **il est i. que ...**, it is undeniable that ..., it cannot be denied that ... .

incontestablement [ɛ̃kɔ̃tɛstabləmɑ̃] *adv* incontestably, undeniably, beyond all doubt.

incontesté [ɛ̃kɔ̃tɛste] *adj* uncontested, undisputed.

incontinence [ɛ̃kɔ̃tinɑ̃s] *nf* **(a)** *Arch & Litt* incontinence, lack of restraint; **(b)** *Méd* incontinence; **i. nocturne**, bedwetting.

incontinent[1] [ɛ̃kɔ̃tinɑ̃] *adj* **(a)** *Arch & Litt* incontinent, unrestrained; **(b)** *Méd* incontinent.

incontinent[2] *adv Arch & Litt* at once, forthwith.

incontournable [ɛ̃kɔ̃turnabl] *adj* **c'est i.**, you can't get away from it; **Harrods est un magasin i.**, Harrods should not be missed, Harrods is a must.

incontrôlable [ɛ̃kɔ̃trolabl] *adj* difficult to verify *or* to check, unverifiable.

incontrôlé [ɛ̃kɔ̃trole] *adj* **(a)** (*non vérifié*) unchecked, unverified; **(b)** (*non surveillé*) uncontrolled.

inconvenance [ɛ̃kɔ̃vnɑ̃s] *nf* impropriety.

inconvenant [ɛ̃kɔ̃vnɑ̃] *adj* improper, indecorous; **il est vraiment i.**, he doesn't know how to behave, he has no manners.

inconvénient [ɛ̃kɔ̃venjɑ̃] *nm* disadvantage, drawback; **les inconvénients qu'il y a à vivre si loin de la ville**, the inconvenience of living so far from town; **je n'y vois pas d'i.**, I can't see any objection(s) (to it), I've got nothing against it; **si vous n'y voyez aucun i., je voudrais ...**, if you have no objection, I'd like to ...; **il n'y a pas d'i. à cela**, that doesn't pose any problem; **pouvez-vous sans i. me prêter ce livre?**, would it be convenient for you to lend me this book?; **nous pouvons sans i. modifier notre itinéraire**, we can easily change our route; **le seul i., c'est que ...**, the only disadvantage is that ... .

inconvertible [ɛ̃kɔ̃vɛrtibl] *adj* inconvertible (*paper money etc*).

incoordination [ɛ̃kɔɔrdinasjɔ̃] *nf* lack of coordination; *Méd* ataxia.

incorporable [ɛ̃kɔrpɔrabl] *adj* (*rare*) incorporable.

incorporalité [ɛ̃kɔrpɔralite] *nf Spéc* incorporeality.

incorporation [ɛ̃kɔrpɔrasjɔ̃] *nf* **(a)** incorporation (**de qch dans qch**, of sth into *or* with sth); **(b)** *Mil* conscription; **sursis d'i.**, deferment of call-up.

incorporéité [ɛ̃kɔrpɔreite] *nf Spéc* incorporeity.

incorporel, -elle [ɛ̃kɔrpɔrɛl] *adj* incorporeal; *Jur* **biens incorporels**, intangible property.

incorporer [ɛ̃kɔrpɔre] **1** *vt* **(a) i. qch à** *ou parfois* **avec qch**, to blend *or* mix *or* incorporate sth into *or* with sth; **(b)** to incorporate (*land*) (**dans un domaine**, in(to) an estate); to insert (*paragraph etc*); **(c)** *Mil* to draft (*troops*). **2 s'incorporer** *vpr* **chercher à s'i. dans un groupe**, to try to join a group.

incorrect [ɛ̃kɔrɛkt] *adj* **(a)** (*impropre*) incorrect, inaccurate, wrong; **(b)** (*défectueux*) defective, faulty; **(c)** (*d'une façon inconvenante*) contrary to etiquette; **tenue incorrecte**, (*débraillé*) slovenly clothes; (*déplacé*) unsuitable clothes; **(d)** (*personne*) impolite, ill-mannered, rude; **être i. avec qn**, to treat s.o. unfairly.

incorrectement [ɛ̃kɔrɛktəmɑ̃] *adv* **(a)** incorrectly, inaccurately, wrongly; **(b)** (*d'une façon défectueuse*) defectively; **(c)** (*d'une façon inconvenante*) in a slovenly manner; unsuitably (*dressed*); **(d)** (*avec impolitesse*) impolitely, rudely; **se conduire i. avec qn**, (*injustement*) to treat s.o. unfairly; (*avec inexactitude*) to treat s.o. impolitely *or* rudely.

incorrection [ɛ̃kɔrɛksjɔ̃] *nf* **(a)** (*inexactitude*) incorrectness, inaccuracy; **(b)** incorrectness, slovenliness; unsuitability (*of clothes*); **(c)** (*impolitesse*) impoliteness, lack of (good) manners, rudeness; **(d)** *Gram* incorrect expression; **(e)** (*action, remarque*) impolite *or* rude remark *or* action.

incorrigibilité [ɛ̃kɔriʒibilite] *nf* incorrigibility.

incorrigible [ɛ̃kɔriʒibl] *adj* incorrigible; **d'une gourmandise i.**, incorrigibly greedy.

incorrigiblement [ɛ̃kɔriʒibləmɑ̃] *adv* (*rare*) incorrigibly.

incorruptibilité [ɛ̃kɔryptibilite] *nf* incorruptibility.

incorruptible [ɛ̃kɔryptibl] *adj* incorruptible.

incorruptiblement [ɛ̃kɔryptibləmɑ̃] *adv* (*rare*) incorruptibly.

incrédibilité [ɛ̃kredibilite] *nf* incredibility.

incrédule [ɛ̃kredyl] **1** *adj* incredulous; *Rel* unbelieving. **2** *n Rel* unbeliever.

incrédulité [ɛ̃kredylite] *nf* incredulity; *Rel* unbelief; **avec i.**, incredulously.

increvable [ɛ̃krəvabl] *adj* **(a)** puncture-proof (*tyre*); **(b)** *Arg* (*personne*) indefatigable, tireless.

incriminatoire [ɛ̃kriminatwar] *adj* incriminating.

incriminé [ɛ̃krimine] *adj* accused (*person*); offending (*object*).

incriminer [ɛ̃krimine] *vt* to incriminate, to accuse, to indict (*s.o.*); to condemn (*sth*).

incrochetable [ɛ̃krɔʃtabl] *adj* unpickable (*lock*); burglar-proof (*safe*).

incroyable [ɛ̃krwajabl] **1** *adj* incredible, unbelievable, beyond belief, extraordinary; **une histoire tout à fait i.**, an altogether incredible story; **il est d'une paresse i.**, he's incredibly lazy. **2** *n Hist Fr* incroyable (*beau or belle of the French Directoire period*).

incroyablement [ɛ̃krwajabləmɑ̃] *adv* incredibly, unbelievably, extraordinarily.

incroyance [ɛ̃krwajɑ̃s] *nf* unbelief.

incroyant, -ante [ɛ̃krwajɑ̃, -ɑ̃t] **1** *adj* unbelieving. **2** *n* unbeliever, non-believer.

incrustation [ɛ̃krystasjɔ̃] *nf* **(a)** (*action*) encrusting; *Menuis* inlaying; **(b)** furring (up) (*of boiler etc*); **(c)** (*ornement*) encrustation; inlay; inlaid work; **avec incrustations de nacre**, inlaid with mother of pearl; **(d)** *Couture* insertion; **i. de dentelle**, lace inlay; **(e)** fur(ring), scale (*in boiler etc*).

incruster [ɛ̃kryste] **1** *vt* **(a)** *Menuis* to inlay (**de**, with); **(b)** to encrust, to form a crust on (*sth*); (*d'eau*) to scale, to fur (up) (*pipes etc*); **(c)** (*pour orner*) to encrust. **2 s'incruster** *vpr* **(a)** (*adhérer*) to become encrusted; **(b)** (*d'un appareil etc*) to fur up; **(c)** *F* **quand on l'invite, il s'incruste**, once you invite him you can't get rid of him.

incubateur, -trice [ɛ̃kybatœr, -tris] **1** *adj* incubating (*apparatus etc*). **2** *nm* incubator.

incubation [ɛ̃kybasjɔ̃] *nf* incubation, hatching (*of eggs*);

sitting (*of hens*); *Méd* **période d'i.,** incubation period (*of disease*).
incube [ɛ̃kyb] *nm* incubus.
incuber [ɛ̃kybe] *vt* to incubate, to hatch (out) (*eggs*).
inculcation [ɛ̃kylkɑsjɔ̃] *nf* inculcating, inculcation.
inculpation [ɛ̃kylpɑsjɔ̃] *nf* indictment, charge.
inculpé, -ée [ɛ̃kylpe] *n Jur* **l'i.,** the accused, the defendant; the prisoner (*in the widest sense*).
inculper [ɛ̃kylpe] *vt* to indict, to charge (**de,** with).
inculquer [ɛ̃kylke] *vt* to inculcate (**à,** in), to instil (**à,** into).
inculte [ɛ̃kylt] *adj* uncultivated, wild (*garden etc*); waste (*land*); unkempt (*beard*); uneducated (*person*).
incultivable [ɛ̃kyltivabl] *adj* untillable, irreclaimable (*land*).
incultivé [ɛ̃kyltive] *adj* untilled, uncultivated (*land*).
inculture [ɛ̃kyltyr] *nf* lack of culture.
incunable [ɛ̃kynabl] *nm Typ* incunabulum, *pl* incunabula.
incurable [ɛ̃kyrabl] **1** *adj* incurable. **2** *n* person with an incurable disease.
incurablement [ɛ̃kyrabləmɑ̃] *adv* incurably.
incurie [ɛ̃kyri] *nf* carelessness, negligence.
incursion [ɛ̃kyrsjɔ̃] *nf* inroad, foray, raid, incursion; *Fig* intrusion, interruption.
incurvation [ɛ̃kyrvɑsjɔ̃] *nf* bend, curve.
incurvé [ɛ̃kyrve] *adj* bent, curved.
incurver [ɛ̃kyrve] *vt & vpr* to bend, to curve.
indatable [ɛ̃databl] *adj* that cannot be dated.
Inde [ɛ̃d] *nf* India; **les Indes,** the Indies; *Hist* **les Indes occidentales,** the West Indies; **les Indes orientales,** the East Indies.
inde [ɛ̃d] *nm* dark blue.
indébrouillable [ɛ̃debrujabl] *adj* inextricable, tangled (*situation etc*).
indécemment [ɛ̃desamɑ̃] *adv* indecently.
indécence [ɛ̃desɑ̃s] *nf* indecency.
indécent [ɛ̃desɑ̃] *adj* indecent, improper.
indéchiffrable [ɛ̃deʃifrabl] *adj* **(a)** indecipherable (*inscription*); illegible (*writing*); **(b)** (*incompréhensible*) unintelligible, incomprehensible; (*personne*) impenetrable, inscrutable.
indéchirable [ɛ̃deʃirabl] *adj* untearable, tearproof.
indécis, -ise [ɛ̃desi, -iz] **1** *adj* **(a)** undecided, unsettled (*question etc*); indecisive, doubtful (*victory etc*); vague, blurred (*outline*); **(b)** (*personne*) indecisive, irresolute; hesitating; **être i. quant au parti à prendre,** to be undecided *or* in two minds how to act. **2** *n* **c'est un i.,** he can never make his mind up.
indécision [ɛ̃desizjɔ̃] *nf* indecision, indecisiveness, irresolution, uncertainty.
indécollable [ɛ̃dekɔlabl] *adj* (*rare*) that cannot be unglued *or* unstuck.
indécomposable [ɛ̃dekɔ̃pozabl] *adj* irresolvable (*element etc*).
indécrottable [ɛ̃dekrɔtabl] *adj* **(a)** *F* incorrigible; hopeless (*dunce etc*); **(b)** (*difficile à nettoyer*) uncleanable.
indéfectibilité [ɛ̃defɛktibilite] *nf Rel* indefectibility (*of the church etc*).
indéfectible [ɛ̃defɛktibl] *adj* **(a)** *Rel* indefectible; **(b)** indestructible (*friendship etc*).
indéfendable [ɛ̃defɑ̃dabl] *adj* indefensible.
indéfini [ɛ̃defini] *adj* **(a)** (*illimité*) indefinite; *Gram* **pronom i.,** indefinite pronoun; **(b)** (*non précis*) undefined.
indéfiniment [ɛ̃definimɑ̃] *adv* indefinitely.
indéfinissable [ɛ̃definisabl] *adj* indefinable, undefinable (*term etc*); indeterminate (*taste etc*).
indéfrisable [ɛ̃defrizabl] *nf Vieilli* permanent wave, perm.
indélébile [ɛ̃delebil] *adj* indelible (*ink, stain*); *Fig* **souvenir i.,** an unfading memory.
indélicat [ɛ̃delika] *adj* **(a)** indelicate, coarse (*nature*); tactless (*action*); **(b)** (*malhonnête*) dishonest, unscrupulous.
indélicatement [ɛ̃delikatmɑ̃] *adv* (*voir adj*) **(a)** indelicately; **(b)** unscrupulously.
indélicatesse [ɛ̃delikatɛs] *nf* **(a)** (*manque de tact*) indelicacy; (*d'une action*) tactlessness; (*acte*) indelicate *or* tactless action; **(b)** (*absence de scrupule*) unscrupulousness; (*acte*) unscrupulous action.
indémaillable [ɛ̃demajabl] *adj* ladderproof, non-run (*tights etc*).
indemne [ɛ̃dɛmn] *adj* **(a)** (*sauf*) uninjured, unhurt, unharmed, unscathed; **elle est sortie i. de l'accident,** she escaped uninjured; **(b)** *Jur Arch* without loss.
indemnisable [ɛ̃dɛmnizabl] *adj* entitled to compensation.
indemnisation [ɛ̃dɛmnizɑsjɔ̃] *nf* indemnification, compensation, indemnity.
indemniser [ɛ̃dɛmnize] *vt* to indemnify, to compensate; **i. qn d'une perte,** to compensate s.o. for a loss; **i. qn en argent,** to pay s.o. compensation in cash.
indemnitaire [ɛ̃dɛmnitɛr] *adj* **prestation i.,** compensation.
indemnité [ɛ̃dɛmnite] *nf* **(a)** indemnity, indemnification, compensation (*for loss sustained*); **i. de guerre,** war indemnity; **(b)** compensation to other party, penalty (*for delay, non-delivery etc*); **(c)** *Admin* allowance, grant; **i. de départ,** (*pour un cadre*) *F* golden handshake; *Can Admin* severance pay; **i. de résidence,** living allowance; **i. de route** *ou* **de déplacement,** travelling expenses; **i. parlementaire,** = M.P.'s salary; *Can* **i. de la vie chère,** cost of living allowance.
indémodable [ɛ̃demɔdabl] *adj* **un tailleur i.,** a classic suit, a suit that will never go out of fashion.
indémontable [ɛ̃demɔ̃tabl] *adj* which cannot be dismantled; **c'est i.,** it doesn't dismantle.
indémontrable [ɛ̃demɔ̃trabl] *adj* undemonstrable, unprovable.
indéniable [ɛ̃denjabl] *adj* undeniable.
indéniablement [ɛ̃denjabləmɑ̃] *adv* undeniably.
indénouable [ɛ̃denwabl] *adj* that cannot be untied *or* unravelled.
indentation [ɛ̃dɑ̃tɑsjɔ̃] *nf* indentation.
indépassable [ɛ̃depasabl] *adj* (*limite*) which cannot be exceeded.
indépendamment [ɛ̃depɑ̃damɑ̃] *adv* independently (**de,** of); **i. de l'ancienneté,** irrespective of seniority.
indépendance [ɛ̃depɑ̃dɑ̃s] *nf* independence; **accéder à l'i.,** to gain independence.
indépendant [ɛ̃depɑ̃dɑ̃] *adj* independent (**de,** of); self-contained (*flat etc*); **circonstances indépendantes de ma volonté,** circumstances beyond my control; **État i.,** free state; **elle est très indépendante,** she's very independent; *Aut* **roues (avant) indépendantes,** independent (front-wheel) suspension; *Gram* **proposition indépendante,** main clause.
indépendantiste [ɛ̃depɑ̃dɑ̃tist] *n Pol* supporter of independence.
indéracinable [ɛ̃derasinabl] *adj* ineradicable.
indéréglable [ɛ̃dereglabl] *adj* foolproof (*mechanism*).
indescriptible [ɛ̃dɛskriptibl] *adj* indescribable.
indésirable [ɛ̃dezirabl] *adj & n* undesirable.
indestructibilité [ɛ̃dɛstryktibilite] *nf* indestructibility.
indestructible [ɛ̃dɛstryktibl] *adj* indestructible.
indéterminable [ɛ̃determinabl] *adj* indeterminable.
indétermination [ɛ̃determinɑsjɔ̃] *nf* **(a)** vagueness (*of ideas*); **(b)** (*d'une personne*) irresoluteness, irresolution.
indéterminé [ɛ̃determine] *adj* **(a)** (*vague*) undetermined; indeterminate, indefinite, vague (*ideas*); **(b)** (*personne*) irresolute, undecided; **elle est encore indéterminée sur ce point,** she still has not made her mind up on the issue.
index [ɛ̃dɛks] *nm* **(a)** *Anat* forefinger, index finger; pointer, needle (*of balance etc*); **(b)** index (*of book*); *Cathol* **l'I.,** the Index; *Fig* **mettre qn/qch à l'i.,** to blacklist s.o./sth.
indexation [ɛ̃dɛksɑsjɔ̃] *nf Écon* indexation, index-linking (*de salaires etc*).
indexé [ɛ̃dɛkse] *adj* (*salaire etc*) index-linked.
indexer [ɛ̃dɛkse] *vt Écon* to index-link, to peg (*prices etc*); **salaires indexés sur l'indice du coût de la vie,** salaries indexed to the cost of living.
indicateur, -trice [ɛ̃dikatœr, -tris] **1** *adj* indicatory; **poteau i.,** signpost; **panneau i. (de route),** road sign. **2** *n Péj* informer. **3** *nm* **(a)** (*livre*) guide; (railway) timetable; (street) directory; **(b)** indicator, pointer (*of barometer etc*); gauge (*of boiler etc*); **i. de niveau (de carburant),** (fuel) gauge; **i. de pression,** pressure gauge; **i. de vitesse,** speed indicator, tachometer; *Aut* speedometer; *Av* airspeed indicator; *Av* **i. d'altitude,** altimeter; *Rad* **i. de direction,** direction finder; **(c)** *Ch & Écon* indicator.
indicatif, -ive [ɛ̃dikatif, -iv] **1** *adj* **(a)** indicative (**de,** of); **(b)** *Gram* **mode i.,** indicative (mood). **2** *nm* **(a)** *Gram* indicative (mood); **à l'i.,** in the indicative; **(b)** *Tél* dialling code; *Rad etc* **i. d'appel,** call sign; **i. du poste,** station signal; **i. (musical),** signature tune, theme tune (*of programme*).
indication [ɛ̃dikɑsjɔ̃] *nf* **(a)** (*action*) indication, indicating, pointing out; **c'est sur l'i. de Jean-Guy que je suis allée voir ce médecin,** it was on Jean-Guy's recommendation that I went to that doctor; **(b)** (*renseignement*) (piece of) information; **fausse i. de revenu,** false declaration of income; **sauf i. contraire,** unless otherwise stated; **à titre**

d'i., for your *or* my *etc* guidance; **c'est une excellente i.,** that's an excellent suggestion; **j'ai décidé de suivre vos indications,** I've decided to take your advice; **(c)** sign, token (*of guilt etc*); **(d) indications topographiques,** survey marks *or* data; **(e) indications,** instruction(s); **indications du mode d'emploi,** directions for use; *Th* **indications scéniques,** stage directions.

indice [ɛ̃dis] *nm* **(a)** (*signe*) indication, sign, mark, token; rating (*of popularity etc*); **c'est l'i. de la reprise,** it's the sign of a recovery; **je vis là un i. de ta fatigue,** to me that was an indication you were tired; **(b)** *Math etc* index (number); **i. inférieur,** suffix; **i. d'octane,** octane rating (*of petrol*); **i. de protection,** protection factor (*of sun cream*); *Écon* **i. du coût de la vie,** cost of living index; **i. des prix de détail,** retail price index; *Rad TV* **i. d'écoute,** ratings; *Rad TV* **avoir un bon i. d'écoute,** to stand high in the ratings, to attract a large listening *or* viewing audience; **l'i. d'écoute a baissé,** the ratings have dropped.

indicible [ɛ̃disibl] *adj* inexpressible, unutterable; unspeakable (*grief, rage*); (*indescriptible*) indescribable; **d'une saleté i.,** indescribably *or* unspeakably filthy.

indiciblement [ɛ̃disibləmɑ̃] *adv* **(a)** (*d'une façon inexprimable*) inexpressibly, unutterably; unspeakably; **(b)** (*d'une façon indescriptible*) indescribably.

indien, -ienne [ɛ̃djɛ̃, -jɛn] **1** *adj* **(a)** Indian; **l'océan i.,** the Indian Ocean; **(b) en** *ou* **à la file indienne,** in Indian *or* single file. **2** *n* **I.,** Indian (*of India, America*). **3** *nf* **indienne (a)** *Tex* cotton print, *surtout US* printed calico; **(b)** *Natation* **nage (à l')indienne,** overarm stroke.

indifféremment [ɛ̃diferamɑ̃] *adv* **(a)** (*sans faire de différence*) indiscriminately, equally; **(b)** *Vieilli* (*avec froideur*) indifferently.

indifférence [ɛ̃diferɑ̃s] *nf* indifference; **répondre avec i.,** to answer with indifference *or* indifferently; **i. à** *ou* **pour,** indifference to, lack of concern *or* of interest in; **son i. pour la politique,** his indifference to *or* lack of interest in politics.

indifférenciation [ɛ̃diferɑ̃sjɑsjɔ̃] *nf* lack of differentiation.

indifférencié [ɛ̃diferɑ̃sje] *adj* undifferentiated.

indifférent [ɛ̃diferɑ̃] *adj* **(a)** (*peu ou pas intéressé*) indifferent (**à,** to); unaffected (**à,** by); unconcerned; **rester i. à tout,** to take no interest in anything; **être i. au sort de qn,** to be indifferent to s.o.'s fate; **il m'est i.,** I'm indifferent to him; **(b)** cold, emotionless (*heart etc*); **cela ne peut vous laisser i.,** it can't leave you indifferent *or* unmoved; **(c)** (*égal*) immaterial, unimportant; **cela m'est i.,** it's all the same *or* it's quite immaterial to me, I don't care either way; **il m'est i. de faire cela ou autre chose,** it doesn't matter to me *or* it's all the same to me whether I do that or something else; **(d)** (*sans importance*) **parler de choses indifférentes,** to chat (about nothing in particular).

indifférer [ɛ̃difere] *vt used with pronoun complement only* (**il indiffère, il indifférera**) *F* **cela m'indiffère,** I couldn't care less about it.

indigence [ɛ̃diʒɑ̃s] *nf* destitution; **être dans l'i.,** to be destitute; **i. d'idées,** total lack of ideas; **avoir une i. d'idées,** to be totally lacking in ideas.

indigène [ɛ̃diʒɛn] **1** *adj Zool Bot etc* indigenous (**à,** to); native (*population etc*); **coutumes indigènes,** indigenous customs. **2** *n* native.

indigent, -ente [ɛ̃diʒɑ̃, -ɑ̃t] **1** *adj* poor, needy, poverty-stricken; **avoir une imagination indigente,** to be totally lacking in imagination. **2** *n* poor person; **les indigents,** the poor, the destitute.

indigeste [ɛ̃diʒɛst] *adj* **(a)** indigestible, stodgy (*food*); **(b)** *Fig* (*fait*) undigested; (*livre*) indigestible.

indigestion [ɛ̃diʒɛstjɔ̃] *nf* indigestion; **avoir une i.,** to have (an attack of) indigestion; *F* **j'en ai une i.,** I'm fed up with it; **comprimés pour l'i.,** indigestion tablets.

indignation [ɛ̃diɲɑsjɔ̃] *nf* indignation; **faire éclater** *ou* **crier son i.,** to give one's indignation free rein; **éclater** *ou* **exploser d'i.,** to explode in indignation; **avec i.,** (*pailer etc*) with indignation, indignantly.

indigne [ɛ̃diɲ] *adj* **(a)** (*ne méritant pas*) unworthy, undeserving; **i. de notre confiance,** unworthy of our confidence; **être i. d'un poste/d'une tâche,** to be unworthy of a position/a task; **ce travail est i. de lui,** this work is not good enough for him *or* is beneath him; **c'est une mère i.,** she's not a fit mother; **(b)** shameful (*action, conduct*); **conduite i. d'une sœur/d'un père,** unsisterly/unfatherly conduct.

indigné [ɛ̃diɲe] *adj* indignant (**de,** at); **d'un air** *ou* **d'un ton i.,** indignantly.

indignement [ɛ̃diɲmɑ̃] *adv* shamefully.

indigner [ɛ̃diɲe] **1** *vt* to rouse (*s.o.*) to indignation, to make (*s.o.*) indignant. **2 s'indigner** *vpr* to become *or* to be indignant; **s'i. de** *ou* **contre qch/qn,** to be indignant at sth/with s.o.; **s'i. que** + *sub ou* **de ce que** + *ind,* to be indignant that ...; **je m'indigne de voir ce crime impuni,** it makes me indignant to see this crime go unpunished.

indignité [ɛ̃diɲite] *nf* **(a)** (*d'une personne*) unworthiness; baseness, vileness (*of an action*); *Jur* **i. nationale,** consorting with the enemy; **(b)** (*action*) shameful action; **souffrir des indignités,** to suffer indignities *or* humiliation.

indigo [ɛ̃digo] *nm & adj inv* indigo(-blue).

indiquer [ɛ̃dike] *vt* **(a)** (*montrer*) to indicate, to point to, to point out; **i. qch du doigt,** to point to *or* at sth, to point sth out (with one's finger); **i. le chemin à qn,** to show s.o. the way, to direct s.o.; **elle m'indiqua comment utiliser cet outil,** she showed me how to use the tool;

(b) (*marquer*) to mark, to show, to give (*information*); **le compteur indique cent,** the meter reads one hundred; **point indiqué sur la carte,** point shown *or* marked on the map; **la maison indiquée sur le bordereau ci-joint,** the firm mentioned on the enclosed slip; **le panneau vert indique la sortie,** the green panel indicates the exit;

(c) (*fournir*) to show, to tell; **indiquez-moi un bon médecin,** can you recommend a doctor?;

(d) (*dénoter*) to point to; **tout dans la maison indique un goût raffiné,** everything in the house indicates *or* shows good taste;

(e) to appoint, to name (*a day etc*); **à l'heure indiquée,** at the appointed *or* scheduled time;

(f) to draw up (*procedure etc*); to prescribe, to lay down (*line of action etc*); **c'était indiqué,** it was the obvious thing to do; **un sujet de plaisanterie tout indiqué,** an obvious subject for jokes; **il est tout à fait indiqué pour ce poste,** he's the very man *or* just the man for the job; **ce n'est pas très indiqué,** it's not very advisable *or* suitable *or* appropriate;

(g) to outline, to sketch (*features, plot etc*).

indirect [ɛ̃dirɛkt] *adj* **(a)** indirect (*route, Gram object etc*); roundabout (*way*); *Jur* collateral (*heirs*); indirect, covert (*attack*); *Gram* **discours i.,** indirect speech, reported speech; **éclairage i.,** concealed lighting; **elle l'a dit d'une façon indirecte,** she said it indirectly *or* in a roundabout way; **je l'ai appris d'une manière indirecte,** I learned of it indirectly; **contributions indirectes,** indirect taxation; **(b)** *Jur* circumstantial (*evidence*).

indirectement [ɛ̃dirɛktəmɑ̃] *adv* indirectly.

indiscernable [ɛ̃disɛrnabl] *adj* indiscernible, scarcely perceptible.

indiscipline [ɛ̃disiplin] *nf* indiscipline, lack of discipline; **faire acte** *ou* **preuve d'i.,** to show a lack of discipline.

indiscipliné [ɛ̃disipline] *adj* undisciplined, unruly; *Fig* **cheveux indisciplinés,** unruly *or* unmanageable hair.

indiscret, -ète [ɛ̃diskrɛ, -ɛt] **1** *adj* **(a)** (*importun*) indiscreet, tactless (*person*); **à l'abri des regards indiscrets,** safe from prying eyes; **une question fort indiscrète,** a very indiscreet question; **je ne voudrais pas être i., mais ...,** I don't want to be indiscreet but ...; **je me méfie des oreilles indiscrètes,** I'm on my guard against eavesdroppers; **(b)** *Arch* indiscreet, imprudent, unguarded. **2** *n* indiscreet *or* tactless person, *F* nosy parker.

indiscrètement [ɛ̃diskrɛtmɑ̃] *adv* indiscreetly.

indiscrétion [ɛ̃diskresjɔ̃] *nf* **(a)** (*curiosité*) indiscretion, indiscreetness; **peut-on vous demander sans i. ...?,** would it be indiscreet *or* rude to ask ...?; **elle a eu l'i. de venir elle-même vérifier,** she was so indiscreet as to come and see for herself; **il a poussé l'i. jusqu'à demander des détails,** he went so far as to ask for details; **(b)** (*action, remarque*) indiscretion; **il lui échappe des indiscrétions,** he blurts out secrets; **commettre une i.,** to be indiscreet.

indiscutable [ɛ̃diskytabl] *adj* indisputable, unquestionable.

indiscutablement [ɛ̃diskytabləmɑ̃] *adv* indisputably, unquestionably.

indiscuté [ɛ̃diskyte] *adj* undisputed, unquestioned, beyond doubt.

indispensable [ɛ̃dispɑ̃sabl] **1** *adj* indispensable (**à qn,** to s.o.; **à, pour qch,** for sth; **pour faire qch,** for doing sth); essential (**à,** for, to); **il est i. que j'aie/d'avoir votre autorisation écrite,** it is essential that I should have *or Am* that I have/it is essential to have your authorization in writing; **une condition i.,** an essential condition; **votre aide m'est i.,** your help is indispensable (to me); **tu te crois donc i.?,** so you think you're indispensable?; **personne n'est i.,** no-one is indispensable; **il nous est i.,** he is indispensable to us, we can't spare him *or* do without him. **2** *nm* the

necessary; **ne prenez que l'i.**, don't take more than is strictly *or* absolutely necessary.
indispensablement [ɛ̃dispɑ̃sabləmɑ̃] *adv* indispensably.
indisponibilité [ɛ̃dispɔnibilite] *nf* **(a)** *Jur* inalienability; **(b)** (*d'une personne*) unavailability.
indisponible [ɛ̃dispɔnibl] *adj* **(a)** *Jur* inalienable (*property*); entailed (*estate*); **(b)** (*personne*) unavailable, not available (*for duty etc*).
indisposé [ɛ̃dispoze] *adj* (*fatigué*) indisposed, unwell, *F* out of sorts; **se sentir vaguement i.**, to feel unwell *or* off colour; **être indisposée,** (*of woman*) to have one's period, *Euph* to be indisposed; **elle est indisposée,** it's her time of the month.
indisposer [ɛ̃dispoze] *vt* **(a)** (*rendre légèrement malade*) to make (*s.o.*) unwell; (*of food etc*) to upset, to disagree with (*s.o.*); **cette odeur m'indispose,** that smell makes me (feel) sick; **(b)** (*contrarier*) to antagonize (*s.o.*); **i. qn contre qn,** to set s.o. against s.o.; **tout l'indispose,** everything annoys him; **elle indispose tout le monde par son attitude,** her attitude antagonises everybody.
indisposition [ɛ̃dispozisjɔ̃] *nf* indisposition, (slight) illness, upset; (*of woman*) (monthly) period.
indissociable [ɛ̃disɔsjabl] *adj* indissociable.
indissolubilité [ɛ̃disɔlybilite] *nf* indissolubility (*of marriage etc*).
indissoluble [ɛ̃disɔlybl] *adj* indissoluble (*bond, friendship*).
indissolublement [ɛ̃disɔlybləmɑ̃] *adv* indissolubly.
indistinct [ɛ̃distɛ̃(kt)] *adj* indistinct; (*visuellement*) hazy, vague, blurred; faint (*inscription*).
indistinctement [ɛ̃distɛ̃ktəmɑ̃] *adv* (*indifféremment*) indiscriminately, without distinction; (*voir*) indistinctly, hazily, vaguely.
individu [ɛ̃dividy] *nm* **(a)** *Biol etc* individual; **tout i. est unique,** every individual is unique; *F* **soigner son i.**, to look after number one; **(b)** *souvent Péj* individual, person, fellow; **i. louche,** shady customer, suspicious character; **quel drôle d'i.!**, what an odd person!, what a funny individual!
individualisation [ɛ̃dividɥalizasjɔ̃] *nf* individualization.
individualiser [ɛ̃dividɥalize] **1** *vt* to individualize; to specify, to particularize (*case etc*). **2 s'individualiser** *vpr* (*d'une personne*) to develop a personality of one's own; *Biol* to take on individual characteristics.
individualisme [ɛ̃dividɥalism] *nm* individualism.
individualiste [ɛ̃dividɥalist] **1** *adj* individualistic. **2** *n* individualist.
individualité [ɛ̃dividɥalite] *nf* individuality.
individuel, -elle [ɛ̃dividɥɛl] *adj* individual; personal (*liberty etc*); private (*fortune etc*); **secrétaire i.**, personal *or* private secretary; **cas i.**, individual case; *Sp* **épreuve individuelle,** individual event.
individuellement [ɛ̃dividɥɛlmɑ̃] *adv* individually, personally.
indivis [ɛ̃divi] *adj Jur* **(a)** undivided, joint (*estate*); **(b)** joint (*owners*); **(c) par i.**, jointly.
indivisément [ɛ̃divizemɑ̃] *adv Jur* jointly.
indivisibilité [ɛ̃divizibilite] *nf* indivisibility.
indivisible [ɛ̃divizibl] *adj* indivisible.
indivisiblement [ɛ̃divizibləmɑ̃] *adv* indivisibly.
indivision [ɛ̃divizjɔ̃] *nf Jur* joint possession.
Indochine [ɛ̃dɔʃin] *nf* Indochina.
indochinois, -oise [ɛ̃dɔʃinwa, -waz] **1** *adj* Indochinese. **2** *n* **I.**, Indochinese.
indocile [ɛ̃dɔsil] *adj* intractable, disobedient.
indocilité [ɛ̃dɔsilite] *nf* intractability, disobedience.
indo-européen, -enne [ɛ̃doøropeɛ̃, -ɛn] (*pl indo-européens, -ennes*) **1** *adj* Indo-European. **2** *n* **I.-E.**, Indo-European. **3** *nm Ling* Indo-European.
indolemment [ɛ̃dɔlamɑ̃] *adv* indolently.
indolence [ɛ̃dɔlɑ̃s] *nf* indolence, apathy, sloth.
indolent [ɛ̃dɔlɑ̃] *adj* **(a)** (*apathique*) indolent, apathetic, slothful; **démarche indolente,** slow *or* lazy walk; **(b)** *Méd* painless, indolent (*tumour*).
indolore [ɛ̃dɔlɔr] *adj* painless.
indomptable [ɛ̃dɔ̃ptabl] *adj* unconquerable (*nation*); untam(e)able (*animal*); unmanageable (*horse*); *Fig* indomitable (*pride*); *Fig* ungovernable, uncontrollable (*passion*); **un appétit i.**, an uncontrollable appetite.
indompté [ɛ̃dɔ̃pte] *adj* unconquered (*nation*); untamed (*animal*); *Fig* uncontrolled (*passion*); *Fig* unbroken (*spirit*); **un appétit i.**, an uncontrollable appetite.
Indonésie [ɛ̃dɔnezi] *nf* Indonesia.
indonésien, -ienne [ɛ̃dɔnezjɛ̃, -jɛn] **1** *adj* Indonesian. **2** *n* **I.**, Indonesian.
indou, -oue [ɛ̃du] *Rel* **1** *adj* Hindu. **2** *n* **I.**, Hindu.
in-douze [induz] *Typ* **1** *adj* duodecimo, (in) twelvemo. **2** *nm inv* duodecimo.
indu [ɛ̃dy] *adj* undue (*haste etc*); unwarranted (*remark etc*); **à une heure indue,** at an ungodly hour; **il rentre à des heures indues,** he comes home at all hours of the night.
indubitable [ɛ̃dybitabl] *adj* beyond doubt, indubitable, undoubted, unquestionable.
indubitablement [ɛ̃dybitabləmɑ̃] *adv* indubitably, undoubtedly, unquestionably.
inductance [ɛ̃dyktɑ̃s] *nf El* inductance.
inducteur, -trice [ɛ̃dyktœr, -tris] *El* **1** *adj* inductive (*capacity etc*); inducing (*current*); **champ i.**, inductive field. **2** *nm* inductor; field magnet (*of dynamo*).
inductif, -ive [ɛ̃dyktif, -iv] *adj* inductive.
induction [ɛ̃dyksjɔ̃] *nf* induction; **raisonner par i.**, to reason by induction; *El* **courant d'i.**, induced current; *El* **bobine d'i.**, induction coil.
induire [ɛ̃dɥir] *vt* (*prp* **induisant**; *pp* **induit**; *pr ind* **j'induis, n. induisons, ils induisent**; *p hist* **j'induisis**; *fu* **j'induirai**) **(a)** (*engager*) to induce; **i. qn à faire qch,** to lead *or* induce *or* tempt s.o. to do sth; **i. qn en erreur,** to lead s.o. astray, to mislead s.o.; **(b)** (*conclure*) to infer, to induce (*conclusion*); **que pouvez-vous en i.?**, what can you infer from that?
induit [ɛ̃dɥi] *El* **1** *adj* induced, secondary (*circuit*). **2** *nm* **(a)** (*circuit*) induced circuit; **charge d'i.**, induced charge; **(b)** armature (*of large dynamo etc*).
indulgence [ɛ̃dylʒɑ̃s] *nf* **(a)** (*tolérance*) indulgence, leniency; **avec i.**, indulgently, leniently; **avoir** *ou* **montrer de l'i. pour** *ou* **envers qn,** to be indulgent with s.o., to make allowances for s.o.; **regard plein d'i.**, indulgent look; **par avance je demande votre i.**, I request your indulgence in advance; *Iron* **faites-moi l'i. de fermer cette porte,** I would be grateful if you closed the door; **(b)** *Rel* indulgence.
indulgent [ɛ̃dylʒɑ̃] *adj* indulgent, lenient, (too) kind; **être i. pour** *ou* **envers qn,** to be indulgent *or* lenient with s.o.
indûment [ɛ̃dymɑ̃] *adv* unduly, improperly.
industrialisation [ɛ̃dystrijalizasjɔ̃] *nf* industrialization.
industrialiser [ɛ̃dystrijalize] **1** *vt* to industrialize. **2 s'industrialiser** *vpr* to become industrialized.
industrialisme [ɛ̃dystrijalism] *nm Hist* industrialism.
industrie [ɛ̃dystri] *nf* **(a)** *Econ* industry, manufacturing; (*entreprise*) industry; **être à la tête d'une i.**, to head an industry; **capitaine d'i.**, captain of industry; **l'i. lourde/légère,** heavy/light industry; **i. de transformation,** processing industry; **i. alimentaire,** food industry; **i. pharmaceutique,** pharmaceuticals; **l'i. automobile,** the motor industry; **l'i. du bâtiment,** the building trade; **i. de pointe,** high technology *or* state-of-the-art industry; **l'i. du spectacle,** the entertainment industry, show business; **(b)** *Arch & Litt* activity; industry (*of bees etc*); (*ingéniosité*) ingenuity, cleverness, skill.
industriel, -elle [ɛ̃dystrijɛl] **1** *adj* industrial (*product etc*); **zone industrielle,** (*d'une ville*) industrial area; *F* **des magazines en quantité industrielle,** vast quantities of magazines. **2** *nm* manufacturer, industrialist.
industriellement [ɛ̃dystrijɛlmɑ̃] *adv* industrially; **vins produits i.**, mass-produced wines.
industrieux, -euse [ɛ̃dystrijø, -øz] *adj Litt* industrious; (*qui montre de l'habileté*) skilful, ingenious.
inébranlable [inebrɑ̃labl] *adj* unshakeable; immovable, solid, firm (*wall etc*); steadfast (*person*); unswerving (*purpose etc*); unwavering (*courage*); **il en a une conviction i.**, he is unshakeably convinced of it, his conviction is unshakeable.
inébranlablement [inebrɑ̃labləmɑ̃] *adv* unshakeably.
inéchangeable [ineʃɑ̃ʒabl] *adj* not exchangeable.
inécoutable [inekutabl] *adj* unbearable, impossible (to listen to).
inécouté [inekute] *adj* unheard, unheeded.
inédit [inedi] **1** *adj* **(a)** unpublished (*book etc*); **(b)** unprecedented; new, original (*show, plan*); **elle a des idées inédites,** she has some original ideas. **2** *nm* **(a)** (*texte*) unpublished work; **un i. de Gide,** an unpublished work by Gide; **(b) l'i.**, the new, the original.
ineffable [inefabl] *adj* ineffable, unutterable.
ineffablement [inefabləmɑ̃] *adv* ineffably.
ineffaçable [inefasabl] *adj* ineffaceable (*mark, memory*); indelible (*stain*).
ineffaçablement [inefasabləmɑ̃] *adv* ineffaceably.
inefficace [inefikas] *adj* ineffective, ineffectual; inefficacious, useless (*remedy*); (*dans son travail*) inefficient.

inefficacement [inefikasmɑ̃] *adv* ineffectively.

inefficacité [inefikasite] *nf* ineffectiveness, ineffectualness; inefficacy (*of remedy*); (*dans son travail*) inefficiency.

inégal, -aux [inegal, -o] *adj* **(a)** unequal (*parts etc*); **(b)** uneven, rough (*ground*); irregular (*pulse etc*); changeable (*wind*); *Fig* (*travail, écrivain*) inconsistent; **d'une humeur inégale,** to be as changeable as the weather.

inégalable [inegalabl] *adj* matchless, incomparable.

inégalé [inegale] *adj* unequalled, unmatched.

inégalement [inegalmɑ̃] *adv* **(a)** (*injustement*) unequally, unevenly; **i. partagé,** unevenly shared; **(b)** (*irrégulièrement*) (*battre*) irregularly.

inégalité [inegalite] *nf* **(a)** (*injustice*) inequality, disparity (**de, entre,** between); **(b)** unevenness (*of ground*); **les inégalités du chemin,** the bumps in the road; *Fig* **i. d'humeur,** capriciousness; **(c)** *Math etc* inequality.

inélastique [inelastik] *adj* (*rare*) inelastic.

inélégamment [inelegamɑ̃] *adv Litt* inelegantly.

inélégance [inelegɑ̃s] *nf Litt* inelegance.

inélégant [inelegɑ̃] *adj Litt* inelegant.

inéligibilité [inelizibilite] *nf* ineligibility.

inéligible [inelizibl] *adj* ineligible.

inéluctable [inelyktabl] *adj* inescapable, *Fml* ineluctable.

inéluctablement [inelyktabləmɑ̃] *adv* inescapably, *Fml* ineluctably.

inemployable [inɑ̃plwajabl] *adj* unusable.

inemployé [inɑ̃plwaje] *adj* unused.

inénarrable [inenarabl] *adj* comical, funny; **dommage que vous ne l'ayez pas vu, c'était i.!,** it was a shame you didn't see it, it was priceless!

inentamé [inɑ̃tame] *adj* intact; uncut (*loaf etc*); **fortune inentamée,** intact fortune.

inéprouvé [inepruve] *adj* **(a)** (*non mis à l'épreuve*) untried, untested; **(b)** (*non ressenti*) not yet experienced *or* felt.

inepte [inɛpt] *adj* inept, foolish, idiotic (*remark etc*).

ineptie [inɛpsi] *nf* **(a)** (*sottise*) ineptitude, ineptness; **(b)** (*action, remarque*) **dire des inepties,** to talk nonsense *or* rubbish; **ce traité est une i.,** the treaty is an absurdity.

inépuisable [inepɥizabl] *adj* inexhaustible; **bavardage i.,** never-ending chatter; **un stock i. d'histoires drôles,** an inexhaustible supply of funny stories; **une imagination i.,** a fertile imagination.

inéquation [inekwɑsjɔ̃] *nf Math* inequation.

inéquitable [inekitabl] *adj* inequitable, unfair.

inerte [inɛrt] *adj* inert (*mass etc*); sluggish (*nature*); dull (*intelligence*); **rester i. pendant un débat,** to remain silent during a debate; **un visage i.,** an expressionless face; **le visage i.,** (*écouter etc*) impassively.

inertie [inɛrsi] *nf* **(a)** *Phys* inertia; **force d'i.,** force of inertia; **moment d'i.,** moment of inertia; **(b)** (*manque de réaction*) passivity; sluggishness, inertness (*of mind, body*); **l'i. de la direction** management's inertia.

inescomptable [inɛskɔ̃tabl] *adj Fin* undiscountable.

inespéré [inɛspere] *adj* unhoped-for, unexpected.

inesthétique [inɛstetik] *adj* unaesthetic.

inestimable [inɛstimabl] *adj* inestimable, invaluable, priceless; **richesse i.,** inestimable weath; **votre aide a été i.,** your help was invaluable.

inévitable [inevitabl] *adj* unavoidable (*accident etc*); inevitable, inescapable (*result*); **c'est i.,** it's inevitable, it's bound to happen; **il est arrivé avec son i. chien,** he arrived with his dog in tow as usual.

inévitablement [inevitabləmɑ̃] *adv* unavoidably, inevitably.

inexact [inɛgzakt] *adj* (*faux*) inexact, inaccurate, incorrect; wrong (*amount etc*); (*manquant de ponctualité*) unpunctual; **des renseignements inexacts,** inaccurate information.

inexactement [inɛgzaktəmɑ̃] *adv* inexactly, inaccurately.

inexactitude [inɛgzaktityd] *nf* **(a)** (*caractère erroné, imprécision*) inaccuracy, incorrectness; (*faute*) mistake; **relever des inexactitudes dans une traduction,** to find mistakes *or* inaccuracies in a translation; **(b)** (*manque de ponctualité*) unpunctuality.

inexaucé [inɛgzose] *adj* unanswered (*prayer*); unfulfilled (*desire*).

inexcusable [inɛkskyzabl] *adj* inexcusable, unwarrantable (*action*); **vous êtes i.!,** you're unforgiveable!

inexécutable [inɛgzekytabl] *adj* (*plan etc*) impracticable, impractical, unworkable; (*ordre*) that cannot be carried out.

inexécuté [inɛgzekyte] *adj* unperformed; (*promesse*) unfulfilled; (*ordre*) not carried out.

inexécution [inɛgzekysjɔ̃] *nf* (*d'un contrat*) non-performance; (*d'une promesse*) non-fulfilment.

inexercé [inɛgzɛrse] *adj* **(a)** (*sans entraînement*) unexercised, untrained; **(b)** (*sans expérience*) unpractised, unskilled, inexperienced (*eye etc*).

inexhaustible [inɛgzostibl] *adj Litt* inexhaustible.

inexistant [inɛgzistɑ̃] *adj* non-existent.

inexistence [inɛgzistɑ̃s] *nf* non-existence.

inexorabilité [inɛgzɔrabilite] *nf* inexorability.

inexorable [inɛgzɔrabl] *adj* inexorable, unrelenting.

inexorablement [inɛgzɔrabləmɑ̃] *adv* inexorably.

inexpérience [inɛksperjɑ̃s] *nf* inexperience.

inexpérimenté [inɛksperimɑ̃te] *adj* **(a)** inexperienced; unpractised, unskilled (*hand etc*); **(b)** untried, untested (*process*).

inexpert [inɛkspɛr] *adj Litt* inexpert, unpractised.

inexpiable [inɛkspjabl] *adj* inexpiable, unatonable.

inexpié [inɛkspje] *adj* unexpiated, unatoned.

inexplicable [inɛksplikabl] *adj* (*comportement*) inexplicable; **le sentiment que j'ai est i.,** I can't explain the feeling I have.

inexplicablement [inɛksplikabləmɑ̃] *adv* inexplicably, unaccountably.

inexpliqué [inɛksplike] *adj* unexplained.

inexploitable [inɛksplwatabl] *adj* unworkable (*mine*).

inexploité [inɛksplwate] *adj* unworked (*mine*); undeveloped (*land*); **ressources inexploitées,** untapped resources.

inexplorable [inɛksplɔrabl] *adj* inexplorable.

inexploré [inɛksplɔre] *adj* unexplored.

inexplosible [inɛksplozibl] *adj* non-explosive.

inexpressif, -ive [inɛkspresif, -iv] *adj* inexpressive, lacking in expression; expressionless (*face*).

inexprimable [inɛksprimabl] *adj* inexpressible, beyond words.

inexprimé [inɛksprime] *adj* unexpressed.

inexpugnable [inɛkspygnabl] *adj* impregnable.

inextensible [inɛkstɑ̃sibl] *adj* inextensible.

in extenso [inɛkstɛ̃so] *adv* in extenso.

inextinguible [inɛkstɛ̃g(ɥ)ibl] *adj* inextinguishable, unquenchable (*fire etc*); *Fig* irrepressible, uncontrollable (*laughter*).

in extremis [inɛkstremis] **1** *adv* at the (very) last minute. **2** *adj* last-minute.

inextricable [inɛkstrikabl] *adj* inextricable.

inextricablement [inɛkstrikabləmɑ̃] *adv* inextricably.

infaillibilité [ɛ̃fajibilite] *nf* infallibility.

infaillible [ɛ̃fajibl] *adj* infallible.

infailliblement [ɛ̃fajibləmɑ̃] *adv* infallibly.

infaisable [ɛ̃fəzabl] *adj* not feasible, impracticable.

infamant [ɛ̃famɑ̃] *adj* **(a)** (*déclaration etc*) defamatory; **(b)** (*ignoble*) ignominious; *Jur* infamous; *Jur* **peine infamante,** penalty involving loss of civil rights.

infâme [ɛ̃fɑm] *adj* infamous; foul (*deed*); unspeakable (*crime etc*); vile, squalid (*slum*).

infamie [ɛ̃fami] *nf* **(a)** infamy; **(b)** (*action, remarque*) infamous action *or* statement; **dire des infamies à** *ou* **de qn,** to vilify *or* slander s.o..

infant, -ante [ɛ̃fɑ̃, -ɑ̃t] *n Spanish Hist* infante, *f* infanta.

infanterie [ɛ̃fɑ̃tri] *nf* infantry; **soldat d'i.,** infantryman, foot soldier; **i. aéroportée** *ou* **de l'air,** airborne infantry; **i. de marine,** Marine Light Infantry.

infanticide¹ [ɛ̃fɑ̃tisid] **1** *n* (*personne*) infanticide. **2** *adj* infanticidal.

infanticide² *nm* (*crime*) infanticide, child murder.

infantile [ɛ̃fɑ̃til] *adj* **(a)** infantile (*disease etc*); **mortalité i.,** infant mortality; **psychiatrie i.,** child psychiatry; **(b)** *Péj* (*attitude etc*) infantile.

infantiliser [ɛ̃fɑ̃tilize] *vt Péj* to cause (*s.o.*) to revert to childhood.

infantilisme [ɛ̃fɑ̃tilism] *nm* **(a)** *Méd* infantilism, retarded development; **(b)** *Péj* **c'est de l'i.,** how infantile!

infarctus [ɛ̃farktys] *nm Méd* infarct, infarction; **i. du myocarde,** myocardial infarction, coronary thrombosis.

infatigable [ɛ̃fatigabl] *adj* indefatigable, untiring, tireless.

infatigablement [ɛ̃fatigabləmɑ̃] *adv* indefatigably, untiringly, tirelessly.

infatuation [ɛ̃fatɥasjɔ̃] *nf* **(a)** (*suffisance*) self-conceit, self-importance; **(b)** *Arch* infatuation.

infatué [ɛ̃fatɥe] *adj* **(a)** (*suffisant*) conceited; **i. (de soi-même),** conceited, full of one's own importance; **(b)** *Arch* infatuated.

infatuer [ɛ̃fatɥe] **1** *vt Arch* to infatuate. **2** **s'infatuer** *vpr* **(a)** **s'i. (de soi-même),** to become full of one's own importance, to become conceited; **(b)** *Vieilli* **s'i. de qn/qch,**

to become infatuated with s.o./sth.

infécond [ɛ̃fekɔ̃] *adj* barren, sterile, infertile; (*terre*) barren, infertile.

infécondité [ɛ̃fekɔ̃dite] *nf* barrenness, sterility, infertility; *Fig* **l'i. d'une politique,** the fruitlessness of a policy.

infect [ɛ̃fɛkt] *adj* stinking (*food*); foul (*air*); noisome, putrid (*smell*); **odeur infecte,** stench; **taudis i.,** filthy hovel; **repas i.,** rotten *or* revolting meal; **temps i.,** filthy *or* foul weather; **elle a été infecte avec sa sœur,** she was rotten to her sister.

infectant [ɛ̃fɛktɑ̃] *adj Méd* infectious (*virus*).

infecter [ɛ̃fɛkte] **1** *vt* **(a)** *Méd* to infect; **(b)** to poison (*the atmosphere*); to contaminate, to taint, to pollute (*water etc*). **2 s'infecter** *vpr* to become infected, to turn *or* go septic.

infectieux, -euse [ɛ̃fɛksjø, -øz] *adj Méd* infectious.

infection [ɛ̃fɛksjɔ̃] *nf* **(a)** *Méd* infection; **i. virale,** viral infection; **(b)** (*puanteur*) stench, stink; **quelle i. dans cette pièce!,** this room stinks!; **(c)** *Péj F* **la télévision, c'est une i.!,** television stinks.

inféodation [ɛ̃feɔdasjɔ̃] *nf Pol* allegiance.

inféoder (s') [sɛ̃feɔde] *vpr Pol* **s'i. à un groupe/un parti,** to give one's allegiance to a group/a party.

inférence [ɛ̃ferɑ̃s] *nf* inference.

inférer [ɛ̃fere] *vt* (**j'infère; j'inférerai**) to infer, to gather (**de,** from).

inférieur, -eure [ɛ̃ferjœr] **1** *adj* **(a)** (*qui est en bas*) lower; **partie inférieure (de qch),** lower part, bottom (of sth); **lèvre inférieure,** lower lip, bottom lip; **membres inférieurs,** lower limbs; **i. au niveau de la mer,** below sea level; *Astron* **planète inférieure,** inferior planet; **i. à la normale,** (*of temperature etc*) below normal; **(b)** (*dans une hiérarchie*) inferior, poor (*quality, goods etc*); **d'un rang i.,** of a lower rank, lower in rank; **elle ne lui est pas inférieure,** she is his equal; **intelligence inférieure,** inferior intelligence; **(c) 6 est i. à 8,** 6 is less than 8; **i. ou égal à 3,** three or less; **note inférieure à douze,** mark below twelve; **i. en nombre,** fewer in number. **2** *n* inferior; **traiter qn comme un i.,** to treat s.o. like an inferior; **être l'i. de qn,** to be s.o.'s inferior.

inférieurement [ɛ̃ferjœrmɑ̃] *adv* **(a)** (*en bas etc*) in a lower position; **(b)** (*moins bien*) in an inferior manner, less well.

infériorité [ɛ̃ferjɔrite] *nf* inferiority; **i. numérique** *ou* **en nombre,** numerical inferiority, inferiority in numbers; *Psy* **avoir un complexe d'i.,** to have an inferiority complex; **i. de niveau,** difference *or* drop in level; **il prend son manque d'expérience comme une i.,** he feels that his lack of experience makes him inferior.

infernal, -aux [ɛ̃fɛrnal, -o] *adj* infernal; **les puissances infernales,** the powers of hell; **machine infernale,** booby trap; *Arch* infernal engine; *F* **cet enfant est i.,** this child's a little devil; **c'est i.!,** it's hellish!, it's sheer hell!

infertile [ɛ̃fɛrtil] *adj* infertile.

infertilité [ɛ̃fɛrtilite] *nf* infertility.

infestation [ɛ̃fɛstasjɔ̃] *nf Méd* infestation.

infester [ɛ̃fɛste] *vt* (*of vermin etc*) to infest, to overrun; **infesté d'insectes,** infested *or* overrun with insects.

infeutrable [ɛ̃føtrabl] *adj* which does not felt *or* mat.

infidèle [ɛ̃fidɛl] **1** *adj* **(a)** (*déloyal*) unfaithful, false, faithless, disloyal (**à,** to); **femme i.,** unfaithful wife; **être i. à sa promesse,** to break one's promise; **(b)** (*inexact*) incorrect, inaccurate; **c'est une traduction i.,** it is not an exact *or* a faithful translation; **mémoire i.,** untrustworthy memory; **(c)** *Rel* infidel. **2** *n Rel* infidel.

infidèlement [ɛ̃fidɛlmɑ̃] *adv* **(a)** (*déloyalement*) unfaithfully; **(b)** (*inexactement*) incorrectly, inaccurately.

infidélité [ɛ̃fidelite] *nf* **(a)** (*déloyauté*) infidelity, unfaithfulness, faithlessness, disloyalty (**à,** to); **faire des infidélités à sa femme,** to be unfaithful to one's wife; **faire une i. à son boucher/sa coiffeur/***etc*, to go to a different butcher/hairdresser/*etc* (*just for once*); **(b)** inaccuracy (*in translation etc*).

infiltration [ɛ̃filtrasjɔ̃] *nf* **(a)** (*d'eau etc*) infiltration, percolation, seepage; **(b)** *Fig* (*de nouvelles idées etc*) infiltration; **(c)** filtering through (*of traffic etc*).

infiltrer [ɛ̃filtre] **1** *vt* to infiltrate; **i. un parti/un pays,** to infiltrate a party/a country. **2 s'infiltrer** *vpr* **(a)** (*of fluid*) to infiltrate, to percolate, to seep (**dans,** into; **à travers,** through); to soak in *or* through, to filter through; **(b)** *Fig* (*of idea etc*) to filter in; **(c)** (*of troops etc*) **s'i. dans un pays,** to infiltrate a country.

infime [ɛ̃fim] *adj* **(a)** tiny, minute; infinitesimal (*number*); **(b)** lowly, mean (*rank etc*).

infini [ɛ̃fini] **1** *adj* infinite; boundless, immeasurable (*space etc*); never-ending, eternal, endless (*bliss etc*); innumerable (*arguments etc*); **prendre d'infinies précautions,** to take innumerable precautions; **bonté infinie,** infinite kindness. **2** *nm Phil* **l'i.,** the infinite; *Phys* infinity; *Phot* **mettre au point sur l'i.,** to focus on infinity; **à l'i.,** to infinity, ad infinitum, boundlessly.

infiniment [ɛ̃finimɑ̃] *adv* infinitely; **i. plus intelligent,** infinitely more intelligent; **se donner i. de peine,** to give oneself an infinite amount of trouble; **je regrette i.,** I'm terribly sorry; **i. petit,** infinitesimally small.

infinité [ɛ̃finite] *nf Math etc* infinity; **l'i. de l'espace,** the infinity *or* boundlessness of space; **une i. de personnes,** (*grand nombre*) an infinite number of people; **une i. de raisons,** an infinite number of reasons.

infinitésimal, -aux [ɛ̃finitezimal, -o] *adj Math etc* infinitesimal.

infinitif, -ive [ɛ̃finitif, -iv] *Gram* **1** *adj* infinitive (*mood*). **2** *nm* infinitive; **à l'i.,** in the infinitive.

infirmation [ɛ̃firmasjɔ̃] *nf Jur* invalidation, nullification, quashing.

infirme [ɛ̃firm] **1** *adj* disabled, crippled; infirm (*old man etc*); *Arch & Litt* weak; **i. du bras gauche,** crippled in the left arm. **2** *n* cripple; (*alité*) invalid; **les infirmes,** the disabled.

infirmer [ɛ̃firme] *vt* **(a)** to show up the weakness of (*proof, argument etc*); to weaken (*s.o.'s authority*); to weaken, to invalidate (*evidence, claim*); **(b)** *Jur* to annul, to quash (*judgment*); to set (*verdict*) aside.

infirmerie [ɛ̃firməri] *nf* (*in prison etc*) infirmary; (*in school, ship*) sick bay.

infirmier, -ière [ɛ̃firmje, -jɛr] *nm* (male) nurse; nurse; *Mil* medical orderly; **i. diplômé(e),** ≈ state-registered nurse; **i. en chef,** matron; *Admin* nursing officer; **i. visiteur, -euse,** district nurse.

infirmité [ɛ̃firmite] *nf* (*invalidité*) infirmity; (*handicap*) physical disability; *Arch & Litt* weakness, frailty.

inflammabilité [ɛ̃flamabilite] *nf* inflammability; *Tech & Am* flammability.

inflammable [ɛ̃flamabl] *adj* inflammable; *Tech & Am* flammable.

inflammation [ɛ̃flamasjɔ̃] *nf Méd* inflammation.

inflammatoire [ɛ̃flamatwar] *adj Méd* inflammatory.

inflation [ɛ̃flasjɔ̃] *nf Écon* inflation; **politique d'i.,** inflationary policy; **l'i. a atteint sept pour cent,** inflation has reached seven per cent.

inflationniste [ɛ̃flasjɔnist] *Écon* **1** *n* inflationist. **2** *adj* inflationary.

infléchi [ɛ̃fleʃi] *adj* **(a)** *Gram* inflected (*vowel etc*); **(b)** inflected, bent (*ray etc*).

infléchir [ɛ̃fleʃir] **1** *vt* **(a)** to bend, to inflect, to curve (*ray etc*); **(b)** to change the direction of (*policy etc*). **2 s'infléchir** *vpr* **(a)** to bend, to curve, to deviate; *Opt* (*of ray*) to be inflected; **(b)** (*of structure*) to cave in.

inflexibilité [ɛ̃flɛksibilite] *nf* inflexibility, rigidity.

inflexible [ɛ̃flɛksibl] *adj* inflexible, unbending, rigid, unyielding; **demeurer i. dans une résolution,** to stick to a resolution; **une règle i.,** an inflexible rule.

inflexiblement [ɛ̃flɛksibləmɑ̃] *adv* inflexibly.

inflexion [ɛ̃flɛksjɔ̃] *nf* **(a)** (*mouvement*) inflexion, inflection; *Math Opt etc* bend(ing); change of direction (*of curve, ray*); bend(ing) (*of body*); **une i. de tête,** a nod; **légère i. du corps,** slight bow; **(b)** modulation (*of voice*); **(c)** *Ling Gram* inflection.

infliger [ɛ̃fliʒe] *vt* (**j'infligeai(s), n. infligeons**) to inflict; **i. une peine/une amende à qn,** to impose a penalty/a fine on s.o.; **il nous a infligé sa présence,** he inflicted himself on us.

inflorescence [ɛ̃flɔresɑ̃s] *nf Bot* inflorescence.

influençable [ɛ̃flyɑ̃sabl] *adj* easily influenced.

influence [ɛ̃flyɑ̃s] *nf* influence; **exercer une i. sur qch/qn,** to have an influence *or* an effect on sth/s.o.; **sous l'i. de qch,** under the influence of sth; **sous l'i. de l'alcool,** under the influence of drink; **sous ton i.,** under your influence; **il a beaucoup d'i.,** he has a lot of influence, he's very influential; **sphère d'i.,** sphere of influence; **trafic d'i.,** corrupt practice.

influencer [ɛ̃flyɑ̃se] *vt* (**j'influençai(s), n. influençons**) to influence, to have an influence on (*s.o., sth*); to influence, to sway (*public opinion*).

influent [ɛ̃flyɑ̃] *adj* influential.

influer [ɛ̃flye] *vi* **i. sur qn,** to influence s.o., to exercise *or* have (an) influence on *or* over s.o.; **i. sur qch,** to have an effect on sth.

influx [ɛ̃fly] *nm* **(a)** *Physiol* **i. nerveux,** nerve impulse; **(b)** (*fluide*) influx.

info [ɛ̃fo] *nf F* = **INFORMATION**.

infographie [ɛ̃fɔgrafi] *nf* computer graphics.

in-folio [infɔljo] **1** *adj inv* folio. **2** *nm inv* folio.

informateur, -trice [ɛ̃fɔrmatœr, -tris] *n* informant.

informaticien, -ienne [ɛ̃fɔrmatisjɛ̃, -jɛn] **1** *n* computer scientist. **2** *adj* **ingénieur i.**, computer engineer.

informatif, -ive [ɛ̃fɔrmatif, -iv] *adj* informative.

information [ɛ̃fɔrmɑsjɔ̃] *nf* **(a)** (*renseignement*) information; news (item); **centre d'i.**, information centre; **une i. de première importance**, a very important piece of information; **c'est la seule i. dont je dispose**, it's the only information I have; **un journal d'i.**, a serious *or* quality newspaper, *F* a heavy; **je vous envoie pour votre i. ...**, I'm sending you for your information ...; **le droit à l'i.**, freedom of information; **mettre la main sur l'i.**, to take control of the media; *Rad TV Journ* **informations**, news (bulletin); *Journ* **informations de la dernière heure**, latest news; **(b)** *Ordinat* data; **traitement de l'i.**, data processing; **théorie de l'i.**, information theory; **(c)** (*enquête*) inquiry; *Jur* preliminary investigation (*of a case*); *Jur* **ouvrir une i.**, to begin legal proceedings.

informatique [ɛ̃fɔrmatik] **1** *nf* data processing; (*science*) computer science, information science, informatics; **travailler dans l'i.**, to be in computers; **société/magazine/***etc* **d'i.**, computer company/magazine/*etc*; **cours d'i.**, computer course, data-processing course; **i. à domicile**, home computing. **2** *adj* (*mobilier, réseau etc*) computer.

informatisation [ɛ̃fɔrmatizɑsjɔ̃] *nf* computerization.

informatiser [ɛ̃fɔrmatize] *vt* to computerize; **service informatisé**, computerized department.

informe [ɛ̃fɔrm] *adj* formless, unformed, shapeless (*mass etc*); crude (*plan*); ill-formed, misshapen (*monster etc*); **un pull i.**, a shapeless sweater.

informé [ɛ̃fɔrme] **1** *adj* informed; **dans les milieux informés**, in informed circles. **2** *nm Jur* result of inquiry; **jusqu'à plus ample i.**, until we have further information *or* are better informed.

informel, -elle [ɛ̃fɔrmɛl] *adj* informal.

informer [ɛ̃fɔrme] **1** *vt* **i. qn de qch**, to inform s.o. of sth, to tell s.o. *or* let s.o. know about sth; to acquaint s.o. with (*a fact*); **veuillez m'en i.**, please let me know; **bien informé**, well informed; **mal informé**, misinformed. **2** *vi Jur* **i. sur un crime**, to investigate *or* inquire into a crime; **i. contre qn**, to inform against s.o.. **3 s'informer** *vpr* to make inquiries; **s'i. de qch**, to inquire *or* ask about sth; **il cherche à s'i.**, he's trying to find out.

informulé [ɛ̃fɔrmyle] *adj* unformulated.

infortune [ɛ̃fɔrtyn] *nf surtout Litt* misfortune, calamity; **compagnons d'i.**, companions in adversity, fellow sufferers; **tomber dans l'i.**, to meet with misfortune, to fall on evil days.

infortuné [ɛ̃fɔrtyne] **1** *adj* unfortunate, unlucky, wretched. **2** *n* **les infortunés**, the unfortunate, the wretched.

infraction [ɛ̃fraksjɔ̃] *nf* **(a)** infringement (*of rights etc*); **(b)** (*violation*) offence; **i. à la loi**, infringement of the law; **i. au devoir**, breach of duty; **i. à un ordre**, violation of an order; **être en i.**, to be committing an offence.

infranchissable [ɛ̃frɑ̃ʃisabl] *adj* impassable; insuperable, insurmountable (*difficulty etc*).

infrangible [ɛ̃frɑ̃ʒibl] *adj Litt* infrangible.

infrarouge [ɛ̃fraruʒ] *adj & nm* infrared.

infrason [ɛ̃frasɔ̃] *nm* infrasonic vibration.

infra(-)sonore [ɛ̃frasɔnɔr] *adj* infrasonic; (*pl infra(-)sonores*).

infrastructure [ɛ̃frastryktyr] *nf* **(a)** *Constr* substructure; *Constr* understructure (*of bridge etc*); *Écon* infrastructure; **(b)** *Tech* infrastructure, basic equipment (*of railways, hospitals etc*); ground environment (*of radar system etc*).

infréquentable [ɛ̃frekɑ̃tabl] *adj* **gens infréquentables**, people one doesn't want to associate with.

infroissable [ɛ̃frwasabl] *adj Tex etc* crease-resistant, uncrushable.

infructueux, -euse [ɛ̃fryktɥø, -øz] *adj* unfruitful, barren (*land etc*); fruitless, unavailing, unsuccessful (*efforts*); unprofitable (*investment*).

infumable [ɛ̃fymabl] *adj* unsmokable (*cigar etc*).

infus [ɛ̃fy] *adj* inborn, innate (*knowledge etc*).

infuser [ɛ̃fyze] **1** *vt* **(a)** (*faire pénétrer*) to instil, to infuse (**à**, into); *Fig* **i. un sang nouveau à un organisme**, to inject new blood into an organization; **(b)** to steep, to infuse (*herbs etc*). **2** *vi* **faire i. le thé**, to infuse *or* brew the tea; **laisser i. le thé**, to let the tea draw *or* brew.

infusible [ɛ̃fyzibl] *adj* infusible, non-fusible.

infusion [ɛ̃fyzjɔ̃] *nf* infusion; infusing (*of herbs, tea*); steeping (*of herbs etc*); (*boisson*) herb tea; **une i. de camomille**, an infusion of camomile, camomile tea.

ingagnable [ɛ̃gaɲabl] *adj* that cannot be won; **la partie est i. pour l'Angleterre**, England can't win.

ingambe [ɛ̃gɑ̃b] *adj* (*physiquement*) nimble, sprightly; (*esprit*) alert.

ingénier (s') [sɛ̃ʒenje] *vpr* **s'i. à faire qch**, to strive *or* make an effort to do sth; **il s'ingénie à me rendre la vie impossible**, he goes out of his way to make my life impossible.

ingénierie [ɛ̃ʒeniri] *nf* engineering.

ingénieur [ɛ̃ʒenjœr] *nm* (graduate, qualified) engineer; **i. (des travaux publics)**, civil engineer; **i. des ponts et chaussées**, = (government) civil engineer; **i. des mines**, mining engineer; **i. électricien**, electrical engineer; **i. mécanicien**, mechanical engineer; **i. électronicien**, electronics engineer; **i. du son**, sound engineer; *Nau* **i. des constructions navales**, naval constructor; **i. de l'artillerie navale**, naval ordnance officer; *Mil* **Corps des Ingénieurs géographes**, = Ordnance Survey; **femme i.**, female engineer.

ingénieusement [ɛ̃ʒenjøzmɑ̃] *adv* ingeniously, cleverly.

ingénieux, -euse [ɛ̃ʒenjø, -øz] *adj* ingenious, clever.

ingéniosité [ɛ̃ʒenjozite] *nf* ingenuity, ingeniousness; cleverness (*of person*).

ingénu, -ue [ɛ̃ʒeny] **1** *adj* ingenuous, artless, simple, naive, unsophisticated (*person*). **2** *n* **faire l'i.**, to affect simplicity. **3** *nf Th* **ingénue**, ingénue.

ingénuité [ɛ̃ʒenɥite] *nf* ingenuousness, artlessness, simplicity, naivety.

ingénument [ɛ̃ʒenymɑ̃] *adv* ingenuously, artlessly, simply, naively.

ingérence [ɛ̃ʒerɑ̃s] *nf* (unwarrantable) interference, meddling; **politique de non i.**, policy of non-interference.

ingérer [ɛ̃ʒere] *v* (**j'ingère**; **j'ingérerai**) **1** *vt Physiol* to ingest (*food*). **2 s'ingérer** *vpr* **s'i. dans une affaire**, to interfere in *or* meddle with a matter.

ingestion [ɛ̃ʒɛstjɔ̃] *nf Physiol* ingestion.

ingouvernable [ɛ̃guvɛrnabl] *adj* **(a)** (*nation etc*) ungovernable; **(b)** unmanageable (*ship etc*).

ingrat, -ate [ɛ̃gra, -at] **1** *adj* ungrateful (**envers**, to, towards); unproductive, unprofitable (*soil etc*); intractable (*material*); thankless (*task*); barren (*subject*); disagreeable, repellent (*work etc*); unattractive, unpleasant (*appearance etc*); **l'âge i.**, the awkward age. **2** *n* ungrateful person.

ingratement [ɛ̃gratmɑ̃] *adv Litt* ungratefully.

ingratitude [ɛ̃gratityd] *nf* ingratitude, ungratefulness.

ingrédient [ɛ̃gredjɑ̃] *nm* ingredient, constituent.

inguérissable [ɛ̃gerisabl] *adj Méd* incurable; inconsolable (*grief*).

ingurgitation [ɛ̃gyrʒitɑsjɔ̃] *nf* (*rare*) ingurgitation.

ingurgiter [ɛ̃gyrʒite] *vt* to ingurgitate; to swallow, to gulp down, *F* to knock back (*drink etc*).

inhabile [inabil] *adj Litt* (*malhabile*) unskilled (**à**, in); unskilful, clumsy; **elle est i. dans ses rapports personnels**, she's a bit clumsy *or* tactless in her dealings with other people; *Jur* **i. à tester**, incompetent to make a will.

inhabilement [inabilmɑ̃] *adv Litt* unskilfully.

inhabileté [inabilte] *nf* lack of skill (**à faire qch**, in doing sth); clumsiness.

inhabilité [inabilite] *nf Jur* incapacity, disability; **i. à succéder**, incompetency to succeed.

inhabitable [inabitabl] *adj* uninhabitable.

inhabité [inabite] *adj* uninhabited; unoccupied (*house*); *Astron* **vol i.**, unmanned flight.

inhabituel, -elle [inabitɥɛl] *adj* unusual; **c'est i. de ne pas les trouver à la maison le dimanche**, it's unusual not to find them at home on a Sunday.

inhalateur, -trice [inalatœr, -tris] **1** *adj* inhaling (*apparatus*). **2** *nm Méd etc* inhaler.

inhalation [inalɑsjɔ̃] *nf* inhalation.

inhaler [inale] *vt* to inhale.

inharmonieux, -ieuse [inarmɔnjø, -jøz] *adj* (*son*) inharmonious, discordant.

inhérence [inerɑ̃s] *nf* inherence, inherency.

inhérent [inerɑ̃] *adj* inherent (**à**, in).

inhiber [inibe] *vt* to inhibit.

inhibiteur, -trice [inibitœr, -tris], **inhibitif, -ive** [inibitif, -iv] **1** *adj* inhibitory (*reflex, nerve etc*). **2** *n* inhibitor.

inhibition [inibisjɔ̃] *nf* inhibition.

inhospitalier, -ière [inɔspitalje, -jɛr] *adj* inhospitable.

inhumain [inymɛ̃] *adj* inhuman.

inhumainement [inymɛnmɑ̃] *adv Litt* inhumanly.

inhumanité [inymanite] *nf Litt* inhumanity.

inhumation [inymasjɔ̃] *nf* burial, interment.
inhumer [inyme] *vt* to bury, to inter.
inimaginable [inimaʒinabl] *adj* unimaginable, inconceivable, unthinkable.
inimitable [inimitabl] *adj* inimitable, matchless.
inimitié [inimitje] *nf* enmity, hostility, ill feeling.
ininflammable [inɛ̃flamabl] *adj* non-(in)flammable, fire-proof.
inintelligemment [inɛ̃teliʒamɑ̃] *adv* unintelligently.
inintelligence [inɛ̃teliʒɑ̃s] *nf* lack of intelligence; **son i. des enfants,** his inability to understand children.
inintelligent [inɛ̃teliʒɑ̃] *adj* unintelligent.
inintelligibilité [inɛ̃teliʒibilite] *nf* unintelligibility.
inintelligible [inɛ̃teliʒibl] *adj* unintelligible.
inintelligiblement [inɛ̃teliʒibləmɑ̃] *adv* unintelligibly.
inintéressant [inɛ̃terɛsɑ̃] *adj* uninteresting.
inintérêt [inɛ̃terɛ] *nm* lack of interest (**pour,** in).
ininterrompu [inɛ̃terɔ̃py] *adj* uninterrupted, unremitting (*efforts*); uninterrupted, unbroken (*sleep etc*); steady (*progress*).
inique [inik] *adj* iniquitous.
iniquement [inikmɑ̃] *adv* iniquitously.
iniquité [inikite] *nf* iniquity.
initial, -aux [inisjal, -o] **1** *adj* initial (*letter, cost etc*); starting (*price*); **vitesse initiale,** (*d'un projectile*) muzzle velocity. **2** *nf* **initiale,** initial (letter).
initialement [inisjalmɑ̃] *adv* initially.
initialiser [inisjalize] *vt Ordinat* to initialize (*a disk*); to boot (up) (*a computer*).
initiateur, -trice [inisjatœr, -tris] **1** *n* initiator; originator, pioneer (*of scheme etc*). **2** *adj* initiatory.
initiation [inisjasjɔ̃] *nf* initiation (**à,** to); **une i. à la musique,** an introduction to music; **rite d'i.,** initiation rite.
initiatique [inisjatik] *adj* initiatory.
initiative [inisjativ] *nf* initiative; **sur l'i. de qn,** on s.o.'s initiative; **prendre l'i. d'une réforme,** to initiate a reform; **prendre l'i. de faire qch,** to take the initiative in doing sth; **faire qch de sa propre i.,** to do sth on one's own initiative; **faire preuve d'i.,** to show initiative; **il n'a aucune i.,** he's got no initiative; **syndicat d'i.,** tourist information bureau; *Mil* **i. de défense stratégique,** strategic defence initiative.
initié, -ée [inisje] *n Rel etc* initiate; (*personne au courant*) person in the know; *Bourse* **délit d'i.,** insider trading.
initier [inisje] **1** *vt* to initiate (*s.o.*) (**à,** into); **c'est moi qui l'ai initié au grec,** it was me who introduced him to Greek. **2 s'initier** *vpr* **s'i. à qch,** to learn *or* be learning sth.
injectable [ɛ̃ʒɛktabl] *adj* injectable.
injecté [ɛ̃ʒɛkte] *adj* congested, inflamed; **yeux injectés de sang,** bloodshot eyes.
injecter [ɛ̃ʒɛkte] **1** *vt* to inject. **2 s'injecter** *vpr* (*of eyes etc*) to become bloodshot.
injecteur, -trice [ɛ̃ʒɛktœr, -tris] **1** *adj* injecting (*tube etc*). **2** *nm* injector; *Av etc* nozzle.
injection [ɛ̃ʒɛksjɔ̃] *nf* injection (*Med of penicillin, Fin of capital etc*); **moteur à i.,** fuel injection engine.
injoignable [ɛ̃ʒwaɲabl] *adj* (*of person*) with whom one cannot get in touch; **elle est i. au téléphone,** she can't be reached on the phone.
injonction [ɛ̃ʒɔ̃ksjɔ̃] *nf* injunction; *Jur* injunction, order.
injure [ɛ̃ʒyr] *nf* (*insulte*) insult; **injures,** abuse; **en venir aux injures,** to start insulting each other; **faire i. à qn,** to insult s.o.; *Litt* **l'i. des ans,** the ravages of time.
injurier [ɛ̃ʒyrje] *vt* to abuse, to insult (*s.o.*).
injurieux, -euse [ɛ̃ʒyrjø, -øz] *adj* insulting, abusive.
injuste [ɛ̃ʒyst] **1** *adj* unjust; unfair (**envers, avec,** to). **2** *nm* **le juste et l'i.,** right and wrong.
injustement [ɛ̃ʒystəmɑ̃] *adv* unjustly.
injustice [ɛ̃ʒystis] *nf* **(a)** (*iniquité*) injustice, unfairness (**envers,** to, towards); **lutter contre l'i.,** to fight (against) injustice; **(b)** (*acte, parole*) injustice; **faire une i. à qn,** to do s.o. an injustice, to wrong s.o..
injustifiable [ɛ̃ʒystifjabl] *adj* unjustifiable.
injustifié [ɛ̃ʒystifje] *adj* unjustified, unwarranted.
inlassable [ɛ̃lasabl] *adj* untiring, unflagging (*efforts etc*); tireless (*person*).
inlassablement [ɛ̃lasabləmɑ̃] *adv* untiringly, tirelessly.
inné [ine] *adj* innate, inborn.
innervation [inɛrvasjɔ̃] *nf Physiol* innervation.
innerver [inɛrve] *vt Physiol* to innervate.
innocemment [inɔsamɑ̃] *adv* innocently.
innocence [inɔsɑ̃s] *nf* innocence; harmlessness (*of joke*); **prouver l'i. de qn,** to prove s.o. innocent, to prove s.o.'s innocence.
innocent, -ente [inɔsɑ̃, -ɑ̃t] **1** *adj* (*non coupable*) innocent, not guilty; (*pur*) innocent, pure; (*naïf*) naive; innocent, inoffensive (*joke*); **i. d'un crime,** innocent of a crime. **2** *n* innocent person; (*idiot*) simpleton; **les (saints) Innocents,** the Holy Innocents; **ne fais pas l'i.!,** don't act so innocent *or* the innocent!; **l'i. du village,** the village idiot; *Prov* **aux innocents les mains pleines,** fortune favours fools.
innocenter [inɔsɑ̃te] *vt* **(a) i. qn (d'une accusation),** to clear s.o. (of a charge); (*d'un juge, d'un jury*) to declare s.o. not guilty; **(b)** (*justifier*) to excuse, to justify (*conduct*).
innocuité [inɔkɥite] *nf* innocuousness, harmlessness.
innombrable [inɔ̃brabl] *adj* innumerable, countless.
innommable [inɔmabl] *adj* (*indéfini*) unnamable; *Péj* unspeakable (*behaviour etc*).
innom(m)é [inɔme] *adj* unnamed, nameless.
innovateur, -trice [inɔvatœr, -tris] **1** *adj* innovatory, innovative. **2** *n* innovator.
innovation [inɔvasjɔ̃] *nf* innovation.
innover [inɔve] **1** *vi* to innovate, to introduce changes *or* innovations, to break new ground. **2** *vt* to introduce, to invent (*something new*).
inobservable [inɔpsɛrvabl] *adj* hardly perceptible *or* noticeable.
inobservance [inɔpsɛrvɑ̃s] *nf* non-observance, inobservance.
inobservation [inɔpsɛrvasjɔ̃] *nf* non-observance, disregard (*of the law*); non-compliance (**de,** with).
inobservé [inɔpsɛrve] *adj* **(a)** (*non observé*) unobserved; (*non remarqué*) unobserved, unnoticed; **(b)** (*de loi*) not kept, not complied with.
inoccupé [inɔkype] *adj* **(a)** (*libre*) unoccupied; vacant (*seat, house*); unoccupied, uninhabited (*house*); **(b)** idle (*person*).
inoculation [inɔkylasjɔ̃] *nf Méd* inoculation.
inoculer [inɔkyle] *vt* **(a) i. une maladie à qn,** to infect s.o. with a disease; *Méd* **i. un virus à qn,** to inoculate s.o. with a virus; *Fig* **elle nous a inoculé sa gaieté,** she infected us with her gaiety; **(b) i. qn (contre une maladie),** to inoculate s.o. (against a disease).
inodore [inɔdɔr] *adj* odourless; *Hum Péj* **incolore, i. et sans saveur,** (*personne*) totally colourless, *F* wishy-washy.
inoffensif, -ive [inɔfɑ̃sif, -iv] *adj* inoffensive, harmless (*person*); harmless, innocuous (*drug etc*).
inondable [inɔ̃dabl] *adj* (*of land*) liable to flooding.
inondation [inɔ̃dasjɔ̃] *nf* flood, *Fml* inundation; (*action*) flooding; deluge (*of questions etc*).
inondé, -ée [inɔ̃de] **1** *adj* flooded; **visage i. de larmes,** face streaming with tears; **i. de lumière,** flooded with light; **i. d'invitations,** inundated *or* swamped with invitations. **2** *n* flood victim.
inonder [inɔ̃de] *vt* to inundate, to flood (*fields etc*); to swamp (*the market*); *Fig* to inundate (*s.o.*) (*with invitations, offers etc*); **nous avons été inondés par l'averse,** we were soaked by the shower; *Fig* **i. un pays de produits importés,** to flood a country with imports.
inopérable [inɔperabl] *adj Chir* inoperable.
inopérant [inɔperɑ̃] *adj* inoperative.
inopiné [inɔpine] *adj* sudden, unexpected.
inopinément [inɔpinemɑ̃] *adv* unexpectedly.
inopportun [inɔpɔrtœ̃, -yn] *adj* inopportune, untimely, ill-timed.
inopportunément [inɔpɔrtynemɑ̃] *adv* inopportunely.
inopportunité [inɔpɔrtynite] *nf Litt* inopportuneness, untimeliness.
inorganique [inɔrganik] *adj* inorganic.
inorganisé [inɔrganize] *adj* (*personne etc*) disorganized; (*main d'œuvre*) unorganized, non-union.
inoubliable [inublijabl] *adj* unforgettable.
inouï [inwi] *adj* unheard-of, extraordinary, incredible; **avec une violence inouïe,** with incredible *or* unprecedented violence; **elle est inouïe!,** she's outrageous!
inox [inɔks] **1** *adj inv* **acier i.,** stainless steel. **2** *nm* stainless steel.
inoxydable [inɔksidabl] **1** *adj* rustproof; **acier i.,** stainless steel. **2** *nm* stainless steel; **évier en i.,** stainless steel sink.
input [input] *nm Ordinat* input.
inqualifiable [ɛ̃kalifjabl] *adj* unspeakable (*behaviour*).
inquiet, -ète [ɛ̃kjɛ, -ɛt] **1** *adj* (*anxieux*) anxious, apprehensive, uneasy, worried; (*agité*) restless; **sommeil i.,** uneasy *or* troubled *or* broken sleep; **i. sur qch/de qn,** uneasy *or* worried about sth/s.o.; **une attente inquiète,** an anxious wait; **une voix inquiète,** an anxious *or* worried voice. **2** *n* anxious person, worrier.
inquiétant [ɛ̃kjetɑ̃, -ɑ̃t] *adj* disturbing, upsetting, worrying.

inquiéter [ɛ̃kjete] *v* (**j'inquiète; j'inquiéterai**) **1** *vt* to worry, to trouble (*s.o.*), to make (*s.o.*) anxious; to harass, to worry (*enemy etc*); *Litt* to disturb (*s.o.'s peace etc*); **la santé de ma mère m'inquiète,** I'm worried about my mother's health. **2 s'inquiéter** *vpr* to become anxious, to get worried; **il n'y a pas de quoi s'i.,** there's nothing to get worried *or* upset about; **ne vous inquiétez pas de cela,** don't worry *or* don't bother about that; **sans s'i. de rien,** without a care in the world.

inquiétude [ɛ̃kjetyd] *nf* **(a)** (*souci*) anxiety, concern, uneasiness; **dissiper les inquiétudes de qn,** to set s.o.'s mind at rest; **état d'i.,** state of anxiety, anxious state of mind; **sois sans i., je m'en occupe,** don't worry (about a thing), I'll take care of it; **éprouver quelques inquiétudes,** to have a few qualms; **(b)** *Arch & Litt* agitation, restlessness.

inquisiteur, -trice [ɛ̃kizitœr, -tris] **1** *nm* inquisitor. **2** *adj* inquisitive, prying (*glance etc*).

inquisition [ɛ̃kizisjɔ̃] *nf* inquisition.

inquisitorial, -aux [ɛ̃kizitɔrjal, -o] *adj* inquisitorial.

inracontable [ɛ̃rakɔ̃tabl] *adj* indescribable.

insaisissable [ɛ̃sezisabl] *adj* **(a)** (*que l'on ne peut attraper*) that cannot be grasped; (*personne*) difficult to catch, elusive; imperceptible (*sound, difference*); **(b)** *Jur* (*of property*) not distrainable, not attachable.

insalissable [ɛ̃salisabl] *adj* dirtproof.

insalubre [ɛ̃salybr] *adj* insalubrious (*climate*); unhealthy (*climate, occupation*); insanitary (*dwelling*).

insalubrité [ɛ̃salybrite] *nf* insalubrity, unhealthiness.

insanité [ɛ̃sanite] *nf* insanity.

insatiabilité [ɛ̃sasjabilite] *nf* insatiability.

insatiable [ɛ̃sasjabl] *adj* (*soif*) insatiable, unquenchable; **curiosité i.,** insatiable curiosity; **d'une curiosité i.,** insatiably curious.

insatiablement [ɛ̃sasjabləmɑ̃] *adv* insatiably.

insatisfaction [ɛ̃satisfaksjɔ̃] *nf* dissatisfaction.

insatisfait [ɛ̃satisfɛ] *adj* (*personne*) dissatisfied; (*désir*) unsatisfied.

inscolarisable [ɛ̃skɔlarizabl] *adj* ineducable.

inscription [ɛ̃skripsjɔ̃] *nf* **(a)** (*action*) writing (down), inscribing; entering, recording (*in diary etc*); (*immatriculation*) registration, enrolment; **droit d'i.,** registration fee, entrance fee; **feuille d'i.,** entry form; **prendre son i.,** (*s'incrire*) to enter one's name; *Jur* **i. hypothécaire,** registry *or* registration of mortgages; **i. de** *ou* **en faux,** plea of forgery; **(b)** inscription (*on tomb etc*); entry (*in account book etc*); directions (*on signpost etc*).

inscrire [ɛ̃skrir] *v* (*prp* **inscrivant**; *pp* **inscrit**; *pr ind* **j'inscris, il inscrit, n. inscrivons**; *p hist* **j'inscrivis**; *fu* **j'inscrirai**) **1** *vt* **(a)** to inscribe, to write down; to take down, to note (down) (*details*); **i. une question à l'ordre du jour,** to put *or* place a question on the agenda; **i. une dépense au budget,** to include an item in the budget;

(b) to register (*marriage etc*); to enrol (*s.o.*); to enter (*s.o.'s*) name; **se faire i. à un cours,** to put one's name down *or* enrol *or* register for a course; **i. un enfant à un club,** to enrol a child in a club;

(c) to inscribe, to engrave (*epitaph etc*);

(d) to inscribe (*triangle etc*) (**dans,** in).

2 s'inscrire *vpr* to put one's name down, to register; (*s'immatriculer*) to enrol; *Jur* **s'i. en faux contre qch,** to dispute the validity of sth, to deny sth; **cette décision s'inscrit dans le cadre de la politique gouvernementale,** this decision is in keeping with the general pattern of the government's policy.

inscrit, -ite [ɛ̃skri, -it] **1** *adj* **(a)** registered (*voter etc*); **(b)** *Math* inscribed. **2** *n* registered person, *surtout* voter. **3** *nm* *Nau* **i. maritime,** = certified navigator.

insécable [ɛ̃sekabl] *adj* indivisible.

insecte [ɛ̃sɛkt] *nm* insect.

insecticide [ɛ̃sɛktisid] **1** *adj* insecticidal; **poudre i.,** insect powder. **2** *nm* insecticide.

insectifuge [ɛ̃sɛktifyʒ] *nm* insect repellent.

insectivore [ɛ̃sɛktivɔr] *Zool* **1** *adj* insectivorous. **2** *nm* insectivore; **insectivores,** Insectivora.

insécurité [ɛ̃sekyrite] *nf* insecurity.

inséminateur, -trice [ɛ̃seminatœr] **1** *adj* inseminating. **2** *nm* inseminator.

insémination [ɛ̃seminasjɔ̃] *nf* insemination; **i. artificielle,** artificial insemination; **i. artificielle avec sperme de donneur,** artificial insemination by donor.

inséminer [ɛ̃semine] *vt* to inseminate.

insensé, -ée [ɛ̃sɑ̃se] **1** *adj* senseless, foolish (*action etc*); extravagant, wild, *F* hare-brained (*scheme etc*); *Vieilli* (*fou*) mad, insane. **2** *n* madman; madwoman.

insensibilisation [ɛ̃sɑ̃sibilizasjɔ̃] *nf* anaesthetization.

insensibiliser [ɛ̃sɑ̃sibilize] *vt* to anaesthetize.

insensibilité [ɛ̃sɑ̃sibilite] *nf* insensitivity.

insensible [ɛ̃sɑ̃sibl] *adj* **(a)** insensitive (**à,** to); **i. à la critique,** impervious to criticism; **(b)** imperceptible, hardly perceptible (*difference etc*).

insensiblement [ɛ̃sɑ̃sibləmɑ̃] *adv* imperceptibly.

inséparable [ɛ̃separabl] **1** *adj* inseparable. **2** *nmpl* **inséparables,** (*oiseaux*) lovebirds; **ce sont les deux inséparables,** (*de personnes*) they are inseparable.

inséparablement [ɛ̃separabləmɑ̃] *adv* inseparably.

insérable [ɛ̃serabl] *adj* insertable.

insérer [ɛ̃sere] (**j'insère; j'insérerai**) **1** *vt* to insert; **i. une annonce dans un journal,** to insert *or* put an advertisement in a paper; **prière d'i.,** for publication (in your columns); (*pour la critique*) publisher's blurb. **2 s'insérer** *vpr* **(a)** to be attached (**sur,** to); **(b)** (*s'attacher*) to fit (**dans,** into).

insertion [ɛ̃sɛrsjɔ̃] *nf* insertion; **l'i. sociale des émigrés,** the (social) integration of immigrants; *Ordinat* **mode d'i.,** insert mode.

insidieusement [ɛ̃sidjøzmɑ̃] *adv* insidiously.

insidieux, -euse [ɛ̃sidjø, -øz] *adj* insidious.

insigne¹ [ɛ̃siɲ] *adj* **(a)** (*remarquable*) distinguished, remarkable; **faveur i.,** signal favour; **(b)** *Péj* notorious; arrant (*liar etc*); **indiscrétion i.,** glaring indiscretion.

insigne² *nm* distinguishing mark, badge; **insignes de la royauté,** insignia of royalty; *Mil* **i. de grade,** badge of rank.

insignifiance [ɛ̃siɲifjɑ̃s] *nf* insignificance, unimportance.

insignifiant [ɛ̃siɲifjɑ̃] *adj* insignificant, unimportant; trivial, trifling (*loss, sum*); nominal (*payment*).

insincère [ɛ̃sɛ̃sɛr] *adj Litt* insincere.

insinuant [ɛ̃sinɥɑ̃] *adj* ingratiating.

insinuation [ɛ̃sinɥasjɔ̃] *nf* insinuation, innuendo.

insinuer [ɛ̃sinɥe] **1** *vt* to insinuate, to suggest, to hint at (*sth*); **que voulez-vous i.?,** what are you hinting *or* getting at? **2 s'insinuer** *vpr* to creep *or* steal in(to); **s'i. dans les bonnes grâces de qn,** to insinuate oneself *or* worm one's way into s.o.'s good books; **s'i. entre les voitures,** to thread one's way through the traffic.

insipide [ɛ̃sipid] *adj* insipid (*food, conversation, story*); insipid, tasteless (*food*); dull, flat, uninteresting (*conversation etc*); tame (*ending*).

insipidité [ɛ̃sipidite] *nf* insipidness (*of food etc*); tameness (*of ending*).

insistance [ɛ̃sistɑ̃s] *nf* insistence (**à faire qch,** on doing sth); **avec i.,** insistently, earnestly.

insistant [ɛ̃sistɑ̃] *adj* insistent.

insister [ɛ̃siste] *vi* to insist; **i. sur un fait,** to stress a fact; **i. sur ses demandes,** to persist in one's claims; **elle a beaucoup insisté,** she was very insistent; **i. pour faire qch,** to insist on doing sth; **i. auprès de qn,** to take up a matter strongly with s.o.; **n'insistez pas trop,** don't put too much emphasis on that; (*ne vous obstinez pas*) don't be too insistent, *F* don't push your luck; **elle a essayé la planche à voile mais elle n'a pas insisté,** she tried windsurfing but soon gave (it) up.

in situ [insity] *adj & adv* in situ.

insociabilité [ɛ̃sɔsjabilite] *nf* insociability.

insociable [ɛ̃sɔsjabl] *adj* unsociable.

insolation [ɛ̃sɔlasjɔ̃] *nf* exposure (*to the sun*); *Méd* sunstroke; **i. annuelle,** (*d'une région etc*) annual hours of sunshine.

insolemment [ɛ̃sɔlamɑ̃] *adv* insolently.

insolence [ɛ̃sɔlɑ̃s] *nf* **(a)** (*impertinence*) insolence, impertinence, impudence; **répondre avec i.,** to answer insolently; **(b)** (*parole, remarque*) insolent remark *or* action.

insolent [ɛ̃sɔlɑ̃] *adj* **(a)** (*impertinent*) insolent, impertinent, impudent, *F* cheeky (**envers, avec,** to); **(b)** haughty, overbearing (*in victory etc*); **(c)** extraordinary (*success etc*); **luxe i.,** indecent *or* blatant luxury.

insolite [ɛ̃sɔlit] **1** *adj* unusual, unwonted, strange. **2** *nm* **l'i.,** the unusual.

insolubilité [ɛ̃sɔlybilite] *nf* insolubility.

insoluble [ɛ̃sɔlybl] *adj* **(a)** insoluble (*substance*); **(b)** insoluble, insolvable (*problem*).

insolvabilité [ɛ̃sɔlvabilite] *nf Com* insolvency.

insolvable [ɛ̃sɔlvabl] *adj Com* insolvent.

insomniaque [ɛ̃sɔmnjak] *adj & n* insomniac.

insomnie [ɛ̃sɔmni] *nf* insomnia, sleeplessness; **nuit d'i.,** sleepless night; **souffrir d'i., avoir des insomnies,** to have insomnia.

insondable [ɛ̃sɔ̃dabl] *adj* **(a)** unfathomable, fathomless (*ocean etc*); **(b)** unfathomable (*mystery*); **(c)** immense,

unbelievable (*stupidity etc*).
insonore [ɛ̃sɔnɔr] *adj* soundproof (*studio, material*).
insonorisation [ɛ̃sɔnɔrizɑsjɔ̃] *nf* soundproofing (*of studio*).
insonoriser [ɛ̃sɔnɔrize] *vt* to soundproof (*a studio*).
insouciance [ɛ̃susjɑ̃s] *nf* **(a)** (*manque de soucis*) freedom from care; (*détachement*) lack of concern, *Litt* insouciance; **(b)** (*inconscience*) thoughtlessness.
insouciant [ɛ̃susjɑ̃] *adj* **(a)** (*sans soucis*) carefree; (*détaché*) unconcerned; **i. de son avenir,** unconcerned about his future; **(b)** (*négligent*) thoughtless, casual, happy-go-lucky.
insoucieux, -euse [ɛ̃susjø, -øz] *adj Litt* heedless (**de,** of).
insoumis, -ise [ɛ̃sumi, -iz] **1** *adj* **(a)** unsubdued (*people etc*); **(b)** refractory, unruly, rebellious, insubordinate (*person*); **(c)** *Mil* absentee (*soldier*). **2** *n* rebellious *or* insubordinate person. **3** *nm Mil* absentee.
insoumission [ɛ̃sumisjɔ̃] *nf* **(a)** insubordination, rebelliousness; **(b)** *Mil* failure to (re)join one's unit, being absent without leave.
insoupçonnable [ɛ̃supsɔnabl] *adj* beyond *or* above suspicion.
insoupçonné [ɛ̃supsɔne] *adj* unsuspected (**de,** by).
insoutenable [ɛ̃sutnabl] *adj* **(a)** untenable (*opinion*); unwarrantable (*assertion*); indefensible (*position*); **(b)** unbearable (*agony, strain, tension*).
inspecter [ɛ̃spɛkte] *vt* to inspect (*troops, school etc*); to survey (*field of battle*); to examine (*work, luggage*).
inspecteur, -trice [ɛ̃spɛktœr, -tris] *n* inspector; overseer (*of works etc*); surveyor (*of mines etc*); examiner (*of business accounts etc*); **i. de la sûreté,** detective inspector; **i. du travail,** factory inspector; **i. des contributions directes,** inspector of taxes; *Scol* **i. d'Académie,** school inspector, *Br* ≈ H.M.I.; **i. (de l'Enseignement) primaire,** primary school inspector; **i. des finances,** ≈ senior Treasury official; **i. de police,** police inspector.
inspection [ɛ̃spɛksjɔ̃] *nf* **(a)** (*examen*) inspection, inspecting; (*de bagages*) inspection, examination, examining; (*revue*) tour of inspection; **faire l'i. de,** to inspect, to examine; *Admin* **i. académique,** school inspection; *Mil etc* **passer l'i.,** (*d'une compagnie etc*) to inspect (*a company etc*); **(b)** (*fonction*) inspectorship, inspectorate; **(c)** (*service*) body *or* board of inspectors, inspectorate; **entrer à l'i. académique,** to become a school inspector.
inspectorat [ɛ̃spɛktɔra] *nm Admin* inspectorate, inspectorship.
inspirateur, -trice [ɛ̃spiratœr, -tris] **1** *adj* **(a)** inspiring (*thought etc*); **(b)** *Anat* inspiratory (*muscle etc*). **2** *n* person who inspires; instigator (*of plot*); **c'était elle mon inspiratrice,** she was my inspiration.
inspiration [ɛ̃spirɑsjɔ̃] *nf* **(a)** (*créatrice*) inspiration; **avoir de l'i.,** to have inspiration; **i. soudaine,** sudden inspiration, *F* brainwave, *Am* brainstorm; **(b)** (*conseil*) prompting; **sous l'i. de qn,** at s.o.'s suggestion *or* instigation; **(c)** *Physiol* inspiration, breathing in; **(d)** (*idée*) inspiration; **elle a eu la bonne i. de venir me chercher,** she had the bright idea *or* was inspired to come for me.
inspiré, -ée [ɛ̃spire] **1** *adj* **(a)** inspired (*writing, poet etc*); **(b) bien/mal i.,** well-/ill-advised. **2** *n* mystic, visionary.
inspirer [ɛ̃spire] **1** *vt* **(a)** (*suggérer*) to inspire; **i. qch à qn,** to inspire s.o. with sth; **contes inspirés de la vie des animaux,** tales drawn from *or* inspired by animal life; *Iron* **cette question ne m'inspire guère,** the subject doesn't exactly inspire me; **i. confiance/le respect,** to inspire confidence/respect; **inspiré par la jalousie,** prompted by jealousy; **(b)** *Physiol* to breathe in (*air etc*). **2** *vi Physiol* to breathe in. **3 s'inspirer** *vpr* **s'i. de qn/qch,** to take *or* draw one's inspiration from s.o./sth, to be inspired by s.o./sth.
instabilité [ɛ̃stabilite] *nf* instability, shakiness, unsteadiness; inconstancy, fickleness, uncertainty (*of fortune etc*); (*de caractère*) instability; (*du temps*) unsettled nature; *Nau* crank (*of ship*); **souffrir d'i.,** (*d'une personne*) to be unstable.
instable [ɛ̃stabl] *adj* **(a)** (*branlant*) unstable, shaky, unsteady, *F* wobbly; **équilibre i.,** unsteady balance; **le plateau est i.,** the tray is wobbling; **(b)** unstable, unreliable, inconstant (*person, nature etc*); **(c)** unsettled, changeable (*weather*); *Nau* crank (*ship*); **la paix est encore i.,** the peace is still fragile.
installateur [ɛ̃stalatœr] *nm* fitter.
installation [ɛ̃stalɑsjɔ̃] *nf* **(a)** installation, installing; setting up (*of machine, house*); fitting up *or* out, equipping (*of workshop*); fixing (*of curtains etc*); induction (*of clergyman*); **fêter son i.,** (*dans une maison*) to celebrate moving in; **prévoir son i. dans une région,** to plan to settle in an area; *Ordinat* **programme d'i.,** installation program; **(b)** fixtures and fittings (*of house etc*); fittings, equipment (*of workshop etc*); *Ind* plant; **l'i. électrique n'est pas conforme,** the wiring is not up to standard; **i. de lavage,** washing bay; **i. (de) radio,** radio installation *or* set; **installations au sol,** (*at aerodrome*) ground installations, facilities.
installer [ɛ̃stale] **1** *vt* to install; to establish, to settle (*one's family etc*); to set up (*machine etc*); to fit up *or* out, to equip (*factory etc*); to fix (*curtains etc*); to induct (*clergyman*); **i. qn dans un fauteuil,** to make s.o. comfortable in an armchair; **i. qn devant la télévision,** to install s.o. in front of the television; **je les ai installés dans la chambre bleue,** I've put them in the blue room; **maison bien installée,** house with all the conveniences; **i. la cuisine/la salle de bain dans une pièce,** to turn a room into a kitchen/bathroom; **i. son cabinet,** (*d'un médecin*) to set up practice.

2 *vi Arg* **en i.,** to show off.

3 s'installer *vpr* (*devant la télé*) to install oneself; (*dans la vie*) to settle (down); (*chez qn*) to make oneself at home; **il finira bien par s'i.,** he'll settle down eventually; **s'i. à la campagne,** to settle in the country; **s'i. comme médecin,** to set (oneself) up as a doctor; **pense-t-elle s'i.?,** (*d'un médecin*) is she going to set up a practice?
instamment [ɛ̃stamɑ̃] *adv* insistently, earnestly; **on demande i. un médecin,** a doctor is urgently required; **ils ont cherché i. à lui faire prononcer un discours,** they urged him to make a speech.
instance [ɛ̃stɑ̃s] *nf* **(a)** (*insistance*) **demander qch à qn avec i.,** to beg *or* plead with s.o. for sth; **prier avec i.,** to pray earnestly; **(b) instances,** requests, entreaties; **j'ai dû plier devant ses instances,** I had to give in to his requests *or* entreaties; **(c)** *Jur* process, suit; **introduire une i. (en justice),** to institute an action; **tribunal d'i.,** *Eng* ≈ magistrates' court; **tribunal de grande i.,** county court; **tribunal de première i.,** court of first instance; **acquitté en seconde i.,** acquitted on appeal; **(d)** (*autorité*) authority; **(e)** (*cours*) **ils sont en i. de divorce,** their divorce proceedings are under way; **être en i. de départ,** to be on the point of departure *or* about to leave; **tout est encore en i.,** everything is still pending.
instant¹ [ɛ̃stɑ̃] *adj Litt* pressing, urgent.
instant² *nm* moment, instant; **à chaque** *ou* **à tout i.,** at every moment; (*sans arrêt*) continually; **par instants,** now and then; **un i. de délai,** a moment's delay; **pendant un i.,** for a moment; **un i.!,** one moment!, wait a moment!; **nous n'avons pas un i. à perdre,** we don't have a moment to lose; **profiter de chaque i.,** to profit from every moment; **elle va arriver d'un i. à l'autre,** she'll be arriving at any moment; **à l'i.,** (*dans le passé*) a moment ago; (*tout de suite*) immediately, instantly, at once; **pour l'i.,** for the moment; **dans un i.,** in a moment; **en un i.,** in no time (at all); **un soin de tous les instants,** unremitting *or* ceaseless care; **dès l'i. que je l'ai vue,** from the moment I saw her; **dès l'i. que tu as réussi tous tes examens,** since *or* seeing that you've passed all your exams.
instantané [ɛ̃stɑ̃tane] **1** *adj* instantaneous (*death etc*); sudden (*fright*); instant (*coffee*). **2** *nm Phot* snapshot, *F* snap.
instantanément [ɛ̃stɑ̃tanemɑ̃] *adv* instantaneously.
instar de (à l') [alɛ̃stardə] *adv Litt* after the fashion *or* manner of, like.
instaurateur, -trice [ɛ̃stɔratœr, -tris] *n Litt* founder, establisher.
instauration [ɛ̃stɔrɑsjɔ̃] *nf Litt* founding, establishment.
instaurer [ɛ̃stɔre] *vt* to found, to establish.
instigateur, -trice [ɛ̃stigatœr, -tris] *n* instigator.
instigation [ɛ̃stigɑsjɔ̃] *nf* instigation, incitement (**à,** to); **agir à l'i. de qn,** to act at *or* on s.o.'s instigation.
instillation [ɛ̃stilɑsjɔ̃] *nf Méd* instillation.
instiller [ɛ̃stile] *vt* to instil; **i. le courage à qn,** to instil courage in(to) s.o.
instinct [ɛ̃stɛ̃] *nm* instinct; **suivre son i.,** to follow one's instincts; **i. maternel,** maternal instinct; **l'i. de conservation,** instinct of self-preservation; **d'i.,** by instinct, instinctively; **avoir l'i. du commerce,** to have a feel for business; **être guidé par un heureux i.,** to be well guided by one's instinct; *Can Pol etc* **i. de tueur,** killer instinct.
instinctif, -ive [ɛ̃stɛ̃ktif, -iv] *adj* (*personne, réaction etc*) instinctive.
instinctivement [ɛ̃stɛ̃ktivmɑ̃] *adv* instinctively.
instit [ɛ̃stit] *n F* (*abrév* **instituteur**) (primary school) teacher.

instituer [ɛ̃stitɥe] *vt* **(a)** (*établir*) to institute; **(b)** to appoint (*official, Jur heir*).
institut [ɛ̃stity] *nm* **(a)** (*établissement*) institute, institution; **i. national de recherche,** national research institute; **I. universitaire de technologie,** technical college (*conferring two-year degrees*), *Br* ≈ polytechnic; **(b) l'I. (de France),** the Institute (composed of the five Académies); **(c) i. de beauté,** beauty salon *or* parlour.
instituteur, -trice [ɛ̃stitytœr, -tris] **1** *n* **(a)** *Scol* (primary school) teacher; **(b)** *Arch* founder (*of hospital etc*). **2** *nf Arch* **institutrice,** governess.
institution [ɛ̃stitysjɔ̃] *nf* **(a)** (*établissement*) institution; *F* **c'est devenu une véritable i.,** it has become an institution; **(b)** *Jur* appointing (*of heir*); **(c)** *Pol* **institutions,** institutions; **(d)** (*d'enseignement*) establishment.
institutionnalisation [ɛ̃stitysjɔnalizasjɔ̃] *nf* institutionalization.
institutionnaliser [ɛ̃stitysjɔnalize] *vt* to institutionalize (*a practice*).
institutionnel, -elle [ɛ̃stitysjɔnɛl] *adj* institutional.
instructeur [ɛ̃stryktœr] **1** *nm* instructor, teacher; *Mil* **sergent i.,** drill sergeant. **2** *adj Jur* **juge i.,** examining magistrate.
instructif, -ive [ɛ̃stryktif, -iv] *adj* instructive.
instruction [ɛ̃stryksjɔ̃] *nf* **(a) instructions,** instructions, directions, orders; **suivre les instructions,** to follow the instructions; **conformément aux instructions,** as directed; **(b)** *Ordinat* instruction; **i.-machine,** machine instruction; **i. d'entrée-sortie,** input/output instruction; **(c)** *Scol* education, schooling; *Mil* training (of troops); *Scol* **i. primaire/secondaire,** primary/secondary education; **i. professionnelle,** vocational training; **avoir de l'i.,** to be well educated; **sans i.,** uneducated; **i. religieuse,** religious instruction; **i. musicale/militaire,** musical/military training; **(d)** *Jur* preliminary investigation (*of case*); **juge d'i.,** examining magistrate; **(e)** (*circulaire*) (official) memo, circular.
instruire [ɛ̃strɥir] *v* (*prp* **instruisant**; *pp* **instruit**; *pr ind* **j'instruis, il instruit, n. instruisons**; *p hist* **j'instruisis**) **1** *vt* **(a)** to teach, to educate, to instruct; **i. qn de qch,** to inform s.o. of sth; **être instruit par l'expérience,** to learn from experience; **(b) i. qn dans** *ou* **en qch/à faire qch,** to instruct s.o. in sth/how to do sth; **(c)** to train, to drill (*troops*); **(d)** *Jur* to examine, to investigate (*case*). **2** *vi* to teach; **i. par le jeu/l'exemple,** to teach through play/by example. **3 s'instruire** *vpr* to educate oneself, to improve one's mind; **s'i. de,** to find out *or* get information about.
instruit [ɛ̃strɥi] *adj* **(a)** (*cultivé*) educated, learned, well-read; **(b)** trained (*soldier etc*); **(c) i. de qch,** acquainted with *or* aware of sth.
instrument [ɛ̃strymɑ̃] *nm* instrument, implement, tool; *Mus* instrument; *Jur* (legal) instrument; **i. de travail,** implement, tool; **i. de navigation,** navigation(al) instrument; *Av* **atterrissage aux instruments,** instrument landing; **i. de chirurgie,** surgical instrument; *Fig* **servir d'i. à la vengeance de qn,** to serve as the instrument *or* tool of s.o.'s vengeance; **être l'i. de qn,** to be s.o.'s instrument; *Mus* **jouer d'un i.,** to play an instrument; **i. à anche/clavier/vent/cordes,** reed/keyboard/wind/string instrument.
instrumentaire [ɛ̃strymɑ̃tɛr] *adj Jur* **témoin i.,** witness to a deed.
instrumental, -aux [ɛ̃strymɑ̃tal, -o] *adj* instrumental (*music etc*).
instrumentation [ɛ̃strymɑ̃tasjɔ̃] *nf Mus* scoring, instrumentation, orchestration.
instrumenter [ɛ̃strymɑ̃te] **1** *vi Jur* to draw up a document; **i. contre qn,** to order proceedings to be taken against s.o.. **2** *vt Mus* to score, to orchestrate (*opera etc*).
instrumentiste [ɛ̃strymɑ̃tist] *n Mus* instrumentalist.
insu [ɛ̃sy] *nm* (*used in the phrase*) **à l'i. de,** without the knowledge of; **à l'i. de ses parents,** without his parents' knowledge; **à mon i.,** without my knowledge.
insubmersible [ɛ̃sybmɛrsibl] *adj* unsinkable.
insubordination [ɛ̃sybɔrdinasjɔ̃] *nf* insubordination.
insubordonné [ɛ̃sybɔrdɔne] *adj* insubordinate.
insuccès [ɛ̃syksɛ] *nm* lack of success, failure.
insuffisamment [ɛ̃syfizamɑ̃] *adv* insufficiently, inadequately.
insuffisance [ɛ̃syfizɑ̃s] *nf* **(a)** (*manque*) insufficiency, deficiency; shortage (*of staff*); inadequacy (*of means*); *Méd* **i. respiratoire,** respiratory insufficiency; *Méd* **i. cardiaque,** cardiac insufficiency, *F* heart failure; **(b)** (*incompétence*) incompetence, inefficiency.
insuffisant [ɛ̃syfizɑ̃] *adj* **(a)** insufficient; inadequate (*means*); short (*measure*); **(b)** (*incapable*) incapable, incompetent.
insufflateur [ɛ̃syflatœr] *nm Méd* insufflator.
insufflation [ɛ̃syflasjɔ̃] *nf Méd* insufflation.
insuffler [ɛ̃syfle] *vt* **(a)** to insufflate; to blow, to breathe (*air into sth*); *Fig* **i. qch à qn,** to inspire s.o. with sth; **(b)** *Méd* to spray (*throat etc*).
insulaire [ɛ̃sylɛr] **1** *adj* insular. **2** *n* islander.
insularité [ɛ̃sylarite] *nf* insularity.
insuline [ɛ̃sylin] *nf Méd* insulin.
insulinothérapie [ɛ̃sylinɔterapi] *nf Méd* insulin therapy.
insultant [ɛ̃syltɑ̃] *adj* insulting, offensive.
insulte [ɛ̃sylt] *nf* insult; **insultes,** abuse; **faire une i. à qn,** to insult s.o.; **c'est une i. à notre famille,** it's an insult to our family; **c'est la pire des insultes,** that's the worst possible insult.
insulté, -ée [ɛ̃sylte] **1** *adj* insulted. **2** *n* injured party.
insulter [ɛ̃sylte] **1** *vt* to insult (*s.o.*). **2** *vi* **i. au malheur,** to jeer at misfortune; **i. au bon goût,** to insult good taste.
insulteur [ɛ̃syltœr] *nm* insulter.
insupportable [ɛ̃sypɔrtabl] *adj* unbearable, unendurable (*pain*); intolerable (*conduct*); unbearable, insufferable (*person*); **cette pensée m'était i.,** the thought was unbearable; **il est i.,** he's infuriating, *F* he's the limit!
insupportablement [ɛ̃sypɔrtabləmɑ̃] *adv* (*voir adj*) unbearably; intolerably; insufferably.
insurgé, -ée [ɛ̃syrʒe] *adj & n* insurgent, insurrectionist, rebel.
insurger (s') [sɛ̃syrʒe] *vpr* (**je m'insurgeai(s), n. n. insurgeons**) to rise (in rebellion), to revolt, to rebel.
insurmontable [ɛ̃syrmɔ̃tabl] *adj* insurmountable, insuperable; unconquerable (*aversion*); **être en proie à des difficultés insurmontables,** to be faced with insurmountable difficulties.
insurmontablement [ɛ̃syrmɔ̃tabləmɑ̃] *adv* insurmountably.
insurpassable [ɛ̃syrpasabl] *adj* unsurpassable.
insurrection [ɛ̃syrɛksjɔ̃] *nf* insurrection, (up)rising, rebellion; **en état d'i.,** insurgent.
insurrectionnel, -elle [ɛ̃syrɛksjɔnɛl] *adj* insurrectional, insurrectionary (*troops etc*).
intact [ɛ̃takt] *adj* intact.
intaille [ɛ̃taj] *nf Spéc* intaglio.
intangibilité [ɛ̃tɑ̃ʒibilite] *nf* intangibility.
intangible [ɛ̃tɑ̃ʒibl] *adj* intangible.
intarissable [ɛ̃tarisabl] *adj* inexhaustible (*well, imagination etc*); endless (*chatter etc*).
intarissablement [ɛ̃tarisabləmɑ̃] *adv* inexhaustibly.
intégrable [ɛ̃tegrabl] *adj Math* integrable.
intégral, -aux [ɛ̃tegral, -o] **1** *adj* **(a)** entire, complete, whole, full-scale; **paiement i.,** payment in full; **texte i.,** full text; **édition intégrale,** (complete and) unabridged edition; **(b)** *Math* **calcul i.,** integral calculus. **2** *nf* **intégrale (a)** *Math* integral; **(b)** *Mus* **l'intégrale des symphonies de Beethoven,** the complete set of Beethoven symphonies.
intégralement [ɛ̃tegralmɑ̃] *adv* wholly, entirely, fully, in full.
intégralité [ɛ̃tegralite] *nf* **l'i.,** the whole; **l'i. de son salaire,** the whole of his salary, his whole salary; **dans son i.,** in its entirety, in full.
intégrant [ɛ̃tegrɑ̃] *adj* integral (*part etc*); **faire partie intégrante de,** to be an integral part of, *F* to be part and parcel of.
intégration [ɛ̃tegrasjɔ̃] *nf* integration; **i. d'un candidat à Polytechnique,** admission of a candidate to the Polytechnic; **i. d'une population,** (social) integration of a group; *Ordinat* **i. à très grande échelle,** very large scale integration.
intègre [ɛ̃tɛgr] *adj* upright, honest; **une femme i.,** a woman of integrity.
intégré [ɛ̃tegre] *adj Ordinat* integrated; **commandes intégrées,** embedded commands; *Can* **système i. de gestion,** management information system.
intégrer [ɛ̃tegre] *v* (**j'intègre; j'intégrerai**) **1** *vt* **(a)** to integrate (**à, dans,** into); **(b)** *Ordinat* to embed (*a command*). **2 s'intégrer** *vpr* to become integrated (**à, dans,** into, with).
intégrisme [ɛ̃tegrism] *nm Rel* fundamentalism.
intégriste [ɛ̃tegrist] *adj & n Rel* fundamentalist.
intégrité [ɛ̃tegrite] *nf* **(a)** (*totalité*) integrity, completeness, entirety; **(b)** (*honnêteté*) integrity, uprightness, honesty.
intellect [ɛ̃telɛkt] *nm* intellect.
intellectualiser [ɛ̃telɛktɥalize] *vt* to intellectualize.
intellectualisme [ɛ̃telɛktɥalism] *nm* intellectualism.
intellectualiste [ɛ̃telɛktɥalist] *adj & n* intellectualist.
intellectualité [ɛ̃telɛktɥalite] *nf Litt* intellectuality.
intellectuel, -elle [ɛ̃telɛktɥɛl] **1** *adj* intellectual; mental (*fatigue etc*); *Péj* highbrow; **travailleur i.,** non-manual

worker, white-collar worker. **2** *n* intellectual; *Péj* highbrow.

intellectuellement [ɛ̃telɛktɥɛlmɑ̃] *adv* intellectually.

intelligemment [ɛ̃teliʒamɑ̃] *adv* intelligently.

intelligence [ɛ̃teliʒɑ̃s] *nf* **(a)** (*compréhension*) understanding, comprehension; **avoir l'i. des affaires,** to have a good head for business; **pour l'i. de ce qui va suivre,** in order to understand what follows; **(b)** (*pensée etc*) intelligence, intellect, mind; **aiguiser l'i. de qn,** to sharpen s.o.'s wits; **le développement de l'i.,** intellectual development; **(c)** (*entente*) **vivre en bonne/mauvaise i. avec qn,** to be on good/bad terms with s.o.; **un air d'i.,** a knowing look; **être d'i. avec qn,** to have an understanding *or* to be in collusion with s.o.; **entretenir des intelligences avec qn,** to keep up a secret correspondence with s.o.; **avoir des intelligences avec l'ennemi,** to have (secret) dealings with the enemy.

intelligent [ɛ̃teliʒɑ̃] *adj* intelligent, bright, clever, *F* brainy; *Ordinat* smart; **une femme intelligente,** an intelligent woman, a woman of intelligence.

intelligentsia [inteliɡ(dʒ)ɛnsja] *nf* **l'i.,** the intelligentsia.

intelligibilité [ɛ̃teliʒibilite] *nf* intelligibility.

intelligible [ɛ̃teliʒibl] *adj* (*compréhensible*) intelligible, understandable; (*clair*) clear, distinct; **à haute et i. voix,** in a loud, clear voice.

intelligiblement [ɛ̃teliʒibləmɑ̃] *adv* intelligibly.

intello [ɛ̃telo] *n F souvent Péj* highbrow, egghead; **je suis un i.,** I'm the intellectual type.

intempérance [ɛ̃tɑ̃perɑ̃s] *nf* intemperance.

intempérant [ɛ̃tɑ̃perɑ̃] *adj* intemperate.

intempérie [ɛ̃tɑ̃peri] *nf* **(a) intempéries,** bad weather; **exposé aux intempéries,** exposed to the elements; **(b)** *Arch* inclemency (*of weather*).

intempestif, -ive [ɛ̃tɑ̃pɛstif, -iv] *adj* untimely, ill-timed, inopportune.

intemporel, -elle [ɛ̃tɑ̃pɔrɛl] *adj* (*hors du temps*) timeless.

intenable [ɛ̃t(ə)nabl] *adj* intolerable, unbearable (*heat*); untenable (*position etc*); *F* **enfant i.,** uncontrollable child; **cette situation est i.,** the situation is unbearable.

intendance [ɛ̃tɑ̃dɑ̃s] *nf* **(a)** *Scol* bursary; (*bureau*) bursar's office; **(b)** *Mil* the Commissariat; **(c)** *Hist Fr* administration (of province); **(d)** *Arch* stewardship (of estate).

intendant, -ante [ɛ̃tɑ̃dɑ̃, -ɑ̃t] **1** *nm* **(a)** *Scol* bursar; **(b)** *Mil* senior Commissariat officer; **(c)** *Hist Fr* administrator (*of province*); **(d)** *Arch* intendant; steward (*of estate*). **2** *nf* **intendante (a)** *Scol* (woman) bursar; **(b)** *Hist Fr* wife of the administrator (*of province*); **(c)** *Rel* Mother Superior (*of certain convents*); **(d)** *Arch* intendant's *or* steward's wife.

intense [ɛ̃tɑ̃s] *adj* intense, severe (*pain*); heavy (*gunfire*); deep (*blue*); **temps d'un froid i.,** intensely cold weather; **circulation i.,** dense *or* heavy traffic.

intensément [ɛ̃tɑ̃semɑ̃] *adv* intensely.

intensif, -ive [ɛ̃tɑ̃sif, -iv] *adj* intensive; *Agr* **culture intensive,** intensive farming *or* cultivation.

intensification [ɛ̃tɑ̃sifikasjɔ̃] *nf* intensification.

intensifier [ɛ̃tɑ̃sifje] *vt* to intensify.

intensité [ɛ̃tɑ̃site] *nf* **(a)** (*d'un regard, d'un sentiment*) intensity, intenseness; force (*of wind*); depth (*of colour*); severity (*of cold*); strength (*of current*); density (*of magnetic field*); **donner plus d'i. à un morceau de musique,** to give more feeling to a piece of music; **(b)** *Ling* **accent d'i.,** stress mark.

intensivement [ɛ̃tɑ̃sivmɑ̃] *adv* intensively.

intenter [ɛ̃tɑ̃te] *vt Jur* **i. une action/un procès à** *ou* **contre qn,** to bring an action against s.o., to institute proceedings against s.o.

intention [ɛ̃tɑ̃sjɔ̃] *nf* **(a)** (*projet*) intention, purpose, design; *Jur* intent; **avec i. délictueuse,** with malicious intent; **sans mauvaise i.,** with no ill intent; **avoir l'i. de faire qch,** to intend *or* mean to do sth; **je n'ai nullement l'i. d'accepter,** I have no intention of accepting; **c'est bien différent de mon i.,** that was not what I intended; **à cette i.,** to that end, with that in mind; **dans l'i. de faire qch,** with a view to *or* with the intention of doing sth; *Prov* **l'enfer est pavé de bonnes intentions,** the road to hell is paved with good intentions; **il a de bonnes intentions,** he means well; **(b) à l'i. de,** in honour *or US* honor of; (*pour*) for the sake of; (*pour aider*) in aid of; **voici une écharpe que j'ai achetée à votre i.,** here's a scarf I bought especially for you; **livres écrits à l'i. des enfants,** books for children.

intentionné [ɛ̃tɑ̃sjɔne] *adj* **bien/mal i.,** well-/ill-disposed (**envers,** towards); **mieux i.,** better disposed; **personne bien intentionnée,** well-intentioned *or* well-meaning person; **c'était une démarche bien intentionnée,** it was well-intentioned.

intentionnel, -elle [ɛ̃tɑ̃sjɔnɛl] *adj* intentional, wilful, deliberate.

intentionnellement [ɛ̃tɑ̃sjɔnɛlmɑ̃] *adv* intentionally.

inter [ɛ̃tɛr] *nm* **(a)** *Fb* **i. droit/gauche,** inside right/left; **(b)** *Tél Vieilli* trunk (line).

interactif, -ive [ɛ̃tɛraktif, -iv] *adj Ordinat* interactive.

interaction [ɛ̃tɛraksjɔ̃] *nf* interaction.

interactivité [ɛ̃tɛraktivite] *nf* interactivity.

interallié [ɛ̃tɛralje] *adj* interallied.

interarmées [ɛ̃tɛrarme] *adj inv Mil* **état-major i.,** joint staff.

interarmes [ɛ̃tɛrarm] *adj inv Mil* combined (*operation etc*).

interastral, -aux [ɛ̃tɛrastral, -o] *adj* (*rare*) interstellar.

interbancaire [ɛ̃tɛrbɑ̃kɛr] *adj* interbank.

intercalaire [ɛ̃tɛrkalɛr] *adj* **(a) feuille i.,** interpolated sheet; **feuillet i.,** insert; **(b) carte i.,** guide (card) (*of card index etc*); **(c)** intercalary (*day, year etc*).

intercalation [ɛ̃tɛrkalasjɔ̃] *nf* interpolation, insertion; *Él* switching in (*of resistance*).

intercaler [ɛ̃tɛrkale] *vt* to interpolate, to insert; *Él* to cut in, to switch in (*resistance*); to intercalate (*day in year etc*); **i. des citations dans un discours,** to intersperse *or* sprinkle a speech with quotations.

intercéder [ɛ̃tɛrsede] *vi* (*conj like* **céder**) to intercede (**auprès de,** with).

intercepter [ɛ̃tɛrsɛpte] *vt* to intercept (*letter, aircraft etc*); to shut *or* cut out (*noise, light*).

intercepteur [ɛ̃tɛrsɛptœr] *nm Av* interceptor.

interception [ɛ̃tɛrsɛpsjɔ̃] *nf* interception (*of a letter, an aircraft*); cutting *or* shutting out (*of noise, light*); *Rad* **i. des émissions,** monitoring; **opérateur d'i.,** monitor; **avion d'i.,** interceptor (aircraft).

intercesseur [ɛ̃tɛrsesœr] *nm Litt* mediator.

intercession [ɛ̃tɛrsesjɔ̃] *nf Litt* intercession.

interchangeable [ɛ̃tɛrʃɑ̃ʒabl] *adj* interchangeable.

interclasse [ɛ̃tɛrklas] *nm Scol* (short) break (between classes).

interclassement [ɛ̃tɛrklasmɑ̃] *nm Ordinat* **i. du courrier,** mail merge.

intercommunication [ɛ̃tɛrkɔmynikasjɔ̃] *nf* intercommunication.

interconnexion [ɛ̃tɛrkɔnɛksjɔ̃] *nf Él* interconnection.

intercontinental, -aux [ɛ̃tɛrkɔ̃tinɑ̃tal, -o] *adj* intercontinental; **fusée intercontinentale,** intercontinental ballistic missile.

intercostal, -aux [ɛ̃tɛrkɔstal, -o] *Anat* **1** *adj* intercostal (*muscle*). **2** *nm* intercostal muscle.

interdépartemental, -aux [ɛ̃tɛrdepartəmɑ̃tal, -o] *adj* interdepartmental.

interdépendance [ɛ̃tɛrdepɑ̃dɑ̃s] *nf* interdependence.

interdépendant [ɛ̃tɛrdepɑ̃dɑ̃] *adj* interdependent.

interdiction [ɛ̃tɛrdiksjɔ̃] *nf* **(a)** (*défense*) prohibition, banning, forbidding; **i. des essais atomiques,** atomic test ban; **i. d'un livre par la censure,** banning of a book by the censor; **i. absolue de toucher à qch,** absolute ban on touching sth; **(b)** *Jur* state of minority declared by court; deprival of control over money; **i. d'un aliéné,** certifying of an insane person; **i. légale,** suspension *or* (temporary) deprivation of civil rights; **i. de séjour,** ban(ning order).

interdigital, -aux [ɛ̃tɛrdiʒital, -o] *adj* interdigital.

interdire [ɛ̃tɛrdir] *v* (*conj like* **dire,** *except pr ind* **v. interdisez** *and imp* **interdisez**) **1** *vt* **(a)** (*défendre*) to forbid, to prohibit, to ban; **i. qch à qn,** to forbid s.o. sth; **la passerelle est interdite aux voyageurs,** passengers are not allowed on the bridge; **le médecin lui a interdit l'alcool,** the doctor has forbidden him to drink; **il nous est interdit de révéler ...,** we are not allowed to reveal ...; **i. à qn de faire qch,** to prohibit s.o. from doing sth, to forbid s.o. to do sth; **je t'interdis de fumer!,** I forbid you to smoke!; **i. à un pilote de voler,** to ground a pilot;

(b) to suspend (*s.o.*) (from his post); *Jur* **faire i. qn,** to have s.o. declared incapable of managing his own affairs;

(c) (*empêcher*) to prevent, to stop; **c'est ce qui nous interdit de penser à une rémission,** that's what stops us from hoping for a remission; **le temps nous interdit de sortir,** the weather is preventing *or* stopping us from going out *or* is making it impossible for us to go out.

2 s'interdire *vpr* **s'i. qch,** to give sth up, to refrain from sth; **il s'interdit d'y penser,** he doesn't let himself think about it.

interdisciplinaire [ɛ̃tɛrdisiplinɛr] *adj* interdisciplinary.

interdit, -ite [ɛ̃tɛrdi, -it] **1** *adj* **(a)** (*non autorisé*) forbidden; **(il est) interdit de fumer,** no smoking; **entrée interdite (au public),** no admittance, no entry; **passage interdit,** no thoroughfare; **c'est un sujet i. ici,** it's a forbidden *or* taboo subject here; **film i. aux moins de 18 ans,** *Br* ≈ (18); **i. de séjour,** (*dans un pays*) banned; *Fig* **être i. de séjour chez qn,** to be extremely unpopular with s.o.; *Ordinat* **i. d'écriture,** (*disquette*) write-protected; **(b)** (*déconcerté*) disconcerted, nonplussed, bewildered, taken aback. **2** *n Jur* **(aliéné) i.,** certified person; **i. de séjour,** ex-convict prohibited from entering a certain area. **3** *nm Rel etc* interdict; *Rel* **des interdits alimentaires,** food forbidden by dietary law; **frapper qn d'i.,** to lay s.o. under an interdict.

intéressant, -ante [ɛ̃terɛsɑ̃, -ɑ̃t] **1** *adj* interesting; **peu i.,** dull, uninteresting; **chercher à se rendre i.,** to try to make oneself interesting, to draw attention to oneself; **prix intéressants,** attractive *or* advantageous prices. **2** *n F* **ne fais pas l'i.!,** stop drawing attention to yourself!

intéressé [ɛ̃terese] **1** *adj* **(a)** (*concerné*) **les parties intéressées,** the interested parties, the persons concerned *or* involved; **(b)** (*égoïste*) selfish, self-seeking; **amour i.,** cupboard love; **agir dans un but i.,** to have an axe to grind; **encore un conseil i.!,** another piece of biased advice! **2** *npl* **les intéressés,** the interested parties, the persons concerned *or* involved; **les premiers intéressés,** those most directly affected; **c'est vous le premier i.,** you are the most closely concerned *or* involved.

intéressement [ɛ̃terɛsmɑ̃] *nm Com Ind* profit(-)sharing (scheme).

intéresser [ɛ̃terese] **1** *vt* **(a)** (*captiver*) to interest, to be interesting to (*s.o.*); **sujet qui m'intéresse beaucoup,** subject which interests me greatly; **ceci peut vous i.,** this may be of interest to you;

(b) (*concerner*) to interest, to affect, to concern; **ça ne m'intéresse pas,** it doesn't interest me, it's of no interest to me; **question qui intéresse le monde entier,** question of worldwide interest;

(c) *Ind Com* **i. qn dans son commerce,** to give s.o. a financial interest *or* a partnership in the business; **i. les employés (aux bénéfices),** to initiate a profit-sharing scheme;

(d) i. qn à qch, to interest s.o. in sth; **savoir i. les enfants,** to know how to get children's interest; **i. un enfant à la musique,** to interest a child in music.

2 s'intéresser *vpr* **(a)** *Ind Com* **s'i. dans une affaire,** to acquire a financial interest in *or* put money into a business;

(b) s'i. à qn/qch, to take an interest in s.o./sth, to be interested in s.o./sth.

intérêt [ɛ̃terɛ] *nm* **(a)** share, stake (*in business etc*); **avoir un i. au jeu,** to have a stake in the game;

(b) (*avantage*) interest, advantage, benefit; **il y a i. à ...,** it is desirable to ...; **j'ai i. à le faire,** it's in my interest to do it; **agir dans son i.,** to act in one's own interest; **ce n'est pas dans mon i.,** it's not in my interest; **i. personnel,** self interest; **il a fait un mariage d'i.,** he married for money; **il sait où se trouve son i.,** he knows where his advantage lies *or F* which side his bread is buttered on; *Rail* **ligne d'i. local,** branch line, local line; *F* **tu n'as pas i. à recommencer!,** you'd better not do it again!;

(c) (*attention, curiosité*) (feeling of) interest; **ressentir de l'i. pour qn,** to feel interested in s.o.; **prendre de l'i. à qch,** to take an interest in sth; **livre sans i.** *ou* **dépourvu d'i.,** uninteresting book; **elle a perdu tout son i. pour son travail/cet ami,** she has lost all interest in her work/boyfriend;

(d) (*importance*) importance; **du plus haut i.,** of the greatest importance; **quelques paroles sans i.,** some unimportant words;

(e) *Fin* **i. simple/composé,** simple/compound interest; **placer son argent à 12% d'i.,** to invest one's money at 12% interest; **prêt à i.,** loan bearing interest; **intérêt(s) couru(s),** accrued interest; *Bourse* **i. de report,** contango.

interface [ɛ̃tɛrfas] *nf Ordinat etc* interface; **i. pour petit système informatique,** small computer system interface; **i.-utilisateur,** user interface.

interférence [ɛ̃tɛrferɑ̃s] *nf Phys Rad etc* interference.

interférent [ɛ̃tɛrferɑ̃] *adj Phys* interfering (*rays etc*).

interférer [ɛ̃tɛrfere] *vi* (**il interfère; il interférait; il interférera**) **(a)** *Phys* (*of light waves etc*) to interfere; **(b)** (*of plans etc*) to interfere with each other.

interféron [ɛ̃tɛrferɔ̃] *nm Biol* interferon.

interfolier [ɛ̃tɛrfɔlje] *vt Tech* to interleave, to interpage.

intergalactique [ɛ̃tɛrgalaktik] *adj* intergalactic.

intergouvernemental, -aux [ɛ̃tɛrguvɛrnəmɑ̃tal, -o] *adj* intergovernmental.

intérieur [ɛ̃terjœr] **1** *adj* interior, inner (*room*); inside (*pocket*); internal (*part*); inland (*sea*); inner (*feelings*); domestic (*administration*); **cour intérieure,** inner courtyard; **vie intérieure,** inner life; **commerce i.,** domestic trade; **(tarif d')affranchissement en régime i.,** inland postage rate; *esp Can Av* **vol i.,** domestic flight.

2 *nm* **(a)** (*dedans*) interior, inside; **à l'i.,** inside, on the inside; (*à la maison*) inside, indoors; **à l'i. de la gare,** inside the station; **la porte était verrouillée à l'i.,** the door was bolted on *or* from the inside; *Cin* **tourné en i.,** shot indoors; *Fig* **une voix à l'i.,** an inner voice; **l'i. du pays,** the interior of the country; **dans l'i. du pays,** inland; **Ministère de l'I.,** ≈ *Br* Home Office, *US* Department of the Interior;

(b) (*maison*) home, house; **vie d'i.,** home life, domestic life; **femme d'i.,** homebody; **vêtements d'i.,** indoor clothes; **un i. douillet,** a cosy interior;

(c) *Fb* **i. gauche/droit,** inside left/right.

intérieurement [ɛ̃terjœrmɑ̃] *adv* inwardly, internally, inside, within; **rire i.,** to laugh to oneself.

interim [ɛ̃terim] *nm* interim; **dans l'i.,** in the interim, (in the) meanwhile; *Fin* **dividende par i.,** interim dividend; **secrétaire par i.,** acting *or* temporary secretary; **assurer l'i. (de qn),** to deputize, to stand in (for s.o.); *Méd* to act as locum (tenens) (for s.o.).

intérimaire [ɛ̃terimɛr] **1** *adj* temporary, provisional (*duty, official etc*); *Pol* **cabinet i.,** caretaker cabinet; **directeur i.,** acting manager; **dividende/rapport i.,** interim dividend/report. **2** *n* deputy; *Méd* locum (tenens); (*secrétaire*) temporary secretary.

intériorisation [ɛ̃terjɔrizasjɔ̃] *nf* interiorization.

intérioriser [ɛ̃terjɔrize] *vt* to interiorize.

interjectif, -ive [ɛ̃tɛrʒɛktif, -iv] *adj* interjectional.

interjection [ɛ̃tɛrʒɛksjɔ̃] *nf* **(a)** *Gram* interjection; **(b)** *Jur* lodging (*of an appeal*).

interjeter [ɛ̃tɛrʒəte] *vt* (*conj like* **jeter**) *Jur* **i. appel (d'un jugement),** to lodge an appeal, to give notice of appeal.

interlignage [ɛ̃tɛrliɲaʒ] *nm Typ* leading out.

interligne [ɛ̃tɛrliɲ] **1** *nm* space between two lines; (*sur machine à écrire*) spacing; *Mus* space (*on the stave*); **dans les interlignes,** between the lines; **écrit à simple/double i.,** typed in single/double spacing, single-/double-spaced. **2** *nf Typ* lead.

interligner [ɛ̃tɛrliɲe] *vt* **(a)** to write between the lines of (*a text*), to interline (*a text*); **(b)** *Typ* to lead out.

interlinéaire [ɛ̃tɛrlineɛr] *adj* interlinear (*notes etc*).

interlocuteur, -trice [ɛ̃tɛrlɔkytœr, -tris] *n* interlocutor; speaker (*engaged in conversation*); **mon i.,** the person I was *or* am speaking to; **i. privilégié,** = person/country etc with whom one/a country etc has a special relationship.

interlocutoire [ɛ̃tɛrlɔkytwar] *Jur* **1** *adj* interlocutory. **2** *nm* interlocutory judgement.

interlope [ɛ̃tɛrlɔp] *adj* unauthorized, illegal (*trade*); suspect, dubious, shady (*house etc*).

interloqué [ɛ̃tɛrlɔke] *adj* disconcerted, nonplussed.

interloquer [ɛ̃tɛrlɔke] *vt* to disconcert, to nonplus (*s.o.*), to take (*s.o.*) aback.

interlude [ɛ̃tɛrlyd] *nm Mus Th* interlude.

intermède [ɛ̃tɛrmɛd] *nm* interval, interlude; *Th* interlude.

intermédiaire [ɛ̃tɛrmedjɛr] **1** *adj* intermediate, intermediary, intervening (*state, time etc*); *MecE* **arbre i.,** countershaft. **2** *n* (*personne*) agent, intermediary, go-between; *Com* middleman. **3** *nm* intermediary, agency; **par l'i. de qn,** through *or* by means of s.o.; **par l'i. de la presse,** through the medium of the press; **sans i.,** without transition, directly.

intermezzo [ɛ̃tɛrmɛdzo] *nm Mus* intermezzo.

interminable [ɛ̃tɛrminabl] *adj* interminable, endless.

interminablement [ɛ̃tɛrminabləmɑ̃] *adv* interminably, endlessly.

interministériel, -ielle [ɛ̃tɛrministerjɛl] *adj* (*entre ministres*) interministerial; (*entre ministères*) interdepartmental, interministerial.

intermission [ɛ̃tɛrmisjɔ̃] *nf*, **intermittence** [ɛ̃tɛrmitɑ̃s] *nf Méd* remission; intermittency, intermittence; (*du cœur*) intermission.

intermittent [ɛ̃tɛrmitɑ̃] *adj* intermittent; irregular (*pulse*); **travail i.,** casual work; *El* **courant i.,** make-and-break current.

intermoléculaire [ɛ̃tɛrmɔlekylɛr] *adj* intermolecular.

internat [ɛ̃tɛrna] *nm* **(a)** living-in (*system, period*); *Scol* boarding; *Méd Br* housemanship, *Am* internship; *Méd* **faire l'i.,** to be a houseman *or Am* an intern; **(b)** (*pensionnat*) boarding school; **(c)** (*pensionnaires*) boarders.

international, -ale, -aux [ɛ̃tɛrnasjɔnal, -o] **1** *adj* international. **2** *n Sp* international (*player*). **3** *nf* **l'Internationale,** the International(e).

internationalement [ɛ̃tɛrnasjɔnalmɑ̃] *adv* internationally.

internationalisation [ɛ̃tɛrnasjɔnalizasjɔ̃] *nf* internationalization.

internationaliser [ɛ̃tɛrnasjɔnalize] *vt* to internationalize.

internationalisme [ɛ̃tɛrnasjɔnalism] *nm* internationalism.

internationaliste [ɛ̃tɛrnasjɔnalist] *adj & n* internationalist.

internationalité [ɛ̃tɛrnasjɔnalite] *nf* internationality.

interne [ɛ̃tɛrn] **1** *adj* internal (*structure, bleeding etc*); inner (*purity etc*); inner (*side*); *Math* interior (*angle*); *Gram* **accusatif i.,** cognate accusative; *Anat* **face i. du bras,** inside of the arm; *Scol* **élève i.,** boarder. **2** *n Scol* boarder; *Méd* house physician, houseman, *Am* intern.

interné, -ée [ɛ̃tɛrne] **1** *adj* interned. **2** *n* internee.

internement [ɛ̃tɛrnəmɑ̃] *nm* internment (*of alien*); confinement (*of the mentally ill*).

interner [ɛ̃tɛrne] *vt* to intern (*alien etc*); to shut up, to confine (*the mentally ill*).

interocéanique [ɛ̃tɛrɔseanik] *adj* interoceanic.

interparlementaire [ɛ̃tɛrparləmɑ̃tɛr] *adj Pol* interparliamentary; **commission i.,** joint committee.

interpellateur, -trice [ɛ̃tɛrpelatœr, -tris] *n* heckler.

interpellation [ɛ̃tɛrpelasjɔ̃] *n* (*question*) question; (*action*) questioning; (*à une réunion etc*) heckling, interruption; (*par sentinelle*) challenge; **les interpellations de la police,** police questioning; **répondre à une i.,** (*au Parlement*) to answer a question.

interpeller [ɛ̃tɛrpele] **1** *vt* **(a)** *Pol* to question, to put a question to (*a minister*); (*à une réunion politique*) to challenge, to heckle; (*d'une sentinelle*) to challenge; (*appeler à*) to call to; **se faire i. par la police,** to be questioned by the police; **i. le ministre pour qu'il s'explique sur sa politique,** to call on *or* challenge the Minister to explain his policy; **(b)** *F* (*toucher*) to affect; **ce film m'interpelle vraiment,** this film really speaks to me. **2 s'interpeller** *vpr* **les deux automobilistes s'interpellaient grossièrement,** the two drivers were exchanging insults.

interpénétration [ɛ̃tɛrpenetrasjɔ̃] *nf Écon etc* interpenetration.

interpénétrer (s') [sɛ̃tɛrpenetre] *vpr* to interpenetrate; **ces deux facteurs s'interpénètrent,** these two factors are interdependent.

interphone [ɛ̃tɛrfɔn] *nm* intercom; **à l'i.,** on the intercom.

interplanétaire [ɛ̃tɛrplanetɛr] *adj* interplanetary; **voyage i.,** space flight.

interpolateur, -trice [ɛ̃tɛrpɔlatœr, -tris] *n* interpolater.

interpolation [ɛ̃tɛrpɔlasjɔ̃] *nf* interpolation.

interpoler [ɛ̃tɛrpɔle] *vt* to interpolate.

interposé [ɛ̃tɛrpoze] *adj* **agir par personnes interposées,** to act through intermediaries; **l'aventure par personnes interposées,** adventure at second hand.

interposer [ɛ̃tɛrpoze] **1** *vt* to interpose, to place. **2 s'interposer** *vpr* to intervene.

interposition [ɛ̃tɛrpozisjɔ̃] *nf* **(a)** (*intervention*) intervention; **(b)** (*situation*) interposition.

interprétable [ɛ̃tɛrpretabl] *adj* interpretable.

interprétariat [ɛ̃tɛrpretarja] *nm* interpretership.

interprétatif, -ive [ɛ̃tɛrpretatif, -iv] *adj* interpretative, explanatory (*note etc*).

interprétation [ɛ̃tɛrpretasjɔ̃] *nf* (*action*) interpreting (*of speech etc*); (*résultat*) interpretation; (*métier*) interpreting; *Mus Th* rendering, rendition; **fausse i.,** misinterpretation, misconstruction (*of statement*); **donner une fausse i. d'un passage,** to misinterpret a passage.

interprète [ɛ̃tɛrprɛt] *n* (*dans une autre langue*) interpreter; *Th Mus etc* interpreter, performer; **servir d'i. à qn,** to act as interpreter to s.o., to interpret for s.o.; *Th* **les interprètes,** the cast; **je ne suis que son i.,** I'm just passing on what he said.

interpréter [ɛ̃tɛrprete] *vt* (**j'interprète; j'interpréterai**) to interpret, to act as interpreter; *Mus Th* to interpret, to perform; to explain, to expound (*text etc*); **i. un discours,** to interpret a speech; **mal i. les paroles de qn,** to misinterpret s.o.'s words; **i. les rêves,** to interpret dreams; **i. des signaux,** to read signals; **mal i. un signal,** to misread a signal.

interpréteur [ɛ̃tɛrpretœr] *nm Ordinat* interpreter.

interprofessionnel, -elle [ɛ̃tɛrprɔfesjɔnɛl] *adj* interprofessional.

interrègne [ɛ̃tɛrrɛɲ] *nm* interregnum.

interrogateur, -trice [ɛ̃tɛrɔgatœr, -tris] **1** *adj* interrogatory, inquiring, questioning. **2** *n* questioner, interrogator; *Scol* (oral) examiner.

interrogatif, -ive [ɛ̃tɛrɔgatif, -iv] **1** *adj* **(a)** inquiring, questioning (*look etc*); **(b)** *Gram* interrogative (*pronoun, sentence etc*). **2** *nm Gram* interrogative (word, pronoun, adjective). **3** *nf Gram* **interrogative,** interrogative (clause).

interrogation [ɛ̃tɛrɔgasjɔ̃] *nf* **(a)** (*d'un prisonnier etc*) interrogation, questioning; *Gram* **point d'i.,** question mark; **(b)** (*question*) question, query; **i. directe/indirecte,** direct/indirect question; *Scol* **i. orale/écrite,** oral/written test.

interrogativement [ɛ̃tɛrɔgativmɑ̃] *adv* interrogatively.

interrogatoire [ɛ̃tɛrɔgatwar] *nm Jur* interrogation, questioning (*of prisoners etc*); cross-examination (*of defendant etc*); **pendant l'i.,** (*le témoin a dit*) under cross-examination.

interroger [ɛ̃tɛrɔʒe] *v* (**j'interrogeai(s); n. interrogeons**) **1** *vt* (*de la police*) to interrogate, to question; *Jur* to cross-examine; to examine (*candidate*); to consult (*history etc*); to examine (*one's conscience*); **i. qn du regard,** to look at s.o. inquiringly, to give s.o. a questioning look. **2 s'interroger** *vpr* to ask oneself, to wonder (**sur,** about; **si,** whether, if).

interrompre [ɛ̃tɛrɔ̃pr] *v* (*conj like* **rompre**) **1** *vt* (*couper la parole à*) to interrupt, to cut in on; to intercept, to interrupt (*flow of river etc*); to stop, to suspend (*traffic etc*); to cut short (*s.o., conversation*); to break off (*negotiations*); to break (*journey*); *El* to break, to switch off (*current*); **je ne voulais pas vous i. dans votre travail,** I didn't want to interrupt you while you were working; **veuillez bien ne pas nous i.,** please don't interrupt; **i. la conversation,** to interrupt *or* break in on the conversation. **2 s'interrompre** *vpr* to break off, to stop (talking).

interrompu [ɛ̃tɛrɔ̃py] *adj* interrupted, broken off; **sommeil i.,** broken sleep.

interrupteur, -trice [ɛ̃tɛryptœr, -tris] **1** *n* interrupter. **2** *nm El* (*commutateur*) switch; (*disjoncteur*) cut-out, circuit breaker, contact breaker; **i. marche-arrêt,** on-off switch; **i. à bascule,** toggle switch; **i. à gradation de lumière,** dimmer (switch); **i. d'escalier,** two-way switch; *Ordinat* **i. à plusieurs positions,** DIP switch.

interruption [ɛ̃tɛrypsjɔ̃] *nf* interruption; breaking in (*on conversation*); severance (*of communication etc*); breaking off (*of negotiations*); *El* disconnection, switching off, breaking (*of current*); **sans i.,** uninterruptedly; (*sans arrêt*) unceasingly, without a break; *Méd* **i. volontaire de grossesse,** abortion; *Ordinat* **fonction d'i.,** interrupt fonction.

interscolaire [ɛ̃tɛrskɔlɛr] *adj* (*match etc*) interscholastic.

intersecté [ɛ̃tɛrsɛkte] *adj* **(a)** *Archit* intersecting, interlacing; **(b)** *Math* intersected (*line etc*).

intersection [ɛ̃tɛrsɛksjɔ̃] *nf* intersection; **point d'i.,** point of intersection.

intersidéral, -aux [ɛ̃tɛrsideral, -o] *adj* intersidereal, interstellar; **course intersidérale,** space race.

interstellaire [ɛ̃tɛrstelɛr] *adj Astron* interstellar.

interstice [ɛ̃tɛrstis] *nm* chink, *Fml* interstice.

interstitiel, -ielle [ɛ̃tɛrstisjɛl] *adj* interstitial.

intersyndical, -aux [ɛ̃tɛrsɛ̃dikal] **1** *adj* interunion. **2** *nf* **intersyndicale,** interunion meeting.

intertropical, -aux [ɛ̃tɛrtrɔpikal, -o] *adj* intertropical.

interurbain [ɛ̃tɛryrbɛ̃] **1** *adj* interurban; *Tél* **lignes interurbaines,** trunk lines; **faire une communication interurbaine,** to call long distance. **2** *nm Tél* trunk (line).

intervalle [ɛ̃tɛrval] *nm* **(a)** (*dans le temps*) interval, period (of time); **un i. d'une heure,** an hour's interval, an interval of an hour, a one-hour interval; **visites à de longs intervalles,** visits at long intervals; **par intervalles,** at intervals, now and then; **dans l'i.,** in the meantime; **(b)** (*dans l'espace*) interval, distance, gap, space; *Mus* interval; **(c)** *Math* interval; **i. ouvert/fermé,** open/closed interval.

intervenant, -ante [ɛ̃tɛrvənɑ̃, -ɑ̃t] *Jur* **1** *adj* intervening. **2** *n* intervening party.

intervenir [ɛ̃tɛrvənir] *vi* (*conj like* **venir,** *aux* **être**) **(a)** (*pour aider*) to intervene, to interpose, to step in; (*ingérer*) to intervene, to interfere; **elle va i. en ta faveur,** she will intervene on your behalf; **au besoin, je pourrais i.,** I could intervene if necessary; **i. dans une conversation,** to break in on a conversation; **faire i. la force armée,** to call out the military, to bring in the army; **(b)** (*arriver*) to happen, to take place, to occur; **un accord est intervenu,** an agreement has been reached; **les changements intervenus depuis 1981,** the changes that have occurred since 1981; **(c)** *Méd* to operate.

intervention [ɛ̃tɛrvɑ̃sjɔ̃] *nf* **(a)** intervention; (*ingérence*) interference; **offre d'i.,** offer of mediation; **i. en faveur de qn,** intervention on behalf of s.o.; **par son i.,** through his intervention; **i. parlementaire,** sponsoring of claims *or* of applications (by members of Parliament); *Mil Av* **i. aérienne,** air strike; **(b)** *Méd* **i. chirurgicale,** (surgical) operation.

interventionnisme [ɛ̃tɛrvɑ̃sjɔnism] *nm Pol etc* interventionism.

interventionniste [ɛ̃tɛrvɑ̃sjɔnist] *adj & n Pol* interventionist.

interversion [ɛ̃tɛrvɛrsjɔ̃] *nf* inversion, transposition, reversal (*of order, dates etc*).

intervertébral, -aux [ɛ̃tɛrvɛrtebral, -o] *adj Anat* intervertebral; **disque i.,** (intervertebral) disc.

intervertir [ɛ̃tɛrvɛrtir] *vt* to invert, to transpose, to reverse (*the order of sth*); **maintenant les rôles sont intervertis,** now the roles are reversed.

interview [ɛ̃tɛrvju] *nf* interview.

interviewé, -ée [ɛ̃tɛrvjuve] *n* interviewee.

interviewer [ɛ̃tɛrvjuve] *vt* to interview.

intervieweu(u)r [ɛ̃tɛrvjuvœr] *nm* interviewer.

intervocalique [ɛ̃tɛrvɔkalik] *adj Ling* intervocalic.

intestat [ɛ̃tɛsta] *adj inv Jur* **mourir i.,** to die intestate.

intestin[1] [ɛ̃tɛstɛ̃] *adj* internal; domestic, civil (*war etc*); **lutte intestine,** infighting.

intestin[2] *nm Anat* **intestin(s),** intestine(s); **gros i.,** large intestine; **i. grêle,** small intestine.

intestinal, -aux [ɛ̃tɛstinal, -o] *adj* intestinal.

intifada [intifada] *nf* intifada.

intimation [ɛ̃timɑsjɔ̃] *nf Jur* notification (*of an order*); **i. de vider les lieux,** notice to quit.

intime [ɛ̃tim] **1** *adj* intimate (*relations, restaurant etc*); cosy (*room*); personal (*hygiene*); private (*secretary*); inward, deep-seated (*grief etc*); **avoir la conviction i. de qch,** to be thoroughly convinced of sth; **elle a l'i. conviction que ...,** she is thoroughly convinced that ...; **pensées intimes,** inmost *or* innermost thoughts; **ami i.,** intimate *or* close friend; **dîner i.,** intimate *or* quiet dinner. **2** *n* intimate *or* close friend.

intimé, -ée [ɛ̃time] *n Jur* respondent, defendant.

intimement [ɛ̃timmɑ̃] *adv* intimately.

intimer [ɛ̃time] *vt* **(a) i. qch à qn,** to notify s.o. of sth; **i. à qn l'ordre de partir,** to give s.o. notice to go; **(b)** *Jur* **i. qn,** to summons s.o. to appear before the Court of Appeal.

intimidable [ɛ̃timidabl] *adj* easily intimidated.

intimidant [ɛ̃timidɑ̃] *adj* intimidating.

intimidateur, -trice [ɛ̃timidatœr, -tris] *adj* intimidating.

intimidation [ɛ̃timidɑsjɔ̃] *nf* intimidation; *surtout Jur* undue influence.

intimider [ɛ̃timide] *vt* **(a)** (*effrayer*) to intimidate; *surtout Jur* to exert undue influence on (*s.o.*); **nullement intimidé,** nothing daunted.

intimisme [ɛ̃timism] *nm Littér Beaux-Arts* intimism.

intimiste [ɛ̃timist] *adj & n Littér Beaux-Arts* intimist.

intimité [ɛ̃timite] *nf* **(a)** intimacy; closeness (*of friendship*); **l'i. du chez-soi,** the privacy of one's own home; **dans l'i.,** in private (life); **le mariage a été célébré dans la plus stricte i.,** it was a very quiet wedding; **(b)** in(ner)most parts, depths (*of one's being etc*); **dans l'i. de sa conscience,** in one's inner conscience.

intitulé [ɛ̃tityle] *nm* title (*of document, book etc*); heading (*of chapter etc*).

intituler [ɛ̃tityle] **1** *vt* to give a title to (*book etc*); **livre intitulé ...,** book entitled ...; **article intitulé ...,** article headed ...; **pourquoi avez-vous intitulé votre livre ...?,** why did you give your book the title ...?, why did you call your book ...? **2 s'intituler** *vpr* to be entitled; *souvent Péj* to call oneself.

intolérable [ɛ̃tɔlerabl] *adj* intolerable, insufferable, unbearable; **vie i.,** life that is not worth living.

intolérablement [ɛ̃tɔlerabləmɑ̃] *adv* intolerably.

intolérance [ɛ̃tɔlerɑ̃s] *nf* intolerance; *Méd* **i. à une substance,** intolerance to a substance.

intolérant [ɛ̃tɔlerɑ̃] *adj* intolerant (**de,** of).

intonation [ɛ̃tɔnɑsjɔ̃] *nf* intonation.

intouchable [ɛ̃tuʃabl] *adj & n* untouchable.

intox [ɛ̃tɔks] *nf Pol F* propaganda.

intoxicant [ɛ̃tɔksikɑ̃] *adj Méd* poisonous, toxic.

intoxication [ɛ̃tɔksikɑsjɔ̃] *nf Méd* intoxication, poisoning; **i. alimentaire,** food poisoning; *F* **regarder la T.V. toute la journée, c'est de l'i.!,** watching television all day is an addiction!

intoxiqué, -ée [ɛ̃tɔksike] *n* addict.

intoxiquer [ɛ̃tɔksike] **1** *vt Méd* to poison; *F* **les médias intoxiquent le public,** the media turn people into zombies *or* brainwash people. **2 s'intoxiquer** *vpr* to poison oneself.

intracellulaire [ɛ̃traselylɛr] *adj Biol* intracellular.

intradermique [ɛ̃tradɛrmik] *adj Anat* intradermic, intradermal.

intrados [ɛ̃trado] *nm Archit* inner surface, soffit, intrados (*of arch*); *Av* undersurface (*of wing*).

intraduisible [ɛ̃tradɥizibl] *adj* untranslatable.

intraitable [ɛ̃trɛtabl] *adj* obstinate, uncompromising, inflexible.

intra-muros [ɛ̃tramyros] *adv* (*habiter*) in town; *esp Univ* **cours donné i.-m.,** intramural course.

intramusculaire [ɛ̃tramyskylɛr] *adj* intramuscular.

intransigeance [ɛ̃trɑ̃ziʒɑ̃s] *nf* intransigence.

intransigeant, -ante [ɛ̃trɑ̃ziʒɑ̃, -ɑ̃t] **1** *adj* intransigent; uncompromising, strict (*moral code etc*); peremptory (*tone*). **2** *n Pol* intransigent.

intransitif, -ive [ɛ̃trɑ̃zitif, -iv] *adj & nm Gram* intransitive.

intransitivement [ɛ̃trɑ̃zitivmɑ̃] *adv Gram* intransitively.

intransmissible [ɛ̃trɑ̃smisibl] *adj* intransmissible.

intransportable [ɛ̃trɑ̃spɔrtabl] *adj* untransportable; (*blessé*) unfit to travel.

intra-utérin [ɛ̃trayterɛ̃] *adj Anat* intrauterine; (*pl intra-utérins, -rines*).

intraveineux, -euse [ɛ̃travɛnø, -øz] *adj* intravenous.

intrépide [ɛ̃trepid] *adj* intrepid, dauntless, undaunted, bold, fearless; **menteur i.,** barefaced liar.

intrépidement [ɛ̃trepidmɑ̃] *adv* intrepidly.

intrépidité [ɛ̃trepidite] *nf* intrepidity, dauntlessness, fearlessness; **avec i.,** fearlessly.

intrigant, -ante [ɛ̃trigɑ̃, -ɑ̃t] **1** *adj* scheming, designing. **2** *n* intriguer, schemer.

intrigue [ɛ̃trig] *nf* (*situation compliquée*) intrigue; (*complot*) plot, scheme; (*liaison amoureuse*) (love) affair; *Th Cin Littér* plot; (*d'une bande dessinée*) plot, story line.

intrigué [ɛ̃trige] *adj* intrigued, puzzled, curious, mystified.

intriguer [ɛ̃trige] **1** *vt* to intrigue, to puzzle (*s.o.*). **2** *vi* to scheme, to plot, to intrigue.

intrinsèque [ɛ̃trɛ̃sɛk] *adj* intrinsic.

intrinsèquement [ɛ̃trɛ̃sɛkmɑ̃] *adv* intrinsically.

introducteur, -trice [ɛ̃trɔdyktœr, -tris] *n* introducer; innovator (*of fashion etc*); usher (*at reception*).

introductif, -ive [ɛ̃trɔdyktif, -iv] *adj Jur* introductory.

introduction [ɛ̃trɔdyksjɔ̃] *nf* introduction (*to a book etc*); introduction, admission, induction (*of steam, gas etc*); introducing, bringing in (*of s.o. into s.o.'s presence etc*); *Rugby* put-in; **l'i. de nouvelles techniques,** the introduction of new techniques; **lettre d'i.,** letter of introduction (**de la part de,** from; **auprès de,** to); **après quelques mots d'i.,** after a few introductory words, after a few words of introduction.

introduire [ɛ̃trɔdɥir] *v* (*prp* **introduisant;** *pp* **introduit;** *pr ind* **j'introduis, il introduit, n. introduisons;** *p hist* **j'introduisis;** *fu* **j'introduirai) 1** *vt* to introduce (*a custom, a reform etc*); to introduce, to insert, to put (*key in lock etc*); *Ordinat* to enter, to input (*data*); to bring in (*goods etc*); to admit, to let in (*steam etc*); to introduce, to launch (*a fashion*); to usher in, to show in (*stranger etc*); **introduisez ce monsieur,** show the gentleman in; **i. qn auprès de qn,** to show s.o. in (to s.o.'s office *etc*); (*présenter*) to introduce s.o. to s.o.

2 s'introduire *vpr* to get in, to enter; **s'i. dans une maison/***etc*, (*d'un intrus*) to get into *or* to enter a house/*etc*; **s'i. dans qch,** to work *or* worm one's way into sth; **l'usage s'en introduit peu à peu,** the custom gradually crept in; **l'eau s'introduit partout,** water is coming in everywhere.

intromission [ɛ̃trɔmisjɔ̃] *nf* intromission.

intronisation [ɛ̃trɔnizɑsjɔ̃] *nf* **(a)** enthroning, enthronement (*esp of bishop*); **(b)** establishment (*of system etc*).

introniser [ɛ̃trɔnize] *vt* **(a)** to enthrone (*king, bishop*); **(b)** to set up, to establish (*new religion etc*).

introspectif, -ive [ɛ̃trɔspɛktif, -iv] *adj* introspective.

introspection [ɛ̃trɔspɛksjɔ̃] *nf* introspection.

introuvable [ɛ̃truvabl] *adj* nowhere to be found; (*produit etc*) unobtainable; **l'assassin reste i.,** the murderer is still at large.

introversion [ɛ̃trɔvɛrsjɔ̃] *nf Psy* introversion.

introverti, -ie [ɛ̃trɔvɛrti] *Psy* **1** *adj* introverted. **2** *n* introvert.

intrus, -use [ɛ̃try, -yz] **1** *adj* intruding. **2** *n* (*dans une réception*) intruder, *F* gatecrasher; *Jur* trespasser.

intrusion [ɛ̃tryzjɔ̃] *nf* intrusion; interference (*in a matter*); *Géol* **roches d'i.,** intrusive rocks.

intuitif, -ive [ɛ̃tɥitif, -iv] **1** *adj* intuitive. **2** *n* intuitionist.

intuition [ɛ̃tɥisjɔ̃] *nf* intuition; **par i.,** intuitively; **avoir une i.,** to have an intuition; **avoir l'i. que ...,** to have an intuition that ... .

intuitivement [ɛ̃tɥitivmɑ̃] *adv* intuitively.

inusable [inyzabl] *adj* everlasting; (*souliers etc*) hard-wearing.

inusité [inyzite] *adj* uncommon, not in common use.

inutile [inytil] *adj* (*qui ne sert à rien*) useless, pointless, unavailing, unprofitable; vain (*effort*); (*non nécessaire*) needless, unnecessary; **je suis i. ici,** I'm (of) no use here; **c'est i.!,** it's pointless!, it's no good!; (*ce n'est pas la peine*) you needn't bother; **bouches inutiles,** useless mouths; **i. de dire que ...,** needless to say ...; **i. d'attendre,** it's no good *or* it's pointless waiting.

inutilement [inytilmɑ̃] *adv* (*sans servir*) uselessly, in vain; (*sans nécessité*) needlessly, unnecessarily; **se déranger i.,** to go to unnecessary trouble; **c'est i. que je lui ai parlé,** it was pointless talking to him, talking to him served no purpose.

inutilisable [inytilizabl] *adj* unserviceable, unusable.

inutilisé [inytilize] *adj* unutilized, unused; untapped (*resources*).

inutilité [inytilite] *nf* uselessness, needlessness, pointlessness.

invaincu [ɛ̃vɛ̃ky] *adj* (*pays*) unconquered; (*armée*) unvanquished; *Sp* unbeaten.

invalidation [ɛ̃validasjɔ̃] *nf Jur* invalidation (*of document, election etc*); unseating (*of elected member*).

invalide [ɛ̃valid] **1** *adj* (*personne*) invalid, infirm; disabled (*soldier etc*). **2** *n* disabled person; (*alité*) invalid.

invalider [ɛ̃valide] *vt Jur* to invalidate (*will, election etc*); to quash (*election*); to unseat (*elected member*).

invalidité [ɛ̃validite] *nf* infirmity; disablement, disability; **pension d'i.,** disability pension.

invariabilité [ɛ̃varjabilite] *nf* invariability.

invariable [ɛ̃varjabl] *adj* invariable, unvarying; **être i. dans ses opinions,** to be unwavering in one's opinions.

invariablement [ɛ̃varjabləmɑ̃] *adv* invariably.

invasion [ɛ̃vazjɔ̃] *nf* invasion; infestation (*by vermin etc*); *Fig* **l'i. des touristes,** the tourist invasion.

invective [ɛ̃vɛktiv] *nf* invective; **invectives,** abuse.

invectiver [ɛ̃vɛktive] **1** *vi* **i. contre qn,** to inveigh *or* rail against s.o. **2** *vt* to hurl abuse at, to abuse (*s.o.*).

invendable [ɛ̃vɑ̃dabl] *adj* unsaleable, unmarketable.

invendu [ɛ̃vɑ̃dy] **1** *adj* unsold. **2** *nm* **invendus,** unsold goods; (*journaux*) unsold copies; (*livres*) remainders.

inventaire [ɛ̃vɑ̃tɛr] *nm* **(a)** inventory; **faire** *ou* **dresser un i.,** to draw up *or* make an inventory; **sous bénéfice d'i.,** conditionally, with reservations; **accepter une succession sous bénéfice d'i.,** to accept an estate without liability to debts beyond the assets descended; **(b)** *Com* stocklist; **(établissement** *ou* **levée d')i.,** stocktaking; **faire** *ou* **dresser l'i.,** to take stock, to stocktake; **(c)** survey (*of ancient monuments, paintings etc*).

inventer [ɛ̃vɑ̃te] **1** *vt* to invent, to devise, to contrive (*machine etc*); (*imaginer*) to dream up; to make up (*story etc*); to coin (*phrase*); *F* **il n'a pas inventé la poudre,** he'll never set the Thames on fire; **mais qu'est-ce qu'il va i. là?,** what's he getting at?, what does he mean?; **i. une histoire,** to spin a yarn; **i. de faire qch,** to hit on the idea of doing sth; **je n'invente rien,** (*c'est vrai*) I'm not making anything up. **2 s'inventer** *vpr* **ça ne s'invente pas,** (*ce don etc*) you've either got it or you haven't.

inventeur, -trice [ɛ̃vɑ̃tœr, -tris] *n* **(a)** inventor, discoverer (*of process etc*); **(b)** *Jur* finder (*of lost object etc*).

inventif, -ive [ɛ̃vɑ̃tif, -iv] *adj* inventive.

invention [ɛ̃vɑ̃sjɔ̃] *nf* **(a)** (*action*) invention, inventing; (*faculté*) inventiveness, imagination; **nécessité est mère d'i.,** necessity is the mother of invention; **(b)** (*découverte*) invention; (*mensonge*) fabrication, lie; **brevet d'i.,** patent (*for an invention*); **pure i. tout cela!,** that's sheer invention, that's nothing but make-believe!; **(c)** *Jur* **i. d'un trésor,** finding of treasure trove.

inventivité [ɛ̃vɑ̃tivite] *nf* inventiveness.

inventorier [ɛ̃vɑ̃tɔrje] *vt* to make an inventory *or* a list of (*goods etc*).

invérifiable [ɛ̃verifjabl] *adj* unverifiable.

inverse [ɛ̃vɛrs] **1** *adj* inverse, inverted, opposite, contrary; **en sens i. (de qch),** in the opposite direction (to sth); **dans l'ordre i.,** in (the) reverse order; *Math* **en raison i. de qch,** in inverse ratio to sth. **2** *nm* opposite, reverse; **faire l'i.,** to do the opposite; **dans mon cas, c'est l'i. qui se passe,** it's the reverse *or* opposite in my case; **à l'i. du bon sens,** unreasonably, against all reason. **3** *nf Math* inverse, reciprocal (*function etc*).

inversement [ɛ̃vɛrsəmɑ̃] *adv* inversely, conversely.

inverser [ɛ̃vɛrse] *vt* to reverse (*current etc*); to invert (*order*); **carburateur inversé,** down-draught carburettor.

inverseur [ɛ̃vɛrsœr] *nm* reverser, reversing device; *El* **i. du courant,** current reverser, change-over switch.

inversion [ɛ̃vɛrsjɔ̃] *nf* **(a)** *Gram Mus etc* inversion; **(b)** reversal, reversing (*of electric current etc*); **i. de marche,** reverse gear.

invertébré [ɛ̃vɛrtebre] *adj & nm* invertebrate.

inverti, -ie [ɛ̃vɛrti] *n* homosexual, *Fml* invert.

investigateur, -trice [ɛ̃vɛstigatœr, -tris] **1** *adj* investigative, investigating; inquiring, searching, scrutinizing (*glance*). **2** *n* investigator.

investigation [ɛ̃vɛstigasjɔ̃] *nf* investigation, inquiry.

investir [ɛ̃vɛstir] **1** *vt* **(a)** to invest (*money, Fig time, energy*); **(b)** *Mil etc* to besiege (*town etc*); to encircle (*building*); **(c) i. qn d'une fonction,** to invest *or* vest s.o. with an office; **i. qn d'une mission,** to entrust s.o. with a mission. **2** *vi Fin* to invest (*dans,* in).

investissement [ɛ̃vɛstismɑ̃] *nm* **(a)** *Fin* investment; (*action*) investing; **i. de l'étranger/à l'étranger,** inward/outward investment; **(b)** *Mil etc* (*d'une ville*) besieging; (*d'un édifice*) encircling.

investisseur [ɛ̃vɛstisœr] *nm Fin* investor.

investiture [ɛ̃vɛstityr] *nf* investiture; induction (*of bishop*); *Pol* nomination (*of candidate*).

invétéré [ɛ̃vetere] *adj* inveterate, deeply rooted (*hatred etc*); inveterate, confirmed (*drunkard, criminal*); intractable (*disease*); **célibataire i.,** confirmed bachelor.

invincibilité [ɛ̃vɛ̃sibilite] *nf* invincibility.

invincible [ɛ̃vɛ̃sibl] *adj* (*armée, adversaire etc*) invincible; (*difficulté*) insuperable.

invinciblement [ɛ̃vɛ̃sibləmɑ̃] *adv* invincibly.

inviolabilité [ɛ̃vjɔlabilite] *nf* inviolability; sacredness (*of office*).

inviolable [ɛ̃vjɔlabl] *adj* inviolable; (*office*) sacred.

inviolablement [ɛ̃vjɔlabləmɑ̃] *adv Litt* inviolably.

inviolé [ɛ̃vjɔle] *adj Litt* inviolate; unbroken (*vow*).

invisibilité [ɛ̃vizibilite] *nf* invisibility.

invisible [ɛ̃vizibl] *adj* invisible; **le village est i. sous le brouillard,** the village is invisible in the mist; *Fig* **il restait i.,** he was nowhere to be seen.

invisiblement [ɛ̃vizibləmɑ̃] *adv* invisibly.

invitant [ɛ̃vitɑ̃] *adj* attractive, inviting.

invitation [ɛ̃vitasjɔ̃] *nf* invitation; **venir à** *ou* **sur l'i. de qn,** to come at s.o.'s invitation *or* request; **venir sans i.,** to come uninvited; **lettre d'i.,** letter of invitation; **envoyer une i. à qn,** to send s.o. an invitation; **une i. à la réflexion,** food for thought.

invite [ɛ̃vit] *nf* invitation, inducement; **répondre à l'i. de qn,** to respond to s.o.'s advances.

invité, -ée [ɛ̃vite] *n* (*pour dîner etc*) guest; (*qui rend visite*) visitor.

inviter [ɛ̃vite] *vt* to invite; **i. qn à dîner,** to invite *or* ask s.o. to dinner; **être déjà invité,** to have a previous engagement; **i. qn à faire qch,** to invite *or* request s.o. to do sth; **tout l'invitait à partir,** everything suggested to him that he should leave; **i. qn à entrer,** to ask s.o. in; **i. à la réflexion,** to give food for thought; **cela invite à penser le contraire,** that inclines me *or* us *etc* to think the opposite.

in vitro [invitro] *adv & adj* **fécondation in v.,** in vitro fertilization.

invivable [ɛ̃vivabl] *adj* unbearable, intolerable; (*vie*) not worth living; *F* (*personne*) impossible to live with.

in vivo [invivo] *adj & adv* in vivo.

invocation [ɛ̃vɔkasjɔ̃] *nf* invocation.

invocatoire [ɛ̃vɔkatwar] *adj Litt* invocatory.

involontaire [ɛ̃vɔlɔ̃tɛr] *adj* involuntary, unintentional; **mouvement i.,** involuntary movement; **c'était tout à fait i.,** (*ce que j'ai fait*) it was quite unintentional; **le témoin i. d'une scène de ménage,** the unwilling witness of a domestic dispute.

involontairement [ɛ̃vɔlɔ̃tɛrmɑ̃] *adv* involuntarily, unintentionally.

involution [ɛ̃vɔlysjɔ̃] *nf* involution.

invoquer [ɛ̃vɔke] *vt* **(a)** to call for; to put forward (*reason etc*); to plead (*forgetfulness etc*); to refer to (*documents*); **(b)** to call upon, to invoke (*the Deity etc*); to invoke, to call forth (*a spirit*); **i. l'aide de la justice,** to appeal to the law.

invraisemblable [ɛ̃vrɛsɑ̃blabl] *adj* unlikely, improbable; *esp Péj* implausible; **histoire i.,** tall story; **chapeau i.,** incredible hat; **ces gens-là sont invraisemblables,** those people are really extraordinary *or* fantastic *or* incredible.

invraisemblablement [ɛ̃vrɛsɑ̃blabləmɑ̃] *adv* improba-

bly; extraordinarily.
invraisemblance [ɛ̃vrɛsɑ̃blɑ̃s] *nf* **(a)** (*improbabilité*) unlikelihood, unlikeliness, improbability; **(b)** (*déclaration etc*) implausible fact *or* statement; **rempli d'invraisemblances,** full of implausibilities.
invulnérabilité [ɛ̃vylnerabilite] *nf* invulnerability.
invulnérable [ɛ̃vylnerabl] *adj* invulnerable.
iode [jɔd] *nm* iodine; **teinture d'i.,** tincture of iodine; **lampe à i.,** tungsten lamp.
iodé [jɔde] *adj* (*eau etc*) iodized.
ioder [jɔde] *vt* to iodize.
iodique [jɔdik] *adj Ch* iodic.
iodler [jɔdle] *vi* to yodel.
iodoforme [jɔdɔfɔrm] *nm Ch* iodoform.
iodure [jɔdyr] *nm Ch* iodide.
ion [jɔ̃] *nm Nucl* ion.
ionien, -ienne [jɔnjɛ̃, -jɛn] **1** *adj* Ionian; Ionic (*dialect etc*). **2** *n* **I.,** Ionian.
ionique¹ [jɔnik] *adj Archit* Ionic (*order*).
ionique² *adj Phys etc* ionic; **accélération i.,** ion acceleration.
ionisant [jɔnizɑ̃] *adj* ionizing.
ionisation [jɔnizɑsjɔ̃] *nf* ionization.
ioniser [jɔnize] *vt Phys Ch* to ionize.
ionosphère [jɔnɔsfɛr] *nf* ionosphere.
iota [jɔta] *nm* iota; *F* **pas un i.,** not a bit, not one iota, not one jot; **on n'y a pas changé un i.,** not an iota of it has been changed.
iourte [jurt] *nf* yourt, yurt.
ipéca(cuana) [ipeka(kwana)] *nm Pharm* ipecac(uanha).
ipso facto [ipsofakto] *adv* ipso facto.
Irak [irak] *nm* Iraq, Irak.
irakien, -ienne [irakjɛ̃, -jɛn] **1** *adj* Iraqi. **2** *nm Ling* Iraqi. **3** *n* **I.,** Iraqi.
Iran [irɑ̃] *nm* Iran.
iranien, -ienne [iranjɛ̃, -jɛn] **1** *adj* Iranian. **2** *nm Ling* Iranian. **3** *n* **I.,** Iranian.
Iraq [irak] *nm* Iraq, Irak.
iraquien, -ienne [irakjɛ̃, -jɛn] *adj & n* = **IRAKIEN.**
irascibilité [irasibilite] *nf Litt* irascibility, testiness.
irascible [irasibl] *adj* irascible, irritable, testy.
iridescent [iridesɑ̃] *adj Litt* iridescent.
iridié [iridje] *adj* **platine i.,** iridioplatinum.
iridium [iridjɔm] *nm Ch* iridium.
iris [iris] *nm* **(a)** *Opt* iris; **(b)** *Anat* iris (*of eye*); *Phot* **(diaphragme) i.,** iris diaphragm; **(c)** (*plante*) iris, flag; **i. jaune** *ou* **des marais,** yellow iris; **racine d'i.,** orris root.
Iris *nf* Iris.
irisation [irizɑsjɔ̃] *nf* iridescence, irisation.
irisé [irize] *adj* iridescent; rainbow-coloured.
iriser [irize] **1** *vt* to make iridescent. **2 s'iriser** *vpr* to become iridescent.
irish coffee [ajriʃkɔfi] *nm* Irish coffee.
irlandais, -aise [irlɑ̃dɛ, -ɛz] **1** *adj* Irish. **2** *nm Ling* Irish, Erse. **3** *n* **I.,** Irishman; Irishwoman; **les I.,** the Irish.
Irlande [irlɑ̃d] *nf* Ireland; **I. du Nord,** Northern Ireland, Ulster; **I. du Sud,** Southern Ireland, Eire.
ironie [irɔni] *nf* irony; **avec une pointe d'i.,** with a touch *or* note of irony; **par une i. du sort,** by an irony of fate; **parler avec i.,** to speak ironically.
ironique [irɔnik] *adj* ironic(al).
ironiquement [irɔnikmɑ̃] *adv* ironically.
ironiser [irɔnize] *vi* to speak ironically, to be ironical (**sur,** about).
ironiste [irɔnist] *n* ironist.
iroquois, -oise [irɔkwa, -waz] **1** *adj* Iroquois, Iroquoian. **2** *nm Ling* Iroquoian. **3** *n* **I.,** Iroquois, Iroquoian.
irradiation [iradjɑsjɔ̃] *nf Phys Méd* (ir)radiation; *Phot* halation.
irradier [iradje] **1** *vi* to (ir)radiate; (*of pain etc*) to spread. **2** *vt* to irradiate, to expose to (atomic) radiation; **aliments irradiés,** irradiated food.
irraisonné [irezɔne] *adj* (*action, crainte*) unreasonable.
irrationalisme [irasjɔnalism] *nm* irrationalism.
irrationalité [irasjɔnalite] *nf* irrationality.
irrationnel, -elle [irasjɔnɛl] **1** *adj* irrational. **2** *nm* **l'i.,** the irrational.
irrationnellement [irasjɔnɛlmɑ̃] *adv* irrationally.
irrattrapable [iratrapabl] *adj* (*délai*) that cannot be made up; (*erreur*) irredeemable; **elle est i.,** (*cette élève*) she'll never catch up.
irréalisable [irealizabl] *adj* (*rêve*) unrealizable; (*projet*) impracticable, unfeasible.
irréalisé [irealize] *adj* unrealized.
irréalisme [irealism] *nm* lack of realism; **faire preuve d'i.,** to be unrealistic.
irréaliste [irealist] *adj* (*proposition etc*) unrealistic.
irréalité [irealite] *nf* unreality.
irrecevabilité [irəsəvabilite] *nf Jur* inadmissibility.
irrecevable [irəsəvabl] *adj Jur* inadmissible (*evidence*); unacceptable (*theory*).
irréconciliable [irekɔ̃siljabl] *adj* irreconcilable.
irrécouvrable [irekuvrabl] *adj* irrecoverable.
irrécupérable [irekyperabl] *adj* irreparable, irremediable (*loss etc*); (*erreur*) irretrievable, irredeemable; **être d'une bêtise i.,** to be incurably stupid.
irrécusable [irekyzabl] *adj* unimpeachable, unexceptionable (*evidence etc*).
irréductibilité [iredyktibilite] *nf* irreducibility.
irréductible [iredyktibl] *adj* **(a)** (*personne, optimisme*) indomitable; unshakeable (*attachment to s.o.*); unyielding, relentless (*opposition*); **un ennemi i. du parti,** an inveterate enemy of the party; **(b)** irreducible (*equation, dislocation*); *Math* **fraction i.,** fraction in its lowest terms.
irréel, -elle [ireɛl] *adj* unreal.
irréfléchi [irefleʃi] *adj* hasty, rash, unthinking; unconsidered, thoughtless (*action*).
irréflexion [irefleksjɔ̃] *nf* thoughtlessness; **faire preuve d'i.,** to be thoughtless.
irréformable [ireformabl] *adj Jur* irrevocable, irreformable (*decision etc*).
irréfutable [irefytabl] *adj* irrefutable, indisputable.
irréfutablement [irefytabləmɑ̃] *adv* irrefutably.
irréfuté [irefyte] *adj* unrefuted.
irrégularité [iregylarite] *nf* irregularity (*of an action, pulse*); unevenness (*of ground, pulse*); **les irrégularités d'une élection,** the irregularities of an election.
irrégulier, -ière [iregylje, -jɛr] **1** *adj* (*verbe, procédure*) irregular; (*terrain*) uneven; (*sommeil*) fitful, broken; (*pouls*) irregular, erratic; **le déroulement de la campagne électorale a été i.,** there were irregularities in the election campaign. **2** *nm Mil* **irréguliers,** irregulars.
irrégulièrement [iregyljɛrmɑ̃] *adv* irregularly.
irréligieux, -ieuse [ireliʒjø, -jøz] *adj* irreligious.
irréligion [ireliʒjɔ̃] *nf* irreligion.
irrémédiable [iremedjabl] **1** *adj* irremediable (*loss*); incurable (*disease*); irreparable (*injury*). **2** *nm* **l'i.,** the inevitable.
irrémédiablement [iremedjabləmɑ̃] *adv* (*voir adj*) irremediably; incurably; irreparably.
irrémissible [iremisibl] *adj Litt* unpardonable (*crime*).
irremplaçable [irɑ̃plasabl] *adj* irreplaceable.
irréparable [ireparabl] *adj* irreparable (*wrong*); irretrievable (*loss, mistake*); (*souliers etc*) beyond repair.
irréparablement [ireparabləmɑ̃] *adv* irreparably.
irrépréhensible [irepreɑ̃sibl] *adj* blameless.
irrépressible [irepresibl] *adj* irrepressible.
irréprochable [ireprɔʃabl] *adj* irreproachable.
irréprochablement [ireprɔʃabləmɑ̃] *adv Litt* irreproachably; faultlessly.
irrésistible [irezistibl] *adj* irresistible; *F* **elle était i. avec son petit chapeau,** she was irresistible in that hat.
irrésistiblement [irezistibləmɑ̃] *adv* irresistibly.
irrésolu [irezɔly] *adj* **(a)** irresolute, indecisive (*nature*); faltering (*steps*); **(b)** unsolved (*problem*).
irrésolution [irezɔlysjɔ̃] *nf* irresolution, irresoluteness, indecision.
irrespect [irɛspɛ] *nm* disrespect.
irrespectueusement [irɛspɛktɥøzmɑ̃] *adv* disrespectfully.
irrespectueux, -euse [irɛspɛktɥø, -øz] *adj* disrespectful (**envers,** to, towards).
irrespirable [irɛspirabl] *adj* unbreathable; *Fig* **l'atmosphère du bureau est devenue i.,** the atmosphere in the office has become unbearable.
irresponsabilité [irɛspɔ̃sabilite] *nf* irresponsibility.
irresponsable [irɛspɔ̃sabl] **1** *adj* irresponsible. **2** *nm* irresponsible person.
irrétrécissable [iretresisabl] *adj* unshrinkable.
irrévérence [ireverɑ̃s] *nf* irreverence.
irrévérencieusement [ireverɑ̃sjøzmɑ̃] *adv* irreverently, disrespectfully.
irrévérencieux, -euse [ireverɑ̃sjø, -øz] *adj* irreverent, disrespectful.
irréversible [ireversibl] *adj* irreversible.
irréversiblement [ireversibləmɑ̃] *adv* irreversibly.
irrévocabilité [irevɔkabilite] *nf* irrevocability.
irrévocable [irevɔkabl] **1** *adj* irrevocable; binding (*agreement*); *Jur* **décret i.,** decree absolute. **2** *nm* **l'i.,** the irrevocable.

irrévocablement [irevɔkabləmɑ̃] *adv* irrevocably.
irrigable [irigabl] *adj* irrigable.
irrigateur [irigatœr] *nm* (a) (*pour arrosage*) (garden) hose; (b) *Méd* irrigator (*for wounds*).
irrigation [irigɑsjɔ̃] *nf* (a) *Agr* irrigation; **canal d'i.,** irrigation canal; (b) *Méd* irrigation.
irriguer [irige] *vt* (a) *Agr* to irrigate; (b) *Méd* to irrigate (*wound*).
irritabilité [iritabilite] *nf* irritability.
irritable [iritabl] *adj* irritable.
irritant [iritɑ̃] **1** *adj* (a) (*énervant*) irritating, exasperating; (b) *Méd* irritant. **2** *nm Méd* irritant.
irritation [iritɑsjɔ̃] *nf* irritation.
irrité [irite] *adj* (a) (*en colère*) irritated (**contre,** with); (b) *Méd* inflamed (*wound*); **avoir la gorge irritée,** to have an inflamed throat.
irriter [irite] **1** *vt* (a) to irritate, to annoy (*s.o.*); *Litt* to excite (*passions etc*); **i. la curiosité de qn,** to excite s.o.'s curiosity; (b) (*of shampoo*) to irritate (*the eyes, skin*); *Méd* to irritate, to inflame (*wound etc*). **2 s'irriter** *vpr* (a) **s'i. contre qn/de qch,** to get irritated *or* annoyed with s.o./at sth; (b) (*of sore etc*) to become irritated *or* inflamed.
irruption [irypsjɔ̃] *nf* (a) (*invasion*) invasion, raid; **faire i. dans une salle,** to burst into a room; **elle a fait i. chez nous à deux heures du matin,** she burst in at two o'clock in the morning; (b) overflow, flood (*of river*); inrush (*of water*); **i. de la mer,** tidal wave.
isabelle [izabɛl] **1** *adj inv* biscuit- *or* cream-coloured; **cheval i.,** light-bay horse, light bay. **2** *nm* light-bay horse, light bay.
Isabelle [izabɛl] *nf* Isabel(la).
Isaïe [izai] *nm Bible* Isaiah.
isard [izar] *nm* izard, wild goat.
Islam [islam] *nm Rel* Islam.
islamique [islamik] *adj* Islamic.
islamisation [islamizɑsjɔ̃] *nf* Islamization.
islamiser [islamize] *vt* to Islamize.
islamisme [islamism] *nm* Islamism.
Islamiste [islamist] *n* Islamic fundamentalist.
islandais, -aise [islɑ̃dɛ, -ɛz] **1** *adj* Icelandic. **2** *nm Ling* Icelandic. **3** *n* **I.,** Icelander.
Islande [islɑ̃d] *nf* Iceland.
isobare [izɔbar] *Météo* **1** *adj* isobaric. **2** *nf* isobar.
isocèle [izɔsɛl] *adj Math* isosceles (*triangle*).
isochrone [izɔkrɔn] *adj* isochronous, isochronal, isochronic.
isoclinal, -aux [izɔklinal, -o] *adj Géol* isoclinal.
isocline [izɔklin] **1** *adj* isoclinal (*line*). **2** *n* isocline, isoclinal line.
isolable [izɔlabl] *adj Ch etc* isolable.
isolant [izɔlɑ̃] **1** *adj* (a) *Constr etc* insulating; **bouteille isolante,** vacuum flask; **cabine isolante,** soundproof box; **matériau i.,** (*contre le froid*) insulation, insulating material; (*contre le bruit*) soundproofing (material); **ruban i.,** insulating tape; (b) isolating (*languages etc*). **2** *nm* (*contre le froid*) insulation (material), insulating material; (*contre le bruit*) soundproofing (material).
isolateur, -trice [izɔlatœr, -tris] *El* **1** *adj* insulating. **2** *nm* insulator.
isolation [izɔlɑsjɔ̃] *nf* (a) *El* insulation; (b) **i. acoustique** *ou* **phonique,** soundproofing; **i. contre le froid,** insulation.
isolationnisme [izɔlasjɔnism] *nm Pol* isolationism.
isolationniste [izɔlasjɔnist] *adj & n Pol* isolationist.
isolé, -ée [izɔle] **1** *adj* (a) isolated; isolated, lonely, remote (*spot etc*); **se sentir i.,** to feel isolated; **c'est un cas i.,** it's an isolated case; (b) *El* insulated (*cable etc*). **2** *n* person who lives *or* works *etc* in isolation.
isolement [izɔlmɑ̃] *nm* (a) isolation; **hôpital d'i.,** isolation hospital; **vivre dans un i. complet,** to live in complete isolation; *Pol* **l'i. diplomatique d'un pays,** the diplomatic isolation of a country; (b) *El* insulation.
isolément [izɔlemɑ̃] *adv* (*interroger des gens*) separately, individually; (*employer un mot*) in isolation.
isoler [izɔle] **1** *vt* (a) to isolate (**de,** from); **sa maladie l'isole,** her illness cuts her off from other people; **se trouver isolé,** to find oneself cut off; (b) *El* to insulate; (c) (*protéger du bruit*) to soundproof. **2 s'isoler** *vpr* (a) (*se séparer*) to become isolated *or* separated; **avoir besoin de s'i. quelques instants,** to need to be alone for a few moments; (b) (*vivre seul*) to isolate oneself.
isoloir [izɔlwar] *nm* polling booth.
isomère [izɔmɛr] *Ch* **1** *adj* isomeric. **2** *nm* isomer.
isométrique [izɔmetrik] *adj Math* isometric(al).
isomorphe [izɔmɔrf] *adj Math etc* isomorphous, isomorphic.
isomorphisme [izɔmɔrfism] *nm Math* isomorphism.
Isorel ® [izɔrɛl] *nm Constr* hardboard.
isotherme [izɔtɛrm] *Météo* **1** *adj* isothermal. **2** *nf* isotherm.
isotope [izɔtɔp] *nm Ch* isotope.
isotrope [izɔtrɔp] *adj Ch Phys* isotropic.
Israël [israɛl] *nm* Israel.
israélien, -ienne [israeljɛ̃, -jɛn] **1** *adj* Israeli. **2** *n* **I.,** Israeli.
israélite [israelit] **1** *adj* Jewish; *Bible* Israelite. **2** *n* **I.,** Jew, *f* Jewess; *Bible* Israelite.
issu [isy] *adj* descended (**de,** from); born (**de,** of); **être i. de,** to stem from.
issue [isy] *nf* (a) exit, way out; outlet (*of tunnel etc*); **i. de secours,** emergency exit; **voie sans i.,** cul-de-sac, dead end; (*sur panneau*) no through road; *Fig* dead end; **la seule i. possible,** the only possible solution; **il n'y a pas d'autre i.,** there is no other way out; **elle est dans une situation sans i.,** there's no way out of her situation; *Fig* **se ménager une i.,** to find a loophole *or* a way out; (b) (*fin*) end, conclusion, outcome; **l'affaire a eu une i. heureuse,** the matter ended happily *or* had a happy ending; **l'i. de la réunion,** at the end *or* close of the meeting.
Istamboul, Istanbul [istɑ̃bul] *n* Istanbul.
isthme [ism] *nm Géog Anat* isthmus.
isthmique [ismik] *adj* Isthmian (*canal, games etc*).
italianisant, -ante [italjanizɑ̃, -ɑ̃t] *n* Italianist.
italianiser [italjanize] *vt* to Italianize.
italianisme [italjanism] *nm Ling* Italianism, Italian phrase *or* idiom.
Italie [itali] *nf* Italy.
italien, -ienne [italjɛ̃, -jɛn] **1** *adj* Italian. **2** *nm Ling* Italian. **3** *n* **I.,** Italian.
italique [italik] **1** *adj* (a) Italic; (b) *Typ* italic (*type*). **2** *nm* (a) *Ling* Italic; (b) *Typ* **en italique(s),** in italic(s). **3** *n Hist* **I.,** Italic.
item [itɛm] **1** *adv* item, likewise, also. **2** *nm* item.
itératif, -ive [iteratif, -iv] *adj* (a) *Jur* reiterated, repeated (*prohibition etc*); (b) *Gram* iterative (*verb*).
Ithaque [itak] *nf* Ithaca.
itinéraire [itinerɛr] *nm* (a) (*chemin*) itinerary, route; **tracer un i.,** to map out a route; **changer d'i.,** to change one's itinerary; **i. touristique,** tourist route; (b) guide (book).
itinérant [itinerɑ̃] *adj* itinerant (*preacher*); **ambassadeur i.,** roving ambassador; **camp (de marche) i. de deux semaines,** two-week hike.
itou [itu] *adv F Vieilli* also, too, likewise; **et moi i.!,** (and) me too!
I.U.T. [iyte] *nm abrév* **Institut universitaire de technologie.**
I.V.C. [ivese] *nf Can* (*abrév* **indemnité de la vie chère**) COLA.
I.V.G. [iveʒe] *nf Méd abrév* **interruption volontaire de grossesse.**
ivoire [ivwar] *nm* (a) (*matière*) ivory; **i. vert,** raw ivory, live ivory; **crucifix d'i.** *ou* **en i.,** ivory crucifix; **noir d'i.,** ivory black; *Fig* **dents d'i.,** teeth like ivory; *Géog* **la Côte d'I.,** the Ivory Coast; *Fig* **tour d'i.,** ivory tower; (b) ivory (*statuette etc*).
ivoirien, -ienne [ivwarjɛ̃, -jɛn] **1** *adj* of the Ivory Coast (Republic). **2** *n* **I.,** inhabitant of the Ivory Coast (Republic).
ivoirier [ivwarje] *nm* worker in ivory.
ivraie [ivrɛ] *nf Bot* **i. vivace, fausse i.,** rye grass; *Fig* **séparer l'i. d'avec le bon grain,** to separate the wheat from the chaff.
ivre [ivr] *adj* drunk; **i. mort,** dead drunk; **i. de joie,** drunk *or* mad with joy; **i. de colère,** drunk with anger.
ivresse [ivrɛs] *nf* drunkenness; (*extase*) rapture, ecstasy; *Jur* **en état d'i. publique,** drunk and disorderly; **conduite en état d'i.,** drunken driving.
ivrogne [ivrɔɲ] **1** *nm* drunkard, alcoholic. **2** *adj* addicted to drink; drunken.
ivrognerie [ivrɔɲri] *nf* habitual drunkenness.
ivrognesse [ivrɔɲɛs] *nf F* drunkard, alcoholic.

J

J, j [ʒi] *nm* (the letter) J, j; *Mil etc* **le jour J,** D day.
j' [ʒ] *pron pers* (*used before a verb beginning with a vowel or h mute; also before* **en, y**) = **JE.**
jabot [ʒabo] *nm* **(a)** (*d'un oiseau*) crop (*of bird*); **enfler** *ou* **gonfler le j.,** (*d'un pigeon*) to pout; *F* (*d'une personne*) to put on airs; **(b)** (*de chemise, blouse*) frill, ruffle, jabot.
jacaranda [ʒakarɑ̃da] *nm* (*plante*) jacaranda.
jacasse [ʒakas] *nf Vieilli* **(a)** (*oiseau*) magpie; **(b)** (*femme bavarde*) chatterbox, gossip.
jacassement [ʒakasmɑ̃] *nm* (*d'une pie*) chatter(ing); (*d'une personne*) chatter(ing), *US* yakking; (*incohérent*) jabber(ing).
jacasser [ʒakase] *vi* (*d'une pie*) to chatter; (*d'une personne*) to chatter, to natter, *US* to yak; (*de façon incohérente*) to jabber.
jacasserie [ʒakas(ə)ri] *nf* chatter(ing), *US* yakking; (*incohérent*) jabber(ing).
jachère [ʒaʃɛr] *nf* fallow (land); **champ en j.,** fallow field; **laisser en j.,** (*un champ*) to leave fallow, to let lie fallow.
jacinthe [ʒasɛ̃t] *nf* **(a)** (*plante*) hyacinth; **j. sauvage** *ou* **des bois,** wild hyacinth, bluebell; **(b)** *Minér Vieilli* jacinth.
jack [ʒak] *nm Él Tél etc* jack.
Jacob [ʒakɔb] *nm* Jacob; **l'échelle de J.,** Jacob's ladder; *F* **bâton de J.,** *Astron* Orion's belt; (*plante*) yellow asphodel.
jacobin, -ine [ʒakɔbɛ̃, -in] **1** *n Rel* Dominican friar *or* nun. **2** *nm Hist* Jacobin. **3** *adj* Jacobin(ic)(al).
jacobite [ʒakɔbit] *adj & nm Hist* Jacobite.
jacquard [ʒakar] **1** *nm* (*métier à tisser*) Jacquard loom; (*tissu*) Jacquard weave; (*pull*) Jacquard. **2** *adj* **pull j.,** Jacquard sweater.
jacquerie [ʒakri] *nf* peasant revolt; *Hist* **J.,** Jacquerie; *Fig* **la j. des agriculteurs français,** the rising up of French farmers.
Jacques [ʒak] *nm* **(a)** James; **(b) Maître J.,** factotum; *Hist* **J. (Bonhomme),** the French peasant; *F* **faire le J.,** (*faire le niais*) to act dumb; (*faire l'idiot*) to act the fool.
jacquet [ʒakɛ] *nm* backgammon.
Jacquot [ʒako] *nm* **(a)** *F* Jim, Jimmy; **(b)** *F* (*perroquet gris*) Polly.
jactance [ʒaktɑ̃s] *nf* **(a)** (*vanité*) boastfulness, boasting, bragging; **(b)** *Arg* jabber(ing).
jacter [ʒakte] *vi Arg* to jabber, *Péj* to spout.
jacuzzi ® [ʒakyzi] *nm* jacuzzi ®.
jade [ʒad] *nm Minér* jade.
jadis [ʒadis] *adv Litt* formerly, in times past; **les chevaliers de j.,** the knights of old; **le temps j.,** the olden days; **contes du temps j.,** tales of long ago.
jaguar [ʒagwar] *nm* jaguar.
jaillir [ʒajir] *vi* to spring (up), to shoot (out); (*of water*) to gush (out, forth); (*of blood*) to spurt; (*of sparks*) to fly; (*of light*) to flash; **la vérité jaillira d'elle-même,** the truth will out.
jaillissant [ʒajisɑ̃] *adj* gushing, spurting (*liquid*); flying (*sparks*).
jaillissement [ʒajismɑ̃] *nm* gush(ing) (out), spurt(ing) (out) (*of liquid*); **j. d'éloquence,** burst of eloquence; *Él* **j. d'étincelles,** sparking.
jaïnisme [ʒainism] *nm Rel* Jainism.
jais [ʒɛ] *nm Minér* jet; **les yeux (noirs) de j.,** jet-black eyes.
jalon [ʒalɔ̃] *nm* **(a)** (*piquet*) (surveyor's) staff *or US* rod; **(b)** (*repère*) landmark, milestone; *Fig* **poser** *ou* **planter des jalons,** to show *or* to pave the way, to blaze a trail; **poser les jalons d'un accord,** to pave the way for *or* to lay the foundations of an agreement.
jalonnement [ʒalɔnmɑ̃] *nm* marking out; (*pour démarquer, séparer*) marking off.
jalonner [ʒalɔne] *vt* (*délimiter*) to lay out, to stake out, to mark out (*line, piece of ground etc*); to peg (out) (*claim*); *Av* to mark out, to stake out (*landing strip*); *Mil* to screen (*enemy advance*); **ils ont jalonné la route pour ceux qui suivront,** they have paved the way *or* blazed the trail for their successors; **événements qui jalonnent la vie de qn,** events that stand out as landmarks *or* milestones in s.o.'s life.
jalonneur [ʒalɔnœr] *nm* (*ouvrier*) & *Mil* marker.
jalousement [ʒaluzmɑ̃] *adv* jealously.
jalouser [ʒaluze] *vt* to envy, to be jealous of (*s.o.*).
jalousie [ʒaluzi] *nf* **(a)** (*sentiment*) jealousy, envy; **j'en crève de j.,** I'm green with envy; **ce sont de petites jalousies,** they're just petty jealousies; **(b)** (*treillis*) (latticework) screen; (*store*) Venetian blind; **(c)** (*plante*) sweet william; **j. des jardins,** rose campion.
jaloux, -ouse [ʒalu, -uz] **1** *adj* (*envieux*) jealous; (*soucieux*) jealous, careful; **j. de sa réputation,** jealous of one's reputation. **2** *n* **c'est un j.,** he's a jealous man; **cela a fait des j.,** it made people jealous.
jamaïcain, -aine, jamaïquain, -aine [ʒamaikɛ̃, -ɛn] **1** *adj* Jamaican. **2** *n* **J.,** Jamaican.
Jamaïque (la) [laʒamaik] *nf* Jamaica.
jamais [ʒamɛ] *adv* **(a)** (*positif*) ever; **plus cher que j.,** dearer than ever; **si j. il revenait,** if he ever came back; **avez-vous j. entendu chose pareille?,** did you ever hear such a thing?; **plus que j.,** more than ever; **avez-vous j. été à Rome?,** have you ever been to Rome?; **à j.,** for ever, for good; **à tout j.,** for ever and ever, for evermore, (for)ever after;

(b) (*négatif*) never; **je ne l'ai j. vu,** I have never seen him; **on ne sait j.,** you never know; **j. homme ne fut plus admiré,** never was a man more admired; **j. le dimanche,** never on a Sunday; **sans j. y avoir pensé,** without ever having thought of it; **c'est le cas ou j.,** it's now or never; **on ne le voit presque j.,** we *etc* hardly ever see him; **on ne le verra plus j.** *ou* **j. plus,** we *etc* shall never see him again; **j. de la vie!,** never!, out of the question!, *F* not on your life!, no fear!; *Prov* **mieux vaut tard que j.,** better late than never; **j., au grand j., je n'admettrai cela,** I shall never, (repeat) never, admit it.
jambage [ʒɑ̃baʒ] *nm* **(a)** jamb (post) (*of door, window, fireplace etc*); **(b)** downstroke (*of written letter*).
jambe [ʒɑ̃b] *nf* **(a)** *Anat Zool etc* leg; **jambes d'un pantalon,** trouser legs; **avoir de bonnes jambes,** to be a good walker; **être jambes nues,** to be bare-legged; **aux longues jambes,** long-legged; **il s'est sauvé à toutes jambes,** he ran off at full *or* at top speed, he ran off as fast as his legs could carry him; **il tire la j.,** (*de fatigue*) he's dragging his feet *or* heels; (*en boitant*) he's dragging one foot behind him; *F* **prendre ses jambes à son cou,** to take to one's heels, to show a clean pair of heels; **il se met dans vos jambes,** he gets under your feet *or* in your way; *F* **travail fait par-dessous** *ou* **par-dessus la j.,** botched work; **traiter qn par-dessous** *ou* **par-dessus la j.,** to be offhand with s.o.; *F* **ça fait une belle j.!,** a (fat) lot of good that will do me!; **avoir les jambes rompues,** to feel one's legs giving way under one, to be on one's last legs; *Fig* **couper les jambes à qn,** (*décourager qn*) to take the wind out of s.o.'s sails; **avoir dix kilomètres dans les jambes,** to have walked ten kilometres; *Fig F* **n'avoir plus de jambes,** to be tired out *or* exhausted; **je n'ai plus mes jambes de vingt ans,** I'm not as young as I was; **rond de j.,** (*danse*) rond de jambe; *Fig Péj* **faire des ronds de j.,** (*se montrer excessivement poli*) to bow and scrape; *Boxe Fb* **jeu de jambes,** footwork;

(b) stem (*of a glass*); leg (*of compasses etc*); **j. de force,** *Constr* strut, prop, brace; *Aut* stay (rod), torque rod; *Nau* **j. de chien,** sheepshank.
jambier, -ière [ʒɑ̃bje, -jɛr] **1** *adj & nm Anat* **(muscle) j.,** leg muscle. **2** *nf* **jambière,** *Cr* pad; *Fb* shin pad *or* guard; (*d'armure*) greave; **jambières,** leggings.
jambon [ʒɑ̃bɔ̃] *nm* **(a)** *Culin* ham; **j. de pays** *ou* **de montagne,** smoked ham; **j. de Parme,** Parma ham; **(b)**

Arg thigh.
jambonneau, -eaux [ʒɑ̃bɔno] *nm* knuckle of ham.
jamboree [ʒɑ̃bɔre] *nm* jamboree.
janissaire [ʒanisɛr] *nm* janissary, janizary.
jansénisme [ʒɑ̃senism] *nm Hist Rel* Jansenism.
janséniste [ʒɑ̃senist] *adj & n Hist Rel* Jansenist.
jante [ʒɑ̃t] *nf* felloe (*of cartwheel*); rim (*of bicycle, car wheel*).
janvier [ʒɑ̃vje] *nm* January; **en j.**, in January; **au mois de j.**, in (the month of) January; **le sept j.**, on the seventh of January, (on) January the seventh, *Am* (on) January seventh.
Japon [ʒapɔ̃] *nm* **(a)** Japan; **être au J.**, to be in Japan; **aller au J.**, to go to Japan; **(b)** (*porcelaine*) Japanese porcelain; **(c)** (*papier*) Japanese vellum.
japonais, -aise [ʒapɔnɛ, -ɛz] **1** *adj* Japanese; **vernis j.**, japan. **2** *nm Ling* Japanese. **3** *n* **J.**, Japanese; **les J.**, the Japanese.
japonaiserie [ʒapɔnɛzri] *nf*, **japonerie** [ʒapɔnri] *nf* piece of Japanese art, Japanese curio.
japonisant, -ante [ʒapɔnizɑ̃, -ɑ̃t] *n* = specialist of Japanese language, civilization or art.
jappement [ʒapmɑ̃] *nm* yelp(ing), yap(ping).
japper [ʒape] *vi* to yelp, to yap.
jappeur, -euse [ʒapœr, -øz] **1** *adj* yelping, yapping (*dog etc*). **2** *n* (*chien*) yelper, yapper.
jaquette [ʒakɛt] *nf* **(a)** (*d'homme*) (man's) morning coat, *Am* cutaway; (*de femme*) (woman's) jacket; **(b)** *Can* nightdress; **(c)** (*de livre*) dust jacket, dust cover; **(d)** (*de dent*) crown, cap.
jardin [ʒardɛ̃] *nm* garden; **j. potager,** kitchen garden; **j. d'agrément,** pleasure garden; **j. à l'anglaise,** landscape garden; **j. botanique,** botanical garden(s), botanics; **j. des plantes,** botanical garden (*in Paris*); **j. alpin,** rock garden; **j. japonais,** miniature Japanese garden; **jardins ouvriers,** allotments; *Scol* **j. d'enfants,** kindergarten; *Th* **côté j.**, prompt side; *Fig* **jeter des pierres dans le j. de qn,** to attack s.o. indirectly.
jardinage [ʒardinaʒ] *nm* **(a)** (*activité*) gardening; **(b)** flaw (*in diamond*).
jardiner [ʒardine] *vi* to garden, to do gardening.
jardinerie [ʒardinri] *nf* garden centre.
jardinet [ʒardinɛ] *nm* small garden.
jardinier, -ière [ʒardinje, -jɛr] **1** *adj* **plantes jardinières,** garden plants. **2** *n* gardener; **j. maraîcher,** market gardener. **3** *nf* **jardinière (a)** (*pour le balcon*) window box; (*à l'intérieur*) jardinière; **(b)** *Culin* **jardinière (de légumes),** mixed vegetables, jardinière; **(c)** *Scol* **jardinière d'enfants,** kindergarten teacher.
jargon [ʒargɔ̃] *nm* **(a)** (*argot*) jargon, lingo; **le j. du palais,** legal jargon; **j. journalistique,** journalese; **(b)** (*baragouin*) gibberish.
jargonner [ʒargɔne] *vi* **(a)** to talk jargon; **(b)** (*baragouiner*) to talk gibberish.
Jarnac [ʒarnak] *nm* **coup de J.**, stab in the back.
jarre [ʒar] *nf* (earthenware) jar.
jarret [ʒarɛ] *nm* **(a)** back of the knee, *F* ham (*of person*); hock (*of horse etc*); **plier le j.**, to bend the knee; **avoir le j. solide,** to have a good pair of legs; **(b)** *Culin* knuckle (*of veal*); shin (*of beef*).
jarretelle [ʒartɛl] *nf* suspender, *US* garter.
jarretière [ʒartjɛr] *nf* **(a)** garter; **Ordre de la J.**, Order of the Garter; **(b)** *Nau* gasket.
jars [ʒar] *nm* (*oiseau*) gander.
jas [ʒa] *nm Nau* stock (*of anchor*); **sans j.**, stockless.
jaser [ʒaze] *vi* **(a)** (*bavarder*) to chatter, to prattle, *F* to gas **(de,** about); **j. comme une pie (borgne),** to talk nineteen to the dozen; **(b)** (*médire*) to gossip; *Péj* to prattle; **cela va faire j.**, that'll set tongues wagging; **(c)** (*moucharder*) to grass, to talk.
jaseur, -euse [ʒazœr, -øz] **1** *adj* chattering, prattling, talkative. **2** *n* chatterbox, gossip. **3** *nm* (*oiseau*) waxwing.
jasmin [ʒasmɛ̃] *nm* (*plante*) jasmine.
jaspe [ʒasp] *nm Minér* jasper; **j. noir,** touch-stone; **j. sanguin,** bloodstone.
jasper [ʒaspe] *vt* to marble, to mottle (*paper etc*).
jaspiner [ʒaspine] *F* **1** *vt* **il jaspine bien l'anglais,** he speaks English well. **2** *vi* to natter, to chatter; **qu'est-ce qu'il jaspine bien!,** what a good talker he is!
jaspure [ʒaspyr] *nf* marbling, mottling.
jatte [ʒat] *nf* (little) bowl, saucer.
jattée [ʒate] *nf* bowlful, saucerful.
jauge [ʒoʒ] *nf* **(a)** gauge, capacity (*of cask etc*); **(b)** *Nau* tonnage, burden (*of ship*); **(c)** *Tech* gauge; *Aut etc* **j. d'essence,** petrol gauge; **j. de niveau d'huile,** dipstick; **j. de vapeur,** steam gauge; **robinet de j.**, gauge cock; *Tex* **bas de j. fine,** fine gauge stockings.
jaugeage [ʒoʒaʒ] *nm* gauging, measuring.
jauger [ʒoʒe] *vt* (**je jaugeai(s); n. jaugeons**) **(a)** (*mesurer*) to gauge, to measure the capacity of (*cask etc*); to measure the tonnage of (*a ship*); **(b)** *Fig* **j. un homme,** to size up a man; **(c)** (*d'un bateau*) **j. 300 tonneaux,** to be of 300 tons burden; **pétrolier qui jauge quarante mille tonneaux,** forty thousand ton tanker; **j. deux mètres d'eau,** to draw two metres of water.
jaugeur [ʒoʒœr] *nm* (*personne*) gauger; (*instrument*) gauge.
jaunâtre [ʒonɑtr] *adj* yellowish (*colour*); sallow, yellowish (*complexion*).
jaune [ʒon] **1** *adj* **(a)** yellow; **j. comme un coing** *ou* **comme un citron,** yellow as a lemon; *Méd* **fièvre j.**, yellow fever; **la race j.**, the yellow-skinned race(s); *Péj* **le péril j.**, the yellow peril;
(b) *Hist* **syndicat j.**, strikebreakers' union;
(c) *Can* (*lâche*) yellow(-bellied).
2 *adj inv* **j. citron,** lemon yellow; **j. d'or,** golden yellow; **j. paille,** straw-coloured; **j. sable,** sandy(-coloured); **j. serin,** canary yellow.
3 *adv* **rire j.**, to force a laugh, to give a forced laugh.
4 *nm* **(a)** (*couleur*) yellow (colour); **tirer sur le j.**, to be yellowish; **porter du j.**, to wear yellow;
(b) (*colorant*) **j. d'ocre,** yellow ochre; **j. de chrome,** chrome yellow;
(c) j. d'œuf, (egg) yolk;
(d) *Ind F* strikebreaker, blackleg, scab;
(e) *Can* (*lâche*) yellow belly.
5 *n Arg* (*terme injurieux*) **J.**, Chink(ie).
jaunet, -ette [ʒonɛ, -ɛt] **1** *adj Vieilli* yellowish. **2** *nm* (*plante*) **j. d'eau,** yellow water lily.
jauni [ʒoni] *adj* yellowed (*by age, sun etc*).
jaunir [ʒonir] **1** *vt* to turn (*sth*) yellow. **2** *vi* to turn *or* become yellow.
jaunissant [ʒonisɑ̃] *adj* yellowing; **blés jaunissants,** ripening corn.
jaunisse [ʒonis] *nf Méd* jaundice; *Fig F* **il en ferait une j.**, he would be mad with jealousy *or* green with envy.
jaunissement [ʒonismɑ̃] *nm* yellowing; (*of wheat*) ripening.
java [ʒava] *nf* **(a)** (*danse*) – type of popular waltz; **(b)** *F* (*fête*) rave-up; **faire la j.**, to live it up, to have a wild time; (*faire du bruit*) to make a racket.
Java [ʒava] *nf* Java.
javanais, -aise [ʒavanɛ, -ɛz] **1** *adj* Javanese. **2** *nm Ling* **(a)** Javan(ese); **(b)** – a form of slang; *F* **c'est du j.**, (*baragouin*) it's double Dutch. **3** *n* **J.**, Javan(ese).
javel (eau de) [odʒavɛl] *nf* bleach.
javelage [ʒavlaʒ] *nm Agr* laying (*of wheat*) in swathes.
javeler [ʒavle] *v* (**je javelle, n. javelons; je javellerai**) **1** *vt Agr* to lay (*cereals*) in swathes. **2** *vi* (*of reaped cereals*) to turn yellow.
javeline [ʒavlin] *nf* javelin.
javelle [ʒavɛl] *nf Agr* swath, loose sheaf (*of wheat etc*).
javellisation [ʒavelizɑsjɔ̃] *nf* chlorination.
javelliser [ʒavelize] *vt* to chlorinate.
javelot [ʒavlo] *nm* javelin.
jazz [dʒaz] *nm* jazz.
jazzman [dʒazman] *nm Mus* jazzman, jazz musician; (*pl jazzmen*).
J.-C. (*abrév* **Jésus Christ**) JC.
je, j' [ʒ(ə)] **1** *pron pers* **(a)** (*unstressed*) **je vois,** I see; **j'ai,** I have, I've; **j'en ai,** I have some; **que vois-je** [vwaʒ] **?,** what do *or* can I see?; **(b)** (*stressed*) *Jur* **je, soussigné ...,** I, the undersigned ... . **2** *nm* **employer le je (dans un récit),** to write in the first person.
jean [dʒin] *nm* jeans; **une paire de jeans,** a pair of jeans.
Jean [ʒɑ̃] *nm* John; **(saint) J.-Baptiste** [batist] , (St) John the Baptist; **la Saint-J.**, Midsummer('s) Day; *Can* **la Saint-J.-Baptiste,** Saint-Jean Baptiste Day (*public holiday in Quebec*).
jean-foutre [ʒɑ̃futr] *nm inv Vulg* good-for-nothing, ne'er-do-well.
Jeanne [ʒan] *nf* Jane, Joan, Jean; **la Papesse J.**, Pope Joan; **J. d'Arc,** Joan of Arc; **cheveux à la J. d'Arc,** bobbed hair with a fringe.
jeannette [ʒanɛt] *nf* **(a)** (*croix*) small gold cross; **(b)** (*de planche à repasser*) sleeveboard; **(c)** (*plante*) **j. jaune,** daffodil; **(d)** (*scoute*) Brownie.
Jeannot [ʒano] *nm F* Johnny, Jack; **J. lapin,** bunny (rabbit).
jeep [(d)ʒip] *nf* jeep.

Jéhovah [ʒeɔva] *nm* Jehovah.
je-m'en-fichisme [ʒmɑ̃fiʃism] *nm F* couldn't-care-less attitude.
je-m'en-fichiste [ʒmɑ̃fiʃist] *n F* person who couldn't care less about anything or anybody.
je-m'en foutisme [ʒmɑ̃futism] *nm Vulg* couldn't-give-a-damn attitude.
je-m'en-foutiste [ʒmɑ̃futist] *n Vulg* person who couldn't give a damn about anything or anybody.
je(-)ne(-)sais(-)quoi [ʒənsɛkwa] *nm inv* **un je-ne-s.-q.,** an indefinable something; **il y a un je-ne-s.-q. qui ne me plaît pas,** there's something about it I don't like.
jennérien, -ienne [ʒenerjɛ̃, -jɛn] *adj Méd* Jennerian.
jenny [ʒeni] *nf Tex* spinning jenny.
jérémiade [ʒeremjad] *nf* whining, complaining.
Jérémie [ʒeremi] *nm* Jeremy; *Bible* Jeremiah.
jerez [ʒerɛs] *nm* **(vin de) j.,** sherry.
Jéricho [ʒeriko] *nm* Jericho.
jerk [djɛrk] *nm (danse)* jerk.
Jéroboam [ʒerɔbɔam] *nm* Jeroboam; **j.,** jeroboam (*of champagne etc*).
jerrican(e), jerrycan [(d)ʒerikan] *nm* jerrycan.
jersey [ʒɛrzɛ] *nm* **(a)** (*corsage*) jersey, jumper, sweater, pullover; **(b)** *Tex* jersey; **j. de laine,** wool jersey; **j. de soie,** silk jersey; *Tricot* **point (de) j.,** stocking stitch.
Jersey [ʒɛrzɛ] *nm* (Island of) Jersey.
jersiais, -aise [ʒɛrzjɛ, -ɛz] **1** *adj* of *or* from Jersey; **(vache) jersiaise,** Jersey cow. **2** *n* **J.,** native *or* inhabitant of Jersey.
jésuite [ʒezɥit] **1** *nm Rel* Jesuit. **2** *adj* **(a)** *Rel* Jesuit, jesuit; **prêtre j.,** Jesuit *or* jesuit priest; **(b)** *Péj* Jesuitic(al), jesuitic(al), hypocritical.
jésuitique [ʒezɥitik] *adj* **(a)** *Rel* Jesuitic, jesuitic; **(b)** *Péj* jesuitic(al), hypocritical.
jésuitisme [ʒezɥitism] *nm* **(a)** *Rel* Jesuitism; **(b)** *Péj* jesuitry, hypocrisy.
jésus [ʒezy] *nm* **(a)** (*statue*) statue of the Christ Child; **(b)** *F* **mon j.,** my little pet; **(c)** *Typ* = super-royal, long royal paper; **grand j.,** = imperial.
Jésus [ʒezy] *nm* Jesus; **J.-Christ** [ʒezykri], Jesus Christ; **en l'an 44 avant/après J.-C.,** in the year 44 B.C./A.D.
jet¹ [ʒɛ] *nm* **(a)** (*action*) throwing (*of stone*); *Arch Litt* casting (*of net, dice etc*); (*résultat*) throw (*of stone*); *Arch Litt* cast (*of net, dice etc*); **à un j. de pierre de nous,** within a stone's throw of us; **force de j.,** impetus; **armes de j.,** missiles, projectiles;
(b) *Métal* cast, casting; **couler qch d'un seul j.,** to cast sth in one piece; *Fig* **faire qch d'un seul j.,** to do sth at one go *or* at one sitting; *Beaux-Arts Littér* **premier j.,** first sketch, rough outline, rough draft;
(c) j. (de marchandises) à la mer, jettison(ing), throwing overboard (of cargo);
(d) jet, gush, stream (*of liquid*); spurt (*of blood*); flash, ray (*of light*); **j. de vapeur,** jet of steam; **j. d'incendie,** jet of water from a fire hose; **j. d'eau,** jet of water; (*fontaine*) fountain; **il parle à j. continu,** he speaks non-stop *or* continuously; **j. de flamme,** jet *or* burst of flame; *Tech* **j. de sable,** sand blast;
(e) *Bot* young shoot (*of tree*); **elle est tout d'un j.,** she is tall and slender;
(f) jet (*of nozzle etc*); spout (*of pump, watering can etc*); **j. de gaz,** gas jet; **diriger le j. de la douche vers le mur,** to turn the shower-head towards the wall.
jet² [dʒɛt] *nm Av F* jet (aircraft); **la j. set,** the jet set.
jetable [ʒətabl(ə)] *adj* disposable.
jeté [ʒ(ə)te] **1** *nm* **(a)** (*danse*) jeté; **(b)** *Tricot* wool over *or* forward; **j. simple/double,** make one/two; **(c)** *Sp* (*haltérophilie*) snatch, jerk; **(d) j. de table,** (table) runner; **j. de lit,** bedspread. **2** *adj F* **(complètement) j.,** crazy.
jetée [ʒ(ə)te] *nf* jetty, pier.
jeter [ʒ(ə)te] *v* **(je jette, n. jetons; je jetterai) 1** *vt* **(a)** (*lancer*) to throw; (*plus fort*) to fling; *Arch Litt* to cast (*nets, dice*); (*loin*) to throw away; **j. qn à la porte,** to throw s.o. out; **j. qch à la tête de qn,** to throw sth at s.o.'s head; *Fig* **elle nous jette à la tête ses diplômes,** she harps on (to us) about her qualifications, she rams her qualifications down our throats; *Fig* **j. des reproches à la tête de qn,** to hurl reproaches at s.o.; **j. qn en prison/à la rue,** to throw s.o. in jail/out (into the street); *Fig* **j. l'éponge,** to throw in the sponge *or* towel;
(b) (*laisser tomber*) to throw down; **j. qch à terre** *ou* **par terre,** to throw sth down to the ground; **j. ses armes,** to throw down one's arms; **il rêve de j. bas le gouvernement,** he dreams of overthrowing *or* bringing down the government;
(c) (*se défaire de*) to throw away, to throw out; **à j.,** to be thrown away; disposable (*nappy etc*); **j. son argent par la fenêtre,** to throw (one's) money away, to throw (one's) money down the drain;
(d) j. un sort à qn, to cast a spell on s.o.; **le sort en est jeté,** the die is cast; *Fig* **j. son dévolu sur qn,** to set one's heart on s.o., to set one's cap at s.o.;
(e) (*émettre*) **j. un cri,** to utter a cry; **j. un soupir,** to heave a sigh; **j. un regard sur qn,** to glance at s.o.; **j. un coup d'œil,** to have a (quick) glance; **ça a jeté un froid,** it cast a chill (*over the proceedings, the conversation etc*);
(f) (*mettre, installer*) **j. qn dans l'embarras,** to throw *or* plunge s.o. into confusion; **j. des racines,** to strike (root); **j. les fondements d'un édifice,** to lay the foundations of a building; **j. un pont sur une rivière,** to throw a bridge over a river; **navires jetés à la côte par la tempête,** ships driven ashore by the storm;
(g) *Métal* **j. (une statue) en fonte,** to cast (a statue); *Nau* **j. le plomb** *ou* **la sonde,** to heave the lead; **j. l'ancre,** to cast anchor; **(faire) j. qch à la mer** *ou* **par-dessus bord,** to jettison sth *or* throw sth overboard; **objets jetés à la mer,** jetsam.
2 se jeter *vpr* to throw oneself; **cours d'eau qui se jette dans la Seine,** stream that flows into the Seine; **se j. à l'eau,** to throw oneself *or* plunge into the water; **se j. par la fenêtre,** to throw oneself out of the window; **se j. aux pieds de qn,** to throw oneself at s.o.'s feet; **se j. sur qn,** to attack s.o., to throw oneself upon *or* at s.o.; **elle s'est jetée sur moi pour m'embrasser,** she rushed up to me and kissed me; **se j. (à corps perdu) dans une entreprise,** to fling oneself (body and soul) into an undertaking.
3 *vi F* **ça jette!,** it's really something!, it's brilliant!; **elle en jette, ta bagnole,** your car's really something, that's some car you've got.
jeteur, -euse [ʒ(ə)tœr, -øz] *n* **j./jeteuse de sort,** wizard/witch.
jeton [ʒ(ə)tɔ̃] *nm* **(a)** *Cartes etc* counter, chip; *Tél etc* token; *F* **faux j.,** hypocrite; **j. de présence,** tally, token (*issued as voucher for attendance at meeting*); *Com* director's fees; **toucher ses jetons,** to draw one's fees; **(b)** *Arg* punch, blow; **avoir les jetons,** to have the jitters *or* the wind up; **ça m'a donné les jetons,** it gave me the jitters, it put the wind up me.
jet-stream [dʒɛtstrim] *nm Météo* jet stream; (*pl jet-streams*).
jeu, *pl* **jeux** [ʒø] *nm* **(a)** (*amusement*) play(ing); *Arch Litt* sport; **jeux éducatifs,** educational games; **salle de jeux,** playroom; **j. de mots,** play on words, pun; **j. d'esprit,** witticism; **j. de main,** horseplay, rough and tumble; *Ordinat* **jeux informatiques,** computer games; **jeux de la fortune,** tricks of fortune; *Fig* **c'est un j. d'enfant,** it's child's play; **se faire (un) j. de (faire) qch,** to make light of (doing) sth, to think nothing of (doing) sth;
(b) *Th Mus etc* (manner of) playing; acting (*of actor*); execution, playing (*of musician*); **j. muet,** dumb show; **jeux de scène,** stage business; *Fig* **être vieux j.,** to be old-fashioned;
(c) (*activité*) **jeux d'adresse,** games of skill; **jeux de société, petits jeux,** parlour games; **jeux de hasard,** games of chance; **j. de rôles,** role-playing; **la règle du j.,** the rules of the game; **j. télévisé,** game show; (*avec questions*) quiz (show); *F* **ce n'est pas du j.,** that's not fair; **jouer le j.,** to play the game, to play fair; *Cartes* **avoir un beau j.** *ou* **du j.,** to have a good hand; **on aurait beau j. de** *ou* **à répondre,** it would be quite easy to answer that; **vous avez beau j.,** now's your chance; *Fig* **faire le j. de qn,** to play into s.o.'s hands; **cacher son j.,** to keep one's cards close to one's chest; **montrer son j.,** to show one's hand *or* one's cards;
(d) *Sp Tennis* **jeux olympiques,** Olympic games; **j., set et match,** game, set and match; **où en est le j.?,** what's the score?; **terrain de jeux,** playing field, sports ground; **en j.,** in play; **mettre la balle en j.,** to bring the ball into play; (*hockey*) to bully off; *Fb* **être hors j.,** (*ballon*) to be out of play; (*joueur*) to be offside;
(e) (*place*) **j. de boules,** (*in France*) bowling ground; (*in Britain*) bowling green; **j. de quilles,** skittle *or* bowling alley;
(f) (*ensemble*) set; **j. d'échecs/de dominos,** chess set/set of dominoes; **j. de cartes,** pack *or* deck of cards; **j. de fiches,** card index; *Mus* **j. d'orgue,** (organ) stop; **j. d'outils,** set of tools; **un j. de clés à molette,** a set of spanners;
(g) le j., gambling; *Fml* gaming; *Bourse* speculating; **maison de j.,** gaming house; **perdre une fortune au j.,** to

gamble away a fortune; **se ruiner au j.,** to ruin oneself gambling; **dettes de j.,** gambling debts; **table de j.,** gaming table, card table; **jouer gros j.,** to play for high stakes; **les jeux sont faits,** (*at roulette*) the stakes are down; *Fig* the die is cast; (*situation critique*) the chips are down; **faites vos jeux!,** place your bets!; **mettre qch en j.,** to stake sth; *Fig* **mettre tout en j.,** to stake one's all, to risk everything; **être en j.,** to be at stake; **les intérêts en j.,** the interests at issue *or* at stake *or* involved; **les forces en j.,** the forces at work, the forces involved; **mettre qch en j.,** to bring sth into play *or* into action; **le j. n'en vaut pas la chandelle,** the game isn't worth the candle; **se prendre au j.,** to get caught up in the game;

(h) (*mise en œuvre*) **j. de lumière,** play of light; *Th* **jeux de lumière,** lighting effects; **le j. de main d'un pianiste,** a pianist's technique; *Sp* **j. de jambes,** (*coureur etc*) leg movements; (*boxeur etc*) footwork; **j. d'eau,** fountain; *Fig* **le j. des alliances,** the (changing) pattern of alliances;

(i) *Tech* **j. d'une serrure,** action of a lock; **j. d'un piston,** length of stroke of a piston; **en j.,** in gear;

(j) *MecE* **j. (utile),** clearance, play; **rattraper le j.,** to tighten sth up; **il y a du j.,** it's rather loose, there's a bit of play; **donner du j. à qch,** to ease *or* slacken sth; **j. (nuisible),** looseness, play, slack; **prendre du j.,** to work free *or* loose; *Fig* **donner du j. à des négociations,** to allow (some) scope for negotiations.

jeu-concours [ʒøkɔ̃kur] *nm Rad TV etc* competition; (*émission*) game show; (*avec questions*) quiz (show); (*pl jeux-concours*).

jeudi [ʒødi] *nm* Thursday; **j. saint,** Maundy Thursday; *F* **la semaine des quatre jeudis,** when pigs begin to fly.

jeun (à) [aʒœ̃] *adj* (*sans avoir mangé*) fasting; (*sans avoir bu*) sober; **être à j.,** (*sans avoir mangé ni bu*) to have eaten or drunk nothing; **boire à j.,** to drink on an empty stomach.

jeune [ʒœn] **1** *adj* **(a)** young (*age*) ; youthful (*appearance etc*); **j. homme,** young man, youth; *F* **elle n'est plus très j.,** she's not so young as she was; **j. fille,** girl, young woman; **jeunes gens,** young people; (*hommes*) young men; **j. aveugle,** blind boy *or* girl; **un j. Français/Anglais,** a French/an English boy; **une j. Indienne,** an Indian girl; **j. détenu,** juvenile offender; **le plus j. de mes frères,** my youngest brother; **je suis plus j. que lui de quatre ans,** I'm four years younger than him *or* he is; **dans son j. âge,** in his young(er) days; **j. d'esprit,** young in mind; **j. marié,** newly-married man, newly-wed; (*le jour du mariage*) bridegroom;

(b) (*en comparaison*) younger; **mon j. frère,** my younger brother; **M. Martin J.,** Mr Martin junior, young Mr Martin;

(c) (*vert*) **vin j.,** new *or* young wine;

(d) *F* (*juste*) **c'est un peu j.!,** it's a bit short *or* thin *or* skimpy (*essay etc*);

2 *n* **(a)** (*personne jeune*) young man *or* woman *or* person, youth; **les jeunes,** young people, the younger generation, youth;

(b) (*d'un animal*) young animal; **jeunes,** young.

3 *adv* **ça fait j.,** it makes you *or* her *etc* look young(er); **s'habiller j.,** to dress in a youthful style.

jeûne [ʒøn] *nm* **(a)** (*période*) fast; **rompre le j.,** to break one's fast; **(b)** (*pratique*) fasting; **jour de j.,** day of fasting, fast day.

jeûner [ʒøne] *vi* to fast, to go without food.

jeunesse [ʒœnɛs] *nf* **(a)** youth; boyhood; girlhood; **je le connais depuis ma j.,** I have known him since childhood *or* since I was young; **dans sa première j.,** in his early youth; **ne pas être de la première j.,** not to be young any longer, to be getting on, to be no longer in one's first flush of youth; **erreurs/péchés de j.,** errors of youth/youthful indiscretions; **(b)** (*fraîcheur*) youthfulness; **la j. de peau,** the fresh, youthful appearance of the skin; **j. d'esprit,** youthful outlook; **(c)** newness (*of wine*); **(d)** (*les jeunes*) youth, young people; **la j. dorée,** the bright young things; *Litt* gilded youth; **club pour la j.,** youth club; **livres pour la j.,** children's books; **la j. du village,** the youth of the village; *F* **salut la j.!,** hi (there), guys!

jeunet, -ette [ʒœnɛ, -ɛt] *adj F Vieilli* youngish.

jeûneur, -euse [ʒønœr, -øz] *n* (*personne*) faster.

jeunot, -otte [ʒœno, -ɔt] *F* **1** *adj* young, youngish, on the young side. **2** *n* youngster.

J.F. *nf abrév* **jeune fille** *ou* **femme**.

J.H. *nm abrév* **jeune homme**.

jingle [dʒingl] *nm Rad* jingle.

jiu-jitsu [ʒyʒitsy] *nm inv Sp* jiu-jitsu.

Jne (*abrév* **jeune**) jr, jnr, jun.

J.O. *nm abrév* **journal officiel**.

joaillerie [ʒɔajri] *nf* **(a)** (*magasin*) jeweller's (shop); **(b)** (*marchandises*) jewellery, *surtout US* jewelry; **(c)** *Com* jewellery trade.

joaillier, -ière [ʒɔaje, -jɛr] *n* jeweller.

job[1] [ʒɔb] *nm F Vieilli* **monter le j. à qn,** to put the wrong idea into s.o.'s head.

job[2] [dʒɔb] *nm F* job, work.

Job [ʒɔb] *nm Bible* Job; **pauvre comme J.,** poor as a church mouse.

jobard, -arde [ʒɔbar, -ard] **1** *adj* gullible, naive. **2** *n* mug, sucker.

jobarderie [ʒɔbard(ə)ri] *nf*, **jobardise** [ʒɔbardiz] *nf* gullibility; **c'est de la j.,** it's a mug's game.

J.O.C. [ʒɔk] *nf abrév* **Jeunesse ouvrière chrétienne**.

jockey [ʒɔkɛ] *nm Courses de chevaux* jockey; *Arch* outrider.

Joconde (la) [laʒɔkɔ̃d] *nf* the Mona Lisa.

jodler [ʒɔdle, jɔ-] *vi* to yodel.

joggeur, -euse [(d)ʒɔgœr, -øz] *n* jogger.

jogging [(d)ʒɔgiŋ] *nm* **(a)** (*vêtement*) jogging suit, track-suit; **(b)** (*activité*) jogging.

joie [ʒwa] *nf* **(a)** joy, delight, gladness; **plein de j.,** full of joy; **elle était folle de j.,** she was wild with delight; **sauter de j.,** to jump for joy; **à ma grande j.,** to my great delight; **une j. profonde,** great pleasure; **accepter avec j.,** to accept with pleasure, to accept gladly; **ma fille faisait ma j.,** my daughter was my (pride and) joy; **le film a fait la j. de Simon,** the film made Simon very happy; **se faire une j. de faire qch,** to delight *or* take a delight in doing sth; **feu de j.,** bonfire; **j. de vivre,** joy of living, joie de vivre; **il se faisait une j. de vous voir,** he was looking forward (so much) to seeing you; **elle vous a fait une fausse j.,** she gave you false cause for celebration; **à cœur j.,** to one's heart's content; *Iron* **les joies de la famille!,** the joys of family life!; **(b) fille de j.,** prostitute.

joignable [ʒwaɲabl] *adj* contactable.

joindre [ʒwɛ̃dr] *v* (*prp* **joignant;** *pp* **joint;** *pr ind* **je joins, il joint, n. joignons, ils joignent;** *impf* **je joignais;** *p hist* **je joignis;** *fu* **je joindrai**) **1** *vt* **(a)** (*réunir*) to join, to bring together; **j. les mains,** to clasp one's hands, to put one's hands together; **j. un tuyau bout à bout,** to join one pipe to the end of another; **j. nos efforts,** to combine *or* unite our efforts; *F* **j. les deux bouts,** to make ends meet;

(b) (*ajouter*) to add (**à,** to); **le bon sens joint à l'intelligence,** common sense combined with intelligence; **j. le geste à la parole,** to suit the action to the word, *F* to put one's money where one's mouth is; **j. l'utile à l'agréable,** to combine business with pleasure; **j. sa voix aux protestations,** to join in the protests; *Com etc* **l'échantillon joint à votre lettre,** the sample enclosed with *or* attached to your letter;

(c) (= **rejoindre**) to meet, to join (*s.o.*); to join (*one's regiment, ship*); **je vous joindrai à l'hôtel,** (*téléphoner*) I shall contact you at the hotel; (*retrouver*) I shall meet *or* join you at the hotel; **comment puis-je vous j.?,** how can I get in touch with you?, how can I reach you?;

(d) (*unir*) to unite, to join; **j. deux jeunes gens par le mariage,** to unite *or* join two young people in marriage.

2 *vi* (*of boards etc*) to meet, to fit; **fenêtre qui joint mal,** window that does not shut properly.

3 se joindre *vpr* to join, to unite; **se j. à la conversation,** to join in the conversation; **voulez-vous vous j. à nous?,** would you like to join us?; **Marie se joint à moi pour vous remercier,** Marie joins (with) me in thanking you.

joint [ʒwɛ̃] **1** *adj* joined, united; **pieds joints,** feet (close) together; **saut à pieds joints,** standing jump; **à mains jointes,** with clasped hands, with hands together; **efforts joints,** combined efforts; **pièces jointes,** (*dans une lettre*) enclosures. **2** *nm* **(a)** *Menuis MecE* joint, join; **j. abouté** *ou* **en about** *ou* **carré** *ou* **plat,** butt joint; **j. biseauté,** scarf joint; **j. d'étanchéité,** gasket, seal; *MecE etc* **j. articulé** *ou* **en charnière,** knuckle (joint); **j. universel** *ou* **brisé** *ou* **de cardan,** universal *or* cardan joint, coupling; **j. sphérique** *ou* **à rotule,** ball(-and socket) joint; **j. à brides,** flange joint; **(b)** *F* **trouver le j.,** to come up with an answer, to find a way; **j'ai du mal à faire le j.,** I've got a little cashflow problem; **(c)** *Arg* (*drogue*) joint.

jointif, -ive [ʒwɛ̃tif, -iv] *adj Tech* joined, placed edge to edge, contiguous.

jointure [ʒwɛ̃tyr] *nf Anat Tech* joint, join; (*d'un cheval*) (*boulet*) fetlock (joint); (*paturon*) pastern; **j. du genou,** knee joint; **les jointures des doigts,** the knuckles.

joker [ʒɔkɛr] *nm Cartes* joker; *Fig* **sortir son j.,** to play one's joker *or* trump card.

joli [ʒɔli] **1** *adj* pretty, attractive, good-looking (*child, girl*); **joli comme un cœur, joli à croquer,** pretty as a picture;

une jolie expression/image, an attractive expression/a nice picture; **il a une jolie fortune,** he's pretty well off; **c'est bien j. tout ça mais ...,** that's all very well and good *or* *F* that's all fine and dandy, but ...; *F Iron* **ce n'est pas j. j.,** that's not very nice; **ah te voilà dans une jolie situation!,** what a fine mess you've got yourself into! **2** *nm* **le j. de l'affaire c'est que ...,** the beauty of the thing *or* the best thing (about it) is that ...; **ah! c'est du j.!,** that's a fine way to do things *or* to behave *etc*!

joliment [ʒɔlimɑ̃] *adv* **(a)** *(bien)* nicely, well; **j. habillé,** well *or* smartly dressed; **c'est j. dit!,** that's neatly put; **(b)** *F* *(extrêmement)* **j. amusant,** awfully *or* terribly funny; **vous avez j. raison,** you're dead right; **on s'est j. amusé(s),** we had a marvellous time.

jonc [ʒɔ̃] *nm* **(a)** *(plante)* rush; **j. fleuri,** flowering rush; **j. des marais,** bulrush; **j. d'Inde,** rattan; **(canne de) j.,** Malacca cane; **(b)** *(vannerie)* rush; *(baguette)* malacca cane, rattan (walking stick); **(c)** *(bijou)* keeper (ring, bangle).

joncher [ʒɔ̃ʃe] *vt* to strew; **j. la terre de fleurs,** to strew the ground with flowers; **les débris de la statue jonchaient le pavé,** fragments of the statue lay strewn about the pavement; **plancher jonché de débris,** floor strewn *or* littered with rubbish.

jonchets [ʒɔ̃ʃɛ] *nmpl* pick-up sticks, jackstraws, spillikins.

jonction [ʒɔ̃ksjɔ̃] *nf* junction; *(fait de joindre)* joining; **point de j.,** meeting point; **j. de deux routes,** junction of two roads; *Tech* **tuyau de j.,** joint pipe; *Rail* **gare de j.,** junction (station); **voie de j.,** crossover; *Mil* **opérer une j.,** *(of troops)* to join forces.

jongler [ʒɔ̃gle] *vi* to juggle (**avec,** with); *Fig* **j. avec les concepts,** to juggle *or* play with concepts.

jonglerie [ʒɔ̃gləri] *nf* juggling.

jongleur, -euse [ʒɔ̃glœr, -øz] *n* **(a)** *(acrobate)* juggler; **(b)** *Arch* *(ménestrel)* jongleur, (medieval) minstrel.

jonque [ʒɔ̃k] *nf Nau* junk.

jonquille [ʒɔ̃kij] **1** *nf* *(plante)* daffodil, jonquil. **2** *nm* bright yellow. **3** *adj inv* bright yellow.

Jordanie [ʒɔrdani] *nf* Jordan.

jordanien, -ienne [ʒɔrdanjɛ̃, -jɛn] **1** *adj* Jordanian. **2** *n* **J.,** Jordanian.

joseph [ʒozɛf] *adj* **papier j.,** fine transparent filter paper.

Josué [ʒozɥe] *nm Bible* Joshua.

jouable [ʒwabl] *adj* playable.

joual [ʒwal] *nm Can Ling* joual *(French Canadian dialect)*.

joubarbe [ʒubarb] *nf* *(plante)* houseleek.

joue [ʒu] *nf* **(a)** cheek *(of person, horse)*; **rouge à joues,** rouge; **danser j. contre j.,** to dance cheek to cheek; **tendre** *ou* **présenter l'autre j.,** to turn the other cheek; **mettre** *ou* **coucher qn en j.,** to aim (a gun) at s.o.; *Culin* **j. de boeuf,** cheek of beef; **(b)** side *(of armchair etc)*; cheek *(of bearing, mortise etc)*; flange *(of wheel)*; web *(of girder etc)*; **(c)** *Arch* **joues,** the bows *(of a ship)*.

jouée [ʒwe] *nf Archit* reveal *(of window)*.

jouer [ʒwe] **1** *vi* **(a)** to play; **j. avec ses lunettes,** to play *or* toy *or* fiddle *or* fidget with one's glasses; **j. sur les mots,** to play on *or* with words; *Fig* **j. avec les sentiments de qn,** to play *or* toy *or* trifle with s.o.'s feelings; **j. avec une idée,** to toy with an idea; **il joue avec son avenir,** he's gambling with *or* risking his future; **cela jouera en sa faveur,** that will act in his favour;

(b) **j. à qch,** to play (at) sth; **j. aux soldats,** to play (at) soldiers; **j. au tennis/aux cartes,** to play tennis/cards; **je ne joue plus!,** I'm not playing any more!; **pour j. l'acteur doit se concentrer,** the actor must concentrate in order to get into his role *or* part *or* character; **c'est à qui de j.?,** whose turn *or* go is it?; *(at chess etc)* whose move is it?; **j. au docteur,** to play doctor;

(c) **j. du piano/de la harpe,** to play the piano/the harp; **j. dans un groupe,** *(d'un musicien)* to play in a group; **j. des coudes,** to elbow one's way (through a crowd); **une fille qui joue de l'œil,** a girl who's making eyes at s.o. *or* who's giving s.o. the eye; **elle joue de son expérience/de sa maladie,** she's taking advantage *or* making the most of her experience/she's exploiting her illness;

(d) *(parier)* to gamble; *Bourse* to speculate; **j. aux courses,** to bet on *or* back horses; **j. à la hausse,** to gamble on a rise in prices, to bull the market; **j. à la baisse,** to gamble on a fall in prices, to bear the market;

(e) *(fonctionner)* to work, to function; **clef qui ne joue pas bien,** key that is hard to turn; **faire j. qch,** to bring sth into play; **faire j. un ressort,** to work *or* trigger *or* release a spring;

(f) *(être effectif)* to be *or* become operative, to operate; **l'augmentation des salaires joue depuis le 1er janvier,** the rise in salaries has been operative since January 1; **cette considération ne joue pas,** that consideration doesn't apply *or* is irrelevant;

(g) *(of wood)* to warp; *(of part)* to fit loosely, to have too much play.

2 *vt* **(a)** *(parier)* to stake; **j. cinq francs,** to stake five francs; **j. le jeu,** to play the game; **j. la revanche,** to play a return match; **j. sa tête,** to risk one's neck;

(b) *Courses de chevaux* to back, to bet on *(horse)*; **j. un cheval gagnant et placé,** to back a horse each way;

(c) to play *(card)*; to move, to play *(pawn)*; *Cartes* **j. trèfle,** to play clubs; *(au début)* to lead clubs; **bien j. ses cartes,** to play one's cards well; *Échecs etc* **j. une pièce,** to move a piece;

(d) *Th* to act, to play, to perform *(role etc)*; **j. (du) Genet,** *(d'une troupe)* to perform *or* put on a Genet play; *(d'un acteur)* to act in a Genet play; **j. Phèdre,** *(d'une actrice)* to play Phaedra; **j. un rôle dans l'affaire,** to play a part in the affair; **j. la surprise,** to feign surprise, to pretend to be surprised;

(e) *Mus* **j. un air au piano/à la flûte,** to play a tune on the piano/flute; **j. du Bach,** to play (some) Bach;

(f) *(duper)* to trick, to fool, to make a fool of *(s.o.)*.

3 se jouer *vpr* **(a)** **faire qch (comme) en se jouant,** to do sth easily *or* without any difficulty; **se j. de qn,** to trifle with s.o.; *(se moquer)* to mock s.o., to make fun of s.o.;

(b) *(au cinéma, théâtre)* to put on, to perform; **qu'est-ce qui se joue actuellement?,** what are they playing *or* what's on at the moment?

jouet [ʒwɛ] *nm* (child's) toy; *(terme plus général)* plaything; *Fig* **être le j. d'une illusion,** to be the victim of an illusion.

jouette [ʒwɛt] *adj Belg* **enfant j.,** child who loves playing.

joueur, -euse [ʒwœr, -øz] **1** *n* **(a)** player *(of game)*; **j. de golf/cricket/football,** golfer/cricketer/footballer; **j. de cartes,** card player; **être bon j.,** to be a good player; **être beau/mauvais j.,** to be a good/bad loser; **(b)** *Mus* player *(of instrument)*; **(c)** gambler; *Bourse* speculator; **j. à la hausse/baisse,** to bull/bear. **2** *adj* **enfant j.,** playful child.

joufflu [ʒufly] *adj* chubby(-cheeked).

joug [ʒu] *nm* **(a)** *Agr* yoke; **mettre les bœufs au j.,** to yoke the oxen; *Fig* **être sous le j. d'un tyran,** to be under the yoke of a tyrant; **secouer le j., s'affranchir du j.,** to throw off the yoke; **(b)** beam *(of balance)*.

jouir [ʒwir] *vi* **(a)** *(profiter)* **j. de la vie,** to enjoy life; **(b)** *(être en possession)* **j. de toutes ses facultés,** to be in full possession of all one's faculties; **j. d'une bonne réputation,** to have a good reputation; **j. d'une bonne santé,** to enjoy good health; **(c)** *(avoir du bon temps)* to enjoy oneself, to have a good time; **gens qui ne pensent qu'à j.,** people who think only of enjoyment *or* pleasure; **ça le fait j. de nous voir peiner,** he gets a kick out of seeing us struggle; **(d)** *(sexuellement)* to have an orgasm, *F* to come.

jouissance [ʒwisɑ̃s] *nf* **(a)** *(plaisir)* enjoyment, pleasure; *(sexuel)* orgasm, climax; **le travail est une j. pour lui,** work is a pleasure to *or* for him; **(b)** *Jur* *(possession)* possession, tenure; **avoir la j. de certains droits,** to enjoy certain rights; **entrer en j. de ses biens,** to enter into possession of one's property; **maison à vendre avec j. immédiate,** house for sale with vacant possession; **avec j. de la cuisine,** *(of accommodation)* with use of kitchen; **j. de passage,** right of way.

jouisseur, -euse [ʒwisœr, -øz] *n* sensualist, *Fml* sybarite.

jouissif, -ive [ʒwisif, -iv] *adj F* enjoyable, pleasure-giving, pleasurable.

joujou, -oux [ʒuʒu] *nm F* toy; *(terme plus général)* plaything; **faire j. avec une poupée,** to play with a doll.

joule [ʒul] *nm Phys* joule.

jour [ʒur] *nm* **(a)** *(clarté)* day, (day)light; **avant le j.,** before dawn, before daybreak; **en plein j.,** in broad daylight; *Fig* publicly; **il fait j.,** it's (getting) light; **il fait à peine j.,** it's hardly light; **le j. se faisait dans mon esprit,** I was beginning to understand *or* to see daylight; **la vérité se fait j. dans son esprit,** the truth is dawning on him; **voyager le** *ou* **de j.,** to travel by day *or* in the day(time); **travailler j. et nuit,** to work day and night *or* night and day; *Min* **travail au j.,** surface work; *Fig* **ils sont le j. et la nuit,** they are as different as chalk and cheese;

(b) *(journée)* day; **huit jours,** a week; **quinze jours,** a fortnight; **c'est à un j. de voyage,** it's a day's journey (away); **quel j. (du mois) sommes-nous?,** what's the date (today)?; **plat du j.,** *(in restaurant)* dish of the day, *F* today's special; **quel j. (de la semaine) sommes-nous?,** what day (of the week) is it (today)?; **plat du j.,** *(au* *restaurant*) dish of the day, *F* today's special; *Prov* **les jours se suivent et ne se ressemblent pas,** who knows what tomorrow holds?; **je l'ai vu l'autre j.,** I saw him the other day; **un j. ou l'autre,** one day, some time (or other); **d'un j. à l'autre, de j. en j.,** day by day, from day to day; **nous l'attendons d'un j. à l'autre,** we're expecting him any day (now); **un j. (alors) que je me promenais,** one day (when) I was out walking; **un (beau) j. je vous le dirai,** one day *or* some day I'll tell you; **tous les jours,** every day; **mes vêtements de tous les jours,** my everyday clothes; **il y a six ans j. pour j.,** six years ago to the (very) day; **vivre au j. le j.,** to live from day to day *or* from hand to mouth; **leur beauté n'est que d'un j.,** their beauty is ephemeral; **mettre/tenir à j.,** to bring/keep up to date; **tenir qn à j. (de qch),** to keep s.o. up to date (about sth), to keep s.o. posted (about sth); **une à deux fois par j.,** once or twice a day; **un de ces jours,** one of these days; *F* **à un de ces jours!,** I'll be seeing you!, see you soon!; *Com* **intérêts à ce jour,** interest to date;

(c) (*date*) day; **j. d'été,** summer's day; **j. de Noël,** Christmas Day; **le j. de mes 20 ans,** my 20th birthday; **j. férié/ouvrable,** public holiday/working day; **prendre j. pour qch,** to fix a day *or* date for sth, to make an appointment for sth; **le grand j.,** the big day; **ce n'est pas son j.,** it's not his day; **il y a les jours avec et les jours sans,** there are good days and (there are) bad days, there are days when everything goes right, and others when everything goes wrong;

(d) (*époque*) **de nos jours,** these days, nowadays; **l'homme du j.,** the man of the moment; **le journal du j.,** today's paper; **vieux jours,** old age; **je l'ai connue dans ses beaux jours,** I knew her in her prime; **mes beaux jours sont passés,** I've had my day;

(e) (*vie*) **donner le j. à un enfant,** to give birth to a child; **il vit le j. à Paris,** he was born in Paris; **mettre qch au j.,** to bring sth to light;

(f) (*éclairage*) light; **vous me cachez le j.,** you're in my light; **jeter le j. sur une affaire,** to throw light on a subject; **voir qch sous un j. nouveau/sous son vrai j.,** to see sth in a new light/in its true light; **présenter une affaire sous un j. favorable,** to present a matter in a favourable light;

(g) (*ouverture*) aperture, opening; **pratiquer un j. dans un mur,** to cut an opening *or* a hole in a wall; **il y a des jours entre les planches,** there are gaps *or* chinks between the planks; **percer à j.,** to bore through *or* go right through (*sth*); *Fig* to see through (*plan etc*);

(h) *Couture* **à j.,** hemstitched; **à jours,** openwork (*trimming, etc*);

(i) *Mil etc* **service de j.,** day duty; **officier de j.,** duty officer; **être de j.,** to be on (day) duty; **pharmacie de j.,** chemist's open (only) during the day; **j. de présence/d'absence,** day on/off duty.

Jourdain [ʒurdɛ̃] *nm* (River) Jordan.

journal, -aux [ʒurnal, -o] *nm* **(a)** (*presse*) (news)paper; **j. de mode,** fashion magazine; **j. sérieux,** quality newspaper; **les journaux,** the Press; **marchand de journaux,** newsagent, *Am* news dealer; (*dans la rue*) (news)paper seller *or* vendor, newsvendor; **livreur de journaux,** paperboy, *Am* newsboy; **dans du (papier) j.,** (wrapped) in newspaper; *Rad* **j. parlé,** radio news; *TV* **j. télévisé,** TV news (programme); **(b)** (*intime*) diary; journal, record (*of events, experiments etc*); **(livre) j.,** account book; **tenir un j.,** to keep a diary; *Nau* **j. de bord,** (ship's) log (book).

journalier, -ière [ʒurnalje, -jɛr] **1** *adj* daily (*task etc*); (*banal*) everyday (*occurrence*). **2** *nm* day labourer, *US* laborer.

journalisme [ʒurnalism] *nm* journalism; **l'influence du j.,** the influence of the press; **faire du j.,** to be a journalist.

journaliste [ʒurnalist] *n* journalist, reporter; **j. politique,** political correspondent *or* journalist.

journalistique [ʒurnalistik] *adj* journalistic; **style j.,** journalese.

journée [ʒurne] *nf* **(a)** (*jour*) day(time); **pendant la j.,** in the daytime, during the day; **toute la j.,** all day (long), the whole day; **il ne fait rien de la j.,** he does nothing all day (long); **je travaillais à longueur de j.,** I worked for days on end; **dans la j.,** in the course of the day;

(b) **j. de travail,** (*jour non chômé*) working day; (*quantité de travail*) day's work; **faire la j. continue,** (*of shop etc*) to remain open at lunchtime; (*d'une personne*) to work through lunch(time); **travailler à la j.,** to work by the day; **homme de j.,** (day) labourer; **femme de j.,** char(woman), daily help, *F* daily; **faire des journées,** (*of charwoman*) to do daily work (*for s.o.*);

(c) (*salaire*) day's wages; **tu as gagné ta j.,** you've earned your (day's) pay;

(d) (*distance*) day's journey;

(e) *Pol Fig* day; **j. d'émeutes,** day of rioting; **gagner la j.,** to win the day.

journellement [ʒurnɛlmɑ̃] *adv* daily, every day.

joute [ʒut] *nf* **(a)** (*combat*) joust, tilt; **j. oratoire,** sparring (match), verbal exchange; **j. sur l'eau,** water tournament; **(b)** *Can* game, match.

jouter [ʒute] *vi* **(a)** (*combattre*) to joust, to tilt; **(b)** (*rivaliser*) to fight; **j. avec qn,** to argue with s.o., to cross swords with s.o..

jouvence [ʒuvɑ̃s] *nf Litt* **Fontaine de J.,** Fountain of Youth.

jouvenceau, -elle [ʒuvɑ̃so, -ɛl] *n Arch* stripling, youth, lad; *f* maiden, damsel.

jovial, -aux [ʒɔvjal, -o] *adj* jovial, jolly, merry.

jovialement [ʒɔvjalmɑ̃] *adv* jovially.

jovialité [ʒɔvjalite] *nf* joviality, jolliness.

joyau, -aux [ʒwajo] *nm* jewel, gem; **les joyaux de la Couronne,** the Crown jewels; *Fig* **j. de la civilisation italienne,** jewel (in the crown) of Italian civilisation.

joyeusement [ʒwajøzmɑ̃] *adv* joyfully; *Litt* joyously.

joyeux, -euse [ʒwajø, -øz] *adj* happy, joyful; *Litt* joyous; **j. Noël!,** merry Christmas!; *Litt* **le j. mois de mai,** the merry month of May; **mine joyeuse,** cheerful expression.

jubé [ʒybe] *nm Archit* rood loft *or* screen, jube.

jubilaire [ʒybilɛr] *adj* **année j.,** jubilee year.

jubilation [ʒybilasjɔ̃] *nf* jubilation.

jubilé [ʒybile] *nm* jubilee.

jubiler [ʒybile] *vi F* to rejoice; (*méchamment*) to gloat.

jucher [ʒyʃe] **1** *vt* to perch. **2 se jucher** *vpr (of birds etc*) to perch; (*pour dormir*) to (go to) roost.

juchoir [ʒyʃwar] *nm* roost(ing place); (*perche*) perch.

judaïque [ʒydaik] *adj* (*loi etc*) Judaic; *Rel* Jewish.

judaïser [ʒydaize] *vi* to Judaize.

judaïsme [ʒydaism] *nm* Judaism.

judas [ʒyda] *nm* **(a)** *Bible* **J.,** Judas (Iscariot); **baiser de J.,** Judas kiss; **(b)** (*traître*) Judas, traitor, betrayer; **(c)** (*ouverture*) Judas (hole, trap); spy hole (*in door*).

Judée [ʒyde] *nf Bible* Judaea; **arbre de J.,** Judas tree.

judéo-allemand [ʒydeɔalmɑ̃] **1** *adj* Yiddish (*pl judéo-allemand(e)s*) **2** *nm Ling* Yiddish.

judéo-chrétien [ʒydeɔkretjɛ̃] *adj* Juda(a)eo-Christian; (*pl judéo-chrétien(ne)s*).

judiciaire [ʒydisjɛr] *adj* judicial; legal (*aid etc*); **casier j.,** record; **avoir un casier j. vierge,** to have a clean record; **enquête j.,** judicial inquiry; **frais judiciaires,** legal charges; **erreur j.,** miscarriage of justice; **vente j.,** sale by order of the court; **poursuites judiciaires,** proceedings; **le pouvoir j.,** judicial power; ≈ the Bench.

judiciairement [ʒydisjɛrmɑ̃] *adv* judicially.

judicieusement [ʒydisjøzmɑ̃] *adv* judiciously.

judicieux, -euse [ʒydisjø, -øz] *adj* judicious; **peu j.,** injudicious, indiscreet.

judo [ʒydo] *nm* judo.

judoka [ʒydɔka] *n* judoka.

juge [ʒyʒ] *nm* **(a)** *Jur* judge; **Monsieur le J.,** Your Honour *or US* honor, *Br* M'Lord, M'Lud; **j. d'instruction,** examining magistrate; **j. d'instance,** *Arch* **j. de paix,** police court magistrate; ≈ Justice of the Peace; *Arch* conciliation magistrate (*in commercial cases*); **les juges,** the bench; **(b)** (*arbitre*) umpire; *Courses de chevaux* judge; **j. de touche,** *Fb* linesman; *Rugby* touch judge; **(c)** *Fig* **être bon j. de qch,** to be a good judge of sth; **je vous en fais j.,** judge for yourself, I leave it to you to judge; **on ne peut pas être j. et partie,** you can't be (the) judge in your own case; **tu es le seul j.,** you alone can judge, only you can be the judge.

jugé [ʒyʒe] *nm* **tirer au j.,** to try a shot in the dark, to fire blind.

jugeable [ʒyʒabl] *adj Jur* subject to a legal decision.

jugement [ʒyʒmɑ̃] *nm* **(a)** *Jur* trial (*of case*); **faire passer qn en j.,** to bring s.o. to trial; **mettre en j.,** to commit for trial; **mise en j.,** arraignment; **passer en j.,** to be brought to trial, to stand trial; **j. par défaut,** judg(e)ment by default; **le (jour du) j. dernier,** the Last Judg(e)ment, doomsday;

(b) (*décision*) decision, award; (*in criminal cases*) sentence; **prononcer un j.,** to pass judg(e)ment; (*in contests etc*) to adjudicate; **rendre un j. arbitral,** to make an award; **j. provisoire,** decree nisi; **j. déclaratif de faillite,** adjudication in bankruptcy;

(c) (*opinion*) opinion, estimation, judg(e)ment; **au j. de bien des gens,** according to many (people); **porter un j. sur qch,** to pass judg(e)ment *or* give an opinion on sth; **j.**

de valeur, value judg(e)ment;

(d) *(discernement)* judg(e)ment, discernment, discrimination; **montrer du j.,** to show sound judg(e)ment *or* good sense; **erreur de j.,** error of judg(e)ment.

jugeote [ʒyʒɔt] *nf F* common sense, gumption, *Sl* nous; **avoir de la j.,** to know what's what.

juger[1] [ʒyʒe] *v* **(je jugeai(s), n. jugeons) 1** *vt* **(a)** *Jur* to try, to judge *(a case)*; to try *(defendant)*; to pass sentence *or* judg(e)ment on *(prisoner)*; to adjudicate, to arbitrate *(claim etc)*;

(b) to judge, to appreciate *(situation)*; to judge, to pass judg(e)ment on, to criticize *(book etc)*; **j. les gens sur la mine,** to judge people by *or* from appearances;

(c) *(croire)* to think, to believe, to be of the opinion; **on le jugeait fou,** people thought him mad; **j. à propos/nécessaire de faire qch,** to think it advisable/necessary to do sth;

(d) j. de qch, to judge sth; **j. de qn/qch,** to form an opinion of s.o./sth; **jugez de ma surprise,** imagine my surprise; **à en j. par ...,** to judge by ..., judging *or* going by ...; **autant que je puisse en j.,** to the best of my judgment; **à vous d'en j.,** it's up to you to draw your own conclusions.

2 se juger *vpr* to be judged; **un homme se juge par ses actions,** a man is judged by his actions.

3 *vi* to judge; **à toi de j.,** it's up to you to form your own opinion; **tu ne peux pas j.,** you're in no position to judge.

juger[2] *nm* = **JUGÉ.**

jugulaire [ʒygylɛr] **1** *adj Anat* jugular *(vein)*. **2** *nf* **(a)** *Anat* jugular; **(b)** chin strap *(of helmet)*.

juguler [ʒygyle] *vt* **(a)** to suppress, to stifle, to repress *(revolt etc)*; to damp down *(inflation)*; to arrest, to halt *(disease)*; **(b)** *Arch* to strangle, to throttle *(s.o.)*.

juif, juive [ʒɥif, ʒɥiv] **1** *adj* Jewish. **2** *n* **J.,** Jew; **Juive,** Jewish woman, Jewish girl, Jew(ess); **le J. errant,** the Wandering Jew. **3** *nm Anat F* **le petit j.,** the funnybone.

juillet [ʒɥijɛ] *nm* July; **en j.,** in July; **au mois de j.,** in (the month of) July; **le sept j.,** on the seventh of July, (on) July the seventh, *Am* (on) July seventh; **le 14 j.,** Bastille Day *(day of national celebration in France)*.

juin [ʒɥɛ̃] *nm* June; **en j.,** in June; **au mois de j.,** in (the month of) June; **le sept j.,** on the seventh of June, (on) June the seventh, *Am* (on) June seventh.

juiverie [ʒɥivri] *nf Arch* Jewry, ghetto.

jujube [ʒyʒyb] *nm Pharm* jujube (lozenge).

juke-box [(d)ʒykbɔks] *nm* jukebox; *(pl juke-boxes)*.

julep [ʒylɛp] *nm Pharm* julep.

jules [ʒyl] *nm* **(a)** *Arg* *(mari, amoureux)* man, guy, boyfriend; **mon j.,** my hubby, my old man; **(b)** *Arg* *(vase de nuit)* chamber-pot, potty, *F* jerry.

Jules [ʒyl] *nm* Julius; **J. César,** Julius Caesar.

julien, -ienne [ʒyljɛ̃, -jɛn] *adj* Julian; **année julienne,** Julian year.

Julien [ʒyljɛ̃] *nm* Julian.

julienne [ʒyljɛn] *nf* **(a)** *(plante)* rocket; **(b)** *Culin* julienne *(soup)*.

Julienne [ʒyljɛn] *nf* Juliana, Gillian.

Juliette [ʒljɛt] *nf* Juliet(te).

jumbo(-jet) [(d)ʒœmbo(dʒɛt)] *nm F* jumbo (jet); *(pl jumbo-jets)*.

jumeau, -elle [ʒymo, -ɛl] **1** *adj* **(a)** twin; **frères jumeaux/sœurs jumelles,** twin brothers/sisters; **vrais jumeaux,** identical twins; **lits jumeaux,** twin beds; **maisons jumelles,** semi-detached houses; **(b)** *(of fruit)* double. **2** *nm Anat* gemellus muscle. **3** *n* *(frère)* twin brother; *(sœur)* twin sister.

jumelage [ʒymlaʒ] *nm* **(a)** *(assemblage)* coupling, pairing; **(b)** twinning *(of towns)*.

jumelé [ʒymle] *adj* **maison jumelée,** semi-detached house; **villes jumelées,** twin(ned) towns; *Aut* **pneus jumelés,** twin *or* dual tyres.

jumeler [ʒymle] *vt* **(je jumelle, n. jumelons; je jumellerai)** to twin *(towns)*; to fish, to reinforce *(mast, beam etc)*.

jumelle [ʒymɛl] *nf* **(a)** *Opt* **(paire de) jumelles,** binoculars; **jumelles de théâtre,** opera glasses; **jumelles de campagne,** field glass(es); **(b)** *MecE* cheeks, side pieces; *Nau* fishes *(of mast)*; *Aut* (spring) shackles.

jument [ʒymɑ̃] *nf* mare; **j. poulinière,** brood mare.

jumping [(d)ʒœmpiŋ] *nm Equitation* show jumping, *F* horse jumping.

jungle [ʒɔ̃gl, ʒœgl] *nf* jungle; *Fig* **c'est une vraie j.,** *(le monde du travail etc)* it's a jungle out there, it's a real rat race, it's dog eat dog; **la loi de la j.,** the law of the jungle.

junior [ʒynjɔr] **1** *adj inv* junior; **M. Martin j.,** Mr Martin junior; *Com* **style** *ou* **mode j.,** youth fashion. **2** *n* junior.

junkie [dʒœnki] *n F* junkie.

Junon [ʒynɔ̃] *nf* Juno.

junte [ʒœ̃t] *nf* junta.

jupe [ʒyp] *nf* **(a)** skirt; *F* **pendu aux jupes de sa mère,** tied to his mother's apron strings; **(b)** *Tech* skirt.

jupe-culotte [ʒypkylɔt] *nf* divided skirt, culotte(s); *(pl jupes-culottes)*.

jupette [ʒypɛt] *nf Sp* skirt.

Jupiter [ʒypitɛr] **1** *nm* Jupiter, Jove. **2** *nf Astron* Jupiter.

jupon [ʒypɔ̃] *nm* **(a)** waist petticoat, underskirt, slip; *F* **il est toujours dans les jupons de sa mère,** he's always hanging on to his mother's apron strings; **(b)** *F* **courir le j.,** to chase after women, to chase the girls, to womanize; **amateur de j.,** womanizer.

Jura [ʒyra] *nm* **le J.,** the Jura (Mountains).

jurassien, -ienne [ʒyrasjɛ̃, -jɛn] **1** *adj* of *or* from the Jura. **2** *n* **J.,** native *or* inhabitant of the Jura.

jurassique [ʒyrasik] *adj & nm* Jurassic.

juratoire [ʒyratwar] *adj* **caution j.,** guarantee given on oath.

juré, -ée [ʒyre] **1** *adj* sworn; **ennemi j.,** sworn enemy; **expert j.,** sworn expert. **2** *n* juryman, *f* jury woman, juror; **les jurés,** the jury; **mesdames, messieurs les jurés,** ladies and gentlemen of the jury.

jurer [ʒyre] **1** *vt* **j. sa foi,** to pledge one's word; **j. sur la Bible,** to swear on the Bible; **j. fidélité à qn,** to swear *or* pledge fidelity to s.o.; **faire j. le secret à qn,** to swear s.o. to secrecy; **j. de faire qch,** to swear *or* vow to do sth; **j. de se venger,** to swear *or* vow revenge; **je vous jure que c'est vrai,** I swear that it's the truth; **j'en jurerais,** I would swear to it; *Prov* **il ne faut j. de rien,** you never can tell. **2** *vi* **(a)** *(blasphémer)* to swear, to curse; *F* **j. comme un charretier,** to swear like a trooper; **(b)** *(of colours etc)* to clash, to jar **(avec,** with).

juridiction [ʒyridiksjɔ̃] *nf* jurisdiction; **sous la j. de ...,** within the jurisdiction of ... .

juridictionnel, -elle [ʒyridiksjɔnɛl] *adj* jurisdictional.

juridique [ʒyridik] *adj* juridical, judicial; legal *(tie, claim etc)*; **conseiller j.,** legal adviser.

juridiquement [ʒyridikmɑ̃] *adv* juridically.

jurisconsulte [ʒyriskɔ̃sylt] *nm* jurisconsult, legal expert.

jurisprudence [ʒyrisprydɑ̃s] *nf* *(doctrine)* jurisprudence; *(décision)* precedent *(of a case)*; *(ensemble des décisions)* case law.

juriste [ʒyrist] *n* *(spécialiste du droit)* jurist, legal expert; *(avocat etc)* lawyer; *(étudiant)* law student; *(professeur)* professor of law.

juron [ʒyrɔ̃] *nm* oath, curse; *(gros mot)* swearword.

jury [ʒyri] *nm* **(a)** *Jur* jury; **dresser la liste du j.,** to empanel the jury; **chef du j.,** foreman of the jury; **membre du j.,** juror, member of the jury; **(b)** selection committee, (panel of) judges *(for exhibition etc)*; **j. d'examen,** examining board, board of examiners.

jus [ʒy] *nm* **(a)** *(de fruit etc)* juice; **j. de fruit,** fruit juice; **plein de j.,** juicy; **un j. d'orange, s'il vous plaît!,** an orange juice, please; **(b)** *Culin* juice *(of meat)*; *(sauce)* gravy; *F* **cuire** *ou* **mijoter dans son j.,** to stew in one's own juice(s); **(c)** *Arg* **il est tombé dans le j.,** he fell in the water *or F* the drink; **(d)** *Arg* *(café)* coffee; **(e)** *(courant électrique)* juice; *(essence)* juice; *Vieilli* **ça vaut le j.,** it's worth it.

jusant [ʒyzɑ̃] *nm* ebb (tide).

jusqu'au-boutisme [ʒyskobutism] *nm inv Pol etc* hard-line attitude; **je n'aime pas son j.'au-b.,** I don't like the way he always has to go the whole hog.

jusqu'au-boutiste [ʒyskobutist] *n* hard liner, extremist; *(fidèle à un parti, des principes)* diehard; *(pl jusqu'au-boutistes)*.

jusque [ʒysk(ə)] **1** *prép* **(a)** *(espace, mesure)* as far as, up to; **jusqu'ici,** up to here, thus far, so far; **venez jusqu'ici,** come over here; **j.-là,** thus far, up to there *or* that point; **jusqu'ici** *ou* **j.-là, c'est très bien,** so far so good; **jusqu'où?,** how far?; **depuis Londres jusqu'à Paris,** all the way from London to Paris; **avoir de l'eau jusqu'à la taille,** to have water (coming) right up to one's waist, to be waist-deep in water; **jusqu'au bout (de la rue),** as far as *or* (up) to the end (of the street); *Fig* **jusqu'à un certain point,** up to a certain point, to a certain extent; *Fig* **jusqu'où ira-t-il?,** how far will he go?, how far will he take the matter?; **aller jusqu'à faire qch,** to go so far as to do sth; **j. chez lui,** up to his very door; **rougir jusqu'aux oreilles,** to blush to the roots of one's hair, to go as red as a beetroot; **la nouvelle est venue jusqu'à lui,** the news reached him; **ce scandale va remonter jusqu'au directeur,** this scandal will reach *or* go as far as the director, this scandal will go right to the top; **compter jusqu'à dix,** to count (up) to ten; **je veux bien mettre jusqu'à 200 francs,** I'm prepared to put in up to 200 francs; **jusqu'à concurrence de 5 000 francs,** (up) to 5,000 francs; **jusqu'à 250 gr.,** not exceeding 250g;

(b) (*temps*) till, until; **attendez jusqu'après les vacances,** wait till after the holidays; **jusqu'ici, jusqu'à maintenant, jusqu'à présent, j.-là,** (*en référence au présent*) until now, up to now, to date, as yet, so far; **j.-là, jusqu'alors,** (*en référence au passé*) until then; **jusqu'à hier/dix heures,** until *or* up to yesterday/ten o'clock; **jusqu'à (l'âge de) 15 ans,** up to the age of 15, up to 15 years old; **jusqu'à aujourd'hui,** until today; **jusqu'à fin mai,** until the end of May; **jusqu'à nouvel ordre,** until further notice; **jusqu'à plus ample informé,** pending further information, until further information is available; **jusqu'à mon dernier jour,** to my dying day; **jusqu'au jour** *ou* **au moment où** *ou* **que ...,** until the time when ..., until (such time as) ...; **si nous remontons jusqu'en** *ou* **jusqu'à 1800,** if we go back as far as 1800;

(c) il sait jusqu'à nos pensées, he knows our very thoughts; **tous jusqu'au dernier,** every last one (of them); **jusqu'à dix personnes l'ont vu,** as many as ten people saw it; **tout en lui, jusqu'à son sourire, a changé,** everything about him, even *or* right down to his smile, has changed; **il a mangé l'oie jusqu'aux os,** he stripped the goose to the carcass; **il se montrait sévère jusqu'à la cruauté,** he was severe to the point of cruelty.

2 *conj* **jusqu'à ce que ...** + *sub, Vieilli* **jusqu'à tant que ...** + *sub,* until ..., till ...; **jusqu'à ce que les portes soient fermées,** until *or* till the doors are shut.

jusques [ʒyskə] *prép Arch & Litt* = **JUSQUE**; **j. et y compris** [ʒyskəzeikɔ̃pri] ..., up to and including ... .

justaucorps [ʒystokɔr] *nm* **(a)** (*pour la gymnastique*) leotard; **(b)** *Arch* jerkin.

juste [ʒyst] **1** *adj* **(a)** (*équitable*) just, right, fair; **esprit j.,** fair mind; **cela n'est pas j.,** it's not fair, it's unfair; **il est en colère, et à j. titre!,** he's angry, and quite right(ly) (so) *or* and with good reason!; **ça n'est qu'une j. récompense,** it's nothing more than he *or* she *etc* deserves; **j. indignation,** righteous indignation; **j. colère,** righteous *or* justified anger; **rien de plus j.,** nothing could be fairer; **être j. envers** *ou* **pour qn,** to be fair to s.o.; **pour être j. envers elle,** to be fair to her, to give her her due; **j. ciel!,** heavens above!;

(b) (*exact*) right, exact, accurate; **quelle est l'heure j.?,** what is the right *or* exact time?; **le mot j.,** the exact *or* right word; **raisonnement j.,** sound reasoning; **se faire une idée j. de la situation,** to get a true picture of the situation; **j. milieu,** happy medium; **votre réponse n'est pas j.,** you've got the answer wrong; **balance j.,** accurate scales; **ma montre est j.,** my watch is right; **arriver à l'heure j.,** to arrive right on time, *F* to arrive on the dot;

(c) *Mus* **quarte j.,** perfect fourth; **ce piano n'est pas j.,** this piano is out of tune;

(d) scanty, bare (*allowance*); tight (*shoes*); tightfitting, skimpy, scanty (*garment*); **c'est tout** *ou* **bien j.,** there's barely enough (*food etc*) to go round; **deux cents francs pour une semaine, c'est un peu j.!,** 200 francs for one week, it's a bit on the short side *or* it's not a lot!; *Com* **au plus j. prix,** at a rock bottom price, at a keen price.

2 *adv* **(a)** (*avec exactitude*) accurately, correctly, rightly; **parler j.,** to speak to the point; **frapper j.,** to strike home; (*bien exprimer un problème etc*) to hit the nail on the head; **chanter j.,** to sing in tune; **sonner j.,** to ring true; **voir j.,** to take a proper view of things; **raisonner j.,** to argue soundly; **deviner** *ou F* **tomber j.,** to guess right;

(b) (*précisement*) exactly, precisely, just; **arriver à dix heures j.,** to arrive on the stroke *or* dot of ten *or* at ten o'clock sharp *or* on the dot; **j. au milieu,** right *or* plumb in the centre; **j. à temps,** just in time, in the nick of time; **c'est j. l'homme qu'il nous faut,** he's exactly the man *or* the very man we want *or* need; **c'est j. ce qu'il faut,** it's the very thing, it's just the job *or* the ticket;

(c) (*seulement, à peine*) barely, just; **c'est tout j. s'il sait lire,** he can barely read; **il ne manque jamais son train, mais c'est tout j.,** he never misses his train, but he cuts it fine *or* it's a close thing; **(n')avoir (que) j. le temps,** to have barely time, to have just (enough) time; **vous avez tout j. le temps,** you haven't a moment to spare; **arriver j. à l'heure,** to arrive just in time; **il échappa tout j. à la mort,** he barely *or* narrowly escaped death;

(d) je ne sais pas au j. si..., I don't exactly know whether...; **comme de j.,** of course, as one would expect; **comme de j., le train est arrivé en retard,** as usual *or* naturally, the train was late.

3 *n* **les justes,** the just, the righteous.

justement [ʒystəmɑ̃] *adv* **(a)** (*exactement*) precisely, exactly, just; **voici j. la lettre que j'attendais,** here is the very letter I was waiting for; **(b)** (*avec justice*) justly, rightly; **être j. récompensé,** to receive a fair reward; **(c)** (*précisement*) precisely, indeed; **et j. le voilà,** and in fact *or* indeed here he is; **j'ai toujours voulu voir Venise — j., on y va,** I've always wanted to visit Venice — well that's just where we're going.

justesse [ʒystɛs] *nf* **(a)** (*précision*) exactness, correctness, precision, accuracy; **j. d'une vis,** exact fit of a screw; **j. d'une opinion,** soundness of an opinion; **j. d'une expression,** aptness *or* appropriateness of an expression; **raisonner avec j.,** to argue soundly *or* rightly; **(b) de j.,** (only) just, by the skin of one's teeth.

justice [ʒystis] *nf* **(a)** justice; **c'est j. que ...** + *sub,* it is only right *or* fair that ...; **faire régner la j.,** to let justice prevail; **il est de toute j. de l'entendre,** it is only fair to give him a hearing *or* to hear him out; **en toute** *ou* **bonne j.,** in all fairness; **avec j.,** justly, deservedly; **faire** *ou* **rendre j. à qn,** to do justice to s.o.; **ce n'est que j.,** it's only just *or* fair; **se faire j. (à soi-même),** to take the law into one's own hands; (*se suicider*) to commit suicide; **faire j. de qch,** to refute *or* challenge sth; **(b)** *Jur* law; **gens de j.,** (*juges*) magistrates; (*avocats etc*) lawyers; **action en j.,** action at law; **aller en j.,** to go to law; **poursuivre qn en j.,** to institute legal proceedings against s.o., to take legal action against s.o..

justiciable [ʒystisjabl] **1** *adj* **j. d'un tribunal,** justiciable to *or* in a court, amenable to a court; *Méd* **cas j. d'un certain traitement,** case in which a certain treatment is indicated. **2** *n* the ordinary individual (in the eyes of the law).

justicier, -ière [ʒystisje, -jɛr] *n* **(a)** dispenser of justice, upholder of the law; **Robin des Bois était un j.,** Robin Hood was a lover of justice *or* a righter of wrongs; **(b)** *Jur Vieilli* dispenser of justice, justiciary.

justifiable [ʒystifjabl] *adj* justifiable.

justificateur, -trice [ʒystifikatœr, -tris] **1** *adj* justifying; *Fml* justificatory. **2** *n Typ* justifier.

justificatif, -ive [ʒystifikatif, -iv] **1** *adj* justificatory; **pièce justificative,** *Com* voucher (copy); (*document écrit*) written proof; *Jur* relevant document. **2** *nm* written proof; *Jur* relevant document.

justification [ʒystifikasjɔ̃] *nf* **(a)** (*explication*) justification, vindication; **(b)** (*preuve*) proof (*of fact, identity*); **(c)** *Typ Ordinat* justification (*of lines*).

justifié [ʒystifje] *adj* **(a)** justified, justifiable (*action*); **peu j.,** unjustifiable, unjustified, unwarranted; **(b)** *Jur* **préjudice j.,** proved damages.

justifier [ʒystifje] *v* (*impf & pr sub* **n. justifiions, v. justifiiez**) **1** *vt* **(a)** to justify, to vindicate (*s.o.'s conduct etc*); to bear out (*statement etc*); to warrant (*action, expenditure*); **son échec ne justifie pas cette crise de nerfs,** his failure doesn't justify *or* warrant such hysterics; **(b)** to prove, to give proof of (*assertion etc*); **(c)** *Typ Ordinat* to justify (*line of type etc*); **j. à droite/gauche,** to right-/left-justify. **2** *vi Jur* **j. de ses mouvements,** to account for one's movements; **j. de son identité,** to prove one's identity. **3 se justifier** *vpr* to justify oneself; **se j. d'une accusation,** to clear oneself *or* one's name of an accusation; **inutile de te j.,** there's no point in trying to justify yourself.

jute [ʒyt] *nm* jute; **toile de j.,** hessian.

juter [ʒyte] *vi* to be juicy, to drip (with) juice.

juteux, -euse [ʒytø, -øz] **1** *adj* juicy; *F* **une affaire juteuse,** a juicy *or* lucrative piece of business. **2** *nm Mil Arg* warrant officer.

juvénile [ʒyvenil] *adj* juvenile; youthful (*appearance etc*).

juvénilité [ʒyvenilite] *nf Litt* juvenility; youthfulness.

juxtalinéaire [ʒykstalineɛr] *adj* **traduction j.,** parallel translation.

juxtaposer [ʒykstapoze] *vt* to juxtapose, to place side by side.

juxtaposition [ʒykstapozisjɔ̃] *nf* juxtaposition.

K

K, k [kɑ] *nm* (the letter) K, k; *Phys* **échelle K. (= Kelvin),** Kelvin *or* absolute scale (*of temperatures*).
k (*abrév* **kilo**) k.
Kaboul [kabul] *nf* Kabul.
kabyle [kabil] **1** *adj* Kabyle. **2** *nm Ling* Kabyle. **3** *n* **K.,** Kabyle.
Kabylie [kabili] *nf* **(la Grande/Petite) K.,** (Great/Lesser) Kabylia.
kafkaïen, -ïenne [kafkajɛ̃, -jɛn] *adj Littér* Kafkaesque.
Kairouan [kɛrwɑ̃] *n* Kairwan.
kaiser [kajzɛr] *nm* kaiser.
kakatoès [kakatɔɛs] *nm* = **CACATOÈS**.
kakémono [kakemɔno] *nm Beaux-Arts* kakemono.
kaki[1] [kaki] *adj inv & nm* khaki, *US* olive-drab.
kaki[2] *nm* (*arbre, fruit*) (Chinese) persimmon.
kaléidoscope [kaleidɔskɔp] *nm* kaleidoscope.
kaléidoscopique [kaleidɔskɔpik] *adj* kaleidoscopic.
kali [kali] *nm* (*plante*) kali, glasswort, (prickly) saltwort.
kalmouk, -ouke [kalmuk] **1** *adj* Kalmuck. **2** *nm Ling* Kalmuck. **3** *n* **K.,** Kalmuck.
kamikaze [kamikaz] **1** *nm* kamikaze; *Fig* **un k. du travail,** workaholic. **2** *adj inv* kamikaze; **opération k.,** kamikaze operation, suicide mission.
Kamtchadale [kamtʃadal] *n* native *or* inhabitant of Kamchatka.
Kamtchatka [kamtʃatka] *nm* Kamchatka.
kanak [kanak] *adj & n* = **CANAQUE**.
kangourou [kɑ̃guru] *nm* kangaroo; **k. de rochers,** wallaby; **île des Kangourous,** Kangaroo Island.
kantien, -ienne [kɑ̃tjɛ̃, -jɛn] *adj Phil* Kantian.
kantisme [kɑ̃tism] *nm Phil* Kantianism, Kantism.
kaolin [kaɔlɛ̃] *nm* kaolin.
kaolinisation [kaɔlinizasjɔ̃] *nf Géol* kaolinization (*of feldspar etc*).
kapok [kapɔk] *nm* kapok.
kapokier [kapɔkje] *nm* (*arbre*) kapok tree.
karakul [karakyl] *nm* caracul, karakul (sheep, wool).
karaté [karate] *nm* karate.
karateka [karateka] *nm* karate expert.
karbau [karbo] *nm* water buffalo.
karité [karite] *nm* (*arbre*) shea(tree).
karma [karma] *nm Rel* karma.
Karpat(h)es [karpat] *nfpl* = **CARPATES**.
karstique [karstik] *adj* karstic.
kart [kart] *nm* (go-)kart, (go-)cart.
karting [kartiŋ] *nm* go-kart racing, karting.
kasba(h) [kazba] *nf* = **CASBA(H)**.
kascher [kaʃɛr] *adj inv Rel* kosher.
Katanga [katɑ̃ga] *nm* Katanga.
kava, kawa [kava] *nf* (*arbuste*) kava; (*boisson*) kava.
kayac, kayak [kajak] *nm* kayak, canoe; **faire du k.,** to (go) canoe(ing).
kéfir [kefir] *nm Culin* kefir.
kelvin [kɛlvin] *Phys* **1** *adj inv* **échelle K.,** Kelvin *or* absolute scale (*of temperatures*). **2** *nm* kelvin.
kendo [kɛndo] *nm* kendo.
képhir [kefir] *nm Culin* kefir.
képi [kepi] *nm* kepi.
kérabau [kerabo] *nm* water buffalo.
kératine [keratin] *nf* keratin, ceratin.
kératite [keratit] *nf Méd* keratitis.
kératoïde [keratɔid] *adj* keratoid, ceratoid.
kératoplastie [keratɔplasti] *nf Chir* keratoplasty, corneal grafting.
kératose [keratoz] *nf Méd Vét* keratosis.
kermès [kɛrmɛs] *nm* **(a)** (*insecte*) kermes; **k. de la vigne,** vine scale; **(b)** (*arbre*) **chêne k.,** kermes oak.
kermesse [kɛrmɛs] *nf* **(a)** (*aux Pays Bas, en Belgique, dans le nord de la France*) kermis, village fair; **(b)** (*fête de bienfaisance*) (charity) fête.
kérosène [kerozɛn] *nm* paraffin (oil), *Am* kerosene; *Av* kerosene.
ketch [kɛtʃ] *nm Nau* ketch.
ketchup [kɛtʃœp] *nm Culin* ketchup.
keufs [kœf] *nmpl Arg* **les k.,** the fuzz.
keynésien, -ienne [kenezjɛ̃, -jɛn] *adj & n Écon* Keynesian.
K.F. [kaɛf] *nm* (*abrév* **kilofrancs**) = a thousand francs; **poste de directeur à 500 K.F.,** director's post, salary 50 K.
kg (*abrév* **kilogramme**) kg.
K.G.B. [kagebe] *nm* KGB.
khâgne [kɑɲ] *nf* = **CAGNE**.
khâgneux, -euse [kɑɲø, -øz] *n* = **CAGNEUX 2 (a)**.
khalifat [kalifa] *nm* = **CALIFAT**.
khalife [kalif] *nm* = **CALIFE**.
khamsin [kamzin] *nm Météo* khamsin.
khan [kɑ̃] *nm* khan.
khédive [kediv] *nm* khedive.
khmer, khmère [kmɛr] **1** *adj* K(h)mer. **2** *nm Ling* K(h)mer. **3** *n* **K.,** K(h)mer.
khôl [kol] *nm* kohl.
kibboutz [kibuts] *nm* kibbutz; (*pl kibbouts, kibboutzim*).
kick(-starter) [kik(startɛr)] *nm* (*for motorbike etc*) kick starter.
kidnapper [kidnape] *vt* to kidnap.
kidnappeur, -euse [kidnapœr, -øz] *n* kidnapper.
kidnapping [kidnapiŋ] *nm* kidnapping.
kieselguhr [kizelgur] *nm Minér* kieselguhr.
kievien, -ienne [kjevjɛ̃, -jɛn] **1** *adj* Kievan; *Hist* **Russie kievienne,** Kievan Russia, Kiev Rus. **2** *n* **K.,** Kievan.
kif [kif] *nm* cannabis, hemp.
kif-kif [kifkif] *adj inv F* same, likewise; **c'est k.-k. (bourricot),** it's all the same, it's six of one and half a dozen of the other, it's as broad as it's long.
kiki [kiki] *nm F* neck, throat; **serrer le k. à qn,** to throttle s.o..
kil [kil] *nm F* litre, *US* liter.
kilo [kilo] *nm F* (= **kilogramme**) kilo.
kilocalorie [kilɔkalɔri] *nf* kilocalorie.
kilocycle [kilɔsikl] *nm* kilocycle.
kilofranc [kilɔfrɑ̃] *nm Fin* = a thousand francs.
kilog [kilɔg] *nm Vieilli* kilogram(me).
kilogramme [kilɔgram] *nm* kilogram(me).
kilohertz [kilɔɛrts] *nm* kilohertz.
kilojoule [kilɔʒul] *nm* kilojoule.
kilométrage [kilɔmetraʒ] *nm* **(a)** measuring (*of road etc*) in kilometres *or US* kilometers; **(b)** marking (*of road*) with kilometre stones; **(c)** (*distance*) length in kilometres, ≈ mileage.
kilomètre [kilɔmɛtr] *nm* kilometre, *US* kilometer; *Rail Admin* **voyageurs-kilomètres,** passenger kilometres; *F* **bouffer** *ou* **avaler du k.,** to eat up the miles.
kilomètre-passager [kilɔmɛtrpasaʒe] *nm Admin Av* passenger-kilometre *or US* -kilometer; (*pl kilomètres-passagers*).
kilométrer [kilɔmetre] *vt* **(je kilomètre, n. kilométrons; je kilométrerai) (a)** to measure (*road etc*) in kilometres *or US* kilometers; **(b)** to mark off (*road*) with kilometre stones.
kilomètre-voyageur [kilɔmɛtrvwajaʒœr] *nm Admin* passenger-kilometre *or US* -kilometer; (*pl kilomètres-voyageurs*).
kilométrique [kilɔmetrik] *adj* kilometric; **borne k.,** kilometre *or US* kilometer stone; ≈ milestone; *Aut* **indemnité k.,** ≈ mileage allowance.
kilo-octet [kilɔɔktɛ] *nm Ordinat* kilobyte; (*pl kilo-octets*).
kilotonne [kilɔtɔn] *nf* kiloton.
kilovolt [kilɔvɔlt] *nm Vieilli* kilovolt.
kilowatt [kilɔwat] *nm* kilowatt.
kilowattheure [kilɔwatœr] *nm Él* kilowatt-hour.
kilt [kilt] *nm* kilt.
kimono [kimɔno] *nm* kimono; **manche k.,** kimono sleeve.
kinase [kinaz] *nf Biol Ch* kinase.

kiné [kine] *n F* physio.
kinésithérapeute [kineziterapøt] *n* physiotherapist.
kinésithérapie [kineziterapi] *nf* physiotherapy.
kinesthésie [kinɛstezi] *nf* kin(a)esthesia, kinesthesis.
king-charles [kiŋʃarl] *nm inv* King Charles spaniel.
kinkajou [kɛ̃kaʒu] *nm* kinkajou, honey bear.
kiosque [kjɔsk] *nm* **(a)** (*pavillon*) kiosk; **k. de** *ou* **à musique,** bandstand; **k. à journaux,** newspaper kiosk; **(b)** (*d'un sous-marin*) conning-tower; **k. de la barre,** (*d'un navire*) wheelhouse; **k. de veille/de navigation,** pilot house, chart house *or* room; **(c)** *Él* **k. de transformation,** transformer box *or* tower.
kipper [kipœr] *nm* kipper.
kir [kir] *nm* kir (= *blackcurrant cordial and white wine*).
kirghise, kirghize [kirgiz] **1** *adj* K(h)irghiz. **2** *nm Ling* K(h)irgiz. **3** *n* **K.,** K(h)irgiz.
kirsch [kirʃ] *nm* kirsch.
kit [kit] *nm* (home assembly) kit; **étagère vendue en k.,** shelf unit sold in kit form, shelf unit sold for home assembly.
kitchenette [kitʃənɛt] *nf* kitchenette.
kit(s)ch [kitʃ] *adj & nm inv* kitsch.
kiwi [kiwi] *nm* **(a)** (*oiseau*) kiwi; **(b)** (*fruit*) kiwi fruit, Chinese gooseberry.
klaxon [klaksɔn] *nm Aut* horn, hooter.
klaxonner [klaksɔne] *vi Aut* to hoot (one's horn), to sound one's horn.
klebs [klɛp(s)] *nm Arg* = **CLEBS**.
kleenex ® [klinɛks] *nm inv* Kleenex ®, paper tissue, paper hanky.
kleptomane [klɛptɔman] *adj & n* = **CLEPTOMANE**.
kleptomanie [klɛptɔmani] *nf* = **CLEPTOMANIE**.
klystron [klistrɔ̃] *nm Électron* klystron.
km (*abrév* **kilomètre(s)**) km.
km/h (*abrév* **kilomètres (à l')heure**) km.p.h.
knock-out [nɔkaut] *Boxe* **1** *adj inv* **mettre (qn) k.-o.,** to knock (s.o.) out; **être k.-o.,** to be knocked out. **2** *nm* knockout.
knout [knut] *nm* knout.
k.o. [kao] *abrév* **knock-out**.
koala [kɔala] *nm* koala (bear).
kobold [kɔbɔld] *nm* kobold.
kola [kɔla] *nm* (*fruit*) cola, kola; **noix de k.,** kola nut.
kolatier [kɔlatje] *nm* (*arbre*) cola (tree), kola (tree).
kolkhoze [kɔlkoz] *nm* kolkhoz, collective farm (*in the USSR*).
komintern [kɔmintɛrn] *nm Pol Hist* comintern.
kopeck [kɔpɛk] *nm* kopeck.
Koran (le) [ləkɔrɑ̃] *nm* = **CORAN**.
korrigan, -ane [kɔrigɑ̃, -an] *n* (*in Brittany*) goblin.
koudou [kudu] *nm* kudu; **grand k.,** greater kudu.
kouglof [kuglɔf] *nm Culin* kugelhopf.
koukri [kukri] *nm* kukri, Gurkha knife.
koulak [kulak] *nm* kulak.
Kourile [kuril] **1** *adj* **les îles Kouriles,** the Kuril(e) Islands. **2** *n* Kurile, Kurilian.
Koweït [kɔwɛjt] *nm* Kuwait.
koweïtien, -ienne [kɔwɛjtjɛ̃, ɛn] **1** *adj* Kuwaiti. **2** *n* **K.,** Kuwaiti.
kraal [kral] *nm* kraal.
krach [krak] *nm* (financial) crash; **il a perdu tout ce qu'il possédait dans le k. de sa banque,** he lost everything when his bank crashed *or* went bust.
kraft [kraft] *nm* kraft; **papier k.,** brown wrapping paper.
kraken [krakɛn] *nm* kraken.
Kremlin (le) [ləkrɛmlɛ̃] *nm* the Kremlin.
kremlinologie [krɛmlinɔlɔʒi] *nf* kremlinology, study of the government of the Soviet Union.
kremlinologue [krɛmlinɔlɔg] *n* Kremlin watcher, Kremlinologist.
kriss [kris] *nm* kris, Malay dagger.
krypton [kriptɔ̃] *nm Ch* krypton.
ksar [ksar] *nm* fortress, fortified village (*in North Africa*); (*pl ksour* [ksur]).
kumquat [kɔmkwat] *nm* (*fruit*) kumquat, cumquat.
Kurde [kyrd] **1** *adj* Kurdish. **2** *nm Ling* kurdish. **3** *n* **K.,** Kurd.
Kurdistan [kyrdistɑ̃] *nm* Kurdistan.
kurtosis [kyrtozis] *nm* kurtosis.
kW *Él* (*abrév* **kilowatt**) kW.
K-way [kawɛ] *nm* waterproof (jacket), cagoule, *Am* K-way.
kWh *El* (*abrév* **kilowatt(s)-heure**) kWh.
kymographe [kimɔgraf] *nm Méd etc* kymograph.
kymrique [kimrik] *adj & nm* = **CYMRIQUE**.
kyrie [kirje] *nm Rel* Kyrie (eleison).
kyrielle [kirjɛl] *nf* **(a)** long string (*of words etc*); **une k. de reproches,** a long list *or* stream of reproaches; **une k. d'insultes,** a torrent of abuse; *F* **une k. de pièces/de photos,** a whole series of rooms/photos; **(b)** *Arch* litany.
kyste [kist] *nm Méd* cyst; **k. synovial,** ganglion.
kystique [kistik] *adj Méd* cystic.

L

L, l [ɛl] *n* **(a)** (the letter) L, l; **(b)** *Ling* **l. mouillé(e),** liquid l, palatal(ized) l; **(c)** *Fin* **L,** £.

l *abrév* **(a)** (**litre**) l; **(b)** (**livre**) bk.

l', la¹ [la] *déf article & pron f see* **LE¹,²**.

la² *nm inv Mus* **(a)** (*note*) A; **donner le la,** to give the *or* an A; *Fig* **les premières lignes donnent le la du livre,** the opening lines set the tone of the book; **(b)** (*tonalité*) lah (*in tonic sol-fa*).

là [la] **1** *adv* **(a)** (*dans un endroit précis*) there; **là où vous êtes,** where you are; **quand il n'est pas là,** when he isn't there *or* here, when he's away; **est-ce que le patron est là?,** is the boss in?; **de là au village il y a un kilomètre,** it's one kilometre from there to the village; **à cinq pas de là se tenait l'agent de police,** five paces away stood the policeman; *F* **ôtez-vous de là!,** get out of there!; **passez par là,** go that way; **là en bas,** down there; *F* **elle a trente-cinq ans, par là,** she's about thirty-five; **il est là,** (*présent*) he's here; **viens là!,** come here!;

(b) (*à ce point*) **les choses en sont là,** that's how things stand at the moment; **la question n'est pas là,** that's not the point;

(c) c'est là qu'il demeure, that's where he lives; **c'est là où nous ne sommes plus d'accord,** that's where we disagree; **c'est là qu'elle fut interrompue,** that's where *or* when she was interrupted, it was at that moment that she was interrupted;

(d) (*à ce moment, ici*) **que vois-je là? mes gants!,** if it isn't my gloves!; **que dites-vous là?,** what's that you're saying?; (*qu'est-ce que vous voulez dire?*) what are you saying?;

(e) ce ...-là, that ...; **ces ... -là,** those ...; **ces gens-là sont ennuyeux,** those people are boring; **il est bête à ce point-là?,** is he (really) that stupid?; *see also* **CE¹ 1, CE² 5; CELUI-LÀ, CELLE-LÀ,** *see* **CELUI 4**;

(f) *Iron* **il se pose là, comme plombier!,** he's an absolutely hopeless plumber!; *F* **il est un peu là,** he makes his presence felt; (*on ne peut éviter de le voir*) you can't miss him; **comme menteur il est un peu là!,** he's a pretty good liar!;

(g) (*ce moment*) then; **d'ici là,** between now and then, in the meantime; **à quelques jours de là,** some days after (that), a few days later;

(h) (*ceci, ça*) **de là à croire que tout est facile, il y a loin,** it's a long way to believing everything is easy; **qu'entendez vous par là?,** what do you mean by that?; **de là on peut conclure que ...,** from this one can conclude that ....

2 *int* **(a)** (*doucement*) **hé là! doucement!,** gently does it!; **là, là! ne vous inquiétez pas,** there now, don't you worry; **là, là!,** (*to child*) there, there;

(b) oh là là!, oh dear!; (*jeeringly*) look at him *or* her!;

(c) alors là, ce n'est pas étonnant!, well, THAT'S not surprising!;

(d) oh là!, s'il vous plaît!, hey, (you,) excuse me!

là-bas [laba] *adv* over there; **le voilà là-b.,** there he is over there.

label [labɛl] *nm* **(a)** *Com* = mark, label (*on article, on published work etc*) certifying that it was manufactured in working conditions of an agreed standard; **le produit porte un l. de qualité/de garantie,** the product has *or* bears a quality/guarantee label; **(b)** *Fig* label, stamp; seal (*of approval*); **cet homme d'affaires a un l. politique très marqué,** this businessman has a very clear political affiliation.

labeur [labœr] *nm* **(a)** *Litt* labour, *Am* labor, toil, hard work; **(b)** *Typ* **imprimerie de l.,** book printing works.

labial, -ale, -iaux [labjal, -jo] **1** *adj* **(a)** *Anat* labial (*muscle etc*); **(b)** *Ling* **consonne labiale,** labial. **2** *nf Ling* **labiale,** labial.

labié [labje] *adj Bot* labiate, lipped.

labiodental, -ale, -aux [labjɔdɑ̃tal, -o] *Ling* **1** *adj* labiodental. **2** *nf* **labiodentale,** labiodental.

labo [labo] *nm F* lab; **l. de langues,** language lab; **les élèves qui font du l.,** pupils doing lab work.

laborantin, -ine [labɔrɑ̃tɛ̃, -in] *n* laboratory assistant.

laboratoire [labɔratwar] *nm* laboratory; **l. de recherche/de langues,** research/language laboratory; **l. d'analyses (médicales),** pathology laboratory; **l. spatial/orbital,** spacelab/orbiting laboratory.

laborieusement [labɔrjøzmɑ̃] *adv* laboriously; **gagner l. sa vie,** to work hard for a living.

laborieux, -euse [labɔrjø, -øz] *adj* **(a)** (*difficile*) arduous, hard; (*détaillé*) painstaking; *Péj* laboured, *Am* labored, laborious (*style etc*); *F* **il n'a pas encore fini? c'est l.!,** hasn't he finished yet? it's taking a long time *or* he's making heavy weather of it!; **(b)** (*travailleur*) hard-working; **les masses laborieuses,** the toiling masses.

labour [labur] *nm Agr* **(a)** (*labourage*) ploughing, *Am* plowing, tilling; **l. à la bêche,** digging; **cheval de l.,** plough horse, *Am* plow horse; **(b) labours,** ploughed *or Am* plowed land; **le semeur dans les labours,** the sower in his ploughed *or Am* plowed fields.

labourable [laburabl] *adj Agr* ploughable, *Am* plowable (*land*).

labourage [laburaʒ] *nm Agr* ploughing, *Am* plowing, tilling.

labourer [labure] **1** *vt* **(a)** *Agr* to plough, *Am* to plow, to till; **l. la terre à la bêche,** to turn over the soil; **le char laboure le chemin,** the tank churns up the ground; **(b)** *Nau* **l. le fond,** (*of ship*) to graze the bottom; (*of anchor*) to drag; **(c) visage labouré de rides,** face furrowed with wrinkles. **2 se labourer** *vpr* **se l. les mains,** to lacerate one's hands.

laboureur [laburœr] *nm Agr* ploughman, *Am* plowman.

labrador [labradɔr] *nm* Labrador (retriever).

labyrinthe [labirɛ̃t] *nm* **(a)** labyrinth, maze; *Fig* **le l. de l'administration,** the administrative labyrinth; **(b)** *Anat* labyrinth (of the ear).

labyrinthique [labirɛ̃tik] *adj* labyrinthine.

lac [lak] *nm Géog* lake; **l. de cirque,** tarn; **les lacs d'Écosse,** the Scottish lochs; **le l. Léman** *ou* **de Genève,** Lake Geneva; **l. artificiel,** (artificial) lake; (*pour fournir de l'eau*) reservoir; **l. de montagne,** mountain lake.

laçage [lasaʒ] *nm* lacing (up) (*of shoes etc*).

lacer [lase] **1** *vt* (**je laçai(s); n. laçons**) to lace (up) (*shoes etc*). **2 se lacer** *vpr* **ce corset se lace sur le côté,** this corset laces (up) at the side.

lacération [laserɑsjɔ̃] *nf* **(a)** laceration; tearing (up), ripping (up); *Méd* lacerating, laceration; (*avec un couteau*) slashing; mauling (*by wild beast*); **(b)** tear; (*blessure*) jagged wound.

lacérer [lasere] *vt* (**je lacère, n. lacérons; je lacérerai**) to tear (*papers, clothes*) (to pieces); (*avec un couteau*) to slash; *Méd* to lacerate; (*d'un animal sauvage*) to maul; **la douleur lui lacère le dos,** the pain is like a knife in his back.

lacet [lasɛ] *nm* **(a)** (*de chaussures*) lace; **chaussures à lacets,** lace-up shoes, lace-ups; **(b)** (*tournant*) (hairpin) bend, sharp bend (*in road*); **sentier en lacets,** winding *or* twisting *or* zigzag path; **la route monte en lacets,** the road winds steeply up; **(c)** *Nau* (*cordage*) swaying, rocking (*of vehicle*); **(d)** *Tech Av* yaw(ing); **axe de l.,** yaw axis; **(e)** *Couture* braid; **(f)** (*piège*) noose, snare (*for rabbits etc*); **tendre un l.,** to set a snare.

lâchage [lɑʃaʒ] *nm* dropping (*of parachutist etc*).

lâche [lɑʃ] *adj* **(a)** (*non serré, large*) loose, slack (*spring, knot etc*); loosely fitting (*garment*); lax (*discipline*); woolly, slipshod, careless (*style*); **(b)** *Litt* (*mou*) weak, feeble (*character etc*); **(c)** *Péj* (*traître*) cowardly; **(d)** *Péj* (*méprisable*) low, despicable.

lâché [lɑʃe] *adj* slovenly, slipshod (*work, style*).

lâchement [lɑʃmɑ̃] *adv* **(a)** (*non serré*) loosely, slackly;

(b) (*sans courage*) like a coward.

lâcher¹ [lɑʃe] **1** *vt* **(a)** (*détendre*) to release; to slacken, to loosen (*spring etc*); *Aut* **l. le frein,** to release the brake; *Fig* **l. la bride à un élève,** to allow a pupil more freedom, to give a pupil his head;

(b) (*ne plus tenir*) to let go (of), to leave go of (*sth*); (*laisser tomber*) to drop (*sth*); *Av* to release, to drop (*bomb, parachutist*); **lâchez-moi!,** let me go!, let go of me!; **l. sa proie,** (*of bird*) to drop its prey; **il ne lâcha pas la corde,** he did not let go of the rope; **l. ses études,** to give up one's studies; **l. pied,** to give way, to give in; *F* **l. qn,** to drop *or* ditch s.o.; to jilt (*a lover*); *F* **il ne m'a pas lâché d'une semelle,** he stuck to me like a leech; *F* **l. des sous,** *Arg* **les l.,** to fork out;

(c) (*libérer*) to set free (*prisoner, bird etc*); to let (*animal*) loose; to let out (*scream etc*); **l. un chien,** to unleash a dog, to let a dog loose; (*à la chasse*) to slip a dog; **l. le chien contre qn,** to set the dog on s.o.; *Arg* **l. le paquet** *ou* **le morceau,** to tell the truth, to come clean.

2 *vi* (*of spring etc*) to slacken; (*of rope*) to break; **mes freins ont lâché,** my brakes failed; *Fig* **ses nerfs ont lâché,** he broke down, his nerves gave way.

lâcher² *nm* release (*of pigeons etc*).

lâcheté [lɑʃte] *nf* **(a)** (*couardise*) cowardice, cowardliness; **il se tait par l.,** he keeps quiet out of cowardice; **(b)** *Litt* (*faiblesse, mollesse*) weakness; (*négligence*) slackness; **(c)** (*bassesse*) cowardice.

lâcheur, -euse [lɑʃœr, -øz] *n F* unreliable person; **c'est un l.,** he's unreliable.

lacis [lasi] *nm* network (*of nerves, wire etc*); **l. de ruelles,** maze of back streets.

laconique [lakɔnik] *adj* laconic.

laconiquement [lakɔnikmɑ̃] *adv* laconically.

laconisme [lakɔnism] *nm* lacon(ic)ism.

lacrymal, -aux [lakrimal, -o] *adj* lachrymal (*duct etc*); **glande lacrymale,** tear gland.

lacrymogène [lakrimɔʒɛn] *adj* **gaz l./grenade l.,** tear gas/tear gas grenade.

lacs [lɑ] *nm* **(a) l. d'amour,** love knot; **(b)** *Arch & Litt* (*piège*) noose.

lactaire [laktɛr] **1** *adj* lacteal. **2** *nm* (*champignon*) lactarius; **l. délicieux,** saffron milk cap.

lactation [laktɑsjɔ̃] *nf* **(a)** *Physiol* lactation; **(b)** (*allaitement*) suckling, nursing.

lacté [lakte] *adj* lacteal, milky; **régime l.,** milk diet; *Astron* **voie lactée,** milky way.

lactifère [laktifɛr] *adj Anat* lactiferous; lacteal (*duct*).

lactique [laktik] *adj Ch* lactic (*acid*).

lactose [laktoz] *nf Ch* lactose.

lacunaire [lakynɛr] *adj* **(a) documentation l.,** incomplete documentation; **des informations lacunaires,** incomplete *or* insufficient information; **(b)** *Anat Bot* (*incomplet*) lacunar(y), lacunal.

lacune [lakyn] *nf* **(a)** (*manque*) lacuna, gap, hiatus (*in text etc*); break (*in succession etc*); blank (*in memory etc*); **cette liste comporte plusieurs lacunes,** there are several items missing on this list; **(b)** *Biol Anat* lacuna; *Bot* air cell.

lacuneux, -euse [lakynø, -øz] *adj* = **LACUNAIRE.**

lacustre [lakystr] *adj* lacustrine, lacustrian (*animal, dwelling*); **habitation l.,** lake dwelling, pile dwelling.

lad [lad] *nm* stable lad, boy.

là-dedans [lad(ə)dɑ̃] *adv* inside; (*dans un lieu, objet indiqué*) in there; (*dans une boîte, un sac*) in it, in this; *F* **debout là-d.!,** rise and shine!

là-dessous [latsu] *adv* under that, under there, underneath; *Fig* **il y a un secret là-d.,** something is being kept secret.

là-dessus [latsy] *adv* on that, on it; **tout le monde est d'accord là-d.,** everybody is agreed about that; **là-d., il est sorti,** thereupon *or* with that he went out; **nous reviendrons là-d.,** we shall come back to that.

ladre [ladr] **1** *adj* **(a)** *Vét* measly, measled (*pig*); **(b)** *Arch* leprous; **(c)** *Arch* (*avare*) niggardly, miserly, stingy. **2** *n Arch* **(a)** (*lépreux*) leper; **(b)** *Litt* (*avare*) niggard, miser, skinflint.

ladrerie [ladrəri] *nf* **(a)** *Vét* measles (*of pigs*); **(b)** *Arch* (*léproserie*) leprosy; **(c)** *Arch & Litt* (*avarice*) meanness, stinginess.

lagon [lagɔ̃] *nm Géog* lagoon.

lagopède [lagɔpɛd] *nm Orn* lagopus; **l. des Alpes,** ptarmigan; **l. d'Écosse,** red grouse.

lagune [lagyn] *nf Géog* lagoon.

là-haut [lao] *adv* up there; (*à un étage supérieur*) upstairs.

lai¹ [lɛ] *nm Littér* lay.

lai² *adj Rel* **frère/sœur lai(e),** lay brother/sister.

laïc [laik] *adj & nm* = **LAÏQUE.**

laîche [lɛʃ] *nf Bot* sedge.

laïcisation [laisizɑsjɔ̃] *nf* laicization, secularization.

laïciser [laisize] *vt* to laicize, to secularize.

laïcisme [laisism] *nm* laicism.

laïcité [laisite] *nf* secularity (*of schools etc*); *Pol* secularism.

laid, laide [lɛ, lɛd] **1 (a)** *adj* ugly (*person, face, building*); ugly, unsightly (*blemish, stain*); *Euph* plain, *Am* homely (*girl, face*); *F* **l. comme un pou** *ou* **à faire peur,** as ugly as sin, *F* plug ugly; **(b)** (*choquant*) mean, low (*action etc*); ugly (*vice etc*); (*to child*) **c'est l. de mentir,** it's very naughty to tell lies. **2** *n* **(a)** (*physiquement*) plain *or Am* homely person; **(b)** *F* (*méchant*) **oh, le l.!/la laide!,** what a naughty boy/girl! **3** *nm* **le l. et le beau,** the ugly and the beautiful.

laidement [lɛdmɑ̃] *adv* **(a)** (*sans goût, mal*) in an ugly way; **(b)** (*ignoblement*) meanly, dishonestly.

laideron, -onne [lɛdrɔ̃, -ɔn] **1** *nm Péj* ugly *or* plain *or Am* homely girl *or* woman; **un petit l.,** an ugly duckling. **2** *adj* **une petite fille laideronne,** a plain little girl.

laideur [lɛdœr] *nf* **(a)** (*physique*) ugliness; unsightliness; plainness, *Am* homeliness (*of girl, features*); **d'une l. épouvantable,** horrifically ugly; **(b)** (*bassesse*) meanness, lowness (*of conduct etc*); **(c) les laideurs de la vie,** the ugly side of life.

laie¹ [lɛ] *nf* (wild) sow.

laie² *nf* forest track, ride.

laie³ *nf Tech* bush hammer.

lainage [lɛnaʒ] *nm* **(a)** (*étoffe*) woollen fabric; **(b)** (*article*) woollen garment *or* article; *F* woolly; **lainages,** woollen goods, woollens; **(c)** *Tex* teaseling; napping; **(d)** (*toison*) fleece.

laine [lɛn] *nf* **(a)** wool; **bêtes à l.,** woolly coated animals; *Tex* **l. cardée,** carding wool; **pure l.,** pure wool; **l. peignée,** worsted; **l. à tricoter,** knitting wool; **l. perlée,** crochet wool; **jupe en** *ou* **de l.,** woollen skirt; **tapis de haute l.,** thick pile wool carpet; **ensemble pure l.,** pure wool outfit; *Fig* **se laisser manger** *ou* **tondre la l. sur le dos,** to (let oneself) be fleeced; **(b) l. de bois,** wood fibre *or Am* fiber; **l. de verre,** glass wool; fibreglass, *Am* fiberglass.

lainer¹ [lɛne] *vt Tex* to teasel, to nap (*cloth*).

lainer² *nm Tex* nap (*of cloth*).

lainerie [lɛnri] *nf* **(a)** (*fabrication*) manufacture of woollens; **(b)** (*usine, atelier*) woollen mill; **(c)** (*magasin de gros*) (wholesale) wool shop.

laineur, -euse [lɛnœr, -øz] *n Tex* teaseler, napper.

laineux, -euse [lɛnø, -øz] *adj* fleecy (*cloth etc*); woolly (*sheep, hair etc*).

lainier, -ière [lɛnje, -jɛr] **1** *adj Com Ind* woollen (*trade etc*); **industrie lainière,** wool industry. **2** *n Ind* worker in a woollen mill; wool worker.

laïque [laik] **1** *adj* lay; secular (*education etc*); **école/enseignement l.,** = (non-religious) state school/education. **2** *n* layman; laywoman; lay person; **les laïques,** the laity.

lais [lɛ] *nm* **(a)** *Géog* **l. (de rivière),** alluvium; **(b)** (*ligne de marée*) foreshore.

laisse¹ [lɛs] *nf* leash, lead; (*à la chasse*) slip; **tenir un chien en l.,** to keep a dog on a lead *or* on the leash; *F* **mener** *ou* **tenir qn en l.,** to keep a tight rein on s.o..

laisse² *nf Géog* foreshore; **l. de haute/basse mer,** high-water/low-water mark.

laissé-pour-compte, laissée-pour-compte [lesepurkɔ̃t] (*pl laissés-pour-compte*) **1** *adj* **(a)** *Com* rejected, returned (*article*); unsold (*goods*); **(b)** (*non-désiré, non-voulu*) rejected, unwanted (*person*). **2** *nm Com* reject; unsold article. **3** *n* unwanted person; **les laissés-pour-compte, tous ceux qui restent seuls à Noël,** unwanted people, all those who are alone at Christmas.

laisser [lese] **1** *vt* **(a)** (*permettre*) to let, to allow; **il le laissa partir,** he let him go, he allowed him to go; **je les ai laissés dire,** I let them speak; **le toit laissait passer la pluie,** the roof let the rain in; **l. faire, l. passer,** live and let live; **l. voir son mécontentement,** to show one's displeasure *or* disapproval; **laisse-moi faire, ça ira plus vite,** (just) leave me to it *or* let me get on with it and it'll soon be done; **l. tomber qch,** to drop sth; *F* **laissez-moi rire!,** don't make me laugh!; **l. sécher la peinture,** to allow the paint to dry; **laissez-les boire un verre de vin,** let them have a glass of wine; **laisse faire,** never mind, don't bother; **laissez-le faire!,** leave it to him, let him get on with it; *F* **l. courir,** to leave (things) alone; **allons, laisse-toi faire!,** go on, be a devil!;

(b) (*quitter*) to leave (*s.o., sth, somewhere*); **vous n'allez pas me l. tout seul?,** you aren't going to leave me all on my own?; **allons, je vous laisse,** well, I'm going *or* I'm off; **merci, vous pouvez nous l.,** thank you, you may leave us *or* you may go; **il a laissé une veuve et trois enfants,** he left a widow and three children; **je vous laisse libre d'agir,** I leave you free to act; **nous l'avions laissé pour mort,** we had left him for dead; **laissez-moi (tranquille)!,** leave me alone!; **elle a laissé son mari,** she has left *or* walked out on her husband; **l. là qn,** to leave s.o. in the lurch; (*donner*) **partir sans l. d'adresse,** to go away without leaving one's address;

(c) (*ne pas prendre*) **l. qch de côté,** to leave sth out; to put sth aside; **laissez-lui son secret,** let him keep his secret; **laissez-lui du gâteau,** leave *or* save some cake for him; **l. le meilleur pour la fin,** to leave *or* save the best till the end; **c'est à prendre ou à l.,** take it or leave it;

(d) (*garder*) to leave, to keep (*s.o., sth in a certain state*); **l. qn derrière soi,** to leave s.o. behind (*in a subject etc*); **l. la fenêtre ouverte,** to leave *or* keep the window open; **laissons cela jusqu'à demain,** let's leave that until tomorrow; **laissez, c'est moi qui paie,** leave that, I'm paying;

(e) (*donner*) **je vous laisse le soin de le faire,** I'll leave it to you (to do it), I'll leave you to do it; **cela nous laisse le temps de ...,** that leaves us time to ...; **l. à qn un héritage,** to leave s.o. a legacy; **laissez-moi vos clefs,** leave me *or* let me have your keys; **je vous le laisse pour 100 francs,** you can have it for 100 francs;

(f) *Litt* **il ne laissera pas d'y aller,** he won't fail to go; **cela ne laisse pas de m'inquiéter,** I feel anxious all the same *or* nevertheless, I can't help worrying about it.

2 se laisser *vpr* **elle se laisse vivre,** she takes life as it comes; **se l. aller,** to let oneself go; **se l. décourager,** to let oneself be discouraged; **ne vous laissez pas aller comme ça!,** pull yourself together!; **se l. emporter par la colère,** to let one's anger get the better of one, to give way to anger; **elle se laissa embrasser,** she allowed herself to be kissed, she let herself be kissed, she let him *or* her *etc* kiss her; *F* **ce vin se laisse boire,** this wine is quite drinkable; **ce livre se laisse lire,** this book is easy to read.

3 *vi* **je vous laisse à penser notre bonheur,** you can imagine how happy we are *or* were; **ce scandale laisse à penser,** this scandal gives one plenty to think about; **cela laisse (beaucoup) à désirer,** it leaves much to be desired.

laisser-aller [lesealе] *nm inv* **(a)** (*désinvolture*) casualness; **le l.-a. des badauds,** the shameless curiosity of the onlookers; **(b)** *Péj* (*relâchement*) carelessness, slovenliness (*of appearance etc*); **il règne un sérieux l.-a. dans ce bureau,** there is a serious lack of discipline in this office.

laisser-faire [lesefɛr] *nm inv Pol* non-interference, laisser-faire, laissez-faire.

laissez-passer [lesepase] *nm inv* pass, permit; *Nau* sea pass.

lait [lɛ] *nm* **(a)** milk; **l. entier,** whole milk; **l. écrémé,** skimmed milk; **l. de beurre,** buttermilk; **petit l.,** whey; *Fig* **boire du petit l.,** to lap it up; **l. condensé,** condensed milk; **l. concentré,** evaporated milk; **l. en poudre,** dried milk; **l. caillé,** curd, curdled milk; **café au l.,** white coffee, *Br* coffee with milk; **chocolat au l.,** milk chocolate; *Culin* **l. de poule,** egg flip, egg nog (*without alcohol*); **vache à l.,** milch cow; *F* (*personne*) mug, sucker; **pot à l.,** milk jug; **l. maternel,** mother's milk; **dents de l.,** milk teeth; **frère/sœur de l.,** foster brother/sister; **cochon de l.,** suckling *or* sucking pig; **(b) l. de coco,** coconut milk; **(c) l. de chaux,** limewater, whitewash; **(d)** (*cosmétique*) **l. démaquillant,** cleansing milk; **l. bronzant,** artificial suntan cream.

laitage [lɛtaʒ] *nm* dairy produce; **on recommande au malade de prendre des laitages,** the patient is being recommended a milk(-based) diet.

laitance [lɛtɑ̃s] *nf*, **laite** [lɛt] *nf* (*de poisson*) milt; *Culin* soft roe.

laité [lete] *adj* soft-roed (*fish*).

laiterie [lɛtri] *nf* **(a)** (*coopérative*) (cooperative) dairy farm; **(b)** (*industrie*) dairy industry; (*usine*) factory producing dairy products; **(c)** (*crémerie*) dairy.

laiteron [lɛtrɔ̃] *nm Bot* sow thistle, milkweed.

laiteux, -euse [lɛtø, -øz] *adj* **(a)** *Méd* lacteal (*disorder etc*); **(b)** *Fig* milk-like; milky(-white) (*light etc*).

laitier[1], -ière [letje, lɛtjɛr] **1** *adj* **l'industrie laitière,** the milk *or* dairy industry; **produits laitiers,** dairy produce; **vache laitière,** milch cow. **2** *nf* **laitière,** milch cow. **3** *n* **(a)** (*livreur, -euse*) milkman; milkwoman; **(b)** *Com* dairyman; dairywoman.

laitier[2] *nm Métal etc* dross, slag.

laiton [lɛtɔ̃] *nm* brass; **(fil de) l.,** brass wire.

laitue [lety] *nf* **(a)** (*légume*) lettuce; **l. romaine,** cos lettuce; **(b)** *Culin* green salad.

laïus [lajys] *nm* **(a)** *F* (*discours*) speech, lecture; **faire un l.,** to make a speech, to hold forth; **(b)** *Péj* (*baratin*) **quel l.!, venons-en au fait!,** what a lot of waffle! let's get to the point!

lama[1] [lama] *nm Rel* (Buddhist) lama; **le Grand l., le dalaï-l.,** the Dalai Lama.

lama[2] *nm Zool Tex* llama.

lamanage [lamanaʒ] *nm Nau* inshore pilotage.

lamaneur [lamanœr] *nm Nau* inshore pilot.

lamantin [lamɑ̃tɛ̃] *nm Zool* manatee, seacow.

lamaserie [lamazri] *nf Rel* lamasery.

lambada [lɑ̃mbada] *nf Mus* lambada.

lambda [lɑ̃bda] *adj inv F* average; **un garçon l.,** an average boy.

lambeau, -eaux [lɑ̃bo] *nm* scrap, bit, shred (*of cloth, paper, flesh etc*); fragment (*of music, conversation etc*); **vêtements en lambeaux,** clothes in rags *or* in tatters; **mettre qch en lambeaux,** to tear sth up, to tear sth to shreds.

lambin, -ine [lɑ̃bɛ̃, -in] *F* **1** *adj* dawdling, slow. **2** *n* dawdler, slowcoach, *Am* slowpoke.

lambiner [lɑ̃bine] *vi F* to dawdle (along).

lambourde [lɑ̃burd] *nf* **(a)** (*d'arbre*) fruit shoot; **(b)** *Constr* wall plate, beam bearing; (*pour parquet*) bridging joist; bearing joist (*of flooring*).

lambrequin [lɑ̃brəkɛ̃] *nm* **(a)** *Hér* mantling, lambrequin; **(b)** (*de rideau*) valance, pelmet.

lambris [lɑ̃bri] *nm Constr* panelling; (*on wall*) wainscot(t)ing (*in wood*); casing, lining (*in marble etc*); **l. d'appui,** dado.

lambrissage [lɑ̃brisaʒ] *nm Constr* wainscot(t)ing, panelling (*of room*).

lambrisser [lɑ̃brise] *vt Constr* **(a)** (*revêtir de lambris*) to wainscot, to panel (*room etc*); **plafond lambrissé,** panelled ceiling; **(b)** to plaster (*wall, ceiling*).

lambswool [lɑ̃bswul] *nm Tex* lambswool; **un pull en l.,** a lambswool pullover.

lame [lam] *nf* **(a)** (*bande plate*) lamina, thin plate, strip, web (*of metal etc*); leaf (*of spring*); slide (*of microscope*); slat (*of venetian blind*); **l. de parquet,** strip of parquet flooring; **(b)** blade (*of sword, knife etc*); **l. de rasoir,** razor blade; **acheter un paquet de lames,** to buy a packet of razor blades; **une l.,** a sword; *Fig* **c'est une fine l.,** he's a fine swordsman; **visage en l. de couteau,** hatchet face; **(c)** *Bot* lamina; gill (*of mushroom*); *Anat* lamina; **(d)** (*vague*) wave; **l. de fond,** ground swell; **l. de houle,** roller, surge; **le creux de la l.,** the trough of a wave.

lamé [lame] **1** *adj* spangled, worked with silver *or* gold; **robe lamée d'or,** gold lamé dress. **2** *nm* **(robe en** *ou* **de) l. (d')or/(d')argent,** gold/silver lamé (dress).

lamellaire [lamelɛr] *adj Minér etc* lamellar, lamellate, foliated.

lamelle [lamɛl] *nf* **(a)** lamella (*of slate etc*); thin sheet, plate (*of iron etc*); scale, flake (*of mica etc*); *Bot* lamella, gill (*of mushroom*); **couper du fromage en lamelles,** to cut cheese into (wafer-) thin slices; **(b)** (*de microscope*) (microscope) slide.

lamellé [lamele], **lamelleux, -euse** [lamelø,-øz] *adj* lamellate(d); foliated, fissile (*slate etc*).

lamentable [lamɑ̃tabl] *adj* **(a)** lamentable, deplorable (*accident etc*); **sort l.,** terrible fate; **(b)** *Péj* (*déplorable, mauvais*) appalling, awful; **orateur l.,** pitiful speaker; **j'ai été l.,** I was hopeless; **(c)** (*triste*) mournful, woeful (*voice etc*).

lamentablement [lamɑ̃tabləmɑ̃] *adv* lamentably, miserably.

lamentation [lamɑ̃tasjɔ̃] *nf* **(a)** (*cri de douleur extrême*) lament; **cri de l.,** wail; **les lamentations d'une femme qui a perdu son enfant,** the wailing of a woman who has lost her child; **le mur des Lamentations,** the Wailing Wall (*in Jerusalem*); **(b)** *Péj* (*plainte, jérémiade*) moaning, complaining; **elle ne cesse de se répandre en lamentations,** she never stops complaining *or* moaning, she is continually pouring out (a stream of) complaints.

lamenter (se) [səlamɑ̃te] *vpr* **se l. sur son sort,** to bemoan *or* lament one's fate; **se l. de son ignorance,** to deplore *or* regret one's ignorance; **cesse donc de te l.!,** stop feeling sorry for yourself!

lamento [lamento] *nm Mus* lamento.

laminage [laminaʒ] *nm Métal* laminating, lamination, rolling, flatt(en)ing (*of metal etc*); **l. à chaude/à froid,** hot-/cold-rolling.

laminer [lamine] *vt* **(a)** (*Métal*) to laminate, to flatten, to roll (*metal*); **(b)** *Fig* (*écraser, diminuer*) **ses revenus sont**

laminés par les impôts, his income is eaten away *or* gobbled up by taxes; **se faire l. par les soucis, être laminé d'inquiétude,** to be worn *or* ground down by worries *or* worry.
lamineur [laminœr] **1** *adj* laminating; **cylindre l.,** roller. **2** *nm* rolling mill operator; laminator.
laminoir [laminwar] *nm* **(a)** *Métal* flatting mill, rolling mill; **l. de finissage,** finishing rolls; *Fig* **faire passer qn au l.,** to put s.o. through the mill; **(b)** (*pour le papier*) plate glazing calender.
lampadaire [lɑ̃padɛr] *nm* **(a)** (*lampe sur haut support*) standard lamp; **(b)** (*réverbère*) street lamp.
lampant [lɑ̃pɑ̃] *adj Pétr* **pétrole l.,** paraffin, *Am* kerosene.
lamparo [lɑ̃paro] *nm Pêche* lamp (*used to attract fish*); **aller à la pêche au l.,** to go fishing by lamplight.
lampe [lɑ̃p] *nf* **(a)** (*appareil d'éclairage*) **l. à huile,** oil lamp, paraffin lamp; *Min* **l. de mineur** *ou* **de sécurité,** miner's (safety) lamp; **l. à pétrole,** oil lamp, paraffin lamp, *Am* kerosene lamp; **l. à gaz,** gas lamp; **l. de camping,** camping gas lamp; **à (la lumière de) la l.,** by lamplight; *Arg* **s'en mettre plein la l.,** to have a good blowout; **(b)** *Él* **l. halogène,** halogen lamp; **l. à incandescence,** incandescent lamp; **l. à arc,** arc lamp; **l. au néon,** neon lamp; **l.-témoin,** pilot light (*on an electrical appliance*); **l. de bureau,** reading light; desk light *or* lamp; **l. de chevet,** bedside lamp; **l. de poche,** (electric) torch, *Am* flashlight; *Cin* **l. à lueurs,** glowlamp; *Phot* **l. éclair,** flashlight; **l. à bronzer,** sun lamp; **(c)** *Électron* **l. (de radio),** (radio) valve *or Am* tube; **l. d'amplification,** amplifying tube; **(d) l. à alcool,** spirit lamp; **l. à souder,** blowlamp, blowtorch.
lampée [lɑ̃pe] *nf F* gulp, swig (*of water, wine etc*); **finir son verre d'une seule l.,** to down (the rest of) one's drink in one.
lamper [lɑ̃pe] *vt* to swig, to toss off, to gulp down.
lampe-tempête [lɑ̃ptɑ̃pɛt] *nf* storm lantern; (*pl lampes-tempêtes*).
lampion [lɑ̃pjɔ̃] *nm* (*lanterne*) fairylight (*for illuminations*); **les lampions des bals populaires,** the paper lanterns *or* Chinese lanterns at local dances; *F* **crier sur l'air des lampions,** to chant (*slogan etc*).
lampiste [lɑ̃pist] *nm* **(a)** *Tech* light maintenance man; *Rail* lampman; **(b)** *Fig* (*subalterne*) *F* underling; (*dupe*) scapegoat, *Am* fall guy; **s'en prendre au l.,** to bully one's subordinate(s); **(c)** *Arch* lamp maker; lamp seller.
lampisterie [lɑ̃pistəri] *nf* **(a)** *Rail etc* lamp room; **(b)** *Arch* (*industrie*) lamp trade; (*fabrique*) lamp works.
lamproie [lɑ̃prwa] *nf* lamprey.
lance [lɑ̃s] *nf* **(a)** (*pique*) spear; **percer un animal d'un coup de l.,** to spear an animal; **fer de l.,** spearhead; **la construction automobile a longtemps été le fer de l. de l'industrie française,** car assembly has long been the flagship of French industry; *Bot* **en fer de l.,** lanceolate; **(b)** *Fig* **rompre une l.** *ou* **des lances avec** *ou* **contre qn,** to cross swords with s.o.; *Fig* **rompre des lances pour qn,** to take up the cudgels for s.o., to defend s.o.; **(c)** *Tech* **l. d'arrosage,** water-hose nozzle; **l. d'incendie,** fire-hose nozzle.
lancé [lɑ̃se] *adj* **train l. à toute vapeur,** train going at full speed; **le voilà l. (dans la vie),** now he's got a start (in life); **la voilà lancée (sur son sujet favori),** *F* now she's off on her pet subject; **jeune homme l.,** young man who has achieved (social) success *or* who has made his name *or F* who has made it.
lance-bombes [lɑ̃sbɔ̃b] *nm inv Av* bomb launcher.
lancée [lɑ̃se] *nf* momentum, impetus; **continuer sur sa l.,** to keep going, to forge ahead.
lance-flammes [lɑ̃sflam] *nm inv Mil* flamethrower.
lance-fusées [lɑ̃sfyze] *nm inv Mil* rocket launcher.
lance-grenades [lɑ̃sgrənad] *nm inv Mil* grenade launcher.
lancement [lɑ̃smɑ̃] *nm* **(a)** (*projection*) throwing, flinging; launching (*of missile, rocket*); dropping, releasing (*of bomb etc*); throwing, launching (*of grenade*); sending up (*of balloon*); **l. du javelot/du disque,** throwing the javelin/the discus; **l. du poids,** putting the shot; **procéder au l. du missile/de la fusée,** to go ahead with the launch(ing) of the missile/rocket; **rampe de l.,** launching ramp; **dégager l'aire de l.,** to clear the launch(ing) area; **(b)** *Nau* launching (*of ship*); **(c)** *MecE* starting (up) (*of engine*); **(d)** *Com* launch(ing) (*of product*); *Bourse* floating (*of company*); **une campagne de l.,** a campaign to launch a new product.
lance-missiles [lɑ̃smisil] *nm inv Mil* missile launcher.
lancéolé [lɑ̃seɔle] *adj Bot* lanceolate.
lance-pierre(s) [lɑ̃spjɛr] *nm inv* catapult; *Fig F* **manger avec un l.-p.,** to wolf one's food (down).
lancer¹ [lɑ̃se] **1** *vt* (**je lançai(s); n. lançons**) **(a)** (*projeter*) to throw, to fling, to hurl; *Litt* to cast; to shoot (*an arrow*); to send up, to launch (*a rocket*); to release (*bomb etc*); to send up (*balloon*); **l. des pierres à qn,** to throw stones at s.o.; **l. des bombes,** (*of aircraft*) to drop bombs; **l. de la fumée,** to puff out smoke; **l. des étincelles,** to shoot out sparks; **le volcan en éruption lance des pierres,** the erupting volcano throws out *or* spews out rocks; *Pêche* **l. la ligne,** to cast the line; **l. qch en l'air,** to toss sth into the air; **une proposition que j'ai lancée à tout hasard,** a suggestion that I made *or* mooted just on the off-chance; **l. un coup d'œil à qn,** to dart *or* shoot a glance at s.o.; **l. un mandat d'arrêt contre qn,** to issue a warrant for s.o.'s arrest; **l. un juron,** to let out a swearword;
(b) *Sp* to throw (*a ball*); *Baseball* to pitch; **l. le disque/le javelot,** to throw the discus/the javelin; **l. le poids,** to put the shot;
(c) (*envoyer*) **l. un cheval,** to start a horse off at full gallop; **l. un chien contre qn,** to set a dog on s.o.; *Fig* **si vous le lancez sur ce sujet il ne s'arrêtera plus,** if you start him (off) on this subject he will never stop;
(d) to launch (*ship, scheme, attack, company*); *Bourse* to float (*company*); to launch (*actor, career etc*); to initiate, to launch, to set (*fashion*); **l. une marchandise,** to launch a (new) product; **l. une souscription,** to start a fund; **l. qn (dans les affaires/etc),** to give s.o. a start, to set s.o. up (in business/*etc*);
(e) (*faire démarrer*) to start (up) (*engine*);
2 *vi* **(a)** to throw; *Cr* to bowl; *Baseball* to pitch;
(b) une douleur qui lance, a throbbing pain.
3 se lancer *vpr* **(a)** (*se jeter*) **le malheureux s'est lancé dans le vide,** the poor wretch threw himself into the abyss; **se l. en avant,** to rush *or* dash *or* shoot forward; **se l. à la poursuite de qn,** to dash off in pursuit of s.o.;
(b) (*s'engager*) **se l. dans les affaires,** to launch out into business; **je reconnais m'être lancée dans cette affaire un peu vite,** I admit that I embarked on *or* got involved in this affair a little too hastily;
(c) (*se faire connaître*) **elle veut se l.,** she wants to make a name for herself.
lancer² *nm* **(a) (pêche au) l.,** casting; **(b)** *Sp* throw; *Baseball* pitch; **l. du javelot,** throwing the javelin; **l. du disque,** discus throwing; **l. du poids,** putting the shot.
lance-roquettes [lɑ̃srɔkɛt] *nm inv Mil* rocket launcher.
lance-satellites [lɑ̃ssatelit] *nm inv* satellite launcher.
lance-torpilles [lɑ̃stɔrpij] *nm inv Mil* **(tube) l.-t.,** torpedo tube.
lancette [lɑ̃sɛt] *nf* **(a)** *Chir* lancet; **(b)** *Archit* **(arc à) l.,** lancet arch.
lanceur, -euse [lɑ̃sœr, -øz] **1** *n* **(a)** (*personne qui jette*) thrower; *Cr* bowler; *Baseball* pitcher; **des petits lanceurs de pierres,** stone-throwing children, children throwing stones; *Sp* **l. de javelot,** javelin thrower; **(b)** *Com* (*promoteur*) promoter; *Bourse* floater (*of company etc*). **2** *nm* launcher (*of satellite, spacecraft etc*).
lancier [lɑ̃sje] *nm* **(a)** *Mil* lancer; **(b) (quadrille des) lanciers,** lancers; **danser les lanciers,** to dance *or* do the lancers.
lancinant [lɑ̃sinɑ̃] *adj* **(a)** (*d'une douleur*) shooting, throbbing; **(b)** (*obsédant*) haunting (*memory*); insistent; *Péj* monotonous (*tune*); **une curiosité lancinante,** (a) burning curiosity.
lanciner [lɑ̃sine] **1** *vi* (*of pain*) to shoot; (*of finger etc*) to throb. **2** *vt* to harass, to trouble.
lançon [lɑ̃sɔ̃] *nm* launce, sand eel.
landais, -aise [lɑ̃dɛ, -ɛz] **1** *adj* **le paysage l.,** the landscape of the Landes (region); **les races landaises,** breeds of cattle *or* sheep from the Landes (region). **2** *n* **L.,** inhabitant of the Landes (region).
landau [lɑ̃do] *nm* **(a)** (*voiture d'enfant*) *Br* pram, *Am* baby carriage; **(b)** *Vieilli* landau.
lande [lɑ̃d] *nf* **(a)** (*de terre*) moor, heath; (*à l'abandon*) waste, *Am* barren; **(b) les Landes,** the Landes (region) (*in south-west France*).
landier [lɑ̃dje] *nm* andiron, fire dog.
land rover ® [landrɔvɛr] *nf Aut* Land Rover ®.
langage [lɑ̃gaʒ] *nm* **(a)** *Ling* language; **l'étude du l.,** the study of language; **l'apprentissage du l.,** language learning, the acquisition of language;
(b) (*style, façon de s'exprimer*) language, speech; *Fig* **il faut traduire cela dans votre l.,** it needs to be translated into words that you can understand; **tenir un l. grossier à qn,** to speak rudely to s.o.; **vous tenez là un drôle de l.,** that's a strange way to talk; **changer de l.,** to change one's

tune; **en voilà un l.!,** that's no way to talk!; **surveillez votre l.!,** watch your language!; **l. administratif/scientifique,** official/scientific language *or Péj* jargon; **l. argotique/populaire,** slang/popular speech;

(c) (*code*) **le l. des fleurs,** the language of flowers; **l. chiffré,** cipher, code; **l. du corps,** body language;

(d) *Ordinat* **l. assembleur** *ou* **d'assemblage,** assembly language; **l. utilisateur,** user language; **l. machine,** machine language; **l. de programmation,** programming language; **l. interactif,** interactive language.

langagier, -ière [lɑ̃gaʒje, -jɛr] **1** *adj* linguistic; **les modes langagières des jeunes,** young people's linguistic fads. **2** *n Can* language professional.

lange [lɑ̃ʒ] *nm Br* nappy, *Am* diaper, *Arch* **langes,** swaddling clothes; *Fig* **être encore dans les langes,** to be still in its infancy.

langer [lɑ̃ʒe] *vt* (**je langeai(s); n. langeons**) to put a *Br* nappy *or Am* diaper on (*a baby*), *Arch* to wrap (*a baby*) in swaddling clothes.

langoureusement [lɑ̃gurøzmɑ̃] *adv* languorously; languishingly.

langoureux, -euse [lɑ̃gurø, -øz] *adj* languorous; (*languissant*) languishing.

langouste [lɑ̃gust] *nf* crayfish, crawfish.

langoustine [lɑ̃gustin] *nf* Dublin Bay prawn; *Culin* **langoustines,** scampi.

langue [lɑ̃g] *nf* **(a)** *Anat* tongue; **tirer la l.,** to stick out one's tongue (**à qn,** at s.o.); *F* to be very thirsty; *F* (*être dans le besoin*) to have one's tongue hanging out (*for sth*); (*se donner du mal*) to huff and puff; *Méd* **l. pâteuse,** coated tongue; *Culin* **l. de bœuf,** ox tongue;

(b) (*parole*) **délier la l. à qn,** to loosen s.o.'s tongue; **avoir la l. bien pendue,** to have a ready tongue *or F* the gift of the gab; **elle a la l. trop longue,** she can't keep her mouth shut, she talks too much; **il sait tenir sa l.,** he can keep a secret; **je l'avais sur le bout de la l.,** I had it on the tip of my tongue; **je donne ma l. au chat,** (*with reference to riddle etc*) I give up, I can't guess; **tu ne dis plus rien? tu as avalé ta l.?,** you've gone all quiet, (has the) cat got your tongue?; *F* **s'en mordre la l.,** to regret bitterly having spoken; **prendre l. avec qn,** to establish *or* make contact with s.o.; *F* **avoir un cheveu sur la l.,** to lisp, to have a (slight) lisp; **une mauvaise l.,** a backbiter, a scandalmonger; **une l. de vipère,** a spiteful gossip;

(c) (*chose allongée*) **langues de feu,** tongues of flame; **l. de terre,** strip *or* spit of land;

(d) *Ling* language, *Litt* tongue; **l. maternelle,** mother tongue; **langues étrangères,** foreign languages; **l. morte,** dead language; **elle parle deux langues couramment,** she speaks two (foreign) languages fluently; **professeur de langues vivantes,** modern language teacher, teacher of modern languages; **avoir le don des langues,** to be a good linguist; **peuples/pays de l. anglaise,** English-speaking people/countries; *Ling* **l. de départ,** source language; **l. d'arrivée** *ou* **cible,** target language; **la l. bien reconnaissable de Marguerite Duras,** the easily recognizable language of Marguerite Duras;

(e) (*jargon*) language; *Péj* jargon; **l. scientifique,** scientific language *or* jargon; **l. verte,** slang; *Fig* **les politiciens qui parlent la l. de bois,** politicians who mouth clichés.

langue-de-bœuf [lɑ̃gdəbœf] *nf* **(a)** (*champignon*) beefsteak fungus; **(b)** (*outil*) (heart-shaped) trowel; (*pl langues-de-bœuf*).

langue-de-cerf [lɑ̃gdəsɛr] *nf Bot* hart's tongue; (*pl langues-de-cerf*).

langue-de-chat [lɑ̃gdəʃa] *nf Culin* (flat) finger biscuit, langue-de-chat; (*pl langues-de-chat*).

languedocien, -ienne [lɑ̃gdɔsjɛ̃, -jɛn] **1** *adj* of Languedoc; **la région languedocienne,** the Languedoc region (*of southern France*). **2** *n* **L.,** inhabitant of the Languedoc (region).

languette [lɑ̃gɛt] *nf* **(a)** (*lichette*) small tongue (*of wood, metal, land, etc*); strip (*of tinfoil etc*); tongue (*of shoe*); thin slice (*of bread*); **(b)** *Menuis* **assemblage à rainure et l.,** feather joint; **(c)** *El* **contact à l.,** snap contact.

langueur [lɑ̃gœr] *nf* **(a)** (*apathie*) languor, languidness; (*sans plaisir*) listlessness; **se mourir de l.,** to pine away; **(b)** (*mélancolie douce, rêverie*) **regard plein de l.,** languishing look; **(c)** *Arch* **(maladie de) l.,** decline.

languide [lɑ̃gid] *adj* languid.

languir [lɑ̃gir] *vi* **(a)** (*désirer, attendre avec impatience*) **l. après qn/qch,** to long *or* pine *or* yearn for s.o./sth; **ne nous faites pas l.,** don't keep us on tenterhooks *or* in suspense; **je languis d'être avec vous,** I am longing *or* pining to be with you; **la conversation languit,** the conversation is flagging; *Région* **les affaires languissent,** business is slack; **(b)** (*se mourir*) to languish, to pine; *Litt* to waste away; (*of plant*) to wilt; **l. d'amour,** to be lovesick.

languissamment [lɑ̃gisamɑ̃] *adv Litt* languidly.

languissant [lɑ̃gisɑ̃] *adj* **(a)** (*ennuyeux, monotone*) languid, listless; lagging, dragging (*conversation*); **(b)** (*amoureux*) languishing (*eyes, look*).

lanière [lanjɛr] *nf* (thin) strap; lash (*of whip*); **découper qch en lanières,** to cut sth in strips.

lanifère [lanifɛr]**, lanigère** [laniʒɛr] *adj* wool-bearing.

lanoline [lanɔlin] *nf* lanoline.

lanterne [lɑ̃tɛrn] *nf* **(a)** lantern; **l. sourde,** dark lantern; **l. vénitienne,** paper lantern; **l. magique,** magic lantern; **l. chinoise,** Chinese lantern; *Fig* **elle veut nous faire prendre des vessies pour des lanternes,** she's trying to pull the wool over our eyes; **l. de projection,** (slide) projector; *F* **éclairer la l. de qn,** to enlighten s.o.; **(b)** (*de véhicule*) (side)light, *Am* parking light; **se mettre en lanternes,** to put one's (side)lights on; *Aut* **l. rouge,** rear *or* tail light (*of convoy*); *Arch* red light (*of brothel*); *Sp* **la l. rouge,** the back-marker, the last man in the race; *Rugby* the wooden spoon; *Fig* **cette équipe de traducteurs est la l. rouge de l'agence,** this team of translators are the slowcoaches of the agency; **(c)** *Arch* (*réverbère*) street lamp; *Hist Fr* (*during the Revolution*) **à la l.!,** string them up!; **(d)** *Archit* ridge turret; **la l. du dôme,** the lantern of the dome.

lanterneau, -eaux [lɑ̃tɛrno] *nm* skylight (*over staircase*).

lanterner [lɑ̃tɛrne] *vi F* (*traînailler*) to dawdle; **faire l. qn,** to keep s.o. hanging about *or* waiting.

laotien, -ienne [laɔsjɛ̃, -jɛn] **1** *adj* Laotian. **2** *n* **L.,** Laotian.

La Palice [lapalis] *nm* **vérité de La P.,** truism, statement of the obvious.

lapalissade [lapalisad] *nf voir* **LA PALICE**.

lapement [lapmɑ̃] *nm* lapping (up) (*of milk etc*).

laper [lape] **1** *vt* (*of dog, cat etc*) to lap (up) (*water, milk etc*). **2** *vi* to lap.

lapereau, -eaux [lapro] *nm* young rabbit.

lapidaire [lapidɛr] **1** *adj* lapidary (*inscription, style etc*); concise (*style*). **2** *nm* lapidary.

lapidation [lapidasjɔ̃] *nf* stoning.

lapider [lapide] *vt* to throw stones at (*s.o.*); (*mettre à mort*) to stone (*s.o.*) to death.

lapin, -ine [lapɛ̃, -in] *n* (buck) rabbit, *f* doe; **l. de garenne,** wild rabbit; **l. domestique** *ou* **de choux,** tame rabbit; *Culin* **un civet de l.,** (a) rabbit stew, jugged rabbit; *Com* **peau de l.,** cony (skin); *F* **poser un l. à qn,** to stand s.o. up; *F* **un drôle de l.,** a queer customer; *F* **un chaud l.,** a don Juan, a Casanova; *F* **c'est un fameux l.,** he's quite a guy; **se sauver** *ou* **courir comme un l.,** to run like hell; **coup du l.,** rabbit punch; *Méd* whiplash injury; **mon petit l.,** my darling, my lamb.

lapiner [lapine] *vi* (*of rabbit*) to litter.

lapinière [lapinjɛr] *nf* rabbit hutch.

lapis [lapis] *nm*, **lapis-lazuli** [lapislazyli] *nm inv* **1** *n Minér* lapis lazuli. **2** *adj inv* **ciel l.-l.,** bright blue sky.

lapon, -one [lapɔ̃, -ɔn] **1** *adj* Lapp. **2** *nm Ling* Lapp, Lappish. **3** *n* **L.,** Lapp, Laplander.

Laponie [lapɔni] *nf* Lapland.

laps¹ [laps] *nm* **un l. de temps,** a lapse *or* space of time.

laps² *adj Rel* (*used only in*) **être l. et relaps,** to have abandoned the Catholic faith.

lapsus [lapsys] *nm* slip (*of the tongue, pen*); **l. de mémoire,** lapse of memory; **faire un l.,** to make a slip (*of the tongue, pen*); **un l. révélateur,** a Freudian slip.

laquage [lakaʒ] *nm* lacquering.

laquais [lakɛ] *nm* flunkey, footman; *Péj* lackey.

laque [lak] **1** *nf* **(a)** (*naturelle*) lac; **l. en écailles,** shellac; **gomme l.,** gum lac; **(b)** (*vernis*) lake; **(c)** (*pour les cheveux*) (hair) lacquer, hair spray. **2** *nm* **(a)** (*vernis*) lacquer; **de** *ou* **en l.,** lacquered; **l. (de Chine),** japan; **(b) des laques,** lacquerware; **un l.,** a piece of lacquerware.

laqué [lake] *adj* **(a)** (*de laque naturelle*) japanned, lacquered; **(b)** (*vaporisé de fixateur*) lacquered (*hair*); **(c)** *Culin* **canard l.,** Peking duck.

laquer [lake] *vt* **(a)** (*de laque*) to lacquer, to japan; **(b)** (*de vernis*) to enamel; **meubles laqués de blanc,** white-enamelled furniture.

laqueur [lakœr] *nm* lacquerer, japanner.

larbin [larbɛ̃] *nm F souvent Péj* servant, flunkey; **je ne suis pas ton l., débrouille-toi tout seul!,** I'm not your servant, sort it out yourself!

larcin [larsɛ̃] *nm* **(a)** *Jur* (petty) theft; **(b)** (*objet volé*) loot;

ses larcins, his loot.

lard [lar] *nm* **(a)** bacon; (*gras*) fat; **barde de l.,** strip of bacon (*on roasting meat*); **l. maigre,** streaky bacon; **l. gras,** fatty bacon; **l. fumé,** smoked bacon; **omelette au l.,** bacon omelette; *Fig* **se demander si c'est du l. ou du cochon,** to wonder what to make of sth; **(b)** *Arg F* (*graisse*) **(se) faire du l.,** to (sit around and) get fat; **gros l.,** big fat slob; **tête de l.,** pigheaded idiot; *Fig* **rentrer dans le l. à qn,** to have a set-to with s.o.; **(c) pierre de l.,** soapstone, steatite; tailor's chalk.

larder [larde] *vt* to lard (*piece of meat*); **l. qn de coups de couteau,** to hack s.o. with a knife; *Tech* **l. un morceau de bois,** to stud a piece of wood with nails; **l. un texte de citations,** to lard *or* pepper a text with quotations.

lardoire [lardwar] *nf* **(a)** *Culin* larding needle, pin; **(b)** *F* sword.

lardon [lardɔ̃] *nm* **(a)** *Culin* lardon; **(b)** *Arg* (*enfant*) kid; **(c)** *Vieilli* jibe, cutting remark.

lare [lar] **1** *adj surtout* **les dieux lares,** lares. **2** *nm Antiq* household god.

largable [largabl] *adj Av* (*of container, equipment*) releasable.

largage [largaʒ] *nm* **(a)** *Av* dropping (*of parachutists, supplies etc*); releasing (*of bomb*); **(b)** *Fig F* (*renvoi*) **le l. d'une secrétaire incompétente,** the sacking of an incompetent secretary.

large [larʒ] **1** *adj* **(a)** (*grand, étendu*) broad, wide; **l. d'épaules,** broad-shouldered; **route l. de dix mètres,** road ten metres wide; **vêtements larges,** loose-fitting clothes; **d'un geste l.,** with a (broad) sweeping gesture; **terme employé dans un sens l.,** term used in a broad sense; **avoir l'esprit l.,** to be broad-minded; *Beaux-Arts* **style l.,** broad *or* bold *or* free style;

(b) (*important, considérable*) large, big; **de larges ressources,** ample resources; **dans une l. mesure, il est responsable,** to a large extent, he is responsible; **il a eu un l. rôle dans le remaniement du pays,** he played a considerable *or* major role in the transformation of the country;

(c) (*généreux*) **mener une vie l.,** to spend freely; **il n'a pas été très l.,** he wasn't very generous.

2 *nm* **(a)** (*espace*) room, space; **être au l.,** to have plenty of room; (*financièrement*) to be well off;

(b) *Nau* open sea; **brise du l.,** sea breeze; *F* **prendre le l.,** to decamp, to beat it; **gagner le l.,** to get to the open sea; **au l.!,** (*to small boat*) keep away!; **au l. de Cherbourg,** off Cherbourg; **trop au l.,** too far from the shore;

(c) (*largeur*) breadth; **route qui a dix mètres de l.,** road ten metres wide; **se promener de long en l.,** to walk up and down *or* to and fro; **il parcourut la pièce en long et en l.,** he walked up and down the room; *F* **il examina la question en long et en l.,** he went into all aspects of the question.

3 *adv* **calculer l.,** to allow a wide margin for error; **cette robe habille l.,** this dress is loose fitting; **voir l.,** to think big; **il n'en mène pas l., il est tout penaud,** he's all uptight and sheepish.

largement [larʒəmɑ̃] *adv* **(a)** (*dans l'espace*) broadly, widely; **la porte était l. ouverte,** the door was wide open; **opinion l. répandue,** widely held opinion; *Beaux-Arts* **peindre l.,** to paint in a free *or* broad style; **(b)** (*généreusement, amplement*) amply; **on l'a l. récompensé,** he has been amply *or* handsomely rewarded; **avoir l. de quoi vivre,** to have ample means; **services l. rétribués,** highly paid services; **avoir l. le temps,** to have plenty of time; **elle a l. quarante ans,** she's at least *or* easily forty (if not more); **il en a eu l. (assez),** he's had (more than) enough.

largesse [larʒɛs] *nf* **(a)** (*générosité*) generosity, largess(e) (**envers,** towards); **avec l.,** generously; **faire des largesses,** to make generous gifts; **(b)** *Arch* bounty; (*prodigalité*) largess(e); **faire l.,** to make handsome presents.

largeur [larʒœr] *nf* breadth, width; span (*of arch*); gauge (*of railway track*); breadth, beam (*of ship*); **avoir trois mètres de l.,** to be three metres wide; **en l., dans la l.,** widthwise, breadthwise; **distance en l.,** distance across; *Fig* **l. de vues/d'esprit,** broadness of outlook/of mind; *F* **dans les grandes largeurs,** in a big way, well and truly.

largo [largo] *Mus* **1** *adv* largo. **2** *nm* largo.

largue [larg] **1** *adj* **(a)** *Nau* (*of rope etc*) loose, slack; **(b)** (*of wind*) free; **naviguer vent l.,** to sail free. **2** *nm* **grand l.,** quartering (wind), (wind) on the quarter; **faire du l.,** to sail free, to sail off the wind, to run free.

larguer [large] *vt* **(a)** *Nau* to let go *or* loose (*rope*); **l. les amarres,** to cast off *or* to slip the mooring ropes; **l. la grand-voile,** to unfurl the mainsail; **(b)** *Av* to drop (*parachutist etc*); **(c)** *F* (*se débarrasser de*) to get rid of, to drop, to chuck (*s.o.*); **l. ses affaires,** to get rid of one's belongings.

larme [larm] *nf* **(a)** (*des yeux*) tear; **fondre en larmes,** to burst into tears, to break down; **verser des larmes de joie,** to weep tears of joy; **pleurer à chaudes larmes,** to weep bitterly; **avoir les larmes aux yeux,** to have tears in one's eyes; **elle était en larmes,** she was in tears; **avec des larmes dans la voix,** in a tearful voice; **au bord des larmes,** on the verge of tears; **avoir toujours la l. à l'œil,** to be easily moved to tears; **il a ri (jusqu')aux larmes,** he laughed till he cried; **larmes de crocodile,** crocodile tears; **(b)** *F* (*petite quantité*) **une l. de rhum,** just a drop of rum.

larmier [larmje] *nm* **(a)** *Anat* inner canthus; corner (of the eye); **(b)** tear bag (*of deer*); temple (*of horse*); **(c)** *Archit* drip (stone); gutter overhang.

larmoiement [larmwamɑ̃] *nm* **(a)** *Méd* watering (*of the eyes*); **(b)** *Péj* (*pleurnicheries*) snivelling.

larmoyant [larmwajɑ̃] *adj* **(a)** *Méd* **yeux larmoyants,** watering eyes; **(b)** (*pleurnicheur*) weepy, tearful, snivelling (*voice etc*); **(c)** *Hist Littér* sentimental (*comedy, drama*); *Péj* maudlin (*story etc*); soppy (*sentimentality*).

larmoyer [larmwaje] *vi* (**je larmoie, n. larmoyons; je larmoierai**) **(a)** (*of the eyes*) to water; **(b)** (*pleurnicher*) to snivel.

larron [larɔ̃] *nm* **(a)** *Arch* robber, thief; *F* **s'entendre comme larrons en foire,** to be as thick as thieves; **l'occasion fait le l.,** opportunity makes the thief; **(b)** *Typ* bite (*in the paper*); **(c)** *Bible* **le bon l. et le mauvais l.,** the thief that was saved and the thief that was damned.

larvaire [larvɛr] *adj* **(a)** larval; **(b)** *Fig* rudimentary, embryonic (*stage etc*).

larve [larv] *nf* larva; grub (*of insect*); *Fig* worm; *Péj* **vivre comme une l.,** to live like the lowest of God's creatures; *F* **ce type, c'est une l.,** he's such a little worm; *F* **ce weekend j'ai été une vraie l.,** I was a real lazy sod this weekend, I did damn-all this weekend.

larvé [larve] *adj* **(a)** *Méd* larvate(d) (*fever etc*); **(b)** *Fig* (*non-déclaré*) insidious, latent (*war etc*).

laryngé [larɛ̃ʒe] *adj Méd* laryngeal (*artery etc*).

laryngectomie [larɛ̃ʒɛktɔmi] *nf Chir* laryngectomy.

laryngien, -ienne [larɛ̃ʒjɛ̃, jɛn] *adj Méd Anat* laryngeal.

laryngite [larɛ̃ʒit] *nf Méd* laryngitis.

laryngologie [larɛ̃gɔlɔʒi] *nf Méd* laryngology.

laryngologiste [larɛ̃gɔlɔʒist] *n*, **laryngologue** [larɛ̃gɔlɔg] *n Méd* laryngologist.

laryngoscope [larɛ̃gɔskɔp] *nm Chir* laryngoscope.

laryngotomie [larɛ̃gɔtɔmi] *nf Chir* laryngotomy.

larynx [larɛ̃ks] *nm Anat* larynx.

las[1] [lɑs] *int Arch* alack!, alas!

las[2]**, lasse** [lɑ, lɑs] *adj* tired, weary; **être l. de qch,** to be (sick and) tired of sth; **de guerre lasse il consentit,** tired of resisting, he agreed; **être l. de tout** *ou* **l. de vivre,** to be tired of life *or* of living.

lasagnes [lazaɲ] *nfpl Culin* lasagna.

lascar [laskar] *nm F* smart *or* streetwise character; **c'est un sacré l.,** he's really streetwise.

lascif, -ive [lasif, -iv] *adj* **(a)** (*sensuel*) sensual, lascivious; **(b)** (*lubrique*) lascivious (*movements*); lascivious, lewd, lecherous (*behaviour*).

lascivement [lasivmɑ̃] *adv* lasciviously, lustfully.

lasciveté, lascivité [lasivte, lasivite] *nf* lasciviousness, lust.

laser [lazɛr] *nm Phys* laser; **disque l.,** compact disc; **rayon l.,** laser beam.

lassant [lɑsɑ̃] *adj* wearisome, tedious.

lasser [lɑse] **1** *vt* to tire, to weary; **ses explications me lassent,** I find his *or* her excuses so tedious; **l. la patience de qn,** to exhaust *or* tax s.o.'s patience. **2 se lasser** *vpr* to tire; **elle se lasse rapidement,** she tires easily; **se l. de qn/qch,** to get tired of s.o./sth; **faire qch sans se l.,** to do sth without tiring; **on ne se lasse pas de l'écouter,** one is never tired of listening to him.

lassitude [lɑsityd] *nf* lassitude, weariness.

lasso [laso] *nm* lasso; **prendre au l.,** to lasso.

latence [latɑ̃s] *nf* latency; **une période** *ou* **un temps de l.,** a period of latency *or* a latent period.

latent [latɑ̃] *adj* latent (*disease, heat etc*); hidden, concealed; **état l.,** latency; *Psy* **le contenu manifeste et le contenu l. du rêve,** the manifest content and the latent content of dreams.

latéral, -ale, -aux [lateral, -o] **1** *adj* **(a)** (*de côté*) lateral; **rue latérale,** side street; **entrée latérale,** side entrance; **(b)** *Ling* **consonne latérale,** lateral (consonant). **2**

nf Ling **latérale,** lateral.
latéralement [lateralmɑ̃] *adv* laterally, on *or* at the side.
latéralisation [lateralizasjɔ̃] *nf Physiol Psy* **l. à droite/à gauche,** right-/left-handedness.
latex [latɛks] *nm Bot Ind* latex.
latifundium [latifɔ̃djɔm] *nf Agr* large farm; (*pl latifundia*).
latin, -ine [latɛ̃, -in] **1** *adj* **(a)** (*qui parle une langue romane*) Latin (*people etc*); **le caractère l.,** (the) Latin temperament; **le Quartier L.,** the Latin Quarter; **Amérique latine,** Latin America; **(b)** *Nau* **voile latine,** lateen sail; **(c)** *Ling* **une version latine,** translation from Latin; **une tournure latine,** a Latin expression. **2** *nm Ling* Latin; **l. classique,** classical Latin; **bas l.,** low Latin; **l. de cuisine,** dog Latin; **j'y perds mon l.,** I can't make head (n)or tail of it. **3** *n* **L.,** Latin.
latinisation [latinizasjɔ̃] *nf* Latinization.
latiniser [latinize] **1** *vt* to Latinize. **2 se latiniser** *vpr* to become Latinized.
latinisme [latinism] *nm* Latinism.
latiniste [latinist] *n* Latinist, Latin scholar.
latinité [latinite] *nf* **(a)** *Ling* (*style*) (style of) Latin; **(b)**(*esprit latin*) Latin civilization; **un trait caractéristique de la l.,** a characteristic feature of Latin civilization *or* the Latin world.
latino-américain, -aine [latinoamerikɛ̃, -ɛn] (*pl Latino-américain(e)s*) **1** *adj* Latin-American. **2** *n* **L.-A.,** Latin-American.
latitude [latityd] *nf* **(a)** (*liberté*) latitude, scope, freedom; **avoir toute l. pour agir,** to have plenty of scope *or* full discretion to act; **vous avez toute l. de dire oui ou non,** you are completely free *or* at liberty to say yes or no; **(b)** *Géog* latitude; **à 30° de l. nord,** at latitude 30° North; **(c)** (*région*) region; **il faut vivre différemment sous ces latitudes,** you have to adopt a different way of life in this part of the world *or* in these latitudes.
latitudinaire [latitydinɛr] *adj & n Litt* latitudinarian.
latrines [latrin] *nfpl* latrines.
lattage [lataʒ] *nm* lathing (*of ceiling, wall etc*).
latte [lat] *nf* lath, batten, slat; **l. volige,** slate lath, roof batten; *Com* **fer en lattes,** slat iron.
latter [late] *vt* to lath (*roof, floor*); to batten (*joints, tiles*).
lattis [lati] *nm* lathing, lathwork.
laudanum [lodanɔm] *nm Pharm* laudanum.
laudateur, -trice [lodatœr, -tris] *n Litt* lauder, praiser.
laudatif, -ive [lodatif, -iv] *adj* laudatory, praising; **un discours l.,** a laudatory speech, a speech in praise (*of sth, s.o.*); **il a été très l.,** he was full of praise (*for sth, s.o.*).
lauréat, -ate [lɔrea, -at] **1** *adj* prizewinning (*pupil etc*). **2** *n* prizewinner; **les lauréats du prix Nobel,** the Nobel prizewinners.
Laurent [lɔrɑ̃] *nm* Lawrence, Laurence; **le (fleuve) Saint L.,** the St Lawrence (River).
lauréole [lɔreɔl] *nf Bot* daphne.
laurier [lɔrje] *nm* **(a)** (*plante*) laurel; **l. commun,** bay laurel, sweet bay; *Culin* **feuille de l.,** bay leaf; **(b)** *Fig* (*gloire*) laurels; **les lauriers de vainqueur,** the victor's laurels; **couronne de lauriers,** laurel wreath; **se reposer** *ou* **s'endormir sur ses lauriers,** to rest on one's laurels.
laurier-rose [lɔrjeroz] *nm* (*plante*) common oleander, rose laurel; (*pl lauriers-roses*).
laurier-sauce [lɔrjesos] *nm Bot Culin* bay; (*pl lauriers-sauce*).
L.A.V. [lav] *nm Méd abrév* **lymphadenopathy associated virus.**
lavable [lavabl] *adj* washable; **l. en machine/à la main,** machine-washable/washable by hand.
lavabo [lavabo] *nm* **(a)** (*appareil sanitaire*) washbasin; **(b)** (*salle de bain*) bathroom, washroom; **(c)** (*toilettes*) toilets; **(d)** *Rel* lavabo.
lavage [lavaʒ] *nm* washing; scrubbing (*of gas*); *Méd* (stomach) wash; **l. de cerveau,** brainwashing; *F* **l. de tête,** dressing-down.
lavallière [lavaljɛr] *nf* **(cravate) l.,** necktie with large bow.
lavande [lavɑ̃d] *nf* (*fleur*) lavender; **(eau de) l.,** lavender water; **bleu l.,** lavender blue.
lavandière [lavɑ̃djɛr] *nf* **(a)** (*blanchisseuse*) washerwoman, laundress; **(b)** (*oiseau*) wagtail.
lavaret [lavarɛ] *nm Région* (*poisson*) lavaret, pollan.
lavasse [lavas] *nf F Péj* watery drink; *Péj* dishwater; **son café, c'est de la l.,** the coffee he *or* she makes tastes like dishwater.
lave [lav] *nf Géol* lava.
lavé [lave] *adj* washed-out; *Tech Beaux-Arts* pale, faint, washy (*colour*); **dessin l.,** wash drawing.
lave-glace [lavglas] *nm Aut Br* windscreen *or Am* windshield washer; (*pl lave-glaces*).
lave-linge [lavlɛ̃ʒ] *nm inv* washing machine.
lave-mains [lavmɛ̃] *nm inv* (small) wash-(hand)basin.
lavement [lavmɑ̃] *nm Méd* (rectal) injection, enema.
laver [lave] **1** *vt* **(a)** (*nettoyer avec un liquide*) to wash; **l. qch à l'eau froide,** to wash sth in cold water; **l. à grande eau,** to swill down; *F* **l. la tête à qn,** to tell s.o. off, to haul s.o. over the coals; **l. à la brosse,** to scrub; **l. la vaisselle,** *Br* to wash up, *Br* to do the washing-up, to wash *or* do the dishes; *Fig* **il faut l. son linge sale en famille,** it doesn't do to wash one's dirty linen in public; **machine à l.,** washing machine; **l. une tache,** to wash out a stain; **l. une plaie,** to bathe *or* cleanse a wound;

(b) *Fig* (*disculper*) **l. qn d'une accusation,** to clear s.o. of an accusation;

(c) (*mélanger d'eau*) to dilute (*paint*); **l. un dessin,** to wash a drawing;

(d) *Tech* **l. un minerai,** to wash an ore; *Ch* **l. un gaz,** to scrub a gas.

2 se laver *vpr* **(a)** (*se nettoyer*) **se l.,** to wash (oneself), to have a wash, *Am* to wash up; **se l. les dents,** to clean *or* brush one's teeth; **se l. la tête,** to wash one's hair; **se l. les mains,** to wash one's hands; *Fig* **je m'en lave les mains,** I wash my hands of it;

(b) (*pouvoir être lavé*) **ce tissu ne se lave pas,** this material won't wash *or* isn't washable; **comment ça se lave, la viscose?,** how should viscose be washed?
laverie [lavri] *nf* **(a)** *Ind* washing plant, washery; **(b) l. automatique,** launderette.
lavette [lavɛt] *nf* **(a)** (*de vaisselle*) dishcloth; **(b)** *Région* (*gant de toilette*) facecloth; **(c)** *Fig F* spineless person, drip, wet.
laveur, -euse [lavœr, -øz] **1** *n* washer; **laveuse (de linge),** washerwoman; **l. de vaisselle,** *Br* washer-up, dishwasher; **l. de vitres,** window cleaner. **2** *nm Ind* scrubber.
lave-vaisselle [lavvɛsɛl] *nm inv* dishwasher.
lavis [lavi] *nm* **(a)** (*procédé*) washing, tinting (*of drawing*); **(b)** (*dessin*) wash drawing.
lavoir [lavwar] *nm* **(a)** (*établissement*) **l. (public),** (public) washhouse; **(b)** (*bassin*) (cement) washtub; **(c)** *Ind* (*machine*) washer; **(d)** (*atelier*) washing plant.
lavomatic [lavomatik] *nm* launderette.
lavure [lavyr] *nf* **(a) l. (de vaisselle),** dishwater; **(b)** *Fig F* (*potage insipide*) insipid *or* watery soup, dishwater; **(c)** *Ind* washing; **(d) lavures,** metal turnings and filings.
laxatif, -ive [laksatif, -iv] *adj & nm Méd* laxative.
laxisme [laksism] *nm* **(a)** (*doctrine morale*) latitudinarianism; **(b)** *Péj* (*laisser-aller*) free-and-easy attitude; **qu'est-ce que c'est que ce l.?,** what kind of free-and-easy attitude is this?
laxiste [laksist] *adj & nm* latitudinarian.
layer¹ [leje] *vt* (**je laie, je laye, n. layons; je laierai, je layerai**) **(a)** (*faire traverser d'une laie*) to open up a path through (*forest*), to blaze a trail through (*forest*); **(b)** (*marquer*) to blaze (*the trees to be left in a cutting*).
layer² *vt* to tool (*a stone*).
layette [lɛjɛt] *nf* baby clothes, layette; *Com* babywear.
layon [lɛjɔ̃] *nm* forest track, trail; (*pour monter à cheval*) bridle path.
lazaret [lazarɛ] *nm* lazaret(to).
lazariste [lazarist] *nm Rel* lazarist (priest).
lazulite [lazylit] *nm Minér* lazulite, blue spar.
lazzi [lazi, ladzi] *nm* jeers, booing, cat calls; (*pl lazzi, lazzis*).
le¹, la¹, les¹ [lə, la, le] *art déf* (**le** *and* **la** *are elided to* **l'** *before a vowel or h mute;* **le** *and* **les** *contract with* **à, de,** *into* **au, aux; du, des**) **(a)** the; (*particularizing the noun or pron*) **ouvrez la porte,** open the door; **il est venu la semaine dernière,** he came last week; **j'apprends le français,** I'm learning French; **la province a perdu le quart/le tiers de ses habitants,** the province has lost a quarter/a third of its inhabitants; **l'un ... l'autre,** (the) one ... the other; **mon livre et le tien,** my book and yours; **j'ai l'impression qu'il ne dit pas tout,** I have the impression *or* a *or* the feeling that there's something he's not saying; **il est arrivé le lundi 12,** he arrived on Monday the 12th; **oh! le beau chat!,** what a beautiful cat!; **debout, les enfants!,** time to get up, children!; **voilà le livre que j'ai préféré,** this is the book that I liked best; **ce n'est plus la Claire que je connaissais,** she's no longer the Claire I used to know; **le Paris de l'après-guerre/que nous aimions,** post-war Paris/the Paris we knew and loved;

(b) la France, France; **l'Afrique,** Africa; **le Mont Blanc,**

Mont Blanc; **les Alpes,** the Alps;

(c) **l'empereur Guillaume,** the Emperor William; **le roi Édouard,** King Edward; **le cardinal Richelieu,** Cardinal Richelieu; *F* **la Marie/le Pierre,** Mary/Peter; *F Région* **il faut rentrer la Marie,** we'll have to bring (old) Marie back inside;

(d) (*with certain Italian names, certain actresses and female singers*) **le Dante,** Dante; **le Tasse,** Tasso; **la Callas,** Callas;

(e) (*in front of proper noun*) **la Renault ® de mon père,** my father's Renault;

(f) (*place names*) **Le Havre,** Le Havre; **La Rochelle,** La Rochelle; **Le Caire,** Cairo; **je reviens du Havre,** I'm just back from le Havre; **je me rends au Caire,** I'm going to Cairo;

(g) (*family names*) **les tableaux de Le Brun,** Le Brun's pictures; **les Curie,** the Curies; **comment vont les Dupond?,** how are the Duponds?;

(h) (*with most feast days*) **la Toussaint,** All Saints' Day; **quand tombe la Saint Simon?,** what day does Saint Simon's day fall on?; *F* **à la Noël,** at Christmas;

(i) (*parts of the body*) **j'ai mal à la gorge,** I've got a sore throat; **elle a les yeux bleus,** she has blue eyes; **hausser les épaules,** to shrug one's shoulders; **elle ferma les yeux,** she closed her eyes; **il s'est pincé le doigt,** he pinched his finger; **le bras me fait mal,** my arm hurts;

(j) *F* (*environ*) **il a téléphoné vers les trois heures,** he phoned (at) about *or* around three o'clock; **ça fera dans les 500 francs,** it'll come to about *or* to something in the region of 500 francs;

(k) (*forming superlatives*) **les jours les plus longs,** the longest days; **le meilleur vin de sa cave,** the best wine in his cellar; **mon amie la plus intime,** my most intimate friend; **c'est elle (qui est) la plus jolie,** she's the prettiest; (*with adverbs*) **c'est elle qui travaille le mieux,** she's the one who works (the) best; (*when there is an absolute superlative*) **c'est lorsqu'elle est seule qu'elle est le plus heureuse,** she's happiest when she's by herself;

(l) (*generalizing the noun*) **je préfère le café au thé,** I prefer coffee to tea; **l'homme est un animal social,** man is a social animal; **elle voudrait bien fumer la pipe,** she would really like to smoke a pipe;

(m) (*distributive*) **trois fois l'an,** three times a year; **cinq francs la livre,** five francs a pound; **il vient le jeudi/les jeudis,** he comes on Thursdays/every Thursday;

(n) (*rendered by the indef art in English*) (*particularizing*) **j'ai le droit de vivre,** I have a right to live; **donner l'exemple,** to set an example; **demander le divorce,** to sue for (a) divorce; **la belle excuse!,** a fine excuse!;

(o) (*avec un adjectif*) **je vous donne les livres neufs et je reprends les vieux,** I'll give you the new books and take back the old ones; **tu préfères la rouge ou la jaune?,** do you prefer the red (one) or the yellow (one)?;

(p) **à la ...,** in the ... mode; **champignons à la grecque,** mushrooms à la grecque; **un travail fait à la va-vite,** a piece of work done in a hurry; **encore une blague à la Marie,** another one of Marie's little jokes;

(q) *partitive* **du, de la, des,** *see* **DE 2.**

le², **la²,** **les²** **1** *pron pers* (*replacing noun*) (*pour un homme*) him; (*pour une femme*) her; (*pour une chose, une idée*) it; (*au pluriel*) them; **je vous le/la présenterai,** I'll introduce him/her to you; **je ne le lui ai pas donné,** I didn't give it to him *or* her; **les voilà!,** there they are!; **ne l'abîmez pas!,** don't spoil it!; **ce pays, je le connais,** I know this country.

2 *pron neut* **(a)** (*replacing adj or noun used as adj*) **malheureux, je l'étais certainement,** I certainly was unhappy; **son frère est médecin, il voudrait l'être aussi,** his brother is a doctor, he would like to be one too; **j'étais fatigué mais maintenant je ne le suis plus,** I was tired, but now I'm not;

(b) (*replacing clause*) **il me l'a dit,** he told me so; **je le pense aussi,** I think so too; **il est plus riche que vous (ne) le pensez,** he's richer than you think (he is); **tiens-le toi pour dit,** take it as read; **tu le sais aussi bien que moi,** you know (it) as well as I do.

lé [le] *nm* width, breadth (*of cloth*); strip (*of wallpaper*).

leader [lidœr] *nm* **(a)** *Pol Sp* leader; **(b)** *Journ* **(article) l.,** leader, editorial.

leasing [liziŋ] *nm Com* leasing; **acheter une auto en l.,** to buy a car on a leasing basis, to lease a car.

léchage [leʃaʒ] *nm* licking; *F* **l. de bottes,** bootlicking.

lèche [lɛʃ] *nf F Péj* bootlicking; **faire de la l. à qn,** to suck up to s.o., to lick s.o.'s boots.

lèche-bottes [lɛʃbɔt] *Arg* **1** *adj inv* **elle est l.-b.,** she's a bootlicker. **2** *n inv* bootlicker, *Am* apple polisher.

lèche-cul [lɛʃky] *nm inv Vulg* arse-licker, brown-nose.

lèchefrite [lɛʃfrit] *nf Culin* dripping pan.

lécher [leʃe] **1** *vt* (**je lèche, n. léchons; je lécherai**) **(a)** to lick; **le chat a léché tout le lait,** the cat lapped up all the milk; **l. le beurre d'une tartine,** to lick the butter off a slice of bread; *Fig* **l. les vitrines,** to go window shopping; *Péj* **l. les bottes** *ou Vulg* **le cul de** *ou* **à qn,** to lick s.o.'s boots; *Vulg* to lick *or* kiss s.o's arse; **(b)** (*fignoler*) to over-polish, to over-finish (*work, style*); **(c)** (*effleurer*) (*vagues*) to lap on, to lap against; (*flammes*) to lick; **les vagues lèchaient le sable,** the waves were lapping on the sand. **2** **se lécher** *vpr* **se l. les doigts,** to lick one's fingers; *F* **il s'en léchait les doigts** *ou* **les babines,** he licked his lips *or* his chops over it.

lécheur, -euse [leʃœr, -øz] *n F Péj* bootlicker, toady.

lèche-vitrines [lɛʃvitrin] *nm F* window-shopping; **faire du l.-v.,** to go window-shopping.

leçon [ləsɔ̃] *nf* **(a)** lesson, class; **l. de choses,** general science (*in primary school*); **leçons particulières,** private lessons, private tuition; **leçons de chant,** singing lessons; *Fig* **donner une l. à qn,** to teach s.o. a lesson; **espérons qu'il en aura tiré une l.,** let's hope he's learnt his lesson; **que cela vous serve de l.,** let that be a lesson *or* a warning to you; **faire la l. à qn,** (*le guider*) to give s.o. instructions, to coach s.o.; (*le réprimander*) to lecture s.o., to give s.o. a lecture; **le bricolage en dix leçons,** DIY in ten (easy) lessons; **(b)** *Scol* (*ce qu'on doit étudier, apprendre*) homework, prep; **il ne connaît pas sa** *ou* **ses leçon(s),** he hasn't learned his lesson(s); **réciter sa l.,** to repeat sth parrot fashion; **(c)** reading (*of a manuscript etc*); **(d)** *Rel* lesson.

lecteur, -trice [lɛktœr, -tris] **1** *n* **(a)** (*personne qui lit*) reader; **c'est un grand l. de romans,** he reads a lot of novels, he's a great novel reader; **(b)** (*dans l'édition*) (publisher's) reader; **(c)** *Univ* foreign language assistant, lector (*in university*). **2** *nm Ordinat* **l. (de disquettes),** (disk) drive; *Cin etc* **l. de son,** sound head, sound reader; **l. optique,** optical reader, visual scanner; **l. de cassettes,** cassette player; **l. de disques compacts,** compact disc player.

lecture [lɛktyr] *nf* **(a)** (*action de lire*) reading; **enseigner la l. à qn,** to teach s.o. to read; **livre de l.,** reading book, reader; **livre d'une l. agréable,** book that makes pleasant reading; **cabinet de l.,** reading room (*of library*); **c'est un homme de grande l.,** he's very well read; **il m'a apporté de la l.,** he brought me something to read; **méthode de l. rapide,** rapid-reading method; *Mus* **l. à vue,** sight reading; **s'informer par la l. des journaux,** to keep oneself informed by reading the newspapers; **table de l.,** reading desk; **l. à haute voix,** reading aloud; **faire la l. à qn,** to read aloud to s.o.; *Pol* **projet repoussé en deuxième l.,** bill rejected at the second reading;

(b) (*interprétation*) **une nouvelle l. de Balzac,** a new reading *or* interpretation of Balzac; **la l. psychanalytique d'une œuvre,** a psychoanalytic(al) reading *or* interpretation of a literary work;

(c) *Ordinat* read(ing);

(d) *Cin* **l. du son,** sound reproduction;

(e) *Tech* **bras de l.,** pick-up arm; **tête de l.,** pick-up (head) (*of a record-player*); reading head, tape reader (*of a tape-recorder*).

ledit, ladite, *pl* **lesdits, lesdites** [lədi, ladit,ledi, ledit] *adj* (*with* **à** *and* **de** *the contractions are as shown under* **LE¹**); **audit, auxdit(e)s, dudit, desdit(e)s,** the aforesaid, the aforementioned, the said.

légal, -aux [legal, -o] *adj* legal; lawful (*action*); statutory (*obligation, amount*); **fête légale,** statutory holiday; **avoir recours aux moyens légaux,** to institute legal proceedings, to take legal action; **suivre la procédure légale,** to follow the legal procedure; **par voies légales,** legally; **médecine légale,** forensic medicine; *Fin* **taux l.,** official rate of interest; **monnaie légale,** legal tender.

légalement [legalmɑ̃] *adv* legally, lawfully.

légalisation [legalizasjɔ̃] *nf* legalization; authentication (*of signature etc*).

légaliser [legalize] *vt* **(a)** (*rendre légal*) to legalize (*practice, drug etc*); **(b)** (*authentifier*) to certify, to authenticate (*signature etc*).

légalité [legalite] *nf* **(a)** legality, lawfulness; **contester la l. d'une mesure,** to contest the legality of a measure; **(b)** (*situation légale*) **rester dans la l.,** to keep within the law; **cet acte l'a fait sortir de la l.,** this act has brought *or* put him *or* her outside the law.

légat [lega] *nm Rel Antiq* legate; **l. du Pape,** Papal Legate.
légataire [legatɛr] *n Jur* legatee, heir; **l. universel,** sole legatee; **l. d'une propriété,** heir to an estate.
légation [legasjɔ̃] *nf* legation.
legato [legato] *adv Mus* **jouer l.,** to play legato.
lège [lɛʒ] *adj Nau* (*of ship*) light.
légendaire [leʒɑ̃dɛr] *adj* **(a)** legendary (*story etc*); **personnage l.,** legendary character; **un amour l.,** a legendary love-affair; **(b)** epic (*combat etc*).
légende [leʒɑ̃d] *nf* **(a)** (*histoire, fable*) legend; **entrer dans la l.,** to become a legend; **la l. de Roland,** the legend of Roland; **la l. napoléonienne,** the Napoleonic legend; **l'histoire dépassée par la l.,** history overtaken by legend; **(b)** inscription, legend (*on coin etc*); caption (*of drawing etc*); key, legend (*to diagram, map etc*); **consulter la l.,** to refer to the key.
légender [leʒɑ̃de] *vt* to provide (*photo*) with a caption, **voir photo légendée,** see photo with caption.
léger, -ère [leʒe, -ɛr] **1** *adj* **(a)** light (*weight etc*); **l. comme une plume,** as light as a feather; **avoir le cœur l.,** to be light-hearted; **avoir le sommeil l.,** to be a light sleeper; **avoir la main légère,** to be gentle with one's hand, to have a delicate touch; (*être habile*) to be clever with one's hands; (*être délicat*) to act with restraint *or* discretion; (*être mesuré*) to rule with a light hand; **conduite légère,** (*en amour*) flighty conduct; **femme légère** *ou* **de mœurs légères,** woman of easy virtue; **propos légers,** frivolous *or* idle talk; **repas l.,** light meal;

(b) slight (*pain, mistake etc*); light, gentle (*breeze*); mild (*tobacco, injury*); light (*wine*); weak (*tea, coffee*); faint (*sound, tint etc*); *Jur* **peine légère,** light sentence, mild punishment; **il y a un l. mieux,** there is a slight improvement, he's *or* she's a shade better; **perte légère,** trivial loss;

(c) *Mil* **les armes légères,** light weaponry; **un croiseur l,** a light cruiser;

(d) (*d'agrément*) **la musique légère,** light music, easy listening music; **c'est un film l.,** it's a light film;

(e) *Péj* (*insuffisant*) **le responsable s'est montré un peu l. sur ce point,** the person in charge was quite off-hand about it; **ça, alors, c'est un peu l.,** it's a bit on the thin side, isn't it?

2 *n* **à la légère,** without due consideration; **parler à la légère,** to speak unthinkingly *or* thoughtlessly; **traiter une affaire à la légère,** to make light of a matter, not to take a matter seriously.

3 *adv F* **il faut y aller l. avec les tranquillisants,** you have to go easy with tranquillizers.
légèrement [leʒɛrmɑ̃] *adv* **(a)** lightly (*dressed etc*); **manger l.,** to eat a light meal; **(b)** slightly (*wounded etc*); **il parut l. surpris,** he seemed a bit *or* slightly taken aback; **(c)** (*avec souplesse*) nimbly, gracefully; **elle se déplace l.,** she moves gracefully; **(d)** *Péj* **agir l.,** to act without due consideration; **traiter qch l.,** to make light of sth.
légèreté [leʒɛrte] *nf* **(a)** lightness (*of gas etc*); nimbleness, agility (*of dancer etc*); **l. de main,** lightness of touch; **(b)** slightness (*of injury etc*); mildness (*of tobacco etc*); weakness (*of tea etc*); **(c)** levity; flightiness (*of conduct*); **(d)** (*en amour*) fickleness.
leggings [legiŋz] *nmpl* leggings.
légiférer [leʒifere] *vi* (**je légifère, n. légiférons; je légiférerai**) to legislate (**sur,** on).
légion [leʒjɔ̃] *nf* legion; **la L. (étrangère),** the Foreign Legion; **la L. d'honneur,** the Legion of Honour *or Am* Honor; *Fig* **l. de moucherons,** host *or* swarm of gnats; **ils sont l.,** they are legion, there are many of them.
légionnaire [leʒjɔnɛr] *nm* **(a)** *Hist* legionary; **(b)** (*in Foreign Legion*) Foreign Legionary, legionnaire; **(c)** (*membre de La Légion d'Honneur*) member of the Legion of Honour *or Am* Honor.
législateur, -trice [leʒislatœr, -tris] *Jur* **1** *n* **(a)** (*personne qui fait les lois*) legislator, lawmaker; **(b)** (*corps législatif, pouvoir*) legislature. **2** *adj* legislative, lawmaking; **puissance législatrice,** legislative power.
législatif, -ive [leʒislatif, -iv] *Jur* **1** *adj* legislative; *Fr Hist* **l'Assemblée législative,** the Legislative Assembly; **élection législative,** parliamentary election; **le pouvoir l.,** the legislature. **2** *nm Pol* **le l.,** legislative power. **3** *nf* **législative (a)** Legislative Assembly; **(b)** *Pol* **les législatives,** parliamentary elections.
législation [leʒislasjɔ̃] *nf Jur* **(a)** (*fait de donner des lois*) legislation; **le droit de l.,** the right to legislate *or* to make laws; **(b) la l.,** legislation, (set of) laws; **l. criminelle,** criminal law; **la l. française/anglaise,** the French/British legislature; **(c)** *Univ* **cours de l.,** course in jurisprudence.
législature [leʒislatyr] *nf Jur* **(a)** (*corps*) legislature, legislative body; **(b)** (*durée*) term of office (*of legislative body*).
légiste [leʒist] **1** *nm Jur* jurist. **2** *adj* **médecin l.,** pathologist.
légitimation [leʒitimasjɔ̃] *nf* **(a)** legitimization (*of child*); **(b)** official recognition (*of delegate, title etc*); **(c)** *Litt* justification (*of conduct*).
légitime [leʒitim] **1** *adj* (*légal, équitable*) legitimate; lawful (*action*); just (*reward*); **propriétaire l.,** legal owner; **union l.,** marriage (*as opposed to living together*); **héritier l.,** rightful heir; **il est tout à fait l. qu'il soit en colère,** he is quite justified in his anger, it's quite legitimate for him to be angry; *Jur* **l. défense,** self-defence. **2** *nf Arg* **ma l.,** the wife, the missus, *Br Sl* her indoors.
légitimement [leʒitimmɑ̃] *adv* legitimately; justifiably (*angry*); rightfully (*belonging to s.o.*); *Jur* lawfully.
légitimer [leʒitime] *vt* **(a)** *Jur* to legitimate, to legitim(at)ize (*child etc*); **(b)** to justify (*action, claim etc*); **il voulait à tout prix l. sa conduite,** he would go to any length(s) to justify his conduct; **(c)** to recognize (*title, power*).
légitimiste [leʒitimist] *adj & n Hist* legitimist.
légitimité [leʒitimite] *nf* **(a)** *Jur* legitimacy (*of child etc*); **(b)** (*bien fondé*) legitimacy, justifiability; justifiable nature, legitimacy (*of a fear*); **la l. d'une démarche/d'une conduite,** the legitimacy *or* justifiability of an action/a course of action.
legs [lɛ, lɛg] *nm* **(a)** *Jur* legacy, bequest; **l. universel,** universal bequest; **faire un l. particulier à son neveu,** to make a specific bequest to one's nephew; **faire un l. à qn,** to leave s.o. a legacy; **(b)** *Fig* (*héritage*) **le l. du passé,** the legacy of the past; **un l. de bons souvenirs,** a store of fond memories.
léguer [lege] *vt* (**je lègue, n. léguons; je léguerai**) **(a)** *Jur* to bequeath, to leave (**à qn,** to s.o.); **(b)** (*transmettre*) to hand down, to pass on (*tradition etc*); **la réputation que lui a légué son père,** the reputation he inherited from his father.
légume [legym] **1** *nm* **(a)** vegetable; *Bot* (*gousse*) legume(n), pod; *Culin* **légumes verts,** green vegetables, greens; **soupe de légumes,** vegetable soup; **légumes secs,** dried vegetables; **(b)** *Fig F* (*personne végétative*) vegetable; **il est devenu un vrai l. après son accident,** he's become a complete vegetable since his accident. **2** *nf Arg* **grosse l.,** *F* bigwig, big shot.
légumier, -ière [legymje, -jɛr] **1** *adj* **jardin l.,** vegetable garden. **2** *nm* vegetable dish. **3** *n Région* greengrocer.
légumineux, -euse [legyminø, -øz] *Bot* **1** *adj* leguminous. **2** *nf* **légumineuse,** leguminous plant.
leitmotiv [laitmɔtiv] *nm Mus etc* leitmotif, leitmotiv; *Fig* recurring theme; (*pl leitmotive*).
lem [lɛm] *nm Astron* lunar exploration module, LEM, *F* moon buggy.
Léman [lemɑ̃] *nm* **le lac L.,** Lake Geneva *or* Leman.
lemme [lɛm] *nm Math Phil* lemma.
lemming [lemiŋ] *nm* lemming.
lémure [lemyr] *nm Antiq* one of the spirits of the dead.
lémuriens [lemyrjɛ̃] *nmpl* (*mammifère*) lemur.
lendemain [lɑ̃dmɛ̃] *nm* next day; **le l. de la bataille,** the day after the battle; **le l. matin,** the next morning, the morning after; **il faut penser au l.,** one must think of the future *or* tomorrow; **il devint célèbre du jour au l.,** he became famous overnight; **au l. de son départ,** soon after *or* in the days following his departure; **des lendemains prometteurs,** a promising future; **des succès sans l.,** short-lived successes; *F* **le l. de cuite,** the morning after the night before.
lénifiant [lenifjɑ̃] *adj* **(a)** *Méd etc* assuaging, soothing; **(b)** *Fig* (*réconfortant*) soothing.
lénifier [lenifje] *vt* (*pr sub & impf* **n. lénifiions, v. lénifiiez**) **(a)** *Méd* to assuage, to soothe, to alleviate; **(b)** *Fig* (*apaiser*) to soothe, to calm.
léninisme [leninism] *nm Pol* Leninism.
léniniste [leninist] *adj & n Pol* Leninist.
lénitif, ive [lenitif, -iv] *adj & nm* lenitive.
lent, lente [lɑ̃, lɑ̃t] *adj* slow (*movement etc*); slow-acting (*poison*); **mort lente,** slow *or* lingering death; **être l. à faire qch,** to be slow to do sth; **avoir l'esprit l.,** to be slow-witted, to be slow in understanding, *F* to be slow on the uptake.
lente [lɑ̃t] *nf* nit; egg (*of louse*).
lentement [lɑ̃tmɑ̃] *adv* slowly; **ruisseau qui coule l.,** slow-flowing stream; **l. mais sûrement,** slowly but surely.
lenteur [lɑ̃tœr] *nf* **(a)** (*développement lent*) slowness;

mettre de la l. à faire qch, to be slow in doing sth; **avec l.,** slowly; (*délibérément*) with due deliberation; **(b) lenteurs,** slowness.

lentigo [lɑ̃tigo] *nm Méd* lentigo.

lentille [lɑ̃tij] *nf* **(a)** *Culin* lentil; **(b) l. d'eau,** duckweed, *Spéc* lemna; **(c)** *Opt* lens; **lentilles de contact,** contact lenses; **lentilles souples/dures,** soft/hard lenses; **(d)** (*grain de beauté*) beauty spot.

lento [lɛnto] **1** *adv Mus* lento. **2** *nm Mus* lento (passage).

Léon [leɔ̃] *nm* Leo, Leon; (*pape*) Leo.

léonin, -ine [leɔnɛ̃, -in] *adj* leonine; **partage l.,** lion's share; *Jur* **société léonine,** = company with advantages accruing to only a small number of shareholders.

Léonore [leɔnɔr] *nf* Leonora.

léopard [leɔpar] *nm* **(a)** leopard; **manteau de l.,** leopard skin coat; **(b)** *Hér* leopard.

L.E.P. [ɛløpe] *nm* (*abrév* **Lycée d'Enseignement Professionnel**) ≈ technical college.

lépidoptère [lepidɔptɛr] **1** *adj* lepidopterous. **2** *nm* (*insecte*) lepidopteran.

lèpre [lɛpr] *nf* **(a)** *Méd* leprosy; **(b)** *Fig* (*pourriture, ce qui ronge*) **mur rongé d'une l.,** rotting wall; **(c)** *Litt* evil; **la l. de la jalousie/de l'arrivisme,** the cancer of jealousy/the vice of ambition.

lépreux, -euse [leprø, -øz] **1** *adj* **(a)** *Méd* leprous; **(b)** *Fig* peeling, scaly, dilapidated (*wall*). **2** *n* leper; **traiter qn comme un l.,** to treat s.o. like a leper.

léproserie [leprozri] *nf* leper hospital.

lepte [lɛpt] *nm* (*insecte*) leptus; **l. automnal,** harvest bug, harvest mite.

lequel, laquelle, lesquels, lesquelles [ləkɛl,lakɛl, lekɛl] *pron* (*contracted with* **à** *and* **de** *to* **auquel, auxquel(le)s, duquel, desquel(le)s**) **1** *pron rel* **(a)** (*personne*) who, whom; (*chose*) which; (*of things after prep*) **l'adresse à laquelle il devait m'écrire,** the address at which he was to write to me; **décision par laquelle ...,** decision whereby ...; **n'importe l. fera l'affaire,** any (one) of them will do;

(b) (*personne*) **ont comparu trois témoins, lesquels ont déclaré ...,** three witnesses appeared, who stated ...; **les deux officiers entre lesquels elle était assise,** the two officers between whom she was sitting; **la dame avec laquelle elle était sortie,** the lady with whom she had gone out; **il y avait beaucoup de gens, parmi lesquels mon cousin Paul,** there were a lot of people, among whom was my cousin Paul; **la dame chez laquelle je l'ai rencontré,** the lady at whose house I met him;

(c) (*pour préciser*) **le père de cette jeune fille, l. est très riche,** the girl's father, who is very rich;

(d) (*adjectival*) **voici cent francs, laquelle somme vous était due par mon père,** here's a hundred francs, (which was) the sum my father owed you; **il écrira peut-être, auquel cas ...,** perhaps he will write, in which case ....

2 *pron interr* which (one); **l. (de ces chapeaux) préférez-vous?,** which (one) (of these hats) do you prefer?; **l. d'entre nous?,** which (one) of us?

lerch(e) [lɛrʃ] *adv Arg* **pas l.,** not much.

lérot [lero] *nm* (*mammifère*) lerot, garden dormouse.

lès [lɛ] *prép* (*occurs only in place names*) near.

lesbien, -ienne [lɛsbjɛ̃, -jɛn] **1** *adj* lesbian. **2** *nf* **lesbienne,** lesbian.

lèse- [lɛz] *adj* injured; **crime de l.-société,** outrage against society.

lèse-majesté [lɛzmaʒɛste] *nf inv Jur* high treason, lese-majesty.

léser [leze] *vt* **(je lèse, n. lésons; je léserai) (a)** (*désavantager*) to wrong (*s.o.*); to wound, to injure; *Jur* **l. les droits de qn,** to encroach upon s.o.'s rights; **la partie lésée,** the injured party; **(b)** (*of action*) to endanger (*s.o.'s interests etc*); **(c)** *Méd* to injure (*organ*).

lésine [lezin] *nf Litt & Vieilli* stinginess.

lésiner [lezine] *vi* to be stingy; to skimp (**sur,** on); **ils n'avaient pas lésiné sur le vin,** they hadn't skimped on the wine.

lésineur, -euse [lezinœr, -øz] *n Vieilli* miser, niggard.

lésion [lezjɔ̃] *nf Méd Jur* lesion; (*blessure*) injury.

lessivable [lesivabl] *adj* washable (*wallpaper etc*).

lessivage [lesivaʒ] *nm* washing (*of linen, wall etc*); *Ch* leaching; *Fig* **on change de structure dans les bureaux, c'est le grand l.,** there's some restructuring going on in the offices, and they're having a big clear-out (of personnel).

lessive [lesiv] *nf* **(a)** (*produit*) detergent, washing powder; *Ch* lye; **(b)** (*action de laver*) wash; **faire la l.,** to do the washing; **jour de l.,** wash(ing) day; **(c)** (*linge sale*) dirty washing; (*plus sale*) soiled linen (*going to the wash*); **(d)** (*linge propre*) (clean) washing.

lessivé [lesive] *adj F* (*fatigué*) washed out.

lessiver [lesive] *vt* **(a)** (*nettoyer*) to scrub, to wash (*floor etc*); **(b)** *Ch* to leach; **(c)** *Arg* (*battre*) to beat, *F* to wipe the floor with (*s.o.*); (*at cards etc*) **se faire l.,** to be cleaned out; **(d)** *Vieilli* to wash, to boil (*linen etc*).

lessiveuse [lesivøz] *nf* copper, boiler.

lest [lɛst] *nm no pl* **(a)** ballast (*of ship, balloon etc*); *Nau* **naviguer sur l., sans cargaison,** to sail in ballast *or* without a cargo; **faire son l.,** to take in ballast; **jeter du l.,** to discharge ballast; *Fig* (*faire des concessions*) to make sacrifices (*in order to attain one's end*); **(b)** *Physiol* **aliment de l.,** food that is filling (but of little nutritional value); *F* stodge.

lestage [lɛstaʒ] *nm* ballasting (*of ship etc*).

leste [lɛst] *adj* **(a)** (*léger*) light; nimble, agile (*person, animal*); smart, brisk (*motion*); **avoir la main l.,** to be quick with one's hands; **(b)** *Fig* (*libre, grivois*) offhand (*manner*); risqué (*jokes*).

lestement [lɛstəmɑ̃] *adv* lightly; nimbly; smartly.

lester [lɛste] **1** *vt* **(a)** to ballast (*ship, balloon*); **(b)** *F* to fill, to cram (*pocket, wallet etc*). **2 se lester** *vpr F* to stuff oneself; **se l. (l'estomac),** to stuff oneself.

létal, ale [letal] *adj* lethal; *Biol* **gène l.,** lethal gene; **dose létale,** lethal dose.

letchi [lɛtʃi] *nm Bot* lychee, litchi.

léthargie [letarʒi] *nf* lethargy; *Méd* coma; **être en l. hypnotique,** to be in a hypnotic trance; **le malade n'est toujours pas sorti de sa l.,** the patient has not yet come out of his coma.

léthargique [letarʒik] *adj* lethargic.

Léthé [lete] *nm Myth* (the river) Lethe.

lette [lɛt] *nm,* **lettique** [lɛtik] *nm Ling* Lettish, Latvian.

letton, -onne [lɛtɔ̃, -ɔn] **1** *adj* Latvian; (*personne*) Lett, Latvian. **2** *nm Ling* Lettish, Latvian. **3** *n* **L.,** Latvian, Lett.

Lettonie [lɛtɔni] *nf* Latvia.

lettrage [lɛtraʒ] *nm Typ* lettering.

lettre [lɛtr] *nf* **(a)** letter (*of the alphabet*); **écrire qch en toutes lettres,** to write sth out in full; **c'est ce qu'il a dit en toutes lettres, sans faire de doute,** that's what he said in unambiguous terms, without leaving any room for doubt; *Typ* **le corps de la l.,** the body of the letter; **c'est écrit en toutes lettres sur son visage,** it's written all over his face; **écrire une somme en (toutes) lettres,** to write an amount in words; *Fig* **c'est gravé en lettres d'or,** it will always be remembered;

(b) selon la l. de la loi, according to the letter of the law; **à la l., au pied de la l.,** to the letter, literally; **traduire à la l.,** to translate word for word; **il prend les choses à la l.,** he takes everything literally; **appliquer des directives à la l.,** to carry out instructions to the letter; **il fut surréaliste avant la l.,** he was a surrealist before the word had been invented;

(c) (*écrit*) letter; **l. d'amour/d'affaires,** love/business letter; **l. recommandée,** registered letter; **l. exprès/par avion,** express/airmail letter; *Journ* **l. ouverte,** open letter; **l. morte,** dead letter; **ce document est resté l. morte,** this document is now useless *or* worthless; *F* **c'est pour moi lettres closes,** it's a mystery to me; *F* **c'est passé comme une l. à la poste,** it went off without a hitch, it went off smoothly;

(d) (*écrit officiel*) **l. de grâce,** reprieve; *Hist* **lettres patentes,** letters patent; *Pol* **lettres de créance,** credentials; **lettres de noblesse,** letters patent of nobility; *Fig* **il a ses lettres de noblesse, c'est un comte,** he's got a noble *or* an aristocratic pedigree, he's a count; *Banque Com* **l. de crédit,** letter of credit;

(e) lettres, literature, *Litt* letters; *Univ* humanities; **homme/femme de lettres,** man/woman of letters; **avoir des lettres,** to be well read; *Univ* **faculté des lettres,** faculty of arts *or* humanities; **lettres classiques,** classics; **lettres modernes,** (*en France*) French studies; (*en Grande-Bretagne*) English studies.

lettré, -ée [letre] **1** *adj* well-read, cultured (*person*). **2** *n* scholar; well-read person.

lettrine [letrin] *nf Typ* **(a)** *Vieilli,* reference letter, superior letter; **(b)** (*at beginning of chapters etc*) dropped initial; **(c)** (*in dictionary*) running head (line).

leu[1] [lø] *nm* (*monnaie*) leu; (*pl lei*).

leu[2] *nm* **à la queue l. l.,** in single file, in Indian file.

leucémie [løsemi] *nf Méd* leuk(a)emia.

leucémique [løsemik] *Méd* **1** *adj* leuk(a)emic. **2** *n* leuk(a)emia sufferer.

leucocytaire [løkɔsitɛr] *adj Physiol* leucocytic.

leucocyte [løkɔsit] *nm Physiol* leucocyte.

leucoma [løkɔma] *nm*, **leucome** [løkom] *nm Méd* leucoma, albugo.
leucorrhée [løkɔre] *nf Méd* leucorrh(o)ea.
leur[1] [lœr] **1** *adj poss* their; **l. oncle et l. tante,** their uncle and (their) aunt; **un(e) de leurs ami(e)s,** a friend of theirs, one of their friends; **elles ont pris leur(s) sac(s),** they picked up their bag(s); **leurs père et mère,** their father and mother. **2** *pron poss* **le l., la l., les leurs,** theirs; **j'ai écrit à mes amis et aux leurs,** I wrote to my friends and to theirs; **notre maison a plus de chambres que la l.,** our house has more rooms than theirs; *Litt* **cette maison qui était l.,** this house of theirs *or* which was theirs; **ils n'y mettent pas du l.,** they don't pull their weight *or* they don't do their share; **les leurs,** their own family *or* friends *etc*; **j'étais des leurs hier soir,** I was with them *or* I joined them last night; **êtes-vous des leurs ou êtes-vous avec nous?,** are you with them or us?, are you on their side or ours?; **ils ont encore fait des leurs,** they've been up to their old tricks again.
leur[2] *pron voir* **LUI[1]**.
leurre [lœr] *nm* **(a)** lure (*for hawks*); **(b)** decoy (*for birds*); (artificial) bait, lure (*for fish*); **(c)** (*illusion*) delusion, deception, illusion; **(d)** *Mil* chaff.
leurrer [lœre] **1** *vt* **(a)** to lure (*hawk etc*); **(b)** (*tromper*) to deceive, to delude (*s.o.*); **il se laisse facilement l.,** he is easily taken in. **2 se leurrer** *vpr* to delude oneself; **il se leurre complètement sur les intentions de son frère,** he's deluding himself completely about his brother's intentions.
lev [lɛv] *nm* (*monnaie*) lev; (*pl leva*).
levage [ləvaʒ] *nm* **(a)** *Tech* lifting (up), hoisting, raising; **câble de l.,** hoisting cable; **cric de l.,** lifting jack; **(b)** *Culin* rising (*of dough etc*).
levain [ləvɛ̃] *nm* leaven; **pain sans l.,** unleavened bread; *Fig* **un l. de révolte,** the seeds of revolt.
levant [ləvɑ̃] **1** *adj* **soleil l.,** rising sun; **il est parti au soleil l.,** he left at sunrise *or surtout US* at sun-up. **2** *nm* **(a) le l.,** the east, the orient; **(b) le L.,** the Levant.
levantin, -ine [ləvɑ̃tɛ̃, -in] **1** *adj* Levantine. **2** *n* **L.,** Levantine.
levé [ləve] **1** *adj* **(a)** (*en l'air*) raised (*hand, fist*); **voter à mains levées,** to vote by a show of hands; **dessin à main levée,** freehand drawing; **pierre levée,** standing stone; **au pied l.,** at a moment's notice; **(b)** *Culin* **pâte bien levée,** well risen dough; **(c)** (*debout*) up; out of bed; (*of sun etc*) up; **je suis l. de bonne heure,** I'm up early, I'm an early riser. **2** *nm* **(a)** plan, survey (*of a piece of land*); **l. aérophotogrammétrique,** aerial survey; **faire le l. d'un terrain,** to survey a piece of land; **(b)** *Mus* up beat.
levée [ləve] *nf* **(a)** (*fait d'enlever*) raising, lifting; *Nau* weighing (*of anchor*); **une l. de boucliers,** collective protest, general outcry;
(b) raising (*of siege*); lifting (*of embargo, punishment etc*); closing, adjourning (*of meeting*); *Jur* **la l. d'option,** the exercising of an option; *Jur* **la l. de séance,** rising (*of court etc*);
(c) removal (*of sth*); breaking (*of seals*); **la l. du corps,** = the beginning of a funeral procession (from the deceased's home);
(d) collecting, gathering (*of crops etc*); levy(ing) (*of troops, taxes*); collection (*of letters*); (*ramassage*) letters *or* mail collected; *Mil* **l. en masse,** levy en masse; **la l. est faite,** the post has been collected *or* has gone; **la l. d'un impôt** *ou* **d'une taxe,** the levying of a tax; *Fin* **l. des actions,** taking (up) (of stock);
(e) *Jur* **l. d'un jugement,** transcript of a verdict;
(f) rising (*of court etc*);
(g) *Nau* **l. de la mer,** rough sea; **l. de la lame,** surge, swell;
(h) (*remblai*) embankment, sea wall; dyke, levee;
(i) *Cartes* trick; **faire une l.,** to take a trick.
lève-glace(s) [lɛvglas] *nm inv Aut* window winder.
lever[1] [ləve] *v* **(je lève, n. levons; je lèverai) 1** *vt* **(a)** (*déplacer vers le haut, soulever*) to lift, to raise; to hold up (*trophy, exhibit*); **l. la main sur qn,** to raise *or* lift one's hand against s.o.; **l. les bras au ciel (dans un geste d'étonnement),** to throw up one's hands (in astonishment); **il ne veut pas l. le petit doigt,** he won't lift a finger, he won't do a thing; **l. la tête,** *Fig* (*se montrer digne*) to hold up one's head, to look up; **l. un malade,** to lift a patient; **l. un enfant,** to help a child get up and dress; **l. les yeux (sur qn),** to look up (at s.o.); **l. son verre,** to raise one's glass (*to s.o.*); *Fig* **l. le coude,** to (be able to) knock it back; *Fig* **on conseille aux automobiliste de l. le pied ce soir sur les routes,** motorists are advised to drive slowly on the roads this evening; **l. l'ancre,** to weigh *or* lift anchor; *Fig* to leave, to go; **l. un lièvre/une perdrix,** to start a hare/to flush a partridge; *Arg* **l. une femme,** to pick up a woman;
(b) (*dresser*) to set upright; **l. une échelle,** to put up a ladder; **l. un étendard,** to raise a standard; **l. un sac,** to stand a sack upright *or* on its end;
(c) to raise (*siege etc*); **l. une option,** to take up an option; to strike, to break (*camp*); to lift (*embargo, punishment etc*); to close, to adjourn (*meeting*);
(d) to remove (*a difficulty, a doubt*); *Fig* **cet article lève le voile sur l'affaire des diamants,** this article reveals the truth about the affair of the diamonds;
(e) to raise, to levy (*troops*); to levy (*tax*); to collect (*letters, mail*); *Fin* to take up (*stock*); *Cartes* **l. (les cartes),** to pick up a trick;
(f) to make, to draw, to get out (*a plan*);
(g) *Culin* **l. les filets,** to remove the fillets;
(h) *Vieilli* to cut off (*from piece of material*).
2 *vi* **(a)** (*of plants*) to shoot;
(b) (*of dough*) to rise.
3 se lever *vpr* **(a)** (*of hands, curtain etc*) to go up;
(b) (*se mettre debout*) to stand up; **levez-vous,** stand up, get up; **se l. de table,** to leave the table;
(c) (*quitter le lit*) to get up (*from bed*); **je me lève de bonne heure,** I'm an early riser, I get up early; **se l. du pied gauche,** to get out of bed on the wrong side;
(d) (*apparaître*) **le jour se lève,** day is breaking *or* dawning; **nous avons vu le soleil se l.,** we saw the sun rise; **le soleil se lève à 7 heures 52,** the sun rises at 7:52; **le vent se lève,** the wind is rising, the wind is getting up;
(e) (*s'éclaircir*) **le temps se lève,** the weather is clearing.
lever[2] *nm* **(a)** getting up (*from bed*), *Fml* rising; levee (*of French king*); **(b)** (*apparition*) **l. du soleil,** sunrise, *Am* sunup; **l. du jour,** daybreak; **(c)** (*montée*) *Th* rising, rise (*of the curtain*); **un l. de rideau,** a curtain raiser; **(d)** (*croquis*) = **LEVÉ 2 (b).**
lève-tard [lɛvtar] *nm inv F* late riser.
lève-tôt [lɛvto] *nm inv F* early riser.
levier [ləvje] *nm* **(a)** *Phys* lever; **bras de l.,** lever arm; **force de l.,** leverage; **ce poids fait l. et permet de bouger la caisse,** this weight acts as a lever and allows the crate to be moved; **(b)** (*outil*) crowbar, lever; **soulever** *ou* **ouvrir** *ou* **forcer qch avec un l.,** to prize *or* prise *or* lever sth up *or* open *or* out; **(c)** (*commande*) lever, handle; *MecE* **l. de commande,** control lever; **être aux leviers de commande,** to be in control *or* in command; **l. de frein,** brake lever; *Aut* **l. (de changement) de vitesse,** gear lever, gear stick, *Am* gearshift; **(d)** *Fig* (*motif d'action*) spur to action; **la jalousie est un excellent l.,** jealousy is an excellent spur to action.
lévitation [levitasjɔ̃] *nf* levitation.
lévite [levit] *n Jew Rel* Levite.
levraut [ləvro] *nm* leveret, young hare.
lèvre [lɛvr] *nf* **(a)** *Anat* lip; **avoir les lèvres charnues** *ou* **pleines/minces,** to have thick *or* full/thin lips; **la l. inférieure,** the lower lip; **se mettre du rouge à lèvres,** to put on lipstick; **il avait un cigare aux lèvres,** he had a cigar between his lips; **j'ai le mot sur le bord des lèvres,** I have the word on the tip of my tongue; **la rumeur est sur toutes les lèvres,** the rumour is on everybody's lips; **manger du bout des lèvres,** to nibble *or* pick at one's food; **il accepta, mais du bout des lèvres,** he grudgingly accepted; **rire du bout des lèvres,** to force a laugh; **il le dit des lèvres, mais le cœur n'y est pas,** he pays lip service (to it); *Fig* **nous étions tous suspendus à ses lèvres,** we were all hanging on his *or* her every word; **pincer les lèvres,** to purse one's lips; **se mordre les lèvres (pour ne pas rire),** to bite one's lips (in order not to laugh);
(b) rim (*of crater*);
(c) lip (*of wound*);
(d) *Bot* lip, labium;
(e) *Anat* **lèvres,** lips, labia (*of vulva*).
levrette [ləvrɛt] *nf* greyhound bitch; **l. (d'Italie),** (small) Italian greyhound.
lévrier [levrije] *nm* greyhound; **l. irlandais** *ou* **d'Irlande,** Irish wolf hound; **l. d'Italie,** Italian greyhound; **l. afghan,** Afghan hound; **l. russe,** borzoi; **courses de lévriers,** greyhound racing.
levure [ləvyr] *nf* yeast; **l. de boulanger,** baker's yeast; **l. de bière,** brewer's yeast; **l. chimique,** = baking powder; **l. en sachet,** yeast in a packet *or* sachet.
lexème [lɛksɛm] *nm Ling* lexeme.
lexical, -aux [lɛksikal, -o] *adj* lexical.
lexicographe [lɛksikɔgraf] *n* lexicographer.

lexicographie [lɛksikɔgrafi] *nf* lexicography.
lexicographique [lɛksikɔgrafik] *adj* lexicographical.
lexicologie [lɛksikɔlɔʒi] *nf* lexicology.
lexicologique [lɛksikɔlɔʒik] *adj* lexicological.
lexicologue [lɛksikɔlɔg] *n* lexicologist.
lexique [lɛksik] *nm* **(a)** (*dictionnaire*) lexicon, small dictionary; (*glossaire*) glossary; vocabulary (*at end of book etc*) **(b)** *Ling* vocabulary, lexis; **le l. de Mallarmé,** the vocabulary of Mallarmé.
lez [le] *prép* (*occurs only in place names*) near.
lézard [lezar] *nm* **(a)** (*reptile*) lizard; **l. gris/des murailles,** grey/wall lizard; **l. vert,** green lizard; **faire le l.,** to bask *or* lounge in the sun; **(b)** (*cuir*) lizard skin.
lézarde [lezard] *nf* crevice, cranny, crack, chink.
lézardé [lezarde] *adj* (*of wall, plaster*) cracked, full of cracks.
lézarder [lezarde] **1** *vt* to crack, split (*plaster etc*). **2 se lézarder** *vpr* (*of wall*) to crack. **3** *vi F* to bask *or* lounge in the sun.
liais [ljɛ] *nm Miner* hard limestone.
liaison [ljɛzɔ̃] *nf* **(a)** (*lien, enchaînement*) joining, binding, connection; **des idées sans l.,** unconnected ideas; **en l. à ce qui a été dit,** in connection with *or* leading on from what has been said;
(b) bonding (*of bricks etc*); mortar, cement; *Constr* **maçonnerie en l.,** bonded masonry;
(c) *Mus* (*moitier*) slur; (*coulée*) tie, ligature;
(d) *Ch* bond;
(e) *Ling* sounding of final consonant before initial vowel sound, liaison; **faire la l.,** to make *or* sound the liaison; *Gram* **mot** *ou* **terme de l.,** linkword;
(f) *Culin* liaison, thickening (*for sauce*);
(g) *Mil* liaison, intercommunications; **agent de l.,** go-between; **être en l. avec ...,** to be in touch with ...; **se mettre en l. avec ...,** to establish (a) liaison *or* to liaise *or* to get in touch with ...; **établir une l. radio,** to establish radio contact;
(h) (*voie, route*) **l. aérienne/maritime/ferroviaire/routière,** air/sea/rail/road link;
(i) (*relation*) (close) contact *or* relationship; **l. d'affaires,** business connection; **travailler en l. (étroite) avec qn,** to work in (close) collaboration with s.o.; **il y a peu de l. entre les 2 villes,** there isn't much contact between the two cities; **l. (amoureuse),** (love) affair, liaison; **je soupçonne le directeur d'avoir une l. avec sa secrétaire,** I suspect the director of having an affair with his secretary.
liaisonner [ljɛzɔne] *vt Constr* **(a)** to bond (*stones etc*); **(b)** to grout, to point (*stonework*).
liane [ljan] *nf Bot* liana; (tropical) creeper.
liant [ljɑ̃] **1** *adj* sociable, friendly; **il est très l.,** he's quick to make friends ; (*dans la vie mondaine*) he's a good mixer. **2** *nm* **(a)** (*ouverture*) engaging manner, sociable disposition; **avoir du l.,** to be sociable; **(b)** (*souplesse*) flexibility, pliability; **(c)** *Tech* binder, binding agent.
liard [ljar] *nm Arch* half farthing; *F* **il n'a pas un l.,** he hasn't (got) a farthing, he hasn't (got) a penny to his name.
lias [ljas] *nm Géol* lias.
liasse [ljas] *nf* bundle, packet (*of letters etc*); wad (*of banknotes*); file (*of papers*); *Com etc* set of multipart forms.
libage [libaʒ] *nm Constr* bastard ashlar.
Liban [libɑ̃] *nm* **le L.,** (the) Lebanon.
libanais, -aise [libanɛ, -ɛz] **1** *adj* Lebanese. **2** *n* **L.,** Lebanese person, native *or* inhabitant of (the) Lebanon.
libation [libasjɔ̃] *nf* **(a)** *Antiq Rel* libation; **(b)** *Fig* **faire des libations,** to drink immoderately *or F* like a fish.
libelle [libɛl] *nm* lampoon, scurrilous satire.
libellé [libele] *nm* wording, terms used (*in document etc*).
libeller [libele] *vt* to draw up, to word (*document etc*); **l. un chèque,** to make out *or* write out a cheque; **télégramme libellé comme suit ...,** telegram worded as follows ... *or* that reads as follows ... .
libellule [libelyl] *nf* (*insecte*) dragonfly.
libérable [liberabl] *Mil* **1** *adj* (*personne*) dischargeable, who can be demobbed; **congé** *ou* **permission l.,** demob leave. **2** *nm* soldier *etc* about to finish his military service.
libéral, -ale, -aux [liberal, -o] **1** *adj* **(a)** (*indépendant*) liberal; **il exerce une profession libérale,** he's a professional man; **défendre la médecine libérale,** to defend private medicine; **(b)** (*généreux*) generous; **(c)** (*tolérant, ouvert*) broadminded; **(d)** *Pol* liberal; **le parti l.,** the Liberal Party; **les doctrines libérales,** liberal doctrines. **2** *n Pol* liberal.
libéralement [liberalәmɑ̃] *adv* liberally.
libéralisation [liberalizasjɔ̃] *nf* liberalization, easing (*of restriction etc*); **l. de la presse,** the liberalization of the press, the easing of restrictions on the press.
libéraliser [liberalize] *vt* to liberalize.
libéralisme [liberalism] *nm Pol & Écon* liberalism.
libéralité [liberalite] *nf* **(a)** liberality; **(b)** (*générosité*) generosity; **(c)** (*cadeau*) (generous) gift; **faire des libéralités à qn,** to give liberally *or* freely to s.o..
libérateur, -trice [liberatœr, -tris] **1** *adj* liberating; **guerre libératrice,** war of liberation; **le pouvoir l. du rire,** the liberating power of laughter. **2** *n* liberator.
libération [liberasjɔ̃] *nf* **(a)** (*mise en liberté*) liberation, freeing, releasing; discharge, release (*of prisoner*); discharge (*of soldier*); **l. conditionnelle,** release (*of prisoner*) on parole; **mouvement de l. de la femme,** women's liberation movement, *F* women's lib; **Front de L. National de la Corse,** Corsican (National) Liberation Front; *Hist Fr* **la L.,** the Liberation (*from the Germans in 1944-45*); **(b)** (*d'une dette*) payment in full, discharge; **l. d'une dette par versements anticipés,** discharge of a debt by means of instalments paid before the due date; **(c)** *Phys* (*émission*) liberation, release; **la l. de chaleur,** the liberation *or* release of heat; *Av* **vitesse de l.,** escape velocity, parabolic velocity.
libératoire [liberatwar] *adj Jur* **paiement l.,** payment in full discharge from debt; (*of money*) **avoir force l.,** to be legal tender.
libéré [libere] **1** *adj* **(a)** (*en liberté*) liberated, free; **(b)** (*soulagé*) relieved, liberated; **c'est une femme libérée,** she's a liberated woman; **(c)** *Fin* (fully) paid-up (*share*). **2** *nm* discharged soldier; discharged prisoner.
libérer [libere] *v* (**je libère, n. libérons; je libérerai**) **1** *vt* **(a)** (*rendre libre*) to liberate, to release; to set (s.o.) free, to free (s.o.); to discharge (*prisoner, soldier*); *Méd* to unblock (*passage*); *Com* to ease (*restriction*); **(b)** (*soulager*) **l. sa conscience,** to free one's conscience; **l. les jeunes du tabou de la sexualité,** to free *or* liberate young people from the taboo of sexuality; **(c)** *Fin* to free (*s.o., an institution etc of debt etc*); **titre de 1 000 francs libéré de 750 francs,** 1000 franc share of which 750 francs are paid (up); **(d)** (*émettre*) to liberate, to release; **la fusion libère de la chaleur,** fusion liberates *or* releases heat. **2 se libérer** *vpr* to free oneself; **se l. (d'une dette),** to redeem *or* liquidate a debt; **se l. pour deux jours,** to (arrange to) take two days off.
Libéria [liberja] *nm* Liberia.
libérien, -ienne [liberjɛ̃, -jɛn] **1** *adj* Liberian. **2** *n* **L.,** Liberian.
libertaire [libertɛr] *adj & n* libertarian.
liberté [liberte] *nf* **(a)** liberty, freedom; **animaux en l.,** animals in the wild, animals running free; **mettre qn/un animal en l.,** to set s.o./an animal free; **être mis en l.,** to be allowed to go free; (*of accused*) to be discharged; **l'assassin est toujours en l.,** the murderer is still at large; **rendre sa l. à un prisonnier,** to set a prisoner free, to release a prisoner; **mise en l.,** liberation, freeing; release (*of prisoner*); *Jur* **(mise en) l. provisoire** *ou* **sous caution,** (release on) bail; **l. conditionnelle,** parole; **avoir pleine l. d'action,** to have full freedom of action, to have a free hand; **les défenseurs de la l.,** the defenders of freedom; **l., égalité, fraternité,** liberty, equality, fraternity; **l. de conscience/de la presse,** freedom of conscience/of the press; **l. de réunion,** freedom of assembly; **l. d'expression/d'opinion,** freedom of expression *or* of speech/freedom of thought; **l. du culte,** freedom of worship;
(b) vous avez toute l. pour organiser la rencontre, you are completely free to organize the meeting as you wish; **parler avec l.** *ou* **en toute l.,** to speak freely *or* without restraint; **j'ai pris la l. de dire ...,** I took the liberty of saying ...; **si je puis prendre une telle l. ...,** if I may be *or* make so bold ...; **faire preuve de l. d'esprit,** to show independence of mind; **se permettre des libertés de langage/de mœurs,** to be rather free in one's use of language/one's standards of behaviour; **prendre des libertés avec qn,** to take liberties with s.o.;
(c) (*loisirs*) **jour de l.,** free day, day off; **avec tout ce travail je n'ai pas beaucoup de l.,** with all this work I haven't (got) much free time.
libertin, -ine [libertɛ̃, -in] **1** *adj* **(a)** (*dissolu*) libertine, dissolute; licentious (*of book etc*); **(b)** *Hist* free-thinking. **2** *n* **(a)** (*personne*) libertine; **(b)** *Hist* free-thinker.
libertinage [libertinaʒ] *nm* **(a)** (*débauche*) licentiousness, dissoluteness, debauchery; **(b)** *Hist* free-thinking.
liberty [liberti] *nm* liberty fabric; **une housse de coussin en l.,** a liberty cushion cover.
libidineux, -euse [libidinø, -øz] *adj Péj* libidinous,

lustful; **des regards libidineux,** lustful *or* lewd *or* lascivious glances.
libido [libido] *nf* libido.
libraire [librɛr] *n Com* bookseller.
libraire-éditeur [librɛreditœr] *nm Com* publisher and bookseller; (*pl libraires-éditeurs*).
librairie [librɛri] *nf* **(a)** *Com* book trade; bookselling; **ouvrages en l.,** published books; **(b)** (*magasin*) bookshop, *US* bookstore; **l. d'art,** art bookshop.
libre [libr] *adj* **(a)** (*indépendant, non soumis*) free; **pays l.,** free country; **traduction l.,** free translation; *Scol* **sujet l.,** free choice of subject (*in essay writing*); **vers l.,** free verse; **laisser qn l. d'agir,** to leave s.o. a free hand, to leave s.o. free to act; **vous êtes l. de le faire, l. à vous de le faire,** you are quite free *or* at liberty to do it; **l. à vous d'essayer,** you're free *or* welcome to try; **l. arbitre,** free will; **l. parole,** free speech; **l. penseur** *ou* **penseuse,** free thinker; **l. pensée,** free thinking, free thought; **l'homme est l.,** man is a free agent; **le monde l.,** the free world; **défendre la l. entreprise,** to defend free *or* private enterprise;
(b) (*disponible*) free, not tied down; (*sentimentalement*) unattached; **je suis l. de onze heures à midi,** I'm free between eleven and twelve; *F* **vous êtes l.?,** (*to taxi driver*) are you free?; **être l. de faire qch,** to be free to do sth; **école l.,** independent (Catholic) school;
(c) (*non attaché*) (*of movement etc*) unrestrained; **robe qui laisse la taille l.,** dress which fits loosely round the waist; **elle a les cheveux libres,** she wears her hair down *or* loose; **donner l. cours à son enthousiasme/sa curiosité,** to give free rein to one's enthusiasm/curiosity;
(d) l. de préjugés, free from prejudice; **l. de soucis,** free from care, carefree;
(e) être l. avec qn, to be free with s.o., to treat s.o. in a familiar way; **allures** *ou* **manières libres,** free and easy manner;
(f) clear, open (*space, road etc*); free, unoccupied (*table, seat*); **avoir du temps de l.,** to have some free *or* spare time, to have some time free *or* to spare; **le lundi est mon jour l.,** Monday is my day off, I have Mondays free; **laisser le champ l.,** to leave the field clear; **je vous laisse le champ l.,** I'll leave you to it, you're free to do as you think best; **la voie est l.,** the coast is clear; *Rail* **voie l.,** line clear; *Tél* **la ligne n'est pas l.,** the line is engaged *or esp Am* busy; **studio à louer, l. de suite,** one-room flat to rent, available immediately; (*taxi sign*) **l.,** for hire; **à l'air l.,** in the open air; **l. possession,** vacant possession;
(g) *Tech* disengaged, running free, out of gear; (*vélo*) *Aut* **roue l.,** freewheel; **descendre une côte en roue l.,** to freewheel *or* coast down a hill;
(h) *Com* **entrée l.,** please come in and look around, no obligation to buy;
(i) *Sp* free, freestyle; **des figures libres,** free figure skating; **la lutte l.,** freestyle wrestling.
libre-échange [libreʃɑ̃ʒ] *nm Écon* free trade.
libre-échangiste [libreʃɑ̃ʒist] **1** *adj Écon* free trade. **2** *nm* free trader; (*pl libre-échangistes*).
librement [librəmɑ̃] *adv* freely, unrestrainedly.
libre-service [librəsɛrvis] *nm* self-service; **(magasin/restaurant) l.-s.,** self-service shop *or US* store/restaurant; **station-essence l.-s.,** self-service petrol *or US* gas station; (*pl libres-services*).
librettiste [libretist] *n Mus* librettist.
libretto [libreto] *nm Mus* libretto; (*pl libretti, librettos*).
Libye [libi] *nf* Libya.
libyen, -enne [libjɛ̃, -jɛn] **1** *adj* Libyan. **2** *n* **L.,** Libyan.
lice [lis] *nf Hist* lists; *Fig* **entrer en l. contre qn,** to enter the lists against s.o..
licence [lisɑ̃s] *nf* **(a)** (*permis*) *Br* licence, *US* license; *Admin* **l. pour vendre qch,** licence to sell sth; **l. de débitant,** licence to sell beer, wines and spirits, *Am* liquor licence; **fabriqué sous l.,** made under licence; **l. d'importation/d'exportation,** import/export licence; **(b)** *Sp* permit, certificate (*giving right of entry into competition*); **(c)** *Univ* bachelor's degree; **l. ès** *ou* **de lettres/ès** *ou* **de sciences/en droit,** bachelor's degree in arts/in science/in law, arts/science/law degree; **passer sa l.,** to take one's degree (exams) *or* one's finals; **(d)** (*liberté*) licence, abuse of liberty; **l. poétique,** poetic licence; **prendre des licences avec qn,** to take liberties with s.o.; **(e)** *Vieilli* (*dérèglement*) licentiousness.
licencié, -ée [lisɑ̃sje] **1** *adj* **(a)** *Univ* **il est l.,** he's a graduate; **professeur l.,** graduate teacher; **(b)** (*renvoyé*) (made) redundant; (*temporairement*) laid off; **un ouvrier l.,** a redundant worker. **2** *n* **(a)** *Univ* **l. ès lettres/ès** *ou* **de sciences/en droit,** bachelor of arts/of science/of law, arts/science/law graduate; **(b)** *Sp* permit holder.
licenciement [lisɑ̃simɑ̃] *nm* disbanding (*of troops*); redundancy (*of workers*); dismissal (*of employee*); **recevoir une lettre de l.,** to receive a redundancy notice; **il y a eu beaucoup de licenciements,** many (people) were made redundant, there were a lot of redundancies.
licencier [lisɑ̃sje] *vt* (*pr sub & impf* **n. licenciions, v. licenciiez**) to disband (*troops*); to make (*workers*) redundant; to dismiss (*employee*).
licencieusement [lisɑ̃sjøzmɑ̃] *adv* licentiously.
licencieux, -euse [lisɑ̃sjø, -øz] *adj* licentious.
lichen [likɛn] *nm* (*parasite*) lichen.
lichette [liʃɛt] *nf F* small slice, nibble (*of bread, cheese etc*).
licite [licit] *adj* licit, lawful, permissible.
licitement [lisitmɑ̃] *adv* licitly, lawfully.
licol [likɔl] *nm* halter.
licorne [likɔrn] *nf* **(a)** *Myth Hér* unicorn; **(b)** *Zool* (*narval*) **l. de mer,** sea unicorn, narwhal.
licou [liku] *nm* halter.
licteur [liktœr] *nm Antiq* lictor.
lido [lido] *nm Géog* sand bar.
lie [li] **1** *nf* dregs; **boire le calice jusqu'à la l.,** to drain the cup to the dregs; **l. (de vin),** lees *or* sediment of wine; *Fig* **la l. de la société,** the dregs of society. **2** *adj inv* **l.(-)de (-)vin,** purplish red, wine-coloured.
lié [lje] *adj* **(a)** (*attaché*) bound; *Litt* **avoir les mains liées,** to have one's hands tied; *Fig* **j'ai les mains liées,** my hands are tied; *Fig* **pieds et poings liés,** bound hand and foot; **avoir la langue liée,** to be bound to keep a secret; **(b)** (*en relation étroite*) **être (très) l. avec qn,** to be (great) friends *or* intimately acquainted with s.o.; **avoir partie liée avec qn,** to be in league with s.o.; **(c)** *Mus* **notes liées,** slurred notes; (*deux notes différentes*) tied notes.
lied [lid] *nm Mus* lied, song; (*pl lieder*).
liège [ljɛʒ] *nm* **(a)** (*matière naturelle*) cork; **semelle de l.,** cork sole; **cigarette à bout de l.,** cork-tipped cigarette; **bouchon de l.,** cork; **(b) (chêne-)l.,** cork oak.
liégeois, -oise [ljeʒwa, -waz] **1** *adj* **(a)** of Liège; **(b)** *Culin* **café/chocolat l.,** iced coffee/chocolate topped with crème Chantilly. **2** *n* **L.,** native *or* inhabitant of Liège.
lien [ljɛ̃] *nm* **(a)** (*attache*) tie, bond; **il s'est libéré de ses liens,** he freed himself from his bonds; **(b)** *Fig* **liens du sang,** blood ties; **l. de parenté,** family relationship; **l. conjugal,** marriage bond; **mes liens de famille,** my family ties; **l. d'amitié,** bond of friendship; **(c)** (*relation*) link, connection; **j'ai du mal à faire le l. avec ce qu'il a dit avant,** I can't see the connection with what he said before; **il y a un l. entre ces événements,** there's a connection *or* link between these events; **(d)** (*pour les cheveux etc*) brace, tie, strap, band.
lier [lje] *v* (*pr sub & impf* **n. liions, v. liiez**) **1** *vt* **(a)** (*attacher*) to bind, to fasten, to tie, to tie up; **l. qch avec une corde,** to bind sth *or* tie sth up with a rope; **l. les pieds et les mains à qn,** to bind s.o. hand and foot; **l. un fagot,** to tie up a bundle of sticks; **on l'a lié à un arbre,** he was tied (up) to a tree; **l. les lacets de ses souliers,** to tie (up) *or* do up one's shoelaces; *Fig* **ce contrat vous lie,** you are bound by this agreement, this agreement binds you *or* is binding on you; **l'intérêt nous lie,** we have common interests; *Fig* **l. les idées,** to connect *or* link ideas; **tout est lié,** (*dans un roman etc*) everything connects; **l. deux mots,** to link two words (in pronunciation), to sound the liaison; *Mus* **l. deux notes,** to slur (two notes); (*entre deux notes différentes*) to tie two notes;
(b) *Culin* to thicken (*sauce*);
(c) l. amitié/conversation avec qn, to strike up a friendship with s.o./to start a *or* enter into conversation with s.o..
2 se lier *vpr* **(a)** (*socialement*) **se l. avec qn,** to form *or* strike up a friendship with s.o.; **il se lie facilement,** he makes friends easily; **je me suis lié d'amitié avec son père,** I have made friends with his father;
(b) (*se mélanger*) **le lait et le jaune d'œuf se lient facilement,** milk and yolk of egg blend easily.
lierre [ljɛr] *nm* (*plante*) ivy; **l. terrestre,** ground ivy.
liesse [ljɛs] *nf* **(a)** *Arch Litt* jubilation, gaiety; **(b) en l.,** jubilant.
lieu, *pl* **lieux** [ljø] *nm* **(a)** (*endroit*) place; **mettre qch en l. sûr,** to put sth in a safe place; **en tous lieux,** everywhere; **en aucun l.,** nowhere; **en haut l.,** in high circles, in high places; **le l. du crime,** the scene of the crime; **la police est sur les lieux de l'accident,** the police are at the scene of the accident; **j'étais sur les lieux,** I was on the spot; **l. mal famé,** disreputable house; **visiter les lieux saints,** to visit

the Holy Places; **l. de rendez-vous,** meeting place, rendezvous; **l. public,** a public place; **l. de travail,** place of work; **en premier l.,** in the first place, first of all, firstly; **en troisième l.,** thirdly; **en dernier l.,** last of all, lastly, finally; **en temps et l.,** at the proper time and place; **en son l.,** in due course;

(b) lieux, premises; **faire un état des lieux,** = to draw up a survey-cum-inventory (of premises); **avant de quitter ces lieux,** before leaving the premises;

(c) *Vieilli* **lieux (d'aisances),** lavatory;

(d) avoir l., to take place; **la réunion aura l. à ...,** the meeting will take place *or* be held at ...;

(e) *(raisons)* ground(s), cause; **il y a (tout) l./j'ai l. de supposer que** + *ind*, there are *or* is/I have (good) grounds *or* (every) reason for supposing that ...; **il y a l. d'attendre,** it would be advisable *or* as well to wait; **je vous écrirai s'il y a l.,** I'll write to you if necessary; **donner l. à des désagréments,** to give rise to trouble; **tout donne l. de croire que ...,** everything leads one *or* us *etc* to believe that ...; **son retour a donné l. à une réunion de famille,** his return was the occasion for a family gathering;

(f) *(function)* **tenir l. de qch,** to take the place of *or* stand instead of sth; **elle lui a tenu l. de mère,** she has been a mother to him; **au l. de,** instead of; *Com & Fml* in lieu of; **au l. d'être satisfait,** instead of being satisfied; **au l. que** + *sub*, instead of + *gerund*;

(g) *Math* **l. géométrique,** locus;

(h) l. commun, commonplace;

(i) *(poisson)* pollack.

lieu(-)dit [ljødi] *nm* (named) place, locality; *(pl lieux (-)-dits)*.

lieue [ljø] *nf* league (= 4 kilometres); *Nau* **l. marine,** = $5\frac{1}{2}$ kilometres; **être à mille lieues de croire qch,** to be far *or* miles from believing sth; **j'étais à cent lieues de penser que ...,** I would never (in a million years) have dreamt that ...; *Vieilli* **il sent son docteur d'une l.,** you can tell he's a doctor a mile off.

lieur, -euse [ljœr, -øz] *Agr* **1** *n* binder *(of sheaves etc)*. **2** *nf* **lieuse,** (mechanical) sheaf binder.

lieutenant [ljøtnɑ̃] *nm* **(a)** *Mil* lieutenant; *Nau* **l. de vaisseau,** lieutenant; *Av* **l. (aviateur),** flying officer, *US* first lieutenant; **(b)** *(Merchant Marine)* mate; **premier l.,** second mate.

lieutenant-colonel [ljøtnɑ̃kɔlɔnɛl] *nm Mil* lieutenant-colonel; *Av* wing commander; *(pl lieutenants-colonels)*.

lièvre [ljɛvr] *nm* hare; *Fig* **c'est vous qui avez levé le l.,** you started it; *Fig* **c'est là que gît le l.,** that's the crucial point, that's the crux of the matter; *Fig* **courir deux lièvres à la fois,** to try to do two things at once; *Fig* **faire lever un l.,** to start a hare; *Fig* **mémoire de l.,** memory like a sieve; *Culin* **pâté de l.,** hare pâté.

lift [lift] *nm* **(a)** *Sp* topspin; **faire un l.,** to give a ball topspin, to put topspin on a ball; **(b)** *F* *(conduite en voiture)* lift, *US* ride; **je te donne un l.?,** can I give you a lift *or US* ride?

lifter [lifte] *vt Sp* to put topspin on; **l. une balle,** to give a ball topspin, to put topspin on a ball.

liftier [liftje] *nm* lift attendant, *Am* elevator operator.

lifting [liftiŋ] *nm Chir* face lift; **elle s'est fait faire un l.,** she's had a face lift.

ligament [ligamɑ̃] *nm Anat* ligament.

ligature [ligatyr] *nf* **(a)** *(fait d'attacher)* tying, binding; **la l. des greffes,** the binding of (the) grafts; **(b)** *Él etc* splice *(in wire, cable)*; **(c)** *Chir Typ* ligature; **l. des trompes,** the tying of tubes.

ligaturer [ligatyre] *vt* **(a)** *(attacher)* to bind, to splice; **(b)** *Chir* to ligature, to tie *(artery etc)*.

lige [liʒ] *adj Hist* liege.

lignage¹ [liɲaʒ] *nm Arch* lineage, descent.

lignage² *nm Typ* linage *(of a text etc)*.

ligne [liɲ] *nf* **(a)** *(fil)* line; (fishing) line; **planter des arbres à la l.,** to plant trees straight by using a line *or* a cord; **l. de sonde,** plumb line; **l. de fond,** ledger line;

(b) *(trait)* line; **l. droite,** straight line; **l. brisée,** broken line; **tracer une l. à main levée,** to draw a line freehand; **les lignes de la main,** the lines of the hand; **votre l. de vie est courte,** you have a short life-line; *Mus* **l. de portée,** stave line; **l. supplémentaire additionnelle,** ledger line; *Fb* **l. de touche,** touch line; *Tennis* **l. de fond/médiane,** base/centre line; *TV* **définition de 625 lignes,** definition of 625 lines; *Aut* **l. blanche,** white line, *US* yellow line;

(c) *(contour, silhouette)* (out)line; **la l. du nez,** the line *or* contour of the nose; **pureté des lignes,** *(in picture)* purity of line; **l. élégante d'une voiture,** elegant lines of a car; *Fig* **grandes lignes d'une œuvre,** broad *or* general outline(s) of a work; **je vais vous expliquer le projet dans ses grandes lignes,** I'll explain the broad outline(s) of the project to you; **garder/soigner sa l.,** to keep/watch one's waistline *or* one's figure; **avoir (de) la l.,** to have a good figure;

(d) *(démarcation, limite)* *Nau* **l. de flottaison,** waterline *(of ship)*; **l. de charge,** load line; *Phys* **l. de force,** line of force; *Mil* **l. de visée** *ou* **de mire,** line of sight; **l. de tir,** line of fire; **la l. du partage des eaux,** watershed; *Nau* **la l. (équatoriale),** the line, the Equator; **passer la l.,** to cross the line; *(filiation)* **descendre en l. directe** *ou* **en droite l. de ...,** to be directly descended from ...; **la l. de démarcation,** demarcation line;

(e) *(rangée)* **l. de maisons,** row of houses; **se mettre en l.,** to line up; **plantés en l.,** planted in a line *or* row; **question qui vient en première l.,** question of primary importance; *Fig* **hors l.,** out of the common; unrivalled, outstanding, incomparable *(artist etc)*; *Fig* **sur toute la l.,** all along all the line;

(f) *(direction)* line; **avancer en l. droite,** to advance in a straight line; *Fig* **redéfinir sa l. d'action,** to adopt a different line *or* course of action; **la l. du parti communiste,** the communist party line;

(g) line *(of writing)*; **écris-moi deux lignes,** drop me a line; *Fig* **lire entre les lignes,** to read between the lines; **aller à la l.,** to begin a new line *or* a new paragraph; *Fig* **entrer en l. de compte,** to come into consideration; *Fig* **cela n'entre pas en l. de compte,** that doesn't come into it; *(in dictating)* **à la l.,** new paragraph, new line; *Fig* **faire entrer un facteur en l. de compte,** to take a factor into account; *Ordinat* **l. de statut,** status line;

(h) *Mil* **l. de front,** front line; *Hist* **L. Maginot,** Maginot Line; **l. d'attaque,** line of attack;

(i) l. de bataille *ou* **de combat,** line of battle, fighting line; **troupe de l.,** troops of the line; **(infanterie de) l.,** line infantry; *Nau Arch* **vaisseau de l.,** ship of the line;

(j) *Rail* line; **grandes lignes,** main lines; **l. maritime/aérienne,** shipping line/airline; **l. d'autobus,** bus service; *(parcours)* bus route;

(k) *Él* (power) line; **l. de haute tension,** high tension wire *or* line; **l. télégraphique,** telegraph line;

(l) l. téléphonique, telephone line; **la l. est occupée,** the line is engaged *or surtout Am* busy; **la l. a été coupée,** I've *or* we've *etc* been cut off; **il y a quelqu'un sur la l.,** there's someone on the line; **vous êtes en l.,** you're connected, you're through; *Tél Pol* **la l. rouge,** the hot line;

(m) *Com* line, range; **BOTÉ lance une nouvelle l. cosmétique,** BOTÉ are launching a new line *or* range of cosmetics; **l. pour hommes,** range for men;

(n) *Can* eighth of an inch (3.175 mm).

lignée [liɲe] *nf* (line of) descendants; *(origine)* line, lineage; **une nombreuse l,** a large number of descendants; **de bonne l. allemande,** of good German stock; *Fig* **un philosophe dans la l. de Russell,** a philosopher in the tradition of Russell.

ligneux, -euse [liɲø, -øz] *adj* ligneous, woody.

lignite [liɲit] *nm Minér* lignite, brown coal.

ligotage [ligɔtaʒ] *nm* binding, tying up *(of s.o.)*.

ligoter [ligɔte] *vt* to tie *(s.o.)* up; to bind *(s.o.)* hand and foot; *Fig* to place restrictions on, to tie down with restrictions, to keep under strict control; **le gouvernement a longtemps ligoté la presse,** the government has kept the press under strict control for a long time.

ligue [lig] *nf* league, confederacy; *Hist* **la L. d'Augsbourg,** the League of Augsburg.

liguer [lige] **1** *vt* to league, to bond *(nations etc)* together; **être ligué avec qn,** to be in league with s.o.. **2 se liguer** *vpr* to league, to form a league **(avec,** with; **contre,** against); **ils se liguent contre moi,** they're conspiring against me.

ligueur, -euse [ligœr, -øz] *n* member of a league.

lilas [lila] **1** *nm Bot* lilac. **2** *adj inv* lilac.

lilial, -iaux [liljal, -jo] *adj Litt* lily-white.

lilliputien, -ienne [lilipysjɛ̃, -jɛn] **1** *adj* Lilliputian. **2** *n* **L.,** Lilliputian.

lillois, -oise [lilwa, -waz] **1** *adj* of *or* from Lille. **2** *n* **L.,** native *or* inhabitant of Lille.

limace [limas] *nf* *(mollusque)* slug; *Arg* **c'est une vraie l.,** he's so slow, he's such a slowcoach *or US* slowpoke.

limaçon [limasɔ̃] *nm* **(a)** *Vieilli* snail; **(b)** *Anat* cochlea *(of the ear)*.

limage [limaʒ] *nm* filing (down, off).

limaille [limaj] *nf* filings; **l. de fer,** iron filings.

limande [limɑ̃d] *nf* **(a)** *(poisson)* dab; **l.-sole,** lemon sole; *F (of woman)* **plate comme une l.,** as flat as a pancake; **(b)** *Menuis* graving piece; **(c)** *(de cordage)* straight edge.

limbe [lɛ̃b] *nm* **(a)** *Astron Math* limb; **(b)** *Bot* lamina, limb (*of leaf*); **(c)** *Rel* **les Limbes,** limbo; **(d)** *Fig* limbo; **le projet est dans les limbes,** the project is as yet undecided *or* is still in (a state of) limbo; **les choses flottent encore dans les limbes, nous n'avons rien décidé,** things are still up in the air, we haven't decided anything.

lime¹ [lim] *nf* **(a)** (*outil*) file; **l. sourde,** dead smooth-file; **l. à ongles,** nail file; **l. émeri,** emery board; **aiguiser un outil à la l.,** to file up a tool; *Fig* **donner un dernier coup de l. à un ouvrage,** to put the finishing touches to a piece of work; **(b)** (*mollusque*) lima.

lime² *nf Bot* lime.

limer [lime] *vt* (*réduire*) to file (down); (*polir*) to file (up); *Fig* to polish (up) (*un projet*); **veste limée aux manches,** jacket worn at the sleeves.

limerick [limrik] *nm Ling* limerick.

limeur, -euse [limœr, -øz] *Tech* **1** *n* filer. **2** *nf* **limeuse,** filing machine.

limier [limje] *nm* (*chien*) bloodhound; *Fig* sleuth.

liminaire [liminɛr] *adj Typ* **pièces** *ou* **feuillets liminaires,** preliminary pages, *F* prelims; **épître l.,** foreword, introduction; *Littér* **la journée l.,** the first day.

limitatif, -ive [limitatif, -iv] *adj* limiting, restrictive, restricting.

limitation [limitɑsjɔ̃] *nf* limitation, restriction; **l. des armements,** arms limitation; **l. des naissances,** birth control, family planning; **l. des salaires,** wage restraint; **l. de vitesse,** speed limit; **il n'y a pas de l. de temps,** there's no time limit.

limite [limit] **1** *nf* **(a)** boundary (*of country, field etc*); **les limites d'un terrain de football,** the boundary (lines) of a football pitch; **marquer les limites du terrain,** to mark out the ground; **à la l. du jardin, il y a une forêt,** just beyond the garden there is a forest;

(b) (*de pouvoir, compréhension etc*) limit; **l. d'âge,** age limit; **fixer** *ou* **imposer des limites à l'autorité de qn,** to set limits *or* bounds on s.o.'s authority; **mettre une l./des limites à ...,** to set a limit/limits to ...; **franchir** *ou* **dépasser les limites,** to go beyond the limits, to go too far; **dans les limites du sujet,** within the limits of the subject; **je ferai tout pour vous aider dans les limites du possible,** I'll do everything I can to help you as far as is humanly possible; **dans une certaine l.,** up to a point; to a certain extent; **à la l., j'accepterais de le voir,** if pushed *or* if I have to, I'll agree to see him; **se battre jusqu'à la dernière l.,** to fight to the death; **il est à la l. de ses forces,** he's completely exhausted; **sans limites,** unbounded, limitless; (*capacité*) **je connais mes limites,** I know my limits *or* what I'm capable of; **il cherche à dépasser ses limites,** he is seeking to go beyond his limits; **ma patience a des limites!,** there are limits to my patience!, my patience is wearing thin!; **il y a des limites!,** there are limits!; **son ambition ne connaît pas de limites,** his ambition knows no bounds; *Boxe* **gagner avant la l.,** to win inside the distance;

(c) *Math* limit, limiting value; *Tech* **l. d'élasticité,** elastic limit; **l. de rupture,** breaking point.

2 *adj* **cas l.,** borderline case; **vitesse l.,** maximum speed; **charge l. d'un pont,** maximum load of a bridge; **date l.,** deadline; (*pour candidature etc*) deadline, closing date; **date l. de vente,** sell-by-date; **50 francs, c'est le prix l.,** 50 francs is the upper limit.

limité [limite] *adj* limited, restricted; **vitesse limitée à 60 km/heure,** speed restricted to 60km/hour; **une conversation limitée par la présence d'une curieuse,** a conversation inhibited by the presence of a curious bystander; *F* **un enfant l.,** a child of limited abilities *or* intelligence.

limiter [limite] **1** *vt* **(a)** (*délimiter*) to bound, to mark the bounds of (*countries etc*); **(b)** (*restreindre*) to limit, to restrict; to set bounds *or* limits to (*s.o.'s power, rights etc*); **l. les dépenses,** to limit expenditure; **l. les dégâts,** to limit the damage. **2 se limiter** *vpr* **il faut apprendre à se l.,** you have to learn to limit yourself *or* to keep within limits; **se l. à ...,** to limit *or* restrict oneself to ....

limitrophe [limitrɔf] *adj* adjacent (**de,** to), bordering (**de,** on); **les pays limitrophes,** the neighbouring *or US* neighboring countries; **être l. d'un autre pays,** to border on another country.

limogeage [limɔʒaʒ] *nm* **(a)** superseding (*of general etc*); **(b)** (*destitution*) dismissal.

limoger [limɔʒe] *vt* **(a)** to supersede (*general etc*); **(b)** (*destituer*) to dismiss (*s.o.*).

limon¹ [limɔ̃] *nm* **(a)** (*alluvium*) silt, alluvium; **le l. employé comme engrais,** silt used as a fertilizer; **(b)** *Géol* limon.

limon² *nm* **(a)** (*brancard*) shaft; **(b)** *Constr* stringboard, stringer (*of staircase*).

limon³ *nm Bot Arch* lemon.

limonade [limɔnad] *nf* **(a)** (*boisson gazeuse*) (fizzy) lemonade; **(b)** *Arch* lemon (and water) drink.

limonadier, -ière [limɔnadje, -jɛr] *n* **(a)** *Ind* soft (fizzy) drinks manufacturer; **(b)** *Arch* (*cafetier*) keeper *or* owner of a café.

limoneux, -euse [limɔnø, -øz] *adj* (*of water etc*) muddy, silty; *Géol* alluvial.

limonier [limɔnje] *nm* shaft horse.

limousin, -ine [limuzɛ̃, -in] **1** *adj* of *or* from (the province of) Limousin. **2** *n* **L.,** native *or* inhabitant of (the province of) Limousin. **3** *nm Ling* Limousin dialect. **4** *nf* **limousine (a)** *Aut Arch* limousine; **(b)** *Vieilli* (*pèlerine*) (shepherd's) rough woollen cloak.

limpide [lɛ̃pid] *adj* limpid, clear (*quartz, water etc*); **un regard l.,** clear *or Litt* limpid expression; clear, lucid (*explanation*); **style l.,** limpid *or* lucid style.

limpidité [lɛ̃pidite] *nf* limpidity, clarity; lucidity.

lin [lɛ̃] *nm* **(a)** (*plante*) flax; **graine de l.,** linseed; **huile de l.,** linseed oil; **(b)** *Tex* **(tissu, toile de) l.,** linen.

linceul [lɛ̃sœl] *nm* winding sheet, shroud; *Fig Litt* **le l. blanc des nuages,** the white shroud formed by the clouds.

linéaire [lineɛr] *adj* **(a)** *Math* linear; **(b) dessin l.,** geometrical drawing; **(c)** *Fig* **récit l.,** linear narrative.

linge [lɛ̃ʒ] *nm* **(a)** linen; **l. de table,** table linen; **l. de maison, gros l.,** household linen; **armoire à l.,** linen cupboard; **(b)** (*dessous*) **l. fin,** frilly underwear; **l. (de corps),** underwear; *Fig F* **c'est du beau l.,** she's a smart-looking woman; **(c)** (*lessive*) washing; **corde à l.,** clothes-line; **corbeille à l.,** laundry basket; **(d)** (*morceau de tissu*) cloth.

lingère [lɛ̃ʒɛr] *nf* linen maid.

lingerie [lɛ̃ʒri] *nf* **(a)** (*dessous féminins*) underwear, lingerie; **(b)** (*pièce réservé à l'entretien du linge*) linen room.

lingot [lɛ̃go] *nm* **(a)** (*masse de métal*) ingot; **l. d'or,** gold bar *or* ingot; *Fin* **or** *ou* **argent en lingots,** bullion; **(b)** *Typ* slug.

lingual, -aux [lɛ̃gwal, -o] *adj Anat Ling* lingual.

linguiste [lɛ̃gɥist] *n* linguist.

linguistique [lɛ̃gɥistik] **1** *adj* linguistic; **un séjour l.,** a stay in a foreign country (*for the purposes of learning the language*); **une communauté l.,** a speech community. **2** *nf* linguistics.

linguistiquement [lɛ̃gɥistikmɑ̃] *adv* linguistically.

linier, -ière [linje, -jɛr] *adj Tex* linen; **industrie linière,** linen industry.

liniment [linimɑ̃] *nm Méd* liniment.

lino [lino] *nm F* (= **linoleum**) lino.

linoléum [linɔleɔm] *nm* linoleum.

linon [linɔ̃] *nm Tex* lawn.

linotte [linɔt] *nf* (*oiseau*) linnet; *F* **tête de l.,** scatterbrain.

linotype ® [linɔtip] *nf Typ* Linotype.

linotypie [linɔtipi] *nf Typ* setting by Linotype.

linotypiste [linɔtipist] *n* Linotype operator.

linteau, -eaux [lɛ̃to] *nm Constr* lintel.

lion, -onne [ljɔ̃, -ɔn] *n* **(a)** lion, *f* lioness; **la part du l.,** the lion's share; **c'est un l.! quel courage!,** he's as brave as a lion!; *F* **il a mangé** *ou Arg* **bouffé du l.,** he's very energetic; (*agressif*) he's very aggressive; **(b) l. de mer,** sea lion; **(c)** *Arch & Litt* celebrity, (literary) lion; **(d)** *Astron* **le L.,** Leo; **les natifs du L.,** those born under (the sign of) Leo, Leos; **(e)** *Fig* **une lionne,** a handsome *or* elegant-looking woman.

lionceau, -eaux [ljɔ̃so] *nm* lion cub.

lipide [lipid] *nm Biol Ch* lipid.

lippe [lip] *nf* (thick) lower lip; **faire la l.,** to pout; (*bouder*) to sulk.

lippu [lipy] *adj* thick-lipped; (*lèvre*) thick.

liquéfaction [likefaksjɔ̃] *nf* liquefaction.

liquéfiable [likefjabl] *adj* liquefiable (*gas*).

liquéfiant, -iante [likefjɑ̃] *adj* liquefactive, liquefying.

liquéfier [likefje] *v* (*pr sub & impf* **n. liquéfiions, v. liquéfiiez**) **1** *vt* to liquefy; *Fig* **cette nouvelle l'a liquéfié,** this piece of news completely sapped his confidence. **2 se liquéfier** *vpr* to liquefy; *Fig* to become drained (of energy); (*avoir peur*) to turn to jelly.

liqueur [likœr] *nf* **(a)** (*spiritueux*) liqueur; **vin de l.,** dessert wine, sweet wine; **je vous propose une l.?,** can I offer you a liqueur?; **verre à l.,** liqueur glass; **l. de cassis,** blackcurrant liqueur; **(b)** *Can* **l. (douce),** soft drink; **(c)** *Ch* solution; **l. titrée,** standard solution.

liquidateur, -trice [likidatœr, -tris] *n Jur* liquidator.
liquidation [likidasjɔ̃] *nf* **(a)** *Jur* liquidation; **l. forcée/volontaire,** compulsory/voluntary liquidation; **entrer en l.,** to go into liquidation; **(b)** settlement, clearing (*of accounts*); *Bourse* settlement; **chambre de l.,** (bankers') clearing house; **(c)** *Com* selling off (*of stocks*); clearance sale.
liquide [likid] **1** *adj* liquid; **la soupe est trop l.,** the soup is too watery *or* too thin; **argent l.,** cash, ready money. **2** *nm* **(a)** (*substance*) liquid, fluid; **il ne pourra prendre que des liquides pendant une semaine,** he will not be able to consume anything but liquids for a week; **(b)** *Fig* (*espèces*) ready cash; **je n'ai pas assez de l.,** I haven't enough cash; **vous payez par chèque ou en l.?,** are you paying by cheque or in cash? **3** *nf Ling* liquid.
liquider [likide] *vt* **(a)** *Jur* to liquidate, to wind up (*a business*); **(b)** to settle (*account*); **(c)** *F* **l. qn,** (*tuer*) to liquidate *or* eliminate s.o.; **c'est liquidé,** it's (all) over; **(d)** to sell off (*stock*).
liquidité [likidite] *nf* liquidity; *Fin* **liquidités,** liquid assets.
liquoreux, -euse [likɔrø, -øz] *adj* liqueur-like (*wine etc*); sweet.
lire[1] [lir] *v* (*prp* **lisant**; *pp* **lu**; *pr ind* **je lis, il lit**; *impf* **je lisais**; *p hist* **je lus**; *fu* **je lirai**) **1** *vt* to read; **l. tout haut** *ou* **à haute voix,** to read aloud; **l. en diagonale,** to scan, to cast a quick eye over (*sth*), to skim through (*sth*); **l. en lecture rapide,** to scan; (*méthode brevetée*) to speed-read; **l. une carte,** to map-read, to read a map; **l. qch dans un livre,** to read sth in a book; **je vais te l. la recette,** I'll read out the recipe to you; **l. de la musique à vue,** to sightread music; **on peut le l. de deux façons différentes,** you can read it two different ways; **avoir beaucoup lu,** to be well read; **l. dans la pensée de qn,** to read s.o.'s thoughts; **l. dans le jeu de qn,** to know s.o.'s game, to know what s.o. is up to; **elle a voulu me l. les lignes de la main,** she wanted to read my hand; *Fml* **dans l'attente de vous l.,** hoping to hear from you soon.
2 se lire *vpr* to read; **ça ne se lit pas bien,** it doesn't read well; **ce livre se lit bien** *ou* **se laisse l.,** it's a readable book, this book is very readable; this book's a good read; **cela se lit sur votre visage/dans vos yeux,** it shows in your face/in your eyes, it's written all over your face/you can read it in your eyes.
lire[2] *nf* (*monnaie*) lira.
lis [lis] *nm* (*plante*) lily; **l. blanc,** white lily; **l. des vallées,** lily of the valley; **l. d'eau** *ou* **d'étang,** water lily; **teint de l.,** lily-white complexion.
Lisbonne [lizbɔn] *nf* Lisbon.
lise [liz] *nf* quicksand.
liseré [lizre] *nm*, **liséré** [lizere] *nm Couture etc* border, edging; piping, binding (*of skirt*); strip (*of different material etc*).
liserer [lizre] **, lisérer** [lizere] *vt* (**je lisère, n. liserons** *or* **n. lisérons; je lisèrerai**) *Couture* **(a)** to border, to edge; to sew an edging on (*sth*); **(b)** (*pour décorer*) to pipe (*trousers, uniform*); to trim (*sth*) with piping.
liseron [lizrɔ̃] *nm* (*plante*) bindweed, convolvulus.
liseur, -euse [lizœr, -øz] **1** *n* reader. **2** *nf* **liseuse (a)** (*couteau à papier*) bookmark(er) and paperknife combined; **(b)** (*couverture amovible*) book cover, (dust) cover, (dust) jacket; **(c)** (*vêtement de femme*) (lady's) bed jacket.
lisibilité [lizibilite] *nf* legibility.
lisible [lizibl] *adj* **(a)** legible (*writing etc*); **(b)** readable, worth reading (*book etc*).
lisiblement [liziblәmɑ̃] *adv* legibly.
lisière [lizjɛr] *nf* **(a)** (*bande de tissu*) selvage, selvedge; **(b)** **tenir qn en lisières,** to keep s.o. on a tight rein; **(c)** edge, border (*of field, forest*).
lissage [lisaʒ] *nm* smoothing, polishing (*of stone etc*); sleeking (*of leather*); glazing (*of paper etc*).
lisse[1] [lis] *nf Nau* **(a)** ribband (*of the hull*); rail, strake; **lisses de l'avant,** harpings; **(b)** handrail (*of the bulwarks*).
lisse[2] *adj* smooth; (*poli*) polished; **cheveux lisses,** sleek hair.
lisser [lise] **1** *vt* to smooth, to polish (*stone etc*); to smooth down (*hair*); to smooth out (*crease*); to sleek (*leather*); to glaze (*paper etc*). **2 se lisser** *vpr* **se l. les plumes,** (*of bird*) to preen its feathers.
lisseur, -euse [lisœr, -øz] **1** *n* smoother, polisher. **2** *nf* **lisseuse,** smoothing machine.
lissoir [liswar] *nm* smoother, polishing iron.
listage [listaʒ] *nm Ordinat* listing.
liste [list] *nf* list; *Mil* roster; **l. officielle des taux,** schedule of charges; **l. électorale,** electoral roll; **l. civile,** Civil List; **l. noire,** blacklist; *Tél F* **être sur la l. rouge,** to have an unlisted number, to be unlisted; **l. d'envoi** *ou* **des abonnés,** mailing list; **l. de mariage,** wedding list; **dresser** *ou* **faire une l.,** to draw up *or* make a list.
listel, -els, -eaux [listɛl, -o] *nm* **(a)** *Archit etc* listel, fillet; **(b)** rim (*of coin*).
lister [liste] *vt Ordinat* to list.
listériose [listerjoz] *nf Méd* listeria.
listing [listiŋ] *nm Ordinat* printout; **papier l.,** listing paper.
lit [li] *nm* **(a)** bed; **l. pour deux personnes, grand l.,** double bed; **lits jumeaux,** twin beds; **l. clos,** box bed; **l. de camp,** camp bed, *Am* cot; **l. pliant,** folding bed; **l. à colonnes,** four-poster (bed); **l. à baldaquin,** canopied four-poster; **lits superposés,** bunk beds, bunks; **l. d'enfant,** cot, *Am* crib; **l. de repos,** couch; **mettre un enfant au l.,** to put a child to bed; **au l. les enfants!,** time for bed children!, bedtime, children!; **aller au l.,** to go to bed; **se mettre au l.,** to get into bed; **rendre visite à qn au saut du l.,** to pay s.o. a visit in the early (hours of the) morning; **être au l.,** to be in bed; **garder le l.,** to stay in bed; **je ne te tire pas du l. au moins?,** I hope I didn't get you out of bed; **faire les lits,** to make the beds; **faire l. à part,** to sleep in separate beds; **un hôtel de 200 lits,** a 200-bed hotel; **chambre à un l./à deux lits,** single-/twin-bedded room; **enfant du second l.,** child by one's second marriage; **être sur son l. de mort,** to be on one's death bed; **mourir dans son l.,** to die of natural causes; **l. de douleur,** sick bed;
(b) (*montant*) **bois de l.,** bedstead; **l. de fer,** iron bedstead; **l. d'époque,** period bed(stead);
(c) *F* (*matelas*) bedding; **l. moelleux/dur,** soft/hard bed *or* mattress; **l. de plume,** feather bed;
(d) bed, layer (*of clay, stone etc*); **l. de cendres,** bed of ashes; *Culin* **placer les filets sur un l. d'épinards,** place the fish on a bed of spinach;
(e) bed (*of river etc*); **l. majeur (d'un fleuve),** flood plain; *HydE* **l. majeur/mineur,** high water/mean water *or* bed;
(f) set (*of the tide etc*); **être dans le l. de marée,** to be in the tideway; *Nau* **dans le l. du vent,** in the wind's eye.
litanie [litani] *nf* **(a)** *Rel* **litanies,** litany; **(b)** *Péj* (rambling) story; **c'est toujours la même l.,** it's the same old story.
lit-bateau [libato] *nm* platform bed; (*pl lits-bateaux*).
lit-cage [likaʒ] *nm* folding bedstead; (*pl lits-cages*).
lit-canapé [likanape] *nm* sofa bed; (*pl lits-canapés*).
litchi [litʃi] *nm* (*fruit*) lychee, litchi.
liteau[1]**, -eaux** [lito] *nm* **(a)** *Constr* batten, rail, ribband; **(b)** *Tex* band, stripe (*on table linen etc*).
liteau[2] *nm* haunt (*of wolves during the day*).
litée [lite] *nf* litter (*of animals*).
literie [litri] *nf* bedding; bed linen.
lithine [litin] *nf Ch* lithia.
lithiné [litine] **1** *adj* **eau lithinée,** lithia water. **2** *nmpl* **lithinés,** lithium salts.
lithium [litjɔm] *nm Ch* lithium.
litho [lito] *nf F* = **LITHOGRAPHIE (b)**.
lithographe [litɔgraf] *n* lithographer.
lithographie [litɔgrafi] *nf* **(a)** (*technique*) lithography; **(b)** (*résultat*) lithograph.
lithographier [litɔgrafje] *vt* (*pr sub & impf* **n. lithographiions, v. lithographiiez**) to lithograph.
lithographique [litɔgrafik] *adj* lithographic.
lithosphère [litɔsfɛr] *nf Géol* lithosphere.
Lithuanie [litɥani] *nf* Lithuania.
lithuanien, -ienne [litɥanjɛ̃, -jɛn] *adj & n* = **LITUANIEN, -IENNE**.
litière [litjɛr] *nf* **(a)** (stable) litter; **la l. du chat,** the cat's litter; *Fig* **faire l. de qch,** to throw sth to the winds; **(b)** *Litt* (*palanquin*) litter, palanquin; **être porté en l.,** to be carried in a litter.
litige [litiʒ] *nm* dispute; (*poursuite*) lawsuit; (*recours à la loi*) litigation; **objet** *ou* **point en l.,** bone of contention; *Jur* subject of the action; **être en l.,** to be in dispute.
litigieux, -euse [litiʒjø, -øz] *adj* litigious (*person*); contentious (*issue*).
litote [litɔt] *nf Littér* litotes, understatement.
litre [litr] *nm* **(a)** (*mesure*) litre, *US* liter; **(b)** (*récipient d'un litre*) litre bottle.
litron [litrɔ̃] *nm Arg* litre *or US* liter of wine.
littéraire [literɛr] **1** *adj* **(a)** literary; **la vie l.,** the literary world, the literary life, life devoted to literature; **avoir l'esprit l.,** to have a literary turn of mind; **(b)** *Litt Péj* insincere, affected. **2** *n* **(a)** (*personne douée pour la littérature*) literary person; **c'est plutôt un l.,** his talents are literary; **(b)** (*étudiant*) arts student; **(c)** (*professeur*) arts teacher; (*de littérature*) teacher of literature.
littérairement [literɛrmɑ̃] *adv* in literary terms.

littéral, -aux [literal, -o] *adj* **(a)** literal (*translation etc*); **le sens l. du mot,** the literal meaning of the word; *Math* **coefficient l.,** literal coefficient; **(b)** (*par écrit*) *Jur* **preuve littérale,** documentary evidence; **arabe l.,** written Arabic.
littéralement [literalmɑ̃] *adv* literally.
littéralité [literalite] *nf Litt* literality, literalness.
littérateur [literatœr] *nm* literary man, man of letters; *Péj* literary hack.
littérature [literatyr] *nf* literature; **se lancer dans la l.,** to embark on a career in literature; **faire carrière dans la l.,** to make a career in writing; *Fig Péj* **tout ça c'est de la l.,** all this is of trifling importance; **on a publié une importante l. sur le sujet,** a considerable amount of literature has been published on the subject.
littoral, -aux [litɔral, -o] **1** *adj* coastal, *Litt* littoral (*region etc*). **2** *nm* coastline, *Litt* littoral.
Lituanie [litɥani] *nf* Lithuania.
lituanien, -ienne [litɥanjɛ̃, -jɛn] **1** *adj* Lithuanian. **2** *nm Ling* Lithuanian. **3** *n* **L.,** Lithuanian.
liturgie [lityrʒi] *nf Rel* liturgy.
liturgique [lityrʒik] *adj Rel* liturgical.
liure [ljyr] *nf Tech* lashing (*of load on cart etc*).
livarde [livard] *nf Nau* sprit; **voile à l.,** spritsail.
livarot [livaro] *nm Culin* Livarot (cheese).
livide [livid] *adj* **(a)** *Litt* livid; **nuages livides,** leaden clouds; **(b)** pallid, ghastly (pale) (*complexion*).
lividité [lividite] *nf* lividness; *Méd* **l. cadavérique,** livor mortis, post-mortem lividity.
living(-room) [liviŋ(rum)] *nm* living room.
livrable [livrabl] *adj* **(a)** *Fin* deliverable; **(b)** *Com* ready for delivery; **marchandises livrables à domicile,** goods delivered to your home.
livraison [livrɛzɔ̃] *nf* **(a)** delivery (*of goods etc*); **l. franco,** free delivery, delivered free; **payable à la l.,** payable on delivery; **l. contre remboursement, paiement à la l.,** cash on delivery, *Am* collect on delivery; **faire l. de qch,** to deliver sth; **prendre l. de qch,** to take delivery of sth; **défaut de l.,** non-delivery; **voiture de l.,** delivery van; *Com* **l. à domicile,** we deliver (anywhere); door-to-door delivery; (*marchandise*) **la l. est arrivée,** the delivery has arrived; **(b)** part (*of book published in parts*).
livre¹ [livr] *nf* **(a)** (*weight*) = pound; half a kilo; *Can* pound (= 0.453kg); **(b) l. (sterling),** pound (sterling); **(c)** *Arch* = franc.
livre² *nm* **(a)** book; **l'industrie du l., le l.,** the book trade; **les ouvriers du l.,** printing and typesetting workers; **l. relié,** bound book; **l. de classe,** schoolbook; **l. de lecture,** reader, reading book; **l. de prix,** prize book; **l. de grammaire,** grammar book; **l. d'images/d'enfant,** picture/children's book; **l. de poche,** paperback; **l. de messe,** missal, prayer book; **l. d'heures,** book of hours; **commencer un l.,** to start (reading/writing) a book; **parler comme un l.,** to talk like a book; **traduire un passage à l. ouvert,** to translate a passage at sight; **le grand l. de la nature,** the Book of Nature;
(b) (*volume contenant des renseignements*) **l. de raison,** family record book; **l. d'or,** visitors' book; *Nau* **l. de bord,** log; **livres de comptabilité** *ou* **de commerce,** account books, the books; **l. de paie,** payroll; *Com* **l. journal,** journal, day book; **tenir les livres,** to keep the accounts *or* the books; **tenue des livres,** book-keeping;
(c) book (*of Bible etc*); **le premier l. des 'Fables' de la Fontaine,** the first book of La Fontaine's Fables.
livre-cassette [livr(ə)kasɛt] *nm* spoken word cassette.
livrée [livre] *nf* **(a)** (*habit de domestique*) livery; **valet en l.,** servant in livery, liveried servant; **porter la l. de qn,** to be in s.o.'s service; **(b)** coat (*of fox etc*); plumage (*of birds*).
livrer [livre] **1** *vt* **(a)** to deliver (*goods etc*); **nous avons bien été livrés,** we acknowledge receipt of the delivery;
(b) (*remettre*) to deliver, to surrender; to give (*s.o., sth*) up; **l. qn à la justice,** to deliver *or* hand over s.o. to justice *or* to the authorities; **il a finalement livré ses complices,** he finally delivered up his accomplices; **livré à soi-même,** left to oneself; **l. un poste à l'ennemi,** to give up a post to the enemy;
(c) (*donner, dévoiler*) **l. un secret,** to betray a secret; **l. ses secrets à qn,** to confide one's secrets to s.o.;
(d) l. passage à qn, to let s.o. pass;
(e) (*exposer à, abandonner à*) to leave (*s.o., sth*) to the mercy of (*s.o., sth*); to abandon (*s.o., sth*) to (*s.o., sth*); **l. un village au pillage,** to abandon a village to pillage; **un épouvantail livré aux vents,** a scarecrow left to the mercy of the four winds;
(f) (*engager*) **l. un assaut à l'ennemi,** to make an attack on the enemy; **l. bataille,** to join battle (**à**, with), to give battle (**à**, to).
2 se livrer *vpr* **(a)** (*se rendre*) to give oneself up; (*of woman*) to surrender (*to a man*); **se l. à la justice,** to surrender to the authorities, to give oneself up;
(b) (*se confier*) to open up; **se l. (à qn),** to confide in s.o.; **il commence à se l., à me parler,** he's beginning to open up and start talking to me;
(c) (*s'abandonner à*) **se l. à un vice,** to indulge in *or* surrender to a vice; **se l. à la boisson,** to take to drink; (*être un alcoolique*) to be a heavy drinker; **se l. au désespoir,** to give way to despair; **se l. à la violence,** (*agresseur*) to behave violently, to turn violent;
(d) to be engaged in (*an occupation*); **se l. à ses occupations habituelles,** to indulge in one's usual activities; **se l. à une enquête,** to proceed with an inquiry, to hold an inquiry; **se l. à l'étude,** to devote oneself to study; **se l. à un sport,** to practise a sport.
livresque [livrɛsk] *adj* **(a)** (*théorique*) acquired from books; **connaissances livresques,** book learning; **(b)** *Péj* bookish (*mind*).
livret [livrɛ] *nm* **(a)** (*petit livre*) small book, booklet; (*d'information*) handbook; *Fin* bank book, passbook; **compte sur l.,** savings account; *Admin* **l. de famille,** family record book for registration of births and deaths; **l. militaire individuel,** service record; **l. scolaire,** school report book; **(b)** *Mus* libretto, book (*of opera*).
livreur, -euse [livrœr, -øz] *n* delivery man *or* boy; delivery girl *or* woman.
Lloyd [lɔjd] *nm* (any) association of marine brokers and underwriters.
lob [lɔb] *nm Tennis* lob.
lobby [lɔbi] *nm Pol* lobby; (*pl lobbies*).
lobe [lɔb] *nm* **(a)** *Anat Bot* lobe; **l. de l'oreille,** ear lobe; **(b)** *Archit* foil.
lobé [lɔbe] *adj* **(a)** *Bot* lobed, lobate; **(b)** *Archit* foiled.
lobectomie [lɔbɛktɔmi] *nf Chir* lobectomy.
lobélie [lɔbeli] *nf Bot* lobelia.
lober [lɔbe] **1** *vi Tennis Fb* to lob. **2** *vt Fb* **l. le goal,** to lob the goalie.
lobotomie [lɔbɔtɔmi] *nf Chir* lobotomy; **on lui a fait une l.,** he's had a lobotomy, he's been lobotomized.
lobulaire [lɔbylɛr] *adj Anat Bot* lobular.
lobule [lɔbyl] *nm Anat* lobule; *Bot* lobelet.
local, -aux [lɔkal, -o] **1** *adj* local (*authority etc*); *Méd* local (*disease, remedy*); **les coutumes locales,** local customs; **averses locales demain dans la matinée,** scattered showers tomorrow morning; **le journal l.,** the local paper; *Méd* **traitement l.,** local treatment; **anesthésie locale,** local anaesthetic, **couleur locale,** local colour. **2** *nm* **(a)** (*lieu, endroit*) premises (*of business, organization*); (*bâtiment*) building; (*salle*) room; **l. d'habitation,** dwelling; **taxe sur les locaux loués/meublés,** tax on rented/furnished property; **l. professionnel,** premises used for professional purposes; *Nau* **locaux affectés au personnel du bord,** crew's quarters; **(b)** (*bureau, permanence*) office(s), premises; **rendez-vous au l. à dix heures pour préparer le matériel,** meeting at the office at ten o'clock to prepare the material; **(c)** *Can Tél* extension.
localement [lɔkalmɑ̃] *adv* locally.
localisation [lɔkalizasjɔ̃] *nf* **(a)** localization, confinement; **(b)** location, locating.
localiser [lɔkalize] **1** *vt* **(a)** to localize, to confine (*epidemic, fire etc*); **(b)** (*repérer*) to locate (*noise etc*); **je n'arrive pas à l. le début du progrès,** I cannot say exactly when things started to improve. **2 se localiser** *vpr* to become localized; **la maladie se localise au scalp,** the disease is confined to the scalp, the disease affects only the scalp.
localité [lɔkalite] *nf* locality, place, spot.
locataire [lɔkatɛr] *n* tenant (*of rented property*); occupier (*of property*); (*chez le propriétaire*) lodger, *Am* roomer; *Jur* lessee, leaseholder.
locatif¹, -ive [lɔkatif, -iv] *adj* concerning the renting or letting of premises; **risques locatifs,** = tenant's obligations and responsibilities (*as regards damage etc*); **valeur locative,** rental (value); **réparations locatives,** repairs incumbent upon the tenant.
locatif², -ive *adj & nm Gram* locative (case).
location [lɔkasjɔ̃] *nf* **(a)** *Br* hire, renting (*of boat etc*); *Br* hiring, renting (*par le locataire*); letting out on hire, *Br* hiring (out), renting (out) (*par le propriétaire*); **donner/prendre qch en l.,** *Br* to hire *or* rent sth out/*Br* to hire *or* rent sth; **l. de voitures (sans chauffeur),** (self-drive) car *Br* hire *or* rental; **voiture de l.,** rented *or Br* hire car, *US*

rental car; **l. de matériel industriel/de piano,** plant-/piano-hire; **(b)** (*de logement*) (*par le locataire*) renting, tenancy; (*par le propriétaire*) *Br* letting, renting (*of house etc*); **prix de l.**, rent; **(c)** *Th etc* booking, reservation (*of seats*); **(bureau de) l.**, box office, booking office.

location-vente [lɔkɑsjɔ̃vɑ̃t] *nf Br* hire purchase, *US* installment plan (*of property, equipment etc*); (*pl locations-ventes*).

loch [lɔk] *nm Nau* (ship's) log; **ligne de l.**, log line; **livre de l.**, log.

loche [lɔʃ] *nf* **(a)** (*poisson*) loach; **(b)** (*mollusque*) grey slug.

lock-out [lɔkaut] *nm inv Ang Ind* lockout.

lock(-)outer [lɔkaute] *vt Ind* to lock out.

locomobile [lɔkɔmɔbil] *nf* (transportable) steam engine.

locomoteur, -trice [lɔkɔmɔtœr, -tris] **1** *adj* locomotor(y) (*organ, disorders etc*). **2** *nf Rail* **locomotrice,** electric engine.

locomotion [lɔkɔmosjɔ̃] *nf* locomotion; **moyens de l.**, means of transport.

locomotive [lɔkɔmɔtiv] *nf* **(a)** *Rail* locomotive, engine; **locomotive diesel (à transmission) électrique,** diesel electric locomotive; **(b)** *Fig* (*élément moteur*) motive force; (*leader*) trendsetter; (*en politique*) political leader.

locuteur, -trice [lɔkytœr, -tris] *n Ling* speaker.

locution [lɔkysjɔ̃] *nf* **(a)** (*expression*) expression, phrase, locution; **l. figée,** set phrase *or* expression; **l. proverbiale,** proverbial expression; **l. vicieuse,** incorrect expression; **(b)** *Gram* **l. adverbiale,** (*groupe de mots*) adverbial phrase; **l. conjonctive,** complex conjunction.

loden [lodɛn] *nm Tex* loden; (*manteau*) loden (coat).

lœss [løs] *nm Géol* loess.

lof [lɔf] *nm Nau* windward side (*of ship*); **venir** *ou* **aller au l.**, to sail into the wind, to luff; **virer l. pour l.**, to wear.

lofer [lɔfe] *vi Nau* to luff.

loft [lɔft] *nm* loft.

logarithme [lɔgaritm] *Math* **1** *nm* logarithm, log; **table de logarithmes,** log(arithm) table. **2** *adj* **fonction l.**, logarithmic function.

logarithmique [lɔgaritmik] *adj Math* logarithmic.

loge [lɔʒ] *nf* **(a)** (*de franc-maçon*) (porter's, freemason's) lodge; **(b)** *Th* box; **première l.**, first-tier box; *Fig* **être aux premières loges,** to have a ringside seat; **(c)** (*d'artiste*) (artist's) dressing room; **(d)** *Beaux-Arts Mus* individual exam room (*for the Prix de Rome*); **(e)** *Archit* loggia; **(f)** *Bot* cell.

logeable [lɔʒabl] *adj* (*of house*) habitable, fit for occupation.

logement [lɔʒmɑ̃] *nm* **(a)** lodging, housing (*of people*); quartering, billeting (*of troops*); stabling (*of horses etc*); **crise du l.**, housing shortage; **(b)** (*appartement etc*) *Br* accommodation, *US* accommodations, lodgings; **l. garni** *ou* **meublé,** furnished rooms *or Br* flat *or Am* apartment; **chercher un l.**, to look for somewhere to live, to look for accommodation; **l. collectif,** *Br* block of flats, *Am* apartment block; **(c)** *Mil* quarters; (*in private house*) billet; **(d)** seating (*of machine part*); housing (*of shaft*).

loger [lɔʒe] *v* **(je logeai(s); n. logeons) 1** *vi* to lodge, to live; (*of troops*) to be quartered *or* billeted; **l. à un hôtel,** to put up *or* stay at a hotel; *Mil* **l. chez l'habitant,** to be billeted (in private houses); **je compte l. chez l'habitant pendant les vacances,** I am intending to stay in a private house when I go on holiday; **être logé et nourri,** to have board and lodging *or* bed and board; **l. à la belle étoile,** to sleep in the open.

2 *vt* **(a)** (*héberger*) to accommodate (*s.o.*); to quarter, to billet (*troops*); to stable (*horses*); **l. un ami pour la nuit,** to put up a friend for the night; **l'auberge de jeunesse peut l. jusqu'à 200 personnes,** the youth hostel can accommodate up to 200 people;

(b) (*placer*) to place, to put; **l. une balle dans qch,** to lodge a bullet in sth; **il faudra bien l. toutes nos affaires dans ce placard,** we'll have to put all our belongings in that cupboard.

3 se loger *vpr* **(a)** (*pour s'installer, dormir*) to find accommodation *or* a house; **nous avons trouvé à nous l.**, we've found somewhere to live; **vous n'aurez pas de mal à vous l. à Rome,** you won't have any trouble finding somewhere to stay in Rome;

(b) (*se placer*) **mon ballon s'est logé sur le toit,** my ball has got stuck on the roof; **la balle se logea dans le mur,** the bullet embedded itself in the wall; **le soupçon se logea dans son cœur,** suspicion became firmly fixed in his mind; **la souris s'est logée sous le lit,** the mouse went and hid under the bed.

logeur, -euse [lɔʒœr, -øz] *n* landlord, landlady (*of furnished apartments*).

loggia [lɔdʒja] *nf Archit* loggia.

logiciel [lɔʒisjɛl] *nm Ordinat* software; **un l. très utile,** a very useful software package; **l. utilisateur,** user software; **les logiciels de traitement de texte,** word-processing software, word-processing software packages.

logicien, -ienne [lɔʒisjɛ̃, -jɛn] *n* logician.

logique [lɔʒik] **1** *adj* **(a)** (*cohérent*) logical (*reasoning etc*); **il est tout à fait l. que tu n'aies pas envie de le revoir,** it is only to be expected that you should not wish to see him again; **une déduction tout à fait l.**, a totally logical deduction; **voyons, soyons logiques,** come on, let's be logical about this; **tu te contredis, tu n'es pas l.!**, you're contradicting yourself!, you're being illogical!;

(b) (*analytique*) logical, methodical; *Ordinat* **analyseur l.**, logic analyser; *Gram* **analyse l.**, analysis (*of sentence*); **le candidat doit avoir l'esprit l.**, the candidate must have a logical mind.

2 *nf* **(a)** *Phil* logic; **faire de la l.**, to do logic; **l. formelle/pure,** formal/pure logic;

(b) (*cohérence, raisonnement*) logic; **la l. des enfants,** childlike logic, the way children's minds work; **c'est sa l., ne posons pas de questions,** that's the way his mind works, let's just leave it at that; **la l. de la passion/de la folie,** the logic of passion/madness; **en toute l., voilà ce qui devrait se passer,** logically, that's what ought to happen; **ça manque de l.**, there's no logic in it, it's illogical; **vous manquez de l.**, you're not being very logical.

logiquement [lɔʒikmɑ̃] *adv* logically.

logis [lɔʒi] *nm* **(a) quitter le l. familial,** to leave the family home; **les femmes au l.**, women who don't go out to work; *Fig* **la folle du l.**, (wild *or* fevered) imagination; **corps de l.**, main (portion of) building; **(b)** *Litt & Vieilli* home, house, dwelling.

logistique [lɔʒistik] **1** *adj* logistic; **soutien l.**, logistic(al) support. **2** *nf Mil etc* logistics.

logo [logo] *nm* (*abrév* **logotype**) logo; **le l. d'une société,** a company logo.

logomachie [lɔgɔmaʃi] *nf* logomachy, battle of words.

loi [lwa] *nf* **(a)** (*autorité, pouvoir*) law; **c'est lui qui fait la l.**, he's the master *or F* the boss; **ce qu'il dit fait l.**, his word is law; **c'est la l. et les prophètes,** it's the absolute *or* gospel truth; **la l. du plus fort,** might is right; **faire la l. à qn,** to lay down the law *or* to dictate to s.o.; **se faire une l. de faire qch,** to make a rule *or* a point of doing sth; **subir la l. de qn,** to be ruled by s.o., to be under s.o.'s thumb;

(b) *Jur* law; **homme de l.**, lawyer, legal practitioner; **tomber sous le coup de la l.**, to come under the law; **projet de l.**, (*émanant de l'initiative gouvernementale*) bill; **proposition de l.**, (*émanant de l'initiative parlementaire*) bill; **l. (votée),** act (of Parliament); **avoir la l. pour soi,** to have the law on one's side; **la l. est dure mais c'est la l.**, the law's the law; **mettre qn hors la l.**, to outlaw s.o.; **l. criminelle,** criminal law; **l. de finances,** Finance Act; **respecter la l.**, to show respect for the law, to obey the law; **nul n'est censé ignorer la l.**, nobody may plead ignorance of the law;

(c) (*règle*) law (*of nature etc*); **lois,** laws (*of game etc*); dictates (*of fashion*); **la l. morale interdit que l'on vole son voisin,** there is a moral law which forbids us to steal from our neighbour; **la l. naturelle,** natural law; *Rel* **la l. divine,** divine law, the law of God; **les lois de la politesse/de l'honneur,** the rules of etiquette/the code of honour;

(d) la l. de la chute des corps, the law of falling bodies, the law of gravity; **les lois économiques,** the laws of economics; **l. phonétique,** a law of phonetics.

loi-cadre [lwakadr] *nf* outline law; (*pl lois-cadres*).

loin [lwɛ̃] **1** *adv* **(a)** (*à une certaine distance*) far; **plus l.**, farther *or* further (on); **moins l.**, less far, not so far; (*of place*) **est-ce l. d'ici?**, is it far (away) from here?; **ce n'est pas l.**, it's not far; **la poste est l.**, the post office is a long way off; **aller très l.**, to go far afield *or* far away; *Fig* **ce jeune homme ira l.**, this young man will go far; **voir l.**, to be far-sighted; *Fig* to be far-sighted *or* shrewd; **l. derrière lui,** far *or* way behind him; *Fig* **laisser ses souvenirs l. derrière soi,** to leave one's memories far behind; *Prov* **l. des yeux, l. du cœur,** out of sight, out of mind; **il y a l. d'ici à Paris,** it's a long way to Paris; *Fig* **de là à l'accuser de mensonge il n'y a pas l.**, that's not far from *or* it's close to calling him a liar; **il ne voit pas plus l. que le bout de son nez,** he can't see any further than the end of his nose, he can't see beyond the end of his nose; *Prov* **il y a**

l. de la coupe aux lèvres, there's many a slip 'twixt cup and lip; **être l. de faire qch,** to be far from doing sth; **il est l. d'avoir compris,** he has completely misunderstood; **ne pas être l. d'une découverte,** to be on the brink of a discovery; **le malade n'ira pas l.,** the patient hasn't long to live; **la voiture est vieille, elle n'ira pas l.,** the car is old and on its last legs; **je ne suis pas fâché, (bien) l. de là!,** I am not angry, far from it *or* anything but!; **vous allez trop l.,** you're going too far; **on pourrait même aller plus l. et dire que ...,** one could even go further and say that ...;

(b) (*dans l'espace*) **je l'ai reconnu de l.,** I recognized him from a distance *or* from a long way off; **admirer qn de l.,** to admire s.o. at *or* from a distance *or* from afar; **ils sont parents, mais de l.,** they are only distantly related; **d'aussi l.** *ou* **du plus l. qu'il les voie/qu'il se souvienne,** as soon as he sees them/as far back as he can remember; *Fig* **de l.,** (*de beaucoup*) by far; **il est de l. plus intelligent que moi,** he is far more intelligent than I am; **c'est de l. son meilleur roman,** it's by far his best novel;

(c) (*dans le temps*) **la famille remonte bien l.,** the family goes back a long way; **voir plus l.,** (*in text*) see further on, see following pages; **il ne devait pas être l. de midi,** it must have been getting on for twelve (o'clock); **ce jour est encore l.,** that day is still distant *or* is still a long way off; **cette époque est bien l.,** (*dans le passé*) those days are long gone; (*dans le futur*) that time is a long way off;

(d) de l. en l., at long intervals, now and then.

2 *nm* **au l.,** in the distance; **apercevoir qn au l.,** to see s.o. a long way away *or* in the distance.

lointain [lwɛ̃tɛ̃] **1** *adj* distant, far off, faraway; remote (*island*); vague (*resemblance*); **ce sont des cousins lointains,** they are distant cousins; **mes souvenirs les plus lointains,** my earliest recollections; **dans un avenir l.,** in the distant future. **2** *nm* distance; **dans le l.,** in the distance; **regard plongé dans le l.,** faraway look; *Beaux-Arts* **les lointains,** the distances (*of a picture*).

loi-programme [lwaprɔgram] *nf Fin Pol* law providing framework for long-term government programme; (*pl lois-programmes*).

loir [lwar] *nm* (*mammifère*) dormouse; **dormir comme un l.,** to sleep like a log.

loisible [lwazibl] *adj* **il lui est l. de refuser,** it is open to him to refuse, he is free *or* entitled to refuse.

loisir [lwazir] *nm* **(a)** (*temps libre*) leisure; **dans mes heures de l., pendant mes loisirs,** in my spare time; **avoir des loisirs,** to have some spare time; **(b)** (*activités*) **les loisirs,** leisure *or* spare time activities; **société de loisirs,** leisure society; **les loisirs sportifs,** sporting activities; **(c)** (*possibilité, temps nécessaire*) opportunity, enough time; **je n'ai pas le l. d'un long entretien,** I have no time for a long conversation; **donner** *ou* **laisser à qn le l. de faire qch,** to give s.o. the opportunity to do sth, to allow s.o. to do sth; **on ne m'a pas laissé le l. de me reposer,** I wasn't given the opportunity *or* any time to rest; **examiner qch à l.,** to examine sth at leisure.

lokoum [lɔkum] *nm* **(rahat-)l.,** Turkish delight.

lolo [lolo] *nm F* **(a)** *Enf* (*lait*) milk; **(b)** (*sein*) boob.

lombago [lɔ̃bago] *nm Méd* lumbago.

lombaire [lɔ̃bɛr] *Anat* **1** *adj* lumbar; **ponction l.,** lumbar puncture. **2** *nf* lumbar.

lombard, -arde [lɔ̃bar, -ard] **1** *adj* Lombard, of *or* from Lombardy; *Hist* **la ligue lombarde,** the Lombard League. **2** *nm Ling* Lombard dialect. **3** *n* **L.,** Lombard.

Lombardie [lɔ̃bardi] *nf* Lombardy.

lombes [lɔ̃b] *nmpl Anat* loins.

lombric [lɔ̃brik] *nm* earthworm.

londonien, -ienne [lɔ̃dɔnjɛ̃, -jɛn] **1** *adj* London. **2** *n* **L.,** Londoner.

Londres [lɔ̃dr] *nm* London.

londrès [lɔ̃drɛs] *nm* Havana cigar.

long, longue [lɔ̃, lɔ̃g] **1** *adj* **(a)** (*dans l'espace*) long; **avoir un long nez/de longues jambes,** to have a long nose/long legs; **elle a les cheveux longs,** she has long hair; **corde longue de 5 mètres,** rope 5 metres long, 5-metre rope; **prendre le chemin le plus l.,** to go the longest way (round); **son explication est trop longue d'un quart,** his explanation is too long by half, his explanation is far too long; **il est l. comme un jour sans pain,** he's a real beanpole; *Fig* **avoir le bras l.,** to be able to pull strings; *Fig* **avoir les dents longues,** to be greedy *or* thirsting (for sth); **phare longue distance,** high-intensity light; **navigation au l. cours,** deep-sea navigation;

(b) (*dans le temps*) (*see also the note to* **prolongé 1**) **un l. hiver,** a long *or* protracted winter; **les jours sont de plus en plus longs,** the days are getting longer (and longer); **discours un peu l.,** somewhat lengthy speech; **longue histoire,** long drawn-out *or* lengthy story; *Ling* **une voyelle longue,** a long vowel; **'a' l.,** long 'a'; **je trouve le temps l.** *ou* **les jours longs,** time seems to drag; **je ne serai pas l.,** I won't be long; **l. soupir,** long-drawn sigh; **c'est un travail l. à faire,** it's slow work, this work takes a long time; **être l. à faire qch,** to take a long time to do sth, to be slow in doing sth; **il s'en sortira, mais ce sera l.,** he'll recover but it'll take a long time;

(c) (*ancien*) long-time, long-standing; **c'est une longue habitude,** it's a habit I've *or* he's *or* she's *etc* had for a long time; **un ami de longue date,** a long-standing friend, a friend of long standing;

(d) (*loin dans l'avenir*) long(-term); **projet à longue échéance,** long-term project; **bail à l. terme,** long lease; **à plus ou moins longue échéance/à plus ou moins l. terme,** sooner or later; **disque (microsillon) de longue durée,** long-playing record;

(e) *Culin* **sauce longue,** thin sauce.

2 *nm* **(a)** (*dans l'espace*) length; **table qui a 2 mètres de l.,** table 2 metres long *or* in length; **en l., de l.,** lengthwise; **de l. en large,** up and down, to and fro; **expliquer qch en l. et en large,** to explain sth in great detail *or* at great length; **racontez-moi cela tout au l.** *ou* **tout du l.,** tell me everything (from beginning to end); **étendu de tout son l.,** stretched out (at) full length; **tout le l. du rivage,** all along the shore; **tomber de tout son l.,** to fall flat on one's face; **le l. de,** along; (*parallèlement, en côtoyant*) alongside; **se faufiler/grimper le l. du mur,** to creep along/to climb up the wall;

(b) (*dans le temps*) **tout le l. du jour,** all day long, throughout the day; **tout au l. de l'entretien,** throughout *or* all through the conversation.

3 *adv* **(a)** (*beaucoup*) **inutile d'en dire plus l.,** I need say no more, there's no need to say any more; **regard qui en dit l.,** meaningful *or* eloquent look; **cette action en dit l. sur ...,** this action speaks volumes for ...; **en savoir l./plus l./trop l.,** to know a lot/more/too much; **il en sait l. sur votre compte,** he knows quite a lot about you;

(b) (*avec des vêtements longs*) **s'habiller l.,** to wear long clothes.

4 *nf* **longue (a)** *Ling* long syllable;

(b) à la longue, in (the course of) time, in the long run, in the end;

(c) *Mus* long note.

longanimité [lɔ̃ganimite] *nf* long-suffering, forbearance.

long-courrier [lɔ̃kurje] (*pl long-courriers*) **1** *adj Nau* ocean-going (*ship*); *Av* long-haul, long-range (*aircraft*). **2** *nm Nau* ocean-going ship, ocean-goer; ocean liner; *Av* long-haul *or* long-range (aircraft).

longe¹ [lɔ̃ʒ] *nf* **(a)** (*pour mener le cheval*) leading rein, halter, tether; **(b)** (*pour le dresser*) lunge, longe.

longe² *nf Culin* loin (*of veal, venison*).

longer [lɔ̃ʒe] *vt* (**je longeai(s); n. longeons**) **(a)** (*suivre*) to go along (*road*); (*parallèlement, en côtoyant*) to go *or* pass alongside; **l. la côte,** to hug the coast; **(b)** (*border*) (*of path etc*) to border, to run alongside; **la route longe un bois,** the road skirts a wood.

longeron [lɔ̃ʒrɔ̃] *nm* **(a)** *Constr* stringer, longitudinal girder; beam, member (*of bridge etc*); **(b)** *Aut* side member, side sill (*of frame*); **(c)** *Av* longeron; spar (*of wing*).

longévité [lɔ̃ʒevite] *nf* longevity, long life; **table de l. d'une population,** life-expectancy table of a population.

longitude [lɔ̃ʒityd] *nf Géog* longitude; **par 10° (de) l. ouest,** at 10° longitude west.

longitudinal, -aux [lɔ̃ʒitydinal, -o] *adj* longitudinal, lengthwise.

longitudinalement [lɔ̃ʒitydinalmɑ̃] *adv* longitudinally, lengthwise, lengthways.

longrine [lɔ̃grin] *nf Tech* **(a)** *Constr* longitudinal beam *or* girder *or* member; **l. de faîtage,** ridge bar; **(b)** *Rail* longitudinal sleeper.

longtemps [lɔ̃tɑ̃] *adv* **(a)** (*pendant un long moment*) a long time; **attendre l.,** to wait for a long time; **cela ne pouvait durer l.,** it couldn't last long; **est-ce que ça va durer l.?,** will it last long?; **ça ne va plus durer l. maintenant,** it won't be long now; *Vieilli* **être l. à faire qch,** to be a long time doing sth; (*avant de s'y mettre*) to be a long time getting round to sth; **rester trop l.,** to stay too long;

(b) (*long espace de temps*) **il y a l.,** long ago, a long time ago; **il n'y a pas l.,** not long ago; **il y a l. qu'il est mort,** he has been dead (for) a long time; *or F* for ages; **il y a l.**

que je ne l'ai vu, it's a long time *or F* ages since I saw him; **mettre l. à faire qch,** to be a long time *or F* to be ages doing sth; **cela existe depuis l.,** it has existed for a long time *or F* for ages; **l. avant/après,** long before/after; **pendant l.,** for a long time; **avant l.,** before long; **cela ne se fera pas avant l.,** it won't happen for a long time to come; **je ne pensais pas vous revoir de l.,** I didn't expect to see you again for a long time; **je n'en ai pas pour l.,** I shan't be long, it won't take me long; **il n'en a plus pour l.,** he hasn't much longer to live.

longuement [lɔ̃gmɑ̃] *adv* **(a)** (*pendant longtemps*) for a long time; (*avec insistance etc*) slowly, deliberately; **il la regarda l.,** he gazed earnestly at her; **(b)** (*en détail*) lengthily, at (great) length; **il faut entrer plus l. dans le détail,** you must go more fully into details; **parler l. avec qn,** to have a (good) long talk with s.o..

longuet, -ette [lɔ̃gɛ, -ɛt] **1** *adj F* rather long, longish (*book, time etc*). **2** *nm Région* bread stick.

longueur [lɔ̃gœr] *nf* **(a)** length; **l. totale, l. hors tout,** length over all, overall length; **mesures de l.,** linear measures; **jardin qui a cent mètres de l.** *ou* **une l. de cent mètres,** garden a hundred metres long; **couper qch en l.** *ou* **dans le sens de la l.,** to cut sth lengthwise; *Sp* **mener/gagner d'une l.,** to lead/win by a length; **la voiture A prend une l. d'avance sur la voiture B,** car A goes one length ahead of car B; *Fig* **la ville de Grenoble avait une l. d'avance sur les autres pour la prévention du sida,** Grenoble had a clear lead over other cities as regards preventive measures against Aids; *Rad* **l. d'ondes,** wavelength; **unité de l.,** unit of length; **traîner en l.,** (*of speech etc*) to drag (on);

(b) à l. de journée/de semaine/d'année, throughout the day/week/year, all day/week/year long; **à l. de journées,** for days on end;

(c) *Péj* **les longueurs de la justice,** the law's delays; **roman plein de longueurs,** novel full of tedious passages.

longue-vue [lɔ̃gvy] *nf* telescope, field glass; (*pl longues-vues*).

loofa [lufa] *nm* (*plante*) loofah.

look [luk] *nm F* look; **soigner son l.,** to pay attention to one's look *or* to the way one looks, to cultivate one's image; **changer de l.,** to change one's look *or* image.

looping [lupiŋ] *nm Av* loop; **faire un l.,** to loop the loop.

lopin [lɔpɛ̃] *nm* **l. de terre,** piece *or* patch *or* plot of ground; (*loué à la municipalité*) allotment.

loquace [lɔkwas, -kas] *adj* loquacious, talkative, garrulous.

loquacité [lɔkwasite, -kasite] *nf* loquacity, talkativeness, garrulousness.

loque [lɔk] *nf* rag; **être en loques,** to be in rags *or* in tatters; **ses vêtements tombent en loques,** his clothes are falling to pieces; *Fig* **je ne suis qu'une l.,** I feel a wreck, I feel like a wet rag; **l'alcool a fait de lui une l.,** alcohol has turned him into a wreck.

loquet [lɔkɛ] *nm* latch (*of door*); **tirer le l.,** to open the door; **fermer la porte au l., pousser le l.,** to put the door on the latch, to keep the door on the latch.

loqueteau, -eaux [lɔkto] *nm* small latch, catch (*for shutter etc*).

loqueteux, -euse [lɔktø, -øz] **1** *adj* (*personne*) in rags; (*vêtements*) in tatters; ragged, tattered (*clothes*); **un vieillard l.,** an old man (dressed) in rags; **un vieux manteau l.,** a tattered old overcoat. **2** *n* ragamuffin.

lord [lɔr] *nm* lord; **la Chambre des lords,** the House of Lords.

lord-maire [lɔrmɛr] *nm* Lord Mayor (*of London etc*); (*pl lords-maires*).

lordose [lɔrdoz] *nf* **(a)** *Anat* (*courbure naturelle*) (natural) curvature of the spine; **(b)** *Méd* lordosis, hollow-back.

lorgner [lɔrɲe] *vt* **(a)** (*regarder indiscrètement*) to eye, to peer at (*sth*); **l. une femme,** to eye up *or* ogle a woman; **l. qch du coin de l'œil,** to cast a sidelong glance at sth; **(b)** (*convoiter*) to have one's eye on (*an inheritance, a post etc*).

lorgnette [lɔrɲɛt] *nf* (pair of) opera glasses; (small) field glasses; *Fig* **regarder** *ou* **voir par le petit bout de la l.,** to have tunnel vision.

lorgnon [lɔrɲɔ̃] *nm* **(a)** (*face à main*) lorgnette; **(b)** (*lunettes*) pince-nez.

loriot [lɔrjo] *nm* (*oiseau*) **l. (jaune),** (golden) oriole.

lorrain, -aine [lɔrɛ̃, -ɛn] **1** *adj* from *or* of Lorraine. **2** *nm Ling* Lorraine dialect. **3** *n* **L.,** inhabitant *or* native of Lorraine. **4** *nf* **la Lorraine,** Lorraine.

lorry [lɔri] *nm Rail* (platelayer's) trolley, pushcar.

lors [lɔr] *adv Litt* **depuis l.,** from that time, ever since then; **dès l., je décidai de ne plus poser de questions,** from that moment on, I decided to ask no more questions; **l. de sa naissance,** at the time of his birth, when he was born; **dès l. qu'elle est arrivée,** (from) the very moment she arrived; (*puisque*) **dès lors que tu refuses, je pars,** since you refuse, I'm leaving; **l. même qu'il souffre, il ne le dit pas,** though he is in pain, he says nothing.

lorsque [lɔrsk(ə)] *conj* (*becomes* **lorsqu'** *before* **il(s), elle(s), on, en, un(e)**) (at the time, moment) when; **l. je suis entré,** when I came in.

losange [lɔzɑ̃ʒ] *nm* **(a)** *Hér* lozenge; **(b) (forme de) l.,** diamond-shaped; **(c)** *Géom* rhomb(us).

losangé [lɔzɑ̃ʒe] *adj* diamond-shaped (*earring etc*); (*dress etc*) with a diamond pattern; *Hér* lozengy.

lot [lo] *nm* **(a)** share (*of estate*); **l. (de terre),** plot (of land); **(b)** (*sort*) lot, fate; **son l. est d'être toujours seul,** he is destined to remain alone all his life; **(c)** prize (*at a lottery*); **gros l.,** first prize, jackpot; *Fig F* **en l'épousant, tu as gagné le gros l.,** by marrying him you've hit the jackpot; *Fin* **emprunt à lots,** lottery loan; **tirage à lots,** prize-drawing; **(d)** batch (*of goods etc*); set (*of towels etc*); **vente par lots séparés,** batch selling; (*at auction*) lot; *Ordinat* **traitement par lots,** batch processing.

loterie [lɔtri] *nf* lottery; **l. nationale,** national lottery; *Fig* **c'est une l.,** it's a lottery *or* matter of chance, it's the luck of the draw.

lotion [losjɔ̃] *nf* lotion; **l. capillaire,** hair lotion; **l. après-rasage,** after-shave (lotion).

lotionner [losjɔne] *vt* to apply lotion to (*sth*).

lotir [lɔtir] *vt* **(a)** (*diviser en lots*) to divide (*sth*) into lots *or* plots *or* batches; **terrains à l.,** development site, building land; **(b)** (*donner*) **l. qn de qch,** to allot sth to s.o.; *Fig* **être bien/mal loti,** to be well/badly off.

lotissement [lɔtismɑ̃] *nm* **(a)** (*résidence*) housing estate *or* development; **(b)** dividing (*of goods etc*) into lots; parcelling out (*of land*); **(c)** sale (*by lots*).

loto [lɔto] *nm* **(a)** (*jeu de hasard*) lotto; **(b)** (*jeu national*) = bingo-style national lottery; **il joue au l. tous les mercredis,** he takes part in *or* enters the national lottery every Wednesday; **(c)** (*matériel*) lotto set.

lotte [lɔt] *nf* (*poisson*) burbot; **l. de mer,** anglerfish.

lotus [lɔtys] *nm* **(a)** (*plante*) lotus; **l. sacré,** Indian lotus; **(b)** (*arbre*) lotus tree; **(c)** *Myth* Lotus.

louable¹ [lwabl] *adj* laudable, praiseworthy, commendable; **des intentions louables,** laudable intentions; **c'est tout à fait l. de ta part,** it is highly commendable on your part.

louable² *adj* rentable; **appartement difficilement l.,** flat difficult to let; **chambre l. à l'année,** a room (that is) let on a yearly basis.

louage [lwaʒ] *nm* **contrat de l.,** rental agreement *or* contract; **l. de services,** contract of employment; **voiture de l.,** rented car, *Br* hire car, *US* rental car.

louange [lwɑ̃ʒ] *nf* (*éloge*) praise; (*officielle*) commendation; **digne de l.,** praiseworthy; **chanter les louanges de qn,** to sing s.o.'s praises; **faire un discours à la l. de qn,** to make a speech in praise of s.o.; **c'est à sa l.,** it's to his credit.

louangeur, -euse [lwɑ̃ʒœr, -øz] *adj Litt* adulatory, laudatory (*poem etc*).

loubar(d), -arde [lubar, -ard] *n F* yob(bo), lout, *surtout US* hoodlum.

louche¹ [luʃ] **1** *adj* **(a)** shady, suspicious (*conduct, character etc*); shifty (*person*); dubious (*situation, remark*); **c'est l.,** it's odd *or* strange; **cela me paraît l.,** it looks suspicious *or F* fishy to me; **il n'y a rien de l. là-dedans,** it is all fair and above board; **(b)** cloudy (*wine etc*); murky (*light etc*); **(c)** *Arch* cross-eyed, squint-eyed (*person*). **2** *nm* **il y a du l. dans cette affaire,** this business is a bit shady.

louche² *nf* (soup) ladle.

loucher [luʃe] *vi* to squint; (*état permanent*) to be cross-eyed, to have a squint; **l. de l'œil gauche,** to have a squint in the left eye; *F* **l. vers** *ou* **sur qch,** to cast longing eyes at sth, to ogle sth; *Fig* **l. sur l'héritage,** to have one's eye on the inheritance.

loucherie [luʃri] *nf* squint(ing).

loucheur, -euse [luʃœr, -øz] *n* cross-eyed *or* squint-eyed person.

louer¹ [lwe] **1** *vt* **(a)** to rent (out), *Br* to let (*room*); *Br* to hire (out), to rent (out) (*equipment, vehicle*) (**à,** to); **maison à l.,** house *Br* to let *or US* for rent; **l. une ferme à bail,** to lease out a farm; **(b)** (*prendre en location*) to rent (*house etc*) (**à,** from); *Br* to hire, to rent (*une voiture*); to reserve, to book (*seat etc*); **l. une maison pour l'été,** to take a house for the summer. **2 se louer** *vpr* **(a)** (*être à louer*) (*maison*) to be *Br* to let *or US* for rent; (*équipement*) to be *Br* for hire *or US* for rent; **cet appartement se loue**

très cher, this flat is very expensive to rent; **(b)** (*of farmhand*) **se l. pour la saison,** to hire oneself out for the season.

louer² **1** *vt* to praise; (*officiellement*) to commend; **il n'a pas cessé de l. tes qualités,** he has had nothing but praise for your qualities; **l. qn de** *ou* **pour qch,** to praise s.o. for sth; **je l'ai loué d'y avoir pensé,** I commended him for having thought of it; **louons le seigneur!, Dieu soit loué!,** thank God! **2 se louer** *vpr* to be very pleased *or* satisfied; **je me loue chaque jour de notre collaboration,** not a day goes by without my realizing the value of our collaboration; **se l. de qch,** to be pleased *or* well satisfied with sth; **se l. d'avoir fait qch,** to congratulate oneself on having done sth; **je n'ai qu'à me louer de lui,** I have nothing but praise for him.

loueur, -euse [lwœr, -øz] *n Br* hirer, *Br* letter, renter; **l. de bateaux,** boat keeper; **l. de chevaux,** person who rents out horses.

loufiat [lufja] *nm Arg Vieilli* waiter (*in a café*).

loufoque [lufɔk] *F* **1** *adj* crazy, loony, barmy; **une histoire l.,** a w(h)acky tale. **2** *n* crackpot, nut, *US* screwball.

loufoquerie [lufɔkri] *nf F* **(a)** (*absurdité*) barminess, craziness; **(b)** (*acte*) crazy act.

lougre [lugr] *nm Nau* lugger.

Louis [lwi] *nm* Lewis, Louis.

louis [lwi] *nm Arch* **l. (d'or),** twenty-franc piece.

Louise [lwiz] *nf* Louisa, Louise.

Louisiane [lwizjan] *nf* Louisiana.

loukoum [lukum] *nm* **(rahat-)l.,** Turkish delight.

loulou, -oute [lulu, -ut] **1** *n* **(a)** *F* (*chéri, chérie*) dear, darling; **(b)** *F* (*voyou*) lout, yob(bo), *Am* hoodlum. **2** *nm* (*chien*) spitz; **l. de Poméranie,** Pomeranian (dog), *F* pom.

loup [lu] *nm* **(a)** wolf; **une horde de loups,** a pack of wolves; **marcher à pas de l.,** to walk stealthily, to creep along, to steal along; *Fig* **avoir une faim de l.,** to be ravenously hungry; *Fig* **il fait un froid de l.,** it's bitterly cold; *Fig F* **se jeter dans la gueule du l.,** to throw oneself into the lion's mouth; *Fig* **il est connu comme le l. blanc,** everybody knows him; *Prov* **quand on parle du l. on en voit la queue,** talk of the devil (and he will appear); *Fig* **avoir vu le l.,** to have lost one's virginity; *Fig* **l'homme est un l. pour l'homme,** it's dog eat dog in this world; *Fig* **les loups ne se mangent pas entre eux,** there is honour among thieves; *Fig* **jeune l.,** young lion; *Fig F* (*term of affection*) **mon petit l., mon gros l.,** my darling, my pet;

(b) (*poisson*) **l. (de mer),** sea perch, sea dace; *Fig F* **l. de mer,** (*marin*) old salt, seadog, jack tar; (*tricot rayé*) striped tee-shirt;

(c) flaw (*in timber etc*); *Ind* defect;

(d) (*demi-masque*) black velvet mask (*worn at a masked ball*).

loupage [lupaʒ] *nm F* failure, flop; **le repas fut un l. complet,** the meal was a total flop.

loup-cervier [lusɛrvje] *nm* lynx; (*pl loups-cerviers*).

loupe [lup] *nf* **(a)** *Méd* wen; **(b)** gnarl (*on tree*); **un meuble en l. de noyer,** a piece of furniture made of burr walnut; **(c)** *Opt* lens, magnifying glass; **l. de philatéliste,** a philatelist's magnifying glass; *Fig F* **tu veux une l.?,** do you want a magnifying glass?; **regarder qch à la l.,** to look at sth through a magnifying glass; *Fig* to put sth under a *or* the microscope.

louper [lupe] *F* **1** *vi* **ça n'a pas loupé,** that's what happened, sure enough. **2** *vt* **(a)** (*ne pas réussir*) to botch, to bungle, to make a botch *or* a mess of (*piece of work*); to fail, *Am* to flunk (*exam*); *Th* to fluff (*one's entrance*); **la soirée est loupée,** the party's a flop; **(b)** (*ne pas prendre*) to miss (*one's turn, opportunity, train*); **il n'en loupe pas une!,** he's always opening his big mouth!; *F* **je ne vais pas le l., je vais lui dire ce que je pense de lui,** I won't let him get away without telling him what I think of him.

loup-garou [lugaru] *nm* (*pl loups-garous*) **(a)** *Myth* werewolf; **(b)** (*pour les enfants*) bogeyman; **si tu ne manges pas ta soupe, attention au l.-g.!,** if you don't eat your soup, the bogeyman will get you!

loupiot, -iote [lupjo, -jɔt] *n F* small child, kid, *Péj* brat.

loupiote [lupjɔt] *nf F* small light, lamp.

lourd, lourde [lur, lurd] **1** *adj* **(a)** heavy (*load, sleep, food etc*); heavily-built, ungainly (*person*); **sol l.,** heavy soil; **le terrain est l. aujourd'hui,** *Sp* the ground *or Horseracing* the going is heavy *or* soft today; **marcher d'un pas l.,** to tread heavily, to walk with a heavy step; **yeux lourds de fatigue,** eyes heavy with tiredness; **avoir le sommeil l.,** to be a heavy sleeper; **j'ai la tête lourde,** my head feels heavy; **avoir l'estomac l.,** to feel bloated; **c'est l. à digérer,** it's difficult to digest, it's heavy on the stomach; **avoir le cœur l.,** to feel very sad, to have a heavy heart; **avoir la main lourde,** (*punir*) to mete out punishment with a heavy hand; (*verser en quantité généreuse*) to be over-generous; **ce travail est trop l. pour elle,** this work is too much for her;

(b) clumsy, awkward (*action etc*); heavy (*movement, style*); **avoir l'esprit l.,** to be slow-witted *or* dull-witted; **faire de lourdes plaisanteries pour gêner qn,** to embarrass s.o. by making clumsy jokes;

(c) (*sérieux, grave*) **lourde erreur,** serious mistake; **lourde perte,** heavy *or* severe loss; **payer de lourdes charges,** to pay quite heavy fees; **une lourde hérédité,** a history of mental (*or* physical) illness in the family; **une lourde tâche,** a weighty task;

(d) **incident l. de conséquences,** incident fraught with consequences; **silence l. de menaces,** ominous silence; **un discours l. de sous-entendus,** a speech full of *or* loaded with innuendos;

(e) close, sultry, muggy (*weather*); **un parfum l.,** a heavy *or* strong fragrance;

(f) *Tech* **poids l.,** heavy lorry *or Am* truck, *Admin* heavy goods vehicle; **artillerie lourde,** heavy artillery; **industrie lourde,** heavy industry.

2 *adv* heavily; **peser l.,** to weigh heavy; **en avoir l. sur le cœur,** to have a heavy heart, to feel very sad; *F* **il n'en reste pas l.,** there isn't much left; there aren't many left; **je n'en fais pas l.,** I don't exactly overwork.

3 *nf Arg* **lourde,** door.

lourdaud, -aude [lurdo, -od] **1** *adj Péj* (*maladroit*) awkward, clumsy; (*bête*) oafish; **des manières lourdaudes,** clumsy *or* oafish manners. **2** *n Péj* (*voyou*) lout; (*bête*) oaf.

lourdement [lurdəmɑ̃] *adv* **(a)** (*avec un matériel pesant*) heavily; **l. chargé,** heavily laden; **(b)** (*gauchement*) awkwardly, clumsily; **elle avance l.,** she lumbers forward; **elle a insisté l. en répétant à plusieurs reprises,** she insisted most emphatically, repeating it several times; **(c)** (*de toute sa force*) heavily; **il est tombé l.,** he fell heavily; *Fig* **ces changements vont peser l. sur notre budget,** these changes will weigh heavy on our budget; **se tromper l.,** to make a big *or* serious mistake; **(d) il se mit à rire l.,** he burst out into coarse laughter.

lourder [lurde] *vt F* to give (*s.o.*) the boot; **se faire l. par sa petite amie,** to get the boot from one's girlfriend, to be given the boot by one's girlfriend.

lourdeur [lurdœr] *nf* heaviness (*of burden etc*); massiveness (*of building*); clumsiness, unwieldiness, awkwardness, ungainliness (*of person, movements*); dullness (*of intellect*); clumsiness (*of style*); severity (*of a loss*); weight (*of a responsibility*); sultriness, closeness (*of the weather*); **avoir des lourdeurs de tête,** to have fits of drowsiness, to feel headachy.

loustic [lustik] *nm F* joker; **il fait le l.,** he's playing the fool *or* fooling around; **c'est un drôle de l.,** he's a strange bloke *or* guy, he's an oddball.

loutre [lutr] *nf* otter; (*fourrure*) **manteau de l.,** otter-skin coat; **l. marine,** sea otter.

louve [luv] *nf* she-wolf.

louveteau, -eaux [luvto] *nm* **(a)** wolf cub; **(b)** (*jeune scout*) cub (scout).

louvoiement [luvwamɑ̃] *nm Nau* tacking; *Fig* hedging, wavering.

louvoyer [luvwaje] *vi* (**je louvoie, n. louvoyons; je louvoierai**) *Nau* to tack, to beat about; to beat to windward; *Fig* **elle louvoyait, incapable de se décider,** she kept wavering, unable to make up her mind.

lover [lɔve] **1** *vt* to coil (*rope*). **2 se lover** *vpr* (*of snake etc*) to coil up; **se l. dans un canapé moelleux,** to curl up on a soft couch.

loxodromique [lɔksɔdrɔmik] *adj Nau* loxodromic (*curve, sailing*); **navigation l.,** plane sailing.

loyal, -ale, -aux [lwajal, -o] **1** *adj* **(a)** (*honnête*) honest, fair, upright, *F* straight (*person etc*); straight (*answer*); **être l. en affaires,** to be upright *or* straightforward in business; **jeu l.,** fair play; **(b)** loyal, faithful (*servant, heart*); true, staunch (*friend*). **2** *nf F* **se battre à la loyale,** to fight cleanly.

loyalement [lwajalmɑ̃] *adv* honestly, fairly; loyally.

loyalisme [lwajalism] *nm Pol* loyalty (*to the Crown etc*); loyalism.

loyaliste [lwajalist] *adj & n* loyalist.

loyauté [lwajote] *nf* **(a)** (*honnêteté*) honesty, uprightness, fairness; **manque de l.,** dishonesty; unfairness; **(b)**

(*fidélité*) loyalty, fidelity (**envers,** to).
loyer [lwaje] *nm* **(a)** rent, rental; **prendre une maison à l.,** to rent a house; **donner à l.,** to rent, *Br* to let (out); **vous êtes encore en retard sur votre l.!,** you're late with your rent again!; **(b)** *Fin* **l. de l'argent,** interest rates, rates of interest.
L.S.D. [ɛlɛsde] *nm Ch* LSD.
lubie [lybi] *nf* whim, fad, craze; **c'est encore une de ses lubies!,** it's another of his crazy ideas!; **il lui prit la l. de manger à 4 heures du matin,** he took it into his head to have something to eat at 4 o'clock in the morning.
lubricité [lybrisite] *nf* lewdness, lust(fulness).
lubrifiant [lybrifjɑ̃] **1** *adj* lubricating. **2** *nm* lubricant.
lubrification [lybrifikɑsjɔ̃] *nf* lubrication, greasing.
lubrifier [lybrifje] *vt* (*pr sub & impf* **n. lubrifiions, v. lubrifiiez**) to lubricate; (*à la graisse*) to grease; (*à l'huile*) to oil.
lubrique [lybrik] *adj* libidinous, lustful, lewd; **un homme l.,** a lecherous man; **des regards lubriques,** lustful glances.
lubriquement [lybrik(ə)mɑ̃] *adv* libidinously, lustfully, lewdly.
Luc [lyk] *nm* Luke.
lucarne [lykarn] *nf* **(a)** (*fenêtre dans un toit*) dormer window, attic window; **l. rampante,** dormer (window); **(b)** (*tabatière*) skylight; **(c)** *Fb* top corner (*of net*).
lucide [lysid] *adj* lucid, clear (*mind, reasoning etc*); lucid, clear-headed, clear-sighted (*person*); *Méd* **elle a des moments lucides, puis se remet à délirer,** she has lucid moments *or* moments of lucidity, then sinks back into delirium.
lucidement [lysidmɑ̃] *adv* lucidly, clearly.
lucidité [lysidite] *nf* lucidity, clearness; clear-mindedness, clear-headedness; *Méd* **des moments de l.,** moments of lucidity.
Lucie [lysi] *nf* Lucy.
Lucien [lysjɛ̃] *nm* Lucian.
Lucienne [lysjɛn] *nf* = Lucy.
Lucifer [lysifɛr] *nm* Lucifer.
luciférien, -ienne [lysiferjɛ̃, -jɛn] **1** *adj* satanic, devilish. **2** *n Hist* Satanist.
Lucile [lysil] *nf* Lucille.
luciole [lysjɔl] *nf* (*insecte*) luciola, firefly.
lucratif, -ive [lykratif, -iv] *adj* lucrative, profitable, paying; **sans but l.,** non-profit-making.
lucrativement [lykrativmɑ̃] *adv* lucratively.
lucre [lykr] *nm Péj* lucre.
ludion [lydjɔ̃] *nm Phys* Cartesian diver.
ludique [lydik] *adj* play; **activité l.,** play activity; **il est très l.,** he is very playful.
ludothèque [lydɔtɛk] *nf* games library; **espace l.,** play area.
luette [lɥɛt] *nf Anat* uvula.
lueur [lɥœr] *nf* **(a)** (*lumière faible*) gleam, glimmer (*of light, hope etc*); **à la l. d'une bougie,** by candlelight; **les premières lueurs de l'aube,** the first light of dawn; **l. soudaine,** flash; **jeter une l.,** to flash; *Fig* **il n'y a plus une l. de vie dans ses yeux,** there isn't the faintest glimmer of life in his eyes any more; **(b)** *Fig* (*moment bref*) spark, flash; **une l. de lucidité/de raison,** a spark *or* flash of lucidity/intelligence.
luffa [lyfa] *nm* (*plante*) loofah.
luge [lyʒ] *nf* toboggan, sledge, sled; **faire de la l.,** to go tobogganing.
lugeur, -euse [lyʒœr, -øz] *n Sp* tobogganer.
lugubre [lygybr] *adj* lugubrious, dismal, gloomy (*atmosphere, mood*); doleful, mournful, (*sound, cry*).
lugubrement [lygybrəmɑ̃] *adv* lugubriously, dismally; dolefully.
lui¹, *pl* **leur** [lɥi, lœr] *pron pers* (*pour un homme*) (to) him; (*pour une femme*) (to) her; (*pour une chose, une idée*) (to) it; (*au pluriel*) (to) them; **je le lui donne,** I give it (to) him/(to) her; **donnez-lui-en,** give him/her some; **cette maison leur appartient,** this house belongs to them; **je lui trouve mauvaise mine,** I think he *or* she looks ill; **je lui ai serré la main,** I shook his *or* her hand; **je lui ai entendu dire cela,** I heard him *or* her say that; **il leur jeta une pierre,** he threw a stone at them; **donnez-le-lui,** give it (to) him *or* her; **montrez-le-leur,** show it to them.
lui², *pl* **eux** [lɥi, ø] *stressed pron pers m* **(a)** (*subject*) (*pour un homme*) he; (*pour une chose*) it; (*au pluriel*) they; **c'est lui,** it's him; (*en le désignant*) that's him; **ce sont eux,** *F* **c'est eux,** it's them; **lui, il a raison, il a raison, lui,** as for him, he's right; (*le seul*) he's the one who is right; **c'est lui-même qui me l'a dit,** he told me so himself; **eux deux/tous,** the two of them/all of them; **Jacques et lui l'ont fait,** he and Jacques did it, *F* Jacques and him did it; **ils le feront, elle bien, lui mal,** they'll both do it, she'll do it well, he'll do it badly;

(b) (*object*) him, it; them; **j'accuse son frère et lui,** I accuse him and his brother; **lui, je le connais, je le connais, lui,** I know him; **lui, je le connais, les autres non,** him I know, but not the others; **elle est plus grande que lui,** she's taller than him *or* than he is; **elle m'a présenté à lui,** she introduced me to him; **elle pense encore à lui,** she still thinks about him; **ce livre est à lui/à eux,** this book is his/theirs; **à lui seul, il n'y arrivera pas,** on his own he won't manage it; **à lui tout seul, il possède déjà deux maisons,** he already owns two houses of his own; **voilà une photo de lui,** here's a photo of him; **c'est pour lui,** it's for him; **c'est par lui que je l'ai su,** it's *or* it was through him that I found out; **j'ai confiance en lui,** I trust him; **c'est à lui de décider,** it's for him to decide; **c'est un ami à lui,** it's a friend of his;

(c) (*réfléchi*) him(self), it(self); them(selves); **il les rassembla autour de lui,** he gathered them round him; **il ne pense qu'à lui,** he thinks only of himself; **chacun d'eux travaille pour lui-même,** each of them works for himself.
lui-même [lɥimɛm] *pron pers* himself, itself; *see* **LUI², MÊME¹ (c)**.
luire [lɥir] *vi* (*prp* **luisant**; *pp* **lui** (*no f*); *pr ind* **il luit, ils luisent**; *p hist* **il luit, ils luirent,** *parfois* **il luisit**; *fu* **il luira**) to shine; (*métal, surface propre*) to gleam, to glow, (*surface de l'eau etc*) to glisten; *Fig* **l'espoir luit,** there's a glimmer of hope.
luisant [lɥizɑ̃] **1** *adj* shining, bright (*star, metal etc*); shiny, glossy (*surface etc*); gleaming (*eyes etc*); glowing (*embers*); **front l. de sueur,** forehead glistening with perspiration; **manteau l. d'usure,** coat shiny with wear; **ver l.,** glow-worm. **2** *nm* shine, gloss sheen.
lumbago [lɔ̃bago] *nm Méd* lumbago.
lumen [lymɛn] *nm* lumen.
lumière [lymjɛr] *nf* **(a)** (*clarté*) light; **l. (du jour), l. du soleil,** daylight, sunlight; **l. électrique,** electric light; **il n'y a plus de l.,** the light's gone out; **la fenêtre donne de la l.,** the window lets in light; (*éclairage électrique*) **allume la l., on n'y voit rien,** put the light on, we can't see anything in here; (*feu*) **les lumières de la ville,** the lights of the city, the city lights; *F* (*phare*) **allume tes lumières, il y a du brouillard,** put your lights on, it's foggy; **à la l. de la lune,** by moonlight;

(b) *Fig* (*compréhension*) light; **appréhender un problème sous une nouvelle l.,** to understand a problem in a new light; **à la l. de son exposé, tout paraît évident,** in the light of his presentation, everything seems clear; **mettre qch en l.,** to bring sth to light; **jeter une l. nouvelle sur qch,** to throw *or* shed a new light on sth; **faire (toute) la l. sur qch,** to clarify sth, to make sth (absolutely) clear;

(c) (*connaissances rationnelles*) **les lumières de la raison,** the light of reason; **avoir des lumières sur qch,** to have some knowledge about sth; **le siècle des lumières,** the Age of Enlightenment;

(d) (*homme de savoir*) **une des lumières de la science,** one of the leading lights in science; *F* **ce n'est pas une l.,** he's not very bright;

(e) (*ouverture*) aperture (*of sighting vane*); ICE slot (*in piston wall*); **l. d'admission/d'échappement,** inlet/exhaust port;

(f) *Phys Astron* **l. oxhydrique,** limelight; *Phys* **l. blanche,** white light; **l. noire** *ou* **de Wood,** black light; *Astron* **l. cendrée,** earthlight, earthshine; **année l.,** light-year; **diffraction de la l.,** diffraction of light.
lumignon [lymiɲɔ̃] *nm* **(a)** (*lampe*) dim light *or* lamp; **(b)** (*bout de mèche*) candle end.
luminaire [lyminɛr] *nm* **(a)** light, lighting (*at party etc*); **(b)** light, candle (*in church*).
luminescence [lyminesɑ̃s] *nf* luminescence.
luminescent, -ente [lyminesɑ̃, -ɑ̃t] *adj* luminescent.
lumineusement [lyminøzmɑ̃] *adv* luminously; brightly; *Fig* clearly.
lumineux, -euse [lyminø, -øz] *adj* luminous (*body, dial*); bright, filled with light (*room*); **montre à cadran l.,** watch with a luminous dial, luminous watch; **couleur très lumineuse,** a very bright *or* intense colour; **regard l.,** radiant look *or* expression; *Fig* **c'est une idée lumineuse,** it's a brilliant idea *or* a brainwave *or Am* brainstorm; **il a une intelligence lumineuse,** he is extremely intelligent; *Phys* **onde lumineuse,** light wave.
luminosité [lyminozite] *nf* luminosity, brightness.
lump [lœp] *nm* (*poisson*) lumpfish; **œufs de l.,** lumpfish

roe.

lunaire [lynɛr] **1** *adj* (*de la lune*) lunar; (*pareil à la lune*) moonlike; **sol l.,** surface of the moon; **cette région ressemble à un paysage l.,** this area resembles a lunar landscape; *Fig* **une visage l.,** a moon-face. **2** *nf* (*plant*) lunaria, *F* honesty, moonwort.

lunaison [lynɛzɔ̃] *nf Astron* lunation, lunar month.

lunatique [lynatik] *adj* whimsical, quirky, temperamental (*person*).

lunch [lœʃ] *nm* buffet lunch; (*pl lunches, lunchs*).

lundi [lœdi] *nm* Monday; **le l. de Pâques/de la Pentecôte,** Easter/Whit Monday.

lune [lyn] *nf* **(a)** *Astron* moon; **on a marché sur la l.,** men have walked on the moon; **la pleine l.,** the full moon; **la nouvelle l.,** the new moon; **les phases de la l.,** the phases of the moon; **clair de l.,** moonlight; **nuit sans l.,** moonless night; **la l. se lève,** the moon is rising; **l. rousse,** April moon; *Fig* **l. de miel,** honeymoon; *Fig* **vieilles lunes,** old times, the past; **il avait un visage en pleine l.,** he had a completely round face *or* a face like a full moon; *Fig* **demander la l.,** to ask for the moon; *Fig* **promettre la l.,** to promise the moon; *Fig F* **être dans la l.,** to be miles away, to be in the clouds; *Fig F* **être bête comme la l.,** to be completely stupid;

(b) *Arch & Littér* month, moon;

(c) (*visage tout rond*) moonface;

(d) *Arg* (*derrière*) bum, backside;

(e) (*humeur*) vagary, caprice, whim; **il est dans une bonne/mauvaise l.,** he is in one of his good/bad moods;

(f) (*plante*) **l. d'eau,** white water-lily;

(g) **l. de mer, poisson l.,** (ocean) sunfish;

(h) **pierre de l.,** moonstone.

luné [lyne] *adj F* **être bien/mal l.,** to be in a good/bad mood.

lunetier, -ière [lyntje, -jɛr] **1** *n* (*fabricant*) spectacle manufacturer. **2** *adj* **industrie lunetière,** spectacle industry.

lunette [lynɛt] *nf* **(a)** *Opt* **l. d'approche,** (refracting) telescope, field glass; *Mil* **l. de pointage,** sighting telescope; **l. astronomique,** astronomical telescope; **(b) (paire de) lunettes,** (pair of) glasses, spectacles, *F* specs, *US* (pair of) eyeglasses; **porter (des) lunettes,** to wear glasses *or* spectacles *or F* specs; **lunettes de protection,** goggles; **lunettes d'écaille,** horn-rimmed glasses; **lunettes noires** *ou* **de soleil,** sunglasses, dark glasses, *F* shades; **serpent à lunettes,** spectacled snake, Indian cobra; *F* **c'est un type à lunettes, facile à reconnaître,** he wears specs, he's easy to recognize; **c'est le type à lunettes,** he's the guy in specs; **(c)** *Archit* lunette; **(d)** lunette (*of guillotine*); **(e)** seat (*of w.c. pan*); **(f)** *Rail* cab window (*of locomotive*); *Aut* **l. arrière,** rear window.

lunetterie [lynɛtri] *nf* spectacle trade.

lunule [lynyl] *nf* **(a)** *Math* lune; **(b)** *Anat* lunula, (half-)moon (*of finger nail*).

lupanar [lypanar] *nm* brothel.

lupin [lypɛ̃] *nm* (*plante*) lupin.

lupus [lypys] *nm Méd* lupus.

lurette [lyrɛt] *nf F* (*used only in*) **il y a belle l.,** a long time ago, *F* ages ago; **il y a belle l. que je ne t'ai pas vu,** I haven't seen you for a long time *or F* for ages, *F* it's been ages since I saw you.

luron, -onne [lyrɔ̃, -ɔn] *n F* **c'est un gai** *ou* **un joyeux l.,** he's quite *or* a bit of a lad *or Vieilli* a gay dog; **c'est une sacrée luronne,** she's quite a girl.

lusitanien, -ienne [lyzitanjɛ̃, -jɛn] *Antiq* **1** *adj* Lusitanian. **2** *n* **L.,** Lusitanian.

lustrage [lystraʒ] *nm* glossing, glazing, lustring (*of cloth etc*); polishing (*of glass*); **l. des fourrures,** lustring of furs.

lustre¹ [lystr] *nm* **(a)** (*lampe*) chandelier; **(b)** (*brillant, éclat*) lustre, polish, gloss; glaze (*of silk etc*); **(c)** *Litt* renown; **il faut redonner du l. à cette ancienne demeure,** some of the splendour needs to be brought back to this stately old dwelling.

lustre² *nm Litt* lustrum, lustre; period of five years; *Fig F* (an) age, ages; **ça fait des lustres qu'on t'attend!,** we've been waiting ages for you!

lustré [lystre] *adj* glazed (*surface, pottery*); glossy (*fur, fabric*); **étoffe lustrée par l'usure,** cloth shiny with wear.

lustrer [lystre] *vt* to glaze, to gloss, to polish (up), to lustre (*leather etc*).

lustrerie [lystrəri] *nf Ind Com* chandelier trade.

lustrine [lystrin] *nf Tex* cotton lustre.

lut [lyt] *nm Cér Ind* lute *or* luting cement.

Lutèce [lytɛs] *nf Antiq* Lutetia.

lutéine [lytein] *nf Biol Ch* lutein.

luter [lyte] *vt Cér Ind* to lute, to seal with luting.

luth [lyt] *nm* **(a)** *Mus* lute; **(b)** *Fig* (*symbole de la poésie*) the poet's pen; **prendre son l.,** to take up one's pen (to write poetry).

luthéranisme [lyteranism] *nm Hist Rel* Lutheranism.

lutherie [lytri] *nf Mus* **(a)** (*fabrication*) stringed instrument industry *or* trade; **(b)** (*ensemble de ces instruments*) stringed instruments.

luthérien, -ienne [lyterjɛ̃, -jɛn] *adj & n Hist Rel* Lutheran.

luthier [lytje] *nm* stringed instrument maker, violin maker.

luthiste [lytist] *nm Mus* lutanist, lutenist, lute player.

lutin [lytɛ̃] **1** *nm* **(a)** (*créature de conte etc*) mischievous sprite, imp, elf, goblin; **(b)** *F* (*of child*) imp. **2** *adj* mischievous, impish.

lutiner [lytine] *vt* **(a)** (*taquiner*) to tease, to plague, to torment (*s.o.*); **(b)** to fondle, to tickle (*woman*).

lutrin [lytrɛ̃] *nm* **(a)** *Rel* lectern; **(b)** *Can* reading stand, music stand; **(c)** (*endroit où se tient le chœur*) choir stall.

lutte [lyt] *nf* **(a)** *Sp* wrestling; **l. libre,** all-in *or* freestyle wrestling; *Sp* **l. de traction à la corde** *ou* **l. à la jarretière,** tug-of-war;

(b) (*combat*) fight, struggle, tussle; (*morale, de guerre*) conflict; **entrer/être en l. avec qn,** to join battle with s.o., to enter into/to be in conflict with s.o.; *Pol Fig* **luttes parlementaires,** parliamentary clashes; **les partis en l.,** the opposing parties; **l. d'intérêts,** clash of interests; **gagner de haute** *ou Litt* **de vive l.,** to win by sheer force *or* by force of arms; **l. à mort,** life and death struggle; fight to the death;

(c) (*action*) **l. contre l'alcoolisme,** fight against alcoholism; **l. pour la liberté,** struggle for freedom; **l. antipollution,** fight against pollution;

(d) *Biol* struggle for survival; **la l. biologique,** survival of the fittest; **l. pour la vie,** natural selection; *Fig* struggle for life; strife; **la l. des classes,** the class struggle;

(e) (*antagonisme*) conflict; **la l. entre le devoir et la passion,** the conflict between duty and passion.

lutter [lyte] *vi* **(a)** (*combattre*) to wrestle (**avec, contre,** with); **(b)** (*se battre*) to struggle, to contend, to fight, to compete; **l. contre la maladie,** to fight against *or* to combat disease; *Fig* **l. contre le vent,** to battle with the wind; **l. contre un incendie,** to fight a fire; **l. pour l'indépendance,** to fight for independence; **(c)** (*rivaliser*) **l. de vitesse avec qn,** to race s.o.; **elles luttent d'adresse pour se faire valoir,** they're using all their skills to outdo each other and get themselves noticed.

lutteur, -euse [lytœr, -øz] *n* **(a)** *Sp* wrestler; **(b)** fighter (*for a cause etc*); **un tempérament de l.,** a fighting *or* fighter's temperament.

lux [lyks] *nm* lux.

luxation [lyksasjɔ̃] *nf Méd* dislocation, luxation (*of joint*); **l. congénitale,** congenital dislocation.

luxe [lyks] *nm* **(a)** (*abondance, richesse*) luxury; luxuriousness, sumptuousness (*of house etc*); **vivre dans le l.,** to live in luxury; **étaler son l.,** to flaunt one's wealth;

(b) (*qualité*) luxury, luxuriousness; **articles de l.,** luxury articles; **édition de l.,** de luxe edition; **train de l.,** first-class and Pullman train; **taxe de l.,** luxury tax;

(c) abundance, profusion (*of food etc*); **l. de précautions,** extravagant precautions;

(d) (*bien superflu, coûteuse*) luxury, indulgence; **goûts de l.,** extravagant tastes; **mon seul l., c'est d'aller au cinéma,** my only luxury *or* indulgence is going to the cinema; **c'est du l.,** that is quite unnecessary *or* a mere luxury; **je me suis payé le l. de le lui dire,** I gave myself the pleasure of telling him so; **se payer le l. d'un cigare,** to indulge in (the luxury of) a cigar; **je vais faire nettoyer ce vieil imperméable, ce ne sera pas du l.,** I'm going to have this old raincoat cleaned, it really needs it.

Luxembourg [lyksɑ̃bur] *nm* (Grand Duchy of) Luxembourg.

luxembourgeois, -oise [lyksɑ̃burʒwa, -waz] **1** *adj* of *or* from Luxembourg. **2** *n* **L.,** Luxembourger.

luxer [lykse] **1** *vt* to dislocate, to luxate (*joint etc*). **2 se luxer** *vpr* to dislocate a joint; **se l. l'épaule,** to dislocate one's shoulder, to put one's shoulder out.

luxueusement [lyksɥøzmɑ̃] *adv* luxuriously, sumptuously.

luxueux, -euse [lyksɥø, -øz] *adj* luxurious, sumptuous.

luxure [lyksyr] *nf Litt* lewdness, lust.

luxuriance [lyksyrjɑ̃s] *nf* luxuriance.

luxuriant [lyksyrjɑ̃] *adj* luxuriant, lush (*vegetation etc*); fertile (*imagination*); **un style l.,** a luxuriant style.

luxurieux, -euse [lyksyrjø, -øz] *adj* lascivious, lewd, lustful, sensual.

luzerne [lyzɛrn] *nf* (*plante*) lucern(e), alfalfa.

lycée [lise] *nm* **(a)** *Scol* = *Br* grammar school, *US* high school, *Br* secondary school; **l. d'enseignement professionnel,** technical high school; **l. technique,** technical high school; **(b)** (*période*) schooldays, high school days; **il se souvient du l. comme de ses meilleures années,** he looks back on his schooldays as the best years of his life; **(c)** *Antiq* **le L.,** the Lyceum.

lycéen, -éenne [liseẽ, -eɛn] *n* = *Br* grammar school *or US* high school *or Br* secondary school pupil.

lydien, -ienne [lidjẽ, -jɛn] *Antiq* **1** *adj* Lydian; *Mus* **(mode) l.,** lydian mode. **2** *n* **L.,** Lydian. **3** *nm Mus* Lydian.

lymphatique [lẽfatik] **1** *adj* **(a)** lymphatic (*gland etc*); **(b)** lethargic, apathetic (*person*). **2** *nm* lymphatic (duct).

lymphe [lẽf] *nf* lymph.

lymphocyte [lẽfɔsit] *nm* lymphocyte.

lymphoïde [lẽfɔid] *adj* lymphoid (*cells, tissue*).

lynchage [lẽʃaʒ] *nm* lynching.

lyncher [lẽʃe] *vt* to lynch.

lynx [lẽks] *nm* lynx; *Fig* **avoir des yeux de l.,** to be sharp-sighted, to have eyes like a hawk.

Lyon [ljɔ̃] *n* Lyons.

lyonnais, -aise [ljɔnɛ, -ɛz] **1** *adj* of *or* from Lyons. **2** *n* **L.,** person from *or* inhabitant of Lyons.

lyophilisation [ljɔfilizasjɔ̃] *nf Tech* freeze-drying.

lyophiliser [ljɔfilize] *vt Tech* to freeze-dry (*coffee etc*); **café lyophilisé,** freeze-dried coffee.

lyre [lir] *nf* **(a)** *Mus* lyre; *Litt* poetry; **prendre sa l.,** to take up (writing) poetry; *F* **toute la l.,** the whole lot (of them), the whole shoot; **(b)** *Astron* Lyra; **(c) (oiseau-)l.,** lyre bird.

lyrique [lirik] **1** *adj* **(a)** lyric(al) (*poem etc*); **poète l.,** lyric poet; **(b)** (*mis en musique*) **drame l.,** lyric drama, opera; **comédie l.,** comic opera, operetta; **théâtre l.,** opera house; **(c)** (*poétique, passionné*) lyrical; **des envolées lyriques,** flights of lyricism; **user du style l.,** to use a lyrical style. **2** *nm* lyric poet.

lyrisme [lirism] *nm* **(a)** lyricism; **(b)** (*exubérance*) excessive enthusiasm.

lys [lis] *nm Arch* = **LIS.**

lysergique [lizɛrʒik] *adj Biol* lysergic; **acide l. (synthétique) diéthylamide,** lysergic acid diethylamide.

M

M, m [ɛm] *nm* (the letter) M, m.

m **(a)** (*abrév* **Monsieur**) Mr; **(b)** (*abrév* **mètre**) m; **(c)** *Gram* (*abrév* **masculin**) masculine; **(d)** (*abrév* **mort**) d.

m' *voir* **ME**.

ma [ma] *voir* **MON**.

maboul, -oule [mabul] *Arg* **1** *adj* (*fou*) crazy, nuts, loony. **2** *n* nut, loony.

macabre [makɑbr] *adj* macabre, gruesome (*discovery, story*); macabre, sick (*humour etc*); **danse m.,** dance of Death.

macache [makaʃ] *adv Arg* not likely!, nothing doing!, no fear!

macadam [makadam] *nm* **(a)** macadam; **m. goudronné,** tarmac(adam); **(b)** (*route*) (macadamized) road.

macadamisage [makadamizaʒ] *nm*, **macadamisation** [makadamizɑsjɔ̃] *nf* tarmacking (*of roads*).

macadamiser [makadamize] *vt* to tarmac (*road*).

macaque [makak] *nm* **(a)** (*singe*) macaque; **m. rhésus,** bandar, rhesus (monkey); **(b)** *F* very ugly person.

macareux [makarø] *nm* puffin.

macaron [makarɔ̃] *nm* **(a)** *Culin* macaroon; **(b) macarons,** (*coiffure*) coils (*over the ears*), *F* earphones; **(c)** (*badge*) badge; (*en tissu*) rosette; (*motif*) (round) motif.

macaroni [makarɔni] *nm* **(a)** *Culin* macaroni; **(b)** *Arg Péj* (*Italien*) wop, *Br* Eyetie.

Macchabée [makabe] *nm* **(a)** *Bible* Maccabaeus; **(b)** *Arg* **m.,** (*mort*) corpse, stiff.

macédoine [masedwan] *nf* **(a)** *Culin* **m. de fruits,** fruit salad; **m. de légumes,** mixed vegetables, macedoine of vegetables; **(b)** *F* (*mélange*) medley, miscellany; *Péj* hotchpotch.

Macédoine [masedwan] *nf* Macedonia.

macédonien, -ienne [masedɔnjɛ̃, -jɛn] **1** *adj* Macedonian. **2** *n* **M.,** Macedonian.

macération [maserɑsjɔ̃] *nf* steeping, soaking.

macérer [masere] *v* (**je macère; je macérerai**) **1** *vt* **(a)** to steep, to soak; **m. des fruits dans de l'eau-de-vie,** to steep *or* soak fruit in brandy; **(b)** *Rel* to mortify (*the flesh*). **2** *vi* to steep, to soak; **la viande doit m. plusieurs jours,** the meat should be left to soak for several days; *Fig F* **laissons-le m.,** let's leave him to stew (in his own juice).

Mach [mak] *nm Av* **(nombre de) M.,** Mach (number).

mâche [mɑʃ] *nf Bot* corn salad, lamb's lettuce, mache.

mâchefer [mɑʃfɛr] *nm Tech* clinker, slag.

mâchement [mɑʃmɑ̃] *nm* chewing, *Fml* mastication.

mâcher [mɑʃe] *vt* to chew, *Fml* to masticate (*one's food*); to munch (*biscuit etc*); (*of animal*) to champ (*fodder*); **papier mâché,** papier mâché; **m. le mors,** (*of horse*) to champ at the bit; *F* **m. son frein,** (*of person*) to champ at the bit; **je ne vais pas m. mes mots,** I won't mince words with you *or* him *etc*; **m. le travail** *ou* **la besogne à qn,** to spoon-feed s.o.; **m. le bois,** (*of blunt tool etc*) to chew up the wood.

machette [maʃɛt] *nf* machete.

Machiavel [makjavɛl] *nm* Machiavelli.

machiavélique [makjavelik] *adj* (*ruse etc*) Machiavellian.

machiavélisme [makjavelism] *nm* Machiavellianism.

mâchicoulis [mɑʃikuli] *nm Archit* machicolation; **à m.,** machicolated.

machin [maʃɛ̃] *nm F* **(a)** (*personne*) **monsieur M.,** Mr whatshisname, what-d'you-call-him, Thingummy; **(b)** (*objet*) **m.(-chouette),** thing(ummy), thingumajig, thingumabob, whatsit(sname), what not, what-d'you-call-it; **qu'est-ce que c'est que ce m.-là?,** what's that (thing *or* gadget)?

machinal, -aux [maʃinal, -o] *adj* mechanical, unconscious (*action*); automatic (*reaction*).

machinalement [maʃinalmɑ̃] *adv* mechanically, unconsciously; (*réagir*) instinctively, automatically.

machination [maʃinɑsjɔ̃] *nf* machination, plot.

machine [maʃin] *nf* **(a)** machine; **m. à coudre,** sewing machine; **m. à laver,** washing machine; **m. à laver la vaisselle,** dishwasher; **m. à écrire,** typewriter; **écrire une lettre à la m.,** to type a letter; **écrit à la m.,** typed, typewritten; *F* **trois pages de m.,** three typewritten pages; **m. à dicter,** dictating machine; **traduction par machine,** machine translation, MT; **m. à calculer,** calculator; (*plus grande*) calculating machine, adding machine; *Ordinat* **langage m.,** machine language; *Ordinat* **exploitable par une m.,** machine-readable; **m. comptable,** accounting machine; **m. à sous,** slot machine, one-armed bandit, *Br* fruit machine; *Ind* **les machines,** the machinery, the plant; **les grosses machines,** the heavy machinery *or* plant; **atelier des machines,** machine shop; **m. à aléser,** boring machine, fine borer; **m. à fraiser,** milling machine; **travailler le métal à la m.,** to machine metal; **fait à la m.,** machine-made; *Constr* **m. à battre** *ou* **à enfoncer les pieux,** pile driver; *Typ* **m. à composer,** typesetting machine; **les machines agricoles,** agricultural machinery *or* machines; **m. à battre,** threshing machine; *Th* **pièce à machines,** play with stage effects; **m. de guerre,** engine of war; *Fig* **la m. administrative,** the administrative machinery; *Fig Péj* **il n'est qu'une m. à penser/à faire de l'argent,** he's nothing but a thinking/money-making machine;
(b) *F* (*véhicule*) machine; **m. volante,** flying machine;
(c) (*moteur*) engine; *Rail* locomotive, engine; **m. thermique,** heat engine; **m. à combustion interne,** internal combustion engine; **m. à gaz,** gas engine; **m. à pétrole,** oil engine; **m. à vapeur,** steam engine; **m. à turbine,** turbine engine; **m. auxiliaire,** donkey engine; **m. motrice,** prime mover; *Rail* **m. de manœuvre,** shunting engine; *Rail* **m. routière,** traction engine; *Nau* **salle des machines,** engine room; **stopper les machines,** to stop the engines; **faire m. arrière,** to reverse the engine; *Fig* to backtrack.

machine-outil [maʃinuti] *nf* machine tool; (*pl machines-outils*).

machiner [maʃine] *vt Vieilli* to scheme, to plot; **affaire machinée d'avance,** put-up job; **qu'est-ce qu'il machine?,** what's he plotting?

machinerie [maʃinri] *nf* **(a)** (*machines*) machinery; *Ind* plant; **(b)** (*salle*) *Ind* machine room; *Nau* engine room.

machinisme [maʃinism] *nm* mechanization (*of agriculture etc*).

machiniste [maʃinist] *nm* **(a)** *Th etc* scene shifter, stagehand; **(b)** *Vieilli* driver (*of bus, electric train etc*).

machisme [matʃism(ə)] *nm* machismo, male chauvinism.

machmètre [makmɛtr] *nm Av* machmeter.

macho [matʃo] **1** *nm* (*phallocrate*) male chauvinist, *F Péj* male chauvinist pig. **2** *adj inv* (*comportement etc*) male chauvinist.

mâchoire [mɑʃwar] *nf* **(a)** *Anat* jaw (*of person, animal*); **la m., les mâchoires,** the jaws; *Arg* **jouer** *ou* **travailler des mâchoires,** (*manger*) to nosh; *F* **bâiller à se décrocher la m.,** to yawn one's head off; **(b)** *MecE* **mâchoires d'un étau,** jaws of a vice; **m. d'une poulie,** flange of a pulley; *Aut* **mâchoires de frein,** brake shoes.

mâchonnement [mɑʃɔnmɑ̃] *nm* chewing.

mâchonner [mɑʃɔne] *vt* **(a)** to chew (*food, cigar*); (*of horse*) to champ (*the bit*); **m. son crayon,** to chew (the end of) one's pencil; **(b)** (*marmonner*) to mutter (*threats etc*); to mumble (*prayer*).

mâchouiller [mɑʃuje] *vt F* to chew away at (*sth*).

mâchure [mɑʃyr] *nf Tex* flaw (*in velvet etc*).

mâchurer¹ [mɑʃyre] *vt* (*noircir*) to soil, to dirty; *Typ* to smudge, to mackle, to blur (*sheet*).

mâchurer² *vt Tech* to dent, to bruise (*metal part in the vice*).

macis [masi] *nm Bot Culin* mace.

mackintosh [makintɔʃ] *nm Vieilli* mackintosh.

macle¹ [makl] *nf* (*crystal*) macle, twin(ned) crystal.

macle² *nf Bot* water chestnut.

maclé [makle] *adj (crystal)* twinned.
macler [makle] *vt Tech* to mix, to stir *(glass)*.
maçon [masɔ̃] **1** *nm* **(a)** *(artisan)* bricklayer; *(avec des pierres)* (stone)mason; **(b)** *(franc-maçon)* (free)mason. **2** *adj* **abeille maçonne** [masɔn] , mason bee.
mâcon [mɑkɔ̃] *nm (also* **vin de M.***)* Mâcon (wine).
maçonnage [masɔnaʒ] *nm* bricklaying; *(avec des pierres)* mason's work.
maçonner [masɔne] *vt (construire)* to build *(wall etc)*; *(recouvrir de pierres)* to face *(wall etc)* with stone; *(condamner)* to wall up, to brick up *(door etc)*.
maçonnerie [masɔnri] *nf* **(a)** brickwork; *(avec des pierres)* masonry, stonework; **(b)** *(organisation secrète)* (free)masonry.
maçonnique [masɔnik] *adj* masonic *(lodge etc)*.
macramé [makrame] *nm* macramé; **faire du m.,** to do macramé; **un set de table en m.,** a set of macramé table-mats.
macre [makr] *nf Bot* water chestnut.
macreuse [makrøz] *nf* **(a)** *(oiseau)* scoter (duck); **(b)** *Culin* shoulder of beef.
macro [makro] *nm Phot Ordinat* macro; *Phot* **se mettre en m.,** to go into macro.
macrobiotique [makrɔbjɔtik] *adj* macrobiotic.
macrocéphale [makrɔsefal] *adj* macrocephalic.
macro-commande [makrɔkɔmɑ̃d] *nf Ordinat* macro (command).
macrocosme [makrɔkɔsm] *nm* macrocosm.
macrocosmique [makrɔkɔsmik] *adj Phil Littér* macrocosmic.
macro-économie [makrɔekɔnɔmi] *nf* macroeconomics.
macro-économique [makrekɔnɔmik] *adj* macroeconomic.
macrographie [makrɔgrafi] *nf Tech* macrography.
macromolécule [makrɔmɔlekyl] *nf Ch* macromolecule.
macrophotographie [makrɔfɔtɔgrafi] *nf Phot* macrophotography, photomacrography.
macropode [makrɔpɔd] **1** *adj Biol* macropodous. **2** *nm (poisson)* paradise fish.
macroscopique [makrɔskɔpik] *adj* macroscopic.
macula [makyla] *nf Anat* macula.
maculage [makylaʒ] *nm (salissure) (action)* soiling, staining; *(tache)* stain, spot; *Typ* off-setting, mackling.
maculature [makylatyr] *nf Typ* waste sheet *(used for packing etc)*; *(feuille intercalaire)* interleaf.
macule [makyl] *nf* **(a)** = **MACULATURE**; **(b)** *Arch & Littér* stain, spot, blemish; **(c)** *Méd* macula; **(d)** *Typ* mackle, blur.
maculer [makyle] **1** *vt Littér* to stain, to spot, to blemish; *Typ* to mackle, to blur. **2** *vi (of paper)* to mackle, to blur; *(of engraving)* to fox.
Madagascar [madagaskar] *nm* Madagascar.
madame, *pl* **mesdames** [madam, medam] *nf* **(a)** Mrs; **M. Martin,** Mrs Martin; **Mesdames Martin,** the Mrs Martin; **M. Veuve Martin,** Mrs Martin, widow of David Martin; **m. la marquise/la comtesse de X,** the Marchioness/the Countess of X; **je voudrais parler à m. la directrice,** *(du magasin)* I would like to speak to the manageress; *(d'un service)* I would like to talk to the manager; *(d'une école)* I would like to speak to the headmistress; *Fml* **comment va m. votre mère?,** how is your mother?;
(b) *(utilisé seul) (pl* **ces dames***)* **voici le chapeau de m.,** here is your hat, madam; **M. se plaint que ...,** *(dit par vendeur)* the lady *or* this lady *or* madam is complaining that ...; *(dit par domestique)* madam is complaining that ...;
(c) *(apostrophe)* madam, *surtout Am* ma'am; *(to titled lady)* your ladyship; *(in police, army etc)* ma'am; **non, m.,** no(, madam); **entrez, mesdames,** come in, ladies; **m. est servie,** dinner is served(, madam);
(d) *(dans une lettre) (always written in full)* **Madame,** (Dear) Madam; **chère Madame,** Dear Mrs Smith;
(e) *F* lady; **jouer à la m.,** to put on airs.
Madeleine [madlɛn] *nf* **(a)** Madeleine; *Bible* Magdalen(e); *F* **pleurer comme une M.,** to cry one's eyes *or* heart out; **(b)** *Culin* **m.,** madeleine.
mademoiselle, *pl* **mesdemoiselles** [madmwazɛl, medmwazɛl] *nf* **(a)** Miss; **M. Martin,** Miss Martin; *Fml Vieilli* **comment va m. votre cousine?,** how is your cousin?; **(b)** *(utilisé seul) (pl* **ces demoiselles***)* **ces demoiselles n'y sont pas,** the young ladies are not at home; **M. se plaint que ...,** *(in shop)* the *or* this young lady is complaining that ...; **(c)** *(apostrophe)* **merci m.,** thank you, miss (Smith); **m. est servie,** dinner is served(, madam); **(d)** *(dans une lettre) (always written in full)* **Mademoiselle,** (Dear) Madam; **chère Mademoiselle,** Dear Miss Smith.
Madère [madɛr] **1** *nf Géog* Madeira. **2** *nm (also* **vin de M.***)* Madeira (wine).
madone [madɔn] *nf* madonna; *Fig* **elle a un visage de m.,** she has a madonna-like face.
Madras [madrɑs] *nm* **(a)** Madras; **(b)** *Tex (tissu)* **m.,** madras (cotton); *(foulard)* (cotton) headscarf.
madré, -ée [madre] **1** *adj* sly, crafty, wily. **2** *n* sly fox.
madrépore [madrepɔr] *nm Zool* madrepore.
madrier [madrije] *nm* (piece of) timber; *(façonné)* thick board *or* plank; *(poutre)* beam.
madrigal, -aux [madrigal, -o] *nm* madrigal.
madrilène [madrilɛn] **1** *adj* of *or* from Madrid. **2** *n* **M,** native *or* inhabitant of Madrid.
maelstrom [malstrɔm] *nm* maelstrom.
maestria [maɛstrija] *nf Beaux-Arts* mastery; **avec m.,** in a masterly manner, brilliantly.
maestro [maɛstro] *nm Mus* maestro.
maf(f)ia [mafja] *nf* mafia.
maf(f)ioso, -si [mafjozo, -zi] *nm* mafioso.
mafflu [mafly] *adj Arch & Litt* heavy-jowled.
magasin [magazɛ̃] *nm* **(a)** shop, *Am* store; **grand m.,** department store; **m. à libre service,** self-service store; **m. à succursales multiples,** chain store; **chaîne de magasins,** chain of shops *or* stores; **employé(e) de m.,** shop assistant, *Am* salesclerk; **courir** *ou* **faire les magasins,** to go shopping; *F* **les magasins sont ouverts!,** *(ta braguette)* your fly's open!; **(b)** *(entrepôt)* store, warehouse; **garçon de m.,** warehouseman, storeman; **marchandises en m.,** stock in hand; **magasins généraux,** bonded warehouse(s); *Mil* **m. à poudre,** powder magazine; **m. d'armes,** armoury, *US* armory; **(c)** magazine *(of rifle, projector)*.
magasinage [magazinaʒ] *nm* **(a)** *Com* warehousing, storing *(of goods)*; **(b)** *Jur* **(droits de) m.,** warehouse dues; storage (charges); **(c)** *Can* **faire du m.,** to go shopping.
magasiner [magazine] *vi Can* to go shopping; **merci d'avoir magasiné chez Simpson,** *(sur panneau)* thank you for shopping at Simpson's.
magasinier [magazinje] *nm* warehouseman, storekeeper.
magazine [magazin] *nm* **(a)** *(journal)* magazine; **un m. féminin,** a women's magazine; **un m. hebdomadaire/mensuel,** a weekly/monthly (magazine); **(b)** *Rad TV* magazine (programme); **le nouveau m. d'information/culturel,** the new current-affairs/arts magazine (programme).
magdalénien, -ienne [magdalenjɛ̃, -jɛn] *adj & nm Hist* Magdalenian.
mage [maʒ] *nm* **(a)** *Antiq* magus; **les trois (Rois) Mages,** *Bible* the Three Magi, the Three Wise Men; *Astron* Orion's belt; *Beaux-Arts Bible* **l'adoration des Mages,** the Adoration of the Magi; **(b)** *(voyant)* seer.
magenta [maʒɛ̃ta] *nm* magenta.
Maghreb [magrɛb] *nm* **le M.,** the Maghreb *(French-speaking North Africa)*.
maghrebin [magrebɛ̃] **1** *adj* of *or* from the Maghreb. **2** *n* **M.,** person from the Maghreb.
magicien, -ienne [maʒisjɛ̃, -jɛn] *n* magician, wizard, sorcerer, *f* sorceress.
magie [maʒi] *nf* magic, wizardry; **m. noire,** black magic; **comme par m.,** as if by magic, magically; *Fig* **c'est la m. du langage,** that's the wonder *or* magic of language.
magique [maʒik] *adj* magic(al); **d'un coup de baguette m.,** with a wave of my *or* his *etc* magic wand; **lanterne m.,** magic lantern; **c'est m.!,** it's magic!
magiquement [maʒikmɑ̃] *adv* magically.
magister [maʒistɛr] *nm* **(a)** *Arch* pedagogue; (village) schoolmaster; **(b)** *Péj* pedant.
magistère [maʒistɛr] *nm* **(a)** *Univ* post-graduate vocational qualification; **(b)** *Fig (autorité morale)* authority; **(c)** *(titre)* Grand Master; **M. de l'Ordre de Malte,** Grand Master of the Order of Malta; **(d)** *Ch Méd* magisterium.
magistral, -aux [maʒistral, -o] *adj* **(a)** *(digne d'un maître)* magisterial, authoritative; **(b)** *(fait par un maître)* authoritative, masterly *(work etc)*; *Fig* colossal, sound *(thrashing)*; *Fig* **une erreur magistrale,** a colossal *or* monumental mistake.
magistralement [maʒistralmɑ̃] *adv* authoritatively; *Fig* soundly, thoroughly.
magistrat [maʒistra] *nm* **(a)** *Jur* magistrate; **il est m.,** he's a magistrate, he sits on the Bench; **m. du parquet,** public prosecutor; **(b)** *Jur Admin Pol* **premier m. de France,** supreme judicial officer of France.
magistrature [maʒistratyr] *nf* magistrature; **la m.**

assise, the judges, the Bench; **la m. debout,** the (body of) public prosecutors; **entrer dans la m.,** (*devenir juge*) to be appointed a judge; (*devenir fonctionnaire public*) to be appointed a public prosecutor.

magma [magma] *nm Ch Géol* magma; *Fig* **un m. informe de pierres,** heap *or* pile of stones; *Fig* **un m. d'idées confuses,** a jumble of confused ideas.

magnanerie [maɲanri] *nf* silkworm breeding, *Spéc* sericulture.

magnanier, -ière [maɲanje, -jɛr] *n* silkworm breeder, *Spéc* sericulturist.

magnanime [maɲanim] *adj* magnanimous; **se montrer m.,** to show magnanimity, to be magnanimous.

magnanimement [maɲanimmɑ̃] *adv* magnanimously.

magnanimité [maɲanimite] *nf* magnanimity.

magnat [magna] *nm* **(a)** *Com Ind* magnate, tycoon; **les magnats du pétrole,** oil magnates *or* tycoons; **(b)** *Hist* magnate, grandee (*of Poland, Hungary*).

magner (se) [s(ə)maɲe] *vpr F* to get a move on.

magnésie [maɲezi] *nf Ch Pharm* magnesia, magnesium oxide; *Pharm* **sulfate de m.,** Epsom salts.

magnésite [maɲezit] *nf Minér* (*magnesium carbonate*) magnesite; (*magnesium silicate*) meerschaum.

magnésium [maɲezjɔm] *nm Ch* magnesium; **éclair de m.,** magnesium light *or* flash.

magnétique [maɲetik] *adj* magnetic; **champ m.,** magnetic field; **enregistrement sur une bande m.,** recording on magnetic tape, tape-recording; **piste m.,** (*d'une carte de crédit*) magnetic strip; **monnaie m.,** plastic money; *Fig* **exercer un pouvoir m.,** to exert a hypnotic *or* magnetic power (**sur,** on, over).

magnétisable [maɲetizabl] *adj* magnetizable; (*personne*) hypnotizable.

magnétisation [maɲetizasjɔ̃] *nf* **(a)** *Phys* magnetization; **(b)** (*de qn*) hypnotizing, mesmerizing.

magnétiser [maɲetize] *vt* **(a)** to magnetize (*iron etc*); **(b)** to mesmerize, to hypnotize (*s.o.*); *Fig* **auditoire magnétisé,** hypnotized *or* spellbound audience.

magnétisme [maɲetism] *nm* **(a)** *Phys* magnetism; **m. terrestre,** the earth's magnetism; **m. rémanent,** residual magnetism; **(b)** (*hypnotisme*) hypnotism, mesmerism; **m. personnel,** personal magnetism; **une personne qui a beaucoup de m.,** a person with a great deal of charisma *or* personal magnetism, a charismatic person.

magnétite [maɲetit] *nf Minér* magnetite, lodestone.

magnéto [maɲeto] **1** *nf Tech* magneto. **2** *nm F* (*magnétophone*) tape recorder; (*magnétoscope*) video recorder.

magnétomètre [maɲetɔmɛtr] *nm Tech* magnetometer.

magnétophone [maɲetɔfɔn] *nm* tape recorder; **m. à cassette(s)** *ou F* **à k7,** cassette recorder.

magnétoscope [maɲetɔskɔp] *nm* video (tape) recorder, *F* video; *Tech* magnetoscope.

magnétoscoper [maɲetɔskɔpe] *vt* to video(-record), to make a video recording of.

magnificat [magnifikat] *nm Rel* magnificat.

magnificence [maɲifisɑ̃s] *nf* (*richesse, éclat*) magnificence, splendour, *US* splendor; *Litt* (*d'une personne*) munificence, lavishness.

magnifier [maɲifje] *vt* (*pr sub & impf* **n. magnifiions, v. magnifiiez**) to magnify, to glorify.

magnifique [maɲifik] *adj* **(a)** magnificent; **un château m.,** a magnificent stately home; **il est m. dans le rôle,** he is magnificent *or* superb *or* brilliant in the role; **quel temps m.!,** what magnificent *or* superb *or* splendid weather!; **on a une vue m. depuis le deuxième étage,** there is a magnificent *or* superb view from the second floor; **(c'est) m.!,** (it's) marvellous *or* great *or* fantastic!; **elle était m. dans sa robe de mariée,** she looked magnificent *or* wonderful *or* superb in her wedding dress; **un bébé m.,** a bonny *or* lovely (little) baby; **(b)** *Vieilli* (*titre pour un prince, un seigneur etc*) Great, Magnificent; (*généreux, prodigue*) liberal, munificent, lavish, princely (*gifts*); **Gatsby le m.,** the Great Gatsby.

magnifiquement [maɲifikmɑ̃] *adv* magnificently, wonderfully, superbly.

magnitude [magnityd] *nf Astron* magnitude (*of star*).

magnolia [maɲɔlja] *nm,* **magnolier** [maɲɔlje] *nm* magnolia (tree).

magnum [magnɔm] *nm* magnum (*of champagne*).

magot¹ [mago] *nm F* hoard, pile (*of money*); (*économies*) savings, nest egg.

magot² *nm* **(a)** Barbary ape, macaque; **(b)** (*figurine*) magot.

magouillage [magujaʒ] *nm,* **magouille** [maguj] *nf F* **faire des magouillages,** to scheme; **je ne trempe pas dans ce genre de m.,** I don't get involved in that kind of shady dealing; **les magouillages électoraux,** pre-election plotting.

magouiller [maguje] **1** *vt* to scheme, to plot; **il magouille un mauvais coup,** he's cooking up a dirty trick. **2** *vi* **il magouille pour se faire bien voir du patron,** he's scheming to get into the boss's good books.

magouilleur, -euse [magujœr, -øz] *n* schemer, plotter.

magret [magrɛ] *nm Culin* (*d'oie, de canard*) fillet, breast.

magyar, -are [magjar] **1** *adj* Magyar. **2** *n* **M.,** Magyar.

maharajah [maaradʒa] *nm* maharaja(h).

maharani [maarani] *nf* maharanee.

mahatma [maatma] *nm* mahatma.

ma(h)-jong [maʒɔ̃g] *nm* mah-jong(g).

Mahomet [maɔmɛ] *nm* Mohammed, Mahomet.

mahométan, -ane [maɔmetɑ̃, -an] *adj & n Vieilli* Mohammedan, Mahometan, Moslem.

mahométisme [maɔmetism] *nm Vieilli* Mohammedanism, Moslemism.

mai [mɛ] *nm* May; **en m.,** in May; **au mois de m.,** in (the month of) May; **le sept m.,** (on) the seventh of May, (on) May the seventh, *Am* (on) May seventh; **le premier m.,** May day; **(arbre de) m.,** maypole.

M.A.I.F. [maif] *nf abrév* **Mutuelle assurance des instituteurs de France.**

maigre [mɛgr] **1** *adj* thin, skinny, lean (*person, animal*); lean (*meat etc*); meagre, *US* meager (*income, diet*); scanty (*vegetation etc*); small (*crop*); infertile, poor (*land etc*); straggling (*beard*); **m. comme un clou,** as thin as a rake; **homme grand et m.,** a tall, thin man; **fromage m.,** low-fat cheese; **m. filet d'eau,** thin trickle of water; **m. repas,** scanty *or* frugal meal; **repas m.,** meatless meal; **jour m.,** day of abstinence; **c'est un peu m.,** (*votre explication*) it's a bit thin; *Typ* **caractères maigres,** lightfaced type.

2 *nm* **(a)** (*personne*) **un grand m.,** a tall, thin man; **c'est une fausse m.,** she's not as thin as she looks;
(b) maigres, shallows (*of river etc*);
(c) un morceau de m., a piece of lean (meat).

maigrelet, -ette [mɛgrəlɛ, -ɛt] *adj & n* thin *or* slight *or* skinny (person).

maigrement [mɛgrəmɑ̃] **1** *adv* meagrely, *US* meagerly, poorly.

maigreur [mɛgrœr] *nf* thinness, leanness, skinniness; *Fig* poorness, meagreness, *US* meagerness, scantiness (*of a meal etc*); baldness (*of style*).

maigrichon, -onne [mɛgriʃɔ̃, -ɔn] **, maigriot, -otte** [mɛgrijo, -ɔt] *adj & n* = **MAIGRELET**.

maigrir [mɛgrir] **1** *vi* to get thin(ner), to lose weight; **elle essaie de m.,** she's slimming; **j'ai maigri de dix kilos,** I've lost ten kilos; **régime pour m.,** (weight-loss) diet. **2** *vt* **(a)** (*of illness*) to make (*s.o.*) thin(ner); (*of garment*) to make (*s.o.*) look thin(ner); **(b)** to thin (*piece of wood etc*).

mail [maj] *nm* **(a)** avenue, promenade; **(b)** (*jeu, lieu*) pall-mall; **(c)** *Vieilli* (*marteau*) mallet.

mailing [mɛliŋ] *nm* **faire un m.,** to do a mailshot.

maillage [majaʒ] *nm* networking.

maille¹ [maj] *nf* **(a)** stitch (*in knitting etc*); **m. à l'endroit,** plain (stitch), knit; **m. à l'envers,** purl (stitch); **m. à l'endroit, m. à l'envers,** knit one, purl one; **m. qui file,** ladder, *Am* run (*in stocking*); **(b)** (*tissu tricoté*) knitwear; **une robe en m. de coton,** a knitted cotton dress; **(c)** link (*of chain*); **cotte de mailles,** coat of mail; **(d)** (*d'un filet*) mesh (*of net etc*); **filet à larges mailles,** wide-mesh net; **passer entre** *ou* **à travers les mailles du filet,** to slip through the net.

maille² *nf* **avoir m. à partir avec qn,** to have an argument *or* set-to with s.o..

maillechort [majʃɔr] *nm* nickel silver.

mailler [maje] *vt* **(a)** to net (*a purse etc*); **(b)** *Tech* (*relier*) to shackle (*two chains*).

maillet [majɛ] *nm* **(a)** (*outil*) mallet; **(b)** *Sp* polo stick *or* mallet; croquet mallet.

mailloche [majɔʃ] *nf* **(a)** (*outil*) beetle, large mallet, maul; **(b)** *Mus* bass drumstick.

maillon [majɔ̃] *nm* **(a)** link (*of a chain*); **m. tournant,** swivel; **être le m. d'une chaîne,** (*d'une personne*) to be a link in the chain; **(b)** *Nau* (*length of chain*) shackle.

maillot [majo] *nm* **(a)** (*pour la danse*) leotard; *Sp* (*football*) top, jersey; (*running, rowing*) vest, singlet; **m. de bain,** swimming costume, swimsuit; **le m. d'une équipe de sport,** the shirt *or* jersey of a sports team; **être m. jaune,** to be the overall leader of the Tour de France; **m. de corps,** (*man's*) vest, undershirt; **(b)** (*pour un bébé*) *Arch* swaddling clothes.

main [mɛ̃] *nf* **(a)** hand; **donner la m. à qn,** to hold s.o.'s hand, to lead s.o. by the hand; **donne la m. à Philippe,** (*pour traverser la rue*) give Philippe your hand, take Philippe's hand; **prendre qn par la m.,** to take s.o's hand, to take s.o. by the hand; **se donner la m.,** to hold hands; **donner d'une m. et reprendre de l'autre,** to give with one hand and take back with the other; **demander la m. d'une jeune fille à ses parents,** to ask a girl's parents for her hand (in marriage); **accorder sa m. à qn,** (*of woman*) to give one's hand in marriage to s.o.; **tendre la m. (à qn),** to hold out one's hand (to s.o.); (*pour l'aider*) to stretch out a hand (to s.o.); **la politique de la m. tendue,** the policy of the out-stretched hand; **je lui ai serré la m.,** I shook hands with him, I shook his hand; **ils se tenaient la m.,** they were holding hands; **la m. dans la m.,** hand in hand; **faire qch de la m. droite/gauche,** to do sth right-handed/left-handed *or* with one's right/left hand; **porter la m. à son chapeau,** (*pour saluer*) to touch one's hat, to tip one's hat; **porter la m. à son portefeuille,** to check one's wallet; *Fig* **on ne le voit pas souvent porter la m. à son portefeuille,** you don't often see him putting his hand in his pocket; **porter la m. sur qn,** to lay hands on s.o.; (*le frapper*) to strike s.o.; **mettre la m. sur qn,** (*de la police*) to catch s.o., *F* to collar *or* nab s.o.; (*le trouver*) to find s.o.; **mettre la m. sur qch,** (*le trouver*) to find sth, to lay *or* put one's hands on sth; (*en prendre possession*) to take possession of sth, to appropriate sth; **je n'en mettrais pas la m. au feu,** I shouldn't like to swear to it; **sac à m.,** handbag; **prendre qn la m. dans le sac,** to catch s.o. red-handed; **en venir aux mains,** to come to blows; **ne pas y aller de m. morte,** (*frapper violemment*) not to pull one's punches; (*exagérer*) to exaggerate, to lay it on; **forcer la m. à qn,** to force s.o.'s hand; **homme de m.,** henchman; **faire m. basse sur qch,** to get one's (greedy) hands on sth; **faire m. basse sur une ville,** to take control of a town; (*la piller*) to pillage a town; **faire m. basse sur les médias,** to take control of the media, to appropriate the media; **haut les mains!,** hands up!; **à bas les mains!,** hands off!; **sous la m.,** within reach; **faire qch (en) sous m.,** to do sth in an underhand way; **donner un coup de m. à qn, prêter la m. à qn,** to lend *or* give s.o. a (helping) hand; *F* **avoir le cœur sur la m.,** to be very generous *or* open-handed; **une m. de fer dans un gant de velours,** an iron hand *or* fist in a velvet glove; **je n'ai que deux mains,** I only have one pair of hands; **rendre un plateau/son courage à deux mains,** to take a tray/one's courage in both hands; **épée à deux mains,** two-handed sword; **attaque à m. armée,** armed attack; **donner de l'argent à pleine(s) main(s),** to dish out money by the handful; **avoir une canne à la m.,** to have a stick in one's hand; **avoir** *ou* **tenir qch dans la m.,** to have *or* hold sth in one's hand; **tenir le succès entre ses mains,** to have success within one's grasp; **de m. en m.,** from hand to hand; **payer de la m. à la m.,** to hand over the money direct (*without receipt or other formality*); **passer de m. en m.,** (*d'un objet*) to pass *or* be passed from hand to hand *or* from person to person; *Fig* (*d'une maison, d'un livre etc*) to go *or* pass through several hands; **passer aux mains de ...,** to pass *or* fall into the hands of ...; **tomber aux mains de l'ennemi,** to fall into enemy hands; **mon avenir est entre vos mains,** my future is in your hands; **être en bonnes mains,** to be in good hands *or* in safe keeping; **remettre qch à qn en mains propres,** to deliver sth to s.o. in person; **prendre une affaire/une situation en m.,** to take a matter/a situation in hand; **mettre le marché en m. à qn,** to force s.o. to choose; **acheter qch de première/seconde m.,** to buy sth firsthand/secondhand; **article de seconde m.,** secondhand article; **renseignements de première m.,** firsthand information; **faire** *ou* **fabriquer qch à la m.,** to do *or* make sth by hand; **fait (à la) m.,** handmade; **scie à m.,** handsaw; **dire adieu de la m. à qn,** to wave goodbye to s.o.; **écrire une lettre de sa propre m.,** to write a letter in one's own hand; **notes écrites à la m.,** handwritten notes; **de m. de maître,** by a master('s) hand; **reconnaître la m. d'un peintre,** to recognize a painter's style; **mettre la m. à la pâte** *ou* **à l'ouvrage,** to lend a hand; *F* to get stuck in; **mettre la dernière m. à qch,** to put the finishing touches to sth; **se faire la m.,** to get one's hand in, to get the knack of sth; **avoir la m.,** to have the knack; **il a perdu la m.,** he's lost the knack *or* his touch; (*d'un sportif, d'un musicien*) he's out of practice; **dessin à m. levée,** freehand drawing; **voter à m. levée,** to vote by a show of hands; **il a sa voiture bien en m.,** he's got the feel of his car; **gagner haut la m.,** *Courses de chevaux* to win in a canter; (*en général*) to win easily *or* hands down; **de longue m.,** for a long time (past); **ami de longue m.,** friend of long standing; *Fig* **se laver les mains de qch,** to wash one's hands of sth; *Fig* **se frotter les mains,** to be rubbing one's hands with anticipation *or* glee; **la m. de Dieu,** the hand of God; *Prov* **jeux de mains, jeux de vilain,** stop fooling around or it'll all end in tears; *Prov* **aux innocents les mains pleines,** fortune favours fools, beginners have all the luck; *Aut* **frein à m.,** handbrake, *Am* emergency brake; *Mus* **morceau à quatre mains,** piece for four hands; duet; *Typ* **m. de papier,** quire of paper; **avoir la m. verte,** to have *Br* green fingers *or Am* a green thumb; **avoir la m. leste,** to be a bit too ready with one's fists;

(b) *Cartes* hand; **avoir la m.,** to have the deal; **passer la m.,** to pass the deal; *Fig* to stand aside, to give someone else a chance; **passer la m. à son fils,** to hand over the reins to one's son, to hand on the business to one's son; **avoir la m. heureuse,** to get *or* be lucky, to have a lucky break;

(c) hand(writing); **avoir une belle m.,** to have good handwriting, to write well; **m. courante,** daybook; *Com* rough book; (*d'escalier*) handrail.

mainate [mɛnat] *nm* myna(h) (bird).

main-d'œuvre [mɛ̃dœvr] *nf* (*personnes, travail*) labour, *US* labor, manpower, workforce; **embaucher de la m.-d'o.,** to take on workers *or* staff; **m.-d'o. étrangère,** foreign labour(ers); **les frais de m.-d'o.,** labour costs.

main-forte [mɛ̃fɔrt] *nf inv* **donner** *ou* **prêter m.-f. à qn,** to come to s.o.'s assistance *or* aid.

mainlevée [mɛ̃lve] *nf Jur* **m. de saisie,** restoration of goods (*taken in distraint*); **m. d'opposition à mariage,** withdrawal of opposition to marriage; *Rel* **m. d'interdit,** removal of interdict.

mainmise [mɛ̃miz] *nf* seizure (**sur,** of); distraint (*upon property*); *Fig* **la m. du gouvernement sur les médias,** the government's appropriation *or* take-over of the media.

maint [mɛ̃, mɛ̃t] *adj Litt* many (a ...); **m. auteur,** many an author; **maintes et maintes fois, à maintes reprises, en m. (et m.) occasion,** time and (time) again.

maintenance [mɛ̃tnɑ̃s] *nf* **(a)** *Ind etc* (*entretien*) maintenance (service); **(b)** *Mil* keeping up to strength (*of unit and equipment*); **(c)** *Arch* (*maintien d'une loi etc*) maintaining (*of law and order etc*).

maintenant [mɛ̃tnɑ̃] *adv* now; **vous devriez être prêt m.,** you ought to be ready by now; **à vous m.,** now it's your turn, your turn next; **dès m., à partir de m.,** from now on(wards), henceforth, in future; **m. que tu es grand,** now (that) you're a big boy; **m. reste à savoir si les employés voudront reprendre le travail,** the question now is whether the employees will be willing to go back to work.

maintenir [mɛ̃tnir] *v* (*conj like* **tenir**) **1** *vt* **(a)** (*soutenir, retenir, tenir fermement*) to keep *or* hold (*sth*) in position; **colonnes qui maintiennent la voûte,** columns that support the vault; **maintiens le piquet pendant que je l'enfonce,** hold the post straight *or* steady while I knock it in; **m. la foule,** to hold back the crowd; **m. son cheval,** to keep one's horse under control;

(b) (*entretenir, garder*) to maintain, to keep, to uphold (*tradition*); to maintain, to keep (*discipline*); to keep, to preserve (*peace etc*); to abide by (*a decision*); **m. qn dans ses fonctions,** to maintain s.o. in office; **m. sa position,** to hold one's own; **je maintiens que c'est faux,** I maintain that it is untrue; **les médecins font tout pour le m. en vie,** the doctors are doing everything possible to keep him alive; **m. qch à température constante,** to keep *or* maintain sth at a constant temperature; **le programme de la chaîne est maintenu malgré la grève de certains techniciens,** the station is maintaining normal service in spite of the fact that some of the technicians are on strike.

2 se maintenir *vpr* to remain, to last; **se m. dans les bonnes grâces de qn,** to keep in favour with s.o.; **se m. contre les attaques de l'ennemi,** to hold one's own *or* one's ground against the enemy; **les prix se maintiennent,** prices remain steady; *F* **comment ça va? — ça se maintient,** how are you? — bearing up; **cela ne peut pas se m. longtemps,** it cannot last long; **le temps se maintient,** the weather is holding.

maintien [mɛ̃tjɛ̃] *nm* **(a)** (*fait de conserver dans le même état*) maintenance; upholding (*of the law, a principle*); keeping (*of order, discipline etc*); **m. de l'ordre,** policing; **(b)** (*allure, posture*) bearing, carriage, deportment; **leçons de m.,** lessons in deportment; *Jur* **m. dans les lieux,** right(s) of a sitting tenant, right(s) of occupancy, security of tenure.

maire [mɛr] *nm* mayor, (*en Écosse*) provost; **monsieur/madame le m.,** the Mayor, His/Her Worship (the Mayor); (*en s'adressant à lui*) Your Worship; *F* **passer devant (monsieur) le m.,** to tie the knot, to get hitched.

mairesse [mɛrɛs] *nf* (*femme maire*) Lady Mayor; (*femme du maire*) mayoress.

mairie [meri] *nf* (*lieu*) town hall, *Am* city hall; (*administration municipale*) town *or* city council, *Am* city hall; **la m. a organisé un voyage pour les personnes âgées de la ville,** the council has organized a trip for the town's senior citizens; **c'est un employé de m.,** he works for the (local) council.

mais [mɛ] **1** *adv* **(a)** (*emphatic*) **m. oui!,** oh yes!, why, certainly!, of course!, *Am* sure!; **m. non!,** oh no!, not at all!, of course not!; **m. qu'avez-vous donc?,** whatever's the matter?; **m. c'est vrai!,** but it's true!, it really is true!; **m. enfin!,** well really!, oh well!; **elle ne fait rien de la journée, m. vraiment rien,** she does nothing all day, absolutely nothing;

(b) *Litt Vieilli* **n'en pouvoir m.,** to be unable to do anything (*about sth*).

2 *conj* but; **famille riche m. honnête,** rich but honest family; **il n'est pas très intelligent mais il est très travailleur,** he's not very intelligent but he's a hard worker; **non seulement ..., m. aussi** *ou* **encore ...,** not only ..., but also ... .

3 *nm* **il y a un m.,** there is one objection; **il n'y a pas de m. (qui tienne),** there are no buts about it.

maïs [mais] *nm* maize, sweetcorn, *Am* corn; **farine de m.,** cornflour, *Am* cornstarch.

maison [mɛzɔ̃] *nf* **(a)** (*habitation*) house; **m. de ville,** town house; **m. de campagne,** (*résidence secondaire*) house in the country, country house; (*de style campagnard*) country cottage; **m. de chasse,** hunting lodge; **m. de rapport,** (block of) flats, apartment block;

(b) (*foyer*) home; **à la m.,** at home; **retournons à la m.,** let's go home, let's go back to the house; **dépenses de la m.,** household expenses; **tenir la m. de qn,** to keep house for s.o.; **il porte des pantoufles dans la m.,** he wears slippers indoors *or* around the house;

(c) (*établissement spécialisé*) **m. centrale** *ou* **de force,** prison; **m. d'arrêt** *ou* **de justice,** prison, gaol (*for prisoners on remand*); **m. de correction,** prison (*where short sentences are served*), *Arch* reformatory (school); **m. de santé,** (*établissement hospitalier*) nursing home; (*psychiatrique*) mental home; **m. de repos/convalescence,** rest/convalescent home; **m. de retraite,** old people's *or* old folk's home; **m. des jeunes et de la culture,** = youth club and arts centre; **m. religieuse,** convent; **m. de jeux,** gambling club, gaming club; **m. close** *ou* **de tolérance** *ou* **de passe,** brothel;

(d) (*entreprise*) firm; **m. de commerce,** business, company; **la M. du Stylo,** the Pen Shop; **m. mère,** head office; *Rel* mother house; **pâté m.,** (*on menu*) home-made pâté; **vin rouge/blanc m.,** house red/white (wine); **l'esprit m.,** the company spirit;

(e) (*famille*) family; **le fils de la m.,** the son of the house; **ami de la m.,** friend of the family; **être de la m.,** to be one of the family; **la maîtresse de m.,** the lady of the house; **faire la jeune fille de la m.,** to pass *or* hand round the snacks (*at a cocktail party etc*);

(f) (*lignée*) **la m. de Bourbon,** the House of Bourbon;

(g) (*domestiques*) household, staff; **la m. du Roi,** the Royal Household; **gens de m.,** servants, (domestic) staff;

(h) *Astrol* house;

(i) *F* extraordinarily good, fantastic; **ça, c'est m.!,** that's excellent *or Am* swell!

Maison-Blanche (la) [lamɛzɔ̃blɑ̃ʃ] *nf* the White House.

maisonnée [mɛzɔne] *nf* household, family.

maisonnette [mɛzɔnɛt] *nf* small house; (*à la campagne*) cottage; (*moderne*) maison(n)ette.

maistrance [mɛstrɑ̃s] *nf Nau* petty officers.

maître, -esse [mɛtr, mɛtrɛs] *n* **(a)** master, *f* mistress; **m./maîtresse de maison,** man/lady of the house; **je veux être m. chez moi,** I insist on being master in my own house; **ce chien n'obéit qu'à son m./sa maîtresse,** this dog obeys nobody but its master/mistress; **parler (à qn) en m.,** to speak authoritatively (to s.o.); **être m. de la situation,** to be master *or* in control of the situation; **un dictateur fou qui veut devenir le m. du monde,** a mad dictator who wants to take over *or* rule the world; **être m. (absolu) de faire qch,** to be (entirely) free to do sth; **laisser qn m. de faire qch,** to leave s.o. free to do sth; **trouver son m.,** to meet one's match; **être m. de soi,** to be self-possessed, to have one's feelings under control; **être m. de sa voiture,** to be in control of one's car; **le conducteur n'était plus m. de sa voiture,** the driver (had) lost control of the car; **navire qui n'est pas m. de sa manœuvre,** ship not under control; **se rendre m. de qch,** (*s'approprier qch*) to take possession of sth; (*conquérir, prendre le contrôle de qch*) to master *or* gain control of sth; **voiture de m.,** chauffeur-driven car;

(b) *Scol* (school)teacher, (school)master, (school) mistress; **m. d'école,** primary *or Am* elementary school teacher; **m. d'internat,** = housemaster; *Univ* **m. assistant,** = assistant lecturer; *Univ* **m. de conférence,** (senior) lecturer, *Am* assistant professor; **m. de danse,** dancing master; **m. d'armes,** fencing master; **m. de chapelle,** choirmaster; **m. nageur,** swimming instructor;

(c) *Tech Art* **m. charpentier/maçon,** master carpenter/mason; **m. queux,** chef; **main de m.,** master hand; **on reconnaît la main du m.,** this is obviously the work of a master; **c'est fait de main de m.,** it's a masterpiece; **tableau de m.,** masterpiece; **les grands maîtres de la peinture flamande/de la musique,** the great masters of Flemish painting/the great composers; **coup de m.,** master stroke; **être passé m. dans l'art de (faire) qch,** to be a past master in sth *or* at doing sth; **m. d'œuvre,** prime contractor; **m. d'ouvrage** *ou* **de l'ouvrage,** contracting authority; **m. de forges,** ironmaster; *Nau* **second m.,** petty officer; **premier m.,** chief petty officer; **m. d'équipage,** boatswain; **être le seul m. à bord,** to be sole master on board; *Fig* to be free to choose, to be free to do whatever one wants; **c'est toi le seul m. à bord,** you're the boss; **m. d'hôtel,** (*dans une maison*) butler; (*dans un restaurant*) head waiter, *Am* maitre d'; *Nau* chief steward; **m. de cérémonies,** master of ceremonies; *F* **m. sot,** utter fool; **m. chanteur,** blackmailer;

(d) (*title given to member of legal profession*) = Mister; (*to painter, writer etc*) Maestro, Master.

maître-autel [mɛtrotɛl] *nm Rel* high altar; (*pl maîtres-autels*).

maître-chien [mɛtrəʃjɛ̃] *nm* dog-handler; (*pl maîtres-chiens*).

maîtresse [mɛtrɛs] *nf* **(a)** mistress; **avoir une m.,** to have a mistress; **être la m. de qn,** to be s.o.'s mistress; **(b)** chief, principal, main; **poutre m.,** main girder *or* beam; **cheville m.,** kingpin; **idée m. d'un ouvrage,** governing idea of a work; **m. femme,** capable woman; *Cartes Ordinat* **carte m.,** master card; *Fig* (*principal atout*) trump card.

maîtrisable [metrizabl] *adj* controllable.

maîtrise [metriz] *nf* **(a)** *Univ* ≈ master's degree, MA; **une m. d'anglais,** ≈ master's degree in English, an MA in English; **(b)** (*contrôle*) mastery (*of one's passions, an art, a subject etc*); **m. de soi,** self-control; *Mil* **m. des mers,** command *or* control of the seas; **(c)** *Ind* **agent de m.,** foreman; **(d)** (*poste*) post of choirmaster (*of cathedral*); (*école*) choir school; (*chorale*) choir (*of cathedral etc*).

maîtriser [metrize] **1** *vt* to control (*a horse etc*); to subdue (*flames, opposition*); to get (*a fire*) under control; to curb, to bridle (*passion*); to control (*epidemic*); to overpower (*s.o.*); to master, to overcome (*one's fears*); to master (*language, subject etc*). **2 se maîtriser** *vpr* to control oneself; **ne pas savoir se m.,** to have no self-control.

majesté [maʒɛste] *nf* **(a)** (*souverain*) majesty; **Sa M. le Roi/la Reine,** His Majesty the King/Her Majesty the Queen; **Leurs Majestés,** their Majesties; *Gram* **pluriel de m.,** royal We; **(b)** majesty, dignity, stateliness (*of bearing*); majesty, grandeur (*of style, landscape*).

majestueusement [maʒɛstɥøzmɑ̃] *adv* majestically.

majestueux, -euse [maʒɛstɥø, -øz] *adj* majestic, stately (*bearing etc*); majestic, imposing (*figure*); **paysage m.,** majestic *or* magnificent landscape.

majeur, -eure [maʒœr] **1** *adj* **(a)** (*plus grand*) greater; **la majeure partie de qch,** the greater *or* major part *or* the bulk *or* the majority of sth; **la majeure partie du temps,** most of the time; **en majeure partie,** for the most part; **prémisse majeure,** major premise; **le lac M.,** Lake Maggiore; *Rel* **les ordres majeurs,** the major sacred orders; **affaire majeure,** matter of great importance; **raison majeure de qch,** chief reason for sth; **être absent pour raison majeure,** to be unavoidably absent; *Jur* **cas de force majeure,** case of absolute necessity *or* force majeure; *Cartes* **couleur majeure,** major suit;

(b) *Jur* of age; **devenir m.,** to attain one's majority, to come of age; *Fig* **un peuple m.,** a mature *or* responsible nation;

(c) *Mus* major (*key etc*); **en sol bémol m.,** in G flat major.

2 *n* person who has come of age *or* reached the age of majority.

3 *nm* middle finger.

4 *nf Cartes* **majeure,** major suit.

majolique [maʒɔlik] *nf Cér* majolica.

major [maʒɔr] *nm* **(a)** *Mil* regimental adjutant (*with administrative duties*); **m. général,** chief of staff (*of a commander-in-chief in the field*); **m. du camp,** camp commandant; *Mil* **(médecin) m.,** medical officer, M.O.; **(b)** *Univ* **sortir m. (d'une grande école),** = to be top of one's year.

majoration [maʒɔrasjɔ̃] *nf* **(a)** (*surestimation*) overestimation, overvaluation (*of assets etc*); **(b)** (*augmentation*) additional charge, surcharge (*on bill*); increase (*in price*).

majordome [maʒɔrdɔm] *nm* major-domo.

majorer [maʒɔre] *vt* **(a)** (*surestimer*) to overestimate, to overvalue (*assets etc*); **(b)** (*augmenter*) to make an additional charge on (*bill*); to raise *or* put up *or* increase the price of (*sth*); **m. les prix de dix pour cent,** to increase *or* put up the prices by ten per cent; **m. une facture de dix pour cent,** to put a surcharge of 10 per cent on an invoice, to increase an invoice by ten per cent.

majorette [maʒɔrɛt] *nf* (drum-)majorette.

majoritaire [maʒɔritɛr] **1** *adj* majority; *Pol* **vote/parti m.,** majority vote/party; *Fin* **actionnaire m.,** majority shareholder. **2** *n* **les majoritaires,** *Pol* members of the majority (party); *Fin* majority (shareholders).

majorité [maʒɔrite] *nf* **(a)** (*supériorité en nombre*) majority; **la m. silencieuse,** the silent majority; **les citoyens en m. pensent que ...,** most citizens *or* the majority of citizens think that ...; **m. gouvernementale,** parliamentary majority; **remporter la m.,** to secure a majority; (*sur un projet*) to carry a vote; **décision prise à la m. (des voix),** decision taken by a majority, majority decision; **élu avec dix voix de m.,** elected by a majority of ten; **être en m., avoir la m.,** to be in a *or* the majority; *Pol* **être dans la m.,** to be a member of the majority party; **m. relative/absolue,** relative/absolute majority; **la majorité des personnes interrogées ...,** the majority of (the) people *or* most of the people questioned ...; **dans la m. des cas,** in the majority of *or* most cases;

(b) *Jur* majority, coming of age; **atteindre la m.,** to attain one's majority, to come of age; **m. légale,** (minimum) voting age; **m. pénale,** = minimum age in law at which a person is deemed capable of distinguishing between right and wrong.

Majorque [maʒɔrk] *nf* Majorca.

majorquin, -ine [maʒɔrkɛ̃, -in] **1** *adj* Majorcan. **2** *n* **M.,** Majorcan.

majuscule [maʒyskyl] **1** *adj* capital (*letter*). **2** *nf* capital letter; *Typ* upper case letter; **majuscules d'imprimerie,** block capitals.

mal¹ [mal] *adj Arch* (= **mauvais**) **bon an, m. an,** year in, year out; **bon gré, m. gré,** willy-nilly.

mal², maux [mal, mo] *nm* **(a)** (*douleur, sensation désagréable*) pain, ache; (*maladie*) illness, sickness; **prendre du m.,** to be taken ill, *F* to catch something; **m. de tête,** headache; **m. de dents,** toothache; **m. de gorge,** sore throat; **m. de cœur,** sickness, nausea; **avoir m. à l'estomac/aux dents/à la tête/à la gorge,** to have stomachache/toothache/a headache/a sore throat; **m. de mer,** seasickness; **avoir le m. de mer,** to be seasick; **m. de l'air,** airsickness; **avoir le m. de la route,** to be travel *or* car sick; **m. des montagnes,** altitude sickness; **m. du pays,** homesickness; **avoir le m. du pays,** to be homesick; **m. des rayons,** radiation sickness; **m. du siècle,** world-weariness; **où avez-vous m.?,** where is the pain?, where does it hurt?; **vous me faites (du) m.,** you're hurting me; **mon genou me fait m.,** my knee hurts; **spectacle qui fait m. (au cœur, au ventre),** painful sight; **être en m. de qch,** to be badly in need of sth; *Prov* **aux grands maux les grands remèdes,** desperate situations call for desperate remedies;

(b) (*préjudice*) harm; (*pénible*) hurt; **faire du m.,** to do harm; **faire du m. à qn,** to harm s.o., to do s.o. harm; *F* **ça me ferait m.!,** (*je ne suis pas d'accord*) you must be joking!; (*refus*) there's no way I'm going to do that; **il fait plus de bruit que de m.,** (*chien, personne*) his bark is worse than his bite; **s'en tirer sans aucun m.,** to escape uninjured *or* unhurt *or* unscathed; **il ne ferait pas de m. à une mouche,** he wouldn't hurt a fly; **je ne lui veux pas de m.,** I mean him no harm; **cela fera plus de m. que de bien,** it will do more harm than good; **le m. est fait,** the harm *or* damage has been done; **souffrir de grands maux,** to suffer great ills; **entre deux maux il faut choisir le moindre,** one must choose the lesser of two evils; **entre deux maux j'ai choisi le moindre,** it was the lesser of two evils; **il n'y a pas de m. à cela,** there's no harm in that; *F* **il n'y a pas de m.,** (*à qn qui s'excuse*) there's no harm done; **m. lui en a pris,** he has had cause to regret it *or* to rue it; **dire du m. de qn,** to speak ill of s.o.; **il a changé en m.,** he has changed for the worse;

(c) (*contraire au bien*) wrong; (*vice etc*) evil; (*mauvaises actions*) wrong(doing); **le bien et le m.,** right and wrong, good and evil; **rendre le bien pour le m.,** to return good for evil; **penser à m.,** to think evil; **il ne pense pas à m.,** he doesn't mean any harm; **quel m. y a-t-il à cela?,** what harm can that do?; *Rel* **délivre-nous du mal,** deliver us from evil; **lutter contre les forces du m.,** to struggle against the forces of evil;

(d) (*difficulté*) **non sans m.,** not without trouble *or* difficulty; **se donner du m. pour faire qch,** to take pains to do sth; **avoir du m. à faire qch,** to have difficulty *or* trouble (in) doing sth; **se donner un m. de chien,** to go to an awful lot of trouble.

mal³ *adv* **(a)** (*contraire aux convenances*) badly; *Fml* ill; **se conduire m.,** to behave badly; **m. à l'aise,** ill at ease; **vous avez m. agi,** you did wrong, you acted badly; *Prov* **bien m. acquis ne profite jamais,** nobody ever profits by ill-gotten gains; **travail m. fait,** badly done work; **tant bien que m.,** (*aussi bien que possible*) as well as is *or* was possible; (*réussir*) after a fashion; **aller de m. en pis,** to go from bad to worse; **s'y prendre m.,** to go about it the wrong way; **m. choisir,** to choose wrongly; **tourner m.,** (*situation*) to turn sour; (*dispute*) to turn ugly; (*personne*) to go to the dogs; **avoir l'esprit m. tourné,** to have a dirty mind; **m. comprendre,** to misunderstand; **m. interpréter,** to misinterpret, to misconstrue, to misread; **s'habiller m.,** to wear the wrong sort of clothes; **on voit m. d'ici,** you can't see (very) well *or* properly from here; **on voit m. comment ...,** it's difficult *or* not easy to see how ...; **vous êtes m. informé,** you are ill-informed; **il a très m. pris la chose,** (*cela l'a blessé, chagriné, irrité*) he took it very badly; **il est** *ou* **s'est mis m. avec sa sœur,** (*en mauvais rapport*) he's on bad terms with his sister; **vous ne feriez peut-être pas m. de ...,** it wouldn't be a bad thing (if you were) to ...;

(b) (*en mauvaise santé*) **se sentir m.,** to feel ill *or* sick; (*près de s'évanouir*) to feel faint; **se trouver m.,** to faint; **aller** *ou* **se porter m.,** to be ill *or* in bad health; **être au plus m.,** to be critically ill *or* at death's door; **elle est** *ou* **elle va très m.,** she's in a very bad way;

(c) (*une certaine quantité de*) **pas m. (de qch),** a fair amount (of sth); **il (n')y en a pas m.,** there are a good many *or* a good few *or* quite a lot (of it *or* them); **cela m'a pris pas m. de temps,** it took me quite a time *or* a fair time; **pas m. de gens,** a good many people;

(d) (*with adj function*) not right; **vous savez ce qui est bien et ce qui est m.,** you know the difference between right and wrong; **c'est très m. de faire ça,** (*en parlant à un enfant*) it's very naughty to do that; **pas m.,** not bad, quite good; **ce n'était pas m. du tout,** it wasn't at all bad; **elle n'est pas m.,** she's quite good-looking; **qu'est-ce que tu penses de ce pull? — pas mal,** what do you think of this pullover? — it's not bad *or* it's OK; **nous ne sommes pas m. ici,** we're quite comfortable *or* not badly off here.

malachite [malakit] *nf Minér* malachite.

malade [malad] **1** *adj* **(a)** (*d'une personne*) ill, sick, unwell; *F* poorly; (*of organ etc*) diseased; **être m.,** to be ill *or F* poorly; **dent m.,** bad *or* sore tooth; **jambe m.,** bad *or F* gammy leg; **j'ai l'estomac m.,** I've got an upset stomach; **tomber m.,** to fall *or* be taken ill *or* sick; **m. de la fièvre typhoïde,** ill with typhoid; **il a été m. comme un chien,** he was as sick as a dog; **être m. du cœur,** to have heart trouble; **être m. d'inquiétude,** to be sick with worry; **ça me rend m. de le voir gâcher sa vie,** it makes me sick to see him waste his life; *F* **il en est m.,** he's really upset about it; **industrie m.,** industry in a bad way; **esprit m.,** sick *or* unhealthy mind; *Mil etc* **se faire porter m.,** to report *or* go sick;

(b) mad, crazy; *F* **t'es pas m.?,** are you off your rocker?

2 *n* sick person; (*invalide*) invalid; *Méd* patient, case; **un grand m.,** a person who is very seriously ill; **les malades,** the sick; **faire le m.,** to pretend that one is ill, to malinger; **un m. mental,** a mentally ill *or* sick person; (*dans un hôpital*) a mental patient; **un m. imaginaire,** a hypochondriac.

maladie [maladi] *nf* **(a)** illness, sickness, disease, ailment; (*maladie particulière*) disorder, complaint; *Vieilli* malady; **m. infantile,** child's illness *or* complaint; **m. sexuellement transmissible,** sexually transmitted disease; **faire une m.,** to be ill; *F* **il en fait une m.,** he's making a song and dance about it; **attraper une m.,** to catch a disease; **par suite de m.,** through illness; **m. de peau** *ou* **cutanée,** skin disease;

m. du foie/du cœur, liver/heart complaint *or* disease; **m. bleue,** blue disease; **m. mentale,** mental illness; **m. du sommeil,** sleeping sickness; **congé de m.,** sick leave; **maladies des plantes,** plant diseases; **(b)** *Vét* **m. (des chiens),** (canine) distemper; **m. des vaches folles** *ou* **de la vache folle,** mad cow disease.
maladif, -ive [maladif, -iv] *adj* sickly (*child*); morbid, unhealthy (*curiosity, thoughts*); **elle était d'une pâleur maladive,** she was deathly pale; **sa maniaquerie est presque maladive,** his fussiness is almost pathological.
maladivement [maladivmɑ̃] *adv* morbidly.
maladresse [maladrɛs] *nf* (*inhabileté*) clumsiness, awkwardness; (*manque de tact*) tactlessness; (*bévue, impair*) blunder; **quelle m. de lui avoir dit que tu n'aimais pas sa robe,** how tactless of you to tell her that you didn't like her dress; **ce devoir est plutôt réussi mais il comporte quelques maladresses de style,** this exercise has been done fairly well in spite of a few awkward *or* clumsy turns of phrase.
maladroit, -oite [maladrwa, -wat] **1** *adj* (*inhabile*) clumsy, awkward (*person*); (*qui manque de tact*) blundering, tactless. **2** *n* (*personne inhabile*) awkward *or* clumsy person; (*personne sans tact*) blunderer, tactless person.
maladroitement [maladrwatmɑ̃] *adv* **(a)** (*de façon gauche*) clumsily; **(b)** (*sans tact*) tactlessly.
malais, -aise [malɛ, -ɛz] **1** *adj* Malay(an). **2** *nm Ling* Malay(an). **3** *n* **M.,** Malay(an).
malaise [malɛz] *nm* **(a)** (*moral*) uneasiness, discomfort; (*social, politique*) unrest; **sa remarque a provoqué un certain m.,** his remark aroused a certain uneasiness; **sentiment de m.,** uneasy feeling; **(b)** (*physique*) feeling of sickness *or* ill-health; **avoir un m.,** to feel faint.
malaisé [maleze] *adj* difficult; **chose malaisée à faire,** difficult thing to do.
malaisément [malezemɑ̃] *adv* with difficulty.
Malaisie [malɛzi] *nf* Malaya.
malappris, -ise [malapri, -iz] **1** *adj* uncouth, ill-bred. **2** *n* ill-bred person, lout.
malard [malar] *nm* drake.
malaria [malarja] *nf* malaria.
malavisé [malavize] *adj Vieilli & Litt* ill-advised, unwise (*action*); unwise, injudicious (*person etc*).
malaxage [malaksaʒ] *nm* kneading (*of dough*); working (*of butter*); mixing (*of cement*); pugging (*of clay*).
malaxer [malakse] *vt* to knead (*dough*); to work (*butter*); to mix (*cement*); to pug (*clay*).
malaxeur [malaksœr] *nm* mixer, mixing machine; (*beurre*) butter worker; (*ciment*) cement mixer; (*argile*) pug mill; **m.-broyeur,** mixing mill.
malchance [malʃɑ̃s] *nf* **(a)** (*guigne*) bad luck, ill luck; **par m.,** as ill luck would have it; **vous jouez de m.,** you're not having much luck; **(b)** (*mésaventure*) mishap, misfortune.
malchanceux, -euse [malʃɑ̃sø, -øz] *adj & n* unfortunate, unlucky (person).
malcommode [malkɔmɔd] *adj* impractical (*appliance*); unsuitable (*clothing*).
maldonne [maldɔn] *nf Cartes* misdeal; **faire m.,** to misdeal; *F* **(il) y a m.,** (*erreur*) there's been a mistake; (*malentendu*) there's been a misunderstanding.
mâle [mɑl] **1** *adj* **(a)** male; cock (*bird*); buck (*rabbit, antelope etc*); dog (*fox, wolf*); bull (*elephant etc*); **un ours m.,** a he-bear; **héritier m.,** male heir; **(b)** manly (*courage*); virile (*style*); **(c)** *Él* **prise m.,** plug; *Tech* **pièce m.,** male component. **2** *n* male; **un beau m.,** (*of animal*) a beautiful male specimen; *Hum* (*of person*) a real he-man.
malédiction [malediksjɔ̃] **1** *nf Litt* (*imprécation*) curse, *Fml* malediction; **une m. pèse sur elle,** she is under a curse, a curse is hanging over her. **2** *int Vieilli* **m.! nous sommes enfermés,** curses! *or* curse it! we're locked in.
maléfice [malefis] *nm* evil spell.
maléfique [malefik] *adj Litt* maleficent; unlucky (*star etc*); evil (*influence*).
malencontreusement [malɑ̃kɔ̃trøzmɑ̃] *adv* unfortunately.
malencontreux, -euse [malɑ̃kɔ̃trø, -øz] *adj* awkward, unfortunate, untoward (*event etc*).
mal(-)en(-)point [malɑ̃pwɛ̃] *adj* in a bad way.
malentendant, -ante [malɑ̃tɑ̃dɑ̃, -ɑ̃t] **1** *n* person who is hard of hearing; **émission sous-titrée pour les sourds et les malentendants,** programme with sub-titles for the deaf and the hearing-impaired. **2** *adj* **enfant m.,** child who is hard of hearing.
malentendu [malɑ̃tɑ̃dy] *nm* misunderstanding, misapprehension.
malfaçon [malfasɔ̃] *nf* (*défaut*) defect.
malfaisance [malfəzɑ̃s] *nf Litt* maleficence, evil-mindedness.
malfaisant [malfəzɑ̃] *adj* evil-minded, harmful (*person*); evil, harmful (*influence*).
malfaiteur, -trice [malfɛtœr, -tris] *n* criminal, lawbreaker; *Litt* wrongdoer; *Fml Vieilli* malefactor; **un dangereux m.,** a dangerous criminal; **association de malfaiteurs,** criminal conspiracy.
malformation [malfɔrmasjɔ̃] *nf* malformation.
malfrat [malfra] *nm F* = **MALFAITEUR.**
malgache [malgaʃ] **1** *adj* Malagasy, Madagascan. **2** *nm Ling* Malagasy. **3** *n* **M.,** Malagasy, Madagascan.
malgracieux, -ieuse [malgrasjø, -jøz] *adj* **(a)** *Vieilli* (*qui manque de politesse*) ungracious, churlish, rude; **(b)** *Littér* (*qui manque d'élégance*) inelegant, ungainly, clumsy.
malgré [malgre] **1** *prép* in spite of, despite; *Fml* notwithstanding; **m. cela, m. tout,** for all that, nevertheless, in spite of everything; (*pourtant*) yet; **m. sa fortune,** for all his wealth; **je l'ai fait m. moi,** I did it in spite of myself. **2** *conj* (*seulement dans* **m. que j'en aie/que tu en aies/***etc*) **m. que vous en ayez,** in spite of all you may say, in spite of all you may do.
malhabile [malabil] *adj* clumsy, awkward; **mains malhabiles,** unskilled hands.
malhabilement [malabilmɑ̃] *adv* clumsily.
malheur [malœr] **1** *nm* **(a)** (*drame, catastrophe*) misfortune; (*accident*) (serious) accident; *Prov* **un m. n'arrive** *ou* **ne vient jamais seul,** misfortunes never come singly, (bad) things come in threes, it never rains but it pours; **un m. est si vite arrivé,** there could easily be an accident; *Prov* accidents will happen; **en cas de m.,** in the event of a fatal accident; **ils ont eu des malheurs,** they have been through difficult times; **quel m.!,** what a tragedy!; **le m. c'est que ...,** the unfortunate thing is that ...; *Prov* **à quelque chose m. est bon,** it's an ill wind that blows nobody any good; **les malheurs de Sophie,** the misfortunes of Sophie; **il n'arrête pas de me raconter ses petits malheurs,** he's forever telling me (about) all his petty cares and woes; *F* **faire un m.,** to do something desperate; **s'il entre ici je fais un m.!,** if he comes in here I'll go mad; **sa nouvelle pièce a fait un m.,** (*a remporté un grand succès*) his latest play was a big hit;
(b) (*chagrin, infortune*) misfortune, unhappiness; **enfant qui fait le m. de ses parents,** child who brings sorrow to his parents; *Prov* **le m. des uns fait le bonheur des autres,** one man's joy is another man's sorrow;
(c) (*mauvaise fortune*) bad luck; **oiseau de m.,** bird of ill omen; **par m.,** unfortunately; **quel m. que je ne l'aie pas su,** what a pity I didn't know (about it); **je le connais pour mon m.,** unfortunately *or* unluckily for me I know him; **porter m. à qn,** to bring s.o. bad luck; **ceux qui ont le m. de le connaître,** those who are unfortunate *or* unlucky enough to know him; **j'ai eu le m. de lui dire que je n'étais pas d'accord avec lui,** I made the (big) mistake of telling him that I didn't agree with him; **jouer de m.,** to be unlucky *or* out of luck; *F* **ces lettres de m.!,** these blasted letters!; **m. à eux!,** woe betide them!
2 *int* hell!
malheureusement [malœrøzmɑ̃] *adv* unfortunately, unhappily, unluckily.
malheureux, -euse [malœrø, -øz] **1** *adj* **(a)** (*qui est à plaindre*) unfortunate, unhappy, wretched (*person, business etc*); poor, badly off (*person*); sad, miserable (*expression etc*); **il a eu une enfance malheureuse,** he had an unhappy childhood; **rendre qn m.,** to make s.o. unhappy *or* miserable; *F* **m. comme les pierres,** wretched, utterly miserable;
(b) (*malchanceux*) unlucky; **candidat m.,** unsuccessful candidate; **m. au jeu,** unlucky at gambling; **avoir la main malheureuse,** to be unlucky; *Prov* **heureux au jeu, m. en amour,** lucky at cards, unlucky in love; **une tentative malheureuse,** an unsuccessful attempt; **un amour m.,** unrequited love;
(c) (*regrettable*) **c'est bien m. pour vous!,** it's hard lines on *or* for you!; **il est bien m. que ...** + *sub*, it's very unfortunate *or* a great pity that ...; *F* **si c'est pas m. tout de même de voir ces enfants obligés de travailler!,** it's such a terrible pity *or* shame to see these children having to work; *F* **le voilà enfin, ce n'est pas m.!,** here he comes at last, and a good job too!;
(d) (*déplacé, malvenu*) **un geste/un mot m.,** an unfortunate gesture/remark;
(e) *F* (*négligeable*) paltry, wretched; **une malheureuse pièce de cinq francs,** a miserable five-franc piece; **tout ça**

pour une malheureuse faute!, all that (trouble) because of a stupid little mistake.

2 *n* **les m.,** the unfortunate, the poor, the needy; **le m./la malheureuse!,** poor man/woman!, poor wretch!; **m.! qu'avez-vous fait?,** you wretch(ed fool)! what have you done?

malhonnête [malɔnɛt] *adj* **(a)** dishonest, *F* crooked (*employee, shopkeeper etc*); **je ne veux pas avoir recours à des procédés malhonnêtes,** I don't want to have to resort to underhand methods; **(b)** *Vieilli* indecent (*gesture*); impolite (*person*); improper (*suggestion*).

malhonnêtement [malɔnɛtmɑ̃] *adv* dishonestly.

malhonnêteté [malɔnɛtte] *nf* **(a)** dishonesty; **j'ai été choqué par la m. de ses procédés,** I was shocked by the underhandedness of his methods *or* by his underhand methods; **(b)** *Vieilli* rudeness, impoliteness; (*remarque impolie*) rude remark.

malice [malis] *nf* **(a)** (*ruse, espièglerie*) mischief, mischievousness, roguishness, naughtiness; **un garçon plein de m.,** a boy who is full of mischief, a mischievous boy; **la m. de ses réflexions,** the mischievousness of his thoughts; **(b)** *Vieilli* (*méchanceté*) malice, spitefulness; **ne pas entendre m. à qch,** (*ne voir rien de mal à qch*) to see no harm in sth; (*ne pas avoir l'intention de faire du mal*) to mean no harm by sth; **sans m.,** harmless, innocent; **(c)** *Vieilli* smart remark; **sac/boîte à malices,** (*of conjuror*) bag/box of tricks; *Fig* **il faut toujours s'attendre à le voir sortir quelque chose de son sac/sa boîte à malices,** you can always count on him to pull something out of his bag/box of tricks.

malicieusement [malisjøzmɑ̃] *adv* mischievously.

malicieux, -ieuse [malisjø, -jøz] *adj* **(a)** (*espiègle*) mischievous, impish, roguish (*person, smile, remark*); **(b)** *Vieilli* malicious.

malien, -ienne [maljɛ̃, -jɛn] **1** *adj* of *or* from Mali, Malian. **2** *n* **M.,** native *or* inhabitant of Mali, Malian.

malignement [maliɲmɑ̃] *adv* maliciously.

malignité [maliɲite] *nf* **(a)** malice, spite(fulness); **(b)** *Méd* malignancy (*of cancer*).

malin, -igne [malɛ̃, -iɲ] **1** *adj* **(a)** (*espiègle, fûté*) shrewd, cunning, sharp; **regard m.,** knowing look; **il est plus m. que ça,** he knows better; **il est m. comme un singe,** he's a crafty devil; (*cet enfant*) he's a little monkey; **elle n'est pas bien maligne** *ou F* **maline,** she's not very clever *or* all that bright; **ce n'est pas la peine de jouer au plus m.,** there's no point in playing tit for tat; **bien m. qui le trouvera!,** it will take a smart one to find it *or* that!; **ce n'était pas très m.,** that wasn't very bright, was it?; **c'est m.! tu as tout gâché!,** *Iron* that was clever! now you've spoiled everything!; *F* **c'est pas bien m.!,** that's not very difficult!, that's simple!;

(b) malicious (*pleasure etc*); *Arch* malignant, evil (-minded), wicked; **l'esprit m.,** the Evil One, the Devil; **éprouver un m. plaisir à faire souffrir qn,** to take a sadistic *or* malicious pleasure in making s.o. suffer;

(c) *Méd* malignant (*cancer etc*).

2 *n* **c'est un m.,** he has his wits about him; *F* he knows what's what; **un petit m.,** a crafty one; *Péj* a smart Aleck; **c'est une petite maligne** *ou F* **maline,** she's a sly one, she's a little imp; **faire le m.,** to show off, to try to be smart; *Iron* **gros m.!,** smarty pants!, smart aleck!, clever Dick *or* clogs!; *Prov* **à m., m. et demi,** there's always somebody cleverer than you.

3 *nm* **le M.,** the Evil One, the Devil.

Malines [malin] *nf* **(a)** (*ville*) Malines, Mechlin; **(b)** (*dentelle*) Mechlin lace.

malingre [malɛ̃gr] *adj* sickly, puny.

malintentionné [malɛ̃tɑ̃sjɔne] *adj* (*d'une personne*) ill-intentioned, spiteful.

mal-jugé [malʒyʒe] *nm Jur* miscarriage of justice; (*pl mal-jugés*).

malle [mal] *nf* **(a)** trunk; *Vieilli* box; **faire sa m.** *ou* **ses malles,** to pack (one's trunk); (*se préparer à partir*) to get ready to leave; *F* **se faire la m.,** to scarper; **(b)** *Aut* boot, *Am* trunk; **la m. arrière,** boot, *Am* trunk; **(c)** *Arch* mail coach; (*service entre Douvres et Calais*) Cross-Channel ferry (*between Dover and Calais*); *Hist* **m. des Indes,** the Indian mail; **(d)** *Can* **mettre une lettre à la m.,** to post *or esp Am* mail a letter.

malléabilité [maleabilite] *nf* malleability.

malléable [maleabl] *adj* malleable.

malle-poste [malpɔst] *nf Arch* (*voiture de la poste*) mail coach; (*pl malles-poste(s)*).

mallette [malɛt] *nf* overnight bag; (*valise*) small (suit)case; (*porte-documents*) attaché case; **une m. en osier,** a wicker (picnic) basket.

malmener [malməne] *vt* (*conj like* **mener**) **(a)** (*brutaliser*) to manhandle (*s.o.*), to treat (*s.o.*) roughly, to give (*s.o.*) a hard *or* rough time; to handle *or* treat (*sth*) roughly; **il malmène sa voiture,** he's really rough with his car; **(b)** (*en paroles*) to slate (*s.o.*), to give (*s.o.*) a hard time; **(c) m. la grammaire,** to misuse grammar, to make grammatical mistakes.

malnutrition [malnytrisjɔ̃] *nf* malnutrition; **des enfants qui souffrent de m.,** children suffering from malnutrition.

malodorant [malɔdɔrɑ̃] *adj* foul-smelling, smelly; *Fml* malodorous.

malotru, -ue [malɔtry] *n* boor, lout.

malouin, -ine [malwɛ̃, -in] **1** *adj* of *or* from Saint-Malo. **2** *n* **M.,** native *or* inhabitant of Saint-Malo.

Malouines [malwin] *nfpl* the Falkland Islands, the Falklands; **la guerre des M.,** the Falklands War *or* conflict; **un habitant des îles M.,** Falkland Islander.

malpoli [malpɔli] *adj F* impolite.

malpropre [malprɔpr] *adj* **(a)** (*sale*) dirty, grubby (*hands etc*); slovenly, untidy (*appearance etc*); slovenly, slipshod (*work*); **(b)** (*inconvenant*) smutty (*story etc*); **(c)** (*malhonnête*) (*individu, conduite etc*) despicable.

malproprement [malprɔprəmɑ̃] *adv* in a slovenly manner.

malpropreté [malprɔprəte] *nf* dirtiness, grubbiness, slovenliness; *Fig* smuttiness (*of story*).

malsain [malsɛ̃] *adj* (*maladif*) unhealthy(-looking) (*person*); (*dangereux pour la santé*) unhealthy, unwholesome (*food*); unhealthy (*climate, house*); (*pernicieux*) unhealthy, pernicious (*literature, person etc*); **une curiosité malsaine,** a morbid curiosity; *Fig* **ça devient m. par ici,** things are *or* it's looking a bit dodgy round here.

malséant [malseɑ̃] *adj Litt* unseemly, unbecoming.

malsonnant [malsɔnɑ̃] *adj* offensive; (*malséant*) unseemly.

malt [malt] *nm* malt.

maltage [maltaʒ] *nm* (*brasserie*) malting.

maltais, -aise [maltɛ, -ɛz] **1** *adj* Maltese. **2** *nm Ling* Maltese. **3** *n* **M.,** Maltese.

Malte [malt] *nf* Malta; **croix de M.,** Maltese cross.

malter [malte] *vt* to malt (*hops*).

malterie [malt(ə)ri] *nf* malt house, malting.

malthusianisme [maltyzjanism] *nm* Malthusianism.

malthusien, -ienne [maltyzjɛ̃, -jɛn] **1** *adj* Malthusian. **2** *n* **M.,** Malthusian.

maltose [maltoz] *nm Ch Ind* maltose.

maltraiter [maltrete] *vt* **(a)** (*brutaliser*) to maltreat, to mistreat, to handle *or* treat roughly, to manhandle; **(b)** (*en paroles*) to slate, *F* to give (*s.o.*) a hard time; **(c)** to misuse (*grammar*).

malveillance [malvɛjɑ̃s] *nf* (*hostilité, animosité*) malevolence, ill will; **avec m.,** malevolently, spitefully; **un incident dû à la m.,** malicious *or* spiteful incident.

malveillant [malvɛjɑ̃] *adj* (*méchant*) malevolent, malicious; (*désobligeant*) spiteful (*remark*).

malvenu [malvəny] *adj* (*déplacé*) ill-advised; (*non-justifié*) unwarranted; (*mal développé*) malformed (*tree etc*).

malversation [malvɛrsasjɔ̃] *nf* professional misconduct, malpractice (*for financial gain*).

malvoisie [malvwazi] *nm* (*also* **vin de M.**) malmsey (wine).

maman [mamɑ̃] *nf* mum(my).

mamelle [mamɛl] *nf* **(a)** udder (*of cow*); teat, dug (*of bitch, sow etc*); *Prov* **labourage et pâturage sont les deux mamelles de la France,** ploughing and grazing are the lifeblood of France; **(b)** *Anat Vieilli* mamma; **enfant à la m.,** child at the breast.

mamelon [mamlɔ̃] *nm* **(a)** *Anat* nipple, teat (*of woman*); **(b)** *Géog* hillock, knoll.

mamelonné [mamlɔne] *adj* mamillate(d); **plaine mamelonnée de collines,** plain covered with rounded hillocks.

mamel(o)uk [mamluk] *nm Hist* mameluke.

m'amie, mamie¹ [mami] *nf F Arch* my dear.

mamie² *nf F* **(a)** grandmother, gran(ny), nan; **(b)** (*vieille dame*) (little) old lady; (*grand-mère*) granny; **il a aidé une petite m. à porter ses sacs,** he helped a little old lady carry her bags.

mamillaire [mamilɛr] *adj Anat* mamillary.

mammaire [mamɛr] *adj* mammary.

mammalogie [mamalɔʒi] *nf* mammalogy.

mammifère [mamifɛr] **1** *adj* mammalian. **2** *nm* mammal.
mammographie [mamɔgrafi] *nf Méd* mammography.
mammouth [mamut] *nm* mammoth.
mamours [mamur] *nmpl F* **faire des m. à qn,** to caress *or* fondle s.o..
M.A.N. [ɛmaɛn] *n Pol Can* (*abrév* **Membre de l'Assemblée Nationale**) MNA.
manade [manad] *nf* (*Provençal dialect*) herd of cattle *or* horses.
management [manaʒmɛnt] *nm Com etc* management.
manager [manadʒɛr] *nm Ind Sp etc* manager; *Cin Th* agent.
manant [manɑ̃] *nm* **(a)** *Hist* peasant, villager; *Arch* yokel; **(b)** *Littér* churl, boor, lout.
manceau, -elle [mɑ̃so, -ɛl] **1** *adj* of *or* from Le Mans. **2** *n* **M.,** native *or* inhabitant of Le Mans.
manche¹ [mɑ̃ʃ] *nf* **(a)** sleeve; **manches longues/courtes,** long/short sleeves; **être en manches de chemise,** to be in one's shirtsleeves; **manches raglan,** raglan sleeves; **robe sans manches,** sleeveless dress; **relever** *ou* **retrousser ses manches,** to roll up one's sleeves; *Fig* to get down to work; *Fig* **avoir qn dans sa m.,** to have s.o. in one's pocket; *Fig* **se faire tirer par la m.,** to be dragged into doing sth; *F* **ça, c'est une autre paire de manches,** that's quite another matter, that's quite a different proposition; *F* **faire la m.,** to beg, to go round with the hat;
(b) *Av* neck (*of balloon*); **m. à air** *ou* **à vent,** *Nau* windsail; *Av* wind sock; *Tech* **m. à eau** *ou* **d'arrosage,** hose (pipe); **m. à incendie,** fire hose;
(c) (*athlétisme*) heat; *Boxe* round; *Tennis* set; *Cartes* hand; (single) game.
manche² *nm* **(a)** handle (*of hammer, saucepan etc*); haft (*of dagger etc*); shaft (*of golf club*); stock (*of whip*); helve (*of axe etc*); neck (*of violin etc*); **m. de** *ou* **à balai,** broomstick; **m. (à balai),** *Av* control column, (joy)stick; *Ordinat* joystick; **couteau à m. d'ivoire,** ivory-handled knife; **m. à gigot,** leg-of-mutton holder (*for carving*); **m. d'un gigot,** knuckle (*of a leg of lamb*); *F* **être du côté du m.,** to be on the strongest *or* the winning side; **branler dans le m.,** to be in a shaky *or* sticky position; **(b)** *F* idiot, clot, nit; **s'y prendre comme un m.,** to go about things in an idiotic way; (*maladroitement*) to go about things in a ham-handed *or* -fisted way; **(c) m. de couteau,** razor clam *or* shell.
Manche (la) [lamɑ̃ʃ] *nf* **(a)** the English Channel; **les îles de la M.,** the Channel Islands; **(b)** La Mancha (*in Spain*).
mancheron¹ [mɑ̃ʃrɔ̃] *nm Couture* **(a)** short sleeve; **(b)** upper part of sleeve.
mancheron² *nm* handle, stilt (*of plough*).
manchette [mɑ̃ʃɛt] *nf* **(a)** (*extrémité de la manche*) cuff; **m. mousquetaire,** double cuff, turn-back cuff (*of shirt*); **boutons de m.,** cufflinks; **(b)** gauntlet (*of glove*); **(c)** (*pour protéger les vêtements*) oversleeve, cuff protector; **(d)** (*lutte*) forearm smash; (*au volley-ball*) dig; **(e)** *Typ* headline (*of newspaper*).
manchon [mɑ̃ʃɔ̃] *nm* (*vêtement*) muff; *Tech* sleeve (*for axle etc*); bush(ing) (*of bearing etc*); socket (*for pivot etc*); **m. d'accouplement,** coupling sleeve; *Aut etc* **m. d'embrayage,** clutch; **m. à incandescence,** incandescent (gas) mantle.
manchot¹, -ote [mɑ̃ʃo, -ɔt] **1** *adj* (*privé d'un bras*) one-armed; (*privé d'une main*) one-handed; (*privé des deux bras*) armless; (*privé des deux mains*) handless, with no hands; *F* **il n'est pas m.,** (*adroit*) he's clever with his hands; (*il peut le faire lui-même*) he's got hands, hasn't he? **2** *n* (*privé d'un bras*) one-armed person; (*privé d'une main*) one-handed person; (*privé des deux bras*) armless person; (*privé des deux mains*) handless person, person with no hands.
manchot² [mɑ̃ʃo] *nm* (*oiseau*) penguin.
mandant [mɑ̃dɑ̃] *nm* **(a)** *Jur* principal (*in transaction*); **(b)** *Pol* **le député et ses mandants,** the member and his constituents.
mandarin [mɑ̃darɛ̃] *nm* **(a)** *Hist* mandarin; *Fig Péj* (*fonctionnaire, intellectuel*) mandarin; **(b)** *Ling* Mandarin (Chinese); **(c)** (*oiseau*) **(canard) m.,** mandarin duck.
mandarinal, -aux [mɑ̃darinal, -o] *adj* mandarin.
mandarinat [mɑ̃darina] *nm Hist* mandarinate; *Fig Péj* **le m.,** the establishment; **les jeunes médecins s'opposent au m.,** young doctors are against the established views of the medical profession.
mandarine [mɑ̃darin] **1** *nf* mandarin(e) (orange), tangerine. **2** *adj inv* tangerine(-coloured).
mandarinier [mɑ̃darinje] *nm* (*arbre*) mandarin(e) (orange) tree, tangerine tree.
mandat [mɑ̃da] *nm* **(a)** (*authority*) & *Hist* mandate; **territoires sous m.,** mandated territories; **m. de député,** member's (electoral) mandate; **m. présidentiel,** president's *or* presidential term of office; **sans m.,** without a mandate; **donner un m. à un député,** to give a mandate to an MP; **(b)** *Jur* power of attorney, proxy; **(c)** *Jur* warrant; **m. de perquisition,** search warrant; **m. d'arrêt,** warrant for arrest; **m. d'amener,** = summons; **m. de comparution,** summons (to appear), *surtout Am* subpoena; **lancer un m.,** to issue a warrant; **m. de dépôt,** committal (*of prisoner*); *Fin* **m. du Trésor,** Treasury warrant; **(d)** (*mode de paiement*) order (to pay), money order; **m. (-poste), m. postal,** = postal order, money order; **m. international,** international money order.
mandataire [mɑ̃datɛr] *n* (*représentant*) representative, mandatory (*of electors etc*); proxy (*at meeting*).
mandat-carte [mɑ̃dakart] *nm* = postal order, money order (*in postcard form*); (*pl mandats-cartes*).
mandater [mɑ̃date] *vt* **(a)** (*charger d'une mission*) to commission (*representative etc*); to give a mandate to (*a member of parliament*); **(b) m. des frais,** (*payer par mandat*) to pay expenses by money order.
mandat-lettre [mɑ̃dalɛtr] *nm* = postal order, money order (*in letter card form*); (*pl mandats-lettres*).
mandat-poste [mɑ̃dapɔst] *nm* = postal order, money order; (*pl mandats-poste*).
mandchou, -oue [mɑ̃dʃu] **1** *adj* Manchu(rian). **2** *nm Ling* Manchu. **3** *n* **M.,** Manchu(rian).
Mandchourie [mɑ̃dʃuri] *nf* Manchuria.
mandement [mɑ̃dmɑ̃] *nm* **(a)** *Arch* mandate, order; **(b)** *Rel* pastoral (letter).
mander [mɑ̃de] *vt Arch* **(a)** (*envoyer chercher qn*) to summon (*s.o.*) to attend; **(b) m. une nouvelle à qn,** to send news (*by letter*) to s.o..
mandibule [mɑ̃dibyl] *nf* mandible.
mandoline [mɑ̃dɔlin] *nf* mandolin(e).
mandorle [mɑ̃dɔrl(ə)] *nf Rel Beaux-Arts* mandorla.
mandragore [mɑ̃dragɔr] *nf* mandrake.
mandrill [mɑ̃dril] *nm* mandrill.
mandrin [mɑ̃drɛ̃] *nm MecE* mandrel (*of lathe*); chuck (*of lathe*); pad (*of brace*); (*to make a hole*) punch; (*to enlarge a hole*) drift.
manécanterie [manekɑ̃tri] *nf* choir school.
manège [manɛʒ] *nm* **(a)** *Equitation* horsemanship, riding; (*dressage*) training, breaking (in) (*of a horse*); **(salle de) m.,** riding school; **m. découvert,** open-air riding school; **maître de m.,** riding instructor *or* master; **(b) m. (de chevaux de bois),** merry-go-round, roundabout, *surtout Am* carousel; **(c)** (*manigances*) ploy, trick; **j'observais leur m.,** I was watching their little game.
mânes [mɑn] *nmpl Antiq Rel* manes, shades, spirits (*of the dead*); **les m. de mes ancêtres,** the spirits of my ancestors.
manette [manɛt] *nf* (hand) lever, switch; *Av* **m. des gaz,** throttle lever.
manganate [mɑ̃ganat] *nm Ch* manganate.
manganèse [mɑ̃ganɛz] *nm Ch* manganese.
manganite [mɑ̃ganit] *nm Ch* manganite.
mangeable [mɑ̃ʒabl] *adj* **(a)** (*comestible*) edible, eatable; **(b)** (*médiocre*) (just about) eatable.
mangeaille [mɑ̃ʒaj] *nf Arch* feed (*for fowls etc*); *F* grub, nosh.
mangeoire [mɑ̃ʒwar] *nf* (feeding) trough; (*pour chevaux, bétail*) manger.
manger¹ [mɑ̃ʒe] *v* **(je mangeai(s); n. mangeons) 1** *vt* to eat; **il a tout mangé,** he's eaten everything (up); **il mange de tout,** he'll eat anything; **mange ta soupe,** eat *or* drink (up) your soup; *F* **j'ai faim, je mangerais bien un morceau,** I'm hungry, I could do with a bite to eat; **m. dans une assiette,** to eat off a plate; **bon à m.,** good to eat; **salle à m.,** dining room; **m. au restaurant,** to eat out, to go out for a meal; **donner à m. à qn,** to give s.o. sth to eat, to feed s.o.; **donner à m. aux poules,** to feed the chickens; **m. comme quatre** *ou* **comme un ogre,** to eat like a horse; **m. à sa faim,** to eat one's fill; **nous avons bien mangé,** we had a very good meal; *Fig* **m. son pain blanc le premier,** to start with the easiest part of a job; **l'appétit vient en mangeant,** eating whets the appetite; *Fig* the more you have the more you want; **ça ne mange pas de pain,** it doesn't cost anything; **m. du curé,** to be violently anticlerical; **on ne vous mangera pas,** they won't eat you; **la rouille mange l'acier,** rust eats into steel; **mangé aux** *ou* **par les mites,** moth-eaten; *F* **chaudière qui mange beaucoup de charbon,** boiler that is very

heavy on coal *or F* that eats up coal; **m. ses mots,** to mumble; **ne pas m. ses mots,** not to mince one's words, to speak frankly, to come out with it; *Arg* **m. le morceau,** (*avouer*) to own up; **m. son argent,** to squander *or* run through one's money.

2 se manger *vpr* **le fromage se mange avec du pain,** cheese is eaten with bread.

manger² *nm* food; **à prendre après m.,** (*of medicine*) to be taken after meals.

mange-tout [mɑ̃ʒtu] **1** *adj inv* **pois m.-t.,** sugar pea, mange-tout; **haricot m.-t.,** French bean, *Am* string bean. **2** *nm inv* (*pois*) sugar pea, mange-tout; (*haricot*) French bean, *Am* string bean.

mangeur, -euse [mɑ̃ʒœr, -øz] *n* eater; **petit m.,** small eater; **gros m., grand m.,** hearty *or* big eater; **les mangeurs d'hommes,** cannibals, man-eating savages.

manglier [mɑ̃glije] *nm* mangrove (tree).

mangouste [mɑ̃gust] *nf* mongoose.

mangue [mɑ̃g] *nf* (*fruit*) mango.

manguier [mɑ̃gje] *nm Bot* mango (tree).

maniabilité [manjabilite] *nf* handiness (*of tool etc*); manoeuvrability, *US* maneuverability (*of aircraft etc*); handling ability (*of vehicle etc*).

maniable [manjabl] *adj* (*valise etc*) manageable; (*véhicule*) easy to handle *or* control *or* drive; (*avion*) easy to control, easy to manœuvre *or US* maneuver; (*outil*) handy; *Fig* **caractère m.,** tractable nature; **peu m.,** awkward.

maniaco-dépressif, -ive [manjakodepresif, -iv] *adj & n* manic-depressive (person).

maniaque [manjak] **1** *adj* finicky, pernickety, picky, fussy. **2** *n* **(a)** (*fou*) maniac, raving lunatic, madman, madwoman; **(b)** (*pointilleux*) fusspot, pernickety person; (*capricieux*) crank, faddy person.

maniaquerie [manjakri] *nf* fussiness, finickiness.

manichéen, -enne [manikeɛ̃, -ɛn] *adj* Manichean.

manichéisme [manikeism] *nm* Manicheism.

manicle [manikl(ə)] *nf* = **MANIQUE.**

manie [mani] *nf* **(a)** *Psy* mania, obsession; **m. de la persécution,** persecution mania *or* complex; **(b)** mania, craze (*for a hobby, type of music*); (*habitude, petite obsession*) odd habit; **avoir la m. de la propreté,** to be obsessed with cleanliness; **elle a la m. de tricoter,** she's a compulsive knitter, *F* she's knitting-mad; **il a ses petites manies,** he has his little ways *or* his little fads; **(c)** *Méd Arch* mental derangement.

maniement [manimɑ̃] *nm* handling (*of tools, business etc*); conduct (*of affairs*); **le m. d'une langue,** a (good) command of a language; **le m. des armes,** the handling of arms; *Mil* **m. d'armes,** drill.

manier [manje] *v* (*impf & pr sub* **n. maniions, v. maniiez**) **1** *vt* **(a)** to handle (*tool, rope etc*); **(b)** (*diriger, contrôler*) to handle, to manage, to control (*horse, business etc*); to control, to manœuvre, *US* to maneuver (*a plane*); **m. les avirons,** to ply *or* pull the oars; **savoir m. la parole,** to know how to handle words, to be good with words; **(c)** *Arch* to feel (*cloth etc*). **2 se manier** *vpr F* (*seulement à l'infinitif*) (*se dépêcher*) to get a move on.

manière [manjɛr] *nf* **(a)** (*façon*) manner, way; **c'est sa m. d'être,** that's the way he is; **laissez-moi faire à ma m.,** let me do it my (own) way; **m. de voir** *ou* **de penser,** way of looking at things; *Iron* **il a l'art et la m. d'embrouiller les situations les plus simples,** he's got a real flair for complicating the simplest situations; **s'y prendre de la bonne m.,** to set about it the right way; **je comprends qu'il t'ait fait une remarque sur ton travail, mais il y a la m.,** I can understand him for wanting to pass criticism on your work, but there are proper ways of going about it; **de cette m.,** in this way; **de m. ou d'autre, d'une m. ou d'une autre,** somehow or other, by some means or other; **de m. à ce que,** in such a way that; **de telle m. que,** in such a way that; **d'une m. générale,** generally speaking; **en aucune m.,** under no circumstances; **de toute m.,** in any case; **d'une certaine m.,** in a manner of speaking, in a sense;

(b) (*conduite*) **manières,** manners; **avoir de bonnes** *ou* **de belles manières,** to be well mannered; **avoir de mauvaises manières,** to be ill mannered; **en voilà des manières!,** that's no way to behave!; **faire des manières,** (*être poseur*) to be affected; (*se faire prier*) to pretend to be reluctant;

(c) *Beaux-Arts Littér etc* **tableau à la m. de Degas,** painting after the manner of Degas.

maniéré [manjere] *adj* **(a)** (*poseur*) affected (*person etc*); **(b)** *Beaux-Arts Littér* mannered (*style*).

maniérisme [manjerism] *nm* **(a)** affectation; **(b)** *Beaux-Arts Littér* mannerism.

manieur, -euse [manjœr, -øz] *n* handler, manager, controller (*of men, business etc*); **m. d'argent,** financier.

manif [manif] *nf F* demo.

manifestant, -ante [manifɛstɑ̃, -ɑ̃t] *n* demonstrator.

manifestation [manifɛstasjɔ̃] *nf* **(a)** manifestation (*of feeling, tendency etc*); **(b)** (*political*) demonstration; **(c)** *Rel* revelation; **(d) m. sportive,** sporting event.

manifeste¹ [manifɛst] *adj* manifest, evident, patent, obvious (*truth etc*); palpable (*error*); **il est m. que ses études ne l'intéressent pas,** it's obvious that he isn't interested in his studies.

manifeste² *nm Pol* manifesto; *Nau Av* manifest.

manifestement [manifɛstəmɑ̃] *adv* manifestly, obviously, patently, palpably.

manifester [manifɛste] **1** *vt* to reveal (*one's intentions*); to show, to exhibit (*confusion*); **m. sa volonté,** to make one's wishes clear. **2** *vi Pol* to demonstrate. **3 se manifester** *vpr* to appear, to become apparent; **leur impatience se manifestait par de bruyantes interruptions,** their impatience showed itself in loud interruptions.

manifold [manifɔld] *nm* duplicate book.

manigance [manigɑ̃s] *nf* scheme, plot; **manigances,** underhand practices.

manigancer [manigɑ̃se] *vt* (**je manigançai(s); n. manigançons**) to scheme, to plot; **qu'est-ce qu'ils manigancent?,** what's their (little) game?, what are they up to?

manille¹ [manij] *nm* (*cigare*) Manil(l)a cheroot.

manille² *nf Cartes* manille.

manille³ *nf Tech* shackle (*of chain*); *Vieilli* shackle (*of prisoner*).

Manille [manij] *n* Manila.

manillon [manijɔ̃] *nm Cartes* ace (*at manille*).

manioc [manjɔk] *nm* manioc, cassava.

manip [manif] *nf F* manipulation.

manipulateur, -trice [manipylatœr, -tris] **1** *n* **(a)** manipulator (*of complicated apparatus, Péj of person*); operator (*of machine*); handler (*of money, goods etc*); **m. de laboratoire,** laboratory technician *or* assistant; **(b)** (*prestidigitateur*) conjuror. **2** *nm Télécom* (sending) key.

manipulation [manipylasjɔ̃] *nf* **(a)** handling (*of chemicals etc*); **(b)** *Méd* manipulation; **m. vertébrale,** manipulation of the spine; **m. génétique,** genetic engineering; **(c)** *Scol* **manipulations,** (*surtout en science*) practical work, experiments; **(d)** (*en prestidigitation*) conjuring; **(e)** *Fig Péj* underhand manœuvre; **manipulations électorales,** vote-rigging.

manipuler [manipyle] *vt* **(a)** to manipulate (*complicated tool, Péj person*); to handle, to operate (*apparatus etc*); *Télécom* to operate; **(b)** *Fig* to rig (*election*); to manoeuvre, *US* to maneuver (*sth*).

manique [manik] *nf* **(a)** (*pour la cuisine*) oven glove (*one of a pair*); **(b)** *Tech* (*gant de protection*) protective glove.

manitou [manitu] *nm* **(a)** manitou (*of American Indians*); **(b)** *F* **(grand) m.,** big shot; (*patron*) big boss, big noise.

manivelle [manivɛl] *nf* **(a)** *MecE* crank; (*pour un vélo*) pedal crank (of bicycle); (*pour un moteur*) crank (handle); *Aut* starting handle; **retour de m.,** backfire; **(b)** *Cin* (*sur les anciennes caméras*) winding handle; *Fig* **dès les premiers tours de m.,** as soon as shooting started, as soon as we started shooting.

manne¹ [man] *nf* **(a)** *Bible* manna; *Fig* (*don inespéré*) godsend, manna from heaven; **(b) m. des poissons,** (mayfly) nymph(s); **(c)** (*substance*) **m. du frêne,** manna.

manne² *nf* basket, hamper.

mannequin¹ *nm* **(a)** *Beaux-Arts* manikin, lay figure; *Couture* dress stand; (*qui a la forme du corps*) dummy, model; **(b)** (*personne*) mannequin, model; **elle est m. chez Chanel,** she works for Chanel as a model.

mannequin² [mankɛ̃] *nm* small (wicker) basket.

manœuvrabilité [manœvrabilite] *nf* manoeuvrability, *US* maneuverability.

manœuvrable [manœvrabl] *adj* manoeuvrable, *US* maneuverable.

manœuvre¹ [manœvr] *nf* **(a)** (*conduite, direction*) working, managing, driving (*of machine etc*); manoeuvring, *US* maneuvering (*of vehicle*); **fausse m.,** false manoeuvre *or US* maneuver;

(b) *Nau* handling, manoeuvring (*of ship*); (*habileté*) seamanship;

(c) *Mil etc* drill, exercise; (*dans une bataille*) manoeuvre; **grandes manœuvres,** army manoeuvres *or* exercises; **m. d'encerclement,** encircling movement; **pivot de m.,** pivot of manoeuvre;

(d) *Rail* shunting, marshalling (*of trains*); **voie de m.,** shunting track, *Am* switching track;
(e) *Fig* scheme, manoeuvre, intrigue; **m. électorale,** vote-catching manoeuvre; **manœuvres,** scheming; *Jur* **manœuvres frauduleuses,** embezzling, *F* swindling;
(f) *Nau* rope; **manœuvres dormantes,** standing rigging; **manœuvres courantes,** running rigging.
manœuvre² *nm* unskilled worker; **travail de m.,** unskilled work; (*manuel*) manual labour *or US* labor.
manœuvrer [manœvre] **1** *vt* (*faire fonctionner*) to work, to operate (*machine etc*); (*conduire, diriger*) to manoeuvre, *US* to maneuver, to handle (*vehicle*); *Rail* to shunt, to marshal (*trucks*); **appareil facile à m.,** apparatus that is easy to operate. **2** *vi* (*faire une manœuvre*) to manoeuvre; *Fig* to manoeuvre, to scheme.
manœuvrier, -ère [manœvrije, -ɛr] *n* **(a)** expert (*soldier, seaman etc*); **(b)** *Fig* manoeuvrer, *US* maneuverer; *Pol* clever *or* wily politician.
manoir [manwar] *nm* (*petit château*) (feudal) manor; (*grande maison*) manor house, country house.
manomètre [manɔmɛtr] *nm* pressure gauge; (*en forme d'U*) manometer.
manométrique [manɔmetrik] *adj Phys* manometric(al); **hauteur m.,** head of water.
manquant¹, -ante [mɑ̃kɑ̃, -ɑ̃t] **1** *adj* (*d'une personne*) missing (*after an accident etc*); absent, missing (*from a class, meeting*); (*d'un objet*) missing; **une pièce manquante d'un puzzle,** a piece missing from a jigsaw (puzzle). **2** *n* absentee; **les manquants,** the missing, those absent.
manquant² *nm Com* **les manquants,** (the) shortages; **éviter des manquants dans la marchandise,** to prevent short delivery.
manque [mɑ̃k] *nm* **(a)** lack (*of food, money, information*); deficiency (*of vitamins*); (*dans un pays etc*) shortage; (*par rapport à un total désiré*) shortfall; **m. d'oxygène,** lack of oxygen; **m. de cœur,** heartlessness; **m. de parole,** breaking one's word, breach of faith; **m. de crédit,** credibility gap; **m. de goût,** lack of taste; **m. d'argent,** lack of money; **par m. de,** through lack of (*foresight etc*); *F* **à la m.,** feeble, pathetic; **espèce de sportif à la m.,** (*tu n'es même pas capable de monter trois étages sans être essouflé*) call yourself a sportsman!; **quelle voiture à la m.!,** what a rust bucket *or* a pile of scrap this car is!; *F* **m. de chance** *ou F* **de pot** *ou* **de bol!,** bad luck (for you *or* him *etc*)!; **je serais bien allé au ciné, m. de bol j'ai du travail,** I would have liked to go to the pictures *or Am* movies but it's just (my) tough *or* rotten luck that I've got work to do; *Com Fin* **m. à gagner,** loss of profit *or* revenue *or* earnings; *Méd* **(crise de) m.,** withdrawal symptoms; **il est en m.,** (*de drogue*) he's got withdrawal symptoms;
(b) manques, (*défauts*) shortcomings, failings.
manqué [mɑ̃ke] **1** *adj* missed (*opportunity etc*); unsuccessful, abortive (*attempt etc*); **coup m.,** (*tir etc*) miss; *Fig* failure; **vie manquée,** wasted life; **c'est un médecin m.,** he ought to have been a doctor; *F* **un garçon m.,** a tomboy. **2** *nm Culin* = biscuit with almond- or fruit-flavoured icing; **un moule à m.,** (round) cake tin.
manquement [mɑ̃kmɑ̃] *nm* **m. à une règle,** violation of a rule; **m. à la discipline,** breach of discipline; **m. au devoir,** breach *or* dereliction of duty.
manquer [mɑ̃ke] **1** *vi* **(a) m. de qch,** to lack *or* be short of sth; **m. de sucre,** to be out of *or* to have run out of sugar; (*avoir peu de*) to have run short of sugar; **m. de courage,** to lack courage; **ne m. de rien,** to have all that one needs; **je trouve qu'il manque de bon sens,** I find him lacking in common sense; *Vieilli* **m. de faire qch,** narrowly to miss doing sth; **il a manqué de tomber,** he nearly *or* almost fell;
(b) (*faire défaut*) to be lacking, to be in short supply; **les vivres/l'eau commence(nt) à m.,** provisions are/water is beginning to run short; **je vais remplacer le bouton qui manque sur ma veste,** I'm going to replace the missing button on my jacket; **les mots me manquent pour exprimer ...,** I'm at a loss for words to express ...; **la place me manque,** I haven't any room (left); *Litt* **ce n'est pas l'envie qui m'en manque,** it's not that I don't want to, I would if I could *or* had the opportunity; *Litt* **le cœur lui manqua,** his heart failed him;
(c) to be absent (*from a class, meeting*); to be missing (*after an accident etc*); **m. à l'appel,** to be absent from rollcall; *Scol* **elle a beaucoup manqué le mois dernier,** she was off (school) a lot *or* missed a lot of classes last month; **m. à qn,** to be missed by s.o.; **sa mère/sa maison lui manque,** he's missing his mother/his house;
(d) (*faillir à qch*) to fall short; **m. à son devoir,** to fail in one's duty; **m. à sa parole,** to break one's word; **m. à la consigne,** to disregard orders; **m. à une règle,** to break *or* violate a rule; **le projet/le coup a manqué,** the plan/the attempt failed; **personne ne peut m. d'avoir observé ...,** no one can fail to have noticed ...; **cela ne pouvait m. d'arriver,** it was bound to happen; **j'étais sûr qu'il allait casser l'assiette, et bien sûr, ça n'a pas manqué,** I was sure he'd break the plate, and sure enough, he did;
(e) (*oublier*) (*à la forme négative*) **ne manquez pas de nous écrire,** don't forget to *or* be sure to write to us; **remerciez bien votre mère! — je n'y manquerai pas,** be sure to thank your mother! — I won't *or* shan't forget.
2 *v impers* **il ne manque pas de candidats,** there's no lack *or* no shortage of candidates; **il ne manquait plus que cela!,** that's all I *or* he *etc* needed!, that's the last straw!; **il manque quelques pages,** there are a few pages missing; **il lui manque un bras,** he has lost an arm; **il me manque dix francs,** I'm ten francs short; **il s'en manque de beaucoup,** far from it.
3 *vt* to miss (*target, train etc*); **j'ai manqué le train de trois minutes,** I missed the train by three minutes; **M. Martin? vous l'avez manqué de peu,** (*il vient de partir*) Mr Martin? you('ve) just missed him; **un film superbe, à ne m. sous aucun prétexte,** a superb film, not to be missed under any circumstances; **m. une occasion,** to lose *or* miss an opportunity; **m. son coup,** (*tir etc*) to miss one's aim *or* stroke *or* shot; *Fig* (*échouer*) to fail (in one's attempt); *F* **il n'en manque pas une,** he's always putting his foot in it; **m. sa vie,** to make a mess of one's life; **il a tout manqué,** he failed completely; **elle a manqué son coup, elle n'a pas réussi à le convaincre que ...,** she failed in her attempt to convince him that ... .
4 se manquer *vpr* to miss each other (*by not being in the same place at the same time*); **ils se sont encore manqués,** they've missed each other again.
mansarde [mɑ̃sard] *nf* (*chambre*) attic; *Archit* **(toit** *ou* **comble en) m.,** mansard roof.
mansardé [mɑ̃sarde] *adj* mansard-roofed; **chambre mansardée,** attic.
mansuétude [mɑ̃sɥetyd] *nf Litt* leniency.
mante [mɑ̃t] *nf* mantis; **m. religieuse,** praying mantis.
manteau, -eaux [mɑ̃to] *nm* **(a)** (*vêtement*) coat; *Fig* **m. de neige,** mantle *or* blanket of snow; *Fig* **sous le m. de la nuit,** under (the) cover of darkness; *Fig* **faire qch sous le m.,** to do sth secretly *or Fml* clandestinely; **(b)** *Zool* mantle (*of mollusc*); **(c) m. (de cheminée),** mantel(piece); **(d)** *Th* **m. d'Arlequin,** proscenium arch.
mantelé [mɑ̃tle] *adj Zool* hooded (*crow*).
mantelet [mɑ̃tlɛ] *nm Rel* mantelletta.
mantille [mɑ̃tij] *nf* mantilla.
manucure [manykyr] **1** *n* manicurist. **2** *nf* manicure; **se faire faire une m.,** to have a manicure.
manucuré [manykyre] *adj* manicured.
manuel¹, -elle [manɥɛl] **1** *adj* manual (*work etc*); **un cours de travaux manuels,** a handicrafts *or Scol* handwork class; **une commande manuelle,** manual controls. **2** *n* **(a)** (*adroit de ses mains*) person who is good with his *or* her hands; **(b)** (*qui exerce une profession manuelle*) manual worker.
manuel² *nm* manual, handbook; **un m. scolaire/d'histoire,** a school/history textbook; **m. de l'utilisateur,** instruction manual.
manufacture [manyfaktyr] *nf* **(a)** *Vieilli* (*usine*) factory; **M. de porcelaine de Sèvres,** the Sèvres porcelain factory; **(b)** *Arch* manufacture.
manufacturer [manyfaktyre] *vt* to manufacture; **la production de produits manufacturés,** the production of manufactured goods; *Écon* manufactures.
manufacturier, -ère [manyfaktyrje, -ɛr] *adj* manufacturing (*town etc*).
manu militari [manymilitari] *adv* by (main) force.
manuscrit [manyskri] **1** *adj* handwritten; **lettre manuscrite,** handwritten letter. **2** *nm* (*texte écrit à la main*) handwritten text; *Littér* manuscript; **il a envoyé son m. chez un éditeur,** he sent his manuscript to a publisher; **retrouver un m. du XIIIe siècle,** to discover a 13th-century manuscript; **m. (dactylographié),** typescript.
manutention [manytɑ̃sjɔ̃] *nf* **(a)** (*action*) handling (of goods); **(b)** *Vieilli* (*lieu*) storehouse, store(s).
manutentionnaire [manytɑ̃sjɔnɛr] *n* packer; (*dans un entrepôt*) warehouseman.
manutentionner [manytɑ̃sjɔne] *vt* to handle (*goods*).
maoïsme [maɔism] *nm Pol* Maoism.
maoïste [maɔist] *adj & n Pol* Maoist.

maori, -ie [maɔri] **1** *adj* Maori. **2** *nm Ling* Maori. **3** *n* **M.,** Maori.

maous, maousse [maus] *adj Arg* massive, enormous.

mappemonde [mapmɔ̃d] *nf* (*carte*) map of the world in two hemispheres; (*globe*) globe.

maquer (se) [səmake] *vpr Arg* **se m. avec qn,** to shack up with s.o..

maquereau[1], -eaux [makro] *nm* mackerel.

maquereau[2], -eaux, [makro, -ɛl] *nm Arg* pimp.

maquerelle [makrɛl] *nf Arg* **(mère) m.,** madam.

maquette [makɛt] *nf* **(a)** *Beaux-Arts* model; **(b)** *Th* model (*of a stage setting*); **(c)** dummy (edition) (*of book*); paste-up (*of page*); **(d)** *Ind* mock up, scale model; **(e)** (*jouet*) model; **il fait des maquettes,** he makes models.

maquettiste [maketist] *n* model maker.

maquignon [makiɲɔ̃] *nm* **(a)** (*marchand de chevaux*) horse trader *or* dealer; **(b)** *Fig* (*entremetteur malhonnête*) dishonest *or* crooked dealer.

maquignonnage [makiɲɔnaʒ] *nm* **(a)** (*vente de chevaux*) horse trading, horse dealing; **(b)** (*trafic*) sharp practice.

maquignonner [makiɲɔne] *vt Péj* **(a)** to fake up (*horse*); **(b)** *Fig* to conduct (*business etc*) dishonestly; **affaire maquignonnée,** put-up job.

maquillage [makijaʒ] *nm* **(a)** (*action*) making up (*of face*); **(b)** (*produits*) make-up; **(c)** (*modification frauduleuse*) disguising (*of stolen car*); forging (*of documents*); faking (*of pictures etc*); **m. des comptes,** fiddling the accounts, cooking the books.

maquiller [makije] **1** *vt* **(a)** to make up (*s.o., face*); **(b)** (*déguiser, falsifier*) to disguise (*stolen car*); to forge (*documents*); to fake (*pictures etc*); to falsify (*accounts*). **2 se maquiller** *vpr* to make (one's face) up.

maquilleur, -euse [makijœr, -øz] *n Th etc* make-up artist *or* assistant *or* man *or* woman; **elle est maquilleuse de studio,** she works at a studio as a make-up assistant.

maquis [maki] *nm* **(a)** *Géog* maquis; *Fig* **le m. de la procédure,** the jungle of legal procedure; **(b)** *Hist* maquis, underground forces (*of the French Resistance in WW II*); **les m. d'Afghanistan,** the Afghan freedom fighters; **prendre le m.,** to go underground; (*fuir à la campagne*) to take to the hills.

maquisard [makizar] *nm* **(a)** member of the maquis, Resistance fighter (*in France in WWII*); **(b) maquisards angolais,** Angolan guerillas.

marabout [marabu] *nm* **(a)** *Rel* marabout (priest, shrine); **(b)** *Arch* (round-bodied) jug; **(c)** (*oiseau*) marabou (stork); (*plume*) marabou (feathers); **(d)** (*sorcier*) witchdoctor.

maraîchage [marɛʃaʒ] *nm* market gardening, *Am* truck farming.

maraîcher, -ère [mareʃe, -ɛr] **1** *adj* **culture maraîchère,** market gardening, *Am* truck farming; **produits maraîchers,** market garden produce. **2** *n* market gardener, *Am* truck farmer.

marais [marɛ] *nm* **(a)** marsh, bog; (*dans un pays chaud*) swamp; (*dans l'est de l'Angleterre*) fen; (*terres marécageuses*) marshland; **m. tourbeux,** peat bog; **gaz des m.,** marsh gas; **m. salant,** saltmarsh; **(b)** (*terrain consacré à la culture maraîchère*) market garden; **(c)** *Fig* **le m. d'une vie sans surprises,** a humdrum, uneventful existence; *Météo* **m. barométrique,** shallow depression.

marasme [marasm] *nm* **(a)** *Méd* marasmus; *Fig* **il était en plein m.,** he was totally drained (*of energy, inspiration*); **(b)** *Écon* stagnation, slump (*in business*); **dans le m. économique actuel,** in the present economic slump.

marasque [marask] *nf* marasca (cherry tree).

marasquin [maraskɛ̃] *nm* maraschino (*liqueur, cherry*).

marathon [maratɔ̃] *nm Sp etc* marathon (race); *Fig* **m. de danse,** dance marathon; **cette réunion a été un véritable m.,** this meeting has been a real marathon.

marathonien, -ienne [maratɔnjɛ̃, -jɛn] *n* marathon runner.

marâtre [marɑtr] *nf* cruel stepmother *or* mother.

maraud, -aude [maro, -od] *n Arch* villain, rascal, rogue, *f* hussy.

maraudage [marodaʒ] *nm* = **MARAUDE (a)**.

maraude [marod] *nf* **(a)** (*vol*) pilfering, petty thieving (*from orchards etc*); **(b) taxi en m.,** cruising taxi.

marauder [marode] *vi* **(a)** to thieve, to pilfer (*from orchards etc*); **(b)** (*of taxi*) to cruise (*in search of fares*).

maraudeur, -euse [marodœr, -øz] **1** *n* pilferer, petty thief. **2** *adj* **(a) taxi m.,** cruising taxi; **(b) loup m.,** prowling wolf.

marbre [marbr] *nm* **(a)** marble; **un escalier en m.,** a marble staircase; **une statue de m.,** a marble statue; **elle est restée de m.,** she remained impassive; **(b)** (*statue*) marble (statue); (*d'une cheminée, d'un meuble etc*) marble top; **(c)** (*in bookbinding*) marbling; **(d)** *MecE* surface plate, face plate; **(e)** *Typ* imposing stone *or* bed (*of press*); **livre sur le m.,** book in type *or* at press; **ne vous inquiétez pas pour l'édition de demain, j'ai du m.,** don't worry about tomorrow's edition, I've got some items left over (from today).

marbré [marbre] *adj* marbled, mottled (*surface, book cover*); mottled, blotchy (*skin*); veined, mottled (*marble*).

marbrer [marbre] *vt* to marble, to mottle (*book cover*); to mottle (*skin*); **le froid lui avait marbré la peau,** his skin was mottled *or* blotchy from the cold.

marbrerie [marbrəri] *nf* **(a)** (*art*) marble working *or* cutting; **m. funéraire,** monumental sculpture *or* masonry; **(b)** (*lieu*) marble mason's yard.

marbrier, -ière [marbrije, -ijɛr] **1** *adj* marble (*industry etc*). **2** *nm* monumental sculptor *or* mason. **3** *nf* **marbrière,** marble quarry.

marbrure [marbryr] *nf* **(a)** (*jaspure*) marbling, veining; **(b)** mottling (*of the skin*); mark, blotch (*of bruise etc*).

marc[1] [mar] *nm* **(a)** (*mesure*) mark; **un m. d'or/d'argent,** a gold/silver mark (coin); **(b)** *Jur Vieilli* **au m. le franc,** pro rata.

marc[2] *nm* **(a)** marc (*of grapes, olives etc*); **(b) (eau de vie de) m.,** marc (brandy); **(c) m. de café/thé,** coffee grounds/(used) tea leaves.

marcassin [markasɛ̃] *nm* young wild boar.

marcassite [markasit] *nf Minér* marcasite.

marchand, -ande [marʃɑ̃, -ɑ̃d] **1** *n* (*dans un magasin*) shopkeeper, *Am* storekeeper; (*qui fait du commerce avec l'étranger*) merchant, trader; **m. au détail,** retailer; **m. en gros,** wholesaler; **m. de chevaux/tableaux,** horse/picture dealer; **m. de légumes,** greengrocer; **aller chez le m. de journaux,** to go to the newsagent's; **m. de tabac,** tobacconist; **m. ambulant,** hawker, travelling *or* door-to-door salesman; **m. des quatre saisons,** barrow boy, *Vieilli* costermonger.

2 *adj* **(a)** commercial; **denrées marchandes,** saleable *or* marketable goods; **prix m.,** trade price; **un tableau sans aucune valeur marchande,** a painting of no saleable *or* marketable value;

(b) une galerie marchande, a shopping centre *or US* center;

(c) marine marchande, merchant navy *or* marine.

marchandage [marʃɑ̃daʒ] *nm* **(a)** bargaining, haggling; *Fig Péj* horse-trading; **(b)** *Jur* illegal subcontracting.

marchander [marʃɑ̃de] **1** *vt* **(a) m. qch avec qn,** to haggle or bargain with s.o. over sth; **(b)** *Fig* **ne pas m. sa peine (pour faire qch),** to make every effort *or* to spare no efforts (to do sth); **elle ne marchande pas ses sentiments,** she is genuinely kind-hearted; **(c)** *Jur* to subcontract illegally. **2** *vi* to haggle.

marchandeur, -euse [marʃɑ̃dœr, -øz] *n* **(a)** haggler; **(b)** *Jur* illegal subcontractor.

marchandisage [marʃɑ̃dizaʒ] *nm* merchandising

marchandise [marʃɑ̃diz] *nf* merchandise, goods, *Vieilli* wares; (*denrée*) commodity; **train de marchandises,** goods train, freight train; **gare de m.,** goods station; **vanter** *ou* **étaler** *ou* **faire valoir sa m.,** to show one's wares to good *or* best advantage; *Fig* to make the most of oneself; **tromper qn sur la m.,** (*fournir un article de qualité inférieure*) to sell s.o. a dud; (*fournir un article différent*) to sell s.o. the wrong thing.

marchant [marʃɑ̃] *adj* **aile marchante,** *Mil* outer flank (*of wheeling movement*); *Fig* leading wing (*of political group etc*).

marche[1] [marʃ] *nf* march(es), border country.

marche[2] *nf* **(a)** (*objet*) step; (*d'un escalier*) stair, step; tread (*of step*); *Tech* (*pédale*) treadle (*of loom etc*); pedal (*of organ etc*); **la m. du bas,** the bottom stair *or* step; **attention à la m.!,** mind the step!; **rater une m.,** to miss a step;

(b) (*action de marcher*) walking, walk; **aimer la m.,** to be fond of walking; **chaussures de m.,** walking shoes; **ralentir sa m.,** to slacken one's pace; **continuer sa m.,** to walk on; **se mettre en m.,** to set off *or* out, to start off *or* out; (*d'un véhicule*) to move off; **deux heures de m.,** two hours' walk(ing); **une m. lente/rapide,** a slow/rapid pace *or* gait; **elle a réglé sa m. sur celle de la vieille dame,** she adjusted her pace to the old lady's;

(c) (*défilé, manifestation*) march; *Mil etc* march; **les grévistes ont organisé une m. silencieuse pour protester contre la mort d'un des leurs,** the strikers organized a silent protest march following the death of one of their comrades; **ouvrir la m.**, to lead the way; **fermer la m.**, to bring up the rear; **colonne en m.**, column on the march; **ordre(s) de m.**, marching orders; *Hist* **la M. sur Rome**, the March on Rome; **en avant, m.!**, forward, march!; **air** *ou* **chanson de m.**, marching tune *or* song; *Mus* **m. nuptiale/funèbre**, wedding/funeral march;

(d) (*mouvement*) running (*of trains etc*); sailing, running (*of ships*); **en m.**, in motion, moving; **m. arrière**, (*pour un véhicule*) reversing, backing; *Fig* backtracking; **faire m. arrière**, (*d'une voiture*) to reverse; *Fig* to backtrack; **entrer dans le garage en m. arrière**, to back *or* reverse into the garage; **navire en m.**, ship under way;

(e) (*fonctionnement*) running, working (*of machine etc*); **être en m.**, (*of machine*) to be running; (*of furnace*) to be in blast; **(re)mettre une machine en m.**, to (re)start an engine; **en état de m.**, in working order; **se mettre en m.**, (*of machine*) to start; **il est responsable de la bonne m. de l'entreprise**, he is responsible for the smooth running of the firm;

(f) course (*of events etc*); march (*of time*); **m. à suivre**, course to be followed, procedure.

marché [marʃe] *nm* **(a)** deal, bargain; (*plus officiel*) contract; **faire** *ou* **conclure un m.**, to strike a deal *or* bargain; **m. de fourniture**, supply contract; **m. conclu**, it's a deal!, *F* done!; **mettre à qn le m. en main**, to invite s.o. to take it or leave it; **par-dessus le m.**, into the bargain, on top of (all) that, as if that wasn't enough; *Fin* **m. au comptant**, spot market; **acheter/vendre qch (à) bon m.**, to buy/sell sth cheaply *or* cheap; **(à) meilleur m.**, more cheaply, cheaper; **articles bon m.**, low-priced *or* cheap goods, bargains; **faire bon m. de qch**, not to think much of sth; **vous vous en êtes tiré à bon m.**, you got off lightly;

(b) (*lieu public de vente*) market; **jour de m.**, market day; **m. aux fleurs/à la volaille**, flower/poultry market; **m. couvert**, covered market; **aller au m.**, to go to (the) market; **faire son m.**, to go shopping *or* to do one's shopping (at the market); **m. aux puces**, junk *or* flea market;

(c) *Com* **lancer un produit sur le m.**, to launch a product; **produit qui n'a pas de m.**, product for which there is no market *or* no sale; **étude de m.**, market research; **conquérir un m.**, to break into a market; **le m. du travail**, the labour market; **le m. mondial des bijoux**, the world market in precious stones; **m. financier** *ou* **des capitaux**, money *or* financial market; **m. des changes**, currency (exchange) market(s); **second m.**, secondary market; **économie de m.**, market economy; **M. commun**, Common Market; **m. noir**, black market; **m. ferme**, steady *or* strong *or* firm market; *Bourse* **le m. de Londres**, the London Stock Market.

marchepied [marʃəpje] *nm* steps (*of altar etc*); step (*of train etc*); *Vieilli* running board (*of a car*); (*escabeau*) (pair of) steps; (*avec plusieurs marches*) stepladder; *Fig* **servir de m. à qn**, to serve as a stepping-stone for s.o..

marcher [marʃe] *vi* **(a)** (*d'une personne*) to walk; **l'enfant ne marche pas encore**, the child isn't walking yet; **il boite en marchant**, he walks with a limp; **façon de m.**, way of walking; **m. à quatre pattes/sur les mains**, to walk on all fours/on one's hands; **m. sur les pieds de qn**, to tread on s.o.'s toes; *Fig* **ne te laisse pas m. sur les pieds**, don't let them walk all over you, don't let yourself be taken advantage of; **défense de m. sur les pelouses**, keep off the grass; *Fig* **m. sur les traces** *ou* **sur les pas de qn**, to follow in s.o.'s footsteps; **l'État marche à la ruine**, the State is heading for ruin; **un peuple qui marche vers la liberté**, a people marching *or* on the march towards liberty *or* freedom; *Mil* **m. contre l'ennemi**, to advance on *or* move against the enemy; *Fig* **faire m. qn**, (*lui faire croire n'importe quoi*) to deceive *or* fool s.o., *F* to pull s.o.'s leg;

(b) (*fonctionner*) (*of machine*) to work, to run, to go; (*of plans etc*) to work, to proceed; **ma montre ne marche plus**, my watch isn't working *or* won't go; **faire m. une machine**, to work *or* operate a machine; **comment ça marche?**, how does it work?; *Fig* **les affaires marchent (bien)**, business is brisk; **les affaires ne marchent plus**, business is at a standstill *or* is (very) slack; **cela fait m. le commerce**, it's good for business; **est-ce que ça marche?**, are you getting along all right?; **ça marche pour ce soir? — ça marche!**, is it OK for this evening *or* are we on for this evening? — definitely!; **je ne marche pas**, I'm having nothing to do with it, count me out; **tu es sûr qu'il va m. dans la combine?**, are you sure he'll come in on it; **on partage les bénéfices 50/50, ça marche?**, we'll share the profits 50/50, (is that) agreed *or* is that OK (with you)?; **ça marche comme sur des roulettes**, it's going like clockwork *or* like a dream *or* really smoothly; **ça ne marche pas si mal**, we're not doing too badly; **la répétition a bien/mal marché**, the rehearsal went well/badly.

marcheur, -euse [marʃœr, -øz] **1** *n* **(a)** walker; **bon m.**, good walker; **(b)** *Péj Vieilli* **vieux m.**, old rake, old roué. **2** *adj* **(a)** *Biol* walking (*animal*); **(b) navire bon m.**, fast ship.

marcotte [markɔt] *nf Bot* layer, runner.

marcotter [markɔte] *vt Bot* to layer.

mardi [mardi] *nm* Tuesday; **M. gras**, Shrove *or* Pancake Tuesday.

mare [mar] *nf* (stagnant) pool; (*dans un parc, une ferme*) pond; **m. aux canards**, duck-pond; **m. de sang**, pool of blood.

marécage [marekaʒ] *nm* marsh, bog; (*dans un pays chaud*) swamp; (*dans l'est de l'Angleterre*) fen; (*terres marécageuses*) marshland.

marécageux, -euse [marekaʒø, -øz] *adj* **(a)** (*de la nature des marécages*) boggy, marshy, swampy; **(b)** (*qui vit dans les marécages*) marsh; **une plante marécageuse**, a marsh plant.

maréchal, -aux [mareʃal, -o] *nm* **(a) m. (de France)**, *Mil* ≈ field marshal; *Hist* ≈ marshal (*of royal household etc*); **(b)** *Mil* **m. des logis**, sergeant; **m. des logis-chef**, sergeant-major.

maréchalat [mareʃala] *nm* ≈ rank of Field Marshal.

maréchale [mareʃal] *nf* wife of field marshal.

maréchalerie [mareʃalri] *nf* (*métier*) horse-shoeing, farriery; (*atelier*) smithy, forge.

maréchal-ferrant [mareʃalferɑ̃] *nm* blacksmith; (*qui ferre les chevaux*) farrier; (*pl maréchaux-ferrants*).

maréchaussée [mareʃose] *nf Hist* corps of mounted constabulary; *F Hum* **la m.**, = the constabulary, the police.

marée [mare] *nf* **(a)** (*mouvement de la mer*) tide; **m. haute/basse**, high/low tide; **m. montante**, flood tide; **m. descendante**, ebb tide; **grande m.**, spring tide; **horaire des marées**, tide tables; **fleuve à m.**, tidal river; *Fig* **contre vents et marées**, come hell or high water; *Fig* **une m. humaine**, a flood of people; **m. noire**, oil slick; **(b)** *Pêche* fresh (sea) fish; **train de m.**, fish train; **arriver comme m. en carême**, (*inévitablement*) to happen inevitably *or* unavoidably; (*au bon moment*) to arrive just at the right moment *or* in the nick of time.

marelle [marɛl] *nf* (*jeu*) hopscotch.

marémoteur, -trice [maremɔtœr, -tris] *adj* tidal (*power etc*); **usine marémotrice**, tidal power station.

marengo [marɛ̃go] **1** *nf Culin* **poulet/veau (à la) m.**, chicken/veal marengo. **2** *nm* (*tissu*) = black cloth with white speckles.

marennes [marɛn] *nf* Marennes oyster.

mareyage [marɛjaʒ] *nm* (the) fish trade.

mareyeur, -euse [marɛjœr, -øz] *n* wholesale fishmonger.

margarine [margarin] *nf* margarine.

marge [marʒ] *nf* **(a)** margin (*of book*); **écrire qch dans la m.**, to write sth in the margin; **laissez une m. de trois centimètres**, leave a margin of three centimetres; **note en m.**, marginal note; *Typ* **illustrations à marges perdues**, bled-off illustrations; **(b)** *Fig* **m. de sécurité**, safety margin; **m. d'erreur**, margin of error; *Ind* **m. de tolérance**, tolerance (margin); **accorder de la m. à qn**, to allow s.o. some latitude, to give s.o. scope; **avoir de la m.**, to have plenty of scope; *Com* **m. bénéficiaire**, profit margin; **(c) en m. de**, outside, apart from; **en m. de l'histoire**, a footnote in history; **vivre en m. (de la société)**, to live on the fringe(s) of society.

margelle [marʒɛl] *nf* coping, curb(stone) (*of a well*).

margeur [marʒœr] *nm Typ* margin stop.

marginal, -aux [marʒinal, -o] **1** *adj* **(a)** (*en bordure*) marginal (*note etc*); *Géog* fringing (*reef*); **(b)** *Écon* **entreprise marginale**, firm that makes only a marginal profit *or* that barely breaks even; **(c)** *Fig* (*secondaire*) marginal; **ce problème n'a qu'une importance marginale**, this problem is of only marginal importance. **2** *n* **c'est un m.**, he's a drop-out; **les marginaux**, the fringe(s) of society.

marginaliser [marʒinalize] *vt* to marginalize; **un groupe social marginalisé**, a marginalized social group, a group on the fringe of society.

marginalité [marʒinalite] *nf* **vivre dans la m.**, to live on the fringe(s) of society.

margoulette [margulɛt] *nf F (visage)* mug; *F* **se casser la m.**, to take a tumble, to come a cropper.

margoulin [margulɛ̃] *nm* rogue; (*homme d'affaires*) swindler.

margrave [margrav] **1** *nm Hist* (*titre de prince*) margrave. **2** *nf* (*femme d'un margrave*) margravine.

margravine [margravin] *nf* (*femme d'un margrave*) margravine.

marguerite [margərit] **(a)** *nf Bot* **(petite) m.,** daisy; **grande m.,** oxeye daisy, marguerite; **effeuiller la m.,** to play she *or* he loves me, she *or* he loves me not; **(b)** (*pour une machine à écrire*) daisy wheel.

Marguerite [margərit] *nf* Margaret.

marguillier [margije] *nm Vieilli* churchwarden.

mari [mari] *nm* husband.

mariable [marjabl] *adj* marriageable.

mariage [marjaʒ] *nm* **(a)** (*union légitime*) marriage; (*cérémonie*) wedding; **m. d'amour,** love match; **faire un m. d'amour,** to marry for love; **m. de raison** *ou* **de convenance,** marriage of convenience; **m. religieux,** church wedding; **m. civil,** civil marriage, registry office wedding; **m. mixte,** mixed marriage; **m. blanc,** unconsummated marriage; **acte de m.,** marriage certificate; **demande en m.,** proposal (of marriage); **liste de m.,** wedding list;

(b) (*état*) matrimony, marriage; **le m. ne lui a pas réussi,** marriage *or* married life didn't suit him; **leur première année de m.,** their first year of married life; **né hors du m.,** born out of wedlock; **anniversaire de m.,** wedding anniversary; **ils ont fêté leurs vingt-cinq ans de m.,** they celebrated their 25th wedding anniversary *or* silver wedding;

(c) combination, association (*of wit and beauty etc*); blend(ing) (*of colours etc*); *Cartes* king and queen (*of a suit*);

(d) *Nau* marrying (*of two ropes*).

Marianne [marjan] *nf* Marian(ne); *Fig* = the (French) Republic.

Marie [mari] *nf* Mary, Maria; *Rel* Mary.

marié, -ée [marje] **1** *adj* married; **non m.,** unmarried, single; **oncle non m./tante non mariée,** unmarried uncle/aunt, bachelor uncle/maiden aunt. **2** *n* married person; **jeune m./mariée,** (*on wedding day*) (bride)groom/bride; (*dans les premiers temps*) newly-married man/woman; **jeunes mariés,** newly-married couple, newlyweds; **robe de mariée,** wedding dress; *Prov* **se plaindre que la mariée est trop belle,** not to know how lucky one is.

marie-couche-toi-là [marikuʃtwala] *nf inv Vieilli* harlot, strumpet.

marier [marje] *v* (*pr sub & impf* **n. mariions, v. mariiez**) **1** *vt* **(a)** (*of priest etc*) to marry (*man and woman*); (*of father*) to marry (off) (*daughter etc*); **fille à m.,** marriageable daughter; **(b)** to join, to unite (*two qualities, companies*); to blend (*colours etc*); **(c)** *Nau* to marry (*ropes*). **2 se marier** *vpr* to marry, to get married; **se m. avec qn,** to marry s.o.; **se m. avec qch,** (*of colour etc*) to blend, to harmonize with sth.

marie-salope [marisalɔp] *nf* (*pl maries-salopes*) **(a)** *Arg* slut; **(b)** *Nau* (mud) dredger.

marieur, -ieuse [marjœr, -jøz] *n* matchmaker.

marigot [marigo] *nm* (*in tropical regions*) backwater (*of river*).

marihuana [mariɥana] *nf,* **marijuana** [mariʒɥana] *nf* marijuana.

marin, -ine [marɛ̃, -in] **1** *adj* **(a)** (*en relation avec la mer*) marine (*plant, engine etc*); **algues marines,** seaweed, *Spéc* marine algae; **sel m.,** sea salt; **monstres marins,** sea monsters; **(b)** (*destiné à la navigation*) **carte marine,** sea chart; **mille m.,** nautical mile; **avoir le pied m.,** to be a good sailor. **2** *nm* sailor, seaman; (*dans la flotte*) (able) seaman; **simple m.,** ordinary seaman, rating; *Litt* seafarer, seafaring man, mariner; **un m. pêcheur,** a (sea) fisherman; **m. d'eau douce,** landlubber; **costume m.,** sailor suit; **col m.,** sailor's collar.

marina [marina] *nf* marina.

marinade [marinad] *nf Culin* **(a)** (*saumure*) pickle; (*avant de faire cuire*) marinade; (*aliment marinés*) pickles; (*viande, poisson*) marinade; **(b)** *Can* **marinades,** pickles.

marinage [marinaʒ] *nm Culin* (*pour préserver*) pickling; (*dans une préparation salée*) salting; (*avant de faire cuire*) marinading, marinating.

marine [marin] **1** *nf* **(a)** navy; **la m. marchande,** the merchant navy, the mercantile marine; **la m. de guerre,** the navy; **officier de m.,** naval officer; **(b)** (*navigation*) seamanship; **terme de m.,** nautical term; **(c)** *Beaux-Arts* seascape, seapiece. **2** *adj* **(bleu) m.,** navy (blue); **un chapeau bleu m.,** a navy(-blue) hat; **une jupe m.,** a navy(-blue) skirt. **3** *nm Mil Br* (Royal) Marine; *US* marine.

mariné [marine] *adj Culin* soused, pickled (*herring etc*).

mariner [marine] *Culin* **1** *vt* to pickle; to marinade, to marinate. **2** *vi* to marinade, to marinate; **un poisson qui doit m. tout une nuit,** a fish that should be left to soak *or* to marinate overnight; *Fig F* **il m'a fait m. pendant deux heures dans son bureau,** he made me hang around in his office for two hours.

maringouin [marɛ̃gwɛ̃] *nm* (*in tropics, Canada*) mosquito.

marinier, -ière [marinje, -jɛr] **1** *adj* **officier m.,** petty officer. **2** *n* waterman, bargee, *Am* bargeman.

marinière [marinjɛr] *nf* **(a)** *Natation* sidestroke; **(b)** (*vêtement*) blouse; **(c)** *Culin* **moules (à la) m.,** moules (à la) marinière (*mussels cooked in white wine*).

mariol(le) [marjɔl] *nm Arg* **faire le m.,** to show off; **quel m.!,** what a clown!

marionnette [marjɔnɛt] *nf* puppet; **m. à gaine,** glove puppet; **m. (à fil),** puppet, marionette; **spectacle/théâtre de marionnettes,** puppet show/theatre.

marionnettiste [marjɔnetist] *n* puppeteer.

marital, -aux [marital, -o] *adj* marital.

maritalement [maritalmɑ̃] *adv* maritally.

maritime [maritim] *adj* maritime (*navigation, plant etc*); **ville m.,** seaside town; **commerce m.,** seaborne trade; **assurance m.,** marine *or* shipping insurance; **courtier m.,** shipbroker; **agent m.,** shipping agent; **arsenal m.,** naval dockyard; *Rail* **gare m.,** harbour station; *Géog Can* **les Provinces Maritimes,** the Maritime Provinces.

maritorne [maritɔrn] *nf Vieilli* sloven, slut, slattern.

marivaudage [marivodaʒ] *nm* (*badinage*) light hearted banter; *Litt* dalliance.

marjolaine [marʒɔlɛn] *nf Bot* (sweet) marjoram.

mark [mark] *nm* (German) mark.

marketing [markətiŋ] *nm* marketing; **faire du m.,** (*étudier*) to do marketing; (*avoir pour profession*) to be in marketing; **elle est chef du m.,** she's (the) head of marketing.

marlou [marlu] *nm Arg* pimp.

marmaille [marmɑj] *nf F* (noisy) kids, brats; **rue pleine de m.,** street swarming with (noisy) kids *or* brats; *Péj* **elle est venue avec toute sa m.,** she brought the whole brood with her.

marmelade [marməlad] *nf* **m. (d'oranges),** (orange) marmalade; **viande en m.,** meat cooked to a pulp; *Fig F* **mettre qch en m.,** to pound sth to a jelly *or* a pulp.

marmite [marmit] *nf* **(a)** (*récipient*) (cooking) pot, pan; (*contenu*) potful, panful; **m. à conserves,** preserving pan; **m. autoclave,** (*cocotte-minute*) pressure cooker; *Fig* **faire bouillir la m.,** to bring home the bacon; **(b)** *Mil F Vieilli* heavy shell; **(c)** *Géol* **m. de géants,** pothole.

marmiter [marmite] *vt Vieilli* to shell (*trenches etc*).

marmiton [marmitɔ̃] *nm* kitchen boy.

marmonnement [marmɔnmɑ̃] *nm* mumbling, muttering.

marmonner [marmɔne] *vt* to mumble, to mutter; **qu'est-ce que tu marmonnes encore?,** what's that you're muttering *or* mumbling (now)?

marmoréen, -enne [marmɔreɛ̃, -ɛn] *adj Litt* marmoreal, marmorean; **blancheur marmoréenne,** marble whiteness.

marmot [marmo] *nm* **(a)** (*enfant*) *F* kid; *Péj* brat; **(b)** *Arch* (*petite figure*) grotesque figure (*especially as a doorknocker*).

marmotte [marmɔt] *nf* marmot; *Fig* **dormir comme une m.,** to sleep like a log *or* a baby.

marmottement [marmɔtmɑ̃] *nm* mumbling, muttering.

marmotter [marmɔte] *vt* to mumble, to mutter.

marmotteur, -euse [marmɔtœr, -øz] *n* mumbler, mutterer.

marnage¹ [marnaʒ] *nm Agr* marling (*of soil*).

marnage² *nm* tidal range.

marne [marn] *nf Géol* marl.

marner [marne] **1** *vt Agr* to marl (*soil*). **2** *vi* **(a)** *Arg* to slave, to slog; **(b)** (*of the sea*) to flow, to rise.

Maroc (le) [ləmarɔk] *nm* Morocco.

marocain, -aine [marɔkɛ̃, -ɛn] **1** *adj* Moroccan. **2** *n* **M.,** Moroccan.

maronner [marɔne] *vi F* to grouse, to grumble.

maroquin [marɔkɛ̃] *nm* **(a)** (*cuir*) morocco (leather); **(b)** *Fig* minister's portfolio.

maroquinerie [marɔkinri] *nf* **(a)** *Ind* (*fabrication du maroquin*) morocco-leather tanning, (*du cuir*) leather working; **(b)** (*atelier*) morocco-leather tannery; **(c)** *Com* (*articles*) (morocco-)leather goods trade; (*magasin*) (fancy) leather shop.

maroquinier [marɔkinje] *nm* **(a)** (*tanneur*) morocco-leather tanner; (*personne qui fabrique des objets en cuir*) leather worker; **(b)** (*commerçant*) dealer in (fancy) leather goods; **chez le m.,** at the leather goods shop.

marotte [marɔt] *nf* **(a)** (*manie, folie*) fad; (*passe-temps*) hobby; **avoir une m.,** to have a bee in one's bonnet; **(b)**

(*milliner's, hairdresser's*) dummy head.

maroufle[1] [marufl] *nm Arch* rogue, scoundrel.

maroufle[2] *nf* (strong) paste.

maroufler [marufle] *vt* to re-mount (*picture*) on a new foundation.

marquage [markaʒ] *nm* marking.

marquant [markɑ̃] *adj* prominent, outstanding (*incident, person etc*); **un épisode m. de son adolescence,** a significant episode in his adolescence; **passages marquants,** (*d'un livre*) purple passages; *Cartes* **carte marquante,** card that counts.

marque [mark] *nf* **(a)** (*signe*) mark; **une m. indélébile,** an indelible mark; **faire une m. dans la marge,** to put a mark in the margin; *Sp* **à vos marques! prêts? partez!,** on your marks! get set! go!; **les roues avaient laissé des marques sur le sable,** the wheels had left marks in the sand; **le cintre a fait une m. sur ce vêtement,** the coat-hanger has left a mark in this garment; **on voit encore la m. du coup qu'elle a reçu,** you can still see the mark where she was hit; **m. laissée par un animal,** (foot)print *or* (paw)mark left *or* made by an animal;

(b) m. (de fabrique), brand; (*sur l'article*) trademark; **m. déposée,** registered trademark; **produits de m.,** branded goods, top quality goods; **m. courante,** standard make; **j'ai eu des voitures de trois marques différentes,** I've had three different makes of car; **les grandes marques d'électroménager,** the main brands of electrical appliance(s); **vin de m.,** wine from a well-known vineyard, choice *or* vintage wine; *Fig* **personnage de m.,** person of distinction, distinguished *or* prominent person;

(c) *Com* (*cachet*) stamp; **un produit qui porte la m. de la douane,** goods that have been stamped at customs; **m. d'orfèvre,** hallmark; **porter la m. du génie,** to bear the stamp *or* the hallmark of genius; *Fig* **marques d'amitié,** tokens of friendship;

(d) *Nau* **la m. de l'amiral,** the admiral's flag;

(e) (*jeux*) score; **tenir la m.,** to keep (the) score;

(f) *Ling* mark, sign; **la m. du pluriel,** the mark *or* sign of the plural.

marqué [marke] *adj* **(a)** (*qui porte une marque, un signe*) marked, bearing a mark; **un drap marqué,** a sheet marked with s.o.'s initials *etc*; **une bague marquée,** a ring bearing s.o.'s initials *etc*; (*gravée*) a ring engraved with s.o.'s initials *etc;* **être m.,** (*d'une personne*) to have a lined *or* furrowed face; **visage m. par la petite vérole/l'âge,** pockmarked face/a face lined with age; *F* **qu'est-ce qu'il y a de m. sur l'enveloppe?,** what does it say on the envelope?, what is there written on the envelope?;

(b) (*prononcé*) marked, decided, unmistakable (*difference etc*); pronounced (*features etc*); distinct (*inclination etc*);

(c) (*ému*) moved; (*impressionné*) impressed; (*influencé*) influenced; **j'ai été très m. par ce film,** the film made a strong impression on me.

marquer [marke] **1** *vt* **(a)** (*faire une marque, un signe*) to leave *or* put a mark on (*sth*); (*enregistrer en écrivant*) to record, to make a note of (*sth*); **m. du bétail,** to brand cattle; *Fig* **m. d'une pierre blanche,** to remember (*a remarkable event, sth that happens very rarely*) **c'est un événement à m. d'une pierre blanche,** it was a remarkable event, it was something that happens once in a blue moon; **il a pris un bout de papier pour m. mon adresse,** he took a piece of paper to make a note of my address (on);

(b) (*délimiter*) to mark; **cette clôture marque l'extrémité de la propriété,** this fence marks the boundary of the property; **m. sa place,** (*in train etc*) to reserve *or F* bag one's seat (*by leaving hat, newspaper etc*); *Fig* **cet événement a marqué la fin de son adolescence,** this event marked the end of his adolescence;

(c) *Sp* **m. un adversaire,** (*le surveiller*) to mark an opponent; **m. un but,** to score a goal; **m. les points,** to keep (the) score; **m. trente points,** to score thirty (points); **ne m. aucun point,** to fail to score (a single point); *Fig* **m. un point,** (*dans une discussion*) to make a good point;

(d) (*indiquer*) to indicate, to show; **la pendule marque dix heures,** the clock says *or* points to ten o'clock; **le thermomètre marque 25°,** the thermometer shows *or* registers 25°; *Mus* **m. la mesure,** to beat time; **m. le pas,** to mark time; **manteau qui marque bien la taille,** coat that shows off the figure; *Fig* **m. le coup,** (*féliciter qch*) to mark the occasion; **elle n'a pas marqué beaucoup d'intérêt pour l'exposition,** she did not show much interest in the exhibition;

(e) (*laisser une forte impression*) **la guerre l'a beaucoup marqué,** the war certainly left its mark on him *or* left a deep impression on him; **ça ne m'a pas marqué,** I wasn't very impressed; **des événements qui marquent l'opinion publique,** events which leave their mark on public opinion.

2 *vi* **(a)** (*écrire*) **crayon qui ne marque pas,** pencil that won't write;

(b) (*laisser une impression*) (*d'un souvenir*) to stand out; (*d'un événement, d'une personne*) to leave *or* make a mark.

marqueté [markəte] *adj* (*bois*) inlaid; (*fourrure*) speckled.

marqueter [markəte] *vt* (**je marquette; je marquetterai**) to spot, to speckle (*fur etc*); to inlay (*table etc*).

marqueterie [markətri] *nf* inlaid work, marquetry.

marqueteur [markətœr] *nm* worker in marquetry, inlayer.

marqueur, -euse [markœr, -øz] **1** *n* **(a)** stamper (*of documents*); brander (*of sheep*); stenciller (*of boxes etc*); **(b)** (*jeux*) scorekeeper, scorer; *Billard* **m. automatique,** scoreboard; **(c)** *Fb etc* **m. (de but),** (goal) scorer. **2** *nm* (felt-tip) marker (pen).

marquis [marki] *nm* marquis, marquess.

marquisat [markiza] *nm* marquisate.

marquise [markiz] *nf* **(a)** (*noble*) marchioness; **(b)** (*véranda*) (overhanging) shelter; (*de toile, tissu*) canopy; (*de verre*) glass porch; (*d'une gare*) glass roof; *Nau* awning (*on pleasure boat etc*); **(c)** (*fauteuil*) sofa, settee (*for two people*); **(d)** (*bague*) marquise (ring).

Marquises [markiz] *nfpl* **les (îles) M.,** the Marquesas (Islands).

marraine [marɛn] *nf* **(a)** (*d'un enfant*) godmother; (*d'un bateau*) christener; **(b)** *Hist* **m. de guerre,** = female correspondent of soldier at the front; **(c)** *Vieilli* presenter (*of débutante*).

marrant, -ante [marɑ̃, -ɑ̃t] **1** *adj F* **(a)** (*drôle*) funny; **(b)** (*bizarre*) odd, strange, funny, queer; **vous êtes m., vous, alors!,** you're the limit! **2** *n* **c'est un m., celui-là,** that guy's a total laugh *or* gas.

marre [mar] *adv F* **en avoir m. de qch/qn,** to be fed up with *or* sick of sth/s.o., to have had enough of sth/s.o.; **j'en ai m.!,** I'm sick of it!

marrer (se) [səmare] *vpr F* to kill oneself laughing.

marri [mari] *adj Arch* sad, sorry, grieved.

marron[1] [marɔ̃] **1** *adj inv* chestnut (brown); **une robe m.,** (a chestnut *or* light) brown dress. **2** *nm* **(a)** chestnut; **m. d'Inde,** horse chestnut; **crème de m.,** (sweet) chestnut purée; **marrons glacés,** candied *or* sugared chestnuts, marrons glacés; *Fig* **tirer les marrons du feu pour qn,** to pull s.o.'s chestnuts out of the fire; **si nous ne faisons pas attention, c'est Pierre qui va tirer les marrons du feu,** (*s'assurer tous les avantages*) if we don't watch out, it'll be Pierre who will reap the benefits; **(b)** *Arg* blow, thump, wallop; **(c)** (*couleur*) chestnut (brown).

marron[2]**, -onne** [marɔ̃, -ɔn] *adj* **(a)** *Hist* **esclave m.,** runaway slave; **(b)** quack (*doctor, lawyer*); unlicensed (*trader*).

marronnier [marɔnje] *nm* chestnut tree; **m. d'Inde,** horse-chestnut tree.

mars [mars] *nm* March; **en m.,** in March; **au mois de m.,** in (the month of) March; **le sept m.,** on the seventh of March, (on) March the seventh, *Am* (on) March seventh; **blé de m., les m.,** spring wheat; **arriver comme m. en carême,** (*inévitablement*) to happen inevitably *or* unavoidably; (*au bon moment*) to arrive just at the right moment *or* in the nick of time.

Mars [mars] *nm Myth Astron* Mars.

marseillais, -aise [marsɛjɛ, -ɛz] **1** *adj* (of) Marseilles. **2** *n* **M.,** person from Marseilles. **3** *nf* **la Marseillaise,** the Marseillaise.

Marseille [marsɛj] *n* Marseilles.

marsouin [marswɛ̃] *nm* **(a)** (*mammifère*) porpoise; **(b)** *Mil F Arch* marine.

marsupial, -iaux [marsypjal, -jo] *adj & nm* marsupial.

marteau, -eaux [marto] **1** *nm* (*outil*) & *Sp* hammer; (*d'un commissaire-priseur*) (auctioneer's) hammer, gavel; (*d'une porte*) (door) knocker; (*d'une horloge*) striker; **m. à panne fendue,** claw hammer; **m. pneumatique,** pneumatic drill; **coup de m.,** hammer stroke; *Fig* **entre l'enclume et le m.,** between the devil and the deep blue sea; *Sp* **lanceur de m.,** hammer thrower; **être premier au lancement de m.,** to come first in the hammer; **requin m.,** hammerhead (shark). **2** *adj F* **il est un peu m.,** he's a bit touched.

marteau-perforateur [martopɛrfɔratœr] *nm* hammer drill; (*pl marteaux-perforateurs*).

marteau-pilon [martopilɔ̃] *nm Métal* power hammer; (*pl*

marteaux-pilons).
marteau-piolet [martopjɔlɛ] *nm Tech* piton hammer; (*pl marteaux-piolets*).
marteau-piqueur [martopikœr] *nm* pneumatic drill; (*pl marteaux-pileurs*).
martel [martɛl] *nm* **(a) se mettre m. en tête,** to be anxious, to worry; **(b)** *Arch* hammer.
martelage [martəlaʒ] *nm* hammering.
martelé [martəle] *adj* hammered; **argent m.,** beaten silver.
martèlement [martɛlmɑ̃] *nm* hammering.
marteler [martəle] *vt* (**je martèle; je martèlerai**) to hammer; *Métal* **m. à froid,** to cold-hammer; *Fig* **idée qui lui martelait la cervelle,** idea that kept hammering in his brain; *Fig* **m. ses mots,** to hammer out one's words; *Fig* **m. un air,** to pound out a tune.
martial, -aux [marsjal, -o] *adj* martial (*music*); warlike (*tribe*); soldierly (*bearing etc*); **arts martiaux,** martial arts; *Mil* **loi martiale,** martial law; *Mil* **code m.,** articles of war; *Mil* **cour martiale,** court martial; **passer devant la cour martiale pour qch,** to be court-martialled for sth.
martialement [marsjalmɑ̃] *adv* martially.
martien, -ienne [marsjɛ̃, -jɛn] *adj & n* Martian.
Martin [martɛ̃] *nm* **(a)** Martin; **(b)** (*name given to a donkey*) ≈ Neddy.
martinet¹ [martinɛ] *nm* **(a)** *Métal* tilt hammer, drop stamp; **(b)** (*fouet*) strap.
martinet² *nm (oiseau)* swift.
martingale [martɛ̃gal] *nf* **(a)** (*pour un cheval*) martingale; (*sur un vêtement*) half belt (*of greatcoat etc*); **(b)** (*jeu*) martingale.
martin-pêcheur [martɛ̃pɛʃœr] *nm* (*oiseau*) kingfisher; (*pl martins-pêcheurs*).
martre [martr] *nf* marten; **m. zibeline,** sable; **m. du Canada,** mink.
martyr, -yre [martir] *n* martyr; **m. d'une cause,** martyr to a cause; **se donner des airs de m., jouer les martyrs,** to put on a martyred expression *or* look, to act the martyr; **un peuple m.,** a martyred people; **ne prends pas cet air de m.,** don't look so martyred, don't act the martyr; **un enfant m.,** an abused child; *Cathol* **commun des martyrs,** common of martyrs.
martyre [martir] *nm* martyrdom; **souffrir le m.,** to suffer martyrdom; *Fig* to suffer agonies; **sa vie de couple a été un vrai m.,** his married life was a real martyrdom; **mettre qn au m.,** to torture s.o..
martyriser [martirize] *vt* to martyr (*s.o.*) (*on account of his faith*); *Fig* (*faire souffrir*) to torture; *Fig* (*punir, exécuter*) to make a martyr of (*a terrorist, lawbreaker*); **il martyrise sa petite sœur,** he bullies his little sister.
marxisme [marksism] *nm* Marxism.
marxiste [marksist] *adj & n* Marxist.
mas [mɑ(s)] *nm* (*en Provence*) farm(house).
mascara [maskara] *nm* (*maquillage*) mascara; **se mettre du m.,** to put on mascara.
mascarade [maskarad] *nf* masquerade; *Fig* sham, masquerade; **cette élection n'est qu'une m.,** the election is nothing but a sham.
mascaret [maskarɛ] *nm* bore, tidal wave (*in estuary*).
mascaron [maskarɔ̃] *nm Archit* grotesque mask (*on keystone of arch etc*).
mascotte [maskɔt] *nf* mascot; *Sp F* **terrain m.,** lucky ground.
masculin [maskylɛ̃] **1** *adj* **(a)** male (*sex, voice etc*); (*qui a les caractères de l'homme*) masculine (*pride, vanity etc*); mannish (*woman*); **mes collègues masculins,** my male colleagues; **(b)** *Gram* masculine; **un nom m.,** a masculine noun; **(c)** (*en poésie*) **rime masculine,** masculine rhyme. **2** *nm Gram* masculine (gender); **ce mot est du m.,** this word is masculine; **au m.,** in the masculine.
masculinité [maskylinite] *nf* masculinity.
maskinongé [maskinɔ̃ʒe] *nm Can (poisson)* muskellunge, *F* muskie.
maso [mazo] *n & adj inv F* (*masochiste*) masochist, glutton for punishment; **tu es complètement m. d'avoir accepté!,** you must be a masochist *or* a glutton for punishment if you agreed!
masochisme [mazɔʃism] *nm Psy* masochism.
masochiste [mazɔʃist] *Psy* **1** *adj* masochistic. **2** *n* masochist.
masque [mask] *nm* **(a)** mask; **un m. de carnaval,** a carnival mask; *Fig* **sa gentillesse n'est qu'un m.,** his kindness is only a façade *or* front; **ôter** *ou* **arracher le m. à qn,** to unmask s.o.; **lever le m.,** to throw off the mask; **m. à gaz,** gas mask; *Méd* **m. de chirurgien,** operating *or* surgeon's mask; *Méd* **m. à oxygène,** oxygen mask; **m. de plongée,** (skin diver's) mask; **m. de soudeur,** welder's (protective) mask *or* face shield; **m. mortuaire,** death mask; **m. (antirides, facial),** (*pour la peau*) face pack; **m. de grossesse,** brown patches on the skin, *Spéc* chloasma; **(b)** *Ordinat* mask; **(c)** (*dispositif de camouflage*) *Mil* shield, hood (*of gun*).
masquer [maske] **1** *vt* to put a mask on, to mask (*s.o.*); (*cacher à la vue*) to mask, to hide, to screen, to conceal (*sth*); (*déguiser*) to disguise, to mask; to shade (*light*); *Nau* to darken (*ship*); **m. une odeur,** to mask a smell; *Mil* **m. une batterie,** to conceal a battery; *Nau* **naviguer à feux masqués,** to steam without lights; **m. ses sentiments,** to mask *or* hide one's feelings; **on ne peut m. la vérité plus longtemps,** the truth cannot be (kept) hidden any longer; **m. ses véritables intentions,** to conceal *or* disguise one's true intentions; **bal masqué,** masked ball. **2 se masquer** *vpr* to put a mask on.
massacrante [masakrɑ̃t] *adj* **être d'une humeur m.,** to be in a filthy *or* vile temper.
massacre [masakr] *nm* **(a)** (*tuerie, boucherie*) massacre, slaughter, butchery; **le m. des indiens d'Amérique,** the massacre *or* slaughter(ing) of the American Indians; **jeu de m.,** ≈ Aunt Sally, *Am* ≈ straw man; **(b)** *Fig F* (right) mess; **ils ont voulu faire un gâteau, c'est un véritable m.,** they wanted to make a cake but they've made a right mess!; **quel m.!** what a mess!; **le match a été un vrai m.,** the match was a real massacre!; **jouer Shakespeare comme cela, c'est un m.,** it's absolutely massacring Shakespeare to perform him like that!; **(c)** *F* (*grand succès*) **cette pièce va faire un m.,** the play will be a smash hit; **(d)** (*tête de daim, de cerf*) stag's head (*displayed as a hunting trophy*).
massacrer [masakre] **1** *vt* **(a)** (*tuer, exterminer*) to massacre, to butcher, to slaughter; **(b)** *F* to bungle, to make a hash of (*work*); to murder, to massacre (*music etc*); to ruin (*clothes*); to hack up (*piece of meat*). **2 se massacrer** *vpr* to massacre *or* slaughter one another; *Fig* **ils se sont fait m.,** (*notre équipe*) they were massacred.
massacreur, -euse [masakrœr, -øz] *n* **(a)** (*tueur*) slaughterer; *Péj* butcher; **(b)** *F* (*gâcheur*) bungler.
massage [masaʒ] *nm* massage; *Méd* **m. cardiaque,** cardiac *or* heart massage; **se faire faire un m.,** to have a massage.
masse¹ [mas] *nf* **(a)** (*d'êtres animés*) mass, crowd (*of people*); (*moins nombreux*) body (*of people*); **culture de m.,** mass *or* popular culture; *F* **il n'y avait pas des masses de gens,** there weren't masses of people there; **la (grande) m. de,** the majority of; **les masses laborieuses,** the (working) masses; *Litt* the toiling masses; **les masses,** the masses; **la m. salariale,** the payroll; **faire partie de la m. salariale,** to be on the payroll; **en m.,** (*en grand nombre*) in large numbers, en masse; **les émigrés italiens sont arrivés en m.,** Italian immigrants arrived in large numbers *or* arrived en masse;

(b) (*d'objets*) mass; **une m. d'eau,** body of water; (*en mouvement*) mass of water; **tomber comme une m.,** to fall heavily *or* in a heap; *Météo* **m. d'air,** mass of air, air mass; **taillé dans la m.,** carved from the block; *Fig F* **un grand type taillé dans la m.,** a big, heavily built sort of chap; **une m. d'ordures,** a pile of rubbish; *F* **il n'y en a pas des masses,** there aren't many; (*du sucre, de la farine etc*) there isn't masses (of it); **il y avait des masses de livres,** there were masses (and masses) of books; **en m.,** in a body, en masse; *Can* **il y en a en m.,** there's masses of it, there are masses of them; **exécutions en m.,** mass executions; *F* **avoir des livres en m.,** to have masses of books; **marchandises en m.,** goods in bulk;

(c) *Fin* fund, stock; **la m. monétaire,** the money supply, (the total amount of) money in circulation; **m. passive,** liabilities; **m. active,** assets; **il faut établir la m. d'équipement dans le budget de cette année,** we have to establish the total amount of (money allowed for) capital goods in this year's budget;

(d) *Phys MecE* mass (*of moving body*); **le kilogramme est l'unité de m.,** the kilogram is the unit of mass; **m. spécifique,** density; *Phys Nucl* **m. critique,** critical mass;

(e) *Él* earth, *Am* ground; **mettre le courant à la m.,** to earth *or Am* ground the current.
masse² *nf* **(a)** (*marteau*) sledgehammer; **m. en bois,** beetle; *Fig F* **coup de m.,** (*dû à une émotion*) crushing *or* sickening blow; (*dû à un prix exorbitant*) (very) nasty shock (*when one sees the bill*); **il a reçu le coup de m.,** (*quand il a appris qu'il était renvoyé*) it came as a crushing blow; **ça a été le coup de m.,** (*quand il nous a annoncé le total*) it came as a very nasty shock; *Fig* **être à la m.,** to have gone

to pieces; **il est complètement à la m.,** (*depuis la mort de sa femme etc*) he's gone completely to pieces; **(b)** (*arme ancienne*) **m. (d'armes),** mace; (*d'un huissier*) (ceremonial) mace; **(c)** *Billard* butt.

massepain [maspɛ̃] *nm* marzipan.

masser¹ [mase] **1** *vt* to mass (*soldiers etc*); *Beaux-Arts* to group (*figures etc*). **2 se masser** *vpr* to mass; to form a crowd; **la foule s'est massée devant le tribunal,** the crowd gathered in front of the court-room.

masser² *vt* to massage; **il lui a massé le dos,** he massaged her back; **elle a massé le patient,** she gave the patient a massage, she massaged the patient.

massette [masɛt] *nf* **(a)** (*outil*) two-handed hammer; **(b)** *Bot* bulrush, reed mace, cat's tail.

masseur, -euse [masœr, -øz] *n* (*personne*) masseur, *f* masseuse; (*appareil*) (vibro-)massager; (*sexuel*) vibrator.

massicot¹ [masiko] *nm Ch* massicot, yellow lead.

massicot² *nm Tech etc* guillotine, trimmer.

massicoter [masikɔte] *vt Tech etc* to guillotine.

massif, -ive [masif, -iv] **1** *adj* **(a)** (*gros, épais*) massive, bulky; (*lourd*) heavy; **(b)** (*plein*) solid (*silver, mahogany etc*); **un meuble en hêtre m.,** a piece of furniture made out of solid beechwood; **(c)** *Fig* (*en masse, en grande quantité*) **action massive,** massive attack; **dose massive,** massive dose. **2** *nm* **(a)** *Archit* solid mass (*of masonry etc*); *Constr* body (*of a pier*); **(b)** clump (*of shrubs etc*); **un m. de fleurs,** a bed of flowers; **(c)** *Géog* massif; **le M. Central,** the Massif Central (= mountain range in central France).

massique [masik] *adj Phys* pertaining to the mass; **puissance m.,** power-to-weight ratio (*of engine*).

massivement [masivmɑ̃] *adv* massively; (*lourdement*) heavily.

mass-media [masmedja] *nmpl* mass media.

massue [masy] *nf* club, bludgeon; **coup de m.,** bludgeon stroke; *Fig* staggering *or* crushing blow; **argument m.,** sledgehammer argument.

mastic [mastic] **1** *nm* **(a)** mastic (resin); (*for windows etc*) putty; (*for wood etc*) filler; **(b)** *Typ* **faire un m.,** to (accidentally) transpose characters. **2** *adj inv* putty-coloured *or US* -colored.

masticage [mastikaʒ] *nm* (*of window*) puttying; (*of wood*) filling.

masticateur, -trice [mastikatœr, -tris] *adj* masticatory (*organ etc*).

mastication [mastikɑsjɔ̃] *nf* chewing, *Fml* mastication.

masticatoire [mastikatwar] *adj & nm* masticatory.

mastiquer¹ *vt* to chew, *Fml* to masticate.

mastiquer² [mastike] **1** *vt* to fill (in) (*cracks etc*); to putty (*window*); **m. des vitres,** to apply putty around window panes. **2** *vi* **couteau à m.,** putty knife.

mastoc [mastɔk] *adj inv F* heavy, lumpish (*person*); clumsy (*construction*).

mastodonte [mastɔdɔ̃t] *nm* **(a)** mastodon; **(b)** *F* (*véhicule*) juggernaut; (*personne*) colossus.

mastoïde [mastɔid] **1** *adj Anat* mastoid (*bone etc*). **2** *nf* mastoid.

mastroquet [mastrɔkɛ] *nm F* **(a)** (*cafetier*) publican; **(b)** (*bistro*) bar, pub.

masturbation [mastyrbɑsjɔ̃] *nf* masturbation; **c'est de la m. intellectuelle,** it's intellectual self-indulgence.

masturber [mastyrbe] **1** *vt* to masturbate. **2 se masturber** *vpr* to masturbate.

m'as-tu-vu, -vue [matyvy] *n inv F* show-off.

masure [mazyr] *nf* tumbledown cottage; *Péj* hovel.

mat¹ [mat] *adj* mat(t), matte, unpolished, dull (*metal*); mat, flat (*colour*); **teint m.,** mat(t) *or* matte complexion; *Fig* **son m.,** (*sourd*) dull sound, thud.

mat² *Échecs* **1** *adj inv* checkmated; **le roi est m.,** the king is checkmated *or* in checkmate. **2** *nm inv* (check)mate; **faire (échec et) m. en trois coups,** to mate in three.

mât [mɑ] *nm* **(a)** *Nau* mast; **grand m.,** mainmast; **m. d'artimon,** mizzenmast; **m. de misaine,** foremast; **m. de hune,** topmast; **m. de charge,** cargo boom, derrick; **navire à trois mâts,** three-masted ship, three-master; **un deux mâts,** a two-masted sailing boat *or Am* sailboat; **(b)** pole; **m. de tente,** tent pole; **m. de cocagne,** greasy pole; *Rail* **m. de sémaphore,** signal post, signal mast.

matador [matadɔr] *nm* matador.

mataf [mataf] *nm Arg* (*matelot*) sailor.

matamore [matamɔr] *nm* braggart, boaster; **faire le m.,** to boast, to brag.

match [matʃ] *nm Sp* match; **m. de boxe,** boxing match; **m. prévu,** fixture; *Fb* **m. de championnat (professionel),** league match; **disputer un m.,** to play a match; **m. retour,** return match; *Rugby Fb* **faire m. nul,** to draw, to tie; (*pl matchs, matches*).

maté [mate] *nm* maté.

matelas [matla] *nm* mattress; **m. pneumatique,** inflatable mattress, air bed; **toile à m.,** ticking; *Tech* **m. de vapeur,** steam cushion; *F* **un m. de billets de banque,** a wad of banknotes.

matelassé [matlase] **1** *adj Tex* quilted; **tissu m.,** quilted material; **un blouson m.,** quilted *or* padded jacket; **porte matelassée,** baize door. **2** *nm* quilted material; **du m. de soie,** quilted silk.

matelasser [matlase] *vt* (*un fauteuil etc*) to stuff, to upholster; (*un tissu*) to quilt; (*recouvrir de tissu matelassé*) to cover with quilted material.

matelassure [matlasyr] *nf* padding, stuffing, wadding (*of mattress, saddle etc*).

matelot [matlo] *nm Nau* **(a)** (*personne*) sailor; **m. (breveté) de première classe,** leading seaman; **m. de deuxième classe,** able seaman; **servir comme simple m.,** to sail before the mast; **(b)** (*bateau*) consort (ship); **m. d'avant/d'arrière,** next ship ahead/next astern.

matelotage [matlɔtaʒ] *nm* **(a)** (*connaissances*) seamanship; **(b)** (*paye*) sailor's pay.

matelote [matlɔt] *nf Culin* = fish stew; **m. de morue,** cod stew; **sauce m.,** red wine and onion sauce.

mater¹ *vt* **(a)** *Échecs* to (check)mate; **(b)** *Fig* (*dresser, dompter*) to subdue, to tame (*s.o.*), to bring (*s.o.*) to heel.

mater² [mate] *vt* **(a)** to mat(t), to dull (*metals, glass etc*); **(b)** to caulk, to hammer (*boiler seams etc*).

mater³ *vt F* to ogle, to leer at (*s.o.*); **se faire m.,** to be ogled, to be leered at.

mâter [mɑte] *vt* to mast (*ship*).

matérialisation [materjalizɑsjɔ̃] *nf* materialization, materializing; **m. d'un projet,** the fruition of a project.

matérialisé [materjalize] *adj Admin* **voie matérialisée,** = section of road delimited by a white line.

matérialiser [materjalize] **1** *vt* to materialize. **2 se matérialiser** *vpr* to materialize.

matérialisme [materjalism] *nm* materialism.

matérialiste [materjalist] **1** *adj* materialistic. **2** *n* materialist.

matérialité [materjalite] *nf* **(a)** (*caractère de ce qui est réel, matériel*) materiality; **(b)** (*matérialisme*) materialism.

matériau [materjo] *nm Constr* (building, construction) material.

matériaux [materjo] *nmpl Constr* material(s); **m. de construction,** building *or* construction material(s); *Fig* material; **il n'a pas tellement de m. pour rédiger sa thèse,** he doesn't have much material for his thesis.

matériel¹, -elle [materjɛl] *adj* **(a)** material; **ne pas avoir le temps m. de faire qch,** to simply not have time to do sth; **être dans l'impossibilité matérielle de bouger,** to find it physically impossible to move; **le plaisir m.,** sensual pleasure; **confort m.,** material comfort; **envoyer une aide matérielle à l'Arménie,** to send material aid to Armenia; **l'incendie n'a causé que des dégâts matériels,** the fire caused only material damage; **besoins matériels,** bodily needs; **(b)** *Fig Péj* materialistic.

matériel² *nm* **(a)** equipment; plant (*of factory*); *Mil* matériel; **m. agricole,** farm equipment *or* machinery; *Rail* **m. roulant,** rolling stock; *Mil* **service du m.,** ordnance; **m. de cuisine,** kitchen equipment; **m. d'école, m. scolaire,** school equipment; **m. de camping,** camping equipment *or* gear; **(b)** *Ordinat* hardware.

matériellement [materjɛlmɑ̃] *adv* materially; **avoir de quoi vivre m.,** to have enough for one's material needs; **chose m. impossible,** physical impossibility; **je ne peux m. pas accepter un travail à temps complet,** it is physically impossible for me to take on a full-time job.

maternel, -elle [matɛrnɛl] *adj* maternal; **le lait m.,** mother's milk; **l'instinct m.,** the maternal instinct; **elle est très maternelle avec ses collègues,** she acts in a very maternal *or* motherly way towards her colleagues; **un cousin du côté m.,** a cousin on one's mother's side; **grand-père m.,** maternal grandfather; **langue maternelle,** mother tongue, native tongue; **centre de protection maternelle et infantile,** mother-and-baby clinic.

maternellement [matɛrnɛlmɑ̃] *adv* maternally.

materner [matɛrne] *vt* to mother (*s.o.*).

maternité [matɛrnite] *nf* **(a)** motherhood, maternity; **un corps déformé par des maternités successives,** a body misshapen by one pregnancy after another; **(b)** (*hôpital*) maternity hospital; **(c)** *Beaux-Arts* Madonna and Child.

math(s) [mat] *nfpl F* maths, *Am* math; *Univ* **m. sup/spé,** = first-/second-year maths class (*for candidates for the*

grandes écoles).
mathématicien, -ienne [matematisjɛ̃, -jɛn] *n* mathematician.
mathématique [matematik] **1** *adj* mathematical; *Fig* mathematical, (very) logical (*mind*). **2** *nfpl* **mathématiques** mathematics; **mathématiques pures/appliquées,** pure/applied mathematics.
mathématiquement [matematikmɑ̃] *adv* mathematically.
matheux, -euse [matø, -øz] *n F* (keen) mathematician.
matière [matjɛr] *nf* **(a)** material; **en quelle m. est ton pantalon?,** what material are your trousers made of?; **matière(s) plastique(s),** plastic(s); **matières grasses,** fats; **m. grise,** grey matter (*of the brain*); *Ind* **matière(s) première(s),** raw material(s); **matières consommables,** consumables; *Fin* **comptabilité matières,** stock record, stores accounts;
(b) *Phys* matter; **m. inanimée,** inanimate matter; **la désintégration de la m.,** the disintegration of matter; *Biol* **m. vivante,** living tissue; *Phil etc* substance;
(c) *Fig* (*sujet, contenu*) subject (matter) (*of speech etc*); subject, topic, theme (*for discussion*); *Scol* (school) subject; **table des matières,** (*d'un livre*) (table of) contents; **faire une entrée en m.,** to introduce one's subject; **il n'y a pas m. à rire,** it's no laughing matter; **cela donne m. à réflexion,** it's food for thought; **en m. de,** as regards; **être bon juge en m. de musique,** to be a good judge of music; **en m. de menuiserie,** as far as woodwork is concerned.
matif [matif] *nm* (*abrév* **marché à terme des instruments financiers**) French financial futures market.
matin [matɛ̃] **1** *nm* morning; **du m. au soir,** from morning till night, morning, noon and night; **quatre heures du m.,** four o'clock in the morning, 4 a.m.; **le jeudi deux au m.,** on the morning of Thursday the second; **c'est le m. que je travaille le mieux,** I work best in the morning(s); **demain m.,** tomorrow morning; **tous les lundis m.,** every Monday morning; **de grand** *ou* **bon m., le m. de bonne heure,** early in the morning, in the early morning; **être du m.,** to be an early bird *or* an early riser; **rentrer au petit m.,** to come home in the wee small hours *or F* with the milk; **un de ces (quatre) matins, un beau m.,** one of these (fine) days. **2** *adv* (early) in the morning; **se lever très m.,** to get up very early.
mâtin, -ine [mɑtɛ̃, -in] **1** *nm* large watchdog, mastiff. **2** *n F* sly dog, *f* minx. **3** *int Arch* by Jove!
matinal, -ale, -aux [matinal, -o] **1** *adj* **(a)** morning (*breeze etc*); **à cette heure matinale,** at this early hour; **promenade matinale,** early morning walk; **(b) être m.,** to be an early riser, **comme tu es m. aujourd'hui!,** you're up very early this morning!, you're an early bird! **2** *n* **c'est un m.,** he's an early riser.
mâtiné [mɑtine] *adj* mongrel; **un teckel m. de caniche,** a cross between a dachshund and a poodle.
matinée [matine] *nf* **(a)** morning; **dans la m.,** in (the course of) the morning; **je ne l'ai pas vu de toute la m.,** I haven't seen him all morning; **une m. de lecture,** a morning (spent) reading; *F* **faire la grasse m.,** to have a lie-in; **(b)** *Th etc* matinée, afternoon performance; *Cin* **on joue ce film en m.,** the film is showing as a matinée.
matines [matin] *nfpl Rel* matins.
matir [matir] *vt* = **MATER²**.
matité [matite] *nf* deadness, dullness (*of sound etc*).
matois, -oise [matwa, -waz] **1** *adj* sly, cunning, crafty. **2** *n* crafty person; **fin m.,** sly devil.
maton, -onne [matɔ̃, -ɔn] *Arg* (*de prison*) screw.
matou [matu] *nm* tom (cat).
matraquage [matrakaʒ] *nm* bludgeoning, *Br F* coshing, *Am* blackjacking; *Fig* **m. idéologique,** ideological brainwashing; **on n'échappe pas au m. publicitaire,** there's no escaping the constant bombardment of adverts; **subir le m. publicitaire,** to be bombarded with advertising.
matraque [matrak] *nf* bludgeon, *Br F* cosh, *Am* blackjack; (*d'agent de police*) *surtout Br* truncheon, *Am* billy (club); *F* **coup de m.,** overcharging (*in restaurant etc*).
matraquer [matrake] *vt* to bludgeon, *Br F* to cosh (*s.o.*); *F* **m. le client,** to fleece *or* rip off the customer; *Fig* **la radio matraque ses annonces/cette chanson toute la journée,** the radio churns out its announcements/that song all day long; *Fig* **m. le public par des campagnes répétitives,** to bombard the public with continuous campaigning; *Fig* **m. qn de questions,** to bombard s.o. with questions.
matriarcal, -aux [matriarkal, -o] *adj* matriarchal.
matriarcat [matriarka] *nm* matriarchy.
matriçage [matrisaʒ] *nm Tech* die stamping.
matrice [matris] *nf* **(a)** *Tech* matrix, die; *Ordinat* array; *Typ* matrix, type mould; (*de disque*) matrix; **(b)** *Admin* original (*of register of taxes*); **(c)** *Anat* uterus, womb.
matricer [matrise] *vt* to stamp (*metal*); **pièce matricée,** stamping.
matricide [matrisid] **1** *adj* matricidal. **2** *n* matricide. **3** *nm* (*crime*) matricide.
matriclan [matriklɑ̃] *nm* matrilinear clan.
matricule [matrikyl] **1** *adj Mil Admin etc* **numéro m.,** (*regimental, administrative*) number. **2** *nm Mil Admin etc* number; *F* **ça risque d'être mauvais pour ton m.,** you'll be in hot water. **3** *nf* **(a)** (*liste*) roll, register, list; *Mil* regimental roll; (*immatriculation*) inscription, registration, enrolment, *US* enrollment; **(b)** (*extrait*) registration certificate.
matriculer [matrikyle] *vt* **(a)** to enter (*s.o.'s*) name on a register; to enrol (*soldier etc*); **(b)** to mark, to stamp (*sth*) with a number.
matrimonial, -iaux [matrimɔnjal, -jo] *adj* matrimonial.
matrone [matrɔn] *nf* matron; *Péj* **vieille m.,** (fat) old woman, old bag.
Matthieu [matjø] *nm* Matthew.
maturation [matyrɑsjɔ̃] *nf* maturation; ripening (*of fruit, cheese*); maturing (*of tobacco etc*).
mâture [mɑtyr] *nf* masts (and spars); **dans la m.,** aloft.
maturité [matyrite] *nf* maturity; ripeness (*of fruit, cheese*); **venir à m.,** to come to maturity; **cette jeune femme ne manque pas de m.,** that young woman is very mature; **sa m. d'esprit est remarquable,** he has a remarkably mature mind.
maudire [modir] *vt* (*prp* **maudissant**; *pp* **maudit**; *pr ind* **je maudis, n. maudissons, v. maudissez, ils maudissent**; *pr sub* **je maudisse**; *p hist* **je maudis**; *fu* **je maudirai**) to curse (*s.o., sth*).
maudit, -ite [modi, -it] **1** *adj* (ac)cursed (*crime etc*); **quel m. temps!,** what filthy weather!; **cette maudite voiture,** that damn(ed) car; **idée maudite,** damn(ed) stupid idea. **2** *n* **le M.,** the Devil; **les maudits,** the accursed, the damned.
maugréer [mogree] *vi* to curse, to fume, to grumble, to grouse (**contre,** about, at).
maure [mɔr] **1** *adj* Moorish; **bain m.,** Turkish bath. **2** *n* **M.,** Moor.
mauresque [mɔrɛsk] **1** *adj* Moorish (*architecture, design etc*). **2** *nf* **(a) M.,** Moorish woman; **(b)** (*boisson*) = pastis with barley water and water.
Maurice [mɔris] *adj* **l'île M.,** Mauritius.
mauricien, -ienne [mɔrisjɛ̃ -jɛn] **1** *adj* Mauritian. **2** *n* **M.,** Mauritian.
Mauritanie [mɔritani] *nf* Mauritania.
mauritanien, -ienne [mɔritanjɛ̃, -jɛn] **1** *adj* Mauritanian. **2** *n* **M.,** Mauritanian.
mausolée [mozɔle] *nm* mausoleum.
maussade [mosad] *adj* **(a)** (*de mauvaise humeur*) surly, sullen; (*triste*) glum; **ça l'a rendu m.,** (*amer*) that disgruntled him; **(b)** (*temps*) dull, gloomy; **paysage m.,** dull countryside.
maussaderie [mosadri] *nf* sullenness, sulkiness, peevishness.
mauvais [mɔvɛ] **1** *adj* **(a)** bad (*breath, dream, advice etc*); **de plus en plus m.,** worse and worse; **le plus m.,** the worst; **m. temps,** bad weather; **mauvaise mer,** rough sea; **être en mauvaise posture,** to be in a difficult situation; **ce n'est qu'un m. moment,** it'll pass; **cela a fait m. effet,** it looked bad, it made a bad impression; **prendre qch en mauvaise part,** to take sth badly *or* in bad part; **elle a reçu une mauvaise nouvelle,** she has had some bad news; **ce n'est pas m.,** it's not bad; **je la trouve mauvaise,** I don't like that (type of thing); **m. pour la santé/la digestion,** bad for the health/the digestion; **elle a mauvaise mine,** she doesn't look well; **mauvaise santé,** bad *or* poor health; **mauvaise vue,** bad *or* poor eyesight; **il a fait une mauvaise bronchite,** he's had a bad attack of bronchitis; **faire de mauvaises affaires,** to be doing badly (in business); **la récolte sera mauvaise,** it will be a bad *or* poor harvest; **je reconnais sa mauvaise écriture,** I recognize his bad *or* poor handwriting; **m. frein,** defective brake; **c'est un m. banquier,** he's bad at figures; **m. en anglais,** bad at *or* poor in *or* at English; **une mauvaise excuse,** a poor excuse; **il est très m. dans ce rôle,** he's very bad in the part;
(b) (*inapproprié*) wrong; **c'est la mauvaise clef,** it's the wrong key; **arriver au m. moment,** to come at a bad *or* an inconvenient time *or* at a bad *or* an awkward moment; **rire au m. endroit,** to laugh in the wrong place; **prendre la mauvaise route,** to take the wrong road; **tenir qch par le**

m. bout, to hold sth by the wrong end; *Tél* **m. numéro,** wrong number;

(c) *(méchant)* bad, evil, wicked *(person)*; bad, ill *(omen)*; **qu'est-ce qu'elle est mauvaise aujourd'hui!,** she's in a nasty mood today!; **mauvaise action,** wrong(doing); **avoir l'air m.,** *(d'une personne)* to look nasty; *(d'un chien)* to look fierce *or* vicious; **c'est un m. sujet** *ou* **un m. garçon,** he's a bad lot; **m. ange,** evil influence; **né sous une mauvaise étoile,** born under an unlucky star; **le m. œil,** the evil eye; **elle n'a pas un m. fond,** underneath *or* at bottom she's not bad; **c'est une mauvaise langue,** he's got a vicious tongue.

2 *adv* **sentir m.,** to smell (bad), to stink; **il fait m.,** the weather's bad.

3 *n* villain, *F* baddie; **dans le film, il joue le rôle du m.,** he plays the baddie in the film.

mauve [mov] **1** *nm (couleur)* mauve. **2** *nf Bot* mallow. **3** *adj* mauve.

mauviette [movjɛt] *nf Fig (physiquement)* puny person; *(moralement)* drip, wet; **quelle m. tu fais!,** you're such a drip *or Am* nerd!

max [maks] *nm inv* **(a)** *(abrév* **maximum**) max; **(b)** *F* **ça lui plaît un m.,** he likes that loads; **il y avait un m. de gens,** there were masses *or* hordes of people there.

maxi [maksi] *F* **1** *adj inv* maxi; **une m.(-)bouteille,** giant- *or* jumbo-size bottle. **2** *nm* maxi (coat *etc*); **la mode du m.,** the maxi fashion. **3** *nf* maxi skirt.

maxillaire [maksilɛr] **1** *adj Anat* maxillary; **os m.,** jawbone, *Spéc* maxilla. **2** *nm* jawbone, *Spéc* maxilla.

maximal, -aux [maksimal, -o] *adj* maximum *(effect etc)*; **pour un confort et une efficacité maximaux,** for maximum comfort and efficiency.

maxime [maksim] *nf* maxim.

maximum [maksimɔm] *(pl maximums, maxima)* **1** *nm* maximum, *pl* maximums, maxima; **m. de rendement,** maximum efficiency; **porter la production au m.,** to raise production to a maximum; **tu dois t'y efforcer au m.,** you must try your very hardest; **m. de la peine,** maximum punishment; **thermomètre à maxima,** maximum thermometer; **on sera 20 au m.,** there will be 20 of us at the most; **nous avons de la place pour 20 personnes au m.,** we have room for a maximum of 20 (people) *or* for 20 (people) at most; *F* **ça lui plaît un m.,** he likes that loads; *F* **un m. des gens ne le savent pas encore,** most people don't know yet. **2** *adj souvent inv* maximum; **rendement m.,** maximum *or* peak output.

maya [maja] **1** *adj* Maya, Mayan. **2** *nm Ling* Mayan. **3** *n* **M.,** Maya, Mayan.

Mayence [majɑ̃s] *nf* Mainz.

mayonnaise [majɔnɛz] *nf Culin* mayonnaise.

mazagran [mazagrɑ̃] *nm* goblet *(of glass, earthenware)*.

mazout [mazut] *nm* (fuel) oil; **chauffage central au m.,** oil-fired central heating.

mazouté [mazute] *adj* polluted with oil; **plage mazoutée,** oil-polluted beach; **oiseaux mazoutés,** oiled birds.

mazurka [mazyrka] *nf* mazurka.

mb. *nm Météo abrév* **millibar.**

m.d. *Mus (abrév* **main droite**) rh.

me, *before a vowel sound* **m'** [m(ə)] *pron pers* **(a)** *(objet direct)* me; **il m'aime,** he loves me; **me voici,** here I am; **(b)** *(objet indirect)* (to) me; **il m'a écrit,** he wrote to me; **il me l'a dit,** he told me so; **donnez-m'en,** give me some; **tu veux bien m'éteindre la lumière?,** would you switch off the light for me?; **(c)** *(verbe pronominal)* myself; **je m'amusais,** I was enjoying myself; **je ne m'en souviens plus,** I don't remember any more; **je me suis dit que ...,** I said to myself that ... .

mea-culpa [meakylpa] *nm inv* **faire** *ou* **dire son m.-c.,** to confess one's sins.

méandre [meɑ̃dr] *nm* meander, loop *(of river)*; bend *(of road)*; *Fig* **se perdre dans les méandres d'un raisonnement,** to get lost in the intricacies of an argument.

mec [mɛk] *nm F* chap, bloke, guy; **t'as raison, mon m.,** you're right, mate *or* chum *or esp Am* man; **son nouveau m.,** her new boyfriend *or* man.

mécanicien, -ienne [mekanisjɛ̃, -jɛn] **1** *n* **(a)** (garage, motor) mechanic; *Nau* engineer; *Av* **m. de bord** *ou* **navigant,** flight engineer; **ouvrier m.,** mechanic; **c'est une bonne mécanicienne.,** she's a good mechanic; **ingénieur m.,** mechanical engineer; **m.-dentiste,** dental technician; **(b)** *Rail* engine driver, *Am* engineer. **2** *nf* **mécanicienne,** machinist *(on sewing machine)*. **3** *adj* **civilisation mécanicienne,** mechanized civilization.

mécanique [mekanik] **1** *adj Tech etc* mechanical; machine-made *(lace, tiles etc)*; clockwork *(railway etc)*; *Fig* automatic; **métier m.,** power loom; **atelier(s) de constructions mécaniques,** engineering works; **un moyen m.,** mechanical means; **nous avons eu des ennuis mécaniques en route,** we had mechanical problems on the way; **moyens mécaniques de contraception,** barrier methods of contraception; *Fig* **un geste m.,** a mechanical *or* an automatic movement; *Fig* **c'est devenu m. pour lui,** it's become automatic for him.

2 *nf* **(a)** (science of) mechanics; **m. des fluides,** fluid mechanics; **m. quantique,** quantum mechanics;

(b) *(génie)* mechanical engineering;

(c) *(mécanisme)* mechanism, piece of machinery; **c'est une belle m., cette moto,** that motorbike's a lovely piece of machinery; *Fig F* **il partit en roulant des mécaniques,** he strutted off.

mécaniquement [mekanikmɑ̃] *adv* mechanically.

mécanisation [mekanizasjɔ̃] *nf* mechanization.

mécaniser [mekanize] *vt* to mechanize.

mécanisme [mekanism] *nm* **(a)** mechanism, machinery; works *(of a watch etc)*; **m. du corps humain,** mechanics of the human body; **m. administratif,** administrative machinery; **(b)** *(de la pensée etc)* mechanics.

mécano [mekano] *nm F* mechanic.

mécanographe [mekanɔgraf] *n* punch operator.

mécanographie [mekanɔgrafi] *nf (procédé)* data processing; *(service)* data processing department.

mécanographique [mekanɔgrafik] *adj* **service m.,** data processing department; **fiche m.,** punch(ed) card.

mécénat [mesena] *nm* sponsorship; *Beaux-Arts* patronage *(of the arts)*; **encourager le m.,** to encourage sponsorship.

mécène [mesɛn] *nm* sponsor; *Beaux-Arts* patron *(of the arts)*.

méchamment [meʃamɑ̃] *adv* **(a)** *(cruellement)* spitefully, maliciously; **(b)** *F (trompé, déçu)* sorely, sadly; **c'est m. vrai/bon,** that's damned true/good.

méchanceté [meʃɑ̃ste] *nf* **(a)** unkindness; *(perverse)* spitefulness, maliciousness; *(d'un enfant)* naughtiness, mischievousness; **faire qch par m.,** to do sth out of spite *or* malice; **la m. de sa remarque m'a blessé,** I was hurt by the spitefulness of his remark; **il l'a dit sans m.,** he didn't mean to be unkind; **(b)** spiteful action *or* remark; **quelle m.!,** what a spiteful *or* a nasty *or* an unkind thing to do *or* say!

méchant, -ante [meʃɑ̃, -ɑ̃t] **1** *adj* **(a)** unpleasant, disagreeable *(business etc)*; **être de méchante humeur,** to be in a (bad) temper;

(b) spiteful, malicious, ill-natured, unkind *(person, remark etc)*; naughty, mischievous *(child)*; vicious, bad-tempered *(animal)*; *F* **pas m.,** harmless; *F* **ce n'est pas m., ça ira chercher dans les 50 francs,** it's not too bad, about 50 francs or so; **attention chien m.,** *(sur panneau)* beware of the dog;

(c) *F (sacré)* great, terrific; **une méchante dégaine,** a snappy look; **une méchante gueule de bois,** a terrific hangover; **une méchante victoire,** a resounding victory;

(d) *Arch* miserable, wretched, poor, sorry *(dwelling etc)*; **un m. billet de cent francs,** a paltry hundred-franc note; **méchante excuse,** lame excuse.

2 *n* **petite méchante!,** you naughty little girl!; *F* **les bons et les méchants,** the goodies and the baddies.

mèche[1] [mɛʃ] *nf* **(a)** wick *(of candle, lamp)*; match *(for firing explosives)*; touch, fuse *(of mine)*; *F* **vendre la m.,** to give the game away, to blow the gaff; **découvrir la m.,** to uncover the plot; **(b)** lock *(of hair)*; wisp, tuft *(of wool etc)*; **elle se fait faire des mèches tous les mois,** she has streaks put in her hair every month; **m. postiche,** hairpiece; (man's) toupee; **(c)** *Chir* tent; **(d)** core, heart *(of cable etc)*; *Nau* mainpiece *(of rudder)*; spindle *(of capstan)*; *Él* **charbon à m.,** cored carbon; **(e)** *Menuis* auger, gimlet; **m. anglaise** *ou* **à trois pointes,** centre bit; **m. hélicoïdale,** twist bit, twist drill; auger bit.

mèche[2] *n inv* **(a)** *F* **être de m. avec qn,** to be in cahoots with s.o.; **(b)** *Arg* **il n'y a pas m.,** nothing doing.

méchoui [meʃwi] *nm Culin* méchoui *(spit-roasted lamb)*.

mécompte [mekɔ̃t] *nm* **(a)** *(erreur)* miscalculation, error; **(b)** *(désillusion)* disappointment; **il a eu un grave m.,** he has been badly let down.

méconnaissable [mekɔnesabl] *adj* unrecognizable.

méconnaissance [mekɔnɛsɑ̃s] *nf* **(a)** failure to recognize *or* appreciate *(s.o.'s talent etc)*; misreading *(of the facts)*; ignoring *(one's obligations)*; **elle a toujours fait preuve d'une m. totale de la politique,** she has never had much of a grasp of politics; **(b)** disavowal, repudiation *(of an action etc)*.

méconnaître [mekɔnɛtr] *vt (conj like* **connaître**) **(a)** to

fail to recognize, to fail to appreciate (*s.o.'s talent etc*); to belittle (*plan etc*); to disregard (*duty*); **m. les faits,** to misread the facts; **(b)** to disown, to repudiate (*action etc*).
méconnu [mekɔny] *adj* unrecognized, unappreciated (*talent etc*).
mécontent, -ente [mekɔ̃tɑ̃, -ɑ̃t] **1** *adj* discontented, displeased, dissatisfied (**de,** with); **je ne suis pas m. de mon sort,** I am not discontented with my lot; **être m. que ...** + *sub,* to be annoyed that ... . **2** *n* grumbler.
mécontentement [mekɔ̃tɑ̃tmɑ̃] *nm* discontent; (*manque de satisfaction*) dissatisfaction (**de,** with); (*déplaisir*) displeasure (**de,** at); **c'est un sujet de m.,** it's a source of discontent *or* dissatisfaction; **marquer** *ou* **exprimer son m.,** to show *or* express one's annoyance *or* displeasure.
mécontenter [mekɔ̃tɑ̃te] *vt* to dissatisfy, to displease (*s.o.*).
Mecque (la) [lamɛk] *nf* Mecca.
mécréant, -ante [mekreɑ̃, -ɑ̃t] **1** *adj* unbelieving. **2** *n* **(a)** (*sans religion*) unbeliever, infidel; **(b)** *F Arch* miscreant, wretch.
médaille [medaj] *nf* **(a)** medal; *Sp* **la m. d'or/d'argent/de bronze,** the gold/silver/bronze (medal); **détenir la m. de,** to hold the medal for; **être m. d'or,** (*d'un sportif*) to be a gold medallist *or* gold medal winner; *Fig* **le revers de la m.,** the other side of the coin; **m. pieuse,** holy medal; **(b)** (*insigne*) (official) badge; **m. d'identité,** (*de chat, chien*) tag.
médaillé [medaje] **1** *adj* holding a medal; (*soldat*) decorated. **2** *n Mil Sp* medal-holder; *Sp* (*récemment décoré*) medallist.
médaillier [medaje] *nm* medal collection (*in cabinet*).
médaillon [medajɔ̃] *nm* **(a)** medallion; **(b)** *Culin* pat (of butter); **m. de foie gras,** medallion of goose liver; **(c)** (*bijou*) medallion; (*avec photo*) locket.
médecin [medsɛ̃] *nm* doctor, physician; **femme m.,** woman doctor; **m. de médecine générale, m. généraliste,** general practitioner, G.P.; **m. consultant,** consultant; **m. légiste,** forensic pathologist; **m. militaire,** army medical officer, M.O.; **m. de bord,** ship's doctor; **m. traitant,** consulting physician; **qui est votre m. (traitant)?,** who is your (regular) doctor?
médecine [medsin] *nf* **(a)** (art of) medicine; **docteur en m.,** doctor of medicine, M.D.; **étudiant en m.,** medical student; *F* **elle fait m.,** she's doing medicine; **école de m.,** medical school; **m. douce,** alternative medicine; **m. du sport/travail,** sports/occupational medicine; **m. légale,** forensic medicine; **service de m. légale,** forensics (department); **(b)** *Arch* (dose of) medicine.
média [medja] *nm* medium, *pl* media; **le pouvoir des médias,** the power of the media; **la télévision est un m. privilégié,** television is the most efficient medium.
médial, -ale, -aux [medjal, -o] **1** *adj Ling* medial (*letter*). **2** *nf* **médiale,** (*en statistique*) median.
médian, -iane [medjɑ̃, -jan] **1** *adj* median (*nerve, line etc*). **2** *nf* **médiane (a)** *Ling* mid vowel; **(b)** (*statistique*) median.
médiateur, -trice [medjatœr, -tris] **1** *adj* mediating, mediatory. **2** *n* mediator; **agir en tant que m.,** to act as mediator.
médiathèque [medjatɛk] *nf* media library.
médiation [medjasjɔ̃] *nf* mediation.
médiatique [medjatik] *adj* media (*coverage, personality etc*); **événement m.,** media event.
médiatiser [medjatize] *vt* to give media coverage to (*sth*); *Péj* to turn (*sth*) into a media event.
médiator [medjatɔr] *nm Mus* plectrum.
médical, -aux [medikal, -o] *adj* medical; **examen m. (complet),** medical examination, check-up; **certificat m.,** medical certificate; **matière médicale,** materia medica.
médicalement [medikalmɑ̃] *adv* medically.
médicalisation [medikalizasjɔ̃] *nf* provision of medical care; **m. des ambulances,** allotting medical staff to ambulances; **m. à outrance,** pill-pushing.
médicaliser [medikalize] *vt* to give medical care to (*person*); to allot medical staff to (*ambulance*); **m. une population,** to make medical care available to a population; **m. la ménopause,** to treat the menopause as a medical issue; **veillez à ne pas m. les enfants trop tôt,** don't get children used to taking medicine too soon.
médicament [medikamɑ̃] *nm* medicine, drug, medication; **est-ce que vous prenez des médicaments?,** are you taking *or* are you on any kind of medication?
médicamenteux, -euse [medikamɑ̃tø, -øz] *adj* medicinal.
médication [medikasjɔ̃] *nf* medication, medical treatment.
médicinal, -aux [medisinal, -o] *adj* medicinal.
Medicis [medisis] *nmpl Hist* Medici (family).
médico-légal, -aux [medikɔlegal, -o] *adj* forensic.
médico-social, -aux [medikɔsɔsjal, -o] *adj* **centre m.-s.,** health centre.
médiéval, -aux [medjeval, -o] *adj* medi(a)eval.
médiéviste [medjevist] *n* medi(a)evalist.
médina [medina] *nf* medina.
médiocre [medjɔkr] **1** *adj* mediocre. **2** *nm* mediocrity.
médiocrement [medjɔkrəmɑ̃] *adv* indifferently, poorly; **m. riche,** not very rich; **elle chante très m.,** she's a very mediocre singer.
médiocrité [medjɔkrite] *nf* mediocrity.
médire [medir] *vi* (*conj like* **dire,** *except pr ind and imp* **médisez**) **m. de qn,** to speak ill of s.o., to run s.o. down; **il médit facilement,** he is always ready to run people down.
médisance [medizɑ̃s] *nf* **(a)** (*action*) slander, scandalmongering; **(b)** (bit of) scandal, slander.
médisant [medizɑ̃] **1** *adj* slanderous, scandalmongering. **2** *n* slanderer, scandalmonger.
méditatif, -ive [meditatif, -iv] *adj* meditative, thoughtful.
méditation [meditasjɔ̃] *nf* meditation; **plongé dans la m.,** lost in thought; **entrer en m.,** to go into meditation; **faire de la m.,** to meditate, to do meditation.
méditer [medite] **1** *vi* to meditate; **m. de faire qch,** to be thinking of doing sth, to be contemplating doing sth. **2** *vt* to contemplate (*sth*); to have (*sth*) in mind; **m. un projet,** to mull over a plan.
Méditerranée [mediterane] *nf* **la (mer) M.,** the Mediterranean (sea); **en M.,** in the Mediterranean.
méditerranéen, -enne [mediteraneɛ̃, -ɛn] **1** *adj* Mediterranean. **2** *n* **M.,** native *or* inhabitant of a Mediterranean country; (*en France*) Southerner.
médium [medjɔm] *nm* **(a)** *Mus* middle register (*of the voice*); **(b)** *Psy* medium.
médius [medjys] *nm Anat* middle finger.
médoc [medɔk] *nm* Médoc (wine).
médullaire [medylɛr] *adj Anat Bot* medullary.
méduse [medyz] *nf* **(a)** jellyfish; *Spéc* medusa; **(b)** *Myth* **M.,** Medusa.
méduser [medyze] *vt F* to stupefy.
meeting [mitiŋ] *nm Pol Sp etc* meeting; **m. d'aviation,** air show.
méfait [mefɛ] *nm* misdeed; *Jur* misdemeanour, *US* misdemeanor; **méfaits d'un orage,** storm damage; **les méfaits de la surinformation,** the evils of over-information; **se déclarer l'auteur du m.,** to own up (to the deed).
méfiance [mefjɑ̃s] *nf* (*manque de confiance*) distrust; (*suspicion*) mistrust; **avoir de la m. envers qn,** to distrust s.o.; (*avoir de la suspicion*) to mistrust s.o.; **regarder qn avec m.,** to eye s.o. distrustfully *or* suspiciously; (*avec suspicion*) to eye s.o. mistrustfully.
méfiant [mefjɑ̃] *adj* distrustful; (*suspicieux*) mistrustful, suspicious (**à l'égard de,** of).
méfier (se) [səmefje] *vpr* (*impf & pr sub* **n.n. méfiions, v.v. méfiiez**) to be on one's guard; **se m. de qn,** to distrust s.o.; (*avoir de la suspicion*) to mistrust s.o.; **méfiez-vous des pickpockets,** beware of pickpockets; **se m. de qch,** to be suspicious *or* wary of sth, to be on one's guard against sth.
méforme [mefɔrm] *nf Sp* poor form *or* condition; **être en m.,** to be off form.
mégacycle [megasikl] *nm Él* megacycle.
mégahertz [megaɛrts] *nm Él* megahertz.
mégalithe [megalit] *nm* megalith.
mégalithique [megalitik] *adj* megalithic.
mégalomane [megalɔman], *F* **mégalo** [megalo] *adj & n* megalomaniac.
mégalomanie [megalɔmani] *nf* megalomania.
mégalopole [megalɔpɔl] *nf* megalopolis.
méga-octet [megaɔktɛ] *nm Ordinat* megabyte.
mégaphone [megafɔn] *nm* megaphone; (*électrique*) loud-hailer, *Am* bullhorn.
mégarde (par) [parmegard] *adv* inadvertently, accidentally.
mégatonne [megatɔn] *nf* megaton.
mégawatt [megawat] *nm Phys* megawatt.
mégère [meʒɛr] *nf* shrew, termagant; **la M. apprivoisée,** The Taming of the Shrew.
mégir [meʒir] **, mégisser** [meʒise] *vt* to taw, to dress (*light skins*).
mégis [meʒi] *adj* **cuir m.,** tawed leather, white leather.

mégot [mego] *nm F* (*de cigarette*) fag end, *Am* butt; (*de cigare*) stump, butt.

mégotage [megɔtaʒ] *nm F* scrimping (and scraping); **mener une vie de m.,** to spend one's life scrimping and scraping.

mégoter [megɔte] *vi F* to scrimp (**sur,** on).

méhari [meari] *nm* racing camel, mehari; (*pl méhara, méharis*).

méhariste [mearist] *nm* camel driver, meharist; *Mil Arch* member of the camel corps (*in Sahara*).

meilleur, -eure [mɛjœr] **1** *adj* **(a)** (*comp of* **bon**) better; **rendre qch m.,** to make sth better, to improve sth; **devenir m.,** to get better, to improve; **je ne connais rien de m.,** I don't know anything better; **les choses prennent une meilleure tournure,** things are taking a turn for the better; **de meilleure heure,** earlier; **m. marché,** cheaper;

(b) (*superl of* **bon**) **le m., la meilleure,** the best (*of several*); the better (*of two*); **m. ami,** best friend; **nous sommes les meilleurs amis du monde,** we're the best of friends; **meilleurs vœux,** (*dans une lettre*) with all good wishes, (with) best wishes.

2 *n* **que le m. gagne,** may the best man win; **j'en passe et des meilleures,** and that's the least of it, and that's not the half of it, and I could go on.

3 *nm* **pour le m. et pour le pire,** for better or (for) worse; **donner le m. de soi-même,** to give of one's best; *Sp* **prendre le m. sur son adversaire,** to get the better *or* best of one's opponent.

4 *adv* **il fait m.,** the weather's better; **il fait m. ici,** it's better here.

méjuger [meʒyʒe] *v* (*conj like* **juger**) **1** *vi* **m. de qn/qch,** to misjudge s.o./sth. **2** *vt* to misjudge. **3 se méjuger** *vpr* to underestimate oneself.

mélancolie [melɑ̃kɔli] *nf* melancholy, gloom; *Méd* melancholia; **elle a une petite crise de m.,** she's (feeling) a bit down in the mouth.

mélancolique [melɑ̃kɔlik] *adj* melancholy, gloomy; *Méd* melancholic.

Mélanésie [melanezi] *nf* Melanesia.

mélanésien, -ienne [melanesjɛ, -jɛn] **1** *adj* Melanesian. **2** *nm Ling* Melanesian. **3** *n* **M.,** Melanesian.

mélange [melɑ̃ʒ] *nm* **(a)** mixing; blending (*of tea etc*); crossing (*of breeds*); **(b)** (*résultat*) mixture; blend (*of tea etc*); intermixture, cross (*of breeds etc*); mix (*of cement etc*); miscellany (*of objects*); **m. pharmaceutique,** pharmaceutical mixture; **sans m.,** unmixed, unadulterated; **m. explosif** *ou* **détonant,** explosive mixture; **pas de whisky après le vin, je me méfie des mélanges,** no whisky after my wine — I don't mix my drinks; **un curieux m. de timidité et d'orgueil,** a strange mixture *or* blend of shyness and arrogance.

mélangé [melɑ̃ʒe] *adj* mixed (*society, breed*); motley (*crowd*).

mélanger [melɑ̃ʒe] *v* (**je mélangeai(s); n. mélangeons**) **1** *vt* to mix, to mingle; to blend (*teas etc*); to mix up (*ideas, documents etc*). **2 se mélanger** *vpr* to mix, to mingle, to blend.

mélangeur [melɑ̃ʒœr] *nm* mixer; *Électron* **m. (de son),** mixer; **(robinet) m.,** mixer tap.

mélanine [melanin] *nf* melanin.

mélanome [melanom] *nm Méd* melanoma; **m. bénin/malin,** benign/malignant melanoma.

mêlant [mɛlɑ̃] *adj Can* **c'est pas m.,** there's no doubt about it.

mélasse [melas] *nf* molasses, treacle; **m. raffinée,** golden syrup; *F* **être dans la m.,** to be in a mess *or* in the soup.

melba [mɛlba] *adj inv Culin* **pêche/poire m.,** peach/pear melba.

mêlé [mele] *adj* **(a)** mixed (*feelings, company*); mingled (*tones*); **(b)** tangled (*skein, hair etc*); tousled (*hair*); involved (*business*).

mêlée [mele] *nf* **(a)** (*conflit*) fray, mêlée; *F* (*bagarre*) scuffle, tussle, free-for-all; *Fig* **au dessus de la m.,** above the fray; **(b)** *Rugby Fb* scrum(mage); *Rugby Fb* **m. ouverte,** ruck.

mêler [mele] **1** *vt* **(a)** to mix, to mingle, to blend; **m. qch à** *ou* **avec qch,** to mix *or* combine sth with sth; **il est mêlé à tout,** he's got a finger in every pie; **m. son vin d'eau,** to put water in one's wine;

(b) (*mettre en désordre*) to mix up, to jumble up, to muddle (up) (*papers etc*); to confuse, to tangle (*ideas etc*); to shuffle (*cards*); *F* **vous avez bien mêlé les cartes!,** a nice mess you've made of it!;

(c) m. qn à qch, to implicate s.o. *or* involve s.o. in sth; **m. qn à la conversation,** to bring s.o. into the conversation; **m. deux races de chien,** to cross two breeds of dog.

2 se mêler *vpr* to mix, to mingle, to blend; **se m. à la foule,** to mingle with *or* blend into the crowd; **se m. à la conversation,** to join in *or* take part in the conversation; **quand l'amour propre se mêle à la colère,** when self-esteem is mingled with anger; **mêlez-vous de ce qui vous regarde,** mind your own business; *F* **mais de quoi je me mêle?,** what business is it of yours?, what's it got to do with you?; **ce n'est pas à moi de m'en m.,** it's not for me to interfere; **se m. de politique,** to dabble in politics.

mélèze [melɛz] *nm* larch (tree).

méli-mélo [melimelo] *nm F* hotchpotch, jumble (*of facts etc*); medley (*of people etc*); **quel m.-m!,** what a mess!; (*pl mélis-mélos*).

mélo [melo] *F* **1** *nm* melodrama. **2** *adj* melodramatic.

mélodie [melɔdi] *nf* **(a)** *Mus* melody, tune; **(b)** melodiousness (*of verse etc*).

mélodieusement [melɔdjøzmɑ̃] *adv* melodiously, tunefully.

mélodieux, -ieuse [melɔdjø, -jøz] *adj* melodious, tuneful.

mélodique [melɔdik] *adj Mus* melodic.

mélodiste [melɔdist] *n* **(a)** melody writer; **(b)** melodist (*as opposed to harmonist*).

mélodramatique [melɔdramatik] *adj* melodramatic.

mélodrame [melɔdram] *nm* melodrama.

mélomane [melɔman] *n* music lover.

melon [məlɔ̃] *nm* **(a)** (*fruit*) melon; **m. cantaloup,** cantaloup(e) (melon), *Am* rock melon; **m. d'hiver** *ou* **de garde,** honeydew melon; **m. d'eau,** water melon; **(b) (chapeau) m.,** bowler (hat), *Am* derby.

melonnière [məlɔnjɛr] *nf* melon bed.

mélopée [melɔpe] *nf Mus* **(a)** (*chant récitatif*) chant, recitative; **(b)** (*chant monotone*) threnody.

MEM [mɛm] *nf Ordinat* (*abrév* **mémoire morte**) ROM.

membrane [mɑ̃bran] *nf* **(a)** *Anat Biol* membrane; **m. poreuse,** porous membrane, diaphragm; **(b)** *Tech* (*in microphone etc*) diaphragm.

membraneux, -euse [mɑ̃branø, -øz] *adj Anat Méd* membranous.

membre [mɑ̃br] *nm* **(a)** member (*of an association*); **membres,** membership; **les états membres,** the member states; **les membres de l'ONU/du Parlement Européen,** the members of the UN/of the European Parliament; *Can* **Membre de l'Assemblée Nationale,** (*du Québec*) Member of the National Assembly; **(b)** *Anat* limb, *Fml* member; **m. viril,** penis; **(c)** (*constituent part*) *Ling Archit* member; *Math* **premier m. d'une équation,** lefthand side of an equation; **(d)** rib, timber (*of ship*).

membrure [mɑ̃bryr] *nf* **(a)** frame(work) (*of building etc*); ribs (*of ship*); **(b)** *Litt* limbs; **homme à forte m.,** strong-limbed *or* powerfully built man; **(c)** *Constr* flange (*of web girder*).

même [mɛm] **1** *adj* **(a)** same; **une seule et m. chose,** one and the same thing; **ils sont du m. âge,** they're the same age; **ce m. jour,** that same day; **tous rassemblés en un m. lieu,** all gathered in the same place; **en m. temps,** at the same time; **les deux concepts sont mêmes,** the two concepts are identical;

(b) (*avant le nom*) very; **aujourd'hui m.,** this very day; **il habite ici m.,** he lives in this very place *or* in this very house; **les enfants mêmes le savaient,** even the children knew it; **c'est cela m.,** that's the very thing; **donner les chiffres mêmes,** to give the actual figures;

(c) ...-m., self; **elle est la bonté m.,** she's kindness itself; **moi-m.,** myself; **toi-m.,** yourself; **lui-m.,** himself, itself; **elle-m.,** herself, itself; **soi-m.,** oneself; **nous-mêmes,** ourselves; **vous-mêmes,** yourselves; **eux-mêmes, elles-mêmes,** themselves; **il l'a fait lui-m.,** he did it himself; **faire qch de soi-m.,** to do sth of one's own accord; **pareille à elle-m.,** she hasn't changed, she's still the same; **la chose n'est pas mauvaise en elle-m.,** the thing is not bad in itself *or* per se; **un autre lui-m.,** a second self.

2 *adv* **(a)** even; **aimer m. ses ennemis,** to love even one's enemies; **je le pense et m. j'en suis sûr,** I think so, in fact I am sure of it; **je n'ai pas m.** *ou* **je n'ai m. pas le prix de mon voyage,** I haven't even enough to pay my fare; **m. lui l'affirme,** even he says so; **m. si je le savais,** even if I knew;

(b) de m., in the same way; **faire de m.,** to do likewise, to do the same; **il en est de m. des autres,** it's the same for the others, the same holds good for the others; **de m. que,** (just) as, like; **tout de m.,** all the same, for all that;

mais tout de m.!, well really!;

(c) boire à m. la bouteille, to drink (straight) out of the bottle; **des maisons bâties à m. le trottoir,** houses built flush with the pavement; **couché à m. le sable,** lying on the bare sand; **taillé à m. la pierre,** cut out of solid rock; **à m. la peau,** next to the skin; **être à m. de faire qch,** to be able *or* in a position to do sth; **il n'est pas à m. de faire le voyage,** he's not up to making the journey; **cela me met à m. de le faire,** that enables me *or* puts me in a position to do it.

3 *pron indéf* **on prend les mêmes et on recommence,** it's always of the same (people)!; **Jean, tu n'es plus le m.!,** you're not the same, Jean!; **cela revient au m.,** it comes (down) *or* amounts to the same thing; *F* **c'est du pareil au m.,** it's all the same, it's the same difference; **elle est toujours la m.,** she's always the same.

mémé [meme] *nf F* gran(ny), nan; *F Péj* **ça fait m. cette robe!,** that dress makes you look like an old woman!

mémento [memẽto] *nm* **(a)** *(de service)* memo(randum), note; **(b)** *(pour se souvenir)* memo, reminder; **(c)** *(livre)* notebook; *Scol* **m. de chimie,** revision notes in chemistry.

mémère [memɛr] *nf F* **(a)** *Enf* grandma, gran(ny), nan; **(b) le petit chien-chien à sa m.,** mummy's little doggie-woggie; **(c)** *Péj* (blousy) middle-aged woman.

mémo [memo] *nm* memo.

mémoire¹ [memwar] *nf* **(a)** memory; **je n'ai pas la m. des noms,** I've no memory for names; **tu perds la m.?,** are you losing your memory?; **il n'a pas de m.,** he's got a bad memory; **rappeler qch à la m. de qn,** to remind s.o. of sth; **je vais lui rafraîchir la m.,** I'll refresh his memory; **réciter qch de m.,** to recite sth from memory; **si j'ai bonne m.,** if I remember rightly, if (my) memory serves me right; **avoir une m. d'éléphant,** to have a long memory *or* a memory like an elephant; **m. collective,** collective memory;

(b) *(souvenir)* memory; **perdre la m. de qch,** to forget sth; **garder la m. de qch,** to keep sth in mind; **avoir m. de qch,** to remember sth; **de m. d'homme,** within living memory; **de m. de pêcheur, je n'en avais jamais vu de si gros,** in all my years as an angler *or* in all my angling career, I've never seen such a big one; **à la m. de qn,** *(of monument etc)* in memory of s.o., to the memory of s.o.; **je signale, pour m., que ...,** I might mention, for the record, that ...; **je vous signale pour m. que ...,** I would remind you that ...;

(c) *Ordinat* memory, store; **mettre un dossier en m.,** to write a file to memory; **m. de 40 méga-octets,** 40 megabyte memory; **carte d'extension de m.,** memory expansion card; **m. tampon,** buffer store; **m. morte,** read-only memory, ROM; **m. vive,** random access memory, RAM; **m. centrale,** main memory.

mémoire² *nm* **(a)** *(rapport)* report; *Jur* (written) statement *(of case)*; *Univ* dissertation, thesis; **(b)** *(contractor's)* account; bill *(of costs)*; **(c) mémoires,** (historical) memoirs; **écrire ses mémoires,** to write one's memoirs; **(d) mémoires,** transactions *(of learned society etc)*.

mémorable [memorabl] *adj* memorable, noteworthy.

mémorandum [memorɑ̃dɔm] *nm* **(a)** memorandum, note; *Admin etc* orders (in brief); *Nau* **m. de combat,** battle orders; **(b)** *(carnet)* notebook.

mémorial, -iaux [memorjal, -jo] *nm* **(a)** *(monument)* memorial; **(b)** *(mémoires)* memoir; **(c)** *Com* daybook.

mémorisation [memorizasjɔ̃] *nf* memorizing; *Ordinat* writing to memory.

mémoriser [memorize] *vt* to memorize *(sth)*, to commit *(sth)* to memory; *Ordinat* to write *(a file)* to memory.

menaçant [mənasɑ̃] *adj* menacing, threatening.

menace [mənas] *nf* threat, menace; *Jur* **menaces,** intimidation; **menaces en l'air,** empty *or* idle threats; **silence lourd de menaces,** ominous silence.

menacé [mənase] *adj* under threat, threatened; **vos jours sont menacés,** your life is in danger.

menacer [mənase] *v* **(je menaçai(s); n. menaçons) 1** *vt* to threaten, to menace; **m. qn du doigt/poing,** to shake one's finger/fist at s.o.; **m. qn d'un procès,** to threaten s.o. with legal proceedings; **m. de faire qch,** to threaten to do sth; **le procès menace d'être long,** the trial threatens to be lengthy. **2** *vi* *(d'une tempête, d'une révolution etc)* to be brewing.

ménade [menad] *nf Myth* maenad, bacchante.

ménage [menaʒ] *nm* **(a)** *(maison)* **jouer au m.,** to play at (keeping) house; **tenir le m. de qn,** to keep house for s.o.; **pain de m.,** large (homemade) loaf; **faire le m.,** to do the housework, *Am* to clean house; **le grand m.,** spring cleaning; *Pol Fig* **faire le m. dans sa maison,** to put one's (own) house in order; *Fig* **faire le (grand) m. dans le parti,** to do some housecleaning in the party; **faire des ménages,** to go out cleaning; **femme de m.,** cleaner, *Br* daily help, *Br F* daily;

(b) monter son m., to furnish one's house; **m. de poupée,** set of doll's furniture;

(c) *(famille)* household, family; **jeune m.,** young (married) couple; **m. à trois,** (matrimonial) triangle; **se mettre en m.,** to set up house; **faire bon/mauvais m. (ensemble),** to get on well/ badly together; *Écon* **la consommation des ménages en France,** French household consumption.

ménagement [menaʒmɑ̃] *nm* care, caution, circumspection; *(tact)* consideration; **avec ménagement(s),** carefully, cautiously; *(avec tact)* considerately, tactfully; **parler sans ménagement(s),** to speak bluntly.

ménager¹, -ère [menaʒe, -ɛr] **1** *adj* household *(equipment etc)*; **travaux ménagers,** housework; **arts ménagers,** domestic science; *Scol* **enseignement m.,** home economics, *Vieilli* domestic science; **eaux ménagères,** waste water; **Salon des Arts Ménagers,** ≈ Ideal Home Exhibition. **2** *nf* **ménagère (a)** housewife; **elle est bonne ménagère,** she's a good housekeeper; **(b)** *Écon* **le panier de la ménagère,** the shopping basket; **(c)** *(service de couverts)* canteen of cutlery.

ménager² *v* **(je ménageai(s); n. ménageons) 1** *vt* **(a)** to use *(sth)* sparingly *or* economically; **elle n'a pas ménagé le sel,** she didn't spare the salt, she was a bit too generous with the salt; **m. sa santé,** to take care of one's health; **m. qn,** to treat s.o. tactfully *or* with consideration; **ne le ménagez pas,** don't spare him; **elle cherche toujours à m. les uns et les autres,** she always tries to do right by everybody; **sans m. ses paroles,** without mincing one's words; *Fig* **m. son cheval,** to spare one's horse;

(b) *(arranger)* to contrive, to arrange; **m. une réconciliation entre deux ennemis,** to bring about a reconciliation between two enemies; **m. une surprise à qn,** to prepare a surprise for s.o.; **m. une ouverture pour les fils,** to make an opening for the wires; **m. une sortie,** to provide an exit.

2 se ménager *vpr* to spare oneself, to take care of oneself; *Péj* to coddle oneself; **se m. une sortie,** to provide oneself with a way out.

ménagerie [menaʒri] *nf* menagerie.

ménagiste [menaʒist] *n Com* *(vendeur)* household appliances dealer; *(fabricant)* manufacturer of household appliances.

mendélien, -ienne [mɛ̃deljɛ̃, -jɛn] *adj Biol* Mendelian.

mendélisme [mɛ̃delism] *nm Biol* Mendelism.

mendiant, -ante [mɑ̃djɑ̃, -ɑ̃t] **1** *adj* mendicant, begging *(friar, order etc)*. **2** *n* beggar(man, -woman); **les quatre mendiants,** *Hist* the four mendicant orders; *Culin* = almonds, raisins, hazelnuts and figs *(served as dessert)*.

mendicité [mɑ̃disite] *nf* begging; **réduit à la m.,** reduced to beggary.

mendier [mɑ̃dje] *v* *(impf & pr sub* **n. mendiions, v. mendiiez) 1** *vi* to beg; **faire son chemin jusqu'à Paris en mendiant,** to beg one's way to Paris. **2** *vt* to beg (for) *(one's bread)*; *Fig Péj* to canvass *(votes)*; **m. des compliments,** to fish for compliments.

mendigo(t), -ote [mɑ̃digo, -ɔt] *n Arg* beggar.

meneau, -eaux [məno] *nm Archit* **m. vertical,** mullion; **m. horizontal,** transom.

menées [məne] *nfpl* schemings *(of political party etc)*; **déjouer les m. de qn,** to thwart *or* outwit s.o..

mener [məne] *v* **(je mène; je mènerai) 1** *vt* **(a)** to take *(s.o. somewhere)*; **m. qn à sa chambre,** to take *or* show s.o. to his room; **m. une ligne entre deux points,** to draw a line between two points;

(b) *(être devant)* to lead, to be *or* go ahead of; **m. le deuil,** to be chief mourner; *Sp* **la France mène la Belgique (par) 2 à 1,** France is leading Belgium by 2 to 1; **m. la danse,** to lead the dance; *Fig* to give orders, to call the tune;

(c) *(conduire)* to lead; **cette petite somme ne te mènera pas bien loin,** this little amount won't get you very far; **cela nous mène à croire que ...,** this leads us to believe that ...; *Fig* **cette affaire peut le m. loin,** this business could get him into deep water;

(d) *(diriger)* to control, to manage; **mari mené par sa femme,** henpecked husband; **m. son personnel au doigt et à l'œil,** to have one's staff under one's thumb;

(e) to steer *(boat)*; **m. de front plusieurs affaires,** to have several irons in the fire; *MecE* **roue menée,** driven wheel;

(f) to manage, to conduct (*business etc*); **m. à bonne fin** *ou* **à bien,** to bring (*sth*) to a successful conclusion; to carry through, to carry out (*plan*); **m. une vie triste,** to lead a sad life; **m. la vie dure à qn,** to give s.o. a hard time.

2 *vi* **chemin qui mène à la ville,** road that leads to the town; **cela ne mène à rien,** this is getting us nowhere; **ne pas en m. large,** to be in a tight corner; (*être gené*) to be embarrassed.

ménestrel [menɛstrɛl] *nm* minstrel.

ménétrier [menetrije] *nm* (strolling) fiddler.

meneur, -euse [mənœr, -øz] **1** *n* leader (*of political party etc*); ringleader (*of revolt*); **m. du jeu,** moving spirit; *TV etc* question master, quiz master; **m. de bœufs,** cattle drover; **m. d'ours,** bear leader; **m. d'hommes,** leader of men; **le grand m. d'hommes que fut De Gaulle,** De Gaulle, that great leader of men. **2** *nf Can Sp* **meneuse de claques,** cheerleader, pom-pom girl.

menhir [menir] *nm* menhir.

méninge [menɛ̃ʒ] *nf Anat* meninx; **les trois méninges,** the three meninges; *F* **se creuser les méninges,** to rack one's brains; **il ne se fatigue pas les méninges,** he doesn't exactly overwork.

méningé [menɛ̃ʒe] *adj Anat* meningeal.

méningite [menɛ̃ʒit] *nf Méd* meningitis.

ménopause [menɔpoz] *nf Physiol* menopause; **faire sa m.,** to be going through the menopause.

ménopausé [menɔpoze] *adj* menopausal.

ménorragie [menɔraʒi] *nf Méd* menorrhagia.

menotte [mənɔt] *nf* **(a)** *Enf* little hand; **(b) menottes,** handcuffs; *Hist* manacles; **mettre** *ou* **passer les menottes à qn,** to put the handcuffs on s.o., to handcuff s.o..

mensonge [mɑ̃sɔ̃ʒ] *nm* **(a)** lie; **faire** *ou* **dire un m.,** to tell a lie; **petit m., m. innocent, pieux m.,** white lie; **gros m.,** downright lie, *F* whopper; *Hum* **c'est vrai, ce m.?,** do you expect me to believe that?, pull the other one *or* leg!; **(b)** (*acte*) lying; **vivre dans le m.,** to live a lie; **détester le m.,** to hate lying *or* lies; **l'amour est un m.,** love is an illusion.

mensonger, -ère [mɑ̃sɔ̃ʒe, -ɛr] *adj* lying, untrue (*story*); deceitful, false (*look*); vain, deceptive, illusory (*hope*).

menstruation [mɑ̃stryasjɔ̃] *nf Physiol* menstruation.

menstruel, -elle [mɑ̃stryɛl] *adj Physiol* menstrual.

menstrues [mɑ̃stry] *nfpl Physiol* menses.

mensualisation [mɑ̃sɥalizasjɔ̃] *nf* monthly payment (*of staff, salaries*); **remboursement par mensualisations,** repayment in monthly instaments.

mensualiser [mɑ̃sɥalize] *vt* to pay (*staff*) monthly.

mensualité [mɑ̃sɥalite] *nf* monthly payment; **payer par mensualités,** to pay monthly *or* by monthly instalments.

mensuel, -elle [mɑ̃sɥɛl] **1** *adj* monthly. **2** *nm* monthly magazine. **3** *n* employee paid monthly.

mensuellement [mɑ̃sɥɛlmɑ̃] *adv* monthly.

mensuration [mɑ̃syrasjɔ̃] *nf* (*action*) measurement, measuring; **prendre les mensurations de qn,** to take s.o.'s measurements; *F* **mensurations,** (*of woman*) vital statistics.

mental, -aux [mɑ̃tal, -o] *adj* mental (*arithmetic, disease etc*); **aliénation mentale,** insanity.

mentalement [mɑ̃talmɑ̃] *adv* mentally.

mentalité [mɑ̃talite] *nf* mentality; **quelle m.!,** what a mentality!

menteur, -euse [mɑ̃tœr, -øz] **1** *adj* lying (*person*); false, deceptive (*appearance*). **2** *n* liar.

menthe [mɑ̃t] *nf* (*plante*) mint; **m. verte,** spearmint, garden mint; **m. anglaise** *ou* **poivrée,** peppermint; **pastilles de m.,** (pepper)mints; **boire une m. à l'eau,** to drink a glass of peppermint cordial; **sirop à la m.,** peppermint cordial.

menthol [mɛ̃tɔl] *nm Ch Pharm* menthol.

mentholé [mɛ̃tɔle] *adj Pharm* mentholated.

mention [mɑ̃sjɔ̃] *nf* **(a)** mention; **faire m. de qn/qch,** to mention *or* refer to s.o./sth; *Scol* **reçu avec m.,** ≈ passed with distinction; **décrocher la m. bien,** ≈ to get a distinction; **(b)** endorsement (*on envelope etc*); **m. inconnu,** stamped not known; **(c)** reference (*at head of letter*).

mentionner [mɑ̃sjɔne] *vt* to mention; **mentionné ci-dessus,** above-mentioned, aforesaid.

mentir [mɑ̃tir] *v* (*prp* **mentant**; *pp* **menti**; *pr ind* **je mens, il ment, n. mentons, ils mentent**; *p hist* **je mentis**; *fu* **je mentirai**) **1** *vi* to lie, to tell lies; **sans m.!,** honestly!; **tu mens comme tu respires,** you're a compulsive liar; **m. à sa réputation,** not to live up to one's reputation; **elle ment à son mari,** she is deceiving her husband. **2 se mentir** *vpr* to fool oneself.

menton [mɑ̃tɔ̃] *nm* chin; **m. en galoche,** jutting chin; **m. fuyant,** receding chin; **double m.,** double chin; *F* **s'en mettre jusqu'au m.,** to stuff oneself, to have a good feed.

mentonnet [mɑ̃tɔnɛ] *nm* **(a)** catch (*of latch etc*); stop (*on moving part of machine*); **(b)** *MecE* tappet, cam; **(c)** *Rail* flange (*of wheel*); **(d)** lug, ear (*of bomb*).

mentonnier, -ière [mɑ̃tɔnje, -jɛr] **1** *adj* of the chin. **2** *nf* **mentonnière,** chinpiece (*of helmet*); *Mil etc* chin strap; *Méd* chin bandage; *Mus* chin rest (*of violin*).

mentor [mɛ̃tɔr] *nm Litt* mentor.

menu¹ [məny] **1** *adj* **(a)** small; fine (*gravel etc*); slender, slim, slight (*figure*); tiny (*fragment*); **m. plomb,** small shot, bird shot; **menue monnaie,** small change; **(b)** trifling, petty (*incident etc*); **menues réparations,** minor repairs; **menus détails,** small *or* minute details; **menus frais, menues dépenses,** minor expenses; **m. peuple,** humble people; **menus propos,** small talk. **2** *adv* small, fine; **hacher m.,** to chop (*meat etc*) up small; (*très fin*) to mince (*meat*); **piler m.,** to crush (*sth*) up small; **écrire m.,** to write small; **il pleuvait dru et m.,** the rain came down in a steady drizzle. **3** *n* **raconter qch par le m.,** to relate sth in detail.

menu² *nm* **(a)** (*repas*) meal; **composer son m.,** to plan one's meal; **m. équilibré,** balanced diet; (*au restaurant*) **m. touristique/gastronomique,** economy/gourmet menu; **prendre le m. (à 75 francs),** to have the (75-franc) set meal; **(b)** *Ordinat* menu; **m. primaire/secondaire/principal,** primary/secondary/main menu; **m. d'impression,** print menu; **m. déroulant,** pull-down menu; **contrôlé par menu(s),** menu driven.

menuet [mənɥɛ] *nm Mus etc* minuet.

menuiser [mənɥize] *vt* **(a)** to cut down, to plane down (*wood to required size*); **(b)** (*travailler le bois*) to do joinery *or* woodwork.

menuiserie [mənɥizri] *nf* **(a)** (*travail*) joinery, woodwork; *Constr* carpentry; **(b)** (*atelier*) joiner's shop; **(c)** (*résultat*) joinery, woodwork, carpentry.

menuisier [mənɥizje] *nm* joiner; **m. en meubles,** cabinet maker; **m. en bâtiments,** carpenter.

méphistophélique [mefistɔfelik] *adj* Mephistophelian.

méphitique [mefitik] *adj* foul, noxious.

méplat [mepla] **1** *adj* flat; *Constr* flat-laid (*joist etc*). **2** *nm* flat part; ledge (*of rock*); *Beaux-Arts* **méplats du visage,** planes that build up the face.

méprendre (se) [səmeprɑ̃dr] *vpr* (*conj like* **prendre**) to be mistaken, to make a mistake (**sur, quant à,** about); **se m. sur un motif,** to mistake *or* misjudge *or* misunderstand a motive; **il n'y a pas à s'y m.,** there can be no mistake about it; **il imitait le maître à s'y m.,** he could give a lifelike imitation of the master.

mépris [mepri] *nm* contempt, scorn; **m. des richesses,** contempt for *or* scorn of wealth; **avoir du m. pour qn,** to despise s.o.; **au m. de qch,** in contempt *or* defiance of sth; **avec m.,** scornfully, contemptuously; **sourire de m.,** contemptuous *or* scornful smile; *Prov* **la familiarité engendre le m.,** familiarity breeds contempt.

méprisable [meprizabl] *adj* contemptible, despicable.

méprisant [meprizɑ̃] *adj* contemptuous, scornful.

méprise [mepriz] *nf* mistake, misapprehension; **par m.,** by mistake.

mépriser [meprize] *vt* to despise, to scorn (*s.o., sth*), to hold (*s.o., sth*) in contempt; **méprisé de** *ou* **par qn,** despised *or* scorned by s.o.; **m. les dangers,** to scorn dangers.

mer [mɛr] *nf* **(a)** sea; **la haute** *ou* **grande m., la m. libre,** the open sea, the high seas; **en haute** *ou* **pleine m.,** (out) at sea; **m. fermée,** inland sea, landlocked sea; **M. Rouge/Noire,** Red/Black Sea; **M. Baltique,** Baltic (Sea); *F* **m. d'huile,** sea as smooth as a millpond; **d'une m. à l'autre,** from coast to coast; **au bord de la m.,** at the seaside; **homme/gens de m.,** seaman/seamen, seafaring man/men; **grosse m.,** heavy sea; **il y a de la m.,** the sea is running high, there's a heavy sea; **essuyer un coup de m.,** to be struck by a heavy sea; **un homme à la m.!,** man overboard!; **servir sur m.,** to serve afloat *or* at sea; **voyage sur m.,** sea voyage; **prendre la m.,** to set sail, to put (out) to sea; **mettre une embarcation à la m.,** to get out *or* lower a boat; **tenir la m.,** (*rester au large*) to remain at sea; (*la contrôler*) to hold the seas, to rule the waves; **navire qui tient bien la m.,** ship that behaves well in a seaway; **droit de la m.,** maritime law; **Conférence de l'ONU sur le droit de la m.,** UN Conference on the Law of the Sea; *F* **ce n'est pas la m. à boire,** it's no big deal; *Fig* **une m. de sable,** a vast expanse of sand; *Fig* **une m. de sang,** a sea of blood;

(b) *(marée)* tide; **m. haute, pleine m.,** high tide; **basse m.,** low tide.

mer-air [mɛrɛr] *adj inv Mil* **missile m.-a.,** sea-to-air missile.

mercanti [mɛrkɑ̃ti] *nm* *(marchand)* bazaar-keeper; *Péj* profiteer, shark.

mercantile [mɛrkɑ̃til] *adj* **(a)** *Péj* **esprit m.,** money-grabbing *or* -making mentality; **(b)** *Arch* mercantile, commercial *(operation etc)*.

mercantilisme [mɛrkɑ̃tilism] *nm* **(a)** *Péj* money-grabbing, profiteering; **(b)** *Hist* mercantilism.

mercenaire [mɛrsənɛr] *adj & n* mercenary.

mercerie [mɛrsəri] *nf* **(a)** *(marchandise)* drapery, haberdashery, *Am* notions; **(b)** *(magasin)* draper's, haberdasher's (shop).

merceriser [mɛrsərize] *vt Tex* to mercerize.

merchandisage [mɛrʃɑ̃dizaʒ] *nm,* **merchandising** [mɛrʃɑ̃dajziŋ] *nm Écon* merchandising.

merci [mɛrsi] **1** *nm* thank you; *(refus)* no thank you; **m. bien, m. beaucoup,** thank you very much; **m. de** *ou* **pour votre offre,** thank you for your offer; *souvent Iron* **grand m.!,** (no) thank you!; **mille mercis de** *ou* **pour votre invitation,** thank you so much for your invitation. **2** *nf* mercy; **être à la m. de qn,** to be at s.o.'s mercy; **crier m.,** to cry for mercy; **sans m.,** merciless(ly), pitiless(ly), ruthless(ly).

mercier, -ière [mɛrsje, -jɛr] *n* draper, haberdasher.

mercredi [mɛrkrədi] *nm* Wednesday; **le m. des Cendres,** Ash Wednesday.

mercure [mɛrkyr] **1** *nm Myth Astron etc* **M.,** Mercury. **2** *nm Ch* mercury.

mercuriale[1] [mɛrkyrjal] *nf Bot* mercury.

mercuriale[2] *nf Litt* reprimand, dressing down.

mercuriale[3] *nf* market price list, market prices *(of cereals etc)*.

mercuriel, -ielle [mɛrkyrjɛl] *adj Pharm* mercurial.

mercurochrome ® [mɛrkyrɔkrɔm] *nm* mercurochrome ®.

merde [mɛrd] *Arg* **1** *nf* shit, *surtout Am* crap; **il est dans la m.,** he's in it up to his bloody neck; **il ne se prend pas pour de la m.,** he's got a bloody high opinion of himself; **c'est de la m.,** *(ce qu'il vient de dire)* that's a load of shit; *(ce que tu viens d'acheter)* it's crap; **avec sa voiture de m.,** with his shitty *or* crappy car; **une idée de m.,** a shitty *or* crappy idea; **c'est la m.,** life is shitty, *Am* this sucks. **2** *int* shit!; **m. alors, je ne m'attendais pas à ça,** oh shit, I didn't expect that; **je te dis m.,** *(bonne chance!)* ≈ break a leg!

merdeux, -euse [mɛrdø, -øz] *Arg* **1** *adj* shitty *(linen etc)*; **c'est un bâton m.,** he's bloody impossible; **elle se sent merdeuse,** she feels shitty. **2** *n* *(personne)* shit; **un petit m.,** a little shit.

merdier [mɛrdje] *nm Arg* **je suis dans un sacré m.,** I'm really in the shit.

merdique [mɛrdik] *adj Arg* shitty, crappy.

merdoyer [mɛrdwaje] *vi* **(je merdoie, n. merdoyons; je merdoierai)** *Arg* to make a balls-up *or* a cock-up.

mère [mɛr] **1** *nf* **(a)** mother; *Zool* dam; **elle est m. de famille,** she is the mother of a family; **elle a été une vraie m. pour son frère,** she's been like a mother to her brother; **sœur par la m.,** half-sister; **enfants sans m.,** motherless children; **m. nourrice,** foster mother; *Arch* wet nurse; **m. célibataire,** unmarried mother; **m. porteuse,** surrogate mother; **m. poule,** mother hen; *F* **la m. Martin,** old Mrs Martin; *Arg* **et dites donc, la petite m.!,** well, missus!; *Rel* **m. abbesse,** abbess; **M. supérieure,** mother superior *(of convent)*;

(b) *(source, origine)* **m. de vinaigre,** mother of vinegar; **l'oisiveté est (la) m. de tous les vices,** the devil finds work for idle hands (to do);

(c) *Beaux-Arts Cér* mould, *Am* mold, matrix *(for plaster casts etc)*; *MecE* die *(of screw thread)*.

2 *adj* **langue m.,** mother tongue; *Biol* **cellule m.,** mother cell; *Com* **maison m.,** parent company; **la Reine M.,** the Queen Mother.

mère-patrie [mɛrpatri] *nf* mother country; *(pl mères-patries)*.

merguez [mɛrgɛz] *nf* *(saucisse)* merguez.

méridien, -ienne [meridjɛ̃, -jɛn] **1** *adj* meridian, meridional *(line etc)*; **chaleur méridienne,** midday heat; **ombre méridienne,** shadow at noon; **cercle m.,** transit (circle). **2** *nm* meridian; **sous le m. de vingt degrés à l'ouest de Greenwich,** twenty degrees West of Greenwich. **3** *nf* **méridienne (a)** *Astron* meridian line; *(altitude)* meridian altitude; **(b)** *(sieste)* midday siesta *or* nap.

méridional, -ale, -aux [meridjɔnal, -o] **1** *adj* **(a)** meridional *(distance etc)*; **(b)** *(du sud)* south(ern). **2** *n* southerner.

meringue [mərɛ̃g] *nf Culin* meringue.

meringuer [mərɛ̃ge] *vt Culin* to enclose *(sweet etc)* in meringue; **pommes meringuées,** apple snow.

mérinos [merinos] *nm* merino *(sheep, cloth etc)*; *Arg* **laisser pisser le m.,** to let things run their course.

merise [məriz] *nf* *(fruit)* wild cherry.

merisier [mərizje] *nm* *(arbre)* wild cherry (tree).

méritant [meritɑ̃] *adj* meritorious, deserving; **peu m.,** undeserving.

mérite [merit] *nm* *(qualité estimable)* merit; *(honneur)* credit; *(valeur)* worth; **par order de m.,** in order of merit; **selon ses mérites,** *(être récompensé)* according to one's merits; **ses remarques avaient le m. d'être franches,** his remarks had the merit of being frank; **au seul m.,** *(promotion)* on merit alone; **régime du m.,** merit system; **augmentation au m.,** merit increase; **chose de peu de m.,** thing of little worth *or* value; **tout le m. lui revient,** the credit is all his, all the credit is due to him; **s'attribuer le m. de qch,** to take the credit for sth; **il faut dire à son m. que ...,** it must be said to his credit that ...; **je n'ai aucun m.,** *(c'est naturel)* I deserve no credit, I can't take any credit (for it); **homme de m.,** man of merit *or* talent *or* ability.

mériter [merite] *vt* **(a)** to deserve, to merit; **il n'a que ce qu'il mérite,** he's got what he deserves, it serves him right; **bien m. de la patrie,** to deserve well of one's country; **livre qui mérite d'être lu,** book worth *or* that merits reading; **cela mérite réflexion,** it's worth thinking about, it merits thinking about; **cela mérite d'être vu/entendu,** it's worth seeing/hearing; **tu mérites qu'on te fasse la même chose,** you deserve to have the same (thing) happen to you; **(b) voilà ce qui lui a mérité cette renommée,** this is what earned *or* merited him this fame.

méritoire [meritwar] *adj* meritorious, deserving.

merlan [mɛrlɑ̃] *nm* *(poisson)* whiting; *F* **faire des yeux de m. frit à qn, regarder qn avec des yeux de m. frit,** *(parce qu'on n'a pas compris)* to gape at s.o.; *(parce qu'on est amoureux de lui)* to look gooey-eyed at s.o..

merle [mɛrl] *nm* *(oiseau)* blackbird; **m. d'eau,** water ouzel; **m. blanc,** white blackbird; *Fig* exceptional creature *or* thing, rare bird; *Fig* **vilain m.,** *Iron* **beau m.,** unpleasant person, nasty piece of work.

merlin[1] [mɛrlɛ̃] *nm Nau* marline, small stuff.

merlin[2] *nm* axe, cleaver; *(pour abattre les arbres)* felling axe; *(pour abattre le bétail)* poleaxe.

merluche [mɛrlyʃ] *nf* **(a)** *(poisson)* hake; **(b)** *Culin* dried (unsalted) cod, stockfish.

mer-mer [mɛrmɛr] *adj inv Mil* **missile m.-m.,** sea-to-sea missile.

mérou [meru] *nm* *(poisson)* grouper.

mérovingien, -ienne [merɔvɛ̃ʒjɛ̃, -jɛn] *Hist* **1** *adj* Merovingian. **2** *nm* **M.,** Merovingian.

mer-sol [mɛrsɔl] *adj inv Mil* **missile m.-s.,** sea-to-ground missile.

merveille [mɛrvɛj] *nf* **(a)** marvel, wonder; **les sept merveilles du monde,** the seven wonders of the world; **faire m.** *ou* **des merveilles,** to work *or* do *or* perform wonders; **ce n'est pas m. qu'il soit parti,** it's not surprising he's left; **à m.,** excellently; **cette robe vous va à m.,** the dress suits you wonderfully (well) *or* down to the ground; **se porter à m.,** to be in excellent health *or* in the best of health; **ce chèque tombe à m.,** the cheque has arrived at exactly the right moment; **(b)** *Culin* = sweet fritter.

merveilleusement [mɛrvɛjøzmɑ̃] *adv* marvellously, wonderfully; **aller m. bien,** to be wonderfully well, to be in excellent health.

merveilleux, -euse [mɛrvɛjø, -øz] **1** *adj* marvellous, wonderful. **2** *nm* **le m.,** the supernatural. **3** *n Hist* ultra-fashionable man *or* woman; *m* fop.

mes [me] *voir* **MON.**

mésalliance [mezaljɑ̃s] *nf* unsuitable marriage; **faire une m.,** to marry beneath oneself.

mésallier (se) [səmezalje] *vt* *(conj like* **allier***)* to marry beneath oneself.

mésange [mezɑ̃ʒ] *nf* *(oiseau)* tit; **m. bleue,** bluetit; **m. charbonnière,** great tit; **m. noire,** coaltit.

mésaventure [mezavɑ̃tyr] *nf* misadventure, mishap, mischance.

mésentente [mezɑ̃tɑ̃t] *nf* disagreement; **climat de m.,** *(entre des gens)* coolness.

mésestimation [mezɛstimasjɔ̃] *nf Litt* underestimation, underrating, undervaluing.

mésestime [mezɛstim] *nf Litt* low esteem; **tenir qn en m.,** to hold s.o. in low esteem.

mésestimer [mezɛstime] *vt* to have a poor *or* low opinion of (*s.o.*); **elle a tendance à m. la difficulté,** she tends to underestimate the difficulty of things.

mésintelligence [mezɛ̃teliʒɑ̃s] *nf* disagreement; **être en m. avec qn,** to be at loggerheads with s.o..

mesmérisme [mɛsmerism] *nm* mesmerism.

méson [mezɔ̃] *nm Nucl* meson.

Mésopotamie [mezɔpɔtami] *nf* Mesopotamia.

mésopotamien, -ienne [mezɔpɔtamjɛ̃, -jɛn] **1** *adj* Mesopotamian. **2** *n* **M.,** Mesopotamian.

mésothérapie [mezɔterapi] *nf Méd* = anti-cellulite treatment involving the use of needles.

mésozoïque [mezɔzɔik] *adj Géol* mesozoic.

mesquin [mɛskɛ̃] *adj* (*caractère, apparence*) mean, shabby; (*excuse etc*) paltry, petty; (*avare*) mean, niggardly, stingy; **un coup m.,** a mean *or* shabby trick.

mesquinement [mɛskinmɑ̃] *adv* meanly.

mesquinerie [mɛskinri] *nf* (*de caractère, procédé*) meanness, pettiness; (*avarice*) niggardliness; **je ne te savais pas capable de telles mesquineries,** I would never have thought you capable of such meanness *or* pettiness, I didn't think you could be so mean *or* petty.

mess [mɛs] *nm Mil* mess.

message [mesaʒ] *nm* message; **m. publicitaire,** advertisement; **chanson/pièce/***etc* **à m.,** song/play/*etc* with a message.

messager, -ère [mesaʒe, -ɛr] **1** *n* messenger; **m. de malheur,** bearer of bad news; *Litt* **m. du printemps,** harbinger of spring. **2** *nm* carrier (*of parcels, cargo*).

messagerie [mesaʒri] *nf* carrying trade; **service de messageries,** parcel delivery; **messageries maritimes/aériennes,** shipping line/air freight company; **bureau de(s) messageries,** (*maritimes*) shipping office; *Rail* parcel(s) office; *Arch* stagecoach office; **m. de presse,** newspaper distributors; **m. électronique,** electronic mail(ing).

messe [mɛs] *nf Rel* (low) mass; **m. des morts,** requiem mass; **célébrer** *ou* **dire la m.,** to celebrate *or* say mass; *Mus* **m. en si mineur,** mass in B minor; *F* **pas de messes basses!,** stop whispering!; **elles font toujours des messes basses,** they're always whispering; **m. noire,** black mass.

messeoir [meswar] *vi* (*prp* **messeyant**; *pp is lacking*; *pr ind* **il messied, ils messeyent**; *pr sub* **il messeye**; *impf* **il messeyait**; *p hist is lacking*; *fu* **il messiéra**) *Arch & Litt* to be unbecoming *or* unseemly; **il lui messied de ...,** it ill becomes him to ... .

messianique [mesjanik] *adj* Messianic.

messianisme [mesjanism] *nm* Messianism.

messidor [mesidɔr] *nm Hist* tenth month of the French Republican calendar (*19-20 June-19-20 July*).

Messie [mesi] *nm* Messiah; *F* **on l'a attendu comme le M.,** we were waiting eagerly for him.

messin, -ine [mesɛ̃, -in] **1** *adj* of Metz. **2** *n* **M.,** native *or* inhabitant of Metz.

messire [mesir] *nm Arch* Sir, Master.

mesurable [məzyrabl] *adj* measurable, *Spéc* mensurable.

mesurage [məzyraʒ] *nm* measuring, measurement.

mesure [məzyr] *nf* **(a)** measurement; (*action*) measurement, measuring; **appareil de m.,** measuring apparatus; **prendre les mesures de qn,** to take s.o.'s measurements, to measure s.o.; **prendre les mesures de qch,** to measure sth; **prendre la m. de qn,** to size s.o. up; **complet (fait) sur mesure(s),** made-to-measure *or Am* custom-made suit; *Fig* **être en m. de faire qch,** to be in a position to do sth; *Fig* **ces vacances, c'est du sur m.,** these holidays are just the ticket *or* suit us down to the ground; *Fig* **donner sa m.,** to show what one is capable of; *Fig* **être à la m. de qn/qch,** to measure up to s.o./sth; *Sp & Fig* **trouver un adversaire à sa m.,** to meet one's match;

(b) dans une certaine m., in some degree, to a certain extent; **dans une large m.,** to a large extent; **dans la m. où,** insofar as; **je vous aiderai dans la m. de mes forces** *ou* **du possible,** I'll help you to the best of my ability *or* as much as I can *or* as best I can;

(c) (au fur et) à m., in proportion; (*l'un après l'autre*) successively, one by one; **je vérifie les chiffres à m.,** I check the figures as I go along; **à m. que,** (in proportion) as; **à m. que je reculais, il s'avançait,** as (fast as) I retreated he advanced;

(d) (*action*) measure, step, action; **m. de sécurité,** safety measure *or* precaution; **prendre des mesures,** to take measures *or* steps *or* action, to adopt measures; **prendre des mesures pour faire qch,** to take measures *or* steps to do sth, to make arrangements for doing sth; **prendre des mesures contre qch,** to take action against sth; **prendre ses mesures,** to make one's arrangements (**pour que,** in order that); **par m. de sécurité/d'hygiène,** for reasons of safety/hygiene; **par m. d'économie,** as a cost-saving measure;

(e) *Math etc* measure; **verser une m. de vin à qn,** to pour s.o. out a measure of wine; **faites-moi bonne m.,** give me good measure; **commune m.,** common measure; *Fig* **il n'y a pas commune m. entre ces deux vins,** there is no comparison between the two wines; **m. de longueur,** measure of length; **m. de surface** *ou* **de superficie,** square measure; **m. de volume,** cubic measure; **poids et mesures,** weights and measures;

(f) required size *or* amount; **pièces qui ne sont pas de m.,** pieces that are not the right size *or* that are not to size; **rester dans la juste m.,** to keep within bounds; **elle n'a pas le sens de la m.,** she has no sense of moderation; **(dé)passer la m.,** to overstep the mark, to overdo it; **ne garder aucune m., oublier toute m.,** to fling aside all restraint, to lose all sense of moderation *or* proportion; **ambition sans m.,** unbounded ambition;

(g) *Escrime* measure, reach, distance;

(h) *Mus* bar; (*temps*) time; **m. à quatre temps,** four-four time, common time; **battre la m.,** to beat time; **barre de m.,** bar line; **en m.,** in (strict) time; **aller en m.,** to keep time; **deux mesures plus loin,** two bars further on;

(i) metre, *US* meter (*of verse*).

mesuré [məzyre] *adj* measured (*tread etc*); temperate, moderate, restrained (*language etc*).

mesurément [məzyremɑ̃] *adv* moderately, with *or* in moderation.

mesurer [məzyre] **1** *vt* **(a)** to measure (*dimensions*); to measure out (*flour, sugar etc*); to measure up (*wood, land*); to measure off (*cloth etc*); to size (*s.o., sth*) up; **m. un client,** to take a customer's measurements; **m. qn des yeux,** to look s.o. up and down; **m. deux mètres,** (*d'une personne*) to be two metres tall; **la colonne mesure dix mètres,** the column measures ten metres *or* is ten metres high; **on mesure le travail au résultat,** the work is judged by results; **m. la nourriture à qn,** to ration s.o.'s food; **le temps vous sera mesuré pour cette épreuve,** you will have a limited amount of time for this test; **m. sa dépense sur ses profits,** to cut one's coat according to one's cloth; **m. la distance à la vue,** to judge *or* estimate *or* gauge distance with one's eyes;

(b) (*ménager, régler*) to calculate, to measure, to weigh (*one's words etc*); **m. le châtiment à l'offense,** to make the punishment fit the crime; **mesure ton vocabulaire!,** moderate your language!; **il ne mesure pas la portée de ses paroles,** he says things without thinking.

2 se mesurer *vpr* **se m. avec** *ou* **à qn,** to measure one's strength against s.o., to measure *or* pit oneself against s.o.; **vous n'êtes pas de force** *ou* **de taille à vous m. avec lui,** you're no match for him; **les adversaires se mesurèrent des yeux,** the opponents sized each other up.

mesureur [məzyrœr] *nm* (*person, device*) measurer; **m. de pression,** pressure gauge.

mésuser [mezyze] *vi* **m. de son bien,** to misuse one's wealth; **m. de son pouvoir,** to abuse one's power.

métabolique [metabɔlik] *adj* metabolic.

métabolisme [metabɔlism] *nm* metabolism.

métacarpe [metakarp] *nm Anat* metacarpus.

métacarpien, -ienne [metakarpjɛ̃, -jɛn] *adj & nm Anat* metacarpal.

métacentre [metasɑ̃tr] *nm Phys* metacentre, *US* metacenter.

métairie [meteri] *nf* small farm (*held on métayage agreement*).

métal, -aux [metal, -o] *nm* **(a)** metal; **métaux précieux,** precious metals; **m. antifriction/blanc,** Babbitt (metal)/white metal; **m. (blanc) anglais,** Britannia metal; **(b)** *Fin* **m. en barres,** bullion.

métalangage [metalɑ̃gaʒ] *nm* metalanguage.

métallifère [metalifɛr] *adj* metalliferous, metal bearing.

métallique [metalik] *adj* metallic; **câble m.,** wire rope; **plume m.,** steel nib; **rendre un son m.,** to clang, to clank; *Fin* **réserve m.,** bullion reserve.

métallisation [metalizasjɔ̃] *nf* **(a)** metallization; converting (*of ore etc*) into metal; **(b)** plating (*with metal*); **(c)** *Phot* bronzing (*of print*).

métallisé [metalize] *adj surtout Aut* metallic (*paint etc*); **voiture bleu m.,** metallic blue car.

métalliser [metalize] *vt* to metallize.

métallo [metalo] *nm F* metalworker.

métallurgie [metalyrʒi] *nf* metallurgy; **crise dans la m.,** crisis in the metallurgical industry.

métallurgique [metalyrʒik] *adj* metallurgic(al).

métallurgiste [metalyrʒist] *nm* **(a)** (*scientifique*) metallurgist; **(b)** (*ouvrier*) metalworker.

métamorphique [metamɔrfik] *adj Géol* metamorphic.

métamorphiser [metamɔrfize] *vt Géol* to metamorphose.

métamorphisme [metamɔrfism] *nm Géol* metamorphism.

métamorphose [metamɔrfoz] *nf* metamorphosis, transformation; *Fig* **quelle m.!,** (*on ne le reconnaît pas*) what a transformation!

métamorphoser [metamɔrfoze] **1** *vt* to metamorphose, to transform; *Fig* **ce voyage l'a métamorphosé,** the journey transformed him. **2 se métamorphoser** *vpr* to change completely, to be transformed.

métaphore [metafɔr] *nf* metaphor, figure of speech, image; **m. disparate** *ou* **incohérente,** mixed metaphor.

métaphorique [metafɔrik] *adj* metaphoric(al), figurative.

métaphoriquement [metafɔrikmɑ̃] *adv* metaphorically, figuratively.

métaphysicien, -ienne [metafizisjɛ̃, -jɛn] *n* metaphysician.

métaphysique [metafizik] **1** *adj* metaphysical. **2** *nf* metaphysics.

métaphysiquement [metafizikmɑ̃] *adv* metaphysically.

métapsychique [metapsiʃik] **1** *adj* psychic (*phenomenon*). **2** *nf* parapsychology.

métastase [metastɑz] *nf Méd* metastasis; **former des métastases,** (*d'un cancer*) to metastasize.

métatarse [metatars] *nm Anat* metatarsus.

métatarsien, -ienne [metatarsjɛ̃, -jɛn] *adj & nm Anat* metatarsal.

métathèse [metatɛz] *nf Ling* metathesis.

métayage [metɛjaʒ] *nm Agr* sharecropping.

métayer, -ère [meteje, -ɛr] *n Agr* sharecropper.

métazoaire [metazɔɛr] *nm Biol* metazoan; **métazoaires,** Metazoa.

métempsycose [metɑ̃psikoz] *nf* metempsychosis.

météo [meteo] *F* **1** *nf* **(a)** weather forecast *or* report; **la m. est mauvaise pour toute la semaine,** the weather forecast is bad for the whole week; **(b)** (= **bureau central de météorologie**) meteorological *or* weather office, met office. **2** *nm F* **Monsieur M.,** the weather man. **3** *adj* meteorological; **bulletin m.,** weather report *or* forecast; **station m.,** meteorological *or* weather station; **frégate** *ou* **navire m.,** weather ship.

météore [meteɔr] *nm* meteor.

météorique [meteɔrik] *adj* meteoric.

météorite [meteɔrit] *n* meteorite.

météorologie [meteɔrɔlɔʒi] *nf* meteorology; **le bureau central de m.,** = the meteorological *or* weather office.

météorologique [meteɔrɔlɔʒik] *adj* = **MÉTÉO 3.**

météorologiste [meteɔrɔlɔʒist], **météorologue** [meteɔrɔlɔg] *n* meteorologist.

métèque [metɛk] *nm* **(a)** *Antiq* metic; **(b)** *F* (*terme injurieux*) wog; (*espagnol*) dago.

méthane [metan] *nm Ch* methane.

méthanier [metanje] *nm Nau* methane tanker.

méthode [metɔd] *nf* **(a)** (*démarche*) method, way; **m. pour faire qch,** method *or* way of doing sth; **elle a sa m.,** she has her own method *or* way of doing things; **il a beaucoup de m.,** he's very methodical; **avec m.,** methodical(ly), systematical(ly); **sans m.,** unmethodical(ly), unsystematical(ly); **je vais changer de m.,** I'm going to change my methods; *F* **c'est la seule m. à suivre,** it's the only way to do it; *F* **il n'y a pas 36 méthodes,** it's the only way; **(b)** (*livre*) primer, grammar; **m. de piano,** piano tutor.

méthodique [metɔdik] *adj* methodical, systematic.

méthodiquement [metɔdikmɑ̃] *adv* methodically, systematically.

méthodisme [metɔdism] *nm Rel* Methodism.

méthodiste [metɔdist] *adj & n Rel* Methodist.

méthodologie [metɔdɔlɔʒi] *nf* methodology.

méthodologique [metɔdɔlɔʒik] *adj* methodological.

méthyle [metil] *nm Ch* methyl.

méthylène [metilɛn] *nm Ch* methylene.

méthylique [metilik] *adj* methyl(ic).

méticuleusement [metikyløzmɑ̃] *adv* meticulously.

méticuleux, -euse [metikylø, -øz] *adj* meticulous, **par trop m.,** over-meticulous; **la maison est d'une propreté méticuleuse,** the house is immaculate *or* spotless(ly clean); **elle est peu méticuleuse dans son travail,** she is not very meticulous about her work.

méticulosité [metikylozite] *nf Litt* meticulousness.

métier [metje] *nm* **(a)** trade, profession, occupation; **quel est votre m.?,** what do you do (for a living)?, what's your job?; **exercer** *ou* **faire un m.,** to carry on a trade *or* a profession; **il est charpentier de son m.,** he's a carpenter by trade; **elle a un bon m.,** she has a good job; **il sent qu'il est temps de changer de m.,** he feels it's time he changed his job; **ils sont du m.,** they're in the trade; *Fig* **ce n'est pas mon m.,** it's not my job; **tours de m.,** tricks of the trade; **parler m.,** to talk shop; *F* **quel m.!,** what a life!; **quel m. de fou!,** you don't have to be crazy to do this job but it helps!; *Hist* **corps de m.,** corporation, g(u)ild; **chacun son m.,** everyone to his trade; *Fig* **c'est le m. qui rentre,** put it down to experience; **il a du m.,** he knows what he's doing; **il manque encore de m.,** he still lacks experience; **homme de m.,** craftsman; **École des Arts et Métiers,** = engineering college (*of university level*); **gens de m.,** experts, professionals; **terme de m.,** technical term; **armée de m.,** regular army;
(b) *Tex* **m. à tisser,** loom; **m. mécanique,** power loom; **m. à filer,** spinning frame; **m. à tapisserie,** tapestry frame; **m. à broder,** embroidery fram, tambour frame; *Fig* **avoir un ouvrage sur le m.,** to have a piece of work in hand.

métis, -isse [meti, -is] **1** *adj* **(a)** (*of person*) halfcaste; (*animal*) crossbreed; (*dog*) mongrel; **plante métisse,** hybrid plant; **(b)** *Tex* **tissu m.,** linen/cotton mixture. **2** *n* (*personne*) halfcaste; *Péj* halfbreed; (*animal*) crossbreed; (*dog*) mongrel. **3** *nm Tex* linen/cotton mixture.

métissage [metisaʒ] *nm* crossbreeding.

métisser [metise] *vt* to cross(breed).

métonymie [metɔnimi] *nf Ling* metonymy.

métrage [metraʒ] *nm* **(a)** (*action*) measuring, measure(ment); *Constr* quantity surveying; **(b)** (*longueur*) (metric) length; **grand/petit m.,** (*tissu*) cut lengthways/crossways; **des métrages de lin,** lengths of linen; **(c)** *Cin* footage, length (*of film*); **long m.,** feature film; **court m.,** short.

mètre[1] [mɛtr] *nm* **(a)** metre, *US* meter; **m. carré/cube,** square/cubic metre; *Sp* **elle se prépare à courir un deux cents mètres (haies),** she's training for the two hundred metres (hurdles); **l'épreuve du 400 mètres,** the 400 metres (race); **(b)** (*ruban etc*) (metre) rule; **m. pliant,** folding rule; **m. à ruban,** tape measure.

mètre[2] *nm Littér* metre, *US* meter.

métré [metre] *nm Constr* measurement(s) (*of building land etc*); (*devis*) bill of quantities.

métrer [metre] *vt* (**je mètre; je métrerai**) **(a)** to measure (by the metre *or US* meter); **(b)** *Constr* to survey (for quantities).

métreur, -euse [metrœr, -øz] *n* **m. (vérificateur),** quantity surveyor.

métrique[1] [metrik] *adj* metric; **adopter le système m.,** to adopt the metric system, *F* to go metric.

métrique[2] *Littér* **1** *adj* metric(al). **2** *nf* prosody, metrics.

métro (le) [ləmetro] *nm F* the underground, *Am* the subway; **le m. de Paris/de Montréal,** the Paris/Montreal metro; **le m. de Londres,** the London underground (system), *F* the tube; **prendre le m.,** to take the underground (railway).

métro-boulot-dodo [metrobulododo] *nm F* the daily grind, the daily routine; **je n'en pouvais plus du m.-b.-d.,** I couldn't take the routine any more; **ma vie se résume au m.-b.-d.,** I'm leading a very humdrum existence *or* dull life.

métrologie [metrɔlɔʒi] *nf* metrology.

métrologique [metrɔlɔʒik] *adj* metrological.

métrologiste [metrɔlɔʒist] *n* metrologist.

métronome [metrɔnɔm] *nm Mus* metronome.

métropole [metrɔpɔl] *nf* **(a)** (*grande ville*) metropolis; (*capitale*) capital; **faire de Marseille une m. d'équilibre,** to turn Marseilles into a second capital; **(b)** (*état*) mother country; **(c)** *Rel* metropolis; see (*of archbishop*).

métropolitain, -aine [metrɔpɔlitɛ̃, -ɛn] **1** *adj* **(a)** *Admin* metropolitan; **armée métropolitaine,** home army; **(b)** *Rel* metropolitan (*church etc*); archiepiscopal. **2** *nm* **(a)** *Admin* underground (railway), *Am* subway; **(b)** *Rel* archbishop; (*de l'Église orthodoxe*) metropolitan.

mets [mɛ] *nm* food.

mettable [metabl] *adj* (*of clothes etc*) wearable; **pas m.,** not fit to wear; **elle dit n'avoir plus rien de m.,** she says she has nothing to wear.

metteur, -euse [metœr, -øz] *n* **m. en scène,** *Th* producer; *Cin* director; *Rad* **m. en ondes,** producer; *Rail*

m. de rails, platelayer, *Am* tracklayer; **m. en œuvre,** mounter (*of jewellery etc*).

mettre [mɛtr] *v* (*prp* **mettant**; *pp* **mis**; *pr ind* **je mets, il met, n. mettons, ils mettent**; *p hist* **je mis**; *fu* **je mettrai**) **1** *vt* **(a)** to put, to lay, to place, to set; **mettez tout cela par terre,** put all that on the floor; **m. la table** *ou* **le couvert,** to lay *or* set the table; **elle a décidé de m. le chauffage central/l'électricité,** she decided to have central heating/electricity installed *or* put in; **m. la main sur qn,** to lay hands on s.o.; **m. un manche à un balai,** to fit a handle to a broom; **m. une annonce dans les journaux,** to put an advertisement in the (news)papers; **m. qn à la porte,** to turn *or* throw s.o. out; (*le renvoyer*) to dismiss *or F* sack s.o.; **je vais vous m. à votre porte,** (*à pied*) I'll see *or* take you home; (*en voiture*) I'll take you home; **m. des enfants au collège,** to send children (away) to school; **m. qn à faire qch,** to set s.o. to do sth; **m. un enjeu,** to lay a stake; **m. de l'argent sur un cheval,** to put *or* stake money on a horse, to back a horse; **qu'est-ce qui vous a mis cela dans la tête?,** what put that into your head?; **m. le feu à qch,** to set fire to sth, to set sth on fire; *Aut* **m. le contact** *ou* **les gaz,** to start the engine *or* car; *F* **j'ai bien envie de lui m. une gifle,** I feel like slapping him; *Arg* **on va leur m. la pâtée,** (*les battre*) we're going to hammer them;

(b) (*consacrer*) **m. du temps à faire qch,** to take time over sth; **j'ai mis deux ans à faire cela,** I took *or* it took me two years to do that; **j'y mettrai tous mes soins,** I'll give it my full attention; **je ne veux pas y m. plus de 50 francs,** I don't want to spend more than 50 francs (on it); **m. cinq cents francs à qch,** to spend 500F on sth, to give 500F for sth;

(c) to put on (*clothes*); **qu'est-ce que je vais m.?,** what shall I wear?; **mettez votre robe bleue,** put your blue dress on; **ne plus m.,** to stop wearing (*a garment*); **j'ai du mal à m. mes souliers,** I find it difficult to get my shoes on; *Arg* **il va falloir les m.!,** we'd better scram *or* run for it!; (*se depêcher*) we'd better get our skates on!;

(d) m. sécher du linge, m. du linge à sécher, to hang the washing up *or* out (to dry); **m. de l'eau à chauffer,** to put some water on to heat (up); **quand on le met à causer,** once you start him *or* get him talking;

(e) to set, to put (*in a condition*); to put on, to turn on, to switch on (*gas, television etc*); **m. une machine en mouvement,** to set a machine going; **m. sa montre à l'heure,** to set one's watch to the correct time; **m. le réveil à cinq heures,** to set the alarm for five o'clock; **m. un texte au propre,** to make a fair copy of a text; **m. qch en œuvre,** to implement sth; **m. qch en marche,** to start sth (up), to set sth in motion; **m. la radio plus fort,** to turn up the radio; **m. des vers en musique,** to set verse to music; **il a fallu m. le texte en espagnol,** the text had to be put into Spanish; **m. le nom au pluriel,** to put the noun into the plural; **m. qch par écrit,** to put sth in writing; **m. son argent en fonds de terre,** to invest one's money in real estate; **ça le met dans tous ses états,** that gets him into a state; **m. qn à la torture,** to put *or* subject s.o. to torture; *Nau* **m. une voile au vent,** to hoist *or* set a sail;

(f) (*admettre*) to admit, to grant; **mettons que vous avez** *ou* **ayez raison,** suppose you're right; **mettons cent francs,** (let's) call it a hundred francs; **mettons qu'il en soit ainsi,** let's assume that that's the case; **mettez que je n'ai rien dit,** pretend I didn't say anything;

(g) (*écrire*) to write; **mettez votre signature au bas de la page,** put your signature at the bottom of the page; **mets que je le remercie,** (*sur la lettre*) tell him thanks.

2 se mettre *vpr* **(a)** (*se placer*) to go, to get; **se m. derrière un arbre,** to go *or* get behind a tree; **se m. au lit,** to get into bed; **se m. à table,** to sit down at (the) table; **se m. contre un mur,** to stand *or* lean against a wall; **mettez-vous auprès du feu,** sit (down) by the fire; **où dois-je me m.?,** where do you want me to stand *or* sit?; *Fig* **je ne savais plus où me m.,** I didn't know where to put myself; **se m. au service de qn,** to enter s.o.'s service;

(b) se m. à (faire) qch, to begin *or* start *or* set about (doing) sth; **se m. au travail,** to start *or* set to work; **il est temps de s'y m.,** we'd better get down to it *or* get on with it; **il s'y est mis de bonne heure,** he started early *or* young; **se m. au régime,** to put oneself on a diet, to go on a diet; **se m. à l'allemand,** to start (learning) German; **se m. à la politique,** to go in for *or* take up politics; **se m. à rire,** to begin *or* start to laugh, to start laughing; **il s'est mis à boire,** he's taken to drink; **il s'est mis à pleuvoir,** it began *or* started to rain, it came on to rain; **se m. en rage,** to get into a rage; **se m. en route,** to start off, to set off, to start on one's way; **on a fini par se m. d'accord,** we finally reached agreement; **se m. au pas,** (*dans un défilé*) to fall into step; to slow down to a walk (*after running*);

(c) (*pour des vêtements*) to dress; **je n'ai rien à me m.,** I haven't got anything to wear, I haven't a thing to wear; **se m. en smoking/en jupe,** to put on a dinner jacket/a skirt; **se m. un pull chaud,** to put on a warm pullover;

(d) le temps se met au beau, the weather's turning out fine; **le temps se met à la pluie,** it's turning to rain;

(e) qu'est-ce qu'ils se sont mis!, they went at it hammer and tongs, they really laid into each other!

3 *vi* **il faudra m. dans les 5 000 francs,** you'll have to spend about 5,000 francs; *Nau* **m. à la voile,** to set sail; *Arg* **qu'est-ce qu'on va lui m.!,** we'll hammer him!

meublant [mœblɑ̃] *adj* **(a)** furnishing (*fabric etc*); **(b)** *Jur* **meubles meublants,** movables.

meuble [mœbl] **1** *adj* movable; *Jur* **biens meubles,** movables, personal estate, chattels, personalty; *Agr* **terre m.,** light *or* running soil. **2** *nm* **(a)** piece of furniture; **meubles,** furniture; **m. d'angle,** corner unit; **m. de bureau,** piece of office furniture; **meubles anciens,** (*antiquités*) antique furniture; (*copies*) reproduction furniture; **être dans ses meubles,** to have a place of one's own; **(b)** *Jur* movable, chattel.

meublé [mœble] **1** *adj* furnished (*room etc*); **non m.,** unfurnished; **pièce pauvrement meublée,** poorly furnished room; **cave bien meublée,** well-stocked cellar. **2** *nm* furnished room; (*appartement*) furnished flat *or Am* apartment; **habiter en m.,** to live in lodgings; (*dans un appartement*) to live in a furnished flat.

meubler [mœble] **1** *vt* to furnish (*room*); to stock (*farm, cellar*) (**de,** with); *Fig* **m. sa tête de choses inutiles,** to fill one's head with useless things; **m. la conversation,** to make conversation. **2 se meubler** *vpr* to furnish one's home.

meuglement [møgləmɑ̃] *nm* lowing, mooing (*of cow*); moaning (*of siren etc*).

meugler [møgle] *vi* (*of cow*) to low, to moo.

meulage [mølaʒ] *nm* grinding (down).

meule [møl] *nf* **(a)** stack, rick (*of hay etc*); clamp (*of bricks*); (*fumier*) mushroom compost; **mettre le foin en m.,** to stack *or* rick the hay; **m. de foin,** haystack, hayrick; **(b)** (*de moulin*) millstone; **m. courante,** runner; **m. à aiguiser,** grindstone; **m. à polir,** buff(ing) wheel; **m. de fromage,** (whole) cheese.

meuler [møle] *vt* to grind (*chisel etc*); to grind (down) (*lens etc*).

meulette [mølɛt] *nf* small haystack.

meulier, -ière [mølje, -jɛr] **1** *adj* pertaining to millstones *or* grindstones; **pierre meulière,** millstone (grit). **2** *nm* millstone maker, grindstone maker. **3** *nf* **meulière (a)** (*carrière*) millstone quarry; **(b)** (*pierre*) millstone (grit).

meunerie [mønri] *nf* **(a)** (*activité*) (flour) milling; **(b)** *Com* milling trade.

meunier, -ière [mønje, -jɛr] **1** *nm* miller; **garçon m.,** millhand. **2** *nf* **meunière (a)** miller's wife; *Culin* **truite m.,** trout meunière (*coated with flour and fried in butter*); **(b)** (*oiseau*) long-tailed tit. **3** *adj* (flour-)milling (*plant, process etc*).

meurt-de-faim [mœrdəfɛ̃] *n inv F* down-and-out.

meurtre [mœrtr] *nm* murder, voluntary manslaughter; **au m.!,** murder!; *Fig* **c'est un m. de retoucher ces tableaux,** it's a crime *or* it's downright vandalism to touch up these pictures; **quel est le mobile du m.?,** what is the motive for the murder?

meurtri [mœrtri] *adj* bruised (*arm, fruit etc*); **visage m.,** battered face; (*par la fatigue*) ravaged face; **être tout m.,** to be black and blue all over.

meurtrier, -ière [mœrtrije, -ijɛr] **1** *adj* **(a)** murderous (*war*); deadly, lethal (*weapon etc*); **colère meurtrière,** murderous rage; **l'imprudence rend la route meurtrière,** reckless driving turns roads into death traps; **(b)** *Arch* (*person*) murderous, guilty of murder. **2** *n* murderer, *f* murderess. **3** *nf* **meurtrière,** loophole.

meurtrir [mœrtrir] *vt* to bruise (*one's arm, fruit etc*); **m. qn de coups,** to beat s.o. black and blue.

meurtrissure [mœrtrisyr] *nf* bruise.

Meuse [møz] *nf* (the river) Meuse, Maas.

meute [møt] *nf* **(a)** pack (*of staghounds etc*); **chiens de m.,** hounds; **lancer la m.,** to loose the pack *or* hounds; **(b)** crowd, mob, pack (*of people in pursuit*).

mévente [mevɑ̃t] *nf* **(a)** slump, stagnation (*of business*); **(b)** sale (*of goods*) at a loss.

mexicain, -aine [mɛksikɛ̃, -ɛn] **1** *adj* Mexican. **2** *n* **M.,** Mexican.

Mexico [mɛksiko] *n* Mexico City.

Mexique (le) [ləmɛksik] *nm* Mexico.

mézigue [mezig] *pron pers Arg (moi)* yours truly; **c'est pour m.,** it's for yours truly; **les plaintes c'est pour m.,** yours truly has to cope with the complaints; **et m.?,** what about me?

mezzanine [mɛdzanin] *nf* **(a)** mezzanine (floor); **(b)** *(fenêtre)* mezzanine window; **(c)** *Th* dress circle, *Am* mezzanine.

mezzo(-soprano) [mɛdzosɔprano] *Mus (pl mezzo-sopranos, -soprani)* **1** *nm* mezzo(-soprano) (voice). **2** *nf (woman)* mezzo(-soprano).

mezzo-tinto [mɛdzotinto] *nm inv* mezzotint.

MF [ɛmɛf] *nf (abrév* **modulation de fréquence***)* FM.

mg *(abrév* **milligramme***)* mg.

Mgr *Rel (abrév* **Monseigneur***)* Mgr.

mi¹ [mi] *adv* **paupières mi-closes,** half-closed eyelids; **la mi-avril/-mai/***etc*, mid-April/-May/*etc*; **à mi-hauteur,** halfway up *or* down; **tissu mi-laine mi-soie,** wool-silk mixture; **faire qch mi de gré mi de force,** to do sth half willingly half unwillingly; **acier mi-doux,** semi-mild steel.

mi² *nm inv Mus* **(a)** (the note) E; **morceau en mi,** piece in E; **(b)** first string, E string *(of violin)*; **(c)** mi *(in the Fixed Do system)*.

miam-miam [mjammjam] **1** *int* yum, yum. **2** *nm Enf* **faire m.-m.,** to eat.

miaou [mjau] *nm* miaow, mew; **faire m.,** *(of cat)* to miaow, to mew.

miasmatique [mjasmatik] *adj* miasmic, miasmatic, miasmal, noxious *(exhalation etc)*.

miasme [mjasm] *nm* miasma.

miaulement [mjolmɑ̃] *nm* mewing, miaowing; *(plus aigu)* caterwauling.

miauler [mjole] *vi* to mew, to miaow; *(de façon plus aiguë)* to caterwaul.

miauleur, -euse [mjolœr, -øz] *adj* mewing, miaowing *(cat)*.

mi-bas [mibɑ] *nm inv* knee(-length) sock; *Com* half-hose.

mi-bois (à) [amibwa] *adv Menuis* **assemblage à mi-b.,** halved joint.

mica [mika] *nm Minér* mica.

mi-carême [mikarɛm] *nf* mid-Lent; *(pl mi-carêmes)*.

micaschiste [mikaʃist] *nm Minér* mica schist.

miche [miʃ] *nf* **(a)** *(pain)* round loaf; *Br* cob (loaf); **(b)** *Arg* **miches,** *(fesses)* bum, *Am* butt; *(seins)* boobs, tits.

Michel [miʃɛl] *nm* Michael; **la Saint-M.,** Michaelmas.

Michel-Ange [mikɛlɑ̃ʒ] *nm* Michelangelo.

micheline [miʃlin] *nf Rail* railcar *(invented and equipped by the Michelin Tyre Company)*.

mi-chemin (à) [amiʃmɛ̃] *adv* halfway, midway.

mi-clos [miklo] *adj* half-closed, half-shut *(eyes etc)*; *(pl mi-clos(es))*.

micmac [mikmak] *nm F* intrigue, scheming; *(résultat)* put-up job; *(désordre)* muddle.

micocoulier [mikɔkulje] *nm Bot* nettle tree.

mi-corps (à) [amikɔr] *adv* **portrait à mi-c.,** half-length portrait; **saisi à mi-c.,** caught round the waist.

mi-côte (à) [amikot] *adv* halfway up *or* down the hill.

mi-course (à) [amikurs] *adv Sp* at the halfway mark.

micro [mikro] **1** *nm F* **(a)** *(microphone)* mike; **parler au m.,** to speak into the mike; **m. caché,** bug; **(b)** *(micro-ordinateur)* micro(computer). **2** *nf* microcomputing.

microanalyse [mikrɔanaliz] *nf Ch* microanalysis.

microbalance [mikrɔbalɑ̃s] *nf Phys* microbalance.

microbe [mikrɔb] *nm* microbe; *(bacterium)* germ, *F* bug; **je ne veux pas que tu me donnes tes microbes,** I don't want your germs; *Fig* **écrase-toi, m.!,** push off, you little squirt!

microbicide [mikrɔbisid] **1** *adj* microbicidal, germ-killing. **2** *nm* microbicide, germ-killer.

microbien, -ienne [mikrɔbjɛ̃, -jɛn] *adj* microbial, microbic *(disease etc)*.

microbiologie [mikrɔbjɔlɔʒi] *nf* microbiology.

microbiologiste [mikrɔbjɔlɔʒist] *n* microbiologist.

micro-canal [mikrɔkanal] *nm Ordinat* **architecture à m.-canaux,** microchannel architecture; *(pl micro-canaux)*.

microcéphale [mikrɔsefal] **1** *adj* microcephalous, microcephalic. **2** *n* microcephalic.

microchirurgie [mikrɔʃiryrʒi] *nf Méd* microsurgery.

microcircuit [mikrɔsirkɥi] *nm Ordinat* microcircuit; **microcircuits,** microcircuitry.

microclimat [mikrɔklima] *nm* microclimate.

microcosme [mikrɔkɔsm] *nm* microcosm; **en m.,** in microcosm; *Fig* **le m.,** *(décideurs etc)* opinion-makers.

micro-édition [mikrɔedisjɔ̃] *nf Ordinat* desktop publishing, DTP.

micro-espacement [mikrɔɛspasmɑ̃] *nm Ordinat* microspacing; *(pl micro-espacements)*.

microfarad [mikrɔfarad] *nm* microfarad.

microfiche [mikrɔfiʃ] *nf Phot* microfiche.

microfilm [mikrɔfilm] *nm Phot* microfilm.

microfilmer [mikrɔfilme] *vt Phot* to microfilm.

microglossaire [mikrɔglɔsɛr] *nm* special language.

micrographie [mikrɔgrafi] *nf* micrography.

micro-informatique [mikrɔɛ̃fɔrmatik] *nf Ordinat* microcomputing.

micromètre [mikrɔmɛtr] *nm* micrometer.

micrométrique [mikrɔmetrik] *adj* micrometric(al); **vis m.,** micrometer screw.

micron [mikrɔ̃] *nm* micron.

micro-onde [mikrɔɔ̃d] *nf* micro-wave; **four à micro-ondes,** microwave oven; *(pl micro-ondes)*.

micro-ondes [mikrɔɔ̃d] *nm (four)* microwave (oven); **faire cuire qch au m.-o.,** to cook sth in the microwave, to microwave sth.

micro-ordinateur [mikrɔɔrdinatœr] *nm Ordinat* micro(computer); *(pl micro-ordinateurs)*.

micro-organisme [mikrɔɔrganism] *nm* micro-organism; *(pl micro-organismes)*.

microphone [mikrɔfɔn] *nm* microphone; mouthpiece *(of telephone)*; **m. électrodynamique,** moving coil microphone; **m. caché,** concealed microphone.

microphotographie [mikrɔfɔtɔgrafi] *nf* **(a)** *(activité)* microphotography, photomicrography; **(b)** *(résultat)* microphotograph, photomicrograph.

microphotographique [mikrɔfɔtɔgrafik] *adj* microphotographic, photomicrographic.

microplaquette [mikrɔplakɛt] *nf Électron* chip.

microprocesseur [mikrɔprɔsesœr] *nm Ordinat* microprocessor.

microscope [mikrɔskɔp] *nm* microscope; **m. électronique,** electron microscope; **m. optique,** light microscope; **regarder au m.,** to look through a microscope; **regarder qch au m.,** to look at sth through *or* under a microscope; **visible au m.,** visible under the microscope.

microscopie [mikrɔskɔpi] *nf* microscopy.

microscopique [mikrɔskɔpik] *adj* microscopic.

microseconde [mikrɔsəgɔ̃d] *nf* microsecond.

microsillon [mikrɔsijɔ̃] *nm* **(a)** *(sillon)* microgroove; **(b)** **(disque) m.,** long-playing record, L.P..

microsociété [mikrɔsɔsjete] *nf* miniature society, society in miniature.

microsociologie [mikrɔsɔsjɔlɔʒi] *nf* – sociology of small groups.

microthermie [mikrɔtɛrmi] *nf* microtherm.

microtome [mikrɔtɔm] *nm* microtome.

miction [miksjɔ̃] *nf* urination, *Spéc* micturition.

midi [midi] *nm no pl* **(a)** *(heure)* midday, (twelve) noon, twelve o'clock; **il est m.,** it's twelve o'clock; **sur le m.,** *F* **sur les m.,** about twelve o'clock *or* noon; **avant m.,** before noon, a.m.; **après m.,** after twelve (noon), p.m.; **m. et demi,** half-past twelve; **repas de m.,** midday meal; *Fig* **chercher m. à quatorze heures,** to look for difficulties where there are none, to complicate matters; *Fig* **être au m. de la vie,** to be in the prime of life; **(b)** *(sud)* south; **chambre au m.,** room facing south; **(c)** southern part, south *(of country)*; *surtout* **le M. (de la France),** the South of France.

midinette [midinɛt] *nf* **(a)** flighty young girl; **(b)** *Vieilli (ouvrière)* office girl, shop girl; *(couturière)* young dressmaker.

mi-distance (à) [amidistɑ̃s] *adv* halfway, midway.

midship(man) [mitʃip(man)] *nm* midshipman; *(pl midshipmen, midships)*.

mie¹ [mi] *nf* crumb *(of loaf, as opposed to crust)*; **pain de m.,** sandwich loaf; *Arg* **à la m. de pain,** not worth a damn.

mie² *nf Arch & Litt (=* **amie***)* **ma m.,** my pet, my love, darling, sweetheart.

miel [mjɛl] **1** *nm* honey; **gâteau de m.,** honeycomb; **m. rosat,** rose honey; *Fig* **elle était tout sucre et tout m.,** she was all sweet and sugary; *Fig* **paroles de m.,** honeyed words; *Fig* **lune de m.,** honeymoon. **2** *int F* **et m.!,** oh, sugar!

miellé [mjele] *adj Litt* honeyed.

mielleusement [mjɛløzmɑ̃] *adv (dire)* in honeyed tones; **sourire m.,** to give a sweet, sugary smile.

mielleux, -euse [mjɛlø, -øz] *adj* **(a)** *(goût)* tasting of honey; **(b)** *Péj* sugary *(speech, smile, person etc)*; smooth *(person)*.

mien, mienne [mjɛ̃, mjɛn] **1** *pron poss* **le m., la mienne, les miens, les miennes,** mine; **j'ai pris ses mains dans les miennes,** I took his hands in mine; **il a**

donné des cadeaux à ses frères et aux miens, he gave presents to his brothers and to mine. **2** *nm* **(a) le m.,** my own (*property etc*); mine; **le tien et le mien,** yours and mine; **votre prix sera le m.,** name your price; **j'ai dû y mettre du m.,** I had to put a lot into it; **(b) les miens,** my (own) family *or* people; **j'ai été renié par les miens,** I've been disowned by my family. **3** *adj poss Litt* mine; **un m. ami,** a friend of mine. **4** *nfpl* **on dit que j'ai encore fait des miennes,** they say I've been up to my old tricks again.

miette [mjɛt] *nf* (*de pain*) crumb; (*morceau*) morsel, scrap; **mettre qch en miettes,** (*un objet*) to smash sth to pieces *or* bits *or* smithereens; **mettre une théorie en miettes,** to reduce a theory to smithereens; **elle m'a laissé quelques miettes de son gâteau,** she left me a few crumbs of her cake; *Fig* **elle n'a pas perdu une m. de la conversation,** not one scrap of the conversation escaped her *or* passed her by.

mieux [mjø] **1** *adv* **(a)** *comp* better; **elle danse m. que moi,** she dances better than I do; **il faut m. les surveiller,** you must watch them more closely; **vous feriez m. de m'écouter,** you'd do better to *or* you'd better listen to me; *Prov* **m. vaut tard que jamais,** better late than never; **il va m.,** he's (feeling) better; **ça va m.,** things are improving; **ça ira m. demain,** it'll be better tomorrow; *Iron* **je vois que ça ne va pas m.!,** you've not improved one bit!; **pour m. dire,** to be more exact; **pour ne pas dire m., pour ne pas m. dire,** to say the least (of it); **de m. en m.,** better and better; **m. encore ...,** better still ...; **(faire qch) à qui m. m.,** to vie with one another (in doing sth); **ils criaient à qui m. m.,** it was a case of who could shout loudest; **tant m.!,** so much the better!, very good!;

(b) le m., (the) best; **la femme le m. habillée de Paris,** the best-dressed woman in Paris; **il s'en est acquitté le m. du monde,** nobody could have done it better.

2 *adj* **c'est on ne peut m.,** it couldn't be better; **tu ne trouveras rien de m.,** you won't find anything better; *F* **c'est tout ce qu'il y a de m.,** it's ideal; **sa famille c'est tout ce qu'il y a de m.,** his family is highly respectable; **ce qu'il y a de m. sur le marché,** the best (there is) on the market; **c'est m. comme ça,** it's better like that; **si tu n'as rien de m. à faire,** if you've nothing better to do; *Iron* **elle n'a trouvé rien de m. que d'aller le répéter à sa mère,** what did she do but go and tell her mother; **ce qui est m., qui m. est ...,** what is better ..., better still ...; **vous serez m. dans ce fauteuil,** you'll be more comfortable in this (arm)chair; **il est m.,** he's (feeling) better; **il est m. que son frère,** he's better-looking *or* more attractive than his brother; **vous ne trouverez pas m. comme hôtel,** you won't find a better hotel; **ce qu'il y a de m. à faire, c'est de ...,** the best thing to do is to ...; **ce que vous avez de m. à faire c'est de ...,** the best thing you can do is to ...; **c'est tout ce qu'il y a de m.,** there's absolutely nothing better; **être le m. du monde** *ou* **au m. avec qn,** to be on the best of terms with s.o.; **c'était la m. des trois sœurs,** she was the best of the three sisters; (*la plus jolie*) she was the best-looking of the three sisters.

3 *nm* **le m. est l'ennemi du bien,** leave well (enough) alone; **faute de m.,** for want *or* lack of something better; **je ne demande pas m.!,** I shall be delighted (*to do so etc*); **j'avais espéré m.,** I had hoped for better things; *Méd etc* **un m., du m.,** a change for the better, an improvement; **faire** *ou* **agir pour le m.,** to act for the best; **le m. serait de ...,** the best plan *or* thing would be to ...; **(en mettant le choses) au m.,** at best; **agir au m. des intérêts de qn,** to act in s.o.'s best interests; **au m., il la vendra 100 francs,** he'll get a hundred francs at most for it; **faire qch de son m.,** to do sth to the best of one's ability; **faire de son m.,** to do one's best, to do the best one can.

mieux-être [mjøzɛtr] *nm no pl* improved condition.

mieux-vivre [mjøvivr] *nm no pl* better *or* higher standard of living; **la lutte pour le m.-v.,** the struggle for a better *or* higher standard of living.

mièvre [mjɛvr] *adj Péj* pretty-pretty.

mièvrerie [mjɛvrəri] *nf Péj* insipid charm *or* prettiness.

mi-fin [mifɛ̃] *adj Com* medium (*grade, quality*); (*pl mi-fins*).

mignard [miɲar] *adj* = **MIGNON**; *Péj* affected.

mignardise [miɲardiz] *nf* **(a)** (*caractère mignon*) charm; *Péj* affectedness; **(b) (œillet) m.,** garden pink.

mignon, -onne [miɲɔ̃, -ɔn] **1** *adj* charming; (*enfant*) darling, *surtout Am* cute; **est-elle mignonne!,** isn't she a darling!; **son péché m.,** his particular weakness; **sois m., va me chercher mes cigarettes,** be a dear *or* an angel and get my cigarettes; *Culin* **filet m.,** filet mignon (*small fillet steak*). **2** *n* **(a)** (*terme d'affection*) pet, darling, dear; **(b)** *Arch* minion.

mignonnement [miɲɔnmɑ̃] *adv Vieilli* daintily.

mignonnette [miɲɔnɛt] *nf* **(a)** (*plante*) (*saxifrage ombreuse*) London pride; (*chicorée sauvage*) wild chicory *or* succory; (*œillet mignardise*) garden pink; **(b)** *Tex* mignonette lace; **(c)** (*poivre*) coarse-ground pepper.

mignoter [miɲɔte] *Vieilli* **1** *vt* to fondle, to caress, to pet (*child*). **2 se mignoter** *vpr* to titivate oneself.

migraine [migrɛn] *nf* migraine, *F* headache; **elle a des migraines,** she has migraines.

migraineux, -euse [migrɛnø, -øz] *n* migraine sufferer.

migrant, -ante [migrɑ̃, -ɑ̃t] **1** *adj* migrant; **travailleur m.,** migrant worker. **2** *n* migrant.

migrateur, -trice [migratœr, -tris] *adj* migrating, migratory (*bird etc*); migrant (*people*).

migration [migrɑsjɔ̃] *nf* migration; **les migrations vacancières,** the holiday exodus.

migratoire [migratwar] *adj* migratory.

migrer [migre] *vi* to migrate (**vers,** to).

mi-jambe(s) (à) [amiʒɑ̃b] *adv* halfway up *or* down the leg(s).

mijaurée [miʒɔre] *nf Péj* conceited *or* affected woman; **ne fais pas la** *ou* **ta m.!,** don't give yourself such airs!

mijoter [miʒɔte] **1** *vt* to simmer (*sth*), to let (*sth*) simmer; *Fig* **m. un projet,** to turn a scheme over in one's mind; **m. un complot,** to hatch a plot. **2** *vi* to simmer. **3 se mijoter** *vpr Fig* **il se mijote quelque chose,** there's something in the wind, something's brewing.

mikado [mikado] *nm* Mikado.

mil¹ [mil] *nm Gym* Indian club.

mil² [mil] *adj* (*used only in writing out dates AD*) thousand; **l'an m. neuf cent quatre-vingt-un,** (the year) nineteen hundred and eighty-one.

mil³ [mij, mil] *nm* (*céréale*) millet.

milady [miledi] *nf* (*titre*) my Lady; (*noble*) titled (English) lady; (*pl miladys*).

milan [milɑ̃] *nm* (*oiseau*) kite.

Milan [milɑ̃] *n* Milan.

mildiou [mildju] *nm* mildew; (*de la vigne*) brown rot; **atteint de m.,** mildewed.

mildiousé [mildjuze] *adj* mildewed (*vine etc*).

mile [majl] *nm* mile.

miliaire [miljɛr] *Méd* **1** *adj* miliary (*gland, fever etc*). **2** *nf* prickly heat, *Spéc* military fever.

milice [milis] *nf* militia.

milicien, -ienne [milisjɛ̃, -jɛn] *n* member of a militia; *m* militiaman.

milieu, -ieux [miljø] *nm* **(a)** middle; **au m. de,** in the middle of, *Litt* amid(st), in the midst of; **au beau m. de la rue/la cour,** right in the middle of the street/the yard; **au m. du navire,** amidships; **il est entré en plein m. d'une discussion,** he came in right in the middle of a discussion; **au m. du courant,** in midstream; **le m. du jour,** midday, noon; **au m. de l'été,** in the middle *or* height of summer; **au m. de l'hiver,** in the middle *or* depth(s) of winter; **au m. de la nuit,** in the middle of the night, *Litt* at dead of night; **vers le m. du mois,** about the middle of the month; **la table du m.,** the middle table;

(b) (*environnement physique*) milieu, environment, surroundings; (*environnement social*) (social) sphere, circle; **les animaux dans leur m.,** animals in their environment; **le m. naturel du loup,** the wolf's natural environment; **je n'appartiens pas à leur m.,** I don't belong to their set *or* circle *or* class; **dans les milieux bien informés,** in well informed circles *or* quarters; **elle ne tient pas à changer de m.,** she's not keen on a change of surroundings; **le m., les gens du m.,** the underworld; **c'est un type du m.,** he's a member of the underworld;

(c) (*moyenne*) middle course, mean; **il n'y a pas de m.,** there's no middle course; **le juste m.,** the happy medium, the golden mean; **tenir le m. entre ... et ...,** to steer a middle course between ... and ...;

(d) *Phys* medium.

militaire [militɛr] **1** *adj* military (*discipline, service etc*); **véhicule m.,** military *or* army vehicle; **à huit heures, heure m.,** at eight o'clock sharp; **la marine m.,** the Navy; **port m.,** naval port. **2** *nm* serviceman, soldier; **les militaires,** the military, the armed forces, the services; **m. de carrière,** career *or* professional soldier.

militairement [militɛrmɑ̃] *adv* militarily; **saluer m.,** to give a military salute; **occuper une ville m.,** to occupy a town by force of arms.

militant, -ante [militɑ̃, -ɑ̃t] **1** *adj* militant; **2** *n* militant; (*du PS etc*) member.

militantisme [militɑ̃tism] *nm* militancy; *Fig* **faire du m.**

culturel, = to tell people what books they should read, what music they should listen to *etc*.
militarisation [militarizasjɔ̃] *nf* militarization.
militariser [militarize] *vt* to militarize.
militarisme [militarism] *nm* militarism.
militariste [militarist] *adj & n* militarist.
militer [milite] *vi* to militate **(pour, en faveur de,** in favour of; **contre,** against); **m. dans le PS,** to be a member of the Socialist Party.
milk-shake [milkʃɛk] *nm* milk shake; **m.-s. à la vanille,** vanilla milk shake; (*pl milk-shakes*).
millage [milaʒ] *nm Can* mileage.
mille¹ [mil] **1** *adj inv* **(a)** thousand; **m. hommes,** a thousand men, one thousand men; **deux m.,** two thousand; **trois cent m. hommes,** three hundred thousand men; **ils sont morts par centaines de m.,** they died in hundreds of thousands; **m. un,** a thousand and one, one thousand and one; **Les M. et une Nuits,** the Arabian Nights; **l'an m.,** the year one thousand; **l'an m. neuf cent avant J.-C.,** (the year) nineteen hundred B.C.;
(b) *Fig* countless, many; **je vous l'ai dit m. fois,** I've told you a thousand times *or* time and time again.
2 *nm inv* **(a)** *Fig* **je te le donne en m.,** you'll never guess in a million years;
(b) *Com* (*chiffre*) thousand; **m. plus m.,** a thousand plus a thousand, one thousand plus one thousand; **un m. de briques,** a thousand bricks;
(c) *Fig* **mettre** *ou* **donner dans le m.,** to hit the bull's eye; *F* **il a des m. et des cents,** he's got pots of money.
mille² *nm* mile (= 1, 609 m); **m. (marin),** nautical mile.
mille(-)feuille [milfœj] (*pl mille-feuilles*) **1** *nf Bot* milfoil, yarrow. **2** *nm Culin* millefeuille, *Am* napoleon.
millénaire [milenɛr] **1** *adj* millennial, millenary. **2** *nm* thousand years, millenary, millennium.
millénium [milenjɔm] *nm* millenium.
mille-pattes [milpat] *nm inv* centipede, millipede.
mille(-)pertuis [milpɛrtɥi] *nm inv Bot* St John's wort.
millésime [milezim] *nm* year of manufacture (*of car etc*); year, vintage (*of wine*); date (*on coin etc*).
millésimé [milezime] *adj* vintage (*wine*); dated (*coin*).
millet [mijɛ] *nm* **(a)** *Bot* millet; **m. long,** canary grass; **(grains de) m.,** birdseed, canary seed; **(b)** *Méd* miliary eruption.
milliaire [miljɛr] *adj Antiq* **borne** *ou* **pierre m.,** milliary column.
milliampère [miliɑ̃pɛr] *nm* milliamp(ere).
milliard [miljar] *nm* one thousand million(s), milliard, *Am* billion.
milliardaire [miljardɛr] *adj & n* multi-millionaire, *Am* billionaire.
milliardième [miljardjɛm] *adj & n* one thousand millionth, *Am* billionth.
milliasse [miljas] *nf F Vieilli* millions and millions; enormous quantity *or* sum (of money).
millibar [milibar] *nm Météo* millibar.
millième [miljɛm] *adj & n* thousandth.
millier [milje] *nm* (about a) thousand, a thousand or so; **des milliers de personnes,** thousands of people; **par milliers,** in thousands.
milligramme [miligram] *nm* milligram(me).
millilitre [mililitr] *nm* millilitre, *US* milliliter.
millimètre [milimɛtr] *nm* millimetre, *US* millimeter.
millimétré [milimetre], **millimétrique** [milimetrik] *adj* **échelle millimétrée,** millimetre *or US* millimeter scale; **papier m.,** graph paper.
million [miljɔ̃] *nm* million; **quatre millions d'hommes,** four million men; **riche à millions,** worth millions.
millionième [miljɔnjɛm] *adj & n* millionth.
millionnaire [miljɔnɛr] *adj & n* millionaire.
millithermie [militɛrmi] *nf Phys* large calorie.
millivolt [milivɔlt] *nm* millivolt.
milord [milɔr] *nm* **(a)** (*titre*) my Lord; (*noble*) (English) nobleman; *Fig* immensely wealthy man; **(b)** *Arch* (*voiture*) victoria.
mi-lourd [milur] *adj & nm Boxe* **(poids) mi-l.,** light heavyweight (boxer); (*pl mi-lourds*).
mime [mim] **1** *nm* mime, (art of) miming. **2** *n* (*personne*) **(a)** mime; **(b)** (*imitateur*) mimic.
mimer [mime] *vt* **(a)** to mime; **m. une scène,** to mime a scene, to act a scene in dumb show; **(b)** (*imiter*) to mimic.
mimétique [mimetik] *adj* mimetic.
mimétisme [mimetism] *nm Zool* mimesis, mimicry; **faire qch par m.,** = unconsciously to do what everyone else is doing; **par m. je commence à passer mes soirées au pub,** I'm spending my evenings in the pub, as people do here, people here spend the evening in the pub, and I'm beginning to do the same; **par m., elle a fini par en faire aussi,** she ended up doing the same thing.
mimi [mimi] *nm Enf* **(a)** (*chat*) pussy (cat), kitty; *F* **mon petit m.,** my darling, my pet; **(b)** (*baiser*) kiss; **fais m. à ta sœur,** give your sister a kiss; **faire un gros m. à qn,** to give s.o. a big kiss.
mimique [mimik] **1** *adj* mimic; **langage m.,** sign language. **2** *nf* **(a)** mimic art, mimicry; **(b)** (*expression*) mime, miming; (*de sourd-muet etc*) sign language.
mimodrame [mimɔdram] *nm Th* mime.
mimosa [mimoza] *nm* mimosa.
mi-moyen [mimwajɛ̃] *adj & nm Boxe* **(poids) mi-m.,** welterweight (boxer); (*pl mi-moyens*).
min. (*abrév* **minimum**) min.
minable [minabl] *Péj* **1** *adj* shabby, seedy(-looking) (*person etc*); pitiable (*appearance etc*); **salaire m.,** mere pittance (of a wage), miserable *or* pathetic wage. **2** *n* failure, washout; **c'est un m., ce type,** that bloke's a dead loss *or* failure; **quelle bande de minables,** what a pathetic *or* useless bunch.
minaret [minarɛ] *nm* minaret.
minauder [minode] *vi* to simper, to mince.
minauderie [minodri] *nf* simpering; **minauderies,** simpering manner.
minaudier, -ière [minodje, -jɛr] **1** *adj* simpering, affected (*person*). **2** *n* simperer.
mince [mɛ̃s] **1** *adj* thin (*person, board, cloth etc*); slender, slight, slim (*person*); **m. revenu,** slender *or* small *or* scanty income; **minces arguments,** poor *or* feeble arguments. **2** *int F* **m. (alors)!,** (*surprise*) well! just fancy that!; (*déception*) blast (it)! **3** *adv* thinly; **peindre m.,** to apply paint thinly.
minceur [mɛ̃sœr] *nf* **(a)** thinness; (*d'une personne*) thinness, slenderness, slimness; **(b)** (*de revenu*) scantiness.
mincir [mɛ̃sir] *vi* to get thinner *or* slimmer, to lose weight.
mine¹ [min] *nf* **(a)** mine; **m. de houille** *ou* **de charbon,** coalmine, colliery, pit; **m. d'or,** goldmine; **m. à ciel ouvert,** opencast mine; **exploitation des mines,** mining; **ingénieur des mines,** mining engineer; *Fig* **une m. de renseignements,** a mine of information; *Fig* **ce travail est loin d'être une m. d'or,** this work doesn't pay at all well; **(b) m. (de crayon),** (pencil) lead; **m. de plomb,** graphite, blacklead; **m. d'étain,** tinstone; **(c)** *Mil etc* mine; **coup de m.,** blast; **faire jouer une m.,** to fire a blast *or* a mine; **attention aux coups de m.!,** (*sur panneau*) danger, blasting; **m. flottante,** floating mine; **poser** *ou* **mouiller une m.,** to lay a mine; **mouilleur de mines,** minelayer; **dragueur de mines,** minesweeper; **champ de mines,** minefield; **m. terrestre,** landmine.
mine² *nf* (*d'une personne*) appearance, look; **mines,** gestures, expressions (*of a baby*); **avoir bonne/mauvaise m.,** to look well/ill; **vous avez meilleure m.,** you're looking better; **il en a une (sale) m.,** he DOES look ill; **m. boudeuse,** sulky expression; **avoir la m. longue,** to have a long face *or* a miserable expression; **faire triste m.,** to look disappointed; **faire bonne m. à qn,** to be pleasant to s.o., to greet s.o. pleasantly *or* with a smile; **faire grise m. à qn,** to give s.o. a poor welcome; **juger les gens sur la m.,** to judge people by *or* on appearances; **plat qui a bonne m.,** appetizing dish, dish that looks good; *Fig* **ça ne paie pas de m.,** it isn't much to look at; **il ne paie pas de m.,** he isn't much to look at, his appearance goes against him; **faire m. d'être fâché,** to pretend to be *or* look as though one is angry; **il a fait m. de me suivre,** he made as if to follow me; *F Iron* **nous avons bonne m. maintenant!,** we DO look silly!; *F* **m. de rien, essaie de vérifier,** without letting on, try to check on it; *F* **m. de rien, l'affaire progresse,** the work is progressing, though you wouldn't think so to look at it; *Péj* **faire des mines,** to simper; **elles font des mines devant le miroir,** they're making faces in the mirror.
miner¹ [mine] *vt* **(a)** (*saper*) to (under)mine (*fortress etc*); **la mer mine les falaises,** the sea is undermining the cliffs *or* is eating the cliffs away; **(b)** *Fig* **la fièvre l'a miné,** fever has undermined *or* sapped his strength; **ses soucis la minent,** her worries are wearing her down; **miné par l'envie,** eaten up *or* consumed with envy.
miner² *vt* (*poser des mines*) to mine (*road etc*).
minerai [minrɛ] *nm* ore; **m. de fer,** iron ore.
minéral, -aux [mineral, -o] **1** *adj* mineral; **chimie minérale,** inorganic chemistry; **eau minérale,** mineral water(s); **source minérale,** mineral spring, spa. **2** *nm* mineral.
minéralier [mineralje] *nm* ore ship.
minéralisation [mineralizasjɔ̃] *nf* mineralization.

minéraliser [mineralize] *vt* to mineralize.
minéralogie [mineralɔʒi] *nf* mineralogy.
minéralogique [mineralɔʒik] *adj* **(a)** *Géol etc* mineralogical; **(b)** *Admin* **numéro m.,** (*d'un véhicule*) registration number, *US* license *or Can* licence number; **plaque m.,** number plate, *US* license *or Can* licence plate.
minéralogiste [mineralɔʒist] *n* mineralogist.
minerve [minɛrv] *nf* **(a)** *Méd* (surgical) collar; **(b)** *Myth* **M.,** Minerva.
minestrone [minɛstrɔn] *nm Culin* minestrone.
minet, -ette [minɛ, -ɛt] **1** *n F* **(a)** (*chat*) pussy (cat), kitty; **mon m., ma minette,** (*terme d'affection*) my darling, my pet; **(b)** *Péj* fashionable young man *or* woman, *F* trendy; **tu as vu la minette là-bas!,** look at her over there! what a cracker! **2** *nf Bot* **minette,** black medic(k).
mineur¹ [minœr] *nm* **(a)** coalminer, collier; **m. de fond,** underground worker; **(b)** *Mil* sapper.
mineur², -eure [minœr] **1** *adj* **(a)** (*inférieur*) minor, lesser; **Asie Mineure,** Asia Minor; **(b)** *Jur* under age; **(c)** *Mus* minor (*note etc*); **gamme mineure,** minor scale; **en ut m.,** in C minor; **(d)** (*de moindre importance*) minor; **ce sont des soucis mineurs,** these are minor worries; **peintre m.,** minor painter. **2** *n Jur* minor; **la consommation de boissons alcooliques est interdite aux mineurs,** no underage drinking. **3** *nm Mus* minor key.
mini [mini] *F* **1** *adj inv* mini; **la mode m. est de retour,** the mini is back (in fashion). **2** *nf* mini(skirt). **3** *adv* **s'habiller m.,** to wear a miniskirt.
miniature [minjatyr] **1** *nf* miniature; **peintre de miniatures,** miniature painter, miniaturist; **en m.,** in miniature, on a small scale. **2** *adj inv* **golf m.,** miniature golf; **yacht m.,** (*maquette*) model yacht; (*de petite taille*) small yacht; **autobus m.,** (*maquette*) toy bus; (*de petite taille*) minibus.
miniaturisation [minjatyrizasjɔ̃] *nf* miniaturization; **la m. de l'informatique,** computer (circuitry) miniaturization.
miniaturiser [minjatyrize] **1** *vt* to miniaturize. **2 se miniaturiser** *vpr* to become miniaturized; **la télévision se miniaturise,** televisions are getting much smaller.
miniaturiste [minjatyrist] *n* miniaturist, miniature painter.
minibus [minibys] *nm* minibus.
mini-cassette [minikasɛt] *nf* mini-cassette; (*pl mini-cassettes*).
mini-chaîne [miniʃɛn] *nf* mini-hifi, compact hifi; (*pl mini-chaînes*).
minier, -ière [minje, -jɛr] **1** *adj* mining (*industry, district etc*). **2** *nf* **minière,** surface *or* opencast mine.
mini(-)jupe [miniʒyp] *nf* miniskirt; (*pl mini(-)jupes*).
minimal, -aux [minimal, -o] *adj* minimal, minimum.
minime [minim] **1** *adj* minimal; minor (*role*); trivial (*loss*); trifling (*value*). **2** *n* **(a)** *Hist Rel* Minim; **(b)** *Sp* junior (*to 15 years old*).
minimiser [minimize] *vt* to minimize, to reduce (*sth*) to the minimum.
minimum [minimɔm] (*pl minima, minimums*) **1** *nm* minimum; **réduire les frais au m.,** to reduce expenses to a minimum; **m. vital,** minimum living wage; **au m.,** as a minimum, at least; **thermomètre à minima,** minimum thermometer; **tu peux y parvenir avec un m. d'effort,** you can get there with a minimum of effort; **je n'y resterai que le m. de temps,** I'll only stay there for as short a time as possible. **2** *adj* **les largeurs minimums** *ou* **minima,** the minimum width(s); **vitesse m.,** minimum speed; **prix m.,** reserve price (*at auction*); *Él* **charge m.,** base load (*of a generator*).
ministère [ministɛr] *nm* **(a)** (*département*) government department; **M. de l'Intérieur,** ≈ Home Office; **M. des Affaires étrangères,** ≈ Foreign (and Commonwealth) Office; *US* ≈ State Department; *Can* ≈ External Affairs Department; **M. de l'Éducation nationale,** ≈ Department of Education; **M. de la Défense (nationale),** ≈ Ministry of Defence; **M. des Travaux publics,** *Can* ≈ Department of public works; *Br Hist* Ministry of public works; **M. de l'Environnement,** ≈ Department of the Environment; **m. du Commerce,** ≈ Department of Trade;
(b) (*gouvernement*) office; **entrer dans un m.,** to take office; **former un m.,** to form a government; **sous le m. Giscard,** under Giscard d'Estaing's government;
(c) *Jur* **le M. public,** ≈ the (Department of the) Director of Public Prosecutions;
(d) *Rel* **le (saint) m.,** the ministry;
(e) *Arch & Litt* agency; **user du m. de qn,** to make use of s.o.'s services; *Jur* **l'accusé a droit au m. d'un avocat,** the accused has the right to counsel *or Am* a lawyer.
ministériel, -ielle [ministerjɛl] *adj* ministerial; *Vieilli* **journal m.,** newspaper supporting the government, government organ; **crise ministérielle,** cabinet crisis; **l'entourage m.,** ministerial entourage; *Jur* **officier m.,** (*avoué, huissier, notaire*) law official.
ministrable [ministrabl] *Pol* **1** *adj* likely to become a minister. **2** *n* likely choice as minister.
ministre [ministr] *nm* **(a)** (*du gouvernement*) minister, secretary (of State); **Premier M.,** Prime Minister; **M. de l'Intérieur** ≈ *Br* Home Secretary; ≈ *US* Secretary of the Interior; **M. des Affaires étrangères** ≈ *Br* Foreign Secretary; *US* ≈ Secretary of State; *Can* ≈ Secretary of State for External Affairs; **M. de l'Éducation nationale** ≈ Secretary of State for Education; **M. de la Défense (nationale)** ≈ Secretary of State for Defence, Minister of Defence; **M. sans portefeuille,** Minister without Portfolio; **M. des Travaux publics,** *Can & Br Hist* ≈ Minister of Public Works; **M. de l'Environnement,** ≈ Secretary of State for the Environment; **M. des Finances,** *Br* ≈ Chancellor of the Exchequer; *US* ≈ Secretary of the Treasury; *Can* ≈ Minister of Finance; **M. de la Justice,** ≈ Lord Chancellor; *US* ≈ Attorney General; *Can* ≈ Minister of Justice and Attorney General; **M. du Commerce** ≈ Secretary of State for Trade and Industry; **papier m.,** petition paper; ≈ official foolscap;
(b) *Rel* (Protestant) minister, clergyman;
(c) *Arch & Litt* servant, agent (*of God, prince etc*).
minitel ® [minitɛl] *nm* = small terminal, connected to telephone, used to consult data banks etc; *Br* ≈ Prestel ®.
minitéliste [minitelist] *n* user of Minitel.
minium [minjɔm] *nm Ch* red lead, minium; (*antirouille*) red lead paint.
minois [minwa] *nm* (pretty) face (*of child, young woman*).
minoration [minɔrasjɔ̃] *nf* decrease.
minorer [minɔre] *vt* **(a)** (*sous-évaluer*) to undervalue, to underestimate; **(b)** to decrease the importance of (*sth*); to lower, to reduce (*figure, sum*).
minoritaire [minɔritɛr] **1** *adj* **parti m.,** minority party; **participation m.,** minority holding. **2** *n* member of a minority.
minorité [minɔrite] *nf* minority; *Jur* minority, nonage, infancy; **être en m.,** to be in the *or* in a minority; **mettre en m.,** to defeat; **m. ethnique,** ethnic minority.
Minorque [minɔrk] *nf* Minorca.
minorquin, -ine [minɔrkɛ̃, -in] **1** *adj* Minorcan. **2** *n* **M.,** Minorcan.
minoterie [minɔtri] *nf* (*moulin*) (large) flour mill; (*activité*) flour-milling.
minotier [minɔtje] *nm* (flour) miller.
minou [minu] *nm F* (*chat*) pussy (cat), kitty; **mon m.,** my darling, my pet.
minuit [minɥi] *nm* midnight, twelve (o'clock) (at night); **m. et demi,** half-past twelve at night; *F* **sur les minuits,** *Vieilli* **sur le m.,** about midnight; **messe de m.,** midnight mass.
minuscule [minyskyl] **1** *adj* **(a)** (*très petit*) tiny, minute, minuscule; **(b) lettre m.,** small letter, *Typ* lower-case letter. **2** *nf* small letter, *Typ* lower-case letter.
minus (habens) [minys(abɛ̃s)] *nm inv F* half-wit, moron.
minutage [minytaʒ] *nm* **(a)** *Mil Th etc* (precision) timing; **(b)** drafting (*of document*).
minute [minyt] *nf* **(a)** minute (*of hour, degree*); **faire qch à la m.,** to do sth at a minute's *or* a moment's notice; **vous êtes à la m.,** you're punctual to the *or* a minute; **êtes-vous à la m?,** are you in a hurry?; **nettoyage-m.,** dry-cleaning while you wait; **réparations (à la) m.,** repairs while you wait; **repas-m.,** convenience meal; **la m. de vérité,** the moment of truth; **il sera là d'une m. à l'autre,** he'll be here any minute now; **ne pas avoir une m. à perdre/de répit,** not to have a moment *or* minute to lose/a moment's *or* minute's rest; *F* **m. (papillon)!,** just a minute! hold on!; **(b)** minute, draft (*of contract etc*); record (*of deed, of judgment*); **faire la m. d'un acte,** to draft an act; **faire la m. d'une réunion,** to draw up the minutes of *or* to minute a meeting.
minuter [minyte] *vt* **(a)** (*dans le temps*) to time; **sa journée est soigneusement minutée,** every minute of his day is carefully planned, his day is run on a tight schedule; **(b)** to minute, to draw up, to draft (*agreement etc*); to record, to enter (*deed, judgment*).
minuterie [minytri] *nf* **(a)** (*appareil*) timer, (automatic) time switch (*of light*); **m. d'enregistrement,** counting mechanism (*of meter*); **(b)** (*mécanisme*) motionwork, train of wheels (*in clock etc*).

minutie [minysi] *nf* **(a)** (*caractère*) meticulousness, attention to detail; **(b)** *Vieilli* minute detail; **minuties,** trifles, petty details, minutiae.
minutieusement [minysjøzmɑ̃] *adv* minutely, meticulously.
minutieux, -ieuse [minysjø, -jøz] *adj* meticulous (*person*); close, thorough, minute, detailed (*inspection etc*).
miocène [mjɔsɛn] *adj & nm Géol* Miocene.
mioche [mjɔʃ] *n F* kid(die), tot; *Péj* brat.
mi-pente (à) [amipɑ̃t] *adv* halfway up *or* down the hill.
mirabelle [mirabɛl] *nf* mirabelle plum.
mirabellier [mirabelje] *nm* mirabelle plum tree.
miracle [mirɑkl] **1** *nm* **(a)** miracle; **faire** *ou* **opérer un m.,** to perform *or* work a miracle; **cela tient du m.,** it's miraculous; **m. d'architecture,** marvel *or* miracle of architecture; **le m. industriel français,** the French industrial miracle; **échapper comme par m.,** to have a miraculous escape; **par m.,** miraculously; **c'est (un) m. que** ... + *sub*, it's a miracle *or* a wonder that ...; **crier (au) m.,** to go into raptures; **(b)** *Littér Hist* miracle (play). **2** *adj inv F* **produit m.,** miracle *or* wonder product.
miraculé [mirakyle] *adj* miraculously healed *or* saved (*person*).
miraculeusement [mirakyløzmɑ̃] *adv* miraculously, by a miracle.
miraculeux, -euse [mirakylø, -øz] *adj* miraculous, wonderful; **remède m.,** miracle cure.
mirador [miradɔr] *nm* **(a)** *Archit* mirador, belvedere; **(b)** *Mil* observation post (*in tree etc*); watchtower (*of prison camp*).
mirage [miraʒ] *nm* mirage.
mire [mir] *nf* **(a)** foresight (*of rifle*); **ligne de m.,** line of sight; *Mil* **angle de m.,** angle of sight; **point de m.,** aim; *Fig* **point de m. de tous les yeux,** (*critiqué*) target for criticism; (*admiré*) cynosure of every eye; **(b)** (*signal*) sighting mark; *TV* test card; **(c)** (*piquet*) (surveyor's) ranging pole; **(d)** *Arch* sighting, aiming (*of firearm*).
mirer [mire] **1** *vt* **(a)** *Vieilli* to aim at, take aim at (*sth*); **(b)** *Litt* to reflect, to mirror; **(c)** to candle (*eggs*). **2 se mirer** *vpr* to look *or* gaze at oneself (*in mirror, water etc*); **les arbres se mirent dans l'eau,** the trees are reflected in the water.
mirette [mirɛt] *nf Arg* (*œil*) (*souvent pl*) **mirettes,** peepers.
mirifique [mirifik] *adj F* wonderful, fabulous.
mirliflor(e) [mirliflɔr] *nm F Hum Vieilli* dandy, fop.
mirliton [mirlitɔ̃] *nm* (*sifflet*) kazoo, mirliton; **vers de m.,** doggerel, bad verse.
mirmidon [mirmidɔ̃] *nm F* whippersnapper, pipsqueak, little runt.
mirobolant [mirɔbɔlɑ̃] *adj F* wonderful, fabulous, marvellous.
miroir [mirwar] *nm* **(a)** mirror, (looking) glass; **m. (pliant) à trois faces,** triple mirror; **m. de courtoisie,** vanity mirror; **m. à** *ou* **aux alouettes,** lark mirror; *Fig* snare, delusion; **m. grossissant,** magnifying mirror; **m. déformant,** distorting mirror; *Fig* **le m. d'une société,** the mirror of a society; **(b)** *Bot* **m. de Vénus,** Venus's looking glass; **(c)** *Culin* **œufs au m.,** fried eggs; **(d)** speculum (*on wing of bird*); eye, ocellus (*on peacock's feather*).
miroitant [mirwatɑ̃] *adj* glistening, gleaming, flashing (*silver etc*); shimmering (*lake etc*); sparkling (*jewel*).
miroité [mirwate] *adj* dappled bay (*horse*).
miroitement [mirwatmɑ̃] *nm* (*of silver etc*) glistening, gleam(ing), flashing; (*of lake etc*) shimmer(ing); (*of jewel*) sparkle, sparkling.
miroiter [mirwate] *vi* to glisten, to gleam, to flash; (*of lake etc*) to shimmer; (*of jewel*) to sparkle; *Fig* **faire m. l'avenir aux yeux de qn,** to lure s.o. with bright prospects.
miroiterie [mirwatri] *nf Com Ind* mirror industry; (*usine*) mirror factory.
miroton [mirɔtɔ̃] *nm Culin* beef boiled in sauce with onions.
mis [mi] *adj Vieilli* **être bien/mal m.,** to be well/badly attired.
misaine [mizɛn] *nf Nau* **(voile de) m.,** (square) foresail; **mât de m.,** foremast.
misanthrope [mizɑ̃trɔp] **1** *nm* misanthropist, misanthrope. **2** *adj* misanthropic.
misanthropie [mizɑ̃trɔpi] *nf* misanthropy.
misanthropique [mizɑ̃trɔpik] *adj Litt* misanthropic.
miscellanées [miselane] *nfpl Litt* miscellany, miscellanea.
miscible [misibl] *adj* miscible.
mise [miz] *nf* **(a)** placing, putting in place; **m. à l'eau,** launching (*of ship*); **m. en bouteilles,** bottling (*of wine etc*); **m. à terre,** landing (*of goods*); **m. bas,** (*d'un animal*) dropping (*of young*); **m. en pratique,** carrying out, putting into practice; **m. en jeu,** bringing into play; **m. en musique d'un poème,** setting of a poem to music; **m. à jour,** bringing to light (*d'un secret etc*); (*réactualisation*) bringing up to date; **m. en garde,** warning, caution; **m. à mort,** kill(ing); **m. en eau (d'un barrage),** filling (of a reservoir); *Typ* **m. en pages,** page-setting; **m. en marche,** starting (*of engine etc*); *Rad etc* **m. en ondes,** production; *Ordinat etc* **m. sous tension,** power-up (*of computer, turbine*); **m. en plis,** setting (*of hair*); **shampooing et m. en plis,** shampoo and set; **m. en liberté,** releasing, release; **m. au net,** final version (*of document etc*); **m. en train,** (*d'un projet etc*) start-up; **m. à la** *ou* **en retraite,** pensioning (off), retiring (*on a pension*);
(b) (*habillement*) dress, clothing, attire; **elle est simple dans sa m.,** she dresses simply; **on voit à sa m. qu'elle n'est pas très riche,** you can see from the way she dresses *or* the clothes she wears that she's not very rich;
(c) *Cartes* stake; bid (*at auction*); **m. à prix,** reserve price, upset price; **son arrivée m'a sauvé la m.,** his arrival got me out of a tight spot;
(d) *Com* **m. de fonds,** putting up of money *or* of capital, (capital) outlay; **m. sociale** *ou* **d'un associé,** partner's holding (*in a business*).
miser [mize] *vt* **(a)** to stake (**sur,** on); **m. sur un cheval,** to back a horse, to (put a) bet on a horse; **m. sur les deux tableaux,** to try to have it both ways; **(b)** *F* (*compter sur*) to count, to bank (**sur,** on).
misérabilisme [mizerabilism] *nm* sordid realism.
misérabiliste [mizerabilist] *adj* sordidly realistic.
misérable [mizerabl] **1** *adj* **(a)** (*indigent*) poor, wretched, impoverished, miserable; **quartier m.,** poverty-stricken district; **la condition m. des paysans,** the wretched condition of the peasantry; **(b)** (*insignifiant*) wretched, miserable, worthless; **un m. salaire,** a miserable wage, mere pittance (of a wage); **pour un m. franc,** for a paltry *or* wretched franc; **(c)** *Vieilli* despicable, mean (*action etc*). **2** *n* (*malheureux*) poor wretch; *Péj* (*fripouille*) scoundrel, wretch, villain.
misérablement [mizerabləmɑ̃] *adv* miserably.
misère [mizɛr] *nf* **(a)** (*indigence*) extreme poverty, destitution; **dans la m.,** poverty-stricken, destitute; **réduire qn à la m.,** to reduce s.o. to destitution; **crier m.,** to plead poverty; **vêtements qui crient m.,** shabby *or* threadbare garments;
(b) (*ennui*) trouble, misfortune; **misères domestiques,** domestic troubles *or* worries; **faire des misères à qn,** to tease s.o. unmercifully;
(c) *Vieilli* (*malheur*) misery; **manger le pain de m.,** to eat the bread of affliction; **reprendre le collier de m.,** to go back to drudgery *or* to the treadmill; **lit de m.,** bed of sickness;
(d) une m., a trifle; **cent francs?, une m.!,** a hundred francs? a mere nothing!; **je l'ai eu pour une m.,** I got it for a song, I got it at a snip of the price;
(e) *Cartes* misère.
miserere, miséréré [mizerere] *nm inv Rel Mus* miserere.
miséreux, -euse [mizerø, -øz] *adj & n* poverty-stricken, destitute (person).
miséricorde [mizerikɔrd] **1** *nf* **(a)** mercy, mercifulness; **crier m.,** to cry for mercy; **faire m. à qn,** to be merciful to s.o.; **(b)** *Nau Arch* **ancre de m.,** sheet anchor. **2** *int Vieilli* mercy on us!, mercy me!, heaven help us!
miséricordieux, -ieuse [mizerikɔrdjø, -jøz] *adj* merciful (**envers,** to).
misogyne [mizɔʒin] **,** *F* **miso** [mizo] **1** *adj* misogynous. **2** *n* misogynist, woman-hater.
misogynie [mizɔʒini] *nf* misogyny.
miss [mis] *nf* (*pl miss(es)*) **(a)** beauty queen; **M. Monde,** Miss World; *F* **voilà, m.,** there you are (miss); **(b)** *Arch* (English) governess.
missel [misɛl] *nm Rel* missal.
missile [misil] *nm* guided missile; **m. à tête chercheuse à infrarouge,** heat-seeking missile; **m. ballistique de moyenne portée,** intermediate-range ballistic missile; **m. de croisière,** cruise missile.
mission [misjɔ̃] *nf* **(a)** *Pol Rel etc* mission; delegation (*of diplomats, businessmen etc*); **avoir m. de faire qch,** to be commissioned to do sth; **ministre en m. spéciale à Paris,** minister on (a) special mission to Paris; **chargé de m.,** official representative; **m. scientifique,** scientific expedition; **partir en m. au pôle nord,** to go on an expedition

to the North Pole; *Mil* **en m.,** on detached service; **en m. de reconnaissance,** on reconnaissance duty; **m. accomplie,** mission accomplished; *Rel* **missions étrangères,** foreign missions; **(b)** (*rôle*) function, task, rôle, aim (*of art etc*); **elle a le sentiment de s'être fixé une m.,** she feels she has found her mission *or* vocation in life; **m. civilisatrice,** civilizing mission; **(c)** *Rel* mission (station).
missionnaire [misjɔnɛr] *adj & n* missionary.
missive [misiv] *nf Litt Hum* missive, letter.
mistigri [mistigri] *nm F* **(a)** (*name given to cat*) puss; **(b)** *Cartes* mistigris.
mistoufle [mistufl] *nf Arg Vieilli* **(a) être dans la m.,** to be broke *or* hard up *or* skint; **(b) faire des mistoufles à qn,** to annoy *or* tease *or* plague s.o..
mistral [mistral] *nm Météo* mistral.
mitaine [mitɛn] *nf Can & Vieilli* (*moufle*) mitten; *F* **mitaines,** (*gants*) gloves, mitts; (*qui laisse les doigts nus*) fingerless gloves.
mite [mit] *nf* **(a)** mite; **m. du fromage,** cheese mite; **(b)** (*petit papillon*) moth; **mangé aux** *ou* **par les mites,** moth-eaten; *Can* **sortir qch des boules à mites,** to take sth out of mothballs, to dust sth off.
mité [mite] *adj* moth-eaten.
mi-temps [mitɑ̃] **1** *nf inv Fb etc* half-time, interval; **première/seconde mi-t.,** first/second half; **la police craint la troisième mi-t.,** the police fear after-match trouble *or* violence. **2** *nm* **emploi à mi-t.,** part-time work *or* employment; *Scol* **mi-t. pédagogique,** part-time teaching position; **travailler à mi-t.,** to work part-time; **l'avantage d'un mi-t.,** the advantage of working part-time.
miter (se) [səmite] *vpr* to become moth-eaten.
miteux, -euse [mitø, -øz] **1** *adj* shabby, tatty (*clothes etc*); seedy-looking (*person*). **2** *n F* shabby *or* down-at-heel *or* seedy-looking person.
Mithridate [mitridat] *nm* Mithridates.
mithridatiser [mitridatize] *vt* to make (*person*) immune (*to poison*).
mitigation [mitigɑsjɔ̃] *nf* mitigation.
mitigé [mitiʒe] *adj* mitigated, modified; **morale mitigée,** lax morals; *Jur* **peine mitigée,** reduced sentence.
mitiger [mitiʒe] *vt* (**je mitigeai(s); n. mitigeons**) *Vieilli* to mitigate (*pain, penalty*); to relax (*rule, law*); **avoir des sentiments mitigés,** to have mixed feelings.
mitigeur [mitiʒœr] *nm* mixer tap.
mitonner [mitɔne] **1** *vt* **(a)** *Culin* to simmer (*soup etc*); **(b)** *Fig* to concoct, to cook up (*project etc*); **(c)** *Fig* to coddle, to pamper, to cosset (*child etc*). **2** *vi* (*of soup etc*) to simmer. **3 se mitonner** *vpr* **je me suis mitonné une bonne petite omelette,** I cooked up a nice little omelette for myself.
mitoyen, -enne [mitwajɛ̃, -jɛn] *adj* intermediate; **mur m.,** party wall; **cloison mitoyenne,** dividing wall (*between two rooms*); **maisons mitoyennes,** semi-detached houses; (*plus de deux*) terraced houses.
mitoyenneté [mitwajɛnte] *nf Jur* joint ownership (*of party wall, hedge etc*).
mitraillade [mitrɑjad] *nf* (volley of) shots, machine-gun fire.
mitraillage [mitrɑjaʒ] *nm* machine-gunning.
mitraille [mitrɑj] *nf* **(a)** *Mil* (*projectiles*) case shot, canister shot, grapeshot; (*décharge*) hail of bullets; **(b)** *F* (*monnaie*) small change.
mitrailler [mitrɑje] *vt* to machine-gun; *Fig* **m. qn de questions,** to fire questions at s.o., to pepper s.o. with questions; **arrête de nous m. avec ton appareil photo!,** stop taking photos all the time!
mitraillette [mitrɑjɛt] *nf* submachine gun, *F* tommy gun.
mitrailleur [mitrɑjœr] **1** *nm* machine-gunner; *Mil Av* **m. arrière,** rear gunner. **2** *adj* **fusil m.,** Bren gun.
mitrailleuse [mitrɑjøz] *nf* machine gun.
mitral, -aux [mitral, -o] *adj* mitral (*valve of the heart*).
mitre [mitr] *nf* **(a)** mitre, *US* miter (*of bishop etc*); **(b)** *Tech* (*chimney*) cowl.
mitré [mitre] *adj* mitred, *US* mitered (*abbot*).
mitron [mitrɔ̃] *nm* baker's boy.
mi-vitesse (à) [amivitɛs] *adv* at half speed.
mi-voix (à) [amivwa] *adv* in an undertone, under one's breath.
mixage [miksaʒ] *nm Cin etc* mixing (*of sounds*).
mixer [mikse] *vt Cin* to mix.
mixe(u)r [miksœr] *nm* mixer; (*pour rendre liquide*) liquidizer.
mixité [miksite] *nf Scol* co-education.
mixte [mikst] *adj* **(a)** mixed; **école m.,** mixed *or* co-educational school; *Tennis* **double m.,** mixed doubles; **(b)** (*combiné*) dual purpose; **train m.,** composite train (*goods and passengers*); **commission m.,** joint commission; **billet m.,** combined rail and road ticket; **mariage m.,** mixed marriage; **cuisinière m.,** gas and electric cooker.
mixtion [mikstjɔ̃] *nf Pharm* (*action*) compounding (*of drugs etc*); (*médicament*) mixture.
mixture [mikstyr] *nf Pharm* mixture; *Culin & Fig* concoction.
ml (*abrév* **millilitre**) ml.
M.L.F. [ɛmɛlɛf] *nm abrév* **Mouvement de libération des femmes.**
Mlle (*abrév* **mademoiselle**) Miss.
Mlles (*abrév* **mesdemoiselles**) Misses.
mm (*abrév* **millimètre(s)**) mm.
MM. (*abrév* **Messieurs**) Messrs.
Mme (*abrév* **Madame**) Mrs.
Mmes *abrév* **Mesdames.**
mnémonique [mnemɔnik] *adj & nf* mnemonic.
mnémotechnie [mnemɔtɛkni] *nf* mnemonics.
mnémotechnique [mnemɔtɛknik] **1** *adj* mnemotechnic. **2** *nf* mnemonics.
Mo [ɛmo] *nm Ordinat* (*abrév* **méga-octet**) Mb.
mob [mɔb] *nf F* = **MOBYLETTE.**
mobile [mɔbil] **1** *adj* **(a)** mobile, movable; (*feuilles etc*) detachable; **album à feuilles mobiles,** loose-leaf album; **fête m.,** movable feast; **(b)** moving, mobile (*person, target etc*); shifting, changing (*expression etc*); **organes mobiles,** sliding *or* working *or* moving parts; **le boxeur est très m.,** the boxer is very nimble *or* quick on his feet; *Hist* **garde m.,** militia (*of 1848, of 1868-71*); **la garde m.,** = (State) security police; **(c)** *Vieilli* unstable, changeable, fickle (*nature*); restless, excitable (*population*). **2** *nm* **(a)** (*raison*) motive (*of crime*); **(b)** *Phys etc* moving body, body in motion; **(c)** *Beaux-Arts* mobile.
mobilier, -ière [mɔbilje, -jɛr] **1** *adj Jur* movable, personal; **biens mobiliers,** personal property, chattels; *Fin* **valeurs mobilières,** stocks and shares, transferable securities. **2** *nm* (*ameublement*) furniture; **m. moderne,** modern furniture; **m. de cuisine,** kitchen furniture; **le développement du m. urbain,** the development of street furniture; *Fig* **tu fais partie du m. maintenant!,** you're a fixture *or* part of the furniture now!; **m. national,** government property.
mobilisateur, -trice [mɔbilizatœr, -tris] *adj* motivating; **slogan m.,** rallying-cry; **le général a lancé un appel m.,** the general launched a recruitment drive.
mobilisation [mɔbilizɑsjɔ̃] *nf* mobilization (*of troops*); raising (*of capital*).
mobilisé, -ée [mɔbilize] **1** *adj* (*of troops*) mobilized, called up. **2** *n* serviceman, *f* servicewoman.
mobiliser [mɔbilize] *vt* to mobilize (*troops*); to call out, to call up (*reservist*); *Fin* to raise (*capital*); **m. toute son énergie,** to summon up all one's strength.
mobilité [mɔbilite] *nf* mobility, moveableness; *Fig* changeableness, instability (*of character*); **la m. de son visage est remarquable,** he has a remarkably lively face.
mobylette ® [mɔbilɛt] *nf* moped.
mocassin [mɔkasɛ̃] *nm* mocassin.
moche [mɔʃ] *adj F* ugly (*individual, thing*); **qu'est-ce qu'elle est m.,** what a sight she is!; **c'est m. ce qu'ils t'ont fait,** it's rotten what they did to you.
mocheté [mɔʃte] *nf F* (*laideur*) ugliness; **c'est d'une m.!,** what an eyesore!; **quelle m., cette fille!,** that girl's a right dog.
modal, -aux [mɔdal, -o] *adj* modal.
modalité [mɔdalite] *nf* **(a)** mode (*of application etc*); *Jur* **modalités,** (restrictive) clauses; **modalités de paiement,** methods of payment; *Fin* **modalités d'une émission,** terms and conditions of an issue; **(b)** *Phil Mus* modality.
mode[1] [mɔd] **1** *nf* **(a)** fashion; **lancer la m. de qch, mettre qch à la m.,** to bring sth into fashion, to set the fashion for sth; **être à la m.,** to be in fashion *or* in vogue, to be all the rage; **ta sœur est très à la m.,** your sister's very fashionable *or F* trendy; **robe à la m.,** fashionable *or* stylish dress; **les mini-jupes sont à la m.,** mini-skirts are in (fashion); **revenir à la m.,** to come back into fashion; **passer de m.,** to go out of fashion; **la m. du long est passée,** long skirts are out (of fashion); **à l'ancienne m.,** in the old style; **journal de m.,** fashion magazine; *Com* **la (haute) m.,** the fashion trade; **à la m. de ...,** after the style *or* manner of ...;

(b) modes, (*clothes*) fashions; **gravures de modes,** fashion plates; **Martine est une vraie gravure de modes,** Martine is a real fashion plate; **(articles de) modes,** millinery; **magasin de modes,** milliner's shop.

2 *adj inv* **coloris m.,** fashion shades *or* colours.

mode² *nm* **(a)** method, mode (*of education etc*); **m. d'emploi,** directions for use; **m. de vie,** way of life; **m. de cuisson,** cooking directions; **m. de gestion,** management style; **(b)** *Phil Vieilli* mode, mood; *Gram* mood; *Mus* mode; *Ordinat* mode; *Ordinat* **le disque dur est utilisable en m. fixe comme en m. portatif,** the hard disk can be used in static as well as in portable mode.
modelage [mɔdlaʒ] *nm (action)* modelling (*in clay etc*); (*résultat*) model.
modèle [mɔdɛl] **1** *nm* **(a)** model, pattern; **m. d'écriture,** handwriting copy; **machines toutes bâties sur le même m.,** machines all built to one pattern *or* on *or* along the same lines; **fabriqué sur trois modèles,** made in three styles; **voiture dernier m.,** car of the latest design; **m. déposé,** registered pattern; **m. réduit** *ou* **à petite échelle,** scale model; **m. réduit de yacht/d'avion,** model yacht/airplane; **prendre qn pour m.,** to take s.o. as one's model, to model oneself on s.o.; **m. de vertu/générosité,** paragon of virtue/ model of generosity;
(b) *Couture* model (*gown, hat*); *Beaux-Arts* (artist's) model; **dessiné d'après (le) m.,** drawn from the model; **servir de m. à un artiste,** to sit *or* model for an artist.
2 *adj* **époux m.,** model *or* exemplary husband; **l'employé m.,** the model employee; **adopter une conduite m.,** to behave in an exemplary manner.
modelé [mɔdle] *nm* **(a)** *Beaux-Arts* relief; (*sculpture*) contours; **(b)** *Géog* relief.
modeler [mɔdle] *v* **(je modèle; je modèlerai) 1** *vt* to model, to mould (*clay etc*); to shape, to mould (*character*); **m. sa personnalité sur celle de qn,** to model oneself on s.o.; **m. la destinée de qn,** to shape s.o.'s destiny. **2 se modeler** *vpr* **se m. sur qn,** to take s.o. as one's model, to model oneself on s.o..
modeleur, -euse [mɔdlœr, -øz] *n* modeller; *Tech* pattern maker.
modélisme [mɔdelism] *nm* modelling.
modéliste [mɔdelist] *n* (*de maquette*) model maker; (*de vêtements*) dress designer.
modem [mɔdɛm] *nm Ordinat* modem; **carte m.,** modem card.
modérateur, -trice [mɔderatœr, -tris] **1** *adj* moderating, restraining. **2** *n* moderator, restrainer. **3** *nm* regulator, governor (*of engine etc*); *Él* damper (*of magnetic needle*); *Nucl* moderator.
modération [mɔderasjɔ̃] *nf* **(a)** (*retenue*) moderation, restraint; **avec m.,** in *or* with moderation; **(b)** (*réduction*) reduction (*in price*); reduction, mitigation (*of penalty*); reduction, diminution (*of taxes*).
modéré [mɔdere] **1** *adj* moderate, restrained, temperate (*person*); reasonable, moderate (*price etc*); subdued (*cheers*). **2** *n Pol* moderate.
modérément [mɔderemɑ̃] *adv* moderately, in moderation; *Iron* **j'ai apprécié m. sa conduite,** I didn't like the way he behaved at all.
modérer [mɔdere] *v* **(je modère; je modérerai) 1** *vt* **(a)** to moderate, to restrain, to curb (*passions etc*); to reduce, to slacken (*speed*); to regulate (*machine*), **(b)** (*réduire*) to reduce (*price*); to mitigate, to reduce (*penalty*). **2 se modérer** *vpr* to control oneself, to calm down.
moderne [mɔdɛrn] **1** *adj* modern, up-to-date (*technology etc*); **studio équipé de tout le confort m.,** studio flat with all modern conveniences; **découverte m.,** recent discovery; **la femme m. travaille,** the modern woman goes out to work; *Hist* **période m.,** the modern period, recent history; **grec m.,** modern Greek; **étudier les lettres modernes,** to study modern literature. **2** *nm* **le m.,** (*choses*) modern things; (*style*) (the) modern style. **3** *n* (*personne*) modern.
modernisation [mɔdɛrnizasjɔ̃] *nf* modernization.
moderniser [mɔdɛrnize] *vt* to modernize, to bring up to date.
modernisme [mɔdɛrnism] *nm* modernism.
moderniste [mɔdɛrnist] *adj & n* modernist.
modernité [mɔdɛrnite] *nf* modernity.
modern style [mɔdɛrnstil] **1** *nm* art nouveau. **2** *adj inv* art nouveau; **balcon m. s.,** art nouveau balcony.
modeste [mɔdɛst] **1** *adj* **(a)** modest (*person, income*); modest, unassuming, self-effacing (*person*); **il fit un m. sourire,** he smiled modestly; **avoir un train de vie m.,** to live quietly, to live a modest life; **avoir des revenus modestes,** to have a modest income; **être d'une origine m.,** to be of humble origin; **un hôtel m.,** a small hotel; **(b)** *Litt Vieilli* (*pudique*) modest. **2** *n* **ne faites pas le m.,** don't be (so) modest.
modestement [mɔdɛstəmɑ̃] *adv* modestly.
modestie [mɔdɛsti] *nf* **(a)** modesty (*of person, income*); **fausse m.,** false modesty; **(b)** *Litt Vieilli* (*pudeur*) modesty.
modicité [mɔdisite] *nf* slenderness (*of means* etc); lowness, reasonableness (*of price*).
modifiable [mɔdifjabl] *adj* modifiable.
modifiant [mɔdifjɑ̃] *adj* modifying (*influence etc*).
modificateur, -trice [mɔdifikatœr, -tris] **1** *adj* modifying, modificatory. **2** *n Vieilli* modifier. **3** *nm Tech* disengaging gear.
modificatif, -ive [mɔdifikatif, -iv] *adj* modifying.
modification [mɔdifikasjɔ̃] *nf* modification, alteration; **apporter** *ou* **faire une m. à qch,** to modify *or* make an alteration to sth; **m. à une convention,** amendment to a convention.
modifier [mɔdifje] *v* (*pr sub & impf* **n. modifiions, v. modifiiez**) **1** *vt* **(a)** to modify (*statement*); to alter, to change (*plan*); to amend (*bill, convention*); *Nau* **m. la route,** to alter course; **(b)** *Gram* to qualify, to modify (*verb*). **2 se modifier** *vpr* to alter, to be modified *or* altered.
modique [mɔdik] *adj* moderate, modest, reasonable (*cost, charge etc*); modest, slender (*income*).
modiquement [mɔdikmɑ̃] *adv* **m. payé,** poorly paid.
modiste [mɔdist] *nf* milliner.
modulaire [mɔdylɛr] *adj* modular.
modulateur, -trice [mɔdylatœr, -tris] *Rad etc* **1** *adj* modulating (*valve etc*). **2** *nm* modulator.
modulation [mɔdylasjɔ̃] *nf* **(a)** *Mus* modulation, transition; *Fig* **une m. des paiements serait souhaitable pour les nouveaux adhérents,** it would be desirable to adjust the rate of payment for new members; **(b)** modulation, inflexion (*of the voice*); **(c)** *Rad etc* modulation; **m. d'amplitude,** amplitude modulation; **m. de fréquence,** frequency modulation.
module [mɔdyl] *nm Archit etc* module; *Math etc* modulus; standard, unit (*of length etc*); *Astronaut* **m. de commande,** command module; **m. d'enseignement,** teaching module.
moduler [mɔdyle] **1** *vt* to modulate (*one's voice, Phys etc amplitude etc*); to inflect (*one's voice*); *Fig* **m. des paiements,** to adjust the rate of payment; **m. la thérapeutique en fonction des résultats obtenus,** to adjust the treatment in the light of results. **2** *vi Mus* to modulate.
modus vivendi [mɔdysvivɛ̃di] *nm inv* modus vivendi.
moelle [mwal] *nf* **(a)** marrow (*of bone*); *Anat* medulla; **os à m.,** marrowbone; *Anat* **m. épinière,** spinal cord; *Fig* **anglais jusqu'à la m. (des os),** English to the backbone; *Fig* **glacé jusqu'à la m. (des os),** frozen to the bone *or* to the marrow; *Fig* **corrompu jusqu'à la m.,** rotten to the core; **(b)** *Bot* pith.
moelleusement [mwaløzmɑ̃] *adv* softly.
moelleux, -euse [mwalø, -øz] **1** *adj* **(a)** soft, velvety (*to the touch*); mellow (*wine, voice*); easy (*motion*); **couverture moelleuse,** soft *or* downy blanket; **(b)** *Bot* pithy; **(c)** *Arch* marrowy (*bone*). **2** *nm* softness (*of colour*); mellowness (*of voice etc*); ease (*of motion*).
moellon [mwalɔ̃] *nm* quarry stone; **m. brut,** rubble(stone); **m. d'appareil,** ashlar.
mœurs [mœr(s)] *nfpl* manners, customs (*of people*); customs, mores (*of country, epoch etc*); habits (*of animals*); **vivre avec les m. de son temps,** to live in tune with the times; **certificat de bonne vie et m.,** certificate of good character; **la police des m.,** *F* **les M.,** = the vice squad; **gens sans m.,** unprincipled people; **femme de m. faciles,** woman of easy virtue; *Arch* **bonnes m.,** morality; *Arch* **avoir des m.,** to be of good moral character.
mofette [mɔfɛt] *nf* **(a)** *Min Arch* choke damp; **(b)** (*mammifère*) skunk.
mohair [mɔɛr] *nm Tex* mohair; **laine m.,** mohair wool.
Mohican [mɔikɑ̃] *nm* Mohican.
moi [mwa] **1** *pron pers* **(a)** (*sujet*) I; **c'est m.,** it's me, *Fml* it is I; **il est plus âgé que m.,** he is older than me *or* than I am; **elle est invitée et m. aussi,** she's invited and so am I; **qui vient avec nous? — m.,** who's coming with us? — I am, me; **m., je veux bien,** for my part, I'm willing; **moi qui vous parle,** I who am talking to you; **je l'ai fait m.-même,** I did it myself;
(b) (*objet*) me; **il accuse mon frère et m.,** he accuses my brother and me; **vous me soupçonnez, m.!,** you suspect ME!; **avec m.,** with me; **venez à m.,** come to me; **à m.!,** help!; **ce livre est à m.,** this book is mine *or* belongs to me; **et m.? vous m'oubliez?,** what about me? have you forgotten me?; **un ami à m.,** a friend of mine; **ces vers ne sont pas de m.,** these verses are not mine;
(c) (*après impératif*) **laissez-m. tranquille,** leave me alone; **donnez-le-m.,** give it (to) me.
2 *nm* ego, self; **culte du m.,** egoism; **la psychanalyse**

nous aide à découvrir notre vrai m., psychoanalysis helps us (to) discover our true self.
moignon [mwaɲɔ̃] *nm* stump (*of amputated limb etc*).
moi-même [mwamɛm] *pron pers* myself; *voir* **MOI, MÊME.**
moindre [mwɛ̃dr] **1** *adj* **(a)** *comp* less(er); lower (*price*); smaller (*quantity*); **au m. reproche, il se met à pleurer,** he bursts into tears at the slightest reproach; **question de m. importance,** question of less(er) importance *or* of minor importance; **(b)** *superl* **le** *ou* **la m.,** the least; **pas la m. chance,** not the slightest *or* remotest *or* faintest chance; **c'est la m. des choses,** it's nothing, it's the least I *or* he *etc* can do; **je ne lui ai pas fait le m. reproche,** I didn't reproach him in the slightest *or* in the least. **2** *n* **de deux maux choisir le m.,** to choose the lesser of two evils; **le dernier, mais non le m.,** last but not least; **un expert, et non des moindres,** no mean expert.
moindrement [mwɛ̃drəmɑ̃] *adv Litt* (*souvent with nég*) less; **je ne suis pas m. atteint que vous,** I'm no less affected than you are; **sans être le m. intéressé,** without being in the least bit interested.
moine [mwan] *nm* **(a)** monk, friar; *Prov* **l'habit ne fait pas le m.,** clothes do not make the man; *Fig* **gras comme un m.,** (as) fat as butter; *Fig* **mener une vie de m.,** to lead the life of Riley; **(b)** *Arch* bed warmer.
moineau, -eaux [mwano] *nm* (*oiseau*) sparrow; *F* **c'est un vilain m.,** he's a bad lot *or* a nasty piece of work; *Com* **têtes de m.,** nuts (*of coal*).
moinillon [mwanijɔ̃] *nm F* young monk.
moins [mwɛ̃] **1** *adv* **(a)** (*comparatif*) less; **je gagne m. que vous,** I earn less than you; **m. encore,** still less, even less; **elle est m. intelligente que sa sœur,** she's not as intelligent as her sister, she's less intelligent than her sister; **beaucoup m. long,** much shorter; **m. d'argent,** less money, not so much money, not as much money; **m. d'hommes/d'occasions,** fewer *or* not so many men/opportunities; **plus on le punit m. il travaille,** the more he's punished the less he works; **il travaille de m. en m.,** he's working less and less; **m. de dix francs,** less than ten francs; **dix francs de m.,** ten francs less; **celui-ci coûte dix francs de m. que l'autre,** this is ten francs less than the other one; **il y a eu 20% de visiteurs de m.** *ou* **en m.,** there have been 20% fewer visitors; **il a m. de trente ans,** he's less than *or* under thirty; **vous compterez cela en m.,** you may deduct that; **il est revenu avec un œil en m.,** he came back minus an eye; **les m. de trente ans,** the under-thirties; **les jeunes et les m. jeunes,** the young and the not so young; **nous étions à m. d'un kilomètre de l'église,** we were less than a kilometre from the church, we were within one kilometre of the church; **en m. de dix minutes,** in less than ten minutes; **en m. de rien,** in less than no time; *F* **en m. de deux,** in no time; **je ne peux pas vous le laisser à m.,** I can't let you have it for less; **dix francs de m.,** ten francs less; **à m. d'accidents,** barring accidents; **à m. d'avis contraire,** unless I *or* you *etc* hear to the contrary; **à m. de partir tout de suite,** unless I *or* you *etc* leave at once; **à m. que ... +** *sub,* unless ...; **à m. que vous (ne) l'ordonniez,** unless you order it; **rien m. que,** nothing less than; **ce n'est rien m. qu'un héros,** he's nothing less than a hero; **ce n'est rien (de) m. qu'un miracle,** it's nothing short of a miracle; **elle mérite des éloges non m. que son frère,** she deserves no less praise than her brother, she deserves praise quite as much as her brother;

(b) (*superlatif*) **le m.,** the least; **les élèves les m. appliqués,** the least industrious pupils; **le m. de gens possible,** the smallest possible number of people, as few people as possible; **pas le m. du monde,** not in the least *or* slightest, by no means; *Prov* **qui peut le plus peut le m.,** you've *or* he's *etc* done much more complicated things in your *or* his *etc* time; **du m.,** at least, that is to say, at all events; **c'est du m. ce qu'il dit,** that's what he says, at least; **au m.,** at least (= *not less than*); **gagner 100 000 francs par an (tout) au m.** *ou* **à tout le m.** *ou* **pour le m.,** to earn 100,000 francs a year at (the very) least *or* to say the least; *F* **tu as fait ton travail, au m.?,** you've done your work, I hope?

2 *prép* minus, less; **une heure m. cinq,** five (minutes) to one; **six m. quatre égale deux,** six minus four equals two; **il fait m. dix (degrés),** it's minus ten (degrees).

3 *nm Math* minus (sign).
moins-value [mwɛ̃valy] *nf* depreciation, drop in value; (*après une vente*) capital loss; (*pl moins-values*).
moirage [mwaraʒ] *nm* watering (*of silk etc*).
moire [mwar] *nf Tex* moire, moiré; **m. de soie,** watered silk.
moiré [mware] *Tex* **1** *adj* watered, moiré (*silk etc*). **2** *nm* = **MOIRURE.**
moirer [mware] *vt* to water (*silk etc*).
moirure [mwaryr] *nf* watered effect, moiré; *TV* shot-silk effect.
mois [mwa] *nm* **(a)** month; **au m. d'août,** in (the month) of August; **louer qch au m.,** to hire sth by the month; **pendant deux m.,** for two months; **cent francs par m.,** a hundred francs a month; **un m. de vacances,** a month's holiday; **le treizième m.,** = month's salary paid as a bonus; **(b)** (*de paie*) month's wages *or* salary; **je dois deux m. à l'épicier,** I haven't paid the grocer for two months.
moïse [mɔiz] *nm* **(a)** (*berceau*) wicker cradle, Moses basket, bassinet; **(b)** *Bible* **M.,** Moses.
moisi [mwazi] **1** *adj* mouldy, *US* moldy; mildewed, mildewy (*wall, fabric etc*); musty, fusty (*taste, smell*). **2** *nm* mould, *US* mold; mildew (*on wall, fabric*); **odeur de m.,** musty smell; **sentir le m.,** to smell musty *or* fusty.
moisir [mwazir] **1** *vt* to make (*sth*) mouldy *or US* moldy. **2** *vi* to go mouldy *or US* moldy, to mildew; *Fig* **j'avais l'impression de m. dans cette ville,** I felt I was mouldering away in that town; *Fig F* **on ne va pas m. ici,** (*partons*) let's not hang about here.
moisissure [mwazisyr] *nf* **(a)** (*sur fromage etc*) mould, *US* mold; **enlever les moississures du fromage,** to remove the mouldy bits from the cheese; **(b)** (*moisi*) mouldiness, *US* moldiness; **une forte odeur de m.,** a strong musty smell.
moisson [mwasɔ̃] *nf* **(a)** (*action*) harvest(ing) (*of cereals*); (*époque*) harvest time; **faire la m.,** to harvest; *Fig* **cela m'a permis de faire une m. d'idées,** that gave me the chance to amass a wealth of ideas; **(b)** (*récolte*) crop, harvest; **rentrer la m.,** to gather in the crops *or* the harvest.
moissonnage [mwasɔnaʒ] *nm* harvesting, reaping.
moissonner [mwasɔne] *vt* **(a)** to reap (*corn, field*); to harvest, to gather (*crops*); *Litt Fig* **m. des lauriers,** to reap *or* win laurels; **(b)** *Litt* **être moissonné dans la fleur de l'âge,** to be cut off in one's prime.
moissonneur, -euse [mwasɔnœr, -øz] **1** *n* harvester, reaper. **2** *nf* **moissonneuse,** reaper, reaping machine.
moissonneuse-batteuse [mwasɔnøzbatøz] *nf* combine (harvester); (*pl moissonneuses-batteuses*).
moissonneuse-lieuse [mwasɔnøzljøz] *nf* reaper-binder; (*pl moissonneuses-lieuses*).
moite [mwat] *adj* moist, sweaty (*hands etc*); muggy (*weather*); **(froid et) m.,** clammy.
moiteur [mwatœr] *nf* moistness, sweatiness (*of hands etc*); **m. froide,** clamminess.
moitié [mwatje] **1** *nf* half; **perdre la m. de son argent,** to lose half one's money; **la m. du temps,** half the time; **la bouteille était à m. pleine/vide,** the bottle was half full/empty; **couper qch par m.,** to cut something in half, to halve sth; **partagé en deux moitiés,** divided into two halves, halved; **vendre qch à m. prix,** to sell sth (at) half price; **s'arrêter à m. chemin,** to stop halfway; **m. plus,** half as much again; **plus grand de m.,** half as big again; **réduit de m.,** reduced by half; **m.-m.,** fifty-fifty; **faire m.-m.,** to go halves; **se mettre** *ou* **être de m., faire m. avec qn dans qch,** to go halves with s.o. in sth, to go fifty-fifty with s.o., to share and share alike; **il y est pour m.,** he was just as much involved; (*c'est sa faute aussi*) he's just as much to blame; *F* **ma (chère) m.,** my better half; **à m.,** half; **à m. mort,** half-dead; **à m. cuit,** half-cooked; **faire les choses à m.,** to half-do things, to do things by halves; **elle ne fait pas les choses à m.,** she doesn't do things by halves.

2 *adv* **m. riant, m. pleurant,** half laughing, half crying; **m. l'un, m. l'autre,** half and half.
moitir [mwatir] *vt Tech* to moisten (*paper etc*).
moka [mɔka] **1** *n Géog* **M.,** Mocha. **2** *nm* (*café*) mocha (coffee); *Culin* mocha cake; **glace au m.,** coffee ice-cream.
mol *voir* **MOU**[1].
molaire[1] [mɔlɛr] *nf* molar.
molaire[2] *adj Phys* molar.
molasse [mɔlas] *nf* = **MOLLASSE**[2].
môle [mol] *nm* (*brise-lames*) breakwater, mole; (*quai*) pier.
moléculaire [mɔlekylɛr] *adj* molecular.
molécule [mɔlekyl] *nf* molecule.
molécule-gramme [mɔlekylgram] *nf* gram(me) molecule; (*pl molécules-grammes*).
molène [mɔlɛn] *nf Bot* mullein.
moleskine [mɔlɛskin] *nf* imitation leather; (*coton*) moleskin.
molestation [mɔlɛstasjɔ̃] *nf* molestation.
molester [mɔlɛste] *vt* to treat (*s.o.*) roughly, to manhandle (*s.o.*); **se faire m. par la police,** to be manhandled by the

police.
moletage [mɔltaʒ] *nm* milling, knurling.
moleter [mɔlte] *vt* (**je molette**; **je moletterai**) to mill, to knurl.
molette [mɔlɛt] *nf* **(a)** serrated roller *or* wheel, knurl; rowel (*of spur*); **clef à m.,** adjustable spanner, *surtout Am* monkey wrench; **m. à briquet,** cigarette lighter wheel; **(b)** cutting wheel (*for glass etc*); *Phot* trimmer (*for prints*); **(c)** *Pharm Arch* small pestle, muller.
mollah [mɔla] *nm Rel* mullah.
mollard [mɔlar] *nm Vulg* (*crachat*) gob.
mollasse¹ [mɔlas] **1** *adj* soft, flabby; (*personne*) slow, lazy. **2** *n* **grand(e) m.,** great lump (of a man, of a woman).
mollasse² *nf Géol* molasse, sandstone.
mollasson, -onne [mɔlasɔ̃, -ɔn] *adj & n F* (*personne*) = **MOLLASSE¹**.
molle *voir* **MOU¹**.
mollement [mɔlmɑ̃] *adv* (*sans énergie*) feebly, weakly; **se plaindre m.,** to whine, to whinge.
mollesse [mɔlɛs] *nf* **(a)** softness (*of cushion etc*); flabbiness (*of flesh etc*); **(b)** slowness; (*manque d'énergie*) weakness, limpness, woolliness (*of style*); laxity (*of government*); (*devant un ennemi, un adversaire*) spinelessness; **la m. du dessin,** the drawing's lack of energy; **sans m.,** briskly, smartly.
mollet, -ette [mɔlɛ, -ɛt] **1** *adj* softish; **pain m.,** (soft) bread roll; **œuf m.,** soft-boiled egg. **2** *nm Anat* calf (*of leg*).
molletière [mɔltjɛr] **1** *adj* **bandes molletières,** puttees. **2** *nf* puttee.
molleton [mɔltɔ̃] *nm* soft thick flannel *or* cotton; (*de table*) table felt.
molletonné [mɔltɔne] *adj* (*gants etc*) fleece-lined.
molletonner [mɔltɔne] *vt* to line (*gloves etc*) with fleece.
mollir [mɔlir] **1** *vi* to soften, to become soft; (*d'un effort etc*) to slacken, to slack off; (*du vent*) to die down, to abate; (*des troupes etc*) to give ground; **mes jambes mollissent,** my legs are giving way (beneath me). **2** *vt Nau* to slacken, to ease, to slack off (*rope*); to ease (*helm*).
mollusque [mɔlysk] *nm* **(a)** mollusc, *US* mollusk; **(b)** *F* (*personne*) great lump.
molosse [mɔlɔs] *nm Litt* watchdog, mastiff.
molybdène [mɔlibdɛn] *nm Minér* molybdenum.
môme [mom] *Arg* **1** *n* (*enfant*) kid, brat, youngster. **2** *nf* woman; (*petite amie*) girlfriend. **3** *adj* **quand j'étais tout m.,** when I was just a kid.
moment [mɔmɑ̃] *nm* **(a)** moment; **le m. venu,** when the time comes *or* has *or* had come; **à ce m.-là,** at that moment, at that time; (*dans le passé*) in those days, then; **à un m. donné,** at a given time; **au m. donné,** at the given *or* appointed time; **c'est le bon m. pour ...,** now is the time to ...; **un m.!,** one moment!, just a moment!; **en ce m.,** at this moment (in time); **il est là en** *ou* **à ce m.,** he's there at the moment *or* (just) now *or* at present; **je suis à vous dans un m.,** I'll be with you in a moment; **il ne me faut rien pour le m.,** I don't need anything at *or* for the moment *or* for the time being; **sur le m. je n'ai pas su que faire,** for a moment I was at a loss; **c'est le m. ou jamais,** it's now or never; **attendre le m. opportun,** to wait for an opportune moment *or* the right moment; **arriver au bon m.,** to arrive at just the right time; **ce n'est qu'un mauvais m.,** it'll soon pass; **un m. de honte/repos,** a moment's shame/rest; **elle n'a pas un m. à elle,** she hasn't a moment *or* minute to herself; **elle en a pour un m. avec ce travail,** the work'll keep her busy for a (good) while; **par moments,** at times, now and again; **d'un m. à l'autre,** (at) any moment *or* time *or* minute; **à tout m., à tous moments,** constantly; **dans un de ses bons moments,** in one of his good moods; **dans un m. de bonté,** in a kind moment; **au m. de partir,** just as I *or* he *etc* was leaving *or* was about to leave; **il attend toujours le dernier m. pour nous dire ce qu'il a décidé,** he always waits till the last minute to tell you what he's decided; **les derniers moments de sa vie,** the last moments of his life; **au m. de sa naissance,** at the time of his birth; **jusqu'au m. où ...,** until (such time as)...;
(b) **du m. que ...,** seeing that ...; **du m. que c'est ce qu'il veut faire,** since that's what he wants to do;
(c) (*époque*) stage; **à quel m. de son développement ...?,** at what stage of *or* point in his development ...?;
(d) *Phys* moment (*of force, inertia etc*); **m. angulaire,** angular momentum.
momentané [mɔmɑ̃tane] *adj* momentary (*effort etc*); temporary (*absence*).
momentanément [mɔmɑ̃tanemɑ̃] *adv* momentarily, temporarily, for a moment.
momerie [mɔmri] *nf Litt Vieilli* mummery; (*pratique insincère*) insincerity.
momie [mɔmi] *nf* mummy.
momification [mɔmifikasjɔ̃] *nf* mummification.
momifier [mɔmifje] *v* (*impf & pr sub* **n. momifiions, v. momifiiez**) **1** *vt* to mummify. **2** **se momifier** *vpr* to become mummified; *Fig* to fossilize.
mon, ma, mes [mɔ̃, ma, me] *adj poss* (**mon** *is used instead of* **ma** *before f words beginning with vowel or h mute*) my; **m. ami, m. amie,** my friend; **m. meilleur ami, ma meilleure amie,** my best friend; **c'est m. affaire à moi,** that's my (own) business; *F* **j'ai m. vendredi,** I've got Friday off; *F* **et voilà m. Simon qui se met à rouspéter,** then old Simon starts grumbling; (*il est plus jeune que moi*) then young Simon starts grumbling; **un de mes amis,** a friend of mine, one of my friends; **m. père et ma mère, mes père et mère,** my father and mother; **non, m. colonel,** no, sir.
monacal, -aux [mɔnakal, -o] *adj* (*vie, calme*) monastic.
monachisme [mɔnaʃism] *nm* monasticism.
monade [mɔnad] *nf Phil etc* monad.
monandre [mɔnɑ̃dr] *adj Bot* monandrous.
monarchie [mɔnarʃi] *nf* monarchy.
monarchique [mɔnarʃik] *adj* monarchic(al).
monarchisme [mɔnarʃism] *nm* monarchism.
monarchiste [mɔnarʃist] *adj & n* monarchist.
monarque [mɔnark] *nm* monarch.
monastère [mɔnastɛr] *nm* monastery; (*couvent*) convent.
monastique [mɔnastik] *adj* monastic.
monaural, -aux [mɔnɔral, -o] *adj* monaural.
monceau, -eaux [mɔ̃so] *nm* heap, pile.
mondain, -aine [mɔ̃dɛ̃, -ɛn] **1** *adj* **(a)** fashionable (*resort etc*); **réunion mondaine,** society gathering; **carnet de la vie mondaine,** diary of social events; *Journ* **chronique mondaine,** society news, gossip column; **la police mondaine,** = the vice squad; **(b)** *Rel* worldly, earthly (*pleasures etc*). **2** *n* socialite. **3** *nf F* **la Mondaine,** = the vice squad.
mondanité [mɔ̃danite] *nf* **(a)** society; **j'avoue n'avoir aucune attirance pour la m.,** I must confess that I don't like going out at all; **mondanités,** social events; *Journ* society news, gossip column; **(b)** *Rel* worldliness.
monde [mɔ̃d] *nm* **(a)** world; **le m. entier,** the whole world; **dans le m. entier,** (*connu, en vente*) world-wide, all over the world, the world over; **le m. des abeilles/de la Nature,** the world of bees/Nature; **le Nouveau M.,** the New World; **le tiers m.,** the Third World; **que le m. est petit!,** it's a small world!; **faire le tour du m.,** to go round the world; **il est allé aux quatre coins du m.,** he's been all over the place; **mettre qn au m.,** to bring s.o. into the world, to give birth to s.o.; **être (encore) au m.,** to be (still) in the land of the living; **être seul au m.,** to be alone in the world; **il est encore de ce m.,** he's still alive; **quand mon grand-père était encore de ce monde,** when my grandfather was (still) alive; **pour rien au m.,** not for the world, not on any account; **je ne te ferais souffrir pour rien au m.,** I wouldn't hurt you for the world; **faire tout au m. pour obtenir qch,** to do everything possible to get sth; **c'est un m.!, il ne fait rien!,** that's a good one *or* that's rich!, he doesn't do anything!; **il n'y a pas de quoi s'en faire un m.,** it's not worth getting worked up about, it's no big deal; **personne au m.,** no man alive; **un des meilleurs hommes du m.,** one of the best men living *or* alive; **vieux comme le m.,** (as) old as the hills; **elle a volé à la face du m.,** she stole things right under everybody's nose; **le bout du m.,** the ends of the earth, the world's end, the back of beyond; *Fig* **ce n'est pas le bout du m.!,** (*de faire ça*) it's not the end of the world, it's no big deal; **il faut de tout pour faire un m.,** it takes all sorts (to make a world); **ainsi va le m.,** it's the way of the world; **l'autre m.,** the next world;
(b) (*milieu*) milieu; **le m. de la haute finance,** the financial world, financial circles; **je ne suis pas de leur m.,** I'm not in their set *or* crowd; **le (beau) m.,** (fashionable) society, *F* the glitterati; **le grand m.,** high society; **aller (beaucoup) dans le m.,** to go out a great deal, to move in fashionable circles; **homme du m.,** society man, man of the world;
(c) (*gens*) people; **tout le m.,** everybody, everyone; **peu de m., pas grand m.,** not many people, not a large crowd; **avoir du m. à dîner,** to have people to dinner; *F* **elle se fout du m.,** she doesn't give a damn about people; **il connaît son m.,** he knows the people he has to deal with; **comment va tout votre m.?,** how is your *or* the family?;
(d) *Arch* servants, men, hands.
mondial, -iaux [mɔ̃djal, -jo] **1** *adj* worldwide (*crisis etc*); **la première/deuxième guerre mondiale,** the First/Second

World War, World War One/Two; **guerre mondiale,** global warfare. **2** *nm Fb* **le M.,** the World Cup.

mondialement [mɔ̃djalmɑ̃] *adv* throughout the world, universally.

mondialisation [mɔ̃djalizasjɔ̃] *nf* globalization.

mondialiser [mɔ̃djalize] **1** *vt* to globalize (*sth*). **2 se mondialiser** *vpr* to become globalized.

mondiovision [mɔ̃djɔvizjɔ̃] *nf TV* satellite television.

monégasque [monegask] **1** *adj* (*native, inhabitant*) of Monaco. **2** *n* **M.,** native *or* inhabitant of Monaco.

monétaire [monetɛr] *adj* monetary; **unité m. d'un pays,** currency of a country; **système m.,** monetary system; *CE* **le serpent m.,** the (currency) snake; **questions monétaires,** monetary questions; **marché m.,** money market; **masse m.,** money supply; **presse m.,** minting press.

monétarisme [monetarism] *nm Écon* monetarism.

monétariste [monetarist] *adj & n Écon* monetarist.

monétiser [monetize] *vt* to monetize, to mint.

mongol, -ole [mɔ̃gɔl] **1** *adj* Mongol, Mongolian. **2** *nm Ling* Mongolian. **3** *n* **M.,** Mongol, Mongolian; *Fig Péj* **il a l'air d'un vrai M.,** he looks really thick.

Mongolie [mɔ̃gɔli] *nf* Mongolia.

mongolien, -ienne [mɔ̃gɔljɛ̃, -jɛn] *Méd* **1** *adj* **bébé m.,** Down's syndrome baby; *Vieilli* mongol baby. **2** *n* person with Down's syndrome; *Vieilli* mongol.

mongolique [mɔ̃gɔlik] *adj* Mongol(ian).

mongolisme [mɔ̃gɔlism] *nm Méd* Down's syndrome; *Vieilli* mongolism.

mongoloïde [mɔ̃gɔlɔid] *Méd* **1** *adj* (*traits*) mongoloid; (*individu*) affected by Down's syndrome. **2** *n* person affected by Down's syndrome; *Vieilli* mongoloid.

moniteur, -trice [monitœr, -tris] **1** *n* **(a)** instructor, *f* instructress; *Sp* coach; **m. d'auto-école/de ski,** driving/ski instructor; **(b)** assistant (*in holiday camp*), *US* (camp) counselor; **(c)** *Rad* (foreign broadcast) monitor. **2** *nm Ordinat etc* monitor; *Méd* **m. cardiaque,** cardiac *or* heart monitor.

monitoire [monitwar] *adj* monitory.

monitorage [monitɔraʒ] *nm* monitoring; **écran de m.,** monitor.

monitorat [monitɔra] *nm* work *or* job of being an instructor; **je déteste le m.,** I hate being an instructor.

monitoring [monitɔriŋ] *nm* monitoring.

monnaie [mɔnɛ] *nf* **(a)** money; **pièce de m.,** coin; **m. légale,** legal tender; **m. scripturale,** bank money, deposit money; **fausse m.,** counterfeit money, coinage; **frapper la m., battre m.,** to coin *or* mint money; *Fig* **(l'hôtel de) la M.,** ≈ the Royal Mint; **m. électronique,** plastic money; **m. de papier,** paper money; **payer qn en m. de singe,** to fob s.o. off, to let s.o. whistle for his money; **c'est m. courante dans ce milieu,** it's common in such circles; **(b)** (*pièces etc*) change; **petite m.,** small change; **donner la m. de mille francs,** to give change for a thousand-franc note; **je dois aller faire de la m.,** I'll have to go and get change; *Fig* **rendre à qn la m. de sa pièce,** to pay s.o. back in his own coin.

monnaie-du-pape [mɔnɛdypap] *nf Bot* honesty; (*pl monnaies-du-pape*).

monnayable [mɔnɛjabl] *adj* convertible into money; *Fig* **cette formation/son expérience est m.,** the training/experience is worth money.

monnayage [mɔnɛjaʒ] *nm* minting, coining.

monnayer [mɔneje] *vt* (**je monnaie; je monnaierai**) **(a)** to coin, to mint (*money*); **(b)** to cash (*a banknote*); *Fig* to cash in on (*one's influence etc*); *Fig* **il faut apprendre à m. son talent,** you must learn to capitalize on your talent.

monnayeur [mɔnɛjœr] *nm* coiner, minter; **faux m.,** counterfeiter.

mono [mɔno] *adj inv* mono (*record etc*).

monoacide [mɔnoasid] *adj Ch* monoacid(ic).

monobloc [mɔnɔblɔk] *adj inv* (*cylinders etc*) made in one piece, cast solid.

monochrome [mɔnɔkrom] *adj* monochrome; *Ordinat* **écran m.,** monochrome screen.

monocle [mɔnɔkl] *nm* monocle.

monocoque [mɔnɔkɔk] **1** *adj* **avion m.,** monocoque; **carrosserie m.,** (*of car*) monocoque body; **bateau m.,** monohull. **2** *nm Nau* monohull.

monocorde [mɔnɔkɔrd] **1** *adj* **(a)** *Mus* single-stringed (*instrument*); **(b)** monotonous (*sound*). **2** *nm* monochord.

monocotylédone [mɔnɔkɔtiledɔn] *nf Bot* monocotyledon.

monoculaire [mɔnɔkylɛr] *adj* monocular (*field glass, vision etc*); **cécité m.,** blindness in one eye.

monoculture [mɔnɔkyltyr] *nf Agr* monoculture.

monocycle [mɔnɔsikl] *nm* monocycle.

monocylindrique [mɔnɔsilɛ̃drik] *adj Aut etc* single-cylinder (*engine*).

monogame [mɔnɔgam] *adj* monogamous.

monogamie [mɔnɔgami] *nf* monogamy.

monogamique [mɔnɔgamik] *adj* monogamic.

monogramme [mɔnɔgram] *nm* monogram.

monographie [mɔnɔgrafi] *nf* monograph.

monokini [mɔnɔkini] *nm* monokini; **faire du m.,** to wear a monokini, to go topless.

monolingue [mɔnɔlɛ̃g] *adj* monolingual.

monolithe [mɔnɔlit] **1** *adj* monolithic. **2** *nm* monolith.

monolithique [mɔnɔlitik] *adj* monolithic; *Fig* **l'attitude m. des syndicats,** the unbending attitude of the unions.

monologue [mɔnɔlɔg] *nm* (*récitation par une seule personne, discours*) monologue; *Th* (*de Hamlet etc*) soliloquy; **m. intérieur,** inner dialogue *or US* dialog (with oneself).

monologuer [mɔnɔlɔge] *vi* (*réciter, faire un discours*) to give a monologue; *Th* to soliloquize, to talk to oneself.

monologueur [mɔnɔlɔgœr] *nm* monologist; *Th* soliloquist.

monomanie [mɔnɔmani] *nf Vieilli* monomania.

monôme [mɔnom] *nm Math* monomial, single term.

monomoteur [mɔnɔmɔtœr] **1** *adj* single-engined. **2** *nm* single-engined aircraft.

mononucléose [mɔnɔnykleoz] *nf Méd* mononucleosis.

monoparental, -aux [mɔnɔparɑ̃tal, -o] *adj* (*famille*) single-parent.

monophasé [mɔnɔfaze] *Él* **1** *adj* single-phase (*current*). **2** *nm* **m. de traction,** single-phase traction current.

monoplace [mɔnɔplas] *adj & n* single-seater (car, aircraft *etc*).

monoplan [mɔnɔplɑ̃] *nm Av* monoplane.

monopole [mɔnɔpɔl] *nm* monopoly; **avoir le m. de la vente,** to have the monopoly of sales; *Fig* **tu n'as pas le m. de ce bureau,** you haven't got a monopoly on this office; **tu n'as pas le m. sur lui,** you haven't got a monopoly on him.

monopolisateur, -trice [mɔnɔpɔlizatœr, -tris] *n* monopolizer, monopolist.

monopolisation [mɔnɔpɔlizasjɔ̃] *nf* monopolization.

monopoliser [mɔnɔpɔlize] *vt* to monopolize, to have the monopoly of (*sth*); **m. la conversation/la cuisine/*etc*,** to monopolize the conversation/the kitchen/*etc*.

monorail [mɔnɔraj] **1** *adj* monorail. **2** *nm* monorail.

monoski [mɔnɔski] *nm Sp* monoski; **faire du m.,** to monoski.

monosyllabe [mɔnɔsilab] **1** *adj* monosyllabic. **2** *nm* monosyllable.

monosyllabique [mɔnɔsilabik] *adj* monosyllabic.

monothéisme [mɔnɔteism] *nm* monotheism.

monothéiste [mɔnɔteist] **1** *adj* monotheistic. **2** *n* monotheist.

monotone [mɔnɔtɔn] *adj* monotonous.

monotonie [mɔnɔtɔni] *nf* monotony.

monotype [mɔnɔtip] *nf Typ* Monotype ® (machine).

monovalent [mɔnɔvalɑ̃] *adj Ch* monovalent, univalent.

monseigneur [mɔ̃sɛɲœr] *nm* **(a)** (*referring to prince*) His Royal Highness; (*to cardinal*) his Eminence; (*to duke, archbishop*) his Grace; (*to bishop*) his Lordship; **m. l'évêque de ...,** the Lord Bishop of ...; (*pl nosseigneurs*); **(b)** (*when speaking to prince*) Your Royal Highness; (*to cardinal*) your Eminence; (*to duke, archbishop*) your Grace; (*to bishop*) my Lord (Bishop), your Lordship; (*pl messeigneurs*); **(c) pince m.,** • (burglar's) jemmy; (*pl monseigneurs*).

monsieur, *pl* **messieurs** [məsjø, mesjø] *nm* **(a) M. Robert Martin,** Mr Robert Martin; **Messieurs Martin et Cie,** Messrs Martin and Co.; **m. le duc/le comte de ...,** the Duke/the Earl of ...; **m. le duc/le comte,** his Grace/his Lordship; **ça n'intéresse pas M. Tout le monde,** that doesn't interest *Br* the man in the street *or Am* Joe Public; **il va encore nous jouer son m.-je-sais-tout,** here he goes again the know-all;

(b) (*to or of small boy*) **M. Robert (Martin),** Master Robert (Martin);

(c) (*utilisé seul*) **voici le chapeau de m.,** (*en s'adressant à lui*) here's your hat, sir; (*sans s'adresser à lui*) here's the gentleman's hat; (*quand on connaît son nom*) here's Mr Smith's hat; **m. n'est pas là,** Mr Smith is out;

(d) (*à un homme*) sir; (*à un duc*) sir, your Grace; (*à un comte*) sir, your Lordship; **bonsoir, messieurs,** goodnight, gentlemen; **m. a sonné?,** you rang, sir?; **que prendront ces messieurs?,** what will you have, gentlemen?; **Mesdames, Messieurs,** ladies and gentlemen; *F* **bonjour,**

Messieurs-Dames!, good morning!;

(e) (*dans une lettre*) **M.,** (*à un étranger*) (Dear) Sir; **M. et cher Confrère, M. et cher Collègue,** Dear Mr Smith; **Cher M.,** (*à une connaissance*) Dear Mr Smith;

(f) (*sur enveloppe*) **M. T. Martin,** Mr T. Martin, *Fml* T. Martin Esq.;

(g) (*homme*) (gentle)man; **deux messieurs que je ne connais pas,** two men I don't know; *Enf* **dis bonjour au m.,** say hello to the gentleman; **il y a un m. qui veut vous parler,** there is a (gentle)man here who wants to speak to you; **c'est un vilain m.,** he's a nasty piece of work.

monstre [mɔ̃str] **1** *nm Myth etc* monster; **les monstres marins,** the monsters of the deep; *Fig* **m. d'ingratitude,** (*personne*) monster of ingratitude; **ces monstres d'hommes,** those brutes of men; *Fig* **m. sacré,** (*du cinéma, de la danse etc*) giant, colossus; *Fig* **le m. sacré de la réforme soviétique,** the leading light of Soviet reform; *F* **cet enfant est un petit m.!,** that child's a little devil *or* a little monster! **2** *adj F* huge, colossal, mammoth; **un travail m.,** a mammoth task.

monstrueusement [mɔ̃stryøzmɑ̃] *adv* monstrously.

monstrueux, -euse [mɔ̃stryø, -øz] *adj* **(a)** (*fantastique*) monstrous, unnatural; **(b)** (*énorme*) huge, colossal; **(c)** (*scandaleux*) shocking, scandalous, dreadful; **elle est d'un égoïsme m.,** she is a monster of selfishness.

monstruosité [mɔ̃stryozite] *nf* monstrosity; monstrousness (*of crime etc*).

mont [mɔ̃] *nm* mount, mountain; **le m. Sinaï,** Mount Sinai; *Fig* **par monts et par vaux,** up hill and down dale; *Fig* **être toujours par monts et par vaux,** to be always on the move; *Fig* **promettre monts et merveilles à qn,** to promise s.o. the earth.

montage [mɔ̃taʒ] *nm* **(a)** setting (*of jewel, specimen etc*); mounting (*of photograph, fishhook etc*); fitting (on) (*of tyre*); fitting up, erecting, assembling, assembly (*of apparatus*); fitting out (*of workshop etc*); hanging (*of door*); *Cin* editing; *Ind* **chaîne de m.,** assembly line; *Cin* **salle de m.,** cutting room; *Écon* **le m. financier d'un projet,** the financial arrangements for a project; **le m. financier a été difficile,** it wasn't easy getting the money together; **le m. financier du projet sera le suivant,** money for the project will be provided as follows; **(b)** taking up, carrying up (*of building materials etc*); **(c)** *Él* connecting up; wiring (up).

montagnard, -arde [mɔ̃taɲar, -ard] **1** *adj* mountain, highland (*people etc*). **2** *n* **(a)** (*habitant*) mountain dweller, highlander; **(b)** *Hist* member of the Montagne.

montagne [mɔ̃taɲ] *nf* **(a)** mountain; (*région*) mountains, mountain region; **une m. très élevée,** a very high mountain; **aimer les paysages de montagnes,** to like mountainous scenery; *CE F* **la m. de beurre,** the butter mountain; *Fig* **une m. de choux,** a huge pile of cabbages; *Fig* **se faire une m. de qch,** to make a mountain out of a molehill; *Fig* **c'est la m. qui accouche d'une souris,** what a lot of fuss for nothing; **montagnes russes,** (*at fair*) big dipper, *surtout Am* roller coaster; **la haute/moyenne m.,** the high mountains/the uplands; *Sp* **faire de la m.,** (*alpinisme*) to do *or* go mountain climbing; (*randonnée*) to do *or* go mountain walking; **jambon de m.,** smoked ham; *F* **c'est de la m. à vaches,** it's just hill-walking; **passer ses vacances à la m.,** to spend one's holiday in the mountains; *Bible* **le sermon sur la m.,** the Sermon on the Mount;

(b) *Hist* (*during the French Revolution*) **la M.,** the Mountain.

montagneux, -euse [mɔ̃taɲø, -øz] *adj* mountainous.

montant [mɔ̃tɑ̃] **1** *adj* rising, ascending; **chemin m.,** uphill road; **marée montante,** rising tide, flood tide; **col m.,** high *or* stand-up collar; *Rail* **train/quai m.,** up train/platform; *Mil* **garde montante,** new guard, relieving guard. **2** *nm* **(a)** amount, sum; **cinq versements d'un m. de 500 francs,** five payments of 500 francs (each); **j'ignore le m. de mes dettes,** I don't know what my debts amount to; **(b)** upright (*of ladder etc*); leg (*of trestle*); column, pillar (*in machine*); pole (*of tent*); stile, jamb (*of door, window*); post (*of gate*); riser (*of stair*); cheek strap (*of bridle*); *Fb* **les montants,** the goalposts.

mont-de-piété [mɔ̃dpjete] *nm Arch* (*now* **crédit municipal**) pawnshop; **mettre qch au m.-de-p.,** to pawn sth; (*pl monts-de-piété*).

monte [mɔ̃t] *nf* **(a)** *Courses de chevaux* mounting (*of horse*); **jockey qui a eu trois montes dans la journée,** jockey who has ridden three times *or* who has had three mounts *or* rides in the day; **(b)** (method of) riding, horsemanship; **m. à l'obstacle,** jumping; **(c)** covering (*of mare*); breeding season, mating season (*of domestic animals*).

monté [mɔ̃te] *adj* **(a)** mounted (*policeman, soldier etc*); *Fig* **il était m.** *ou* **il avait la tête montée contre elle,** he had it in for her; **(b)** set (*jewel*); mounted (*gun etc*); equipped, fitted, appointed (*ship etc*); **photographies non montées,** unmounted photographs; **pièce mal montée,** badly produced play; **cave/boutique bien montée,** well stocked cellar/shop; **coup m.,** put-up job; (*pour accuser qn*) frame-up; **j'ai été victime d'un coup m.,** it was a put-up job; (*pour m'incriminer*) I've been framed; **(c)** *Arg* **bien m.,** (*homme*) well-hung.

monte-charge [mɔ̃tʃarʒ] *nm inv* hoist, goods lift, *Am* goods elevator.

montée [mɔ̃te] *nf* **(a)** rise; rising; **pendant la m.,** as I *or* we *etc* were climbing *or* going up; *HydE etc* **tuyau de m.,** uptake pipe, riser; **m. des eaux,** (*in reservoir*) inflow; **la m. des prix,** the rise in prices, rising prices; **(b)** *Aut Av* **essai de m.,** climbing test; **vitesse en m.,** climbing speed; *Aut Rail* speed on a gradient; **(c)** (*côte*) slope, hill (*in road*); **en haut de la m.,** at the top of the slope *or* hill; **il y a une méchante m. avant d'arriver chez lui,** there's a stiff climb before you reach his house.

monte-en-l'air [mɔ̃tɑ̃lɛr] *nm inv F* cat burglar.

monte-plats [mɔ̃tpla] *nm inv* (*in restaurant*) service lift *or Am* elevator, hoist, dumb waiter.

monter [mɔ̃te] **1** *vi* (*aux souvent* **être**, *parfois* **avoir**) **(a)** (*se déplacer vers le haut*) to go up, to climb (up); (*en haut de l'escalier*) to go upstairs; (*d'un oiseau*) to soar; (*d'un avion*) to climb; **m. à** *ou* **sur un arbre/une échelle,** to climb (up) a tree/a ladder; **m. en haut d'une colline,** to climb *or* go up (right) to the top of a hill; **m. en courant/en rampant/***etc*, to run/crawl/*etc* up; **m. se coucher,** to go (up) to bed; **faire m. qn,** to show s.o. up(stairs); **montez chez moi,** come up to my room; **après ses études, il est monté à Paris,** after college, he moved to Paris; **elle monte souvent à Paris pour voir sa sœur,** she often goes to Paris to see her sister; *Mil* **m. en ligne,** to go to the front (line); **m. à l'assaut,** to go into the attack; *Tennis* **m. au filet,** to come *or* go to the net; *Nau* **faire m. tous les hommes,** to order all hands on deck;

(b) (*pour s'installer etc*) to climb *or* get on *or* into (*sth*); (*dans le train, l'autobus etc*) to get on; **où êtes-vous monté?,** where did you get on?; **m. sur une chaise,** to stand on a chair; **m. en chaire,** to ascend the pulpit; **m. à cheval,** to get on a horse, to mount (a horse); (*faire de l'équitation*) to ride; **montez-vous (à cheval)?,** do you ride?; *F* **m. sur ses grands chevaux,** to get on one's high horse; **m. à** *ou* **en bicyclette,** to ride a bicycle; **m. en voiture,** to get into a car; *Nau Av* **m. à bord,** to board, to go on board; **faire m. qn (en voiture) avec soi,** to give s.o. a lift; **le ministre va m. à la tribune pour s'expliquer,** = the minister will give an explanation to the House; **m. sur les planches,** to go on the stage;

(c) (*d'un ballon, du soleil etc*) to rise; (*d'un prix, baromètre etc*) to rise, to go up; (*de marée*) to rise, to come in; **les frais montent,** the costs are mounting (up); **la somme monte à cent francs,** the total amounts *or* comes to a hundred francs; **faire m. les prix,** to increase *or* raise prices; **empêcher les prix de m.,** to stop prices rising, to keep prices down; **le sang lui monta à la tête,** the blood rushed to his head; **faire m. les larmes aux yeux de qn,** to bring tears to s.o.'s eyes; *Fig* **m. comme une soupe au lait,** to flare up; **faire m. qn,** to get a rise out of s.o.;

(d) (*d'une route etc*) to climb, to slope up; **la rue va en montant,** the street climbs;

(e) (*d'une personne etc*) **m. dans l'estime de qn,** to go up *or* rise in s.o.'s estimation; **faire m. qn dans l'estime de qn,** to raise s.o. in s.o.'s estimation.

2 *vt* (*aux* **avoir**) **(a)** to climb (up), to go up, to come up (*hill, stairs etc*); **m. la rue en courant,** to run up the street; **m. un fleuve,** to go up a river;

(b) to bring *or* carry up; **m. du vin de la cave,** to fetch *or* bring wine up from the cellar; **m. le courrier,** (*d'un concierge etc*) to bring the post; **m. le son,** to turn up the volume; **m. le gaz,** to turn up the gas; *Fig* **m. (la tête à) qn contre qn,** to set s.o. against s.o.;

(c) to set, to mount (*jewel*); to mount (*photo, fishhook etc*); to fit (on) (*tyre*); to set up, to fit up, to erect (*apparatus etc*); to hang (*door*); to fit out, to equip (*workshop etc*); to assemble, to erect (*machine*); *Th* to set (*scene*); to stage, to put on, to produce (*play*); *Cin etc* to edit (*film*); *Couture* to make up (*garment*); **m. un magasin,** to set up *or* open a shop; **elle commence à m. son trousseau,** she's beginning to put her trousseau together; **m. un complot/un coup,** to hatch a plot/to plan a burglary; *F* **m. le coup à**

qn, to deceive s.o., to take s.o. in; *F* **ses copains lui ont monté la baraque avec Rosalie,** his mates fixed him up with Rosalie; *Tricot* **m. les mailles,** to cast on (the stitches);

(d) *Mil etc* **m. la garde,** to mount *or* keep guard;

(e) to ride (*horse*);

(f) être bien monté en vaisselle, to be well-supplied with crockery;

(g) *Él* to connect up, to wire (up).

3 se monter *vpr* **(a)** (*d'un prix etc*) to amount; **à combien se monte tout cela?,** how much does all this add up to *or* come to?;

(b) (*s'équiper*) to equip oneself, to fit oneself out (**en,** with); **se m. en vaisselle,** to supply oneself with crockery; **se m. en affaires,** to set up (in business) on one's own;

(c) *F* to lose one's temper; **elle s'est montée contre lui,** she's got it in for him;

(d) (*d'un cheval*) to be ridden; **Flicka se monte facilement,** Flicka is easy to ride.

monteur, -euse [mɔ̃tœr, -øz] *n* setter (*of jewels*); mounter (*of pictures etc*); *Cin* editor; *MecE etc* fitter; *F* **c'est un sacré m. d'affaires,** he's a first-rate fixer.

monticule [mɔ̃tikyl] *nm* (*petite colline*) hillock, mound; (*plus petit*) hummock; *Can Baseball* mound; **m. de neige/terre/***etc*, mound of snow/earth/*etc*.

mont(-)joie [mɔ̃ʒwa] *nf* cairn, heap of stones; (*pl monts-joie, montjoies*).

montoir [mɔ̃twar] *nm* mounting block, horse block; **côté (du) m.,** nearside (*of horse*); **côté hors (du) m.,** offside.

montrable [mɔ̃trabl] *adj* fit to be seen, presentable.

montre [mɔ̃tr] *nf* **(a)** watch; **m. (de poignet),** (wrist)watch; **m. à recouvrement,** hunter; **m. à guichet,** half hunter; **m. marine,** ship's chronometer; **à ma m. il est midi,** by my watch it's midday; **cela lui a pris dix minutes m. en main,** it took him ten minutes by the clock; **course contre la m.,** race against time; *Fig* **on est dans une course contre la m.,** we're racing against time; **(b)** (*preuve*) show, display; **faire m. d'un grand courage,** to display great courage; *Litt* **faire qch pour la m.,** to do sth merely for show; **(c)** (*vitrine*) shop window, display window; (*dans meuble*) showcase; **mettre qch en m.,** to put sth in the window *or* on show *or* on display.

Montréal [mɔ̃real] *n* Montreal.

montréalais, -aise [mɔ̃realɛ, -ɛz] **1** *adj* (of) Montreal. **2** *n* **M.,** Montrealer.

montre-bracelet [mɔ̃trəbraslɛ] *nf* wristwatch; (*pl montres-bracelets*).

montrer [mɔ̃tre] **1** *vt* (*révéler, faire preuve de*) to show, to display, to exhibit; (*désigner*) to show, to point out; **il a montré un grand courage,** he showed *or* displayed great courage; **elle nous montre ses plus beaux dessins,** she shows us her best drawings; **on n'ose plus m. ses jambes avec le froid!,** you don't feel like going about bare-legged in this cold!; **une robe décolletée qui montre les épaules,** a low-cut dress which leaves the shoulders bare; **elle a montré une jolie paire de jambes en s'asseyant,** she showed a pretty pair of legs as she sat down; **il n'y montre jamais le nez,** he never shows his face there; **m. qn/qch du doigt,** to point s.o./sth out (with one's finger), to point to s.o./sth; **m. le chemin à qn,** to show s.o. the way; **m. la ville à qn,** to show s.o. round the town; **cela te montre qu'il faut être prudent,** that (just) shows that you have to be careful; **l'histoire montre que tout est relatif,** history shows that everything is relative; **m. à qn à faire qch,** to show s.o. how to do sth; **montre-lui la manière de le faire,** show him how to do it *or* how it's done.

2 se montrer *vpr* **(a)** to appear; **il n'ose plus se m.,** he doesn't dare show himself *or* his face;

(b) des taches brunes se montrent sur la peau, brown marks appear on the skin;

(c) il se montra prudent, he showed prudence; **il s'est montré très gentil,** he was very kind; **il s'est montré très courageux,** he displayed great courage.

montreur, -euse [mɔ̃trœr, -øz] *n* showman, *f* showwoman (*at fair etc*); exhibitor (*of wild beasts*); **m. d'ours,** bear leader.

montueux, -euse [mɔ̃tɥø, -øz] *adj* hilly.

monture [mɔ̃tyr] *nf* **(a)** mounting (*of photograph etc*); mount (*of picture etc*); setting (*of jewel*); frame (*of saw, umbrella, spectacles etc*); stock (*of gun, pistol*); handle, guard (*of sword*); **lunettes sans m.,** rimless spectacles; **(b)** (*horse etc*) mount, (saddle) horse.

monument [mɔnymɑ̃] *nm* **(a)** monument, memorial; **m. funéraire,** monument (over a tomb); **m. aux morts,** war memorial; **(b)** (*édifice public*) public *or* historic building; **(c)** *F* **cette armoire est un m.,** it's an enormous cupboard; **ce livre est un m.,** the book is a masterpiece; **ce recueil est un m. d'absurdité,** this collection is monumentally absurd.

monumental, -aux [mɔnymɑ̃tal, -o] *adj* monumental; **commettre une erreur monumentale,** to commit a monumental blunder; **elle est d'une bêtise monumentale,** she's monumentally stupid.

mope [mɔp] *nf Can* (*balai*) mop.

moquer [mɔke] **1** *vt Arch* to mock. **2 se moquer** *vpr* **se m. de qn/qch,** to mock *or* make fun of *or* laugh at *or* poke fun at s.o./sth; **vous vous moquez,** you're joking, you're not serious; **se faire m. de soi,** to make a fool of oneself; **il se moque du tiers comme du quart,** he doesn't care *or* give a damn about anybody or anything; **elle s'en moque éperdument,** she just couldn't care less; *F* **je m'en moque comme de l'an quarante** *ou* **comme de ma première chemise,** I don't care two hoots *or* a tinker's cuss *or* a tinker's damn; **vous vous moquez** *ou* **c'est se m. du monde!,** it's the height of impertinence!, what a cheek!

moquerie [mɔkri] *nf* mockery, jeering, ridicule.

moquette [mɔkɛt] *nf* **(a)** (fitted) carpet; **(b)** *Tex* moquette.

moquetter [mɔkəte] *vt* to carpet.

moqueur, -euse [mɔkœr, -øz] **1** *adj* **(a)** (*remarque etc*) mocking, jeering, scoffing; **rires moqueurs,** mocking *or* derisive laughter; **(b)** (*personne*) given to mockery. **2** *n* mocker, scoffer. **3** *nm* (*oiseau*) mockingbird.

moqueusement [mɔkøzmɑ̃] *adv* mockingly.

moraillon [mɔrajɔ̃] *nm* hasp, clasp (*of lock*).

moraine [mɔrɛn] *nf Géol* moraine.

moral, -aux [mɔral, -o] **1** *adj* **(a)** moral; **courage m.,** moral courage; **sens m.,** moral sense; **victoire morale,** moral victory; **certitude morale,** moral certainty; **cette histoire n'est pas morale,** this is not a very edifying story; **science morale,** ethics; **facultés morales,** ability to distinguish between right and wrong; **(b)** *Jur* **personne morale,** legal entity, corporation. **2** *nm* morale; **c'est bon pour le m.,** it's good for morale; **le m. est bas,** morale is low; **son m. est bas,** his spirits are low; *F* **avoir le m. à zéro,** to be fed up; **remonter le m. de** *ou* **à qn,** to raise s.o.'s spirits, to cheer s.o. up.

morale [mɔral] *nf* **(a)** (*bien*) morals; **contraire/conforme à la m.,** immoral/moral; **(b)** (*conduite*) ethics; **tu ne vas quand même pas me faire une leçon de m., si?,** you're not going to start lecturing me, are you now?; **faire (de) la m. à qn,** to lecture s.o.; **adopter une m. d'ascète,** to adopt an ascetic philosophy *or* way of life; **(c)** moral (*of story*).

moralement [mɔralmɑ̃] *adv* morally; **m. tu ne peux pas lui faire ça,** morally (speaking) you can't do that to him.

moralisateur, -trice [mɔralizatœr, -tris] **1** *adj* **(a)** *Péj* moralizing (*person*); **(b)** elevating, edifying (*principles*). **2** *n* moralizer.

moralisation [mɔralizɑsjɔ̃] *nf Arch* moralization (*of community etc*).

moraliser [mɔralize] **1** *vi* to moralize. **2** *vt* **(a)** to clean up (*politics, the financial market etc*); **(b)** to lecture (*s.o.*).

moraliste [mɔralist] **1** *adj* moralistic. **2** *n* moralist.

moralité [mɔralite] *nf* **(a)** (*mérite*) morality; (good) moral conduct; **certificat de m.,** character reference; **(b)** (*attitude*) morals, honesty; **elle est d'une m. douteuse,** her morals are dubious, she has dubious morals; **(c)** moral (*of story*); **(d)** *Hist Littér* morality (play).

morasse [mɔras] *nf Typ* brush proof (*of newspaper*).

moratoire [mɔratwar] *Jur* **1** *adj* moratory (*agreement etc*); (*payment*) delayed by agreement; **intérêts moratoires,** interest on overdue payments. **2** *nm* moratorium.

moratorium [mɔratɔrjɔm] *nm Jur* moratorium.

morbide [mɔrbid] *adj* morbid.

morbidement [mɔrbidmɑ̃] *adv* morbidly.

morbidité [mɔrbidite] *nf* morbidity, morbidness.

morbleu [mɔrblø] *int Arch* 'sdeath!, zounds!

morceau, -eaux [mɔrso] *nm* **(a)** piece, bit (*of food*); **m. de choix,** choice morsel; **bas morceaux,** cheap(er) cuts (*of meat*); **aimer les bons morceaux,** to like good things (to eat); *F* **manger un m.,** to have a bite to eat *or* a snack; **emporter le m.,** to win (*in deal etc*); *F* **lâcher le m.,** to give the game away; **(b)** piece, bit (*of soap, cloth, wool etc*); *Mus* piece; piece, bit, scrap, fragment (*of paper etc*); lump (*of sugar etc*); piece, bit, patch (*of land etc*); piece, bit, length (*of string*); **sucre en morceaux,** lump sugar, cube sugar; **mettre qch en morceaux,** to pull sth to pieces *or* to bits; **tomber en morceaux,** to fall *or* be falling to pieces *or* bits; *Mus* **m. au trombone,** piece for the trombone; *Litt* **morceaux choisis,** selected passages *or* extracts; *F* **cette fille, c'est un beau m.,** she's a bit of all right, that girl.

morceler [mɔrsəle] *vt* (**je morcelle; je morcellerai**) to cut (*sth*) up into small pieces; **m. une propriété,** to break up *or* parcel out an estate.
morcellement [mɔrsɛlmɑ̃] *nm* breaking up, parcelling out, cutting up, division (*of estate etc*).
mordache [mɔrdaʃ] *nf* clamp, claw (*of vice*); jaw, clip, grip, dog (*of chuck*).
mordacité [mɔrdasite] *nf Litt* mordancy (*of critic etc*).
mordant [mɔrdɑ̃] **1** *adj* mordant, biting, caustic, scathing (*wit, speech etc*); cutting, caustic, scathing (*remark etc*); penetrating, piercing (*sound*); **froid m.,** biting cold. **2** *nm* mordancy (*of wit etc*); keenness (*of troops etc*); bite (*of file etc*); (*for dyeing*) mordant; *Mus* mordent.
mordicus [mɔrdikys] *adv F* stoutly, doggedly; **elle l'affirme m.,** she's quite dogged about it.
mordieu [mɔrdjø] *int Arch* 'sdeath!, zounds!
mordillage [mɔrdijaʒ] *nm* nibbling.
mordiller [mɔrdije] *vi & vt* to nibble.
mordoré [mɔrdɔre] *adj & n* bronze (colour).
mordorer [mɔrdɔre] *vt* to bronze (*leather etc*).
mordorure [mɔrdɔryr] *nf* bronze finish (*on leather etc*).
mordre [mɔrdr] **1** *vt* **(a)** (*d'un chien etc*) to bite; **le froid lui mordait les doigts,** the cold was nipping his fingers; *F* **m. la poussière,** to bite the dust; *Fig* **approche, je ne vais pas te m.,** come on, I won't bite you;
(b) (*accrocher*) to bite into; **acide qui mord les métaux,** acid that bites (into) *or* eats away *or* acts on metals.
2 *vi* **(a)** to bite; **m. à** *ou* **dans une pomme,** to bite into *or* take a bite out of an apple; **m. sur qch,** to encroach (up)on sth; **la route mord sur mon terrain,** the road encroaches on my land; *Tennis* **m. sur la ligne,** to have one's foot (just) over the line; **m. à l'appât** *ou* **à l'hameçon,** to rise to *or* swallow the bait; **le public a bien mordu,** the public responded well; *F* **il mord au latin,** he's taking to Latin; *Pêche* **ça mord,** I've got a bite;
(b) (*accrocher*) to catch, to engage; **lime/vis qui mord,** file/screw that bites *or* has a good bite; **l'ancre ne mord pas,** the anchor won't hold *or* grip;
(c) (faire) m. une planche, to etch a plate.
3 se mordre *vpr* to bite oneself; **se m. la langue,** to bite one's tongue; **se m. la langue d'avoir parlé,** to regret bitterly having spoken; **se m. les lèvres,** to bite one's lips; **il s'en mord les lèvres,** he bitterly regrets it.
mordu, -e [mɔrdy] **1** *adj* bitten; *F* madly in love; *F* **elle est mordue de ski,** she's been bitten by the skiing bug, she's mad on skiing. **2** *n* fan; **m. du bridge/cinéma/***etc*, bridge/film/*etc* fanatic.
more [mɔr] = **MAURE**.
morelle [mɔrɛl] *nf Bot* nightshade.
moresque [mɔrɛsk] = **MAURESQUE**.
morfil [mɔrfil] *nm* wire edge (*on tool*).
morfondre (se) [səmɔrfɔ̃dr] *vpr* (*s'ennuyer*) to be bored to death; (*être triste*) to mope; **se m. à la porte de qn,** to hang around at s.o.'s door.
morfondu [mɔrfɔ̃dy] *adj* gloomy.
morganatique [mɔrganatik] *adj* morganatic.
morganatiquement [mɔrganatikmɑ̃] *adv* morganatically.
morgeline [mɔrʒəlin] *nf Bot* scarlet pimpernel; (*à fleurs blanches*) chickweed.
morgue¹ [mɔrg] *nf* (*insolence*) pride, haughtiness, arrogance; **regard plein de m.,** haughty *or* arrogant look.
morgue² *nf* (*dans un hôpital etc*) mortuary, morgue.
moribond, -onde [mɔribɔ̃, -ɔ̃d] **1** *adj* moribund, dying, at death's door. **2** *n* **les moribonds,** the dying.
moricaud, -aude [mɔriko, -od] *F Péj* **1** *adj* dark-skinned, dusky, swarthy. **2** *n* dark-skinned person.
morigéner [mɔriʒene] *vt* (**je morigène; je morigénerai**) to lecture (*s.o.*), to take (*s.o.*) to task, to give (*s.o.*) a good talking to.
morille [mɔrij] *nf Culin* morel.
morillon [mɔrijɔ̃] *nm* **(a)** (*oiseau*) tufted duck; **(b)** (*pierre précieuse*) rough emerald.
mormon, -one [mɔrmɔ̃, -ɔn] **1** *n* Mormon, Latter-Day Saint. **2** *adj* Mormon (*church etc*).
mormonisme [mɔrmɔnism] *nm* Mormonism.
morne [mɔrn] *adj* dismal, dejected, gloomy (*person, silence etc*); gloomy, dreary, dull (*weather etc*).
mornifle [mɔrnifl] *nf F* (*gifle*) slap, backhander.
morose [mɔroz] *adj* morose, moody, surly, sullen.
morosité [mɔrozite] *nf* moroseness, moodiness, surliness.
Morphée [mɔrfe] *nm* Morpheus; **dans les bras de M.,** in the arms of Morpheus.
morphème [mɔrfɛm] *nm Ling* morpheme.
morphine [mɔrfin] *nf* morphine, *parfois* morphia.
morphinisme [mɔrfinism] *nm Méd* morphinism.
morphinomane [mɔrfinɔman] **1** *adj* addicted to morphine. **2** *n* morphine addict.
morphinomanie [mɔrfinɔmani] *nf* addiction to morphine.
morphologie [mɔrfɔlɔʒi] *nf* morphology.
morphologique [mɔrfɔlɔʒik] *adj* morphological.
morphologiquement [mɔrfɔlɔʒikmɑ̃] *adv* morphologically.
morpion [mɔrpjɔ̃] *nm* **(a)** *Arg* (*pou*) crab; **(b)** *Arg* (*gamin*) child, kid, brat; **(c)** (*jeu*) noughts and crosses, *US* tick-tack-toe.
mors [mɔr] *nm* **(a)** (*d'un étau*) jaw; **(b)** (*de livre*) joint; **(c)** (*de harnais*) bit; **prendre le m. aux dents,** (*d'un cheval*) to take the bit in its teeth, to bolt; *Fig* (*d'une personne*) to take the bit between one's teeth, to be carried away.
morse¹ [mɔrs] *nm* walrus.
morse² *nm Télécom* Morse (*code etc*).
morsure [mɔrsyr] *nf* **(a)** bite; **une m. de chien,** a dog bite; **une m. profonde,** a deep bite; **(b)** (*d'acide etc*) biting.
mort¹, morte [mɔr, mɔrt] **1** *adj* **(a)** dead (*person, leaf, language etc*); lifeless (*expression etc*); **m. et enterré,** dead and buried, dead and gone; **je le veux m. ou vif,** I want him, dead or alive; **il est m.,** he's dead; **il est m. hier,** he died yesterday; **m. pour la France,** (*soldier etc*) who died for France; *Prov* **morte la bête, m. le venin,** dead men tell no tales; **m. de peur,** frightened to death; **elle avait le regard m.,** she had a lifeless look; **plus m. que vif,** half-dead with fright; *Com* **marché m.,** dead market; **la mer Morte,** the Dead Sea; *F* **je n'en peux plus, je suis m. (de fatigue),** I can't go on, I'm dead tired;
(b) temps m., *Sp* stoppage time, injury time (*in match*); lull (*in work, conversation*); *MecE* **poids m.,** dead weight; *Constr* dead load; **point m.,** dead centre *or US* center (*of piston stroke*); neutral position (*of lever etc*); *Aut* neutral gear; *Aut* **mettre le levier au point m.,** to put the (gear) lever into neutral; **arriver à un point m.,** to come to a standstill; **les pourparlers sont arrivés à un point m.,** the talks have come to a standstill *or* reached deadlock; **angle m.,** (*in car etc*) blind spot; **œuvres mortes,** dead works; **eau morte,** stagnant water; *Beaux-Arts* **nature morte,** still life; **balle morte,** spent bullet.
2 *n* dead person; **le nombre des morts sur la route,** the number of deaths on the roads; **les morts,** the dead; *Rel* **jour** *ou* **fête des Morts,** All Souls' day; **l'office des morts,** the burial service; **faire le m.,** to pretend to be dead, to play dead; **je lui ai écrit pour me plaindre il y a trois semaines, mais depuis, il fait le m.,** I wrote to him to complain three weeks ago but since then he's been as silent as the grave *or* I haven't heard a thing; **tête de m.,** death's head; (*pavillon*) skull and crossbones, Jolly Roger; *Aut* **la place du m.,** the passenger seat; *Fig* **c'est un m. vivant,** he's half dead.
3 *nm Cartes* dummy; **faire le m.,** to be dummy.
mort² *nf* **(a)** death; **pâle comme la m.,** as pale as death; **il n'y a pas eu m. d'homme,** there was no loss of life; **mettre qn à m.,** to put s.o. to death; **condamner qn à m.,** to condemn *or* sentence s.o. to death; **sentence** *ou* **arrêt de m.,** death sentence, sentence of death; **à m. les traîtres!,** death to the traitors!; *Arg* **m. aux vaches!,** down with the cops!; **blessé à m.,** mortally wounded; **lutte à m.,** fight to the death *or* end; *F* **freiner à m.,** to jam on the brakes; **se donner la m.,** to take one's (own) life; *F* **vous allez attraper la m.!,** you'll catch your death (of cold)!; **mourir de sa belle m.** *ou* **de m. naturelle,** to die a natural death, to die of natural causes; **être à la m.** *ou* **à l'article de la m.,** to be at death's door; **à la m. de son père,** on his father's death; **haïr qn à m.,** to loathe and detest s.o.; **ennemis à m.,** deadly enemies; **silence de m.,** deadly *or* deathlike silence *or* hush; **il avait la m. dans l'âme,** he was sick at heart, he had a heavy heart; **partir la m. dans l'âme,** to leave with a heavy heart; **souffrir m. et passion,** to suffer agonies; **je m'en souviendrai jusqu'à la m.,** I'll remember it until my dying day; **à la vie, à la m.,** for ever, for life; **le monopole est la m. de l'industrie,** monopoly means the end *or* is the ruin of industry; **ce fut un arrêt de m. pour notre entreprise,** it spelt the end *or* was the deathknell for our company;
(b) *Bot* **m. aux loups,** wolfsbane; **m. aux poules,** henbane.
mortadelle [mɔrtadɛl] *nf* mortadella.
mortaise [mɔrtɛz] *nf* slot; *Menuis* mortise; **assemblage à tenon et à m.,** mortise (and tenon) joint; *MecE etc* **m. de clavette,** keyway.
mortaiser [mɔrtɛze] *vt* to slot, to mortise.

mortalité [mɔrtalite] *nf* **(a)** mortality, death rate; **taux de m.,** mortality *or* death rate; **m. infantile,** child *or* infant mortality; **(b)** *Arch* mortal nature.

mort-aux-rats [mɔrora] *nf inv* rat poison.

mort-bois [mɔrbwa] *nm* underwood, brushwood; (*pl morts-bois*).

morte-eau [mɔrto] *nf* neap tide; (*pl mortes-eaux*).

mortel, -elle [mɔrtɛl] **1** *adj* **(a)** (*qui tue*) mortal; fatal, mortal (*wound etc*); **coup m.,** mortal blow, lethal blow, death blow; **poison m.,** deadly poison; **rayon m.,** death ray; **il a fait une chute mortelle de 100 mètres,** he fell 100 metres to his death; **(b)** *F* deadly dull, boring; **je l'ai attendu deux mortelles heures,** I waited two solid *or* whole hours for him; **le sport, je trouve ça m.,** I find sport deadly dull; **(c)** deadly (*hatred, sin etc*); **ennemi m.,** deadly enemy, mortal enemy; **d'une pâleur mortelle,** deathly pale. **2** *n* mortal.

mortellement [mɔrtɛlmɑ̃] *adv* mortally, fatally (*wounded etc*); **pécher m.,** to commit a mortal sin; **m. pâle,** deathly pale; **m. offensé,** mortally offended; *F* **s'ennuyer m.,** to be bored to death; **m. ennuyeux,** deadly dull *or* boring.

morte-saison [mɔrt(ə)sɛzɔ̃] *nf Com etc* slack period, off season; (*pl mortes-saisons*).

mortier [mɔrtje] *nm* **(a)** *Culin etc* mortar; **pilon et m.,** mortar and pestle; **(b)** *Mil* mortar; **obus de m.,** mortar shell; **(c)** *Constr* **m. ordinaire,** lime mortar; **m. hydraulique,** hydraulic cement *or* mortar; **m. liquide** *ou* **clair,** grout(ing); **planche à m.,** mortarboard.

mortifiant [mɔrtifjɑ̃] *adj* mortifying.

mortification [mɔrtifikɑsjɔ̃] *nf* **(a)** mortification, chastening (*of flesh, passions etc*); **(b)** (*humiliation*) mortification, humiliation; **(c)** *Culin* hanging (*of game etc*); **(d)** *Méd Vieilli* gangrene, mortification (*of limb etc*).

mortifié [mɔrtifje] *adj* **(a)** mortified, humiliated; **(b)** *Méd Vieilli* gangrenous.

mortifier [mɔrtifje] *v* (*pr sub & impf* **n. mortifiions, v. mortifiiez**) **1** *vt* **(a)** to mortify (*flesh, passions etc*); **(b)** to mortify, to humiliate (*s.o.*); **(c)** *Culin* to hang (*game etc*); **(d)** *Méd Vieilli* to make gangrenous, to cause (*limb etc*) to mortify. **2 se mortifier** *vpr* to mortify oneself.

mortinatalité [mɔrtinatalite] *nf* rate of stillbirths.

mort-né, -née [mɔrne] (*pl mort-né(e)s*) **1** *adj* stillborn (*child etc*); *Fig* **projet m.-né,** plan destined to fail. **2** *n* stillborn child.

mortuaire [mɔrtɥɛr] *adj* mortuary (*urn etc*); **drap m.,** pall; **registre m.,** register of deaths; **avis m.,** announcement of death (*in papers etc*); **la maison m.,** the house of the deceased; **chambre m.,** death chamber; **dépôt m.,** mortuary.

morue [mɔry] *nf* **(a)** (*poisson*) cod; **huile de foie de m.,** cod-liver oil; **(b)** *Vulg* (*prostituée*) tart.

morutier, -ière [mɔrytje, -jɛr] **1** *adj* cod-fishing (*industry etc*). **2** *nm* **(a)** (*bateau*) cod-fishing boat; **(b)** (*pêcheur*) cod-fisher(man).

morve [mɔrv] *nf* **(a)** *Vét* glanders; **(b)** (*du nez*) (nasal) mucus, *F* snot.

morveux, -euse [mɔrvø, -øz] **1** *adj* **(a)** *Vét* glandered; **(b)** (*d'un enfant etc*) **être m.,** to have a runny *or F* snotty nose; *Prov* **qui se sent m. se mouche,** if the cap fits wear it. **2** *n F* (*gamin*) kid, *Péj* brat; (*plus âgé*) snot, (little) jerk.

mosaïque[1] [mɔzaik] *adj Bible* Mosaic (*law etc*).

mosaïque[2] *nf Beaux-Arts etc* mosaic; **dallage en m.,** mosaic flooring; *TV* **m. photoélectrique,** photoelectric mosaic; **m. des plantes,** virus disease; *Fig* **le marché forme une m. de couleurs,** the market is a kaleidoscope of colours.

mosaïste [mɔzaist] *n Beaux-Arts* worker in mosaic.

Moscou [mɔsku] *n* Moscow.

moscoutaire [mɔskutɛr] *Péj Vieilli* **1** *adj* Communist, *F* Commie. **2** *n* **M.,** Communist, *F* Commie.

moscovite [mɔskɔvit] **1** *adj* Muscovite. **2** *n* **M.,** Muscovite.

mosquée [mɔske] *nf* mosque.

mot [mo] *nm* word; **répéter qch m. pour m.,** to repeat sth word for word *or* verbatim; **traduire m. à m., faire du m. à m.,** to translate word for word *or* literally; **prendre qn au m.,** to take s.o. at his word; **groupe de mots,** word group; *Ordinat* **m. de 6 bits,** 6-bit byte; **sans m. dire,** without (saying) a word; **qui ne dit m. consent,** silence means consent; **ne pas souffler m. de qch,** not to breathe a word about sth; **dire un m.** *ou* **deux mots à qn,** to have a word with s.o.; **dire un m. pour** *ou* **en faveur de qn,** to put in a good word for s.o.; **avoir des mots avec qn,** to have words with s.o.; **vous avez dit le m.!,** you've hit the nail on the head!, you said it!; **avoir le dernier m.,** to have the last word; **j'ignore le premier m.** *ou* **je ne sais pas un (traître) m. de latin,** I don't know the first thing about Latin; **sur ces mots, il se leva,** and so saying, he got up; **en d'autres mots,** in other words; **en un m., en peu de mots, en quelques mots,** briefly, in a word; **en un m. comme en cent,** in a nutshell; **au bas m.,** at the lowest estimate; **gros m.,** swear word; **ne dis pas de gros mots!,** don't swear!; **le m. de l'énigme,** the key to the enigma; **voilà le fin m. de l'affaire!,** so that's what's at the bottom of it!; **faire comprendre qch à qn à mots couverts,** to give s.o. a hint of sth; *Ordinat etc* **m. de passe,** password; *Mil* **m. de ralliement,** password; **m. d'ordre,** *Mil* password; keynote (*of policy*); watchword, slogan (*of political party etc*); **mots croisés,** crossword puzzle(s), crossword(s); **envoyer** *ou* **écrire un (petit) m. à qn,** to drop s.o. a line, to write s.o. a note; **avoir son m. à dire,** to have one's say; **je ne pouvais pas placer un m.,** I couldn't get a word in edgeways; **il a toujours le m. pour rire,** he's always ready with a joke; **m. historique,** historic remark, memorable saying; **bon m.,** witty remark, witticism, one-liner.

motard [mɔtar] *nm F* **(a)** biker; **(b)** (*de la police*) motorcycle policeman, speed cop; **m. d'escorte,** police outrider.

mot-clé [mokle] *nm* keyword; (*pl mots-clé(s)*).

motel [mɔtɛl] *nm* motel.

motet [mɔtɛ] *nm Mus* motet.

moteur, -trice [mɔtœr, -tris] **1** *adj* **(a)** motive, propulsive, driving (*power etc*); **arbre m.,** drive shaft, main shaft; *MecE* **unité motrice,** power pack *or* unit; **force motrice,** driving force; **roue motrice,** driving wheel; **voiture à roues avant motrices,** car with front-wheel drive; **temps m.,** power stroke;

(b) *Anat* motor (*nerve etc*); **cet enfant souffre de troubles moteurs,** this child suffers from motor deficiences.

2 *nm* **(a)** motor, engine; **m. à vapeur,** steam engine; **m. à combustion interne** *ou* **à explosion,** internal combustion engine; **m. diesel,** diesel engine; **m. à gaz,** gas engine; **m. à pistons,** piston engine; **m. à deux/quatre temps,** two-/four-stroke engine; **m. à refroidissement par air,** air-cooled engine; **m. à réaction,** jet engine; **m. électrique,** electric motor; **commandé par m.,** motor(-driven), power(-driven); **à moteurs multiples** *ou* **à plusieurs moteurs,** multi-engine(d) (*aircraft etc*); **m. d'avion,** aero-engine;

(b) (prime) mover, instigator (*of plot*).

3 *nf Rail* **motrice,** motor coach, *surtout US* motor car.

motif [mɔtif] *nm* **(a)** motive, incentive, reason; **m. de mécontentement,** cause *or* grounds for discontent; **avoir un m. pour faire qch,** to have a motive in *or* for doing sth; **c'est un faux m.,** that's not the real reason; *F Vieilli* **courtiser qn pour le bon m.,** to court s.o. with honourable intentions; **quel m. avez-vous de vous plaindre?,** what grounds have you for complaint?; **quel est le m. de ce coup de téléphone?,** what is the reason for *or* behind this telephone call?; **soupçons sans m.,** groundless *or* unfounded suspicions; **insulter qn sans m.,** to insult s.o. gratuitously; *Jur* **motifs d'un jugement,** grounds upon which a judgment has been delivered;

(b) *Mil Jur* charge; **porter le m.,** to put on a charge;

(c) *Beaux-Arts* motif; *Couture* design, pattern, motif (*for embroidery etc*); *Mus* theme, motto, figure.

motilité [mɔtilite] *nf* motivity.

motion [mosjɔ̃] *nf* motion, proposal; **faire une m.,** to propose a motion, to move a proposal; **la m. a été adoptée,** the motion was carried; **m. de censure,** motion of censure; **présenter une m.,** to table a motion.

motivant [mɔtivɑ̃] *adj* motivating; **on leur laisse voir un avenir m.,** they are presented with a future full of promise.

motivation [mɔtivɑsjɔ̃] *nf Psy etc* motivation; **étudier les motivations du consommateur,** to study consumer motivation.

motivé [mɔtive] *adj* **(a)** motivated (*person*); **élève très m.,** very keen *or* motivated pupil; **(b)** justified (*action*); **refus m.,** justifiable refusal; **opinion motivée,** considered opinion; **non m.,** unjustified, unwarranted; *Jur* **sentence arbitrale motivée,** = award stating the reasons on which it is based; **avis m.,** counsel's opinion.

motiver [mɔtive] *vt* **(a)** to motivate (*an action*); **l'ambition les motivent,** they are motivated by ambition; **(b)** to justify, to warrant (*sth*); to state the reason for (*refusal etc*); **la situation motive nos craintes,** the situation gives us cause for concern.

moto [mɔto] *nf F* motorbike.

motocross [mɔtɔkrɔs] *nm Sp* motocross.
motoculteur [mɔtɔkyltœr] *nm Agr* motor cultivator.
motoculture [mɔtɔkyltyr] *nf* mechanized farming.
motocycle [mɔtɔsikl] *nm Admin* motorcycle.
motocyclette [mɔtɔsiklɛt] *nf* motorcycle, *F* motorbike.
motocycliste [mɔtɔsiklist] *nm* motorcyclist; *Mil* dispatch rider.
motofaucheuse [mɔtofoʃøz] *nf* motor scythe.
motonautique [mɔtɔnotik] *adj* **sport m.,** motorboating.
motonautisme [mɔtɔnotism] *nm* motorboating.
motoneige [mɔtɔnɛʒ] *nf* snowmobile; *surtout Can* skidoo.
motopompe [mɔtɔpɔ̃p] *nf* motor(-driven) pump.
motorisation [mɔtɔrizasjɔ̃] *nf* motorization, mechanization.
motorisé [mɔtɔrise] *adj* motorized; *Mil* **les troupes motorisées,** mechanized troops; *F* **vous êtes m.?,** have you got a car *or* transport?, are you mobile?; **la ville la plus motorisée de France,** the town with the greatest number of cars in France.
motoriser [mɔtɔrize] *vt* to motorize, to mechanize.
motoriste [mɔtɔrist] *nm* engine manufacturer.
mot-outil [mouti] *nm Ling* form word, link word; (*pl mots-outils*).
motrice *voir* **MOTEUR.**
motricité [mɔtrisite] *nf Biol* motivity; *Psy* motor function.
motte [mɔt] *nf* **(a)** clod, lump (*of earth*); ball (*left on roots of tree*); **m. de gazon,** sod, turf; **m. de tourbe,** (turf of) peat; **m. de beurre,** pat *or* block of butter; **(b)** *Archéol* motte.
motteux [mɔtø] *nm* (*oiseau*) wheatear, stonechat.
motus [mɔtys] *int* mum's the word!
mou[1], mol, *f* **molle** [mu, mɔl] **1** *adj* (*the masc form* **mol** *is used before vowel or h mute*) soft (*substance*); lifeless, spineless (*person*); slack (*rope*); flabby, soft (*flesh, hand*); soft, flaccid (*muscle*); woolly, limp (*style*); feeble (*attempt*); lax (*government*); **j'ai les jambes molles,** my legs are giving way; **rayons mous,** soft X-rays; **m. au toucher,** soft to the touch; **un mol (et doux) oreiller,** a (soft and) downy pillow; *F* **il est m. comme une chiffe** *ou* **comme une chique,** he's completely spineless; *F* **je ne me sens pas bien, je suis tout m.,** I'm not well, I feel all limp; **il fait de molles excuses,** he makes (some) lame *or* feeble excuses.
2 *n* spineless person; *F* **c'est une molle,** she's spineless.
3 *nm* slack (*of rope etc*); **donner du m. à un cordage,** to slacken a rope; **prendre du m.,** (*of rope*) to slacken.
4 *adv* **elle joue trop m.,** she doesn't put enough verve into her playing.
mou[2] *nm* lights, lungs (*of slaughtered animal*).
mouchage [muʃaʒ] *nm* **(a)** (*du nez*) wiping *or* blowing s.o.'s *or* one's nose; **(b)** snuffing (out) (*of candles*).
mouchard [muʃar] *nm F* **(a)** (*informateur*) informer, police spy, stool pigeon; *Scol* sneak; **oh le m.!,** (what a) sneak!; **(b)** *Tech* (*tachymètre*) spy in the cab; **(c)** (*contrôleur*) watchman's clock; **(d)** *Av* observation plane.
mouchardage [muʃardaʒ] *nm F* sneaking, grassing, squealing.
moucharder [muʃarde] *vt F* to grass *or* squeal on (*s.o.*).
mouche [muʃ] *nf* **(a)** fly; **m. domestique,** housefly; **m. de la viande, m. bleue,** blowfly, bluebottle; **m. à feu,** firefly; **m. à miel,** honey bee; **m. tse'-tse',** tsetse fly; *Vulg* **m. à merde,** (*bleue*) bluebottle; (*verte*) greenbottle; **faire d'une m. un éléphant,** to make a mountain out of a molehill; **on aurait entendu voler une m.,** you could have heard a pin drop; **prendre la m.,** to fly into a temper, to take offence; **quelle m. vous pique?,** what's the matter with you?, what's bitten you?; **elle ne ferait pas de mal à une m.,** she wouldn't hurt *or* harm a fly; **tomber comme des mouches,** to drop like flies; **c'est une fine m.,** he's a sharp customer; *Pêche* **m. mouillée,** wet fly; *Pêche* **m. à saumon,** salmon fly; **pêche à la m. sèche,** dry-fly fishing; *Boxe* **poids m.,** flyweight;
(b) bull's eye (*of target*); **faire m.,** to hit the bull's eye, to score a bull; *Fig* **il a fait m. avec cette proposition,** he hit the jackpot *or* he scored with that suggestion;
(c) **bateau m.,** river bus, bateau mouche;
(d) beauty spot; *Hist* patch (*on face*); tuft of hair (*on chin*);
(e) *Escrime* covering of foil button; button (*on sword*);
(f) *Arch* spot, speck; stain (*on garment etc*).
moucher [muʃe] **1** *vt* **(a)** to wipe, to blow (*child's etc*) nose; **(b)** to snuff (out) (*candle*); *F* to put (*s.o.*) in his place, to snub (*s.o.*); (*le rembarrer*) to tell (*s.o.*) off. **2 se moucher** *vpr* to blow one's nose; *F* **il ne se mouche pas du coude,** he thinks a lot of himself.
moucheron[1] [muʃrɔ̃] *nm* gnat, midge.
moucheron[2] *nm* snuff (*of candle*).
moucheronner [muʃrɔne] *vi* (*of fish*) to be rising, to be on the rise.
moucheté [muʃte] *adj* **(a)** spotty, speckled, flecked; **cheval m.,** flea-bitten horse; **chat m.,** tabby cat; **blé m.,** smutty wheat; **mer mouchetée d'écume,** foam-flecked sea; **nez moucheté de taches de rousseur,** freckled nose; **(b)** *Escrime* buttoned (*sword*).
moucheter [muʃte] *vt* (**je mouchette; je mouchetterai**) **(a)** (*avec des taches*) to spot, to speckle, to fleck; **(b)** *Escrime* **m. un fleuret,** to cover the button of a foil; **m. une épée,** to put a button on a sword, to button a sword.
mouchette [muʃɛt] *nf* **(a) mouchettes,** (pair of) snuffers (*for candles*); **(b)** *Archit* outer fillet (*of dripstone*).
moucheture [muʃtyr] *nf* spot, speck, speckle, fleck.
mouchoir [muʃwar] *nm* handkerchief; (*autour du cou*) kerchief; **m. (de tête),** headscarf; **m. en papier,** paper handkerchief; *Fig* **je vais faire un nœud à mon m.,** I'll tie a knot in my handkerchief; **jardin grand comme un m. (de poche),** pocket handkerchief (of a) garden.
mouchure [muʃyr] *nf* **(a)** (*du nez*) nasal mucus; **(b)** snuff (*of candle*).
moudjahiddin [mudʒa(j)idin] *nm* mujaheddin, mujahedeen.
moudre [mudr] *vt* (*prp* **moulant;** *pp* **moulu;** *pr ind* **je mouds, il moud, n. moulons, ils moulent;** *pr sub* **je moule;** *p hist* **je moulus;** *fu* **je moudrai**) **(a)** to grind, to mill (*corn etc*); to grind (*coffee, pepper*); *Fig* **on l'a moulu de coups,** he was beaten up; **(b)** *Vieilli* to grind out (*tune*) (*on barrel organ*).
moue [mu] *nf* pout; **faire la m.,** to pout, to look sulky; **faire une m.,** to purse one's lips; **faire une vilaine m.,** to scowl; *Fig* **elle n'a pas fait la m. lorsqu'on lui a proposé de venir,** she didn't object at all when we suggested she could come along.
mouette [mwɛt] *nf* (sea)gull.
mouf(f)ette [mufɛt] *nf* skunk.
moufle[1] [mufl] **1** *nf* (*gant*) mitten, mitt. **2** *n Tech* **(a)** tackle block; pulley block (*with several sheaves*); **(b)** (= **palan**) (block and) tackle.
moufle[2] *nm Ch Cér* muffle; **(four à) m.,** muffle (furnace).
mouflet, -ette [muflɛ, -ɛt] *n F* (*enfant*) kid, brat.
mouflon [muflɔ̃] *nm* mouf(f)lon, wild sheep.
mouillage [mujaʒ] *nm* **(a)** (*d'un tissu etc*) moistening, damping; (fraudulent) watering down (*of wine*); **(b)** *Nau* anchoring (*of ship*); laying, mooring (*of mine*); putting down (*of buoy*); **(c)** *Nau* (*emplacement*) anchorage, moorage; **être au m.,** to be riding at anchor; **prendre son m.,** to anchor; **m. forain,** open berth.
mouillé [muje] *adj* **(a)** moist, damp, wet; **m. jusqu'aux os,** wet through, soaked to the skin; *F* **poule mouillée,** (*personne*) drip; *surtout Br Pol* wet; **(b)** *Nau* (*ship*) (lying) at anchor, moored; **(c)** *Ling* palatalized (*consonant*).
mouillement [mujmɑ̃] *nm Ling* palatalization.
mouiller [muje] **1** *vt* **(a)** to wet, to moisten, to damp; *Culin* to add liquid to (*stew*); to dilute, to water down (*wine etc*); **on s'est fait m. par l'averse,** we got soaked in the downpour; **(b)** *Nau* to cast, to drop (*anchor*); to anchor (*ship*); **(c)** *Nau* to lay (*mine*); to put down (*buoy*); **(d)** *Ling* to palatalize (*consonant*). **2** *vi Nau* to anchor; (*d'un navire*) to lie at anchor; **mouillez!,** let go (the anchor)! **3 se mouiller** *vpr* **(a)** to become *or* get wet; (*of eyes*) to fill with tears; **se m. les pieds,** to get one's feet wet; **(b)** *F* to get involved (*in crime etc*); **il ne veut pas se m.,** (*prendre parti*) he doesn't want to commit himself *or* to stick his neck out.
mouillette [mujɛt] *nf* finger (*of bread etc*).
mouilleur [mujœr] *nm* **(a)** *Nau* **m. de mines/filets,** minelayer/net layer; **(b)** damper (*for stamps etc*); **(c)** *Nau* timber (*of anchor*).
mouillure [mujyr] *nf* **(a)** *Typ etc* damping, wetting; **(b)** (*marque*) damp mark, stain; **(c)** *Ling* palatalization (*of consonant*).
mouise [mwiz] *nf Arg* poverty; **être dans la m.,** to be hard up *or* in dire straits.
moujik [muʒik] *nm* moujik.
moujingue [muʒɛ̃g] *n Arg* (*enfant*) kid, brat.
moukère [mukɛr] *nf F* (*femme*) woman.
moulage[1] [mulaʒ] *nm* grinding, milling.
moulage[2] *nm* **(a)** casting, moulding, *US* molding; founding (*of iron*); **m. à cire perdue,** lost wax process; **(b) m. au** *ou* **en plâtre,** plaster cast.
moule[1] [mul] *nm* mould, *US* mold; *Tech* matrix; **m. à gelée,** jelly mould; **m. à gâteaux,** cake tin; **m. à beurre,**

butter print; **jeter qch en** *ou* **dans un m.,** to cast sth; *Fig* **des comme lui on n'en fait plus, on a cassé le m.,** they broke the mould when they made him; *Fig* **une fille faite au m.,** a girl with a great figure; *Fig* **elle a rejeté le m. de son éducation,** she has broken out of the mould of her upbringing.

moule² *nf* **(a)** mussel; **(b)** *Arg* (*personne molle*) drip, wet; (*idiot*) fool, idiot.

moulé [mule] *adj* cast, moulded, *US* molded; **statue de plâtre m.,** plaster cast; **pain m.,** tin loaf; **écriture moulée,** copperplate handwriting; **lettres moulées,** (hand) printing; **je me trouve trop moulée dans cette robe,** this dress clings too much.

mouler [mule] **1** *vt* **(a)** to cast (*statue etc*); to found (*iron*); **(b)** to mould, *US* to mold (*statue etc*); **robe qui moule la taille,** tightly fitting *or* figure-hugging dress, dress that clings to the figure; *Fig* **m. sa conduite sur qn,** to model one's behaviour on s.o.. **2 se mouler** *vpr Fig* **elle se moule sur sa sœur,** she models herself on her sister.

mouleur [mulœr] *nm* caster, moulder, *US* molder.

moulière [muljɛr] *nf* mussel bed.

moulin [mulɛ̃] *nm* **(a)** mill; **m. à vent,** windmill; *Fig* **se battre contre des moulins à vent,** to tilt at windmills (*like Don Quixote*); **m. à eau,** watermill; **roue de m.,** millwheel; **constructeur de moulins,** millwright; **ça fait venir de l'eau au m.,** it's (all) grist to the mill; **on y entre comme dans un m.,** anybody can go in; **m. à minerai,** ore crusher; **m. à huile,** oil crusher; **m. à poivre,** pepper mill; **m. à légumes,** food mill; **m. à café,** coffee grinder; (*manuel*) coffee mill; *Rel* **m. à prières,** prayer wheel; *F* **m. à paroles,** chatterbox, windbag; **(b)** *F* (*de voiture*) engine.

mouliner [muline] *vt* **(a)** *Culin F* to pass through a food mill; **(b)** *Tex* to throw (*silk*); *Pêche* to reel in (*the line*).

moulinet [mulinɛ] *nm* **(a)** *Tech* winch; *Pêche* reel; *Pêche* **m. à cliquet,** click reel; **(b) faire des moulinets (avec sa canne),** to twirl one's stick; **faire des moulinets (avec les bras),** to wave one's arms around.

moulinette ® [mulinɛt] *nf* food mill; **passer la soupe à la m.,** to put the soup through the food mill; *Fig* **il m'a passé à la m.,** he put me through it *or* through the mill; **le metteur en scène passe 'l'Avare' à la m.,** the producer is turning 'L'Avare' into a travesty (of itself).

moulu [muly] *adj* ground (*coffee etc*); *Fig* very tired, dead-beat; **m. (de coups),** black and blue, aching all over; **on se sent m. après une longue marche,** you feel dead-beat *or* worn out after a long walk.

moulure [mulyr] *nf Archit Menuis* (ornamental) moulding, *US* molding, profile, profiling.

moulurer [mulyre] *vt* to cut a moulding *or US* molding on (*sth*); **profils moulurés,** mouldings.

mourant, -ante [murɑ̃, -ɑ̃t] **1** *adj* dying; faint (*voice*). **2** *n* dying man, *f* dying woman; **les mourants,** the dying.

mourir [murir] *v* (*prp* **mourant;** *pp* **mort;** *pr ind* **je meurs, il meurt, n. mourons, ils meurent;** *pr sub* **je meure, nous mourions;** *p hist* **il mourut;** *fu* **je mourrai** [murre] ; *aux* **être**) **1** *vi* **(a)** (*d'une personne, d'un animal, d'une plante*) to die; **il est mort hier,** he died yesterday; **m. de faim,** to die of starvation, to starve to death; (*avoir très faim*) to be starving; **m. dans son lit,** to die in one's bed; **il est mort de vieillesse,** he died of old age; **m. de sa belle mort,** to die of natural causes; **m. accidentellement,** to die in an accident; **m. de mort naturelle,** to die a natural death; **elle l'aimait à en m.,** she was desperately in love with him; **m. avant l'âge,** to die before one's time; **m. à la peine,** to die in harness; **au moment de m.,** in the hour of death; **il est mort assassiné,** he was murdered; **elle est morte seule,** she died alone; **m. martyr d'une cause,** to die a martyr to a cause; **faire m. qn,** to put s.o. to death; **faire m. qn à petit feu,** to keep s.o. on tenterhooks; *F* **il me fera m.,** he'll be the death of me; **vous me faites m. d'impatience,** the suspense is killing me; **je mourais de peur,** I was dying of fright, I was frightened to death; **m. d'inquiétude,** to be worried to death; **m. de chagrin,** to be weighed down with grief, to be grief-stricken; (*littéralement*) to die of grief; **ennuyer qn à m.,** to bore s.o. to death; **m. d'envie de faire qch,** to be dying to do sth; **j'ai cru m. de rire,** I thought I would die laughing, I nearly died laughing; *Fig* **tu ne vas pas en m., tout de même,** it won't kill you, you know!;
(b) (*d'un feu, d'une habitude etc*) to die out; *Min* (*d'un filon*) to peter out; (*d'une voix*) to trail off; **les vagues qui viennent m. sur la plage,** the waves which die away on the beach.
2 se mourir *vpr Litt* to be dying; (*d'un feu, d'une habitude*) to die out; **je sens que je me meurs,** I feel that I am dying; **la lampe se mourait,** the lamp was fading *or* giving out.

mouroir [murwar] *nm F Péj* **ces foyers de personnes âgées sont des mouroirs,** these homes are just places where old people are left to die; **on a découvert des mouroirs de vieillards dans un grand hôpital,** in a large hospital, places were found where old people were simply left to die.

mouron [murɔ̃] *nm Bot* **m. rouge** *ou* **des champs,** scarlet pimpernel; **m. blanc** *ou* **des oiseaux,** chickweed; **m. d'eau,** water pimpernel, brookweed; *Arg* **se faire du m.,** to worry oneself to death.

mousquet [muskɛ] *nm* musket.

mousquetaire [muskətɛr] *nm* musketeer; **gants (à la) m.,** gauntlets, gauntlet gloves.

mousqueterie [muskətri] *nf* musketry; **feu de m.,** rifle fire.

mousqueton [muskətɔ̃] *nm* **(a)** *Mil* (*fusil court*) carbine; *Arch* cavalry magazine rifle; **(b)** (*d'escalade etc*) karabiner.

moussaillon [musajɔ̃] *nm F* young ship's boy.

moussaka [musaka] *nf Culin* moussaka.

moussant [musɑ̃] *adj* frothing, foaming.

mousse¹ [mus] *nf* **(a)** moss; **couvert de m.,** moss-grown, mossy; *Prov* **pierre qui roule n'amasse pas m.,** a rolling stone gathers no moss; *Tricot* **point m.,** moss stitch; **(b)** froth, foam (*of sea etc*); head (*on glass of beer*); lather (*of soap*); *Culin* mousse; *Culin* **m. au chocolat,** chocolate mousse; *F* **se faire de la m.,** to fret, to worry; **(c)** *Ch* **m. de platine,** platinum sponge; **caoutchouc m.,** foam rubber.

mousse² *nm* ship's boy.

mousse³ *adj Tech* blunt (*blade, point etc*).

mousseline [muslin] *nf* **(a)** *Tex* muslin; **m. de soie,** chiffon; **(b) verre m.,** muslin glass; **(c)** *Culin* **pommes (de terre) m.,** puréed potatoes.

mousser [muse] *vi* to froth, to foam; (*of soapy water*) to lather; (*of wine etc*) to sparkle, to fizz; *Arg* **faire m. qn,** to make s.o. lose his temper *or* flare up.

mousseron [musrɔ̃] *nm* edible mushroom; *surtout* St George's agaric.

mousseux, -euse [musø, -øz] **1** *adj* **(a)** (*écumeux*) frothy, foaming; **(b)** sparkling (*wine*). **2** *nm* sparkling wine.

moussoir [muswar] *nm* whisk.

mousson [musɔ̃] *nf* monsoon.

moussu [musy] *adj* mossy, mossgrown.

moustache [mustaʃ] *nf* **(a) la m., les moustaches,** moustache; **m. à la gauloise,** walrus moustache; **m. en brosse,** toothbrush moustache; **(b)** whiskers (*of cat etc*).

moustachu [mustaʃy] *adj* with a large moustache.

moustiquaire [mustikɛr] *nf* mosquito net; *Can* (*à la fenêtre*) screen.

moustique [mustik] *nm* (*insecte*) mosquito; *F* (*personne insignifiante*) weed; *F* (*enfant*) nipper.

moût [mu] *nm* must (*of grapes*); wort (*of beer*).

moutard [mutar] *nm Arg* (*enfant*) kid, nipper.

moutarde [mutard] *nf* mustard; **graine de m.,** mustard seed; **la m. lui est montée au nez,** he lost his temper *or* flared up; **gaz m.,** mustard gas; **(jaune) m.,** mustard (yellow).

moutardier [mutardje] *nm* **(a)** mustard maker *or* seller; *F* **il se croit le premier m. du pape,** he's too big for his boots; **(b)** (*pot*) mustard pot.

moutier [mutje] *nm Arch* monastery.

mouton, -onne [mutɔ̃, -ɔn] **1** *nm* **(a)** sheep; *Culin* mutton; **éleveur de moutons,** (*pour la viande*) sheep farmer; (*pour la laine*) woolgrower; **doux comme un m.,** as gentle as a lamb; **revenons à nos moutons,** let's get back to the subject; **c'est un m. à cinq pattes,** he's a rare bird; **c'est un vrai m.,** he's a sheep; **ils ont tous suivi comme des moutons,** they all followed like sheep; **saut de m.,** (*d'un cheval*) buck; *Culin* **ragoût de m.,** mutton stew; **(peau de) m.,** sheepskin;
(b) *F* (*dans les prisons*) (police) spy;
(c) moutons, white horses (*on waves*); **la mer fait des moutons,** there are white horses on the sea;
(d) moutons, fluff, *Am* dust bunnies (*under bed etc*);
(e) *Constr etc* drop hammer; ram, monkey (*of pile driver*); head (*of beetle, rammer*); tup (*of steam hammer*).
2 *adj Fig* sheeplike.

moutonnant [mutɔnɑ̃] *adj* (*sea*) covered with white horses, foam-flecked.

moutonné [mutɔne] *adj* fleecy (*cloud etc*); **tête moutonnée,** curly *or* frizzy head of hair.

moutonnement [mutɔnmɑ̃] *nm* (*of sea*) breaking into white horses, frothing.

moutonner [mutɔne] **1** *vi* (*of sea*) to break into white

horses, to froth. **2 se moutonner** *vpr* (*of sky*) to become covered with fleecy clouds.
moutonneux, -euse [mutɔnø, -øz] *adj* **(a)** (*sea*) foam-flecked, covered with white horses; **(b)** (*sky*) covered with fleecy clouds.
moutonnier, -ière [mutɔnje, -jɛr] *adj* (*foule*) sheeplike; (*personne*) easily led.
mouture [mutyr] *nf* **(a)** grinding, milling (*of corn*); **(b)** milling dues; **tirer deux moutures d'un sac,** to get double profit out of sth; **(c)** *Agr* maslin; **(d)** *Péj* rehash (*of article etc*); **c'est la deuxième m. du texte,** this is the second go at the text.
mouvance [muvɑ̃s] *nf* **(a)** (*d'un pays*) sphere of influence; **relever de la m. d'un pays,** to come within *or* be part of a country's sphere of influence; *Fig* **se marquer davantage dans la m. du parti socialiste,** to move closer towards the socialist party's line; **(b)** (*instabilité*) flux, constant change; **tout est en m.,** everything's in a state of flux.
mouvant [muvɑ̃] *adj* moving, mobile; **sable m.,** driftsand; **sables mouvants,** quicksand.
mouvement [muvmɑ̃] *nm* **(a)** movement, motion; (*geste*) gesture; **m. en arrière,** backward movement *or* motion; **rester sans m.,** to stand motionless *or* stockstill; **faire un m.,** to move; **il aime le m.,** (*voyager*) he likes change, he can't stay in one place; **répondre d'un m. de tête,** (*pour dire non*) to answer with a shake of the head, to shake one's head; (*pour dire oui*) to answer with a nod, to nod; **il a eu un m. de recul/dégoût,** he recoiled *or* started backward/he was seized with distaste; **mettre en m., imprimer un m. à,** to put *or* set (*sth*) in motion, to set (*sth*) going; to start (*engine*); **se mettre en m.,** to start off, to move off; **être toujours en m.,** to be always on the move; **elle est allée faire ses mouvements de gymnastique,** she's gone to do her exercises; **on ne pouvait pas faire un m.,** you couldn't move; **le m. d'une grande ville,** the bustle *or* activity of a large town; **petite ville sans m.,** lifeless *or* dull little town; *Mus* **presser/ralentir le m.,** to quicken/slow the tempo; **symphonie à trois mouvements,** symphony in three movements; *MecE* **m. acquis,** impressed motion; **m. perpétuel,** perpetual motion; **quantité de m.,** momentum, impulse; **pièces en m.,** moving parts (*of machine*); **vérifier le m. des marchandises/des capitaux,** to check the flow of goods/capital; *Mil* **m. de troupes,** troop movement; **guerre de m.,** mobile warfare; **par un m. audacieux, ils ont pris possession du village,** a daring move put them in possession of the village; **un bon m.,** a kind gesture;
(b) (*changement*) change, modification; *Géog* fall, rise (*in sea level*); **m. de terrain,** undulation; **m. de personnel,** staff changes; **suivre le m.,** to go with the flow; **le m. des idées,** the evolution of ideas; **le m. des naissances,** the trend in the birthrate; *F* **être dans le m.,** to be in the swim *or* abreast of the times *or* up to date;
(c) premier m., first impulse; **il a eu un m. d'éloquence,** he had a burst of eloquence; **m. d'humeur,** outburst of temper *or* petulance; **de son propre m.,** of one's own accord; **avoir un bon m.,** to act on a kindly impulse; **dans un m. de colère,** in a fit of anger;
(d) *Pol etc* movement; **le m. syndical,** the union movement; **M. de libération des femmes,** Women's Liberation Movement, *F* Women's Lib; **M. pacifiste,** peace movement; **les cheminots vont reconduire leur m. de grève,** the railwaymen want to extend their strike action; **lancer un m. de grève/révolte,** to launch a strike/revolt; **m. insurrectionnel,** uprising.
(e) line(s) (*of drapery etc*);
(f) traffic (*on road, in port etc*); *Rail* **mouvements des trains,** train arrivals and departures; **chef de m.,** traffic manager; **mouvements des navires,** shipping intelligence;
(g) works, movement (*of clock etc*); **m. d'horlogerie,** clockwork.
mouvementé [muvmɑ̃te] *adj* **(a)** animated, lively (*discussion etc*); thrilling (*voyage etc*); eventful (*day*); **une partie mouvementée,** an exciting game; **ville/rue mouvementée,** busy town/street; **vie mouvementée,** eventful life; **(b) terrain m.,** undulating ground.
mouvementer [muvmɑ̃te] *vt* to enliven, to animate.
mouvoir [muvwar] *v* (*prp* **mouvant**; *pp* **mû, mue**; *pr ind* **je meus, il meut, n. mouvons, ils meuvent**; *pr sub* **je meuve, n. mouvions, ils meuvent**; *p hist* **je mus** (*rare*); *fu* **je mouvrai**) **1** *vt* **(a)** to drive, to actuate (*machine etc*); to propel (*ship etc*); **mû à la vapeur,** propelled by steam, steam-driven; *Fig* **mû par la colère/l'intérêt,** moved *or* prompted by anger/prompted by interest; **(b)** to move. **2 se mouvoir** *vpr* to move, to stir.
moyen[1], -enne [mwajɛ̃, -ɛn] *adj* **(a)** middle; **les classes moyennes,** the middle class(es); *Hist* **le m. âge,** the Middle Ages; **coutumes du m. âge,** medi(a)eval customs; **point m.,** midpoint; *Scol* **cours m.,** intermediate class;
(b) average, mean (*pressure, speed etc*); average, medium (*quality etc*); average, moderate (*price*); **le Français m.,** the average Frenchman, the man in the street; **temps m. de réaction,** mean reaction time; **m. terme,** middle term; **prendre un m. terme,** to take a middle course; **la durée moyenne de travail du Français,** the average French working week; **de taille** *ou* **grandeur moyenne,** medium-sized; **femme de taille moyenne,** woman of average height; *Péj* **travail d'une qualité très moyenne,** work of a very indifferent quality, very average work; **élève m.,** average pupil.
moyen[2] *nm* **(a)** means; *Prov* **la fin justifie les moyens,** the end justifies the means; **par tous les moyens,** by fair means or foul; **employer les grands moyens,** to take extreme measures; **j'emploierai tous les moyens,** I'll use whatever means I have to; **au m.** *ou* **par (le) m. de qch,** by means of *or* with the help of sth; **y a-t-il m. de le faire?,** is there any way it can be done?, is it possible (to do it)?; **il n'y a pas m.,** it can't be done, it's impossible; **il n'y a pas m. de le lui faire comprendre,** there's no way of making him understand; *F* **pas m.!,** no way!; **le m. d'y aller?,** how do we get there?; **trouver (le) m. de faire qch,** to find a means *or* a way of doing sth; **inventer un m. de s'échapper,** to invent a means of escape; **faire qch par ses propres moyens,** to do sth on one's own, to draw (up)on one's own resources (to do sth); **m. de transport,** means of transport; **arriver par ses propres moyens,** to arrive under one's own steam; **avec les moyens du bord,** with the means at one's disposal; **voies et moyens,** ways and means; **dans la (pleine) mesure de mes moyens,** to the best *or* to the utmost of my ability; **enfant qui a des moyens,** bright *or* talented child; **elle me fait perdre tous mes moyens,** she really bowls me over; **faire perdre tous ses moyens à qn,** to disconcert s.o.;
(b) *Fin* **moyens,** means; **vivre au-dessus de ses moyens,** to live beyond one's means; **il a largement les moyens de faire construire,** he can well afford to build; **je n'en ai pas les moyens,** I can't afford it.
moyen(-)âge [mwajɛnɑʒ] *nm* Middle Ages; **le haut m. (-)â.,** the early Middle Ages.
moyenâgeux, -euse [mwajɛnɑʒø, -øz] *adj* medi(a)eval; *Fig Péj* medi(a)eval, old-fashioned, outdated.
moyen-courrier [mwajɛ̃kurje] *Av adj & nm* medium-range (aircraft); (*pl moyens-courriers*).
moyennant [mwajɛnɑ̃] *prép* (in return) for; **louer qch m. cent francs par jour,** to hire sth for *or* at (a charge of) a hundred francs a day; **faire qch m. finance,** to do sth for a consideration; **m. paiement de dix francs,** on payment of ten francs; **m. quoi,** in return for which, in consideration of which; *Litt* **m. que ...,** provided that ... .
moyenne [mwajɛn] *nf* average; *Math* mean; *Scol* pass mark; **en m.,** on (an) average; *Aut* **m. (horaire),** average (speed); **faire du 100 de m.,** to do an average of *or* to average 100 kilometres per hour; **travail au-dessus/au-dessous de la m.,** work above/below average *or* above/below par; **enfant d'une intelligence au-dessus de la m.,** child of above average intelligence.
moyennement [mwajɛnmɑ̃] *adv* moderately, fairly; **travailler m.,** to work fairly well.
Moyen-Orient [mwajɛ̃nɔrjɑ̃] *nm* Middle East.
moyen-oriental [mwajɛ̃nɔrjɑ̃tal] *adj* Middle Eastern.
moyette [mwajɛt] *nf Agr* shock (*of corn*).
moyeu, -eux [mwajø] *nm* hub (*of car wheel*); nave (*of cartwheel etc*); boss (*of propeller etc*).
mozarabe [mɔzarab] *Hist* **1** *adj* Mozarabic. **2** *n* **M.,** Mozarab.
mozzarella [mɔdʒarɛla] *nm* mozzarella.
M.S.T. [ɛmɛste] *nf Méd* (*abrév* **maladie sexuellement transmissible**) STD.
mu [my] *nm* mu.
mû *voir* **MOUVOIR**.
muance [mɥɑ̃s] *nf Arch* **(a)** *Mus* mutation; **(b)** breaking (*of voice at puberty*).
mucilage [mysilaʒ] *nm* mucilage, gum.
mucilagineux, -euse [mysilaʒinø, -øz] *adj* mucilaginous, viscous.
mucosité [mykozite] *nf* mucus, mucosity.
mucus [mykys] *nm* mucus.
mue [my] *nf* **(a)** moult(ing), *US* molt(ing) (*of birds, mammals, crustaceans*); shedding *or* casting of the antlers (*of a deer etc*); sloughing (*of reptiles*); (*époque*) moulting season; (*dépouille*) feathers *etc* moulted *or US* molted;

antlers shed; slough (*of snakes*); **serin en m.,** moulting canary; **(b)** *Physiol* breaking of the voice (*at puberty*); **(c)** mew (*for hawks*); coop (*for poultry*).

muer [mɥe] **1** *vt Litt* to change (**en,** into); **m. sa tête,** (*of stag*) to shed *or* cast its antlers. **2** *vi* **(a)** (*of bird, mammal, crustacean*) to moult, *US* to molt; (*of deer etc*) to shed *or* cast its antlers; (*of reptile*) to slough, to cast its skin; **(b)** (*of voice*) to break (*at puberty*); **il commence à m.,** his voice is breaking. **3 se muer** *vpr* **se m. (en),** to be transformed, to change (oneself) (into).

müesli [mɥ(yɛ)sli] *nm* muesli.

muet, -ette [mɥɛ, -ɛt] **1** *adj* (*personne*) dumb; (*taciturne*) silent, dumb, mute; silent (*film, Th part*); blank (*map etc*); *Ling* silent (*letter*); **m. de naissance,** born dumb; *Fig* **la stupeur m'a rendu m.,** I was struck dumb with astonishment; **j'écoutais, m. d'étonnement,** I listened speechless with astonishment *or* in mute astonishment; **m. de colère,** speechless with anger; **rester m.,** to remain silent; **m. comme une tombe,** (as) silent as the grave; **le cinéma m.,** silent cinema *or* films; **jeu m.,** dumb show. **2** *n* mute. **3** *nm Cin* **le m.,** silent films.

mufle [myfl] *nm* **(a)** muffle, (hairless part of) muzzle (*of ox, bison etc*); nose, *F* snout (*of lion etc*); **(b)** *F* (*homme*) lout, boor.

muflerie [myfləri] *nf F* **(a)** (*caractère*) boorishness; **(b)** (*action*) low-down trick.

muflier [myflije] *nm Bot* antirrhinum, snapdragon; **m. bâtard,** linaria.

mufti [myfti] *nm Rel* mufti.

muge [myʒ] *nm* (*poisson*) mullet.

mugir [myʒir] *vi* **(a)** (*d'une vache*) to low, to moo; (*d'un taureau*) to bellow; **(b)** (*du vent, de la mer*) to roar, to boom, to moan; (*du vent*) to howl.

mugissement [myʒismɑ̃] *nm* **(a)** lowing, mooing (*of cow*); bellowing (*of bull*); **(b)** roaring, booming, moaning (*of sea, wind*); howling (*of wind*).

muguet [mygɛ] *nm* **(a)** (*plante*) lily of the valley; **(b)** *Méd* thrush.

mulassier, -ière [mylasje, -jɛr] *adj & nf* **(jument) mulassière,** mule-breeding (mare).

mulâtre [mylɑtr] **1** *adj* mulatto, half-caste. **2** *n* (*f* **mulâtre, mulâtresse** [mylɑtrɛs]) mulatto.

mule¹ [myl] *nf* (she-)mule.

mule² *nf* (*slipper*) mule; **la m. du Pape,** the Pope's slipper; **baiser la m. du Pape,** to kiss the Pope's toe.

mulet¹ [mylɛ] *nm* (he-)mule.

mulet² *nm* (*poisson*) grey mullet.

muletier, -ière [myltje, -jɛr] **1** *adj* **équipage m.,** mule train. **2** *nm* mule driver, muleteer.

mulot [mylo] *nm* field mouse.

multicellulaire [myltiselylɛr] *adj* multicellular.

multicolore [myltikɔlɔr] *adj* multicoloured, *US* multicolored.

multicoque [myltikɔk] *nm Nau* multihull.

multiculturalisme [myltikyltyralism] *nm* multiculturalism.

multiculturel, -elle [myltikyltyrɛl] *adj* multicultural.

multidimensionnel, -elle [myltidimɑ̃sjɔnɛl] *adj* multidimensional; *Fig* (*expérience, compétence etc*) multifaceted.

multidisciplinaire [myltidisiplinɛr] *adj* multidisciplinary.

multiflore [myltiflɔr] *adj Bot* multiflora.

multifonction [myltifɔ̃ksjɔ̃] *adj* multi-functional; *Ordinat* **clavier m.,** multi-functional keyboard.

multiforme [myltifɔrm] *adj* multiform.

multilatéral, -aux [myltilateral, -o] *adj* (*accord etc*) multilateral.

multimédia [myltimedja] *adj* multimedia.

multimilliardaire [myltimiljardɛr], **multimillionnaire** [myltimiljɔnɛr] *adj & n* multimillionaire.

multinational, -ale, -aux [myltinasjɔnal, -o] **1** *adj* multinational. **2** *nf* **multinationale,** multinational (company).

multipare [myltipar] **1** *adj* multiparous. **2** *nf* multipara.

multipiste [myltipist] *adj* multitrack.

multiplace [myltiplas] **1** *adj* **avion m.,** = passenger aircraft. **2** *nm* passenger aircraft.

multiple [myltipl] **1** *adj* multiple, *Fml* manifold; **les causes sont multiples,** the reasons are many *or Fml* manifold; **mourrir de blessures multiples,** to die of multiple injuries; **maison à succursales multiples,** multiple store, chain store; *Aut* **klaxon à sons multiples,** multitone horn; **pour utilisateurs multiples,** multi-user; *Ordinat* **à accès m.,** multi-access. **2** *nm Math* multiple; **le plus petit commun m.,** the lowest common multiple.

multiplex [myltiplɛks] *adj inv & nm Rad etc* multiplex.

multipliable [myltiplijabl] *adj* multipli(c)able.

multiplicande [myltiplikɑ̃d] *nm Math* multiplicand.

multiplicateur, -trice [myltiplikatœr, -tris] **1** *adj* multiplying; **engrenage m.,** step-up gear. **2** *nm Math Él* multiplier.

multiplicatif, -ive [myltiplikatif, -iv] *adj* multiplicative, multiplying.

multiplication [myltiplikasjɔ̃] *nf* **(a)** *Math etc* multiplication; **la m. des crimes/des clubs sportifs,** the increase in crime/in the number of sports clubs; *Bible* **la m. des pains,** the miracle of the loaves and fishes; **(b)** *MecE* gear (ratio); step-up, stepdown (*of gear*); **grande/petite m.,** high/low gear; **m. du levier,** leverage.

multiplicité [myltiplisite] *nf* multiplicity.

multiplié [myltiplije] *adj* multiplied, multiple.

multiplier [myltiplije] *v* (*pr sub & impf* **n. multipliions, v. multipliiez**) **1** *vt* **(a)** *Math etc* to multiply (**par,** by); **(b)** *MecE* **m. la vitesse de révolution,** to gear up. **2 se multiplier** *vpr* **(a)** to multiply, to increase; **les crimes se multiplient,** crime is on the increase; **les lapins se multiplient rapidement,** rabbits multiply rapidly; **(b)** *Fig* to be in half a dozen places at once; **se m. pour aider qn,** to do one's utmost in order to help s.o..

multipolaire [myltipɔlɛr] *adj Él Biol* multipolar.

multiprocesseur [myltiprɔsesœr] *nm Ordinat* multiprocessor.

multiprogrammation [myltiprɔgramasjɔ̃] *nf Ordinat* multiprogramming.

multipropriété [myltiprɔprijete] *nf* time-share; **acheter un appartement/un maison/***etc* **en m.,** to buy a time-share (flat/house/*etc*).

multiracial, -aux [myltirasjal, -o] *adj* multiracial.

multirisque [myltirisk] *adj* **assurance m.,** comprehensive insurance.

multistandard [myltistɑ̃dar] *adj inv* multistandard.

multitâche [myltitɑʃ] *adj Ordinat* multitasking.

multitraitement [myltitrɛtmɑ̃] *nm* multiprocessing.

multitude [myltityd] *nf* multitude (**de,** of).

munichois, -oise [mynikwa, -waz] **1** *adj* (of) Munich. **2** *n* **M.,** native *or* inhabitant of Munich.

municipal, -aux [mynisipal, -o] *adj* municipal; **conseil m.,** town council, local council; **bibliothèque municipale,** public library; **loi municipale,** by-law; *Arch* **la garde municipale,** the military police (*of Paris*).

municipalisation [mynisipalizasjɔ̃] *nf* municipalization; **la m. des sols a été votée,** there has been a vote in favour of placing land under municipal control.

municipaliser [mynisipalize] *vt* to municipalize.

municipalité [mynisipalite] *nf* **(a)** (*ville*) municipality; **(b)** (*région*) local administrative area; **(c)** (*maire etc*) corporation, local council.

munificence [mynifisɑ̃s] *nf Litt* munificence.

munificent [mynifisɑ̃] *adj Litt* munificent.

munir [mynir] **1** *vt* to supply, to fit, to equip, to provide, to furnish (**de,** with); **muni des sacrements de l'Église,** fortified with the rites of the Church. **2 se munir** *vpr* to provide oneself (**de,** with).

munition [mynisjɔ̃] *nf* **(a) munitions (de guerre),** ammunition, munitions; **(b)** *Arch* munitioning, provisioning (*of an army*); **munitions de bouche,** provisions; **(c)** *Mil* **pain de m.,** ration bread.

munitionnaire [mynisjɔnɛr] *nm Mil Arch* commissary, supply officer.

muphti [myfti] *nm Rel* mufti.

muqueux, -euse [mykø, -øz] **1** *adj* mucous (*membrane etc*). **2** *nf* **muqueuse,** mucous membrane.

mur [myr] *nm* wall; **m. de clôture,** enclosing wall; **m. d'appui,** low wall; **m. de soutènement,** retaining wall; **m. de refend,** partition (wall); **m. mitoyen,** party wall; **gros murs,** main walls; **maison aux murs de briques,** brick (- built) house; **ne laisser que les quatre murs,** to leave only the four walls (standing); *Fig* **mettre qn au pied du m.,** to put s.o. on the spot, to drive s.o. into a corner, to have s.o. with his back to the wall; *Fig* **il est à présent dans nos murs,** he is in town at the moment; *Fig* **se taper la tête contre les murs,** to hit one's head against a (brick) wall; *Fig* **se heurter à un m. d'incompréhension,** to come up against a wall *or* a barrier of incomprehension; *Fig* **Alain est un m., on ne peut pas lui parler,** you can't talk to Alain, it's like talking to a wall; *Fig* **les murs ont des oreilles,** walls have ears; *Hist* **le m. de Berlin,** the Berlin wall; **franchir le m. du son,** (*of aircraft etc*) to break the sound barrier.

mûr [myr] *adj* **(a)** ripe (*fruit etc*); mellow (*wine etc*); mature (*age, mind etc*); **après mûre réflexion,** after mature consideration; **m. pour qch,** (*personne*) fit *or* ready for sth; **il est très m. pour son âge,** he is very mature for his age; **(b)** *Arg* (*saoul*) canned.

murage [myraʒ] *nm* walling (in) (*of town*); walling up, bricking up, blocking up (*of doorway etc*).

muraille [myrɑj] *nf* **(a)** (high defensive) wall; **la Grande M. de Chine,** the Great Wall of China; **les murailles de la ville,** the town walls; **m. de glace,** ice barrier; **(b)** side (*of ship*).

mural, -aux [myral, -o] *adj* mural; **peinture murale,** mural, wall painting; **pendule murale,** wall clock; **carte murale,** wall map; *Archit* **console murale,** wall bracket.

mûre [myr] *nf* **(a) m. sauvage** *ou* **de ronce,** blackberry; **(b)** (*fruit*) mulberry.

mûrement [myrmɑ̃] *adv* with mature consideration; **après avoir m. réfléchi,** after careful consideration.

murène [myrɛn] *nf* (*poisson*) moray (eel).

murer [myre] **1** *vt* to wall in (*town etc*); to wall up, to block up, to brick up (*doorway etc*). **2 se murer** *vpr* to shut oneself away; **elle se mure dans le silence/la solitude,** she has retreated into silence/solitude.

muret [myrɛ] *nm*, **murette** [myrɛt] *nf* low wall; (*de pierres posées les unes sur les autres*) dry stone wall.

mûrier [myrje] *nm* **(a)** mulberry (tree, bush); **(b) m. (sauvage),** bramble, blackberry bush.

mûrir [myrir] **1** *vt* to ripen, to mature; to bring (*abscess*) to a head; **m. une question,** to give a question careful consideration. **2** *vi* to ripen, to mature; (*of abscess*) to come to a head; **cet enfant a beaucoup mûri,** the child has greatly matured.

mûrissant [myrisɑ̃] *adj* ripening.

mûrissement [myrismɑ̃] *nm* (*de fruits*) ripening; *Fig* (*d'un projet etc*) development.

murmure [myrmyr] *nm* murmur, murmuring; babbling (*of stream*); **murmures,** murmurs, murmuring; (*plaintes*) muttering, grumbling; **un m. d'approbation,** a murmur of approval; **ce fut accepté sans un m. (de réprobation),** this was accepted without a murmur (of complaint).

murmurer [myrmyre] **1** *vt* to murmur. **2** *vi* to grumble, to complain; **m. entre ses dents,** to mutter.

mûron [myrɔ̃] *nm* wild raspberry.

musaraigne [myzarɛɲ] *nf* shrew (mouse).

musard, -arde [myzar, -ard] *F* **1** *adj* dawdling, idling. **2** *n* dawdler, idler.

musarder [myzarde] *vi* to dawdle, to idle.

musarderie [myzardəri] *nf*, **musardise** [myzardiz] *nf* dawdling, idling.

musc [mysk] *nm* musk.

muscade [myskad] *nf* **(a) (noix) m.,** nutmeg; **fleur de m.,** mace; **(b)** (*d'escamoteur*) conjuror's vanishing ball *or* pea; **passez m.!,** hey presto!

muscadier [myskadje] *nm Bot* nutmeg (tree).

muscadin [myskadɛ̃] *nm Arch* dandy, fop.

muscardin [myskardɛ̃] *nm* dormouse.

muscat [myska] **1** *adj* muscat; **raisin m.,** muscat grape, muscatel grape; **vin m.,** muscatel (wine). **2** *nm* (*raisin*) muscat *or* muscatel grape; (*vin*) muscatel (wine).

muscle [myskl] *nm* muscle; *F* **allez, du m.!,** come on, put your back into it!; *F* **avoir du m.,** to have plenty of brawn.

musclé [myskle] *adj* muscular; **il est bien m.,** he is very muscular, he has well developed muscles; *Fig* **la plume musclée d'un écrivain,** an author's sinewy style; *Fig* **un café m.,** a good strong cup of coffee; *Fig* **lancer une campagne électorale musclée,** to launch a punchy electoral campaign; *Fig* **un nouveau parti libéral m.,** a new liberal party with some muscle; *Fig* **politique musclée,** red-blooded policy.

muscler [myskle] **1** *vt* to develop the muscles of; *Fig* **tout faire pour m. l'industrie française,** to do everything to give French industry some muscle. **2** *vi F* **ça muscle, le sport,** sport builds up your muscles. **3 se muscler** *vpr* to develop one's muscles; **elle se muscle depuis qu'elle fait partie de ce club de natation,** she's developed her muscles since she joined the swimming club; *Fig* **l'industrie sidérurgique s'est bien musclée depuis 1970,** the iron and steel industry has grown greatly in strength *or* has developed some muscle since 1970.

muscu [mysky] *nf F* = **MUSCULATION**.

musculaire [myskylɛr] *adj* muscular (*system, tissue, strength*); **fibre m.,** muscle fibre.

musculation [myskylɑsjɔ̃] *nf* body-building; **faire de la m.,** to do body-building.

musculature [myskylatyr] *nf* musculature.

musculeux, -euse [myskylø, -øz] *adj* muscular (*person, arm etc*).

muse [myz] *nf* muse; **invoquer sa m.,** to invoke *or* call on one's muse.

museau, -eaux [myzo] *nm* muzzle, snout (*of animal*); *F* (*visage*) face; **vilain m.,** ugly mug.

musée [myze] *nm* museum; **m. (de peinture, d'art),** art gallery; *Fig* **son bureau est un véritable m.,** his office is a regular museum; **Venise, ville-m.,** the historical city of Venice; *F* **quel m. des horreurs!,** (*ce groupe*) what a chamber of horrors!

museler [myzle] *vt* (**je muselle; je musellerai**) to muzzle (*dog etc*); *Fig* to muzzle, to gag (*the press, s.o.*).

muselière [myzəljɛr] *nf* (*for animal*) muzzle; **mettre une m. à un chien,** to muzzle a dog.

musellement [myzɛlmɑ̃] *nm* muzzling (*of animal, newspaper*); gagging (*of person*).

muser [myze] *vi Arch & Litt* to idle, to dawdle, to moon about.

muserolle [myzrɔl] *nf* noseband.

musette [myzɛt] *nf* **(a)** *Mus* **orchestre m.,** = accordion band; **bal m.,** popular dance (hall) (*with accordion band*); **(b) m. (mangeoire),** (horse's) nosebag; **(c)** *Arch* (*sac*) (schoolboy's) satchel; *Mil etc* haversack.

muséum [myzeɔm] *nm* natural history museum.

musical, -aux [myzikal, -o] *adj* musical (*sound, evening etc*); **l'art m.,** music; **avoir l'oreille musicale,** to have an ear for music.

musicalement [myzikalmɑ̃] *adv* musically.

musicalité [myzikalite] *nf* musicality, musical quality.

music-hall [myzikol] *nm* music hall; **numéros de m.-h.,** variety turns; (*pl music-halls*).

musicien, -ienne [myzisjɛ̃, -jɛn] **1** *adj* musician; **elle est musicienne,** (*a le sens de la musique*) she is musical; (*elle joue*) she's a musician; **elle est bonne musicienne,** she's a good musician. **2** *n* member of a band; (*classique*) member of an orchestra; *Mil etc* bandsman.

musicographe [myzikɔgraf] *n* musicographer.

musicologie [myzikɔlɔʒi] *nf* musicology.

musicologue [myzikɔlɔg] *n* musicologist.

musicothérapie [myzikɔterapi] *nf* music therapy.

musique [myzik] *nf* music; **mettre des paroles en m.,** to set words to music; **instrument de m.,** musical instrument; **boîte à m.,** music(al) box; **m. de chambre,** chamber music; **m. d'ambiance** *ou* **de fond,** background music; **m. de supermarché,** Muzak ®; **faire de la m.,** to make music, to play; **elle sait lire la m.,** she can read music; **jouer sans m.,** to play without music; *F* **il connaît la m.,** he knows what's what, he's up to all the tricks; *F* **avec elle, c'est toujours la même m.,** she never changes the record; **il veut acheter la m. du film,** he wants to buy the soundtrack of the film; *Can* **faire face à la m.,** to face the music; **chef de m.,** bandmaster.

musiquette [myzikɛt] *nf Péj* piped music, muzak ®.

musoir [myzwar] *nm* pierhead, jetty head.

musqué [myske] *adj* **(a)** musky, scented with musk; **rose musquée, rosier m.,** musk rose; **(b) bœuf m.,** musk ox; **rat m.,** muskrat, musquash; **canard m.,** Muscovy duck, musk duck; **(c)** *Arch* affected (*poet, style etc*).

mussif [mysif] *nm* **or m.,** mosaic gold, disulphide of tin.

must [mœst] *nm F* must; **l'informatique, c'est un m.,** data processing is a must.

mustang [mystɑ̃g] *nm* mustang.

musulman, -ane [myzylmɑ̃, -an] **1** *adj* Moslem, Muslim. **2** *n* **M.,** Moslem, Muslim.

mutabilité [mytabilite] *nf* mutability.

mutable [mytabl] *adj* changeable, mutable.

mutation [mytɑsjɔ̃] *nf* (*changement*) change, alteration; *Mus Biol* mutation; *Ling* gradation (*of vowel*); shift (*of consonant*); *Jur* change of ownership; transfer (*of property*); transfer (*of personnel, Fb of players*); **l'Europe de l'Est est en pleine m. politique,** Eastern Europe is undergoing profound political change.

muter [myte] *vt* to transfer (*personnel*).

mutilateur, -trice [mytilatœr, -tris] **1** *n* mutilator. **2** *adj* mutilative.

mutilation [mytilɑsjɔ̃] *nf* mutilation, maiming (*of person*); mutilation, defacement (*of book, statue etc*).

mutilé, -ée [mytile] **1** *adj* mutilated, maimed (*person*); **il est m. du bras,** he's lost an arm; **m. de la face,** disfigured. **2** *n* **mutilés de guerre,** disabled ex-servicemen; **les grands mutilés,** the severely disabled.

mutiler [mytile] *vt* to mutilate, to maim (*s.o.*); to mutilate, to deface (*book, statue etc*).

mutin, -ine [mytɛ̃, -in] **1** *adj* **(a)** full of fun; **sourire m.,**

cheeky grin; **(b)** *Arch* insubordinate; disobedient, unruly, unbiddable (*child*). **2** *nm* **(a)** (*soldat*) mutineer; **(b)** (*enfant*) unruly child.
mutiné [mytine] **1** *adj* rebellious; mutinous (*troops*). **2** *nm* mutineer.
mutiner (se) [səmytine] *vpr* to rise in revolt, to rebel; *Nau Mil & Hum* to mutiny.
mutinerie [mytinri] *nf* rebellion; *Nau Mil & Hum* mutiny.
mutique [mytik] *adj Méd* (*personne*) suffering from mutism.
mutisme [mytism] *nm* dumbness, muteness, mutism; **les responsables observent un m. absolu,** the officials are maintaining total silence; **se renfermer dans le m.,** to maintain a stubborn silence.
mutité [mytite] *nf Méd* mutism.
mutualisme [mytɥalism] *nm Biol Écon* mutualism.
mutualiste [mytɥalist] **1** *adj* mutualistic. **2** *n* **(a)** *Écon* mutualist; **(b)** member of a mutual insurance company.
mutualité [mytɥalite] *nf* **(a)** mutual insurance; **société de m.,** friendly society; **(b)** *Litt* mutuality, reciprocity.
mutuel, -elle [mytɥɛl] **1** *adj* mutual; **un amour m.,** a mutual love; **ils ont fini par faire des compromis mutuels,** they ended up by making mutual compromises; **société d'assurance mutuelle,** mutual insurance company, friendly society. **2** *nf* **mutuelle,** (*société*) mutual insurance company, friendly society; (*assurance*) private insurance; **prendre une mutuelle,** to take out private insurance.
mutuellement [mytɥɛlmɑ̃] *adv* mutually.
Mycènes [misɛn] *n Hist* Mycenae.
mycénien, -ienne [misenjɛ̃, -jɛn] *adj Hist* Mycenaean.
mycologie [mikɔlɔʒi] *nf Bot* mycology.
myéline [mjelin] *nf Anat* myelin(e).
myélite [mjelit] *nf Méd* myelitis.
myélome [mjelom] *nm Méd* myeloma.
mygale [migal] *nf* (*araignée*) trapdoor spider.
myocarde [mjɔkard] *nm Anat* myocardium.
myocardite [mjɔkardit] *nf Méd* myocarditis.
myologie [mjɔlɔʒi] *nf Anat* myology.
myome [mjom] *nm Méd* myoma.
myope [mjɔp] **1** *adj* myopic, shortsighted; *Fig* **m. comme une taupe,** as blind as a bat. **2** *n* myope, shortsighted person.
myopie [mjɔpi] *nf Méd* myopia, shortsightedness.
myosotis [mjɔzɔtis] *nm* (*fleur*) myosotis, forget-me-not.
myriade [mirjad] *nf* myriad.
myriapode [mirjapɔd] *nm* myriapod; **myriapodes,** Myriapoda.
myrmidon [mirmidɔ̃] *nm F* whippersnapper, little runt.
myrrhe [mir] *nf* myrrh.
myrte [mirt] *nm* (*plante*) myrtle; **m. des marais,** sweet gale, bog myrtle.
myrtille [mirtij] *nf* (*baie*) bilberry, whinberry.
mystère [mistɛr] *nm* **(a)** mystery; **on n'a jamais pénétré ce m.,** this mystery has never been fathomed (out); **elle aime le m.,** she likes to be mysterious; *Fig F* **m. et boule de gomme,** wouldn't you like to know; (*je n'en ai aucune idée*) search me; *Fig* **je n'en fais pas m.,** I make no mystery *or* no secret of it; **(b)** *Hist Littér* mystery (play); **m. de la Passion,** Passion play.
mystérieusement [misterjøzmɑ̃] *adv* mysteriously.
mystérieux, -euse [misterjø, -øz] *adj* mysterious.
mysticisme [mistisism] *nm* mysticism.
mystifiable [mistifjabl] *adj* gullible.
mystifiant [mistifjɑ̃] *adj* deceptive.
mystificateur, -trice [mistifikatœr, -tris] **1** *adj* deceptive. **2** *n* deceiver; (*qui fait des farces*) hoaxer.
mystification [mistifikɑsjɔ̃] *nf Péj* (*tromperie*) deception; (*farce*) hoax, practical joke; **m. collective,** mass deception.
mystifier [mistifje] *vt* (*impf & pr sub* **n. mystifiions, v. mystifiiez**) *Péj* (*tromper*) to deceive; (*faire une farce à*) to hoax, to fool, to bamboozle (*s.o.*), to play a practical joke on (*s.o.*), to pull (*s.o.'s*) leg; **se laisser m. par qch,** to be taken in *or* fooled by sth.
mystique [mistik] **1** *adj* mystic(al). **2** *n* mystic.
mystiquement [mistikmɑ̃] *adv* mystically.
mythe [mit] *nm* myth, legend.
mythique [mitik] *adj* mythical.
mythologie [mitɔlɔʒi] *nf* mythology.
mythologique [mitɔlɔʒik] *adj* mythological.
mythologiquement [mitɔlɔʒikmɑ̃] *adv* mythologically.
mythologue [mitɔlɔg] *n* mythologist.
mythomane [mitɔman] *adj & n* pathological (liar); *Psy* mythomaniac.
mythomanie [mitɔmani] *nf Psy* mythomania.
mytiliculteur [mitilikyltœr] *nm* mussel farmer.
mytiliculture [mitilikyltyr] *nf* mussel farming.
myxœdème [miksedɛm] *n Méd* myxoedema, *US* myxedema.
myxomatose [miksɔmatoz] *nf* myxomatosis.
myxomycètes [miksɔmisɛt] *nm* myxomycetes.

N

N, n [ɛn] *nm* (the letter) N, n.
na [na] *int F* so there!
nabab [nabab] *nm* nabob; **n. de la drogue,** drug baron.
nabot, -ote [nabo, -ɔt] **1** *n* dwarf, midget. **2** *adj* dwarfish, tiny (*person*).
Nabuchodonosor [nabykɔdɔnɔzɔr] *nm Bible Hist* Nebuchadnezzar.
nacelle [nasɛl] *nf* **(a)** basket (*of balloon*); aerial work platform (*for cleaning windows etc*); gondola, car (*of airship*); nacelle (*of aircraft*); pod (*of aircraft engine*); **(b)** *Vieilli* (*bateau*) skiff, wherry.
nacre [nakr] *nf* mother of pearl.
nacré [nakre] *adj* (*lustre etc*) pearly.
nadir [nadir] *nm Astron* nadir.
nævus [nevys] *nm Med* naevus, *US* nevus.
nage [naʒ] *nf* **(a)** swimming; stroke (*in swimming*); **se sauver à la n.,** to swim to safety; **traverser une rivière à la n.,** to swim across a river; *F* **être (tout) en n.,** to be bathed in perspiration; **n. sur le dos,** backstroke; **n. libre,** freestyle; **faire de la n.,** to swim; **(b)** (*aviron*) rowing, sculling; **banc de n.,** thwart; **chef de n.,** stroke.
nageoire [naʒwar] *nf* **(a)** fin (*of fish*); flipper (*of dolphin etc*); **n. caudale,** caudal fin, tail fluke; **(b)** float, water wings (*to support swimmer*); float (*of seaplane*).
nager [naʒe] *vi* (**je nageais; n. nageons**) **(a)** to swim; (*of wood, cork*) to float; **n. vers la côte,** to swim for the shore; **n. la brasse,** to swim breaststroke; **tu sais n.?,** can you swim?; **n. debout,** to tread water; **légumes qui nagent dans le beurre,** vegetables swimming in butter; *Fig* **n. dans le sang,** to be bathed in blood; *Fig F* **n. comme un poisson dans l'eau,** (*être à l'aise*) to be like a fish in water; **n. entre deux eaux,** to be floating beneath the surface; *Fig* not to commit oneself; **n. dans l'abondance,** to be rolling in money; **n. dans le bonheur,** to be blissfully happy; *F* **tu nages dans ce costume,** the suit drowns you; *F* **je nage,** I'm all at sea;
(b) to row; **nagez partout!,** pull away!; **n. en arrière** *ou* **à culer,** to back water; **n. plat,** to feather; **n. à** *ou* **en couple,** to (double) scull; **n. en pointe,** to row.
nageur, -euse [naʒœr, -øz] **1** *n* **(a)** swimmer; **être bon/mauvais n.,** to be a good/bad swimmer, to swim well/badly; **n. de combat,** frogman; **(b)** (*rameur*) oarsman, rower; **n. de l'arrière,** stroke; **n. de l'avant,** bow (oar). **2** *adj* swimming (*animal*).
naguère [nagɛr] *adv Litt* not long ago, a short time ago, lately.
naïade [najad] *nf* naiad, water nymph.
naïf, -ïve [naif, -iv] **1** *adj* **(a)** (*innocent*) naive, ingenuous, innocent; **elle était assez naïve pour croire ses mensonges,** she was naive enough to believe his lies; *Art* **un peintre n.,** a naive painter; **(b)** *Péj* (*peu sophistiqué*) simple-minded, credulous, unsophisticated, *F* green. **2** *n* **vous me prenez pour un n.!,** what sort of a fool do you take me for?; **jouer les naïfs** *ou* **les naïves,** to act *or* play the innocent.
nain, naine [nɛ̃, nɛn] **1** *n* dwarf; midget; *Cartes* **N. jaune,** Pope Joan. **2** *adj* dwarf(ish); **haricots nains,** dwarf beans.
naissain [nɛsɛ̃] *nm* (*of oyster, mussel*) spawn, spat.
naissance [nɛsɑ̃s] *nf* **(a)** birth; **sourd de n.,** deaf from birth, born deaf; **jour de n.,** birthday; **lieu de n.,** birthplace; **donner n. à un enfant,** to give birth to a child; **acte de n.,** birth certificate; **extrait de n.,** = (copy of) birth certificate; **contrôle des naissances,** birth control; **français de n.,** French by birth; *Fig* **la n. du printemps,** the birth of spring; **la n. du jour,** dawn, daybreak, the break of day; **donner n. à une rumeur,** to give rise to a rumour; **prendre n.,** to originate, to start; **(b)** root (*of tongue, nail etc*); source (*of river*); *Archit* spring (*of pillar, arch*); **point de n.,** point of origin; **n. du cou,** nape of the neck; **cicatrice à la n. des cheveux,** scar just where the hair begins *or* at the hairline.
naissant [nɛsɑ̃] *adj* newborn; dawning (*day*); nascent (*beauty*); **à l'aube naissante,** at break of day; **barbe naissante,** incipient beard; *Ch* **à l'état n.,** nascent.
naître [nɛtr] *vi* (*prp* **naissant**; *pp* **né**; *pr ind* **je nais, il naît, n. naissons, ils naissent**; *pr sub* **je naisse**; *p hist* **je naquis**; *fut* **je naîtrai**; *aux* **être**) **(a)** to be born; **il naquit** *ou* **est né en 1880,** he was born in 1880; **enfant/poussin qui vient de n.,** newly-born child/newly-hatched chick; **né de parents anglais,** of English parentage; **enfant à n.,** unborn child; **il naît plus de filles que de garçons,** more girls than boys are born; **être né pour qch,** to be cut out for sth; **il est né pour être musicien/réussir,** he was born *or* destined to be a musician/to succeed; **être né l'un pour l'autre,** to be made for one another *or* each other; **il est né poète,** he is a born poet; **je l'ai vu n.,** I have known him from birth *or* since he was a baby; **Christine Thomas, née Martin,** Christine Thomas, née Martin; **je ne suis pas né d'hier** *ou* **de la dernière pluie,** I wasn't born yesterday;
(b) (*of hopes, fears etc*) to be born, to (a)rise, to spring up; **faire n.,** to give rise to, to raise, to breed (*hope, anxiety, suspicion*); to arouse (*suspicion*); to give rise to (*doubt*); to provoke (*smile*);
(c) (*of plants*) to begin to grow *or* come up, to appear; (*of day*) to dawn; (*of project*) to originate.
naïvement [naivmɑ̃] *adv* naively, ingenuously.
naïveté [naivte] *nf* **(a)** (*innocence*) naivety, simplicity, ingenuousness; **elle a eu la naïveté de croire à ses promesses,** she was naive enough to believe his promises; **(b)** (*remarque*) naive *or* ingenuous remark.
Namibie [namibi] *nf* Namibia.
namibien, -ienne [namibjɛ̃, -jɛn] **1** *adj* Namibian. **2** *n* **N.,** Namibian.
nana [nana] *nf F* girl (friend); **une n. qu'elle a rencontrée cet été,** a girl she met last summer; **il est venu avec sa n.,** he came with his girlfriend.
nanisme [nanism] *nm* dwarfism.
Nankin [nɑ̃kɛ̃] **1** *n* **(a)** Nanking; **(b)** *Tex* nankeen. **2** *adj inv Tex* nankeen.
nanoseconde [nanɔsəgɔ̃d] *nf* nanosecond.
nansouk [nɑ̃zuk] *nm Tex* nainsook.
nanti, -ie [nɑ̃ti] **1** *adj* (*personne, pays*) well-off, rich. **2** *n* **les nantis,** the well-off, the rich.
nantir [nɑ̃tir] **1** *vt* **(a) n. qn de qch,** to provide s.o. with sth; **être bien nanti,** to be well off *or* well provided for; **(b)** to give security to (*creditor*). **2 se nantir** *vpr* **se n. d'un parapluie,** to provide *or* arm oneself with an umbrella.
nantissement [nɑ̃tismɑ̃] *nm Jur* pledge, collateral, security, cover; **déposer des titres en n.,** to lodge stock as security.
napalm [napalm] *nm* napalm; **bombe au n.,** napalm bomb.
naphtaline [naftalin] *nf,* **naphtalène** [naftalɛn] *nm* naphthalene; *Can Fig* **sortir qch de la n.,** to take sth out of mothballs; **boules de n.,** mothballs.
naphte [naft] *nm* naphtha, mineral oil; **n. de goudron,** coal-tar naphtha.
Napoléon [napɔleɔ̃] *nm* **(a)** Napoleon; **fauteuil/table/***etc* **N.,** Empire chair/table/*etc*; **(b)** (*pièce*) twenty-franc piece (*bearing the effigy of Napoleon*).
napoléonien, -ienne [napɔleɔnjɛ̃, -jɛn] *adj* Napoleonic.
napolitain, -aine [napɔlitɛ̃, -ɛn] **1** *adj* Neapolitan; **tranche napolitaine,** Neapolitan ice (cream). **2** *n* **N.,** Neapolitan.
nappage [napaʒ] *nm Culin* coating (with sauce).
nappe [nap] *nf* **(a)** tablecloth; **mettre/ôter la n.,** to lay/remove the cloth; **n. à thé,** tea cloth; *Rel* **n. d'autel,** altar cloth; **(b)** *Fig* sheet (*of ice, fire*); **n. d'eau,** sheet of water; *Géol* **n. phréatique,** water table; **n. de mazout,** oil slick; **n. éruptive,** lava flow; **n. pétrolifère,** oil layer.
napper [nape] *vt* **(a)** *Culin* to coat (with sauce); **(b)** to

cover with a cloth.

napperon [naprɔ̃] *nm* (small linen) cloth, mat; **n. de plateau,** traycloth; **n. individuel,** place mat.

narcisse [narsis] *nm* **(a)** (*plante*) narcissus; **n. sauvage** *ou* **des prés,** daffodil; **n. des poètes,** pheasant's eye; **(b)** *Psy* narcissist.

Narcisse [narsis] *nm Myth* Narcissus.

narcissique [narsisik] *adj Psy* narcissistic.

narcissisme [narsisism] *nm Psy* narcissism.

narco-dollars [narkɔdɔlar] *nmpl* drug money.

narcose [narkoz] *nf Méd* narcosis.

narcotique [narkɔtik] *Méd* **1** *adj* narcotic. **2** *nm* narcotic; *Old-Fashioned* opiate; **faire prendre un n. à qn,** to drug s.o.

narco-trafiquant, -ante [narkɔtrafikɑ̃, -ɑ̃t] *n* drug trafficker.

nard [nar] *nm Bot Pharm* spikenard, nard.

narguer [narge] *vt* to scoff at (*sth, s.o.*).

narguilé, narghilé, narghileh [nargile] *nm* hookah, narghile.

narine [narin] *nf* nostril.

narquois [narkwa] *adj* mocking (*tone, smile*).

narquoisement [narkwazmɑ̃] *adv* mockingly; (*dire*) in a mocking tone.

narrateur, -trice [naratœr, -tris] *n* narrator; teller (*of story*), storyteller.

narratif, -ive [naratif, -iv] *adj* narrative.

narration [narɑsjɔ̃] *nf* **(a)** narrating, narration; *Gram* **présent de n.,** historic present; **(b)** narrative, account (*of event*); *Scol* narrative composition.

narrer [nare] *vt Litt* to narrate, to relate.

narval [narval] *nm* narwhal, unicorn whale; (*pl narvals*).

nasal, -ale, -aux [nazal, -o] **1** *adj* nasal (*bone, sound*). **2** *nf Ling* **nasale,** nasal.

nasaliser [nazalize] *vt* to nasalize (*sound*).

nase [naz] *adj F* (*person*) dead beat, shattered; (*car etc*) done for, clapped out.

naseau, -eaux [nazo] *nm* nostril (*of horse, ox*); *F* **les naseaux,** the nose.

nasillard [nazijar] *adj* nasal; **ton n.,** (nasal) twang; **parler d'une voix nasillarde,** to talk through one's nose.

nasillement [nazijmɑ̃] *nm* **(a)** speaking through one's nose; **(b)** (nasal) twang.

nasiller [nazije] *vi* to speak through one's nose *or* with a twang.

nasique [nazik] *nm* (*mammifère*) proboscis monkey.

nasse [nas] *nf* eel pot, lobster pot; hoop net (*for birds*); trap (*for rats*); *Fig* **tomber dans la n.,** to fall into a trap.

natal, -als [natal] *adj* (*rarely used in pl*) native; **ville natale,** birthplace, *F* home town; **mon pays n.,** my native land; **ma maison natale,** the house where I was born.

nataliste [natalist] *adj* **politique n.,** policy to increase the birthrate, pro-birth policy.

natalité [natalite] *nf* birthrate; **forte n.,** high birthrate.

natation [natɑsjɔ̃] *nf* swimming; **école de n.,** swimming baths.

natatoire [natatwar] *adj Zool* natatory, natatorial (*organ, membrane*); **vessie n.,** (*de poisson*) swim bladder, air bladder.

natif, -ive [natif, -iv] **1** *adj* **(a)** native; **je suis n. de Londres,** I'm a Londoner (by birth); **(b)** *Minér etc* native, virgin (*gold etc*); **(c)** (*inné*) natural, inborn; **bon sens n.,** mother *or* native wit. **2** *n* native.

nation [nɑsjɔ̃] *nf* nation; *Nau* **pavillon de n.,** national flag.

national, -ale, -aux [nasjɔnal, -o] **1** *adj* national; **l'hymne n.,** national anthem; **Assemblée nationale,** National Assembly. **2** *n* **nationaux,** nationals (*of a country*). **3** *nf* **nationale,** main road; *Br* ≈ A road.

nationalement [nasjɔnalmɑ̃] *adv* nationally.

nationalisation [nasjɔnalizɑsjɔ̃] *nf* nationalization.

nationaliser [nasjɔnalize] *vt* to nationalize (*industry*).

nationalisme [nasjɔnalism] *nm Pol* nationalism.

nationaliste [nasjɔnalist] **1** *n Pol* nationalist. **2** *adj* nationalist; *Péj* nationalistic; **la Chine n.,** Nationalist China.

nationalité [nasjɔnalite] *nf* nationality; *Nau* **acte de n.,** (ship's) certificate of registry; **les personnes de n. française,** people of French nationality, French nationals.

national-socialisme [nasjɔnalsɔsjalism] *nm Pol Hist* National Socialism.

Nations Unies [nɑsjɔ̃zyni] *nfpl Pol F* **les N. U.,** the UN.

nativement [nativmɑ̃] *adv* innately, naturally.

nativité [nativite] *nf Rel Beaux-Arts* nativity.

natron [natrɔ̃] *nm,* **natrum** [natrɔm] *nm Minér* natron, native soda.

natte [nat] *nf* **(a)** plait, braid (*of hair, gold thread etc*); **porter des nattes,** to wear one's hair in plaits; **porter** *ou* **avoir une n.,** to have a pigtail; **(b)** mat, matting (*of rush, straw*).

natter [nate] *vt* **(a)** to plait, to braid (*hair, straw etc*); **(b)** to cover (*wall etc*) with mats.

naturalisation [natyralizɑsjɔ̃] *nf* **(a)** *Admin* naturalization; **(b)** naturalizing, acclimatizing (*of plant, animal*); adoption (*of word, idea, art*); **la n. d'un concept étranger,** the adoption of a foreign concept; **(c)** preservation, mounting (*of botanical specimen etc*); **n. d'animaux,** taxidermy.

naturalisé, -ée [natyralize] **1** *adj* naturalized. **2** *n* naturalized subject *or* citizen.

naturaliser [natyralize] *vt* **(a)** *Admin* to naturalize; **se faire n. français,** to become a naturalized Frenchman; **(b)** to naturalize, to acclimatize (*plant, animal*); to adopt (*word, idea, art*); **n. des expressions anglaises,** to absorb English expressions into the language; **(c)** to preserve, to mount (*botanical specimen*); to mount, to stuff (*animal*).

naturalisme [natyralism] *nm* naturalism.

naturaliste [natyralist] **1** *n* **(a)** (*savant*) naturalist; **(b)** (*artisan*) taxidermist. **2** *adj* naturalistic.

nature [natyr] **1** *nf* **(a)** (*environnement*) nature; **les lois de la n.,** the laws of nature; **laisser faire la n.,** to let nature take its course; **vice contre n.,** unnatural vice; **à l'état de n.,** in a state of nature; in the natural state; **plus grand que n.,** larger than life; **peindre d'après n.,** to paint from nature *or* from life; **n. morte,** still life (painting); *F* **se perdre** *ou* **disparaître dans la n.,** to vanish into thin air; *Aut F* **partir dans la n.,** to run *or* smash into a tree *or* bank *etc*;

(b) (*caractère*) nature; **n. du climat/du sol,** nature of the climate/soil; **faits de n. à nous étonner,** facts of an astonishing nature, astonishing facts; **ce n'est pas dans ma n.,** it's not in my nature; **être d'une n. douce,** to be gentle; **être timide de** *ou* **par n., être d'une n. timide,** to be naturally shy *or* shy by nature; **c'est une bonne n.,** he's *or* she's a kindly (sort of) man *or* woman; **une n. violente,** a naturally violent person; *F* **c'est une n.,** he's *or* she's a real personality; *F* **c'est une petite n.,** he's *or* she's a weakly sort of person;

(c) **payer en n.,** to pay in kind.

2 *adj inv* **(a)** *Culin* plain; **bœuf/pommes n.,** (plain) boiled beef/potatoes; **thé n.,** tea without milk; **yaourt n.,** plain yogurt;

(b) (*conforme à la réalité*) **grandeur n.,** full-scale, life-size(d);

(c) (*personne*) natural, unaffected.

naturel, -elle [natyrɛl] **1** *adj* **(a)** natural (*history, law*); **mort naturelle,** death from natural causes; **enfant n.,** natural *or* illegitimate child; **de grandeur naturelle,** life-size(d); **c'est n. de le faire,** it's only natural *or* reasonable to do so; **mais c'est tout n.,** it was a pleasure, *Am* you're welcome;

(b) native (*wit*); natural, innate (*gift*); natural, unaffected (*person*); simple, straightforward (*answer*); **il lui est n. de peindre,** painting comes naturally to him; **alcool n.,** raw spirit; **vin n.,** unfortified wine; **soie naturelle,** pure *or* real silk; *Mus* **note naturelle,** natural.

2 *nm* (*tempérament*) nature, character, disposition; **d'un bon n.,** of a kind disposition; *Prov* **chassez le n., il revient au galop,** what's bred in the bone will come out in the flesh;

(b) (*simplicité, spontanéité*) naturalness; **elle joue la comédie avec beaucoup de n.,** she's a natural (as a) comic actor;

(c) (*d'après la réalité*) **voir les choses au n.,** to see things as they are; **peindre qch au n.,** to paint sth true to life *or* realistically; *Culin* **thon au n.,** tuna (packed) in brine.

naturellement [natyrɛlmɑ̃] *adv* naturally; **n. timide,** naturally shy, shy by nature; **se conduire n.,** to behave naturally *or* without affectation; **vous vous en êtes fâché? — n.!,** you resented it? — naturally! *or* of course (I did)!

naturisme [natyrism] *nm* naturism; **adepte du n.,** naturist, nudist.

naturiste [natyrist] **1** *n* naturist, nudist. **2** *adj* naturist.

naufrage [nofraʒ] *nm* (ship)wreck; **faire n.,** (*of ship*) to be wrecked; (*of sailor*) to be shipwrecked; *Fig* (*of company*) to go bankrupt; **périr dans un n.,** to be lost at sea.

naufragé, -ée [nofraʒe] **1** *adj* (*ship*) wrecked; (*sailor*) shipwrecked, castaway. **2** *n* castaway, shipwrecked man; shipwrecked woman.

naufrageur, -euse [nofraʒœr, -øz] *n* wrecker (*of ships*);

bateau n., wrecker.

nauséabond [nozeabɔ̃] *adj* nauseous, nauseating (*smell, conduct*); evil-smelling (*person, room*).

nausée [noze] *nf* **(a)** (*envie de vomir*) nausea; **avoir la n.** *ou* **des nausées,** to feel sick *or Am* nauseous; **donner des nausées à qn,** to nauseate s.o.; **(b)** *Fig* disgust; **l'hypocrisie me donne la n.,** hypocrisy makes me sick *or* nauseates me.

nauséeux, -euse [nozeø, -øz] *adj* **(a)** nauseating, nauseous; **odeur nauséeuse,** nauseating smell; **(b)** *Fig* loathsome, nauseating (*hypocrisy etc*).

nautique [notik] *adj* nautical (*term, instrument etc*); **sports nautiques,** water sports; **carte n.,** (sea) chart.

nautisme [notism] *nm Sp* sailing.

naval, -ale, -als [naval] **1** *adj* naval; nautical; **termes navals,** nautical terms; **armée navale,** fleet, naval force; **architecture navale,** naval architecture; **construction navale,** shipbuilding; **chantier n.,** shipyard; **base navale,** naval base; **les forces navales,** the navy; **l'École navale,** the Naval College. **2** *nf* **la Navale,** the Naval College.

navarin [navarɛ̃] *nm Culin* lamb stew *or* casserole.

navet [navɛ] *nm* **(a)** turnip; **n. de Suède,** swede; **(b)** *F* (*film, play*) flop, *Am* turkey.

navette¹ [navɛt] *nf* **(a)** *Tex* shuttle; *Av etc* shuttle (service); **faire la n. entre deux endroits,** (*of vehicle*) to ply *or* shuttle back and forth between two places; (*of person*) to go to and fro, to shuttle back and forth; *Rail* to commute; **navettes fréquentes entre la gare et la ville,** frequent (shuttle) service between station and town; *Astronaut* **n. spatiale,** space shuttle; **(b)** *Rel* incense boat; incense box.

navette² *nf Bot* rape; **(huile de) n.,** rape (seed) oil, colza oil.

navigabilité [navigabilite] *nf* **(a)** navigability (*of river etc*); **(b) (état de) n.,** seaworthiness (*of ship*); airworthiness (*of aircraft*); **en (bon) état de n.,** (*ship*) seaworthy; (*aircraft*) airworthy.

navigable [navigabl] *adj* **(a)** navigable (*river*); **(b)** seaworthy (*ship*); airworthy (*aircraft*).

navigant, -ante [navigɑ̃, -ɑ̃t] **1** *adj* **personnel n.,** navigation crew. **2** *n* **les navigants,** navigation crew.

navigateur [navigatœr] **1** *nm* navigator (*of ship, aircraft etc*); *Litt* navigator, seafarer. **2** *adj* **peuple n.,** seafaring people.

navigation [navigɑsjɔ̃] *nf* navigation; **n. sur arc de grand cercle,** great circle sailing *or* navigation; **n. à l'estime,** dead reckoning; **n. côtière,** coastal navigation; **n. au long cours, n. hauturière,** deep-sea *or* ocean navigation; **n. intérieure** *ou* **fluviale,** inland navigation; **n. à voile,** sailing; **n. de plaisance,** sailing, yachting; **école de n. (de la marine marchande),** nautical school; **compagnie de n.,** shipping company; **permis de n.,** ship's passport, sea letter; **journal de n.,** log(book); *Av* **n. à vue/aux instruments,** visual/instrument flying; **n. spatiale,** space navigation, astronautics.

naviguer [navige] **1** *vi* (*of ship, seaman*) to sail (**vers,** to); **n. au commerce,** to be in the merchant service; **n. au long cours,** to be in the foreign trade; **navire qui navigue bien,** ship that behaves well at sea; *Fig F* **il a beaucoup navigué,** he's seen the world; *Fig F* **elle sait n.,** she can take care of herself. **2** *vt* to navigate (*ship, aircraft*).

navire [navir] *nm* ship, vessel; **n. à voiles,** sailing ship; **n. à vapeur,** steamship, steamer; **n. frère, n. jumeau,** sister ship, twin ship; **n. de commerce, n. marchand,** merchantman, merchant ship; **n. de plaisance,** pleasure boat; **n. de pêche,** fishing boat; **n. au long cours,** ocean-going ship; **n. de guerre,** warship; **n. de combat,** battleship; **n. météo(rologique),** weather ship; *US* ocean station vessel; **les navires dans le port,** the shipping in the harbour.

navire-citerne [navirsitɛrn] *nm Nau* tanker; (*pl navires-citernes*).

navire-école [navirekɔl] *nm* training ship; (*navires-écoles*).

navrant [navrɑ̃] *adj* heartrending, heartbreaking; **c'est n.,** it's very distressing; **un film n. de bêtise,** an incredibly stupid film; **un contretemps n.,** an unfortunate *or* regrettable mishap.

navré [navre] *adj* heartbroken (*person*); woebegone (*expression*); **être n. de qch,** to be (deeply) grieved at sth; **je suis n. de l'apprendre,** I'm terribly sorry to hear it.

navrer [navre] *vt* to grieve (*s.o.*) deeply, to break (*s.o.'s*) heart.

nazaréen, -enne [nazareɛ̃, -en] *adj & n Bible* Nazarene.

naze [naz] *adj F voir* **NASE**.

nazi, -e [nazi] *adj & n Hist Pol* Nazi.

nazisme [nazism] *nm Hist Pol* Nazism.

N.B. [ɛnbe] *abrév* NB.

ne, n' [n(ə)] *adv* **(a)** (*forming neg verb with* **pas**) **je ne la connais pas,** I don't know her; **il ne m'avait pas vu,** he hadn't seen me; (*for the use of* **ne** *in conjunction with* **aucun, aucunement, goutte, guère, jamais, mie, mot, personne, plus, point, que (ne ... que), rien,** *see these words*);

(b) (*used alone, chiefly in literary style with* **cesser, oser, pouvoir, savoir, importer,** *and often as an archaism with other verbs*) **il ne cesse de parler,** he is for ever talking; **je n'ose lui parler,** I dare not speak to him *or* her; **je ne puis vous le promettre,** I cannot promise you that; **je ne sais que faire,** I don't know what to do; **je ne saurais vous le dire,** I cannot tell you; (*always used without* **pas** *in*) **n'importe,** never mind, it doesn't matter;

(c) (*in the following constructions*) **qui ne connaît cette œuvre célèbre?,** who does not know this famous work?; **que ne ferait-elle pour vous?,** what would she not do for you?; **je n'ai d'autre désir que celui de vous plaire,** I have no other desire than to please you; **si je ne me trompe,** unless I am mistaken; **voilà six mois que je ne l'ai vue,** it is now six months since I (last) saw her, I haven't seen her for six months; **il n'y a personne à qui il ne se soit adressé,** there is no one to whom he did not apply; **il n'eut garde d'y aller,** he took good care not to go; **qu'à cela ne tienne!,** by all means!; **je n'ai que faire de votre aide,** I don't need your help;

(d) (*used optionally in literary style with a vague negative connotation*) **je crains qu'elle (ne) prenne froid,** I am afraid she may catch cold; **évitez** *ou* **prenez garde qu'on (ne) vous voie,** take care not to be seen; **peu s'en fallut qu'elle (ne) tombât,** she nearly fell; **je ne nie pas que cela (ne) soit vrai,** I don't deny that it's true; **il est plus vigoureux qu'il (ne) paraît,** he is stronger than he looks; **elle agit autrement qu'elle ne parle,** her actions belie her words.

né [ne] *adj* born; **c'est un conteur né,** he's a born storyteller; **enfant né d'un premier mariage,** child of a first marriage; **né d'une famille bourgeoise,** born into a middle-class family; *Fig* **un film né de la rencontre d'un réalisateur et d'une actrice,** a film that grew out of a meeting between a director and an actress; **Mme Martin, née Dupond,** Mrs Martin, née Dupond; **on dirait qu'il est né pour se battre,** he's a born fighter; **être bien né,** to be of noble birth.

néanmoins [neɑ̃mwɛ̃] *adv* nevertheless, nonetheless, yet.

néant [neɑ̃] *nm* **(a)** nothing; *Litt* nought, naught; **sortir du n.,** to rise from nothing; **réduire qch à n.,** to reduce sth to nothing *or* to nought; **(b)** worthlessness, uselessness (*of s.o., sth*); **le n. des grandeurs humaines,** the vanity of human greatness; **(c)** (*on form, tax return etc*) none, nil.

nébuleux, -euse [nebylø, -øz] **1** *adj* nebulous, cloudy, hazy, misty (*sky, view*); nebulous, vague, hazy (*ideas*); obscure (*writer, theory*). **2** *nf Astron* **nébuleuse,** nebula.

nébuliseur [nebylizœr] *nm* nebuliser.

nébulosité [nebylozite] *nf* nebulousness, cloudiness, haziness (*of sky, idea etc*); *Météo* **forte n.,** heavy cloud cover.

nécessaire [nesesɛr] **1** *adj* necessary, requisite; **n. à** *ou* **pour qch/qn,** necessary *or* required for sth/s.o.; **n. pour faire qch,** necessary for doing sth; **se rendre n. à qn,** to make oneself indispensable to s.o.; **avoir l'argent n.,** to have the necessary money; **il n'est pas n. d'être impoli,** there is no need to be rude; **ils n'ont pas jugé n. de venir s'excuser,** they didn't think *or* deem it necessary to come and apologize; **il est n. que vous teniez compte de cela,** you really must take notice of this; **peu n.,** needless, unnecessary. **2** *nm* **(a)** necessities, necessaries; **le strict n.,** bare necessities; **se refuser le n.,** to deny oneself the necessities of life; **faire le n.,** to do what is necessary; **(b)** outfit, kit (*of tools*); **n. de réparation,** repair kit; **n. de toilette,** dressing case, toilet case; **n. de voyage,** overnight bag.

nécessairement [nesesɛrmɑ̃] *adv* necessarily, of necessity.

nécessité [nesesite] *nf* **(a)** necessity; **de (toute) n.,** necessarily, of necessity; **il est de toute n. de faire quelque chose,** it is essential to do something, we simply must do something; **être dans la n. de faire qch,** to be compelled to do sth; **ce voyage est une n.,** this journey is essential; **quelle n. y avait-il de faire cela?,** what need was there to do that?; **faire qch par n.,** to do sth out of necessity, to be compelled to do sth; **faire de n. vertu,** to make a virtue (out) of necessity; **(b)** (*besoin*) need, want;

les nécessités de la vie, the necessities of life; **objets de première n.** *ou* **de toute n.,** essential items, essentials; **denrées de première n.,** essential foodstuffs; **selon les nécessités,** as circumstances require; **c'est une n.,** it's a must; **être dans la n.,** (*être pauvre*) to be in need *or* in straitened circumstances.

nécessiter [nesesite] *vt* to require, to demand, to necessitate, to entail (*sth*).

nécessiteux, -euse [nesesitø, -øz] **1** *adj* needy, in need. **2** *n* **les n.,** the needy, the poor, the destitute.

nécrologe [nekrɔlɔʒ] *nm* obituary list, necrology, death roll.

nécrologie [nekrɔlɔʒi] *nf* obituary (notice); *Journ* deaths (column), the obituary column, the obituaries.

nécrologique [nekrɔlɔʒik] *adj* obituary (*notice*).

nécromancie [nekrɔmɑ̃si] *nf* necromancy.

nécromancien, -ienne [nekrɔmɑ̃sjɛ̃, -jɛn] *n* necromancer.

nécrophore [nekrɔfɔr] *nm* carrion beetle, scavenger beetle.

nécropole [nekrɔpɔl] *nf* necropolis.

nécrose [nekroz] *nf Biol* necrosis.

nécroser [nekroze] *vt Biol* to cause necrosis in (*tissue*).

nectaire [nɛktɛr] *nm Bot* nectary.

nectar [nɛktar] *nm* nectar.

nectarine [nɛktarin] *nf* (*fruit*) nectarine.

néerlandais, -aise [neɛrlɑ̃dɛ, -ɛz] **1** *adj* Dutch, (of the) Netherlands; **le Gouvernement n.,** the Dutch Government, the Government of the Netherlands. **2** *nm Ling* (*in the Netherlands*) Dutch; (*in Belgium*) Flemish. **3** *n* **N.,** Dutchman; Dutchwoman.

nef [nɛf] *nf* **(a)** nave (*of church*); **n. latérale,** aisle; **(b)** *Litt* ship.

néfaste [nefast] *adj* luckless, ill-omened, inauspicious; **jour n.,** ill-fated *or* evil day; **influence n.,** harmful *or* very bad influence.

nèfle [nɛfl] *nf* (*fruit*) medlar; **n. du Japon,** loquat; *Fig* **des nèfles!,** no fear!, nothing doing!

néflier [neflije] *nm* (*arbre*) medlar (tree); **n. du Japon,** loquat (tree).

négateur, -trice [negatœr, -tris] *Litt* **1** *adj* denying; **une doctrine négatrice,** a negative doctrine. **2** *n* denier.

négatif, -ive [negatif, -iv] **1** *adj* (*réponse, attitude, résultat*) & *Math Phys etc* negative; *Phot* épreuve négative, negative. **2** *nm Phot* negative. **3** *nf Gram* **négative,** negative; **je réponds par la négative,** my answer is no *or* in the negative.

négation [negɑsjɔ̃] *nf* **(a)** negation, denial; **(b)** *Gram* negative.

négativement [negativmɑ̃] *adv* (*répondre*) negatively, in the negative; *Phys* **un électron chargé n.,** a negatively charged electron.

négligé [negliʒe] **1** *adj* **(a)** neglected (*opportunity etc*); **épouse négligée,** neglected wife; **(b)** careless, slovenly (*dress, appearance, style*). **2** *nm* **(a)** carelessness (*in one's appearance*), slovenliness; **(b)** (*vêtement*) négligé(e).

négligeable [negliʒabl] *adj* negligible, insignificant, inconsiderable.

négligemment [negliʒamɑ̃] *adv* **(a)** (*habillé*) negligently, carelessly; **(b)** (*répondre*) casually, nonchalantly.

négligence [negliʒɑ̃s] *nf* negligence; neglect (*of s.o., of duty*); (*nonchalance*) carelessness, lack of care; **n. à faire qch,** (*nonchalance*) carelessness in doing sth; (*omission*) remissness in doing sth, failure to do sth; *Jur* **n. coupable** *ou* **criminelle,** criminal negligence; **négligences de style,** carelessness of style; **par n.,** through an oversight.

négligent [negliʒɑ̃] *adj* (*parent*) negligent; careless, neglectful (**de,** of); (*remarque*) indifferent, casual.

négliger [negliʒe] *v* (**je négligeai(s); n. négligeons**) **1** *vt* **(a)** (*délaisser*) to neglect, to be neglectful of (*one's health, duty, children*); to be careless about (*one's appearance, dress*); **n. de faire qch,** to neglect *or* fail to do sth, to leave sth undone; **(b)** (*omettre, oublier*) to disregard (*advice etc*); to miss (*an opportunity*); **ne rien n. pour obtenir qch,** to leave no stone unturned (in order) to get sth. **2 se négliger** *vpr* to neglect oneself.

négoce [negɔs] *nm* trade, trading, business; **faire du n.,** to be in trade *or* business; **le petit/le haut n.,** small/big business.

négociabilité [negɔsjabilite] *nf Fin* negotiability.

négociable [negɔsjabl] *adj Fin* negotiable, transferable (*bond, bill etc*).

négociant, -ante [negɔsjɑ̃, -ɑ̃t] *n* (*wholesale*) merchant, dealer; **n. en gros,** wholesaler; **n. en vins,** wine merchant.

négociateur, -trice [negɔsjatœr, -tris] *n* negotiator (*of treaty, deal etc*).

négociation [negɔsjɑsjɔ̃] *nf* **(a)** negotiation, negotiating (*treaty, bill*); **en n.,** under negotiation; **entamer des négociations,** to enter into negotiations; **(b)** *Com* negotiation, transaction.

négocier [negɔsje] *v* (*impf & pr sub* **n. négociions**) **1** *vi* **(a)** (*traiter, discuter*) to negotiate (**avec,** with); **(b)** *Arch* to trade. **2** *vt* **(a)** to negotiate (*loan, bill etc*); **(b)** *Aut* **n. un virage,** to negotiate a bend.

nègre, négresse [nɛgr, negrɛs] **1** *n* **(a)** *Péj* negro, *f* negress; **la traite des nègres,** the slave trade; **travailler comme un n.,** to work like a slave; **parler petit n.,** to talk pidgin (French *etc*); **(b)** *Fig* drudge; ghost (writer) (*of author*); devil (*of barrister*). **2** *adj* **(a)** (*f* **nègre**) negro (*art, race*); **(b)** *inv* ((*couleur*) nigger(-brown); *F* **propos n. blanc,** double talk.

négrier [negrije] **1** *nm* **(a)** (*dans la traite des nègres*) slave trader; *F* owner of sweat shop; (*employeur, surveillant*) slave driver; **(b)** (*bateau*) slave ship. **2** *adj* **vaisseau n.,** slave ship.

négrillon, -onne [negrijɔ̃, -ɔn] *n Péj* piccaninny.

négroïde [negrɔid] *adj* negroid.

neige [nɛʒ] *nf* **(a)** snow; **la saison des neiges,** the snowy season; **neiges éternelles** *ou* **perpétuelles,** perpetual snow; **tempête de n.,** blizzard; **amas de n.,** snowdrift; *Can* **banc de n.,** snow bank; **être bloqué par la n.,** to be snowed up *or* snowbound; **n. fondue,** (*qui tombe*) sleet; (*par terre*) slush; **n. artificielle,** artificial snow; **boule de n.,** snowball; **histoire qui fait boule de n.,** story that snowballs; **faire un bonhomme de n.,** to make a snowman; *Fig* **fondre comme n. au soleil,** to melt (like snow in sunshine); **train de n.,** winter sports train; **classe de n.,** = class temporarily transferred to winter resort; **barbe de n.,** snowy beard; **blanc comme (la) n.,** white as snow, snow-white; *Fig* **être blanc comme n.,** to be as pure as the driven snow; *Culin* **blancs d'œufs battus en n.,** stiffly-beaten egg whites; *Culin* **œufs à la n.,** floating islands; *Ind* **n. carbonique,** (carbon dioxide) snow, dry ice; **(b)** *Arg* (*cocaïne*) snow.

neiger [neʒe] *v impers* (**il neigeait**) to snow.

neigeux, -euse [nɛʒø, -øz] *adj* **(a)** snowy (*peak, weather*); snow-covered (*roof etc*); **(b)** *Fig* (*barbe*) snow-white, snowy.

nématode [nematɔd] *nm Zool* nematode (threadworm).

nénuphar [nenyfar] *nm* water lily, nenuphar; **n. des étangs, n. jaune,** yellow pond lily.

néo-calédonien, -ienne [neɔkaledɔnjɛ̃, -jɛn] (*pl néo-calédoniens, -iennes*) **1** *adj* New Caledonian. **2** *n* **N.-C.,** New Caledonian.

néo-classicisme [neɔklasisism] *nm* neoclassicism.

néo-colonialisme [neɔkɔlɔnjalism] *nm* neocolonialism.

néo-fascisme [neɔfasism, -ʃism] *nm* neofascism.

néo-gallois, -oise [neɔgalwa, -waz] (*pl néo-gallois, -oises*) **1** *adj* of New South Wales. **2** *n* **N.-G.,** native *or* inhabitant of New South Wales.

néo-gothique [neɔgɔtik] *adj & nm Archit* neo-gothic; (*pl néo-gothiques*).

néo-hébridais, -aise [neɔebridɛ, -ɛz] (*pl néo-hébridais, -aises*) **1** *adj* of the New Hebrides. **2** *n* **N.-H.,** native *or* inhabitant of the New Hebrides.

néo-impressionnisme [neɔɛ̃prɛsjɔnism] *nm Beaux-Arts* neoimpressionism.

néolithique [neɔlitik] *adj & nm* Neolithic (Age).

néologisme [neɔlɔʒism] *nm* neologism.

néon [neɔ̃] *nm Ch* neon; **tube au n.,** neon tube.

néo-natal [neɔnatal] *adj Méd* neonatal; (*pl néo-natals*).

néonazi, -ie [neɔnazi] *adj & n* néo-Nazi.

néonazisme [neɔnazism] *nm* neo-Nazism.

néophyte [neɔfit] *n* **(a)** *Rel* (*converti*) neophyte; **(b)** *Fig* (*novice*) novice, tyro.

néo-réalisme [neɔrealism] *nm* neorealism.

néo-réaliste [neɔrealist] *adj* (*film, cinéaste*) neorealist.

néo-zélandais, -aise [neɔzelɑ̃dɛ, -ɛz] (*pl néo-zélandais, -aises*) **1** *adj* New Zealand (*government, butter*). **2** *n* **N.-Z.,** New Zealander.

népérien, -ienne [neperjɛ̃, -jɛn] *adj* Napierian (*logarithms*).

néphrétique [nefretik] **1** *adj* nephritic, renal (*pain, colic*). **2** *n* sufferer from nephritis, nephritic.

néphrite [nefrit] *nf* **(a)** *Méd* nephritis; **n. chronique,** Bright's disease; **(b)** *Minér* nephrite, jade, greenstone.

népotisme [nepɔtism] *nm* nepotism.

néréide [nereid] *nf* nereid, sea nymph.

nerf [nɛr] *nm* **(a)** (*optic, spinal*) nerve; **crise de nerfs,** (fit of) hysterics; **il a les nerfs en pelote** *ou* **à vif** *ou* **en**

boule, his nerves are on edge; **porter** *ou* **taper** *ou Can* **tomber sur les nerfs à qn,** to get on s.o.'s nerves; **avoir les nerfs à fleur de peau,** to be irritable *or* touchy; **je suis à bout de nerfs,** my nerves are frayed; **c'est un paquet de nerfs,** he is a bundle of nerves; **être** *ou* **vivre sur les nerfs,** to live on one's nerves; **passer ses nerfs sur qn/qch,** to work off one's irritation on s.o./sth; **guerre des nerfs,** war of nerves;

(b) *F* (*in sing always at the end of the word group*) sinew, tendon, ligament; **un peu de n.!,** look a bit more lively!; **mets-y du n.!** put some energy *or* guts into it!; **caractère sans n.,** weak character; **avoir du n.,** to have stamina; *Prov* **l'argent est le n. de la guerre,** = money is the sinews of war; **n. de bœuf,** *Arch* life preserver; *F* cosh; *Am* blackjack;

(c) (*reliure*) band, cord.

nerprun [nɛrprœ̃] *nm Bot* buckthorn.

nervation [nɛrvɑsjɔ̃] *nf Bot Zool* nervation, venation.

nervé [nɛrve] *adj Bot* nervate, veined.

nerveusement [nɛrvøzmɑ̃] *adv* **(a)** (*avec énergie*) energetically; **(b)** (*avec irritation*) impatiently, irritably; (*avec excitation*) excitedly, hysterically; **rire n.,** to laugh excitedly *or* hysterically.

nerveux, -euse [nɛrvø, -øz] **1** *adj* **(a)** nervous (*system etc*); **centre n.,** nerve centre; **dépression nerveuse,** nervous breakdown; **(b)** sinewy, wiry (*arm, body*); stringy (*meat*); vigorous, terse (*style etc*); **moteur n.,** responsive engine; **(c)** (*émotif, excité*) excitable, highly-strung, *F* nervy; **elle est nerveuse aujourd'hui,** she is on edge today; **rire n.,** hysterical laugh. **2** *n* nervous person.

nervi [nɛrvi] *nm* henchman, thug.

nervosité [nɛrvozite] *nf* irritability, state of nerves, edginess.

nervure [nɛrvyr] *nf* nervure, rib, vein (*of leaf, insect wing*); flange, rib (*on casting etc*); gill (*of radiator etc*); *Av* rib (*of wing*); rib, raised band (*on back of book*); *Tech* **n. de renfort,** stiffening rib; **n. de refroidissement,** cooling flange *or* fin; *Archit* **voûte à nervures,** ribbed vault; **plafond à nervures,** filleted ceiling; *Couture* **nervures,** pin tucks.

nervuré [nɛrvyre] *adj* ribbed.

net, nette [nɛt] **1** *adj* **(a)** (*propre*) clean, spotless (*plate etc*); flawless (*stone*); clear, sound (*conscience*); **en avoir le coeur n.,** to have (got) it off one's chest; *Fig* **j'ai les mains nettes,** my hands are clean, I had nothing to do with it; **faire place nette,** to tidy up, to put things away; *Fig* **on m'a demandé de faire place nette,** I was asked to leave; **rente nette de tout impôt,** income free of tax; **cassure nette,** clean break; *Cartes etc* **faire tapis n.,** to sweep the board;

(b) (*clair, précis*) clear (*sight, idea, style*); distinct (*print*); sharp (*outline*); plain, straight (*answer*); **division nette,** clear-cut division; **écriture nette,** neat handwriting; *Phot* **image nette,** sharp image; **sa réponse a été claire et nette,** his answer was unequivocal, he made it quite plain; **elle a gardé des souvenirs très nets de sa petite enfance,** she remembers her childhood quite clearly *or* vividly;

(c) net (*weight, price*); net, clear (*profit*).

2 *adv* **(a)** (*d'une manière précise, brutale*) plainly, flatly, outright; **parler n.,** to speak plainly; **refuser qch (tout) n.,** to refuse sth point-blank *or* flatly; **s'arrêter n.,** to stop dead; **coupé n.,** cut clean through;

(b) (*avec clarté*) clearly, distinctly;

(c) *Com* **cent francs n.,** a hundred francs net.

3 *nm* **mettre un devoir au n.,** to make a fair copy of an exercise.

nettement [nɛtmɑ̃] *adv* (*proprement*) cleanly; (*distinctement*) clearly, distinctly; (*clairement*) plainly, flatly; **profil n. découpé,** clear-cut *or* sharp-cut profile; **il est arrivé n. en retard,** he was more than a little late, he arrived quite late; **partagé n. en deux classes,** sharply divided into two classes; **ce livre est n. pacifiste,** this book is definitely *or* markedly pacifist; **parler n.,** to speak plainly *or* straight out.

netteté [nɛtte] *nf* **(a)** (*précision*) cleanness (*of break*); **écrit avec n.,** neatly written; **(b)** (*clarté*) clearness (*of thought, style*); distinctness (*of vision, object*); sharpness (*of image*); vividness (*of memory*); flatness (*of refusal*).

nettoiement [nɛtwamɑ̃] *nm* cleaning (*of streets*); cleaning, clearing (*of ground*); clearing (*of forest*); **service du n.,** refuse collection.

nettoyage [nɛtwajaʒ] *nm* **(a)** cleaning; **n. à sec,** dry cleaning; **n. par le vide,** vacuum cleaning; **faire le n.,** to clean up; **le grand n. de printemps,** spring cleaning; *Mil* **opérations de n.,** mopping-up operations; **(b)** (*action de débarrasser*) cleaning *or* clearing out; **(c)** *F* (*renvoi brutal*) abrupt dismissal.

nettoyer [nɛtwaje] *v* (**je nettoie; je nettoierai**) **1** *vt* **(a)** to clean (*room, clothes, wound*); to scour (*pan, deck*); to swab (*deck*); to wash out (*bottle*); to clean (*corn*); **n. à grande eau,** to swill (down); **n. une pièce à fond,** to turn out a room; **n. à sec,** to dry-clean; **(b)** *Fig F* (*of burglar*) to strip, to clean out (*a house*); **se faire n. au jeu,** to get cleaned out gambling; **n. un endroit de voleurs,** to rid a place of thieves; *Mil* **n. les poches de résistance,** to mop up. **2 se nettoyer** *vpr* **se n. les dents,** to clean one's teeth; **le four se nettoie automatiquement,** the oven is self-cleaning.

nettoyeur, -euse [nɛtwajœr, -øz] **1** *n* (*personne*) cleaner; **n. de vitres,** window cleaner. **2** *nf* **nettoyeuse,** (*machine*) cleaning machine, cleaner; *Ind* scrubber.

neuf¹ [nœf] **1** *adj* (*at the end of the word group* [nœf]; *before* **ans** *and* **heures** [nœv], *otherwise before vowel sounds* [nœf]; *before a noun or adj beginning with a consonant often* [nœf]) nine; **j'en ai n.** [nœf], I have nine; **il a n. ans** [nœvɑ̃] , he is nine (years old); **n. et demi** [nœfədmi] , nine and a half. **2** *nm* (*always* [nœf]) **le n. mai,** the ninth of May; **Louis N.,** Louis the Ninth; **deux neufs,** two nines; **le n. de carreau,** the nine of diamonds; *Math* **faire la preuve par n.,** to cast out the nines.

neuf², neuve [nœf, nœv] **1** *adj* (brand-)new (*garment*); new (*thought, subject*); **à l'état n.,** in new condition, as new; (*postage stamp, book*) in mint condition, unused; **faire peau neuve,** (*d'un serpent*) to shed its skin; *Fig* to turn over a new leaf; **regarder qch d'un œil n.,** to take a fresh view of sth; **approche neuve d'un problème,** new approach to a problem; **herbe neuve,** new grass; **la curiosité (toute) neuve d'un enfant,** a child's newly awakened curiosity; **être n. dans un métier,** to be new to a job; **n. aux affaires,** new to business; *F* **qu'est-ce qu'il y a** *ou* **quoi de n.?,** what's new?; **il n'y a rien de n.,** there's nothing new.

2 *nm* **vendre du n. et de l'occasion,** to sell new and second-hand goods; **habillé de n.,** wearing new clothes; **meublé de n.,** newly furnished; **trouver du n.,** to find sth new; **à n.,** anew; **refaire un mur à n.,** to rebuild a wall; **remettre à n.,** to make (*sth*) as good as new; to recondition, to renovate (*a machine*); to do (*sth*) up.

neurasthénie [nørasteni] *nf Méd* neurasthenia; **faire de la n.,** to be (clinically) depressed.

neurasthénique [nørastenik] *adj & n Méd* (clinically) depressed (person); *Vieilli* neurasthenic.

neurobiologie [nørɔbjɔlɔʒi] *nf* neurobiology.

neuroblaste [nørɔblast] *nm Biol* neuroblast.

neurochirurgie [nørɔʃiryrʒi] *nf Chir* neurosurgery.

neurochirurgien, -ienne [nørɔʃiryrʒjɛ̃, -jɛn] *n Chir* neurosurgeon.

neuroleptique [nørɔlɛptik] *Méd* **1** *adj* neuroleptic (*drug*). **2** *nm* neuroleptic drug, *F* tranquillizer; **être sous neuroleptiques,** to be on tranquillizers.

neurologie [nørɔlɔʒi] *nf Méd* neurology.

neurologiste [nørɔlɔʒist], **neurologue** [nørɔlɔg] *n Méd* nerve specialist, neurologist.

neurone [nørɔn] *nm Physiol* neuron.

neuronique [nørɔnik] *adj* neuronic.

neuropsychiatrie [nørɔpsikjatri] *nf* neuropsychiatry.

neuropsychologie [nørɔpsikɔlɔʒi] *nf* neuropsychology.

neurotique [nørɔtik] *adj Méd* neurotic.

neutralisation [nøtralizɑsjɔ̃] *nf* neutralization, neutralizing (*of country, acid etc*); *Mil* **tir de n.,** neutralizing fire.

neutraliser [nøtralize] **1** *vt* to neutralize (*effort, country, acid etc*). **2 se neutraliser** *vpr* (*s'annuler réciproquement*) to cancel each other out.

neutralisme [nøtralism] *nm Pol* neutralism, nonalignment.

neutraliste [nøtralist] **1** *adj* neutralist; **les pays neutralistes,** the non-aligned countries. **2** *n* neutralist.

neutralité [nøtralite] *nf Pol Ch Él etc* neutrality; **garder la n.,** to remain neutral; **sortir de la n.,** to take sides; **violer la n. d'un État,** to violate a country's neutrality.

neutre [nøtr] **1** *adj* **(a)** (*ni masculin, ni féminin*) neuter; *Gram* **pronom n.,** neuter pronoun; **abeille n.,** neuter *or* working bee; **(b)** (*qui n'a pas pris position*) neutral (*nation, ship, Ch salt, El wire*); *Mil* **la zone n.,** no-man's land; **rester n.,** to remain neutral; **je resterai tout à fait n.,** I won't take sides; **(c)** (*sans caractéristique distinctive*) neutral (*tone of voice, colour*). **2** *nm* **(a)** neutral; *Gram* **au n.,** in the neuter; **(b)** *Can Aut* neutral; **se mettre sur le n.,** to go into neutral.

neutron [nøtrɔ̃] *nm Phys* neutron.
neuvaine [nœvɛn] *nf Rel* novena, neuvaine.
neuvième [nœvjɛm] **1** *adj* ninth. **2** *nm* ninth (part). **3** *nf Mus* ninth; *Scol* first form *or US* grade (*of junior school*).
neuvièmement [nœvjɛmmɑ̃] *adv* ninthly.
névé [neve] *nm Géol* névé, granular ice.
neveu, -eux [nəvø] *nm* nephew; **n. à la mode de Bretagne,** first cousin once removed.
névralgie [nevralʒi] *nf* neuralgia.
névralgique [nevralʒik] *adj* neuralgic.
névrite [nevrit] *nf* neuritis.
névritique [nevritik] *adj* neuritic.
névropathe [nevrɔpat] *n* neuropath.
névrose [nevroz] *nf Méd* neurosis.
névrosé, -ée [nevroze] *adj & n* neurotic (patient).
névrotique [nevrɔtik] *adj Méd* neurotic (*disorder etc*).
newyorkais, -aise [njujɔrkɛ, -ɛz] **1** *adj* (of) New York. **2** *n* **N.,** New Yorker.
nez [ne] *nm* **(a)** (*d'un être humain*) nose; **parler/chanter du n.**, to speak/sing through one's nose; **ça se voit comme le n. au milieu de la figure,** it is as plain as the nose on your face; **mener** *ou* **conduire qn par le bout du n.,** to lead s.o. by the nose, to push s.o. around; **fourrer** *ou* **mettre le n. dans les affaires d'autrui,** to poke one's nose *or* pry into other people's business; **baisser le n.,** to look ashamed; **cela lui pend au n.,** it may well happen to him any day; **faire un pied de n. à qn,** to cock a snook at s.o.; *Arg* **je l'ai dans le n.,** I can't stand him, *Br* he gets up my nose; **avoir un verre dans le n.,** to be a bit drunk *or* tipsy; **cela lui est passé sous le n.,** it slipped by *or* eluded him; **elle ne voit pas plus loin que le bout de son n.,** she can't see beyond the end of her nose; **montrer le bout de son n.,** to peek out; **se trouver n. à n. avec qn,** to find oneself face to face with s.o.; **regarder qn sous le n.,** to look defiantly at s.o.; **dire qch au n. de qn,** to say sth to s.o.'s face; **se bouffer le n.,** (*de deux personnes*) to be constantly arguing; **fermer la porte au n. (et à la barbe) de qn,** to shut the door in s.o.'s face; **à vue de n.,** at first sight, at a guess, at a rough estimate; **le n. au vent,** sniffing the wind; **se casser le n.,** to come a cropper; **il fait un temps à ne pas mettre le n. dehors,** it's not the kind of weather to be out in; **ton n. remue,** (*tu mens*) your nose is getting longer; **sentir à plein n.,** to smell to high heaven; **ça sent l'entourloupe à plein n.,** there's something very fishy going on;
(b) sense of smell; (*of dogs*) scent; **avoir du n.** *ou* **le n. fin,** (*avoir un bon odorat*) to have a good nose *or* a keen sense of smell; *F* (*avoir de l'intuition*) to be shrewd *or* far-seeing;
(c) (*d'un objet*) nose, bow, head (*of ship*); nose (*of aircraft*); nosing (*of step*); nosepiece (*of engine*); *Av* **piquer du n.,** to nosedive.
ni [ni] *conj* (**ne** *is either expressed or implied*) nor; **ni moi (non plus),** nor I *or F* me (either), *F* me neither; neither do *or* did *or* shall I; **sans argent ni bagages,** without money or luggage; **il ne mange ni ne boit,** he neither eats nor drinks; **il est parti sans manger ni boire,** he left without (either) eating or drinking; **ni ... ni,** neither ... nor; **ni Pierre ni Henri ne sont** *ou* **n'est là,** neither Peter nor Henry is there; **je n'ai ni femme ni enfant ni amis,** I have neither wife nor child nor friends; **ni l'un ni l'autre ne l'a vu,** neither (of them) saw it.
niais, -aise [njɛ, -ɛz] **1** *adj* simple, foolish (*person, answer, air*); inane (*smile*); **je ne suis pas assez n. pour le lui dire,** I know better than to tell him, I'm not fool enough to tell him. **2** *n* fool, simpleton; **petite niaise!,** you stupid little fool!
niaisage [njɛzaʒ] *nm Can* idleness.
niaisement [njɛzmɑ̃] *adv* foolishly; **rire n.,** to give a silly laugh.
niaiser [njɛze] *Can* **1** *vt* (*faire tourner en bourrique*) to drive (*s.o.*) crazy; (*se moquer de*) to laugh at (*s.o.*); (*raconter des histoires à*) to pull s.o.'s leg. **2** *vi* (*ne rien faire*) to hang around doing nothing.
niaiserie [njɛzri] *nf* **(a)** (*bêtise*) silliness, foolishness; **(b) dire des niaiseries,** (*une bêtise, une ânerie*) to talk nonsense, to make silly remarks.
niaiseux, -euse [njɛzø, -øz] *adj Can* idiotic, stupid.
Nicée [nise] *nf Antiq* Nicaea; **le symbole de N.,** the Nicene Creed.
niche¹ [niʃ] *nf* **(a)** niche, nook, recess; **(b) n. à chien,** dogkennel.
niche² *nf F* trick, prank.
nichée [niʃe] *nf* nest(ful) (*of birds*); brood (*of birds, children*); litter (*of mice, puppies*).
nicher [niʃe] **1** *vi* (*of birds*) to build a nest, to nest; *F* (*of person*) to hang out; **maison nichée dans un bois,** cottage nestling *or* hidden away in a wood; **niché dans un fauteuil,** curled up in an armchair. **2 se nicher** *vpr* (*of birds*) to (build a) nest.
nichet [niʃɛ] *nm* (*œuf factice*) nest egg.
nichoir [niʃwar] *nm* breeding cage, coop, nesting box.
nichons [niʃɔ̃] *nmpl Arg* (*d'une femme*) boobs, tits.
nickel [nikɛl] **1** *nm Métal* nickel. **2** *adj F* **c'est n.!,** it's super clean!
nickelage [niklaʒ] *nm* nickelling, nickel plating.
nickelé [nikle] *adj* nickelled, nickel-plated; *F* **avoir les pieds nickelés,** to sit tight, to refuse to budge.
nickeler [nikle] *vt* (**je nickelle, n. nickelons; je nickellerai**) to nickel.
nickélifère [nikelifɛr] *adj* nickel-bearing.
niçois, -oise [niswa, -waz] **1** *adj* of Nice; *Culin* **salade niçoise,** salad niçoise. **2** *n* **N.,** inhabitant of Nice.
nicotine [nikɔtin] *nf Ch* nicotine.
nictation [niktɑsjɔ̃] *nf*, **nictitation** [niktitɑsjɔ̃] *nf* nictation, nictitation.
nictitant [niktitɑ̃] *adj Zool* nictitating (*membrane*).
nid [ni] *nm* nest (*of bird, mouse, ant etc*); **n. d'aigle,** eyrie; **trouver la pie au n.,** to have a lucky find; **mettre une poule au n.,** to set a hen; *Couture* **nid(s) d'abeilles,** smocking, honeycomb stitch; **un torchon nid(s) d'abeilles,** a honeycomb cloth; **n. d'ange,** (*pour les bébés*) baby's sleeping bag, *Am* bunting (bag); *Prov* **petit à petit l'oiseau fait son n.,** great oaks from little acorns grow; **n. de brigands,** robbers' den; **n. d'amoureux,** love nest; **n. à rats,** poky little place; **n. de poule,** pothole (*in road*); **n. à poussière,** dust trap; *Mil* **n. de mitrailleuses,** nest of machine guns; *Nau* **n. de corbeau** *ou* **de pie,** crow's nest.
nièce [njɛs] *nf* niece; **n. à la mode de Bretagne,** first cousin once removed.
niellage [njɛlaʒ] *nm* inlaying with niello, niello work.
nielle¹ [njɛl] *nf* smut, blight (*of wheat*).
nielle² *nf* **n. des blés,** corn cockle.
nielle³ *nm Métal* niello.
niellé [njele] *adj* **blé n.,** blighted wheat.
nieller [njele] *vt* to inlay with niello.
nielleur [njɛlœr] *nm* niello worker.
niellure [njelyr] *nf* niello work.
nier [nje] *v* (*impf & pr sub* **n. niions**) **1** *vt* to deny (*a fact, God, the evidence*); **je nie l'avoir vue,** I deny having seen her; **je nie qu'il m'ait vu,** I deny that he saw me; **il n'y a pas à le n.,** there is no denying it *or F* no getting away from it; **n. une dette,** to repudiate a debt. **2** *vi* **l'accusé nie,** the accused denies the charge.
nigaud, -aude [nigo, -od] **1** *n* simpleton, *F* clot, twit. **2** *adj* silly, simple, *F* clottish.
nigelle [niʒɛl] *nf* (*fleur*) nigella, love-in-a-mist.
Niger [niʒɛr] *nm* Niger.
Nigéria [niʒerja] *nm* Nigeria.
nigérien, -ienne [niʒerjɛ̃, -ɛn] **1** *adj* Nigerian. **2** *n* **N.,** Nigerian.
nihilisme [niilism] *nm Phil* nihilism.
nihiliste [niilist] *Phil* **1** *adj* nihilist(ic). **2** *n* nihilist.
Nil (le) [lənil] *nm* the (river) Nile; **vert (de) N.,** (*colour*) eau-de-nil.
nilgau(t) [nilgo] *nm* (*mammifère*) nilgai.
nilotique [nilɔtik] *adj* of the Nile, Nilotic.
nimbe [nɛ̃b] *nm* halo, nimbus.
nimbé [nɛ̃be] *adj* haloed, nimbused.
nimbus [nɛ̃bys] *nm Météo* nimbus.
ninas [ninas] *nm inv* small cigar.
nippes [nip] *nfpl F* **(a)** (shabby, old) clothes; **tu ne pourrais pas mettre autre chose que tes vieilles n.?,** haven't you got anything else to put on apart from those old rags?; **(b)** (*fringues*) gear; **à part les n., rien ne l'intéresse,** he isn't interested in anything apart from clothes, *Am* he's a clotheshorse.
nipper [nipe] *vt F* to fit (*s.o.*) out, to rig (*s.o.*) out; **bien nippé,** well turned out.
nippon, -one [nipɔ̃, -ɔn] **1** *adj* Nipponese, Japanese. **2** *n* **N.,** Nipponese, Japanese.
nique [nik] *nf Vulg* (*used only in*) **faire la n. à qn,** to cock a snook at s.o..
niquer [nike] *vt Vulg* to screw, to lay.
nitouche [nituʃ] *nf F* **sainte n.,** little hypocrite; **c'est une sainte n.,** butter wouldn't melt in her mouth.
nitrate [nitrat] *nm Ch* nitrate.
nitre [nitr] *nm Ch* nitre, saltpetre, *US* niter, saltpeter.
nitré [nitre] *adj Ch* nitrated; **composé n.,** nitro compound.
nitrer [nitre] *vt Tech* to nitrate.
nitreux, -euse [nitrø, -øz] *adj* nitrous.

nitrifier [nitrifje] *vt Ch* to nitrify.
nitrique [nitrik] *adj Ch* nitric (*acid*).
nitrobenzine [nitrɔbɛ̃zin] *nf Ch* nitrobenzine.
nitrocellulose [nitrɔselyloz] *nf Ch* nitrocellulose.
nitroglycérine [nitrɔgliserin] *nf Ch* nitroglycerine.
nitrure [nitryr] *nm Ch* nitride.
niveau, -eaux [nivo] *nm* **(a)** (*instrument*) gauge; **n. à bulle d'air,** air *or* spirit level; **n. de maçon/à plomb,** vertical/plumb level; **n. à lunette,** surveyor's level; **(b)** (*intensité, hauteur*) level; **n. d'eau/d'huile,** water/oil level; **n. de bruit,** noise level; *Rad* **n. de transmission,** transmission level; **le n. de l'eau/de la mer,** water/sea level; **n. des basses/hautes eaux,** low-water/high-water mark; **jardin à trois niveaux,** garden on three levels; **immeuble à dix niveaux,** ten-storey building; **être de n.,** to be level; **à franc n.,** (on a) dead level; **mettre qch de n.,** to level sth; **navire de n.,** boat on an even keel; **passage à n.,** level crossing, *US* grade crossing; **carburateur alimenté par différence de n.,** gravity-fed carburettor; **elle a une cicatrice au n. de la cuisse,** she has a scar on her leg at about thigh-level; **au n. régional,** at regional level; **(c)** (*degré*) standard, level; **n. de vie,** standard of living; **n. des études,** academic standard; **tous les élèves ne sont pas du même n.,** not all the pupils are *or* have reached the same (academic) standard, not all the pupils are of the same level of ability; **être à n.,** to be at the same level; **évaluer le n. des candidats,** to evaluate the candidates' level of ability *etc*; **n. de langue,** level of language, register; **être au n. de qch/qn, être de n. avec qch/qn,** to be on a level *or* on a par with sth/s.o; **ils sont d'un n. social différent,** they are from different social strata; **les salaires augmentent régulièrement à tous les niveaux,** there are regular salary increases for all grades *or* at all levels.
nivelage [niv(ə)laʒ] *nm* levelling.
niveler [nivle] *vt* **(je nivelle; je nivellerai) (a)** to take the level of, to survey (*ground*); **(b)** to level, to even up (*ground, fortunes*); **n. par le bas,** to level down.
niveleur, -euse [nivlœr, -øz] **1** *adj* levelling. **2** *n* (*personne*) leveller. **3** *nm* small harrow. **4** *nf Constr* **niveleuse,** grader.
nivellement [nivɛlmɑ̃] *nm* levelling (*of ground, social classes*); **repère de n.,** (*dans l'arpentage*) bench mark.
nivéole [niveɔl] *nf* (*plante*) snowflake.
nivôse [nivoz] *nm Hist Fr* = fourth month of Republican calendar (*Dec.-Jan.*).
nobiliaire [nɔbiljɛr] **1** *adj* **almanach n.,** peerage (list); **particule n.,** nobiliary particle. **2** *nm* peerage (list).
noble [nɔbl] **1** *adj* **(a)** noble (*family*); **(b)** (*imposant*) stately, lofty (*air*); *Th* **père n.,** heavy father; **(c)** (*généreux*) highminded; **il n'est animé que par de nobles sentiments,** he is acting out of noble sentiments; **(d)** (*précieux*) noble; **la soie est une matière n.,** silk is a noble fabric. **2** *n* noble(man); noblewoman; **les nobles,** the nobility, the nobles.
noblement [nɔbləmɑ̃] *adv* nobly.
noblesse [nɔblɛs] *nf* **(a)** nobility; **famille de n. récente,** recently ennobled family; **la haute et la petite n.,** the nobility and gentry; **se marier dans la n.,** to marry into nobility, to marry a title; **n. oblige,** noblesse oblige; **(b)** nobility, nobleness (*of style, conduct*).
noce [nɔs] *nf* **(a)** wedding; (*fête*) wedding festivities; (*ensemble des assistants*) wedding party; **repas de n.,** wedding breakfast; **nuit de noces,** wedding night; **voyage de noces,** honeymoon (trip); **noces d'argent/de vermeil/d'or/de diamant,** silver/ruby/golden/diamond wedding; **il l'avait épousée en secondes noces,** she was his second wife; **(b)** *F* **faire la n.,** to go on a binge, to live it up; **usé par la n.,** worn out by dissipation; **je n'étais pas à la n.,** it was no picnic.
noceur, -euse [nɔsœr, -øz] *n F* **(a)** reveller, roisterer; **(b)** fast liver.
nocif, -ive [nɔsif, -iv] *adj* injurious, harmful.
nocivité [nɔsivite] *nf Fml* harmfulness; noxiousness.
noctambule [nɔktɑ̃byl] **1** *adj* noctambulant. **2** *n* **(a)** (*somnambule*) somnambulist, sleepwalker; **(b)** *F* night bird.
noctuelle [nɔktɥɛl] *nf Ent* noctua, owlet moth.
nocturne [nɔktyrn] **1** *adj* nocturnal (*animal*); night (*attack, visit*); *Bot* night-flowering; **évasion n.,** escape by night. **2** *nm* **(a)** *Rel* nocturn; **(b)** *Art Mus* nocturne; **(c)** *Sp* **match (disputé) en n.,** evening game. **3** *nf* late evening opening (*of shop etc*). **4** *nmpl* **nocturnes,** night birds (of prey).
nodal, -aux [nɔdal, -o] *adj* nodal (*point, line*).
nodosité [nɔdozite] *nf* **(a)** nodosity; **(b)** *Bot Med* node, nodule.
nodule [nɔdyl] *nm Géol Méd etc* nodule.
Noé [noe] *nm Bible* Noah.
Noël [nɔɛl] *nm* **(a)** Christmas; **à la (fête de) N., à N.,** at Christmas (time); **le jour de N.,** Christmas Day; **la nuit** *ou* **la veillée de N.,** Christmas Eve; **bûche de N.,** yule log; **le Père N.,** Father Christmas, Santa Claus; **croire au Père N.,** to believe in Father Christmas *or* Santa Claus; *Fig F* to believe in Father Christmas *or* Santa Claus *or* fairies; **(b) un n.,** a Christmas carol; **(c) (petit) n.,** Christmas present.
Noémi [nɔemi] *nf* Naomi.
nœud [nø] *nm* **(a)** knot; *Nau* hitch, bend; **n. coulant,** (*pour serrer*) slip knot; (*pour étrangler*) noose; **n. de grappin,** fisherman's bend; **n. droit** *ou* **plat,** reef knot; **n. de vache,** carrick bend; **n. de bois,** timber hitch; **corde à nœuds,** knotted rope; **faire** *ou* **serrer un n.,** to make *or* tie a knot; **faire son n. de cravate,** to knot one's tie; **faire un n. à son mouchoir,** to tie a knot in one's handkerchief; **les nœuds de l'amitié,** the bonds *or* ties of friendship; **trancher le n. gordien,** to cut the Gordian knot; *Fig* **le n. de la question,** the crux *or* rub of the matter; **(b)** coil (*of snake*); **(c)** bow; **faire un n.,** to tie a bow; **n. papillon,** bow tie; **n. de diamants,** diamond cluster; **(d)** node (*of orbit, curve, oscillation*); **(e)** knot, knur(l) (*in timber*); node, joint, knot (*in bamboo etc*); **n. de voies ferrées,** railway junction; **(f)** *Nau* (*vitesse*) knot; **filer** *ou* **faire tant de nœuds,** to do so many knots.
noir, noire [nwar] **1** *adj* black; **robe noire,** black dress; **n. comme de l'ébène/comme de l'encre,** as black as ebony, ebony black/inky black, as black as ink; **n. comme (du) jais,** jet black; **n. comme poix,** pitch-black; **des yeux noirs,** dark eyes; **race noire,** negro race; **un quartier n.,** a black neighbourhood; **la mer Noire,** the Black Sea; *Av* **boîte noire,** black box; **(b)** dark, swarthy (*skin, complexion*); *F* **être n. de coups,** to be black and blue; **pain/blé n.,** black bread/buckwheat; **il est rentré tout n. de ses vacances,** he was as brown as a berry when he came back from his holidays; **(c)** dark (*night, cell*); gloomy (*weather, thoughts*); grim (*irony*); dire (*poverty*); *Phot* **chambre noire,** darkroom; **il faisait n.** *ou* **nuit noire** *ou* **n. comme dans un four,** it was pitch-dark; **avoir des idées noires,** to be down in the dumps, to have the blues; **être d'une humeur noire,** to be depressed *or* in a black mood; **humour n.,** black *or* sick humour; *Fig* **ma bête noire,** my pet aversion *or* hate, my bete noire; *F* **série noire,** chapter of accidents, run of bad luck; **roman série noire,** thriller; **film n.,** thriller; **(d)** dirty, grimy, black (*hands, linen*); **(e)** base (*ingratitude*); wicked (*slander*); heinous (*crime*); foul (*deed*); black (*magic*); **liste noire,** black list; **le (marché) n.,** the black market; **caisse noire,** slush fund; **(f)** *Arg* dead drunk.
2 *n* **N.,** black (man); **Noire,** black (woman); *Arch* **traite des Noirs,** slave trade.
3 *nm* **(a)** black; **d'un n. d'ébène,** as black as ebony; **c'était écrit n. sur blanc,** it was there in black and white; *Fig* **voir tout en n.,** to look on the dark side of everything; *F* **le travail au n.,** *F* moonlighting, *Sl* work(ing) on the black; **il a été engagé au n.,** he was employed illegally *or* on the black; **il est chauffeur de taxi au n.,** he moonlights as a taxi-driver; **aller du blanc au n.,** to go from one extreme to the other; **être vêtu de n., être en n.,** to be dressed (all) in black; **broyer du n.,** to be down in the dumps; **n. de Chine,** India(n) ink; **se mettre du n. aux yeux,** to put mascara *or* eye-liner on; **avoir peur du n.** *ou* **dans le n.,** to be afraid of the dark; **(b)** bull's eye (*of target*);
4 *nf Mus* **noire,** crotchet.
noirâtre [nwarɑtr] *adj* blackish, darkish.
noiraud, -aude [nwaro, -od] *adj & n* swarthy (man, woman).
noirceur [nwarsœr] *nf* **(a)** blackness (*of ink etc*); darkness, gloominess (*of weather etc*); heinousness, foulness (*of crime*); **(b)** *Can* dark(ness); **avoir peur dans la n.,** to be afraid of the dark; **(c)** black spot; smudge (*on the face etc*); **(d)** *Litt* base action; dirty trick.
noircir [nwarsir] **1** *vi* to grow *or* become *or* turn black *or* dark, to darken. **2** *vt* to blacken (*sth*), to make (*sth*) black; *F* **n. du papier,** to scribble; **n. la réputation de qn,** to blacken s.o.'s character; **n. la situation,** to paint things blacker than they are. **3 se noircir** *vpr* to grow black *or* dark; (*of sky*) to darken, to become overcast; *Fig F* (*se

soûler) to get blind drunk; **se n. le visage,** to black one's face; *Th* to black up.
noircissement [nwarsismɑ̃] *nm* blackening.
noircissure [nwarsisyr] *nf* black spot, smudge.
noise [nwaz] *nf* (*only in*) **chercher n. à qn,** to try to pick a quarrel with s.o..
noisetier [nwaztje] *nm* hazel (tree *or* bush).
noisette [nwazɛt] **1** *nf* **(a)** hazel nut; *Culin* **n. de beurre,** knob *or* nut of butter; **(b) (couleur de) n.,** hazel, nut-brown. **2** *adj inv* **yeux n.,** hazel eyes.
noix [nwa] *nf* **(a)** walnut; *Arg* (*tête*) nut; *Culin* **n. de beurre,** knob *or* nut of butter; **n. d'Amérique** *ou* **du Brésil,** Brazil nut; **n. d'acajou,** cashew nut; **n. vomique,** nux vomica; **n. de coco,** coconut; *Arg* **à la n.,** useless; *Arg* **excuses à la n.,** trivial excuses; **travail à la n.,** shocking piece of work; *Arg* **quelle n.!,** what a nit!; **(b)** *Culin* eye (*of cutlet*); pope's eye (*of leg of mutton*).
nom [nɔ̃] *nm* **(a)** name; **traiter qn de tous les noms,** to call s.o. names; **quelqu'un dont je tairai le n.,** someone who shall be nameless; **je le ferai ou j'y perdrai mon n.,** I'll do it or my name isn't Jones *or* Smith *etc*; **n. de famille,** surname; **n. de baptême,** Christian name, first name, given name; **n. et prénoms,** full name; **n. de jeune fille,** maiden name; **n. de femme mariée** *ou* **de mariage,** married name; **porter le n. de qn,** to be named *or* called after s.o.; **n. de guerre,** assumed name, pseudonym; (*d'un écrivain*) pseudonym, pen name; (journalist's) pen name; (*d'un acteur*) stage name; **n. de théâtre** *ou* **de scène,** stage name; **n. d'emprunt,** assumed name; **voyager sous un faux n.,** to travel under an alias; **on le connaissait sous le n. de Leduc,** he went by the name of Leduc; **appeler les choses par leur n.,** to call a spade a spade; **impolitesse qui n'a pas de n.,** unspeakable rudeness; *F* **n. de n.!, n. d'une pipe!, n. d'un chien!, n. de Dieu!,** hell!; *Com* **n. déposé,** registered (trade) name; **se faire un n.,** to win fame, to make a name for oneself; **n'être maître que de n.,** to be master in name only; **ne connaître qn que de n.,** to know s.o. only by name; **au n. de la loi,** in the name of the law; **faire une proposition au n. de qn,** to make a proposal for s.o. *or* on behalf of s.o.; **parler en son n.,** to speak for oneself; *Bible* **un homme du n. de Pierre,** a man named Peter;
(b) *Gram* noun.
nomade [nɔmad] **1** *adj* nomadic, wandering (*life, tribe*); migratory (*game*); roving (*instinct*). **2** *nmpl* **nomades,** nomads, wandering tribes; *Jur* gypsies.
nombre [nɔ̃br] *nm* **(a)** number; **n. entier,** whole number, integral number, integer; **n. premier,** prime number; **n. atomique,** atomic number; **(bon) n. de gens, un certain n. de gens, un assez grand n. de gens,** a number of *or* a good many people; **le plus grand n. est de cet avis,** the majority are of this opinion; **un grand/petit n. d'entre nous,** many/(a) few of us; **ils ont vaincu par le n.,** they conquered by force of numbers; **surpasser en n.,** to outnumber; **être en n. suffisant,** to have a quorum (*at meeting*); **sans n.,** countless, numberless, without number; **venez pour faire n.,** come and help make up the numbers; **en n. écrasant,** by an overwhelming majority; **ils sont au n. de huit,** there are eight of them; **être au n.** *ou* **du n. des élus,** to be one of *or* among the elect; **mettre** *ou* **compter qn au n. de ses intimes,** to number s.o. among one's friends; **sur le n.,** among *or* out of (all) those people; **sur le n. il y aura bien quelqu'un pour me ramener en voiture,** out of all those people there's bound to be someone who can give me a lift home; *Bible* **Le Livre des Nombres,** (the Book of) Numbers;
(b) *Gram* number.
nombreux, -euse [nɔ̃brø, -øz] *adj* numerous, many (*members, objects*); large (*family, army, group*); **réunion peu nombreuse,** small party; **auditoire peu n.,** thin audience; **pendant de nombreuses générations,** for many generations; **nous sommes peu n.,** there are very few of us.
nombril [nɔ̃bri(l)] *nm* **(a)** navel; *F* **être décolletée jusqu'au n.,** (*d'une femme*) to be showing a lot of cleavage; **il avait une chemise ouverte jusqu'au n.,** his shirt was open to the waist; *F* **il se prend pour le n. du monde,** he thinks he's God's gift to the world; *Fig* **se regarder le n.,** to contemplate one's navel; **(b)** *Bot* hilum.
nombrilisme [nɔ̃brilism] *nm* self-absorption.
nombriliste [nɔ̃brilist] *adj* self-absorbed.
nomenclature [nɔmɑ̃klatyr] *nf* **(a)** (*ensemble de termes techniques*) nomenclature; **(b)** (*liste des objets d'une collection etc*) list, catalogue.
nominal, -aux [nɔminal, -o] *adj* **(a)** nominal (*price, horse-power, authority*); *Fin* **valeur nominale,** face value; *El* **courant n.,** rated current (*of machine*); **(b)** (*relatif au nom*) nominal; **appel n.,** roll call, callover.
nominalement [nɔminalmɑ̃] *adv* nominally.
nominalisme [nɔminalism] *nm Phil* nominalism.
nominatif, -ive [nɔminatif, -iv] **1** *adj* **état n.,** list of names, nominal roll; **votre carte bancaire est nominative,** (*inscription sur carte*) this banker's card may be used only by the authorized signatory *or* by the person whose name it bears; *Fin* **titres nominatifs,** registered securities. **2** *nm Gram* nominative (case); **au n.,** in the nominative.
nomination [nɔminasjɔ̃] *nf* **(a)** nomination (*for an appointment*); **poste à la n. du ministre,** post in the gift of the Minister; **(b)** appointment (*to a position*); **recevoir sa n.,** to be appointed; **n. à un grade supérieur,** promotion; **(c)** (*pour une remise de récompense*) nomination, recommendation; **ce film a trois nominations pour les Césars,** this film has received three César nominations.
nominativement [nɔminativmɑ̃] *adv* by name.
nominé [nɔmine] *adj* (*film etc*) nominated (**à une récompense**/*etc*, for an award/*etc*).
nommément [nɔmemɑ̃] *adv* **(a)** namely; (*spécialement*) especially, in particular; **(b) mentionner qn n.,** to mention s.o. by name.
nommer [nɔme] **1** *vt* **(a)** (*appeler*) to name (*s.o., sth*), to give a name to (*s.o., sth*); **on le nomma Jean,** they named *or* called him John; **on nomme aumôniers les prêtres attachés à un régiment,** priests attached to a regiment are called *or* styled chaplains;
(b) (*désigner*) to name (*s.o.*), to mention (*s.o.*) by name; **un homme que je ne nommerai pas,** a man who shall be nameless; **n. un jour,** to appoint a day; **à jour nommé,** on the appointed day; **elle est arrivée à point nommé,** (*au bon moment*) she arrived just at the right moment *or* just when she was needed;
(c) (*à un poste*) to appoint (*s.o.*); *Mil* to commission (*an officer*); **être nommé au grade supérieur,** to be promoted; **n. qn à un emploi,** to nominate s.o. for a job.
2 se nommer *vpr* **(a)** (*s'identifier*) to give one's name; **(b)** (*s'appeler*) to be called *or* named; **comment vous nommez-vous?,** what is your name?
non [nɔ̃] **1** *adv* **(a)** (*no liaison with a following word*) no; **répondre par oui ou n.,** to answer yes or no; **c'est dégoûtant, n.?,** isn't it disgusting?; **il a commencé comme éboueur — n.!,** he started as a dustman – really!; **mais n.!, dame n.!, mon Dieu n.!, que n.!,** oh dear, no!, no indeed!; **n. pas!,** not so!, not at all!; **n., je vous en prie,** please don't!; **je pense que n.,** I don't think so, I think not; **je dis que n.,** I say no; **faire signe que n.,** (*de la tête*) to shake one's head; (*au doigt*) to refuse with a gesture; **qu'elle vienne ou n.,** whether she comes or not; **n. (pas) que je le craigne,** not that I fear him; **n. que je ne vous plaigne,** not that I don't pity you;
(b) not; **n. loin de la ville,** not far from the town; **n. sans raison,** not without reason; **n. seulement ..., mais encore** *ou* **aussi ...,** not only ..., but also ... .
2 *nm inv* **répondre par un n.,** to answer in the negative; **les n. l'emportent,** the noes have it; **se fâcher pour un oui, pour un n.,** to flare up at the least (little) thing.
non-activité [nɔnaktivite] *nf* non-activity; **mettre en n.-a.,** to suspend (*employee*); *Mil* to put (*officer*) on half pay; **mise en n.-a.,** suspension (*of employee*); *Mil* placing (*of officer*) on half pay.
nonagénaire [nɔnaʒenɛr] *adj & n* nonagenarian.
non-agression [nɔnagresjɔ̃, nɔ̃-] *nf* nonaggression.
non-aligné [nɔnaliɲe, nɔ̃-] *adj Pol* (*pays*) nonaligned; (*pl non-alignés*).
non-alignement [nɔnaliɲmɑ̃, nɔ̃-] *nm Pol* nonalignment.
nonante [nɔnɑ̃t] *adj & nm inv Belg Suisse* ninety.
non-arrivée [nɔ̃arive, nɔn-] *nf* non-arrival.
non-assistance [nɔ̃asistɑ̃s, nɔn-] *nf Jur* **n.-a. à personne en danger,** = failure to render assistance to a person in danger.
non-belligérance [nɔ̃beliʒerɑ̃s] *nf* nonbelligerency.
nonce [nɔ̃s] *nm* **n. du Pape,** Papal Nuncio.
nonchalamment [nɔ̃ʃalamɑ̃] *adv* nonchalantly, unconcernedly; **marcher n.,** to saunter along.
nonchalance [nɔ̃ʃalɑ̃s] *nf* nonchalance, indifference.
nonchalant [nɔ̃ʃalɑ̃] *adj* nonchalant, unconcerned.
nonciature [nɔ̃sjatyr] *nf* **(a)** (*charge d'un nonce*) nunciature; **(b)** (*résidence*) nuncio's residence.
non-combattant [nɔ̃kɔ̃batɑ̃] *adj & nm* noncombatant; (*pl non-combattants*).
non-conformisme [nɔ̃kɔ̃fɔrmism] *nm* nonconformity.

non-conformiste [nɔ̃kɔ̃fɔrmist] (*pl non-conformistes*) **1** *adj* **(a)** *Rel* nonconformist; **(b)** unconventional. **2** *n* nonconformist.
non-dit [nɔ̃di] *nm* unvoiced remark; **un film riche en n.-dits,** a film full of meaningful silences.
none [nɔn] *nf Antiq* (*heure*) ninth hour; **nones,** (*jour*) nones.
non-être [nɔnɛtr] *nm Phil* nonentity, nonexistence.
non-exécution [nɔnɛgzekysjɔ̃] *nf* nonfulfilment (*of agreement etc*); nonperformance (*of contract*).
non-existant [nɔnɛgzistɑ̃, nɔ̃-] *adj* nonexistent; (*pl non-existants*).
non-existence [nɔnɛgzistɑ̃s, nɔ̃-] *nf* nonexistence.
non-ferreux, -euse [nɔ̃fɛrø, -øz] *adj Métal* nonferrous; (*pl non-ferreux, -euses*).
non-fumeur, -euse [nɔ̃fymœr, -øz] *adj & n* (*personne, voiture de train etc*) nonsmoker; **fumeur ou n.-f.?**, smoking or nonsmoking?
non-inscrit [nɔnɛ̃skri, nɔ̃-] *nm Pol* independent; (*pl non-inscrits*).
non-intervention [nɔnɛ̃tɛrvɑ̃sjɔ̃] *nf* nonintervention, noninterference.
non-interventionniste [nɔnɛ̃tɛrvɑ̃sjɔnist] *adj & n* noninterventionist; (*pl non-inverventionnistes*).
non-lieu [nɔ̃ljø] *nm Jur* **ordonnance** *ou* **arrêt** *ou* **déclaration de n.-l.,** nonsuit; (*pl non-lieux*).
non-livraison [nɔ̃livrɛzɔ̃] *nf* nondelivery (*of goods*).
nonne [nɔn] *nf Rel* nun.
non-négociable [nɔ̃negɔsjabl] *adj* non-negotiable; (*pl non-négociables*).
nonnette [nɔnɛt] *nf* **(a)** *Rel F* young nun; **(b)** *Culin* small cake of iced gingerbread; **(c)** (*oiseau*) tit, tomtit.
nono, -ote [nɔno, -ɔt] *n Can F* idiot.
nonobstant [nɔnɔpstɑ̃] *prép & adv Arch* notwithstanding; **ce n.,** this notwithstanding.
non-paiement [nɔ̃pɛmɑ̃] *nm* nonpayment.
nonpareille [nɔ̃parɛj] *nf Typ* six-point type, nonpareil.
non-pesanteur [nɔ̃pəzɑ̃tœr] *nf* weightlessness.
non-recevoir [nɔ̃r(ə)səvwar] *nm Jur* **opposer une fin de n.-r. à une réclamation,** to put in a plea in bar of a claim; to traverse a claim.
non-récupérable [nɔ̃rekyperabl] *adj* expendable, disposable; (*pl non-récupérables*).
non-retour [nɔ̃r(ə)tur] *nm* **point de n.-r.,** point of no return.
non-sens [nɔ̃sɑ̃s] *nm inv Scol* (*dans une traduction*) meaningless word *or* phrase; **c'est un n.-s.,** it's meaningless *or* (a) nonsense.
non-stop [nɔnstɔp] *adv F* **faire qch n.-s.,** to do sth non-stop.
non-syndiqué, -ée [nɔ̃sɛ̃dike] (*pl non-syndiqués, -ées*) **1** *adj* non-union, *Am* non-unionized (*employee*). **2** *n* non-unionist.
non-usage [nɔnyzaʒ] *nm* disuse; *Jur* non-user.
non-valable [nɔ̃valabl] *adj Jur* invalid (*clause etc*); (*ticket etc*) not valid; (*pl non-valables*).
non-valeur [nɔ̃valœr] *nf* unproductiveness; *Fin* bad debt; *Jur* unproductive asset; **terres en n.-v.,** unproductive land; *Fig* **pour nous c'est une n.-v.,** he's no use *or F* a dead loss to us; (*pl non-valeurs*).
non-violence [nɔ̃vjɔlɑ̃s] *nf* non-violence.
non-violent, -ente [nɔ̃vjɔlɑ̃, - ɑ̃t] **1** *n* person who does not believe in violence. **2** *adj* (*manifestation*) nonviolent.
non-voyant, -ante [nɔ̃vwajɑ̃, -ɑ̃t] *n* blind person.
nopal, -als [nɔpal] *nm Bot* nopal; cochineal cactus, cochineal fig.
nord [nɔr] **1** *nm* (*no pl*) **(a)** north; **au n., dans le n.,** in the North; **au n. de Madrid,** (to the) north of Madrid; **dans le n. de Madrid,** in North Madrid; **borné au n. par la Belgique,** bounded on the north by Belgium; **maison exposée au n.,** house facing north; **voyager vers le n.,** to travel north-(ward(s)); **du n.,** of *or* from the north; northern (*province*); northerly, north (*wind*); **la mer du N.,** the North Sea; **l'Amérique du N.,** North America; **l'Irlande du N.,** Northern Ireland; **le grand N.,** the frozen North; *F* **perdre le n.,** (*s'égarer*) to lose one's bearings; (*paniquer*) to lose one's head; **les gens du N.,** northerners; **les industriels du N.,** northern industrialists; **(b)** *Nau* **le n.,** the north wind. **2** *adj inv* north; **le Pôle N.,** the North Pole.
nord-africain, -aine [nɔrafrikɛ̃, -ɛn] (*pl nord-africains, -aines*) **1** *adj* North African. **2** *n* **N.-A.,** North African.
nord-américain, -aine [nɔramerikɛ̃, -ɛn] (*pl nord-américains, -aines*) **1** *adj* North American. **2** *n* **N.-A.,** North American.
nord-est [nɔrɛst] *nm* **(a)** north-east; **(b)** (*vent*) north east-wind, north-easter, *F* nor'easter.
nordique [nɔrdik] **1** *adj* Nordic; *Hist* Norse. **2** *nm* Norse (language). **3** *n* **N.,** Scandinavian (person).
nordir [nɔrdir] *vi Nau* (*of the wind*) to veer north(ward).
nordiste [nɔrdist] **1** *adj* **(a)** *US Hist* northerner; **(b)** *Sp* northern (*club*). **2** *nm US Hist* northerner.
nord-nord-est [nɔrnɔrɛst] *nm & adj inv* north-north-east.
nord-nord-ouest [nɔrnɔrwɛst] *nm & adj inv* north-north-west.
nord-ouest [nɔrwɛst] *nm* **(a)** north-west; **(b)** (*vent*) north-west wind, north-wester, *F* nor'wester.
noria [nɔrja] *nf* **(a)** chainpump, bucketchain, noria; **(b)** bucket conveyor.
normal, -aux [nɔrmal, -o] **1** *adj* **(a)** normal (*state, course, speed*); **c'est bien n.,** it's quite normal; **elle n'est pas dans son état n.,** she's not her normal *or* usual self; **en temps n.,** in *or* under normal circumstances; **c'est tout à fait n. que la jeunesse se rebelle,** it's only natural for youth to rebel; *Scol* **École normale,** (for primary, *Am* elementary school teachers) teacher training college; *Univ* **École normale supérieure,** = university level college that prepares students for senior posts in teaching and other professions;
(b) standard; **poids n.,** standard weight; **échantillon n.,** average sample; **vitesse normale,** rated speed.
2 *nf* **normale (a) la normale,** (the) normal; **la température est revenue à la normale,** the temperature is back to normal; *Golf* **la normale du parcours,** par for the course;
(b) *Univ F* **Normale Sup,** = **École normale supérieure.**
normalement [nɔrmalmɑ̃] *adv* normally, in the ordinary course of things *or* events.
normalien, -ienne [nɔrmaljɛ̃, -jɛn] *n Scol* student *or* former student of a teacher training college; *Univ* student *or* former student of the École normale supérieure.
normalisation [nɔrmalizɑsjɔ̃] *nf Pol* normalization.
normaliser [nɔrmalize] *vt* to normalize (*relations*); to standardize (*equipment*).
normalité [nɔrmalite] *nf* normality.
normand, -ande [nɔrmɑ̃, -ɑ̃d] **1** *adj* **(a)** Norman, (of) Normandy; **faire le trou n.,** = to have a drink of spirits, traditionally Calvados, between the courses of a meal; **(b)** *Hist* Norman; **la conquête normande,** the Norman conquest. **2** *n* **(a) N.,** Norman; **c'est un fin N.,** he's shrewd; **réponse de N.,** non-committal *or* equivocal *or* evasive answer; **à N. N. et demi,** set a thief to catch a thief; **(b) les Normands,** the Norsemen.
Normandie [nɔrmɑ̃di] *nf* Normandy.
norme [nɔrm] *nf* **(a)** norm, standard; **n. de conduite,** rule of conduct; **qui échappe à la n.,** (*situation*) exceptional, abnormal; **être d'une intelligence qui échappe à la n.,** to be exceptionally intelligent; **(b)** *Ind Com* standard; **jouet conforme aux normes de sécurité,** a toy which conforms to safety standards.
norois, noroît [nɔrwa] *nm* (*vent*) north-west wind, north-wester, *F* nor'wester.
Norvège [nɔrvɛʒ] *nf* Norway.
norvégien, -ienne [nɔrveʒjɛ̃, -jɛn] **1** *adj* Norwegian. **2** *nm Ling* Norwegian. **3** *n* **N.,** Norwegian. **4** *nf* **norvégienne,** round-stemmed rowing-boat.
nos *voir* **NOTRE.**
nostalgie [nɔstalʒi] *nf* nostalgia; (*mal du pays*) homesickness; **avoir la n. du foyer,** to pine *or* long *or* yearn for home, to be homesick.
nostalgique [nɔstalʒik] **1** *adj* nostalgic (*mood, memories*); homesick (*person*); **des sentiments nostalgiques,** feelings of nostalgia. **2** *n* nostalgic person.
nostalgiquement [nɔstalʒikmɑ̃] *adv* nostalgically.
nota [nɔta] *nm inv* footnote; (*en marge*) marginal note; **n. bene,** [nɔtabene], please note, nota bene.
notabilité [nɔtabilite] *nf* (*caractère*) person of distinction; (*person*) notability.
notable [nɔtabl] **1** *adj* notable, worthy of note; considerable; (*personne*) eminent, distinguished. **sans variation n.,** without appreciable change. **2** *n* eminent *or* distinguished person, person of distinction; **les notables de la ville,** the leading citizens, the local worthies.
notablement [nɔtabləmɑ̃] *adv* notably, appreciably.
notaire [nɔtɛr] *nm* **(a)** *Jur* notary; *Scot* notary public; **par-devant n.,** before a notary; **(b)** *Rel* **n. apostolique,** apostolical notary.
notamment [nɔtamɑ̃] *adv* notably, more particularly; especially, in particular.
notarié [nɔtarje] *adj Jur* **acte n.,** deed executed by a

notary.

notation [nɔtɑsjɔ̃] *nf* **(a)** notation; **(b)** *Scol* marking (*of work*).

note [nɔt] *nf* **(a)** note; **prendre des notes,** to take (down) notes; **jeter quelques notes sur le papier,** to jot down a few notes; **peux-tu me passer tes notes?,** can you lend me your notes?; **s'aider de notes dans un discours,** to speak from notes; **prendre n. de qch, prendre qch en n.,** to note sth, to make a note of sth; **prendre bonne n. de qch,** to take due note of sth; *Admin* **n. de service,** memorandum; **n. diplomatique,** diplomatic note; *Constr* **n. de cubage,** statement of measurement; **n. en** *ou* **au bas de la page,** footnote;

(b) *Scol etc* mark, *Am* grade; **bonne/mauvaise n.,** good/bad mark; **notes trimestrielles,** (end-of-term) report; **carnet** *ou* **relevé de notes,** school report;

(c) *Mus* note; **fausse n.,** wrong note; *Fig* contretemps, jarring note; **donner la n.,** to sound the keynote (*to singers etc*); *Fig* to call the tune; **chanter sur une autre n., changer de n.,** to change one's tune; **forcer la n.,** to exaggerate; (*faire du zèle*) to overdo it; **sa robe n'était pas dans la n.,** her dress didn't suit the occasion *or* struck the wrong note; **une n. d'originalité,** a touch *or* note of originality;

(d) *Com* invoice; (*in hotel etc*) bill, *US* check.

noté [nɔte] *adj* **être bien/mal n.,** to have a good/bad record.

noter [nɔte] *vt* **(a)** (*remarquer*) to note (*sth*), to take notice of (*sth*); **chose à n.,** thing worthy of notice; **notez bien cela,** take good note of this, note this well; **cela est à n.,** this is worth noting *or* remembering; **notez bien ce que je vous dis,** mark my words; **avez-vous noté l'heure?,** did you note *or* notice the time?; **(b)** (*mettre par écrit*) to put *or* jot (*sth*) down, to take *or* make a note of (*sth*); **n. la consommation de combustible,** to keep track of the fuel consumption; **n. un passage d'un trait,** to mark a passage; **(c)** *Scol* to mark, *Am* to grade (*work*).

notice [nɔtis] *nf* **(a)** (*exposé*) notice, account; **(b)** review (*of book etc*); **(c)** instructions, directions; (*livret*) book(let), handbook, manual; **n. d'emploi,** directions for use; **n. publicitaire,** (*livret*) advertising brochure; advertisement (*in newspaper*).

notification [nɔtifikɑsjɔ̃] *nf Jur* notification, notice; **recevoir n. de qch,** to be notified of sth.

notifier [nɔtifje] *vt* (*impf & pr sub* **n. notifiions**) **n. qch à qn,** to notify s.o. of sth; **n. son consentement,** to signify one's consent; *Jur* **on lui notifia qu'il aurait à déménager dans les vingt-quatre heures,** he received notice to quit within twenty-four hours.

notion [nosjɔ̃] *nf* notion, concept, idea; **l'amitié est une n. abstraite,** friendship is an abstract concept; **perdre la n. du temps/de la réalité,** to lose track of time/all sense of reality; **j'ai une vague n. de ce que ça veut dire,** I've a vague idea of what it means; **avoir des notions de chimie,** to have a smattering of chemistry.

notoire [nɔtwar] *adj* well-known (*fact, public figure*); *Péj* notorious (*criminal*); **son avarice est n.,** his miserliness is notorious *or* legendary.

notoirement [nɔtwarmɑ̃] *adv* manifestly; *Péj* notoriously.

notoriété [nɔtɔrjete] *nf* **(a)** notoriety (*of fact*); reputation (*of person*); **avoir de la n.,** to be well known, to have a good reputation; **il est de n. publique que ...,** it is public *or* common knowledge that ...; **(b)** *Jur* **acte de n.,** attested affidavit.

notre, nos [nɔtr, no] *adj poss* our; (*de roi, reine*) Our; **nos père et mère,** our father and mother; **n. meilleur ami,** our best friend.

nôtre [notr] **1** *adj poss* ours; **sa maison est n.,** his house is ours. **2** *pron poss* **le n., la n., les nôtres,** ours, our own; **il préfère vos tableaux aux nôtres,** he prefers your pictures to ours. **3** *nm* **le n.,** our own, what is ours; **il faut y mettre du n.,** we all have to make an effort *or* pitch in; **les nôtres,** our own (friends, family, folk *etc*); **est-il des nôtres?,** is he one of us?; **vous serez des nôtres, n'est-ce pas?,** you will join us, won't you?

Notre-Dame [nɔtrədam] *nf Rel* Our Lady; **la fête de N.-D.,** the feast of the Assumption.

nouba [nuba] *nf* **(a)** *Arg* **faire la n.,** to paint the town red; **(b)** Algerian military band.

noue¹ [nu] *nf* marshy meadow, water meadow.

noue² *nf Constr* **(a)** valley (*of roof*); **(b)** gutter lead, flashing.

nouer [nwe] **1** *vt* to tie, to knot; **n. qch serré,** to knot sth tightly, to make a tight knot in sth; **n. ses cheveux,** to tie up one's hair; **n. qch dans qch,** to tie up *or* fasten sth in sth; *Couture* **point noué,** lock stitch (*on machine*); **avoir la gorge nouée,** to have a lump in one's throat; **n. conversation avec qn,** to enter into conversation with s.o.; **n. des relations avec qn,** to establish relations with s.o.; **n. l'intrigue d'un roman,** to bring the action of a novel to a head *or* climax; **pièce bien nouée,** well plotted play. **2** *vi* (*of blossom*) to set. **3 se nouer** *vpr* **(a)** (*of cord, thread*) to become knotted; to kink; **(b)** *Littér Th Cin* to take shape; **l'intrigue se noue dès le premier acte,** the plot takes shape as early as Act One; **(c) se n. à qch,** to fasten on *or* cling to sth; **(d)** (*of blossom*) to set; **(e) se n. les cheveux,** to tie up one's hair.

noueux, -euse [nwø, -øz] *adj* knotty (*string, wood*); gnarled (*tree trunk, hands*).

nougat [nuga] *nm* nougat.

nouille [nuj] *nf* **(a)** *Culin* **nouilles,** (ribbon) noodles; **(b)** *F* idiot; **c'est une n.,** he's an idiot *or* a drip.

nounou [nunu] *nf Enf F* nanny.

nounours [nunurs] *nm* teddy (bear).

nourri [nuri] *adj* **(a)** (*alimenté*) fed; (*sainement*) nourished; **bien n.,** well fed; **mal n.,** undernourished, underfed; **(b)** (*riche*) rich, copious (*style*); broad, firm (*line in drawing*); full (*tone, sound*); sustained (*applause*); **discussion nourrie,** heated debate, lively discussion; *Mil* **feu n.,** brisk *or* sustained fire.

nourrice [nuris] *nf* **(a)** child minder; **(b)** *Tech* auxiliary tank, service tank; *Aut* spare can (*of petrol, Am gasoline*); **(c)** (wet) nurse; **mettre un enfant en n.,** to put out a child to nurse; **mise en n.,** fosterage; **épingle de n.,** safety pin.

nourricier, -ière [nurisje, -jɛr] **1** *adj* (*sève, suc*) nutritive; (*artère, canal*) nutrient; (*terre*) nourishing. **2** *n* **(père) n.,** foster father; **(mère) nourricière,** foster mother.

nourrir [nurir] **1** *vt* **(a)** to bring up, to rear (*children etc*); (*avec soin, tendresse*) to nurture; **nourri dans la misère,** reared in poverty; **être logi et nourri,** to get (one's) bed and board;

(b) to feed (*people, animals*) (**de, avec,** with, on); to feed (*fire*); **n. sa famille,** to maintain *or* keep *or* feed one's family; **n. des employés/des élèves,** to board workers/pupils; **travail qui nourrit son homme,** job that provides a living; **avoir tant par mois logé et nourri,** to get so much a month with board and lodging; **le lait nourrit,** milk is nourishing; **lectures qui nourrissent l'esprit,** reading that improves the mind; *Mus* **n. le son,** to give fullness *or* body to the tone;

(c) to foster (*hatred*); to harbour (*thoughts*); to cherish, to harbour, to entertain (*hope*);

(d) to suckle, to nurse (*infant*); **nourri au biberon,** bottle-fed.

2 se nourrir *vpr* **se n. de lait,** to live *or* subsist on milk; **se n. de rien,** to eat next to nothing.

nourrissage [nurisaʒ] *nm* rearing, feeding (*of cattle*).

nourrissant [nurisɑ̃] *adj* nourishing, nutritious; satisfying, substantial (*meal, amount of food*); *Biol* nutritive.

nourrisseur [nurisœr] *nm* **(a)** (*de bétail, de boucherie*) stockbreeder; (*de vaches laitières*) dairyman; **(b)** *Tech* feed roll (*of various machines*).

nourrisson [nurisɔ̃] *nm* baby at the breast, infant; *Arch* nurs(e)ling.

nourriture [nurityr] *nf* **(a)** (*aliments*) food; (*saine*) nourishment; **priver qn de n.,** to starve s.o.; **n. de l'esprit,** food for the mind; **les nourritures terrestres,** the fruits of the earth; **(b)** (*repas*) board, keep; **il ne gagne pas sa n.,** he isn't worth *or* doesn't earn his keep; **(c)** *Arch* feeding, suckling (*of infant*).

nous [nu] *pron pers* **(a)** (*subject*) we;

(b) (*direct object*) us; (*indirect object*) to us; **il ne n. connaît pas,** he does not know us; **lisez-le-n.,** read it to us; **elle n. en a parlé,** she spoke to us about it;

(c) (*reflexive*) **n. n. réchauffons,** we are warming ourselves; **n. n. sommes versé du vin,** we poured ourselves some wine; **n. n. battions avec l'ennemi,** we were fighting the enemy;

(d) (*reciprocal*) **n. n. connaissons,** we know each other;

(e) n. deux/tous, (*subject*) we two/we all, both of us/all of us; (*object*) us two/us all, all of us; **c'est n. qui sommes fautifs,** it is we who are to blame; **n. autres Anglais,** we English; **un ami à n.,** a friend of ours; **ce livre est à n.,** that book is ours *or* belongs to us; **c'est à n. de jouer,** it's our turn (to play); **il était avec n.,** he was with us; **entre n. soit dit,** (this is) between ourselves;

(f) (*royal or editorial we, with concords in the singular*) **n. sommes désolé de l'apprendre,** we are grieved to hear it.

nous-même(s) [numɛm] *pron pers* **(a) n.-mêmes,** ourselves; **nous l'avons fait n.-mêmes,** we did it ourselves; **(b)** (*following royal, editorial we*) ourself; *voir* **MÊME 1 (c)**.

nouveau, -el, -elle, -eaux [nuvo, -ɛl] **1** *adj* (**nouvel** *is used before m sing nouns beginning with a vowel or h mute*) **(a)** (*récent*) new; **les nouvelles voitures,** new (models of) cars; **livres nouveaux,** new books *or* publications; **manteau n.,** coat of a new cut; **du vin n.,** new *or* young wine; **l'herbe nouvelle,** young grass; **je suis n. dans ce métier,** I'm new to this business; **tout n. tout beau,** new and exciting *or* attractive; **il n'y a rien de n.,** there's nothing new, there are no new developments, there's no news;

(b) (*qui succède à un autre*) fresh, another; **un n. chapitre,** a new *or* fresh chapter; **une nouvelle raison,** a further *or* additional reason; **jusqu'à nouvel ordre,** until further notice; **la nouvelle génération,** the new *or* rising generation; **le Nouvel An,** the New Year; **la nouvelle lune,** the new moon; **le Nouveau testament,** the New Testament; **le n. roman,** the nouveau roman, the new novel; **la nouvelle Marilyn Monroe,** the new Marilyn Monroe; **vêtu à la nouvelle mode,** dressed in the latest fashion; **acheter une nouvelle voiture,** to buy a new *or* another car; **il met tous les jours une nouvelle chemise,** he wears a different shirt every day;

(c) (*with adv function*) **le nouvel arrivé, les nouveaux arrivés,** the newcomer(s); **les nouveaux pauvres,** the new poor; *Péj* **les nouveaux riches,** the nouveaux riches; **les nouveaux convertis,** the new converts, the newly converted;

(d) à n., (once) again; *Banque* **solde à n.,** balance brought forward; **de n.,** (over) again, afresh.

2 *nm* **j'ai appris du n.,** I've heard something new; **c'est du n.,** that's news to me.

3 *nmpl* **les nouveaux,** the newcomers; *Scol* the new pupils *or* students.

nouveau-né, -née [nuvone] *adj & n* newborn (child); (*pl nouveau-nés, -nées*).

nouveauté [nuvote] *nf* **(a)** newness, novelty; **(b)** (*changement*) change, innovation; **voilà une n. de sa part!,** that's a change *or* something new for him; **(c)** (*produit récent*) new invention, new publication *etc*; **vous trouverez ce disque/livre au rayon nouveautés,** you'll find the record/book in the new releases rack/on the new titles shelf; **(d)** *Vieilli* **nouveautés,** fancy goods; **magasin de nouveautés,** draper's shop, *Am* dry goods store; **les nouveautés de printemps,** the spring fashions.

nouvelle [nuvɛl] *nf* **(a)** (piece of) news; **nouvelles,** news (**de qn,** of, about s.o.); **bonne/mauvaise n.,** good/bad news; **première n.!,** that's the first I've heard of it!; **quelles nouvelles?,** what is the news?; **la n. de sa mort,** the news of his death; **la n. a été confirmée par le gouvernement,** the news *or* report was confirmed by the government; **vous connaissez la n.?,** have you heard the news *or* the latest?; *Journ* **dernières nouvelles,** late news; **tu as écouté les nouvelles ce matin?,** did you listen to the news this morning?; **demander** *ou* **(aller) prendre des nouvelles de (la santé de) qn,** to inquire *or* ask about s.o.('s health); **envoyez-moi de vos nouvelles,** let me hear from you; **on n'eut plus jamais de ses nouvelles,** he was never heard of again; **goûtez cela, vous m'en direz des nouvelles,** taste this, I'm sure you'll like it; **vous aurez de mes nouvelles!,** I'll give you something to think about!; *Prov* **pas de nouvelles, bonnes nouvelles,** no news is good news;

(b) *Littér* short story.

Nouvelle-Angleterre [nuvɛlɑ̃glətɛr] *nf* New England.

Nouvelle-Calédonie [nuvɛlkaledɔni] *nf* New Caledonia.

Nouvelle-Ecosse [nuvɛlekɔs] *nf* Nova Scotia.

Nouvelle-Galles du Sud [nuvɛlgaldysyd] *nf* New South Wales.

Nouvelle-Guinée [nuvɛlgine] *nf* New Guinea.

nouvellement [nuvɛlmɑ̃] *adv* newly, lately, recently.

Nouvelle-Orléans [nuvɛlɔrleɑ̃] *nf* New Orleans.

Nouvelles-Hébrides [nuvɛlzebrid] *nfpl* New Hebrides.

Nouvelle-Zélande [nuvɛlzelɑ̃d] *nf* New Zealand.

nouvelliste [nuvelist] *n* short-story writer.

nova, *pl* **novæ** [nɔva, -ə] *nf Astron* nova.

novateur, -trice [nɔvatœr, -tris] **1** *adj* innovative. **2** *n* innovator.

novembre [nɔvɑ̃br] *nf* November; **en n.,** in November; **au mois de n.,** in (the month of) November; **le premier n.,** (on) the first of November, (on) November the first.

novice [nɔvis] **1** *n* novice, beginner; (*in convent*) novice; (*in profession*) probationer; (*scout*) tenderfoot; *Nau* **n. au commerce,** apprentice to the merchant service; ordinary seaman. **2** *adj* **être n. à** *ou* **dans qch,** to be new to *or* inexperienced in sth.

noviciat [nɔvisja] *nm* noviciate, novitiate.

noyade [nwajad] *nf* **(a)** drowning (fatality); **sauver qn de la n.,** to save s.o. from drowning; **mort par n.,** death by drowning; **(b)** *Hist Fr* execution by drowning.

noyau, -aux [nwajo] *nm* **(a)** stone (*of fruit*); **n. de cerise,** cherry stone *or* pit; **fruit à n.,** stone fruit; **enlever** *ou* **retirer le n. d'un fruit,** to stone *or* pit a fruit; **(b)** (*centre*) nucleus (*of atom, cell, comet, colony*); core (*of the earth*); **n. de bombe nucléaire,** (nuclear) bomb core; *F* **un petit n. de joueurs,** a small knot of players; **un petit n. d'amis,** a small circle of friends; *Pol* **n. communiste,** communist cell; **le n. dur,** the hard core; **noyaux de résistance,** pockets of resistance; **(c)** *Archit* newel (*of stairs*); **escalier à n. plein,** winding staircase; *El* core (*of armature*); *Métal* core (*of mould*); *Géol* **n. volcanique,** volcanic bomb.

noyautage [nwajotaʒ] *nm Pol* infiltration.

noyauter [nwajote] *vt Pol* to infiltrate, to set up cells in (*trade union etc*).

noyé, -ée [nwaje] **1** *adj* (*mort*) drowned; (*en train de se noyer*) drowning; *Géol* **roche noyée,** sunken rock; **yeux noyés,** swimming eyes; *Fig* **j'ai déniché ce vase n. dans un tas de vieilleries,** I found this vase buried in a pile of old junk. **2** *n* **secours aux noyés,** first aid for the drowning; **on a repêché un n. dans la rivière,** a drowned man was fished out of the river.

noyer¹ [nwaje] *nm* walnut (tree, wood); **n. (blanc) d'Amérique,** hickory.

noyer² *v* (**je noie, n. noyons; je noierai**) **1** *vt* to drown (*s.o.*); to swamp, to inundate, to deluge (*the earth etc*); to flood (*bunker, carburettor*); to sink (*sth*) in cement; to countersink (*screw*); to drive (*nail*) in flush; **yeux noyés de larmes,** eyes brimming with tears; **noyé dans la foule,** lost in the crowd; **n. son chagrin (dans l'alcool),** to drown one's sorrows (in drink); **n. son vin,** to put too much water into *or* to drown one's wine; **n. la sauce,** to make the sauce too thin; **n. le poisson,** (*à la ligne*) to play the fish; *F* to tire out one's opponent. **2 se noyer** *vpr* to drown oneself; (*as an accident*) to be drowned, to drown; **elle se noierait dans un verre d'eau,** she makes a mountain out of a molehill; **se n. dans les détails,** to get bogged down in details; **se n. dans l'alcool,** to hit the bottle, to drink oneself to death.

nu [ny] **1** *adj* **(a)** naked (*person*); bare (*shoulders, limbs, wire*); *Beaux-Arts* nude (*figure*); **mettez-vous torse nu,** strip to the waist; **se baigner tout nu,** to bathe in the nude; **nu comme la main** *ou* **comme un ver,** stark naked, in the buff; (**NOTE nu** *before the noun that it qualifies is invariable and is joined to the noun by a hyphen*); **aller tête nue** *ou* **nu-tête,** to go bareheaded *or* without anything on one's head; **aller pieds nus** *ou* **nu-pieds,** to go barefoot(ed); **visible à l'œil nu,** visible to the naked eye;

(b) *Fig* uncovered, undisguised; unsheathed, naked (*sword*); **la vérité (toute) nue,** the plain *or* naked truth; **châssis nu,** stripped chassis; *El* **fil nu,** open wire;

(c) bare (*country, tree, room*).

2 *nm Beaux-Arts* (the) nude; **des nus,** nude studies, nudes; **à nu,** bare, naked; **mettre à nu,** to lay bare, to expose, to uncover (*sth*); to clear (*land*); to strip (*tree, wire*); to lay bare (*one's heart*); **monter un cheval à nu,** to ride (a horse) bareback.

nuage [nɥaʒ] *nm* **(a)** cloud; **n. en queue de vache,** cirrus, mare's tail; **nuages pommelés,** mackerel sky; **ciel couvert de nuages,** overcast sky; **sans nuages,** cloudless (*sky*); *Fig* unclouded (*life, future*); *Fig* **bonheur sans nuages,** perfect bliss; **n. de poussière/fumée,** cloud of dust/smoke; **n. artificiel,** smoke screen; *Fig* **être** *ou* **se perdre dans les nuages,** to have one's head in the clouds, to be daydreaming; **(b)** *Fig* gloom, shadow; **un n. de tristesse assombrissait son front,** her face was clouded with sadness; **(c)** dash, tiny drop (*of milk in a cup of tea*).

nuageux, -euse [nɥaʒø, -øz] *adj* **(a)** cloudy (*weather*); overcast (*sky*); **(b)** *Fig* hazy (*thought, ideas*); **explication nuageuse,** unclear explanation.

nuance [nɥɑ̃s] *nf* **(a)** shade (of colour), hue; *Mus* **il joue sans nuances,** he plays without any light and shade; **(b)** gradation, slight difference, shade (*in meaning, tone*); **une n. d'amertume/de mépris,** a touch *or* tinge *or* suggestion of bitterness/contempt; **je ne saisis pas la n.,** I don't quite see the difference.

nuancé [nɥɑ̃se] *adj* (*couleur, ton*) subtle; (*discours*) full of nuances; **ses réponses sont toujours très nuancées,** he always qualifies his answers.

nuancer [nɥɑ̃se] *vt* (**je nuançai(s); n. nuançons**) **(a)** to shade (*colours*); (*mélanger*) to blend (**de,** with); **(b)** to vary (*tone etc*); to moderate, to qualify (*refusal*); *Mus* **n. son jeu,** to introduce light and shade into one's playing.

nuancier [nɥɑ̃sje] *nm Com* sample card, chart (*of colours*).

nubile [nybil] *adj* nubile, marriageable; **âge n.,** age of consent.

nubilité [nybilite] *nf* nubility, marriageable age.

nucléaire [nykleɛr] **1** *adj* (*armes, énergie etc*) *& Biol Phys* nuclear; *Phys* **particule n.,** elementary particle; **hiver n.,** nuclear winter. **2** *nm* nuclear power.

nucléé [nyklee] *adj Biol etc* nucleate(d) (*cell etc*).

nucléique [nykleik] *adj* nucleic (*acid*).

nucléole [nykleɔl] *nm Biol* nucleolus.

nucléon [nykleɔ̃] *nm Phys* nucleon.

nucléonique [nykleɔnik] *Phys* **1** *adj* nucleonic. **2** *nf* nucleonics.

nucléus [nykleys] *nm* nucleus.

nudisme [nydism] *nm* nudism.

nudiste [nydist] *n* nudist.

nudité [nydite] *nf* **(a)** nudity, nakedness (*of person*); bareness (*of rock, wall*); **(b)** *Beaux-Arts* nude (figure).

nue [ny] *nf Arch & Litt* high cloud(s); **nues,** skies; *Fig* **porter** *ou* **élever qn/qch aux nues,** to laud *or* praise s.o./sth to the skies; **se perdre dans les nues,** to be lost in the clouds *or* in daydreams, to have one's head (completely) in the clouds; *Fig* **tomber des nues,** to be thunderstruck.

nuée [nɥe] *nf* cloud (*of insects*); host (*of enemies*); *Litt* (*large*) cloud, storm cloud; **n. ardente,** (*d'un volcan*) nuée ardente (*cloud of ash*).

nuire [nɥir] *v* (*ppr* **nuisant**; *pp* **nui**; *pr ind* **je nuis, n. nuisons**; *pr sub* **je nuise**; *p hist* **je nuisis**; *fu* **je nuirai**) **1** *vi* **n. à qn/à qch,** to be harmful *or* injurious *or* prejudicial to s.o./to sth, to harm s.o./sth; **cela ne nuira en rien,** that will do no harm; **cela nuira à sa réputation,** it will damage his reputation; **n. aux intérêts de qn,** to prejudice s.o.'s interests; *Jur* **dans l'intention de n.,** maliciously; *Prov* **abondance de biens ne nuit pas,** ≈ you can't have too much of a good thing. **2 se nuire** *vpr* to do oneself (a great deal of) harm; to damage one's own interests.

nuisance [nɥizɑ̃s] *nf* (*cause of*) nuisance, harm; harmful effect.

nuisette [nɥizɛt] *nf* baby doll (nightie).

nuisibilité [nɥizibilite] *nf* harmfulness, injuriousness.

nuisible [nɥizibl] *adj* harmful; (*chagrinant*) hurtful (**à,** to); **plantes nuisibles,** noxious plants; **animaux nuisibles,** vermin.

nuisiblement [nɥiziblәmɑ̃] *adv* harmfully, injuriously.

nuit [nɥi] *nf* **(a)** night; **la n. dernière,** last night; **cette n.,** tonight; (*passée*) last night; **veiller jusqu'à une heure avancée de la n.,** to sit up far into the night; **passer la n. à faire qch,** to stay *or* sit up all night doing sth; *F* **on a passé la n. à faire la fête,** we made a night of it; **passer la n. chez des amis,** to stay overnight *or* the night with friends; **passer la n. à l'hôtel,** to spend *or* stay the night at the hotel; **payer une n. d'hôtel,** to pay for a night at a hotel; **bonne n.!,** good night!; **le bateau de n.,** the night boat *or* ferry; **vêtements de n.,** nightwear; **oiseau de n.,** nightbird; *Beaux-Arts* **effet de n.,** night effect, night piece; *Cin* **n. américaine,** day for night; **voyager de n.** *ou* **la n.,** to travel by night *or* at night; **être de n.,** to be on night shift *or* night duty *or F* nights; **n. et jour** [nɥiteʒur], night and day; **je n'ai pas dormi de la n.,** I never slept *or* I didn't sleep a wink all night; **n. blanche,** sleepless night; **passer une n. blanche,** to spend a sleepless night; (*volontairement*) to stay up all night; *Fig* **c'est le jour et la n.,** they're like chalk and cheese; *Prov* **la n. porte conseil,** = it would be best to sleep on it;

(b) darkness; **il commence à faire n.,** night is falling, it is growing *or* getting dark; **il fait déjà n.,** it is dark already; **à la n. tombante,** at nightfall, at dusk; **après la tombée de la n., à (la) n. tombée,** after dark; *Prov* **la n. tous les chats sont gris,** all cats are grey at night; *Fig* **la n. de l'ignorance,** the darkness of ignorance; **perdu dans la n. des temps,** lost in the mists of time.

nuitamment [nɥitamɑ̃] *adv* by night.

nuitée [nɥite] *nf* overnight stay (*in hotel etc*).

nul, nulle [nyl] **1** *adj indéf* (*with* **ne** *expressed or understood*) no, not one; **n. espoir,** no hope; **il n'a nulle cause de se plaindre,** he has no reason to complain; **sans nulle vanité,** without boasting.

2 *adj* **(a)** (*following noun*) worthless (*argument, effort*); empty (*mind*); **homme n.,** man of no account, nonentity; **elle est nulle ta blague,** your joke is rubbish *or* useless; *Scol* **il est n. en mathématiques,** he is hopeless *or* useless at mathematics; *Jur* **n. et de n. effet, n. et sans effet, n. et non avenu,** invalid, null and void; **bulletin (de vote) n.,** spoilt paper; *Sp* **course** *ou* **manche nulle,** dead heat; **faire match n.,** to draw (a game); **partie nulle,** drawn game, draw;

(b) non-existent (*funds etc*); nil; **le solde est n.,** the balance is nil; *Phys* **tension nulle,** zero tension.

3 *pron indéf* no one, nobody; **n. autre que moi ne le sait,** none but I knows of it.

nullard, -arde [nylar, -ard] *Arg* **1** *adj* useless, hopeless (*person*). **2** *n* dud.

nullement [nylmɑ̃] *adv* (*with* **ne** *expressed or understood*) not at all, by no means; **nous ne sommes n. surpris,** we are not in the least surprised; **il n'est n. sot,** he is by no means a fool.

nullification [nylifikɑsjɔ̃] *nf* nullification.

nullité [nylite] *nf* **(a)** *Jur* nullity, invalidity (*of deed, marriage etc*); **frapper une clause de n.,** to render a clause void; **lors d'un mariage, la bigamie est une cause de n.,** bigamy is grounds for annulment; **(b)** (*de qn*) incompetence; incapacity; **(c)** *F* (*personne*) nonentity, nobody; **c'est une vraie n.,** he's a dead loss; **cette blague est d'une totale n.,** that joke is a dead loss.

nûment [nymɑ̃] *Litt adv* frankly, without embellishments.

numéraire [nymerɛr] **1** *adj* (*coins*) legal; **valeur n.,** legal-tender value. **2** *nm* metallic currency, specie, current coin; **payer en n.,** to pay in cash.

numéral, -aux [nymeral, -o] *adj & nm* numeral.

numérateur [nymeratœr] *nm Math* numerator.

numération [nymerɑsjɔ̃] *nf Math* numeration; notation; *Méd* **n. globulaire,** blood count.

numérique [nymerik] *adj* **(a)** numerical (*value, superiority etc*); **(b)** *Ordinat* digital (*computer, data*); **balance à affichage n.,** digital scales; **enregistrement/disque n.,** digital recording/record.

numériquement [nymerikmɑ̃] *adv* numerically.

numéro [nymero] *nm* **(a)** (*chiffre*) number; **n. d'ordre,** running number, serial number; **tirer un bon n.,** to draw a lucky *or* winning number; *Fig* to have a stroke of luck; **j'habite au n. 10,** I live at number 10; **la chambre n. 20,** room (number) 20; *F* **priorité n. un,** number one priority; **tenue n. un,** best clothes; **n. de téléphone** *ou* **d'appel,** telephone number; *Tél* **n. vert,** *Br* ≈ Freephone, *Can* ≈ Zenith, *US* ≈ 0-800 number; **(b)** number, issue (*of periodical*); **n. du jour** *ou* **de la semaine** *ou* **du mois, dernier n.,** current issue *or* number; **ancien n., n. déjà paru,** back issue *or* number; **vente au n.,** single copies sold; **(c)** *Th* act, number, turn; **n. de cirque,** circus act; *F* **il aime faire son petit n.,** he likes doing his little act; *Fig* **quel n.!,** what a character!; **(d)** *Com* number (*of sewing cotton etc*); count (*of yarn*); size (*in stock sizes*).

numérotage [nymerɔtaʒ] *nm*, **numérotation** [nymerɔtɑsjɔ̃] *nf* numbering (*of houses etc*); page numbering, pagination (*of book*).

numéroter [nymerɔte] *vt* to number (*houses etc*); to page, to paginate (*book*); *Mil* **numérotez-vous (à partir de la droite)!,** (from the right) number!

numéroteur [nymerɔtœr] *nm* numbering machine, numbering stamp.

numismate [nymismat] *n* numismatist.

numismatique [nymismatik] **1** *adj* numismatic. **2** *nf* numismatics, numismatology.

nummulaire [nymylɛr] *nf Bot* moneywort, creeping Jenny.

nunuche [nynyʃ] *adj F* silly.

nuptial, -iaux [nypsjal, -jo] *adj* bridal, nuptial; **anneau n.,** wedding ring; **marche nuptiale,** wedding march; **chambre nuptiale,** bridal suite; **messe nuptiale,** nuptial mass.

nuptialité [nypsjalite] *nf* marriage rate.

nuque [nyk] *nf* nape *or* back of the neck; **elle veut une coupe de cheveux qui dégage bien la n.,** she wants her hair cut short at the back; **saisir qn par la n.,** to catch hold of s.o. by the scruff of the neck.

nurse [nœrs] *nf* nanny, (children's) nurse.

nursery [nœrsәri] *nf* nursery; (*pl nurseries*).

nutation [nytɑsjɔ̃] *nf* nutation.

nutritif, -ive [nytritif, -iv] *adj* nutritive; nourishing (*food*); **valeur nutritive,** food *or* nutritional value.

nutrition [nytrisjɔ̃] *nf* nutrition; **une mauvaise n.,** a bad *or* unbalanced diet.

nutritionniste [nytrisjɔnist] *n* nutritionist, dietician, dietitian.

nyctalope [niktalɔp] *adj* hemeralopic, day-blind.

nylon [nilɔ̃] *nm* nylon; **bas (de) n.**, nylon stockings, nylons.

nymphe [nɛ̃f] *nf* **(a)** *Myth* nymph; **(b)** *Ent* nymph, pupa, chrysalis.

nymphéa [nɛ̃fea] *nm* nymphea, white water lily.

nymphomane [nɛ̃fɔman] *adj & nf Méd* nymphomaniac; *F* **elle est vraiment n.**, she's a real nympho(maniac), she's sex mad.

nymphomanie [nɛ̃fɔmani] *nf Méd* nymphomania.

O

O, o [o] *nm* **(a)** (the letter) O, o; **(École des) langues o,** *Br* ≈ School of Oriental Studies; **(b)** (*abrév* **ouest**) W.

ô [o] *int Litt* O!

O.A.A. [oɑɑ] *nf* (*abrév* **Organisation de l'alimentation et l'agriculture**) FAO.

O.A.C.I. [oɑsei] *n* (*abrév* **Organisation de l'aviation civile internationale**) ICAO.

O.A.S. [oɑɛs] *n Hist abrév* **Organisation de l'armée secrète.**

oasien, -ienne [ɔazjɛ̃, -jɛn] **1** *adj* oasis (*vegetation etc*). **2** *n* oasis dweller.

oasis [ɔazis] *nf* (*parfois m*) (*dans le désert*) oasis; *Fig* **une o. de calme,** a haven of peace.

obédience [ɔbedjɑ̃s] *nf* **(a)** *Cathol* obedience; **(b)** (*soumission*) **musulman de stricte o.,** strict Moslem; **pays d'o. communiste,** countries under Communist rule; **(c)** *Litt* (*obéissance*) obedience.

obéir [ɔbeir] *vi* **o. à qn,** to obey s.o.; (*régulièrement, toujours*) to be obedient to s.o.; **o. à qn au doigt et à l'œil,** to be at s.o.'s beck and call; **la voiture obéit au doigt et à l'œil,** the car responds at a touch; **il est obéi (de ses enfants),** he is obeyed (by his children); **se faire o.,** to command obedience; **o. à qch,** to yield *or* submit to sth; **o. à un ordre,** to obey *or* comply with an order; **o. à la force,** to yield to force; **o. à son instinct,** to follow *or* obey one's instinct; **o. à sa conscience,** to follow (the dictates of) *or* obey one's conscience; **o. à la mode,** to follow the dictates of fashion; *Nau* **o. à la barre,** to answer the helm; *Av* **o. aux commandes,** to respond to the controls.

obéissance [ɔbeisɑ̃s] *nf* obedience (**à,** to); **refus d'o.,** insubordination; **devoir o. à qn,** to owe s.o. obedience *or* allegiance; **jurer o. au roi,** to swear allegiance to the king.

obéissant [ɔbeisɑ̃] *adj* obedient (*child, husband, animal etc*).

obel, obèle [ɔbɛl] *nm Typ* obelus, obelisk.

obélisque [ɔbelisk] *nm Archit* obelisk; **l'o. de Cléopâtre,** Cleopatra's Needle.

obérer [ɔbere] *vt* (**j'obère; j'obérerai**) to involve (*s.o.*) in debt; to burden (*s.o., sth*) with debt; **finances fort obérées,** heavily encumbered finances.

obèse [ɔbɛz] *adj & n* obese (person).

obésité [ɔbezite] *nf* obesity.

obier [ɔbje] *nm* (*arbuste*) guelder rose, snowball tree.

obituaire [ɔbitɥɛr] *adj & nm Rel* **(registre) o.,** obituary list, register of deaths.

objecter [ɔbʒɛkte] *vt* (*rétorquer*) to raise *or* interpose (*sth*) as an objection; **je n'ai rien à o. à la proposition,** I have no objection to the proposal, I have nothing (to say) against the proposal; **o. qch à qn,** to bring something up against s.o.; **on lui objecta sa jeunesse,** they took exception to his youth, his youth counted against him.

objecteur [ɔbʒɛktœr] *nm* **o. de conscience,** conscientious objector.

objectif, -ive [ɔbʒɛktif, -iv] **1** *adj* objective, unbiased; **observateur o.,** neutral *or* objective observer. **2** *nm* **(a)** (*but*) aim, object(ive), end; *Mil etc* objective; (*cible*) target; **atteindre son o.,** to attain one's object(ive); **(b)** *Phys* object glass, objective (*of microscope etc*); *Phot* lens; *Phot* **régler l'o.,** to adjust the lens *or* focus; *Phot* **braquer son o. sur qn,** to train the camera(s) on s.o..

objection [ɔbʒɛksjɔ̃] *nf* objection; **faire** *ou* **formuler** *ou* **soulever** *ou* **dresser une o.,** to object, to make *or* raise an objection (**à,** to); *Jur* **o. votre honneur!,** objection *or* I object, m'lud *or US* your honor!; **o. de conscience,** conscientious objection.

objectivement [ɔbʒɛktivmɑ̃] *adv* objectively.

objectivité [ɔbʒɛktivite] *nf* objectivity, objectiveness.

objet [ɔbʒɛ] *nm* **(a)** article, thing, object; **o. de luxe,** luxury article *or* item; **o. de première nécessité,** essential *or* basic item; **je suis allé aux objets trouvés,** I went to the lost-property *or* lost-and-found office *or* department; **o. d'art,** objet d'art; *Astron* **o. volant non identifié,** unidentified flying object; **quel o. affreux!,** what a dreadful object!;
(b) *Gram* object, complement; **o. direct/indirect,** direct/indirect object;
(c) *Phil* object; **la femme-o.,** woman as (an) object;
(d) subject, (subject) matter; **l'o. de la conversation,** the subject of the conversation; **cela fera l'o. de ma conférence,** this will be the subject of my lecture; **l'o. de ma visite,** the purpose of my visit; **o. de pitié/haine,** object of pity/hatred;
(e) (*but*) object, aim, purpose (*of action*); **remplir son o.,** to attain one's end; **sans o.,** aimless(ly), purposeless(ly), pointless(ly);
(f) *Ordinat* object.

objurgation [ɔbʒyrgɑsjɔ̃] *nf* objurgation.

oblat, -ate [ɔbla, -at] *n Rel* oblate.

oblation [ɔblɑsjɔ̃] *nf Rel* oblation, offering.

obligataire [ɔbligatɛr] *Fin* **1** *n* bondholder, debenture holder. **2** *adj* **emprunt o.,** debenture loan.

obligation [ɔbligɑsjɔ̃] *nf* **(a)** (moral) obligation, duty; **je me sens dans l'o. de vous avertir,** I feel it's my duty *or* I feel compelled to warn you; **faire honneur/manquer à ses obligations,** to meet/to fail to meet one's obligations; **avoir des obligations envers qn,** to be under an obligation to s.o.; **je me vois dans l'o. de me taire,** I find myself obliged to keep silent; *Rel* **fête d'o.,** day of obligation; **o. du service militaire,** liability to military service; **(b)** *Jur* recognizance, bond; **o. alimentaire,** maintenance order; **contracter une o. irrévocable,** to enter into a binding agreement; **(c)** *Fin* bond, debenture, redeemable stock; **o. convertible** *ou* **échangeable,** convertible bond; **o. au porteur,** bearer bond.

obligatoire [ɔbligatwar] *adj* obligatory, mandatory, compulsory; binding (*agreement*); **école laïque, gratuite et o.,** free, compulsory and non-religious education; **l'uniforme est o.,** uniform must be worn; *F* **c'était o.,** it HAD to happen, it was inevitable.

obligatoirement [ɔbligatwarmɑ̃] *adv* compulsorily; **vous devez o. montrer votre passeport à la frontière,** you are required to show your passport at the frontier.

obligé, -ée [ɔbliʒe] **1** *adj* **(a)** (*contraint*) obliged, bound, compelled (**de faire qch,** to do sth); **(b)** (*indispensable*) indispensable, necessary; **(c)** *F* (*inévitable*) inevitable, sure to happen; **c'est o. qu'il rate son examen,** he's bound to fail his exam; **(d)** (*reconnaissant*) obliged, grateful (**de,** for); **je vous serais très o. de ...,** (*dans une lettre*) I would be most obliged *or* grateful (to you) if you would ...; **(e)** *Mus* **récitatif o.,** recitative ob(b)ligato. **2** *n* person under obligation; *Jur* obligee; *Vieilli* **je suis votre o.,** I am in your debt.

obligeamment [ɔbliʒamɑ̃] *adv* obligingly; **il m'a o. aidé à porter ma valise,** he (very) obligingly *or* kindly helped me to carry my suitcase.

obligeance [ɔbliʒɑ̃s] *nf* obligingness; **ayez** *ou* **veuillez avoir l'o. de fermer la porte,** would you be so kind as to *or* would you be good enough to close the door.

obligeant [ɔbliʒɑ̃] *adj* obliging, helpful, kind; (*poli*) civil; **c'est très o. de votre part,** it's very obliging *or* kind *or* civil of you.

obliger [ɔbliʒe] *v* (**j'obligeai(s); n. obligeons**) **1** *vt* **(a)** (*contraindre*) to oblige, to bind, to compel, *Fml* to constrain; **ma signature m'y oblige,** my signature binds me *or* holds me to it; **votre devoir vous y oblige,** you are duty bound to do it; **o. qn à faire qch,** to compel *or* force s.o. to do sth, *F* to make s.o. do sth; **être obligé de faire qch,** to be obliged *or* compelled to do sth, *F* to have to do sth; **rien ne t'y oblige,** you don't have to; **(b)** (*rendre service à*) to oblige (*s.o.*), to do (*s.o.*) a favour. **2 s'obliger** *vpr* **s'o. à faire qch,** to bind oneself *or* undertake to do sth; (*ne pas manquer de faire*) to make a point of doing sth.

oblique [ɔblik] **1** *adj* oblique (*line etc*); slanting (*stitch*); skew (*arch*); **regard o.,** sideways *or* sidelong glance; **manœuvre o.,** (*malhonnête*) underhand move; *Gram* **cas o.,** oblique case. **2** *nm Anat* oblique muscle. **3** *nf* oblique line; **pluie qui tombe en o.,** slanting rain.

obliquement [ɔblikmɑ̃] *adv* obliquely, slantwise; **regarder qn o.,** to look sideways *or* sidelong at s.o.; **tourner o.,** to veer.

obliquer [ɔblike] *vi* **obliquez à gauche/à droite!,** bear left/ right!

obliquité [ɔblikɥite] *nf* obliqueness.

oblitérateur, -trice [ɔbliteratœr, -tris] **1** *adj Tech* obliterating. **2** *nm* cancel (*for stamps etc*).

oblitération [ɔbliterɑsjɔ̃] *nf* **(a)** *Méd* obstruction; **(b)** obliteration; cancelling, cancellation (*of stamps etc*); **(cachet d')o.,** postmark.

oblitérer [ɔblitere] *v* **(j'oblitère, n. oblitérons; j'oblitérerai) 1** *vt* **(a)** to cancel (*stamp*); **timbre oblitéré,** used stamp; **(b)** *Méd* (*obstruer*) to obstruct; **(c)** *Litt Fig* to obliterate (*marks, the past etc*). **2 s'oblitérer** *vpr Litt* **peu à peu le passé s'oblitérait dans sa mémoire,** little by little, every trace of the past disappeared from his memory.

oblong, -ongue [ɔblɔ̃, -ɔ̃g] *adj* **(a)** oblong; **un coquillage de forme oblongue,** an oblong shell; **(b)** (*livres etc*) **format o.,** oblong format.

obnubiler [ɔbnybile] *vt* **(a)** (*obséder*) to obsess (*s.o.*); **(b)** to cloud (*mind*); (*rendre perplexe*) to bemuse (*s.o.*).

obole [ɔbɔl] *nf* **(a)** small offering; (*dans la Bible*) widow's mite; **chacun a apporté son o.,** everyone made a contribution; **(b)** *Hist* (*Greek*) obolus; (*French*) obole.

obscène [ɔpsɛn] *adj* obscene, *F* smutty (*language, book*); obscene, lewd (*gesture*).

obscénité [ɔpsenite] *nf* obscenity, *F* smuttiness (*of language, book*); obscenity, lewdness (*of gesture*).

obscur [ɔpskyr] *adj* **(a)** (*sombre*) dark (*night, room*); gloomy (*weather*); **(b)** (*inexplicable, confus*) obscure, difficult to understand, abstruse (*subject*); **(c)** (*vague*) indistinct, dim (*horizon etc*); vague, dim (*forebodings*); **(d)** (*inconnu*) obscure, unknown; (*humble*) lowly, humble (*parentage*); **un o. écrivain,** an unknown *or* obscure writer.

obscurantisme [ɔpskyrɑ̃tism] *nm* obscurantism.

obscurcir [ɔpskyrsir] **1** *vt* **(a)** (*assombrir*) to obscure; to darken (*room*); to darken, to cloud (*sky*); **yeux obscurcis par les larmes,** eyes dimmed with tears; **(b)** (*rendre confus*) **o. un texte,** to make a text obscure *or* unintelligible. **2 s'obscurcir** *vpr* to darken, to grow dark; (*of sky*) to cloud over; (*of sight, faculty*) to grow dim.

obscurcissement [ɔpskyrsismɑ̃] *nm* obscuring (*of light, meaning*); darkening (*of room, sky*); dimming (*of mind*).

obscurément [ɔpskyremɑ̃] *adv* obscurely, dimly.

obscurité [ɔpskyrite] *nf* obscurity; (*noirceur*) darkness; (*confusion*) unintelligibility, abstruseness; dimness (*of a memory etc*); **vivre dans l'o.,** to live in obscurity; **sortir de l'o.,** to emerge from obscurity, to become known.

obsédant [ɔpsedɑ̃] *adj* haunting (*memory*); obsessive (*thought*).

obsédé, -ée [opsede] *n* fanatic, maniac; **un o. sexuel,** a sex maniac.

obséder [ɔpsede] *vt* **(j'obsède; j'obséderai)** (*of thought, memory*) to obsess (*s.o.*).

obsèques [ɔpsɛk] *nfpl* funeral.

obséquieusement [ɔpsekjøzmɑ̃] *adv* obsequiously.

obséquieux, -euse [ɔpsekjø, -øz] *adj* obsequious.

obséquiosité [ɔpsekjozite] *nf* obsequiousness.

observance [ɔpsɛrvɑ̃s] *nf* observance (*of rule*); **communiste de stricte o.,** hardline communist.

observateur, -trice [ɔpsɛrvatœr, -tris] **1** *n* **(a)** observer (*of events, phenomena, enemy's movements etc*); *Mil etc* spotter; **o. des Nations Unies,** United Nations observer; **(b)** observer, keeper (*of rules, laws*). **2** *adj* observant.

observation [ɔpsɛrvɑsjɔ̃] *nf* **(a)** (*surveillance*) observation; **être en o.,** to be on the lookout *or* on the watch; (*à l'hôpital*) to be under observation; **(main)tenir qn en o.,** to keep s.o. under observation; **malade en o.,** patient under observation; **poste d'o.,** observation *or* lookout post; **avion d'o.,** spotter plane; **observations par satellite,** satellite observations; **il a l'esprit d'o.,** (*rien ne lui échappe*) he is very observant; **(b)** (*remarque*) observation, remark; **si je puis me permettre une o.,** if I may be allowed to make an observation *or* to say something; **il faisait toujours des observations à ses élèves,** he was always finding fault with his pupils; **observations sur un auteur,** comments *or* notes on an author; **(c)** (*respect*) observance, keeping (*of laws*); **(d)** (*étude*) observation (*of stars etc*).

observatoire [ɔpsɛrvatwar] *nm Astron* observatory; *Mil* observation post.

observer [ɔpsɛrve] *vt* **(a)** (*surveiller, regarder*) to watch (*sth, s.o.*); **on nous observe,** we are being watched; **je l'observais faire,** I watched him doing it;

(b) (*remarquer*) to note, to notice; **faire o. qch à qn,** to draw s.o.'s attention to sth, to point sth out to s.o.;

(c) (*suivre, respecter*) to observe, to keep (to), to comply with, to adhere to (*rules, laws etc*); **o. une stricte économie,** to practise strict economy; **ne pas o. la loi/le dimanche,** to break the law/the sabbath; **o. le silence,** to keep silent; **o. une minute de silence,** to observe a minute's silence; **o. une promesse,** to keep a promise; **faire o. la loi,** to enforce (obedience to) the law;

(d) (*étudier*) to observe, to study (*the stars*); to take, to read (*an angle*); *Nau* **o. le soleil,** to take the sun, to take a sight at the sun.

obsession [ɔpsesjɔ̃] *nf* obsession (*by idea, emotion*).

obsessionnel, -elle [ɔpsesjɔnɛl] *adj Psy* obsessional; **une névrose obsessionnelle,** an obsessional neurosis.

obsidienne [ɔpsidjɛn] *nf Minér* obsidian; *F* volcanic glass.

obsidional, -aux [ɔpsidjɔnal, -o] *adj* **fièvre obsidionale,** mass psychosis (*of people under siege*); *Psy* **délire o.,** persecution complex.

obsolescence [ɔpsɔlesɑ̃s] *nf* obsolescence.

obsolescent [ɔpsɔlesɑ̃] *adj* obsolescent.

obsolète [ɔpsɔlɛt] *adj* obsolete; **un mot devenu o.,** a word that has become obsolete, an obsolete word.

obstacle [ɔpstakl] *nm* obstacle; *Fig* impediment, hurdle, hindrance; **il continua sa route sans rencontrer d'o.,** he continued on his way unimpeded; **faire o. à qch/qn,** to stand in the way of sth/s.o.; **je n'y vois pas d'o.,** I don't see any difficulty (in *or* about it); **course d'obstacles,** *Courses de chevaux* steeplechase; *Sp* hurdle race.

obstétrical, -aux [ɔpstetrikal, -o] *adj* obstetric(al).

obstétrique [ɔpstetrik] *nf* obstetrics.

obstination [ɔpstinɑsjɔ̃] *nf* obstinacy, stubbornness; *F Péj* pigheadedness.

obstiné [ɔpstine] *adj* obstinate, stubborn, headstrong; *F Péj* pigheaded (*person*); stubborn, dogged (*resistance*).

obstinément [ɔpstinemɑ̃] *adv* obstinately, stubbornly.

obstiner (s') [sɔpstine] *vpr* **s'o. sur qch** *ou* **à faire qch,** (*continuer*) to persist in (doing) sth; (*vouloir*) to be bent on (doing) sth; **s'o. dans son silence,** to remain stubbornly *or* obstinately silent.

obstruction [ɔpstryksjɔ̃] *nf* obstruction, blocking (*of street, passage*); blockage, clogging (*of drain*); *Méd* **o. intestinale,** stoppage of the bowels; **faire de l'o.,** *Pol* to filibuster; *Fb etc* to obstruct.

obstructionnisme [ɔpstryksjɔnism] *nm Pol* filibustering.

obstructionniste [ɔpstryksjɔnist] *Pol* **1** *nm* filibusterer. **2** *adj* filibustering (*tactics*).

obstruer [ɔpstrye] *vt* to obstruct, to block (*street, pipe*).

obtempérer [ɔptɑ̃pere] *vi* **(j'obtempère, n. obtempérons; j'obtempérerai) o. à,** to obey (*summons, order*); to comply with (*order*); *Jur* **refus d'o.,** refusal to comply (*with a police officer's instructions etc*).

obtenir [ɔptənir] *v* (*conj like* **tenir**) **1** *vt* to obtain, *F* to get (*goods, permission*); to obtain, to secure (*promise*); to obtain, to gain, *F* to get (*s.o.'s consent etc*); to obtain, to achieve, *F* to get (*result*); **o. qch de qn,** to obtain *or F* get sth from s.o.; **j'ai obtenu de le voir,** I obtained *or F* got permission to see him; **j'ai obtenu qu'elle revienne,** (*je l'ai décidée à revenir*) I got her to come back; (*j'ai convaincu d'autres personnes qui l'empêchaient de revenir*) I arranged for her to come back.

2 s'obtenir *vpr* **où cela s'obtient-il?,** where can you get it?

obtention [ɔptɑ̃sjɔ̃] *nf* obtaining; **pour l'o. de qch,** (in order) to obtain sth.

obturateur, -trice [ɔptyratœr, -tris] **1** *adj* closing; *Anat* obturator (*vein, muscle*). **2** *nm* **(a)** *Anat Chir* obturator (*of aperture*); **(b)** (*volet etc*) shutter, stopcock, stop valve; *Aut* throttle; *Phot* shutter; *Phys* **o. à neutrons,** neutron shutter; **o. de plaque,** focal-plane shutter; **o. au diaphragme,** diaphragm shutter.

obturation [ɔptyrɑsjɔ̃] *nf* closing (*of cavity*); sealing (*of pipe*); filling (*of tooth*); **pâte d'o. (dentaire),** (dental) filler.

obturer [ɔptyre] *vt* to stop, to seal (*pipe, aperture*); to close (*cavity*); to fill (*tooth*).

obtus [ɔpty] *adj* **(a)** obtuse (*angle*); **(b)** dull, dim-witted (*person*); **(c)** *Vieilli* blunt (*point*); rounded (*leaf*).

obus [ɔby, oby] *nm Mil* shell; **o. armé,** live shell; **o. non**

explosé, unexploded shell; **o. à balles** *ou* **à mitraille,** shrapnel (shell).

obusier [ɔbyzjɛ] *nm Mil* howitzer.

obvier [ɔbvje] *vi* (*impf & pr sub* **n. obviions**) **o. à qch,** to prevent sth; **o. à un accident,** to take precautions *or* to guard against an accident.

oc [ɔk] *adv Ling Hist* **la langue d'oc,** langue d'oc (*language of southern France*).

O.C. [ose] *nfpl Rad* (*abrév* **ondes courtes**) S.W..

occase [ɔkaz] *nf F* bargain.

occasion [ɔkazjɔ̃] *nf* **(a)** opportunity, occasion, chance; **saisir une o.,** to take *or* seize an opportunity; *F* **sauter sur l'o.,** to jump at the chance; **avoir l'o. de faire qch,** to have the opportunity of doing *or* to do sth; **si l'o. se présente, si vous en trouvez l'o.,** if the opportunity arises, if the opportunity comes your way, *F* if you get the chance; **attendre l'o.,** to bide one's time; **suivant l'o.,** according to the occasion; **à l'o.,** when the opportunity presents itself; **voir qn à l'o.,** to see s.o. from time to time; **venez boire un coup à l'o.,** come for a drink when you get a *or* the chance; **à la première o.,** at the first *or* earliest opportunity; **à plusieurs occasions,** on several occasions; **pour l'o.,** for the occasion; **s'habiller pour l'o.,** to dress for the occasion; **à l'o. de son mariage,** on the occasion of his marriage; **par occasions.,** now and then, occasionally; **en pareille o.,** in similar circumstances; **en cette o.,** at this juncture; **dans les grandes occasions,** on great occasions; **(b)** (*affaire*) bargain; **vente d'o.,** (*soldes*) sale; **marchandises d'o.,** job lot; **faire le neuf et l'o.,** to sell new and secondhand goods; **voitures/livres/meubles d'o.,** secondhand cars/books/furniture; **ça, c'est une o.!,** it's a bargain!; **(c)** (*motif*) motive, reason, cause, occasion; **o. d'une dispute,** cause of a dispute.

occasionnel, -elle [ɔkazjɔnɛl] *adj* occasional; chance (*meeting*); casual (*help*); **une situation tout à fait occasionnelle,** (*qui ne se reproduira pas*) a quite exceptional *or* a one-off situation; **cause occasionnelle d'une révolte,** event that led to a revolt.

occasionnellement [ɔkazjɔnɛlmɑ̃] *adv* (*se voir etc*) occasionally; (*par hasard*) accidentally.

occasionner [ɔkazjɔne] *vt* to cause, to give rise to, to bring about, *Fml* to occasion.

occident [ɔksidɑ̃] *nm* west; *Fml & Litt* occident; *Pol* **l'O.,** the West.

occidental, -ale, -aux [ɔksidɑ̃tal, -o] **1** *adj* west, western; **côte occidentale,** west coast; **l'Europe occidentale,** Western Europe; **les Indes occidentales,** the West Indies. **2** *n* Westerner; *Fml & Litt* Occidental.

occidentalisation [ɔksidɑ̃talizasjɔ̃] *nf* westernization.

occidentaliser [ɔksidɑ̃talize] **1** *vt* to westernize. **2 s'occidentaliser** *vpr* to become westernized.

occipital, -aux [ɔksipital, -o] *adj & nm Anat* occipital (bone).

occiput [ɔksipyt] *nm Anat* occiput.

occire [ɔksir] *vt* (*used only in inf & pp* **occis**) *Arch & Hum* to slay, to kill.

occlusif, -ive [ɔklysif, -iv] *Ling* **1** *adj* occlusive. **2** *nf* **occlusive,** occlusive consonant, stop.

occlusion [ɔklyzjɔ̃] *nf* occlusion; obstruction, stoppage (*of bowel*).

occultation [ɔkyltasjɔ̃] *nf Astron* occultation; **feu à occultations,** occulting *or* intermittent light.

occulte [ɔkylt] *adj* occult (*science*); secret (*accounts*); hidden (*cause*); clandestine, covert (*role*); **les sciences occultes,** the occult; (*magie noire*) the black arts.

occulter [ɔkylte] *vt* to occult (*heavenly body, light, signal*); *Fig* **o. des informations,** to conceal information.

occultisme [ɔkyltism] *nm* occultism.

occupant, -ante [ɔkypɑ̃, -ɑ̃t] **1** *adj* occupying (*tenant, forces*); in possession (*of property*); **2** *n* occupier, occupant (*of house*); occupant (*of post*); *Jur* **premier o.,** occupant; *Mil* **l'o.,** the occupying power.

occupation [ɔkypasjɔ̃] *nf* **(a)** (*fait d'être ou de rester quelque part*) occupancy, occupation; (*fait de posséder ou d'entrer en possession*) possession (*of house etc*); *Mil* occupation (*of conquered country*); **armée d'o.,** army of occupation; **l'O.,** the Occupation (1940); **grève avec o. des lieux,** sit-in strike; **(b)** (*besogne, ouvrage*) work, employment; **avoir de l'o.,** to be busy, to have things to do; **ne pas avoir d'o.,** (*être oisif*) to have nothing to do; **vaquer à ses occupations,** to go about one's business.

occupé [ɔkype] *adj* **(a)** (*personne*) (*travaillant*) busy; (*avec un autre client etc*) engaged; **o. aux préparatifs du départ,** busy with the preparations for departure, busy getting ready to leave; **c'est un homme fort o.,** he's a very busy man; **je suis o.,** I am busy; **(b)** (*place*) taken; *Tél* (*ligne*) engaged, *Am* busy; (*sur la porte des toilettes*) engaged; *Fig* **en territoire o.,** in occupied territory.

occuper [ɔkype] **1** *vt* **(a)** to inhabit, to reside in, to occupy (*house etc*);
(b) *Mil etc* to occupy, to hold, to take possession of (*town, building*); **les ouvriers ont décidé d'o. l'usine,** the workers have decided to occupy the factory;
(c) (*remplir*) to occupy, to fill, to take up (*time, space*); **faire qch pour o. le temps,** to do sth to fill in *or* occupy (the) time;
(d) to have, to hold (*an important job etc*);
(e) to give employment to (*s.o.*); **o. vingt ouvriers,** to employ twenty workmen; **o. qn,** to give s.o. something to do; (*matière à réfléchir*) to give s.o. something to think about.
2 s'occuper *vpr* **(a)** to keep oneself busy; **s'o. à faire qch,** to be engaged in *or* busy doing sth; **s'o. en lisant,** to spend one's time reading;
(b) s'o. de , (*être intéressé par qch*) to go in for *or* be interested in (*photography etc*); (*se charger de*) to apply oneself to *or* to attend to (*sth*); **cette maison s'occupe surtout d'argenterie,** this firm specialises in (making) silverware; **il s'occupe de trop de choses,** he takes on too much, he has too many irons in the fire; **nous allons maintenant nous o. du bilan,** we will now turn (our attention) to the balance sheet; **je m'en occuperai,** I'll see to it, I'll deal with it; **qui s'occupe de ce qu'il dit?,** who cares (about) what he says?; **occupe-toi de ce qui te regarde!,** mind your own business!; *F* **t'occupe (pas)!,** forget it!, not to worry!; **s'o. de qn,** to attend to *or* look after s.o.; *Com* **est-ce qu'on s'occupe de vous?,** are you being attended to *or* being served?

occurrence [ɔkyrɑ̃s] *nf* **(a)** (*circonstance*) occurrence, event; **en l'o.,** in the event, as it is *or* was; **(b)** *Ling* (*apparition*) occurrence; **on note une grande o. du mot,** the word occurs frequently.

O.C.D.E. [osedeø] *n* (*abrév* **Organisation de coopération et de développement économique**) OECD.

océan [ɔseɑ̃] *nm* ocean; **d'un o. à l'autre,** from coast to coast; **les plages de l'O.,** (*en France*) the Atlantic resorts; *Fig* **un o. de fleurs,** a sea of blossom.

Océanie [ɔseani] *nf* Oceania.

océanien, -ienne [ɔseanjɛ̃, -jɛn] **1** *adj* Oceanian. **2** *n* **O.,** Oceanian; (*de Polynésie, Mélanésie*) South Sea Islander.

océanique [ɔseanik] *adj* ocean (*current etc*).

océanographie [ɔseanɔgrafi] *nf* oceanography.

océanographique [ɔseanɔgrafik] *adj* oceanographic(al).

océanologie [ɔseanɔlɔʒi] *nf* oceanology.

ocelle [ɔsɛl] *nm Zool* ocellus, simple eye (*of insect*); ocellus, eye (*on feather, insect's wing*).

ocelot [ɔslo] *nm* (*mammifère*) ocelot.

ocre [ɔkr] *nf & adj inv* ochre, *US* ocher.

octaèdre [ɔktaɛdr] **1** *adj* octahedral. **2** *nm* octahedron.

octaédrique [ɔktaedrik] *adj* octahedral.

octane [ɔktan] *nm Ch* octane; **essence à haut indice d'o.,** high-octane petrol *or US* gasoline.

octave [ɔktav] *nf Mus etc* octave.

octet [ɔktɛ] *nm Ordinat* byte; **milliard d'octets,** gigabyte.

octobre [ɔktɔbr] *nm* October; **en o.,** in October; **au mois d'o.,** in (the month of) October; **le premier o.,** (on) October (the) first, (on) the first of October; *Hist* **les journées d'o.,** = October 5th and 6th 1789 (when Louis XVI was forced to return to Paris); **la Révolution d'o.,** the October Revolution.

octogénaire [ɔktɔʒenɛr] *adj & n* octogenarian.

octogonal, -aux [ɔktɔgɔnal, -o] *adj* octagonal.

octogone [ɔktɔgɔn] *nm* octagon.

octopode [ɔktɔpɔd] *adj & nm* (*mollusque etc*) octopod.

octosyllabe [ɔktɔsilab] **1** *adj* octosyllabic. **2** *nm* octosyllable.

octroi [ɔktrwa] *nm* **(a)** (*concession*) concession, grant(ing) (*of favour*); **(b)** *Hist* (*impôt*) town dues, city toll (*on goods*); (*bureau qui percevait cet impôt*) tollhouse.

octroyer [ɔktrwaje] *v* (**j'octroie, n. octroyons; j'octroierai**) **1** *vt* **o. qch à qn,** to grant *or* concede sth to s.o.; **o. du temps/une grâce/une permission/des faveurs,** to allow (*s.o.*) time/to grant (*s.o.*) mercy/permission/to bestow favours (*on s.o.*). **2 s'octroyer** *vpr* **il s'est octroyé (le droit de prendre) un jour de vacances supplémentaire,** he gave *or* awarded himself (the right to take) an extra day's holiday.

octuor [ɔktyɔr] *nm Mus* octet, octette.

octuple [ɔktypl] **1** *adj* octuple; eightfold (*amount*). **2** *nm* octuple.

oculaire [ɔkylɛr] **1** *adj* **(a)** (*visuel*) **témoin o.**, eyewitness; **(b)** (*de l'œil*) **hygiène o.**, eye care, care of the eyes; **globe o.**, eyeball. **2** *nm Opt* eyepiece, ocular.

oculiste [ɔkylist] *n* ophthalmologist.

odalisque [ɔdalisk] *nf* odalisque, odalisk.

ode [ɔd] *nf Litt* ode.

odeur [odœr] *nf* smell; (*généralement désagréable*) odour, *US* odor; (*agréable*) scent; **o. de brûlé,** smell of burning; **je sentais une o. de brûlé,** I could smell something burning; **sans o.,** odourless, *US* odorless; **bonne o.,** pleasant smell; **mauvaise o.,** bad smell, *F* stench; *Fig* **mourir en o. de sainteté,** to die in the odour of sanctity; **ne pas être en o. de sainteté auprès de qn,** to be in s.o.'s bad books; *Prov* **l'argent n'a pas d'o.,** money has no smell.

odieusement [ɔdjøzmɑ̃] *adv* odiously, hatefully.

odieux, -euse [ɔdjø, -øz] *adj* odious, hateful (*person, vice*); odious, abominable (*crime*).

odomètre [ɔdɔmɛtr] *nm* (*pour véhicule*) odometer; (*pour piéton*) pedometer.

odontologie [ɔdɔ̃tɔlɔʒi] *nf Méd* odontology.

odorant [ɔdɔrɑ̃] *adj* (*agréable*) sweet-smelling, fragrant; (*désagréable*) smelly, stinking.

odorat [ɔdɔra] *nm* (sense of) smell; **avoir l'o. fin,** to have a keen sense of smell.

odoriférant [ɔdɔriferɑ̃] *adj* sweet-smelling, *Litt* odoriferous.

odyssée [ɔdise] *nf* **(a)** *Littér* **l'O.,** the Odyssey; **(b)** *Fig* odyssey; **ce voyage a été une véritable o.,** it was a truly epic journey.

œcuménique [ekymenik] *adj Rel* (o)ecumenical.

œdème [edɛm] *nm Med* oedema, *US* edema.

Œdipe [edip] *nm Littér* Oedipus; *Psy* **complexe d'O.,** Oedipus complex.

œil, *pl* **yeux** [œj, jø] *nm* **(a)** eye; **o. de verre,** glass eye; **avoir les yeux bleus,** to have blue eyes; **hôpital pour les maladies des yeux,** opthalmic *or* eye hospital; **visible à l'o. nu,** visible to the naked eye; **voir qch de ses (propres) yeux,** to see sth with one's own eyes; *F* **avoir un o. qui dit zut** *ou* **merde à l'autre,** to be cross-eyed, to have a squint; **fermer/ouvrir les yeux,** to close/open one's eyes; **je n'ai pas fermé l'o. de la nuit,** I didn't sleep a wink all night; **ne dormir que d'un o.,** to be only half-asleep; **faire qch les yeux fermés,** to do sth with one's eyes shut; *Fig* **je pourrais le faire les yeux fermés,** I could do it with my eyes shut *or* closed; **ouvrir de grands yeux,** (*de surprise*) to open one's eyes wide; (*par curiosité*) to stare; **avoir les yeux qui brillent,** (*de joie, plaisir*) to have sparkling eyes, to have a twinkle in one's eye; (*de fièvre*) to have sparkling eyes; (*de malice, complicité*) to have a gleam in one's eye; **faire les gros yeux,** to glare; **lever les yeux au ciel,** (*d'exaspération*) to raise one's eyes heavenward *or* to heaven; **baisser les yeux,** (*par timidité*) to lower one's gaze, to look down; **avoir les** *ou* **des petits yeux,** (*avoir sommeil*) to be unable to keep one's eyes open; **avoir un o. au beurre noir,** to have a black eye; **regarder qn entre les (deux) yeux** *ou* **dans les yeux** *ou* **dans le blanc des yeux,** to look s.o. full in the face *or* straight in the eye; **entre quatre yeux,** *F* **entre quat'z'yeux** [katzjø] **,** in private, between you and me (and the gatepost); **les yeux dans les yeux,** face to face; (*avec franchise*) (wo)man to (wo)man; **n'avoir d'yeux que pour une personne,** to have eyes only for a certain person; *Prov* **o. pour o., dent pour dent,** an eye for an eye, a tooth for a tooth; **épouser une femme pour ses beaux yeux,** to marry a woman for her (good) looks; **il ne travaille pour les beaux yeux de personne,** he doesn't do anything for love *or* for nothing; **avoir des yeux de merlan frit,** to have a ridiculous, love-lorn expression on one's face, to look like a lovesick calf; **coûter les yeux de la tête,** to cost a fortune *or* an arm and a leg; **avoir les yeux plus gros que le ventre,** to have eyes (that are) bigger than one's belly; **n'avoir plus que ses** *ou* **les yeux pour pleurer,** to have nothing left apart from the clothes on one's back; **chose qui saute aux yeux,** something obvious *or* that stares you in the face; **ça crève les yeux qu'il est amoureux d'elle,** it's painfully *or* glaringly obvious that he's in love with her; *F* **battre de l'o.,** to be sleepy *or* drowsy; **je m'en bats l'o.,** I don't give a hoot, I couldn't care less; *F* **mon o.!,** my foot!; **tourner de l'o.,** (*s'évanouir*) to faint; *F* **entrer à l'o.,** to get in free *or* gratis; **le mauvais o.,** the evil eye; **avoir un o. critique sur qch,** to be watching sth with a critical eye; **nous voyons ça du même o.,** we see eye to eye with each other about it; **ne pas en croire ses yeux,** not (to be able) to believe one's eyes; **faire les yeux doux à qn,** *F* **faire de l'o. à qn,** to make eyes at s.o.; *F* **taper dans l'o. à qn,** to take s.o.'s fancy;

(b) (*vue*) sight; **avoir de bons/mauvais yeux,** to have good/bad eyesight; **s'user** *ou* **s'abîmer les yeux,** to ruin one's eyes *or* eyesight; **fatiguer les yeux,** to strain one's eyes; **dès que j'eus jeté les yeux sur lui,** as soon as I had set eyes on him; **se consulter des yeux,** to exchange glances; **chercher qn des yeux,** to look about for s.o.; *F* **se rincer l'o.,** to get an eyeful; **elle n'a pas froid aux yeux,** she's not afraid of anything; **aux yeux de la loi/de Dieu,** in the eyes of the law/in the sight of God; **à mes yeux,** in my opinion; **l'accident s'est déroulé sous mes yeux,** the accident happened right before my eyes; **avoir qch sous les yeux,** to have sth right in front of one's eyes; *Tennis etc* **avoir la balle dans l'o.,** to have one's eye in;

(c) (*attention*) attention, notice; **avoir** *ou* **garder l'o. ouvert** *ou* **les yeux ouverts,** to be observant *or* sharp-eyed; **avoir l'o. sur qch,** to keep an eye on sth; **avoir l'o. sur qn, avoir qn à l'o.,** to keep an eye on s.o.; **avoir l'o. à tout,** to see to everything; **ouvrir l'o. (et le bon),** to keep one's eyes peeled *or* skinned; **ne pas avoir les yeux en face des trous,** to be half-asleep; *F* **elle n'a pas les yeux dans sa poche,** she is very observant, she keeps her eyes open; **fermer les yeux sur qch,** (*par indulgence*) to turn a blind eye to sth; (*par refus de la réalité*) to close one's eyes to sth; **ouvrir les yeux à qn sur qch,** to open s.o.'s eyes to sth; **coup d'o.,** glance; **au** *ou* **du premier** *ou* **d'un seul coup d'o.,** at first sight, at the outset; **jeter un coup d'o. sur qch,** to run one's eye over sth, to glance through *or* at sth; **il y a un joli coup d'o. d'ici,** (*vue*) there's a lovely view from here; **avoir le coup d'o.,** to have good judgement; **ça vaut** *ou* **ça mérite le coup d'o.,** it's worth a look; **voir** *ou* **regarder qn/qch d'un mauvais o.,** to look unfavourably *or* disapprovingly on s.o./sth, to frown on s.o./sth;

(d) eye (*of needle etc*); (screw-)hole (*of hinge*); eye (splice) (*on rope*); hole (*in bread, gruyère*); globule *or* speck of fat (*on soup*);

(e) *Typ* (*pl* **œils**) face (*of letter*); **piton à o.,** eye bolt; **lettre d'un autre o.,** wrong fount; *Ordinat* **o. d'un caractère,** type face;

(f) *El TV* **o. électrique,** electric eye; **o. magique, o. cathodique,** magic eye, cathode eye, electron ray tube;

(g) *Météo* eye (*of cyclone*).

œil-de-bœuf [œjdəbœf] *nm* bull's-eye (window); (*pl œils-de-bœuf*).

œil-de-chat [œjdəʃa] *nm Minér* cat's eye; (*pl œils-de-chat*).

œil-de-perdrix [œjdəperdri] *nm* soft corn; (*pl œils-de-perdrix*).

œillade [œjad] *nf* glance; **lancer/jeter une o. à qn,** to glance meaningfully at s.o.; **lancer des œillades à qn,** to make eyes at s.o..

œillère [œjɛr] *nf* **(a)** (*pour un cheval*) blinker, eye flap, *US* blinder; **avoir des œillères,** (*être borné*) to be narrow-minded; (*ignorer la réalité*) to wear blinkers; **(b)** *Méd* eyebath, *surtout US* eyecup.

œillet [œjɛ] *nm* **(a)** (*fleur*) pink; **o. des fleuristes,** clove pink, carnation; **o. de poète,** sweet william; **o. des prés,** ragged robin; **o. d'Inde,** French marigold; **avoir/porter un o. à la boutonnière,** to have/wear a carnation in one's buttonhole; **(b)** (*trou*) eyelet (*of boot, sail etc*); **(c)** (*papeterie*) (gummed) reinforcement.

œilleton [œjtɔ̃] *nm Opt* eyepiece (*of viewfinder*); (*d'une plante*) eye (bud).

œillette [œjɛt] *nf* oil poppy, opium poppy; **huile d'o.,** poppy seed oil.

œnologie [enɔlɔʒi] *nf* oenology, *US* enology, **cours d'o.,** wine-appreciation course.

œnologique [enɔlɔʒik] *adj* oenological, *US* enological.

œnologue [enɔlɔg] *n* oenologist.

œsophage [ezɔfaʒ] *nm Anat* oesophagus, *US* esophagus, gullet.

œstre [østr] *nm* (*mouche*) gadfly, warble (fly), bot(t) fly.

œstrogène [ɛstrɔʒɛn] *adj & nm Physiol* oestrogen, *US* estrogen.

œstrus [ɛstrys] *nm Physiol* œstrus, *US* estrus.

œuf, *pl* **œufs** [œf, ø] *nm* **(a)** egg; **blanc/jaune d'o.,** egg white/yolk; **o. frais,** fresh egg; **o. du jour,** freshly-laid egg; **o. en poudre,** dried *or* dehydrated *or* powdered egg; *Culin* **o. à la coque,** boiled egg; **o. mollet,** soft-boiled egg; **o. dur,** hard-boiled egg; **œufs brouillés,** scrambled eggs; **o. sur le plat** *ou* **au plat,** fried egg; *Culin* **œufs à la neige,** whipped egg-whites; *Culin* **œufs au lait,** egg custard; **o. de Pâques,** Easter egg; **en forme d'o.,** egg-shaped; *Fig*

mettre tous ses œufs dans le même panier, to put all one's eggs in one basket; *F* **marcher sur des œufs,** to tread on thin ice; **il tondrait un o.,** he's a skinflint; **faire d'un o. un bœuf,** to make a mountain out of a molehill; *Prov* **qui vole un o. vole un bœuf,** he that will steal a penny will steal a pound; **tuer la poule aux œufs d'or,** to kill the goose that lays the golden egg(s); *F* **quel o.!,** what an idiot *or* fool!; *F* **va te faire cuire un o.!,** go jump in the lake!;

(b) *Biol* ovum; egg (*of insect*); berry (*of crayfish, lobster*); **œufs,** spawn (*of frog, fish etc*); hard roe (*of fish*); *F* **étouffer** *ou* **tuer qch dans l'o.,** to nip sth in the bud;

(c) *Couture* **o. à repriser,** darning egg.

œufrier [œfrije] *nm* egg holder *or* stand (*for boiling eggs*).

œuvé [œve] *adj* hard-roed (*fish*); berried (*lobster*).

œuvre [œvr] **1** *nf* **(a)** (*travail*) work; **faire o. utile,** to do useful work; **leur rencontre était son o.,** (*grâce à lui*) it was thanks to him that they met; (*à cause de lui*) it was because of him that they met; **être à l'o.,** to be working *or* at work; **mettre qn à l'o.,** to set s.o. to work; **se mettre à l'o.,** to get down to *or* set to work; **quand le médecin arriva, la mort avait déjà fait son o.,** by the time the doctor arrived the patient had already died; **mettre en o.,** to use, to make use of (*sth*); to bring (*sth*) into operation *or* play; to implement (*a treaty*); **mettre tout en o.,** to leave no stone unturned (*in search, enquiry*); to take all possible steps (*to ensure sth is done*); **bois d'o.,** timber; **main d'o.,** manpower; (*d'une usine etc*) workforce; **exécuteur des hautes œuvres,** executioner, hangman; **o. de bienfaisance** *ou* **de charité,** charitable society *or* institution, charity; **les bonnes œuvres,** charitable work; **quête au profit d'une o.,** collection in aid of a charity;

(b) (*création*) work, production; **œuvres d'un peintre,** works of a painter; **l'o. de Molière/Mozart,** the works of Molière/Mozart; **œuvres complètes/choisies,** complete/selected works; **o. d'art,** work of art;

(c) *Nau* **œuvres vives,** quick works, vitals; **œuvres mortes,** dead works, upper works, topsides.

2 *nm* **gros o. (d'un bâtiment),** fabric (of a building); *Constr* **à pied d'o.,** on site; *Fig* ready to start work.

3 *n Beaux-Arts Littér* works (*of an artist, painter etc*); **l'o. entier** *ou* **entière de Beethoven,** the complete works of Beethoven.

œuvrer [œvre] *vi* **(a)** (*faire des bonnes œuvres*) to do charitable *or* voluntary work; **il œuvre pour les enfants handicapés,** he does charitable work for handicapped children; **(b)** *Litt* to work.

offensant [ɔfɑ̃sɑ̃] *adj* offensive, insulting.

offense [ɔfɑ̃s] *nf* **(a)** offence, *US* offense; **faire une o. à qn,** to offend s.o.; **soit dit sans o.,** with all due respect; *F* **il n'y a pas d'o.,** no offence taken; **(b)** *Rel* transgression, sin, trespass; **pardonne-nous nos offenses,** forgive us our trespasses; **(c)** *Jur* **o. à la Cour,** contempt of Court.

offensé, -ée [ɔfɑ̃se] *adj & n* offended, injured (person).

offenser [ɔfɑ̃se] **1** *vt* **(a) o. qn,** to offend s.o., to give offence *or US* offense to s.o.; **sans vous o.,** without wishing to offend, *F* no offence intended; **(b)** to offend against (*good taste etc*); **o. les regards,** to be an eyesore. **2 s'offenser** *vpr* to be offended (**de,** by); to take offence (**de,** at).

offenseur [ɔfɑ̃sœr] *nm* offending person *or* party.

offensif, -ive [ɔfɑ̃sif, -iv] *adj* offensive (*war, weapon*).

offensive [ɔfɑ̃siv] *nf* offensive; **passer à l'o.,** to go on the *or* over to the offensive; *Fig* **o. de l'hiver/du froid,** onset of winter/sudden cold spell, cold snap; **o. diplomatique,** diplomatic offensive.

offensivement [ɔfɑ̃sivmɑ̃] *adv* offensively.

offertoire [ɔfɛrtwar] *nm Rel Mus* offertory.

office [ɔfis] **1** *nm* **(a)** (*charge*) office, functions, duty; **faire o. de secrétaire,** to act as secretary; **la pilule a rempli son o.,** the pill did its job; **d'o.,** (*membre*) ex officio; (*automatiquement*) automatically, as a matter of routine; *Jur* **avocat nommé d'o.,** barrister appointed by the court; **(b)** (*assistance*) service, turn; **accepter les bons offices de qn,** to accept s.o.'s good offices; **(c)** *Rel* service, office (*for the day etc*); **l'o. des morts,** the burial service, the Office for the Dead; **livre d'o.,** prayer book; **aller à l'o.,** to go to church *or* chapel; **(d)** (*établissement*) bureau, office; **o. du tourisme,** tourist (information) office. **2** *nf* **(a)** (butler's) pantry; **(b)** *Vieilli* back kitchen, scullery; (*pour domestiques*) servants' hall.

officialisation [ɔfisjalizasjɔ̃] *nf* officialization, officializing.

officialiser [ɔfisjalize] *vt* to officialize.

officiant [ɔfisjɑ̃] *Rel* **1** *adj* officiating (*priest*). **2** *nm* officiant.

officiel, -ielle [ɔfisjɛl] **1** *adj* official (*statement, language, visit, source*); **la version officielle est le suicide,** the official version is suicide; **c'est o.,** it's official; **à titre o.,** officially, formally; **congé o.,** national holiday; **le Journal O.,** *CE* Official Journal; *Br* = the (official) Gazette. **2** *nm* **(a)** official; **(b) l'O.,** = the (official) Gazette; *Mil Nau* **être à l'O.,** to be gazetted.

officiellement [ɔfisjɛlmɑ̃] *adv* officially; **o. il a donné sa démission,** (*en fait il s'est fait renvoyer*) officially, he resigned; **il a donné sa démission o.,** (*dans les formes*) he formally resigned.

officier¹ [ɔfisje] *nm* **(a)** (*fonctionnaire*) officer; **o. de l'état** *ou* **d'état civil,** = registrar (of births, marriages and deaths); **o. ministériel,** (*notaire*) notary (public); (*huissier*) officer of the court; **(b)** *Mil* (commissioned) officer; **o. supérieur,** field officer, *US* senior officer; **o. général,** general officer, *Nau* flag officer; **o. de marine,** naval officer; *Nau* **o. de pont,** deck officer; **o. de port,** harbour master; **(c)** *Fr* **O. de la Légion d'Honneur,** Officer of the Legion of Honour *or US* Honor.

officier² *vi* (*impf & pr sub* **n. officiions**) to officiate; *Hum Fig* to do the honours.

officieusement [ɔfisjøzmɑ̃] *adv* unofficially.

officieux, -euse [ɔfisjø, -øz] *adj* unofficial (*information etc*); *Journ* **note d'origine officieuse,** inspired piece; **à titre o.,** unofficially.

officinal, -aux [ɔfisinal, -o] *adj Pharm* officinal (*preparation*); medicinal (*plant*).

officine [ɔfisin] *nf* **(a)** *Pharm* dispensary, pharmacy; **(b)** *Fig* hotbed (*of intrigue*); nest (*of spies*).

offrande [ɔfrɑ̃d] *nf* **(a)** offering, gift; **apporter son o.,** to make a donation; **(b)** *Rel* offertory; **o. votive,** votive offering.

offrant [ɔfrɑ̃] *nm* **le plus o.,** the best offer; (*at auction*) the highest bidder; **vendre au plus o.,** to sell to the highest bidder.

offre [ɔfr] *nf* offer, proposal; tender (*for contract*); bid (*at auction sale*); **faire o. de qch,** to offer sth; **recevoir/accepter une o.,** to receive/accept an offer *or* a bid; **faire des offres de service à qn,** to offer to help s.o.; *Com* to solicit orders; **o. d'emploi,** job offer; *Journ* **offres d'emploi,** vacancies; *Fin* **o. publique d'achat,** takeover bid; **faire** *ou* **lancer une o. publique d'achat,** to make a takeover bid; **o. publique d'achat à crédit,** leveraged buy-out; *Fin* **o. publique d'échange,** offer for exchange of stock; *Écon* **l'o. et la demande,** supply and demand.

offrir [ɔfrir] *v* (*prp* **offrant**; *pp* **offert** [ɔfɛr] ; *pr ind* **j'offre, n. offrons**; *p hist* **j'offris**; *fu* **j'offrirai**) **1** *vt* to give (*a present*); to offer up (*a sacrifice*); **c'est pour o.,** it's for a present; **c'est pour offrir?,** would you like it (gift) wrapped?; **o. un déjeuner à qn,** to invite s.o. to lunch, to offer s.o. lunch; **je t'offre un verre,** I'll buy *or* stand you a drink; **on lui a offert une place de mécanicien,** he was offered a job as a mechanic; **o. la main de sa fille à qn,** to offer one's daughter's hand in marriage to s.o.; **o. une résistance acharnée,** to put up stiff *or* fierce resistance; **o. de faire qch,** to offer to do sth; **o. son nom à une femme,** to propose to a woman; **o. mille francs (pour** *ou* **de qch),** to offer a thousand francs (for sth); (*aux enchères*) to bid a thousand francs (for sth); **la campagne offre des vues splendides,** the countryside offers *or Fml* affords magnificent views; **l'histoire en offre plusieurs exemples,** history gives *or Fml* affords several examples of it.

2 s'offrir *vpr* **(a) s'o. comme guide,** to offer oneself *or* one's services as a guide; **s'o. à faire qch,** to offer *or* volunteer to do sth; **s'o. aux regards,** (*d'un spectacle*) to meet *or* greet one's *etc* eyes; (*d'une personne*) to present *or* reveal oneself to the public gaze; *Péj* to flaunt oneself;

(b) s'o. un bon cigare, to treat oneself to a good cigar; **ne pas pouvoir s'o. qch,** to be unable to afford sth; **je ne peux pas m'o. une secrétaire,** I can't afford a secretary.

off-shore [ɔfʃɔr] **1** *adj Sp* **bateau o.-s.,** speedboat, powerboat; **course o.-s.,** speedboat *or* powerboat race; *Pétr* **plateforme o.-s.,** (offshore) oilrig. **2** *nm* (*bateau*) speedboat, powerboat; (*course*) speedboat *or* powerboat racing.

offusquer [ɔfyske] **1** *vt* to offend, to shock (*s.o.*). **2 s'offusquer** *vpr* **s'o. de qch,** to take offence at sth; **il s'offusque d'un rien,** he takes offence at the drop of a hat.

ogival, -aux [ɔʒival, -o] *adj Archit* ogival; gothic (*architecture*).

ogive [ɔʒiv] *nf* **(a)** *Archit* (diagonal) rib; **voûte d'ogives,** ribbed vault; **(b)** *Mil* head (*of shell*); nose cone (*of rocket*); **o. nucléaire,** nuclear warhead.

ogre, *f* **ogresse** [ɔgr, ɔgrɛs] *n* ogre, *f* ogress; **manger comme un o.,** to eat like a horse.

oh [o] *int* oh!; **oh! hisse!,** yo-heave-ho!
ohé [ɔe] *int* hi!, hullo!; *Nau* **o. du navire!,** ship ahoy!
ohm [om] *nm Él* ohm.
ohmique [omik] *adj Él* ohmic.
ohmmètre [ommɛtr] *nm Él* ohmmeter.
oïdium [ɔidjɔm] *nm* oidium, (vine) mildew.
oie [wa] *nf* goose; *Culin* **confit d'o.,** = goose preserved in goose fat; **graisse d'o.,** goose fat; **o. sauvage,** wild goose; **conte de ma mère l'O.,** Mother Goose story; *F* **ne faites pas l'o.,** don't be silly *or* an idiot; *F* **une o. blanche,** a naive young girl; **pas de l'o.,** goose step; **jeu de l'o.,** ≈ snakes and ladders.
oignon [ɔɲɔ̃] *nm* **(a)** (*légume*) onion; **petits oignons,** (*pour les salades*) spring onions; (*pour les conserves*) pickling onions; **aux petits oignons,** *Culin* with baby onions; *F* (*parfait*) first-rate; **se mettre en rang d'oignons,** to form up in a row; *Arg* **occupe-toi** *ou* **mêle-toi de tes oignons,** mind your own business; **(b)** *Bot* bulb; **(c)** *Méd* bunion; **(d)** (*montre*) turnip (watch).
oïl [ɔil] *adv Ling Hist* **la langue d'o.,** langue d'oïl (*language of northern France*).
oindre [wɛ̃dr] *vt* (*conj like* **craindre**) **(a)** *Vieilli* to (rub with) oil; **(b)** *Rel* to anoint (*king etc*).
oint [wɛ̃] *adj & nm* anointed; **l'O. du Seigneur,** the Lord's anointed.
oiseau, -eaux [wazo] *nm* bird; **oiseaux de basse-cour,** poultry; **o. de proie,** bird of prey; **oiseaux de volière** *ou* **d'appartement,** cage birds; **o. de passage,** bird of passage; *Fig* **o. de malheur** *ou* **de mauvais augure,** bird of ill omen; *Fig* **être comme l'o. sur la branche,** to be here today and gone tomorrow; *Prov* **petit à petit l'o. fait son nid,** from little acorns mighty oaks do grow; **avoir un appétit d'o.,** to eat like a bird; **à vol d'o.,** as the crow flies; *F* **l'o. s'est envolé,** the bird has flown; *F* **drôle d'o.,** (*personne*) odd type *or* sort *or* customer; **c'est l'o. rare,** he's a rare bird; **mon petit o.,** my pet; **donner à qn des noms d'o.,** to shout insults at s.o., to call s.o. names.
oiseau-mouche [wazomuʃ] *nm* hummingbird; (*pl oiseaux-mouches*).
oiseler [wazle] *v* (**il oiselle, n. oiselons; il oisellera**) **1** *vi* to go bird-catching. **2** *vt* to fly (*a hawk*).
oiseleur [wazlœr] *nm* fowler, bird catcher.
oiselier [wazəlje] *nm* bird seller.
oiselle [wazɛl] *nf* hen bird; *F* naive young girl.
oisellerie [wazɛlri] *nf* (*élevage*) bird breeding; (*vente*) bird selling.
oiseux, -euse [wazø, -øz] *adj* idle (*talk*); pointless (*discussion*); **explication oiseuse,** explanation that doesn't cut any ice *or* gets you nowhere.
oisif, -ive [wazif, -iv] **1** *adj* idle, unoccupied; **vie oisive,** idle life. **2** *n* person of leisure.
oisillon [wazijɔ̃] *nm* fledgling.
oisivement [wazivmɑ̃] *adv* idly.
oisiveté [wazivte] *nf* idleness; *Prov* **l'o. est (la) mère de tous les vices,** the Devil finds work for idle hands (to do).
oison [wazɔ̃] *nm Orn* gosling.
O.I.T. [oite] *nf* (*abrév* **Organisation internationale du travail**) ILO.
okapi [ɔkapi] *nm* okapi.
oléagineux, -euse [ɔleaʒinø, -øz] **1** *adj* oleaginous, oil-yielding; **graines oléagineuses,** oilseeds. **2** *nmpl* oilseeds.
oléiculteur [ɔleikyltœr] *nm* olive grower.
oléiculture [ɔleikyltyr] *nf* olive growing.
oléifère [ɔleifɛr] *adj* oil-producing.
oléique [ɔleik] *adj Ch* oleic (*acid*).
oléoduc [ɔleɔdyk] *nm* (oil) pipeline.
olé-olé [ɔleɔle] *adj inv F* close to the bone, near the knuckle, risqué; **il y a quelques scènes o.-o. dans ce spectacle,** the performance contains a few scenes which are a bit close to the bone.
olfactif, -ive [ɔlfaktif, -iv] *adj* olfactory (*nerves etc*).
olibrius [ɔlibrijys] *nm F Péj* oddball.
olifant [ɔlifɑ̃] *nm Litt* ivory (hunting) horn.
oligarchie [ɔligarʃi] *nf* oligarchy.
oligarchique [ɔligarʃik] *adj* oligarchic(al).
oligarque [ɔligark] *nm* oligarch.
oligo-élément [ɔligɔelemɑ̃] *nm Biol* trace element; (*pl oligo-éléments*).
oligopole [ɔligɔpɔl] *nm Écon Pol* oligopoly.
oliphant [ɔlifɑ̃] *nm Littér* ivory (hunting) horn.
olivaie [ɔlivɛ] *nf* olive plantation *or* grove.
olivâtre [ɔlivɑtr] *adj* olive(-coloured, *US* -colored); sallow (*complexion*).
olive [ɔliv] **1** *nf* olive; *Él* switch; *Archit* olive moulding *or US* molding; **huile d'o.,** olive oil. **2** *adj inv* olive green.
oliveraie [ɔlivrɛ] *nf* olive plantation *or* grove.
olivette [ɔlivɛt] *nf* **(a)** (*raisin*) olive-shaped grape; (*tomate*) plum tomato; **(b)** (*olivaie*) olive plantation *or* grove.
olivier [ɔlivje] *nm* **(a)** (*arbre*) olive (tree); **le Mont des Oliviers,** the Mount of Olives; **se présenter un rameau d'o. à la main,** to hold out the olive branch; **(b)** (*bois*) olive (wood), **un saladier en o.,** an olive-wood salad bowl.
Olivier [ɔlivje] *nm* Oliver.
ollé-ollé [ɔleɔle] *adj inv F* = **OLÉ-OLÉ.**
olographe [ɔlɔgraf] *adj Jur* holograph.
O.L.P. [ɔɛlpe] *n* (*abrév* **Organisation de libération de la Palestine**) PLO.
Olympe [ɔlɛ̃p] *nm Myth* (Mount) Olympus; **les dieux de l'O.,** the gods of Olympus.
olympiade [ɔlɛ̃pjad] *nf* olympiad.
olympien, -ienne [ɔlɛ̃pjɛ̃, -jɛn] **1** *adj* Olympian; *Fig* **calme o.,** olympian calm. **2** *n* **O.,** Olympian.
olympique [ɔlɛ̃pik] *adj* olympic (*games, champion*); **Comité international o.,** International Olympics Committee.
ombelle [ɔ̃bɛl] *nf Bot* umbel; **en o.,** umbellate.
ombellifère [ɔ̃belifɛr] *Bot* **1** *adj* umbelliferous. **2** *nfpl* **ombellifères,** Umbelliferae, umbellifers.
ombilic [ɔ̃bilik] *nm Anat* umbilicus, navel; *Bot* hilum.
ombilical, -aux [ɔ̃bilikal, -o] *adj* umbilical; **cordon o.,** umbilical cord; *Astronaut* umbilical tether (*of space suit*); *Fig* **couper le cordon o.,** to cut the umbilical cord.
omble [ɔ̃bl] *nm* (*poisson*) **o.(-chevalier),** char.
ombrage [ɔ̃braʒ] *nm* **(a)** shade (*of trees*); **(b) prendre o. de qch,** (*of person*) to take offence *or US* offense *or* umbrage at sth; (*of horse*) to shy at sth; **porter** *ou* **faire o. à qn,** to give umbrage to s.o..
ombragé [ɔ̃braʒe] *adj* shaded, shady.
ombrager [ɔ̃braʒe] *vt* (**il ombrageait**) (*d'un arbre*) to shade, to protect (*sth*) against the sun.
ombrageusement [ɔ̃braʒøzmɑ̃] *adv* (*of person*) touchily; (*of horse*) skittishly.
ombrageux, -euse [ɔ̃braʒø, -øz] *adj* (*person*) easily offended, touchy, quick to take offence *or US* offense; (*cheval*) skittish.
ombre¹ [ɔ̃br] *nf* **(a)** shadow; **projeter une o.,** to cast a shadow; **suivre qn comme son o.,** to follow *or* stick to s.o. like their shadow; *Fig* **avoir peur de son o.,** to be frightened at *or* of one's own shadow; **lâcher la proie pour l'o.,** to catch at shadows; **ombres chinoises,** shadow theatre *or* show;
(b) (*d'un arbre*) shade; **se reposer à l'o. d'un arbre,** to rest in *or* under the shade of a tree; **quarante degrés à l'o.,** forty degrees in the shade; *Fig* **il a vécu à l'o. de son village natal,** he never lived more than a stone's throw away from the village where he was born; **elle a grandi à l'o. de la Tour Eiffel,** she grew up in the shadow of *or* within a stone's throw of the Eiffel Tower; *Arg* **mettre qn à l'o.,** to put s.o. inside *or* behind bars; **jeter une o. sur la fête,** to cast a shadow *or* a gloom over the festivities; **vivre dans l'o. de qn,** to be (always) overshadowed by s.o., to live in s.o.'s shadow; **faire de l'o. à qn,** to put s.o. in the shade;
(c) (*obscurité*) darkness; **à l'o. de la nuit,** under the cover of darkness;
(d) (*être de l'au-delà*) ghost; **le royaume des ombres,** the nether world; *Fig* **n'être plus que l'o. de soi-même,** to be a mere shadow of one's former self;
(e) (*trace*) **vous n'avez pas l'o. d'une chance,** you haven't the ghost of a chance; **il n'y a pas l'o. d'un doute,** there isn't the *or* a shadow of a doubt; **une o. de méchanceté,** a hint *or* touch of malice;
(f) *Astron* umbra;
(g) *Beaux-Arts* **l'o. et la lumière,** light and shade; *Fig* **il y a une o. au tableau,** there's a fly in the ointment;
(h) (*maquillage*) **o. à paupières,** eye shadow.
ombre² *nf* **terre d'o.,** umber.
ombre³ *nm* (*poisson*) **o. (-chevalier),** char; **o. de rivière,** grayling.
ombrelle [ɔ̃brɛl] *nf* sunshade, parasol; *Zool* umbrella (*of jellyfish*).
ombrer [ɔ̃bre] *vt* to shade (*greenhouse, drawing*).
ombreux, -euse [ɔ̃brø, -øz] *adj Litt* shady (*walk, grove*).
Ombrie [ɔ̃bri] *nf* Umbria.
omelette [ɔmlɛt] *nf* omelette, *US* omelet; **o. au jambon,** ham omelette; *Culin* **o. norvégienne,** baked Alaska; *Fig* **on ne fait pas d'o. sans casser des œufs,** you can't make an omelette without breaking eggs.
omettre [ɔmɛtr] *vt* (*conj like* **mettre**) to omit, to miss out,

to leave out (*word, detail*); **o. de faire qch,** to fail *or* omit *or* neglect to do sth.

omission [ɔmisjɔ̃] *nf* (*d'un mot, détail*) omission; (*oubli*) oversight; **péché/mensonge par o.,** sin of/lying by omission; *Typ* **signe d'o.,** caret.

omnibus [ɔmnibys] **1** *nm* (*train*) slow *or* stopping train; *Arch* (*bus*) (omni)bus. **2** *adj inv* **train o.,** slow *or* stopping train; *El* **barre o.,** busbar.

omnidirectionnel, -elle [ɔmnidirɛksjɔnɛl] *adj* omnidirectional (*antenna*).

omnipotence [ɔmnipɔtɑ̃s] *nf* omnipotence.

omnipotent [ɔmnipɔtɑ̃] *adj* omnipotent, all powerful.

omnipraticien, -ienne [ɔmnipratisjɛ̃, -jɛn] *n Méd* general practitioner, *Br F* GP.

omniprésence [ɔmniprezɑ̃s] *nf* omnipresence.

omniprésent [ɔmniprezɑ̃] *adj* omnipresent.

omniscience [ɔmnisjɑ̃s] *nf* omniscience.

omniscient [ɔmnisjɑ̃] *adj* omniscient.

omnisports [ɔmnispɔr] *adj inv* **stade/centre o.,** (multi-purpose) sports stadium/centre.

omnium [ɔmnjɔm] *nm* **(a)** *Écon* combine; *Bourse* **o. de valeurs,** = investment trust; **(b)** *Sp* open; *Courses de chevaux* open handicap.

omnivore [ɔmnivɔr] **1** *adj* omnivorous. **2** *nm* omnivore.

omoplate [ɔmɔplat] *nf* shoulder blade, scapula.

O.M.S. [oɛmɛs] *nf* (*abrév* **Organisation mondiale de la santé**) WHO.

on [ɔ̃] *pron indéf* (*sometimes becomes* **l'on,** *especially after vowel sound*) **(a)** (*indéterminé*) one, people; you, we, they *etc*; **on ne sait jamais,** you never know, you never can tell; **on n'en sait rien,** nobody knows anything about it; **on n'aime pas à être traité comme ça,** people don't like to be treated like that; **partout où l'on trouve de ces fossiles,** wherever these fossils are found; **on ne connaît jamais son bonheur,** you never know how lucky you are; **quand on demande à une femme d'être sa** *ou* **votre femme,** when a man asks a woman to be his wife, when you ask a woman to be your wife; **on était le sept mars,** it was the seventh of March; **on dit qu'elle est folle,** it's said *or* they *or* people say that she's mad, she's said to be mad; **on frappe à la porte,** someone's *or* somebody's (knocking) at the door, there's a knock at the door; **on a enfoncé la porte,** the door was burst open; **on demande une bonne cuisinière,** (*annonce*) wanted, a good cook;

(b) (*précisé*) (*a following adj, noun or pp agrees in gender and number as the sense requires*) **on parlait très peu au déjeuner,** we didn't talk much over lunch; **on ne s'était jamais séparés,** we had never been separated; **on n'est pas toujours jeune et belle,** women can't be young and beautiful for ever; **où va-t-on?,** where are we going?; **alors, on s'en va comme ça?,** are you really leaving just like that?; **nous, on est tous égaux,** we're all equal here.

onagre[1] [ɔnagr] *nf* (*fleur*) evening primrose.

onagre[2] *nm* (*mammifère*) onager, wild ass.

once[1] [ɔ̃s] *nf* ounce.

once[2] *nf* (*mammifère*) ounce, snow leopard.

oncle [ɔ̃kl] *nm* uncle; **o. à la mode de Bretagne,** first cousin once removed; (*famille éloignée*) distant relation; *Fig* **un o. d'Amérique,** rich uncle; **O. Sam,** Uncle Sam.

onction [ɔ̃ksjɔ̃] *nf* (*suavité*) unction; *Méd* = massage or rubbing with oil; *Rel* **l'extrême o.,** extreme unction.

onctueusement [ɔ̃ktɥøzmɑ̃] *adv* unctuously.

onctueux, -euse [ɔ̃ktɥø, -øz] *adj* (*yaourt, sauce*) smooth, creamy; (*peinture etc*) smooth; *Péj* (*manières*) unctuous, smooth.

onctuosité [ɔ̃ktɥozite] *nf* (*de yaourt, d'une sauce*) smoothness, creaminess.

onde [ɔ̃d] *nf* **(a)** *Phys etc* wave; **o. calorifique/lumineuse/sonore,** heat/light/sound wave; *Av* **o. de choc,** shock wave; *Rad* **ondes courtes,** short wave; **ondes moyennes, petites ondes,** medium wave; **grandes ondes,** long waves; **les ondes,** the radio; **sur les ondes,** on the air *or* the radio; **passer sur les ondes,** (*d'une émission*) to be broadcast *or Am* aired; *Fig F* **nous ne sommes pas sur la même longueur d'o.,** we're not on the same wavelength; **(b)** *Métal* corrugation; **(c)** *Litt* wave, water, tide; **sur la terre et sur l'o.,** on land and water; **les ondes de la foule,** the surging of the crowd.

ondé [ɔ̃de] *adj Litt* wavy (*hair*); watered (*silk*).

ondée [ɔ̃de] *nf* sudden downpour.

ondemètre [ɔ̃dmɛtr] *nm Rad* wavemeter.

ondin, -ine [ɔ̃dɛ̃, -in] *n Myth* water sprite.

on-dit [ɔ̃di] *nm inv* rumour, *US* rumor, hearsay.

ondoiement [ɔ̃dwamɑ̃] *nm* **(a)** undulation, wavy motion (*of reeds, corn etc*); **(b)** *Rel* = baptism conducted in cases of emergency.

ondoyant [ɔ̃dwajɑ̃] *adj* **(a)** undulating (*ground*); wavy (*line, horizon*); swaying (*crowd, motion*); waving, swaying (*reeds*); **(b)** changeable (*disposition*).

ondoyer [ɔ̃dwaje] *v* (**j'ondoie; j'ondoierai**) **1** *vi* to undulate, to wave, to ripple; (*of flames etc*) to billow. **2** *vt Rel* to baptize (*in cases of emergency*).

ondulant [ɔ̃dylɑ̃] *adj* undulating (*landscape*); waving (*reeds*); flowing (*mane*).

ondulation [ɔ̃dylasjɔ̃] *nf* undulation (*of water, ground etc*); wave (*in hair*).

ondulatoire [ɔ̃dylatwar] *adj Phys* undulatory; **mouvement o.,** wave motion.

ondulé [ɔ̃dyle] *adj* undulating, rolling (*ground*); wavy, waved (*hair*); corrugated (*iron, cardboard*); **route ondulée,** switchback road; **trait o.,** wavy line.

onduler [ɔ̃dyle] **1** *vi* to undulate, to ripple. **2** *vt* to wave (*the hair*); to corrugate (*iron, cardboard*).

onduleux, -euse [ɔ̃dylø, -øz] *adj* = **ONDULANT**.

onéreux, -euse [ɔnerø, -øz] *adj* onerous (*task*); burdensome (*tax*); heavy (*expenditure*); **à titre o.,** subject to certain liabilities *or* to payment.

ongle [ɔ̃gl] *nm* (finger)nail; claw (*of animal*); talon (*of bird of prey*); **ongles des orteils,** toenails; **coup d'o.,** scratch; **se faire les ongles,** (*les couper*) to cut one's nails; (*les vernir*) to varnish *or* do one's nails; *Méd* **o. incarné,** ingrowing nail; **se ronger les ongles,** to bite one's nails; *Fig* **avoir les ongles crochus,** to be mean *or* tight-fisted; **connaître** *ou* **savoir qch sur le bout des ongles,** to know sth perfectly; **il est français jusqu'au bout des ongles,** he's French to his finger tips, he's every inch a Frenchman.

onglée [ɔ̃gle] *nf* tingling, aching (*of numbed finger tips*); **j'ai l'o.,** my fingers are numb with cold.

onglet [ɔ̃glɛ] *nm* **(a)** guard (*of a book*); tab (*of thumb index*); thumbnail groove (*of penknife*); **dictionnaire à onglets,** thumb-indexed dictionary; **(b)** *Bot* unguis, claw (*of petal*); **(c)** *Menuis* mitre, **boîte à onglets,** mitre box; **tailler à o.,** to mitre; **(d)** *Culin* (*du bœuf*) flank of beef.

onglier [ɔ̃glije] *nm* (*trousse*) manicure set.

onguent [ɔ̃gɑ̃] *nm* unguent, ointment.

onguiculé [ɔ̃gikyle] *adj Biol* unguiculate.

ongulé [ɔ̃gyle] *adj & nm Zool* ungulate.

onirique [ɔnirik] *adj Litt* oneiric.

onirisme [ɔnirism] *nm* (state of) hallucination.

onirologie [ɔnirɔlɔʒi] *nf* oneirology.

onomatopée [ɔnɔmatɔpe] *nf* onomatopoeia.

ontogenèse [ɔ̃tɔʒənɛz] *nf* ontogenesis, ontogeny.

ontogénétique [ɔ̃tɔʒenetik] *adj* ontogenetic, ontogenic.

ontologie [ɔ̃tɔlɔʒi] *nf Phil* ontology.

ontologique [ɔ̃tɔlɔʒik] *adj Phil* ontological.

O.N.U. [ɔny] *nf* (*abrév* **Organisation des Nations unies**) UN(O).

onusien, -ienne [ɔnyzjɛ̃, -jɛ̃n] **1** *adj* (of the) UN; **la politique onusienne,** UN policy. **2** *n* UN official.

onyx [ɔniks] *nm Minér* onyx; **marbre o.,** onyx marble.

onze [ɔ̃z] (*the* **e** *of* **le** *and* **de** *is not, as a rule, elided before* **onze** *and its derivatives*) **1** *adj inv* eleven; **o. cent trente,** eleven hundred and thirty; **nous n'étions que o.** [kəɔ̃z], **nous n'étions qu'o.,** there were only eleven of us; **le o. avril,** the eleventh of April; **Louis O.,** Louis the Eleventh. **2** *nm inv Fb Cr* **le o.,** the eleven, the team.

onzième [ɔ̃zjɛm] **1** *adj* eleventh; **le o. jour,** the eleventh day. **2** *n* eleventh. **3** *nm* eleventh (part). **4** *nf Mus* eleventh.

onzièmement [ɔ̃zjɛmmɑ̃] *adv* in (the) eleventh place.

oolithe [ɔɔlit] *nm Minér* oolite.

oolithique [ɔɔlitik] *adj Minér* oolitic.

O.P.A. [opea] *nf* (*abrév* **offre publique d'achat**) takeover bid; **faire** *ou* **lancer une OPA,** to make a takeover bid (**sur,** for); **OPA à crédit,** leveraged buy-out.

opacité [ɔpasite] *nm* opacity (*of body*); cloudiness (*of liquid*); darkness, denseness (*of forest*).

opale [ɔpal] **1** *nf* opal. **2** *adj inv* opalescent; **verre o.,** opal glass; *El* **ampoule o.,** pearl bulb.

opalescence [ɔpalesɑ̃s] *nf* opalescence.

opalescent [ɔpalesɑ̃] *adj* opalescent.

opalin, -ine [ɔpalɛ̃, -in] **1** *adj* opaline (*hue, reflection*). **2** *nf* opaline.

opaque [ɔpak] *adj* opaque; **collant o.,** opaque tights; **o. aux rayons X,** impervious to X-rays; *Ling* **mot o.,** opaque word.

O.P.E. [opeø] *nf abbr* **offre publique d'échange.**

open [ɔpɛn] **1** *adj inv* open; **une compétition o.,** an open competition; **un billet o.,** an open ticket. **2** *n Sp* **un o. de tennis,** a tennis open.

O.P.E.P. [ɔpɛp] *nf* (*abrév* **Organisation des pays**

exportateurs de pétrole) OPEC.
opéra [ɔpera] *nm* **(a)** opera; **il aime beaucoup l'o.,** he loves opera; **c'est une chanteuse d'o.,** she's an opera-singer; **grand o.,** grand opera; **o. bouffe,** opera bouffe, comic opera; **(b)** (*lieu*) opera house; **l'O. (de Paris),** the Paris Opera House; **les petits rats de l'O.,** = ballet pupils at the Paris Opera House.
opérable [ɔperabl] *adj Chir* operable (*patient, tumour*).
opéra-comique [ɔperakɔmik] *nm* opéra comique (*opera with spoken dialogue*); (*pl opéras-comiques*).
opérande [ɔperɑ̃d] *nm Ordinat* operand.
opérant [ɔperɑ̃] *adj* effective; **les mesures ont été opérantes,** the measures (taken) were effective.
opérateur, -trice [ɔperatœr, -tris] **1** *n* (machine) operator; *Typ* machine setter; *Tél* operator; *Cin* cameraman; **o. de radio,** radio operator; *Ordinat* **o. de saisie,** computer operator *or* keyboarder; *Fin* **o. boursier,** stock-exchange dealer. **2** *nm* **(a)** *Math* operator; **(b)** working piece (*of a machine*).
opération [ɔperasjɔ̃] *nf* **(a)** *Chir* **o. (chirurgicale),** (surgical) operation; **subir une o.,** to undergo *or* have an operation; **salle d'o.,** operating theatre *or US* room; **o. à chaud,** emergency operation (*for appendicitis etc*); **(b)** *Math Mil* operation; *Fin* (commercial) transaction; **opérations militaires,** military operations; **o. publicitaire,** advertising campaign; **opérations de Bourse,** Stock Exchange dealings *or* business *or* transactions; **(c)** operation, process; **par l'o. du Saint-Esprit,** by the operation of the Holy Ghost; *F* by magic.
opérationnel, -elle [ɔperasjɔnɛl] *adj* operational.
opératoire [ɔperatwar] *adj Chir* operative (*procedure etc*); **médecine o.,** surgery; **choc o.,** post-operative shock; **bloc o.,** operating wing (*in hospital*).
opercule [ɔpɛrkyl] *nm* cover, lid, cap; *Biol* operculum, gill cover (*of fish*); *Nau* **o. de hublot,** deadlight.
operculé [ɔpɛrkyle] *adj Biol* operculate(d).
opéré, -ée [ɔpere] *n* patient (who has had an operation).
opérer [ɔpere] *v* (**j'opère; j'opérerai**) **1** *vt* to bring about, to work, to effect; to perform (*multiplication, Ch synthesis etc*); **o. une réforme,** to carry out a reform; **o. une retraite,** to (effect a) retreat; **o. un sondage,** to sink a borehole; (*d'opinion*) to carry out *or* conduct an opinion poll; *Chir* **o. un malade/un abcès,** to operate on a patient/an abscess; **être opéré de l'appendicite,** to be operated on for appendicitis; **se faire o.,** to undergo *or* have an operation. **2** *vi* (*d'un médicament*) to take effect; **laisser o. la nature,** to let nature take its course; **son éloquence opéra sur la foule,** his eloquence swayed the crowd; **la façon dont les cambrioleurs ont opéré,** the way the burglars operated *or* went to work. **3 s'opérer** *vpr* to come about, to take place; **un changement complet s'est opéré dans sa vie,** his life has changed completely.
opérette [ɔperɛt] *nf* operetta; **chanteuse d'o.,** operetta singer; *Fig* **héros d'o.,** cardboard *or* two-dimensional *or* conventional hero.
ophidien, -ienne [ɔfidjɛ̃, -jɛn] *adj & nm* ophidian.
ophite [ɔfit] *nm Minér* ophite, serpentine.
ophrys [ɔfris] *nm* ophrys; **o. abeille,** bee orchid; **o. araignée,** spider orchid.
ophtalmie [ɔftalmi] *nf Méd* ophthalmia; **o. des neiges,** snow blindness.
ophtalmique [ɔftalmik] *adj Méd* ophthalmic.
ophtalmo [ɔftalmo] *n Méd F* ophthalmologist.
ophtalmologie [ɔftalmɔlɔʒi] *nf Méd* ophthalmology.
ophtalmologiste [ɔftalmɔlɔʒist], **ophtalmologue** [ɔftalmɔlɔg] *n Méd* ophthalmologist.
ophtalmoscope [ɔftalmɔskɔp] *nm Méd* ophthalmoscope.
opiacé [ɔpjase] *adj* containing opium.
opiacer [ɔpjase] *vt* (**j'opiaçai(s); n. opiaçons**) to mix with opium.
opiner [ɔpine] *vi* **o. pour/contre qch,** to pronounce oneself in favour of/against sth; **o. sur qch,** to give one's opinion on sth; *Fig* **o. du chef** *ou* **de la tête** *ou* **du bonnet,** to nod (one's) approval, to signify (one's) assent.
opiniâtre [ɔpinjɑtr] *adj* (*tenace*) obstinate, stubborn (*person*); persistent (*cough*); unyielding (*opposition*); stout, dogged (*resistance*).
opiniâtrement [ɔpinjɑtrəmɑ̃] *adv* obstinately, stubbornly; (*to resist*) stoutly, doggedly.
opiniâtreté [ɔpinjɑtrəte] *nf Vieilli* (*obstination*) obstinacy, stubbornness; (*persévérance*) perseverance, determination.
opinion [ɔpinjɔ̃] *nf* opinion (**de,** of; **sur,** about); **opinions politiques,** political opinions *or* views; **liberté d'o.,** freedom of thought *or* opinion; **journal d'o.,** = political weekly or monthly (with a particular stance); **o. publique,** public opinion; **créer un mouvement d'o.,** to create a groundswell of opinion; **sondage d'o.,** opinion poll; **émettre une o.,** to express an opinion; **sans o.,** (*dans un sondage*) Don't know; **les opinions sont partagées,** opinion is divided; **partager l'o. de qn,** to agree with s.o.; **partager les opinions de qn,** to share s.o.'s opinion(s) *or* views, to think the same way as s.o.; **avoir le courage de ses opinions,** to have the courage of one's convictions; **amener qn à son o.,** to bring s.o. round to one's way of thinking; **avoir bonne/mauvaise o. de qn,** to have a good/bad opinion of s.o.; **donner bonne o. de soi,** to make a good impression.
opiomane [ɔpjɔman] *n* opium addict.
opium [ɔpjɔm] *nm* opium; *Fig* **la religion est l'o. du peuple,** religion is the opium of the people; *Hist* **guerre de l'o.,** opium war.
opossum [ɔpɔsɔm] *nm* (*marsupial*) opossum.
opportun, -une [ɔpɔrtœ̃, -yn] *adj* **(a)** opportune, timely, well-timed (*arrival*); convenient (*time*); **arriver au moment o.,** to arrive at an opportune *or* the right moment; **(b)** expedient, advisable (*course of action*).
opportunément [ɔpɔrtynemɑ̃] *adv* opportunely, at the right moment.
opportunisme [ɔpɔrtynism] *nm* opportunism.
opportuniste [ɔpɔrtynist] **1** *adj* opportunist(ic). **2** *n* opportunist.
opportunité [ɔpɔrtynite] *nf* opportuneness, timeliness (*of arrival etc*); expediency, advisability (*of project etc*).
opposant, -ante [ɔpozɑ̃, -ɑ̃t] **1** *adj* opposing, adverse (*party etc*). **2** *n* opponent; *Pol* member of the Opposition.
opposé [ɔpoze] **1** *adj* **(a)** opposing, opposed (*armies, characters etc*); opposite (*side, shore, direction*); conflicting (*interests, advice*); **angles opposés par le sommet,** vertically opposite angles; **leurs opinions sont diamétralement opposées,** their views are poles apart *or* diametrically opposed; **tons opposés,** contrasting colours;
(b) être o. à une mesure/à ce que qch se fasse, to oppose *or* be opposed to *or* be against a measure/sth being done.
2 *nm* **(a) l'o.,** the contrary *or* reverse *or* opposite (*of sth*); **à l'o.,** on the contrary; **le deuxième film de ce réalisateur est vraiment l'o. du premier,** the director's second film is the complete opposite of *or* is in complete contrast to his first, **à l'o. de ce que nous attendions,** contrary to expectation *or* what we expected;
(b) la gare est à l'o., the station is in the opposite direction.
opposer [ɔpoze] **1** *vt* to oppose; **o. qch à qch,** to set sth against *or* opposite sth; **je n'ai rien à o. à ce raisonnement,** I have no objection to this argument; **o. une vigoureuse résistance,** to put up *or* offer vigorous resistance, *F* to resist tooth and nail; **o. son veto,** to exercise one's veto; **o. le vice à la vertu,** to contrast vice with virtue; **cette course oppose les meilleurs athlètes de toute l'Europe,** this race brings together Europe's finest athletes.
2 s'opposer *vpr* **s'o. à qch,** to oppose sth, to be opposed to sth; **s'o. résolument à qch,** to be resolutely opposed to sth; **s'o. à un projet/à un mariage,** to oppose *or* be against a plan *or* scheme/marriage; (*faire obstacle*) to stand in the way of a scheme/a marriage; **il n'y a pas de loi qui s'y oppose,** there is no law against it; **rien ne s'oppose à votre succès,** nothing stands between you and success; **les meilleurs joueurs d'échecs s'opposent dans ce tournoi,** this tournament pits the best chess players against one another, the best chess players come up against each other in this tournament.
opposite [ɔpozit] *nm* **à l'o. de,** opposite, facing.
opposition [ɔpozisjɔ̃] *nf* **(a)** opposition; **mettre o. à qch,** to oppose sth; **agir en o. avec la loi,** to contravene the law; *Pol* **l'o.,** the Opposition; **faire o. à un chèque,** to stop payment of a cheque; **(b)** *Jur* caveat; **o. sur titre,** attachment against securities; **jugement susceptible d'o.,** judgment liable to stay of execution; **(c)** (*contraste*) contrast, antithesis; **c'est en o. totale avec les principes qu'il expose dans ses livres,** it is in total contradiction to *or* it totally contradicts the principles that he puts forward in his books; **par o. à qch,** as opposed to sth; **couleurs en o.,** contrasting colours; **(d)** *Astron* opposition (*of planets*).
oppressant [ɔpresɑ̃] *adj* (*chaleur, sentiment*) oppressive.
oppresser [ɔprese] *vt* **(a)** to cause (*s.o.*) difficulty in breathing; **(b)** (*de problèmes, responsabilités*) to weigh (*s.o.*) down; **(c)** = **OPPRIMER**.
oppresseur [ɔpresœr] **1** *nm* oppressor. **2** *adj* oppressive, tyrannical.
oppressif, -ive [ɔpresif, -iv] *adj* oppressive (*government*

etc).

oppression [ɔprɛsjɔ̃] *nf* **(a)** (*d'un peuple*) oppression; **(b)** *Méd* **o. de la poitrine,** tightness of the chest, difficulty in breathing.

oppressivement [ɔprɛsivmɑ̃] *adv* oppressively, tyrannically.

opprimé, -ée [ɔprime] **1** *adj* oppressed, down-trodden; **un peuple opprimé qui se rebelle,** an oppressed people in revolt. **2** *n* **les opprimés,** the oppressed.

opprimer [ɔprime] *vt* to oppress (*a people, a nation*); to suppress (*freedom*).

opprobre [ɔprɔbr] *nm Litt* opprobrium; **jeter l'o. sur qn,** to cast opprobrium on s.o.; **accabler** *ou* **couvrir qn d'o.,** to heap opprobrium on s.o..

optatif, -ive [ɔptatif, -iv] *adj & nm Ling* optative (mood).

opter [ɔpte] *vi* to opt; **o. entre deux choses,** to choose between two things; **o. pour qch,** to opt for sth; **tu devras o. pour l'une des deux choses,** you'll have to opt for one of two things.

opticien, -ienne [ɔptisjɛ̃, -jɛn] *n* optician.

optimal, -aux [ɔptimal, -o] *adj* optimum, optimal.

optimisme [ɔptimism] *nm* optimism; **il faut voir les choses avec o.,** we must look at things optimistically; **il fait preuve de beaucoup d'o.,** he shows a great deal of optimism.

optimiste [ɔptimist] **1** *adj* optimistic; **sois un peu o., les choses vont s'arranger,** try to be optimistic *or* look on the bright side, everything will work out fine in the end; **nous ne sommes pas très optimistes quant à la guérison de ce malade,** we're not very optimistic about the patient's chances of recovery *or* that the patient will recover. **2** *n* optimist.

optimum [ɔptimɔm] (*pl optimums, parfois optima*) **1** *adj* optimum (*conditions*); **la température o.** *ou* **optima ne dépassera pas 5 degrés,** the maximum temperature will not exceed 5 degrees. **2** *nm* optimum; **o. de population,** optimum population density.

option [ɔpsjɔ̃] *nf* option, choice (**de,** of; **entre,** between); **sur ce modèle d'appareil photo, le flash est en o.,** on this model of camera, the flash is an optional extra; *Bourse* **o. d'achat** *ou* **pour acheter,** call (option); *Bourse* **o. de vente,** put (option); *Bourse* **jour d'o.,** option day; **o. pour un sujet de film,** option on the film rights (*of a book*); *Scol* **matières à o.,** optional *or* elective subjects; **il a passé le latin en o. au baccalauréat,** he took Latin as an option *or* an optional subject *or* an elective (subject) for the baccalauréat.

optionnel, -elle [ɔpsjɔnɛl] *adj* optional.

optique [ɔptik] **1** *adj* optic (*nerve*); optic, visual (*angle*); optical (*microscope*); **télégraphie o.,** visual signalling; **verre o.,** optical glass. **2** *nf* **(a)** optics; **instruments d'o.,** optical instruments; **o. électronique,** electron optics; **transmettre par o.,** to communicate by visual signals; **(b)** (*perspective*) point of view; (*manière de voir*) way of looking at things; **o. du théâtre,** stage perspective; **(c)** optical system (*of projector etc*).

optométriste [ɔptɔmetrist] *n* optometrist.

opulence [ɔpylɑ̃s] *nf* opulence, affluence; *Fig* fullness, ampleness (*of bosom, form etc*); **nager dans l'o.,** to be rolling in money.

opulent [ɔpylɑ̃] *adj* opulent (*furnishings, surroundings*); rich, monied, wealthy, affluent (*person*); abundant (*harvest*); buxom (*figure*); **une poitrine opulente,** an ample bosom.

opuscule [ɔpyskyl] *nm* (*brochure*) opuscule.

or¹ [ɔr] *nm* **(a)** gold; **la ruée vers l'or,** the gold rush; **chercheur d'or,** gold-prospector; *Fig* gold-digger; **mine d'or,** gold-mine; *Fig* **cette boutique est une véritable mine d'or pour les collectionneurs,** this shop is a real gold mine *or* treasure trove for collectors; **or noir,** oil, black gold; **or en barre,** ingot gold, (gold) bullion; *Fig* **c'est de l'or en barres,** it's as safe as the Bank of England *or* as houses; *Fin* **étalon or,** gold standard; **poudre d'or,** gold dust; **montre en or** *ou* **d'or,** gold watch; **bracelet doré à l'or fin,** a fine gold (plated) bracelet; **en or massif,** (in) solid gold; *F* **j'ai une femme en or,** I've a wonderful wife; **or en feuille(s),** gold foil; **feuille d'or,** gold leaf; **payer qch à prix d'or,** to pay a fortune for sth; **affaire en or,** (*achat*) excellent bargain; (*commerce, combine*) lucrative line of business; **il vaut son pesant d'or,** he's worth his weight in gold; **l'âge d'or,** the golden age; **cœur d'or,** heart of gold; **parler d'or,** to speak words of wisdom; **livre d'or,** (official) visitors' book; **rouler sur l'or, être (tout) cousu d'or,** to be rolling in money, to have money coming out of one's ears; *Prov* **tout ce qui brille n'est pas or,** all that glitters or glistens is not gold; **le silence est d'or,** silence is golden; **(b)** (*couleur*) gold (colour, *US* color); *Hér* or; **vieil or,** old gold; **chevelure d'or,** golden hair.

or² *conj* now (then); (*pour conclure*) well (then); **or, pour revenir à ce que nous disions,** now to come back to what we were saying; **or..., donc...,** now..., therefore...; **avant de le lire, je pensais que le livre était bon — or, il ne l'était pas,** before reading it, I thought the book was good — well, it wasn't; **je n'achète jamais de chocolats, o., la semaine dernière j'en ai acheté une grosse boîte,** I never buy chocolates, and then, last week, I bought a huge box.

oracle [ɔrɑkl] *nm* oracle; **parler d'un ton d'o.,** to speak with assurance.

orage [ɔraʒ] *nm* (thunder)storm; **le temps est à l'o.,** the weather's thundery, there's thunder in the air; **il va faire de l'o., il y a de l'o. dans l'air,** there's a storm brewing; **o. magnétique,** magnetic storm; *Fig* **tenir tête à l'o.,** to face the music.

orageusement [ɔraʒøzmɑ̃] *adv* stormily.

orageux, -euse [ɔraʒø, -øz] *adj* thundery, stormy (*weather etc*); stormy (*season, sea*); stormy, tempestuous (*life etc*); heated (*discussion*).

oraison [ɔrɛzɔ̃] *nf* prayer; **faire** *ou* **dire** *ou* **réciter une o.,** to say one's prayers; **o. funèbre,** funeral oration.

oral, -aux [ɔral, -o] **1** *adj* oral (*tradition, teaching, examination*); oral, verbal (*deposition, communication*); *Anat* oral (*cavity*); **par voie orale,** (*transmettre des traditions*) orally, by word of mouth; *Méd* orally; *Psy* **stade o.,** oral stage. **2** *nm* oral examination; *surtout Univ* viva voce examination, *F* oral, viva.

oralement [ɔralmɑ̃] *adv* (*transmettre des traditions*) orally, by word of mouth; *Méd* orally.

orange [ɔrɑ̃ʒ] **1** *nf* orange; **o. amère,** bitter orange, Seville orange; **o. sanguine,** blood orange; **o. pressée,** freshly-squeezed orange drink; **peau d'o.,** orange peel. **2** *nm* orange (colour, *US* color). **3** *adj inv* orange(-coloured, *US* -colored); **carte o.,** (*pour les transports parisiens*) = monthly season (ticket).

orangé [ɔrɑ̃ʒe] *adj & nm* orange (colour, *US* color); orange-coloured *or US* -colored.

orangeade [ɔrɑ̃ʒad] *nf* orangeade.

oranger [ɔrɑ̃ʒe] *nm* orange tree; **fleur d'o.,** orange blossom; **eau de fleur d'o.,** orange-flower water.

orangeraie [ɔrɑ̃ʒrɛ] *nf* orange grove.

orangerie [ɔrɑ̃ʒri] *nf* orangery.

orang-outan(g) [ɔrɑ̃utɑ̃] *nm* orang-outang, orang-utan; (*pl orangs-outans*).

orateur, -trice [ɔratœr, -tris] *n* orator; (*at dinner etc*) speaker.

oratoire¹ [ɔratwar] *adj* oratorical (*talent, gesture*); **l'art o.,** (the art of) oratory, public speaking; **il a pris des précautions oratoires,** he chose his remarks carefully.

oratoire² *nm Rel* **(a)** oratory, chapel for private prayer; **(b) l'O.,** the Oratory.

oratorio [ɔratɔrjo] *nm Mus* oratorio.

orbe¹ [ɔrb] *nm* orb.

orbe² *adj* **mur o.,** blind wall.

orbitaire [ɔrbitɛr] *adj Anat* orbital (*nerve etc*).

orbital, -aux [ɔrbital, -o] *adj* orbital (*motion*).

orbite [ɔrbit] *nf* **(a)** orbit (*of planet, spacecraft, electron*); **en** *ou* **sur o.,** orbiting, in orbit; **mettre un satellite en** *ou* **sur o.,** to put a satellite in *or* into orbit; **(b)** orbit, (sphere of) influence; **(c)** *Anat* socket, orbit (*of the eye*).

orbiter [ɔrbite] *vi* to orbit.

Orcades (les) [lezɔrkad] *nfpl* the Orkneys, the Orkney Islands.

orchestral, -aux [ɔrkɛstral, -o] *adj* orchestral.

orchestration [ɔrkɛstrasjɔ̃] *nf* **(a)** *Mus* orchestration, scoring; **faire une nouvelle o. d'un morceau,** to re-orchestrate a piece; **(b)** orchestration, organization (*of campaign*).

orchestre [ɔrkɛstr] *nm Mus* orchestra; **diriger un o.,** to conduct an orchestra; **chef d'o.,** conductor; **o. de chambre,** chamber orchestra; **o. de jazz,** jazz band; *Th* **(fauteuil d')o.,** (seat in the) stalls.

orchestrer [ɔrkɛstre] *vt Mus* to orchestrate (*piece of music*); to score (*opera etc*); *Fig* (*organiser*) to orchestrate, to organize (*campaign etc*).

orchidée [ɔrkide] *nf* orchid.

orchis [ɔrkis] *nm* orchis, wild orchid; **o. militaire,** military *or* soldier orchid; **o. à deux feuilles,** butterfly orchid.

ordalie [ɔrdali] *nf Hist* ordeal; **o. par l'eau/le feu,** ordeal by water/fire.

ordinaire [ɔrdinɛr] **1** *adj* ordinary, usual, normal, common; **vêtements ordinaires,** ordinary *or* everyday clothes; **vin o.,** table *or US* jug wine; **peu** *ou* **pas o.,** unusual, uncommon, out of the ordinary; **gens ordinaires,** ordinary *or* common people; *F* **celle-là n'est pas o.!,** that's a bit much!; *Math* **fractions ordinaires,** vulgar fractions; *Fin* **actions ordinaires,** ordinary shares; **votre fournisseur o.,** your normal *or* regular *or* usual supplier; **médecin o. du roi,** physician in ordinary to the king; **évêque o.,** diocesan bishop; **de taille o.,** ordinary-sized, average-sized; (*une personne*) of average height; **vin très o.,** very ordinary wine.

2 *nm* **(a)** (*habitude*) custom, usual practice; **comme à son o.,** as he usually does; **d'o., à l'o.,** usually, as a rule; **comme à l'o., comme d'o.,** as usual;

(b) (*moyenne*) usual state of things; **cela sort de l'o.,** it's unusual *or* out of the ordinary; **intelligence au-dessus de l'o.,** above-average intelligence;

(c) standard menu (*at inn etc*); *Mil* (company) mess; **auberge où l'o. est excellent,** inn where the food is excellent; *Mil* **fonds d'o.,** mess fund;

(d) *Cathol* **l'o. de la messe,** the ordinary of the mass.

ordinairement [ɔrdinɛrmɑ̃] *adv* as a rule, ordinarily, usually.

ordinal, -aux [ɔrdinal, -o] *adj* ordinal (*adjective etc*).

ordinateur [ɔrdinatœr] *nm* **(a)** computer; **o. autonome,** stand-alone computer; **o. personnel** *ou* **individuel,** personal computer; **o. portable,** portable (computer); **o. central,** mainframe computer; **(b)** *Rel* ordainer.

ordination [ɔrdinasjɔ̃] *nf Rel* ordination.

ordonnance [ɔrdɔnɑ̃s] *nf* **(a)** (*disposition*) order, (general) arrangement (*of building etc*); disposition, grouping (*in a picture etc*); **(b)** (*ordre*) statute, enactment, ordinance, order; *Jur* order, ruling (*of judge sitting alone*); **o. d'amnistie,** amnesty ordinance; **o. de police,** police regulation; *Fin* **o. de paiement,** order *or* warrant for payment; **(c)** *Méd* prescription; **délivré seulement sur o.,** available only on prescription; **(d)** *Mil* orderly; *Mil* **habit d'o.,** uniform; **bottes d'o.,** issue boots; **revolver d'o.,** service revolver; **officier d'o.,** aide-de-camp; *Nau* flag lieutenant.

ordonnancement [ɔrdɔnɑ̃smɑ̃] *nm Admin* order to pay; *Ind* scheduling (*of production*).

ordonnancer [ɔrdɔnɑ̃se] *vt* (**j'ordonnançai(s); n. ordonnançons**) *Admin* to authorize.

ordonnateur, -trice [ɔrdɔnatœr, -tris] *n* **(a)** director; (*à un spectacle*) master of ceremonies; **o. des pompes funèbres,** funeral director (*at the funeral itself*); **(b)** *Admin* person authorized to pass accounts.

ordonné, -ée [ɔrdɔne] **1** *adj* **(a)** orderly, well ordered (*life, arrangement*); *Ordinat* **traitement non o.,** random processing; **(b)** (*person*) of regular habits; tidy (*person*). **2** *nf Math* **ordonnée,** ordinate; **axe des ordonnées,** Y-axis.

ordonner [ɔrdɔne] *vt* **(a)** (*mettre de l'ordre*) to arrange (*sth*); to set (*sth*) to rights; *Math* to arrange (*terms*) in ascending *or* descending order; **(b)** (*donner un ordre*) to order, to command, to direct; **o. à qn de faire qch,** to order s.o. *or* give s.o. orders to do sth; **o. à qn de se taire,** to tell s.o. to be quiet; **o. une grève,** to call a strike; **o. une enquête,** to order an enquiry; *Méd* **o. un remède à qn,** to prescribe a remedy for s.o.; **(c)** *Jur* (*statuer*) to ordain, to rule; *Rel* **o. qn prêtre,** to ordain s.o. as a priest.

ordre [ɔrdr] *nm* **(a)** (*organisation*) order; **o. alphabétique/chronologique,** alphabetical/chronological order; **procéder par o.,** to do things in order; *Th* **distribution par o. d'entrée en scène** *ou Cin TV* **par o. d'apparition de l'écran,** cast in order of appearance; **numéro d'o.,** serial number; *Fig* **c'est dans l'o. des choses,** it's in the nature of things; *Mil* **o. de bataille,** battle array; **avec o.,** methodically; **travail sans o.,** untidy *or* unmethodical work; **travailler sans o.,** to work unmethodically; **manque d'o.,** untidiness; **en bon o.,** (*de façon réglée*) in (an) orderly manner; (*comme cela doit être*) in good order; **homme d'o.,** orderly man; (*être pour l'ordre public*) law and order man; **avoir de l'o.,** (*ranger ses affaires*) to be tidy; (*être méthodique*) to be methodical *or* systematic; **(re)mettre de l'o. dans qch,** to put (*sth*) (back) in order; (*ranger ses affaires*) to tidy (up) (*room*); **mettre de l'o. dans ses affaires, mettre ses affaires en o.,** (*arranger, régler*) to put one's affairs in order, to settle one's affairs; *Fig* to set one's house in order; **tout est en o.,** everything is in order; **en o. de marche,** (*machine etc*) in working order; **o. du jour,** agenda (*of meeting*); *Mil* general orders, order of the day; *Mil* **cité à l'o. du jour,** = mentioned in despatches; *Fig* **la guerre froide est à l'o. du jour,** the cold war is very much in the news;

(b) (*discipline*) orderliness, discipline; **o. public,** law and order; **atteinte à l'o. public,** breach of the peace; **troubler l'o. public,** to cause a breach of the peace; **assurer l'o.,** to preserve (law and) order; **maintenir l'o.,** to maintain order; **rétablir l'o.,** to restore order; **les forces de l'o.,** the forces of law and order, the police (*especially at demonstration etc*); **rappeler qn à l'o.,** to call s.o. to order; **tout est rentré dans l'o.,** everything has returned to normal; (*après une émeute etc*) order has been restored; **idées qui renversent l'o. établi,** ideas that upset the established order (of things);

(c) (*catégorie*) *Biol Archit* order; **ordres grecs,** classical orders; **o. des carnivores,** order of carnivores; *Hist* **les trois ordres (de l'État),** the three orders *or* classes (of the State); **de premier o.,** first-class, first-rate; **hôtel de troisième o.,** third-rate hotel; **tireur de premier o.,** crack shot; **renseignement d'o. général,** general information; **d'o. privé,** of a private nature; **dans un tout autre o. d'idées,** in a quite different connection, of a quite different nature; **de l'o. de dix tonnes,** in the order of *or* in the region of *or* about ten tonnes;

(d) (*communauté*) order; **o. religieux,** religious *or* monastic order; **o. de chevalerie,** order of knighthood; **o. de la Légion d'Honneur,** Order of the Legion of Honour *or US* Honor; **o. des avocats,** ≈ the Bar; **o. des médecins,** ≈ the (British, American *etc*) Medical Association; *Rel* **les ordres,** holy orders; **entrer dans les ordres,** to take holy orders;

(e) (*acte d'autorité*) order, command; **o. d'exécution,** death warrant; *Ind etc* order to perform; **donner o. à qn de faire qch,** to order s.o. to do sth; **donner des ordres à qn,** to give s.o. orders, to order s.o. about; **par o.** *ou* **sur l'o. de qn,** on the order of s.o.; **n'obéir qu'aux ordres du patron,** to take orders only from the boss; **se mettre aux ordres de qn,** to put oneself at s.o.'s disposal; **être aux ordres de qn,** to be at s.o.'s disposal; **jusqu'à nouvel o.,** until further orders *or* notice; (*pour le moment*) for the time being; **à moins d'o.** *ou* **sauf o. contraire,** in the absence of orders to the contrary, unless otherwise directed; **mot d'o.,** watchword; *Mil* **o. d'appel (sous les drapeaux),** call-up papers; **o. de comparaître,** summons to attend; **à vos ordres, mon général!,** (*to a general*) yes sir!;

(f) *Fin Com* order; **payez à l'o. de J. Martin,** pay to the order of J. Martin; **o. d'achat,** purchase order; **billet à o.,** bill of exchange payable to order; **o. de bourse,** Stock Exchange order;

(g) *Ordinat* instruction, statement.

ordure [ɔrdyr] *nf* **(a)** (*crasse*) dirt, filth, muck; **(b)** (*objets*) **ordures,** rubbish, refuse; **ordures ménagères,** household rubbish *or* refuse *or Am* garbage; **boîte à ordures** *ou* **aux ordures,** dustbin, refuse bin, *Am* trash can, garbage can; **jeter** *ou* **mettre aux ordures,** to throw in the bin; **(c)** (*in talk, writing*) filthiness, smut; **dire/écrire des ordures,** to talk/write smut; **se vautrer dans l'o.,** to wallow in filth; **(d)** *Fig Péj* **il exploite tout le monde, c'est vraiment une o.,** he exploits everybody, he's a real shit.

ordurier, -ière [ɔrdyrje, -jɛr] *adj* smutty, filthy, foul (*book, song, language*).

oréade [ɔread] *nf Myth* oread.

orée [ɔre] *nf* **à l'o. de la forêt/du bois,** on the edge of the forest/wood.

oreillard [ɔrɛjar] *nm* **(a)** *Zool* long-eared bat; **(b)** (*d'un fauteuil*) wing.

oreille [ɔrɛj] *nf* **(a)** ear; *Anat* **o. externe/moyenne/interne,** outer/middle/inner ear; **avoir mal à l'o.** *ou* **aux oreilles,** to have earache; **aux oreilles courtes,** short-eared; **à longues oreilles,** long-eared; **mettre** *ou* **porter son chapeau sur l'o.,** to cock one's hat, to wear one's hat over one ear; **baisser l'o., avoir l'o. basse,** to be crestfallen; **il partit l'o. basse,** he went off with his tail between his legs; **coucher les oreilles,** (*d'un cheval*) to set *or* lay its ears back; **tirer les oreilles à qn,** to pull *or* tweak s.o.'s ears; *Fig* to give s.o. a telling off; *F* **il s'est (bien) fait tirer l'o.,** he took a lot of coaxing; **il ne s'est pas fait tirer l'o.,** he didn't have to be asked twice; **montrer le bout de l'o.,** to show one's true colours; **rougir jusqu'aux oreilles,** to go as red as a beetroot; **n'écouter que d'une o.,** to listen with half an ear; *F* **ça lui entre par une o. et ça sort par l'autre,** it goes in one ear and out the other; **dire** *ou* **souffler qch à l'o. de qn** *ou* **dans le creux de l'o. de qn,** to whisper sth in s.o.'s ear; **dresser** *ou* **tendre l'o.,** to prick up one's ears; **être tout oreilles,** to be all ears; **prêter l'o. à qn,** to lend an ear to s.o.; **je n'en crois pas mes oreilles,** I can't believe my ears *or* what I'm hearing; **faire la sourde o.,** to turn a deaf ear; **ce n'est pas tombé dans**

l'o. d'un sourd, it did not fall on deaf ears; **il n'entend pas de cette o.-là,** he is deaf in that ear; *Fig* **il ne l'entend pas de cette o.-là,** he won't hear of it; *F* **(é)chauffer les oreilles à qn,** to annoy s.o., to get on s.o.'s nerves; **casser les oreilles à qn,** (*with noise*) to split s.o.'s eardrums *or* drive s.o. crazy; (*with questions*) to drive s.o. crazy; **dire de bouche à o.,** to tell by word of mouth; **c'est le bouche à o. qui a fait le succès de ce film,** it was word of mouth that made this film a hit; **mettre la puce à l'o. à qn,** to set s.o. thinking, to make s.o. suspicious; **rebattre les oreilles à qn de qch,** to din sth into s.o.'s ears; **être dur d'o.,** to be hard of hearing; *Fig* **vous pouvez dormir sur vos deux oreilles,** you can sleep easily in your bed; **avoir l'o. juste, avoir de l'o.,** (*pour la musique*) to have a good ear *or* an ear for music;

(b) wing (*of armchair*); handle (*of dish, vase*); ear flap (*of cap*); **écrou à oreilles,** butterfly nut.

oreiller [ɔreje] *nm* pillow; **taie d'o.,** pillow case; **sur l'o.,** in bed; **confidences sur l'o.,** pillow talk.

oreillette [ɔrɛjɛt] *nf* **(a)** *Anat* auricle (*of the heart*); **(b) fauteuil à oreillettes,** wing chair; **casquette à oreillettes,** cap with ear flaps.

oreillons [ɔrɛjɔ̃] *nmpl Méd* mumps.

Orénoque (l') [lɔrenɔk] *nm* the Orinoco (river).

ores [ɔr] *adv Arch* now; (*still used in*) **d'o. et déjà,** (*désormais*) from now on; (*à ce moment précis*) here and now.

orfèvre [ɔrfɛvr] *nm* goldsmith, silversmith; **être o. en la matière,** to be an expert in the matter.

orfèvrerie [ɔrfɛvrəri] *nf* (*métier*) goldsmith's trade; (*magasin*) goldsmith's shop; (*objet*) (gold, silver) plate.

orfraie [ɔrfrɛ] *nf Orn* sea eagle; *F* **pousser des cris d'o.,** to shriek at the top of one's voice.

organdi [ɔrgɑ̃di] *nm Tex* organdie.

organe [ɔrgan] *nm* **(a)** *Physiol* organ; **les organes genitaux,** the genital organs, the genitals, the genitalia; **(b)** (*élément*) part, component (*of machine*); **organes de transmission,** transmission gear; *Ordinat* **o. d'entrée,** input unit; **(c)** (*instrument*) organ; **o. de publicité,** advertising agency; **o. de presse,** (*publication*) organ of the press, newspaper; **l'o. officiel du parti,** the official organ of the party; **(d)** (*voix*) voice; **o. mâle et sonore,** manly voice.

organigramme [ɔrganigram] *nm* organization chart; *Ordinat* (data) flow chart.

organique [ɔrganik] *adj* organic (*disease, chemistry, law*).

organiquement [ɔrganikmɑ̃] *adv* organically.

organisateur, -trice [ɔrganizatœr, -tris] **1** *adj* organizing. **2** *n* organizer; promoter (*of boxing match etc*).

organisation [ɔrganizɑsjɔ̃] *nf* **(a)** (*planification*) organization, organizing, planning; **qualités d'o.,** organizing ability; *Ordinat* **o. des données,** data organization; **o. scientifique du travail,** organization and methods;

(b) (*business etc*) organization; **o. de voyage,** travel agent's, tour company; **o. politique/syndicale,** political/trade-union organization; **O. de l'alimentation et l'agriculture,** Food and Agriculture Organization; *Hist* **O. de l'armée secrète,** Secret Army Organization (= *right-wing group opposed to Algerian independence*); **O. de l'aviation civile internationale,** International Civil Aviation Authority; **O. de coopération et de développement économique,** Organization for Economic Cooperation and Development; **O. internationale du travail,** International Labour Organization; **O. de libération de la Palestine,** Palestine Liberation Organization; **O. mondiale de la santé,** World Health Organization; **O. des Nations unies,** United Nations Organization; **O. des Nations unies pour l'éducation, la science et la culture,** United Nations Educational, Scientific and Cultural Organization; **O. des pays exportateurs de pétrole,** Organization of Petroleum Exporting Countries; **O. du traité de l'Atlantique Nord,** North Atlantic Treaty Organization; **O. de l'unité africaine,** Organization of African Unity;

(c) *Biol* structure (*of human body etc*).

organisationnel, -elle [organizasjɔnɛl] *adj* organizational.

organisé [ɔrganize] *adj* **(a)** (*planifié*) organized; **voyage o.,** conducted tour; *F* **c'est du vol o.,** it's daylight robbery; **bien o.,** (*personne*) systematic; **les manifestants n'étaient pas organisés,** the demonstrators were not organized; **(b)** *Biol* organic (*being etc*).

organiser [ɔrganize] **1** *vt* to organize, to arrange (*meeting, business, entertainment*); to organize, to plan (*a journey, one's time*). **2 s'organiser** *vpr* to get organised; (*pour travailler*) to get *or* settle down to work.

organisme [ɔrganism] *nm* **(a)** *Biol* organism; *Anat* (the) system; **(b)** (*organisation*) organization, body.

organiste [ɔrganist] *n Mus* organist.

organothérapie [ɔrganɔterapi] *nf Méd* organotherapy.

orgasme [ɔrgasm] *nm* orgasm.

orge [ɔrʒ] **1** *nf* barley; **sucre d'o.,** barley sugar. **2** *nm* **o. mondé,** hulled barley; **o. perlé,** pearl barley.

orgeat [ɔrʒa] *nm* **sirop d'o.,** barley water.

orgelet [ɔrʒəlɛ] *nm* stye (*on the eye*).

orgiaque [ɔrʒjak] *adj* orgiastic.

orgie [ɔrʒi] *nf* (*sexuelle*) orgy; (*avec excès de boissons*) drunken feast; *Fig* **une o. de couleurs,** a riot of colour.

orgue [ɔrg] *nm* (*nfpl* **orgues**) **(a)** *Mus* organ; **un bel o., de belles orgues,** a fine organ; **o. du chœur** *ou* **d'accompagnement,** choir organ; **tenir l'o.** *ou* **les orgues,** to be at *or* to be playing the organ; **o. de Barbarie,** barrel organ; **joueur d'o.,** organ grinder; **point d'o.,** pause; *Fig* **le point d'o. de la réunion,** the climax *or* high point of the meeting; **(b)** *Géol* **orgues de basalte,** basalt columns.

orgueil [ɔrgœj] *nm* pride, arrogance; **péché d'o.,** sin of pride; **être gonflé d'o.,** to be swollen with pride; **mettre son o. à faire qch,** to take a pride in doing sth; **tirer o. de qch,** to take a pride in sth; **être l'o. et la joie de qn,** to be s.o.'s pride and joy; **par o., il ne veut pas admettre son erreur,** he is too proud to admit his error.

orgueilleusement [ɔrgœjøzmɑ̃] *adv* proudly; *Péj* arrogantly, haughtily.

orgueilleux, -euse [ɔrgœjø, -øz] **1** *adj* proud; *Péj* arrogant, haughty. **2** *npl* **les o.,** the proud.

oriel [ɔrjɛl] *nm* oriel (window), bay window.

orient [ɔrjɑ̃] *nm* **(a)** east; *Litt* orient; **L'O.,** the Orient; **le proche/le moyen/l'extrême O.,** the Near/Middle/Far East; **en O.,** in the East; **pays/peuples d'O.,** Eastern *or* Oriental nations/peoples; **tapis d'O.,** oriental carpet; *Hist* **l'Empire d'O.,** the Eastern (Roman) Empire; (*plus tard*) the Byzantine Empire; **(b)** (*reflet nacré*) water, orient (*of pearl*).

orientable [ɔrjɑ̃tabl] *adj* swivelling (*chair*); adjustable (*lamp, aerial*).

oriental, -ale, -aux [ɔrjɑ̃tal, -o] **1** *adj* eastern (*region*); east (*coast*); oriental (*language*); *Hist* **les Indes orientales,** the East Indies. **2** *n* **O.,** Oriental.

orientaliste [ɔrjɑ̃talist] *n* orientalist.

orientateur, -trice [ɔɔrjɑ̃tatœr, -tris] *n* = **ORIENTEUR, -EUSE 1.**

orientation [ɔrjɑ̃tɑsjɔ̃] *nf* **(a)** orientation; **table d'o.,** orientation *or* panoramic table; **avoir le sens de l'o.,** to have a (good) sense of direction; **course d'o.,** orienteering course; **(b)** *Scol* **o. professionnelle,** careers advice *or* guidance; **conseiller d'o. professionnelle, conseiller d'o. pédagogique,** careers adviser; **(c)** swivelling, steering (*of crane etc*); positioning (*of aerial*); **o. d'un canon,** training of a gun; **à o. libre,** free-moving, adjustable; (*qui tourne*) rotatable; **(d)** (*situation*) orientation, aspect (*of house*); **l'o. de la politique,** the trend of politics; **o. des voiles,** set *or* trim of the sails.

orienté [ɔrjɑ̃te] *adj* **(a)** (*disposé*) facing; **pièce orientée au sud,** room with a southerly aspect, room facing south; **(b)** (*peu objectif*) **ouvrage o. politiquement,** work with a political bias *or* slant.

orienter [ɔrjɑ̃te] **1** *vt* **(a)** to orient(ate) (*building*); to train (*gun*); to point, to direct (*telescope*); to trim (*sail*);

(b) (*mener*) to direct, to guide; **o. un élève vers la chimie,** to encourage a pupil to take up chemistry; **o. une revue vers les goûts féminins,** to aim *or* angle a magazine towards women readers; **o. la conversation vers d'autres sujets,** to turn the conversation to other topics;

(c) to set (*map*) by the compass;

(d) *Math* **o. une droite,** to indicate the direction of a straight line (*with an arrow*).

2 s'orienter *vpr* **(a)** to orientate oneself, to take *or* find one's bearings; (*avec une boussole*) to take a (compass) bearing;

(b) (*se destiner*) to take a direction (**vers,** towards); **il s'oriente vers la carrière diplomatique,** he is preparing to enter the diplomatic service; **cette politique s'oriente vers le communisme,** this policy is tending *or* moving towards Communism.

orienteur, -euse [ɔrjɑ̃tœr, -øz] **1** *n* careers adviser. **2** *nm* (*instrument*) orientator. **3** *adj Mil* **officier o.,** interviewing officer (*for candidates for military service*).

orifice [ɔrifis] *nm* aperture, opening; orifice (*of the body*); mouth (*of well, shaft*).

oriflamme [ɔriflam] *nf* **(a)** *Hist* oriflamme; **(b)** streamer, banner.

origan [ɔrigɑ̃] *nm* oregano, marjoram.

originaire [ɔriʒinɛr] *adj* **(a)** (*provenance*) originating (**de**, from, in); (*personne*) native (**de**, of); **il est o. de Russie/du Havre,** he comes *or* hails from Russia/Le Havre; **(b)** (*initial*) original, founding (*member*).

originairement [ɔriʒinɛrmɑ̃] *adv* originally, at the beginning.

original, -ale, -aux [ɔriʒinal, -o] **1** *adj* **(a)** (*premier*) original (*text, manuscript*); *Typ* top (*copy*); **édition originale,** first edition; *Cin* **copie originale (du film),** master print; **(b)** (*nouveau*) original (*style, idea*); **(c)** (*excentrique*) odd, eccentric. **2** *nm* original; *Typ* top copy; **copier qch d'après l'o.,** to copy sth from the original; **lire un auteur dans l'o.,** to read an author in the original (language). **3** *n* eccentric person; **c'est un o.,** he's (quite) a character.

originalité [ɔriʒinalite] *nf* **(a)** (*nouveauté*) originality; **(b)** (*excentricité*) eccentricity, oddity; **(c)** (*trait original*) original *or* special feature.

origine [ɔriʒin] *nf* **(a)** (*création, début*) origin, beginning; **l'o. de l'univers,** the origin of the universe; **dès l'o.,** from the very beginning, from the outset; **à l'o.,** originally, in the beginning; **des origines à nos jours,** from the earliest times to the present day;

(b) (*ascendance*) origin, extraction, birth; **être d'o. illustre,** to be of noble descent; **la colonie devait son o. aux baleiniers,** the colony was founded by whalers; **il est d'o. anglaise, il est anglais d'o.,** he is English by birth; **il a des origines anglaises,** he is of English extraction *or* has English origins;

(c) (*source*) origin, source; origin, derivation (*of word*); origin (*of custom*); **tirer son o. de qch,** to originate from sth; **bureau d'o.,** office of dispatch; **certificat d'o.,** certificate of origin; **vins d'o.,** vintage wines; **appellation d'o. contrôlée d'un vin,** = official quality guarantee of a wine;

(d) *Math* **(point) o.,** zero point.

originel, -elle [ɔriʒinɛl] *adj* original (*sin, grace*); original, primary (*cause, meaning*).

originellement [ɔriʒinɛlmɑ̃] *adv* originally.

orignal, -aux [ɔriɲal, -o] *nm Zool* moose.

oripeau, -eaux [ɔripo] *nm* **(a)** *Tech* tinsel, foil; **(b)** (*ornement d'or faux*) tawdry *or* cheap finery; **(c) oripeaux,** (*haillons*) rags, old clothes; (*vêtements voyants*) loud *or* gaudy clothes.

ORL [oɛrɛl] *n Méd* (*abrév* **oto-rhino-laryngologiste**) ENT specialist.

orléaniste [ɔrleanist] *adj & n Hist Fr* Orleanist.

ormaie [ɔrmɛ] *nf* elm grove.

orme [ɔrm] *nm* **(a)** elm (tree); **o. blanc, o. de(s) montagne(s),** wych elm; **o. champêtre** *ou* **à petites feuilles,** common elm, English elm; **maladie des ormes,** (Dutch) elm disease; **(b)** elm (wood).

ormeau, -eaux [ɔrmo] *nm* (*arbre*) (young) elm.

orné [ɔrne] *adj* ornate, florid (*style*); **lettre ornée,** illuminated initial (letter).

ornement [ɔrnəmɑ̃] *nm* ornament; (*détail*) embellishment; (*parure*) adornment; **sans o.,** plain, unadorned; **plantes d'o.,** ornamental plants; *Rel* **ornements sacerdotaux,** vestments; *Mus* **notes d'o.,** grace notes.

ornemental, -aux [ɔrnəmɑ̃tal, -o] *adj* ornamental, decorative.

ornementation [ɔrnəmɑ̃tasjɔ̃] *nf* ornamentation, decoration.

ornementer [ɔrnəmɑ̃te] *vt* to ornament, to decorate.

orner [ɔrne] *vt* to ornament, to decorate; **o. une robe de dentelles,** to trim a dress with lace.

ornière [ɔrnjɛr] *nf* rut; *Fig* **sortir de l'o.,** (*de la routine*) to get out of the rut; (*d'une situation difficile*) to get out of trouble *or* a fix.

ornithologie [ɔrnitɔlɔʒi] *nf* ornithology.

ornithologique [ɔrnitɔlɔʒik] *adj* ornithological.

ornithologiste [ɔrnitɔlɔʒist] **, ornithologue** [ɔrnitɔlɔg] *n* ornithologist.

ornithorynque [ɔrnitɔrɛ̃k] *nm Zool* duck-billed platypus, *Spéc* ornithorhynchus.

orogénèse [ɔrɔʒenɛz] *nf Géol* orogenesis.

orographie [ɔrɔgrafi] *nf* orography.

oronge [ɔrɔ̃ʒ] *nf Bot* royal agaric, Caesar's mushroom; **fausse o.,** fly agaric.

orpaillage [ɔrpajaʒ] *nm* gold washing *or* panning.

Orphée [ɔrfe] *nm Myth* Orpheus.

orphelin, -ine [ɔrfəlɛ̃, -in] **1** *n* orphan. **2** *adj* orphan(ed); **o. de père,** fatherless; **o. de mère,** motherless.

orphelinat [ɔrfəlina] *nm* orphanage, children's home.

orphéon [ɔrfeɔ̃] *nm* **(a)** band; **(b)** *Arch* choral society.

orphéoniste [ɔrfeɔnist] *n* **(a)** (*d'une fanfare*) member of a band; **(b)** (*d'une chorale*) member of a choral society.

orphie [ɔrfi] *nf Zool* garfish, garpike.

orpiment [ɔrpimɑ̃] *nm Tech* orpiment, yellow arsenic.

orpin [ɔrpɛ̃] *nm Bot* stonecrop.

orque [ɔrk] *nf Zool* orc, grampus.

Orsay [ɔrsɛ] **le Quai d'O.,** = the French Foreign Office.

orteil [ɔrtɛj] *nm* toe; **(gros) o.,** big toe.

O.R.T.F. [oɛrteɛf] *nm* (*abrév* **Office de la radiodiffusion et télévision française**) *Br* ≈ BBC.

orthochromatique [ɔrtɔkrɔmatik] *adj Phot* orthochromatic.

orthodontie [ɔrtɔdɔ̃ti] *nf* orthodontics.

orthodoxe [ɔrtɔdɔks] **1** *adj* orthodox (*church, doctrine, opinion*); **peu o.,** unorthodox, unconventional. **2** *n* person of orthodox beliefs; *Rel* Orthodox; *Pol* member who follows the (official) party line.

orthodoxie [ɔrtɔdɔksi] *nf* orthodoxy.

orthogénie [ɔrtɔʒeni] *nf Méd* birth control, family planning.

orthogonal, -aux [ɔrtɔgɔnal, -o] *adj* orthogonal.

orthogonalement [ɔrtɔgɔnalmɑ̃] *adv* orthogonally, at right angles.

orthographe [ɔrtɔgraf] *nf* spelling; **faute d'o.,** spelling mistake; **réforme de l'o.,** spelling reform; **o. d'usage/d'accord,** literal/grammatical spelling; **être bon en o., avoir une bonne o.,** to be good at spelling.

orthographier [ɔrtɔgrafje] *vt* (*impf & pr sub* **n. orthographiions**) to spell (*word*); **mal o.,** to spell (*word*) incorrectly, to misspell (*word*).

orthographique [ɔrtɔgrafik] *adj* **(a)** *Gram* orthographic(al); **réforme o.,** spelling reform; **(b)** orthographic (*projection etc*).

orthopédie [ɔrtɔpedi] *nf* orthop(a)edics.

orthopédique [ɔrtɔpedik] *adj* orthop(a)edic; **chaussures/semelles orthopédiques,** orthop(a)edic shoes/built-up soles.

orthopédiste [ɔrtɔpedist] *n* **(a)** (*médecin*) orthop(a)edist; **(b)** (*fabricant*) maker of orthop(a)edic apparatus.

orthophonie [ɔrtɔfɔni] *nf* speech therapy.

orthophoniste [ɔrtɔfɔnist] *n* speech therapist.

ortie [ɔrti] *nf* nettle; **o. brûlante,** stinging nettle; **o. blanche,** dead nettle.

ortolan [ɔrtɔlɑ̃] *nm Orn* ortolan (bunting).

orvet [ɔrvɛ] *nm Zool* slow-worm, blindworm.

os [ɔs, *pl* o] *nm* **(a)** bone; **à** *ou* **aux gros os,** big-boned; **n'avoir que la peau sur les os, n'être qu'un sac d'os,** to be nothing but skin and bone, to be just a bag of bones; **voir qn en chair et en os,** to see s.o. in the flesh; **mouillé** *ou* **trempé jusqu'aux os,** soaked to the skin, wet through; **casser** *ou* **rompre les os à qn,** to beat s.o. black and blue; **il ne fera pas de vieux os,** he's not long for this world, he won't make old bones; *Fig* **ronger jusqu'à l'os,** to bleed (*s.o.*) white *or* dry; **os à moelle,** marrow bone; **viande avec os,** meat on the bone; **viande sans os,** meat off the bone, boned meat; **cuiller en os,** bone spoon; **os de seiche,** cuttlebone; **(b)** *F* snag, hitch; **tomber sur un os,** to run up against a difficulty *or* a snag; **il y a un os,** there's a snag.

O.S. [oɛs] *nm abrév* **ouvrier spécialisé.**

oscar [ɔskar] *nm Cin* (*récompense*) Oscar.

oscillant [ɔsilɑ̃] *adj* **(a)** oscillating (*pendulum, Él discharge*); rocking (*shaft*); jigging (*sieve etc*); *Rad* **circuit o.,** oscillatory circuit; **(b)** *Fin* fluctuating (*market*).

oscillateur [ɔsilatœr] *nm Rad Electron* oscillator; oscillating coil.

oscillation [ɔsilasjɔ̃] *nf* **(a)** oscillation; swing (*of pendulum*); *Rad etc* **oscillations amorties/entretenues,** damped/sustained oscillations; **(b)** rocking (*of boat*); **(c)** *MecE* vibration; **(d)** fluctuation (*of the market etc*); **oscillations d'un extrême à l'autre,** swings from one extreme to the other.

oscillatoire [ɔsilatwar] *adj* oscillatory (*movement, circuit*).

osciller [ɔsile] *vi* **(a)** to oscillate; (*d'un mouvement plus large*) to sway; (*of pendulum*) to swing; (*of speedometer needle*) to flicker; (*of boat*) to rock; **(b)** (*hésiter*) **o. entre deux opinions,** to waver between two opinions; **(c)** *Fin* (*of market*) to fluctuate.

oscillographe [ɔsilɔgraf] *nm* oscillograph; **o. cathodique,** cathode ray tube.

oscilloscope [ɔsilɔskɔp] *nm* oscilloscope.

osculateur, -trice [ɔskylatœr, -tris] *adj* osculatory, osculating (*curve*).

osculation [ɔskylasjɔ̃] *nf* osculation (*of curves*).

osé [oze] *adj* daring, audacious (*person etc*); risqué (*joke*); **c'était une tentative plutôt osée de sa part,** it was a rather bold attempt on his part; **être trop o.,** to go too far; **certaines scènes du film sont un peu osées,** certain scenes in the film go a little too far.

oseille [ozɛj] *nf* **(a)** *Bot* sorrel; *Arg* **la faire à l'o. à qn,** to trick s.o., to put a fast one over on s.o.; **(b)** *Arg* (*argent*) dough, lolly; **avoir de l'o.,** to have bags *or* pots of money, to be loaded; **il a gagné suffisamment d'o. pour s'acheter une caisse,** he's earned enough dough to buy himself some wheels; **prends l'o. et tire-toi,** take the money and run.

oser [oze] *vt* **o. faire qch,** *Litt* **o. qch,** to dare *or* venture to do sth; **je n'ose pas le faire,** I am afraid to do it; **je n'ose le faire,** I hesitate to do it; **les mots qu'il n'a jamais osé dire,** the words he never dared (to) say; **comment ose-t-il répondre à son père?,** I don't know how he has the audacity to answer his father back; **approchez si vous osez!,** come over here if you dare!; **vous n'oseriez (pas)!,** you wouldn't dare!; **j'ose espérer qu'il va me remercier,** I dare say he won't thank me; **si j'ose (le) dire,** if I may venture to say so.

oseraie [ozrɛ] *nf* osier bed.

osier [ozje] *nm* **(a)** *Bot* osier; **brin d'o.,** withy; **(b)** wicker; (*objets en osier*) wickerwork; **panier d'o.,** wicker basket.

osmonde [ɔsmɔ̃d] *nf Bot* **o. royale,** royal fern.

osmose [ɔsmoz] *nf* osmosis.

ossature [ɔsatyr] *nf* **(a)** *Biol* frame, skeleton (*of man, animal*); **d'une o. puissante,** powerfully built, of powerful build; **(b)** *Fig* (*structure*) frame(work) (*of building etc*); main girders (*of bridge*); **l'o. sociale,** the social structure.

osselet [ɔslɛ] *nm* knucklebone (*of sheep*); **jouer aux osselets,** to play at knucklebones; *Anat* **les osselets de l'oreille,** the ossicles of the ear, the otic bones.

ossements [ɔsmɑ̃] *nmpl* bones (*of dead men, animals*).

osseux, -euse [ɔsø, -øz] *adj* bony (*face, hand*); osseous (*tissue*); **système o.,** bone structure; **greffe osseuse,** bone graft.

ossification [ɔsifikasjɔ̃] *nf Méd* ossification.

ossifier [ɔsifje] **1** *vt* to ossify. **2 s'ossifier** *vpr* to become ossified, to ossify.

ossu [ɔsy] *adj* big-boned, raw-boned.

ossuaire [ɔsɥɛr] *nm* ossuary, charnel house.

ostensible [ɔstɑ̃sibl] *adj* open, public; *Péj* ostentatious.

ostensiblement [ɔstɑ̃sibləmɑ̃] *adv* openly, publicly; *Péj* ostentatiously; (*évidemment*) obviously, patently, visibly.

ostensoir [ɔstɑ̃swar] *nm Rel* monstrance.

ostentation [ɔstɑ̃tasjɔ̃] *nf* ostentation, show, display; **faire o. de sa misère,** to parade one's poverty; **agir par** *ou* **avec o.,** to do sth (in order) to show off.

ostentatoire [ɔstɑ̃tatwar] *adj* ostentatious.

ostéoarthrite [ɔsteoartrit] *nf Méd* infectious osteoarthritis.

ostéologie [ɔsteɔlɔʒi] *nf* osteology.

ostéomyélite [ɔsteɔmjelit] *nf Méd* osteomyelitis.

ostéopathe [ɔsteɔpat] *n Méd* osteopath.

ostéoporose [ɔsteɔpɔroz] *nf Méd* osteoporosis.

ostracisme [ɔstrasism] *nm* **(a)** ostracism; **frapper qn d'o.,** to ostracize s.o.; **(b)** (*hostilité, attitude de rejet*) hostility; **les autres membres du club faisaient preuve de beaucoup d'o. à son égard,** the other club members showed a great deal of hostility towards him.

ostréicole [ɔstreikɔl] *adj* **l'industrie o.,** oyster farming; **parc o.,** oyster bed; **la région est l'un des plus grands parcs ostréicoles de la France,** it is one of the largest oyster-producing regions in France.

ostréiculteur, -trice [ɔstreikyltœr, -tris] *n* oyster farmer.

ostréiculture [ɔstreikyltyr] *nf* oyster farming.

ostrogot(h), -ot(h)e [ɔstrɔgo, -ɔt] *n Hist* Ostrogoth; *Fig* **quel o.!,** what a boor!

otage [ɔtaʒ] *nm* hostage (**de,** for); **prendre qn en o.,** to take s.o. (as) hostage; **servir d'o.,** to serve as a hostage; **une prise d'o.,** the taking *or* seizing *or* seizure of a hostage; **libération d'un o. politique,** release of a political hostage.

otalgie [ɔtalʒi] *nf Méd* otalgia, earache.

O.T.A.N. [ɔtɑ̃] *nf* (*abrév* **Organisation du traité de l'Atlantique Nord**) NATO.

otarie [ɔtari] *nf* otary, sea lion, eared seal.

ôter [ote] **1** *vt* to remove, to take away; to take off (*garment*); to take out (*stain*); **ô. le couvert,** to clear away, to clear the table; **ô. qch à qn,** to take sth away from s.o.; **cela n'ôte rien à sa valeur,** that detracts in no way from its value; **ô. qch de qch,** to take sth away from sth; **ôtez trois de cinq,** take away *or* subtract three from five; **cela me l'a ôté tout à fait de l'esprit,** that drove *or* put it entirely out of my head; **ô. le pain de la bouche à qn,** to take the bread out of s.o.'s mouth; **ô. la vie à qn,** to take s.o.'s life. **2 s'ôter** *vpr* to remove oneself, to move away; *F* **ôtez-vous de là!,** get out (of here)!; **ôte-toi de là que je m'y mette!,** get out and make room for me!

otique [ɔtik] *adj Anat* otic (*nerve etc*).

otite [ɔtit] *nf Méd* otitis.

otologie [ɔtɔlɔʒi] *nf* otology.

oto-rhino [ɔtɔrino] *n Méd F* ENT specialist; (*pl oto-rhinos*).

oto-rhino-laryngologiste [ɔtɔrinɔlarɛ̃gɔlɔʒist] *n* ear, nose and throat specialist; (*pl oto-rhino-laryngologistes*).

otoscope [ɔtɔskɔp] *nm Méd* otoscope, ear speculum.

ottoman, -ane [ɔtɔmɑ̃, -an] **1** *adj & n Hist* Ottoman. **2** *nm* (*étoffe*) grogram. **3** *nf* **ottomane,** (*meuble*) divan, ottoman.

ou [u] *conj* or; **voulez-vous du bœuf ou du jambon?,** would you like beef or ham?; **trois ou quatre fois par jour,** three or four times a day; **l'un ou l'autre,** one or the other; **entrez ou sortez,** either come in or go out; **vous ou moi, nous lui en parlerons,** (either) you or I will speak to him about it; **lui ou son frère va** *ou* **vont vous aider,** he or his brother will help you; **l'un ou l'autre devait forcément être le chef,** one or the other was bound to take the lead; **j'appelle tout de suite ou j'attends demain,** (*statement*) I'll either call straight away or wait till tomorrow; (*question*) shall I call straight away or wait till tomorrow?; **ou ... ou (bien) ...,** either ... or (else) ...; **ou vous payez ou j'appelle la police,** either you pay up or (else) I call the police; *Ordinat* **circuit OU,** OR circuit.

où [u] *adv* **(a)** (*interr*) where; **où habite-t-il?,** where does he live?; **où allez-vous?,** where are you going?; **où en êtes-vous?,** how far have you got (with it)?; **par où est-il passé?,** which way did he go?; **jusqu'où les a-t-il suivis?,** how far did he follow them?; **(b)** (*rel*) where; **j'irai où vous voudrez,** I'll go where(ever) you wish; **partout où il va,** wherever he goes; **vous le trouverez là où vous l'avez laissé,** you will find it where you left it; **d'où on conclut qu'il est coupable,** from which one concludes that he is guilty; **où que vous soyez,** wherever you may be; **mettez-le n'importe où,** put it down anywhere; **(c)** (*quand*) when; **dans le temps où il était jeune,** in the days when he was young; **(d)** (= **dans lequel, auquel** *etc*) **la maison où il habite,** the house in which he lives, the house he lives in.

O.U.A. [ɔya] *nf* (*abrév* **Organisation de l'unité africaine**) OAU.

ouache [waʃ] *nf Can* bear's den.

ouaille [waj] *nf Bible Litt* sheep; **le pasteur et ses ouailles,** the minister and his flock.

ouais [wɛ] *int* **(a)** *F* yeah!, *surtout Am* yep!; (*sceptical*) oh yeah?; **(b)** *Arch* (*of surprise*) what!, my word!

ouananiche [wananiʃ] *nf Can* freshwater salmon.

ouaouaron [wawarɔ̃] *nm Can* bullfrog.

ouate [wat] *nf* (*souvent* **la ouate,** *parfois* **l'ouate**) **(a)** wadding, padding; **doublé d'o.,** wadded, quilted; **(b)** (*pour soins*) cotton wool; **o. hydrophile,** (absorbent) cotton wool; **(c) o. de verre,** fibreglass, *US* fiberglass.

ouaté [wate] *adj* wadded, padded; *Fig* fleecy (*cloud, snow*); soft (*footstep*); woolly (*outlines*); **robe de chambre ouatée,** quilted dressing gown.

ouater [wate] *vt* to wad, to pad; (*matelasser*) to quilt.

ouatine [watin] *nf Tex* quilting (material).

ouatiné [watine] *adj* quilted (*material*); *Fig* cosy (*life*).

oubli [ubli] *nm* **(a)** (*acte d'oublier*) forgetting; (*défaillance de la mémoire*) forgetfulness; (*négligence*) neglect (*of duty*); **par o.,** inadvertently, by *or* through an oversight; **l'o. de soi-même,** (*désintéressement, abnégation*) selflessness; **(b)** (*général*) oblivion; **tomber dans l'o.,** to sink *or* fall into oblivion, to be forgotten; **sortir de l'o.,** to emerge from oblivion; **(c)** (*omission, négligence*) omission, oversight; **réparer un o.,** to rectify an omission.

oubliable [ublijabl] *adj* forgettable.

oublier [ublije] *v* (*impf & pr sub* **n. oubliions**) **1** *vt* **(a)** to forget; **j'ai oublié son nom,** I have forgotten his name, his name has slipped my memory; **o. le passé,** to forget the past, to let bygones be bygones; **faire o. son passé,** to live down one's past; **o. de faire qch,** to forget to do sth; **on ne nous le laissera pas o.,** we shall never hear the last of it *or* be allowed to forget it, we'll never live it down; **il mourut oublié de tous,** he died forgotten by all, he died in obscurity; **n'oubliez pas à qui vous vous adressez,** remember who you're talking to;

(b) to overlook (*an appointment*); to neglect (*duty*); to leave (*sth*) out *or* behind; **o. l'heure,** to lose count of time.

2 s'oublier *vpr* to forget one's manners, to forget oneself; **le chien s'est oublié sur le tapis,** the dog's made a mess on the carpet; **s'o. à rêver,** to lose oneself in a daydream; *F* **il ne s'oublie pas,** he's no altruist, he always looks after number one; **les langues étrangères s'oublient facilement quand on ne les pratique pas,** foreign languages are easily forgotten when one doesn't use them.

oubliette [ublijɛt] *nf* oubliette, secret dungeon; *F* **mettre qch aux oubliettes,** to shelve sth indefinitely.

oublieux, -euse [ublijø, -øz] *adj* forgetful; neglectful (*of duty*).

oued [wɛd] *nm Géog* wadi.

Ouessant [wɛsɑ̃] *nm* Ushant.

ouest [wɛst] **1** *nm* west; **les provinces de l'O.,** the western provinces; **vent d'o.,** westerly wind; **le vent d'o.,** the west wind; **à l'o. de qch,** (to the) west *or* (to the) westward of sth; **à l'o., dans l'o.,** in the west; **vers l'o.,** westward(s); **une pièce exposée plein o.,** a room that faces due west; *Pol* **l'O.,** the West; **les rapports entre l'Est and l'O. sont moins tendus qu'ils ne l'ont été,** East-West relations are less tense than they were. **2** *adj inv* west (*coast*); westerly (*wind*); western (*province*).

ouest-allemand, -ande [wɛstalmɑ̃, -ɑ̃d] (*pl ouest-allemand(e)s*) **1** *adj* West German. **2** *n* **O.-A.,** West-German.

ouf [uf] *int* ah!, what a relief!; **pousser un o. de soulagement,** to heave a sigh of relief; **o., on étouffe ici!,** phew!, it's stifling in here; *F* **il n'a pas eu le temps de dire o.!,** he didn't even have time to catch his breath.

Ouganda [ugɑ̃da] *nm* Uganda.

oui [wi] **1** *adv* yes; **vient-il? — o.,** is he coming? — yes (he is); **je crois que o.,** I think so; **faire signe que o., faire o. de la tête,** to nod in agreement; **mais o., bien sûr que o.,** (yes,) of course, naturally; **o., o., allez toujours,** yes, (yes,) get on with it; **êtes-vous content de partir? — o. et non,** are you happy to be leaving? — yes and no; **eh! o.! c'est encore moi!,** yes! it's me again!; *Nau* **o., commandant!,** aye, aye, sir!; **ah, o.?,** really?, is that so?; **tu viens, o.?,** you're coming, aren't you?; **tu viens, o. ou non?,** are you coming or not?, are you coming or aren't you?, are you coming, yes or no?

2 *nm inv Pol* **deux cents o. et trois cents non,** two hundred ayes and three hundred noes; *F* **se quereller pour un o. pour un non,** to quarrel about nothing; **changer d'avis pour un o. pour un non,** to change one's mind at the drop of a hat.

ouï-dire [widir] *nm inv* hearsay; **je ne le sais que par o.-d.,** I know it only by *or* from hearsay.

ouïe [wi] *nf* **(a)** (sense of) hearing; **avoir l'o. fine,** to have keen *or* sharp ears, to have excellent hearing; **avoir l'o. défectueuse,** to be hard of hearing; **à portée de l'o.,** within earshot, within hearing distance; **être tout o.,** to be all ears *or* all attention; **(b)** *Mus* **ouïes,** sound holes (*of violin etc*); **(c)** *Tech* ear (*of ventilator etc*); *Zool* **ouïes,** gills (*of fish*).

ouille [uj] *int* ouch!, ooh!

ouïr [wir] *vt* (*only used in inf, pp* **ouï**, *compound tenses, prp* **oyant** *and imp* **oyez**; *p hist* **j'ouïs** *and fu* **j'ouïrai** *sometimes used*) *Arch* to hear; **nous l'avons ouï dire à notre père,** we have heard our father say so; *Jur* **o. les témoins,** to hear the witnesses; *Arch* **oyez, oyez braves gens ...,** oyez, oyez *or* now hear this, good people ... .

ouistiti [wistiti] *nm Zool* marmoset.

ouragan [uragɑ̃] *nm* hurricane; **entrer comme un o. dans une pièce,** to burst into a room; **o. politique,** political storm; **sa déclaration a déclenché un o.,** his statement caused an uproar.

Oural (l') [lural] *nm* **(a)** the Ural (river); **(b)** the Ural Mountains, the Urals.

ourdir [urdir] *vt* **(a)** *Tex* to warp (*linen, cloth*); **(b)** to plait (*straw*); **(c)** *Fig* to hatch, to weave (*plot*).

ourdissage [urdisaʒ] *nm Tex* warping.

ourdisseur, -euse [urdisœr, -øz] *n* **(a)** *Tex* warper; **(b)** *Fig* plotter.

ourdou [urdu] *nm Ling* Urdu.

ourler [urle] *vt* **(a)** *Couture* to hem; **o. à jour,** to hemstitch; **(b)** to edge, to border (**de,** with); **(c)** *Tech* to lap joint (*metal sheets*).

ourlet [urlɛ] *nm* **(a)** *Couture* hem; **o. à jour,** hemstitched hem; **faux o.,** false hem; **point d'o.,** hemming; (*individuel*) hemstitch; **(b)** (*repli, rebord*) edge (*of crater*); helix, rim (*of ear*); **(c)** *Tech* lap joint, hem (*of metal sheets*).

ours, ourse [urs] **1** *n* bear, *f* she bear; **o. blanc** *ou* **polaire,** polar bear; **o. brun,** brown bear; **o. gris d'Amérique,** grizzly bear; **Grand Lac de l'O.,** Great Bear Lake; **combats d'o.,** bear baiting; **o. en peluche,** teddy bear; *F* **o. mal léché,** uncouth individual; **quel o.!,** what a boor!; *Prov* **il ne faut pas vendre la peau de l'o. avant de l'avoir tué,** don't count your chickens before they are hatched; **o. marin,** sea bear, fur seal; *Bot* **raisin d'o.,** bearberry. **2** *nf Astron* **la Grande Ourse,** (*constellation*) the Great Bear; (*sept étoiles*) the Plough, *Am* the Big Dipper; **la Petite Ourse,** the Little Bear, *Am* the Little Dipper.

oursin [ursɛ̃] *nm* sea urchin.

ourson [ursɔ̃] *nm* bear cub.

oust(e) [ust] *int Arg* **allez o.!,** (*avance!*) get a move on!; (*va-t'en!*) hop it!, scram!

out [awt] *adj inv* out (of fashion); **ce chanteur est déjà o.,** that singer is already out of fashion.

outarde [utard] *nf Orn* **(a)** bustard; **(b)** *Can* Canada goose.

outil [uti] *nm* (*d'un ouvrier, artisan etc*) tool; (*de cuisine etc*) implement; **o. à main,** hand tool; **o. à moteur,** power tool; **o. coupant** *ou* **de coupe** *ou* **tranchant,** cutting tool; (*pour bords ou bordures*) edging tool.

outillage [utijaʒ] *nm* **(a)** (*ensemble d'outils*) set of tools; *Aut etc* tool kit; **(b)** (*équipement*) gear, plant, equipment (*of factory*).

outiller [utije] **1** *vt* to equip *or* supply (*workman*) with tools; to equip *or* fit out *or* supply (*factory*) with plant; **être bien outillé en livres,** to be well provided with books. **2 s'outiller** *vpr* (*d'une usine*) to equip itself; (*d'un bricoleur*) to obtain *or* buy *etc* the tools (*to do sth*).

outrage [utraʒ] *nm* **(a)** *Jur* **o. (à agent),** insulting behaviour; **o. (à magistrat),** = contempt of court; **o. aux bonnes mœurs** *ou* **à la pudeur,** public indecency; **(b)** (*injure*) outrage; flagrant insult (*to morals, good taste etc*); **faire o. aux convenances,** to offend against propriety; *Euph* **faire subir les derniers outrages à une femme,** to violate a woman; *Litt Fig* **l'o. des ans,** the ravages of time.

outrageant [utraʒɑ̃] *adj* insulting (*offer, refusal*); offensive (*joke*); scurrilous (*accusation*); **propos o.,** offensive remarks.

outrager [utraʒe] *vt* (**j'outrageai(s)**) **(a)** (*insulter*) to insult; **o. un homme dans son honneur/dignité,** to offend against *or* violate a man's honour/dignity; **(b)** *Fig* (*porter atteinte à*) to outrage, to violate (*the truth*); **ses propos outragent le bon sens,** his words are an offence against *or* to common sense.

outrageusement [utraʒøzmɑ̃] *adv* **(a)** outrageously, insultingly; **(b)** (*excessivement*) excessively (*stupid etc*).

outrageux, -euse [utraʒø, -øz] *adj Vieilli* insulting.

outrance [utrɑ̃s] *nf* excess; **faire des outrances de langage,** to use outrageous language; **à o.,** to the utmost; **combat à o.,** fight to the death; **attaque à o.,** all-out attack; **industrialisme à o.,** out and out industrialization; **travailler à o.,** to work excessively.

outrancier, -ière [utrɑ̃sje, -jɛr] *adj* extreme (*views, left-winger*); out-and-out (*thief, liar*); extremist (*views, slogans*).

outre¹ [utr] *nf* wine skin; (*en peau de chèvre*) goatskin bottle.

outre² **1** *prép* **(a)** (*in a few set phrases*) beyond; **o. mesure,** beyond measure, inordinately, unduly, overmuch; **se fatiguer o. mesure,** to overtire oneself; **(b)** in addition to; **o. cette somme,** in addition to that sum; **o. cela,** in addition to that; (*d'ailleurs*) besides; (*encore*) furthermore. **2** *adv* further, beyond; **passer o., aller o.,** to go on, to proceed further; **passer o. à une interdiction,** to disregard *or* take no notice of *or* ignore a prohibition; **passer o. à la loi,** to override the law; **en o.,** (*d'ailleurs*) besides, moreover; (*encore*) further(more), also, again; (*de plus, de trop*) over and above; **j'ai, en o., deux neveux,** I have, besides, two nephews. **3** *conj* **o. (le fait) qu'il est riche,** apart from the fact that he's rich, apart from *or* besides *or* in addition to being rich.

outré [utre] *adj* **(a)** indignant; **o. de colère,** beside oneself with anger; **(b)** *Litt* exaggerated, extravagant, overdone (*praise*); overstated (*value, argument*); **d'une activité outrée,** hyperactive.

outre-Atlantique [utratlɑ̃tik] *adv* on the other side of the Atlantic, across the Atlantic; **d'o.-A.,** transatlantic.

outrecuidance [utrəkɥidɑ̃s] *nf* presumptuousness, effrontery.

outrecuidant [utrəkɥidɑ̃] *adj* **(a)** (*orgueilleux*) presumptuous; **(b)** (*insolent*) impertinent.

outre-Manche [utrəmɑ̃ʃ] *adv* on the other side of the Channel, across the Channel in Britain *or* France.

outremer [utrəmɛr] **1** *nm* **(a)** *Minér* lapis lazuli; **(b)** **(bleu d')o.,** ultramarine (blue). **2** *adj* **un pull o.,** an ultramarine *or* bright blue pullover.

outre-mer [utrəmɛr] *adv* overseas; **commerce d'o.-m.,** oversea(s) trade; **nos collègues d'o.-m.,** our colleagues from abroad; *Admin* **territoires d'o.-m.,** overseas territories.

outrepasser [utrəpase] *vt* to exceed; to go beyond (*a limit, one's rights*).

outrer [utre] *vt* **(a)** (*exagérer*) to exaggerate; to overdo (*a rôle*); **(b)** (*mettre en colère*) to infuriate.

outre-Rhin [utrərɛ̃] *adv* beyond the Rhine, in Germany.

outre-tombe (d') [dutrətɔ̃b] *adv Fig Hum* from beyond the grave; **une voix d'o.-t.,** in a grave, booming voice.

outsider [awtsajdœr] *nm Courses de chevaux etc* outsider; **le cheval gagnant fait partie des outsiders,** the winning horse was one of the outsiders.

ouvert [uvɛr] *adj* **(a)** open; **porte grande ouverte,** wide-open door; **plaie ouverte,** gaping wound; *Chir* **opérer à cœur o.,** to perform open-heart surgery; **accueillir qn à bras ouverts,** to welcome s.o. with open arms; **faire qch les yeux ouverts,** to do sth with one's eyes open; **fleur ouverte,** flower in bloom; **il va travailler chemise ouverte,** (*sans cravate*) he doesn't wear a tie to work; **voyelle ouverte,** open vowel; *Fb* **jeu o.,** open *or* loose game; **traduire à livre o.,** to translate off the cuff; **ville ouverte,** open *or* unfortified town; **o. de 10 heures à 5 heures,** open (from) 10 to 5; **collection ouverte au public,** collection open to the public; **o. à la navigation,** open to navigation; *Banque* **compte o.,** open account, open credit; **guerre ouverte,** open warfare; *F* **l'épicier du coin reste o. jusqu'à minuit,** the grocer on the corner stays open till midnight; **ils se sont disputés de façon ouverte,** they quarrelled in public; **déchaîner une campagne ouverte contre un candidat présidentiel,** to launch a public campaign against a presidential candidate; **le gaz est o.,** the gas is on; **le robinet est o.,** the tap is (turned) on; **la séance est ouverte,** I declare the meeting open; **la chasse est ouverte depuis 15 jours,** the hunting *or* open season began two weeks ago;

(b) *Fig* (*franc, sans préjugé*) **elle est très ouverte,** she's very open-minded; **caractère o.,** frank *or* open nature; **avoir l'esprit o.,** to be open-minded; **parler à cœur o.,** to speak freely.

ouvertement [uvɛrtəmɑ̃] *adv* openly, frankly; overtly (*hostile*).

ouverture [uvɛrtyr] *nf* **(a)** opening (*of door, book, session, shooting season etc*); **o. des hostilités,** outbreak of hostilities; **o. d'un compte/d'un crédit,** opening of an account/a credit; **conférence d'o.,** opening lecture; *Rugby* **il est demi d'o.,** he plays stand-off *or* fly-half;

(b) ouvertures, overtures; **faire des ouvertures à qn,** to make ouvertures to s.o.; **le chef d'état attend qu'on lui fasse des ouvertures de paix,** the country's leader is waiting for peace overtures to be made to him;

(c) *Mus* overture (*of opera etc*);

(d) heures d'o., opening hours (*of shop etc*); opening times (*of museum*); banking hours (*of bank*);

(e) (*accès*) opening, aperture (*in wall etc*); mouth (*of cave*); gap, break (*in hedge*); **flacon à large o.,** wide-mouthed flask; **ouvertures d'une machine,** (steam) ports of an engine;

(f) (*écartement*) width, span (*of arch etc*); spread (*of compass legs*); *Él* **o. d'induit,** armature gap;

(g) *Phot* aperture;

(h) *Fig* **o. de cœur,** frankness; **o. d'esprit,** open-mindedness; *Pol* **le Président pratique une nouvelle politique d'o. politique et sociale,** the President is following a new policy of conciliation in political and social affairs.

ouvrable [uvrabl] *adj* **jour o.,** working day; **heures ouvrables,** business hours, working hours.

ouvrage [uvraʒ] **1** *nm* **(a)** (*travail*) work; **se mettre à l'o.,** to set to work; **mettre qn à l'o.,** to set s.o. to work; **avoir du cœur à l'o.,** to work with a will;

(b) *Tech* (*construction*) workmanship; **entreprise spécialisée dans les ouvrages de maçonnerie,** firm specializing in masonry work; **l'ouvrier fait le gros de l'o.,** the workman does the bulk of the work; **faire des ouvrages d'art pour développer le réseau de communications d'une région,** to carry out civil engineering works to develop the communications system of a region;

(c) (*résultat*) piece of work, product; (*livre*) book, work; **o. en prose,** prose work; **un o. de philosophie/de géographie,** a work of philosophy, a philosophy/geography book; **ouvrages de dames,** needlework; (*brodure, crochet*) fancywork; **corbeille/boîte à o.,** work basket/workbox; *Fig* **son succès est l'o. de sa patience,** his success is due to (his) patience.

2 *nf F* **c'est de la belle o.,** that's a nice bit of work.

ouvragé [uvraʒe] *adj* **(a)** = **OUVRÉ**; **(b)** (*orné*) elaborate.

ouvrager [uvraʒe] *vt* (**j'ouvrageai(s)**) to work (*metal, jewel(le)ry*); (*orner*) to figure (*brocade*).

ouvrant [uvrɑ̃] **1** *adj Aut* **toit o.,** sun roof, sliding roof. **2** *nm Beaux-Arts* (*panneau*) panel (*of a triptych*).

ouvré [uvre] *adj* **(a)** *Tech* worked (*timber*); wrought (*iron*); **produits ouvrés et semi-ouvrés,** finished and semi-finished products; **(b)** (*orné*) decorated; embroidered (*tablecloth*).

ouvre-boîte(s) [uvrəbwat] *nm* can opener, tin opener; **un o.-b. électrique,** an electric can *or* tin opener; (*pl ouvre-boîtes*).

ouvre-bouteille(s) [uvrəbutɛj] *nm* bottle opener; (*pl ouvre-bouteilles*).

ouvre-huître(s) [uvrɥitr] *nm* oyster knife; (*pl ouvre-huîtres*).

ouvre-lettres [uvrəlɛtr] *nm inv* letter opener.

ouvrer [uvre] *vt* **(a)** *Tech* to work (up) (*wood, copper etc*); **(b)** (*orner*) to work, to embroider (*tablecloth etc*).

ouvreur, -euse [uvrœr, -øz] *n Cartes* player who opens the bidding.

ouvreuse [uvrøz] *nf Th Cin* usherette.

ouvrier, -ère [uvrije, -ɛr] **1** *adj* **(a)** (*prolétaire*) **la classe ouvrière, les classes ouvrières,** the working class(es); **agitation ouvrière,** industrial unrest, labour unrest; **contrôle o.,** workers' control; **syndicat o.,** trade union; **quartier o.,** working class district; **(b)** *Zool* **abeille ouvrière,** worker bee; **fourmi ouvrière,** worker ant. **2** *n* (*prolétaire*) worker, working man *or* woman; (*de réparation, de travaux publics*) workman; operative (*of machine*); **o. en bois/sur métaux,** woodworker/metalworker; **o. agricole,** agricultural labourer, farm worker; **o. qualifié,** skilled worker, craftsman; **o. spécialisé,** semi-skilled worker; *Rail* **o. de la voie,** platelayer, *Am* tracklayer; **ouvrière couturière,** seamstress; *Litt Fig* **il est l'o. de sa fortune,** he is a self-made man. **3** *nf Zool* **ouvrière,** worker (bee, ant *etc*).

ouvriérisme [uvrijerism] *nm Pol* (*autogestion*) control by the workers; (*syndicalisme*) trade unionism.

ouvrir [uvrir] *v* (*prp* **ouvrant**; *pp* **ouvert**; *pr ind* **j'ouvre**; *pr sub* **j'ouvre**; *p hist* **j'ouvris**) **1** *vt* **(a)** to open (*a door, a box*); to unfasten (*a bolt, a catch*); (*avec une clef*) to unlock; **o. sa maison à qn,** to throw open one's house to s.o.; **il n'a pas ouvert la bouche,** *F* **il ne l'a pas ouverte,** he didn't open his mouth; **o. le lit,** to turn down the bed(clothes); **o. un robinet/le gaz,** to turn on a tap/the gas; **o. l'électricité,** to switch on (the electricity); *F* **o. le poste,** to switch on the radio *or* the television; *Él* **o. le circuit,** to break *or* switch off the current; *Fig* **o. la porte aux abus,** to open the door *or* the way to abuses;

(b) *Fig* (*découvrir*) **o. son cœur à qn,** to open one's heart to s.o., to unburden oneself to s.o.; **cette expérience lui a ouvert l'esprit,** this experience has broadened his mind;

(c) (*tracer*) to cut through (*wall etc*); to open up (*mine etc*); to cut (*canal*); to cut open (*box etc*); *Méd* to open, to lance (*abscess*);

(d) (*commencer, lancer*) to open; **o. un débat,** to open *or* start a debate; **o. le bal,** to open the ball; **o. une école/une boutique,** to open a school/a shop; **o. boutique,** to set up shop; **o. la marche,** to lead the way; **ils ont décidé de ne pas o. la piste bleue,** they decided not to open the blue run; **o. un compte chez qn,** to open an account with s.o.; **cela ouvre l'appétit,** it sharpens *or* whets the appetite.

2 *vi* to open; **o. à qn,** to answer the door to s.o., to let s.o. in; **la scène ouvre par un chœur,** the scene opens with a chorus; **le salon ouvrait sur le jardin,** the drawing room opened on(to) the garden; **les magasins n'ouvrent pas les jours de fête,** the shops do not open on public holidays.

3 s'ouvrir *vpr* **(a)** (*devenir ouvert*) to open; **la porte s'ouvrit en coup de vent,** the door flew open; **les yeux du chaton vont bientôt s'o.,** the kitten's eyes will soon open; **les fenêtres s'ouvrent sur le jardin,** the windows look out *or* open onto the garden; *Fig* **un gouffre s'ouvrait sous mes pieds,** a chasm opened out *or* yawned under my feet; **s'o. un chemin à travers la foule,** to push one's way through the crowd; *Fig* **les nouvelles perspectives qui s'ouvrent aux jeunes diplômés,** the new prospects that are opening up for young graduates; **la séance s'ouvre par un discours,** the meeting opens with a speech; **le bal s'ouvrit par une valse,** the ball opened *or* began *or* started with a waltz;

(b) (*se confier*) **s'o. à qn,** to unburden oneself to s.o., to confide in s.o..

ouvroir [uvrwar] *nm* **(a)** (*salle de couvent*) workroom, sewing room; **(b)** (*fondation charitable*) (ladies') work party, *Am* sewing bee.

ovaire [ɔvɛr] *nm Anat Bot* ovary; **kyste de l'o.,** ovarian cyst.

ovale [ɔval] **1** *adj* oval, egg-shaped; *Sp F* **ballon o.,** rugger ball; (*rugby*) rugger; **les adeptes du ballon o.,** rugger fans. **2** *nm* oval; **en o.,** oval.

ovalisation [ɔvalizasjɔ̃] *nf Tech* ovalization (*of cylinders*).

ovalisé [ɔvalize] *adj Tech* ovalized (*cylinder*).

ovaliser [ɔvalize] *vt Tech* **l'usure ovalise les cylindres,** cylinders become ovalized through wear.

ovarien, -ienne [ɔvarjɛ̃, -jɛn] *adj Anat Bot* ovarian.

ovation [ɔvasjɔ̃] *nf* ovation; **faire une o. à qn,** to give s.o. an ovation.

ovationner [ɔvasjɔne] *vt* to give (*s.o.*) an ovation.

ové [ɔve] *adj* egg-shaped, ovate (*fruit etc*).

overdose [ɔvœrdoz] *nf* overdose; **mourir d'une o.,** to die of *or* from an overdose.

ovidés [ɔvide] *nmpl Zool Agr* Ovidae.

oviducte [ɔvidykt] *nm* oviduct.

ovin [ɔvɛ̃] *Agr* **1** *adj* ovine (*species etc*). **2** *nmpl* **ovins,** sheep.

ovipare [ɔvipar] *adj & nm Zool* oviparous (animal).

ovni [ɔvni] *nm* (*abrév* **objet volant non identifié**) UFO.

ovoïde [ɔvɔid] *adj* ovoid, egg-shaped; *Él* **maillon o.,** egg insulator.

ovovivipare [ɔvɔvivipar] *adj & nm* ovoviviparous (animal).

ovulaire [ɔvylɛr] *adj* ovular.

ovulation [ɔvylasjɔ̃] *nf* ovulation.

ovule [ɔvyl] *nm* **(a)** *Biol* ovule; **(b)** *Pharm* **ovules gynécologiques,** (vaginal) pessaries.

oxalate [ɔksalat] *nm Ch* oxalate.

oxalide [ɔksalid] *nf*, **oxalis** [ɔksalis] *nm Bot* oxalis, wood sorrel.

oxalique [ɔksalik] *adj Ch* **acide o.,** oxalic acid.

oxford [ɔksfɔrd] *Tex* **1** *nm* **une chemise en o.,** an Oxford shirt. **2** *adj* **de la flanelle o.,** Oxford.

oxhydrique [ɔksidrik] *adj* oxyhydrogen (*burner*).

oxyacétylénique [ɔksiasetilenik] *adj Tech* oxyacetylene (*gas, welding*).

oxycoupage [ɔksikupaʒ] *nm Métal* oxygen cutting; oxyacetylene cutting out.

oxydable [ɔksidabl] *adj* **(a)** *Ch* oxidizable; **(b)** (*d'un métal*) liable to rust.

oxydant [ɔksidɑ̃] **1** *adj* oxidizing. **2** *nm* oxidizer, oxidizing agent.

oxydation [ɔksidasjɔ̃] *nf Ch* oxidizing, oxidation.

oxyde [ɔksid] *nm Ch* oxide; **o. de carbone,** carbon monoxide.

oxyder [ɔkside] **1** *vt Ch* to oxidize. **2** **s'oxyder** *vpr* to become oxidized; (*d'un métal*) to rust.

oxygénation [ɔksiʒenasjɔ̃] *nf Ch* **(a)** (*fait de respirer de l'air pur*) **elle manque d'o.,** she doesn't get enough fresh air; **(b)** (*application d'eau oxygénée*) **les méfaits de l'o. sur les cheveux,** the damaging effects of bleach on the hair.

oxygène [ɔksiʒɛn] *nm* **(a)** *Ch* oxygen; *Méd* **tente à o.,** oxygen tent; **(b)** *F* **j'ai besoin d'o.,** (*j'étouffe*) I need fresh air *or* room to breathe.

oxygéné [ɔksiʒene] *adj Ch* oxygenated; **eau oxygénée,** hydrogen peroxide; **cheveux oxygénés,** peroxide blonde hair, bleached hair.

oxygéner [ɔksiʒene] *v* (**il oxygène; il oxygénera**) **1** *vt* **(a)** *Ch* to oxygenate, to oxygenize (*liquid, living tissue*); to oxidize (*element, chemical*); **(b)** to bleach (*hair*). **2** **s'oxygéner** *vpr* **(a)** *F* (*respirer*) to take *or* get a breath of fresh air; **(b)** (*se blondir*) **s'o. les cheveux,** to bleach one's hair.

oxyton [ɔksitɔ̃] *nm Ling* oxytone.

oxyure [ɔksjyr] *nm Méd* oxyuris.

oyat [ɔja] *nm Bot* marram grass.

ozalid [ɔzalid] *nm Typ* ozalid ®.

ozone [ɔzɔn] *nf Ch* ozone; **couche d'o.,** ozone layer.

ozonisation [ɔzɔnizasjɔ̃] *nf Ch Tech* ozonization.

ozoniser [ɔzɔnize] *vt* to ozonize.

P

P, p [pe] *nm* (the letter) P, p.
pacage [pakaʒ] *nm Agr* **(a)** (*champ*) pasture(land); **(b)** (*action de faire paître*) pasturing, grazing; *Jur* **droit(s) de p.,** grazing rights, common of pasture.
pacager [pakaʒe] *vt* (**je pacageai(s), n. pacageons**) to pasture, to graze (*beasts, field*).
pacane [pakan] *nf* pecan (nut); *Culin* **tarte aux pacanes,** pecan pie.
pacemaker [pɛsmɛkœr] *nm Sp Méd* pacemaker.
pacha [paʃa] *nm* pasha; *F* **mener une vie de p., faire le p.,** to lead an easy life.
pachyderme [paʃidɛrm] *nm* pachyderm; *Fig F* (*personne*) fat lump, tub of lard; **une allure de p.,** an elephantine *or* lumbering gait.
pacificateur, -trice [pasifikatœr, -tris] **1** *adj* pacifying. **2** *n* peacemaker.
pacification [pasifikasjɔ̃] *nf* pacification.
pacifier [pasifje] *vt* (*impf & pr sub* **n. pacifiions, v. pacifiiez**) to pacify.
pacifique [pasifik] **1** *adj* peaceful; **utilisation p. d'une découverte,** peaceful application of a discovery; **manifestation p.,** peaceful demonstration; **mener une existence p.,** to lead a quiet *or* peaceful life; **l'océan P.,** the Pacific (Ocean); *Jur* **possesseur p.,** uncontested owner. **2** *n Bible* **bienheureux les pacifiques,** blessed are the peacemakers. **3** *nm* **le P.,** the Pacific.
pacifiquement [pasifikmɑ̃] *adv* peacefully, quietly.
pacifisme [pasifism] *nm Pol* pacifism.
pacifiste [pasifist] *adj & n Pol* pacifist.
pack [pak] *nm* **(a)** (ice)pack (*of the polar seas*); **(b)** *Rugby Fb* pack; **(c)** (*lot*) pack; **cannettes de bière en p. de 6,** a six-pack (of beer).
package deal [pakɛdʒdil] *nm* package deal.
pacotille [pakɔtij] *nf Péj* **(marchandises de) p.,** shoddy goods; **c'est de la p.,** it's junk; **bijoux de p.,** paste jewellery; **de p.,** shoddy, third-rate; **exotisme de p.,** third-rate exoticism.
pacte [pakt] *nm* pact; **p. à quatre,** four-power pact; *Jur* **p. de famille,** family settlement; **p. de préférence,** preference clause; **signer un p. avec le diable,** to sign a pact with the Devil.
pactiser [paktize] *vi* **p. avec l'ennemi,** (*se mettre d'accord*) to come to terms with the enemy; *Fig* **p. avec sa conscience,** to make a compromise with one's conscience; **p. avec un crime,** to compound a felony.
pactole [paktɔl] *nm* gold mine; **ce travail est un bon p.,** this type of work is a real gold mine.
paddle [padœl] *nm Sp* paddle tennis.
paddock [padɔk] *nm* paddock; *Arg* **se mettre au p.,** (*se coucher*) to hit the sack.
paddy [padi] *nm inv* paddy.
Padoue [padu] *nf* Padua.
paella [paela] *nf Culin* paella.
paf [paf] **1** *int* slap!, bang! **2** *adj inv Arg* **être p.,** (*saoul*) to be tight.
pagaie [pagɛ] *nf* paddle (*for canoe*).
pagaïe, pagaille [pagaj] *nf F* disorder, clutter (*of objects*); **en p.,** in a mess; (*papiers*) in disorder; **tout ramasser en p.,** to bundle everything up; **je les ai mis en p.,** (*ces livres etc*) I've just bundled them up, they're not in any particular order; **quelle p.!,** what a mess!, what a shambles!; **il y en a en p.,** there's lots *or* loads of it *or* of them.
paganisme [paganism] *nm* paganism.
pagayer [pageje] *vi & vt* (**je pagaie, je pagaye**) to paddle.
pagayeur, -euse [pagɛjœr, -øz] *n* paddler.
page¹ [paʒ] *nf* page (*of book etc*); **un livre de 250 pages,** a 250-page book; **p. blanche,** blank page; *Typ* **mettre en pages,** to make up; **mise en pages,** making up, page setting; *Typ* **pages de départ,** prelims; **une des plus belles pages de Victor Hugo,** one of Victor Hugo's finest passages; *F* **être à la p.,** to be in the know; (*à la mode*) to be up to date; **ne pas être à la p.,** to be behind the times; *Fig* **une des plus célèbres pages de l'histoire,** one of the most famous pages *or* chapters in history.
page² *nm* page(boy).
page³, pageot [paʒo] *nm Arg* (*lit*) sack, *Br* pit.
pagination [paʒinasjɔ̃] *nf* pagination.
paginer [paʒine] *vt* to paginate.
pagne [paɲ] *nm* loincloth.
pagnoter (se) [sepaɲɔte] *vpr Arg* (*se coucher*) to hit the sack.
pagode [pagɔd] *nf* **(a)** *Archit* pagoda; **toit en p.,** pagoda roof; **manches p.,** pagoda sleeves; **(b)** *Arch* (*nodding toy*) mandarin.
paie [pɛ] *nf* **(a)** pay; (*par semaine*) wages; **feuille** *ou* **bulletin de p.,** pay (advice) slip; **(b)** (*fait de donner ou toucher l'argent*) payment; **jour de p.,** pay day; **faire la p.,** to pay (out) the wages.
paiement [pɛmɑ̃] *nm* payment; payment, discharge (*of debt*); **gros p.,** heavy disbursement; **p. d'avance,** payment in advance, prepayment; **p. contre livraison,** cash on delivery, C.O.D.; **p. à termes** *ou* **par acomptes,** payment by *or* in instalments; *Fig* **voilà donc le p. de mon aide!,** so that's what I get for helping you!
païen, -ïenne [pajɛ̃, -jɛn] *adj & n* pagan, heathen.
paillage [pɑjaʒ] *nm Agr* mulching.
paillard, -arde [pajar, -ard] **1** *adj* ribald, bawdy; **regard p.,** leer. **2** *n Arch* debauchee; *m* rake.
paillardise [pajardiz] *nf* **(a)** ribaldry, bawdiness; **(b)** (*parole*) bawdy joke *or* story; **(c)** *Arch* debauchery.
paillasse [pajas] **1** *nf* **(a)** (*matelas*) straw mattress, paillasse, palliasse; **(b)** (*de l'évier*) draining board. **2** *nm* clown, buffoon.
paillasson [pajasɔ̃] *nm* (*tapis-brosse*) (door)mat; *Fig* doormat; **mettre la clef sous le p.,** to clear out, *Br F* to (do a) flit.
paille [pɑj] **1** *nf* **(a)** straw; **botte de p.,** truss of straw; **p. de litière,** loose straw; **menue p., p. d'avoine,** chaff; **p. de riz** *ou* **d'Italie,** rice straw; **chapeau de p.,** straw hat; **chaise de p.,** straw-bottomed chair; *Fig* **homme de p.,** man of straw, *Am* straw man; *Fig* **feu de p.,** flash in the pan; *Fig* **être sur la p.,** to be destitute; *Fig* **voir la p. dans l'œil du prochain,** to see the mote in one's brother's eye; **tirer à la courte p.,** to draw lots; **(b)** (*pour boire*) (drinking) straw; **boire qch avec une p.,** to drink sth through *or* with a straw; **(c) p. de fer,** steel wool; **(d)** (*défaut*) flaw (*in gem etc*). **2** *adj inv* straw-coloured *or US* -colored; *Culin* **pommes p.,** = deep-fried straw potatoes.
paillé¹ [pɑje] *nm* stable litter.
paillé² *adj* **(a)** (*couleur*) straw-coloured *or US* -colored; **(b)** (*chaise etc*) straw-bottomed; **(c)** flawed (*metal, gem etc*); scaly (*metal*).
pailler¹ [pɑje] *nm* (*hangar*) farmyard, straw yard; (*meule*) straw stack.
pailler² *vt* **(a)** *Agr* to protect *or* mulch with straw; **(b)** to put a straw bottom in (*a chair*).
paillet [pajɛ] *nm Nau* mat, fender; **p. d'abordage, p. makarov,** collision mat.
pailleté [pajte] *adj* spangled (**de,** with).
pailleter [pajte] *vt* (**je paillette; je pailletterai**) to spangle.
paillette [pajɛt] *nf* **(a)** spangle, sequin; **(b)** grain of gold dust (*in stream*); flake (*of mica etc*); **savon en paillettes,** soap flakes; **(c)** flaw (*in gem*).
pailleux, -euse [pɑjø, -øz] *adj* **(a)** (*qui contient de la paille*) strawy (*manure*); **(b)** flawy (*iron, glass*).
paillis [pɑji] *nm Agr* mulch.
paillon [pɑjɔ̃] *nm* **(a)** (*de métal*) (large) spangle; **(b)** (*de soudure*) (jeweller's) foil; **(c)** wisp of straw; **(d)** straw case (*for bottle*).
paillote [pajɔt] *nf* straw hut.

pain [pɛ̃] *nm* **(a)** (*aliment*) bread; (*unité*) loaf, *pl* loaves; **quelle sorte de p. devrais-je acheter?,** what kind of bread should I buy?; **achète deux pains de mie,** buy two sandwich loaves; **p. de seigle,** rye bread; **p. noir,** buckwheat bread, black rye bread; **p. bis,** brown bread; **p. complet,** wholemeal bread; **p. viennois,** wheaten bread; **p. frais/rassis,** fresh bread/stale bread; **p. de ménage,** (homemade) loaf; **p. de mie,** sandwich loaf; **p. de campagne, p. paysan,** farmhouse loaf; **p. grillé,** toast; **mettre qn au p. et à l'eau** *ou* **au p. sec,** to put s.o. on bread and water *or* on dry bread; **p. azyme,** unleavened bread; *Rel* **le p. et le vin,** the bread and wine; **bon comme bon p.,** kind-hearted, good-natured; *Fig* **acheter qch pour une bouchée de p.,** to buy sth for a song *or* for next to nothing; *Fig* **il ne vaut pas le p. qu'il mange,** he isn't worth his salt; *Fig* **manger son p. blanc le premier,** (to) live now, pay later; *Fig* **avoir du p. sur la planche,** to have plenty of work to do, to have a lot on one's plate; *Fig* **gagner son p.,** to earn one's living; *Fig* **ôter à qn le p. de la bouche,** to take the bread out of s.o.'s mouth; *Fig* **je ne mange pas de ce p.-là,** I'd rather starve (than get involved in that); *Bot* **arbre à p.,** breadfruit tree;

(b) p. perdu, (*cuit à la poêle*) French toast; (*cuit au four*) = dessert consisting of stale bread soaked in milk and cooked with eggs, sugar and raisins; **p. d'épices,** ≈ gingerbread; **p. de Gênes,** Genoa cake; **petit p.,** (bread) roll; **p. au chocolat,** chocolate-filled roll; **pain au lait,** sweet roll; **p. aux raisins,** currant bun; *Fig* **ça se vend comme des petits pains,** it sells *or* it's selling like hot cakes; *Culin* **p. de poisson,** fish loaf;

(c) bar, cake (*of soap*); bar (*of wax*); **p. de sucre,** sugar loaf; *Géog* **(montagne en) p. de sucre,** sugar loaf (mountain);

(d) *Arg* (*coup de poing*) punch; **flanque-lui un p.,** sock him one;

(e) *Arch* **p. à cacheter,** (sealing) wafer.

pair [pɛr] **1** *adj* even (*number*); **jours pairs,** even dates; *Ordinat* **parité paire,** even parity; **jouer p.,** to bet on the even numbers; *Rail* **voie paire,** up line.

2 *nm* **(a)** (*égal*) equal, peer; *Litt* **être avec qn** *ou* **traiter qn de p. à compagnon,** to treat s.o. as an equal; **sans p.,** unequalled, peerless; **hors (de) p.,** unrivalled, beyond compare; **aller de p. (avec),** to be on a par *or* on an equal footing (with); (*au même moment*) to happen at the same time (as); **le chômage va de p. avec les crises économiques,** unemployment and economic crises go hand in hand;

(b) peer (of the realm); *Br* **Chambre des Pairs,** House of Lords;

(c) *Fin* par; **p. du change,** par of exchange; **au-dessous/au-dessus du p.,** below/above par; **au p.,** at par;

(d) travailler au p., to work au pair, to do au pair work; **(jeune fille) au p.,** au pair (girl);

(e) le p. et l'impair, odd and even.

paire [pɛr] *nf* pair (*of shoes, spectacles, scissors etc*); brace (*of game birds, pistols*); **p. de bœufs,** yoke of oxen; *F* **une belle p. de fesses,** (*de femme*) a nice piece of ass; (*d'homme*) nice buns; *Fig F* **ça, c'est une autre p. de manches,** that's another story; *F* **les deux font la p.,** they're two of a kind; *Arg* **se faire la p.,** to clear out, to beat it.

pairesse [pɛrɛs] *nf Br* peeress.

pairie [peri] *nf* peerage.

paisible [pezibl] *adj* peaceful; **silence p.,** peaceful *or* undisturbed silence; *Jur* **p. possesseur d'un bien,** uncontested owner of a piece of property.

paisiblement [peziblәmɑ̃] *adv* peacefully.

paître [pɛtr] *v* (*prp* **paissant**; *pr ind* **je pais, il paît, n. paissons**; *pr sub* **je paisse**; *impf* **je paissais**; *fu* **je paîtrai**; *no p hist; pp* **pu** *is used only in the phrase shown under* **2**) **1** *vt* (*of animals*) to feed on (*leaves etc*); to crop (*grass*); *Arch & Litt* to feed, to graze (*cattle*). **2** *vi* (*of animals*) to feed; (*manger de l'herbe*) to graze, to pasture; (*manger des feuilles*) to browse; **faucon qui a pu,** hawk that has fed; *Fig F* **je l'ai envoyé p.,** I sent him packing.

paix [pɛ] *nf* peace; **faire la p.,** to make peace; **faire la p. avec qn,** to make one's peace with s.o., to make it up with s.o.; *Pol* **demander la p.,** to sue for peace; **rester en p. avec un pays,** to remain at peace with a country; **vivre en p. avec ses voisins/sa conscience,** to live at peace with one's neighbours/conscience; **en temps de p.,** in peacetime; **observer/troubler la p.,** to keep/break the peace; **climat de p. sociale,** (*absence de grèves*) climate of industrial peace; *Jur* **juge de p.,** magistrate, justice of the peace; **la p. du tombeau,** the quiet of the grave; **avoir besoin de p. pour se concentrer,** to need peace and quiet to concentrate; **dormir en p.,** to sleep peacefully; **laissez-moi en p.,** leave me alone *or* in peace; *F* **fiche-moi la p.!,** don't bother me!, shut up!; **la p.!,** hush!, be quiet!

Pakistan [pakistɑ̃] *nm* Pakistan.

pakistanais, -aise [pakistanɛ, -ɛz] **1** *adj* Pakistani. **2** *n* **P.,** Pakistani.

pal [pal] *nm* **(a)** (*pieu*) pale, stake; *Arch* **le (supplice du) p.,** impalement; **(b)** (*plantoir*) planter, dibber.

palabre [palabr] *nf* (*souvent pl*) **palabres,** palaver, (interminable) discussion.

palabrer [palabre] *vi* to palaver, to talk interminably.

palace [palas] *nm* luxury hotel.

paladin [paladɛ̃] *nm* paladin; (*itinérant*) knight-errant.

palais¹ [palɛ] *nm* **(a)** palace (*of king etc*); **le P. Bourbon,** the Assemblée nationale; **le P. de l'Élysée,** the Elysée (Palace) (*residence of the French President*); **(b)** *Jur* **P. de Justice, le P.,** the law courts; **gens du** *ou* **de P., le P.,** lawyers; **terme de P.,** legal term.

palais² *nm* **(a)** *Anat* palate; **voûte du p., p. dur,** hard palate; **voile du p., p. mou,** soft palate; **p. fendu,** cleft palate; **(b)** (*goût*) (sense of) taste; **avoir le p. fin,** to have a fine palate.

palan [palɑ̃] *nm* hoist, hoisting gear; *Tech Nau* pulley block, purchase tackle, whip.

palanche [palɑ̃ʃ] *nf* yoke (*for carrying buckets etc*).

palanque [palɑ̃k] *nf* (timber) stockade.

palanquer [palɑ̃ke] *vi* to stockade.

palanquin [palɑ̃kɛ̃] *nm* palanquin.

palastre [palastr] *nm* box (*of lock*); **serrure à p.,** rim lock.

palatal, -ale, -aux [palatal, -o] **1** *adj* **(a)** *Ling* palatal; **voyelle palatale,** front vowel; **(b)** *Anat* palatal (*bones etc*). **2** *nf Ling* **palatale,** palatal.

palatalisation [palatalizasjɔ̃] *nf Ling* palatalization.

palataliser [palatalize] *vt Ling* to palatalize.

palatin, -ine [palatɛ̃, -in] **1** *adj* **(a)** *Hist* palatine; **Comte p.,** Count Palatine; **(b) Le Mont P.,** the Palatine Hill (*in Rome*). **2** *n Hist* palatine. **3** *nf Hist* **La Palatine,** the Princess Palatine.

Palatinat (le) [lәpalatina] *nm Hist* the Palatinate.

pale¹ [pal] *nf* **(a)** blade (*of oar, propeller*); vane (*of fan etc*); **hélice à trois/quatre pales,** three-/four-bladed propeller; **(b)** sluice (gate); hatch (*of mill*).

pale² *nf Rel* pall(a), chalice cover.

pâle [pɑl] *adj* **(a)** (*livide, blafard*) pale; *Litt Méd* pallid; **p. comme un linge** *ou* **comme la mort,** as white as a sheet, deathly pale; **être p. de colère,** to be livid with rage; *Mil F* **se faire porter p.,** to report sick; **(b)** pale (*colour, sky*); pale, faint (*light*); **les Visages pâles,** the Palefaces; **un sourire p.,** a wan *or* faint smile; **style p.,** colourless style; **une p. imitation de Vermeer,** a pale *or* poor imitation of Vermeer; *F* **c'est un p. crétin,** he's a complete idiot *or* fool.

palefrenier [palfrәnje] *nm* groom; *Arch* (*d'auberge*) ostler.

palefroi [palfrwa] *nm Hist* palfrey.

paléographe [paleɔgraf] *n* palaeographer, *surtout US* paleographer.

paléographie [paleɔgrafi] *nf* palaeography, *surtout US* paleographer.

paléographique [paleɔgrafik] *adj* palaeographic, *surtout US* paleographic.

paléolithique [paleɔlitik] **1** *adj* Palaeolithic, *surtout US* Paleolithic. **2** *nm* Palaeolithic *ou surtout US* Paleolithic age.

paléontologie [paleɔ̃tɔlɔʒi] *nf* palaeontology, *surtout US* paleontology.

paléontologique [paleɔ̃tɔlɔʒik] *adj* palaeontological, *surtout US* paleontological.

paléontologiste [paleɔ̃tɔlɔʒist], **paléontologue** [paleɔ̃tɔlɔg] *n* palaeontologist, *surtout US* paleontologist.

paleron [palrɔ̃] *nm* shoulder blade, blade bone (*of horse, ox etc*); *Culin* **p. de bœuf,** chuck.

Palestine [palɛstin] *nf* Palestine.

palestinien, -ienne [palɛstinjɛ̃, -jɛn] **1** *adj* Palestinian. **2** *n* **P.,** Palestinian.

palet [palɛ] *nm* **(a)** (*anneaux*) quoit; **jouer au(x) palet(s),** to play at quoits; **(b)** (*for ice hockey*) puck; (*for curling*) stone.

paletot [palto] *nm* (short) overcoat; *Arg* **tomber sur le p. de qn,** to attack s.o., to jump on s.o.; (*pour lui parler*) to buttonhole s.o., to nab s.o..

palette [palɛt] *nf* **(a)** (painter's) palette; *Fig* (*éventail*) range (*of activities, products etc*); **la p. de Matisse,** the range of colours used by Matisse; **(b)** (*pour la manutention*) pallet; **(c)** *Culin* shoulder (*of mutton, pork*); **(d)** (*aube*) paddle, float board (*of paddle wheel*); **(e)** (*raquette de bois*) (wooden) battledore.

palettisation [paletizasjɔ̃] *nf Tech* palletization.

palettiser [paletize] *adj Tech* to palletize.

palétuvier [paletyvje] *nm* mangrove.

pâleur [pɑlœr] *nf* paleness, pallor; **d'une p. mortelle,** deathly pale.

palier [palje] *nm* **(a)** *Archit* landing (*of stairs*); **nous sommes voisins de p.,** we live on the same floor; **p. intermédiaire,** half-landing; **(b)** (*étape*) stage; **procéder par paliers,** to proceed in stages; **(c)** *Aut Rail etc* level stretch; *Math etc* plateau (*of graph*); *Aut Rail etc* **vitesse en p.,** speed on the level *or* on the flat; *Av* **voler en p.,** to fly level; **le taux des naissances a atteint un p.,** the birthrate has reached a plateau *or* has levelled off; **(d)** *Tech* bearing; **p. d'arbre,** shaft bearing.

palière [paljɛr] *adj* **porte p.,** landing door, door opening onto the landing; **marche p.,** top step.

palindrome [palɛ̃drom] *nm Ling* palindrome.

palinodie [palinɔdi] *nf* **(a)** *Litt* palinode; **(b)** *Péj* recantation.

pâlir [pɑlir] **1** *vi* to become pale, to grow pale; (*of light, star etc*) to fade, to grow dim; (*of colour*) to fade; **p. d'horreur,** to turn pale *or* go white with horror; **ses joues ont pâli,** his cheeks have lost their colour; **faire p. qn de jalousie,** to make s.o. green with envy; *Fig* **p. sur un travail,** to slave over a piece of work. **2** *vt* to turn (*s.o., sth*) pale.

palis [pali] *nm* **(a)** (*clôture*) (picket) fence; **(b)** (*espace entouré*) enclosure, pale; **(c)** (*pieu*) picket.

palissade [palisad] *nf* **(a)** (*clôture*) fence; *Mil* palisade; **(b)** (*de jardin*) hedge.

palissader [palisade] *vt* to fence in, to rail in, to enclose; *Mil* to palisade.

palissandre [palisɑ̃dr] *nm* (*bois*) Brazilian rosewood.

pâlissant [pɑlisɑ̃] *adj* (*face*) turning pale; fading, waning (*light*); fading (*colour*).

palladium¹ [paladjɔm] *nm Myth* Palladium; *Fig* (*garantie*) safeguard.

palladium² *nm Ch* palladium.

palliatif, -ive [paljatif, -iv] **1** *adj* palliative. **2** *nm Méd & Fig* palliative; *Fig* stopgap measure.

pallier [palje] *v* (*impf & pr sub* **n. palliions, v. palliiez**) **1** *vt* to palliate (*pain, disease*); to extenuate (*offence, mistake*); (*cacher, dissimuler*) to cover up (*offence, mistake*). **2** *vi* **p. aux conséquences d'une faute,** to mitigate the consequences of an error; **p. à un manque de matière première,** to compensate *or* make up for the lack of raw material.

palmarès [palmarɛs] *nm Scol etc* honours *or US* honors list; (*à une distribution de prix*) prize list; *Sp* (list of) medal winners; *Mus Rad etc* **p. (de la chanson),** (the) charts, the top twenty *or* thirty *etc*; **être** *ou* **figurer au p.,** to be among the (prize) winners; *Mus* to be in the charts; **avoir un beau p.,** (*d'un sportif*) to be having a good season *or* year.

palme [palm] *nf* **(a)** palm (branch); *Fig* (*symbole de la victoire*) palm; **le dimanche des Palmes,** Palm Sunday; **p. du martyre,** martyr's crown, crown of martyrdom; **palmes (académiques),** = decoration given by the Ministry of Education; **avec p.,** (*decoration*) ≈ with bar; **(b)** *Arch* palm (tree); **huile/vin de p.,** palm oil/wine; **(c)** (*pour nager*) flipper.

palmé [palme] *adj* **(a)** *Bot* palmate (*leaf*); **(b)** *Orn* web-footed; **pied p.,** webbed foot.

palmer [palmɛr] *nm Tech* micrometer.

palmeraie [palmərɛ] *nf* palm grove.

palmette [palmɛt] *nf Archit* palmette.

palmier [palmje] *nm* **(a)** palm (tree); **cœur de p.,** palm (tree) heart; **(b)** *Culin* = small sweet pastry in shape of palm leaf.

palmipède [palmipɛd] *Orn* **1** *adj* web-footed, *Spéc* palmiped(e). **2** *nm* web-footed bird, *Spéc* palmiped(e).

palmiste [palmist] *nm* (*plante*) cabbage palm *or* tree; **chou p.,** palm tree heart.

palombe [palɔ̃b] *nf Région* ringdove, wood pigeon.

palonnier [palɔnje] *nm* (*de voiture*) swingletree, whippletree; *Av* rudder bar; *Aut* **p. de freinage,** compensator.

pâlot, -otte [pɑlo, -ɔt] *adj* rather pale, peaky; sickly-looking (*child*).

palourde [palurd] *nf* (*mollusque*) clam.

palpable [palpabl] *adj* **(a)** (*que l'on peut toucher*) palpable, tangible; **(b)** (*réel, vérifiable*) palpable (*error, lie*); obvious, easily perceived, plain (*truth etc*).

palper [palpe] **1** *vt* to feel (*sth*); to examine (*sth*) by feeling; *Méd* to palpate. **2** *vi F* to receive money, to be paid; **qu'est-ce qu'il a dû p.!,** he must have made a mint!; **j'ai palpé 500 balles,** I was paid *or* got 500 francs; **quand est-ce que je vais p.?,** when am I going to get my money?, when am I going to get paid?

palpeur [palpœr] *nm* (*de cuisinière*) (heat) sensor.

palpitant [palpitɑ̃] **1** *adj* palpitating, fluttering (*heart*); quivering (*with emotion etc*); **roman p. (d'intérêt),** thrilling *or* exciting novel. **2** *nm Arg* (*cœur*) ticker.

palpitation [palpitɑsjɔ̃] *nf* palpitation (*of heart*); fluttering (*of heart, eyelid, pulse*); **avoir des palpitations,** to have palpitations.

palpiter [palpite] *vi* (*of heart*) to palpitate; (*of heart, pulse, eyelid*) to flutter; (*of light etc*) to flicker; **il palpitait de peur,** he was quivering with fear.

paluche [palyʃ] *nf Arg* (*main*) mitt, paw.

paludéen, -enne [palydeɛ̃, -ɛn] *adj* marsh (*plant, land etc*); *Méd* malarial.

paludisme [palydism] *nm* malaria.

palustre [palystr] *adj* marsh (*plant etc*); *Méd* malarial.

pâmer (se) [səpɑme] *vpr* **(a) se p. de rire,** to be convulsed with laughter, to split one's sides (with laughter); **se p. d'admiration,** to be in raptures (**sur,** over), to be overcome with admiration (**sur,** for); **(b)** *Arch* (*s'évanouir*) to swoon, to faint.

pâmoison [pɑmwazɔ̃] *nf Arch* swoon; *Iron* **tomber en p.,** to swoon; **tomber en p. devant qch,** to go into raptures over sth.

pampa [pɑ̃pa] *nf* pampas (*of South America*).

pamphlet [pɑ̃flɛ] *nm* satirical tract, lampoon.

pamphlétaire [pɑ̃fletɛr] *n* lampooner.

pamplemousse [pɑ̃pləmus] *nm* **(a)** (*fruit*) grapefruit; **(b)** (*arbre*) shaddock.

pampre [pɑ̃pr] *nm* vine branch (*with grapes*).

pan¹ [pɑ̃] *nm* **(a)** (*de chemise, manteau*) tail; (*de jupe*) panel; **se promener en p. de chemise,** to wander about in one's shirt-tails; **(b)** (*morceau*) section, piece; **p. de mur,** section of wall; **p. de bois,** timber framing; **p. de comble,** side *or* panel of a roof; **p. de ciel,** patch of sky; **p. de voûte,** severy; **(c)** face, side (*of angular building etc*); **tour à huit pans,** eight-sided *or* octagonal tower; **p. coupé,** cant; **en p. coupé,** with the corner cut off.

pan² *int* **(a)** bang!, crash!, wham!; **(b)** *Enf* **je vais te faire p. p.!,** I'll smack you!

Pan [pɑ̃] *nm Myth* Pan.

panacée [panase] *nf* panacea.

panachage [panaʃaʒ] *nm* **(a)** mixing (*of colours* etc); **(b)** *Pol* = splitting one's vote between candidates from different parties.

panache [panaʃ] *nm* **(a)** (*aigrette*) plume, panache; plume, tuft (*of feathers etc*); **p. de fumée,** plume *or* wreath *or* trail of smoke; *F* **faire p.,** (*of rider, cyclist*) to take a header; **(b)** (*brio, éclat*) ostentation, panache; **il a du p.,** he has panache; **(c)** *Archit* panache (*of pendentive*).

panaché [panaʃe] **1** *adj* variegated, multicoloured, *US* multicolored (*bird, flower*); motley (*crowd*); *Pol* **liste panachée,** = ballot paper in which votes are split among candidates from different parties; *Culin* **salade panachée,** mixed salad; **glace panachée,** = selection of various flavours of ice cream; **bière panachée,** shandy. **2** *nm* shandy.

panacher [panaʃe] *vt* **(a)** (*bigarrer*) to variegate (*with different colours*); **(b)** *Pol* **p. une liste électorale,** to split one's votes (among candidates from different parties).

panade [panad] *nf Culin* bread soup; *F* **être dans la p.,** to be in the soup *or* in a fix; (*ne pas avoir d'argent temporairement*) to be short of cash.

panafricain [panafrikɛ̃] *adj Pol* Pan-African.

panafricanisme [panafrikanism] *nm Pol* Pan-Africanism.

panais [panɛ] *nm* (*légume*) parsnip.

Panama [panama] *nm* **(a)** Panama; **le canal de P.,** the Panama Canal; **(b)** (*chapeau*) panama hat.

Paname [panam] *nm Arg* Paris.

panaméen, -enne [panameɛ, -ɛn] **1** *adj* Panamanian. **2** *n* **P.,** Panamanian.

panaméricain [panamerikɛ̃] *adj Pol* Pan-American.

panaméricanisme [panamerikanism] *nm Pol* Pan-Americanism.

panarabisme [panarabism] *nm Pol* Pan-Arabism.

panard [panar] **1** *adj* (*horse*) knock-kneed, cow-hocked. **2** *nm Arg* (*pied*) foot; **panards,** feet, *Br* plates (of meat); **quel p.!,** great!, terrific!, fantastic!

panaris [panari] *nm Méd* whitlow.

pancarte [pɑ̃kart] *nf* sign, notice; (*affiche*) placard.

pancréas [pɑ̃kreas] *nm Anat* pancreas.

pancréatique [pɑ̃kreatik] *adj Anat* pancreatic.

panda [pɑ̃da] *nm* panda.

pandémie [pɑ̃demi] *nf Méd* pandemic.
pandémonium [pɑ̃demɔnjɔn] *nm (lieu de corruption)* den of vice *or* iniquity; *(lieu de désordre)* pandemonium.
pandit [pɑ̃di] *nm (Indian title)* pandit, pundit.
pané [pane] *adj Culin* coated with breadcrumbs, breaded.
panégyrique [paneʒirik] *nm* panegyric; **faire le p. de qn,** to extol s.o.'s virtues *or* merits.
panégyriste [paneʒirist] *nm* panegyrist, eulogist.
panel [panel] *nm* panel; *(échantillon)* sample (group).
paner [pane] *vt Culin* to cover *or* coat *(meat, fish etc)* with breadcrumbs.
paneterie [pantri] *nf* bread store *(in barracks, schools etc)*.
panetière [pantjɛr] *nf* bread bin.
pangermanisme [pɑ̃ʒɛrmanism] *nm Pol* Pan-Germanism.
panier [panje] *nm* **(a)** *(corbeille)* basket; basket(ful) *(of fruit etc)*; **p. à anse(s),** basket; **mettre** *ou* **jeter qch au p.,** to throw sth away *or* out; *(littéralement)* to throw sth in the wastepaper basket; **p. à provisions,** shopping basket; **p. à salade,** salad shaker; *F (convoi cellulaire)* prison van, *Br Vieilli* Black Maria; **p. à bouteilles,** bottle carrier; *Fig* **mettre tous ses œufs dans le même p.,** to put all one's eggs in one basket; *Fig* **moi, les hommes je les mets tous dans le même p.,** men are all alike *or* the same, as far as I'm concerned; *Fig* **il faut pas les mettre tous dans le même p.,** you can't lump them all together, they're not all tarred with the same brush; *F* **p. percé,** spendthrift; *Écon* **le p. de la ménagère,** the shopping basket; *Écon Fig* **p. des devises,** basket of currencies; *Fig* **le dessus du p.,** the pick of the bunch; *Fig* **c'est un p. de crabes,** they're always fighting *or* at each other's throats;
(b) *(nasse)* lobster pot;
(c) *Sp (basketball)* basket; **réussir** *ou* **marquer un p.,** to score (a basket);
(d) *(de tondeuse)* grass box;
(e) *(pour diapositives)* slide magazine;
(f) *(de crinoline)* hoop.
panier-repas [panjerəpɑ] *nm (panier)* lunch basket; *(repas)* packed lunch; *(pl paniers-repas)*.
panifiable [panifjabl] *adj (cereals etc)* suitable for making bread.
panifier [panifje] *vt (impf & pr sub* **n. panifiions, v. panifiiez***)* to turn *(flour)* into bread.
panique [panik] **1** *adj* panic *(terror)*. **2** *nf* panic; **pris de p.,** panic-stricken; **pris de p. ils s'enfuirent,** they fled in a panic; **ne pas céder à la p.,** not to let oneself be panicked, not to give way to panic; *F* **pas de p., c'est pas la fin du monde!,** don't panic, it's not the end of the world!
paniquer [panike] *F* **1** *vt* to get *(s.o.)* into a panic. **2** *vi* to (get into a) panic, to get panicky.
panislamisme [panislamism] *nm Pol* Pan-Islamism.
panne¹ [pan] *nf* **(a)** *Tex* panne, plush; **(b)** *(gras)* fat, lard; *Fig (of person)* flab; *Fig* **tu as de la p.,** you're flabby.
panne² *nf* **(a)** *(arrêt de fonctionnement)* (mechanical) breakdown; *Él* (power) failure, outage; **en p.,** out of order; **p. de courant** *ou* **d'électricité,** power failure, power cut, blackout; *Rad TV* **p. d'émission,** technical fault *or* hitch; **p. de moteur,** engine failure; **tomber en p. d'essence, tomber en p. sèche,** to run out of petrol *or Am* gas; *F* **il m'a fait le coup de la p.,** he pretended we'd run out of petrol *or Am* gas; **vous êtes en p.?,** *(to motorist)* have you broken down?; *F* **être en p.,** *(of person)* to be *or* get stuck; *F* **rester en p. devant une difficulté,** to be *or* get stuck over a difficulty; *F* **laisser qn en p.,** to leave s.o. in the lurch, to let s.o. down; *F* **je suis en p. d'allumettes,** I've run out of matches; *F* **avoir une p. d'oreiller,** to oversleep;
(b) *Nau* **en p.,** hove to; **mettre un navire en p.,** to bring a ship to.
panne³ *nf Constr* purlin *(of roof)*.
panne⁴ *nf Tech* peen, pane *(of hammer)*.
panneau, -eaux [pano] *nm* **(a)** *(pour afficher)* board; **p. d'affichage,** *Br* notice *or Am* bulletin board; *(de publicité)* (advertisement) hoarding, *Am* billboard; *Ordinat* bulletin board; *Aut* **p. indicateur,** signpost, direction sign; **p. de signalisation (routière),** roadsign; **panneaux électoraux,** noticeboards for election posters; **(b)** *(élément plan)* panel; **panneaux,** panelling; **porte à panneaux,** panelled door; **p. vitré,** glass panel; **p. mobile/coulissant,** movable/sliding panel; *Nau etc* **p. d'écoutille, p. de cale,** hatch cover; **(c)** snare, net *(for game)*; *Fig* **tomber** *ou* **donner dans le p.,** to fall into the trap.
panneau-réclame [panoreklam] *nm* (advertisement) hoarding, *Am* billboard; *(pl panneaux-réclame)*.
panneton [pantɔ̃] *nm* web, bit *(of key)*.
panonceau, -eaux [panɔ̃so] *nm* **(a)** *(de notaire etc)* plaque; **(b)** *(pancarte)* sign; **(c)** *Arch* escutcheon.
panoplie [panɔpli] *nf (armure)* panoply; *(assortiment)* set *(of tools)*; *Fig* panoply, array; **p. de soldat/d'infirmière/etc,** soldier's/nurse's/*etc* outfit *or* costume *(for child)*; **j'ai eu droit à toute la p.,** I got the works.
panorama [panɔrama] *nm* panorama; *Fig* **p. des théories actuelles,** overview of current theories.
panoramique [panɔramik] **1** *adj* panoramic; **voiture avec carrosserie p.,** car with panoramic *or* wrap-round windows; **vue p.,** panoramic view. **2** *nm Cin TV* panning.
pansage [pɑ̃saʒ] *nm* grooming *(of horse etc)*.
panse [pɑ̃s] *nf* **(a)** *F (ventre)* belly, paunch, pot; **s'en mettre plein la p.,** to gorge *or* stuff oneself; **(b)** first stomach, paunch, rumen *(of ruminant)*; **(c)** belly, bulge *(of bottle etc)*; sound bow *(of bell)*.
pansement [pɑ̃smɑ̃] *nm Méd* **(a)** *(action)* dressing *(for wound)*; **faire un p.,** to dress a wound, to apply a dressing; **(b)** *(élément protecteur)* dressing; *(enroulé autour d'une blessure)* bandage; **p. (adhésif),** (sticking) plaster; **il est couvert de pansements,** he's all bandaged up; **il faut mettre un p.,** you ought to put a bandage on it.
panser [pɑ̃se] *vt* **(a)** to dress, to put a dressing on *(a wound)*; to bandage *(a limb)*; to put a plaster on *(a finger)*; **p. un blessé,** to dress s.o.'s wounds; **(b)** to groom, to rub down *(horse)*.
panslavisme [pɑ̃slavism] *nm Pol* Pan-Slavism.
pansu [pɑ̃sy] *adj* potbellied *(person, bottle etc)*; paunchy *(person)*.
pantagruélique [pɑ̃tagryelik] *adj* pantagruelian *(meal etc)*.
pantalon [pɑ̃talɔ̃] *nm* **(a)** (pair of) trousers, *Am* pants; **mettre un p.,** to put on a pair of trousers; **mettre son p.,** to put on one's trousers; **p. de golf,** plus-fours; **p. de ski,** (a pair of) ski pants; **p. fuseau,** tapering trousers, ski pants; **elle porte des pantalons,** she wears trousers; *Fig* **c'est elle qui porte le p.,** she wears the trousers; **(b)** *Th* **P.,** Pantaloon.
pantalon-jupe [pɑ̃talɔ̃ʒyp] *nm* palazzo pants; *(pl pantalons-jupes)*.
pantalonnade [pɑ̃talɔnad] *nf* **(a)** *Th Hist* burlesque farce; **(b)** *(hypocrisie)* piece of hypocrisy.
pantelant [pɑ̃tlɑ̃] *adj* **(a)** panting, gasping; **être p. d'émotion,** to be panting with emotion; **la nouvelle m'a laissé p.,** the news left *or* had me gasping; **(b)** quivering, twitching *(dying animal, body)*; **chair pantelante,** twitching flesh *(of dying animal)*.
panteler [pɑ̃tle] *vi* (**je pantelle, n. pantelons; je pantellerai**) to pant, to gasp; **p. d'émotion,** to be panting with emotion.
pantène, pantenne [pɑ̃tɛn] *nf* **(a)** *(de chasse)* draw net; **(b)** *Nau* **en p.,** in disorder; **vergues en p.,** yard apeak, scandalized *(as sign of mourning)*.
panthéisme [pɑ̃teism] *nm Phil* pantheism.
panthéiste [pɑ̃teist] *Phil* **1** *adj* pantheistic(al). **2** *n* pantheist.
panthéon [pɑ̃teɔ̃] *nm* pantheon; **le p. grec,** the Greek pantheon; **faire partie du p. des hommes célèbres,** to have a place in the hall of fame.
panthère [pɑ̃tɛr] *nf* panther.
pantin [pɑ̃tɛ̃] *nm (poupée)* jumping jack; *Péj (fantoche)* puppet, stooge; **elle a fait de son époux un p.,** she has her husband wrapped around her little finger.
pantographe [pɑ̃tɔgraf] *nm Rail* pantograph.
pantois [pɑ̃twa] *adj* astounded, *F* flabbergasted; **j'en suis tout p.,** I'm astounded *or* speechless *or F* flabbergasted; **en rester p.,** to be speechless *or F* flabbergasted.
pantomime [pɑ̃tɔmim] *nf* **(a)** *Th (art)* mime; *(spectacle)* mime show; **(b)** *Péj (comédie)* scene; **que signifie cette p.?,** what on earth are you playing at?
pantouflard, -arde [pɑ̃tuflar, -ard] *adj & n F* stay-at-home.
pantoufle [pɑ̃tufl] *nf* slipper; **il était en pantoufles,** he was wearing *or* he was in his slipppers; **les pantoufles de vair de Cendrillon,** Cinderella's glass slippers; *Fig* **passer sa vie dans ses pantoufles,** to live a quiet life; *Fig* **raisonner comme une p.,** to talk through one's hat.
pantoufler [pɑ̃tufle] *vi F (d'un fonctionnaire)* to join the private sector.
panure [panyr] *nf Culin* breadcrumbs.
PAO [peao] *nf Ordinat (abrév* **publication assistée par ordinateur***)* DTP.
paon [pɑ̃] *nm* **(a)** *(oiseau)* peacock; **pousser des cris de p.,** to screech like a peacock; **se parer des plumes du p.,** to take all the credit; **être vaniteux comme un p.,** to be as

vain as a peacock; **faire le p.,** to strut about; **(b)** (*insecte*) peacock butterfly.

paonne [pan] *nf* peahen.

paonneau, -eaux [pano] *nm* peachick.

papa [papa] *nm* dad; *surtout Enf* daddy; *surtout Am* pa, pop; **p. gâteau,** indulgent father; **c'est un fils à p.,** he's a daddy's boy; *F* **faire qch à la p.,** to do sth in a leisurely fashion; *Aut Fig* **aller à la p.,** to potter along; *F Péj* **de p.,** old-fashioned, behind the times; *F Péj* **c'est un film de p.,** the film is old-fashioned *or* behind the times.

papal, -aux [papal, -o] *adj* papal.

papauté [papote] *nf* papacy.

papaye [papaj] *nf* pa(w)paw, papaya.

papayer [papaje] *nm* pa(w)paw, papaya (tree).

pape [pap] *nm* **(a)** *Rel* pope; **plus catholique que le p.,** more Catholic than the Pope; *F* **heureux comme un p.,** happy as a sandboy, happy as Larry; *F* **sérieux comme un p.,** deadly serious; **(b)** (*d'une association, un mouvement etc*) leading light.

papelard¹, -arde [paplar, -ard] *Péj* **1** *adj* sanctimonious, smarmy (*voice etc*); **il a un air p.,** he looks as if butter wouldn't melt in his mouth. **2** *n* sanctimonious *or* self-righteous person, hypocrite.

papelard² *nm F* (piece of) paper; (*journal*) (news)paper.

paperasse [papras] *nf Péj* papers; (*fiches à remplir*) forms, *F* red tape; **il y a plein de p. sur mon bureau,** my desk is covered in paper; **c'est de la p.!,** it's just a lot of (old) papers!; **j'ai horreur de toutes ces paperasses,** I hate all this red tape.

paperasserie [paprasri] *nf Péj* (accumulation of) papers; (*à remplir*) forms, *Br F* bumf, bumph; **la p. (administrative),** red tape; **il y a trop de p.,** (*dans ce travail*) there's too much paperwork; (*pour obtenir un visa etc*) there's too much paperwork *or* red tape (involved).

paperassier, -ière [paprasje, -jɛr] *Péj* **1** *adj* (*personne*) fond of paperwork; (*procédure*) cluttered up with red tape. **2** *n* **(a)** (*personne qui amasse les papiers*) hoarder of (old) papers, *Am F* pack rat; **(b)** (*fonctionnaire*) bureaucrat.

papeterie [papetri] *nf* **(a)** *Ind* paper manufacturing; (*usine*) paper mill; **(b)** (*magasin*) stationer's (shop); (*articles*) stationery; **librairie-p.,** bookshop and stationer's.

papetier, -ière [paptje, -jɛr] *n* **(a)** *Ind* paper manufacturer; **(b)** *Com* stationer.

papetier-libraire [paptjelibrɛr] *nm Com* bookseller and stationer; (*pl papetiers-libraires*).

papier [papje] *nm* **(a)** (*matière*) paper; **pâte à p.,** pulp; **p. pelure,** India paper; **p. buvard,** blotting paper; **p. carbone,** carbon paper; *Ordinat* **p. continu,** continuous paper *or* stationery; *Ordinat* **p. continu plié en accordéon,** fanfold paper; **p. couché,** art paper; **p. glacé,** glazed paper; **p. émeri,** emery paper; **p. de verre,** glasspaper, sandpaper; **p. gommé,** gummed paper; **p. gris,** brown paper; **p. kraft,** kraft (paper); **p. filtre,** filter paper; **p. journal,** newsprint; (*vieux journaux*) newspaper; **p. de soie,** tissue paper; **p. parcheminé,** greaseproof paper; **p. à cigarettes,** cigarette paper; *Phot* **p. sensible,** sensitized paper; **p. calque,** tracing paper; **p. ministre,** official paper; **p. à lettres,** notepaper, writing paper; **p. à en-tête,** headed notepaper; **p. machine,** typing paper; **p. à dessin,** drawing paper; **p. réglé,** ruled *or* lined paper; **p. à musique,** manuscript paper; **être réglé comme du p. à musique,** to be as regular as clockwork; **p. d'emballage,** wrapping paper; **p. hygiénique, p. toilette,** toilet paper, *F* loo paper, *Euph* bathroom tissue; *Arg* **p. cul,** bog paper; **p. peint,** wallpaper; **p. mâché,** papier mâché; **avoir une mine de p. mâché,** to look green about the gills; **un p.,** a sheet *or* piece of paper; **notez plutôt cela dans votre carnet que sur un p.,** put it down in your notebook rather than on a scrap of paper; **son bureau est couvert de papiers,** his desk is covered in paper(s); *F* **être dans les petits papiers de qn,** to be in s.o.'s good books; *F* **rayez cela de vos papiers,** don't count on it, (you can) forget it; **classer ses papiers,** to put one's papers in order; **jeter des idées sur le p.,** to put some ideas down on paper; **gratter du p.,** (*comme métier*) to be a pen-pusher; (*en utiliser beaucoup*) to use a lot of paper; **noircir du p.,**to scribble; **sur le p.,** on paper, in theory;

(b) papiers, (*documents*) papers, documents; *Jur* **papiers d'une affaire,** documents relating to a case; **les papiers de la vente/de la voiture,** the sale/car documents; *Admin* **papiers (d'identité),** (identity) papers; **mes papiers sont en règle,** my papers are in order; **vos papiers, s'il vous plaît!,** can I see your (identity) papers, please?; *Aut* can I see your driving licence *or Am* driver's license, please?;

(c) *Jur* **p. timbré,** stamped paper (*for official and legal documents*);

(d) *Fin* bill(s); **p. de commerce,** commercial *or* trade paper; **p. long** *ou* **à long terme,** long(-dated) bill;

(e) *Journ* article; **il a fini son p.,** he has finished his article;

(f) p. d'aluminium, aluminium foil, tinfoil; **p. d'argent/d'étain,** silver foil *or* paper/tinfoil.

papier-monnaie [papjemɔnɛ] *nm Fin* paper money; (*pl papiers-monnaie*).

papillaire [papilɛr] *adj Anat etc* papillary.

papille [papij, -il] *nf Anat Bot* papilla; **p. gustative,** taste bud.

papillon [papijɔ̃] *nm* **(a)** (*insecte*) butterfly; **p. de nuit,** moth; **c'est un p.,** she's flighty; **esprit p.,** butterfly mentality; *F* **minute p.!,** just a minute!, hold on a minute!; **nœud p.,** bow tie; *Natation* **brasse p.,** butterfly stroke; **(b)** (*dans un livre*) inset; (*prospectus*) handbill; **(c)** *Aut* (parking) ticket; **je me suis encore pris un p.,** I got another (parking) ticket; **(d)** *Tech* (*de réglage*) butterfly valve; (*écrou*) thumb screw, butterfly nut, wing nut.

papillonnant [papijɔnɑ̃] *adj* fluttering, flitting; *Fig* (*inconstant, changeant*) fickle.

papillonnement [papijɔnmɑ̃] *nm* fluttering; flitting (*from place to place, person to person*).

papillonner [papijɔne] *vi* to flit about (*from person to person*); to pass rapidly (*from one subject to another*).

papillotage [papijɔtaʒ] *nm* **(a) p. des yeux,** blinking (of the eyes); **(b)** *Typ* mackling, slurring.

papillote [papijɔt] *nf* **(a)** *Culin* = buttered paper (*for cooking chops etc*); **cailles en papillotes,** quails en papillote; **(b)** (*papier*) twist of paper; frill (*round knuckle of ham etc*); **tu peux en faire des papillotes,** you can throw it away; **(c)** *Arch* paper (*for hair*).

papillotement [papijɔtmɑ̃] *nm* twinkling; *Cin* flickering; (*des yeux*) blinking.

papilloter [papijɔte] **1** *vi* **(a)** (*of eyes*) to blink; (*of light*) to twinkle; *Cin etc* to flicker; **(b)** (*scintiller*) to glitter; (*plus brillamment*) to dazzle; **(c)** *Typ* to mackle, to slur. **2** *vt Arch* to put (*hair*) into curl papers.

papisme [papism] *nm* (Roman) Catholicism; *Péj* popery, papism.

papiste [papist] *n* (Roman) Catholic; *Péj* papist.

papoter [papɔte] *vi F* to chatter, to have a natter.

papou, -oue [papu] (*pl papous, -oues*) **1** *adj* Papuan. **2** *nm Ling* Papuan. **3** *n* **P.,** Papuan.

papouille [papuj] *nf F* tickle; (*caresse*) squeeze; **faire des papouilles à qn,** to hug and squeeze s.o..

paprika [paprika] *nm Bot Culin* paprika.

papule [papyl] *nf F* pimple; *Méd* papule; weal (*of urticaria*).

papyrus [papirys] *nm* papyrus; (*feuille*) sheet of papyrus; **écrire sur des p.,** to write on papyrus.

pâque [pɑk] **1** *nf Rel Juive* **P.,** Passover. **2** *nfpl* **pâques,** Easter; **joyeuses pâques,** happy Easter; **faire ses pâques,** to take the sacrament at Easter. **3** *nm* (*contraction of* **jour de Pâques,** *used without article*) **Pâques,** Easter; **le lundi de Pâques,** Easter Monday; **œufs de Pâques,** Easter eggs; *F* **remettre qch à Pâques ou à la Trinité,** to put sth off indefinitely.

paquebot [pakbo] *nm Nau* (steam)ship; (*gros*) liner.

pâquerette [pɑkrɛt] *nf* daisy.

paquet [pakɛ] *nm* **(a)** (*pour produit etc*) packet; (*pour la poste*) parcel, package; (*ballot, liasse*) bundle; **p. de linge/lettres,** bundle of linen/letters; **expédier un p.,** to send (off) a parcel; **faire un p.,** to make up *or* tie up a parcel; **p.-cadeau,** gift-wrapped parcel; **est-ce que je vous fais un p.-cadeau?,** would you like it gift-wrapped?; **p. de café,** bag of coffee; **du riz/du café/***etc* **en p.,** packaged rice/coffee/*etc*; **p. de cigarettes,** packet *or Am* pack of cigarettes; **il fume un p. par jour,** he smokes twenty a day; **faire son p.** *ou* **ses paquets,** to pack one's bags, to get ready to leave; *Fin* **p. d'actions,** parcel of shares; **p. de billets,** wad of notes; *F* **il a touché un joli p.,** he's made a packet; *F* **des livres** *etc* **en p.,** heaps *or* piles of books *etc*; **p. de neige,** heap of snow; (*poussé par le vent*) snowdrift; **des paquets d'eau tombaient,** the rain was coming down in sheets; **p. de mer,** (*vague*) big wave; **embarquer des paquets de mer,** (*d'un bateau*) to take on a lot of water; **c'est un p. de nerfs/d'os,** he's a bundle of nerves/he's all skin and bone; **mettre le p.,** to go all out, to pull out all the stops; *F* **risquer le p.,** to risk *or* chance the lot; *F* **donner** *ou* **lâcher son p. à qn,** to give s.o. a piece of one's mind; **il a eu son p.,** I *or* she *etc* told him what I *or* she *etc* thought of him;

(b) *Rugby Fb* **p. (d'avants),** pack; **(c)** *Typ* type matter.

paquetage [paktaʒ] *nm Mil etc* (soldier's) pack; **faire son p.,** to get one's kit ready.

par [par] **1** *prép* **(a)** (*à travers*) **on y arrive p. un escalier,** the place is reached by a flight of stairs; **jeter qch/ regarder p. la fenêtre,** to throw something/to look out of the window; **il entra p. la fenêtre,** he came in through the window; **p. monts et p. vaux,** over hill and dale; **p. 10º de latitude nord,** at a latitude of 10º North; **passer p. Calais,** to travel *or* go via Calais *or* by way of Calais; **venez p. ici/ allez p. là,** come this way/go that way; **c'est p. ici,** this is the way, it's this way; **p. où est-il passé?,** which way did he go?;

(b) (*dans*) **il court p. les rues,** he runs through the streets; **p. tout le pays,** throughout the country; **de p. le monde,** throughout the world;

(c) (*pendant, durant*) **p. un jour d'hiver,** on a winter's day; **ne sortez pas p. cette chaleur,** don't go out in this heat; **p. le passé,** in the past; **je l'ai averti p. trois fois,** I warned him three times;

(d) (*agent*) **il a été puni p. son père,** he was punished by his father; **accablé p. l'inquiétude,** overcome by *or* with anxiety; **faire qch p. soi-même,** (*seul*) to do sth unaided; (*de sa propre volonté*) to do sth on one's own initiative; **elle est remarquable p. sa beauté,** she is remarkable for her beauty; **examiner/juger qch p. soi-même,** to examine/ judge sth (for) oneself; **j'ai appris p. les Martin que vous étiez malade,** I heard through *or* from the Martins that you were ill; **faire faire qch p. qn,** to have sth done by s.o.;

(e) (*motif*) **faire qch p. habitude,** to do sth out of habit; **j'ai fait cela p. amitié/respect pour vous,** I did it out of friendship/respect for you; **p. pitié!,** for pity's sake!; **p. hasard/erreur,** by chance/mistake;

(f) (*au moyen de*) **il fut salué p. des acclamations,** he was hailed with cheers; **attacher qch p. une chaîne,** to fasten sth with a chain; **conduire/prendre qn p. la main,** to lead/take s.o. by the hand; **envoyer qch p. la poste,** to send sth by post *or* through the post; **répondre p. oui ou p. non,** to answer yes or no; **ça commence p. un 't',** it begins with (a) 't'; **je suis venu p. le train,** I came by train; **commencer p. le commencement,** to begin at the beginning; **commencer p. la salade,** to begin *or* start with salad; **il a essayé p. tous les moyens,** he tried (by) every possible means, he tried everything; **mon cousin p. alliance,** my cousin by marriage; **société p. actions,** joint-stock company; **obtenir qch p. la force,** to obtain sth by force; **appeler qn p. son nom,** to call s.o. by his name;

(g) (*selon*) according to; **classer les livres p. taille,** to arrange the books according to (their) size; **des dossiers rangés p. ordre alphabetique,** files (arranged) in alphabetical order;

(h) (*distributif*) **entrer deux p. deux,** to come in two by two, to come in in twos; **trois fois p. jour,** three times a day; **10 000 francs p. an,** 10,000 francs a year *or* per annum; **il gagne 1 000 francs p. semaine,** he earns 1,000 francs a *or* per week; **un guide p. groupe de six,** one guide per group of six *or* for each group of six;

(i) commencer *ou* **débuter/finir** *ou* **achever** *ou* **terminer p. faire qch,** to begin/end by doing sth; **il va finir p. m'agacer!,** I've had enough of him!;

(j) (*au nom de*) (= *Arch* **de part**) **de p. le Roi,** by order of the King, in the name of the King.

2 *adv* **p. trop,** far too, much too; *Litt* **vous êtes p. trop aimable,** you are far *or* much too kind; **elle est p. trop sûre d'elle,** she's far *or* much too self-assured.

para [para] *nm F* para.

parabole [parabɔl] *nf* **(a)** (*allégorie*) parable; **parler par p.,** to speak in parables; **(b)** *Math* parabola.

parabolique [parabɔlik] **1** *adj* parabolic; **radiateur p.,** electric fire (with parabolic reflector). **2** *nm* electric fire (with parabolic reflector).

parachèvement [paraʃɛvmɑ̃] *nm* finishing, completion; (*perfectionnement*) perfecting, perfection.

parachever [paraʃve] *vt* (*conj like* **achever**) to complete (*sth*), to finish (*sth*) off; (*perfectionner*) to perfect.

parachutage [paraʃytaʒ] *nm* parachuting, dropping (by parachute); parachute landing (*of men, supplies*); *Can Pol* (*d'un candidat*) parachuting in; **son p. dans le bureau,** the way he was foisted on the office.

parachute [paraʃyt] *nm* **(a)** (*appareil de saut*) parachute; **p. dorsal/ventral,** back(-pack)/lap-pack parachute; **saut en p.,** parachute jump; **faire du p.,** to go parachuting; **(b) p. de mine,** safety device (*of pitshaft cage*).

parachuter [paraʃyte] *vt* to parachute, to drop by parachute; *F* (*nommer, désigner*) to pitchfork (*s.o.*) (into a job); *Can Pol* to parachute (*a candidate*) in.

parachutisme [paraʃytism] *nm* parachuting.

parachutiste [paraʃytist] **1** *n* parachutist. **2** *nm Mil* paratrooper; **parachutistes,** paratroops. **3** *adj* parachute; **détachements parachutistes,** parachute detachments.

parade¹ [parad] *nf* **(a)** (*défilé*) parade; **faire la p.,** to parade; *Nau* **faire p.,** to dress ship; **p. de cirque,** circus parade; **p. nuptiale,** (*des animaux*) courtship dance *or* ritual; **(b)** (*exhibition*) show, ostentation; **faire p. de ses bijoux/ses connaissances,** to display *or* show off one's jewels/knowledge; **habits de p.,** full-dress *or* ceremonial clothes; *Fig* **sourire de p.,** insincere *or* forced smile; **(c)** *Équitation* stopping, pulling up (*of horse*);

parade² *nf* **(a)** *Escrime* parade, parry; *Boxe* parry; **(b)** (*réplique*) riposte; **faire une p.,** to riposte.

parader [parade] *vi* to make a display, to show off; (*en se promenant*) to strut about.

paradigmatique [paradigmatik] *Ling* **1** *adj* paradigmatic. **2** *nf* study of paradigmatic relationships.

paradigme [paradigm] *nm Ling* paradigm.

paradis [paradi] *nm* paradise, heaven; **le P. terrestre,** the garden of Eden; **cette île est un p. terrestre,** this island is heaven on earth; **l'enfer et le p.,** heaven and hell; **aller au** *ou* **en p.,** to go to heaven *or* paradise; **il ne l'emportera pas au** *ou* **en p.,** he won't get away with it; **p. fiscal,** tax haven; **un p. pour les enfants,** a paradise for chidren; *Th F* **le p.,** the gods; **oiseau de p.,** bird of paradise.

paradisiaque [paradizjak] *adj* paradisiac(al), paradisaical.

paradisier [paradizje] *nm* (*oiseau*) bird of paradise.

paradoxal, -aux [paradɔksal, -o] *adj* paradoxical.

paradoxalement [paradɔksalmɑ̃] *adv* paradoxically.

paradoxe [paradɔks] *nm* paradox; **le p. du menteur,** the Cretan liar paradox.

parafe [paraf] *nm* = **PARAPHE**.

parafer [parafe] *vt* = **PARAPHER**.

paraffinage [parafinaʒ] *nm* paraffining.

paraffine [parafin] *nf Ch* paraffin; *Com* paraffin (wax); *Méd* **huile de p.,** liquid paraffin.

paraffiner [parafine] *vt* to paraffin.

parafiscal [parafiskal] *adj* **taxe parafiscale,** indirect tax.

parafiscalité [parafiskalite] *nf* indirect taxation.

parage¹ [paraʒ] *nm Arch* birth, descent; **de haut p.,** of high lineage, high-born.

parage² *nm* **(a)** (*des sols*) dressing of the ground (*before the winter*); **(b)** trimming (*of joints of meat*).

parage³ *nm* **(a)** *Nau* (*souvent pl*) **parages,** waters, region(s); **les parages du Cap Horn,** the waters off Cape Horn; **se trouver dans les parages du Cap Horn,** to be off Cape Horn; **(b)** (*toujours pl*) **dans les parages de ...,** in the vicinity of ..., near ...; **que faites-vous dans ces parages?,** what are you doing here *or* in these parts?; **est-ce qu'il est dans les parages?,** is he around?; **il est dans les parages,** he's around somewhere.

paragraphe [paragraf] *nm* **(a)** paragraph; **(b)** *Typ* section mark, paragraph.

Paraguay [paragwɛ] *nm* Paraguay.

paraguayen, paraguéen, -enne [parag(w)ɛjɛ̃, -ɛn] **1** *adj* Paraguayan. **2** *n* **P.,** Paraguayan.

paraître¹ [parɛtr] *nm* **l'être et le p.,** being and seeming, reality and appearance.

paraître² *v* (*prp* **paraissant**; *pp* **paru**; *pr ind* **je parais, il paraît, n. paraissons**; *impf* **je paraissais**; *p hist* **je parus**; *fu* **je paraîtrai**) **1** *vi* **(a)** (*se montrer*) to appear; (*of star, moon etc*) to appear, to come out; (*of actor*) to appear, to come on; **le jour commençait à p.,** day was dawning; **elle n'a pas paru de la journée,** she hasn't been seen all day, nobody's seen her all day; **lorsque l'enfant paraît,** when the baby arrives;

(b) (*of book etc*) to be published, to come out; (*of periodical*) to appear, to come out; **faire p. un livre,** to publish a book; **vient de p.,** just out; (*livre*) just published;

(c) (*se voir, être visible*) to show, to be visible *or* apparent; **cette tache paraît à peine,** the stain is hardly visible, the stain hardly shows; **laisser p. ses sentiments,** to show one's feelings; (*malgré soi*) to betray one's feelings; **faire p. qch,** to show sth, to display sth; **p. en public,** to appear in public; *Th* **c'est alors qu'elle parut sur la scène,** it was at that moment that she appeared on stage; **elle aime un peu trop p.,** she likes to show off;

(d) (*sembler, faire*) to seem, to look; **il paraissait furieux,** he looked furious; (*à l'entendre*) he sounded furious; **l'endroit lui parut familier,** the place seemed familiar to him; **il ne paraît pas remarquer leur pré-**

sence, he doesn't seem to notice their presence.

2 *v impers* **je suis très mal — il n'y paraît pas,** I'm very ill — you don't look it; **demain il n'y paraîtra plus,** there'll be no trace of it tomorrow; **sans qu'il y paraisse,** without its being apparent; **il paraît qu'elle s'en va, elle s'en va, paraît-il,** it seems *or* appears (that) she's leaving, apparently she's leaving, she's leaving apparently; **il me paraît que ...,** it seems to me *or* it strikes me that ...; **à ce qu'il paraît,** apparently, it would seem so; **il paraît que oui/non,** so it appears, it appears *or* seems so/it appears not, it seems not.

3 *vt* **(a) il paraît (avoir) trente ans,** he looks about thirty; (*de qn de plus âgé*) he looks no more than thirty; **elle a quarante ans, mais elle ne les paraît pas,** she is forty, but she doesn't look it; **elle paraît son âge,** she looks her age;

(b) (*se faire passer pour*) to pass for, to appear to be; **il veut p. ce qu'il n'est pas,** he wants to pass for *or* he wants to appear to be something that he isn't.

parallaxe [paralaks] *nf Astron etc* parallax.

parallèle [paralɛl] **1** *adj* parallel (**à**, to, with); *Ordinat* **imprimante/interface p.,** parallel printer/interface; *Gym* **barres parallèles,** parallel bars; **rue qui est p. à la rivière,** street that runs parallel to *or* with the river; **droites parallèles à l'infini,** parallel straight lines extending into infinity; **mener une action p.,** to take parallel *or* similar action; **deux expériences parallèles,** two very similar experiences (*of two different people*); **mener une vie p.,** to lead a secret life; **circuits parallèles de vente,** parallel sales networks; *Écon* **marché p.,** unofficial *or* illegal market.

2 *nf* parallel (line); *Él* **montage en p.,** parallel connection.

3 *nm Géog* parallel (*of latitude*); (*comparaison*) comparison, parallel; **mettre qn en p. avec qn,** to compare s.o. with s.o.; **établir un p. entre ... et ...,** to establish *or* draw a parallel between ... and ... .

parallèlement [paralɛlmɑ̃] *adv* parallel (**à**, to, with); (*en même temps*) concurrently; (*de la même façon*) in the same way.

parallélépipède [paralelepipɛd] *nm* parallelepiped.

parallélisme [paralelism] *nm* parallelism; *Aut* (wheel) alignment.

parallélogramme [paralelɔgram] *nm Géom* parallelogram.

paralysant [paralizɑ̃] *adj* paralysing.

paralysé, -ée [paralize] **1** *adj* paralysed. **2** *n* person who is paralysed; **les paralysés,** the paralysed.

paralyser [paralize] *vt* (*rendre infirme*) to paralyse; (*empêcher d'agir, de fonctionner*) to paralyse, to incapacitate; to cripple (*economy etc*); **paralysé des deux jambes,** paralysed in both legs; **le froid paralyse ses mains,** his hands are numbed *or* paralysed by the cold; **paralysé par la peur,** paralysed *or* helpless with fear.

paralysie [paralizi] *nf Méd & Fig* paralysis; **p. agitante,** Parkinson's disease; **p. générale (progressive),** creeping paralysis.

paralytique [paralitik] *adj & n* paralytic.

paramètre [paramɛtr] *nm Math* parameter.

paramilitaire [paramilitɛr] *adj* paramilitary.

parangon [parɑ̃gɔ̃] *nm Litt* paragon.

parano [parano] **1** *adj F* paranoid; **il est complètement p.!,** he's completely paranoid! **2** *nf F* paranoia; **elle fait de la p.!,** she's being paranoid!; **arrête ta p.!,** stop being paranoid!

paranoïa [paranɔja] *nf Psy* paranoia.

paranoïaque [paranɔjak] *adj & n Psy* paranoiac.

paranoïde [paranɔid] *adj* paranoid.

paranormal, -aux [paranormal, -o] *adj* paranormal.

parapente [parapɑ̃t] *nf* paragliding.

parapet [parapɛ] *nm* parapet.

paraphe [paraf] *nm* **(a)** (*ajouté à la signature*) flourish, paraph; **(b)** initials (*of one's name*).

parapher [parafe] *vt* to initial.

paraphrase [parafraz] *nf* paraphrase; **faire de la p.,** to paraphrase.

paraphraser [parafraze] *vt* to paraphrase.

paraplégie [parapleʒi] *nf Méd* paraplegia.

paraplégique [parapleʒik] *adj & n Méd* paraplegic.

parapluie [paraplɥi] *nm* umbrella; **p. nucléaire** *ou* **atomique,** nuclear umbrella.

parasitaire [parazitɛr] *adj* parasitic(al).

parasite [parazit] **1** *nm Biol* parasite; *Fig* parasite, hanger-on, sponger; *Rad TV* **parasites,** interference; (*causés par des phénomènes atmosphériques*) atmospherics. **2** *adj Biol* parasitic (*insect, plant etc*); *Rad TV* **bruits parasites,** interference.

parasiter [parazite] *vt Biol* to parasitize; *Fig F* (*profiter de*) to leech off.

parasitique [parazitik] *adj* parasitic(al).

parasitisme [parazitism] *nm* parasitism.

parasol [parasɔl] *nm* parasol, sunshade; (*sur la plage*) beach umbrella; **pin p.,** parasol pine, umbrella pine.

paratonnerre [paratɔnɛr] *nm* lightning conductor.

paratyphoïde [paratifɔid] *adj & nf Méd* paratyphoid (fever).

paravent [paravɑ̃] *nm* screen; *Fig* **ce n'est qu'un p.,** it's just a smoke screen *or* front.

parbleu [parblø] *int Vieilli* good Lord, yes! of course!

parc [park] *nm* **(a)** (*jardin*) park; grounds (*of castle etc*); **p. zoologique,** zoological gardens; **p. naturel,** nature reserve; **p. maritime,** marine wildlife park; **(b)** enclosure (*for special purposes*); **p. de stationnement,** car park, *Am* parking lot; **p. scientifique,** science park; **p. d'attractions,** amusement park, *Br* funfair; **p. à bestiaux,** cattle pen; **p. à moutons,** sheepfold; **p. à huîtres/moules,** oyster/mussel bed; **p. (pour enfants),** playpen; *Mil* **p. d'artillerie,** artillery park; *Mil* **p. de munitions,** ammunition depot; **(c)** fleet (*of buses, cars etc*); *Rail* rolling stock; **p. automobile,** number of cars on the roads; **le p. des téléviseurs couleurs,** the total number of colour televisions owned by the population; **p. immobilier,** housing stock.

parcage [parkaʒ] *nm* parking (*of car*); enclosing, penning (*of cattle*); folding (*of sheep*).

parcellaire [parsɛlɛr] *adj* (*land*) divided into small portions *or* into parcels; **travail p.,** work divided into sections.

parcelle [parsɛl] *nf* (small) fragment; particle (*of gold etc*); parcel (*of land*); *Fig* **il n'a pas la moindre p. de jugement,** he hasn't a scrap of common sense.

parcellisation [parsɛlizɑsjɔ̃] *nf* parcelling (*of land*); breakdown (*of work etc*) into sections.

parcelliser [parsɛlize] *vt* to divide (*land*) into small portions; to break down (*work etc*) into sections.

parce que [parskə] *conj* because; **je le dis p. q. c'est vrai,** I say so because it is true; **p. qu'on lui dit de le faire, il le fait,** (just) because he's told to do it, he does it; **pourquoi ne viens-tu pas? — p. q.,** why aren't you coming? — (just) because (I'm not).

parchemin [parʃəmɛ̃] *nm* parchment; (*de livre*) vellum; **papier p.,** vegetable parchment, parchment paper; **un p.,** a parchment, a document; *Univ* a diploma; **des parchemins,** titles of nobility.

parcheminé [parʃəmine] *adj* parchment-like.

parcheminer [parʃəmine] **1** *vt* to give a parchment finish to (*paper*). **2 se parcheminer** *vpr* to shrivel up; (*of skin*) to become shrivelled.

parcimonie [parsimɔni] *nf* thrift; **avec p.,** thriftily.

parcimonieusement [parsimɔnjøzmɑ̃] *adv* thriftily.

parcimonieux, -euse [parsimɔnjø, -øz] *adj* thrifty.

par-ci, par-là [parsiparla] *adv* (*dans l'espace*) here and there; (*dans le temps*) now and then, from time to time.

parcmètre, parcomètre [parkmɛtr, parkɔmɛtr] *nm* parking meter.

parcourir [parkurir] *vt* (*conj like* **courir**) **(a)** to travel through (*a stretch of country*); **p. les rues,** to wander (through) the streets; **p. les mers,** to sail the seas; *Fig* **un frisson me parcourut,** a shiver went through me; **p. une distance de plusieurs kilomètres,** to cover a distance of several kilometres; **p. une distance en deux heures,** to cover a distance in two hours; **(b)** (*regarder*) to examine (cursorily); **p. un texte,** to go through a text; **p. qch des yeux** *ou* **du regard,** to glance at *or* over sth; **p. un livre,** to glance *or* skim through a book.

parcours [parkur] *nm* route (*of procession, bus etc*); course (*of river*); *Sp* circuit, course; *Golf* course, links; (*distance*) distance covered; **p. de 10 kilomètres,** run of 10 kilometres; **le car fait le p. entre la ville et la côte,** the bus runs between the town and the coast; **payer le p.,** to pay the fare; *Mil* **p. du combattant,** obstacle course; *Fig* **incident de p.,** (temporary) hitch.

par-delà [pardəla] *prép & adv* beyond.

par-derrière [pardɛrjɛr] **1** *prép* behind, round the back of. **2** *adv* behind, round the back; **entrer p.-d.,** to come in the back way, to come in the back door.

par-dessous [pardəsu] *prép & adv* under, beneath, underneath; **je suis passé p.-d.,** I crept underneath.

pardessus [pardəsy] *nm* overcoat.

par-dessus [pardəsy] *prép & adv* over (the top of); **sauter p.-d. (la table),** to leap over (the table); **jeter qch p.-d.**

bord, to throw sth overboard; **p.-d. le marché,** into the bargain; (*comble des misères etc*) on top of it all; **j'en ai p.-d. la tête,** I've had just about enough.

par-devant [pardəvɑ̃] **1** *prép* in front of; **passer p.-d. la maison,** to pass the house; *Jur* **acte signé p.-d. (le) notaire,** deed signed in the presence of a lawyer. **2** *adv* in front.

par-devers [pardəvɛr] *prép* **(a) p.-d. soi,** in one's possession; **(b) p.-d. le juge,** before the judge.

pardi [pardi] *int F* of course!, naturally!

pardon [pardɔ̃] *nm* **(a)** (*grâce*) pardon; forgiveness (*of an offence*); *Jur* (free) pardon; **accorder son p. à qn,** to forgive s.o.; **demander p. à qn,** to apologize to s.o.; **(je vous demande) p.,** I beg your pardon, (I'm) sorry; (*pour avertir, attirer l'attention de qn*) excuse me; **p., j'y suis allé,** (*expressing contradiction*) I'm sorry *or* excuse me, but I DID go; **p.?,** (*in conversation*) I beg your pardon?, what did you say?; *Arg* **on dit qu'il n'est pas très malin, mais alors son fils, p.!,** they say he's not very clever, but no way can you say that about his son!; **(b)** *Rel* (*in Brittany*) religious festival; *Rel Juive* **Grand P., jour du P.,** Day of Atonement, Yom Kippur.

pardonnable [pardɔnabl] *adj* pardonable, forgivable, excusable; **il s'est trompé mais c'est p.,** he made a mistake, but he can be pardoned for it.

pardonner [pardɔne] **1** *vt* to pardon, to forgive, to excuse; **p. qn,** to forgive s.o.; **pardonnez-moi si je vous contredis,** excuse me for contradicting you. **2** *vi* to forgive; **elle pardonne vite,** she is quick to forgive; **maladie/faute qui ne pardonne pas,** fatal illness/mistake. **3 se pardonner** *vpr* **je ne me le pardonnerai jamais,** I'll never forgive myself; **c'est une erreur qui ne se pardonne pas,** it's an unforgivable mistake.

paré [pare] *adj* **(a)** (*prêt*) ready; **être p. contre le froid,** to be prepared for the cold (weather); **vous voilà p.!** you're all set!; *Nau* **p. à virer!,** ready about!; **(b)** (*orné*) decorated, ornamented (**de,** with); (*personne*) dressed (up) (**de,** in); (*femme*) wearing jewels, covered in jewels; **(c)** *Culin* (*viande*) dressed.

pare-avalanches [paravalɑ̃ʃ] *nm inv* avalanche barrier, avalanche wall.

pare-balles [parbal] *adj inv* bullet-proof; **gilet p.-b.,** bullet-proof vest.

pare-boue [parbu] *nm inv* mudguard; (*derrière la roue*) mudflap.

pare-brise [parbriz] *nm inv Aut etc* windscreen, *Am* windshield.

pare-chocs [parʃɔk] *nm inv Aut* bumper, *Am* fender.

pare-éclats [parekla] *nm inv Mil* splinter proof shield (*on trench parapet etc*).

pare-étincelles [paretɛ̃sɛl] *nm inv* fireguard.

pare-feu [parfø] *nm inv* **(a)** (*dans la forêt*) firebreak; **(b)** (*de cheminée*) fireguard.

parégorique [paregɔrik] *adj & nm Pharm* paregoric.

pareil, -eille [parɛj] **1** *adj* **(a)** (*semblable*) like, alike, similar; **ce n'est pas p.,** it's not the same (thing); **en voici un tout p.,** here's one exactly like it; **p. que** *ou* **à,** the same as, just like; **et lui, qu'est-ce qu'on lui donne? — p., une orange,** and what shall we give him? — the same (thing), an orange; **ses deux chaussettes ne sont pas pareilles,** his socks don't match; **l'an dernier à pareille époque,** this time last year;

(b) (*tel*) such; (*suivant le nom*) like that; **en p. cas,** in a case like this, in such cases; **comment a-t-il pu faire une chose pareille!,** how could he do such a thing!; **qu'a-t-il donc fait pour avoir une pareille chance?,** how did he manage to get so lucky?; **j'ignorais que tu y portais un p. interêt,** I didn't realize you were so interested.

2 *n* (*pair*) equal match; **elle n'a pas sa pareille au monde,** there's no one like her, she's second to none; **il n'a pas son p. pour le travail,** there's no one to equal him for work; **sans p.,** unparalleled, matchless; **occasion sans pareille,** unparalleled opportunity; **méchanceté sans pareille,** unparalleled wickedness; **mes pareils,** my equals; **lui et ses pareils,** him and people like him.

3 *nf* **rendre la pareille à qn,** to retaliate, to give s.o. tit for tat, to pay s.o. back in his own coin; **si on me frappe je rends la pareille,** if any one hits me I hit back.

4 *nm F* **c'est du p. au même,** it's just the same, it comes (down) to the same thing.

5 *adv F* **faire p.,** to do the same; **ils s'habillent p.,** they dress the same; **ça se prononce p.,** it's pronounced the same.

pareillement [parɛjmɑ̃] *adv* **(a)** (*de la même manière*) in a similar manner, in the same way; **(b)** (*aussi*) also, likewise; *F* (*en réponse à des vœux*) the same to you!; **et moi p.!,** same here!

parement [parmɑ̃] *nm* **(a)** (*décoration*) ornament, decoration; *Couture Tex* (*de manche, col*) facing; **p. d'autel,** (altar) frontal; **(b)** *Constr* (*d'un mur*) face, facing; (*de la pierre*) (dressed) face.

parementer [parmɑ̃te] *vt Constr* to face (*wall etc*).

parenchyme [parɑ̃ʃim] *nm Anat Bot* parenchyma.

parent, -ente [parɑ̃, -ɑ̃t] **1** *nm* **(a)** (*always pl*) **parents,** (*père et mère*) parents, mother and father; **les parents sortent ce soir,** my parents *or F* (my) mum and dad are going out this evening; **parents adoptifs,** adoptive parents; **parents biologiques,** biological parents;

(b) *Litt* (*always pl*) **parents,** (*ancêtres*) forefathers, forebears;

(c) *Biol* parent.

2 *n* (*personne appartenant à la proche famille*) relative, (blood) relation; **proche p./p. éloigné,** close/distant relative; **être p. avec** *ou* **de qn,** to be related to s.o.; **c'est une parente,** she's a relation *or* a relative; **nous sommes parents par alliance/par mon père,** we are related by marriage/on my father's side; *Fig* **traiter qn en p. pauvre,** to treat s.o. like a poor relation; *Fig* **le Larzac, le p. pauvre du Massif Central,** the Larzac region, the poor relation of the Massif Central.

3 *adj* related; (*semblable*) similar; **sciences parentes,** related sciences; **leurs œuvres révèlent des intelligences/sensibilités parentes,** their work shows a similar intelligence/sensitivity.

parental, -aux [parɑ̃tal, -o] *adj* parental (*authority etc*).

parenté [parɑ̃te] *nf* **(a)** relationship; *Spéc* (*en sociologie*) kinship; relationship, affinity (*between two languages etc*); **il n'y a entre eux aucune p.,** they are not related in any way; **liens de p.,** family connections; **(b)** (*famille*) family, relations.

parenthèse [parɑ̃tɛz] *nf* **(a)** *Gram* parenthesis; *Fig* (*digression*) parenthesis, digression; **cette époque a été une p. dans sa vie,** that period was an interlude in his life; **je voudrais ouvrir une p.,** (*pour aborder cette question*) I would like to digress for a moment; **(b)** *Typ* bracket; **mettre un mot entre parenthèses,** to put a word in brackets, to bracket a word; **entre parenthèses,** incidentally, by the way; **il faut mettre ce problème entre parenthèses,** (*de côté*) this problem has to be put to one side.

paréo [pareo] *nm* pareo.

parer[1] [pare] **1** *vt* **(a)** (*éviter*) to fend off (*an attack*); to parry, to ward off (*blow*); (*en esquivant*) to dodge (*blow*); *Nau* **p. un abordage,** to avoid *or* fend off a collision; *Nau* **p. un cap,** to clear *or* double a headland; **(b)** (*protéger*) to protect; **p. les enfants contre les difficultés de la vie,** to protect children against life's difficulties; **p. une maison du froid,** to protect a house from *or* against the cold. **2** *vi* **p. à,** to provide *or* guard against (*sth*); to avert (*accident*); to avoid (*difficulty, problem*); to ward off, to stave off (*defeat, disaster*); **p. à toute éventualité,** to be prepared for anything; **on ne peut pas p. à tout,** you can't guard against everything; **p. au plus pressé,** to attend to the most urgent things first.

parer[2] **1** *vt* **(a)** (*arranger*) to dress, to trim (*meat, leather*); *Nau* to clear (*cable, anchor etc*); **(b)** (*vêtir*) to deck out, to adorn (*s.o.*) (**de,** with); (*décorer*) to decorate, to embellish; to arrange (*room etc*) with care *or* taste; **p. la mariée,** to dress the bride; **p. qn de toutes les qualités,** to attribute every quality to s.o.. **2 se parer** *vpr* to dress oneself up; to deck oneself out, to adorn oneself (*with jewels*); **se p. d'un faux titre,** to assume a false title.

pare-soleil [parsɔlɛj] *nm inv Aut etc* sun visor.

paresse [parɛs] *nf* **(a)** (*indolence*) laziness, idleness; **par pure p.,** out of sheer laziness; **(b)** (*lenteur*) **p. d'esprit** *ou* **intellectuelle,** sluggishness of mind; *Méd* **p. intestinale,** sluggishness of the bowels.

paresser [parese] *vi* to laze (about, around).

paresseusement [paresøzmɑ̃] *adv* (*voir adj*) **(a)** idly, lazily; **(b)** sluggishly.

paresseux, -euse [parɛsø, -øz] **1** *adj* **(a)** (*indolent*) lazy; (*oisif*) idle; *Fml* indolent; **p. comme une couleuvre,** bone idle; **prendre la solution paresseuse,** to take the line of least resistance, to take the easy way out; **il est p. pour se lever,** you can't get him out of bed (in the morning); **(b)** (*lent*) sluggish (*bowels, mind*); **un fleuve p.,** a slow-moving *or* flowing river. **2** *n* lazy person, *F* lazybones. **3** *nm* sloth.

parfaire [parfɛr] *vt* (*conj like* **faire**; *used chiefly in inf and pp*) to finish off, to complete, to round off (*one's work etc*); to make up (*a sum*); **p. ses connaissances,** to perfect one's knowledge.

parfait [parfɛ] **1** *adj* **(a)** (*irréprochable*) perfect; faultless (*performance*); flawless (*diamond, reputation*); **beauté parfaite,** incomparable beauty; **en ordre p.,** in perfect order; **il est loin d'être p.,** he's far from perfect, he's no saint; **vous avez été p.,** you were wonderful *or* splendid; **(c'est** *ou* **voilà qui est) p.!,** (that's) splendid!, fine!, wonderful!, *F* great!; **p., passons à autre chose,** fine *or* good, let's go on to something else; **(b)** (*complet*) perfect, complete; thorough (*examination, explanation*); **un p. orateur,** an accomplished speaker; *F* **un p. imbécile,** a perfect idiot, an utter fool, a downright *or* complete idiot; **en p. accord,** in full *or* perfect agreement; *Mus* **accord p.,** perfect chord; **une ressemblance parfaite,** a close *or* great resemblance. **2** *nm* **(a)** *Gram* perfect (tense); **(b)** *Culin* parfait; **p. au café,** coffee parfait.

parfaitement [parfɛtmɑ̃] *adv* **(a)** (*admirablement*) perfectly, to perfection; **cela m'ira p.,** that will suit me perfectly *or* just fine; **elle s'occupe de ses enfants p.,** she looks after her children wonderfully well; **(b)** (*totalement*) completely, thoroughly; **je comprends p.,** I quite *or* perfectly understand; **il est p. idiot,** he's a perfect idiot; **il a p. le droit de le dire,** he has a perfect right to say so; **(c)** (*tout à fait*) certainly, exactly; **vous dites que vous l'avez vu? — oui, p.,** you say you saw it? — indeed I did *or* yes, I most definitely did.

parfois [parfwa] *adv* sometimes, at times; (*moins souvent*) occasionally, (every) now and then; **p. elle lit, p. elle tricote,** sometimes she reads, other times she knits.

parfum [parfœ̃] *nm* **(a)** (*senteur, odeur*) perfume, fragrance, scent (*of flower*); bouquet, aroma (*of wine*); whiff (*of scandal*); **(b)** (*à base d'essences*) perfume, *Br* scent; **(c)** *Culin* flavour, *US* flavor (*of ice cream*); **(d)** *F* **être au p.,** to be in the know, to be wise to sth; *F* **mettre qn au p.,** to fill s.o. in; to put s.o. wise (*to a trick etc*).

parfumé [parfyme] *adj* scented, fragrant, sweet-smelling (*flower*); fragrant (*wine, air*); (*au goût*) sweet-tasting; **des fruits très parfumés,** fruit that is full of flavour *or US* flavor; **glace parfumée au cafe,** coffee-flavoured ice-cream; **l'air p. du soir,** the balmy evening air; **elle est trop parfumée,** she wears too much perfume *or* scent.

parfumer [parfyme] **1** *vt* **(a)** (*embaumer*) to scent, to perfume; **les fleurs parfument la pièce,** the flowers scent the room; **(b)** *Culin* to flavour, *US* to flavor (**à,** with); **(c)** (*mettre du parfum sur*) to scent a (*handkerchief*); to perfume (*a drawer*). **2 se parfumer** *vpr* to wear *or* use perfume.

parfumerie [parfymri] *nf* (*magasin*) & *Ind* perfumery; (*rayon*) perfume counter; (*produit*) perfumery, perfumes.

parfumeur, -euse [parfymœr, -øz] *n* perfumer.

pari [pari] *nm* **(a)** (*convention*) bet; *Vieilli* wager; **faire un p.,** to make *or* lay a bet; **tenir un p.,** to take (up) a bet; *Fig* **les paris sont ouverts,** it's anyone's guess (how it will end); **(b)** (*jeu*) betting; **p. mutuel,** *Br* ≈ totaliz(at)or system, *F* the tote; *Am* ≈ pari-mutuel.

paria [parja] *nm* (*in India*) pariah; *Fig* pariah, (social) outcast.

parier [parje] *v* (*impf & pr sub* **n. pariions, v. pariiez**) **1** *vt* to bet, *Fml* to wager (*sth*); **je parie une bouteille de vin qu'il ne viendra pas,** I bet a bottle of wine he won't come; **il y a gros à p. que ...,** it's virtually certain that ..., the odds are that ...; **je te parie tout ce que tu veux ...,** I bet you anything (you like) ...; **je l'aurais parié,** I might have known (it); *F* **tu en as assez, je parie?,** you've had enough, I bet. **2** *vi* to bet; **p. sur un cheval,** to bet on *or* back a horse; **p. avec qn,** to bet with s.o..

pariétal, -aux [parjetal, -o] **1** *adj* **(a)** *Anat* parietal (*bone etc*); **(b)** *Beaux-Arts* **art p.,** cave painting. **2** *nm Anat* parietal bone.

parieur, -euse [parjœr, -øz] *n* better, *F* punter; *Sp surtout Courses de chevaux* backer; (*au jeu*) gambler.

parigot, -ote [parigo, -ɔt] *Arg Péj* **1** *adj* Parisian. **2** *n* **P.,** Parisian.

Paris [pari] *nm* Paris.

parisien, -ienne [parizjɛ̃, -jɛn] **1** *adj* Parisian; *Péj* **esprit p.,** superior Parisian outlook; **le Bassin p./la banlieue parisienne,** the Paris Basin/suburbs. **2** *n* **P.,** Parisian.

paritaire [paritɛr] *adj Ind* with parity of representation.

parité [parite] *nf* **(a)** (*égalité*) parity; equality (*of rank, value*); *Fin* **p. de change,** parity; **(b)** *Math* parity; *Ordinat* **p. paire/impaire,** even/odd parity.

parjure [parʒyr] **1** *nm* perjury. **2** *n* perjurer. **3** *adj* faithless (*person*).

parjurer (se) [səparʒyre] *vpr* to perjure oneself, to be guilty of *or* commit perjury.

parka [parka] *n* parka.

parking [parkiŋ] *nm* (*stationnement*) parking; (*emplacement*) car park, *Am* parking lot; **place de p.,** parking place *or* spot, place to park; **mettre sa voiture au p.,** to put one's car in the car park; **p. payant/gratuit,** paying/free car park; **p. de dissuasion,** park-and-ride (facilities).

parlant [parlɑ̃] *adj* **(a)** speaking; lifelike (*portrait*); eloquent, meaningful (*gesture*); vivid (*description*); **cinéma p.,** talking pictures, *F* talkies; *Tél* **l'horloge parlante,** the speaking clock, *Br F* Tim; **(b)** *F* (*bavard*) talkative, garrulous.

parlé [parle] **1** *adj* spoken (*language, word*); *TV Rad* **journal p.,** news broadcast *or* programme *or US* program. **2** *nm* spoken part (*in opera*).

parlement [parləmɑ̃] *nm* **(a)** parliament; **(b)** *Hist* high judicial court (*in Paris and provinces*).

parlementaire¹ [parləmɑ̃tɛr] **1** *adj Pol* parliamentary (*government etc*). **2** *n Pol* member of Parliament; *US* congressman.

parlementaire² *n Mil* negotiator, mediator.

parlementarisme [parləmɑ̃tarism] *nm Pol* parliamentary government.

parlementer [parləmɑ̃te] *vi* **(a)** (*négocier*) to negociate (**avec,** with); *Vieilli* to parley, to hold a parley (**avec,** with); **(b)** *F* to talk at length (**avec,** with).

parler¹ [parle] **1** *vi* **(a)** to speak, to talk; (*avouer*) to talk, to reveal information; **le bébé ne parle pas encore,** the baby hasn't learnt to talk yet; **elle parle bien pour son age,** she talks well for her age; **il parle bien/avec style,** (*d'un orateur*) he's a good/stylish speaker; **p. haut,** to talk loudly; **p. bas,** to speak *or* talk quietly *or* in a low voice; **p. entre ses dents,** to mumble; **parlez plus haut** *ou* **plus fort!,** speak up!; **p. du nez,** to talk through one's nose; **s'enrouer à force de p.,** to talk oneself hoarse; **p. par gestes,** to use sign language; **le président va p.,** the president is about to speak; **parlez-vous sérieusement?,** are you serious?, do you really mean it?; **laissez-le p.,** let him have his say; **elle aime s'écouter p.,** she likes the sound of her own voice; **p. pour ne rien dire,** to talk for the sake of talking; **p. à tort et à travers,** to talk drivel; **parlons franc,** let's talk frankly, let's be frank; **généralement parlant,** generally speaking; **on parlait très peu au petit déjeuner,** there was very little talking over breakfast; **c'est une façon de p.,** it's a way of speaking, don't take it literally; **une chance, façon de p.,** a piece of luck so to speak; *Arg* **tu parles!,** you're telling me!, you bet!; (*pas question*) you must be joking!, no way!; **tu parles si c'est utile!,** a fat lot of use that is!; **je ne peux pas le faire p.,** I can't get him to talk, I can't get a word out of him; **parlons peu mais parlons bien,** let's be brief and to the point;

(b) p. à qn, to talk *or* speak to s.o.; **p. de qn/qch,** to mention *or* refer to *or* speak of *or* talk about s.o./sth; **n'en parlez à personne,** don't tell anyone about it; *F* **ne m'en parlez pas!,** you're telling me!; *Fig* **c'est p. à un mur,** it's like talking to a brick wall; **nous ne nous parlons pas,** (*nous nous sommes disputés*) we are not talking (to each other), we are not on speaking terms; (*nous ne nous connaissons pas*) we are not on speaking terms; *Nau* **p. à un navire,** to speak a ship; *F* **moi qui vous parle, je peux vous aider,** I'm the one who can help you; **en avez-vous parlé aux autres?,** have you spoken to the others about it?; **il n'en parle jamais,** he never talks about it; **nous en parlerons après déjeuner,** we can talk it over *or* talk about it after lunch; **n'en parlons plus,** let's drop the subject, let's say no more about it; **cela ne vaut pas la peine d'en p.,** it isn't worth talking about; **on parle d'organiser une fête,** there's some talk about (organizing) a party; **mal p. de qn,** to criticize s.o., to run s.o. down; **j'entends beaucoup p. de lui,** I hear a good deal about him; **mon père ne veut pas en entendre p.,** my father won't hear of it; **je n'en ai jamais entendu p.,** I've never heard of it; **faire p. de soi,** to get talked about; **son dernier film parle de la guerre,** his latest film is about the war; **ça parle de quoi?,** what's it about?; **on ne parle que de cela,** everyone's talking about it; **sans p. de,** to say nothing of ..., not to mention ...; **sans p. de mal, elle a peut-être eu un accident?,** I hope I'm not tempting fate, but perhaps she's had an accident?; *Arg* **tu parles d'une occasion!,** talk about an opportunity!; *Arg* **tu parles d'un idiot!,** talk about an idiot!; **les résultats parlent d'eux-mêmes,** the results speak for themselves; **cette peinture parle à l'imagination,** this painting fires the imagination; **p. pour/contre qn,** to speak for/against s.o..

2 *vt* **p. (le) français,** to speak French; **elle parlait**

français, she was speaking *or* talking French; **p. affaires, p. boutique,** to talk business *or F* shop.

3 se parler *vpr* **(a)** to be spoken; **l'anglais se parle partout,** English is spoken everywhere;

(b) se p. à soi-même, to talk to oneself.

parler² *nm* speech; (*régional*) dialect; **il a un p. rude,** he's got a coarse way of speaking.

parleur, -euse [parlœr, -øz] *n Péj* **beau p.,** glib *or* smooth talker.

parloir [parlwar] *nm* parlour, *US* parlor, visiting room (*of school, convent etc*).

parlot(t)e [parlɔt] *nf F* gossip, chitchat, natter; **faire la p. avec qn,** to have a natter with s.o..

Parme [parm] *nf* Parma.

Parmentier [parmɑ̃tje] *n Culin* **hachis P.,** ≈ cottage pie.

parmesan [parməzɑ̃] *nm Culin* parmesan (cheese).

parmi [parmi] *prép* among, amongst; **p. les arbres,** among the trees; **p. la foule,** among *or* in the crowd; **nous souhaitons vous voir bientôt p. nous,** we hope that you'll soon be with us; **c'est une solution p. d'autres,** that's one solution; **les inégalités p. les hommes,** inequalities between men.

Parnasse (le) [ləparnas] *nm* **(a)** *Antiq* Parnassus; **(b)** *Litt Hist* the Parnassian School (of poetry).

parnassien, -ienne [parnasjɛ̃, -jɛn] *adj & nm Litt Hist* Parnassian.

parodie [parɔdi] *nf* (*pastiche*) parody; (*simulacre*) parody, mockery.

parodier [parɔdje] *vt* (*impf & pr sub* **n. parodiions, v. parodiiez**) to parody, to make a mockery of (*sth*); to parody, to imitate (*s.o.*), to take (*s.o.*) off.

parodique [parɔdik] *adj Littér* parodic(al).

paroi [parwa] *nf* **(a)** (*cloison*) partition (wall) (*between rooms*); **(b)** (*mur*) wall (*of rock, tent etc*); (inner) wall (*of house*); (*rock*) face; *Biol* (*cell*) wall; **(c)** (*face intérieure*) lining (*of tunnel, stomach*); inner side *or* surface (*of vase etc*).

paroisse [parwas] *nf* **(a)** (*territoire*) parish; **il n'est pas de la p.,** he's not from here; **(b)** (*habitants*) parishioners.

paroissial, -aux [parwasjal, -o] *adj* parish; **église paroissiale,** parish church; **salle paroissiale,** church hall.

paroissien, -ienne [parwasjɛ̃, -jɛn] **1** *n* parishioner. **2** *nm* prayer book.

parole [parɔl] *nf* **(a)** (*mot*) (spoken) word; **paroles,** lyrics (*of song*); **elle n'a pas dit une p. de la journée,** she hasn't spoken *or* said a word all day; **ce sont ses propres paroles,** those are his very words; **assez de paroles! des actes!,** that's enough talk(ing)!, let's see some action!, **romance sans paroles,** song without words; **la p. de Dieu,** the word of God; **p. blessante,** hurtful remark; *Iron* **belles paroles,** fine words; **voilà une bonne p.!,** well said!;

(b) *Fig* (*engagement*) promise, word; **tenir (sa) p.,** to keep one's promise *or* word; **manquer à sa p.,** to break one's promise *or* word; **il est (homme) de p., il a sa p., il n'a qu'une p.,** he's a man of his word; **(je vous donne ma) p!, p. d'honneur!,** I give you my word (of honour)!; **je l'ai cru sur p.,** I took his word for it; **prisonnier sur p.,** prisoner on parole;

(c) la p., speech, speaking; (*manière, diction*) delivery; **avoir la p. facile,** to have the gift of the gab; **avoir le don de la p.,** to be a good speaker; **perdre la p.,** to lose the power of speech; **si les animaux avaient l'usage de la p.,** if animals could speak *or* talk; **addresser la p. à qn,** to speak to s.o.; **couper la p. à qn,** to cut s.o. short, to interrupt s.o.; **prendre la p.,** (to begin) to speak; **taisez-vous, vous n'avez pas la p.,** be quiet, it's not your turn to speak; **la p. est à M. Renault,** Mr Renault will now speak;

(d) *Cartes* **p.!,** pass!; (*in bridge*) no bid!

parolier, -ière [parɔlje, -jɛr] *n* songwriter, lyric writer; (*d'opéra*) librettist.

paronyme [parɔnim] *nm* paronym.

paronymie [parɔnimi] *nf* paronymy.

paroxysme [parɔksism] *nm* paroxysm (*of anger, pain*); *Méd* crisis (point) (*of illness*); **être au p. de la joie,** to be ecstatically happy; **atteindre son p.,** to reach its highest point.

parpaing [parpɛ̃] *nm Constr* breeze block; (*à travers un mur*) perpend, parpend, *US* parpen.

Parque [park] *nf Myth* Fate; **les Parques,** the Parcae, the Fates.

parquer [parke] **1** *vt Ordinat* to park (*disk*); to pen (*cattle*); to fold (*sheep*); to confine, to pack in (*soldiers*); to park (*artillery, cars etc*); **on nous a parqués comme des moutons dans la salle d'attente,** we were herded into the waiting room. **2 se parquer** *vpr Aut* to park.

parquet [parkɛ] *nm* **(a)** *Jur* public prosecutor's office; **(membres du) p.,** public prosecutor and his deputies; **déposer une plainte au p.,** to lodge a complaint in court; **(b)** *Bourse* **le P.,** the floor, *Am* the pit; **(c)** *Constr* (wooden *or* parquet) floor, flooring; (wooden) backing (*of mirror*); **lame de p.,** floorboard; *Nau* **p. de chargement,** dunnage; *Nau* **p. de chauffe,** stokehold platform.

parquetage [parkətaʒ] *nm* **(a)** (*fabrication, installation*) making *or* laying of (wooden *or* parquet) floors; **(b)** (*sol*) (wooden, parquet) flooring, floor.

parqueter [parkəte] *vt* (**je parquette, n. parquetons; je parquetterai**) to lay a (wooden *or* parquet) floor in (*room etc*); to parquet (*a room*).

parqueterie [parkətri] *nf* making *or* laying of (wooden *or* parquet) floors.

parqueteur [parkətœr] *nm* (*fabricant*) parquet maker; (*installateur*) parquet layer; ≈ flooring contractor.

parrain [parɛ̃] *nm Rel & Fig Péj* godfather; sponsor (*of child in Third World etc*); sponsor, proposer (*of new member for club*); namer (*of ship*); patron (*of foundation*); *Rel* **être p.,** to stand godfather (**de,** to).

parrainage [parɛnaʒ] *nm* sponsorship (*of child in Third World etc*); proposing (*for membership*); naming (*of ship*); patronage (*of foundation*).

parrainer [parene] *vt Rel* to act as godfather to (*a child*); to sponsor (*a child in the Third World*); to sponsor, to propose (*a new member*); to name (*a ship*); to act as patron of (*a foundation*).

parricide [parisid] **1** *n* parricide. **2** *nm* (*crime*) parricide. **3** *adj* parricidal.

parsec [parsɛk] *nm Astron* parsec.

parsemé [parsəme] *adj* **ciel p. d'étoiles,** sky studded *or* spangled with stars; **champ p. de pâquerettes,** field sprinkled *or* dotted with daisies; **texte p. de coquilles,** text riddled with misprints; **un visage p. de taches de rousseur,** a freckled face; **ses affaires sont parsemées sur son lit,** his things are scattered *or* strewn all over his bed.

parsemer [parsəme] *vt* (*conj like* **semer**) to strew (*with papers*) (**with,** de); to sprinkle (*with sugar*) (**with,** de); to scatter (*with seeds*) (**with,** de); **des feuilles parsemaient le chemin,** the path was scattered *or* covered with leaves.

parsi, -ie [parsi] *adj & n Rel* Parsee.

part [par] *nf* **(a)** (*portion*) share, part, portion; **diviser un gâteau en parts,** to divide a cake into portions; **la p. du lion,** the lion's share; **faire la p. du feu,** to cut one's losses; **avoir/vouloir sa p. du gâteau,** to have/to want one's share *or* slice of the cake; *Fin* **p. de fondateur,** founder's share(s); **avoir sa p. de qch,** to come in for a share *or* one's share of sth; **professeur à p. entière,** fully-qualified teacher, *F* full(y)-fledged teacher; **ils viennent pour une bonne p. des environs de Lille,** they come very largely from the Lille area; **une grande p. d'entre elles,** a large proportion of them; **pour ma p.,** for my part, as for me, as far as I am concerned, speaking for myself; **prendre qch en bonne/mauvaise p.,** to take sth in good/bad part;

(b) (*participation*) share, participation; **avoir p. à qch,** to have a hand *or* a share in sth; **avoir p. au gâteau,** to be involved in sth, to have a finger in the pie; **prendre p. à,** to take part in (*sth*); to join in (*a game*); to share in (*the honours*); **prendre p. à la conversation,** to take part *or* join in the conversation; **prendre p. à la joie de qn,** to share in s.o.'s joy; **je n'y ai pris aucune p.,** I had nothing to do with it; **faire p. de qch à qn,** to inform s.o. of sth, to tell s.o. about sth; **lettre de faire-p.,** announcement (*of wedding, death etc*); **faire la p. de qch,** to take sth into account *or* into consideration, to make allowance(s) for sth; **faire la p. des choses,** to make allowances;

(c) nulle p., nowhere; **autre p.,** somewhere else, *Fml* elsewhere; **nulle p. ailleurs,** nowhere else; **quelque p.,** somewhere; *Euph* **aller quelque p.,** (*aux toilettes*) to go somewhere; (*d'une femme*) to (go and) powder one's nose; **de p. et d'autre,** here and there; **faire des concessions de p. et d'autre,** to make concessions on both sides; **de toute(s) part(s),** on all sides; **de p. en p.,** through and through, right through; **d'une p./d'autre p.,** on the one hand/on the other hand;

(d) de la p. de, from; **je viens de la p. de ...,** I represent ...; (*c'est ... qui m'envoie*) I've come on behalf of ...; *Tél* **c'est de la p. de qui?,** who's speaking *or* calling?; **dites-lui de ma p. que ...,** tell him from me that ...; **ce serait bien aimable de votre p.,** it would be very kind of you; **cela m'étonne de sa p.,** that surprises me, coming from him;

(e) à p., apart, separately; **prendre qn à p.,** to take s.o.

aside; **mettre de l'argent à p.,** to put money by *or* aside; **plaisanterie à p.,** joking apart; **c'est une femme à p.,** she's an exceptional woman, she's one of a kind; **un cas à p.,** a special case; **et à p. lui?,** who besides him?; **et à p. lui qui connais-tu?,** who do you know apart from *or* besides him?; **je me disais à p. moi que ...,** I was saying to myself that ...; **à p. quelques exceptions/quelques pages,** with a few exceptions/with the exception of a few pages; **à p. cela tout va bien,** apart from that everything is fine; *F* **à p. que ...,** apart from the fact that ... .

partage [partaʒ] *nm* **(a)** (*action*) division; *Jur* partition (*of property*); **faire le p. de qch,** to divide sth, to share sth out; **un amour sans p.,** undivided love; **il y a p. d'opinions,** opinions are divided; **p. des voix,** division of the votes; *Géog* **ligne de p. des eaux,** watershed, *Am* divide; **(b)** (*lot*) share, portion; **donner/recevoir qch en p.,** to give/receive sth in a will; **la souffrance est le p. du genre humain,** suffering is the lot of mankind.

partagé [partaʒe] *adj* **(a)** (*incertain*) divided; **elle est partagée,** (*elle n'aime pas à choisir*) she's torn; **les avis sont partagés,** opinions are divided; **(b)** (*entre plusieurs personnes*) shared; **amour p.,** mutual love.

partageable [partaʒabl] *adj* divisible, which can be divided.

partager [partaʒe] *v* (**je partageai(s); n. partageons**) **1** *vt* **(a)** to divide (*into shares, groups etc*); to parcel out (*land*); to divide, to apportion (*property etc*); to divide, to share (out) (*loot etc*); **p. son temps entre deux occupations,** to divide one's time between two occupations; **le fleuve partage le pays en deux,** the river divides *or* cuts the country in two;

(b) (*avoir ou mettre en commun*) to share; **p. qch avec qn,** to share sth with s.o.; **p. la joie/l'avis de qn,** to share s.o.'s joy/opinion; **p. le repas de qn,** to share s.o.'s meal, to share a meal with s.o.;

(c) être bien partagé, to be well provided for.

2 *vi* to share; **elle n'aime pas p.,** she doesn't like sharing.

3 se partager *vpr* **(a)** to divide, to be divided; **le gâteau peut se p. en quatre morceaux,** the cake can be cut into four portions;

(b) (*faire un partage entre*) to share; **ils se sont partagé les bénéfices,** they shared *or* divided the profits between them;

(c) (*faire en même temps*) to divide one's time; **elle se partage entre ses enfants et son travail,** she divides her time between her children and her work.

partageur, -euse [partaʒœr, -øz] *adj* willing to share; **il n'est pas p.,** he doesn't like sharing.

partance [partɑ̃s] *nf* **en p.,** (*train*) about to leave; (*aircraft*) about to take off; (*ship*) about to sail; **en p. pour Bordeaux,** bound for Bordeaux; **train en p. pour Londres,** train for London, London train.

partant[1] [partɑ̃] *adv Litt* consequently, therefore.

partant[2] **1** *adj* departing. **2** *nm* (*personne*) person leaving, departing traveller *etc*; *Courses de chevaux etc* runner; **les arrivants et les partants,** the arrivals and departures; *F* **je suis p.,** you can count me in; *F* **je suis toujours p. pour ce genre de choses,** you can always count me in for that type of thing.

partenaire [partənɛr] *n* partner; **partenaires sociaux,** employers and trade unions *or US* labor unions.

parterre [partɛr] *nm* **(a)** *F* (*sol*) floor; **(b)** (*de fleurs*) flower bed; (*plate-bande*) border; **(c)** *Th* (*places, le public*) (the) pit.

parthe [part] *Antiq* **1** *adj* Parthian. **2** *n* **P.,** Parthian; **la flèche du P.,** the Parthian shot.

parthénogénèse [partenɔʒenɛz] *nf Biol* parthenogenesis.

parthénogénétique [partenɔʒenetik] *adj Biol* parthenogenetic.

Parthénon (le) [ləpartenɔ̃] *nm Antiq* the Parthenon.

parti[1] [parti] *nm* **(a)** (*camp*) party; **le p. (communiste),** the Communist Party; **prendre le p. de qn,** to take s.o.'s side *or* part; **prendre p. pour/contre qn,** to side with/against s.o.; **se mettre** *ou* **se ranger du p. de qn,** to side with s.o., to take sides with s.o.;

(b) (*marriageable person*) **un bon** *ou* **beau p.,** a good match;

(c) (*choix, décision*) decision, choice; **prendre p.,** to come to a decision, to make up one's mind; **mon p. est pris,** my mind's made up; **en prendre son p.,** (*se résigner*) to resign oneself to the inevitable; (*en tirer ce qu'on peut*) to make the best of it; **prendre le p. de faire qch,** to decide *or* resolve to do sth; **il ne savait quel p. prendre,** he did not know what course to take; **p. pris,** bias (*in favour of or against a competitor etc*); (*préjugé*) prejudice; **de p. pris,** bias(s)ed, prejudiced; **sans p. pris,** unbias(s)ed;

(d) (*profit*) advantage, profit; **tirer p. de qch,** to make (good) use of sth, to turn sth to (good) account, to take advantage of sth; **tirer le meilleur p. possible de ...,** to make the best possible use of ...;

(e) faire un mauvais p. à qn, to ill-treat s.o., to handle s.o. roughly.

parti[2] *adj F* (*qui a bu*) tipsy, tight; (*qui a pris de la drogue*) high.

partial, -aux [parsjal, -o] *adj* partial, bias(s)ed (*judge*); bias(s)ed, one-sided (*view, article*).

partialement [parsjalmɑ̃] *adv* in a bias(s)ed way.

partialité [parsjalite] *nf* partiality (**envers,** for, to); bias (**envers,** in favour of; **contre,** against).

participant [partisipɑ̃] **1** *adj* participating. **2** *n* participant (*in meeting, action*); member (*of club*); *Sp etc* competitor; **les participants à la manifestation,** those taking part in the demonstration.

participation [partisipɑsjɔ̃] *nf* **(a)** (*collaboration*) participation (**à,** in); (*aux élections*) turnout; **cela s'est fait sans ma p.,** I didn't take any part in it, I had no hand in it; **représentation avec la p. de plusieurs vedettes,** show with appearances by several stars; **mauvaise p. d'un élève en classe,** poor level of participation by a pupil; **p. aux frais,** (financial) contribution; **taux de p. électorale,** voter turnout; **(b)** *Com* share, interest (**à,** in); **p. aux bénéfices,** profit sharing; **p. majoritaire,** major shareholding; **p. ouvrière,** worker participation.

participe [partisip] *nm Gram* participle.

participer [partisipe] *vi* **(a) p. à,** to take part in (*meeting, game etc*); to participate in, to take part in (*discussion etc*); (*of actor*) to appear in (*show*); to be involved in, to be (a) party to (*plot etc*); **p. à la joie/au chagrin de qn,** to share (in) s.o.'s joy/sadness; **(b) p. à,** (*financièrement*) to contribute (money) to (*sth*); **(c) p. à,** (*partager*) to share in (*profits etc*); **(d)** *Litt* **p. de qch,** to partake of sth, to have some of the characteristics of sth.

participial, -ale, -aux [partisipjal, -o] **1** *adj Gram* participial (*phrase etc*). **2** *nf* **participiale,** participial clause.

particularisation [partikylarizɑsjɔ̃] *nf* particularization.

particulariser [partikylarize] **1** *vt* (*définir par ses particularités*) to particularize; (*donner des précisions*) to give particulars *or* details of (*sth*). **2 se particulariser** *vpr* to distinguish oneself from others; to be distinguished (**par,** by).

particularisme [partikylarism] *nm Pol Rel etc* particularism.

particularité [partikylarite] *nf* **(a)** (*spécificité*) particularity, special nature (*of sth*); **(b)** (*caractéristique*) characteristic, (distinctive) feature; (*qui sort de l'ordinaire*) peculiarity; **(c)** *Litt* detail, particular.

particule [partikyl] *nf* **(a)** particle; **panneau de particules,** particle board; *Nucl* **p. alpha/bêta,** alpha/beta particle; **(b)** *Gram* particle; **avoir un nom à p.,** to belong to the nobility, *F* to have a handle to one's name; **dictionnaire des particules nobiliaires,** *Br* ≈ Burke's Peerage ®.

particulier, -ière [partikylje, -jɛr] **1** *adj* **(a)** (*spécial*) particular, special; (*propre*) peculiar, characteristic; **signes particuliers,** (*on passport*) distinguishing features; **attitude qui lui est particulière,** attitude that is characteristic of *or* peculiar to him; **sa démarche bien particulière,** his own particular way of walking; **les besoins particuliers à l'enfant,** the special *or* specific needs of children; **revenir sur un point p.,** to come back to a specific point;

(b) (*remarquable*) unusual, exceptional; (*assez bizarre*) peculiar; **cas p.,** special case; **faire un travail avec un soin p.,** to carry out a piece of work with particular care; *Péj* **ce style est un peu p.,** the style is rather peculiar; **mœurs particulières,** peculiar (sexual) tendencies;

(c) (*privé*) private (*room, life etc*); personal (*account*); **secrétaire p.** *ou* **particulière,** private secretary; **leçons particulières,** private lessons, tuition; **j'ai des raisons particulières pour le désirer,** I have my own (private) reasons *or* I have reasons of my own for wishing it; **à titre p.,** in a private capacity.

2 *n* (*individu*) private person, private individual; **simple p.,** ordinary person; *Péj* **il y a un p. en bas qui désirerait vous parler,** there's a person downstairs who would like to speak to you; **que nous veut ce p.?,** what does that character want?

3 *nm* **le p. ne l'intéresse pas,** he's not interested in specific details; **aller du p. au général,** to go from the specific to the general.

4 *adv* **en p.**, in particular; **notez en p. que ...,** note particularly that ...; **recevoir qn en p.,** (*en privé*) to receive s.o. privately *or* in private; **prendre qn en p.,** to take s.o. aside.

particulièrement [partikyljɛrmɑ̃] *adv* **(a)** (*surtout*) particularly, (e)specially; **il aime tous les arts et p. la peinture,** he is fond of all the arts (and) especially painting; **(b)** (*spécialement*) particularly, outstandingly, exceptionally; **j'attire tout p. votre attention sur cette question,** I would particularly like to draw your attention to this question; **(c)** (*d'une façon intime*) intimately; **je ne la connais pas p.,** I don't know her very well.

partie [parti] *nf* **(a)** (*morceau*) part (*of a whole*); **la plus grande p. du chemin,** the best part of the way; **une bonne p. du papier est abîmée,** a good *or* great deal of the paper is damaged; **les parties du corps,** the parts of the body; **les parties génitales,** *F* **les parties,** the genitals, *F* the private parts, the privates; *Gram* **parties du discours,** parts of speech; **une dissertation en trois parties,** a dissertation in three parts *or* sections; **en p.,** partly, in part; **en grande** *ou* **majeure p.,** largely, to a great extent, for the most part; **il dépense la plus grande p. de son argent,** he spends most of *or* the best part of his money; **faire p. de qch,** to be *or* form part of sth; **cela ne fait pas p. de mes responsabilités,** that isn't part of *or* one of my responsibilities; **je ne fais plus p. de ce cercle,** I don't belong to this club any longer; **faire p. de la famille,** to be part of *or* one of the family; **parties par million,** parts per million;

(b) comptabilité en p. simple/double, single/double entry book- keeping;

(c) (*domaine*) field, subject; line, particular branch (*of a business, profession*); **ce n'est pas (de) ma p., je ne suis pas de la p.,** that's not (in) my line; **les ordinateurs, ce n'est pas ma p.,** computers are not (in) my line;

(d) *Mus* (*of voice, instrument*) part; **parties d'orchestre,** orchestral parts;

(e) (*fête, réunion*) party; **p. de plaisir,** trip, outing; **ce n'est pas une p. de plaisir!,** it's no picnic!, it's not my idea of fun!; **p. de chasse,** shooting party; **voulez vous être-de la p.?,** will you join us?; **je n'étais pas de la p.,** I wasn't invited;

(f) (*jeu*) game; **faire une p. de cartes/d'échecs,** to have *or* play a game of cards/chess; **p. nulle,** draw; **gagner la p.,** to win the game; **la p. se trouve égale,** it's a close *or* even match; *Fig* **ce n'est que p. remise,** it's only a temporary postponement;

(g) (*combat*) struggle; (*pour un point d'honneur*) duel; **p. inégale,** uneven struggle;

(h) *Jur* party (*to dispute, in contract etc*); **être juge et p.,** to be judge in one's own case; **entendre les avocats des deux parties,** to hear counsel on both sides; **p. civile,** plaintiff claiming damages (in criminal case);

(i) (*adversaire*) opponent; **les parties belligérantes,** the belligerent parties; **avoir affaire à forte p.,** to have a powerful opponent *or* *F* a tough customer to deal with;

(j) prendre qn à p. (de qch/d'avoir fait qch), to take s.o. to task, to call s.o. to account (for sth/for doing sth);

(k) avoir p. liée avec qn, to make common cause with s.o..

partiel, -elle [parsjɛl] **1** *adj* partial; **paiement p.,** part payment; **travailler à temps p.,** to have a part-time job, to work part time; *Pol* **élection partielle,** by-election; *Univ* **épreuve partielle,** class exam. **2** *nm Univ* class exam.

partiellement [parsjɛlmɑ̃] *adv* partly, in part, partially (*finished, cooked*).

partir [partir] *vi* (*prp* **partant**; *pp* **parti**; *pr ind* **je pars, il part, n. partons, ils partent**; *pr sub* **je parte**; *impf* **je partais**; *p hist* **je partis**; *fu* **je partirai**) (*aux* **être**) **(a)** (*s'en aller*) to depart, to leave; (*commencer un voyage*) to start, to set out, to set off; (*sans destination particulière*) to go off, to go away; (*à pied*) to walk off *or* away; (*de bateau*) to leave, to sail; (*d'avion*) to leave, to take off; (*d'automobiliste*) to drive off; (*de cavalier*) to ride off; **je pars de la maison à huit heures,** I leave home at eight o'clock; **il est temps que je parte,** it's time I went *or* I left *or* I was off; **p. pour Paris/le Canada/la France/la campagne, p. à Paris/au Canada/en France/à la campagne,** to leave for Paris/Canada/France/the country; **p. en vacances,** to go (away) on holiday; **p. faire ses courses,** to (go and) do one's shopping, to go out (to do one's) shopping; **p. chez qn,** to set out for s.o.'s house; **nous partons demain,** we're leaving tomorrow; **l'avion va p. dans une heure,** the plane leaves *or* takes off in an hour; **partez!,** get out!; *Sp* go!; *Fig* **p. de ce monde,** to die, to depart this life; **p. à toute vitesse** *ou* **comme une flèche,** to set off at full speed, to be off like a shot; **cette affaire est bien/mal partie,** this business has got off to a good/bad start; *Arg* **c'est parti, mon kiki!,** off we go!, here we go!; **nous sommes partis pour une période de prospérité,** we are in for a period of prosperity; **p. de zéro,** to start from scratch; *Aut* **le moteur est parti du premier coup,** the engine started first time; **le fusil est parti,** the gun went off; **p. gagnant/battu d'avance,** to be a winner/ loser right from the start; **p. à rire, p. d'un éclat de rire,** to burst out laughing; **il est parti pour être malheureux,** he'll end up being unhappy, he's riding for a fall; **quand elle part sur ce sujet, on ne l'arrête pas,** once she's off *or* started on that subject, there's no stopping her;

(b) (*disparaître*) (*of pain*) to go; (*of button etc*) to come off; (*of paint etc*) to peel; **la tache ne part pas,** the stain won't come off;

(c) (*venir*) to emanate, to spring, to proceed (**de,** from); **mot qui part du cœur,** word (which comes) from the heart; **en partant du principe qu'il a raison,** assuming that he's right; **le chemin part du village,** the path starts at the village; **ça part pourtant d'un bon sentiment,** it was for the best of motives;

(d) à p. d'aujourd'hui, from today (onwards); **à p. du 15,** from the 15th (onwards), on and after the 15th; **à p. de la route, il courut,** he started running when he got to road; *Com* **robes à p. de 200 francs,** dresses from 200 francs (upwards); **c'est fait à p. de céréales,** it's made from cereals;

(e) faire p., to remove, to get out (*stain etc*); to fire (*gun*); to let off (*fireworks*); to send off (*the mail*); to touch off (*mine*); to start (*engine*).

partisan, -ane [partizɑ̃, -an] **1** *n* partisan, follower (*of s.o.*); advocate, supporter (*of policy etc*). **2** *nm Mil* partisan; **guerre de partisans,** guer(r)illa warfare. **3** *adj* **querelles partisanes,** sectarian quarrels; **être p. de (faire) qch,** to be in favour *or* *US* favor of (doing) sth; **je suis p. de la réforme,** I'm all for reform.

partitif, -ive [partitif, -iv] *adj & nm Gram* partitive (noun, article).

partition [partisjɔ̃] *nf* **(a)** *Pol* partition, division; **(b)** *Mus* score; **p. d'orchestre,** full score; **elle joue sans p.,** she plays without music.

partouse [partuz] *nf Arg* orgy.

partout [partu] *adv* **(a)** everywhere; **chercher qch p.,** to look everywhere for sth, to hunt high and low for sth; **p. où,** wherever; **p. ailleurs,** anywhere else; **un peu p.,** all over the place; **souffrir de p.,** to feel pain all over; **j'ai mal p.,** I ache all over; **je ne peux pas être p. à la fois,** I can't be everywhere *or* in two places at once; **(b)** *Tennis* all; **30 p.,** 30 all; **40 p.,** deuce.

partouze [partuz] *nf Arg* orgy.

partouzer [partuze] *vi Arg* to have an orgy.

parturiente [partyrjɑ̃t] *nf Méd* woman in parturition.

parturition [partyrisjɔ̃] *nf Méd* parturition.

parure [paryr] *nf* **(a)** (*vêtements et bijoux*) costume, finery; **(b)** (*décoration*) ornament; (*ensemble*) set (*of jewel(le)ry, lingerie etc*); **p. de diamants,** set of diamonds; **p. de table,** table linen; **(c)** parings (*of leather etc*); trimmings (*of meat*).

parution [parysjɔ̃] *nf* appearance, publication, issue (*of book, article etc*).

parvenir [parvənir] *vi* (*conj like* **venir**; *aux* **être**) **(a)** (*arriver*) to arrive; **p. à un endroit,** to arrive at *or* reach a place; **votre lettre m'est parvenue,** I received your letter; **la lettre leur est parvenue,** the letter reached them, they received the letter; **votre demande doit nous p. avant le 4,** your application must be in *or* reach us by the 4th; **faire p. qch à qn,** to send *or* forward sth to s.o.; **écrits anciens qui sont parvenus jusqu'à nous,** ancient writings which have come down to us; **(b)** (*atteindre*) to attain, to reach (*a great age etc*); (*réussir*) to succeed; **p. à faire qch,** to manage to do sth, to succeed in doing sth; **p. à la gloire/la célébrité,** to achieve glory/fame; **(c)** (*s'élever socialement*) to succeed *or* get on in life.

parvenu, -ue [parvəny] *n Péj* parvenu, upstart.

parvis [parvi] *nm Archit* parvis (*in front of a church*).

pas[1] [pa] *nm* **(a)** (*enjambée*) step, pace; (*plus long*) stride; (*que l'on entend*) footstep; (*allure*) pace; *Mil* step; **à chaque p.,** at every step; **p. à p.,** step by step, little by little; **allonger le p.,** to lengthen one's stride; **aller à p. comptés,** to walk with measured tread; **aller** *ou* **avancer** *ou* **marcher à grands p.,** to stride along; *Fig* **avancer à**

grands p., to make great strides (forward), to make great progress; **marcher à petits p.**, (*of child etc*) to toddle (along); **marcher d'un p. lourd**, to walk with a heavy tread; **faire un p.**, to take a step; **faire un p. en avant/en arrière**, to step forward/back; **faire deux p. en avant**, to take two steps *or* paces forward; **faire les cent p.**, to pace up and down; **faux p.**, slip, stumble; *Fig* faux pas, (social) blunder; *Fig* **il n'y a que le premier p. qui coûte**, once you've taken the first step, that's the hardest part over, the longest journey starts with a single step; *Fig* **elle a fait un grand p. en avant**, she has made great progress; *Fig* **faire le premier p.**, to take the first step, to make the first move; **j'y vais de ce p.**, I'm going at once; **entendre des p.** *ou* **un bruit de p.**, to hear footsteps; **je l'ai reconnu à son p.**, I knew him by his step; **ils habitent à deux p. d'ici**, they live a few yards away *or* (within) a stone's throw from here; **il était à deux p. de nous**, he was within a couple of paces *or* feet of us; **au p.**, (*lentement*) at a walking pace; **roulez au p.**, (*sur panneau*) dead slow; **mettre son cheval au p.**, to walk one's horse; *Fig* **mettre qn au p.**, to bring s.o. into line; **marcher au p.**, to march in step *or* in time; **se mettre au p.**, to get in step; **marquer le p.**, to mark time; **changer le p.**, to change step; **hâter** *ou* **presser le p.**, to quicken one's pace; **ralentir le p.**, to slow down; **p. ordinaire**, normal pace; *Mil* marching step; **p. redoublé**, double time; **marcher au p. cadencé**, to march in quick time; **p. de gymnastique**, jog trot; *Mil* double time; **p. de l'oie**, goose step; **p. de valse**, waltz step; **p. de deux**, (*en danse*) pas de deux; **p. de bourrée**, (*en danse*) pas de bourrée; **avoir** *ou* **prendre le p. sur qn**, to have *or* take precedence over s.o.; **céder le p. à qn**, to give s.o. precedence;
(b) (*trace*) footprint; **marcher sur les p. de qn**, to follow in s.o.'s tracks; *Fig* to follow in s.o.'s footsteps; **arriver sur les p. de qn**, to arrive just after s.o.; **revenir sur ses p.**, to retrace one's steps;
(c) *Arch* step (*of stair*); **p. de la porte**, doorstep; **il est sur le p. de la porte**, he's standing on the doorstep; **p. de porte**, key money;
(d) (*passage*) passage; (*de montagne*) (mountain) pass; (*détroit*) strait; **le p. de Calais**, the Straits of Dover; *Fig* **tirer qn d'un mauvais p.**, to get s.o. out of a hole *or* fix; *Fig* **sauter le p.**, to take the plunge; *Litt* to die;
(e) *Tech* pitch, thread (*of screw*); pitch (*of propeller*); distance, spacing (*between seats on aeroplane, bus etc*); **sièges au p. de 980 mm**, seats 980 mm apart.

pas² *adv* **(a)** not; (*avant un nom*) no; **je ne sais p.**, I don't know; **je ne l'ai p. encore vue**, I haven't seen her yet; **je n'en dis p. plus**, I won't say another word; **ne p. parler au conducteur**, (please) do not speak to the driver; **p. du tout, absolument p.**, not at all, by no means, *F* not a bit of it, absolutely not; **pourquoi p.?**, why not?; **p. moi**, not me; **qu'il vienne ou p. cela m'est égal**, it's all the same to me whether he comes or not; **elle est libre, lui p.**, she's free, he isn't; *F* **tu es heureuse, p. vrai?**, you're happy, aren't you?; **tu m'écriras, p.?**, (*n'est-ce pas*) you'll write, won't you?; **p. tant que ça**, not that much, not as much as that; *F* **p. si fort, la radio!**, turn that radio down!; **p. d'argent, p. de voiture**, no money, no car; **allez, p. d'histoires!**, come on, don't make a fuss!; **viendra?, viendra p.?/passera?, passera p.?/***etc*, will he come or won't he?, will he or won't he (come)?/will he make it or won't he ?, will he *or* won't he (make it)?/*etc*; *F* **c'est p. vrai!**, you're kidding!, no kidding!; *F* **connais p.!**, I don't know him; *F* **si c'est p. malheureux!**, isn't that a shame!; **p. possible!**, no! incredible!; **affaibli mais non p. découragé**, weakened but not discouraged; **ce n'est p. qu'il soit beau**, he's not exactly handsome;
(b) (*qualifying an adj*) **des lilas p. fleuris**, lilac not yet in bloom;
(c) p. un mot ne fut dit, not a word was spoken; **fier comme p. un**, prouder than anyone; **il est menteur comme p. un**, he's a terrible liar.

pascal, -aux [paskal, -o] *adj* paschal (*lamb*); (*de la fête de Pâques chrétienne*) Easter (*communion etc*).

paso-doble [pasɔdɔbl] *nm* paso doble.

passable [pasabl] *adj* passable, tolerable, acceptable; *Scol* **mention p.**, ≈ (average to below average) pass; (*in degree exam*) *Br* ≈ third class; **c'est p.**, it's not too bad.

passablement [pasabləmɑ̃] *adv* passably, tolerably; **dessiner p.**, to draw tolerably well; **c'est p. long**, it's rather *or* fairly long; **il a p. voyagé**, he has travelled a lot.

passade [pasad] *nf* **(a)** (*engouement, liaison courte*) passing fancy, whim; **(b)** *Équitation* passade.

passage [pasaʒ] *nm* **(a)** crossing (*of road, river*); passing over *or* across (*a stretch of land*); passing through (*a doorway*); going past (*a place*); *Nau* passage; **la rivière est de p. facile**, the river is easy to cross; **elle guette le p. du facteur**, she's watching *or* on the lookout for the postman; **j'attends le p. de l'autobus**, I'm waiting for the bus (to come); **chacun sourit sur son p.**, every one smiles as he goes by; **il y a toujours du p. ici**, there are always a lot of people (coming and going) here; **livrer p.**, to make way; **p. interdit (au public)**, no entry, no thoroughfare; **lieu de p.**, (*dans une maison*) heavy traffic area; **oiseau de p.**, bird of passage; **droit de p.**, right of way; **être de p. dans une ville**, to be passing through a town; **voyageur de p. à Paris**, traveller passing through Paris; **clientèle de p.**, *F* **le p.**, casual trade; *Mus* **note de p.**, passing note; **il m'a saisi au p.**, he caught me as I went past; *Fig* **et au p. je te ferai remarquer ceci ...**, and incidentally, let me draw your attention to this ...; *Él* **p. du courant**, flow of current; *Nau* **payer son p.**, to pay for one's passage; **p. du jour à la nuit**, transition *or* change from day to night; **avec le p. du temps**, with the passage of time, as the days passed, as time went on *or* by; *Scol* **le p. d'un élève en classe supérieure**, the moving up of a child into a higher class; **examen de p.**, end-of-year exam; *F* **p. à tabac**, beating up;
(b) (*chemin*) passage, way; (*ruelle*) alley(way); (*magasins*) (shopping) arcade, *Am* mall; *Nau* channel; **se frayer** *ou* **se faire un p.**, to force *or* elbow one's way through; **barrer le p. à qn**, to stand in *or* block s.o.'s way, to block s.o.'s passage;
(c) *Rail* **p. à niveau**, level crossing, *Am* grade crossing; **p. souterrain**, subway, underpass, *Am* underground passage; **p. clouté**, pedestrian crossing; **p. pour piétons**, pedestrian crossing; (*sous-terrain*) pedestrian subway; *Aut* **p. protégé**, priority over secondary roads;
(d) passage (*of book etc*); passage, piece (*of music etc*);
(e) p. à vide, (*trouble physique*) (funny) turn; **avoir un p. à vide**, (*physique*) to have a (funny) turn), to come over all funny; (*moral*) to be a bit down, to go through a bad patch; (*être sans ressources*) to be at a loss; **elle a eu un p. à vide en mai**, (*ma fille, cette athlète etc*) she went through a bad patch in May; **il a eu un p. à vide dans la cote**, (*ce cycliste, ce coureur*) he lost it on the hill;
(f) *Météo* **p. nuageux/pluvieux**, cloudy/rainy spell.

passager, -ère [pasaʒe, -ɛr] **1** *adj* **(a) oiseau p.**, bird of passage; **(b)** fleeting, short-lived, transitory (*beauty etc*); momentary (*pain etc*); **état p.**, passing phase; **(c)** (*passant*) busy; **rue passagère**, busy street. **2** *n* passenger (*by sea, air*); **p. clandestin**, stowaway.

passagèrement [pasaʒɛrmɑ̃] *adv* temporarily, for a short while.

passant, -ante [pasɑ̃, -ɑ̃t] **1** *adj* busy (*road etc*). **2** *n* passer-by. **3** *nm* keeper, guide; **p. de courroie**, strap loop.

passation [pasɑsjɔ̃] *nf Jur* drawing up, signing (*of agreement*); (*en comptabilité*) entering (*of items*); *Pol* **p. des pouvoirs**, transfer of power.

passavant [pasavɑ̃] *nm* **(a)** *Nau* (fore-and-aft) gangway, catwalk; **(b)** *Jur* transire.

passe¹ [pɑs] *nf* **(a) mot de p.**, password; **(b)** (*manipulation*) **passes magnétiques**, mesmeric *or* hypnotic passes; **(c)** *Fb etc* pass; *Escrime* pass, thrust; *Escrime & Fig* **p. d'armes**, passage of arms; *Fb* **p. en avant**, forward pass; **(d)** *Métal* cut (*on lathe*); **(e) maison de p.**, hotel used by prostitutes and their clients; **(f)** (*at roulette*) any number above 18; *Escrime* pass, thrust; *Escrime & Fig* **p. d'armes**, passage of arms; **(g)** *Nau* (*chenal*) pass, channel; **p. étroite**, narrows; **(h) être en p. de faire qch**, to be on the way to doing sth; **il est en p. de faire fortune**, he looks as though he will make a fortune; **être dans une mauvaise p.**, to be in a fix *or* tight corner; (*du point de vue moral*) to be in a bad way; **elle est dans une bonne p.**, everything's going right for her; **(i)** *Typ* **(main de) p.**, overs, over sheets, overplus; **exemplaires de p.**, surplus copies (of book), over copies.

passe² *nm F* pass key, skeleton key, master key.

passé [pase] **1** *adj* **(a)** (*écoulé*) past, gone by; **la semaine passée**, last week; **il est quatre heures passées**, it's gone four, it's after four; **il a quarante ans passés**, he's over forty; **(b)** (*fini*) over; **l'orage est p.**, the storm is over; **(c)** (*éteint, décoloré*) faded (*colour*). **2** *nm* **(a) le p.**, the past; **comme par le p.**, as in the past; **avoir un p. chargé**, to have a shady *or* chequered past; **oublions le p.**, let bygones be bygones; **(b)** *Gram* past (tense); **p. simple**, preterite, past historic; **p. composé**, perfect (tense). **3** *prép* beyond; **p. les arbres pas un abri**, beyond the trees there's no shelter; **p. cette date**, after this date; **p. la première impression**, once the first impression has worn off.

passe-droit [pɑsdrwa] *nm* (undeserved) privilege, favour,

US favor; **le fils du patron a eu un p.-d., on a fait un p.-d. au fils du patron,** the boss's son got preferential treatment; (*pl passe-droits*).

passéisme [paseism] *nm Péj* attachment to *or* nostalgia for the past.

passéiste [paseist] *adj & n* (person) attached to the past.

passe-lacet [paslasɛ] *nm* bodkin; *Fig F* **raide comme un p.-l.,** (as) stiff as a poker; (*pl passe-lacets*).

passement [pasmɑ̃] *nm Tex* (gold, silver, silk) braid(ing).

passementer [pasmɑ̃te] *vt* to braid.

passementerie [pasmɑ̃tri] *nf Tex* **(a)** *Com* haberdashery trade, *Am* notions trade; **(b)** (*accessoire décoratif*) braid.

passementier, -ière [pasmɑ̃tje, -jɛr] *Tex* **1** *adj* haberdashery, *Am* notions (*trade etc*). **2** *n* haberdasher, *Am* dealer in notions.

passe-montagne [pasmɔ̃taɲ] *nm* balaclava (helmet); (*pl passe- montagnes*).

passe-partout [paspartu] **1** *nm inv* **(a)** (*clef*) pass key, skeleton key, master key; *Fig* **il ne répond que par p.-p.,** he gives nothing but stock replies *or* answers; **(b)** (*outil*) cross-cut saw; **(c)** (*cadre*) (*photograph etc*) frame (with removable back). **2** *adj inv* all-purpose, stock; **réponse p.-p.,** stock reply *or* response *or* answer; **tenue p.-p.,** outfit that can be worn anywhere.

passe-passe [paspas] *nm no pl* (*illusions magiques*) legerdemain, sleight of hand; *Fig* (*tromperie*) confidence trick , *F* con trick; *surtout* **tour de p.-p.,** conjuring trick.

passe-plats [paspla] *nm inv* service hatch.

passepoil [paspwal] *nm* braid, piping (*for garments*).

passepoiler [paspwale] *vt* to braid, to pipe (*garment*); **poche passepoilée,** welted pocket.

passeport [paspɔr] *nm Admin & Fig* passport; *Nau* passport, sea letter; **les enfants sont sur le p. de leur mère,** the children are on their mother's passport.

passer [pase] **1** *vi* **(a)** (*se déplacer, circuler*) to pass; to go (on, by, along); *Fml* to proceed; **p. sur un pont,** to cross (over) a bridge; **il est passé devant le magasin,** he went by *or* passed (by) the shop; **p. par-dessus/par-dessous qch,** to get over/under sth; **la voiture lui est** *ou* **a passé(e) sur les jambes,** the car ran over his legs; *Fig* **p. sur le corps de qn pour parvenir à qch,** to trample all over s.o. to attain sth; **la bouteille est** *ou* **a passé(e) de main en main,** the bottle was passed round; **faire p. les gâteaux,** to hand *or* pass round the cakes; **par où est-il passé?,** which way did he go?; **je regardais p. la procession,** I was watching the procession; **p. sur une difficulté,** to pass over a difficulty; **passons!,** well, let's leave it at that!; **en passant,** by the way; **dire qch en passant,** to mention sth in passing; **soit dit en passant,** by the way, incidentally;

(b) (*aller d'un lieu à un autre, changer*) **p. à l'ennemi,** to go over to the enemy; (*d'un espion*) to defect; **passons à la salle à manger,** let's go into the dining room; *Scol* **p. dans la classe supérieure,** to move up, to be moved up (a class); **passons à autre chose,** let's move on to other matters; (*changeons de sujet*) let's change the subject; *Aut* **p. en seconde,** to go *or* change into second (gear); **il est passé du rire aux larmes,** his laughter changed to tears; *Fig* **il passe sans cesse du rire aux larmes,** one day he's up, the next day he's down;

(c) (*se transmettre*) **p. à la postérité,** to be remembered by posterity; **l'héritage est passé à sa fille,** the inheritance went to his daughter; **le mot est passé dans l'usage,** the word is in common use;

(d) (*traverser*) **la route passe par le village,** the road runs *or* goes through the village; **mon dîner ne passe pas,** my dinner won't go down; **je ne peux pas p.,** I can't get by *or* past; **on ne passe pas,** no thoroughfare; **défense de p.,** no entry; **laisser p.,** to let in (*light, air etc*); to let through (*person etc*); *Fig* **laisser p. une erreur,** to overlook a mistake; **cette histoire n'a pas passé,** I *or* he *etc* still hasn't got over it; **passez par la fenêtre,** go through the window; **faire p. un tuyau à travers le mur,** to run a pipe through the wall; **faire p. des gens d'un pays à un autre,** to smuggle people out of one country and into another; *Fig* **il est passé par l'université,** he did a university course; **il dit tout ce qui lui passe par la tête,** he says anything *or* the first thing that comes into his head; **la première chose qui m'a** *ou* **m'est passé(e) par la tête,** the first thing that came into my head; **sa chemise passait,** his shirt was hanging out; **il faut que le café passe très lentement, the** coffee has to filter very slowly; *Can* **j'ai passé tout droit,** I overslept;

(e) *Rad* **cette chanson n'est pas passée à la radio,** this song hasn't been played on the radio; *TV Cin* **ce film est passé la semaine dernière,** the film was on *or* was shown last week; *TV Cin etc* **qu'est-ce qui passe ce soir?,** what's on this evening?;

(f) (*aux* **être**) (*aller*) **p. chez qn,** to call on s.o.; **je passerai chez vous ce soir,** I'll come round this evening; **en passant, je suis entré dire bonjour,** I just looked in *or* dropped in on my way past; **il est passé prendre le courrier,** he dropped by to pick up the mail; **je ne fais que p. pour demander de vos nouvelles,** I just called to see how you were; **est- ce que le facteur est passé?,** has the postman been?, has the post come?;

(g) (*subir*) to go through, *Fml* to undergo; **il est passé par des difficultés,** he has had a difficult *or* bad time; **je suis passé par là,** I've been through it; **tout le monde y passe,** it happens to everybody *or* to us all; *F* **il a failli y p.,** (*mourir*) he nearly died; **toute sa fortune y a** *ou* **y est passé(e),** he spent his entire fortune on it;

(h) (*disparaître, finir*) to disappear, to cease; **la douleur a** *ou* **est passé(e),** the pain has gone; **le vert est passé de mode,** green is out of fashion; **le plus dur est passé,** the worst is over; **ça lui passera (avec l'âge),** he'll grow out of it; **couleurs qui passent,** colours that fade; **il faut laisser p. l'orage,** we must let the storm blow over; **cela a fait p. mon mal de tête,** it has cured my headache; **laisser p. sa dernière chance,** to miss one's last chance;

(i) (*s'écouler*) to elapse, to go by; **des années ont passé depuis ...,** years have passed *or* it's been years since ...; **à mesure que les années passent,** as the years go by; **comme le temps passe (vite)!,** how time flies!; **faire p. le temps,** to pass the time; **tout passe, tout lasse, tout casse,** nothing lasts, everything comes to an end;

(j) (*devenir*) to become; **ce mot est passé en proverbe,** the saying has become a proverb; **le chiffre d'affaires est passé de deux à trois millions,** our turnover has gone up from two to three million;

(k) (*aux* **avoir**) (*être considéré comme*) to be considered, to pass for; **p. pour riche,** to be considered rich; **p. pour avoir fait qch,** to be credited with having done sth; **ceci passe pour vrai,** everyone believes this is true; **se faire p. pour ...,** to pass oneself off as, to pose as ...;

(l) (*aux* **avoir**) (*être accepté*) to be accepted; **la loi a passé,** the bill has been carried *or* has gone through; **passe encore qu'il revienne demain, mais ..., qu'il revienne demain, passe encore mais ...,** if he comes back tomorrow that's one thing *or* (that's all) well and good, but ...; **cela peut p./cela ne passe pas,** it will/won't do; *F* **cette histoire-là ne passe pas,** that story won't wash;

(m) (*aux* **être**) *Jur* **p. en jugement,** to come up for judgment; **l'affaire passera demain/en janvier,** the case will be heard tomorrow/in January;

(n) *Cartes* **passe!,** pass!; (*at bridge*) no bid!

2 *vt* **(a)** to cross, to go over (*bridge, river*); to go through, to pass through (*a doorway, a gate*); to go through, to clear (*customs*); to cross (*a frontier*); *Fig* to pass, to go beyond, to exceed, to surpass; **vous avez passé la maison,** you've gone past the house; *Fig* **il a passé la soixantaine,** he's in his sixties; *Fig* **cela passe les limites** *ou* **les bornes,** that's going too far; *Fig* **le vieux ne passera pas l'hiver,** the old man won't last (through) the winter; **p. son chemin,** to go one's way;

(b) (*transporter*) to convey across, to carry across; to ferry (*goods, passengers*) over (*a river*); **p. des marchandises en fraude,** to smuggle goods;

(c) (*mettre en circulation*) to pass; **p. des faux billets,** to pass forged banknotes;

(d) (*donner*) to pass; **p. qch à qn,** to pass *or* hand sth to s.o.; **voulez-vous me p. l'eau, s'il vous plaît,** please pass me the water; **p. un message,** to pass on a message; **il m'a passé son rhume,** he gave me his cold, I caught his cold; *Sp* **p. le ballon,** to pass the ball; **p. la parole à qn,** to hand (s.o.) over to s.o.; *Tél* **allô, je vous passe M. Robert/Paris,** hello, I'm putting you through to Mr Robert/ to Paris; *Tél* **passez-moi M. Robert,** give me *or* put me through to Mr Robert; *Tél* **passez-moi un coup de fil demain,** call me tomorrow, give me a call *or Br* ring tomorrow; **p. sa colère sur qn,** to vent one's anger on s.o.;

(e) (*mettre, faire aller*) **p. une éponge sur le tableau,** to wipe the blackboard; *Fig* **passons l'éponge là-dessus,** let's say no more about it; **p. le tapis à l'aspirateur, p. l'aspirateur sur le tapis,** to vacuum the carpet; **p. sa tête par la fenêtre,** to put one's head out of the window; **je lui ai passé mon bras autour de la taille,** I slipped my arm round his waist; **p. une chemise/une robe,** to slip on a shirt/a dress; *Aut* **p. la seconde/la troisième,** to go *or* change into second/third (gear); *Nau* **p. une manœuvre,** to reeve a rope; **qu'est-ce que je vais lui p.!,** I won't half tell him off!, he won't half catch it!; **je l'ai sentie p.,** I really caught it; **p. un couteau à la meule,** to sharpen a knife; **p. un parquet à la cire,** to polish a (parquet) floor; **p. des troupes en revue,** to inspect *or* review troops;

(f) *Cin TV* to show (*film*); **salle qui passe Hamlet,** cinema showing Hamlet; **p. un disque,** to play a record;

(g) to pass, to spend (*time, one's life*); **on y passera le temps nécessaire,** we'll spend as much time on it as necessary; **pour p. le temps,** (in order) to while away *or* pass the time;

(h) (*pardonner*) to excuse (*fault etc*); **on ne lui passe rien,** he doesn't get away with anything; **passez-moi l'expression,** (if you'll) pardon the expression;

(i) (*omettre*) to omit, to leave out; **p. sous silence,** to make no mention of (*sth*); to keep quiet about (*an embarrassing fact, a guilty secret*); **j'en passe, et des meilleures,** and that's not all *or* not the half of it; **il est beau, intelligent, instruit, et j'en passe,** he's handsome, intelligent, cultured, and that's not all;

(j) *Jur* to reach (*an agreement*); to enter into, to sign (*a contract*); **p. un accord,** to conclude an agreement, to enter into an agreement; **p. une commande,** to place an order **(de qch à qn,** for sth with s.o.); **p. une loi,** to pass a law; **p. un article en compte,** (*en comptabilité*) to post an entry;

(k) p. un examen, to sit for *or* to take an exam(ination);

(l) to strain (*liquid*); to sift (*flour*); **p. le café,** to filter the coffee;

(m) (*devenir*) **p. capitaine,** to be promoted to captain; **elle est passée maître dans l'art du collage/l'art du mentir,** she's a past master at collage/lying.

3 se passer *vpr* **(a)** (*se produire, arriver*) to happen; **cela s'est passé il y a dix ans,** it happened ten years ago; **que se passe-t-il?, qu'est-ce qui se passe?,** what's going on?, what's happening?; **tout s'est bien passé,** everything went (off) smoothly; **mon histoire se passe en France,** my story is set in France; *F* **ça ne se passera pas comme ça,** I won't stand for it;

(b) (*cesser*) to cease; (*of time*) to elapse, to go by; **nos ennuis finiront par se p.,** our troubles will come to an end eventually; **le temps s'est passé depuis que ...,** much time has passed since ...; **mon mal de tête se passe,** my headache is going;

(c) se p. de qn/qch, to do without s.o./sth, to dispense with s.o./sth; **je m'en passerai,** I'll do *or* manage without it; **ces faits se passent de commentaires,** these facts need no comment;

(d) se p. la main dans les cheveux, to run one's fingers through one's hair;

(e) se p. une fantaisie, to indulge a whim.

passereau, -eaux [pasro] *nm* (*oiseau*) **(a)** *Arch* sparrow; **(b) passereaux,** passerines, passeriformes.

passerelle [pasrɛl] *nf* **(a)** (*au-dessus d'une rue, d'un ruisseau*) footbridge; **(b)** *Nau* **p. (de commandement),** bridge; **p. de navigation,** navigation bridge; **(c)** (*pont incliné*) **p. de débarquement** *ou* **d'embarquement,** *Nau* gangway, gangplank; *Av* (*amovible*) steps; (*fixe*) passenger bridge; **(d)** *Fig* (*intermédiaire*) intermediate stage *or* link; **ce cours est une p. entre les deux niveaux,** this course bridges the two levels.

passe-temps [pastɑ̃] *nm inv* pastime, hobby.

passe-thé [paste] *nm inv* tea strainer.

passeur, -euse [pasœr, -øz] *n* ferryman, ferrywoman; **il est p. (de frontière),** (*de marchandises*) he's a smuggler; (*de gens*) he smuggles people across the border.

passible [pasibl] *adj* liable **(de,** to, for); **p. d'une amende,** liable to a fine; **p. de l'impôt,** (*personne*) liable for tax.

passif, -ive [pasif, -iv] **1** *adj* passive (*obedience etc*); **rester p.,** to remain (im)passive; *Pol* **faire de la résistance passive,** to offer passive resistance; *Gram* **forme passive,** passive; *Com* **dettes passives,** liabilities; *Mil* **défense passive,** civil defence. **2** *nm Gram* passive; *Com* liabilities, debt.

passing-shot [pɑsiŋʃɔt] *nm Sp* passing shot; (*pl passing-shots*).

passion [pɑsjɔ̃] *nf* **(a)** passion; **p. pour la musique,** passion for music; **vivre une p.,** to have a passionate love affair, to be passionately in love; **aimer qn à la** *ou* **avec p.,** to love s.o. passionately; **il a la p. des voitures,** he has a passion for cars; **la moto est sa p.,** he's mad about motorbikes; **parler avec/sans p.,** to speak passionately/dispassionately; **lutter contre ses passions,** to struggle against one's passions; **déclencher des passions,** to unleash passions *or* strong emotions; **(b)** *Rel* **la P.,** the Passion (of Christ); **semaine de la P.,** Passion Week; *Mus* **la P. selon saint Jean,** the St John Passion; **fruit de la p.,** passion fruit.

passionnant [pasjɔnɑ̃] *adj* exciting, fascinating, gripping, thrilling (*story etc*).

passionné, -ée [pasjɔne] **1** *adj* passionate, impassioned (*plea*); **débat p.,** heated *or* impassioned debate; **amour p.,** passionate love; **p. de** *ou* **pour qn/qch,** passionately fond of s.o./sth. **2** *n* enthusiast; **c'est une passionnée de moto(s),** she's mad about motorbikes, she's a motorbike fanatic.

passionnel, -elle [pasjɔnɛl] *adj* of passion, passionate; **état p.,** state of passion, passionate state; **crime p.,** crime of passion.

passionnément [pasjɔnemɑ̃] *adv* passionately.

passionner [pasjɔne] **1** *vt* **(a)** (*inspirer intérêt très vif*) to interest passionately; *Litt* to impassion; **le sport la passionne,** she is passionately fond of sport, sport is her passion; **livre qui passionne,** fascinating book; **(b)** (*animer*) to heat up. **2 se passioner** *vpr* **se p. de** *ou* **pour qch,** to become passionately fond of sth, to become (madly) enthusiastic about sth, to conceive a passion for sth.

passivement [pasivmɑ̃] *adv* passively.

passivité [pasivite] *nf* passivity, passiveness.

passoire [paswar] *nf Culin* strainer; **p. à légumes,** colander; **sa mémoire est une p.,** he's got a memory *or* a head like a sieve; **cette frontière est une vraie p.,** the border has as many holes in it as a sieve.

pastel [pastɛl] *nm* **(a)** *Beaux-Arts* pastel; (*dessin*) pastel drawing; **tableau au p.,** picture in pastel; **bleu p.,** pastel blue; **je n'aime pas les (tons) pastels,** I don't like pastels; **(b)** *Bot* woad.

pastelliste [pastelist] *n Beaux-Arts* pastellist.

pastèque [pastɛk] *nf* (*fruit*) water melon.

pasteur [pastœr] *nm* **(a)** *Litt* shepherd; *Fig* leader; **peuple p.,** pastoral people; *Fig* **un p. d'hommes,** (*conducteur*) a leader of men; *Rel* **le bon P.,** the Good Shepherd; **(b)** *Rel* pastor, *surtout* (Protestant) minister.

pasteurisation [pastœrizɑsjɔ̃] *nf* pasteurization.

pasteuriser [pastœrize] *vt* to pasteurize.

pastiche [pastiʃ] *nm* pastiche.

pasticher [pastiʃe] *vt* to do a pastiche of.

pastille [pastij] *nf* **(a)** (*bonbon, pilule*) (*molle*) pastille; (*dure*) lozenge; **p. contre la toux,** cough drop, cough sweet, throat pastille; **p. de menthe,** (pepper)mint; **(b)** (*motif*) circle.

pastis [pastis] *nm* pastis; *F* fix, trouble; *F* **être dans le p.,** to be in a fix; *F* **quel p.!,** what a mess!

pastoral, -ale, -aux [pastɔral, -o] **1** *adj* pastoral. **2** *nf* **pastorale,** *Littér* pastoral (play, poem); *Mus* pastoral(e).

pastorat [pastɔra] *nm* pastorate.

pastoureau, -elle, -eaux [pasturo, -ɛl] **1** *n Arch & Litt* shepherd lad, shepherd lass. **2** *nf* **pastourelle,** *Mus* pastourelle; (*danse*) fourth figure of the quadrille.

pat [pat] *nm inv Échecs* stalemate; **faire p.,** to stalemate.

patachon [pataʃɔ̃] *nm Arg* **mener une vie de p.,** to lead a wild life.

Patagonie [patagɔni] *nf* Patagonia.

patapouf [patapuf] **1** *int* flop! **2** *nm Enf* **gros p.,** fat lump.

pataquès [patakɛs] *nm F* **(a)** (*faute de liaison*) faulty liaison; **(b)** (*faute de langage*) serious mistake (*in pronunciation etc*).

patata [patata] *int voir* **PATATI.**

patate [patat] *nf* **(a)** *F* (*pomme de terre*) spud; *F* idiot, clot; **la corvée de patates,** peeling the spuds; *esp Mil* spud-bashing; *Fig* **en avoir gros sur la p.,** to be down in the mouth, to be down in the dumps; **(b) p. (douce),** sweet potato; **(c)** *Math* = set diagram (*used for teaching young children*).

patati [patati] *int F* **et p. et patata,** and so on and so forth.

patatras [patatra] *int F* crash!

pataud, -aude [pato, -od] **1** *nm* puppy with big paws. **2** *n Vieilli* lump. **3** *adj F* heavy, clumsy (*person*); clumsy, awkward (*appearance, gait*).

pataugeoire [patoʒwar] *nf* paddling pool.

patauger [patoʒe] *vi* **(je pataugeai(s); n. pataugeons)** (*dans la boue*) to squelch in the mud; (*dans l'eau*) to paddle (in the water); *Fig F* (*s'embrouiller*) to become embarrassed, to flounder (*in speech, situation etc*).

patchouli [patʃuli] *nm* patchouli.

patchwork [patʃwork] *nm* patchwork quilt.

pâte [pɑt] *nf* **(a)** *Culin* (*de tarte*) pastry; (*de pain, gâteau*) dough; **p. à pain,** dough; **p. brisée,** short(crust) pastry; **p. à choux,** choux pastry; **p. feuilletée,** flaky *or* puff pastry; **p. à frire,** batter; **p. à crêpes,** pancake batter; **pâtes (alimentaires),** pasta; **des pâtes fraîches,** fresh pasta; *Fig*

être de la p. dont on fait les héros, to be the stuff that heroes are made of; *Fig* **c'est une bonne p.,** he's a good sort; *Fig* **une p. molle,** a wimp; *Fig* **mettre la main à la p.,** to get down to it; *Fig* **être comme un coq en p.,** to be in clover; **(b)** (*mélange, composition*) **fromage à p. dure/molle,** hard/soft cheese; **p. de fruits,** fruit jelly; **p. d'amandes,** almond paste; **p. à papier,** pulp; **p. dentifrice,** toothpaste; **p. à modeler,** modelling clay; **(c)** *Beaux-Arts* paint, colours, *US* colors; (*plus épais*) paste; **(d)** *Typ* (printer's) pie; **caractères tombés en p.,** pied type.

pâté [pɑte] *nm* **(a)** *Culin* (*terrine*) pâté; **p. de foie,** liver pâté; **p. de campagne,** pâté de campagne (*coarse pâté made with pork*); **p. en croûte,** meat *etc* pie; **p. impérial,** spring roll; **p. (de sable),** sandpie; **(b)** (*bloc*) block (*of houses*); **(c)** (*tache*) blot, blob (*of ink*).

pâtée [pɑte] *nf* **(a)** (*pour volaille, cochon*) mash; (*pour chat ou chien*) pet food, dog *or* cat food; **(b)** *Arg* (*correction*) thrashing, good hiding.

patelin [patlɛ̃] **1** *adj Vieilli Péj* (*personne, manière, air*) unctuous. **2** *nm F* village, small place; **mon p.,** my village; **quel sale p.!,** what a dump!, what a hole!

patelle [patɛl] *nf* **(a)** (*mollusque*) limpet; **(b)** *Archéol* patella.

patène [patɛn] *nf Rel* paten.

patenôtre [patnotr] *nf F* prayer; *Arch* paternoster; *Fig* (*paroles incompréhensibles*) gibberish.

patent [patɑ̃] *adj* **(a)** (*clair*) obvious, evident; **erreur patente,** obvious mistake; **il est p. que ...,** it is patently obvious that ...; **(b) lettres patentes,** letters patent.

patentable [patɑ̃tabl] *adj Admin* (*trade etc*) subject to a licence, requiring a licence.

patente [patɑ̃t] *nf* **(a)** *Com* (*licence*) licence (*to exercise a trade or profession*); (*impôt*) tax (*paid by merchants and professional men*); **payer p.,** to be duly licensed; **(b)** *Nau* **p. (de santé),** bill of health.

patenté [patɑ̃te] *adj Com* licensed; *Fig F* **imbécile/menteur p.,** out- and-out fool/liar.

patenter [patɑ̃te] *vt Com* to license.

pater [patɛr] *nm inv* **(a)** *Rel* the Lord's prayer; *Cathol* (*surtout en latin*) Paternoster; (*grain du chapelet*) paternoster (bead); **(b)** *F* (*père*) the old man, *Am* pop, *Br Vieilli* pater.

patère [patɛr] *nf* (coat) peg.

paternalisme [patɛrnalism] *nm Péj* paternalism.

paternaliste [patɛrnalist] *adj Péj* paternalistic.

paterne [patɛrn] *adj Litt* benevolent.

paternel, -elle [patɛrnɛl] **1** *adj* paternal; (*protecteur, bienveillant*) fatherly, kindly (*tone, advice*); fatherly (*care*); **du côté p.,** on the father's side; **le domicile p.,** (the family) home; **image paternelle,** father figure; **l'amour p.,** paternal *or* fatherly love. **2** *nm F* **le p.,** the old man, *Am* pop.

paternellement [patɛrnɛlmɑ̃] *adv* paternally, in a fatherly way.

paternité [patɛrnite] *nf* paternity, fatherhood; *Jur* **p. légitime/naturelle,** legitimate/natural paternity; *Jur* **recherche de la p.,** affiliation; **il vit mal sa p.,** he's finding fatherhood difficult, he's finding it difficult being a father; *Fig* **revendiquer/désavouer la p. d'un livre,** to claim/to repudiate authorship of a book.

pâteux, -euse [pɑtø, -øz] *adj* **(a)** pasty; doughy (*bread*); **langue pâteuse,** coated *or* furred tongue; **bouche pâteuse,** dry mouth; **(b)** (*trop épais*) muddy (*ink*); *Péj* **style p.,** woolly style.

pathétique [patetik] *Litt* **1** *adj* **(a)** pathetic, touching, moving (*story, situation, tone*); **(b)** *Anat* pathetic (*muscle*). **2** *nm* pathos.

pathétiquement [patetikmɑ̃] *adv* pathetically, movingly.

pathétisme [patetism] *nm* pathos.

pathogène [patɔʒɛn] *adj Méd* pathogenic.

pathologie [patɔlɔʒi] *nf Méd* pathology.

pathologique [patɔlɔʒik] *adj Méd* pathological.

pathologiquement [patɔlɔʒikmɑ̃] *adj Méd* pathologically.

pathologiste [patɔlɔʒist] *n Méd* pathologist.

pathos [patos] *nm Littér* pathos.

patibulaire [patibylɛr] *adj* **(a)** (*sinistre*) **avoir une mine p.,** to have a sinister look, to look sinister; **(b)** *Vieilli* **fourches patibulaires,** gibbet.

patiemment [pasjamɑ̃] *adv* patiently.

patience¹ [pasjɑ̃s] *nf* **(a)** patience; (*en supportant un mal, une souffrance*) long-suffering; **avoir de la p., prendre p.,** to have patience, to be patient; **montrer de la p. envers qn,** to be patient with s.o.; **attendre avec p.,** to wait patiently; **ma p. est à bout, je suis à bout de p.,** my patience is exhausted *or* is at an end; **(prenez) p.!,** (have) patience!, be patient!, *F* hang on (a moment)!; **perdre p.,** to lose (one's) patience; **garder p.,** not to lose one's patience; **jeu de p.,** (jigsaw) puzzle; *Fig* painstaking task; **(b)** *Cartes* patience, *Am* solitaire; **faire des patiences,** to play patience *or Am* solitaire.

patience² *nf Bot* patience (dock); spinach dock.

patient, -ente [pasjɑ̃, -ɑ̃t] **1** *adj* patient; (*qui endure une épreuve*) long-suffering. **2** *n Méd* patient.

patienter [pasjɑ̃te] *vi* to wait; **faire p. qn,** to ask s.o. to wait; **pour vous faire p. je vais vous passer un film,** I'll show you a film while you're waiting *or* to pass the time for you; **p. en lisant le journal,** to read the newspaper to while away *or* pass the time.

patin [patɛ̃] *nm* **(a)** skate; (*de traîneau*) runner; **patins à glace/à roulettes,** ice/roller skates; **nous allons faire du p. à glace,** we're going (ice)skating; **sais-tu faire du p. à glace?,** can you (ice)skate?; **(b)** (*sur parquet*) cloth pad; *Arch* (*chaussure*) patten; **(c)** *Tech* shoe; **p. (de frein),** (brake) shoe; **(d)** *Arg* French kiss; **rouler un p. à qn,** to give s.o. a French kiss.

patinage¹ [patinaʒ] *nm* **(a)** skating; **p. artistique,** figure skating; **p. de vitesse,** speed skating; **(b)** (*d'une roue*) spinning.

patinage² *nm* patination (*of bronze etc*).

patine [patin] *nf* patina.

patiner¹ [patine] *vi* **(a)** (*faire du patinage*) to skate; **(b)** (*d'une roue*) to spin; (*of belt, clutch*) to slip; *Fig* **la nouvelle organisation patine,** the new organization hasn't found its feet yet.

patiner² *vt* to give a patina to (*bronze etc*).

patinette [patinɛt] *nf* (child's) scooter.

patineur, -euse [patinœr, -øz] *n* skater.

patinoire [patinwar] *nf* skating rink, ice rink; *Fig* **cette route est une vraie p.,** this road is like a skating rink *or* an ice rink.

patio [patjo] *nm Archit* patio.

pâtir [pɑtir] *vi Arch* to suffer (**de,** because of).

pâtis [pɑti] *nm Agr* grazing ground, pasture.

pâtisserie [pɑtisri] *nf* **(a)** *Culin* (*gâteau*) pastry, (small) cake; (*gâteaux*) pastries; *Com* confectionery; **elle fait de la bonne p.,** she makes good cakes; **(b)** (*confection de gâteaux*) pastry making; **(c)** (*magasin*) cake shop; (*p.-confiserie*) confectioner's.

pâtissier, -ière [pɑtisje, -jɛr] **1** *n* (*métier*) pastrycook, pastry chef; (*confisier*) confectioner; **Papa est très bon p.,** Dad makes very good cakes. **2** *adj* **crème pâtissière,** confectioner's custard.

patois [patwa] **1** *nm* patois, provincial dialect. **2** *adj* patois (*word etc*).

patouiller [patuje] *F* **1** *vi* to flounder (in the mud). **2** *vt* to paw (*sth*).

patraque [patrak] *adj F* (*person*) out of sorts, under the weather; **se sentir p.,** to feel out of sorts *or* under the weather.

pâtre [pɑtr] *nm Litt* (*pour bétail*) herdsman; (*pour moutons*) shepherd.

patriarcal, -aux [patriarkal, -o] *adj* patriarchal.

patriarcat [patriarka] *nm* **(a)** patriarchy; **(b)** *Rel* patriarchate.

patriarche [patriarʃ] *nm* patriarch.

patricien, -ienne [patrisjɛ̃, -jɛn] *adj & n* patrician.

patrie [patri] *nf* (*nation*) native country; (*localité de naissance*) birthplace; **mère p.,** mother country; **mourir pour la p.,** to die for one's country; *Fig* **la p. des arts/de la musique,** the cradle *or* birthplace of the arts/music.

patrimoine [patrimwan] *nm* heritage; (*d'un ancêtre*) patrimony; **faire partie du p.,** to be part of our *or* one's *etc* heritage; **p. familial,** family wealth *or* heritage; *Fig* (*génétique etc*) family heritage; **p. artistique,** artistic heritage; *Biol* **p. héréditaire,** genotype.

patrimonial, -aux [patrimɔnjal, -o] *adj Jur* patrimonial.

patriotard, -arde [patrijɔtar, -ard] *Péj* **1** *adj* jingoistic. **2** *nm* jingoist.

patriote [patrijɔt] **1** *adj* patriotic (*person*). **2** *n* patriot.

patriotique [patrijɔtik] *adj* patriotic.

patriotiquement [patrijɔtikmɑ̃] *adv* patriotically.

patriotisme [patrijɔtism] *nm* patriotism.

patron, -onne [patrɔ̃, -ɔn] **1** *n* **(a)** (*personne qui dirige*) boss (*of firm, business*); (*propriétaire*) owner (*of firm, business*); proprietor, proprietress (*of hotel*); master, mistress (*of house*); *Univ* **p. de thèse,** thesis supervisor; **oui, p.,** yes, boss, *Am* yes, chief; **il faut parler au p.,** you'll *etc* have to speak to the boss; **(b)** (*protecteur*) protector, protectress; patron, patroness (*of a society, the arts, an artist*); **le**

p. d'une ville/d'un club, the patron of a city/a club; **(c)** *Rel* patron saint; **le saint p.,** the patron saint; **la patronne des musiciens,** the patron saint of musicians; **(d)** *Méd* senior consultant (*in teaching hospital*); **les grands patrons,** leading specialists *or* consultants; **(e)** *Nau* skipper, master (*of small vessel*); coxswain (*of boat*). **2** *nm* (*sewing, knitting*) pattern; **p. (ajuré),** stencil (plate).

patronage [patrɔnaʒ] *nm* **(a)** (*parrainage*) patronage; *Com* custom; **(b)** (*organisation*) (church) youth club; (*siège, endroit*) meeting place *or* headquarters of youth club; *Péj Fig* **roman de p.,** moralizing *or F* preachy novel.

patronal, -aux [patrɔnal, -o] *adj* **(a)** (*de l'employeur*) (of) employers; **syndicat p.,** employers' association; **(b)** (*relatif au saint patron*) of the patron saint; **fête patronale,** = town or village festival marking the patron saint's name day.

patronat [patrɔna] *nm* (body of) employers; (*syndicat*) employers' organization; *Br* ≈ Confederation of British Industry; **être en dispute avec le p.,** to be arguing with the bosses.

patronner [patrɔne] *vt* to support (*hospital, charity etc*); to sponsor (*artist, candidate*); to protect (*person*); **p. une candidature,** to support a candidacy; (*avec aide financière*) to sponsor a candidacy.

patronnesse [patrɔnɛs] *adj & nf souvent Iron* **(dame) p.,** patroness.

patronyme [patrɔnim] *nm* patronymic.

patronymique [patrɔnimik] *adj* patronymic.

patrouille [patruj] *nf Mil etc* patrol; **aller en p.,** to go on patrol; **être de p.,** to be on patrol; *Av* **p. de chasse,** fighter patrol.

patrouiller [patruje] *vi* to patrol, to be on patrol.

patrouilleur [patrujœr] *nm* soldier *or* guard *etc* on patrol; *Av* patrol aircraft; *Nau* patrol boat *or* ship.

patte [pat] *nf* **(a)** (*de chien, chat etc*) paw; (*d'oiseau*) foot; (*d'insecte*) leg; *F* (*jambe*) pin; *F* (*main*) hand; *Péj* paw; **se dresser sur ses pattes,** (*d'un chien*) to sit up and beg; **pattes de devant,** forelegs, forepaws; **pattes de derrière,** hind legs; **marcher à quatre pattes,** to walk on all fours; **avoir une p. folle,** to have a gammy leg; *Fig* **retomber sur ses pattes,** to land on one's feet; *Fig* **tirer dans les pattes de qn,** to give s.o. a bad time; **bas** *ou* **court sur pattes,** short-legged; **faire p. de velours,** (*of cat*) to draw in its claws; *Fig* to be in a conciliatory mood; **coup de p.,** scratch; *Fig* cutting remark, *F* dig; **le chat m'a donné un coup de p.,** the cat scratched me; *F* **pattes de mouche(s),** cramped *or* spidery handwriting; **p. de lapin,** rabbit foot; *F* **pattes (de lapin),** (*cheveux*) sideboards, sideburns; *F* **avoir le coup de p.,** (*of painter*) to have talent; *F* **tenir qn sous sa p.,** to have s.o. at one's mercy *or* under one's thumb; *F* **tomber dans les pattes de qn,** to fall into s.o.'s clutches; *F* **bas les pattes!,** hands off!; *F* **graisser la p. à qn,** to grease s.o.'s palm; **pantalon à pattes d'éléphant,** bell-bottomed *or* flared trousers;
(b) (*rabat*) flap (*of pocket, envelope*); tongue (*of wallet, shoe*);
(c) (*attache*) clamp, clip, fastening; *Nau* fluke, palm (*of anchor*); *Nau* claw (*of grapnel*);
(d) *Couture etc* strap (*on garment*); **pattes d'épaule,** shoulder straps.

patte-d'oie [patdwa] *nf* (*pl pattes-d'oie*) **(a)** (*carrefour*) crossroads; **(b)** (*wrinkle*) crow's foot; **(c)** *Bot* goose foot.

pattemouille [patmuj] *nf* damping cloth (*for ironing*).

pattu [paty] *adj* **(a)** (*qui a de grosses pattes*) large-pawed (*dog etc*); **(b)** (*dont la patte porte des plumes*) feather-legged (*pigeon*).

pâturage [pɑtyraʒ] *nm* **(a)** grazing; *Jur* grazing rights; **(b)** (*endroit*) pasture, grazing ground; **pâturages,** pasture land.

pâture [pɑtyr] *nf* **(a)** (*nourriture*) food, feed, fodder (*of animals*); *Fig* **p. intellectuelle,** food for the mind; *Fig* **donner qn/qch en p. au public,** to serve s.o./sth up for public consumption; **(b)** (*pâturage*) pasture; *Jur* **vaine p.,** (right of) common.

pâturer [pɑtyre] **1** *vi* (*of cattle etc*) to graze, to feed. **2** *vt* (*of cattle etc*) to graze (on) (*meadow*).

pâturin [pɑtyrɛ̃] *nm Bot* meadow grass.

paturon [patyrɔ̃] *nm* pastern (*of horse*).

paume [pom] *nf* **(a)** *Anat* palm (*of hand*); **(b) (jeu de) p.,** real tennis; (*terrain*) real tennis court.

paumé, -ée [pome] **1** *adj* lost; *Fig* **il est complètement p.,** he hasn't got a clue. **2** *n F* (*person*) loser.

paumelle [pomɛl] *nf* **(a)** *Nau etc* (sailmaker's) palm; **(b)** (*pièce métallique*) plate (*of door hinge*).

paumer [pome] *F* **1** *vt* to lose. **2 se paumer** *vpr* to get lost.

paupérisation [poperizasjɔ̃] *nf* impoverishment.

paupérisme [poperism] *nm* pauperism.

paupière [popjɛr] *nf Anat* eyelid.

paupiette [popjɛt] *nf Culin* (meat) olive; **paupiettes de veau,** veal olives.

pause [poz] *nf* **(a)** (*arrêt*) pause; *Fb etc* half time; *Ind etc* meal break; **p.-café,** coffee break; **p.-repas,** meal break; **faire une p.,** to pause, to have a break; **(b)** *Mus* semibreve rest.

pauvre [povr] **1** *adj* **(a)** (*qui manque de biens*) poor; **p. comme Job,** poor as a church mouse; **p. d'esprit,** half-witted; **minerai p. en métal,** ore with a low metal content; *Aut* **mélange p.,** weak mixture; **(b)** (*malheureux*) poor, unfortunate; **le p. homme!,** poor chap!; **p. de moi!,** poor old me!; **p. Pierre,** poor (old) Pierre; **(c)** (*misérable*) shabby (*dress, furniture etc*); paltry (*excuse*); pathetic, weak (*argument etc*); bad (*speaker*); **c'est un p. type,** he's pathetic, he's a poor sod; **p. idiot!,** silly fool!; **(d)** (*stérile*) barren (*land*); poor (*soil*); **des terres pauvres,** barren lands. **2** *n* poor man, poor woman; **les pauvres et les riches,** the rich and the poor; *Fig* **p. d'esprit,** half-wit; **le p., il n'a pas de chance!,** poor chap, he hasn't much luck!; **mon p.,** my dear (friend).

pauvrement [povrəmɑ̃] *adv* poorly; **p. vêtu,** poorly *or* shabbily dressed; **il lit p.,** he's a poor reader.

pauvresse [povrɛs] *nf* poor woman.

pauvret, -ette [povrɛ, -ɛt] *n F Iron* **le p., la pauvrette,** the poor little thing.

pauvreté [povrəte] *nf* poverty; *Fig* poorness (*of language*); *Fig* baldness (*of style etc*); *Rel* **vœu de p.,** vow of poverty; **p. du sol,** (*stérilité*) poorness of the soil.

pavage [pavaʒ] *nm* **(a)** (*action*) paving; (*aux pavés ronds*) cobbling; **(b)** (*revêtement*) paving; (*rond*) cobblestones.

pavane [pavan] *nf Mus* pavan(e).

pavaner (se) [səpavane] *vpr* to strut about.

pavé [pave] *n* **(a)** (*morceau de grès*) paving stone; (*rond*) cobblestone; *F Journ* prominent article; *F Péj* (*livre, thèse*) brick; *Fig* **un p. dans la mare,** a (nice) bit of scandal; *Fig* **avoir un p. sur l'estomac,** to feel a weight on one's stomach; **p. de viande,** slab of meat; **p. publicitaire,** prominent advertisement; **(b)** (*revêtement*) pavement, paving; (*rue*) paved road; *Fig* (*rues*) the street, the streets; **brûler le p.,** to run very fast; (*in car*) to race along; **tenir le haut du p.,** to belong to the upper class; (*diriger, être en tête*) to be the leader *or* the boss; **battre le p.,** to loaf about the streets; **être sur le p.,** to be on the street.

pavement [pavmɑ̃] *nm* (ornate) paving, pavement.

paver [pave] *vt* to pave (*street etc*); (*avec des pavés ronds*) to cobble; **cour pavée,** paved *or* cobbled yard.

paveur [pavœr] *nm* paver, paviour, *US* pavior.

pavillon [pavijɔ̃] *nm* **(a)** (*petite maison*) (small) bungalow; **p. d'entrée (d'une propriété),** (gate) lodge; **p. de jardin,** summerhouse, pavilion; **p. de chasse,** shooting lodge;
(b) (*d'un hôpital etc*) pavilion, block, wing;
(c) (*partie évasée*) horn (*of hooter, loudspeaker, siren*); bell (*of brass instrument*); mouth (*of funnel*); *Tél* **p. d'écouteur,** earpiece; *Anat* **p. de l'oreille,** pavilion, auricle, external ear;
(d) *Nau* (*drapeau*) flag, colours, *US* colors; **p. de départ** *ou* **de partance,** Blue Peter; **p. noir,** Jolly Roger; **p. de quarantaine,** yellow flag; **p. de complaisance,** flag of convenience; **p. de détresse,** flag of distress; **hisser** *ou* **arborer son p.,** to hoist one's colours; **battre un p.,** to fly a flag; **amener** *ou* **baisser le p.,** *Nau* to strike one's flag, to surrender; *Fig* (*céder*) to admit defeat;
(e) *Mil Arch* tent, pavilion.

pavillonnaire [pavijɔnɛr] *adj* **banlieue p.,** suburbia.

pavois [pavwa] *nm* **(a)** *Nau* (*d'un navire*) bulwark; **(b)** *Nau* **petit** *ou* **grand p.,** flags (*for dressing ship*), dressing; **mettre** *ou* **hisser le grand p.,** to dress over all; **(c)** *Hist* (*grand bouclier*) (body) shield, pavis(e).

pavoiser [pavwaze] **1** *vt* (*décorer*) to deck (*house etc*) with flags; to put out bunting in (*a street etc*); *Nau* to dress (*ship*). **2** *vi* (*décorer*) to put out the flags; *Nau* to dress ship; *F* (*se réjouir*) to crow; *F* **il n'y a vraiment pas de quoi p.!,** there's nothing to crow about!

pavot [pavo] *nm* (*fleur*) poppy; **p. somnifère,** opium poppy; **tête de p.,** poppyhead; **graine(s) de p.,** poppy seed.

payable [pɛjabl] *adj* payable; *Com* **p. à la livraison,** payable on delivery; **p. à vue,** payable at *or* on sight.

payant [pɛjɑ̃] *adj* (*qui paie*) paying (*guest etc*); (*où il faut payer*) charged for; **spectateur p.,** spectator who pays (for admission); **élèves payants,** paying pupils; **spectacle p.,** show with charge for admission; **toutes les places sont payantes,** no free seats; *Fig* **affaire payante,** (*bénéfique*) paying proposition; *Fig* **ça s'est avéré p.,** it turned out to be worth it.

payer [peje] *v* **(je paye, je paie; je payerai, je paierai) 1** *vt* **(a)** (*remettre (à qn) ce qu'on lui doit*) to pay; **p. qn,** to pay s.o.; **combien vous a t-il fait p.?,** how much did he charge you?; **p. qn de ses services,** to pay s.o. for his services; **trop/trop peu payé,** overpaid/underpaid; **se faire p.,** to get paid; **p. qn de paroles** *ou* **de mots,** to put s.o. off with fine words;

(b) (*acquitter, régler*) to pay, to settle, to discharge (*debt etc*); **p. son loyer,** to pay one's *or* the rent; **p. la note,** to pay the bill; *Com* **p. un effet,** to honour *or US* honor a bill; **la prime de déplacement ne paie pas tous les frais de voyage,** the relocation allowance doesn't cover all the travel costs; **congés payés,** paid holidays, holidays with pay; *Admin* paid leave;

(c) (*acquérir contre de l'argent*) to pay for (*sth*); **la viande a été payée,** the meat's (been) paid for; **combien tu l'as payé?,** how much did you pay for it?; **elle ne l'a pas payé très cher,** she bought *or* got it quite cheaply, she didn't pay a lot for it; **p. qch à qn,** to pay s.o. for sth; **ses parents lui paient tout ce qu'il veut,** his parents pay for everything he wants, his parents buy him anything he wants; **je le lui ai payé cent francs,** I paid him a hundred francs for it; **p. le dîner à qn,** to treat s.o. to dinner; **c'est moi qui paie la tournée,** it's my round; **port payé,** (*colis*) carriage paid; (*lettre*) post paid; *Télécom* **réponse payée,** answer prepaid;

(d) *Fig* (*expier*) to pay for (*sth*); **il a payé sa témérité de sa vie,** he paid for his rashness with his life; **faire p. ses méfaits à qn,** to bring s.o. to account; **vous me le paierez!,** you'll pay for this!; *F* **je suis payé pour le savoir,** I've learnt (it) the hard way; **je ne suis pas payé pour ça,** that's not my job; **il l'a payé cher,** he paid dearly for it.

2 *vi* **(a)** (*verser de l'argent*) to pay; **p. cash** *ou* **comptant,** to pay cash; **p. en liquide/par chèque/par carte (de crédit),** to pay (in) cash/by cheque/by credit card; **c'est toujours moi qui paie,** I'm always the one who pays, I always end up paying the bill; **p. rubis sur l'ongle,** to pay on the nail;

(b) p. de ses dernières économies, to sacrifice the last of one's savings; *Fig* **p. de sa personne,** to bear the brunt (*of the work etc*); **p. d'audace** *ou* **d'effronterie,** to brazen it out, to put a bold face on it; **il ne paie pas de mine, mais il est doué,** he doesn't look it, but he's very clever, he doesn't look very clever but he is;

(c) (*rapporter*) to pay; **le crime ne paie pas,** crime doesn't pay; **la traduction en free-lance, ça ne paie pas,** freelance translation doesn't pay; **ça a payé,** (*cette affaire*) it was worth it.

3 se payer *vpr* **(a) voilà monsieur, payez-vous,** (*when offering large note in payment*) here you are, take it out of that; *Fig* **se p. de mots,** to talk a lot of fine words;

(b) (*s'offrir*) **je me suis payé une glace,** I treated myself to an ice cream; *Fig* **se p. la tête de qn,** to make fun of s.o.; **se p. le luxe de sortir deux fois par semaine,** to treat oneself to two nights out a week; **se p. le luxe de partir sans régler ses dettes,** to have the nerve to leave without paying one's debts; *F* **s'en p. une tranche,** to have a good time;

(c) le bonheur cela ne se paie pas, you can't buy happiness.

payeur, -euse [pɛjœr, -øz] *n* payer; *Admin etc* pay clerk; *Mil etc* paymaster.

pays[1] [pei] *nm* (*nation*) country, land; (*région*) region, district, locality; **pays riches/en voie de développement,** rich/developing countries; **visiter des p. étrangers,** to visit foreign countries *or* lands; **voir du p.,** to see the world, to travel (around) a lot; **p. du rêve,** dreamland; **vous n'êtes donc pas de ce p.?,** so you're not from these parts?; **p. perdu,** out-of-the-way place; **être en p. de connaissance,** to be among friends; **denrées du p.,** home(grown) produce; **vin de p.** *ou* **du p.,** local wine; **le p.,** native region, village *etc*; **revenir au p.,** to go back home; **avoir le mal du p.,** to be homesick; **p. de montagne(s),** hill country; *pl* **p. bas,** lowlands.

pays[2], payse [pei, peiz] *n Région* fellow-countryman, -woman; **nous sommes p.,** we're from the same area *or* place.

paysage [peizaʒ] *nm* **(a)** landscape; (*vue*) scenery; *Fig* (*ensemble*) scene, set-up; **le p. urbain,** the urban landscape; **le p. audiovisuel français,** the broadcasting set-up in France; **(b)** *Beaux-Arts* landscape (painting); *F* **cela fait bien dans le p.,** that looks good there.

paysager, -ère [peizaʒe, -ɛr] *adj* (*jardin, espace*) landscaped; **bureau p.,** open-plan office; *Fig* **vocation paysagère,** desire to travel *or* to see the world.

paysagiste [peizaʒist] *nm* **(a)** (*peintre*) landscape painter; **(b) (jardinier) p.,** landscape gardener.

paysan, -anne [peizɑ̃, -an] **1** *adj* peasant (*life, family*); rustic (*lifestyle, manners*). **2** *n* person who lives in the country, country dweller; (*agriculteur*) (small) farmer; *Hist* peasant; *Péj* peasant, country bumpkin; *Hum Péj* rustic; *Agr* **p. (propriétaire),** farmer; **les paysans,** country people; *Hist* the peasants, the peasantry.

paysannerie [peizanri] *nf* **(a)** (*ensemble des paysans*) country people; **(b)** *Littér* story of peasant life.

Pays-Bas (les) [lepeiba] *nmpl* the Netherlands.

p.c. (*abrév* **pour cent**) per cent.

P.C. [pese] *nm* **(a)** (*abrév* **parti communiste**) CP; **(b)** *abrév* **poste de commandement.**

p.c.c. [pesese] *abrév* **pour copie conforme.**

P.C.V. [peseve] *nm Tél* (*abrév* **payable chez vous**) reverse-charge call, *Am* collect call; **appeler en P.C.V.,** to make a reverse-charge call, *Am* to call collect.

p.d. *Com abrév* **port dû.**

P-D.G., P-d.g. [pedeʒe] *nm abrév* **Président-directeur général.**

péage [peaʒ] *nm* **(a)** (*droit*) toll; **pont à p.,** toll bridge; *Arch* **barrière de p.,** turnpike; **(b)** (*installation*) *Aut* tollbooth; *Arch* tollhouse.

péager, -ère [peaʒe, -ɛr] *n Arch* toll collector.

péagiste [peaʒist] *n Aut* tollbooth attendant.

péan [peɑ̃] *nm Antiq* paean, song of triumph.

peau, -eaux [po] *nf* **(a)** (*derme*) skin; **avoir la p. blanche/noire,** to be white/black; **une belle p.,** a beautiful skin *or* complexion; **avoir la p. grasse/sèche/mixte,** to have greasy/dry/combination skin; **beauté à fleur de p.,** beauty that is skin-deep; *Fig* **avoir la p. dure,** to have a thick skin, to be thick-skinned; *Fig* **prendre qn par la p. du cou,** to take s.o. by the scruff of the neck; *Fig* **faire p. neuve,** to turn over a new leaf; **elle n'a que la p. et les os,** she's nothing but skin and bone; **je ne voudrais pas être dans sa p.,** I wouldn't like to be in his shoes; **se mettre dans la p. de qn,** to put oneself in s.o.'s shoes; *Th* **entrer dans la p. d'un personnage,** to get right inside a part, *F* to get into the skin of a character; *Fig* **j'ai ça dans la p.,** it's in my blood; *Fig F* **avoir qn dans sa p.,** to be crazy about s.o.; *F* **se sentir mal dans sa p.,** to feel uncomfortable; **c'est un garçon mal dans sa p.,** he's all mixed-up; **risquer sa p.,** to risk one's neck; **sauver sa p.,** to save one's skin *or* bacon; **craindre pour sa p.,** to fear for one's life; *F* **se faire crever la p.,** to get killed *or* bumped off; *F* **j'aurai sa p.!,** I'll get him!; *F* **la p.!, p. de balle** *ou* **de zébi!,** nothing doing!, no way!; *Arg Vieilli* **vieille p.,** old hag, old bag;

(b) (*dépouille*) skin, hide (*of animal*); pelt, fur (*of fur-bearing animal*); **p. de lapin,** rabbit skin, cony(skin);

(c) (*cuir*) prepared hide, leather; **p. de mouton,** sheepskin; **p. de chamois,** shammy (leather); **p. de chevreau,** kid; **p. de daim,** buckskin; **p. de veau,** calfskin, box calf; **p. de requin,** shagreen; **p. de serpent,** snakeskin; *Fig F* **p. de chagrin,** diminishing asset; *F* **p. d'âne,** diploma; *Arg* **c'est une p. de vache,** (*cet homme*) he's a bastard; (*cette femme*) she's a cow;

(d) peel, skin (*of fruit*); **p. de banane,** banana skin; *Fig* **p. d'orange,** cellulite;

(e) (*pellicule*) film, skin (*of milk*);

(f) (*envie*) hangnail.

peaucier [posje] *adj & nm Anat* **(muscle) p.,** platysma.

peaufiner [pofine] *vt* to clean with a shammy leather; *Fig F* (*fignoler*) to polish up, to add the final touches to (*a text*).

Peau-Rouge [poruʒ] *adj & n Vieilli* (*amérindien*) Red Indian, redskin; (*pl Peaux-Rouges*).

peausserie [posri] *nf* **(a)** skin trade; **(b)** (*marchandise*) leatherwear, leather goods.

peaussier [posje] *nm* skinner, skin dresser.

pébroc, pébroque [pebrɔk] *nm F* (*parapluie*) brolly.

pécari [pekari] *nm* peccary.

peccadille [pekadij] *nf* peccadillo.

pechblende [pɛʃblɛ̃d] *nf Minér* pitchblende.

pêche[1] [pɛʃ] *nf* **(a)** peach; **p.-abricot,** yellow-fleshed peach; **p. Melba,** peach Melba; *Fig* **peau de p.,** (soft and) velvety skin; **murs p.,** peach(-coloured, *US* -colored) walls; **(b)** *F* (*coup*) blow, clout; **(c)** *F* **se fendre la p.,** to laugh, to burst out laughing; **(d)** *F* (*forme*) feeling of being on top of the world; **avoir la p.,** to be feeling on top of the world, to be on top form; **ça va te donner la p.,** it'll make you feel on top of the world.

pêche[2] *nf* **(a)** (*activité*) fishing; **aller à la p.,** to go fishing;

p. à la truite, trout fishing; **p. (à la ligne),** angling; **p. à la mouche,** fly fishing; **grande p.,** deep-sea fishing; **petite p.,** coastal *or* inshore fishing; **p. à la baleine,** whaling; **canne à p.,** fishing rod; **(b)** (*produits pêchés*) catch; **faire une heureuse p.,** to get a good haul; *Bible* **la p. miraculeuse,** the miraculous draught of fishes; **(c)** (*endroit*) fishing ground(s); **p. gardée,** restricted fishing area; **p. privée,** private fishing ground.

péché [peʃe] *nm* sin, *Fml* transgression; **le p. originel,** original sin; **p. mortel,** mortal sin; **les sept péchés capitaux,** the seven deadly sins; **vivre dans le p.,** *Rel* to live in a state of sin, to lead a sinful life; (*of unmarried person*) to live in sin; **p. mignon,** peccadillo; **à tout p. miséricorde,** there is no sin that cannot be forgiven; **péchés de jeunesse,** youthful indiscretions; *F* **ce n'est pas un p.!,** it's not a crime!

pécher [peʃe] *vi* (**je pèche, n. péchons; je pécherai**) to sin, *Fml* to transgress; **p. par orgueil,** to commit the sin of pride; **il pèche par trop de timidité,** his failing is his excessive shyness; **cette enquête pèche sur un point,** the inquiry falls down on one point; **p. par excès/défaut,** to exceed/fall short of what is required; **p. par omission,** to sin by omission; **p. contre l'honnêteté,** to act dishonestly.

pêcher[1] [peʃe] *nm* peach tree.

pêcher[2] **1** *vt* **(a)** to fish for (*trout etc*); **p. le corail,** to dive for coral; **p. la baleine,** to hunt whales; **(b)** *F* (*trouver*) **où avez-vous pêché cela?,** where did you pick that up?, where did you get hold of that? **2** *vi* **p. à la ligne,** to angle (with rod and line); **p. à la mouche,** to fly-fish; **p. en mer,** to go sea fishing; *Fig* **p. en eau trouble,** to fish in troubled waters.

pêcherie [pɛʃri] *nf* fishery, fishing ground.

pécheur, pécheresse [peʃœr, peʃrɛs] **1** *n Rel* sinner, *Fml* transgressor. **2** *adj Rel* sinful.

pêcheur, -euse [peʃœr, -øz] **1** *n* fisherman, -woman; **p. à la ligne,** angler; **p. de baleines,** whaler; **p. de perles,** pearl diver. **2** *adj* **bateau p.,** fishing smack.

pécore [pekɔr] *nf F* silly and stuck-up girl *or* woman.

pecquenaud, -aude [pekno, -od] *n Péj* peasant, country bumpkin.

pectine [pɛktin] *nf* pectin.

pectique [pɛktik] *adj* pectic (*acid*).

pectoral, -aux [pɛktɔral, -o] **1** *adj* pectoral (*muscle, fin etc*); *Méd* **sirop p.,** expectorant; *Méd* **pastille de pâte pectorale,** cough lozenge. **2** *nm Anat* pectoral muscle.

pécule [pekyl] *nm* **(a)** (*économies*) savings, *F* nest egg; **(b)** *Mil Nau* gratuity (*on discharge*).

pécuniaire [pekynjɛr] *adj* financial, *Fml* pecuniary (*advantage*); financial (*position*); **être dans un embarras p.,** to be short of money, *Hum & Vieilli* to be in pecuniary difficulties.

pécuniairement [pekynjɛrmɑ̃] *adv* financially.

pédagogie [pedagɔʒi] *nf* pedagogy, pedagogics; **manquer de p.,** (*de professeur*) to lack teaching skills; *Fig* to lack tact.

pédagogique [pedagɔʒik] *adj* (*voyage, sortie etc*) educational; (*méthode*) teaching; *Fml* pedagogical.

pédagogiquement [pedagɔʒikmɑ̃] *adv* pedagogically.

pédagogue [pedagɔg] *n* educationalist; *Fml Arch* pedagogue.

pédale [pedal] *nf* **(a)** pedal (*of cycle, car, piano etc*); *MecE* pedal, treadle (*of lathe etc*); **appuyer sur les pédales,** (*à vélo*) to pedal hard; **p. d'embrayage,** clutch pedal; *Fig F* **perdre les pédales,** to get all mixed up; (*se paniquer*) to lose one's head, to get in a tizzy; **(b)** *Mus* **(note de) p.,** pedal (note); **(c)** *Arg* (*homme*) gay; *Péj* homo, queer, poof(ter); **il est de la p.,** he's gay.

pédaler [pedale] *vi* **(a)** to pedal; (*faire du vélo*) to cycle; **(b)** *F* (*se dépêcher*) to hurry, to rush along.

pédaleur, -euse [pedalœr, -øz] *n* cyclist.

pédalier [pedalje] *nm* **(a)** (*de vélo*) crank gear; **(b)** (*clavier d'orgue*) pedal board.

pédalo [pedalo] *nm* pedal boat, pedalo.

pédant, -ante [pedɑ̃, -ɑ̃t] **1** *n* pedant. **2** *adj* pedantic.

pédanterie [pedɑ̃tri] *nf* pedantry.

pédantesque [pedɑ̃tɛsk] *adj* pedantic.

pédantisme [pedɑ̃tism] *nm* pedantry.

pédé [pede] *nm F* (*homosexuel*) gay; *Péj* homo, queer, poof(ter).

pédéraste [pederast] *nm* homosexual; *Péj Vieilli* p(a)ederast.

pédérastie [pederasti] *nf* homosexuality; *Péj Vieilli* p(a)ederasty.

pédestre [pedɛstr] *adj* (*journey*) on foot; **chemin p.,** footpath.

pédiatre [pedjatr] *n Méd* paediatrician, *US* pediatrician.

pédiatrie [pedjatri] *nf Méd* paediatrics, *US* pediatrics.

pédicelle [pedisɛl] *nm Biol Bot* pedicel, pedicle.

pédicule [pedikyl] *nm Biol Anat* pedicle, peduncle.

pédicure [pedikyr] *n* chiropodist.

pedigree [pedigri] *nm* (*of animal, Fig of person*) pedigree.

pédomètre [pedɔmɛtr] *nm* pedometer.

pédoncule [pedɔ̃kyl] *nm Biol* peduncle.

pédophile [pedɔfil] *adj* paedophiliac, *US* pedophiliac.

pédophilie [pedɔfili] *nf* paedophilia, *US* pedophilia.

pedzouille [pɛdzuj] *nm F* peasant, country bumpkin.

peeling [piliŋ] *nm* (*gommage*) face scrub; *Méd* exfoliation treatment; **se faire un p.,** to give oneself a face scrub; *Méd* **se faire faire un p.,** to have one's skin peeled.

pègre [pɛgr] *nf* the underworld.

peignage [pɛɲaʒ] *nm Tex* combing, carding (*of wool etc*).

peigne [pɛɲ] *nm* **(a)** (*demêloir, barrette*) comb; **p. fin,** fine-tooth comb; *Fig* **passer qch au p. fin,** to go through sth with a fine-tooth comb; **se donner un coup de p.,** to run a comb through one's hair, to give one's hair a comb; **(b)** *Tex* card (*for wool*); hackle (*for hemp*); **p. de métier à tisser,** reed; **(c)** (*mollusque*) pecten, scallop.

peigné [peɲe] **1** *adj* **(a)** (*personne*) combed; **bien p.,** well groomed (*person*); **mal p.,** unkempt (*person*); tousled (*hair*); **(b)** *Tex* worsted (*yarn*). **2** *nm* worsted (yarn).

peigne-cul [pɛɲky] *nm Péj F* creep; (*pl peigne-culs*).

peignée [peɲe] *nf* **(a)** *Tex* cardful (*of wool, flax, hemp*); **(b)** *F* (*râclée*) thrashing, good hiding.

peigner [peɲe] **1** *vt* **(a)** (*coiffer*) to comb (out) (*hair etc*); **p. un enfant,** to comb a child's hair; *F* **p. la girafe,** to waste one's time; **(b)** *Tex* to card, to comb (*wool*); to hackle (*hemp*). **2 se peigner** *vpr* to comb one's hair.

peignoir [pɛɲwar] *nm* **(a)** (*vêtement d'intérieur*) housecoat; (*robe de chambre*) dressing gown; (*pour après le bain*) bath robe; **(b)** (*chez le coiffeur*) cape, overall.

peinard [pɛnar] *adj Arg* (*poste, situation*) cushy; **rester p.,** to take things easy; **tiens-toi p.,** keep quiet, keep your nose clean; **il est bien p.,** he's having an easy time of it.

peindre [pɛ̃dr] *v* (*prp* **peignant**; *pp* **peint**; *pr ind* **je peins, il peint, n. peignons**; *impf* **je peignais**; *p hist* **je peignis**; *fu* **je peindrai**) **1** *vt* to paint; **p. qch en vert,** to paint sth green; **p. qch à la chaux,** to whitewash sth; **papier peint,** wallpaper; **p. son nom sur sa boutique,** to paint one's name above one's shop *or* on one's shop window; **p. un coucher de soleil,** to paint a sunset; *Fig* **elle peint la situation avec justesse,** she gives an accurate account *or* description of the situation; *Fig* **p. tout en rose,** to paint everything in rosy colours. **2** *vi* to paint. **3 se peindre** *vpr Fig* **l'innocence se peint sur son visage,** innocence is written on his face.

peine [pɛn] *nf* **(a)** (*sanction*) punishment, penalty; **p. capitale,** capital punishment; **la p. de mort,** the death penalty; **p. de prison,** prison sentence; **défense d'entrer sous p. d'amende,** trespassers will be prosecuted; **errer comme une âme en p.,** to wander about like a lost soul;

(b) (*chagrin*) sorrow, sadness; (*tourment*) distress; **j'ai beaucoup de p.,** I feel very upset, I'm very distressed; **faire de la p. à qn,** to grieve *or* distress s.o.; **je m'en suis séparé avec beaucoup de p.,** I was very sorry to part with it; **cela fait p. à voir,** it's painful to see; **être dans la p.,** to be in distress;

(c) (*effort*) trouble, pains; **se donner de la p. pour faire qch,** to take trouble *or* pains to do sth; **se donner beaucoup de p. pour faire qch,** to take great pains over sth, to go to a lot of trouble to do sth; **donnez-vous** *ou* **prenez la p. de vous asseoir,** please take a seat; **en vous donnant un peu de p. vous y arriverez,** with a little effort you'll manage it; **c'est p. perdue,** it is a waste of time; **elle n'est pas au bout des ses peines,** her troubles aren't over yet; **en être pour sa p.,** to have all one's trouble for nothing; **il lui a donné 100 francs pour sa p.,** he gave him 100 francs for his trouble; **cela vaut la p. d'essayer,** it's worth trying; **cela vaut la p. que tu viennes,** it's (well) worth your while coming; **cela ne vaut pas la p.,** it's not worth the trouble; **ce n'est pas la p. de changer de robe,** you needn't bother to change (your dress); *Iron* **c'était bien la p. de venir!,** we might just as well have stayed at home!;

(d) (*difficulté*) difficulty; **j'ai eu toutes les peines du monde à le trouver,** I had the utmost difficulty in finding it; **elle a de la p. à parler,** (*après une opération*) she has difficulty speaking, she finds it difficult to speak; **elle a de la peine à en parler,** it's difficult for her to talk about it, she finds it difficult to talk about; **j'ai p. à croire que ... +** *sub*, I find it hard to believe that ...; **avoir p. à retenir ses larmes,** to have difficulty holding back one's tears; **ne**

jamais être en p. de trouver une excuse, never to be at a loss for an excuse; **avec p., à grand-p.,** with (great) difficulty; **sans p.,** easily; **(e) à p.,** hardly, barely, scarcely; **on tient à p. debout, il y a du vent!,** it's so windy, we're nearly blown off our feet!; **c'est à p. si je le connais,** I hardly know him; **il est à p. 3 heures,** it's barely 3 o'clock; **à p. étions-nous sortis qu'il se mit à pleuvoir,** we had only just gone out when it began to rain, we were scarcely out of the door before it started to rain.

peiner [pene] **1** *vt* to pain, to grieve, to upset, to distress (*s.o.*); **cette nouvelle m'a beaucoup peiné,** I was very saddened by the news; **d'un ton peiné,** in an aggrieved tone. **2** *vi* to toil, to labour, *US* to labor; **il peinait sur son travail,** he was struggling over his work; **p. à marcher,** to have trouble *or* difficulty walking; *Aut* **le moteur peine,** the engine is labouring.

peintre [pɛ̃tr] *nm* **(a)** (*artiste*) painter; **(artiste) p.,** artist; **une femme p.,** a woman artist; **p. de portraits,** portrait painter, portraitist; **(b)** (*ouvrier, artisan*) **p. en bâtiment(s),** (house) painter; **p. décorateur,** painter and decorator; *Th* **p. de décors,** scene painter; **(c)** *Fig* portrayer; **cet auteur est un p. de la société parisienne,** this author is a portrayer of *or* portrays Parisian society.

peinture [pɛ̃tyr] *nf* **(a)** (art of) painting; **p. figurative,** figurative painting; **musée de p.,** art gallery, picture gallery; **faire de la p.,** to paint; **p. à l'huile/à l'aquarelle** *ou* **à l'eau,** oil painting/watercolour, *US* watercolor (painting); **p. en bâtiments,** (house) painting; **p. au pistolet,** spray painting; **(b)** (*tableau*) picture, painting; *Fig* **p. des mœurs de l'époque,** portrayal *or* description of the customs of the period; *Fig* **je ne peux pas le voir en p.,** I can't stand the sight of him; **(c)** (*matière*) paint; **attention p. fraîche!, attention à la p.!,** wet paint; **p. à la colle/en détrempe,** size/distemper; **p. mate,** matt emulsion (paint); **p. brillante** *ou* **laquée,** gloss (paint); **(d)** (*surface peinte*) paintwork; **il faudra refaire les peintures,** the paintwork will have to be redone.

peinturlurer [pɛ̃tyrlyre] *vt F* to daub (*canvas, wall, piece of paper etc*) (with paint).

péjoratif, -ive [peʒɔratif, -iv] **1** *adj* pejorative (*word, sense*); disparaging (*comment, tone*). **2** *nm* pejorative.

péjorativement [peʒɔrativmɑ̃] *adv* pejoratively.

pékin [pekɛ̃] *nm* **(a)** *Tex* Pekin (fabric); **(b)** *Mil F* civilian; **être en p.,** to be in civvies.

Pékin [pekɛ̃] *nm* Peking, Beijing.

pékinois, -oise [pekinwa, -waz] **1** *adj* of *or* from Peking *or* Beijing. **2** *nm* **(a)** (*dog*) pekin(g)ese, *F* peke; **(b)** (*dialecte*) Mandarin (Chinese), Pekinese. **3** *n* **P.,** Pekin(g)ese.

pelade [pəlad] *nf Méd* alopecia.

pelage [pəlaʒ] *nm* coat, fur (*of animal*); wool (*of sheep*).

pélagique [pelaʒik] *adj* pelagic, pelagian (*fauna etc*).

pélargonium [pelargɔnjɔm] *nm* pelargonium, *F* geranium.

pelé, -ée [pəle] **1** *adj* bald; hairless (*skin*); *Fig* bare (*countryside*); threadbare (*material*). **2** *n F* baldie; **il n'y avait que trois pelés et un tondu,** there was hardly anyone there.

pêle-mêle [pɛlmɛl] **1** *adv* higgledy-piggledy; **tout est entassé p.-m.,** everything is piled up higgledy-piggledy *or* any old how; **mettre tout p.-m.,** to jumble everything up. **2** *nm inv* jumble; (*état d'une personne, d'une situation*) muddle.

peler [pəle] **1** *vt* to peel, to skin (*vegetables, fruit*). **2 se peler** *vpr* to peel; **la pêche se pèle facilement,** peaches peel easily *or* are easy to peel. **3** *vi* (*of skin etc*) to peel; **j'ai le nez qui pèle,** my nose is peeling.

pèlerin, -ine [pɛlrɛ̃, -in] **1** *n* pilgrim. **2** *nm* **(a) (requin) p.,** basking shark; **(b) (faucon) p.,** peregrine falcon.

pèlerinage [pɛlrinaʒ] *nm* (*action*) pilgrimage; (*lieu*) place of pilgrimage.

pèlerine [pɛlrin] *nf* cape, cloak; (*à capuche*) hooded cape.

pélican [pelikɑ̃] *nm* pelican.

pelisse [pəlis] *nf Arch* pelisse.

pellagre [pelagr] *nf Méd* pellagra.

pelle [pɛl] *nf* (child's, gardener's) spade; shovel (*for coal, ashes*); scoop (*for cereal, nuts etc*); **p. à charbon,** coal shovel; **p. à tarte,** tart slice; **p. à ordures,** dustpan; **ramasser qch à la p.,** to shovel sth up; *Fig* **remuer/ramasser l'argent à la p.,** to be rolling in money/to be raking it in; *F* **ramasser une p.,** to fall flat on one's face; *F* **il y en a à la p.,** there's masses *or* loads (of it *or* them); *Constr etc* **p. mécanique,** mechanical shovel; (*drague*) shovel dredger; *Fig* **rouler une p. à qn,** (*l'embrasser*) to give s.o. a French kiss.

pelle-pioche [pɛlpjɔʃ] *nf* pick and shovel in one; (*pl pelles-pioches*).

pelletée [pɛlte] *nf* shovelful, spadeful; *Fig F* **une p. d'injures,** a mouthful *or* stream of insults.

pelleter [pɛlte] *vt* (**je pellette** [pɛlt], **n. pelletons; je pelletterai** [pɛltre]) to shovel (up).

pelleterie [pɛltri] *nf* **(a)** (*fourrure*) pelt; **(b)** (*confection*) fur making; *Com* fur trade, furriery.

pelleteuse [pɛltøz] *nf Constr* mechanical shovel.

pelletier, -ière [pɛltje, -jɛr] *n* furrier.

pellicule [pelikyl] *nf* **(a)** (*de glace, peinture*) thin layer; (*sur un liquide*) film; *Spéc* pellicle; **(b)** (*enveloppe du raisin*) grape skin; **(c)** *Phot* film; **(d) pellicules,** dandruff; **avoir des pellicules,** to have dandruff.

Pélopon(n)èse (le) [ləpelɔpɔnɛz] *nm* (the) Peloponnese.

pelotage [p(ə)lɔtaʒ] *nm F* petting, necking.

pelotari [p(ə)lɔtari] *nm* pelota player.

pelote [p(ə)lɔt] *nf* **(a)** ball (*of wool, string*); **p. (à épingles),** pincushion; *Fig F* **faire sa p.,** to make one's pile; (*aux dépens d'autrui*) to feather one's nest; *Fig* **avoir les nerfs en p.,** to be on edge, to be nervy; **(b) p. (basque),** pelota.

peloter [p(ə)lɔte] **1** *vt* **(a)** *F* to pet s.o.; **(b)** *Arch* to wind (*wool, string etc*) into a ball. **2 se peloter** *vpr* to neck, to pet.

peloteur, -euse [p(ə)lɔtœr, -øz] **1** *adj F* **mains peloteuses,** wandering hands. **2** *n* **(a)** *F* **c'est un sacré p.,** he's got wandering hands; **(b)** *Tex* (*ouvrier*) ball winder. **3** *nf Tex* **peloteuse,** balling machine.

peloton [p(ə)lɔtɔ̃] *nm* **(a)** ball (*of wool, string etc*); **(b)** group (*of people*); cluster (*of bees, caterpillars*); *Sp* **le p.,** the main body (of runners), the bunch; **le p. de tête,** the leading group *or* bunch; **(c)** *Mil troop (of cavalry)*; platoon (*of tanks etc*); **p. d'instruction,** training unit; **p. de discipline** *ou* **de punition,** punishment squad; **p. d'exécution,** firing squad.

pelotonner [p(ə)lɔtɔne] **1** *vt* to wind (*wool, string etc*) into a ball. **2 se pelotonner** *vpr* to curl up (into a ball), to roll oneself up; (*pour avoir chaud*) to huddle up; **se p. dans un fauteuil,** to curl up in an armchair; **se p. contre la cheminée,** to huddle up to the fire; **se p. dans les bras de qn,** to snuggle into s.o.'s arms.

pelouse [p(ə)luz] *nf* lawn; *Courses de chevaux* the public enclosures, the ground within the track.

peluche [p(ə)lyʃ] *nf* **(a)** *Tex* plush; **jouet en p.,** soft toy, cuddly toy; **(b)** (*flocon, poil*) (piece of) fluff; (*de pullover*) pilling; **c'est plein de peluches,** it's all pilled.

peluché [p(ə)lyʃe] *adj* pilled (*material*).

pelucher [p(ə)lyʃe] *vi* (*of worn material*) to pill.

pelucheux, -euse [p(ə)lyʃø, -øz] *adj* fluffy; downy (*chick, cheeks*).

pelure [p(ə)lyr] *nf* **(a)** (*peau*) peel, skin (*esp of fruit*); peelings (*of vegetables*); **p. d'oignon,** dark rosé wine; *Com* **(papier) p.,** flimsy; **(b)** *F* (*vêtement*) (old) coat.

pelvien, -ienne [pɛlvjɛ̃, -jɛn] *adj Anat* pelvic.

pelvis [pɛlvis] *nm Anat* false pelvis.

pénal, -aux [penal, -o] *adj* penal (*code*); **clause pénale,** penalty clause (*in contract*).

pénalisation [penalizasjɔ̃] *nf Sp* penalization, penalizing.

pénaliser [penalize] *vt Sp* to penalize.

pénalité [penalite] *nf* **(a)** (*système pénal*) penal system; **(b)** *Jur Sp etc* (*sanction*) penalty; *Fb* **coup de pied de p.,** penalty (kick); **donner le coup de pied de p.,** to take the penalty (kick).

penalty [penalti] *nm Fb* penalty; (*pl penalties*).

pénates [penat] *nmpl* (*dieux domestiques*) penates; *Fig* **regagner ses p.,** to return home.

penaud [pəno] *adj* sheepish; **d'un air p.,** sheepishly.

penchant [pɑ̃ʃɑ̃] *nm* **(a)** (*tendance*) propensity, penchant (*for sth*); tendency (*to do sth*); (*préférence*) leaning (*towards sth*); **p. à faire qch,** inclination to do sth, penchant for doing sth; **un p. à la boisson,** a fondness *or* partiality for drink; **il a un p. pour** *ou* **à la paresse,** he tends to be lazy; **avoir un p. pour qn,** to be rather fond of s.o.; **(b)** *Arch & Litt* slope; **p. de la colline,** hillside.

penché [pɑ̃ʃe] *adj* (*incliné*) leaning; sloping, slanting (*handwriting*); **la Tour penchée de Pise,** the leaning Tower (of Pisa); *Fig* **prendre des airs penchés,** to pretend to be lost in thought; **p. sur le berceau,** bending over the cradle.

pencher [pɑ̃ʃe] **1** *vt* to bend; **p. une assiette/une bouilloire/un verre/***etc*, to tilt a plate/a kettle/a glass/*etc*; **p. la tête en avant,** to bend *or* lean forward; **p. les épaules,** to stoop. **2** *vi* (*s'écarter de la position verticale*) to lean (over); **le navire penche sur le côté,** the ship is listing; **faire p. la balance,** to tip the scales, to swing the balance; **le tableau penche vers la droite,** the picture is tilting to the right; *Fig* **p. vers** *ou* **pour qch,** to incline *or* lean towards sth; *Fig* **p. pour cette solution,** to prefer *or* favour *or US* favor this solution. **3 se pencher** *vpr* to bend, to stoop, to lean; **se p. en avant,** to bend forward; **se p. (en, au) dehors,** to lean out; **se p. à** *ou* **par la fenêtre,** to lean out (of) the window; *Fig* **se p. sur un problème,** to look into a problem; *Fig* **se p. sur qn,** to take care of s.o..

pendable [pɑ̃dabl] *adj* outrageous, abominable (*trick etc*); *Arch* (*crime*) for which the penalty is hanging; **cas p.,** reprehensible action; **le cas n'est pas p.,** it's nothing serious.

pendaison [pɑ̃dɛzɔ̃] *nf* hanging; **p. de la crémaillère,** housewarming (party).

pendant[1] [pɑ̃dɑ̃] **1** *adj* **(a)** (*qui pend*) hanging, *Fml* pendent; dangling (*legs*); drooping (*moustache*); **oreilles pendantes,** floppy ears; **(b)** (*en attente*) pending. **2** *nm* **(a)** (*objet*) pendant; **p. (d'oreille),** drop earring; *Mil* **p. de ceinturon,** sword-belt sling, frog; **(b)** counterpart, match (*of picture etc*); **ces deux tableaux (se) font p.,** these two pictures make a pair.

pendant[2] **1** *prép* during; **p. l'été,** during the summer, in summer; **restez là p. quelques minutes,** stay there for a few minutes; **route bordée d'arbres p. un kilomètre,** road lined with trees for a kilometre. **2** *conj* **p. que,** while, *Fml* whilst; **elle lisait p. que je repassais,** she was reading while I was ironing, she read while I ironed; **p. que j'y pense,** while I think of it; **p. que vous y êtes,** while you're at *or* about it. **3** *adv* **avant la classe et p.,** before and during the class.

pendard, -arde [pɑ̃dar, -ard] *n F Arch* rogue, scoundrel.

pendeloque [pɑ̃dlɔk] *nf* (*de bijou*) pendant; (*de lustre*) pendant, crystal.

pendentif [pɑ̃dɑ̃tif] *nm* **(a)** (*bijou*) pendant; **(b)** *Archit* pendentive.

penderie [pɑ̃dri] *nf* wardrobe, *Am* closet.

pendiller [pɑ̃dije] *vi* to dangle.

pendoir [pɑ̃dwar] *nm* hook (*for hanging meat*).

pendouiller [pɑ̃duje] *vi F* to hang loosely *or* untidily, to dangle.

pendre [pɑ̃dr] **1** *vt* **(a)** (*accrocher*) to hang (*sth*) (up); **p. du linge pour le faire sécher,** to hang the washing out to dry; **p. la crémaillère,** to give a housewarming party; **(b)** (*mettre à mort*) to hang; *Fig F* **qu'il aille se faire p. ailleurs,** let him go hang *or* go to hell; *Fig* **je veux être pendu si ...,** I'll be hanged if ... . **2** *vi* to hang; (*of hair etc*) to hang down; **les voiles pendaient le long des mâts,** the sails were flapping idly against the masts; **jupe qui pend par derrière,** skirt that hangs down *or* dips at the back; *F* **cela lui pend sur la tête,** it's hanging over him *or* threatening him; *F* **ça lui pend au nez,** he's got it coming to him. **3 se pendre** *vpr* **(a)** (*se suicider*) to hang oneself; **(b)** (*s'accrocher*) **se p. à qch,** to hang on *or* cling to sth; **se p. au cou de qn,** (*par affection*) to hug s.o..

pendu, -ue [pɑ̃dy] **1** *adj* hung, hanging; hanged (*man*); **p. aux jupes de sa mère,** clinging to his mother's skirts; *Fig* **avoir la langue bien pendue,** to be a great talker, to be very talkative; **il est toujours p. au téléphone,** he's never off the phone. **2** *n* hanged man, hanged woman.

pendulaire [pɑ̃dylɛr] *adj* swinging, pendular (*motion*).

pendule [pɑ̃dyl] **1** *nm* pendulum. **2** *nf* clock; **p. à coucou,** cuckoo clock; *Fig* **remettre les pendules à l'heure,** to get things straight.

pendulette [pɑ̃dylɛt] *nf* small clock; (*réveil-matin*) travelling clock, travel alarm.

pêne [pɛn] *nm* latch, bolt (*of lock*).

pénéplaine [peneplɛn] *nf Géol* peneplain.

pénétrabilité [penetrabilite] *nf* penetrability.

pénétrable [penetrabl] *adj* **(a)** (*perméable*) penetrable; **(b)** (*compréhensible*) understandable.

pénétrant [penetrɑ̃] *adj* penetrating; piercing (*wind, cold*); drenching (*rain*); pervasive, obtrusive, strong (*smell*); penetrating, searching, keen (*look*); shrewd (*mind*); **plaie pénétrante,** perforating wound.

pénétration [penetrasjɔ̃] *nf* **(a)** penetration (*of chemical, bullet etc*); *Fig* **la p. d'idées nouvelles,** the penetration of new ideas; **(b)** (*clairvoyance*) penetration, insight, shrewdness (*of person*); acuteness (*of mind*).

pénétré [penetre] *adj* penetrated, imbued (**de,** with); **p. d'humidité,** (*mur etc*) riddled with damp; *Fig* **p. d'un sentiment/d'une idée,** imbued with a feeling/an idea; *Péj* **il est p. de son importance,** he's full of his own importance; **d'un ton p.,** in an earnest tone, earnestly; **d'un air p.,** with an earnest air, earnestly.

pénétrer [penetre] *v* (**je pénètre, n. pénétrons; je pénétrerai**) **1** *vi* to penetrate; **la baïonnette pénétra jusqu'au poumon,** the bayonet penetrated to the lung; **un cambrioleur a pénétré dans la maison,** a burglar broke into the house; **l'eau avait pénétré partout,** the water had penetrated *or* got in everywhere; **p. dans la pensée de l'auteur,** to fathom what the author is thinking.

2 *vt* to penetrate; **la balle pénétra l'os,** the bullet penetrated *or* pierced the bone; **p. un secret,** to fathom a secret; **p. la pensée** *ou* **les intentions de qn,** to fathom s.o.'s thoughts *or* intentions.

3 se pénétrer *vpr* **(a)** (*of substances*) to combine; **(b)** (*s'imbiber*) to become imbued (**de,** with); **se p. d'une idée,** to let an idea sink in.

pénible [penibl] *adj* **(a)** (*qui demande de l'effort*) laborious, arduous, hard (*task etc*); laboured, *US* labored, heavy (*breathing, style*); rough (*road*); **vie p.,** hard *or* difficult life; **(b)** (*dérangeant, insupportable*) painful, distressing (*spectacle, news etc*); **l'idée m'est trop p.,** the idea is too painful; **p. à voir,** painful to see; **(c)** *F* (*personne*) difficult; **ce qu'elle est p.!,** she's a pain!

péniblement [penibləmɑ̃] *adv* laboriously, arduously, with difficulty; (*douloureusement*) painfully; **avancer** *ou* **aller** *ou* **marcher p.,** to plod *or* trudge along; **respirer p.,** to breathe heavily.

péniche [peniʃ] *nf Nau* pinnace; (*de transport fluvial*) barge; (*pour transporter le charbon*) coal barge; (*pour embarquer des marchandises*) lighter; *Mil* **p. de débarquement,** landing craft.

pénicilline [penisilin] *nf Pharm* penicillin.

péninsulaire [penɛ̃sylɛr] *adj* peninsular.

péninsule [penɛ̃syl] *nf* peninsula; **P. Ibérique,** Iberian Peninsula.

pénis [penis] *nm Anat* penis.

pénitence [penitɑ̃s] *nf* **(a)** penitence, repentance; **(b)** (*peine*) penance; (*punition*) punishment; **faire p.,** to do penance (**de,** for); **mettre un enfant en p.,** to punish a child, *surtout* to put a child in the corner; **il est en p.,** he's in disgrace; **(c)** (*aux jeux*) forfeit.

pénitencier [penitɑ̃sje] *nm* **(a) grand p.,** penitentiary (priest); **(b)** (*maison d'arrêt*) prison, *Am* penitentiary.

pénitent, -ente [penitɑ̃, -ɑ̃t] *adj & n Rel* penitent.

pénitentiaire [penitɑ̃sjɛr] *adj* penitentiary (*system*).

pénitentiel, -ielle [penitɑ̃sjɛl] **1** *adj* penitential. **2** *nm* penitential (book).

penne [pɛn] *nf* (*d'un oiseau*) quill; (*d'une flèche*) feather.

Pennsylvanie [pɑ̃silvani, pɛ̃-] *nf* Pennsylvania.

pénombre [penɔ̃br] *nf* (*lumière faible*) half-light, semi-darkness, shadowy light; *Astron Phys* penumbra; **rester dans la p.,** to remain inconspicuous *or* in the background.

pensable [pɑ̃sabl] *adj* thinkable; **ce n'est pas p.,** it's unthinkable.

pensant [pɑ̃sɑ̃] *adj* thinking (*man, woman*); **bien p.,** orthodox, right-thinking; **écologiste bien p.,** die-hard ecologist; **mal p.,** unorthodox.

pense-bête [pɑ̃sbɛt] *nm F* memory jogger; (*pl pense-bêtes*).

pensée[1] [pɑ̃se] *nf* (*fleur*) pansy.

pensée[2] *nf* (*réflexion*) thought; (*esprit*) thought, mind; (*opinion*) thought, view; **absorbé** *ou* **perdu dans ses pensées,** lost in thought *or* in one's thoughts; **se représenter clairement qch par la p.,** to have a clear conception *or* a clear idea of sth; **entrer dans la p. de qn,** to understand s.o.'s thinking; **dire sa p.,** to speak one's mind, to say what one thinks; **saisir la p. de qn,** to grasp s.o.'s meaning; **il partage ma p.,** he shares my opinion, he thinks the same way I do; **libre p.,** free thought, free thinking; **la p. des vacances,** the thought of the holidays; **la p. que tu seras là,** the thought that you will be there; **la p. marxiste,** Marxist thought; **en p., par la p.,** in one's mind; **je suis avec vous en p.** *ou* **par la p.,** my thoughts are with you, I am with you in thought; *Fml* **pensées affectueuses,** (*dans une lettre*) fond(est) regards.

penser[1] [pɑ̃se] *nm Arch & Litt* thought.

penser[2] **1** *vi* **(a)** to think; **p. à qn/qch,** to think of *or* about s.o./sth; **il pense à elle,** he's thinking of her; **à quoi pensez-vous?,** what are you thinking of *or* about?; (*où avez-vous la tête?*) what are you thinking of?, how could you (think of such a thing)?; **p. tout haut,** to think aloud; **je l'ai fait sans y p.,** I did it without thinking; **pensez-vous!,** what an idea!, don't you believe it!; **est-ce qu'il a donné un bon pourboire? — pensez-vous!,** did he give a good tip? — what do YOU think *or* you're joking! *or* no fear! *or* what him!; **vous n'y pensez pas!,** you don't mean it!; **n'y pensez plus,** forget about it; **ah, j'y pense!,** by the way!;

rien que d'y p., ça me donne des frissons, I shiver at the mere thought (of it), just thinking of it gives me the shivers; **elle l'a fait sans p. à mal,** she didn't mean any harm by it; **p. à faire qch,** (*envisager*) to think of doing sth; (*se souvenir*) to remember to do sth; **il me fait p. à mon frère,** he reminds me of my brother;

(b) (*réfléchir*) to think; **manière de p.,** attitude of mind; **il pense par lui-même,** he thinks for himself; **je pense comme vous,** I think like you *or* as you do, I agree with you; **voilà ma façon de p.,** that's my way of thinking, that's the way I see it; **pensez donc!,** just fancy!;

(c) p. vacances, to think (about) holidays; **il faut p. européen,** we must think European.

2 *vt* **(a) p. qch,** to think *or* believe sth; (*imaginer*) to imagine *or* picture sth; **je le pensais bien,** I thought as much, I thought so; **comment peux-tu p. une chose pareille?,** how can you think such a thing?; **je pense que oui/non,** I think so/not; **pensez si j'étais furieux,** you can imagine how angry I was; **je ne savais plus que p.,** I no longer knew what to think; **je le pense fou,** I think he's mad;

(b) p. qch de qn/qch, to think sth of s.o./sth; **qu'est-ce que tu penses de lui?,** what do you think of him?; **qu'en penses-tu?,** what do you think (of it)?; **j'en pense le plus grand bien,** I have a very high opinion of him *or* her *or* it; **p. du mal de qn,** to have a poor opinion of s.o.; **je lui ai dit carrément ce que j'en pensais** *ou* **ce que je pensais** *ou* **ma façon de p.,** I told him straight what I thought; (*en se fâchant*) I gave him a piece of my mind;

(c) p. faire qch, to expect to do sth; **je pense le voir demain,** I expect *or* hope to see him tomorrow; *Litt* **j'ai pensé mourir de rire,** I thought I would die laughing;

(d) (*concevoir*) **p. qch,** to think sth out; **p. la ville en fonction des habitants,** to think of the city in terms of its inhabitants; **les plans ont été mal pensés,** the plans were badly thought out; **p. l'actualité en démocrate,** to view current events from a democratic standpoint.

penseur, -euse [pɑ̃sœr, -øz] *n* thinker; **libre p.,** free thinker.

pensif, -ive [pɑ̃sif, -iv] *adj* thoughtful, pensive.

pension [pɑ̃sjɔ̃] *nf* **(a)** (*allocation*) pension, allowance; **p. de retraite,** (retirement, old age) pension; **p. viagère,** life annuity; **p. alimentaire,** (*dans un divorce*) maintenance, alimony; **(b) être en p. chez qn,** to board with s.o.; **p. complète,** full board, *US* American plan; **sept jours en p. complète,** seven days full board *or US* American plan; **prendre la demi-p.,** to take half-board; **chambre et p.,** board and lodging; **p. de famille,** boarding house; **(c)** (*pensionnat*) (private) boarding school; (*élèves*) boarders; **mettre un enfant en p.,** to send a child to boarding school.

pensionnaire [pɑ̃sjɔnɛr] *n* **(a)** boarder (*in boarding house, at school*); resident (*in hotel*); paying guest, lodger (*in private house*); resident (*of old people's home*); inmate (*of prison*); **(b)** (*personne qui reçoit une pension*) pensioner; **p. de la Comédie-Française,** member of the Comédie Française company; **p. de la Villa Médicis,** = scholarship student at the Villa Medicis.

pensionnat [pɑ̃sjɔna] *nm Scol* (*établissement*) boarding school; (*élèves*) (school) boarders.

pensionné, -ée [pɑ̃sjɔne] **1** *adj* pensioned (*soldier, employee*). **2** *n* pensioner.

pensionner [pɑ̃sjɔne] *vt* to pension.

pensivement [pɑ̃sivmɑ̃] *adv* pensively, thoughtfully.

pensum [pɛ̃sɔm] *nm Scol Vieilli* imposition; (*lignes*) lines.

pentagonal, -aux [pɛ̃tagɔnal, -o] *adj Math* pentagonal.

pentagone [pɛ̃tagɔn] **1** *adj Math* pentagonal. **2** *nm* **(a)** *Math* pentagon; **(b)** *US Mil* **le P.,** the Pentagon.

pentamètre [pɛ̃tamɛtr] *adj & nm Littér* pentameter.

Pentateuque (le) [ləpɛ̃tatøk] *nm Bible* the Pentateuch.

pentathlon [pɛ̃tatlɔ̃] *nm Sp* pentathlon.

pente [pɑ̃t] *nf* **(a)** (*inclinaison*) slope; *Spéc* (*d'une colline*) gradient, *Am* grade; **p. ascendante,** upwards slope, slope up, *Am* upslope; *Spéc* rising gradient, *Am* upgrade; **p. descendante,** downwards slope, slope down, *Am* downslope; *Spéc* falling gradient, *Am* downgrade; **à faible/forte p.,** gently/steeply sloping; **colline à vingt cinq-pour cent de p.,** hill with a gradient of one in four; *Aut* **p. 10%,** slope of 10%, hill 1 in 10; **en p.,** sloping; shelving (*beach, coastline*); **rue en p.,** steep street; **p. d'une rivière,** fall of a river; *Arg* **avoir la dalle en p.,** to be a bit of a boozer; *Fig F* **être sur une mauvaise p.,** to be going downhill, to be on a slippery slope, to be on a downward path; *Fig* **remonter la p.,** to get back on one's feet; **(b)** (*cambrure*) camber (*of road*); pitch (*of roof*); *Math* slope (*of a curve*); **angle de p.,** (*sur un plan*) angle of slope; **(c)** *Av* slope (*of flight path*).

Pentecôte [pɑ̃tkot] *nf Rel* Pentecost; *Br* (*jours fériés*) Whitsun(tide); **dimanche de la P.,** *Br* Whit Sunday.

pentu [pɑ̃ty] *adj* (*chemin*) sloping.

penture [pɑ̃tyr] *nf Tech* strap hinge (*of door etc*); **p. et gond,** hook and hinge; *Nau* **pentures du gouvernail,** rudder braces.

pénultième [penyltjɛm] *adj & nf* penultimate.

pénurie [penyri] *nf* scarcity (*of money etc*).

pep [pɛp] *nm* pep; **avoir du p.,** to be full of pep.

pépé [pepe] *nm F* grandad, grandpa, *surtout US* gramp(s); (*vieil homme*) old man, grandad.

pépée [pepe] *nf Arg* (*fille*) bird, chick, *Am* broad.

pépère [pepɛr] *F* **1** *nm* **(a) c'est un gros p.,** he's an old fatty; (*of child*) he's a chubby little chap; **(b)** (*grand-père*) grandad, grandpa, *surtout US* gramp(s). **2** *adj* **(a)** (*endroit, repas*) quiet, relaxed; **un petit coin p.,** a nice quiet little spot; **(b) il est p., tranquille,** he's got it easy; **un travail p.,** a cushy little job *or* number. **3** *adv Aut* **rouler p.,** to potter along.

pépettes, pépètes [pepɛt] *nfpl Arg* (*argent*) lolly, dough.

pépie [pepi] *nf* (*oiseau*) pip; *F* **avoir la p.,** (*avoir soif*) to be parched.

pépiement [pepimɑ̃] *nm* cheep(ing), chirp(ing).

pépier [pepje] *vi* to cheep, to chirp.

pépin¹ [pepɛ̃] *nm* **(a)** pip (*of apple, grape etc*); **sans pépins,** seedless; **(b)** *F* (*ennui*) hitch; **avoir un p.,** to be in trouble *or* in difficulties; **elle a eu un gros p.,** (*avec son fils etc*) she had some trouble *or* problems.

pépin² *nm F* (*parapluie*) brolly.

pépinière [pepinjɛr] *nf* **(a)** nursery (*of young trees*); **(b)** (*berceau*) training ground.

pépiniériste [pepinjerist] *n* nursery gardener.

pépite [pepit] *nf* nugget (*of gold*).

pepsine [pɛpsin] *nf Biol Ch* pepsin.

peptique [pɛptik] *adj* peptic.

peptone [pɛptɔn] *nf Physiol Ch* peptone.

péquenaud, -aude [pekno, -od] *n F* peasant, country bumpkin, yokel.

péquenot [pekno] *nm Arg* = **PÉQUENAUD**.

péquiste [pekist] *Can Pol* **1** *adj* (of the) Parti Québécois, PQ. **2** *n* member *or* supporter of the Parti Québécois *or* PQ.

perçage [pɛrsaʒ] *nm* piercing (*of cloth, skin*); boring (*of large hole*); drilling (*of smaller hole*).

percale [pɛrkal] *nf Tex* percale.

percaline [pɛrkalin] *nf* percaline.

perçant [pɛrsɑ̃] *adj* piercing, penetrating (*eyes, shriek*); penetrating, *Péj* shrill (*voice*); keen, sharp (*wits*); **vent p.,** biting wind.

perce [pɛrs] *nf* **(a)** (*machine*) borer; (*outil*) drill; (*poinçon*) punch; **(b)** hole (*of wind instrument*); **(c) mettre en p.,** to broach, to tap (*wine etc*).

percé [pɛrse] *adj* (*d'un petit trou*) pierced; (*d'un grand trou*) bored; (*d'un vêtement etc*) in holes; **p. de vers,** worm-eaten (*fruit, wood*); **oreilles percées,** pierced ears; **pantalon p.,** trousers with a hole in the seat; *Fig* **complot p. à jour,** plot brought to light.

percée [pɛrse] *nf* **(a)** (*ouverture*) opening; (*dans mur*) opening, breach, gap; (*dans forêt*) cutting; (*clairière*) glade; **faire une p. dans un bois,** to cut a passage through a wood; **(b)** *Mil Sp & Fig* breakthrough; **faire une p.,** to make a breakthrough, to break through; **p. technologique,** technological breakthrough.

percement [pɛrs(ə)mɑ̃] *nm* boring (*of hole, passage*); opening (*of street*); cutting (*of canal*); driving (*of tunnel*).

perce-muraille [pɛrs(ə)myraj] *nf Bot* wall pellitory; (*pl perce-murailles*).

perce-neige [pɛrs(ə)nɛʒ] *n inv Bot* snow-drop.

perce-oreille [pɛrsɔrɛj] *nm* earwig; (*pl perce-oreilles*).

perce-pierre [pɛrs(ə)pjɛr] *nf* (*plante*) samphire, sea fennel; (white, meadow) saxifrage; (*pl perce-pierres*).

percepteur, -trice [pɛrsɛptœr, -tris] **1** *adj* perceiving, discerning; (*organe*) of perception. **2** *nm Admin* tax collector, *F* tax man.

perceptibilité [pɛrsɛptibilite] *nf* perceptibility.

perceptible [pɛrsɛptibl] *adj* **(a)** (*que l'on peut percevoir*) perceptible (**à,** by, to); discernible; **p. à l'oreille,** audible; **(b)** *Admin* collectable (*tax*).

perceptiblement [pɛrsɛptibləmɑ̃] *adv* perceptibly; (*à l'oreille*) audibly.

perceptif, -ive [pɛrsɛptif, -iv] *adj* perceptive.

perception [pɛrsɛpsjɔ̃] *nf* **(a)** perception (*through the senses*); **(b)** *Admin* collection (*of taxes, duties, rent*); levying (*of taxes*); **(bureau de) p.,** tax inspector's office, revenue office.

percer [pɛrse] *v* **(je perçai(s); n. perçons) 1** *vt* **(a)** (*transpercer*) to pierce, to go through (*sth*); *Fig* **vous me percez les oreilles,** you're deafening me; **p. la foule,** to make *or* elbow one's way through a crowd; **p. un abcès,** to lance an abscess; **le soleil perce les nuages,** the sun is breaking through *or* piercing the clouds; **p. qn d'un coup de couteau,** to stab s.o.; **p. le cœur à qn,** to cut s.o. to the quick; **p. l'avenir,** to foresee the future; **p. un complot,** to uncover a plot; **p. qch à jour,** to find sth out;
(b) (*trouer*) to make a hole *or* an opening in (*sth*); to drill, to bore (*hole*); to drive (*tunnel*); to open (*street*); to cut (*canal*); **p. un mur,** to make a hole in a wall; **p. un tonneau,** to broach *or* tap a cask; **p. une porte dans un mur,** to make *or* open a door in a wall; **se faire p. les oreilles,** to have one's ears pierced.
2 *vi* to come through, to break through; **le soleil commence à p.,** the sun is breaking through *or* coming out; **ses dents percent,** his teeth are coming through, he is cutting his teeth; **l'abcès a percé,** the abscess has burst; *Fig* **rien n'a percé de leur entretien,** nothing has emerged about their meeting; **auteur qui commence à p.,** author who is beginning to make a name (for himself); **laisser p. ses sentiments,** to show one's feelings.

perceur, -euse [pɛrsœr, -øz] **1** *n* driller; puncher (*of sheet metal etc*). **2** *nf* **perceuse,** boring *or* drilling machine; (*outil*) drill. **3** *nm* **p. de coffres-forts,** safe breaker.

percevable [pɛrsəvabl] *adj* **(a)** (*perceptible*) perceivable; **(b)** *Admin* collectable, leviable (*tax*).

percevoir [pɛrsəvwar] *vt* (*prp* **percevant;** *pp* **perçu;** *pr ind* **je perçois, n. percevons, ils perçoivent;** *pr sub* **je perçoive, n. percevions, ils perçoivent;** *impf* **je percevais;** *p hist* **je perçus;** *fu* **je percevrai) (a)** (*prendre conscience de*) to perceive, to discern (*with the senses, the intellect*); **p. un bruit,** to hear *or* catch a sound; **(b)** *Admin* to collect (*taxes, rents etc*); to levy (*taxes*); **(c)** (*toucher*) to receive, to be paid (*interest etc*).

perche¹ [pɛrʃ] *nf* (thin) pole; *F* (*personne*) beanpole; *Rail* coupling pole; **p. à houblon,** hop pole; *Sp* **saut à la p.,** pole vault(ing); *Cin TV* **p. (à son),** boom; **conduire un bateau à la p.,** to punt a boat; *Fig* **tendre la p. à qn,** to give s.o. a helping hand; (*donner une indication*) to give s.o. a broad hint.

perche² *nf* (*poisson*) perch.

perche-man [pɛrʃman] *nm* ski-lift attendant.

percher [pɛrʃe] **1** *vi* (*of birds*) to perch; (*pour la nuit*) to roost; *Fig F* **il perche au quatrième,** he lives up on the fourth floor; **où perchez-vous?,** where do you hang out? **2** *vt F* **p. un vase sur une armoire,** to perch *or* stick a vase on top of a wardrobe. **3 se percher** *vpr* **se p. sur une branche,** (*of bird*) to perch on a branch; *Fig F* **il s'est perché sur le mur pour mieux voir,** he perched himself on the wall to see better.

percheron [pɛrʃərɔ̃] *nm* Percheron.

percheur, -euse [pɛrʃœr, -øz] *adj* perching; roosting (*bird*).

perchiste [pɛrʃist] *n Sp* pole vaulter; *Cin TV* boom operator.

perchlorate [pɛrklɔrat] *nm Ch* perchlorate.

perchlorique [pɛrklɔrik] *adj Ch* perchloric.

perchoir [pɛrʃwar] *nm* (bird's) perch, roost.

perclus [pɛrkly] *adj* (*paralysé*) (partly) paralysed, *surtout US* paralyzed; (*raide*) stiff (*leg etc*); **il est p. de sa jambe gauche,** he has lost the use of his left leg; **p. de rhumatismes,** crippled with rheumatism; *Fig* **p. de terreur,** paralysed with fright.

perçoir [pɛrswar] *nm* (*outil*) awl, gimlet, broach.

percolateur [pɛrkɔlatœr] *nm* (coffee) percolator.

percussion [pɛrkysjɔ̃] *nf* impact; *Tech* percussion; *Méd* sounding (by percussion), percussion; **fusil à p.,** percussion gun; *Mus* **instruments à** *ou* **de p.,** percussion instruments; *Mus* **aux percussions, Jack,** on percussion, Jack.

percussionniste [pɛrkysjɔnist] *n Mus* percussionist.

percutant [pɛrkytɑ̃] **1** *adj* **(a)** (*qui percute*) percussive; *Mil* **obus p.,** percussion fuse shell; **(b)** *Fig* forceful (*speech*); incisive (*style*). **2** *nm Mil* percussion fuse shell.

percuter [pɛrkyte] **1** *vt* **(a)** (*heurter violemment*) to strike (*sth*) sharply; **p. l'amorce,** (*sur une arme*) to strike the primer; **l'avion percuta une colline,** the plane crashed into a hillside; **(b)** *Méd* to sound (*chest*) by percussion, to percuss (*chest*). **2** *vi* **l'avion percuta contre le sol,** the plane crashed to the ground; **la voiture est allée p. contre un arbre,** the car crashed into a tree.

percuteur [pɛrkytœr] *nm* striker, hammer (*of gun, fuse*); needle (*of rifle*); firing pin (*of machine gun*).

percuti-réaction [pɛrkytireaksjɔ̃] *nf Méd* percutaneous reaction; (*pl percuti-réactions*).

perdant, -ante [pɛrdɑ̃, -ɑ̃t] **1** *adj* losing; **billet p.,** (*de loterie*) losing ticket, blank (ticket). **2** *n* loser.

perdition [pɛrdisjɔ̃] *nf* **(a)** *Rel* perdition; **lieu de p.,** den of vice *or* iniquity; **(b)** *Nau* **navire en p.,** ship in distress.

perdre [pɛrdr] **1** *vt* **(a)** to lose; (*ne pas saisir*) to lose, to miss; **j'ai perdu mes clés,** I've lost my keys; **vous êtes en train de p. votre écharpe,** you're losing your scarf; **un enfant perdu dans un magasin,** a child lost in a store; **p. un ami après une dispute,** to lose a friend after a quarrel; **p. son père,** to lose one's father; **p. du terrain,** to lose ground; **p. pied,** (*of swimmer*) *& Fig* to get out of one's depth; (*of climber*) to lose one's footing; **p. la partie,** to lose the game; **il perd son pantalon,** his trousers are too big for him; **p. ses cheveux,** to be losing one's hair, to be going bald; **p. la raison** *ou* **la tête** *ou F* **le nord** *ou* **la boule,** to go mad, *F* to go round the bend, *Am* to go bananas; **p. le fil,** to lose the thread (of the conversation); **p. haleine,** to get out of breath; **p. courage/patience,** to lose heart/patience; **faire p. une habitude à qn,** to break s.o. of a habit; **vous ne perdrez rien pour attendre,** you will lose nothing by waiting; **tu ne perds rien pour attendre!,** just you wait!; **n'avoir rien à p.,** to have nothing to lose; **p. son chemin,** to lose one's way; **p. son temps,** to waste (one's) time; **faire qch sans p. de temps,** to do sth without losing any time, to lose no time in doing sth; **il n'y a pas de temps à p.,** there is no time to lose; **il n'y a pas un instant à p.,** there isn't a moment to lose; **elle ne perd pas un mot de la conversation,** she isn't missing a (single) word of the conversation; **p. une occasion,** to miss an opportunity; **p. qn/qch de vue,** to lose sight of s.o./sth; **vous n'y perdez rien,** you're not missing *or* losing anything (by it);
(b) (*ruiner*) to ruin, to destroy; **l'ambition l'a perdu,** ambition was his undoing *or* his downfall; **des lectures qui perdent la jeunesse,** the kind of reading that is ruining our youth;
(c) *Obst* **elle a perdu les eaux,** her waters have broken.
2 *vi* **(a) la marée perd,** the tide is ebbing;
(b) fût qui perd, leaking cask;
(c) *Nau* to fall *or* drop astern;
(d) (*ne pas remporter une partie, bataille etc*) to lose; **il a perdu,** he lost.
3 se perdre *vpr* **(a)** (*disparaître*) to disappear, to be lost; **le navire se perdit corps et biens,** the ship was lost with all hands; **se p. dans la foule,** to disappear into the crowd, to lose oneself in the crowd; **cela se perd facilement,** it's easily lost, it's easy to lose; **cet usage se perd,** the custom is dying out;
(b) (*of mechanical power etc*) to be wasted, to run to waste; (*of food*) to go bad; **il y a des fessées qui se perdent,** he *or* she needs a good spanking;
(c) (*s'égarer*) to lose one's way; **il s'est perdu dans le bois,** he got lost in the wood; **se p. en conjectures,** to get lost in conjecture; *F* **je m'y perds,** I can't make head (n)or tail of it.

perdreau, -eaux [pɛrdro] *nm* young partridge.

perdrix [pɛrdri] *nf* partridge; **p. des neiges,** ptarmigan.

perdu, -ue [pɛrdy] **1** *adj* **(a)** lost; (*égaré*) lost, missing; (*que l'on ne gagne pas*) lost; **p. dans ses pensées,** lost in thought; **je suis p.,** I'm lost; *Fig* I'm lost, I'm totally confused; **ma tête est perdue,** I'm going mad; **les causes perdues d'avance,** causes lost right from the start; **un match p.,** a defeat; **il habite un trou p.,** he lives at the back of beyond; **à mes moments perdus, à mes heures perdues,** in my spare time; **c'est peine perdue,** it's a waste of time *or* effort; *Com* **emballage p.,** non-returnable *or* throw-away *or* disposable packing; **ce n'est pas p. pour tout le monde,** (*cet objet*) somebody's making good use of it; (*en trouvant qch*) finders keepers (losers weepers); (*cette situation*) their loss is our gain;
(b) (*abîmé*) ruined; (*personne*) ruined, destroyed; **ma robe est perdue,** my dress is ruined; **un homme p. par le scandale/la maladie,** a man ruined by scandal/ravaged by illness; **âme perdue,** lost soul;
(c) à corps p., without restraint, recklessly; **se jeter à corps p. dans la mêlée,** to hurl oneself into the fray.
2 *n* **crier comme un p.,** to shout like a madman.

père [pɛr] *nm* **(a)** (*géniteur*) father; **de p. en fils,** from father to son, from generation to generation; *Prov* **tel p. tel fils,** like father like son; **M. Martin p.,** Mr Martin senior; **p. de famille,** father, family man; **en bon p. de famille,** wisely; **p. nourricier,** foster father; **p. naturel,** natural father; *Th* **p. noble,** heavy father; **nos pères,** our forefathers, our ancestors; *F* **gros p.,** a big chap; *F* **c'est un p.**

tranquille, he's a quiet sort (of chap); *F* **petit p.,** old chap, *Am* old buddy; **le p. Jean,** old John; *Fig* **il a été un vrai p. pour moi,** he was like a father to me; *Fig* **le p. du cubisme,** the father *or* founder of cubism;

(b) *Rel* father; **le Saint-P.,** the Holy Father; **p. spirituel,** *Rel* father confessor; *Fig (d'un mouvement)* father; **les Pères Blancs,** the White Friars, the Carmelites; **le (Révérend) P. Martin,** Father Martin; **mon p.,** father;

(c) *Rel* (*Dieu*) **notre P. qui êtes aux cieux,** our Father who art in heaven; **le P., le Fils et le Saint Esprit,** the Father, the Son, and the Holy Ghost;

(d) (*dans un élévage*) sire.

pérégrination [peregrinasjɔ̃] *nf Litt* peregrination.

péremption [perɑ̃psjɔ̃] *nf* **(a)** *Jur* lapsing; time limitation (*in a suit*); **(b) date de p.,** (*d'aliments etc*) use-by date.

péremptoire [perɑ̃ptwar] *adj* **(a)** peremptory (*tone*); **argument p.,** unanswerable argument; **(b)** *Jur* **délai p.,** strict time limit.

péremptoirement [perɑ̃ptwarmɑ̃] *adv* peremptorily.

pérenniser [perenize] *vt* to perpetuate.

pérennité [perenite] *nf* (*d'une théorie, une verité*) timelessness, everlastingness.

péréquation [perekwasjɔ̃] *nf Admin Écon* equalization (*of taxes, salaries*); *Rail* standardizing (*of freight charges, tariffs*); *Can Admin* **fonds de p.,** equalization fund.

perestroïka [perestrɔika] *nf Pol* perestroika.

perfectibilité [pɛrfɛktibilite] *nf Litt* perfectibility.

perfectible [pɛrfɛktibl] *adj* perfectible.

perfectif, -ive [pɛrfɛktif, -iv] *adj & nm Gram* perfective.

perfection [pɛrfɛksjɔ̃] *nf* **(a)** perfection; **atteindre la p.,** to achieve perfection; **à la p.,** to perfection, perfectly; **(b)** *F* **une p.,** a jewel, a gem, a pearl.

perfectionnement [pɛrfɛksjɔnmɑ̃] *nm* **(a)** (*action*) perfecting; (*amélioration*) improving; (*formation*) (further) training; **brevet de p.,** patent relating to improvements; *Scol* **cours de p.,** refresher course; **(b)** (*résultat*) **un/des perfectionnement(s),** an improvement/improvements.

perfectionner [pɛrfɛksjɔne] **1** *vt* to perfect; (*améliorer*) to improve; **p. son français,** to improve *or* brush up one's French. **2 se perfectionner** *vpr* to improve; (*apprendre davantage*) to increase one's knowledge; **se p. en allemand,** to improve one's German.

perfectionnisme [pɛrfɛksjɔnism] *nm* perfectionism.

perfectionniste [pɛrfɛksjɔnist] *adj & n* perfectionist.

perfide [pɛrfid] **1** *adj* treacherous (**envers,** to); *Litt* perfidious; **la p. Albion,** perfidious Albion. **2** *n Arch & Litt* traitor.

perfidement [pɛrfidmɑ̃] *adv* treacherously; *Litt* perfidiously.

perfidie [pɛrfidi] *nf Litt* **(a)** (*déloyauté*) perfidiousness; **(b)** (*action*) perfidy.

perforage [pɛrfɔraʒ] *nm* punching (*of leather*); perforation (*of paper*); boring (*through wood, wall etc*).

perforant [pɛrfɔrɑ̃] *adj* perforating; **obus p.,** armour-piercing shell; *Méd* **ulcère p.,** perforated ulcer.

perforateur, -trice [pɛrfɔratœr, -tris] **1** *adj* perforating; *Tech* perforative. **2** *n* punch card operator. **3** *nf* **perforatrice (a)** *Constr* rock drill, driller, borer; drilling machine; **(b)** (**pince**) **p.,** ticket punch; **(c)** perforator; (*pour cuir*) punch; **(d)** *Ordinat* card punch, (key) punch; **p. de bande,** tape perforator, tape punch. **4** *nm Chir* perforator.

perforation [pɛrfɔrasjɔ̃] *nf* **(a)** (*action*) perforation, perforating; *Ordinat* punching, perforation; **(b)** (*trou*) perforation; *Ordinat* punch (hole); *Méd* **p. intestinale,** perforation of the intestine.

perforer [pɛrfɔre] *vt* **(a)** (*trouer*) to perforate (*paper*); to bore (through), to drill (*wood, wall*); to punch (*leather etc*); **(b)** *Ordinat* (*of machine*) to perforate (*tape etc*); to punch hole in (*card*); (*of person*) to key punch; **carte perforée,** punch card; **bande perforée,** punched card.

perforeuse [pɛrfɔrøz] *nf* perforator; *Ordinat* card punch.

performance [pɛrfɔrmɑ̃s] *nf Sp etc* performance; *Fig* (*exploit*) feat, achievement; *Tech* **les performances d'une voiture,** a car's performance; **la p. éblouissante d'un acteur,** the dazzling performance of an actor; *Fig* **quelle p.!,** what an achievement!, what a feat!

performant [pɛrfɔrmɑ̃] *adj* (*machine, entreprise*) high performance; **des résultats performants,** outstanding *or* impressive results.

perfusion [pɛrfyzjɔ̃] *nf Méd* perfusion.

pergola [pɛrgɔla] *nf* pergola.

péri [peri] *n* peri.

péricarde [perikard] *nm Anat* pericardium.

péricardite [perikardit] *nf Méd* pericarditis.

péricliter [periklite] *vi* (*of business, undertaking*) to be in danger *or* in jeopardy; **ses affaires périclitent,** his business is about to collapse.

péridot [perido] *nm* (*pierre*) peridot, chrysolite.

péridural, -ale, -aux [peridyral, -o] **1** *adj Méd* epidural; **anesthésie péridurale,** epidural anaesthesia *or US* anesthesia, *F* epidural. **2** *nf Méd* **péridurale,** epidural; **s'accoucher sous p.,** to give birth under an epidural.

périgée [periʒe] *nm Astron* perigee.

périglaciaire [periglasjɛr] *adj Géog* periglacial.

périhélie [perieli] *nm Astron* perihelion.

péri-informatique [periɛ̃fɔrmatik] *nf Tech* computer-related technologies.

péril [peril] *nm* peril, danger; (*particulier*) risk, hazard; **au p. de sa vie,** at the risk of one's life; **en p.,** in danger, in peril; **il y aurait p. à prendre cette voiture,** it would be unsafe to use that car; **mettre qch en p.,** to imperil *or* endanger *or* jeopardize sth; **les périls de cette affaire,** the risks involved in this affair; **à ses risques et périls,** at one's own risk.

périlleusement [perijøzmɑ̃] *adv* perilously.

périlleux, -euse [perijø, -øz] *adj* perilous, hazardous, dangerous; **saut p.,** somersault.

périmé [perime] *adj* out-of-date (*coupon etc*); expired (*bill*); (*ticket, passport*) no longer valid, out of date; lapsed (*money order, ticket etc*); **votre passeport est p.,** your passport has expired *or* is out of date; **marchandises périmées,** goods that are past their sell-by date; **conceptions périmées,** outdated concepts.

périmer [perime] **1** *vi* to lapse, to become out of date; **laisser p. un passeport,** to let a passport expire. **2 se périmer** *vpr Jur* to lapse; (*of passport, ticket*) to expire.

périmètre [perimɛtr] *nm* perimeter.

périnatal, -aux [perinatal, -o] adj Méd perinatal.

périnatalité [perinatalite] *nf Méd* perinatal period.

périnatologie [perinatɔlɔʒi] *nf Méd* perinatal medicine.

périnée [perine] *nm Anat* perineum.

période [perjɔd] **1** *nf* **(a)** period (*of time*); **p. de changements sociaux,** period of social change; *Biol* **p. d'incubation,** incubation period; **longue p. de beau temps,** long spell of fine weather; **la p. bleue de Picasso,** Picasso's Blue Period; **la p. classique,** the Classical Period *or* Age; **première p. de l'existence,** early stages of life; *Mil* **p. (d'instruction),** (completion of) training; **pendant la p. électorale,** during the elections; **aller en France en pleine p. électorale,** to go to France in the middle of elections;

(b) period (*of recurring phenomenon, of cycle*); **nombre de périodes par seconde,** frequency (*of sound wave etc*); *Ch* **p. de radioactivité,** half life; *Math* **p. d'une fraction décimale,** repetend of a (recurring) decimal; *Phys* **p. d'une onde,** period of a wave;

(c) *Gram* period, complete sentence; *Mus* **p. (musicale),** phrase.

2 *nm Litt* **le plus haut p. (de la gloire/***etc***),** the highest point *or* pitch *or* degree (of glory/*etc*), the height (of glory/*etc*).

périodicité [perjɔdisite] *nf* periodicity.

périodique [perjɔdik] **1** *adj* **(a)** periodic; **phases périodiques de récession et de progrès,** periodic *or* cyclical phases of recession and economic progress; **presse p.,** periodical publications; *Math* **fraction p.,** recurring decimal; *Math* **fonction p.,** periodic function; *Méd* **fièvre p.,** recurrent fever; **(b)** (*hygiénique*) **tampons/serviettes périodiques,** tampons/sanitary towels *or US* napkins. **2** *nm* periodical.

périodiquement [perjɔdikmɑ̃] *adv* at regular intervals.

périoste [perjɔst] *nm Anat* periosteum.

péripatéticien, -ienne [peripatetisjɛ̃, -jɛn] **1** *adj Phil* peripatetic. **2** *n Phil* peripatetic. **3** *nf F* **péripatéticienne,** prostitute, street walker.

péripétie [peripesi] *nf Litt* **(a)** sudden change of fortune (*in novel, in life*); **(b) péripéties,** mishaps, adventures; vicissitudes, ups and downs (*of life*).

périphérie [periferi] *nf* **(a)** periphery; *Géom* circumference; **(b)** (*banlieue*) outskirts; **vivre à la p. de Paris,** to live on the outskirts of Paris.

périphérique [periferik] **1** *adj* **(a)** (*situé autour*) peripheral; **boulevard p.,** ring road; *Rad* **radio p.,** = radio station broadcasting from outside national territory; *Anat* **système nerveux p.,** peripheral nervous system; **(b)** *Ordinat* peripheral. **2** *nm* **(a)** (*ceinture routière*) ring road; **(b)** *Ordinat* peripheral.

périphrase [perifraz] *nf* circumlocution; *Gram* periphrasis, periphrase.

périphrastique [perifrastik] *adj* circumlocutory; *Gram*

periphrastic.
périple [peripl] *nm* (*voyage*) (long) tour, journey; (*par mer*) sea voyage.
périr [perir] *vi* (*aux* **avoir**) (*of person*) to perish, to die (unnaturally); (*of object*) to be destroyed; (*of ship*) to be wrecked *or* lost; (*of empire*) to fall into ruin; **p. dans un incendie,** to die *or* perish in a fire; **p. noyé,** to drown, to be drowned; **p. victime d'un accident,** to die as a result of an accident; **faire p. qn,** to kill s.o.; *Fig* **p. d'ennui,** to die of boredom; *Fig* **s'ennuyer à p.,** to be bored to death; **son nom ne périra pas,** his name will live (on).
périscolaire [periskɔlɛr] *adj* extracurricular.
périscope [periskɔp] *nm* periscope.
périscopique [periskɔpik] *adj* periscopic.
périssable [perisabl] *adj* perishable; **denrées périssables,** perishable foodstuffs.
périssoire [periswar] *nf* (single-seater river) canoe.
péristaltique [peristaltik] *adj Physiol* peristaltic (*motion*).
péristaltisme [peristaltism] *nm Physiol* peristalsis.
péristyle [peristil] *nm Archit* peristyle.
péritoine [peritwan] *nm Anat* peritoneum.
péritonite [peritonit] *nf Méd* peritonitis.
péri-urbain, -aine [periyrbɛ̃, -ɛn] *adj* suburban (*housing estate*); out-of-town (*parking, shopping*).
perle [pɛrl] *nf* **(a)** (*naturelle*) pearl; *Fig* (*personne*) jewel, gem, treasure; **p. fine,** real pearl; **p. de culture,** cultured pearl; **fil de perles,** string of pearls; **nacre de p.,** mother-of-pearl; *Fig* **jeter des perles aux pourceaux,** to cast pearls before swine; **c'est la p. des frères,** he's the best brother in the world; **ma bonne est une p.,** my maid is a gem *or* a treasure; **(b)** *Scol* howler; **(c)** bead (*of glass, metal etc*); *Fig F* **enfiler des perles,** to waste one's time on futilities; **p. de rosée,** dewdrop; **perles de sang,** drops of blood; **perles de sueur,** beads of sweat.
perlé [pɛrle] *adj* **(a)** set with pearls; (*de perles de verre*) beaded; *Fig* pearl-like; **gris p.,** pearl gray; **riz p.,** husked *or* polished rice; **orge p.,** pearl barley; **verre p. de rosée,** glass beaded with moisture; *Fig* **dents perlées,** pearly teeth; *Fig* **rire p.,** rippling laughter; **(b)** (*needlework*) tastefully *or* exquisitely done; *Mus* clear-cut.
perler [pɛrle] **1** *vt* to execute (*piece of embroidery*) to perfection; *Mus* to play (*piece*) in clear-cut fashion. **2** *vi* (*of tears, sweat etc*) to form in beads; **la sueur perlait sur son front,** sweat beaded his forehead, beads of sweat stood out on his forehead.
perlier, -ière [pɛrlje, -jɛr] *adj* containing *or* producing pearls, pearl-bearing; **huître perlière,** pearl oyster.
perlimpinpin [pɛrlɛ̃pɛ̃pɛ̃] *nm* **poudre de p.,** miracle powder.
perlingual, -aux [pɛrlɛ̃gwal, -o] *adj Méd* **à prendre par voie perlinguale,** place under the tongue.
permanence [pɛrmanɑ̃s] *nf* **(a)** (*continuité*) permanence; **assemblée en p.,** permanent assembly; **en p.,** permanently, continuously; **(b)** (*service d'accueil d'un organisme*) reception; **la p. est assurée le dimanche,** there is someone on duty on Sundays; **être de p.,** to be on duty; **p. électorale,** (parliamentary candidate's) committee rooms; **p. de police,** police station open night and day; **(c)** *Scol* prep room.
permanent, -ente [pɛrmanɑ̃, -ɑ̃t] **1** *adj* standing (*order, committee*); continuous (*performance*); permanent (*court etc*); **en direct de notre envoyé p. à New York,** live from our New York correspondent *or* from our permanent correspondent in New York; *Ordinat* **mémoire permanente,** permanent memory; **cinéma p.,** (cinema *or Am* movie theater with) continuous showings. **2** *nf* **permanente,** permanent wave, *F* perm. **3** *nm Pol* official representative, permanent representative.
permanenter [pɛrmanɑ̃te] *vt* to perm; **se faire p.,** to have a perm.
permanganate [pɛrmɑ̃ganat] *nm Ch* permanganate.
perme [pɛrm] *nf F* **(a)** *Mil* leave; **(b)** *Scol* prep room.
perméabilité [pɛrmeabilite] *nf* permeability, perviousness; *Fig* susceptibility (*to influence etc*).
perméable [pɛrmeabl] *adj* permeable, pervious (**à,** to); *Fig* sensitive, susceptible (**à,** to).
permettre [pɛrmɛtr] *v* (*conj like* **mettre**) **1** *vt* to allow, to permit; **p. qch à qn,** to allow s.o. sth; **p. à qn de faire qch,** to allow s.o. to do sth, to let s.o. do sth; **mes moyens ne me le permettent pas,** I can't afford it; **est-il permis d'entrer?,** may I come in?; **s'il est permis de s'exprimer ainsi,** if I *or* we may say so; **autant qu'il est permis d'en juger,** as far as one can tell; **il se croit tout permis,** he thinks he can do anything he likes; **il n'est pas permis à tout le monde de ...,** not everyone can *or* is able to ...; **permettez-moi de vous dire que vous avez tort,** excuse me, but you're wrong; **permettez-moi de vous présenter ma sœur,** allow me to introduce you to my sister, may I introduce you to my sister?; **permettez!,** excuse me!, not so fast!, if you don't mind!; **vous permettez?,** may I?, do you mind?; **si le temps le permet,** weather permitting.
2 se permettre *vpr* **(a) se p. de faire qch,** to take the liberty of doing sth, to venture to do sth; **je me permets d'attirer votre attention sur ...,** I venture to draw *or* I take the liberty of drawing your attention to ...; **(b) se p. qch,** to allow oneself sth, to indulge in sth; **il se permet bien des choses,** he takes a lot of liberties.
permis [pɛrmi] **1** *adj* allowed, permitted; **il n'est pas p. de stationner là,** you're not allowed *or* permitted to park there, parking there isn't allowed *or* permitted; **il n'est pas p. de marcher sur la pelouse,** (*sur panneau*) keep off the grass; **est-ce qu'il est p. de rapporter six bouteilles de vin?,** am I allowed to bring back six bottles of wine?, are six bottles of wine allowable?; **cela ne devrait pas être p.,** that (type of thing) shouldn't be allowed; *Hum* **être aussi beau que ça, ça ne devrait pas être p.,** nobody's got a right to be that gorgeous.
2 *nm Admin* permit, licence, *US* license; **p. de chasse,** shooting licence, game licence; **p. de séjour,** (*pour des étrangers*) residence permit; **p. d'inhumer,** burial certificate; **p. de construire,** planning permission; *Aut* **p. (de conduire),** driving licence, *Can* driver's licence, *US* driver's license; (*examen*) driving test.
permissif, -ive [pɛrmisif, -iv] *adj* **(a)** permissive (*attitude etc*); **(b)** *Rail* **bloc p.,** permissive block.
permission [pɛrmisjɔ̃] *nf* **(a)** (*autorisation*) permission; *Jur* leave; **demander/donner la p. de faire qch,** to ask/give permission to do sth; **il n'a pas même demandé la p.,** he didn't even ask permission; **avec votre p.,** with your permission, if I may; **(b)** *Mil etc* leave (of absence); (*certificat*) pass; **en p.,** on leave; **il s'est marié pendant sa p.,** he got married during his leave *or* while (he was) on leave.
permissionnaire [pɛrmisjɔnɛr] **1** *nm* **(a)** (*détenteur d'un permis*) licence *or US* license holder; **(b)** *Mil etc* man on leave; *Nau* liberty man. **2** *adj* **officier p.,** officer on leave.
permissivité [pɛrmisivite] *nf* permissiveness.
permutabilité [pɛrmytabilite] *nf* permutability, interchangeability.
permutable [pɛrmytabl] *adj* permutable, interchangeable.
permutation [pɛrmytasjɔ̃] *nf* **(a)** (*échange*) exchange of posts; *Mil* transfer; **(b)** transposition (*of figures, letters*); *Math etc* permutation; **(c)** *Ling* metathesis.
permuter [pɛrmyte] **1** *vt* **(a)** *Math etc* to permute; **(b)** *Vieilli* to exchange (*post*) (**avec qn,** with s.o.). **2** *vi* to exchange posts (with colleague).
pernicieusement [pɛrnisjøzmɑ̃] *adv* perniciously.
pernicieux, -ieuse [pɛrnisjø, -jøz] *adj* pernicious, injurious, harmful; *Méd* **anémie pernicieuse,** pernicious anaemia *or US* anemia.
péroné [perɔne] *nm Anat* fibula.
péroraison [perɔrɛzɔ̃] *nf* peroration.
pérorer [perɔre] *vi Péj* to hold forth, to speechify, to spout.
Pérou (le) [ləperu] *nm* Peru; *Fig* **ce n'est pas le P.,** (*ce prix*) that's cheap; (*cet objet*) it's not worth very much; (*ce travail*) it's not highly paid.
peroxyde [pɛrɔksid] *nm Ch* peroxide.
perpendiculaire [pɛrpɑ̃dikylɛr] **1** *adj* perpendicular (**à, sur,** to). **2** *nf Géom* perpendicular (line); **tirer une p.,** to drop *or* draw a perpendicular (**à, sur,** to).
perpendiculairement [pɛrpɑ̃dikylɛrmɑ̃] *adv* perpendicularly; **p. à,** perpendicular to.
perpète, perpette (à) [apɛrpɛt] *adv F* for ever; **condamné à p.,** sentenced for life; **envoyer qch à p.,** to send sth flying off into the distance; **vivre à P.-les-Oies,** to live at *or* in the back of beyond *or* in the sticks *or Am* the boonies.
perpétration [pɛrpetrasjɔ̃] *nf Jur* perpetration.
perpétrer [pɛrpetre] *vt* (**je perpètre; je perpétrerai**) to perpetrate (*crime etc*).
perpétuation [pɛrpetɥasjɔ̃] *nf* perpetuation.
perpétuel, -elle [pɛrpetɥɛl] *adj* perpetual; everlasting (*God, love*); permanent (*secretary etc*); **rente perpétuelle,** (rent in) perpetuity; **mouvement p.,** perpetual motion; **crainte perpétuelle,** perpetual *or* constant fear; **commentaire p.,** running commentary; **de perpétuels reproches,** perpetual *or* constant *or* endless reproaches.
perpétuellement [pɛrpetɥɛlmɑ̃] *adv* perpetually.
perpétuer [pɛrpetɥe] **1** *vt* to perpetuate, to carry on (*name etc*); **p. le souvenir de qn,** to perpetuate s.o.'s

memory, to keep s.o.'s memory alive. **2 se perpétuer** *vpr* to remain, to survive; **se p. dans son œuvre,** to live on in one's work.

perpétuité [perpetɥite] *nf* perpetuity; **à p.,** in perpetuity, for ever; (*penal servitude*) for life.

perplexe [pɛrplɛks] *adj* perplexed, puzzled.

perplexité [pɛrplɛksite] *nf* perplexity; **être dans la plus complète p.,** to be completely baffled *or* utterly perplexed.

perquisition [pɛrkizisjɔ̃] *nf Jur* search; **mandat de p.,** search warrant; **faire une p. chez qn,** to search s.o.'s premises.

perquisitionner [pɛrkizisjɔne] *vi Jur* to make *or* conduct *or* carry out a search (*of premises etc*); **p. au domicile de qn,** to search s.o.'s house.

perré [pere] *nm Constr* stone pitching *or* facing (*of road, embankment*).

perron [pɛrɔ̃] *nm Archit* (flight of) steps (*leading to building*), perron; *Am* (*surtout d'une maison*) stoop.

perroquet [pɛrɔkɛ] *nm* **(a)** (*oiseau*) parrot; **répéter qch comme un p.,** to repeat sth parrot fashion; **(b)** (*boisson*) pastis with mint; *Vieilli* absinthe; **(c)** *Nau* topgallant (*sail*).

perruche [pɛryʃ] *nf* **(a)** (*oiseau*) parakeet; (*femelle du perroquet*) hen parrot; *F* (*femme bavarde*) natterer, gossip; **p. (ondulée),** budgerigar; **(b)** *Nau* mizzen topgallant sail.

perruque [pɛryk] *nf* **(a)** (*postiche*) wig; *Hist* periwig, peruke; **(b)** *Pêche* tangled line, *F* bird's nest.

perruquier, -ière [pɛrykje, -jɛr] *n* wig maker.

pers [pɛr] *adj Litt* (*vert*) blue-green; (*gris*) blue-grey.

persan, -ane [pɛrsɑ̃, -an] **1** *adj* Persian; **chat p.,** Persian cat; **tapis p.,** Persian rug *or* carpet. **2** *nm Ling* Farsi; *Hist* Persian. **3** *n* **P.,** Persian.

perse [pɛrs] **1** *nf* **P.,** Persia; **tapis de P.,** Persian rug *or* carpet. **2** *adj* of ancient Persia, Persian. **3** *n* **P.,** Persian. **4** *nm Ling Arch* Persian. **5** *nf Tex* chintz.

persécuté, -ée [pɛrsekyte] **1** *adj* persecuted (*person*). **2** *n* **(a)** *Psy* sufferer from persecution mania; **(b)** (*victime*) victim of persecution.

persécuter [pɛrsekyte] *vt* (*martyriser*) to persecute (*s.o.*) (**à cause de,** because of; **pour,** for); **arrête de p. ta petite soeur,** stop bullying your little sister.

persécuteur, -trice [pɛrsekytœr, -tris] **1** *n* persecutor. **2** *adj* persecuting.

persécution [pɛrsekysjɔ̃] *nf* persecution; *Psy* **manie** *ou* **folie** *ou* **délire de p.,** persecution mania.

persévérance [pɛrseverɑ̃s] *nf* perseverance.

persévérant [pɛrseverɑ̃] *adj* persevering.

persévérer [pɛrsevere] *vi* (**je persévère, n. persévérons; je persévérerai**) to persevere (**dans,** in); **il n'a guère persévéré,** he didn't show much perseverance.

persicaire [pɛrsikɛr] *nf* (*plante*) persicaria, lady's thumb.

persienne [pɛrsjɛn] *nf* (slatted) shutter.

persiflage [pɛrsiflaʒ] *nm* banter; (*raillerie*) mockery.

persifler [pɛrsifle] *vt* to ridicule (*s.o.*); to make fun of (*s.o.*).

persifleur, -euse [pɛrsiflœr, -øz] **1** *n* banterer; (*railleur*) mocker. **2** *adj* derisive, mocking (*tone etc*).

persil [pɛrsi] *nm* parsley.

persillade [pɛrsijad] *nf Culin* beef salad (*seasoned with chopped parsley etc*); (*sauce*) sauce seasoned with parsley, garlic *etc*.

persillé [pɛrsije] *adj Culin* **(a) fromage à pâte persillée,** blue cheese; **(b)** (*meat*) marbled; **(c)** (*assaisonné de persil*) sprinkled with chopped parsley.

persique [pɛrsik] *adj* (ancient) Persian; **le Golfe P.,** the Persian Gulf.

persistance [pɛrsistɑ̃s] *nf* **(a)** (*constance*) persistence, persistency (**à faire qch,** in doing sth); **avec p.,** persistently; **p. dans le mensonge,** persistent lying; **(b)** persistence, continuance (*of fever etc*).

persistant [pɛrsistɑ̃] *adj* **(a)** persistent (*efforts etc*); **(b)** lasting, enduring (*perfume etc*); *Bot* (*leaves*) persistent, indeciduous.

persister [pɛrsiste] *vi* **(a)** (*persévérer*) to persist; **il faut p.,** you must persevere *or* keep going *or* keep it up; **p. dans sa résolution/décision,** to persist in one's resolve/to stick to one's decision; **p. à faire qch,** to persist in doing sth; **p. à croire qch,** to persist in thinking sth, to continue to believe sth; **il (y) persiste,** he persists in it, he sticks to it; **(b)** (*continuer*) to persist, to continue; **la fièvre persiste,** the fever continues.

persona grata [pɛrsɔnagrata] *adj inv Pol* **être p. g. à l'étranger,** to be persona grata in foreign countries.

personnage [pɛrsɔnaʒ] *nm* **(a)** (*personne importante*) personage, person of rank *or* of distinction; **p. connu,** celebrity; **un grand p.,** a great figure; **les personnages de l'histoire,** the great names in history; **il est devenu un p.,** he's become quite an important person *or F* quite a big shot; **(b)** *Péj* person, individual; **un curieux p.,** an odd (sort of) character; **c'est un triste p.,** he's a poor specimen; **(c)** (public) image, persona (*of politician etc*); **(d)** *Th Littér* character (*in play, novel*); **personnages,** dramatis personae; *Fig* **jouer un p.,** to play a part *or* role, to put on an act; **(e)** *Beaux-Arts* figure (*in a painting*).

personnalisation [pɛrsɔnalizasjɔ̃] *nf* personalization.

personnalisé [pɛrsɔnalize] *adj* (*voiture, crédit*) customized; **accueil p.,** a welcome with that personal touch.

personnaliser [pɛrsɔnalize] *vt* to personalize; to give a personal touch to (*a room etc*); **p. une voiture,** to customize a car; **p. sa retraite,** to adapt one's pension to one's personal needs; **p. ses draps,** to personalize one's sheets; **p. l'image de marque du personnel,** to give staff a corporate identity.

personnalité [pɛrsɔnalite] *nf* **(a)** (*caractère*) personality; **trouble de la p.,** personality disorder; **avoir de la p.,** to be full of personality; **c'est une forte p.,** he has a strong personality; *Pol* **culte de la p.,** personality cult; **(b)** (*personnage important*) personage, personality; **les personnalités politiques,** the key political figures; **c'est une p.,** he's an important man, *F* he's somebody; **(c)** *Jur* **p. juridique,** legal personality *or* status.

personne [pɛrsɔn] **1** *nf* **(a)** (*individual*) person; **la p. dont je parlais,** the person I was talking about *or Fml* of whom I was speaking; **une assemblée de trois cents personnes,** an assembly of three hundred people; **une tierce p.,** a third party; **cela coûte 3 francs par p.,** it costs 3 francs a *or* per head; **une p. âgée,** an elderly person; **grande p.,** adult, grown-up; *Jur* **personnes physiques ou morales,** individual and legal entities; **il y a erreur sur la p.,** you've got the wrong person; **personnes à la charge,** dependants; **la p. et l'œuvre,** the man and his work; *Fig Péj* **il est encore avec cette (horrible) p.,** he's still with that (horrible) creature;

(b) (*one's own self*) **être satisfait/faire grand cas de sa (petite) p.,** to be self-satisfied/to be full of (one's own) self-importance; **en p.,** in person, personally; **le roi est venu en p.,** the king came in person, the king himself came; **il est la bonté en p.,** he is kindness itself, he is kindness personified; **elle est bien de sa p.,** she's very attractive *or* good-looking; **exposer sa p.,** to expose oneself to danger, to risk death;

(c) *Gram person;* **écrire à la troisième p. du singulier,** to write in the third person singular;

(d) *Psy Phil* (*individu conscient*) person; **le respect de la p. (humaine),** respect for the individual's rights.

2 *pron indéf m inv* **(a)** (*quiconque*) anyone, anybody; **il le sait aussi bien** *ou* **mieux que p.,** nobody knows it better than he does; **il est exclu que p. parle,** nobody is allowed to speak; **elle danse comme p.,** no-one dances *or* can dance like her, she dances *or* can dance better than anyone; **je ne dois rien à p.,** I don't owe anyone anything *or* anything to anyone; (*argent*) I don't owe anyone a penny; **sans nommer p.,** without naming anybody, naming no names, without naming names;

(b) (*with* **ne** *expressed or understood*) no(-)one, nobody; **p. n'est venu,** no(-)one *or* nobody has come; **qui est là? — p.,** who's there? — no(-)one *or* nobody; **que p. ne sorte,** no(-)one *or* nobody is to leave; **il n'y a p. de blessé,** no (-)one *or* nobody has been injured, there are no casualties; **p. d'autre n'était à bord,** there was no(-)one else *or* nobody else on board; **dans cette maison p. ne se connaissait,** in this house no(-)one knew anyone else *or* nobody knew anybody else; **je n'y suis pour p.,** I'm not at home to anybody *or* anyone, if anybody *or* anyone calls I'm not at home; **je ne connais p. de plus hypocrite,** I don't know anybody *or* anyone (who is) more hypocritical.

personnel, -elle [pɛrsɔnɛl] **1** *adj* **(a)** personal (*letter, business, Gram pronoun*); not transferable (*ticket*); **objets personnels,** personal belongings; **fortune personnelle,** private means, private income; **verbe p.,** verb that takes a personal subject;

(b) (*égoïste*) selfish; *Sp* **joueur p.,** selfish player; **intérêt p.,** self-interest.

2 *nm* personnel, staff (*of institution, school, firm*); workforce (*of factory, in industry*); employees (*of boss, firm*); *Mil* personnel, manpower; *Nau* complement; **p. de bureau,** clerical staff, office staff, secretarial staff; **p. réduit,** reduced staff, skeleton staff; **faire partie du p. de ...,** to be on the staff of ...; **manquer de p.,** to be understaffed; **directeur du p.,** personnel manager; **le p. politique/artistique,** the political/artistic staff; *Av* **p. au**

sol, p. rampant, ground personnel, ground staff, ground crew; **service du p.,** personnel (department).

personnellement [pɛrsɔnɛlmɑ̃] *adv* personally.

personnification [pɛrsɔnifikɑsjɔ̃] *nf* personification, embodiment.

personnifier [pɛrsɔnifje] *vt* (*impf & pr sub* **n. personnifiions, v. personnifiiez**) to personify (*inanimate object, virtue, vice, etc*); **elle personnifie toute la bonté humaine,** she is the embodiment *or* personification of all human kindness; **il personnifie son pays,** he typifies his country.

perspectif, -ive [pɛrspɛktif, -iv] *adj* perspective (*plan*).

perspective [pɛrspɛktiv] *nf* **(a)** outlook, view, prospect; **en p.,** in the future, in prospect; **avoir qch en p.,** to have sth in view; **j'envisage avec plaisir la p. de le revoir,** I am looking forward to seeing him again; **perspectives d'avenir,** future prospects; **(b)** *Beaux-Arts etc* (linear) perspective; **p. à vol d'oiseau,** bird's-eye view; **dessin en p.,** drawing in perspective; **(c)** (*point de vue*) viewpoint; **dans une p. marxiste,** from the Marxist point of view.

perspicace [pɛrspikas] *adj* perspicacious, shrewd.

perspicacité [pɛrspikasite] *nf* perspicacity, shrewdness, insight, acumen.

persuader [pɛrsɥade] **1** *vt* **(a) p. qn,** to persuade *or* convince s.o.; **p. qn de qch/de faire qch,** to persuade *or* convince s.o. of sth/to persuade s.o. to do sth; **j'ai fini par les p.,** I convinced *or* persuaded them in the end, I talked them round in the end; **être persuadé de qch,** to be sure *or* convinced of sth; **être persuadé que ...,** to be sure *or* convinced that ...; **j'en suis tout à fait persuadé,** I am quite convinced of it; **je n'en suis pas persuadé,** I'm not sure *or* convinced;

(b) *Vieilli* **p. qch à qn,** to persuade s.o. of sth, to make s.o. believe sth.

2 *vi* **p. à qn de faire qch,** to persuade *or* induce s.o. to do sth.

3 se persuader *vpr* (*convaincre*) to persuade *or* convince oneself; **ils se sont persuadé(s) que ...,** they have convinced themselves that ... .

persuasif, -ive [pɛrsɥazif, -iv] *adj* persuasive, convincing.

persuasion [pɛrsɥazjɔ̃] *nf* **(a)** (*fait ou action de persuader*) persuasion; **(b)** (*conviction, certitude*) conviction, belief.

perte [pɛrt] *nf* **(a)** loss (*of money, relative, lawsuit, sight, reason etc*); **des pertes importantes,** considerable *or* significant losses; **pertes et profits,** profit and loss; **vendre qch à p.,** to sell sth at a loss; **être en p.,** to be out of pocket; **p. sèche,** dead loss; **p. de connaissance,** loss of consciousness; **à p. de vue,** as far as the eye can see; *Fig* **discuter à p. de vue,** to argue till the cows come home;

(b) (*gaspillage*) waste; **p. de temps,** waste of time; **expliquer qch à qn en pure p.,** to waste one's time *or* breath trying to explain sth to s.o.; **dépense en pure p.,** wasteful expenditure;

(c) (*déperdition*) loss; leakage (*from pipe, container*); **p. de chaleur,** heat loss, loss of heat; *Él* **p. de charge,** drop in voltage; *Él* **p. à la terre,** earth leakage; *Av* **avion en p. de vitesse,** plane that is losing speed; *Fig* **le président/le cinéma semble en p. de vitesse,** the President/the film industry seems to be running out of steam; *Méd* **pertes (de sang),** loss of blood, *Spéc flooding; Méd* **pertes blanches,** vaginal discharge, *Spéc* leucorrhoea, *esp US* leukorrhea;

(d) (*destruction*) ruin, destruction; **jurer la p. de qn,** to swear to ruin s.o.; **il court à sa p.,** he is heading for disaster; *Nau* **p. corps et biens,** loss of vessel with all hands.

pertinemment [pɛrtinamɑ̃] *adv* **(a)** pertinently, to the point; **(b) savoir qch p.,** to know sth for a fact.

pertinence [pɛrtinɑ̃s] *nf* pertinence, pertinency, relevance.

pertinent [pɛrtinɑ̃] *adj* pertinent, relevant (**à,** to).

pertuis [pɛrtɥi] *nm* **(a)** (*canal*) sluice; **(b)** (*d'un fleuve*) narrows; (*détroit*) strait(s), (narrow) channel.

perturbateur, -trice [pɛrtyrbatœr, -tris] **1** *adj* disturbing, upsetting; **éléments perturbateurs,** disruptive elements. **2** *n* troublemaker.

perturbation [pɛrtyrbɑsjɔ̃] *nf Astron* disturbance; perturbation; disruption (*of public services*); **p. (atmosphérique),** (atmospheric) disturbance; **perturbations du service aérien,** disruption of air travel.

perturber [pɛrtyrbe] *vt* to disrupt (*public services etc*); (*de nouvelles*) to perturb, to upset (*s.o.*); *Astron* to perturb.

péruvien, -ienne [peryvjɛ̃, -jɛn] **1** *adj* Peruvian. **2** *n* **P.,** Peruvian.

pervenche [pɛrvɑ̃ʃ] *nf* **(a)** (*plante*) periwinkle; **(bleu) p.,** periwinkle blue; **(b)** *F* (woman) traffic warden.

pervers, -erse [pɛrvɛr, -ɛrs] **1** *adj* perverse (*idea*); perverted (*mind, sexual practices*); **goûts p.,** unnatural tastes; **conseils p.,** evil advice. **2** *n* twisted person; (*sexuel*) pervert.

perversion [pɛrvɛrsjɔ̃] *nf* perversion (*of taste, morals*); warping (*of the mind*); *F* **c'est de la p.!,** that's twisted *or* perverted!; **p. sexuelle,** sexual perversion.

perversité [pɛrvɛrsite] *nf* perversity, depravity.

perverti, -ie [pɛrvɛrti] **1** *adj* perverted, depraved (*person*). **2** *n* pervert.

pervertir [pɛrvɛrtir] **1** *vt* to pervert (*person, taste, meaning*); to deprave (*person*); to corrupt (*person, morals*). **2 se pervertir** *vpr* (*of person, taste, meaning*) to become perverted; (*of person*) to become depraved; (*of person, morals*) to become corrupt(ed).

pesage [pəzaʒ] *nm* **(a)** (*pesée*) weighing; **(b)** *Courses de chevaux* weigh-in; (*lieu*) weighing room.

pesamment [pəzamɑ̃] *adv* heavily; **marcher p.,** to walk with a heavy tread.

pesant [pəzɑ̃] **1** *adj* heavy (*suitcase, tread*); ponderous, clumsy (*style, writer*); sluggish (*mind*); deep (*sleep*); **silence p.,** heavy silence; **marcher à pas pesants,** to walk heavily; **elle trouve le temps p.,** time hangs heavy on her hands. **2** *nm* **cela vaut son p. d'or,** it's worth its weight in gold.

pesanteur [pəzɑ̃tœr] *nf* **(a)** weight; *Phys* gravity; **p. spécifique,** specific gravity; **(b)** heaviness; inelegance, unwieldiness (*of movement, walk*); slowness, sluggishness (*of mind*); **j'ai une p. d'estomac,** there is something lying heavy on my stomach; **pesanteurs intellectuelles,** intellectual baggage *or* impedimenta; **pesanteurs économiques,** economic impedimenta.

pèse-alcool [pɛzalkɔl] *nm* alcoholometer; (*pl pèse-alcools*).

pèse-bébé [pɛzbebe] *nm* baby scales; (*pl pèse-bébés*).

pesée [pəze] *nf* **(a)** weighing; *Boxe Courses de chevaux* weigh-in; **faire la p. de qch,** to weigh sth; **cette balance a une p. de 150 kilos,** the scale(s) can weigh up to 150 kilos; **(b)** (*pression*) force, leverage, effort; **exercer une p. sur une porte,** to try to force a door.

pèse-lait [pɛzlɛ] *nm inv* lactometer; (*pl pèse-laits*).

pèse-lettre(s) [pɛzlɛtr] *nm* letter scales; (*pl pèse-lettres*).

pèse-personne [pɛzpɛrsɔn] *nm* scales; (*pl pèse-personnes*).

peser [pəze] *v* (**je pèse, n. pesons; je pèserai**) **1** *vt* to weigh (*parcel etc*); *Fig* **p. ses paroles,** to weigh one's words, to think before one speaks; *Fig* **réponse bien pesée,** considered *or* careful answer; *Fig* **p. une décision,** to ponder a decision; **p. le pour et le contre,** to weigh up the pros and cons; *Sp* **se faire p.,** to weigh in.

2 se peser *vpr* to weigh oneself.

3 *vi* (*faire, avoir comme poids*) to weigh; (*être lourd*) to be heavy; (*of argument etc*) to carry weight; **il ne pèse pas lourd,** he doesn't weigh much; *Fig* he doesn't count for much; **paquet qui pèse deux kilos,** parcel weighing two kilos; **cela me pèse de vous le demander,** it isn't easy for me to ask you; **le temps lui pèse,** time hangs heavy on his hands; **p. sur qch,** to press on sth; **p. sur un levier,** to press (down) *or* pull a lever; *Can* **p. sur un bouton,** to push a button; **aliment qui pèse sur l'estomac,** food that lies heavy on the stomach; *Fig* **un silence pesait sur l'assemblée,** a heavy silence hung over the meeting; **une lourde responsabilité pèse sur lui,** he is weighed down by a heavy responsibility; **ça lui pèse sur la conscience,** it lies heavy on his conscience; *Fig* **p. sur un choix,** to weigh up *or* mull over a choice; *Fig* **p. sur un mot,** to lay stress on *or* to stress a word; **p. une échelle contre un mur,** to lean a ladder against a wall.

peseta [pezeta] *nf* peseta.

pèse-vin [pɛzvɛ̃] *nm* oenometer; (*pl pèse-vins*).

peson [pəzɔ̃] *nm* balance.

pessaire [pesɛr] *nm Méd* pessary.

pesse [pɛs] *nf*, **pessereau** [pɛsro] *nm* (*plante*) horse tail; *Spéc* equisetum.

pessimisme [pesimism] *nm* pessimism.

pessimiste [pesimist] **1** *adj* pessimistic. **2** *n* pessimist.

peste [pɛst] *nf* **(a)** *Méd* plague; *Litt Arch* pestilence; **p. bubonique** *ou* **noire,** bubonic plague; *Hist* the Black Death; **p. bovine/porcine,** cattle plague/swine fever; **être atteint de la p.,** to have the plague, to be stricken with the plague; *F* **fuir qch/qn comme la p.,** to avoid sth/s.o. like the plague; *Litt Vieilli* **p.!,** good gracious!, heavens!; *Arch & Litt* **p. soit du vieux fou!,** a plague on the old fool!; **(b)** *Fig Péj* (*enfant*) pest, nuisance; **petite p.,** little devil *or* pest;

(c) *Litt Fig Péj* (*chose dangereuse*) curse; **l'ambition est la p. de ce milieu,** ambition is the curse of this group of people.

pester [pɛste] *vi* **p. contre qn/qch,** to curse *or* rave at s.o./sth; **il pestait,** he was cursing.

pesticide [pɛstisid] **1** *adj* pesticidal. **2** *nm* pesticide.

pestiféré, -ée [pɛstifere] **1** *adj* plague-stricken. **2** *n* plague victim; **fuir qn comme un p.,** to avoid s.o. like the plague.

pestilence [pɛstilɑ̃s] *nf* stench, stink.

pestilentiel, -elle [pɛstilɑ̃sjɛl] *adj* stinking, f(o)etid.

pet [pɛ] *nm Arg* **(a)** fart; **faire un p.,** to fart; **ça ne vaut pas un p. (de lapin),** it isn't worth a damn *or* a monkey's fart; **(b)** *Vieilli* **il va y avoir du p.,** there's going to be trouble; (*scandale*) there's going to be a nice bit of scandal; **p.! le voilà!,** look out! he's coming!; **faire le p.,** to be on the watch *or* on the lookout; **(c)** [pɛt] **ta voiture a pris un p.,** your car's had a bash.

pétainiste [petenist] *Hist* **1** *adj* Pétainist. **2** *n* follower of Pétain, Pétainist.

pétale [petal] *nm* petal.

pétanque [petɑ̃k] *nf* (*in the Midi*) game of bowls.

pétant [petɑ̃] *adj Arg* **à neuf heures pétantes,** on the stroke *or* dot of nine o'clock, at nine o'clock sharp.

pétarade [petarad] *nf* **(a)** (*of horse*) (succession of) farts; **(b)** crackling (*of fireworks, firearms*); **(c)** (*de voiture, mobylette etc*) backfiring, backfire.

pétarader [petarade] *vi* **(a)** (*of horse*) to let off a succession of farts; **(b)** (*of fireworks, firearms*) to crackle; **(c)** (*de voiture, mobylette etc*) to backfire.

pétard [petar] *nm* **(a)** (*firework*) cracker, banger; *Min* shot, blast; *Mil* explosive charge; *Arch* petard; *Rail* fog signal; *Arg* (*pistolet*) shooter, *US* gat; **faire partir un p.,** to let off a banger; **(b)** (*bruit*) din, racket; **il va y avoir du p.,** there's going to be a hell of a row; **faire du p.,** to raise a stink; **être en p.,** to be in a flaming temper; **(c)** *Arg* (*derrière*) bum, *Am* ass, fanny; **(d)** *F* (*drogue*) joint, reefer.

pétaudière [petodjɛr] *nf* bedlam, bear garden; **la réunion a tourné en p.,** the meeting turned into a bear garden.

pet-de-nonne [pɛd(ə)nɔn] *nm Culin* (type of) fritter; (*pl pets-de-nonne*).

péter [pete] *v* (**je pète, n. pétons; je péterai**) **1** *vi* **(a)** *Arg* to fart; **il l'a envoyé p.,** he told him to piss off; **p. dans la soie,** to live in the lap of luxury; **p. plus haut que son cul,** to be big-headed *or* conceited;

(b) (*of burning wood etc*) to crack, to crackle; (*of cork etc*) to pop;

(c) *F* (*casser*) to fall apart, to break; (*of string etc*) to snap; **ça va lui p. entre les mains,** it'll fall apart in his hands; **tous les boutons étaient prêts à p.,** all the buttons were about to pop off;

(d) *F* **p. de joie/santé,** to be jumping for joy/bouncing with health.

2 *vt* **(a)** *F* **p. le feu** *ou* **des flammes,** to be bursting with energy *or* vitality; **ça va p. des flammes,** there's going to be a hell of a row;

(b) *Arg* (*casser*) to bust (*sth*);

(c) *Arg* **être (complètement) pété,** (*saoul*) to be rat-arsed.

3 se péter *vpr* **il s'est pété la gueule,** he had an accident.

pète(-)sec [pɛtsɛk] *nm inv F* martinet, disciplinarian.

péteux, -euse [petø, -øz] *n F Péj* (*lâche*) yellow-belly; **c'est un petit p.,** he's yellow.

pétillant [petijɑ̃] *adj* crackling (*fire*); sparkling (*wine*); fizzy (*water*); sparkling (*eyes, wit*); sprightly (*wit*).

pétillement [petijmɑ̃] *nm* crackling (*of burning wood*); sparkling, fizzing, bubbling (*of champagne*); sparkling (*of the eyes*).

pétiller [petije] *vi* (*of burning wood*) to crackle; (*of drink*) to sparkle, to fizz, to bubble; (*of eyes*) to sparkle; **p. de joie,** to bubble over with joy; **p. d'esprit,** to sparkle with wit.

pétiole [pesjɔl] *nm Bot* petiole.

petiot, -ote [pətjo, -ɔt] *F* **1** *adj* tiny, wee. **2** *n* tiny child; **ma petiote,** my little girl; **viens ici, p.,** come here, little chap.

petit, -ite [p(ə)ti, -it] **1** *adj* **(a)** (*de taille réduite*) little, small; **un p. homme,** a short *or* little man; **c'est un homme p.,** he's small *or* short; **une toute petite maison,** a tiny little house; **p. bois,** kindling wood; **petite distance,** short distance; **mes chaussures sont trop petites,** my shoes are too small (for me); **en p.,** on a small scale, in miniature; **p. à p.,** little by little, bit by bit, gradually; **se faire tout p.,** to make oneself as inconspicuous as possible; (*s'abaisser*) to cower (**devant,** before, in front of); *Fig* **le monde est p.,** it's a small world; *F* **le p. coin,** the toilet, *Br* the loo, *Am* the john; **petits fours,** petits fours; **petits pois,** (garden) peas; **p. déjeuner,** breakfast; **p. doigt,** little finger, *Am & Scot* pinkie; **p. salé,** = streaky bacon;

(b) p. misérable!, little wretch!;

(c) (*affectueux*) **mais ma petite Louise ...,** but my dear Louise ...; *Fig* **les petites phrases des grands hommes,** the utterances of important men; **p. ami/petite amie,** boyfriend/girlfriend; **un p. coup de rouge,** a drop of red wine; **fumer une bonne petite cigarette,** to have a quiet smoke;

(d) (*de niveau inférieur*) lesser, minor; **les petits talents,** the lesser talents; *Scol* **les petites classes,** the lower forms; **le p. personnel,** junior staff; **la petite industrie,** light industry; **p. commerçant,** small shopkeeper; **les petits propriétaires,** the small landowners; *Com* **petite caisse,** petty cash;

(e) (*de moindre importance*) small, little, minor, insignificant (*problem, mistake etc*); insignificant, unimportant (*fact*); *Péj* petty (*complaint, affair*); minor (*character, event*); **petites routes,** minor roads; **ce n'est pas une petite affaire,** that's no small matter; **p. accident,** minor accident; **j'ai un p. rhume,** I've a slight cold *or* a bit of a cold; **les petites gens,** people in humble circumstances; **faire de petits profits,** to make (only) a small profit; **rouler à petite vitesse,** to drive slowly; **un p. moment,** a brief moment; *F* a tick; **à p. feu,** over a low heat; **le p. jour,** daybreak, the early hours;

(f) (*(plus) jeune*) little, young(er, -est); **mon p. frère,** my little brother; **tu es trop p. pour ça,** you're too young for that; **quand tu étais p.,** when you were little *or* small *or* young; **p. cousin, petite cousine,** second cousin; **p. enfant,** little child; **petite fille,** little girl; **un p. Anglais,** an English boy; **les petits Thomas,** the Thomas children;

(g) (*faible*) poor (*health*); **il a une petite santé,** he's never really well;

(h) (*borné*) narrow-minded; (*mesquin*) petty; mean, petty (*remark, action*); ungenerous (*in one's praise, in defeat*); **c'est vraiment p.,** that's really mean *or* petty; **c'est un p. esprit,** he's petty-minded.

2 *n* little boy; little girl; **pauvre petit(e),** poor little thing; *Scol* **les petits,** the juniors; **le p.,** the youngest (boy); *F* (*term of affection*) *F* **bonjour, mon p.,** (*to woman, child*) good morning, my dear.

3 *nm* young (*of animal*); **petits du chien/du chat,** (dog's) puppies/(cat's) kittens; **faire des petits,** to have young; (*of bitch*) to pup, to whelp; (*of lion etc*) to whelp; (*of sow*) to farrow; (*of cat*) to kitten; (*of wolf*) to cub; *Fig F* (*of money*) to increase, to multiply; *Iron* **le vase a fini par faire des petits, il est tombé,** the vase ended up in pieces when it fell.

petit-beurre [pətibœr] *nm Culin* = butter biscuit, *Am* butter cookie.

petit-bourgeois, petite-bourgeoise [p(ə)tiburʒwa, p(ə)titburʒwaz] (*pl petit(e)s-bourgeois(es)*) **1** *adj* lower middle class, petit-bourgeois; *Péj* narrow-minded. **2** *n* member of the lower middle class; **les petits-bourgeois,** the petty bourgeoisie.

petite-fille [p(ə)titfij] *nf* grand-daughter; (*pl petites-filles*).

petitement [pətitmɑ̃] *adv* **(a)** (*dans la pauvreté*) poorly; **(b)** (*bassement*) meanly, pettily; **(c) elle est logée p.,** she lives in cramped accommodation.

petite-nièce [p(ə)titnjɛs] *nf* great-niece; (*pl petites-nièces*).

petitesse [p(ə)titɛs] *nf* **(a)** smallness, small size (*of any object*); slenderness (*of figure*); **(b)** *Péj* (*mesquinerie*) meanness, pettiness; paltriness (*of meal, sum of money*); **p. d'esprit,** narrow-mindedness; **(c)** *Péj* (*action mesquine*) shabby deed; **faire des petitesses,** to do mean *or* shabby things.

petit-fils [p(ə)tifis] *nm* grandson; (*pl petits-fils*).

petit-gris [p(ə)tigri] *nm* (*pl petits-gris*) **(a)** *Zool* Siberian squirrel; (*sa fourrure*) squirrel (fur); **(b)** *Culin* = edible brown snail.

pétition [petisjɔ̃] *nf* petition; **adresser une p. à qn,** to petition s.o.; **faire signer une p.,** to set up a petition; **p. de principe,** begging the question; *Spéc* petitio principii.

pétitionnaire [petisjɔnɛr] *n* petitioner.

petit-lait [p(ə)tilɛ] *nm* whey; (*pl petits-laits*).

petit-maître [p(ə)timɛtr] *nm Arch* fop, dandy; (*pl petits-maîtres*).

petit-nègre [pətinɛgr] *nm Ling F* **(a)** (*mauvais français*) ungrammatical French, bad French; **(b)** *Vieilli* (*français parlé dans les colonies*) pidgin French.

petit-neveu [p(ə)tinvø] *nm* great-nephew; (*pl petits-neveux*).
petite-nièce [pətitnjɛs] *nf* great-niece; (*pl petites-nièces*).
petits-enfants [p(ə)tizɑ̃fɑ̃] *nmpl* grandchildren.
pétoche [petɔʃ] *nf F* (blue) funk; **avoir la p.,** to be scared *or* in a blue funk.
pétoire [petwar] *nf* **(a)** (*sarbacane*) (child's) peashooter; **(b)** (*mauvais fusil*) poor sort of gun, popgun.
peton [pətɔ̃] *nm Enf* tootsy-wootsy; **petons,** tootsies.
pétoncle [petɔ̃kl] *nm* scallop.
Pétrarque [petrark] *nm* Petrarch.
pétrel [petrɛl] *nm* petrel; **p. tempête,** storm(y) petrel.
pétri [petri] *adj* kneaded, moulded, *US* molded (**de,** out of); **un homme p. d'orgueil,** a man puffed up with pride; **p. d'ignorance,** steeped in ignorance.
pétrifiant [petrifjɑ̃] *adj* petrifying, petrifactive.
pétrification [petrifikɑsjɔ̃] *nf* petrification, petrifaction; *Fig* **p. du cœur,** hardening of the heart.
pétrifier [petrifje] *v* (*impf & pr sub* **n. pétrifiions, v. pétrifiiez**) **1** *vt* **(a)** *Minér* to petrify; *Fig* **pétrifié de peur,** petrified, paralysed *or US* paralyzed with fear; **(b)** (*couvrir de calcaire*) to encrust with lime. **2 se pétrifier** *vpr* to petrify, to become petrified; *Fig* **son sourire se pétrifia,** his smile became fixed.
pétrin [petrɛ̃] *nm* kneading trough; **p. mécanique,** kneading machine; *Fig* **se mettre dans le p.,** to get into trouble *or* a mess *or* into a fix; *Fig* **être dans le p.** *ou* **dans un beau p.,** to be in a jam *or* a tight corner *or* in a mess.
pétrir [petrir] *vt* (*brasser*) to knead (*dough, bread*); (*façonner*) to knead, to shape, to mould, *US* to mold (*clay*); *Fig* **p. l'esprit de qn,** to mould *or* shape a person's character; *Méd* **p. un muscle,** to knead a muscle; *Fig* **p. les doigts de qn en lui disant bonjour,** to greet s.o. with a vice-like *or US* vise-like handshake.
pétrissage [petrisaʒ] *nm* kneading.
pétrisseur, -euse [petrisœr, -øz] **1** *n* kneader; **ouvrier p.,** dough mixer. **2** *nf* **pétrisseuse,** kneading machine.
pétrochimie [petrɔʃimi] *nf* petrochemistry.
pétrochimique [petrɔʃimik] *adj* petrochemical.
pétrochimiste [petrɔʃimist] *n* petrochemist.
pétrodollar [petrodɔlar] *nm Fin* petrodollar.
pétrographie [petrɔgrafi] *nf Géol* petrography.
pétrole [petrɔl] *nm* petroleum, (mineral) oil; **p. brut,** crude (oil); **p. lampant,** paraffin (oil), *Am* kerosene; **gisement de p.,** oil deposit, oilfield; **puits de p.,** oil well; **lampe à p.,** oil lamp; **bleu p.,** petrol blue; **vert p.,** deep turquoise.
pétrolette [petrɔlɛt] *nf F* moped.
pétroleuse [petrɔløz] *nf* ardent *or* committed feminist; *Hist* (1871) incendiary.
pétrolier, -ière [petrɔlje, -jɛr] **1** *adj* **l'industrie pétrolière,** the petroleum *or* oil industry; **société pétrolière,** oil company; **pays p.,** oil-producing country; **navire p.,** (oil) tanker. **2** *nm* **(a)** (*financier, industriel*) oil magnate, oilman; (*technicien*) petroleum engineer; **(b)** (*navire*) (oil) tanker.
pétrolifère [petrɔlifɛr] *adj* petroliferous, oil-bearing; **gisement p.,** oilfield.
pétulance [petylɑ̃s] *nf* liveliness, exuberance.
pétulant [petylɑ̃] *adj* lively, exuberant, irrepressible.
pétunia [petynja] *nm* petunia.
peu [pø] **1** *adv* **(a)** (*(en) petite quantité*) little; **p. ou point,** little or none; **manger p. (ou point),** to eat little (or nothing); **p. de viande,** not much meat, very little meat; **pour p. qu'il pleuve, je resterai à la maison,** even if it only rains a little I'll stay at home; **ce n'est pas p. dire,** that's saying a good deal; **quelque p.,** somewhat, rather; **je suis quelque p. surpris,** I am somewhat *or* rather surprised; **si tu m'aimais tant soit p.,** if you loved me at all *or* even a little; **si tu es tant soit p. fatigué,** if you're at all *or* the least bit tired; **p. s'en faut pour que je me mette en colère,** I'm on the verge of losing my temper; **p. de chose,** (very) little, not much; **pour si p. de chose,** for such a small thing; **p. à p.,** gradually, little by little; **fort p.,** very little; *F* **très p. pour moi!,** not for me!;
(b) few; **p. de gens,** few people; **p. en garderont un souvenir,** few people will remember it; **p. d'entre eux avaient voyagé,** few of them had travelled; **nous en savons p. de choses,** we know little about it, we don't know much about it; **il suffirait de p. de choses pour que ça fonctionne,** it wouldn't need much to get it to work; **en p. de mots,** in a few words;
(c) (*pas (très)*) not very; **p. utile,** not very useful; **p. intelligent,** unintelligent; **p. honnête,** dishonest; **p. profond,** shallow;
(d) (*de temps*) **p. après,** shortly after(wards), not long after(wards); **sous p., dans p., avant p., d'ici p.,** soon, before long; **depuis p.,** lately, recently; **j'ai manqué le train de p.,** I just missed the train; **il y a p.,** not (very) long ago, recently.
2 *nm* **(a)** (*petite quantité*) little, bit; **c'est p. d'y penser,** (*il faut encore agir*) it's not enough to think about it; **le p. qu'il y a est à votre disposition,** you are welcome to the little there is; **son p. d'éducation,** what little education he has had; **il a p. fait pour nous,** he has done (very) little for us;
(b) un peu, a little, a bit; **il nous reste un p. de temps/sucre,** we still have a little time/sugar left; **elle a un p. moins/un p. plus de quarante ans,** she's a little under/over forty; **un p. de vin,** a little wine, a bit of wine; **un tout petit p.,** a very little, a tiny bit *or* drop; **encore un p.,** a little more; (*encore quelques-uns*) a few more; **il sait un p. d'anglais,** he knows a little English, he has a smattering of English; **vous êtes allé un p. loin!,** you went a bit far!; **je suis un p. en retard,** I'm a bit or a little late; *F* **ça, c'est un p. fort!,** that's a bit much!; **un p. plus et il tombait dans l'eau,** he very nearly fell in the water; **pour un p. je l'aurais jeté dehors,** I all but *or* I nearly threw him out; **écoutez un p.,** just listen; *F* **je vous demande un p.!,** I ask you!; *F* **tu ferais ça? — un p.!,** you'd do that? — you bet!;
(c) (*de temps*) **restez encore un p.,** stay a bit longer, stay a little (while) longer.
peuchère [pøʃɛr] *int Région* strewth!, heavens!
peuh! [pø] *int* pooh!, bah!
peuplade [pœplad] *nf* small tribe (*of primitive peoples*).
peuple [pœpl] **1** *nm* **(a)** (*nation*) people, nation; **le p. français,** the French people; **le p. élu,** the chosen race; **(b)** (*ensemble des citoyens*) people (*considered as a political entity*); **dans une démocratie le p. gouverne,** in a democracy it is the people who govern; **le roi et son p.,** the king and his people *or* subjects; **le p.,** the people, the masses; **les gens du p.,** *Vieilli* **le bas** *ou* **petit p.,** the lower classes, the working classes; **(c)** crowd (of people); **quel p.!,** what a crowd!, what a lot of people!; **ça fait du p.,** that's one hell of a lot of people; *Fig* **elle se fiche** *ou* **se fout du p.,** who does she think she is! **2** *adj inv F Péj* **ça fait p.,** that's vulgar, that's common.
peuplé [pœple] *adj* inhabited; **très/peu p.,** densely/sparsely populated.
peuplement [pœpləmɑ̃] *nm* peopling, populating (*of a region*); stocking (*of fish pond, game preserve etc*); planting (*with trees*); **régions à faible p.,** sparsely populated areas.
peupler [pœple] **1** *vt* **(a)** (*pourvoir d'habitants*) to populate, to people (*country*); to stock (*fish pond etc*); to plant (with trees); **(b)** (*occuper*) to inhabit; **les gens qui peuplent la terre,** the world's inhabitants; **rue peuplée de gens,** crowded street; **Fig ville peuplée de souvenirs,** town full of memories. **2 se peupler** *vpr* to become populated; **la rue s'est peuplée peu à peu,** the street gradually filled (up) with people.
peupleraie [pøplərɛ] *nf* poplar plantation.
peuplier [pøplije] *nm* poplar; **p. tremble,** aspen.
peur [pœr] *nf* fear; (*subite*) fright; **avoir p.,** to be *or* feel afraid *or* frightened; **avoir p. du chien,** to be afraid of the dog; **ne pas avoir p. de mourrir,** not to be afraid of dying; **il ne faut pas avoir p. de le lui dire,** you mustn't be afraid of telling him so; **j'ai p. pour lui,** I'm afraid for him; **n'ayez pas p.!,** don't be afraid!; *F* **vous n'avez pas p.!,** (*vous vous obstinez*) you're not easily put off!; (*vous avez du culot*) you've got a nerve!; **prendre p.,** to take fright; *F* **avoir une p. bleue,** to be in a blue funk, to be scared to death; **avoir une p. panique des voyages en avion,** to be terrified of flying; **je n'avais qu'une p., qu'il dise oui,** my only fear was that he might say yes; **en être quitte pour la p.,** to get off with a fright; **il a eu plus de p. que de mal,** he was more frightened than hurt; **faire p. à qn,** to frighten s.o., to give s.o. a fright; **il m'a fait une de ces peurs,** he gave me such a fright!; (*je me suis inquiété pour lui*) he gave me such a fright, I was terrified for him!; **être laid à faire p.,** to be horrifically ugly, to be as ugly as sin; **sans p.,** fearless, fearlessly; **j'avais p. de vous gêner,** I was afraid I might be in your way; **j'en ai bien p.,** I'm afraid so; **j'ai p. qu'il (ne) soit en retard,** (*je suis inquiété*) I'm worried in case he is *or Fml* should be late; (*formule de politesse*) I'm afraid he may be late; *Fig* **ne pas avoir p. de mots,** to call a spade a spade, not to mince one's words; **la p. des élèves (devant leur professeur),** the children's fear (of their teacher); **la p. de s'engager,** the fear of committing oneself; **de p. de,** for fear of (*sth*); **de p. que ... (ne)** +

sub, in case ..., for fear that ... .
peureusement [pœrøzmɑ̃] *adv* fearfully.
peureux, -euse [pœrø, -øz] **1** *adj* timid, fearful, *Fml* timorous (*person, glance*). **2** *n* fearful *or* timid person; **quel p.!**, what a coward!, *F* what a wimp!
peut-être [pøtɛtr] *adv* perhaps, maybe, possibly; **p.-ê. que oui, p.-ê. que non,** perhaps, perhaps not, maybe, maybe not; **elle est p.-ê. rentrée chez elle,** she may have gone home; **p.-ê. finiras-tu par lui pardonner,** perhaps you'll forgive him in the end, you may forgive him in the end; **p.-ê. bien qu'il viendra,** he may very well come; *Iron* **tu le sais mieux que moi, p.-ê.?**, you think you know better, do you?; **je ne sais pas faire la cuisine, p.-ê.?**, you think I can't cook?
p. ex. (*abrév* **par exemple**) eg.
pèze [pɛz] *nm Arg* (*argent*) dough, lolly.
pff [pf], **pfft** [pft], **pffut** [pfyt] *int* (*indicating scorn*) pooh!
P.G. [peʒe] *nm* (*abrév* **prisonnier de guerre**) POW.
phacochère [fakɔʃɛr] *nm* warthog.
phaéton [faetɔ̃] *nm* phaeton.
phagocyte [fagɔsit] *nm Biol* phagocyte.
phagocyter [fagɔsite] *vt Fig* to swallow up, to engulf; **les zones industrielles phagocytent la banlieue,** the suburbs are being swallowed up *or* engulfed by industrial estates.
phagocytose [fagɔsitoz] *nf Fig* swallowing up.
phalange [falɑ̃ʒ] *nf* **(a)** *Antiq Mil* phalanx; *Litt* host, army; *Hist Pol* **la P.**, the Falange, Falangist party; **(b)** *Anat* phalanx.
phalangette [falɑ̃ʒɛt] *nf Anat* top joint, *Spéc* ungual phalanx (*of finger, toe*).
phalangien, -ienne [falɑ̃ʒjɛ̃, -jɛn] *adj Anat* phalangeal.
phalangiste [falɑ̃ʒist] *n Hist Pol* Falangist.
phalanstère [falɑ̃stɛr] *nm Hist Econ* phalanstery; *Fig* **un p. de philosophes,** a community of philosophers.
phalène [falɛn] *nf* (*parfois nm en poésie*) geometrid (moth).
phallique [falik] *adj* phallic.
phallo [falo] *nm Péj* (= **phallocrate**) MCP.
phallocrate [falɔkrat] *nm F* male chauvinist (pig).
phallocratie [falɔkrasi] *nf* male supremacy; (*attitude, opinions*) male chauvinism.
phallocratique [falɔkratik] *adj* male chauvinist (*person, attitude*); male-dominated (*profession, sport*).
phalloïde [falɔid] *adj Biol* phalloid; **amanite p.**, (*champignon vénéneux*) amanita phalloides, death cap.
phallus [falys] *nm* phallus.
phantasme [fɑ̃tasm] *nm* phantasm.
pharamineux, -euse [faraminø, -øz] *adj F* staggering, fantastic, colossal.
pharaon [faraɔ̃] *nm* **(a)** *Hist* Pharaoh; **(b)** *Cartes* faro.
pharaonique [faraɔnik], **pharonien, -ienne** [faraɔnjɛ̃, -jɛn] *adj Hist* Pharaonic.
phare [far] *nm* **(a)** (*tour lumineuse*) lighthouse; **p. à éclats,** flashing light; **p. à feu fixe/à feu tournant,** fixed/revolving light; **gardien de p.**, lighthouse keeper; **(b)** *Av* beacon; **p. d'atterrissage,** landing light; **(c)** *Aut etc* headlight; **mettre les phares en code** *ou* **en veilleuse,** to dip *or Am* dim the headlights; **p. code,** dipped *or Am* dimmed headlight; **rouler pleins phares,** to drive on full beam *or* full headlights *or Am* high beams; **p. anti- brouillard,** foglamp; **p. de recul,** reversing light.
-phare [far] *suff* **personnalité-p.**, leading light; **film-p.**, seminal film.
pharisaïque [farizaik] *adj* **(a)** *Péj* (*hypocrite*) hypocritical; *Litt* pharisaic(al); **(b)** *Hist Rel* Pharisaic(al).
pharisien, -ienne [farizjɛ̃, -jɛn] **1** *n* **(a)** *Péj* hypocrite; *Vieilli & Litt* pharisee; **(b)** *Hist Rel* Pharisee. **2** *adj* **(a)** *Péj* (*pointilleux*) self-righteous; **(b)** *Hist Rel* Pharisaic(al).
pharmaceutique [farmasøtik] *adj* pharmaceutic(al); **société p.**, pharmaceutical company; **l'industrie p.**, the pharmaceutical industry, pharmaceutics.
pharmacie [farmasi] *nf* **(a)** (*science*) pharmacy, pharmaceuticals; **(b)** (*commerce, magasin*) chemist's (shop); *Vieilli* pharmacy; *Am* drugstore, pharmacy; (*dispensaire*) dispensary; **la p. de l'hôpital,** the hospital dispensary; **(c)** (*médicaments*) pharmaceuticals; **(armoire à) p.**, medicine chest *or* cabinet; **p. de voyage/de premiers soins,** travelling *or US* traveling first-aid kit/first-aid kit.
pharmacien, -ienne [farmasjɛ̃, -jɛn] *n* pharmacist, *Br* (dispensing) chemist, *Am* druggist.
pharmaco [farmako] *adj* **p. dépendance,** drug dependency; **p.-vigilance,** = monitoring the side-effects of drugs.
pharmacologie [farmakɔlɔʒi] *nf* pharmacology.
pharmacologique [farmakɔlɔʒik] *adj* pharmacological.
pharmacopée [farmakɔpe] *nf* pharmacopoeia.
pharyngé [farɛ̃ʒe], **pharyngien, -ienne** [farɛ̃ʒjɛ̃, -jɛn] *adj Méd Anat* pharyng(e)al.
pharyngite [farɛ̃ʒit] *nf Méd* pharyngitis.
pharynx [farɛ̃ks] *nm Anat* pharynx.
phascolome [faskɔlɔm] *nm Zool* wombat.
phase [fɑz] *nf* (*période*) phase, stage (*of an illness etc*); *Astron Ch Phys* phase; *Phys* **en p.**, in phase, in step; **décalage de p.**, difference of phase, phase displacement; *El* **(conducteur de) p.**, phase conductor.
phatique [fatik] *adj Ling* **fonction p.**, phatic function.
Phebus [febys] *nm Myth* Phoebus.
Phèdre [fɛdr] *nf Myth* Phaedra.
Phénicie [fenisi] *nf* Phoenicia.
phénicien, -ienne [fenisjɛ̃, -jɛn] *Hist* **1** *adj* Phoenician. **2** *nm Ling* Phoenician. **3** *n* **P.**, Phoenician.
phénix [feniks] *nm Myth* phoenix; *Fig Litt* (*personne unique en son genre*) paragon.
phénol [fenɔl] *nm Ch* phenol; *Com* carbolic acid.
phénoménal, -aux [fenɔmenal, -o] *adj Phil & F* (*incroyable*) phenomenal.
phénoménalement [fenɔmenalmɑ̃] *adv* phenomenally.
phénomène [fenɔmɛn] *nm* (*expérience, fait, personne*) phenomenon, *pl* phenomena; (*in fairs etc*) freak (*of nature*); **quel sacré p.!**, (*il est drôle*) what a character!
phénoménologie [fenɔmenɔlɔʒi] *nf Phil* phenomenology.
philanthrope [filɑ̃trɔp] *n* philanthropist.
philanthropie [filɑ̃trɔpi] *nf* philanthropy.
philanthropique [filɑ̃trɔpik] *adj* philanthropic(al).
philatélie [filateli] *nf*, **philatélisme** [filatelism] *nm* philately, stamp collecting.
philatélique [filatelik] *adj* philatelic.
philatéliste [filatelist] *n* philatelist, stamp collector.
philharmonie [filarmɔni] *nf* philharmonic society.
philharmonique [filarmɔnik] *adj* philharmonic (*society, orchestra etc*).
philhellène [filelɛn] **1** *nm* Philhellene. **2** *adj* philhellenic.
philhellénisme [filelenism] *nm* philhellenism.
Philippe [filip] *nm* Philip.
philippin, -ine [filipɛ̃, -in] **1** *adj* Filipino, Philippine. **2** *n* **P.**, Filipino.
Philipines (les) [lefilipin] *nfpl* the Philippines.
philistin [filistɛ̃] *adj & nm Péj* philistine.
philo [filo] *nf Scol F* philosophy.
philodendron [filɔdɛ̃drɔ̃] *nm* philodendron.
philologie [filɔlɔʒi] *nf* philology.
philologique [filɔlɔʒik] *adj* philological.
philologiquement [filɔlɔʒikmɑ̃] *adv* philologically.
philologue [filɔlɔg] *n* philologist.
philosophale [filɔzɔfal] *adj* **la pierre p.**, the philosophers' stone.
philosophe [filɔzɔf] **1** *n* philosopher; **prendre une déception en p.**, to react philosophically to a disappointment. **2** *adj* philosophical.
philosopher [filɔzɔfe] *vi* to philosophize.
philosophie [filɔzɔfi] *nf* **(a)** (*science*) philosophy; *Scol* art subjects; **la p. de l'histoire/des sciences,** the philosophy of history/science; **supporter une épreuve avec p.**, to suffer a hardship philosophically; *F* **c'est ma p.**, that's my philosophy, that's my outlook on life; *Scol* **(classe de) p.**, philosophy class (*Eng* ≈ upper sixth).
philosophique [filɔzɔfik] *adj* philosophical.
philosophiquement [filɔzɔfikmɑ̃] *adv* philosophically.
philtre [filtr] *nm* philtre, *US* philter, love potion.
phlébite [flebit] *nf Méd* phlebitis.
phlébologie [flebɔlɔʒi] *nf Méd* phlebology.
phlébotomie [flebɔtɔmi] *nf Méd* phlebotomy.
phlegmon [flɛgmɔ̃] *nm Méd* phlegmon.
phlox [flɔks] *nm* phlox.
pH-mètre [peaʃmɛtr] *nm Tech* pH meter.
phobie [fɔbi] *nf Psy Méd* phobia, morbid fear; *Fig F* **avoir la p. des gendarmes,** to be terrified of policemen.
phobique [fɔbik] *adj & n Psy Méd* phobic.
phonation [fɔnasjɔ̃] *nf Physiol Ling* phonation.
phonatoire [fɔnatwar] *adj* phonatory.
phone [fɔn] *nm Phys* phon.
phonème [fɔnɛm] *nm Ling* phoneme.
phonémique [fɔnemik] *adj Ling* phonemic.
phonéticien, -ienne [fɔnetisjɛ̃, -jɛn] *n* phonetician.
phonétique [fɔnetik] **1** *adj* phonetic. **2** *nf* phonetics.
phonétiquement [fɔnetikmɑ̃] *adv* phonetically.
phoniatre [fɔnjatr] *n Méd* speech therapist.
phoniatrie [fɔnjatri] *nf Méd* speech therapy.

phonie [fɔni] *nf Rad Électron* wireless telegraphy, radiotelegraphy.
phonique [fɔnik] *adj* acoustic; *Vieilli* phonic; **isolation p.,** soundproofing, sound insulation.
phono [fɔno] *nm F Vieilli* = **PHONOGRAPHE**.
phonographe [fɔnɔgraf] *nm (gramophone) Vieilli* record player, gramophone, *Am & Arch* phonograph.
phonographique [fɔnɔgrafik] *adj* phonographic.
phonologie [fɔnɔlɔʒi] *nf Ling* phonology.
phonologique [fɔnɔlɔʒik] *adj Ling* phonologic(al).
phonologue [fɔnɔlɔg] *n Ling* phonologist.
phonothèque [fɔnɔtɛk] *nf* sound archives.
phoque [fɔk] *nm* seal; **souffler comme un p.,** to (puff and) wheeze *or* blow like a grampus; *Vulg* **il est pédé comme un p.,** he's a real queer *or* poofter; **(b)** *Com* sealskin.
phosgène [fɔsʒɛn] *nm Ch* phosgene (gas).
phosphatage [fɔsfataʒ] *nm Agr* treating *(of the soil etc)* with phosphates.
phosphate [fɔsfat] *nm Ch* phosphate; **sans phosphates,** phosphate free.
phosphaté [fɔsfate] *adj Ch* phosphatic, phosphated; **bouillie phosphatée,** phosphate-enriched feed.
phosphater [fɔsfate] *vt* to treat with phosphates, to phosphate.
phosphène [fɔsfɛn] *nm Physiol* phosphene.
phosphore [fɔsfɔr] *nm Ch* phosphorus; **p. blanc,** yellow phosphorus.
phosphoré [fɔsfɔre] *adj* phosphorated.
phosphorer [fɔsfɔre] *vi F* to have one's thinking cap on; **ils phosphorent,** *(pour résoudre un problème)* they're having a brainstorming session; **alors, ça phosphore?,** working hard, are we?
phosphorescence [fɔsfɔresɑ̃s] *nf* phosphorescence.
phosphorescent [fɔsfɔresɑ̃] *adj* phosphorescent.
phosphoreux, -euse [fɔsfɔrø, -øz] *adj Ch* phosphorous.
phosphorique [fɔsfɔrik] *adj Ch* phosphoric.
phosphure [fɔsfyr] *nm Ch* phosphide.
phot [fɔt] *nm Phys* phot.
photo [foto] *nf* photo, snap(shot); **prendre qn en p.,** to take a photo *or* snap(shot) of s.o.; **une p. de mes vacances,** a photo from my holidays *or Am* vacation, one of my holiday snaps; *F* **tu veux ma p.?,** who do you think you're staring at?, what are you staring or gawping at?; **appareil p.,** camera.
photocalque [fɔtɔkalk] *nm Ind* phototype *(from tracing)*.
photochimie [fɔtɔʃimi] *nf* photochemistry.
photochimique [fɔtɔʃimik] *adj* photochemical.
photocomposer [fɔtɔkɔ̃poze] *vi & vt Br* to filmset, to photoset, *surtout Am* to photocompose.
photocomposeuse [fɔtɔkɔ̃pozøz] *nf* filmsetter, photosetter, *surtout Am* photocomposer.
photocomposition [fɔtɔkɔ̃pozisjɔ̃] *nf* filmsetting, photosetting, *surtout Am* photocomposition, phototypesetting.
photocopie [fɔtɔkɔpi] *nf* photocopy.
photocopier [fɔtɔkɔpje] *vt (conj like* **copier***)* to photocopy.
photocopieur [fɔtɔkɔpjœr] *nm*, **photocopieuse** [fɔtɔkɔpjøz] *nf* photocopier.
photo(-)électricité [fɔtɔelɛktrisite] *nf* photo-electricity.
photo(-)électrique [fɔtɔelɛktrik] *adj* photoelectric *(cell, effect)*.
photo-finish [fɔtɔfiniʃ] *nf inv Sp* photo finish; *(appareil)* photo-finish camera.
photofission [fɔtɔfisjɔ̃] *nf Phys Nucl* photonuclear fission.
photogénique [fɔtɔʒenik] *adj Phot* photogenic.
photogrammétrie [fɔtogrametri] *nf* photogrammetry.
photographe [fɔtɔgraf] *n* **(a)** *(professionnel de la photo)* photographer; **reporter p.,** press photographer; **(b)** *(commerçant)* camera dealer.
photographie [fɔtɔgrafi] *nf* **(a)** *(technique, hobby etc)* photography; **faire de la p.,** to be an amateur photographer; **(b)** *(cliché)* photograph; **prendre une p. de qn,** to take s.o.'s photograph *or* a photograph of s.o..
photographier [fɔtɔgrafje] *vt (impf & pr sub* **n. photographiions, v. photographiiez***)* to photograph, to take a photograph of *(sth)*; **se faire p.,** to have one's photograph taken.
photographique [fɔtɔgrafik] *adj* photographic *(reproduction, description etc)*; **appareil p.,** camera.
photographiquement [fɔtɔgrafikmɑ̃] *adv* photographically.
photograveur [fɔtɔgravœr] *nm* photoengraver.
photogravure [fɔtɔgravyr] *nf* photoengraving; *(process, print)* photogravure.
photo-interprétation [fɔtɔɛ̃tɛrpretɑsjɔ̃] *nf Tech* = photomapping.
photolithographie [fɔtɔlitɔgrafi] *nf* photolithography.
photolyse [fɔtɔliz] *nf Ch* photolysis.
photomaton [fɔtomatɔ̃] *nm* (automatic) photo machine *or* booth.
photomécanique [fɔtɔmekanik] *adj Tech* photomechanical *(process etc)*.
photomètre [fɔtɔmɛtr] *nm Tech* photometer.
photométrie [fɔtɔmetri] *nf Phys* photometry.
photométrique [fɔtɔmetrik] *adj Phys* photometric(al).
photomontage [fɔtɔmɔ̃taʒ] *nm* photomontage.
photon [fɔtɔ̃] *nm* photon.
photopériodisme [fɔtɔperjɔdism] *nm Bot* photoperiodism.
photophobie [fɔtɔfɔbi] *nf Méd* photophobia.
photophore [fɔtɔfɔr] *nm* **(a)** *(lampe)* reflective lamp *(esp of miner)*; **(b)** *(pour bougie)* candle holder with glass shade.
photopile [fɔtɔpil] *nf Tech* solar cell.
photoreportage [fɔtɔrəpɔrtaʒ] *nm* photojournalism.
photo-robot [fɔtɔrɔbo] *nm* Identikit ® picture; *(pl photos-robots)*.
photosensible [fɔtɔsɑ̃sibl] *adj* photosensitive.
photosphère [fɔtɔsfɛr] *nf Astron* photosphere.
photostat [fɔtɔsta] *nm Tech* photostat.
photostoppeur, -euse [fɔtɔstɔpœr, -øz] *n Com* street photographer.
photostylo [fɔtɔstilo] *nm Ordinat* light pen.
photosynthèse [fɔtɔsɛ̃tɛz] *nf Biol* photosynthesis.
photothèque [fɔtɔtɛk] *nf* photo(graphic) library.
photothérapie [fɔtɔterapi] *nf Méd* phototherapy.
phototypie [fɔtɔtipi] *nf Tech* collotype (process).
photovoltaïque [fɔtɔvɔltaik] *adj* photovoltaic; **cellule p.,** photovaltaic cell; **effet p.,** photovoltaic effect.
phragmite [fragmit] *nm* **(a)** *Bot* reed; **(b)** *(oiseau)* sedge warbler.
phrase [fraz] *nf* **(a)** *Gram* sentence; **p. toute faite,** stock phrase; *Fig* **faire des phrases,** to mouth empty phrases; **sans phrases,** straight out, without mincing one's words; *Gram* **membre de p.,** phrase; **(b)** *Mus* phrase.
phrasé [fraze] *nm Mus* phrasing.
phraséologie [frazeɔlɔʒi] *nf (syntax)* phraseology; *Péj (verbiage)* flowery *or* high-flown language.
phraser [fraze] **1** *vt Mus* to phrase. **2** *vi* to use high-flown language.
phréatique [freatik] *adj Géol* phreatic; **nappe p.,** ground water.
phrénologie [frenɔlɔʒi] *nf Arch* phrenology.
phrénologique [frenɔlɔʒik] *adj Arch* phrenological.
phrénologiste [frenɔlɔʒist] *nm Arch* phrenologist.
phrygane [frigan] *nf Ent (trichoptère)* caddis fly; *(éphémère)* mayfly; **larve de p.,** caddis worm.
Phrygie [friʒi] *nf Antiq* Phrygia.
phrygien, -ienne [friʒjɛ̃, -jɛn] **1** *adj Antiq* Phrygian; *Hist* **bonnet p.,** Phrygian cap *(in French Revolution)*. **2** *n Antiq* **P.,** Phrygian.
phtisie [ftizi] *nf Méd Arch* consumption; *Spéc* phthisis; **p. galopante,** galloping consumption.
phylactère [filaktɛr] *nm* **(a)** *Rel Juive* phylactery; **(b)** *Beaux-Arts* scroll; **(c)** *(de bande dessinée)* speech balloon.
phylloxéra, phylloxera [filɔksera] *nm Ent* phylloxera.
physicien, -ienne [fizisjɛ̃, -jɛn] *n* physicist; **p. de l'atome,** nuclear physicist.
physico-chimie [fizikɔʃimi] *nf (no pl)* physical chemistry.
physico-chimique [fizikɔʃimik] *adj* physicochemical; *(pl physico-chimiques)*.
physico-mathématique [fizikomatematik] **1** *nf* mathematical physics. **2** *adj* relating to mathematical physics.
physiocrate [fizjɔkrat] *nm Écon Hist* physiocrat.
physiocratie [fizjɔkrasi] *nf Écon Hist* physiocracy.
physiologie [fizjɔlɔʒi] *nf* physiology.
physiologique [fizjɔlɔʒik] *adj* physiological.
physiologiquement [fizjɔlɔʒikmɑ̃] *adv* physiologically.
physiologiste [fizjɔlɔʒist] *n* physiologist.
physionomie [fizjɔnɔmi] *nf Vieilli Fml* physiognomy; *Littér* countenance; appearance, aspect; **jeux de p.,** mimicry.
physionomiste [fizjɔnɔmist] *n* good judge of faces; *(savant)* physiognomist; **je ne suis pas p.,** I've no memory for faces.
physique [fizik] **1** *adj* physical; **douleur p.,** physical pain; **culture p.,** physical training; *Scol* physical education; **le monde p.,** the physical *or* material world. **2** *nf (science)*

physics; *Scol Vieilli* physics textbook; **p. nucléaire,** nuclear physics; *Géog* **p. du globe,** geophysics. **3** *nm* physique (*of person*); (*apparence*) external appearance; **le p. et le moral,** the mind and the body; **au p.,** to look at (him, her *etc*); **soigner son p.,** to take care of *or* look after oneself; **il a le p. de l'emploi,** he looks the part.

physiquement [fizikmɑ̃] *adv* physically.

phytosanitaire [fitɔsanitɛr] *adj* **produits phytosanitaires,** = fertilizers, herbicides etc.

phytothérapie [fitɔterapi] *nf* herbal medicine.

pi [pi] *nm Math etc* pi.

piaf [pjaf] *nm Arg* (*oiseau*) sparrow.

piaffement [pjafmɑ̃] *nm Equitation* pawing (the ground).

piaffer [pjafe] *vi* (*d'un cheval*) to paw the ground; *Fig* (*trépigner*) to stamp one's feet; **p. d'impatience,** to fidget.

piaillard, -arde [pjɑjar, -ard] *adj & n F* = **PIAILLEUR, -EUSE.**

piaillement [pjɑjmɑ̃] *nm F* cheeping (*of bird*); *Fig* squalling, squealing (*of child*); squawking (*of person complaining*).

piailler [pjɑje] *vi F* (*of small birds*) to cheep; *Fig* (*of children*) to squall, to squeal; (*complain*) to squawk.

piaillerie [pjɑjri] *nf F* = **PIAILLEMENT.**

piailleur, -euse [pjɑjœr, -øz] *F* **1** *adj* cheeping (*bird*); squalling, squealing (*child*). **2** *n* cheeping bird; *Fig Péj* (*enfant*) squaller, squealer; (*qui se plaint*) squawker.

pianiste [pjanist] *n* pianist; **un p. (de) jazz,** a jazz pianist.

piano¹ [pjano] *nm* piano; **p. à queue,** grand piano; **p. demi-queue,** baby grand; **p. droit,** upright piano; **p. mécanique,** player piano; **jouer du p.,** to play the piano; *F* **faire son p.,** (*étudier*) to learn (to play) the piano; (*faire ses exercices*) to do one's piano practice.

piano² *adv & nm Mus* piano; *Fig F* **allez-y p.,** gently does it; **allez-y p. avec lui,** go easy with *or* on him; **vas-y p. avec le café,** go easy with *or* on the coffee.

piano-forte [pjanɔfɔrte] *nm Hist Mus* antique piano (*dating from around 1800*).

pianotage [pjanɔtaʒ] *nm F* tinkling away (*on piano*); drumming (*of fingers*).

pianoter [pjanɔte] *vi F* **(a)** (*mal jouer du piano*) to tinkle away (on the piano); **(b)** (*tapoter*) to drum one's fingers; **ses doigts pianotent sur la nappe,** his fingers are drumming on the tablecloth.

piastre [pjastr] *nf* piastre; *Can Arg* (*dollar*) buck.

piaule [pjol] *nf Arg* pad.

piaulement [pjolmɑ̃] *nm* cheep(ing) (*of chicks*); *Fig F* whimpering, whining (*of children*).

piauler [pjole] *vi* (*of chicks*) to cheep; *Fig F* (*of children*) to whine, to whimper.

P.I.B. [peibe] *nm Écon* (*abrév* **produit intérieur brut**) GDP.

pic¹ [pik] *nm* **(a)** (*pioche*) pick, pickaxe, *US* pickax; **p. pneumatique,** pneumatic drill; **p. de mineur,** miner's pick; **(b)** (*sommet*) (mountain) peak; **à p.,** perpendicular, sheer (*drop, cliffs*); (*to drop*) perpendicularly; (*to stop, to end, to fall away*) abruptly; **sentier à p.,** steep path; **promontoire à p.,** sheer headland, bluff; **couler à p.,** (*of ship etc*) to sink like a stone; *F* **tomber à p.,** to happen at the right moment; *F* **il est arrivé** *ou* **tombé à p.,** he turned up just at the right moment; (*au dernier moment*) he turned up (just) in the nick of time.

pic² *nm* (*oiseau*) woodpecker.

picador [pikadɔr] *nm* picador.

picaillons [pikajɔ̃] *nmpl Arg* (*argent*) dough, ackers.

picard, -arde [pikar, -ard] **1** *adj* of Picardy; *Culin* **ficelle picarde,** = ham and cheese pancake. **2** *nm Ling* Picardy dialect. **3** *n* **P.,** person from Picardy.

Picardie [pikardi] *nf* Picardy.

picaresque [pikarɛsk] *adj* picaresque (*novel*).

pic(c)olo [pikɔlo] *nm Mus* piccolo.

pichenette [piʃnɛt] *nf* flip, flick (of the finger).

pichet [piʃɛ] *nm* (small) jug, *esp US* pitcher.

pickles [pikɔlz] *nmpl* pickles.

pickpocket [pikpɔkɛt] *nm* pickpocket.

pick-up [pikœp] *nm* **(a)** (*bras de lecture*) pick-up (arm); *Vieilli* (*électrophone*) record player; **(b)** (*véhicule*) pick-up (truck).

picoler [pikɔle] *vi F* to tipple, to booze.

picorer [pikɔre] **1** *vi* (*of bird etc*) to pick *or* scratch about (*for food*); (*mordre*) to peck; (*manger*) to feed; *Fig* (*manger à peine*) to peck *or* pick at one's food. **2** *vt* (*par manque d'appétit*) to peck *or* pick at (*food*); *Fig* (*grignoter*) to nibble (on) (*sth*); **on a eu des sandwichs à p.,** (*à cette soirée*) we had sandwiches to nibble, that's all.

picot [piko] *nm* **(a)** (*pointe*) splinter (of wood); **(b)** (*marteau*) pick hammer; **(c)** *Couture* picot; **(d)** *Pêche* fishing-net (*for flatfish*).

picoté [pikɔte] *adj* pock-marked, pitted.

picotement [pikɔtmɑ̃] *nm* pricking, tingling, smarting (sensation); **j'ai des picotements dans les yeux,** my eyes are stinging *or* smarting.

picoter [pikɔte] **1** *vt* **(a)** (*faire des petits trous dans*) to prick tiny holes in (*sth*); **(b)** (*of bird*) to peck (at) (*fruit etc*); **(c)** (*irriter*) to produce a tingling sensation in (*sth*); to tickle (*throat*); to prickle (*skin*); **la fumée me picotait les yeux,** the smoke made my eyes sting *or* smart. **2** *vi* (*of eyes etc*) to smart, to sting; (*of throat*) to tickle; (*of skin*) to prickle.

picotin [pikɔtɛ̃] *nm Agr* **(a)** (*mesure*) peck (*of oats*); **(b)** (*ration*) feed, ration (*of oats*).

picrate [pikrat] *nm* **(a)** *Arg* (*vin*) plonk; **(b)** *Ch* picrate.

Pictes [pikt] *nmpl Hist* Picts.

pictogramme [piktɔgram] *nm Ling* pictogram.

pictographie [piktɔgrafi] *nf Ling* pictography.

pictographique [piktɔgrafik] *adj Ling* pictographic.

pictural, -aux [piktyral, -o] *adj* pictorial.

pic(-)vert [pikvɛr] *nm* green woodpecker; (*pl pics-(-)verts*).

pie¹ [pi] **1** *nf* **(a)** magpie; *F* chatterbox; *F* **bavarder comme une p.,** to chatter like a magpie; **(b) fromage à la p.,** cream cheese with herbs. **2** *adj inv* **cheval/jument p.,** piebald (horse/mare), *Am* pinto (horse/mare); **vache p.,** black and white cow; *Vieilli* **voiture p. (de la police),** patrol car; *Br* ≈ Panda car.

pie² *adj Arch* pious, charitable; (*still used in*) **œuvre(s) pie(s),** charitable deed(s) *or* work(s), good deed(s) *or* work(s).

Pie [pi] *nm* Pius.

pièce [pjɛs] *nf* **(a)** (*salle, chambre*) room (*of house*); **un (appartement de) trois pièces,** a three-room(ed) flat *or Am* apartment; **un trois-pièces cuisine,** a three-room(ed) flat with kitchen;

(b) (*élément*) piece; **p. de musée,** museum piece; **p. de bétail/gibier,** head of cattle/game; **p. de blé,** wheatfield; **p. d'eau,** ornamental lake; (*plus petite*) ornamental pond; **p. de vin,** barrel *or* cask of wine; **service complet de trente-six pièces,** a complete thirty-six piece dinner service; *Fin* **p. (de monnaie),** coin; **p. de dix francs,** ten-franc piece; **donner la p. à qn,** to give s.o. a tip, to tip s.o.; **les pièces d'un uniforme,** the items of a uniform; **costume deux- pièces/trois-pièces,** two-piece/three-piece suit; **(maillot de bain) une p.,** one-piece swimsuit; *Culin* **p. montée,** ornamental cake; **p. de résistance,** pièce de résistance, main dish; **ils coûtent dix francs (la) p.,** they cost ten francs each *or* apiece; **ils se vendent à la p.,** they are sold singly *or* separately; **marchandises à la p.,** piece goods; **travailler aux pièces,** to do piece work; *F* **on n'est pas aux pièces,** we're not in a hurry;

(c) p. (de théâtre), play; **monter une p.,** to put on a play;

(d) *Mus Littér* piece; **une p. de Couperin/en vers,** a piece by Couperin/of verse;

(e) tout d'une p., all of a piece; *Fig* **être tout d'une p.,** to be blunt; **histoire inventée de toutes pièces,** made-up story;

(f) *MecE* part (*of machine, clock etc*); component part; **p. rapportée,** patch, insert; **pièces de rechange, pièces détachées,** replacement parts, spare parts, spares; **p. de charpente,** beam; (*sous le plancher*) joist;

(g) (*raccord*) patch; **mettre** *ou* **poser une p. à un vêtement,** to put a patch on *or* to patch a garment;

(h) (*morceau, débris*) fragment, bit; **vêtements en pièces,** tattered clothes; **mettre en pièces,** to smash (*a vase*) to bits *or* to pieces; to pull *or* tear (*a book*) to pieces; to tear (*garment etc*) to pieces; **mettre une voiture à pièces,** to take a car to pieces; **tailler l'ennemi en pièces,** to cut the enemy to pieces; **p. à p.,** bit by bit, piece by piece;

(i) *Jur Admin etc* (*document*) document, paper; **p. justificative,** *Jur* document in proof; (*reçu*) voucher; **p. à conviction,** exhibit (*in criminal case*); **p. à l'appui,** supporting document; **p. jointe,** enclosure; **p. d'identité,** identity paper(s), proof of identity; **juger sur pièces,** to judge on the evidence;

(j) (*quantité déterminée*) **p. de bœuf,** joint of beef; **p. d'étoffe,** roll of material;

(k) *Echecs* (chess) piece; (*dames*) draught(sman), *Am* checker;

(l) *Mil* **p. (d'artillerie),** piece of ordnance; **p. de campagne,** field gun; **chef de p.,** number one, squad leader, *US* chief of (piece) section;

(m) *Hér* piece, ordinary, charge; **p. honorable,** honourable ordinary, *US* honorable ordinary.

piécette [pjesɛt] *nf* small coin.

pied [pje] *nm* **(a)** foot (*of person*); **p. bot/plat,** club/flat foot; **doigts de p.,** toes; **sauter à pieds joints/sur un p.,** to jump with (one's) feet together/to hop (on one foot); **être pieds nus,** to be barefoot, to be in bare feet; **il n'avait pas de chaussures aux pieds,** he had no shoes on (his feet); (*pieds nus*) he was barefoot; **se jeter aux pieds de qn,** to throw oneself at s.o.'s feet; **avoir bon p. bon œil,** to be hale and hearty; **se lever du p. gauche,** to get out of bed on the wrong side, to get out of the wrong side of bed; **il ne peut pas mettre un p. devant l'autre,** (*il est faible*) he can hardly put one foot in front of the other; **de la tête aux pieds, de p. en cap** [dəpjetɑ̃kap], from head to foot, from top to toe; *Fig* **faire des pieds et des mains pour ...,** to do one's utmost to ..., to move heaven and earth to ...; *F* **être bête comme ses pieds,** to be unbelievably stupid; *F* **faire du p. à qn,** (*pour avertir*) to give s.o. a kick; (*par jeu*) to play footsie with s.o.; *F* **ça lui fera les pieds!,** that'll serve him right!; *F* **elle me casse les pieds,** (*elle m'ennuie*) she bores the pants off me; (*elle m'agace*) she gets on my wick; **il me casse les pieds pour que je fasse quelque chose,** he's on my back to get me to do something; **mettre p. à terre** [pjetatɛr], to get out (*of car etc*); to dismount (*from horse*); **tomber sur ses pieds,** to fall *or* land on one's feet; *Fig* **une fois de plus il est retombé sur ses pieds,** he's landed on his feet yet again; **je ne remettrai jamais les pieds chez lui,** I'll never set foot in his house again; **je n'ai pas mis le p. dehors de toute la journée,** I haven't set foot outside all day; *F* **mettre les pieds dans le plat,** to put one's foot in it; **attention où vous mettez les pieds!,** tread carefully!, watch your step!; **avoir un p. dans la tombe,** to have one foot in the grave; *F* **ne pas savoir sur quel p. danser,** not to know which way to turn; **marcher sur les pieds de qn,** to tread *or* stand on s.o.'s toes; *F* **lever le p.,** to run off, *Br F* to scarper; **faire qch au p. levé,** to do sth straight off, to do sth at a moment's notice; **frapper du p.,** to stamp (one's foot); **pousser qch du p.,** to kick sth; **coup de p.,** kick; **donner** *ou* **envoyer un coup de p. à qn,** to kick s.o., to give s.o. a kick; **chasser qn à coups de p.,** to kick s.o. out; **enfoncer une porte à coups de p.,** to kick a door in;

(b) à p., on foot; **aller à p.,** to walk, to go on foot; **faire deux kilomètres à p.,** to walk two kilometres; **vous en avez pour vingt minutes à p.,** it will take you twenty minutes to walk (there) *or* twenty minutes on foot; **course à p.,** (running, walking) race; **mettre qn à p.,** to suspend s.o.;

(c) sur p., standing, on one's feet; **elle est sur p. de bonne heure,** she's up early; **mettre une affaire sur p.,** to set up *or* start a business; **il est de nouveau sur p.,** he's up and about again, he's getting about again; **portrait en p.,** full-length portrait;

(d) *F* **jouer comme un p.,** to be a terrible player; **il conduit comme un p.,** he's a bloody awful driver;

(e) *Fig* (*assise, équilibre*) footing; (*appui*) foothold; **avoir le p. marin,** to be a good sailor; **avoir p.,** (*d'un nageur*) to be within one's depth; **perdre p.,** to get out of one's depth; *Fig* to be confused, to be at a loss; **prendre p.,** to get a foothold; **lâcher p.,** to give in (*to opponent*);

(f) *F* **prendre son p.,** to get a kick (out of sth); *Arg* (*sexuellement*) to come; *F* **c'est le p.!,** it's fantastic!, it's great!;

(g) *Fig* (*rang*) **nous sommes sur le même p., lui et moi,** he and I are on an equal footing (with each other); **être sur un p. d'égalité avec qn,** to be on an equal footing with s.o.; **vivre sur un grand p.,** to live on a grand scale;

(h) (*patte*) hoof (*of horse*); (*trace*) footprint; (*piste*) track(s) (*of animal*); *Culin* **p. de veau/mouton/porc,** knuckle of veal/leg of mutton/pigs' trotter;

(i) (*partie inférieure*) foot (*of stocking, tree, staircase, bed*); foot, base (*of column, wall*); (*bas*) foot (*of mountain*); *Math* foot (*of a perpendicular*); *Constr etc* **à p. d'œuvre,** on site;

(j) (*support*) leg (*of chair, table etc*); (*de téléscope*) stand, rest; (*partie élancée d'un verre*) stem; *Phot* foot; **p. (à trois branches),** tripod; **p. de lampe** *ou* **de lampadaire,** lampstand;

(k) (*plant*) stalk (*of plant*); stock (*of vine*); **p. de céleri/d'asperges/de salade,** head of celery/asparagus/lettuce;

(l) *Nau* step, heel (*of mast*); (*reliure*) tail (*of book*);

(m) (*mesure*) foot; *Littér* (metrical) foot; **p. carré/cube,** square/cubic foot; **au petit p.,** (in) miniature; **p. à p.** [pjeapje], step by step; **p. à coulisse,** calliper square.

pied-à-terre [pjetatɛr] *nm inv* pied-à-terre.

pied-bot [pjebo] *nm* club-footed person; (*pl pieds-bots*).

pied-d'alouette [pjedalwɛt] *nm Bot* larkspur, delphinium; (*pl pieds-d'alouette*).

pied-de-biche [pjedbiʃ] *nm* (*poignée de sonnette*) bell pull; (*outil*) nail extractor, nail claw; *Tech* (*pièce coudée*) presser foot (*of sewing machine*); (*pied de meuble galbé*) cabriole leg (*of chair, table etc*); (*pl pieds-de-biche*).

pied-de-poule [pjedpul] *adj & nm Tex* broken check, houndstooth (material); (*pl pieds-de-poule*).

pied-de-roi [pjedərwa] *nm Can* folding rule; (*pl pieds-de-roi*).

pied-droit [pjedrwa] *nm Constr* pier (*of arch, of bridge*); *Archit* engaged pier; (*pl pieds-droits*).

piédestal, -aux [pjedɛstal, -o] *nm* pedestal.

pied-noir [pjenwar] (*pl pieds-noirs*) **1** *n F* Algerian-born Frenchman *or* Frenchwoman. **2** *adj inv F* French Algerian, Algerian French.

piédouche [pjeduʃ] *nm* small pedestal.

piédroit [pjedrwa] *nm* = **PIED-DROIT**.

piège [pjɛʒ] *nm* **(a)** (*pour les animaux*) trap, snare; **dresser** *ou* **tendre un p.,** to set a trap (**à,** for); **prendre un animal au p.,** to trap an animal, to catch an animal in a trap; **(b)** *Fig* (*embuscade*) trap, ambush; **attirer l'ennemi dans un p.,** to draw the enemy into a trap *or* an ambush; **donner/tomber dans le p.,** to walk/fall into the trap; **être pris à son propre p.,** to be caught in one's own trap, *Prov* to be hoist by one's own petard; **dictée pleine de pièges,** dictation full of pitfalls; *Vulg* **p. à cons,** mug's game.

piégeage [pjeʒaʒ] *nm* trapping (*of animals*).

piéger [pjeʒe] *vt* (**je piège, n. piégeons; je piégeai(s); je piégerai**) **(a)** (*attraper*) to trap (*animal, person*); *Fig* **p. qn,** to trap s.o.; (*tromper*) to dupe s.o.; **les électeurs ont été piégés,** the voters have been duped; **se faire p.,** to fall into a trap; **(b)** (*installer un piège dans*) to set a trap in (*a yard, a forest*); **(c)** (*placer un explosif dans*) to booby-trap.

piégeur [pjeʒœr] *nm* trapper.

pie-grièche [pigrijɛʃ] *nf* (*pl pies-grièches*) **(a)** *Orn* shrike; **(b)** *F Vieilli* (*woman*) shrew.

pie-mère [pimɛr] *nf Anat* pia mater; (*pl pies-mère*).

Piémont [pjemɔ̃] *nm* Piedmont.

piémontais, -aise [pjemɔ̃tɛ, -ɛz] **1** *adj* Piedmontese. **2** *nm Ling* Piedmont (dialect). **3** *n* **P.,** native *or* inhabitant of Piedmont.

piéride [pjerid] *nf* pierid; **p. du chou,** cabbage white (butterfly).

pierraille [pjɛraj] *nf* broken stones, loose stones, rubble.

pierre [pjɛr] *nf* **(a)** stone; (*bloc rocheux*) stone; (*rocher*) rock, boulder; *Minér* **p. ponce,** pumice (stone); **p. à chaux,** limestone; **pierres de gué,** stepping stones; **p. d'achoppement,** stumbling block; *Prov* **p. qui roule n'amasse pas mousse,** a rolling stone gathers no moss; **assaillir qn à coups de pierres,** to pelt s.o. with stones; **jeter une p. à qn,** to throw a stone at s.o.; *Fig* **jeter la p. à qn,** to reproach s.o.; *Fig* **c'est une p. dans votre jardin,** that's a dig at you; *Fig* **faire d'une p. deux coups,** to kill two birds with one stone; **malheureux comme les pierres,** bitterly unhappy; *Fig* **avoir un cœur de p.,** to have a heart of stone; *Constr* **p. à bâtir,** building stone; **p. de taille,** ashlar, freestone; **p. angulaire,** corner stone; **mur de p.,** stone wall; **mur en pierres sèches,** drystone wall; **maison de** *ou* **en p.,** stone dwelling; **p. à p.,** stone by stone; **ils n'ont pas laissé p. sur p.,** they didn't leave a stone standing; *Fig* **apporter sa p. à l'édifice,** to make a contribution to sth; **poser la première p.,** to lay the foundation stone; *Fig* to lay the foundation (*for sth*); *Hist* **Âge de (la) p.,** Stone Age; **outils en p.,** flint implements; **Âge de la p. taillée/polie,** Old/New Stone Age;

(b) gem; **p. précieuse,** precious stone, gem; **p. fine,** semi-precious stone;

(c) *Tech* **p. à affûter/à aiguiser,** whetstone/grindstone; **p. à briquet,** (lighter) flint;

(d) (*concrétion*) piece of grit; **des fruits pleins de pierres,** fruit full of grit; **p. à fusil,** gun flint; **p. de touche,** touchstone; **p. philosophale,** philosopher's stone.

Pierre [pjɛr] *nm* Peter.

pierreries [pjɛr(ə)ri] *nfpl* precious stones, jewels, gems.

pierreux, -euse [pjɛrø, -øz] *adj* **(a)** (*couvert de pierres*) stony (*ground, road etc*); gravelly (*bed of river*); **(b)** (*qui contient des concrétions*) gritty (*pear*); **(c)** *Méd* calculous (*formation*).

pierrot [pjɛro] *nm* **(a)** *Th* **P.,** Pierrot; **(b)** *F* (*oiseau*) sparrow; **(c) P.,** Pete.

pietà [pjeta] *nf inv* pietà.

piétaille [pjetɑj] *nf Mil F* rank and file, infantrymen; *Fig* (*piétons*) pedestrians.

piété [pjete] *nf* **(a)** (*ferveur religieuse*) piety; **articles de p.,** devotional objects; **(b)** (*affection*) **p. filiale,** filial piety *or* devotion.

piétinement [pjetinmɑ̃] *nm* (*bruit*) stamping; (*marche sur place*) standing around; *Fig* (*stagnation*) lack of progress; **à cause du p. de l'enquête,** because the enquiry is at a standstill.

piétiner [pjetine] **1** *vt* **(a)** (*en trépignant*) to stamp on (*sth*); (*en marchant*) to trample on (*sth*); (*écraser*) to trample (*sth*) down; to tread (*leaves*) underfoot; *Fig* **p. un cadavre,** to speak ill of the dead; **(b)** *Fig* (*malmener*) to have no respect for (*s.o.'s convictions etc*). **2** *vi* (*frapper des pieds*) **p. d'impatience,** to stamp one's feet impatiently *or* with impatience; **p. (sur) place,** to mark time; *Fig* **l'instruction piétine,** the judge's investigation is making no headway.

piétisme [pjetism] *nm Hist Rel* Pietism.

piétiste [pjetist] *adj & n Hist Rel* Pietist.

piéton, -onne [pjetɔ̃, -ɔn] **1** *n* pedestrian; **sentier pour piétons,** footpath. **2** *adj* **sentier p.,** footpath; **zone piétonne,** pedestrian precinct.

piétonisation [pjetɔnizɑsjɔ̃] *nf* pedestrianization.

piétoniser [pjetɔnize] *vt* to pedestrianize.

piétonnier, -ière [pjetɔ̃nje, -jɛr] *adj* pedestrian.

piètre [pjɛtr] *adj Litt* wretched, poor (*fellow*); lame, paltry (*excuse*); **faire p. figure,** to cut a poor figure; **p. consolation,** cold comfort.

piètrement [pjɛtrəmɑ̃] *adv* wretchedly, poorly.

pieu[1]**, -ieux** [pjø] *nm* (*piquet*) stake, post; *Constr etc* pile; **p. creux,** tubular pile; **enfoncer** *ou* **battre un p.,** to drive (in) a pile; **p. de fondation,** foundation pile.

pieu[2] *nm F* (*lit*) pit; **se mettre au p.,** to hit the hay *or* the sack.

pieusement [pjøzmɑ̃] *adv* (*dévotement*) piously, reverently; (*avec grand respect*) dutifully.

pieuter (se) [səpjøte] *vpr F* to hit the hay *or* the sack.

pieuvre [pjœvr] *nf* octopus; *Fig Péj* (*personne*) leech; *Fig* **la p. bureaucratique,** the tentacles of bureaucracy.

pieux, -euse [pjø, -øz] *adj* **(a)** (*religieux*) pious, devout; **p. mensonge,** white lie; **(b)** (*dévoué*) dutiful, devoted, reverent.

pif[1] [pif] *int* bang!, crack!, smack!

pif[2] *nm F* (*nez*) conk, hooter; *Fig* **faire qch au p.,** to do sth by guesswork.

pif(f)er [pife] *vt F* **je peux pas le p.,** I can't stand (the sight of) him, I can't stomach him.

pifomètre [pifɔmɛtr] *nm F* nose (for sth); **en politique, il n'y a que le p. qui compte,** in politics, having a nose for things is all-important; **au p.,** at a rough guess.

pige [piʒ] *nf* **(a)** (*mesure*) measuring rod; *Typ* take; = amount of copy to be set up in a given time; *Journ* **être payé à la p.,** to be paid by the line; **(b)** *F* year; **il a 45 piges,** he's 45; **à 60 piges,** at 60; **(c)** *F* **faire la p. à qn,** to go one better than s.o..

pigeon [piʒɔ̃] *nm* **(a)** pigeon; **p. mâle/femelle,** cock/hen pigeon; **p. voyageur,** carrier pigeon, homing pigeon; **p. colombin** *ou* **bleu,** stock dove; **p. ramier,** ring dove, wood pigeon; **p. paon,** fantail; **p. d'argile,** clay pigeon; **le tir aux pigeons d'argile,** (*sport*) clay-pigeon shooting; (*événement*) clay-pigeon shoot; **p. vole,** = children's game with forfeits; ≈ Simon says; **(b)** *F Péj* (*personne*) sucker, mug, *Am* fall guy, patsy; **(c)** *Constr* builder's plaster; (*morceau de pierre dans la chaux*) hard lump, nodule (*in lime*).

pigeonnant [piʒɔnɑ̃] *adj F* (*of bust*) high; **soutien-gorge p.,** (lift and) support *or* cross-your-heart bra.

pigeonne [piʒɔn] *nf* (hen, female) pigeon.

pigeonneau, -eaux [piʒɔno] *nm* young pigeon, squab.

pigeonner [piʒɔne] *vt F* to dupe; to swindle, to cheat (*out of money*); **je me suis laissé** *ou* **fait p.,** I've been had *or* suckered.

pigeonnier [piʒɔnje] *nm* **(a)** pigeon house, dovecot(e); **(b)** *F Fig* garret, attic.

piger [piʒe] *v* (**je pigeai(s); n. pigeons**) **1** *vt* **(a)** *Région* to measure; **(b)** *Arg* to understand; **tu piges la combine?,** d'you get what they're *or* we're *etc* up to?; **pige-moi ça!,** take a butcher's at that! **2** *vi* **tu piges?,** get it?; **il a pigé,** he's twigged, the penny's dropped.

pigiste [piʒist] *n Journ* = journalist paid at a rate per line; freelance journalist.

pigment [pigmɑ̃] *nm Biol Tech* pigment.

pigmentaire [pigmɑ̃tɛr] *adj Biol* pigmentary.

pigmentation [pigmɑ̃tɑsjɔ̃] *nf* pigmentation.

pigmenter [pigmɑ̃te] *vt Tech* to pigment.

pigne [piɲ] *nf* (*pin*) pine cone; (*sapin*) fir cone; (*graine*) pine kernal.

pignocher [piɲɔʃe] *vi Vieilli* to pick at one's food.

pignon[1] [piɲɔ̃] *nm Constr* gable (end); **avoir p. sur rue,** to have premises in a desirable location; *Fig* to be in a position of some standing.

pignon[2] *nm MecE* gear; (*la plus petite de deux roues*) pinion; **p. de chaîne,** sprocket wheel, chain sprocket (*of motor cycle etc*); **grand p.,** front chain wheel (*of bicycle*).

pignon[3] *nm Bot* pine kernel.

pignouf [piɲuf] *nm Arg* yob(bo).

pilaf [pilaf] *nm Culin* pilaf, pilaw, pilau; **riz p.,** pilau rice.

pilage [pilaʒ] *nm* pounding, crushing, grinding.

pilaire [pilɛr] *adj* of the hair.

pilastre [pilastr] *nm Archit* pilaster; newel (*at bottom of handrail*).

pilchard [pilʃar] *nm* pilchard.

Pilate [pilat] *nm Hist* **Ponce P.,** Pontius Pilate.

pile[1] [pil] *nf* **(a)** pile, stack (*of books etc*); (*en désordre*) heap; **mettre en p.,** to heap, to stack, to pile (up); **(b)** (*pilier*) pier (*of bridge*); **(c)** *El* battery; *Spéc* cell; **p. sèche,** dry cell; **p. de rechange,** spare battery (*for torch etc*); **(d)** *Phys Nucl Vieilli* **p. atomique,** atomic pile, nuclear reactor.

pile[2] *nf F* **(a)** (*volée de coups*) belting, beating, thrashing; **flanquer** *ou* **donner une p. à qn,** to give s.o. a thrashing *or* hiding *or* licking; **(b)** (*défaite*) crushing defeat, hammering; **recevoir** *ou* **prendre une p.,** to take a hammering, to be beaten hollow, to be murdered; **flanquer une p. à une équipe,** to hammer a team, to walk all over a team.

pile[3] **1** *nf* reverse (*of coin*); **p. ou face,** heads or tails; **jouer à p. ou face,** to toss (up) for it. **2** *adj* **côté p.,** reverse side (*of coin*). **3** *adv* **s'arrêter p.,** (*s'arrêter brusquement*) to come to a dead stop, to stop dead; **s'arrêter p. au feu,** to stop dead at the lights; *Fig* **vous tombez p.,** you've come just at the right moment; (*au dernier moment*) you've come in the nick of time; **ça tombait p.,** that's just what was wanted *or* just what the doctor ordered; **tu seras p. à l'heure,** you'll be (there) right on time, you'll be (there) on the dot; **à six heures p.,** on the dot of six; **ma montre est p. à l'heure,** my watch is dead on *or* bang on (time).

piler [pile] **1** *vt* **(a)** (*broyer*) to pound, to crush, to grind (*in mortar, mill etc*); to powder, to pestle (*drug*); to grind (*almonds*); **poivre pilé,** ground pepper; **(b)** *F* (*battre*) to thrash (*s.o.*); **notre équipe s'est fait p.,** our team got a good thrashing *or* hammering. **2** *vi F* to slam on the brakes.

pilet [pilɛ] *nm* **(canard) p.,** pintail (duck).

pileux, -euse [pilø, -øz] *adj Anat* hair(y); *Spéc* pilose; **follicule p.,** hair follicle; **système p.,** hair.

pilier [pilje] *nm* **(a)** (*colonne*) pillar, column; (*poteau, pieu*) post; **(b)** *Rugby Fb* prop (forward); **(c)** *Fig* (*soutien*) support, mainstay; **ce point est le p. de notre théorie,** our theory rests on that point, that point is the mainstay of our theory; **p. de l'Église/de la démocratie,** (*personne, journal*) bastion *or* pillar of the church/of democracy; *F Péj* **c'est un p. de cabaret** *ou* **de bistrot,** he's always propping up the bar.

pillage [pijaʒ] *nm* **(a)** (*ravage*) pillage, looting, plunder(ing); **mettre une ville au p.,** to sack a town; **(b)** (*chapardage, vol*) pilfering, filching; **(c)** *Fig* (*d'œuvre etc*) plagiarism.

pillard, -arde [pijar, -ard] **1** *adj* **(a)** pillaging, looting; **(b)** (*chapardeur*) thieving, pilfering. **2** *n* pillager, plunderer; (*lors d'une émeute*) looter.

piller [pije] *vt* **(a)** (*dévaster, ravager*) to pillage, to plunder (*village*); to loot (*shop*); to sack (*Rome etc*); to ransack (*house, room*); **(b)** (*voler*) to rob (*s.o.*); **(c)** *Fig* **p. un auteur,** to plagiarize an author, to steal from an author.

pilleur, -euse [pijœr, -øz] **1** *adj* pillaging, plundering, looting. **2** *n* pillager, plunderer; (*lors d'une émeute*) looter; **c'est un p. d'idées,** he's always stealing ideas from people; *Nau* **p. d'épaves,** wrecker.

pilon [pilɔ̃] *nm* **(a)** *Pharm etc* pestle; *Tech* (earth) rammer, punner; **p. mécanique,** power hammer; *Fig* **mettre un livre au p.,** to pulp a book; **(b)** (*cuisse (de poulet)*) drumstick; **(c)** (*jambe de bois*) wooden leg.

pilonnage [pilɔnaʒ] *nm* pounding, ramming; *Spéc* punning; *Mil* heavy bombing, shelling.

pilonner [pilɔne] *vt* **(a)** (*écraser*) to pound (*drugs etc*); to pulp (*paper*); to ram, to beat, to pun (*earth, concrete etc*); **(b)** *Mil* to shell, to bombard.

pilori [pilɔri] *nm* pillory; *Fig* **clouer** *ou* **mettre qn au p.,** to pillory s.o..

pilo-sébacé, -ée [pilosebase] *adj Anat* pilosebaceous.

pilosité [pilozite] *nf Anat* hairiness; *Spéc* pilosity; **p.**

normale/excessive, normal/excessive hair growth; **p. faciale,** facial hair.

pilot [pilo] *nm* **(a)** *Constr* pile; **p. de pont,** bridge pile; **(b)** *Tech* (*chiffons*) = cloth used in paper-making.

pilotage [pilɔtaʒ] *nm* **(a)** *Nau* pilotage, piloting; **(droits** *ou* **frais de) p.,** pilotage (dues); **(b)** *Av* pilotage, piloting, flying; **poste de p.,** cockpit; (*in larger aircraft*) flight deck; **p. automatique,** automatic piloting; **école de p.,** flying school; **le p. d'un jumbo-jet ne s'apprend pas en un mois,** you can't learn to fly a jumbo jet in the space of a month.

pilote [pilɔt] *nm* **(a)** *Av Nau* pilot; (*conducteur*) driver (*of racing car etc*); *Av* **p. d'essai,** test pilot; *Av* **p. de ligne,** airline pilot; **p. breveté,** *Av* licensed pilot; *Mil Av* certified pilot; **p. automatique,** automatic pilot, *F* George; **bateau p.,** pilot boat, cutter; *Fig* **usine/installation p.,** pilot factory/plant; **université p.,** experimental university; **(b)** (*poisson*) pilot fish.

piloter [pilɔte] *vt Nau* to pilot (*ship*); *Av* to pilot, to fly (*aircraft*); (*conduire*) to drive, to pilot (*racing car etc*); *F* **p. qn dans Londres,** to guide *or* show s.o. round London.

pilotis [pilɔti] *nm Constr* piling; **bâti sur p.,** built on piles.

pilou [pilu] *nm Tex* flannelette, cotton flannel.

pilulaire [pilylɛr] *adj Pharm* pilular.

pilule[pilyl] *nf Pharm* pill, tablet; **la p. abortive,** the abortion pill; **la p.,** (*contraceptive*) the pill; **elle prend la p.,** she's on the pill; *Fig F* **prendre une** *ou* **la p.,** to have a crushing defeat, to take a hammering, to be beaten hollow; *Fig* **avaler la p.,** to bite the bullet; *Fig* **la p. était amère,** it was a bitter pill to swallow; *Fig* **dorer la p.,** to sugar the pill.

pimbêche [pɛ̃bɛʃ] **1** *nf* girl *or* woman who puts on airs. **2** *adj* **elle est un peu p.,** *F* she's a bit stuck-up.

piment [pimɑ̃] *nm Bot* pimento, capsicum; *Fig* (*piquant*) piquancy, spice; *Culin* **p. rouge,** red chilli, pimento; **p. doux,** red pepper; **une fille qui ne manque pas de p.,** a girl with something striking about her; **donner du p. à une histoire,** to add piquancy *or* spice to a story.

pimenté [pimɑ̃te] *adj Culin* spicy, highly spiced, hot; *Fig* spicy (*story*).

pimenter [pimɑ̃te] *vt Culin* to season (*sth*) with pimento *or* with red pepper; *Fig* (*relever*) to give piquancy *or* spice to (*a story*).

pimpant [pɛ̃pɑ̃] *adj* smart, spruce, trim (*dress, person*); **une ville pimpante,** a neat, elegant town.

pimprenelle [pɛ̃prənɛl] *nf Bot* burnet, bloodwort.

pin [pɛ̃] *nm* **(a)** (*arbre*) pine (tree); **p. maritime,** maritime pine; **p. d'Écosse** *ou* **sylvestre,** Scots pine; **p. pignon** *ou* **parasol,** umbrella pine; **p. de montagne,** silver pine, white pine; **p. de Virginie,** scrub pine; **pomme de p.,** (*pin*) pine cone; (*sapin*) fir cone; **(b)** (*bois*) pine(wood).

pinacle [pinakl] *nm* pinnacle; *Fig* **porter qn au p.,** to praise s.o. to the skies; **être au p.,** to be at the top.

pinacothèque [pinakɔtɛk] *nf* picture gallery, art gallery.

pinaillage [pinajaʒ] *nm F* quibbling, hair-splitting.

pinailler [pinaje] *vi F* to quibble, to split hairs, to be finicky (*over a piece of work*); **p. sur les détails,** to quibble over details.

pinailleur, -euse [pinajœr, -øz] *F* **1** *adj* quibbling, nit-picking. **2** *n* quibbler, nitpicker.

pinard [pinar] *nm F* wine, vino; (*de qualité inférieure*) plonk.

pinasse [pinas] *nf Nau* pinnace, shallop.

pinçage [pɛ̃saʒ] *nm* pinching off, nipping off (*of buds*).

pince [pɛ̃s] *nf* **(a)** (*outil*) pliers; (*aux mâchoires recourbées*) pincers; *Tech* tongs; *Chir* forceps; **p. à épiler,** tweezers; **pince(s) coupante(s),** cutting pliers, wire cutters; **p. universelle,** (universal) pliers;
(b) (*pincette*) clip; **p. de cravate,** tie pin *or* clip; **p. à vélo,** bicycle clip; **p. à sucre,** sugar tongs; **p. à ongles,** nail clippers; **p. à papier,** paper clip; **p. à linge,** clothes peg; *Chir* **p. hémostatique,** artery clip; *El* **p. de raccordement,** connecting clamp, connector; **p. pour fil terminal,** terminal clamp;
(c) (*pied de chèvre*) crowbar;
(d) (*patte*) pincer, claw, nipper (*of crab etc*);
(e) *F* (*main*) paw, mitt;
(f) incisor (*of herbivorous animal*);
(g) *F* toe, point (*of horse's hoof or shoe*); *F* **aller à pinces,** to foot it;
(h) *Couture* dart, pleat.

pincé [pɛ̃se] *adj* stiff, starchy; (*serré*) tight, stiff; **sourire p.,** tight-lipped smile; **répondre d'un ton p.,** to answer stiffly *or* starchily; **nez p.,** thin nose; **les lèvres pincés,** with pursed lips *or* lips pursed, tight-lipped; **instrument à cordes pincées,** plucked stringed instrument.

pinceau, -eaux [pɛ̃so] *nm* **(a)** (*brosse*) (paint)brush; **coup de p.,** brush stroke; **(b)** *Fig* (*technique, manière*) brushwork; **(c)** *F Vieilli* (*pied*) foot; **(d)** *Opt* **p. de lumière,** pencil of light.

pincée [pɛ̃se] *nf* pinch (*of salt, snuff etc*).

pince-fesses [pɛ̃sfɛs] *nm inv F* shindig, knees-up, bash.

pincement [pɛ̃smɑ̃] *nm* **(a)** (*fait de pincer*) pinching, nipping; **(b)** *Fig* (*sensation vive, douloureuse*) pang, twinge (*of regret etc*); **il a eu un p. au cœur,** his heart missed a beat; **(c)** *Mus* plucking (*of guitar strings etc*); **(d)** pinching off, nipping off (*of buds*).

pince-monseigneur [pɛ̃smɔ̃sɛɲœr] *nf* (burglar's) jemmy; (*pl pinces-monseigneur*).

pince-nez [pɛ̃sne] *nm inv* pince-nez.

pincer [pɛ̃se] *v* **(je pinçai(s); n. pinçons) 1** *vt* **(a)** to pinch, to nip; **son grand-père lui pinça la joue,** his grandfather pinched his cheek; *F* **ça pince dur ce matin!,** it's pretty nippy this morning; **p. les lèvres,** to purse one's lips; **(b)** to nip off (*buds*); to top (*plant*); **(c)** *Mus* to pluck (*harp strings etc*); **(d)** *Couture* to put darts in (*a garment*); **(e)** *F* (*attraper*) to grip, to hold firm(ly); **p. un voleur,** to catch a thief; **se faire p.,** to get caught *or* nicked, to cop it; *F* **en p. pour qn,** to be keen on *or* crazy about s.o.. **2 se pincer** *vpr* **se p. le doigt dans la porte,** to catch one's finger in the door; **se p. le nez,** to hold one's nose.

pince-sans-rire [pɛ̃ssɑ̃rir] **1** *n inv* person of dry (and ironical) humour. **2** *adj* **répondre d'un air p.-s.-r.,** to answer drily *or* deadpan.

pincette [pɛ̃sɛt] *nf* (*petite pince*) tweezers; **pincettes,** (fire) tongs, pair of (fire) tongs; *Fig F* **il n'est pas à prendre avec des pincettes,** (*il est sale*) I wouldn't touch him with a bargepole *or Am* with a ten foot pole; (*il est de très mauvaise humeur*) he's like a bear with a sore head.

pinçon [pɛ̃sɔ̃] *nm* pinch mark.

pindarique [pɛ̃darik] *adj Hist Litt* Pindaric (*ode*).

pinéal, -aux [pineal, -o] *adj Anat* pineal.

pineau [pino] *nm* = (type of) apéritif made from wine and brandy.

pinède [pinɛd] *nf,* **pineraie** [pinrɛ] *nf* pine forest, pinewood.

pingouin [pɛ̃gwɛ̃] *nm* penguin; (*de la famille des macareux*) auk; **p. royal,** king penguin.

ping-pong [piŋpɔ̃g] *nm* (*no pl*) ping pong, table tennis.

pingre [pɛ̃gr] **1** *adj Péj* miserly, mean, stingy. **2** *n Péj* miser, skinflint, *Am* tightwad.

pingrerie [pɛ̃grəri] *nf Péj* stinginess, niggardliness.

pinot [pino] *nm* Pinot grape.

pin's [pinz] *nm inv* lapel pin, *Br* badge.

pinson [pɛ̃sɔ̃] *n* finch; **être gai comme un p.,** to be as happy as a lark.

pintade [pɛ̃tad] *nf* guinea fowl; **p. mâle,** guinea cock; **p. femelle,** guinea hen.

pintadeau, -eaux [pɛ̃tado] *nm* young guinea fowl, guinea poult.

pinte [pɛ̃t] *nf* **(a)** *Arch* pint (0.93 litres); *Eng US* pint; *Can* quart; **(b)** *F Vieilli* **se payer une p. de bon sang,** to have a good time *or* a good laugh.

pinter [pɛ̃te] *Arg* **1** *vi* to booze; to swill (*beer, wine*). **2 se pinter** *vpr* to booze; (*s'enivrer*) to get tight *or* sozzled *or* plastered; **il (s')est pinté,** he's tight *or* sozzled *or* plastered.

pin up [pinœp] *nf inv* (*en photo*) pinup (girl); (*jolie fille*) dolly bird.

pinyin [pinjin] *nm Ling* Pinyin.

pioche [pjɔʃ] *nf* **(a)** (*outil*) pickaxe, *US* pickax, pick; *Agr* mattock; *Fig F* **tête de p.,** pig-headed person; **(b)** (*dominos*) stock, pile.

piocher [pjɔʃe] **1** *vt* **(a)** (*creuser*) to dig (with a pick), to pick; **(b)** *F* (*travailler*) to grind at, to swot up (*sth*); **p. son allemand,** to swot up *or* mug up one's German. **2** *vi* **(a)** (*fouiller*) to dig, to delve (**dans,** into); **(b)** (*dominos*) to draw from the stock.

piocheur, -euse [pjɔʃœr, -øz] **1** *adj F* hardworking. **2** *n Scol F Vieilli* slogger; *Péj* swot. **3** *nf Constr* **piocheuse,** digger, mechanical excavator.

piolet [pjɔlɛ] *nm* ice axe.

pion [pjɔ̃] *nm* **(a)** *Scol F* prefect (*paid to supervise pupils*); **(b)** *Échecs* pawn; **(c)** (*dans d'autres jeux*) piece; (*aux dames*) draught(sman), *US* checker; *Fig* **n'être qu'un p. (sur l'échiquier),** to be only a pawn in the game.

pioncer [pjɔ̃se] *vi* **(je pionçai(s); n. pionçons)** *Arg* to have a kip *or* a snooze *or* forty winks *or* some shut-eye.

pionne [pjɔn] *nf Scol F* prefect (*paid to supervise pupils*).

pionnier [pjɔnje] *nm* pioneer; **le p. du cinéma parlant,** the pioneer of talking pictures; **j'admire son esprit p.,** I admire his pioneering spirit.

pipe¹ [pip] *nf* **(a)** pipe; **p. de bruyère/en terre,** briar/clay pipe; **fumer la p.,** to smoke a pipe; *Fig F* **casser sa p.,** to kick the bucket; **nom d'une p.!,** heavens above!; *F* **20 francs par tête de p.,** 20 francs a head; *F* **se fendre la p.,** to split one's sides laughing, to laugh one's head off; *Vulg* **tailler une p. à qn,** to give s.o. a blowjob; **(b)** *(contenu)* pipeful (of tobacco); **(c)** *Arg Vieilli (cigarette)* ciggy, *Br* fag; **(d)** *Région (futaille)* (large) cask, barrel.

pipe² [pajp] *nm (tuyau)* pipe(-line) *(for liquid, gas)*.

pipeau, -eaux [pipo] *nm* **(a)** *Mus* (reed) pipe; **p. de chasse,** bird call; **(b) pipeaux,** limed twigs *(to snare birds)*.

pipée [pipe] *nf* bird snaring, bird catching *(with bird calls and limed twigs)*.

pipelet, -ette [piplɛ, -ɛt] **1** *n F Vieilli* concierge, porter, *esp US* janitor. **2** *nf* **une pipelette,** a gossip, a chatterbox.

pipe(-)line [piplin, pajplajn] *nm* pipeline; *(pl pipe(-)lines)*.

piper [pipe] **1** *vi F* **ne pas p. (mot),** not to say a word, to keep silent, to keep mum. **2** *vt* **(a)** *(attraper avec des appeaux)* to lure *(birds) (by means of bird calls)*; *Fig* **se faire p.,** to be taken in; **(b)** *(truquer)* to load *(dice)*; to mark *(cards)*; *Fig* **les dés sont pipés,** the dice are loaded.

piperade [pip(ə)rad] *nf*, **pipérade** [piperad] *nf Culin* = (kind of) omelette with peppers and tomatoes.

pipi¹ [pipi] *nm F* pee; *Enf* wee-wee; **faire p.,** to piddle, to pee; *Enf* to wee-wee, to have a wee-wee; **aller faire p.,** to go to the loo, to go for a pee; **il y a du p. de chien sur le tapis,** the dog's made a puddle on the carpet; *F Péj* **c'est du p. de chat,** *(ce thé, ce café)* it's dishwater.

pipi² *nm*, **pipit** [pipit] *nm* pipit; **p. des prés,** meadow pipit, meadow titlark.

pipistrelle [pipistrɛl] *nf Zool* (small) bat, pipistrelle.

piquage [pikaʒ] *nm* (machine) stitching.

piquant [pikɑ̃] **1** *adj* **(a)** *(pointu)* prickling *(sensation)*; pointed *(object)*; prickly, thorny *(plant)*; stinging *(nettle)*; bristly, prickly *(beard)*;

(b) biting *(wind)*;

(c) piquant, spicy, hot *(taste)*; *Culin* **sauce piquante,** piquant sauce; **moutarde piquante,** hot mustard; *F* **eau piquante,** fizzy water;

(d) *Fig (caustique)* mordant; **remarques piquantes,** cutting remarks;

(e) *Fig (qui stimule la curiosité, l'intérêt)* piquant, striking *(beauty)*; **une petite brune piquante,** a striking little brunette.

2 *nm* **(a)** *(épine)* prickle, thorn *(of plant)*; quill, spine *(of porcupine)*; bristle *(of hedgehog)*; spike, barb *(of barbed wire etc)*;

(b) *F (agrément)* piquancy, pungency *(of style)*; **cette fille a du p.,** that girl is rather striking *or* strikingly attractive; **le p. du changement,** the attraction of change; **le changement donne du p. à la vie,** variety is the spice of life.

pique¹ [pik] **1** *nf Arch (armement)* pike; *(of picador)* lance. **2** *nm Cartes* spade(s); **valet de p.,** jack of spades; **il me reste encore trois piques,** I still have three spades left (in my hand).

pique² *nf* **(a)** *(méchanceté)* taunt, spiteful remark, *F* dig; **envoyer** *ou* **lancer des piques à qn,** to get at s.o., to have a dig *or* a go at s.o.; **(b)** *Vieilli (brouille)* pique, ill-feeling.

piqué, -ée [pike] **1** *adj* **(a)** quilted *(coverlet, garment)*; **p. à la machine,** machine-stitched; *(matelassé)* machine-quilted;

(b) *(marqué par les vers)* wormeaten *(wood, book)*; *(marqué par l'humidité)* (damp *or* rust *or* mould-) spotted *(mirror etc)*; foxed *(page, engraving)*; pitted *(metal)*; *Fig* **ciel p. d'étoiles,** sky studded with stars; **une histoire qui n'est pas piquée des hannetons** *ou* **des vers,** one heck of a story; **une recette qui n'est piquée des hannetons** *ou* **des vers,** a recipe that couldn't be bettered, one heck of a (good) recipe;

(c) *F* batty, barmy, loony; **il faudrait être p. pour ne pas en profiter,** you'd (have to) be crazy not to take advantage of it;

(d) *(acide)* sour, tart *(wine)*;

(e) *Mus* staccato *(notes)*.

2 *nm* **(a)** *Av* **descente en p.,** vertical dive, nose dive; **bombardement en p.,** dive bombing;

(b) *Tex (matelassure)* quilting piqué.

3 *n F* nutter, loony; **c'est une vieille piquée,** she's an old nutter *or* loony.

pique-assiette [pikasjɛt] *n inv F* scrounger, sponger; *US* freeloader.

pique-bœuf [pikbœf] *nm* beefeater, oxpecker; *(pl pique-bœufs* [pikbø]*)*.

pique-feu [pikfø] *nm inv* poker.

pique-fleurs [pikflœr] *nm inv* (glass) flower holder.

pique-nique [piknik] *nm* picnic; **faire un p.-n.,** to go for a picnic, to (have a) picnic; *(pl pique-niques)*.

pique-niquer [piknike] *vi* to (have a) picnic.

pique-niqueur, -euse [piknikœr, -øz] *n* picnicker; *(pl pique-niqueurs, -euses)*.

piquer [pike] **1** *vt* **(a)** *(percer avec pointe)* to prick; *(d'une guêpe etc)* to sting; *(d'une puce)* to bite; *(aiguillonner)* to spur on *(horse)*; to goad *(ox)*; *F* **quelle mouche vous pique?,** what's eating you?, what's getting (at) you?; **p. un cheval de l'éperon,** to prick *or* spur a horse; **p. des deux,** to spur on one's horse; *(s'en aller à cheval)* to gallop off; *Fig* to rush *or* dash off; **la fumée me pique les yeux,** the smoke makes my eyes sting *or* smart;

(b) *Méd* to give *(s.o.)* an injection; **se faire p. contre qch,** to be vaccinated against sth; *F* **p. un chien,** to put a dog down;

(c) *(offenser, froisser)* to pique, to offend *(s.o.)*; **p. qn au vif,** to cut s.o. to the quick; **p. l'amour-propre de qn,** to hurt *or* wound s.o.'s self-esteem *or* pride;

(d) *(exciter)* to arouse, to excite; **p. l'attention,** to arouse the attention; **p. la curiosité de qn,** to arouse *or* excite s.o.'s curiosity;

(e) *(trouer) (acide, vers)* to eat into; *(tacheter)* to spot, to mark; **mains piquées de taches de rousseur,** freckled *or* freckly hands;

(f) *(coudre)* to prick, to puncture; *Couture* to (back) stitch; to quilt *(bedspread etc)*; **p. du cuir,** to stitch leather; **p. (à la machine),** to machine (stitch);

(g) *Culin* **p. de la viande,** to lard meat; **rôti piqué d'ail,** joint stuck with garlic; **p. des petits pois,** to stab peas;

(h) *Mus* **p. une note,** to play a note staccato; *Nau* **p. l'heure,** to strike the hour;

(i) *F* to pinch, to swipe **(qch à qn,** sth from s.o.);

(j) *(accrocher)* to stick, to insert *(sth into sth)*; **p. une photo au mur,** to pin a photo on *or* to the wall;

(k) *F* **p. un cent mètres,** to sprint (off), to go into a sprint; **p. un plongeon** *ou* **une tête,** to take a header, to dive; **p. un roupillon,** to have forty winks; **p. une crise,** to throw a fit; **p. une crise de larmes,** to burst into tears; **p. un soleil** *ou* **un fard,** to go bright red, to blush.

2 *vi* **(a)** *Av* **p. (du nez),** to nosedive; *Nau* **p. de l'avant,** to go down by the bows;

(b) *(qui picote)* to make a thing sting *or* smart; **moutarde qui pique,** hot mustard; *F* **eau qui pique,** fizzy water; **vent qui pique,** keen *or* biting wind; **ça pique,** it stings; *(to unshaven man)* you're all bristly;

(c) les abeilles piquent, les mouches ne piquent pas, bees sting, flies don't.

3 se piquer *vpr* **(a)** *(se blesser)* to prick oneself; *(se faire une piqûre)* to give oneself an injection; *(se droguer)* to inject oneself; **il se pique,** he's a needle-user;

(b) *(se froisser)* to take offence, to get irritated;

(c) se p. de faire qch, to pride oneself on doing sth; **se p. de littérature,** to pride oneself on one's knowledge of literature; **se p. au jeu,** to get excited over *or* to get into a game;

(d) *(se couvrir de taches)* to get *or* go *or* become spotted *(with rust, mould etc)*; *(of metals)* to pit; *(of wood)* to get *or* become wormeaten, to get woodworm; *(of clothes etc)* to get *or* become motheaten; *(devenir acide) (of wine)* to turn acid, to (turn) sour.

piquet¹ [pikɛ] *nm* **(a)** *(pieu)* stake, post; *(plus petit)* peg; **mettre** *ou* **attacher les chevaux au p.,** to tether the horses; **p. de tente,** tent peg; **droit/raide comme un p.,** as straight as a ramrod/as stiff as a poker; **(b)** *Mil etc* picket; **p. d'incendie,** fire picket; **piquets de grève,** strike pickets; **p. volant,** flying picket; **(c)** *Scol* **envoyer qn au p.,** to send s.o. to stand in the corner; **être au p.,** = to stand in the corner.

piquet² *nm Cartes* piquet; **faire un p.,** to play a hand at piquet.

piquetage [piktaʒ] *nm Tech* staking (out).

piqueter [pikte] *vt* **(je piquette, n. piquetons; je piquetterai) (a)** *(jalonner)* to stake out, to mark out *(ground etc)*; **(b)** *(marquer)* to spot, to dot; **piqueté de noir,** dotted *or* speckled with black.

piquette [pikɛt] *nf* **(a)** marc diluted with water; *Péj* cheap (and nasty) wine, *F* plonk; *F* **ça n'était pas de la p.,** that was no small matter; **(b)** *Arg (râclée)* thrashing, hammering; **prendre une p.,** to get a good thrashing, to get a hammering.

piqueur, -euse [pikœr, -øz] **1** *nm* **(a)** *(à la chasse)* whipper-in; *Equitation* groom; **(b)** *Min etc* hewer, pickman;

(c) *Rail* platelayer, *US* tracklayer. **2** *n Ind* (leather) stitcher. **3** *adj Zool* **insecte p.,** stinging insect.
piquoir [pikwar] *nm Tech* (draughtsman's) needle.
piqûre [pikyr] *nf* **(a)** (*petite blessure*) sting, bite (*of insect*); **p. d'épingle,** pinprick; **(b)** *Méd* (hypodermic) injection, *F* shot, jab; **faire une p. à qn,** to give s.o. an injection; **(c)** (*trou*) puncture, small hole; pit (*in metal etc*); **p. de vers,** wormhole (*in wood,* book); **p. de mites,** moth-hole (*in garment*); **p. d'aiguille,** pinhole (*in leather etc*); **(d)** *Couture* (back)stitching (*of material, leather*); **(point de) p.,** lockstitch (*of sewing machine*); **(e)** (*tache*) spot, speck (*of rust, dust, mould*); foxing (*of paper*); pitting (in metal).
piranha [pirana] *nm* piranha (fish).
piratage [pirataʒ] *nm* pirating; **p. informatique,** hacking; **p. de cassettes,** bootlegging; **p. d'un livre,** plagiarizing a book.
pirate [pirat] **1** *nm* **(a)** (*des mers*) pirate; **p. de l'air,** hijacker, skyjacker; **(b)** (*voleur, filou*) pirate, shark; (*écrivain, artiste*) plagiarist. **2** *adj Fig* clandestine; *Rad* **station p.,** pirate station.
pirater [pirate] *vt* to pirate (*recording*); to bootleg (*cassette*); to plagiarize (*author, essay*); *Ordinat* to hack.
piraterie [piratri] *nf* **(a)** (act of) piracy; *Av* **p. aérienne,** hijacking, skyjacking; **(b)** *Fig* (*escroquerie*) piracy; **c'est de la p.,** it's daylight robbery.
pire [pir] **1** *adv* worse; **je chante/cuisine encore p. que lui,** I sing/cook even worse than he (does). **2** *adj* **(a)** (*comp*) worse; **cela est bien p.,** that's much worse; **le remède est p. que le mal,** the cure is worse than the disease; *Prov* **il n'est p. eau que l'eau qui dort,** still waters run deep; **rien n'est p. que ...,** nothing is worse than ...; **ce qui est p.,** what is worse; **(b)** (*superl*) worst; **le p., la p., les pires,** the worst; **un voyou de la p. espèce,** a lout of the worst kind; **nos pires erreurs,** our worst mistakes. **3** *nm* **le p. de l'histoire, c'est que ...,** the worst thing about it is that ...; **pour le meilleur et pour le p.,** for better or for worse; **s'attendre au p.,** to expect the worst.
Pirée (le) [ləpire] *nm* Piraeus.
piriforme [pirifɔrm] *adj* pyriform.
pirogue [pirɔg] *nf* pirogue, (dugout) canoe.
piroguier [pirɔgje] *nm* boatman (*in a pirogue*).
pirouette [pirwɛt] *nf* **(a)** (*danse*) *& Equitation* pirouette; *Fig F* **répondre par une p.** *ou* **des pirouettes,** to sidestep *or* dodge the question, to give a facetious answer; **(b)** *Fig* (*revirement*) reversal *or* change of opinion, about-turn, volte-face, turnaround.
pirouetter [pirwete] *vi* to pirouette.
pis[1] [pi] *nm* udder (*of cow etc*).
pis[2] **1** *adv comp* **p. que tout cela,** worse than all that; **il y a p.,** there is *or* are worse; **de p. en p.,** worse and worse; **aller de mal en p.,** to go from bad to worse; **tant p.!,** it can't be helped, never mind! **2** *adj* **(a)** (*comp*) **cela serait encore p.,** that would be worse still; **et qui p. est,** and what is worse; **le malade est p. que jamais,** the patient is worse; **(b)** (*superl*) **ce qu'il y a de p.,** what is worst; (*ce qu'il y a de pire*) the worst there is. **3** *n* **(a)** (*comp*) **pour ne pas dire p.,** to say no more; **il a fait tout cela et p.,** he did all that and (something even) worse; **dire p. que pendre de qn,** to badmouth s.o.; **(b)** (*superl*) **le p.,** the worst; **faire p.,** to do the worst; **en mettant les choses au p.,** if the worst comes to the worst; **au p. aller,** at the very worst.
pis(-)aller [pizale] *nm inv* makeshift; (*solution temporaire*) stopgap; (*dernier recours*) last resort.
piscicole [pisikɔl] *adj* piscicultural.
pisciculteur, -trice [pisikyltœr, -tris] *n* fish breeder, *Fml* pisciculturist.
pisciculture [pisikyltyr] *nf* fish breeding, *Fml* pisciculture.
pisciforme [pisifɔrm] *adj* pisciform.
piscine [pisin] *nf* **(a)** (*bassin de natation*) swimming pool; **p. couverte/en plein air,** indoor/open-air *or* outdoor swimming pool; **p. publique,** swimming baths; **(b)** *Rel* piscina.
piscivore [pisivɔr] *adj* piscivorous.
Pise [piz] *nf* Pisa.
pisé [pize] *nm Constr* cob.
pissaladière [pisaladjɛr] *nf Culin Région* = (open) onion and tomato tart, garnished with anchovies or sardines and olives.
pissat [pisa] *nm* urine (*of horse, donkey etc*).
pisse [pis] *nf Vulg* piss, pee.
pisse-froid [pisfrwa] *nm inv F* (*personne morose*) wet blanket.
pissenlit [pisɑ̃li] *nm* dandelion; *F* **manger les pissenlits par la racine,** to be pushing up the daisies.
pisser [pise] *Vulg* **1** *vi* **(a)** to (have a) piss, to (have a) pee: **il a pissé dans sa culotte,** he's pissed *or* peed *or* wet his pants; **c'est comme si je pissais dans un violon,** it's like peeing into the wind; **laisse p.!,** leave it!, forget it!; **(b)** *F* (*fuir*) to leak; (*en plus grande quantité*) to gush out; **tonneau qui pisse,** leaky barrel. **2** *vt* **p. du sang,** to pass blood with the urine; **son bras pissait le sang,** there was blood gushing *or* pouring from his arm, his arm was pouring with blood. **3** *v impers* **ça pisse dur,** it's pissing down.
pissette [pisɛt] *nf Ch* wash(ing) bottle.
pisseur, -euse [pisœr, -øz] *Vulg* **1** *n* **(a) c'est un p.,** he's always going for a piss *or* pee, he's got a weak bladder; **(b)** *Journ Péj* **p. de copie,** writer who churns out rubbish. **2** *nf* **pisseuse,** little girl; *Péj* brat.
pisseux, -euse [pisø, -øz] *adj F* **(a)** (*qui sent l'urine*) smelling of urine; (*taché par l'urine*) stained with urine, urine-stained; **(c)** *Fig* (*passé, jauni*) faded, washed out, wishy-washy, yellowy.
pisse-vinaigre [pisvinɛgr] *nm F* (*avare*) skinflint; (*qui se plaint toujours*) grumbler, grouser.
pissoir [piswar] *nm,* **pissotière** [pisɔtjɛr] *nf F* (public) urinal; (*dans la rue*) street urinal.
pistache [pistaʃ] **1** *nf* pistachio (nut); *Culin* **glace à la p.,** pistachio ice-cream. **2** *adj inv* pistachio (green).
pistachier [pistaʃje] *nm* pistachio tree.
pistage [pistaʒ] *nm* tracking, trailing, tailing.
pistard [pistar] *nm Cyclisme* track racer.
piste [pist] *nf* **(a)** track, trail, scent; **suivre la p.,** to follow the track *or* the footprints; **être sur la p. de qn/qch,** to be on the track of s.o./sth; **la police a plusieurs pistes,** the police have several leads; **brouiller les pistes,** to confuse the issue; **suivre une fausse p.,** to be on the wrong track; **être sur la bonne p.,** to be on the right track;
(b) *Sp* racetrack; (*athlétisme*) running track; (*course automobile*) racing track; **p. cendrée,** cinder track; **tour de p.,** lap; *Aut etc* **p. de vitesse,** racing track; **p. d'essai,** test track; *Sp* **p. de patinage,** skating rink; **p. de ski,** (ski) piste, (ski)run; **p. artificielle,** artificial *or* dry ski slope; **p. de danse,** dance floor; **p. (de cirque),** (circus) ring; **en p.!,** into the ring!; *Fig* (*au travail*) get cracking!;
(c) *Av* runway; **p. d'envol,** take-off strip; **p. d'atterrissage,** landing strip;
(d) (*path*) track, trail; **p. pour cavaliers, p. cavalière,** bridle path; **p. cyclable,** cycle track;
(e) track (*of tape recorder*); **magnéto 4 pistes,** 4-track tape recorder; *Cin* **p. sonore,** soundtrack.
pister [piste] *vt* to track, to trail; **p. qn,** to follow *or* tail *or* shadow s.o..
pisteur [pistœr] *nm* ski run attendant *or* supervisor.
pistil [pistil] *nm Bot* pistil.
pistole [pistɔl] *nf* pistole.
pistolet [pistɔlɛ] *nm* **(a)** (*arme à feu*) pistol, (hand) gun; *Hist* **p. d'arçon,** horse pistol; *Mil etc* **p. de tir,** firing pistol; **p. à air comprimé,** air pistol; *Sp* **p. de starter,** starting pistol; **p. à bouchon,** popgun; **p. à eau,** water pistol; *Tech* **p. (à peinture), p. (vaporisateur),** paint gun, spray gun; **peinture au p.,** spray painting, spraying; **(b)** *Culin* (milk) roll; **(c)** (*instrument*) French curve; **(d)** *F* bedpan; **(e)** (*type bizarre*) queer *or* odd sort *or F* fish.
pistolet-mitrailleur [pistɔlɛmitrajœr] *nm* submachine gun, sten gun, tommy gun; (*pl pistolets-mitrailleurs*).
pistoleur [pistɔlœr] *nm Tech* paint-gun *or* spray-gun worker.
piston [pistɔ̃] *nm* **(a)** *MecE* piston (*of machine, pump, jack etc*); **p. à air/eau,** air/water piston; **tête de p.,** piston head; *Tech* **p. plongeur,** plunger (*of force pump etc*); ram (*of hydraulic press*); **(b)** *Fig* (*recommandation*) string-pulling; **avoir du p.,** to have friends in the right places, to have clout; **il a eu une place par p.,** someone pulled strings to get him the job; **(c)** *Mus* valve (*of cornet etc*); **cornet à pistons** *ou* **p.,** valve cornet.
pistonner [pistɔne] *vt* to use one's influence *or* one's clout to help (*s.o.*), to pull strings *or* wires for (*s.o.*); **il s'est fait p.,** he got someone to pull strings for him.
pistou [pistu] *nm Culin* pesto; **soupe de** *ou* **au p.,** vegetable soup served with pesto.
pitance [pitɑ̃s] *nf* **(a)** *Arch* (*in convent etc*) allowance (of food); **(b)** *Péj Vieilli* sustenance, food; **se faire une maigre p.,** to eke out a living.
pitchoun, -oune [pitʃun] *n Région* (*enfant*) bairn.
pitchpin [pitʃpɛ̃] *nm Bot* pitch pine.
piteusement [pitøzmɑ̃] *adv* piteously, miserably.
piteux, -euse [pitø, -øz] *adj* piteous, woeful, pitiable, miserable; **faire piteuse mine,** to look crestfallen; **p. résultat,** poor *or* miserable result; **être dans un p. état,** to

be in a poor way *or* a sorry state.

pithécanthrope [pitekɑ̃trɔp] *nm* pithecanthrope.

pithiviers [pitivje] *nm Culin* = puff pastry containing rum and almond-flavoured cream.

pitié [pitje] *nf* **(a)** (*compassion*) pity, compassion; **avoir p. de qn,** to pity s.o.; (*s'apitoyer*) to take *or* have pity on s.o.; (*épargner*) to have mercy on s.o.; **prendre p. de qn, prendre qn en p.,** to take pity on s.o.; **sans p.,** pitiless(ly), merciless(ly), ruthless(ly); **par p.,** out of pity; (*en implorant*) for pity's sake; **p.!,** (have) mercy!, for pity's sake!; **faire p.,** to arouse pity *or* compassion; **il me faisait p.,** I felt sorry for him; **cela faisait p. à voir,** it was pitiable to see (it); *Vieilli* **c'est p. qu'il soit resté seul,** it's sad that he should have been left alone; **(b)** (*commisération mêlée de mépris*) pity; **c'est à faire p.!,** it's lamentable!, it's pitiful!

piton [pitɔ̃] *nm* **(a)** *Tech* (metal) eye (bolt); **p. (d'alpiniste),** piton, peg; **p. à vis,** screw eye; **p. à boucle,** ring bolt; **(b)** (*sommet*) peak (*of mountain*).

pitoyable [pitwajabl] *adj* **(a)** (*digne de pitié*) pitiable, pitiful, piteous, lamentable (*tale, condition etc*); **(b)** *Péj* (*lamentable*) pathetic, lamentable (*excuse, joke etc*).

pitoyablement [pitwajabləmɑ̃] *adv* pitifully; **échouer p.,** to fail miserably.

pitre [pitr] *nm* (*bouffon*) (circus) clown; (*fou*) clown, buffoon; **faire le p.,** to clown (around), to play the fool.

pitrerie [pitrəri] *nf* clowning, (tom)foolery, buffoonery.

pittoresque [pitɔrɛsk] **1** *adj* picturesque; colourful, *US* colorful, graphic (*description, style*). **2** *nm* picturesqueness; vividness (*of style etc*).

pituitaire [pitɥitɛr] *adj Anat* pituitary.

pituite [pitɥit] *nf Anat* (*vomissement*) bile; *Arch* phlegm.

pivert [pivɛr] *nm* green woodpecker.

pivoine [pivwan] *nf Bot* peony; *Fig* **rouge comme une p.,** red as a beetroot.

pivot [pivo] *nm* **(a)** pivot; *MecE* pin, axis; swivel (*of gun etc*); fulcrum (*of lever*); (*in dentistry*) pivot, post; **p. à rotule,** ball pivot; **p. de compas** *ou* **de boussole,** centre pin of a compass; **à p., monté sur p.,** pivoted, swivelling; **canon à p.,** swivel gun; **(b)** *Fig* (*élément central*) mainspring, central figure (*of drama etc*); **(c)** *Bot* tap root.

pivotant [pivɔtɑ̃] *adj* **(a)** (*qui tourne*) pivoting, swivelling, revolving; **fauteuil p.,** swivel chair; **base pivotante,** swivel base; **(b)** *Bot* tap-rooted (*tree, plant*); **racine pivotante,** tap root.

pivoter [pivɔte] *vi* **(a)** (*tourner*) to pivot, to swivel, to revolve; to turn, to hinge (**sur,** (up)on); *Mil etc* (*of troops*) to wheel; **faire p. qch,** to turn *or* swivel sth round; **p. sur ses talons,** to swing round *or* pivot on one's heels; **(b)** *Bot* (*of plant*) to form a tap root.

pixel [piksɛl] *nm Ordinat* pixel.

pizza [pidzɑ] *nf* pizza.

pizzéria [pidzerja] *nf* pizzeria.

pizzicato [pidzikato] *nm Mus* pizzicato (passage); (*pl pizzicati*).

P.J. [peʒi] *nf F* (*abrév* **Police Judiciaire**) *Br* ≈ CID.

placage [plakaʒ] *nm* **(a)** (*fait de recouvrir*) veneering (*of wood*); facing (*of stone*); plating (*of metal*); **p. au chrome,** chrome *or* chromium plating; **(b)** (*matériau*) veneer; **bois de p.,** veneer; **(c)** *Rugby Fb* tackle.

placard [plakar] *nm* **(a)** (*armoire murale*) (wall) cupboard; *F* (*emploi, situation*) cushy job *or* number; *Fig* **un p. doré,** a gilded cage; *Fig* **mettre qn au p.,** to give s.o. a cushy job; **(b)** (*affichage*) poster, bill; *Journ* **p. publicitaire** *ou* **de publicité,** advertisement (*in newspaper*); **(c)** *Typ* **(épreuve en) p.,** galley (proof); **(d)** *Nau* patch (*on sail*); **(e)** *Tech* panel (*of door*); **(f)** *F* thick layer *or* coating.

placarder [plakarde] *vt* **(a) p. une affiche,** to stick a bill *or* poster on a wall; **p. un mur,** to stick bills *or* posters on a wall; **(b)** *Typ* to run to galley proofs.

placardeur [plakardœr] *nm Vieilli* billsticker, billposter.

place [plas] *nf* **(a)** (*lieu, endroit*) place, position; (*emplacement*) place; **changer sa chaise de p.,** to move *or* shift one's chair; **mettre en p.,** to put (*sth*) in its place; to put (*a gun, movie camera etc*) in position; **mise en p.,** putting into place *or* into position, setting, fitting, mounting (*of part of equipment*); **tout est à sa p.,** everything's in its place; **p. de parking,** parking place *or* space; **je n'ai pas trouvé de p. en ville,** I couldn't find any parking places *or* spaces in town; **remettez vos livres à leur p.,** put your books away; **ils y sont à leur p.,** they are not out of place there; **voulez-vous prendre ma p.?,** would you like to change places with me?; **il ne peut pas rester en p.,** he can't keep still; **il ne tient pas en p. aujourd'hui,** he is very fidgety today; **sur p.,** on the spot; *Constr* on site; **faire du sur p.,** to mark time, to stand still; **il lut la lettre sur p.,** he read the letter there and then *or* then and there; **personnel engagé sur p.,** staff employed locally; **rester sur p.,** to stay put; **la police sera sur p. dans quelques minutes,** the police will be on the scene *or* spot in a few minutes; **on trouve tout sur p.,** everything we *etc* need is here *or* will be there; **son nom a pris p. dans l'histoire,** his name has found a place in history;

(b) *Fig* (*condition, situation*) place; *Fig* **avoir sa p. au soleil,** to have one's place in the sun; **il finira par trouver sa p. dans ce milieu,** he'll eventually find a niche among those people; **je viens à la p. de mon père,** I've come instead of my father *or* in my father's place *or Fml* stead; **remettre qn à sa p.,** to put s.o. in his place; **à votre p. je ...,** in your place *or* if I were you I ...; **mets-toi à sa p.!,** put yourself in his position, look at things from his point of view;

(c) (*espace*) room; **occuper beaucoup de p.,** to take up a great deal of room; **nous n'avons pas de p. pour mettre un piano,** we have no room for a piano; **gagner de la place,** to make some (extra) room for oneself; **faire p. à qn/qch,** to make room *or* way for s.o./sth; *Vieilli* **(faites) p.!,** stand aside!; **faites-lui un peu de p.,** make room for him; **céder** *ou* **laisser la p. à qn,** to give way to s.o.;

(d) (*siège*) seat; **à vos places!,** take your seats!; **restez à votre p.,** stay in your seat, remain seated; **louer deux places au théâtre,** to book two seats at the theatre; **il n'y avait pas une p.,** there wasn't a seat to be found *or* to be had; **p. avant/arrière,** front/back seat (*in car*); **voiture à deux/à quatre places,** two-/four-seater (car); *Aut* **une deux places,** a two-seater; **prix des places,** (*transports publics*) fares; *Th etc* admission prices; **payer p. entière,** (*transports publics*) to pay full fare; *Th etc* to pay full price;

(e) (*appartenance, rôle*) place; **la p. de l'homme dans le monde,** man's place in the world; **sa famille tient une grande p. dans sa vie,** his family holds an important place in his life; **il aura toujours une p. dans mon cœur,** he'll always have a place in my heart;

(f) (*emploi, poste*) situation, post; **quitter/perdre sa p.,** to leave/to lose one's job; *Fig* **une personne en p.,** a person in high office; *Fig* **les gens en p.,** people in high places, people with influence; **le gouvernement en p.,** the government in office *or* power;

(g) (*lieu public*) square; **la p. Rouge,** Red Square; **p. du marché,** market place; **p. d'armes,** drill ground, parade ground;

(h) *Com Fin* market; **achats sur p.,** local purchases; **prix sur p.,** loco price; **être bien connu sur la p.,** to be a well-known player in the market; **avoir du crédit sur la p.,** to have credit (facilities) locally; *Banque Fin* **affaires sur la p. de Paris,** business on the Paris market;

(i) *Mil* **p. (forte, de guerre),** fortified place; (*ville*) fortress *or* fortified town;

(j) (*rang*) place, placing; **il a eu une bonne p. au concours,** he was well placed in the competition; **une p. d'honneur,** a place of honour.

placé [plase] *Courses de chevaux* **1** *adj* placed (*horse*); **arriver p.,** to be placed. **2** *nm* placed horse.

placebo [plasebo] *nm* placebo.

placement [plasmɑ̃] *nm* **(a)** (*fait de donner un emploi*) placing; (*fait d'attribuer un siège*) seating; **bureau** *ou* **agence de placement(s),** employment bureau *or* agency; **(b)** *Fin* investing (*of money*); (*argent*) investment; **faire des placements,** to invest (money), to make investments; **p. avantageux,** good investment; *F* **p. de père de famille,** blue chip (investment), gilt-edged investment.

placenta [plasɛ̃ta] *nm Obst* placenta; (*expulsé après accouchement*) after-birth, placenta.

placentaire [plasɛ̃tɛr] *adj Obst* placental.

placer [plase] *v* (**je plaçai(s); n. plaçons**) **1** *vt* **(a)** (*mettre à sa place*) to place, to put, to set (down); to seat (*spectators, guests etc*); **p. des invités autour d'une table,** to sit guests around a table; *Th etc* **p. qn,** to show s.o. to his seat; *Fig* **vous êtes mieux placés que moi pour en juger,** you're better placed than I (am) to judge; *Fig* **vous êtes bien placés pour le savoir,** you're in a position to know, you ought to know; **p. une sentinelle,** to post a soldier on sentry duty; **maison bien placée,** well situated house; **p. l'honnêteté au plus haut rang,** to put *or* set *or* place a high value on honesty, **confiance mal placée,** misplaced confidence;

(b) (*procurer un emploi*) to place (*s.o.*), to find a post *or* a job for (*s.o.*); **p. qn comme apprenti chez qn,** to apprentice s.o. to s.o.;

(c) (*vendre*) to sell (*goods*); **valeurs difficiles à p.,** bills difficult to negotiate;

(d) (*situer*) to set; **le lieu où Racine place l'action,** the place where Racine sets the action of the play;

(e) *(dire)* to get in; **il voulait à tout prix p. son histoire,** he was determined to get his anecdote in *(to the conversation etc)*; *F* **avec elle, on ne peut pas en p. une!,** with her, it's impossible to get a word in edgeways *or US* edgewise; **je n'ai pas pu p. un mot,** I couldn't get a word in edgeways *or US* edgewise;

(f) *Fin* to invest *(money)*.

2 se placer *vpr* **(a)** *(prendre sa place)* to take one's seat *or* one's place *(at table etc)*; *Mil Sp etc* to take up one's position; **dites-moi où me p.,** tell me where to sit; **si je me place à votre point de vue,** if I look at things from your point of view, *F* if I put myself in your shoes; **marchandises qui se placent facilement,** goods that sell readily;

(b) *(trouver un emploi)* to obtain *or* find a job; **se p. comme vendeuse,** to get a job as a salesgirl.

placet [plasɛ] *nm* **(a)** *Arch* petition, address; **(b)** *Jur* (plaintiff's) claim.

placette [plasɛt] *nf* (small) square.

placeur, -euse [plasœr, -øz] *n* **(a)** *(personne qui tient un bureau de placement)* employment agent *or* consultant; **(b)** steward *(at public meetings)*; *Cin Th* usher, *f* usherette.

placide [plasid] *adj* placid, calm.

placidement [plasidmɑ̃] *adv* placidly, calmly.

placidité [plasidite] *nf* placidity, calmness.

placier [plasje] *nm Com* **(a)** travelling salesman, traveller; **(b)** = person who allocates stall space in market.

plafond [plafɔ̃] *nm* **(a)** *Archit* ceiling; **p. à caissons,** coffered ceiling; **chambre haute/basse de p.,** high-/low-ceilinged room; *Fig F* **avoir une araignée au p.,** to have bats in the belfry; **(b)** *(toit)* roof *(of car, of cave)*; **(c)** *(maximum)* ceiling; **prix p.,** maximum price, ceiling (price); **fixer un p. à un budget,** to fix a ceiling to a budget; **p. des charges budgétaires,** spending limit, budgetary limit; **(d)** *Av* ceiling, flying height *(of aircraft)*; *Aut* top *or* maximum speed; *Météo* **p. (nuageux),** ceiling *(of clouds)*.

plafonnage [plafɔnaʒ] *nm Constr* ceiling work.

plafonnement [plafɔnmɑ̃] *nm* peaking, levelling off, *US* leveling off; **la production automobile est en plein p.,** car production has reached its ceiling *or* has peaked.

plafonner [plafɔne] **1** *vt* to put a ceiling in *(room)*. **2** *vi* **(a)** *Av* to fly at the ceiling; *Aut* to go at maximum *or* top speed; **(b)** *Fig (of price etc)* to reach a ceiling *or* a maximum, to peak; **la fréquentation des cinémas plafonne,** cinema attendance has reached a peak *or* is levelling off.

plafonneur [plafɔnœr] *nm Tech* plasterer of ceilings.

plafonnier [plafɔnje] *nm* ceiling light; *Aut* courtesy *or* interior light.

plage [plaʒ] *nf* **(a)** *(grève)* beach; **être/aller à la p.,** to be on/to go to the beach; **p. de sable/de galets,** sandy/pebble beach; **(b)** *(lieu touristique)* seaside resort; **(c)** *Nau* freeboard deck *(of battleship)*; **p. arrière,** *Nau* quarter deck; *Aut* window shelf; **(d)** area; *Opt* **p. lumineuse,** light area, high light; **(e)** *(durée)* time, period; *TV Rad* (time) segment *(of broadcast)*; **p. horaire très écoutée/regardée,** peak listening/viewing time *or* period; *Can* **p. fixe,** *(dans un horaire variable)* core time; **(f)** *Fig (éventail)* range; *Rad* **p. de réception (d'un appareil),** tuning range; *Com* **p. de prix,** price range; **(g)** track, band *(of gramophone record)*; **(h)** *(écart)* range; **p. de trafic du R.E.R.,** varying frequency of suburban train services *(in Paris)*.

plagiaire [plaʒjɛr] *n* plagiarist.

plagiat [plaʒja] *nm* plagiarism.

plagier [plaʒje] *vt (impf & pr sub* **n. plagiions, v. plagiiez)** to plagiarize.

plagiste [plaʒist] *n* beach attendant.

plaid [plɛd] *nm* travelling rug.

plaidable [plɛdabl] *adj Jur* pleadable.

plaidant [plɛdɑ̃] *adj Jur* pleading *(counsel)*; **les parties plaidantes,** the litigants.

plaider [plede] **1** *vt* to plead *(a cause)*; **p. la cause de qn,** to speak in favour of *or* defend s.o.; **son défenseur va p. la folie,** his counsel will plead insanity *or* will put forward a plea of insanity; **p. le faux pour savoir le vrai,** to make a false allegation in order to get at the truth; **p. coupable/non coupable,** to plead guilty/not guilty. **2** *vi (avocat)* to plead **(pour,** for; **contre,** against); *(plaignant)* to go to court, to litigate; **p. contre qn,** to take s.o. to court, to take proceedings against s.o.; *Fig* **p. pour** *ou* **en faveur de qn/qch,** to speak for s.o./sth, to defend s.o./sth. **3 se plaider** *vpr* **la cause s'est plaidée hier,** the case was heard yesterday.

plaideur, -euse [plɛdœr, -øz] *n* litigant.

plaidoirie [plɛdwari] *nf* counsel's speech.

plaidoyer [plɛdwaje] *nm Jur* address to the Court; *(esp by counsel for the defence)* speech for the defence; *Fig (défense passionnée)* defence plea.

plaie [plɛ] *nf* **(a)** *(blessure) & Fig* wound, sore; *(coupure)* cut; **rouvrir d'anciennes plaies,** to reopen old wounds; **retourner** *ou* **remuer le couteau** *ou* **le fer dans la p.,** to twist *or* turn the knife in the wound; **mettre le doigt sur la p.,** to put one's finger on the source of the trouble; **(b)** *(fléau)* affliction, evil, scourge; *(personne, chose)* pest, menace; **quelle p.!,** what a pest!; **les dix plaies d'Égypte,** the ten plagues of Egypt.

plaignant, -ante [plɛɲɑ̃, -ɑ̃t] *Jur* **1** *adj* **partie plaignante,** plaintiff, complainant, litigant. **2** *n* plaintiff, litigant.

plain [plɛ̃] **1** *adj* flat, level, even *(ground, surface)*; plane *(surface, geometry)*. **2** *nm* **le p.,** high tide.

plain-chant [plɛ̃ʃɑ̃] *nm Mus* plainsong, plainchant; *(pl plains-chants)*.

plaindre [plɛ̃dr] *v (prp* **plaignant**; *pp* **plaint**; *pr ind* **je plains, il plaint, n. plaignons, ils plaignent**; *pr sub* **je plaigne**; *impf* **je plaignais**; *p hist* **je plaignis**; *fu* **je plaindrai) 1** *vt* **(a)** *(témoigner de la compassion à)* to pity; **il est fort à p.,** he is greatly to be pitied; **elle n'est pas à p.,** *(elle n'a pas besoin de se faire des soucis)* she hasn't anything to worry about; *(elle ne mérite pas qu'on la plaigne)* she doesn't deserve any sympathy;

(b) *Arch & Région* to (be)grudge; **on n'a pas plaint l'argent,** there was no stint of money; **il ne plaint pas sa peine,** he spares himself no trouble.

2 se plaindre *vpr* to complain; *(se lamenter)* to moan, to groan; **se p. de qn/qch,** to complain of *or* about s.o./sth; *(critiquer)* to find fault with s.o./sth; **il n'y a pas de quoi vous p., vous n'avez pas à vous p.,** you have nothing to complain about, you shouldn't grumble; **se p. (de ce) que** (+ *sub*), to complain (about the fact) that ... .

plaine [plɛn] *nf* **(a)** *Géog* plain; **(b)** *Hist* **la P.,** the Plain (= *moderate deputies during the French Revolution*).

plain-pied [plɛ̃pje] *adv* **de p.-p.,** on a level; *(au même étage)* on one floor; **salon de p.-p. avec le jardin,** sitting room on a level with *or* at the same level as the garden; **deux surfaces de p.-p.,** two surfaces which are flush with (each other); *Fig* **nous sommes de p.-p.,** we are on an equal footing (with each other).

plainte [plɛ̃t] *nf* **(a)** *(cri, gémissement)* moan, groan; **(b)** *(revendication, protestation)* complaint; **sujet de p.,** subject of a complaint; **(c)** *Jur* indictment, complaint; **porter p., déposer une p. (contre qn),** to lodge a complaint (against s.o.) **(auprès de,** with); **p. en diffamation,** action for libel.

plaintif, -ive [plɛ̃tif, -iv] *adj* plaintive *(tone)*.

plaintivement [plɛ̃tivmɑ̃] *adv* plaintively.

plaire [plɛr] *v (prp* **plaisant**; *pp* **plu**; *pr ind* **je plais, il plaît, n. plaisons, ils plaisent**; *pr sub* **je plaise**; *impf* **je plaisais**; *p hist* **je plus**; *fu* **je plairai) 1** *vi* **p. à qn,** to please s.o.; **cet homme me plaît,** I like this man; **ce livre m'a plu,** I liked *or* enjoyed this book; **la nouvelle robe lui plaît beaucoup,** she's very pleased with the new dress; **cette offre devrait lui p.,** this offer should appeal to him; **chercher à p. à qn,** to try to please s.o.; **elle ne lui plaît pas,** he's not attracted to her, *F* he doesn't fancy her; *(du point de vue de son caractère à elle)* he doesn't care for her; **cela ne me plaît pas du tout,** I don't like that at all; **c'est ce qui plaît en ce moment,** it's what people seem to like just now; **il plaît,** people like him, he's popular; **je le ferai si cela me plaît,** I'll do it if I want to *or* if I feel like it.

2 *v impers* **s'il vous plaît,** please, *Vieilli* if you please; *F (pour insister)* if you please; **et pas n'importe qui, s'il vous plaît,** and not just anybody, if you please *or* if you don't mind; **vous plairait-il de nous accompagner?,** would you like to come with us?; *Vieilli & Région* **plaît-il?,** I beg your pardon?, what did you say?; **comme il vous plaira,** (just) as you like *or* please; **plaise à Dieu qu'il vienne!,** God grant *or* please God that he may come!; **à Dieu ne plaise (que ...),** God forbid (that ...); **plût au ciel que ...!,** would to heaven that ...!

3 se plaire *vpr* **(a)** *(s'aimer soi-même)* to admire oneself, *F* to fancy oneself; **elle se plaît dans cette robe,** she likes wearing that dress;

(b) *(s'aimer)* to be attracted to each other, *F* to fancy each other; **je crois qu'ils se plaisent,** I think they are attracted to each other, *F* I think they fancy each other;

(c) *(se trouver bien)* **je me plais beaucoup à Paris,** I enjoy *or* I love being in Paris; **se p. à faire qch,** to enjoy doing sth; **il ne se plaît pas ici,** he doesn't like it *or* he's unhappy here; **la vigne se plaît sur les coteaux,** the vine thrives *or* does well on hillsides; **ils se plaisent dans leur maison,** they like being in their house.

plaisamment [plɛzamɑ̃] *adv* **(a)** (*agréablement*) pleasantly; **(b)** (*drôlement*) funnily, amusingly; **(c)** *Litt* (*d'une façon ridicule*) ridiculously.

plaisance [plɛzɑ̃s] *nf* **(a) bateau de p.,** pleasure boat; **maison de p.,** country house; **navigation de p., la p.,** yachting; **(b)** *Arch* pleasure.

plaisancier [plɛzɑ̃sje] **1** *n* yachtsman. **2** *adj* yacht, for yachts; **voie plaisancière,** yacht lane.

plaisant [plɛzɑ̃] **1** *adj* **(a)** (*agréable*) pleasant, agreeable; **p. à l'œil,** pleasing to the eye; **(b)** (*drôle*) funny, amusing; (*d'un humour sec ou ironique*) droll; **(c)** *Vieilli* (*always before the noun*) ridiculous, absurd, ludicrous (*person, answer*). **2** *nm* **(a) le (plus) p. de l'affaire c'est que ...,** the funniest thing about it is that ...; **(b)** *Arch* wag, joker; **faire le p.,** to play *or* act the comedian; **mauvais p.,** person who plays nasty tricks.

plaisanter [plɛzɑ̃te] **1** *vi* **(a)** (*s'amuser, rire*) to joke, to jest; **elle aime bien p.,** she enjoys a joke; **il faut bien p., n'est-ce pas?,** we all have to have a joke from time to time, don't we?; **dire qch en plaisantant,** to say sth as a joke *or* in jest; **(b)** (*dire par jeu*) to joke; **vous plaisantez!,** you're joking!, you don't mean it!; **je ne plaisante pas,** I'm serious, I'm not joking; **c'est un homme avec qui on ne plaisante pas,** he is not a man to be trifled with; **on ne plaisante pas avec la justice,** the law is not to be trifled with; **il ne plaisante pas là-dessus** *ou* **sur ces choses-là,** he doesn't joke about things like that. **2** *vt* to tease (*s.o.*) (**sur qch,** about sth); to poke fun at (*s.o.*), to make fun of (*s.o.*).

plaisanterie [plɛzɑ̃tri] *nf* (*blague*) joke, jest; (*activité*) joking, jesting; **une fine p.,** a subtle joke; **faire des plaisanteries,** to tell *or* crack jokes; **faire des plaisanteries à qn,** to play tricks *or* (practical) jokes on s.o.; **une mauvaise p.,** a silly joke *or* prank; (*méchante*) a spiteful trick; **il nous a raconté une p. qui n'était pas drôle,** he told us a bad joke *or* a joke that wasn't funny; **tourner une chose en p.,** to laugh something off; **entendre la p.,** to know how to take a joke; **par p.,** for fun, for a joke.

plaisantin [plɛzɑ̃tɛ̃] *nm* practical *or* malicious joker; *Fig Péj* **c'est un p.,** (*on ne peut pas lui faire confiance*) he's a tricky customer.

plaisir [plezir] *nm* **(a)** (*sensation plaisante*) pleasure, delight; **j'apprends avec p. que vous êtes de mon avis,** I'm delighted *or* so glad to hear you agree with me; **faire p. à qn,** to please s.o.; **cela m'a fait p. de le revoir,** it gave me great pleasure to see him again; **cela me fait grand p. de vous voir,** I'm delighted to see you; **cela fait p. à voir,** it's a pleasure to see; **faire à qn le p. de ...,** to do s.o. the favour *or US* favor of ...; **voulez-vous me faire le p. de vous taire!,** will you PLEASE be quiet!; **ils vous prient de leur faire le p. de dîner avec eux,** they request the pleasure of your company at dinner; **j'ai le p. de vous apprendre que ...,** I have pleasure in informing you that ..., I'm pleased to be able to tell you that ...; **le p. d'offrir/de recevoir,** the pleasure of giving/receiving; **au p. de vous revoir,** goodbye, I hope we'll meet again; *F* **au p.!,** goodbye!, see you (again)!; **prendre p. à qch,** to enjoy sth; **prendre p.** *ou* **avoir du p. à faire qch,** to enjoy doing sth; **avec p.!,** with pleasure!;

(b) (*agrément*) pleasure, fun; **c'est par p. que vous faites cela?,** are you doing that because you like it *or* for the fun of it?; **parler pour le p. de parler,** to talk for talking's sake; **elle travaille pour le p.,** she works because she enjoys it; **se tourmenter à p.,** to worry for the sake of worrying; *Fig Iron* **je vous souhaite bien du p.,** the best of luck (to you)!, you'll need it!;

(c) (*distraction*) amusement, enjoyment; **menus plaisirs,** amusement(s), entertainment; (*passe-temps*) pastimes; **je ne partage pas ses goûts, mais c'est son p.,** it's not to my taste, but he enjoys it; **prendre son p. comme on peut,** to take one's pleasure where one finds it; **s'accorder un petit p. (défendu),** to indulge in a little (forbidden) pleasure; **jouer (aux cartes** *etc*) **pour le p.** *ou* **pour son p.,** to play (cards *etc*) for pleasure *or* enjoyment *or* fun; **c'est un p. coûteux, le planeur,** it's an expensive pastime, gliding; **partie de p.,** outing, trip; (*pique-nique*) picnic; *Fig Iron* **ce n'est pas une partie de p.,** it's no picnic;

(d) *Littér* **le p., les plaisirs,** dissipation; **lieu de p.,** place of amusement; (*où l'on s'amuse la nuit*) night haunt;

(e) le p. (sexuel), (sexual) pleasure; **prendre du p.,** to obtain pleasure.

plan¹ [plɑ̃] **1** *adj* even, level, flat (*ground, surface*); plane (*surface, geometry*).

2 *nm* **(a)** *Math etc* plane; **p. incliné,** inclined plane; *Constr* **p. de référence,** datum plane *or* level; *Opt* **p. focal,** focal plane;

(b) (*surface aménagée*) **p. d'eau,** stretch of water; reach (*of a river*); **p. de travail,** work(ing) surface, worktop (*of kitchen unit*); **p. de cuisson,** stove top;

(c) *Beaux-Arts etc* **premier p.,** foreground; **second p.,** middle ground; **au second p.,** in the middle distance; *Fig* **ce problème occupe le premier p.,** this question is very much to the fore; *Fig* **reléguer qn au second p.,** to push s.o. into the background *or* out of the limelight; *Fig* **un artiste de premier p.,** an artist of the first rank, a first-rate artist; **sur le même p.,** at *or* on the same level; **sur le p. politique,** in the political field *or* sphere; (*d'un point de vue politique*) from the political point of view; *Phot Cin* **p. rapproché,** close shot, close-up; **faire un gros p.,** to take *or* shoot a close-up;

(d) *Av* **p. de sustentation,** aerofoil, *US* airfoil; **p. fixe horizontal,** tail plane; **p. supérieur,** upper wing *or* plane (*of biplane*).

plan² *nm* **(a)** (*relevé*) plan, drawing; draft, draught (*of construction*); *Constr Tech* blueprint; (*de ville*) plan, map; **p. géométral,** ground plan; **tracer un p.,** to draw a plan; **relever le p. d'une région,** to survey *or* map out an area; **p. d'un moteur,** plan of an engine;

(b) *Fig* (*projet*) plan, scheme, project; **faire** *ou* **arrêter le p. de qch,** to plan sth; *Fig* **tirer des plans sur la comète,** to build castles in Spain *or* in the air; **p. d'occupation des sols,** land-use plan; **sans p. arrêté,** without any set plan; **p. de travail,** plan *or* schedule of work; **p. antihausse,** anti-inflation policy; **p. d'études,** study plan *or* programme, curriculum; *Ordinat* **p. calcul,** = plan to establish a computer industry in France; *Av* **p. de vol,** flight plan; **p. comptable,** accounting plan; **p. économique,** economic plan, plan for the economy; **p. quinquennal,** five-year plan; **quels sont vos plans pour les années à venir?,** what are your plans for the future?; **p. d'un roman/d'un devoir,** plan of *or* for a novel/essay plan.

plan³ *nm F* **laisser qn en p.,** to leave s.o. in the lurch; (*sans moyen de transport*) to leave s.o. stranded; **laisser son travail en p.,** to leave one's work unfinished.

planage [planaʒ] *nm Tech* planing (*of wood*); planishing (*of metal*).

planche [plɑ̃ʃ] *nf* **(a)** (*pièce de bois*) board; (*moins large*) plank; (*étagère*) shelf; *F* (*ski*) plank; **p. à dessin,** drawing board; *Fig* **c'est ma p. de salut,** it's my sheet anchor; (*dernier espoir*) it's my last hope; *Natation* **faire la p.,** to float on one's back; **p. à pain,** breadboard; **p. à découper** *ou* **à hacher,** chopping board; **p. à laver,** washboard; **p. à pâtisserie,** pastry board; **p. à fromage,** cheeseboard; **p. à repasser,** ironing board; *Fig* **avoir du pain sur la p.,** to have enough on one's plate; *Fig F* **c'est une p. à pain** *ou* **à repasser,** she's flat-chested, *F* she's as flat as a pancake;

(b) *Nau* **p. (de débarquement),** gangplank; **jour de p.,** lay day; **passer à la p.,** to walk the plank;

(c) *Th* **les planches,** the stage; **monter sur les planches,** to go on the stage; **être sur les planches,** to be on the stage, *F* to tread the boards; **l'amour des planches,** love of the stage;

(d) *Beaux-Arts etc* (metal) plate, block (*for printing, etching etc*); **p. à billets,** printing press (*for printing banknotes*); *Fig* **faire fonctionner la p. à billets,** to print (too much) money; **planches en couleurs,** colour *or US* color plates;

(e) (*de jardin potager*) bed;

(f) *Sp* **p. (de surf),** surfboard; **p. (à voile),** sailboard, windsurfer; **faire de la p. (à voile),** to go windsurfing, to windsurf; **p. à roulettes,** skateboard.

planchéiage [plɑ̃ʃejaʒ] *nm* boarding, planking (*of partition, deck*); flooring (*of room etc*).

planchéier [plɑ̃ʃeje] *vt* (*impf & pr sub* **n. planchéiions**) (*poser les planches*) to board (*partition etc*); to board over, to plank over (*deck*); to floor (*room etc*).

plancher¹ [plɑ̃ʃe] *nm* **(a)** (*sol*) floor; *F* **le p. des vaches,** dry land, terra firma; **(b)** *Fig* (*minimum*) minimum, lower limit; **le p. des versements,** the minimum deposit; **prix p.,** bottom price; **(c)** *Tech* planking (*of deck*); floorplates (*of engine room*); flooring (*of trench*); *Aut Fig* **mettre le pied au p.,** to put one's foot down; *Fig F* **débarrassez-moi le p.!,** get out!, clear out!, beat it!, scram!; **(d)** *Tech* bottom (*of lock*); *Anat* floor (*of cavity*).

plancher² *vi Scol F* to be called up to the blackboard (*for questioning etc*); *Fig* (*présenter un rapport*) to (present a) report; **les ministres planchent sur ce problème,** the

ministers are to present a report on the matter; (*travailler sur*) the ministers are working on the matter.
planchette [plɑ̃ʃɛt] *nf* (*petite planche*) small board, plank; (*étagère*) (small) shelf; *Spéc* (*de topographe*) plane table; *Phot* **p. d'objectif,** lens panel.
planchiste [plɑ̃ʃist] *n Sp* windsurfer.
plançon [plɑ̃sɔ̃] *nm* (*jeune arbre*) sapling; (*plante*) set, slip.
plan-concave [plɑ̃kɔ̃kav] *adj Opt* plano-concave (*lens*); (*pl plan-concaves*).
plan-convexe [plɑ̃kɔ̃vɛks] *adj Opt* plano-convex (*lens*); (*pl plan-convexes*).
plancton [plɑ̃ktɔ̃] *nm* plankton.
plane [plan] *nf Tech* drawing knife.
plané [plane] *adj Av* **vol p.,** gliding; **descendre en vol p.,** to glide down; *F* **faire un vol p.,** to fall (heavily).
planéité [planeite] *nf* evenness, flatness.
planer¹ [plane] *vt Tech* to plane (*wood*); to planish (*metal*).
planer² *vi* **(a)** (*d'un oiseau*) to glide, to soar; (*voltiger*) to hover; (*d'un ballon*) to float; (*d'un planeur*) to glide; (*de la brume, fumée*) to hover, to hang; *Fig* **p. sur qch/qn,** to hang *or* hover over sth/s.o.; **(b)** *Litt* to look down (*from the air, from on high*) (**sur,** upon); **(c)** *Fig F* (*être particulièrement bien*) to be *or* feel on top of the world, to be on cloud nine; (*perdre le sens des réalités*) to have one's head in the clouds; (*après s'être drogué*) to be high; **ça plane pour moi!,** I'm feeling on top of the world!
planétaire [planetɛr] *adj* **(a)** *Astron* planetary (*system etc*); **(b)** *MecE* **engrenage p.,** planet gear; **(c)** *Phys* orbital, orbiting (*electrons*); **(d)** (*expansion, action*) on a worldwide *or* global scale.
planétairement [planetɛrmɑ̃] *adv* **voir les choses p.,** to look at things on a worldwide basis.
planétarisation [planetarizasjɔ̃] *nf* globalization; **la p. économique,** the growth of a world economy.
planétarisé [planetarize] *adj* on a world-wide *or* global scale; **conscience planétarisée,** global awareness.
planétarium [planetarjɔm] *nm Astron* planetarium.
planète [planɛt] *nf Astron* planet; (*Terre*) (the) Planet; *Fig* **être né sous une bonne p.,** to be born under a lucky star; **planètes inférieures/supérieures,** inner/outer planets; **sur toute la p.,** over the whole planet, all over the planet.
planétisation [planetizasjɔ̃] *nf* = **PLANÉTARISATION**.
planétoïde [planetɔid] *nm Astron* planetoid.
planétologie [planetɔlɔʒi] *nf* planetology.
planeur¹, -euse [planœr, -øz] *n Tech* planisher.
planeur² *nm Av* glider.
planeuse [planøz] *nf Tech* planing machine; (*pour métal*) planishing machine.
planifiable [planifjabl] *adj Écon* that can be planned (for).
planificateur, -trice [planifikatœr, -tris] *Econ etc* **1** *adj* planning (*authority etc*). **2** *n* planner.
planification [planifikasjɔ̃] *nf Écon* planning.
planifier [planifje] *vt* (*impf & pr sub* **n. planifiions**) *Écon* to plan.
planisme [planism] *nm Écon* planning.
planisphère [planisfɛr] *nm* planisphere.
planning [planiŋ] *nm* **(a)** planning; (*programme de travail*) work schedule; **(b) p. familial,** family planning.
planque [plɑ̃k] *nf F* **(a)** (*cachette*) hiding place, hideout; **la police est en p. devant la maison,** the police are staking out the house; **(b)** (*travail facile*) cushy job *or* number.
planquer [plɑ̃ke] *F* **1** *vt* to hide, to stash (*sth*) (away). **2 se planquer** *vpr* to hide; (*à cause des coups de fusil*) to take cover.
plant [plɑ̃] *nm* **(a)** (*pépinière*) (nursery) plantation (*of trees, bushes*); **(b)** (*carré*) patch, bed; **p. de choux,** cabbage patch; **(c)** (*bouture*) (*d'un arbre*) sapling; (*d'une plante*) set, slip; **jeunes plants,** seedlings.
plantain [plɑ̃tɛ̃] *nm Bot* plantain.
plantaire [plɑ̃tɛr] *adj Anat* plantar; **voûte p.,** plantar arch.
plantard [plɑ̃tar] *nm* = **PLANÇON**.
plantation [plɑ̃tasjɔ̃] *nf* **(a)** (*fait de planter*) planting (*of trees, seeds*); **(b)** (*exploitation*) (*sugar, tea*) plantation; **p. d'oranges,** orange grove; **(c)** *Th* **p. de décors,** erection of scenery; **(d) p. de cheveux,** head of hair; **avoir une curieuse p. de cheveux,** to have a strange-looking haircut.
plante¹ [plɑ̃t] *nf Anat* sole (of the foot).
plante² *nf* plant; **p. potagère,** (*herbe*) herb; (*légume*) vegetable; **p. marine,** seaweed; **p. à fleurs,** flowering plant; **plantes vertes** *ou* **à feuilles persistantes,** evergreens; **p. d'appartement,** pot *or* house plant; **p. de serre,** hothouse plant; **Jardin des Plantes,** Botanical Gardens; *Fig F* **cette fille, quelle belle p.!,** she's a nice bit of stuff, that girl!
planté [plɑ̃te] *adj* **(a)** (*garni*) planted; **colline plantée d'arbres,** hill planted with trees; **(b)** (*situé*) situated, placed; **maison bien plantée,** pleasantly situated house; **(c)** (*bâti*) built; **enfant bien p.,** sturdy *or* healthy child; **bien p. sur ses jambes,** sturdily built; **(d)** (*debout*) standing; **il était p. au milieu de la pièce,** he had planted himself *or* he was standing right there in the middle of the room; *F* **ne la laissez pas plantée là,** don't leave her standing there.
planter [plɑ̃te] **1** *vt* **(a)** to plant, to set (*seeds, flowers, trees*);
(b) (*enfoncer*) to fix, to set (up); **p. un pieu dans le sol,** to drive *or* stick a stake in the ground; **p. un drapeau,** to put up *or* hoist *or* raise a flag; **avoir les dents bien/mal plantées,** to have straight/crooked teeth; **p. une échelle contre le mur,** to stand a ladder against the wall; **p. sa tente,** to put up *or* pitch one's tent; *Fig* **p. les personnages,** to build up *or* give substance to the characters; *F* **p. son chapeau sur la tête,** to put *or* stick one's hat on one's head; **p. un baiser sur la joue de qn,** to plant a kiss on s.o.'s cheek;
(c) *Fig* (*donner brusquement*) to fix, to set; **p. son regard sur qn,** to fix one's gaze on s.o.; *F* **p. là qn,** to leave s.o. in the lurch; (*abandonner*) to desert s.o.; **il veut tout p. là,** he wants to drop everything *or* give it all up.
2 se planter *vpr* **(a)** to stand (firmly); **se p. devant qn,** to plant oneself *or* stand squarely in front of s.o.;
(b) se p. dans ses calculs, to get one's calculations wrong.
planteur [plɑ̃tœr] *nm* planter, grower (*of vegetables etc*); (*exploitant dans un pays tropical*) planter, settler (*in new colony*).
planteuse [plɑ̃tøz] *nf Agr Tech* potato planting machine.
plantigrade [plɑ̃tigrad] *adj & nm Zool* plantigrade (animal).
plantoir [plɑ̃twar] *nm* dibber, dibble.
planton [plɑ̃tɔ̃] *nm Mil* orderly; **être de p.,** to be on orderly duty; *F* **faire le p.,** to kick one's heels, hang around.
plantureusement [plɑ̃tyrøzmɑ̃] *adv* copiously.
plantureux, -euse [plɑ̃tyrø, -øz] *adj* **(a)** (*copieux*) copious, abundant; (*repas*) copious, lavish; (*femme*) buxom; **poitrine plantureuse,** ample bosom; **(b)** (*fécond*) fertile (*countryside*).
plaquage [plakaʒ] *nm* **(a)** *Rugby* tackle; **(b)** *F* chucking, ditching, packing in (*esp of lover*).
plaque [plak] *nf* **(a)** (*feuille rigide*) plate, sheet (*of metal*); slab (*of marble etc*); block (*of chocolate*); patch, sheet (*of ice etc*); layer (*of snow*); **p. de blindage,** armour *or US* armor plate; **p. de cheminée,** fireback; **p. de propreté,** fingerplate (*of door*); **p. chauffante,** hotplate; **p. de four,** baking sheet *or* tray, *Am* cookie sheet; **p. de trou d'homme, p. d'égout,** manhole cover; *Constr* **p. d'assise,** wall plate; *Tech* **p. (de fond),** base plate; *Rail* **p. tournante,** turntable; *Fig* **c'est la p. tournante du projet,** the plan hinges on it; **cet aéroport est une p. tournante pour les industries régionales,** this airport is the hub of industrial activity in the region; *Él* **p. d'accumulateur,** accumulator plate; **p. à grille,** grid plate; **p. photographique,** photographic plate; **appareil à plaques,** plate camera; **p. stéréoscopique,** stereo slide;
(b) *Rad* plate, anode; **tension de p.,** plate voltage, anode voltage;
(c) (*portant une inscription*) (ornamental) plaque; (*insigne*) badge (*of office*); star (*of an order*); **p. commémorative,** commemorative plaque *or* tablet; **p. funéraire** *ou* **mortuaire** *ou* **en cuivre,** church brass; **p. de porte,** door plate; (*avec nom*) name plate; **p. indicatrice de rue,** name plate (of street), street sign; **p. d'identité,** (soldier's) identification plate, identity disc, *esp US* dog tag; **p. d'identification,** (*avec nom*) name plate; (*avec numéro*) number plate (*of machine*); *Aut etc* **p. d'immatriculation** *ou* **de police, p. minéralogique,** number plate, *US* license plate;
(d) *Méd* plaque, patch (*on skin*); **plaques muqueuses,** mucous plaque; **p. (dentaire),** plaque; **sclérose en plaques,** multiple sclerosis; **p. sanguine,** red blood disc;
(e) *Fig F* **être à côté de la p.,** to be off-target, to miss the point.
plaqué [plake] *nm* **(a)** (*articles*) plated goods; (*fabriqué à électrolyse*) (electro)plate; **(métal) p.,** plated metal; **p. or,** gold-plate; **montre en p. or,** gold-plated watch; **(b) (bois)**

p., veneered wood.
plaquemine [plakmin] *nf Bot* persimmon.
plaqueminier [plakminje] *nm Bot* persimmon (tree).
plaquer [plake] **1** *vt* **(a)** *(appliquer une plaque)* to veneer *(wood)*; to plate *(metal)*; to flash *(glass)*; to lay on *(plaster)*; **(b)** *(mettre à plat)* to plaster down *(hair)*; **le vent lui plaquait son manteau sur les jambes,** the wind blew his coat against his legs; **p. qn contre un mur,** to flatten s.o. against a wall; **il avait les épaules plaquées au mur,** he stood with his shoulders (pinned *or* pressed) to the wall; **(c)** *Rugby* to tackle, to bring down *(opponent)*; **(d)** *Mus* **p. un accord,** to strike (and hold) a chord; **(f)** *F* to ditch, to chuck *(s.o.)*, to pack *(s.o.)* in; **tout p.,** to chuck it all in, to give it all up. **2 se plaquer** *vpr* **se p. au sol/contre un mur,** to lie flat on the ground/to flatten oneself against a wall.
plaquette [plakɛt] *nf* **(a)** *(petite plaque)* small plate *(of metal etc)*; small plaque *(with name, inscription etc)*; *(bloc)* block *(of metal etc)*; *Ordinat* circuit board; **p. de circuits imprimés,** printed circuit board, PCB; **(b)** *(petit livre)* booklet; **(c) plaquettes sanguines,** blood platelets.
plaqueur [plakœr] *nm* **(a)** *(sur métaux)* plater *(of metal)*; **(b)** *(sur bois)* veneerer.
plasma [plasma] *nm* **(a)** *Biol* plasma; **p. sanguin,** blood plasma; **(b)** *Ordinat* **p. gazeux,** gas plasma.
plastic [plastik] *nm* plastic explosive.
plasticage [plastikaʒ] *nm* plastic bomb attack.
plasticien, -ienne [plastisjɛ̃, -jɛn] *n* **(a)** *Tech* plastics technician; **(b)** *Méd* plastic surgeon.
plasticité [plastisite] *nf* plasticity.
plastifiant [plastifjɑ̃] *nm* plasticizer.
plastifier [plastifje] *vt (impf & pr sub* **n. plastifiions)** to plasticize; **jaquette plastifiée,** laminated jacket.
plastiquage [plastikaʒ] *nm* = **PLASTICAGE**.
plastique [plastik] **1** *adj (mou)* plastic, malleable; **arts plastiques,** plastic art(s); **chirurgie plastique,** plastic surgery; **aux formes plastiques,** with a fine figure. **2** *nf* **(a)** *Beaux-Arts etc* plastic art, art of modelling; **(b)** *(harmonie des formes)* figure, physique *(of actress, dancer)*. **3** *nm* plastic.
plastiquer [plastike] *vt* to bomb *(sth) (using plastic explosive)*.
plastiqueur, -euse [plastikœr, -øz] *n* bomber *(using plastic explosive)*.
plastron [plastrɔ̃] *nm* **(a)** *(pièce d'armure)* breastplate *(of cuirass)*; *(d'escrimeur)* (fencer's) platron, pad; **(b)** front *(of dress etc)*; (man's) shirt front, dick(e)y.
plastronner [plastrɔne] **1** *vt* to put a plastron on *(s.o.)*. **2** *vi* to throw out one's chest; *Fig* to strut, swagger.
plat [pla] **1** *adj* **(a)** *(qui a peu de relief)* flat, level; **pays p.,** flat country; **chaussure plate,** low-heeled *or* flat shoe; **avoir la poitrine plate/les pieds plats,** to be flat-chested/-footed; **cheveux plats,** straight hair; **mer plate,** smooth sea; **calme p.,** dead calm; **eau plate,** still water; **vis à tête plate,** screw with countersunk head; **assiette plate,** plate *(as opposed to dish)*; *Ordinat* **écran p.,** flat screen;
(b) *Fig (ennuyeux)* flat, dull, insipid, tame; **style p.,** commonplace style; **vin p.,** dull *or* flat *or* insipid wine;
(c) à p., flat; **couché à p. sur le sol,** lying flat on the ground; **dormir à p.,** to sleep without a pillow; *Fig* **tomber à p.,** *(of play etc)* to fall flat, *F* to be a flop; **sa proposition est tombée à p.,** his suggestion fell flat; **tomber à p. ventre,** to fall flat on one's face; *Péj Fig* **se mettre à p. ventre devant qn,** to grovel to s.o.; **pneu à p.,** flat tyre *or US* tire; **accu à p.,** flat battery; *F* **être à p.,** *(épuisé)* to be exhausted *or* all in; *(en mauvaise santé)* to be run down; *Aut* to have a flat (tyre); **cette maladie l'a mis à p.,** this illness has taken it out of him.
2 *nm* **(a)** *(partie plate)* flat *(of hand etc)*; blade *(of oar)*; face *(of hammer)*;
(b) *Sp* **le p.,** flat racing; *Natation* **faire un p.,** to do a bellyflop;
(c) *F* **faire du p. à qn,** to make advances to s.o.;
(d) *Culin (contenant, contenu)* dish; **mettre les petits plats dans les grands,** to put on a marvellous spread; *Fig* **mettre les pieds dans le p.,** to put one's foot in it; *F* **en faire tout un p.,** to make a great fuss about sth, to pile on the agony; **p. à barbe,** shaving dish; **p. de quête,** *(in church)* collection plate;
(e) *Culin* course *(at dinner etc)*; **p. de résistance,** main course, main dish; **p. cuisiné,** ready-cooked dish; *(à emporter)* takeaway dish.
platane [platan] *nm* plane tree.
plat-bord [plabɔr] *nm Nau* gunwale, gunnel; **hauteur au-dessus du p.-b.,** height above the hull; *(pl plats-bords)*.
plate [plat] *nf Nau* punt, flat-bottomed (fishing) boat.
plateau, -eaux [plato] *nm* **(a)** tray; **p. d'argent,** silver salver; **p. à** *ou* **de fromages,** cheeseboard; **p.-repas,** meal on a tray *(on aeroplane etc)*; *Fig* **servi sur un p.,** (served) on a plate; **ça ne va pas t'arriver servi sur un p.,** you're not going to get it served up on a plate; **(b)** pan *(cf scales)*; turntable *(of record deck)*; *(grand panneau)* shelf *(of oven etc)*; top *(of table)*; **(c)** *Géog* plateau; **hauts-plateaux,** high plateaus *or* plateaux; **p. continental,** continental shelf; **(d)** *Méd* dead level *(of a disease)*; **(e)** *Th* floor *(of the stage)*; *Cin* set; **p. tournant,** revolving stage; **(f)** *Rail etc* flat *or* open truck; **(g)** *MecE etc* plate, disc, *US* disk; *Cyclisme* **p. de pédalier,** front chain wheel; *Aut etc* **raccordement à plateaux,** flange assembly; **p. d'embrayage,** clutch plate.
plate-bande [platbɑ̃d] *nf* flower bed; *Fig F* **ne marchez pas sur mes plates-bandes,** keep off my patch.
plate-forme [platfɔrm] *nf (pl plates-formes)* **(a)** *(partie ouverte)* platform *(of bus etc)*; flat roof *(of house)*; footplate *(of locomotive)*; **(b)** *Géog* **p.-f. continentale,** continental shelf; **(c)** *Rail etc* flat *or* open truck; **(d)** *Mil* **p.-f. de tir,** gun platform; **p.-f. tournante,** turntable; **(e)** *Pol* platform.
plate-longe [platlɔ̃ʒ] *nf (pièce pour empêcher le cheval de ruer)* kicking strap; *(longe)* leading rein; *(pl plates-longes)*.
platement [platmɑ̃] *adv* flatly, dully.
platinage [platinaʒ] *nm* platinum plating.
platine¹ [platin] *nf Tech* plate *(of lock, watch etc)*; lock (plate) *(of rifle)*; platen *(of printing press, typewriter)*; stage *(of microscope)*; turntable *(of record deck)*; *F* **s'acheter une nouvelle p.,** *(tourne-disque)* to buy oneself a new deck.
platine² **1** *nm* platinum. **2** *adj inv* platinum; **cheveux (blonds) p.,** platinum blond hair.
platiné [platine] *adj* **(a)** *(recouvert de platine)* platinum-plated, platinized; *Aut* **vis platinées,** points; **(b) cheveux platinés,** platinum blond hair; **une blonde platinée,** a platinum blond.
platiner [platine] *vt* to plate with platinum, to platinize.
platitude [platityd] *nf* **(a)** *(de personnalité)* flatness, dullness; *(de style)* vapidity; **ce film est d'une p.,** this film is so dull; **(b)** *(propos)* commonplace remark, platitude; **débiter des platitudes,** to platitudinize; *Arch* **faire des platitudes à qn,** to grovel to s.o..
Platon [platɔ̃] *nm* Plato.
platonicien, -ienne [platɔnisjɛ̃, -jɛn] **1** *adj* Platonic *(school, philosopher)*. **2** *n* Platonist.
platonique [platɔnik] *adj* **(a)** platonic *(love etc)*; **(b)** *(vain)* useless, futile, vain *(attempt etc)*.
platonisme [platɔnism] *nm* Platonism.
plâtrage [plɑtraʒ] *nm* plastering *(of wall etc)*; *Constr* plasterwork.
plâtras [plɑtra] *nm (débris)* (plaster) rubble; *(morceau)* lump of plaster.
plâtre [plɑtr] *nm* **(a)** plaster; **p. de moulage,** plaster of Paris; **enduire qch de p.,** to plaster over sth; **plâtres,** plasterwork *(on house etc)*; *Fig F* **essuyer les plâtres,** *(d'une maison)* to be the first occupant of a house; *(subir des conséquences fâcheuses)* to be the first to suffer; **(b)** *(ouvrage)* plaster cast; **(c)** *Méd* plaster; *(moule)* plaster cast; **poser un p.,** to put a plaster cast on; **avoir la jambe dans le p.,** to have one's leg in plaster.
plâtrer [plɑtre] **1** *vt* **(a)** *(enduire de plâtre)* to plaster *(wall, ceiling)*; to plaster up *(hole, crack)*; **(b)** *Méd* to put *(leg etc)* in plaster; **(c)** *Agr* to dress *(soil)* with sulphate. **2 se plâtrer** *vpr F* **se p. (le visage),** to plaster one's face with make-up.
plâtrerie [plɑtrəri] *nf (usine)* plasterworks; **travaux de p.,** plasterwork, plastering.
plâtreux, -euse [plɑtrø, -øz] *adj (wall etc)* covered with plaster; *Fig* chalky *(water, cheese)*; **teint p.,** pasty *or* chalky complexion.
plâtrier [plɑtrije] *nm* plasterer.
plâtrière [plɑtrijɛr] *nf (carrière)* gypsum quarry; *(four)* plaster kiln, gypsum kiln.
plausibilité [plozibilite] *nf* plausibility.
plausible [plozibl] *adj* plausible.
plausiblement [ploziblәmɑ̃] *adv* plausibly.
play-back [plɛbak] *nm inv* miming; **chanter en p.-b.,** to mime to a record *etc*.
play-boy [plɛbɔj] *nm* playboy; *(pl play-boys)*.
plèbe [plɛb] *nf* **(a)** *Hist* **la p.,** the plebs; **(b)** *Péj* **la p.,** the lower orders, the common people, the plebs; **les goûts de la p.,** plebeian tastes.
plébéien, -ienne [plebejɛ̃, -jɛn] *adj & n* plebeian.
plébiscite [plebisit] *nm* plebiscite.
plébisciter [plebisite] *vt* **(a)** *(élire par plébiscite)* to vote

for (*s.o., sth*) by plebiscite; **(b)** (*élire à une très forte majorité*) to elect (*s.o.*) by a large majority.

plectre [plɛktr] *nm* plectrum.

pléiade [plejad] *nf* **(a)** *Astron* Pleiades; **(b)** *Litt* pleiad; *Fig* **une p. de gens célèbres,** a galaxy of famous people.

plein [plɛ̃] **1** *adj* **(a)** full (**de,** of); (*contenant*) filled (**de,** with); *Fml* (*bien nourri, fourni*) replete (**de,** with); **bouteille pleine,** full bottle; **pleine bouteille,** bottleful; **p. comme un œuf,** chock-full, chock-a-block; **l'autobus est p.,** the bus is full; *F* **être p.,** (*ivre*) to be drunk, to have had a skinful; **salle pleine à craquer,** room full to bursting; **avoir le ventre p.,** to be full (up), to have eaten one's fill; **ne parle pas la bouche pleine,** don't speak with your mouth full; **entreprise pleine de dangers,** enterprise fraught with danger(s); **il a les doigts pleins d'encre,** his fingers are covered with ink;

(b) (*of animal*) pregnant; **jument/brebis/chèvre pleine,** mare in foal/ewe with lamb/goat in kid;

(c) (*complet*) complete, entire, whole; **pleine lune,** full moon; **p. sud,** due south; **la chambre est (en) p. ouest,** the room faces due west; **pleine mer,** (*marée haute*) high tide; **en pleine mer,** out at sea, on the open sea; **reliure pleine peau,** full leather binding; **p. pouvoir,** full power; *Jur* power of attorney; **de son p. gré,** of one's own free will;

(d) (*solide, qui occupe toute la masse*) solid (*tyre, axle etc*); continuous (*line*); **table en acajou p.,** solid mahogany table; **joues pleines,** full *or* plump cheeks; *Fig* **son p.,** full sound; *Fig* **à p. temps,** full-time; **travailler à p. temps,** to work full-time; **un p. temps,** a full-time job;

(e) en p. visage, full *or* right in the face; **en p. hiver,** in the depth *or* the middle of winter; **en p. air,** in the open (air); **restaurant en p. air,** open-air restaurant; **marché en p. vent,** open-air market; **en p. jour,** in broad daylight; **s'arrêter en p. milieu de la place,** to stop right in the middle of the square; **en pleine nuit,** in the middle of the night, at dead of night; **en pleine saison,** at the height of the season; **en p. tribunal,** in open court; **être en p. travail,** to be hard at work; **respirer à pleine poitrine, à pleins poumons,** to breathe deeply; **boire à p. verre,** to drink deeply; **crier à pleine gorge,** to shout at the top of one's voice; **apporter des fleurs à pleins bras,** to bring armfuls of flowers; **être en pleine possession de ses moyens,** to be in full possession of one's faculties; **à pleines voiles,** with all sails set, under full sail; *Fig* **avoir le cœur p.,** to have a heavy heart, to be weighed down by sorrow; **être p. de certitudes,** to be full of certainty in one's own beliefs; **suffit, j'ai la tête pleine!,** that's enough, I've had it up to here!

2 *adv* **il avait des larmes p. les yeux,** his eyes were full of tears; **il a des livres p. ses poches,** his pockets are stuffed with books; **avoir de l'argent p. les poches,** to have plenty of money; **à p.,** at full capacity; **l'argument/la remarque porte à p.,** the argument/remark has had the desired effect; **elle est mignonne tout p.,** she's awfully sweet; *F* **il y avait p. de gens,** there were lots of people; *Nau* **porter p.,** to keep her full.

3 *nm* **(a)** (*fait de remplir*) **faire le p. (d'un réservoir),** to fill (up) (a tank); *Aut* **faire le p. (d'essence),** to fill up (with petrol); **faites le p., s'il vous plaît,** fill her up, please!; **avoir son p.,** (*of ship*) to be fully laden; **faire le p. dans un supermarché,** to fill up one's trolley at a supermarket;

(b) (*phase maximale*) full extent, full height *etc*; **le p. (de la mer),** high tide; **battre son p.,** (*de la marée*) to be at the full; *Fig* **la saison bat son p., c'est le p. de la saison,** the season is at it's height *or* is in full swing;

(c) en p. dans le centre, full *or* right in the middle;

(d) (*trait épais*) downstroke (*in writing*); *Typ* thick stroke.

pleinement [plɛnmɑ̃] *adv* fully, entirely; (*to enjoy sth*) to the full.

plein-emploi [plɛnɑ̃plwa] *nm inv* full employment.

pléistocène [pleistɔsɛn] *adj & nm Géol* Pleistocene.

plénier, -ière [plenje, -jɛr] *adj* **(a)** *Arch* full, complete; absolute; **(b)** plenary (*court, indulgence*).

plénipotentiaire [plenipɔtɑ̃sjɛr] *adj & nm* plenipotentiary.

plénitude [plenityd] *nf* plenitude, fullness (*of emotion, experience, power etc*); completeness (*of victory etc*); **la p. d'un son,** the fullness *or* rich quality of a sound.

plénum [plenɔm] *nm* plenum.

pléonasme [pleɔnasm] *nm* pleonasm; **par p.,** pleonastically.

pléonastique [pleɔnastik] *adj* pleonastic.

plésiosaure [plezjɔzɔr] *nm* plesiosaurus.

pléthore [pletɔr] *nf* plethora.

pléthorique [pletɔrik] *adj* **(a)** *Méd Vieilli* full-blooded, plethoric; **(b)** (*très abondant*) superabundant; (*trop*) excessive; **classe p.,** over-crowded class.

pleur [plœr] *nm Litt* tear; **verser des pleurs,** to shed tears; **fondre en pleurs,** to dissolve into tears; **cessez vos pleurs,** dry your tears; **être tout en pleurs,** to be bathed in tears.

pleurage [plœraʒ] *nm Tech* wow; **niveau de p.,** wow level.

pleural, -aux [plœral, -o] *adj Anat* pleural.

pleurant, -ante [plœrɑ̃, -ɑ̃t] **1** *adj Arch* crying, weeping. **2** *n Beaux-Arts* weeper, mourner (*on a tomb*).

pleurard, -arde [plœrar, -ard] **1** *adj Péj Vieilli* whimpering, fractious (*child*); whining, whimpering, tearful (*voice*). **2** *n Péj Vieilli* whimperer, *F* crybaby.

pleurer [plœre] **1** *vt* **(a) p. qn/qch,** to weep for s.o./sth; (*regretter*) to lament s.o./sth; **p. ses vingt ans,** to weep for *or* over one's lost youth; **mourir sans être pleuré,** to die unmourned;

(b) (*laisser couler*) to cry; **p. toutes les larmes de son corps,** to cry one's eyes out; **p. misère,** to complain; (*donner la pauvreté comme excuse*) to plead poverty;

(c) *Fig F Vieilli* (*ménager*) to spare; **elle ne pleure pas ses efforts/ses conseils,** she spares no effort/she's generous with her advice.

2 *vi* **(a)** (*verser des larmes*) to cry, to weep, to shed tears (**sur,** over; **pour,** for); **p. sur soi-même** *ou* **sur son sort,** to bewail *or* bemoan one's fate; **p. de joie,** to weep for joy; **p. à chaudes larmes,** to sob *or* to cry one's heart out; **s'endormir en pleurant,** to cry oneself to sleep; **c'est à faire p.,** it's enough to make you weep *or* cry;

(b) (*des yeux*) to water, to run;

(c) *Fig Péj* (*supplier*) to grovel; **(aller) p. auprès de qn,** to grovel to s.o.; **p. après une faveur,** to grovel for a favour *or US* favor.

pleurésie [plœrezi] *nf Méd* pleurisy.

pleurétique [plœretik] *Méd* **1** *adj* pleuritic (*pain*). **2** *n* person with pleurisy.

pleureur, -euse [plœrœr, -øz] **1** *n Vieilli* person who weeps easily. **2** *nf* **pleureuse,** hired mourner. **3** *adj Péj* whimpering; **saule p.,** weeping willow.

pleurite [plœrit] *nf Méd* dry pleurisy.

pleurnichard, -arde [plœniʃar, -ard(ə)] *n* = **PLEURNICHEUR.**

pleurnichement [plœrniʃmɑ̃] *nm* = **PLEURNICHERIE.**

pleurnicher [plœrniʃe] *vi F* to whimper, to whine, to snivel, to grizzle.

pleurnicherie [plœrniʃri] *nf F* whimpering, whining, snivelling, grizzling.

pleurnicheur, -euse [plœrniʃœr, -øz] *F* **1** *n* whiner, sniveller; (*qui pleure facilement*) crybaby. **2** *adj* whimpering, whining, snivelling.

pleurote [plœrɔt] *nf* oyster mushroom.

pleutre [pløtr] *Litt Péj* **1** *adj* cowardly. **2** *nm* coward.

pleuvasser [pløvase], **pleuviner** [pløvine] *v impers* to drizzle.

pleuvoir [pløvwar] *v* (*prp* **pleuvant**; *pp* **plu**; *pr ind* **il pleut, ils pleuvent**; *impf* **il pleuvait**; *p hist* **il plut**; *fu* **il pleuvra**) **1** *v impers* to rain; **il pleut à verse** *ou* **à seaux,** it's raining hard, it's pouring (down) (with rain); **il pleut à petites gouttes,** it's drizzling; **les jours où il pleut,** on wet *or* rainy days; *Fig* **il pleut des cordes,** it's bucketing down, it's coming down in buckets; *Fig* **il pleuvait des coups,** blows fell thick and fast *or* rained down. **2** *vi* **faire p. des coups sur qn,** to rain blows (down) on s.o., to shower s.o. with blows; **les invitations pleuvent sur lui,** invitations are pouring in to him, he's being inundated with invitations.

pleuvoter [pløvɔte] *v impers* = **PLEUVASSER.**

plèvre [plɛvr] *nf Anat* pleura.

plexiglas ® [plɛksiglɑs] *nm* perspex, *US* lucite; (*comme verre de sécurité*) Plexiglass ®.

plexus [plɛksys] *nm Anat* plexus; **p. solaire,** solar plexus.

pleyon [plɛjɔ̃] *nm Agr* withe, osier tie.

pli [pli] *nm* **(a)** (*rabat*) pleat; fold (*in curtains etc*); *Couture* **p. creux** *ou* **rentré** *ou* **inverti, double p.,** box pleat, inverted pleat; **p. couché,** knife pleat; **petit p.,** tuck; **jupe à plis,** pleated skirt; **faire des plis à une robe,** to pleat a dress;

(b) mise en plis, set; **faire une mise en plis à qn,** to set s.o.'s hair;

(c) (faux) p., (*ondulation d'un tissu*) wrinkle, crease; **faire le p. d'un pantalon,** (*by ironing*) to put a crease in a pair of trousers; *Fig* **ça ne fait pas un p.,** (there's) no doubt about it; **prendre le p. de faire qch,** to get into the habit of doing sth; *Géol* **p. de terrain,** undulation;

(d) bend (*of the arm, leg*); **p. du jarret,** hollow of the knee;

(e) (*bourrelet de peau*) fold (*of skin*); (*petit*) wrinkle; **les plis du front,** the lines on the forehead;

(f) (*pliure*) cover, envelope (*of letter*); **sous p. séparé,** under separate cover; **nous vous envoyons sous ce p. ...,** we are sending you herewith ..., please find enclosed ...; *Nau* **p. cacheté,** sealed orders; *Nau etc* **plis consulaires,** consular packages;

(g) *Cartes* **faire un p.,** to take a trick.

pliable [plijabl] *adj* foldable (*chair, bed*); pliable, flexible (*material*); **canot p.,** folding boat.

pliage [plijaʒ] *nm* folding (*of material*).

pliant [plijɑ̃] **1** *adj* folding (*chair etc*); collapsible (*table etc*); **pied p.,** folding tripod. **2** *nm* folding chair; (*sans dossier*) folding stool; (*de camping*) camping stool.

plie [pli] *nf* plaice.

plié [plije] *nm* (*danse*) plié.

plier [plije] *v* (*impf & pr sub* **n. pliions**) **1** *vt* **(a)** (*mettre en double*) to fold (*sheet, clothes*); to turn down (*page*); to furl (*sail*); (*rabattre*) to fold up *or* away (*umbrella*); **p. ses affaires,** to pack up one's belongings; *Fig* **p. bagage,** to pack one's bags;

(b) (*faire une flexion*) to bend (*bough, knee etc*); **plié en deux,** (*personne*) bent double, doubled up; *Fig F* **être plié de rire,** to be doubled up laughing *or* with laughter, to be bent double with laughter; **p. la tête,** (*courber*) to bow one's head; *Fig* to submit; **p. qn à la discipline,** to impose discipline on s.o..

2 *vi* **(a)** (*se courber*) to bend (over); **poutre qui plie sous le poids,** beam that bends *or* gives *or* sags under the weight;

(b) (*se soumettre*) to submit, to yield; (*of troops in battle*) to give in, to give way; **tout plie devant lui,** he carries all before him; **elle ne pliera pas devant lui,** she will not submit *or* give in to him.

3 se plier *vpr* to fold (up); **se p. aux circonstances/à la discipline,** to yield *or* bow *or* submit to circumstances/to submit *or* conform to discipline; **se p. aux lois,** to obey the law.

plieur, -euse [plijœr, -øz] **1** *n* (*personne*) folder. **2** *nf* **plieuse,** folding machine.

Pline [plin] *nm Littér* Pliny.

plinthe [plɛ̃t] *nf* **(a)** *Archit* plinth (*of column*); **(b)** (*bande*) skirting(board), *Am* baseboard.

pliocène [plijɔsɛn] *adj & nm Géol* Pliocene.

plioir [plijwar] *nm* **(a)** (*coupe-papier*) paper knife; **(b)** (*planchette*) winder (*for fishing line*).

plissage [plisaʒ] *nm* pleating (*of material*).

plissé [plise] **1** *adj* **(a)** *Couture* pleated (*dress etc*); **(b) lèvres plissées,** puckered lips; **front p.,** wrinkled brow. **2** *nm Couture* pleat(ing), pleats, tucks; **p. soleil,** sunray pleat.

plissement [plismɑ̃] *nm* **(a)** (*pli*) pleating (*of material*); folding (*of paper etc*); corrugation (*of metal, cardboard*); **(b)** (*froissement*) creasing, crumpling, crinkling (*of paper, material*); **(c)** (*froncement*) puckering (*of lips*); screwing up (*of the eyes*); **(d)** *Géol* fold; **le p. hercynien,** the Armorican *or* Hercynian fold.

plisser [plise] **1** *vt* **(a)** (*plier*) to pleat (*skirt etc*); to fold (*paper etc*); to corrugate (*metal, cardboard*); **(b)** (*froisser*) to crease, to crumple, to crinkle (*paper, material*); **(c)** (*froncer*) to wrinkle (*face*); to pucker (*lips*); **un sourire plissait sa figure/ses lèvres,** a smile wrinkled his face/puckered his lips; **p. les yeux,** to screw up one's eyes. **2** *vi* (*d'un vêtement etc*) to crease, to crumple; (*des lèvres*) to pucker; (*du front*) to wrinkle. **3 se plisser** *vpr* (*d'une étoffe*) to crease; **la soie se plisse facilement,** silk creases easily; **ses yeux se plissent quand elle sourit,** she screws up her eyes when she smiles.

plisseur, -euse [plisœr, -øz] **1** *n* (*personne*) pleater, folder. **2** *nf* **plisseuse,** pleating machine.

plissure [plisyr] *nf* pleats.

pliure [plijyr] *nf* (*action*) folding (*of paper etc*); (*résultat*) fold (*in material etc*); bend (*in knee*).

ploc [plɔk] *int* splosh!; (*objet plus petit*) plop!; (*contre qch de solide*) splat!

ploiement [plwamɑ̃] *nm* bending.

plomb [plɔ̃] *nm* **(a)** (*métal*) lead; **p. laminé** *ou* **en feuilles,** sheet lead; **tuyau de p.,** lead pipe; **blanc de p.,** white lead; *Fig* **sommeil de p.,** deep *or* heavy sleep; *Fig* **ciel de p.,** leaden sky; *Fig* **teint de p.,** livid complexion; *Fig* **soleil de p.,** blazing (hot) sun; *Fig* **n'avoir pas de p. dans la tête,** to be scatterbrained;

(b) (*poids*) lead (weight); *Pêche* sinker; *Nau* **jeter** *ou* **lancer le p. (de sonde),** to heave the lead; **fil à p.,** plumb line; **à p.,** upright, vertical(ly); **le soleil donnait à p. sur nous,** the sun was beating straight down on our heads;

(c) *Archit* **plombs,** leadwork, leads (*of window*); **mise en p.,** leading;

(d) *Typ* type, metal; (*de chasse*) shot; **petit** *ou* **menu p.,** small shot; **gros p.,** buckshot;

(e) *Arch* **plombs,** (housemaid's) sink;

(f) (*sceau*) lead seal (*on meter etc*); *Él* **p. (fusible),** fuse; **faire sauter les plombs,** to blow the fuses.

plombage [plɔ̃baʒ] *nm* **(a)** (*fait de garnir avec du plomb*) covering (*sth*) with lead; *Cér* lead glazing; **(b)** (*fait de mettre des plombs*) weighting (*sth*) with lead; **(c)** filling (*of tooth*).

plombagine [plɔ̃baʒin] *nf Minér* black lead, graphite.

plombe [plɔ̃b] *nf Arg* hour; **voilà quatre plombes,** it's striking four; **on ne va pas l'attendre pendant des plombes,** we're not going to wait for him for ever(more).

plombé [plɔ̃be] *adj* leaded (*window etc*); lead (-covered) (*roof etc*); *Fig* leaden, livid (*complexion, sky*); leaden (*sky*).

plomber [plɔ̃be] **1** *vt* **(a)** (*couvrir de plomb*) to cover (*sth*) with lead; *Cér* to glaze; **(b)** (*mettre des plombs à*) to weight (*sth*) with lead; **(c)** *Fig* (*rendre livide*) to turn (*complexion, sky*) livid; **(d)** (*faire un plombage*) to fill, to stop (*tooth*); **le dentiste m'a plombé une dent,** the dentist gave me a filling; **(e)** *Constr* to plumb (*wall*). **2 se plomber** *vpr* (*of complexion, sky*) to become leaden *or* livid.

plomberie [plɔ̃bri] *nf* (*installations, métier*) plumbing; (*atelier*) plumber's shop.

plombier [plɔ̃bje] *nm* (*technicien*) plumber; *Fig F Péj* (*policier spécialiste de l'écoute clandestine*) snooper, eavesdropper; (*au téléphone*) phone-tapper.

plombières [plɔ̃bjɛr] *nf Culin* tutti-frutti (ice-cream).

plonge [plɔ̃ʒ] *nf F* washing up, dishwashing (*in restaurant*); **faire la p.,** to do the washing up, to be a dishwasher (*in a restaurant*).

plongeant [plɔ̃ʒɑ̃] *adj* plunging (*fire, neckline etc*); **vue plongeante,** view from above, bird's eye view.

plongée [plɔ̃ʒe] *nf* **(a)** (*fait de plonger*) diving; **faire de la p.,** to dive, to go in for diving; **p. sous-marine,** skin *or* scuba diving; **(b)** (*de sous-marin*) dive, diving, submersion; **effectuer sa p.,** to dive, to submerge; **p. raide,** crash-dive; **(c)** *Cin TV* high angle shot; (*verticale*) bird's eye view.

plongeoir [plɔ̃ʒwar] *nm* diving board.

plongeon [plɔ̃ʒɔ̃] *nm* **(a)** (*oiseau*) diver, *US* loon; **(b)** (*fait de plonger*) dive; **p. de haut vol,** high dive; **faire un p.,** (*d'un nageur, gardien de but*) to dive; *Fig F* **faire un p.,** to suffer a heavy loss (*in business*).

plonger [plɔ̃ʒe] *v* (**je plongeai(s); n. plongeons**) **1** *vi* **(a)** (*s'immerger*) (*d'un nageur, avion, sous-marin etc*) to dive; **p. dans une rivière,** to plunge into a river; (*d'une position assez haute*) to dive into a river; *Fig* **p. dans sa poche pour y prendre de la monnaie,** to thrust *or* plunge one's hand in(to) one's pocket for change; **p. raide,** (*d'un sous-marin*) to crash-dive;

(b) *Fig* (*descendre*) to plunge; **les murs plongent dans le fossé,** the walls plunge *or* run steeply down into the moat; **son regard plongea sur nous,** he gazed down at us; *Fig* **p. dans le sommeil,** to fall into a deep sleep; **p. du nez,** (*d'un navire*) to pitch; (*d'une rue*) to dip.

2 *vt* to plunge, to thrust (**dans,** in(to)); **p. la main dans sa poche,** to thrust one's hand into one's pocket; *Fig* **être plongé dans ses pensées,** to be immersed *or* lost *or* deep in thought; *Fig* **être plongé dans le noir/l'angoisse,** to be plunged into darkness/to be overcome by anguish; **il plongea son regard sur nous,** he stared at us.

3 se plonger *vpr* to immerse oneself (**dans,** in); *Fig* **se p. dans l'étude,** to bury *or* immerse oneself in one's studies; **se p. dans son travail,** to throw oneself into *or* to immerse oneself in one's work; *Fig* **se p. dans Proust,** to become absorbed *or* engrossed in Proust; **se p. sur un problème,** to become absorbed in *or* to go thoroughly into a problem; *Fig* **se p. dans le vice,** to enter the world of vice.

plongeur, -euse [plɔ̃ʒœr, -øz] **1** *adj* diving (*bird etc*). **2** *n* **(a)** (*personne qui plonge dans l'eau*) diver; **cloche à plongeurs,** diving bell; **p. sous-marin,** skin *or* scuba diver; **(b)** *F* (*personne qui fait la vaisselle*) washer-up, bottlewasher (*in restaurant*). **3** *nm* **(a)** *Orn* diver, diving bird; **(b)** *Tech* plunger (*of pump*).

plosive [ploziv] *nf Ling* plosive.

plot [plo] *nm Él* contact (stud).

plouc [pluk] *Péj* **1** *nm* yokel, (country) bumpkin; **quel p., celui-là!,** what a prat he is! **2** *adj Péj* yokel, yokelly; **pas de chaussures de sport!, ça fait p.!,** don't wear trainers, that's really naff!

plouf [pluf] *int* plop!; (*objet plus lourd*) splosh!

ploutocrate [plutɔkrat] *nm* plutocrat.

ploutocratie [plutɔkrasi] *nf* plutocracy.

ploutocratique [plutɔkratik] *adj* plutocratic.

ployable [plwajabl] *adj* pliable, flexible.

ployage [plwajaʒ] *nm* bending (*of branch etc*).

ployer [plwaje] *v* (**je ploie, n. ployons; je ploierai**) **1** *vt* to bend (*branch, knee*). **2** *vi* (*courber*) to bend; (*d'une corde etc*) to sag; (*se casser, s'effondrer*) to give (way); to bow (*under yoke, burden*); (*de troupes*) to give in, to give way; *Litt* to submit, to yield.

pluches [plyʃ] *nfpl Mil F* **(corvée de) p.,** spud-bashing.

pluie [plɥi] *nf* **(a)** rain; **p. battante** *ou* **torrentielle,** pouring *or* pelting rain; **p. fine,** drizzle; **goutte de p.,** raindrop; **eau de p.,** rainwater; **le temps est à la p.,** it looks like rain; **temps de p.,** rainy *or* wet weather; **jour sans p.,** dry day; **sous la p.,** in the rain; *Fig* **parler de la p. et du beau temps,** to talk about nothing in particular; *Fig F* **il n'est pas tombé de la dernière p.,** he wasn't born yesterday; *Prov* **après la p. le beau temps,** it's a long road that has no turning; *F* **faire la p. et le beau temps,** to be the boss, to rule the roost; **la saison des pluies,** the rainy season; **p. d'orage,** downpour, cloudburst; *Météo* thundery shower; **p. acide, pluies acides,** acid rain;
(b) shower (*of blows etc*); hail (*of bullets etc*); **p. d'or,** shower of gold; (*feu d'artifice*) golden rain; **une p. de reproches/compliments,** a stream of criticism/compliments.

plumage [plymaʒ] *nm* (*ensemble des plumes*) plumage, feathers; (*fait de plumer*) plucking.

plumard [plymar] *nm Arg* sack, pit; **aller au p.,** to hit the sack, to crash (out).

plum-cake [plumkɛk] *nm Vieilli* fruit cake; (*pl plum-cakes*).

plume¹ [plym] *nf* **(a)** feather; **oiseau sans plumes,** callow *or* unfledged bird; **gibier à plumes,** game birds; *F* **il y a laissé des plumes,** he didn't get away unscathed; *Fig F* **on lui a volé dans les plumes,** they laid into him; **léger comme une p.,** (as) light as a feather; *Prov* **la belle p. fait le bel oiseau,** fine feathers make fine birds; **lit de plume(s),** feather bed; *Boxe* **poids p.,** featherweight;
(b) (*de stylo*) (pen) nib; **p. (d'oie),** quill (pen); **p. à dessin,** drawing pen; *Fig* **les idées se pressent sous sa p.,** he can't write his ideas down quickly enough, his ideas are coming thick and fast; **écrire au courant** *ou* **au fil de la p.,** to write down (*words, ideas etc*) as they come into one's head; **dessin à la p.,** pen (and ink) drawing; **trait de p.,** stroke of the pen; **prendre la p.,** to put pen to paper; *Fig* **vivre de sa p.,** to make one's living by writing, to live by one's pen; *Fig* **avoir la p. facile,** to have a gift for writing;
(c) *Méd* **p. à vaccin,** vaccine point.

plume² *nm* = **PLUMARD.**

plumeau, -eaux [plymo] *nm* (*ustensile de ménage*) feather duster; (*touffe de poils*) tuft (*of hair etc*).

plumer [plyme] **1** *vt* to pluck (*poultry*); to scrape (*asparagus*); *F* to rob, to fleece, to skin (*s.o.*). **2** *vi* to feather. **3 se plumer** *vpr Arg* to hit the hay, to crash (out).

plumet [plymɛ] *nm* plume (*of helmet etc*); ostrich feather (*as ornament*).

plumetis [plymti] *nm Couture* **(a) broderie au p.,** raised *or* satin stitch; **(b)** (*étoffe*) Swiss muslin.

plumeux, -euse [plymø, -øz] *adj* feathery.

plumier [plymje] *nm* (*ouvert*) pen tray; (*à couvercle*) pencil box, pencil case.

plum(-pudding) [plum(pudiŋ)] *nm* plum pudding, Christmas pudding; (*pl plum(s)-puddings*).

plupart (la) [laplypar] *nf* most, the majority, *Fml* the greater part; (*de plusieurs quantités*) the greatest part; **la p. des hommes,** most (of the) men, the majority (of the) men; **la p. d'entre eux,** most of them; **la p. du temps,** most of the time; (*en général*) in most cases, generally; **pour la p.,** for the most part, mostly.

plural, -aux [plyral, -o] *adj* plural (*vote etc*).

pluralisme [plyralism] *nm Pol Phil* pluralism; **p. politique,** political pluralism, multi-party system.

pluraliste [plyralist] **1** *adj* pluralist(ic); **elections pluralistes,** multi-party elections. **2** *n* pluralist.

pluralité [plyralite] *nf* (*multiplicité*) plurality, multiplicity; *Rel* **p. des bénéfices,** pluralism; *Arch* **élu à la p. des voix,** elected by a majority.

pluriannuel, -elle [plyrianɥɛl] *adj* **récolte pluriannuelle,** crop harvested every few years; **contrat p.,** contract valid for a number of years.

pluridisciplinaire [plyridisiplinɛr] **1** *adj* multidisciplinary (*approach, studies*). **2** *nm* **le technicien doit être un p.,** the technician must possess a range of skills.

pluridisciplinarité [plyridisiplinarite] *nf* **favoriser la p. dans les études universitaires,** to encourage students to take up a range of subjects.

plurinational, -aux [plyrinasjɔnal, -o] *adj Vieilli* multinational.

pluriel, -elle [plyrjɛl] **1** *adj* plural. **2** *nm* plural; **au p.,** in the plural.

pluripartisme [plyripartism] *nm Pol* multi-party system.

plus [ply] (*often* [plys] *at the end of a word group*; [plyz] *before a vowel* **plus on est de fous, plus on rit** [plyzɔ̃nɛdfuplyzɔ̃ri]) **1** *adv* **(a)** (*davantage*) more; **soyez p. réaliste!,** be more realistic!; **ils sont (beaucoup) p. nombreux,** there are (far) more of them; **c'est sa mère, en p. jeune,** she looks just like her mother, only younger; **il est p. grand que moi,** he's taller than I (am) *or* than me; **je ne suis pas p. grand que lui,** I'm no taller than he (is) *or* than him; **elle écoute p. attentivement,** she listens more attentively; **une fenêtre p. haute que large,** a window higher than it is wide; **il a p. de patience que moi,** he has more patience than I have *or* than me; **deux fois p. grand,** twice as big; *F* **c'est p. que bien,** it's more than just good; **des résultats p. que satisfaisants,** more than satisfactory results; **je gagne p. que vous,** I earn more than you (do); **p. qu'à moitié** (*souvent* [plyskamwatje]), more than half (*done etc*); **en vouloir toujours p.,** to be always wanting more; **p. d'une fois,** more than once; **p. de dix hommes,** more than ten men; **il a p. de vingt ans,** he's over twenty; **pendant p. d'une heure,** for over *or* for more than an hour; **p. loin,** further *or* farther (on); **p. tôt,** sooner, earlier; **p. ... (et) p. ...,** the more ..., the more ...; **p. on est de fous p. on rit,** the more the merrier; **p. je lis, moins je retiens,** the more I read the less I remember; **et qui p. est** [plyzɛ], and what is more, and moreover; **j'en ai trois fois p. qu'il ne m'en faut,** I've (got) three times as much *or* as many as I need; **il y en a tant et p.,** there's an awful lot (of it *or* them); **c'est d'autant p. vrai qu'il l'a dit lui-même,** it must be true, he said so himself;
(b) (le) p., (the) most; **la p. longue rue** *ou* **la rue la p. longue de la ville,** the longest street in the town; **la p. belle femme que j'aie jamais vue,** the most beautiful woman I've ever seen; **c'est vous qui avez fait le p. de fautes,** you've made (the) most mistakes; **le p. vite possible,** as quickly as possible; **c'est à trente ans qu'elle a été la p. belle,** she was at her most beautiful *or* best at thirty; **ce que je désire le p.,** what I most desire; **le p. drôle, ce qu'il y a de p. drôle,** the funniest thing; **crier le p. fort,** to shout (the) loudest; **faites le p. que vous pourrez,** do the most you can, do your utmost; **(tout) au p.,** at the (very) most, at the (very) outside, at (the very) best; **c'est tout au p. s'il est midi,** it's twelve o'clock at the latest; **c'est tout ce qu'il y a de p. simple,** nothing could be simpler; **c'était des p. réussi,** (*extrêmement*) it was eminently successful;
(c) (*négation*) **ne... p.,** no more, no longer; **je (ne) le ferai p.,** I won't do it again; **je (ne) veux p. de cela,** I don't want any more of that; **je (ne) la verrai p. (jamais),** I'll never see her again; *Litt* **il n'est p.,** (*mort*) he is no more; **je n'ai** *ou F* **j'ai p. d'argent,** I haven't any money left, I've (got) no more money; **sans p. attendre,** without further ado; **p. de doute,** there is no longer any doubt about it; **il n'y a p. de jeunesse!,** young people aren't what they used to be; **p. d'espoir!,** there's no hope (now); **p. de potage, merci,** no more soup, thank you; **il (n')y en a p.,** there's no more (left), there's none left; **il (n')y a p. rien,** there's nothing left; (*c'est tout ce que j'offre etc*) there's nothing more; **p. que dix minutes!,** only ten minutes left!; **on procède non p. par ordre alphabétique, mais par thème,** we shall no longer proceed in alphabetical order, but according to theme; **pas p. que,** no more than; **pas p. qu'on ne doit voler, on ne doit mentir,** it is no more acceptable to lie than it is to steal;
(d) non p., either (*in negative sentences*); **je n'en ai pas non p.,** I haven't got any either; **(ni) moi non p.,** neither do I, neither did I *etc*, I don't, I didn't *etc* either; **jamais non p. je n'avais songé à ...,** nor had I ever thought of ...; **vous n'en avez guère non p.,** you haven't got much either;
(e) [plys] *esp Math* plus; **sept p. neuf p. un,** seven plus nine plus one; **il fait p. 20 (degrés),** it's plus 20 (degrees); **500 francs d'amende, p. les frais,** 500 francs fine and *or*

plus costs; *Golf* **p. quatre** [plyskatr], plus four;

(f) de p., more; **une journée de p.**, one day more, one more day; **il a trois ans de p. que moi,** he's three years older than I am *or* than me; **rien de p., merci,** nothing more *or* nothing else, thank you; **de p. en p.**, more and more; **de p. en p. froid,** colder and colder;

(g) en p., in addition, into the bargain; (*en sus*) extra; **la même maison, avec un balcon en p.**, the same house, but with a balcony; (*avec un autre balcon*) the same house, but with an extra *or* additional balcony; **le vin est en p.**, wine is extra; **il y en a trois en p. de lui,** there are three more besides him; **en p. de sa maison, elle s'occupe de son entreprise,** in addition to her house, she looks after her business (as well); **en p. de ce qu'il me doit,** over and above what he owes me; **sans p.**, (just that and) nothing more; **sans p. il les mit à la porte,** without further *or* more ado he turned them out; **elle a été aimable, sans p.**, she was pleasant, but no more than that;

(h) p. ou moins [plyzumwɛ̃], more or less; **elle joue p. ou moins bien,** she plays fairly well, she's not a bad player; **c'est un mensonge, ni p. ni moins,** it's nothing more nor less than a lie, it's purely and simply a lie; **ni p. ni moins,** neither more nor less.

2 *nm* **(a)** more; **qui peut le p. peut le moins,** you have *or* he has *etc* done more difficult things than that before;

(b) *Math* (*signe*) plus (sign);

(c) *Golf* **le p.** [ləplys], the odd;

(d) *Fig* (*atout*) advantage, asset, *F* plus; **c'est un p. pour vous,** that's a plus for you.

plusieurs [plyzjœr] *adj & pron* several; **p. personnes l'ont remarqué,** a number of people (have) noticed it; **de p. manières,** in more ways than one; **j'en ai p.**, I have several; **on s'y est mis à p.**, several *or* a number of us got together (to do it); **un ou p.**, one or more.

plus-que-parfait [plyskəparfɛ] *nm Gram* pluperfect, past perfect; (*pl plus-que-parfaits*).

plus-value [plyvaly] *nf* **(a)** *Econ Fin etc* increase in value, appreciation (*of goods, land etc*); (*excédent*) surplus, excess yield (*of tax etc*); **les recettes présentent une p.-v. de ...,** the receipts show an increase of ...; **impôt sur les p.-values,** capital gains tax; **(b)** *Phil* surplus (value), plus value.

plutonium [plytɔnjɔm] *nm Ch* plutonium.

plutôt [plyto] *adv* **(a)** rather, sooner; **p. la mort que l'esclavage,** sooner death than slavery; **p. souffrir que mentir,** it is better to suffer than to lie; **il récite p. qu'il ne chante,** he recites rather than sings; **p. que de partir,** instead of leaving; (*expression d'une préférence*) rather than leave; **demande p. à ta mère,** (you'd) better ask your mother (instead); **ne pleurez pas, riez p.**, don't cry, laugh instead;

(b) (*pour préciser*) rather, on the whole; **il faisait p. froid (que chaud),** the weather was cold if anything; **elle n'est pas bête, p. étourdie,** she's not so much stupid as confused, she's not stupid, just confused; **ses parents, ou p. son père,** his parents, or rather *or* or more precisely his father; **il n'est pas satisfait, mais p. soulagé,** he's not exactly satisfied, relieved rather;

(c) (*assez*) fairly, quite, rather, *F* pretty, *esp Fml* somewhat; **son discours était p. long,** his speech was somewhat long *or* was on the long side; *F* **il est p. bien, ce type!,** he's not bad-looking at all, that guy; **je suis en retard? – oui p.!**, am I late? – not half! *or* you can say that again!

pluvial, -iaux [plyvjal, -jo] *adj Géog* pluvial; rainy (*season etc*); **eau pluviale,** rainwater.

pluvier [plyvje] *nm (oiseau)* plover.

pluvieux, -ieuse [plyvjø, -jøz] *adj* rainy; wet, rainy (*weather, day*).

pluviner [plyvine] *vi* = **PLEUVASSER.**

pluviomètre [plyvjɔmɛtr] *nm Météo* rain gauge, pluviometer.

pluviôse [plyvjoz] *nm Hist Fr* Pluviôse (= *fifth month of the French Republican calendar*) (*Jan 20, 21-Feb 18, 19*).

pluviosité [plyvjozite] *nf Météo* rainfall.

P.M.E. [peɛmø] *nf(pl) (abrév* **petite(s) et moyenne(s) entreprise(s)**) small business.

P.M.I. [peɛmi] *nf* (*abrév* **petite et moyenne industrie**) = small industrial companies.

P.M.U. [peɛmy] *nm* (*abrév* **Pari Mutuel Urbain**) = state-run betting system; *Br* ≈ the Tote.

P.N.B. [peɛnbe] *nm Écon* (*abrév* **Produit national brut**) GNP.

pneu [pnø] *nm* **(a)** tyre, *US* tire; **p. à carcasse radiale,** radial tyre; **p. à carcasse croisée,** cross ply tyre; **(b)** (*lettre exprès*) *express letter;* **envoyer un p.**, to send an express letter (*through the pneumatic despatch system*).

pneumatique [pnømatik] **1** *adj* pneumatic; air (*pump etc*); inflatable (*raft etc*); **marteau p.**, pneumatic drill; **canot p.**, rubber dinghy. **2** *nm* = **PNEU.**

pneumocoque [pnømɔkɔk] *nm Biol* pneumococcus.

pneumologie [pnømɔlɔʒi] *nf Méd* pneumology.

pneumologue [pnømɔlɔg] *n Méd* chest specialist.

pneumonie [pnømɔni] *nf Méd* pneumonia.

pneumothorax [pnømotɔraks] *nm Méd* pneumothorax.

P.O. **(a)** (*abrév* **par ordre**) by order; **(b)** *Rad* (*abrév* **petites ondes**) MW.

Pô (le) [ləpo] *nm* the (river) Po.

pochade [pɔʃad] *nf* rapid sketch.

pochard, -arde [pɔʃar, -ard] *n F* drunk(ard), boozer.

poche¹ [pɔʃ] *nf* **(a)** (*partie de vêtement*) pocket; **p. de poitrine,** breast pocket; **p. intérieure,** inside (breast) pocket; **p. revolver,** hip pocket; **p. carnier,** poacher pocket; **p. plaquée,** patch pocket; *F* **faire les poches à qn,** to rifle *or* go through s.o.'s pockets; **calculateur de p.**, pocket calculator; **carnet de p.**, pocket book; **livre de p.**, paperback; **argent de p.**, pocket money; **avoir les poches vides,** to have empty pockets; *Fig* to be penniless; **avoir toujours la main à la p.**, to be always paying out, to be always putting one's hand in one's pocket; **j'en suis de ma p.**, I'm out of pocket by it; **payer de sa p.**, to pay out of one's own pocket *or* money; *Fig* **se remplir les poches,** to make a packet; **j'ai cent francs en p.**, I've (got) a hundred francs on me; **mettre qch dans sa p.**, to put sth in one's pocket, to pocket sth; *F* **mettez ça dans votre p. (et votre mouchoir dessus),** put that in your pipe and smoke it; **connaître qn/qch comme sa p.**, to know s.o./sth inside out *or* like the back of one's hand; *Fig* **les mains dans les poches,** with one's eyes shut, with one's hands tied behind one's back; **il n'a pas sa langue dans sa p.**, he's got plenty to say for himself; **mettre qn dans sa p.**, to get s.o. eating out of one's hand, to twist s.o. round one's little finger; *F* **c'est dans la p.**, it's in the bag;

(b) (*sac*) bag; (*plus grand*) sack; (*for tobacco etc*) pouch; **p. à cartes,** map case *or* holder; *Fig* **acheter chat en p.**, to buy a pig in a poke;

(c) (*amas de substance*) pocket; *Min* **p. d'eau,** feeder of water, water feeder; **p. de pétrole,** pocket of crude oil; **p. d'air,** *Av* air pocket; (*dans une pipe*) airlock;

(d) (*déformation*) bag; **pantalon qui fait des poches aux genoux,** trousers that are baggy at the knees; **poches sous les yeux,** bags under the eyes;

(e) *Biol Méd* sac; pouch (*of kangaroo etc*); *Anat* sac; **p. des eaux,** amniotic sac;

(f) (*filet de chasse*) purse net, bag net (*for catching rabbits*); **p. d'un chalut,** (*de pêche*) purse seine;

(g) *Fig* (*secteur*) pocket; **p. de résistance/pauvreté,** pocket of resistance/deprivation.

poche² *nf Tech* **p. à couler** *ou* **de coulée,** casting ladle.

poche³ *nm F* paperback; **paru en (collection de) p.**, published in paperback.

poché [pɔʃe] *adj* **(a)** *Culin* **œuf p.**, poached egg; **(b) œil p.**, black eye.

pocher¹ [pɔʃe] **1** *vt* **(a)** *Culin* to poach (*eggs, fish*); **(b)** *F* **p. l'œil à qn,** to give s.o. a black eye; *Arg* **la ferme, ou je te poche un œil!,** shut up, or I'll sock you one! **2** *vi* (*of clothes*) to get baggy.

pocher² *vt* to dash off (*sketch etc*).

pochette [pɔʃɛt] *nf* **(a)** (*enveloppe*) pouch; envelope (*for papers etc*); case (*for instruments etc*); sleeve (*of record*); **p. d'allumettes,** book of matches; **p.-surprise,** lucky bag; *Fig F* **la vie est une p.-surprise,** life is full of surprises; **(b)** (*petit mouchoir*) (breast pocket) handkerchief.

pocheuse [pɔʃøz] *nf* (egg) poacher.

pochoir [pɔʃwar] *nm* stencil (plate); **passer qch au p.**, to stencil sth; **décorer un plancher de motifs au p.**, to stencil a floor; **brosse à p.**, stencil(ling) brush.

pochon [pɔʃɔ̃] *nm Région* **(a)** (*sac*) bag; **(b)** (*grande louche*) ladle.

podagre [pɔdagr] *Arch* **1** *nf* gout. **2** *n* gout-sufferer. **3** *adj* suffering from gout.

podium [pɔdjɔm] *nm* podium; *Sp* rostrum; **monter sur le p.**, to mount the podium *or Sp* rostrum.

podologie [pɔdɔlɔʒi] *nf Méd* chiropody, *US* podiatry.

podologue [pɔdɔlɔg] *n Méd* chiropodist, *US* podiatrist.

podomètre [pɔdɔmɛtr] *nm* pedometer.

poêle¹ [pwal] *nf* frying pan, *esp US* skillet; **passer qch à la p.**, to fry sth.

poêle² *nm* **(a)** *Litt Arch* canopy (*in Catholic wedding*); **(b)** (funeral) pall; **porteurs des cordons du p.**, pall bearers.

poêle[3] *nm* stove; **p. à feu continu,** slow-burning stove; **p. à bois/à mazout,** wood(-burning) stove/oil stove.

poêlée [pwale] *nf* panful.

poêler [pwale] *vt* to cook in a frying pan, to fry.

poêlon [pwalɔ̃] *nm* casserole (dish).

poème [pɔɛm] *nm* poem; **p. symphonique/en prose,** symphonic/prose poem; *F* **c'est tout un p.,** (*personne*) he's quite a character; (*situation*) it's quite a carry-on.

poésie [pɔezi] *nf Littér* **(a)** (*art*) poetry; **faire de la p.,** to write poetry; *Fig* **la p. du style,** the poetic quality of the style; **une région pleine de p.,** a region full of (poetic) charm; **la p. des grandes villes américaines,** the romance of the great American cities; **(b)** (*poème*) poem, piece of poetry.

poète [pɔɛt] **1** *nm* poet; (*personne douée pour la poésie*) romantic (figure), poet; **elle est devenue le grand p. de son temps,** she became the greatest poet of her age. **2** *adj* **femme p.,** woman poet, poetess.

poétesse [pɔetɛs] *nf* woman poet, poetess.

poétique [pɔetik] **1** *adj* poetic (*inspiration, licence etc*); **l'art p.,** the art of poetry. **2** *nf* poetics.

poétiquement [pɔetikmɑ̃] *adv* poetically.

poétiser [pɔetize] *vt* to poet(ic)ize.

pogne [pɔɲ] *nf Arg* (*main*) paw, mitt.

pognon [pɔɲɔ̃] *nm F* (*argent*) lolly, dough.

pogrom(e) [pɔgrɔm] *nm* pogrom.

poids [pwa] *nm* **(a)** weight; (*lourdeur*) heaviness; **de tout son p.,** with all *or* with the whole of one's weight; **surveiller son p.,** to watch one's weight; **perdre du p.,** to lose weight; **vendre au p.,** to sell by weight; **ajouter qch pour faire le p.,** to throw sth in as a makeweight; **être plié sous le p. d'un sac,** to be weighed down by a sack; **p. utile,** live weight; *Av* payload; **p. mort,** dead weight; *Fig* **il ne sert à rien, c'est un p. mort,** he's useless, he's a dead weight; **p. brut,** gross weight; **p. net,** net weight; **p. en charge,** laden weight; *Aut* **p. lourd,** heavy lorry, *Am* truck; *Fml* heavy goods vehicle;

(b) (*masse*) weight; **p. atomique,** atomic weight; **p. spécifique,** *Phys* specific weight; *Ch* specific gravity;

(c) *Boxe* **p. coq,** bantamweight; **p. lourd,** heavyweight; **p. moyen,** middleweight; **p. mouche,** flyweight; **p. plume,** featherweight; **p. léger,** lightweight; **p. welter** *ou* **mi-moyen,** welter-weight; **ne pas faire le p.,** to fail to come up to weight *or* to make the (minimum) weight; *Fig F* **il ne fait pas le p.,** he's not up to the job *or* up to scratch *or* up to it;

(d) *Fig* (*importance*) importance; **donner du p. à qch,** to give weight to sth; **cette région dynamique finira par avoir autant de p. que Paris,** this dynamic region will eventually become as important as Paris; **faire le p. face à la concurrence,** to measure up to the competition; **le parti ne fait pas le p. devant le problème,** the party does not measure up to the problem; **son opinion a du p.,** his opinion carries weight;

(e) (*charge*) weight (*in clock etc*); **un p. de 20 kilos,** a 20-kilo weight; *Admin* **poids et mesures,** weights and measures; **étalonnage des p.,** standardization of weights; *Sp* **lancer le p.,** to put the shot;

(f) *Fig* (*charge pénible, écrasante*) load, burden; *Litt* **le p. des ans,** the weight of the years; **le p. des impôts,** the burden of taxation.

poignant [pwaɲɑ̃] *adj* poignant (*moment, thought*); harrowing (*experience, sight, reading etc*).

poignard [pwaɲar] *nm* dagger; **coup de p.,** stab; **donner un coup de p. à qn,** to stab s.o..

poignarder [pwaɲarde] *vt* to stab (*s.o.*); *F* to knife (*s.o.*).

poigne [pwaɲ] *nf* grip, grasp; *Fig* **homme à p.** *ou* **qui a de la p.,** strong *or* forceful *or* firm man; *Fig* **un chef d'état à p.,** a strong head of state, a head of state with a firm grip.

poignée [pwaɲe] *nf* **(a)** (*quantité contenue dans une main*) handful (*of flour etc*); fistful (*of banknotes*); **à** *ou* **par poignées,** in handfuls, by the handful; **(b)** (*petit nombre*) handful; **p. d'hommes,** handful of men; **(c) p. de main,** handshake; **donner une p. de main à qn,** to shake hands with s.o.; **(d)** handle (*of door etc*); grip (*of pistol*); hilt (*of sword*); pull (*of bell etc*).

poignet [pwaɲɛ] *nm* **(a)** *Anat* wrist; *Fig* **faire qch à la force du p.,** to do sth by sheer strength; (*à force de travail*) to do sth by sheer hard work; **(b)** (*d'une chemise etc*) cuff; (*bracelet, brassard*) wristband.

poil [pwal] *nm* **(a)** (*of animal*) hair, fur; **poils de chat,** cat hairs; **p. de chameau,** camel hair; **à p. long,** long-haired, shaggy; *Fig* **tomber sur le p. à qn,** to attack *or* to go for s.o.; *Arch* **monter un cheval à p.,** to ride a horse bareback; **les poils d'une brosse,** the bristles of a brush;

(b) (*fourrure*) coat (*of animals*); **cheval d'un beau p.,** sleek horse; **chien au p. rude/à p. dur,** wire-haired/rough-coated dog; *Fig* **caresser qn dans le sens du p.,** to rub s.o. up the right way;

(c) *Tex* nap (*of cloth*); pile (*of velvet*);

(d) *Anat* (body)hair; **p. du visage,** facial hair; **poils follets,** down; *F* **à p.,** starkers, (stark) naked, in the raw; **se mettre à p.,** to strip off; *F* **avoir un p. dans la main,** to be workshy *or* bone idle; *F* **ne pas avoir un p. sur le caillou,** to be as bald as a coot; *F* **avoir du p. aux pattes,** to have hairy legs; *Fig* **reprendre du p. de la bête,** to regain (one's) strength, to pick up; *Fig F* **des spécialistes de tous poils,** specialists on every subject under the sun; *F* **être de bon/de mauvais p.,** to be in a good/bad mood; *F* **(fait) au quart de p.,** perfectly (done); **à un p. près,** as near as dammit; **un p. plus vite,** a fraction faster; **au p.!,** wonderful!, super!;

(e) (*foin*) hair, bristle; **les poils d'artichaut,** the hairs on an artichoke; **p. à gratter,** itching powder.

poilant [pwalɑ̃] *adj F* hilarious, killingly *or* screamingly funny.

poiler (se) [səpwale] *vpr F* to kill oneself laughing.

poilu [pwaly] **1** *adj* (*qui a des poils*) hairy, shaggy; **p. comme un singe,** hairy as an ape; **une femme poilue,** a woman with a lot of (body) hair, a hairy woman. **2** *nm F* French soldier (1914-1918).

poinçon [pwɛ̃sɔ̃] *nm* **(a)** (*pointeau*) (engraver's) style, burin; (*de cordonnier*) awl, bradawl; *Couture* bodkin; (embroiderer's) stiletto; (sailmaker's) stabber; **p. à glace,** ice pick; **(b)** (*estampille, perforateur*) (perforating) punch; **(coup de) p. sur un billet,** punch hole in a ticket; **(c)** (*matrice*) die, stamp; **p. à chiffrer,** number punch; **(d)** (*marque*) stamped mark; **p. de contrôle,** hallmark (stamp).

poinçonnage [pwɛ̃sɔnaʒ] *nm,* **poinconnement** [pwɛ̃sɔnmɑ̃] *nm* stamping, boring, punching; (*contrôle par perforation*) punching (*of ticket etc*); (*fait de marquer*) stamping, hallmarking.

poinçonner [pwɛ̃sɔne] *vt* to prick (*small hole*); to bore (*large hole*); to punch (*metal, leather*); (*contrôler*) to punch, to clip (*ticket etc*); (*estampiller*) to stamp, to hallmark.

poinçonneur, -euse [pwɛ̃sɔnœr, -øz] **1** *n* (*personne*) *Ind* puncher; (*à la gare*) ticket collector. **2** *nf* **poinçonneuse,** stamping *or* punching machine; (ticket) punch.

poindre [pwɛ̃dr] *vi* (*prp* **poignant**; *pp* **point**; *pr ind* **il point, ils poignent**; *impf* **il poignait**; *p hist* **il poignit**; *fu* **il poindra**; *used esp in third person and in inf*) (*of daylight*) to dawn, to break; (*of plants etc*) to come up, to sprout, to come out; **p. à l'horizon,** (*of ship*) to heave in sight.

poing [pwɛ̃] *nm Anat* fist; **poings nus,** bare knuckles; **sabre/revolver au p.,** sword/revolver in hand; **serrer les poings,** to clench one's fists; **menacer qn du p., montrer le p. à qn,** to shake one's fist at s.o.; **dormir à poings fermés,** to sleep soundly *or* like a log; **coup de p.,** punch; **donner un coup de p. à qn,** to punch s.o.; *F* **envoyer son p. dans la figure de qn,** to give s.o. a punch in the face, *F* to bash s.o.'s face in; **taper du p. sur la table,** to bang one's fist (down) on the table; *Fig* **lever le p. (en signe de protestation),** to give a raised-fist salute; **il est tombé sur eux à coups de p.,** he laid into them with his fists; **coup de p. (américain),** knuckleduster.

point[1] [pwɛ̃] *nm* **(a)** (*dans l'espace*) point; **p. de départ,** starting point *or* place; **p. d'eau,** waterhole (*in desert*); tap (*in campsite*); **p. de vue,** (*panorama*) viewpoint, view; *Fig* (*opinion*) point of view, viewpoint, standpoint; **à tous les points de vue,** in all respects, in every respect; **en tous points,** in every way, in all respects; **au** *ou* **du p. de vue international,** from an international angle *or* point of view *or* viewpoint; **du** *ou* **au p. de vue caractère,** as far as (his *etc*) character is concerned; **p. chaud,** (*in war etc*) hot spot; *Fig* **les points chauds de l'actualité,** the most topical issues of the day; *Tech* **p. critique,** critical point; *Av* **essai au p. fixe,** ground run; **p. d'appui,** *Mil etc* base of operations; *Nau* outlying station; *Fig* strong point (*of argument etc*); *Tech* fulcrum (*of lever*); *Nau* **p. d'attache,** mooring (post); *Fig* **cette maison/ville est mon p. d'attache,** this house/city is my home base; *Aut* **p. mort,** neutral (gear); *Fig* **la production est au p. mort,** production is at a standstill; *MecE* **p. de graissage,** lubricating point; *Com* **p. de vente,** stockist;

(b) (*dans le temps*) point; **le p. du jour,** daybreak; **être sur le p. de faire qch,** to be on the point of doing sth, to be about to do sth; **sur le p. de mourir,** at *or* on the point of death; **arriver à p. nommé** *ou* **juste à p.,** to arrive just at the right moment *or* in the nick of time; **tout vient à p. à qui sait attendre,** everything comes to him who waits;

(c) (*question*) point, particular; **p. de droit,** point of law; **le p. capital,** the main point; **traiter un problème en trois points,** to deal with a problem in three stages; **mettre son p. d'honneur à ne pas céder,** to make it a point of honour not to yield; **n'ayez aucune crainte sur ce p.,** don't worry on that score *or* on that count; **exécuter un ordre de p. en p.,** to carry out an order exactly *or* to the letter;

(d) *Couture* stitch; **p. devant** *ou* **glissé** *ou* **coulé,** running stitch; **p. arrière,** backstitch; **p. de chausson,** herringbone stitch; **p. noué,** knot stitch; **p. de chaînette,** chainstitch; **p. roulé,** whipping; **p. croix, p. croisé,** cross-stitch; **p. de languette/de feston,** blanket/buttonhole stitch; **p. de Bruxelles,** Brussels lace; **p. perdu,** blind stitch, slip stitch; **coudre qch à points perdus,** to blindstitch *or* slipstitch sth; **faire un p. à un vêtement,** to put a few stitches in a garment;

(e) *Tricot* **p. de riz,** moss stitch; **p. mousse,** plain knitting, garter stitch;

(f) **p. de côté,** (*douleur*) stitch (in the side); **avoir un p. au dos,** to have a stabbing pain in one's back;

(g) *Nau Av etc* **p. estimé,** dead reckoning (position); **faire le p.,** to take bearings, to find one's position (on a map);

(h) *Opt* **au p.,** in focus; **mettre au p.,** to focus (*lens etc*); to perfect (*design etc*); to tune (*engine*); to adjust (*sth*); to finalize (*arrangements*); **mise au p.,** focusing (*of lens*); perfecting (*of technique etc*); tuning (*of engine*); adjusting (*of mechanism*); finalizing, finalization (*of arrangements*); restatement (*of question*); *Fig* **cette question reste à mettre au p.,** this question remains to be settled; **faire le p. (d'une question),** to take stock (of a question); **le p. sur l'affaire Martin,** an in-depth look at the Martin affair; *Vieilli* **recherche et mise au p.,** research and development;

(i) *Typ* dot; pip (*on dice etc*); **mettre les points sur les i,** to dot one's i's; *Fig* to make one's meaning perfectly plain; **p. (final),** full stop, *Am* period; **deux points,** colon; **p. d'interrogation,** question mark; *Fig* **ce qu'il lui a dit? on ne sait pas, c'est le p. d'interrogation,** what did he say to him? we don't know, that's the question we're all asking; **p. d'exclamation,** exclamation mark *or Am* point; *F* **tu restes ici, un p., c'est tout!,** you're staying here and that's that!, *esp Am* you're staying here, period!; *Télécom* **points et traits,** dots and dashes (*of Morse alphabet*); *Typ* **caractères de huit points,** eight-point type;

(j) (*marque visible*) speck, spot, dot; **le navire n'est qu'un p. à l'horizon,** the ship is a mere speck on the horizon; **p. noir,** (*on skin*) blackhead; *Fig* problem; (*à l'avenir*) cloud on the horizon; (*embouteillage*) blackspot (on the road), serious traffic build-up;

(k) (*phase, degré*) point, stage; (*étendue*) degree, extent; **p. d'ébullition,** boiling point; **p. d'éclair,** flash point; **p. de fusion/de congélation,** melting/freezing point; **jusqu'à un certain p.,** to a certain extent, up to a certain point; **au p. où en sont les choses,** as matters stand; **à ce p. que, à tel p. que, au p. que ...,** to such a point *or* an extent that ..., so much so that ...; **vous n'êtes pas malade à ce p.-là,** you're not as ill as all that; **au dernier p.,** to *or* in the last degree;

(l) **mal en p.,** ill, *F* in a bad way; *Vieilli* **en bon p.,** in good condition; **à p.,** in the right condition; *Culin* done to a turn; (*steak*) medium;

(m) (*de jeux*) point; (*total des points*) score; *Scol* mark; **marquer les points,** to keep (the) score; **elle a marqué 10 points,** she scored 10 points; *Boxe* **gagner aux points,** to win on points; **rendre des points à qn,** to give s.o. points; *Fig* to be more than a match for s.o.; *Scol* **bon/mauvais p.,** good/bad mark;

(n) (*unité*) point; *Géog* **points cardinaux,** cardinal points (of the compass); *Math* **points limites,** limiting points, limits; **p. d'intersection,** (point of) intersection; **l'indice de prix gagne/perd deux points,** the retail price index has gone up/down (by) two points;

(o) *Mus* **p. d'orgue,** pause, fermata.

point[2] *adv Vieilli Litt & Dial* = **PAS**[2]; **peu ou p.,** little or not at all; **le connaissez-vous? — p.,** do you know him? — not at all; **depuis plusieurs semaines, p. de nouvelles,** there's been no news (at all) for several weeks.

pointage [pwɛ̃taʒ] *nm* **(a)** (*contrôle*) checking, ticking off (*of names on list etc*); scrutiny (*of votes etc*); *Nau* pricking (*of chart*); plotting (*of position on map*); (*à l'usine etc*) timekeeping; *Sp* (*à l'arrivée*) clocking in; (*au départ*) clocking out; **(b)** *Mus* dotting (*of note*); **(c)** pointing, levelling, training (*of telescope etc*); (*tir*) aiming, training (*of gun etc*).

pointe [pwɛ̃t] *nf* **(a)** point (*of pin, knife etc*); tip, head (*of arrow, lance*); nose (*of bullet*); toe (*of shoe*); top (*of spire*); **p. d'aiguille,** needlepoint; *Rail* point of a switchblade; **coup de p.,** thrust; **à la p. de l'épée,** at the point of a sword; *Fig* by force; **p. d'asperge,** asparagus tip; **en p.,** pointed, tapering; **aller en p.,** to taper; **tailler un crayon en p.,** to sharpen a pencil; **barbe en p.,** pointed beard, goatee beard; **p. de lance,** spearhead; **marcher/se tenir sur la p. des pieds,** to walk/stand on tiptoe; **entrer sur la p. des pieds,** to tiptoe in; **faire des pointes,** to dance on point(s);

(b) (*moment d'intensité*) peak (*Math of curve, El of load, Méd of fever*); *Sp etc* **p. de vitesse,** spurt, sprint; **vitesse de p.,** highest speed; **heures** *ou* **période de p.,** peak period, rush hour; **les pointes de trafic,** the peak periods of traffic; *Litt* **p. du jour,** daybreak;

(c) *Mil* point (*of advanced guard*); *Fig* **pousser une p. sur ...,** to launch a spearhead against ...; **nous avons poussé une p. jusqu'à Paris,** we pressed on to Paris; *Nau* **tir en p.,** firing ahead; **être à la p. de qch,** to set the pace *or* lead in sth, to be in the forefront of sth, to be at the cutting edge of sth; **être à la p. de la lutte,** to be in the forefront of the struggle; *Fig* **les secteurs de p.,** high-tech industries, the most advanced sectors of industry; **industrie de p.,** high-tech *or* state-of-the-art industry; **technologie de p.,** state-of-the-art technology, leading edge technology;

(d) (*petite quantité, trace*) hint, touch, tinge; **parler avec une p. d'accent (étranger),** to speak with a hint of a foreign accent; **p. d'ironie,** touch of irony; **p. d'ail/de vanille,** touch of garlic/dash of vanilla;

(e) (*raillerie*) witty phrase, quip; **lancer des pointes à qn,** to make digs at s.o.;

(f) *Nau* gore (*of sail*); **p. de canot,** canvas;

(g) *Géog* **p. (de terre),** foreland, head(land);

(h) (*outil*) (stonemason's) point; *Menuis* **p. carrée,** bradawl; **p. à tracer,** scribe; **p. (sèche),** (dry) point, etching needle; **la p. sèche,** dry-point (etching);

(i) (*clou*) nail; (*pour tapis*) tack; *Sp* spike (*on shoe*); **chaussures à pointes,** spiked shoes, spikes;

(j) *Méd* **pointes de feu,** ignipuncture;

(k) (*lange*) nappy, *Am* diaper; (*écharpe, foulard*) (triangular) scarf.

pointeau, -eaux [pwɛ̃to] *nm* **(a)** *MecE* centre punch, *US* center punch; (*carburateur*) needle; **(b)** *Vieilli* (*personne*) timekeeper.

pointer[1] [pwɛ̃te] **1** *vt* **(a)** (*vérifier*) to check, to tick off (*names on list etc*); to scrutinize (*votes etc*); *Nau etc* to prick (*the chart*); to plot (*position*) (on the map);

(b) (*dresser*) **le cheval pointa les oreilles,** the horse pricked up its ears; **il pointa son nez à la porte,** his face appeared around the door, he peeped around the door;

(c) (*diriger*) to point, to level, to train (*telescope etc*); to aim, to train (*gun*); to train (*searchlight*) (**sur,** on);

(d) *Mus* to dot (*a note*); **note pointée,** dotted note;

(e) (*aiguiser*) to point (*needle*); to sharpen (*pencil*);

(f) *Vieilli* (*piquer*) to stab (*with sword etc*); to prick (*with needle etc*);

2 *vi* **(a)** **p. (à l'arrivée/à la sortie),** (*à l'usine*) to clock in/out;

(b) (*apparaître*) to appear; (*of plant*) to come up; (*of bird*) to soar; (*of horse*) to rear;

(c) (*au jeu de boules*) to get one in (= *to get one's ball nearest to the jack*).

3 se pointer *vpr F* to turn up, to show up.

pointer[2] [pwɛ̃tɛr] *nm* (*chien*) pointer.

pointeur, -euse [pwɛ̃tœr, -øz] **1** *n* (*contrôleur*) checker; *Ind* timekeeper; *Sp etc* marker, scorer; *Mil* gun-layer. **2** *nf* **pointeuse,** (time)clock.

pointillage [pwɛ̃tijaʒ] *nm Beaux-Arts etc* dotting; (*plus serré*) stippling.

pointillé [pwɛ̃tije] **1** *adj* dotted (*line*); stippled (*engraving*); *Tex* pinhead (*cloth*). **2** *nm* **(a)** (*trait*) dotted line; (*sur une feuille détachable etc*) perforations; **détacher suivant le p.,** tear along the dotted line; **(b)** (*technique de dessin*) stippling, stipple; **dessin en p.,** stippled design.

pointiller[1] [pwɛ̃tije] *vt* **(a)** (*percer de petits trous*) to dot; **roue à p.,** dotting wheel; **(b)** *Beaux-Arts* to stipple.

pointiller[2] *vi Péj Arch* to cavil (over trifles), to split hairs.

pointilleux, -euse [pwɛ̃tijø, -øz] *adj* particular, fastidious, finicky, *F* pernickety (**sur,** about).

pointillisme [pwɛ̃tijism] *nm Beaux-Arts* pointillism.

pointilliste [pwɛ̃tijist] *adj & n Beaux-Arts* pointillist.

pointu [pwɛ̃ty] **1** *adj* **(a)** (*aigu*) (sharp-)pointed (*knife etc*);

shrill (*voice*); **(b)** *Fig* (*susceptible*) touchy (*tone of voice, mood*); **(c)** *Fig* (*spécialisé*) in-depth; **être p. sur la question,** to be an expert on the question. **2** *adv Région F* **parler p.,** to speak with a Parisian accent.

pointure [pwɛ̃tyr] *nf* size (*in shoes, gloves etc*); **quelle est votre p. (de gants)?,** what size (gloves) do you take?

point-virgule [pwɛ̃virgyl] *nm* semicolon; (*pl points-virgules*).

poire [pwar] *nf* **(a)** pear; **entre la p. et le fromage,** at the end of the meal; *Fig* **j'irai lui en parler entre la p. et le fromage,** I'll talk to him about it when he's got a bit more time (to himself); *Fig* **garder une p. pour la soif,** to put something by for a rainy day; *Fig* **couper la p. en deux,** to compromise; (*faire la moyenne entre deux quantités*) to split the difference; **(b)** (*objet en forme de poire*) (pear-shaped) bulb (*of camera shutter etc*); (pear-shaped) switch (*of electric light*); **p. à lavement,** enema bag; **(c)** *F* (*tête*) mug; **il a une bonne p.,** he's got a nice enough face, he looks nice enough; **(d)** *F* (*idiot*) mug, sucker; **je ne suis pas une p.!,** I'm no mug!

poiré [pware] *nm* perry.

poireau, -eaux [pwaro] *nm* (*légume*) leek; *F* **faire le p.,** to be kept waiting, *F* to kick *or* cool one's heels.

poireauter [pwarote] *vi F* to be kept waiting, *F* to kick *or* cool one's heels.

poirée [pware] *nf Bot* white beet.

poirier [pwarje] *nm* **(a)** (*arbre*) pear tree; *Gym* **faire le p.,** to do a headstand; **(b)** (*bois*) pear-tree wood.

pois [pwa] *nm* **(a)** (*plante*) pea; **p. de senteur,** sweet pea; **(b)** *Culin* **petits p.,** garden peas; **p. chiche,** chickpea; **p. carré,** marrowfat pea; **p. cassés,** split peas; **purée de p.,** thick pea soup; (*avec morceaux de viande*) pease pudding; *F* (*brouillard*) peasouper; **(c)** (*pastille rond*) spot, polka dot; **cravate bleue à p. blancs,** blue tie with white spots, blue polka dot tie; **tissu à p.,** spotted *or* polka dot material.

poiscaille [pwɑskɑj] *n Arg* fish.

poison [pwazɔ̃] **1** *nm* **(a)** (*substance fatale*) poison; **(b)** *Fig F* (*thing*) **quel p.!,** how boring!, what a bind! **2** *n F* (*personne*) pest, horror.

poissard, -arde [pwasar, -ard] **1** *adj* vulgar, coarse. **2** *nf Vieilli Péj* **poissarde,** fishwife.

poisse [pwas] *nf F* bad luck; **c'est la p.!,** just my luck!; **porter la p.,** to bring bad luck.

poisser [pwase] **1** *vt* **(a)** (*engluer*) to pitch; **fil poissé,** waxed thread; **(b)** (*salir avec une matière gluante*) to make (*hands etc*) sticky (*with jam etc*); **(c)** *Arg Vieilli* to nab (*s.o.*). **2** *vi* (*of substance*) to be sticky.

poisseux, -euse [pwasø, -øz] *adj* sticky.

poisson [pwasɔ̃] *nm* **(a)** fish; **p. d'eau douce/de mer,** freshwater/saltwater fish; **p. chat,** catfish; **p. lune,** sunfish; **p. pilote,** pilot fish; **p. plat,** flat fish; **p. rouge,** goldfish; **p. volant,** flying fish; **prendre un/du p.,** to catch a/some fish; **je n'aime pas le p.,** I don't like fish; **p. d'avril!,** April fool!; **être (heureux) comme un p. dans l'eau,** to be as happy as a sandboy, to be in one's element; *F* **engueuler qn comme du p. pourri,** to shoot one's mouth off at s.o., to give s.o. a real mouthful; **(b)** *Astron* **les Poissons,** Pisces; **(c)** *Ent* **p. d'argent,** silver fish.

poissonnerie [pwasɔnri] *nf* (*magasin*) fish shop, fishmonger's; (*marché*) fish market.

poissonneux, -euse [pwasɔnø, -øz] *adj* (*of lake etc*) full of fish.

poissonnier, -ière [pwasɔnje, -jɛr] **1** *n Com* fishmonger, woman fishmonger, *Vieilli* fishwife. **2** *nm* (*bateau*) = small boat used by fishmongers to buy fish direct from fishing boats. **3** *nf* **poissonnière,** (*ustensile*) fish kettle.

poitrail [pwatraj] *nm* **(a)** *Constr* breastsummer; **(b)** (*partie du corps de certains animaux*) breast (*of horse*); *Fig F* (*poitrine*) chest; **un homme au p. découvert,** a man with a bare chest *or* torso; **(c)** breast strap, breastplate.

poitrinaire [pwatrinɛr] *adj & n Vieilli* consumptive (person).

poitrine [pwatrin] *nf* **(a)** (*thorax*) chest; **rhume de p.,** chest(y) cold; **chanter à pleine p.,** to sing at the top of one's voice; *Mus* **voix de p.,** chest voice; *Arch* **s'en aller de la p.,** to be dying of consumption; **(b)** (*poitrail*) chest; *Litt* breast; (*de femme*) bosom; **serrer qn contre** *ou* **sur sa p.,** to hold *or* press *or* clasp s.o. to one's breast; **tour de p.,** (*of man, child*) chest (measurement); (*of woman*) bust (measurement); **avoir une belle/forte p.,** to have a shapely bosom/to be well-endowed; **avoir la p. plate,** to be flat-chested; **elle n'a pas encore de p.,** her bust hasn't started to develop yet; **(c)** *Culin* breast (*of veal*); brisket (*of beef*); belly (*of pork*).

poivrade [pwavrad] *nf Culin* (*sauce*) highly peppered salad dressing; **manger des artichauts à la p.,** to eat artichokes (raw) with salt and pepper.

poivre [pwavr] *nm* pepper; **p. blanc/noir,** white/black pepper; **p. de Cayenne,** Cayenne pepper, chilli pepper; *Culin* **steak au p.,** pepper steak ; **grain de p.,** peppercorn; **p. et sel,** pepper-and-salt (*hair*).

poivré [pwavre] *adj* **(a)** (*assaisonné au poivre*) peppery (*food*); pungent (*smell*); **(b)** *Fig* (*grivois*) spicy, ribald (*story*).

poivrer [pwavre] **1** *vt* to (put) pepper (on), to season with pepper. **2 se poivrer** *vpr F* to get plastered *or* smashed.

poivrier [pwavrije] *nm* **(a)** *Bot* pepper plant; **(b)** (*petit pot*) pepper pot.

poivrière [pwavrijɛr] *nf* **(a)** (*plantation*) pepper plantation; **(b)** (*boîte*) pepper pot; **(c)** *Archit* pepperbox (turret).

poivron [pwavrɔ̃] *nm Bot* (sweet) pepper, capsicum; **p. vert/rouge/jaune,** green/red/yellow pepper.

poivrot, -ote [pwavro, -ɔt] *n Arg* drunk(ard), wino, boozer.

poix [pwa] *nf* pitch; **p. sèche,** resin; **noir comme (de la) p.,** pitch black; **p. liquide,** tar.

poker [pɔkɛr] *nm Cartes* poker; **p. d'as,** poker dice; *Fig* **une partie de p.,** a game of bluff (and counter-bluff).

polaire [pɔlɛr] **1** *adj* polar; **l'étoile p.,**the pole star; **froid p.,** intense *or* Arctic cold; **expédition p.,** polar expedition, expedition to the (North, South) Pole. **2** *nf Math* polar; **la p.,** the pole star.

polar [pɔlar] *nm F* (*livre*) thriller, whodunnit.

polarimètre [pɔlarimɛtr] *nm Phys* polarimeter.

polarisable [pɔlarizabl] *adj* polarizable.

polarisant [pɔlarizɑ̃] *adj* polarizing.

polarisation [pɔlarizɑsjɔ̃] *nf* **(a)** *Phys* polarization, polarizing (*of light, electrodes*); *Electron* **p. de grille,** grid bias; **résistance de p. de grille,** bias resistor; **(b)** *Fig* (*focalisation*) focusing (*of attention, energies etc*).

polariscope [pɔlariskɔp] *nm Opt* polariscope.

polariser [pɔlarize] **1** *vt Electron* to polarize; *Fig* to draw, to attract; **ce phénomène polarise l'attention de tous,** this phenomenon has been the focus of everybody's attention. **2 se polariser** *vpr F* (*de l'attention*) to focus; **se p. sur une question,** to focus one's attention on a question.

polariseur [pɔlarizœr] *nm Opt* polarizer.

polarité [pɔlarite] *nf* polarity.

polaroïd ® [pɔlarɔid] *nm Phot* polaroid ® (camera).

polatouche [pɔlatuʃ] *nm Zool* flying squirrel.

polder [pɔldɛr] *nm Géog* polder.

pôle [pol] *nm* **(a)** *Géog* pole; *Géog* **P. Nord/Sud,** North/South Pole; *Phys* **pôles semblables,** like poles; **pôles contraires,** opposite poles; **pôles magnétiques,** (*de la Terre*) magnetic poles; **(b)** *Fig* **p. d'intérêt/d'attraction,** focus of interest/centre of attention; *Écon Pol* **les pôles de croissance,** the main centres of economic growth; *Aut Sp* **être en p. position,** to be in pole position.

polémique [pɔlemik] **1** *adj* polemic(al). **2** *nf* polemic; (*situation controversée*) controversy.

polémiquer [pɔlemike] *vi* to engage in polemic.

polémiste [pɔlemist] *n* polemicist.

polémologie [pɔlemɔlɔʒi] *nf* the study of war.

polenta [pɔlɛnta] *nf Culin* polenta.

poli[1] [pɔli] **1** *adj* **(a)** (*lisse*) polished, burnished (*steel etc*); polished, buffed (*leather, shoes*); **(b)** *Vieilli* (*élégant*) polished, elegant (*style, writer*). **2** *nm* polish, gloss.

poli[2] *adj* (*courtois*) polite (*person, manners*); polite, civil (*person, answer*); **être très p. avec qn,** to be very polite *or* very courteous to s.o.; **peu p.,** rude, discourteous.

police[1] [pɔlis] *nf* **(a)** (*maintien de l'ordre*) maintenance of law and order; (*par la police*) policing; **exercer** *ou* **faire la p.,** to maintain law and order, to keep order; **p. du roulage** *ou* **de la circulation,** traffic regulations; *Vieilli* **numéro de p. d'un véhicule,** registration number *or Can* licence *or US* license number of a vehicle; **intervention des forces de p.,** police intervention, action by the police; *Jur* **tribunal de (simple) p.,** magistrate's court; *Mil* **salle de p.,** guard-room;

(b) la p., the police (force); **p. de la circulation,** traffic police; **p. administrative,** = administrative branch of the police; **p. judiciaire,** *Br* ≈ Criminal Investigation Department; **p. mondaine** *ou* **des mœurs,** ≈ vice squad; **appeler la p.,** to call the police; **agent de p.,** police officer; (*de circulation*) traffic policeman; **inspecteur de p.,** = (police) inspector; **commissaire de p.,** = (police) superintendent; **préfet de p.,** = chief commissioner of the Paris police; **appeler p. secours,** ≈ to dial *Br* 999 *or Am* 911 (for the police); **être de** *ou* **dans la p.,** to be in the police, to be a member of the police force; **remettre qn en-**

tre les mains de la p., to give s.o. up to the police; **la p. est à vos trousses,** the police are after you.
police² *nf* **(a)** *Jur* (insurance) policy; **p. d'assurance (sur la) vie/(contre l')incendie,** life insurance/fire insurance policy; **prendre une p.**, to take out a policy; **(b)** *Typ Ordinat* font.
policé [pɔlise] *adj* civilized.
policeman [pɔlisman] *nm* (British) policeman.
policer [pɔlise] *vt* **(je poliçai(s); n. poliçons) (a)** *Arch* (*gouverner*) to bring (*country*) under orderly government; **(b)** *Arch & Litt* to civilize.
polichinelle [pɔliʃinɛl] *nm* **(a)** (Mr) Punch; **théâtre de p.,** ≈ Punch and Judy show; **secret de p.**, open secret; *Fig F* **avoir un p. dans le tiroir,** (*être enceinte*) to have a bun in the oven; **(b)** *Fig Péj* buffoon; **faire le p.**, to act the fool.
policier, -ière [pɔlisje, -jɛr] **1** *adj* police (*enquiry, state, dog etc*); detective (*novel*). **2** *nm* **(a)** (*officier de police*) policeman, police officer; **femme p.**, policewoman; **(b)** *F* (*roman etc*) detective novel, whodunnit.
policlinique [pɔliklinik] *nf* = **POLYCLINIQUE.**
poliment [pɔlimɑ̃] *adv* politely, courteously.
polio [poljo] *Méd* **1** *nf F* polio. **2** *n* polio victim.
poliomyélite [pɔljɔmjelit] *nf Méd* poliomyelitis.
poliomyélitique [pɔljɔmjelitik] *Méd* **1** *adj* (*virus etc*) polio. **2** *n* polio victim.
polir [pɔlir] **1** *vt* **(a)** (*poncer*) to burnish, to buff (*metal etc*); **poli par l'usage,** shiny with use; **(b)** (*perfectionner*) to polish (up) (*style, speech etc*); to refine (*manners*). **2 se polir** *vpr* **se p. les ongles,** to polish *or* buff one's nails.
Polisario [pɔlisarjɔ] *nm Pol* **le Front P.**, the Polisario.
polissage [pɔlisaʒ] *nm* burnishing (*of metal*); buffing (*of metal, fingernails*).
polisseur, -euse [pɔlisœr, -øz] **1** *n* polisher. **2** *nf* **polisseuse,** polishing machine.
polissoir [pɔliswar] *nm Tech* buffing wheel; (*de graveur*) grinding disc; (*pour les ongles*) nail buffer.
polissoire [pɔliswar] *nf* **(a)** (*brosse*) polishing brush (*for shoes*); **(b)** *Ind* polishing shop.
polisson, -onne [pɔlisɔ̃, -ɔn] **1** *n* **(a)** (*galopin*) naughty child, *F* rascal, scamp; **(b)** *Vieilli* street urchin. **2** *adj* **(a)** (*méchant*) naughty, mischievous (*child*); **(b)** (*coquin, grivois*) smutty; **regard p.**, leer.
polissonner [pɔlisɔne] *vi Vieilli* (*of child*) to be mischievous *or* naughty.
polissonnerie [pɔlisɔnri] *nf* **(a)** (*espièglerie*) (child's) mischievous trick; **(b)** (*parole*) smutty remark; (*plaisanterie*) smutty joke.
politesse [pɔlitɛs] *nf* politeness, good manners, courtesy; **formules de p.**, = conventional polite phrases; (*dans une lettre*) customary salutation and close; **il l'a dit par p.**, he said it out of politeness *or* to be polite; **brûler la p. à qn,** to leave s.o. abruptly, to leave without saying goodbye to s.o.; **une p.**, a polite remark; **faire des politesses à qn,** to treat s.o. courteously *or* politely; **faire échange de politesses,** to exchange compliments.
politicaillerie [pɔlitikajri] *nf F* political manoeuvring *or US* maneuvering.
politicard, -arde [pɔlitikar, -ard] *F* **1** *n* political manoeuverer *or US* maneuverer. **2** *adj* scheming.
politicien, -ienne [pɔlitisjɛ̃, -jɛn] **1** *n* politician, *surtout US* politico. **2** *adj Péj* politicking; **politique politicienne,** politicking; **faire de la politique politicienne,** to politick.
politique [pɔlitik] **1** *adj* **(a)** (*de la société, du gouvernement*) political; **homme** *ou* **femme p.**, politician; **le corps p.**, the body politic; **détenu p.**, political prisoner; **il existe une connivence p. entre eux,** they have similar politics; **économie p.**, economics, *Vieilli* political economy; **(b)** *Arch & Litt* politic (*answer, choice, conduct*).
2 *nf* **(a)** (*du gouvernement etc*) policy; **p. intérieure/extérieure,** domestic *or* home/foreign policy; **suivre une nouvelle p.**, to follow *or* adopt a new policy; **la p. d'autriche,** burying one's head in the sand;
(b) (*affaires publiques*) politics; **se lancer dans la p.**, to go into politics; *Fig* **p. fiction,** political fantasy *or* fiction; **scénario de p. fiction,** scenario belonging to the realms of political fantasy *or* fiction.
3 *nm* **(a)** (*personne*) politician, statesman;
(b) *Fig* (*domaine*) politics; **le p. francais,** French politics; **limiter le p. aux questions nationales,** to restrict (political) discussions to national issues.
politiquement [pɔlitikmɑ̃] *adv* **(a)** politically, from a political angle; **(b)** *Litt* prudently, diplomatically.
politiquer [pɔlitike] *vi Arch F* to talk politics.
politisation [pɔlitizɑsjɔ̃] *nf* politicization.
politiser [pɔlitize] *vt* to politicize (*s.o., sth*); to bring politics into (*sth*).
polka [pɔlka] *nf* polka.
pollen [pɔlɛn] *nm* pollen; **taux du p.**, pollen count.
pollinisation [pɔlinizɑsjɔ̃] *nf* pollination.
polluant [pɔlɥɑ̃] **1** *adj* polluting; **produit p.**, pollutant. **2** *nm* pollutant; **polluants atmosphériques,** air pollution.
pollué [pɔlɥe] *adj* polluted; **région fortement polluée,** highly polluted region, region with a high level of pollution.
polluer [pɔlɥe] *vt* **(a)** (*infester*) to pollute (*atmosphere etc*); **(b)** *Arch & Litt* to pollute, to defile (*holy place*).
pollueur, -euse [pɔlɥœr, -øz] **1** *n* polluter. **2** *adj* polluting.
pollution [pɔlysjɔ̃] *nf* **(a)** (*dégradation de l'environnement*) pollution (*of the air, etc*); **p. atmosphérique,** atmospheric *or* air pollution; **(b)** *Arch & Litt* pollution, defilement (*of holy place*); **(c)** *Méd* **pollutions nocturnes,** wet dreams, *Méd* nocturnal emissions.
polo [polo] *nm* **(a)** *Sp* polo; **(b)** (*chemise*) polo shirt.
polochon [pɔlɔʃɔ̃] *nm F* bolster; **combat à coups de polochons,** pillow fight.
Pologne [pɔlɔɲ] *nf* Poland.
polonais, -aise [pɔlɔnɛ, -ɛz] **1** *adj* Polish. **2** *nm Ling* Polish. **3** *n* **P.**, Pole; *F* **soûl comme un P.**, as drunk as a lord. **4** *nf Mus* **polonaise,** polonaise.
poltron, -onne [pɔltrɔ̃, -ɔn] **1** *adj* cowardly. **2** *n* coward.
poltronnerie [pɔltrɔnri] *nf* cowardice.
polyacide [pɔliasid] *Ch* **1** *adj* polyacid. **2** *nm* polyacid.
polyamide [pɔliamid] *nm Ch* polyamide.
polyandre [pɔljɑ̃dr] *adj* polyandrous.
polyandrie [pɔljɑ̃dri] *nf* polyandry.
polyarthrite [pɔliartrit] *nf Méd* polyarthritis.
polychrome [pɔlikrom] *adj* polychrome, polychrom(at)ic.
polychromie [pɔlikrɔmi] *nf* polychromy.
polyclinique [pɔliklinik] *nf Méd* health centre; (*annexe d'hôpital*) outpatients' clinic *or* department.
polycopie [pɔlikɔpi] *nf* stencilling *or* duplicating process.
polycopié [pɔlikɔpje] **1** *adj* duplicated, cyclostyled. **2** *nm* duplicate; *Scol Univ* duplicated course material.
polycopier [pɔlikɔpje] *vt* to duplicate, to cyclostyle.
polyculture [pɔlikyltyr] *nf Agr* mixed farming.
polydactyle [pɔlidaktil] *adj* polydactyl.
polyèdre [pɔliɛdr] *Math* **1** *adj* polyhedral. **2** *nm* polyhedron.
polyédrique [pɔliedrik] *adj Math* polyhedral, polyhedric.
polyester [pɔliɛstɛr] *nm Ch* polyester.
polyéthylène [pɔlietilɛn] *nm* polythene; *surtout Am* polyethylene.
polygame [pɔligam] **1** *adj* polygamous. **2** *n* polygamist.
polygamie [pɔligami] *nf* polygamy.
polyglotte [pɔliglɔt] *adj & n* polyglot.
polygonal, -aux [pɔligɔnal, -o] *adj* polygonal.
polygone [pɔligɔn] *nm* **(a)** *Math* polygon; **(b)** *Mil* experimental range, shooting range.
polymérisable [pɔlimerizabl] *adj Ch* that can be polymerized.
polymère [pɔlimɛr] *Ch* **1** *adj* polymeric. **2** *nm* polymer.
polymérisation [pɔlimerizɑsjɔ̃] *nf Ch* polymerization.
polymorphe [pɔlimɔrf] *adj Biol Ch* polymorphous, polymorphic.
polymorphie [pɔlimɔrfi] *nf*, **polymorphisme** [pɔlimɔrfism] *nm Biol Ch* polymorphism.
Polynésie [pɔlinezi] *nf* Polynesia.
polynésien, -ienne [pɔlinezjɛ̃, -jɛn] **1** *adj* Polynesian. **2** *n* **P.**, Polynesian.
polynôme [pɔlinom] *nm Math* polynomial.
polynucléaire [pɔlinykleɛr] *adj Biol* polynuclear.
polype [pɔlip] *nm* **(a)** *Zool* polyp; **(b)** *Méd* polyp(us).
polypétale [pɔlipetal] *adj Bot* polypetalous.
polypeux, -euse [pɔlipø, -øz] *adj Méd* polypous.
polyphasé [pɔlifaze] *adj El* polyphase, multiphase (*system*).
polyphonie [pɔlifɔni] *nf Mus* polyphony.
polysémie [pɔlisemi] *nf* polysemy.
polysémique [pɔlisemik] *adj Ling* polysemous.
polysoc [pɔlisɔk] *nm Agr* multiple plough *or US* plow.
polystyle [pɔlistil] *adj Archit* Polystyle (*hall, temple*).
polystyrène [pɔlistirɛn] *nm Ch* polystyrene.
polysyllabe [pɔlisilab] **1** *adj* polysyllabic (*word*). **2** *nm* polysyllable.
polysyllabique [pɔlisilabik] *adj* polysyllabic.
polytechnicien, -ienne [pɔlitɛknisjɛ̃, -jɛn] *n* student at the École polytechnique; (*diplômé*) graduate of the École polytechnique.
polytechnique [pɔlitɛknik] **1** *adj* **(a)** *Arch* polytechnic; **(b)** **École p.**, = university institution specializing in

engineering. **2** *nf* **la P.**, = university institution specializing in engineering.
polythéisme [pɔliteism] *nm* polytheism.
polythéiste [pɔliteist] **1** *n* polytheist. **2** *adj* polytheistic, polytheist.
polythène [pɔlitɛn] *nm* polythene.
polyuréthane [pɔliyretan] *nm Ch* polyurethane.
polyvalence [pɔlivalɑ̃s] *nf Ch* polyvalence, polyvalency, multivalence.
polyvalent [pɔlivalɑ̃] **1** *adj* **(a)** *Ch* polyvalent, multivalent; **(b)** *(salle, outil)* multi-purpose; *(outil etc)* versatile; **elle est polyvalente,** she's very versatile; *Admin* **inspecteur p.,** tax inspector. **2** *nm Admin* tax inspector.
polyvinyle [pɔlivinil] *nm Ch* polyvinyl; **chlorure de p.,** polyvinyl chloride.
polyvinylique [pɔlivinilik] *adj Ch* polyvinyl.
pomélo [pɔmelo] *nm* pomelo.
pomiculteur [pɔmikyltœr] *nm* fruit grower.
pommade [pɔmad] *nf Méd* ointment; *Arch* pomade *(for the hair etc)*; **p. pour les lèvres,** lip salve; *Fig* **passer de la p. à qn,** to butter s.o. up.
pommader [pɔmade] *vt Arch* to pomade.
Pommard [pɔmar] *nm* Pommard.
pomme [pɔm] *nf* **(a)** *(fruit)* apple; **p. à cuire,** cooking apple, cooker; **p. à couteau,** eating apple; **p. à cidre,** cider apple; **p. sauvage,** crab apple; **compote de pommes,** stewed apples, apple purée; *Fig* **p. de discorde,** bone of contention; *F* **moi, sa p. et toi,** me, him and you; *F* **haut comme trois pommes,** *(enfant)* knee-high to a grasshopper; *F* **tomber dans les pommes,** to pass out, to faint; *Anat* **p. d'Adam,** Adam's apple; **p. épineuse,** thorn apple; **p. de chêne,** oak apple; **p. de pin,** pine cone, fir cone;
(b) **p. de terre,** potato; *Culin* **pommes (à la) vapeur/à l'anglaise,** steamed/boiled potatoes; **pommes chips,** potato crisps, *Am* chips; **bifteck aux pommes,** steak and chips; *Fig F* **c'est un vrai sac de pommes de terre, cette femme,** she's a real sack of potatoes, that woman;
(c) *(cœur)* heart *(of lettuce, cabbage)*;
(d) *(partie arrondie)* knob *(of bedstead, walking stick etc)*; rose *(of watering can)*; *Nau* truck *(of mast)*; **canne à p. d'or,** gold-headed stick; **p. de douche,** shower head.
pommé [pɔme] *adj* **(a)** *(cabbage etc)* well rounded, round; **laitue pommée,** cabbage lettuce; **choux bien pommés,** fine heads of cabbage; **(b)** *F Vieilli* complete, downright *(fool, blunder etc)*.
pommeau, -eaux [pɔmo] *nm* pommel *(of sword, saddle)*; butt *(of fishing rod)*; knob *(of walking stick)*.
pommelé [pɔmle] *adj* dappled, mottled; **gris p.,** dapple-grey *(horse)*; **ciel p.,** mackerel sky.
pommeler (se) [səpɔmle] *vpr* (**il se pommelle; il se pommellera**) **(a)** *(of sky)* to become covered *or* dappled with small fleecy clouds; **(b)** *(devenir rond)* = **POMMER**.
pommelle [pɔmɛl] *nf* grating, strainer *(over drainpipe etc)*.
pommer [pɔme] *vi (of cabbage etc)* to form a head *or* heart, to heart (up).
pommeraie [pɔmrɛ] *nf* apple orchard.
pommette [pɔmɛt] *nf* **(a)** *Anat* cheekbone; **avoir les pommettes saillantes,** to have high cheekbones; **(b)** *(partie, chose ronde)* knob.
pommier [pɔmje] *nm* apple tree; **p. sauvage,** crab (apple) tree.
pompage [pɔ̃paʒ] *nm* pumping (up, out *etc*); **station de p.,** pumping station.
pompe¹ [pɔ̃p] *nf* *(cérémonie)* pomp, ceremony, display; **en grande p.,** with great (pomp and) ceremony; **ordonnateur** *ou* **entrepreneur de pompes funèbres,** undertaker, funeral director, *surtout US* mortician.
pompe² *nf* **(a)** pump; **p. aspirante,** suction pump, lift pump; **p. (re)foulante,** force pump; **p. aspirante et foulante,** lift-and-force pump; **p. à incendie,** fire engine, *Am* fire truck; **p. à air, p. pneumatique,** air pump, pneumatic pump; **p. à vide,** vacuum pump; **p. de bicyclette,** bicycle pump; **p. d'alimentation** *ou* **alimentaire,** feed pump; **p. à chaleur,** heat pump; **épuiser l'eau à la p.,** to pump out the water; **eau de p.,** pump water; *F Iron* **Château-la-P.,** Adam's ale, tap water; *F* **avoir le coup de p.,** to be fagged out; **une barre de chocolat pour le coup de p. de onze heures,** a chocolate bar for when you get that sinking feeling; *F* **à toutes pompes,** like lightning, at top speed; *F* **faire des pompes,** to do press-ups *or Am* push-ups; *MecE* **p. à graisse,** grease gun; **p. à essence,** *(de moteur)* fuel pump; *(distributeur)* petrol pump, *Am* gas pump; *(station-service)* petrol station, *Am* gas station;
(b) *Mus* **p. d'accord,** (tuning) slide *(of wind instrument)*;
(c) **serrure à p.,** Bramah lock;
(d) *F* **pompes,** shoes; **ça, c'est de la p.!,** those are some shoes!; **en avoir plein les pompes,** to have had it up to here; **être à côté de ses pompes,** to be on one's uppers, to be flat broke;
(e) *Arg Mil* **(soldat de) deuxième p.,** *Br* squaddie, *US* grunt.
Pompée [pɔ̃pe] *nm Antiq* Pompey.
Pompéi [pɔ̃pei] *nf* Pompeii.
pompéien, -enne [pɔ̃pejɛ̃, -jɛn] **1** *adj* Pompeiian. **2** *n* **P.,** Pompeiian.
pomper [pɔ̃pe] **1** *vt* **(a)** *(puiser)* to pump *(water, air)*; *Fig F (épuiser)* to do *(s.o.)* in; **des parasites qui pompent le sang,** parasites that suck the blood; *F* **être pompé,** to be fagged out; *F* **tu me pompes l'air,** you're getting on my wick; **(b)** *Arg* to knock back *(a drink)*. **2** *vi* **(a)** *(faire marcher une pompe)* to pump; **(b)** *Scol Arg* to copy (**sur qn,** from s.o.).
pompette [pɔ̃pɛt] *adj F* tipsy, merry.
pompeusement [pɔ̃pøzmɑ̃] *adv Péj* pompously.
pompeux, -euse [pɔ̃pø, -øz] *adj Péj* pompous.
pompier¹ [pɔ̃pje] *nm* fireman, *Am* fire fighter; **p. de service,** fire officer; **les pompiers,** *Br* the fire brigade, *Am* the fire fighters.
pompier², -ière [pɔ̃pje, -jɛr] *Beaux-Arts Péj* **1** *adj* hackneyed *(art, style)*. **2** *nm* artist with a hackneyed style.
pompiste [pɔ̃pist] *n Aut* (petrol, *Am* gas) pump attendant, forecourt attendant.
pompon [pɔ̃pɔ̃] *nm* pompom, *F* bobble; *F* **ça, c'est le p.!,** that's the limit!, that takes the biscuit; *Iron* **avoir le p.,** to be the limit, to take the biscuit; *F Vieilli* **avoir son p.,** to be tipsy.
pomponner (se) [səpɔ̃pɔne] *vpr F* to doll oneself up.
ponçage [pɔ̃saʒ] *nm* **(a)** *(action de poncer)* pumicing; *(au papier de verre)* sandpapering; *(de peinture)* rubbing down, sanding down; **(b)** *Beaux-Arts* pouncing.
ponce [pɔ̃s] *nf* **(a)** **(pierre) p.,** pumice (stone); **(b)** *Beaux-Arts* pouncing bag.
ponceau¹, -eaux [pɔ̃so] *nm* culvert.
ponceau², -eaux 1 *nm* **(a)** *Bot* (corn) poppy; **(b)** **(rouge) p.,** poppy red. **2** *adj inv* **(rouge) p.,** poppy-red, flame red.
Ponce Pilate [pɔ̃spilat] *nm Bible* Pontius Pilate.
poncer [pɔ̃se] *vt* (**je ponçai(s); n. ponçons**) **(a)** *(passer à une substance abrasive)* to pumice; *(au papier de verre)* to sandpaper; to rub down, to sand down *(paint)*; **(b)** *Beaux-Arts* to pounce.
ponceur [pɔ̃sœr] *nm* polisher.
ponceuse [pɔ̃søz] *nf* sanding machine, sander.
poncho [pɔ̃tʃo] *nm* poncho.
poncif [pɔ̃sif] *nm* **(a)** *Beaux-Arts* pouncing pattern; **(b)** *(banalité, évidence)* banality, commonplace.
ponction [pɔ̃ksjɔ̃] *nf Méd* puncture; tapping *(of lung etc)*; pricking *(of blister)*.
ponctionner [pɔ̃ksjɔne] *vt Méd* to puncture; to tap *(lung, patient)*; to prick *(blister)*.
ponctualité [pɔ̃ktɥalite] *nf* punctuality.
ponctuation [pɔ̃ktɥasjɔ̃] *nf* punctuation.
ponctuel, -elle [pɔ̃ktɥɛl] *adj* **(a)** *(régulier)* punctual; **(b)** *Phys* **source ponctuelle de chaleur,** pinpoint flame; **source lumineuse ponctuelle,** point source; **projecteur p.,** spotlight; **(c)** *Fig (qui ne concerne qu'un point)* **intervention ponctuelle du gouvernement,** exceptional action by the government; **c'est un changement p.,** the change is due to exceptional circumstances; **avoir des connaissances ponctuelles dans un domaine,** to have detailed knowledge of one subject; **aide ponctuelle,** assistance given on a one-off basis; **opération ponctuelle,** one-off operation.
ponctuellement [pɔ̃ktɥɛlmɑ̃] *adv* selectively.
ponctuer [pɔ̃ktɥe] *vt* to punctuate *(sentence)*; to emphasize, to accentuate *(one's words in speaking)*; **elle ponctua ses explications de silences,** her explanation was punctuated with silences.
pondaison [pɔ̃dɛzɔ̃] *nf* egg-laying time.
pondérable [pɔ̃derabl] *adj Tech* weighable.
pondérateur, -trice [pɔ̃deratœr, -tris] *adj* balancing, stabilizing.
pondération [pɔ̃derasjɔ̃] *nf* **(a)** *(d'une personne)* levelheadedness; *(symétrie, équilibre)* balance; **parler/agir avec p.,** to speak/act calmly *or* with poise; **(b)** *Econ* weighting *(of index)*; *Math* **coefficient de p.,** weighting.
pondéré [pɔ̃dere] *adj* **(a)** *(équilibré, calme)* well balanced *(mind)*; cool, levelheaded, poised *(person)*; **(b)** *Econ* **indice**

p., weighted index.
pondérer [pɔ̃dere] *vt* (**je pondère; je pondérerai**) **(a)** (*équilibrer*) to balance (*powers etc*); **(b)** *Econ* to weight (*index*).
pondéreux, -euse [pɔ̃derø, -øz] *adj Tech* heavy (*goods etc*).
pondeur, -euse [pɔ̃dœr, -øz] **1** *adj* (egg-)laying; **poule pondeuse,** laying hen. **2** *nf* **pondeuse,** (*poule*) (good) layer; *Fig Péj* (*femme*) brood mare. **3** *nm Péj* **p. de prose,** prolific author.
pondoir [pɔ̃dwar] *nm* nest box.
pondre [pɔ̃dr] *vt* **(a)** (*of birds etc*) to lay (*eggs*); **œuf frais pondu,** new laid egg; **(b)** *Fig F* (*of writer etc*) to churn out (*novel etc*); **elle a pondu une de ces traductions!,** she produced an awful translation.
poney [pɔnɛ] *nm* pony.
pongiste [pɔ̃ʒist] *n Sp* table tennis player.
pont [pɔ̃] *nm* **(a)** *Constr* bridge; **p. pour piétons,** footbridge; **p. volant,** flying bridge; **p. tubulaire,** box (girder) bridge; **p. suspendu,** suspension bridge; **p. cantilever** *ou* **à consoles** *ou* **en encorbellement,** cantilever bridge; **p. basculant** *ou* **à bascule,** drawbridge, bascule bridge; **p. tournant** *ou* **pivotant,** swing bridge; **p. de bateaux,** floating bridge, pontoon bridge; *Admin* **les Ponts et Chaussées,** = the Roads *or* Highways Department; *Mil* **tête de p.,** bridgehead; *Ind* **p. roulant,** travelling crane; (*support*) gantry; *Ind* **p. de décharge** *ou* **à chariots culbuteurs,** tipping stage; **p. élévateur,** (*in garage*) (repair) ramp; **p. de graissage,** (*in garage*) ramp; *El* **p. de Wheatstone,** Wheatstone's bridge; **p. aérien/maritime,** airlift/sealift; **vivre sous les ponts,** to be a tramp; *Fig* **il est passé de l'eau sous les ponts,** a lot of water has passed *or* flowed under the bridge; **p. aux ânes** [pɔ̃tozan], common knowledge; *Fig* **faire le p.,** to take the intervening working day(s) off; (*en fin de semaine*) to make a long weekend of it; *Fig* **le p. de la Pentecôte,** the (long) Whitsun Bank Holiday weekend; *Fig* **faire un p. d'or à qn,** to give s.o. a golden hello;
(b) *Nau* deck (of ship); **p. avant,** foredeck; **p. arrière,** after deck; **p. principal,** main deck; **p. supérieur, p. des gaillards,** upper deck; **p. inférieur,** lower deck; **navire à un p.,** single-decker (ship), single-deck ship; **navire à deux/trois ponts,** two-/three-decker; **homme** *ou* **matelot de p.,** deck hand; (*dans la marine*) upper-deck rating; **monter sur le p.,** to go *or* come on deck; **être sur le p.,** to be on deck; **tout le monde sur le p.!,** all hands on deck!; (*dans la marine*) clear lower deck!; **commander tout le monde sur le p.,** to pipe up all hands; **passage** *ou* **voyage sur le p.,** deck passage, *Com* **sur p.,** free on board, f.o.b; **faux p.,** orlop deck; **p. des embarcations,** boat deck; **p. des emménagements, p. des premières,** saloon deck; **p. promenade,** promenade deck, sun deck, hurricane deck (*on liner*); **p. de manœuvre,** hurricane deck; **p. d'envol,** flight deck (*of aircraft carrier etc*);
(c) *MecE* live axle; *Aut* **p. arrière,** rear axle, back axle;
(d) *Cartes* bridge (*in a card*);
(e) *Fig* link, bridge; **assurer un p. entre Paris et la province,** to provide a link between Paris and the provinces; **il faut couper les ponts,** you must break it off; **elle a coupé les ponts avec ce milieu,** she broke off all relations *or* severed all links *or* ties with that circle.
Pont (le) [ləpɔ̃] *nm Antiq* **(a)** the (Kingdom of) Pontus; **(b) le P.-Euxin,** the Euxine Sea, the Black Sea.
pontage [pɔ̃taʒ] *nm* **(a)** bridge building; (*travaux*) bridging; **(b)** *Nau* decking; **(c)** *Méd* (*greffage*) bypass operation; **on lui a fait un p.,** he's had a bypass, he's had bypass surgery.
pont-bascule [pɔ̃baskyl] *nm* drawbridge, bascule bridge; (*pour peser les poids lourds etc*) weighbridge; (*pl ponts-bascules*).
ponte[1] [pɔ̃t] *nf* **(a)** (*pondaison*) laying (of eggs); **(b)** (*œufs*) eggs (laid).
ponte[2] *nm* **(a)** (*à la roulette etc*) punter; **(b)** *F* big shot, bigwig.
ponté [pɔ̃te] *adj* decked (*boat*); **non p.,** open (*boat*).
pontée [pɔ̃te] *nf Nau* deck load, deck cargo.
ponter[1] [pɔ̃te] *vt* **(a)** *Nau* to lay the decks of, to deck (*vessel*); **(b)** (*installer un pont sur*) to bridge (*river etc, esp with pontoon bridge*).
ponter[2] *vi* (*à la roulette etc*) to punt.
pontier [pɔ̃tje] *nm Tech* keeper of swing bridge.
pontife [pɔ̃tif] *nm* pontiff; *F* bigwig; **le souverain P.,** (*the Pope*) the Supreme Pontiff; *F* **les pontifs de l'hôpital,** the bigwigs *or* top brass at the hospital.
pontifiant [pɔ̃tifjɑ̃] *adj F Péj* pontificating.
pontifical, -aux [pɔ̃tifikal, -o] **1** *adj* pontifical, papal. **2** *nm* pontifical.
pontificat [pɔ̃tifika] *nm* pontificate; **sous le p. de Jean-Paul II,** during the pontificate of John-Paul II.
pontifier [pɔ̃tifje] *vi* (*impf & pr sub* **n. pontifiions; v. pontifiiez**) to pontificate.
pont-l'Évêque [pɔ̃levɛk] *nm inv* Pont l'Évêque cheese.
pont-levis [pɔ̃l(ə)vi] *nm* drawbridge (*of castle etc*); **p.-l. à fléau** *ou* **à balancier,** lever drawbridge; (*pl ponts-levis*).
Pont-Neuf [pɔ̃nœf] *nm Fig* **être solide comme le P.-N.,** to have the constitution of an ox, to be as fit as a fiddle.
ponton [pɔ̃tɔ̃] *nm* **(a)** (*construction flottante*) pontoon; **p. d'incendie,** fire float; **p. d'atterrissage,** (floating) landing stage; **(b)** *Nau Vieilli* (*prison flottante*) prison ship; **p. à mâture,** sheer hulk.
pontonnier [pɔ̃tɔnje] *nm* **(a)** *Mil* pontoneer, pontonier; **(b)** (*gardien*) keeper of swing bridge.
pool [pul] *nm* **(a)** *Econ etc* pool, common stock, common fund; (*investisseurs*) pool, combine, syndicate; **(b)** (*équipe*) **p. de dactylos,** typing pool.
pop [pɔp] *adj inv & nm* **(musique) p.,** pop (music); **chanteur p.,** pop singer.
pop'art [pɔpart] *nm Beaux-Arts* pop art.
pop-corn [pɔpkɔrn] *nm inv* popcorn.
pope [pɔp] *nm Rel* pope (of the Orthodox church).
popeline [pɔplin] *nf Tex* poplin.
popote [pɔpɔt] **1** *nf* **(a)** *F* (*cuisine*) cooking; **faire la p.,** to do the cooking; **(b)** *Mil etc* canteen; (*mess*) officers' mess. **2** *adj inv F souvent Péj* stay-at-home (*person*).
popotin [pɔpɔtɛ̃] *nm Arg* bum, *Am* ass; **se manier le p.,** to get a move on; *Br Vulg* to get one's arse in gear.
populace [pɔpylas] *nf Péj* rabble, riff-raff.
populacier, -ière [pɔpylasje, -jɛr] *adj* common, vulgar, low.
populage [pɔpylaʒ] *nm* marsh marigold.
populaire [pɔpylɛr] *adj* popular; *Pol etc* of the people; **démocratie p.,** people's democracy; **manifestation p.,** mass demonstration; **chanson p.,** folk song; **expression p.,** slang expression; **un roman p.,** a popular *or* low-brow novel; **les classes populaires,** the working classes; **quartier p.,** working class district; **bal p.,** (local) dance (*open to the public*); *Th etc* **places populaires,** cheap seats; **se rendre p.,** to make oneself popular.
populairement [pɔpylɛrmɑ̃] *adv* (*s'exprimer, parler*) in the vernacular.
populariser [pɔpylarize] *vt* to popularize.
popularité [pɔpylarite] *nf* popularity; **la cote de p.,** popularity rating.
population [pɔpylasjɔ̃] *nf* population.
populationnisme [pɔpylasjɔnism] *nm* = policy of population growth.
populationniste [pɔpylasjɔnist] *adj* **politique p.,** policy of population growth; **gouvernement p.,** government in favour of population growth.
populeux, -euse [pɔpylø, -øz] *adj* populous, densely populated.
populisme [pɔpylism] *nm Littér* naturalism.
populiste [pɔpylist] *adj Littér* naturalist.
populo [pɔpylo] *nm F* **(a) le p.,** the (common) people; *Péj* the rabble; **(b)** (*foule*) crowd (*of people*).
poquet [pɔkɛ] *nm Agr* seed hole.
porc [pɔr] *nm* **(a)** pig, *Am* hog; *F* (*personne*) pig, swine; (*homme grossier*) pig, slob; **gardeur de porcs,** pig keeper, pigman; *Arch* swineherd; **p. sauvage,** wild boar; **(peau de) p.,** pigskin; **être sale comme un p.,** (*physiquement, mentalement*) to be a filthy pig; **manger comme un p.,** to eat like a pig; **(b)** *Culin* pork; **côtelette de p.,** pork chop.
porcelaine [pɔrsəlɛn] *nf* **(a)** *Cér* porcelain, china(ware); **p. de Chine,** china; **p. de Saxe,** Dresden china; **p. tendre (anglaise),** bone china; **(b)** (*mollusque*) cowrie, porcelain shell.
porcelainier, -ière [pɔrsəlɛnje, -jɛr] **1** *adj* **industrie porcelainière,** porcelain industry. **2** *nm* porcelain manufacturer.
porcelet [pɔrsəlɛ] *nm* young pig, piglet.
porc-épic [pɔrkepik] *nm* porcupine; *F* (*personne*) prickly customer; (*pl porcs-épics* [pɔrkepik]).
porche [pɔrʃ] *nm* porch.
porcher, -ère [pɔrʃe, -ɛr] *n* pig keeper, pigman; *Arch* swineherd.
porcherie [pɔrʃəri] *nf* piggery; (*enclos*) pigsty, *Am* pigpen; *Fig Péj* **quelle p.!,** what a pigsty!
porcin, -ine [pɔrsɛ̃, -in] **1** *adj* porcine; **élevage p.,** pig breeding; **peste porcine,** swine fever, *Am* hog cholera; *Fig Péj* **un visage p.,** a piggy face. **2** *nmpl* **porcins,** pigs,

swine, *Am* hogs.

pore [pɔr] *nm* pore (*of skin, plant, stone*); **avoir les pores dilatés,** to have open pores; *Fig* **elle exprime son bonheur par tous les pores,** happiness is written all over her (face), she exudes happiness.

poreux, -euse [pɔrø, -øz] *adj* porous.

porion [pɔrjɔ̃] *nm* overseer, foreman (*in coalmine*).

porno [pɔrno] *F* **1** *adj* porn(o). **2** *n* **le p.,** porn(o).

pornographe [pɔrnɔgraf] *n* pornographer.

pornographie [pɔrnɔgrafi] *nf* pornography.

pornographique [pɔrnɔgrafik] *adj* pornographic.

porosité [pɔrozite] *nf* porosity, porousness.

porphyre [pɔrfir] *nm Minér* porphyry.

porridge [pɔridʒ] *nm Culin* porridge.

port¹ [pɔr] *nm* (*abri*) harbour, *US* harbor; (*plus important*) port; **p. naturel,** natural harbour; **p. à** *ou* **de marée,** tidal harbour; **p. de toute marée, p. en eau profonde,** deep-water harbour; **capitaine de p.,** harbour master; **droits de p.,** harbour dues, port charges; **p. de commerce,** commercial port; **p. de transit,** port of transit; **p. artificiel,** artificial port; **p. d'attache,** home port, port of commissioning; **p. d'entrée,** port of entry; *Com* **p. franc,** free port; **entrer dans le p.,** to enter harbour; **entrer au p.,** to come into port; **quitter le p.,** to leave port, to clear the harbour; **arriver à bon p.,** to come safe into port; *F* **le p. des navires perdus,** = Davy Jones' locker; **Dunkerque est le premier p. de France,** Dunkirk is the largest port in France; **p. de mer, p. maritime,** seaport; **p. fluvial,** river port; **p. militaire** *ou* **de guerre,** naval port, naval base; **p. de pêche,** fishing port; *Nau* **les ports de la métropole,** the home ports; **p. d'armement,** port of registry, *US* port of documentation.

port² *nm* **(a)** (*fait de porter*) (act of) carrying; **permis de p. d'armes,** permit for carrying firearms; *Mil* **se mettre au p. d'armes,** to shoulder arms; **le p. du casque est obligatoire,** (*sur panneau*) safety helmets must be worn;
(b) (*fait de mettre*) wearing (*of uniform etc*); manner of carrying (*sword etc*);
(c) (*prix du transport*) cost of transport; porterage, carriage (*of goods*); postage (*of parcel, letter*); delivery charge (*of telegram*); *Com* **ports de lettres, frais de p.,** postage, postal charges; **franc(o) de p., p. payé** *ou* **perçu,** carriage paid, post paid; **en p. dû,** carriage forward;
(d) (*allure*) bearing, gait, carriage (*of person*); **un p. de reine,** a regal *or* queenly bearing; **un gracieux p. de tête,** a graceful manner of holding one's head;
(e) *Bot* habit (*of plant*);
(f) *Nau* burden, tonnage (*of ship*);
(g) *Mus* **p. de voix,** glide, portamento.

port³ *nm* pass (*in the Pyrenees*).

portable [pɔrtabl] **1** *adj* **(a)** (*facilement transportable*) portable (*typewriter, computer etc*); **(b)** (*mettable*) wearable, presentable (*garment etc*); **(c)** *Jur* payable at the address of the payee. **2** *n Ordinat TV* portable.

portage [pɔrtaʒ] *nm* **(a)** (*transport*) porterage, conveyance, transport (*of goods*); portage (*of boat*); **frais de p.,** porterage; **(b)** (*partie d'un fleuve*) portage.

portager [pɔrtaʒe] *vi Can* to portage.

portail [pɔrtaj] *nm* portal (*of church etc*).

portance [pɔrtɑ̃s] *nf Av* lift (per unit area).

portant [pɔrtɑ̃] **1** *adj* **(a)** (*qui soutient*) bearing, carrying; **mur p.,** load-bearing wall; **à bout p.,** point-blank; *Av* **surface portante,** aerofoil, *Am* airfoil; *Nau* **vent p.,** fair wind; **(b) être bien p.,** to be in good health; **être mal p.,** to be in poor health, to be unwell. **2** *nm* **(a)** *Tech* upright; (*support*) supporter, stay, strut; **(b)** *Vieilli* (*anse*) (lifting) handle (*of trunk etc*); **(c)** (*partie que l'on place sous un aimant*) armature, keeper (*of magnet*); **(d)** (*chenille*) tread (*of wheel*); **(e)** (*présentoir*) rack (*in clothes shop*); **(f)** *Nau* oar support.

portatif, -ive [pɔrtatif, -iv] **1** *adj* portable (*typewriter etc*); **armes portatives,** small arms; **glaces portatives,** ice cream to take away. **2** *n Ordinat TV* portable.

porte [pɔrt] *nf* **(a)** (*entrée*) door (*of house, cupboard etc*); **p. d'entrée,** front door; **p. de sortie,** way out, exit; *Fig* way out, means of escape; **p. de derrière/de service,** back door/tradesmen's entrance; **à ma p.,** on my doorstep; *Fig* **journée portes ouvertes,** open day, *Am* open house; *F* **entrer dans une profession par la petite p.,** to get into a profession by the back door; **p. à deux battants,** double door; **p. battante,** swing door; **p. tournante,** revolving door; **p. roulante, p. coulissante,** sliding door; **p. vitrée,** glass door; **aller ouvrir la p.,** to answer the door; *Fig* **c'est la p. ouverte à toutes les atrocités,** it leaves the door wide open to all sorts of atrocities; **gagner** *ou* **prendre la p.,** to make off; *F* **je lui ai parlé entre deux portes,** I spoke to him for a brief moment; **trouver p. close,** to find nobody at home; *Fig* to be refused entrance; **mettre qn à la p.,** to throw *or* kick s.o. out; (*d'un emploi*) to fire *or* to sack s.o.; **tais-toi ou tu vas prendre la p.,** be quiet or I'll put you out; **refuser** *ou* **fermer** *ou* **défendre sa p. à qn,** to refuse s.o. admission; **habiter p. à p.,** to be next-door neighbours;
(b) (*voie d'entrée*) gateway (*to a park etc*); doorway, entrance (*in building*); gate (*at airport*); **portes d'une ville,** gates of a town; **l'ennemi est à nos portes,** the enemy is at the gates; **p. cochère** *ou* **charretière,** carriage entrance *or* gateway; **les portes de l'enfer,** the gates of hell; **être aux portes de la mort,** to be at death's door; *Econ* **politique de la p. ouverte,** open-door policy; *Hist* **la (Sublime-)P., la P. ottomane,** the (Sublime) Porte, the Turkish government; **la campagne est à vos portes,** the countryside is on your doorstep; *Tech* **p. de visite,** inspection door; (*d'égout*) manhole door, cover; *Min etc* **p. d'aérage,** air gate, trap (*door*); *Tech* **p. d'écluse,** (lock) gate;
(c) (*portière*) door (*of car, train*); **attendre l'ouverture complète des portes,** wait until the doors are fully open;
(d) *Ski* gate, pair of flags;
(e) (*fente*) eye (*of hook and eye*);
(f) (*usu pl*) **portes,** (*dans la roche*) gorge; (*passage étroit*) defile, pass.

porte à porte [pɔrtapɔrt] *nm* **faire du p. à p.,** to go from door to door (*selling, canvassing etc*).

porté [pɔrte] *adj* inclined, disposed; **être p. à l'indulgence,** to be inclined to be indulgent; **être p. à la colère,** to be quick- tempered; **p. à faire qch,** inclined to do sth, given to doing sth; **être p. à oublier,** to be apt to forget; **p. sur qn/qch,** fond of s.o./sth.

porte(-)à(-)faux [pɔrtafo] *nm inv* overhang; *Constr* cantilever; **en p. à f.,** overhanging; *Fig* **situation en p. à f.,** uncertain *or* unstable position.

porte-affiche(s) [pɔrtafiʃ] *nm* notice board, *Am* bulletin board; (*pl porte-affiches*).

porte-aiguille [pɔrteɡɥij] *nm Chir* needle holder; (*pl porte- aiguille(s)*).

porte-aiguilles [pɔrteɡɥij] *nm inv Couture* needle case.

porte-allumettes [pɔrtalymɛt] *nm inv* match holder.

porte-amarre [pɔrtamar] *nm inv Nau* line-throwing apparatus; **flèche p.-a.,** line-throwing rocket; (*pl porte-amarre(s)*).

porte-avions [pɔrtavjɔ̃] *nm inv Nau* aircraft carrier.

porte-bagages [pɔrtbagaʒ] *nm inv* luggage rack; *Aut etc* (luggage) carrier; (*au toit d'une automobile*) roof rack.

porte-baïonnette [pɔrtbajɔnɛt] *nm* bayonet frog; (*pl porte-baïonnette(s)*).

porte-balais [pɔrtbalɛ] *nm inv Él* brush holder (*of dynamo etc*).

porte-bébé(s) [pɔrtbebe] *nm inv* baby carrier; (*pl porte-bébés*).

porte-billets [pɔrtbijɛ] *nm inv* notecase, *Am* billfold.

porte-bombes [pɔrtbɔ̃b] *nm inv Mil Av* bomb rack.

porte-bonheur [pɔrtbɔnœr] *nm inv* (lucky) charm; (*animal, enfant*) mascot; **petit cochon p.-b.,** lucky pig.

porte-bouteilles [pɔrtbutɛj] *nm inv* bottle rack, wine rack.

porte-brosses [pɔrtbrɔs] *nm inv* **p.-b. (à dents),** toothbrush holder.

porte-carte(s) [pɔrtəkart] *nm inv* **(a)** (*à cartes de crédit, de visite*) card holder, wallet; **(b)** (*à cartes géographiques*) map case *or* holder.

porte-chapeaux [pɔrtʃapo] *nm inv* hat stand.

porte-chars [pɔrtəʃar] *nm inv Mil* tank transporter.

porte-cigares [pɔrtsigar] *nm inv* cigar case.

porte-cigarettes [pɔrtsigarɛt] *nm inv* cigarette case.

porte-clefs [pɔrtəkle] *nm inv* **(a)** key ring; **(b)** *Arch* turnkey, prison warder.

porte-conteneurs [pɔrtkɔ̃tnœr] *nm inv Tech* container ship.

porte-copie [pɔrtkɔpi] *nm Typ* copy holder; (*pl porte-copie(s)*).

porte-couteau [pɔrtkuto] *nm* knife rest; (*pl porte-couteau(x)*).

porte-croix [pɔrtəkrwa] *nm inv Rel* cross bearer.

porte-documents [pɔrtdɔkymɑ̃] *nm inv* document case; (*serviette*) briefcase.

porte-drapeau [pɔrtdrapo] *nm Mil* colour bearer, *US* color bearer; *Fig* standard bearer; (*pl porte-drapeau(x)*).

portée [pɔrte] *nf* **(a)** (*petits*) litter, brood (*of animal*); farrow (*of sow*);
(b) (*amplitude*) reach (*of arm etc*); radius (*of crane jib*

etc); range (*of gun, radio station etc*); scope (*of treaty etc*); range, compass (*of voice etc*); **à p. (de tir),** within range; **à p. de fusil,** within rifle range, within gunshot; **à p. de canon,** within gun range; **(à) courte p., (à) petite p.,** (at) short range; **(à) grande p., (à) longue p.,** (at) long range; **canon à longue p.,** long-range gun; **à p. de (la) voix,** within calling distance; **à p. d'oreille,** within hearing (distance), within earshot; **hors de p. de voix,** out of earshot; **à p. de (la) vue,** within sight; **des chaussures à la p. de toutes les bourses,** shoes to suit every budget; **c'est à ma p.,** (*cet objet*) it's within my reach; (*ce livre*) I can understand it; (*ce travail*) I can do it; **hors de ma p.,** (*dans l'espace*) beyond my reach; (*de voix*) beyond the reach *or* range; *Fig* (*de compréhension*) beyond my understanding; **hors de p.,** out of reach *or* range, beyond reach; **à mettre hors de p. des enfants,** keep out of the reach of children; **à p. de la main,** (*pas très loin*) within reach, to hand; **j'ai toujours un tube d'aspirine à p. de la main,** I always have *or* keep some aspirin(s) handy; **livre à la p. de tout le monde,** (*facile à lire*) book that anyone can understand;

(c) *Mus* stave; staff;

(d) *Fig* (*force*) bearing, (full) significance (*of a statement*); implication, import (*of words*); **conséquences d'une p. incalculable,** far-reaching consequences;

(e) (*charge*) *Constr* bearing (*of beam*); span (*of roof bridge*); *Nau* **p. en lourd** *ou* **en poids,** deadweight (capacity);

(f) *MecE* bearing surface; **portées d'un arbre,** (main) journals;

(g) *MecE etc* (*point d'appui*) boss (*on shaft etc*).

porte-étendard [pɔrtetɑ̃dar] *nm inv Arch* standard bearer (*in cavalry*).

portefaix [pɔrtəfɛ] *nm Arch* (street) porter.

porte-fenêtre [pɔrtfənɛtr] *nf* French window; (*pl portes-fenêtres*).

portefeuille [pɔrtəfœj] *nm* **(a)** (*pour l'argent*) wallet, *Am* billfold; *Fig* **avoir un p. bien garni,** to be rich; **lit en p.,** apple pie bed; **jupe p.,** wrapover *or* wrapround *or* wraparound skirt; **(b)** (*cartable*) portfolio (*for drawings etc*); *Com* **p. d'assurances,** portfolio (*of insurance broker*); **p. d'actions,** share portfolio; **(c)** *Fin* **effets en p.,** bills in hand, holdings; **p. (titres),** investments, securities; **(d)** *Fig Pol* (*fonction de ministre*) portfolio; **ministre sans p.,** minister without portfolio.

porte-greffe(s) [pɔrtəgrɛf] *nm inv* stock; (*pl porte-greffe(s)*).

porte-hélicoptères [pɔrtelikɔptɛr] *nm inv Nau* helicopter carrier.

porte-jarretelles [pɔrtʒartɛl] *nm inv* suspender belt.

porte-journaux [pɔrtʒurno] *nm inv* newspaper rack.

porte-jupe [pɔrtəʒyp] *nm* skirt hanger; (*pl porte jupe(s)*).

porte-malheur [pɔrtmalœr] *nm inv* bringer of bad luck, Jonah.

portemanteau, -eaux [pɔrtmɑ̃to] *nm* **(a)** coat(-and-hat) rack *or* stand, hallstand; *Fig* **avoir des épaules en p.,** to be broad-shouldered, to have muscular shoulders; **(b)** *Arch* portmanteau.

portement [pɔrtəmɑ̃] *nm* **p. de croix,** (Christ's) bearing of the Cross.

porte-menu [pɔrtməny] *nm inv* menu holder.

porte(-)mine [pɔrt(ə)min] *nm* propelling pencil; (*pl porte-mine(s)*).

porte-monnaie [pɔrtmɔnɛ] *nm inv* purse.

porte-musique [pɔrtmyzik] *nm inv* music case, music folio.

porte-objet [pɔrtɔbʒɛ] *nm* (*de microscope*) (object) slide; (*platine*) stage; (*pl porte-objet(s)*).

porte-outil [pɔrtuti] *nm* tool holder (*of machine tool*); chuck (*of drill*); slide rest (*of lathe*); (*pl porte-outil(s)*).

porte-papier [pɔrtpapje] *nm inv* **p.-p. (hygiénique),** toilet roll holder.

porte-parapluies [pɔrtparaplɥi] *nm inv* umbrella stand.

porte-parole [pɔrtparɔl] *nm inv* spokesperson, spokesman, *f* spokeswoman; mouthpiece (*of deputation etc*); organ (*of political party etc*).

porte-pipes [pɔrtəpip] *nm inv* pipe rack.

porte-plat [pɔrtəpla] *nm* (dish) stand; (*pl porteplat(s)*).

porte-plume [pɔrtəplym] *nm inv* penholder.

porter [pɔrte] **1** *vt* **(a)** (*soutenir*) to carry (*a suitcase, a child etc*); to bear, to support (*weight, load*); **p. qn en triomphe,** to carry s.o. shoulder high; **p. la tête haute,** to hold *or* carry one's head high; **ces abus portent en eux leur propre châtiment,** these abuses carry their own punishment; **elle porte bien son âge,** she's wearing well; **elle porte/ne porte pas son âge,** she looks/doesn't look her age; **mes jambes ne me portent plus,** my legs won't carry me any further; **p. qn dans son cœur,** to have a great affection for s.o., to be very fond of s.o.; *Iron* **je ne le porte pas dans mon cœur,** he's not exactly my favourite *or US* favorite person; *Mil* **portez armes!,** shoulder arms!; *Nau* **p. tout dessus,** (*of ship*) to have all sails set;

(b) (*produire*) to produce; **p. des fruits,** to bear fruit; **terres qui portent du blé,** wheat-producing land; **argent qui porte intérêt,** money that bears *or* brings in interest; **cela vous portera bonheur,** that will bring you luck; *Prov* **la nuit porte conseil,** sleep on it;

(c) (*avoir avec ou sur soi*) to wear (*garment etc*); **p. des lunettes/une bague/du noir,** to wear glasses/a ring/black; **p. une moustache,** to have a moustache; **p. des cicatrices,** to bear scars; *Fig* **p. la soutane,** to have taken one's vows, to be a priest; **il porte le nom de son oncle,** he's called after his uncle; **le chameau porte deux bosses,** the camel has two humps;

(d) (*transporter*) to carry, to take (*sth somewhere*); **p. qch dans la maison/dehors,** to take *or* carry sth into the house/outside; **p. une lettre à la poste,** to (go and) post *or Am* mail a letter; **p. le lait à domicile,** to deliver milk to the door; **il porta le verre à ses lèvres,** he raised *or* lifted the glass to his lips; **p. qn en terre,** to carry s.o. to his grave; **courant qui porte au sud,** current that sets to the south;

(e) (*diriger*) **p. un coup à qn, p. la main sur qn,** to strike s.o., to aim a blow at s.o.; **il porta la main à sa casquette,** he touched his cap; **p. ses regards sur qn,** to look at s.o.; **p. son attention sur qch,** to give sth one's attention; *Fig* **p. un différend devant un tribunal,** to take a dispute to a court; *Fig* **p. une accusation contre qn,** to bring *or* lay a charge against s.o.; *Fig* **p. un toast à qn,** to drink *or* offer a toast to s.o., to toast s.o.; **p. témoignage,** to bear witness; **p. qch à la connaissance de qn,** to bring sth to s.o.'s attention, to make sth known to s.o., to let s.o. know sth;

(f) (*inscrire*) to mark, to enter; **p. une position sur une carte,** to mark *or* show a position on a map; **p. une somme au crédit de qn/d'un compte,** to credit s.o. with a sum, to credit a sum to s.o./to an account; **p. une somme au débit de qn,** to debit s.o. with a sum; **se faire p. malade,** to report sick; *Mil etc* **p. qn manquant à l'appel,** to report s.o. absent from roll call; **p. qn déserteur,** to declare s.o. a deserter; *Nau* **p. un homme au rôle de l'équipage,** to enter a seaman on the ship's books;

(g) (*être revêtu ou marqué de*) to bear; **la lettre porte la date du 2 juin,** the letter is dated June 2nd,

(h) (*inciter à*) to induce, to incline, to prompt; **p. qn à qch,** to incite s.o. to sth; **tout me porte à croire que ...,** everything leads *or* inclines me to believe that ...; **être porté sur l'alcool,** to drink (a bit too much); *F* **être porté sur la chose,** to have a one-track mind;

(i) (*monter, transformer*) to raise, to carry; **p. la température à 100°,** to raise the temperature to 100°; **p. un inconnu au pouvoir,** to bring an unknown person to power; **p. une pièce classique à l'écran,** to bring *or* transfer a classical drama to the screen; **p. la production au maximum,** to raise *or* increase production to a maximum;

(j) to show (*interest, affection for s.o., sth*); **par la tendresse que je vous porte,** by the love I bear you;

(k) (*donner*) to provide, to offer; **p. secours à un bateau en détresse,** to come to the aid of a boat in distress; **p. assistance à toute personne en danger,** to provide *or* offer assistance to all those in danger;

(l) (*mentionner*) to declare, to state; **le rapport ne porte rien de tout cela,** the report makes no mention of any of that; **la loi porte que cet usage est interdit,** this practice is expressly forbidden by law; *Mil etc* **la décision porte que ...,** it is stated in orders that ... .

2 *vi* **(a)** (*appuyer*) to rest, to bear; **tout le poids porte sur cette poutre,** all the weight bears on this beam; **croyez-vous que la glace porte?,** do you think the ice will hold?; **la discussion porte toujours sur le même sujet,** the discussion always turns on the same subject; **faire p. son attention sur qch,** to bring one's mind to bear on sth; **la perte a porté sur nous,** we had to stand the loss;

(b) (*atteindre*) to hit, to reach (*target, mark*); **sa tête a porté sur le trottoir,** his head hit *or* struck the pavement; **aucun des coups n'a porté,** none of the blows had any effect; **chaque coup/mot a porté,** every shot/word hit home *or* told; **coup qui porte** *ou* **qui a porté,** telling blow; **son discours a porté sur ses auditeurs,** his speech made an impact on his audience; **sa voix porte bien,** his voice carries well; *F* **ce bruit me porte sur les nerfs,** that noise gets on my nerves;

(c) *Nau* (*of sail*) to fill, to draw; **portez plein!,** keep her full!;

(d) *Nau* **laisser p.,** to bear away; **laisser p. sur un navire,** to bear down upon *or* run down a ship;

(e) (*être en gestation*) **les juments portent onze mois,** the gestation period of a mare is eleven months.

3 se porter *vpr* **(a)** (*aller*) to go, *Fml* to proceed (*to a place*); **se p. au secours de qn,** to go to s.o.'s assistance; **la foule s'est portée vers la gare,** the crowd made for the station;

(b) (*se livrer à*) to commit; **se p. à des voies de fait/à des extrémités,** to commit acts of violence/to go to extremes;

(c) (*se diriger*) to turn; **son regard se portait vers son frère,** his eyes were turned towards his brother; *Mil* **se p. en avant,** to advance; **la conversation s'est portée sur l'Extrême-Orient,** the conversation turned to the Far East;

(d) se p. bien/à merveille, to be well, to be in good health/to enjoy the best of health; **comment vous portez-vous?,** how are you?; **je ne m'en porte pas plus mal,** I'm none the worse for it;

(e) (*se présenter comme*) to offer oneself; **se p. candidat/caution,** to offer oneself *or* stand as candidate/as surety;

(f) (*devoir être porté*) to be worn; (*être à la mode*) to be fashionable; **le sabre se porte à gauche,** the sabre is worn on the left; **le nœud papillon se porte de plus en plus,** more and more people are wearing bow-ties, bow-ties are becoming more and more fashionable; **le bleu se porte beaucoup cette année,** blue is being worn a lot *or* is very fashionable this year; **les mini-jupes se porteront cet été,** mini-skirts will be fashionable *or* in fashion this summer.

porte-revues [pɔrtrəvy] *nm inv* newspaper *or* magazine rack.

porterie [pɔrtəri] *nf* gatehouse (*of convent etc*).

porte-savon [pɔrtsavɔ̃] *nm* soapdish; (*pl porte-savon(s)*).

porte-serviettes [pɔrtsɛrvjɛt] *nm inv* towel rail.

porte-toasts [pɔrtətost] *nm inv* toast rack.

porteur, -euse [pɔrtœr, -øz] **1** *n* **(a)** bearer, carrier (*of message etc*); **p. de nouvelles,** bearer *or* bringer of news; **j'arrivais p. d'heureuses nouvelles,** I arrived bringing good news; **par p.,** by messenger;

(b) (*employé*) (*railway etc*) porter; **p. d'eau,** water carrier; **chaise à porteurs,** sedan chair;

(c) *Méd* **p. de germes,** (germ) carrier;

(d) (*détenteur*) holder; *Fin* bearer, endorsee, payee (*of a cheque*); **p. de papiers volés,** person carrying stolen identity papers; **p. de titres,** holder of stock, stockholder; **p. d'actions,** shareholder; **payable au p.,** payable to bearer; **effets au p.,** bearer stock(s).

2 *adj* **(a)** *Tech* **essieu p.,** bearing axle, carrying axle; **câble p.,** suspension cable; *El* **fréquence porteuse,** carrier frequency; **onde porteuse,** carrier wave;

(b) *Méd* **les individus porteurs du virus,** individuals who carry the virus, (individuals who are) carriers of the virus;

(c) *Fig* (*industrie, marché, créneau*) growth.

porte-vent [pɔrtəvɑ̃] *nm inv* air duct; wind chest (*of organ*); **(b)** *Méd* blast pipe.

porte-voix [pɔrtəvwa] *nm inv* megaphone; (*électrique*) loudhailer, *Am* bullhorn; **mettre ses mains en p.-v.,** to cup one's hands round one's mouth.

portfolio [pɔrtfoljo] *nm* portfolio.

portier, -ière [pɔrtje, -jɛr] *n* **(a)** (*gardien*) porter, doorman, doorkeeper; commissionaire (*at hotel*); **p. de nuit,** night porter; **(b)** *Litt* gatekeeper (*of estate etc*); **(c)** *Rel* **(frère) p.,** porter; **(sœur) portière,** portress.

portière [pɔrtjɛr] *nf* **(a)** door (*of car, railway carriage, Am railroad coach*); **(b)** (*rideau*) door curtain; **(c)** raft, cut (*of pontoon bridge*).

portillon [pɔrtijɔ̃] *nm* wicket (gate); *Rail* side gate (*at level crossing*); gate, barrier (*at station*); *Fig* **cela se bouscule au p.,** he can't get his words out.

portion [pɔrsjɔ̃] *nf* portion, share (*of cake, money*); portion, section (*of group, population etc*); portion, part (*of region, country, book*); **p. de viande,** portion *or* helping of meat.

portique [pɔrtik] *nm* **(a)** *Archit* portico, porch; **(b)** *Gym* (cross)beam (*for hanging apparatus*); **(c)** *Rail* **p. à signaux,** signal gantry; **(d)** *Tech* **grue à p.,** travelling gantry crane.

portland [pɔrtlɑ̃d] *nm Tech* Portland cement.

Porto [pɔrto] *nm* **(a)** *Géog* Oporto; **(b)** (*wine*) port.

portoricain, -aine [pɔrtɔrikɛ̃, -ɛn] **1** *adj* Puerto Rican. **2** *n* **P.,** Puerto-Rican.

Porto Rico [pɔrtoriko] *nm* Puerto Rico.

portrait [pɔrtrɛ] *nm* **(a)** (*représentation*) portrait; (*ressemblance*) likeness; **p. en pied/buste,** full-/half-length portrait; **faire le p. de qn,** to do *or* paint a portrait of s.o.; (*au crayon*) to draw a portrait of s.o.; *Fig* **c'est le p. vivant de son père,** he's the spitting image of his father; *Fig* **p. en prose,** portrait in prose, word portrait; *Phot* **p. en noir et blanc/en couleurs,** black-and-white/colour photograph (*of a person*); **p. littéraire,** character sketch; **(b)** *Arg* (*visage*) face, *Br* clock, dial; **il s'est fait abîmer le p.,** his face is a real mess; **(c)** *Beaux-Arts* portrait painting, portraiture; **l'art du p.,** the art of portraiture.

portraitiste [pɔrtretist] *n* portrait painter.

portrait-robot [pɔrtrɛrobo] *nm* (*photomontage*) Photofit ® (picture); *Fig* **faire le p.-r. du candidat idéal,** to draw up a profile of the ideal candidate; (*pl portraits-robots*).

portraiturer [pɔrtretyre] *vt* to portray.

portuaire [pɔrtɥɛr] *adj* **installations portuaires,** port facilities *or* installations.

portugais, -aise [pɔrtygɛ, -ɛz] **1** *adj* Portuguese. **2** *nm Ling* Portuguese. **3** *n* **P.,** Portuguese. **4** *nf* **portugaise (a)** Portuguese oyster; **(b)** *F* (*oreille*) lughole; **tu as les portugaises ensablées ou quoi ?,** have you got cotton-wool in your ears or what?

Portugal [pɔrtygal] *nm* Portugal.

pose [poz] *nf* **(a)** placing; putting up, hanging (*of curtain etc*); hanging (*of picture etc*); laying (*of bricks, carpet etc*); setting (*of stones etc*); fitting (*of watchglass etc*); installation (*of apparatus, appliance etc*); **p. de câbles,** cable laying; **(b)** (*attitude*) pose, posture; *Beaux-Arts Phot etc* pose; **prendre une p.,** to assume *or* strike a pose; **(c)** *Péj* (*airs*) posing, affectation, posturing; **sans p.,** unaffected(ly); **(d)** *Golf* lie (*of a ball*); **(e)** *Phot* exposure; **temps de p.,** exposure time; **p. instantanée,** instantaneous exposure.

posé [poze] *adj* **(a)** (*réfléchi, calme*) staid, serious, calm, grave, sedate (*person*); steady (*bearing etc*); sober (*appearance*); **écrire à main posée,** to write slowly *or* carefully; *Mus* **voix bien posée,** even *or* steady voice; **(b)** (*en train de couver*) sitting (*bird*).

posément [pozemɑ̃] *adv* sedately, calmly; (*to proceed, move*) steadily, deliberately.

posemètre [pozmɛtr] *nm Phot* exposure meter.

poser [poze] **1** *vi* **(a)** (*porter*) (*of beam etc*) to rest, to lie (*on sth*);

(b) to pose (*as artist's model*); to sit (*for one's portrait*);

(c) *Péj* (*prendre des airs*) to show off, to pose; **p. pour la galerie,** to play to the gallery; *F* **je ne pose pas à l'ange,** I don't pretend to be an angel.

2 *vt* **(a)** (*mettre*) to put, to place, to lay, to set (*sth*) (down) (*somewhere*); **pose-le sur la table,** put it (down) on the table; **p. les armes,** to lay down one's arms; **p. un avion,** to land an aircraft; **p. sa candidature,** to stand (as a candidate) **(aux élections,** in the elections); to apply **(à un poste,** for a job);

(b) (*formuler*) **p. une question à qn,** to ask s.o. a question, to put a question to s.o.; **p. la question de confiance,** to table a motion of confidence; **p. un problème,** to pose a problem; **p. un problème à qn,** to pose a problem for s.o., to set s.o. a problem; **p. une règle de conduite,** to lay down a rule of conduct;

(c) (*écrire*) to put; *Math* **p. un chiffre,** to put *or* set down a number; **je pose deux et je retiens un,** put down two (and) carry one;

(d) to put up, to hang (*curtain etc*); to hang (*picture etc*); to lay (*bricks, carpet, foundation stone, rails etc*); to set (*stones, rivets, boiler*); to fit (*watchglass etc*); **p. une vitre,** to put in a pane of glass; **p. l'électricité,** to install electricity; **p. des jalons,** to prepare the ground, to put down markers; **p. la première pierre à qch,** to lay the foundation stone for sth; *Fig* to lay the foundation(s) for sth;

(e) p. qn, to establish s.o.'s reputation (*as an author etc*);

(f) (*supposer, établir*) to suppose, to admit, to grant; **p. des principes,** to lay down principles; **posons le cas que cela soit,** supposing *or* assuming *or* let's suppose *or* assume that that is the case; **cela posé,** assuming this to be true;

(g) *Mus* **bien p. la voix,** to pitch (one's voice) correctly;

(h) p. son regard sur qn, to look at s.o..

3 se poser *vpr* **(a)** (*of bird etc*) to settle, to alight **(sur,** on); (*of aircraft etc*) to land;

(b) (*apparaître*) to come up, to crop up, to arise; (*d'une question*) to be asked; **un nouveau problème se pose,** we are faced with a new problem; **la question se posera toujours,** it's a perennial question;

(c) (*se prétendre*) **se p. comme prêtre,** to pretend to be *or* pose as a priest; **se p. en réformateur,** to set oneself up as *or* to claim to be a reformer;

(d) (*devoir être posé*) to be put *or* laid *or* placed *or* set; **cette potiche se pose par terre,** this vase should be (placed) on the ground;

(e) se p. des questions, to ask oneself questions; **tu te poses trop de questions,** you ask yourself too many questions; **je finis par me p. des questions,** (*sur sa compétence etc*) I'm beginning to have my doubts;

(f) *F* **comme enquiquineur, il se pose là!,** he's a real pain in the neck!

poseur, -euse [pozœr, -øz] *n* **(a)** *Tech* layer (*of cables etc*); **p. d'affiches,** billsticker, billposter; *Rail* **p. de rails** *ou* **de voie,** platelayer, *Am* tracklayer; *Nau* **p. de mines,** minelayer; **(b)** *Péj* (*pédant*) show-off, poser; *Litt* poseur; **il est p.,** he's always putting on airs, he's rather affected; **des airs de p.,** airs and graces; **c'est une poseuse,** she's a show-off.

positif, -ive [pozitif, -iv] **1** *adj* **(a)** (*sûr, certain*) positive, actual, real (*fact etc*); *Méd* positive (*reaction, test*); **c'est p.,** it's a positive fact; **(b)** *Math Él etc* positive (*number, pole etc*); *Phot* **épreuve positive,** proof; **(c)** (*pratique*) practical, unsentimental, matter-of-fact (*person*); **esprit p.,** practical mind; **(d)** (*enthousiaste*) positive (*remark, attitude, person*); **(e)** *Jur* **droit p.,** statute law. **2** *nm* **(a)** *Mus* choir organ (*of full organ*); **(b)** *Phot* positive (print).

position [pozisjɔ̃] *nf* **(a)** (*emplacement*) position (*of ship, aircraft etc*); *Golf* lie (*of the ball*); **p. stable/horizontale,** stable/horizontal position; **le coureur français est en première p.,** the French runner is in the lead *or* in first place; *Aut* **feux de p.,** sidelights; **p. d'atterrissage,** (*of aircraft*) landing attitude;

(b) *Mil etc* **p. clef,** key position; **p. masquée,** position behind cover; **p. défensive** *ou* **de défense,** defensive position; **p. de repli** *ou* **de recueil,** fall-back position;

(c) (*attitude corporelle*) posture, attitude (*of the body etc*); (*debout*) stance; position (*of the feet*); **première/troisième p.,** (*en danse*) first/third position; **p. debout,** standing position; *Hum* **p. du missionnaire,** missionary position;

(d) (*opinion, avis*) position; **quelle est votre p. sur la guerre?,** what is your position on the war?, what position do you take on the war?; **expliquer sa p.,** to explain one's position; **elle est restée sur ses positions,** she refused to back down; **prise de p.,** strong line; **la prise de p. de notre pays,** our country's strong line, the strong line taken by our country;

(e) condition, circumstances; **dans sa p., il ne peut pas se permettre ces choses-là,** he can't afford to do things like that in his position; **p. sociale,** social standing *or* position *or* status;

(f) (*situation*) **p. gênante,** embarrassing situation; **voici ma p.,** this is how things stand with me; **être en p. de faire qch,** to be in a position to do sth; *F* **être dans une p. intéressante,** to be pregnant, *Vieilli* to be in an interesting situation;

(g) *Fin* account; **demander sa p.,** to ask for one's balance; **feuille de p.,** bank statement, statement of account, balance slip.

positionnement [pozisjɔnmɑ̃] *nm* **(a)** *Tech* positioning; **(b)** *Fin* calculation of the balance (*on an account*); **(c)** *Com* positioning.

positionner [pozisjɔne] *vt* **(a)** *Tech* to position; **(b)** *Fin* to calculate the balance of (*an account*); **(c)** *Com* to position (*a product*).

positivement [pozitivmɑ̃] *adv* positively; **je ne le sais pas p.,** I don't know it for certain; *Él* **chargé p.,** positively charged.

positivisme [pozitivism] *nm Phil* **(a)** *Hist* positivism; **(b)** (*relativisme*) materialism.

positiviste [pozitivist] *adj & n Phil* positivist.

positivité [pozitivite] *nf Él Phil* positivity.

positon [pozitɔ̃] *nm*, **positron** [pozitrɔ̃] *nm Nucl* positron.

posologie [pozɔlɔʒi] *nf Méd etc* dosage (*of drug*); (*science*) posology.

possédant, -ante [pɔsedɑ̃, -ɑ̃t] *adj & n* **les possédants, les classes possédantes,** the propertied *or* moneyed classes, the wealthy.

possédé, -ée [pɔsede] **1** *adj* possessed (**de,** by); dominated (*by passion etc*); **p. du diable,** possessed by the devil. **2** *n* person possessed; *Fig* madman, madwoman, maniac.

posséder [pɔsede] *v* (**je possède; je posséderai**) **1** *vt* **(a)** (*avoir*) to possess, to own, to have (*property etc*); **p. un titre,** to hold *or* have a title; **p. un million,** to be worth a million;

(b) (*connaître*) to have a thorough knowledge of, to be master of (*subject etc*); **p. une vérité,** to be aware of a basic truth;

(c) (*maîtriser*) to curb, to control (*one's tongue etc*); **p. son métier,** to know one's trade inside out; **p. un grand talent,** to possess a great talent; **p. son âme en paix,** to possess one's soul in peace;

(d) (*dominer*) (*of demon etc*) to possess (*s.o.*); **ils étaient tous possédés de la même illusion,** they all laboured under the same delusion;

(e) *F* (*tromper*) to fool (*s.o.*); **je me suis fait p.,** I've been had;

(f) p. une femme, to possess a woman, *F* to have a woman.

2 se posséder *vpr* to control oneself *or* one's temper; **elle ne se possédait plus de joie,** she was beside herself with joy.

possesseur [pɔsesœr] *nm* possessor, owner; **il se croit le p. de la vérité,** he thinks he knows everything.

possessif, -ive [pɔsesif, -iv] **1** *adj* **(a)** *Gram etc* possessive; **(b)** *Psy* possessive (*mother, husband*); **il est trop p. avec sa femme,** he's too possessive with *or* towards his wife. **2** *nm Gram* possessive.

possession [pɔsesjɔ̃] *nf* **(a)** (*fait de détenir, d'avoir*) possession, ownership; **être en p. de qch,** to be in possession of sth, to own sth; *Jur* to be possessed of sth; **être en p. de toutes les données,** to be in possession of *or* to possess all the facts; *Com* **nous sommes en p. de votre lettre du 4 mars,** we are in receipt of *or* have received your letter of 4th March; **avoir qch en sa p.,** to have sth in one's possession; **entrer en p. d'un héritage,** to enter into possession of an inheritance; **entrée en p. d'un patrimoine,** accession to an estate; **prendre p. de,** to take possession of (*a flat, a car etc*); **rentrer en p. de qch,** to gain possession of sth; **la p. vaut titre,** possession is nine points *or* tenths of the law;

(b) (*bien*) possession; *surtout* property, estate; **avoir quelques possessions,** to have a few possessions;

(c) *Psy* possession (*by evil spirit*);

(d) (*maîtrise*) self-possession, self-control; **reprendre p. de soi-même,** to regain *or* recover one's self-control *or* composure; **être en p. de ses facultés,** to be in (full) possession of one's faculties; **elle était en pleine p. de ses moyens,** she was at the peak of her powers *or* her abilities.

possessivité [pɔsesivite] *nf* possessiveness.

possessoire [pɔseswar] *Jur* **1** *adj* **intenter une action p.,** to undertake an action for possession (of land). **2** *nm* right of possession (*of property*).

possibilité [pɔsibilite] *nf* **(a)** (*éventualité*). possibility; feasibility (*of plan, operation*); **voir la p. de faire qch,** to see the possibility of doing sth, to consider it possible to do sth; **il faut prendre en compte la p. du rejet (de greffe),** we have to allow for the possibility of rejection *or* for the possibility that the transplant will be rejected;

(b) (*cas*) possibility; **c'est une p. que je n'avais pas envisagée,** it's a possibility that I hadn't envisaged;

(c) (*moyen*) opportunity, chance; **c'est la première fois qu'elle a la p. de le faire,** this is the first chance she's had to do it *or* of doing it; **si j'ai la p. de lui écrire,** if it's possible for me *or* if I can manage to write to him;

(d) possibilités, (*of person*) capabilities, capacity; **connaître ses possibilités,** to be aware of one's (own) capabilities; **chacun doit payer selon ses possibilités,** from each according to his means.

possible [pɔsibl] **1** *adj* **(a)** (*faisable*) possible; feasible (*plan, operation*); **c'est (bien) p.,** it's (quite) possible, it's quite likely, (very) possibly, very likely; **est-ce p.?, ce n'est pas p.!,** *F* **pas p.!,** it's not possible!, impossible!, you can't mean it!; **si (c'est) p.,** if possible; **est-il p. de faire des fautes pareilles?,** how can people make such mistakes?; **il ne m'est pas p. de le faire,** I can't possibly do it; **il ne m'est guère p. de le faire,** it's a bit difficult for me (to do it); **il est p. qu'il soit mort,** it's possible that he's dead, he may *or* might be dead; **il n'est pas p. que j'y aille,** (*je ne peux pas*) it's impossible for me to go (there); (*il n'est pas question*) there's no possibility of my going there; **aussitôt que p., dès que p.,** as soon as possible; **est-ce que tu viens? – p.,** are you coming? – possibly; **est-ce qu'il te serait p. de travailler demain?,** would it be possible for you to work tomorrow?, could you possibly work tomorrow?;

(b) (*existant, maximum, minimum*) **le moins souvent p.,** as infrequently as possible; **le moins de détails possible(s),** as few details as possible; **tous les détails possibles,** every possible detail; **la boîte la plus grande p.,** the largest box possible, the largest possible box; **elle a eu tous les ennuis possibles et imaginables,** she's had every problem you can think of; **dans la plus large mesure p.,** as far as possible; *Fml* **le plus tôt qu'il vous sera p.,** at your earliest convenience;

(c) (*éventuel*) possible, potential; **danger p.,** possible *or* potential danger; **il est p. qu'il y pense à la dernière minute,** he may well think of it at the last minute;

(d) *F* (*supportable*) **cette fille n'est pas p.!,** that girl is impossible!; **ça n'est plus p.,** I can't take (it) any more, I've had enough.

2 *nm* **(a)** what is possible; **dans la mesure du p.,** as far as possible; **faire tout son p. pour ...,** to do all *or* everything one (possibly) can (do) to ..., to do one's utmost *or* best to ..., to make every endeavour *or* *US* endeavor to ..., to try one's hardest to...; **il s'est montré aimable au p.,** he was extremely pleasant, he couldn't have been kinder *or* nicer;

(b) (*chose réalisable*) possibility; **envisageons tous les possibles,** let's consider all the possibilities.

postal, -aux [pɔstal, -o] *adj* postal, *Am* mail (*service etc*); **sac p.,** mailbag; **carte postale,** postcard.

postcombustion [pɔstkɔ̃bystjɔ̃] *nf Tech* afterburning, reheat (*of rocket, turbojet*); **dispositif de p.,** afterburner.

postcommunion [pɔstkɔmynjɔ̃] *nf Rel* postcommunion.

postcure [pɔstkyr] *Méd* **elle est en p.,** she's being monitored.

postdater [pɔstdate] *vt* to postdate (*cheque etc*).

poste¹ [pɔst] *nf* **(a)** *Admin* post, *Am* mail; **les Postes et Télécommunications,** the postal services, = the Post Office; **envoyer une lettre par la p.,** to post *or Am* mail a letter; **(bureau de) p.,** post office; **p. principale, grande p.,** main post office (*in a town*); **aller à la p.,** to go to the post office; **receveur, -euse des postes,** postmaster, postmistress; **p. restante,** poste restante; **(b)** *Arch* (*relais de chevaux*) post, relay; **chevaux de p.,** posthorses; **maître de p.,** postmaster; **aller en p.,** to travel post; **courir la p.,** to go posthaste.

poste² *nm* **(a)** (*fonction*) position, appointment, job; **il y a des postes vacants,** there are (job) vacancies; **un p.-clé,** a key position; **occuper un p. de confiance,** to have a position of trust; *Ind* **p. de jour/nuit,** day/night shift;

(b) (*installation*) **p. d'essence,** petrol station, filling station, *Am* gas station; **p. d'incendie,** (*équipement*) fire equipment; **p. de contrôle,** checkpoint; *Av* **p. de pilotage,** cockpit, flight deck; *Rail* **p. d'aiguillage,** signal box; **p. de signaux,** signal tower;

(c) *Rad etc* **p. (de) radio,** radio set; **p. de télévision,** television set; **p. récepteur,** receiver, receiving set; *F* **ouvrir/fermer le p.,** to switch the radio *or* television on/off;

(d) *Rad* **p. émetteur,** (*endroit*) broadcasting station; (*équipement*) transmitter;

(e) *Tél* extension, *Am* local; **p. 35,** extension 35; **le p. est occupé,** the extension *or* line is engaged;

(f) (*bureau*) post; **p. de la Croix-Rouge,** Red Cross station; **p. de secours,** first aid post;

(g) (*salle*) quarters, wardroom; **p. d'équipage,** crew's quarters; (*in merchant service*) forecastle; *Nau* **p. des maîtres,** warrant officers' wardroom; **p. des aspirants,** gunroom;

(h) (*en comptablité*) entry, item;

(i) *Mil* post, station (*of soldier etc*); *Mil* **p. avancé,** advanced *or* outlying post; **p. d'écoute,** listening station; **p. d'observation,** observation post; *Mil Nau* **chef de p.,** guard commander; **à vos postes!,** take post!, to your post!, stand by!; **p. de police,** police station; *Mil* **p. de police** *ou* **de garde,** guardroom; **p. de commandement,** headquarters, *US* command post; *Nau* control room; **postes de combat,** action stations; **être à son p.,** to be at one's post; *Fig* **être solide au p.,** to be still going strong;

(j) *Nau* (*lieu*) berth; **p. de mouillage,** anchoring berth; **p. d'amarrage,** mooring berth, mooring(s); **mettre les ancres à p.,** to stow the anchors.

posté, -ée [pɔste] **1** *adj* **travail p.,** shift work; **ouvrier p.,** shift worker. **2** *n* shift worker.

poster¹ [pɔste] **1** *vt* to post (*sentry etc*); to station (*men, troops*). **2 se poster** *vpr* to take up a position, to station oneself.

poster² *vt* to post, *Am* to mail (*letter etc*).

poster³ [pɔstɛr] *nm* poster.

postérieur, -ieure [pɔsterjœr] **1** *adj* **(a)** (*of time*) subsequent (**à,** to); later; **p. à son décès,** after his death; **la rechute est très postérieure à son opération,** the relapse came a long time after the operation; **avoir lieu à une date postérieure,** to be held at a later date; **être remis à une date postérieure,** to be postponed to a later date; **(b)** (*of place*) hind, back; **partie postérieure de la tête,** back part of the head. **2** *nm F* (*derrière*) bottom, backside, *Am* fanny; *Hum* posterior.

postérieurement [pɔsterjœrmɑ̃] *adv* subsequently (**à,** to); at a later date.

postériorité [pɔsterjɔrite] *nf* posteriority.

postérité [pɔsterite] *nf* posterity; (*famille, descendance*) descendants; **mourir sans (laisser de) p.,** to die without issue; **nous travaillons pour la p.,** we are working for future generations; *Fig* **la p. du nouveau-roman,** the legacy of the nouveau roman; **entrer dans la p.,** to go down in history.

postface [pɔstfas] *nf* postscript.

postglaciaire [pɔstglasjɛr] *adj Géol* postglacial.

posthume [pɔstym] *adj* posthumous.

postiche [pɔstiʃ] **1** *adj* false (*hair, eyelashes etc*). **2** *nm* hairpiece.

posticheur [pɔstiʃœr] *nm* wig-maker.

postier, -ière [pɔstje, -jɛr] *n* post office employee.

postillon [pɔstijɔ̃] *nm* **(a)** *Arch* postilion; **(b)** (*salive*) **postillons,** shower(s) of spit; **envoyer des postillons,** to splutter, to sputter (*in speaking*).

postillonner [pɔstijɔne] *vi* to splutter, to sputter (*in speaking*).

post-industriel, -ielle [pɔstɛ̃dystrijɛl] *adj* post-industrial.

postmodernisme [pɔstmɔdɛrnism] *nm* postmodernism.

postnatal, -als [pɔstnatal] *adj* postnatal.

postopératoire [pɔstɔperatwar] *adj Méd* postoperative (*care etc*).

postposition [pɔstpozisjɔ̃] *nf Gram* postposition.

postscolaire [pɔstskɔlɛr] *adj* continuation (*classes etc*); **enseignement p.,** further education.

post-scriptum [pɔstskriptɔm] *nm inv* postscript, P.S..

postsynchronisation [pɔstsɛ̃krɔnizasjɔ̃] *nf Cin* postsynchronization.

postsynchroniser [pɔstsɛ̃krɔnize] *vt Cin* to postsynchronize.

postulant, -ante [pɔstylɑ̃, -ɑ̃t] *n* **(a)** (*candidat*) candidate, applicant (*for post*); **(b)** *Rel* postulant.

postulat [pɔstyla] *nm Phil* postulate, assumption.

postuler [pɔstyle] **1** *vt* **(a)** (*demander*) to apply for (*post etc*); **(b)** *Phil* to postulate. **2** *vi Jur* **p. pour un client,** (*of lawyer*) to act on behalf of a client.

posture [pɔstyr] *nf* **(a)** (*attitude*) posture, attitude (*of the body etc*); **(b)** (*condition*) position (*in society etc*); **être en p. de faire qch,** to be in a position to do sth; **être en bonne/mauvaise p. (pour faire qch),** to be in a good/bad position, to be well/badly placed (to do sth).

pot [po] *nm* **(a)** (*récipient*) pot; **p. de terre,** earthenware pot; **p. d'étain,** pewter tankard; **p. de chambre,** chamber pot; *F* **(petit) p.,** (*for child*) potty; **le petit va sur le p. tout seul,** the little boy can use the potty all on his own; **mettre en p.,** to pot (*plant, meat etc*); **p. de fleurs,** flowerpot, plant pot; **p. de colle,** pot of glue; *Fig* **quel p. de colle (il est)!,** I can't shake him off, I can't get rid of him; **quel p. de colle tu fais aujourd'hui!,** stop annoying *or* bugging me!; **il est gentil mais c'est un p. de colle,** he's nice but he tends to cling; *F* **payer les pots cassés,** to carry the can; **p. à tabac,** tobacco jar; *Fig F* (*personne petite et grosse*) short, stocky person; **pot(s) à eau,** water jug(s); **p. à lait, p. au lait,** milk jug; (*en métal*) milk can; **p. de confiture,** pot *or* jar of jam; *Fig* **découvrir le p. aux roses** [potoroz], to find out what's been going on; *F* **c'est le p. de terre contre le p. de fer,** he's more than met his match; *Nau* **le p. au noir,** the doldrums;

(b) (*contenu*) pot, jar; **finir un p. de confiture,** to finish a pot *or* jar of jam; *F* **allons prendre un p.,** let's go for a drink;

(c) *F* (*derrière*) bum, *Am* fanny; **se manier** *ou* **se bouger le p.,** to get a move on;

(d) *Culin* (*marmite*) (cooking) pot; **manger à la fortune du p.,** to take pot luck; **en trois coups de cuiller à p.,** in a twinkling; *Fig* **tourner autour du p.,** to beat about the bush; **sourd comme un p.,** as deaf as a post;

(e) *F* (*chance*) **avoir du p.** *ou* **un coup de p.,** to be lucky, to have a stroke of luck; **manque de p., pas de p.,** hard luck; **elle a vraiment pas de p.,** she has no luck at all;

(f) p. d'échappement, exhaust (system); *(tuyau)* exhaust (pipe); **p. catalytique,** catalytic converter.

potable [pɔtabl] *adj* **(a)** *(que l'on peut boire)* drinkable, fit to drink; **eau p.,** drinking water; **(b)** *F (correct)* fair, good enough; **travail p.,** fairly good work.

potache [pɔtaʃ] *nm Scol F* schoolboy *(attending collège or lycée)*.

potage [pɔtaʒ] *nm* **(a)** *(soupe)* soup; **p. aux légumes,** vegetable soup; **(b)** *Arch & Litt* **pour tout p.,** all told, (all) in all.

potager, -ère [pɔtaʒe, -ɛr] **1** *adj* **herbes potagères,** pot herbs; **plante potagère,** vegetable; **jardin p.,** vegetable *or* kitchen garden. **2** *nm* vegetable *or* kitchen garden.

potasse [pɔtas] *nf Ch* potash; **chlorate de p.,** potassium chlorate.

potasser [pɔtase] *F* **1** *vt* to swot up; **p. une question,** to swot up a question. **2** *vi* to swot.

potassique [pɔtasik] *adj Ch* (of, containing) potassium; potassic *(salt)*.

potassium [pɔtasjɔm] *nm Ch* potassium.

pot-au-feu [pɔtofø] **1** *nm inv Culin* = boiled beef with vegetables. **2** *adj inv F* stay-at-home *(person)*.

pot-de-vin [podvɛ̃] *nm* bribe, sweetener, backhander; *(pl pots-de-vin)*.

pote [pɔt] *nm Arg* mate, pal, *US* buddy.

poteau, -eaux [pɔto] *nm* **(a)** post, pole, stake; *Min* pit prop; *Sp* goalpost; **p. indicateur,** signpost; **p. télégraphique,** telegraph pole; *Sp* **p. de départ,** starting post; *Sp* **p. d'arrivée,** finishing post, winning post; **rester au p.,** *(of horse)* to be left at the post; *F* **avoir des jambes comme des poteaux,** to have legs like tree-trunks; **(b) p. (d'exécution),** execution post *(for s.o. about to be shot)*; **mettre qn au p.,** to put s.o. up against a wall (and shoot them); **le général au p.!,** down with the general!; **(c)** *Arg Vieilli* mate, pal, *US* buddy.

potée [pɔte] *nf* **(a)** *Vieilli* potful; jugful *(of milk etc)*; **(b)** *Culin* stew *(esp cabbage and carrots with pork etc)*; **(c)** *F Vieilli (grande quantité)* swarm *(of children etc)*; **j'en ai une p.,** I've (got) lots *or* loads of them; **(d)** *Tech* **p. d'émeri,** emery powder; **p. d'étain,** putty powder.

potelé [pɔtle] *adj* chubby.

potence [pɔtɑ̃s] *nf* **(a)** *(gibet)* gallows, gibbet; **mettre qn à la p.,** to hang s.o. on the gallows; **échapper à la p.,** to cheat the gallows; **gibier de p.,** gallows bird; **(b)** *(charpente)* support, arm, crosspiece, bracket; jib *(of crane)*; stem *(of handlebar of bicycle)*; **en p.,** T-shaped; **(c)** *Nau Mil* davit.

potentat [pɔtɑ̃ta] *nm* potentate.

potentialiser [pɔtɑ̃sjalize] **1** *vt* **(a)** *Pharm* to potentiate, **(b)** *Fig* to maximize. **2 se potentialiser** *vpr* to maximize one's potential.

potentialité [pɔtɑ̃sjalite] *nf* potentiality; **une p. inutilisée,** unused potential.

potentiel, -elle [pɔtɑ̃sjɛl] **1** *adj* potential; *Gram* **préfixe/sens p.,** potential prefix/meaning; *MecE* **énergie potentielle,** potential energy. **2** *nm* **(a)** *(puissance)* potential; potentialities *(of a situation)*; **p. de guerre,** war establishment; **(b)** *El* potential; *Rad* **p. de grille,** grid potential; **(c)** *Gram* potential (mood).

potentiellement [pɔtɑ̃sjɛlmɑ̃] *adv* potentially.

potentille [pɔtɑ̃tij] *nf Bot* **p. (rampante),** cinquefoil.

potentiomètre [pɔtɑ̃sjɔmɛtr] *nm Electron* potentiometer; *Cin* fader *(of sound)*.

poterie [pɔtri] *nf* **(a)** *(usine)* pottery (works); *(atelier)* potter's workshop *or* studio; *(art, techniques)* pottery, potter's art; **cours de p.,** pottery class; **faire de la p.,** to do *or* make pottery; **(b)** piece of pottery; *(objets)* pottery; **p. (de terre),** earthenware; **p. de grès,** stoneware; **(c)** *Tech* **p. d'étain,** pewter(ware).

poterne [pɔtɛrn] *nf* postern (gate).

potiche [pɔtiʃ] *nf* **(a)** *(vase)* (large) vase *(esp of Chinese or Japanese porcelain)*; **(b)** *Fig* figurehead.

potier [pɔtje] *nm* potter.

potin [pɔtɛ̃] *nm F* **(a) potins,** gossip, tittle tattle; **(b)** *(bruit)* row, rumpus; **faire du p.,** to kick up a row *or* rumpus, to make a din.

potiner [pɔtine] *vi* to gossip.

potion [posjɔ̃] *nf Méd etc* potion; *Hum* concoction.

potiron [pɔtirɔ̃] *nm* pumpkin.

pot-pourri [popuri] *nm Mus etc* pot pourri, medley; *(pl pots-pourris)*.

potron-minet [pɔtrɔ̃minɛ] *nm F Arch* **dès p.-m.,** at daybreak, at the crack of dawn.

pou, *pl* **poux** [pu] *nm* louse, *pl* lice; **p. de pubis,** pubic louse, *F* crab (louse); **œuf de p.,** nit; **p. de mouton,** sheep tick; **p. de mer,** *(crustacé)* sea louse; *F* **laid comme un p.,** as ugly as sin; **fier** *ou* **orgueilleux comme un p.,** as proud as a peacock; *F* **chercher des poux dans la tête de qn,** to pick a quarrel with s.o. (about nothing).

pouah [pwa] *int* ugh!

poubelle [pubɛl] *nf* dustbin, (refuse) bin, *Am* garbage can, trash can; **p. à pédale,** pedal bin; **jeter qch à la p.,** to put sth in the dustbin, to throw sth in the bin *or* away; *Fig F* to reject sth as rubbish.

pouce [pus] *nm* **(a)** *Anat* thumb; **sucer son p.,** to suck one's thumb; *F* **donner un coup de p. à qn/qch,** to help s.o./sth (along); **donner le coup de p. à qch,** to put the finishing touches to sth; *F* **manger sur le p.,** to have a (quick) snack; **se tourner les pouces,** to twiddle one's thumbs; **mettre les pouces,** to give in, to knuckle under; *Arg* **et le p.,** and the rest; *(un peu plus)* and a bit more besides; *Scol Arg* **p.!,** pax!; **(b)** *(gros orteil)* big toe; **(c)** *Can & Vieilli* inch; **ne pas bouger d'un p.,** not to move an inch.

Poucet [pusɛ] *nm* **le Petit P.,** Tom Thumb.

poucettes [pusɛt] *nfpl Arch* = metal rings attached to the thumbs of prisoners.

poucier [pusje] *nm* **(a)** *(doigtier)* thumbstall; **(b)** *Tech* thumb piece *(of door latch)*.

pouding [pudiŋ] *nm Culin (plum etc)* pudding.

poudingue [pudɛ̃g] *nm Géol* conglomerate, puddingstone.

poudrage [pudraʒ] *nm Tech* powdering.

poudre [pudr] *nf* **(a)** *(substance)* powder; **réduire qch en p.,** to reduce sth to powder, to powder sth, to pulverize sth; **p. d'or,** gold dust; **p. dentifrice,** tooth powder; **p. à récurer,** scouring powder; **café en p.,** instant coffee; **sucre en p.,** caster sugar; **p. de savon,** soap powder; **lessive en p.,** washing powder; **p. à éternuer,** sneezing powder; **p. (de riz),** (face) powder;

(b) *(explosif)* (explosive) powder; **p. à canon,** gunpowder; *Fig* **être vif comme la p.,** to be volatile; *Fig* **mettre le feu aux poudres,** to spark off a crisis; **la nouvelle s'est répandue comme une traînée de p.,** the news spread like wildfire; **faire parler la p.,** to let one's guns do the talking; *Fig F* **il n'a pas inventé la p.,** he won't set the Thames on fire;

(c) *Arch* dust; *Fig* **jeter de la p. aux yeux de qn,** to dazzle *or* impress s.o..

poudrer [pudre] **1** *vt* to powder, to sprinkle with powder; **p. ses cheveux,** to put powder on one's hair; **une femme poudrée,** a woman with a powdered face. **2** *vi Can* **il poudre,** it's snowing slightly. **3 se poudrer** *vpr* to powder one's face *or* nose *etc*.

poudrerie [pudrəri] *nf* **(a)** *(fabrique de poudre)* (gun)powder factory; **(b)** *Can* blowing snow.

poudreux, -euse [pudrø, -øz] **1** *adj* **(a)** *(qui a la consistance de la poudre)* powdery, powdered; **la neige poudreuse,** powder snow; **(b)** *Vieilli (couvert de poussière)* dusty. **2** *nf* **poudreuse (a)** *(neige)* powder (snow); **(b)** *(sucrier)* sugar sprinkler *or* castor.

poudrier [pudrije] *nm* powder box; *(porté dans un sac à main etc)* (powder) compact.

poudrière [pudrijɛr] *nf (entrepôt)* powder magazine; *Fig (région)* powder keg.

poudrin [pudrɛ̃] *nm* spindrift.

poudroiement [pudrwamɑ̃] *nm* dust haze *(on road etc)*.

poudroyer [pudrwaje] *vi Litt* **(il poudroie; il poudroiera)** to form clouds of dust; **la route poudroie,** the dust whirls up from the road.

pouf [puf] **1** *int* bump!, thud!; *(coup de poing etc)* wham! **2** *nm* **(a)** *(meuble)* pouf(fe); **(b)** *Belg* **à p.,** on tick; **taper à p.,** *(au hasard)* to make a wild guess.

pouffer [pufe] *vi* **p. (de rire),** to burst out laughing; *(rire bruyamment)* to guffaw.

pouffiasse [pufjas] *nf Vulg* whore, tart; *Péj Vulg* **une grande p.,** a (great) fat cow, *Br Sl* a fat slag.

pouillerie [pujri] *nf* squalor; *(lieu)* filthy place, lousy hole.

pouilleux, -euse [pujø, -øz] **1** *adj* **(a)** *(couvert de vermine)* lousy, verminous; **(b)** *(misérable)* wretched, miserable; **quartier p.,** slum; **(c)** *Géog* **Champagne pouilleuse,** = barren part of the Champagne region. **2** *n* **(a)** *(personne couverte de vermine)* louse-ridden *or* flea-bitten person; **(b)** *(mendiant)* tramp, beggar, *Am* bum.

pouillot [pujo] *nm (oiseau)* warbler.

poujadisme [puʒadism] *nm Pol Hist* Poujadism (= lower middle-class, populist movement in the 1950s and 60s); *Fig Péj* narrow-minded *or* shopkeeper mentality.

poujadiste [puʒadist] *nm Pol Hist* Poujadist(e); *Fig Péj* small-town, narrow-minded.

poulailler [pulaje] *nm* **(a)** *(basse-cour)* hen house, hen roost; **(b)** *Th F* **le p.,** the gods.

poulain [pulɛ̃] *nm* **(a)** colt, foal; **(b)** *Sp etc* trainee; protégé (*of manager etc*); **(c)** *Tech* **p. (de chargement),** skid (*for unloading barrels etc*).

poulaine [pulɛn] *nf* **(a)** *Nau* (ship's) head; **(b)** *Nau* **les poulaines,** the latrines (*for crew*); **(c) soulier à la p.,** long pointed shoe.

poularde [pulard] *nf Culin* fattened pullet.

poulbot [pulbo] *nm* street urchin (of Montmartre).

poule[1] [pul] *nf* **(a)** hen; *Culin* (boiling) fowl; **p. pondeuse,** laying hen; **p. au pot,** boiled chicken; *Fig* **ma (petite) p.!,** my dear!, my pet!; *Fig* **la p. aux œufs d'or,** the goose that laid the golden eggs; *Fig* **mère p.,** mother hen, mother who fusses over her children; *Fig Péj* **p. mouillée,** (*personne*) softie, wimp; **se coucher comme** *ou* **avec les poules,** to go to bed early; **lait de p.,** (non-alcoholic) egg flip, egg nog; *Fig* **quand les poules auront des dents,** when pigs can fly; **p. d'eau,** moorhen; **p. faisane,** hen pheasant; **petite p. de bruyère,** grey hen;

(b) *Arg Péj* (*fille*) chick, bird, tart, *Am* broad.

poule[2] *nf* **(a)** (*enjeu*) pool, kitty; **(b)** *Escrime etc* pool, tournament; *Rugby* group; **(c)** *Courses de chevaux* **p. d'essai,** = early-season race for three-year olds.

poulet [pulɛ] *nm* **(a)** chicken; *Culin* **p. fermier** *ou* **de grain,** free-range chicken; **p. aux hormones** *ou* **(élevé) en batterie,** battery (-farmed) chicken; **cuisse de p.,** chicken leg; **p. rôti,** roast chicken; **(b) mon (petit) p.,** my darling, my pet; **(c)** *F* cop; **(d)** *Arch* (witty, amorous) letter.

poulette [pulɛt] *nf* **(a)** *Vieilli* young hen, pullet; *Culin* **sauce (à la) p.,** = rich white sauce (*with onions, mushrooms, white wine etc*); **(b)** *Vieilli* filly, wench; *Am F* dame, broad; *F* **ma p.,** my darling, my pet.

pouliche [puliʃ] *nf* filly.

poulie [puli] *nf* pulley; **p. simple/double,** single/double block; **p. fixe,** fixed pulley, standing block; **p. folle,** loose pulley.

pouliner [puline] *vi* (*of mare*) to foal.

poulinière [pulinjɛr] *adj & nf* **(jument) p.,** brood mare.

pouliot[1] [puljo] *nm Bot* pennyroyal.

pouliot[2] *nm* windlass (*on dray etc*).

poulot, -otte [pulo, -ɔt] *n Enf* (my) pet, (my) darling.

poulpe [pulp] *nm* octopus.

pouls [pu] *nm* pulse; **tâter le p. de qn,** to feel s.o.'s pulse; *Fig* to sound s.o. (out); **prendre le p. à qn,** to take s.o.'s pulse; *Fig* **prendre le p. de l'économie,** to take the pulse of the economy.

poumon [pumɔ̃] *nm Anat* lung; **p. d'acier,** iron lung; **respirer à pleins poumons,** to take a deep breath; **crier à pleins poumons,** to shout at the top of one's voice; **cracher ses poumons,** to cough one's guts up *or* out.

poupard, -arde [pupar, -ard] **1** *nm* **(a)** (*gros bébé*) chubby baby; **(b)** *Vieilli* baby doll. **2** *adj Vieilli* chubby (-cheeked); **visage p.,** baby face.

poupart [pupar] *nm* edible crab.

poupe [pup] *nf Nau* stern, poop; **avoir le vent en p.,** to have the wind aft; *Fig* to be in luck, to be favoured *or US* favored by fortune.

poupée [pupe] *nf* **(a)** (*jouet*) doll; *Enf* dolly; **maison de p.,** doll's house; *Fig* doll's house, shoebox; **jouer à la p.,** to play with dolls; **(b)** *F* (*jolie fille*) bird, doll, chick; **(c)** (*pantin*) **p. (mannequin),** dummy; (milliner's) block; **(d)** (*pansement au doigt*) finger bandage; (*le doigt lui-même*) bandaged finger; **(e)** *Tech* headstock, poppet (head) (*of lathe*); *Nau* **p. de cabestan,** capstan head; *Nau* **p. d'amarrage,** bollard, belaying pin.

poupin, -ine [pupɛ̃, -in] *adj* chubby(-cheeked); **visage p.,** baby face.

poupon [pupɔ̃] *nm* (tiny) baby.

pouponner [pupɔne] *vi* to play the doting (little) mother.

pouponnière [pupɔnjɛr] *nf* nursery (*for children up to three years old*).

pour [pur] **1** *prép* **(a)** (*à la place de*) for; **allez-y p. moi,** go for me *or* instead of me; *Fml* go in my stead; **agir p. qn,** to act on s.o.'s behalf; **p. le Président,** on behalf of the President;

(b) (*comme*) for; **il la veut p. femme,** he wants her for *or* as his wife; **tenir qn p. fou,** to regard s.o. as a madman; **prendre qn p. un autre,** to take s.o. for s.o. else; **laisser qn p. mort,** to leave s.o. for dead; **une attitude p. le moins étrange,** a somewhat strange attitude, a strange attitude, to say the least; *F* **c'est p. de bon** *ou* **p. de vrai,** I mean it, I'm serious, really; **ça compte p. du beurre, on rejoue,** that doesn't count, let's play again;

(c) (*direction*) for; **je pars p. la France,** I'm off to *or* setting out for France; **le train p. Paris,** the Paris train, the train to *or* for Paris;

(d) (*temps*) for; **je vais en Suisse p. quinze jours,** I'm going to Switzerland for a fortnight; **p. dans trois jours,** (with)in three days, in three days' time; **p. toujours,** for ever, for good; **p. le moment,** for the time being; **il sera ici p. quatre heures,** he'll be here for four hours; (*à quatre heures*) he'll be here by four o'clock; **j'en ai p. une heure,** it'll take me an hour, I'll be an hour;

(e) (*contre*) for; **il a acheté son vélo p. 50 francs,** he bought his bike for 50 francs; **il me l'a vendu p. trois fois rien,** he sold it to me for next to nothing; **trente p. cent,** thirty per cent *or* percent; **10 p. 1000,** one per cent *or* percent; **mot p. mot,** word for word; **jour p. jour,** to the (very) day; **donnez-moi p. 100 francs d'essence,** give me 100 francs' worth of petrol *or Am* gas; **j'en ai p. mon argent,** I've got my money's worth; **être p. beaucoup/peu dans une affaire,** to count for much/little in an affair;

(f) (*cause, but*) for; **vêtements p. hommes,** clothes for men; **livres p. enfants,** children's books, books for children; **j'épargne p. quand je serai vieux,** I'm saving for my old age; **je suis ici p. affaires,** I'm here on business; **je viens p. la machine à laver,** I've come about the washing machine; **pommade p. les démangeaisons,** ointment to relieve itching; *F Ordinat* **moniteur p. graphismes,** graphics monitor; **c'est p. cela qu'il est venu,** that's why he came; **p. l'amour de Dieu,** for God's sake, for heaven's sake, for Pete's sake; **faites-le p. moi,** do it for me *or* my sake; **j'avais peur p. lui,** I was nervous on his account; **mourir p. sa patrie,** to die for one's country; **être bon pour les animaux,** to be kind to animals; **l'art p. l'art,** art for art's sake; **p. la forme,** for form's sake; **beaucoup de bruit p. rien,** a lot of fuss about *or* over nothing, *Litt* much ado about nothing; **tant pis p. moi,** hard luck on me;

(g) (*en faveur de*) for, in favour *or US* favor of; **parler p. qn,** to speak in favour of s.o.; **je suis p. la libération de la femme,** I'm all for women's liberation; **moi, je suis p.,** I'm all for it, I'm in favour of it;

(h) (*quant à, en ce qui concerne*) for; **p. mon compte,** for my part, as far as I'm concerned; **il est grand p. son âge,** he's tall for his age; **p. ce qui est de ...,** as regards ..., with regard to ...; **p. (ce qui est de) moi,** as for me, for my part, as far as I'm concerned; **p. moi c'est absurde,** in my opinion it's ridiculous; **ce ne sera une surprise p. personne,** it will come as a surprise to nobody; **p. moi, je veux bien,** personally, I'm willing; **p. cela,** for all that; **en tout et p. tout,** in total, all included; *F* **p. de la chance, c'est de la chance,** you're in luck and no mistake;

(i) p. + *inf*, (in order) to; **il faut manger p. vivre,** one must eat to live; **p. ainsi dire,** so to speak; **c'était p. rire,** it was just for a laugh; **il s'en va p. ne jamais revenir,** he's going away for good, he's leaving never to return; **nous nous sommes dépêchés p. ne pas être en retard,** we hurried so as not to be late;

(j) p. que + *sub*, in order that, so that; **je vous dis cela p. que vous soyez sur vos gardes,** I'm telling you this in order to put you on your guard; **il est trop tard p. qu'elle sorte,** it is too late for her to go out; **mettez-le là, p. qu'on ne l'oublie pas,** put it there so that it won't be forgotten;

(k) (*ayant pour résultat*) **p. ma déception, il n'est pas venu,** to my disappointment, he didn't come; **cela n'est pas p. me surprendre,** that does not come as a surprise to me; **cette amitié n'était pas p. lui plaire,** the friendship was not to his liking;

(l) (*after* **assez, trop**) **assez intelligent p. comprendre,** intelligent enough to understand; **être trop faible p. marcher,** to be too weak to walk; **trop beau p. être vrai,** too good to be true;

(m) *Litt* considering; **il est bien ignorant p. avoir étudié si longtemps,** he's very ignorant considering how long he's studied;

(n) *Litt* (*concession*) (al)though; **p. être petit, il n'en est pas moins brave,** though small, he is none the less brave;

(o) *F* **être p. partir,** to be about to start out *or* set off, to be on the point of starting out *or* setting off;

(p) mourir p. mourir, if I *or* we *etc* must die; **ennuis p. ennuis, je préfère les miens,** as troubles go, I prefer my own;

(q) p. peu que + *sub*, if only, if ever; **p. peu que vous hésitiez vous êtes fichu,** if you hesitate for a moment *or* hesitate at all, you've had it;

(r) (*à cause de*) for, on account of; **on l'apprécie p. sa gentillesse,** he is liked on account of his kindness; **fermeture p. raisons familiales,** closed for family reasons; **p. un rien,** over nothing; **p. un peu c'était trop tard,** it was very nearly too late; **merci p. tout,** thank you for everything; **être puni p. avoir désobéi,** to be punished for having disobeyed *or* for disobeying *or* for disobedience; **je le sais p. l'avoir vu,** I know from having seen it; **il est mort p. avoir trop travaillé,** he died of overwork(ing).

2 *nm* **peser le p. et le contre,** to weigh (up) the pros and cons; **entendre le p. et le contre,** to hear both sides.

pourboire [purbwar] *nm* tip; *Fml* gratuity; **donner un p. au porteur,** to tip the porter.

pourceau, -eaux [purso] *nm* hog, pig, swine; *Fig* **jeter des perles aux pourceaux,** to cast pearls before swine.

pourcentage [pursɑ̃taʒ] *nm* percentage; rate (*of interest*); commission (*for salesman etc*); *Constr* **rampe à fort p.,** steep gradient.

pourchasser [purʃase] *vt* to pursue; to pursue, to hunt (down) (*criminal*); *Vieilli* to harry (*debtor*); **pourchassé de rue en rue,** hounded from street to street.

pourlécher [purleʃe] *v* (**je pourlèche; je pourlécherai**) **1** *vt* **(a)** *Arch* to lick (*sth*) (all) over; **(b)** *Vieilli* to polish up (*verses etc*). **2 se pourlécher** *vpr* **se p. (les babines),** to lick one's lips.

pourparler [purparle] *nm* (*souvent pl*) **pourparlers,** (*tractation, discussion*) talks; **entrer en pourparlers,** to enter into *or* begin negotiations (**avec,** with).

pourpier [purpje] *nm Bot* purslane.

pourpoint [purpwɛ̃] *nm* pourpoint, doublet.

pourpre [purpr] **1** *nf* **(a)** (*teinte naturelle*) purple (dye) (*of the ancients*); **(b)** *Fig* (*symbole de haute dignité*) royal *or* imperial dignity; **né dans la p.,** born in *or* to the purple. **2** *nm* crimson, rich red (colour); **le p. lui monta au visage,** he turned crimson; *Physiol* **p. rétinien,** red pigment, visual purple. **3** *adj* crimson; (*of person*) crimson, purple (**de rage,** with rage).

pourpré [purpre] *adj Litt* purple, crimson.

pourquoi [purkwa] **1** *adv & conj* why; **p. faire?,** what for?; **p. cela?,** why?; **p. êtes-vous venu?,** what have you come for?; **dis-moi p.,** tell me why; **mais p. donc?,** what on earth for?; **je voulais savoir p. (il était parti),** I wanted to know why (he had left); **voilà p.,** that's (the reason) why; **c'est p. ...,** and that's why ..., and so ...; **p. pas?, p. non?,** why (ever) not? **2** *nm inv* **je ne sais pas le p.,** I don't know the reason why; **les p. et les comment,** the whys and wherefores; **les p. des enfants,** the questions that children ask.

pourri [puri] **1** *adj* rotten (*fruit, wood*); rotten, decayed (*tooth*); putrid (*flesh*); rotten, addle(d), bad (*egg*); damp (*climate*); wet (*weather*); (*corrompu*) rotten; **il est p. de vices,** he's rotten to the core; **gouvernement p.,** corrupt government; **ils sont pourris d'argent,** they're stinking rich, they're rolling in money, they've got money coming out of their ears. **2** *nm* **(a)** (*décomposition*) rotten *or* bad *or* decayed part (*of an apple etc*); **sentir le p.,** to smell rotten; **(b)** *F* (*personne*) swine, *Br* sod, *Br* git; **bande de pourris!,** you bunch of rotten swines!

pourrir [purir] **1** *vi* to rot, to decay; (*of body*) to putrefy, to decompose; (*of food*) to go rotten, to go bad; (*of egg*) to go rotten, to go bad, to addle; *Fig* **p. en prison,** to rot in prison; **faire p.,** to rot (*wood etc*); *Fig* **laisser p. la situation,** to allow the situation to deteriorate; **laisse-le p. dans son orgueil,** leave him to stew *or* wallow in his own pride. **2** *vt* **(a)** (*gâter*) to rot; **(b)** *Fig F* (*corrompre*) to spoil; **elle pourrit ses enfants en leur donnant tant d'argent,** she's spoiling her children by giving them so much money.

pourrissement [purismɑ̃] *nm Fig* deterioration (*of a situation*).

pourrissoir [puriswar] *nm* **(a)** *Litt* muck heap; **(b)** *Tech* steeping vats.

pourriture [purityr] *nf* **(a)** (*décomposition*) rotting, rot, decay; **p. sèche (du bois),** dry rot; **en p.,** rotting; **(b)** (*état de décomposition*) rottenness; *Fig* corruption; **(c)** *F* (*personne*) swine, *Br* sod.

poursuite [pursɥit] *nf* **(a)** (*chasse*) pursuit; chase (*of enemy ship*); hunt(ing), tracking (*of criminal*); **être à la p. de qch,** to be in pursuit of sth; *Fig* **la p. du bonheur/de la sagesse,** the pursuit of happiness/wisdom; **se mettre** *ou* **se lancer à la p. de qn,** to set off in pursuit of s.o., to chase after s.o.; **(b)** (*continuation*) continuation; **p. d'un travail,** carrying out of a piece of work; *Com* **p. du client,** follow-up system; **(c)** *Electron* tracking (*of aircraft, missile etc*); **radar de p.,** tracking radar; **(d)** *Jur* (*souvent pl*) **poursuites,** lawsuit, action; prosecution (*of criminal*); suing (*of debtor*); **engager** *ou* **entamer** *ou* **intenter des poursuites (judiciaires) contre qn,** to take *or* institute (legal) proceedings against s.o., to take legal action against s.o..

poursuiteur [pursɥitœr] *nm Cyclisme* pursuit cyclist.

poursuivant, -ante [pursɥivɑ̃, -ɑ̃t] **1** *adj Jur* prosecuting (*party*). **2** *n* **(a)** *Jur* plaintiff, prosecutor; **(b)** (*personne qui poursuit*) pursuer.

poursuivre [pursɥivr] *v* (*conj like* **suivre**) **1** *vt* **(a)** (*pourchasser*) to pursue, to go after, to chase, to hunt (down) (*s.o., an animal*); to seek for *or* after (*sth*); **ce songe me poursuit,** that dream haunts me; **poursuivi par la guigne,** dogged by bad luck;

(b) (*relancer*) to hound, to harry (*debtor*); *Mil* to harry (*enemy*);

(c) (*harceler*) to assail (**de,** with); **p. une femme de ses assiduités,** to force one's attentions on a woman; **p. qn de sa colère,** to vent *or* unleash one's anger on s.o.;

(d) *Jur* **p. (en justice),** to sue (*s.o.*), to take proceedings against (*s.o.*); to prosecute (*criminal*);

(e) (*continuer*) to pursue, to continue, to proceed with, to go on with (*story etc*); **p. un travail,** to carry on (with) a piece of work; **p. un avantage,** to follow up *or* press an advantage; **p. un but,** to work towards an end.

2 *vi* **poursuivez,** go on, continue (*your story etc*).

3 se poursuivre *vpr* to be continuing, to be going on *or* ahead; **les préparatifs se poursuivent,** preparations are continuing *or* going on *or* going ahead.

pourtant [purtɑ̃] *adv* nevertheless, however, still, (and) yet; **un homme mûr et p. plein de fantaisie,** a man who, though mature, is full of imagination; **vous n'allez p. pas nous quitter?,** you're surely not going to leave us?, you're not going to leave us though, are you?

pourtour [purtur] *nm* periphery, circumference, compass (*of building etc*); precincts (*of a cathedral*); **mur de p.,** enclosure wall (*of prison, town etc*).

pourvoi [purvwa] *nm Jur* appeal; **p. en grâce,** petition for mercy.

pourvoir [purvwar] *v* (*prp* **pourvoyant;** *pp* **pourvu;** *pr ind* **je pourvois, n. pourvoyons;** *pr sub* **je pourvoie;** *impf* **je pourvoyais;** *p hist* **je pourvus;** *fu* **je pourvoirai**) **1** *vi* **p. aux besoins de qn,** to provide for *or* cater for *or* supply s.o.'s needs; (*de façon plus immédiate*) to attend to *or* see to s.o.'s needs; **p. à un emploi,** to fill a job; **on n'y a pas pourvu,** no provision has been made for it. **2** *vt* **p. qn de,** to supply *or* provide *or* furnish s.o. with (*sth*); to equip s.o. with (*tools*); **p. qn d'une charge,** to invest s.o. with *or* to appoint s.o. to an office; **être pourvu de tout l'équipement nécessaire,** to be supplied *or* provided *or* furnished with all the necessary equipment. **3 se pourvoir** *vpr* **(a)** (*se munir*) to provide oneself (**de,** with); **(b)** *Jur* to appeal, to lodge an appeal; **se p. en grâce,** to petition for mercy.

pourvoyeur, -euse [purvwajœr, -øz] *n* supplier, provider; *Fml* purveyor; *Constr* contractor; (*en provisions alimentaires*) caterer.

pourvu que [purvykə] *conj* (+ *sub*) provided (that), so *or* as long as; **p. qu'il ne fasse pas de gaffes!,** I only hope he won't make any blunders!

poussage [pusaʒ] *nm Tech* pushing.

poussa(h) [pusa] *nm* (*jeu*) tumbler; *Fig* (*gros homme*) wobbly man, potbellied man.

pousse [pus] *nf* **(a)** (*croissance*) growth (*of leaves, hair, feathers*); cutting (*of teeth*); **(b)** *Bot* (young) shoot, sprout; **p. de bambou,** bamboo shoot.

poussé [puse] *adj elaborate* (*ornamentation etc*); deep, searching, exhaustive, extensive (*study*); **il aboutit à un scepticisme assez p.,** he carries scepticism to some lengths *or* rather far; **faire des études très poussées,** to pursue one's studies to a very advanced level; *Phot* **cliché trop p.,** over-developed negative; *Aut* **moteur p.,** hotted-up *or* souped-up engine.

pousse-café [puskafe] *nm inv* (glass of) liqueur (*after coffee*).

poussée [puse] *nf* **(a)** (*pression*) thrust; (*de liquide*) buoyancy; (*de la mer*) heave; **p. du vent,** wind pressure; **centre de p.,** aerodynamic centre, centre of pressure; (*de liquide*) centre of buoyancy; *Phys* **axe de p.,** aerodynamic axis; **force de p.,** upward thrust; **la p. de la foule,** the pushing of the crowd;

(b) (*geste, fait de pousser qn*) thrust; (*coup de coude etc*) push, shove; **écarter qch d'une p.,** to push *or* shove sth aside; **p. vitale,** vital impetus;

(c) (*fait de croître*) growth; *Méd* (*accès*) eruption, outbreak (*of pimples etc*); **p. de croissance,** a spurt of growth; **p. de fièvre,** sudden rise of *or* in temperature;

(d) *Fig* (*augmentation soudaine*) upsurge (*of passion etc*); bulge (*in profits etc*); **forte p. en hausse,** strong upward tendency (*of the market etc*).

pousse-pousse [puspus] *nm inv* rickshaw.

pousser [puse] **1** *vt* **(a)** (*soumettre qch à une force*) to push; (*rudement*) to shove; (*loin, en avant*) to thrust; to drive (*cattle*); to push, to wheel (*bicycle*); (*du vent*) to blow, to drive (*boat etc*); **ne poussez pas!,** don't push!; **p. qn du coude/du genou,** to nudge s.o. (with one's elbow/knee); **p. la porte,** to push the door open; **p. du fond,** to punt; **p. une charrette,** to push (along) *or* wheel a cart;

(b) (*inciter*) to drive (on), to impel, to urge; **p. qn à faire qch,** to induce s.o. *or* lead s.o. to do sth; (*contre son gré*) to push s.o. into doing sth; (*encourager*) to egg s.o. on to do sth; *Litt* **poussé par la pitié,** prompted by pity; **il faut le p.,** he needs to be pushed;

(c) (*continuer*) to push on (with) (*piece of work*); to pursue (*studies*); to urge on (*horse*); **p. une attaque à fond,** to push *or* thrust *or* drive an attack home; **p. une promenade jusqu'à la ville,** to walk on *or* push on as far as the town; **p. trop loin une plaisanterie,** to take *or* carry a joke too far; **p. la guerre jusqu'au bout,** to carry the war to its conclusion; **p. la vente de qch,** to push the sale of sth; *Tech* **p. les feux,** to raise steam, to stoke up;

(d) *Litt* (*produire*) to put out, to grow (*leaves, roots*); (*of child*) to cut (*teeth*);

(e) (*exprimer*) to utter (*cry*); to give (*cheer*); **p. un cri,** to shout; **p. un soupir,** to (heave a) sigh; *F* **il nous en a poussé une,** he gave us a song.

2 *vi* **(a)** (*écarter de soi*) to push; **p. à la roue,** to put one's shoulder to the wheel; *Fig F* (*exagérer*) to overdo it, to go (a bit) too far; **faut pas p.!,** don't (let's) overdo it!, that's going a bit too far!; **la mère n'eut pas besoin de p.,** the mother didn't need to push when she gave birth;

(b) (*continuer, avancer*) to push on (*to a place*); *Mil* to push forward; **p. jusqu'au bois,** to push on as far as the wood;

(c) (*croître*) (*d'une plante*) to grow, to sprout, to spring up; (*des cheveux, des ongles*) to grow; (*des dents*) to come through; **laisser p. sa barbe,** to grow a beard; **ses dents commencent à p.,** his teeth are beginning to come through, he's beginning to cut his teeth; *Fig* **tous ces enfants poussent,** these children are all shooting up;

(d) (*inciter à*) to press; **p. à la hausse,** to have an inflationary effect; **p. au changement,** to press for change.

3 se pousser *vpr* **(a)** (*se mettre en vue*) to push oneself forward; to make one's way (*in society etc*); (*à coups de coude etc*) to shove *or* elbow one's way (*to the front of a crowd*);

(b) (*se presser*) to move up (*to make room*).

poussette [pusɛt] *nf* (*voiture d'enfants*) (child's) push-chair; (*caddie*) shopping trolley.

pousseur [pusœr] *nm* **(a)** (*bateau*) tug; **(b)** *Astron* booster rocket.

poussier [pusje] *nm* coal dust, screenings; (*charbon*) slack.

poussière [pusjɛr] *nf* dust; **p. d'or,** gold dust; **enlever la p. des meubles,** to dust the furniture; **couvert de p.,** dusty, covered in dust; **s'en aller** *ou* **tomber en p.,** to crumble (in)to dust; **réduire qch en p.,** to reduce sth to dust; *Fig* to smash sth to atoms; **mordre la p.,** to bite the dust; **une p.,** a speck of dust; *F* **10 francs et des poussières,** ten francs plus (a bit); **poussières radioactives,** radioactive dust.

poussiéreux, -euse [pusjerø, -øz] *adj* dusty.

poussif, -ive [pusif, -iv] *adj* wheezy, short-winded (*person*); broken-winded (*horse*); wheezy (*engine*).

poussin [pusɛ̃] *nm* chick; *Culin* spring chicken; *F* **mon p.,** pet.

poussinière [pusinjɛr] *nf* chicken coop; (*éleveuse*) brooder, incubator.

poussivement [pusivmɑ̃] *adv* breathlessly.

poussoir [puswar] *nm* push button (*of electric bell etc*); *MecE* push rod (*of a valve etc*); **p. à ressort,** trigger.

poutrage [putraʒ] *nm* framework of beams, joist framing.

poutre [putr] *nf* **(a)** (*madrier*) (wooden) beam; **grosse p.,** ba(u)lk; **p. de faîte,** ridge piece, roof tree; **p. de plancher,** ceiling joist; **poutres apparentes,** exposed beams; **(b)** *Constr* (metal) girder; **p. à âme pleine,** plate girder; **p. à caisson,** box girder.

poutrelle [putrɛl] *nf Constr* girder.

poutser [putse] *vt Région F* to clean (up).

pouvoir¹ [puvwar] *nm* **(a)** (*possibilité*) power, ability, capacity; **il n'est pas en mon p. de ...,** it is not within *or* it is beyond my power to ...; **je ferai tout ce qui est en mon p.,** I'll do everything in my power; **avoir le p. de faire qch,** to have the power *or* the ability to do sth; **il a des pouvoirs surnaturels,** he has supernatural powers;

(b) (*propriété*) *Ch Phys etc* **p. calorifique,** calorific value; **p. rayonnant,** radiating capacity; *Écon* **p. d'achat,** purchasing power;

(c) (*puissance*) power; **p. politique,** political power; **p. absolu,** absolute power; **avoir un p. absolu sur qn,** to have complete power over s.o.; **le p. des sens/des images,** the power of the senses/of images; **tomber au p. de l'ennemi,** to fall into enemy hands; **elle est en son p.,** she's in his power; **abuser de son p.** *ou* **de ses pouvoirs,** to abuse one's authority; **ambitionner le p.,** to aim for *or* at power; **prendre le p.,** to assume power; (*après élections etc*) to come into *or* take office; **le parti au p.,** the party in power; **quand les Libéraux sont au p.,** when the Liberals are in (power); *Fig* **une affaire qui concerne le p.,** a government matter; **les pouvoirs publics,** the authorities; **p. exécutif,** executive power; **p. législatif,** legislative power; **p. judiciaire,** judicial power; (*les juges*) the judiciary;

(d) *Jur* power of attorney; **avoir/recevoir plein(s) pouvoir(s) pour agir,** to have full powers/to be (fully) empowered *or* authorized to act; **se présenter sans pouvoirs réguliers,** to come without full credentials; **bon pour p.,** good for proxy.

pouvoir² *v* (*prp* **pouvant**; *pp* **pu**; *pr ind* **je peux, je puis** (*always* **puis-je** [pɥiʒ]), **tu peux, il peut, n. pouvons, ils peuvent**; *pr sub* **je puisse, n. puissions**; *impf* **je pouvais**; *p hist* **je pus**; *fu* **je pourrai** [pure]) **1** *vt* **(a)** (*être capable de*) to be able; **si je peux,** if I can; **je ne peux (pas) le faire,** I cannot *or* can't do it, I'm unable to do it; **cela ne peut (pas) se faire,** it cannot *or* can't be done; **comment a-t-il pu dire cela?,** how could he say that?; **il aurait pu le faire s'il avait voulu,** he could have done it if he had wanted to; **si vous aviez pu le voir,** if you'd been able to see him, if you could have seen him; **il ne pouvait pas l'accompagner,** he couldn't go with him, he wasn't able *or* he was unable to go with him; **faire tout ce qu'on peut,** to do one's (level) best *or* the best one can *or* all *or* everything one can; **j'ai fait toutes les démarches que j'ai pu,** I took every step that I possibly could; **j'ai pu le revoir,** I managed *or* was able to see him again; **je n'y peux rien,** I can't help it; **on n'y peut rien,** it can't be helped, there's nothing that can be done about it; **il a été on ne peut plus grossier,** he was as rude as could be, he was extremely rude; **il travaille on ne peut mieux,** he's as good a worker as it's possible to be; **il n'en peut plus (de fatigue),** he's quite exhausted *or* worn out *or* tired out; **elle peut beaucoup,** she's very capable; **sauve qui peut,** every man for himself; **on ne peut pas ne pas l'admirer,** you can't not admire him, you can't help admiring him, you have to admire him; **je viendrai aussitôt que je pourrai,** I'll come as soon as I can; **qu'est-ce qu'il peut bien me vouloir?,** what(ever) can he want?; **où pouvait-il bien être à cette heure?,** where(ver) could he be at this time?; **la loi ne peut rien contre lui,** the law can't touch him;

(b) (*avoir le droit, la permission (de)*) to be allowed to; **vous pouvez partir,** you can *or Fml* may go; **elle ne peut pas sortir seule,** she can't go out alone, she isn't allowed out alone; **puis-je entrer?,** can *or Fml* may I come in?; **quand pourrai-je emménager?,** when can I move in?, when will I be able to move in?;

(c) (*être possible*) to be possible *or* probable; **la porte a pu se fermer toute seule,** the door may have *or* could have closed on its own; **on peut se tromper, n'est-ce pas?,** after all, we could be wrong; **nous pourrions le trouver si nous nous dépêchions,** we might find him if we hurry; **elle peut bien s'excuser, je ne lui pardonnerai pas,** she can apologize all she likes, but I shan't forgive her; **tout de même vous auriez (bien) pu faire moins de bruit,** all the same you could have *or* might have made less noise;

(d) *Litt* **puisse-t-il défendre nos lois!,** may he defend our laws!

2 *v impers* **cela se peut (bien),** it may be *or* it could well be (the case), it's quite possible, maybe, possibly; **cela ne se peut pas,** it can't be done, that's impossible; **advienne que pourra,** come what may; **autant que faire se peut,** as much as can *or* could be done; **il peut se faire** *ou* **il peut arriver que ...,** + *sub*, it may be *or* may happen that ...; **il se peut qu'il ne soit pas coupable,** he may not *or* might not be guilty; **il se peut qu'il vienne,** he may come, he could well come.

p.p. *abrév* **port payé.**

PPCM [pepeseem] *nm Math* (*abrév* **plus petit commun multiple**) LCM.

ppm [pepeem] (*abrév* **parties par million**) ppm.

PQ [peky] *nm* **(a)** *Can Pol* (*abrév* **Parti Québécois**) Parti québécois; **(b)** *F* (*papier hygiénique*) loo paper.

P.R. *abrév* **poste restante**.
pragmatique [pragmatik] *adj* pragmatic.
pragmatisme [pragmatism] *nm* pragmatism.
pragmatiste [pragmatist] *adj & n* pragmatist.
praire [prɛr] *nf* clam.
prairial [prɛrjal] *nm Hist Fr* = ninth month of the French Republican Calendar (*May 20-June 18*).
prairie [preri] *nf* (*pré, champ*) meadow; (*large étendue*) grassland, *Am* prairie; **p. artificielle,** cultivated grassland; *Géog* **la P.**, the Prairies.
pralin [pralɛ̃] *nm*, **praline** [pralin] *nf Culin* praline, sugared almond; *Péj F* **cucul la p.**, nutty, *Br* dotty; **elle est cucul la p.**, she's (a bit) nutty *or* dotty *or* cuckoo.
praliné [praline] *adj Culin* containing ground praline; **amandes pralinées,** sugared almonds.
praliner [praline] *vt Culin* to brown (*almonds etc*) in sugar.
praticable [pratikabl] **1** *adj* (*possible, réalisable*) practicable; feasible (*plan, idea etc*); passable, negotiable (*road etc*); *Th* practicable (*door, window*). **2** *nm Th Tech* movable platform (*for camera or projectors*).
praticien, -ienne [pratisjɛ̃, -jɛn] *n* **(a)** *Jur* (legal) practitioner; *Méd* (medical) practitioner; **(b)** (*technicien, expert*) expert; **(c)** (*ouvrier*) sculptor's assistant.
pratiquant, -ante [pratikɑ̃, -ɑ̃t] *Rel* **1** *adj* practising; **catholique p.**, practising Catholic. **2** *n* (regular) churchgoer.
pratique [pratik] **1** *adj* practical, useful (*method etc*); practical, handy (*gadget etc*); convenient (*time etc*); practical (*person*); **avoir l'esprit p.**, to have a practical turn of mind; **sens p.**, practical common sense.

2 *nf* **(a)** (*application*) practice; **mettre en p.**, to put (*sth*) into practice; to apply (*system etc*); **c'est une p. courante,** it's common practice, it's quite usual; **la théorie et la p.**, theory and practice; **en p.**, in practice;

(b) (*expérience, exercice*) practice, experience; *Litt* practising (*of virtue*); **p. du théâtre,** theatrical experience; **la p. du golf coûte cher,** golfing *or* (playing) golf costs a lot; **la p. du football m'a valu une jambe cassée,** I got a broken leg *or* broke my leg (through) playing football; **perdre la p. de qch,** to lose the knack of sth; (*d'un sport, d'une activité*) to get out of practice; **avoir une longue p. de qch,** to have a lot of practical experience of sth;

(c) *Jur* practice (*of the law*); **terme de p.**, legal term;

(d) *Arch* **il avait vécu dans la p. des hauts fonctionnaires,** he had associated with high-ranking civil servants;

(e) (*exercice, action*) practice; **pratiques religieuses,** religious practices *or* observances; **pratiques clandestines,** underhand practices; *Jur* **libre p.**, free exercise (*of one's religion etc*); *Nau* **avoir libre p.**, to be out of quarantine;

(f) practice (*of lawyer, doctor*); custom, business (*of tradesman*);

(g) *Vieilli* (*clientèle*) (*lawyer's*) clients; (*doctor's*) patients; (*tradesman's*) customers.
pratiquement [pratikmɑ̃] *adv* (*dans l'expérience*) in practice; (*en fait*) in actual fact; (*presque*) practically, virtually.
pratiquer [pratike] **1** *vt* **(a)** (*exercer*) to practise (*virtues, witchcraft etc*); to put (*plan*) into practice; to employ, to use (*method etc*); **il pratique le football,** he plays football; **elle pratique la natation,** she's a (keen) swimmer, she swims; **voilà comment on le pratique ici,** that's how it's usually done here; *Com* **les cours pratiqués,** the ruling prices; **p. les conseils de qn,** to put s.o.'s advice into practice;

(b) *Méd* **p. une intervention,** to operate, to carry out an operation;

(c) (*observer, faire l'exercice de*) to observe, to practice; **il ne pratique pas (sa religion),** he doesn't practise his religion;

(d) (*travailler*) to practise; **médecin qui pratique dans cette ville,** doctor who practises in this town; **il ne pratique plus,** he's no longer in practice;

(e) (*ménager*) to make; **p. une ouverture dans un mur,** to make an opening in a wall; **p. un sentier,** to make *or* open up a path;

(f) *Arch* to frequent, to associate with (*s.o.*);

(g) to study (*book, author*).

2 se pratiquer *vpr* to be done; **voilà comment ça se pratique,** that's how it's done.
praxis [praksis] *nf* praxis.
pré [pre] *nm* meadow; *Arch* **aller sur le p.**, to fight a duel.
préalable [prealabl] **1** *adj* **(a)** (*antérieur*) previous, prior (**à**, to); **formalités préalables au débat,** formalities that precede the debate; **(b)** preliminary (*agreement etc*); **à titre de mesure p.**, as a preliminary (measure). **2** *nm* **(a)** (*condition*) prerequisite, condition; **au p.**, to begin with, first (of all); (*auparavant*) beforehand; **(b)** *Arch* (*préparation*) preliminary.
préalablement [prealabləmɑ̃] *adv* first (of all); (*auparavant*) beforehand); **p. à ...**, prior to ... .
préalpes (les) [leprealp] *nfpl* the foothills of the Alps.
préalpin [prealpɛ̃] *adj* of the foothills of the Alps.
préambule [preɑ̃byl] *nm* (*d'un discours*) preamble (**de**, to); (*d'une action*) prelude; **il a abordé le sujet sans p.**, he (dispensed with preliminaries and) came straight to the point.
préamplificateur [preɑ̃plifikatœr] *nm Electron* preamplifier.
préapprentissage [preaprɑ̃tisaʒ] *nm* pre-apprenticeship training.
préau, -aux [preo] *nm* **(a)** (*cour intérieure*) (court)yard (*esp of prison*); open space (*of cloister*); **(b)** (*partie couverte*) covered (part of) playground.
préavis [preavi] *nm* (previous, advance) notice; **sans p.**, without notice *or* warning; **p. de licenciement,** redundancy notice; **exiger un p. de trois mois,** to require three months' notice.
prébende [prebɑ̃d] *nf Rel* prebend; *Fig* sinecure.
prébendé [prebɑ̃de] *adj Rel* prebendal.
prébendier [prebɑ̃dje] *nm Rel* prebendary.
précaire [prekɛr] *adj* precarious (*tenure, position, state of health etc*); delicate (*health*); precarious, rickety (*dwellings*).
précairement [prekɛrmɑ̃] *adv* precariously.
précambrien, -ienne [prekɑ̃brijɛ̃, -ijɛn] *adj Géol* Precambrian, Pre-Cambrian.
précarité [prekarite] *nf* precariousness.
précaution [prekosjɔ̃] *nf* **(a)** (*mesure*) precaution; **prendre des** *ou* **ses précautions,** to take precautions (**pour,** for); **mesures de p.**, precautionary measures; **par (mesure de) p.**, as a precaution; **(b)** (*soin*) caution, wariness, care; **avec p.**, cautiously, warily, carefully.
précautionner [prekosjɔne] **1** *vt Arch* to warn, to caution (**contre,** against). **2 se précautionner** *vpr* to take precautions; **se p. contre qch,** to take precautions *or* guard against sth.
précautionneusement [prekosjɔnøzmɑ̃] *adv* cautiously, warily, carefully.
précautionneux, -euse [prekosjɔnø, -øz] *adj* cautious, wary, careful.
précédemment [presedamɑ̃] *adv* previously, already, before.
précédent [presedɑ̃] **1** *adj* preceding, previous, former; **le jour p.**, the day before, the previous day. **2** *nm* precedent; **créer un p.**, to create *or* set a precedent; **sans p.**, unprecedented, without precedent.
précéder [presede] *v* (*conj like* **céder**) **1** *vt* (*arriver avant*) to precede, to go *or* come before; **la musique précède les troupes,** the band marches in front of the troops; **l'antichambre qui précède le salon,** the antechamber leading to the drawing room; **faire p. un concert d'un discours,** to preface a concert with a speech; **je l'ai précédé de 10 minutes,** I got there ten minutes before he did *or* before him *or* ahead of him; *Fig* **le scandale a précédé la révélation de l'affaire,** the scandal occurred before the affair came to light; **p. qn (en dignité)**, to have precedence over s.o.. **2** *vi* **la page qui précède,** the preceding *or* previous page, the page before; **ce qui précède,** the foregoing.
précepte [presɛpt] *nm* precept.
précepteur, -trice [presɛptœr, -tris] *n* (private) tutor, teacher.
préceptoral, -aux [presɛptɔral, -o] *adj* tutorial.
préceptorat [presɛptɔra] *nm* tutorship.
précession [presesjɔ̃] *nf Astron etc* precession.
préchambre [preʃɑ̃br] *nf Tech* precombustion chamber (*of diesel engine*).
prêche [prɛʃ] *nm* sermon.
prêcher [preʃe] **1** *vt* **(a)** (*enseigner*) to preach (*the Gospel etc*) (**à**, to); **p. l'économie,** to preach economy; **(b)** (*conseiller*) to preach to (*s.o.*); *Fig* to lecture (*s.o.*), to tell (*s.o.*) off; **p. un converti,** to preach to the converted. **2** *vi* **(a)** (*prononcer un sermon*) to preach; **p. dans le désert,** to preach in the wilderness; **(b)** *Fig* (*moraliser*) to preachify, to sermonize; **p. d'exemple,** to practise what one preaches.
prêcheur, -euse [prɛʃœr, -øz] **1** *adj Rel* **(a)** preaching (*friar*); **(b)** (*moralisateur*) sermonizing (*person*). **2** *n Fig Péj* sermonizer, preacher.
prêchi-prêcha [preʃipreʃa] *nm inv F Péj* preaching,

preachifying, sermonizing.
précieusement [presjøzmɑ̃] *adv* **(a)** (*avec soin*) very carefully; **garder qch p.,** to treasure sth; **(b)** *Litt* (*avec préciosité*) preciously, affectedly.
précieux, -euse [presjø, -øz] **1** *adj* **(a)** (*d'une grande valeur*) precious; **pierre précieuse,** precious stone; **(b)** valuable (*advice, time etc*) (**à,** to); **(c)** *Litt* affected, mannered (*style*). **2** *nf Hist Littér Fr* **précieuse,** = pedantic woman.
préciosité [presjozite] *nf Litt* affectation, affectedness, preciousness.
précipice [presipis] *nm* chasm, abyss; (*bord d'une falaise, d'un ravin etc*) precipice.
précipitamment [presipitamɑ̃] *adv* hurriedly, hastily, *Fml* precipitately; **entrer/sortir p.,** to rush *or* hurry *or* dash in/out; **agir trop p.,** to be too hasty *or* precipitate, to act too hastily *or* precipitately.
précipitation [presipitɑsjɔ̃] *nf* **(a)** (*grande hâte*) great hurry *or* haste, *Fml* precipitation; **sortir avec p.,** to hurry *or* rush *or* dash out; **(b)** *Ch Phys* precipitation; **(c)** *Météo* (*surtout pl*) **précipitations,** precipitation, rain(fall).
précipité [presipite] **1** *adj* hasty, hurried, *Fml* precipitate; headlong (*flight etc*); hasty, hurried, abrupt (*departure*); racing (*pulse*); **s'avancer à pas précipités,** to rush forward *or* along; **un bruit de pas précipités,** hurried *or* quick footsteps. **2** *nm Ch etc* precipitate.
précipiter [presipite] **1** *vt* **(a)** (*entraîner*) to throw down, to hurl down; **p. qn dans le désespoir,** to plunge s.o. into despair; **p. un peuple dans la guerre,** to plunge a nation into war; **(b)** (*dépêcher, hâter*) to hurry, to hasten, to rush; to precipitate (*events*); **il ne faut rien p.,** we mustn't rush things, we mustn't be overhasty; **(c)** *Ch* to precipitate (*substance*). **2** *vi Ch* (*of substance*) to precipitate, to form a precipitate. **3 se précipiter** *vpr* **(a)** (*se hâter*) to dash, to rush (headlong) (**sur,** at); **le fleuve se précipite dans la mer,** the river rushes into the sea; **(b)** *Ch* to precipitate.
précis [presi] **1** *adj* precise, exact, accurate, definite; **exiger d'une façon précise que ...,** to call unambiguously for ...; **à deux heures précises,** at two o'clock precisely *or* sharp; **je suis parti sans raison précise,** I left for no definite reason *or* for no particular reason; **en termes p.,** in distinct terms, distinctly; **il est très p. dans son travail,** he's very meticulous in his work; **des gestes p.,** precise movements. **2** *nm* abstract, summary, précis (*of document etc*); **p. d'histoire de France,** short history of France.
précisément [presizemɑ̃] *adv* **(a)** (*exactement*) precisely, exactly, accurately; (*sans aucun doute*) definitely; **ce n'est pas p. une réussite,** it's not exactly a success, it's not (exactly) what you'd call a success; **a-t-il dit cela? – oui p.,** did he say that? – yes, those were his very words; **(b)** (*justement*) **c'est p. l'homme que je cherche,** he's just the man I'm looking for; **c'est p. ce que je lui disais,** that's just *or* exactly what I said to him, **p. il m'en fallait un aujourd'hui,** as it happens *or* as a matter of fact, I needed one today.
préciser [presize] **1** *vt* **(a)** (*déterminer*) to specify, to state (*sth*) precisely *or* specifically; **il faut p. vos affirmations,** you must be (more) explicit *or* specific in your statements; **(b)** (*rendre plus net*) to clarify; **p. les détails,** to go into more detail; **je tiens à p. que ...,** I wish to make it clear that ...; **p. la date de la réunion,** to give the exact *or* precise date of the meeting. **2** *vi* to be precise *or* explicit. **3 se préciser** *vpr* to become clear(er) *or* (more) explicit; (*of ideas*) to take shape; **les vacances se précisent,** the holiday plans are taking shape.
précision [presizjɔ̃] *nf* **(a)** (*exactitude*) precision, preciseness (*of information, movements*); exactness, accuracy (*of information, description, piece of work*); **avec p.,** precisely, accurately; **p. de tir,** accuracy of fire; **instruments de p.,** precision instruments; **(b) une p.,** a (precise) detail, (a point of) clarification; **donner** *ou* **apporter des précisions sur qch,** to give precise details about sth; **demander des précisions sur qch,** to ask for more information *or* for full particulars about sth.
précité [presite] *adj* aforesaid, aforementioned; (*plus haut sur une page, dans un document*) above(-mentioned).
préclassique [preklasik] *adj Hist* preclassical.
précoce [prekɔs] *adj* precocious; early (*fruit, frost etc*); premature (*senility etc*); **enfant p. pour son âge,** child who is advanced *or* precocious for his age.
précocement [prekɔsmɑ̃] *adv Litt* precociously.
précocité [prekɔsite] *nf* precocity, precociousness; earliness (*of fruit, season etc*); **p. sexuelle,** sexual precociousness.
précolombien, -ienne [prekɔlɔ̃bjɛ̃, -jɛn] *adj Hist* pre-Columbian.
précombustion [prekɔ̃bystjɔ̃] *nf Tech* precombustion.
précompte [prekɔ̃t] *nm* deduction (*from an account, salary*).
précompter [prekɔ̃te] *vt* to deduct (*income tax etc from s.o.'s salary etc*).
préconception [prekɔ̃sɛpsjɔ̃] *nf* preconception; (*contre qn, qch*) prejudice.
préconçu [prekɔ̃sy] *adj* preconceived; *Péj* **idée préconçue,** preconceived idea.
préconiser [prekɔnize] *vt* to recommend, to advocate.
précontraint [prekɔ̃trɛ̃] *adj & nm Tech* **(béton) p.,** prestressed concrete.
précuit [prekɥi] *adj* pre-cooked, ready-cooked (*food*).
précurseur [prekyrsœr] **1** *nm* precursor, forerunner; *Litt* harbinger (*of spring etc*). **2** *adj* precursory; (*qui laisse prévoir l'avenir*) premonitory (*sign*); **signe p.,** forewarning, portent.
prédateur, -trice [predatœr, -tris] **1** *adj* predatory; **oiseau p.,** bird of prey. **2** *nm* predator; (*oiseau*) bird of prey; *Litt* (*animal*) beast of prey.
prédécéder [predesede] *vt* (*conj like* **décéder**) to predecease.
prédécesseur [predesesœr] *nm* predecessor.
prédélinquant, -ante [predelɛ̃kɑ̃, -ɑ̃t] *n* potential delinquent.
prédestination [predɛstinɑsjɔ̃] *nf* predestination.
prédestiné [predɛstine] *adj* predestined, fated (**à,** to).
prédestiner [predɛstine] *vt* to predestine (**à,** to).
prédétermination [predetɛrminɑsjɔ̃] *nf* predetermination.
prédéterminer [predetɛrmine] *vt* to predetermine.
prédicant [predikɑ̃] *nm Rel* predicant.
prédicat [predika] *nm Gram* predicate.
prédicateur, -trice [predikatœr, -tris] *n* preacher.
prédicatif, -ive [predikatif, -iv] *adj Gram* predicative.
prédication [predikɑsjɔ̃] *nf Rel* **(a)** preaching; **(b)** (*sermon*) sermon.
prédiction [prediksjɔ̃] *nf* **(a)** (*action de prédire*) prediction, predicting, foretelling; **(b)** (*ce qui est prédit*) prediction, forecast.
prédigéré [prediʒere] *adj* predigested.
prédilection [predilɛksjɔ̃] *nf* predilection, partiality, fondness; **auteur de p.,** favourite author; **avoir une p. pour qch,** to be (very) partial to sth.
prédire [predir] *vt* (*conj like* **dire** *except pr ind & imp* **(v.) prédisez**) to predict, to prophesy, to foretell.
prédisposer [predispoze] *vt* to predispose; **être prédisposé aux accidents,** to be accident-prone.
prédisposition [predispozisjɔ̃] *nf* predisposition (**à,** to); **p. au vice,** propensity to vice.
prédominance [predɔminɑ̃s] *nf* predominance, prevalence.
prédominant [predɔminɑ̃] *adj* predominant, prevailing, prevalent.
prédominer [predɔmine] *vi* to predominate, to prevail; to have the upper hand (*over an opponent*) (**sur,** over); (*d'une préoccupation*) to be uppermost.
pré-électoral, -aux [preelɛktɔral, -o] *adj Pol* pre-electoral, pre-election.
pré-emballé [preɑ̃bale] *adj* pre-packed.
prééminence [preeminɑ̃s] *nf* pre-eminence.
prééminent [preeminɑ̃] *adj* pre-eminent.
préemption [preɑ̃psjɔ̃] *nf* pre-emption.
pré(-)encollé [preɑ̃kɔle] *adj* pre-pasted, ready-to-hang (*wallpaper*).
préétablir [preetablir] *vt* to pre-establish.
préexistant [preɛgzistɑ̃] *adj* pre-existent.
préexistence [preɛgzistɑ̃s] *nf* pre-existence.
préexister [preɛgziste] *vi* to pre-exist; **p. à qch,** to exist *or* be in existence before sth.
préfabrication [prefabrikɑsjɔ̃] *nf* prefabrication.
préfabriqué [prefabrike] **1** *adj* prefabricated; *Fig Péj* **idée préfabriquée,** preconceived notion; **candidat p.,** packaged candidate. **2** *nm* prefab.
préface [prefas] *nf* **(a)** (*avant-propos*) preface, foreword (**à, de,** to); **(b)** *Rel* preface.
préfacer [prefase] *vt* to write a preface to *or* for (*a book*); to preface (*speech*).
préfacier [prefasje] *nm* preface writer.
préfectoral, -aux [prefɛktɔral, -o] *adj Admin* prefector(i)al, of the prefect.
préfecture [prefɛktyr] *nf Admin* prefecture; **les bureaux de la p.,** the prefector(i)al offices, the offices of the Departmental administration; **la P. de police (de Paris**

etc), the headquarters of the (Paris *etc*) police; **p. maritime,** area under command of a port admiral; (*bureau*) naval superintendent's office, port admiral's office.
préférable [preferabl] *adj* preferable (**à,** to); **il serait p. de le revoir** *ou* **qu'on le revoie,** it would be preferable *or* better to see him again.
préférablement [preferabləmɑ̃] *adv* preferably.
préféré, -ée [prefere] *adj & n* favourite, *US* favorite.
préférence [preferɑ̃s] *nf* preference; **de p.,** preferably; **de p. à ...,** in preference to ...; **donner** *ou* **accorder la p. à qn,** to give s.o. preference (**sur,** over); **il n'a pas de p.,** he has no (particular) preference; *Jur* **droits de p.,** priority rights; *Fin* **actions de p.,** preference shares, *Am* preferred stock.
préférentiel, -elle [preferɑ̃sjɛl] *adj* preferential; *Jur* **vote p.,** preferential voting (system).
préférer [prefere] *vt* (**je préfère; je préférerai**) to prefer (**à,** to); **je préfère du thé,** I prefer (to have) tea; **je préférerais que vous veniez,** I would prefer *or* rather you came; **il préféra mourir plutôt que de se rendre,** he preferred death to surrender, he died rather than surrender.
préfet [prefɛ] *nm Admin* prefect; **p. de police,** prefect of the Paris police (= chief commissioner); *Nau* **p. maritime,** port admiral, commander-in-chief of the port.
préfète [prefɛt] *nf* prefect's wife; *F* (*female*) prefect.
préfiguration [prefigyrɑsjɔ̃] *nf* prefiguration, foreshadowing.
préfigurer [prefigyre] *vt* to prefigure, to foreshadow.
préfinancement [prefinɑ̃smɑ̃] *nm Fin* advance funding.
préfixe [prefiks] *nm Gram etc* prefix.
préfixer [prefikse] *vt* to prefix.
préformation [preformɑsjɔ̃] *nf* preformation.
préglaciaire [preglasjɛr] *adj Géol* pre-glacial.
préhellénique [preelenik] *adj* pre-Hellenic.
préhenseur [preɑ̃sœr] *adj* prehensile.
préhensile [preɑ̃sil] *adj* prehensile.
préhension [preɑ̃sjɔ̃] *nf* gripping.
préhistoire [preistwar] *nf* prehistory.
préhistorique [preistɔrik] *adj* prehistoric.
pré-industriel, -ielle [preɛ̃dystrijɛl] *adj* pre-industrial.
préjudice [preʒydis] *nm* prejudice, detriment (*to a cause, s.o.'s situation etc*); (moral) injury, wrong (*to a person*); damage (*to s.o.'s prospects etc*); *Jur* tort; **porter p. à qn,** to inflict injury *or* loss on s.o.; (*of action*) to be prejudicial to s.o.'s interests; **au p. de qn,** to the prejudice *or* detriment of s.o.; **sans p. de ...,** without prejudice to ... .
préjudiciable [preʒydisjabl] *adj* prejudicial, injurious, detrimental, harmful (**à,** to).
préjudiciel, -elle [preʒydisjɛl] *adj Jur* interlocutory (*question etc*); prejudicial (*action*).
préjudicier [preʒydisje] *vi* (*pr sub & impf* **n. préjudiciions**) *Arch & Litt* to be detrimental *or* prejudicial (**à,** to).
préjugé [preʒyʒe] *nm* (*opinion toute faite*) prejudice; preconception (*about sth*); **avoir un p. pour** *ou* **envers qn/qch,** to be prejudiced *or* have a prejudice in favour of s.o./sth; **gens sans préjugés,** unprejudiced *or* unbias(s)ed people; **p. favorable,** preconceived favourable opinion.
préjuger [preʒyʒe] *v* (*conj like* **juger**) *Litt* **1** *vi* **p. de qch,** to prejudge sth; **autant qu'on peut p.,** as far as one can judge beforehand *or* in advance. **2** *vt* **p. qch,** to prejudge sth.
prélart [prelar] *nm Nau etc* tarpaulin.
prélasser (se) [səprelase] *vpr* to lounge, to loll (*in an armchair etc*); to bask (*in the sun*).
prélat [prela] *nm* prelate.
prélature [prelatyr] *nf Litt* prelacy.
prélavage [prelavaʒ] *nm* prewash.
prèle, prêle [prɛl] *nf Bot* horsetail.
prélèvement [prelɛvmɑ̃] *nm* **(a)** (*déduction*) deduction in advance; setting apart (*of a portion*); **p. d'échantillons,** sampling; *Méd* **p. de sang,** taking of blood (*for a test*); **p. sur le capital** *ou* **sur la fortune,** capital levy; **(b)** (*échantillon*) sample; *Méd* swab; **(c)** *Fin* amount deducted; *Banque* standing order.
prélever [prelve] *vt* (*conj like* **lever**) to deduct *or* set apart (*portion*) in advance; to levy (*tax*); **p. une commission de deux pour cent,** to deduct *or* charge a commission of two per cent; **p. un échantillon,** to take a sample (*of blood etc*).
préliminaire [preliminɛr] **1** *adj* preliminary; **vue p.,** preview. **2** *nm* **préliminaires,** preliminaries.
préliminairement [preliminɛrmɑ̃] *adv* preliminarily.
prélude [prelyd] *nm Mus & Fig* prelude (**de, à,** to).
préluder [prelyde] *vi Mus* to play a prelude; *Fig* **p. à qch,** to serve as a prelude to sth.
prématuré, -ée [prematyre] **1** *adj* premature; premature, untimely (*death*). **2** *n* premature baby.
prématurément [prematyremɑ̃] *adv* prematurely.
prématurité [prematyrite] *nf* prematureness, prematurity.
prémédication [premedikɑsjɔ̃] *nf Méd* premedication, *F* premed.
préméditation [premeditɑsjɔ̃] *nf* premeditation; **avec p.,** deliberately; *Jur* with premeditation, with malice aforethought.
préméditer [premedite] *vt* to premeditate; **insulte préméditée,** deliberate *or* premeditated insult; **elle n'avait pas prémédité de lui demander de rester,** she hadn't planned *or* intended to ask him to stay.
prémenstruel, -elle [premɑ̃stryɛl] *adj* premenstrual; **syndrome p.,** premenstrual tension.
prémices [premis] *nfpl* **(a)** *Arch Litt* first fruits; **(b)** *Vieilli Litt* (*début*) early beginnings.
premier, -ière [prəmje, -jɛr] **1** *adj* **(a)** (*initial*) first; **le p. jour du mois,** the first day of the month; **les trois premières années,** the first three years; **les premières heures après minuit,** the (wee) small hours (*of the morning*); **première éducation,** early education; **dans les premiers temps,** in early times, in former times; **les premiers temps elle n'osait pas parler,** at first she didn't dare speak; **en p. (lieu),** in the first place, first, firstly; **la première fois,** the first time; **dès le p. jour,** from the first day, from the beginning *or* the outset; **du** *ou* **au p. coup,** at the first attempt; **les premiers venus,** the first to arrive; **le p. venu vous dira cela,** anybody will tell you that; **ce n'est pas le p. venu,** he isn't just anybody *or* anyone; **au p. de ces messieurs,** (*at hairdresser's etc*) next (customer), please; **il n'a pas le p. sou,** he hasn't (got) two halfpennies to rub together; **p. voyage,** maiden voyage; *Fin* **p. cours,** opening price; *Aut* **première (vitesse),** first (gear); *Typ* **première (épreuve),** first proof; *Ordinat* **p. modèle,** entry-level model; *Scol* **p. cycle,** = first three years of secondary school; *Univ* = first two years of undergraduate course;
(b) (*original*) primary, original; **sens p. d'un mot,** original meaning of a word; **cause première d'un malheur,** prime *or* primary cause of a misfortune; **vérité première,** basic truth; *Ind* **matières premières,** raw materials;
(c) (*dans un ordre*) **habiter au p. (étage),** to live on the first *or Am* the second floor; **p. plan,** foreground; *Fig* forefront; **première marche,** bottom stair; *Th* **premières loges,** first tier boxes; *Fig* **être aux premières loges,** to have a ringside seat; *Sp* **p. de cordée,** leader; **au p. rang,** in the first rank; **au tout p. rang,** in the forefront; **le tout p.,** the foremost; *Sp etc* **prendre la première place,** to take the lead;
(d) (*placé au sommet de la hiérarchie*) **le p. chirurgien de Paris,** the leading *or* top surgeon in Paris; **P. Ministre,** Prime Minister, Premier; **p. commis,** principal clerk, head clerk; *Nau* **p. maître,** chief petty officer; **capitaine en p.,** senior captain; **p. choix,** best quality; **de première importance,** of the highest importance, of prime importance; **de première nécessité,** essential; *Rail etc* **billet de première classe,** first-class ticket; **voyager en première classe,** to travel first class; *Th etc* **p. rôle,** leading part, lead; **première danseuse,** leading dancer; *Arg* **de première,** first-rate, first-class;
(e) (*non défini*) given (*term*) (*in logic*); **nombre p.,** prime number.
2 *n* **(a)** (*dans un classement*) first; **il/elle est le p./la première de sa classe,** he's/she's (the) top of his/her class; **arriver le p.** *ou* **la première** *ou* **en p.,** to arrive first; **elle était la première à arriver,** she was the first to arrive; **nous sommes arrivés les premiers,** we were the first to arrive, we arrived first; **arriver bon p.,** to come in an easy first; **être le p. à faire qch,** to be (the) first to do sth;
(b) *Th* **jeune p.,** (young) romantic lead *or* hero; **jeune première,** (young) romantic lead *or* heroine; *Fig* **il a des airs de jeune p.,** he looks like a matinée idol *or* film star.
3 *nf* **première (a)** *Couture etc* forewoman;
(b) *Th etc* first performance, first night, première;
(c) (*ascension*) first ascent;
(d) (*Av Rail etc*) first class; **billet de première,** first-class ticket; **voyager en première,** to travel first class;
(e) *Fin* **première de change,** first of exchange;
(f) *Scol Br* ≈ lower sixth (form);
(g) (*vitesse*) first (gear), bottom (gear); **passer en première,** to go into first gear;
(h) (*de chaussure*) inner sole, insole.
4 *nm* **(a)** (*date*) **le p. janvier,** the first of January, January

(the) first; **le p. de l'an,** New Year's Day;
(b) (*premier étage*) first floor, *Am* second floor.
premièrement [prəmjɛrmɑ̃] *adv* first, firstly, in the first place.
premier-né, première-née [prəmjene, prəmjɛrne] *adj & n* firstborn; (*pl premiers-nés, premières-neés*).
prémilitaire [premilitɛr] *adj* premilitary.
prémisse [premis] *nf Phil* premise, premiss.
prémolaire [premɔlɛr] *nf Anat* premolar (tooth).
prémonition [premɔnisjɔ̃] *nf* premonition.
prémonitoire [premɔnitwar] *adj* premonitory.
prémunir [premynir] **1** *vt Vieilli* **p. qn contre qch,** to caution *or* forewarn *or* put s.o. on his guard against sth. **2 se prémunir** *vpr* **se p. contre qch,** (*en se servant de qch*) to provide against sth; (*être vigilant*) to be on one's guard against sth; **se p. contre le rhume,** to take precautions against (catching) a cold.
prenable [prənabl] *adj* pregnable (*town, fort*).
prenant [prənɑ̃] *adj* **(a)** *Fin* **partie prenante,** payee; recipient (*of money, goods*); **il n'est plus p., la voiture ne l'intéresse plus,** he's not interested in the car any more, so there's no deal; **(b)** *Zool* prehensile (*tail*); **(c)** engaging, captivating (*voice etc*); fascinating, compelling (*book etc*); absorbing, captivating (*personality*).
prénatal, -als [prenatal] *adj* antenatal, prenatal.
prendre [prɑ̃dr] *v* (*prp* **prenant**; *pp* **pris**; *pr ind* **je prends, il prend, n. prenons, ils prennent**; *pr sub* **je prenne, n. prenions**; *impf* **je prenais, n. prenions**; *p hist* **je pris, n. prîmes**; *fu* **je prendrai**) **1** *vt* **(a)** (*saisir*) to take; **il l'a prise par le bras,** he took her (by the) arm; **p. les armes,** to take up arms; **p. brusquement qch,** to snatch sth (up), to seize sth; **p. qn par les cheveux,** to grasp *or* grab s.o. by the hair; **je suis allé p. mon parapluie,** I went to get my umbrella; **p. qch avec des pincettes,** to pick sth up with a pair of tongs; **je sais comment le p.,** I know how to handle him; (*le persuader*) I know how to get round him; **p. qch dans un tiroir,** to take *or* get sth out of a drawer; **p. qch sur la table,** to take sth from *or* off the table; **je l'ai prise dans mes bras,** I took her in my arms; **p. qn dans un coin,** to take s.o. into a corner; **où avez-vous pris cela?,** where did you get that (from)?; (*cette idée*) where did you get that idea (from)?;
(b) (*prendre la responsabilité de*) to take (in) (*lodgers etc*); **p. qch sur soi,** to take responsibility for sth; **p. sur soi de faire qch,** to take it upon oneself to do sth;
(c) (*accepter, recevoir*) **vous avez mal pris mes paroles,** you took me *or* what I said the wrong way; **il a très mal pris la chose,** he took it very badly;
(d) (*enlever*) to take (*sth*) (away); **p. qch à qn,** to take sth from s.o.; (*voler*) to steal sth from s.o., to rob s.o. of sth; (*priver*) to deprive s.o. of sth; **cela me prend tout mon temps,** it takes (up) all my time; **ça m'a pris deux heures,** it took me two hours; **mon temps est entièrement pris,** I haven't a free minute, my time is completely taken up; **c'est autant de pris,** so far so good; **j'ai dû p. sur mes économies,** I had to draw on my savings;
(e) (*en argent*) **prenez ce que je vous offre,** take what I'm offering you; **dites-moi ce que vous prenez pour cela,** how much do you charge?; *F* **il prend cher,** he charges a lot, he's expensive;
(f) (*s'approprier*) to take; **c'est à p. ou à laisser,** take it or leave it; **j'en prends et j'en laisse,** I'm taking that with a pinch of salt;
(g) (*considérer*) **à tout p.,** on the whole, all in all; **à bien p. les choses,** rightly speaking; **prenons qu'il en soit ainsi,** let's assume that this is the case;
(h) (*s'emparer de*) to catch, to capture, to seize (*fugitive*); to take, to capture, to seize (*city*); to seize (*illegal goods*); **p. une ville d'assaut,** to take a town by storm, to storm a town; **p. un poisson/un voleur,** to catch a fish/a thief; *Prov* **tel est pris qui croyait p.,** it's a case of the biter bit; **se faire p.,** to be *or* get caught; **se laisser p.,** to let oneself be *or* get caught; *Fig* to let oneself be taken in; **il s'y est laissé p.,** he fell into the trap; **p. qn à voler,** to catch s.o. stealing; **être pris à faire qch,** to be caught doing sth; **p. qn sur le fait,** to catch s.o. in the act; **que je vous y prenne!,** just *or* don't let me catch you (at it) again!; **on ne m'y prendra plus,** I won't be caught (out) *or* taken in again; **être pris par le brouillard,** to be caught in the fog; **il s'est pris le pied contre une racine,** he caught his foot on a root; **être/rester pris,** to get/be stuck;
(i) **elle a été prise d'une crise de larmes,** she burst into tears; **le vin lui** *ou* **le prend à la tête,** wine goes to his head; **l'envie lui a pris de partir,** he was seized with a desire to leave; **si jamais l'envie vous en prenait,** if ever you should feel so inclined; *F* **ça te prend souvent?,** do you often feel like that?, do you get like that often?; **qu'est-ce qui lui prend?,** what's come over him?, what's up with him?; **bien lui en a pris,** it was lucky for him that he did;
(j) (*emmener*) to call for, to collect, to fetch (*s.o.*); (*of taxi etc*) to pick (*s.o.*) up; **prends ton frère avec toi,** take your brother with you; **p. des marchandises,** (*of boat*) to take in cargo; *Nau* **p. de l'eau douce,** to fill up with fresh water; **le bateau prend l'eau,** the boat is leaking, the boat is letting in water;
(k) (*acheter*) to buy, to book (*tickets etc*); **p. un billet direct pour Londres,** to book (straight) through to London; **p. une chambre,** (*in hotel*) to book *or* take a room;
(l) **p. sa retraite,** to retire; **tu as mauvaise mine, tu devrais p. quelques jours,** you don't look too good, you ought to take a few days off; **il n'a pas pris de vacances l'année dernière,** he didn't take *or* have a holiday *or* any holidays last year;
(m) (*s'informer de*) **p. des renseignements,** to make inquiries;
(n) (*noter*) **p. des notes/quelques notes,** to take notes/to take down a few notes; **p. le pouls/la température de qn,** to take s.o.'s pulse/temperature;
(o) (*embaucher*) to engage, to take on (*staff*);
(p) **p. qn comme exemple,** to take s.o. as an example;
(q) **p. qn/qch pour ...,** to mistake *or* take s.o./sth for ...; **on le prenait pour un colonel,** we (mis)took him for a colonel, we took him to be a colonel;
(r) to eat, to have (*food*); to take (*medicine*); to take, to have (*bath*); **qu'est-ce que vous pren(dr)ez?,** what will you have (to drink)?; **il prend du sucre dans son thé,** he takes *or* has sugar in his tea; **il prend toujours un petit verre avant d'aller se coucher,** he always has a nightcap *or* a small glass of something before going to bed; **à ne pas p. à jeun,** not to be taken on an empty stomach;
(s) *F* (*recevoir*) **qu'est-ce que tu vas p.!,** you're for it!, you'll catch it!;
(t) (*attraper*) to catch (*illness*); to acquire (*accent, habits*); **p. froid,** to catch cold;
(u) (*se mettre à avoir*) to take on, to assume (*appearance*); to strike (*attitude*); **p. un ton sévère,** to put on a severe manner; **p. du poids,** to put on *or* gain weight; **p. de l'âge,** to be getting old *or* on; **prendre ses distances,** to distance oneself;
(v) *Méd* **p. du sang,** to draw off blood;
(w) (*utiliser*) to take, to go by (*train, bus etc*); **prenez une chaise,** take *or* have a seat, sit down; **p. le chemin de** *ou* **pour Paris,** to take the road to Paris; **p. à travers champs,** to strike across the fields; *Aut* **p. un virage,** to take a bend; *Nau* **p. le large,** to take to the open sea; **p. le trot,** (*d'un cheval*) to break into a trot.
2 *vi* **(a)** (*of mortar, jelly etc*) to set; (*of milk*) to curdle; (*of river etc*) to freeze; (*of soup, stew etc*) to stick (*to bottom of pan*);
(b) (*of plant etc*) to take (root);
(c) (*of fire*) to take, to catch; (*of match*) to strike, to light; **le feu a pris à sa robe,** her dress caught fire;
(d) (*réussir, marcher*) **le vaccin a pris,** the vaccine has taken (effect); **cette mode ne prendra pas,** this fashion won't catch on; *F* **ce truc-là prend toujours,** this trick is always successful; **cela ne prend pas avec moi!,** you can't fool me!, it won't wash with me!;
(e) (*aller*) **p. à gauche,** to bear (to the) left, to fork left; **p. par la vieille ville,** to go via the old town.
3 se prendre *vpr* **(a)** (*s'accrocher*) **son manteau s'est pris dans la porte/à un clou,** her coat (got) caught in the door/on a nail; **ils se sont pris par la taille,** they put their arms around each other('s waists); **se p. par la main,** to take hold of each other by the hand, to hold hands;
(b) *Vieilli* (*of jelly etc*) to set; (*of river etc*) to freeze;
(c) (*qui peut être pris en main*) to be held; (*être attrapé*) to be caught; **le verre se prend par son pied,** you hold the glass by its *or* the stem; **médicament qui se prend le soir,** medicine to be taken in the evening;
(d) (*se considérer*) to take oneself, to consider oneself (to be); **se p. au sérieux,** to take oneself seriously; **il se prend pour un héros,** he thinks he's a hero; *Vulg* **il ne se prend pas pour une** *ou* **de la merde,** he thinks he's God's gift, he thinks the sun shines out of his arse;
(e) **se p. de,** to develop, to form (*friendship, dislike*); **se p. d'amitié pour qn,** to take a liking to s.o.; (*devenir ami*) to form a friendship with s.o.; **se p. de dégoût pour qch,** to take a (strong) dislike to sth;
(f) *Litt* **se p. à faire qch,** to begin *or* start to do sth, to begin *or* start doing sth;

(g) s'en p. à qn, (*physiquement, verbalement*) to attack s.o.; (*moralement*) to blame s.o., to put *or* lay the blame on s.o.; **ne vous en prenez pas à moi,** don't take it out on me; **ne t'en prends qu'à toi-même,** you've only (got) yourself to blame;

(h) il sait comment s'y p., he knows how to go *or* set about it; **je sais comment m'y p. avec lui,** I know how to deal with him *or* handle him; **vous vous y prenez mal,** you're going about it (in) the wrong way; **il s'y prend bien,** he sets *or* goes about it (in) the right way; **s'y p. à deux fois,** to make two attempts, to have two goes (at sth).

preneur, -euse [prənœr, -øz] *n* **(a)** *Com Fin* buyer, purchaser; payee (*of cheque*); **je suis p.**, I'll take it; **(b)** *Jur* lessee, leaseholder; **(c)** *Courses de chevaux* **les preneurs,** the takers of odds.

prénom [prenɔ̃] *nm* first name, *surtout US* given name; (*dans les pays chrétiens*) Christian name.

prénommé [prenɔme] **1** *adj* called, named; *Jur* said, abovenamed, aforesaid; **le p. Victor,** the man called Victor. **2** *n Jur* **le p.**, (the) abovenamed, (the) aforesaid.

prénommer [prenɔme] **1** *vt* to give (*a child*) a (Christian *etc*) name. **2 se prénommer** *vpr* **il se prénomme Adam,** his first name *or* Christian name *or esp US* given name is Adam.

prénuptial, -aux [prenypsjal, -o] *adj* prenuptial.

préoccupant [preɔkypɑ̃] *adj* worrying.

préoccupation [preɔkypɑsjɔ̃] *nf* **(a)** (*obsession*) preoccupation (**de,** with); **ma seule p. a été d'assurer ...,** my only concern has been to ensure...; **(b)** (*torment*) anxiety, worry; **préoccupations matérielles,** worries about material things.

préoccupé [preɔkype] *adj* preoccupied (**de,** with); **d'un ton p.**, (*pensant à autre chose*) absentmindedly; (*inquiet*) in a worried tone.

préoccuper [preɔkype] **1** *vt* to preoccupy, to engross (*s.o.*); **être préoccupé par qch,** to be preoccupied with sth, to have sth on one's mind; **elle a quelque chose qui la préoccupe,** she's got something on her mind, she's preoccupied (with something); **sa santé me préoccupe,** I'm anxious about his health. **2 se préoccuper** *vpr* **se p. de,** to give one's attention to (*sth*); to attend *or* see to (*a task*); (*s'intéresser, se passionner*) to care about (*sth*).

préparateur, -trice [preparatœr, -tris] *n* **(a)** (*assistant*) assistant (*in laboratory*); *Ind* demonstrator; **p. en pharmacie,** (dispensing) chemist's assistant; **(b)** *Arch* preparer.

préparatifs [preparatif] *nmpl* preparations (**de,** for); **faire ses p. de départ,** to prepare for departure.

préparation [preparɑsjɔ̃] *nf* **(a)** (*fait de préparer, de se préparer*) preparation, preparing, getting ready (**à,** for); making, cooking, *surtout Am* fixing (*of meal etc*); **parler sans p.**, to speak ad lib *or* extempore *or F* off the cuff; **discours sans p.**, ad lib *or* impromptu speech; **annoncer une nouvelle sans p.**, to blurt out a piece of news; *Mil* **p. militaire,** training (course) in preparation for military service; **p. au mariage,** preparation for marriage; **(b)** *Ind* dressing (*of raw material*); **(c)** *Scol* preparation (*of an exercise etc*); *Pharm etc* preparation; *Culin* **p. pour gâteau,** cake mix; **(d)** (*composition, chose préparée*) exercise, piece of work; **(e)** (*organisation*) preparation, planning, arranging.

préparatoire [preparatwar] *adj* preparatory, preliminary; *Scol* **cours p.**, = first year infants' class; **classes préparatoires,** preparatory classes; **école p.**, = school that prepares students for higher education; **travail p.**, preliminary work.

préparer [prepare] **1** *vt* **(a)** (*organiser, apprêter*) to prepare, to get ready; to make preparations *or* arrangements for, to arrange (*meeting etc*); to make (up) (*bed*); *Pharm* to make up (*prescription*); **elle prépare le déjeuner,** she's getting (the) lunch ready, she's preparing *or* cooking *or esp Am* fixing (the) lunch; **plats préparés,** ready-cooked meals, convenience foods;

(b) *Ind* to dress (*raw materials*);

(c) p. qn à qch, to prepare s.o. for sth; (*entraîner*) to train *or* coach s.o. for sth; **p. qn à une nouvelle,** to prepare s.o. for a piece of news;

(d) *Univ* to prepare, to study for (*exam*);

(e) (*prévoir, ébaucher*) to plan, to arrange, to prepare; **p. un coup,** to hatch something, to cook something up; **p. ses vacances,** to plan *or* arrange one's holidays *or Am* vacation; **p. un discours,** to prepare a speech; **p. son avenir,** to prepare for one's future; **cette découverte a été préparée par toute une tradition scientifique,** a whole scientific tradition prepared the ground *or* paved the way for this discovery;

(f) (*amener*) **p. ses effets/la surprise,** to calculate one's effects in advance/to prepare a surprise.

2 se préparer *vpr* **(a)** (*être imminent*) to be in the offing; **un orage se prépare,** a storm is brewing; **il se prépare quelque chose,** there's something in the air; (*mauvais coup etc*) there's something afoot, there's something fishy going on;

(b) (*s'apprêter*) **se p. à qch/à faire qch,** to prepare (oneself) *or* to get ready for sth/to do sth, **se p. à** *ou* **pour un voyage,** to get ready for a journey; *Mil etc* **se p. au combat,** to prepare for action *or* combat; **il est dans la salle de bain, il se prépare,** he's in the bathroom getting ready.

prépayé [prepeje] *adj* prepaid.

prépondérance [prepɔ̃derɑ̃s] *nf* preponderance (**sur,** over).

prépondérant [prepɔ̃derɑ̃] *adj* preponderant; **voix prépondérante,** casting vote.

préposé, -ée [prepoze] *n* (*employé, agent*) employee; *Admin* official; attendant (*in cloakroom, toilet etc*); **p. (des postes),** postman, *esp Am* mailman; **p. des douanes,** customs officer; *Jur* **commettant et p.**, principal and agent.

préposer [prepoze] *vt* **p. qn à une fonction,** to appoint s.o. to an office; **il a été préposé au poste de chargé des relations publiques,** he was put in charge of public relations, he was appointed public relations officer.

prépositif, -ive [prepozitif, -iv] *adj Gram* prepositional (*phrase*).

préposition [prepozisjɔ̃] *nf Gram* preposition.

prépositionnel, -elle [prepozisjɔnɛl] *adj Gram* prepositional.

prépuce [prepys] *nm Anat* foreskin.

préraphaélite [prerafaelit] *adj & nm Beaux-Arts* Pre-Raphaelite.

préretraite [prerətrɛt] *nf* early retirement; **partir en p.**, to take early retirement; **être mis en p.**, to be given early retirement, to be pensioned off, *F* to be put out to grass.

prérogative [prerɔgativ] *nf* prerogative; **p. parlementaire,** parliamentary privilege.

préromantique [prerɔmɑ̃tik] *adj Hist Littér* pre-Romantic.

préromantisme [prerɔmɑ̃tism] *nm Hist Littér* pre-Romanticism.

près [prɛ] **1** *adv* **(a)** near; **il habite tout p.**, he lives nearby *or* close by *or* near here *or* close at hand; **vous êtes trop p.**, you're too close; **plus p.**, nearer; **à (qch) p.**, with the exception of sth, except for sth, apart from sth; **à cela p.**, except on that point, with that one exception; **à ce détail p.**, except for this detail; **à cela p. que ...,** except that ...; **à peu d'exceptions p.**, with (a) few exceptions; **à cinq centimètres p.**, to within five centimetres; **il devinerait votre poids à un milligramme p.**, he would guess your weight to the nearest milligram; **nous n'en sommes pas à un ou deux jours p.**, a day or two more or less doesn't matter; **je ne suis pas à cela p.**, I haven't come to that (yet); **je l'ai raté à deux minutes p.**, I missed him by two minutes;

(b) à peu de choses p., about, approximately; **un chef-d'œuvre à peu de chose p.**, little short of a masterpiece; **à peu p.**, (*pas tout à fait*) nearly; (*approximately*) about, approximately; **le travail est à peu p. achevé,** the work is almost *or* just about *or* more or less completed; **il était à peu p. certain que ...,** it was fairly certain that ...;

(c) à beaucoup p., by far; **le mieux équipé à beaucoup p.**, by far the best equipped; **ce n'est pas à beaucoup p. la somme qu'il me faut,** that's nothing like *or* nowhere near the amount I need; *Nau* **courir au plus p.**, to sail on a wind *or* close to the wind *or* on a bowline;

(d) de p., close, near; (*voir qch etc*) (from) close to *or* up; **tirer de p.**, to fire at close range; **examiner qch de p.**, to examine sth closely; **suivre qn de p.**, to follow s.o. closely; (*ne pas être loin derrière*) to follow hard *or* close on s.o. *or* on s.o.'s heels; **quand je l'ai vu de p.**, when I saw him close up *or* at close quarters; *Fig* **connaître qn de p.**, to know s.o. very well.

2 *prép* **p. de qn/qch,** near (to) *or* close to s.o./sth; **p. de là,** nearby; **p. de chez eux,** near (to) them, near (to) where they live; **tout p. de moi,** very close to me; *Admin* **ambassadeur p. le gouvernement français,** ambassador to the French government; *Nau* **courir p. du vent,** to sail close to the wind; **il est p. de midi,** it's nearly *or* almost twelve (o'clock) *or* midday; **elle était p. d'éclater en sanglots,** she was on the brink *or* the verge of tears; **il y a**

p. de dix ans, close on *or* nearly ten years ago; **p. de 10% sont pour,** almost 10% are for *or* are in favour; **p. de partir,** on the point *or* verge of leaving, about to leave; **nous ne sommes pas p. de le revoir,** it will be a long time before we see him again; **est-il p. d'avoir fini?** is he anywhere near finished?; *F* **être p. de ses sous,** to be mean, to be tight-fisted.

présage [prezaʒ] *nm* omen, sign, *Litt* presage, portent; (*de malheur*) foreboding; **p. de crise,** sign of an approaching crisis; **mauvais p.,** bad *or* ill omen; **oiseau de mauvais p.,** bird of ill omen.

présager [prezaʒe] *vt* (**je présageai(s); n. présageons**) **(a)** (*annoncer*) to be an omen of, *Litt* to presage, to portend; to (fore)bode (*misfortune*); **cela ne présage rien de bon,** it bodes no good, nothing good will come of it, it's very ominous; **(b)** (*prédire*) (*d'une personne*) to predict; (*d'une chose*) to augur.

présalaire [presalɛr] *nm* (student's) grant.

pré-salé [presale] *nm* (*mouton*) salt-meadow sheep; (*viande*) salt-meadow lamb; (*pl prés-salés*).

présanctifié [presɑ̃ktifje] *adj Rel* presanctified.

presbyte [prɛzbit] *adj* long-sighted; *Spéc* presbyopic.

presbytère [prɛzbitɛr] *nm* presbytery.

presbytérianisme [prɛzbiterjanism] *nm* Presbyterianism.

presbytérien, -ienne [prɛzbiterjɛ̃, -jɛn] *adj & n* Presbyterian.

presbytie [prɛsbisi] *nf* long-sightedness; *Spéc* presbyopia.

prescience [presjɑ̃s] *nf* prescience; foreknowledge (*of crime etc*).

prescient [presjɑ̃] *adj* prescient.

préscolaire [preskɔlɛr] *adj* preschool.

prescripteur, -trice [preskriptœr, -tris] *n* **le p. d'une ordonnance,** the writer of a prescription.

prescription [prɛskripsjɔ̃] *nf* **(a)** *Jur* prescription; **invoquer la p.,** to raise a defence under the statute of limitations; **(b)** *Méd* prescription, direction(s) (for treatment); **(c)** (*instruction*) regulation(s), instructions.

prescrire [prɛskrir] *v* (*conj like* **écrire**) **1** *vt* **(a)** (*ordonner*) to prescribe (*duty*); to lay down, to fix (*time etc*); to stipulate, to lay down (*conditions etc*); to prescribe (*remedy*); **à la date prescrite,** on the prescribed date, on the date fixed; **(b)** *Jur* to prescribe, to bar by the statute of limitations; **(c)** (*réclamer*) to demand, to require; **ce que l'honneur prescrit,** the demands *or* dictates of honour *or US* honor. **2 se prescrire** *vpr Jur* **ces dettes se prescrivent par cinq ans,** these debts are barred at the end of five years.

préséance [preseɑ̃s] *nf* precedence, priority (**sur,** over); **avoir la p. sur qn,** to take precedence over s.o..

présélecteur [preselɛktœr] *nm Tech* preselector.

présélection [preselɛksjɔ̃] *nf* **(a)** (*premier choix*) preselection, preselecting (*for specialized training etc*); shortlisting (*for a job*); **(b)** *Aut* **boîte de vitesses à p.,** preselector gearbox.

présélectionner [preselɛksjɔne] *vt Tech* to preselect.

présence [prezɑ̃s] *nf* **(a)** (*fait d'être dans un lieu*) presence, attendance; **je désire sa p.,** I want him to come *or* be here; **il ignore votre p.,** he doesn't know you're here; **faire acte de p.,** to show up; (*pour la forme*) to put in an appearance; *Scol* **régularité de p.,** regular attendance; **feuille de p.,** attendance register; *Ind* time card;

(b) (*personnalité*) presence; **avoir de la p.,** to have great presence (*on public occasions etc*); **la p. du chef d'orchestre,** the conductor's imposing presence; **la p. de Descartes dans la philosophie contemporaine,** the continuing influence of Descartes in contemporary philosophy;

(c) en p., face to face, facing one another; **mettre les deux parties en p.,** to bring the two parties together; **en p. de la mort,** in the presence of death; **en p. de ces faits,** in view of these facts, faced with these facts; **cela s'est fait en ma p.,** it was done in my presence; **cela s'est dit en ma p.,** it was said in my hearing;

(d) (*existence*) presence; **la p. de sang dans les urines,** the presence of blood in the urine; **expliquez-moi la p. de cette arme ici,** explain to me how this weapon came to be here; *Fig* **p. d'esprit,** presence of mind; *Rel* **p. réelle,** real presence.

présent¹, -ente [prezɑ̃, -ɑ̃t] **1** *adj* **(a)** (*qui est dans le lieu dont on parle*) present; **les personnes présentes,** those present; **être p. à un spectacle,** to be present at a performance; **Jacques Martin, ici p., vous le dira,** Jacques Martin, who is here with us, will tell you; (*à l'école*) **Tardi? — oui! p.!,** Tardi? – here! *or* present!; **cela m'est toujours p. à l'esprit,** it's always present in my mind; (*d'un conseil, d'un danger etc*) I always keep it in mind; **p. par la pensée,** here *or* there *or* present in spirit;

(b) (*attentif, disponible*) attentive, paying attention; **esprit p.,** alert *or* quick mind; (*sens de l'humour*) ready wit;

(c) (*actuel*) present (*situation, moment*); **vivre dans l'instant p.,** to live for the moment *or* the present; **la présente convention,** this convention; *Jur* **par la présente lettre,** hereby, by these presents;

(d) *Gram* present; **le temps p.,** the present (tense);

(e) à p., at present, (just) now, currently; **jusqu'à p.,** up to now *or* the present (time), until now; (*de qch qui ne s'est pas encore produit*) as yet; **dès à p.,** from now on, henceforth; **à p. que ...,** now that ... .

2 *n* (*témoin*) person (who is) present; **le nom des présents à la réunion,** the names of those present at the meeting.

3 *nm* **(a)** *Gram* present (tense); **le p. du subjonctif,** the present subjunctive; **mettre le texte au p.,** to put the text into the present tense;

(b) (*partie du temps*) present; **nous n'avons rien à lui reprocher à p.,,** at present *or* at the moment *or* at this moment in time we have nothing to reproach him for; **vivre dans le p.,** to live for the present.

4 *nf Jur Admin* **par la présente** *ou* **les présentes,** (*par cette lettre, ce texte*) hereby, by these presents.

présent² *nm Litt* present, gift; **faire p. de qch à qn,** to make a present of sth to s.o.; to present s.o. with (*prize*).

présentable [prezɑ̃tabl] *adj* presentable.

présentateur, -trice [prezɑ̃tatœr, -tris] *n* **(a)** (*démonstrateur de produits*) demonstrator; **(b)** *Rad TV* presenter (*of a programme*); (*entre les émissions*) announcer; **(c)** introducer (*of person into society*); **(d)** *Rel* .patron (*of a living*).

présentation [prezɑ̃tasjɔ̃] *nf* **(a)** presentation (*of facts, piece of work etc*); **la p. des idées d'un pamphlet,** the way the ideas are presented *or* the presentation of the ideas in a political pamphlet; *Banque* **p. à l'encaissement d'un chèque,** clearance of a cheque *or US* check; *Com* **payable à p.,** payable on demand *or* on presentation *or* at sight;

(b) appearance, presentation; *Ordinat etc* display; **soigner la** *ou* **sa p.,** to take care over one's appearance *or* over how one looks; **recherche hôtesses, excellente p.,** hostesses required, must have smart, attractive appearance; **livre de bonne p.,** well-produced book;

(c) *Obst* presentation; **p. par les pieds,** breach delivery;

(d) (*de personnes*) introduction (**à qn,** to s.o.); presentation (*at court*); **lettre de p.,** letter of introduction; **je vous laisse faire les présentations,** I'll leave you to make the introductions;

(e) *Rel* **la P. de la Vierge,** (Feast of) the Presentation (of the Blessed Virgin Mary);

(f) (*à un public*) *Mil* **p. du drapeau,** trooping the colour; **p. des objets dans une vitrine,** the presentation *or* (putting on) display of items in a shop window; *Com* **p. de collections,** fashion show *or* parade; **la p. du nouveau modèle diesel,** the unveiling *or* presentation of the new diesel model;

(g) *Cin* trailer, *US* preview;

(h) *Av* **p. trop courte,** undershoot; **p. trop longue,** overshoot.

présenter [prezɑ̃te] **1** *vt* **(a)** (*montrer*) to show, to produce, to present; **p. qch à qn,** to present s.o. with sth, to present sth to s.o; **p. un spectacle/un film,** to put on a performance/to present a film; **p. ses pièces d'identité,** (*au commissariat etc*) to submit proof of identity; **p. son passeport,** to produce *or* show one's passport; *Mil* **p. les armes,** to present arms; **présentez armes!,** present arms!; **p. sa main à qn,** to hold out one's hand to s.o.;

(b) (*dire, exprimer*) **p. une excuse à qn,** to offer an apology to s.o.; **p. ses hommages à qn,** to pay one's respects to s.o.; **p. ses arguments ,** to present *or* put forward one's argument.

(c) (*soumettre*) to put in (*witness, claim*); *Scol* **p. le français (à un examen),** to take *or* offer French (as one of one's subjects at an examination);

(d) (*faire connaître*) to table (*motion*); to put (*case*); *TV etc* to compere, to emcee (*show*); **il m'a présenté tous les faits,** he set out *or* put *or* laid before me all the facts of the case; **p. des conclusions,** to submit conclusions (*at a meeting*); **p. un projet de loi,** to bring in *or* introduce a bill; **son travail est bien présenté,** his work is well presented *or* set out;

(e) p. qn à qn, to introduce *or* present s.o. to s.o.; **nous**

n'avons pas été présentés, we haven't been introduced; **je voudrais vous p. ma cousine,** I'd like you to meet my cousin, *Fml* allow me to introduce my cousin (to you); **p. qn comme candidat,** to put s.o. forward as a candidate; **il a été présenté pour ce poste,** he has been put forward *or* proposed for this post; **p. les meilleurs élèves pour le concours d'entrée,** to enter the best pupils *or* put the best pupils forward for the entrance examination.

2 *vi F* **il présente bien,** he's a man of good appearance.

3 se présenter *vpr* **(a)** (*se produire*) **une occasion se présente (de faire qch),** an opportunity presents itself *or* occurs (for doing sth); **un beau spectacle s'est présenté à mes yeux,** a beautiful sight met my eyes; **si le cas se présente,** if the case arises; **attendre que quelque chose se présente,** to wait for something to turn up; **la chose se présente bien,** things look promising; **l'affaire se présente sous un jour nouveau,** the matter appears in a new light;

(b) (*se porter candidat*) to present oneself; *Mil etc* to report; **se p. à un examen,** to go in for *or* sit *or* enter for *or* take an examination; **se p. chez qn,** to call on s.o.; **se p. à qn,** to introduce oneself to s.o.; **se p. aux élections,** to stand (as a candidate) at the elections; **se p. comme candidat,** to come forward as a candidate; **il se présente bien,** he makes a good impression;

(c) *Obst* to present; **l'enfant se présente mal,** the child is presenting badly.

présentoir [prezɑ̃twar] *nm Com* display unit.

présérie [preseri] *nf Tech* test series, pilot series.

préservateur, -trice [prezɛrvatœr, -tris] **1** *adj Arch* preservative; preventive (*measures*). **2** *nm* preservative (*in food etc*).

préservatif, -ive [prezɛrvatif, -iv] **1** *adj* preservative; preventive (**contre,** of); protective (*layer, clothing*). **2** *nm* (*condom*) (contraceptive) sheath, condom, Durex ®; **p. féminin,** barrier contraceptive (*for women*); (*stérilet*) IUD; (*diaphragme*) cap, diaphragm.

préservation [prezɛrvɑsjɔ̃] *nf* preservation, protection (*of crops etc*); protection (*of person*).

préserver [prezɛrve] **1** *vt* to preserve, to protect (**de,** from); **le ciel m'en préserve!,** heaven forbid!; **à p. de l'humidité,** to be kept dry. **2 se préserver** *vpr* to protect oneself; **se p. de l'humidité,** to keep (oneself) dry.

présidence [prezidɑ̃s] *nf* **(a)** *Pol* presidency; **sous sa p.,** under *or* during his presidency; **(b)** (*de club etc*) chairmanship; **prendre la p.,** (*à une réunion*) to take the chair; **(c)** (*habitation*) president's house.

président, -ente [prezidɑ̃, -ɑ̃t] *n* **(a)** *Pol* president (*of republic etc*); **le P., la Présidente,** the President; *Vieilli* **la Présidente,** the President's wife; *US* the First Lady; **(b)** (*d'assemblée etc*) chairperson, chairman, chairwoman; **être élu p.,** to be voted into the chair; **Monsieur le p./Madame la présidente, permettez-moi de ...,** Mr/Madam Chairman, allow me to ...; **(c)** *Pol Hist* **p. du Conseil,** Prime Minister; **(d) p. du jury,** *Jur* foreman of the jury; *Scol* chief examiner; (*dans un concours*) chairman of the adjudicating committee; **(e)** *Ind Com* **p.-directeur général,** chairman and managing director; **(f)** (*magistrat*) president (*of legal tribunal etc*); presiding judge.

présidentiable [prezidɑ̃sjabl] *n* presidential hopeful.

présidentiel, -elle [prezidɑ̃sjɛl] **1** *adj* presidential; **l'élection présidentielle,** the presidential election, the election for president; **régime p.,** presidency. **2** *nfpl* **présidentielles,** presidential elections.

présider [prezide] **1** *vt* **(a)** (*diriger, conduire le débat*) to preside over (*council*); to chair (*meeting*); **(b)** (*être à la place d'honneur*) to be the guest of honour at (*a banquet*). **2** *vi* **(a)** (*diriger*) to preside, to be in the chair; **p. à une réunion,** to preside at *or* over a meeting; **(b)** (*veiller*) **p. à** to preside over (*sth*); **p. aux destinées de ...,** to preside over the destinies of ...; **(c)** (*régler*) **p. à** to govern; **les codes qui président à ces cérémonies,** the codes that govern these ceremonies.

présomptif, -ive [prezɔ̃ptif, -iv] *adj* **héritier p.,** heir presumptive; (*fils aîné*) heir apparent.

présomption [prezɔ̃psjɔ̃] *nf* **(a)** (*supposition*) presumption; *Jur* presumptive evidence; *Jur* **preuve par p.,** circumstantial evidence; **(b)** (*suffisance*) presumption, presumptuousness.

présomptueusement [prezɔ̃ptɥøzmɑ̃] *adv* presumptuously.

présomptueux, -euse [prezɔ̃ptɥø, -øz] **1** *adj* presumptuous. **2** *n* **un jeune p.,** a presumptuous young man.

présonorisation [presɔnɔrizɑsjɔ̃] *nf TV etc* playback.

presque [prɛsk(ə)] *adv* **(a)** (*à peu près*) almost, nearly; **c'est p. impossible,** it's almost *or* next to *or* all but *or* well nigh impossible; **je les ai p. tous,** I have nearly all of them; **c'est p. de la folie,** it's little short of madness; *Litt* **c'est une p. certitude,** it's well nigh certain, it's virtually certain; **(b)** (*with negative*) scarcely, hardly; **p. jamais,** hardly ever, almost never; **p. rien,** scarcely anything, next to nothing; **p. personne,** hardly anyone.

presqu'île [prɛskil] *nf* peninsula.

pressage [prɛsaʒ] *nm* pressing (*of grapes, laundry, gramophone records etc*).

pressant [prɛsɑ̃] *adj* pressing, urgent (*need etc*); insistent (*creditor etc*); **en termes pressants,** in pressing terms; **cas p.,** urgent case.

press-book [presbuk] *nm* press book; (*model's, artist's etc*) portfolio.

presse [prɛs] *nf* **(a)** (*ensemble des imprimés, des textes*) press; (*journaux*) newspapers; (*revues*) magazines; **photographe de p.,** press photographer; *Fig* **avoir bonne/mauvaise p.,** to have a good/bad press; **service de p.,** publicity (department); **agence de p.,** news agency; **la p. du cœur,** romance magazines; **la p. à sensations,** the popular press, the tabloids; *Péj* the gutter press; **la grande p.,** national daily (quality) newspapers; **la liberté de la p.,** the freedom of the press; **délits de p.,** infringements of press laws; **exemplaire de service de p.,** press copy, review copy;

(b) *Tech* press; *Typ* (printing) press; **p. mécanique,** power press; **p. à copier,** letter press, copying press; **travailler du métal à la p.,** to stamp metal; **p. à imprimer** *ou* **d'imprimerie,** printing press; **p. à bras,** hand press; **p. à rogner,** guillotine; **livre sous p.,** book that has gone to press; **prêt à mettre sous p.,** (*livre*) ready for press; (*journal*) ready to put to bed;

(c) *Arch & Litt* press, crowd, throng; **fendre la p.,** to force one's way through the crowd;

(d) *Nau Arch* press (gang);

(e) *Ind Com* haste, urgency; **il n'y a pas de p.,** there's no hurry; **moments de p.,** busy periods.

pressé [prese] **1** *adj* **(a)** (*comprimé*) pressed; compressed (*gas etc*); **citron p.,** fresh(ly squeezed) lemon juice; **p. à froid,** cold-pressed; **fromage à pâte pressée,** cheese with a rind; **(b)** (*serré*) crowded, close together; **pressés les uns contre les autres,** crowded *or* packed *or* squashed together; (*objets*) pressed *or* packed *or* squashed together; **(c)** (*à la hâte*) in a hurry, hurried; **je suis très p.,** I'm in rather a hurry, I'm very pressed for time; **p. de partir,** in a hurry to go; **avoir un air p.,** to look (as though one is) in a hurry; **on n'est pas p.,** there's no rush, we're not in a hurry; **(d)** (*urgent*) urgent, pressing (*work etc*); **ce n'est pas p.,** it's not urgent, there's no hurry. **2** *nm* **aller au plus p.,** to deal with the most urgent thing(s) first.

presse-agrumes [prɛsagrym] *nm inv* (electric) juice extractor *or* press, (electric) juicer (*for citrus press*).

presse-ail [prɛsaj] *nm inv* garlic press *or* crusher.

presse-bouton [prɛsbutɔ̃] *adj inv* push-button (*war etc*).

presse-citron [prɛssitrɔ̃] *nm inv* (electric) lemon squeezer.

presse-étoupe [prɛsetup] *nm inv Tech* stuffing box.

presse-fruits [prɛsfrɥi] *nm inv (electric)* juice extractor *or* press, (electric) juicer.

presse-livres [prɛslivr] *nm inv* book ends.

pressentiment [presɑ̃timɑ̃] *nm* presentiment; (*d'un malheur*) foreboding; (*vision etc*) premonition; (*préavis*) forewarning; **j'ai comme un p. que ...,** I have a feeling that ...; **avoir le p. que quelque chose va se passer,** to have a (funny) feeling that something is going to happen.

pressentir [presɑ̃tir] *vt* (*conj like* **sentir**) **(a)** to have a presentiment of (*sth*); (*sentir*) to sense (*sth*); to have a foreboding of (*misfortune*); **p. que quelque chose va se passer,** to have a (funny) feeling that something is going to happen; **faire** *ou* **laisser p. qch,** to foreshadow *or* portend sth; (*misfortune*) to forebode sth; **faire p. qch à qn,** to give s.o. an inkling *or* a hint of sth; **(b) p. qn (sur** *ou* **pour qch),** to sound s.o. out (about sth); (*être interrogé, approché*) to approach s.o. (about sth).

presse-papiers [prɛspapje] *nm inv* paperweight.

presse-purée [prɛspyre] *nm inv* vegetable masher (*for potatoes etc*).

presser [prese] **1** *vt* **(a)** (*exprimer*) to press, to squeeze (*lemon, sponge etc*); to press (*record*); **p. à froid,** to cold-press; **p. du raisin/des pommes,** to press grapes/apples; **p. un vêtement,** to (steam-)press a garment; **p. qn contre son cœur,** to clasp s.o. in one's arms; **il m'entraînait en me pressant le bras,** he dragged me off clutching me by the arm;

(b) (*appuyer sur*) to press, to push (*switch, button*); *Ordinat* to hit;

(c) (*harceler*) **pressé par ses créanciers,** hard pressed by his creditors; **p. l'ennemi,** to press the enemy; **p. qn de questions,** to ply *or* bombard s.o. with questions; **p. qn de faire qch,** to press *or* urge s.o. to do sth;

(d) (*dépêcher*) to hurry (*s.o.*) (up); to accelerate, to speed up (*work, movement*); **p. le pas,** to quicken one's pace; **p. le départ de qn,** to hasten s.o.'s departure; **qu'est-ce qui vous presse?,** why are you in such a hurry?, what's the hurry?, what's the rush?

2 *vi* **le temps presse,** there isn't much time (left); **l'affaire presse,** the matter is urgent; **il n'y a rien qui presse, rien ne presse,** *F* **ça ne presse pas,** there's no hurry *or* rush.

3 se presser *vpr* **(a)** (*s'entasser*) to press, to crowd, to throng; to squash up, to crush (*against railings etc*); **on s'y presse toujours à six heures,** there's always a crowd there at six o'clock;

(b) (*se serrer*) **elle s'est pressée contre lui,** she pressed (herself) against him; (*de façon affectueuse*) she snuggled (up) against him, she snuggled up to him;

(c) (*se dépêcher*) to hurry (up); **pressez-vous!,** hurry up!; **répondre sans se p.,** to answer deliberately *or* leisurely; **faire qch sans se p.,** to take one's time over doing sth; **il faut se p. d'oublier,** we must forget as quickly as we can; **se p. d'entrer/de descendre,** to hurry in/down.

presse-raquette [presrakɛt] *nm inv* racket press.

presseur, -euse [prɛsœr, øz] **1** *adj* **rouleau p.,** roller. **2** *n* presser; **p. d'étoffes,** presser of materials.

pressing [presiŋ] *nm* **(a)** (*repassage à la vapeur*) steam pressing; (*nettoyage à sec*) dry cleaning; **(b)** (*magasin*) dry cleaner's.

pression [prɛsjɔ̃] *nf* **(a)** (*action insistante*) pressure; **exercer une p. sur qn,** to bring pressure to bear on s.o., to pressurize *or* put pressure on s.o.; **faire p. sur qn,** to pressurize s.o., to put pressure on s.o.; **groupe de p.,** pressure group; *Fig* **être sous p.,** to be under pressure; **un bouton (à) p., une p.,** a press stud, a snap fastener, *F* a popper;

(b) *Tech* tension (*of steam*); (*action de presser*) pressure; **vis de p.,** binding screw;

(c) *Phys* **p. atmosphérique/artérielle,** atmospheric/blood pressure; **bière (à la) p.,** draught *or US* draft beer; **un demi p.,** = a half of (draught) beer *or US* draft beer; *Aut etc* **jauge de p.,** pressure gauge (*for tyres etc*); *Tech* **machine à haute/basse p.,** high-/low-pressure engine; **mettre sous p.,** to pressurize; **mettre (la chaudière) sous p.,** to get up steam; **cabine sous p.,** (*d'un avion*) pressurized cabin; *Météo* **zone de hautes pressions,** area of high pressure.

pressoir [prɛswar] *nm* **(a)** (*presse*) (*pour faire du vin*) wine press; (*pour faire du cidre*) cider press; (*pour huile*) oil press; **(b)** (*lieu*) press house, press room.

pressurage [presyraʒ] *nm* pressing (*of fruit etc*).

pressurer [presyre] *vt* (*presser*) to press (*fruit etc*); *Fig* (*exploiter*) to squeeze.

pressurisation [presyrizɑsjɔ̃] *nf* pressurization.

pressuriser [presyrize] *vt* to pressurize.

prestance [prɛstɑ̃s] *nf* presence; **avoir de la p.,** to have (great) presence.

prestant [prɛstɑ̃] *nm Mus* diapason (stop) (*of organ*).

prestataire [prɛstatɛr] **1** *adj* **société p. de services,** company that provides a service. **2** *nm Admin* person receiving benefits *or* allowances; **p. de service,** provider of a service.

prestation [prɛstɑsjɔ̃] *nf* **(a)** (*allocation*) benefit; *Admin* allowance; (*sécurité sociale*) benefit; **prestations familiales,** ≈ family allowance; **prestations sociales,** national insurance benefits; **p. compensatoire,** (*en cas de divorce*) compensation; **(b) p. de service,** provision of a service; **(c)** (*résultat, performance*) performance; **la p. d'un homme politique au journal télévisé,** the performance put up by a politician on the TV news; **les prestations médiocres d'une entreprise,** the poor performance of a firm; **(d)** *Jur* **p. de serment,** taking the oath; *Hist* **p. de foi,** oath of fealty; **(e) p. en nature,** = work done without payment.

preste [prɛst] *adj* quick, sharp, nimble; (*pour remarquer qch etc*) alert; **avoir la main p.,** to be skilful *or US* skillful *or* nimble with one's hands.

prestement [prɛstəmɑ̃] *adv* quickly, promptly.

prestidigitateur, -trice [prɛstidiʒitatœr, -tris] *n* conjurer.

prestidigitation [prɛstidiʒitɑsjɔ̃] *nf* conjuring; *Fig* sleight of hand, legerdemain, **tour de p.,** conjuring trick; *Fig* **c'est de la p.!,** it's just like magic!

prestige [prɛstiʒ] *nm* **(a)** prestige (*of important person, office etc*); (*séduction, attrait*) glamour, *US* glamor (*of movie star, lifestyle etc*); **sans p.,** undistinguished; **publicité de p.,** prestige advertising; **le p. de l'uniforme,** the glamour of the uniform; **(b)** *Arch* marvel.

prestigieux, -euse [prɛstiʒjø, -øz] *adj* **(a)** (*qui a du renom*) prestigious; **un nom p.,** a great name; **des artistes/produits p.,** famous *or* renowned artists/prestige products; **(b)** *Litt* marvellous, wonderful, amazing.

presto [prɛsto] *adv* **(a)** *Mus* presto; **(b)** *F* double-quick, at *or* on the double.

présumable [prezymabl] *adj* presumable.

présumer [prezyme] *vt* (*supposer*) to presume, to assume; **tu viens aussi, je présume?,** I presume you're coming too (are you)?; **p. qn innocent,** to presume *or* assume s.o. (to be) innocent; **le coupable présumé, le présumé coupable,** the supposed culprit; **le voleur présumé,** the alleged thief; **il est à p.** *ou* **on présume qu'il est mort,** he is assumed to be dead; **trop p. de soi,** to presume too much, to be overconfident; **trop p. de ses forces,** to overestimate *or* overrate one's strength.

présupposé [presypoze] **1** *adj* presupposed. **2** *nm* presupposition.

présupposer [presypoze] *vt* to presuppose.

présupposition [presypozisjɔ̃] *nf* presupposition.

présure [prezyr] *nf* rennet.

prêt¹ [prɛ] *adj* ready, prepared; **c'est p.!,** (*repas etc*) it's ready!; **p. à l'emploi,** ready for use; **p. à servir,** ready to serve; **se tenir p.,** to be ready; **être p. à tout,** to be ready *or F* game for anything; (*pour parvenir à son but*) to be prepared to do anything; **p. à partir,** ready to leave *or* go, ready for the off; **être p. à commencer,** to be all set (to begin); **p. à rendre service,** willing to help.

prêt² *nm* **(a)** (*action*) loaning, lending; (*somme*) loan; **p. de 1 000 francs,** loan of 1,000 francs; **p. à court terme,** short (-term) loan; **p. d'honneur,** loan on trust; **p. hypothécaire,** mortgage loan; **p. sur titres,** loan on securities; **p. sur gage(s),** pawnbroking; **à titre de p.,** (*money etc*) as a loan; (*equipment etc*) on loan; **(b)** *Mil* pay; **(c)** (*avance sur salaire*) advance (*on wages*).

prêt-à-porter [prɛtapɔrte] *nm* ready-made *or* ready-to-wear clothes; **en p.-à-p.,** *Br* off the peg, *Am* off the rack.

prêté [prete] **1** *adj* borrowed. **2** *nm* **c'est un p. pour un rendu,** it's tit for tat.

prétendant, -ante [pretɑ̃dɑ̃, -ɑ̃t] **1** *n* applicant, candidate (**à,** for); claimant (*to property, a title*); pretender (*to a throne*). **2** *nm* suitor; **elle a beaucoup de prétendants,** she's got lots of admirers.

prétendre [pretɑ̃dr] **1** *vt* **(a)** (*déclarer*) to maintain, to assert, to claim; **je prétends que ce n'est pas vrai,** I maintain that it is not true; **on prétend que ...,** people say that ..., it is said that ...; **à ce qu'il prétend,** according to him; **ils prétendent être de nos amis,** they claim to be friends of ours; **on le prétend fou,** they say he's mad; **il ne prétend pas être artiste,** he doesn't pretend to be artistic, he lays no claim to being an artist;

(b) (*vouloir*) to mean; **je prétends être obéi,** I expect to be obeyed; **prétendez-vous me faire la loi?,** do you think you have the right to dictate to me?; **je ne prétends pas lui faire comprendre,** I don't pretend to be able to make him understand;

(c) *Vieilli* (*demander*) to claim (as a right); (*exiger*) to require; **que prétendez-vous de moi?,** what do you require *or* want of me?

2 *vi* **p. à qch,** to lay claim to sth; **p. aux honneurs,** to aspire to honours *or US* honors; *Litt* **p. à la main de qn,** to aspire to marry s.o..

3 se prétendre *vpr* to claim to be; **elle se prétend incomprise,** she claims to be *or* that she's misunderstood.

prétendu, -ue [pretɑ̃dy] **1** *adj* alleged (*culprit, thief etc*); would-be (*hero, celebrity etc*); **p. voleur,** alleged thief; **un p. baron,** a self-styled *or* bogus baron; **prétendus progrès,** so-called progress. **2** *n Arch & Région* **mon p./ma prétendue,** my fiancé/my fiancée.

prête-nom [prɛtnɔ̃] *nm Fig* figurehead; *Péj* man of straw; (*pl prête-noms*).

prétentaine [pretɑ̃tɛn] *nf* **courir la p.,** to be a womanizer.

prétentieusement [pretɑ̃sjøzmɑ̃] *adv* pretentiously.

prétentieux, -euse [pretɑ̃sjø, -øz] **1** *adj* pretentious (*writer, person, words*); showy (*dress, appearance, person*). **2** *n* pretentious person; **un jeune p.,** a conceited young idiot; **regarde-la, quelle prétentieuse!,** look at her, she really fancies herself.

prétention [pretɑ̃sjɔ̃] *nf* **(a)** (*revendication, ambition*) pretension, claim (**à**, to); **je n'ai pas la p. de remporter le prix,** I don't for a moment suppose I shall get the prize; **je n'ai pas la p. de vous être supérieur,** I don't pretend *or* claim to be better than you are; **renoncer à ses prétentions,** to renounce one's claims; **il n'a aucune p. à l'esprit,** he doesn't pretend to be witty, he lays no claim to being witty; **(b)** (*fait d'être prétentieux*) pretentiousness, pretension; **homme sans prétention(s),** unassuming *or* unpretentious man; **écrire avec p.,** to write pretentiously *or* in a pretentious style; **(c)** (*condition*) condition (*in a contract etc*); **les prétentions du vendeur,** the vendor's conditions; **envoyer curriculum vitae et prétentions,** send curriculum vitae and state salary required.

prêter [prete] **1** *vt* **(a)** (*fournir temporairement*) to lend, *surtout Am* to loan; **p. qch à qn,** to lend sth to s.o., to lend s.o. sth; **p. sur gage(s),** to lend against security;

(b) (*donner*) to give, to lend; **p. son appui** *ou* **son concours à qn,** to give *or* lend s.o. one's support; **p. la main à qn,** to give *or* lend s.o. a hand; **p. l'oreille,** to listen, to lend an ear; **p. attention,** to pay attention; **p. serment,** to take an oath; **p. le flanc à la critique,** to lay oneself open *or* expose oneself to criticism; **p. son nom,** to lend one's name, to allow one's name to be used;

(c) (*attribuer*) to attribute, to ascribe (**à**, to); **on me prête des discours que je n'ai jamais tenus,** I am credited with speeches which I never made.

2 *vi* **(a) p. à qch,** to give rise to sth; **privilège qui prête aux abus,** privilege that lends itself to *or* that is open to *or* that invites abuse;

(b) (*of gloves, material etc*) to give, to stretch.

3 se prêter *vpr* **(a)** (*consentir*) to lend oneself, to be a party (**à**, to); **se p. à un accommodement,** to consent to *or* to fall in with an arrangement;

(b) (*permettre*) to lend itself (**à**, to); **roman qui se prête à des interprétations différentes,** novel which lends itself to different interpretations; **domaine d'étude qui se prête à des développements variés,** area of study that can be developed in different ways; **j'aurais voulu lui parler de ses enfants, mais la situation ne se prêtait pas à cela,** I'd have liked to talk to him about his children, but it was neither the time nor the place.

prétérit [preterit] *nm Gram* preterite (tense).

préteur [pretœr] *nm Antiq* praetor.

prêteur, -euse [prɛtœr, -øz] **1** *n* lender; **p. sur gages,** pawnbroker. **2** *adj* ready *or* willing to lend; **je ne suis pas p.,** I don't believe in lending.

prétexte [pretɛkst] **1** *nm* pretext, excuse; *Fml* plea; **sous p. de ...,** on *or* under (the) pretext of ...; *Fml* on a plea of ...; (*apparemment pour ...*) ostensibly to ...; **sous p. d'amitié,** under the pretext of friendship; **sous aucun p.,** on no account, under no circumstances; **prendre p. de qch pour faire qch,** to use sth as a pretext *or* to make a pretext of sth for doing sth. **2** *nf Antiq* toga praetexta. **3** *adj Antiq* **la toge p.,** toga praetexta.

prétexter [pretɛkste] *vt* to use *or* give (*sth*) as a pretext; **il a prétexté qu'il était malade,** he gave the excuse that he was ill; **p. la fatigue,** to plead fatigue, to give fatigue as an excuse.

prétoire [pretwar] *nm* **(a)** *Jur* (floor of the) court; **(b)** *Antiq* praetorium.

prétorien, -ienne [pretɔrjɛ̃, -jɛn] *Antiq* **1** *adj* praetorian. **2** *nm* (member of the) praetorian (guard); *Fig* (*de dictature*) military bodyguard (*of dictator*).

prêtre [prɛtr] *nm* priest; **grand p.,** high priest; **se faire (ordonner) p.,** to be ordained (a priest), to become a priest.

prêtre-ouvrier [prɛtruvrije] *nm* worker priest; (*pl prêtres-ouvriers*).

prêtresse [prɛtrɛs] *nf* priestess.

prêtrise [pretriz] *nf* priesthood; **recevoir la p.,** to take (holy) orders.

preuve [prœv] *nf* **(a)** proof, evidence; token, proof (*of friendship, good intentions*); **ils sont arrivés ensemble, mais ce n'est pas une p.,** they arrived together but that proves nothing *or* doesn't prove anything; **faire la p. de qch,** to prove sth; **faire p. d'intelligence,** to show intelligence; **faire ses preuves,** to prove oneself, to show one's mettle; **cette méthode a fait ses preuves,** this method has stood the test of time; **fournir la p. contraire,** to produce proof to the contrary; **comme p.,** by way of proof, as proof; **cette confusion est une p. de mauvaise organisation,** this confusion is evidence *or* proof of poor organization; *F* **le directeur est incapable, à p. le déficit de la maison,** the manager is incompetent, witness the firm's deficit; **à p. que ...,** witness the fact that ...;

(b) *Math* **faire la p. d'une opération,** to prove *or* test the validity of a mathematical operation; **la p. par neuf,** casting out the nines;

(c) *Jur* evidence; **p. directe,** direct evidence; **p. indirecte,** circumstantial evidence; **preuves testimoniales,** (witnesses') evidence; **le soin** *ou* **l'obligation de faire la p.,** the onus *or* burden of proof.

preux [prø] *Arch & Litt* **1** *adj* gallant, valiant. **2** *nm* valiant knight.

prévaloir [prevalwar] *v* (*conj like* **valoir**, *except pr sub* **je prévale**) **1** *vi* to prevail (**sur,** over; **contre,** against); **ce principe prévaut sur tous les autres,** this principle takes precedence over all others; **faire p. son droit,** to assert one's rights; **faire p. son opinion,** to win acceptance for one's opinion. **2 se prévaloir** *vpr* **se p. de,** to avail oneself of, to take advantage of (*sth*); to exercise (*a right*); to presume on (*one's birth, wealth*).

prévaricateur, -trice [prevarikatœr, -tris] *Jur* **1** *adj* unjust, dishonest (*judge etc*). **2** *n* unjust judge; (*dans une gestion*) betrayer of trust.

prévarication [prevarikasjɔ̃] *nf Jur* breach of trust; (*dans une organisation*) maladministration.

prévariquer [prevarike] *vi Jur* to depart from justice; *Com Admin* to betray one's trust.

prévenance [prɛvnɑ̃s] *nf* kindness, consideration; (*d'un geste, d'une bonne idée*) thoughtfulness; **une acte de p.,** a kindly *or* thoughtful act *or* deed, an act of kindness; **une p.,** a thoughtful *or* kind act *or* deed; **avoir des prévenances pour qn,** to show consideration towards s.o..

prévenant [prɛvnɑ̃] *adj* **(a)** (*personne*) kind, considerate (**envers,** to); (*geste, idée*) thoughtful (**envers,** towards); **(b)** pleasing, prepossessing (*manner, appearance*).

prévenir [prɛvnir] *vt* (*conj like* **venir** *but with aux* **avoir**) **(a)** (*informer*) to inform, to tell; (*avertir*) to warn; (*à l'avance*) to forewarn; **p. qn de qch,** to give s.o. notice of sth, to let s.o. know about sth; **je vais le p. que vous êtes ici,** I'll let him know *or* tell him you're here; **on m'avait prévenu que la police était à mes trousses,** I had been warned that the police were after me; **vous auriez dû m'en** *ou* **me p.,** you should have told me (about it) beforehand; **je l'ai prévenue, si ça ne s'améliore pas, c'est la porte!,** I've warned her, if there's no improvement she'll be out of a job;

(b) (*empêcher*) to prevent, to ward off, to stave off (*illness, danger*); to avert (*danger, accident*); *Prov* **mieux vaut p. que guérir,** prevention is better than cure;

(c) (*devancer*) to anticipate (*s.o., s.o.'s desires etc*); to forestall (*s.o., question, objection*);

(d) (*agir, influencer*) to predispose, to bias; **p. qn en faveur de qn,** to predispose s.o. in favour of s.o., to bias s.o. *or* make s.o. bias(s)ed towards s.o.; **p. qn contre qn,** to prejudice s.o. against s.o., to bias s.o. *or* make s.o. bias(s)ed against s.o.; **son visage prévient en sa faveur,** he has a prepossessing face.

préventif, -ive [prevɑ̃tif, -iv] *adj* preventive (*medicine etc*); **à titre p.,** as a preventive (measure); **exercer un effet p.,** to act as a deterrent; *Cartes* **ouverture préventive,** pre-emptive bid; *Jur* **détention préventive,** detention awaiting trial, committal for trial; **être en détention préventive,** to be in custody.

prévention [prevɑ̃sjɔ̃] *nf* **(a)** prevention (*of disease etc*); **p. routière,** road safety (measures); **(b)** *Jur* **être en état de p.,** to be in custody, to be committed for trial; **mise en p.,** committal for trial; **(c)** (*opinion, avis*) predisposition (**en faveur de,** in favour *or US* favor of), bias (**en faveur de,** towards); prejudice, bias (**contre,** against); **observateur sans p.,** unprejudiced *or* unbias(s)ed observer.

préventivement [prevɑ̃tivmɑ̃] *adv* **(a)** (*pour traitement etc*) as a preventive (measure); **(b)** *Jur* **arrêter qn p.,** to arrest s.o. on suspicion; **détenu p.,** committed for trial.

préventorium [prevɑ̃tɔrjɔm] *nm* tuberculosis sanatorium.

prévenu, -ue [prɛvny] **1** *adj* **(a)** (*qui a une opinion*) prejudiced, bias(s)ed; **(b)** *Jur* **p. de vol,** accused of theft; (*inculpé*) charged with theft. **2** *n Jur* **le p., la prévenue,** the prisoner, the accused.

prévisible [previzibl] *adj* foreseeable.

prévision [previzjɔ̃] *nf* anticipation, expectation; (*description d'un événement futur*) forecast, prediction; **en p. de qch,** in the expectation *or* in anticipation of sth; **selon toute p.,** in all likelihood; **contre toute p.,** contrary to all expectations; **dépasser les prévisions,** to exceed all expectations; **prévisions météorologiques** *ou* **du temps,** weather forecast; *Fin* **p. boursière,** stock-exchange forecast; **prévisions budgétaires,** budget estimates.

prévisionnel, -elle [previzjɔnɛl] *adj* estimated; **la gestion prévisionnelle des entreprises,** management by objectives.

prévoir [prevwar] *vt* (*conj like* **voir** *except in fu and cond* **je prévoirai, je prévoirais**) **(a)** (*penser, imaginer*) to foresee (*the future, disaster*); to forecast (*the weather, prices etc*); to anticipate (*s.o.'s actions*); **tout laisse prévoir ...,** everything points *or* all signs point to ...; **rien ne fait p. un changement de temps,** there appears to be no prospect of a change in the weather; **comment aurais-je pu p. que ça n'allait pas me plaire?,** how could I have foreseen *or* known in advance *or* anticipated that I wouldn't like it?;

(b) (*organiser*) to take (*measures*) beforehand, to provide for (*sth*); **dépenses prévues au budget,** expenses provided for in the budget; **la loi n'a pas prévu un cas semblable,** the law makes no provision for a case of this kind; **la réunion est prévue pour demain,** the meeting is arranged *or* planned *or* scheduled for tomorrow; **le personnel prévu dans le contrat,** the personnel provided for *or* laid down *or* stipulated in the contract; **on ne peut pas tout p.,** you can't think of *or* provide for everything; **elle prévoit de demander une augmentation,** she's planning to ask for *or* planning on asking for a rise; **p. des rectifications,** to allow for adjustments; **comme prévu,** as (was) planned; **cela s'est passé comme p.,** it went according to plan; **vitesse prévue,** (*of ship*) designed speed; **charge prévue,** (*of lorry etc*) specified load.

prévôt [prevo] *nm* **(a)** *Escrime* **p. de salle** *ou* **d'armes,** assistant fencing master; **(b)** *Mil* assistant provost marshal; **grand p.,** provost marshal; **(c)** *Hist & Jur* provost.

prévoyance [prevwajɑ̃s] *nf* (*précaution*) precaution; (*dans le futur*) foresight, forethought; **il ne manque pas de p.,** he thinks well ahead; **fonds de p.,** contingency fund, reserve fund; **société de p.,** provident society.

prévoyant [prevwajɑ̃] *adj* provident (*fate, parents, state*); far-sighted (*planner, administration etc*).

prie-Dieu [pridjø] *nm inv* prie-dieu, prayer stool.

prier [prije] *v* (*impf & pr sub* **n. priions, v. priiez**) **1** *vt* **(a)** *Rel* to pray to (*God etc*); **je prie Dieu qu'il en soit ainsi,** I pray (to) God that it may be so;

(b) (*supplier*) to beg; *Fml & Litt* to beseech, to entreat; **elle a accepté l'invitation après s'être fait un peu p.,** she accepted the invitation after a little persuasion; **se faire p.,** to require a great deal of persuasion; **il ne s'est pas fait p.,** he didn't need *or* take much persuading, he didn't need to be asked twice; **sans se faire p.,** readily, willingly;

(c) *Fml* (*demander*) to ask, to request; **p. qn de faire qch,** to ask s.o. to do sth; **je te prie de ne pas t'occuper de ça!,** I'd be obliged if you minded your own business; **puis-je vous p. de vouloir bien fermer la porte?,** would you be so kind as to close the door?; **p. qn d'entrer,** to ask s.o. (to come) in; **p. qn de sortir,** to ask s.o. to come out; (*de partir*) to ask s.o. to leave; **dites-moi, je vous prie,** would you please tell me; **je vous en prie,** (*faites-le*) please do!, of course!; (*ne le faites pas*) please don't!; (*il n'y a pas de quoi*) it's *or* it was a pleasure, you're welcome!, that's all right!; *Fml* **je vous prie de bien vouloir recevoir l'assurance de mes sentiments les meilleurs,** (*dans une lettre*) yours sincerely;

(d) (*formal invitation*) **Monsieur et Madame Hugo prient Monsieur et Madame Adam de leur faire l'honneur d'assister à ...,** Mr and Mrs Hugo request the pleasure of Mr and Mrs Adam's company at ...; *Arch & Litt* **p. qn à dîner,** to invite s.o. to dinner.

2 *vi* to pray (**pour,** for); **nous avons prié pour qu'il revienne vivant,** we prayed that he might return alive, we prayed for his safe return.

prière [prijɛr] *nf* **(a)** (*formule*) prayer; **faire** *ou* **dire ses prières,** to say one's prayers; *Hum* **tu peux faire ta p.,** say your prayers; **(b)** (*acte de prier*) **faire la p.,** to offer prayer; **être en prières,** to be praying *or* at prayer; **p. avant le repas,** grace; **(c)** (*demande*) request; *Fml & Litt* entreaty; **à la p. de qn,** at s.o.'s request; **p. de ne pas fumer,** please *or* kindly do not smoke, you are requested not to smoke; **p. de fermer la porte,** please close the door; **être accessible aux prières,** to be open to requests.

prieur, -eure [prijœr] *n* prior, *f* prioress.

prieuré [prijœre] *nm* (*couvent*) priory.

primage [primaʒ] *nm Tech* priming.

prima donna [prima dɔna] *nf* prima donna; (*pl prime donne, prima donna*).

primaire [primɛr] **1** *adj* **(a)** primary (*school, colour etc*); **(b)** *Jur* **délinquant p.,** first offender; **(c)** *Géol* **ère p.,** primary era; **(d)** *Él Tech* **circuit p.,** primary; **(e)** *Écon* **secteur p.,** primary sector; **(f)** *Péj* (*simpliste*) of limited outlook, simple-minded. **2** *nm* **(a)** *Scol* primary education; **(b)** *Géol* primary era; **(c)** *Él* primary (winding); **(d)** *Écon* primary sector; **(e)** (*personne*) person of limited outlook.

primat [prima] *nm* **(a)** *Rel* primate; **(b)** *Phil* primacy.

primate [primat] *nm Zool* primate.

primauté [primote] *nf* **(a)** *Rel etc* primacy; **(b)** (*supériorité*) priority.

prime¹ [prim] **1** *adj Arch & Litt* first; **de p. abord,** to begin with, at first, at the outset; **elle n'est plus dans sa p. jeunesse!,** she's no spring chicken! **2** *nf* **(a)** *Rel* prime; **chanter p.,** to sing the prime; **(b)** *Escrime* prime; **(c)** *Math* **B p.,** (*noté B'*) B prime.

prime² *nf* **(a)** *Fin* (*d'assurance*) premium; **p. d'émission,** issue premium; *Fig* **faire p.,** to be at a premium; *Bourse* **marché à p.,** option market; **(b)** *Com Admin etc* grant; (*sur salaire*) bonus; **p. de déménagement/de vie chère,** removal *or* relocation/cost-of-living allowance; *Ind* **p. de rendement,** productivity bonus; **p. à la construction,** building subsidy *or* grant (*for people building their own houses*); *Mil* **p. de démobilisation,** demobilization gratuity; **(c)** *Com* free gift; *Fig* **en p.,** as a bonus, into the bargain.

primer¹ [prime] **1** *vt* to surpass, to outdo; (*avoir la priorité*) to take precedence over (*s.o., sth*); **considération qui prime toutes les autres,** consideration of the first importance, consideration that outweighs all others. **2** *vi Fig* **le courage prime (sur toutes les autres qualités),** courage takes first place (over all other qualities).

primer² *vt* **(a)** (*donner un prix honorifique à*) to award a prize to (*cattle at show etc*); **taureau primé,** prize bull; **roman primé,** prizewinning novel; **(b)** (*donner une allocation à*) to give *or* award a subsidy *or* grant to, to subsidize (*s.o., sth*); **industrie primée,** subsidized industry.

primerose [primroz] *nf* (*fleur*) hollyhock.

primesautier, -ière [primsotje, -jɛr] *adj* impulsive, spontaneous (*person*); ready, quick (*wit, reply*).

primeur [primœr] *nf* **(a) primeurs,** (early) fruit and vegetables; **marchand de primeurs,** greengrocer (*selling early produce*); **cultiver des primeurs,** to grow early produce *or* early vegetables (and/fruit); **(b)** *Arch & Litt* newness, freshness; **avoir la p. d'une nouvelle,** to be the first to hear a piece of news.

primevère [primvɛr] *nf* (*fleur*) primula; **p. à grandes fleurs,** primrose; **p. officinale,** mountain primrose; **p. commune,** cowslip; **p. des jardins,** polyanthus.

primipare [primipar] **1** *adj* primiparous. **2** *nf* primipara.

primitif, -ive [primitif, -iv] **1** *adj* **(a)** (*qui est le plus près de l'origine*) primitive; *Opt* **couleurs primitives,** primary colours *or US* colors; *Géol* **terrains primitifs,** primitive strata, primitive terrain; *Gram* **temps primitifs,** primary tenses; **(b)** (*premier*) first, original; **la forme primitive d'une société,** the earliest form of (a) society; **économie primitive,** primitive economic system; **(c)** *Péj* (*rudimentaire*) primitive (*tool*); primitive, crude (*methods, customs etc*). **2** *nm* **(a)** *Beaux-Arts* primitive, early master; **(b)** *Vieilli* primitive tribesman.

primitivement [primitivmɑ̃] *adv* originally.

primitivisme [primitivism] *nm* primitivism.

primo [primo] *adv* first(ly), in the first place.

primogéniture [primɔʒenityr] *nf Jur* primogeniture.

primo-infection [primɔɛ̃feksjɔ̃] *nf Méd* primary infection.

primordial, -aux [primɔrdjal, -o] *adj* **(a)** (*premier*) primordial, primeval; **c'est un besoin p. que de communiquer,** communication is one of our most basic needs; **(b)** (*capital*) **une question primordiale,** a question of the utmost importance; **d'une nécessité/importance primordiale,** of prime necessity/importance.

prince [prɛ̃s] *nm* prince; **p. héritier** *ou* **royal** *ou* **impérial,** crown prince; **le fait du p.,** high-handed government action; **p. consort,** prince consort; *Fig* **il est habillé comme un p.,** he's dressed like a king; **le p. des ténèbres,** the prince of darkness; *Fig* **être bon p.,** to be generous *or* open-handed.

prince de galles [prɛ̃sdəgal] *adj & nm inv Tex* Prince of Wales check.

princeps [prɛ̃sɛps] *adj inv* **édition p.,** first edition.

princesse [prɛ̃sɛs] *nf* princess; **p. royale,** princess royal.

princier, -ière [prɛ̃sje, -jɛr] *adj* princely.

princièrement [prɛ̃sjɛrmɑ̃] *adv* (*to dine*) like a prince, in princely fashion; **nous avons été reçu p.,** we were given right royal treatment.

principal, -ale, -aux [prɛ̃sipal, -o] **1** *adj* principal, chief, leading (*person*); principal, main (*question, building*); **associé p.,** senior partner; **agent p.,** head agent; **but p.,** main object; **un des principaux actionnaires,** a major shareholder; *Gram* **proposition principale,** main clause. **2** *nm* **(a) le p.,** the principal thing, the main thing, the main point; **le p. est de réussir,** the main *or* most important thing is to succeed; **(b)** principal, capital sum; (*de l'impôt*) = original amount of tax payable (before surcharges); **(c)** *Mus* principal. **3** *n* principal, chief; *Scol* principal, head (teacher), headmaster, headmistress (*of college etc*).

principalement [prɛ̃sipalmɑ̃] *adv* principally.

principauté [prɛ̃sipote] *nf* principality.

principe [prɛ̃sip] *nm* **(a)** (*fondement, loi*) principle; **aboutir à un accord de p.,** to reach an agreement in principle; **poser qch en p.,** to lay sth down as a principle; **p. de nos actions,** mainspring of our actions; **les principes de la géométrie,** the principles of geometry;

(b) *Ch* element, constituent (*of a substance*); **p. actif,** active principle *or* constituent;

(c) principes, rudiments; **avoir des principes de philosophie,** to have a rudimentary knowledge of philosophy;

(d) (*règle de conduite*) principle; **déclaration de principes,** statement *or* declaration of principle; **elle doit rembourser cet argent, ne serait-ce que pour le p.,** she must pay that money back, even if only for the principle of the thing; **par p.,** on principle; **en p.,** in principle, theoretically, in theory; **avoir pour p. de ...,** to make it a matter of principle to ...;

(e) principes (moraux), (moral) principles; **avoir des principes,** to have (high) principles; **manquer à ses principes,** to fail to live up to one's standards; **sans principes,** unprincipled.

printanier, -ière [prɛ̃tanje, -jɛr] *adj* spring (*flowers etc*); spring-like (*temperature etc*); **comme tu es printanière avec cette robe!,** how (fresh and) spring-like you look in that dress!

printemps [prɛ̃tɑ̃] *nm* spring; **au p.,** in (the) spring (time); *Can F* **avoir la fièvre du p.,** to have spring fever; *Fig* **le p. de la vie,** the springtime of one's life; *Fig F* **elle n'a que 26 p.,** she's only 26; *Fig Pol* **le p. de la démocratie,** the flowering of democracy.

prioritaire [priɔritɛr] **1** *n* person with priority. **2** *adj* (that has) priority; **être p.,** to have priority; **droits prioritaires,** priority rights; *Fin* **action p.,** preference share; **le véhicule venant de la droite est p.,** the vehicle coming from the right has (the) right of way *or* has priority.

priorité [priɔrite] *nf* priority; **une question qui vient en p.,** a question which comes before all others, a question which has priority; **régler une question en p.,** to settle a question as a (matter of) priority; **droits de p.,** priority rights; *Fin* **actions de p.,** preference shares, *Am* preferred stock; **réclamer la p.,** to claim the right to speak first; **avoir la p. sur,** to take priority *or* precedence over; **une carte de p.,** = pass giving s.o. priority to move to the head of a queue; *Aut* **p. (de passage),** right of way, priority; **route à p.,** major road; **p. à droite,** (*sur panneau*) ≈ *Br* give way *or Am* yield to vehicles coming from the right.

pris [pri] *adj* **(a)** (*siège*) occupied, taken; **tout est p.,** all seats *or* rooms *etc* are booked; **avoir les mains prises,** to have one's hands full; **(b)** (*occupé*) engaged, occupied, busy; **je suis très p. ce matin,** I'm very busy this morning, I've got a lot on this morning; **(c) p. de peur,** panic-stricken, seized with fear; **p. de remords,** smitten with remorse; **p. de colère,** in a rage; **p. de boisson,** the worse for drink; *Fml & Jur* under the influence (of alcohol); **(d)** (*gelée etc*) set; (*rivière etc*) frozen (over); **avoir le nez p.,** to have a blocked nose; **avoir la gorge prise,** to have a sore throat; **(e) bien p.,** (*femme*) well-proportioned, shapely; **(f)** (*attrapé*) caught, captured.

prise [priz] *nf* **(a)** taking, capture, seizure (*of town, prisoners etc*); catch (*of fish*); dose (*of medicine*); pinch (*of snuff*); sample (*of ore etc*); *Méd* **faire une p. de sang,** to take a blood sample; *Mil etc* **p. d'armes,** parade under arms; *Jur* **p. de corps,** arrest; **la p. de la Bastille,** the fall *or* storming of the Bastille; *Echecs* **p. de la dame par le fou,** the capture *or* taking of the queen by the bishop; **p. de colis à domicile,** collection of parcels;

(b) *El* **p. de courant,** (*mâle*) plug; (*femelle*) socket, plug *or* power point, outlet; *El* **p. multiple,** adaptor; *El* **p. de terre,** earth, *Am* ground (connection); **faire une p. à une rivière/sur un câble,** to tap a river/a cable; **p. d'air,** ventilation aperture; (*de moteur*) air intake *or* inlet; *Av* air scoop; **p. d'eau,** intake of water; (*dispositif*) cock, tap, valve; (*à incendie*) (fire) hydrant; (*point d'alimentation*) offtake (*of canal, from river etc*);

(c) *Phot Cin TV* **p. de vue(s),** taking of photographs; *Cin TV* shooting; (*cliché*) shot; (*de filmage continu*) take; *TV* **p. de vues en direct,** live broadcast; *Cin TV* **p. de son,** sound recording;

(d) p. en charge, (*par taxi*) picking up (*of passenger*); (*par sécurité sociale*) (guaranteed) reimbursement;

(e) *Fig* **p. de conscience,** awareness, realization; **la p. en considération de facteurs importants,** the taking into consideration *or* account of important factors;

(f) *Tech* engagement, mesh(ing); **en p.,** in gear, engaged; **mettre en p.,** to engage, to put into gear; *Aut* **en p. (directe),** in top (gear); **p. directe,** direct drive; *Fig* **en p. (directe) sur** *ou* **avec qch,** in touch *or* in contact with sth; **hors de p.,** out of gear;

(g) (*solidification*) solidification, congealing, setting; **faire p.,** (*of cement*) to set;

(h) (*pour se retenir*) hold; (*plus ferme*) grasp, grip; (*en escalade*) hold; (*pour le pied*) foothold; **trouver (une) p. à** *ou* **sur qch,** to get a grip *or* a hold on *or* of sth; *Fml Tech* to gain a purchase on sth; **avoir p. sur qn,** to have a hold on *or* over s.o.; *Fig* **la morale n'a aucune p. sur ce garçon,** preaching has no effect *or* makes no impression on that boy; **lâcher p.,** to lose one's hold; **donner p. aux reproches,** to lay oneself open to reproaches; **je n'avais pas de p. (pour me hisser),** I had no purchase (with which to pull myself up);

(i) (*lutte etc*) hold; **être** *ou* **en venir aux prises avec qn/qch,** to come to grips with s.o./sth, to grapple with s.o./sth; **mettre aux prises des intérêts,** to bring interests into conflict;

(j) *Nau* prize; **être de bonne p.,** to be (a) lawful prize; **part de p.,** prize money; **cour des prises,** prize court; **équipage de p.,** prize crew.

prisée [prize] *nf Jur* valuation (*of goods*).

priser[1] [prize] **1** *vt* to snuff (*sth*) up (*through the nose*). **2** *vi* to take snuff; **tabac à p.,** snuff.

priser[2] *vt* **(a)** *Litt* to set a (high) value on, to prize, to value (*sth*); **(b)** *Arch* to appraise, to value (*goods*).

priseur[1], -euse [prizœr, -øz] *n* snuff-taker.

priseur[2] *nm* (official) valuer; (*pour les ventes aux enchères*) auctioneer.

prismatique [prismatik] *adj* prismatic.

prisme [prism] *nm* prism; **jumelles à p.,** prism(atic) binoculars; *Fig* **elle voit la situation à travers un p.,** she has a distorted view of the situation.

prison [prizɔ̃] *nf* **(a)** (*lieu de détention*) prison, jail; **être/aller en p.,** to be in/to go to prison *or* jail; **mettre qn en p.,** to put s.o. in prison *or* jail, to imprison s.o.; **gardien de p.,** prison warder, prison officer; **s'échapper de p.,** to escape from *or* break out of prison *or* jail; **tenir qn en p.,** to keep s.o. imprisoned; *Péj F* **aimable comme une porte de p.,** as friendly as a slap in the face; *Fig* **cette école est une vraie p.,** this school is like a prison; **(b)** (*peine*) imprisonment; **faire de la p.,** to be in prison *or* jail, to serve a prison *or* jail sentence; **cinq ans de p.,** five years' imprisonment; **il a été condamné à cinq ans de prison ferme/avec sursis,** he was given a five-year prison *or* jail sentence/a five-year suspended prison sentence; **il risque la p.,** he risks going to prison *or* jail; *Arch* **p. pour dettes,** debtors' prison.

prisonnier, -ière [prizɔnje, -jɛr] **1** *n* prisoner; **p. de guerre,** prisoner of war, POW; **camp de prisonniers,** prison camp; **camp de prisonniers de guerre,** prisoner-of-war camp; **faire qn p.,** to take s.o. prisoner; **se constituer p.,** to give oneself up; **il a été constitué p.,** he was remanded in custody. **2** *adj* imprisoned, in prison; (*pris, attrapé*) captive; *Fig* **être p. de ses principes,** to be a slave to one's principles.

privatif, -ive [privatif, -iv] **1** *adj* **(a)** *Gram* privative; **(b)** (*particulier*) private; **jardin p.,** private garden. **2** *nm Gram* privative prefix.

privation [privasjɔ̃] *nf* **(a)** (*perte, manque*) deprivation; **p. d'un droit/de la liberté,** loss of a right/of liberty; **(b) privations,** privation, hardship; **s'imposer des privations,** to deprive oneself, to go without.

privatique [privatik] *nf* home video equipment.

privatisable [privatizabl] *adj* privatizable.

privatisation [privatizasjɔ̃] *nf* privatization.

privatiser [privatize] *vt* to privatize.

privautés [privote] *nfpl* (undue) familiarity; **prendre des p. avec qn,** to be over-familiar with s.o..

privé [prive] **1** *adj* **(a)** (*individuel*) private (*life, individual, enterprise etc*); **se réunir en séance privée,** to sit in private (session) *or* closed session; **renseignements**

privés, inside information; **visite privée,** private *or* unofficial visit; *Hist* **le Conseil p.,** the Privy Council; **(b)** (*libre*) private (*school, patient etc*). **2** *nm* **(a)** (*vie etc*) private life; **parler à qn en p.,** to speak to s.o. in private; **connaître qn dans le p.,** to know s.o. in private life; **(b)** *Ind Scol Méd* **le p.,** (*secteur libre*) the private sector.

priver [prive] **1** *vt* **p. qn de qch,** to deprive s.o. of sth; **tu seras privé de dessert,** you'll have to go without your pudding, there'll be no pudding for you; **j'ai été privé de sommeil,** I didn't get any sleep; **je ne vous en prive pas?,** can you spare it? **2 se priver** *vpr* **se p. de,** to do *or* go without (*sth*); to go short of (*food etc*); to deprive oneself of, to deny oneself (*a pleasure etc*); **toi, tu n'aimes pas te p.!,** you certainly don't like to go *or* do without, do you!; **il ne se prive pas de le lui dire,** he never misses a chance to tell her so.

privilège [privilɛʒ] *nm* **(a)** (*avantage, droit*) privilege; **jouir du p.** *ou* **avoir le p. de faire qch,** to be privileged to do sth, to enjoy the privilege of doing sth; *Hist* **abolition des privilèges,** abolition of privileges; *Iron* **il a le p. de me déplaire,** I have a particular dislike for him; **(b)** licence, grant; charter (*of bank*); **(c)** *Jur* preferential claim.

privilégié, -ée [privileʒje] **1** *adj* (*favorisé*) privileged; **elle est privilégiée par son expérience,** she enjoys an advantage on account of her experience; **banque privilégiée,** chartered bank; **créancier p.,** preferential creditor; **action privilégiée,** preference share. **2** *n* privileged person; **quelques privilégiés l'ont vu,** a privileged few have seen it.

privilégier [privileʒje] *vt* (*pr sub & impf* **n. privilégiions, v. privilégiiez**) to privilege.

prix [pri] *nm* **(a)** (*valeur*) value, worth; (*coût*) cost; *Fig* **à tout p.,** at all costs, at any price; **faire qch à p. d'argent,** to do sth for money; **se vendre à p. d'or,** (*of goods*) to fetch huge prices; **à aucun p.,** not on any terms, not at any price; *Fig* **au p. de,** at the price of; **au p. de sa vie,** at the cost of his life; **attacher beaucoup de p.** *ou* **un grand p. à qch,** to set a high value on sth, to set great store by sth; **il attache beaucoup de p.** *ou* **un grand p. à l'apparence de sa voiture,** he sets great store by his car's appearance, he prizes his car's appearance;

(b) (*en argent*) price; **acheter qch à bas p./à juste p.,** to buy sth at a low/a fair price; **p. de vente,** selling price; **p. au comptant,** cash price; **p. courant,** current price, market price; **p. initial,** prime cost; **à** *ou* **au p. coûtant, au p. de revient,** at cost price; **p. de gros,** wholesale price; **p. de détail,** retail price; **vous pouvez l'acheter si vous y mettez le p.,** you can buy it at a price; *F* **faire un p. à qn,** to quote s.o. a price; **je vous ferai un p. (d'ami),** I'll let you have it cheap; **une voiture dans mes p.,** a car I can afford *or* within my means *or* within my price range; **c'est plus dans mes p.,** that's more in my line; *Bourse* **actions cotées au p. de ...,** shares quoted at the rate of ...; **(repas à) p. fixe,** set (price) meal; **articles de p.,** expensive goods; **coûter un p. fou,** to cost the earth; **c'est hors de p.,** the price is prohibitive; **ne pas avoir de p.,** to be priceless; **mettre à p. la tête de qn,** to put a price on s.o.'s head; **mise à p. d'une propriété,** upset price of an estate; **mise à p.,** (*at auction*) reserve price (*of article*); *Écon* **hausse/baisse des p.,** rise/fall in prices; **c'est mon dernier p.,** that's my final offer;

(c) (*tarif*) charge; **p. d'un voyage,** fare; **quel est le p. du billet?,** how much do the tickets cost?; (*transports*) what is the fare?;

(d) (*récompense*) prize; (*d'une bonne action*) reward; **avoir** *ou* **remporter le p.,** to win *or* carry off the prize; **le p. Nobel,** the Nobel Prize; **un/le p. Nobel,** (*personne*) a/the Nobel prizewinner *or Am* laureate; **distribution des p.,** prizegiving; *Br Scol* speech day, prizegiving; *Scol* **livre de p.,** prize book;

(e) (*œuvre, ouvrage primé*) prizewinning work; **j'ai lu le dernier p. Médicis,** I've read the latest Prix Médicis;

(f) *Sp* race; **Grand p. (automobile),** Grand Prix.

prix-courant [prikurɑ̃] *nm Com* price list; (*avec plus d'informations*) catalogue; (*pl prix-courants*).

pro [pro] *n inv Sp etc F* pro; **elle l'a fait en p.,** she did it like a pro ; **c'est une vraie p.,** she's a real pro.

probabilité [prɔbabilite] *nf* probability, likelihood; **selon toute p.,** in all likelihood, most probably; *Math* **calcul des probabilités,** theory of probability.

probable [prɔbabl] *adj* probable, likely; **il est p. qu'elle viendra,** she'll probably come; **peu p.,** improbable, unlikely; **il est peu p.** *ou* **il n'est pas p. qu'elle vienne,** she's not likely *or* she's unlikely to come; **c'est très p.,** (it's) very likely; **c'est plus que p.,** it's more than likely; *F* **tu pourras rester avec nous?, — p.,** will you be able to stay with us? — probably; **p. qu'elle ne se souvient plus de ce que je lui ai dit,** she probably doesn't remember what I told her.

probablement [prɔbabləmɑ̃] *adv* probably.

probant [prɔbɑ̃] *adj* convincing, conclusive (*evidence etc*); *Fml* probative; **peu p.,** unconvincing.

probation [prɔbasjɔ̃] *nf Jur Rel* probation.

probatoire [prɔbatwar] *adj* **stage p.,** trial *or* probationary period; *Scol* **examen p.,** grading examination; *Jur* **délai p.,** probation.

probe [prɔb] *adj Litt* honest, upright.

probité [prɔbite] *nf* probity, integrity.

problématique [prɔblematik] **1** *adj* problematic(al); questionable (*morals etc*). **2** *nf* set of problems; *Phil* problematics.

problématiquement [prɔblematikmɑ̃] *adv* problematically.

problème [prɔblɛm] *nm* problem; **soulever un p.,** to raise a problem; **il faut trouver une solution à ce p.,** a solution to this problem needs to be found; *Scol* **faire des problèmes,** to do sums; **un p. d'algèbre,** an algebra problem; *F* **(il n'y a) pas de p.,** (*bien sûr!*) no problem!; **ce n'est pas un p.,** it's not a problem, that's no problem; **cette nouvelle organisation pose p.,** this new organization is posing *or* creating a problem; *Psy* **un adolescent qui a des problèmes,** a problem teenager; *F* **encore un type à problèmes,** another guy with problems; **avoir des problèmes familiaux,** to have family problems.

procédé [prɔsede] *nm* **(a)** (*comportement*) proceeding, dealing, conduct; **échange de bons procédés,** (*de formules de politesse*) exchange of courtesies *or* civilities; (*de petits services*) exchange of friendly services; **c'est un échange de bons procédés,** one good turn deserves another; **(b)** process; method (*of working*); **p. de travail,** operating procedure; **p. de fabrication,** manufacturing process; **ça sent le p.,** it seems rather artificial; **(c)** tip (*of billiard cue*).

procéder [prɔsede] *vi* (*conj like* **céder**) **(a)** (*venir de*) to proceed (**de,** from); to originate (**de,** in); **sa maladie procède de l'intempérie du climat,** his illness is attributable to the bad climate; **(b)** (*agir*) to proceed, to act; **p. avec méthode,** to proceed methodically; **(c) p. à une enquête,** to institute *or* initiate an enquiry.

procédure [prɔsedyr] *nf* **(a)** *Jur etc* procedure; **terme de p.,** legal term; **(b)** (*démarche*) proceedings; **engager une p. de divorce,** to begin *or* institute divorce proceedings; **vice de p.,** procedural irregularity; *Av* **la p. d'atterrissage,** landing sequence.

procédurier, -ière [prɔsedyrje, -jɛr] **1** *adj* quibbling, *F* nit-picking; pettifogging (*lawyer etc*). **2** *n* quibbler, *F* nit-picker; (*surtout avocat*) pettifogger.

procès [prɔsɛ] *nm* **(a)** *Jur* (legal) proceedings, action (at law); **p. civil,** lawsuit; **p. criminel,** (criminal) trial; **engager un p.,** to engage in a lawsuit; **faire** *ou* **intenter un p. à qn,** to bring an action against s.o., to institute proceedings against s.o., to sue s.o.; to prosecute (*offender*); **être en p. avec qn,** to be involved in legal proceedings with s.o.; **intenter un p. en divorce à qn,** to institute divorce proceedings against s.o.; **le dossier du p.,** the brief; **gagner/perdre son p.,** to win/lose one's case; *Fig* **faire le p. de qn/qch,** to criticize s.o./sth; *Fig* **sans autre forme de p.,** without (any) further ceremony, without further ado; *Fig* **c'est un p. contre la société,** the whole of society is on trial; **(b)** *Anat Vieilli* process.

processeur [prɔsesœr] *nm Ordinat* processor.

processif, -ive [prɔsesif, -iv] *adj* progressive (*measures etc*).

procession [prɔsesjɔ̃] *nf* procession; **aller en p.,** to go *or* walk *etc* in procession; *Fig* **une p. de mendiants/d'étudiants,** a procession of beggars/students.

processionnaire [prɔsesjɔnɛr] **1** *adj* processionary. **2** *nf Ent* **chenille p.,** processionary caterpillar.

processionnel, -elle [prɔsesjɔnɛl] *adj* processional (*hymn, march*).

processionnellement [prɔsesjɔnɛlmɑ̃] *adv Litt* in procession.

processus [prɔsesys] *nm* **(a)** (*évolution*) progress, course, process; **Gorbatchev a instauré un p. de changement,** Gorbachov has initiated a process of change; **(b)** (*méthode*) method, process; **le p. est toujours le même,** the method of operation *or* the process is always the same; **l'introduction de nouveaux p.,** the introduction of new methods; **(c)** *Anat* process.

procès-verbal [prɔsɛvɛrbal] *nm* (*pl procès-verbaux*) **(a)**

Jur policeman's report (*about an offence*); **avoir un p.-v.,** to get a (parking) ticket; **dresser le p.-v. d'une contravention** *ou* **dresser (un) p.-v. à** *ou* **contre qn,** to report *or F* to book s.o.; **(b)** (*rapport*) (official) report; proceedings, minutes (*of meeting*); record (*of evidence etc*); **approbation du p.-v.,** approval of the minutes; **registre des p.-verbaux,** minute book.

prochain, -aine [prɔʃɛ̃, -ɛn] **1** *adj* **(a)** (*qui suit immédiatement*) next; **dimanche p.,** next Sunday; **la semaine prochaine,** next week; **le p. numéro,** the next issue (*of magazine*); **son p. départ, son départ p.,** his approaching *or* impending departure; **dans un avenir p.,** in the near future, before long; **à la prochaine fois!,** be seeing you!, *F* see you (soon)!; **(b)** *Vieilli* (*proche*) nearest. **2** *n* neighbour, *US* neighbor; (*tout être humain*) fellow human being; **l'amour du p.,** love for one's fellow humans. **3** *nf F* **à la prochaine!,** see you (soon)!

prochainement [prɔʃɛnmɑ̃] *adv* shortly, soon.

proche [prɔʃ] **1** *adv* **tout p.,** close at hand, nearby, close by; **de p. en p.,** step by step, by degrees; **p. de mourir,** near(ing) death; **p. de la ruine,** on the verge of ruin.

2 *adj* near (**de,** to); neighbouring, *US* neighboring; **la ville la plus p.,** the nearest town; **l'heure est p.,** the hour is near *or* at hand; **sa fin est p.,** he is close *or* near to death; **la fin est p.,** the end is nigh; **cela me paraît pourtant si p.!,** it seems like only yesterday!; **l'italien est p. du français,** Italian is close to French; **ses proches parents,** his close relations; *Jur & Fml* his next of kin; **ils sont proches parents,** they are closely related; **je me sens p. de lui,** I feel close to him.

3 *n* **réunir ses proches,** to gather one's nearest and dearest (around one).

Proche-Orient (le) [ləprɔʃɔrjɑ̃] *nm* the Middle East; *Vieilli* the Near East.

proclamateur, -trice [prɔklamatœr, -tris] *n Litt* proclaimer.

proclamation [prɔklamɑsjɔ̃] *nf* proclamation.

proclamer [prɔklame] *vt* to proclaim, to declare; **p. le résultat du scrutin,** to declare the poll; **on proclama que …,** it was given out that …; **p. son innocence,** to proclaim *or* protest one's innocence; **p. qn roi,** to proclaim s.o. king.

proclitique [prɔklitik] *adj & nm Ling* proclitic.

proconsul [prɔkɔ̃syl] *nm Hist* proconsul.

proconsulaire [prɔkɔ̃sylɛr] *adj Hist* proconsular.

proconsulat [prɔkɔ̃syla] *nm Hist* proconsulate.

procréateur, -trice [prɔkreatœr, -tris] *Hum & Vieilli* **1** *adj* procreative. **2** *n* procreator.

procréation [prɔkreɑsjɔ̃] *nf* procreation; *Arch* begetting (*of children*).

procréatique [prɔkreatik] *nf* artificial birth technology.

procréer [prɔkree] *vt Litt* to procreate, *Arch* to beget.

procurateur [prɔkyratœr] *nm Hist* procurator.

procuration [prɔkyrɑsjɔ̃] *nf Com Fin Jur* procuration, proxy, power of attorney; **par p.,** by proxy, *Spéc* per pro(curationem); **voter par p.,** to vote by proxy; *Fig* **elle avait le sentiment de vivre par p.,** she felt she was living by proxy; **donner (la) p. à qn,** to confer powers of attorney on s.o..

procuratrice [prɔkyratris] *nf Jur* procurator, proxy.

procurer [prɔkyre] **1** *vt* **p. qch à qn,** to procure *or* obtain *or* get sth for s.o.; **la joie que lui procure le sport,** the pleasure he finds in *or* gets from sport; **cet emploi vous procure une excellente sécurité,** this post will provide you with excellent job security. **2 se procurer** *vpr* to procure, to obtain, to get; **se p. de l'argent,** to raise *or* obtain *or* find money; **où peut-on se p. ce livre?,** where can you get this book?; **impossible à se p.,** unobtainable.

procureur [prɔkyrœr] *nm Jur* procurator, proxy; **p. de la République,** *Eng* ≈ public prosecutor; *Scot* ≈ procurator fiscal; *US* ≈ district attorney; **p. général,** ≈ Attorney General.

prodigalité [prɔdigalite] *nf* prodigality, lavishness, extravagance; wealth, abundance (*of detail*); *Fig* **prodigalités,** (*dépenses*) lavish *or* reckless expenditure.

prodige [prɔdiʒ] **1** *nm* wonder, marvel; (*personne*) prodigy; **faire des prodiges,** to do *or* work wonders; **un p. d'ingéniosité,** a wonderful piece of ingenuity; **tenir du p.,** to be extraordinary; (*être inexplicable*) to be inexplicable; **c'est un p.,** (*personne*) he's a prodigy; (*fait*) it's amazing *or* incredible. **2** *adj* **enfant p.,** child prodigy.

prodigieusement [prɔdiʒjøzmɑ̃] *adv* prodigiously.

prodigieux, -euse [prɔdiʒjø, -øz] *adj* prodigious, extraordinary (*amount, strength*); *F* (*incroyable*) phenomenal, stupendous; *Iron* **sa bêtise est prodigieuse,** his stupidity knows no bounds.

prodigue [prɔdig] **1** *adj* **(a)** prodigal; lavish, unsparing (**de,** of); **il est p. pour ses enfants,** he's very generous towards his children; **p. d'excuses,** profuse in apologies; **être p. de son argent,** to spend lavishly, to be free with one's money; **(b)** *Péj* wasteful, spendthrift; **il est très p. de conseils,** he's very free with his advice; *Bible* **l'enfant p.,** the prodigal son. **2** *n* spendthrift, squanderer.

prodiguer [prɔdige] *vt* **(a)** (*donner abondamment*) to give freely; *Litt* to be prodigal *or* lavish of (*sth*); **p. qch à qn,** to lavish sth on s.o.; **p. ses conseils,** to be generous *or* free with one's advice; **(b)** *Péj* to waste, to squander.

prodrome [prɔdrom] *nm* premonitory symptom (*of disease*); preamble (*to a treatise*).

producteur, -trice [prɔdyktœr, -tris] **1** *adj* productive (**de,** of); producing; **pays p. de blé/pétrole,** wheat-growing/oil-producing country; *Cin* **société productrice,** production company. **2** *n* (*entreprise etc*) *& Rad TV Cin* producer.

productible [prɔdyktibl] *adj* producible.

productif, -ive [prɔdyktif, -iv] *adj* productive.

production [prɔdyksjɔ̃] *nf* **(a)** *Ind* production, producing; generation (*of electricity etc*); **la p. du dernier modèle d'ordinateur,** (the) production of the latest model of computer; **moyens de p.,** means of production; **coût de p.,** cost of production, production cost; **augmenter la p.,** to increase production *or* output; *Cin* **directeur de p.,** producer; **(b)** (*produit*) product; **productions,** *Agr* produce; yield (*of mine etc*); output (*of factory*); **p. littéraire,** literary output; *Cin* **une p. franco-russe,** a Franco-Russian (co-)production; **p. du génie,** work of genius; **(c)** production; *Jur etc* exhibiting; **p. des pièces,** exhibition of documents.

productique [prɔdyktik] *nf* production engineering.

productivisme [prɔdyktivism] *nm Péj* obsession with productivity.

productiviste [prɔdyktivist] *adj Péj* that emphasizes productivity to an obsessive degree.

productivité [prɔdyktivite] *nf* productivity, productiveness; productive capacity (*of factory*); **accroissement de la p.,** increase in productivity.

produire [prɔdɥir] *v* (*prp* **produisant;** *pp* **produit;** *pr ind* **je produis, n. produisons;** *impf* **je produisais;** *p hist* **je produisis;** *fu* **je produirai**) **1** *vt* **(a)** *Ind Agr* to produce; *Litt* to bring forth, to bear (*offspring etc*); to generate (*heat etc*); *Cin etc* to produce (*film etc*); **argent qui produit de l'intérêt,** money that yields interest; *Écon* **p. cent voitures par jour,** to produce *or* to turn out a hundred cars a day;

(b) to produce, to bring about (*result, effect*); **p. une impression favorable,** to produce *or* create *or* make a favourable impression; **cela risque de p. une grande surprise,** there is a risk that it will cause a major surprise;

(c) (*créer*) to produce, to turn out; **elle vient de p. son premier roman,** she's just produced *or* written *or* turned out her first novel;

(d) *Jur etc* to produce, to bring forward (*evidence etc*); **p. des témoins,** to produce witnesses.

2 se produire *vpr* **(a)** to occur, to happen, to arise; (*of event*) to take place; (*of organization, relationship*) to come into being; **il pourrait se p. des incidents,** there might be trouble;

(b) (*of actor etc*) to appear.

3 *vi* **(a)** *Écon* to produce, to be productive; **p. plus,** to be more productive;

(b) *Jur* **sommation de p.,** order *or* requirement to present one's ID papers *or* driving licence *etc*.

produit [prɔdɥi] *nm* **(a)** (*marchandise*) product; *Agr* **produits,** produce; **produits agricoles,** agricultural produce; **le p. de la terre,** the produce of the land; **produits de marque,** branded goods; **p. manufacturé,** manufactured product; **les services et les produits,** goods and services; **produits ménagers** *ou* **d'entretien,** (household) cleaning products, household goods; **produits chimiques,** chemicals; **produits de beauté,** cosmetics;

(b) (*profit*) yield; **p. brut,** gross earnings *or* proceeds; *Écon* **p. intérieur brut,** gross domestic product; *Écon* **p. national brut,** gross national product; **p. d'une vente,** proceeds of a sale; *Com* **le p. de la journée,** the day's takings *or* receipts; **le p. de dix années de travail,** the product *or* result of ten years' work;

(c) *Math* product (*of multiplication*);

(d) (*création*) product; **c'est le p. de son imagination,** it's the *or* a product of his imagination.

proéminence [prɔeminɑ̃s] *nf* (*état*) prominence; (*ce qui fait saillie*) protuberance.

proéminent [prɔeminɑ̃] *adj* prominent; projecting

(*rock*); protuberant (*nose, growth*).

prof [prɔf] *n F* (school)teacher; (*maître de conférences*) prof; (*maître assistant*) lecturer.

profanateur, -trice [prɔfanatœr, -tris] *Litt* **1** *adj* profanatory. **2** *n* profaner.

profanation [prɔfanɑsjɔ̃] *nf* profanation, desecration; desecration, violation (*of grave etc*).

profane [prɔfan] **1** *adj* profane; secular (*music etc*); unhallowed (*burial ground*); *Fig* **elle est p. (en la matière)**, she's unversed in *or* unfamiliar with that particular subject; *Fig* **je n'ai jamais fait de ski, je suis un p.,** I've never skied, I'm a complete beginner. **2** *n Fig* uninitiated person, layman.

profaner [prɔfane] *vt* to profane; to desecrate (*church etc*); to desecrate, to violate (*grave etc*); to misuse, to degrade (*one's talent etc*); to defile (*innocence*).

proférer [prɔfere] *vt* (**je profère; je proférerai**) to utter; **sans p. une (seule) parole,** without (so much as) a word.

profès, -esse [prɔfɛ, -ɛs] *Rel* **1** *adj* professed. **2** *n* professed monk *or* nun.

professer [prɔfese] **1** *vt* **(a)** to profess (*religion, opinion*); to hold (*views*); **(b)** (*enseigner*) to teach; **il professe la physique au lycée,** he teaches physics at the lycée. **2** *vi* (*être titulaire d'une chaire*) to be a professor; (*comme maître assistant*) to be a lecturer; (*dans une école*) to be a teacher; **il professe à la Sorbonne,** he's a professor *or* lecturer *or* he teaches at the Sorbonne.

professeur [prɔfɛsœr] *nm* (school)teacher; (*dans une école privée*) master, *f* mistress; (*at university*) professor; (*maître assistant*) lecturer; (*surtout à Oxford, Cambridge*) don; **elle est p. de piano,** she's a piano teacher, she teaches (the) piano; **p. principal** *ou* **de classe,** class *or* form teacher; (*dans une école privée*) form master *or* mistress; **p. de terminale,** sixth-form teacher; **c'est un bon/mauvais p.,** he's a good/bad teacher; **p. de chant,** singing teacher; **p. de natation,** swimming instructor.

profession [prɔfɛsjɔ̃] *nf* **(a)** (*métier*) profession, occupation; (*pour artisans*) trade; **p. libérale,** (liberal) profession; **médecin de (sa) p.,** doctor by profession; **menuisier de p.,** carpenter by trade; **ballerine de p.,** professional ballet dancer; *Fig F* **rouspéteur de p.,** professional grumbler, full-time grumbler; **sans p.,** unemployed; **(b) p. de foi,** profession of faith; **faire p. de qch,** to profess sth.

professionnalisation [prɔfɛsjɔnalisɑsjɔ̃] *nf* professionalization; (*d'un sportif*) turning professional.

professionnaliser (se) [səprɔfɛsjɔnalize] *vpr* (*d'un sportif*) to turn professional.

professionnalisme [prɔfɛsjɔnalism] *nm* professionalism.

professionnel, -elle [prɔfɛsjɔnɛl] **1** *adj* **(a)** professional; vocational (*training etc*); **maladies professionnelles,** occupational diseases; **syndicat p.,** trade association; **déformation professionnelle,** = (bad) habit(s) acquired through the type of work one does; **faire preuve de conscience professionnelle,** to be conscientious (in one's work); **cela n'est pas très p.,** it's not very professional; **(b)** professional (*footballer etc*); **écrivain p.,** writer by profession. **2** *n* **(a)** *Sp* professional; **(b)** *Ind etc* skilled worker.

professionnellement [prɔfɛsjɔnɛlmɑ̃] *adv* professionally.

professoral, -aux [prɔfɛsɔral, -o] *adj aussi Fig* professorial.

professorat [prɔfɛsɔra] *nm* teaching profession (*esp higher education*); **choisir le p.,** to chose teaching as a *or* one's profession.

profil [prɔfil] *nm* **(a)** (*de personne*) profile; **dessiner qn de p.,** to draw s.o. in profile; **vue de p.,** side view; *Fig* **adopter un p. bas,** to adopt a low profile; **(b)** profile, contour, outline; (*dessin, technique*) section; **p. en travers,** cross section; **p. de l'horizon,** skyline; *Géol* **le p. d'une rivière,** the profile of a river; **p. psychologique,** psychological profile; **le p. de l'employé idéal,** the profile of the ideal employee; *Fig* **elle a tout à fait le p. de l'emploi,** her experience suits her perfectly for the job, she's exactly the type of person that's needed (for the job); **p. médical,** medical history.

profilage [prɔfilaʒ] *nm Beaux-Arts* profiling; *Tech* shaping; streamlining (*of car body etc*).

profilé [prɔfile] **1** *adj shaped (metal etc)*; *Tech etc* streamlined (*car etc*); **fers profilés,** sectional irons, iron sections. **2** *nm Tech* **profilés en acier,** steel sections, sectional steel.

profiler [prɔfile] **1** *vt* **(a)** (*représenter de profil*) to profile; (*dessin, technique*) to draw (*sth*) in section; **(b)** to shape (*a piece of metal*); to streamline (*car etc*). **2 se profiler** *vpr* to stand out in profile, to be outlined, to be silhouetted (**à, sur, contre,** against); *Fig* **ses vacances se profilent,** his holiday plans are taking shape.

profit [prɔfi] *nm* **(a)** (*avantage*) profit, benefit; **faire (son) p. de qch,** to profit by *or* from sth; **mettre qch à p.,** to turn sth to (good) account; **tirer p. de qch,** to take advantage of sth, to derive benefit from sth; (*utiliser qch*) to make use of sth; *F* **sa vieille auto m'aura fait du p.,** his old car has served me well; **j'en ai eu peu de p.,** I gained little advantage from it; **travail sans p.,** unprofitable *or* profitless work; **elle ne cherche que son p.,** she's only interested in personal gain; **au p. de qn,** on behalf of s.o., for the benefit of s.o.; **au p. des pauvres,** in aid of the poor; **concert donné au p. des orphelins,** benefit concert for orphans; **les socialistes perdront au p. des communistes,** votes will swing from the Socialists to the Communists, the Communists will pick up votes from the Socialists;

(b) *Écon* **un p.,** a profit; **profits et pertes,** profit and loss; **vendre à p.,** to sell at a profit; **il n'y a pas de petits profits,** every little helps; **p. de 12%,** 12% profit.

profitable [prɔfitabl] *adj* profitable; advantageous (*situation*); beneficial (*experience, exercise*).

profitablement [prɔfitabləmɑ̃] *adv* profitably.

profiter [prɔfite] *vi* **(a) p. de qch,** to take advantage of sth, to turn sth to (good) account, to (derive) benefit from sth; **il est de bon humeur aujourd'hui, il faut en p.,** he's in a good mood today, we'd better make the most of it; **p. de l'occasion,** to seize *or* make the most of the opportunity; **p. de la vie/de sa jeunesse,** to enjoy life (to the full)/to make the most of one's youth; **il a profité de ce que tout le monde dormait encore pour s'esquiver,** he took advantage of the fact that everyone was still asleep to slip away; **il a profité de mon offre,** he took me up on my offer;

(b) *Écon* **p. sur une vente,** to make a profit on a sale;

(c) p. à qn, to be to s.o.'s advantage, to (be of) benefit (to) s.o.; **ses idées révolutionnaires ne lui ont pas profité,** his revolutionary ideas did not do him any good (in the end), his revolutionary ideas were of no benefit to him; *Prov* **bien mal acquis ne profite jamais,** ill-gotten goods never prosper; *F* **ces chaussures m'ont bien profité,** these shoes have lasted me a long time;

(d) *F* (*of child, plant etc*) to thrive, to grow.

profiterole [prɔfitrɔl] *nf Culin* profiterole.

profiteur, -euse [prɔfitœr, -øz] *n Péj* profiteer; **les profiteurs de guerre,** war profiteers.

profond [prɔfɔ̃] **1** *adj* **(a)** deep; **puits p. de six mètres,** well six metres deep; **ces étagères ne sont pas profondes,** these shelves are not very deep; **un décolleté p.,** a plunging neckline; **forêt profonde,** dense *or* thick forest; **révérence profonde, p. salut,** low bow; **voix profonde,** deep voice; **peu p.,** shallow;

(b) profound (*dislike*); deep-seated (*prejudice, dislike etc*); underlying (*cause etc*); **des marques profondes, ineffaçables,** deep, indelible scars;

(c) *Fig* profound (*wisdom, scholarship etc*); thorough (*knowledge etc*); deep, sound (*sleep*); (*pénétrant*) profound, meaningful (*words*); **un bleu p.,** a deep blue; **silence p.,** profound *or* heavy silence; **p. soupir,** heavy sigh; **elle me lança un p. regard,** she cast a meaningful look in my direction; **p. dégoût,** profound or deep disgust; **un homme p.,** a man who thinks deeply, a deep thinker; **un esprit p.,** a mind of great depth; **ses intentions profondes étaient honorables,** deep down his intentions were honourable.

2 *adv* **creuser p.,** to dig deep.

3 *nm* **au plus p. de mon cœur,** in my heart of hearts; **au plus p. de la nuit,** at dead of night, in the middle of the night.

profondément [prɔfɔ̃demɑ̃] *adv* profoundly, deeply; **dormir p.,** to sleep soundly; **p. endormi,** sound *or* fast asleep; **s'incliner p.,** to make a deep *or* low bow; **j'en suis p. certain,** I am convinced of it; **se comprendre p.,** to have a profound *or* deep understanding of each other; **elle l'aimait p.,** she loved him deeply.

profondeur [prɔfɔ̃dœr] *nf* **(a)** depth (*of water, hole in the ground etc*); deepness (*of voice etc*); **avoir dix mètres de p.,** to be ten metres deep, to be ten metres in depth; **en p.,** in depth; *Fig* **travailler en p.,** to be working in depth; **des changements en p.,** in-depth *or* profound changes; **peu de p.,** shallowness; **(b)** (*de sentiment*) depth; (*d'esprit etc*) profoundness, profundity; **un film sans p.,** a film with no depth, a shallow *or* superficial film; **(c) profondeurs,** (*de*

l'être) depths, recesses (*of the mind*); **la psychologie des profondeurs,** psychoanalysis.
pro forma [prɔfɔrma] *adj inv* **facture p.f.,** pro forma invoice.
profus [prɔfy] *adj Litt* profuse.
profusément [prɔfyzemɑ̃] *adv Litt* profusely.
profusion [prɔfyzjɔ̃] *nf* profusion, abundance; **à p.,** in profusion; **des bouteilles à p.,** an abundance of bottles, bottles galore; **donner de l'argent à p.,** to give a great deal of money.
progéniture [prɔʒenityr] *nf* progeny, progeniture, offspring; *Fig F* **il nous a présenté sa p.,** he introduced his offspring to us.
progestatif, -ive [prɔʒɛstatif, -iv] *Biol Ch* **1** *adj* **corps p.,** corpus luteum. **2** *nm* progestin, progestogen.
progestérone [prɔʒɛsterɔn] *nf Biol Ch* progesterone.
progiciel [prɔʒisjɛl] *nm Ordinat* software package.
prognathe [prɔgnat] *adj* undershot, underhung (*jaw*); *Spéc* prognathous, prognathic.
programmable [prɔgramabl] *adj Electron* programmable.
programmateur, -trice [prɔgramatœr, -tris] **1** *n Rad TV* programme planner, scheduler. **2** *nm Tech* automatic control (device).
programmation [prɔgramɑsjɔ̃] *nf* **(a)** *TV etc* programme planning, scheduling; **un changement de p.,** a change to the advertised *or* scheduled programme; **(b)** *Ordinat* programming; **langage de p.,** programming language.
programme [prɔgram] *nm* **(a)** programme, *Am* program (*of concert etc*); **hors p.,** not on *or* in the programme; *Rad TV* **un changement des programmes,** a change to the advertised *or* scheduled programme; **changement de p., on ne part plus,** there's been a change of plan, we're not going away after all; **(b)** *Scol* **p. (d'études),** curriculum; syllabus (*of course*); **ne pas sortir du p.,** not to depart from the syllabus; **cela n'est pas au p.,** that's not in the syllabus; **les auteurs au** *ou* **du p.,** the set books; **(c)** programme, *Am* program, platform (*of political party*); **p. de réformes sociales,** programme of social reform; **p. électoral,** (electoral) platform; **(d)** *Ordinat* program; **p. de commande,** driver; **p. traducteur,** interpreter.
programmer [prɔgrame] **1** *vt* **(a)** *Ordinat* to program; **(b)** *TV Rad* to schedule (*programme*); **(c)** (*organiser, mettre au point*) to plan (*holiday, changes*). **2** *vi* **(a)** *TV Rad* to draw up a schedule; **(b)** *Ordinat* to program.
programmeur, -euse [prɔgramœr, -øz] *n Ordinat* programmer; **analyste-p.,** systems analyst.
progrès [prɔgrɛ] *nm* **(a)** progress; progress, advance (*of army etc*); progress, spread(ing) (*of epidemic etc*); **la maladie fait du p.,** the disease is making progress *or* is making headway;
(b) progress, advancement, improvement; **faire des p.,** (*of pupil etc*) to make progress, to improve, to get on well; **le malade fait des p. satisfaisants,** the patient is making satisfactory progress *or* is progressing satisfactorily; **un p. sensible vers la démocratie,** a significant step *or* advance towards democracy; *F* **il y a du p.,** there's definitely an improvement; **la science a fait de grands p.,** science has made great progress *or* great strides (forward); **suivre les p. d'un malade/d'un élève,** to follow *or* monitor a patient's/pupil's progress; **suivre les p. d'une science,** to keep abreast of a science; **suivre les p. d'une affaire,** to keep track of a matter;
(c) le p., (economic, scientific *etc*) progress; **croire au p.,** to believe in progress; *Pol* **parti du p.,** progressive party.
progresser [prɔgrese] *vi* to progress, to advance; to make progress *or* headway (*in enquiry etc*); to gain ground (*in contest, of epidemic etc*); (*d'un élève etc*) to make progress, to improve; **son cancer progresse,** his cancer is spreading *or* getting worse.
progressif, -ive [prɔgresif, -iv] *adj* progressive; gradual (*growth etc*); *Ling* **la forme progressive en anglais,** the progressive *or* continuous form in English; **impôt p.,** progressive *or* graduated tax.
progression [prɔgrɛsjɔ̃] *nf* **(a)** (*mouvement*) progress(ion), moving forward; **la p. des marcheurs,** the walkers' progress; **(b)** (*développement*) advance (*of army*); advancement (*in career, society*); **la p. de la délinquance/du sida,** the spread of delinquency/AIDS; **(c)** *Math* **p. arithmétique,** arithmetical progression; *Mus* **p. harmonique,** harmonic progression.
progressiste [prɔgresist] *adj & n* progressive.
progressivement [prɔgresivmɑ̃] *adv* progressively.
progressivité [prɔgresivite] *nf* progressiveness.
prohiber [prɔibe] *vt* to prohibit, to forbid; **p. à qn de faire qch,** to forbid s.o. to do sth; **p. le tabac à qn,** to forbid s.o. tobacco; **marchandises prohibées,** prohibited goods; **temps prohibé,** close season (*for hunting etc*).
prohibitif, -ive [prɔibitif, -iv] *adj* **(a)** prohibitive (*price etc*); **(b)** prohibitory (*law etc*).
prohibition [prɔibisjɔ̃] *nf* prohibition; *Hist* **pendant la p.,** during Prohibition.
prohibitionnisme [prɔibisjɔnism] *nm Econ etc* prohibition(ism).
prohibitionniste [prɔibisjɔnist] *adj & n Econ etc* prohibitionist.
proie [prwa] *nf* prey; (*à la chasse*) quarry; **oiseau de p.,** bird of prey; **faire sa p. de qch,** (*of animal*) to prey on sth; *Fig* **c'est une p. facile,** he's easy prey *or* meat; **être la p. de qn,** to be the prey *or* victim of s.o.; **les enfants sont la p. de la publicité,** children are the victims of advertising; **être en p. aux remords,** to be (a) prey to remorse, to be tormented by remorse; **tomber en p. à la tentation,** to fall prey to temptation.
projecteur [prɔʒɛktœr] *nm* **(a)** *Cin Phot* (slide, film) projector; **(b)** searchlight; floodlight (*on building etc*); *Th* spotlight; **illuminé par des projecteurs,** floodlit.
projectif, -ive [prɔʒɛktif, -iv] *adj* projective; **espace p.,** projective space; *Psy* **test p.,** projective test.
projectile [prɔʒɛktil] *nm* projectile; (*lancé par un agresseur etc*) missile.
projection [prɔʒɛksjɔ̃] *nf* **(a)** projection; throwing forward *or* up *or* out (*of heavy body etc*); sp(l)atter(ing), splash(ing) (*of liquid*); *Géol* **projections volcaniques,** (volcanic) ejecta; **(b)** *Cin etc* projection; **appareil de p.,** (slide *or* film) projector; **la p. durera 45 minutes,** it will take 45 minutes to show the film, the showing will last 45 minutes; **cabine de p.,** projection room; **p. par transparence,** rear projection; **conférence avec projections,** lecture (illustrated) with slides; **(c)** beam (*of light*); **(d)** *Math Archit etc* projection, plan; **p. horizontale,** ground plan; **(e)** (*image*) (outward) manifestation; *Psy* projection (**dans,** onto); **cette expression est la p. de sa pensée,** that expression is the outward manifestation of his thought, that expression reveals what he is thinking.
projectionniste [prɔʒɛksjɔnist] *n Cin* projectionist.
projet [prɔʒɛ] *nm* **(a)** (*plan*) plan, project, scheme; (*chantier, travaux*) & *Scol Univ* project; **faire des projets,** to make plans; **faire** *ou* **former un p.,** to make *or* devise a plan; **former le p. de faire qch,** to plan to do sth; **(b)** plan (*of building etc*); blueprint (*of machine etc*); **p. de contrat,** draft agreement; **p. de loi,** (draft) bill; **à l'état de p.,** at the planning stage; **ça n'est resté qu'à l'état de p.,** it never got off the ground; **p. d'architecture,** architectural project.
projeter [prɔʒte] *v* (*conj like* **jeter**) **1** *vt* **(a)** (*lancer*) to project; **le train projette des gravillons en passant,** the train throws up loose stones as it passes; **(b)** to cast (*shadow*); **(c)** (*of volcano*) to eject (*ash*); **l'explosion les a projetés au loin,** the explosion flung *or* hurled them far away; **(d)** *Cin* to show, to screen (*film*); **(e)** to plan, to contemplate (*journey etc*); **je projette de partir demain,** I'm thinking of leaving *or* I'm planning to leave tomorrow; **(f)** *Psy* to project; **le patient projette ses angoisses sur son analyste,** the patient projects his anxieties onto his analyst. **2 se projeter** *vpr* to stand out; (*d'un rocher*) to project, to jut out; **une ombre s'est projetée sur le mur,** a shadow fell *or* was cast on the wall.
projeteur [prɔʒtœr] *nm Tech* planner; designer (*of machine etc*); **concepteur-p.,** creative designer.
projo [prɔʒo] *nm F* projector.
prolapsus [prɔlapsys] *nm Méd* prolapse.
prolétaire [prɔletɛr] *adj & n* proletarian.
prolétariat [prɔletarja] *nm* proletariat.
prolétarien, -ienne [prɔletarjɛ̃, -jɛn] *adj* proletarian.
prolétarisation [prɔletarizasjɔ̃] *nf* proletarianization.
prolétariser [prɔletarize] *vt* to proletarianize.
prolifération [prɔliferasjɔ̃] *nf* proliferation.
prolifère [prɔlifɛr] *adj Biol* proliferous.
proliférer [prɔlifere] *vi* (**il prolifère; il proliférera**) to proliferate; **la petite délinquance prolifère,** petty crime is on the increase.
prolifique [prɔlifik] *adj* prolific.
prolixe [prɔliks] *adj* wordy; *Fml* prolix, verbose.
prolixement [prɔliksəmɑ̃] *adv* at great length.
prolixité [prɔliksite] *nf* prolixity, verbosity.
prolo [prɔlo] *Péj F* **1** *adj* plebby (*accent, tastes*). **2** *n* pleb, prole, oik.
prologue [prɔlɔg] *nm* prologue (**de,** to).

prolongation [prɔlɔ̃gasjɔ̃] *nf* prolongation, protraction (*of discussions*); prolongation, lengthening (*of stay*); prolongation, extension (*of leave*); *Fb* **jouer les prolongations,** to play extra time *or Am* overtime.

prolonge [prɔlɔ̃ʒ] *nf* **(a)** *Rail etc* lashing rope; **(b)** *Mil* ammunition wagon; **p. d'artillerie,** gun carriage (*at military funeral*).

prolongé [prɔlɔ̃ʒe] *adj* **(a)** prolonged (*absence etc*); **soupir p.,** long-drawn-out sigh; **applaudissements prolongés,** prolonged *or* sustained applause; **(b)** *Math* prolate (*ellipsoid*).

prolongement [prɔlɔ̃ʒmɑ̃] *nm* **(a)** prolongation, continuation (*of street etc*); prolongation, lengthening, extension (*of wall, railway etc*); **je veux installer le frigidaire dans le p. de la paillasse,** I want the fridge in line with the worktops; *Fig* **ce départ était dans le p. de sa toute première décision,** the departure was in line with *or* consistent with his original decision; **(b) prolongements,** developments, consequences (*of an action etc*); **quels seront les prolongements de ce débat?,** what will the fallout of the debate be?

prolonger [prɔlɔ̃ʒe] *v* (**je prolongeai(s); n. prolongeons**) **1** *vt* to prolong, to extend (*stay*); to prolong, to protract, to spin out (*argument etc*); **visite très prolongée,** very lengthy visit; *Rail* **p. un billet,** to extend a ticket; **p. un mur,** to extend a wall; *Math* **p. une droite,** to continue *or* produce a line. **2 se prolonger** *vpr* to be prolonged; (*of road etc*) to continue, to extend; **la guerre s'est prolongée jusqu'à l'année suivante,** the war went on *or* carried on until the following year.

promenade [prɔmnad] *nf* **(a)** walking; (*balade*) walk; (*courte*) stroll; (*en voiture etc*) outing, trip; **faire une p. (à pied),** to go for a walk; **faire une p. en voiture,** to go for a drive; **faire une p. à bicyclette,** to go for a bicycle ride; **faire une p. à cheval,** to go (horse)riding, to go for a ride; **p. en bateau,** (*en canot*) row; (*en voilier*) sail; **être en p.,** to be out walking, to be out for a walk; **faire faire une p. à qn,** to take s.o. (out) for a walk; *Mus* **concert p.,** promenade concert, prom; **p. militaire,** route march; **(b)** (*avenue*) promenade (*on the seafront*); (*dans certains noms de rues*) parade.

promener [prɔmne] *v* (**je promène; je promènerai**) **1** *vt* **(a)** (*faire aller, conduire*) to take (*s.o.*) (out) for a walk; (*en voiture*) to take (*s.o.*) (out) for a drive; **p. son chien,** to take one's dog for a walk; **p. son cheval,** to exercise one's horse; **cela vous promènera un peu,** that will get you out a bit; **p. des amis à travers Paris,** to show *or* take friends round Paris;

(b) (*faire aller*) to pass, to run; **p. sa main sur qch,** to pass *or* run one's hand over sth; **p. ses yeux sur qch,** to run one's eye(s) over sth.

2 se promener *vpr* **(a)** (*se balader*) to walk; **je vais me p.,** I'm going (out) for a walk *or* stroll; **se p. en Auvergne,** to tour Auvergne; **se p. dans sa chambre,** to pace up and down in one's room; *F* (*avec omission de* **se**) **mener p. les enfants,** to take the children (out) for a walk; *F* **envoyer p. qn,** to send s.o. packing; **va te p.!,** get out!, *F* buzz off!;

(b) (*of eyes, thoughts etc*) to wander; *Fig F* **cette vieille chaise s'est promenée dans toute la maison avant d'aller à la poubelle,** that old chair found its way into every room in the house before it was thrown out; *F* **il laisse p. ses affaires partout,** he leaves his things lying around all over the place.

promeneur, -euse [prɔmnœr, -øz] **1** *n* walker, stroller (*in a park etc*); (*randonneur*) walker, rambler. **2** *nf Vieilli* **promeneuse d'enfants,** mother's help (*who takes children for a walk*).

promenoir [prɔm(ə)nwar] *nm* promenade, (covered) walk; lobby (*of law courts etc*); *Th Vieilli* lounge.

promesse [prɔmɛs] *nf* **(a)** (*serment*) promise; **faire une p.,** to make a promise; **tenir sa p.,** to keep one's promise; **tu as ma p.,** you have my word *or* promise; **manquer à sa p.,** to break one's promise; *Fig* **plein de promesses,** full of promise, that shows a great deal of promise, very promising; **entreprise pleine de promesses,** promising undertaking; **(b)** *Com etc* undertaking to pay; **p. d'achat/de vente,** agreement *or* undertaking to purchase/undertaking *or* promise to sell.

prométhéen, -enne [prɔmeteɛ̃, -ɛn] *adj Litt* Promethean.

prometteur, -euse [prɔmɛtœr -øz] *adj* promising, full of promise; attractive (*invitation*).

promettre [prɔmɛtr] *v* (*conj like* **mettre**) **1** *vt* **(a)** to promise; **p. qch à qn,** to promise s.o. sth, to promise sth to s.o.; **on promet une forte récompense,** a handsome reward is being offered; **p. à qn de faire qch,** to promise s.o. to do sth; **il m'a promis qu'il le ferait,** he promised me he'd do it; *F* **tu le regretteras, je te le promets,** you'll regret it, mark my words; *F* **je vous promets qu'on s'est amusé,** we had a really great time; **le médecin promet un prompt rétablissement,** the doctor predicts a speedy recovery;

(b) (*faire espérer*) **le temps promet de la chaleur,** it promises to be hot, it looks as though it will be hot; **il promet d'éclipser tous ses rivaux,** he looks set to eclipse all his rivals.

2 *vi* **les vignes promettent,** the vines look promising; **enfant qui promet,** promising child, child who shows promise; **c'est un projet qui promet,** the plan has possibilities; *F* **ça promet!,** (*avant, au début d'une affaire*) that looks promising!; *Iron* that doesn't look too good.

3 se promettre *vpr* **(a)** (*à qn d'autre*) to promise (to) each other; **ils se sont promis de ne plus se disputer,** they promised (each other) not to *or* that they wouldn't quarrel any more;

(b) se p. qch, to promise oneself sth; **se p. des plaisirs nouveaux,** to anticipate new pleasures;

(c) (*décider*) **se p. de travailler,** to make up one's mind *or* to resolve to work.

promis, -ise [prɔmi, -iz] **1** *adj* promised; **la Terre promise,** the Promised Land; **p. à,** destined for; **il est p. à un grand avenir,** he is destined for a great future, he has a great future ahead of him. **2** *n Vieilli & Région* fiancé(e), betrothed.

promiscuité [prɔmiskɥite] *nf* promiscuity; (*beaucoup de personnes*) overcrowding; **je ne supportais plus la p. de cet apartement,** I couldn't take the overcrowding in the flat any more; **je déteste la p. des transports en commun,** I hate the crowding on public transport.

promontoire [prɔmɔ̃twar] *nm* promontory, headland; (*plus grand*) cape.

promoteur, -trice [prɔmɔtœr, -tris] *n* **(a) p. (immobilier),** property developer; **(b)** (*créateur*) originator **(de,** of); **(c)** *Ch* promoter.

promotion [prɔmosjɔ̃] *nf* **(a)** (*avancement*) promotion (*to a higher position*); *Rel* preferment; **p. à l'ancienneté,** promotion by seniority; **(b)** *Univ* (students of the same) year; *Am* ≈ class; **camarade de p.,** fellow student; **le premier de sa p.,** the first in his year, top of his year; **(c)** *Com* **p. des ventes,** sales promotion; **articles en p.,** items on offer *or* on promotion; **notre p. de la semaine,** this week's special offer; **faire de la p. immobilière,** to go in for property development.

promotionnel, -elle [prɔmosjɔnɛl] *adj* **(a)** *Com* **vente promotionnelle,** special offer; **(b) l'aspect p. d'une profession,** the promotion prospects in a profession.

promouvoir [prɔmuvwar] *vt* (*conj like* **mouvoir**) **(a)** (*donner un avancement*) to promote; **elle a été promue chef du personnel,** she's been promoted to personnel manager; *Fig* **p. les relations entre l'Est et l'Ouest,** to further *or* promote good relations between East and West; **(b)** *Com* to promote; (*à prix réduit*) to put (*sth*) on (special) offer.

prompt [prɔ̃] *adj* prompt, quick, swift (*reaction, condemnation*); **esprit p.,** quick mind; (*sens de l'humour*) ready wit; **être d'humeur prompte,** to be quick-tempered; **il est p. à la colère** *ou* **à se fâcher,** he loses his temper *or* flares up easily; **p. à agir,** quick to act; **avoir la main/repartie prompte,** to be quick to raise one's hand/to be quick with the answers, *Fml* to have a ready wit; **p. à la riposte,** prompt *or* quick in one's repartee; **prompte vengeance,** speedy *or* swift revenge; **nous vous souhaitons un p. rétablissement,** we wish you a speedy recovery.

promptement [prɔ̃tmɑ̃] *adv Litt* promptly, quickly.

prompteur ® [prɔ̃ptœr] *nm* teleprompt(er) ®, autocue ®.

promptitude [prɔ̃tityd] *nf Litt* promptness, quickness, swiftness (*of reaction etc*); (*vigilance*) alertness; **avec toute la p. possible,** with all possible dispatch.

promu, -ue [prɔmy] **1** *adj* (who has been) promoted. **2** *n* person who has been promoted; *Scol* **les nouveaux promus,** = this year's graduates (of a grande École).

promulgation [prɔmylgasjɔ̃] *nf* promulgation.

promulguer [prɔmylge] *vt* to promulgate (*law*); to publish, to issue (*decree*).

prône [pron] *nm Rel* sermon, homily.

prôner [prone] *vt* to praise, to extol; **dans cette situation je prône la patience,** I would strongly recommend *or* urge patience.

pronom [prɔnɔ̃] *nm Gram* pronoun.

pronominal, -aux [prɔnɔminal, -o] *adj Gram* pronominal.
pronominalement [prɔnɔminalmɑ̃] *adv* pronominally.
prononçable [prɔnɔ̃sabl] *adj* pronounceable.
prononcé [prɔnɔ̃se] **1** *adj* pronounced (*feature*); pronounced, decided, marked (*taste, feature etc*); **courbe prononcée,** sharp curve; **accent étranger très p.,** strong *or* marked foreign accent; **peu p.,** faint. **2** *nm Jur* decision; **p. du jugement,** verdict.
prononcer [prɔnɔ̃se] *v* (**je prononçai(s); n. prononçons**) **1** *vt* **(a)** to utter, to say (*word*); **sans p. un mot,** without (uttering) a word; **il a prononcé quelques mots entre ses dents,** he muttered a few words; **il ne faut jamais p. son nom,** you must never mention him *or* his name;
(b) (*déclarer*) to deliver, to make (*speech*); *Jur* **p. une sentence,** to pass *or* pronounce sentence; **p. un divorce,** to pronounce *or* declare a couple divorced;
(c) (*articuler, dire*) to pronounce (*word*); **mal p. un mot,** to mispronounce a word;
(d) (*marquer*) to make (*facial features*) more pronounced.
2 *vi* **(a)** (*articuler*) to pronounce (one's words); **apprendre à p.,** to learn to pronounce one's words properly, to learn proper pronunciation;
(b) (*s'exprimer*) to pronounce (**sur qch,** on sth); **p. en faveur de qn,** to decide *or* declare in favour of s.o.; **p. sur une question,** to adjudge *or* adjudicate a question.
3 se prononcer *vpr* **(a)** (*être articulé*) to be pronounced; **ça s'écrit comme ça se prononce,** it is written as it is pronounced; **cette lettre ne se prononce pas,** this letter is not pronounced;
(b) (*apparaître*) to become (more) pronounced; **leurs différences de caractère se prononcent,** their character differences are becoming more pronounced;
(c) (*s'exprimer*) to give an opinion *or* a decision; **le médecin ne s'est pas encore prononcé,** the doctor has not yet given his verdict.
prononciation [prɔnɔ̃sjasjɔ̃] *nf* **(a)** (*articulation*) pronunciation; **défaut de p.,** speech defect; **faute de p.,** mispronunciation; **système de p.,** pronunciation system; **(b)** delivery (*of speech*); *Jur* passing (*of sentence*).
pronostic [prɔnɔstik] *nm* **(a)** (*prévision*) forecast, prediction, *Fml* prognostication; **(b)** *Méd* prognosis.
pronostiquer [prɔnɔstike] *vt* **(a)** (*prévoir*) to forecast, to predict; *Fml* to prognosticate; **(b)** *Méd* **p. un prompt rétablissement,** to predict a speedy recovery; **p. au plus grave,** to give a very serious prognosis.
pronostiqueur, -euse [prɔnɔstikœr, -øz] *n* forecaster, pundit; *Sp* tipster.
pronunciamento [prɔnunsjamɛnto] *nm Pol* pronunciamento.
propagande [prɔpagɑ̃d] *nf* publicity; *Péj* propaganda; *Com* **faire de la p.,** to advertise.
propagandiste [prɔpagɑ̃dist] **1** *adj* propagandist, sloganeering. **2** *n* propagandist.
propagateur, -trice [prɔpagatœr, -tris] *n* propagator, spreader (*of news, disease etc*); disseminator (*of ideas*).
propagation [prɔpagasjɔ̃] *nf* spread(ing) (*of an epidemic*); propagation (*of rumour, new ideas*); dissemination (*of news, ideas*); *Phys* **la vitesse de p. d'une onde,** velocity of propagation of a wave; **p. d'une espèce,** propagation of a species.
propager [prɔpaʒe] *v* (**je propageai(s); n. propageons**) **1** *vt* to propagate (*plant, rumour*); to spread (*disease, rumour, news*); to disseminate (*ideas, news*); *Litt* to spread abroad; **p. une mode,** to spread *or* popularize a fashion. **2 se propager** *vpr* **(a)** (*of disease etc*) to spread; **(b)** (*of light, sound*) to be propagated; **(c)** *Biol* (*of plant etc*) to propagate, to reproduce.
propane [prɔpan] *nm Ch* propane.
propanier [prɔpanje] *nm Nau* propane tanker.
propédeutique [prɔpedøtik] *nf* **(a)** (*enseignement préparatoire*) propaedeutics; **(b)** *Vieilli* first year of university course.
propène [prɔpɛn] *nm Tech* propene.
propension [prɔpɑ̃sjɔ̃] *nf* propensity, tendency, inclination (**à,** to).
propergol [prɔpɛrgɔl] *nm Tech* (rocket) propellant.
prophase [prɔfɑz] *nf Biol* prophase.
prophète, prophétesse [prɔfɛt, prɔfetɛs] *n* prophet, *f* prophetess; *Litt* seer; **il a été bon p.,** his prophecy *or* prophecies turned out to be true *or* came true; **p. de malheur,** prophet of doom, Jeremiah.
prophétie [prɔfesi] *nf* prophecy.
prophétique [prɔfetik] *adj* prophetic(al).
prophétiquement [prɔfetikmɑ̃] *adv* prophetically.
prophétiser [prɔfetize] *vt* to prophesy, to foretell.
prophylactique [prɔfilaktik] *adj Méd* prophylactic.
prophylaxie [prɔfilaksi] *nf Méd* prophylaxis.
propice [prɔpis] *adj* propitious (**à,** to); auspicious (*sign, beginning*); favourable, *US* favorable (*conditions*); **né sous une étoile p.,** born under a lucky star; **peu p.,** unpropitious; inauspicious (*moment etc*); **si la fortune nous est p.,** if Fortune smiles on us.
propitiation [prɔpisjasjɔ̃] *nf Rel* propitiation.
propitiatoire [prɔpisjatwar] *adj Rel* propitiatory.
proportion [prɔpɔrsjɔ̃] *nf* **(a)** proportion; *Math* ratio; **la p. du tronc et des jambes,** the size of the trunk (as) compared with the legs; **varier en p. directe/inverse,** to vary in direct proportion *or* ratio/in indirect proportion *or* inverse ratio; **p. d'alcool dans un vin,** percentage of alcohol in a wine; **dans quelle p. faut-il ajouter le sel?,** in what proportions should salt be added?; **à p., en p. (de),** proportionally, proportionately, in proportion (to); **tout augmente, et les salaires à p.,** everything is going up, and salaries are keeping pace; **à p. que** + *ind*, as; **hors de (toute) p. avec,** out of (all) proportion to; *Fig* **cette dispute est sans p. avec son objet,** this argument is out of all proportion to the issue; **des travaux hors de p.,** roadworks of huge proportions; **défaut de p.,** disproportion (**entre,** between); **toute(s) proportion(s) gardée(s),** all things considered, making all due allowance;
(b) proportions, size, proportions; **salle de vastes proportions,** hall of vast proportions *or* dimensions; **dans de plus vastes proportions,** on a greater *or* wider scale; **si les commandes diminuent dans de sérieuses proportions,** if orders should decrease to any great extent.
proportionné [prɔpɔrsjɔne] *adj* **(a) bien p.,** well-proportioned (*body etc*); **(b)** proportionate, proportional (**à,** to); (*de la même échelle, du même degré*) commensurate (**à,** with); **la cotisation est proportionée à vos revenus,** payment is in proportion *or* proportional to your income; **salaire p. aux qualifications,** salary commensurate with qualifications.
proportionnel, -elle [prɔpɔrsjɔnɛl] **1** *adj* proportional (**à,** to); *Pol* **représentation proportionnelle,** proportional representation; *Ordinat* **espacement p.,** proportional spacing; **inversement p.,** inversely proportional, in inverse ratio (**à,** to); **impôt p. (au revenu),** fixed-rate *or* fixed-percentage income tax. **2** *nf* **proportionnelle (a)** *Math* proportional; **(b)** *Pol* proportional representation.
proportionnellement [prɔpɔrsjɔnɛlmɑ̃] *adv* proportionally, proportionately, in proportion (**à,** to).
proportionner [prɔpɔrsjɔne] *vt* to proportion, to adjust, to adapt (**à,** to).
propos [prɔpo] *nm* **(a)** subject, matter; **à ce p., à p.,** talking of that, in connection with that, while we're on the subject; **à p., avez-vous lu ce livre?,** by the way *or* that reminds me, have you read this book?; **à tout p.,** at every turn; **dire qch à p.,** to say sth to the point, to say sth suitable *or* appropriate; **mot jeté à p.,** timely word; **remarque faite à p.,** apt *or* relevant *or* pertinent *or* apposite remark; **faire qch à p.,** to do sth at the right moment; **arriver fort à p.,** to arrive at just the right moment *or* in the nick of time; **juger à p. de ...,** to consider it advisable to ..., to see fit to ...; **mal à p.,** at the wrong time *or* moment, inopportunely; **hors de p.,** ill-timed, irrelevant (*remark*); **c'était hors de p.,** it was out of place; **à p. de,** in connection with, with regard to, on the subject of, apropos of; **à p. de rien,** for nothing at all, for no reason whatever; **à p. de quoi?, à quel p.?,** what about?;
(b) (*intention*) purpose, intention, resolution; **avoir le ferme p. de faire qch,** to have the firm intention of doing sth, to be resolved to do sth; **de p. délibéré,** deliberately, on purpose;
(c) (*parole*) remark; **des p.,** talk, words; **p. méchants/désagréables,** nasty/unpleasant remarks; **des p. de table,** table talk; **changer de p.,** to change the subject.
proposer [prɔpoze] **1** *vt* to propose, to suggest (*plan*); to propose, to propound (*theory*); to propose, to move, to put forward (*amendment*); **p. une définition pour un mot,** to suggest a definition for a word; **p. qn comme modèle,** to hold *or* set s.o. up as a model; **p. de l'argent à qn,** to offer s.o. money; **être proposé pour un emploi,** to be suggested *or* proposed *or* recommended for a job; **p. un candidat,** to put forward *or* put up *or* propose a candidate; **p. que l'on fasse qch,** to propose *or* suggest that sth should be done; **je propose que nous commencions par le problème du Brésil,** (*en ouverture de discours*) I propose to start with the

problem of Brazil; **je lui ai proposé de le faire,** I proposed *or* suggested that he (should) do it.

2 *vi* to propose; **je le laisse p.,** I leave him to make the suggestions; **l'homme propose et Dieu dispose,** man proposes and God disposes.

3 se proposer *vpr* **(a)** (*se présenter*) to propose oneself, to come forward, to offer one's services; **se p. comme secrétaire,** to offer to act as secretary;

(b) se p. qch, to have sth in view; **il s'est proposé cet objectif,** he set himself this objective; **se p. de faire qch,** to mean *or* intend *or* propose to do sth.

proposition [prɔpozisjɔ̃] *nf* **(a)** proposal, proposition; offer (*to give, buy sth*); **faire une p.,** to make a proposal; (*in an assembly*) to put *or* propose a motion; **faire des propositions à une femme,** to proposition a woman; **mettre une p. aux voix,** to put a motion to the vote; **propositions de paix,** peace proposals; **(b)** *Phil Math etc* proposition; **(c)** *Gram* clause.

propre [prɔpr] **1** *adj* **(a)** (*exact*) proper; **signification p. d'un mot,** proper meaning of a word; **chercher le mot p.,** to try to find the exact word *or* the mot juste; **dans votre p. intérêt,** in your own interest; **ce sont là ses propres paroles,** these are his very words;

(b) (*particulier*) peculiar, proper (**à,** to); **une façon de marcher à lui p.,** his own particular *or* characteristic way of walking;

(c) *Phys* **fréquence p.,** natural frequency;

(d) (*personnel*) own; **mon p. argent,** my own money; **ses idées lui sont propres,** his ideas are his own; **voir avec ses propres yeux,** to see with one's own eyes; **je le lui ai remis en main(s) propre(s),** I delivered it to him personally; **à remettre en main p.,** to be delivered to the addressee in person;

(e) (*convenable*) appropriate, suitable, proper, fit(ting); **p. à qch,** adapted *or* fitted *or* suited to sth; **l'endroit le plus p. au camping,** the best *or* most suitable place for camping; **exercice p. à aiguiser l'intelligence,** exercise calculated to sharpen the wits; **p. à tout,** fit for anything; **p. à rien,** good for nothing;

(f) (*impeccable*) clean; neat (*desk, appearance*); (*soigné, bien présenté*) neat, tidy (*work*); (*non polluant*) clean, non-polluting (*engine, car*); **une énergie p.,** a clean form of energy; **chambre p. et nette,** clean and tidy room; **je n'ai plus rien de p.,** I haven't (got) anything clean left to wear; **p. comme un sou neuf,** as clean as a new pin, *F* spick and span; **être p. sur soi,** to be clean, to have clean habits; *F* **nous voilà propres!,** we're in a nice mess!; **le chat est très p.,** the cat is a very clean animal; **mon bébé était p. à vingt mois,** my baby was dry at twenty months; **cette copie n'est pas très p.,** this isn't a very clean copy;

(g) *Fig* spotless (*reputation*); clear (*conscience*); **ce n'est pas p., ces affaires,** there's something shady *or* not quite kosher about the business; **ce n'est pas très p. tout ça,** (*du point de vue moral*) that's a bit tacky.

2 *nm* **(a)** property, attribute, characteristic (*of nation, person etc*); (*caractère, nature*) nature; **le p. de l'homme,** man's distinguishing feature;

(b) au p., in the literal sense; **employer un mot au p.,** to use a word in its literal sense *or* literally;

(c) avoir qch en p., to possess sth in one's own right; **la maison m'appartient en p.,** the house is mine, the house belongs to me; **il a un exemplaire en p.,** he has a copy of his own;

(d) *Scol* **passer au p.,** to make a neat copy of sth, to copy sth out neatly; **recopier son devoir au p.,** to make a fair copy of an exercise, to copy an exercise (neatly);

(e) c'est du p.!, what a mess!

propre(-)à(-)rien [prɔprarjɛ̃] *n* good-for-nothing, ne'er-do-well; (*pl propres(-)à(-)rien*).

proprement [prɔprəmɑ̃] *adv* **(a)** (*d'une manière propre*) cleanly; **une maison p. tenue,** a house that is kept clean (and tidy); **manger p.,** not to make a mess when eating; **(b)** *F* (*convenablement*) well; (*de façon efficace*) efficiently; **assez p.,** tolerably well; **(c)** (*avec honnêteté*) fairly, decently; **se tirer d'affaire p.,** to get out of a difficult situation with one's honour *or US* honor intact; **(d) à p. parler,** strictly speaking; **pas à p. parler,** not exactly; **p. dit,** actual; **pierres précieuses p. dites,** precious stones according to the strictest definition of the term; **(e)** (*strictement*) strictly (speaking); **cette maison lui appartient p.,** this house is his and his alone.

propret, -ette [prɔprɛ, -ɛt] *adj* neat, tidy.

propreté [prɔprəte] *nf* **(a)** (*hygiène, soin*) cleanliness; cleanness (*of clothes, crockery*); neatness, tidiness (*of room, work*); **produits pour la p. de la maison,** household cleansers; *Nau* **postes de p.,** cleaning stations; **(b)** (*de moteur etc*) cleanness.

propriétaire [prɔprietɛr] *n* **(a)** owner (*of car, property etc*); proprietor, *f* proprietress (*of business, hotel*); **se rendre p. de qch,** to acquire sth; **p. (de maison),** householder; **qui est le p. de cette terre?,** who owns this land?; **p. foncier,** landowner; **être p.,** to be a man of property *or* a landowner; (*de maison*) to be a property owner, to have a house of one's own; **(b)** (*qui loue*) landlord, *f* landlady.

propriété [prɔpriete] *nf* **(a)** ownership, proprietorship; (*chose possédée*) property; (*terres*) property, estate; **p. privée/publique,** private/public property; **p. foncière (perpétuelle et) libre,** freehold; **titres de p.,** title deeds; **p. littéraire,** literary property; (*droit*) copyright; **p. industrielle,** patent rights; **p. foncière,** landed property, landed estate; **propriétés immobilières,** real estate, *surtout Am* realty; **(b)** property, characteristic, peculiar quality (*of metal, plant etc*); **(c)** propriety, correctness (*of language etc*).

proprio [prɔprio] *nm F* landlord.

propulser [prɔpylse] **1** *vt* to propel. **2 se propulser** *vpr F* to come; to go.

propulseur [prɔpylsœr] **1** *adj* propellent, propulsive, propelling; **gaz p.,** propellant, propellent. **2** *nm* **(a)** *Av etc* propeller; **p. à hélice,** screw propeller; **(b)** (*gaz*) propellant, propellent.

propulsif, -ive [prɔpylsif, -iv] *adj* = **PROPULSEUR 1.**

propulsion [prɔpylsjɔ̃] *nf* propulsion, propelling; **réacteur de p.,** propulsion jet; **sous-marin à p. nucléaire,** nuclear-powered submarine; **véhicule à p. électrique,** electrically powered vehicle.

propylène [prɔpilɛn] *nm Ch* propylene.

pro rata [prɔrata] *nm inv* proportional part, proportion; **paiement au p. r.,** payment pro rata; **au p. r. de qch,** in proportion to sth.

prorogatif, -ive [prɔrɔgatif, -iv] *adj* proroguing.

prorogation [prɔrɔgasjɔ̃] *nf* **(a)** *surtout Jur* extension of time; **(b)** prorogation (*of parliament*).

proroger [prɔrɔʒe] *vt* **(je prorogeai(s); n. prorogeons) (a)** to extend (*time limit*); **(b)** to prorogue, to adjourn (*parliament*).

prosaïque [prozaik] *adj* prosaic, commonplace, pedestrian.

prosaïquement [prozaikmɑ̃] *adv* prosaically.

prosaïsme [prozaism] *nm* prosaic nature *or* quality, prosaicness.

prosateur [prozatœr] *nm* prose writer.

proscenium [prɔsenjɔm] *nm Th* **(a)** *Antiq* proscenium (arch); **(b)** (*avant-scène*) proscenium, apron.

proscription [prɔskripsjɔ̃] *nf* proscription (*of s.o., sth*); outlawing, banishment, exile (*of s.o.*); forbidding, condemning (*of sth*).

proscrire [prɔskrir] *vt* (*conj like* **écrire**) to proscribe (*s.o., sth*); to outlaw, to banish, to exile (*s.o.*); to forbid, to condemn (*sth*); **p. qn de la société,** to proscribe *or* ostracize s.o. from society.

proscrit, -ite [prɔskri, -it] **1** *adj* proscribed. **2** *n* outlaw.

prose [proz] *nf* prose; **en p.,** in prose; **poème en p.,** prose poem; *F* **j'ai lu sa p.,** I've read his (piece of) nonsense.

prosélyte [prɔzelit] *n* proselyte; *Fig* convert; *Fig* **faire des prosélytes,** to make *or* gain converts.

prosélytisme [prɔzelitism] *nm* proselytism, proselytizing.

prosodie [prɔzɔdi] *nf* prosody.

prosodique [prɔzɔdik] *adj* prosodic.

prospect [prɔspɛ] *nm* prospective customer, prospect.

prospecter [prɔspɛkte] *vt* **(a)** *Min* to prospect; **(b)** *Com* to canvass.

prospecteur, -trice [prɔspɛktœr, -tris] *n* **(a)** *Min* prospector; **(b)** *Com* canvasser.

prospectif, -ive [prɔspɛktif, -iv] *adj* prospective; **analyse prospective,** (*en affaires*) forecast.

prospection [prɔspɛksjɔ̃] *nf* **(a)** *Min* prospecting; **(b)** canvassing.

prospectus [prɔspɛktys] *nm* **(a)** prospectus; **(b)** (*de publicité*) handbill, leaflet; (*avec plusieurs pages*) brochure.

prospère [prɔspɛr] *adj* prosperous, thriving, flourishing; **les années prospères de sa vie,** the prosperous period in his life.

prospérer [prɔspere] *vi* **(je prospère; je prospérerai)** to prosper, to thrive, to flourish, to do well.

prospérité [prɔsperite] *nf* prosperity, prosperousness; *Com* **vague de p.,** boom; **cette industrie est en pleine p.,** the industry is thriving.

prostaglandine [prɔstaglɑ̃din] *nf Méd* prostaglandin.

prostate [prɔstat] *nf Anat* prostate (gland).
prostatique [prɔstatik] **1** *adj Anat* prostatic. **2** *nm* prostate sufferer.
prostatite [prɔstatit] *nf Méd* prostatitis.
prosternation [prɔstɛrnɑsjɔ̃] *nf Litt* prostration; *Fig Péj* grovelling, kowtowing.
prosterné [prɔstɛrne] *adj* prostrate.
prosternement [prɔstɛrnəmɑ̃] *nm* prostration; (*état*) prostrate attitude.
prosterner [prɔstɛrne] **1** *vt* to bend, to bow (*head etc*). **2 se prosterner** *vpr* (*se courber*) to prostrate oneself (**devant,** before); *Fig Péj* (*s'abaisser*) to grovel, to kowtow (**devant,** to).
prostituée [prɔstitɥe] *nf* prostitute.
prostituer [prɔstitɥe] **1** *vt* to prostitute (*person, talent etc*). **2 se prostituer** *vpr* to prostitute oneself.
prostitution [prɔstitysjɔ̃] *nf* prostitution; *Fig* **c'est de la p.,** (*ton attitude*) you're just prostituting yourself.
prostration [prɔstrɑsjɔ̃] *nf* **(a)** prostration; **(b)** *Méd* (nervous) exhaustion.
prostré [prɔstre] *adj* prostrate(d); (*épuisé*) exhausted; *Fig* **notre économie est prostrée,** our economy is on its knees.
protagoniste [prɔtagɔnist] *nm* protagonist.
prote [prɔt] *nm Typ* foreman, overseer.
protecteur, -trice [prɔtɛktœr, -tris] **1** *n* **(a)** (*personne*) protector, *f* protectress; *Can Admin* **Bureau du p. du citoyen,** Office of the Ombudsman; *Vieilli* **cet homme est son p.,** this man is her protector; **(b)** patron, *f* patroness (*of the arts etc*). **2** *nm* protector, shield; guard (*for machine tool etc*). **3** *adj* protective (*device, tariff etc*); patronizing (*tone etc*); **société protectrice des animaux,** = society for the prevention of cruelty to animals; **des mesures économiques protectrices,** measures designed to protect the economy.
protection [prɔtɛksjɔ̃] *nf* **(a)** protection (**contre,** from, against); protection, conservation (*of the environment etc*); **p. civile,** civil defence; **p. de l'enfance,** child welfare; **sous la p. de la police,** under police protection; **dispositif de p.,** safety device, protective device; **écran/visière de p.,** protective screen/visor; *Can Admin* **Commissaire à la p. de la vie privée,** Privacy Commissioner; **(b)** patronage; (*mécénat*) patronage, sponsorship (*of the arts etc*); **prendre qn sous sa p.,** to take s.o. under one's wing; *Péj* **par p.,** through influence; **(c)** *Écon Pol* protection(ism).
protectionnisme [prɔtɛksjɔnism] *nm Écon* protection(ism).
protectionniste [prɔtɛksjɔnist] *adj & n* protectionist.
protectorat [prɔtɛktɔra] *nm* protectorate.
protégé, -ée [prɔteʒe] **1** *adj* protected; *Aut* **'passage p.',** priority (over vehicles entering from minor road ahead). **2** *n* (*jeune artiste, sportif etc*) protégé, *f* protégée.
protège-cahier [prɔtɛʒkaje] *nm* exercise-book cover; (*pl protège-cahiers*).
protège-dents [prɔtɛʒdɑ̃] *nm inv Boxe* gum shield.
protéger [prɔteʒe] *v* (**je protège, n. protégeons; je protégeai(s); je protégerai**) **1** *vt* **(a)** to protect, to shelter, to shield, to guard (**contre,** against, from); **p. un peuple contre l'adversaire,** to protect a nation against the enemy; **les verres fumés protègent bien les yeux,** tinted lenses offer good protection for the eyes; **cette combinaison vous protègera de tout germe,** these overalls will protect you from any germs; **p. les droits acquis,** to protect *or* defend hard-won rights;
(b) *Écon* to protect (*industry etc*); to give (*s.o.*) one's support;
(c) to patronize, to be a patron of (*the arts etc*); **on la protège en haut-lieu,** she has friends in high places.
2 se protéger *vpr* **se p. de,** to protect oneself from (*sth*); to guard against (*disease, over-confidence*); **se p. contre les intempéries/du soleil,** to protect oneself against bad weather/the sun's rays.
protège-tibia [prɔtɛʒtibja] *nm Sp* shin guard; (*pl protège-tibias*).
protège-tympan [prɔtɛʒtɛ̃pɑ̃] *nm inv* earplug(s).
protéiforme [prɔteifɔrm] *adj Litt* protean (*organisms*); ever-changing (*moods, opinions etc*).
protéine [prɔtein] *nf* protein; **surveiller les protéines dans son alimentation,** to watch one's protein intake; **alimentation faible en protéines,** food that is low in protein, low-protein food.
protéique [prɔteik] *adj Ch* protein(ic).
protestable [prɔtestabl] *adj Jur* which may be protested.
protestant, -ante [prɔtɛstɑ̃, -ɑ̃t] *adj & n Rel* Protestant.
protestantisme [prɔtɛstɑ̃tism] *nm Rel* Protestantism; (*ensemble des protestants*) (the) Protestant churches, (the) Protestant community.
protestataire [prɔtɛstatɛr] **1** *adj* (*letter etc*) of protest. **2** *n* protester, protestor.
protestation [prɔtɛstɑsjɔ̃] *nf* **(a)** (*affirmation*) protestation, declaration, affirmation; **faire une p.** *ou* **des protestations de son innocence,** to protest *or* declare one's innocence; **(b)** (*reproche, déclaration opposée*) protest; **faire une p. contre qch,** to make a protest *or* to protest about *or* against sth, *Am* to protest sth; **élever des protestations énergiques,** to raise a strong protest; **voulez-vous signer notre p.?,** will you sign our protest?; **réunion de p.,** protest meeting.
protester [prɔtɛste] **1** *vt* **(a)** (*affirmer*) to protest, to declare; **(b)** *Jur* to protest (*bill*). **2** *vi* to protest; **je proteste!,** I protest!; **p. de son innocence,** to protest one's innocence; **p. contre qch,** (*en manifestant*) to protest *or* make a protest about *or* against sth, *Am* to protest sth; (*devant la justice*) to challenge (*ruling*); **elle a protesté auprès du directeur,** she complained to the manager.
protêt [prɔtɛ] *nm Com Jur* protest; **dresser un p.,** to make a protest.
prothèse [prɔtɛz] *nf* **(a)** *Chir* prosthetics, prosthesis; **(b) (appareil de) p.,** prosthesis; **p. dentaire,** (*complet*) false teeth, denture(s); (*partiel*) bridge; *Spéc* dental prosthesis.
prothésiste [prɔtezist] *n* prosthesis maker.
protide [prɔtid] *nm* protein.
protocolaire [prɔtɔkɔlɛr] *adj* formal, pertaining to protocol *or* etiquette; **clauses protocolaires d'accord,** formal provisions of agreement.
protocole [prɔtɔkɔl] *nm* **(a)** (*procédés diplomatiques*) protocol; (*usage*) etiquette, formalities, social conventions; **le chef du p.,** the chief of protocol; **(b)** *Typ* list of proofreading symbols.
proto-étoile [prɔtɔetwal] *nf Astron* protostar.
protohistoire [prɔtɔistwar] *nf* protohistory.
proton [prɔtɔ̃] *nm Nucl* proton.
protoplasma [prɔtɔplasma] *nm,* **protoplasme** [prɔtɔplasm] *nm Biol* protoplasm.
prototype [prɔtɔtip] *nm* prototype.
protoxyde [prɔtɔksid] *nm Ch* monoxide; **p. d'azote,** nitrous oxide.
protozoaire [prɔtɔzɔɛr] *nm Zool* protozoan, protozoon; **les protozoaires,** the Protozoa.
protractile [prɔtraktil] *adj* protractile.
protrusion [prɔtryzjɔ̃] *nf* protrusion.
protubérance [prɔtyberɑ̃s] *nf* protuberance; knob (*on stick etc*); *Anat* bump (*on the skull*); *Astron* (solar) prominence.
protubérant [prɔtyberɑ̃] *adj* protuberant.
protuteur, -trice [prɔtytœr, -tris] *n Jur* acting guardian (*of minor*).
prou [pru] *adv* **peu ou p.,** more or less; (*pas beaucoup*) not much; not many.
proue [pru] *nf* prow, stem, bow(s) (*of ship*).
prouesse [pruɛs] *nf* **(a)** *Litt* (*acte*) prowess, valour, *US* valor; **(b)** feat, achievement (*in sport etc*); *Iron* **quelle p!,** that's quite *or* what a feat *or* an achievement!
prouvable [pruvabl] *adj* provable; **c'est facilement p.,** it's easy to prove.
prouver [pruve] **1** *vt* **(a)** (*établir comme vrai*) to prove (*fact*); **la police n'a rien pu p.,** the police couldn't prove anything; **p. le bien-fondé d'une réclamation,** to substantiate a claim, to make good one's claim; **(b)** (*être la preuve de*) **p. sa capacité,** to prove *or* show one's ability, to give *or* show proof of one's ability. **2 se prouver** *vpr* **(a)** to prove to oneself; **que cherche-t-il à se p.?,** what's he trying to prove to himself?; **(b)** (*à qn*) **nous nous sommes prouvé que les deux versions étaient correctes,** we proved to each other that both versions were correct; **(c)** (*qui peut être prouvé*) **ça ne se prouve pas,** (*c'est une intuition*) you can't prove it, it's not the sort of thing you can prove.
provenance [prɔvnɑ̃s] *nf* source, origin; **de p. anglaise,** of English origin, English in origin; **pays de p.,** country of origin; **train en p. de Bordeaux,** train from Bordeaux.
provençal, -ale, -aux [prɔvɑ̃sal, -o] **1** *adj* Provençal, of Provence. **2** *nm Ling* Provençal. **3** *n* **P.,** person from Provence.
provende [prɔvɑ̃d] *nf* (*pour élevage*) provender, fodder.
provenir [prɔvnir] *vi* (*conj like* **venir**) to proceed, to result, to arise, to come, to derive, to be derived (**de,** from); (*tirer son origine*) to originate (**de,** in); **des produits provenant du Japon,** products from Japan; **les difficultés qui proviennent de cette situation,** the difficulties arising from the situation; *Jur* **les enfants provenant** *ou*

provenus de ce mariage, the children issuing from this marriage, the children of this marriage.

proverbe [prɔvɛrb] *nm* proverb; **passer en p.,** to become a proverb.

proverbial, -aux [prɔvɛrbjal, -o] *adj* proverbial; **une femme d'une beauté proverbiale,** a woman of legendary beauty.

proverbialement [prɔvɛrbjalmɑ̃] *adv* proverbially.

providence [prɔvidɑ̃s] *nf* providence; **c'est un secret de la p.,** it's in the hands of providence; **être la p. de qn,** to be s.o.'s guardian angel; **l'État P.,** the Welfare State.

providentiel, -elle [prɔvidɑ̃sjɛl] *adj* providential; **par une circonstance providentielle,** by an act of providence.

providentiellement [prɔvidɑ̃sjɛlmɑ̃] *adv* providentially.

provignage [prɔviɲaʒ] *nm,* **provignement** [prɔviɲmɑ̃] *nm* layering (of vine).

provigner [prɔviɲe] *vt* to layer (*vine*).

provin [prɔvɛ̃] *nm* layered branch, stock.

province [prɔvɛ̃s] **1** *nf* **(a) la p.,** the provinces; (*la campagne*) the country; **sa p. (d'origine),** the part of the country where he was born; **vivre en p.,** to live in the provinces; **vie de p.,** provincial life, life in the provinces; *Péj* **mentalité de p.,** small-town *or* provincial mentality; **cousin de p.,** country cousin; **aller en p.,** to leave town; **(b)** *Admin* province; *Can Géog* **les Provinces Maritimes,** the Maritime Provinces, *F* the Maritimes; **(c)** *Rel* **p. ecclésiastique,** (ecclesiastical) province. **2** *adj inv F Péj* provincial, parochial.

provincial, -ale, -aux [prɔvɛ̃sjal, -o] **1** *adj* provincial; **la vie provinciale,** provincial life, life in the provinces; *Péj* provincial, countrified (*manners etc*); provincial, parochial (*outlook*); **manières provinciales,** small-town *or* provincial ways. **2** *n* provincial. **3** *nm Rel* provincial.

provincialisme [prɔvɛ̃sjalism] *nm Ling* provincialism.

proviseur [prɔvizœr] *nm Scol* headmaster (*of a lycée*).

provision [prɔvizjɔ̃] *nf* **(a)** provision, store, stock, supply; **faire p. de charbon,** to lay in a stock of coal; *Vieilli* **provisions de bouche,** food; **placard à provisions,** food cupboard; **provisions de guerre,** munitions; **faire ses provisions,** to go shopping; **sac à provisions,** shopping bag; **(b)** *Com* funds, cover, reserve, margin; **verser une p.** *ou* **des provisions,** to pay a deposit; **faire p. pour une lettre de change,** to provide for a bill; **insuffisance de p.,** insufficient funds (*to meet cheque etc*); **chèque sans p.,** bad *or F* dud *or Sl* rubber cheque, cheque that bounced; **faire un chèque sans p.,** to write out a dud cheque; **il m'a fait un chèque sans p.,** his cheque bounced; **par p.,** provisionally; **(c)** *Jur* retaining fee (*paid to lawyer*).

provisionnel, -elle [prɔvizjɔnɛl] *adj Jur* provisional (*division of estate etc*); **tiers p.,** = one third of income tax paid in advance.

provisoire [prɔvizwar] **1** *adj* provisional; *Fml* provisory; temporary (*halt, arrangement etc*); **nommé à titre p.,** appointed provisionally; **dividende p.,** interim dividend; **habitation p.,** emergency *or* temporary accommodation; *Jur* **détention p.,** (temporary) custody; *Jur* **être en liberté p.,** to be on bail, to have been released on bail. **2** *nm* something temporary; **s'installer dans le p.,** to treat something temporary as permanent; **ça n'est que du p.,** it's only temporary, it's only for the time being.

provisoirement [prɔvizwarmɑ̃] *adv* provisionally, temporarily.

provitamine [prɔvitamin] *nf Biol Ch* provitamin.

provocant [prɔvɔkɑ̃] *adj* **(a)** (*agressif*) provocative, aggressive (*language etc*); **(b)** provocative, tantalizing, alluring (*smile etc*).

provocateur, -trice [prɔvɔkatœr, -tris] **1** *adj* provocative; **agent p.,** agent provocateur. **2** *n* **(a)** (*agresseur*) aggressor; **(b)** instigator (*of disturbance etc*).

provocation [prɔvɔkasjɔ̃] *nf* **(a)** (*défi*) provocation; **lancer des provocations à qn,** to hurl defiance at s.o.; **c'est de la p.!,** it's (a) deliberate provocation!; **p. en duel,** challenge to a duel; **(b)** *Jur* instigation; **p. au crime,** incitement to crime.

provoquer [prɔvɔke] *vt* **(a)** (*défier*) to provoke (*s.o.*); (*sexuellement*) to lead (*s.o.*) on; **p. qn en duel,** to challenge s.o. to a duel; **(b)** (*inciter*) to induce, to instigate; **p. qn au crime,** to incite s.o. to crime; **p. les jeunes à la violence,** to incite young people to violence *or* to act violently; **(c)** to cause, to bring about (*desired result etc*); to provoke, to give rise to (*criticism etc*); to provoke, to produce (*response*); **p. un courant d'air,** to create a draught; **p. le sommeil/la sueur,** to induce sleep/perspiration; **p. la curiosité,** to arouse curiosity; **p. la gaieté,** to cause *or* provoke cheerfulness; **p. un sourire,** to raise a smile.

proxénète [prɔksenɛt] *n Jur* procurer, *f* procuress; *Litt & Arch* pander.

proxénétisme [prɔksenetism] *nm* pimping; *Jur* procuring.

proximité [prɔksimite] *nf* proximity, nearness, closeness; imminence, proximity (*of event*); **la p. de la ville,** the proximity of the town; **à p.,** near at hand, close by; **à p. de qch,** close to sth, in the vicinity of sth; **p. de parenté,** near relationship.

proyer [prwaje] *nm* (*oiseau*) **(bruant) p.,** bunting.

prude [pryd] *Péj* **1** *adj* prudish. **2** *nf* prude; **ne fais pas la p.!,** don't be such a prude!

prudemment [prydamɑ̃] *adv* prudently, carefully, cautiously.

prudence [prydɑ̃s] *nf* prudence, carefulness, cautiousness, caution; prudence, wisdom (*of decision etc*); **agir avec p.,** to act prudently; **une p. forte bien pensée,** a prudent, well thought-out action; *Prov* **p. est mère de sûreté,** discretion is the better part of valour.

prudent [prydɑ̃] *adj* prudent, careful, cautious (*person etc*); prudent, wise, well advised (*decision etc*); prudent, advisable (*course of action*); **vous avez raison, c'est plus p.,** you're right, it's safer *or* more sensible; **il faut être très p. en ...,** the greatest care must be taken in ...

pruderie [prydri] *nf Péj* prudery, prudishness.

prud'homme [prydɔm] *nm* **conseil des prud'hommes,** conciliation board (*in industrial disputes*); **aller devant les prud'hommes,** ≈ to go to an industrial tribunal.

prudhommerie [prydɔmri] *nf Péj* pomposity, sententiousness.

pruine [prɥin] *nf* bloom (*on fruit*).

prune [pryn] **1** *nf* (*fruit*) plum; **p. de Damas,** damson; **verre de p.,** a glass of plum brandy; *Fig F* **pour des prunes,** for nothing; *Fig F* **des prunes!,** no fear!, not (bloody) likely! **2** *adj inv* plum(-coloured, *US* -colored).

pruneau, -eaux [pryno] *nm* **(a)** (*fruit*) prune; **(b)** *Arg* (rifle) bullet.

prunelle [prynɛl] *nf* **(a)** (*fruit*) sloe; **(liqueur de) p.,** sloe gin; **(b)** *Anat* pupil (*of the eye*); *Fig* **comme la p. de ses yeux,** like the apple of one's eye; **j'y tiens comme à la p. de mes yeux,** it's the apple of my eye, it's my pride and joy; *F* **jouer de la p.,** to flutter one's eyelashes.

prunellier [prynelje] *nm* blackthorn, sloe (bush).

prunier [prynje] *nm* plum tree; *F* **secouer qn comme un p.,** to give s.o. a good shaking; *Fig* to give s.o. a good telling off.

prunus [prynys] *nm* (*arbre*) prunus, Japanese flowering cherry.

prurigineux, -euse [pryriʒinø, -øz] *adj Méd* pruritic.

prurit [pryrit] *nm Méd* pruritus.

Prusse [prys] *nf Hist* Prussia; **bleu de P.,** Prussian blue; *Fig F* **travailler pour le roi de P.,** to work for nothing *or* for peanuts.

prussiate [prysjat] *nm Ch* cyanide.

prussien, -ienne [prysjɛ̃, -jɛn] *Hist* **1** *adj* Prussian. **2** *n* **P.,** Prussian.

prytanée [pritane] *nm* military school (for sons of officers).

P.S. [peɛs] **(a)** (*abrév* **post-scriptum**) P.S.; **(b)** (*abrév* **Parti socialiste**) Socialist Party.

psallette [psalɛt] *nf* choir school.

psalmiste [psalmist] *nm* psalmist.

psalmodie [psalmɔdi] *nf* **(a)** *Rel* psalmody; **(b)** (*déclamation, formule monotone*) droning.

psalmodier [psalmɔdje] *v* (*pr sub & impf* **n. psalmodiions, v. psalmodiiez**) **1** *vt* **(a)** *Rel* to intone, to chant (*office etc*); **(b)** (*dire avec monotonie*) to drone out (*sth*), to recite (*sth*) monotonously. **2** *vi* **(a)** *Rel* to intone, to chant; **(b)** (*parler avec monotonie*) to drone (on, away).

psaltérion [psalterjɔ̃] *nm Mus* psaltery.

psaume [psom] *nm* psalm.

psautier [psotje] *nm* psalter, psalm book.

pseudo- [psødo] *préf* pseudo; **des p.-intellectuels,** pseudo-intellectuals.

pseudo-membrane [psødɔmɑ̃bran] *nf Méd* pseudomembrane, false membrane; (*pl pseudo-membranes*).

pseudonyme [psødɔnim] *nm* pseudonym, assumed name; (*pour un écrivain*) pseudonym; **elle a pris un p.,** (*cette écrivain*) she writes under a pseudonym.

pseudo-rubis [psødɔrybi] *nm inv Minér* rose quartz.

pseudo-saphir [psødɔsafir] *nm Minér* blue quartz; (*pl pseudo- saphirs*).

psi [psi] *nm* psi.

psitt [psit] *int* psst!

psittacose [psitakoz] *nf Méd Vét* psittacosis.
psoriasis [psjɔrazis] *nf Méd* psoriasis.
pst [pst] *int* psst!
psy [psi] *F* **1** *adj* = **psychiatrique**; **psychologique**; **psychanalytique.** **2** *nf* = **psychiatrie**; **psychologie**; **psychanalyse.** **3** *n* (*psychologue, psychanalyste*) shrink.
psychanalyse [psikanaliz] *nf* psychoanalysis; **être en p.,** to be in *or* undergoing (psycho)analysis.
psychanalyser [psikanalize] *vt* to psychoanalyse; **p. des rêves/des lettres,** to (psycho)analyse dreams/letters.
psychanalyste [psikanalist] *n* psychoanalyst.
psychanalytique [psikanalitik] *adj* psychoanalytic(al).
psyché [psiʃe] *nf* **(a)** *Myth* **P.,** Psyche; **(b)** *Phil* psyche; **(c)** (*miroir*) cheval glass, swing mirror.
psychédélique [psikedelik] *adj* psychedelic; *F* **la mode p.,** the fashion for psychedelia.
psychiatre [psikjatr] *n* psychiatrist.
psychiatrie [psikjatri] *nf* psychiatry.
psychiatrique [psikjatrik] *adj* psychiatric; mental (*hospital etc*).
psychique [psiʃik] *adj* psychic.
psychisme [psiʃism] *nm* psyche, inner mind.
psycho [psiko] *nf* = **PSYCHOLOGIE**.
psychodrame [psikɔdram] *nm* psychodrama.
psychologie [psikɔlɔʒi] *nf* psychology; **tu manques de p.,** you're not much of a psychologist, you don't have much idea of how people's minds work; **la p. des descriptions chez Proust,** the psychological insights offered by Proust's descriptions; **une p. très fragile,** a very fragile personality.
psychologique [psikɔlɔʒik] *adj* (*roman, film etc*) psychological; **le moment p.,** the psychological moment.
psychologiquement [psikɔlɔʒikmɑ̃] *adv* psychologically.
psychologue [psikɔlɔg] **1** *n* psychologist. **2** *adj* **elle n'est pas très p.,** she's not much of a psychologist, she doesn't understand how people's minds work.
psychonévrose [psikɔnevroz] *nf* psychoneurosis.
psychopathe [psikɔpat] *n Vieilli* psychopath.
psychopathie [psikɔpati] *nf Vieilli* psychopathy.
psychopathologie [psikɔpatɔlɔʒi] *adj* psychopathology.
psychopédagogie [psikɔpedagɔʒi] *nf* application of experimental psychology to education.
psychopharmacologie [psikɔfarmakɔlɔʒi] *nf* psychopharmacology.
psychophysiologie [psikɔfizjɔlɔʒi] *nf* psychophysiology.
psychose [psikoz] *nf* **(a)** *Psy* psychosis; **p. traumatique,** shellshock; **(b)** (*obsession*) obsession; **p. de guerre,** fear of war.
psychosociologie [psikɔsɔsjɔlɔʒi] *nf* social psychology.
psychosomatique [psikɔsɔmatik] *adj Méd* psychosomatic.
psychotechnique [psikɔteknik] **1** *adj* psychotechnical. **2** *nf* psychotechnology, psychotechnics.
psychothérapeute [psikɔterapøt] *n* psychotherapist.
psychothérapie [psikɔterapi] *nf* (psycho)therapy; **p. analytique,** analytical (psycho)therapy; **p. familiale,** family therapy; **faire de la p. de groupe,** to go to *or* do group therapy.
psychothérapique [psikɔterapik] *adj* psychotherapeutic; **intervention p.,** psychotherapeutic treatment.
psychotique [psikɔtik] *adj & n* psychotic.
psychotonique [psikɔtɔnik] *adj Pharm* psychoactive, psychotropic.
psychotrope [psikɔtrɔp] *nm Pharm* psychotropic drug.
psychromètre [psikrɔmɛtr] *nm Météo* psychrometer.
ptérodactyle [pterɔdaktil] *nm* pterodactyl.
ptérosaurien [pterɔsɔrjɛ̃] *nm* pterosaur.
Ptolémée [ptɔleme] *nm Antiq* Ptolemy; *Astron* **système de P.,** Ptolemaic system.
ptomaïne [ptɔmain] *nf Bio Ch* ptomaine.
P.T.T. [petete] *nfpl* (*abrév* **Poste, Télécommunications et Télédiffusion**) Post Office.
puant [pɥɑ̃] *adj* **(a)** (*qui sent mauvais*) stinking, foul-smelling; *Ch F* **gaz p.,** hydrogen sulphide; *F* stink bomb gas; **boule puante,** stink bomb; **(b)** *Fig* (*odieux*) (offensively) pretentious, conceited.
puanteur [pɥɑ̃tœr] *nf* stink, stench.
pub¹ [pyb] *nf F* **(a)** (*publicité*) publicity; *Com* advertising; **faire de la p.,** to advertise; (*comme profession*) to be in advertising; **faire de la p. pour un savon,** (*d'un acteur*) to advertise a soap; (*d'une agence*) to do the advertising for a soap; **faire de la p. pour une société internationale,** to do (the) advertising for an international company; **une agence de p.,** an ad(vertising) agency; **(b)** *TV Rad* ad(vert), commercial; *Journ* ad(vert); *TV* **regarder les pubs à la télévision,** to watch the TV ads *or* the ads *or* commercials on television.
pub² [pœb] *nm* pub.
pubère [pybɛr] *adj* pubescent.
puberté [pybɛrte] *nf* puberty.
pubescent [pybesɑ̃] *adj Bot* pubescent, downy.
pubien, -ienne [pybjɛ̃, -jɛn] *adj Anat* pubic.
pubis [pybis] *nm Anat* pubis, pubes; (*os*) pubic bone.
publiable [pybliabl] *adj* fit for publication.
public, -ique [pyblik] **1** *adj* public; public, open (to the public) (*meeting*); **la chose publique,** the public welfare; (*gouvernement*) state, government, commonwealth, *Fml* res publica; **service p.,** public utility (service), *Am* utility; **travailler pour le bien p.,** to work for the common good; **force publique,** (civil) police; **la dette publique,** the national debt; *Admin* **ministère p.,** = public prosecutor; **la voie publique,** the public highway; **il est de notoriété publique que ...,** it is public *or* common knowledge that ... .
2 *nm* **le p.,** the public; **'interdit au p.',** 'no admittance *or* admission to the public', 'keep out'; **le grand p.,** the general public; **un p. cultivé,** a cultured *or* an educated audience; (*lecteurs*) cultured *or* discerning readers; **cette chanteuse a encore son p.,** this singer still has a following; **en p.,** in public, publicly.
publicain [pyblikɛ̃] *nm Antiq* tax gatherer; *Bible* publican.
publication [pyblikasjɔ̃] *nf* **(a)** (*fait de rendre public*) publication, publishing; publication, bringing out (*of book*); issue (*of an order*); **p. de vente aux enchères,** notice of sale by auction; **date de p.,** date of publication; **(b)** (*magazine etc*) publication; **p. périodique,** periodical; **p. trimestrielle,** quarterly (publication).
publicisation [pyblisizasjɔ̃] *nf Pol* nationalization (*of an industry*); bringing (*of a private school*) into the state system.
publiciser [pyblisize] *vt* **(a)** *Pol* to nationalize (*an industry*); to bring (*private school*) into the state system; **(b)** (*faire connaître*) to make (*a candidate*) known to the public.
publiciste [pyblisist] *n* publicist; publicity agent (*of an entertainer etc*).
publicitaire [pyblisitɛr] **1** *adj* (concerned with) publicity; *Com* (concerned with) advertising; **campagne p.,** publicity campaign; *Com* advertising campaign; **agence p.,** advertising agency; **vente p.,** promotional sale. **2** *n* publicity agent, *F* adman.
publicité [pyblisite] *nf* **(a)** (*informations au public*) = **PUB¹ (a)**; **(b)** *TV Rad Journ* = **PUB¹ (b)**; **(c)** (*caractère public*) public nature; **la p. des débats à l'Assemblée,** the public nature of the debates in the National Assembly.
public-relations [pœblikrileʃənz] **1** *nf* public relations, *F* PR; **le service de p.-r.,** the public relations department, *F* PR. **2** *n* public relations officer, *F* PR man *or* woman.
publier [pyblije] *vt* (*pr sub & impf* **n. publiions, v. publiiez**) **(a)** (*rendre public*) to publish, to make public, to make known (*trade figures etc*); to proclaim (*decree*); to issue (*an order*); **les bans ont-ils été publiés?,** have the banns been published?; **p. la nouvelle que ...,** to release the news that ...; **(b)** to publish, to bring out (*book*); **ce journal est publié sur seize pages,** the paper runs to sixteen pages.
publipostage [pyblipɔstaʒ] *nm* mailshot; **logiciel de p.,** mail merge software; **faire un p.,** to do a mailshot.
publiquement [pyblikmɑ̃] *adv* publicly, in public; (*ouvertement*) openly; **se faire ridiculer p.,** to hold oneself up to public ridicule.
puce [pys] **1** *nf* **(a)** flea; **piqûre de p.,** fleabite; **marché aux puces, les puces,** flea market; **les puces de Paris,** the Paris flea market; *Fig* **mettre la p. à l'oreille à qn,** to arouse s.o.'s suspicions; *F* **secouer les puces à qn,** to give s.o. a good telling off; **c'est une p.,** (*elle est minuscule*) she's tiny; *F* **mais oui ma p.,** yes (my) dear *or* (my) love *or* (my) pet; **jeu de p.,** tiddlywinks; **p. de mer,** sand hopper, sand flea; **herbe aux puces,** fleawort; **(b)** *Ordinat* (micro)chip. **2** *adj inv* puce(-coloured, -colored).
puceau, -eaux [pyso] *nm & adj m F* virgin.
pucelage [pyslaʒ] *nm Hum* virginity; **perdre son p.,** to lose one's virginity.
pucelle [pysɛl] **1** *adj* virgin. **2** *nf* virgin; *Arch & Euph* maid(en); *Hist* **la P. d'Orléans,** the Maid of Orleans.
puceron [pysrɔ̃] *nm* plant louse, greenfly, aphid.
pucier [pysje] *nm Arg* (*lit*) pit.
pudding [pudiŋ] *nm Culin* (plum) pudding, Christmas pudding; (*gâteau*) = rich cake with icing.
puddlage [pydlaʒ] *nm Métal* puddling.
puddler [pydle] *vt Métal* to puddle.

pudeur [pydœr] *nf* (*réserve*) modesty; **sans p.,** unblushing(ly), shameless(ly); **rougir de p.,** to blush with shame; **par p. il n'a pas abordé le sujet,** out of a sense of decency *or* propriety he did not mention the subject.
pudibond [pydibɔ̃] *adj* easily shocked, prudish.
pudibonderie [pydibɔ̃dri] *nf* prudishness.
pudicité [pydisite] *nf Litt* modesty.
pudique [pydik] *adj* modest; **une allusion p.,** a discreet reference.
pudiquement [pydikmɑ̃] *adv* modestly.
puer [pɥe] **1** *vi* to stink, to reek; **ça pue!,** what a stink! **2** *vt* to stink *or* reek of (*sth*); **p. l'ail,** to smell *or* stink of garlic; **il puait le vin,** he reeked of wine.
puéricultrice [pɥerikyltris] *nf* nursery nurse.
puériculture [pɥerikyltyr] *nf* child care, infant welfare.
puéril [pɥeril] *adj* puerile, childish.
puérilement [pɥerilmɑ̃] *adv* childishly.
puérilité [pɥerilite] *nf* puerility, childishness.
puerpéral, -aux [pɥɛrperal, -o] *adj Obst* puerperal.
puffin [pyfɛ̃] *nm* (*oiseau*) shearwater.
pugilat [pyʒila] *nm* **(a)** (*combat de boxeurs*) boxing, *Fml* pugilism; **(b)** (*dispute, bataille*) fight, brawl, *F* set-to.
pugiliste [pyʒilist] *nm* boxer, *Fml* pugilist.
pugnace [pygnas] *adj Litt* pugnacious.
pugnacité [pygnasite] *nf Litt* pugnacity, pugnaciousness.
puîné, -ée [pɥine] *Vieilli* **1** *adj* (*de deux*) younger; (*de plusieurs*) youngest. **2** *n* younger *or* youngest brother *or* sister.
puis [pɥi] *adv* then; **tourner à droite p. à gauche,** turn right (and) then left; **et p. c'est tout,** and that's all (there is to it); **et p.,** and then; (*d'ailleurs*) moreover, (and) besides; **et p. qu'est-ce qui s'est passé?,** then what happened?, what happened then *or* next?; **et p. (quoi)?, et p. après?,** then what?, what next?; *F* (*qu'est-ce que ça peut faire*) so what?
puisage [pɥizaʒ] *nm* drawing (up) (*of water*).
puisard [pɥizar] *nm* sunk draining trap; (*pour ordures*) cesspool, sink; *Min Tech etc* sump, well.
puisatier [pɥizatje] *nm* (*ouvrier*) well maker, well sinker; *Min* shaft sinker.
puisement [pɥizmɑ̃] *nm* = **PUISAGE**.
puiser [pɥize] **1** *vt* to draw (*water*) (**à, dans,** from); *Fig* **p. une idée chez un auteur,** to take *or* get *or* derive an idea from an author; **p. aux sources,** to draw on the original authorities, to go to the source; *Litt & Hum* to go to the fountainhead. **2** *vi* **elle puise dans ses réserves,** she's drawing on her reserves; **p. dans son sac,** to dip into one's bag.
puisque [pɥisk(ə)] *conj* since, as, seeing that; **je le ferai, puisqu'il le faut,** I'll do it, since I must; **p. tu veux savoir, je vais te le dire,** since *or* seeing that you want to know, I'll tell you; **p. je te dis que je l'ai vu!,** but I'm telling you I DID see it!
puissamment [pɥisamɑ̃] *adv* powerfully; **p. riche,** exceedingly rich.
puissance [pɥisɑ̃s] *nf* **(a)** power; force (*of habit*); strength (*of wind etc*); **il est en votre p. de décider,** it is in your power to decide; **p. d'une machine,** power of an engine; *Mil* **p. de** *ou* **du feu,** fire power; **p. en chevaux,** horsepower; **p. au frein,** brake horsepower; *Admin* **p. fiscale d'une voiture,** engine rating of a car for road tax purposes; *Rad* **p. d'antenne,** aerial capacity; **poste émetteur de haute p.,** high-power radio transmitter;
(b) *Math* power; **élever un nombre à la nième p.,** to raise a number to the nth power; **dix (à la) p. quatre (10^4),** ten to the fourth, ten to the power of four;
(c) (*autorité*) power; **avoir qn en sa p.,** to have s.o. in one's power; **la volonté de p.,** the desire for power; **être en p. de mari,** to be under a husband's control *or* authority; **p. paternelle,** paternal authority;
(d) *Pol* **les grandes puissances,** the great powers;
(e) *Fig* **les puissances célestes,** the powers above; **les puissances des ténèbres,** the powers of darkness;
(f) **en p.,** potential(ly).
puissant [pɥisɑ̃] **1** *adj* **(a)** powerful (*army, engine, car*); strong (*man, wind etc*); *Iron* **ah c'est drôle, c'est p.,** oh very funny; **(b)** potent (*remedy etc*); **en p. relief,** in bold relief; **une des plus puissantes maisons du pays,** one of the leading firms in the country; **(c)** (*fort*) powerful (*voice*). **2** *nmpl* **les puissants,** the powerful, the mighty (ones).
puits [pɥi] *nm* **(a)** (*pour l'eau*) well; **p. de sondage,** boring; **p. artésien,** artesian well; **p. à ciel ouvert,** open well; **p. naturel,** natural well; **p. absorbant, p. perdu,** cesspool; *Fig* **c'est un p. de science,** he's a mine of information; (*d'un esprit plus profond*) he's a fount of knowledge; **(b)** shaft, pit (*of mine*); **p. d'aération, d'aérage,** air shaft, ventilation shaft; **p. du pétrole,** oil well; **p. d'extraction,** winding shaft; **(c)** *Ind* **p. de montage,** erecting pit; **(d) p. de lancement,** launching silo.
pull [pyl] *nm F* pullover.
pullman [pulman] *nm Rail* Pullman (car).
pull-over [pulɔvœr] *nm* pullover; (*pl pull-overs*).
pullulation [pylylasjɔ̃] *nf*, **pullulement** [pylylmɑ̃] *nm* **(a)** pullulation, rapid multiplication (*of organisms etc*); **(b)** swarm(ing) (*of children etc*).
pulluler [pylyle] *vi* **(a)** (*se reproduire*) to pullulate, to multiply rapidly; **(b)** (*être en profusion*) to be found in profusion; (*en mouvement*) to swarm; **la rue pullule de monde,** the street is swarming with people.
pulmonaire [pylmɔnɛr] **1** *adj* pulmonary; **congestion p.,** pulmonary congestion. **2** *nf* lungwort.
pulpe [pylp] *nf* **(a)** (*de fruit*) pulp; **réduire qch en p.,** to reduce sth to a pulp, to pulp sth; **(b)** (*partie molle*) pad (*of finger or toe*); (*des dents*) pulp.
pulpeux, -euse [pylpø, -øz] *adj* (*lèvres*) fleshy; **une fille pulpeuse,** a sexy female.
pulsar [pylsar] *nm Astron* pulsar.
pulsation [pylsasjɔ̃] *nf* (*fait de battre*) throbbing, pulsating (*of sore*); beating, pulsating (*of the heart etc*); (*battement*) throb; (heart)beat.
pulsative [pylsativ] *adj Méd* **douleur p.,** throbbing pain; *Spéc* pulsatory pain.
pulser [pylse] *vt* to force (*air*) (*into a room, an engine*).
pulsion [pylsjɔ̃] *nf Psy* impulse; **p. sexuelle,** sex drive; **p. de mort,** death wish.
pulsionnel, -elle [pylsjɔnɛl] *adj* impulsive, impulse; **phénomène p.,** impulsive action, instinctive action; **c'était plus p. que réfléchi,** it was more of a reflex *or* an impulse than a conscious act; **un achat p.,** an impulse buy *or* purchase.
pulsomètre [pylsɔmɛtr] *nm Ind* pulsometer, (steam-condensing) vacuum pump.
pulsoréacteur [pylsɔreaktœr] *nm Av* pulse jet.
pulvérisable [pylverizabl] *adj* (*poudre etc*) pulverizable; (*liquid*) that can be sprayed.
pulvérisateur [pylverizatœr] *nm* **(a)** pulverizer (*of hard substances*); **(b)** (*de liquide*) spray(er); *Tech* vaporizer, atomizer.
pulvérisation [pylverizasjɔ̃] *nf* **(a)** pulverization, pulverizing, crushing (*of hard substances*); **(b)** spray(ing), atomization, atomizing, vaporization (*of liquids*).
pulvériser [pylverize] *vt* **(a)** to pulverize (*rock*); to grind *or* reduce (*substance*) to powder; **(b)** to spray, to atomize, to vaporize (*liquid*); **(c)** *Fig* to pulverize (*s.o.*), to knock (*s.o.*) into a cocked hat; *Sp F* to smash (*record*).
pulvériseur [pylverizœr] *nm Agr* disc *or US* disk harrow.
pulvérulence [pylverylɑ̃s] *nf* powderiness, dustiness.
pulvérulent [pylverylɑ̃] *adj* powdery, dusty; *Tech* pulverulent.
puma [pyma] *nm* puma, cougar, mountain lion.
punaise [pynɛz] *nf* **(a)** (*insecte*) bug; **p. des lits,** bed bug, house bug; **p. des bois,** stinkbug; *F* **p. de sacristie,** bigoted churchwoman; *F & Dial* **oh p!,** goodness!, gosh!; **(b)** (*pour accrocher*) drawing pin, *Am* thumbtack.
punaiser [pyneze] *vt F* to pin (up); **p. des affiches au mur,** to pin posters to the wall.
punch¹ [pɔ̃ʃ] *nm Culin* punch; **bol à p.,** punchbowl.
punch² [pœnʃ] *nm Boxe & F* punch; *Fig* **elle ne manque pas de p.,** (*quelle énergie!*) she's full of energy; **un slogan qui a du p.,** punchy *or* catchy slogan; **cette aide de l'état a donné du p. à notre organisation,** the government's assistance was a shot in the arm.
punching-ball [pœnʃiŋbol] *nm Boxe* punchball; (*pl punching-balls*).
punique [pynik] *adj Hist* Punic (*wars etc*); *Litt* **foi p.,** Punic faith, treachery.
punir [pynir] *vt* to punish; *Litt* to avenge (*crime*); **p. qn de mort/prison,** to punish s.o. with death/imprisonment; **p. qn d'un crime/pour un mensonge,** to punish s.o. for a crime/for a lie; **ça te punira de ta curiosité!,** that'll teach you to be nosey!; **être puni par où l'on a péché,** to reap what one has sown; **être puni de ses crimes,** to be punished *or* pay the penalty for one's crimes; **me voilà puni de ma gourmandise!,** it serves me right for being greedy!, that'll teach me to be greedy!; *Mil* **homme puni,** defaulter.
punissable [pynisabl] *adj* punishable.
punitif, -ive [pynitif, -iv] *adj* punitive; **expédition punitive,** punitive expedition.

punition [pynisjɔ̃] *nf* punishment, punishing; **p. corporelle,** corporal punishment; **proportionner la p. à l'offense,** to make the punishment fit the crime; **donner une p. à un enfant,** to punish a child; **en p. de qch,** as (a) punishment for sth; **par** *ou* **pour p.**, for punishment, by way of punishment, as a punishment.

punk [pœ̃k] **1** *adj* punk (*music etc*). **2** *n* punk.

pupe [pyp] *nf* **(a)** (*enveloppe*) pupa case; **(b)** (*chrysalide*) pupa, chrysalis.

pupillaire[1] [pypilɛr] *adj Jur* pupil(l)ary, pertaining to a ward.

pupillaire[2] *adj Anat* pupil(l)ary (*membrane etc*).

pupillarité [pypilarite] *nf Jur* pupil(l)age.

pupille[1] [pypil, -ij] *n Jur* ward; **pupilles de la Marine/de l'Air,** children whose fathers have died while serving in the Navy/Air Force; *Vieilli* **pupilles de la Nation,** war orphans; **p. de l'État,** child in (state) care.

pupille[2] *nf Anat* pupil (*of the eye*).

pupitre [pypitr] *nm* **(a)** (*d'écolier etc*) desk; **p. à musique,** music stand; **(b)** *Mus* group (*of instruments*); **chef de p.**, front desk player; **(c)** *Ordinat* **p. (de commande),** console (desk); **p. de visualisation,** visual display unit.

pupitreur, -euse [pypitrœr, -øz] *n Ordinat* console operator.

pur, pure [pyr] **1** *adj* **(a)** (*pas mélangé*) pure; **or p.**, pure gold; **whisky p.**, straight *or* neat whisky; **elle boit son whisky p.**, she drinks her whisky straight *or* neat; **air p.**, pure air; **ciel p.**, clear sky; **liquide p. de tout mélange,** liquid free from all admixture;

(b) (*total*) pure; **p. hasard,** pure chance, mere chance; **la pure vérité,** the simple *or* plain *or* honest *or* unvarnished truth; **la vérité pure et simple,** the pure and simple truth; **l'invitation est de pure forme,** the invitation is purely for form's sake; **par pure malice,** out of pure *or* sheer malice; **c'est de la folie pure (et simple),** it's pure folly, it's sheer madness; **travailler en pure perte,** to work for nothing *or* to no purpose; **un style p.**, a lean style; **cheval p. sang,** thoroughbred horse;

(c) *Fig* (*moralement*) pure, untarnished; **conscience pure,** clear conscience; **p. d'esprit,** pure-minded;

(d) (*théorique*) pure (*science, mathematics etc*).

2 *n Pol etc* **un p.**, a diehard.

purée [pyre] **1** *nf Culin* purée; **p. (de pommes de terre),** mashed *or* creamed potato(es), *Br F* mash, potato purée; **p. de carottes,** pureed carrots; *F* **être dans la p.**, to be down on one's luck. **2** *int F* (*colère etc*) hell!, blast (it)!; (*surprise*) wow!

purement [pyrmɑ̃] *adv* purely.

pureté [pyrte] *nf* purity; clearness (*of the sky*); *Fig* **la p. de sa voix,** the purity of his voice.

purgatif, -ive [pyrgatif, -iv] *Méd* **1** *adj* purgative. **2** *nm* purgative, purge.

purgation [pyrgɑsjɔ̃] *nf* purging, purgation.

purgatoire [pyrgatwar] *nm Rel* purgatory.

purge [pyrʒ] *nf* **(a)** *Méd* purge, purgative; **(b)** *Tex* cleaning (*of yarn*); **(c)** *Pol* purge; **(d)** draining (*of liquid*); **robinet de p.**, drain *or* bleed cock; **vis de p.**, bleed screw; **(e)** *Jur* redemption, paying off (*of mortgage*).

purgeoir [pyrʒwar] *nm* purifying tank, filtering tank (*of water supply etc*).

purger [pyrʒe] *v* (**je purgeai(s); n. purgeons**) **1** *vt* **(a)** *Méd* to purge, to clean, to cleanse, to clear; **p. un malade,** to purge a patient; **p. les intestins,** to purge the system, to clear out the bowels; *Fig* **p. un pays de voleurs,** to rid a country of bandits; **p. ses terres de dettes,** to clear *or* disencumber one's estate of debt; *Nau* **p. la quarantaine,** to clear one's quarantine; **(b)** *Jur* to redeem, to pay off (*mortgage*); **p. sa peine,** to serve one's sentence; **(c)** to blow off (*steam*); to blow out, to drain (*cylinder etc*); to bleed (*brakes etc*). **2 se purger** *vpr* **(a)** *Méd* to take a purgative *or* a laxative; **(b)** *Fig* **se p. d'une accusation,** to clear oneself of an accusation.

purgeur [pyrʒœr] *nm* drain cock, bleed cock; **p. de vapeur,** blow-off cock; (*qui capte de l'eau*) steam trap.

purifiant [pyrifjɑ̃] *adj* purifying, cleansing.

purificateur, -trice [pyrifikatœr, -tris] **1** *adj* purifying, cleansing. **2** *nm* purifier, cleanser; **p. d'air** *ou* **d'atmosphère,** air purifier.

purification [pyrifikɑsjɔ̃] *nf* purification; purifying (*of metals etc*); cleansing, purging (*of the blood etc*).

purifier [pyrifje] *v* (*pr sub & impf* **n. purifiions, v. purifiiez**) **1** *vt aussi Fig* to purify, to cleanse; to refine (*metal*); to purge (*blood etc*); **p. la langue,** to purify the language. **2 se purifier** *vpr* to become pure, to be purified.

purin [pyrɛ̃] *nm Agr* liquid manure; **fosse à p.**, manure pit, sump.

purisme [pyrism] *nm* purism (*of language etc*).

puriste [pyrist] *n* purist.

puritain, -aine [pyritɛ̃, -ɛn] **1** *n* puritan; *Hist* Puritan. **2** *adj* puritan(ical); *Hist* Puritan.

puritanisme [pyritanism] *nm* puritanism.

purotin [pyrɔtɛ̃] *nm Arg Vieilli* down-and-out, loser.

purpura [pyrpyra] *nm Méd* purpura.

purpurin, -ine [pyrpyrɛ̃, -in] *adj Litt* deep crimson.

pur-sang [pyrsɑ̃] *nm inv* thoroughbred (horse).

purulence [pyrylɑ̃s] *nf Méd* purulence.

purulent [pyrylɑ̃] *adj Méd* purulent; **foyer p.**, abscess.

pus [py] *nm Méd* pus, matter.

push-pull [puʃpul] *El* **1** *nm* push-pull. **2** *adj inv* push-pull; **montage p.-p.**, push-pull assembly.

pusillanime [pyzilanim] *adj Litt* pusillanimous, faint-hearted.

pusillanimité [pyzilanimite] *nf Litt* pusillanimity, faint-heartedness.

pustule [pystyl] *nf* pustule; (*de crapauds*) wart.

pustuleux, -euse [pystylø, -øz] *adj* pustulous.

putain [pytɛ̃] *Arg Vulg* **1** *nf* **(a)** whore, *Am* hooker; **(b) cette p. de guerre/machine,** this bloody *or Vulg* fucking war/machine. **2** *int* (*colère etc*) shit!; (*surprise*) Christ!

putassier, -ière [pytasje, -jɛr] *adj Arg Vulg* (*area*) full of whores; (*dress*) tarty; **avoir un air/un langage p.**, to look/talk like a whore; **avoir des manières putassières,** to act like a whore.

putatif, -ive [pytatif, -iv] *adj* putative, supposed, presumed.

pute [pyt] *nf Arg Vulg* = **PUTAIN 1 (a)**; **la p.!**, (*elle m'a menti etc*) the bitch!

putois [pytwa] *nm* **(a)** polecat; **p. (d'Amérique)**, skunk; *F* **crier comme un p.**, to squeal like a pig; (*fourrure*) polecat (fur); **(b)** (*brosse*) paintbrush.

putréfaction [pytrefaksjɔ̃] *nf* putrefaction; **matière en p.**, putrefying matter.

putréfier [pytrefje] **1** *vt* to putrefy, to rot. **2 se putrifier** *vpr* to putrefy, to become putrid.

putrescence [pytresɑ̃s] *nf* putrescence.

putrescent [pytresɑ̃] *adj* putrescent.

putrescible [pytresibl] *adj* liable to putrefy.

putride [pytrid] *adj* putrid, tainted; **fermentation p.**, putrefactive fermentation.

putridité [pytridite] *nf Litt* putridity, putridness.

putsch [putʃ] *nm Pol* putsch.

putschiste [putʃist] *Pol* **1** *adj* putsch. **2** *nm* person involved in a putsch.

puy [pɥi] *nm Géol* puy.

puzzle [pœzl] *nm* (jigsaw) puzzle; *Fig* **le p. commence à prendre forme dans son esprit,** the pieces of the puzzle are beginning to fall into place.

P.-V. [peve] *nm F* (*abrév* **procès-verbal**) (parking) ticket; **j'ai attrapé un p.-v. ce matin,** I got a ticket this morning.

P.V.C. [pevese] *nm Tech* (*abrév* **polychlorine de vinyle**) PVC; **siège en P.V.C.,** PVC seat.

pyélite [pjelit] *nf Méd* pyelitis.

pygmée [pigme] *nm* pygmy, pigmy.

pyjama [piʒama] *nm* pyjamas, *Am* pajamas; **un p.**, a pair of pyjamas; **c'est un vrai p.**, (*ce vêtement*) it's loose and comfortable.

pylône [pilon] *nm* **(a)** *Él* pylon; lattice mast (*supporting telegraph wires etc*); **p. électrique,** electricity pylon; **grue à p.**, tower crane; **(b)** *Archit* pylon (*of Egyptian temple*).

pylore [pilɔr] *nm Anat* pylorus.

pyorrhée [pjɔre] *nf Méd* pyorrhoea, *US* pyorrhea.

pyramidal, -aux [piramidal, -o] *adj* pyramidal; *F Arch* **succès p.**, tremendous *or* colossal success.

pyramide [piramid] *nf* pyramid; **entasser des oranges en p.**, to pile up oranges in a pyramid.

pyrénéen, -enne [pireneɛ̃, -ɛn] **1** *adj* Pyrenean. **2** *n* **P.**, Pyrenean.

Pyrénées (les) [lepirene] *nfpl* the Pyrenees.

pyrèthre [pirɛtr] *nm* (*plante*) feverfew, pyrethrum; **poudre de p.**, pyrethrum (powder), insect powder; pellitory of Spain.

pyrex ® [pirɛks] *nm* Pyrex ®; **plat en p.**, pyrex dish.

pyrexie [pirɛksi] *nf Méd* pyrexia, fever.

pyrite [pirit] *nf Minér* (iron) pyrites; **p. de cuivre,** copper pyrites.

pyrogallique [pirɔgalik] *adj Ch* pyrogallic.

pyrogallol [pirɔgalɔl] *nm Ch* pyrogallol.

pyrograveur, -euse [pirɔgravœr, -øz] *n* pyrographer.

pyrogravure [pirɔgravyr] *nf* poker work; (*gravure*) pyrograph.

pyromane [pirɔman] *n Psy* pyromaniac; *Jur* (*incendiaire*) arsonist.
pyromanie [pirɔmani] *nf Psy* pyromania.
pyromètre [pirɔmɛtr] *nm Phys Tech* pyrometer.
pyrométrie [pirɔmetri] *nf Phys* pyrometry.
pyrosis [pirɔzis] *nm Méd* pyrosis, heartburn.
pyrotechnie [pirɔtɛkni] *nf* pyrotechnics.
pyrotechnique [pirɔtɛknik] *adj* pyrotechnic(al).
pyrrhonien, -ienne [pirɔnjɛ̃, -jɛn] *Phil* **1** *adj* Pyrrhonist. **2** *n* **P.**, Pyrrhonist.
pyrrhonisme [pirɔnism] *nm Phil* Pyrrhonism.
Pythagore [pitagɔr] *nm* Pythagoras; **théorème de P.**, Pythagoras' theorem.
pythagoricien, -ienne [pitagɔrisjɛ̃, jɛn] *Phil* **1** *adj* Pythagorean. **2** *n* **P.**, Pythagorean.
pythagorisme [pitagɔrism] *nm Phil* Pythagoreanism.
Pythie [piti] *nf* **(a)** **P. de Delphi**, Pythia of Delphi; **(b)** *Litt* prophetess, oracle.
python [pitɔ̃] *nm* python.
pyxide [piksid] *nf* **(a)** *Bot* pixidium, pyxis; **(b)** *Rel* pyx.

Q

Q, q [ky] *nm* (the letter) Q, q.

Q.C.M. [kysɛɛm] *nm inv abrév* **questionnaire à choix multiple.**

Q.G. [kyʒe] *nm inv Mil F* (*abrév* **quartier général**) H.Q.; **les Q.G. ont été transportés dans une autre ville,** the H.Q. has been moved to another town.

Q.I. [kyi] *nm* (*abrév* **quotient intellectuel**) I.Q..

quadragénaire [kwadraʒenɛr] *adj & n* quadragenarian.

Quadragésime [kwadraʒezim] *nf Rel* **(le dimanche de) la Q.,** Quadragesima (Sunday).

quadrangulaire [kwadrɑ̃gylɛr] *adj* quadrangular, four-angled; four-cornered (*building*).

quadrant [k(w)adrɑ̃] *nm Math* quadrant.

quadratique [kwadratik] *adj* **(a)** *Math* quadratic; **(b)** *Minér* quadratic, tetragonal.

quadrature [kwadratyr] *nf* **(a)** *Math* quadrature, squaring (*esp* of the circle); *Fig* **chercher la q. du cercle,** to try to square the circle; **(b)** *Astron Phys* quadrature; **marées de q.,** neap tides, neaps.

quadrichromie [kwadrikrɔmi] *nf* four-colour printing.

quadriennal, -aux [kwadrijenal, -o] *adj* **(a)** quadrennial, lasting for four years, four-year (*plan, term*); **(b)** quadrennial, occurring every four years, four-yearly (*festival*).

quadrifolié [kwadrifɔlje] *adj* four-leaved, quadrifoliate.

quadrijumeaux [kwadriʒymo] *nmpl* quadruplets.

quadrilatère [k(w)adrilatɛr] *nm Math Mil etc* quadrilateral.

quadrillage [kadrijaʒ] *nm* **(a)** cross ruling, squaring (*of paper, map*); *Mil etc* partitioning (*of zone in search operations*); **la police a établi un q. du quartier,** the police have the district under tight surveillance, the police are combing the area; **(b)** (*motif*) (pattern of) checks, squares; (*sur une carte*) grid.

quadrille [kadrij] *nm* quadrille; **q. des lanciers,** lancers.

quadrillé [kadrije] *adj* squared, cross-ruled (*paper*); **carte quadrillée,** grid map; *Aut* **zone quadrillée,** box junction.

quadriller [kadrije] *vt* **(a)** to rule in squares, to cross-rule (*paper*); **le quartier est quadrillé par un réseau de ruelles,** the district is criss-crossed by a network of alleys; **(b)** to comb (*district for criminals etc*).

quadrimoteur, -trice [k(w)adrimɔtœr, -tris] *adj & nm* four-engined (aircraft).

quadriparti [kwadriparti], **quadripartite** [kwadripartit] *adj* quadripartite (*corolla, treaty*); four-party, four-power (*conference*).

quadriréacteur [k(w)adrireaktœr] *nm Av* four-engined jet aircraft.

quadrisyllabe [kwadrisilab] *nm* quadrisyllable.

quadrisyllabique [kwadrisilabik] *adj* quadrisyllabic.

quadrumane [k(w)adryman] *Zool* **1** *adj* quadrumanous, four-handed (*animal*). **2** *nm* quadrumane.

quadrupède [k(w)adrypɛd] **1** *adj* quadruped, four-footed (*animal*). **2** *nm* quadruped.

quadruple [k(w)adrypl] **1** *adj* quadruple, fourfold. **2** *nm* **être payé au q.,** to be repaid fourfold; **payer le q. du prix,** to pay four times the price.

quadrupler [k(w)adryple] *vt & vi* to quadruple, to increase fourfold.

quadruplés, -ées [k(w)adryple] *npl* quadruplets, *F* quads.

quai [ke] *nm* **(a)** *Nau* quay; (*for loading, unloading*) wharf; (*built out over water*) pier; **amener un navire à q.,** to bring a ship alongside, to berth a ship; **q. des pétroliers,** oil wharf; **droits de q.,** wharfage; *Com* **livrable à q.,** (*goods*) ex-quay, ex-wharf; **(b)** embankment (*along river*); *F* **le Q. d'Orsay,** the French Foreign Office; **(c)** *Rail* platform; **accès aux quais,** = to the trains; **q. d'arrivée/de départ,** arrival/departure platform; **le train est à q.,** the train is in; **(d)** *Rail etc* **q. de chargement,** loading platform *or* bay.

quaker, -eresse [kwɛkœr, -(ə)rɛs; kwa-] *n* Quaker, Quakeress, Friend.

quakerisme [kwɛkrism, kwak(ə)rism] *nm* Quakerism.

qualifiable [kalifjabl] *adj* (*que l'on peut qualifier*) definable; **conduite peu q.,** indescribable conduct.

qualificatif, -ive [kalifikatif, -iv] *Gram* **1** *adj* qualifying (*adjective etc*). **2** *nm* qualifier, epithet.

qualification [kalifikasjɔ̃] *nf* **(a)** qualification, **q. professionnelle,** professional qualifications; *Sp* **obtenir sa q.,** to qualify; **match de q.,** qualifying match; **il court les épreuves de q.,** he's running in the heats; **leur q. est assurée,** they are sure to qualify; **(b)** (*nom*) designation, name, title; **s'attribuer la q. de colonel,** to call oneself colonel; **(c)** *Gram* qualifying (*of noun etc*); *Jur* legal definition (*of crime etc*).

qualifié, -ée [kalifje] **1** *adj* **(a) q. pour faire qch,** qualified to do sth; **ouvrier q./non q.,** skilled/unskilled worker; **le ministre q.,** the competent minister; **je suis certainement q. pour en parler,** I am certainly qualified to speak about it; **(b)** *Jur* aggravated (*offence*); **(c)** *Sp* **cheval** *ou* **coureur q.,** qualifier; **équipe qualifiée,** qualifying team. **2** *n Sp* qualifier.

qualifier [kalifje] *v* (*impf & pr sub* **n. qualifiions**) **1** *vt* **(a) q. qn à faire qch,** to qualify s.o. to do sth; **(b)** (*appeler*) to style, to call, to term, to qualify; **acte qualifié (de) crime,** action termed a crime; **q. qn de son titre** *ou* **de son grade,** to address *or* designate s.o. by his correct title; **q. qn de charlatan,** to call s.o. a quack; **conduite qu'on ne saurait q.,** unspeakable conduct; **(c)** *Gram* to qualify. **2 se qualifier** *vpr* **(a) se q. pour une fonction,** to qualify for an office; *Sp* **il s'est qualifié pour la finale,** he qualified for *or* got through to the finals; **(b) se q. colonel,** to call *or* style oneself colonel.

qualitatif, -ive [kalitatif, -iv] *adj* qualitative; *Ch* **analyse qualitative,** qualitative analysis.

qualité [kalite] *nf* **(a)** quality; **bonne/mauvaise q.,** good *or* high/bad quality, **de première q.,** high-grade, first rate; **blé de première q.,** prime wheat; **vin de première q.,** choice wine; **chocolat de q. supérieure,** extra fine chocolate; **minerai de q. inférieure,** low-grade ore; *Ordinat* **q. courrier,** (near) letter quality; **vin qui a de la q.,** wine that has quality; **elle n'achète que des produits de q.,** she buys only quality products; **homme qui a beaucoup de qualités,** man with many good qualities *or* points; **améliorer la q. de la vie,** to improve the quality of life;

(b) (*propriété*) quality, property; **qualités fébrifuges,** antifebrile properties;

(c) (*occupation*) profession, occupation; (*fonction*) capacity; **décliner ses titres et qualités,** to enumerate one's titles and qualifications; *Admin* **nom, prénom et q.,** surname, forename and occupation; **il nous révéla sa q. de prêtre,** he disclosed the fact that he was a priest; **agir en q. de tuteur,** to act (in one's capacity) as guardian; **ès qualités,** ex officio; **avoir q. pour agir,** to have authority to act; **qualités de gestionnaire,** management *or* managerial qualities; **avoir les qualités requises pour un emploi,** to have the necessary qualifications *or* to be qualified for a job;

(d) *Vieilli* **gens de q.,** people of quality, gentlefolk.

quand [kɑ̃] **1** *conj* **(a)** when; **je lui en parlerai q. je le verrai,** I'll mention it to him when I see him; *F* **je me souviens de q. tu as commencé à travailler,** I remember when you started to work; *F* **q. je pense que le voyage devait être annulé,** when I think that they were going to cancel the trip; *F* **q. je vous le disais!,** didn't I tell you so!;

(b) q. (même), even if, even though, although; *Litt* **q. il me l'affirmerait je n'en croirais rien,** even if he assured me of it I wouldn't believe it; *Litt* **je n'en voudrais pas q. (bien) même on me le donnerait,** I wouldn't have it as a gift; **je le ferai q. même,** I'll do it all the same *or* in spite of everything; *F* **q. même, ça serait plus gentil de la chercher à la gare,** even so, it would be nicer to meet her at the station; **c'est q. même gentil de sa part,** even so, it's nice of him; **tu aurais pu me le dire q. même,** you MIGHT have told me; **elle ne sait pas compter — q. même!,** she can't count — you're joking!; **ça y est q. même, ce n'est pas trop tôt!,** and not before time either!

2 *adv* when; **q. viendra-t-il?,** when will he come?; **dites-moi q. il viendra,** tell me when he will come; **n'importe q.,** no matter when, at any time; **jusqu'à q. serez-vous à Paris?,** how long will you be in Paris?; **depuis q. êtes-vous à Paris?,** how long have you been in Paris?; **à q. le mariage?,** when will the wedding be?, when is the wedding?; **de q. est ce journal?,** what is the date of this paper?; **pour q. est la réunion?,** when is the meeting?

quant à [kɑ̃ta] *prép* as for; **q. à moi,** as for me, for my part, as far as I am concerned; **q. à cela,** as to that, for that matter; **q. à l'avenir,** as for the future; **q. à le demander, je n'y aurais pas songé,** as for asking for it, I wouldn't have dreamt of it.

quant-à-soi [kɑ̃taswa] *nm inv* dignity, reserve; **rester sur** *ou* **tenir son q.-à-s.,** to stand on one's dignity; (*garder ses distances*) to keep oneself to oneself.

quantième [kɑ̃tjɛm] *nm Litt* day of the month; **quel q. (du mois) sommes-nous?,** what is the date?

quantifiable [kwɑ̃tifjabl] *adj* quantifiable; **donnés non-quantifiables,** unquantifiable data.

quantification [kwɑ̃tifkɑsjɔ̃] *nf Phil* quantification; *Phys* quantization.

quantifier [kwɑ̃tifie] *vt Phys* to quantify.

quantique [kwɑ̃tik] *adj Phys etc* quantum (*theory, mechanics, number etc*).

quantitatif, -ive [kɑ̃titatif, -iv] *adj* quantitative (*analysis etc*).

quantitativement [kɑ̃titativmɑ̃] *adv* quantitatively.

quantité [kɑ̃tite] *nf* **(a)** (*somme, dose*) quantity, amount; **en grande/petite q.,** in large/small quantities *or* amounts; **q. négligeable,** negligible quantity *or* amount; *F* **il faut la considérer comme q. négligeable,** what she thinks is of no consequence, her opinion is neither here nor there; **dans la q. prescrite,** in the prescribed dose; **en q.,** in quantity, in bulk; **nous en avons en q.,** we have plenty of them; **q.** *ou* **des quantités de gens,** a lot *or* a great number of people; **(b)** *Phys etc* quantity; *Math* **q. variable,** variable quantity; *Phys* **q. de mouvement,** momentum, impulse.

quantum [kwɑ̃tɔm] *nm* (*pl quanta*) **(a)** *Phys* quantum; **théorie des quanta,** quantum theory; **(b)** (*quantité*) amount, proportion, ratio; **fixer le q. des dommages-intérêts,** to fix the amount of damages, to assess the damages.

quarantaine [karɑ̃tɛn] *nf* **(a)** (*environ quarante*) (about) forty, some forty; **une q. de personnes,** about forty people; **approcher de la q.,** (*âge*) to be getting on for forty, to be almost forty; **(b)** (*isolement*) quarantine; **pavillon de q.,** quarantine flag; **purger la q.,** to clear one's quarantine; **mettre un navire en q.,** to quarantine a ship, to put a ship in quarantine; **mettre qn en q.,** to quarantine s.o., to put s.o. in quarantine; *F* to send s.o. to Coventry; **être en q.,** to be in quarantine.

quarante [karɑ̃t] *nm inv* forty; **page q.,** page forty; **habiter au numéro q.,** to live at number forty; **la semaine de q. heures,** the forty-hour week; *F* **je m'en fiche comme de l'an q.,** I couldn't care less, I don't care a damn; *Tennis* **q. à** *ou* **partout,** deuce; **les années q.,** the (nineteen) forties; **les Q.,** the Forty, the French Academy.

quarante-cinq [karɑ̃tsɛ̃kt] *nm* **q.-c. tours,** single.

quarantenaire [karɑ̃tnɛr] *adj* **(a)** quarantine (*regulations etc*); **(b)** *Jur* lasting for forty years.

quarantième [karɑ̃tjɛm] *adj & n* fortieth.

quart¹ [kar] *nm* fourth person *or* party; **le tiers et le q.,** everybody and anybody; *F* **il se fiche du q. comme du tiers,** he doesn't give a damn for anybody; **le q. monde,** the Fourth World.

quart² *nm* **(a)** quarter, fourth part; **donner un q. de tour à une vis,** to give a screw a quarter turn; *F* **c'est parti au q. de tour,** (*d'un moteur*) it started first time *or* right away; (*d'une discussion, d'un débat*) it got off to a great start, it took off right away; **il est parti au q. de tour,** he blew up; **il part au q. de tour,** he's got a short fuse; *F* **elle a compris au q. de tour,** she twigged right away; *Com* **remise du q.,** discount of 25%; **un q. de siècle,** a quarter century, twenty-five years; **q. d'heure,** quarter of an hour; **dans un petit q. d'heure,** in ten minutes or so; **pour le q. d'heure,** for the time being, for the moment; *F* **passer un mauvais q. d'heure,** to have a bad time; **trois quarts,** three quarters; **la mode du trois quarts,** the fashion for three-quarter length skirts *etc*; **manteau trois quarts,** three-quarter length coat; **les trois quarts du temps,** most of the time; *F* **être aux trois quarts ivre/mort,** to be three parts drunk/all but dead; **il est deux heures et q.** *ou* **deux heures un q.,** it's (a) quarter past *or Am* after two; **six heures moins le q., cinq heures trois quarts,** (a) quarter to *or Am* of six; **q. de cercle,** quadrant; *Mus* **q. de soupir,** semiquaver rest; *Sp* **q. de finale,** quarter final; **l'équipe va jouer en q. de finale,** the team will play in the quarter final; **un q. de beurre,** a quarter of a kilo of butter;

(b) (*bouteille*) quarter litre *or US* liter bottle; *Mil* (*gobelet*) quarter litre *or US* liter mug;

(c) *Nau* **q. (de vent),** point of the compass; **nord-est q. est,** north-east by east;

(d) *Nau* (*veille*) watch; **q. en bas,** watch below; **q. en haut,** watch on deck; **petit q.,** dog watch; **officier de q.,** officer of the watch; **homme de q.,** watch keeper; **être de q.,** to be on watch; **faire le q.,** to keep watch; *F* (*of prostitute*) to walk her beat; **battre son q.,** (*of policeman*) to pound the beat, to be on one's beat;

(e) *Arg* police station.

quart-arrière [kararjɛr] *nm Fb* quarterback.

quarte [kart] *nf* **(a)** *Mus* fourth; **(b)** *Escrime* quart, quarte, carte; **parer en q.,** to parry in carte.

quarté [karte] *nm* = system of betting on four horses in the same race.

quarteron, -onne [kart(ə)rɔ̃, -ɔn] *adj & n Vieilli* quadroon.

quartier [kartje] *nm* **(a)** (*quart*) quarter, fourth part; **bois de q.,** quartered logs; **q. de pomme,** piece of apple; **la lune est au premier q.,** the moon is in the first quarter; *Culin* **q. d'agneau/de bœuf,** quarter of lamb/of beef; **cinquième q.,** offal; *Hér* **quartiers de l'écusson,** quarters *or* quarterings of the shield;

(b) (*morceau*) part, piece; portion (*of cake*); segment (*of orange*); plot (*of land*); **mettre qch en quartiers,** to tear sth to pieces; **q. de lard,** gammon of bacon; **q. de chevreuil,** haunch of venison;

(c) (*d'une ville*) district, neighbourhood, *US* neighborhood; *Admin* ward (*of town*); **les quartiers nord de la ville,** the north side of (the) town; **q. des spectacles,** theatreland, theatre district; **ils habitent les beaux quartiers,** they live in the well-off part of town; **q. réservé,** red-light district; **je ne suis pas du q.,** I don't belong to this district, I'm not local; **demandez aux gens du q.,** ask the locals; **médecin/cinéma de q.,** local doctor/cinema;

(d) *Mil* quarters; **rentrer au q.,** to return to quarters *or* barracks; **avoir q. libre,** to be off duty; *Fig* **vous avez q. libre jusqu'à dix-huit heures,** you're free until 6 o'clock, take a break until 6 o'clock, your time's your own till 6 o'clock; **quartiers d'hiver,** winter quarters; *Fig* **un endroit idéal pour prendre nos quartiers d'hiver,** an ideal place to spend the winter; **Q. général,** headquarters; **Grand Q. général,** General Headquarters;

(e) **faire q. à qn,** to give s.o. quarter; **demander q.,** to ask for quarter; **il ne fait de q. à personne,** he spares nobody.

quartier-maître [kartjemɛtr] *nm Nau* leading seaman; (*pl quartier(s)-maîtres*).

quartile [kwartil] *nm* quartile.

quartz [kwarts] *nm Minér* quartz, rock crystal; *Électron* quartz crystal; **piloté par q.,** crystal-controlled; **horloge/montre à q.,** quartz clock/watch.

quartzeux, -euse [kwartsø, -øz] *adj Minér* **sable q.,** quartz sand.

quartzite [kwartsit] *nf Minér* quartzite, quartz rock.

quasar [kazar] *nm Astron* quasar.

quasi¹ [kazi] *nm Culin* chump end (*of loin of veal, beef*).

quasi² *adv* almost, virtually, quasi; **q. aveugle,** almost *or* virtually blind; **je n'ai q. rien senti,** I scarcely felt anything; **j'en ai la q.-certitude,** I am practically certain of it; *Jur* **q.-contrat,** implied contract; **q.-délit,** technical offence; **la q. totalité du budget,** almost the entire budget.

quasiment [kazimɑ̃] *adv F* almost, to all intents and purposes; **q. guéri,** as good as cured.

Quasimodo [kazimɔdo] *nf* First Sunday after Easter, Low Sunday; **le lundi de (la) Q.,** Low Monday.

quassia [kwasja] *nm* **(a)** *Bot* quassia (tree); **(b)** *Pharm* quassia; **q. en copeaux,** quassia chips.

quaternaire [kwatɛrnɛr] *adj Ch Géol etc* quaternary.

quatorze [katɔrz] *nm inv* fourteen; **le q. juillet,** the fourteenth of July, Bastille Day; **page q.,** page fourteen; **Louis Q.,** Louis the Fourteenth; **vivre au q. de la place,** to live at number fourteen, the square.

quatorzième [katɔrzjɛm] **1** *adj & n* fourteenth. **2** *nm* fourteenth (part).

quatorzièmement [katɔrzjɛmmɑ̃] *adv* in the fourteenth

place.
quatrain [katrɛ̃] *nm Littér* quatrain.
quatre [katr] *nm inv* four; **Henri Q.,** Henry the Fourth; *Sp* **il est arrivé q. ou cinquième,** he came in fourth or fifth; **il est q. heures,** it's four o'clock; *F* **ton q. heures,** your afternoon snack; **le q. août,** the fourth of August, August (the) fourth; **habiter au numéro q.,** to live at number four; **pain de q. livres,** quartern loaf; **q. barré,** (*à l'aviron*) a coxed four; **par q.,** in fours; **se mettre par q.,** to form fours; *Fig* **se mettre en q. pour faire qch,** to do one's utmost to accomplish sth; *Fig* **il se couperait** *ou* **se mettrait en q. pour vous,** he would do anything for you; *Fig* **se mettre en q. pour plaire à qn,** to bend over backwards to please s.o.; *Fig* **clair comme deux et deux font q.,** as clear as daylight; **monter l'escalier q. à q.,** to go upstairs four at a time, to rush upstairs; *Fig* **avoir la tête en q.,** to have a splitting headache; *Fig* **je me tenais à q. pour ne pas rire,** it was all I could do not to laugh; *Fig* **pull/livre/** *etc* **de q. sous,** cheap *or* inexpensive sweater/book/*etc*; *Cartes* **le q. de pique,** the four of spades.
Quatre-Cantons [katr(ə)kɑ̃tɔ̃] *nmpl* **lac des Q.-C.,** Lake Lucerne.
quatre-cent-vingt-et-un [katrəsɑ̃vɛ̃teœ̃] *nm inv* = dice game in which the aim is to throw 4 - 2 - 1.
quatre-mâts [katrəmɑ] *nm inv Nau* four-masted ship, four master.
quatre-quarts [katrkar] *nm Culin* ≈ pound cake.
quatre-quatre [katkatr] *n inv Aut* four-wheel drive.
quatre-saisons [katrəsɛzɔ̃] *nf inv* **(a) marchand des q.-s.,** street merchant (*selling fresh fruit and vegetables*); **(b)** (*fraise*) perpetual-fruiting strawberry.
Quatre-Temps [katrətɑ̃] *nmpl Rel* Ember days.
quatre-vingt-dix [katrəvɛ̃dis] *nm* ninety.
quatre-vingt-dixième [katrəvɛ̃dizjɛm] *adj & n* ninetieth.
quatre-vingtième [katrəvɛ̃tjɛm] *adj & n* eightieth.
quatre-vingts [katrəvɛ̃] *nm* (*omits the final* **s** *when followed by another number or when used as an ordinal*) eighty; **ils étaient q.-v.,** there were eighty of them; **page q.-vingt,** page eighty; **q.-vingt-un,** eighty-one; **q.-vingt-onze,** ninety-one; **ça fait q.-v.,** that comes to eighty; **habiter au q.-vingt,** to live at number eighty.
quatrième [katrijɛm] **1** *adj* fourth; **habiter au q. étage,** to live on the fourth *or Am* the fifth floor. **2** *nf* **(a)** *Cards* sequence of four; **(b)** *Scol* **(classe de) q.,** *Br* ≈ third form (*of secondary school*), *Am* ≈ seventh or eighth grade. **3** *nm* **monter au q.,** to go up to the fourth *or Am* fifth floor.
quatrièmement [katrijɛmmɑ̃] *adv* fourthly, in the fourth place.
quatuor [kwatɥɔr] *nm Mus* quartet(te).
quayage [kejaʒ] *nm Tech* quayage, wharfage.
que¹ [k(ə)] *pron rel* **(a)** (*often omitted in English*) (*person*) that, whom; (*thing*) that, which; **l'homme q. vous voyez,** the man (whom, that) you see; **montrez-moi les livres q. vous avez achetés,** show me the books (that, which) you have bought; **c'est le meilleur q. nous ayons,** it is the very best (that) we have; **il n'est venu personne q. je sache,** no one has come as far as I know; **il faut attendre le temps qu'elle se prépare,** you'll need to wait till she's ready; **advienne q. pourra,** come what may; **coûte q. coûte,** at all costs;
(b) (*attribut*) **il mourut en brave soldat qu'il était,** he died like the gallant soldier he was; **idiot q. je suis,** fool that I am; **menteur q. tu es!,** you liar!; **couvert qu'il était de poussière,** covered with dust as he was; **purs mensonges q. tout cela!,** that's all a pack of lies!; **c'est une théorie intéressante q. la vôtre,** yours is an interesting theory;
(c) les jours qu'il fait chaud, on hot days; **un jour q. j'étais de service,** one day when I was on duty; **du** *ou* **au temps q. les automobiles n'existaient pas,** before cars existed; **depuis trois mois q. j'habite Paris,** for the three months I have been living in Paris; **les trois ans q. j'ai habité à Paris,** the three years (during which) I lived in Paris.
que² *pron interr* **(a)** what; **q. voulez-vous?,** what do you want?; **q. dit Jean?,** what does John say?; **qu'y a-t-il à voir dans cette ville?,** what is there to see in this town?; **q. faire?,** what can I *or* we *or* one do?, what's to be done?; **q. dire?,** what could I say?; **il ne savait q. penser,** he didn't know what to think; **qu'en sait-elle?,** what does she know (about it)?; **je n'ai q. faire de vos souhaits,** I don't want your good wishes; **q. prendrez-vous, du lait ou de la crème?,** what would you like, *or* which will you take, milk or cream?; **qu'est-il arrivé?, q. s'est-il passé?,** what has happened?; **qu'est-ce?,** what is it?; **q. devenir?,** what's to become of us *or* him *etc*?;
(b) q. ne le disiez-vous?, why didn't you say so?; **qu'il est beau!,** how handsome he is!; **q. c'est bien vrai!,** how true!; **q. de déceptions!,** how many *or* what a lot of disappointments!
que³ *conj* **(a)** that (*often omitted in English*); **je vois qu'il me trompe,** I see (that) he's deceiving me; **je ne doute pas qu'elle (ne) consente,** I have no doubt she will consent; **je désire qu'il vienne,** I want him to come; **j'ai peur qu'il ne vienne,** I'm afraid he will come; **je pense q. non,** I think not;
(b) (*imp or optative*) **qu'elle entre!,** let her come in!; **q. Dieu lui pardonne!,** may God forgive him!; **q. je vous y reprenne!,** just let me catch you at it again!;
(c) (*hypothetical*) **q. la machine chauffe, et il y aura un accident,** let the machine run hot and there will be an accident; **qu'il essaie encore une fois, et il ...!,** just let him try again and he'll ...!;
(d) (soit) qu'il pleuve ou qu'il fasse du vent, whether it rains or blows; **q. tu le veuilles ou non,** whether you wish *or* like it or not;
(e) (*linking up two verbs in the conditional*) **il l'affirmerait q. je ne le croirais pas,** even if he said it was true, I would not believe it;
(f) *Litt* **il ne se passe jamais une année qu'il ne nous écrive,** a year never goes by without his writing to us;
(g) (*equivalent to* **afin que, alors que, avant que, depuis que, puisque, sans que, tant que** *etc*) **approchez qu'on vous entende,** come nearer so that we can hear you; **à peine étais-je rentré q. le téléphone a sonné,** I'd scarcely come in when the telephone rang; **je ne le quitterai pas q. l'affaire ne soit terminée,** I will not leave him till the matter has been settled; **il y a trois jours q. je ne l'ai vue,** it is three days since I saw her; *Litt* **ne partez pas q. je ne vous aie parlé,** don't go before I have had a talk with you;
(h) (*to avoid repetition of another conj*) **quand il entrera et qu'il vous trouvera ici,** when he comes in and finds you here; **quoiqu'il pleuve et qu'il fasse froid,** although it is rainy and cold; **si on vient et qu'on veuille me consulter,** if anyone comes and wants to consult me;
(i) (*in comparison*) **aussi/plus grand q. moi,** as tall as/taller than I (am) *or F* me; **tout autre q. moi,** anyone but me; **un autre parapluie q. celui-là,** another umbrella besides that one; **vous écrivez plus correctement q. vous (ne) parlez,** you write more correctly than you speak; **il habite la même maison q. moi,** he lives in the same house as I do *or* as me;
(j) ne ... q., only; **il n'est q. blessé,** he is only wounded; **il n'a qu'une jambe,** he has only one leg; **il n'a fait qu'entrer et sortir,** he just slipped in and out again; **elle ne fait q. de sortir,** she has only just gone out; **je n'en ai q. trop,** I have all too many; **il n'y a pas qu'elle qui le sache,** she is not the only one who knows it; **l'homme ne vit pas q. de pain,** man does not live by bread alone; **il ne me reste plus q. vingt francs,** I have only twenty francs left; **je ne bois jamais q. de l'eau,** I never drink anything but water;
(k) *Arch & Litt* **q. si vous savez la vérité, il est de votre devoir de la révéler,** if you know the truth, it is your duty to reveal it;
(l) *F* **ah! q. non!/q. si** *ou* **oui!,** ah! surely not!/yes indeed!; **il va au cercle — qu'il dit!,** he goes to the club — so he says!; **ton manteau est dans un état, q. c'est une horreur!,** your coat is in a terrible state!
Québec [kebɛk] *nm* Quebec.
québécisme [kebesism] *nm Ling* Quebecism (*expression peculiar to Quebec French*).
québécitude [kebesityd] *nf* Quebec identity.
québécois, -oise [kebekwa, -waz] **1** *adj* Quebecer, native *or* inhabitant of Quebec. **2** *nm Ling* Quebec French. **3** *n* **Q.,** Quebecer.
quel, quelle [kɛl] **1** *adj* **(a)** *rel* what, which; **q. que soit le résultat,** whatever the result may be; **quelle que soit mon affection pour vous,** however great my affection for you, much as I love you; **quels que soient ces hommes,** whoever these men may be; **q. que soit l'endroit où,** wherever, no matter where; **à quelle époque que ce soit,** at whatever time; **il l'a rendu tel q.,** he gave it back the way (it was when) he got it; **mettez-moi à n'importe quelle table,** put me at any table you like.
(b) *interr* **quelle réponse a-t-elle faite?,** what was her reply?; **quelle heure est-il?,** what time is it?, what's the

time?; **dites-moi quelle heure il est,** tell me the time, tell me what time it is; **q. livre avez-vous pris?,** what *or* which book did you take?; **q. homme?,** which man?; **q. genre d'homme est-ce?,** what sort of a man is he?; **si tu savais à q. point il tient à cette montre,** if you knew how fond he is of this watch; **quels sont ces messieurs?,** who are these gentlemen?; **de ces deux projets q. est le plus sûr?,** which is the safer of these two plans?;

(c) (*exclamatory*) **q. homme!,** what a man!; **quelle bonté!,** how kind!; **q. dommage que personne n'en ait rien su,** what a shame no-one knew anything about it.

2 *pron interr* which (one); **de vous trois, q. est le plus rapide?,** which (one) of you three is the fastest?

quelconque [kɛlkɔ̃k] *adj* **(a)** (*n'importe lequel*) any (whatever); **décrire un cercle passant par trois points quelconques,** to describe a circle passing through any three points; **pour une raison q. le projet peut échouer,** the plan can fail for any (of a) number of reasons;

(b) (*insignifiant, médiocre*) ordinary, commonplace; **répondre d'une façon q.,** to make some sort of reply; **parler de choses quelconques,** to talk about one thing and another; **une femme très q.,** a very plain-looking woman, a very nondescript sort of woman; **on ne peut pas lui donner un emploi q.,** we can't give him an ordinary job *or F* any old job; **son travail est q.,** his work isn't up to much; **un q. général Alain,** some General Alain or other.

quelque [kɛlk(ə)] **1** *adj* **(a)** some, some little, a few; **pendant q. temps,** for some time; **il y a quelques jours,** a few days ago; **je ressentais q. inquiétude,** I felt some *or* a slight uneasiness; **avec quelques amis,** with some friends, with a few friends; **cent et quelques mètres,** a hundred metres plus *or* and a bit; **nous étions quarante et quelques,** there were rather more than forty of us, there were forty or so of us;

(b) (*correlative to* **qui, que** + *sub*) **q. ambition qui l'agite,** whatever ambition moves him; **quelques erreurs qu'elle ait commises,** whatever mistakes she has made; **sous q. prétexte que ce soit,** under any pretext whatever; **tout traité de q. nature qu'il soit,** every treaty of whatsoever character; **de q. côté que vous regardiez,** whichever way you look;

(c) (*un*) some, any; **il arrivera q. jour,** he will arrive some day; **adressez-vous à q. autre,** apply to someone else; **avez-vous q. ami qui puisse vous aider?,** have you some *or* a friend who can help you?

2 *adv* **(a)** some, about; **q. dix ans,** some *or* about ten years; **les q. mille francs qu'il m'a prêtés,** the thousand francs or so *or* or thereabouts that he lent me;

(b) (*correlative to* **que** + *sub*) **q. grandes que soient ses fautes,** however great his faults may be; **q. méchant qu'il fût,** wicked as he was.

quelque chose [kɛlkəʃoz] *pron indéf inv* something; (*dans les phrases interrogatives ou conditionnelles*) something, anything; **q. c. me dit qu'elle viendra,** something tells me she will come; **avez-vous q. c. à dire?,** have you anything to say?; **q. c. de nouveau/d'autre,** something new/else; **tu veux q. c. à manger/boire?,** would you like something to eat/drink?; F **il a q. c.,** there's something the matter with him; **il y a q. c.,** there's something up *or* afoot; *F* **ah mais c'est q. c., ça!,** that's a bit stiff!; **il y est pour q. c.,** he has something to do with it; **cela m'a fait q. c.,** I felt it a good deal; **ça te ferait vraiment q. c. si je m'en allais?,** would it really matter to you if I went away?; **c'est déjà q. c.,** that's always something, anyhow that's something; *F* **q. c. comme deux ans,** about *or* something like two years; *F* **je lui ai offert un petit q. c.,** (*cadeau*) I gave him a little something.

quelquefois [kɛlkəfwa] *adv* sometimes, now and then.

quelque part [kɛlkəpar] *adv* **(a)** somewhere; **on ira q. p. où tu n'es jamais allé,** we'll go somewhere you've never been before; **cela doit bien venir de q. p.,** it must come from somewhere; **(b)** *Litt Vieilli* (*correlative to* **que** + *sub*) **q. p. qu'il fouillât,** wherever he searched.

quelqu'un, quelqu'une [kɛlkœ̃, kɛlkyn], *pl* **quelques-uns, -unes** [kɛlkəzœ̃, -yn] **1** *pron indéf* **(a)** **quelques-uns des magasins,** some of the shops; **j'ai lu quelques-unes des lettres,** I have read a few of the letters; **quelques-un(e)s d'entre nous,** a few of us;

(b) *Arch* **quelqu'une de ces dames va s'en occuper,** one of the ladies will see to it.

2 *nm* someone, somebody; (*dans les phrases interrogatives ou conditionnelles*) someone, somebody, anyone, anybody; **q. me l'a dit,** someone told me; **de la part de q. qui pense à vous,** from someone who is thinking of you; **si q. vient,** if anybody *or* somebody comes; **q. de plus,** someone extra; **q. de trop,** one too many; **y a-t-il eu q. de blessé?,** was anyone hurt?; **il faudra q. d'assez fort,** it will need someone fairly strong; *F* **ça intéresse q.?,** anyone *or* anybody interested?; *F* **est-il q.?,** is he anybody?; **ils sont q. dans leur village,** they are somebody in their village.

quémander [kemɑ̃de] **1** *vt* **q. qch à qn,** to beg for *or* solicit sth from s.o. **2** *vi Arch* to beg (from door to door).

quémandeur, -euse [kemɑ̃dœr, -øz] *n Litt* (*qui demande de l'argent*) beggar; (*tapeur*) cadger.

qu'en-dira-t-on (le) [ləkɑ̃diratɔ̃] *nm inv* gossip, tittle-tattle; **se moquer du q.,** not to care what people say.

quenelle [kənɛl] *nf Culin* quenelle.

quenotte [kənɔt] *nf Enf* tooth.

quenouille [kənuj] *nf* **(a)** *Tex* distaff; *Fig* **succession qui tombe en q.,** succession that falls to the distaff side; **(b)** bedpost (*of four-poster bed*).

quéquette [kekɛt] *nf Enf Vulg* willy.

querelle [kərɛl] *nf* quarrel, dispute, *F* row; **chercher q. à qn,** to try to pick a quarrel with s.o.; **avoir une q. avec qn,** to have a quarrel *or* a row with s.o.; **q. d'Allemand,** trumped-up quarrel; **querelles de famille,** family squabbles; **q. d'amoureux,** lovers' tiff; **q. d'ivrognes,** drunken brawl; **familles en q. ouverte,** families in open feud; **épouser la q. de qn,** to take up *or* espouse s.o.'s cause.

quereller [kərele] **1** *vt Vieilli* to quarrel with (*s.o.*); to nag, to scold (*s.o.*). **2 se quereller** *vpr* to quarrel, to wrangle; to fall out (**avec,** with); (*d'amoureux*) to have a tiff.

querelleur, -euse [kərɛlœr, -øz] **1** *n* quarreller; *f* scold. **2** *adj* quarrelsome.

quérir [kerir] *vt* (*used only in the inf after* **aller, venir, envoyer**) **aller q. qn/qch,** to go and fetch s.o./sth.

qu'est-ce que [kɛskə] *pron interr* what; **q. q. vous voulez?,** what do you want?; **q. q. la grammaire?,** what is grammar?; **q. q. c'est que ça?,** what's that?; *F* **q. qu'il fait beau!,** how fine it is!; **q. qu'on rigole** *ou* **a rigolé!,** what a laugh!; *F* **q. q. tu avais besoin d'aller lui dire ça?,** why did you have to go and tell him that?

qu'est-ce qui [kɛski] *pron interr* **(a)** (*subject*) what; **q. q. est arrivé?,** what (has) happened?; **(b)** *F* who; **q. q. est là?,** who's there?; **je ne savais pas q. q. était là,** I didn't know who was there.

question [kɛstjɔ̃] *nf* **(a)** question, query (**sur,** about, on); *Ordinat* query; **faire** *ou* **poser** *ou* **adresser une q. à qn,** to ask s.o. a question, to put a question to s.o.; **sa fidélité ne fait pas q.,** there is no doubt *or* question about his loyalty; **quelle q.!,** what a question!, what a thing to ask!; **tu te poses trop de questions,** you worry too much; **mettre en q.,** to question (*sth*); to challenge (*statement*); **elle ne cesse de tout remettre en q.,** she questions absolutely everything; **le voyage est remis en q.,** there's a question mark hanging over the trip; **voici un point qui fait q.,** this is a debatable *or* moot point; **il n'y a pas de q.,** there is no doubt about it; **c'est une q.(-)piège,** it's a trick question;

(b) (*affaire*) question, matter, point, issue; **je voudrais vous consulter sur une q. d'affaires,** I would like to consult you on a business matter; **questions d'actualité,** current affairs; **ce n'est qu'une q. d'argent,** it is simply a question of money; **c'est une q. de minutes/d'habitude,** it's a matter of minutes/force of habit; **il ne saurait être q. de les inviter,** we couldn't think of *or* there can be no question of inviting them; **la personne en q.,** the person in question; *F* **la q. alcoolisme,** the problem of alcoholism; *F* **q. argent, ce n'est pas rose,** moneywise, things are pretty grim; **ce n'est pas là la q.,** that is not the point; **sortir de la q.,** to wander from the point; **rappeler qn à la q.,** to call s.o. to order; **de quoi est-il q.?,** what is it all about?; *Iron* **c'est bien la q.!,** that's completely beside the point!; **qu'il n'en soit plus q.,** let us say no more about it, let's drop the subject; **il est q. de lui élever une statue,** there is some talk of putting up a statue to him; **il n'en est pas q.,** it's out of the question; *F* **alors là, pas q.,** no way, no chance;

(c) *Jur* (point at) issue; **q. de fait/droit,** issue of fact/law;

(d) *Hist* **appliquer la q. à qn, mettre qn à la q.,** to torture s.o..

questionnaire [kɛstjɔnɛr] *nm* questionnaire; **q. à choix multiple,** multiple choice question paper.

questionner [kɛstjɔne] *vt* to question (*s.o.*), to ask (*s.o.*) questions (**sur,** about).

questionneur, -euse [kɛstjɔnœr, -øz] **1** *adj* (*air*) inquiring; *Péj* inquisitive. **2** *n* inquisitive person.

quête [kɛt] *nf* **(a)** quest, search; **se mettre en q. de qch, aller à la q. de qch,** to set out *or* go in search of sth; **gens en q. de plaisirs,** pleasure seekers; **(b)** beating (*for game*); (*of hounds*) tracking, scenting; **(c)** (*collecte*) collection;

faire la q., to make a collection (*for a fund*); *F* to pass the hat round; *Rel* to take the collection.

quêter [kete] **1** *vt* **(a)** to collect (*money etc*); **(b)** to seek (*approval, praise*); to fish for, to angle for (*compliments*); (*of hounds*) to seek (*game*). **2** *vi* **(a)** (*faire la quête*) to collect money, to raise funds; **(b)** (*of hounds*) to quarter.

quêteur, -euse [ketœr, -øz] *n* fund-raiser; *Rel* taker of the collection.

quêteux [ketø] *nm Can* beggar.

quetsche [kwɛtʃə] *nf* **(a)** (*prune*) dark-red plum; **(b)** (*eau-de-vie*) = plum liqueur similar to kirsch.

queue [kø] *nf* **(a)** tail; **couper la q. à un cheval,** to dock a horse *or* a horse's tail; **cheval à longue q.,** longtailed horse; **cheval à q. écourtée,** bobtail (horse); **q. de renard,** fox's brush; **q. de rat,** rat's tail; **q. de cheval,** (*coiffure*) pony tail; **avoir une q. de cheval,** to have a pony tail, to wear one's hair in a pony tail; **le conducteur m'a fait une q. de poisson,** the driver cut right in front of me; *F* **finir en q. de poisson,** (*of play, novel etc*) to tail off, to fizzle out; **sans q.,** tailless; **à la q. gît le venin,** the sting is in the tail; **il s'en retourna la q. entre les jambes,** he went off with his tail between his legs; *F* **pas la q. d'un** *ou* **d'une,** not a blessed one;

(b) tail (*of comet, kite, letter*); trail (*of meteor*); stem (*of crotchet, quaver*); handle (*of pan*); stalk (*of fruit, flower*); shank (*of button*); pin (*of brooch*); tailpiece (*of violin*); train (*of dress*); fang, tang, shank (*of tool*); rod, stem (*of valve*); **la q. d'une marguerite,** the stem of a daisy; **avion sans q.,** tailless aircraft; **bouton à q.,** shanked button; **habit à q.,** tail coat; **piano à q.,** grand piano; *Typ* **lettre à q. inférieure,** descending letter;

(c) (tail) end (*of a procession, book, winter, piece of material etc*); tailings (*of ore, grain, etc*); **venir en q. (du cortège),** to bring up the rear; *Courses de chevaux* **arriver en q.,** to come in at the tail end; **être à la q. de la classe,** to be at the bottom of the class; *Fig* **une histoire sans q. ni tête,** a story one cannot make head nor tail of; **voiture en q. de train** *ou* **du train,** carriage *or* coach in the rear of the train; **wagon de** *ou* **en q.,** end carriage; **ils vont avoir la q. de l'orage,** they'll catch *or* get the tail-end of the storm; **attaquer une armée en q.,** to attack an army in the rear;

(d) queue, *Am* line (*of people*); **faire (la) q.,** to form a queue, to queue up, *Am* to stand in line; **faire une heure de q.,** to queue *or* stand in a queue *or Am* stand in line for an hour;

(e) *Billard* cue; **faire fausse q.,** to miscue;

(f) *Vulg* (*pénis*) prick, *Br* dick.

queue-d'aronde [kødarɔ̃d] *nf Menuis* dovetail, fantail; **assemblage à q.-d'a.,** dovetail(ed) joint; (*pl queues-d'aronde*).

queue-de-chat [kødʃa] *nf* (*pl queues-de-chat*) **(a)** (*fouet*) cat-o'-nine-tails; **(b)** (*nuage*) mare's tail.

queue-de-cochon [kødkɔʃɔ̃] *nf* (*outil*) auger bit, gimlet (*pl queues-de-cochon*).

queue-de-morue [kødmɔry] *nf* (*pl queues-de-morue*) **(a)** (**habit à**) **q.-de-m.,** tail coat, *F* tails; **(b)** (*brosse*) (painter's) flat brush;

queue-de-pie [kødpi] *nf* = **QUEUE-DE-MORUE (a)**; (*pl queues-de-pie*).

queue-de-rat [kødra] *nf* (*pl queues-de-rat*) **(a)** (*lime*) rat tail, rat-tailed file; **(b)** (*pour les trous*) reamer.

qui¹ [ki] *pron rel* **(a)** (*sujet*) who, that; (*chose*) which, that; **homme/femme q. parle français,** man/woman who speaks French; **phrases q. ne sont pas françaises,** sentences that are not French; **vous q. êtes libres,** you who are free; **c'est la plus âgée q. a répondu,** it was the eldest who answered; **il y a peu de gens q. sachent cela,** there are few people who know that; **il n'y a personne q. ne comprenne cela,** there is no one who does not understand that; **dans ce match, q. était son premier, l'équipe a fait preuve de résistance,** in this their first match, the team showed staying power; **je le vois q. vient,** I see him coming; **c'est une femme charmante, et q. a du talent,** she is a charming woman, and talented;

(b) (= **celui qui**) **q. vivra verra,** time will tell; **tout vient à point à q. sait attendre,** all things come to him who waits; **sauve q. peut,** every man for himself; **adressez-vous à q. vous voudrez,** apply to anyone you like; *F* **comme q. dirait,** so to speak, in a way;

(c) (= **ce qui**) **q. plus est,** what is more; **q. pis est,** what is worse; **voilà q. me plaît,** this is what I like;

(d) ce q., *voir* **CE**;

(e) (*après prép*) (*peut être omis en anglais*) who, *surtout Fml* whom; **voilà l'homme à q. je pensais,** there is the man (who) I was thinking of *or* the man of whom I was thinking; **il cherche quelqu'un avec q. jouer,** he is looking for someone to play with;

(f) (*indéf*) some; **on se dispersa, q. d'un côté, q. d'un autre,** we scattered, some going one way, some another;

(g) q. que, who(so)ever; (*complément d'objet ou après prép*) whom(so)ever; **q. que ce soit q. sonne, ne laissez pas entrer,** whoever rings *or* no matter who rings don't let him in; **q. que ce soit,** anyone; **je défie q. que ce soit de le prouver,** I challenge anyone to prove it; **je n'ai pas trouvé q. que ce soit,** I found no one at all.

qui² *pron interr m sing* who; (*complément d'objet ou après prép*) who, *surtout Fml* whom; **q. a dit cela?,** who said that?; **savez-vous q. a dit cela?,** do you know who said that?; **q. désirez-vous voir?,** who(m) do you wish to see?; **q. vient à la réunion?,** who is coming to the meeting?; **devinez q. est arrivé le premier,** guess who was here first; **de q. parlez-vous?,** of whom are you speaking?, who are you talking about?; **à q. est ce canif?,** whose knife is this?, whose is this knife?; **de q. êtes-vous le fils?,** whose son are you?; **q. d'autre?,** who(m) else?; *F* **q. ça?,** who did you say?; **c'est à q. entrera le premier,** it's a question of who comes in first; **c'était à q. l'aiderait,** they vied with *or* outdid each other in helping him; *F* **il est là, — q. donc?,** he's there — who?; **q. de vous me suivra?,** which of you will follow me?

quia (à) [akɥija] *adv* **être à q.,** to be in a quandary; **réduire** *ou* **mettre qn à q.,** to nonplus *or* floor *or* stump s.o..

quiche [kiʃ] *nf Culin* quiche, flan; **q. lorraine,** quiche lorraine.

quiconque [kikɔ̃k] *pron indéf m sing* **(a)** who(so)ever, anyone who, anybody who; **q. désobéira sera puni,** whoever disobeys *or* anyone who disobeys will be punished; **(b)** (= **qui que ce soit**) anyone (else), anybody (else); **q. de mes amis,** any of my friends.

quidam [k(ɥ)idam] *nm* someone, somebody, an individual.

qui est-ce que [kiɛskə] *pron interr* whom?; **qui est-ce que vous désirez voir?,** who(m) do you wish to see?

qui est-ce qui [kiɛski] *pron interr* who?

quiet, -ète [kjɛ, -ɛt] *adj Arch* calm.

quiétisme [kjietism] *nm Hist Rel* quietism.

quiétiste [kjietist] *adj & n Hist Rel* quietist.

quiétude [kjietyd] *nf* peace(fulness); **en toute q.,** with an easy mind.

quignon [kiɲɔ̃] *nm* chunk, hunk (*of bread*).

quille¹ [kij] *nf* **(a)** ninepin, skittle; **jeu de quilles,** set of skittles; *Fig* **être reçu comme un chien dans un jeu de quilles,** to be treated as an intruder; *Fig* **se tenir droit comme une q.,** to hold oneself ramrod straight *or* as straight as a ramrod; **(b)** *Arg* leg, pin; **il ne tient pas sur ses quilles,** he's shaky on his pins; **(c)** *Mil F* **à nous la q.!,** civvy street, here we come!; **la q., c'est dans cent cinquante jours,** we'll be back in civvy street in a hundred and fifty days.

quille² *nf* keel; **fausse q.,** false keel, outer keel; **q. de roulis, q. latérale,** bilge keel; **poser la q. d'un navire,** to lay down a ship.

quilleur, euse [kijœr, -øz] *n Can* skittle player.

quillier [kije] *nm* set of skittles.

quincaillerie [kɛ̃kajri] *nf* **(a)** (*ustensile*) hardware, *Br* ironmongery; *Fig F* **elle a mis toute sa q.,** she's wearing all her hardware *or* every bit of jewellery she has; **(b)** *Ind* hardware business; *Com* hardware shop, *Br* ironmonger's.

quincaillier, -ière [kɛ̃kaje, -jɛr] *n* hardware merchant, *Br* ironmonger.

quinconce [kɛ̃kɔ̃s] *nm* quincunx; **rivetage en q.,** staggered *or* zigzag riveting.

quinine [kinin] *nf* (sulphate of) quinine.

quinquagénaire [k(ɥ)ɛ̃k(w)aʒenɛr] *adj & n* quinquagenarian.

Quinquagésime [k(ɥ)ɛ̃kwaʒezim] *nf Rel* Quinquagesima (Sunday).

quinquennal, -aux [kɛ̃kenal, -o] *adj* quinquennial; five-year (*plan*); five-yearly (*festival*).

quinquennat [kɛ̃kena] *nm* five-year period.

quinquet [kɛ̃kɛ] *nm* **(a)** *F* **ouvrez/fermez les quinquets!,** open/close your eyes!; **(b)** (*lampe*) oil lamp.

quinquina [kɛ̃kina] *nm* **(a)** *Pharm* cinchona, quinquina (bark, tree); **(b) (vin de) q.,** (apéritif) tonic wine.

quint [kɛ̃] *adj Arch* fifth; *Hist* **Charles-Q.,** Charles the Fifth (Holy Roman Emperor).

quintal, -aux [kɛ̃tal, -o] *nm* quintal (= 100 kg).

quinte [kɛ̃t] *nf* **(a) q. de toux,** fit of coughing; **(b)** *Mus* fifth, quint; **q. juste,** perfect fifth; **(c)** *Cartes* quint; **(d)** *Escrime* quinte; **(e)** *Vieilli* fit of bad temper.

quintefeuille [kɛ̃tfœj] **1** *nf Hér Bot* cinquefoil. **2** *nm*

Archit cinquefoil.

quintessence [kɛ̃tesɑ̃s] *nf* quintessence.

quintessencié [kɛ̃tesɑ̃sje], **quintessenciel, -elle** [kɛ̃tesɑ̃sjɛl] *adj* quintessential.

quintette [k(ɥ)ɛ̃tɛt] *nm Mus* quintet(te).

quinteux, -euse [kɛ̃tø, -øz] *adj* capricious, crotchety (*person*); restive (*horse*).

quintuple [kɛ̃typl] **1** *adj* fivefold, quintuple. **2** *nm* **être payé au q.,** to be repaid fivefold; **trente est (le) q. de six,** thirty is five times (as much as) six.

quintuplés, -ées [kɛ̃typle] *npl* quintuplets, *F* quins.

quintupler [kɛ̃typle] **1** *vt* to increase (*sth*) fivefold; to quintuple (*sth*); to multiply (*sth*) by five. **2** *vi* to increase fivefold, to quintuple.

quinzaine [kɛ̃zɛn] *nf* **(a)** (*environ quinze*) (about) fifteen, some fifteen; **une q. de francs,** fifteen francs or so; **(b)** (*deux semaines*) fortnight, *Am* two weeks; **remettre une cause à q.,** to adjourn a case for a fortnight; **(c)** (*salaire*) fortnight's *or Am* two weeks' pay *or* wages.

quinze [kɛ̃z] *nm inv* **(a)** fifteen; **Louis Q.,** Louis the Fifteenth; **le q. mai,** (on) the fifteenth of May, (on) May (the) fifteenth; **demeurer au numéro q.,** to live at number fifteen; *Tennis* **q. partout,** fifteen all; **(b) q. jours,** a fortnight; **demain en q.,** a fortnight (from) tomorrow, tomorrow fortnight; **tous les q. jours,** every fortnight, once a fortnight, fortnightly, every other week; *Rugby* **le q. de France,** the French fifteen.

quinzième [kɛ̃zjɛm] **1** *adj & n* fifteenth. **2** *nm* fifteenth (part).

quinzièmement [kɛ̃zjɛmmɑ̃] *adv* fifteenthly, in the fifteenth place.

quiproquo [kiprɔko] *nm* (*taking of one person or thing for another*) mistake.

quittance [kitɑ̃s] *nf* receipt, discharge; **q. de loyer,** rent receipt; **q. pour solde,** receipt in full.

quittancer [kitɑ̃se] *vt* **(je quittançai(s))** to receipt (*bill*).

quitte [kit] **1** *adj* **(a)** (*libéré*) free, quit, rid **(de,** of); discharged **(de,** from); **être q. de dettes,** to be out of debt; **je suis q. envers vous,** I am no longer in your debt; **nous sommes quittes,** we are quits *or* all square; **tenir qn q. de qch,** to release s.o. from sth, to let s.o. off sth; **je vous tiens q. du reste,** never mind the rest; **il en a été q. pour la peur,** he got off *or* escaped with a fright; **ils en ont été quittes à bon compte,** they came off *or* got off lightly; **jouer (à) q. ou double,** to play double or quits; **(b) q. à,** even if it entails; **je le ferai, q. à être grondé,** I'll do it even if I'm scolded, I'll do it and chance the scolding; **il abandonne ce travail, q. à le reprendre plus tard,** he's giving up this work but may resume it later. **2** *nm* **un q. ou double,** double or quits.

quitter [kite] **1** *vt* to leave, to quit (*place, person*); to vacate (*office*); **q. la grande route,** to turn off the main road; *Ordinat* **q. le système,** to quit (the system); **q. les rails,** (*of train*) to jump the rails; *Nau* **q. la jetée** *ou* **le quai,** to cast off; **q. le service,** to leave *or* quit the service; **q. le théâtre,** to give up the stage; **q. les affaires,** to retire from business; **q. ses mauvaises habitudes,** to leave off *or* give up one's bad habits; **un ami très cher vient de nous q.,** a very dear friend has just passed away; **q. la vie,** to depart this life; **quel plaisir de tout q.!,** how nice to get away from it all!; **il ne l'a pas quittée des yeux,** he never took his eyes off her; **ne le quittez pas des yeux,** keep your eye on him, don't let him out of your sight, don't take your eyes off him; **elle veut q. son mari,** she wants to leave her husband; **elle ne quitte pas sa mère,** (*elle n'est pas indépendante*) she won't leave her mother, she never leaves her mother's side; **vous ne quittez pas votre veste?,** won't you take off your jacket?; *Tél* **ne quittez pas (l'écoute)!,** hold on!, hold the line!; **q. la partie,** to give up, *F* to throw in the towel *or* sponge.

2 se quitter *vpr* to part, to say goodbye; **ils se sont quittés bons amis,** they parted good friends; **il est tard, nous devons nous q.,** it's late, we have to say goodbye now.

quitus [k(ɥ)itys] *nm* receipt in full; *Jur* quietus, final discharge (*from debt, liability etc*).

qui-vive [kiviv] *nm inv* **être** *ou* **se tenir sur le q.-v.,** to be on the alert *or* the qui vive.

quoi¹ [kwa] *pron rel* **(a)** what; **ce sur q. l'on discute,** what is being discussed; **ce à q. je m'oppose,** what I object to; **c'est en q. vous vous trompez,** that is where you are wrong; **après q.,** after which; **travaille, sans q. tu ne mangeras pas,** work, otherwise you won't eat;

(b) il a bien autre chose à q. penser!, he has other things to think about!; **un autre fait, à q. vous n'avez pas pris garde,** another fact, which you have left out of consideration; **il a de q. vivre,** he has enough to live on; *F* **il a de q.,** he's well *or* comfortably off; **il y a de q. vous faire enrager,** it's enough to drive you mad; **il n'y a pas de q. être fier,** there's nothing to be proud of; **je suis en colère — je vous comprends, il y a de q.,** I'm angry – I understand, you've every right to be; **il n'y a pas de q.,** (*when receiving thanks, apologies*) don't mention it, not at all, you're welcome!; **avez-vous de q. écrire?,** have you anything *or* something to write with?; **il faut trouver de q. allumer le feu,** we must find something to light the fire with;

(c) voilà comme q. je me suis trouvé là, that's how I happened to be there; *F* **comme q. ça n'était pas la peine de s'énerver,** so it wasn't worth getting worked up about;

(d) (*correlative to* **qui, que** + *sub*) **q. qui survienne, restez calme,** whatever happens, keep calm; **q. qu'il en soit,** however that may be; **q. qu'on fasse, il n'est jamais content,** no matter what you do *or* whatever you do he's never satisfied; **q. que ce soit,** anything (whatever); **puis-je vous être utile en q. que ce soit?,** can I be of use to you in any way?; **avez-vous dit q. que ce soit?,** did you say anything (at all)?; **q. que ce soit qui l'en empêche,** whatever may be preventing him.

quoi² **(a)** *pron interr* what; **qui ou q. vous a donné cette idée?,** who or what gave you that idea?; **q. d'autre?,** what else?; **q. de nouveau?,** what's new?; **q. de plus simple?,** what could be simpler *or* easier?; **eh bien! q.?,** well, what about it?; **vous désirez q.?,** what is it you want?; **les journaux ne savent (pas) q. ébruiter,** the papers don't know what to disclose; **de q. parlez-vous?,** what are you talking about?; **à q. pensez-vous?,** what are you thinking of *or* about?; **en q. puis-je vous être utile?,** how can I help you?; **à q. bon (faire qch)?,** what's the use *or* good (of doing sth)?; **en q. est-ce?, c'est en q.?,** what's it made of?;

(b) *int* **(mais) q.! q. donc!,** what! what's that?; **q., c'est vous!,** what, is it you?; *F* **q.?, je n'entends rien!,** what?, I can't hear you!; **mais alors q.? tout est annulé?,** don't tell me it's all off!; **enfin q.! il ne peut pas se désister comme ça?,** wait a minute, he can't back out like that!; **on ne va pas y passer la nuit q.!,** we're not going to spend the night there!

quoique [kwak(ə)] *conj* (*souvent* + *sub*) (al)though; **quoiqu'il soit pauvre il est généreux,** although he is poor he is generous; **je suis heureux q. garçon,** I am happy though a bachelor; *F* **nous recevons souvent des coups, q., vous savez, nous en donnons aussi,** we often receive blows, but then, of course, we hit back.

quolibet [kɔlibɛ] *nm* gibe; **poursuivre qn de quolibets,** to gibe *or* jeer at s.o..

quorum [k(w)ɔrɔm] *nm* quorum.

quota [k(w)ɔta] *nm* quota; **q. d'importation,** import quota.

quote-part [kɔtpar] *nf* share, quota, portion; (*pl quotes-parts*).

quotidien, -ienne [kɔtidjɛ̃, -jɛn] **1** *adj* daily, everyday; **la vie quotidienne,** everyday life. **2** *nm* **(a)** *Journ* **les quotidiens,** the daily papers, the dailies; **(b) au q.,** on a day-to-day basis; **vivre ses nouvelles résolutions au q.,** to try to keep one's new resolutions one day at a time; **la science-fiction au q.,** science fiction in the everyday world.

quotidiennement [kɔtidjɛnmɑ̃] *adv* daily, every day.

quotidienneté [kɔtidjɛnte] *nf* everyday life, day-to-day life.

quotient [kɔsjɑ̃] *nm* **(a)** *Math etc* quotient; **(b) q. électoral,** electoral quota; **q. intellectuel,** intelligence quotient, I.Q.; **son q. intellectuel est de 120,** he has an IQ of 120.

quotité [kɔtite] *nf* quota, share, proportion; *Jur* **q. disponible,** disposable portion of estate.

R

R, r [ɛr] *nm* (the letter) R, r; **rouler les r,** to roll one's r's.
r. (*abrév* **route**) Rd.
rab [rab] *nm Arg* (*nourriture*) extra (food); (*travail*) extra (time); **il reste du poulet en r.,** there's some chicken left for the asking *or* going spare *or* up for grabs; **elle fait du r.,** (*des heures supplémentaires*) she's doing extra work *or* overtime.
rabâchage [rabaʃaʒ] *nm* (tedious) repetition.
rabâcher [rabaʃe] **1** *vi* to say the same thing over and over again. **2** *vt* **ils rabâchent toujours la même chose,** they're always harping on the same string *or* the same old thing; **r. une leçon,** to learn a lesson by going over it again and again.
rabâcheur, -euse [rabaʃœr, -øz] *n & adj* repetitive (person); **il est très r.,** he's always repeating himself *or* harping on the same thing.
rabais [rabɛ] *nm* discount; reduction (*in price*); **r. en cas de paiement comptant,** discount for cash; **faire un r. sur qch,** to give a discount on sth, to make a reduction *or* an allowance on sth; **vendre qch au r.,** to sell sth at a discount *or* at a reduced price.
rabaissement [rabɛsmɑ̃] *nm* **(a)** lowering (*of blind, price*); **(b)** (*critique*) disparagement.
rabaisser [rabese] **1** *vt* **(a)** to lower (*sth*); to reduce, to lower (*price*); **(b)** to depreciate, to disparage, to belittle (*s.o., talent etc*); to humble, to belittle (*s.o.*), *F* to put (*s.o.*) down. **2 se rabaisser** *vpr* to humble *or* lower oneself, *F* to put oneself down.
rabane [raban] *nf Tex* raffia (fabric); *F* **mettre les rabanes sur le sable,** to put (raffia) mats down on the sand.
rabat [raba] *nm* **(a)** flap (*of handbag etc*); bands (*of official costume*); **(b)** beating (*for game*).
rabat-joie [rabaʒwa] **1** *nm inv* killjoy, *F* spoilsport, *F* wet blanket, *F* party pooper. **2** *adj inv* **elle est r.-j.,** she's a killjoy *or* a spoilsport *or* a wet blanket *or* a party pooper.
rabattable [rabatabl] *adj* that can be folded back; *Aut* **capote r.,** folding roof, drophead.
rabattage [rabataʒ] *nm* beating (*for game*); driving (*of game*); heading off (*of fugitives*).
rabatteur, -euse [rabatœr, -øz] *n* **(a)** (*à la chasse*) beater; **(b)** *Fig* tout.
rabattre [rabatr] *v* (*conj like* **battre**) **1** *vt* **(a)** to fold (*sth*) back; to shut (*lid*); to lower, to pull down, to shut (*blind*); to turn down (*collar*); to tilt back (*seat*); **r. une couture,** to press down *or* flatten a seam; **r. le bord d'une tôle,** to flange a plate; **porte rabattue contre la paroi,** door folded back to the wall; **le vent rabat la fumée,** the wind is driving down the smoke; *Sp* **r. la balle,** to smash the ball; **r. la foule vers la place,** to drive the crowd back towards the square;
(b) (*diminuer*) to reduce, to lessen, to diminish; to cut back (*tree, branch*); **r. tant du prix,** to take *or F* knock so much off the price; **je n'en rabattrai pas un sou,** I won't take a penny less for it; **r. l'orgueil de qn,** to humble s.o.'s pride; **r. de ses prétentions, en r.,** to climb down; *Tricot* **r. les mailles,** to cast off;
(c) to drive *or* head off (*game, fugitives*).
2 *vi* **il faut r. à droite,** you must turn off *or* bear to the right.
3 se rabattre *vpr* **(a) table qui se rabat,** folding *or* drop-leaf table;
(b) l'armée se rabattit sur la ville, the army fell back on the town;
(c) ayant épuisé ce sujet, il se rabattit sur la politique, having exhausted this subject, he fell back on politics; **elle finira par se r. sur ce qu'on lui propose,** she'll end up accepting what they're offering her;
(d) *Sp Aut* to cut in (*after overtaking*).
rabattu [rabaty] *adj* turned-down; **col r.,** turn(ed)-down collar; **chapeau r.,** slouch hat; **couture rabattue,** run and fell seam.
rabbin [rabɛ̃] *nm* rabbi; **grand r.,** Chief Rabbi.
rabbinique [rabinik] *adj* rabbinical.
rabbinisme [rabinism] *nm* rabbinism.
rabbiniste [rabinist] *n* rabbinist.
rabdomancie [rabdɔmɑ̃si] *nf* water divining, *Spéc* rhabdomancy.
rabelaisien, -ienne [rablɛzjɛ̃, -jɛn] *adj Littér* Rabelaisian.
rabibochage [rabibɔʃaʒ] *nm F* patching up, repairing, mending; (*entre amis*) making up, reconciliation.
rabibocher [rabibɔʃe] *F* **1** *vt* to patch up, to repair; **j'ai réussi à les r.,** I managed to patch things up between them. **2 se rabibocher** *vpr* to patch things up, to make it up.
rabiot [rabjo] *nm Arg* **(a)** (*supplément de nourriture*) extra (food); **un r. de poulet,** a second helping *or* seconds of chicken; **(b)** (*supplément de temps*) overtime; **faire du r.,** to work overtime; **récupérer un r. de cinq minutes,** to have an extra five minutes.
rabioter [rabjɔte] **1** *vi Arg* **(a)** to scrounge, to cadge (*surplus food etc*); **(b)** (*financièrement*) to make a bit on the side, to be on the fiddle. **2** *vt* to wangle (*sth*); **j'ai réussi à r. cinq minutes,** I managed to snatch *or* steal an extra five minutes.
rabique [rabik] *adj* rabies (*virus*).
râble¹ [rɑbl] *nm* back (*of hare, rabbit*); *Culin* **r. de lièvre,** saddle of hare; *F* **il m'a sauté sur le r.,** he jumped on me.
râble² *nm* fire rake.
râblé [rable] *adj* broad-backed, strong-backed, strapping (*fellow*).
rabot [rabo] *nm Menuis* plane; **r. à languette,** grooving plane, tongue plane.
rabotage [rabɔtaʒ] *nm Menuis* planing.
raboter [rabɔte] *vt* to plane (*wood*); to scrape, to rub (*surface*); *Fig* **r. son style,** to polish one's style.
raboteur [rabɔtœr] *nm Menuis* (*personne*) planer.
raboteuse [rabɔtøz] *nf Menuis* planing machine, planer.
raboteux, -euse [rabɔtø, -øz] *adj* rough, uneven (*surface*); knotty (*wood*); bumpy, uneven (*road*); *Fig* unpolished (*style*).
rabougri [rabugri] *adj* stunted (*plant, person*).
rabougrir [rabugrir] **1** *vt* to stunt (the growth of) (*sth*). **2 se rabougrir** *vpr* to become stunted.
rabouter [rabute] *vt* to join end to end.
rabrouer [rabrue] *vt* to snub (*s.o.*), to brush (*s.o.*) off.
racaille [rakaj] *nf* rabble, riff-raff, scum.
raccommodable [rakɔmɔdabl] *adj* mendable, repairable.
raccommodage [rakɔmɔdaʒ] *nm* **(a)** (*action*) mending, repairing (*of garments etc*); darning, mending (*of stocking*); **faire du r.,** to do some darning *or* mending; **(b)** (*résultat*) mend, repair; darn (*of stocking*).
raccommodement [rakɔmɔdmɑ̃] *nm F* reconciliation.
raccommoder [rakɔmɔde] **1** *vt* **(a)** to mend, to repair (*dress, watch etc*); to darn (*stocking*); **(b)** *F* to reconcile (*two people*). **2 se raccomoder** *vpr* to make it up, to patch things up; **ils se sont raccommodés,** they made it up *or* patched things up *or* became friends again.
raccommodeur, -euse [rakɔmɔdœr, -øz] *n* mender, repairer.
raccompagner [rakɔ̃paɲe] *vt* to accompany (*s.o.*) back; **je vais vous r.,** I'll take you back, I'll go back with you, I'll see you home; **r. qn à la porte,** to see *or* show s.o. to the door.
raccord [rakɔr] *nm* **(a)** join (*in a building, picture etc*); **papier sans raccords,** (wall)paper with no pattern repeat; **faire des raccords (de peinture),** to touch up (the paintwork); **faire un r. à une bande magnétique,** to splice a tape; *F* **faire un r.,** (*de maquillage*) to touch up one's make-up; **(b)** (*pièce d'assemblage*) connection, coupling, joint; *El* **r. mâle et femelle,** plug and socket

connection; **bouchon de r.,** adapter; **r. de lampe,** lamp adapter *or* connector; **r. de graissage,** grease nipple; **(c)** (*action*) linking up.

raccordement [rakɔrdəmɑ̃] *nm* **(a)** (*en ajustant*) adjusting; *Rail Constr* **rayon de r. d'une courbe,** transition radius of a curve; **(b)** (*pour relier*) joining, linking (up), connecting; **pièces de r.**, making-up lengths (*of piping etc*); *Rail* **voie de r.**, junction line, loop line; service siding (*to factory etc*); *El* **boîte de r.**, junction box (*for cables etc*).

raccorder [rakɔrde] **1** *vt* **(a)** (*brancher*) to join (up), to connect, to unite, to couple; to link up (*buildings, roads*); *El* **r. à la masse** *ou* **à la terre,** to earth, *Am* to ground; **(b)** to bring (*parts*) into line; to make (*parts*) flush; **(c)** to splice (*a tape*). **2 se raccorder** *vpr* to fit together, to link up.

raccourci [rakursi] *nm* **(a)** (*route plus courte*) short cut; **prendre un r.,** to take a short cut; **(b)** (*résumé*) abridgment, shortened version; **en r.,** briefly, in brief; **voici l'histoire en r.,** this, in brief, is the story, these are the outlines of the story; **la famille est la société en r.,** the family is society in miniature, the family is a microcosm of society; **(c)** *Beaux-Arts* foreshortening; **bras en r.,** foreshortened arm.

raccourcir [rakursir] **1** *vt* **(a)** to shorten, to reduce the length of (*sth*); to take up (*sleeve etc*); **r. ses pas,** to take shorter steps, to shorten one's stride; *Fig* **tomber à bras raccourcis sur qn,** to pitch into s.o., to go for s.o. tooth and nail; **r. son chemin,** to take a short cut; **(b)** to shorten, to abridge (*speech etc*); **(c)** *Beaux- Arts* to foreshorten. **2** *vi* to grow shorter, to shorten; **les jours raccourcissent,** the days are growing shorter *or* drawing in; *F* **les jupes raccourcissent encore cet hiver,** skirts are getting even shorter this winter.

raccourcissement [rakursismɑ̃] *nm* **(a)** shortening, reducing (in length); **(b)** (*pour abréger*) shortening, abridging, abridgment; **(c)** *Beaux-Arts* foreshortening; **(d)** (*of skirts*) growing shorter; (*of cloth*) shrinking; (*of days*) drawing in.

raccroc [rakro] *nm* fluke, lucky stroke; **par r.,** by a fluke.

raccrochage [rakrɔʃaʒ] *nm* accosting, soliciting, touting.

raccrocher [rakrɔʃe] **1** *vt* **(a)** to hook *or* hang (*sth*) up again, to put (*sth*) back on the hook; *Tél* **r. l'appareil,** to put down the receiver, to ring off, to hang up; *F* **ce boxeur devrait r. les gants,** it's time this boxer hung up his gloves; **(b)** *F* (*rattraper*) to recover (*sth*), to get hold of (*s.o., sth*) again; **r. une commande,** to save *or* rescue an order; **(c)** to stop (*s.o. in the street etc*); (*of prostitute*) to accost (*passer-by*). **2** *vi Tél* to hang up; **il m'a raccroché au nez,** he hung up on me. **3 se raccrocher** *vpr* **(a) se r. à qch,** to catch hold of sth, to catch on to sth; **se r. à une espérance,** to cling to a hope; **se r. à tout,** to clutch at every straw; **(b)** *F* to recoup one's losses; **(c)** (*se rapporter*) to be linked, to be connected; **cette idée ne se raccroche pas du tout au sujet,** that idea has nothing to do with the subject, that idea is totally unrelated to the subject.

raccrocheuse [rakrɔʃøz] *nf* street walker.

race [ras] *nf* **(a)** (*famille*) ancestry, descent; **de r. noble,** of noble blood *or* descent *or* extraction; *Fig* **être de la r. des gagnants,** to be a born winner; **il chasse de r.,** he's a chip off the old block; **être fin de r.,** to be decadent; **elle a de la r.,** she's distinguished *or* aristocratic, she's got breeding; **(b)** (*ethnie*) race; **la r. blanche/noire,** the white/black race; **la r. humaine,** the human race; **(c)** *Zool* breed; **la r. chevaline,** the horse species; **améliorer/croiser les races,** to improve/to cross breeds; **chien/taureau de r.** *ou* **qui a de la r.,** pure-bred dog/bull, pedigree dog/bull; **cheval de r.,** thoroughbred (horse); *Prov* **bon chien chasse de r.,** what's bred in the bone comes out in the flesh.

racé [rase] *adj* (*animal*) thoroughbred, pure bred; (*personne*) aristocratic, distinguished; *F* **profil r.,** clean *or* elegant lines (*of car, yacht*).

racème [rasɛm] *nm Bot* raceme.

rachat [raʃa] *nm* **(a)** repurchase, buying back; **pacte de r.,** covenant of redemption; **avec faculté de r.,** with option of repurchase *or* redemption; **r. des captifs,** ransom of the prisoners; **r. d'une société par la direction,** management buy-out; **(b)** (*en assurances*) surrender (*of policy*); **valeur de r.,** surrender value; **(c)** *Rel* **r. d'un péché,** atonement for a sin.

rachetable [raʃtabl] *adj* **(a)** redeemable (*stock*); **(b)** atonable (*sin*).

racheter [raʃte] *v* (*conj like* **acheter**) **1** *vt* **(a)** to repurchase, to buy (*sth*) back; (*acheter davantage*) to buy some more of (*sth*); **je n'ai plus de café, je dois en r.,** I've no coffee left, I'll have to buy some more; **(b)** (*en assurances*) to surrender (*policy*); to redeem (*annuity*); **(c)** to redeem (*debt, pledge*); to make up for, to compensate for (*a fault*); to ransom (*prisoner*); **r. des otages,** to ransom *or* pay a ransom for hostages; **Jésus-Christ est mort pour r. les hommes,** Christ died to redeem mankind; **r. ses péchés,** to atone for one's sins; **r. son honneur,** to retrieve one's honour. **2 se racheter** *vpr* to redeem oneself; **que puis-je faire pour me r.?,** what can I do to make up for it?, how can I redeem myself?

rachidien, -ienne [raʃidjɛ̃, -jɛn] *adj Anat* rachidian (*bulb, canal*).

rachis [raʃis] *nm Anat Bot* rachis.

rachitique [raʃitik] *adj Méd* rickety, *Spéc* rachitic.

rachitisme [raʃitism] *nm Méd* rickets, *Spéc* rachitis.

racial, -aux [rasjal, -o] *adj* racial.

racine [rasin] *nf* **(a)** root (*of plant, hair, nail, tooth etc*); *Bot* **r. pivotante,** tap root; **r. de gingembre,** root ginger; **cultiver des racines,** to grow root vegetables; **jeter** *ou* **pousser des racines,** to throw out roots; **prendre r.,** (*d'une plante, Fig d'une personne*) to take root; *Fig* **couper le mal à la r.,** to strike at the root of the evil; *Fig* **manger les pissenlits par la r.,** to be pushing up the daisies; **(b)** *Math* **r. carrée/cubique,** square/cube root; **(c)** *Ling* **r. d'un mot,** root of a word; **(d)** *Fig* (*origine*) root; **elle n'a plus de r.,** she's lost her roots, she doesn't belong anywhere any more; **être à la recherche de ses racines,** to be searching for one's roots.

raciner [rasine] *vt* to marble (*the covers of book*).

racisme [rasism] *nm* rac(ial)ism; *Fig* **c'est du r. anti-vieux,** that's ageism, it's a case of prejudice against old people.

raciste [rasist] *adj & n* rac(ial)ist.

racket [rakɛt] *nm F* racket; **faire du r.,** to run a racket.

racketter [rakɛte] *vt* to extort money from (*s.o.*), to subject (*s.o.*) to a protection racket.

racketteur [rakɛtœr] *nm F* racketeer.

raclage [raklaʒ] *nm* scraping.

raclée [rakle] *nf F* thrashing, hiding; **flanquer** *ou* **administrer une r. à qn,** to give s.o. a thrashing *or* hiding; *Fig* **son parti/son équipe a pris une belle r.,** his party/team got a good thrashing *or* hiding *or* licking.

raclement [rakləmɑ̃] *nm* scraping (noise).

racler [rakle] **1** *vt* to scrape (*skin, carrot etc*); **r. une casserole,** to scrape (out) a saucepan; **r. une allée,** to rake a drive; *F* **r. les fonds de tiroirs,** to scrape (the bottom of) the barrel; *Fig F* **r. du** *ou* **le violon,** to scrape *or* saw on the fiddle; **ce vin racle la gorge,** this wine's (a bit) rough on the throat. **2 se racler** *vpr* **se r. la gorge,** to clear one's throat.

raclette [raklɛt] *nf* **(a)** (*petit racloir*) scraper; **(b)** *Phot etc* squeegee; **(c)** (*de jardin*) hoe; **(d)** *Culin* raclette (= *Savoyard dish of potatoes and melted cheese*).

racloir [raklwar] *nm* **(a)** scraper; **(b)** *Phot etc* squeegee.

racolage [rakɔlaʒ] *nm* **(a)** soliciting, accosting; **faire du r.,** to tout for custom, to ply for trade, to solicit; **(b)** *Hist* press-ganging (*into army, navy*); **r. de partisans,** enlisting of supporters.

racoler [rakɔle] **1** *vt* **(a)** to solicit, to accost; **(b)** *Hist* to press-gang (*men into army, navy*); **r. des partisans,** to enlist *or* tout for supporters. **2** *vi* to tout for custom, to solicit.

racoleur, -euse [rakɔlœr, -øz] **1** *adj* **publicité racoleuse,** eye-catching advertising. **2** *n* **(a)** (*politicien*) propagandist; (*commerçant*) tout; **(b)** *Hist* crimp. **3** *nf* **racoleuse,** street walker.

racontable [rakɔ̃tabl] *adj* relatable, tellable.

racontar [rakɔ̃tar] *nm F* story, piece of gossip; **ce ne sont que des racontars,** it's just tittle-tattle.

raconter [rakɔ̃te] **1** *vt* to tell, to relate, to narrate, to recount; **r. de longues histoires,** to spin long yarns; **il en a raconté de belles,** he told some fine *or* tall stories; **qu'est-ce qu'il raconte là?,** what is he talking about?; **allez, racontez!,** come on, out with it! **2 se raconter** *vpr* to talk about oneself; **je ne tiens pas à me r. devant tout le monde,** I'm not keen on talking about myself in front of lots of people.

raconteur, -euse [rakɔ̃tœr, -øz] *n* storyteller, narrator.

racoon [rakun] *nm* rac(c)oon.

racornir [rakɔrnir] **1** *vt* to make (*sth*) hard *or* tough (*as horn*). **2 se racornir** *vpr* **(a)** (*des ongles*) to grow horny; (*du papier*) to grow brittle; **(b)** *Fig* to shrivel up.

racornissement [rakɔrnismɑ̃] *nm* hardening, toughening (up).

racquitter (se) [sərakite] *vpr* to recoup oneself, to retrieve one's losses.

radar [radar] *nm* radar; **r. à ondes entretenues,**

continuous-wave radar; **balayage r.,** radar scan; **écho r.,** radar echo; **r. d'autoguidage,** homing radar; *Fig F* **ce matin je suis** *ou* **j'avance au r.,** I'm like a zombie this morning, I'm on auto-pilot this morning; *Fig* **l'intuition est mon plus sûr r.,** intuition is the best guide.
radariste [radarist] *n* radar operator.
rade[1] [rad] *nf Nau* roadstead; **r. foraine** *ou* **ouverte,** open roadstead; **r. fermée,** sheltered roadstead; **navire en r.,** ship in the roads; **mettre un navire en r.,** to lay up a ship; *Fig* **mettre qn/un projet en r.,** to leave s.o. in the lurch/to jettison a project.
rade[2] *nm Arg* (*comptoir*) bar, counter; (*bistro*) bar.
radeau, -eaux [rado] *nm* raft; **r. de sauvetage,** life raft.
radial, -ale, -aux [radjal, -o] **1** *adj* **(a)** radial; **pneumatique à carcasse radiale,** radial(-ply) tyre; **(b)** *Anat* radial (*muscle, nerve*). **2** *nf* **radiale (a)** radial road, urban motorway; **(b)** *Anat* radial.
radian [radjɑ̃] *nm Math* radian.
radiance [radjɑ̃s] *nf* radiance.
radiant [radjɑ̃] **1** *adj* radiant (*heat, beauty etc*); **pouvoir r.,** radiating capacity. **2** *nm Astron* radiant (point).
radiateur [radjatœr] *nm* radiator; **r. à eau chaude,** hot-water radiator; **r. électrique,** electric fire *or* radiator; **r. soufflant,** fan heater; *Aut etc* **r. à nid d'abeilles,** honeycomb radiator.
radiation[1] [radjɑsjɔ̃] *nf* **(a)** striking out, crossing out; cancellation (*of debt*); **(b)** striking off the roll(s); disbarment (*of barrister*); striking off (*of solicitor*).
radiation[2] *nf Phys* radiation; **r. cosmique,** cosmic radiation; *Électron* **r. (de) haute fréquence,** high-frequency radiation; *Nucl* **r. alpha/bêta,** alpha/beta radiation, alpha-ray/beta-ray emission.
radical, -ale, -aux [radikal, -o] **1** *adj* **(a)** *Math Bot Pol* radical; **signe r.,** radical *or* root sign; **politicien r.,** radical politician; **(b)** (*fondamental*) radical, complete; **réformes radicales,** radical *or* sweeping reforms; **changement r.,** radical change; **elle a été radicale, il n'y a rien d'autre à faire,** she was adamant, there's nothing else for it. **2** *n Pol* radical; **r. de droite/de gauche,** right-wing/left-wing radical. **3** *nm Ling* root, radical; *Math* radical *or* root sign; *Ch* radical; **radicaux libres,** free radicals.
radicalement [radikalmɑ̃] *adv* radically.
radicalisation [radikalizɑsjɔ̃] *nf Pol* radicalisation.
radicaliser [radikalize] *Pol* **1** *vt* to radicalise. **2 se radicaliser** *vpr* to radicalise, to become (more) radical.
radicalisme [radikalism] *nm Pol* radicalism.
radical-socialisme [radikalsɔsjalism] *nm Pol* radical socialism.
radical-socialiste [radikalsɔsjalist] *adj & n Pol* radical socialist; (*pl radicaux-socialistes*).
radicelle [radisɛl] *nf Bot* radicel, rootlet.
radicule [radikyl] *nf Bot* radicle.
radier[1] [radje] *nm Constr* frame, floor, bed; sill (*of lock gate*); apron (*of dock*); **r. de fondation,** foundation raft.
radier[2] *vt* (*impf & pr sub* **n. radiions**) to erase (*sth*), to strike (*sth*) out; to strike (*sth, s.o.*) off, to cross (*sth, s.o.*) off (*a list etc*).
radiesthésie [radjɛstezi] *nf* dowsing, divination.
radiesthésiste [radjɛstezist] *n* dowser, diviner.
radieux, -euse [radjø, -øz] *adj* radiant (*sun, eyes*); dazzling (*sun*); beaming (*with joy*).
radin [radɛ̃] *adj & n Arg* mean, stingy (person).
radiner [radine] *Arg* **1** *vi* to turn up, to show up, to roll up. **2 se radiner** *vpr* to turn up, to show up, to roll up.
radio [radjo] *F* **1** *nf* **(a)** radio (set), *Br Vieilli* wireless; **à la r.,** on the radio; **écouter la r.,** to listen to the radio; **faire de la r.,** to be *or* work as a radio presenter; **travailler à la r.,** to work for (the) radio; **r. libre,** independent local radio (station); **r. pirate,** pirate radio (station); **passer à la r.,** to broadcast, to go on the air *or* radio; **(b)** (*radiotéléphonie*) radiotelephony; **(c)** *Méd* X-ray (photograph); **passer une r.** *ou* **à la r.,** to be X-rayed. **2** *nm Vieilli* **(a)** (*télégramme*) radio(gram); **(b)** (*opérateur*) radio operator.
radioactif, -ive [radjɔaktif, -iv] *adj* radioactive.
radioactivité [radjɔaktivite] *nf* radioactivity.
radioalignement [radjɔaliɲ(ə)mɑ̃] *nm Av Nau* radio-beacon route; **voler par r.,** to fly airways.
radioastronomie [radjɔastrɔnɔmi] *nf* radio astronomy.
radiobalisage [radjɔbalizaʒ] *nm* radio-beacon navigation; *Av* airways navigation.
radiobalise [radjɔbaliz] *nf* radio beacon, marker beacon.
radiocassette [radjɔkasɛt] *nf* radio cassette (player).
radiocommunication [radjɔkɔmynikɑsjɔ̃] *nf* radiocommunication.
radiocompas [radjɔkɔ̃pɑ] *nm Av* radio compass.
radioconducteur [radjɔkɔ̃dyktœr] *nm* radio conductor.
radiodermite [radjɔdɛrmit] *nf Méd* radiodermatitis, X-ray dermatitis.
radiodiagnostic [radjɔdjagnɔstik] *nm Méd* X-ray diagnosis.
radiodiffuser [radjɔdifyze] *vt Rad* to broadcast.
radiodiffusion [radjɔdifysjɔ̃] *nf Rad* broadcasting.
radioélectricien, -ienne [radjɔelɛktrisjɛ̃, -jɛn] *n* radio (and television) technician.
radiogénique [radjɔʒenik] *adj F* **il a une voix r.,** he has a good broadcasting voice.
radiogoniomètre [radjɔgɔnjɔmɛtr] *nm* radiogoniometer, direction finder.
radiogoniométrie [radjɔgɔnjɔmetri] *nf* radiogoniometry, direction finding.
radiogramme [radjɔgram] *nm* **(a)** *Méd* radiograph, X-ray photograph; **(b)** (*message*) radio telegram, radiogram.
radiographe [radjɔgraf] *n Méd* radiographer.
radiographie [radjɔgrafi] *nf Méd* **(a)** (*technique*) radiography, X-ray photography; **(b)** (*cliché*) X-ray photograph, radiograph.
radiographier [radjɔgrafje] *vt* (*impf & pr sub* **n. radiographiions**) *Méd* to radiograph, to X-ray.
radiographique [radjɔgrafik] *adj Méd* radiographic; **examen r.,** X-ray examination.
radioguidage [radjɔgidaʒ] *nm Av Nau* radio control, radio direction, radio guidance; (*de missile etc*) homing; *Rad* traffic information (*for motorists*).
radioguidé [radjɔgide] *adj* radio-controlled; guided (*missile*).
radio(-)journal [radjɔʒurnal] *nm Rad* news, news bulletin; (*pl radio(-)journaux*).
radiologie [radjɔlɔʒi] *nf Méd* radiology.
radiologique [radjɔlɔʒik] *adj Méd* radiological; **examen r.,** X-ray examination.
radiologue [radjɔlɔg] **, radiologiste** [radjɔlɔʒist] *n Méd* radiologist.
radiomètre [radjɔmɛtr] *nm Phys* radiometer.
radionavigant [radjɔnavigɑ̃] *nm Nau Av* radio officer.
radionavigation [radjɔnavigɑsjɔ̃] *nf* navigation by radar.
radiophare [radjɔfar] *nm Nau Av* radio beacon.
radiophonie [radjɔfɔni] *nf* radio(tele)phony, wireless telephony.
radiorepérage [radjɔrəperaʒ] *nm* radiolocation.
radioreportage [radjɔrəpɔrtaʒ] *nm Rad* radio reporting *or* commentary.
radioreporter [radjɔrəpɔrtɛr] *nm Rad* reporter, commentator.
radioscopie [radjɔskɔpi] *nf Méd* radioscopy, X-ray examination.
radioscopique [radjɔskɔpik] *adj Méd* **examen r.,** X-ray examination.
radiosondage [radjɔsɔ̃daʒ] *nm Météo* radiosonde exploration.
radiosonde [radjɔsɔ̃d] *nf* **(a)** *Météo* radiosonde; **(b)** *Av* radio altimeter.
radio-taxi [radjɔtaksi] *nm* radiocab, radiotaxi; (*pl radio-taxis*).
radiotechnique [radjɔtɛknik] *nf* radiotechnology.
radiotélégramme [radjɔtelegram] *nm* radio telegram.
radiotélégraphie [radjɔtelegrafi] *nf* radio telegraphy, wireless telegraphy.
radiotélégraphier [radjɔtelegrafje] *vt* (*conj like* **télégraphier**) to radio (*a telegram*).
radiotélégraphique [radjɔtelegrafik] *adj* radiotelegraphic, wireless.
radiotéléphonie [radjɔtelefɔni] *nf* radio(tele)phony, wireless telephony.
radiotélescope [radjɔtelɛskɔp] *nm* radio telescope.
radiotélévisé [radjɔtelevize] *adj* broadcast on both radio and television.
radiothérapeute [radjɔterapøt] *n Méd* radiotherapist.
radiothérapie [radjɔterapi] *nf Méd* radiotherapy, X-ray treatment.
radis [radi] *nm* radish; *F* **ne pas avoir un r.,** to be (stony) broke, not to have a bean; **je ne dépense pas un r. de plus,** I'm not spending a penny more.
radium [radjɔm] *nm* radium.
radius [radjys] *nm Anat* radius.
radotage [radɔtaʒ] *nm* twaddle, drivel; rambling talk (*of old person etc*).
radoter [radɔte] *vi* to ramble on (incoherently); (*rabâcher*) to keep on repeating oneself; **il commence à r.,** he's getting a bit gaga.
radoteur, -euse [radɔtœr, -øz] *n Vieilli* dotard; **c'est un**

r., he's always rambling on.

radoub [radu] *nm Nau* refitting, graving (*of ship*); **navire en r.,** ship under repair *or* in dry dock; **bassin de r.,** graving dock, dry dock.

radouber [radube] *vt* **(a)** to repair the hull of (*ship*); to dock (*ship in dry dock*); **(b)** to mend, to repair (*net*); *F* to patch (*sth*) up.

radoucir [radusir] **1** *vt* to calm, to soften; to calm (*s.o.*) down, to mollify (*s.o.*); **la pluie a radouci le temps,** the rain has brought milder weather. **2 se radoucir** *vpr* to calm down; (*of weather*) to become milder.

radoucissement [radusismɑ̃] *nm* **(a)** softening (*of voice etc*); calming down (*of person*); **(b)** *Météo* milder spell, change for the better.

rafale [rafal] *nf* squall, strong gust, blast (*of wind*); burst (*of gunfire*); **vent à rafales,** blustering *or* gusty wind; **temps à rafales,** squally weather.

raffermir [rafɛrmir] **1** *vt* **(a)** to firm up, to make (*sth*) firm(er); **crème qui raffermit la peau,** cream which tones up the skin; **(b)** to confirm, to reinforce, to strengthen (*authority, resolution*); to fortify, to restore (*courage, spirit*); to steady (*prices, nerves*). **2 se raffermir** *vpr* (*of ground*) to harden, to get firmer; (*of muscle etc*) to firm up, to get firmer; (*of health*) to improve; (*of prices*) to steady; **ses jambes se raffermissent,** his legs are growing stronger again; **son autorité se raffermit,** he is recovering *or* regaining his authority; **il se raffermit dans sa résolution,** he is more determined than ever.

raffermissement [rafɛrmismɑ̃] *nm* **(a)** firming (up), making firm(er); improvement, building up (*of health*); **(b)** steadying (*of prices*); **(c)** strengthening, confirmation, reinforcement (*of authority, power*).

raffinage [rafinaʒ] *nm* (*oil, sugar etc*) refining.

raffiné [rafine] *adj* **(a)** refined (*sugar etc*); **(b)** subtle, refined (*mind*); delicate, refined (*taste etc*); refined, polished (*manners, style*).

raffinement [rafinmɑ̃] *nm* refinement (*of manners*); refinement, subtlety, nicety (*of language*); subtlety, refinement (*of thought, policy*); refinement (*of luxury, cruelty*); **le comble du r.,** the height of refinement.

raffiner [rafine] **1** *vt* to refine (*sugar, oil etc*); **r. ses manières,** to refine *or* polish one's manners. **2** *vi* to be overmeticulous; **r. sur la propreté,** to carry cleanliness to extremes; **vous raffinez!,** you're being too subtle!

raffinerie [rafinri] *nf* (oil, sugar) refinery.

raffineur, -euse [rafinœr, -øz] *n* (oil, sugar) refiner; **un r. de la langue anglaise,** (*connaisseur*) a refiner of the English language.

raffoler [rafɔle] *vi F* **r. de qn/qch,** to dote on *or* adore *or* be mad about s.o./sth.

raffut [rafy] *nm F* din, racket, row.

raffûter [rafyte] *vt* to (re)sharpen, to (re)set (*tool*).

rafiau, rafiot [rafjo] *nm Nau* skiff (*with lateen sail*); **vieux r.,** old tub.

rafistolage [rafistɔlaʒ] *nm F* patching up; **ça n'ira pas loin, c'est du r.,** it won't last long, it's just a makeshift *or* patched-up job.

rafistoler [rafistɔle] *vt F* to patch up.

rafle [rafl] *nf* **(a)** looting; *F* clean sweep (*by burglars etc*); **r. d'étalage avec bris de devanture,** smash-and-grab raid; **(b)** round-up, raid (*by the police*).

rafler [rafle] *vt F* to swipe, to nick (*contents of house etc*); **ils m'ont tout raflé,** they've cleaned me out totally, they've swiped the lot.

rafraîchir [rafrɛʃir] **1** *vt* **(a)** (*rendre frais*) to cool (*sth*) (down); to air (*room*) **(b)** to freshen up (*colour*); to do up, to renovate (*picture*); to touch up (*edged tool*); **r. les cheveux à qn,** to trim s.o.'s hair, to give s.o.('s hair) a trim; **r. la mémoire à qn,** to refresh *or* jog s.o.'s memory; **je vais te r. les idées,** I'll jog your memory for you. **2** *vi* **mettre le vin à r. à la cave,** to put the wine to cool in the cellar. **3 se rafraîchir** *vpr* **(a)** (*du temps*) to grow *or* turn cooler; **(b)** to freshen oneself up; *F* (*en buvant*) to have a refreshing drink.

rafraîchissant [rafrɛʃisɑ̃] *adj* refreshing, cooling (*breeze, drink*); **simplicité rafraîchissante,** refreshing simplicity.

rafraîchissement [rafrɛʃismɑ̃] *nm* **(a)** cooling (*of temperature, liquid etc*); **(b)** freshening up (*of colour*); **(c)** (*boisson*) cold drink; **rafraîchissements,** refreshments.

raga [raga] *nm inv Mus* raga.

ragaillardir [ragajardir] **1** *vt* (*physiquement*) to revive (*s.o.*), to make (*s.o.*) feel better; (*encourager*) to cheer (*s.o.*) up. **2 se ragaillardir** *vpr* to cheer up, *F* to buck up.

rage [raʒ] *nf* **(a)** *Méd* rabies; **(b)** *Fig* rage, fury, frenzy; (*passion*) passion (*for sth*); **la tempête fait r.,** the storm is raging; **l'incendie faisait r.,** the fire was blazing *or* raging (furiously); **cette mode fait r. chez** *ou* **parmi les jeunes,** this fashion is all the rage with the young; **avoir la r. du jeu/d'écrire,** to have a passion for gambling/writing; *F* **c'est pas de l'amour, c'est de la r.,** that's not love, it's madness; **r. de dents,** raging toothache.

rageant [raʒɑ̃] *adj F* infuriating.

rager [raʒe] *vi* (**je rageai(s); n. rageons**) *F* to rage, to be in a rage, to fume; **ça me fait r. de voir ça!,** it makes me wild *or* mad to see it!, seeing that makes my blood boil!

rageur, -euse [raʒœr, -øz] *adj* violent, furious, infuriated (*tone*).

rageusement [raʒøzmɑ̃] *adv* furiously.

raglan [raglɑ̃] **1** *nm* raglan coat. **2** *adj inv* **manches r.,** raglan sleeves.

ragondin [ragɔ̃dɛ̃] *nm Zool* coypu; (*fourrure*) nutria.

ragot¹, -ote [rago, -ɔt] **1** *nm* (*sanglier*) boar in its third year. **2** *adj & n* dumpy, squat (person).

ragot² *nm* piece of gossip; **faire des ragots,** to gossip; **c'est un méchant r.,** it's just ill-natured gossip.

ragoter [ragɔte] *vi F* to gossip.

ragoût [ragu] *nm Culin* stew, ragout; **r. de mouton,** mutton stew; **(faire) cuire qch en r.,** to stew sth.

ragoûtant [ragutɑ̃] *adj* (*with neg*) **peu** *ou* **pas r.,** unpleasant, disgusting, uninviting.

ragréer [ragree] *vt* **(a)** to finish off (*stonework, woodwork*); to clean up, to trim up (*joint etc*); **(b)** to clean (*façade of building*).

rag-time [ragtajm] *nm* (*danse*) & *Mus* ragtime.

rahat-lokoum [raatlokum], **rahat-loukoum** [raatlukum] *nm* Turkish delight.

rai [rɛ] *nm* ray; **des rais de lumière passaient sous la porte,** rays of light filtered through under the door.

raid [rɛd] *nm* **(a)** *Mil* raid; **(b)** *Sp* endurance test; (*en automobile*) long-distance rally; (*en avion*) long-distance flight.

raide [rɛd] **1** *adj* **(a)** stiff (*limb, joints*); taut, tight (*rope*); **corde r.,** tightrope; **mettre un câble au r.,** to take up the slack in a cable; **cheveux raides,** straight hair; **assis r. sur sa chaise,** sitting bolt upright on his chair; *F* **r. (comme un passe-lacet),** (stony) broke; **(b)** stiff (*manner*); inflexible, unbending, unyielding (*character etc*); **réponse r.,** brusque reply; **(c)** steep (*stair, slope*); **(d)** *F* **histoire r.,** tall story; **ça c'est un peu r.!,** that's a bit thick!; **il en a vu de raides,** he's had some queer experiences. **2** *adv* **(a)** (*monter*) steeply; **(b) tuer qn r.,** to kill s.o. outright; **tomber r. mort,** to drop dead; **il y avait une odeur à tomber r. mort,** it stank to high heaven, the smell (just about) knocked me *or* him *etc* out; **tomber r. par terre,** to drop to the ground.

raider [rɛdœr] *nm Fin* (corporate) raider.

raideur [rɛdœr] *nf* **(a)** stiffness (*of limb, joints, movement*); tightness (*of rope*); **donner plus de r. à qch,** to stiffen sth (up); **(b)** stiffness, starchiness (*of manner*); inflexibility (*of character*); **(c)** steepness, abruptness (*of slope*)

raidillon [rɛdijɔ̃] *nm* steep path; (short and steep) rise (*in a road*).

raidir [redir] **1** *vt* to stiffen (*cloth*); to make (*sth*) stiff *or* hard; to tighten, to pull taut (*rope etc*); to brace (*one's arms*); to stiffen (*resistance etc*). **2 se raidir** *vpr* **(a)** (*of limbs, joints*) to stiffen, to grow stiff(er); (*of cable*) to tauten, to grow taut; **(b)** (*of person*) to grow tense *or* rigid; **elle se raidit sur sa chaise,** she tensed up on her chair; **il se raidit,** he grew tense *or* rigid; *Fig* **se r. contre le malheur,** to steel *or* brace oneself against misfortune.

raidissement [rɛdismɑ̃] *nm* stiffening; (*de corde*) tautening; *Fig* **r. des rapports internationaux,** increase of tension in international relations.

raidisseur [rɛdisœr] *nm Tech* wire stretcher.

raie¹ [rɛ] *nf* **(a)** stripe; line, stroke (*on paper etc*); **(b)** *Opt* **raies du spectre, raies spectrales,** spectrum lines; **(c)** parting, *Am* part (*in the hair*); **porter la r. à droite/à gauche/de côté/au milieu,** to part one's hair on the right/on the left/at the side, to have a side parting/to part one's hair in the centre; **(d)** *Agr* furrow.

raie² *nf* (*poisson*) ray, skate; **r. bouclée,** thornback; *Culin* **r. au beurre noir,** skate in brown butter sauce.

raifort [rɛfɔr] *nm* horseradish.

rail [rɑj] *nm* **(a)** rail; **rails mobiles,** movable rails, switch rails; **r. conducteur,** conductor rail, live rail (*of electrified railway*); **quitter les rails, sortir des rails,** (*d'un train*) to be derailed, to go off the rails; *Fig* **remettre l'économie sur les rails,** to put the economy (back) on its feet again; **il faut le remettre sur les rails,** we'll have to put him back on the rails *or* straighten him out; **le président va mettre un train de réformes sur les rails,** the president is going to initiate a series of reforms *or* set a series of reforms in motion; **dans cette voiture, on est comme sur des rails,** this car's so smooth, you'd think you were running on rails; **on l'a mis sur des rails à la sortie du lycée,** a path was mapped out for him when he left school;

(b) (*chemins de fer*) railways, *US* railroads; **travailleurs du r.**, railwaymen, *US* railroaders;

(c) (*glissière*) crash barrier; **r. de sécurité,** crash barrier;

(d) (*itinéraire*) lane; **les bateaux se déplacent sur quatre rails au large d'Ouessant,** boats sail along four sea lanes off Ushant; **le respect des rails aériens,** the respect of air (traffic) lanes *or* air corridors.

railler [rɑje] **1** *vt* to laugh at, to make fun of (*s.o.*); **elle le raille de** *ou* **sur sa timidité,** she mocks *or* scoffs *or* jeers at his shyness; **2** *vi* **je ne raille pas,** I'm not joking. **3 se railler** *vpr* **se r. de qn/qch,** to laugh *or* scoff at *or* make fun of s.o./sth.

raillerie [rɑjri] *nf* (*plaisanterie*) joking, banter; **il n'entend pas r. là-dessus,** he is very touchy on that point; **sans r.**, joking apart, seriously; **recueillir des railleries,** to be scoffed at *or* made fun of.

railleur, -euse [rɑjœr, -øz] **1** *adj* mocking, bantering. **2** *n* scoffer, banterer.

railleusement [rɑjøzmɑ̃] *adv* mockingly.

rainer [rene] *vt* to groove.

rainette [rɛnɛt] *nf* **(a)** (*grenouille*) tree frog; **(b)** (*pomme*) pippin; **r. grise,** russet.

rainure [renyr] *nf* **(a)** groove; **r. de clavette,** keyway, key slot; **à rainure(s),** grooved; **(b)** *Astron* rille (*on the moon*).

rainurer [renyre] *vt* to groove.

raiponce [rɛpɔ̃s] *nf Bot* rampion.

raisin [rɛzɛ̃] *nm* **(a) (grain de) r.**, grape; **grappe de r.**, bunch of grapes; **raisin(s) de table,** dessert grapes; **manger du r.**, to eat grapes; **raisins secs,** raisins; **raisins de Corinthe,** currants; **raisins de Smyrne,** sultanas; **(b)** *Bot* **r. de renard,** herb Paris; **(c)** (*mollusque*) **r. de mer,** sea grapes, cuttle-fish eggs; **(d) grand r.**, (*papier*) ≈ royal.

raisiné [rɛzine] *nm* fruit preserved in grape jelly.

raison [rɛzɔ̃] *nf* **(a)** (*motif*) reason, motive, ground (**de,** for); **ce n'est pas une r. (pour faire qch),** that's no reason to do sth; **pour des raisons de convenance,** for reasons of *or* on grounds of expediency; **pour quelle r.?,** why? what for?; **sans r.**, without (any) reason, for no reason, needlessly; **en** *ou* **pour r. de qch,** by reason of *or* on account of sth; **en r. de son âge,** because of *or* due to his age; **en r. d'un deuil récent,** owing to a recent bereavement; **je me rends à vos raisons,** I admit *or* can see you're right; **à plus forte r.**, with greater reason, all the more reason; **r. de plus,** all the more reason; **r. de plus pour venir avec nous,** all the more *or* yet another reason to come with us; **r. d'être de qch,** raison d'être of *or* object of *or* reason for sth; **c'est ma seule r. d'être,** it's my whole life *or* raison d'être; **sa petite fille est sa r. d'être,** his granddaughter is his entire reason for living *or* his only raison d'être; **c'est la r. d'être de cet organisme,** that's the whole point of *or* reason for that institution; **la r. pour laquelle il est venu,** the reason (why) he came;

(b) (*entendement*) reason; **il n'a pas toute sa r.**, he is not quite sane, he's not quite in his right mind; **revenir** *ou* **se mettre à la r.**, to come to one's senses, to see reason; **vous perdez la r.!,** have you taken leave of your senses?; **entendre r.**, to listen to reason; **rendre r. de qch,** to give an explanation of sth, to account for sth; **l'âge de r.**, the age of reason; **mariage de r.**, marriage of convenience;

(c) avoir r., to be right; **avoir r. de faire qch,** to be justified *or* right in doing sth; **donner r. à qn,** to admit that s.o. is right; **l'événement lui donna r.**, in the event, he was proved right; **ce n'est pas r. d'agir ainsi,** there is no justification for such an action; **se faire une r.**, to accept the inevitable, to resign oneself; **le travail n'était pas bon, mais il a bien fallu se faire une r.**, the work wasn't well done but we had to make the best of a bad job; **avec r.**, rightly; **boire plus que de r.**, to drink too much *or* more than is reasonable; **comme de r.**, as a matter of course, as one might expect;

(d) (*satisfaction*) satisfaction, reparation; **demander r. d'un affront,** to demand satisfaction for an insult; **se faire r. à soi-même,** to take the law into one's own hands; **avoir r. de qn/qch,** to get the better of s.o./sth; **elle ne partira pas tant qu'elle n'aura pas eu r. de cet appareil,** she won't leave until she's got that machine going *or* sorted that machine out;

(e) *Com* **r. sociale,** (company) name;

(f) *Math* ratio; **r. géométrique/arithmétique,** geometrical/arithmetical ratio; **r. directe/inverse,** direct/inverse ratio *or* proportion; **le poids est en r. directe du volume,** the weight is directly proportional to the volume; **travail payé à r. de cinquante francs l'heure,** work paid at the rate of fifty francs an hour; **à r. de deux par minute,** at the rate of two per *or* a minute; **à r. de huit mots par ligne,** on the basis of eight words to a line.

raisonnable [rɛzɔnabl] *adj* **(a) être r.**, rational being; **soyez r.!,** be sensible *or* reasonable!, listen to reason!; **à son âge il devrait être plus r.**, he is old enough to know better; **(b)** (*sensé*) according to reason; **interprétation r.**, reasonable interpretation; **l'homme est un aminal r.**, man is a reasoning animal; **tu ne peux pas sortir** ET **travailler, ce n'est pas r.!,** you can't go out (all the time) AND work, it's daft!; **(c) prix r.**, reasonable *or* moderate *or* fair price; **d'une grandeur r.**, reasonably large, decent-sized.

raisonnablement [rɛzɔnabləmɑ̃] *adv* **(a)** (*logiquement*) reasonably, rationally; **tout ce qu'on pouvait r. demander,** all that one could reasonably ask for; **(b)** (*assez*) reasonably, fairly (*large etc*); (*manger etc*) moderately, in moderation; *F* (*travailler etc*) fairly well, reasonably well.

raisonné [rɛzɔne] *adj* reasoned (*argument*); rational, analytical (*grammar*); *Com* **catalogue r.**, descriptive catalogue.

raisonnement [rɛzɔnmɑ̃] *nm* (*pensée etc*) reasoning; **homme de r. juste,** man of sense; **je comprends ton r.**, I understand your reasoning *or* (line of) argument; **r. irréfutable,** irrefutable argument *or* (chain of) reasoning; **pas de raisonnements!,** don't argue!

raisonner [rɛzɔne] **1** *vi* **(a)** (*penser*) to reason (**sur,** about, upon); **r. par induction/déduction,** to reason by induction *or* inductively/by deduction *or* deductively; **(b)** (*discuter*) to argue (**sur,** about); **on ne peut r. avec ce genre de personnes,** you can't reason with people like that; **ne raisonnez pas tant!,** don't be so argumentative! **2** *vt* **(a)** to reason with (*s.o.*); **je vais essayer de le r.**, I'll try and reason with him *or* make him see sense; **(b)** *Litt* **r. ses actions,** to consider *or* study one's actions. **3 se raisonner** *vpr* to make oneself see reason, to reason with oneself; **la jalousie ne se raisonne pas,** jealousy cannot be reasoned with *or* knows no reason; **raisonne-toi donc!,** try to be reasonable!

raisonneur, -euse [rɛzɔnœr, -øz] **1** *adj* **(a)** reasoning, rational; **(b)** (*qui discutaille*) argumentative. **2** *n* **(a)** reasoner; **(b)** (*discutailleur*) arguer.

raja(h) [raʒa] *nm* raja(h).

rajeunir [raʒœnir] **1** *vt* **(a)** to rejuvenate (*s.o.*); **ce chapeau la rajeunit de dix ans,** this hat makes her look ten years younger; **ça me rajeunit,** it makes me feel younger; **ça ne nous rajeunit pas!,** it brings it home *or* makes you realize that we're not getting any younger; **tu la rajeunis, elle a passé la trentaine,** she's not as young as you think, she's over thirty; **(b)** to renovate, to do up (*clothes etc*); to revive (*expression etc*); **r. une organisation,** to modernise an organization; **le comité a besoin d'être rajeuni,** the committee needs new blood. **2** *vi* to grow young again, to get younger. **3 se rajeunir** *vpr* (*pour paraître plus jeune*) to make oneself look younger; (*se dire, prétendre plus jeune*) to make oneself out (to be) younger than one is.

rajeunissant [raʒœnisɑ̃] *adj* rejuvenating; **traitement/crème rajeunissant(e),** rejuvenating treatment/cream.

rajeunissement [raʒœnismɑ̃] *nm* rejuvenation.

rajout [raʒu] *nm* addition; **on ne peut plus faire de r.**, nothing else can be added, we can't add anything else.

rajouter [raʒute] *vt* to add (*sth*), to add more of (*sth*).

rajustement [raʒystəmɑ̃] *nm* readjustment.

rajuster [raʒyste] **1** *vt* to readjust (*sth*), to put (*sth*) straight; **r. les salaires,** to bring wages into line with the cost of living. **2 se rajuster** *vpr* to tidy *or* straighten oneself up; **elle est allée se r.**, she's gone to smarten herself up.

râle[1] [rɑl] *nm* (*oiseau*) **r. d'eau,** water rail; **r. de genêts,** corncrake.

râle[2] *nm*, **râlement** [rɑlmɑ̃] *nm* rattle (*in the throat*); **le r. (de la mort),** the death rattle; *Méd* **on lui a découvert un r. au poumon,** they've discovered a crepitation in his lung.

ralenti [ralɑ̃ti] **1** *adj* slow(er); **au trot r.**, at a slow trot. **2** *nm* **(a)** slow motion; *Aut* **prendre un virage au r.**, to take a corner slowly; *Cin* **scène au** *ou* **en r.**, scene in slow motion; *Ind* **travail au r.**, go-slow; *F* **elle travaille au r.**, (*elle ne fait presque plus rien*) she's just marking time; **la malade a l'impression de vivre au r.**, the patient feels he's living in slow motion *or* hardly living at all; **(b)** (*de moteur*) idling, slow running; **tourner au r.,** to idle, to tick over.

ralentir [ralɑ̃tir] **1** *vt* to slacken, to reduce (*speed*); **r. la marche,** to reduce speed; **r. ses efforts,** to ease up. **2** *vi* to slow down, to reduce speed; **la progresion ralentit,** progress is slowing; *Aut* **ralentis, il y a de la glace!,** slow down, there's ice! **3 se ralentir** *vpr* (*of movements*) to slow down; (*of enthusiasm*) to flag, to wane; **j'ai dû me r.,** (*je travaillais trop*) I had to slow down.

ralentissement [ralɑ̃tismɑ̃] *nm* slowing up, slowing down; waning, flagging (*of enthousiasm*); **périodes de r. dans les affaires,** slack times in business.

ralentisseur [ralɑ̃tisœr] *nm Aut* speed bump, *Br F* sleeping policeman; *MecE* retarder; *Nucl* moderator.

râler [rɑle] *vi* **(a)** *F* (*d'une personne*) to grouse, to moan, to grumble; **r. en silence,** to fume; **ça me fait r. de voir ce gaspillage!,** it really makes me fume *or* see red *or* makes my blood boil to see all this waste; **laisse-le r.,** let him moan; **elle râle contre notre retard,** she's moaning about our being late; **elle passe son temps à r.,** she spends her whole time grumbling *or* grousing; **(b)** (*de douleur*) to moan, to groan; (*d'un mourant*) to be at one's last gasp; **(c)** (*d'un tigre*) to growl.

râleur, -euse [rɑlœr, -øz] *F* **1** *adj* grumbling, moaning, grousing; **elle est très râleuse,** what a moaner *or* a grumbler she is. **2** *n* grumbler, moaner, grouser.

ralingue [ralɛ̃g] *nf Nau* bolt rope (*of sail*); **tenir les voiles en r.,** to keep the sails shivering.

ralinguer [ralɛ̃ge] *Nau* **1** *vt* to rope (*a sail*). **2** *vi* (*of sails*) to shiver.

ralliement [ralimɑ̃] *nm* **(a)** rally(ing) (*of troops, ships*); **mot de r.,** password; **point de r.,** rallying point; **signe de r.,** rallying sign; **(b)** homing (*of aircraft*); **(c) winning over** (*of adherents*); **son r. à notre parti fut immédiat,** he immediately came over *or* was won over to our party.

rallier [ralje] *v* (*impf & pr sub* **n. ralliions**) **1** *vt* **(a)** to rally (*troops, ships etc*); *Fig* **r. l'opinion autour d'une idée commune,** to mobilise *or* rally *or* unite public opinion around a common idea; **(b)** *Mil etc* to rejoin (*unit*); to make one's way back to (*base*); *Nau* **r. le bord,** to rejoin one's ship; **(c)** to win (*s.o.*) over, to bring (*s.o.*) round (*to a party, opinion*); *Fig* **les groupuscules ont rallié le groupe majoritaire,** the small groups have united with *or* joined the majority group; **cette proposition a rallié tous les suffrages,** this proposal has won unanimous approval *or* has unanimous support. **2 se rallier** *vpr* **(a)** (*of troops etc*) to rally; **(b) se r. à un parti,** to join a party; **se r. à une opinion,** to come round to an opinion.

rallonge [ralɔ̃ʒ] *nf* **(a)** extension leaf (*of table*); extension piece (*of lifting jack etc*); *Can* runoff (*of desk*); **table à rallonge(s),** extending table; *F* **nom à r.,** double-barrelled name; **(b)** (*électrique*) extension flex *or* lead *or* cord; **(c)** *F* additional *or* extra time *or* payment *etc*; **une r. de trois jours,** an additional *or* an extra three days.

rallongement [ralɔ̃ʒmɑ̃] *nm* lengthening, extension.

rallonger [ralɔ̃ʒe] *v* (**je rallongeai(s); n. rallongeons**) **1** *vt* to lengthen (*sth*), to make (*sth*) longer. **2** *vi F* **les jours rallongent,** the days are lengthening *or* getting longer *or* drawing out.

rallumer [ralyme] **1** *vt* to relight (*lamp, fire*); to rekindle (*fire*); *Fig* to rekindle, to revive (*anger, hope etc*). **2 se rallumer** *vpr* (*d'un feu*) to flare up *or* blaze up again, to rekindle; (*d'une lampe*) to come on *or* go on again; *Fig* (*d'une guerre, dispute*) to flare up again; *Fig* (*de l'espoir etc*) to rekindle, to revive.

rallye [rali] *nm Sp* (car) rally.

Ramadan [ramadɑ̃] *nm Rel* Ramadan; **respecter le R.,** to observe Ramadan.

ramage [ramaʒ] *nm* **(a)** (*motif*) floral design; **(b)** song, twittering, chirping (*of birds*).

ramas [ramɑ] *nm F* = **RAMASSIS**.

ramassage [ramasaʒ] *nm* gathering, collecting, picking up; **r. à la pelle,** shovelling up; **r. scolaire,** school bus service; **car de r. scolaire,** school bus.

ramassé [ramase] *adj* **(a)** (*pelotonné*) thick-set, stocky; **(b)** compact (*machine, style*).

ramasse-miettes [ramasmjɛt] *nm inv* crumb tray *or* scoop, table tidy.

ramasse-monnaie [ramasmɔnɛ] *nm inv* change tray.

ramasse-poussière [ramaspusjɛr] *nm inv* dustpan.

ramasser [ramase] **1** *vt* **(a)** to pick (up), to gather, to collect; **r. son mouchoir,** to pick up one's handkerchief; **r. des coquillages,** to collect shells; **r. les pommes de terre,** to dig (up) potatoes; **r. des champignons,** to pick *or* gather mushrooms; **r. son courrier,** to pick up *or* collect one's mail; **r. à la pelle,** to shovel up; **r. qn,** to help s.o. up *or* to his feet; *Fig* **être à r. à la petite cuillère,** to be worn out *or* fit to drop; *F* **r. une bûche/une pelle,** to come a cropper; **r. une engueulade,** to get a bawling out; *Arg* **se faire r.,** to be run in *or* picked up (*by the police*); *Aut F* **r. un procès-verbal,** to get a ticket;

(b) to collect, to gather (*several things*); **r. les cartes,** to pick up the cards; **r. ses affaires,** to collect one's belongings; **r. les assiettes/les copies,** to collect the dishes/the papers *or* scripts; **r. de l'argent,** to collect money; *F* to make one's pile; **le car qui ramasse les enfants,** the bus which picks up the children; **r. des bribes de connaissances,** to pick up scraps of knowledge;

(c) to gather (*sth*) together (in a mass); **village ramassé autour de son église,** village clustering round its church; **le tigre ramasse son corps avant de bondir,** the tiger crouches *or* gathers itself before springing; **r. toutes ses forces,** to gather *or* muster all one's strength; **r. ses cheveux dans une natte,** to gather one's hair in a pigtail.

2 se ramasser *vpr* **(a)** to gather oneself (*for an effort*); (*d'un tigre*) to crouch (*before springing*);

(b) to pick oneself up (*after a fall*); *Fig F* (*échouer*) to come a cropper.

ramassette [ramasɛt] *nf Belg* dustpan.

ramasseur, -euse [ramasœr, -øz] *n* collector, gatherer; **r. de lait,** collector of milk (*from farms*).

ramassis [ramasi] *nm Péj* heap, pile, jumble (*of things*); bunch (*of people*).

rambarde [rɑ̃bard] *nf Nau etc* (guard) rail.

ramdam [ramdam] *nm F* row, racket; **faire du** *ou* **un sacré r.,** to make a heck of a din *or* racket.

rame¹ [ram] *nf* stick, cane (*for growing peas etc*); **haricots à rames,** stick beans; *F* **elle n'en fiche pas une r.,** she does damn all, she never does a stroke (of work).

rame² *nf* (*aviron*) oar; **aller à la r.,** to row; **faire force de rames,** to row hard; **faire fausse r.,** to catch a crab.

rame³ *nf* **(a)** ream (*of paper*); **une r. de 500 feuilles,** a ream of 500 sheets; **(b)** string, tow (*of barges*); *Rail* **r. (de wagons),** made-up train; **la r. directe pour Tours,** the through coach(es) for Tours; **r. (de métro),** underground train; **la dernière r. passe à minuit,** the last train leaves at midnight.

rameau, -eaux [ramo] *nm* **(a)** (*d'arbre*) (small) branch *or* bough; *Rel* **le dimanche des Rameaux, les Rameaux,** Palm Sunday; **(b)** branch (*of family, language*); **(c)** *Anat* ramification.

ramée [rame] *nf* **(a)** *Litt & Vieilli* green *or* leafy boughs (*of tree*); **(b)** (*branches coupées*) cut branches; **(c)** *F* **il n'en fiche pas une r.,** he does damn all, he never does a stroke (of work).

ramener [ramne] *v* (*conj like* **mener**) **1** *vt* **(a)** to bring (*s.o., sth*) back (again); **r. qn chez lui en voiture,** to drive s.o. home; **r. la paix,** to restore peace; **la faim le ramènera,** he'll come back when he's hungry; **r. un malade à la vie,** to bring a patient round; **r. la conversation sur un sujet,** to lead *or* bring the conversation back to a subject; **r. le compteur à zéro,** to reset the speedometer at zero; **il a ramené des bijoux de son voyage,** he brought back jewels from his journey *or* travels; *Arg* **r. sa gueule** *ou* **sa fraise, la r.,** to kick up a fuss *or* a stink; (*interférer*) to stick *or* shove one's oar in;

(b) (*réduire*) to reduce; **r. tout à un seul principe,** to reduce everything to a single principle; **r. une fraction à sa plus simple expression,** to reduce a fraction to its simplest terms;

(c) (*remettre, baiser*) to draw *or* pull down *or* up; **r. son chapeau sur ses yeux,** to pull one's hat down over one's eyes; **r. la couverture sur le bébé,** to pull the blanket up over the baby.

2 se ramener *vpr* **(a) voici à quoi se ramène son raisonnement,** this is what his argument amounts to *or F* boils down to;

(b) *F* (*arriver*) to roll up.

ramequin [ramkɛ̃] *nm Culin* ramekin, ramequin.

ramer¹ [rame] *vt* to stake (*peas etc*).

ramer² *vi* (*aviron*) to row, *Litt* to pull (at the oar); **r. en couple,** to scull; **r. à rebours,** to back water; *Fig F* **qu'est-ce qu'on a ramé!,** we didn't half (have to) work hard *or* struggle.

rameur, -euse [ramœr, -øz] *n* (*à l'aviron*) rower, oarsman, *f* oarswoman; **r. de couple,** sculler.

rameux, -euse [ramø, -øz] *adj* ramose, branching.

rami [rami] *nm Cartes* rummy.

ramie [rami] *nf Bot* ramie; **(toile de) r.,** grass cloth.

ramier [ramje] *adj inv & nm* **(pigeon) r.,** ring dove, wood pigeon.

ramification [ramifikasjɔ̃] *nf* ramification, branch, branching (out); **secte ayant des ramifications dans toutes les grandes villes,** sect with branches in all major towns; **les ramifications d'une famille,** the branches of a family.

ramifier (se) [səramifje] *vpr* to ramify, to branch out; **cette organisation se ramifie dans plusieurs pays du monde,** this organization has branches in several countries.

ramille [ramij] *nf* twig.

ramolli, -ie [ramɔli] **1** *adj (beurre)* soft; *F (personne)* soft in the head. **2** *n F* dodderer.

ramollir [ramɔlir] **1** *vt* to soften. **2 se ramollir** *vpr* to soften, to grow soft; *F* **son cerveau se ramollit,** he has softening of the brain.

ramollissement [ramɔlismɑ̃] *nm* softening.

ramollo(t) [ramɔlo] *F* **1** *adj* soft in the head. **2** *nm* **un vieux r.,** an old dodderer, an old fogey.

ramonage [ramɔnaʒ] *nm* chimney sweeping; cleaning (*of boiler tubes*).

ramoner [ramɔne] **1** *vt* to sweep (*chimney*); to take out (*flue*); to clean (*fire tubes*). **2** *vi* to clean *or* sweep a chimney.

ramoneur [ramɔnœr] *nm* (chimney) sweep.

rampant [rɑ̃pɑ̃] *adj* **(a)** creeping (*plant*); crawling (*animal*); *Av F* **personnel r.,** ground staff; **(b)** *Péj* grovelling, cringing (*person, character*); pedestrian (*style*); **(c)** *Hér* **lion r.,** lion rampant; **(d)** *Archit* **arche/voûte rampante,** rampant arch/vault.

rampe [rɑ̃p] *nf* **(a)** banisters, handrail (*of stair*); *Arg* **lâcher la r.,** to kick the bucket, to snuff it; *F* **tenir bon la r.,** to be still going strong; **(b)** slope, incline, rise; gradient (*of road*); *Aut* **vitesse en r.,** speed when (hill) climbing *or* going uphill; **(c)** (*passerelle etc*) ramp, gangway; **r. d'accès,** access ramp (*of bridge*); **r. mobile,** portable ramp, movable gangway; **r. de lancement,** (*de projectile*) launching ramp; **(d)** bank (*of projectors etc*); *Av* **r. (lumineuse) d'atterrissage,** illuminated landing strip; **r. de graissage,** lubricating rack, oil distributor; **(e)** *Th* footlights, float(s); **être sous les feux de la r.,** to be in the limelight; **pièce qui ne passe pas la r.,** play that fails to get across.

rampement [rɑ̃pmɑ̃] *nm* creeping, crawling.

ramper [rɑ̃pe] *vi* to creep, to crawl; (*d'une plante*) to creep, to trail; **entrer/sortir en rampant,** to crawl in/out; **r. à quatre pattes,** to creep *or* crawl on all fours; *Péj* **r. devant les chefs,** to crawl *or* grovel to the bosses.

ramure [ramyr] *nf* **(a)** (*d'arbre*) branches, boughs, foliage; **(b)** (*d'un cerf*) antlers.

rancard [rɑ̃kar] *nm Arg* **(a)** (*rendez-vous*) date, meet(ing); **j'ai r. avec lui à 2 heures,** I've got a date with him *or* I'm meeting him at two o'clock; (*avec le médecin*) I've got an appointment with him at *or* for two o'clock; **(b)** (*renseignement*) info, gen, low-down.

rancart [rɑ̃kar] *nm* **mettre au r.,** to discard (*sth*); to shelve (*project*); **la mise au r. de notre projet,** the scrapping of our project.

rance [rɑ̃s] **1** *adj* rancid, rank. **2** *nm* **sentir le r.,** to smell rancid.

ranch [rɑ̃ʃ] *nm* ranch; **exploiter un r.,** to ranch.

rancidité [rɑ̃sidite] *nf* rancidness.

rancir [rɑ̃sir] *vi* to become *or* grow rancid.

rancissement [rɑ̃sismɑ̃] *nm* growing *or* becoming rancid.

rancœur [rɑ̃kœr] *nf* rancour, bitterness, resentment; **j'ai de la r. contre lui,** I feel resentment towards him.

rançon [rɑ̃sɔ̃] *nf* ransom; **mettre qn à r.,** to hold s.o. to ransom; **payer la r. de qn,** to ransom s.o.; **la r. du progrès/de la gloire,** the price of progress/glory.

rançonner [rɑ̃sɔne] *vt* to hold (*s.o.*) to ransom; to hold up (and rob) (*traveller*); *F* to fleece (*customer etc*).

rancune [rɑ̃kyn] *nf* rancour, spite, malice; **garder r. à qn, avoir de la r. contre qn,** to harbour resentment against s.o., to have a grudge against s.o., to bear s.o. malice; **par r.,** out of spite; **sans r.!,** no ill *or* hard *or* bad feelings!; **il y a de vieilles rancunes entre eux,** there is bad blood between them.

rancunier, -ière [rɑ̃kynje, -jɛr] *adj & n* vindictive, spiteful (person).

randonnée [rɑ̃dɔne] *nf* (*en voiture*) outing, run, trip, excursion; (*à vélo*) run, ride; (*en montagne*) hill-walking; (*en haute montagne*) climbing, mountaineering; (*à ski de fond*) cross-country skiing; (*avec peau de phoque*) ski-mountaineering; **r. à pied,** hike; **chemin de grande r.,** long-distance footpath *or* walk.

randonneur, -euse [rɑ̃dɔnœr, -øz] *n* rambler, hiker, walker; (*en montagne*) hill-walker; (*à ski*) cross-country skier; (*avec peau de phoque*) ski-mountaineer.

rang [rɑ̃] *nm* **(a)** row, line (*of trees, seats etc*); row (*of onions, knitting*); bank (*of oars*); *Mil* rank; **fauteuil au premier r.,** front-row seat; *Fig* **je le sais, j'étais au premier r. (pour le voir),** I should know, I have first-hand experience; **le photographe nous a demandé de nous mettre en r. d'oignons,** the photographer asked us to stand (close together) in a line; **machine à quatre rangs de touches,** four-bank typewriter; **r. de perles,** string *or* rope of pearls; **sur deux rangs,** in two ranks, two deep; **par rangs de trois,** three abreast; **formez vos rangs!,** fall in!; *Mil & Fig* **serrer les rangs,** to close ranks; **en rangs serrés,** in close order; *Mil & Fig* **rompre les rangs,** to break ranks; **sortir des rangs,** to fall out (of line), to break rank; **homme du r.,** private; **officier sorti du r.,** officer promoted from the ranks;

(b) (*classement*) rank, place; (*social*) station; *Mil* rank; **r. élevé,** high rank; **dame de haut r.,** lady of rank; **r. social,** social status; **il faut tenir notre r.,** we have to keep up our position; **avoir r. de colonel,** to hold the rank of colonel; **de premier r.,** first-class, first-rate; **il est au r. des meilleurs,** he ranks amongst the best; **il est au premier r. de sa profession,** he is at the top of (the tree in) his profession; **par r. d'âge,** according to age; **être mis sur le même r.,** to be placed on the same footing; **occuper un r. supérieur à qn,** to rank above s.o.; **prendre** *ou* **avoir r. avant/après qn,** to rank before/after s.o.; **il a pris r. parmi les grands poètes,** he has taken his place *or* is counted among the great poets; **prendre r. dans un parti,** to join a party; **sortir d'une école avec un bon r.,** to leave a school with a good grade; **venir au** *ou* **en troisième r.,** to rank third; **arriver au premier r.,** to come to the front; *Fig* **se mettre sur les rangs,** to enter the lists, to come forward (as a candidate), to put in for the job; **servir dans les rangs des mécontents,** to serve in the ranks of the malcontents; **grossir les rangs des révoltés,** to swell the ranks of the rebels; **il y avait déjà quelqu'un sur les rangs,** there was already someone in the field;

(c) *Can* concession road; (*quartier*) concession, rural district.

rangé [rɑ̃ʒe] *adj* **(a)** (*en ordre*) tidy, orderly; well-ordered, orderly (*life*); steady, orderly, (well-)ordered (*person*); **fille rangée,** dutiful daughter; *F* **être r. des voitures,** to be a reformed character, to have settled *or* steadied down; **(b) bataille rangée,** pitched battle.

rangée [rɑ̃ʒe] *nf* row, line (*of persons, buttons, seats, trees*); tier (*of seats on a slope*).

rangement [rɑ̃ʒmɑ̃] *nm* **(a)** (*action*) tidying, putting in order; *surtout Ordinat* storage; **la manie du r.,** mania for tidiness; **volume de r.,** storage space; **(meuble de) r.,** storage unit; **r. de cuisine,** kitchen cabinet; **faire du r. (dans son bureau),** to do some tidying up (in one's office); **(b)** (*disposition*) arrangement; **r. rationnel,** logical arrangement.

ranger [rɑ̃ʒe] *v* **(je rangeai(s); n. rangeons) 1** *vt* **(a)** to arrange, to tidy (*room etc*); to set (*things*) to rights;

(b) (*classer*) to put (*sth*) away, to put (*sth*) back in its place; to stow away, to tidy away (*objects*); to stow (*goods*); *Ordinat* **r. en mémoire,** to store; *Aut* **r. une voiture,** to pull in to the side;

(c) r. qn parmi les grands écrivains, to rank *or* count s.o. amongst the great writers; *Nau* **r. la côte,** to run along the shore, to hug the coast;

(d) to arrange; to draw up, to marshal (*troops etc*).

2 se ranger *vpr* **(a) se r. (de côté),** to get out of the way, to draw to one side, to stand aside; **on se rangea pour nous laisser passer,** they stood aside *or* made way for us; *Aut* **la voiture s'est rangée contre le mur,** the car pulled in alongside the wall; *Nau* **se r. à quai,** to berth;

(b) se r. du côté de qn, to take sides with s.o., to side with s.o.; **se r. à l'opinion de qn,** to fall in with *or* come round to s.o.'s opinion;

(c) *Mil* to draw up, to line up;

(d) *F* **il s'est rangé,** he has steadied *or* settled down.

rani [rani] *nf* ranee.

ranimation [ranimasjɔ̃] *nf* resuscitation, reanimation.

ranimer [ranime] **1** *vt* to revive, to put new life into (*s.o., sth*); to bring (*s.o.*) back to life; to bring (*fainting person*) round; to revive (*plant, colour*); to stir up (*the fire*); to reawaken, to rekindle (*anger, hope*); to liven up (*the conversation*); to cheer (*s.o.*) up again, to hearten (*s.o.*). **2 se ranimer** *vpr* to revive; (*d'un feu*) to rekindle, to flicker into life; **elle ne fut pas longue à se r.,** she soon came round.

Raoul [raul] *nm* Ralph.

rap [rap] *nm Mus* rap.

rapace [rapas] **1** *adj* predatory; *Fig* rapacious, grasping (*person*); **oiseau r.,** bird of prey. **2** *nm* bird of prey.

rapacité [rapasite] *nf* rapacity; *Fig* rapaciousness, rapacity; **avec r.,** rapaciously.

râpage [rɑpaʒ] *nm* grating (*of nutmeg, carrot etc*); rasping (*of metal, wood*).

rapatrié, -ée [rapatrije] *adj & n* repatriate.

rapatriement [rapatrimɑ̃] *nm* repatriation.

rapatrier [rapatrije] *vt* to repatriate (*s.o.*); **se faire r.,** to get *or* be repatriated; *Fig* **r. des capitaux (de l'étranger),** to repatriate capital.

râpe [rɑp] *nf* **(a)** (*de cuisine*) grater; **r. à muscade/à fromage,** nutmeg/cheese grater; **(b)** *Tech* rasp.

râpé [rɑpe] **1** *adj* **(a)** grated (*cheese, carrot etc*); **(b)** (*usé*) worn out, threadbare (*garment*); **(c)** *F* (*raté*) **c'est r. pour le weekend,** we've had it for the weekend. **2** *nm* **(a)** (*vin*) rape wine; **(b)** (*fromage*) grated cheese.

râper [rɑpe] *vt* to rasp (*wood, metal*); to grate (*carrot, nutmeg etc*); to grind (*snuff*); **ce vin râpe la gorge,** this wine is rough *or* harsh on the throat.

rapetassage [raptasaʒ] *nm F* patching up.

rapetasser [raptase] *vt F* to patch up, to do up (*garment*).

rapetissement [raptismɑ̃] *nm* reducing, diminishing.

rapetisser [raptise] **1** *vt* to make (*sth*) smaller, to reduce; to shorten (*garment*); to shrink (*material*); **la distance rapetisse les objets,** distance makes things look smaller. **2** *vi* to shorten, to become smaller *or* shorter, to shrink. **3 se rapetisser** *vpr* to grow smaller *or* shorter, to shrink.

râpeux, -euse [rɑpø, -øz] *adj* raspy (*tongue*); harsh (*wine*); rasping, grating (*noise*).

raphia [rafja] *nm* raphia (palm); (*fibre*) raffia.

rapiat, -ate [rapja, -at] *F* **1** *adj* stingy, miserly, tight-fisted. **2** *n* miser, skinflint.

rapide [rapid] **1** *adj* **(a)** rapid, swift, fast (*current etc*); speedy, rapid, swift, fast (*recovery*); fast (*runner, film*); **r. comme une flèche,** as swift as an arrow; **faire des progrès rapides,** to make rapid progress; **fusil à tir r.,** quick-firing rifle; *Aut* **voie r.,** fast lane; *Sp* **piste r.,** fast track; **(b)** steep (*slope*). **2** *nm* **(a)** rapid (*in river*); **(b)** express (train).

rapidement [rapidmɑ̃] *adv* rapidly, swiftly; **le temps passe r.,** time flies; **trop r.,** too quickly; **travailler r.,** to work quickly *or* fast; **je l'ai lu r.,** I read through it quickly, I had a quick read through it.

rapidité [rapidite] *nf* **(a)** rapidity, swiftness (*of actions*); **(b)** steepness (*of slope*).

rapiéçage [rapjesaʒ] *nm*, **rapiècement** [rapjɛsmɑ̃] *nm* patching (up), mending (*of garment*).

rapiécer [rapjese] *vt* (**je rapièce, n. rapiéçons; je rapiécerai**) to patch, to put a patch on (*garment*).

rapière [rapjɛr] *nf* rapier; **traîneur de r.,** swashbuckler.

rapin [rapɛ̃] *nm F Péj* (*peintre*) dauber.

rapine [rapin] *nf* rapine, pillage, depradation; **habitudes de r.,** predatory habits.

raplapla [raplapla] *adj inv F* (*person*) dead beat, washed out, all in.

rappareiller [rapareje] **, rapparier** [raparje] *vt* (*impf & pr sub* **n. rappariions**) to match, to complete (*pair*); to pair (*two things*).

rappel [rapɛl] *nm* **(a)** calling to mind, recalling (*of incident etc*); (*pour se souvenir*) reminder; **lettre de r.,** (letter of) reminder; **r. de traitement** *ou* **de solde,** back pay; **(b)** recall (*of general, ambassador, reservists*); **lettres de r.,** letters of recall; **(c)** *Com* calling in (*of sum advanced*); **(d)** *Méd* **injection de r.,** booster injection; **(e) r. à l'ordre,** call(ing) to order; **(f)** *Th* curtain call; (*à un concert*) encore; **(g)** (*retour*) back motion, return; **ressort de r.,** return spring, drawback spring; **(h)** *Tech* readjustment; **vis de r.,** adjusting screw; **r. de l'usure,** taking up of the wear; **fil de r.,** bracing wire, straining wire; **tige de r.,** stay rod; **(i)** abseil; **faire une descente** *ou* **descendre en r., faire du r.,** to abseil down; **(j)** *Mil* **battre le r.,** to call *or* beat to arms.

rappeler [raple] *v* (*conj like* **appeler**) **1** *vt* **(a)** (*oralement*) to call (*s.o.*) again; *Tél* to ring *or* call *or* phone (*s.o.*) again;

(b) (*faire revenir*) to recall (*ambassador*); to call *or* summon (*s.o.*) back; *Th* **être rappelé trois fois,** to take three curtain calls; **r. son chien,** to call off one's dog; **r. qn à l'ordre,** to call s.o. to order; **r. qn à la vie,** to restore s.o. to life, to resuscitate s.o., to bring s.o. round;

(c) r. son courage, to summon up one's courage (again);

(d) (*pour se souvenir*) to recall (*sth*); *Ordinat* to recall; **rappelez-moi votre nom,** what was your name again?; **r. qch à qn,** to remind s.o. of sth; **vous me rappelez mon oncle,** you remind me of my uncle; **cela me rappelle mon enfance,** it brings back my childhood to me, it reminds me of my childhood; **puis-je te r. que tu me dois 200 francs?,** may I remind you that you owe me 200 francs?; **rappelez-moi à son bon souvenir,** remember me (kindly) to him; **choses qu'il vaut autant ne pas r.,** things best forgotten; *Com* **prière de r. ce numéro,** in reply please quote this number;

(e) to draw back (*machine part etc*); *Typ* **r. le chariot,** to return the carriage; (*de quelques espaces*) to backspace;

(f) (*of guy rope*) to brace back; (*of tie rod*) to tie, to stay.

2 se rappeler *vpr* **(a) se r. qch,** to recall *or* recollect *or* remember sth, to call sth to mind; **un rêve dont je ne me rappelle presque plus rien,** a dream I can remember almost nothing about; **se r. (d')avoir promis qch,** to remember having promised sth; **rappelez-vous que ce n'est qu'une enfant,** remember *or* bear in mind that she is only a child;

(b) *F* **on se rappelle la semaine prochaine,** (*au téléphone*) we'll give each other a ring next week.

rappliquer [raplike] *vi Arg* to turn up, to show (up); **il va r. avec ses copains,** he's going to turn *or* roll up with his pals; **r. à la maison,** to roll back home.

rapport [rapɔr] *nm* **(a)** (*relation*) relations (*between people*); **mettre qn en r. avec qn,** to bring s.o. into contact *or* put s.o. in touch with s.o.; **avoir des rapports avec qn,** (*officiels*) to have dealings *or* relations with s.o.; (*amicaux*) to be in touch with s.o.; (*sexuels*) to have sexual intercourse *or* sex with s.o.; **les couples qui n'ont plus de rapports,** couples who no longer have sexual relations *or* sex; **avoir de bons rapports avec qn,** to be on good terms with s.o.; **cesser tout r. avec qn,** to break off all relations with s.o.; *Pol* **les rapports entre Est et Ouest,** East-West relations; **entretenir des rapports de bon voisinage avec les pays européens,** to maintain good relations with European countries;

(b) (*lien*) relation, connection (**avec,** with); **sans r. avec le sujet,** without any bearing on *or* unconnected with *or* irrelevant to the subject; **sa décision est sans r. avec ce qui se passe ici,** his decision is unrelated to *or* has nothing to do with what's going on here; **avoir r. à qch,** to relate *or* refer to sth; **un métier en r. avec ses goûts,** a trade in line *or* harmony with his tastes; **question qui a un r. très étroit avec une autre,** question that is closely connected with another; **rôle en r. avec votre dignité,** role in keeping with your dignity; **par r. à qch,** with regard *or* respect to sth, in relation to sth; (*en comparaison*) in comparison with *or* compared with sth; **par r. au mark,** against the German mark; **sous ce r.,** in this respect; **sous tous les rapports,** in all respects, in every respect; **homme bien sous tous rapports,** attractive man in all respects *or* in every way; **je ne vois pas le r.,** I don't see the connection;

(c) (*proportion*) ratio, proportion; **le résultat n'est pas en r. avec l'effort fourni,** the result is not proportional to the effort expended; *Math* **r. arithmétique/géométrique,** arithmetical/geometrical ratio; **dans le r. de un à trois,** in the ratio of one to three; **le r. maître-élèves est de 1 pour 20,** the staff-student ratio is 1 to 20; *Aut* **r. des engrenages,** gear ratio;

(d) (*écrit etc*) account, report, statement; return (*of expenses etc*); **au r. de notre représentant,** according to our representative; **r. officiel,** official report; **faire** *ou* **rédiger un r. sur qch,** to make *or* draw up a report on sth; **r. de gestion,** annual report (*of company*); **r. financier,** treasurer's report; *Nau* **r. de mer,** (ship's) protest;

(e) *Fin etc* yield, return, profit; **capital en r.,** interest-bearing *or* productive capital; **arbre fruitier en plein r.,** fruit tree in full yield; **immeuble de r.,** rental property; **d'un bon r.,** profitable, that brings in a good return, that pays well; **les rapports du tiercé,** winnings on the 'tiercé';

(f) *Mil* daily parade for issue of orders; **salle des rapports,** orderly room;

(g) terres de r., made ground, artificial soil; **pièces de r.,** built-up parts (*of machinery*).

rapportable [rapɔrtabl] *adj* **(a) pièces rapportables,** pieces that fit together; **(b)** (*attribuable*) referable, attributable (**à,** to).

rapportage [rapɔrtaʒ] *nm Scol F* taletelling, sneaking.

rapporté [rapɔrte] *adj* **(a) terre rapportée,** made ground; **(b)** built-up (*machine*); compound (*girder*); **(c) étau à mâchoires rapportées,** vice with detachable *or* inserted jaws; *Couture* **manche rapportée,** set-in sleeve; **poches rapportées,** patch pockets; **bout r.,** toecap.

rapporter [rapɔrte] **1** *vt* **(a)** (*pour rendre*) to bring back, to carry back; to return (*borrowed article*); (*d'un chien*) to retrieve (*game*); **rapportez-moi un kilo de sucre,** bring me back a kilo of sugar; **il n'en a rapporté que la honte,** all he got out of it was disgrace;

(b) r. qch à une cause, to attribute *or* ascribe sth to a cause; **r. un événement à une époque,** to assign *or* refer an event to a period; **r. tout à soi** *ou* **à ses intérêts,** to view everything in terms of (one)self;

(c) to report, to give an account of (*sth*); **vous n'auriez pas dû le r.,** you shouldn't have repeated it; **je vous rapporte ses paroles,** I'm telling you what he said; **l'histoire rapporte que ...,** history relates that ...;

(d) to add, to put in, to insert (*pieces to build up a machine*); to sew on (*a binding*); **r. des terres,** to carry in earth (*to build up terrace*);

(e) *Fin etc* to bring in, to bear, to yield; **placement qui rapporte dix pour cent,** investment that brings in *or* returns ten per cent; **arbres qui rapportent beaucoup,** trees that yield well; **cela ne rapporte rien,** it doesn't pay;

(f) *Jur etc* to rescind, to revoke (*decree*); to withdraw, to cancel (*order*); **r. un ordre de grève,** to call off a strike;

(g) to plot, to set off, to lay off (*angle*); *Géom* **r. des mesures à une autre échelle,** to plot measurements on a different scale;

(h) (*en comptabilité*) to post (*item*).

2 se rapporter *vpr* **(a)** to refer, to relate to have reference (**à,** to); **les documents qui se rapportent à l'affaire,** the relevant documents;

(b) s'en r. à qn/au témoignage de qn, to rely on *or* to put one's faith in s.o./s.o.'s evidence; **je m'en rapporte à vous,** I'll take your word for it;

(c) *Tech* (*d'une pièce*) to fit (**avec,** with);

(d) to agree, to tally (**avec,** with); **couleurs qui se rapportent bien,** colours that go well together.

3 *vi* **(a) la publicité rapporte,** it pays to advertise; **affaire qui rapporte,** profitable business, business that pays;

(b) (*en secret*) to tell tales, to sneak; **r. sur le compte de qn,** to tell on s.o.;

(c) r. sur un projet, to report on a plan.

rapporteur, -euse [rapɔrtœr, -øz] **1** *adj* telltale, sneaky, tattling. **2** *n* telltale, sneak, tattler. **3** *nm* **(a)** reporter, recorder; *Pol* **r. d'une commission,** chairman of a committee; **r. d'une conférence,** rapporteur of a conference; **(b)** *Mil* judge advocate (*at court martial*); **(c)** *Math* protractor; **r. à limbe complet,** circular protractor.

rapprendre [raprɑ̃dr] *vt* (*conj like* **prendre**) **(a)** (*apprendre*) to learn (*sth*) (over) again; **elle a dû r. à marcher après son accident,** she had to learn to walk (all over) again after her accident; **(b)** (*enseigner*) to teach (*sth*) again.

rapproché [raprɔʃe] *adj* near (*in space, time*); **maisons très rapprochées,** houses very close *or* near to one another; **des examens très rapprochés,** exams occurring very close together *or* to each other; **faits rapprochés dans le temps,** events occurring close together (in time); **yeux rapprochés,** close-set eyes; **espèces rapprochées,** closely related species; *Phot Cin* **plan r. sur un visage,** close-up on a face.

rapprochement [raprɔʃmɑ̃] *nm* **(a)** (*lien*) setting side by side, putting together, comparing (*of facts, ideas*); **il n'a pas fait le r.,** he didn't make the connection; **je ne peux m'empêcher de faire un r. entre ces deux faits,** I can't help making a connection between *or* linking the two facts; **(b)** bringing *or* placing together (*of two things*); bringing together, reconciling (*of two persons*); **(c)** nearness, proximity, closeness (*of two objects*); **(d)** (*réconciliation*) reconciliation, *surtout Pol* rapprochement.

rapprocher [raprɔʃe] **1** *vt* **(a)** to bring (*objects*) nearer *or* closer together; to bring (*sth*) near (again); **r. les lèvres d'une plaie,** to draw together *or* join the lips of a wound; **r. une chaise du feu,** to draw up a chair to the fire; **une lunette rapproche les objets,** a field-glass makes objects look nearer; **il va falloir r. les rendez-vous,** we'll have to make our meetings more frequent, we'll have to meet more often; **chaque jour les rapproche de la fin,** each day brings them nearer the end; **je te déposerai sur la place, ça te rapprochera (de chez toi),** I'll drop you off in the square, that'll get you a bit nearer home;

(b) to bring (*two people*) together; **un intérêt commun les rapproche,** a common interest unites them *or* brings *or* draws them together; **cette épreuve nous a rapprochés,** that ordeal drew *or* brought us together *or* made us closer;

(d) (*lier*) to put together *or* side by side; to compare (*facts, ideas*).

2 se rapprocher *vpr* **(a) se r. de qch,** to draw near(er) to sth; **rapproche-toi de lui, il n'entend pas,** move closer to him, he can't hear;

(b) *Fig* **se r. de son idéal,** to come close to one's ideal; **son costume se rapprochait d'un uniforme,** his clothes looked almost like *or* came near to being a uniform; **se r. de la vérité,** to approximate *or* come close to the truth; **ça n'est pas tout à fait ça, mais ça s'en approche,** that's not quite it but it's something close *or* similar;

(c) se r. de qn, to become reconciled *or* to make it up with s.o.; **elles se sont rapprochées depuis la mort de leur père,** they have become closer since the death of their father; **la France et l'Espagne s'étaient rapprochées,** a rapprochement had taken place between France and Spain.

rapsodie [rapsɔdi] *nf* rhapsody.

rapt [rapt] *nm* abduction, kidnapping.

râpure [rɑpyr] *nf Tech* raspings, gratings, filings.

raquer [rake] *vt Arg* to fork out, to cough up, to stump up.

raquette [rakɛt] *nf* **(a)** (*tennis*) racket, racquet; (*table tennis, ping pong*) bat; *Aut F* **coups de r.,** jolts; *Fig* **une des meilleures raquettes du monde,** one of the best tennis players in the world; **(b)** regulating lever (*of watch*); **(c)** (*pour marcher dans la neige*) snowshoe; **(d)** *Bot F* prickly pear.

rare [rar] *adj* **(a)** rare (*book, insect etc*); **visites rares et éloignées,** visits few and far between; **je suis un des rares à aimer la pluie,** I am one of the few people who like rain; **se faire r.,** to be seldom seen; **vous devenez r. comme les beaux jours,** you are quite a stranger, we seldom see you (these days); **la main-d'œuvre/l'argent était r.,** there was a shortage of labour/money; *F* **ça n'aurait rien de r.,** that wouldn't be anything out of the ordinary; **ça n'a rien de r. de sa part,** that's by no means unusual for him; **(b)** rare, uncommon, exceptional (*merit, beauty*); **r. courage,** rare *or* singular courage; **(c)** *Litt* thin, sparse, scanty (*hair etc*); *Phys* rare (*atmosphere*); **il faisait un jour r.,** the light was very dim *or* weak.

raréfaction [rarefaksjɔ̃] *nf* **(a)** rarefaction (*of gas, air*); **(b)** depletion (*of supplies*); growing scarcity (*of product, money*).

raréfier [rarefje] **1** *vt* **(a)** *Phys* to rarefy; **(b)** to deplete (*sth*), to make (*sth*) scarce. **2 se raréfier** *vpr* **(a)** *Phys etc* to become rarefied, to rarefy; **(b)** (*moins fréquent*) to become scarce *or* infrequent.

rarement [rarmɑ̃] *adv* rarely, seldom, infrequently.

rareté [rarte] *nf* **(a)** rarity, tenuity (*of gas etc*); **(b)** scarceness, scarcity, dearth (*of objects*); infrequency (*of visits*); **(c)** novelty, singularity, unusualness (*of phenomenon*); **(d) cabinet plein de raretés,** cabinet full of rare objects *or* of rarities *or* curiosities; **(e)** rare occurrence (*of word etc*).

ras [rɑ] **1** *adj* **(a)** close-cropped (*hair, head*); close-shaven (*beard, chin*); short-napped (*velvet*); short-pile (*carpet*); **couper r. les cheveux,** to crop the hair short *or* close; **chien à poil r.,** short-haired dog;

(b) (*vide*) bare, blank; **en rase campagne,** in the open country; **faire table rase de qch,** to make a clean sweep of sth; **faire table rase du passé,** to erase the past; **pull r. du cou,** crew-neck *or* round-neck sweater;

(c) mesure rase, full (level) measure; **verser du vin à qn à r. bord,** to fill s.o.'s glass to the brim.

2 *adv* **à** *ou* **au r. de,** (on a) level *or* flush with; **vaisseau chargé au r. de l'eau,** vessel laden to the water line; **voler au r. du sol,** to fly close to the ground, to skim (along) the ground; *F* **son humour vole** *ou* **reste au r. des pâquerettes,** his sense of humour is pretty basic *or* low (brow).

rasade [razad] *nf* glassful (*of wine*).

rasage [razaʒ] *nm* shaving; *Tex* shearing; **lotion après-r.,** after-shave lotion.

rasant [razɑ̃] *adj* **(a) tir r.,** grazing fire; **trajectoire rasante,** flat trajectory; **vol r.,** flight that skims the ground; **lumière rasante,** oblique *or* (almost) horizontal light; **(b)** *F* boring (*person, speech*).

rascasse [raskas] *nf* scorpion fish.

rasé [raze] *adj* shaven; **r. de près,** close-shaven; **(entièrement) r.,** (*visage*) (clean-)shaven; (*tête*) shaven.

rase-mottes [razmɔt] *nm inv Av* **vol en r.-m.,** *F* hedge hopping; **faire du** *ou* **voler en r.-m.,** to skim the ground, *F* to hedge hop.

raser [raze] **1** *vt* **(a)** to shave (*head, beard*); to shave off (*moustache*); *Tex* to shear (*cloth*); **raser qn,** to shave s.o., to give s.o. a shave; **(b)** to raze (*building*) (to the ground), to pull down (*building*); *Nau* to dismast, *Arch* to razee (*ship*); **(c)** (*frôler*) to graze, to brush, to skim (over); **l'hirondelle rase le sol,** the swallow skims the ground; **r. la côte/le mur,** to hug the shore/the wall; **(d)** *F* to bore (*s.o.*). **2 se raser** *vpr* **(a)** to shave; **je dois me r.,** I need a shave; **(b)** *F*

to be bored.
raseur, -euse [razœr, -øz] *n* **(a)** *Tex* shearer; **(b)** *F* bore.
rasibus [razibys] *adv F* **couper r.,** to cut quite close; **la balle est passée r.,** the bullet whizzed past very close.
ras-le-bol [ralbɔl] **1** *nm* **(a) j'en ai** *ou* **il y en a r.-le-b. (de tes histoires),** I'm fed up (with your nonsense), I'm sick to the back teeth (of your nonsense); **(b)** (*sentiment*) discontent, dissatisfaction; **le r.-le-b. généralisé qui s'empare des professeurs,** the widespread dissatisfaction to which teachers are falling prey; **le r.-le-b. des jeunes,** the dissatisfaction of the young. **2** *int* enough!; **tu ne vas pas recommencer!, r.-le-b.!,** don't you start again!, enough's enough!
rasoir [razwar] **1** *nm* **(a)** razor; **r. de sûreté,** safety razor; **r. électrique,** electric razor *or* shaver; **pierre à r.,** hone; **cuir à r.,** strop; **savoir** *ou* **dire son texte au r.,** to know *or* recite one's text off by heart; **(b)** *F* (*personne*) bore. **2** *adj inv* boring.
Raspoutine [rasputin] *nm* Rasputin.
rassasié [rasazje] *adj* (*repu*) satisfied; *Fig F* full, sated (**de,** with).
rassasiement [rasazimɑ̃] *nm* satisfying (*of hunger*); *Fig* satiety, surfeit.
rassasier [rasazje] **1** *vt* **(a)** to satisfy (*hunger, curiosity, passion*); **r. qn,** to satisfy s.o.'s hunger; **les fruits ne rassasient pas,** fruit does not satisfy your hunger *or* fill your stomach, fruit is not very filling; **(b)** *Fig* to sate, to satiate (**de,** with); **r. son regard à contempler qch,** to feast one's eyes on sth. **2 se rassasier** *vpr* to eat one's fill; **se r. d'un mets/de plaisirs,** to take one's fill of *or* gorge oneself on a dish/to take one's fill of pleasures.
rassemblement [rasɑ̃bləmɑ̃] *nm* **(a)** assembling, collecting, gathering (*of documents, troops, tools*); *Mil* fall in, parade; **sonner le r.,** to sound the assembly; **r.!,** fall in!, form up!; *Pol* **le r. de la gauche,** the union of the left; **(b)** (*foule*) crowd, gathering; **provoquer un r.,** to draw *or* attract a crowd.
rassembler [rasɑ̃ble] **1** *vt* **(a)** to reassemble, to bring together again (*persons, pieces of machinery*); **(b)** to assemble, to muster (*troops*); to collect, to gather together, to get together (*persons, things*); **r. ses idées,** to collect one's thoughts; **r. toutes les pièces d'un procès,** to bring together all the documents of a case; *Fig* **r. son courage/toutes ses forces,** to muster *or* summon up one's courage/all one's strength; *Équitation* **r. un cheval,** to gather a horse. **2 se rassembler** *vpr* (*s'assembler*) to assemble, to come together, to get together, to gather; *Mil* to fall in, to muster; **les ouvriers se rassemblent sous l'égide du syndicat,** the workers are gathering *or* banding together under the aegis of the union.
rasseoir [raswar] *v* (*conj like* **asseoir**) **1** *vt* to seat (*s.o.*) again; **r. une statue sur sa base,** to replace a statue on its base. **2 se rasseoir** *vpr* **(a)** (*de personne*) to sit down again; **faire r. qn,** to make s.o. sit down again; **(b)** (*de liquide*) to settle; **laisser r. le vin,** to let the wine settle.
rasséréner [raserene] *v* **(je rassérène, n. rassérénons; je rassérénerai) 1** *vt* to calm (*s.o.*), to restore (*s.o.'s*) equanimity *or* peace of mind. **2 se rasséréner** *vpr* **(a)** (*du ciel*) to clear (up); **(b)** (*de personne*) to recover one's serenity.
rassir [rasir] **1** *vi* to go *or* get stale; **j'ai laissé r. mon pain,** I have let my bread go stale. **2 se rassir** *vpr* to go *or* get stale.
rassis [rasi] *adj* **(a) pain r.,** stale bread; **(b)** *Fig* settled, calm, sober (*disposition*); **faire qch de sens r.,** to do sth coolly.
rassortir [rasɔrtir] *vt* = **RÉASSORTIR.**
rassurant [rasyrɑ̃] *adj* reassuring, heartening; **peu r.,** disquieting.
rassurer [rasyre] **1** *vt* to reassure, to cheer, to hearten; **je suis assez peu rassuré,** I have my misgivings; **cela me rassure (de savoir que ...),** it reassures me (to know that ...); **ah, tu me rassures!,** well, that's a relief! **2 se rassurer** *vpr* to feel reassured; **rassurez-vous là-dessus,** make yourself easy *or* set your mind at rest on that point.
rasta [rasta] *adj & n* Rasta(farian).
rastaquouère [rastakwɛr] *nm F* **un drôle de r.,** a real flash Harry.
rat [ra] **1** *nm* **(a)** rat; **r. surmulot,** brown *or* Norway rat; **r. noir,** black rat; **mort aux rats,** rat poison; **chasse aux rats,** rat catching; **preneur de rats,** ratcatcher, *Admin* rodent operator; **r. des champs,** field mouse; **r. d'eau,** water vole; **r. musqué,** muskrat, musquash; **r. géant (des Indes),** bandicoot; **r. d'Égypte** *ou* **de Pharaon,** mongoose; **r. d'Amérique,** coypu; *Fig* **r. d'église,** constant church-goer; **pauvre comme un r. d'église,** (as) poor as a church mouse; **r. d'hôtel,** hotel thief; **r. de bibliothèque,** bookworm (*who spends his time in libraries*); *F* **petit r. (d'Opéra),** young ballet pupil; *F* **mon petit r.,** darling; *F* **être fait comme un r.,** to be caught like a rat in a trap; *Arg* **face de r.,** ratbag;
(b) (*avare*) miser, skinflint; *F* **c'est un r.,** he's stingy *or* a miser;
(c) *Can* tricky customer.
2 *adj inv F* **(a)** stingy, tight; **ce qu'il est r.!,** what a skinflint!
(b) *Can* wily, sly.
rata [rata] *nm Arg* grub, nosh, chow.
ratafia [ratafja] *nm* (*boisson*) ratafia.
ratage [rataʒ] *nm F* botching, bungling, messing up.
rataplan [rataplɑ̃] *nm* roll (*of a drum*).
ratatiné [ratatine] *adj* **(a)** shrivelled, shrunken (*apple, face*); **petite vieille ratatinée,** wizened little old woman; **(b)** *F* smashed-up (*car*).
ratatinement [ratatinmɑ̃] *nm* shrivelling (up).
ratatiner [ratatine] **1** *vt* **(a)** to shrivel (up); **(b)** *Arg* (*tuer*) to bump (*s.o.*) off; (*battre*) to beat (*s.o.*) up. **2 se ratatiner** *vpr* to shrivel up; (*of parchment*) to wrinkle up; **une vieille dame qui se ratatine,** a shrunken little old lady.
ratatouille [ratatuj] *nf Culin* ratatouille.
rate¹ [rat] *nf* spleen; *F* **se dilater la r.,** to have a good laugh, to split one's sides laughing; **ne pas se fouler la r.,** to take things pretty easy.
rate² *nf* female rat.
raté, -ée [rate] **1** *n* (*personne*) failure. **2** *nm* misfire (*of gun, engine*); **le moteur avait des ratés,** the engine was misfiring.
râteau, -eaux [rɑto] *nm* **(a)** (*de jardin*) rake; **r. mécanique,** raker; **r. faneur,** tedder; **(b)** *Nau* **r. de pont,** squeegee; **(c)** (*de croupier*) rake; **(d)** *F* comb; **(e)** wards (*of a lock*).
râtelage [rɑtlaʒ] *nm* raking.
râteler [rɑtle] *vt* **(je râtelle, n. râtelons; je râtellerai)** to rake up (*hay etc*).
râtelier [rɑtəlje] *nm* **(a)** rack (*in stable*); *F* **quand il n'y a plus de foin dans le r.,** when we're broke; **manger au r. de qn,** to live off s.o.; **il mange à tous les râteliers,** it's all grist to his mill; **(b) r. d'armes/à outils/à pipes/à seaux,** arm/tool/pipe/bucket rack; **(c)** *F* (set of) false teeth.
rater [rate] **1** *vi* (*d'un fusil*) to misfire, to fail to go off; (*d'un moteur*) to misfire; (*d'une enterprise*) to backfire. **2** *vt* **(a) r. son coup,** to miss one's shot, to miss the mark; *Golf* to foozle (*one's shot*); **coup raté,** miss, *F* fluff; *Av* **atterrissage raté,** bad landing; **(b)** *F* **r. un** *ou* **son coup,** to fail in an attempt, not to bring it off; *Fig* **j'ai raté mon coup, elle avait déjà ce disque,** I blew it *or* fluffed it, she already had the record; **r. son train,** to miss one's train; **r. son bac,** to fail in one's baccalauréat; **j'ai raté l'occasion,** I missed *or* lost the chance; **je ne vais pas le r.,** I'm really going to sort him out; **elle n'en rate pas une!,** she's always putting her foot in it!
ratiboiser [ratibwaze] *vt Arg* **(a) r. qch à qn,** to do s.o. out of sth; **(b)** to swindle, to rook (*s.o.*), to clean (*s.o.*) out; **je suis complètement ratiboisé,** I'm flat broke *or Br* stony broke *or* skint.
raticide [ratisid] *nm* rat poison.
ratier [ratje] *adj & nm* **(chien) r.,** ratter.
ratière [ratjɛr] *nf* rat trap.
ratification [ratifikasjɔ̃] *nf* ratification; **accord sous réserve de r.,** agreement subject to ratification *or* confirmation.
ratifier [ratifje] *vt* to ratify (*treaty, act*); to confirm (*decision*).
ratio [rasjo] *nm* ratio.
ratiocination [rasjɔsinasjɔ̃] *nf Litt* hair-splitting, quibbling.
ratiociner [rasjɔsine] *vi Litt* to split hairs.
ration [rasjɔ̃] *nf* ration(s); (*pour bête*) feed; **r. de combat,** iron rations; **rations imposées en temps de guerre,** wartime rations; **r. calorique,** calorie intake; *F* **ça va!, j'ai eu ma r. de critiques,** that'll do! I've had enough *or* my share of criticism.
rationalisation [rasjɔnalizasjɔ̃] *nf* rationalization; rationalizing (*of industry*).
rationaliser [rasjɔnalize] *vt* to rationalize.
rationalisme [rasjɔnalism] *nm* rationalism.
rationaliste [rasjɔnalist] *adj & n* rationalist.
rationalité [rasjɔnalite] *nf* rationality.
rationnel, -elle [rasjɔnɛl] *adj* **(a)** rational (*system,*

quantity); theoretical (*mechanics*); **(b)** (*logique*) rational, reasonable, sensible.
rationnellement [rasjɔnɛlmɑ̃] *adv* rationally, sensibly.
rationnement [rasjɔnmɑ̃] *nm* rationing.
rationner [rasjɔne] *vt* to ration (*population, patient, supplies*).
ratissage [ratisaʒ] *nm* **(a)** (*du jardin*) raking; **(b)** (*au casino*) raking in (*of the stakes*); **(c)** *F* combing, thorough search (*of district, by police etc*).
ratisser [ratise] **1** *vt* **(a)** to rake (*path*); to rake (up) (*leaves*); **(b) r. les mises,** (*au casino*) to rake in the stakes; **(c)** *F* to search, to comb (*a district*); **(d)** *F* to swindle, to rook, to fleece (*s.o.*); (*ruiner*) to ruin (*s.o.*). **2** *vi Pol* **pour obtenir une majorité, le parti socialiste a dû r. large,** to obtain a majority the Socialist Party had to cast its net as wide as possible.
ratissoire [ratiswar] *nf* hoe, scuffle.
raton [ratɔ̃] *nm* young rat; **r. laveur,** raccoon.
ratonnade [ratɔnad] *nf* (*contre des Maghrébins etc*) attack; *Br* ≈ Paki-bashing.
ratoureux, -euse [raturø, -øz] *Can* **1** *adj* wily, devious; **parfois le bonheur est un peu r.,** sometimes happiness is not all it seems. **2** *n* shady customer.
R.A.T.P. [ɛratepe] *nf* (*abrév* **Régie autonome des transports parisiens**) = Parisian municipal transport system.
rattachement [rataʃmɑ̃] *nm* re-attachment; **le r. de l'Alsace à la France,** the return of Alsace to France.
rattacher [rataʃe] **1** *vt* (*attacher de nouveau*) to fasten *or* tie (up) (*sth*) again, to refasten; **rattachez le chien,** tie up the dog (again); **r. l'Alsace à la France,** to (re)unite Alsace with France; *Fig* **les liens qui vous rattachent à la famille,** the ties that bind you to your family; **c'est tout ce qui le rattache à la vie,** that's all he's living for; **r. qch à qch,** to link up *or* connect sth with sth; *Mil* **unité rattachée,** attached unit. **2 se rattacher** *vpr* **se r. à qch,** to be connected with sth; **ce problème se rattache à ce qui a été dit,** this problem is connected with what's been mentioned.
rattrapage [ratrapaʒ] *nm* **(a)** *MecE* **r. du jeu,** taking up of play; compensation for play; **(b)** *Scol* **cours de r.,** remedial class; **(c) r. des salaires/des prix,** the catching up of wages/prices.
rattrape-jeu [ratrapʒø] *nm inv MecE* **(dispositif) r.-j.,** device for taking up play.
rattraper [ratrape] **1** *vt* **(a)** to recapture (*s.o., sth*); to catch (*s.o., sth*) again; *F* **on ne m'y rattrapera pas!,** you won't catch me doing that again!;
(b) to overtake, to catch (*s.o.*) up; **je vous rattraperai à l'angle de la rue,** I'll catch you up at the corner (of the street); **se faire r. par la police,** to get caught by the police;
(c) r. son argent/sa santé, to recover one's money/health; **r. le temps perdu,** to make up for lost time; **r. l'arriéré de besogne,** to catch up with arrears of work;
(d) *MecE* **r. le jeu/l'usure,** to take up the play/the wear;
(e) to correct, to retrieve (*mistake etc*); *Culin* **r. une mayonnaise,** to retrieve *or* salvage a (curdled) mayonnaise; **comment r. cette erreur/imprudence?,** how can I make up for this mistake/carelessness?
2 se rattraper *vpr* **se r. à une branche,** to save oneself by catching hold of a branch; *Fig F* **se r. aux branches,** to clutch at straws; **se r. de justesse,** to just stop oneself falling; **se r. (avant de faire une erreur),** to stop oneself (before making a mistake); **je me suis rattrapé en l'invitant,** I've made up for it *or* I made amends by inviting him; **pas de soleil depuis 3 mois, je vais me r.!,** no sun for three months, I'm going to make up for it now; **elle s'est bien rattrapeée depuis,** she's really made up for it since; **se r. auprès de qn,** to get back into favour with s.o., to get back into s.o.'s favour; **se r. de ses pertes,** to make good one's losses, to recoup oneself.
3 *vi F* to catch up; **ça va lui permettre de r.,** that will enable him to catch up.
rature [ratyr] *nf* erasure, deletion, crossing out; **faire une r.,** to cross out *or* delete a word.
raturer [ratyre] *vt* to erase, to cross out, to delete (*word*).
raucité [rosite] *nf* raucousness, hoarseness.
raugmenter [rogmɑ̃te] *vi Arg* (*d'un prix*) to rise, to go up again.
rauque [rok] *adj* hoarse, raucous, rough, harsh (*voice, etc*).
ravage [ravaʒ] *nm* (*souvent pl*) **ravages,** havoc, devastation; ravages (*of war, disease*); **faire des ravages,** to wreak havoc; *Fig* **cette mode fait des ravages parmi les jeunes,** this fashion is all the rage among the young.
ravagé [ravaʒe] *adj* **(a)** ravaged; **pays r.,** devastated country; **visage r.,** ravaged *or* haggard face; **(b)** *F* (*fou*) mad, cracked; **tu es complètement r.!,** you're completely nuts *or* potty!
ravager [ravaʒe] *vt* (**je ravageai(s); n. ravageons**) to ravage, to devastate, to lay waste (*town, country etc*); **visage ravagé par la petite vérole/l'alcool,** face pitted with *or* ravaged by smallpox/face ravaged by alcohol.
ravageur, -euse [ravaʒœr, -øz] **1** *adj* ravaging; devastating (*storm*); destructive (*birds*). **2** *n* ravager, destroyer, devastator.
ravalement [ravalmɑ̃] *nm* **(a)** *Constr* repointing (*of stonework*); (*en recrépissant*) roughcasting; (*enduit*) (coat of) roughcast; **(b)** cutting back (*of tree*); **(c)** *Vieilli* disparagement, depreciation (*of s.o.*).
ravaler [ravale] **1** *vt* **(a)** to swallow (*sth*) again, to swallow (*sth*) down; **r. un sanglot/sa colère,** to choke (down) a sob/to suppress *or* stifle one's anger; **r. des larmes,** to choke back one's tears; **je lui ferai r. ses paroles,** I'll make him eat his words; **(b)** (*abaisser*) to degrade, to lower (*s.o.*); (*dévaluer*) to disparage (*s.o.*); **(c)** to cut back (*tree*); **(d)** *Constr* to repoint (*stonework*); to roughcast (*wall*). **2 se ravaler** *vpr* to degrade *or* lower *or* debase oneself; **vous ne vous ravaleriez pas jusque-là,** you would not stoop to that.
ravaleur [ravalœr] *nm* roughcaster, plasterer.
ravaudage [ravodaʒ] *nm* **(a)** (*action*) mending, repairing (*of clothes*); darning, mending (*of socks*); (*ratage*) botching, bungling (*of work*); **(b)** (*résultat*) mend, repair (*of garment*); darn, mend (*of sock*); *F* (*d'objet*) botch(-up).
ravauder [ravode] *vt* **(a)** to mend, to repair (*clothes*); to darn, to mend (*socks*); **(b)** *F* to botch, to bungle (*work*).
ravaudeur, -euse [ravodœr, -øz] *n* (*de vêtements*) mender; (*de chaussettes*) darner.
rave [rav] *nf* (*colza*) rape; (*radis*) radish; (*navet*) turnip; **céleri r.,** celeriac.
ravi [ravi] *adj* delighted (**de,** with); **je suis r. de vous voir,** I'm delighted to see you; **d'un air r.,** delightedly.
ravier [ravje] *nm* hors-d'œuvres dish.
ravigotant [ravigɔtɑ̃] *adj F* refreshing, invigorating; **un verre de calva r.,** a revitalizing glass of calvados.
ravigote [ravigɔt] *nf Culin* =hard-boiled eggs served with ravigote sauce and herbs; **sauce r.,** ravigote sauce (*highly seasoned oil and vinegar dressing*).
ravigoter [ravigɔte] *vt F* to cheer (*s.o.*) up, to buck (*s.o.*) up.
ravin [ravɛ̃] *nm* ravine, gully.
ravine [ravin] *nf* **(a)** (*petit ravin*) gully; **(b)** (*rivière*) (mountain) torrent.
ravinement [ravinmɑ̃] *nm* gullying, channelling (*by running water*).
raviner [ravine] *vt* (*d'orage, de torrent*) to gully, to channel (*the ground*); to furrow, to cut up (*road*).
ravioli(s) [ravjɔli] *nm(pl) Culin* ravioli.
ravir [ravir] *vt* **(a)** (*plaire*) to delight; **belle à r.,** ravishingly beautiful; **elle chante à r.,** she sings charmingly *or* delightfully; **cela te va à r.,** it suits you beautifully, you look delightful in it; **(b)** *Litt* to ravish, to carry off (*s.o.*); **r. qch à qn,** to rob s.o. of sth, to steal sth from s.o..
raviser (se) [səravize] *vpr* to change one's mind.
ravissant [ravisɑ̃] *adj* ravishing, entrancing, delightful.
ravissement [ravismɑ̃] *nm* **(a)** (*extase*) rapture, ecstasy, delight; **être dans le r.,** to be in raptures; **(b)** *Litt* carrying off, *Arch* ravishment.
ravisseur, -euse [ravisœr, -øz] **1** *adj* predatory. **2** *n* abductor, kidnapper, *Arch* ravisher.
ravitaillement [ravitajmɑ̃] *nm* **(a)** *Mil etc* supply(ing), provisioning (**en,** with); **r. (en carburant),** refuelling; **r. en munitions,** ammunition supply; **distribution du r.,** issue of supplies; **convoi de r.,** supply column; **r. à la mer,** replenishment *or* refuelling at sea; **r. en vol,** in-flight refuelling; **le r. des grandes villes est un des problèmes de la guerre,** maintaining supplies in large cities is one of the problems of war; *F* **aller au r.,** to go shopping; **(b)** supplies (*of food, fuel etc*).
ravitailler [ravitaje] **1** *vt* to (re)supply, to (re)provision (**en,** with); **r. un avion en vol,** to refuel an aircraft in flight. **2 se ravitailler** *vpr* to take in (fresh) supplies; **se r. (en carburant),** to refuel; *F* **se r. dans le voisinage,** to shop *or* stock up locally.
ravitailleur [ravitajœr] **1** *nm Mil etc* (*camion*) supply truck; (*bateau*) supply ship; (*avion*) supply aircraft. **2** *adj* **navire r.,** supply ship.
ravivage [ravivaʒ] *nm* brightening up (*of colour*); cleaning (*of metal surfaces*).

raviver [ravive] **1** *vt* **(a)** to revive (*fire, memory, pain*); **(b)** to brighten up, to touch up (*colour*); to clean (*surfaces to be soldered*); **r. une plaie,** *Méd* to trim a wound; *Fig* to reopen an old sore. **2 se raviver** *vpr* to revive.

ravoir [ravwar] *vt* (*only in inf*) **(a)** (*récupérer*) to have (*sth*) (once) again; to get (*sth*) back again; **(b)** *F* (*in neg*) to clean (up); **je n'arrive pas à r. cette casserole,** I can't get this pan properly clean.

rayage [rɛjaʒ] *nm* **(a)** scratching, scoring (*of glass etc*); **(b)** ruling (*of paper etc*); **(c)** striping (*of fabric*); **(d)** rifling (*of gun*); **(e)** striking out (*of word etc*); striking off (*of name from list*).

rayé [reje] *adj* **(a)** striped, stripy; **pantalon r.,** striped *or* stripy trousers; **tablier r. rouge et bleu,** red and blue striped *or* stripy apron; **chat roux r.,** orange tabby cat; **(b)** lined, ruled (*paper*); **(c)** rifled, grooved (*gun*); **âme rayée,** rifle(d) bore.

rayer [reje] *vt* (**je raie, je raye, n. rayons; je raierai, je rayerai**) **(a)** to scratch (*glass etc*); to score (*surface*); **(b)** to rule, to line (*paper*); **(c)** to stripe (*fabric*); **(d)** to rifle (*gun*); to groove (*cylinder*); **(e)** to strike out, to cross out, to delete (*word etc*); **on vous a rayé** *ou* **on a rayé votre nom de la liste,** you have *or* your name has been struck off the list; *Fig* **tu ne peux pas r. cet événement de ta vie,** you can't banish *or* blot out that event from your life; **il voudrait me r. de sa vie,** he'd like to erase *or* banish me from his life; *Mil* **r. qn des contrôles,** to strike s.o. off the strength.

rayon¹ [rɛjɔ̃] *nm* **(a)** ray (*of light, hope*); beam (*of light*); **un faible r. de lumière,** a faint gleam of light; **r. de soleil,** sunbeam; *Opt* **r. visuel,** line of sight; **rayons cosmiques,** cosmic rays; **rayons X,** X-rays; *Méd* **mal des rayons,** radiation sickness; **r. électronique,** electron beam; **(b)** radius (*of circle*); *Aut* **r. de braquage,** radius of turning circle, steering lock; **(c)** (*périmètre*) range; **dans un r. de deux kilomètres,** within a radius of two kilometres; **r. d'action,** (*of aircraft*) range of action *or* operation; **avion à grand r. d'action,** long-range aircraft; **r. d'action d'une campagne publicitaire,** coverage *or* range of an advertising campaign; **cette entreprise a étendu son r. d'action,** this firm has extended its scope; **(d)** spoke (*of wheel*); **(e) étoile à cinq rayons,** five-point(ed) star; **(f)** *Bot* ray.

rayon² *nm* **(a)** (*in shop*) department, counter; **r. des soldes,** bargain counter; **r. hommes/femmes,** mens' wear/ladies' wear (department); **chef de r.,** head *or* buyer of department; **magasin à rayons multiples,** department store; *Fig* **ce n'est pas mon r.,** (*ça ne me concerne pas*) that's nothing to do with me, that's none of my business; (*ça n'est pas dans mes compétences*) that's not in my line; *Fig* **c'est son r.,** that's right up his street; *Fig* **elle en connaît un r. (sur la question),** she's well clued up (on the subject); **(b)** shelf (*of cupboard etc*); **rayons,** set of shelves; **(c) r. de miel,** honeycomb.

rayon³ *nm Agr* drill; **r. d'oignons,** row of onions.

rayonnage [rɛjɔnaʒ] *nm* shelving, (set of) shelves.

rayonnant [rɛjɔnɑ̃] *adj* **(a)** radiant (*heat, sun*); **(b)** radiant, beaming (*face*); **r. de santé,** glowing with health; **(c)** *Bot* radiating; **(d)** *Archit* rayonnant.

rayonne [rɛjɔn] *nf Tex* rayon.

rayonnement [rɛjɔnmɑ̃] *nm* **(a)** *Phys* radiation; **protection contre le r.,** glow screen; **(b)** radiance (*of sun etc*); *Fig* influence; **un r. intérieur l'habite,** he has an inner radiance.

rayonner¹ [rɛjɔne] *vi* **(a)** *Phys* to radiate; *Rad* **r. dans l'antenne,** to howl; **(b)** to beam, to shine; **il rayonnait de joie,** he was radiant *or* beaming with joy; **(c)** to radiate (*from a centre*); **une douleur qui rayonne,** a spreading pain; **r. autour d'Avignon,** to make Avignon the centre (*for excursions*).

rayonner² *vt* to fit with shelves, to shelve (*room etc*).

rayure [rejyr] *nf* **(a)** (*bande*) stripe, streak; **tissu à rayures,** striped *or* stripy material; **(b)** (*éraflure*) scratch, score; **(c)** groove (*of rifling*).

raz [ra] *nm* **r. (de courant),** strong current (*in estuary*); **r. de marée,** tidal wave; *Fig* **cette nouvelle a eu l'effet d'un r. de marée,** the news caused great upheaval; *Pol Fig* **ça a été un r. de marée pour les socialistes,** it was a landslide (victory) for the Socialists, it was a Socialist landslide.

razzia [razja] *nf* (*attaque*) incursion, raid, *Hist* razzia; *F* **faire (une) r. sur les articles en solde,** to make a clean sweep of *or* to snap up the bargains.

R.D. [ɛrde] *nf abrév* **route départementale**.

R.D.A. [ɛrdea] *nf* (*abrév* **République démocratique allemande**) GDR.

r.d.c. *abrév* **rez-de-chaussée**.

ré [re] *nm inv Mus* **(a)** (the note) D; **(b)** re (*in the Fixed Do system*).

réa [rea] *nm* sheave, pulley wheel.

réabonnement [reabɔnmɑ̃] *nm* renewal of subscription.

réabonner [reabɔne] **1** *vt* to renew (*s.o.'s*) subscription (**à,** to). **2 se réabonner** *vpr* to renew one's subscription.

réabsorber [reapsɔrbe] *vt* to reabsorb.

réabsorption [reapsɔrpsjɔ̃] *nf* reabsorption.

réac [reak] *adj & n Pol F Péj* reactionary.

réaccoutumer [reakutyme] **1** *vt* to reaccustom (**à,** to). **2 se réaccoutumer** *vpr* to become reaccustomed, to reaccustom oneself.

réactance [reaktɑ̃s] *nf Él* reactance.

réacteur [reaktœr, -tris] *nm* **(a)** (*moteur*) jet engine, reaction engine; **(b)** (*avion*) jet aircraft; **(c)** *Nucl* (atomic, nuclear) reactor, pile; **r. propulseur de navire,** ship-propulsion reactor.

réactif, -ive [reaktif, -iv] **1** *adj* reactive; **non r.,** non-reactive; *Ch* **papier r.,** reagent paper, test paper; *Él* **courant r.,** reactive current; **couplage r.,** feedback coupling. **2** *nm Ch* reagent; **r. à base de mercure,** mercury reagent.

réaction [reaksjɔ̃] *nf* **(a)** *Ch Phys* reaction; **faire la r. des alcaloïdes,** to test for alkaloids; **r. en chaîne,** chain reaction;

(b) *Él* reaction, feedback; *Rad* **amplificateur** *ou* **récepteur à r.,** regenerative receiver; **r. dans l'antenne,** howling;

(c) (*de machines etc*) reaction; (*de fusil*) kick; **r. réciproque,** interaction; **tube de r.,** torque tube; **moteur à r.,** jet engine, reaction engine *or* motor; **propulsion par r.,** jet propulsion, reaction propulsion; *F* **la voiture a de très bonnes réactions (sur la glace),** the car responds well *or* handles well (on ice); **avion à r.,** jet(-propelled) aircraft, jet plane, jet;

(d) *Physiol* reaction, response (*of organ etc*); **r. cutanée,** cutaneous *or* skin reaction; *Méd* skin test;

(e) reaction; **r. à une situation nouvelle,** reaction to a new situation; **r. de peur,** reaction of fear; **faire qch par r.,** to do sth as a reaction; **en r. à sa famille,** in reaction to his family; **rester sans r.,** to show no reaction; **qu'a-t-il répondu?, — rien, aucune r.,** what did he reply?, — nothing, he didn't react at all; **avoir des réactions lentes,** to be slow to react; **psychologie de r.,** behaviourism;

(f) *Pol* **la r.,** reactionary attitude; (*personnes*) reactionaries.

réactionnaire [reaksjɔnɛr] *adj & n Pol* reactionary.

réactiver [reaktive] *vt* to revive, to regenerate; to reactivate (*catalyst, serum*); **r. le feu,** to revive *or* poke (up) the fire.

réactivité [reaktivite] *nf* reactivity.

réactualiser [reaktyalise] *vt* to bring up to date, to update.

réadaptation [readaptasjɔ̃] *nf* **(a)** rehabilitation (*of invalid, prisoner*); **(b)** readjustment (*of projects etc*).

réadapter [readapte] **1** *vt* **(a)** to rehabilitate (*invalid, prisoner*); **(b)** to readjust (*projects*). **2 se réadapter** *vpr* to readjust, to become readjusted.

réadmettre [readmɛtr] *vt* (*conj like* **mettre**) to readmit.

réadmission [readmisjɔ̃] *nf* readmission.

réaffecter [reafɛkte] *vt* **r. qn à son premier emploi,** to reinstate s.o. in his former job; **r. une subvention à sa destination première,** to reallocate funds to their original use.

réaffirmer [reafirme] *vt* to reaffirm.

réagir [reaʒir] *vi* to react (**sur,** on; **contre,** against; **à,** towards); **on verra comment il va r.,** we'll see how he reacts.

réajuster [reaʒyste] *vt* = **RAJUSTER**.

réal, -aux [real, -o] *nm* (*monnaie*) real.

réalisable [realizabl] *adj* realizable, feasible (*plan*); *Fin* realizable (*assets*); *Fig* attainable (*dream*).

réalisateur, -trice [realizatœr, -tris] **1** *adj* **il a l'esprit r.,** he can get things done *or* get results. **2** *n Cin Rad* producer; **r. de télévision/de radio,** television/radio producer.

réalisation [realizasjɔ̃] *nf* **(a)** realization, carrying out, accomplishment (*of plan etc*); creation (*of work of art*); **la dernière r. de Picasso,** Picasso's final *or* last creation; **(b)** *Cin TV* production; **(c)** *Fin* realization.

réaliser [realize] **1** *vt* **(a)** to achieve, to realize (*an ambition, success*); to attain (*dream*); to carry out, to implement (*plan*); to effect (*cure*); to create (*work of art*);

(b) *Cin etc* to produce (*film, programme*);

(c) *Fin* to realize (*asset*), to convert (*asset*) into cash; to make (*profit*);

(d) *F* to understand (*mistake, situation*); **je ne réalisais pas l'importance de la situation,** I didn't realize *or* understand the seriousness of the situation; **elle n'arrive pas à r. que cela est vrai,** she's not able to see *or* realize it's true.

2 se réaliser *vpr* **(a)** (*d'un projet etc*) to materialize; (*d'une prédiction etc*) to come true;

(b) (*d'une personne*) to fulfil oneself.

3 *vi F* to understand, to realize, *F* to twig; **laisse-lui le temps de r.,** give him time for it to sink in.

réalisme [realism] *nm* realism; **le r. d'une description,** the realism of a description; **faire preuve de r. politique,** to demonstrate political realism *or* pragmatism.

réaliste [realist] **1** *adj* realistic; **ce n'est pas r.,** it's not realistic. **2** *n* realist.

réalité [realite] *nf* reality, actuality; **en r.,** in reality, really, actually, as a matter of fact; **elle n'a pas le sens des réalités,** she has no sense of reality, she doesn't live in the real world; **c'est une r.,** it's a reality *or* fact.

réanimation [reanimasjɔ̃] *nf Méd* resuscitation; **service de r.,** intensive care (unit).

réanimer [reanime] *vt Méd* to resuscitate (*s.o.*).

réapparaître [reaparɛtr] *vi* (*conj like* **apparaître**; *aux often* **être**) to reappear.

réapparition [reaparisjɔ̃] *nf* reappearance.

réapprovisionnement [reaprɔvizjɔnmɑ̃] *nm* restocking.

réapprovisionner [reaprɔvizjɔne] **1** *vt* to replenish (*s.o.'s*) supplies (**en,** of); to restock (*shop*) (**en,** with). **2 se réapprovisionner** *vpr* to stock up again, to restock (**en,** with).

réargenter [rearʒɑ̃te] *vt* to resilver.

réarmement [rearməmɑ̃] *nm* **(a)** rearming, rearmament; *Pol* **r. moral,** moral rearmament; **(b)** *Nau* refitting, recommissioning.

réarmer [rearme] *vt* **(a)** *Pol* to rearm; **(b)** to recock (*gun*); to reset (*camera shutter etc*); **(c)** *Nau* to refit, to recommission. **2 se réarmer** *vpr Pol* to rearm. **3** *vi Pol* to rearm.

réassort [reasɔr] *nm* (*d'une boutique*) restocking.

réassortiment [reasɔrtimɑ̃] *nm* **(a)** (re)matching (*of colours etc*); **(b)** (*d'une boutique*) restocking; (*stock*) new stock.

réassortir [reasɔrtir] *v* (*conj like* **assortir**) **1** *vt* **(a)** to obtain a match for (*sth, a set*); **(b)** to restock (*shop*). **2 se réassortir** *vpr* to restock.

réassurance [reasyrɑ̃s] *nf* reinsurance.

réassurer [reasyre] *vt* to reinsure.

réassureur [reasyrœr] *nm* reinsurer.

rebaisser [r(ə)bese] *vi* (*de prix, température*) to come down again.

rebaptiser [rəbatize] *vt* to rename (*street etc*).

rébarbatif, -ive [rebarbatif, -iv] *adj* (*sujet, tâche*) forbidding, daunting; (*visage, mine*) forbidding, unprepossessing; (*style*) off-putting.

rebâtir [rəbatir] *vt* to rebuild (*house*); *Couture* **r. par le pied,** to underpin.

rebattre [rəbatr] *vt* (*conj like* **battre**) **(a)** to beat (*sth*) again; **(b)** *Cartes* to reshuffle; **(c)** *F* **r. les oreilles à qn de qch,** to shove sth down s.o.'s throat.

rebattu [r(ə)baty] *adj* hackneyed, trite (*story*).

rebelle [rəbɛl] **1** *adj* rebellious (*person, spirit etc*); stubborn, obstinate (*fever*); intractable, unworkable (*material*); **pour les mèches rebelles,** for unruly *or* unmanageable hair; **r. à toute discipline,** unamenable to discipline. **2** *n* rebel.

rebeller (se) [sərəbele] *vpr* to rebel, to revolt (**contre,** against); (*protester*) to protest.

rébellion [rebeljɔ̃] *nf* rebellion, (up)rising, revolt; **en état de r.,** insurgent.

rebiffer (se) [sərəbife] *vpr F* to strike *or* hit back.

rebiquer [r(ə)bike] *vi F* to stick up; **le col de ta chemise rebique,** your shirt collar's sticking up.

reblochon [rəblɔʃɔ̃] *nm* reblochon (= type of cheese from Savoie).

reboire [rəbwar] *vt* (*conj like* **boire**) to drink again; **jamais je ne reboirai de ce vin,** I'll never drink *or* touch that wine again.

reboisement [rəbwazmɑ̃] *nm* (re)afforestation.

reboiser [rəbwaze] *vt* to (re)afforest.

rebond [rəbɔ̃] *nm* (*d'un ballon*) bounce; (*avec renvoi*) rebound.

rebondi [rəbɔ̃di] *adj* round, chubby (*cheeks*); plump, chubby (*person*); **ventre r.,** paunch.

rebondir [rəbɔ̃dir] *vi* **(a)** (*d'un ballon*) to bounce; (*avec renvoi*) to rebound; **(b)** *Fig* to start off *or* up again; **faire r. l'intrigue/la conversation,** to get the plot/conversation moving again; **le dollar a rebondi,** the (value of the) dollar has shot back up again; *Can* **son chèque a rebondi,** his cheque bounced.

rebondissement [rəbɔ̃dismɑ̃] *nm* **(a)** rebound(ing), bounce; **(b)** *Fig* new development (*in a case etc*).

rebord [rəbɔr] *nm* **(a)** edge, border, rim; hem (*of garment*); lip (*of cup*); **r. d'une fenêtre,** window sill *or* ledge; **(b)** (*surélevé*) raised edge, flange.

reborder [rəbɔrde] *vt* **(a)** to put a new edging *or* border *or* hem on *or* to (*garment*); **(b) r. qn dans son lit,** to tuck s.o. up (in bed) again.

reboucher [rəbuʃe] **1** *vt* **(a)** to stop *or* block (*sth*) up again; to recork (*bottle*); **(b)** to stop out (*woodwork*) (with putty). **2 se reboucher** *vpr* to become filled in again, to get blocked again; **l'évier s'est rebouché,** the sink's got blocked up again; **la bouteille se rebouche mal,** the bottle doesn't recork very well.

rebours [rəbur] *nm* wrong way (*of the grain, nap*); **à r.,** against the grain, the wrong way; **prendre qn à r.,** to rub s.o. up the wrong way; **compter à r.,** to count backwards; **compte à r.,** countdown; **le compte à r. a commencé,** the countdown has started; **compliment à r.,** backhanded compliment; **prendre à r. une rue à sens unique,** to go the wrong way along a one-way street; **prendre tout à r.,** to take everything the wrong way, to misconstrue everything; **elle fait tout à r.,** she does everything the wrong way round *or* back to front.

rebouter [rəbute] *vt F* to set (*broken limb*); to reduce (*dislocation*).

rebouteur, rebouteux, -euse [rəbutœr, rəbutø, -øz] *n F* bonesetter.

reboutonner [rəbutɔne] **1** *vt* to rebutton, to button up again. **2 se reboutonner** *vpr* to do oneself up again, to do up one's buttons again.

rebrousse-poil (à) [arəbruspwal] *adv* **brosser un chapeau à r.-p.,** to brush a hat against the nap *or* the wrong way; **caresser le chat à r.-p.,** to stroke the cat the wrong way *or* against the fur; *F* **prendre qn à r.-p.,** to rub s.o. up the wrong way.

rebrousser [rəbruse] *vt* **(a)** to turn up, to brush up (*hair, nap*); **(b) r. chemin,** to retrace one's steps, to turn back.

rebuffade [rəbyfad] *nf* rebuff, snub; **essuyer une r.,** to receive a snub, to suffer a rebuff, to be snubbed *or* rebuffed.

rébus [rebys] *nm* rebus; *Fig* enigma, puzzle.

rebut [rəby] *nm* **(article de) r.,** reject; **papier de r.,** waste paper; **habits de r.,** cast-off clothing, cast-offs; *Ind* **pièces de r.,** rejects, throw-outs; **marchandises de r.,** rubbishy goods, trash; **mettre au r.,** to throw (*sth*) away; to scrap (*a car*); **bureau des rebuts,** dead-letter office; *Fig* **le r. de la population/du genre humain,** the dregs of the population/ of the human race.

rebutant [rəbytɑ̃] *adj* **(a)** tiresome, irksome; disheartening (*work*); **(b)** disagreeable (*manner*); unprepossessing (*person*).

rebuter [rəbyte] **1** *vt* **(a)** to rebuff, to repulse (*s.o.*); **(b)** to reject, to discard (*sth*); **(c)** (*décourager*) to dishearten, to discourage; **(d)** (*choquer*) to shock, to disgust. **2 se rebuter** *vpr* to lose heart, to be put off.

recacheter [rəkaʃte] *vt* to reseal.

recalage [rəkalaʒ] *nm F* failure (*in an exam*).

recalcification [rəkalsifikasjɔ̃] *nf* recalcification, recalcifying.

recalcifier [rəkalsifje] *vt* to (re)calcify.

récalcitrance [rekalsitrɑ̃s] *nf* recalcitrance, refractoriness.

récalcitrant, -ante [rekalsitrɑ̃, -ɑ̃t] **1** *adj* recalcitrant, refractory, obstinate (*person, horse*). **2** *n* recalcitrant.

recalé, -ée [rəkale] *n F* failed candidate, failure.

recaler [rəkale] *vt F* to fail (*s.o. in exam*); **être recalé, se faire r. (au baccalauréat/en maths),** to fail, *F* to flunk (the baccalauréat/(in) maths).

récapitulatif, -ive [rekapitylatif, -iv] *adj* recapitulatory, recapitulative; *Ordinat* **carte récapitulative,** summary card.

récapitulation [rekapitylasjɔ̃] *nf* **(a)** recapitulation, summing up, *F* recap; **faire la r. des points importants,** to recapitulate *or* sum up the important points; **(b)** (*résumé*) summary, résumé, *F* recap.

récapituler [rekapityle] **1** *vt* to recapitulate, to sum up, *F* to recap (*proceedings*); *Scol* to revise. **2** *vi* **je récapitule,** to recapitulate, to sum up.

recaser [rəkaze] *F* **1** *vt* **(a)** (*dans une entreprise*) to find another job for (*s.o.*); **(b)** (*dans un logement*) to rehouse (*s.o.*). **2 se recaser** *vpr* to find a new job.

recel [rəsɛl] *nm Jur* receiving (and concealing) (*of stolen goods*); harbouring (*of criminal*).

receler [rəs(ə)le] *vt* (**je recèle, n. recelons; je recèlerai**) **(a)** *Jur* to receive (*stolen goods*); to harbour (*criminal*); to conceal (*child*); **(b) la terre recèle de grands trésors,** great treasures lie hidden in the earth; *Litt* **cette femme recèle un grand secret,** this woman is harbouring *or* concealing a deep secret.

recéler [rəsele] *vt* (**je recèle, n. recélons; je recélerai**) = **RECELER.**

receleur, -euse [rəs(ə)lœr, -øz] *n Jur* receiver (*of stolen goods*), *F* fence.

récemment [resamɑ̃] *adv* recently, lately, of late; **je le constatai encore r.,** I noticed it again recently.

recensement [rəsɑ̃smɑ̃] *nm* **(a)** census; return (*of population, horses, resources*); counting (*of votes*); *Mil* registration; **r. du contingent,** registration of those eligible for military service; **faire un r.,** to take a census; **agent chargé du r.,** recording official; **(b)** *Com* new inventory.

recenser [rəsɑ̃se] *vt* **(a)** to take the census of (*town etc*); to count (*votes*); *Mil* to register; **(b)** (*dans un magasin*) to check off (*goods*); to make an inventory (*of belongings*).

recenseur, -euse [rəsɑ̃sœr, -øz] *n* census taker; counter, teller (*of votes*).

récent [resɑ̃] *adj* recent.

recéper [rəsepe] *vt* (**je recèpe, n. recépons; je recéperai**) to cut back (*tree, vine stock*) to the stump.

récépissé [resepise] *nm* **(a)** (acknowledgement of) receipt; **r. d'entrepôt,** warehouse receipt; **(b)** acknowledgement (*of complaint etc*).

réceptacle [resɛptakl] *nm* **(a)** receptacle; **(b)** *Bot* receptacle.

récepteur, -trice [resɛptœr, -tris] **1** *adj* receiving (*apparatus, set*). **2** *nm* **(a)** *Physiol* receptor (*of stimulus*); **(b)** *MecE* driven part (*of machine*); **(c)** *Tél* receiver; (*radio, TV, radar*) receiver, set; *Tél* **décrocher le r.,** to lift the receiver; *Télécom* **r. Morse,** Morse receiver; *Ordinat* **r. de données,** data receiver.

réceptif, -ive [resɛptif, -iv] *adj* receptive (**à,** to).

réception [resɛpsjɔ̃] *nf* **(a)** receipt (*of letter, order, goods*); taking delivery (*of goods*); **accuser r. de qch,** to acknowledge receipt of sth; *Sp* **il s'est blessé à la r.,** (*d'un sauteur etc*) he hurt himself on landing; **la r. du ballon,** controlling the ball;

(b) admission (*to membership etc*);

(c) welcome; **faire une bonne r. à qn,** to welcome s.o. warmly, to give s.o. a good reception; **séance de r. de M. Yourcenar à l'Académie Française,** M. Yourcenar's induction *or* welcoming ceremony at the Académie Française;

(d) (*soirée*) (*official, court*) reception; **salle de r.,** reception room; **frais de r.,** entertainment expenses; **jour de r.,** at-home day;

(e) (hotel) reception (desk);

(f) *Tél Télécom Rad TV Electron* receiving, reception; **appareil** *ou* **poste de r.,** receiving set; **la r. est bonne/mauvaise ici,** the reception is good/bad here, you get good/bad reception here.

réceptionnaire [resɛpsjɔnɛr] *n* **(a)** *Com Ind* receiving agent *or* clerk; **(b)** receiver, consignee (*of goods*).

réceptionner [resɛpsjɔne] *vt* to check and sign for (*goods on delivery*).

réceptionniste [resɛpsjɔnist] *n* receptionist.

réceptivité [resɛptivite] *nf* receptivity; susceptibility (*to infection*).

récessif, -ive [resesif, -iv] *adj Biol* recessive.

récession [resesjɔ̃] *nf Econ* recession.

recette [rəsɛt] *nf* **(a)** *Fin* receipts, returns, takings; *Sp* gate money; **dépenses et recettes,** expenses and receipts, outgoings and incomings; *Th Cin* **faire r.,** to be a (box office) success; **(b)** collection (*of moneys due*); **garçon de r.,** bank messenger; **(c)** receiving; receipt (*of stores*); acceptance (*from contract*); **prendre qch en r.,** to accept *or* take delivery of sth; **(d)** *Admin* receivership, collectorship (*of rates and taxes etc*); (*bureau*) receiver's office, collector's office; **(e)** *Culin* recipe; *Pharm* formula; **livre de r.,** cookery book, recipe book; **recettes de métier,** tricks of the trade; **quelle est la r. du succès?,** what's the recipe for success *or* the secret of success?

recevable [rəsəvabl] *adj* admissible, acceptable (*excuse*); (*goods*) fit for acceptance; *Jur* admissible (*evidence*); *Fml* **être r. dans une demande,** to be entitled to proceed with a claim.

receveur, -euse [rəsəvœr, -øz] **1** *n* **(a)** receiver; recipient (*of letter, blood transfusion*); *Méd* **r. universel,** universal recipient; **(b)** collector (*of taxes, excise, customs*); **r./receveuse des Postes,** postmaster/postmistress; **r. buraliste,** tobacconist; **(c)** *Vieilli* (bus) conductor, *f* conductress. **2** *nm Can* **(a)** *Base-ball* receiver; **(b)** *Fb* (*éloigné*) wide receiver; (*rapproché*) tight end; (*inséré*) slotback.

recevoir [rəsəvwar] *v* (*prp* **recevant;** *pp* **reçu;** *pr ind* **je reçois, il reçoit, n. recevons, ils reçoivent;** *pr sub* **je reçoive, n. recevions;** *impf* **je recevais;** *p hist* **je reçus;** *fu* **je recevrai**) **1** *vt* **(a)** to receive, to get (*letter, present*); **r. qch de qn,** to receive *or* get sth from s.o.; **r. un conseil,** to receive *or* be given advice; **elle ne sait pas r. les compliments,** she doesn't know how to take *or* accept compliments; *Rel* **r. la communion/l'absolution,** to receive communion/absolution; **nous avons bien reçu votre lettre,** we are in receipt of your letter;

(b) to get, to receive (*punishment, wound*); to get, to incur (*blame*); **r. un coup de pieds aux fesses,** to receive *or* get a kick in *or* up the backside; *F* **arrête ou tu vas r. une gifle,** stop it *or* you'll get a slap;

(c) to receive, to welcome (*s.o.*); **être mal reçu,** to meet with a poor reception;

(d) to entertain (*friends*); to receive (*clients*); **r. des amis à dîner,** to have friends (round) to dinner; **ils reçoivent très peu,** they don't do much entertaining, they don't have friends round much *or* often; **elle reçoit des pensionnaires,** she takes (in) boarders *or* lodgers; **cet hôtel peut r. jusqu'à 200 clients,** this hotel can take *or* accommodate up to 200 guests; **le médecin reçoit à 6 heures,** the doctor is available for consultation at 6 o'clock, the doctor's surgery is at 6 o'clock;

(e) (*admettre*) to receive, to admit; **elle a été reçue à l'Académie française,** she was admitted to the Académie Française; *Scol* **élèves reçus en première,** pupils admitted *or* promoted to the top form; **être reçu à un examen,** to pass an exam(ination); **être reçu premier,** to be *or* come (out) first *or* top; **être reçu médecin,** to qualify as a doctor; *Nau* **être reçu capitaine,** to get one's captain's certificate;

(f) (*prendre*) to receive, to take; **r. de l'eau dans un vase,** to catch water in a vessel; **le Rhône reçoit l'Isère et la Sorgue,** the Isère and the Sorgue flow into the Rhône;

(g) *Rad* to receive (*transmission*);

(h) to accept, to admit (*opinion, excuse*).

2 se recevoir *vpr* **(a)** *Sp* to land (*after jump*);

(b) (*s'inviter*) to visit one another, to go to each other's houses.

3 *vi* **(a)** (*donner des réceptions*) to entertain;

(b) (*consulter*) to be available for consultation;

(c) *F* **tu vas r.!,** you're asking for it!, you're going to get it!

rechange [rəʃɑ̃ʒ] *nm* replacement; **linge de r.,** change of linen; **r. de vêtements,** change of clothes, spare set of clothes; **trousse de r.,** duplicate set (*of tools etc*); *Aut etc* **pièces de r./rechanges,** spare parts/spares; **pile de r.,** spare battery (*for torch*).

rechanger [rəʃɑ̃ʒe] *vt* (*conj like* **changer**) to change *or* exchange (*sth*) again.

rechanter [rəʃɑ̃te] *vt* to sing again.

rechapage [rəʃapaʒ] *nm* retreading, remoulding (*of tyre*).

rechaper [rəʃape] *vt* to retread, to remould (*tyre*); **pneu rechapé,** retread, remould.

réchappé, -ée [reʃape] *n Litt* survivor (*of disaster, wreck*); **r. de potence,** gallows bird.

réchapper [reʃape] *vi* (*aux* **avoir** *or* **être**) to escape (**de,** from); **il a réchappé du naufrage,** he survived the wreck; **il n'en réchappera pas,** it is all up with him; **r. à une crise,** to come through *or* survive a crisis.

recharge [rəʃarʒ] *nf* **(a)** refill (*for ball-point pen etc*); **(b)** recharging (*of battery*); **mettre l'accumulateur en r.,** to put the battery on charge.

rechargeable [rəʃarʒabl] *adj* (*briquet*) refillable; (*pile*) rechargeable; (*arme*) reloadable.

rechargement [rəʃarʒəmɑ̃] *nm* **(a)** recharging (*of accumulator*); reloading (*of vehicle, gun, ship*); **(b)** remetalling (*of road*); reballasting (*of railway track*).

recharger [rəʃarʒe] *vt* (*conj like* **charger**) **(a)** to recharge (*accumulator*); *Fig* **r. ses batteries,** to recharge one's batteries; **(b)** to reload (*lorry, gun, camera*); to refill (*pen, lighter*); to make up (*the fire*); **(c)** to remetal (*road*); to reballast (*railway track*).

rechasser [rəʃase] *vt* to chase (*s.o.*) out again; to drive back (*ball*).

réchaud [reʃo] *nm* **(a)** stove; **r. à gaz,** gas ring; **r. à alcool,** spirit lamp; **(b)** (*chauffe-plat*) hot plate, plate warmer.

réchauffage [reʃofaʒ] *nm* reheating, warming up (*of food*).

réchauffé [reʃofe] **1** *adj* **(a)** (*plat*) reheated, warmed-up; *Péj* rehashed; **(b)** *Fig F* (*plaisanterie*) stale, old. **2** *nm* **(a)** (*plat*) warmed-up *or* reheated *or Péj* rehashed food; **(b)** *Fig F* **c'est du r.,** (*plaisanterie*) that's an old *or* a stale joke; (*nouvelles*) that's stale news *or* old hat; (*politique*) it's the same old thing.

réchauffement [reʃofmɑ̃] *nm* warming (up); **r. de la planète** *ou* **de l'atmosphère,** global warming.

réchauffer [reʃofe] **1** *vt* to reheat (*sth*); to warm (*sth*) (up) again, to warm up (*s.o., food*); *Fig* **r. une vieille histoire,** to revive an old story; **r. le courage de qn,** to rekindle s.o.'s courage; **r. le cœur à qn,** to put new heart into s.o.; **cela me réchauffe le cœur,** it does my heart good, it's heart-warming; *Agr* **r. une couche,** to put fresh manure on a hot bed. **2 se réchauffer** *vpr* to get warm (again); **l'atmosphère se réchauffe,** the atmosphere is getting warmer *or* warming (up).

réchauffeur [reʃofœr] *nm* heater; **r. d'eau d'alimentation,** feed-water heater; **serpentin r.,** heating coil.

réchauffoir [reʃofwar] *nm* plate warmer (*in stove*).

rechausser [rəʃose] **1** *vt* **(a)** to put (*s.o.'s*) shoes *or* boots on again (for them); **(b) r. une voiture,** to fit a car with new tyres; **(c)** to underpin (*structure*); to bank up the foot of (*tree etc*). **2 se rechausser** *vpr* to put one's shoes on again; (*acheter de nouvelles chaussures*) to buy (oneself) new shoes.

rêche [rɛʃ] *adj* harsh, rough (*surface, wine*); prickly, cross-grained (*person*).

recherche [rəʃɛrʃ] *nf* **(a)** search, quest; **la r. de la vérité,** the search for *or* after (the) truth; **r. des plaisirs,** pleasure-seeking, the pursuit of pleasure; **la r. de la gloire,** the pursuit of glory, the quest for glory; **r. de débouchés,** market research, marketing; **r. de filons,** prospecting; **r. pétrolifère,** oil prospecting; *Él* **r. de dérangements,** locating of faults; **être à la r. de qn/qch,** to be looking for *or* in search of s.o./sth; **j'ai couru à la r. d'un médecin,** I ran for *or* to find a doctor;

(b) (*scientifique etc*) research; **faire de la r.,** to do research, to be engaged in research, to be a research worker; **r. développement,** research and development; **faire des recherches sur qch,** to do research on sth, to research sth;

(c) (*par la police*) searching; **droit de r.,** right of search (*at sea*);

(d) (*effort*) affectation, studied elegance, meticulous care; **style sans r.,** straightforward *or* unaffected style; **mettre de la r. dans la présentation d'un document,** to take (a lot of) trouble over the presentation of a document.

recherché [rəʃɛrʃe] *adj* **(a)** much sought-after, in (great) demand (*used after noun*); **(b)** choice, elaborate (*dress etc*); studied (*speech*); **d'un travail r.,** of exquisite workmanship; **(c)** *Péj* strained, affected (*style*); **(d)** (*criminel etc*) wanted.

rechercher [rəʃɛrʃe] *vt* **(a)** to search for, to seek (*s.o., sth*); to search *or* inquire into (*causes etc*); *Ordinat* **r. qch,** to search *or* do a search for sth; *Tél etc* **r. un dérangement,** to try to locate a fault; **homme recherché par la police/pour meurtre,** man wanted by the police/for murder; **r. un mot dans le dictionnaire,** to look up a word in the dictionary; **(b)** to seek (after), to try to obtain (*favours etc*); to court (*praise*).

rechigné [rəʃiɲe] *adj* sour-tempered, sullen.

rechigner [rəʃiɲe] *vi F* to grimace, to look sour; **faire qch en rechignant,** to do sth with bad grace; **faire qch sans r.,** to do sth willingly *or* gladly; **r. à la besogne,** to jib *or* ba(u)lk at work; **r. à faire qch,** to ba(u)lk *or* jib at doing sth.

rechute [rəʃyt] *nf Méd* relapse; *Fig* **r. dans le vice,** relapse into vice.

rechuter [rəʃyte] *vi Méd* to (have a) relapse.

récidivant [residivɑ̃] *adj Méd* recurring, recurrent (*disease*).

récidive [residiv] *nf* **(a)** repetition of an offence, relapse (*into crime*); **(b)** *Méd* recurrence (*of a disease*).

récidiver [residive] *vi* **(a)** to repeat an offence; **il a récidivé,** he has relapsed into crime; **(b)** (*d'une maladie*) to recur.

récidiviste [residivist] *n* habitual criminal, repeat offender, *Fml* recidivist.

récidivité [residivite] *nf Méd* recurrent nature (*of disease*).

récif [resif] *nm* reef; **r. (en) barrière,** barrier reef; **r. de corail** *ou* **corallien,** coral reef.

récipient [resipjɑ̃] *nm* container, receptacle; receiver (*of air pump, retort etc*); **r. cylindrique,** drum.

réciprocité [resiprɔsite] *nf* reciprocity.

réciproque [resiprɔk] **1** *adj* **(a)** reciprocal, mutual (*benefits, love etc*); **(b)** (*logique*) *& Gram Math* reciprocal, inverse (*ratio*); reversible (*motion*); *Math* converse (*propositions*). **2** *nf* **(a) rendre la r. à qn,** to pay *or* get s.o. back, to get *or* be even with s.o.; **et la r. est vraie,** and the reverse is true; **(b)** (*logique*) *& Math* converse; *Math* reciprocal.

réciproquement [resiprɔkmɑ̃] *adv* reciprocally; (*mutuellement*) mutually; **ils s'aident r.,** they help one another; **et r.,** and vice versa, conversely.

récit [resi] *nm* **(a)** narration, narrative; relation (*of events*); **il nous fit le r. de ses aventures,** he gave us an account of his adventures; **(b)** *Mus* solo; **jeux de r.,** solo organ; **clavier de r.,** swell organ.

récital, -als [resital] *nm* (poetry) recital.

récitant, -ante [resitɑ̃, -ɑ̃t] *n* **(a)** *Mus* (*voice, instrument*) solo; **(b)** (*lecteur*) narrator.

récitatif [resitatif] *nm Mus* recitative.

récitation [resitasjɔ̃] *nf* (*action*) recitation, reciting; *Scol* **apprendre une r.,** to learn a text by heart.

réciter [resite] *vt* to recite (*poem etc*); *F* **r. la même leçon,** to tell the same story.

réclamant, -ante [reklamɑ̃, -ɑ̃t] *n* claimant.

réclamation [reklamasjɔ̃] *nf* **(a)** (*orale*) complaint, objection, protest; **(b)** (*écrite*) claim; **faire** *ou* **déposer une r.,** to make *or* put forward a claim; **prouver le bien-fondé d'une r.,** to substantiate a claim; **r. d'indemnité,** claim for compensation; *Sp* **r. contre un joueur,** complaint about a player.

réclame [reklam] *nf* **(a)** (*publicité*) advertising; **faire de la r.,** to advertise; *Fig* **faire de la r. pour qn,** to push s.o.; **article (en) r.,** special offer; **vente r.,** sale; **cela ne lui fera pas de r.,** that won't be a very good advert(isement) for him; **(b)** (*panneau etc*) advertisement; **r. lumineuse,** illuminated sign.

réclamer [reklame] **1** *vi* to complain; **r. contre qch,** to protest against sth, to object to sth; to appeal against (*decision*); *F* **cet enfant ne cesse de r.,** that child's never satisfied. **2** *vt* **(a)** to lay claim to (*sth*); to claim (*a right*); to (re)claim (*lost property*); **r. son argent,** to ask for one's money back; **r. de l'argent à qn,** to dun s.o.; **(b)** (*exiger*) to call for (*s.o., sth*); **r. qch/qn à grands cris,** to clamour for sth/s.o.; **(c) plante qui réclame des soins continuels,** plant that requires continual care. **3 se réclamer** *vpr* **il se réclame de droite/de Londres,** he says he is right-wing/he says he comes *or* is from London, he says he's a Londoner.

reclassement [rəklasmɑ̃] *nm* reclassifying, reclassification; regrading (*of staff*).

reclasser [rəklase] *vt* to reclassify, to regroup, to rearrange; to regrade (*staff*).

reclouer [rəklue] *vt* to nail (*sth*) (up) again.

reclus, -use [rəkly, -yz] **1** *adj* secluded, cloistered. **2** *n* **(a)** (*ermite*) hermit, recluse; *Rel* cloistered monk *or f* nun; **(b)** *Fig* recluse; **vivre en r.,** to live like a hermit, to live the life of a recluse, to be a recluse.

réclusion [reklyzjɔ̃] *nf* **(a)** reclusion, seclusion; **(b)** *Jur* imprisonment; **r. à perpétuité,** life sentence.

réclusionnaire [reklyzjɔnɛr] *n Jur* prisoner, convict (*serving long term*).

récognition [rekɔgnisjɔ̃] *nf Phil* recognition, identification.

recoiffer [rəkwafe] **1** *vt* **r. qn,** to do s.o.'s hair again. **2 se recoiffer** *vpr* **(a)** to do one's hair again; **se r. avant de sortir,** to do *or* comb one's hair before going out; **(b)** (*remettre son chapeau etc*) to put on one's hat again.

recoin [rəkwɛ̃] *nm* nook, recess; **coins et recoins,** nooks and crannies.

recollage [rəkɔlaʒ] *nm* gluing (again), sticking together (again).

récollection [rekɔlɛksjɔ̃] *nf Rel* recollection, meditation.

recoller [rəkɔle] **1** *vt* to paste *or* glue (*sth*) together again, to repaste, to restick. **2** *vi Sp* to catch up. **3 se recoller** *vpr* **(a)** (*d'un os cassé*) to knit; **(b)** *Arg* **ils se sont recollés,** they are back together again *or* living together again.

récoltable [rekɔltabl] *adj* ready for harvesting *or* picking.

récolte [rekɔlt] *nf* **(a)** harvesting, gathering (*of crops*); vintaging (*of grapes*); **faire une r.,** to produce a crop; **faire la r. du blé,** to harvest the wheat; **(b)** collecting, gathering (*of specimens etc*); **(c)** (*produits*) harvest, crop(s); vintage (*of grapes*); **une belle r.,** a good harvest *or* crop; **rentrer la r.,** to get in *or* bring in *or* gather in the harvest *or* the crops;

(d) collection (*of objects*).

récolter [rekɔlte] **1** *vt* to harvest, to gather in, to get in (*crop*); *Prov* **qui sème le vent récolte la tempête,** he who sows the wind shall reap the whirlwind; *F* **je n'en ai récolté que des injures,** all I got out of it was insults. **2 se récolter** *vpr Agr* **ces fraises se récoltent en juin,** these strawberries are ready for picking in June.

recommandable [rəkɔmɑ̃dabl] *adj* **(a)** commendable; **peu r.,** undesirable; **hôtel peu r.,** poor *or* shabby hotel; **(b)** (*que l'on conseille*) advisable; **vu votre santé, ce n'est pas r.,** given your state of health, it's not advisable.

recommandation [rəkɔmɑ̃dɑsjɔ̃] *nf* **(a)** recommendation, recommending; **(lettre de) r.,** letter of recommendation *or* of introduction; **(b)** (*conseil*) recommendation, advice; **suivre les recommandations de qn,** to follow s.o.'s advice; **(c)** registration (*of letter*).

recommandé [rəkɔmɑ̃de] **1** *adj* registered. **2** *nm* **envoi en r.,** *F* **un r.,** registered letter *or* parcel.

recommander [rəkɔmɑ̃de] **1** *vt* **(a)** to recommend (*hotel, product*); **r. qn à un employeur,** to recommend s.o. to an employer; **r. son âme à Dieu,** to commend one's soul to God; **(b)** (*conseiller*) to advise; **r. la prudence à qn,** to advise s.o. to be prudent; **je vous recommende de rester,** I advise you to stay; **je te le recommande fortement,** I highly *or* strongly recommend it to you; **(c)** to register (*letter, parcel*). **2 se recommander** *vpr* **(a) se r. à Dieu,** to commend oneself to God; **(b) se r. de qn,** to give s.o. as a reference; **(c) se r. par qch,** to have sth in one's favour; **elle se recommande par son efficacité,** her efficiency is a strong point in her favour.

recommencement [rəkɔmɑ̃smɑ̃] *nm* beginning *or* starting again.

recommencer [rəkɔmɑ̃se] *v* **(je recommençai(s); n. recommençons) 1** *vt* to begin *or* start (*sth*) (over) again, *Fml* to recommence; **r. sa vie,** to make a new *or* fresh start in life, to start life afresh; **r. à faire qch,** to begin *or* start to do *or* doing sth again; **tout est à r.,** we shall have to begin *or* start all over again, *F* we'll have to go back to square one. **2** *vi* to do it again, to begin again, to start afresh; **ne recommencez pas!,** don't (you) do it again!; **le voilà qui recommence!,** he's at it again!; **qui parle?, ça recommence?,** who's talking?, that chatter's not going to start again, is it?

récompense [rekɔ̃pɑ̃s] *nf* reward, recompense; **mille francs de r.,** a thousand francs reward; **en r. de vos services,** as a reward for your services, in return for your services; **la juste r. de ses crimes,** just retribution for his crimes; **distribution des récompenses,** giving out of the awards *or* prizes.

récompenser [rekɔ̃pɑ̃se] *vt* to reward, to recompense; **r. qn de qch,** to reward s.o. for sth; **son travail a été bien récompensé,** his work was well *or* amply rewarded.

recomposer [rəkɔ̃poze] *vt* **(a)** *Ch* to recompose, to recombine (*elements*); **(b)** *Typ* to reset (*matter*).

recomposition [rəkɔ̃pozisjɔ̃] *nf* **(a)** *Ch* recombining; **(b)** *Typ* resetting.

recompter [rəkɔ̃te] *vt* to recount, to count again.

réconciliateur, -trice [rekɔ̃siljatœr, -tris] *n* reconciler.

réconciliation [rekɔ̃siljɑsjɔ̃] *nf* reconciliation; **amener une r. entre deux personnes,** to bring about a reconciliation *or* to heal the breach between two people.

réconcilier [rekɔ̃silje] **1** *vt* to reconcile (*persons, inconsistencies*); **ce voyage m'a réconcilié avec la marche,** the trip renewed my appetite for walking. **2 se réconcilier** *vpr* to be *or* become reconciled; **se r. avec qn,** to make it up *or* be friends again with s.o., to patch things up with s.o.; **se r. avec Dieu,** to make one's peace with God; **se r. avec soi-même,** to be *or* feel a peace with oneself.

reconductible [rəkɔ̃dyktibl] *adj* renewable; **bail r.,** renewable lease.

reconduction [rəkɔ̃dyksjɔ̃] *nf* **(a)** *Jur* renewal (*of lease*); **tacite r.,** renewal by tacit agreement; **(b)** continuation (*of budget, measures*); **voter la r. de la grève,** to vote for the continuation of the strike *or* for continued strike action.

reconduire [rəkɔ̃dɥir] *vt* (*conj like* **conduire**) **(a)** to see *or* escort *or* take (*s.o.*) home; to accompany *or* take *or* bring (*s.o.*) back; **(b)** (*jusqu'à la porte*) to see *or* show (*s.o.*) out *or* to the door; **(c)** to renew (*lease etc*); *Admin* to continue (*temporary measure*); **r. une grève,** to continue a strike.

réconfort [rekɔ̃fɔr] *nm* comfort, consolation; **paroles de r.,** comforting words; *F* **une petite goutte de r.,** a little drop of comfort.

réconfortant [rekɔ̃fɔrtɑ̃] **1** *adj* **(a)** strengthening, stimulating; tonic (*medicine*); **(b)** comforting, cheering (*words*). **2** *nm* tonic, stimulant.

réconforter [rekɔ̃fɔrte] *vt* **(a)** to strengthen, to fortify, to refresh (*s.o.*); **(b)** (*moralement*) to comfort (*s.o.*), to cheer (*s.o.*) up; **ça me réconforte de voir que je ne suis pas la seule,** it cheers me up *or* I'm glad to see I'm not the only one. **2 se réconforter** *vpr* to cheer oneself up.

reconnaissable [rəkɔnɛsabl] *adj* recognizable (**à,** by, from, through); **style r. entre tous,** unmistakeable style; **c'est difficilement r.,** it's hardly *or* scarcely recognizable; **il n'est plus r.,** he's unrecognizable, you wouldn't recognize him any more.

reconnaissance [rəkɔnɛsɑ̃s] *nf* **(a)** recognition (*of s.o., sth*); *Ordinat* **r. optique des caractères,** optical character recognition; *Mil* **signal de r.,** recognition signal;

(b) acknowledgement (*of promise, debt*); recognition, acknowledgement (*of government*); **r. d'un enfant né hors mariage,** acknowledgement of a child born out of wedlock;

(c) (*gratitude*) gratitude; **témoigner de la r. à qn,** to show gratitude to s.o.; **avec r.,** gratefully; **r. de** *ou* **pour qch,** gratitude *or* thankfulness for sth; *F* **c'est la r. du ventre,** that's cupboard love; **en r. à votre invitation,** in gratitude for your invitation;

(d) *Com* note of hand, promissory note; **donner une r. à qn,** to give s.o. an I.O.U.; **r. (de dépôt de gage),** pawn ticket;

(e) *Mil* reconnaissance, reconnoitring, *F* recce; **détachement/avion de r.,** reconnaissance party/aircraft; **être en r.,** to be reconnoitring *or* on (a) reconnaissance;

(f) inspection, exploration, examination (*of ground, site*); *Min* prospecting; (*topographie*) surveying, charting; **levé de r.,** exploratory survey.

reconnaissant [rəkɔnɛsɑ̃] *adj* **(a)** grateful; **être r. à qn de qch,** to be grateful to s.o. for sth; **votre fils r.,** (*dans une lettre*) your grateful *or* loving *or* devoted son; **(b)** (*pour remercier*) grateful, thankful (**de,** for); **je vous serai r. de ne plus en parler,** I'd thank you not to mention it again, I'd be grateful if you didn't mention it again.

reconnaître [rəkɔnɛtr] *v* (*conj like* **connaître**) **1** *vt* **(a)** to recognize; to identify (*s.o., aircraft, body*); **r. qn à sa démarche,** to recognize *or* know *or* tell s.o. by his walk; **ils se ressemblent tant qu'on ne peut les r.,** they are so alike that you can't tell them apart; **je vous reconnais bien là!,** that's just like you!, that's you all over!;

(b) *Nau* **r. la terre,** to sight land;

(c) to recognize, to acknowledge (*truth, right, government*); to acknowledge, to admit (*mistake*); **r. qn pour chef,** to acknowledge s.o. as leader; **r. qch comme vrai,** to acknowledge sth to be true, to admit the truth of sth; **reconnu pour** *ou* **comme incorrect,** admittedly incorrect; **r. qu'on s'est trompé, r. s'être trompé,** to admit *or* own that one was mistaken; **je reconnais mon erreur,** I admit *or* acknowledge my mistake;

(d) *Jur* **r. un enfant,** to acknowledge *or* own a child;

(e) *Mil etc* to reconnoitre, to make a reconnaissance of (*a position etc*); to explore (*the ground*);

(f) *Min* to prospect.

2 se reconnaître *vpr* **(a)** (*soi-même*) to recognise oneself; **le bébé ne se reconnait pas encore,** the baby doesn't *or* can't recognise itself yet; **je ne me reconnais pas sur cette photo,** I don't recognise myself in that photo;

(b) (*se retrouver*) to find one's way about *or* around; **ce n'est pas facile de se r. dans Tokyo,** it's not easy to find your way about *or* to find your bearings in Tokyo; **c'est à ne pas s'y r.,** it's all very confusing;

(c) gaz qui se reconnaît à son odeur, gas recognizable by its smell.

reconquérir [rəkɔ̃kerir] *vt* (*conj like* **conquérir**) to regain, to recover, to reconquer (*province*); to regain (*esteem*).

reconquête [rəkɔ̃kɛt] *nf* reconquest.

reconsidérer [rəkɔ̃sidere] *vt* (*conj like* **considérer**) to reconsider.

reconsolider [rəkɔ̃solide] *vt* to reconsolidate.

reconstituant [rəkɔ̃stitɥɑ̃] *adj & nm Méd* tonic.

reconstituer [rəkɔ̃stitɥe] *vt* to reconstitute (*army, government*); to reconstruct (*a crime, a system*); to restore (*health, damaged building*).

reconstitution [rəkɔ̃stitysjɔ̃] *nf* reconstitution, reconstruction (*of government, company*); restoration (*of building etc*); **r. d'un crime,** reconstruction of a crime.

reconstruction [rəkɔ̃stryksjɔ̃] *nf* reconstruction, rebuilding.

reconstruire [rəkɔ̃strɥir] *vt* (*conj like* **construire**) to reconstruct, to rebuild.

reconventionnel, -elle [rəkɔ̃vɑ̃sjɔnɛl] *adj Jur*

demande reconventionnelle, counterclaim.
reconversion [rəkɔ̃vɛrsjɔ̃] *nf* **(a)** reconversion (*of factory etc*); *Fig* **r. culturelle/politique,** cultural/political conversion; **(b)** redeployment (*of workers*); **stage de r.,** re-training course.
reconvertir [rəkɔ̃vɛrtir] **1** *vt* **(a)** to reconvert (*factory etc*); **(b)** to redeploy (*staff*). **2 se reconvertir** *vpr* to change one's occupation; **se r. dans la publicité,** to start a new career in advertising.
recopier [rəkɔpje] *vt* (*conj like* **copier**) **(a)** (*en double*) to recopy, to take another copy of (*sth*); **(b)** (*au propre*) to make a fair copy of (*draft*).
recoquillé [rəkɔkije] *adj* wrinkled, cockled (*paper, cloth*); dog-eared (*page*).
record [rəkɔr] **1** *nm Sp etc* record; **battre le r.,** to break *or* beat the record; **détenir le r.,** to hold the record; *Fig* **il bat tous les records d'impolitesse,** he takes some beating for rudeness. **2** *adj* **vitesse r.,** record speed; **dans** *ou* **en un temps r.,** in record time; **attirer une affluence r.,** to draw record crowds; **chiffre r. d'accidents,** record accident figure; **atteindre le chiffre r. de 5 000,** to reach the record figure of 5,000.
recorder [rəkɔrde] *vt* to rope up (*bale*) again; to retie (*packet*); to restring (*racket*).
recordman [rəkɔr(d)man] *nm* (men's) record holder; (*pl recordmen*).
recordwoman [rəkɔr(d)woman] *nf* (women's) record holder; (*pl recordwomen*).
recorriger [rəkɔriʒe] *vt* to recorrect, to correct again (*proofs, homework etc*); (*d'un professeur*) to mark (*homework*) again.
recors [rəkɔr] *nm Jur Arch F* bailiff's man; **les r. de la justice,** the minions of the law.
recoucher [rəkuʃe] **1** *vt* **(a)** to put (*s.o.*) to bed again; **(b)** to lay (*person, object*) down again. **2 se recoucher** *vpr* to go to bed again, to go back to bed. **3** *vi F* **r. avec qn,** to sleep *or* have sex with s.o. again.
recoudre [rəkudr] *vt* (*conj like* **coudre**) to sew up (*tear, wound*); to sew (*button*) on again; *F* **il a fallu me r.,** they had to stitch me up again.
recoupement [rəkupmɑ̃] *nm* **(a)** *Constr* batter (*of wall*); **(b)** crosschecking (*of information*); **je l'ai compris par r.,** I found out by crosschecking.
recouper [rəkupe] **1** *vt* **(a)** (*à nouveau*) to cut again; **je vous recoupe une tranche de gâteau?,** will I cut you another slice *or* piece of cake?; **(b)** *Constr* to step (*wall*); **(c)** to (re)blend (*wines etc*); **(d)** (*coïncider*) to confirm, to support. **2 se recouper** *vpr* to agree, to tally; **les deux témoignages se recoupent,** the two statements tally.
recourbé [rəkurbe] *adj* bent, curved; (*bec*) curved, hooked; **nez r.,** hook nose.
recourber [rəkurbe] *vt* to bend down *or* back *or* round.
recourir [rəkurir] *v* (*conj like* **courir**) **1** *vi* **(a)** to run again; **r. jusque chez soi,** to run back home (*for sth*); *Sp* **elle n'a pas recouru depuis les Jeux Olympiques,** she hasn't run since the Olympic Games; **(b) r. à (l'aide de) qn,** to appeal to s.o. for help, to turn to s.o.; **r. à qch,** to have recourse to sth; **r. à la violence,** to resort to violence; **r. à la justice,** to take legal proceedings; **(c)** *Jur* **r. en cassation,** to appeal. **2** *vt Sp* to rerun, to run again.
recours [rəkur] *nm* **(a)** recourse, resort; **en dernier r.,** as a last resort; **c'est sans r.,** there's nothing else for it, there's no other option; **avoir r. à qn,** to have recourse to s.o.; **avoir r. à qch,** to have recourse to sth, to resort to sth; **(b)** *Jur* **r. en cassation,** appeal; **r. en grâce,** petition for reprieve; **s'assurer contre le r. des tiers,** to insure against a third party claim; *Can* **r. collectif,** class action.
recouvrable [rəkuvrabl] *adj* recoverable, retrievable (*debt etc*).
recouvrement[1] [rəkuvrəmɑ̃] *nm* **(a)** recovery (*of health etc*); **(b)** recovery, collection (*of debts, bill*); collection (*of tax*); **r. par la poste,** payment by cash on delivery.
recouvrement[2] *nm* **(a)** re-covering; (*pour la première fois*) covering; **tôle de r.,** covering plate; **(b)** (over)lapping; lap (*of slates*); overlap (*of map sheets, strata*); **à r.,** lapped, lap-jointed; **en r.,** overlapping; **planches à r.,** weatherboarding; *Géol* **lambeau de r.,** outlier; **(c)** *Tech* cover; lap, cover (*of slide valve*).
recouvrer [rəkuvre] *vt* **(a)** to recover, to retrieve, to get back (*one's property*); to regain, to get back (*strength, freedom*); **(b)** (*percevoir*) to recover, to collect (*debts, taxes*); **créances à r.,** outstanding debts.
recouvrir [rəkuvrir] *v* (*conj like* **couvrir**) **1** *vt* **(a)** to re-cover (*umbrella, roof*); **(b)** (*tapisser*) to cover (over) (**de,** with); **fauteuil recouvert de velours,** armchair covered in velvet; **(c)** (*masquer*) to cover up, to hide (*faults*); **(d)** to (over)lap (*slates etc*); *Fig* **cette étude recouvre les thèmes abordés en cours d'année,** this study goes over *or* covers the subjects dealt with in the course of the year. **2 se recouvrir** *vpr* (*of sky*) to cloud over (again).
recracher [rəkraʃe] **1** *vt* to spit (*sth*) out (*again*). **2** *vi* to spit again.
récré [rekre] *nf Scol F* break; (*pour les plus jeunes*) playtime.
récréatif, -ive [rekreatif, -iv] *adj* entertaining, amusing (*occupation*); **lecture récréative,** light reading; **séance récréative,** entertainment.
récréation [rekreasjɔ̃] *nf* **(a)** (*détente*) recreation, amusement, relaxation; **(b)** *Scol* recreation, break, *Am* recess; (*pour les plus jeunes*) playtime; **cour de r.,** playground; **pendant la r.,** during *or* at playtime *or* break.
recréer [rəkree] *vt* to re-create (*sth*); **ce film recrée le climat de l'époque,** this film re-creates the atmosphere of the period.
recrépir [rəkrepir] *vt* to roughcast again, to renew the roughcast of, to replaster, to repoint (*wall*).
recrépissage [rəkrepisaʒ] *nm* replastering.
recreuser [rəkrøze] *vt* to hollow (*sth*) out again; *Fig* to dig *or* go deeper into (*question etc*).
récrier (se) [sərekrije] *vpr* (*conj like* **crier**) **(a) se r. contre** *ou* **sur qch,** to cry out *or* expostulate *or* protest against sth; **ils n'ont pas manqué de se r.,** they didn't fail to protest *or* complain; **(b)** (*of hounds*) to be in full cry.
récriminateur, -trice [rekriminatœr, -tris] *adj* recriminatory, recriminative.
récrimination [rekriminasjɔ̃] *nf* recrimination.
récriminer [rekrimine] *vi* to reproach (**contre qn,** s.o.).
récrire [rekrir] *v* (*conj like* **écrire**) **1** *vt* to rewrite (*sth*), to write (*sth*) (over) again. **2** *vi* to write (*to s.o.*) again.
recroquevillé [rəkrɔkvije] *adj* **(a) r. dans un fauteuil,** curled up *or* huddled (up) in an armchair; **(b)** knotted (*fingers*); **(c)** shrivelled, curled up (*leaf etc*).
recroqueviller (se) [sərəkrɔkvije] *vpr* **(a)** (*of person, animal*) to curl up, to huddle (up); **(b)** (*of leaf*) to shrivel (up), to curl up; (*of flower*) to wilt.
recru [rəkry] *adj* **r. (de fatigue),** tired out, worn out.
recrudescence [rəkrydesɑ̃s] *nf* renewed *or* fresh outbreak, *Fml* recrudescence (*of fire, disease*).
recrudescent [rəkrydesɑ̃] *adj* recrudescent.
recrue [rəkry] *nf* recruit, new member (*of party, team*); *Mil* recruit; *Can Sp* rookie; **jeune r.,** raw recruit.
recrutement [rəkrytmɑ̃] *nm* recruiting, recruitment (*of soldiers, staff etc*); *Pol* **campagne de r.,** recruitment *or* membership drive; **agence de r.,** recruiting *or* recruitment agency.
recruter [rəkryte] **1** *vt* to recruit (*regiment, men, supporters*); **notre directeur a été recruté par un chasseur de têtes,** our director was headhunted. **2 se recruter** *vpr* to be recruited. **3** *vi* to recruit; **r. par voie de concours,** to recruit by means of a competitive entry examination.
recruteur [rəkrytœr] *adj* recruiting (*officer*).
recta [rɛkta] *adv* punctually; **payer r.,** to pay on the nail; **arriver r.,** to arrive punctually *or* on the dot.
rectal, -aux [rɛktal, -o] *adj Anat* rectal.
rectangle [rɛktɑ̃gl] **1** *adj* right-angled. **2** *nm* rectangle; *TV* **r. blanc,** 'for adults only' sign.
rectangulaire [rɛktɑ̃gylɛr] *adj* rectangular; *Math* right-angled (*co-ordinates*).
recteur, -trice [rɛktœr, -tris] **1** *nm* **(a)** *Scol* (*in France*) rector (*of educational district*); **(b)** *Rel Arch* rector (*of Jesuit college*). **2** *adj Orn* **penne rectrice,** tail feather. **3** *nf Orn* **rectrice,** tail feather.
rectificateur [rɛktifikatœr] *nm Ch* rectifier; *Él* (current) rectifier.
rectificatif, -ive [rɛktifikatif, -iv] **1** *adj* rectifying, correcting; **facture rectificative,** amended invoice. **2** *nm* correction, *Fml* corrigendum.
rectification [rɛktifikasjɔ̃] *nf* **(a)** amendment, correction (*of document, text*); rectification, correction (*of calculation, mistake*); adjustment (*of account, instrument*); rectification (*of curve, boundary*); straightening (*of alignment*); **je voudrais faire une r.,** I'd like to make a correction; **(b)** tru(e)ing (*of work on lathe*); **(c)** rectifying, redistilling (*of alcohol, petroleum*); **(d)** *Él* rectification (*of current*).
rectifier [rɛktifje] *vt* **(a)** to amend, to correct (*document, text*); to rectify, to correct (*calculation, mistake*); to put (*mistake*) right; to adjust (*account, prices, instrument*); to amend (*account*); to rectify (*boundary, curve*); to straighten (*alignment*); *Mil* **r. l'alignement,** to dress the

ranks; **(b)** *MecE* to true, to grind (true); **(c)** *Ch* to rectify, to re-distil (*alcohol, petroleum*); **(d)** *El* to rectify (*current*); **(e)** *Arg* (*tuer*) to bump (*s.o.*) off.

rectiligne [rɛktiliɲ] *adj* rectilinear, in a straight line.

rectilinéaire [rɛktilineɛr] *adj Phot* rectilinear (*lens*).

rectitude [rɛktityd] *nf* **(a)** straightness (*of line*); **(b)** *Fig* (*honnêteté*) rectitude, uprightness, integrity; correctness, soundness (*of judgment*).

recto [rɛkto] *nm* recto, right-hand side (*of page*); view side, front (*of picture postcard*).

rectorat [rɛktɔra] *nm Admin* rectorship, rectorate.

rectum [rɛktɔm] *nm Anat* rectum; **cancer du r.,** rectal cancer, cancer of the rectum.

reçu [rəsy] **1** *adj* received, accepted, recognised (*opinion, custom*); **idées reçues,** preconceived ideas. **2** *nm* receipt, voucher (*for goods, money*); **je vous fais un r.?,** would you like a receipt?; **r. pour solde de tout compte,** receipt in full settlement, 'paid in full'.

recueil [rəkœj] *nm* collection, compilation (*of poems etc*); compendium (*of laws*); **r. de morceaux choisis,** selection, anthology.

recueillement [rəkœjmɑ̃] *nm* meditation, contemplation; **r. d'esprit,** composure; **écouter de la musique avec r.,** to listen contemplatively to music.

recueilli [rəkœji] *adj* meditative, contemplative, rapt.

recueillir [rəkœjir] *v* (*conj like* **cueillir**) **1** *vt* **(a)** to collect, to gather (*anecdotes, curios*); to collect, to make a collection of (*author's works*); **r. l'eau de pluie,** to collect *or* catch (the) rainwater; **r. des renseignements,** to collect *or* gather information; **r. ses forces,** to collect *or* gather all one's strength; **r. ses idées,** to collect one's thoughts; **(b)** to get in, to gather (*crops*); to recover (*by-products*); to win (*votes, praise*); **r. le fruit de ses travaux,** to reap the fruit of one's labours; **r. un héritage,** to inherit; **(c)** to take (*s.o.*) in, to shelter (*s.o.*), to give (*s.o.*) a home. **2 se recueillir** *vpr* to meditate; **se r. sur la tombe d'un ami,** to meditate beside a friend's grave.

recuire [rəkɥir] *vt* (*conj like* **cuire**) **(a)** *Culin* to cook *or* bake (*sth*) again; *Cér* to rekiln; **(b)** to anneal, to temper (*steel*); to anneal (*glass*).

recuisson [rəkɥisɔ̃] *nf* **(a)** *Culin* recooking, rebaking; **(b)** tempering (*of steel*); annealing (*of glass*).

recuit [rəkɥi] *nm* reheating; tempering (*of steel*); annealing (*of steel, glass*); **r. blanc,** bright annealing.

recul [rəkyl] *nm* **(a)** retreat (*of glacier, army*); backing (*of horse*); backward movement, return (*of control lever*); **le r. de la mortalité,** the downturn *or* decline in the death-rate; **il eut un brusque mouvement de r.,** he recoiled, he started back; *Aut* **phare de r.,** reversing light; **(b)** recoil (*of cannon*); recoil, kick (*of rifle*); *Nau* slip (*of propeller*); **(c)** (*distance*) room to move back; **manquer de r.,** to be too close for a proper view; **je manque de r. pour juger,** I'm too closely involved to be able to judge; **considérer la situation avec r.,** to consider the situation with detachment; **tu devrais prendre du r.,** you should try to look at it (more) objectively.

reculade [rəkylad] *nf* retreat, backward movement; *Fig Péj* climb(ing) down.

reculé [rəkyle] *adj* distant, remote (*time, place*); early (*times*).

reculement [rəkylmɑ̃] *nm* **(a)** backing (*of carriage etc*); **(b)** (*de harnais*) breech band.

reculer [rəkyle] **1** *vi* to move back, to step back, to draw back, to recede; *Mil* to fall back, to retreat; (*d'une épidémie etc*) to lose ground; (*d'un cheval, une voiture*) to back; (*d'un fusil, un canon*) to recoil; **r. contre qch,** to back into sth; **faire r. un cheval,** to back a horse; *Fig* **faire r. la maladie,** to get the disease under control; **faire r. la pauvreté,** to reduce (the level of) poverty; **ses affaires ont reculé,** his business has fallen off; **r. devant qch,** to draw back *or* shrink from sth; **r. devant des menaces,** to give way in the face of threats; **r. devant une obligation,** to shirk an obligation; **il ne recule devant rien,** nothing daunts him; **il est trop tard pour r.,** it's too late to draw back *or* pull out; **cela en a fait r. plus d'un,** that's put off *or* daunted more than one person; *F* **r. pour mieux sauter,** to put off the evil day.

2 *vt* **(a)** to move back (*chair*); to back (*horse*); *Fig* **r. les frontières de la science,** to push forward *or* roll back *or* extend the frontiers of science;

(b) (*remettre*) to postpone, to defer, to put off (*payment, decision*); **r. le moment de décider,** to put off (making) a decision.

3 se reculer *vpr* to draw *or* stand *or* step *or* move back.

reculons (à) [ar(ə)kylɔ̃] *adv* **marcher à r.,** to walk backwards; (*régresser*) to move *or* go backwards; **sortir à r.,** to back out.

récupérable [rekyperabl] *adj* recoverable; **ferraille r.,** scrap metal.

récupérateur [rekyperatœr] *nm Ind* regenerator, recuperator; *Mil* recuperator; **r. d'huile,** oil extractor.

récupération [rekyperasjɔ̃] *nf* **(a)** recovery (*of debt, book, spacecraft etc*); **(b)** *Ind* recovery, salvage (*of waste products*); **four à r.,** regenerative furnace; *Fig* **la r. d'une manifestation par un parti politique,** the exploitation *or* harnessing of a demonstration by a political party, the exploitation *or* takeover of a demonstration for political ends; **(c)** recovery (*from illness*).

récupérer [rekypere] *v* (**je récupère, n. récupérons; je récupérerai**) **1** *vt* **(a)** to recover (*debt, book etc*); to get back, to retrieve (*book etc*); to collect, to pick up (*s.o.*); *Ordinat* to recover; **r. ses forces,** to recover (one's strength), to regain one's strength; **(b)** to recover, to salvage (*waste products*); *Fig* to rehabilitate, to find alternative employment for (*s.o.*); *Pol Fig* to exploit (*s.o.*); to make capital out of (*sth*); **r. de la ferraille,** to collect scrap; **(c)** to retrieve, to recoup (*a loss*); to make up (*lost time*). **2** *vi* to recuperate, to recover (one's strength).

récurage [rekyraʒ] *nm* scouring.

récurer [rekyre] *vt* to scour, to clean (*pots and pans*).

récureur, -euse [rekyrœr, -øz] **1** *n* scourer. **2** *nm* scourer, scouring agent.

récurrence [rekyrɑ̃s] *nf* recurrence.

récurrent [rekyrɑ̃] *adj* **(a)** *Anat* recurrent (*nerve, vein*); **(b)** *Méd etc* recurrent, recurring; **fièvre récurrente,** recurrent fever; *Math* **série récurrente,** recurrent series; *Ordinat* **processus r.,** recursive process.

récusable [rekyzabl] *adj Jur* challengeable (*juryman*); impugnable (*evidence*).

récusation [rekyzasjɔ̃] *nf Jur* **r. de juré/d'arbitre,** challenge of *or* exception to *or* objection to a juryman/an arbitrator; **r. de témoignage,** impugnment of evidence.

récuser [rekyze] **1** *vt* to challenge, to take exception to, to object to (*witness etc*); to impugn (*evidence*); to challenge (*authority*). **2 se récuser** *vpr Jur* to decline to give an opinion, to disclaim competence.

recyclage [rəsiklaʒ] *nm* **(a)** *Ind* retraining (*of staff*); readaptation (*to new techniques etc*); *Scol* reorientation (*of student*); (*cours*) refresher course(s); **(b)** (*de matériaux*) recycling.

recycler [rəsikle] **1** *vt* **(a)** *Scol* to reorient(ate) (*pupil's studies*); *Ind* to retrain (*staff*); **(b)** to recycle (*paper, glass etc*). **2 se recycler** *vpr Scol* to change one's course of study; *Ind* to retrain.

rédacteur, -trice [redaktœr, -tris] *n* **(a)** writer, drafter (*of deed, communiqué*); **r. d'un dictionnaire,** dictionary compiler; **(b)** *Journ* member of editorial staff, sub-editor; **r. en chef,** editor; **r. aux actualités,** news editor; **r. politique,** political editor.

rédaction [redaksjɔ̃] *nf* **(a)** drafting, drawing up, writing (*of deed* etc); **(b)** *Journ* editing; (*poste*) editorship; (*personnel*) editorial staff; (*bureau*) (newspaper) office(s); **note de la r.,** editor's note; **(c)** *Scol* essay, composition.

rédactionnel, -elle [redaksjɔnɛl] *adj* editorial.

reddition [redisjɔ̃, rɛddi-] *nf* **(a)** surrender (*of town, army*); **r. sans condition,** unconditional surrender; **(b)** rendering (*of account*).

redécouvrir [rədekuvrir] *vt* (*conj like* **couvrir**) to rediscover.

redemander [rədmɑ̃de] *vt* **(a)** (*pour la deuxième fois*) to ask for (*sth*) again; (*pour en avoir plus*) to ask for more *or* a second helping of (*sth*); **(b)** (*pour récupérer*) to ask for (*sth*) back (again).

rédempteur, -trice [redɑ̃ptœr, -tris] **1** *adj* redeeming. **2** *n* redeemer.

rédemption [redɑ̃psjɔ̃] *nf* redemption, redeeming.

redescendre [rədesɑ̃dr, -de-] **1** *vi* to come *or* go down again; *Nau* (*of the wind*) to back. **2** *vt* **(a)** (*apporter*) to take *or* bring *or* let (*sth*) down again; **(b)** (*descendre*) to come *or* go down (*stairs, river*) again.

redevable [rəd(ə)vabl] *adj* **être r. de qch à qn,** to be indebted to s.o. for sth; **je vous suis r. de cent francs,** I still owe you a hundred francs.

redevance [rəd(ə)vɑ̃s] *nf TV* licence fee; **redevances d'auteur,** author's royalties; **r. pétrolière,** oil royalty.

redevenir [rədəvnir] *vi* (*conj like* **devenir**) **r. jeune,** to become *or* grow young again; **r. malade,** to fall ill again.

redevoir [rəd(ə)vwar] *vt* (*conj like* **devoir**) to owe a balance of (*a sum*); **il me redoit dix francs,** he still owes me ten francs.

rédhibitoire [redibitwar] *adj* **(a)** *Jur* **vice r.,** redhibitory defect; **(b) être petit est r.,** it's a handicap being small, being small puts you at a disadvantage.

rediffuser [rədifyze] *vt Rad TV* to repeat, to broadcast again.

rediffusion [rədifyzjɔ̃] *nf Rad TV* repeat (broadcast); **il n'y a que des rediffusions ce soir,** there's nothing on tonight but repeats.

rédiger [rediʒe] *vt* (**je rédigeai(s)**; **n. rédigeons**) **(a)** to draw up, to draft, to write (out) (*agreement, letter etc*); to write (*article*); **(b)** *Journ* to edit (*periodical*).

redingote [rədɛ̃gɔt] *nf* (*pour hommes, femmes*) redingote; (*pour femmes*) fitted coat.

redire [rədir] *vt* (*conj like* **dire**) **(a)** to tell *or* say (*sth*) again, to repeat (*sth*); **(b) trouver à r.,** to complain; **trouver à r. à qch,** to find fault with *or F* pick holes in sth; **il n'y a rien à r. à cela,** there's nothing to be said against that.

rediscuter [rədiskyte] *vt* to have further discussion on, to discuss again.

redistribuer [rədistribɥe] *vt* to redistribute, to re-allocate; *Cartes* to redeal (*cards*).

redistribution [rədistribysjɔ̃] *nf* redistribution, reallocation.

redite [rədit] *nf* (useless) repetition.

redondance [rədɔ̃dɑ̃s] *nf* redundancy.

redondant [rədɔ̃dɑ̃] *adj* redundant (*word, style, Ordinat code*).

redonner [rədɔne] **1** *vt* **(a)** to give (*sth*) again; *Cartes* to redeal; **on redonne Hamlet,** Hamlet is on again; **(b)** (*davantage*) to give more of (*sth*); **(c)** (*rendre*) to give (*sth*) back, to return (*sth*); **cela m'a redonné du courage,** that put new heart into me *or* restored my courage; **ça m'a redonné envie de voyager,** that made me want to travel again. **2** *vi* **r. dans des excès,** to fall into excesses again; **r. dans l'exagération,** to exaggerate again.

redorer [rədɔre] *vt* to regild; *Fig* **r. son blason,** (*d'un noble*) to restore the family fortunes by marrying money.

redormir [rədɔrmir] *vi* (*conj like* **dormir**) to sleep *or* go to sleep again.

redoublant, -ante [rədublɑ̃, -ɑ̃t] *n Scol* pupil who remains a second year in the same class.

redoublé [rəduble] *adj* **rime redoublée,** double rhyme; **battre qn à coups redoublés,** to thrash s.o. soundly.

redoublement [rədubləmɑ̃] *nm* **(a)** redoubling (*of joy etc*); **avec un r. de zèle,** with renewed *or* redoubled zeal; **(b)** *Ling* reduplication.

redoubler [rəduble] **1** *vt* **(a)** to increase (*dose*); **r. ses efforts,** to redouble one's efforts; **r. le chagrin de qn,** to add to s.o.'s grief; **r. ses cris,** to redouble one's cries, to shout louder than ever; *Scol* **r. une classe,** to repeat a class; **(b)** to reline (*garment*). **2** *vi* to redouble; *Scol* to repeat a class; **la pluie redoubla,** the rain came on worse *or* came down harder than ever, the rain came down twice as hard; **r. d'efforts,** to redouble one's efforts.

redoutable [rədutabl] *adj* redoubtable, formidable, dangerous (*enemy*); **un adversaire r.,** a formidable opponent.

redoute [rədut] *nf* **(a)** (*fortification*) redoubt; **(b)** *Arch* gala evening (*at dance hall*).

redouter [rədute] *vt* to fear, to dread (*sth*); to be in awe of (*s.o.*); **r. d'apprendre qch,** to dread hearing sth; **je redoute surtout de devenir aveugle,** the thing *or* what I fear *or* dread most is going blind.

redoux [rədu] *nm Météo* rise in temperature.

redresse [rədrɛs] *nf Nau* **palans de r.,** righting tackle; *Arg* **c'est un type à la r.,** he's got his wits about him.

redressement [rədrɛsmɑ̃] *nm* **(a)** righting, setting up again (*of fallen object*); righting (*of boat*); *Opt* erecting (*of inverted image*); **(b)** rectification, correction (*of account, mistake*); tru(e)ing (*of a surface*); **r. économique,** economic recovery; **plan de r.,** recovery plan; *Hist* **maison de r.,** ≈ approved school, reformatory; **(c)** *El* rectification (*of alternating current*); **valve de r.,** rectifying valve.

redresser [rədrese] **1** *vt* **(a)** to right (*sth*), to set (*sth*) upright again; to right (*boat*); to straighten up, to lift the nose of (*aircraft*); *Opt* to erect (*inverted image*); **(b)** to redress, to right (*wrong, grievance*); to rectify (*mistake*); to adjust (*account*); to straighten (out) (*bent wood, warped metal*); to true (*surface*); **r. la tête,** to hold up one's head; (*la lever*) to raise *or* lift one's head, to look up; **il est le seul capable de r. la situation,** he's the only one who can correct *or* rectify the situation; **r. l'équilibre des forces,** to redress the balance of power; **(c)** *El* to rectify (*current*). **2 se redresser** *vpr* **(a)** to stand up (straight) again; (*avec fierté*) to draw oneself up, to hold one's head high; **se r. sur son séant,** to sit up straight (again); **(b)** (*of economy etc*) to recover.

redresseur, -euse [rədrɛsœr, -øz] **1** *n* **r. de torts,** righter of wrongs; (*chevalier*) knight errant. **2** *nm El* rectifier (*of current*). **3** *adj* **(a)** *El* rectifying (*device*); **(b)** *Opt* erecting (*prism*); **viseur r.,** reversal finder.

redû [rədy] *nm* balance due.

réducteur, -trice [redyktœr, -tris] **1** *adj* reducing; *Ch* **agent r.,** reducing agent; *MecE* **ensemble r.,** reduction gear assembly. **2** *nm* reducer; *Ch* reducing agent; *MecE* reduction gear *or* unit; *Th* **r. d'éclairage,** dimmer; **r. de têtes,** head shrinker.

réductible [redyktibl] *adj* reducible.

réduction [redyksjɔ̃] *nf* **(a)** reduction, cutting down (*of expenditure*); mitigation (*of penalty*); writing down (*of capital*); setting (*of fracture*); gearing down (*of machinery*); stepping down (*of voltage*); **réductions de salaires,** reductions in wages, wage cuts; **carte de r.,** = card entitling the holder to a reduction in train fares, theatre tickets etc; **cette carte donne droit à une r.,** this card entitles the holder to a reduction; **grandes réductions de prix,** big (price) reductions; *Mus* **r. pour piano,** short score (*of opera etc*); **bateau en r.,** scale model of a ship; **(b)** capture (*of town*).

réduire [redɥir] *v* (*prp* **réduisant**; *pp* **réduit**; *pr ind* **je réduis, il réduit, n. réduisons**; *impf* **je réduisais**; *p hist* **je réduisis**; *fu* **je réduirai**) **1** *vt* to reduce (*pressure, amount, speed*); to reduce, to lower, to bring down, to cut (*price*); to reduce, to lower (*interest rate*); to reduce, to curtail, to cut down (*expenses*); to restrict (*freedom*); to write down (*capital*); *El to step down (voltage*); *Ch* to reduce (*oxide*); *Math* to reduce (*fractions*); *Méd* to reduce (*fracture, dislocation*); **il faut r. les dépenses/les frais,** expenditure/costs must be reduced *or* cut; **billet à prix réduit,** cheap *or* cut-price ticket; **édition réduite,** abridged edition; **modèle réduit,** scale model; **r. un homme à un grade inférieur,** *Mil* to reduce a man; *Nau* to disrate a man; **r. du bois en cendres,** to reduce wood to ashes; **r. qch en miettes,** to smash sth to pieces; **r. des francs/kilogrammes en centimes/grammes,** to convert *or* reduce francs/kilograms to centimes/grams; *Culin* **r. une sauce,** to reduce a sauce; *Mus* **r. une partition,** to arrange a score for the piano; **r. qn à la misère/au désespoir,** to reduce s.o. to poverty/to drive s.o. to despair; **r. qn à demander pardon,** to compel s.o. to ask for forgiveness; **j'en suis réduit à le faire moi-même,** I'm reduced to doing it myself; **r. qn par la famine,** to starve s.o. into submission.

2 se réduire *vpr* **(a) se r. au strict nécessaire,** to confine oneself to what is strictly necessary;

(b) les frais se réduisent à peu de chose, the expenses come to very little; **à quoi se réduit tout cela?,** what does all that amount to *or* boil down to?; **se r. en poussière,** to crumble into dust; **la sauce s'est réduite,** the sauce has reduced.

3 *vi* **faire r. un sirop,** to reduce a syrup.

réduit [redɥi] *nm* **(a)** (*petit logement*) small *or* poor room *or* quarters, hovel; **(b)** *Arch* keep, redoubt.

réduplication [redyplikasjɔ̃] *nf* reduplication.

réécriture [reekrityr] *nf* rewriting.

réédification [reedifikasjɔ̃] *nf* rebuilding, re-erection.

réédifier [reedifje] *vt* (*conj like* **édifier**) to rebuild, to reerect.

rééditer [reedite] *vt* to republish, to re-issue (*book*); *Fig F* to rake up (*old story*).

réédition [reedisjɔ̃] *nf* re-issue (*of book etc*); *Fig F* repeat; **c'est une r. de leur dispute de la semaine dernière,** it's a repeat *or* a re-run of the argument they had last week, it's last week's argument all over again; **c'est une r. du match France-Écosse,** it's a repeat of the France-Scotland match, it's the France-Scotland match all over again.

rééducatif, -ive [reedykatif, -iv] *adj* **thérapie rééducative,** occupational therapy.

rééducation [reedykasjɔ̃] *nf* **(a)** *Méd* re-education (*of muscle after paralysis etc*); rehabilitation (*of person*); **r. de la parole,** speech therapy; **centre de r. (professionnelle),** rehabilitation centre; **faire de la r.,** (*chez un kinésithérapeute*) to have physio(therapy); **(b)** rehabilitation (*of delinquents*).

rééduquer [reedyke] *vt* to rehabilitate (*the disabled, delinquents*); *Méd* to re-educate (*a muscle*).

réel, -elle [reel] **1** *adj* **(a)** real, actual (*fact, person*); *Math* real (*number*); *Opt* true (*image*); **salaire nominal et salaire r.,** nominal wage rate and net earnings; **offre réelle,** cash offer; **(b)** (*before noun*) real, great (*pleasure etc*). **2**

nm Math real number; **le r.**, reality.
réélection [reelɛksjɔ̃] *nf* re-election.
rééligible [reeliʒibl] *adj* re-eligible.
réélire [reelir] *vt* (*conj like* **élire**) to re-elect.
réellement [reɛlmɑ̃] *adv* really, in reality, actually.
réembarquer [reɑ̃barke] *vt* to re-embark.
réembaucher [reɑ̃boʃe] *vt* to take on (*workers*) again, *Am* to rehire (*workers*).
réémetteur [reemɛtœr] *nm TV Rad* relay transmitter.
réemploi [reɑ̃plwa] *nm* re-employment.
réemployer [reɑ̃plwaje] *vt* to re-employ.
réensemencer [reɑ̃s(ə)mɑ̃se] *vt* to resow (*field*).
réentendre [reɑ̃tɑ̃dr] *vt* to listen to (*record, tape etc*) again.
rééquilibrage [reekilibraʒ] *nm* (*de pneus*) balancing; *Pol* **tout faire pour le r. de la gauche,** to do everything to restore the balance between left and right.
réescompter [reɛskɔ̃te] *vt Fin* to rediscount (*bill*).
réévaluation [reevalɥasjɔ̃] *nf* revaluation.
réévaluer [reevalɥe] *vt* to revalue.
réexpédier [reɛkspedje] *vt* (*conj like* **expédier**) **(a)** to send on, to forward, to redirect (*letters, goods*); **(b)** (*pour rendre*) to send (*sth*) back, to return (*sth*) (*to the sender*).
réexpédition [reɛkspedisjɔ̃] *nf* **(a)** sending on, forwarding, redirection (*of letter etc*); **(b)** sending back, return(ing) (*to sender*).
réexportation [reɛkspɔrtɑsjɔ̃] *nf* re-exportation.
réexporter [reɛkspɔrte] *vt* to re-export.
refaçonner [rəfasɔne] *vt* to remake, to refashion.
réfaction [refaksjɔ̃] *nf* allowance, rebate (*on damaged or substandard goods*).
refaire [rəfɛr] *v* (*conj like* **faire**) **1** *vt* **(a)** to do (*one's homework, a translation etc*) again; to make (*journey, dress etc*) again; to remake (*a film*); **r. sa malle,** to pack one's trunk again; **c'est à r.,** it will have to be done again; **passer la nuit à r. le monde,** to spend the night putting the world to rights; **elle a refait sa vie avec cet homme,** she has made a new life for herself with that man;
(b) (*réparer*) to repair, to mend; to do up, to renovate (*flat, house*); to recover (*one's strength*);
(c) *F* (*d'un marchand*) to do, to diddle (*s.o.*); (*duper*) to take (*s.o.*) in; **on vous a refait,** you've been had.
2 se refaire *vpr* **(a)** to recover (one's health); *F* **elle se refait une beauté,** she's doing her face again; **une soirée comme ça, ça ne se refera pas,** a party like that doesn't happen twice;
(b) (*se changer*) to change one's ways; **on ne se refait pas,** I *etc* can't change the way I *etc* am (made);
(c) (*se rétablir*) to retrieve *or* recoup one's losses.
réfection [refɛksjɔ̃] *nf* **(a)** remaking; (*de bâtiment*) rebuilding; (*réparation*) repair(ing); (*d'un appartement, une maison*) restoration, doing up; **route en r.,** road under repair; **(b)** (*repas*) meal.
réfectoire [refɛktwar] *nm* refectory, dining hall.
refend [rəfɑ̃] *nm* **(a) bois de r.,** wood in planks; **(b) pierre de r.,** corner stone; **mur de r.,** partition (wall).
refendre [rəfɑ̃dr] *vt* to split, to cleave (*slates*); to slit (*leather*); to rip (*timber*).
référé [refere] *nm Jur* summary procedure; **(ordonnance de) r.,** provisional order.
référence [referɑ̃s] *nf* **(a)** reference; **livre de r.,** reference book; **faire r. à un ouvrage,** to refer to a work *or* a book; **références au bas des pages,** footnotes; **r. topographique,** map reference; **plan de r.,** datum plane, plane of reference; *F* **ce n'est pas une r.,** don't take my *or* his *etc* word for it, don't go by what I *or* he *etc* say(s); **le film a été primé à Cannes mais ce n'est pas une r.,** the film won a prize at Cannes but that's no recommendation; **(b)** reference (*on letter, document*); **r. à rappeler,** in replying please quote; **en r. à,** with reference to; **(c) références,** (employee's) reference, testimonial; (*contact*) referee; **est-ce que vous voulez me servir de r.?,** may I use you as a reference?
référencé [referɑ̃se] *adj Com F* bearing a reference number.
référencié [referɑ̃sje] *adj* (*quotation*) with a reference.
referendum, référendum [referɛ̃dɔm] *nm* referendum; **faire un r.,** (*voter*) to vote in a referendum; (*l'organiser*) to hold a referendum.
référer [refere] *v* (**je réfère, n. référons; je référerai**) **1** *vi* **r. à qn d'une question,** to refer a matter to s.o.; **en r. à la cour,** to report *or* submit the case to the court; **en r. à son supérieur,** to refer a matter to one's superior. **2 se référer** *vpr* **se r. à qch,** to refer to sth; **se r. à** *ou* **s'en r. à qn d'une question,** to refer a matter to s.o..
refermer [rəfɛrme] **1** *vt* to shut *or* close (up) again; **il referma la porte sur lui,** he closed the door after him. **2 se refermer** *vpr* to close (again); (*of wound*) to close up, to heal.
refiler [rəfile] *vt Arg* **r. qch à qn,** to palm sth off on s.o., to foist *or* unload sth on s.o..
réfléchi [refleʃi] *adj* **(a)** reflective, thoughtful (*person*); deliberate, considered (*action, opinion*); **c'est tout r.,** that's settled; **tout bien r.,** all things considered, after due consideration; **(b)** *Gram* reflexive (*verb, pronoun*).
réfléchir [refleʃir] **1** *vt* **(a)** to reflect, to throw back (*image, light, sound*); to bend back (*light*);
(b) il réfléchit que son argent ne suffirait pas, it occurred to him that he would not have enough money.
2 *vi* to think; **je réfléchis,** I'm thinking; (*avant de décider*) I'm thinking about it; **prends le temps de r.,** (take time to) think about it; **donne-moi le temps de r.,** give me time to think; **r. à** *ou* **sur qch,** to think about sth, to reflect on sth, to ponder *or* consider *or* weigh sth, to turn sth over in one's mind; **réfléchissez-y,** think about it, think it over; **je demande à r.,** I would like to think about it *or* think it over; **donner à r. à qn,** to give s.o. food for thought, to make s.o. think twice; **parler sans r.,** to speak without thinking *or* hastily.
3 se réflechir *vpr* (*of light, heat, sound etc*) to be reflected *or* thrown back, to reverberate.
réfléchissement [refleʃismɑ̃] *nm* reflection, reflecting (*of light etc*).
réflecteur, -trice [reflɛktœr, -tris] **1** *adj* reflecting (*mirror, panel*). **2** *nm* reflector; (*miroir*) reflecting mirror; (*télescope*) reflector, reflecting telescope.
réflectif, -ive [reflɛktif, -iv] *adj* **(a)** (*de la réflexion*) reflective; **(b)** *Physiol* reflex.
réflectorisé [reflektɔrize] *adj* reflective; **casque r.,** reflective helmet.
reflet [rəflɛ] *nm* reflection; sheen (*of silk etc*); **r. des eaux,** gleam on the waters; **les reflets de la lune sur le lac,** the reflection of the moon on the lake; **chevelure à reflets d'or,** hair with glints of gold; **r. des glaces,** ice blink; **reflets changeants,** play of colours; *Fig* **être le r. de qch,** to reflect *or* be a reflection *or* an indication of sth; **ce n'est que le r. du temps des colonies,** it is a pale reflection of colonial times.
refléter [rəflete] *v* (**je reflète, n. reflétons; je refléterai**) **1** *vt* to reflect (*scattered light, Fig s.o.'s embarrassment*). **2 se refléter** *vpr* to be mirrored *or* reflected; **le Louvre se reflète dans la Seine,** the Louvre is mirrored *or* reflected in the Seine.
refleurir [rəflœrir] **1** *vi* **(a)** to flower *or* blossom again; **(b)** *Fig* (*of art, literature*) to flourish again, to revive. **2** *vt* to put fresh flowers on (*grave*).
reflex [rəflɛks] *adj & n* **(appareil) r.,** reflex (camera).
réflexe [reflɛks] **1** *adj Phys Physiol* reflex. **2** *nm Physiol* reflex; (*réaction*) reflex, reaction; **r. rotulien,** knee reflex *or* jerk; **avoir de bons réflexes,** to have good reflexes, to react quickly; **ça a été un r.,** it was a reflex, it was automatic; **c'est devenu un r.,** it's become automatic.
réflexif, -ive [reflɛksif, -iv] *adj Phil Math* reflexive.
réflexion [reflɛksjɔ̃] *nf* **(a)** (*pensée*) reflection, thought; **agir sans r.,** to act hastily *or* without thinking; **(toute) r. faite, à la r.,** (*finalement*) on reflection; (*après changement d'avis*) on further consideration, on second thoughts; **à la r. vous changerez d'avis,** on reflection *or* when you think it over, you'll change your mind; **(b)** (*remarque*) remark; **une r. désobligeante,** an unpleasant remark; **elle ne supporte pas qu'on lui passe la moindre r.,** she cannot stand even the slightest criticism; **(c)** reflexion, *Phys* reflection (*of image, light, sound*); **angle de r.,** angle of reflection.
refluer [rəflye] *vi* to flow back; (*of tide*) to ebb; **le sang lui reflua au visage,** the blood surged to his cheeks; **la foule a reflué vers la ville,** the crowd swept back towards the town.
reflux [rəfly] *nm* reflux, flowing back; ebb(ing) (*of tide*); (*recul*) surging back; **le flux et le r.,** the ebb and flow.
refondre [rəfɔ̃dr] **1** *vt* **(a)** to recast (*metal, a bell*); to recoin, to remint (*money*); **(b)** to rewrite (*poem*); **r. un ouvrage,** to rewrite a work. **2** *vi* (*of snow*) to melt again.
refonte [rəfɔ̃t] *nf* **(a)** recasting (*of metal*); recoinage (*of money*); **(b)** rewriting (*of poem, play*); remodelling, reorganization (*of factory*).
réformable [refɔrmabl] *adj* reformable.
reformater [rəfɔrmate] *vt Ordinat* to reformat (*page*).
réformateur, -trice [refɔrmatœr, -tris] **1** *adj* reforming. **2** *n* reformer.
réformation [refɔrmɑsjɔ̃] *nf* reformation, reform; *Hist Rel* **la R.,** the Reformation.

réformatoire [refɔrmatwar] *adj* reformatory, reformative.

réforme [refɔrm] *nf* **(a)** reform (*of abuses, calendar*); **la r. de l'orthographe,** spelling reform; **climat de r. politique et sociale,** climate of political and social reform; *Hist Rel* **la R.,** the Reformation; **(b)** *Mil* discharge, invaliding out (*for physical unfitness*); rejection (*of recruit*); **r. temporaire,** deferment (*of military service*); **commission de r.,** special medical board; **mettre à la r.,** to discharge (*man, officer*) from the service, to invalid (*man, officer*) out (of the service); *Ind* **matériel en r.,** scrapped plant.

réformé, -ée [refɔrme] **1** *adj* **(a)** *Rel* Protestant; reformed (*church*); **(b)** *Mil* (*exempté*) discharged for unfitness; rejected (*recruit*). **2** *n* **(a)** *Rel* Protestant; **(b)** *Mil* **r. temporaire,** deferred recruit.

reformer [rəfɔrme] **1** *vt* to form again, to re-form; **r. les rangs,** to fall into line again. **2 se reformer** *vpr* to re-form; **l'opposition se reformait,** the opposition was re-forming.

réformer [refɔrme] *vt* **(a)** to reform (*abuse, law*); (*pour améliorer*) to improve, to reform; *Jur* to reverse (*decision*); **(b)** to condemn, to scrap (*equipment*); *Mil Nau* to discharge as unfit, to invalid out (of the service); to reject (*recruit*).

réformisme [refɔrmism] *nm Pol* reformism.

réformiste [refɔrmist] *adj & n* reformist.

refoulé, -ée [rəfule] *Psy* **1** *adj* repressed (*feelings*); repressed, inhibited (*person*). **2** *n* repressed *or* inhibited person.

refoulement [rəfulmɑ̃] *nm* **(a)** pressing *or* driving *or* forcing back; driving in *or* out (*of pin, bolt*); backing (*of train*); upsetting (*of metal*); tamping (*of earth*); **(b)** delivery, discharge, output (*of pipe*); **soupape de r.,** delivery valve (*of pump*); **tuyau de r.,** exhaust pipe; **(c)** *Psy* (unconscious) repression.

refouler [rəfule] **1** *vt* **(a)** to drive back, to force back, to press back; *Admin* to expel, to turn back (*an alien*); to drive *or* force in *or* out (*bolt, pin*); (*of ship*) to stem (*the tide*); to back (*train*); to upset (*metal*); to tamp (*earth*); to deliver, to discharge (*water*); **pompe refoulante,** force pump; **(b)** to repress *or* suppress *or* contain (*one's feelings*); to force back (*tears*); *Psy* to repress (*an instinct*); **r. son agressivité,** to repress one's aggressiveness. **2** *vi MecE* **(a)** (*of pin*) to go the wrong way; **(b)** (*of sink*) to back up.

refouloir [rəfulwar] *nm* tamping tool; *Mil Arch* rammer.

réfractaire [refraktɛr] **1** *adj* refractory, rebellious, insubordinate; *Tech* refractory (*ore*); fireproof, fire (*brick, clay*); *Hist Fr* **prêtre r.,** non-juring priest; **r. à.,** resistant to; **être r. aux influences,** to be resistant to influence; **r. aux acides,** acid-proof; **le coton est r. à la teinture,** cotton does not dye well; **r. à la loi,** unwilling to accept the law; *Méd* **maladie r.,** refractory disease. **2** *n* rebel; *Mil Jur* defaulter.

réfracter [refrakte] *vt* to refract, to bend (*rays etc*).

réfracteur, -trice [refraktœr, -tris] **1** *adj* refracting. **2** *nm* refractor.

réfraction [refraksjɔ̃] *nf* refraction, bending (*of ray*); **indice de r.,** index of refraction, refractive index.

refrain [rəfrɛ̃] *nm* **(a)** refrain, burden (*of song*); **chanter de vieux refrains,** to sing old songs *or* old ditties; *F* **c'est toujours le même r.,** it's (always) the same old story; **(b) r. en chœur,** chorus.

réfrangible [refrɑ̃ʒibl] *adj Phys* refrangible.

refréner [rəfrene] *vt* (**je refrène, n. refrénons; je refrénerai**) to curb, to restrain, to control (*feelings*).

réfrigérant [refriʒerɑ̃] **1** *adj* refrigerating, cooling (*action, apparatus*); freezing (*mixture*); *Fig* chilly (*reception*). **2** *nm* (*mélange*) refrigerant, coolant; refrigerator, condenser (*of still*); **r. à cheminée,** cooling tower.

réfrigérateur [refriʒeratœr] *nm* refrigerator, *F* fridge; *Fig* **mettre un projet au r.,** to shelve a plan, to put a plan on ice.

réfrigération [refriʒerasjɔ̃] *nf* refrigeration, chilling (*of meat, drinks etc*); **appareils de r.,** refrigeration appliances; **r. industrielle,** industrial refrigeration.

réfrigérer [refriʒere] *vt* (**je réfrigère, n. réfrigérons; je réfrigérerai**) to refrigerate; **viande réfrigérée,** chilled meat; **camion réfrigéré,** refrigerated van, reefer; *Fig* **son accueil me réfrigéra,** I received a chilly welcome.

réfringence [refrɛ̃ʒɑ̃s] *nf Phys* refringency.

réfringent [refrɛ̃ʒɑ̃] *adj* refringent.

refroidi [rəfrwadi] *nm F* (*cadavre*) stiff.

refroidir [rəfrwadir] **1** *vt* **(a)** to cool, to chill (*water*); to cool (*engine, fluid*); to quench (*metal*); **refroidi par (l')air,** air-cooled; **(b)** *Fig* to cool, to chill (*friendship etc*); to cool (off), to dash (*enthusiasm*); **(c)** *Arg* (*tuer*) to bump (*s.o.*) off. **2** *vi* to grow cold, to cool down *or* off; **laisser r. son thé,** to let one's tea get cold; **dépêchez-vous!, ça va r.!,** hurry up! it's getting cold!; **le temps a refroidi,** it *or* the weather has got *or* grown colder. **3 se refroidir** *vpr* **(a)** to cool; **le temps se refroidit,** it's *or* the weather's getting colder; **(b)** *Méd* to catch a chill.

refroidissement [rəfrwadismɑ̃] *nm* **(a)** cooling, chilling (*of water*); cooling (*of engine*); quenching (*of metal*); **r. du temps,** fall in temperature; **agent de r.,** cooling agent, coolant; **(b)** *Méd* **attraper un r.,** to catch a chill; **(c)** *Fig* cooling off (*of friendship*).

refroidisseur [rəfrwadisœr] *nm* cooler, refrigerator unit; *Nucl* cooler, coolant; **système r.,** cooling system.

refuge [rəfyʒ] *nm* **(a)** refuge, shelter; **(lieu de) r.,** place of refuge; *Fig* **le sport est son r.,** he takes refuge in sport; **r. anti-bombe,** air-raid shelter; **pays-r.,** country of refuge; **valeur-r.,** hedge against inflation; **(b)** (*en montagne*) (mountain) hut, refuge; (*d'oiseau*) (bird) sanctuary; (*sur la route*) traffic island; **(c) Dieu est mon r.,** God is my refuge.

réfugié, -ée [refyʒje] *n* refugee; **r. politique,** political refugee.

réfugier (se) [sərefyʒje] *vpr* to take refuge, to find shelter, to shelter; **se r. dans les mensonges/le sport,** to take refuge in lying/sport.

refus [rəfy] *nm* refusal, denial; **essuyer un r.,** to meet with a refusal; **r. d'obéissance,** insubordination; *Jur* contempt of court; *F* **ce n'est pas de r.,** I won't say no; **je n'admettrai pas de r.,** I won't take no for an answer; **visser** *ou* **serrer un boulon à r.,** to screw a bolt home *or* tight.

refusé, -ée [rəfyze] *n Scol* failed candidate; *Beaux-Arts* **salon des refusés,** Impressionists.

refuser [rəfyze] **1** *vt* **(a)** to refuse, to decline (*sth*); to refuse, to decline, to turn down (*offer*); **r. mille francs d'un tableau,** to refuse *or* turn down a thousand francs for a picture; **r. qch à qn,** to refuse *or* deny s.o. sth; **on ne peut rien lui r.,** you can refuse him nothing, you can't refuse him anything; **r. toute qualité à qn,** to refuse to see any good in s.o.; **r. la porte à qn,** to refuse to let s.o. in, *Fml* to deny s.o. admittance; **r. l'obstacle,** (*of horse*) to refuse, to ba(u)lk; *Mil* **r. le combat,** to decline battle; **r. de faire qch,** to refuse to do sth; **je refuse de lui obéir,** I refuse to obey him; **r. de virer,** (*of ship*) not to obey the helm;

(b) to turn (*s.o.*) down; *Mil* to reject (*a man*) for military service; *Scol* to fail (*candidate*); *Scol* **être refusé,** to fail; **r. du monde,** to turn people away.

2 *vi* to refuse; (*of horse*) to refuse, to ba(u)lk; *Nau* (*of wind*) to veer forward; **non! je refuse!,** no! I refuse!; **r. tout net,** to refuse point blank.

3 se refuser *vpr* **se r. à l'évidence,** to shut one's eyes to the facts; **se r. à faire qch,** to refuse to do sth; **je me refuse à ce genre de pratique,** I refuse to get involved in that kind of thing.

réfutation [refytasjɔ̃] *nf* refutation, rebuttal.

réfuter [refyte] *vt* to refute, to rebut, to disprove.

rég. *Mil* (*abrév* **régiment**) Rgt.

regagner [rəgaɲe] *vt* **(a)** to regain, to recover, to win *or* get back (*confidence etc*); to win *or* get (*s.o.*) back; to recover, to win *or* get back (*money etc*); **r. le temps perdu,** to make up for lost time; **(b)** to get back to (*a place*), to reach (*a place*) again; **r. son foyer,** to get back home.

regain [rəgɛ̃] *nm* **(a)** renewal (*of interest*); revival (*of activity*); **connaître un r. de vie,** to have a new lease of life; **(b)** *Agr* aftermath.

régal, -als [regal] *nm* delicious dish, treat; **les marrons glacés, c'est mon r.,** marrons glacés are my favourite treat, I adore marrons glacés; **c'est un vrai r. de l'écouter,** it is a treat *or* a pleasure to listen to him; **c'est un r. pour les yeux,** it's a feast for the eyes.

régalade [regalad] *nf F* **boire à la r.,** to pour a drink down one's throat without the bottle touching one's lips.

régale [regal] *adj Ch* **eau r.,** aqua regia.

régaler¹ [regale] *vt* to level (*ground*).

régaler² **1** *vt F* to entertain (*friends*); **r. qn de qch,** to regale s.o. with sth, to treat s.o. to sth. **2** *vi F* to stand treat; **c'est moi qui régale,** I'm standing treat, (it's) my treat. **3 se régaler** *vpr F* to feast (**de,** on); to treat oneself (**de,** to); **on s'est bien régalé,** we had a slap-up meal; *Fig* **elle se régale avec ses petits-enfants,** she's having the time of her life with her grandchildren.

regard [rəgar] *nm* **(a)** look, glance, gaze; **r. appuyé,** fixed *or* intent gaze; **r. de côté,** sidelong glance; **r. vitreux,** glassy stare; **je sentis son r. se poser sur moi,** I felt his gaze on me; **jeter un r. à qn,** to glance at s.o.; **jeter** *ou* **lancer un r. sur qch,** to (cast a) glance at *or* over sth;

chercher qn du r., to look round for s.o.; **interroger qn du r., lancer à qn un r. interrogateur,** to give s.o. a questioning look, to look at s.o. inquiringly; **lancer un r. furieux à qn,** to glare at s.o.; **lancer un r. noir à qn,** to give s.o. a black look; **détourner le r.,** to look away, to avert one's eyes; **exposé aux regards,** exposed to view; **caché aux regards,** out of sight; **attirer le(s) regard(s),** to attract attention, to be conspicuous; **en r. de qch,** opposite *or* facing sth; (*comparé à*) compared with sth; **texte avec illustration en r.,** text with illustration (on the) opposite (page); **au r. de nos livres de comptabilité,** on looking at *or* examining our accounts; **au r. de la loi elle est coupable,** she is guilty in the eyes of the law;
(b) r. (d'accès, de visite), inspection hole; manhole (*of sewer*);
(c) peephole (*of oven, door*); draught hole (*of furnace*);
(d) (*contrôle*) control; *Jur* **droit de r.,** right of inspection.

regardant [rəgardɑ̃] *adj* (*avare*) tightfisted, stingy (*person*); (*exigeant*) concerned; **elle n'est pas regardante sur la présentation,** she's not concerned *or* bothered about the presentation.

regarder [rəgarde] **1** *vt* **(a)** to look at (*sth, s.o.*); to watch (*game etc*); **r. qn dans les yeux,** to look s.o. in the eyes; **r. qn fixement,** to stare at s.o.; **r. qn de travers,** to look askance at s.o.; **r. qn avec méfiance,** to look at *or* eye s.o. suspiciously; **se faire r.,** to attract attention, to make oneself conspicuous; **r. qn faire qch,** to watch s.o. doing sth; *F* **regarde voir si ce n'est pas cuit,** (check and) see if it's cooked yet; **regarde-moi ça!,** (*viens voir*) (come and) look at this!; *F* **regarde-moi ça, c'est ce que tu appelles du travail fini!,** look at that — is that what you call a job well done!; *F* **non, mais tu ne m'as pas regardé!,** what d'you take me for?;
(b) (*considérer*) to regard, to consider (*s.o., sth*); **r. qch comme un crime,** to regard sth *or* look on sth as a crime, to consider sth (to be) a crime; **il faut r. la vie en face/les choses telles qu'elle sont,** you've got to face up to life/to see things as they are; **ne r. que ses intérêts,** to consider only one's own interests;
(c) (*concerner*) to concern (*s.o.*); **cela ne vous regarde pas,** that doesn't concern you, that's no concern of yours, that's none of your business; **en ce qui me regarde,** as far as I am concerned.
2 *vi* **(a) r. par la fenêtre,** (*du dedans*) to look out of the window; (*du dehors*) to look in (through) the window; *F* **r. à la fenêtre,** to look out of the window; **r. à sa montre,** to look at one's watch *or* at the time; **puis-je r.?,** may I have a look?; **r. par le trou de la serrure,** to peep through the keyhole;
(b) r. sur, to look on to, to face (*sth*); **fenêtre qui regarde sur le jardin,** window that looks on to the garden;
(c) r. à qch, to pay attention to sth; **sans r. à la dépense,** regardless of expense; **je ne regarde pas à vingt francs,** I am not worried about twenty francs more *or* less; **à y bien r.,** on thinking it over; **y bien r.** *ou* **y r. à deux fois avant de faire qch,** to think twice before doing sth; **je n'y regarde pas de si près,** I'm not as particular *or* fussy as all that.
3 se regarder *vpr* (*d'une seule personne*) to look at oneself; (*de deux personnes*) to look at each other; **ils se regardaient en chiens de faïence,** they were glaring at each other; **nos deux maisons se regardent,** our houses face *or* are opposite each other; **ça se regarde dans les deux sens,** there are two ways of looking at that; *F* **elle ne s'est pas regardée!,** if only she could see herself.

regarnir [rəgarnir] *vt* to re-stock (*larder, shelves*); **il faut que je regarnisse mon portefeuille,** I must get some money *or* cash.

régate [regat] *nf* **(a)** regatta; **faire de la r.,** to race; **r. à voiles,** yacht races; **r. à l'aviron,** boat races; **(b)** (*nœud*) (narrow) sailor-knot tie.

régatier, -ière [regatje, -jɛr] *n Nau* racing yachtsman *or f* yachtswoman; (*à l'aviron*) racing oarsman *or f* oarswoman.

regazonner [rəgazɔne] *vt* to returf.

regel [rəʒɛl] *nm* renewed frost.

regeler [rəʒle] *vi* (**il regèle; il regèlera**) to freeze again.

régence [reʒɑ̃s] **1** *nf* regency; *Hist Fr* **la R.,** the Regency (*1715-1723*). **2** *adj inv* **style R.,** Regency (style); **meubles style R.,** Regency furniture; *F* **elle est très r.,** she's very genteel.

régénérateur, -trice [reʒeneratœr, -tris] **1** *adj* regenerating, regenerative; *Rel* **eau régénératrice,** baptismal water; *Nucl* **pile régénératrice,** breeder reactor. **2** *nm Ind* regenerator, regenerating plant *or* furnace.

régénération [reʒenerɑsjɔ̃] *nf* **(a)** regeneration; **(b)** *Ind* reconditioning; *Nucl* breeding.

régénérer [reʒenere] *v* (**je régénère, n. régénérons; je régénérerai**) **1** *vt* **(a)** to regenerate; **(b)** to reactivate (*catalyst*). **2 se régénérer** *vpr* (*de l'enthousiasme, intérêt*) to re-awaken.

régent, -ente [reʒɑ̃, -ɑ̃t] **1** *n* **(a)** regent; **(b)** *Fin* director; **(c)** *Belg* (secondary) schoolmaster; **(d) le R.,** the Regent diamond. **2** *adj* **reine régente/prince r.,** Queen/Prince Regent.

régenter [reʒɑ̃te] *vt* to domineer over, to dictate to (*s.o.*); **il veut tout r.,** he wants to run everything *or* the show.

régicide [reʒisid] **1** *n* regicide. **2** *nm* (*crime*) regicide. **3** *adj* regicidal.

régie [reʒi] *nf* **(a)** *Admin* management, control; administration, stewardship (*of property*); **en r.,** in the hands of trustees; **r. du dépôt légal,** copyright department; *Can* **R. des Loyers,** ≈ rental board; **(b)** (*entreprise publique*) public corporation, state-owned company; **(c) r. des impôts indirects,** excise (administration); **(d)** *Hist* Customs and Excise; **employé de la r.,** exciseman; **(e)** *Th* management; *Cin* production; *TV* central control room.

regimbement [rəʒɛ̃b(ə)mɑ̃] *nm* refractoriness.

regimber [rəʒɛ̃be] *vi* (*of person*) to jib, to ba(u)lk (**contre,** at), to kick (**contre,** against); (*of horse*) to kick (**contre,** at, against); **il est toujours à r.,** he's always protesting about something.

regimbeur, -euse [rəʒɛ̃bœr, -øz] *adj* refractory, recalcitrant.

régime [reʒim] *nm* **(a)** *Pol Admin* form of government *or* administration, regime; **r. des hôpitaux,** hospital regulations *or* rules; **le r. du travail,** the organization of labour; **le r. féodal,** the feudal system; *Hist Fr* **l'ancien r.,** the old regime (*before 1789*); **r. parlementaire,** parliamentary regime *or* system; **le r. actuel,** the present order of things; **sous le r. de Pompidou/Thatcher/***etc*, during the Pompidou/Thatcher/*etc* administration;
(b) *Tech* **r. (nominal),** rating (*of engine, motor, generator*); **r. de marche normal,** normal working *or* operating conditions; **charge de r.,** rated load; **puissance de r.,** normal power; *Av Nau Aut* **r. de croisière,** cruising speed; *Aut* **r. de ville,** town conditions; **elle fait trois litres au cent en r. de ville,** she does 100 km to three litres in town; **à ce r., on aura fini dans trois jours,** at this rate, we'll be finished in three days; **gardez ce r.,** keep to this speed; *Él* **r. de charge (d'un accumulateur),** charging rate; **variations de r.,** load variations;
(c) *Géog* (rate of) flow (*of river etc*); **r. climatique,** climatic conditions; **r. thermique,** temperature pattern;
(d) (*alimentaire*) diet; **r. lacté,** milk diet; **être au r.,** to be on a diet, to be dieting; **se mettre au r.,** to go on a diet; **je dois faire un r.,** I must go on a diet; *Sp* **r. d'entraînement,** training;
(e) *Gram* object; **cas r.,** objective case; **r. direct/indirect,** direct/indirect object;
(f) bunch, stem (*of bananas, dates*).

régiment [reʒimɑ̃] *nm Mil* regiment; *F* **aller au r.,** to join the army; **quand j'étais au r.,** when I was in the army, when I was doing my military service; **un r. d'admirateurs,** a host *or* swarm of admirers; *F* **il y en a pour un r.,** there's enough for a whole army.

régimentaire [reʒimɑ̃tɛr] *adj* regimental.

région [reʒjɔ̃] *nf* region; **r. militaire,** military district, = (*northern etc*) command; **dans la r. de Nantes,** in the Nantes area; **je ne connais pas la r.,** I don't know the area; **habiter en** *ou* **la r.,** to live in the provinces; **les régions polaires,** the polar regions; **r. du coton,** cotton-growing area, cotton belt; *Anat* **la r. lombaire,** the lumbar region.

régional, -aux [reʒjɔnal, -o] **1** *adj* regional (*expressions, cooking, development etc*); local (*committee*). **2** *nm Tél* area telephone system.

régionalisation [reʒjɔnalizɑsjɔ̃] *nf* regionalization.

régionaliser [reʒjɔnalize] *vt* to regionalize.

régionalisme [reʒjɔnalism] *nm* regionalism.

régionaliste [reʒjɔnalist] **1** *adj* **(a)** regional (*novel etc*); **(b)** regional (*policy*). **2** *n* **(a)** (*écrivain*) regional writer; **(b)** *Pol etc* regionalist.

régir [reʒir] *vt* **(a)** to govern, to rule; to manage (*estate*); **(b)** *Gram* to govern (*case, noun*).

régisseur [reʒisœr] *nm* manager; agent, steward (*of estate*); bailiff (*of farm*); *Th* stage manager; *Cin* assistant director; *TV* **r. de plateau,** floor manager.

registre [rəʒistr] *nm* **(a)** (*livre*) register, record; (*de comptes*) account book; (*des délibérations*) minute book; **rapporter un article sur un r.,** to post *or* enter an item in a register; **s'inscrire au r. du commerce,** to enter oneself in the trade register; **signer le r.,** (*d'un hôtel*) to sign the register; **les registres de l'état civil,** the registers of births, marriages and deaths; **r. des chevaux,** stud book; **r. d'une machine,** log book of a machine; **(b)** *Mus* register; (*étendue totale*) compass; **(c)** *Typ* register (*of page with page*); **(d) r. d'aérage,** ventilation flap; **r. de cheminée,** register, damper (*of furnace, chimney*); **(e)** *Tech* regulator lever, throttle (valve); **(f)** draw stop (*of organ*); **(g)** *Ordinat* register.

réglable [reglabl] *adj* adjustable.

réglage [reglaʒ] *nm* **(a)** regulating, adjusting, adjustment, setting (*of apparatus*); rating (*of chronometer*); **r. automatique,** automatic control; **à r. automatique,** self-adjusting; **vis de r.,** set screw; **r. de la vitesse,** speed control; *Mil* **r. du tir,** ranging; **(b)** *Rad etc* adjustment, control, tuning; **réglages,** dial readings; **r. de la luminosité,** brightness control; **(c)** ruling (*of paper*).

règle [rɛgl] *nf* **(a)** rule (*of conduct, art, grammar etc*); **les règles de l'honneur,** the code of honour; **les règles de la politesse exigent que ...,** courtesy demands that ...; *Rel* **r. d'un ordre,** rule of an order; *Nau* **règles de route,** rule of the road (*at sea*); **les règles du jeu,** the rules of the game; *Fig* **c'est la r. du jeu,** that's the rule of the game; *Fig* **ce n'est pas la r. du jeu,** that's (just) not done; *Fig* **le gouvernement a encore changé les règles du jeu,** the government have moved the goalposts again; *Com* **pour la bonne r.,** for order's sake; **se faire une r. de se coucher de bonne heure,** to make it a rule to go to bed early; **je suis en r. avec lui,** I'm all square with him; **être en r. avec sa conscience,** to have a clear conscience; **mettre qch en r.,** to put sth in order *or* to rights; **tout est en r.,** everything is in order *or* correct; **votre passeport est-il en r.?,** is your passport in order?; **reçu en r.,** formal receipt; **bataille en r.,** *Mil* battle according to the rules; *Fig* regular set-to; **en r. générale,** as a general rule; **agir dans les règles,** to act according to rule; **jouer selon les règles,** to play according to the rules; *Fig* **selon les règles de l'art,** by *or* according to the book; *Fig* **elle fait la bouillabaisse selon les règles de l'art,** she makes a classic *or* traditional bouillabaisse; *Fig* **boire du champagne selon les règles de l'art (avec des fraises),** to drink champagne in the traditional way; **comme c'est la r., comme de r.,** as is the rule; **r. d'or,** golden rule; *Math Vieilli* **r. de trois,** rule of three;

(b) rule, ruler; (*d'arpenteur*) measuring rod; **r. à araser,** straight edge; **r. divisée,** scale; **r. à calcul,** slide rule;

(c) prendre qn pour r., to take s.o. as a guide *or* an example;

(d) *Physiol* period; **avoir ses règles,** to have one's period; **absence de règles,** amenorrhoea; **règles abondantes,** heavy periods.

réglé [regle] *adj* **(a)** ruled (*paper*); **papier non r.,** plain paper; **(b)** (*organisé*) regular, well-ordered, fixed, steady; **vie réglée,** well-ordered life; **à des heures réglées,** at set hours; *F* **r. comme du papier à musique,** as regular as clockwork.

règlement [rɛgləmɑ̃] *nm* **(a)** payment, settlement (*of account*); settlement (*of difficulty*); **r. judiciaire,** rule of Court; **r. à l'amiable,** amicable settlement; **faire un r. par chèque,** to pay by cheque; **pour r. de tout compte,** in full settlement; *Fig* **un r. de compte(s),** a settling of accounts; **(b)** (*statut*) regulation(s); statutes (*of university*); rules (*of a society*); **règlements de police,** by(e)-laws; **les règlements militaires,** army regulations.

réglementaire [rɛgləmɑ̃tɛr] *adj* statutory, prescribed; **tenue r.,** regulation uniform; **ce n'est pas r.,** it's against the rules.

réglementariste [rɛgləmɑ̃tarist] **1** *adj* (*attitude, professeur etc*) pernickety; **un fonctionnaire r.,** a civil servant who goes by the book. **2** *n* pernickety person.

réglementation [rɛgləmɑ̃tasjɔ̃] *nf* **(a)** regulating, regulation; **r. du trafic des changes,** exchange control; **(b) la r.,** the regulations, the rules.

réglementer [rɛgləmɑ̃te] *vt* to regulate, to make rules for (*sth*); **r. le droit de grève,** to control the right to strike.

régler [regle] *vt* **(je règle, n. réglons; je réglerai) 1** *vt* **(a)** to rule (*paper*);

(b) to regulate, to order (*one's life, conduct etc*); to readjust, to adjust, to set (*mechanism*); to adjust (*compass*); to rate (*chronometer*); **r. sa journée,** to plan one's day; **r. ses dépenses sur son revenu,** to cut one's coat to suit one's cloth; *Sp* **r. l'allure,** to set the pace; *Mil* **r. le tir,** to range; **r. une montre,** to regulate a watch; **la pendule est bien réglée,** the clock keeps good time; **r. l'allumage/le moteur,** to adjust the timing/to tune the engine;

(c) to settle (*question, quarrel, account*); to settle, to pay (*bill*); **r. ses affaires,** to put one's affairs in order; **r. les livres,** to balance *or* make up the books; **r. son compte** *ou* **ses comptes à qn,** to settle one's account(s) *or* one's bill(s) with s.o.; (*se venger*) to settle accounts with s.o.; **r. de vieux comptes,** to pay off old scores; **r. le boulanger,** to pay the baker; **r. la note,** to pay the bill.

2 *vi* to pay; **r. en espèces,** to pay (in) cash; **c'est moi qui règle,** I'm paying, *F* this is on me.

3 se régler *vpr* **(a)** (*of mechanism*) to be adjustable;

(b) (*se finir*) to be concluded *or* settled; **ça s'est réglé à l'amiable,** it was settled amicably.

réglette [reglɛt] *nf* small ruler.

régleur, -euse [reglœr, -øz] **1** *n* (*personne*) regulator, adjuster (*of mechanism*). **2** *nf* **régleuse,** ruling machine (*for paper*).

réglisse [reglis] **1** *nf Bot* liquorice. **2** *nm* **bâton de r.,** stick of liquorice.

réglo [reglo] *adj inv F* OK, in order; **ça n'est pas très r.,** that's a bit dodgy; **elle a été très r.,** she was very straight; **un contrat r.,** a bona fide contract.

réglure [reglyr] *nf* ruling (*of or on paper*).

règne [rɛɲ] *nm* **(a)** reign (*of king*); **sous le r. de Louis XIV,** in the reign of Louis XIV; **c'est le r. de l'argent/de la technologie,** money/technology reigns supreme; **(b)** (*naturel*) (*vegetable, animal*) kingdom.

régner [reɲe] *vi* **(je règne, n. régnons; je régnerai) (a)** (*of monarch*) to reign, to rule; (*of conditions, opinion*) to prevail, to be prevalent, *Fml* to obtain; **il règne une ambiance de suspicion,** suspicion is prevalent; *Iron* **la confiance règne!,** there's trust *or* confidence for you!; **r. sur l'opinion,** to dominate opinion; **(b) une galerie règne le long du bâtiment,** a gallery runs *or* extends along the building.

regonfler [rəgɔ̃fle] **1** *vt* to reinflate (*balloon*); to blow up, to pump up (*tyre*); *F* to put new life into (*s.o.*). **2** *vi* (*of river*) to swell, to rise (again).

regorger [rəgɔrʒe] *vi* **(je regorgeai(s); n. regorgeons)** to abound **(de,** in**)**; **les trains regorgent de gens,** the trains are packed (with people); **les rues regorgeaient de monde,** the streets were teeming *or* swarming with people; **sa maison regorge de livres,** his house is cram full of books; **elle regorge de santé,** she is bursting with health.

regratter [rəgrate] *vt Constr* to scrape, to rub down (*wall*).

regreffer [rəgrefe] *vt* to regraft.

régresser [regrese] *vi* **(a)** to regress; to diminish (*in intensity*); **la gauche regresse,** the Left is losing ground; **(b)** *Psy* to regress.

régressif, -ive [regresif, -iv] *adj* regressive; *Biol* **forme régressive,** throwback; *Géol* **érosion régressive,** headwater erosion.

régression [regresjɔ̃] *nf* **(a)** regression; **r. marine,** recession of sea (*from the coast*); *Math* **coefficient de r.,** regression coefficient; **(b)** *Biol* retrogression; *Psy* regression; **(c)** decline (*in business*); drop (*in sales*); **épidémie en r.,** epidemic on the decline.

regret [rəgrɛ] *nm* **(a)** regret **(de,** for**)**; **exprimer le r. de ne pouvoir être présent,** to express regret at not being able to be present; **avoir du r.,** to feel regret, to be sorry; **avoir r. de qch/d'avoir fait qch,** to regret sth/having done sth; **j'ai r. à vous quitter,** I am sorry to leave you; **j'ai le r.** *ou* **je suis au r. de vous annoncer que ...,** I regret *or* am sorry to inform you that ...; **j'en suis au r.,** I am sorry; **faire qch à r.,** to do sth with regret *or* regretfully *or* reluctantly; **à mon (grand) r.,** (much) to my regret; *F* **sans r.?,** (you have) no regrets?, you're quite happy about it?; *F* **tous mes regrets!,** sorry!, my apologies!; **(b) le r. de la patrie,** homesickness; **mourir sans laisser de regrets,** to die unlamented.

regrettable [rəgrɛtabl] *adj* regrettable, unfortunate (*mistake etc*).

regrettablement [rəgrɛtabləmɑ̃] *adv* regrettably.

regretter [rəgrete] *vt* **(a)** to regret (*sth*); **r. d'avoir fait qch,** to regret *or* be sorry for having done sth; **je regrette qu'elle soit parti si tôt,** I am sorry that she left so early, I wish she hadn't left so early; **tu ne le regretteras pas!,** you won't regret it; **vous le regretterez,** you'll regret it, you'll be sorry (for it); **je regrette!,** (I'm) sorry!; **(b)** to miss (*s.o., sth*); **r. un absent,** to miss an absent friend; **mourir regretté de tous,** to die regretted by all; **il sera regretté de tous,** he'll be greatly missed; **r. Paris,** to miss Paris; **r. son argent,** to wish one had one's money back.

regrèvement [regrɛvmɑ̃] *nm* increase in tax(ation).

regrimper [rəgrɛ̃pe] **1** *vt* to climb (up) again; **r. l'escalier,** to climb the stairs again. **2** *vi* to climb up again; **r. à l'arbre,** to climb the tree again.

regrossir [rəgrosir] *vi* to put on weight again.

regroupement [rəgrupmɑ̃] *nm* regrouping; **r. de plusieurs sociétés,** amalgamation of several companies; **r. parcellaire,** consolidation (*of land holdings*).

regrouper [rəgrupe] **1** *vt* to rally (*people*); *Mil* to regroup (*men*); to amalgamate (*companies*); **les dernières œuvres de Dali ont été regroupées,** (*pour cette exposition*) Dali's last paintings have been brought together. **2 se regrouper** *vpr* (*of people*) to rally; *Mil* (*of men*) to regroup; (*of companies*) to amalgamate.

régularisation [regylarizɑsjɔ̃] *nf* **(a)** (*de litige*) regularization, regularizing; (*des papiers*) putting in order; **ses papiers sont en voie de r.,** his papers are (in the process of) being put in order; **(b)** regulation, regulating (*of river, mechanism*); **r. de la circulation,** traffic control.

régulariser [regylarize] *vt* **(a)** to regularize, to make regular; to put (*document*) into proper form; to put (*papers*) in order; **r. la pente d'une route,** to grade a road; **r. une situation,** to regularize a situation; **(b)** to regulate (*the running of a machine*); **r. un fleuve,** to regulate the flow of a river; **r. la circulation,** to regulate *or* control the traffic.

régularité [regylarite] *nf* **(a)** regularity (*of features, shape, habits*); steadiness, evenness, regularity (*of motion*); **épreuve de r.,** reliability trial; **(b)** (*ponctualité*) punctuality; **avec une r. d'horloge,** as regular as clockwork.

régulateur, -trice [regylatœr, -tris] **1** *adj* regulating (*force, mechanism*); **soupape régulatrice,** governor valve. **2** *nm* **(a)** *Tech* regulator; regulator, governor, balance wheel (*of clock*); regulator, governor (*of steam engine, turbine*); throttle valve (*of steam engine*); *Nau* governor (*of log*); **r. de marge,** margin stop; *Th* **r. d'éclairage de scène,** stage dimmer; **(b)** *Rail* controller, *Am* dispatcher; dispatcher (*of taxis*); *Nau* guide (*of the fleet*); **r. aérien,** air traffic controller.

régulation [regylɑsjɔ̃] *nf* **(a)** regulation, readjustment (*of compass*); **(b)** (*contrôle*) control, regulation; **r. des naissances,** birth control; **r. de la circulation,** traffic control; *MecE* **dispositif** *ou* **système de r. (du carburant/de la pression** *etc***),** (fuel/pressure *etc*) control system; *Él* **r. de la tension,** voltage regulation.

régulier, -ière [regylje, -jɛr] **1** *adj* **(a)** regular (*features, polygon*); **quittance régulière,** receipt in due form, proper receipt; *Gram* **verbe r.,** regular verb; **ce n'est pas r.,** that's not according to the rules; **(b)** steady (*pulse, increase*); even (*motion*); regular (*bus service*); steady, ordered (*life*); steady (*work, worker*); **des coups réguliers,** regular *or* steady blows; **être r. dans ses habitudes,** to be regular in one's habits; **humeur régulière,** even temper; **(c)** regular (*priest, soldier*); **troupes régulières,** regular troops, regulars. **2** *n* regular (customer); **un r. du bar,** a regular (at the bar).

régulièrement [regyljɛrmɑ̃] *adv* **(a)** (*uniformément*) regularly; (*respirer*) steadily, evenly; **je la vois r.,** I see her regularly *or* at regular intervals; **(b)** (*selon la loi*) regularly, in accordance with the regulations; **membres r. désignés,** properly elected members.

régurgitation [regyrʒitɑsjɔ̃] *nf* regurgitation.

régurgiter [regyrʒite] *vt* to regurgitate (*food*).

réhabilitation [reabilitɑsjɔ̃] *nf* **(a)** rehabilitation (*of delinquent, invalid etc*); discharge (*of bankrupt*); re-establishment (*of reputation*); **(b)** rehabilitation (*of slum district*).

réhabilité, -ée [reabilite] *n* rehabilitated person; *Fin* discharged bankrupt.

réhabiliter [reabilite] **1** *vt* **(a)** to rehabilitate (*a delinquent, an invalid, a politician*); to clear (*s.o., s.o.'s good name*); to discharge (*bankrupt*); **r. qn dans ses droits,** to reinstate s.o. in his rights; **(b)** to renovate (*old building*); to rehabilitate (*slum district*). **2 se réhabiliter** *vpr* to rehabilitate oneself, to re-establish one's good name.

réhabituer [reabitɥe] **1** *vt* to reaccustom (**à,** to); **r. qn à faire qch,** to get s.o. used *or* accustomed to doing sth again. **2 se réhabituer** *vpr* **se r. à faire qch,** to get used *or* accustomed to doing sth again.

rehaussement [rəosmɑ̃] *nm* raising, heightening (*of wall, of picture on wall etc*); **r. fiscal,** tax increase.

rehausser [rəose] *vt* **(a)** to raise, to heighten (*wall etc*); to make (*sth*) higher; **(b)** to enhance, to set off (*colour, complexion*); **r. une veste de jalons,** to liven up *or* brighten up a jacket with braid; **r. un détail,** to accentuate a detail.

rehaut [rəo] *nm Beaux-Arts* touch-up (*to a picture*); **les rehauts,** the highlights.

réimperméabiliser [reɛ̃pɛrmeabilize] *vt* to reproof (*raincoat*).

réimplantation [reɛ̃plɑ̃tɑsjɔ̃] *nf Chir* reimplantation.

réimplanter [reɛ̃plɑ̃te] *vt Chir* to reimplant.

réimportation [reɛ̃pɔrtɑsjɔ̃] *nf* **(a)** reimportation; **(b)** (*marchandise*) reimport.

réimporter [reɛ̃pɔrte] *vt* to reimport.

réimposer [reɛ̃poze] *vt* **(a)** to tax (*s.o.*) again; to reimpose (*tax*); **(b)** *Typ* to reimpose.

réimposition [reɛ̃pozisjɔ̃] *nf* **(a)** further taxation; reimposition (*of tax*); **(b)** *Typ* reimposition.

réimpression [reɛ̃presjɔ̃] *nf* **(a)** (*action*) reprinting; **(b)** (*livre etc*) reprint.

réimprimer [reɛ̃prime] *vt* to reprint.

Reims [rɛ̃s] *nm* Rheims.

rein [rɛ̃] *nm* **(a)** *Anat* kidney; **r. artificiel,** kidney *or* dialysis machine; **(b) reins,** back; **la chute** *ou* **le creux des reins,** the small of the back; **douleur** *ou* **mal aux reins,** backache; *Fig* **casser les reins à qn,** to ruin s.o.; *Fig* **il a les reins solides,** he's tough; *F* **se faire un tour de reins,** to rick one's back.

réincarcération [reɛ̃karserɑsjɔ̃] *nf* reimprisonment, *Fml* reincarceration.

réincarcérer [reɛ̃karsere] *vt* to reimprison, *Fml* to reincarcerate.

réincarnation [reɛ̃karnɑsjɔ̃] *nf* reincarnation.

réincarner (se) [səreɛ̃karne] *vpr* to be reincarnated (**en qch/qn,** as sth/s.o.).

réincorporer [reɛ̃kɔrpɔre] *vt* to reincorporate.

reine [rɛn] *nf* **(a)** queen; **elle a un port** *ou* **un maintien de r.,** she has a queenly *or* regal bearing; **la r. Anne,** Queen Anne; **r. mère,** queen mother; *F* (*belle-mère*) mother-in-law; **(b)** (*abeille*) queen (bee); **(c)** *Échecs* queen; **(d) r. de beauté,** beauty queen; **la r. du bal,** the belle of the ball.

reine-claude [rɛnklod] *nf* greengage; (*pl reines-claudes*).

reine-des-prés [rɛndepre] *nf Bot* meadowsweet; (*pl reines-des-prés*).

reine-marguerite [rɛnmargərit] *nf Bot* China aster; (*pl reines-marguerites*).

reinette [rɛnɛt] *nf* pippin; **r. grise,** russet.

réinfection [reɛ̃fɛksjɔ̃] *nf* reinfection.

réinfecter [reɛ̃fɛkte] *vt* to reinfect.

réinjecter [reɛ̃ʒɛkte] *vt* to reinject, to make a fresh injection of (*money*).

réinscrire [reɛ̃skrir] *vt* (*conj like* **inscrire**) to re-register.

réinsérer [reɛ̃sere] **1** *vt* to reintegrate. **2 se réinsérer** *vpr* to be reintegrated.

réinsertion [reɛ̃sɛrsjɔ̃] *nf* reintegration; **r. sociale,** rehabilitation.

réinstaller [reɛ̃stale] **1** *vt* to reinstall, to reinstate. **2 se réinstaller** *vpr* **il s'est réinstallé à Reims,** he has moved to Rheims.

réintégration [reɛ̃tegrɑsjɔ̃] *nf* **(a)** reinstatement (*of official etc*); restoration (*of area*); **r. des démobilisés dans la vie civile,** rehabilitation of ex-servicemen; **(b) r. de domicile,** resumption of residence; *Jur* **r. du domicile conjugal,** restitution of conjugal rights.

réintégrer [reɛ̃tegre] *vt* (*conj like* **intégrer**) **(a) r. qn (dans ses fonctions),** to reinstate s.o., to restore s.o. to his position *or* office; **(b) r. son domicile,** to resume possession of one's domicile, to return to one's home.

réintroduction [reɛ̃trɔdyksjɔ̃] *nf* reintroduction.

réintroduire [reɛ̃trɔdɥir] *vt* (*conj like* **introduire**) to reintroduce.

réitératif, -ive [reiteratif, -iv] *adj* reiterative.

réitération [reiterɑsjɔ̃] *nf* reiteration.

réitérer [reitere] *vt* (**je réitère, n. réitérons; je réitérerai**) to reiterate, to repeat.

reître [rɛtr] *nm Litt* ruffianly soldier.

rejaillir [rəʒajir] *vi* **(a)** to gush out, to spurt *or* splash up *or* out, to spout; **(b)** *Fig* **sa honte a rejailli sur nous,** his disgrace rebounded on us; **tout ceci rejaillit sur moi,** it all reflects on me.

rejaillissement [rəʒajismɑ̃] *nm* **(a)** springing (up), gushing (out), spurting (up, out), splashing, spouting (*of liquid*); **(b)** *Fig* reflection (*of glory*).

rejet [rəʒɛ] *nm* **(a)** (*action*) throwing out, throwing up; (*terre*) spoil (earth); *Géol* throw (*of fault*); *Géol* **r. horizontal,** heave; **(b)** rejection (*of proposal, Méd of transplant*); setting aside (*of claim*); dismissal (*of claim, an appeal*); *Fig F* **faire un r. sur l'école/les sports/***etc*, to hate school/sports/*etc*; **(c)** (*de plante*) shoot; **(d)** (*en poésie*) enjambment.

rejeter [rəʒte] *v* (*conj like* **jeter**) **1** *vt* **(a)** to throw again; **r. un poisson à l'eau,** to throw a fish back; **elle rejette ses cheveux en arrière,** she wears her hair back; **r. son chapeau en arrière,** to tilt one's hat back; *Fig* **r. le blâme sur d'autres,** to shift the blame on to others, to put *or* lay the blame on others;

(b) (*ne pas admettre*) to reject (*s.o., sth*); to reject, to dismiss, to turn down (*an offer*); to disallow (*an expense*); **elle croit qu'on la rejette,** she feels rejected; *Méd* **r. une greffe,** to reject a transplant; **elle a rejeté la nourriture,** her stomach rejected the food, she couldn't keep the food down; **r. un projet de loi,** to reject *or* throw out a bill; *Jur* **r. un pourvoi,** to dismiss an appeal; *Tricot* **r. les mailles,** to cast off.

2 se rejeter *vpr* to fall back (**sur,** on); **se r. sur les circonstances,** to lay the blame on circumstances; **se r. en arrière,** to leap *or* spring back(wards); (*of horse*) to shy.

rejeton [rəʒtɔ̃] *nm* **(a)** (*de plante*) shoot, sucker; **(b)** *F* offspring (*of family*); **il avait emmené ses rejetons avec lui,** he had brought his offspring (with him).

rejoindre [rəʒwɛ̃dr] *v* (*conj like* **joindre**) **1** *vt* **(a)** to rejoin, to reunite, to join (together) again; to connect (*streets, rivers etc*); **sa pensée rejoint la mienne,** his ideas are akin to mine; **cela rejoint ce que je disais tout à l'heure,** that fits in with what I was saying just now; **(b) r. qn,** to join s.o.; (*avec un effort*) to catch s.o. up; **je vous rejoindrai plus tard,** I'll meet *or* join you later; **r. son régiment,** to (re)join one's regiment; **il a évité de r. la grande route,** he avoided (joining) the main road. **2 se rejoindre** *vpr* to meet; **les droites se rejoignent au point P,** the straight lines meet at the point P; **on se rejoindra ce soir,** we'll meet up this evening.

rejointoyer [rəʒwɛ̃twaje] *vt* (*conj like* **jointoyer**) *Constr* to (re)joint, to (re)point (*walls*).

rejouer [rəʒwe] **1** *vt* to replay (*match*); to play (*piece of music*) again. **2** *vi Cartes* to play again.

réjoui [reʒwi] *adj* jolly, cheerful, merry.

réjouir [reʒwir] **1** *vt* to delight, to gladden, to cheer (*s.o.*); **cela me réjouit le cœur de l'entendre,** it does my heart good *or* it makes my heart glad to hear it; **r. l'œil,** to delight the eye. **2 se réjouir** *vpr* **(a)** to rejoice (**de,** at, in); to be glad (**de,** of), to be delighted (**de,** at); **je me réjouis de le revoir,** I am delighted to see him again; **il faut se r. que tout se passe bien,** we can be glad that everything is going well; **(b)** *Vieilli* (*s'amuser*) to enjoy oneself.

réjouissance [reʒwisɑ̃s] *nf* rejoicing; **réjouissances publiques,** public festivities; **le programme des réjouissances,** the programme of festivities; *Iron* the list of treats in store.

réjouissant [reʒwisɑ̃] *adj* cheering, heartening (*news, prospect etc*); **cela n'a rien de r.,** it's a gloomy prospect.

relâche [rəlɑʃ] **1** *nm* **(a)** (*arrêt*) respite, rest; **travailler sans r.,** to work without respite *or* without a break; **elle le répète sans r.,** she repeats it continually; **prendre un peu de r., se donner r.,** to have a rest; *Th* **il y a r. ce soir,** there is no performance this evening; *Th* **faire r.,** to be closed; *Th* **r.,** (*sur panneau*) closed; **(b)** slackening, loosening (*of rope*). **2** *nf Nau* (*arrêt*) call; (*port*) port of call; **faire r. dans un port,** to call at *or* put into a port.

relâché [rəlɑʃe] *adj* slack, loose (*rope*); loose, lax (*morals, conduct*).

relâchement [rəlɑʃmɑ̃] *nm* **(a)** slackening, loosening (*of rope*); relaxation, falling off (*of discipline*); looseness, laxity (*of morals*); **le r. de l'attention des élèves,** the wavering of the pupils' attention; **(b)** release (*of prisoner*).

relâcher [rəlɑʃe] **1** *vt* **(a)** to loosen, to slacken (*rope etc*); to relax (*muscle*); to loosen (*the bowels*); to relax (*discipline, morals*); **j'ai relâché mon attention pendant un instant,** my attention slackened *or* wavered for a moment; **(b)** to release, to let go (*prisoner, caged bird*); *Fig* **je vous relâche,** I'll let you get along *or* go. **2** *vi Nau* to put into port. **3 se relâcher** *vpr* (*of rope*) to slacken; (*of shoelace*) to come loose *or* undone; (*of worker*) to become slack; (*of zeal*) to flag, to fall off; (*of morals*) to grow lax; **son attention se relâche,** his attention slackens *or* wavers; **cet élève s'est complètement relâché,** this pupil has completely slacked off; **se r. dans son travail,** to slacken *or* ease off.

relais¹ *nm* **(a)** shift (*of workmen*); relay (*of post horses, runners, hounds*); **ouvriers de r.,** shift workers; **travail sans r.,** unrelieved (spell of) work; **ville-r.,** stopover (town); *Sp* **course de r.,** relay race; **prendre le r.,** to take over (**de qn,** from s.o.); **l'homéopathie prend le r. de la médecine traditionnelle,** homeopathy is taking over from traditional medicine; **ce poste lui a servi de r. pour se présenter aux élections,** this position was a springboard for him in his bid for office; **chevaux de r.,** post horses;

(b) (*auberge*) coaching inn, post house; **r. gastronomique,** restaurant with a reputation for good food; *Aut* **r. routier,** service station (with café); **prochain r. routier: 10 km,** (*sur panneau*) ≈ *Br* services: 5 miles;

(c) *MecE etc* relay (unit); *Él* relay; *Rad* **r. de radiodiffusion,** relay broadcasting station; **r. de télévision,** television relay station.

relais² [rəlɛ] *nm* (*vase*) silt, warp; sandbank (*along river*); sand flats (*along shore*).

relance [rəlɑ̃s] *nf* **(a)** fresh start; revival (*of economy etc*); **plan de r.,** recovery plan; **r. de la natalité,** upturn in the birth rate; **(b)** *Com* following up (*of customer*); **lettre de r.,** follow-up letter; **(c)** *Cartes* raise; **poker sans maximum de r.,** poker with no ceiling.

relancement [rəlɑ̃smɑ̃] *nm* **(a)** throwing again; relaunch (*of spacecraft*); **(b)** restarting (*of machine etc*); boosting (*of production etc*).

relancer [rəlɑ̃se] *v* (*conj like* **lancer**) **1** *vt* **(a)** to throw (*sth*) again; (*pour rendre*) to throw (*sth*) back; *Tennis* to return (*the ball*); **(b)** to boost (*trade*); to restart (*engine*); to start (*quarry*) again; **r. un projet,** to relaunch a project; **(c)** to give (*s.o.*) a reminder; (*harasser*) to badger (*s.o.*); to harass (*debtor*). **2** *vi Cartes etc* to increase the stake, to raise the bid.

relanceur, -euse [rəlɑ̃sœr, -øz] *n Tennis* person receiving the service; **avantage au r.,** (*qui s'appelle Dupont*) advantage Dupont.

relaps, -e [rəlaps] *adj & n* relapsed (heretic).

rélargir [relarʒir] *vt* to widen (*sth*), to make (*sth*) wider.

relater [rəlate] *vt* to relate, to state (*facts*).

relatif, -ive [rəlatif, -iv] **1** *adj* relative (*position, value, Gram pronoun, clause*); **avoir la majorité relative,** to have a relative majority; *Mus* **tons relatifs,** related keys; **questions relatives à un sujet,** questions related to *or* connected with a subject; **vivre dans un luxe r.,** to live in comparative luxury; **tout est r.,** everything is relative. **2** *nm* **(a)** *Gram* relative pronoun; **(b) le r.,** the relative.

relation [rəlasjɔ̃] *nf* **(a)** relation; **les relations humaines,** human relations; **nos relations avec la Hollande,** our relations with Holland; **entamer des relations, se mettre** *ou* **entrer en relation(s) avec qn,** to enter into a relationship with s.o.; **avoir** *ou* **entretenir des relations avec qn,** to be in touch *or* to have dealings with s.o.; **être en r. avec qn,** to be in touch *or Fml* in communication with s.o.; **je vais les mettre en r.,** I'll put them in touch (with each other); **être en relation(s) d'amitié avec qn,** to be on friendly terms with s.o.; **nos relations sont très chaleureuses,** we are on very good terms (with one another); **elle a de mauvaises relations avec lui,** she is not on good terms with him; **des relations épistolaires,** correspondence; **relations d'affaires,** business dealings; **entretenir des relations de bon voisinage avec les pays d'Europe/sa belle-famille,** to be on neighbourly *or* good terms with European countries/on good terms with one's in-laws; **elle a relations,** she is well connected, she has influential friends; **c'est une r. de travail,** he's a colleague; **faire jouer ses relations,** to pull strings; *Pol* **cesser ses relations,** to break off relations (**avec,** with); **cesser ses relations avec qn,** to drop s.o.'s acquaintance; **relations publiques,** public relations; **il travaille dans les relations publiques,** he works in *or* he's in public relations; **elle est chargée des relations publiques,** she's in charge of public relations; *Pol* **encourager les relations internationales,** to encourage international relations; **les relations culturelles/diplomatiques,** cultural/diplomatic relations; **r. entre la cause et l'effet, r. de cause à effet,** relationship *or* connection between cause and effect; **r. étroite entre deux faits,** close relationship *or* connection between two facts; **c'est sans r. avec le sujet,** it bears no relation to the subject; *Rail* **r. entre Paris et Lille,** service between Paris and Lille; *Anat* **relations de deux organes,** relative positions of two organs;

(b) (*récit*) account, report, narrative, statement; **faire la r. de qch,** to give an account of sth.

relationnel, -elle [rəlasjɔnɛl] *adj* relational; *Ordinat* **base de données relationnelles,** relational data base.

relativement [rəlativmɑ̃] *adv* **(a)** (*d'une façon relative*) relatively; **c'est r. fréquent,** it is relatively frequent; **(b)** (*en relation*) in relation (**à,** to); **(c)** (*en comparaison*) comparatively.

relativiser [rəlativize] *vt* to relativize.

relativisme [rəlativism] *nm* relativism.

relativiste [rəlativist] *adj & n* relativist.

relativité [rəlativite] *nf* relativity.

relaver [rəlave] *vt* to wash (*sth*) again.

relax [rəlaks] **1** *adj* laid back, relaxed; **elle est très r.** *ou* **relaxe,** she's very laid back *or* relaxed; **fauteuil-r.,** reclining chair; **baby-r.,** baby chair. **2** *nm* relaxation.

relaxant [rəlaksɑ̃] *adj* relaxing; **bain r. (aux plantes),** herbal foam bath.

relaxation [rəlaksɑsjɔ̃] *nf* relaxation.

relaxe¹ [rəlaks] *nf* release, discharge (*of accused person*).

relaxe² *adj* **fauteuil r.,** reclining chair.

relaxer [rəlakse] **1** *vt* **(a)** to relax; **(b)** *Jur* to release, to discharge (*prisoner*). **2 se relaxer** *vpr* to relax.

relayer [rəleje] *v* (**je relaie, je relaye, n. relayons; je relaierai, je relayerai**) **1** *vt* **(a)** to relay, to relieve, to take turns with, to change with (*s.o.*); to take over from (*s.o.*); **je te relaierai à 8 heures,** I'll take over (from you) at 8 o'clock, I'll relieve you at 8 o'clock; **(b)** *TV Rad* to relay (*broadcast*). **2** *vi Arch* to relay, to change horses.

relayeur, -euse [rəlejœr, -øz] *n Sp* relay runner.

relecture [rəlɛktyr] *nf* (*d'épreuves*) proofreading; (*d'un livre*) re-reading; **la r. de Stendhal m'a pris deux mois,** it took me two months to re-read Stendhal.

relégation [rəlegɑsjɔ̃] *nf Jur* transportation.

reléguer [rəlege] *vt* (*conj like* **léguer**) **(a)** *Sp* to relegate (*team*); **r. un tableau au grenier,** to relegate *or* consign a picture to the attic; **se trouver relégué au second plan,** to find oneself relegated to *or* pushed into the background; **(b)** to transport (*convict*).

relent [rəlɑ̃] *nm* (*odeur*) musty *or* unpleasant *or* stale smell; (*goût*) musty taste; *Fig* **un r. de scandale entoure ce politicien,** there is a whiff of scandal about this politician.

relevable [rəlvabl] *adj* adjustable (*for height*); hinged (*counter flap etc*); *Av* **train d'atterrissage r.,** retractable undercarriage; **accoudoir r.,** folding armrest.

relevage [rəlvaʒ] *nm* raising, lifting; **dispositif de r.,** luffing gear (*of crane*).

relevailles [rəlvaj] *nfpl Vieilli* churching (*of woman after childbirth*); **faire ses r.,** to be churched.

relève [rəlɛv] *nf* **(a)** (*action*) *Mil* relief (*of troops, sentry*); changing (*Mil of the guard, Ind of shift*); **troupes de r., la r.,** relieving troops; **prendre la r. de qn,** to relieve s.o., to take over from s.o.; *Fig* **prendre la r.,** to take over; **(b)** (*de personnel*) relief (driver *etc*).

relevé [rəlve] **1** *adj* **(a)** raised, erect (*head etc*); turned up (*collar, sleeve*); **chapeau r.,** off-the-face hat; **pantalon à bords relevés,** turn-up trousers, turn-ups, *Am* pants with cuffs; **(b)** exalted, high (*position*); noble (*sentiment*); lofty (*style*); **(c)** highly-seasoned (*sauce*). **2** *nm* **(a)** abstract, summary, account, statement; **r. d'identité bancaire,** = document giving details of one's bank account; **r. de consommation (du gaz),** meter reading; **r. des naissances,** table *or* summary of births; **r. de compte,** bank statement; **(b)** (*en topographie*) survey; **faire le r. d'un terrain,** to plot a piece of land.

relèvement [rəlɛvmɑ̃] *nm* **(a)** (*action*) raising up, setting up again (*of fallen object*); raising, heightening (*of picture, wall*); recovery, revival (*of business*); increase (*in wages*); raising (*of tariff, tax*); **(b)** *Com* statement; **(c)** (*de terrain*) *&* *Nau* position; bearing (*by compass*); **r. radio(goniométrique),** radio bearing *or* *F* fix; **faire** *ou* **prendre un r.,** to take a bearing, to take bearings.

relever [rəlve] *v* (*conj like* **lever**) **1** *vt* **(a)** to raise *or* lift (*sth*) up again, to right (*sth*); to set (*s.o.*) on his feet again, to pick s.o. up; to right (*a ship*); (*ramasser*) to pick up (*from the ground*); (*reconstruire*) to rebuild (*wall*); *Fig* **r. le gant,** to take up the gauntlet *or* challenge, to accept the challenge; **r. le défi,** to take up *or* accept the challenge; *Scol* **r. les compositions,** to take in *or* collect the essays;

(b) (*plus haut*) to raise, to heighten (*sth*); to turn up (*one's collar*); to tuck up, to roll up (*one's sleeves*); *Tricot* to pick up (*stitch*); to raise, to refloat (*sunken ship*); **r. ses cheveux,** to put one's hair up; **r. sa voilette,** to lift *or* raise one's veil; **r. les yeux,** to raise one's eyes; **r. la tête,** to look up, to raise one's head; *Fig* to hold up one's head (again); **r. les salaires/les prix,** to raise *or* increase wages/prices; **r. les espérances,** to raise *or* revive hopes; **r. la fortune de qn,** to restore s.o.'s fortune; **r. l'économie,** to revive the economy; **r. le niveau de vie,** to raise the standard of living;

(c) (*signaler*) to call attention to (*sth*), to point (*sth*) out; to challenge (*statement*); **on n'a relevé aucune preuve contre elle,** no evidence has been found against her;

(d) (*mettre en valeur*) to throw (*sth*) into relief; to enhance, to heighten, to set off (*colour etc*); to season, to add condiments to (*sauce*); to enliven, to liven up (*story*);

(e) (*remplacer*) to relieve (*troops, a sentry*); **r. qn,** to take s.o.'s place, to take over (from s.o.);

(f) (*libérer*) **r. qn d'un vœu,** to release s.o. from a vow; **r. qn de ses fonctions,** to relieve s.o. of his office, to dismiss s.o.;

(g) (*noter*) to note, to record (*temperature*); to take down (*statement etc*); to make out (*account*); to read (*meter*); **r. le gaz,** to read the gas meter; **r. des empreintes digitales,** to take fingerprints;

(h) *Nau* to take the bearings of (*a place*); *Nau* to sight (*land*); (*d'un arpenteur*) to survey, to plot (*piece of land*); *Math* to plot (*graph*).

2 *vi* **(a) r. de maladie,** to be recovering from an illness; **(b) r. de qn,** to be answerable *or* responsible to s.o.; **cette affaire ne relève pas de nous,** this matter is not our responsibility; **r. de l'article 7,** to come under article 7; **son cas relève de la folie,** he must be mad.

3 se relever *vpr* **(a)** to rise to one's feet (again); (*après avoir été à genoux*) to get up from one's knees; (*d'un navire*) to right itself; **l'accoudoir se relève,** the armrest lifts up;

(b) (*of trade, courage*) to revive, to recover; **se r. de qch,** to recover from sth; **le pays doit se r. de 20 ans de gestion anarchiste,** the country has to recover from 20 years of anarchist rule; **il ne s'en relèvera pas,** he will never get over it.

releveur, -euse [rəlvœr, -øz] **1** *adj & nm Anat* **(muscle) r.,** levator (muscle). **2** *n* (*personne*) meter reader.

relief [rəljɛf] *nm* **(a)** *Beaux-Arts Archit* relief, *Spéc* relievo; *Géog* relief; **carte en r.,** relief *or* raised map; **cinéma/photographie en r.,** stereoscopic cinema/photography; *Fig* **mettre en r., donner du r. à,** to throw (*sth*) into relief; to bring out (*contrast*); to set off (*beauty*); **style sans r.,** flat style; **position très en r.,** prominent position; **(b)** *Vieilli* **reliefs,** remains (*of meal*).

relier [rəlje] *vt* (*impf & pr sub* **n. reliions**) **(a)** (*attacher*) to tie together; **(b)** (*joindre*) to connect, to link, to join (*objects, points, persons etc*); **r. les bords d'une brèche,** to bridge a gap; **(c)** to bind (*book*); **r. un livre de nouveau,** to rebind a book; **relié en veau,** bound in calf; **(d)** to hoop (*cask*).

relieur, -euse [rəljœr, -øz] *n* (book)binder.

religieusement [rəliʒjøzmɑ̃] *adv* **(a)** (*avec attention*) religiously; **(b)** (*selon la religion*) piously, religiously; **se marier r.,** to get married in church; **(c)** (*scrupuleusement*) scrupulously.

religieux, -euse [rəliʒjø, -øz] **1** *adj* religious; sacred (*music, art*); devotional (*books*); **mariage r.,** church wedding; **communauté religieuse,** religious community; **soin r.,** religious *or* scrupulous care; **silence r.,** respectful silence. **2** *nm* (*moine*) monk, friar. **3** *nf* **religieuse (a)** (*nonne*) nun; **(b)** (*gâteau*) cream puff.

religion [rəliʒjɔ̃] *nf* **(a)** religion; **avoir de la r.,** to be religious; **mourir en r.,** to die in the faith; **entrer en r.,** to take one's vows; **minorités de r.,** religious minorities; **la r. chrétienne/juive/buddhiste,** the Christian/Jewish/Buddhist religion *or* faith; **(b)** *Fig* **se faire une r. de qch,** to make a religion of sth, to make sth a point of conscience; **la r. du serment,** the sanctity of the oath.

religiosité [rəliʒjozite] *nf* religiosity.

reliquaire [rəlikɛr] *nm* reliquary, shrine.

reliquat [rəlika] *nm* **(a)** (*reste*) remainder (*of sum of money etc*); balance (*of an account*); **(b)** *Méd* aftereffects (*of an illness*).

relique [rəlik] *nf* relic (*of saint*); **garder qch comme une r.,** to treasure sth; **les reliques de sa gloire,** the relics *or* remnants of his glory.

relire [rəlir] *v* (*conj like* **lire**) **1** *vt* to re-read, to read (over) again. **2 se relire** *vpr* to read (over) what one has written.

reliure [rəljyr] *nf* **(a)** (*activité, art*) bookbinding; **atelier de r.,** bindery; **donner un livre à la r.,** to send a book for binding *or* to be bound; **(b)** (*couverture*) **r. anglaise** *ou* **en toile,** cloth binding; **r. pleine,** full leather binding.

relogement [rəlɔʒmɑ̃] *nm* rehousing.

reloger [rəlɔʒe] *vt* (*conj like* **loger**) to rehouse.

relouer [rəlue] *vt* **(a)** (*donner en location*) to rent (out) again, *Br* to relet, to let (out) again (*house etc*) (**à,** to); **(b)** (*prendre en location*) to rent again (*house etc*).

reluire [rəlɥir] *vi* (*conj like* **luire**) to shine, to glitter, to gleam; **faire r. qch,** to polish *or* shine sth up; **brosse à r.,** shoebrush; *Fig F* **manier la brosse à r.,** to do some soft-soaping *or* buttering-up; *Prov* **tout ce qui reluit n'est pas or,** all that glitters is not gold.

reluisant [rəlɥizɑ̃] *adj* shining, gleaming, glossy; **visage r.**

de propreté, scrubbed and shining face; *Fig F* **cela n'est pas très r.**, it's not all that wonderful; **c'est une perspective peu reluisante,** it's hardly a glowing prospect.

reluquer [rəlyke] *vt F* to eye (*stranger, s.o.'s fortune etc*); **r. les filles,** to eye (up) *or* ogle the girls.

rem [rɛm] *nm* (*abrév* **Roentgen Equivalent Man**) rem.

remâcher [rəmɑʃe] *vt* **(a)** to chew again; **(b)** *Fig* to ruminate on (*sth*), to turn (*sth*) over in one's mind, to brood over (*sth*).

remailler [rəmaje] *vt* to mend (the meshes of), to re-mesh (*net*); to darn, to mend a run *or Br* ladder in (*stocking*); to darn (*sweater etc*).

remake [rimek] *nm* (*de disque*) *& Cin* remake; *Cin* **faire un r.**, to do a remake.

rémanence [remanɑ̃s] *nf* remanence, residual magnetism; *Opt* **r. des images visuelles,** persistence of vision.

rémanent [remanɑ̃] *adj* (*en magnétisme*) *& Él* residual, remanent; *Opt* persistent (*image*).

remanger [rəmɑ̃ʒe] *vt* (*conj like* **manger**) to eat again; **j'en ai remangé,** I had some more; **je n'en ai jamais remangé,** I've never eaten any since *or* again.

remaniement [rəmanimɑ̃] *nm* **(a)** (*action*) altering, reshaping; **(b)** (*changement*) alteration, modification, change; **apporter des remaniements à un ouvrage,** to make changes to a work; *Pol* **r. ministériel,** cabinet reshuffle.

remanier [rəmanje] *vt* (*impf & pr sub* **n. remaniions**) to alter, to change (*literary work, speech etc*); to make changes in (*team*); *Pol* to reshuffle (*cabinet*).

remaquiller [rəmakije] **1** *vt* **r. qn,** to make s.o. up again. **2 se remaquiller** *vpr* (*de nouveau*) to make oneself up again; (*en retouchant*) to touch up one's make-up.

remarcher [rəmarʃe] *vi* **(a)** (*of person*) to walk again; **(b)** (*of machine etc*) to work again.

remariage [rəmarjaʒ] *nm* remarriage.

remarier [rəmarje] **1** *vt* to marry (*one's daughter*) again. **2 se remarier** *vpr* to remarry, to marry again.

remarquable [rəmarkabl] *adj* **(a)** remarkable, noteworthy (*event, book etc*) (**par,** for); remarkable, outstanding (*person*); remarkable (*change, result*); **faits remarquables de la semaine,** highlights *or* outstanding events of the week; **d'un courage r.**, remarkably brave; **(b)** (*étrange*) strange, astonishing; **il est r. qu'il n'ait rien entendu,** it's strange *or* astonishing *or* a wonder that he heard nothing.

remarquablement [rəmarkabləmɑ̃] *adv* remarkably.

remarque [rəmark] *nf* **(a)** (*observation*) remark; **faire une r.**, to make *or* pass a remark; (*critique*) to make a critical observation *or* remark; **faire la r. de qch,** to remark on sth; **je dois lui en faire la r.**, I must remark on it to him; **digne de r.**, noteworthy; **texte avec remarques,** text with notes *or* comments; **(b)** (*sur une gravure*) inset engraving.

remarqué [rəmarke] *adj* **entrée/absence très remarquée,** conspicuous entrance/absence; **discours très r.**, speech that attracted considerable attention.

remarquer [rəmarke] **1** *vt* **(a)** (*constater*) to notice; **elle a été remarquée par un réalisateur de télévision,** she was spotted *or* noticed by a television director; **je n'ai pas remarqué son absence,** I didn't notice his absence; **faire r. qch à qn,** to point sth out to s.o., to call s.o.'s attention to sth; **je n'avais pas remarqué,** I hadn't noticed; *F* **remarque, il n'est pas le seul,** mind (you), he's not the only one; **r. qn dans la foule,** to notice s.o. in the crowd; **je remarque que personne n'en a parlé,** I notice *or* note that no-one has spoken about it; **se faire r.**, to attract attention, to get noticed; **(b)** (*dire*) to remark, to observe, to say; **(c)** to mark (*linen*) again. **2 se remarquer** *vpr* (*of stain, scar, Fig anger etc*) to be noticeable, to show.

remballage [rɑ̃balaʒ] *nm* repacking.

remballer [rɑ̃bale] *vt* to repack, to pack (*goods*) (up) again; *Fig F* **tu peux r. les compliments,** you can keep your compliments to yourself.

rembarquement [rɑ̃barkəmɑ̃] *nm* re-embarking, re-embarkation (*of passengers, troops*); reshipping, reshipment (*of goods*).

rembarquer [rɑ̃barke] **1** *vt* to re-embark (*passengers, troops*); to re-ship (*goods*); to hoist in (*boat*). **2 se rembarquer** *vpr* to re-embark, to go on board again. **3** *vi* = **2** *vpr*.

rembarrer [rɑ̃bare] *vt F* to rebuff, to snub (*s.o.*); (*mettre à sa place*) to put (*s.o.*) in his place; **se faire r.**, to be rebuffed *or* snubbed; (*mis à sa place*) to be put in one's place.

remblai [rɑ̃blɛ] *nm Constr* **(a)** (*action*) filling up, filling in (*with earth etc*); (*pour levée de terre*) embanking, banking (up); **(b)** (*terre etc*) filling (material); **(c)** (*levée de terre*) embankment, bank; **route en r.**, embanked road.

remblayage [rɑ̃blɛjaʒ] *nm* = **REMBLAI (a)**.

remblayer [rɑ̃bleje] *vt* (**je remblaie, je remblaye, n. remblayons; je remblaierai, je remblayerai**) *Constr* **(a)** to fill (up), to pack (*sunken part of ground*); **(b)** (*pour levée de terre*) to embank, to bank (up) (*road, railway line*).

rembobinage [rɑ̃bɔbinaʒ] *nm* (*de film etc*) rewinding.

rembobiner [rɑ̃bɔbine] *vt* to rewind (*film, typewriter ribbon, magnetic tape*).

remboîtage [rɑ̃bwataʒ] *nm* re-casing (*of book*).

remboîtement [rɑ̃bwatmɑ̃] *nm* **(a)** re-casing (*of book*); **(b)** *Chir* putting back into place, *Spéc* reduction (*of dislocated bone*).

remboîter [rɑ̃bwate] *vt* **(a)** to re-case (*book*); **(b)** to reassemble, to fit (*pieces etc*) together again; **(c)** *Chir* to put (*dislocated bone*) back into place, *Spéc* to reduce (*dislocated bone*).

rembourrage [rɑ̃buraʒ] *nm* **(a)** (*action*) stuffing, padding; **(b)** (*matériau*) stuffing *or* padding material.

rembourrer [rɑ̃bure] *vt* to stuff, to pad (*chair, mattress, cushion etc*); to pad (*shoulders of garment*); *F* **bien rembourré,** plump, well-padded (*person*).

remboursable [rɑ̃bursabl] *adj* repayable, reimbursable, refundable (*expenses*); redeemable (*annuity, bond*); repayable (*loan*).

remboursement [rɑ̃bursəmɑ̃] *nm* repayment, refunding, reimbursing (*of expenses*); redeeming, redemption (*of annuity, bond*); repayment (*of loan*); **emprunt de r.**, refunding loan; **livraison contre r.**, payment *or* cash on delivery, C.O.D..

rembourser [rɑ̃burse] **1** *vt* **(a)** to repay, to refund, to reimburse (*expenses*); to redeem, to pay off (*annuity, bond*); to repay, to pay back (*loan*); **(b) r. qn de qch,** to reimburse s.o. for sth; **puis-je être remboursé?,** (*dans un magasin etc*) can I have *or* get my money back?; **je me suis fait remboursé, on m'a remboursé,** I got my money back, I was reimbursed; *Th F* **remboursez!,** we want our money back! **2 se rembourser** *vpr* to get one's money back; **elle s'est remboursée dans la caisse,** she paid herself back out of the till.

rembrayer [rɑ̃breje] *vi Aut* to let the clutch in again; *Fig F* to start work again.

rembrunir [rɑ̃brynir] **1** *vt* **(a)** to make (*sth*) dark(er), to darken (*sth*); **(b)** *Fig* to cast a gloom over (*the company*). **2 se rembrunir** *vpr* **(a)** (*of the sky*) to cloud over, to grow dark; **(b)** *Fig* (*of person, face*) to become gloomy; (*of face*) to cloud over.

rembucher [rɑ̃byʃe] *vt* (*à la chasse*) to drive (*quarry*) to covert.

remède [rəmɛd] *nm Méd & Fig* remedy, cure (**à, pour, contre,** for); **r. de bonne femme,** old wives' remedy; **le r. est pire que le mal,** the cure is worse than the disease; **porter r. à qch,** to find a remedy *or* cure for sth; **r. héroïque,** kill-or-cure remedy; *Prov* **aux grands maux les grands remèdes,** desperate ills call for desperate remedies; **c'est sans r.**, it is past *or* beyond remedy, there's no help for it.

remédier [rəmedje] *vi* (*impf & pr sub* **n. remédiions**) **r. à,** to remedy, to put right (*mistake, situation*); to remedy, to cure (*problem*); *Méd* to cure (*disease*); **r. à l'usure,** to make good the wear and tear.

remembrement [rəmɑ̃brəmɑ̃] *nm Admin* re-allocation, regrouping (*of land*).

remembrer [rəmɑ̃bre] *vt Admin* to re-allocate, to regroup (*land*).

remémorer [rəmemɔre] **1** *vt* **r. qch à qn,** to remind s.o. of sth. **2 se remémorer** *vpr* to remember sth, to recall sth, to call sth to mind.

remerciement [rəmɛrsimɑ̃] *nm* **remerciements,** thanks; (*dans un livre*) acknowledgements; **lettre de r.**, letter of thanks; **faire ses remerciements à qn pour qch,** to thank s.o. for sth; **tous mes remerciements à vos parents,** (give) my thanks to your parents.

remercier [rəmɛrsje] *vt* (*impf & pr sub* **n. remerciions**) **(a)** (*dire merci à*) to thank (**de, pour,** for); **je vous remercie de m'avoir aidé,** thank you for helping me; **remerciez-les bien de ma part,** give them my sincere thanks; **il me remercia d'un sourire,** he smiled his thanks, he thanked me with a smile; **(non,) je vous remercie,** no thank you; **(b)** (*congédier*) to dismiss (*employee*).

remettant [rəmɛtɑ̃] *nm Fin* remitter.

remetteur, -euse [rəmɛtœr, -øz] **1** *adj* remitting (*bank etc*). **2** *n* remitter.

remettre [rəmɛtr] *v* (*conj like* **mettre**) **1** *vt* **(a)** (*replacer*) to put back (again); **r. son chapeau/son manteau,** to put one's hat/coat on again; **r. qch à sa place,** to replace sth, to put sth back in its place *or* where it belongs; *F* **r. qn à sa place,** to put s.o. in his place; *F* **je n'y ai plus jamais remis les pieds,** I never set foot in there again; **r. qn sur le trône,** to restore s.o. to the throne; *Ordinat* **r. à zéro,** to reset; *Fb* **r. le ballon en jeu,** to throw the ball (back) in(to play); *Tennis* **balle à r.,** let (ball); **r. un os,** to put a bone back in place, *Spéc* to reduce a bone; **r. qn dans son chemin/sur la bonne voie,** to set s.o. on his way again/on the right path; **r. qch en usage,** to bring sth into use again *or* back into use; **r. un manche à un balai,** to put a new handle on a broom; **r. une doublure à un habit,** to reline a coat; **r. qch en cause** *ou* **en question,** to call sth into question; **r. en état,** to repair, to mend; **r. en marche,** to restart (*engine, machine*); **il a été remis en liberté,** he was set free *or* freed *or* released; **r. une pièce au théâtre,** to put on a play again, to revive a play; **r. à la voile,** to set sail again; **on ne pourra r. l'eau/le gaz/le téléphone avant demain,** we can't connect (up) the water/gas/telephone again until tomorrow;

(b) *Fig* **r. l'esprit de qn,** to put s.o.'s mind at rest; **r. qn (sur pied),** to restore s.o. to health, to put s.o. on his feet again;

(c) to recall, to recollect; **il faut le lui r. en mémoire,** he'll have to be reminded of it; **je ne vous remets pas,** I don't remember you, I can't place you;

(d) r. bien ensemble des personnes brouillées, to bring together *or* reconcile people who have quarrelled;

(e) (*rendre*) to hand over, to deliver (*letter, parcel etc*); to send in (*application*); **r. qn à la justice** *ou* **entre les mains de la police,** to hand *or* turn s.o. over to the police; **r. son âme à Dieu,** to commit one's soul to God; **r. sa charge à qn,** to hand over one's duties to s.o.;

(f) to remit, to cancel (*debt*); to remit (*penalty*); to pardon, to forgive (*offence*); to allow (*discount*);

(g) (*différer*) to postpone, to put off (*meeting etc*); **r. une affaire au lendemain,** to put off *or* postpone *or* defer a matter till the next day; *Jur* **r. une cause à huitaine,** to adjourn *or* remand a case for a week; **r. qch à plus tard,** to put sth off (till later); *Échecs etc* **partie remise,** draw, drawn game; *Fig* **c'est partie remise,** there'll be another time for it, the opportunity will arise again;

(h) *F* **remettons ça!,** let's begin again!; (*boisson*) let's have another drink!;

(i) *F* **en r.,** to lay it on (a bit) thick.

2 se remettre *vpr* **(a) se r. au lit,** to go back to bed; **se r. en route,** to set off again; **le temps se remet (au beau),** the weather is clearing up (again); *F* **elle s'est remise avec lui,** she has made it up with him; **se r. bien ensemble,** to make it up again;

(b) se r. au travail *ou* **à travailler,** to start *or* set to work again; **elle s'est remise à boire,** she('s) started drinking again; **se r. au français/au tennis/***etc*, to take up French/tennis/*etc* again;

(c) se r. d'une maladie/d'un choc, to recover from *or* get over an illness/a shock; *Fig* **voyons, remettez-vous!,** come on, pull yourself together!; *Fig* **elle ne s'en est pas remise!,** she couldn't get over it!;

(d) s'en r. à qn de qch, to rely on s.o. for sth; **je m'en remets à vous,** I'll leave it to you, it's up to you.

remeubler [rəmœble] **1** *vt* to refurnish (*house etc*). **2 se remeubler** *vpr* to refurnish one's house *etc*.

rémige [remiʒ] *nf Orn* wing quill.

remilitarisation [rəmilitarizasjɔ̃] *nf* remilitarization.

remilitariser [rəmilitarize] **1** *vt* to remilitarize. **2 se remilitariser** *vpr* to become remilitarized.

réminiscence [reminisɑ̃s] *nf* **(a)** *Phil Psy* reminiscence; **(b)** (*souvenir vague*) vague recollection; **il y a des réminiscences de Mozart là-dedans,** there are echoes of Mozart in it, it is reminiscent of Mozart.

remise [rəmiz] *nf* **(a)** putting back (*of sth in its place*); *Fb* **r. en jeu,** throw-in; *Rugby* **r. en jeu à la touche,** line-out;

(b) r. en état, repairing, mending; **r. à neuf,** (*d'appareils ménagers etc*) reconditioning; **r. en ordre,** putting in order; **r. en marche,** restarting;

(c) delivery (*of letter etc*); **payable contre r. du coupon,** payable on presentation of the coupon; **r. des clefs,** handing over of the keys (*of flat etc*);

(d) remission (*of penalty, debt, tax*); **faire r. d'une dette,** to remit *or* cancel a debt;

(e) r. (de fonds), remittance; **faire une r. (de fonds) à qn,** to send s.o. a remittance;

(f) (*rabais*) discount, reduction; **r. sur marchandises,** trade discount; **vous avez droit à une r. de 25%,** you are entitled to a discount *or* reduction of 25%; **faire une r. sur un article,** to allow a discount *or* make a reduction on an article;

(g) (*appentis*) shed, outhouse; *Rail* engine shed; *Arch* (*pour carrosses*) coachhouse; **voiture de (grande) r.,** hired car (with chauffeur); *Arch* **(voiture de) r.,** (*carrosse*) hired *or* livery carriage;

(h) (*ajournement*) postponement; **je partirai demain sans r.,** I shall start tomorrow without fail.

remiser [rəmize] *vt* **(a)** to garage (*car*); *Rail* to put (*engine*) in the shed; **r. sa valise/***etc*, to put one's case/*etc* away; **(b)** to put (*carriage*) in the coachhouse; **(c)** *Arg* (*rembarrer*) to put (*s.o.*) in his place, to take (*s.o.*) down a peg or two.

remisier [rəmizje] *nm Bourse* half-commission man.

rémissible [remisibl] *adj* remissible.

rémission [remisjɔ̃] *nf* **(a)** remission (*of sin, debt*); **sans r.,** (*travailler etc*) unremittingly, without a break; (*payer*) without delay; **tous sans r.,** all without exception; **(b)** *Méd* remission, abatement (*of fever*); remission (*of illness*); abatement (*of pain*).

rémittent [remitɑ̃] *adj Méd* remittent.

remmaillage [rɑ̃majaʒ] *nm* = **REMAILLAGE**.

remmailler [rɑ̃maje] *vt* = **REMAILLER**.

remmancher [rɑ̃mɑ̃ʃe] *vt* to put a new handle on (*sth*).

remmener [rɑ̃mne] *vt* (*conj like* **mener**) to take (*s.o.*) back; **il fut remmené en prison,** he was taken back to prison.

remodelage [rəmɔdlaʒ] *nm* remodelling; (*réorganisation*) restructuring, reorganization.

remodeler [rəmɔdle] *vt* (*conj like* **modeler**) **(a)** (*refaçonner*) to remodel; **(b)** (*réorganiser*) to restructure, to reorganize.

rémois, -oise [remwa, -waz] **1** *adj* of *or* from Rheims. **2** *n* **R.,** native *or* inhabitant of Rheims.

remontage [rəmɔ̃taʒ] *nm* **(a)** winding up, rewinding (*of clock, watch*); **montre à r. automatique,** self-winding watch; **(b)** (*assemblage*) putting together again, reassembling (*of parts of machinery etc*).

remontant [rəmɔ̃tɑ̃] **1** *adj* **(a)** invigorating (*drink*); **(b)** remontant (*rose*). **2** *nm* tonic, *F* pick-me-up.

remonte [rəmɔ̃t] *nf* **(a)** run (*of fish to spawn*); ascent (*of boat going upstream*); **(b)** *Mil* remounting (*of cavalry*); **cheval de r.,** remount.

remontée [rəmɔ̃te] *nf* **(a)** ascent (*of hill, river etc*); *Sp etc* **une belle r.,** a good recovery; **faire une r.,** to make a recovery; **(b)** *Ski* **r. mécanique,** ski lift; **(c)** *Min* raising (to the surface).

remonte-pente [rəmɔ̃tpɑ̃t] *nm* T-bar; (*pl remonte-pentes*).

remonter [rəmɔ̃te] **1** *vi* (*the aux is usu* **être**, *sometimes* **avoir**) **(a)** (*dans l'espace*) to go *or* come up again, to go *or* come back up; **je suis remonté lui parler,** I went upstairs again *or* back upstairs to speak to him; **r. sur son cheval,** to remount one's horse; **r. en voiture,** to get into one's car again; **r. à la surface,** to resurface, to come back up to the surface; **r. vers la source de la rivière,** to sail *or* row (up) towards the source of the river *or* upstream; **la route remonte avant d'accéder au pont,** the road rises again before it gets to the bridge; **le baromètre remonte,** the barometer is rising again; **le soleil remonte,** the sun is getting higher; **mon soutien-gorge remonte,** my bra is riding up; **les actions pétrolières ont remonté,** oil shares have gone up *or* risen again; *Fig F* **ses actions remontent,** things are looking up for him, his stock is rising; *Fig* **r. dans l'estime de qn,** to go up again in s.o.'s estimation;

(b) (*dans le temps*) to go back; **r. à l'origine de qch,** to go back to the origin of sth; **il fait r. sa famille aux Croisades,** he can trace his family back to the Crusades; **cette dette remonte à plusieurs années,** this debt dates back *or* goes back several years; **une amitié qui remonte au déluge,** a friendship that is as old as the hills;

(c) (*of the tide*) to flow;

(d) *Nau* **r. au** *ou* **dans le vent,** to beat up to windward;

(e) *Équitation* **r. (à cheval),** to ride again, to go riding again.

2 *vt* (*aux* **avoir**) **(a)** to go *or* come *or* climb back up (*hill, stairs etc*), to go *or* come *or* climb up (*hill, stairs etc*) again; **r. la rue,** to go *or* walk *or* drive *or* ride back up the street; **r. la rivière,** to go *or* row *or* sail *or* swim upstream; (*of fish*) to run upstream; *Fig* **r. la pente,** to get back on one's feet (again);

(b) (*hausser etc*) to take *or* bring (*sth*) back up, to take *or* bring (*sth*) up again; *Min* to raise (*miners, coal*); **r. ses**

chaussettes, to pull up one's socks; **r. son pantalon,** to hitch up *or* pull up one's trousers; **r. un mur,** to heighten a wall;
(c) *Mil* to remount, to provide fresh mounts for (*cavalry*);
(d) r. une horloge/montre, to wind (up) *or* rewind a clock/watch; **r. (les forces de) qn,** to put new life into s.o.; **ça m'a remonté le moral,** it raised my spirits, it cheered me up; **un verre de vin vous remontera,** a glass of wine will cheer you up *or* do you good;
(e) r. un vin en alcool, to fortify a wine;
(f) (*assembler*) to put together again, to reassemble (*parts of machine etc*);
(g) to restock (*shop*); to replenish (*one's wardrobe*);
(h) *Th* to put (*play*) on again, to revive (*play*).
3 se remonter *vpr* **(a) se r. en vin/***etc*, to get in fresh supplies of wine/*etc*; **se r. en vêtements/***etc*, to get some new clothes/*etc*;
(b) (*moralement etc*) to recover one's strength *or* one's spirits; **prendre qch pour se r.,** to take a tonic.

remontoir [rəmɔ̃twar] *nm* winder (*of watch*).

remontrance [rəmɔ̃trɑ̃s] *nf* remonstrance; **faire des remontrances à qn,** to remonstrate with s.o., to admonish s.o..

remontrer [rəmɔ̃tre] **1** *vt* **(a)** to show (*sth*) again; **(b) en r. à qn,** to give advice to s.o., to put s.o. right; **il en remontrerait au diable,** he could teach the devil a trick or two. **2 se remontrer** *vpr* to show oneself again.

rémora [remɔra] *nm* (*poisson*) remora.

remordre [rəmɔrdr] **1** *vt* to bite again. **2** *vi* **r. à qch,** to bite at sth again; *Fig* to have another go *or* stab at sth; *Fig F* **r. à l'hameçon,** to be taken in again by the same trick.

remords [rəmɔr] *nm* remorse; **avoir du** *ou* **des r.,** to feel remorse; **un r.,** a twinge of remorse; **des r. de conscience,** twinges of conscience; **atteint de r.,** conscience-stricken; **r. d'un crime,** remorse for a crime.

remorquage [rəmɔrkaʒ] *nm* towing (*of car, trailer, barge etc*); towing, tugging (*of ship*); pulling, hauling (*of train*); **barre de r.,** tow bar (*of glider*).

remorque [rəmɔrk] *nf* **(a)** (*traction*) towing; **prendre un navire/une voiture en** *ou* **à la r.,** to take a ship/a car in tow, to tow a ship/a car; **croc de r.,** tow hook; **timon de r.,** tow bar; **être en** *ou* **à la r.,** to be in *or* on tow; **sortir du port à la r.,** to be towed out of harbour; *Fig* **se mettre** *ou* **être à la r. de qn,** to follow in s.o.'s wake, to follow s.o.'s lead; (*être en retard*) to trail behind *or* after s.o.; **politique à la r.,** follow-my-leader policy; **(b) (câble de) r.,** towline, towrope; *Nau* **donner la r.,** to give *or* pass the tow line; **(c)** (*bateau*) tow, vessel under tow *or* being towed; **(d)** (*véhicule*) trailer; **r. de plaisance, r. (de) camping,** *Br* caravan, *Am* (camping) trailer; **(e)** *Rail* **rame r.,** slip portion; **voiture r.,** slip coach.

remorquer [rəmɔrke] *vt* to tow (*car, trailer etc*); to tug, to tow (*ship*); to tow (*barge*); to pull, to haul (*train*); *Fig* **elle remorque toute sa famille,** she has her whole family in tow, she drags her whole family along.

remorqueur, -euse [rəmɔrkœr, -øz] **1** *adj* towing (*boat etc*); *Rail* relief (*engine*). **2** *nm* tug(boat), towboat.

remoudre [rəmudr] *vt* (*conj like* **moudre**) to regrind (*cereals, coffee etc*), to grind (*cereals, coffee etc*) again.

remouiller [rəmuje] *vt* **(a)** to wet *or* moisten (*sth*) again; **(b)** *Nau* **r. (l'ancre),** to drop *or* cast anchor again.

rémoulade [remulad] *nf Culin* **(sauce) r.,** remoulade (sauce) (*mayonnaise sauce with mustard, herbs etc*); **céleri r.,** celeriac in a remoulade (sauce).

remoulage¹ [rəmulaʒ] *nm* recasting (*of statue etc*).

remoulage² *nm* **(a)** regrinding, remilling (*of cereals*); **(b)** (*farine*) bran.

remouler [rəmule] *vt* to recast (*statue etc*).

rémouleur [remulœr] *nm* knife grinder.

remous [rəmu] *nm* eddy (*of river*); wash, backwash (*of ship*); swirl (*of the tide*); *Fig* bustle, bustling, milling (*of crowd*); **r. d'eau,** whirlpool; *Av* **r. d'air,** eddy; *Fig* **ce livre va provoquer des r.,** this book is going to cause a stir.

rempaillage [rɑ̃pajaʒ] *nm* re-seating, re-bottoming (*of rush-bottomed chairs*).

rempailler [rɑ̃paje] *vt* to re-seat, to re-bottom (*rush-bottomed chair*).

rempailleur, -euse [rɑ̃pajœr, -øz] *n* upholsterer, chair-bottomer.

rempaqueter [rɑ̃pakte] *vt* (*conj like* **paqueter**) to rewrap, to wrap up again.

rempart [rɑ̃par] *nm* rampart; *Fig* **le r. de nos libertés,** the bulwark *or* bastion of our liberties; **faire un r. de son corps à qn,** to shield s.o. with one's body.

rempiéter [rɑ̃pjete] *vt* (**je rempiète, n. rempiétons; je rempiéterai**) *Constr* to underpin (*wall*).

rempiler [rɑ̃pile] **1** *vt* to stack *or* pile up again. **2** *vi Mil F* to re-enlist; (*pour un emploi*) to sign on again.

remplaçable [rɑ̃plasabl] *adj* replaceable.

remplaçant, -ante [rɑ̃plasɑ̃, -ɑ̃t] *n* (*personne*) substitute, replacement; *Sp* reserve, substitute, *F* sub (*for team*); locum (tenens) (*of doctor, clergyman*); *Scol* supply teacher; *Th* understudy.

remplacement [rɑ̃plasmɑ̃] *nm* **(a)** replacing, replacement, substitution; **en r. de qch/qn,** in place *or* lieu of sth/s.o., as a replacement *or* substitute for sth/s.o.; **faire un r.,** to act as a replacement *or* substitute, to stand in; **dactylo qui fait des remplacements,** temporary typist, *F* temp; **(b) de r.,** spare (*tyre*); substitute (*food*); alternative (*facilities*); **pile de r.,** replacement battery; **valeur de r.,** replacement value.

remplacer [rɑ̃plase] *v* (*conj like* **placer**) **1** *vt* **(a)** (*succéder à, tenir lieu de*) to take the place of, to replace, to take over from (*sth, s.o.*); (*temporairement*) to stand in for, to substitute for (*s.o.*); **(b)** (*changer*) to replace (*broken pane, old car etc*); **r. qch par qch d'autre,** to replace sth by sth else, to put sth else in place of sth. **2 se remplacer** *vpr* to be replaceable; **un ami comme toi, ça ne se remplace pas,** friends like you are irreplaceable *or* can't be replaced, friends like you are hard to come by.

remplage [rɑ̃plaʒ] *nm Archit* tracery (*of Gothic window*).

rempli [rɑ̃pli] **1** *adj* full (**de,** of); **visage (bien) r.,** full face; **r. de son importance,** full of one's own importance. **2** *nm Couture* tuck.

remplir [rɑ̃plir] **1** *vtr* **(a)** to fill (**de,** with); to fill (up) (*glass etc*); (*à nouveau*) to refill (*glass etc*); to fill in (*gap, space*); **cela a rempli mon temps,** it occupied *or* took up all my time; **cela ne peut r. votre vie entièrement,** it can't be the only thing in your life; **r. qn de joie/colère/***etc*, to fill s.o. with joy/anger/*etc*; **les étrangers remplissaient la ville,** the town was filled with *or* full of strangers; **r. l'air de ses cris,** to fill the air with one's cries; **(b)** to fill in *or* out, to complete (*form etc*); **(c)** to fulfil (*promise, condition*); to carry out (*order, instructions*); to do, to perform (*one's duty*); **r. le but,** to serve *or* answer the purpose; *Th* **r. un rôle,** to fill *or* sustain a part. **2 se remplir** *vpr* to fill (up).

remplissage [rɑ̃plisaʒ] *nm* **(a)** filling (up) (*of cask, reservoir*); filling (in) (*of hole, gap*); **(b)** padding (*of literary work*); **faire du r.,** to pad.

remplisseur, -euse [rɑ̃plisœr, -øz] **1** *n* (*ouvrier*) filler (in). **2** *nf Ind* **remplisseuse,** bottle-filling machine.

remploi [rɑ̃plwa] *nm* **(a)** (*réutilisation*) re-use; **(b)** *Fin* re-investment.

remployer [rɑ̃plwaje] *vt* (*conj like* **employer**) **(a)** (*réutiliser*) to re-use; **(b)** *Fin* to re-invest (*money*).

remplumer (se) [sərɑ̃plyme] *vpr* **(a)** (*of bird*) to get new feathers *or* new plumage; **(b)** *F* (*financièrement*) to be in funds again; **(c)** *F* (*grossir*) to put on weight again.

rempocher [rɑ̃pɔʃe] *vt* to put (*sth*) back in one's pocket.

remporter [rɑ̃pɔrte] *vt* **(a)** (*reprendre*) to take (*sth*) back *or* away; **(b)** (*gagner*) to win, to carry off (*prize*); to achieve (*success*); to win, to gain (*victory, advantage*) (**sur,** over); **r. la première place,** to obtain first place.

rempotage [rɑ̃pɔtaʒ] *nm* repotting.

rempoter [rɑ̃pɔte] *vt* to repot (*plant*).

remprunter [rɑ̃prœ̃te] *vt* to borrow again.

remuant [rəmɥɑ̃] *adj Pej* overactive (*person*); (*turbulent*) restless (*child*).

remue-ménage [rəmymenaʒ] *nm inv* commotion, confusion, hubbub; **faire du r.-m.,** to create a commotion *or* hubbub.

remue-méninges [rəmymenɛ̃ʒ] *nm inv* brainstorming.

remuement [rəmymɑ̃] *nm* moving, movement (*of chairs, feet, lips etc*).

remuer [rəmɥe] **1** *vt* **(a)** to move (*one's head, legs etc*); to move, to shift (*furniture etc*); **r. la queue,** (*of dog*) to wag its tail; **(b)** to stir (*sauce, coffee etc*); to turn up, to turn over, to disturb (*the ground*); **r. ciel et terre,** to move heaven and earth, to leave no stone unturned; **r. qn/le cœur de qn,** to move *or* touch s.o./to touch s.o.'s heart. **2** *vi* (*of person*) to move, to stir; **ne remue pas tout le temps!,** don't fidget!, keep still!; **dent qui remue,** loose tooth. **3 se remuer** *vpr* (*bouger*) to move, to stir; (*se déplacer*) to bustle about; (*être actif*) to be active; **remuez-vous un peu!,** get a move on!; **il a fallu se r. pour obtenir sa signature,** we had to go to great lengths *or* to a lot of trouble to get his signature *or* to get him to sign.

rémunérateur, -trice [remyneratœr, -tris] **1** *adj* remunerative, profitable (*work etc*). **2** *n* remunerator.

rémunération [remynerasjɔ̃] *nf* remuneration, payment

(**de**, for).

rémunératoire [remyneratwar] *adj Jur* granted as remuneration *or* payment.

rémunérer [remynere] *vt* (**je rémunère, n. rémunérons; je rémunérerai**) to remunerate, to pay (*s.o.*); to pay for (*work, services etc*).

renâcler [rənakle] *vi* **(a)** (*renifler*) (*of horse etc*) to snort; (*of person*) to sniff, to snort; **(b)** (*rechigner*) to show reluctance, to hang back; **r. à la besogne** *ou* **devant le travail,** to be workshy, to jib at one's work; **il a accepté en renâclant,** he accepted grudgingly.

renaissance [rənɛsɑ̃s] **1** *nf* **(a)** *Rel* rebirth; **(b)** *Fig* renaissance, revival (*of letters, arts etc*); **r. du printemps,** reappearance of spring; *Beaux-Arts Littér* **la R.,** the Renaissance. **2** *adj inv* **R.,** Renaissance (*art, castle etc*).

renaissant [rənɛsɑ̃] *adj* **(a)** reviving (*strength, economy, industry etc*); **problèmes/***etc* **sans cesse renaissants,** constantly recurring problems/*etc*; **(b)** (*de la Renaissance*) (of the) Renaissance.

renaître [rənetr] *vi* (*conj like* **naître,** *but pp* **rené** *and compound tenses not in use and p hist* **je renaquis** *rare*) **(a)** *Rel* to be born again; **ville qui renaît de ses cendres,** town that is rising again from its ashes; **r. à la vie,** to take on a new lease of life; **(b)** (*réapparaître*) to return, to reappear; (*of plants*) to grow again, to spring up again; (*of nature, industry, the arts etc*) to revive; (*of hope*) to revive, to be reborn; **faire r. les espérances de qn,** to revive s.o.'s hopes.

rénal, -aux [renal, -o] *adj Anat* renal; **calcul r.,** kidney stone.

renard [rənar] *nm* **(a)** (*animal*) fox; **r. argenté,** silver fox; **la chasse au r.,** fox-hunting; *Fig* **c'est un fin r.,** he's as sly as a fox; **(b)** (*fourrure*) fox (fur); **(c)** *Tech* leak, fissure (*in boiler, dam etc*).

renarde [rənard] *nf* vixen.

renardeau, -eaux [rənardo] *nm* fox cub.

renardière [rənardjɛr] *nf* **(a)** (*tanière*) foxhole, (fox's) earth; **(b)** *Can* (*élevage*) fox farm.

renauder [rənode] *vi Arg* (*se plaindre*) to grouch, to grumble.

rencaissage [rɑ̃kɛsaʒ] *nm* putting (*of plants*) in boxes *or* tubs again.

rencaissement [rɑ̃kɛsmɑ̃] *nm* putting back (*of money*) in the till.

rencaisser [rɑ̃kese] *vt* **(a)** to put (*plants*) in boxes *or* tubs again; **(b)** to put (*money*) back in the till.

rencard, rencart [rɑ̃kar] *nm Arg* **(a)** (*rendez-vous*) date, rendezvous; **(b)** (*information*) (a piece of) info, *Br* gen, lowdown.

rencarder [rɑ̃karde] *vt Arg* **(a)** (*donner rendez-vous à*) to fix up a date *or* rendezvous with; **(b)** (*renseigner*) to give the info *or Br* gen to.

renchéri, -ie [rɑ̃ʃeri] *adj & n* particular, fastidious, fussy (person).

renchérir [rɑ̃ʃerir] **1** *vt* to make (*sth*) dearer, to raise the price of (*sth*). **2** *vi* **(a)** (*of prices, rents, goods*) to get dearer; **(b)** (*dire ou faire plus qu'un autre*) to go one better, to go further; **r. sur une histoire/***etc*, to improve on a story/*etc*; **r. sur une citation,** to cap a quotation.

renchérissement [rɑ̃ʃerismɑ̃] *nm* (*de marchandises*) rise *or* increase in price; (*de prix, loyers*) rise, increase (**de,** in).

rencogner [rɑ̃kɔɲe] *F* **1** *vt* to push *or* drive (*s.o.*) into a corner. **2 se rencogner** *vpr* to huddle up; **il s'est rencogné contre sa mère,** he huddled *or* snuggled up against his mother.

rencontre [rɑ̃kɔ̃tr] *nf* **(a)** meeting, encounter (*of persons*); meeting (*of streams*); junction (*of roads*); collision (*between two cars*); conjunction (*of circumstances*); **faire la r. de qn,** to meet s.o.; **aller à la r. de qn,** to go to meet s.o.; **faire une mauvaise r.,** to have an unpleasant encounter; **connaissance de r.,** chance acquaintance; **(b)** *Tech* **roue de r.,** balance wheel (*of clock*); **(c) r. de pétrole,** strike *or* striking of oil; **(d)** encounter, meeting (*of opponents*); (*duel*) duel; *Sp* match, meeting; *Boxe* fight; *Mil* **une r. avec l'ennemi,** a brush *or* skirmish with the enemy; **(e)** *Arch & Litt* **par r.,** by chance.

rencontrer [rɑ̃kɔ̃tre] **1** *vt* **(a)** (*par hasard*) to meet, to encounter, to come across, *F* to bump into (*s.o.*); to come across, to encounter (*sth*); to encounter, to meet with (*opposition, difficulty etc*); **r. qn sur son chemin,** to run *or* come across *or F* bump into s.o.; **r. l'ennemi,** to encounter the enemy; **r. les yeux de qn,** to meet s.o.'s glance; **la voiture a rencontré un autobus,** the car collided with *or* ran into a bus; **un thème que l'on rencontre souvent chez Genet,** a theme that one encounters *or* comes across often in Genet; **r. un indice,** to hit upon a clue; **c'est un ami comme on n'en rencontre plus,** he's the sort of friend you don't find any more; **r. le bonheur auprès de qn,** to find happiness with s.o.;

(b) (*avoir un rendez-vous avec*) to meet; **je vais le r. ce matin,** I shall (be) meet(ing) him this morning; *Sp* **r. une autre équipe,** to meet *or* play against another team.

2 se rencontrer *vpr* **(a)** (*of people, rivers, Sp teams etc*) to meet; **leurs yeux se rencontrèrent,** their eyes met;

(b) (*se heurter*) to collide, to run into each other;

(c) (*se trouver*) to occur, to be found; **comme cela se rencontre!,** how lucky!;

(d) (*of ideas*) to agree, to tally.

rendement [rɑ̃dmɑ̃] *nm* **(a)** yield (*of land, mine, tax*); return, profit (*on investment*); **actions à gros r.,** shares that yield high interest; **(b)** output (*of workers*); output, production (*of works*); throughput (*of computer*); **r. individuel,** output per man; **travailler à plein r.,** (*of works*) to work to full capacity; (*of machine*) to work at full load; **(c)** efficiency, performance (*of machine etc*); **machine à grand r.,** heavy-duty machine; **(d)** *Sp* **r. de temps,** time handicap.

rendez-vous [rɑ̃devu] *nm inv* **(a)** (*rencontre*) appointment; (*d'amoureux*) date; **donner (un) r.-v.** *ou* **fixer un r.-v. à qn, prendre r.-v. avec qn.,** to arrange to meet s.o., *esp Fml* to make *or* fix an appointment with s.o., **j'ai (un) r.-v. à huit heures,** I'm meeting someone at eight o'clock; **r.-v. social,** meeting between employers and unions; **se rencontrer sur r.-v.,** to meet by appointment; **'ne reçoit que sur r.-v.',** 'by appointment only'; **r.-v. d'affaires,** business appointment; **r.-v. spatial,** docking in space; **(b)** (*endroit*) meeting place; **r.-v. de chasse,** venue of the meet.

rendormir [rɑ̃dɔrmir] *v* (*conj like* **dormir**) **1** *vt* to send (*s.o.*) to sleep again. **2 se rendormir** *vpr* to fall asleep again, to go (off) *or* drop off to sleep again.

rendre [rɑ̃dr] **1** *vt* **(a)** (*restituer*) to give back, to return, to restore; to repay, to pay back (*money*); to take back, to return (*a purchase*); to return (*invitation*); **r. son salut à qn,** to return s.o.'s greeting; **r. qn à la santé,** to restore s.o. to health; **r. la monnaie d'un billet de cent francs,** to give change for a hundred-franc note; **r. le bien pour le mal,** to return good for evil; *F* **je le lui rendrai!,** I'll get even with him!, I'll get him back!;

(b) r. hommage à qn, to pay homage to s.o.; **r. grâce à qn,** to give thanks to s.o.; **il faut lui r. sa liberté,** he must be given his freedom; **r. service à qn,** to render *or* do s.o. a service; **r. la justice,** to dispense *or* administer justice; **nous allons leur r. visite,** we're going to pay them a visit;

(c) (*of land, taxes etc*) to produce, to yield; **placement qui rend 10%,** investment that brings in *or* yields 10%; **terre qui ne rend rien,** unproductive land;

(d) (*livrer*) to deliver; **r. des marchandises à destination,** to deliver goods (to their destination); **prix rendu,** delivery price;

(e) (*vomir*) to bring up, to throw up (*food etc*); **r. l'âme** *ou* **la vie,** to breathe one's last, *F* to give up the ghost;

(f) *Mil* to give up, to surrender (*one's arms, a fortress etc*);

(g) (*prononcer*) to issue, to pronounce (*decree*); to deliver (*judg(e)ment*); to bring in, to return (*verdict*);

(h) (*exprimer*) to render, to express; **r. le sens de l'auteur,** to render *or* convey the author's meaning; **r. le sens du mot en anglais,** to render *or* express (the meaning of) the word in English; **elle rend très bien Chopin,** she plays Chopin very well;

(i) (+ *adj*) **le homard me rend malade,** lobster makes me ill; **r. les choses difficiles,** to make things difficult; **vous me rendez fou!,** you're driving me mad!

2 se rendre *vpr* **(a)** (*aller*) **se r. dans un lieu,** to go *or* make one's way to a place; **se r. en toute hâte à un endroit,** to hurry to a place; **se r. chez qn,** to call on s.o.;

(b) (*en perdant*) to surrender; **se r. (prisonnier),** to give oneself up; *Fig* **se r. à la raison,** to give in *or* yield to reason;

(c) il se rend ridicule, he is making himself (look) ridiculous.

3 *vi* (*of land etc*) to be productive; **le moteur rend bien,** the engine runs *or* performs well.

rendu [rɑ̃dy] **1** *adj* **(a)** (*arrivé*) **être r.,** to have arrived; **nous voilà rendus à Manchester,** here we are in Manchester; *Fig F* **on n'est pas r.,** (*il y a encore beaucoup à faire*) we're not there yet; **(b) r. (de fatigue),** exhausted, tired out. **2** *nm* **(a)** *Beaux-Arts* rendering (*of subject*); **r. exact des couleurs,** exact reproduction of colour; **(b)** *Com*

returned article, return.
rêne [rɛn] *nf* rein; **fausses rênes,** bearing rein, check rein; **rênes de bride,** bit reins; **rênes de mors,** curb reins; **à bout de rênes,** with reins slack; **lâcher les rênes,** to loosen the reins, to give a horse his head; *Fig (abandonner)* to let go; *Fig* **tenir les rênes du gouvernement,** to hold the reins of government.
renégat, -ate [rənega, -at] *n* renegade, turncoat; *Rel* renegade.
reneiger [rənɛʒe] *v impers* to snow again.
renégociation [rənegɔsjasjɔ̃] *nf* renegotiation.
renégocier [rənegɔsje] *vt* to renegotiate.
renfaîtage [rɑ̃fɛtaʒ] *nm* new-ridging (*of roof*).
renfaîter [rɑ̃fete] *vt* to new-ridge (*roof*).
renfermé [rɑ̃fɛrme] **1** *adj* uncommunicative, withdrawn (*person*). **2** *nm* **odeur de r.,** stuffy *or* musty smell; **sentir le r.,** to smell stuffy *or* musty.
renfermer [rɑ̃fɛrme] **1** *vt* **(a)** (*enfermer*) to shut (*sth, s.o.*) up; (*de nouveau*) to shut (*sth, s.o.*) up again; *El* **fusible renfermé,** enclosed fuse; **(b)** (*contenir*) to contain; **livre qui renferme des idées nouvelles,** book that contains new ideas; **le genre renferme l'espèce,** the genus includes the species. **2 se renfermer** *vpr* **(a) se r. en soi-même/dans le silence,** to withdraw into oneself/into silence; **(b) se r. dans ses instructions,** to limit *or* confine oneself to one's instructions.
renfiler [rɑ̃file] *vt* to rethread, to restring (*beads etc*); to rethread (*needle*).
renflé [rɑ̃fle] *adj* bulging; *Nau* bluff-bowed (*ship*).
renflement [rɑ̃fləmɑ̃] *nm* bulge (*of pillar etc*).
renfler [rɑ̃fle] **1** *vt* to make (*sth*) bulge. **2 se renfler** *vpr* to bulge.
renflouage [rɑ̃fluaʒ] *nm*, **renflouement** [rɑ̃flumɑ̃] *nm* floating off, refloating (*of stranded ship*); *Fig* refloating (*of business*).
renflouer [rɑ̃flue] *vt* to float off, to refloat (*stranded ship*); *Fig* **r. une entreprise,** to refloat a business, to set a business on its feet again; *Fig* **r. qn,** to keep s.o. afloat (financially).
renfoncement [rɑ̃fɔ̃smɑ̃] *nm* **(a)** (*creux*) hollow, recess; **r. d'une porte,** doorway; **(b)** *Géol* downcast fault; **(c)** *Typ* indentation (*of line*).
renfoncer [rɑ̃fɔ̃se] *v* (*conj like* **enfoncer**) **1** *vt* **(a)** to drive (*nail etc*) further in; to pull down (*one's hat*); **r. ses larmes,** to choke back one's tears; **(b)** *Constr* to recess, to set back (*façade etc*); *Typ* to indent (*line*). **2 se renfoncer** *vpr* to sink in; *Beaux-Arts* (*of background*) to recede.
renforçage [rɑ̃fɔrsaʒ] *nm* **(a)** strengthening, reinforcing (*of wall, seam etc*); **(b)** *Phot* intensification.
renforcement [rɑ̃fɔrsəmɑ̃] *nm* **(a)** strengthening, reinforcement (*of beam, team etc*); **(b)** intensifying, reinforcing (*of sound*); *Phot* intensification.
renforcer [rɑ̃fɔrse] *v* (*conj like* **forcer**) **1** *vt* **(a)** to reinforce, to strengthen (*wall, beam, seam, army, team etc*); to back (*map*); to strengthen (*a law*); **(b)** to reinforce, to intensify (*sound*); to intensify (*colour*); to reinforce (*suspicion, fear etc*); to back up (*statement*); **r. qn dans ses opinions,** to confirm s.o. in his opinions. **2** *vi* (*of wind*) to grow stronger. **3 se renforcer** *vpr* to grow stronger.
renfort [rɑ̃fɔr] *nm* **(a) renforts,** (*personnes*) reinforcements; (*matériel*) fresh supplies; **des soldats envoyés en r.,** reinforcements; **régiment de r.,** supporting *or* back-up regiment; **cheval de r.,** extra horse, trace horse; **à grand r. d'épingles/de conseils,** with (the help of) lots of pins/advice; **(b)** (*pièce*) reinforcement, strengthening piece; backing (*of sail*); *Menuis* tusk (*of tenon*); **plaque** *ou* **tôle de r.,** stiffening plate.
renfrogné [rɑ̃frɔɲe] *adj* frowning (*brow, face*); sullen, scowling (*person*); glum, sullen (*look*).
renfrogner (se) [sərɑ̃frɔɲe] *vpr* to frown, to scowl.
rengagé [rɑ̃gaʒe] *Mil* **1** *adj* re-enlisted. **2** *nm* re-enlisted soldier.
rengagement [rɑ̃gaʒmɑ̃] *nm* re-engagement (*of staff*); *Mil* re-enlistment.
rengager [rɑ̃gaʒe] *v* (*conj like* **engager**) **1** *vt* to re-engage (*staff*); to renew (*combat*). **2 se rengager** *vpr Mil* to re-enlist. **3** *vi* **(a)** to re-enlist; **(b)** (*recommencer*) to begin again.
rengaine [rɑ̃gɛn] *nf* cliché; (*morceau de musique*) catchy tune; **vieille r.,** old refrain; *F* **c'est toujours la même r.,** it's (always) the same old story.
rengainer [rɑ̃gene] *vt* to sheathe, to put up (*one's sword*); *F* **r. son compliment,** to save one's compliments, to keep one's compliments to oneself.
rengorger (se) [sərɑ̃gɔrʒe] *vpr* (*conj like* **engorger**) (*of bird*) to strut; (*of person*) to strut, to swagger, to throw out one's chest.
rengraisser [rɑ̃grɛse] *vi* to grow fat again, to put on weight again.
reniement [rənimɑ̃] *nm* **(a)** disowning (*of friend etc*); denial (*of Christ*); disavowal (*of action*); **(b)** repudiation (*of opinions etc*); abjuration (*of faith*).
renier [rənje] *v* (*conj like* **nier**) **1** *vt* **(a)** to disown, to renounce, to repudiate (*friend, father etc*); to deny (*Christ*); to disavow (*action*); **(b)** to repudiate (*opinion, idea*); to abjure (*one's faith*). **2 se renier** *vpr* to repudiate one's opinions.
reniflement [rənifləmɑ̃] *nm* **(a)** (*action*) sniffing; (*de cheval*) snorting; **(b)** (*bruit*) sniff; (*de cheval*) snort.
renifler [rənifle] **1** *vi* to sniff; (*of horse*) to snort; *Fig* **r. sur qch,** to sniff at *or* turn up one's nose at sth; **r. sur l'avoine,** (*of horse*) to be off its feed. **2** *vt* to sniff (up) (*snuff etc*); to sniff (*flower, smell etc*); **il sait r. une bonne affaire,** he's got a (good) nose for a bargain.
renifleur, -euse [rəniflœr, -øz] **1** *adj* sniffling. **2** *n* sniffler.
renne [rɛn] *nm* reindeer.
renom [rənɔ̃] *nm* (*popularité*) renown, fame; **en r.,** famous, renowned, celebrated; **produit de r.,** famous *or* renowned *or* celebrated product; **médecin en grand r.,** doctor with a great reputation; **aïeux de grand r.,** famous *or* renowned *or* celebrated ancestors.
renommé [rənɔme] *adj* renowned, famous, celebrated (**pour,** for).
renommée [rənɔme] *nf* **(a)** (*popularité*) renown, fame; **connaître qn de r.,** to know s.o. by repute; **(b)** *Jur* **(preuve par) commune r.,** hearsay evidence.
renommer [rənɔme] *vt* to re-appoint; (*élire*) to re-elect.
renonce [rənɔ̃s] *nf Cartes* **(a)** renounce, inability to follow suit; **avoir une r. à cœur,** to be short of hearts; **(b) fausse r.,** revoke; **faire une fausse r.,** to revoke.
renoncement [rənɔ̃smɑ̃] *nm* **(a)** renouncing, renouncement (**à,** of); **(b) r. (à soi-même),** self-denial; **vie de r.,** a life of renunciation.
renoncer [rənɔ̃se] *v* (**je renonçai(s); n. renonçons**) **1** *vi* **(a) r. à qch,** to renounce sth; **r. à qn,** to drop s.o.; **r. à faire qch,** to give up *or* forgo doing sth; (*projet*) to give up *or* drop the idea of doing sth; **r. à un droit,** to waive a right; **r. à un voyage,** to give up all idea of a journey; **r. à une réclamation,** to withdraw *or* renounce a claim; **r. à la lutte,** to give up *or* renounce the struggle; **r. à sa carrière,** to give up *or* abandon one's career; **y r.,** to give up; **deux des coureurs ont renoncé,** two of the runners dropped out; **vous allez devoir r. au chocolat,** you're going to have to give up chocolate; **r. à sa religion,** to renounce *or* abnegate one's religion;
(b) *Cartes* to renounce, to fail to follow suit; (*faire une fausse renonce*) to revoke.
2 *vt* to renounce, to disown, to repudiate (*s.o.*); **r. sa foi,** to renounce *or* abnegate one's faith.
renonciation [rənɔ̃sjasjɔ̃] *nf* renunciation (**à,** of); *Jur* **r. à un droit,** renunciation *or* disclaimer *or* waiver of a right.
renoncule [rənɔ̃kyl] *nf Bot* ranunculus; (*sauvage*) (wild) buttercup; **r. flottante,** water crowfoot; **fausse r.,** lesser celandine.
renouée [rənwe] *nf Bot* knotgrass, polygonum.
renouer [rənwe] **1** *vt* **(a)** to tie (up) (*ribbon, shoelace etc*) again; to do up *or* knot (*tie*) again; **(b)** *Fig* to renew, to resume (*conversation etc*); **r. une amitié avec qn,** to renew one's friendship with s.o.. **2** *vi* **r. avec qn,** to make friends with s.o. again; **cet auteur renoue avec la tradition de la littérature courtoise,** this author is reviving the tradition of courtly literature.
renouveau [rənuvo] *nm* **(a)** (*printemps*) springtide, spring (*of the year*); **(b)** *Fig* (*renaissance*) revival; **r. de vie,** new lease of life; **r. religieux/des arts,** religious/artistic revival; **un r. de succès,** renewed success; **connaître un r.,** to enjoy *or* experience a revival.
renouvelable [rənuvlabl] *adj* renewable (*contract, energy etc*); repeatable (*experience*).
renouveler [rənuvle] *v* (**je renouvelle, n. renouvelons; je renouvellerai**) **1** *vt* **(a)** to renew (*one's wardrobe etc*); to renew, to replace (*stock, equipment*); **r. ses pneus,** to get a new set of tyres; **r. l'air d'une salle,** to air a room;
(b) to change (*method, team, staff*) completely; **r. la face du pays,** to alter the whole appearance of the country, to transform the country;
(c) to renew (*promise, alliance, lease, contract, passport*); to revive (*custom, tradition etc*); to repeat (*experience*); to renew (*acquaintance, a quarrel*); **r. le**

souvenir de qch, to refresh one's memory about sth; *Com* **r. une commande,** to repeat an order; **r. sa demande,** to renew *or* repeat one's request.

2 *vi* **(a) la lune vient de r.,** the moon is new;

(b) r. de zèle, to act with renewed zeal.

3 se renouveler *vpr* **(a)** (*se reformer*) (*of skin etc*) to be renewed;

(b) (*se produire*) to recur, to happen again; **que cela ne se renouvelle pas!,** don't let it happen again!;

(c) (*changer*) to change; **il ne se renouvelle pas,** it's always the same with him;

(d) (*être remplacé*) to be replaced.

renouvellement [rənuvɛlmɑ̃] *nm* **(a)** replacement, renewal (*of stock, equipment*); **r. échelonné du matériel,** phasing out of equipment; **(b)** reform (*of system*); revival (*of tradition etc*); **(c)** renewing, renewal (*of treaty, lease etc*); increase (*of zeal etc*).

rénovateur, -trice [renɔvatœr, -tris] **1** *adj* reforming. **2** *n* (*personne*) reformer (*of method etc*); reviver (*of artistic genre*). **3** *nm* (*produit*) restorer.

rénovation [renɔvɑsjɔ̃] *nf* **(a)** renovation, restoring, restoration (*of building, furniture etc*); **(b)** *Fig* revival (*of artistic genre*); reform(ing) (*of method etc*).

rénover [renɔve] *vt* **(a)** to renovate, to restore (*building, furniture etc*); **(b)** *Fig* to revive (*artistic genre*); to reform (*method, institution etc*).

renseigné [rɑ̃seɲe] *adj* **bien/mal r.,** well-/ill-informed (**sur,** about).

renseignement [rɑ̃sɛɲmɑ̃] *nm* (piece of) information; *Mil etc* (piece of) intelligence; *Tél etc* **renseignements,** enquiries, *surtout Am* inquiries; **pardon Monsieur, c'est pour un r.,** excuse me, could you give me some information?; **donner des renseignements sur qch,** to give (some) information *or* particulars about sth; **prendre des renseignements sur qch,** to make enquiries *or* to enquire about sth; **aller aux renseignements,** to go to find out *or* to make enquiries; **bons renseignements sur qn,** favourable report on s.o.; **embaucher qn sans renseignements,** to engage s.o. without references; **bureau de renseignements,** information bureau *or* office; **renseignements (techniques),** data; **service de r.,** intelligence branch *or* service *or* department; **organes de renseignements et de sécurité,** security; **agent de** *ou* **du r.,** (intelligence) agent.

renseigner [rɑ̃seɲe] **1** *vt* **r. qn,** to give s.o. some information; **r. qn sur qch,** to inform s.o. *or* give s.o. information about sth; **on vous a mal renseigné,** you have been misinformed; **être bien renseigné sur qch,** to be well informed about sth; **je vais vous r. sur lui,** I'll tell you something about him. **2 se renseigner** *vpr* to make inquiries, to inquire; (*obtenir des renseignements*) to find out, to get information (**sur,** about).

rentabilisation [rɑ̃tabilizɑsjɔ̃] *nf* making profitable.

rentabiliser [rɑ̃tabilize] **1** *vt* to make (*firm etc*) profitable. **2 se rentabiliser** *vpr* to become profitable.

rentabilité [rɑ̃tabilite] *nf* profitability.

rentable [rɑ̃tabl] *adj* profitable; **ce n'est pas r.,** it doesn't pay; **loyer r./peu r.,** economic/uneconomic rent.

rente [rɑ̃t] *nf* **(a) rentes,** (*revenue*) (unearned, private) income; **vivre de ses rentes,** to live on one's private income; **(b)** (*pension*) annuity, pension, allowance; **r. viagère,** life annuity; **r. de situation,** guaranteed income; **faire une r. à qn,** to make an (annual) allowance to s.o.; **on lui a fait une r.,** he has been pensioned off; **(c) rentes (sur l'État),** (government) stocks, funds, bonds; **(d)** *Fig F* **c'est une r., ce bateau,** this boat costs a fortune (to run).

rentier, -ière [rɑ̃tje, -jɛr] *n* person of private means *or* with a private income; **petit r.,** small investor; **mener une vie de r.,** to live a life of leisure *or* a leisured life.

rentoiler [rɑ̃twale] *vt* to remount (*map*); to put a new canvas to (*painting*).

rentrant, -ante [rɑ̃trɑ̃, -ɑ̃t] **1** *adj* **(a)** *Math* **angle r.,** reflex angle; *Phot* **monture rentrante,** sunken mount; **(b)** *Av* **train d'atterrissage r.,** retractable undercarriage. **2** *n* new player; *Cartes* cutter-in.

rentré [rɑ̃tre] *adj* **(a)** hollow, sunken (*cheeks*); sunken (*eyes*); **(b)** suppressed (*laughter, rage*).

rentrée [rɑ̃tre] *nf* **(a)** return, return home (*of holidaymakers, cars etc*); *Astronaut* **r. atmosphérique,** re-entry into the atmosphere; *Mus* **r. d'un motif/d'un instrument,** re-entry of a theme/an instrument;

(b) re-opening (*of schools, law courts, theatres*); **r. (parlementaire),** re-assembly, re-opening (of Parliament); *Scol* **la r. (des classes),** the beginning of term; **le jour de la r.,** the first day of (the new) term; **la r. des élèves et la r. des professeurs,** the start of the new school term; **la r. sociale,** the start of the social calendar; **faire sa r. politique,** to make one's political comeback; **cet acteur a fait une r. très inattendue,** this actor made an unexpected comeback; **la r. littéraire,** this autumn's new books;

(c) taking in, receipt (*of money*); **faire des rentrées d'argent,** to get some money in;

(d) getting in (*of crops*);

(e) *Fb* **r. en touche,** throw-in.

rentrer [rɑ̃tre] **1** *vi* (*aux* **être**) **(a)** (*entrer de nouveau*) to re-enter, to come *or* go in again; (*of spacecraft*) to re-enter (the atmosphere); **r. dans sa chambre,** to go back into one's room; **lorsqu'il rentra en France/à Paris,** when he returned to France/Paris; **r. au port,** to return *or* put back to port; **r. dans l'armée,** to rejoin the army; **r. dans les bonnes grâces de qn,** to regain favour with s.o.; **r. dans ses droits,** to recover one's rights; **r. dans ses frais,** to be reimbursed (for one's expenses); **r. en correspondance avec qn,** to resume correspondence with s.o.; **r. dans son bon sens,** to recover one's senses; **r. dans le bon chemin,** to mend one's ways, to turn over a new leaf; **r. en scène,** (*of actor*) to come on again;

(b) (*à la maison*) to return home, to go *or* come (back) home; **je rentre chez moi,** I'm going *or* returning home; **il est l'heure de r.,** it's time we went home, it's time to go home; **r. dîner,** to go home to dinner *or* for dinner; **elle rentre de Paris,** she is just home from Paris;

(c) (*reprendre ses occupations*) (*of school, law courts etc*) to re-open, to resume; (*of Parliament*) to re-assemble, to re-open; (*of pupil, teacher*) to go back to school; (*of actor*) to return to the stage, to make a comeback; **r. en fonction(s),** (*of official*) to resume one's duties;

(d) (*d'objets*) to go in; **cela ne pourra pas r. dans mon sac,** it won't go in my bag; **faire r. qch dans sa boîte,** to put sth back into its box;

(e) (*d'argent etc*) to come in; **faire r. ses fonds,** to call in one's money;

(f) (*forme emphatique* **d'entrer**) to enter, to come *or* go in; *Cartes* to cut in; **r. en soi-même,** to retire *or* withdraw into oneself; **elle m'est rentrée dedans,** she ran into *or* collided with me; **ils se sont rentrés en plein dedans,** they ran *or* went slap (bang) into each other; **tubes qui rentrent les uns dans les autres,** tubes that fit into one another; **je ne rentre plus dans mon pantalon!,** I can't get into my trousers any more!; *F* **les jambes me rentrent dans le corps,** I'm too tired to stand; **cela ne rentre pas dans mes fonctions,** that doesn't come within my remit *or* province, that's not part of my job; **r. dans une catégorie,** to fall into a category;

(g) *Typ* **faire r. une ligne,** to indent a line.

2 *vt* (*aux* **avoir**) **(a)** to take in, to bring in, to get in (*sth*); *Nau* to heave in, to haul in (*rope*); to haul down, to strike (*the colours*); to ship (*the oars*); to take (*anchor*) aboard; to haul up (*boat*); *Av* to retract, to raise (*landing gear*); **rentre ton ventre,** pull in your stomach; **r. la récolte,** to get in *or* gather in the harvest; **r. sa chemise,** to tuck in one's shirt; **r. un désir,** to repress a desire;

(b) (*à la maison*) to take (*s.o., sth*) home.

renversant [rɑ̃vɛrsɑ̃] *adj F* astounding, staggering (*news etc*); astounding, amazing (*person*).

renverse [rɑ̃vɛrs] *nf* **(a)** shift, turn (*of tide, current*); change round (*of the wind*); **(b) à la r.,** on one's back; **tomber à la r.,** to fall (over) backwards *or* on one's back; *Fig* to be staggered *or* bowled over *or* knocked for six.

renversé [rɑ̃vɛrse] *adj* **(a)** (*à l'envers*) inverted, reversed (*image etc*); inverted (*arch, pyramid*); **écriture renversée,** backhanded writing; **tête renversée en avant/en arrière,** head tipped *or* tilted forward/back; *Culin* **crème renversée,** custard mould; *F* **c'est le monde r.!,** what's the world coming to!; **(b)** (*tombé*) overturned, upset (*chair etc*); **(c)** (*déconcerté*) staggered, astounded.

renversement [rɑ̃vɛrsəmɑ̃] *nm* **(a)** reversal; inversion (*of image, proposition, Mus of interval, chord*); **r. des valeurs,** inversion of values; **r. d'une situation,** reversal of a situation; **r. des rôles,** role reversal; **r. des alliances,** reversal of alliances; **(b)** turn(ing) (*of the tide*); shift(ing), backing (*of the wind*); **r. de la vapeur,** reversing (*of engine*); **(c)** (*à l'envers*) turning upside down; **charrette à r.,** tip-up cart; *Tech* **couple de r.,** torque (reaction); *Fig* **le r. de mes projets,** the disruption of my plans; **(d)** overthrow (*of regime, government etc*).

renverser [rɑ̃vɛrse] **1** *vt* **(a)** to reverse, to invert (*image, proposition, Mus interval, chord*); **r. les fusils,** to reverse arms; **r. la tête en avant/en arrière,** to tip *or* tilt one's head forward/back; *Nau* **r. la ligne,** to turn the line; **r. un levier,** to throw over a lever; **r. la marche,** to reverse (the engine); *Aut* to go into reverse; **r. la vapeur,** to reverse steam; *Fig* to go back on one's decision, to backpedal; **r. les rôles,** to turn the tables on s.o.; **r. la situation,** to reverse *or* turn round the situation;

(b) (*à l'envers*) to turn upside down; **'ne pas r.'**, 'this side up';

(c) (*faire tomber*) to knock (*s.o., sth*) over *or* down; to overturn, to upset (*pail*); to capsize (*boat*); to spill (*liquid*); **il fut renversé par une auto,** he was knocked down *or* over by a car; *Fig* **cela renverse tous mes projets,** that disrupts all my plans; **elle est parvenue à r. tous les obstacles,** she managed to overcome *or* surmount all the obstacles;

(d) to overthrow (*regime, government etc*);

(e) (*déconcerter*) to stagger, to astound (*s.o.*).

2 *vi* (*of vehicle*) to overturn; (*of boat*) to capsize; (*of liquid*) to spill; (*of tide*) to turn.

3 se renverser *vpr* (*of object*) to fall over, to fall down; (*of vehicle*) to overturn; (*of boat*) to capsize; **se r. sur sa chaise,** to lean back on one's chair, to tilt one's chair back.

renvoi [rɑ̃vwa] *nm* **(a)** sending back, return(ing) (*of goods etc*); return (*of ball*); *Ordinat* feedback; **(b)** dismissal, *Br* sacking (*of employee*); discharge (*of troops*); expulsion (*of pupil*); **(c)** (*ajournement*) putting off, postponement; **(d)** referring, reference (*to committee etc*); *Jur* transfer (*of case to another court*); **(e)** *Typ* reference (mark), cross reference; **r. en marge,** marginal alteration; **(f)** *Tech* **r. de mouvement,** counter gear(ing) *or* motion, reverse motion; **r. de commande,** shafting; **levier de r.,** reversing lever; **engrenage de r.,** reversing gear; **poulie de r.,** return pulley; **(g) r. de courant,** cross current; **(h)** (*éructation*) burp, belch; **donner des renvois,** (*of food*) to repeat.

renvoyer [rɑ̃vwaje] *vt* (*conj like* **envoyer**) **(a)** (*faire retourner*) to send back, to return (*gift, letter etc*); to return (*ball*); to send (*s.o.*) back; to throw back, to re-echo (*sound*); to reflect (*heat, light*); *Cartes* to return (*suit*);

(b) (*faire partir*) to send *or* turn (*s.o.*) away; *Jur* to discharge (*defendant*); **r. des troupes dans leurs foyers,** to discharge *or* dismiss troops; *F* **r. qn bien loin,** to send s.o. packing;

(c) (*licencier*) to dismiss, *Br* to sack (*employee*), *Br* to give (*employee*) the sack; to send down (*university student*); to expel (*pupil from school*);

(d) (*différer*) to put off, to postpone, to defer (*matter, debate*); *Jur* **r. une affaire à huitaine,** to put off *or* postpone *or* defer a case for a week; *Jur* **r. le prévenu à une autre audience,** to remand the accused;

(e) (*reporter*) to refer (*s.o., a matter*) (**à,** to); *Pol* **r. un projet à une commission,** to send a bill to a committee; **les numéros renvoient (le lecteur) aux notes,** the numbers refer to the notes.

réoccupation [reɔkypɑsjɔ̃] *nf* reoccupation, reoccupying (*of territory etc*).

réoccuper [reɔkype] *vt* to re-occupy (*territory etc*); **r. une fonction,** to resume an office.

réorganisateur, -trice [reɔrganizatœr, -tris] *n* reorganizer.

réorganisation [reɔrganizɑsjɔ̃] *nf* reorganization.

réorganiser [reɔrganize] **1** *vt* to reorganize. **2 se réorganiser** *vpr* to be reorganized.

réorientation [reɔrjɑ̃tasjɔ̃] *nf* reorientation.

réorienter [reɔrjɑ̃te] *vt* to reorient(ate).

réouverture [reuvɛrtyr] *nf* reopening (*of theatre, shop etc*); **r. des débats,** resumption of proceedings.

repaire [rəpɛr] *nm* den, lair (*of lions, thieves*); nest (*of pirates*); haunt (*of criminals*).

repairer [rəpere] *vt* (*of game*) to have gone to earth, to be in cover(t).

repaître [rəpɛtr] *v* (*prp* **repaissant**; *pp* **repu**; *pr ind* **je repais, n. repaissons**; *pr sub* **je repaisse**) **1** *vt* **(a)** to feed (*animals*); **(b)** *Fig* **r. ses yeux de qch,** to feast one's eyes on sth. **2 se repaître** *vpr* **(a)** (*of animal*) to eat its fill; **(b)** *Fig* **se r. de sang,** to wallow in blood; **se r. de chimères,** to indulge in vain imaginings.

répandre [repɑ̃dr] **1** *vt* **(a)** (*verser*) to pour out; (*faire tomber*) to spill (*salt, wine etc*); to shed (*tears, blood*);

(b) (*disperser*) to spread, to scatter; to shed (*light*); to give off, to give out (*heat, scent*); to strew (*flowers*); to sprinkle (*sand*); **r. du sable sur le plancher,** to sprinkle sand on the floor *or* the floor with sand; **r. la terreur,** to spread terror; **cette nouvelle répandit la tristesse dans la ville,** this news cast a gloom over *or* spread gloom throughout the town; **r. une nouvelle,** to spread *or* circulate a piece of news; **r. une mode,** to spread a fashion;

(c) to lavish (*benefits etc*).

2 se répandre *vpr* **(a)** (*of liquid, smoke, sand etc*) to spill; (*of smell, panic, rumour*) to spread; **la foule se répandit dans la rue,** the crowd spilled into the street; **les touristes se répandent dans la ville,** tourists are invading *or* overrunning the town; **cette opinion/cette pratique se répand,** this opinion/this practice is gaining ground *or* is spreading; **la nouvelle s'est répandue peu à peu,** the news spread gradually; **l'usage de cet article s'est répandu,** this article is now widely used;

(b) se r. en explications, to launch forth into explanations; **se r. en excuses,** to apologize profusely, to be full of apologies; **se r. sur un sujet,** to give forth *or* expatiate on a subject;

(c) *Vieilli* **se r. dans le monde,** to lead a social life; **il faut vous r.,** you should get about more.

répandu [repɑ̃dy] *adj* **(a)** widespread, prevalent (*method, prejudice etc*); widely read (*magazine*); widely held (*opinion*); **(b)** *Vieilli* widely known (*person*), (*person*) much in evidence; **il est très r. dans les milieux politiques,** he is well known in political circles.

réparable [reparabl] *adj* **(a)** repairable, mendable (*shoe, machine etc*); **(b)** reparable (*mistake, loss*).

reparaître [rəparɛtr] *vi* (*conj like* **paraître**; *aux often* **avoir**) to reappear; (*of disease*) to recur.

réparateur, -trice [reparatœr, -tris] **1** *adj* refreshing (*sleep*); **chirurgie réparatrice,** reconstructive surgery. **2** *n* repairer, mender.

réparation [reparɑsjɔ̃] *nf* **(a)** repair(ing), mending (*of shoe, machine*); repair(ing) (*of house etc*); restoring, restoration (*of one's strength*); **réparations d'entretien,** maintenance; **être en r.,** to be under repair; **route en r.,** road up for repairs; **faire des réparations,** to make repairs; **(b)** (*satisfaction*) reparation, amends, redress; *Arch* (*par les armes*) satisfaction (*by duel*); **la r. des dégâts,** making good the damage; **en r. d'un tort,** in reparation of *or* in atonement for a wrong; **réparations de guerre,** war reparations; *Jur* **r. légale,** legal redress; **r. civile,** compensation; *Fb* **coup de pied de r.,** penalty kick; *Fb* **surface de r.,** penalty area.

réparer [repare] *vt* **(a)** to repair, to mend (*shoe, machine etc*); to repair (*house etc*); to refit (*ship*); **r. ses forces,** to restore one's strength; **r. le désordre,** to put things in order, to restore order; **r. ses pertes,** to repair *or* make good one's losses; **la maison a besoin d'être réparée,** the house is in need of repair *or* needs to be repaired; **(b)** (*remédier à*) to make atonement *or* amends for (*misdeed*); to repair, to rectify, to put right (*mistake*); to make good, to rectify (*omission*); to redress (*wrong*); to make good (*damage*).

reparler [rəparle] **1** *vi* **r. de qch,** to speak about sth again; **il ne faut plus en r.,** it must not be mentioned again; **r. à qn,** to speak to s.o. again. **2 se reparler** *vpr* to speak to each other again.

repartager [rəpartaʒe] *vt* (*conj like* **partager**) to share (out) *or* divide (up) again.

repartie [rəparti] *nf* retort, rejoinder; **avoir l'esprit de r., avoir la r. prompte, avoir de la r.,** to be quick at repartee.

repartir [rəpartir] *vi* (*conj like* **partir**) **(a)** (*aux* **être**) (*of traveller, train etc*) to set *or* start off again; (*of fire, machine etc*) to start (up) again; **je repars pour Paris,** I'm off to Paris again; **r. à zéro,** to start from scratch again, to go back to square one; **r. à rire,** to burst out laughing again; *F* **ça repart, ils se disputent encore!,** they're off arguing again!; **(b)** (*aux* **avoir**) (*répondre*) to retort, to reply.

répartir [repartir] *v* (**je répartis, n. répartissons**) **1** *vt* **(a)** (*partager*) to distribute, to divide (up), to share (out) (**entre,** among); to distribute (*weight, load*); to spread (out) (*courses, payments etc*); **r. un dividende,** to distribute a dividend; **versements répartis sur plusieurs années,** payments spread (out) over several years; **charge uniformément répartie,** evenly distributed load; *Couture* **r. le surplus du col,** to ease the collar (onto the neckband);

(b) (*déterminer*) to apportion, to allocate (*expenses etc*); to assess (*taxes*); to allot, to allocate (*shares*); **r. une avarie,** to adjust an average.

2 se répartir *vpr* to split (up); **ils se répartissent le travail,** they are dividing (up) *or* sharing (out) the work among themselves; **les sommes se répartissent ainsi,** the amounts are divided (up) *or* split (up) like this.

répartiteur [repartitœr] *nm* distributer, apportioner; **(commissaire) r.,** assessor of taxes.

répartition [repartisjɔ̃] *nf* **(a)** (*manière de partage*) (manner of) distribution; **r. de la population par groupes d'âge,** breakdown of the population according to age group; **(b)** (*partage*) distribution, dividing up, sharing out **(entre**

plusieurs personnes, among several people); apportionment, allocation (*of expenses, liabilities etc*); assessment (*of taxes*); *Bourse* allotment, allocation (*of shares*); (*dividende*) dividend; **r. d'avarie,** adjustment of average; *Bourse* **(lettre d')avis de r.,** letter of allotment *or* allocation; **première et unique r.,** first and final dividend; **dernière r.,** final dividend.

repas [rəpɑ] *nm* meal; (*d'animal*) feed, feeding; **faire trois r. par jour,** to have three meals a day; **r. de noce,** ≈ wedding breakfast; **faire un r.,** to have a meal; **léger r., petit r.,** light meal, snack; **aux heures de r.,** at meal times; **prendre ses r. chez qn/chez soi,** to board with s.o./to eat at home; **colis-r.,** packed meal; **plateau-r.,** meal on a tray.

repassage [rəpasaʒ] *nm* ironing (*of clothes*); **faire du r.,** to do some ironing; **n'exigeant aucun r.,** non-iron; **table de r.,** ironing board.

repasser [rəpase] **1** *vi* (*aux* **avoir** *ou* **être**) **(a)** (*devant qch ou un lieu*) to pass (by) again, to go by again, to come by again; **r. chez qn,** to call on s.o. again; **une idée me repasse dans l'esprit,** an idea keeps running through my mind; *F* **il peut toujours r.!,** he's got another think coming!;

(b) *Ordinat* to rerun; **faites r. la dernière phrase,** (*de bande magnétique*) play back the last sentence; **ce film repasse au Royal,** the film is showing again *or* is on again at the Royal.

2 *vt* **(a)** (*franchir*) to pass over *or* cross (over) (*mountain, frontier etc*) again; **r. la mer,** to cross the sea again;

(b) (*répéter*) to replay, to play back (*tape, record*); to show (*film*) again; **r. qch dans son esprit,** to go over sth in one's mind; **r. une leçon/un rôle,** to look over *or* go over a lesson/a part; **r. un examen,** to resit an exam, to take *or* sit an exam again;

(c) (*transporter*) to take *or* convey over again; **le batelier nous repassera,** the boatman will ferry us back;

(d) (*donner*) **r. un plat à qn,** to pass s.o. a dish again; **r. une fausse pièce à qn,** to palm off *or* foist *or* unload a dud coin on s.o.;

(e) (*aiguiser*) to sharpen, to whet, to grind (*knife, tool*); **r. un rasoir sur le cuir,** to strop a razor;

(f) (*avec un fer*) to iron (*clothes*); **fer à r.,** iron; **planche à r.,** ironing board.

repasseur, -euse [rəpasœr, -øz] **1** *nm* (knife) grinder. **2** *nf* **repasseuse,** (*personne*) ironer; (*machine*) ironing machine.

repavage [rəpavaʒ] *nm,* **repavement** [rəpavmɑ̃] *nm* repaving.

repaver [rəpave] *vt* to repave.

repayer [rəpeje] *vt* (*conj like* **payer**) to pay again.

repêchage [rəpɛʃaʒ] *nm* **(a)** fishing out (*from water*); **(b)** *Fig* helping, rescuing (*of person in difficulties*); **épreuve de r.,** *Scol* supplementary examination (*for candidates who have failed*); *Sp* repechage, extra heat (*for runners-up*); *Can* selectors' meeting (*to pick young competitors*).

repêcher [rəpeʃe] *vt* **(a)** (*retirer de l'eau*) to fish out; **(b)** *Fig* to rescue, to help (out) (*s.o. in difficulties*); *Scol* **r. un candidat à l'oral,** to let a candidate scrape through at the oral; *Sp* **r. un concurrent,** to let a competitor go through; **ceux qui ont échoué au mois de juillet peuvent être repêchés en octobre,** those who failed in July may sit the exam again in October.

repeindre [rəpɛ̃dr] *vt* (*conj like* **peindre**) to repaint.

repeint [rəpɛ̃] *nm Beaux-Arts* touched-up area.

repenser [rəpɑ̃se] **1** *vi* to think again (**à,** about); **j'y repenserai,** I shall think it over *or* think about it again *or* give it some more thought; **je n'y ai pas repensé,** I haven't given it another thought *or* thought about it again. **2** *vt* to reconsider (*problem, plan etc*); to rethink (*concept*); **r. le transport/***etc*, to rethink the whole question of transport/*etc*.

repentant [rəpɑ̃tɑ̃] *adj* repentant.

repenti, -ie [rəpɑ̃ti] **1** *adj* repentant. **2** *adj & nf* **(fille) repentie,** reformed prostitute.

repentir[1] [rəpɑ̃tir] *nm Rel* repentance; *Fig* regret.

repentir[2] (se) [sərəpɑ̃tir] *vpr* (*prp* **se repentant**; *pp* **repenti**; *pr ind* **je me repens, il se repent**; *pr sub* **je me repente**; *p hist* **je me repentis**) *Rel* to repent; **se r. de qch/d'avoir fait qch,** to repent of sth/of having done sth; *Fig* to repent *or* regret *or* be sorry for sth/for having done sth.

repérage [rəperaʒ] *nm* **(a)** (*action de marquer, jalonnement*) marking off *or* out; **(b)** (*action de trouver*) locating (*of fault, target etc*); identifying, *F* spotting (*of enemy aircraft*); **r. radio,** radio location, radio fix; *Cin* **faire des repérages avant de faire un film,** to check the location(s) before making a film; **partir en r.,** to go to check the location(s).

repercer [rəpɛrse] *vt* (*conj like* **percer**) *Tech* to pierce (*metal*).

répercussion [repɛrkysjɔ̃] *nf* **(a)** reverberation (*of sound*); **(b)** *Fig* repercussion (**sur,** on).

répercuter [repɛrkyte] **1** *vt* **(a)** to reverberate, to reflect back (*sound*); to reflect (*light, heat*); **(b)** to pass on (*an order, a price increase etc*); **r. l'augmentation des salaires sur les prix,** to pass the wage increase on to prices. **2 se répercuter** *vpr* (*of sound*) to reverberate; (*of light*) to reflect; *Fig* to have repercussions (**sur,** on).

reperdre [rəpɛrdr] *vt* to lose again.

repère [rəpɛr] *nm* **(a)** reference, guide; (*marque*) reference mark, guide mark; (*en arpentage*) bench mark; (*balise, jalon*) marker; *Tech* **r. de montage/d'ajustage,** assembly/line-up mark; **(b) point de r.,** landmark; *Fig* **les points de r. dans la vie,** the landmarks *or* reference points in one's life.

repérer [rəpere] *v* (**je repère, n. repérons; je repérerai**) **1** *vt* **(a)** (*marquer, jalonner*) to mark off *or* out; **(b)** (*trouver*) to locate (*fault, target, place etc*); to identify, *F* to spot (*aircraft*); **r. qn dans la foule,** to spot s.o. *or* pick s.o. out in the crowd; *Courses de chevaux* **r. les gagnants,** to pick the winners; **se faire r.,** to attract attention. **2 se repérer** *vpr* to get one's bearings, to find one's way about; **je n'arrive pas à me r. dans ce problème,** I can't make head (n)or tail of this problem.

répertoire [repɛrtwar] *nm* **(a)** (*liste*) index, list; (*table*) table; (*catalogue*) catalogue; *Ordinat* directory; **r. à onglets,** thumb index; **r. d'adresses,** directory; (*carnet*) address book; **r. des rues,** street index; **(b)** *Th Mus* repertoire, repertory; **pièce de** *ou* **du r.,** stock piece; **le r. classique,** the classical repertoire *or* repertory; **il a un r. de trois discours,** he has three stock speeches *or* a repertoire of three speeches.

répertorier [repɛrtɔrje] *vt* (*impf & pr sub* **n. répertoriions**) to index, to list (*item*).

repeser [rəpəze] *vt* (*conj like* **peser**) to reweigh.

répété [repete] *adj* repeated.

répéter [repete] *v* (**je répète, n. répétons; je répéterai**) **1** *vt* **(a)** to repeat (*words, secret, action, experience etc*); **r. que,** to repeat that; **je t'ai répété cent fois de ne pas le faire,** I've told you a hundred times not to do it; **je ne me le ferai pas r.,** I shall not need to be told twice; **(b)** to rehearse (*play*); to practice (*piece of music*); to learn (*part, lesson*). **2 se répéter** *vpr* (*of person*) to repeat oneself; (*of event etc*) to recur, to happen again. **3** *vi Th* to rehearse.

répétiteur, -trice [repetitœr, -tris] **1** *n Scol* (private) tutor, coach. **2** *nm Nau* (signal) repeater.

répétitif, -ive [repetitif, -iv] *adj* repetitive.

répétition [repetisjɔ̃] *nf* **(a)** repetition (*of word, action etc*); *Ordinat* **fonction de r.,** repeat function; **fusil à r.,** repeating rifle; **des laryngites à r.,** repeated bouts of laryngitis; **montre à r.,** repeater (watch); **(b)** *Th* rehearsal; *Mus* practice; **r. générale** *ou* **en costume,** dress rehearsal; **mettre une pièce en r.,** to put a play into rehearsal; **(c)** *Scol* private lesson.

repeuplement [rəpœpləmɑ̃] *nm* repopulation (*of country etc*); restocking (*of pond*); replanting (*of forest*).

repeupler [rəpœple] **1** *vt* to repopulate (*country etc*); to restock (*pond*); to replant (*forest*). **2 se repeupler** *vpr* to be repopulated, to become repopulated; **la ville se repeuple,** the population of the town is increasing again.

repincer [rəpɛ̃se] *vt* (*conj like* **pincer**) *F* **on ne m'y repincera pas,** you won't catch me at it again.

repiquage [rəpikaʒ] *nm* **(a)** *Couture* restitching; **(b)** mending, repairing (*of road*); **(c)** pricking out, planting out (*of seedlings*); **(d)** subculturing (*of bacteria*); **(e)** re-recording (*of record*); **(f)** *Phot* retouching.

repiquer [rəpike] **1** *vt* **(a)** (*percer*) to prick *or* pierce (*sth*) again; **(b)** to mend, to repair (*road*); **(c)** *Couture* to restitch; **(d)** to prick out, to plant out (*seedlings*); **plant à r.,** bedding plant; **(e)** to dress (*millstone*); **(f)** to subculture (*bacteria*); **(g)** to re-record (*record, tune*); **(h)** *Phot* to retouch; **(i)** *F* (*reprendre*) to catch (*s.o.*) again; **et que je ne te repique pas à faire ça!,** don't let me catch you doing that again! **2** *vi F* **r. au plat,** to have a second helping; *F* **r. au truc,** to be at it again.

répit [repi] *nm* respite, breathing space; *Com* **jours de r.,** days of grace; **ne laisser aucun r. à qn,** to give s.o. no respite; **laisser un moment de r. à qn,** to give s.o. a breather; **prendre un moment de r.,** to take a breather; **sans r.,** without a break, continuously; **souffrir sans r.,** to have no respite from pain.

replacement [rəplasmɑ̃] *nm* **(a)** replacement, replacing (*of object etc*), putting back (*of object etc*) in its place *or* where it belongs; **(b)** reinvestment (*of funds*); **(c) r. de qn,** finding a new job for s.o..

replacer [rəplase] *v* (*conj like* **placer**) **1** *vt* **(a)** to replace (*object etc*), to put (*object etc*) back in its place *or* where it belongs; *Fig* to put (*event etc*) in context; **(b)** to reinvest (*funds*); **(c)** to find fresh employment *or* a new job for (*s.o.*). **2 se replacer** *vpr* to find (oneself) a new job.

replanter [rəplɑ̃te] *vt* to replant; **r. une forêt en sapins,** to replant a forest with firs.

replat [rəpla] *nm* (*de versant*) shelf.

replâtrage [rəplɑtraʒ] *nm* **(a)** replastering (*of wall*); **(b)** (*pour camoufler*) patching up; **(c)** (*réparation grossière*) superficial repair; **(d)** *Fig* (*réconciliation superficielle*) patched-up *or* makeshift peace.

replâtrer [rəplɑtre] *vt* **(a)** to replaster (*wall*); **(b)** to patch up (*sth unsound*); **(c)** *Fig* to patch up (*quarrel, friendship*).

replet, -ète [rəplɛ, -ɛt] *adj* stoutish, podgy, dumpy (*person*); chubby, podgy (*face*).

réplétion [replesjɔ̃] *nf* repletion.

repleuvoir [rəplœvwar] *v impers* to rain again.

repli [rəpli] *nm* **(a)** fold, turn (*in cloth*); **replis du terrain,** folds in the ground; *Fig* **les plis et les replis du cœur,** the innermost recesses of the heart; **une attitude de r.,** a withdrawn attitude; **(b)** winding, bend, meander (*of river*); coil (*of rope, snake, intestine*); **(c)** *Mil* falling back, withdrawal.

repliable [rəplijabl] *adj* folding.

repliement [rəplimɑ̃] *nf* **(a)** folding up (*of object*); **(b)** *Mil* falling back, withdrawal; **(c)** (*sur soi-même*) withdrawal, withdrawing (into oneself).

replier [rəplije] *v* (*conj like* **plier**) **1** *vt* **(a)** to fold up (*newspaper, sheet, blade of penknife etc*) (again); to turn *or* fold down (*edge, corner*); to roll up (*one's sleeves*); to tuck up (*one's legs*); (*of bird*) to fold (*wings*); **(b)** *Mil* to withdraw, to pull back (*troops*). **2 se replier** *vpr* **(a)** (*of object*) to fold up; (*of snake*) to coil up; **(b)** (*of stream, path*) to wind, to turn, to meander; **(c) se r. sur soi-même,** to withdraw into oneself; **(d)** (*of troops*) to fall back, to withdraw.

réplique [replik] *nf* **(a)** (*réponse*) retort, rejoinder; **avoir la r. prompte,** to be ready with an answer; **preuve qui ne souffre aucune r.,** incontrovertible proof; **argument sans r.,** unanswerable argument; **obéir sans r.,** to obey without a word; *F* **et pas de r.!,** don't answer (me) back!; **(b)** *Th* line(s); **manquer sa r.,** to miss one's cue; **donner la r. à un acteur,** to play opposite an actor; **(c)** (*copie*) replica; (*sosie*) double.

répliquer [replike] **1** *vt* **r. qch à qn,** to say sth in answer to s.o.; **'pas de danger!', répliqua-t-il,** 'not likely!', he retorted. **2** *vi* (*répondre*) to retort, (*avec impertinence*) to answer back; **r. à qn,** to answer s.o. back; **il répliqua par un coup de pied,** he answered with a kick.

replisser [rəplise] *vt* to re-pleat (*skirt*).

replonger [rəplɔ̃ʒe] *v* (*conj like* **plonger**) **1** *vt* to plunge again (**dans,** into). **2 se replonger** *vpr* **se r. dans l'étude/***etc*, to become immersed again in study/*etc*. **3** *vi* to dive (in) again.

repolir [rəpɔlir] *vt* to repolish; *Fig* to polish up (*one's style*).

répondant, -ante [repɔ̃dɑ̃, -ɑ̃t] *nm* **(a)** (*responsable, garant*) surety, security, guarantor; *F* **avoir du r.,** to have plenty of money stashed away; **(b)** *Rel* server (*at mass*).

répondeur, -euse [repɔ̃dœr, -øz] **1** *adj* given to answering back, impertinent. **2** *nm* **r. (téléphonique), r. enregistreur,** (telephone) answering machine.

répondre [repɔ̃dr] **1** *vt* **(a)** to answer, to reply; to answer *or* reply with (*remark, letter, etc*); **r. que,** to answer *or* reply that; **qu'est-ce qu'elle vous a répondu?,** what was her answer *or* reply (to you)?, what did she tell you (in reply)?; **je n'ai rien répondu,** I made no reply, I gave no answer *or* reply; **il répondit n'en rien savoir,** he answered *or* replied that he knew nothing about it; *Pol* **Londres a immédiatement répondu présent,** London immediately signalled its readiness to help;

(b) *Rel* **r. la messe,** to make the responses at Mass.

2 *vi* **(a)** to answer, to reply; **r. à,** to answer, to reply to (*person, letter etc*); to return, to acknowledge (*greeting*); to answer (*accusation*); to comply with, to fall in with (*request*); **r. par écrit,** to reply in writing, to write back; **elle ne m'a pas encore répondu,** she hasn't answered me *or* replied to me yet, I haven't had an answer *or* a reply from her yet; **r. à l'appel,** to answer the roll *or* to one's name; **r. à un coup de sonnette,** to answer the bell; **r. à l'amour de qn,** to respond to *or* return s.o.'s love; **les freins n'ont pas répondu,** there was no response from the brakes, the brakes didn't respond; **le chien répond à son nom,** the dog responds *or* answers to his name; *Tél* **ça ne répond pas,** there's no answer;

(b) r. à qch, to answer, to meet; to fulfil (*need, purpose*); to come up to (*standard, expectations*); to comply *or* agree with (*formula*); **ne pas r. à l'attente,** to fall short of expectation;

(c) r. de qn/qch, to answer for s.o./sth, to be answerable *or* accountable *or* responsible for s.o./sth; **il va revenir, je vous en réponds,** he will come back, I assure you *or* take my word for it; **j'en répondrais,** I'd stake my life on it; **je ne réponds de rien,** I'm promising nothing, I'm making no promises.

répons [repɔ̃] *nm Rel* response.

réponse [repɔ̃s] *nf* **(a)** answer, reply; **avoir** *ou* **trouver r. à tout,** to have *or* find an answer for everything, never to be at a loss for an answer; **rendre r. à qn,** to return s.o. an answer, to reply to s.o.; **faire une r. de Normand,** to give a non-committal *or* an evasive reply; **argument sans r.,** unanswerable argument; **elle fait toujours les questions et les réponses,** she always does all the talking; **pour toute r., elle éclata en sanglots,** her only answer was to break into sobs; *F* **j'ai sonné plusieurs fois, mais pas de r.,** I've rung several times, but there's no answer; **en r. à votre lettre,** in answer *or* reply to your letter; **lettre restée sans r.,** letter left unanswered; **bulletin-/carte-r.,** reply coupon/card; **r. payée,** reply paid; *Jur* **droit de r.,** right to reply (*in the press*);

(b) response (*to an appeal*);

(c) *Physiol* responsiveness, response (*to stimulus*);

(d) response (*of engine, brakes etc*);

(e) *Ordinat* answering; **r. automatique,** unattended answering;

(f) (*solution*) answer (**à,** to).

repopulation [rəpɔpylɑsjɔ̃] *nf* repopulation, repopulating (*of region etc*).

report [rəpɔr] *nm* **(a)** (*en comptabilité*) carrying forward, bringing forward (*of total*); **le r. d'un rendez-vous à une date ultérieure,** the postponement of an appointment until a later date; **le r. des voix au second tour,** the transfer of votes to the second-round candidate; **(b)** (*somme*) amount carried forward, carry forward, carry over; **(c)** *Bourse* contango(ing), continuation; **prendre des actions en r.,** to take in stock; **(taux de) r.,** contango (rate), continuation rate; **(d)** *Phot* transfer; **papier (à) r.,** transfer paper; **(e)** *Typ* lines carried over; **(f)** *Rad* plot(ting); **table de r.,** plotting board; **(g)** *Ordinat* carry; **(h)** *Courses de chevaux* double.

reportage [rəpɔrtaʒ] *nm Journ Rad TV* **(a)** (*article, émission*) report; (*en direct*) (live) commentary (*on a match etc*); **r. en exclusivité,** scoop, exclusive report; **(b)** (*activité*) reporting; **faire du r.,** to do some reporting; (*métier*) to be a reporter.

reporter¹ [rəpɔrtɛr] *nm Journ Rad TV* reporter; **r. photographe,** press photographer.

reporter² [rəpɔrte] **1** *vt* **(a)** (*pour rendre*) to take (*sth*) back; **r. un livre à qn,** to take a book back to s.o.;

(b) (*dans le temps etc*) to take *or* carry (*s.o.*) back; to trace back (*origins*);

(c) r. qch à plus tard, to postpone *or* put off *or* defer sth until later;

(d) (*comptabilité*) to carry forward, to bring forward, to carry over (*total*); **à r.,** carried forward;

(e) *Bourse* to contango; **(faire) r. des titres,** to take in stock;

(f) (*transcrire*) *& Phot* to transfer (**sur,** to).

2 se reporter *vpr* **(a) se r. à un document,** to refer *or* turn to a document; **se r. à ...,** (*dans un livre etc*) the reader is referred to ..., see ...;

(b) se r. au passé/à la période de l'après-guerre/*etc*, to look back *or* think back to the past/to the post-war period/*etc*;

(c) (*se déplacer*) to be transferred; **sa colère s'est reportée sur moi,** his anger has been transferred to me.

repos [rəpo] *nm* **(a)** rest, *Fml* repose; **au** *ou* **en r.,** at rest; **se donner** *ou* **prendre du r.,** to take a rest; **maison de r.,** rest home, convalescent home; **le dimanche est mon unique jour de r.,** Sunday is my only day off; **le r. éternel,** eternal rest; **terre au r.,** fallow land; *Mil* **r.!,** (stand) at ease!; **(b)** *Tech* **au r.,** (*rifle*) at halfcock; (*mechanism*) in neutral (position); (*machine*) out of gear; **(c)** *Littér* pause, rest (*in a verse*); **(d)** (*quiétude*) peace, tranquillity (of mind); **être en r. au sujet de qn,** to feel easy in one's mind about s.o.; **laisser qn en r.,** to leave s.o. alone *or* in peace; **de tout r.,** absolutely safe; **valeur de tout r.,** safe investment, gilt-edged security; **vivre avec lui, ce n'est pas de tout r.!**, living with him is no bed of roses!

reposant [rəpozɑ̃] *adj* restful, relaxing (*holiday etc*); refreshing (*sleep*); soothing (*colour*).

reposé [rəpoze] *adj* **(a)** rested, refreshed (*person, mind*); fresh (*face*); **s'éveiller bien r.**, to awake refreshed; **(b) je le ferai à tête reposée**, I'll do it when my mind's clearer; **laissez-moi y réfléchir à tête reposée**, give me time to think it over.

repose-bras [rəpoʒbra] *nm inv* armrest.

repose-pied [rəpozpje] *nm inv* footrest (*of motorcycle, chair*).

reposer [rəpoze] **1** *vt* **(a)** (*à sa place*) to put (*sth*) back (down), to replace (*sth*); *Mil* **reposez arme!**, order arms!;

(b) to re-lay (*railway line*);

(c) (*détendre*) to rest; **r. l'esprit**, to rest *or* refresh the mind; **couleur qui repose les yeux**, colour that is restful *or* soothing to the eyes;

(d) to restate (*problem*); to ask (*question*) again.

2 *vi* **(a)** (*of person*) to rest; (*être étendu*) to lie; **le corps reposait sur son lit de parade**, the body was lying in state; **ici repose ...**, here lies (buried) ...; *F* **ça repose, le sauna**, a sauna is restful;

(b) r. sur, to be built on (*rock etc*); *Fig* to be based on; (*dépendre de*) to depend on; **le commerce repose sur le crédit**, commerce is based on credit;

(c) (*of liquid*) to settle; **faire r. ses chevaux**, to rest one's horses; **laisser r. la terre**, to let the ground rest *or* lie fallow.

3 se reposer *vpr* **(a)** (*se relaxer*) to rest, to take a rest; *Fig* **il ne faut pas se r. sur ses lauriers**, you must not rest on your laurels;

(b) se r. sur qn/qch, to rely upon s.o./sth, to put one's trust in s.o./sth; **se r. sur qn du soin de qch**, to rely upon s.o. to look after sth.

repose-tête [rəpoztɛt] *nm inv* headrest.

reposoir [rəpozwar] *nm* (*en plein air*) wayside altar; (*dans l'église*) temporary altar.

repoussage [rəpusaʒ] *nm* embossing, repoussé work.

repoussant [rəpusɑ̃] *adj* repulsive, repellent (*appearance etc*); offensive, repulsive (*smell*).

repousse [rəpus] *nf* regrowth, regrowing (*of hair, plants, lawn etc*).

repoussé [rəpuse] *Tech* **1** *adj* embossed, repoussé; **cuivre r.**, spun copper. **2** *nm* embossing, repoussé.

repoussement [rəpusmɑ̃] *nm* recoil, kick (*of firearm*).

repousser [rəpuse] **1** *vt* **(a)** (*écarter*) to push (*object*) aside *or* away; (*en arrière*) to push (*object*) back; to repel, to beat off (*enemy, attack*); to reject, to turn down (*offer, proposal*); **r. qn**, to push s.o. aside; *Fig* (*rabrouer*) to turn s.o. away; **repoussé de tout le monde**, spurned by all; **r. un projet de loi**, to throw out a bill; **(b)** (*différer*) to postpone, to put off (*event*); **(c)** (*dégoûter*) to be repellent to, to repel (*s.o.*); **(d)** to emboss, to work (*metal, leather*) in repoussé. **2** *vi* (*of tree, plant*) to shoot (up) again, to spring up again; (*of hair, leaves*) to grow again; **elle se fait r. les cheveux**, she's letting her hair grow again.

repoussoir [rəpuswar] *nm* **(a)** (*pour chasser un clou etc*) drift; (*ciseau*) embossing punch; (*de manucure*) cuticle pen; **(b)** *Beaux-Arts* strong piece of foreground; **servir de r. à la beauté de qn**, to set off *or* to serve as a foil to s.o.'s beauty; **quel r.!**, (*personne laide*) what an ugly devil!

répréhensible [repreɑ̃sibl] *adj* reprehensible.

répréhension [repreɑ̃sjɔ̃] *nf* reprehension.

reprendre [rəprɑ̃dr] *v* (*conj like* **prendre**) **1** *vt* **(a)** to retake, to recapture (*town, escaped prisoner*);

(b) r. du pain/vin/*etc*, to take *or* have some more bread/wine/*etc*;

(c) (*récupérer*) to get (*sth*) back; **je suis allé r. mon parapluie**, I went to get back *or* recover my umbrella; **r. sa place**, to resume one's seat; **r. connaissance**, to recover consciousness, to come to; **je vous reprendrai en passant**, I'll pick you up again as I go by;

(d) *Fig* **la fièvre l'a repris**, he has had another bout of fever; **sa timidité l'a repris**, his shyness got the better of him again; *F* **on ne m'y reprendra plus**, I shan't be had *or* caught again *or* another time; **que je ne vous y reprenne plus!**, don't let me catch you at it again!;

(e) to take back (*gift, unsold goods, sale item etc*); to re-engage (*employee*); to retract (*promise*); to go back on (*one's word*); **le garagiste me l'a repris à l'achat de la nouvelle**, the man at the garage took it off me in part exchange *or* as a trade-in for the new car;

(f) (*recommencer*) to resume, to take up again (*conversation, habits, work*); **reprenons les faits**, let us go over the facts again *or* recapitulate (the facts); **r. l'affaire à son origine**, to go back to the beginning; **r. du goût pour qch**, to recover one's taste for sth; **r. la route**, to take (to) the road again; **r. son cours**, to continue *or* carry on as before; **r. une pièce**, to revive a play; **r. des forces**, to regain strength; **r. courage**, to take courage again; **r. la parole**, to resume, to go on (talking, speaking); **r. un refrain en chœur**, to take up *or* join in a chorus; **'oui', reprit-il**, 'yes', he replied; **r. les choses en main**, to take things in hand again;

(g) (*réparer*) to repair, to mend; (*corriger*) to redo (*text*); to retouch (*painting*); *Couture* to alter; **r. un mur en sous-œuvre**, to underpin a wall;

(h) (*critiquer*) to reprove, to reprimand (*s.o.*) (**de**, for); to find fault with (*sth*).

2 *vi* **(a)** (*recommencer*) to start *or* begin again; (*of fashion*) to return, to be revived; (*of patient, business*) to recover, to pick up again; **les cours reprennent à quatorze heures**, classes start *or* begin again at two o'clock; **le froid a repris**, the cold weather has set in again;

(b) (*of plant*) to take (root) again, to strike (root).

3 se reprendre *vpr* **(a)** (*se ressaisir*) to recover, to pull oneself together; **reprends-toi!**, pull yourself together!, get a grip on yourself!; **donnez-moi le temps de me r.**, give me time to collect myself *or* my thoughts;

(b) (*se corriger*) to correct oneself (*in speaking*);

(c) se r. à faire qch, to begin *or* start to do sth again; **se r. à la vie**, to get a new lease of life;

(d) s'y r. à plusieurs fois pour faire qch, to make several attempts *or* have several goes at doing sth (*before succeeding*).

représailles [rəprezaj] *nfpl* reprisals, retaliation; **en r. pour** *ou* **de qch**, as a reprisal for sth; **expédition de r.**, punitive expedition; **user de r.**, to take reprisals.

représentable [rəprezɑ̃tabl] *adj* representable.

représentant, -ante [rəprezɑ̃tɑ̃, -ɑ̃t] *n* **(a)** representative; **être le r. de l'opinion publique**, to represent public opinion; **r. syndical**, (trade-)union representative; *US* **la Chambre des représentants**, the House of Representatives; *Pol* **le r. de la France à Londres**, France's representative in London; **(b)** *Com* (sales) representative, *F* (sales) rep (**en**, for); **(c)** *Jur* representative (heir).

représentatif, -ive [rəprezɑ̃tatif, -iv] *adj* **(a)** representative; **symbole r. du pouvoir**, symbol representative of *or* representing power; **(b)** *Vieilli* (*imposant*) dignified, impressive (*person*).

représentation [rəprezɑ̃tasjɔ̃] *nf* **(a)** *Pol Jur etc* representation; (*représentants*) representatives; *Pol* **r. proportionnelle**, proportional representation; **r. syndicale**, (trade-)union representation; (*représentants*) (trade-) union representatives; **(b)** *Com* (sales) representation; **faire de la r., être dans la r.**, to be a (sales) representative *or F* a (sales) rep; **(c)** representation (*of concept, facts, object etc*); **c'est sa r. de la situation**, that's his idea of the situation, that's how he sees the situation; *Psy* **faculté de la r. spatiale**, space perception; **(d)** *Jur* production (*of documents etc*); **(e)** *Th* performance; **troupe en r.**, company on tour; **droits de r.**, performing rights; **(f) frais de r.**, entertainment allowance; *F* **être en r.**, to be trying to impress.

représentativité [rəprezɑ̃tativite] *nf* representativeness.

représenter [rəprezɑ̃te] **1** *vt* **(a)** (*présenter de nouveau*) to present (*sth*) again; **je voudrais r. ce candidat (au concours)**, I would like to re-enter this candidate (for the exam);

(b) *Jur* to produce (*documents etc*);

(c) (*figurer*) to represent; **tableau représentant un moulin**, picture representing a mill; **r. qn comme un imposteur**, to represent s.o. as an impostor; **il me représente son père**, he puts me in mind of *or* he reminds me of his father;

(d) (*pour qn*) to represent (*s.o.*); **se faire r.**, to appoint *or* send a representative; *Pol* **r. une circonscription**, to represent *or* sit for a constituency; **il représente la France aux Jeux Olympiques**, he's representing France in the Olympic Games; **r. une maison de commerce**, to represent a firm; *Jur* **r. qn en justice**, to appear for s.o.;

(e) (*correspondre à*) to represent (*amount, number etc*); **ceci représente de nombreuses heures de travail**, this represents many hours of work; **cela ne représente pas une grosse somme** *ou* **beaucoup pour lui**, this does not mean much to him;

(f) *Th* to perform, to put on (*play*);

(g) r. qch à qn, to point out sth to s.o..

2 *vi* (*en imposer*) **r. (bien)**, to impress people, to cut a fine figure, to have a good presence; **il ne représente pas au physique,** he's not very impressive physically.

3 se représenter *vpr* **(a) se r. à un examen,** to resit an exam; **se r. aux élections,** *Br* to stand for *or Am* to run for election again;

(b) *(of opportunity)* to occur again, to recur;

(c) se r. comme officier/*etc*, to describe oneself as an officer/*etc*;

(d) *(s'imaginer)* to imagine; **représentez-vous mon étonnement,** (just) imagine my astonishment.

répressif, -ive [represif, -iv] *adj* repressive *(law, parents etc)*.

répression [represjɔ̃] *nf* repression; **mesures de r.,** repressive measures.

réprimandable [reprimɑ̃dabl] *adj* reproachable, blameworthy, *Fml* reprovable.

réprimande [reprimɑ̃d] *nf* reprimand, *Fml* reproof; **faire une r. à qn,** to reprimand s.o., *Fml* to reprove s.o., *F* to tell s.o. off; **air de r.,** reproving look.

réprimander [reprimɑ̃de] *vt* to reprimand, *Fml* to reprove, *F* to tell *(s.o.)* off.

réprimer [reprime] *vt* to repress, to suppress, to check *(crime, desire, anger etc)*; to suppress, to hold back *(laughter, sob, tears)*; to repress, to suppress, to quell, to put down *(revolt)*.

reprint [rəprint] *nm (livre)* reprint.

repris [rəpri] *nm* **r. de justice,** habitual criminal *or* offender.

reprisage [rəprizaʒ] *nm* mending, darning *(of garment)*.

reprise [rəpriz] *nf* **(a)** *Mil* retaking, recapture *(of position etc)*;

(b) *Com* taking back *(of unsold goods, sale items etc)*; *Jur* **droit de r.,** right to recover possession; **r. jusqu'à 5 000 francs,** part exchange *or* trade-in (allowance) up to 5,000 francs;

(c) resumption *(of work, debate)*; renewal, resumption *(of negotiations)*; return, revival *(of fashion)*; *Th* revival *(of play)*; *Cin* rerun *(of film)*; *Rad TV* repeat; *Ordinat* rerun;

(d) renewal *(of activity)*; return *(of cold weather)*; fresh bout *(of fever)*; **r. des affaires,** recovery *or* revival of business; **mouvement de r.,** upward movement;

(e) r. (de vitesse), pick-up, acceleration *(of engine)*; **cette voiture a une très bonne r.,** this car accelerates quickly *or* has good acceleration;

(f) *Boxe* round; *Escrime* bout; *Fb* second half *(of game)*; *Équitation* lesson; *(groupe de cavaliers)* riders;

(g) faire qch à plusieurs reprises, to do sth several times *or* repeatedly *or* on several occasions; **à trois reprises,** three times, on three occasions;

(h) *Mus* repeat; re-entry *(of theme, instruments)*;

(i) *Couture (action)* darning, mending *(of sock)*; mending *(of garment)*; *(raccord)* darn, mend; **r. perdue,** invisible mend;

(j) *Constr* **r. en sous-œuvre,** underpinning;

(k) *(somme payée à un locataire)* = money paid for fittings and improvements *(paid to outgoing tenant)*.

repriser [rəprize] *vt* to mend *(garment)*; to darn, to mend *(sock)*; **aiguille/coton/œuf à r.,** darning needle/cotton/egg *or* mushroom.

réprobateur, -trice [reprɔbatœr, -tris] *adj* reproving.

réprobation [reprɔbɑsjɔ̃] *nf* reprobation.

reproche [rəprɔʃ] *nm* **(a)** *(remontrance)* reproach; **faire des reproches à qn,** to reproach *or* censure *or* upbraid s.o.; **je ne vous fais pas de reproches,** I am not blaming you; **elle est un r. vivant pour moi,** she is a constant reproach to me; **ton de r.,** reproachful tone; **vie sans r.,** blameless life; **le seul r. qu'on puisse faire à ce roman, c'est ...,** the only criticism one can make about *or* the only thing wrong with this novel is ...; **(b)** *Jur* **r. de témoin,** objection to witness.

reprocher [rəprɔʃe] **1** *vt* **(a)** to reproach; **r. qch à qn,** to reproach s.o. for sth; **je ne vous reproche rien,** I'm not blaming you for anything; **r. qn d'avoir fait qch,** to reproach *or* blame s.o. for having done sth; **qu'est-ce que vous reprochez à ce livre?,** what do you find wrong with this book?; **(b)** *Jur* to object to *(witness, evidence)*. **2 se reprocher** *vpr* **se r. qch,** to reproach oneself with sth, to blame oneself for sth; **je me reproche de lui avoir fait confiance,** I reproach *or* blame myself for having trusted him.

reproducteur, -trice [rəprɔdyktœr, -tris] **1** *adj* **(a)** reproductive *(organ, cell etc)*; **(b)** *(animal)* kept for breeding; stud *(horse)*. **2** *nm (animal)* breeder; **reproducteurs,** breeding stock, breeders; **r. d'élite,** pedigree sire.

reproductif, -ive [rəprɔdyktif, -iv] *adj* reproductive.

reproduction [rəprɔdyksjɔ̃] *nf* **(a)** *(génération)* reproduction; **les organes de la r.,** the reproductive organs; **animaux élevés en vue de la r.,** animals reared for breeding; **r. sexuée/asexuée,** sexual/asexual reproduction; **(b)** reproduction, reproducing *(of document, picture, sound etc)*; *(image)* reproduction; **droits de r.,** reproduction rights; **droits de r. en feuilleton,** serial rights; **(c)** *(copie)* copy, reproduction.

reproduire [rəprɔdɥir] *v (conj like* **produire***)* **1** *vt* to reproduce *(sound, picture, document etc)*; *Journ* to reprint *(article)*. **2 se reproduire** *vpr* **(a)** *(of animals etc)* to reproduce, to breed, to multiply; **(b)** *(of events)* to recur, to happen again; **et que cela ne se reproduise plus!,** don't let it happen again!

reprographie [rəprɔgrafi] *nf* duplicating *(of documents)*, *Spéc* reprography.

reprographier [rəprɔgrafje] *vt* to duplicate *(document)*.

réprouvé, -ée [repruve] *n* outcast, reprobate; *Rel* reprobate.

réprouver [repruve] *vt* **(a)** to condemn *(crime, attitude)*; to disapprove of *(s.o.)*; **(b)** *Rel* to damn.

reps [rɛps] *nm Tex* rep(p).

reptation [rɛptɑsjɔ̃] *nf* crawling.

reptile [rɛptil] *nm* reptile; *(serpent)* snake; *Fig F (personne)* reptile.

repu [rəpy] *adj* satiated, full; *Fig* **être r. de qch,** to have had one's fill of sth.

républicain, -aine [repyblikɛ̃, -ɛn] *adj & n* republican.

républicanisme [repyblikanism] *nm* republicanism.

république [repyblik] *nf* **(a)** *Pol* republic; *F* **on est en r.,** it's a free country; **la R. de Saint-Marin,** the Republic of San Marino; **la R. française,** the French Republic; **R. démocratique allemande,** German Democratic Republic; **(b)** *Fig* **la r. des lettres,** the republic *or* world of letters.

répudiation [repydjɑsjɔ̃] *nf* **(a)** repudiation *(of wife, opinion, duty etc)*; **(b)** *Jur* renunciation *(of succession, nationality)*.

répudier [repydje] *vt (impf & pr sub* **n. répudiions***)* **(a)** to repudiate *(wife, opinion, duty etc)*; **(b)** *Jur* to renounce, to relinquish *(succession, nationality)*.

répugnance [repyɲɑ̃s] *nf* **(a)** repugnance (**pour,** for); aversion (**pour,** to); loathing (**pour,** of, for); **avoir de la r. pour,** to have a loathing of *or* for; **(b) r. à faire qch,** reluctance *or* unwillingness to do sth; **avec r.,** reluctantly, unwillingly.

répugnant [repyɲɑ̃] *adj* repugnant, loathsome, disgusting.

répugner [repyɲe] **1** *vi* **(a) r. à qch,** to feel repugnance for sth; **r. à faire qch,** to be reluctant *or* lo(a)th to do sth; **(b) r. à qn,** to be repugnant to s.o.. **2** *v impers* **il me répugne de le faire,** I am reluctant *or* lo(a)th to do it. **3** *vt* to be repugnant to *(s.o.)*.

répulsif, -ive [repylsif, -iv] *adj Phys & Fig* repulsive.

répulsion [repylsjɔ̃] *nf* **(a)** *Phys* repulsion; **(b)** *(aversion)* repulsion; **éprouver de la r. pour qn,** to feel repulsion for s.o., to be repelled by s.o..

réputation [repytɑsjɔ̃] *nf* reputation; **jouir d'une bonne r.,** to have a good reputation *or* name, to be well spoken of; **cela a fait sa r.,** it made his name; **sa r. de chirurgien,** his reputation as a surgeon; **connaître qn de r.,** to know s.o. by reputation *or* by repute; **il a (une) mauvaise r.,** he has a bad reputation *or* a bad name; **elle a la r. d'une femme d'affaires/d'être généreuse,** she has a reputation as a businesswoman/for being generous *or* for her generosity; **maison de mauvaise r.,** disreputable house, house of ill repute.

réputé [repyte] *adj* well-known, famous, renowned *(expert, restaurant, wine etc)*; **r. très intelligent/***etc*, reputed *or* considered to be very intelligent/*etc*; **r. pour qch,** well known *or* famous *or* renowned for sth.

réputer [repyte] *vt* to consider, to think, to deem; **il est réputé ne rien ignorer de cette science,** he is reputed to know everything about this science.

requérant, -ante [rəkerɑ̃, -ɑ̃t] *Jur* **1** *adj* **partie requérante,** applicant, claimant. **2** *n* applicant, claimant.

requérir [rəkerir] *vt (conj like* **acquérir***)* **(a)** to solicit, to seek *(favour)*; to request *(s.o.'s presence, assistance)*; to require, to call for *(explanation, care etc)*; to demand *(s.o.'s attention)*; **opération qui requiert des mains habiles,** operation that requires *or* calls for skilled hands; **(b)** to conscript *(civilians) (for a public service)*; **(c)** *Jur (of prosecution)* to demand, to call for *(sentence)*.

requête [rəkɛt] *nf* **(a)** *(demande)* request; **adresser une r. à qn,** to petition s.o.; **à** *ou* **sur la r. de qn,** at s.o.'s request; **(b)** *Jur* petition; **r. en cassation,** appeal.

requiem [rekɥijɛm] *nm inv* requiem; **messe de r.,**

requiem (mass).
requin [rəkɛ̃] *nm* shark; **peau de r.**, shagreen.
requinquer [rəkɛ̃ke] *F* **1** *vt* to buck *or* perk (*s.o.*) up; **le voilà requinqué,** he's (back to) his old self again. **2 se requinquer** *vpr* to buck *or* perk up.
requis [rəki] **1** *adj* required, requisite, necessary. **2** *nm* (*civil*) labour conscript.
réquisition [rekizisjɔ̃] *nf* **(a)** *Admin* requisitioning, commandeering (*of provisions, vehicles etc*); **r. civile,** (*de personne*) conscription for a public service; **mettre en r.,** to requisition, to commandeer; **(b)** *Jur* (*plaidoirie*) prosecution address.
réquisitionner [rekizisjɔne] *vt* to requisition, to commandeer (*provisions, vehicles etc*); to conscript (*civilians*); **elle nous a réquisitionnés pour faire la vaisselle,** she conscripted us to do the washing-up.
réquisitoire [rekizitwar] *nm Jur* prosecution address; *Fig* indictment (**contre,** against).
R.E.R. [ɛrəɛr] *nm Rail* (*abrév* **Réseau express régional**) = express rail network serving Paris and its suburbs.
resaler [rəsale] *vt Culin* to put more salt in, to add more salt to.
resalir [rəsalir] **1** *vt* to (get) dirty again. **2 se resalir** *vpr* to get oneself dirty again, to dirty oneself again.
rescapé, -ée [rɛskape] **1** *adj* surviving (*person*). **2** *n* survivor (*of disaster, shipwreck etc*).
rescinder [resɛ̃de] *vt Jur* to rescind, to annul.
rescision [resizjɔ̃] *nf Jur* rescission, annulment.
rescousse [rɛskus] *nf* **aller** *ou* **venir à la r. de qn,** to go *or* come to the rescue of s.o.; **appeler qn à la r.,** to call to s.o. for help *or* assistance.
rescrit [rɛskri] *nm* rescript.
réseau, -eaux [rezo] *nm* **(a)** netting, network (*of threads etc*); *Archit* tracery; *Anat* plexus (*of nerves*); *Biol* (nuclear) meshwork; *Opt* diffraction grating; *Phys Nucl* lattice (*of reactor*); *Mil* **r. de barbelés,** barbed wire entanglement; **(b)** network, system (*of roads, railways, rivers etc*); *Rad TV* network; *Tél* network, system; *Rail* **r. express national,** = suburban train network in Paris; *Él* **r. national,** national grid system; **r. de distribution urbain,** town mains; *Tél* **r. urbain,** local area network; *Tél* **r. interurbain,** trunk network; **(c) r. d'espionnage,** spy ring *or* network; **r. de résistance,** resistance network; **r. d'amis/de relations,** network of friends/relatives; **(d)** *Ordinat* **r. de données,** data network; **r. local,** local area network, LAN; **mise en r.,** networking.
réséda [rezeda] **1** *nm Bot* reseda; **r. odorant,** mignonette. **2** *adj inv & nm* (*couleur*) reseda, mignonette.
réservation [rezɛrvasjɔ̃] *nf* **(a)** (*de place, à l'hôtel etc*) reservation, booking; **bureau de r.,** booking office; **(b)** *Jur* reservation; **r. faite de tous mes droits,** without prejudice to my rights.
réserve [rezɛrv] *nf* **(a)** (*restriction*) reservation; **faire des réserves,** to have reservations (**sur,** about); **apporter une r. à un contrat,** to enter a reservation in respect of an agreement; **à la r. de ...,** except for ...; **sous r. de qch,** subject to sth; *Jur* **sous r.,** without prejudice; **sous toutes réserves,** without committing oneself; **sans r.,** without reservation, unreservedly; **éloges sans r.,** unqualified praise;
(b) (*discrétion*) reserve; **se tenir** *ou* **demeurer sur la r.,** to refuse to commit oneself; **être sur la r.,** to be on one's guard; **son attitude manque de r.,** his attitude is lacking in caution; **quand il sort de sa r.,** when he breaks through his reserve;
(c) reserve (*of provisions, troops, equipment, money etc*); **réserves mondiales,** world reserves (*of oil etc*); **réserves bancaires,** bank reserves; **puiser dans les réserves,** to draw on the reserves; **en r.,** in reserve; **mettre qch en r.,** to reserve sth, to put sth by; **tenir qch en r.,** to keep sth in reserve *or* in store; **fonds de r.,** reserve fund; **vivres de r.,** reserve *or* emergency rations, iron rations; **pièces de r.,** spare parts;
(d) *Mil* reserve; **r. de l'armée active,** reserve of the regular army; **officier de r.,** officer of the reserve;
(e) *Jur* **r. légale,** legal share (*of inheritance*);
(f) (*parc*) reserve; (*pour gibier*) preserve; **réserves (indiennes),** (Indian) reservation; **r. naturelle,** nature reserve;
(g) (*local*) storehouse, storeroom; (*de bibliothèque*) reserve (collection);
(h) *Tech* resist.
réservé [rezɛrve] *adj* **(a)** reserved (*room, seat etc*); **place réservée aux personnes âgées,** seat reserved for the elderly; **salle réservée aux réunions,** room reserved *or* kept for meetings, meeting room; **(b) tous droits réservés,** all rights reserved; **(c)** reserved, guarded, cautious (*person*); guarded, cautious (*attitude*); **avis r.,** qualified opinion.
réserver [rezɛrve] **1** *vt* to reserve (**à, pour,** for); to set aside, to put by, to save (*goods, money etc*) (**à, pour,** for); (*louer*) to reserve, to book (*room, seat etc*); **r. une place à qn,** to keep *or* save a seat for s.o.; **place réservée,** reserved seat; **r. du bois pour l'hiver,** to store wood for the winter; **r. son courage pour plus tard,** to save (up) one's courage for later; **r. son jugement,** to reserve (one's) judgment; *Cathol* **cas réservé,** reserved sin; *Jur* **biens réservés de la femme mariée,** married woman's separate estate; **'chasse/pêche réservée',** 'private hunting/fishing'; *Admin* **quartier réservé,** red-light district; **le sort que la vie nous réserve,** the fate that life has in store for us.
2 se réserver *vpr* **se r. un droit,** to reserve oneself a right; **je me réserve,** I shall wait and see, I'll bide my time; **je préfère me r. pour la dessert,** I prefer to save myself *or* my appetite for the dessert.
3 *vi* (*au théâtre, à l'hôtel etc*) to book.
réserviste [rezɛrvist] *nm Mil* reservist.
réservoir [rezɛrvwar] *nm* **(a)** (*bassin*) reservoir; **r. de barrage,** storage basin; **(b)** (*pour poissons*) fish pond; **(c)** (*cuve*) tank; **r. à gaz,** gasholder, gasometer; **r. à minerai,** ore bin *or* bunker; **r. à mazout,** fuel-oil tank; **r. d'essence,** *Br* petrol *or Am* gas tank.
résidant [rezidɑ̃] *adj* resident.
résidence [rezidɑ̃s] *nf* **(a)** (*état*) residence; **certificat de r.,** residence permit; **lieu de r.,** place of residence; *Jur* **en r. surveillée,** under house arrest; **(b)** (*demeure*) residence, home; **r. secondaire,** second home; **r. principale,** main residence *or* home; **changer de r.,** to change one's residence, to move (house); **r. médicalisée (pour personnes âgées),** nursing home; **(c)** (*immeuble*) *Br* block of luxury flats, *Am* luxury apartment building.
résident, -ente [rezidɑ̃, -ɑ̃t] *n* **(a)** (*diplomate*) resident; **ministre r.,** minister resident; **(b)** (*étranger*) (foreign) resident.
résidentiel, -elle [rezidɑ̃sjɛl] *adj* residential.
résider [rezide] *vi* **(a)** (*vivre*) to reside, to live (**à, dans, en,** in); **les chanoines ne résidaient pas,** the canons were non-resident; **(b)** *Fig* to rest, to lie; **toute la difficulté réside en ceci,** all the difficulty rests *or* lies in this.
résidu [rezidy] *nm* **(a)** residue, residuum; **résidus,** remnants; (*déchets*) waste; **résidus urbains,** town refuse; **résidus de fission,** radioactive waste; **(b)** *Math* remainder.
résiduaire [rezidɥɛr] *adj* waste; *Ind* **eaux résiduaires,** waste water, process water.
résiduel, -elle [rezidɥɛl] *adj* residual.
résignation [reziɲasjɔ̃] *nf* (*soumission*) resignation; **avec r.,** resignedly, with resignation.
résigné [reziɲe] *adj* resigned (**à,** to); **je suis r.,** I'm resigned to it.
résigner [reziɲe] **1** *vt* to resign, to give up (*position, possessions*); **r. sa charge** *ou* **ses fonctions,** to give up *or* relinquish one's appointment, to resign; **r. le pouvoir,** to lay down office. **2 se résigner** *vpr* **se r. à qch/à faire qch,** to resign oneself to sth/to doing sth; **il faut se r.,** one has to resign oneself to it.
résiliable [reziljabl] *adj* annullable, cancellable.
résiliation [reziljasjɔ̃] *nf* cancellation, annulment, termination (*of contract*).
résilience [reziljɑ̃s] *nf* resilience, impact strength.
résilient [reziljɑ̃] *adj* resilient.
résilier [rezilje] *vt* to annul, to cancel, to terminate (*agreement, contract etc*).
résille [rezij] *nf* **(a)** (*pour cheveux*) hairnet; **bas r.,** fishnet stockings; **(b)** (*de vitrail*) cames, lattice.
résine [rezin] *nf* resin.
résiné [rezine] *adj & nm* **(vin) r.,** retsina.
résiner [rezine] *vt* **(a)** (*enduire de résine*) to resin, to dip in resin; **(b)** (*extraire la résine de*) to tap (*tree*) for resin.
résineux, -euse [rezinø, -øz] **1** *adj* resinous (*smell etc*); coniferous (*tree, forest*). **2** *nm* conifer.
résistance [rezistɑ̃s] *nf* **(a)** *Pol etc* resistance, opposition (**à,** to); **n'offrir aucune r.,** to offer *or* make no resistance; **r. passive,** passive resistance; *Hist* **la R.,** the Resistance (movement);
(b) r. à la maladie/à la contagion, resistance to disease/to contagion;
(c) *Phys* resistance; **r. de l'air,** resistance of the air; **r. à l'avancement,** drag;
(d) *Él* resistance; (*conducteur*) element (*of appliance*); **unité de r.,** unit of resistance; **r. à curseur,** rheostat;

(e) *Tech* resistance, strength, toughness (*of materials*); **r. à la flexion,** bending strength; **r. à la traction,** tensile strength; **r. au choc,** impact resistance; **limite de la r.,** yield point; **acier à haute r.,** high-resistance *or* high-tensile steel; **tissu qui n'a pas de r.,** flimsy material;

(f) (*endurance*) resistance, staying power, stamina, endurance; **il a une bonne r. à la fatigue,** he doesn't tire easily;

(g) pièce de r., *Culin* main course *or* dish, pièce de résistance; *Fig* principal feature *or* item, pièce de résistance (*of entertainment etc*).

résistant, -ante [rezistɑ̃, -ɑ̃t] **1** *adj* **(a)** strong, tough, resistant; fast (*colour*); **r. à l'acide,** acid-proof; **r. à la chaleur,** heatproof, heat-resistant; **r. au choc,** shockproof; **r. à l'usure,** hard-wearing; **(b)** (*robuste*) strong, tough, hardy (*person*); hardy (*plant*); **(c)** *Pol etc* rebellious. **2** *n* **(a)** *Pol etc* rebel; **(b)** *Hist* member of the Resistance movement.

résister [reziste] *vi* **(a)** (*se débattre, s'opposer*) to resist; **r. à qn/à la justice/***etc*, to resist *or* offer resistance to s.o./the law/*etc*; **r. à faire qch,** to resist doing sth; **ces couleurs ne résistent pas,** these colours are not fast; *Fig* **on ne peut pas te r.,** it's impossible to refuse you; **(b) r. à,** to resist (*temptation, fatigue*); to hold out against, to resist (*attack*); to bear (up against), to withstand (*pain*); to stand up to (*ill treatment etc*); **r. à l'analyse,** (*d'un argument etc*) to stand up to analysis.

résolu [rezɔly] *adj* resolute, determined (*person*); **elle est résolue à le faire,** she is resolved *or* determined to do it.

résoluble [rezɔlybl] *adj* **(a)** solvable, resoluble (*problem*); **(b)** *Jur* annullable, cancellable, terminable (*contract*).

résolument [rezɔlymɑ̃] *adv* resolutely, determinedly.

résolution [rezɔlysjɔ̃] *nf* **(a)** resolution (*of substance, dissonance, television screen etc*); **écran à haute r.,** high-resolution screen; **(b)** solution, resolution (*of problem*); **(c)** *Jur* annulment, cancellation, termination (*of contract*); **(d)** resolution; **prendre la r. de faire qch,** to resolve *or* determine to do sth; *Pol* **prendre une r.,** to pass a resolution; **quelles sont vos nouvelles résolutions?,** (*au début de l'année nouvelle*) what are your New Year resolutions?; **(e)** (*détermination*) resoluteness, determination, strength of will.

résonance [rezɔnɑ̃s] *nf* **(a)** resonance; *Mus* **caisse de r.,** sound box; *Méd* **r. magnétique nucléaire,** nuclear magnetic resonance, NMR; **(b)** *Fig* (*effet*) response, echo; **(c)** (*repercussion*) repercussion.

résonateur [rezɔnatœr] *nm Él* resonator.

résonnant [rezɔnɑ̃] *adj* **(a)** resonant, resounding, sonorous (*voice etc*); **r. de,** resonant *or* resounding *or* echoing with; **(b)** *Phys* resonant.

résonner [rezɔne] *vi* (*of sound, footsteps etc*) to resound, to resonate, to echo; (*of voice, room*) to echo; **l'air résonnait de leurs cris,** the air rang *or* resounded *or* echoed with their cries.

résorber [rezɔrbe] **1** *vt* **(a)** *Méd* to resorb; **(b)** to absorb (*surplus, deficit*); **r. la crise économique,** to solve the economic crisis from within. **2 se résorber** *vpr* **(a)** *Méd* to be resorbed; **(b)** (*of surplus, deficit*) to be absorbed.

résorption [rezɔrpsjɔ̃] *nf* **(a)** *Méd* resorption; **(b)** absorption (*of surplus, deficit*).

résoudre [rezudr] *v* (*prp* **résolvant**; *pp* **résolu**, *parfois* **résous, -oute**; *pr ind* **je résous, il résout, n. résolvons**; *impf* **je résolvais**; *p hist* **je résolus**; *fu* **je résoudrai**) **1** *vt* **(a)** (*transformer*) **r. qch en qch,** to resolve *or* break up sth into sth; **(b)** *Jur* to annul, to cancel, to terminate (*contract etc*); **(c)** to resolve, to clear up (*difficulty*); to solve (*equation*); to solve, to resolve, to work out (*problem*); to resolve, to settle (*question*); *Mus* **r. une dissonance,** to resolve a discord; **(d) r. qn à faire qch,** to induce *or* persuade *or* prevail upon s.o. to do sth; **(e)** (*décider*) to decide on, to determine on (*sth*); **r. de partir,** to decide to go. **2 se résoudre** *vpr* **(a) se r. en qch,** to resolve *or* break up into sth; **(b) se r. à faire qch,** to resolve *or* make up one's mind to do sth.

respect [rɛspɛ] *nm* respect; **elle inspire le r.,** she inspires respect; **avoir le r. des lois,** to respect *or* have respect *or* regard for the law; **parler avec r.,** to speak respectfully *or* with respect; **r. de soi,** self-respect; **r. humain,** deference to the opinions of others, common decency; **le r. de la nature/des morts,** respect for nature/the dead; **faire qch par r. pour qn,** to do sth out of respect for s.o.; **manquer de r. envers qn,** to be disrespectful to s.o., to show a lack of respect towards s.o.; **tenir qn en r.,** to keep s.o. at a respectful distance; **sauf le r. que je vous dois, sauf votre r.,** with all due respect, with all due deference (to you); **rendre** *ou* **présenter ses respects à qn,** to pay one's respects to s.o..

respectabilité [rɛspɛktabilite] *nf* respectability.

respectable [rɛspɛktabl] *adj* **(a)** (*digne de respect*) respectable, worthy of respect; **(b)** (*digne de considération*) respectable, fairly large; **un nombre r. de spectateurs,** a respectable *or* fairly large *or* fair number of spectators.

respecter [rɛspɛkte] **1** *vt* to respect, to have respect *or* regard for (*sth, s.o.*); **r. la loi,** to abide by the law; **faire r. la loi,** to enforce the law; **se faire r.,** to command respect; **le feu ne respecta rien,** the fire spared nothing. **2 se respecter** *vpr* to respect oneself; **il se respecte trop pour faire cela,** he's above doing that; **un professeur qui se respecte ne ferait pas cela,** no self-respecting teacher would do that.

respectif, -ive [rɛspɛktif, -iv] *adj* respective.

respectivement [rɛspɛktivmɑ̃] *adv* respectively.

respectueusement [rɛspɛktɥøzmɑ̃] *adv* respectfully.

respectueux, -euse [rɛspɛktɥø, -øz] *adj* respectful (**de,** of); **r. des lois,** respectful of the law, law-abiding; **être r. des opinions d'autrui,** to show respect for the opinions of others; **se tenir à distance respectueuse,** to keep at a respectful distance; **veuillez agréer mes sentiments r.,** (*dans une lettre*) yours sincerely.

respirable [rɛspirabl] *adj* breathable; *Fig* **l'atmosphère n'était plus r.,** the atmosphere had become oppressive *or* suffocating.

respirateur [rɛspiratœr] *nm* respirator.

respiration [rɛspirɑsjɔ̃] *nf* breathing, *Spéc* respiration; (*de plante*) respiration; **r. artificielle,** artificial respiration; *Méd* **r. contrôlée/assistée,** controlled/assisted respiration; **avoir la r. difficile,** to have trouble *or* difficulty breathing; **couper la r. à qn,** to wind s.o.; *Fig* to take s.o.'s breath away, to flabbergast s.o..

respiratoire [rɛspiratwar] *adj* respiratory (*organ etc*); breathing (*apparatus, exercise*); **troubles respiratoires,** breathing *or* respiratory trouble; **casque r.,** (fireman's) smoke helmet.

respirer [rɛspire] **1** *vi* to breathe; (*of plant*) to respire; **r. longuement,** to draw a long breath; **r. par le nez/la bouche,** to breathe through the nose/mouth; **laissez-moi r.,** let me get my breath (back), let me catch my breath; **je n'ai pas respiré de la journée,** I haven't had time to breathe all day; *Fig F* **ouf! je respire!,** (*soulagement*) ah! I can breathe again! **2** *vt* **(a)** to breathe (in), to inhale; **aller r. un peu d'air,** to go for a breath of air; **(b) r. la vengeance,** to breathe (out *or* forth) vengeance; **elle respire la santé,** she radiates health; **ici tout respire la paix/la confiance,** here everything breathes peace/confidence.

resplendir [rɛsplɑ̃dir] *vi* to shine, to gleam; **r. de joie/santé,** (*of face*) to be shining with joy/glowing with health; (*of person*) to radiate joy/health.

resplendissant [rɛsplɑ̃disɑ̃] *adj* shining, gleaming; **r. de joie/santé,** (*face*) shining with joy/glowing with health; (*person*) radiant with joy/health.

responsabiliser [rɛspɔ̃sabilize] *vt* to remind (*s.o.*) of his responsibilities; (*rendre responsable*) to make (*s.o.*) responsible.

responsabilité [rɛspɔ̃sabilite] *nf* responsibility; (*légale*) liability (**de,** for); **r. de l'employeur,** employer's liability; **accepter une r.,** to assume *or* accept *or* take on a responsibility; **j'ai la r. de l'entretien de la maison,** I am responsible for the upkeep of the house; **fuir les responsabilités,** to evade *or* avoid responsibility; **être appelé à de hautes responsabilités,** to be given important responsibilities; **faire qch sous sa (propre) r.,** to do sth on one's own responsibility; **r. civile/au tiers,** civil/third-party liability; *Pol* **r. ministérielle,** ministerial accountability.

responsable [rɛspɔ̃sabl] **1** *adj* responsible (**de,** for); (*légalement*) liable (**de,** for); **r. pour ses enfants,** responsible *or* answerable for one's children; **le ministre est r. devant** *ou* **envers les Chambres,** the Minister is responsible *or* answerable *or* accountable to Parliament; **rendre qn/qch r. d'un malheur,** to hold s.o./sth responsible for a misfortune, to blame s.o./sth for a misfortune. **2** *n* **(a)** (*coupable*) person responsible (**de,** for); **qui est le r. de cette plaisanterie idiote?,** who is responsible for this silly prank?; **(b)** (*personne en charge*) person in charge; (*dirigeant élu*) official.

resquillage [rɛskijaʒ] *nm,* **resquille** [rɛskij] *nf* (*au théâtre etc*) sneaking in without paying; (*dans l'autobus, le métro etc*) fare-dodging.

resquiller [rɛskije] **1** *vi* (*au théâtre, au concert etc*) to sneak in without paying; (*dans l'autobus, le métro etc*) to dodge paying one's fare. **2** *vt* to get (*theatre seat etc*) without paying, to sneak into (*theatre etc*) (without paying).

resquilleur, -euse [rɛskijœr, -øz] *n* **(a)** (*au théâtre etc*) person who has sneaked in without paying; (*dans l'autobus, le métro etc*) fare-dodger; **(b)** (*dans une queue*) queue-jumper.
ressac [rəsak] *nm Nau* undertow.
ressaisir [rəsezir] **1** *vt* to recapture (*fugitive etc*); to recover (possession of) (*property*); to seize (*power*) again; **la peur l'a ressaisi,** fear gripped him again. **2 se ressaisir** *vpr* to regain one's self-control, to pull oneself together; **ressaisissez-vous!,** pull yourself together!; **cet élève s'est ressaisi au second trimestre,** this pupil recovered *or* rallied in the second term.
ressasser [rəsɑse] *vt* (*dans son esprit*) to turn over in one's mind; (*répéter*) to keep coming out with; **r. la même histoire,** to hark back to the same old story; **plaisanterie ressassée,** (old) chestnut.
ressaut [rəso] *nm* **(a)** *Archit* projection; *Tech* swell, lug; *Géol* rock step; **faire r.,** to project; **(b)** sharp rise, bump (*in the ground*); **(c)** *Équitation* rise (*in the saddle*); **(d)** bounce (*of vehicle*); **les sauts et ressauts de la conversation,** sudden changes in conversation.
ressauter [rəsote] **1** *vi* to jump again. **2** *vt* to jump (over) again.
ressemblance [rəsɑ̃blɑ̃s] *nf* resemblance, likeness; (*trait*) resemblance; **avoir de la r. avec qn/qch,** to bear *or* show a resemblance to s.o./sth; **classement par r. de forme,** classification according to similarity of form; **il y a une r. frappante entre la mère et la fille,** there is a striking resemblance between (the) mother and (the) daughter.
ressemblant [rəsɑ̃blɑ̃] *adj* **portrait bien r.,** lifelike portrait, good likeness; **elle est très ressemblante,** (*sur une photo etc*) it is very like her.
ressembler [rəsɑ̃ble] **1** *vi* **r. à qn/qch,** (*physiquement*) to resemble *or* to be like *or* to look like s.o./sth; (*moralement*) to resemble *or* to be like s.o./sth; *F* **cela ne ressemble à rien,** it's like nothing on earth; (*ça ne veut rien dire*) it just doesn't make sense; **cela lui ressemble tout à fait!,** that's just like him!, that's him all over!; **cela ne lui ressemble pas de se plaindre,** it's not like him to complain. **2 se ressembler** *vpr* to be alike, to resemble each other; **ils se ressemblent comme deux gouttes d'eau,** they are as like as two peas (in a pod); *Prov* **qui se ressemble s'assemble,** birds of a feather flock together.
ressemelage [rəsəmlaʒ] *nm* resoling.
ressemeler [rəsəmle] *vt* (*conj like* **semeler**) to resole (*shoes*).
ressentiment [rəsɑ̃timɑ̃] *nm* resentment (**de,** at; **contre,** against); **avec r.,** resentfully.
ressentir [rəsɑ̃tir] *v* (*conj like* **sentir**) **1** *vt* to feel (*pain, anger, sympathy, effect, insult etc*); to feel, to experience (*shock, sensation*); **r. de l'affection pour qn,** to be fond of s.o., to have (great) affection for s.o.; **r. vivement la perte de qn,** to feel deeply *or* to be deeply affected by the loss of s.o.. **2 se ressentir** *vpr* **(a) se r. de,** to feel the effects of (*accident, illness, war etc*); to show the effects of (*work, effort etc*); **(b)** *F* **s'en r. pour qch,** to feel fit for *or* up to sth.
resserre [rəsɛr] *nf* (*pour outils*) tool shed; (*pour stocker*) storeroom; **r. à légumes,** vegetable rack.
resserré [rəsere] *adj* narrow, confined.
resserrement [rəsɛrmɑ̃] *nm* **(a)** (*contraction*) narrowing (*of valley etc*); **r. du crédit,** credit squeeze, tightening of credit; **(b)** tightening (*of knot, bolt etc*); *Fig* strengthening (*of friendship, bonds*).
resserrer [rəsere] **1** *vt* **(a)** (*contracter*) to squeeze together (*objects*); to close, to constrict (*pores*); *Fig* to squeeze, to tighten (*credit*); **r. un récit,** to condense a story; **(b)** to tighten (*knot, belt, nut, bolt*); *Fig* to strengthen (*friendship, bonds*). **2 se resserer** *vpr* **(a)** (*of valley etc*) to narrow, to become narrower *or* more confined; (*of pores*) to close; **(b)** (*of knot*) to tighten; *Fig* (*of bonds*) to strengthen, to grow stronger; **l'énigme se resserre,** the plot thickens, the mystery deepens.
resservir [rəsɛrvir] *v* (*conj like* **servir**) **1** *vt* **(a)** (*servir de nouveau*) to serve (*diner etc*) again; **r. un plat,** to serve up a dish again; **(b)** (*servir en plus*) to give (*diner etc*) some more *or* another helping; to serve another helping of (*fish etc*). **2** *vi* to be used again. **3 se resservir** *vpr* (*of diner etc*) to have some more, to have another helping; **resservez-vous du riz,** help yourself to *or* have some more rice *or* another helping of rice.
ressort [rəsɔr] *nm* **(a)** (*élasticité*) elasticity, springiness; **faire r.,** to spring back, to fly back; *Fig* **avoir du r.,** to be resilient *or* buoyant;
(b) (*pièce*) spring; **r. de sommier,** bed spring; **r. de montre,** watch spring; **r. à boudin** *ou* **en spirale,** coil spring, spiral spring; **r. à feuilles** *ou* **à lames,** leaf *or* laminated spring; **r. moteur, grand r.,** mainspring; **actionné** *ou* **mû par r.,** spring-driven; **verrou à r.,** spring bolt; **suspendu à ressort(s),** sprung (*cart etc*); **sans ressort(s),** unsprung; *Fig F* **faire jouer tous les ressorts,** to pull all the strings;
(c) *Fig* (*motivation*) motive; **l'intérêt est un puissant r.,** self-interest is a powerful motive;
(d) *Jur* (*compétence*) province, scope, competence; (*étendue de juridiction*) jurisdiction; **être du r. de la cour,** to be *or* fall within the competence of the court; **cela n'est pas de son r.,** that does not fall within his province, that's not his responsibility;
(e) *Jur* **en dernier r.,** without appeal; *Jur Fig* as a last resort.
ressortir¹ [rəsɔrtir] *v* (*conj like* **sortir**) **1** *vi* (*aux* **être**) **(a)** (*d'un lieu*) to come *or* go out again; **elle est ressortie de chez elle,** she came *or* went out of her house again; **(b)** (*se détacher*) to stand out; **faire r. des couleurs,** to bring out *or* set off colours; **faire r. un fait,** to emphasize *or* accentuate *or* stress a fact; **faire r. le sens de qch,** to bring out the meaning of sth; **(c)** (*résulter*) to emerge, to be evident (**de,** from); **il en ressort que ...,** it emerges *or* is evident from this that ...; **le prix moyen ressort à vingt francs,** the average price works out at twenty francs. **2** *vt* (*aux* **avoir**) to get out (*umbrella, clothes etc*) again; *Fig* **elle ressort toujours le même genre d'histoires,** she always comes out with the same old stories.
ressortir² *vi Jur* **r. à,** to come under the jurisdiction of; **ces affaires ressortissent au tribunal d'instance,** these cases belong to *or* come before *or* come under the jurisdiction of a magistrate's court; *Fig* **concepts qui ressortissent à la géométrie/***etc*, concepts that belong to *or* come within the province of geometry/*etc*.
ressortissant, -ante [rəsɔrtisɑ̃, -ɑ̃t] **1** *adj Jur* **r. à,** under the jurisdiction of. **2** *n* (*d'un pays*) national, citizen.
ressouder [rəsude] **1** *vt* to resolder; (*par la soudure autogène*) to reweld. **2 se ressouder** *vpr* (*of bone*) to knit again, to join again.
ressource [rəsurs] *nf* **(a)** (*habileté*) resourcefulness; **personne de r.,** resourceful person; **elle a de la r.,** she is resourceful; **(b) ruiné sans r.,** irretrievably *or* irremediably ruined; **sans r. et sans espoir,** helpless and hopeless; **(c)** (*moyen*) expedient; **avoir mille ressources,** to be very resourceful; **les ressources de la langue française,** the resources of the French language; **je n'avais d'autre r. que la fuite,** I had no choice but to run away, there was no course open to me but flight; **en dernière r.,** in the last resort; **(d) ressources,** (*argent*) resources, means; (*agricoles, pétrolières etc*) resources; **être à bout de ressources,** to be at the end of one's resources; **ressources personnelles,** private means; **(e)** *Av* flattening out, pull-out (*from dive*).
ressouvenir (se) [sərəsuvnir] *vpr* (*conj like* **venir**) **se r. de qch,** to remember *or* recollect sth (*from long ago*); **faire r. qn de qch,** to remind s.o. of sth.
ressusciter [resysite] **1** *vt* **(a)** to resuscitate (*s.o.*), to restore (*s.o.*) to life; **r. les morts,** to raise the dead; **ce vin me ressuscite,** this wine is putting new life into me; **(b)** *Fig* to revive (*quarrel, fashion, memory etc*). **2** *vi* to revive, to come to life again; *Rel* to rise from the dead; **ressuscité d'entre les morts,** risen from the dead.
restant [rɛstɑ̃] **1** *adj* **(a)** remaining, left; **les vingts francs restants,** the remaining twenty francs, the twenty francs remaining *or* left; **(b) poste restante,** *Br* poste restante, *Am* general delivery. **2** *nm* remainder, rest; **restants,** remains, leftovers, remnants (*of meal*); **un r. d'étoffe,** a left-over piece of material; *Com* **r. d'un compte,** balance of an account.
restau [rɛsto] *nm F* restaurant; **r. U(niversitaire),** university canteen *or* refectory.
restaurant [rɛstɔrɑ̃] *nm* restaurant; **manger au r.,** to eat out; **r. libre-service,** self-service restaurant; **r. universitaire,** university canteen *or* refectory; **r. routier,** *Br* transport café, *Am* truck stop.
restaurateur, -trice [rɛstɔratœr, -tris] *n* **(a)** restorer (*of buildings, pictures*); *Litt* restorer (*of régime, dynasty etc*); **(b)** (*de restaurant*) restaurateur, restaurant owner *or* manager.
restauration [rɛstɔrasjɔ̃] *nf* **(a)** restoration (*of building, statue, dynasty etc*); restoring, re-establishment (*of discipline etc*); **(b)** (*métier*) catering; **r. rapide,** fast food; **chaîne de r. rapide,** fast-food chain; **(c)** (*en Suisse*) (*restaurant*)

restaurant.

restaurer [rɛstɔre] **1** *vt* **(a)** to restore (*building, picture, dynasty, health etc*); **r. la discipline/l'autorité,** to re-establish *or* restore discipline/authority; **(b)** (*faire manger*) to give (*s.o.*) some refreshment. **2 se restaurer** *vpr* (*manger*) to take some refreshment.

restauroute [rɛstorut] *nm* roadside restaurant; (*sur l'autoroute*) *Br* motorway *or Am* freeway restaurant.

reste [rɛst] *nm* **(a)** rest, remainder (*of work, money, wine etc*); *Math* remainder; **le r. de la vie,** the rest *or* remainder of one's life; **le r. du temps,** the rest of the time; **le r. des professeurs/***etc*, the rest *or* remainder of the teachers/*etc*; **le r. (des gens),** the rest, the others; **avoir un r. d'espoir,** to have still some hope left; **il y avait un r. de beurre/lait,** there was a bit of butter/milk left over; **elle a de beaux restes,** she still has some of her beauty; **jouir de son r.,** to make the most of what is left *or* of one's remaining time; **ne pas demander son r.,** to have had enough of it; **partir sans demander son r.,** to leave without further ado; **je ferai le r.,** I shall do the rest; **pour le r.,** as for the rest; **et (tout) le r.,** and everything else, and so on, and so forth; **payer le r. par acomptes,** to pay the balance in instalments; **être en r.,** to be indebted (**avec qn,** to s.o.); **de r.,** (to) spare, left (over); **quand j'ai du temps de r.,** when I have some spare time *or* time to spare; **avoir de l'argent de r.,** to have more than enough money; **du** *ou* **au r.,** besides, moreover;

(b) restes, leftovers, remains, remnants (*of meal*); remains (*of ancient city, fortune etc*); remnant (*of army*); **restes mortels,** mortal remains.

rester [rɛste] *vi* (*aux* **être**) **(a)** (*subsister*) to remain, to be left; **les cinq francs qui restent,** the remaining five francs, the five francs left (over); **il me reste cinq francs,** I have *or* I've got five francs left; **il ne me reste qu'à vous remercier,** it only remains for me to thank you; **(il) reste à savoir s'il a raison,** it remains to be seen whether he's right; **il n'en reste pas moins que ...,** it is nevertheless the case that ...; **dix-neuf divisé par cinq, je pose 3, reste 4,** nineteen divided by five makes 3, and 4 over;

(b) (*demeurer*) to remain, to stay; **il est resté à travailler,** he stayed (behind) to work; **mon sac a dû r. sur le comptoir,** I must have left my bag on the counter; **les mots lui restèrent dans la gorge,** the words stuck in his throat; **il restait là à me regarder,** he sat *or* stood there looking at me; **restez où vous êtes,** keep *or* stay where you are; **r. assis,** to remain *or* stay seated *or* sitting; **r. au lit,** to stay *or* remain in bed; **je pars — non, reste!,** I'm going — no, stay!; **r. (à) dîner,** to stay to *or* for dinner; **le plus dur reste à faire,** the hardest part remains *or* is still to be done; **r. sur place,** to stay where one is, to stay put; *F* **j'y suis, j'y reste,** here I am and here I stay; *F* **y r.,** (*mourir*) to peg out, to snuff it; **le nom lui est resté,** the name stayed with him; **en r. là,** to proceed no further; **restons-en là pour aujourd'hui,** let's leave it there *or* at that for today; **où en sommes-nous restés (de notre lecture/***etc***)?,** where did we leave off (in our reading/*etc*)?; **la chose en resta là,** there the matter rested *or* remained; **que cela reste entre nous,** this is strictly between ourselves; **cela m'est resté sur l'estomac,** (*of food*) it's lying heavy on my stomach; *Fig* it still rankles with me, *F* it still bugs me;

(c) (*dans un état*) to stay, to remain; **r. tranquille/calme,** to stay *or* keep *or* remain still/calm; **r. en bonne santé,** to remain *or* keep in good health; **la cuisinière est restée allumée,** the cooker stayed *or* remained lit; **r. bien avec qn,** to remain *or* keep on good terms with s.o.;

(d) (*durer*) to last, to endure.

restituable [rɛstitɥabl] *adj* returnable, repayable (*sum of money*).

restituer [rɛstitɥe] *vt* **(a)** (*reconstituer*) to restore (*inscription, text*); **(b)** (*vendre*) to restore, to return, to hand back (*stolen goods etc*); to return, to refund (*money*) (**à,** to); **(c)** to release (*energy*); to reproduce (*sound*).

restitution [rɛstitysjɔ̃] *nf* **(a)** (*reconstitution*) restoration (*of text, monument*); **(b)** (*fait de rendre*) restitution, return(ing) (*of stolen goods etc*); return(ing), refunding (*of money*).

resto [rɛsto] *nm F* = **RESTAU.**

restoroute [rɛstɔrut] *nm* = **RESTAUROUTE.**

restreindre [rɛstrɛ̃dr] *v* (*prp* **restreignant;** *pp* **restreint;** *pr ind* **je restreins, il restreint, n. restreignons;** *p hist* **je restreignis;** *fu* **je restreindrai**) **1** *vt* to restrict, to curb (*ambition, number of people etc*); to cut down, to restrict, to limit (*production*); to limit (*authority*); **r. les dépenses,** to restrict *or* cut down *or* curtail expenses; **offre restreinte aux abonnés,** offer limited *or* restricted to subscribers. **2 se restreindre** *vpr* **(a)** (*réduire ses dépenses*) to cut down; **(b)** (*of area of research etc*) to become restricted, to narrow.

restreint [rɛstrɛ̃] *adj* restricted, limited (*production, number of people, vocabulary etc*); confined, limited (*space*); narrow (*limits*); **dans un sens r.,** in a restricted *or* limited *or* qualified sense; **édition à tirage r.,** limited edition.

restrictif, -ive [rɛstriktif, -iv] *adj* restrictive (*term, clause etc*).

restriction [rɛstriksjɔ̃] *nf* restriction, limitation; **faire des restrictions,** to express (some) reservations; **r. mentale,** mental reservation; **apporter des restrictions à la consommation,** to place restrictions *or* limitations on consumption; **sans r.,** unreservedly; **période de r.,** restrictive period, period of restriction; **r. des naissances,** birth restrictions.

restructuration [rəstryktyrɑsjɔ̃] *nf* restructuring.

restructurer [rəstryktyre] **1** *vt* to restructure. **2 se restructurer** *vpr* to be restructured.

resucée [rəsyse] *nf F* **(a)** (*de vin etc*) drop; **(b)** *Péj* (*répétition*) rehash (*of play, book etc*).

résultant, -ante [rezyltɑ̃, -ɑ̃t] **1** *adj* resultant, resulting (**de,** from). **2** *nf* **résultante,** consequence, result; *Math* resultant.

résultat [rezylta] *nm* result (*of calculation*); result, outcome (*of action, investigation etc*); result, effect (*of disease, treatment*); **résultats,** results (*of examination, contest*); **attendre le r. des courses,** to wait for the racing results; *Fig* to wait and see what happens; **sans r.,** without result; inconclusive (*experiment*); ineffective (*remedy*); *Com* **résultats de l'exercice** *ou* **de l'exploitation,** trading results; **ces révélations eurent pour r. la chute du Gouvernement,** these revelations led to *or* resulted in the fall of the Government; **donner des résultats,** to yield results; *F* **r.: il a été licencié,** as a result he was dismissed.

résulter [rezylte] *vi* (*used only in the inf, third person & prp; aux often* **être**) to result, to arise (**de,** from); **qu'en a-t-il résulté?,** what was the result of it?, what came of it?, what was the outcome?; **il en résulte que ...,** the result of this is that ... .

résumé [rezyme] *nm* summary, résumé; **faire le r. de,** to summarize; *Jur* **r. des débats,** summing up; **en r.,** (*en peu de mots*) in short, in brief; (*à tout prendre*) to sum up.

résumer [rezyme] **1** *vt* to summarize, to give a summary of (*article, s.o.'s ideas etc*); to sum up (*situation, argument*); *Jur* **r. les débats,** to sum up; **pour r. les faits,** to sum up; **voilà toute l'affaire résumée en un mot,** that's the whole thing in a nutshell. **2 se résumer** *vpr* (*of speaker etc*) to sum up; **pour me r.,** to sum up; **voilà à quoi tout cela se résume,** that's what it all amounts to *or F* boils down to.

résurgence [rezyrʒɑ̃s] *nf* resurgence (*of subterranean stream*).

résurgent [rezyrʒɑ̃] *adj* resurgent (*stream*).

resurgir [rəsyrʒir] *vi* to reappear suddenly.

résurrection [rezyrɛksjɔ̃] *nf* **(a)** *Rel* resurrection; **(b)** *Fig* revival (*of the arts, past etc*).

retable [rətabl] *nm* retable, reredos, altarpiece.

rétabli [retabli] *adj* (*après une maladie*) recovered.

rétablir [retablir] **1** *vt* **(a)** to re-establish, to restore (*order, communications, dynasty, relations, reputation etc*); **r. sa santé,** to recover one's health; **r. un malade,** to restore a patient to health; **(b)** to re-establish (*facts, truth*); to restore (*text*); **(c)** to reinstate (*official etc*); **r. un officier dans son commandement,** to restore an officer to his command. **2 se rétablir** *vpr* **(a)** (*après une maladie*) to recover, to get well again; (*après un saut*) to heave oneself up; **(b) l'ordre se rétablit,** order is being restored; **le silence s'est rétabli,** silence returned; **(c) se r. dans les bonnes grâces de qn,** to re-establish oneself in s.o.'s good graces.

rétablissement [retablismɑ̃] *nm* **(a)** re-establishment, restoration (*of order, dynasty, communications etc*); reinstatement (*of official etc*); restoration (*of text*); **r. de la religion,** religious revival; **(b)** recovery (*after illness*); **(c)** *Gym* pull-up; **faire un r.,** to heave oneself up.

retailler [rətɑje] *vt* to cut (*garment*) again; to prune (*tree*) again; to (re-)sharpen (*pencil*).

rétamage [retamaʒ] *nm* re-tinning (*of pan etc*); re-silvering (*of mirror*).

rétamé [retame] *adj F* (*ivre*) canned; (*fatigué*) worn *or* tired out; (*financièrement*) broke; (*démoli*) wrecked.

rétamer [retame] *vt* **(a)** to re-tin (*pan etc*); **(b)** to re-silver (*mirror*); **(c)** *F* (*enivrer*) to get canned; (*fatiguer*) to wear *or* tire out; (*au jeu*) to clean out; (*démolir*) to wreck.

rétameur [retamœr] *nm* **(a)** (*de casserole etc*) tinsmith; **(b)** (*de glace*) silverer.
retapage [rətapaʒ] *nm F* doing up (*of old house, car etc*); straightening (*of bed*); touching up (*of speech etc*).
retape [rətap] *nf F* **faire la r.,** (*of prostitute*) to solicit; (*of salesman*) to tout (for business).
retaper [rətape] **1** *vt* **(a)** *F* to do up (*old house, car etc*); to straighten (*bed*); to touch up (*speech etc*); **r. qn,** to buck up *or* pick s.o. up; **(b)** (*à la machine*) to retype (*letter etc*), to type (*letter etc*) again. **2 se retaper** *vpr F* **(a)** (*après une maladie*) to recover; **(b) se r. le moral,** to buck up; **se r. les cheveux,** to tidy one's hair; **on se retape une belote?,** shall we have another game of belote?
retapisser [rətapise] *vt* to repaper (*room etc*).
retard [rətar] *nm* **(a)** delay; (*de personne attendue*) lateness; **une heure de r.,** an hour's delay; **agir sans r.,** to act without delay; **le train a du r.,** the train is (running) late; **le train a dix minutes de r.** *ou* **est en r. de dix minutes,** the train is ten minutes late; **ma montre prend du r.,** my watch is slow; **apporter du r. à faire qch,** to be slow in doing sth; **mettre qn en r.,** to make s.o. late, to delay s.o.; **arriver en r.,** to arrive late; **être en r.,** to be late; (*sur un programme*) to be behind(hand); (*of clock*) to be slow; **compte en r.,** account outstanding *or* overdue; **après plusieurs retards le contrat a été signé,** after several delays the contract was signed;
(b) (*dans son développement*) backwardness; **r. mental,** mental retardation, backwardness; **élève/pays en r. sur les autres,** backward pupil/country; **en r. sur son siècle,** behind the times; **mesures en r. sur les événements,** out-of-date measures; **être en r. pour** *ou* **dans qch,** to be *or* lag behind in sth; **être en r. de dix ans par rapport aux autres pays industrialisés,** to be (lagging) ten years behind (the) other industrialized countries;
(c) lag (*of tides etc*); *Tech* **r. à l'admission,** retarded *or* late admission, admission lag; **r. à l'allumage,** retarded ignition; *El* **r. d'aimantation,** magnetic lag;
(d) *Mus* retardation.
retardataire [rətardatɛr] **1** *adj* **(a)** (*qui arrive en retard*) late; **(b)** (*dans son développement*) backward (*pupil etc*); out-of-date (*ideas etc*). **2** *n* latecomer.
retardateur, -trice [rətardatœr, -tris] *adj* retarding; delaying (*tactics*).
retardé, ée [rətarde] **1** *adj* **(a)** delayed (*departure*); **(b)** (*mentalement*) backward, retarded (*child*); *Scol* backward (*pupil*). **2** *n Scol* backward pupil.
retardement [rətardəmɑ̃] *nm* delay; *Mil* **action de r.,** delaying action; **bombe à r.,** time bomb; *Fig* **comprendre une allusion à r.,** to be slow in taking *or* to take a hint.
retarder [rətarde] **1** *vt* **(a)** (*faire arriver en retard*) to delay, to hold up (*person, train etc*); **(b)** (*différer*) to delay, to put off (*event, departure etc*); to defer (*payment*); **(c)** to put back (*watch, clock*) (**de,** by). **2** *vi* **(a) l'horloge retarde,** the clock is slow; **ma montre retarde** *ou F* **je retarde de dix minutes,** my watch is ten minutes slow; **pendule qui retarde dix minutes par jour,** clock that loses ten minutes a day; **il retarde sur son siècle,** he is behind the times; *F* **vous retardez,** (*vous n'êtes pas au courant*) you're not up to date; **(b)** *Tech* to lag.
retâter [rətɑte] **1** *vt* to feel (*sth*) again. **2** *vi F* **r. de qch,** to have another taste of sth; *F* **r. de la prison,** to do another stretch.
reteindre [rətɛ̃dr] *vt* (*conj like* **teindre**) to redye.
retéléphoner [rətelefɔne] **1** *vi* to ring (*s.o.*) up *or* call (*s.o.*) (up) again. **2 se retéléphoner** *vpr* to speak to each other on the phone again.
retendre [rətɑ̃dr] *vt* **(a)** to stretch (*sth*) again; *Mus* to tighten (*strings*) again; to reset (*trap*); **(b)** to hold out (*one's hand*) again.
retenir [rətnir] *v* (*conj like* **tenir**) **1** *vt* **(a)** (*faire rester*) to hold back, to detain, to delay (*s.o.*); **r. l'attention,** to hold *or* arrest the attention; **r. qn à dîner,** to keep s.o. for dinner; **elle m'a retenu par le bras,** she held me back by the arm; **r. la foule,** to keep back *or* hold back the crowd; **r. qn prisonnier,** to keep *or* hold s.o. prisoner; **je ne vous retiens pas,** I mustn't keep you; **qu'est-ce qui vous retient?,** what's keeping you?; *Nau* **retenu par les glaces,** ice-bound;
(b) (*maintenir en place*) to hold in position, to secure; **r. l'eau,** to hold water, to be watertight;
(c) (*garder*) to retain; **r. une somme sur le salaire de qn,** to keep back *or* deduct so much from s.o.'s wages;
(d) ah! je le retiens, ton ami!, oh! I won't forget your friend in a hurry!; (*se souvenir de*) to remember (*lesson, name etc*); **retenez ce numéro,** remember *or* don't forget the number;
(e) (*réserver*) to reserve, to book (*seat, room, table etc*); to engage (*staff*);
(f) *Math* **je pose 2 et je retiens 5,** put down 2 and carry 5;
(g) to restrain, to curb, to check (*one's anger*); to keep back, to hold back (*one's tears*); to stifle (*a cry*); **r. son souffle,** to hold one's breath; **r. qn de faire qch,** to restrain s.o. *or* to hold s.o. back from doing sth.
2 se retenir *vpr* **(a) se r. à qch,** to hold on to sth;
(b) (*se contenir*) to restrain *or* control *or* contain oneself; **se r. de faire qch,** to stop oneself (from) doing *or* refrain from doing sth;
(c) une comptine qui se retient facilement, a counting rhyme that is easy to remember.
rétenteur, -trice [retɑ̃tœr, -tris] *adj* retaining (*force*); *Anat* **muscle r.,** retentor (muscle).
rétention [retɑ̃sjɔ̃] *nf* holding back; *Méd* retention (*of water etc*); *Jur* **droit de r.,** lien (**de,** on); **faire de la r. d'information,** to hold back *or* withhold information.
retentir [rətɑ̃tir] *vi* **(a)** to (re)sound, to echo, to ring; (*of horn*) to sound; **le champ retentit de leurs cris,** the field resounded *or* echoed *or* rang with their shouts; **(b)** *Fig* **r. sur,** to have an effect on, to have repercussions on.
retentissant [rətɑ̃tisɑ̃] *adj* resounding, ringing (*voice, noise*); resounding (*success*); dismal (*failure*); **discours r.,** speech that arouses wide interest.
retentissement [rətɑ̃tismɑ̃] *nm* **(a)** (*bruit*) resounding *or* echoing sound *or* noise; **(b)** *Fig* repercussion (*of event etc*); **procès qui a eu un grand r.,** lawsuit that aroused wide interest *or* that made a great stir.
retenu [rət(ə)ny] *adj* **(a)** (*réservé*) prudent, circumspect, cautious (*words etc*); **(b)** (*empêché*) detained; **elle a été retenue par des obligations/un incident,** she has been detained by her commitments/an incident; **(c)** *Scol* **élève r.,** pupil in detention; **vous êtes r. samedi matin,** you'll be kept in on Saturday morning.
retenue [rət(ə)ny] *nf* **(a)** deduction, stoppage (*from wages etc*); **faire une r. de 5% sur les salaires,** to stop *or* deduct 5% from the wages; **r. à la source,** deduction at source; **(b)** *Math* carry over; **(c)** *Scol* detention; **mettre un élève en r.,** to keep a pupil in, to give a pupil detention; **(d)** (*discrétion*) reserve, restraint; **manger avec r.,** to eat sparingly; **s'exprimer sans r.,** to express oneself unreservedly; **(e)** holding back (*of water*); **clapet de r.,** back-pressure *or* non-return valve; **(f)** (*fait de garder*) holding (*of goods by Customs*); **(g)** (*barrage*) dam; **(h)** (*eau*) water (*retained in reservoir*); **(i)** (*cordage*) stay, guy.
réticence [retisɑ̃s] *nf* **(a)** (*réserve*) reticence, reserve; **sans r.,** unreservedly; **(b)** (*hésitation*) hesitation, unwillingness; **après bien des réticences, il a dit oui,** after much hesitation he said yes; **(c)** (*omission*) omission.
réticent [retisɑ̃] *adj* **(a)** (*réservé*) reticent, reserved; **(b)** (*hésitant*) hesitant, unwilling.
réticulaire [retikylɛr] *adj* reticular.
réticule [retikyl] *nm* **(a)** (*sac*) (small) ladies' handbag, reticule; **(b)** *Opt* reticle, cross wires.
réticulé [retikyle] *adj* reticulate(d).
rétif, -ive [retif, -iv] *adj* restive, stubborn (*horse*); recalcitrant (*person*).
rétine [retin] *nf Anat* retina.
rétinien, -ienne [retinjɛ̃, -jɛn] *adj Anat* retinal.
retirable [rətirabl] *adj* withdrawable.
retirage [rətiraʒ] *nm* reprinting (*of book, photograph etc*).
retiré [rətire] *adj* **(a)** secluded, remote (*place*); solitary (*life*); **vivre r.,** to live in seclusion, to live a solitary life; **(b)** (*à la retraite*) retired.
retirer [rətire] **1** *vt* **(a)** (*faire sortir*) to take out; (*enlever*) to take off (*coat, gloves, glasses etc*); **r. un enfant du collège,** to remove a child *or* take a child away from school; **r. de l'argent d'une banque,** to withdraw money from a bank; **r. des marchandises de la douane,** to take goods out of bond, to clear goods; **r. des bagages,** to take out *or* collect luggage; **r. un bouchon,** to pull out a cork; **r. ses mains de ses poches,** to take one's hands out of one's pockets; **on ne lui retirera pas de l'idée qu'il mérite mieux,** he won't be persuaded *or* convinced that he doesn't deserve better;
(b) r. un profit de qch, to derive *or* draw *or* get a profit from sth; **combien en avez-vous retiré?,** how much did you get out of it?; **quel plaisir peut-il en r.?,** what pleasure can he get *or* derive from it?; **elle dit n'avoir retiré que des ennuis de cet accord,** she says she got nothing but trouble out of this agreement;
(c) to extract (*oil from shale etc*);

(d) r. qch à qn, to withdraw sth from s.o., to take away sth from s.o.; **r. le permis de conduire à qn,** to take away *or* withdraw s.o.'s driving licence, to disqualify *or* ban s.o. from driving;

(e) to withdraw, to take back (*remark, promise*); **r. sa candidature,** to withdraw one's candidature, to stand down; *Jur* **r. une plainte,** to withdraw an action;

(f) to fire (*gun*) again; *Typ* to reprint (*book*).

2 se retirer *vpr* **(a)** (*s'en aller*) to retire, to withdraw; **se r. dans sa chambre,** to retire to one's bedroom; **vous pouvez vous r.,** you may go; **se r. à la campagne,** to retreat *or* withdraw to the country; **se r. de la lutte,** to retire from the field; **se r. en faveur de qn,** (*of candidate*) to stand down in favour of s.o.;

(b) se r. des affaires, to retire from business; **se r. du barreau,** to retire from the bar;

(c) (*of cloth*) to shrink;

(d) (*of floods*) to subside; (*of sea*) to recede; (*of tide*) to ebb.

retombant [rətɔ̃bɑ̃] *adj* hanging.

retombée [rətɔ̃be] *nf* **(a)** *Archit* spring(ing) (*of arch*); **(b) retombées radioactives,** radioactive fallout; **(c)** (*répercussion*) repercussion; **la grève aura des retombées sur les prix,** the strike will have repercussions *or* a knock-on effect on prices.

retombement [rətɔ̃bmɑ̃] *nm* falling down (again); *Fig* (*dans le désespoir etc*) relapse.

retomber [rətɔ̃be] *vi* (*aux souvent* **être**) **(a)** to fall (down) again; (*of rain, bombs etc*) to fall again; **l'attention est retombée,** attention has fallen off *or* slackened; *F* **tu ne retomberas jamais sur une pareille occasion,** you'll never come across an opportunity like it again;

(b) (*après un saut etc*) to land; *Fig* **il retombe toujours sur ses pieds,** he always falls *or* lands on his feet; **r. toujours dans la même situation,** always to end up *or* land in the same situation; **éviter que la conversation retombe sur le même sujet,** to prevent the conversation from coming round to the same subject again;

(c) r. dans le vice, to relapse into vice; **r. en enfance,** to lapse into one's second childhood; **r. malade,** to fall *or* become ill again;

(d) (*en bas, en arrière*) **r. dans son fauteuil,** to fall back *or* sink back into one's armchair; **faire r. un store,** to let down *or* pull down a blind; **laisser r. ses bras,** to drop one's arms; **le blâme retombera sur lui,** the blame will fall on him; **faire r. le blâme sur qn,** to put *or* lay the blame on s.o.; **la responsabilité retombe sur moi,** the responsibility falls on me; *F* **tout ça retombera sur moi,** it'll all come back on me;

(e) (*of hair, curtains*) to hang (down).

retordre [rətɔrdr] *vt* **(a)** to wring out (*washing*) again; **(b)** *Tex* to twist (*thread, yarn*); **machine à r.,** twisting machine, twister; *F* **il vous donnera du fil à r.,** he will give you trouble; **vous avez là du fil à r.,** you've got your work cut out.

rétorquer [retɔrke] *vt* **(a) r. que,** to retort that; **(b)** to cast back, to hurl back (*accusation*); **r. un argument contre qn,** to turn s.o.'s argument against them.

retors, -orse [rətɔr, -ɔrs] *adj* **(a)** *Tex* twisted (*thread, cord*); **(b)** curved (*beak*); **(c)** crafty, wily, devious (*person*).

rétorsion [retɔrsjɔ̃] *nf Jur Pol* retaliation, *Spéc* retortion; **mesures de r.,** retaliatory measures.

retouche [rətuʃ] *nf* (*action*) touching up, retouching (*of picture, photograph etc*); altering (*of text, garment*); (*résultat*) (*of picture, photograph etc*) retouch; (*of text, garment*) alteration; **faire des retouches à un vêtement,** to make alterations to a garment.

retoucher [rətuʃe] **1** *vt* to retouch, to touch up (*picture, photograph etc*); to touch up, to alter (*text*); to alter, to make alterations to (*garment*). **2** *vi* **votre article est bien, n'y retouchez pas,** your article is good, don't alter a word of it *or* leave it alone.

retoucheur, -euse [rətuʃœr, -øz] *n* **(a)** *Beaux-Arts Phot* retoucher; **(b)** (*en confection*) alteration hand.

retour [rətur] *nm* **(a)** turn, bend, angle (*of wall*); **tours et retours,** twists and turns; **en r. d'équerre,** at right angles;

(b) reversal (*of fortune, opinion*); (*changement d'avis*) change of mind; **r. de conscience,** qualms of conscience; **faire un r. sur le passé,** to look back on the past;

(c) (*de voyage*) return, going back, coming back; **être de r.,** to be back (again); **un journaliste (de) r. de Paris,** a reporter just back from Paris; **de r. chez moi, je lui écrivis,** on my return home I wrote to him; **être sur son r.,** to be about to return *or* on the point of returning; **à mon r.,** on my return; **partir sans esprit de r.,** to depart with no thought of return(ing); **être perdu sans r.,** to be irretrievably lost; **point de non-r.,** point of no return; *F* **cheval de r.,** old offender, old lag; **voyage de r.,** return journey *or* trip; **billet de r.** *ou* **d'aller et r.,** return ticket; **coupon de r.,** return half; **par r. (du courrier),** by return (of post); **le r. de l'hiver/d'une maladie,** the return of winter/recurrence of a disease; *Mil* **r. offensif,** counter attack, counter stroke; *Cin* **r. en arrière,** flashback; **r. à la nature/au calme,** return to nature/a state of calm; *Biol* **r. à un type,** reversion to (a) type; **par un juste r. des choses, celui qui l'a fait a été puni,** as was only fair in the end, the one who did it was punished; **être sur le r.,** to be past middle age *or* past one's prime; **beauté sur le r.,** beauty on the wane; **le r. d'âge,** (*d'une femme*) the change of life;

(d) return (*of machine part*); **course de r.,** back stroke (*of piston*); **r. de carburateur,** backfire; **avoir des retours,** to backfire; **r. de manivelle,** backfire kick; *Fig* **il y a eu un r. de manivelle,** it backfired; **r. de chariot,** (*de machine à écrire*) carriage return; **touche r.,** return key; **appuyez sur touche r.,** press return; **r. arrière,** backspace; **r. automatique de ruban,** automatic ribbon reverse; *Ordinat* **r. d'information,** feedback;

(e) *Él* **conducteur de r.,** return conductor; **r. à la terre** *ou* **à la masse,** *Br* earth connection, *Br* earthing, *Am* grounding;

(f) return (*of goods, letter*); **marchandises de r.,** *F* **retours,** returns; **vendu avec faculté de r.,** on sale or return;

(g) *Jur* reversion; **faire r. à un ascendant,** to revert to an ascendant;

(h) (*locutions*) **payer qn de r.,** to repay s.o. in kind; **payer de r. l'affection de qn,** to return s.o.'s affection; **aimer qn en r.,** to return s.o.'s love; **en r. tu ne diras rien à personne,** in return you won't say anything to anyone; **en r. de sa participation,** in return for his participation; **à beau jeu beau r.,** one good turn deserves another; *Sp* **match r.,** return match.

retournement [rəturnəmɑ̃] *nm* reversal (*of situation*); *Fig* **votre brusque r. est incompréhensible,** your sudden about-turn *or Am* about-face is incomprehensible.

retourner [rəturne] **1** *vt* **(a)** (*en mettant la face intérieure à l'extérieur*) to turn (*a skin, an umbrella, a garment*) inside out; **retournez vos poches,** turn out your pockets;

(b) (*verticalement*) to turn over; to turn over *or* up (*the soil*); to turn (*hay, omelette*); to turn up (*card*); **on avait retourné la pièce pour trouver la lettre,** they had ransacked the room *or* turned the room upside down to find the letter; *Fig* **r. une idée,** to turn over an idea; **tourner et r. qch,** to turn sth over and over (again); **r. une question dans tous les sens,** to thrash out a question; *F* **votre récit m'a tout retourné,** (*bouleversé*) your story upset me *or* gave me quite a turn;

(c) (*horizontalement*) to turn (*sth*) round; **r. la tête,** to turn one's head, to look round; **il retourna l'arme contre moi et tira,** he turned the gun on me and fired; **r. un argument contre qn,** to turn an argument against s.o.; **r. une situation,** to reverse a situation; *F* **r. qn,** (*faire changer d'avis*) to make s.o. change his mind *or* alter his views;

(d) r. qch à qn, to return sth to s.o., to send sth back to s.o.; **r. le compliment,** to return the compliment.

2 *vi* (*aux* **être**) **(a)** to return, to go back; **sa fortune retourne à sa famille,** his fortune reverts to his family; **r. déjeuner chez soi,** to go home to lunch; **r. sur le passé,** to go back *or* revert to the past; *Biol* **r. à un type,** to revert to (a) type; **r. à ses premières amours,** to return *or* go back to one's first love; **r. sur qn,** (*of crime, mistake*) to return *or* come back *or* recoil on s.o.;

(b) de quoi retourne-t-il?, *Cartes* what are trumps?; *F* what's it all about?, what's up?

3 se retourner *vpr* **(a)** (*of car, sleeping person etc*) to turn over; *Fig* **ne pas avoir le temps de se r.,** not to have time to look round; *F* **laisse-lui le temps de se r.,** give him time to sort himself out; *Fig F* **il doit se r. dans sa tombe,** he must be turning in his grave;

(b) (*tourner la tête*) to turn (round); **on se retourne sur son passage,** all heads turn when he goes by;

(c) se r. contre qn, (*of person*) to turn against s.o., to round on s.o.; **cela finira par se r. contre lui,** it'll eventually backfire on him;

(d) s'en r. à un endroit, to return *or* go back to a place; **il s'en retourna sans dire un mot,** he went off without saying a word.

retracer [rətrase] *vt* (*conj like* **tracer**) **(a)** to redraw, to retrace (*a line*); to mark out (*path*) again; **(b)** to retrace, to

recount (*event, life etc*).
rétractation [retraktɑsjɔ̃] *nf* retraction, recantation; *Jur* rescinding (*of sentence*).
rétracter¹ [retrakte] **1** *vt* to retract, to draw in (*claws etc*). **2 se rétracter** *vpr* (*se contracter*) to shorten; (*of materials*) to shrink; (*of muscle*) to retract.
rétracter² **1** *vt* to retract, to withdraw, to take back (*words*); to withdraw, to retract, to go back on (*opinion*); **r. un arrêt,** to rescind *or* retract a decree. **2 se rétracter** *vpr* (*se dédire*) to retract, to recant, *F* to eat one's words.
rétracteur [retraktœr] *adj & nm* **(muscle) r.,** retractor (muscle).
rétractile [retraktil] *adj* retractile.
rétraction [retraksjɔ̃] *nf* retraction.
retraduction [rətradyksjɔ̃] *nf* retranslation.
retraduire [rətradɥir] *vt* (*conj like* **traduire**) to retranslate.
retrait [rətrɛ] *nm* **(a)** shrinkage, shrinking (*of wood, cement etc*); **(b)** subsiding (*of flood*); retreat (*of glacier*); **(c)** withdrawal (*of order, candidature, troops etc*); cancelling (*of licence*); scratching (*of horse in race*); **r. des bagages,** baggage (re)claim; **r. du permis de conduire,** disqualification from driving, driving ban; **r. de fonds,** withdrawal of money invested; **r. d'un ordre de grève,** calling off a strike; **(d)** recess (*in wall etc*); **en r.,** recessed (*shelves etc*); sunken (*panel*); **maison en r.,** house standing back *or* set back from the road; **rester en r.,** (*of person*) to be *or* stay in the background; *Typ* **ligne en r.,** indented line.
retraite [rətrɛt] *nf* **(a)** *Mil etc* retreat, withdrawal; **battre en r.,** to beat a retreat, to retire; **battre** *ou* **sonner la r.,** to beat *or* to sound the retreat; *Nau* **tirer en r.,** to fire astern; **en ordre de r.,** in retiring order; **faire r.,** to withdraw (*in argument*);
(b) (*fanfare*) tattoo; *Nau* **coup de canon de r.,** evening gun; **r. aux flambeaux,** torchlight tattoo *or* procession;
(c) retirement (*from active life*); **caisse de r.,** superannuation fund, pension fund; **être à la** *ou* **en r.,** to be retired; (*of army officer*) to be on the retired list; **prendre sa r.,** to retire; **prendre sa r. anticipée,** to take early retirement; **militaire en r.,** army pensioner; **mettre qn à la r.,** to retire s.o., to pension s.o. off;
(d) (*pension*) retirement pension; **indemnité r.,** retirement allowance; **jouir d'une petite r.,** to have a small pension;
(e) maison de r. (pour vieillards), old people's home;
(f) *Rel* retreat; **faire une r.,** to go into retreat;
(g) (*abri*) retreat, refuge; lair, haunt (*of wild beasts*); hideout (*of thieves*);
(h) *Archit* offset (*of wall, between storeys*); recess (*in wall*).
retraité, -ée [rətrete] **1** *adj* (*à la retraite*) retired; on the retired list (*army officer*); **soldat r.,** army pensioner. **2** *n* (*old age*) senior citizen, pensioner, OAP.
retraitement [rətrɛtmɑ̃] *nm* reprocessing (*of nuclear waste*); **usine de r.,** reprocessing plant.
retraiter *vt* to reprocess (*nuclear waste*).
retranchement [rətrɑ̃ʃmɑ̃] *nm Mil* entrenchment; *Fig* **forcer qn dans ses (derniers) retranchements,** to drive s.o. to the wall.
retrancher [rətrɑ̃ʃe] **1** *vt* **(a) r. qch de qch,** to cut off sth from sth; **r. un passage d'un livre,** to cut a passage out of a book; **r. un nombre d'un autre,** to subtract one *or* a number from another; **r. qch sur une somme,** to deduct sth from a sum of money; **(b) r. qch à qn,** to dock s.o. sth, to dock sth from s.o.; **r. le superflu,** to cut out everything superfluous; **(c)** *Mil* to entrench (*post*). **2 se retrancher** *vpr* **(a)** *Mil* to entrench oneself, to dig in; **(b) se r. dans le silence,** to take refuge in silence.
retranscription [rətrɑ̃skripsjɔ̃] *nf* retranscription.
retranscrire [rətrɑ̃skrir] *vt* to retranscribe.
retransmetteur [rətrɑ̃smetœr] *nm Rad* (*appareil*) relay.
retransmettre [rətrɑ̃smɛtr] *vt* (*conj like* **transmettre**) to retransmit.
retransmission [rətrɑ̃smisjɔ̃] *nf* retransmission.
retravailler [rətravaje] **1** *vt* to work on (*speech etc*) again; to work (*clay, dough etc*) again. **2** *vi* to work again (**à qch,** at sth); **je veux r.,** I want to go back to work.
retraverser [rətraverse] *vt* to recross.
rétréci [retresi] *adj* narrow (*road etc*); shrunken (*garment*); limited (*ideas*); **esprit r.,** narrow mind.
rétrécir [retresir] **1** *vt* **(a)** (*rendre plus étroit*) to narrow (*street, the mind etc*); to take in (*garment*); **(b)** (*au lavage*) to shrink (*garment*). **2** *vi* (*of garment, cloth*) to shrink. **3 se rétrécir** *vpr* to narrow, to become narrower; **le chemin continue en se rétrécissant,** the path gets narrower and narrower.
rétrécissement [retresismɑ̃] *nm* **(a)** (*action*) narrowing; shrinking (*of garment, cloth*); **(b)** *Méd* stricture; **(c)** (*partie*) narrow part (*of tube etc*).
retrempe [rətrɑ̃p] *nf* retempering (*of steel*).
retremper [rətrɑ̃pe] **1** *vt* **(a)** to soak *or* steep (*linen etc*) again; **(b)** to retemper (*steel*); **(c)** *Fig* to reinvigorate (*s.o.*); **cela lui retrempera le caractère!,** that will toughen up his character!, that will be character-building for him!; **r. son énergie à,** to gain new energy from. **2 se retremper** *vpr* **(a)** (*dans l'eau*) to bathe again; **(b) se r. dans un milieu sympathique/le milieu familial,** to get new strength from a congenial atmosphere/the family atmosphere.
rétribuer [retribɥe] *vt* to remunerate, to pay (*employee etc*); to pay for (*work, service*); **travail rétribué,** paid work.
rétribution [retribysjɔ̃] *nf* **(a)** (*paie*) remuneration, payment (*for services*); **fonctions sans r.,** honorary duties; **(b)** (*récompense*) recompense (**de,** for).
retrier [rətrije] *vt* to re-sort.
retriever [retrivœr] *nm* (*chien*) retriever.
rétro [retro] **1** *nm* **(a)** *Billard* pull-back, screwback (stroke); **(b)** = **RÉTROVISEUR**; **(c)** (*style*) pre-1960s style. **2** *adj inv* pre-1960s style (*film, dress, fashion, music etc*). **3** *adv* in pre-1960s style.
rétroactif, -ive [retrɔaktif, -iv] *adj* retroactive, retrospective (*law etc*); **augmentation avec effet r. au 1er juillet,** increase backdated to July 1st.
rétroaction [retrɔaksjɔ̃] *nf* **(a)** (*de décret etc*) retroaction, retrospective effect; **(b)** *Électron Rad* feedback.
rétroactivement [retrɔaktivmɑ̃] *adv* retroactively, retrospectively.
rétroactivité [retrɔaktivite] *nf* retroactivity, retrospective effect.
rétrocéder [retrɔsede] *v* (*conj like* **céder**) **1** *vt* to retrocede (*right etc*); (*revendre*) to resell. **2** *vi Méd* to retrocede.
rétrocession [retrɔsesjɔ̃] *nf* retrocession.
retrochargeuse [retrɔʃarʒøz] *nf* back loader.
rétrofusée [retrɔfyze] *nf* retrorocket.
rétrogradation [retrɔgradɑsjɔ̃] *nf* **(a)** *Astron* retrogradation; **(b)** (*dans un développement*) retrogression; **(c)** reduction, demotion (*of N.C.O.*) to a lower rank; demotion (*of official*) to a lower grade.
rétrograde [retrɔgrad] **1** *adj* retrograde, backward (*motion*); *Billard* **effet r.,** pull back, screw back; **amnésie r.,** retrograde amnesia; **phrase r.,** palindrome; *Pol* **politique/mesure r.,** retrograde *or* reactionary policy/measure. **2** *n Pol* reactionary.
rétrograder [retrɔgrade] **1** *vi* **(a)** to move backwards; (*of planet, glacier*) to retrograde; *Mil* to fall back, to retreat; *Fig* (*dans son développment*) to retrogress; **(b)** *Aut* to change down (gear); **r. de troisième en seconde,** to change down from third to second. **2** *vt* to reduce *or* demote (*N.C.O.*) to a lower rank; to demote (*official*) to a lower grade.
rétrogression [retrɔgresjɔ̃] *nf* (*mouvement*) retrogression.
rétropédalage [retrɔpedalaʒ] *nm Cyclisme* back-pedalling.
rétropédaler [retrɔpedale] *vi Cyclisme* to back-pedal.
rétroprojecteur [retrɔprɔʒɛktœr] *nm* overhead projector.
rétropropulsion [retrɔprɔpylsjɔ̃] *nf Astronaut* reverse thrust.
rétrospectif, -ive [retrɔspɛktif, -iv] **1** *adj* retrospective. **2** *nf Beaux-Arts* **rétrospective,** retrospective (exhibition); *Cin* **rétrospective René Clair,** René Clair retrospective. **3** *nm Cin TV* flashback.
rétrospection [retrɔspɛksjɔ̃] *nf* retrospection.
rétrospectivement [retrɔspɛktivmɑ̃] *adv* retrospectively, in retrospect.
retroussé [rətruse] *adj* **nez r.,** snub *or* turned-up *or Litt* retroussé nose.
retroussement [rətrusmɑ̃] *nm* turning up, rolling up (*of sleeves, trousers*); tucking up (*of shirt*); curling (*of the lips*).
retrousser [rətruse] **1** *vt* to turn up, to roll up (*one's sleeves, trousers*); to tuck up (*one's skirt*); to curl (up) (*one's lip*). **2 se retrousser** *vpr* (*of woman*) to tuck up one's skirt(s); (*of moustache*) to curl up.
retroussis [rətrusi] *nm* **(a)** (*de vêtement*) turned-back facings; **bottes à r.,** topboots; **(b)** curl(ing) (*of hair, lips*).
retrouvable [rətruvabl] *adj* recoverable, retrievable; **facilement r.,** easy to find, easily found.

retrouvaille [rətruvɑj] *nf* finding again; **retrouvailles,** reunion.

retrouver [rətruve] **1** *vt* **(a)** to find *(again)*; *(rencontrer)* to meet again; *(découvrir)* to rediscover; **r. son chemin,** to find one's way again; *Prov* **un(e) de perdu(e), dix de retrouvé(e)s,** there are (plenty) more fish in the sea; **la clef a été retrouvée,** the key has been found; **r. la parole/sa santé,** to regain *or* recover one's speech/one's health; **on retrouve chez lui la curiosité de sa grand-mère,** he has his grandmother's curiosity; **on ne retrouve plus cet auteur dans son dernier roman,** we don't recognize this author in his last novel, this author's last novel is uncharacteristic; **tu ne retrouveras jamais une telle occasion,** you'll never come across an opportunity like it again;

(b) *(rejoindre)* **aller r. qn,** to go and join s.o.; **je vous retrouverai ce soir,** I shall see you again this evening.

2 se retrouver *vpr* **(a) se r. dans la même position,** to find oneself *or* to be in the same position again; **se r. à Paris,** to be back in Paris; **tu vas te r. sans un sou,** you're going to find yourself *or* be penniless again;

(b) *(retrouver son chemin)* to find one's bearings; *Fig* **je ne peux m'y r.!,** I can't make it out!; *F* **s'y r.,** *(financièrement)* to cover one's expenses, to break even;

(c) *(entre personnes)* to meet again; **comme on se retrouve!,** fancy meeting you!, it's a small world!; **on se retrouvera!,** I'll get even (with you)!;

(d) *(en soi-même)* to find oneself again;

(e) *(exister)* to exist; **ce mot se retrouve dans de nombreuses langues,** this word exists in numerous languages; **ça ne se retrouvera pas,** you won't find anything like it again.

rétroversion [retrɔvɛrsjɔ̃] *nf Méd* retroversion.

rétrovirus [retrɔvirys] *nm Méd* retrovirus.

rétroviseur [retrɔvizœr] *nm Aut* (rear-view) mirror; **r. extérieur,** *Br* wing mirror, *Am* outside mirror.

rets [rɛ] *nm* (hunting) net; *Litt* **prendre qn dans ses r.,** to catch s.o. in one's toils.

réuni [reyni] *adj* **(a)** *(rassemblé)* put together; **plus forts que nous et les Anglais réunis,** stronger than us and the English (put) together *or* combined; **(b)** *Com* amalgamated, united *(dairies etc)*.

réunification [reynifikɑsjɔ̃] *nf Pol* reunification.

réunifier [reynifje] *vt Pol* to reunify.

réunion [reynjɔ̃] *nf* **(a)** *(action de rassembler)* putting *or* bringing together *(of objects)*; gathering (together) *(of facts, information etc)*; bringing together *(of people, family etc)*; *(à nouveau)* reunion *(of family, political party etc)*; *(action de joindre)* joining together; **r. d'une province à la France,** union of a province with France; **(b)** *(action de se rassembler)* coming *or* gathering together; **droit de r.,** right of assembly; **salle de r.,** assembly room; **(c)** *(assemblée)* meeting; session, sitting *(of a commission)*; **r. de famille,** family gathering; **r. électorale,** election meeting; **le directeur est en r.,** the manager is in a meeting; **r. publique,** public meeting.

Réunion (La) [lareynjɔ̃] *nf* Réunion.

réunionnais, -aise [reynjɔnɛ, -ɛz] **1** *adj* of *or* from Réunion. **2** *n* **R.,** native *or* inhabitant of Réunion.

réunir [reynir] **1** *vt* **(a)** *(rassembler)* to put *or* bring *(objects)* together; to gather (together) *(facts, information etc)*; to bring *(people, family etc)* together; *(à nouveau)* to reunite *(family, political party etc)*; *(joindre)* to join together; **r. qch à qch,** to join sth to sth; **r. une somme,** to collect *or* get together a sum of money; **r. une armée,** to raise an army; **r. un comité,** to convene a committee, to call a committee together;

(b) *(comporter)* to combine; **il réunit de grandes qualités,** he combines great qualities.

2 se réunir *vpr* **(a)** *(of persons)* to meet, to gather together; **l'assemblée se réunit une fois par semaine,** the assembly meets once a week; **se r. autour d'une personnalité,** to gather *or* congregate around a famous person;

(b) *(of banks etc)* to amalgamate; *(of churches, states etc)* to unite; **tout se réunissait contre nous,** everything combined against us.

réussi [reysi] *adj* successful; *Iron* **c'est r.!, la voilà en larmes!,** well done *or* very clever!, she's in tears now!; **mal r.,** unsuccessful.

réussir [reysir] **1** *vi* to be successful, to be a success, to succeed; *(of plant)* to thrive; **le projet avait mal réussi,** the plan had proved a failure; *F* **le homard ne me réussit pas,** lobster doesn't agree with me; **r. dans qch,** to succeed *or* be successful at *or* in sth; **r. à un examen,** to pass an examination; *Scol* **r. de justesse,** to scrape through; **r. à faire qch,** to succeed in doing sth; *Iron* **elle a réussi à déranger tout le monde,** she managed to disturb everybody; **c'est un garçon qui réussira,** he's a boy who will do well *or* succeed *or* be successful; **ne pas r. à faire qch,** to be unsuccessful at *or* in doing sth, to fail to do sth; **tout lui réussit,** he's successful in everything; **ce truc-là ne réussira pas,** that trick won't work *or* won't come off.

2 *vt* to make a success of *(sth)*, to be successful with *(sth)*; **elle réussit (bien) les omelettes,** she makes very good omelettes; *Cartes* **r. son contrat,** to make one's contract; *F* **r. son coup,** to do the trick, to bring it off.

réussite [reysit] *nf* **(a)** *(succès)* success; *(d'entreprise etc)* success, successful result; **cette soirée est une belle r.!,** this party is a great success; **r. sociale,** social success; **(b)** *Cartes* patience; **faire une r.,** to play patience.

réutilisation [reytilizɑsjɔ̃] *nf* reuse.

réutiliser [reytilize] *vt* to reuse.

revaccination [rəvaksinɑsjɔ̃] *nf* revaccination.

revacciner [rəvaksine] *vt* to revaccinate.

revaloir [rəvalwar] *vt* *(conj like* **valoir**; *used chiefly in the fu)* **je vous le revaudrai!, je vous revaudrai cela!,** *(menace)* I'll pay you back for that!; *(reconnaissance)* I'll do the same for you another time!

revalorisation [rəvalɔrizɑsjɔ̃] *nf* **(a)** revaluation *(of currency)*; raising *(of pensions, prices etc)*; **(b)** *Fig* re-emphasis on the importance of *(idea, profession etc)*.

revaloriser [rəvalɔrize] *vt* **(a)** to revalue *(currency)*; to raise *(pensions, prices etc)*; **(b)** *Fig* to re-emphasize the importance of *(idea, profession etc)*.

revanchard, -arde [rəvɑ̃ʃar, -ard] *adj & n Pol Péj* revanchist.

revanche [rəvɑ̃ʃ] *nf* **(a)** *(vengeance)* revenge; **prendre sa r. sur qn,** to take one's revenge on s.o., to get one's own back on s.o., to get even with s.o.; **je prendrai ma r. un jour,** it will be my turn one day; **(b)** *Sp* return match *or* game; **(c)** *Fig* **en r.,** *(en compensation)* in return, in compensation; *(par contre)* on the other hand; **à charge de r.,** on condition that I do the same for you.

revancher (se) [sərəvɑ̃ʃe] *vpr Vieilli* to revenge oneself, to be revenged.

revanchisme [rəvɑ̃ʃism] *nm Pol* revanchism.

revanchiste [rəvɑ̃ʃist] *adj & n Pol* revanchist.

rêvasser [rɛvase] *vi* to daydream, to let one's mind wander, to muse.

rêvasserie [rɛvasri] *nf* musing, daydreaming; **rêvasseries,** daydreams.

rêvasseur, -euse [rɛvasœr, -øz] **1** *adj* daydreaming. **2** *n* (day)dreamer.

rêve [rɛv] *nm* **(a)** *(de dormeur)* dream; **faire un r.,** to (have a) dream; **voir qch en r.,** to see sth in a dream *or* in one's dreams; **ça s'est passé comme dans un r.,** it happened as (if) in a dream; **faites de beaux rêves!,** pleasant *or* sweet dreams!; **la psychologie du r.,** the psychology of dreams *or* of dreaming; **(b)** *(idéal)* dream; **rêves de gloire,** dreams of glory; **maison/voiture/***etc* **de r.,** dream house/car/*etc*; **la maison de nos rêves,** the house of our dreams, our dream house; **c'est le r.!,** it's all you could wish for!, it's ideal!

rêvé [reve] *adj* perfect, ideal.

revêche [rəvɛʃ] *adj* **(a)** *(hargneux)* bad-tempered, cantankerous; **(b)** *Vieilli* harsh, rough *(cloth etc)*.

réveil [revɛj] *nm* **(a)** waking, awakening; *Fig* awakening; **à mon r., au r,** on waking; **le r. de la nature,** the awakening of Nature; **avoir un fâcheux r.,** to have a rude awakening; **le r. d'un volcan,** the renewed rumblings of a volcano; **(b)** *Mil* reveille; **sonner le r.,** to sound reveille; **(c)** *(pendulette)* alarm (clock); **mettre le r.,** to set the alarm; **radio-r.,** radio alarm, clock radio.

réveillé [reveje] *adj* awake; **je suis mal r.,** I haven't woken up (properly) yet, I'm still half asleep.

réveille-matin [revɛjmatɛ̃] *nm inv* alarm clock.

réveiller [reveje] **1** *vt* **(a)** *(tirer du sommeil)* to wake (up), to (a)waken; **réveillez-moi à sept heures,** wake me (up) at seven o'clock; **un bruit à r. les morts,** a noise to wake the dead; *Prov* **ne réveillez pas le chat qui dort,** let sleeping dogs lie; **(b)** *Fig* to stir up, to rouse *(s.o.)*; to awaken *(memories)*; to revive *(memory, courage)*. **2 se réveiller** *vpr* **(a)** *(of sleeper)* to wake (up), to awake; **se r. d'un sommeil agité,** to wake out of *or* from a troubled sleep; *Fig* **réveille-toi! tout a changé!,** wake up! everything has changed!; **(b)** *(of feelings)* to be awakened *or* roused *or* stirred (up); **(c)** *(of nature, vegetation)* to revive.

réveillon [revɛjɔ̃] *nm* *(repas)* midnight supper; *(réjouissances)* midnight party *(after midnight mass on Christmas Eve or New Year's Eve)*.

réveillonner [revɛjɔne] *vi* to see Christmas *or* the New

Year in (*with a midnight supper and party*).

réveillonneur, -euse [revɛjɔnœr, -øz] *n* (Christmas Eve *or* New Year's Eve) party-goer.

révélateur, -trice [revelatœr, -tris] **1** *adj* revealing, telltale (*sign, attitude, silence etc*); *Ch* tracer (*substance*); **signe r. d'un changement,** sign revealing a change; **c'est très r.,** it is very revealing; **c'est r. de ...,** it reveals ... . **2** *n* revealer, discoverer (*of plot, crisis etc*). **3** *nm Phot* developer.

révélation [revelɑsjɔ̃] *nf* **(a)** revelation, disclosure (*of secret, intention etc*); **(b) ce fut une r.!,** that was a revelation *or* an eye-opener!; **la dernière r. du ballet français,** the latest discovery *or* find in French ballet; **ce jeune musicien est la r. des années 90,** this young musician is the discovery *or* find of the 90's; **(c)** *Rel* revelation; **la r. divine,** the revealed religion.

révélé [revele] *adj* revealed (*religion, truth*).

révéler [revele] *v* (**je révèle, n. révélons; je révélerai**) **1** *vt* **(a)** (*dévoiler*) to reveal, to disclose (*secret, intention etc*); **il révéla maladroitement la vérité,** he let out the truth; **somme dont le montant n'a pas été révélé,** undisclosed amount; **l'enquête révèle que ...,** the survey reveals that ...; **(b)** (*témoigner de*) to show (*talent*); to reveal, to show (*kindness, good humour*); to betray, to reveal (*faults*); **(c)** *Phot* to develop. **2 se révéler** *vpr* **(a)** (*of person*) to reveal oneself *or* one's character; **se r. difficile,** to prove difficult; **il s'est révélé un bon ami,** he proved (to be) *or* showed himself (to be) a good friend; **(b)** (*of mystery*) to be revealed; (*of fact*) to come to light.

revenant, -ante [rəvnɑ̃, -ɑ̃t] **1** *adj Vieilli* (*avenant*) pleasing, prepossessing. **2** *n* ghost; **histoire de revenants,** ghost story; *F* **voilà une revenante!,** you're *or* he's *etc* a stranger!

revendeur, -euse [rəvɑ̃dœr, -øz] *n Com* retailer; (*d'articles d'occasion*) secondhand dealer.

revendicateur, -trice [rəvɑ̃dikatœr, -tris] **1** *adj* (*speech, letter etc*) supporting one's claims *or* demands. **2** *n* protestor.

revendicatif, -ive [rəvɑ̃dikatif, -iv] *adj* protest (*movement etc*); **journée revendicative,** day of protest.

revendication [rəvɑ̃dikɑsjɔ̃] *nf* **(a)** (*action*) claiming; **(b)** (*demande*) claim, demand (**sur,** on); **les revendications ouvrières,** the demands of labour, labour demands; *Jur* **(action en) r.,** action for recovery of property.

revendiquer [rəvɑ̃dike] *vt* **(a)** (*demander*) to claim, to demand; to assert, to insist on (*one's rights*); to lay claim to (*territory*); **(b)** (*assumer*) to claim (*responsibility*); **l'attentat n'a pas été revendiqué,** nobody has claimed responsibility for the attack.

revendre [rəvɑ̃dr] *vt* (*après achat*) to resell; (*vendre de nouveau*) to sell again; *Fig* **j'en ai à r.,** I have more than enough of it *or* them.

revenez-y [rəvnezi] *nm inv F* **(a)** going back, return (to the past); **un r.-y de tendresse,** a return *or* renewal of affection; **(b) ce gâteau a un goût de r.-y,** this cake tempts you to take more *or F* is very moreish.

revenir [rəvnir] *vi* (*conj like* **venir,** *aux* **être**) **(a)** (*rentrer*) to come back, to return; (*venir de nouveau*) to come back, to come again; **r. à la hâte,** to hurry back; **je reviens tout de suite,** I'll be back immediately; **r. de voyage,** to come back *or* return from a journey *or* trip; **je l'ai rencontré en revenant de l'église,** I met him on my way back from church; **r. sur ses pas,** to retrace one's steps, to turn back; **le temps passé ne revient plus,** time that is past will never come again; **l'herbe reviendra,** the grass will come *or* grow again; **ce nom/sujet revient souvent dans la conversation,** this name/subject often turns up *or* crops up in conversation; **fête qui revient tous les dix ans,** festival that occurs *or* recurs *or* comes round every ten years; **esprit qui revient,** ghost that walks; **r. à ses premières amours,** to go back *or* return to one's first love; **vous y reviendrez!,** (*à une méthode etc*) you'll go back *or* come back to it!; **je suis revenu au régime lacté,** I have gone back to a milk diet; **r. sur ses aveux/une promesse,** to retract one's confession/go back on a promise; **r. sur son opinion,** to reconsider one's opinion; **r. sur un sujet,** to bring up a subject again; **revenons à nos moutons,** let's get back to the subject; **en r. à qch,** to revert to sth; **pour en r. à la question,** to come back to our subject; **r. sur le passé,** to rake up the past; **il n'y a pas à y r.,** there is no going back on it;

(b) (*of strength, courage etc*) to return, to come back (**à qn,** to s.o.); **il ne faudrait pas que ces paroles lui reviennent,** don't let this get back to him; **la mémoire me revient,** my memory is coming back; **honneur qui me revient,** honour that falls to me by right; **à chacun ce qui lui revient,** to each his due;

(c) cela me revient à la mémoire, I am beginning to recall it, it's coming back to me; *F* **ça me revient maintenant,** I have it *or* I've got it now; **votre nom ne me revient pas,** your name escapes me *or* has slipped my memory, I can't think of your name;

(d) son visage ne me revient pas, I don't like the look of him;

(e) r. de sa surprise/d'une maladie, to recover from *or* get over one's surprise/an illness; **r. d'une théorie,** to abandon a theory; **r. d'une erreur,** to realize one's mistake; **je suis revenu de toutes mes illusions,** I have lost all my illusions; **elle est revenue de tout,** she doesn't care about anything any more; **je n'en reviens pas!,** (*étonnement*) I can't get over it!; **r. à la santé,** to recover *or* regain one's health; **il revient de loin,** (*il a failli mourir*) he has been at death's door; **r. à soi,** to recover consciousness, to come round, to come to;

(f) *Culin* **faire r.,** to brown;

(g) r. à, (*coûter*) to cost (*s.o.*); **sa maison lui est revenue à une forte somme,** his house cost him a lot of money; **r. cher,** to work out expensive, to cost a lot;

(h) *Fig* **cela revient au même,** it amounts *or* comes to the same thing; **cela revient à dire que ...,** that amounts to saying that ... .

2 se revenir *vpr F* **s'en r.,** to return, to make one's way back.

3 *v impers* **il me revient encore 100 francs,** I have still 100 francs to get; **c'est à elle qu'il revient de faire la demande,** it is up to *or* down to her to make the request; **il me revient que vous dites du mal de moi,** I hear *or* I have been told that you are speaking ill of me.

revente [rəvɑ̃t] *nf* resale; **objet de r.,** secondhand article.

revenu [rəv(ə)ny] *nm* **(a)** income (*of person*); revenue (*of the State*); **r. du travail,** earned income; **r. national brut,** gross national income; **impôt sur le r.,** income tax; **politique des revenus,** incomes policy; **(b)** yield (*of investment, capital*); **(c)** *Métal* tempering (*of steel*).

rêver [reve] **1** *vi* **(a)** (*of sleeper*) to dream (**de,** about); **on croirait r.!,** it can't be true!, I can't believe it!; *Fig* **j'en rêve la nuit,** I dream about it at night; **(b)** (*rêvasser*) to dream (**à,** of); **r. creux,** to daydream; **je ne rêve pas, il l'a bien dit!,** I'm not dreaming *or* imagining things, he did say it!; **(c)** (*souhaiter*) **r. de,** to dream of; **r. de faire,** to dream of doing. **2** *vt* (*of sleeper*) to dream of (*sth*); *Fig* (*souhaiter*) **r. mariage/la gloire,** to dream of marriage/glory; **vous l'avez rêvé!,** you must have imagined *or* dreamt it!; **j'ai rêvé que ...,** I dreamt that ... .

réverbération [reverberɑsjɔ̃] *nf* reflection (*of light, heat*); reverberation (*of sound*).

réverbère [reverbɛr] *nm* **(a)** (*lampe*) street lamp *or* light; **(b)** (*réflecteur*) (heat) reflector.

réverbérer [reverbere] *vt* (**il réverbère; il réverbérera**) to reflect, to throw back (*heat, light*); to make (*sound*) reverberate.

reverdir [rəverdir] **1** *vi* to grow *or* turn green again. **2** *vt* to make (*sth*) green again; (*peindre*) to paint (*sth*) green again.

révérence [reverɑ̃s] *nf* **(a)** (*déférence*) reverence (**envers, pour,** for); **r. parler,** with all due respect; **(b) Votre R.,** your Reverence; **(c)** (*salut*) bow (*of man*); curtsey (*of woman*); **faire la r. à qn,** (*of man*) to bow to s.o.; (*of woman*) to curtsey to s.o.; **tirer sa r. (à la compagnie),** to bow out; *Fig* **je vous tire ma r.,** I must take my leave.

révérenciel, -ielle [reverɑ̃sjɛl] *adj Litt* **il m'inspire une crainte révérencielle,** I live in holy fear of him.

révérencieusement [reverɑ̃sjøzmɑ̃] *adv Litt* reverently.

révérencieux, -euse [reverɑ̃sjø, -øz] *adj Litt* reverent; **peu r.,** irreverent.

révérend [reverɑ̃] *Rel* **1** *adj* reverend; **le r. père Martin,** Reverend Father Martin; **la révérende mère supérieure,** the Reverend Mother Superior. **2** *nm* reverend; **oui, mon R.,** yes, Reverend.

révérer [revere] *vt* (**je révère, n. révérons; je révérerai**) to revere; **maître révéré,** revered master.

rêverie [rɛvri] *nf* (*activité*) reverie, dreaming, musing; (*moment*) reverie; *Litt* **plongé dans de vagues rêveries,** in a brown study; **ces rêveries ne vous mèneront nulle part,** these dreams *or* illusions will lead you nowhere.

revernir [rəvernir] *vt* to revarnish.

revers [rəvɛr] *nm* **(a)** reverse (side) (*of coin, medal etc*); wrong side (*of material*); other side, back (*of page*); **r. de la main,** back of the hand; **donner un r. de main à qn,** to deal s.o. a backhanded blow; **(coup de) r.,** *Tennis* backhand (stroke); *Escrime* reverse; *Mil* **prendre une position à r.,** to capture a position in the rear; *Fig* **c'est le r. de la médaille,** that's the other side of the coin; **(b)** lapel (*of coat*); turnover (*of sock*); top (*of boot*); cuff (*of sleeve*); **r. de pantalon,** trouser *Br* turn-up *or Am* cuff; **habit à r. de velours,** coat faced with velvet; **bottes à r.,** top boots; **(c) r. (de fortune),** reversal (of fortune), setback; **les succès et les r. de la vie,** the ups and downs of life.

reverser [rəvɛrse] *vt* **(a)** (*servir de nouveau*) to pour (*sth*) out again; **je vous reverse un verre?,** shall I pour you another glass?; **(b)** (*remettre*) to pour (*sth*) back; **(c)** *Fig* to shift (*blame*); **(d)** *Fin* to transfer (*sum*) (**sur,** to).

réversibilité [revɛrsibilite] *nf* reversibility; *Jur* revertibility (*of pension etc*).

réversible [revɛrsibl] *adj* **(a)** reversible (*process, garment etc*); *Fig* **l'histoire n'est pas r.,** you can't put the clock back; **(b)** *Jur* revertible (*pension etc*).

réversion [revɛrsjɔ̃] *nf Jur Biol* reversion.

revêtement [rəvɛtmɑ̃] *nm* **(a)** *Tech* covering; (*enduit*) coating; (*à l'intérieur*) lining; *Av* skin (*of fuselage*); *Menuis* veneer; **r. de sol,** floor covering; **câble à r. en caoutchouc,** rubber-covered cable; **r. calorifuge,** lagging (*of boiler etc*); **(b)** *Constr* facing (*of wall*); revetment (*of embankment*); surface (material) (*of road*).

revêtir [rəvetir] *v* (*conj like* **vêtir**) **1** *vt* **(a)** (*habiller*) to clothe, to dress; **r. qn de qch,** to dress s.o. in sth; *Fig* **r. qn d'une dignité/d'une autorité,** to invest s.o. with a dignity/an authority; **pièce revêtue de votre signature,** document bearing your signature; *Litt* **revêtu de verdure,** verdure-clad;

(b) *Tech* (*couvrir*) to cover; (*enduire*) to coat; (*à l'intérieur*) to line (**de,** with); *Constr* to face (*wall*); to revet (*embankment*); to surface (*road*); to lag (*boiler*); **murs revêtus de boiseries,** panelled walls; **route non revêtue,** unsurfaced road;

(c) (*endosser*) to put on (*uniform, robes etc*); *Fig* **r. la forme humaine/un caractère particulier,** to assume human shape/take on a particular character; **fait qui revêt de l'importance,** fact that takes on importance.

2 se revêtir *vpr* **se r. de qch,** to put on, to dress oneself in (*uniform, robes etc*); to assume (*dignity*).

rêveur, -euse [rɛvœr, -øz] **1** *adj* dreamy; **ces résultats me laissent r.,** these results are bewildering. **2** *n* dreamer.

rêveusement [rɛvøzmɑ̃] *adv* dreamily; (*avec perplexité*) with bewilderment.

revient [rəvjɛ̃] *nm* **(a) (prix de) r.,** cost price; **(b)** *Métal* tempering.

revigorant [rəvigɔrɑ̃] *adj* reviving (*drink*).

revigorer [rəvigɔre] *vt* to reinvigorate; (*of drink, food*) to revive (*s.o.*).

revirement [rəvirmɑ̃] *nm* **(a)** *Nau* tacking about, going about; **(b)** sudden change (*of fortune*); reversal (*of feeling*); (*changement d'avis*) about-turn, *Am* about-face; **r. d'opinion,** (sudden) change in public opinion.

révisable [revizabl] *adj Jur* reviewable (*case*); **prix r.,** price subject to modification *or* open to offer.

réviser [revize] *vt* **(a)** to revise (*text etc*); to audit (*accounts*); *Jur* to review, to reconsider (*case*); *Fig* to reappraise (*belief etc*); **r. son jugement,** to revise one's judgment; **(b)** *Scol* to revise; **(c)** *Tech* to service (*car, engine etc*).

réviseur [revizœr] *nm* reviser; *Typ* proofreader; **r. (comptable),** auditor.

révision [revizjɔ̃] *nf* **(a)** revision (*of text etc*); *Typ* proofreading; **(b)** auditing (*of accounts*); **(c)** *Scol* revision; **faire des révisions,** to revise; **(d)** review, reconsideration (*of legal case*); *Fig* re-appraisal (*of belief etc*); **r. déchirante,** agonizing re-appraisal; **(e)** *Tech* service, servicing (*of car, engine etc*).

révisionnisme [revizjɔnism] *nm Pol* revisionism.

révisionniste [revizjɔnist] *adj & n Pol* revisionist.

réviso [revizo] *n Pol F Péj* revisionist.

revisser [rəvise] *vt* to screw back (again).

revitalisant [rəvitalizɑ̃] *adj* revitalizing (*shampoo etc*).

revitalisation [rəvitalizasjɔ̃] *nf* revitalization.

revitaliser [rəvitalize] *vt* to revitalize (*skin, region etc*).

revivifier [rəvivifje] *vt* (*impf & pr sub* **n. revivifiions, v. revivifiiez**) to revive (*memory, feeling*).

revivre [rəvivr] *v* (*conj like* **vivre**) **1** *vi* (*après la mort*) to live again, to come to life again; *Fig* (*recouvrir son énergie*) to come alive again; **elle revit dans sa fille,** she lives on in her daughter; **se sentir r.,** to feel oneself restored to life; **faire r. qn,** to bring s.o. to life again, to revive s.o.; **faire r. une coutume,** to revive a custom. **2** *vt* to relive (*the past*); to relive (*experience etc*), to live through (*experience etc*) again.

révocabilité [revɔkabilite] *nf* revocability (*of contract etc*); removability (*of official*).

révocable [revɔkabl] *adj* revocable (*contract etc*); removable (*official*).

révocation [revɔkasjɔ̃] *nf* revocation (*of testament, edict, contract etc*); removal, dismissal (*of official*).

révocatoire [revɔkatwar] *adj Jur* revocatory.

revoici [rəvwasi] *prép F* **me r.!,** here I am again!, it's me again!; **nous r. à Paris,** here we are in Paris again *or* back in Paris.

revoilà [rəvwala] *prép F* **le r.!,** there he is again!; **nous r. en Angleterre,** here we are in England again *or* back in England.

revoir[1] [rəvwar] *v* (*conj like* **voir**) **1** *vt* **(a)** (*voir ou regarder de nouveau*) to see (*s.o., sth*) again; (*rencontrer*) to see *or* meet (*s.o.*) again; **je revois encore ma maison d'enfance,** (*en souvenir*) I (can) see my childhood home again; **(b)** (*examiner*) to revise (*text, lesson*); to re-examine (*accounts, manuscript*), to look over (*accounts, manuscript*) again; to read (*proofs*). **2 se revoir** *vpr* **(a)** (*se rencontrer*) to see each other *or* meet again; **on se reverra!,** we shall see each other *or* meet again!; **(b)** (*en souvenir*) to see oneself.

revoir[2] (au) [orəvwar] **1** *int* goodbye. **2** *nm inv* goodbye; **des au r. sans fin,** endless goodbyes; **dis au r. au monsieur,** say goodbye to the gentleman.

révoltant [revɔltɑ̃] *adj* revolting, sickening, shocking (*sight, procedure etc*); outrageous, appalling (*behaviour*); appalling (*injustice*).

révolte [revɔlt] *nf* **(a)** (*émeute, indignation*) revolt, rebellion; **en r.,** in revolt (**contre,** against); **sentiment de r.,** rebellious feeling; **(b)** (*mutinerie*) mutiny.

révolté, -ée [revɔlte] **1** *adj* **(a)** (*indigné*) outraged, appalled (**de voir,** to see); **(b)** (*en révolte*) rebellious, insurgent; **r. contre,** in revolt against. **2** *n* rebel, insurgent; (*mutiné*) mutineer.

révolter [revɔlte] **1** *vt* **(a)** (*inciter à la révolte*) to induce (*s.o.*) to revolt; **(b)** (*indigner*) to revolt, to appal, to shock (*s.o.*). **2 se révolter** *vpr* **(a)** to revolt, to rebel (**contre,** against); (*se mutiner*) to mutiny; **(b) le bon sens se révolte contre une telle supposition,** common sense revolts against such a supposition.

révolu [revɔly] *adj* past (*days, moments etc*); **avoir quarante ans révolus,** to be over forty years of age; **quand le temps sera r.,** in the fullness of time; **une époque révolue,** a past *or* bygone age.

révolution [revɔlysjɔ̃] *nf* **(a)** (*rotation*) revolution (*of the earth, a wheel*), **(b)** *Pol etc* revolution; **toute la ville est en r.,** the whole town is in revolt *or* up in arms; *Hist* **la R.,** the French Revolution (*1789*); **r. culturelle/industrielle,** cultural/industrial revolution; **r. de palais,** palace revolution.

révolutionnaire [revɔlysjɔnɛr] *adj & n* revolutionary.

révolutionner [revɔlysjɔne] *vt* **(a)** (*transformer*) to revolutionize (*industry, theory etc*); **(b)** (*mettre en émoi*) to stir up (*person, village etc*).

revolver [revɔlvɛr] *nm* **(a)** (*arme*) revolver, *F* gun; **r. à six coups,** six-shooter; **(b) (porte-outils) r.,** revolving tool holder; *Tech* **tour (à) r.,** turret lathe, capstan lathe; **poche-r.,** hip pocket; **(c)** revolving nosepiece (*of microscope*).

revolvériser [revɔlverize] *vt F* to gun down.

révoquer [revɔke] *vt* **(a)** to dismiss, to remove (*official*) (from office); **(b)** to revoke, to repeal, to rescind (*decree, contract etc*); **(c) r. qch en doute,** to call sth into question.

revoter [rəvɔte] **1** *vt* to vote again for (*law etc*). **2** *vi* to vote again.

revouloir [rəvulwar] *vt F* (*conj like* **vouloir**) to want (*sth*) again; **en reveux-tu?,** would you like some more?

revoyure (à la) [alarvwajyr] *int Arg* see you!, bye!

revue [rəvy] *nf* **(a)** (*examen*) review, survey, inspection; *Mil* review, inspection (*of troops*); inspection (*of barracks*); **r. de presse,** review of the papers *or* the press; **r. de santé,** medical inspection; **faire la r. des troupes,** to review *or* inspect the troops; **passer en r.,** to review, to go over (*problems, possibilities etc*); *Mil* to review, to inspect (*troops*); *F* **je suis encore de la r.,** I've had all this trouble for nothing; **(b)** (*magazine*) review, magazine; **r. scientifique/littéraire/***etc*, scientific/literary/*etc* journal; **(c)** *Th* revue; **(d)** *F Vieilli* **nous sommes (des gens) de r.,** we shall meet again.

révulsé [revylse] *adj* **yeux révulsés,** eyes with the whites showing.

révulser [revylse] **1** *vt* **(a)** *F* (*dégoûter*) to revolt, to disgust (*s.o.*); **(b)** *Méd* to counter-irritate. **2 se révulser** *vpr* (*of face*) to contort; **son regard se révulsa, ses yeux se révulsèrent,** he showed the whites of his eyes.
révulsif, -ive [revylsif, -iv] *adj & nm Méd* revulsive, counter-irritant.
révulsion [revylsjɔ̃] *nf Méd* revulsion, counter-irritation.
rewriter¹ [rirajtœr, rərajtœr] *nm* rewriter.
rewriter² [rirajte, rərajter] *vt* to rewrite.
rewriting [rirajtiŋ, rərajtiŋ] *nm* rewriting.
rez-de-chaussée [redʃose] *nm inv* **(a)** (*niveau*) *Br* ground floor, *Am* first floor; **au r.-de-c.,** on the *Br* ground *or Am* first floor; **(b) (appartement en) r.-de-c.,** *Br* ground-floor flat, *Am* first-floor apartment.
rez-de-dalle [redədal] *nm inv* (*niveau*) *Br* ground floor, *Am* first floor (*opening on to a central concourse*); **(appartement en) r.-de-d.,** *Br* ground floor flat, *Am* first floor apartment.
rez-de-jardin [redʒardɛ̃] *nm inv* (*niveau*) garden level; **appartement en r.-de-j.,** garden *Br* flat or *Am* apartment.
R.F. [ɛrɛf] *nf abrév* **République française.**
R.F.A. [ɛrɛfa] *nf* (*abrév* **République fédérale allemande**) FRG.
r.g. *abrév* **rive gauche**.
rhabillage [rabijaʒ] *nm* **(a)** (*de meuble etc*) repairing, overhaul; **(b)** (*de personne*) getting dressed again.
rhabiller [rabije] **1** *vt* **(a)** (*réparer*) to repair (*watch, furniture etc*); **(b)** (*habiller*) **r. qn,** to dress s.o. again, to put s.o.'s clothes on again; **(c)** *Fig* to give a new look to (*building, old idea etc*). **2 se rhabiller** *vpr* **(a)** (*mettre ses vêtements*) to put on one's clothes again, to get dressed again; *F* **il peut aller se r.,** he'd better give up!; *F* **va te r.!,** get lost!; **(b)** (*s'acheter de nouveaux vêtements*) to buy (some) new clothes.
rhabilleur [rabijœr] *nm* repairer (*of clocks etc*).
rhapsode [rapsɔd] *nm Antiq* (*chanteur*) rhapsode, rhapsodist.
rhapsodie [rapsɔdi] *nf* rhapsody.
rhapsodique [rapsɔdik] *adj* rhapsodic.
rhénan, -ane [renɑ̃] **1** *adj* Rhenish, (of *or* from the) Rhine. **2** *n* **R.,** Rhinelander, native *or* inhabitant of the Rhine.
Rhénanie [renani] *nf* **la R.,** the Rheinland; **R.-Palatinat,** Rheinland-Palatinate.
rhénium [renjɔm] *nm Ch* rhenium.
rhéostat [reɔsta] *nm Él* rheostat; **r. de démarrage,** rheostatic starter (*of electric motor*).
rhésus [rezys] *nm* **(a)** *Zool* rhesus monkey; **(b)** *Physiol* **facteur r.,** rhesus *or* Rh factor; **r. positif/négatif,** rhesus *or* Rh positive/negative; **incompatibilité r.,** rhesus *or* Rh incompatibility.
rhéteur [retœr] *nm* **(a)** *Antiq* (*professeur*) rhetor; **(b)** (*orateur*) rhetorician.
rhétoricien, -ienne [retɔrisjɛ, -jɛn] *n* rhetorician.
rhétorique [retɔrik] **1** *nf* **(a)** *Littér* rhetoric; **figure de r.,** figure of speech; **(b)** *Scol Arch* **(classe de) r.,** = sixth form; **(c)** (*emphase*) rhetoric. **2** *adj* rhetorical (*effect etc*).
rhéto-roman, -ane [retɔrɔmɑ̃, -an] *adj & nm Ling* Rhaeto-Romanic.
Rhin (le) [lərɛ̃] *nm* the (river) Rhine.
rhinite [rinit] *nf Méd* rhinitis, coryza.
rhinocéros [rinɔserɔs] *nm* rhinoceros, *F* rhino.
rhinologie [rinɔlɔʒi] *nf Méd* rhinology.
rhinopharyngé [rinɔfarɛ̃ʒe] **, rhinopharyngien, -ienne** [rinɔfarɛ̃ʒjɛ̃, -jɛn] *adj Méd* nose-and-throat, *Spéc* rhinopharyngeal.
rhinopharyngite [rinɔfarɛ̃ʒit] *nf Méd* inflammation of the nose and throat, *Spéc* rhinopharyngitis.
rhinopharynx [rinɔfarɛ̃ks] *nm Anat* nose and throat, *Spéc* rhinopharynx.
rhinoplastie [rinɔplasti] *nf Chir* rhinoplasty.
rhinoscopie [rinɔskɔpi] *nf Méd* rhinoscopy.
rhizome [rizom] *nm Bot* rhizome.
rhodanien, -ienne [rɔdanjɛ̃, -jɛn] *adj* of the Rhone.
Rhodes [rɔd] *nf* Rhodes.
Rhodésie [rɔdezi] *nf Hist* Rhodesia.
rhodésien, -ienne [rɔdezjɛ̃, -jɛn] **1** *adj* Rhodesian. **2** *n* **R.,** Rhodesian.
rhodium [rɔdjɔm] *nm Ch* rhodium.
rhododendron [rɔdɔdɛ̃drɔ̃] *nm Bot* rhododendron.
rhombique [rɔ̃bik] *adj* rhombic.
rhomboïdal, -aux [rɔ̃bɔidal, -o] *adj* rhomboid.
rhomboïde [rɔ̃bɔid] *nm* rhomboid.
Rhône (le) [lərɔn] *nm* the (river) Rhone.
rhubarbe [rybarb] *nf* rhubarb.
rhum [rɔm] *nm* rum; **r. blanc,** white rum.
rhumatisant, -ante [rymatizɑ̃, -ɑ̃t] *adj & n Méd* rheumatic.
rhumatismal, -aux [rymatismal, -o] *adj Méd* rheumatic (*pain, fever etc*).
rhumatisme [rymatism] *nm Méd* rheumatism; **r. articulaire,** rheumatoid arthritis; **r. déformant,** polyarthritis; **avoir des rhumatismes,** to have rheumatism; *F* **être perclus de rhumatismes,** to be crippled with rheumatism.
rhumatoïde [rymatɔid] *adj Méd* rheumatoid.
rhumatologie [rymatɔlɔʒi] *nm Méd* rheumatology.
rhumatologiste [rymatɔlɔʒist], **rhumatologue** [rymatɔlɔg] *n* rheumatologist.
rhume [rym] *nm Méd* cold; **gros r.,** heavy cold; **r. de cerveau,** head cold; **r. des foins,** hay fever; **prendre** *ou* **attraper un r.,** to catch (a) cold; **avoir un r.,** to have a cold.
rhumerie [rɔmri] *nf* rum distillery.
ria [rija] *nf Géog* ria; **côte à rias,** ria coast.
riant [rijɑ̃] *adj* **(a)** smiling, cheerful (*face*); **(b)** cheerful, pleasant (*atmosphere etc*).
rib [rib] *nm F* (*abrév* **relevé d'identité bancaire**) = document giving details of one's bank account.
ribambelle [ribɑ̃bɛl] *nf F* long string (*of insults, names etc*); herd (*of animals*); **r. d'enfants,** swarm *or* whole lot of children.
ribaud, -aude [ribo, -od] *Arch & Litt* **1** *adj* debauched (*person*). **2** *n* debauchee.
riboflavine [ribɔflavin] *nf* riboflavin, vitamin B2.
ribonucléique [ribɔnykleik] *adj* ribonucleic (*acid*).
ribote [ribɔt] *nf F Vieilli* drunken bout, binge; **être en r.,** to be tipsy *or* tight.
ribouldingue [ribuldɛ̃g] *nf Arg Vieilli* spree, binge; **faire la r.,** to go on a spree *or* a binge.
ricain, -aine [rikɛ̃, -ɛn] *F* **1** *adj* Yank, American. **2** *n* **R.,** Yank, American.
ricanement [rikanmɑ̃] *nm* **(a)** (*rire*) (*sarcastique*) snigger; (*bête*) giggle; **(b)** (*action*) (*sarcastique*) sniggering; (*bête*) giggling.
ricaner [rikane] *vi* (*sarcastiquement*) to snigger; (*bêtement*) to giggle.
ricaneur, -euse [rikanœr, -øz] **1** *adj* (*sarcastique*) sniggering; (*bête*) giggling; **air r.,** sneering look. **2** *n* (*sarcastique*) sniggerer; (*bête*) giggler.
richard, -arde [riʃar, -ard] *n Péj* (*personne riche*) moneybags.
Richard [riʃar] *nm* Richard; **R. Cœur de Lion,** Richard the Lionheart.
riche [riʃ] **1** *adj* **(a)** (*personne*) rich, wealthy, well-off; **être r. à millions,** to be worth millions; **les pays riches,** (the) rich *or* wealthy countries; **r. d'espérances,** rich in hope; **r. de possibilités,** rich in possibilities; *F* **ça fait r.,** it looks posh; **musée r. en tableaux,** museum rich in paintings; **un repas trop r.,** too rich a meal; **r. en protéine,** rich *or* high in protein, with a high protein content; **faire un r. mariage,** to marry into a wealthy family, *F* to marry money; **langue r.,** rich language; **rime r.,** rich rhyme; **végétation r.,** rich *or* luxuriant vegetation;

(b) rich, sumptuous (*furniture, carpet etc*); valuable, handsome (*gift*); rich (*ore*); rich, abundant (*harvest*); *Com* **article r.,** superior article; *Aut* **mélange r.,** rich mixture; **une r. nature,** a person full of vitality; **livre/expérience r. d'enseignements,** very instructive book/experience; *F* **une r. idée,** a splendid idea; *F* **ce n'est pas r.,** it's not up to much.

2 *n* rich *or* wealthy person; **les riches,** the rich, the wealthy; **nouveau r.,** nouveau riche; *Péj* **fils** *ou* **gosse de r.,** little rich kid.
richelieu [riʃəljø] *nm* lace-up shoe, Oxford (shoe); (*pl richelieu, richelieux*).
richement [riʃmɑ̃] *adv* **(a)** richly; **pourvoir r. ses enfants,** to make abundant provision for one's children; **marier r. sa fille,** to marry one's daughter into a wealthy family; **(b)** (*luxueusement*) richly, sumptuously; **(c)** (*copieusement*) copiously.
richesse [riʃɛs] *nf* **(a)** (*of person, country*) wealth; **la r. publique,** public wealth; **r. en matières premières,** resources of raw materials; **vivre dans la r.,** to be wealthy; **(b) richesses,** riches, wealth; *Fig* riches (*of poem etc*); **musée plein de richesses,** gallery full of treasures *or* valuable objects; **(c)** richness, sumptuousness (*of furniture, carpet etc*); fertility (*of soil*); exuberance (*of vegetation*); richness (*of experience, description, imagination*).

richissime [riʃisim] *adj F* extremely rich, rolling in money.
ricin [risɛ̃] *nm* castor-oil plant; **huile de r.,** castor oil.
ricocher [rikɔʃe] *vi* **(a)** to rebound; (*sur l'eau*) to bounce (**sur,** off); **(b)** (*of bullet*) to ricochet (**sur,** off).
ricochet [rikɔʃɛ] *nm* **(a)** rebound; (*sur l'eau*) bounce; **faire des ricochets (sur l'eau),** to play at ducks and drakes; **(b)** ricochet (*of bullet*); *F* **apprendre qch par r.,** to hear of sth indirectly.
ric-rac [rikrak] *adv F* **payer r.-r.,** to pay to the very last penny; **être r.-r.,** to be broke.
rictus [riktys] *nm* grin, grimace, rictus.
ride [rid] *nf* **(a)** wrinkle (*on the face, on fruit*); **front creusé de rides profondes,** deeply lined *or* furrowed brow; *Fig F* **cela n'a pas pris une r.,** it's still just as good; **(b)** ripple (*on water, sand*); ridge (*of sand*); *Nau* (shroud) lanyard.
ridé [ride] *adj* wrinkled; **pomme ridée,** wrinkled *or* shrivelled apple.
rideau, -eaux [rido] *nm* **(a)** screen, curtain (*of trees etc*); *Mil* **r. de troupes,** screen of troops; **r. de feu,** fire curtain; **r. de fumée,** smoke screen; **(b)** (*d'intérieur*) curtain, *Am* drape; **rideaux de fenêtre,** window curtains; **lit garni de rideaux,** curtained bed; **rideaux de lit,** bed hangings; **tirer les rideaux,** to draw the curtains; *F* **tirer le r. sur qch,** to draw a veil over sth; **(c)** *Th* curtain; **r. d'entr'acte,** act drop; **r. à huit heures précises,** the curtain rises at eight sharp; *Arg* **r.!,** let's call it a day!; **(d) r. de fer,** *Th* safety curtain; metal shutter (*of shop*); *Pol* Iron Curtain; **(e)** register, blower (*of fireplace*); roll top (*of desk*); **classeur à r.,** roll-shutter cabinet.
ridelle [ridɛl] *nf* rack, rail (*of cart, lorry*).
rider [ride] **1** *vt* **(a)** to wrinkle, to line (*forehead*); to wrinkle, to shrivel (*skin, fruit*); **(b)** to ripple (*water, sand etc*); **(c)** *Nau* to set up, to tighten (*the shrouds*). **2 se rider** *vpr* **(a)** (*of skin*) to wrinkle; (*of forehead*) to become wrinkled *or* lined; (*of apple*) to shrivel up; **(b)** (*of water*) to ripple.
ridicule [ridikyl] **1** *adj* ridiculous, absurd, ludicrous; **il serait r. d'annuler la fête,** it would be ridiculous *or* ludicrous *or* absurd to cancel the party; **que c'est r. de se fâcher pour si peu!,** how ridiculous *or* ludicrous *or* absurd to get worked up about such a small thing!; **une quantité r. de beurre,** a ridiculous amount of butter; **se rendre r.,** to make a fool of oneself, to make oneself look ridiculous.
2 *nm* **(a)** (*absurdité*) ridiculousness, absurdity; **c'est d'un r. achevé,** it is perfectly ridiculous *or* the height of absurdity; **tomber dans le r.,** to make oneself ridiculous; **se couvrir de r.,** to make a fool of oneself, to make oneself look ridiculous;
(b) (*dérision*) ridicule; **craindre le r.,** to fear ridicule; **tourner qn en r.,** to hold s.o. up to ridicule, to ridicule s.o.;
(c) (*chose ridicule*) **les ridicules de notre époque,** the absurdities of our time.
ridiculement [ridikylmɑ̃] *adv* ridiculously, absurdly, ludicrously.
ridiculiser [ridikylize] **1** *vt* to ridicule, to hold up to ridicule. **2 se ridiculer** *vpr* to make oneself look ridiculous, to make a fool of oneself.
ridule [ridyl] *nf* (little) wrinkle.
rien [rjɛ̃] **1** *pron indéf* **(a)** (*quelque chose*) (*in questions* **rien** *is preferred to* **quelque chose** *when a negative answer is expected*) anything; **y a-t-il r. de plus triste?,** is there anything more depressing?;
(b) (*with* **ne** *expressed*) nothing, not anything; **r. ne l'intéresse,** nothing interests him; **je n'ai r. vu,** I saw nothing, I didn't see anything; **il n'a r. mangé depuis hier,** he has eaten nothing *or* not eaten anything since yesterday; **je n'ai r. à faire,** I have nothing to do, I don't have anything to do; **il n'y a r. à faire,** it can't be helped; *F* **r. à faire, ça ne marche pas,** it's no good, it's not working; **il ne faut r. lui dire,** he mustn't be told anything, he must be told nothing; **personne n'osa r. dire,** nobody dared say anything; **n'en dites r.,** don't say anything *or* a word about it, say nothing about it; **il n'est r. de tel que de se bien porter,** there is nothing like feeling well; **je n'ai r. de nouveau à vous dire,** I have nothing *or* I don't have anything new to tell you; **il ne vous faut r. d'autre?,** do you require anything else?; **elle veut ça et r. d'autre,** she wants that and nothing else; **ce n'est r.,** it's nothing; **ça ne fait r.,** it doesn't matter, it makes no difference *or F* no odds; **cela ne fait r. à l'affaire,** that is nothing to do with it; **si cela ne vous fait r.,** if you don't mind; **comme si de r. n'était,** as if nothing had happened; **il n'en est r.!,** nothing of the kind!; **je n'en ferai r.,** I shall do nothing of the kind *or* sort; **elle n'est r. pour moi,** she is *or* means nothing to me; **sa fille n'a r. de lui,** his daughter doesn't take after him in any way; **il n'était pour r. dans l'affaire,** he had nothing to do with *or* had no hand in the matter; *F* **il ne sait r. de r.,** he knows nothing at all *or* nothing about anything;
(c) (*with* **ne** *understood*) **que faites-vous? — r./presque r.,** what do you do? — nothing/hardly anything; **r. du tout,** nothing at all; **c'est tout ou r.,** it's all or nothing; **avoir qch pour r.,** to get sth for (next to) nothing; **parler pour r.,** to waste one's breath; **tout cet effort pour r.!,** all that effort for nothing *or* in vain; **jouer pour r.,** to play for fun; **pourquoi demandez-vous cela? — pour r.,** why do you ask that? — no reason *or* I just wondered; **se fâcher de r.,** to get angry about nothing; **merci, monsieur — de r.,** thank you (very much) — it's a pleasure *or* you're welcome *or* (please) don't mention it; **en moins de r.,** in less than no time, in no time at all; **une affaire de r. (du tout),** an insignificant matter; **femme de r.,** loose woman; **une petite pièce de r. du tout,** a wretched little room; **un homme de r. du tout,** a man of no account, a nobody; **un** *ou* **une r. (-)du(-)tout,** a (mere) nobody; **une coupure de r. du tout,** a superficial cut; *F* **un moins que r.,** (*personne*) a dead loss, a hopeless case; **pour trois fois r.,** for next to nothing; **faire qch comme (un) r.,** to do sth easily *or* without any trouble at all; *Tennis* **quinze à r.,** fifteen love;
(d) (*the negation is expressed or implied elsewhere in the sentence*) **il est inutile de r. dire,** you needn't say anything; **avant qu'elle ait r. dit,** before she said anything; **sans r. faire,** without doing anything; **sans nous gêner en r.,** without troubling us at all *or* in the slightest;
(e) r. que, nothing but, only, merely; **je frémis r. que d'y songer,** the mere thought (of it) *or* just thinking of it makes me shudder; **r. que pour aller à un bal,** for the sake of going *or* just to go to a dance; **il m'a confié le secret, r. qu'à moi,** he told the secret just to me *or* to me alone; **r. que cela?,** is that all?;
(f) (*with* **ne ... pas**) on ne peut pas vivre de r., you can't live on nothing; **ce n'est pas r.!,** that's something!
2 *adv Arg* right, *Br* not half; **elle est r. chic!,** she's right smart!, *Br* she isn't half smart!
3 *nm* **(a)** (*bagatelle*) trifle, (mere) nothing; **elle s'habille d'un r.,** she looks good (dressed) in anything; **se piquer d'un r.,** to take offence at the slightest thing; **perdre son temps à des riens,** to waste one's time with trifles; **dire des riens,** to indulge in small talk; **il court 400 mètres comme un r.,** he runs 400 metres just like that *or* with no trouble (at all);
(b) un r. de, (*un petit peu de*) (just) a little; **en un r. de temps,** in no time (at all), in less than no time; **un r. de femme,** a tiny little woman;
(c) un r., (*un peu*) a bit, a trifle; **il est un r. pédant,** he is a bit *or* a trifle pedantic.
rieur, -euse [rijœr, -øz] **1** *adj* cheerful. **2** *n* laugher; **avoir les rieurs de son côté** *ou* **avec soi,** to have the last laugh.
riesling [rislin] *nm* (*vin*) riesling.
rififi [rififi] *nm Arg* brawl, free-for-all.
riflard¹ [riflar] *nm Tech* (*lime*) coarse file; (*ciseau*) paring chisel; (*rabot*) jackplane.
riflard² *nm F* (*parapluie*) umbrella, *Br* brolly.
rifler [rifle] *vt Tech* (*avec une lime*) to plane; (*avec un ciseau*) to pare; (*avec un rabot*) to plane.
rigide [riʒid] *adj* **(a)** rigid; tense (*muscle*); fixed (*axle*); **couverture r.,** stiff cover (*of book*); **(b)** *Fig* rigid, inflexible (*person, rule, system etc*).
rigidement [riʒidmɑ̃] *adv* rigidly.
rigidifier [riʒidifje] *vt* to rigidify, to make rigid.
rigidité [riʒidite] *nf* **(a)** rigidity; tenseness (*of muscles*); **r. cadavérique,** rigor mortis; **(b)** *Fig* rigidity, inflexibility (*of person, rule, system etc*).
rigolade [rigɔlad] *nf F* fun; (*chose ridicule*) farce, joke; **ça n'est pas de la r.,** it's no laughing matter *or* joke; **prendre qch à la r.,** to treat sth as a joke, to make a joke out of sth.
rigolard, -arde [rigɔlar, -ard(ə)] *F* **1** *adj* (*personne*) fond of a lark *or* a laugh; jolly (*look*). **2** *n* **c'est une rigolarde,** she's fond of a lark *or* a laugh.
rigole [rigɔl] *nf* (*caniveau*) channel; (*filet d'eau*) rivulet.
rigoler [rigɔle] *vi F* **(a)** (*rire*) to laugh; **(b)** (*s'amuser*) to have some fun *or* a laugh, to enjoy oneself; **(c)** (*plaisanter*) to joke (**avec,** about); **il ne faut pas r. avec le feu,** you shouldn't mess about with fire.
rigolo, -ote [rigɔlo, -ɔt] *F* **1** *adj* **(a)** (*drôle*) funny; **ce n'est pas r.,** it's no laughing matter *or* joke; **(b)** (*curieux*) funny, queer, odd. **2** *n* (*personne amusante*) joker; (*fumiste*) phoney, fraud. **3** *nm* (*revolver*) revolver.
rigorisme [rigɔrism] *nm* rigorism, strictness.
rigoriste [rigɔrist] **1** *adj* rigorous, strict. **2** *n* rigorist, rigid

moralist.

rigoureusement [rigurøzmɑ̃] *adv* **(a)** *(avec dureté)* rigorously, severely, harshly; **(b)** *(strictement)* strictly; **à parler r., ce n'est pas vrai,** strictly speaking, it is not true; **r. exact,** absolutely correct; **informations r. établies,** rigorously established information.

rigoureux, -euse [rigurø, -øz] *adj* **(a)** *(dur)* rigorous, severe, harsh *(punishment, measures etc)*; hard *(winter)*; **(b)** *(strict)* strict; **observer une neutralité rigoureuse,** to observe strict neutrality; **au sens r. du mot,** in the strict sense of the word.

rigueur [rigœr] *nf* **(a)** *(dureté)* rigour, harshness, severity; **prendre des mesures de r.,** to take rigorous *or* harsh *or* severe measures; **r. du temps,** harshness *or* severity of the weather; **avant les rigueurs de l'hiver,** before the worst of the winter sets in; **user de r. avec qn,** to be severe with *or* hard on s.o.; **tenir r. à qn,** not to forgive s.o.; **(b)** strictness *(of rules etc)*; **la r. d'un raisonnement,** the closeness *or* exactness of an argument; **style qui manque de r.,** sloppy style; **être de r.,** to be compulsory *or* obligatory; **délai de r.,** deadline; **l'habit n'est pas de r.,** evening dress is optional; **à la r.,** if need be, if really necessary; **à la r. on peut se servir d'un succédané,** at a pinch one may use a substitute.

rillettes [rijɛt] *nfpl Culin* potted mince *(made from pork, rabbit, goose etc)*.

rimailler [rimaje] *vi Péj Vieilli* to versify.

rimailleur, -euse [rimajœr, -øz] *n Péj Vieilli* versifier, rhymster, poetaster.

rimaye [rimɑj] *nf* bergschrund.

rime [rim] *nf* rhyme; **rimes croisées** *ou* **alternées,** alternate rhymes; **rimes plates** *ou* **suivies,** couplet rhymes; **dictionnaire de rimes,** rhyming dictionary; *F* **sans r. ni raison,** without rhyme or reason.

rimer [rime] **1** *vt* to put into verse, to versify *(tale etc)*; **poésie rimée,** rhyming verse. **2** *vi* **(a)** *(of word etc)* to rhyme (**avec,** with); *F* **à quoi cela rime-t-il?,** what sense *or* what meaning is there in that?; **cela ne rime à rien,** there's no sense *or* neither rhyme nor reason in it; **(b)** *(faire des vers)* to write verse *or* poetry.

rimeur, -euse [rimœr, -øz] *n Péj* rhymer, rhymester.

rimmel ® [rimɛl] *nm* mascara.

rinçage [rɛ̃saʒ] *nm* *(action)* rinsing; *(opération)* rinse; *(pour les cheveux)* (colour *or US* color) rinse.

rinceau, -eaux [rɛ̃so] *nm Archit* foliated scroll.

rince-bouteilles [rɛ̃sbutɛj] *nm inv* bottle-washing machine.

rince-doigts [rɛ̃sdwa] *nm inv* finger bowl.

rincée [rɛ̃se] *nf* **(a)** *Arg* *(coups)* thrashing; **(b)** *F* *(averse)* downpour.

rincer [rɛ̃se] *v* **(je rinçai(s); n. rinçons) 1** *vt* to rinse *(clothes)*; to rinse (out) *(glass etc)*; *Arg* **se faire r.,** *(au jeu)* to be cleaned out. **2 se rincer** *vpr* **se r. la bouche,** to rinse one's mouth (out); *Arg* **se r. le gosier** *ou* **la dalle,** *(boire)* to wet one's whistle; *Arg* **se r. l'œil,** to get an eyeful.

rincette [rɛ̃sɛt] *nf Arg* nip of brandy *etc* *(put into emptied cup or glass)*.

rinceur, -euse [rɛ̃sœr, -øz] **1** *n* *(personne)* rinser. **2** *nf* **rinceuse,** *(machine)* bottle-washing machine.

rinçure [rɛ̃syr] *nf* *(eau sale)* rinsing water; *F* *(mauvaise boisson)* dishwater.

ring [riŋ] *nm Boxe* ring; **le r.,** *(la boxe)* boxing; **monter sur le r.,** to go into the ring; *(faire de la boxe)* to take up boxing.

ringard[1] [rɛ̃gar] *nm* *(tisonnier)* poker.

ringard[2], **-arde** [rɛ̃gar, -ard] *F* **1** *adj* *(démodé)* old-fashioned *(person, song, style etc)*. **2** *n* fuddy-duddy.

ripage [ripaʒ] *nm* **(a)** scraping, polishing *(of stones)*; **(b)** sliding along *(of load etc)*; **(b)** *(glissement)* slipping; *(de véhicule)* skidding.

ripaille [ripaj] *nf F* feast, blow-out; **faire r.,** to have a feast *or* blow-out.

ripailler [ripaje] *vi F* to feast, to have a (good) blow-out.

ripailleur, -euse [ripajœr, -øz] *n F* reveller.

ripaton [ripatɔ̃] *nm Arg* *(pied)* foot.

riper [ripe] **1** *vt* **(a)** *(polir)* to scrape, to polish *(stone)*; **(b)** *(faire glisser)* to slide along *(load etc)*; *Rail* to shift *(the track)*. **2** *vi* to slip; *(of wheels)* to skid; *(of cargo)* to shift; **(b)** *Arg* *(s'en aller)* to clear off.

ripolin ® [ripɔlɛ̃] *nm* enamel (paint).

ripoliner [ripɔline] *vt* to enamel, to paint with enamel.

riposte [ripɔst] *nf* **(a)** *(coup)* counterstroke; *Boxe Escrime* riposte, counter; **(b)** *(réponse)* riposte, retort; **(c)** *(représailles)* counterattack.

riposter [ripɔste] *vi* **(a)** *Boxe Escrime* to riposte, to counter; *Fig* **je riposterai,** I'll give as good as I get; **(b)** *(répondre)* to retort, to riposte; **(c)** *(user de représailles)* to counterattack.

riquiqui [rikiki] *adj inv F* *(mesquin)* stingy, mean *(portion etc)*; *(pauvre)* shabby, tatty *(garment etc)*; **ça fait r.,** *(mesquin)* it looks a bit stingy *or* mean; *(pauvre)* it looks a bit shabby *or* tatty.

rire[1] [rir] *nm* laughter, laughing; **un r.,** a laugh; **éclat de r.,** burst of laughter; **avoir un accès de fou r.,** to laugh uncontrollably; *Arg* *(sur scène)* to corpse; **provoquer** *ou* **exciter des rires,** to cause laughter; **r. moqueur,** sneer; **il eut un r. d'incrédulité,** he laughed incredulously; **un gros r. bruyant,** a horse laugh, a guffaw.

rire[2] *v* *(prp* **riant**; *pp* **ri**; *pr ind* **je ris, n. rions, ils rient**; *pr sub* **je rie**; *p hist* **je ris**; *fu* **je rirai) 1** *vi* **(a)** to laugh; **se tenir les côtes de r., r. comme un bossu,** to be doubled up *or* convulsed with laughter, to split one's sides laughing; **r. bruyamment,** to guffaw; **r. en soi-même, r. tout bas,** to laugh to oneself, to chuckle; **r. en dedans,** to laugh up one's sleeve; **r. faux** *ou* **pointu,** to give a forced laugh; **r. bêtement,** to giggle, to titter; **dire qch en riant,** to say sth laughingly *or* with a laugh; *(en blaguant)* to say sth by way of *or* as a joke; **il a ri (jusqu')aux larmes,** he laughed till he cried; **c'était à mourir** *ou F* **à crever de r.,** we nearly died laughing; **ne pas avoir le cœur à r.,** not to be in a laughing mood; **il n'y a pas de quoi r.,** it's no laughing matter *or* no joke; **cela nous a souvent fait r.,** we have often laughed about it, we have had many a laugh over it; **il nous faisait tordre** *ou* **mourir de r.,** he made us split our sides laughing; *F* **j'étais mort de r.,** I was killing myself laughing; **r. de qn,** to laugh at s.o., to make fun of s.o.; **r. d'une histoire,** to laugh over *or* at a story; **il rit de vos menaces,** he laughs at *or* scoffs at *or* makes light of your threats; **il prête à r.,** he makes himself a laughing stock; **vous me faites r.!,** nonsense!, you must be joking!; **laissez-moi r.!, ne me faites pas r.!,** don't make me laugh!;

(b) *(s'amuser)* to have (some) fun, to have a laugh *or* some laughs; **vous voulez r.!,** are you joking?, do you really mean it?; **prendre qch en riant,** to laugh sth off; **pour r.,** for fun, for a joke; **non mais sans r.!,** no, but seriously!; **sans r., c'est vrai,** honestly or seriously, it's true; *F* **c'était pour de r.,** it was only for fun; **roi pour r.,** sham king; **soldats pour r.,** make-believe soldiers; **je l'ai fait histoire de r.,** I did it for a joke *or* for fun;

(c) *(of eyes, landscape)* to smile; **la fortune lui rit,** fortune smiles on him.

2 se rire *vpr* **se r. de qn,** to laugh at *or* make fun of s.o.; **se r. de qch,** to laugh at *or* make light of sth.

ris[1] [ri] *nm Litt* laughter.

ris[2] *nm Nau* reef *(in sail)*; **prendre un r.,** to take in a reef; **larguer un r.,** to shake out a reef.

ris[3] *nm Culin* **r. (de veau),** (calf's) sweetbread.

risée [rize] *nf* **(a)** *(moquerie)* mockery, derision; **s'exposer à la r. publique,** to expose oneself to public scorn *or* derision; **(b)** *(objet de moquerie)* laughing stock; **nous étions la r. de tous,** we were a public laughing stock *or* the butt of everyone's jokes; **(c)** *Nau* *(brise)* light squall, flurry (of wind).

risette [rizɛt] *nf* *(d'enfant)* (little) laugh, smile; **fais (la) r. à papa!,** now smile for daddy!

risible [rizibl] *adj* laughable, ridiculous *(mistake, conduct etc)*; ridiculous *(person)*.

risiblement [riziblәmɑ̃] *adv* ridiculously.

risotto [rizɔto] *nm Culin* risotto.

risque [risk] *nm* risk; **courir un r.,** to run a risk; **prendre un r./des risques,** to take a risk/risks; **groupe à haut r.,** high-risk group; **vous le faites à vos risques et périls,** you do it at your own risk; **avoir le goût du r.,** to like taking risks; **au r. de sa vie,** at the risk *or* peril of his life; **il y a un r. de rechute,** there's a risk of relapse; **le r. de se voir trahi,** the risk of seeing oneself betrayed; **au r. de manquer le train,** at the risk of missing the train; **risques du métier,** occupational hazards; **police tous risques,** comprehensive *or* all-risks policy; **r. d'incendie,** fire risk; **souscrire un r.,** to underwrite a risk.

risqué [riske] *adj* **(a)** *(dangereux)* risky, hazardous *(business etc)*; **(b)** *(osé)* risqué, *F* near the knuckle *(joke etc)*.

risquer [riske] **1** *vt* to risk *(one's life, reputation, job etc)*; **il faut r. le combat,** we must risk a battle; **je ne veux rien r.,** I am not taking any risks *or* any chances; **r. gros,** to play for big stakes; *Prov* **qui ne risque rien n'a rien,** nothing venture, nothing gain; **r. le coup,** to chance it; **il risquait de tout perdre,** he risked *or* ran the risk of losing everything; **la grève risque de durer longtemps,** the strike may (well) go on for a long time; *F* **il risque de gagner,** he has a good chance of winning; **r. un œil,** to peep out. **2 se**

risquer *vpr* to take a risk, to take risks; **je ne m'y risquerais pas,** I wouldn't risk it; **se r. à faire qch,** to venture to do sth; **se r. dans une maison abandonnée,** to venture into an abandoned house; *Prov* **qui ne risque rien n'a rien,** nothing ventured nothing gained.
risque-tout [riskətu] **1** *n inv* daredevil. **2** *adj inv* **il est r.-t.,** he's a daredevil.
rissole [risɔl] *nf Culin* rissole.
rissoler [risɔle] *vt & vi Culin* to brown; **pommes (de terre) rissolées,** sauté potatoes.
ristourne [risturn] *nf* refund, rebate; *Com* (*rabais*) discount; **faire une r. à qn,** to give s.o. a refund *or* rebate; *Com* to give s.o. a discount.
ristourner [risturne] *vt* to refund, to return (*amount overpaid*) (**à qn,** to s.o.).
Rital, -ale, -als [rital] *n F Péj* (*Italien*) wop, *Br* Eyetie.
rite [rit] *nm* rite; *Fig* (*habitude*) ritual; **les rites de la vie quotidienne,** the ritual of everyday life.
ritournelle [riturnɛl] *nf Mus* ritornello; *F* **c'est toujours la même r.,** it's (always) the same old story.
ritualisme [ritɥalism] *nf Rel* ritualism.
ritualiste [ritɥalist] **1** *adj* ritualistic. **2** *n* ritualist.
rituel, -elle [ritɥɛl] **1** *adj* ritual. **2** *nm* **(a)** (*habitudes*) ritual; **selon le r.,** according to ritual; **r. d'initiation,** initiation ritual; **(b)** *Rel* (*livre*) ritual (book).
rituellement [ritɥɛlmɑ̃] *adv* **(a)** (*habituellement*) invariably; **(b)** *Rel* virtually.
rivage [rivaʒ] *nm* (*de mer, lac*) shore; (*plage*) beach; *Litt* (*de rivière*) bank.
rival, -ale, -aux [rival, -o] *adj & n* rival; **sans r.,** unrivalled.
rivaliser [rivalize] *vi* **r. avec qn,** to compete *or* vie with s.o.; **r. d'adresse,** to vie in skill (**avec qn,** with s.o.).
rivalité [rivalite] *nf* rivalry.
rive [riv] *nf* **(a)** bank (*of river*); shore (*of lake, sea*); **la R. gauche,** the Left Bank (*of the Seine*); **(b)** *Tech* lip (*of oven*).
river [rive] *vt* **(a)** (*attacher*) to rivet; *Fig* **être rivé à un emploi,** to be stuck *or* fixed in a job; **(b)** to clinch (*nail*); *F* **r. son clou à qn,** to leave s.o. speechless.
riverain, -aine [rivrɛ̃, -ɛn] **1** *adj* (*de rivière*) riverside, waterside; (*de lac*) lakeside, waterside (*owner, property etc*); (*de route*) roadside, bordering (on) the road (*property etc*). **2** *n* (*de rivière*) riverside resident; (*de lac*) lakeside resident; **les riverains de cette rue,** the people who live in *or* along this street; **'route interdite sauf aux riverains',** 'access only'.
rivet [rivɛ] *nm* rivet.
rivetage [rivtaʒ] *nm* riveting.
riveter [rivte] *vt* (**je rivette, n. rivetons**) to rivet.
riveteuse [rivtøz] *nf* riveting machine.
rivière [rivjɛr] *nf* **(a)** river; **pêche en r.,** river fishing; **(b)** *Équitation* water jump; **(c) r. de diamants,** diamond rivière.
rivoir [rivwar] *nm* (*marteau*) riveting hammer; (*machine*) riveting machine.
rivure [rivyr] *nf* (*action*) riveting; (*joint*) rivet(ed) joint; (*tête*) rivet head.
rixe [riks] *nf* brawl, scuffle.
riz [ri] *nm* rice; **r. en paille,** paddy; **r. décortiqué,** husked rice; **r. étuvé** *ou* **incollable,** non-stick rice; **r. brun,** brown rice; **eau de r.,** rice water; **r. au lait,** rice pudding; **poudre de r.,** face powder.
riziculteur, -trice [rizikyltœr, -tris] *n* rice grower.
riziculture [rizikyltyr] *nf* rice growing.
rizière [rizjɛr] *nf* rice field, paddy field.
riz-pain-sel [ripɛ̃sɛl] *nm inv Mil Arg* commissariat.
RN [ɛrɛn] *nf abrév* **route nationale**.
robe [rɔb] *nf* **(a)** (*de femme*) dress, frock; **r. du soir,** evening gown *or* dress; **r. de grossesse,** maternity dress; **r.-tablier,** *Br* pinafore dress, *Am* jumper; **(b) r. d'intérieur,** housecoat; **r. de baptême,** christening robe; **r. de chambre,** dressing gown, *Am* robe; *Hum* **vieux comme mes robes,** (*histoire*) as old as the hills; *Culin* **pommes de terre en r. de chambre** *ou* **des champs,** jacket potatoes, potatoes in their jackets; **(c)** robe, gown (*of lawyer etc*); **les gens de r., la r.,** the legal profession; **(d)** skin (*of onion*); husk (*of bean*); wrapper (leaf) (*of cigar*); **(e)** (*pelage*) coat (*of horse etc*); **(f)** colour, *US* color (*of wine*).
robert [rɔbɛr] *nm Arg* (*sein*) tit, boob.
Robert [rɔbɛr] *nm* Robert.
robin [rɔbɛ̃] *nm Péj* lawyer.
robine [rɔbin] *nf Can Arg* methylated spirits, *Br* meths.
robinet [rɔbinɛ] *nm* tap, *Am* faucet; **r. d'eau froide,** cold-water tap *or Am* faucet; **r. mélangeur,** mixer tap *or Am* faucet; **r. d'arrêt** *ou* **de fermeture,** stopcock, shut-off (valve); **r. de vidange** *ou* **de purge,** drain cock; **r. à flotteur,** ballcock; *Nau* **r. de prise d'eau à la mer,** seacock; **ouvrir/fermer le r.,** to turn on/off the tap *or Am* faucet; **problèmes de robinets,** sums about filling baths and tanks.
robinetterie [rɔbinɛtri] *nf* (*robinets*) (system of) taps.
robineux [rɔbinø] *nm Can Arg* tramp, methylated spirits *or Br* meths drinker.
robinier [rɔbinje] *nm Bot* robinia, false acacia.
robot [rɔbo] *nm* robot, automaton; **r. (ménager),** food processor; **avion r.,** drone.
robot-cuisine [rɔbokɥizin] *nm* food processor.
robotique [rɔbɔtik] *nf* robotics.
robotisation [rɔbɔtizasjɔ̃] *nf* automation.
robotiser [rɔbɔtize] *vt* to automate; *Fig* to turn (*s.o.*) into a robot *or* an automaton.
robre [rɔbr] *nm Cartes* rubber.
robusta [rɔbysta] *nm* (*café*) robusta.
robuste [rɔbyst] *adj* robust (*person, health*); stout (*faith*); hardy (*plant*); sturdy (*bicycle, machine etc*).
robustesse [rɔbystɛs] *nf* robustness (*of person*); hardiness (*of plant*); sturdiness (*of bicycle, machine etc*).
roc [rɔk] *nm* rock; **bâti sur le r.,** built on rock; **ferme comme un r.,** as firm *or* solid as a rock; **Jules, c'est un r.,** Jules is a sturdy sort.
rocade [rɔkad] *nf* (*route*) bypass; *Mil* communications line.
rocaille [rɔkaj] **1** *nf* **(a)** (*arrangement*) rock work; **(jardin de) r.,** rockery, rock garden; **(b)** (*pierraille*) (loose) stones *or* rocks; **(c)** (*terrain*) stony *or* rocky ground. **2** *adj inv Beaux-Arts* rocaille (*style, table etc*).
rocailleux, -euse [rɔkajø, -øz] *adj* **(a)** (*pierreux*) rocky, stony; **(b)** *Fig* rugged, harsh (*style etc*); harsh, rough (*voice*).
rocambole [rɔkɑ̃bɔl] *nf Bot* Spanish garlic.
rocambolesque [rɔkɑ̃bɔlɛsk] *adj* fantastic, incredible (*adventures, story etc*).
rochassier, -ière [rɔʃasje, -jɛr] *n* rock climber.
roche [rɔʃ] *nf* (*matière, rocher*) rock; *Géol* **roches ignées/sédimentaires/métamorphiques,** igneous/sedimentary/metamorphic rocks; **r. de fond,** bedrock; **eau de r.,** clear spring water; *Fig* **clair comme de l'eau de r.,** as clear as crystal; **avoir un cœur de r.,** to have a heart of stone; **homme de la vieille r.,** one of the old school.
rocher [rɔʃe] *nm* **(a)** (*masse de pierre*) rock; (*escarpé*) crag; **r. branlant,** rocking stone, logan(stone); **côte hérissée de rochers,** rockbound coast; **le R. de Gibraltar,** the Rock of Gibraltar, *F* the Rock; **(b) r. artificiel,** rockery; **(c)** (*paroi*) rock face; **faire du r.,** to go rock climbing; **(d)** (*bouchée de chocolat*) chocolate (*containing nuts*).
rochet[1] [rɔʃɛ] *nm* **(a)** *Tech* ratchet; **roue à r.,** ratchet wheel; **(b)** *Tex* (large) bobbin.
rochet[2] *nm* (*surplis*) rochet.
rocheux, -euse [rɔʃø, -øz] *adj* rocky; **masse/paroi rocheuse,** rock mass/face; **les (montagnes) Rocheuses,** the Rocky Mountains, the Rockies.
rock (and roll) [rɔk(ɛnrɔl)] *Mus* **1** *nm* rock (and roll); (*danse*) jive. **2** *adj inv* rock.
rocker [rɔkœr] *n* (*musicien*) rock musician; (*enthousiaste*) rock (music) fan.
rocking-chair [rɔkiŋtʃɛr] *nm* rocking chair; (*pl rocking-chairs*).
rococo [rokoko] **1** *nm & adj inv Beaux-Arts* rococo. **2** *adj inv* (*démodé*) old-fashioned.
rodage [rɔdaʒ] *nm* **(a)** grinding in (*of glass stopper, valve*); running in (*of car engine*); *Ordinat* burn-in; *Aut* **en r.,** running in.
rodeo, rodéo [rɔdeo] *nm* rodeo.
roder [rɔde] *vt* **(a)** *Tech* to grind in (*glass stopper, valve*); **poudre à r.,** abradant; **(b)** *Aut* to run in (*new car*); *Ordinat* to burn in; *Fig* to let (*business, team etc*) get into its stride; *Th* to run in (*show*); **être rodé,** (*of business etc*) to be in its stride; *Th* to be run in; (*of person*) to be broken in (*to a job*).
rôder [rode] *vi* **(a)** to prowl, to be on the prowl; **r. dans les rues,** to prowl about *or* hang about the streets; *Fig F* **il rôde autour de moi depuis quelques jours,** he has been hanging around me for a few days; **un pauvre chien qui rôde,** a poor dog roaming around; **(b) r. sur son ancre,** (*of ship*) to veer at anchor.
rôdeur, -euse [rodœr, -øz] **1** *adj* prowling. **2** *n* prowler.
rodoir [rɔdwar] *nm* grinding tool.
Rodolphe [rɔdɔlf] *nm* Rudolph, Rudolf.
rodomontade [rɔdɔmɔ̃tad] *nf* **rodomontade(s),** boasting, bragging; **faire des rodomontades,** to boast, to brag.

Rodrigue [rɔdrig] *nm* Roderigo, Roderick.
Rogations [rɔgɑsjɔ̃] *nfpl Rel* Rogations.
rogatoire [rɔgatwar] *adj Jur* rogatory.
rogaton [rɔgatɔ̃] *nm F* scrap (of food), leftover.
Roger [rɔʒə] *nm* Roger.
rognage [rɔɲaʒ] *nm* (*action*) clipping, trimmng (*of claws, fingernails*); trimming, paring (*of leather, metal etc*).
rogne [rɔɲ] *nf F* bad temper; **être en r.,** to be cross *or* in a (bad) temper; **mettre qn en r.,** to make s.o. cross, to put s.o. in a (bad) temper; **se ficher en r.,** to see red.
rogner [rɔɲe] *vt* to clip, to trim (*claws, fingernails*); to trim, to pare (*leather, metal etc*); to clip (*coin*); (*of inflation*) to eat away at (*savings etc*); **r. les tranches,** to cut *or* trim the edges (*of a book*); *Fig* **r. la pension de qn,** to whittle down s.o.'s allowance; **r. (sur) les dépenses,** to cut down *or* curtail *or* reduce expenses.
rognoir [rɔɲwar] *nm* paring *or* trimming tool, parer, trimmer.
rognon [rɔɲɔ̃] *nm Culin* kidney.
rognonner [rɔɲɔne] *vi F* to grumble, to grouse.
rognures [rɔɲyr] *nfpl* (*déchets*) clippings (*of claws, fingernails*); trimmings, parings (*of leather, metal etc*); scraps (*of meat*).
rogomme [rɔgɔm] *nm F* **voix de r.,** (drunkard's) husky voice.
rogue [rɔg] *adj* arrogant, haughty.
roi [rwa] **1** *nm* **(a)** (*souverain*) king; **le r. Louis XIII,** (King) Louis XIII; *Bible* **les rois (mages),** the three wise men, the three kings, the Magi; **le R. Soleil,** the Sun King; **jour** *ou* **fête des Rois,** Twelfth Night; *Rel* Epiphany; **tirer les rois,** to eat Twelfth Night cake; **plat de r.,** dish fit for a king; **heureux comme un r.,** as happy as a sandboy; **(b) le r. des animaux,** (*lion*) the king of beasts; **r. des resquilleurs,** champion gatecrasher; **le r. du plastique/des pizzas,** the plastics/pizza king; **(c)** *Cartes Échecs* king. **2** *adj inv* **bleu r.,** royal blue.
roide [rwad] **, roideur** [rwadœr] **, roidir** [rwadir] *Arch* = **RAIDE, RAIDEUR, RAIDIR.**
roitelet [rwatlɛ] *nm* **(a)** *Péj* petty king; **(b)** (*oiseau*) wren; **r. huppé,** goldcrest.
Roland [rɔlɑ̃] *nm* Roland.
rôle [rol] *nm* **(a)** (*liste*) list, register; *Jur* roll (*of court*); **à tour de r.,** in turn, by turns, in rotation; **faire qch à tour de r.,** to take turns (in) doing sth, to do sth in turns; **les rôles de l'armée active,** the active list; *Nau* **r. de l'équipage,** list of the crew, muster roll; *Admin* **r. des impôts** *ou* **d'impôt,** assessment book;
(b) *Th* part, role; *Fig* role; **r. titre,** title role; **premier r.,** lead, leading man *or* lady; **second r.,** supporting part *or* role; **répéter son r.,** to learn one's part *or* role; **Mme Oldani dans le r. de la Tosca,** Mme Oldani as Tosca; **assigner un r. à qn,** to cast s.o. in a part; **distribution des rôles,** (*action*) casting; (*liste*) cast (list); **jouer le r. de Macbeth,** to play (the part of) Macbeth; *F* **jouer un r. secondaire,** to play second fiddle; **tu as le beau r.,** it's easy *or* all right for you; **les femmes n'ont pas toujours un r. facile,** a woman's role is not always easy; **le r. du médécin,** the doctor's role *or* function *or* job; **le r. du sport dans l'éducation,** the role *or* function of sport in education; **elle a joué un grand r. dans la politique internationale,** she played an important role in international politics; **un r. de premier plan,** a leading role; **jeu de rôles,** role playing; **ce n'est pas son r. de te conseiller,** it's not his job to advise you; **elle sort de son r.,** it's out of character for her.
rollier [rɔlje] *nm* (*oiseau*) roller.
rollmops [rɔlmɔps] *nm inv Culin* rollmop.
roll on-roll off [rɔlɔnrɔlɔf] *adj & nm inv* **(navire) r. on-r. off,** roll-on/roll-off ship.
romain, -aine [rɔmɛ̃, -ɛn] **1** *adj* Roman; **l'Empire r.,** the Roman Empire; **l'Église romaine,** the Church of Rome; **chiffres romains,** Roman numerals; *Typ* **caractère r.,** roman type. **2** *n* **R.,** Roman. **3** *nm Typ* roman.
romaine¹ [rɔmɛn] *adj & nf* **(balance) r.,** steelyard.
romaine² *nf* (*laitue*) cos (lettuce), *Am* romaine; *Fig F* **être bon comme la r.,** (*bienveillant*) to be too kind for words; (*destiné à être victime*) to be sure to get it in the neck.
romaïque [rɔmaik] *adj & nm Ling* Romaic, modern Greek.
roman¹ [rɔmɑ̃] *nm* **(a)** (*en prose*) novel; **r. policier,** detective novel; **r. noir,** thriller; **r. cycle, r.-fleuve,** saga (novel); **r.-photo,** story told in photographs; **r.-feuilleton,** serial (story); **votre histoire, c'est du r.,** your story is just a fairy tale; *Fig* **l'histoire de notre rencontre est tout un r.,** the story of our meeting is quite a romance; **le nouveau r.,** the antinovel, the nouveau roman; **(b)** *Hist* (*poème*) romance; **le R. de la Rose,** the Romance of the Rose.
roman² [rɔmɑ̃] **1** *adj* **(a)** *Ling* Romance, Romanic; **(b)** *Archit* Romanesque; (*en Angleterre*) Norman. **2** *nm* **(a)** *Ling* Romance, Romantic; **(b)** *Archit* Romanesque style; (*en Angleterre*) Norman style.
romance [rɔmɑ̃s] *nf* (*chanson*) (sentimental) song, drawing-room ballad.
romancer [rɔmɑ̃se] *vt* to fictionalize.
romanche [rɔmɑ̃ʃ] *adj & nm Ling* Romans(c)h.
romancier, -ière [rɔmɑ̃sje, -jɛr] *n* novelist.
romand [rɔmɑ̃] **1** *adj* **la Suisse romande,** French (-speaking) Switzerland. **2** *nmpl* **les Romands,** the French (-speaking) Swiss.
romanesque [rɔmanɛsk] *adj* **(a)** romantic (*person, adventure*); **(b)** *Littér* novelistic (*technique etc*).
romanichel, -elle [rɔmaniʃɛl] *n Péj* **(a)** (*tsigane*) gipsy, *pl* gipsies, romany; **(b)** (*vagabond*) tramp, vagrant.
romaniser [rɔmanize] *vt* to Romanize.
romaniste [rɔmanist] *nm* **(a)** *Rel Jur* Romanist; **(b)** *Ling* Romanist, student of the Romance languages.
romano [rɔmano] *n F Péj* (*tsigane*) gippo.
romantique [rɔmɑ̃tik] *Beaux-Arts Littér* **1** *adj* Romantic. **2** *n* Romantic(ist).
romantisme [rɔmɑ̃tism] *nm Beaux-Arts Littér etc* Romanticism.
romarin [rɔmarɛ̃] *nm Bot Culin* rosemary.
rombière [rɔ̃bjɛr] *nf Arg* **(vieille) r.,** old biddy.
Rome [rɔm] *nm ou f* Rome; *Prov* **tous les chemins mènent à R.,** all roads lead to Rome.
Roméo [rɔmeo] *nm* Romeo; **R. et Juliette,** Romeo and Juliet.
rompre [rɔ̃pr] *v* (*pr ind* **je romps, il rompt, ils rompent**) **1** *vt* **(a)** (*casser*) to break; (*en deux parties*) to break in two; to snap (*stick, string*); (*en plusieurs parties*) to break (up); (*d'un ruisseau etc*) **r. ses digues,** to burst its banks; *Th* **applaudir à tout r.,** to bring down the house; *Mil* **r. les rangs,** to disperse, to dismiss; **r. le silence,** to break the silence; **r. une promesse,** to break a promise; **r. un choc,** to deaden a shock;
(b) (*interrompre*) to break off (*conversation engagement, diplomatic relations*); to call off (*deal*); to break (*a spell*); **r. un tête-à-tête,** to interrupt *or* break in on a private conversation; *Él* **r. un circuit,** to break a circuit; **r. l'équilibre,** to upset the balance; **r. les chiens,** to call off the hounds; *Fig* to change the subject;
(c) r. un cheval, to break in a horse; **r. qn à la discipline/à la fatigue,** to break s.o. in to discipline/inure s.o. to fatigue.
2 *vi* **(a)** (*casser*) to break; (*of stick, string*) to break, to snap; *Fig* **r. avec qn,** to break with s.o.; **r. avec une habitude,** to break (oneself of) a habit; **r. avec sa vie passée,** to break with one's past life;
(b) (*of troops*) **r. devant l'ennemi,** to break before the enemy;
(c) *Boxe Escrime* to break.
3 se rompre *vpr* **(a)** (*se casser*) to break; (*of stick, string*) to break, to snap; (*of ice*) to break (up); **son cœur battait à se r.,** his heart was throbbing violently *or* fit to burst; **se r. le cou,** to break one's neck; **se r. une artère,** to burst an artery;
(b) *Fig* **se r. à qch,** to break oneself in *or* accustom oneself to sth; **se r. à la fatigue,** to inure oneself to fatigue.
rompu [rɔ̃py] *adj* **(a)** broken; **chemin r.,** road full of potholes; **être r. de fatigue,** to be worn out *or* tired out; **r. de travail,** worn out *or* tired out by work; **couleur rompue,** colour with a shot effect; **(b) r. à,** experienced in; **être r. aux affaires,** to be experienced in business.
romsteck [rɔmstɛk] *nm* rump steak.
ronce [rɔ̃s] *nf* **(a)** (*arbuste*) bramble(s), blackberry bush; (*branche*) bramble (branch); **(b) ronce(s) artificielle(s),** barbed wire; **(c)** curl (*in grain of wood*); **r. de noyer,** bur(r) walnut.
ronceraie [rɔ̃srɛ] *nf* bramble patch.
ronchon [rɔ̃ʃɔ̃] *F* **1** *adj* grouchy, grumpy. **2** *n* grumbler, grouser, grouch.
ronchonnement [rɔ̃ʃɔnmɑ̃] *nm F* grumbling, grousing, grouching.
ronchonner [rɔ̃ʃɔne] *vi F* to grumble, to grouse, to grouch.
ronchonneur, -euse [rɔ̃ʃɔnœr, -øz] *adj & n F* = **RONCHON.**
roncier [rɔ̃sje] *nm*, **roncière** [rɔ̃sjɛr] *nf* (thick) bramble bush.
rond, ronde [rɔ̃, rɔ̃d] **1** *adj* **(a)** round (*ball, table etc*);

rounded (*arm*); plump (*person, cheeks, figure*); **écriture ronde,** round hand(writing); **avoir le dos r.,** to be round-shouldered; **tuiles rondes,** curved *or* rounded tiles; **le ballon r.,** (association) football, *Br* soccer;

(b) voix ronde, full voice; **vent r.,** brisk wind; **en chiffres ronds,** in round figures; **deux cents francs tout ronds,** a round two hundred francs, exactly two hundred francs; **compte r.,** round sum; *F* **homme tout r.,** straightforward man; **être r. en affaires,** to be straightforward where business is concerned;

(c) *Arg* (*ivre*) tipsy.

2 *adv* **tourner r.,** (*of wheel*) to run true; (*of engine, factory, business etc*) to run smoothly; *F* **cela ne tourne pas r.,** there's something the matter; (*ça va mal*) it's not going well; *F* **elle ne tourne pas r.,** there's something up *or* the matter with her.

3 *nm* **(a)** (*figure*) circle; **le chat se met en r.,** the cat curls up *or* coils itself up; **danser/s'asseoir en r.,** to dance/sit in a circle *or* a ring; **tourner en r.,** to go round in a circle *or* ring; *Fig* to go round in circles; **r. de jambe,** sweep of the leg; *F* **faire des ronds de jambe,** to bow and scrape; **r. de serviette,** napkin ring; *F* **en baver des ronds de chapeau,** to be absolutely flabbergasted;

(b) (*tranche*) slice (*of sausage*); pat (*of butter*); **r. de cuir,** (*coussin*) (round leather) chair cushion; *Arg* **il n'a pas un r.,** he hasn't a penny.

4 *nf* **ronde (a)** (*danse*) round (dance); (*chanson*) round, roundelay;

(b) *Mil etc* (*visite de surveillance*) round(s); (*de policier*) beat; **faire la ronde,** to go the rounds; (*de policier*) to be on the beat; *Arch* **la ronde de nuit,** (*hommes, veille*) the night watch; **chemin de ronde,** parapet walk, rampart walk;

(c) (*écriture*) round hand(writing);

(d) *Mus* (*note*) *Br* semibreve, *Am* whole note;

(e) à la ronde, around; **à dix lieues à la ronde,** for thirty miles (a)round; **(faire) passer le vin à la ronde,** to pass the wine round, to hand round the wine; **boire à la ronde,** to drink in turn.

rond-de-cuir [rɔ̃dkɥir] *nm F Péj* penpusher, clerk; (*pl ronds-de-cuir*).

rondeau, -eaux [rɔ̃do] *nm* **(a)** *Littér* rondeau; **(b)** *Mus* rondo.

ronde(-)bosse [rɔ̃dbɔs] *nf Beaux-Arts* sculpture in the round; **en r.(-)b.,** in the round; (*pl rondes-bosses*).

rondelet, -ette [rɔ̃dlɛ, -ɛt] *adj* plump, chubby, podgy (*person*); podgy (*fingers*); **somme rondelette,** good (round) sum, tidy sum.

rondelle [rɔ̃dɛl] *nf* **(a)** disc (*of cardboard etc*); slice (*of lemon, sausage, gherkin etc*); *Can* **r. (de hockey),** puck; **(b)** ring (*of umbrella etc*); **(c)** (*de vis, d'ecrou etc*) washer; **r. de robinet,** tap washer.

rondement [rɔdmɑ̃] *adv* **(a)** (*promptement*) briskly, promptly, smartly; **mener r. les choses,** to make short work of things, to deal with things briskly *or* promptly; **(b)** (*carrément*) bluntly, frankly; **il nous a dit r. qu'il n'était pas d'accord,** he told us straight *or* bluntly *or* frankly that he didn't agree.

rondeur [rɔ̃dœr] *nf* **(a)** roundness; (*de personne, joues etc*) plumpness; **rondeurs,** rounded forms *or* lines; (*de femme*) curves; **(b)** (*franchise*) straightforwardness, plain dealing; **avec r.,** in a straightforward manner.

rondin [rɔ̃dɛ̃] *nm* log; **cabane en rondins,** log cabin; **chemin de rondins,** corduroy road.

rondo [rɔ̃do] *nm Mus* rondo.

rondouillard [rɔ̃dujar] *adj F* plump, chubby, podgy (*person*).

rond-point [rɔ̃pwɛ̃] *nm* circus (*where several roads meet*); (*à sens giratoire*) roundabout, *Am* traffic circle; (*pl ronds-points*).

ronéo ® [rɔneo] *nf* Roneo ®.

ronéotyper [rɔneɔtipe] *vt* to Roneo ®.

ronflant [rɔ̃flɑ̃] *adj* **(a)** *Méd* **râle r.,** rhonchus; **(b)** roaring (*wind, fire*); booming (*organ*); humming (*top*); whirring, purring (*engine*); **(c)** *Fig Péj* high-sounding, sonorous (*title*); bombastic (*speech, style*); high-flown (*promise*).

ronflement [rɔ̃fləmɑ̃] *nm* **(a)** (*de dormeur*) snoring; **(b)** *Fig* (*de vent, feu*) roaring; (*d'orgue*) booming; (*de toupie*) humming; (*de moteur*) whirring, purring.

ronfler [rɔ̃fle] *vi* **(a)** (*de dormeur*) to snore; **(b)** *Fig* (*de vent, feu*) to roar; (*d'orgue*) to boom; (*de toupie*) to hum; (*de moteur*) to whirr, to purr.

ronflette [rɔ̃flɛt] *nf F* snooze.

ronfleur, -euse [rɔ̃flœr, -øz] **1** *n* (*personne*) snorer. **2** *nm Tél* buzzer.

rongeant [rɔ̃ʒɑ̃] *adj* **(a)** corroding (*acid*); rodent (*ulcer*); **(b)** *Fig* gnawing (*anxiety*).

ronger [rɔ̃ʒe] *v* **(je rongeai(s); n. rongeons) 1** *vt* **(a)** (*of mouse etc*) to gnaw (at), to nibble (at); **r. un os,** (*of dog*) to gnaw a bone; (*of person*) to pick a bone, to gnaw (at) *or* nibble (at) a bone; **rongé par les vers,** worm-eaten; **(b)** (*of acid, rust*) to corrode, to eat away (*metal etc*); (*of the sea*) to erode (*cliffs*); **être rongé de chagrin,** to be consumed *or* tormented with grief. **2 se ronger** *vpr* **(a)** to worry, to fret; **se r. de chagrin, se r. le cœur** *ou* **les sangs,** to eat one's heart out; **(b) se r. les ongles,** to bite one's nails.

rongeur, -euse [rɔ̃ʒœr, -øz] **1** *adj* rodent(-like), gnawing (*animal*); *Fig* gnawing (*anxiety*). **2** *nm* rodent.

ronron [rɔ̃rɔ̃] *nm* (*de chat*) purr(ing); (*de moteur*) purr(ing), whirr(ing); (*d'avion*) drone, droning; (*de machine*) whirr(ing); **faire r.,** (*of cat*) to purr; *Fig* **le r. de la vie quotidienne,** the humdrum nature of everyday life.

ronronnement [rɔ̃rɔnmɑ̃] *nm* (*de chat*) purring; (*de moteur*) purr(ing), whirr(ing); (*d'avion*) drone, droning; (*de machine*) whirr(ing).

ronronner [rɔ̃rɔne] *vi* (*de chat*) to purr; (*de moteur*) to purr, to whirr; (*d'avion*) to drone; (*de machine*) to whirr.

roque [rɔk] *nm Échecs* castling; **petit/grand r.,** castling on the king's/queen's side.

roquefort [rɔkfɔr] *nm* (*fromage*) Roquefort.

roquer [rɔke] *vi* **(a)** *Échecs* to castle; **(b)** (*au croquet*) to croquet the ball.

roquet [rɔkɛ] *nm Péj* (*chien*) cur; (*personne*) nasty little squirt.

roquette¹ [rɔkɛt] *nf Bot* rocket; **r. des jardins,** winter-cress.

roquette² *nf Mil* (*projectile*) rocket.

rorqual [rɔrkwal] *nm* rorqual, finback (whale).

rosace [rozas] *nf Archit* **(a)** rose (window); **(b) r. de plafond,** ceiling rose.

rosacé [rozase] *Bot* **1** *adj* rosaceous, rose-like. **2** *nfpl* **rosacées,** Rosaceae, rosaceous plants.

rosaire [rozɛr] *nm Rel* rosary; **dire** *ou* **réciter son r.,** to tell one's beads, to say the rosary.

rosâtre [rozɑtr] *adj* pinkish.

rosbif [rɔzbif] *nm* **(a)** *Culin* (*rôti*) roast beef; (*à rôtir*) roast beef; **(b)** *Arg* (*Britannique*) (*terme injurieux*) Brit.

rose [roz] **1** *nf* **(a)** rose; **r. incarnate,** damask rose; **r. mousseuse,** moss rose; **r.-thé,** tea rose; **r. sauvage,** wild rose, dog rose; **eau de r.,** rosewater; *F* **roman à l'eau de r.,** sugary *or* sentimental novel; **essence de roses,** attar *or* otto of roses; **lèvres de r.,** rosy lips; *Prov* **(il n'est) pas de r. sans épines,** no rose without a thorn; *F* **découvrir le pot aux roses** [pɔtoroz] , to find out the secret; *F* **envoyer qn sur les roses,** to send s.o. packing;

(b) bois de r., rosewood;

(c) *Archit* rose (window);

(d) *Nau* **r. des vents,** compass card; **dire la r.,** to box the compass; **r. mobile,** floating dial;

(e) (*diamant*) rose (diamond), rose-cut diamond.

2 *adj* pink (*dress etc*); rosy (*complexion*); **des rubans rose pivoine,** peony-red ribbons; **tout n'est pas r. dans ce monde,** life is not a bed of roses; **ce n'est pas bien r., cette histoire-là,** it's a pretty grim story.

3 *nm* pink; **voir la vie** *ou* **tout en r.,** to see everything through rose-coloured glasses *or* spectacles.

rosé [roze] **1** *adj* pinkish; **vin r.,** rosé. **2** *nm* (*vin*) rosé.

roseau, -eaux [rozo] *nm* reed; **r. aromatique,** sweet flag, sweet rush.

rose-croix [rozkrwa] *nm inv* Rosicrucian.

rosée [roze] *nf* dew; **goutte de r.,** dewdrop; **couvert** *ou* **humecté de r.,** dewy (*grass etc*); *Phys* **point de r.,** dew point.

roselet [rozlɛ] *nm* (*fourrure*) ermine.

roselier, -ière [rozəlje, -jɛr] **1** *adj* reed-bearing (*marsh*). **2** *nf* **roselière,** reed bed.

roséole [rozeɔl] *nf Méd* roseola.

roser [roze] *vt Litt* to make (*sth*) pink.

roseraie [rozrɛ] *nf* rosery, rose garden.

rosette [rozɛt] *nf* **(a)** bow (*of ribbon*); **(b)** (*insigne*) rosette (*esp of the Legion of Honour*); **recevoir la r.,** to be awarded the Legion of Honour; **(c) r. de Lyon,** = sort of slicing sausage.

Rosette [rozɛt] *n* **la pierre de R.,** the Rosetta stone.

rosier [rozje] *nm* rose tree, rose bush; **r. sur tige,** standard rose; **r. sauvage,** briar.

rosière [rozjɛr] *nf Hist* = maiden awarded a wreath of roses by her village for her virtuous conduct; *Fig Iron* **ce n'est pas une r.,** she's no angel.

rosiériste [rozjerist] *n* rose grower.

rosir [rozir] **1** *vt* to turn pink. **2** *vi* **(a)** to become *or* turn

pink; **(b)** (*d'émotion*) to blush.
rosse [rɔs] **1** *nf* **(a)** *Péj Vieilli* (*cheval*) nag; **(b)** *F Péj* (*homme*) beast, swine; (*femme*) bitch, beast. **2** *adj F Péj* nasty, horrid (*person, conduct*); nasty, dirty (*trick*); nasty, spiteful (*remark*).
rossée [rɔse] *nf F* beating, thrashing, hiding.
rosser [rɔse] *vt F* to beat, to thrash (*s.o.*), to give (*s.o.*) a (good) hiding.
rosserie [rɔsri] *nf F* **(a)** (*caractère*) nastiness; **(b)** (*mauvaise action*) nasty *or* dirty trick; **faire une r. à qn,** to play a nasty *or* dirty trick on s.o.; **(c)** (*parole*) nasty *or* spiteful remark.
rossignol [rɔsiɲɔl] *nm* **(a)** (*oiseau*) nightingale; **(b)** (*clef*) skeleton key; **(c)** *F* (*objet*) old unsaleable article, white elephant; **vieux rossignols,** old stock.
rossinante [rɔsinɑ̃t] *nf Péj Vieilli* (*cheval*) old worn-out hack.
rostre [rɔstr] *nm Antiq* (*éperon de navire*) rostrum.
rot [ro] *nm F* belch, burp; (*de bébé*) burp; **faire un r.,** to belch, to burp; **faire faire son r. à un bébé,** to burp a baby.
rôt [ro] *nm Arch* roast (meat).
rotarien [rɔtarjɛ̃] *nm* Rotarian.
rotatif, -ive [rɔtatif, -iv] **1** *adj* rotary (*pump, engine etc*). **2** *nf* **rotative,** rotary (printing) press.
rotation [rɔtɑsjɔ̃] *nf* **(a)** *Phys Tech* rotation; spin (*of projectile*); **mouvement de r.,** rotational *or* rotating motion; **corps en r.,** rotating body; **pièce à r.,** revolving part; **axe de r.,** axis of rotation; *Math* **faire faire une r. de 90° à une droite,** to rotate a line through an angle of 90°; **(b) r. des cultures,** crop rotation, rotation of crops; **(c)** turnround (*of ship, buses etc*); turnover (*of stocks, capital, staff*).
rotatoire [rɔtatwar] *adj* **(a)** rotatory (*movement*); rotational (*force*); **(b)** rotary (*polarization*).
roter [rɔte] *vi F* to belch, to burp.
rôti [roti] **1** *nm* roast (meat), joint; (*à rôtir*) (roasting) joint; **r. de porc,** (joint of) roast pork; *F* **ne vous endormez pas sur le r.,** don't dawdle. **2** *adj* roast; **poulet r.,** roast chicken; *Fig F* **ça ne va pas te tomber tout r. dans la bouche,** it's not going to just fall into your lap.
rôtie [roti] *nf* (slice of) toast.
rotin¹ [rɔtɛ̃] *nm* **(a)** *Bot* rattan; **sièges en r.,** cane *or* rattan chairs; **(b)** (*canne*) rattan walking stick.
rotin² *nm F* (*sou*) **pas un r.!,** not a penny!
rôtir [rotir] **1** *vt* **(a)** to roast (*meat, chestnut*); to toast (*bread*); **(b)** *F* (*of the sun*) to scorch, to dry up (*grass etc*). **2 se rôtir** *vpr* **se r. au soleil,** to roast in the sun. **3** *vi Culin* to roast; *F* **on rôtit ici,** it's scorching (hot) here.
rôtisserie [rotisri] *nf* **(a)** (*restaurant*) grill(room), steakhouse; **(b)** (*boutique*) = shop selling roast meat.
rôtisseur, -euse [rotisœr,-øz] *n* **(a)** (*restaurateur*) grill-room proprietor; **(b)** (*commerçant*) = seller of roast meat.
rôtissoire [rotiswar] *nf Culin* (rotating) spit, rotisserie.
rotogravure [rɔtɔgravyr] *nf Typ* rotogravure.
rotonde [rɔtɔ̃d] *nf* **(a)** *Archit* rotunda; **(b)** *Rail* (circular) engine shed, roundhouse.
rotondité [rɔtɔ̃dite] *nf* **(a)** (*de la Terre etc*) rotundity, roundness; **(b)** (*embonpoint*) plumpness; **rotondités,** (*de femme*) full curves.
rotor [rɔtɔr] *nm El* rotor (*of dynamo, turbine*); *Av* rotor (*of helicopter*).
rotule [rɔtyl] *nf* **(a)** *Anat* kneecap, *Spéc* patella; *F* **être sur les rotules,** to be dead beat *or* on one's last legs; **(b)** *Tech* knee joint, ball(-and-socket) joint; *Aut* **r. de direction,** steering knuckle.
rotulien, -ienne [rɔtyljɛ̃, -jɛn] *adj Anat* patellar.
roture [rɔtyr] *nf Hist* **(a) terre en r.,** land held by a commoner; **(b) la r.,** (*condition*) the common rank; (*gens*) the commonalty, the commons.
roturier, -ière [rɔtyrje, -jɛr] *Hist* **1** *adj* common, of the common people. **2** *n* commoner.
rouage [rwaʒ] *nm* **(a)** (*ensemble des roues*) wheels, wheelwork, gear work; **rouage(s) d'une montre,** works *or* train of wheels of a watch; **r. d'horloge,** clockwork; *Fig* **les rouages de l'administration,** the wheels of government; **organisation aux rouages bien huilés,** smooth-running organization; **(b)** (*roue*) (toothed) wheel, cog wheel.
rouan , -anne [rwɑ̃, -an] **1** *adj* roan (*horse*). **2** *nm* roan.
roublard, -arde [rublar, -ard] *F* **1** *adj* wily, crafty, cunning (*person*). **2** *n* wily *or* crafty *or* cunning devil; **un fin r.,** an old fox.
roublardise [rublardiz] *nf F* **(a)** (*caractère*) cunning, wiliness, craftiness; **(b)** (*acte*) crafty *or* cunning trick.
rouble [rubl] *nm* (*monnaie russe*) rouble.
roucoulement [rukulmɑ̃] *nm* cooing (*of pigeon etc*); *Fig* billing and cooing (*of lovers*).
roucouler [rukule] **1** *vi* (*of pigeon etc*) to coo; *Fig* (*of lovers*) to bill and coo. **2** *vt* to coo (*endearments*); to warble (*song*).
roudoudou [rududu] *nm F* = coloured toffee (*to be licked out of a mould*).
roue [ru] *nf* wheel; **véhicule à quatre roues,** four-wheeled vehicle; **interdit aux deux roues,** (*sur panneau*) no two wheeled vehicles; **r. de secours,** spare wheel; **rouler en r. libre,** to coast; *Fig* to do as one likes; *F* **la cinquième r. du carosse,** an entirely useless person *or* thing, *Am* fifth wheel; *Fig* **pousser à la r.,** to put one's shoulder to the wheel, to lend a helping hand; **sans roues,** wheelless, without wheels; *Nau* **la r. du gouvernail,** the wheel; **faire la r.,** (*of peacock*) to spread its tail; *Péj* (*parader*) to strut, to swagger; (*acrobatie*) to turn cartwheels *or* a cartwheel; **r. à corde,** cable pulley; **r. à aile, r. volante,** flywheel; **r. dentée, r. d'engrenage,** toothed wheel, cogwheel, gear (wheel); **r. de commande, r. de transmission, r. motrice,** driving wheel; **r. de turbine,** turbine wheel, impeller; **r. à eau, r. hydraulique,** water wheel, hydraulic wheel; **r. en dessous,** undershot (water)wheel; **r. en dessus,** overshot (water)wheel; **r. de moulin,** mill wheel; *Nau* **bateau à roues,** paddle boat; **la r. de la fortune,** the wheel of fortune; **r. à feu,** Catherine wheel; *Arch* **condamner un criminel à la r.,** to condemn a criminal to the wheel.
roué, -ée [rwe] **1** *adj* cunning, sly (*person*). **2** *n* (*roublard*) cunning *or* sly devil. **3** *nm Hist* (*débauché*) rake, roué.
rouelle [rwɛl] *nf* round slice (*of lemon, carrot etc*); **r. de veau,** fillet of veal.
rouennais, -aise [rwanɛ, -ɛz] **1** *adj* of *or* from Rouen. **2** *n* **R.,** native *or* inhabitant of Rouen.
rouer [rwe] *vt* **(a)** *F* **r. qn de coups,** to beat s.o. black and blue; **(b)** *Arch* (*supplicier*) to break (*s.o.*) on the wheel.
rouerie [ruri] *nf* **(a)** (*acte*) cunning *or* sly trick; **(b)** (*caractère*) cunning, slyness.
rouet [rwɛ] *nm* **(a)** (*de fileuse*) spinning wheel; **(b)** *Tech* sheave (*of pulley*); scutcheon (*of lock*).
rouf [ruf] *nm Nau* deck house.
rouflaquettes [ruflakɛt] *nfpl F* (*favoris*) *Br* sideboards, *Am* sideburns.
rouge [ruʒ] **1** *adj* **(a)** red; *Pol* red; **fer r.,** red-hot iron; **fruits rouges,** berries and currants; **viande r.,** red meat; **être r. de honte,** to be red *or* to blush with shame; **être r. comme une tomate,** (*of person*) to be as red as a beetroot; **avoir les yeux rouges,** to have red eyes, to be red-eyed; **être r. comme une écrevisse,** (*brûlé par le soleil*) to be as red as a lobster; *Rel* **le chapeau r.,** the cardinal's (red) hat; *Pol* **le drapeau r.,** the red flag; **porto r.,** ruby port;
(b) (*inv in compounds*) **des rubans rouge cerise,** cherry-red ribbons; **r. sang,** blood-red; **r. drapeau,** pillar-box red.
2 *adv* **se fâcher tout r.,** to lose one's temper completely; **voir r.,** to see red.
3 *nm* **(a)** (*couleur*) red; **peindre qch en r.,** to paint sth red; **porter le fer au r.,** to make the iron red-hot; **le r. lui monte aux joues,** he is going red in the face; *Prov* **r. le soir, espoir,** red sky at night (is the) shepherd's delight;
(b) (*cosmétique*) rouge; **r. à lèvres, bâton de r.,** lipstick; **r. à joues,** blusher;
(c) r. d'Angleterre *ou* **de Prusse,** (jewellers') rouge;
(d) (*vin*) red wine; **gros r.,** coarse red wine;
(e) *Fig* **mon compte/le commerce extérieur est dans le r.,** my account/foreign trade is in the red.
4 *n* (*communiste*) Red.
rougeâtre [ruʒɑtr] *adj* reddish.
rougeaud, -eaude [ruʒo] *adj & n* red-faced (person).
rouge-gorge [ruʒgɔrʒ] *nm* robin (redbreast); (*pl rouges-gorges*).
rougeoiement [ruʒwamɑ̃] *nm* red glow.
rougeole [ruʒɔl] *nf Méd* measles; **avoir la r.,** to have (the) measles.
rougeoleux, -euse [ruʒɔlø, -øz] *Méd* **1** *adj* suffering from (the) measles. **2** *n* person with measles.
rougeoyant [ruʒwajɑ̃] *adj* glowing (red).
rougeoyer [ruʒwaje] *vi* (**il rougeoie; il rougeoiera**) **(a)** (*briller*) to glow red; **(b)** (*devenir rouge*) to turn red, to redden.
rouge-queue [ruʒkø] *nm* (*oiseau*) redstart; (*pl rouges-queues*).
rouget [ruʒɛ] *nm* (*poisson*) red mullet; **r. grondin,** gurnard.
rougeur [ruʒœr] *nf* **(a)** (*causée par la chaleur, l'émotion*) flush(ing); (*causée par la honte, la gêne*) blush(ing); **(b)** *Méd* (*tache*) red spot *or* blotch; **(c)** (*couleur*) redness.

rougir [ruʒir] **1** *vt* **(a)** to redden, to turn (*sky, leaves etc*) red; **eau rougie,** water with a little red wine; *Fig* **r. ses mains,** (*commettre un crime*) to get blood on one's hands; **(b) fer rougi au feu,** iron heated red-hot; **r. le fer au blanc,** to make iron white-hot; **(c)** to flush (*the face*). **2** *vi* **(a)** (*of sky, leaves etc*) to redden, to turn red; **faire r. un métal,** to heat a metal red-hot; **(b)** (*of person*) to turn *or* go red, to flush; (*de honte, gêne*) to blush, to redden, to turn *or* go red; **r. jusqu'aux oreilles,** to blush to the roots of one's hair; **r. d'un faux pas,** to be ashamed of an indiscretion; **r. de qn,** to blush for s.o.; **r. de colère,** to flush with anger.

rougissant [ruʒisɑ̃] *adj* **(a)** reddening (*sky etc*); **(b)** blushing (*person, face*).

rougissement [ruʒismɑ̃] *nm* **(a)** reddening (*of sky*); **(b)** (*sous l'émotion*) flush(ing); (*sous la honte, la gêne*) blush(ing).

rouille [ruj] **1** *nf* **(a)** rust; **tache de r.,** iron stain, iron mould (*on cloth*); **(b)** *Agr* rust, mildew, blight. **2** *adj inv* rust(-coloured).

rouillé [ruje] *adj* **(a)** rusty, rusted (*metal etc*); **(b)** (*coloré*) rust-coloured; **(c)** *Fig* rusty, out of practice; **(d)** *Agr* mildewed (*plant*).

rouiller [ruje] **1** *vt* to rust, to make (*iron etc*) rusty. **2** *vi* (*of metal, lock etc*) to rust (up), to get rusty. **2 se rouiller** *vpr* **(a)** (*of metal, lock etc*) to rust (up), to get rusty; **(b)** *Fig* **je me rouille,** I am getting rusty *or* out of practice; **(c)** *Agr* (*of plant*) to become mildewed.

rouillure [rujyr] *nf* **(a)** rustiness (*of metal, lock etc*); **(b)** *Agr* rust, blight (*of plants*).

rouir [rwir] **1** *vt* to steep, to ret (*flax etc*). **2** *vi* to steep, to ret.

rouissage [rwisaʒ] *nm* steeping, retting (*of flax etc*).

roulade [rulad] *nf* **(a)** roll (*in the dust, downhill etc*); **(b)** *Mus* roulade; **(c)** *Culin* roulade.

roulage [rulaʒ] *nm* **(a)** rolling (*of ploughed land, of metal etc*); **(b)** (*transport de marchandises*) haulage; **entrepreneur de r.,** carrier, *Br* haulier, *Am* hauler; **cheval de r.,** cart horse, draught horse.

roulant, -ante [rulɑ̃, -ɑ̃t] **1** *adj* **(a)** sliding (*door*); travelling (*crane*); **escalier r.,** escalator; **allure roulante,** rolling gait; **voiture bien roulante,** smooth-running car; *Rail* **matériel r.,** rolling stock; **personnel r.,** train *or* lorry *or* bus *etc* crews; **(b) chemin bien r.,** good road; **(c)** *Com* **affaire roulante,** going concern; **fonds r.,** working capital; **(d)** *F* (*drôle*) hilarious (*person, joke, story etc*). **2** *nf Mil F* **roulante,** field kitchen.

roulé [rule] **1** *adj* rolled; **col r.,** roll collar, polo neck, turtle neck; **elle est bien roulée,** she has a great figure. **2** *nm* **(a)** (*viande*) rolled joint; **(b) r. à la confiture,** Swiss roll.

rouleau, -eaux [rulo] *nm* **(a)** *Tech* roller; *Typ* (ink) roller; *Phot* roller (squeegee); **roulements à rouleaux,** roller bearings; **r. compresseur,** road roller; **r. à vapeur,** steamroller; **r. pour gazon,** garden roller; **passer le gazon au r.,** to roll the lawn; **r. à pâtisserie,** rolling pin; **r. porte-serviettes,** towel-roller; *Typ* **r. porte-papier,** impression roller; **r. à mise en plis,** (hair) roller; **(store sur) r.,** roller blind; **r. à peinture,** paint roller;

(b) (*bande*) roll (*of paper etc*); roll, spool (*of film*); coil (*of rope*); twist (*of tobacco*); scroll (*of parchment*); **r. de réglisse,** liquorice roll; *Fig* **être au bout de son** *ou* **du r.,** (*sans argent*) to be short (of money); (*exaspéré*) to be at the end of one's tether; (*près de la mort*) to be on one's last legs;

(c) (*lame*) billow, roller;

(d) *Sp* (*saut en hauteur*) roll; **r. ventral,** straddle;

(e) *Culin* **r. de printemps,** spring roll.

roulé-boulé [rulebule] *nm* roll (*executed tucked up in a ball*); (*pl roulés-boulés*).

roulée [rule] *nf Arg* thrashing, beating.

roulement [rulmɑ̃] *nm* **(a)** rolling (*of ball etc*); **r. d'yeux,** rolling of the eyes; **(b)** (*circulation*) movement (*of vehicle*); *Av* taxiing; **bande de r.,** tread (*of tyre*); **train de r.,** bogie; **galet de r.,** bogie wheel; **(c)** (*bruit*) rumbling (*of wagon, thunder*); rattle (*of vehicle on stones*); rolling (*of drum*); **(d)** *Tech* (*pièce*) bearing; **r. à billes,** ball bearing; **r. à galets** *ou* **à rouleaux,** roller bearing; **(e)** *Com* **r. de fonds,** circulation of capital; **(f)** (*rotation*) rotation, alternation, taking turns (*in duties etc*); **par r.,** in rotation.

rouler [rule] **1** *vt* **(a)** to roll (*stone, cask, furniture etc*) (along); to throw, to roll (*dice*); *Min* to haul (*coal*); **r. le bébé dans sa poussette,** to push the baby (along) in its pushchair; **r. les yeux,** to roll one's eyes; **r. les hanches,** to sway *or* swing one's hips; **r. un projet dans sa tête,** to turn over a plan in one's mind; **r. de mauvaises pensées,** to think evil thoughts;

(b) *F* **r. qn,** (*duper*) to take s.o. in; **il m'a roulé de deux mille francs,** he has done me out of two thousand francs;

(c) to roll up (*map, one's sleeves, umbrella etc*); to roll (*meat, fish, cigarette*); to roll out (*pastry*);

(d) r. un champ/un tennis, to roll a field/a tennis court;

(e) r. les r, to roll one's r's;

(f) r. qn dans une couverture, to roll *or* wrap s.o. up in a blanket; *F* **se faire r. dans la farine,** to be made a fool of.

2 *vi* **(a)** (*of ball, falling person etc*) to roll; (*of car, train*) to go; **r. sur une pente,** to roll down a slope; **r. (en voiture),** to drive; **nous avons roulé toute la nuit,** we drove *or* travelled all night; **cette voiture a peu roulé,** this car has a low mileage; *Av* **r. sur le sol,** to taxi; *F* **ça roule,** (*tout va bien*) everything's fine; **je ne roule pas sur l'or,** I'm not rolling in money; *Fin* **l'argent roule,** money is circulating freely; **la conversation roulait sur le sport,** the talk was about sport; **r. dans tous les pays,** to knock about the world; *Prov* **pierre qui roule n'amasse pas mousse,** a rolling stone gathers no moss;

(b) (*of thunder*) to roll, to rumble; (*of drum*) to roll;

(c) *Nau* (*of ship*) to roll;

3 se rouler *vpr* **(a)** to roll (about); **se r. par terre,** to roll (about) on the ground; *Fig* **se r. (par terre),** (*rire*) to be convulsed with laughter;

(b) le hérisson se roule en boule, the hedgehog rolls up into a ball;

(c) se r. les pouces, to twiddle one's thumbs; *Arg* **se les r.,** to have a cushy time.

roulette [rulɛt] *nf* **(a)** (*de meuble etc*) caster, roller; **chaise à roulettes,** chair on casters *or* rollers; **patins à roulettes,** roller skates; **ça marche** *ou* **va comme sur des roulettes,** things are going like clockwork; *Av* **r. de nez/queue,** nose/tail wheel; **(b)** *Tech* (*de relieur*) fillet; (*de cordonnier*) pricking wheel; *Couture* tracing wheel, tracer; *Culin* pastry wheel; **(c)** *F* (*de dentiste*) drill; **(d)** (*jeu*) roulette; **r. russe,** Russian roulette.

rouleur, -euse [rulœr, -øz] **1** *nm* **(a)** (*vagabond*) rolling stone; *F* **r. de cabarets,** pub crawler; **(b)** *Cyclisme* **un bon r.,** a good performer on the flat; **(c)** *Nau* ship that rolls heavily. **2** *nf Ent* **rouleuse,** leaf roller, leaf crumpler.

roulier [rulje] *nm Hist* wagoner.

roulis [ruli] *nm Nau* roll(ing); **coup de r.,** roll, lurch; **quille de r.,** rolling chock, bilge keel; **table à r.,** fiddle.

roulotte [rulɔt] *nf* (*de bohémiens*) caravan; (*de camping*) *Br* caravan, *Am* trailer; *F* **vol à la r.,** theft from parked cars.

roulotté [rulɔte] *adj & nm Couture* **(ourlet) r.,** rolled hem.

roulure [rulyr] *nf Arg* (*terme injurieux*) (*prostituée*) whore.

roumain, -aine [rumɛ̃, -ɛn] **1** *adj* Rumanian, Ro(u)manian. **2** *nm Ling* Rumanian, Ro(u)manian. **3** *n* **R.,** Rumanian, Ro(u)manian.

Roumanie [rumani] *nf* Rumania, Ro(u)mania.

round [rawnd, rund] *nm Boxe* round.

roupie¹ [rupi] *nf* (*monnaie*) rupee.

roupie² *nf F* **avoir la r.,** to have a drippy nose; **c'est de la r. de sansonnet,** it's worthless rubbish.

roupiller [rupije] *vi F* to sleep; (*faire un petit somme*) to have a snooze, to take a nap.

roupillon [rupijɔ̃] *nm F* nap, snooze; **faire** *ou* **piquer un r.,** to take a nap, to have a snooze.

rouquin, -ine [rukɛ̃, -in] **1** *adj F* red-haired, ginger-haired (*person*). **2** *n F* (*personne*) redhead. **3** *nm Arg* (*vin*) (cheap) red wine.

rouscailler [ruskaje] *vi Arg* (*protester*) to grouse, to bellyache.

rouspétance [ruspetɑ̃s] *nf F* grousing, bellyaching.

rouspéter [ruspete] *vi* **(je rouspète; je rouspéterai)** *F* to grouse, to bellyache (**contre,** about).

rouspéteur, -euse [ruspetœr, -øz] *F* **1** *adj* grumpy, grouchy. **2** *n* grumbler, grouser.

roussâtre [rusatr] *adj* reddish.

rousse *voir* **ROUX.**

rousserolle [rusrɔl] *nf* (*oiseau*) reed warbler.

roussette [rusɛt] *nf* **(a)** (*poisson*) spotted dogfish; **(b)** (*chauve-souris*) flying fox; **(c)** (*grenouille*) common frog.

rousseur [rusœr] *nf* redness (*of hair etc*); **tache de r.,** freckle; **couvert de taches de r.,** freckled; **rousseurs,** (*dans un livre etc*) foxing.

roussi [rusi] *nm* **ça sent le r.,** there's a smell of (something) burning; *Fig* there's trouble ahead.

roussin [rusɛ̃] *nm Hist* (*cheval*) charger.

roussir [rusir] **1** *vt* **(a)** to turn (*sth*) brown; *Culin* to brown (*meat etc*); **(b)** (*en brûlant*) to scorch, to singe (*linen etc*). **2** *vi* **(a)** (*of leaves, trees etc*) to turn brown or russet; **(b)** *Culin*

faire r., to brown.

routage [rutaʒ] *nm* sorting and routing (*of printed papers etc*).

routard, -arde [rutar, -ard] *n F* (young) hitchhiker.

route [rut] *nf* **(a)** road; **r. nationale, grande r.,** main road, major road, *Am* highway, *Br* ≈ A road; **r. départementale,** secondary road, *Br* ≈ B road; **prendre la r. de Paris,** to take the road for *or* to Paris; **r. à double voie,** dual carriageway; **par la r.,** by road; **code de la r.,** highway code; **les accidents de la r.,** road accidents; **chanson de r.,** marching song; **l'état des routes,** road conditions; **(b)** (*chemin à suivre*) route, way; *Nau* course; *Av Nau* (*ligne*) route; **se mettre en r.,** to start out, to set out; (*of ship*) to get under way; *Nau* **suivre une r.,** to steer a course; *Nau* **faire r. sur Calais,** to steer *or* make for Calais; **navire en r. pour l'étranger,** ship outward bound; **en r.!,** (*allons*) let's be off!, let's go!; (*allez*) off you go!; **faire r. ensemble,** to travel together; **marchandises avariées en cours de r.,** goods damaged in transit; **frais de r.,** travel(ling) expenses; **barrer la r. à qn,** to bar s.o.'s way; *Fig* to stand in s.o.'s way; **montrer la r. à qn,** to show s.o. the way; **r. de mer,** sea route; **r. de navigation,** (shipping) lane, ocean lane; **r. terrestre,** (over)land route; **r. commerciale,** trade route; **(c)** *Fig* path; **nos routes se croiseront un jour,** our paths will cross one day; **ta r. est tracée,** your path is marked out *or* set out (for you); **(d)** (*marche*) **mettre le moteur en r.,** to start up the engine; **mettre des travaux en r.,** to start operations; *F* **ils ont un bébé en r.,** they've got a baby on the way.

router [rute] *vt* to sort and route (*printed papers etc*).

routier¹, -ière [rutje, -jɛr] **1** *adj* **(a)** *Nau Av* **livre r.,** track chart; **(b) carte routière,** road map; **police routière,** traffic police; **pont r.,** road bridge; **bicyclette routière,** roadster; **locomotive routière,** traction engine; **transports routiers,** road transport; **gare routière,** bus *or* coach station. **2** *nm* **(a)** (*camion*) **gros r.,** heavy (goods) lorry, *Am* heavy truck; **(b)** (*conducteur*) *Br* long-distance lorry driver, *Am* teamster, truck driver; **(c)** (*vélo*) roadster; **(d)** (*cycliste*) road racer; **(e)** (*restaurant*) *Br* transport café, *Am* roadside café (*used by truck drivers*). **3** *nf* **routière,** (*voiture*) tourer, *Am* touring car.

routier² *nm* **(a) vieux r.,** (*homme experimenté*) old hand (**de,** at); **(b)** (*scout*) rover.

routine [rutin] *nf* routine; **examen de r.,** routine examination; **faire qch par r.,** to do sth as a matter of routine.

routinier, -ière [rutinje, -jɛr] **1** *adj* routine (*duties etc*); routine-minded (*person*), (*person*) who sticks to routine. **2** *n* slave to routine.

rouvrir [ruvrir] *v* (*conj like* **ouvrir**) *vt & vi*, **se rouvrir** *vpr* to reopen.

roux, rousse [ru, rus] **1** *adj* russet, reddish-brown (*leaves, animal's coat etc*); **chevelure blond r.,** sandy hair; *Culin* **beurre r.,** brown butter. **2** *n* (*personne*) red-haired person, redhead. **3** *nm* **(a)** (*couleur*) russet, reddish-brown; **(b)** *Culin* roux.

royal, -aux [rwajal, -o] *adj* royal; (*digne d'un roi*) regal, kingly (*magnificence etc*); magnificent, fit for a king (*gift, meal etc*); **prince r.,** crown prince; *Fig* **la voie royale,** the royal road; **une paix royale,** a blissful peace; **un mépris r.,** a lofty contempt.

royalement [rwajalmɑ̃] *adv* royally, regally; *F* **s'amuser r.,** to enjoy oneself immensely *or* hugely; *F* **je m'en fiche r.,** I couldn't care less about it.

royalisme [rwajalism] *nm* royalism.

royaliste [rwajalist] **1** *adj* royalist; **être plus r. que le roi,** to be more Catholic than the Pope. **2** *n* royalist.

royalties [rwajalti] *nfpl* royalties (*on patent, oil or for use of pipeline*).

royaume [rwajom] *nm* kingdom, realm; *Fig* realm; **le r. des cieux** *ou* **de Dieu,** the kingdom of heaven.

Royaume-Uni (le) [lərwajomyni] *nm* the United Kingdom.

royauté [rwajote] *nf* (*monarchie*) monarchy; (*dignité*) kingship.

R.P. [ɛrpe] *nfpl* (*abrév* **relations publiques**) PR.

RPR [ɛrpeɛr] *nm Pol* (*abrév* **Rassemblement pour la République**) = right of centre political party.

ruade [rɥad] *nf* lashing out, kick (*of horse*); **allonger** *ou* **décocher** *ou* **lancer une r.,** to lash out (**à,** at).

Ruanda [rwɑ̃da] *nm* Rwanda.

ruandais, -aise [rwɑ̃dɛ, -ɛz] **1** *adj* Rwandan. **2** *n* **R.,** Rwandan.

ruban [rybɑ̃] *nm* **(a)** ribbon; **r. de chapeau,** hatband; **le r. rouge,** the red ribbon (*of the Legion of Honour*); *Nau* **le r. bleu,** the Blue Riband; **r. de fil,** tape; **mètre à** *ou* **en r.,** measuring tape; **r. adhésif,** adhesive tape; **r. magnétique,** magnetic *or* recording tape; **r. encreur,** (*de machine à écrire*) inking ribbon; *Él* **r. isolant,** insulating tape; **(b) r. d'acier,** steel band; **fer à r.,** hoop iron; **scie à r.,** band saw, belt saw.

rubané [rybane] *adj* **(a)** *Biol* striped; *Minér* **agate rubanée,** ribbon agate, banded agate; **(b) canon r.,** strip-wound gun barrel.

rubaner [rybane] *vt* **(a)** (*orner*) to trim (*sth*) with ribbon(s); **(b)** *Él* to tape (*wire*); **(c)** to cut (*sth*) into ribbons *or* strips.

rubanerie [rybanri] *nf* (*fabrication*) ribbon manufacture; (*commerce*) ribbon trade.

rubato [rubato] *adv & nm Mus* rubato.

rubéole [rybeɔl] *nf Méd* German measles, *Spéc* rubella.

rubican [rybikɑ̃] *adj* roan (*horse*).

rubicond [rybikɔ̃] *adj* rubicond, florid (*complexion*).

rubidium [rybidjɔm] *nm Ch* rubidium.

rubis [rybi] *nm* ruby; (*de montre, d'horloge*) jewel; **r. balais,** balas ruby; **r. spinelle,** spinel ruby; **r. de Bohème,** rose quartz; **montre montée sur r.,** jewelled watch; *F* **faire r. sur l'ongle,** to drink to the last drop; **payer r. sur l'ongle,** to pay cash on the nail.

rubrique [rybrik] *nf* **(a)** *Rel Jur* rubric; **(b)** (*dans un livre*) imprint; **(c)** *Journ* (*titre*) heading; (*articles*) column; **il tient la r. de la mode au Figaro,** he writes the fashion column in the Figaro; **sous la même r.,** under the same heading.

ruche [ryʃ] *nf* **(a)** (bee)hive; (*abeilles*) hive; **r. en paille,** (bee-)skep; *Fig* **r. d'industrie,** (regular) hive of industry; **(b)** *Couture* ruche, ruching.

ruché [ryʃe] *nm Couture* ruche, ruching.

ruchée [ryʃe] *nf* (*abeilles*) hive.

rucher¹ [ryʃe] *nm* apiary.

rucher² *vt Couture* to ruche.

rude [ryd] *adj* **(a)** (*primitif*) uncouth, unpolished, primitive (*people, manners*); **un r. montagnard,** a rugged mountain dweller; **(b)** (*au toucher, au goût etc*) rough (*skin, cloth, wine*); stiff, hard (*brush*); harsh, grating (*voice*); **(c)** (*pénible*) hard, severe (*winter*); stiff, arduous (*task*); heavy, severe (*blow*); rude (*shock*); steep (*path*); stiff, steep (*climb*); **être mis à r. épreuve,** to be severely tested *or* tried; **il a été à r. école,** he had a strict upbringing; **(d)** (*sévère*) severe, harsh (*person*); **(e)** *F* (*remarquable*) **r. appétit,** hearty appetite; **un r. gaillard,** (*courageux*) a stout fellow; **faire une r. gaffe,** to put one's foot in it in no uncertain manner.

rudement [rydmɑ̃] *adv* **(a)** (*sévèrement*) roughly, harshly, severely; **être r. éprouvé,** to be severely tested *or* tried; **travailler r.,** to work hard; **(b)** (*frapper, heurter etc*) hard; **(c)** (*très*) awfully, terribly; **je suis r. fatigué,** I'm awfully *or* terribly tired.

rudesse [rydɛs] *nf* **(a)** roughness, ruggedness (*of a surface, style*); coarseness (*of material*); roughness (*of wine*); harshness (*of voice*); **(b)** severity (*of winter, task*); **(c)** severity, harshness (*of person*); **traiter qn avec r.,** to treat s.o. harshly.

rudiment [rydimɑ̃] *nm* **(a)** rudiment (*of organ etc*); **(b) rudiments,** rudiments (*of knowledge*); beginnings (*of scheme*); **établir les rudiments d'une théorie,** to establish the basis *or* the first principles of a theory.

rudimentaire [rydimɑ̃tɛr] *adj* rudimentary.

rudoyer [rydwaje] *vt* (**je rudoie; je rudoierai**) to treat (*s.o.*) roughly *or* harshly.

rue¹ [ry] *nf* **(a)** (*voie*) street; **r. principale,** main street; **la grande r.,** the main street, *Br* the high street; **petite r. écartée,** back street; **le peuple descendit dans la r.,** people came out on the streets (*to protest etc*); **manifestation de r.,** street demonstration; **être à la r.,** to find oneself out on the street; **mettre qn à la r.,** to put s.o. out on the street; **courir les rues,** to roam the streets; (*of news etc*) to be common knowledge; (*of rumour*) to be rife; **ça ne court pas les rues,** you don't find that very often, that's hard to come by; **l'homme de la r.,** the man in the street; **(b)** *Th* **rues,** slips.

rue² *nf Bot* rue; **r. des murailles,** wall rue.

ruée [rɥe] *nf* rush; **la r. sur** *ou* **vers les plages,** the rush for the seaside; **la r. vers l'or,** the gold rush.

ruelle [rɥɛl] *nf* **(a)** (*allée*) lane, alley; **(b)** (*entre le lit et le mur*) = space between the bed and the wall; **(c)** *Hist Littér* = (part of) room used by ladies to hold salons in the 17th century.

ruer [rɥe] **1** *vi* (*of horse etc*) to kick, to lash out. **2 se ruer**

vpr **se r. sur qn/qch,** to hurl *or* fling oneself at s.o./sth; **les invités se sont rués sur le buffet,** the guests made a dash for *or* pounced on the buffet; **se r. à l'attaque,** to throw oneself into the attack; **se r. à la porte,** to rush *or* make a rush for the door.

ruf(f)ian [ryfjɑ̃] *nm Arch* (*souteneur*) procurer.

rugby [rygbi] *nm* rugby (football), *F* rugger; **r. à treize/quinze,** rugby league/union.

rugbyman, *pl* **-men** [rygbiman, -mɛn] *nm* rugby player.

rugir [ryʒir] **1** *vi* (*of lion, person etc*) to roar; (*of wind, storm*) to howl; **r. de colère,** to roar with rage. **2** *vt* to roar out (*insults etc*).

rugissant [ryʒisɑ̃] *adj* roaring (*lion etc*); howling (*wind, storm*).

rugissement [ryʒismɑ̃] *nm* roar(ing) (*of lion etc*); howl(ing) (*of wind, storm*); **un r. de colère,** a roar of anger.

rugosité [rygozite] *nf* **(a)** (*caractère*) roughness; **(b)** (*point*) rough spot.

rugueux, -euse [rygø, -øz] *adj* rough (*skin, cloth etc*) rough, gnarled (*tree, bark*).

Ruhr [rur] *nf* **la R.,** the Ruhr.

ruine [rɥin] *nf* **(a)** (*écroulement*) ruin (*of building etc*); **menacer r.,** to threaten to collapse; **tomber en r.,** to fall into ruin(s); **maisons qui tombent en r.,** tumbledown houses; **tout tombe en r.,** everything is going to (w)rack and ruin; **(b)** *Fig* ruin, downfall (*of person, society etc*); **aller** *ou* **courir à la r.,** to be on the road to ruin; **la société est au bord de la r.,** society is threatened with ruin; **cette maison, quelle r.!,** this house will be the ruin of me!, this house is ruinously expensive!; **ce sera sa r.,** it will be the ruin *or* the ruination of him; **l'alcool a fait d'elle une r.,** alcohol has been her ruin *or* ruination; **(c)** (*vestige*) ruin; **les ruines de Troie,** the ruins of Troy; **leur château est une vieille r.,** their castle is an old ruin; *Fig* **se relever de ses ruines,** to rise from the ruins.

ruiner [rɥine] **1** *vt* to ruin; **r. qn,** to ruin s.o., to bankrupt s.o.; **un homme ruiné,** a ruined *or* broken man; **r. les espoirs de qn,** to ruin *or* wreck s.o.'s hopes; *F* **ce n'est pas ça qui va te r.,** (*ce n'est pas cher*) it won't ruin you, it won't break the bank. **2 se ruiner** *vpr* to ruin *or* bankrupt oneself; (*dépenser beaucoup*) to spend a (small) fortune; **se r. la santé,** to ruin one's health.

ruineusement [rɥinøzmɑ̃] *adv* ruinously.

ruineux, -euse [rɥinø, -øz] *adj* ruinously expensive; **dépenses ruineuses,** ruinous expenditure; **ce n'est pas r.,** it won't ruin you *or* us *etc*, it won't break the bank.

ruisseau, -eaux [rɥiso] *nm* **(a)** (*cours d'eau*) brook, (small) stream; **(b)** stream (*of blood, lava*); flood (*of tears*); **(c)** (*le long du trottoir*) gutter; *Fig* **calomnie ramassée dans le r.,** slander picked up in the gutter; *Fig* **sortir qn du r.,** to pull s.o. out of the gutter; *Fig* **pousser qn au r.,** to throw s.o. into the gutter; *Fig* **tomber dans le r.,** to fall into the gutter.

ruisselant [rɥislɑ̃] *adj* streaming, dripping (wet) (**de,** with); **eaux ruisselantes,** running water; (*en filets*) trickling water.

ruisseler [rɥisle] *vi* (**il ruisselle; il ruissellera**) **(a)** (*of liquid*) to stream, to run; (*en filets*) to trickle; **l'eau ruisselait par la porte,** the water was streaming *or* pouring in *or* out at the door; **(b)** (*of surface*) to run, to drip; **le parquet ruisselait,** the floor was running with water; **front ruisselant de sueur,** forehead dripping *or* streaming with sweat.

ruisselet [rɥislɛ] *nm* brooklet, rivulet, rill.

ruissellement [rɥisɛlmɑ̃] *nm* **(a)** streaming, running (*of water etc*); (*en filets*) trickling; *Géog* runoff; **(b)** shimmer (*of jewellery, light etc*).

rumba [rumba] *nf* (*danse, musique*) rumba.

rumen [rymɛn] *nm no pl* rumen (*of ruminant*).

rumeur [rymœr] *nf* **(a)** (*bruit confus*) confused *or* distant murmur; hum (*of traffic*); **(b)** (*protestation*) din, uproar, clamour, *US* clamor; **tout est en r.,** everything is in an uproar; **(c)** (*on-dit*) rumour, *US* rumor; **r. publique,** common report; **la r. court qu'il est ruiné,** it is rumoured *or* rumour has it *or* the rumour is that he's ruined.

ruminant [ryminã] *adj & nm Zool* ruminant.

rumination [ryminasjɔ̃] *nf Zool* rumination, ruminating.

ruminer [rymine] **1** *vi* (*of animal*) to ruminate, to chew the cud. **2** *vt* **(a)** (*of animal*) to ruminate, to chew; **(b)** *Fig* to ruminate on *or* over, to chew over (*idea, plan etc*).

rumsteck [rɔmstɛk] *nm* rump steak.

runabout [rœnabawt] *nm Nau* runabout, speedboat.

rune [ryn] *nf* rune.

runique [rynik] *adj* runic.

rupestre [rypɛstr] *adj* **dessins rupestres,** rock drawings; **peintures rupestres,** cave paintings; **plantes rupestres,** rock plants.

rupin, -ine [rypɛ̃, -in] *Arg* **1** *adj* (*riche*) loaded (*person*); plush (*apartment etc*). **2** *n* **c'est un r.,** he's loaded; **les rupins,** the rich, the well-off.

rupiner [rypine] *vi Arg* **r. à un examen,** to do well in an examination.

rupteur [ryptœr] *nm Él* contact breaker, circuit breaker; *Aut* **r. (d'allumage),** make-and-break.

rupture [ryptyr] *nf* **(a)** breaking (*of rope, beam etc*); bursting (*of dam etc*); rupture (*of blood vessel, ligament*); fracture (*of bone*);

(b) breaking up (*of surface etc*); *Mil* **obus de r.,** armour-piercing shell;

(c) *Fig* breaking off (*of battle, negotiations*); calling off (*of a deal*); breach (*of contract, of promise of marriage*); **la r. de fiançailles,** the breaking off of the engagement; **r. de charge,** transhipment of cargo; *El* **r. du circuit,** breaking of *or* break in the circuit; **r. de stock,** stock outage; **magasin en r. de stock,** shop that is out of stock; *Pol* **être en r. avec le parti,** to be at odds with *or* in disagreement with the party; **il y a eu r. entre eux,** they've quarrelled, there's been a split between them; **scène de r.,** (*entre époux etc*) break-up scene; **la r. de la princesse et de son époux,** the break-up *or* split-up between the princess and her husband.

rural, -ale, -aux [ryral, -o] **1** *adj* rural; **vie rurale,** country *or* rural life; **chemin r.,** country lane. **2** *n* country person; **les ruraux,** country people.

ruse [ryz] *nf* ruse, trick, wile; **la r.,** (*habileté*) cunning; **r. de guerre,** stratagem (of war); *Fig* **r. d'Indien,** crafty *or* cunning trick; **obtenir qch par r.,** to obtain sth by a ruse *or* by cunning.

rusé, -ée [ryze] **1** *adj* crafty, sly, cunning. **2** *n* **c'est une (petite) rusée,** she's a crafty *or* sly *or* cunning little thing.

ruser [ryze] *vi* to use trickery *or* cunning.

rush [rœʃ] *nm* **(a)** *Sp* sprint, spurt (*at end of race*); **(b)** *F* rush (*of people*); **(c)** *Cin* **rushes,** rushes.

russe [rys] **1** *adj* Russian. **2** *nm Ling* Russian. **2** *n* **R.,** Russian.

Russie [rysi] *nf* Russia; **R. blanche,** White Russia.

russification [rysifikasjɔ̃] *nf* Russianization.

russifier [rysifje] *vt* (*pr sub & impf* **n. russifiions**) to Russianize.

russule [rysyl] *nf* (*champignon*) russula.

rustaud, -aude [rysto, -od] **1** *adj* boorish, uncouth. **2** *n* boor, bumpkin, *Am* hick.

rusticité [rystisite] *nf* **(a)** rusticity; **(b)** *Agr* hardiness (*of plant*).

rustine ® [rystin] *nf* repair patch (*for mending inner tube of bicycle*).

rustique [rystik] **1** *adj* **(a)** rustic (*manners, life etc*); **danse r.,** country dance; **mobilier r.,** rustic(-style) *or* country-style furniture; **petit pont de bois r.,** little rustic bridge; **(b)** *Constr* **ouvrage r.,** rustic (stone)work; **(c)** *Agr* hardy (*plant*). **2** *nm* rustic *or* country style.

rustre [rystr] *Péj* **1** *adj* boorish, loutish. **2** *nm* boor, lout.

rut [ryt] *nm Zool* rut(ting) (*of male*); heat (*of female*); **en r.,** rutting; (*femelle*) in *or* on heat.

rutabaga [rytabaga] *nm* swede, *Am* rutabaga.

Ruth [ryt] *nf* Ruth.

ruthénium [rytenjɔm] *nm Ch* ruthenium.

rutilance [rytilɑ̃s] *nf* gleam(ing); (*rouge*) red glow.

rutilant [rytilɑ̃] *adj* gleaming; (*rouge*) glowing red.

rutilement [rytilmɑ̃] *nm* gleam(ing); (*rouge*) red glow.

rutiler [rytile] *vi* to gleam; (*rouge*) to glow red.

rythme [ritm] *nm Mus Littér* rhythm; **r. respiratoire,** breathing rate; **le r. de la vie moderne,** the tempo *or* pace of modern life; *Mus* **marquer le r.,** to beat time; *Com* **r. des livraisons,** delivery rate; **au r. de trois par semaine/***etc*, at the rate of three a week/*etc*; **à ce r., nous n'aurons pas fini ce soir,** at this rate we won't have finished by this evening.

rythmé [ritme] *adj* rhythmic(al).

rythmer [ritme] *vt* to put rhythm into (*movement, sentence etc*); to mark the rhythm of (*tune*).

rythmique [ritmik] **1** *adj* rhythmic(al). **2** *nf* rhythmics.

S

S, s [ɛs] *nm* (the letter) S, s; **faire des s,** to zigzag; **en S,** S-shaped; **sentier en s,** winding path.
S **(a)** (*abrév* **Sud**) S; **(b)** (*abrév* **seconde**) sec.
S.A. [ɛsa] *nf* (*abrév* **Société Anonyme**) Ltd.
Saba [saba] *nf* Sheba.
sabaye [sabɛj] *nf Nau* mooring rope; (*pour remorquer*) towline.
sabayon [sabajɔ̃] *nm Culin* zabaglione.
sabbat [saba] *nm* **(a)** (Jewish) Sabbath; **jour du s.,** Sabbath day; **observer/violer le s.,** to keep/break the Sabbath; **(b)** (*assemblée nocturne*) (*witches'*) sabbath; *F* **faire un s. de tous les diables,** to make a hell of a row; **s. de chats,** caterwauling.
sabbatique [sabatik] *adj* sabbatical (*year etc*); **prendre trois mois sabbatiques,** to take *or* do a three-month sabbatical.
sabin, -ine [sabɛ̃, -in] *Antiq* **1** *adj* Sabine. **2** *n* **S.,** Sabine; **l'enlèvement des Sabines,** the rape of the Sabine women.
sabir [sabir] *nm Ling* lingua franca.
sablage [sablaʒ] *nm* **(a)** *Ind* sandblasting (*of building*); **(b)** sanding, gritting (*of icy road*).
sable[1] [sabl] **1** *nm* sand; **sables mouvants,** quicksands; *Nau* **fond de s.,** sandy bottom; **une plage de s.,** a sandy beach; **tempête de s.,** sandstorm; **bac à s.,** (*pour enfants*) sandpit; *Constr* **s. liant** *ou* **mordant,** sharp sand; *F* **être sur le s.,** (*sans travail*) to be out of work *or* a job; (*démuni*) to be down and out; *Fig* **bâtir sur du s.,** to build on sand; *Fig* **semer sur le s.,** to sew on stony ground; **un grain de s. dans l'engrenage,** a spanner in the works; **avoir du s. dans les yeux,** to be sleepy; *Fig* **le marchand de s. passe,** the sandman is coming; **s. de fer,** fine iron filings. **2** *adj inv* sandy.
sable[2] *nm Hér etc* sable.
sablé [sable] **1** *adj* **(a)** sanded, gravelled (*path etc*); **(b)** **pâte sablée,** short(crust) pastry. **2** *nm Culin* = shortbread.
sabler [sable] *vt* **(a)** to sand, to gravel (*path etc*); to sand, to grit (*icy road*); **(b)** to cast (*medal etc*) in a sand mould *or US* mold; **(c)** *F* **s. le champagne,** to celebrate with champagne, to break open a bottle of champagne; **(d)** to sandblast (*building*).
sableur, -euse[1] [sablœr, -øz] **1** *n* sand moulder *or US* molder. **2** *nf* **sableuse,** sandblaster, sand jet.
sableux, -euse[2] [sablø, -øz] *adj* sandy.
sablier [sablije] *nm* hourglass; *Culin* egg timer.
sablière[1] [sablijɛr] *nf* **(a)** (*carrière*) sand quarry; **(b)** (*de locomotive*) sand box.
sablière[2] *nf Const etc* (lengthwise) beam, stringer, templet.
sablon [sablɔ̃] *nm* scouring sand; welding sand.
sablonner [sablɔne] *vt* to sand.
sablonneux, -euse [sablɔnø, -øz] *adj* sandy.
sablonnière [sablɔnjɛr] *nf* sand quarry.
sabord [sabɔr] *nm Nau* porthole; **s. d'aération,** air port; **s. de charge,** cargo door; **faux s.,** deadlight; *Arg Vieilli* **mille sabords!,** shiver my timbers!
sabordage [sabɔrdaʒ] *nm,* **sabordement** [sabɔrdəmɑ̃] *nm Nau* scuttling.
saborder [sabɔrde] **1** *vt* to scuttle (*ship, plan etc*); *Fig* (*détruire*) to ruin, to destroy (*plan*). **2 se saborder** *vpr Nau* to scuttle one's ship; *Fig* (*s'anéantir*) to wind up, *F* to pack in.
sabot [sabo] *nm* **(a)** wooden shoe, clog, sabot; *Arg* old *or* useless article; old tub (*of a ship*); old crock (*of a car*); *Fig* **je vous entends** *ou* **vois venir avec vos gros sabots,** I can see what you're after, I can see you coming a mile off; *F* **elle n'a pas les deux pieds dans le même s.,** there are no flies on her; **il joue/chante comme un s.,** he can't play/sing to save his life; **elle travaille comme un s.,** she makes a botch of everything;
(b) hoof (*of horse etc*);
(c) *Tech* shoe, sabot (*of pile etc*); caster socket (*of furniture*); **s. d'enrayage,** drag, skid, shoe, trig (*of wheel*); **s. d'arrêt,** chock; **s. de frein,** brake block, brake shoe; *Aut* **s. de Denver,** Denver boot, wheel clamp; **mettre un s. de Denver à une voiture,** to (wheel-)clamp a car; *Aut* **s. (de pare-chocs),** overrider; **s. de pompe,** pump piston, bucket; *Phot* **s.-contact,** hot shoe;
(d) (*toupie*) whipping top;
(e) *Bot* **s. de Vénus,** lady's slipper;
(f) (*coquillage*) turban shell.
sabotage [sabɔtaʒ] *nm* **(a)** *F* (*d'un travail*) botching; (*travail*) botched (up) job; **(b)** (act of) sabotage; *Typ* intentional garbling (*of copy*); **(c)** *Rail* chairing (*of sleepers*).
saboter [sabɔte] *vt* **(a)** *F* to botch, to make a mess of (*a job*); to murder (*a song etc*) **(b)** to sabotage (*a car, a policy*); **(c)** *Tech* to shoe (*a pile etc*); **(d)** *Rail* to chair (*sleeper*).
saboteur, -euse [sabɔtœr, -øz] *n* **(a)** (*de son travail*) bungler, botcher; **(b)** (*malfaiteur*) saboteur.
sabre [sabr] *nm* sabre, *US* saber; **traîner** *ou* **faire sonner son s.,** to rattle one's sabre; **s. d'abordage,** cutlass; **s. au clair,** (with) drawn sword.
sabrer [sabre] *vt* **(a)** to cut (*s.o.*) down with a sword; *F* to slash, to make drastic cuts in (*a manuscript, a play*); *F* (*critiquer*) to slate (*s.o., a play*); *F* (*renvoyer*) to sack (*employee*); **(b)** *F* (*gâcher*) to botch (*a job*).
sabreur [sabrœr] *nm* **(a)** (dashing) swordsman; **(b)** *F* **s. de besogne,** slapdash worker.
sac[1] [sak] *nm* **(a)** bag; (*plus grand*) sack; **s. de** *ou* **en papier,** paper bag *or* sack; **s. de plastique,** plastic bag; **s. à blé,** grain sack; **contre trois sacs de blé,** for three sacks of wheat; **s. à main,** handbag, *Am* purse; **s. à** *ou* **en bandoulière,** shoulder bag; **s. à provisions,** shopping bag; **s. à ouvrage,** workbag; **s. à outils,** tool bag; **s. de voyage/nuit,** travel/overnight bag; **s. de plage,** beach bag; **s. à dos, s. de campeur,** rucksack, *Am* backpack; **partir s. au dos,** to set off with one's rucksack on one's back *or Am* with one's backpack; **s. alpin (de scout),** knapsack; **course en s.,** sack race; *Mil* **s. de fantassin** *ou* **de soldat,** pack, knapsack; *Mil* **s. à munitions,** cartridge pouch; **s. (d'écolier),** schoolbag; **s. de couchage,** sleeping bag; **s. de sable** *ou* **de terre,** sandbag; *Nau* **s. (de) marin,** kitbag; *F* **s. d'os,** bag of bones; *F* **un s. (de nœuds),** a muddle; *Boxe F* **travailler le s.,** to practise with the punchball; **s. à fourrages,** nosebag; **s. à poussière,** dustbag (*for vacuum cleaner etc*); **s. de sauvetage,** canvas escape chute; *F* **s. percé,** spendthrift; *F* **habillé comme un s.,** dressed like a tramp; **robe s.,** (*mode*) sack (dress); *F* **s. à vin,** boozer; *Arg* **homme de s. et de corde,** out-and-out scoundrel; *Arg* **ils ont le s., il y a le s.,** they've got (pots *or* bags of) money; *Arg* **faire** *ou* **gagner son s.,** to make one's pile; *Arg* **épouser le (gros) s.,** to marry money; *F* **vous êtes tous dans le même s.,** you're all in the same boat; *F* **prendre qn la main dans le s.,** to catch s.o. red-handed; *F* **vider son s.,** to get it off one's chest; (*avouer*) to come clean; *Arg* **remplir son s.,** to fill one's belly; *F* **mettez ça dans votre s.!,** put that in your pipe and smoke it!; *F* **l'affaire est dans le s.,** it's in the bag; *Nau* **faire s.,** (*d'une voile*) to bag, to belly; *Arch* **s. à papier!,** damn it!;
(b) *Arg* ten francs;
(c) *Anat Bot* sac;
(d) pouch (*of marsupial*);
(e) (*filet*) poke net;
(f) *Av* **s. à vent,** windsock;
(g) *Géol* **s. de minerai,** pocket of ore;
(h) *Tex* (*jute*) sackcloth; **sous le s. et la cendre,** in sackcloth and ashes;
(i) *Can Fb* quarterback sack.
sac[2] *nm* sack(ing), pillage; **mettre à s. une ville,** to sack *or* plunder a town; **faire le s. d'une maison,** to ransack a house; **mise à s. d'une maison,** ransacking of a house.

saccade [sakad] *nf* jerk, jolt; *MecE* backlash; **s. de bride,** sharp jerk of the bridle; **par saccades,** in *or* by fits and starts.
saccadé [sakade] *adj* jerky, abrupt (*movement, style*); **d'une voix saccadée,** in a jerky *or* staccato voice; **style s.,** jerky *or* staccato style; **respiration saccadée,** irregular breathing.
saccader [sakade] *vt* to jerk (*a horse's rein*).
saccage [sakaʒ] *nm* havoc.
saccager [sakaʒe] *vt* (**je saccageai(s); n. saccageons**) to sack, to pillage (*town*); to ransack (*house etc*); **ils ont tout saccagé,** (*mis en désordre*) they turned everything upside down.
saccageur, -euse [sakaʒœr, -øz] *n* plunderer.
saccharifier [sakarifje] *vt* (*pr sub & impf* **n. saccharifiions, v. saccharifiiez**) *Ch* to saccharify.
saccharimètre [sakarimɛtr] *nm* **(a)** *Ch* saccharimeter; **(b)** (*de brasserie*) saccharometer.
saccharin [sakarɛ̃] *adj* saccharine.
saccharine [sakarin] *nf Ch etc* saccharin(e).
saccharomètre [sakarɔmɛtr] *nm* saccharometer.
saccharose [sakaroz] *nm Ch* saccharose.
sacerdoce [sasɛrdɔs] *nm* priesthood, ministry (*of the Church*); **durant son s.,** during his priesthood *or* ministry; *Fig* **pour lui, c'est un s.,** for him, it's a vocation, he is dedicated; **le s. de la médecine,** dedication to medicine.
sacerdotal, -aux [sasɛrdɔtal, -o] *adj* priestly.
sachem [saʃɛm] *nm* sagamore, sachem (*North American Indian chief*).
sachet [saʃɛ] *nm* sachet, (small) bag; **s. de lavande,** lavender bag *or* sachet; **s. de thé,** teabag; **thé en sachets,** teabags; **je n'achète jamais mon thé en sachets,** I never buy teabags.
sacoche [sakɔʃ] *nf* **(a)** (*de vélo etc*) saddlebag; **(b)** (*besace*) bag; **s. du facteur,** postman's bag; **s. en toile/cuir,** canvas/leather bag; **s. à outils,** tool bag; **(c)** *Belg Can* handbag, *Am* purse.
sacquer [sake] *F* **1** *vt* **(a)** (*renvoyer*) to sack (*s.o.*); **(b)** (*noter sévèrement*) to be a tough marker (*of student*); **(c)** *F* **je ne peux pas les s.,** I hate their guts. **2** *vi* (*d'un professeur*) to be a tough marker.
sacral, -aux [sakral, -o] *adj* sacral.
sacraliser [sakralize] *vt* to make *or* consider (*sth, s.o.*) sacred; **s. la liberté,** to consider freedom to be sacred, to consider freedom as something sacred.
sacramentel, -elle [sakramɑ̃tɛl] *adj Rel* sacramental; *Fig* solemn, binding.
sacrant [sakrɑ̃] *adj Can Sl* **au plus s.,** pdq (= *pretty damn quick*).
sacre [sakr] *nm* (*célébration*) rite; anointing (*of king*); consecration (*of bishop*); *Fig* **recevoir le prix Goncourt, c'est le s. pour un écrivain,** being awarded the prix Goncourt is the crowning achievement of a writer's career.
sacré¹ [sakre] **1** *adj* **(a)** *Rel* holy (*scripture etc*); sacred, consecrated (*vessel, place etc*); **art s.,** sacred art; **musique sacrée,** sacred music; **les ordres sacrés,** holy orders; **pour lui rien n'est s.,** to him nothing is sacred; **elle a le feu s.,** she is truly inspired; **il n'a pas le feu s.,** his heart isn't in it; **(b)** sacred (*duty, trust etc*); **(c)** *F* damn(ed), bloody; **votre s. chien,** your damned *or* bloody dog; **s. imbécile,** damned *or* bloody fool; **il a une sacrée chance,** he's damn(ed) *or* bloody lucky; **s. nom de Dieu** *ou* **d'un chien** *ou* **d'une pipe!,** damn and blast it! **2** *nm* the sacred.
sacré² *adj Anat* sacral.
Sacré-Cœur [sakrekœr] *nm Rel* Sacred Heart (of Jesus).
sacredieu [sakrədjø], **sacrebleu** [sakrəblø], **sacredié** [sakrədje] *int Vieilli* good God!
sacrement [sakrəmɑ̃] *nm Rel* sacrament; **le saint S.,** the Blessed Sacrament; *Fig F* **elle le promène comme le saint S.,** she shows it off as if it was the crown jewels; **recevoir les sacrements,** to receive the sacraments; **fréquenter les sacrements,** to be a regular communicant.
sacrément [sakremɑ̃] *adv F* damn(ed), bloody; **il fait s. chaud,** it's damn(ed) *or* bloody hot; **elle a s. bien répondu,** she gave a damn(ed) *or* bloody good answer.
sacrer [sakre] **1** *vt* to anoint (*a king*); to consecrate (*a bishop*); **s. qn roi/empereur,** to anoint *or* crown s.o. king/emperor; *Fig* **il a été sacré meilleur acteur de l'année 1991,** he was named best actor of 1991. **2** *vi F* to curse and swear.
sacret [sakrɛ] *nm* (*oiseau*) sakeret.
sacrifiable [sakrifjabl] *adj* expendable.
sacrificateur, -trice [sakrifikatœr, -tris] *n* sacrificer; **grand s.,** (Jewish) High Priest.
sacrifice [sakrifis] *nm* sacrifice; *Rel* **le saint s.,** mass; **ça a dû être un s.,** that must have been a sacrifice; **offrir qch en s.,** to offer up sth as a sacrifice; **faire à qn le s. de sa vie,** to sacrifice one's life for s.o.; **faire des sacrifices,** to make sacrifices; **esprit de s.,** spirit of self-sacrifice; **je n'ai pas le goût du s.,** I have no taste for self-sacrifice.
sacrifier [sakrifje] *v* (*impf & pr sub* **n. sacrifiions, v. sacrifiiez**) **1** *vt* to sacrifice (*victim*); to sacrifice, to give up (*time, money, career etc*) (**à,** to); *Com* **s. des marchandises,** to sell goods at a loss; **il a réussi en sacrifiant sa santé,** he succeeded at the cost of his health; **s. sa vie pour son pays,** to sacrifice *or* lay down one's life for one's country; **s. sa vie à une cause,** to devote one's (entire) life to a cause. **2** *vi* **s. aux idoles,** to sacrifice to idols; **s. à la mode,** to conform to fashion. **3 se sacrifier** *vpr* to sacrifice oneself; **elle s'est sacrifiée pour vous,** she sacrificed herself for you; **se s. pour la bonne cause,** to sacrifice oneself for the right cause.
sacrilège¹ [sakrilɛʒ] *nm* sacrilege; **ce serait un s. que de ...,** it would be sacrilege to ... .
sacrilège² **1** *adj* sacrilegious (*action, thought etc*). **2** *n* sacrilegious person.
sacristain [sakristɛ̃] *nm* **(a)** *Rel* sacristan; sexton; **(b)** *Culin* = small flaky pastry.
sacristi [sakristi] *int Arch* good Lord!
sacristie [sakristi] *nf Rel* sacristy, vestry.
sacro-saint [sakrosɛ̃] *adj* sacrosanct; *Iron* precious.
sacrum [sakrɔm] *nm Anat* sacrum.
sadique [sadik] **1** *adj* sadistic. **2** *n* sadist.
sadisme [sadism] *nm* sadism.
sadomasochisme [sadɔmazɔʃism] *nm Psy* sadomasochism.
sadomasochiste [sadɔmazɔʃist] *Psy* **1** *adj* sadomasochistic. **2** *n* sadomasochist.
saducéen, -enne [sadyseɛ̃, -ɛn] *n* Sadducee.
safari [safari] *nm* safari; **en s.,** on safari; **s. photo,** photographic safari; **vestes s.,** safari jackets.
safran¹ [safrɑ̃] **1** *nm* **(a)** *Bot* saffron, crocus; **(b)** *Culin etc* saffron; **riz au s.,** saffron rice. **2** *adj inv* saffron (yellow).
safran² *nm Nau* rudder blade.
safrané [safrane] *adj* saffron(-coloured, -flavoured, *US* -colored, -flavored).
safraner [safrane] *vt Culin* to flavour *or US* flavor with saffron.
saga [saga] *nm Littér* saga.
sagace [sagas] *adj* sagacious, acute, shrewd.
sagacement [sagasmɑ̃] *adv* sagaciously, shrewdly.
sagacité [sagasite] *nf* sagacity, shrewdness; **avec s.,** sagaciously.
sagaie [sagɛ] *nf* assegai.
sage [saʒ] **1** *adj* **(a)** (*avisé*) wise, sensible (*policy, person etc*); **une politique peu s.,** an unwise policy, not a very sensible policy; **il serait plus s. de faire ceci,** it would be wiser *or* more sensible to do this; **être s. après l'heure,** to be wise after the event, *Am F* to be a Monday-morning quarter back; **(b)** well-behaved, good (*child*); quiet, docile (*animal*); modest, sober (*dress, conduct*); **sois s.!,** be good!; **s. comme une image,** as good as gold; **(c)** (*chaste*) sexually unaware. **2** *nm* wise man; *Phil* sage; **comité des sages,** committee of wise men.
sage-femme [saʒfam] *nf* midwife; (*pl sages-femmes*).
sagement [saʒmɑ̃] *adv* **(a)** (*raisonnablement*) wisely, sensibly; **(b)** (*tranquillement*) quietly.
sagesse [saʒɛs] *nf* **(a)** (*prudence, connaissance*) wisdom; **agir avec s.,** to act wisely *or* sensibly; **dent de s.,** wisdom tooth; **écoute-la, elle est la voix de la s.,** listen to her, she is the voice of reason; **la s. d'un chef d'État,** the wisdom of a head of state; **(b)** (*d'enfant*) good behaviour *or US* behavior; **(c)** modesty, chastity (*of a woman*).
sagittaire [saʒitɛr] *nm Astron Hér* Sagittarius.
sagou [sagu] *nm* sago.
sagouin [sagwɛ̃] *nm* **(a)** (*singe*) squirrel monkey; **(b)** *F* slovenly *or* dirty fellow; **vieux s.,** revolting old man.
Sahara (le) [ləsaara] *nm* the Sahara (Desert).
saharien, -ienne [saarjɛ̃, -jɛn] **1** *adj* Saharan; desert (*troops*); **température saharienne,** scorching *or* sizzling temperature. **2** *n* **S.,** Saharan. **3** *nf* **saharienne,** bush jacket *or* shirt.
Sahel [saɛl] *nm* Sahel.
sahib [saib] *nm* sahib.
sahraoui, -ie [sarawi] **1** *adj* of the Western Sahara. **2** *n* **S.,** native of the Western Sahara.
saïga [saiga] *nm* saiga antelope.
saignant [sɛɲɑ̃] *adj* **(a)** bleeding, raw (*wound etc*); **(b)** *Culin* rare (*meat*).
saignée [seɲe] *nf* **(a)** *Méd Arch* blood-letting; *Fig* drain (*on*

one's resources); *Méd* **faire une s. à qn,** to bleed s.o.; **faire une s. dans un arbre,** to tap a tree (*for gum etc*); **(b)** *Anat* (*pli*) bend of the arm *or* the knee; **(c)** (*rigole*) (drainage) trench, ditch; *MecE* groove (*for oil etc*); *Constr* hole (*in a wall, for pipe, cable etc*).

saignement [sɛɲmɑ̃] *nm* bleeding; **s. de nez,** nosebleed; **elle souffre de saignements de nez,** she suffers from nosebleeds.

saigner [seɲe] **1** *vi* (*of person, wound etc*) to bleed; **mon doigt saigne,** my finger is bleeding; **je saigne du nez,** my nose is bleeding, I have a nosebleed; *Fig Litt* **le cœur m'en saigne,** it makes my heart bleed; **c'est une plaie qui saigne encore,** it's an open wound, it still rankles. **2** *vt Méd Arch & Fig* to bleed (*s.o.*); **s. un porc,** to bleed *or* stick a pig; **s. un poulet,** to bleed a chicken; **s. à blanc,** to bleed (*an animal, Fig s.o.*) white; **s. un arbre,** to tap a (gum) tree; **s. un fossé,** to drain a ditch; **s. une rivière,** to divert water from a river. **3 se saigner** *vpr* **se s. aux quatre membres** *ou* **aux quatre veines,** to sacrifice oneself, to bleed oneself white.

saigneur [sɛɲœr] *nm* **(a)** (*d'animaux*) slaughterman; **(b)** (*de caoutchouc*) collector of rubber.

saillant [sajɑ̃] **1** *adj* projecting, jutting out (*roof, cornice etc*); prominent, high (*cheekbones*); protruding (*teeth*); bulging (*muscles*); *Fig* salient, striking, outstanding (*feature, point etc*); **angle s.,** (*d'une fortification*) salient angle. **2** *nm Mil* salient.

saillie [saji] *nf* **(a)** (*partie en avant*) protrusion; *Archit Constr* projection, ledge, set-off; **en s.,** projecting, jutting out; **s. du mollet,** swell of the calf; **faire s.,** to project, to jut out; (*of pockets*) to bulge; (*of knees of trousers*) to bag; **menton qui fait s.,** protruding chin; **(b)** (*dans l'élevage*) covering (*by male*); **(c)** *Litt* sally, flash of wit; **(d)** *Arch* spurt, bound.

saillir [sajir] **1** *vt* (*prp* **saillissant**; *pp* **sailli**; *pr ind* **je saillis, n. saillissons**; *fu* **je saillirai**) (*dans l'élevage*) to cover (*female*). **2** *vi* (*used only in prp* **saillant**; *pp* **sailli**; *pr ind* **il saille, ils saillent**; *fu* **il saillera**) to project, to jut out (**sur,** over); **la poutre saille de 25 cm,** the beam projects 25 cm.

sain, saine [sɛ̃, sɛn] *adj* **(a)** healthy (*person*); sound (*horse, fruit, timber etc*); sound, clear (*judgment*); healthy, wholesome (*food*); healthy, sound (*economy*); **gestion saine,** (*d'une entreprise etc*) sound management; **climat/exercice s.,** healthy climate/exercise; **un esprit s. dans un corps s.,** a sound mind in a sound body; **s. et sauf,** safe and sound; **s. de corps et d'esprit,** sound in body and mind; **(b)** *Nau* clear, safe (*coast, anchorage*).

sainbois [sɛ̃bwa] *nm Bot* spurge flax.

saindoux [sɛ̃du] *nm Culin* lard.

sainement [sɛnmɑ̃] *adv* **(a)** (*salubrement*) healthily; **(b)** (*raisonnablement*) sanely.

sainfoin [sɛ̃fwɛ̃] *nm Bot Agr* sainfoin.

saint, sainte [sɛ̃, sɛ̃t] **1** *adj* **(a)** *Rel* holy; saintly, godly (*person, life*); **la Sainte Église,** the Holy Church; **guerre sainte,** holy war; **semaine sainte,** Holy Week; **le Vendredi s.,** Good Friday; **être saisi** *ou* **pris d'une sainte colère/indignation,** to be seething with righteous anger/indignation; **une sainte action,** a pious deed; *F* **j'en ai une sainte horreur!,** I loathe it!; **lieu s.,** holy place; **la Terre sainte,** the Holy land; *F* **toute la sainte journée,** the whole blessed day; **le s. patron des horlogers,** the patron saint of watch-makers;

(b) s. Pierre, St Peter; **sainte Catherine,** St Catherine; **l'église S.-Pierre,** St Peter's (church); **la S. Georges,** St George's day; *Can F* **du mouvement, Sainte Bénite!,** *F* get a move on, for Pete's sake!

2 *n* saint; **s. d'une ville,** patron saint of a town; **c'est un petit s. (de bois),** he's a little prig; **sa femme est une sainte,** his wife is a saint; **il lasserait la patience d'un s.,** he would try the patience of a saint; **elle prêche pour son s.,** she has an axe to grind; **ne savoir plus à quel s. se vouer,** to be at one's wits' end; *Rel* **les Saints du dernier jour,** the Latter-day Saints.

3 *nm* **le S. des Saints,** the Holy of Holies; *Fig* the inner sanctum, *Hum* the holy of holies, the sanctum sanctorum.

saint-bernard [sɛ̃bɛrnar] *nm inv* St Bernard (*dog*); *F* **c'est un vrai s.-b.,** he's a good Samaritan.

Saint-Cyr [sɛ̃sir] *nm* Saint-Cyr military academy.

Saint-Cyrien [sɛ̃sirjɛ̃] *nm* cadet training at Saint-Cyr; (*pl Saint-Cyriens*).

Saint-Domingue [sɛ̃dɔmɛ̃g] *nm* Santo Domingo.

Sainte-Croix [sɛ̃tkrwa] *n* **l'île S.-C.,** Santa Cruz island.

Sainte-Hélène [sɛ̃telɛn] *n* St Helena.

Saint-Elme [sɛ̃tɛlm] *nm* **feu S.-E.,** St Elmo's fire.

Sainte-Lucie [sɛ̃tlysi] *n* St Lucia.

saintement [sɛ̃tmɑ̃] *adv* righteously; **mourir s.,** to die a godly death.

Saint-Esprit [sɛ̃tɛspri] *nm* **le S.-E.,** the Holy Ghost, the Holy Spirit.

sainteté [sɛ̃tte] *nf* holiness, saintliness (*of person*); sanctity (*of the law, of a vow*); *Rel* **sa S.,** His Holiness (the Pope); *Fig* **être en odeur de s. auprès de qn,** to be in s.o.'s good books; *Fig* **je ne suis pas en odeur de s.,** I'm not popular, *F* I'm not flavour of the month.

Sainte-Touche [sɛ̃ttuʃ] *nf F* pay day.

saint-frusquin [sɛ̃fryskɛ̃] *nm no pl Arg* **tout le s.-f.,** the whole kit and caboodle, the whole damn lot.

Saint-Glinglin [sɛ̃glɛ̃glɛ̃] *adv F* **jusqu'à la S.-G.,** till the cows come home, till doomsday; **on sera payé à la S.-G.,** we'll be paid when there are two blue moons in the sky.

Saint-Graal (le) [ləsɛ̃gral] *nm Littér* the (holy) Grail.

saint-honoré [sɛ̃tɔnɔre] *nm* Saint-Honoré (*choux pastry ring filled with confectioner's sugar*); (*pl saint-honoré(s)*).

Saint-Jean (la) [lasɛ̃ʒɑ̃] *nf* Midsummer Day.

Saint-Laurent (le) [ləsɛ̃lɔrɑ̃] *nm Can Géog* the St Lawrence (river); **la Voie maritime du S.-L.,** the St Lawrence Seaway.

Saint-Lundi [sɛ̃lœ̃di] *nf F* **faire la S.-L.,** to take Monday off.

Saint-Marin [sɛ̃marɛ̃] *n* (the Republic of) San Marino.

Saint-Martin (la) [lasɛ̃martɛ̃] *nf* St Martin's day, Martinmas; **été de la S.-M.,** Indian summer.

Saint-Michel (la) [lasɛ̃miʃɛl] *nf* Michaelmas.

Saint-Office [sɛ̃tɔfis] *nm* **(a)** *Cathol* the Holy Office; **(b)** *Hist* the Inquisition.

Saint-Père (le) [ləsɛ̃pɛr] *nm Rel* the Holy Father.

saint-pierre [sɛ̃pjɛr] *nm inv* (*poisson*) John Dory.

Saint-Siège (le) [ləsɛ̃sjɛʒ] *nm Rel* the Holy See.

Saint-Simonisme [sɛ̃simɔnism] *nm Écon* Saint Simonianism, Saint-Simonism.

Saint-Sylvestre (la) [lasɛ̃silvɛstr] *nf* New Year's Eve, *Scot* Hogmanay; **faire la veillée de la S.-S.,** to see the New Year in.

saisi [sezi] *nm Jur* distrainee.

saisie [sezi] *nf* seizure (*of contraband goods etc*); *Jur* distraint, execution; foreclosure, foreclosing (*of a mortgage*); *Nau* embargo; **procès-verbal de s.,** warrant (for seizure of property); *Ordinat* **s. de données,** data capture; *Ordinat* **s. automatique/manuelle,** automatic/manual input.

saisie-arrêt [seziarɛ] *nf Jur* attachment, garnishment; *Écosse* arrestment; (*pl saisies-arrêts*).

saisir [sezir] **1** *vt* **(a)** (*attraper*) to seize, to grasp, to grab (*s.o., sth*), to take *or* catch hold of (*s.o., sth*); *Jur* to seize, to attach (*real estate, a ship*); to distrain upon (*goods*); **s. qn par le bras/au collet,** to seize *or* catch s.o. by the arm/by the collar; **s. un trône/une ville,** to seize *or* take possession of a throne/a town; **s. l'occasion (de faire qch),** to seize *or* grasp *or* jump at the opportunity (to do sth); **s. un prétexte pour faire qch,** to use a pretext to do something; *Fig* **s. la balle au bond,** to jump at the opportunity; **être saisi d'étonnement,** to be startled *or* staggered; **être saisi par le froid/la peur,** to be struck by the cold/to be overcome *or* stricken with fear; **être saisi de panique,** to be panic-stricken; *Jur* **s. une hypothèque,** to foreclose on a mortgage;

(b) to perceive, to grasp (*the truth, s.o.'s meaning*); **je n'ai pas saisi son nom,** I didn't catch his name; **mal s. qch,** to misunderstand sth; **l'artiste a bien saisi la ressemblance,** the artist has caught *or* captured the likeness;

(c) *Ordinat* to capture (*data*);

(d) *Jur* **s. un tribunal d'une affaire,** to refer a matter to a court, to lay a matter before a court; **nous sommes saisis de deux questions,** we have two questions before us; **s. la chambre d'un projet de loi,** to table a bill;

(e) *Culin* to seal (*meat*);

(f) *Nau* to stow, to secure (*the anchors, the boats*).

2 *vi* **je ne saisis pas (bien),** I don't (quite) get the idea; **il saisit vite,** he's quick (on the uptake).

3 se saisir *vpr* **se s. de qn/qch,** to seize on s.o./sth; **se s. d'un marché,** to corner a market.

saisissable [sezisabl] *adj* **(a)** perceptible, distinguishable; **(b)** *Jur* distrainable, attachable.

saisissant, -ante [sezisɑ̃, -ɑ̃t] **1** *adj* **(a)** biting (*cold*); striking (*resemblance*); gripping (*words*); thrilling (*spectacle*); **(b)** *Jur* distraining (*party*). **2** *n Jur* distrainer.

saisissement [sezismɑ̃] *nm* **(a)** (*frisson*) sudden chill; **(b)** (*émotion*) shock; **pâle de s.,** pale with emotion.

saison [sɛzɔ̃] *nf* season; **les quatres saisons,** the four seasons; **très tôt en s.,** very early in the season; **en cette s.,** at this time of year; **en toute(s) saison(s),** all (the) year round; **la s. nouvelle,** spring (time); **la mauvaise/la belle, s.,** the winter/summer months; **l'arrière-s.,** late autumn; **marchand de quatre saisons,** street merchant (*selling fruit and vegetables*); **la saison sèche/des pluies,** the dry/rainy season; **la s. des semailles,** sowing time; **la haute/basse s.,** the high/low season; **faire une bonne/mauvaise s.,** to have a good/bad season; **la s. bat son plein,** the season is in full swing *or* at its height, it is the height of the season; **la s. musicale/sportive,** the music/sporting season; **la s. de grand travail, le fort de la s.,** the busy season *or* time (of the year); **la s. creuse, la morte s.,** the off season, the slack season; **prendre ses vacances à la s. creuse,** to take one's holidays off season; **voyager pendant la s. creuse,** to travel off season; **de s.,** in season, seasonable; **le pull est de s.,** it's the weather for pullovers; **hors de s.,** (*légumes etc*) out of season; (*temps*) unseasonable; *Fig* (*remarque etc*) ill-timed, inopportune; **faire une s.,** to take a cure (*at a spa*); **travailler en s.,** *F* **faire les saisons,** to do seasonal work (*in resorts*).

saisonnier, -ière [sɛzɔnje, -jɛr] **1** *adj* seasonal. **2** *n* seasonal worker.

sajou [saʒu] *nm Zool* capuchin monkey.

saké [sake] *nm*, **saki[1]** [saki] *nm* (*boisson*) saké, saki.

saki[2] *nm Zool* saki (monkey).

salade[1] [salad] *nf* **(a)** salad; **panier à s.,** salad shaker; *Br F Vieilli* Black Maria; **faire une s.,** to make a salad; **s. de fruits,** fruit salad; **s. de homard,** lobster salad; **s. russe,** Russian salad; **haricots verts en s.,** green bean salad; *F* **mettre tout en s.,** to throw everything into confusion; **quelle s.!,** what a shambles!; *F* **salades,** (*mensonges*) lies; (*absurdités*) nonsense; **(b)** *Bot Culin* lettuce *etc*; **s. verte,** green salad.

salade[2] *nf Hist Mil* sallet, salade.

saladier [saladje] *nm* salad bowl.

salage [salaʒ] *nm* salting.

salaire [salɛr] *nm* **(a)** pay; (*mensuel*) salary; (*surtout hebdomadaire*) wage(s); **s. à la tâche** *ou* **aux pièces,** piece wage(s); **s. à forfait,** job wages; **s. au rendement,** incentive pay; **s. indexé,** index-linked pay; **s. de base,** basic wage; **s. légal,** legal rate of pay; **s. brut/net,** gross/net salary *or* wage; **s. minimum interprofessionnel de croissance,** = guaranteed minimum wage; **s. indirect,** fringe benefits; *Prov* **toute peine mérite s.,** the labourer *or US* laborer is worthy of his hire; **(b)** (*récompense*) reward, recompense, retribution; **le s. du péché,** the wages of sin.

salaison [salɛzɔ̃] *nf* (*action*) salting; (*degré*) (degree of) salinity.

salamalec [salamalɛk] *nm F* **faire des salamalecs à qn,** to bow and scrape to s.o..

salamandre [salamɑ̃dr] *nf* **(a)** salamander; **s. aquatique,** newt; **(b)** (*outil*) salamander (stove), slow-burning *or* slow-combustion stove.

salami [salami] *nm* salami.

salant [salɑ̃] *adj* salt (*marsh etc*).

salarial, -aux [salarjal, -o] *adj* **masse salariale,** wages bill, payroll; **politique salariale,** wages policy.

salariat [salarja] *nm* **(a)** wage-earning; **je préfère le s. au travail free-lance,** I'd rather work nine to five than freelance; **(b)** (*employés*) wage earners.

salarié, -ée [salarje] **1** *adj* **(a)** wage-earning; **(b)** paid (*work*). **2** *n* wage earner.

salaud [salo] *Arg* **1** *nm* bastard; **tour de s.,** dirty trick; **ah mon s.! tu ne te plains plus maintenant,** so, you old bugger, you're not complaining now. **2** *adj* rotten; **un mec s.,** a bastard; **ce qu'il est s.!,** what a bastard he is!

sale[sal] **1** *adj* **(a)** dirty; (*répugnant*) filthy; offensive, filthy, coarse (*word, story*); **de l'eau s.,** dirty water; *Phys Nucl* **bombe s.,** dirty bomb; **industrie s.,** dirty industry; *Arg* **c'était pas s.!,** it was pretty good!, it was quite something!; **(b)** *F* (*always before the noun*) nasty; **c'est un s. boulot!,** it's a rotten job; **être dans une s. affaire,** to be caught up in a dirty business; **il a une s. tête,** (*antipathique*) he looks really nasty; (*malade*) he looks rotten; **ne fais pas cette s. tête** *ou F* **gueule!,** take that look off your face!; **s. individu, s. type,** louse; **s. fasciste!,** filthy Fascist!; **s. coup,** low blow; (*action*) dirty trick; **s. temps,** filthy weather; **ah la s. bête!,** (*cet animal*) bloody animal; (*cette personne*) the beast!, the rotten thing!

2 *nm F* **mettre du linge au s.,** to put dirty clothes in the wash.

3 *n* **oh! le s.!,** what a mess you're in!

salé [sale] **1** *adj* **(a)** salt (*fish etc*); salted (*butter, nuts*); **eau salée,** salt water; (*pour conserver*) brine; **le Grand Lac S.,** the Great Salt Lake; **le potage est trop s.,** the soup is too salty; **pain s.,** lick, *Am* salt lick; **prés salés,** saltings, salt meadows; **(b)** *Fig* spicy, risqué (*tale, joke*); *F* stiff (*price, sentence*); *Arch* witty. **2** *nm* **du s.,** salt pork; **petit s.,** streaky bacon; *Arg* **un (petit) s., un morceau de s.,** (*enfant*) a brat.

salement [salmɑ̃] *adv* **(a)** dirtily; (*parler, manger*) in a disgusting manner; **(b)** *Arg* (very) badly; **j'ai s. besoin d'argent,** I'm badly in need of money; **s. difficile,** bloody difficult; **ça m'aiderait s.,** it would be a big help; **je suis s. fatigué,** I'm dog-tired, I'm pooped.

saler [sale] *vt* **(a)** to salt (*sth*), to season (*sth*) with salt; **(b)** *F* to fleece (*customers*); **s. la note,** to bump up the bill; **on nous a salés,** we were stung; **on l'a salé,** (*sanctionné*) he got a tough sentence; **(c)** to salt, to cure (*bacon etc*).

saleté [salte] *nf* **(a)** dirtiness, filthiness (*of person, street, clothes etc*); (*crasse*) dirt, filth; (*désordre*) mess; **le chat a fait ses saletés par terre,** the cat made a mess on the floor; **(b)** (*camelote*) trashy goods, rubbish, junk; (*nourriture*) junk food; **(c)** (*obscenité*) obscenity; (*remarque*) obscenity, obscene remark; (*blague*) obscene joke; **il m'a dit des saletés,** he used obscenities to me; **(d)** *F* (*personne*) bastard; **quelle s.!, il m'a roulé!,** the bastard, he's conned me!

saleur, -euse [salœr, -øz] *n* salter.

salicoque [salikɔk] *nf* prawn.

salicorne [salikɔrn] *nf Bot* glasswort, saltwort.

salicylate [salisilat] *nm Ch* salicylate.

salicylique [salisilik] *nm Ch* salicylic (acid).

salière [saljɛr] *nf* **(a)** salt cellar; (*de cuisine*) salt box; **(b)** eye socket (*of horse*); **(c)** *F* (*de clavicule*) salt cellar.

salifier [salifje] *vt* (*impf & pr sub* **n. salifiions, v. salifiiez**) *Ch* to salify.

saligaud, -aude [saligo, -od] *n Arg* (*personne sale*) dirty beast, *f* slut; *Fig* (*salaud*) bastard, *f* bitch.

salin, -ine [salɛ̃, -in] **1** *adj* saline (*solution*); salty (*taste*). **2** *nm* **(a)** (*marais*) salt marsh; **(b)** *Ch Ind* salin(e). **3** *nf* **saline (a)** (*entreprise*) salt works; **(b)** (*marais*) salt marsh.

salinage [salinaʒ] *nm* **(a)** (*entreprise*) salt works; **(b)** (*solution*) saturated solution of salt; (*concentration*) concentrating of the brine.

salingue [salɛ̃g] *Arg* **1** *adj* filthy. **2** *n* filthy *or* disgusting person.

salinier, -ière [salinje, -jɛr] **1** *adj* salt (*industry etc*). **2** *nm* (*propriétaire*) salt-mine owner; *Com* salt merchant, salter.

salinité [salinite] *nf* saltness, salinity (*of sea water etc*).

salique [salik] *adj Hist* Salic (*law*).

salir [salir] **1** *vt* to dirty, *Fml* to soil (*one's hands, clothes etc*); to make (*ship's bottom etc*) foul; **attention, ça salit les mains,** careful, it gets your hands dirty; **s. le plancher,** to make the floor dirty; (*of animal*) to make a mess on the floor; **s. sa réputation,** to tarnish *or* sully one's reputation; **s. l'idée de l'amour,** to debase the idea of love. **2 se salir** *vpr* to get dirty; to dirty *or Fml* soil one's clothes; *Fig* **elle n'aime pas se s. les mains,** she doesn't like to get her hands dirty.

salissant [salisɑ̃] *adj* **(a)** soiling, that dirties; **travail s.,** dirty *or* messy work; **(b)** easily soiled (*material etc*); **c'est peu s.,** it doesn't show the dirt.

salissure [salisyr] *nf* stain, dirty mark.

salivaire [salivɛr] *adj* salivary (*gland etc*).

salivation [salivasjɔ̃] *nf* salivation.

salive [saliv] *nf* saliva; *F* **perdre sa s.,** to waste one's breath; **pas la peine de dépenser ta s.,** don't waste your breath, save your breath.

saliver [salive] *vi* to salivate.

salle [sal] *nf* **(a)** room; *Sp* **partie en s.,** indoor game; **les salles du Louvre,** the galleries of the Louvre; **travailler en s.,** (*d'un restaurant*) to work in the dining room, to be a member of the dining room staff; **s. de séjour,** living room; **s. à manger,** dining room; (*meubles*) dining room suite; *Can* **s. à dîner,** dining room; **s. de bain(s),** bathroom; **s. d'eau,** shower room; *Scol* **s. de classe,** classroom; **s. de cours** *ou* **de conférences,** lecture room; **s. des professeurs,** staff room; **s. de restaurant,** dining room; **personnel de s.,** (*d'un restaurant*) dining room staff; **s. des fêtes,** = community hall; (*d'un village*) village hall; **s. de bal,** ballroom; **s. de récréation,** recreation room; **s. d'attente,** waiting room; **s. de départ,** departure lounge; **s. du conseil,** council room *or* chamber; *Ind etc* boardroom; **s. des dactylo(graphe)s,** typing pool; **s. de rédaction,** (*newspaper*) office; *Com etc* **s. d'exposition,** showroom; **s. de** *ou* **des ventes,** saleroom; *Ind* **s. de dessin,** drawing office; **s. des chaudières,** boiler room; **s. des machines,**

engine room; **s. d'exploitation radar,** radar operations room; **s. de contrôle,** (*of spacecraft*) control room; **s. de cinéma,** cinema; **les salles obscures,** the cinema, the movies; *Cin TV* **s. de régie,** control room; *Cin* **s. de projection** *ou* **de vision,** viewing room; **s. des pas perdus,** concourse (*of railway station etc*); lobby (*of Houses of Parliament*); waiting hall (*of law courts*); **s. d'hôpital,** (hospital) ward; **s. d'opérations,** operating theatre *or Am* room; *Mil* **s. de garde,** guardroom; **s. de service,** orderly room; **s. des opérations,** operations room;

(b) *Th etc* auditorium, house; **s. pleine,** (*sur panneau*) full house; **on joue à s. pleine depuis un mois,** we've been playing to full houses for a month; **faire s. comble,** to have a full house; **toute la s. applaudit,** the whole house *or* audience applauded.

salmigondis [salmigɔ̃di] *nm* hotchpotch.

salmis [salmi] *nm Culin* salmi (*game half-cooked by roasting then stewed in a wine sauce*).

salmonella [salmɔnɛla] *nf inv*, **salmonelle** [salmɔnɛl] *nf Méd* salmonella.

salmonellose [salmɔneloz] *nf Méd Vét* salmonellosis, *F* salmonella poisoning.

salmoniculteur, -trice [salmɔnikyltœr, -tris] *n* salmon farmer.

salmoniculture [salmɔnikyltyr] *nf* salmon farming.

saloir [salwar] *nm* **(a)** (*pour salaisons*) salting tub; **(b)** *Vieilli* (*salière*) salt sprinkler.

Salomon [salɔmɔ̃] *nm* Solomon; **les îles S.,** the Solomon Islands.

salon [salɔ̃] *nm* **(a)** sitting room, *surtout Br* lounge, drawing room; **petit s.,** morning room; (*meubles*) three- piece suite; **s. réservé,** (*in hotel etc*) private room; **jeux de s.,** parlour *or US* parlor games; **(b)** saloon, cabin (*in ship etc*); saloon car (*in train*); **(c)** *Com* **s. de thé,** tea room(s); **s. de coiffure,** hairdressing salon; **(d)** (*art etc*) exhibition; (*motor, boat, trade*) show; **s. de livre,** book fair; **(e)** *Littér Hist* salon.

saloon [salun] *nm* saloon; **porte de s.,** saloon door.

salop, -ope [salo, -ɔp] *Arg* **1** *n* bastard, *f* bitch. **2** *nf* **salope,** prostitute, tart.

salopard [salɔpar] *nm* **(a)** *Arg* bastard; **(b)** *Hist* rebel fighter.

saloper [salɔpe] *vt Arg* to botch (*a piece of work*).

saloperie [salɔpri] *nf F* **(a)** (*désordre*) mess; (*camelote*) rubbish, junk; **tu ne vas pas manger cette s.!,** you're not going to eat that rubbish *or* junk!; **(b)** (*coup bas*) dirty trick; **(c) dire des saloperies,** to talk smut, to talk dirty.

salopette [salɔpɛt] *nf* dungarees, overalls, *Am* coverall(s).

salpêtrage [salpɛtraʒ] *nm* **(a)** (*formation*) manufacture *or* formation of saltpetre *or US* saltpeter; **(b)** (*traitement*) treatment with saltpetre *or US* saltpeter.

salpêtre [salpɛtr] *nm* **(a)** *Ch* saltpetre, *US* saltpeter; **(b)** (*sur les murs*) saltpetre *or US* saltpeter rot.

salpêtrer [salpetre] *vt* **(a)** to cover *or* treat (*ground*) with saltpetre *or US* saltpeter; **(b)** to rot (*walls*).

salpicon [salpikɔ̃] *nm Culin* = meat or fish and diced vegetables in sauce, used as filling for vol-au-vent etc.

salpingite [salpɛ̃ʒit] *nf Méd* salpingitis.

salsa [salsa] *nf* salsa.

salse [sals] *nf Geol* salse, mud volcano.

salsepareille [salsəparɛj] *nf Bot Pharm* sarsaparilla.

salsifis [salsifi] *nm Bot Culin* salsify.

saltatoire [saltatwar] *adj Ent Méd* saltatory.

saltimbanque [saltɛ̃bɑ̃k] *n* acrobat.

salubre [salybr] *adj* healthy (*climate, diet*).

salubrité [salybrite] *nf* healthiness (*of climate etc*); **s. publique,** public health.

saluer [salɥe] **1** *vt* **(a)** to greet (*s.o.*); (*faire la révérence*) to bow to (*s.o.*); **s. qn d'un coup de chapeau,** to raise one's hat to s.o.; **s. qn de la main,** to wave to s.o.; **passer qn sans le s.,** to cut s.o. (dead); *Th* **s. le public,** to bow to the audience; *Billard* **s. la bille,** to miss; **s. qn par un vivat,** to cheer s.o.; **la loi a été froidement saluée par l'opposition,** the bill got a cool reception from the opposition; **saluez-le de ma part,** give him my regards; *Bible* **Je vous salue, Marie ...,** hail, Mary; **s. qn comme ...,** to hail s.o. as ...; **je salue en lui notre sauveur,** I salute him as our saviour;

(b) *Nau* **s. un grain,** to reduce sail for a squall.

2 *vi* **s. en se découvrant,** to raise one's hat in greeting; *Mil etc* **s. du drapeau,** to lower the colour, *US* to droop the color; *Nau* **s. (du pavillon),** to dip (the flag); **s. de vingt coups,** to fire a twenty gun salute.

3 se saluer *vpr* to great each other.

salure [salyr] *nf* saltness.

salut [saly] *nm* **(a)** (*sauvegarde*) safety; saving (*of lives, souls*); *Rel* salvation; **chercher son s. dans la fuite,** to fly for one's life; **port de s.,** haven of refuge; **c'est sa seule planche de s.,** it's his only lifeline; **faire son s.,** to find salvation; **travailler à son s.,** to work out one's own salvation; **l'Armée du S.,** the Salvation Army;

(b) (*salutation*) greeting, salutation; **adresser un s. à qn,** (*de la main*) to wave to s.o., to give s.o. a wave; (*en se découvrant*) to raise one's hat to s.o.; *F* **s. (à tous)!,** hullo, hello, hi(, everybody)!; (*on leaving*) so long (everybody)!; *F* **bonjour, s.!,** hullo, how are you?;

(c) *Mil etc* salute; **faire un s.,** to give a salute; **faire le s. militaire,** to salute; **s. du drapeau,** lowering of the colour, *US* drooping of the color; *Nau* **s. du pavillon,** dipping of the flag;

(d) *Cathol* Benediction (of the Holy Sacrament).

salutaire [salytɛr] *adj* salutary, beneficial.

salutation [salytɑsjɔ̃] *nf* salutation, greeting; **agréez** *ou* **veuillez agréer mes meilleures salutations,** (*dans une lettre*) yours sincerely; **salutations distinguées,** (*dans une lettre*) yours sincerely.

salutiste [salytist] *n* member of the Salvation Army, Salvationist.

salvateur, -trice [salvatœr, -tris] *adj Litt* saving.

salve [salv] *nf Mil* (*de petites armes*) salvo, volley; **tirer une s. (d'honneur),** to fire a salute; **s. d'applaudissements,** burst of applause.

samare [samar] *nf Bot* (*sycamore etc*) key.

samaritain, -aine [samaritɛ̃, -ɛn] *Bible* **1** *adj* Samaritan. **2** *n* **S.,** Samaritan; **le bon S.,** the good Samaritan; *Fig* **faire le bon S.,** to be a good Samaritan.

samedi [samdi] *nm* Saturday; **le S. saint,** (the) Saturday before Easter, Holy Saturday.

samizdat [samizdat] *nm* samizdat.

samouraï, samurai [samuraj] *nm Hist Japonaise* samurai.

samovar [samɔvar] *nm* samovar.

sampan(g) [sɑ̃pɑ̃] *nm* sampan.

SAMU [samy] *nm* (*abrév* **service d'aide médicale d'urgence**) = emergency ambulance service; **appelez le S.!,** ≈ call an ambulance!

sana [sana] *nm F* sanatorium.

sanatorium [sanatɔrjɔm] *nm* sanatorium.

sanctificateur, -trice [sɑ̃ktifikatœr, -tris] **1** *adj* sanctifying. **2** *n* sanctifier; **le S.,** the Holy Ghost, the Sanctifier.

sanctification [sɑ̃ktifikɑsjɔ̃] *nf* sanctification.

sanctifier [sɑ̃ktifje] *vt* (*impf & pr sub* **n. sanctifiions, v. sanctifiiez**) to sanctify, to make holy; **que Ton nom soit sanctifié,** hallowed be Thy Name.

sanction [sɑ̃ksjɔ̃] *nf* **(a)** (*approbation*) sanction, approval, assent; **(b) s. (pénale),** sanction, penalty, punishment; *Pol* **prendre des sanctions contre un pays/contre des grévistes,** to impose sanctions on a country/to take action against strikers; **la s. de la paresse,** the price *or* consequence of laziness; **c'est la s. du succès,** that's the price of success.

sanctionner [sɑ̃ksjɔne] *vt* **(a)** (*approuver*) to sanction, to approve; **sanctionné par l'usage,** sanctioned by custom; **(b)** to sanction, to penalize (*offence, person*); to attach a penalty to (*decree*).

sanctuaire [sɑ̃ktɥɛr] *nm* sanctuary; **ce s. qu'est l'ambassade,** the sanctuary offered by the embassy.

sanctus [sɑ̃ktys] *nm Rel Mus* sanctus.

sandale [sɑ̃dal] *nf* sandal.

sandalette [sɑ̃dalɛt] *nf* light sandal.

sandow ® [sɑ̃do] *nm* **(a)** *Gym* chest expander; **(b)** *MecE Av etc* rubber extensible spring.

sandwich [sɑ̃dwi(t)ʃ] *nm* sandwich; **s. au jambon,** ham sandwich; **homme(-)s.,** sandwich man; **verre s.,** laminated glass; *F* **pris en s.,** stuck, sandwiched (**entre,** between); (*pl sandwich(e)s*).

sandwicherie [sɑ̃dwi(t)ʃəri] *nf* sandwich bar.

sang [sɑ̃] *nm* **(a)** blood; **animaux à s. chaud/froid,** warm-blooded/cold-blooded animals; **coup de s.,** stroke; **yeux injectés de s.,** bloodshot eyes; **répandre** *ou* **verser le s.,** to shed blood; **battre qn jusqu'au s.,** to punch s.o. till he bleeds; **il y a du s. versé entre eux,** there's bad blood between them; **verser du s. pour la patrie,** to shed one's blood for one's country; **victoire sans effusion de s.,** bloodless victory; **le pays a été mis à feu et à s.,** the country was put to fire and sword; **laver un outrage par le s.,** to avenge an insult with blood; **le prix du sang,** blood money; **écoulement de s.,** bleeding, haemorrhage, *US* hemorrhage; **je n'arrive pas à arrêter le s.,** I can't stop the bleeding; **donner son s.,** to give blood; **donneur de s.,** blood donor; **il était tout en s.,** he was covered with blood; **avoir du s. sur les mains,** to have blood on one's hands; **taché de s.,** bloodstained; *Fig* **il est tâché de s.,** he has blood on his hands, he's a killer; **avoir le rythme dans le s.,** to have a(n innate) sense of rhythm; *Fig* **avoir le s. chaud,** to be hot-blooded; **le s. lui monta au visage,** the blood rushed to his face; **cela fait bouillir le s.,** it makes your blood boil; **cela me glace le s.,** it makes my blood run cold; **il n'a pas de s. dans les veines,** he's gutless; **avoir du s. de navet,** to be spineless, to be a yellow-belly; **se faire du mauvais s., se manger les sangs,** to worry; **se faire un s. d'encre,** to worry oneself sick; **suer s. et eau** [sɑ̃keo], to sweat blood; **cela m'a fouetté le s.,** that got my adrenalin going; **conte à tourner les sangs,** bloodcurdling tale; **tout mon s. n'a fait qu'un tour,** my heart missed a beat; *Ind etc* **apport en s. frais,** new blood; *(argent)* fresh *or* additional capital; *Arg* **bon s. (de bon soir)!, bon s. de bon Dieu!,** damn and blast it!; *Arg* **bon s. d'imbécile!,** (you) bloody fool!;

(b) *(race, lignée)* blood; **Indiens pur s.,** full-blooded Indians; **(homme de) s. mêlé,** half-caste; **avoir du s.,** *(of horse)* to be blooded; **cheval de s.,** blood horse; **cheval pur s.,** thoroughbred; **c'est dans le s.,** it's in his *or* our *etc* blood; **son propre s.,** one's own flesh and blood; **s. bleu,** blue blood; **c'est un s. bleu,** he's an aristocrat, he has blue blood (in his veins); **droit du s.,** birthright.

sang-froid [sɑ̃frwa] *nm no pl* coolness, composure, *Litt* sang-froid; **garder** *ou* **conserver son s.-f.,** to keep (one's) cool; **perdre son s.-f.,** to lose one's self-control; **faire qch de s.-f.,** to do sth calmly *or* coolly; **tuer qn de s.-f.,** to kill s.o. in cold blood.

sanglant [sɑ̃glɑ̃] *adj* **(a)** bloody *(wound, battle, tale)*; bloodstained *(handkerchief etc)*; **(b)** cruel *(reproach etc)*; **critique sanglante,** scathing criticism; **affront s.,** deadly insult.

sangle [sɑ̃gl] *nf* strap; *(harnais)* girth; *(de meuble)* webbing; **lit de s.,** camp bed.

sangler [sɑ̃gle] *vt* to girth *(horse)*; **sanglé dans son uniforme,** buttoned up tight in his uniform.

sanglier [sɑ̃glije] *nm* (wild) boar.

sanglot [sɑ̃glo] *nm* sob; **pousser un s.,** to give a sob; **éclater en sanglots,** to burst into sobs *or* tears; **il pleurait à gros sanglots,** he was sobbing his heart out; **avec des sanglots dans la voix,** in a tearful voice, strangling a sob.

sangloter [sɑ̃glɔte] *vi* to sob.

sang-mêlé [sɑ̃mele] *nm inv* person of mixed blood, half-caste; *(in South Africa)* coloured, *US* colored (person).

sangria [sɑ̃grija] *nf* sangria.

sangsue [sɑ̃sy] *nf* leech.

sanguin, -ine [sɑ̃gɛ̃, -in] **1** *adj* **(a)** *Anat* (of) blood; **groupe s.,** blood group; **produits sanguins,** blood products; **transfusion sanguine,** blood transfusion; **(b)** sanguine *(temperament)*; ruddy *(complexion)*. **2** *nm Bot* dogwood. **3** *nf* **sanguine (a)** *(craie)* red chalk, sanguine; **(b)** *Minér* bloodstone; **(c)** *(orange)* blood orange.

sanguinaire [sɑ̃ginɛr] *adj* bloodthirsty *(man)*; bloody *(fight)*.

sanguinelle [sɑ̃ginɛl] *nf Bot* dogwood.

sanguinolent [sɑ̃ginɔlɑ̃] *adj* **(a)** tinged with blood; **(b)** *Biol* blood-red.

sanie [sani] *nf Med* pus, *Spéc* sanies.

sanitaire [sanitɛr] **1** *adj* **(a)** medical *(staff, equipment)*; health *(measures)*; *Mil etc* **voiture s.,** ambulance; **(b)** sanitary *(equipment, engineering)*; **bloc s.,** *(dans un camping)* toilet *or* sanitary block; **système s.,** sanitation. **2** *nm* **le s.,** *F* **les sanitaires,** sanitary installations, (the) plumbing; *F* **aller aux sanitaires,** to use the facilities, *Hum* to inspect the plumbing. **3** *nf Mil etc* ambulance.

sans [sɑ̃] *prép* **(a)** without; **s. queue,** without a tail; **partez s. moi,** go without me; **il est revenu s. argent** *ou* **s. un sou** *ou* **s. le sou,** he came back without any money *or* without a penny; **elle arriva s. argent ni bagages,** she arrived without any *or* either money or luggage; **s. faute,** without fail; **demain s. faute,** tomorrow without fail; **suffisant, s. plus,** adequate but no more (than that); **s. parler,** without speaking; **cela va s. dire,** it goes without saying; **il va s. dire que c'est une réussite,** it's a success, needless to say; **vous n'êtes pas s. le connaître,** you must know him; **tu n'es pas s. savoir que ...,** you know very well that ...; **ces questions n'étaient pas s. m'embarrasser,** these questions were naturally somewhat embarrassing; **sans plus attendre,** without further delay, immediately; **non s. difficulté,** not without difficulty; *F* **que ferais-tu s.?,** how would you manage without?;

(b) **s. que** + *sub*, without + *gerund*; **s. que nous le sachions,** without our knowing; **il ne parlait jamais s. qu'on lui parlât,** he never spoke unless he was spoken to;

(c) -less, -lessly, -free; un-; **plaintes s. fin,** endless complaints; **se plaindre s. fin,** to complain endlessly; **être s. le sou,** to be broke *or* penniless; **couple sans enfants,** childless couple; **s. sel/phosphates/***etc*, salt/phosphate/*etc*-free; **baignade s. danger,** safe bathing; **s. cesse,** unceasingly; **s. mot dire, s. dire un mot,** without saying a word; **regarder qn s. mot dire,** to look at s.o. without saying a word; **s. hésiter,** unhesitatingly, without hesitating;

(d) **s. vous je ne l'aurais jamais fait,** if it hadn't been for you *or* but for you, I would never have done it; **s. cela, s. quoi,** otherwise; *F* **sois sage, s. ça tu seras puni!,** be good or (else) you'll be punished!

sans-abri [sɑ̃zabri] *n inv* homeless person.

sans-cœur [sɑ̃kœr] *n inv F* heartless person.

sanscrit [sɑ̃skri] *adj & nm Ling* Sanskrit.

sans-culotte [sɑ̃kylɔt] *nm Hist (Fr Revolution)* sans culotte *(person with extreme republican sympathies)*; *(pl sans-culottes)*.

sans-emploi [sɑ̃zɑ̃plwa] *n inv* unemployed *or* jobless person; **le nombre des s.-e. augmente,** the unemployment *or* jobless figure is rising.

sans-façon [sɑ̃fasɔ̃] **1** *nm* bluntness *(of speech etc)*; *(naturel)* informality; *(indifférence)* offhand manner. **2** *adj (naturel)* informal; *(indifférent)* offhand.

sans-faute [sɑ̃fot] *nm inv Sp* clear round; **accomplir** *ou* **faire un s.-f.,** *(d'un cheval)* to have a clear round; *Fig (d'un candidat)* to turn in a faultless performance, not to put a foot wrong.

sans-fil [sɑ̃fil] *Vieilli* **1** *nf inv* wireless. **2** *nm inv* radio *or* wireless message.

sans-gêne [sɑ̃ʒɛn] **1** *nm* offhandedness. **2** *adj inv* offhand *(person)*; **qu'est-ce qu'il est s.-g.!,** he's got a cheek!

sanskrit [sɑ̃skri] *adj & nm Ling* Sanskrit.

sans-le-sou [sɑ̃ləsu] *F* **1** *adj inv* broke. **2** *n inv* **c'est un s.-le-s.,** he's broke.

sans-logis [sɑ̃lɔʒi] *n inv* homeless person.

sansonnet [sɑ̃sɔnɛ] *nm (oiseau)* starling; *F* **c'est de la roupie de s.,** it's rubbish.

sans-parti [sɑ̃parti] *n inv Pol* independent.

sans-patrie [sɑ̃patri] *n inv* stateless person.

sans-soin [sɑ̃swɛ̃] *n inv F* careless person.

sans-souci [sɑ̃susi] *adj inv* happy-go-lucky.

santal [sɑ̃tal] *nm* sandalwood.

santé [sɑ̃te] *nf* health; **être en bonne s.,** to be well, to be in good health; **s. de fer,** iron constitution; **ne pas avoir de s., avoir une s. fragile** *ou* **délicate,** *F* **avoir une petite s.,** to have poor health, to be delicate; *F* **comment va la s.?,** how's things?, how's tricks?; **respirer la s.,** to look the picture of health; **absent pour raison de s.,** absent for health reasons *or* on medical grounds; **maison de s.,** (private) nursing home, clinic; **boire à la s. de qn,** to drink s.o.'s health; **à votre s.!,** your health!, *F* cheers!; *Suisse F* **s.!,** *(when s.o. sneezes)* bless you!; *Admin* **Ministère de la S. et de la Sécurité sociale,** Department of Health and Social Security; **médecin de la s.,** medical officer of health; *Nau* **agent de (la) s.,** quarantine officer.

santiag [sɑ̃tjag] *nf* cowboy boot.

santon [sɑ̃tɔ̃] *nm (in Provence)* clay *or* carved wood figure *(in Christmas crib)*.

saoul [su] **, saoulard** [sular] **, saouler** [sule] = **SOÛL, SOÛLARD, SOÛLER**.

sapajou [sapaʒu] *nm Zool* sapajou.

sape [sap] *nf* **(a)** undermining *(of wall, tower etc)*; *Mil* sapping; **(b)** *(tranchée)* sap, trench; **(c)** *(outil)* mattock; **(d)** *pl Arg* **sapes,** *(vêtements)* togs.

saper [sape] **1** *vt* **(a)** *Mil etc & Fig* to undermine; **s. le moral de qn,** to sap s.o.'s morale; **(b)** *Arg* to dress; **être bien sapé,** to be well dressed. **2 se saper** *vpr* to get dolled up.

saperlipopette [sapɛrlipɔpɛt] **, saperlotte** [sapɛrlɔt] *int Arch* gad!

sapeur [sapœr] *nm Mil* sapper; *F* **fumer comme un s.,** to smoke like a chimney.

sapeur-pompier [sapœrpɔ̃pje] *nm Admin* fireman, *Am* fire fighter; **les sapeurs-pompiers,** the fire brigade, *Am* the fire fighters.

saphique [safik] *adj* Sapphic.

saphir [safir] *nm* sapphire.

saphisme [safism] *nm* sapphism.

sapin [sapɛ̃] *nm* **(a)** fir (tree); *Com* **(bois de) s.,** deal; **(b)** *F (cercueil)* coffin; **sentir le s.,** to have one foot in the grave; **toux qui sent le s.,** churchyard cough; **(c)** *Can* **se faire**

passer un s., (*se faire avoir*) to be taken for a ride.
sapine [sapin] *nf* **(a)** (*planche*) deal board; **(b)** *Constr* crane tower; **(c)** (*en viticulture*) deal tub.
sapinière [sapinjɛr] *nf* fir plantation.
saponacé [sapɔnase] *adj* saponaceous.
saponaire [sapɔnɛr] *nf Bot* soapwort.
saponifiant [sapɔnifjɑ̃] *Ch* **1** *adj* saponifying. **2** *nm* saponifier, saponifying agent.
saponification [sapɔnifikɑsjɔ̃] *nf* saponification.
saponifier [sapɔnifje] *vt* (*impf & pr sub* **n. saponifiions, v. saponifiiez**) to saponify.
saponite [sapɔnit] *nf Minér* saponite.
sapristi [sapristi] *int F* good heavens!
saprophage [saprɔfaʒ] *adj Ent* saprophagous.
saprophyte [saprɔfit] *nm Biol* saprophyte.
saquebute [sakbyt] *nf Mus Arch* sackbut.
saquer[1] [sake] *vt Nau* to jerk (*heavy body*) along.
saquer[2] *vt F* = **SAQUER**.
sarabande [sarabɑ̃d] *nf* (*danse*) *& Mus* saraband; *F* uproar, bedlam; **ils ont fait la s. toute la nuit,** they kicked up a racket all night long.
sarbacane [sarbakan] *nf* blowpipe; (*toy*) peashooter.
sarcasme [sarkasm] *nm* (piece of) sarcasm.
sarcastique [sarkastik] *adj* sarcastic.
sarcelle [sarsɛl] *nf* teal.
sarclage [sarklaʒ] *nm* weeding.
sarcler [sarkle] *vt* **(a)** to weed (*garden etc*); to hoe (*soil, crop*); to clean (*field*); **plante sarclée,** root crop; **(b)** to hoe (*weeds*) up *or* out.
sarclet [sarklɛ] *nm*, **sarclette** [sarklɛt] *nf* (weeding) hoe.
sarcloir [sarklwar] *nm* (weeding) hoe.
sarcome [sarkom] *nm Méd* sarcoma; **s. de Kaposi,** Kaposi's sarcoma.
sarcophage [sarkɔfaʒ] **1** *nm* sarcophagus. **2** *nf Ent* bluebottle.
sarcoplasme [sarkɔplasm] *nm Anat* sarcoplasm(a).
sarcopte [sarkɔpt] *nm Zool* sarcoptid.
Sardaigne [sardɛɲ] *nf* Sardinia.
sarde [sard] **1** *adj* Sardinian. **2** *n* **S.,** Sardinian. **3** *nf* (*poisson*) bonito.
sardine [sardin] *nf* **(a)** sardine; **boîte de sardines,** tin of sardines; *F* **serrés comme des sardines,** packed like sardines; **(b)** *Mil F* N.C.O.'s stripe; **(c)** (*de tente*) tent peg.
sardinerie [sardinri] *nf* sardine cannery.
sardinier, -ière [sardinje, -jɛr] **1** *n* (*pêcheur*) sardine fisher; (*ouvrier*) sardine packer. **2** *nm* (*filet*) sardine net; (*bateau*) sardine boat.
sardonique [sardɔnik] *adj* sardonic.
sardonyx [sardɔniks] *nf Minér* sardonyx.
sargasse [sargas] *nf* sargasso, gulf weed; **la mer des Sargasses,** the Sargasso Sea.
sari [sari] *nm* sari.
sariette [sarjɛt] *nf Bot Culin* savory.
sarigue [sarig] *nf* opossum.
S.A.R.L. [ɛsaɛrɛl] *nf* (*abrév* **société anonyme à responsabilité limitée**) = limited liability company; *Br* ≈ Ltd; (*coté en Bourse*) plc.
sarment [sarmɑ̃] *nm* (*tige*) bine; (*de vigne*) vine shoot.
sarmenteux, -euse [sarmɑ̃tø, -øz] *adj* climbing (*plant*).
sarong [sarɔ̃] *nm* sarong.
sarrasin, -ine [sarazɛ̃, -in] **1** *adj Hist* Saracen. **2** *n Hist* **S.,** Saracen. **3** *nm Agr* buckwheat. **4** *nf* **sarrasine,** portcullis.
sarrau [saro] *nm* overall, smock.
Sarre (la) [lasar] *nf* the Saar.
sarriette [sarjɛt] *nf Bot Culin* savory.
sas[1] [sɑ] *nm* sieve; **passer qch au s.,** to sift *or* sieve sth.
sas[2] *nm* **(a)** *HydE* lock chamber, coffer; **(b)** *Constr Nau Astronaut* airlock.
sassafras [sasafrɑ] *nm Bot* sassafras.
sassage[1] [sasaʒ] *nm* sifting, sieving.
sassage[2] *nm* passing (*of a boat*) through a lock.
sassement [sasmɑ̃] *nm* = **SASSAGE**[1,2].
sasser[1] [sase] *vt* to sift (*flour*); to bolt, to screen (*flour, plaster*); to winnow (*grain*); *Min* to jig (*ore*).
sasser[2] *vt* to pass (*a boat*) through a lock.
sasseur, -euse [sasœr, -øz] *n* sifter.
Satan [satɑ̃] *nm* Satan.
satané [satane] *adj F* confounded; **s. temps!,** filthy weather!
satanique [satanik] *adj* satanic; fiendish (*cruelty, idea, grin etc*).
satanisme [satanism] *nm* satanism.
satellisation [satelizɑsjɔ̃] *nf* **(a)** *Astron* putting into orbit (*of satellite, spacecraft*); **programme de s.,** space programme; **(b)** *Pol* (*of country*) becoming a satellite (state); making (*of a country*) into a satellite state.
satelliser [satelize] **1** *vt* **(a)** *Astron* to put (*satellite, spacecraft, man etc*) into orbit; **(b)** *Fig Pol* to make (*a country*) into a satellite (state). **2 se satelliser** *vpr* **(a)** *Astron* to go into orbit; **(b)** *Fig Pol* to become a satellite (state).
satellite [satelit] **1** *nm* **(a)** *Astron* satellite; **s. artificiel,** artificial satellite; **s. terrestre/lunaire,** earth-orbiting/moon-orbiting satellite; **s. de télécommunications,** (tele)communications satellite, *F* comsat; *TV* **retransmis par s.,** transmitted by satellite; **émission retransmise par s.,** satellite broadcast; **télévision par s.,** satellite television; **s. météorologique,** weather *or* meteorological satellite, *F* metsat; **(b)** *Fig Pol* satellite (state); **(c)** *Tech* planet wheel, bevel gear; **engrenage à satellites,** (sun-and-)planet gear. **2** *adj* **(a)** *Anat* **veines satellites,** companion veins; **(b)** *Fig Pol* **pays s.,** satellite state; **agglomération s.,** satellite town.
satiété [sasjete] *nf* satiety; **manger/boire à s.,** to eat/drink one's fill; **se détendre à s.,** to relax fully *or* completely; **j'ai ri/parlé à s.,** I laughed/talked until I couldn't laugh/talk any more.
satin [satɛ̃] *nm* **(a)** *Tex* satin; **(b) bois de s.,** satinwood; **(c)** *Bot* **s. blanc,** honesty.
satinage [satinaʒ] *nm* satining (*of ribbon, cloth*); glazing (*of leather*); hot pressing (*of paper, linen*); surfacing (*of paper*); *Phot* burnishing, enamelling (*of print*).
satiné [satine] **1** *adj* satiny, satin-like (*material*); glazed (*leather, paper*); **peinture satinée,** gloss (paint). **2** *nm* gloss; (*d'un tissu*) smoothness.
satiner [satine] *vt* to give a glossy surface to (*material etc*); to glaze (*leather*).
satinette [satinɛt] *nf Tex* sateen, satinet(te).
satire [satir] *nf* satire (**contre,** on; **de,** of); **trait de s.,** epigram; **faire la s. de son époque,** to satirize one's times.
satirique [satirik] **1** *adj* satiric(al). **2** *n* satirist.
satiriquement [satirikmɑ̃] *adv* satirically.
satiriser [satirize] *vt* to satirize.
satisfaction [satisfaksjɔ̃] *nf* **(a)** satisfaction; **la s. du travail bien fait,** the satisfaction of a job well done; **s. par le travail,** job satisfaction; **donner de la s. à qn,** to give s.o. satisfaction; **donner s. aux vœux de qn,** to satisfy s.o.'s desires; **avoir la s. de faire qch,** to have the satisfaction of doing sth; **nous avons la s. de pouvoir dire que ...,** it gives us great satisfaction to be able to say that ...; **je n'ai pas trouvé** *ou* **obtenu entière s. avec ce nouveau produit,** I was not entirely satisfied with the new product; **à la s. générale,** to everyone's satisfaction; **j'ai eu une s. aujourd'hui,** one good thing happened today; **(b)** reparation, amends (**pour, de,** for); *Rel* atonement.
satisfaire [satisfɛr] *v* (*conj like* **faire**) **1** *vt* **(a)** to satisfy, to please (*s.o.*); to satisfy, to gratify (*one's curiosity etc*); (*sexuellement*) to satisfy (*s.o.*); **s. le désir de qn,** (*l'accomplir*) to carry out s.o.'s wish; **s. l'attente de qn,** to come up to s.o.'s expectations; **de manière à vous s.,** to your satisfaction; **s. sa faim,** to appease one's hunger; **s. ses interlocuteurs,** to satisfy one's questioners;

(b) to make amends to (*s.o.*); *Rel* to make atonement for, to atone for.

2 se satisfaire *vpr* **(a) se s. de peu,** to be content with very little;

(b) (*de ses besoins naturels*) to relieve oneself; (*de ses besoins sexuels*) to achieve satisfaction.

3 *vi* **(a) s. à,** to satisfy, to meet (*demand, requirement, condition, objection*); to satisfy, to fulfil, to carry out (*one's wishes*); to comply with (*regulation etc*); **s. à une examen,** to satisfy the examiners;

(b) *Arch* **s. à qn,** to give s.o. satisfaction (*in duel*).
satisfaisant [satisfəzɑ̃] *adj* satisfactory (*reply, work*); satisfying (*meal*).
satisfait, -aite [satisfɛ, -ɛt] **1** *adj* satisfied; (*désir, vœu*) fulfilled; *Iron* **vous voilà s.!,** well, you asked for it!; **je n'en suis pas s.,** I'm not satisfied, I'm not pleased with it *or* not happy about it; **être s. de sa nouvelle voiture,** to be satisfied *or* pleased *or* happy with one's new car; *Com* **j'espère que vous en serez entièrement s.,** I trust it will give you complete satisfaction; **femme satisfaite,** (*sexuellement*) satisfied woman; **mal s.,** dissatisfied (**de,** with). **2** *n* satisfied *or* contented person.
satsuma [satsyma] **1** *nm Cér* Satsuma ware. **2** *nf* satsuma (orange).
saturable [satyrabl] *adj* saturable.
saturant [satyrɑ̃] *adj* saturating, saturant; **vapeur saturante,** saturated vapour.
saturateur [satyratœr] *nm Ch Ind* saturator;

(*humidificateur*) humidifier.

saturation [satyrasjɔ̃] *nf* saturation; **arriver à s.,** to reach saturation point; **campagne de s.,** (*in advertising*) saturation campaign; **s. du marché,** market saturation.

saturé [satyre] *adj* saturated (*solution, compound*); *Com* **le marché est s.,** the market is saturated *or* has reached saturation point; **ville saturée,** overcrowded city; **j'en suis s.,** I'm sick of it *or* them.

saturer [satyre] *vt* to saturate (**de,** with); *Fig* **elle nous sature d'anecdotes,** she's forever telling us stories.

saturnales [satyrnal] *nfpl Antiq & Fig* saturnalia.

Saturne [satyrn] *nm Myth Astron* Saturn.

saturnie [satyrni] *nf Ent* emperor moth.

saturnien, -ienne [satyrnjɛ̃, -jɛn] *adj* saturnine.

saturnin, -ine [satyrnɛ̃, -in] *adj Méd* **intoxication saturnine,** lead poisoning.

saturnisme [satyrnism] *nm Méd* lead poisoning.

satyre [satir] *nm* **(a)** *Myth Ent* satyr; **(b)** *F* sex maniac.

satyrique [satirik] *adj Antiq* satyric.

sauce [sos] *nf* **(a)** *Culin* sauce; **s. aux champignons,** mushroom sauce; **rallonger la s.,** to water down the sauce; *Fig F* to pad out a book; to spin out a story; *F* **accommoder un même sujet à toutes les sauces,** to dish up the same subject in every shape; *F* **on l'a mis à toutes les sauces,** they put him to good use, they used him at every opportunity; *F* **il suffit de varier la s.,** all that's needed is to change the presentation a little; *Fig* **à quelle s. sera-t-il mangé?,** how shall we deal with it *or* him?; *F* **c'est la même politique servie à une autre s.,** same meat, different gravy!; *F* **être dans la s.,** to be in the soup; **(b)** (*craie noire*) soft black crayon, black chalk, lamp black; **(c)** *Fig F* (*pluie*) shower.

saucée [sose] *nf F* (*pluie*) downpour; **recevoir une s.,** to get soaked *or* a soaking.

saucer [sose] *vt* (**je sauçai(s); n. sauçons**) **(a)** to mop up the sauce from (*one's plate*); **(b)** *F* **se faire s.,** to get soaked *or* wet through, to get a soaking.

saucette [sosɛt] *nf Can F* **faire une s.,** to have a quick screw *or* a quickie; **faire une s. à Québec,** to make a quick trip to Quebec City, to pop over to Quebec City.

saucier [sosje] *nm* sauce cook.

saucière [sosjɛr] *nf* sauce boat.

sauciflard [sosiflar] *nm Arg* (*saucisse*) sausage, *Br* banger.

saucisse [sosis] *nf* **(a)** sausage; *F* **il n'attache pas son chien avec des saucisses,** he's careful with his money; **(b)** *Arg* idiot, *Br* nit; **(c)** *Mil F* barrage balloon.

saucisson [sosisɔ̃] *nm* **(a)** sausage; **s. à l'ail,** garlic sausage; *F* **elle est toujours ficelée comme un s.,** she's always bulging *or* bursting out of her clothes; **(b)** *Arg* idiot, *Br* nit; **(c)** (*pain*) cylindrical loaf; **(d)** (*de poudre*) powder hose.

saucissonné [sosisɔne] *adj F* trussed up; **s. dans son collant,** poured into her tights.

saucissonner [sosisɔne] *F* **1** *vt* to tie up like a sausage. **2** *vi* to picnic, to eat a snack.

saucissonneur, -euse [sosisɔnœr, -øz] *n F* picnicker.

sauf¹, sauve [sof, sov] *adj* safe, unscathed, unhurt; **sain et s.,** safe and sound; **s'en tirer la vie sauve,** to come off unscathed; **l'honneur est s.,** honour is saved *or* intact.

sauf² *prép* except (for); **il est indemne s. une écorchure au bras,** he is unhurt except for *or* apart from *or* save for a grazed arm; **elle n'a rien s. son salaire,** she has nothing except (for) *or* apart from her wages; **s. correction,** subject to correction; **s. avis contraire,** unless you *or* I *etc* hear to the contrary; **s. indication contraire,** unless otherwise stated *or* specified; **s. de rares exceptions,** with very few exceptions; **s. accidents, s. imprévu,** barring accidents, unless anything unforeseen occurs; **s. erreur ou omission,** errors and omissions excepted; **s. cas de force majeure,** except in cases of force majeure; **je consens, s. à revenir sur ma décision,** I consent, but I reserve the right to reconsider my decision; **s. le respect que je vous dois, s. votre respect, s. votre honneur,** with all due respect; **s. s'il pleut,** unless it rains, if it doesn't rain; **je n'ai rien fait, s. d'écrire des lettres,** I've done nothing except write *or* apart from writing some letters; *F* **s. que** + *ind,* except that; **tout s'est bien passé, s. que la mariée est arrivée en retard,** everything went off well, apart from the fact that the bride was late.

sauf-conduit [sofkɔ̃dɥi] *nm* safe conduct, pass; (*pl sauf-conduits*).

sauge [soʒ] *nf* **(a)** *Bot Culin* sage; **(b)** *Bot* salvia.

saugrenu [sogrəny] *adj* absurd, preposterous.

saule [sol] *nm* willow; **s. pleureur,** weeping willow.

saumâtre [somɑtr] *adj* **(a)** brackish, briny (*taste, water*); **(b)** *F* (*person*) bitter, sour; **je la trouve s.,** I think it's a bit thick *or* a bit much.

saumon [somɔ̃] *nm* **1 (a)** salmon; **darne de s.,** salmon steak; **s. fumé,** smoked salmon; **(b)** ingot (*of tin etc*); pig (*of lead etc*). **2** *adj inv* **rubans s.,** salmon-pink ribbons; **rose s.,** salmon pink.

saumoné [somɔne] *adj* **truite saumonée,** sea trout, salmon trout.

saumure [somyr] *nf* (pickling) brine.

saumuré [somyre] *adj* pickled (*in brine*).

saumurer [somyre] *vt* to pickle.

sauna [sona] *nm* sauna.

saupiquet [sopikɛ] *nm Culin* = spicy stew.

saupoudrage [sopudraʒ] *nm* sprinkling, dredging.

saupoudrer [sopudre] *vt* **(a)** to sprinkle, to dust, to dredge (**de,** with); *Fig* **s. des crédits/des subventions,** to hand *or* dish out credit/subsidies (left, right and centre *or* to all and sundry); **(b)** *Arch* to sprinkle (*sth*) with salt.

saupoudreuse [sopudrøz] *nf,* **saupoudroir** [sopudrwar] *nm* dredger, caster, sifter.

saur [sɔr] *adj m* **hareng s.,** kipper, red herring.

saurer [sɔre] *vt* to kipper (*herrings*); to smoke (*fish, bacon*).

saurien [sɔrjɛ̃] *adj & nm* saurian.

saut [so] *nm* **(a)** jump; *Sp* **s. en longueur/en hauteur,** long *or Am* broad jump/high jump; *Sp* **s. à la perche,** pole vault; **s. en** *ou* **à skis,** ski jump *or* (*activité*) jumping; **s. en parachute,** parachute jump *or* (*activité*) jumping; **s. à la corde,** skipping; **faire un s.,** to take a leap; **la voiture a fait un s. de 50 mètres dans la mer,** the car plunged 50 metres into the sea; **entrer/se lever d'un s.,** to dash *or* rush in/to jump *or* leap up; **au s. du lit,** on getting out of bed; **de plein s.,** at one bound; **un s. dans l'inconnu,** a leap into the unknown; *Fig* **faire le (grand) s.,** to take the plunge; **s. périlleux,** somersault; **s. de l'ange,** swallow dive; **par sauts et par bonds,** jerkily, in fits and starts; **faire un s. à Paris/chez le boulanger,** to pop over to Paris/round to the baker's; **il n'y a qu'un s. d'ici là,** it's only a stone's throw (away); **s. de température,** sudden rise *or* jump in temperature;

(b) *Mus* skip;

(c) *Ordinat* jump, skip (instruction);

(d) (*en élevage*) covering;

(e) (*de cours d'eau*) waterfall.

saut-de-lit [sodli] *nm* (light) dressing gown; (*pl sauts-de-lit*).

saut-de-loup [sodlu] *nm* sunken fence, ha-ha; (*pl sauts-de-loup*).

saut-de-mouton [sodmutɔ̃] *nm* overpass, *Br* flyover; (*pl sauts-de-mouton*).

saute [sot] *nf* (sudden) change (*of wind, mood*); jump (*in temperature, price*).

sauté [sote] *adj & nm Culin* sauté.

saute-mouton [sotmutɔ̃] *nm no pl* leapfrog; **jouer à s.-m.,** to play leapfrog.

sauter [sote] *v* (*aux* **avoir**) **1** *vi* **(a)** to jump; **s. à la perche,** to pole-vault; **s. à la corde,** to skip, *Am* to skip rope; **s. du lit/à cheval,** to jump *or* leap out of bed/on to one's horse; *Equitation* **le cheval refuse de s.,** the horse is refusing (the jump *or* fence); **s. par la fenêtre,** to jump *or* leap out (of) the window; **s. à terre,** to jump down; **s. du coq à l'âne,** to skip from one subject to another; **s. à la gorge de qn,** to jump on s.o.; (*d'un chien*) to fly at s.o. *or* at s.o.'s throat; **cela saute aux yeux,** it's obvious; *F* **et que ça saute!,** and make it snappy!, step on it!; **s. au cou de qn,** to fling one's arms round s.o.'s neck; **s. au plafond,** (*du bouchon de champagne etc*) to hit the ceiling; (*de peur*) to jump out of one's skin; (*de joie*) to be overjoyed; (*de colère*) to hit the roof; **s. de joie,** to jump for joy; **s. sur qn,** to fly *or* fling oneself at s.o.; **s. sur une offre/sur l'occasion,** to jump at an offer/at the opportunity;

(b) to explode, to blow up; (*of business, government etc*) to collapse; (*of button etc*) to come off, to fly off; (*of rivet*) to start; *El* (*of fuse*) to blow, *F* to go; **faire s.,** to blast (*rock*); to blow up (*bridge etc*); to explode (*mine*); to burst (*boiler*); to wreck (*plan etc*); to bring down (*government etc*); to sack, to fire (*official*); to dandle (*child*); *Culin* to sauté (*potatoes*); *Culin* to toss (*pancake*); **faire s. une serrure,** to burst a lock (open); **faire s. un piège,** to spring a trap; **faire s. le bouchon,** to pop the cork (*of a bottle*); **se faire s. la cervelle,** to blow one's brains out; **faire s. la banque,** to break the bank; *El* **faire s. les plombs,** to blow the fuses.

2 *vt* **(a)** to jump (over), to leap over, to clear (*ditch, fence* *etc*); *Fig* **s. le pas,** to take the plunge;

(b) (*omettre*) to skip (*page*); to leave out (*line in copying etc*); *Tricot* to drop (*a stitch*); *Scol* **s. une classe,** to skip a class *or* year; *Typ* **s. un mot,** to make an out; *F Vieilli* **je la saute,** I'm not eating; (*j'ai faim*) I'm ravenous;

(c) (*of stallion*) to cover (*mare*); *Arg* to lay (*a girl*).

sauterelle [sotrɛl] *nf Ent* grasshopper; (*noisible*) locust; *Fig F* (*fille maigre*) beanpole; **invasion de sauterelles,** invasion of locusts; **grande s. d'Orient,** locust.

sauterie [sotri] *nf Vieilli* party, *F* hop.

saute-ruisseau [sotrɥiso] *nm inv F Arch* errand boy.

sauteur, -euse [sotœr, -øz] **1** *adj* leaping, jumping (*insect etc*). **2** *n* **(a)** *Sp* jumper; **s. en longueur,** long jumper; **s. à la perche,** pole vaulter; **(b)** *Fig F* weathercock. **3** *nf* **sauteuse (a)** (*casserole*) frying pan; **(b)** *Arg* prostitute, tart.

sautillant [sotijɑ̃] *adj* hopping (*bird*); skipping (*child*); *Fig* **style s.,** jerky style; **discussion sautillante,** discussion that moves from one topic to another.

sautillement [sotijmɑ̃] *nm* hop(ping); *Fig* **le s. de sa conversation,** the twists and turns of his conversation.

sautiller [sotije] *vi* to hop (about).

sautoir [sotwar] *nm* **(a)** St Andrew's cross; *Hér* saltire; **porté en s.,** worn on a chain *or* ribbon round the neck; **(b)** (*long collier*) (long) chain; **(c)** *Sp* jumping area.

sauvage [sovaʒ] **1** *adj* **(a)** wild (*plant, animal*); savage, brutal (*person, attack*); **chat s.,** wildcat; *Can* raccoon; **lieu s.,** wild *or* uninhabited spot; **la côte ouest est restée très s.,** the west coast has remained very wild *or* unspoiled; **(b)** *Vieilli* primitive (*people*); **(c)** *Fig* (*timide*) unsociable; **(d)** (*spontané*) unauthorized; **grève s.,** wildcat strike; **camping s.,** unauthorised camping; **urbanisation s.,** uncontrolled growth; **psychanalyse s.,** amateur psychoanalysis; **(e)** **soldes sauvages,** prices slashed. **2** *n* (*f parfois* **sauvagesse**) **(a)** *Vieilli* savage; *Can Péj* (American) Indian; *F* **on n'est pas des sauvages!,** we're not savages!; **(b)** *Fig* unsociable person; **c'est un s.,** he's unsociable.

sauvagement [sovaʒmɑ̃] *adv* savagely; **pousser s.,** (*d'une plante*) to grow in the wild.

sauvageon, -onne [sovaʒɔ̃, -ɔn] **1** *nm* wild stock (*for grafting*). **2** *n* (*enfant*) little savage.

sauvagerie [sovaʒri] *nf* **(a)** savagery, brutality, barbarity; **(b)** *Fig* unsociability.

sauvagin, -ine [sovaʒɛ̃, -in] **1** *adj* (*taste, smell*) of wildfowl. **2** *nf* **chasse à la sauvagine,** wildfowling.

sauvegarde [sovgard] *nf* **(a)** safeguard (**contre,** against); **sous la s. de qn,** under s.o.'s protection; **clause de s.,** saving clause; **la s. des forêts/du patrimoine national,** the safeguarding *or* protection of the forests/the nation's heritage; **(b)** *Ordinat* saving; **faire la s. d'un fichier,** to save a file; **(c)** *Nau* (*corde*) oar lanyard; (*chaîne*) rudder chain.

sauvegarder [sovgarde] *vt* **(a)** to safeguard (**contre,** against); **(b)** *Ordinat* to save (*file*).

sauve-qui-peut [sovkipø] *nm inv* stampede, headlong flight.

sauver [sove] **1** *vt* **(a)** to save, to rescue (*s.o.*) (**de,** from); *Rel* to save (*s.o., s.o.'s soul*); **s. qn de la misère/d'une situation désagréable,** to save *or* rescue s.o. from misery/from an unpleasant situation; *Fig* **tu me sauves!,** you're a lifesaver!; **le malade est sauvé,** the patient is out of danger; **s. la vie à** *ou* **de qn,** to save s.o.'s life; **Dieu sauve le roi!,** God save the King!; *F* **il n'y a que la foi qui sauve,** faith is a marvellous thing!, isn't faith marvellous!;

(b) to salvage (*ship, goods*); *F* **s. les meubles,** to save something from the wreck; **s. les apparences,** to keep up appearances; **s. la face,** to save face; *F* **s. sa peau** *ou* **sa tête,** to save one's skin; *Fig* **ce qui le sauve, c'est que ...,** his saving grace is that ...; **la fin sauve le film** it's the end that saves *or* rescues the film.

2 se sauver *vpr* **(a)** to escape (**de,** from); **sauve qui peut!,** every man for himself!;

(b) (*s'enfuir*) to run away, to be off; **il se fait tard, je me sauve,** it's getting late, I'm off *or* I must fly; **se s. à toutes jambes,** to take to one's heels, to beat a hasty retreat, *Br F* to scarper;

(c) (*of milk etc*) to boil over.

sauvetage [sovtaʒ] *nm* **(a)** rescue; **s. aérien en mer,** air-sea rescue; **il a fait plusieurs sauvetages en mer,** he has saved several lives at sea; **appareil de s.,** life-saving *or* rescue apparatus; **ceinture de s.,** life-belt; **gilet de s.,** life jacket; **bouée de s.,** lifebuoy; **ligne de s.,** lifeline; **canot** *ou* **embarcation de s.,** lifeboat; **échelle de s.,** fire escape; *Fig* **le s. d'une entreprise,** the rescue of a company; **(b)** salvage (*of ship, goods*).

sauveteur [sovtœr] **1** *nm* rescuer. **2** *adj m* **bateau s.,** lifeboat.

sauvette (à la) [alasovɛt] *adv* in a hurry; *Péj* furtively; **vendre à la s.,** to peddle on the streets (*illegally*); **marchand à la s.,** illicit street vendor.

sauveur, salvatrice [sovœr, salvatris] **1** *n* saviour, *US* savior. **2** *adj* saving.

savamment [savamɑ̃] *adv* **(a)** (*avec érudition*) learnedly; **elle expose s. ses connaissances,** she presents her knowledge in a learned manner; **(b)** (*en connaissance de cause*) knowingly; **j'en parle s.,** I know what I'm talking about; **(c)** (*habilement*) cleverly, skilfully, *US* skillfully; **elle sait s. convaincre son monde,** she's very good at convincing the people she deals with.

savane [savan] *nf* **(a)** *Géog* savanna(h); **(b)** *Can* swamp.

savant, -ante [savɑ̃, -ɑ̃t] **1** *adj* **(a)** well informed, knowledgeable (**en,** about); (*érudit*) erudite, scholarly; learned (**en,** in); **(b)** skilful, clever, able; **s. calcul,** clever calculation; **chien s.,** performing dog; **grâce à de savantes manœuvres,** thanks to some skilful manoeuvres. **2** *n* scientist; (*érudit*) scholar.

savarin [savarɛ̃] *nm Culin* savarin.

savate [savat] *nf* **(a)** (*vieille chaussure*) old *or* worn-out shoe; *F* **traîner la s.,** to be down at heel; **(b)** *Tech* sole (plate); **(c)** *Sp* kick boxing; **(d)** *F* clumsy oaf; **comme une s.,** abominably, very badly.

saveur [savœr] *nf* **(a)** taste, flavour, *US* flavor; **sans s.,** tasteless, insipid; **(b)** *Fig* spice, pungency.

Savoie [savwa] *nf* Savoy; *Culin* **biscuit de S.,** = sponge cake.

savoir[1] [savwar] *v* (*prp* **sachant**; *pp* **su**; *pr ind* **je sais, il sait, n. savons, ils savent**; *pr sub* **je sache, n. sachions, ils sachent**; *imp* **sache, sachons, sachez**; *impf* **je savais**; *p hist* **je sus**; *fu* **je saurai**) **1** *vt & vi* **(a)** to know; **s. qch par cœur,** to know sth by heart; **s. une langue/le chemin,** to know a language/the way; **il en sait des choses** *ou* **plus d'une,** he knows a thing or two;

(b) (*être conscient de*) to know; **je ne savais pas cela,** I didn't know *or* was not aware of that; **je le sais bien!,** I know!; **elle est jolie, et elle le sait bien,** she's pretty, and doesn't she know it!; **ce n'est pas bien, tu sais!,** it isn't right, you know!; **je n'en sais rien,** I know nothing about it; (*je ne sais pas*) I don't know; **en s. trop,** to know too much; **je n'en sais trop rien,** I'm not (very) sure; **comment le saurais-je?, qu'est-ce j'en sais?,** how should I know?; **peut-on s.?,** what's it (all) about?, can you tell me about it?; **saura-t-on un jour?,** will we ever know?; **qu'en savez-vous?,** what do you know about it?; **il sera peut-être là, qui sait?,** perhaps he'll be there, who knows?; **je ne veux pas s.,** I don't want any explanations, I don't want to know (anything about it); *F* **je ne veux pas le s.,** that's nothing to do with me; *F* **est-ce que je sais(, moi)?,** I haven't a clue!, don't ask me!; *Litt* **je ne sais,** I do not know; **sans le s.,** unconsciously, unwittingly, without being aware of it; **je voudrais bien s. pourquoi,** I'd like to know why, I wonder why; **reste à s. si ...,** it remains to be seen whether ... *or* if ...; **je crois s. qu'il est ici,** I understand he is here; **il n'a rien voulu s.,** he wouldn't listen to us; **faire s. qch à qn,** to tell s.o. sth, to inform s.o. of sth; **je le sais par ma sœur,** I heard it from my sister; **vous auriez dû le lui faire s.,** you should have told him, you should have let him know; **(à) s.,** i.e., that is to say, namely, to wit, viz.; **il y a quatre possibilités, à s. ...,** there are four possibilities, (namely) ...; **pas que je sache,** not to my knowledge; **(à ce) que je sache,** so far as I know; **(pour) autant que je sache,** as far as I know; (*quand on ne sait rien*) for all I know; **pour autant que je sache il pourrait très bien être au Canada,** he could be in Canada for all I know; **la question est de s. si elle viendra,** the question is whether she will come; **on ne sait pas,** there is no saying *or* knowing; **on ne sait jamais,** you never know, you never can tell; **si jeunesse savait!,** if youth but knew!; **si j'avais su,** if I had known, had I known; *Litt* (*in first person only*) **je ne sache pas qu'on vous ait invité,** I am not aware that you have been invited;

(c) *Litt* (*connaître*) to know (of) (*s.o.*); **je sais un bon horloger,** I know (of) a good watchmaker; *Péj* **avec la fille que vous savez,** with you know who; **c'est encore une lettre de qui vous savez,** it's another letter from you know who;

(d) (*être certain*) to know; **des parents que je sais venir de Londres,** relatives who I know come from London; **il sait ce qu'il veut,** he knows what he wants, he knows his own mind; **je ne sais (pas) où le trouver,** I don't know where to find him; **ne s. que faire/que dire,** not to know *or* to be at a loss what to do/to say; **je ne sais que penser,** I don't know what to think; **sachez que ...,** I would have you know that ...; **ne pas s. où se mettre,** not to know where to put oneself;

(e) (*être capable de*) to know how, to be able (*to do sth*); **savez-vous nager?,** can you swim?; **s. écouter,** to be a good listener; **il sait parler aux femmes!,** he knows how to talk to women!; **il faut s. être patient,** you have to learn to be patient; **je ne saurais vous conseiller,** I wouldn't know what advice to give you; **on ne saurait se souvenir de tout,** you can't remember everything; **je sais y aller,** I know how to go *or* get there; **je crois que je saurai le faire,** I think I can manage it; **s. vivre,** to know how to behave; *F* **elle sait y faire avec les enfants,** she's good with children; *F* **s. s'y prendre avec qn,** to know how to handle s.o.; **je ne saurais guère vous le dire,** I'm afraid I can't tell you;

(f) (*locutions*) **je ne sais qui,** somebody or other; **je ne sais qui de ses amis,** some friend or other of his; **un je ne sais quoi de déplaisant,** something vaguely unpleasant; **c'est je ne sais quoi qu'elle a mangé,** it's something she's eaten; **je ne sais quelle maladie,** some illness or other; **c'est un Monsieur/Madame je sais tout (mieux),** he's/she's a real know-all; **je suis tout je ne sais comment,** I feel very odd; **il y a je ne sais combien de temps,** ages ago, heaven knows how long ago; **des robes, des chapeaux, des gants, que sais-je?,** dresses, hats, gloves, and what have you *or* and goodness knows what else; **il a des amis, Dieu sait,** God knows, he has plenty of friends!; **Dieu sait comment,** God knows how; **Dieu sait si je le lui ai répété,** God knows how often I've told him.

2 se savoir *vpr* **je me savais très malade,** I knew I was very ill; **ça se saura vite,** it'll soon get out, everyone will know about it soon; **ça se saurait si c'était possible,** if it was possible, everyone would know about it.

savoir² *nm* knowledge, learning.

savoir-faire [savwarfɛr] *nm inv* (*social*) savoir-faire; (*technique*) expertise, know-how.

savoir-vivre [savwarvivr] *nm inv* savoir-vivre, good manners; **manquer de s.-v.,** to be uncouth.

savon [savɔ̃] *nm* soap; **(pain de) s.,** bar *or* tablet *or* cake of soap; **s. liquide/en paillettes,** liquid soap/soap flakes; **s. à barbe,** shaving soap; **s. de Marseille,** = household soap; **eau de s.,** soap suds; **ça partira avec du s.,** it will come off with soap, soap will take it off *or* out; **acheter des savons,** to buy soap; *F* **donner** *ou* **flanquer** *ou* **passer un s. à qn,** to give s.o. a telling-off; *Minér* **s. blanc** *ou* **minéral** *ou* **de montagne,** mountain soap, rock soap; **s. naturel** *ou* **des soldats,** smectic clay; **pierre de s.,** soapstone; *Spéc* steatite.

savonnage [savɔnaʒ] *nm* soaping, washing (*of clothes etc*).

savonner [savɔne] **1** *vt* **(a)** to soap (*sth*); to soap, to lather (*chin before shaving*); *Aut* **piste savonnée,** skidpan; **(b)** *Tech* to rub, to grind (*glass with glass soap*). **2 se savonner** *vpr* to wash oneself with soap.

savonnerie [savɔnri] *nf* soap factory.

savonnette [savɔnɛt] *nf* bar of (toilet) soap.

savonneux, -euse [savɔnø, -øz] *adj* soapy.

savourer [savure] *vt* to relish, to enjoy.

savoureusement [savurœzmɑ̃] *adv* with relish.

savoureux, -euse [savurø, -øz] *adj* tasty (*dish*); full-flavoured, *US* -flavored (*wine*); *Fig* spicy (*story*).

Saxe [saks] **1** *nf* Saxony; **porcelaine de S.,** Dresden china. **2** *nm* **s.,** (piece of) Dresden china.

saxhorn [saksɔrn] *nm Mus* saxhorn; **s. basse,** euphonium.

saxifrage [saksifraʒ] *nf* saxifrage.

saxo [sakso] *nm F* sax.

saxon, -onne [saksɔ̃, -ɔn] **1** *adj Hist Géog* Saxon. **2** *nm Ling* Saxon. **3** *n* **S.,** Saxon.

saxophone [saksɔfɔn] *nm Mus* saxophone.

saxophoniste [saksɔfɔnist] *n Mus* saxophonist.

saynète [sɛnɛt] *nf Th* playlet, short comedy.

sbire [sbir] *nm F Péj* (*policier*) pig; (*voyou*) thug.

scab [skab] *nm* (*briseur de grève*) scab.

scabieux, -ieuse [skabjø, -jøz] **1** *adj* scabby. **2** *nf Bot* **scabieuse,** scabious.

scabreux, -euse [skabrø, -øz] *adj* **(a)** (*indécent*) indecent, shocking, *Fml* scabrous; **(b)** *Litt* difficult, tricky.

scalaire¹ [skalɛr] *nf* (*poisson*) angel fish.

scalaire² *adj & nm Math* scalar.

scalène [skalɛn] *adj Math Anat* scalene.

scalp(e) [skalp] *nm* scalp; (*action de scalper*) scalping.

scalpel [skalpɛl] *nm Chir* scalpel.

scalper [skalpe] *vt* to scalp.

scandale [skɑ̃dal] *nm* (*politique, financier etc*) scandal; **faire (un) s., causer du s.,** to create a scandal; **il a fait tout un s. parce que ...,** he made a tremendous scene *or* kicked up a tremendous fuss because ...; **au grand s. de ses parents,** to the great indignation *or* disgust of his parents; **c'est un s.!,** it's a scandal!, it's scandalous!; **crier au s.,** to protest vociferously, *F* to raise the roof.

scandaleusement [skɑ̃daløzmɑ̃] *adv* scandalously.

scandaleux, -euse [skɑ̃dalø, -øz] *adj* scandalous; **prix s.,** scandalous prices.

scandaliser [skɑ̃dalize] **1** *vt* to scandalize, to shock. **2 se scandaliser** *vpr* to be scandalized *or* shocked; **il ne se scandalise de rien,** nothing shocks him.

scander [skɑ̃de] *vt* to scan (*verse*); *Mus* to mark, to stress (*a phrase*); **s. un slogan,** to chant a slogan.

scandinave [skɑ̃dinav] **1** *adj* Scandinavian. **2** *n* **S.,** Scandinavian.

Scandinavie [skɑ̃dinavi] *nf* Scandinavia.

scandium [skɑ̃djɔm] *nm Ch* scandium.

scanner [skanɛr] *nm Méd Ordinat* scanner; **faire un s.,** to have a scan; *Typ* to scan.

scanographie [skanɔgrafi] *nf Méd* **(a)** (*science*) scanning; **(b)** (*cliché*) scan.

scansion [skɑ̃sjɔ̃] *nf* scansion, scanning.

scaphandre [skafɑ̃dr] *nm* **(a)** diving suit; **s. autonome,** aqualung, scuba; **(b)** *Astron* space suit.

scaphandrier [skafɑ̃drije] *nm* diver (*in diving suit*).

scaphoïde [skafɔid] *adj & nm Anat Biol* scaphoid.

scapulaire [skapylɛr] *adj & nm* scapular.

scarabée [skarabe] *nm* scarab.

scare [skar] *nm* (*poisson*) parrot fish, scar.

scarificateur [skarifikatœr] *nm Agr* harrow, scarifier; *Chir* scarificator.

scarifier [skarifje] *vt* (*impf & pr sub* **n. scarifiions, v. scarifiiez**) *Agr Chir* to scarify; *Biol* to abrade.

scarlatine [scarlatin] *nf Med* scarlet fever, *Spéc* scarlatina; **avoir la s.,** to have scarlet fever.

scarlatineux, -euse [skarlatinø, -øz] *adj & n* (patient) suffering from scarlet fever.

scarole [skarɔl] *nf Bot* endive.

scato [skato] *adj F* dirty; **plaisanterie s.,** dirty joke; **humour s.,** lavatory humour.

scatologie [skatɔlɔʒi] *nf* scatological *or* lavatorial humour *or US* humor; (*livres*) scatology, scatological literature.

scatologique [skatɔlɔʒik] *adj* scatological (*literature*).

scatophage [skatɔfaʒ] **1** *adj* scatophagous (*fish, insect*). **2** *nm* dung fly, *Spéc* scatophage.

scatophagie [skatɔfaʒi] *nf* scatophagy.

sceau, *pl* **sceaux** [so] *nm* seal; **S. de l'État,** State seal; **mettre** *ou* **apposer son s. à un document,** to set one's seal to a document; **mettre le s. à la réputation de qn,** to set the seal on s.o.'s reputation; **s. du génie,** mark *or* stamp of genius; **sous le s. du secret,** under the seal of secrecy; *Bot* **s. de Salomon,** Solomon's seal.

scélérat, -ate [selera, -at] *Arch & Litt* **1** *adj* wicked. **2** *n* scoundrel.

scellé [sele] **1** *adj* sealed, under seal. **2** *nm Jur* (imprint of official) seal; **mettre/lever les scellés,** to put on/remove the seals.

scellement [sɛlmɑ̃] *nm Constr* sealing, setting; fixing, bedding (*of a post in stone, in concrete*); end (*of post etc, fitting in socket*); **vingt centimètres de s.,** bedded to a depth of twenty centimetres.

sceller [sele] *vt* **(a)** to seal; (*ratifier*) to ratify, to confirm; **s. un pacte,** to set the seal on an agreement; **(b)** *Constr* to bed, to fasten, to fix in.

scénario [senarjo] *nm* scenario; *Cin TV* script, screenplay; *Fig* **le s. de la déclaration de guerre,** the background to the declaration of war.

scénariste [senarist] *n Cin TV* scriptwriter.

scène [sɛn] *nf Th* **(a)** stage; (*le théâtre*) stage, theatre, *US* theater; **entrer en s.,** to appear, to come on; *Fig* to appear on the scene; **être en s.,** (*of actor*) to be on; **en s. pour le un!,** beginners please!; **mise en s.,** staging, production; (*décor*) setting; **metteur en s.,** producer; **mettre qch en s.,** to stage sth; **porter qch à la s.,** to adapt sth for the theatre; **elle a la folie de la s.,** she's stage-struck; **quitter la s.,** to retire from the stage *or* from acting; *Fig* **la s. politique/internationale,** the political/international scene *or* arena;

(b) (*décor, action*) scene; **changement de s.,** change of scene; **le tableau représente une s. de chasse,** the painting represents a hunting scene; **une s. d'amour,** a love scene; **la grande s. du II,** the big scene in Act II; **troisième s. du second acte,** act two scene three; **la s. se passe au moyen âge,** the scene *or* action takes place in the middle ages; **revoir les scènes de sa jeunesse,** to revisit the

scenes of one's youth; **ce fut une s. pénible,** it was a painful scene; **scènes de la vie des camps,** scenes of camp life; **imagine la s.!,** just picture it!, imagine *or* picture the scene!;
(c) *F* scene, row; **faire une s.,** to make a scene; **s. de ménage,** domestic squabble; **tu ne vas pas nous faire une s.!,** you're not going to make a scene!
scénique [senik] *adj* theatrical, (of the) stage; **éclairage s.,** stage lighting; **indications scéniques,** stage directions.
scéniquement [senikmɑ̃] *adv* from the theatrical point of view, theatrically speaking.
scénographe [senɔgraf] *n* scenographer.
scénographie [senɔgrafi] *nf* **1** *Beaux-Arts etc* scenography. **2** *Th* scenecraft.
scepticisme [sɛptisism] *nm* scepticism, *US* skepticism.
sceptique [sɛptik] **1** *adj* sceptic(al), *US* skeptic(al). **2** *n* sceptic, *US* skeptic.
sceptiquement [sɛptikmɑ̃] *adv* sceptically, *US* skeptically.
sceptre [sɛptr] *nm* sceptre, *US* scepter; *Fig* **s. de fer,** rod of iron.
schako [ʃako] *nm Mil* shako.
scheik [ʃɛk] *nm* sheik.
schelem [ʃlɛm] *nm Cartes* slam; **petit/grand s.,** little/grand slam.
schéma [ʃema] *nm* **(a)** diagram, plan, schema; **(b)** project, plan (*for a book etc*); **s. directeur,** master plan.
schématique [ʃematik] *adj* diagrammatic, schematic; *Péj* oversimplified.
schématiquement [ʃematikmɑ̃] *adv* schematically, diagrammatically; (*en gros*) in outline, in a simplified manner.
schématisation [ʃematizɑsjɔ̃] *nf* schematization, reduction to essentials.
schématiser [ʃematize] *vt* to schematize (*sth*), to make a diagram of (*sth*); *Péj*) to simplify (*sth*).
schématisme [ʃematism] *nm Phil* schematism; *Péj* simplification.
schème [ʃɛm] *nm Phil Psy* schema; *Beaux-Arts etc* design.
scherzando [skɛrtsando, skɛrdz-] *adv Mus* scherzando.
scherzo [skɛrtso, -dzo] *Mus* **1** *nm* scherzo. **2** *adv* scherzando.
schibboleth [ʃibɔlɛt] *nm* shibboleth.
schilling [ʃiliŋ] *nm* (*monnaie autrichienne*) schilling.
schismatique [ʃismatik] *adj & n* schismatic.
schisme [ʃism] *nm* schism.
schiste [ʃist] *nm Géol* schist, shale.
schisteux, -euse [ʃistø, -øz] *adj Géol* schistose.
schistoïde [ʃistɔid] *adj* schistoid.
schistosomiase [ʃistɔzomjaz] *nf Méd* schistosomiasis.
schizogamie [skizɔgami] *nf Biol* schizogamy.
schizoïde [skizɔid] *adj & n Psy* schizoid.
schizoïdie [skizɔidi] *nf Psy* schizoidism, schizothymia.
schizoïdique [skizɔidik] *adj Psy* schizoid.
schizophasie [skizɔfazi] *nf Psy* schizophasia.
schizophrène [skizɔfrɛn] *adj & n Psy* schizophrenic.
schizophrénie [skizɔfreni] *nf Psy* schizophrenia.
schizophrénique [skizɔfrenik] *adj & n Psy* schizophrenic.
schizothymie [skizɔtimi] *nf Psy* schizothymia.
schizothymique [skizɔtimik] *adj Psy* schizothymic.
schlass [ʃlas] *adj inv Arg* (*soûl*) tight, sozzled, *Br* rat-arsed.
schlinguer [ʃlɛ̃ge] *vi Arg* to stink, *Br* to pong.
schlittage [ʃlitaʒ] *nm* transporting on a timber sledge.
schlitte [ʃlit] *nf* (timber) sledge (*for transporting lumber*), *US* dray.
schlitter [ʃlite] *vt* to transport (*lumber*) on a timber sledge.
schnaps [ʃnaps] *nm* schnapps.
schnau(t)zer [ʃnawzɛr] *nm* (*chien*) schnauzer.
schnock, schnoque [ʃnɔk] *adj & n Arg* mad, batty, crazy, daft (person).
schnorchel, schnorkel [ʃnɔrkɛl] *nm* snorkel.
schnouff [ʃnuf] *nf F* (*drogue*) dope, junk.
schofar [ʃɔfar] *nm Rel Mus* shophar.
schooner [skunœr, ʃunɛr] *nm Nau* schooner.
schorre [ʃɔr] *nm* salt meadow.
schuss [ʃus] *nm Ski* schuss; **descendre la piste en s.,** to shuss down the slope.
sciage [sjaʒ] *nm* sawing.
sciant [sjɑ̃] *adj Arg* boring; **il est s.,** he's a damn nuisance; (*ennuyeux*) he bores me stiff.
sciaphile [sjafil] *adj Biol* shade-loving.
sciatique [sjatik] **1** *adj Anat* sciatic (*nerve, artery etc*). **2** *nm* sciatic nerve. **3** *nf Méd* sciatica.
scie [si] *nf* **(a)** saw; **s. à bois,** wood saw; **s. à métaux,** hacksaw; **s. mécanique,** power saw; **s. circulaire,** circular saw, *Am* buzz saw; **s. articulée, s. à chaîne(tte),** chain saw; **s. à chantourner,** (*manuelle*) bowsaw, turning saw; (*mécanique*) jigsaw, scroll saw; **s. à découper, s. anglaise,** (*manuelle*) fret saw; (*mécanique*) jigsaw; **en dents de s.,** serrate(d); **jeu de la s.,** cat's cradle; *Méd* **bruit de s.,** rasping murmur; **(b) (poisson) s.,** sawfish; **mouche à s.,** sawfly; **(c)** *F* (*personne ennuyeuse*) bore; (*formule*) catchphrase; (*rengaine*) hit tune.
sciemment [sjamɑ̃] *adv* knowingly, on purpose, wittingly.
science [sjɑ̃s] *nf* **(a)** (*savoir*) knowledge, learning; **s. infuse,** intuition; *Fig* **il croit avoir la s. infuse,** he thinks he knows everything; **avoir la s. des couleurs,** (*d'un peintre*) to know how to use colour; **(b)** science; **la s. n'a pas de patrie,** science knows no frontiers; **homme de s.,** scientist; **doué pour les sciences,** good at science; **préparer une licence ès sciences,** to be studying for a science degree; **les sciences exactes** *ou* **pures,** the exact sciences; **sciences physiques/naturelles/appliquées,** physical/natural/applied science; **sciences humaines,** humanities; **sciences expérimentales,** experimental science; **sciences sociales,** social science(s); **les sciences occultes,** the occult sciences.
science-fiction [sjɑ̃sfiksjɔ̃] *nf* science fiction; **roman/film de s.-f.,** science fiction novel/film.
scientifique [sjɑ̃tifik] **1** *adj* scientific. **2** *n* scientist.
scientifiquement [sjɑ̃tifikmɑ̃] *adv* scientifically.
scientisme [sjɑ̃tism] *nm* **(a)** scientism; **(b)** (doctrines of) Christian Science.
scientiste [sjɑ̃tist] **1** *adj* scientistic. **2** *n* **(a)** (*adept of scientism*) scientist; **(b) s. chrétien(ne),** Christian Scientist.
scier¹ [sje] *vt* (*pr sub & impf* **n. sciions, v. sciiez**) to saw (*wood*); to saw off (*branch etc*); *F* **s. qn,** to amaze s.o..
scier² *vi* (*à l'aviron*) to back water, to back the oars.
scierie [siri] *nf* sawmill.
scieur [sjœr] *nm* sawyer; **s. de long,** (pit) sawyer.
scieuse [sjøz] *nf* mechanical saw.
scille [sil] *nf* **(a)** *Bot* scilla, squill; **s. maritime,** sea onion; **(b)** *Pharm* squills.
scinder [sɛ̃de] **1** *vt* to divide, to split up. **2 se scinder** *vpr* to split up.
scinque [sɛ̃k] *nm Zool* skink.
scintillant [sɛ̃tijɑ̃] **1** *adj* scintillating, twinkling; *Fig* scintillating, sparkling (*wit*). **2** *nm* tinsel decoration(s).
scintillation [sɛ̃tijɑsjɔ̃] *nf* = **SCINTILLEMENT**.
scintillement [sɛ̃tijmɑ̃] *nm* scintillation (*of star etc*); *Cin TV* flicker(ing); sparkling, twinkling (*of eyes, stars, jewellery etc*).
scintiller [sɛ̃tije] *vi* to scintillate, to sparkle; (*of star*) to twinkle; *Électron TV Cin* to flicker; *Fig* **esprit qui scintille,** scintillating *or* sparkling wit.
scion [sjɔ̃] *nm* **(a)** scion, shoot; **(b)** tip (*of fishing rod*).
scirpe [sirp] *nm Bot* club rush, bulrush.
scissile [sisil] *adj Phys Nucl* fissionable (*material*).
scission [sisjɔ̃] *nf* **(a)** *Pol etc* split, division; **faire s.,** to secede; **(b)** *Ch* scission, cleavage; *Phys Nucl* fission, splitting; **s. nucléaire,** nuclear fission.
scissionniste [sisjɔnist] *adj & n* secessionist.
scissipare [sisipar] *adj Biol* fissiparous.
scissiparité [sisiparite] *nf Biol* schizogenesis, fissiparity.
scissure [sisyr] *nf Anat etc* fissure, cleavage, cleft.
sciure [sjyr] *nf* **s. (de bois),** sawdust; **s. de marbre,** marble dust.
scléral, -aux [skleral, -o] *adj Anat* scleral, sclerotic.
sclérenchyme [sklerɑ̃ʃim] *nm Biol* sclerenchyma.
scléreux, -euse [sklerø, -øz] *adj Méd* sclerous, sclerosed, hard (tissue).
sclérifié [sklerifje] *adj Biol* sclerosed, hardened (*tegument etc*).
sclérodermé [sklerɔdɛrme] *adj Zool* sclerodermatous, sclerodermic.
sclérodermie [sklerɔdɛrmi] *nf Méd* scleroderma.
sclérogène [sklerɔʒɛn] *adj Méd* sclerogenic.
sclérome [sklerom] *nm Méd* scleroma.
scléromètre [sklerɔmɛtr] *nm Phys* sclerometer.
sclérophylle [sklerɔfil] *Bot* **1** *adj* sclerophyllous. **2** *nm* sclerophyll.
scléroprotéine [sklerɔprɔtein] *nf* scleroprotein.
sclérose [skleroz] *nf Méd* sclerosis; *Fig* ossification, (mental) sclerosis; **s. vasculaire** *ou* **des artères,** arteriosclerosis; **s. en plaques,** multiple sclerosis, MS; *Fig* **s. d'un parti,** sclerosis *or* creeping paralysis of a party.

sclérosé [skleroze] *adj Méd* sclerosed; *Fig* rigid, hidebound, ossified.

scléroser [skleroze] **1** *vt Méd* to sclerose, to harden. **2** *Fig* **se scléroser** *vpr* to become hidebound *or* ossified.

sclérotique [sklerɔtik] *Anat* **1** *adj* sclerotic. **2** *nf* sclerotic, sclera (*of the eye*).

scolaire [skɔlɛr] *adj* **(a)** academic, scholastic (*achievements, success*); educational (*reform, organization*); **vie s.**, school life; **année s.**, school *or* academic year; **enfant d'âge s.**, child of school age; **frais scolaires,** school fees; **livres scolaires,** school books, text books; **(b)** *Péj* scholastic, bookish; (*style*) laboured, *US* labored.

scolairement [skɔlɛrmɑ̃] *adv Péj* (*réciter, écrire*) in a laboured *or US* labored style.

scolarisable [skɔlarizabl] *adj* of school age.

scolarisation [skɔlarizɑsjɔ̃] *nf* **(a)** school attendance; **(b)** (*éducation*) education, schooling.

scolariser [skɔlarize] *vt* to provide education for (*children*); to equip *or* provide (*an area*) with schools.

scolarité [skɔlarite] *nf* **s. obligatoire,** compulsory schooling; **prolongation de la s.,** raising of the school-leaving age; **s. à temps partiel** = day release classes; **taux de s.,** percentage of children in full-time education; **certificat de s.,** = certificate of attendance (*at school or university*); **frais de s.,** school fees.

scolasticat [skɔlastika] *nm* theological training; (*établissement*) theological college.

scolastique [skɔlastik] **1** *adj* scholastic (*philosophy etc*). **2** *nm* scholastic. **3** *nf* scholasticism.

scolex [skɔlɛks] *nm inv Zool* scolex, head (*of tape-worm*).

scoliaste [skɔljast] *nm* scholiast.

scoliose [skɔljoz] *nf Méd* scoliosis, lateral curvature of the spine.

scolopendre¹ [skɔlɔpɑ̃dr] *nf* centipede, *Spéc* scolopendrid.

scolopendre² *nf Bot* hart's tongue, *Spéc* scolopendrium.

scombéroïde [skɔ̃berɔid] *nm* scombroid.

scombre [skɔ̃br] *nm* scombrid.

sconse [skɔ̃s] *nm* skunk; (*fourrure*) skunk (fur).

scoop [skup] *nm Journ* scoop; *Fig* **c'est un s.!,** well I never!; **j'ai un s.,** I've got some news.

scooter [skutɛr] *nm* (motor) scooter.

scootériste [skuterist] *n* scooter rider.

scopie [skɔpi] *nf Arg Méd* radioscopy.

scopolamine [skɔpɔlamin] *nf Ch Pharm* scopolamine, hyoscine.

scops [skɔps] *nm* scops owl.

scorbut [skɔrbyt] *nm Méd* scurvy, *Spéc* scorbutus.

scorbutigène [skɔrbytiʒɛn] *adj Méd* scurvy-producing (*diet*).

scorbutique [skɔrbytik] *adj & n Méd* scorbutic.

score [skɔr] *nm Sp* score; **s. électoral,** share of the vote; **faire un bon s.,** to turn in a good performance, to perform creditably.

scoriacé [skɔrjase] *adj Métal Géol etc* slaggy.

scorie [skɔri] *nf* **(a)** *Métal* **scories,** slag, cinders, scoria; (*de fer*) (iron) dross; (*de charbon*) clinker; **(b)** *Géol* **scories (volcaniques),** scoria, volcanic slag; **(c)** *Fig* mediocre *or* inferior part (*of sth*).

scorpène [skɔrpɛn] *nf* scorpion fish.

scorpioïde [skɔrpjɔid] *adj Bot* scorpioid.

scorpion [skɔrpjɔ̃] *nm* **(a)** scorpion; *Astron* **le S.,** Scorpio; **(b) s. aquatique** *ou* **d'eau,** water scorpion; **s. de mer,** scorpion fish.

scorsonère [skɔrsɔnɛr] *nf,* **scorzonère** [skɔrzɔnɛr] *nf* black salsify, *Spéc* scorzonera.

scotch [skɔtʃ] *nm* **(a)** scotch (whisky); **un double s.,** a double scotch; (*pl scotches*); **(b) Scotch ®,** self-adhesive tape, *Br* ≈ Sellotape ®, *Am* ≈ Scotchtape ®.

scotcher [skɔtʃe] *vt* to sellotape.

scotch-terrier [skɔʃterje] *nm* Scotch terrier; (*pl scotch-terriers*).

scotie [skɔti] *nf Archit* scotia (*of pillar*).

scotome [skɔtom] *nm Méd* scotoma.

scotopique [skɔtɔpik] *adj Méd* scotopic.

scottish-terrier [skɔtiʃterje] *nm* Scotch terrier; (*pl scottish-terriers*).

scout [skut] *nm* (boy) scout.

scoutisme [skutism] *nm* scouting.

Scrabble ® [skrabl] *nm* Scrabble ®; **jouer au S.,** to play scrabble.

scratch [skratʃ] (*pl scratches*) *Sp* **1** *nm* (*course*) scratch race; (*joueur*) scratch (player); **partir s.,** to start (at) scratch. **2** *adj* **course s.,** scratch race; **joueur s.,** scratch (player).

scratcher [skratʃe] *vt Courses de chevaux etc* to scratch (*horse, competitor*).

scribe [skrib] *nm Antiq* scribe; *Péj* pen-pusher.

scribouillard, -arde [skribujar, -ard] *n Péj* pen-pusher.

script¹ [skript] *nm Fin* scrip.

script² **1** *nm* (*handwriting*) script; *Cin F* film script; **écriture s.,** script printing; **2** *nf Cin F* continuity girl.

script-girl [skriptgœrl] *nf Cin* continuity girl; (*pl script-girls*).

scriptural, -aux [skriptyral, -o] *adj* scriptural; *Banque* **monnaie scripturale,** bank or other forms of financial credit.

scrofulaire [skrɔfylɛr] *nf Bot* figwort.

scrofule [skrɔfyl] *nf Méd* scrofula; *Arch* **les scrofules,** scrofula, *Arch* the king's evil.

scrofuleux, -euse [skrɔfylø, -øz] *adj & n Méd* scrofulous (person).

scrotum [skrɔtɔm] *nm Anat* scrotum.

scrupule [skrypyl] *nm* **(a)** scruple (**sur,** about); **sans scrupules,** unscrupulous(ly); **se faire (un) s. de faire qch, avoir des scrupules à faire qch,** to have scruples about doing sth; **il ne se fait pas s. d'emprunter à la caisse,** he has no scruples about borrowing from the till; **je n'aurai aucun s. à le lui dire,** I'll have no scruples about telling him so; **exact jusqu'au s.,** scrupulously exact; **(b)** *Arch* (*unité de poids*) scruple.

scrupuleusement [skrypyløzmɑ̃] *adv* scrupulously.

scrupuleux, -euse [skrypylø, -øz] *adj* scrupulous (**sur,** about, over, as to; **à faire qch,** in doing sth); **peu s.,** unscrupulous.

scrutateur, -trice [skrytatœr, -tris] **1** *adj Litt* searching (*mind, look*). **2** *n* teller, scrutineer (*of a ballot, poll*).

scruter [skryte] *vt* to scrutinize (*sth*), to examine (*sth*) closely.

scrutin [skrytɛ̃] *nm* **(a)** poll; **s. d'arrondissement,** = constituency poll; **s. secret,** secret vote *or* ballot; **s. découvert,** open vote *or* ballot; **dépouiller le s.,** to count the votes; **résultat du s.,** result of the vote *or* ballot; **(b) tour de s.,** ballot, round (of voting); **s. de ballotage,** second ballot; **voter au s.,** to ballot; **élire qn au s.,** to ballot for s.o.; **(c)** voting (*in an assembly*); (*parliamentary*) division; **procéder au s.,** to take the vote; *Br Parl* to divide; **s. uninominal,** system of voting for a single candidate; **s. proportionnel** *ou* **de liste,** system of voting by proportional representation *or* by lists; **s. majoritaire,** first-past-the-post system; **demander le s.,** to ask for a count; **projet adopté sans s.,** bill passed without a division.

scrutiner [skrytine] *vi* to vote, to go to the polls; (*avec ballotage*) to ballot.

scull [skyl, skœl] *nm Sp Nau* scull, skiff; (*activité*) sculling.

sculpter [skylte] *vt* to sculpture, to sculpt; (*dans du bois*) to carve (**dans,** in, out of); **bois sculpté,** carved wood.

sculpteur [skyltœr] *nm* sculptor; **femme s.,** woman sculptor, sculptress; **s. sur bois,** woodcarver.

sculptural, -aux [skyltyral, -o] *adj* sculptural (*art*); statuesque (*figure, beauty*).

sculpture [skyltyr] *nf* (*œuvre, art*) sculpture; **s. sur bois,** woodcarving; **faire de la s.,** to sculpt, to (do) sculpture.

scutellaire [skytelɛr] *nf Bot* skull cap; *Spéc* scutellaria.

scutum [skytɔm] *nm Ant Ent* scutum.

scyphoméduse [sifɔmedyz] *nf Zool* scyphomedusan; **scyphoméduses,** Scyphomedusae.

scythe [sit] **1** *adj* Scythian. **2** *n* **S.,** Scythian.

Scythie [siti] *nf* Scythia.

SDF [ɛsdeɛf] (*abrév* **sans domicile fixe**) of no fixed abode.

se [s(ə)] *pron* (**s'** *before vowel or mute h*) **(a)** (*complément direct*) himself; (*sujet femelle*) herself; (*non humain*) itself; (*indéfini*) oneself, *Am* himself; (*pl*) themselves; (*complément indirect*) to himself; to herself; to itself; to oneself; to themselves; **se flatter,** to flatter oneself; **il se rase,** he is shaving; **elle s'est coupée au doigt** *ou* **s'est coupé le doigt,** she has cut her finger; **il se parle (à lui-même),** he's talking to himself; **ils se sont fait mal,** they hurt themselves;

(b) (*réciproque*) each other; (*plus de deux personnes*) one another; (*indirect*) to each other; (*plus de deux personnes*) to one another; **se nuire (l'un à l'autre),** to hurt each other *or* one another; **ils** *ou* **elles se parlent,** they talk to each other *or* one another; **il est dur de se quitter,** it is hard to part;

(c) (*passif*) **la clef s'est retrouvée,** the key has been found; **cet article se vend partout,** this article is sold *or* is on sale everywhere; **la porte s'est ouverte,** the door opened *or* came open;

(d) (*avec v impers*) **il se peut qu'elle vienne,** (it's possible that) she might come; **comment se fait-il que ...?,** how is it that ...? (*Note that* **se** *is often omitted before an infinitive dependent on* **faire, laisser, mener, envoyer, voir**; *eg* **se taire; faire taire les enfants**).

séance [seɑ̃s] *nf* **(a)** (*réunion*) sitting, session, meeting (*of assembly etc*); **être en s.,** to be sitting *or* in session; **la s. s'ouvrira/sera levée à huit heures,** the meeting will open/adjourn at eight o'clock; **en s. publique,** at an open meeting; *Jur* in open court; **s. d'information,** briefing; **s. de spiritisme,** seance;

(b) *Cin Th* performance, show; *Cin* **s. privée,** private showing;

(c) sitting (*for one's portrait etc*); **faire une longue s. à table,** to sit a long time over one's meal; *Méd* **traitement de trois séances,** course of three treatments; *Méd* **s. de rééducation,** physiotherapy session;

(d) (*période*) period, session; **s. de travail/d'entraînement,** working/training period *or* session;

(e) **s. tenante,** straight away, at once;

(f) *F Péj* (*scène*) performance; **il nous a fait une s. de larmes,** he turned on the waterworks.

séant [seɑ̃] **1** *adj Arch & Litt* becoming (**à,** to), fitting; **il ne serait pas s. de se contredire,** it would not be fitting to contradict each other. **2** *nm* **se mettre sur son s.,** to sit up (*in bed etc*); **être sur son s.,** to be in a sitting position; **tomber sur son s.,** to sit down with a bump.

seau, *pl* **seaux** [so] *nm* bucket, pail; **s. à glace** *ou* **à rafraîchir,** ice bucket; **s. à incendie,** fire bucket; **s. à charbon,** coal scuttle; **s. à biscuits,** biscuit barrel; **s. à champagne,** champagne bucket; **apporter un s. d'eau,** to bring a bucket(ful) *or* pail(ful) of water; *F* **il pleut à seaux,** it's pouring down, it's bucketing down.

sébacé [sebase] *adj* sebaceous (*gland*).

sébile [sebil] *nf* (wooden begging) bowl.

séborrhée [sebɔre] *nf Méd* seborrhoea, *US* seborrhea.

sébum [sebɔm] *nm Anat* sebum.

sec, sèche [sɛk, sɛʃ] **1** *adj* **(a)** dry (*weather, ground, throat, skin, wine etc*); dried (*cod, fruit etc*); seasoned, matured (*wood, cigar*); **regarder d'un œil s.,** to look on dry-eyed; **avoir la gorge sèche,** (*avoir soif*) to be dry *or* parched; **mettre qn au pain s. et à l'eau,** to put s.o. on bread and water; **mur de pierres sèches,** drystone wall; *Aut* **être en panne sèche,** to have run out of petrol *or Am* gas; **traverser un torrent à pied s.,** to cross a torrent without getting one's feet *or* shoes wet; **s. comme une allumette,** bone dry; *Admin* **le régime s.,** (*sans boisson*) prohibition; **pays secs,** (*sans boisson*) dry countries, prohibitionist countries; **perte sèche,** dead loss; **en cinq s.,** in no time; *F* **je l'ai s.!,** (*j'ai soif*) I'm dry *or* parched!; *Fig* am I annoyed!;

(b) (*maigre*) spare, gaunt (*person*); lean (*figure, horse*); **s. et nerveux,** wiry; **s. comme un coup de trique,** as thin as a rake;

(c) sharp, curt (*remark, answer*); incisive (*tone*); sharp (*blow*); unsympathetic, unfeeling (*heart etc*); dry, bald (*narrative, style*); **casser qch d'un coup s.,** to snap sth; **frapper à la porte d'un coup s.,** to rap on the door; **faire un accueil très s. à qn,** to give s.o. a very cool reception; **mine sèche,** sour face.

2 *adv* **(a)** **boire s.,** to drink one's spirits neat *or* straight; (*beaucoup*) to drink a lot, to be a heavy drinker;

(b) (*rudement*) hard, sharply; **la voiture a viré très s.,** the car swung round sharply; *Aut* **démarrer s.,** to shoot off, to tear off; **sonner s.,** (*of coin etc*) to chink; **fermer s. le couvercle,** to slam down the lid;

(c) **à s.,** dry; (*asseché*) dried up; *F* (*sans argent*) hard up, broke; *F* **au bout de cinq minutes il était à s.,** he dried up after five minutes; **nettoyage à s.,** dry cleaning; **maçonnerie à s.,** dry masonry; **navire à s.** *ou* **au s.,** ship aground *or* high and dry; **filer** *ou* **courir** *ou* **fuir à s. (de toile),** (*of ship*) to run under bare poles;

(d) **tout s.,** only, merely; *Arg* **aussi s.,** at once, straight away, right away.

3 *nm* dryness; **tenir au s.,** keep in a dry place.

4 *nf Arg* **sèche,** (*cigarette*) *Br* fag, *US* butt.

5 *n* **un vieux s.,** a wizened old man.

sécable [sekabl] *adj* divisible.

secam [sekam] *adj & nm TV* secam.

sécant, -ante [sekɑ̃, -ɑ̃t] *Math* **1** *adj* secant, cutting (*line, surface*). **2** *nf* **sécante,** secant.

sécateur [sekatœr] *nm* pruning shears, *Br* secateurs.

sécession [sesesjɔ̃] *nf* secession; **faire s.,** to secede (**de,** from).

sécessionniste [sesesjɔnist] *adj & n* secessionist.

séchage [seʃaʒ] *nm* drying (*of hay, clothes etc*); seasoning (*of wood*).

sèche-cheveux [sɛʃʃəvø] *nm inv* hair drier.

sèche-linge [sɛʃlɛ̃ʒ] *nm inv* (*appareil*) tumble dryer; (*armoire*) airing cupboard.

sèche-mains [sɛʃmɛ̃] *nm inv* (hot-air) hand drier.

sèchement [sɛʃmɑ̃] *adv* **(a)** (*avec dureté*) curtly, tartly; **(b)** **écrire s.,** to write in a bald style; **traiter un sujet s.,** to treat a subject baldly.

sécher [seʃe] *v* (**je sèche, n. séchons; je sécherai**) **1** *vt* to dry (*clothes, surface etc*); to dry up (*stream etc*); **le vent sèche la peau,** wind dries (out) the skin; **se sécher les cheveux,** to dry one's hair; **s. ses larmes,** to dry one's tears; *F* **s. un verre,** (*le vider*) to drain a glass; *Scol etc F* **s. un cours,** to skip *or* cut a class. **2** *vi* **(a)** (*of clothes, surface etc*) to (become) dry; **faire s. du bois,** to dry *or* season wood; **faire s. du linge,** to dry clothes; **s. d'impatience/d'ennui,** to be consumed with impatience/boredom; **s. sur pied,** (*of plant, Fig of person*) to wilt; **(b)** *F* (*ne pouvoir répondre*) to dry up; *Scol* to be stumped (*by an examiner*).

sécheresse [seʃrɛs, sɛ-] *nf* **(a)** dryness (*of the air, ground, throat etc*); **(b)** (*absence de pluie*) drought; **(c)** curtness (*of manner etc*); coldness, unfeelingness (*of heart etc*); dryness, baldness (*of style*); **parler avec s.,** to speak curtly.

sécherie [seʃri, sɛ-] *nf* (*appareil*) drying machine, drier; (*lieu*) drying area.

sécheur [seʃœr] *nm Tech* drying machine, drier.

séchoir [seʃwar] *nm* **(a)** (*appareil*) drier; **s. (à cheveux),** hair drier; *Ind* **s. à vapeur,** steam drier; **(b)** (*dispositif pliant*) clothes horse; **(c)** *Tech* (*lieu*) drying area; **s. à houblon,** oast house.

second, -onde [səgɔ̃, -ɔ̃d] **1** *adj* second; *Com* junior (*partner*); *Th* supporting, minor (*role*); **une seconde fois,** a second time; **en s. lieu,** in the second place, secondly; **seconde nature,** second nature (**chez qn,** with s.o.); **au s. étage,** on the second *or Am* third floor; **votre ami est un s. Sherlock Holmes,** your friend is another *or* a second Sherlock Holmes; **donner un s. souffle à l'économie,** to revitalize the economy; *Sp & Fig* **trouver son s. souffle,** to get one's second wind; *Mus* **les seconds violons,** the second violins; *Gram* **la seconde personne du singulier,** the second person singular; **de seconde main,** secondhand; **au s. plan,** in the background; *Rail* **seconde classe,** second class; **le don de seconde vue,** the gift of second sight; *Nau* **commandant** *ou* **officier en s.,** executive officer; **commander en s.,** to be second in command; *Jur* **signer en s.,** (*of notary*) to countersign (*deed*); *F* **ça passe en s.,** that comes second *or* takes second place; **de s. ordre** *ou* **choix,** second-rate; *Sp* **prendre la seconde place,** to come second, to take second place; *Phil etc* **causes secondes,** second causes; *Méd* **état s.,** semi-conscious state (*of a sleepwalker*); (*anormal*) trance, daze.

2 *nm* **(a)** (*assistant*) principal assistant; *Mil & F* second in command; *Nau* first mate; (*de duelliste*) second;

(b) (*étage*) second *or Am* third floor; **habiter au s.,** to live on the second *or* third floor.

3 *nf* **seconde (a)** *Typ* second proof; *Aut* second (gear); *Aut* **passer en seconde,** to change (up *or* down) into second; *Rail etc* **voyager en seconde,** to travel second class; *Scol* **(classe de) seconde,** *Br* ≈ fifth form, *Am* ≈ 12th grade; **élève de seconde,** *Br* ≈ fifth-former, *Am* ≈ 12th grader; *Mus* **seconde majeure/mineure,** major/minor second;

(b) second (*of time, arc, angle*); **aiguille des secondes,** second hand (*of a watch*); **j'en ai pour une seconde,** I'll only be a second *or* moment; **(attendez) une seconde!,** just a second!, just a moment!; **en un quart** *ou* **une fraction de seconde,** in a split second, in no time.

4 *n* second; *Sp* **finir bon s.,** to finish a good second; **la seconde est française,** the competitor in second place is French; **mon s.,** (*enfant*) my second child *or* son; **sans s.,** second to none; **intelligence sans seconde,** exceptional intelligence.

secondaire [səgɔ̃dɛr] **1** *adj* **(a)** *Scol* secondary; **établissement d'enseignement s.,** secondary school; **centre d'études secondaires,** ≈ *Br* comprehensive school; **(b)** (*peu important*) secondary, subordinate, of minor importance; *Rail* **voie s.,** side track; *Ling* **accent s.,** secondary accent, secondary stress; *Mus* **temps s.,** weak beat; *Th Littér* **intrigue s.,** sub-plot; **personnage s.,** minor character; **(c)** *Écon* secondary (*activities*); *Géol* **l'ère s.,** the secondary era. **2** *nm* **(a)** *Él* secondary winding; *Rad* secondary (*of transformer*); **(b)** **le s.,** *Géol* the secondary era; *Écon* the secondary sector, secondary activities.

secondairement [səgɔ̃dɛrmɑ̃] *adv* secondarily.

secondement [səgɔ̃dmɑ̃] *adv* secondly, in the second place.

seconder [səgɔ̃de] *vt* **(a)** to second, to back up, to support (*s.o.*); **(b)** to forward, to further, to promote (*s.o.'s interests, plans etc*).

secouement [səkumɑ̃] *nm* shaking; shake (*of the head*).

secouer [səkwe] **1** *vt* **(a)** to shake (*tree, one's head etc*); to plump up, to shake up (*cushion, pillow*); (*of shock, illness, news etc*) to shake, to affect (*s.o.*); (*of wind*) to buffet (*boat*); **nous avons été secoués pendant la traversée,** we had a rough crossing; *Fig* **il est impossible de s. son indifférence,** it is impossible to shake him out of his indifference; **il faut la s. pour qu'elle s'en sorte,** we have to shake her out of it; *F* **s. (les puces à) qn,** (*réprimander*) to tell s.o. off; (*pousser à agir*) to rouse s.o. to action; **(b)** (*se débarrasser de*) to shake off (*the yoke, the dust*). **2** *vi* **voiture qui secoue,** bumpy *or* jolting car. **3 se secouer** *vpr* (*agir*) to shake oneself *or* snap out of it, to pull oneself together.

secourable [səkurabl] *adj* helpful, willing to help; **main s.,** helping hand; **peu s.,** unhelpful.

secourir [səkurir] *vt* (*conj like* **courir**) to help, to aid (*s.o.*).

secourisme [səkurism] *nm Méd* first aid; **brevet de s.,** first-aid certificate.

secouriste [səkurist] *n* first-aid worker.

secours [səkur] *nm* help, relief, aid, assistance; (*financier, matériel*) aid; *Mil* relief; **crier au s.,** to call for help; **appel au s.,** call for help; **au s.!,** help!; *Méd* **premiers s.,** first aid; **boîte/trousse de s.,** first-aid box/kit; **poste de s.,** first-aid post; **s. en montagne,** mountain rescue; **les s. vont arriver,** help will arrive; *Mil* relief will arrive; **porter** *ou* **prêter (du) s. à qn,** to help *or* assist s.o.; **demander (du) s.,** to ask for help *or* assistance; **aller** *ou* **se porter au s. de qn,** to go to s.o.'s assistance; *Mil* **se porter au s. d'un bataillon,** to go in support of a battalion; **cela m'a rendu grand s., cela m'a été d'un grand s.,** it has been a great help (to me); **puis-je vous être d'aucun s.?,** can I be of (some) help *or* assistance?; **sa présence ne m'a été d'aucun s.,** his presence was of no help (to me); **le s. aux enfants,** child welfare work; **caisse de s.,** relief fund; **société de s. mutuels,** benefit society, friendly society; **sortie** *ou* **porte de s.,** emergency exit; *Fig* **c'est sa seule porte de s.,** it's his only way out; *Aut* **roue de s.,** spare wheel; **éclairage de s.,** emergency lighting (system); *Mil* **troupes de s., des s.,** relief troops, relieving force; *Rail* **corvée de s.,** breakdown gang; *Rail* **locomotive/train de s.,** relief engine/train.

secousse [səkus] *nf* shake, shaking; (*cahot*) jolt, jerk; *Fig* (*morale*) shock; **s. sismique,** (earth) tremor; **les secousses de la route/de la voiture,** the bumps in the road/the jolting of the car; **s. électrique,** electric shock; **se dégager d'une s.,** to jerk *or* wrench *or* shake oneself free; **sans s.,** smoothly; **par secousses,** (*avancer etc*) jerkily; (*travailler*) in fits and starts; (*respirer*) in gasps; **s. politique,** political upheaval; *Fig* **se remettre d'une s.,** to recover from a shock; *Fig* **ce serait une terrible s. pour lui,** it would be a terrible shock for him.

secret¹, -ète [səkrɛ, -ɛt] **1** *adj* secret (*orders, signal, treaty, door etc*); secret, hidden (*feelings, thoughts*); occult (*science*); *Fig* (*cachottier*) secretive, reticent (*person*); **la raison secrète d'un acte,** the secret *or* real reason for an action; *Admin* **très s., ultra-s.,** top secret; **la police secrète,** the secret police. **2** *nf* **la secrète,** (*police*) the secret police.

secret² *nm* **(a)** secret; **garder un s.,** to keep a secret; **trahir un s.,** to betray a secret; **mettre qn dans le s.,** to let s.o. into *or* in on the secret; **être du s.** *ou* **dans le s.,** to be in on the secret, *F* to be in the know; **n'avoir point de s. pour qn,** (*d'une personne*) to have no secrets from s.o.; **les ordinateurs n'ont pas de secrets pour elle,** computers hold no secrets for her; **s. d'État,** state secret; *Fig* **ce n'est pas un s. d'État!,** it's not a state secret!; **s. de fabrication,** trade secret; **ce n'est un s. pour personne,** it's no secret; **le s. du bonheur,** the secret of happiness; **trouver le s. pour faire qch,** to find the knack of doing sth; **c'est un des secrets de la nature,** it's one of nature's secrets; **elle a le s. des soirées réussies,** she knows the secret for giving successful parties; **bureau à s.,** desk with a secret compartment;

(b) (*discrétion*) secrecy; **dire qch à qn sous le sceau du s.,** to tell s.o. sth under pledge of secrecy; **en s.,** in secret, privately; **je vous demande le (plus grand) s.,** I'm asking you to keep this (strictly) secret; **abuser du** *ou* **trahir le s. professionnel,** to commit a breach of confidence; *Rel* **le s. de la confession,** the secrecy of the confessional;

(c) mettre qn au s., (*l'enfermer*) to put s.o. in solitary confinement; (*l'informer*) to let s.o. into *or* in on the secret.

secrétaire [səkretɛr] **1** *n* secretary; **s. bilingue/trilingue,** bilingual/trilingual secretary; **s. particulier,** private secretary; **s. médicale,** medical secretary; (*de dentiste*) dentist's secretary; **s. d'État,** Secretary of State; **s. d'ambassade,** secretary; *Journ* **s. de rédaction,** sub-editor; **s. général,** Secretary General; *Com* company secretary; *Admin* **s. de direction,** executive secretary, personal assistant; **s. d'administration,** (*fonctionnaire*) ≈ *Br* assistant principal; **s. de mairie,** ≈ town clerk; (*de village*) = mayor's secretarial assistant. **2** *nm* **(a)** *Orn* secretary bird; **(b)** (*meuble*) writing desk, secretaire.

secrétariat [səkretarja] *nm* **(a)** (*fonction*) secretaryship; **(b)** (*bureau*) secretary's office, secretariat; **(c)** (*métier*) secretarial work.

secrète [səkrɛt] *nf Rel* (*oraison*) secret.

secrètement [səkrɛtmɑ̃] *adv* secretly, in secret.

sécréter [sekrete] *vt* (**il sécrète; il sécrétera**) (*of gland etc*) to secrete; *Fig* **s. l'ennui,** to exude boredom.

sécréteur, -trice, *parfois* **-euse** [sekretœr, -tris, -øz] *adj* secreting, secretory (*gland etc*).

sécrétion [sekresjɔ̃] *nf Physiol* secretion; **glande à s. externe/interne,** exocrine/endocrine gland.

sécrétoire [sekretwar] *adj Physiol* secretory.

sectaire [sɛktɛr] *adj & n* sectarian.

sectarisme [sɛktarism] *nm* sectarianism.

secte [sɛkt] *nf* sect.

secteur [sɛktœr] *nm* **(a)** (*zone*) area, district; *Mil* sector, area (*of responsibility, attack etc*); **s. français de Berlin,** French sector of Berlin; *Com* **s. de vente,** sales area; **s. de surveillance,** *Rad etc* surveillance sector *or* area; (*de policier*) beat; *Él* **secteur (de distribution électrique),** mains; *Él* **branché sur le s.,** plugged into the mains; *Él* **se brancher sur le s.,** to run off the mains; *Él* **panne de s.,** mains failure;

(b) *Écon etc* sector, field (*of activity*); **le s. privé,** the private sector, private enterprise; **le s. public,** the public sector; **s. primaire/secondaire/tertiaire,** primary/secondary/tertiary sector; *F* **changer de s.,** to move (somewhere else); *F* **ce n'est pas mon s.,** that's not my line;

(c) *Astron Math* sector; *Ordinat* sector; *Tech* sector, quadrant; **graphique à secteurs,** pie chart; *Aut etc* **s. de direction,** steering sector; *Aut* **s. de frein,** quadrant *or* ratchet of the handbrake; *Nau* **s. dangereux,** dangerous quadrant (*of storm*).

section [sɛksjɔ̃] *nf* **(a)** (*action de couper*) section, cutting; *Vét* docking (*of tail*); **s. des tendons,** cutting of the tendons;

(b) (*division*) section (*of chapter, building etc*); *Admin* branch (*of a department, political party etc*); *Mil* platoon (*of infantry*); *Mil* section (*of artillery*); *Nau* sub-division (*of fleet*); *Biol* section (*of a genus*); *Mus* **la s. rythmique,** the rhythm section; **s. (électorale),** ward; **s. de vote,** polling station; *Mil* **chef de s.,** platoon commander; *Mil Av* flight commander; *Mil Av* **s. de bombardiers,** bomber flight;

(c) *Math* section; (*intersection*) intersection; *Archit Tech* (*dessin*) section, profile; *Math* **point de s.,** point of intersection; *Él* **s. morte,** idle coil; *Phys Nucl* **s. efficace,** cross section;

(d) stage (*on bus route etc*); **changement de s.,** ≈ *Br* fare stage; *Rail* **s. de block,** block section;

(e) *Scol* course.

sectionnement [sɛksjɔnmɑ̃] *nm* **(a)** division into sections; **(b)** (*coupe*) severing.

sectionner [sɛksjɔne] **1** *vt* **(a)** (*fractionner*) to divide (*district etc*) into sections; **(b)** (*couper*) to sever. **2 se sectionner** *vpr* to be severed.

sectionneur [sɛksjɔnœr] *nm Él* disconnecting switch, isolating switch.

sectoriel, -ielle [sɛktɔrjɛl] *adj* sector-related.

sectorisation [sɛktɔrizasjɔ̃] *nf* division into sectors.

sectoriser [sɛktɔrize] *vt* to divide into sectors.

sécu [seky] *nf F abrév* **sécurité sociale.**

séculaire [sekylɛr] *adj* **(a)** centennial (*event*); *Astron* secular; **année s.,** last year of the century; **(b)** (*très ancien*) centuries-old, age-old (*tree, tradition etc*).

sécularisation [sekylarizasjɔ̃] *nf* secularization.

séculariser [sekylarize] *vt* to secularize; to deconsecrate (*church*).

séculier, -ière [sekylje, -jɛr] **1** *adj* secular (*clergy, jurisdiction etc*); (*laïque*) lay, laic; **le bras s.,** the secular

arm. **2** *n* secular.
secundo [səgɔ̃do, sɛk-] *adv* secondly, in the second place.
sécurisant [sekyrizɑ̃] *adj* reassuring.
sécuriser [sekyrize] *vt* to reassure (*s.o.*), to make (*s.o.*) feel secure; **s. les rues,** to make the streets safe.
sécurit ® [sekyrit] *nm* safety glass.
sécuritaire [sekyritɛr] *adj* **mesures sécuritaires,** (*pour la protection des informations etc*) security measures; (*contre le danger physique*) safety measures.
sécurité [sekyrite] *nf* **(a)** (*ordre, stabilité*) security; (*sentiment*) (feeling of) security; **en s. contre ...,** safe *or* secure from ...; **être en s.,** to be safe *or* secure; **s. matérielle/affective,** material/emotional security; **je veille à sa s.,** I'm making sure he's safe; **s. de l'emploi,** security of employment; *Admin* **S. sociale,** Social Security, *Am* Welfare;
(b) (*absence de danger*) safety; **s. de la route** *ou* **routière,** road safety; *Admin* **s. publique,** public safety; **services de s.,** *Mil* security forces; stewards (*at demonstration etc*); security officers (*in firm etc*); **s. nationale/internationale,** national/international security; *Nau* **officier de s.,** officer in charge of fire precautions; *Tech Constr Ind* **marge de s.,** safety margin; **règles de s.,** safety rules *or* code; **cran de s.,** safety catch; **dispositif de s.,** safety device; **verre de s.,** safety glass, splinterproof glass; *Él* **éclairage de s.,** emergency lighting;
(c) (*dispositif*) safety catch; **porte munie d'une s.-enfants,** door with a childproof lock.
sédatif, -ive [sedatif, -iv] *adj & nm Méd* sedative.
sédation [sedɑsjɔ̃] *nf Méd* sedation.
sédentaire [sedɑ̃tɛr] *adj* sedentary (*occupation, life, work, person*); settled (*population*); garrison(ed) (*troops*); non-migrant (*bird*).
sédentairement [sedɑ̃tɛrmɑ̃] *adv* sedentarily.
sédentariser [sedɑ̃tarize] **1** *vt* to make (*population etc*) settle. **2 se sédentariser** *vpr* to settle.
sédiment [sedimɑ̃] *nm* sediment, deposit.
sédimentaire [sedimɑ̃tɛr] *adj Géol etc* sedimentary.
sédimentation [sedimɑ̃tɑsjɔ̃] *nf* sedimentation.
séditieux, -euse [sedisjø, -øz] **1** *adj* seditious (*speech, assembly*); seditious, rebellious (*troops etc*); **tenir des propos s.,** to talk treason. **2** *nm* rebel.
sédition [sedisjɔ̃] *nf* sedition.
séducteur, -trice [sedyktœr, -tris] **1** *n* seducer, *f* seductress. **2** *adj* seductive.
séduction [sedyksjɔ̃] *nf* **(a)** (*action*) (*sexuelle*) seduction; (*par son charme*) charming; **(b)** (*moyen de séduire*) attraction; **séductions physiques,** physical attractions; **exercer une s. mystérieuse/irrésistible sur qn,** to exercise a mysterious/an irresistible attraction over s.o.; **la s. des richesses,** the lure *or* attraction of wealth.
séduire [sedɥir] *v* (*conj like* **conduire**) **1** *vt* **(a)** (*sexuellement*) to seduce (*s.o.*); **(b)** (*gagner par son charme*) to charm (*s.o.*); (*of plan, words etc*) to attract (*s.o.*), to appeal to (*s.o., the imagination etc*); **cela m'a séduit du premier coup,** it took my fancy *or* attracted me *or* appealed to me at once. **2** *vi* to exercise one's charm.
séduisant [sedɥizɑ̃] *adj* attractive, appealing.
segment [sɛgmɑ̃] *nm* segment; *Tech* **s. de piston,** piston ring, packing ring; *Aut* **s. de frein,** brake shoe; *Aut* **frein à segments,** segmented brake.
segmentation [sɛgmɑ̃tɑsjɔ̃] *nf* segmentation.
segmenter [sɛgmɑ̃te] **1** *vt* to segment, to divide into segments; *Ordinat* to partition, to section, to segment. **2 se segmenter** *vpr* to segment, to divide into segments.
ségrégation [segregɑsjɔ̃] *nf* segregation.
ségrégationnisme [segregasjɔnism] *nm Pol* (policy of) racial segregation.
ségrégationniste [segregasjɔnist] *adj & n Pol* segregationist.
séguedille [segədij] *nf* (*danse, musique*) seguidilla.
seiche[1] [sɛʃ] *nf* (*mollusque*) cuttlefish; **os de s.,** cuttlebone.
seiche[2] *nf Géog* seiche.
seigle [sɛgl] *nm* rye; **pain de s.,** rye bread.
seigneur [sɛɲœr] *nm* **(a)** (*maître*) lord; (*d'un manoir*) lord of the manor, ≈ *Br* squire; *Hist* (*homme noble*) nobleman, noble; **mon s. et maître,** my lord and master; **le s. de Sercq,** the seigneur of Sark; (*femme*) the dame of Sark; *Hist* **les seigneurs,** the nobility; **à tout s. tout honneur,** honour where honour is due; **mener une vie de grand s.,** to live like a lord; **ne faites pas le grand s.,** don't try and lord it over us; **en grand s.,** in grand style; **(b)** *Rel* **le S.,** the Lord (God); **Notre-S.,** our Lord; **le jour du S.,** the Lord's day; *F* **S.!, S. Dieu!,** good Lord!; **(c)** (*poisson*) lumpfish.
seigneurial, -aux [sɛɲœrjal, -o] *adj* (*magnifique*) stately, lordly; *Hist* seigneurial (*rights etc*).
seigneurie [sɛɲœri] *nf Hist* (*terre, pouvoir*) seigneury; **votre S.,** (*titre*) your Lordship; *Iron* **sa S.** his lordship, *Arg* his nibs.
sein [sɛ̃] *nm* (*de femme*) breast; *Litt* (*d'homme*) breast, bosom; **serrer qn sur son s.,** to press s.o. to one's bosom *or* heart; **donner le s. à un enfant,** to breast-feed a child; **danseuse aux seins nus,** topless dancer; **au s. de la famille,** in the bosom of the family; **au s. du luxe,** in the lap of luxury; **au s. de la commission,** within the committee; *Litt* **enfant que j'ai porté dans mon s.,** child that I carried in my womb; **le s. de la terre,** the bowels of the earth.
seine [sɛn] *nf Pêche* seine, draw net.
Seine [sɛn] *nf* **la S.,** the Seine.
seing [sɛ̃] *nm Jur* **acte sous s. privé,** private agreement (*without legal certification*).
séisme [seism] *nm* earthquake; *Fig Litt* upheaval.
séismique [seismik] *adj* seismic.
séismo- [seismɔ-] *préf* = **SISMO-.**
seize [sɛz] **1** *adj inv* sixteen; **Louis S.,** Louis the Sixteenth; **numéro s.,** number sixteen. **2** *nm inv* sixteen; **le s. mai,** (on) the sixteenth of May, (on) May the sixteenth, *Am* (on) May sixteenth; **demeurer au s.,** to live at number sixteen.
seizième [sɛzjɛm] **1** *adj num* sixteenth. **2** *n* sixteenth. **3** *nm* (*fraction*) sixteenth (part).
séjour [seʒur] *nm* **(a)** (*résidence*) residence; (*arrêt*) stay; **droit de s.,** right of residence *or* abode; **carte** *ou* **permis de s.,** residence permit; **s. de quinze jours,** two week(s') *or Br* fortnight's stay; **(salle de) s.,** living room; **(b)** *Litt* (*lieu*) abode.
séjourner [seʒurne] *vi* (*of person*) to stay; (*of snow etc*) to lie.
sel [sɛl] *nm* **(a)** salt; **s. de cuisine,** cooking salt; **s. fin,** fine salt; **gros s.,** coarse salt; **s. marin,** sea salt; **régime sans s.,** salt-free diet; *F* **mettre** *ou* **mêler son grain de s.,** to butt in; *Fig* **le s. de la terre,** the salt of the earth; *Pharm* **s. d'Angleterre** *ou* **d'Epsom,** Epsom salts; **s. pour bains,** bath salts; **sels (volatils) anglais,** smelling salts; *Ch* **s. double,** double salt; **(b)** *Fig* (*esprit*) piquancy, wit.
select, sélect [selɛkt] *adj F* select (*gathering, clientele etc*); **le monde s.,** high society.
sélecteur [selɛktœr] *nm Ordinat Él etc* selector; (*de motocyclette*) gear(-change) pedal.
sélectif, -ive [selɛktif, -iv] *adj* selective; *Rad* **récepteur s.,** selective receiver.
sélection [selɛksjɔ̃] *nf* **(a)** selection; **faire** *ou* **opérer une s. parmi ...,** to make a selection from among ...; **s. professionnelle,** professional recruitment; *Sp* **match de s.,** trial game; *Biol* **s. naturelle,** natural selection; **(b)** *Mus* selection (**sur,** from).
sélectionné [selɛksjɔne] **1** *adj* selected (*player, product etc*). **2** *n Sp* selected player.
sélectionner [selɛksjɔne] *vt* to select.
sélectionneur, -euse [selɛksjɔnœr, -øz] *n* selector.
sélectivité [selɛktivite] *nf Rad* selectivity.
sélénieux [selenjø] *adj m Ch* selenious (*acid*).
sélénique [selenik] *adj Ch* selenic (*acid*).
sélénite [selenit] **1** *n* (*habitant de la lune*) inhabitant of the moon. **2** *adj* of the moon.
sélénium [selenjɔm] *nm Ch* selenium.
sélénographie [selenɔgrafi] *nf* selenography.
sélénographique [selenɔgrafik] *adj* selenographic(al) (*map etc*).
self [sɛlf] **1** *nm F* self-service restaurant. **2** *nf Él* self-induction; **(bobine de) s.,** self-induction coil.
self-control [sɛlfkɔ̃trɔl] *nm* self-control.
self-inductance [sɛlfɛ̃dyktɑ̃s] *nf Él* self inductance.
self-induction [sɛlfɛ̃dyksjɔ̃] *nf Él* self induction.
self-made-man [sɛlfmɛdman] *nm* self-made man; (*pl self-made-men*).
self-service [sɛlfsɛrvis] *nm* self-service restaurant; (*pl self-services*).
selle [sɛl] *nf* **(a)** (*de cheval, bicyclette*) saddle; **se mettre en s.,** to mount; **être bien en s.,** to have a good seat; *Fig* to be firmly in the saddle; **aider qn à monter en s.,** to help s.o. into the saddle; *Fig F* to give s.o. a leg up *or* a helping hand; **monter sans s.,** to ride bareback; **(b)** *Physiol* stool; **aller à la s.,** (*déféquer*) to pass *or* have a motion; **les selles du bébé,** the baby's stools *or* motions; **(c)** *Culin* **s. de mouton,** saddle of mutton; **s. de bœuf,** baron of beef; **(d)** (*de sculpteur*) turntable.
seller [sele] *vt* to saddle (*horse*).

sellerie [sɛlri] *nf* **(a)** (*selles, métier*) saddlery; **(b)** (*salle*) harness room, tack room.

sellette [sɛlɛt] *nf* **(a)** *F* **mettre qn/être sur la s.,** to have s.o./to be in the hot seat *or* under examination; **(b)** (*d'ouvrier de bâtiment*) cradle; **(c)** (*de sculpteur*) turntable; **(d)** (*de cheval de trait*) saddle.

sellier [selje] *nm* saddler, harness maker.

selon [s(ə)lɔ̃] *prép* **(a)** according to; **s. lui,** according to him; **s. moi,** in my opinion *or* view, as I see it; **s. toute vraisemblance,** in all likelihood *or* probability; **s. le cas,** as the case may be; **varier s. les cas/les saisons/***etc*, to vary from case to case/season to season/*etc*; *F* **c'est s.,** it all depends; **(b) s. que** + *ind*, depending on whether.

Seltz [sɛls] *nm* **eau de S.,** soda water, Seltzer (water).

semailles [səmɑj] *nfpl* **(a)** sowing; **(le temps des) s.,** sowing time; **(b)** (*graines*) seeds.

semaine [s(ə)mɛn] *nf* **(a)** week; (*jours ouvrés*) (working) week; **deux fois par s.,** twice a week; **une s. de vacances,** a week's holiday; **fin de s.,** weekend; *Can* **bonne fin de s.!,** have a good weekend!; *Scol* **pensionnaire à la s.,** weekly boarder; *F* **politique à la petite s.,** shortsighted policy; *F* **la s. des quatre jeudis,** never (in a month of Sundays); **jour de s.,** weekday; **la s. seulement,** weekdays only; **il est toujours à Paris en s.,** he is always in Paris during the week; **faire la s. anglaise,** to work a five-day week; **s. de trente-cinq heures,** thirty-five-hour week; **(b)** (*salaire*) week's pay *or* wages; **(c)** *Mil etc* (*tour de service*) week's duty; **officier de s.,** duty officer for the week.

semainier, -ière [s(ə)menje, -jɛr] **1** *n* person on duty for the week; *Mil* duty officer for the week. **2** *nm* **(a)** (*meuble*) chest of seven drawers; **(b)** (*agenda*) desk diary.

sémantème [semɑ̃tɛm] *nm Ling* semanteme.

sémanticien, -ienne [semɑ̃tisjɛ̃, -jɛn] *n* semanticist.

sémantique [semɑ̃tik] *Ling* **1** *adj* semantic. **2** *nf* semantics.

sémaphore [semafɔr] *nm Rail* semaphore signal; *Nau* signal station (*on land*).

semblable [sɑ̃blabl] **1** *adj* similar; **être semblables,** to be similar *or* alike; **s. à qch,** similar to sth; **deux cas tout à fait semblables,** two cases absolutely alike; **s. à son père,** like his father; **triangles semblables,** similar triangles; **de semblables projets,** such plans, plans like that; **je n'ai rien dit de s.,** I said nothing of the sort, I said no such thing. **2** *n* **(a)** fellow; **vous et vos semblables,** you and people like you, you and your kind *or* sort; **(b)** (*être humain*) fellow man *or* creature; **nos semblables,** our fellow men, our fellow creatures.

semblant [sɑ̃blɑ̃] *nm* semblance, appearance (**de,** of); **faux s.,** pretence, sham; **elle portait un s. de jupe,** she was wearing an apology for a skirt; **faire un s. de résistance,** to make a show of resistance; **faire s. de faire qch,** to pretend to do sth; **tu fais s.?,** are you pretending?; **sans faire s. de rien,** without seeming to take any notice, as if nothing had happened.

sembler [sɑ̃ble] *v* (*aux* **avoir**) **1** *vi* to seem; **elle semblait malade,** she seemed (to be) ill; **il me semble vieux,** he seems *or* looks old to me; **s. être/faire,** to seem to be/do. **2** *v impers* **il me semblait rêver,** it seemed to me *or* I thought (that) I was dreaming; **il me semble avoir entendu son nom,** I seem to have heard his name; **à ce qu'il me semble ...,** it strikes me (that) ...; **faites comme bon vous semble(ra),** do as you think best; **il semble que** + *ind or sub*, it seems that ..., it looks as if ...; **il me semble que** + *ind*, it seems to me that ... .

sème [sɛm] *nm Ling* sememe.

semé [s(ə)me] *adj* **s. de,** strewn with (*rocks etc*); dotted with (*daisies etc*); studded with (*diamonds etc*); sprinkled with (*quotations etc*); **s. d'embûches** *ou* **de pièges,** full of traps.

séméio- [semejɔ-] *préf* = **SÉMIO-**.

semelle [s(ə)mɛl] *nf* **(a)** sole (*of shoe*); foot (*of stocking, sock*); **s. intérieure,** insole, inner sole; **chaussures à semelles de caoutchouc,** rubber-soled shoes; **remettre une s. à une chaussure,** to resole a shoe; **ne pas avancer d'une s.,** to make no progress; **il ne reculera pas d'une s.,** he won't give an inch; **il ne me quitte pas d'une s.,** he's always at my heels; **(b)** *Tech* bed plate (*of machine, lathe*); shoe (*of anchor, sledge*); **s. de poutre,** girder flange; **s. de coussinet de rail,** chair foot; **(c)** *Nau* **s. de dérive,** leeboard.

semence [s(ə)mɑ̃s] *nf* **(a)** *Agr* seed; *Physiol* semen; *Agr* **blé de s.,** seed corn; *Fig* **semences de discorde,** seeds of discord; **s. de perles,** seed pearls; **s. de diamants,** diamond sparks; **(b)** (*clou*) (tin)tack.

semer [s(ə)me] *vt* (**je sème, n. semons; je sèmerai**) **(a)** to sow (*seeds*); **(b)** to strew, to scatter (*flowers etc*); to spread (*news, discord*); **s. de l'argent,** to spend money recklessly, to throw money about; **(c)** *F* (*distancer*) to shake (*s.o.*) off, to get rid of (*s.o.*); (*laisser tomber*) to lose, to shed (*sth*).

semestre [s(ə)mɛstr] *nm* **(a)** (*six mois*) half-year; **(b)** (*paiement*) half-yearly *or* six-monthly payment; **(c)** *Scol Univ* semester.

semestriel, -elle [səmɛstrijɛl] *adj* half-yearly, six-monthly.

semestriellement [səmɛstrijɛlmɑ̃] *adv* half-yearly, every six months; *Scol Univ* every semester.

semeur, -euse [s(ə)mœr, -øz] *n Agr* sower; *Fig* spreader, disseminator (*of news etc*); *Fig* sower (*of discord*).

semi- [səmi] *préf* semi-; NOTE *in the plural of compound words prefixed by* **semi-**, **semi-** *remains invariable and the following noun or adj takes the pl form.*

semi-automatique [səmiɔtɔmatik] *adj* semiautomatic.

semi-chenillé [səmiʃənije] *adj & nm* **(véhicule) s.-c.,** half-track (vehicle).

semi-circulaire [səmisirkylɛr] *adj* semicircular.

semi-conducteur, -trice [səmikɔ̃dyktœr, -tris] *Él* **1** *adj* semiconducting. **2** *nm* semiconductor.

semi-conserve [səmikɔ̃sɛrv] *nf* semi-preserved food; **semi-conserves,** semi-preserved goods.

semi-consonne [səmikɔ̃sɔn] *nf* semivowel, semiconsonant.

semi-fini [səmifini] *adj Écon* semifinished (*product*).

semi-fixe [səmifiks] *adj* semi-fixed.

semi-historique [səmiistɔrik] *adj* semi-historical.

semi-illettré [səmiiletre] *adj* semiliterate.

sémillant [semijɑ̃] *adj* lively, bright (*child, wit*); bright, engaging (*glance*).

semi-lunaire [səmilynɛr] *adj* half-moon-shaped.

semi-mensuel, -elle [səmimɑ̃sɥɛl] *adj* bi-monthly, *surtout Br* fortnightly (*periodical etc*).

séminaire [seminɛr] *nm* **(a)** *Univ* seminar; (*conférence*) seminar, conference; **(b)** *Rel* **(grand) s.,** (Roman Catholic) seminary, training college (*for the priesthood*); **petit s.,** secondary school (*staffed by priests*).

séminal, -aux [seminal, -o] *adj Biol* seminal.

séminariste [seminarist] *nm Rel* seminarist.

semi-nomade [səminɔmad] **1** *adj* seminomadic. **2** *n* seminomad.

semi-officiel, -ielle [səmiɔfisjɛl] *adj* semiofficial.

sémiologie [semjɔlɔʒi] *nf Méd Ling* sem(e)iology.

sémiologique [semjɔlɔʒik] *adj Méd Ling* sem(e)iological.

semiologue [semjɔlɔg] *n Méd Ling* sem(e)iologist.

sémiotique [semjɔtik] **1** *adj* semiotic. **2** *nf* semiotics.

semi-perméable [səmipɛrmeabl] *adj* semipermeable.

semi-portique [səmipɔrtik] *nm* semi-portal bridge crane.

semi-précieux, -ieuse [səmipresjø, -jøz] *adj* semiprecious (*stone*).

semi-public, -ique [səmipyblik] *adj Jur* semipublic.

sémique [semik] *adj Ling* semic.

semi-remorque [səmir(ə)mɔrk] **1** *nf* (*remorque*) semitrailer, *Am F* semi. **2** *nm* (*poids lourd*) semitrailer, *Am F* semi.

semi-rigide [səmiriʒid] *adj* semirigid (*airship*).

semis [s(e)mi] *nm Agr* **(a)** (*action*) sowing; **(b)** (*plant*) seedbed; **(c)** (*jeune plante*) seedling.

sémite [semit] **1** *adj* Semitic. **2** *n* Semite.

sémitique [semitik] *adj* Semitic.

sémitisant, -ante [semitizɑ̃, -ɑ̃t] **, sémitiste** [semitist] *n* Semitic scholar, Semitist.

sémitisme [semitism] *nm* Semitism.

semi-ton [səmitɔ̃] *nm Mus* semitone.

semi-voyelle [səmivwajɛl] *nf Ling* semivowel.

semoir [s(ə)mwar] *nm Agr* **(a)** (*sac*) seed bag; **(b)** (*machine*) sowing machine, seeder.

semonce [səmɔ̃s] *nf* **(a)** (*réprimande*) reprimand, scolding, lecture; **une verte s.,** a good telling-off; **(b)** *Nau* **coup de s.,** warning shot.

semoule [səmul] *nf* semolina; **sucre s.,** caster sugar.

sempiternel, -elle [sɛ̃pitɛrnɛl] *adj* eternal, never-ending.

sempiternellement [sɛ̃pitɛrnɛlmɑ̃] *adv* eternally, endlessly.

sénat [sena] *nm* senate; (*édifice*) senate (house).

sénateur [senatœr] *nm* senator.

sénatorial, -aux [senatɔrjal, -o] *adj* senatorial.

séné [sene] *nm Bot Pharm* senna.

sénéchal, -aux [seneʃal, -o] *nm Hist* seneschal.

sénéchaussée [seneʃose] *nf Hist* (*juridiction*) seneschalsy, seneschal's jurisdiction; (*tribunal*) seneschal's court.
séneçon [sɛnsɔ̃] *nm Bot* groundsel.
Sénégal [senegal] *nm* Senegal.
sénégalais, -aise [senegalɛ, -ɛz] **1** *adj* Senegalese. **2** *n* **S.,** Senegalese.
Sénégambie [senegɑ̃bi] *nf* Senegambia.
Sénèque [senɛk] *nm* Seneca.
sénescence [senesɑ̃s] *nf Biol* senescence.
sénescent [senesɑ̃] *adj Biol* senescent.
sénevé [senve] *nm* **(a)** *Bot* mustard; **(b)** (*graine*) mustard seed.
sénile [senil] *adj Méd & F Péj* senile.
sénilité [senilite] *nf* senility, senile decay.
senior [senjɔr] *adj & n Sp* senior.
senne [sɛn] *nf Pêche* seine, draw net.
señorita [senjɔrita] *nm* small cigar, whiff.
sens [sɑ̃s] *nm* **(a)** sense (*of touch, sight, beauty, time, rhythm etc*); **le sixième s.,** the sixth sense; **perdre/reprendre ses s.,** to lose/regain consciousness; **s. moral,** moral sense, conscience; **avoir le s. de l'humour/du ridicule/***etc*, to have a sense of humour/the ridiculous/*etc*; **avoir le s. des affaires,** to have good business sense; **plaisir des s.,** sensual pleasures; **éveiller les s.,** to excite the senses;
(b) (*jugement*) sense; **s. commun/bon s.,** common sense/good sense; **un homme de bon s.,** a sensible man; **gros** *ou* **robuste** *ou* **bon s.,** elementary common sense; **cela n'a pas de s. (commun)** *ou* **bon s.,** there's no sense to *or* in it; **en dépit du bon s.,** contrary to common sense; **le bon s. veut que ...,** it stands to reason that ...; **vous avez perdu le s. commun,** you've taken leave of your senses; **rentrer dans son bon s.,** to come to one's senses (again); **s. pratique,** practical (common) sense; **il n'a aucun s. pratique,** he's completely unpractical, he's not practically minded; **à mon s.,** to my mind, in my view *or* opinion; **j'abonde dans votre s.,** I entirely agree with you; **cela tombe sous le s.,** it's perfectly obvious;
(c) (*signification*) meaning, sense (*of a word etc*); **s. propre/figuré,** literal *or* basic/figurative meaning *or* sense; **au s. ordinaire du mot,** in the ordinary meaning *or* sense of the word; **mot à double s.,** word with a double meaning; **faire un faux s.,** to misinterpret, to misunderstand; **ces paroles n'ont pas de s. pour moi,** these words mean *or* convey nothing to me; **en ce s. que ...,** in (the sense) that ...;
(d) (*direction*) direction; (*position*) way; **dans le bon/mauvais s.,** in the right/wrong direction; (*position horizontale*) the right/wrong way round; (*position verticale*) the right/wrong way up; **en s. inverse,** in the opposite direction; **dans le s. du courant,** with the current, with the stream; **dans le s. de la longueur,** lengthwise, lengthways; **dans le s. de la largeur,** widthwise, breadthwise, across; **dans les deux s.,** both ways; **tailler dans le s. du bois,** to cut wood in the direction of the grain *or* along the grain; **dans le s. inverse du grain,** against *or* across the grain; **dans le s. des aiguilles d'une montre,** clockwise; **dans le s. inverse des aiguilles d'une montre,** anticlockwise, *Am* counterclockwise; **courir dans tous les s.,** to run in all directions; **s. de la circulation,** direction of the traffic; **rue à double s.,** street with two-way traffic; **s. unique,** (*sur panneau*) one-way (street); **s. interdit,** (*sur panneau*) no entry; *Aut* **s. giratoire,** roundabout, *Am* traffic circle; *Rail* **voyager dans le s. de la marche,** to travel facing the engine; *Math* **s. direct,** positive direction; *Math* **s. rétrograde,** negative direction; *Ordinat* **s. de déroulement,** flow direction; **s. dessus dessous** [sɑ̃tsytsu] , upside down, the wrong way up; (*en désordre*) upside down, in a mess, in a muddle, in a state of confusion; **s. devant derrière,** back to front, the wrong way round.
sensas(s) [sɑ̃sas] *adj F* fantastic, great.
sensation [sɑ̃sasjɔ̃] *nf* **(a)** sensation; (*impression*) feeling; **avoir la s. que ...,** to have a *or* the feeling that ...; **cela donne la s. de ...,** it feels like ...; **(b)** (*scandale*) **presse à s.,** gutter press; **roman/nouvelles à s.,** sensational novel/news; **faire s.,** to create a sensation.
sensationnel, -elle [sɑ̃sasjɔnɛl] *adj* sensational (*news, novel etc*); *F* (*remarquable*) fantastic, great.
sensé [sɑ̃se] *adj* sensible (*person, action, remark etc*).
senseur [sɑ̃sœr] *nm Électron* sensor, sensing device.
sensibilisateur, -trice [sɑ̃sibilizatœr, -tris] **1** *adj Phot etc* sensitizing. **2** *nm Phot* sensitizer, sensitizing bath. **3** *nf Biol* **sensibilisatrice,** sensitizer.
sensibilisation [sɑ̃sibilizasjɔ̃] *nf Phot Méd* sensitization; *Fig* growing awareness (**à,** of); **la s. de l'opinion,** (*action*) heightening public awareness; (*résultat*) heightened *or* increased public awareness.
sensibiliser [sɑ̃sibilize] **1** *vt Phot Méd etc* to sensitize; *Fig* **s. qn à,** to heighten s.o.'s awareness of, to make s.o. aware *or* sensitive to (*problem etc*); **s. l'opinion,** to heighten *or* increase public awareness (**à,** of). **2 se sensibiliser** *vpr* **se s. à,** to become aware of *or* sensitive to.
sensibilité [sɑ̃sibilite] *nf* sensitiveness, sensitivity (*of person*); (*compassion*) compassion, feeling; sensitiveness (*of skin, film etc*); sensitivity (*of an instrument*); **s. à fleur de peau,** hypersensitivity; **enfant d'une grande s.,** extremely sensitive child; **la s. romantique/wagnérienne,** (the) Romantic/Wagnerian sensibility; **avoir de la s.,** to be compassionate *or* soft-hearted.
sensible [sɑ̃sibl] **1** *adj* **(a)** sensitive (*person*); **s. à,** sensitive to (*ridicule, charm etc*); susceptible to (*pain, influence*); aware of (*danger*); **s. sur,** sensitive about; **peu s.,** insensitive, *F* thick-skinned; **avoir l'oreille s.,** to have a keen sense of hearing; **avoir la peau s.,** to have sensitive skin; *Fig F* to be thin-skinned; **ouïe peu s.,** dull hearing; **être s. au froid,** to feel the cold; (*of plant*) to be tender; **être s. aux bontés de qn,** to appreciate s.o.'s kindness; **être s. à la musique,** to have a feeling for music; *Mus* **la note s.,** the leading note; *Fig* **toucher la note** *ou* **la corde s.,** to appeal to the emotions;
(b) (*compatissant*) compassionate, sympathetic; **cœur s.,** tender heart; **peu s.,** callous; **peu s. à,** impervious to;
(c) sensitive (*plate, balance, thermometer etc*);
(d) (*douloureux*) tender, painful, sore (*feet etc*); sensitive (*tooth*); **s. au toucher,** tender *or* painful to the touch; **toucher qn à un endroit s.,** to touch s.o. on a tender spot *or* on the raw; *Fig* **blesser qn à l'endroit s.,** to tread on s.o.'s corns;
(e) (*perceptible*) perceptible (*sound etc*); appreciable, considerable (*difference, progress etc*); **le monde s.,** the tangible world; **d'une manière s.,** perceptibly, appreciably; **dommages sensibles,** serious damage; **un vide s.,** a noticeable gap; **éprouver un plaisir s.,** to feel a keen pleasure;
(f) (*sentant*) sentient.
2 *nf Mus* leading note.
sensiblement [sɑ̃sibləmɑ̃] *adv* **(a)** (*notablement*) appreciably, perceptibly; **(b)** (*à peu près*) approximately, roughly, more or less.
sensiblerie [sɑ̃sibləri] *nf Péj* sentimentality.
sensitif, -ive [sɑ̃sitif, -iv] **1** *adj* **(a)** *Litt* oversensitive; **(b)** *Physiol* sensory. **2** *nf Bot* **sensitive,** sensitive plant, mimosa pudica.
sensoriel, -ielle [sɑ̃sɔrjɛl] *adj* sensorial, sensory.
sensorimoteur, -trice [sɑ̃sɔrimɔtœr, -tris] *adj Méd* sensorimotor.
sensualisme [sɑ̃sɥalism] *nm Phil* sensualism, sensationalism.
sensualiste [sɑ̃sɥalist] *adj & n Phil* sensualist, sensationalist.
sensualité [sɑ̃sɥalite] *nf* sensuality.
sensuel, -elle [sɑ̃sɥɛl] *adj* sensual (*person, pleasure etc*); sensual, sensuous (*lips etc*).
sentant [sɑ̃tɑ̃] *adj* sentient.
sente [sɑ̃t] *nf* (*sentier*) (foot)path.
sentence [sɑ̃tɑ̃s] *nf* **(a)** (*jugement*) sentence, judgment; **(b)** *Vieilli* (*maxime*) maxim.
sentencieusement [sɑ̃tɑ̃sjøzmɑ̃] *adv* sententiously.
sentencieux, -ieuse [sɑ̃tɑ̃sjø, -jøz] *adj* sententious.
senteur [sɑ̃tœr] *nf* **(a)** *Litt* scent; **(b)** *Bot* **pois de s.,** sweet pea.
senti [sɑ̃ti] **1** *adj* heartfelt (*words etc*); **quelques mots bien sentis,** a few well chosen words. **2** *nm Phil* sense datum.
sentier [sɑ̃tje] *nm* (foot)path; *Fig* path; **s. pour cavaliers,** bridle path; **s. battu,** beaten track; *Fig* **sur le s. de la guerre,** on the warpath.
sentiment [sɑ̃timɑ̃] *nm* **(a)** (*sensation*) feeling, sensation (*of joy, relief, hunger etc*);
(b) sense (*of beauty, duty*); **avoir le s. que ...,** to have a *or* the feeling that ...; **privé de s.,** devoid of feeling; numb (*limb etc*); **juger par s.,** to judge by one's impressions;
(c) faire appel aux bons sentiments de qn, to appeal to s.o.'s finer feelings; *F* **c'est parti d'un bon s.,** it was well meant, the intention was good;
(d) (*émotion*) feeling; **le s. de la nature,** a feeling for nature; **ses sentiments vis-à-vis de moi,** his feelings towards me; *Mus* **jouer avec s.,** to play with feeling; *F* **allons, du s.!,** come on, give it some feeling!; **faire du s.,**

to sentimentalize; **je ne fais pas de s. en affaires,** I don't let sentiment interfere with business; **allons! pas de s.!,** come on, don't be sentimental!; *F* **le faire au s.,** to appeal to the emotions; **avoir qn au s.,** to win s.o. over by appealing to his feelings; **prendre qn par les sentiments,** to appeal to s.o.'s feelings;

(e) avoir du s. pour qn, to be drawn to s.o., to feel attracted to s.o.;

(f) veuillez agréer (l'expression de) mes sentiments distingués, yours faithfully; **veuillez bien recevoir l'expression de mes sentiments les meilleurs,** yours sincerely;

(g) *Litt* (*opinion*) feeling, opinion.

sentimental, -ale, -aux [sɑ̃timɑ̃tal, -o] **1** *adj* **(a) vie sentimentale,** love life; **intrigue sentimentale,** love affair; **(b)** (*romantique*) sentimental. **2** *n* **c'est une sentimentale,** she is sentimental.

sentimentalement [sɑ̃timɑ̃talmɑ̃] *adv* sentimentally.

sentimentalisme [sɑ̃timɑ̃talism] *nm* sentimentalism, sentimentality.

sentimentaliste [sɑtimɑ̃talist] *adj & n* sentimentalist.

sentimentalité [sɑ̃timɑ̃talite] *nf* sentimentality.

sentine [sɑ̃tin] *nf Nau* bilge (*of ship*); *Litt* **s. de tous les vices,** sink of iniquity.

sentinelle [sɑ̃tinɛl] *nf Mil* **(a)** (*soldat*) sentry; **(b)** (*veille*) guard(ing), watch; **en s.,** on guard, on sentry duty.

sentir [sɑ̃tir] *v* (*prp* **sentant**; *pp* **senti**; *pr ind* **je sens, il sent, n. sentons, ils sentent**; *pr sub* **je sente**; *impf* **je sentais**; *p hist* **je sentis**; *fu* **je sentirai**) **1** *vt* **(a)** to feel (*pain, hunger, cold, joy, sorrow etc*); **je sentais trembler le plancher,** I could feel the floor trembling; **je sens l'hiver qui vient,** I can feel winter coming; **on ne sent pas la différence,** you can't feel the difference; **s. quelque chose pour qn,** to feel something for s.o., to feel drawn to s.o.; **je ne sens rien pour lui,** I feel nothing towards him; *F* **s. ses bras/ses jambes,** to feel pains in one's arms/one's legs; **je ne sens plus mes jambes/mes pieds,** I can hardly feel my legs/my feet;

(b) (*être conscient de*) to be conscious of, to feel (*insult, one's strength etc*); to be aware of *or* conscious of (*danger*); **s. grandir son influence,** to feel one's influence growing; **je sens que vous avez raison,** I have a *or* the feeling that you are right; **ce sont des choses que l'on sent,** you can sense *or* feel things like that; **sa façon de s. les choses,** how he feels about things; **s. la barre,** (*of ship*) to answer to the helm; **il m'a fait s. que ...,** he gave me to understand that ...; **faire s. son autorité,** to make one's authority felt; **l'effet se fera s.,** the effect will be felt;

(c) (*par l'odorat*) to smell (*odour, flower etc*); **je ne sens rien,** I can't smell anything; *F* **je ne peux pas le s.,** (*supporter*) I can't bear him, I can't stand (the sight of) him; *Fig* **s. le cadavre,** to scent disaster, to smell ruin; **s. qch de loin,** to feel sth coming; **s. qn de loin,** to see through s.o.;

(d) (*avoir l'odeur de*) to smell of (*sth*); (*avoir un goût de*) to taste of (*sth*); **cela sent le brûlé,** there's a smell of burning; **ça sent bon le pain frais,** there's a delicious smell of fresh bread; **vin qui sent le bouchon,** corked wine; **la pièce sent l'humidité,** the room smells *or* feels damp; **la salle sentait le tabac à plein nez,** the room was reeking of tobacco; *Fig* **il sentait l'acteur à plein nez,** he had actor written all over him; *Fig* **ce livre sent le labeur,** a lot of hard work has obviously gone into this book, *Péj* this book reeks of effort; *Fig* **il sent le cadavre,** he looks as if he is on his last legs.

2 *vi* **(a) s. bon/mauvais,** to smell good/bad; **fleurs qui sentent bon,** sweet-smelling flowers;

(b) *F* (*sentir mauvais*) to smell (bad); **il sent des pieds,** his feet smell.

3 se sentir *vpr* **(a) cela se sent,** it is something that you feel *or* sense *or* that needs no explanation;

(b) se s. bien/fatigué/*etc*, to feel well/tired/*etc*; **se s. dix ans de moins,** to feel ten years younger; **elle se sentait mourir/revivre,** she felt she was dying/coming alive again; **se s. du courage,** to feel brave *or* full of courage; **je ne m'en sens pas le courage,** I don't feel equal *or* up to it; **tu t'en sens capable?,** do you think you can manage it?, do you feel capable of it?;

(c) il ne se sent pas de joie, he is beside himself with joy; *F* **tu ne te sens plus?,** have you taken leave of your senses?

seoir [swar] *vi Litt* (*used only in prp* **seyant**, **séant**; *pr ind* **il sied, ils siéent**; *pr sub* **il siée, ils siéent**; *impf* **il seyait, ils seyaient**; *fu* **il siéra, ils siéront**) to suit, to become; **cette robe vous sied bien,** that dress suits you *or* is very becoming; **il lui sied mal de ...,** it ill becomes him to ...; **comme il sied,** as is fitting.

Séoul [seul] *n* Seoul.

sépale [sepal] *nm Bot* sepal.

séparable [separabl] *adj* separable (**de,** from); **deux théories difficilement séparables,** two theories which are *or* which it is difficult to separate.

séparateur, -trice [separatœr, -tris] **1** *adj* separating, separative; *Opt* resolving (*power*). **2** *nm Tech* separator; *Ordinat* delimiter.

séparation [separɑsjɔ̃] *nf* (*action*) separation; (*cloison*) partition, division; *Fig* boundary; **s. d'avec qn,** (*fait d'être séparé*) separation from s.o.; (*fait de se séparer*) parting from s.o.; **la s. de l'erreur et de la vérité,** distinguishing between error and truth; **s. de la tête du corps,** severance of the head from the body; **s. de corps,** legal separation (*of husband and wife*); **s. de fait, s. amiable,** de facto separation; *Jur* **s. de biens,** = marriage settlement under which husband and wife administer their separate properties; **s. de l'Église et de l'État,** separation of Church and State; **mur de s.,** dividing wall; **s. en bois,** wooden partition.

séparatisme [separatism] *nm Pol* separatism.

séparatiste [separatist] *adj & n Pol* separatist, secessionist.

séparé [separe] *adj* **(a)** (*distinct*) separate, distinct; **(b)** (*désuni*) separated; **nous vivons s. l'un de l'autre,** we live apart.

séparément [separemɑ̃] *adv* separately.

séparer [separe] **1** *vt* to separate (**de,** from); (*partager*) to divide; **s. les bons d'avec les mauvais,** to separate the good from the bad; **s. une chambre en trois,** to divide a room into three; **s. deux combattants,** to part *or* separate two fighters; *Boxe* **séparez!,** break!; **personne ne peut nous s.,** no one can separate *or* come between us; **le fleuve sépare la ville en deux,** the river divides the town in two; **mur qui sépare deux champs,** wall separating two fields; **la guerre sépare des familles,** war separates families *or* keeps families apart; **leurs opinions politiques les séparent,** their political opinions divide them.

2 se séparer *vpr* (*se quitter*) to separate, to part (**de,** from); (*of crowd, assembly etc*) to break up, to disperse; (*of river, road etc*) to divide, to branch off; **nous ne nous séparerons jamais,** we shall never part; **se s. de** *ou* **d'avec sa femme,** to separate from one's wife; **l'armée se sépara,** the army disbanded; **elle a dû se s. de son vieux chat,** she had to part with her old cat; *Fig* **ici je me sépare entièrement de vous,** here I disagree *or* part company with you; *Ch* **se s. à l'état cristallin,** (*of salt*) to crystallize out.

sépia [sepja] **1** *nf* (*couleur, matière colorante*) sepia. **2** *adj inv* sepia.

sept [sɛt] **1** *adj inv* seven; **le s. mai,** (on) the seventh of May, (on) May (the) seventh, *Am* (on) May seventh; **Édouard S.,** Edward the Seventh. **2** *nm inv* seven; **le s. du mois,** the seventh of the month; *Cartes* **le s. de cœur,** the seven of hearts.

septain [sɛtɛ̃] *nm Littér* seven-line stanza.

septante [sɛptɑ̃t] **1** *adj inv Belg Suisse* seventy. **2** *nm inv Bible* **la version des S.,** the Septuagint.

septembre [sɛptɑ̃br] *nm* September; **en s., au mois de s.,** in September; **le premier/le sept s.,** (on) the first/seventh of September, (on) September the first/seventh, *Am* (on) September first/seventh.

septennal, -aux [sɛptɛnal, -o] *adj* septennial, seven-year (*period, parliament etc*).

septennat [sɛptɛna] *nm* seven-year term (*of president etc*).

septentrion [sɛptɑ̃trijɔ̃] *nm Litt* north.

septentrional, -aux [sɛptɑ̃trijɔnal, -o] **1** *adj* northern. **2** *nmpl* **septentrionaux,** northerners.

septicémie [sɛptisemi] *nf Méd* septic(a)emia, *US* septicemia, blood poisoning.

septicémique [sɛptisemik] *adj Méd* septic(a)emic, *US* septicemic.

septième [sɛtjɛm] **1** *adj* seventh; **être au s. ciel,** to be in seventh heaven; **s. étage,** seventh *or Am* eighth floor. **2** *n* (*personne, objet, événement etc*) seventh (one); **habiter au s.,** to live on the seventh *or Am* eighth floor. **3** *nm* (*fraction*) seventh (part); **trois septièmes,** three sevenths. **4** *nf* **(a)** *Mus* seventh; **(b)** *Scol* = top form of primary school.

septièmement [sɛtjɛmmɑ̃] *adv* in the seventh place, seventhly.

septique [sɛptik] *adj* septic; **fosse s.,** septic tank.

septuagénaire [sɛptɥaʒenɛr] *adj & n* septuagenarian,

seventy-year-old.
septuagésime [sɛptɥaʒezim] *nf Rel* Septuagesima.
septum [sɛptɔm] *nm Anat Bot* septum.
septuor [sɛptɥɔr] *nm Mus* septet(te).
septuple [sɛptypl] **1** *adj* sevenfold, septuple. **2** *nm* septuple; **au s.,** sevenfold; **le s. de deux,** seven times two; **payer le s.,** to pay seven times as much.
septupler [sɛptyple] *vt & vi* to increase sevenfold.
sépulcral, -aux [sepylkral, -o] *adj* sepulchral.
sépulcre [sepylkr] *nm* sepulchre; **le saint s.,** the Holy Sepulchre; *Fig* **s. blanchi,** whited sepulchre.
sépulture [sepyltyr] *nf* **(a)** *Litt* (*inhumation*) burial; **refuser la s. à qn,** to refuse Christian burial to s.o.; **(b)** (*lieu*) burial place; **sépultures militaires,** war cemeteries.
séquelles [sekɛl] *nfpl* after-effects; (*de guerre etc*) aftermath.
séquence [sekɑ̃s] *nf* sequence; *Cartes* run.
séquentiel, -ielle [sekɑ̃sjɛl] *adj* sequential.
séquestration [sekɛstrasjɔ̃] *nf* **(a)** *Jur* sequestration (*of goods*); **(b)** confinement (*of s.o.*).
séquestre¹ [sekɛstr] *nm Jur* (*action*) sequestration; *Nau* embargo; **mettre en** *ou* **sous s. les biens de qn,** to sequester *or* sequestrate s.o.'s property.
séquestre² *nm Jur* depository, trustee, administrator (*of sequestrated property*).
séquestrer [sekɛstre] **1** *vt* **(a)** to sequester, to sequestrate (*property*); *Nau* to lay an embargo upon (*ship*); **(b)** to keep (*s.o.*) locked up; *Jur* to confine (*s.o.*) illegally. **2 se séquestrer** *vpr* to cut oneself off from the world.
séquoia [sekɔja] *nm* (*arbre*) sequoia.
sérac [serak] *nm Géol* serac.
sérail [seraj] *nm* seraglio.
séraphin [serafɛ̃] *nm* seraph.
séraphique [serafik] *adj* seraphic, angelic.
serbe [sɛrb] **1** *adj* Serb, Serbian. **2** *n* **S.,** Serb, Serbian.
Serbie [sɛrbi] *nf* Serbia.
serbo-croate [sɛrbɔkrɔat] **1** *adj* Serbo-Croat(ian). **2** *nm Ling* Serbo-Croat.
Sercq [sɛrk] *nm* Sark.
serein¹ [sərɛ̃] *adj* serene, calm (*person, face, day etc*); **jugement s.,** calm judgment.
serein² *nm* evening dew.
sereinement [sərɛnmɑ̃] *adv* serenely, calmly.
sérénade [serenad] *nf* **(a)** *Mus* serenade; **donner une s. à qn,** to serenade s.o.; **(b)** *F* (*tapage*) racket.
sérénité [serenite] *nf* serenity, calmness; **avec s.,** with serenity, serenely, calmly.
séreux, -euse [serø, -øz] *adj Anat Méd* serous.
serf, serve [sɛrf, sɛrv] *Hist* **1** *n* serf. **2** *adj* **condition serve,** serfdom; **terre serve,** land in bondage *or* in villein tenure.
serfouette [sɛrfwɛt] *nf* combined hoe and fork.
serge [sɛrʒ] *nf Tex* (woollen) serge.
sergent¹ [sɛrʒɑ̃] *nm Mil* sergeant; **s. fourrier, s. comptable,** quartermaster sergeant; **s. instructeur,** drill sergeant; *Can* **s. d'armes,** sergeant at arms; *Arch* **s. de ville,** policeman.
sergent² *nm Tech* cramp, clamp.
sergent-chef [sɛrʒɑ̃ʃɛf] *nm Mil* quartermaster sergeant; (*pl sergents-chefs*).
séricicole [serisikɔl] *adj* sericultural.
sériciculteur [serisikyltœr] *nm* silkworm breeder, *Spéc* sericulturist.
séri(ci)culture [seri(si)kyltyr] *nf* silkworm breeding, *Spéc* sericulture.
série [seri] *nf* **(a)** series, succession (*of events etc*); *Sp* (*épreuve*) heat; *Billard* break; *Billard* run (*of cannons*); **s. de catastrophes, s. noire,** series *or* chapter of accidents, run of bad luck; **livre de s. noire,** (crime) thriller; **s. de jours chauds,** spell of hot weather; **s. de conférences,** series *or* course of lectures; *Rad TV* **s. (d'émissions),** (radio *or* television) series; *Sp* **s. éliminatoire,** qualifying heat;

(b) series (*of press articles, postage stamps etc*); set (*of documents, tools etc*); range (*of sizes, samples etc*); *Ind Com* range, line (*of goods etc*); *Math Ch Phys Nucl* series; **en** *ou* **par série(s),** in series, serially; *F* **elle en a toute une s.,** she has a whole collection of them; **fabrication** *ou* **production en (grande(s)) série(s),** mass production; **chaîne de fabrication en s.,** production line; **voiture de s.,** standard car; *Admin etc* **prix de s.,** contract price (*for public works etc*); *Com* **fins de séries,** ends of lines, oddments, remnants; (*livres invendus*) remainders; **article hors s.,** custom-made *or* custom-built article; **numéro hors s.,** (*magazine*) special issue; *Fig* **c'est tout à fait hors s.,** it's quite exceptional; **une personnalité hors s.,** an exceptional personality; *El* **en s.,** in series;

(c) (*groupe*) group, category; *Sp* rank; *Boxe* **s. poids plumes,** featherweight rating; *Cin* **film de s. B,** B (-category) film; *Péj* **film de s. Z,** nth grade film;

(d) *Scol* specialization; **choisir une s.,** to decide what one is going to specialize in.
sériel, -ielle [serjɛl] *adj* serial; *Mus* twelve-tone, serial, dodecaphonic.
sérier [serje] *vt* (*impf & pr sub* **n. sériions, v. sériiez**) to arrange in series; **s. les questions,** to take the questions one by one.
sérieusement [serjøzmɑ̃] *adv* (*avec sérieux*) seriously, solemnly; (*sincèrement*) seriously, in earnest, genuinely; (*gravement*) seriously, gravely (*ill, wounded*); **parlez-vous s.?,** are you serious?, do you really mean it?
sérieux, -euse [serjø, -øz] **1** *adj* (*qui ne plaisante pas*) serious; (*sincère*) serious, genuine (*offer, purchaser etc*); reliable (*information*); responsible, reliable, serious (*person, firm etc*); (*important*) serious, important (*matter etc*); serious (*illness, situation*); **des lectures sérieuses,** serious reading; *F* **s. comme un pape,** as solemn as a judge; **êtes-vous s.?,** are you serious *or* in earnest?, do you mean it?; **d'un ton** *ou* **d'un air s.,** seriously; **peu s.,** irresponsible (*person*); **voyons, ce n'est pas s.,** come on, you're not serious *or* you don't mean it; **pas s. s'abstenir,** (*dans une petite annonce*) genuine replies only; *Com* **client s.,** good customer.

2 *nm* seriousness; **garder son s.,** to keep a straight face; **se prendre au s.,** to take oneself seriously; **je vous ai pris au s.,** I took you seriously, I thought you were serious, I thought you meant it; **on ne peut pas la prendre au s.,** you can't take her seriously; **manque de s.,** irresponsibility; **avec s.,** seriously.
sérigraphie [serigrafi] *nf* silk-screen printing.
sérigraphié [serigrafje] *adj* silk-screen(-printed).
serin, -ine [sərɛ̃, -in] **1** *nm Orn* canary. **2** *adj inv* **jaune s.,** canary yellow. **3** *adj F* silly, stupid, idiotic (*person*). **4** *n F* (*idiot*) idiot.
seriner [sərine] *vt* **(a)** *Fig Péj* **s. qch à qn,** to drum sth into s.o.; **s. à qn que ...,** to drum it into s.o. that ...; **(b) s. un air à un oiseau,** to teach a bird to sing by using a bird organ.
seringa(t) [sərɛ̃ga] *nm Bot* seringa.
seringue [sərɛ̃g] *nf* syringe; **s. de jardin,** garden syringe; *Méd* **s. à injections,** hypodermic syringe; **s. jetable,** disposable syringe; *Aut* **s. à graisse,** grease gun.
seringuer [sərɛ̃ge] *vt Méd* to syringe, to inject; (*au jardin*) to spray.
serment [sɛrmɑ̃] *nm* (solemn) oath; *Pol* **s. politique,** oath of allegiance; *Admin* **s. professionnel,** oath of office (*of magistrates, lawyers, police etc*); **déclaration sous s.,** sworn statement; **prêter s. (entre les mains de qn),** to take an oath *or* to be sworn (before s.o.); (*of jury etc*) to be sworn in; **faire prêter s. à qn,** to administer the oath to s.o.; **déclarer sous s.,** to state *or* declare under oath; **violer un s.,** to break an oath; **être sous la foi du s.,** to be on oath; **faire s. de faire qch,** to swear to do sth; **certifier qch sous s.,** to declare sth on oath; **faire un faux s.,** to commit perjury; *Fig* **s. d'ivrogne,** empty promise.
sermon [sɛrmɔ̃] *nm Rel* sermon (**sur,** on); *F Péj* (*remontrance*) sermon, lecture, talking-to; *Bible* **le S. sur la Montagne,** the Sermon on the Mount.
sermonner [sɛrmɔne] *vt F Péj* to lecture (*s.o.*), to give (*s.o.*) a lecture *or* talking-to.
sermonneur, -euse [sɛrmɔnœr, -øz] *F* **1** *adj* sermonizing. **2** *n* sermonizer.
sérodiagnostic [serɔdjagnɔstik] *nm Méd* serodiagnosis.
sérologie [serɔlɔʒi] *nf* serology.
seronégatif, -ive [serɔnegatif, -iv] *Méd* **1** *adj* HIV negative. **2** *n* person who is HIV negative.
séropositif, -ive [serɔpɔzitif, -iv] *Méd* **1** *adj* HIV positive. **2** *n* person infected with the HIV virus, HIV victim *or* sufferer.
séropositivité [serɔpɔzitivite] *nf Méd* infection with the HIV virus; **taux de s.,** HIV positive rate; **il était renvoyé à cause de sa s.,** he was dismissed for being HIV positive.
sérosité [serozite] *nf* serous fluid.
sérothèque [serɔtɛk] *nf Méd* serum collection.
serpe [sɛrp] *nf* billhook.
serpent [sɛrpɑ̃] *nm* **(a)** (*reptile*) snake; *CE Fin* (currency) snake; **s. femelle,** female snake; **s. d'eau,** grass snake; **s. de verre,** slow-worm; **s. à coiffe** *ou* **à lunettes,** (Indian) cobra; **s. à sonnettes,** rattlesnake, *Am F* rattler; **s. à**

sonnettes cornu, horned rattlesnake, *US F* sidewinder; **s. de mer,** *Myth* sea serpent; (*poisson*) pipe fish; *Journ* stock article; *Bible* **le s.,** the Serpent; *Fig* **s. de fumée,** wreath *or* coil of smoke; **(b)** *Hist Mus* serpent.

serpentaire[1] [sɛrpɑ̃tɛr] *nf Bot* serpentaria; **s. de Virginie,** snakeroot.

serpentaire[2] *nm Orn* serpent eater, secretary bird.

serpentant [sɛrpɑ̃tɑ̃] *adj* winding, snaking, meandering (*stream, road etc*).

serpenteau, -eaux [sɛrpɑ̃to] *nm* **(a)** *Zool* young snake; **(b)** (*fusée volante*) serpent.

serpenter [sɛrpɑ̃te] *vi* (*of river, road etc*) to wind, to snake, to meander; **le chemin monte/descend en serpentant,** the road winds *or* snakes *or* meanders up/down the hill.

serpentin, -ine [sɛrpɑ̃tɛ̃, -in] **1** *adj* serpentine; **marbre s.,** serpentine (marble), ophite. **2** *nm* **(a)** coil (*of tubing etc*); **(b)** (*ruban*) paper streamer (*as used at parties*). **3** *nf Minér* **serpentine,** serpentine, ophite.

serpette [sɛrpɛt] *nf* pruning knife.

serpillière [sɛrpijɛr] *nf* floorcloth; **passer la s. dans la cuisine,** to mop the kitchen floor.

serpolet [sɛrpɔlɛ] *nm Bot* wild thyme.

serrage [sɛraʒ] *nm Tech* tightening (*of screw, nut, knot etc*); clamping (*of joint*); **s. des freins,** application of the brakes, braking; **vis de s.,** set screw, locking screw.

serre [sɛr] *nf* **(a)** (*construction*) greenhouse; (*qui fait partie d'une maison*) conservatory; **s. chaude,** hothouse; **s. de palmiers,** palm house; **plante de s. chaude,** hothouse plant; **plantes sous s.,** plants under glass; *Écol* **effet de s.,** greenhouse effect; *Écol* **gaz à effet de s.,** greenhouse gas; **(b)** (*action*) pressing, squeezing (*of grapes etc*); **(c) serres,** claws, talons (*of bird of prey*).

serré [sɛre] **1** *adj* tight (*boots, clothes, knot, screw etc*); close (*texture*); serried, closed (*ranks*); dense (*formation*); closely argued (*discussion*); closely reasoned (*argument*); tight (*schedule*); *Géog* narrow (*pass*); **un café noir bien s.,** a strong black coffee; **pluie serrée,** teeming rain; **deux pages d'une écriture serrée,** two closely written pages; **budget s.,** tight budget; **les dents serrées, les lèvres serrées,** with clenched teeth; **maisons serrées,** houses huddled together; **serrés comme des harengs** *ou* **des sardines,** packed like sardines; **avoir le cœur s.,** to be sad at heart, to have a heavy heart; **avec la gorge serrée,** with a lump in one's throat; **surveillance serrée,** close supervision; **étude serrée,** intensive study (*of a text*); **style s.,** concise style; *Sp* **la partie va être serrée,** it's going to be a tight *or* close game; *Sp etc* **arrivée serrée,** close finish.

2 *adv* **écrire s.,** to have closely written handwriting; *Fig* **jouer s.,** to play a cautious game, to take no chances; **on a joué très s.,** it was a close-run thing.

serre-frein(s) [sɛrfrɛ̃] *nm inv Rail* brakeman.

serre-joint(s) [sɛrjwɛ̃] *nm inv* (*outil*) clamp.

serre-livres [sɛrlivr] *nm inv* book end.

serrement [sɛrmɑ̃] *nm* **(a) s. de main,** handshake; **s. de cœur,** pang; **(b)** *Min* dam, partition (*to keep out water*).

serrer [sɛre] **1** *vt* **(a)** (*saisir, tenir*) to clasp, to grip; (*presser*) to squeeze, to press; **s. la main à** *ou* **de qn,** to shake hands with s.o.; **tenir qch sans s.,** to hold sth loosely; **s. qn entre ses bras,** to clasp s.o. in one's arms, to hug s.o.; **s. le cou à qn,** to strangle s.o.; **cela me serre le cœur,** it wrings my heart; *Équitation* **s. un cheval,** to keep a horse well in hand;

(b) (*of garment, shoes etc*) to be too tight for (*s.o.*); **s. les pieds à qn,** to pinch s.o.'s feet, **cette jupe me serre (à) la taille,** this skirt is too tight round the waist;

(c) to tighten (*knot, screw, belt etc*); to clamp (*joint*); to furl, to take in (*sails*); to clench (*one's fists, teeth*); **s. les freins,** to apply *or* put on the brakes; *Mus* **en serrant,** stringendo;

(d) (*rapprocher*) to close up, to put close together; *Mil & Fig* to close (*ranks*); **s. son style,** to condense one's style; *Typ* **s. une ligne,** to reduce the spaces in a line;

(e) (*être près de*) to keep close to (*s.o., sth*); to hug (*Nau the shore, Aut the kerb*); *Sp* (*pousser*) to jostle (*a competitor*); **s. qn de près,** to follow s.o. closely; **s. une question de près,** to focus narrowly on a question.

2 *vi* **serrez à droite!,** keep to the right!

3 se serrer *vpr* **(a)** (*se rapprocher*) to squeeze up *or* together; **se s. les uns contre les autres,** to huddle together; **se s. contre qn,** to snuggle up to s.o.; (*pour être protégé*) to cling to s.o.;

(b) mon cœur se serra, my heart sank;

(c) *Fig* **se s. (la ceinture),** to tighten one's belt; *F* **se s. les coudes,** to back one another up.

serre-tête [sɛrtɛt] *nm inv* **(a)** (*bandeau*) headband; (*pour les cheveux*) hairband; **(b)** *Sp* (*bonnet*) cap; *Av* helmet.

serrure [sɛryr] *nf* lock; **s. de sûreté,** safety lock; **trou de la s.,** keyhole.

serrurerie [sɛryrri] *nf* **(a)** (*métier*) locksmithing, locksmith's trade; (*magasin*) locksmith's (shop); **(b)** (*travail, ouvrages*) iron work, metal work; **s. d'art,** art metal work; **grosse s.,** heavy ironwork.

serrurier [sɛryrje] *nm* **(a)** (*de serrures*) locksmith; **(b)** (*de métaux*) ironsmith.

sertir [sɛrtir] *vt* to set (*precious stone*); to crimp (*cartridge, can etc*).

sertissage [sɛrtisaʒ] *nm* setting (*of precious stone*); crimping (*of cartridge, can etc*).

sertisseur, -euse [sɛrtisœr, -øz] **1** *n* (*ouvrier*) setter (*of precious stones*); crimper (*of cartridges, can etc*). **2** *nm* (*appareil*) crimper (*for cans etc*).

sertissure [sɛrtisyr] *nf* (*action, manière*) setting (*of precious stone*); (*partie de chaton*) bezel.

sérum [serɔm] *nm* **(a)** *Physiol Méd* serum; **s. sanguin,** blood serum; **s. de vérité,** truth serum, *F* truth drug; **(b) s. (lactique),** whey.

servage [sɛrvaʒ] *nm Hist* serfdom, bondage; *Fig* bondage.

serval [sɛrval] *nm Zool* serval; (*pl servals*).

servant, -ante [sɛrvɑ̃, -ɑ̃t] **1** *adj* **frère s.,** lay brother; **cavalier** *ou* **chevalier s.,** faithful admirer. **2** *nm* **(a)** *Mil* gunner; **(b)** *Tennis* server; **(c)** *Rel* **s. (de messe),** server. **3** *nf* **servante (a)** (*domestique*) (maid)servant; **(b)** (*table*) side table; **(c)** *Tech* (adjustable) support.

serve [sɛrv] *adj & n voir* **SERF**.

serveur, -euse [sɛrvœr, -øz] **1** *n* **(a)** (*dans un bar*) *surtout Am* bartender; (*homme*) barman; (*femme*) *Br* barmaid; (*dans un restaurant*) *Am* waitperson; (*homme*) waiter; (*femme*) waitress; **(b)** *Cartes* dealer; **(c)** *Tennis* server. **2** *nm Ordinat* **s. de fichiers,** file server.

serviabilité [sɛrvjabilite] *nf* obligingness, helpfulness.

serviable [sɛrvjabl] *adj* obliging, helpful.

service [sɛrvis] *nm* **(a)** service; **le s. est désastreux,** (*dans ce restaurant*) the service here is appalling; **s. (non) compris,** service (not) included; **libre s.,** self-service (*in shop etc*); *Com* **s. après vente,** after-sales service; **s. clients,** customer service; *Écon* **services,** services; **les biens et les services,** goods and services; **société de services,** service company; **entrer en s. (chez qn),** to go into (s.o.'s) service; **gens de s.,** domestic staff; **être au s. de qn,** to be in s.o.'s service; **se passer des services d'un employé,** to dispense with an employee's services; **mourir au s. du roi,** to die in the king's service; **escalier de s.,** back stairs; **porte de s.,** tradesmen's entrance; *Admin* **s. contractuel,** contract service; **indications de s.,** service instructions; *Admin Mil* **états de s.,** service record; *Tél* **communication** *ou* **conversation de s.,** service call; *Mil etc* **s. militaire (obligatoire),** (compulsory) military service; **faire son s.,** to do one's military service; **en s. actif, en activité de s.,** on the active list; **service(s) de guerre,** active service; **en s. aux armées,** on active service; **(in)apte au s.,** (un)fit for service; **être libéré du s.,** to be discharged; **libération du s.,** discharge; *Fin* **s. des intérêts,** interest charges;

(b) *Tennis* service; **faire un** *ou* **le s.,** to serve; **au s., Martin,** Martin to serve;

(c) (*fonction*) duty; **s. de jour,** day duty; **s. de nuit,** night duty; *Nau* orders for the night; **être de s./ne pas être de s.,** to be on/off duty; **tableau de s.,** duty chart *or* list *or* roster; **à quelle heure prenez-vous/quittez-vous votre s.?,** at what time do you go on duty/off duty?; *Mil etc* **mort en s. commandé,** killed on active service; **s. de corvée,** *Mil* fatigue duty; *Nau* duty; **s. d'ordre,** (*police*) police; (*d'une manifestation etc*) stewards; **s. de garde,** guard duty; **planton de s.,** duty orderly; **officier/sous-officier de s.,** duty/non-commissioned officer; *F* **être s. s.,** to be a stickler for rules and regulations;

(d) (*département*) *Admin Com* department; *Mil* corps, service; *Méd etc* service; **chef de s.,** head of department; **s. vente/marketing/***etc*, sales/marketing/*etc* department; **s. central,** headquarters; **s. de renseignements,** information office; *Tél* directory enquiries, *Am* information; **les services publics,** public utilities, *Am* utilities; *TV* **s. public,** public-service broadcasting (network); **s. des eaux,** = water board; **s. des postes, s. postal,** postal service, *surtout Am* mail service; **S. Régional de la Police Judiciaire,** ≈ *Br* regional crime squad; **s. gouvernemental,** government agency *or* department; **correspondance de s.,** official correspondence; *Méd* **s. des contagieux,** isolation ward; **s. technique,** technical branch, engineering department; *Journ* **s. des informations,** information service;

(e) operation (*of machine etc*); **s. à bras** *ou* **manuel,** hand *or* manual operation; **en s.,** (*machine*) in service, in use, in operation; (*aircraft, ship*) in commission; **aptitude au s.,** serviceability; **en (bon) état de s., propre au s.,** in (good) working order, serviceable; **hors (de) s.,** (*machine, mechanism*) out of order; (*gun etc*) out of action; (*ship etc*) disabled; **mettre en s.,** to bring *or* put (*machine etc*) into service; to bring *or* put (*aircraft, ship*) into commission; **retirer du s.,** to withdraw from service *or* from use; to decommission (*aircraft, ship*); **retirer graduellement du s.,** to phase out;

(f) service (*of train, liner, aircraft etc*); **assurer** *ou* **faire le s. entre ... et ...,** to operate between ... and ...; **s. assuré toute l'année,** year-round service; **s. de marchandises,** goods *or* freight service; **s. de voyageurs,** passenger service;

(g) (*aide*) favour, *US* favor, service; **rendre (un) s. à qn,** to do s.o. a favour *or* a service *or* a good turn; **rendre un bon/un mauvais s. à qn,** to do s.o. a good/a bad turn; **demander un s. à qn,** to ask s.o. a favour; **les services qu'il a rendus à l'enseignement,** his services to education; **à votre s.,** at your service; **qu'y a-t-il pour votre s.?,** what can I do for you?; **ce manteau m'a fait un bon s.,** this coat has worn well, I've had a lot of wear out of this coat; **ce livre m'a rendu grand s.,** this book was very useful to me;

(h) (*en élevage*) service (*of stallion*);

(i) (*ensemble de repas*) sitting; *Rail etc* **dernier s. à deux heures,** last sitting (for lunch) at two o'clock;

(j) set (*of utensils, table linen etc*); **s. (de table),** (*assiettes etc*) dinner service; (*linge*) set of table linen; **s. à découper,** carving knife and fork; **s. américain,** set of table mats.

serviette [sɛrvjɛt] *nf* **(a) s. (de table),** (table) napkin, serviette; **s. d'enfant,** feeder, bib; **(b) s. (de toilette),** (hand) towel; **s. sans fin,** roller towel; **s. hygiénique,** *Br* sanitary towel, *Am* sanitary napkin; **(c)** (*sac*) briefcase.

serviette-éponge [sɛrvjetepɔ̃ʒ] *nf* terry towel; (*pl serviettes-éponges*).

servile [sɛrvil] *adj* servile; slavish (*imitation, translation*).

servilement [sɛrvilmɑ̃] *adv* servilely; (*imiter, traduire*) slavishly.

servilité [sɛrvilite] *nf* servility; (*d'imitation, de traduction*) slavishness.

servir [sɛrvir] *v* (*prp* **servant**; *pp* **servi**; *pr ind* **je sers, il sert, n. servons**; *pr sub* **je serve**; *impf* **je servais**; *p hist* **je servis**; *fu* **je servirai**) **1** *vi* **(a)** (*être utile*) to be useful *or* of use (**à qn,** to s.o.); **la machine peut encore s.,** the machine can still be used *or* is still fit for use; **cela peut s. un de ces jours,** it may come in handy *or* be of use one day; **toujours prêt à s.,** always ready for use;

(b) s. à qch/à faire qch, to be useful *or* used for sth/for doing sth; **ne s. à rien,** to be (of) no use *or* useless; **à quoi cela sert-il?,** what is the good *or* the use *or* the point of that?; *F* **à quoi sert ce truc-là?,** what's that gadget (used) for?; **ça ne servira pas à grand-chose,** that won't be much good *or* much use; **cela ne sert qu'à l'irriter,** it only irritates him; **je ne vois pas à quoi sert d'y aller,** I don't see the good *or* the point of going; **à quoi sert qu'on l'attende?,** what's the point *or* use of waiting for him?;

(c) s. de, (*of object*) to serve as, to be used as; (*of person*) to act as; **les pupitres servent de tables,** the desks serve *or* are used as tables; **s. de prétexte,** to serve as a pretext; **elle lui a servi de mère,** she has been a mother to him;

(d) *Tennis* to serve;

(e) to serve (*in army, government etc*) (**sous,** under); *Mil* **en âge de s.,** of military age; **s. à table,** to wait at table, *Am* to wait table.

2 *v impers* **il ne sert à rien de pleurer,** it's no good *or* use crying.

3 *vt* **(a)** to serve (*s.o., dinner, fish etc*); to serve, to attend to (*customer*); to wait on, to serve (*diner*); (*of tradesman*) to supply (*s.o. with goods*); **s. Dieu,** to serve God; **est-ce qu'on vous sert?,** are you being served *or* attended to?; **madame est servie,** dinner is served, madam; *F* **en fait de pluie, nous sommes servis,** as far as rain goes, we get more than our share; **s. qch chaud,** to serve sth hot; **s. à qn d'un plat,** to help s.o. to a dish; **s. à boire à qn,** to give s.o. a drink *or* something to drink; **s. sa patrie/une cause,** to serve one's country/a cause; **nous sommes très bien servis,** we have very good (domestic) help; **ce cours d'eau sert le moulin,** this stream drives the mill; **s. une rente à qn,** to pay an annuity to s.o.; **tout le monde est servi?,** (*dans l'autobus*) any more fares please?; *Rel* **s. la messe,** to serve at mass;

(b) (*aider*) to help, to assist, to be of service to (*s.o.*); to serve, to further (*s.o.'s interests*); **en quoi puis-je vous s.?,** what can I do for you?, how can I help you *or* be of service to you?; **sa mémoire l'a mal servi,** his memory served him badly;

(c) *Tennis* to serve (*ball*); *Cartes* **à vous de s.,** (it's) your deal;

(d) (*of stallion*) to serve, to cover (*mare*);

(e) to serve (*gun*);

(f) (*à la chasse*) to dispatch (*animal*).

4 se servir *vpr* **(a) se s. d'un plat,** to help oneself to a dish; **servez-vous!,** help yourself!;

(b) *Com* **se s. chez Martin,** to shop at Martin's;

(c) se s. de qch/qn, (*utiliser*) to use sth/s.o., to make use of sth/s.o..

serviteur [sɛrvitœr] *nm* servant; **s. de l'État,** civil servant; *Arch* **votre s.,** (*dans une lettre*) your obedient servant; **personne ne le sait mieux que votre s.,** no one knows it better than yours truly.

servitude [sɛrvityd] *nf* **(a)** (*asservissement*) servitude; (*contrainte*) constraint; **la s. de la mode,** the tyranny *or* constraints of fashion; **(b)** *Jur* easement; **s. de passage,** right of way.

servocommande [sɛrvɔkɔmɑ̃d] *nf* *Av Aut etc* servo(control).

servofrein [sɛrvɔfrɛ̃] *nm Aut etc* servobrake.

servomécanisme [sɛrvɔmekanism] *nm Tech* servomechanism, servo system.

servomoteur [sɛrvɔmɔtœr] *nm* servomotor.

ses [se] *adj poss voir* **SON**[1].

sésame [sezam] *nm* **(a)** *Bot* sesame; **(b) s., ouvre-toi!,** open, sesame!

sessile [sɛsil] *adj Biol* sessile (*leaf, horn etc*).

session [sesjɔ̃] *nf* **(a)** *Parl Jur* session, sitting; **(b)** *Univ* (*exam*) session.

sesterce [sɛstɛrs] *nm Antiq* (*monnaie*) sestertius, sesterce; **grand s.,** sestertium.

set [sɛt] *nm* **(a)** *Tennis* set; **gagner en deux sets,** to win in two sets; **(b) s. (de table),** set of table mats.

sétacé [setase] *adj Biol* setaceous, bristly.

séton [setɔ̃] *nm Chir Vét* seton.

setter [setɛr] *nm* (*chien*) setter.

seuil [sœj] *nm* **(a)** (*entrée*) doorway, threshold; (*dalle etc*) doorstep; *Fig* threshold (*of death etc*); *Phys Psy etc* threshold; **franchir le s.,** to cross the threshold; **sur le s.,** on the threshold; **au s. de la nouvelle année,** on the threshold of the new year; **être au s. de la célébrité,** to stand on the threshold of fame; *Écon* **s. de rentabilité,** break-even point; *Physiol* **s. de sensibilité,** threshold of sensitivity *or* of response; *Psy* **s. de la conscience,** threshold of consciousness; **(b)** *Géog* **s. continental,** continental shelf; **(c)** sill (*of dry dock, lock*).

seul, -e [sœl] **1** *adj* **(a)** (*preceding the noun*) (*unique*) only, single, sole; **un s. homme,** (*pas plus qu'un*) a single man; (*d'entre tous les autres*) only one man; **son s. exécuteur testamentaire,** his sole executor; **son s. souci,** his one *or* only *or* sole care; **il ne suffit pas d'un s. exemple,** a single example *or* one example alone will not suffice; **il suffit d'une seule fois,** once is enough; **mon s. et unique stylo,** my one and only pen; **un s. mot, et je te quitte,** one word from you and I'll go; **la seule pensée m'effraie,** the mere *or* very thought frightens me;

(b) (*following the noun or used predicatively*) (*séparé des autres*) alone, by oneself, on one's own; **se sentir très s,** to feel very lonely; **enfin seuls!,** alone at last!; **une femme seule,** a woman on her own; **être garçon s.,** (*of bachelor*) to be unattached; **il peut marcher tout s. maintenant,** he can walk by himself now; **faire cavalier s.,** to act alone, to go it alone; **parler s. à s. à qn,** to speak to s.o. tête-à-tête, to have a private conversation with s.o.; **s. (à s.) avec soi-même,** alone with one's thoughts; **l'œuvre seule de ...,** the sole *or* exclusive work of ...; **j'ai une cachette que moi s. connais,** I have a hiding place which no-one else knows about *or* *Fml* which I alone know; **je l'ai fait tout s.** *ou* **à moi s.,** I did it (by) myself *or* all on my own *or* single-handed; **cela va tout s.,** it's plain sailing; **cela ne va pas tout s.,** it isn't easy, it isn't all plain sailing; **parler/chanter/***etc* **tout s.,** to talk/sing/*etc* to oneself; *Mus* **passage pour violin s.,** passage for unaccompanied *or* solo violin;

(c) (*following the noun or preceding the article or poss adj*) (*seulement*) alone, only; **la violence seule** *ou* **seule la**

violence le contraindrait, only violence *or* violence alone *or* nothing short of violence would compel him; **seule la chasse les fait vivre,** hunting is their only *or* sole source of food; **s. un expert pourrait nous conseiller,** only an expert could advise us; **nous sommes seuls à le savoir,** we are the only ones *or* people who know about it.

2 *n* **un s.,** (*pas plus qu'un*) a single person; (*chose*) a single one; (*d'entre tous les autres*) only one person; (*chose*) only one; **le gouvernement d'un s.,** absolute rule; **pas un s.,** (*chose*) not (a single) one; (*personne*) not a single person; **vous êtes le s. qui puissiez m'aider,** you are the only one who can help me, *Fml* you alone can help me; **il était le s. à nous encourager,** he was the only one who encouraged us, *Fml* he alone encouraged us.

seulement [sœlmɑ̃] *adv* **(a)** (*juste*) only; **nous sommes s. deux,** there are only *or* just two of us; **je te demande s. un peu de patience,** I'm just asking you to be a bit patient; **venir s. de faire qch,** to have only just done sth; **non s. ..., mais aussi ...** *ou* **mais encore ...,** not only ..., but also...; **(b)** (*uniquement*) only, solely, merely; **il y va s. pour vous faire plaisir,** he is only going to please you, he is going just *or* merely *or* solely to please you; *F* **entrez s.,** do come in; *F* **essaie s.!,** just (you) try!; **(c)** (*même*) even; **sans s. me regarder,** without even looking at me; **il ne m'a pas s. regardé,** he didn't even *or* so much as look at me; **si s. ...!,** if only ...!; **(d)** (*with conj force*) **je viendrais bien, s. ...,** I should like to come, but ... *or* only ...; **elle est gentille, s. elle est un peu sotte,** she is kind, but *or* only she is a bit silly.

sève [sɛv] *nf Bot* sap (*of plant*); *Fig Litt* vitality, *Br* vigour, *US* vigor; *Bot & Fig* **la s. monte,** the sap is rising.

sévère [sevɛr] *adj* **(a)** (*dur*) severe, harsh (*judge, criticism, punishment etc*); stern, severe (*face, look*); severe (*beauty*); **climat s.,** severe *or* hard climate; **être s. envers** *ou* **pour** *ou* **avec qn/pour les fautes de qn,** to be severe *or* hard on s.o./on s.o.'s failings; **mener un train s.,** to set a gruelling pace; **(b)** strict, rigid (*discipline, morals*); **architecture/style s.,** severe architecture/style; **morale peu s.,** lax morals; **des pertes sévères,** severe losses.

sévèrement [sevɛrmɑ̃] *adv* **(a)** (*durement*) severely, harshly; **(b)** (*strictement*) strictly, rigidly; **(c)** (*gravement*) severely; **s. atteint,** severely affected.

sévérité [severite] *nf* **(a)** severity, harshness (*of judge, measure, criticism, punishment etc*); sternness, severity (*of face, look*); strictness (*of discipline*); **avec s.,** with severity, severely; **(b)** severity (*of style etc*).

sévices [sevis] *nmpl* brutality, cruelty; **s. (sexuels) à enfant,** child abuse.

Séville [sevil] *n* Seville.

sévir [sevir] *vi* **(a)** (*agir avec rigueur*) to act ruthlessly; **s. contre qn/qch,** to deal ruthlessly with s.o./sth; **(b)** (*of epidemic, war etc*) to rage; (*of hooligans*) to wreak havoc; **la crise qui sévit actuellement,** the present crisis.

sevrage [səvraʒ] *nm* **(a)** (*de nourrisson, drogué etc*) weaning; *Méd* **symptômes de s.,** withdrawal symptoms; **(b)** *Bot* separating (*of layer, scion*).

sevrer [səvre] *vt* **(je sèvre, n. sevrons; je sèvrerai)** **(a)** to wean (*child, lamb, drug addict etc*); *Litt* **s. qn de qch,** to deprive s.o. of sth; **(b)** *Bot* to separate (*layer, scion*).

sèvres [sɛvr] *nm* (*porcelaine*) Sèvres (porcelain).

sexage [sɛksaʒ] *nm* sexing (*of poultry*).

sexagénaire [sɛgzaʒenɛr] *adj & n* sexagenarian.

Sexagésime [sɛgzaʒezim] *nf Rel* Sexagesima (Sunday).

sex-appeal [sɛksapil] *nm F* sex appeal.

sexe [sɛks] *nm* **(a)** (*classement*) sex; **le (beau) s.,** the fair sex; **le s. faible, le deuxième s.,** the weaker sex; **le s. fort,** the stronger sex; **(b)** (*parties sexuelles*) genitals; **(c)** (*sexualité*) sex; **problèmes de s.,** sex problems.

sexisme [sɛksism] *nm* sexism.

sexiste [sɛksist] *adj & n* sexist.

sexologie [sɛksɔlɔʒi] *nf* sexology.

sexologique [sɛksɔlɔʒik] *adj* sexological.

sexologue [sɛksɔlɔg] *n* sexologist.

sex-shop [sɛksʃɔp] *nm* sex shop; (*pl sex-shops*).

sextant [sɛkstɑ̃] *nm Nau Math* sextant.

sextuor [sɛkstɥɔr] *nm Mus* sextet(te).

sextuple [sɛkstypl] **1** *adj* sixfold, sextuple. **2** *nm* sextuple; **au s.,** sixfold; **le s. de deux,** six times two; **payer le s.,** to pay six times as much.

sextuplé, -ée [sɛkstyple] *n* sextuplet.

sextupler [sɛkstyple] *vt & vi* to increase sixfold.

sexualisation [sɛksɥalizɑsjɔ̃] *nf* sexualization.

sexualiser [sɛksɥalize] *vt* to sexualize.

sexualité [sɛksɥalite] *nf* sexuality.

sexué [sɛksɥe] *adj* sexed (*plant, animal*); sexual (*reproduction*).

sexuel, -elle [sɛksɥɛl] *adj* sexual; **vie sexuelle,** sex life; **acte s.,** sex act.

sexuellement [sɛksɥɛlmɑ̃] *adv* sexually; **maladie s. transmissible,** sexually transmitted disease; **être attiré s. par qn,** to be sexually attracted to s.o..

sexy [sɛksi] *adj inv F* sexy.

seyant [sɛjɑ̃] *adj* becoming (*garment*).

Seychelles [seʃɛl] *nfpl* **les S.,** the Seychelles.

shah [ʃa] *nm* shah.

shake-hand [ʃɛkɑ̃d] *nm inv Arch & Hum* handshake.

shaker [ʃɛkœr] *nm* cocktail shaker.

shakespearien, -ienne [ʃɛkspirjɛ̃, -jɛn] *adj* Shakespearian, Shakespearean.

shako [ʃako] *nm Mil* shako.

shampooiner [ʃɑ̃pwine] *vt* to shampoo.

shampooineur, -euse [ʃɑ̃pwinœr, -øz] **1** *n* (*employé*) shampooer. **2** *nf* **shampooineuse (à moquette),** carpet shampooer.

shampooing [ʃɑ̃pwɛ̃] *nm* **(a)** (*action*) shampoo; **faire** *ou* **donner un s. à qn,** to shampoo s.o.('s hair), to give s.o. a shampoo; **(b)** (*produit*) shampoo; **s. sec,** dry shampoo; **s. pour cheveux secs/gras,** shampoo for dry/greasy hair; **s. aux œufs,** egg shampoo; **s. à moquettes,** carpet shampoo.

shampouiner [ʃɑ̃pwine] *vt* to shampoo.

shampouineur, -euse [ʃɑ̃pwinœr, -øz] *n* = **SHAMPOOINEUR.**

shant(o)ung [ʃɑ̃tuŋ] *nm Tex* shantung.

sharia [ʃarja] *nf* (*loi islamique*) sharia.

sheik [ʃɛk] *nm* sheik.

shérif [ʃerif] *nm* sheriff.

sherpa [ʃɛrpa] *n* Sherpa.

sherry [ʃeri] *nm* sherry.

shetland [ʃɛtlɑ̃d] **1** *nmpl* **les (îles) S.,** the Shetland Islands, the Shetlands. **2** *nm Tex* Shetland wool; **(pull en) s.,** shetland sweater.

shilling [ʃiliŋ] *nm* shilling.

shimmy [ʃimi] *nm Aut* shimmy.

shinto [ʃɛ̃to] *nm*, **shintoïsme** [ʃɛ̃tɔism] *nm* Shinto, Shintoism.

shocking [ʃɔkiŋ] *adj inv Hum & Vieilli* shocking.

shogoun [ʃɔgun] *nm Hist* shogun.

shoot [ʃut] *nm* **(a)** *Fb* shot; **(b)** *Arg* (*de drogue*) shot; **se faire un s. (d'héroïne),** to give oneself a shot (of heroin), to shoot up (heroin).

shooter [ʃute] **1** *vi Fb* to shoot. **2** *vt* **(a)** *Fb* **s. un pénalty,** to take a penalty (kick); **(b)** *Arg* (*avec de la drogue*) to shoot (*s.o.*) up. **3 se shooter** *vpr Arg* to shoot (up); **se s. à l'héroïne,** to shoot (up) heroin.

shopping [ʃɔpiŋ] *nm* shopping; **faire du s.,** to go shopping.

short [ʃɔrt] *nm* (pair of) shorts.

show [ʃo] *nm* show; **s. aérien,** air show.

show-business [ʃobiznɛs] *nm* show business.

showroom [ʃorum] *nm* showroom.

shunt [ʃœt] *nm Él Chir* shunt.

shunter [ʃœte] *vt Él* to shunt.

si¹ [si] **1** *conj* (*by elision* **s'** *before* **il, ils**) **(a)** if; **je ne sortirai pas s'il pleut,** I won't go out if it rains; **s'il n'avait pas plu, nous serions partis,** if it hadn't rained we would have gone; **si on ne le surveille pas, il s'échappera,** he will escape unless he is watched *or* if he is not watched; **s'il vient, vous m'avertirez,** if he comes, let me know; **j'aurais été soldat, si je n'étais poète,** I would have been a soldier if I were not a poet; **si j'avais su,** if I'd known, had I (but) known; **si ce n'est toi, c'est donc ton frère,** if it is not you, then it is your brother; **qui le fera si ce n'est moi?,** who will do it if I don't *or* unless I do?; **si ce n'était que je l'ai vu moi-même,** if I hadn't seen it (for) myself; **un des plus grands, si ce n'est le plus grand,** one of the biggest, if not the biggest; **si ce n'était mon rhumatisme, je vous accompagnerais,** if it weren't for my rheumatism I would go with you; **s'il fait beau et si je suis libre je sortirai,** if it's fine and (if) I'm free, I'll go out; **oui, si on veut,** yes, if you like; **si je ne m'abuse, si je ne me trompe,** if I am not mistaken; **si seulement j'étais à Paris!,** if only I were in Paris!; *Fml* **si tant est que** + *sub*, provided that ...;

(b) (*concession*) **si je me plains, c'est que j'en ai sujet,** if I complain, it's for good reason; **s'il est malheureux et s'il a des ennuis, c'est bien de sa faute,** if he is unhappy and in trouble, it is entirely his own fault; **s'il fut sévère, il fut juste,** he was just though severe; **ce fut à peine s'il put distinguer l'heure à sa montre,** he could scarcely see the hands of his watch; **c'est tout au plus si l'on peut compter jusqu'à vingt femmes dans la salle,** at (the) most there are only about twenty women in the hall; **le père Martin, (un) brave homme s'il en fut,** old Martin, a good chap if ever there was one.

(c) (*question indirecte*) if, whether; **je me demande si c'est vrai/s'il viendra,** I wonder if *or* whether it is true/he will come; **je lui ai demandé s'il était marié et s'il avait des enfants,** I asked him if *or* whether he was married, and if *or* whether he had a family; *F* **si je connais Paris?,** do I know Paris?; *F* **si c'est pas malheureux de voir ça!,** isn't it dreadful to see that!;

(d) (*combien*) how much; **pensez si j'étais furieux!,** you can imagine how angry I was!;

(e) (*supposition*) what if, suppose; **et si elle l'apprend?,** and what if she hears of it?; **si nous changions de sujet?,** suppose we change the subject?; **si on faisait une partie de bridge?,** what about *or* how about a game of bridge?

2 *nm* **tes si et tes mais,** your ifs and buts; *Prov* **avec des si on mettrait Paris dans une bouteille,** if ifs and ands were pots and pans there'd be no need for tinkers.

si² *adv* **(a)** (*tellement*) so; **ne courez pas si vite,** don't run so fast; **il est si faible que ...,** he is so weak that ...; **un si bon dîner,** such a good dinner; **de si bons dîners,** such good dinners; **il n'est pas si à plaindre que cela,** he is not to be as pitied as all that; **ce n'est pas si facile,** it's not so easy;

(b) (= *'aussi' dans une proposition négative*) **il n'est pas si beau que vous,** he is not as handsome *or* not so handsome as you;

(c) donnez-m'en si peu que vous voudrez *ou* **si peu que rien,** give me just a (very) little;

(d) si bien que ..., with the result that ..., so that in the end ...; **il dépensa sans regarder, si bien qu'en fin de compte il fut ruiné,** he spent recklessly, with the result that *or* so that in the end he was ruined;

(e) (*concession*) **si ... que** + *sub*, however; **si jeune qu'il soit,** however young he may be, young as he is; **aucun médecin, si habile soit-il,** no doctor, however capable; **si peu que ce soit,** however little (it may be); **votre méthode, si parfaite soit-elle ...,** your method, however perfect ...; **si bien qu'il s'y prenne,** however skilfully he sets about it;

(f) (*réponse à une question négative*) yes; **si fait,** yes indeed; **ça ne fait rien — si, ça fait quelque chose,** it doesn't matter – yes, it does (matter); **il n'est pas parti? — si/je crois que si,** he hasn't gone? – yes, he has/yes, I think he has, yes, I think so; **mais si, je l'ai vue,** yes, I did see her; **il ne s'en remettra pas — que si!,** he won't get over it – yes, he will!; *F* **tu ne t'en souviens, plus, je pense? — si, si,** you probably don't remember – yes, I do; **vous en voulez? — merci — mais si!,** would you like some? – no, thank you – oh go on!

si³ *nm inv Mus* (*note*) B; (*en chantant la gamme*) te, ti; **morceau en si,** piece in B; **en si bémol,** in B flat.

Siam [sjam] *nm* Siam.

siamois, -oise [sjamwa, -waz] **1** *adj* Siamese; **chat s.,** Siamese cat; **frères s., sœurs siamoises,** Siamese twins. **2** *n* **S.,** Siamese. **3** *nm* **(a)** (*chat*) Siamese (cat); **(b)** *Ling* Siamese.

Sibérie [siberi] *nf* Siberia; **chien de S.,** Siberian dog.

sibérien, -ienne [siberjɛ̃, -jɛn] **1** *adj* Siberian; *Fig* **il fait un froid s.,** it's like Siberia. **2** *n* **S.,** Siberian.

sibilant [sibilɑ̃] *adj Méd* sibilant, hissing.

sibylle [sibil] *nf Antiq* sibyl.

sibyllin [sibilɛ̃] *adj* **(a)** *Antiq* sibylline; **(b)** *Litt* (*énigmatique*) cryptic, enigmatic.

sic [sik] *adv* sic; *F* **la sincérité-s., le socialisme-s.,** so-called sincerity/socialism, sincerity/socialism quote-unquote.

SICAV [sikav] *n Fin* (*abrév* **société d'investissment à capital variable**) = mutual fund.

siccatif, -ive [sikatif, -iv] *adj & nm* siccative.

Sicile [sisil] *nf* Sicily.

sicilien, -ienne [sisiljɛ̃, -jɛn] **1** *adj* Sicilian. **2** *n* **S.,** Sicilian. **3** *nf Mus* **sicilienne,** siciliano.

sicle [sikl] *nm Hist* (*monnaie, poids*) shekel.

Sida, SIDA [sida] *nm Méd* Aids, AIDS; **avoir le s.,** to have Aids.

sidatique [sidatik] *adj & n Péj* = **SIDÉEN.**

side-car [sidkar] *nm* (*habitacle*) sidecar; (*véhicule*) motorcycle and sidecar, *Br* combination; (*pl side-cars*).

sidéen, -enne [sideɛ̃, -ɛn] *Méd* **1** *adj* suffering from Aids. **2** *n* Aids sufferer *or* victim.

sidéral, -aux [sideral, -o] *adj* sidereal.

sidérant [siderɑ̃] *adj F* staggering (*news, story etc*).

sidéré [sidere] *adj* **(a)** *F* flabbergasted, staggered; **(b)** *Vieilli* struck dead *or* down (*by lightning, apoplexy*).

sidérer [sidere] *vt* (**il sidère; il sidérera**) **(a)** *F* to flabbergast, to stagger (*s.o.*); **(b)** *Vieilli* (*of lightning, apoplexy etc*) to strike (*s.o.*) dead, to strike (*s.o.*) down.

sidérose [sideroz] *nf* **(a)** *Minér* siderite; **(b)** *Méd* siderosis.

sidérostat [siderɔsta] *nm Astron* siderostat.

sidérurgie [sideryrʒi] *nf* metallurgy of iron and steel; (*industrie*) iron and steel industry.

sidérurgique [sideryrʒik] *adj* **industrie s.,** iron and steel industry; **usine s.,** iron and steel works.

sidérurgiste [sideryrʒist] *n* iron and steel metallurgist.

sidi [sidi] *nm Arg* (*terme injurieux*) Arab, *Br* wog (*native of N Africa living in France*).

siècle [sjɛkl] *nm* **(a)** (*cent ans*) century; **au vingtième s.,** in the twentieth century; **cette maison a au moins un s.,** this house is at least a hundred years old; **lit vieux d'un bon s.,** bed at least a hundred *or* a good hundred years old;

(b) (*époque*) age; **le s. de Louis XIV, le grand s.,** the age of Louis XIV; **notre s.,** our century, the age we live in, the present time; **c'est un homme de son s./d'un autre s.,** he's a man of his times/he belongs to another age *or* another century; **vivre dans** *ou* **avec sa s.,** to be in tune with one's times; **le mal du s.,** the scourge of our times; **jusqu'à la fin des siècles,** to the end of (all) time; *Rel* **pour les siècles des siècles,** world without end; *F* **il y a un s.** *ou* **ça fait des siècles que je ne vous ai vu,** I haven't seen you for ages, it's ages since I saw you;

(c) *Rel* **le s.,** the world, worldly life.

siège [sjɛʒ] *nm* **(a)** (*centre*) seat, centre, *US* center (*of learning, government, activity etc*); *Min* workings; **s. social,** head office, registered office (*of a company*); **avoir son s. à Londres,** (*d'une société etc*) to have its head office *or* headquarters in London, to be headquartered in London; **chef de s.,** engineer in charge (*of mine etc*); *Rel* **s. épiscopal,** see;

(b) *Mil* siege; **mettre le s. devant une ville, faire le s. d'une ville,** to lay siege to *or* besiege a town; **lever le s.,** to raise the siege; *F* (*partir*) to get up and go; **état de s.,** state of siege;

(c) (*meuble*) seat; (*de cocher*) box; *Parl* seat; **s. à la Chambre,** seat in Parliament; **le s. du juge,** the judge's bench; *Aut* **s. avant/arrière,** front/back seat; **prenez un s.,** take a seat, (do) sit down; **elle occupe un s. important,** she holds an important position;

(d) (*de chaise, de W.-C., de personne*) seat; *Av* **s. éjectable,** ejector seat; **bain de s.,** sitz bath, hip bath; *Obst* **accouchement par le s.,** *F* **un s.,** breech delivery; **le bébé se présente par le s.,** the baby is in the breech position;

(e) *Tech* seating (*of valve etc*).

siège-baquet [sjɛʒbakɛ] *nm Aut* bucket seat; (*pl sièges-baquets*).

siéger [sjeʒe] *vi* (**je siège, n. siégeons; je siégeai(s); je siégerai**) **(a) s. à Londres,** (*of company etc*) to have its head office *or* headquarters in London, to be headquartered in London; **après avoir siégé à Bayeux pendant dix ans,** (*of bishop*) having held the see of Bayeux for ten years; *Méd & Fig* **c'est là que siège le mal,** that is the root of the problem; **(b)** (*of court of law, judge, assembly etc*) to sit; **(c) s. à la Chambre,** to have a seat *or* to sit in Parliament; *Jur* **s. au tribunal,** to be on the bench.

sien, sienne [sjɛ̃, sjɛn] **1** *adj poss* (*d'homme etc*) his; (*de femme etc*) hers; (*de bébé*) his, hers; (*d'animal, de nation, de chose etc*) its; (*après un sujet indéfini*) one's own; **adopter qch comme s.,** to adopt sth as one's own; **faire s.,** to accept as one's own; **un s. ami,** a friend of his *or* hers.

2 *pron poss* **le s., la sienne, les siens, les siennes,** (*d'homme etc*) his; (*de femme etc*) hers; (*de bébé*) his, hers; (*d'animal, de nation, de chose etc*) its; (*après un sujet indéfini*) one's own; **ma sœur est plus intelligente que la sienne,** my sister is more intelligent than his *or* hers; **il prit mes mains dans les (deux) siennes,** he took my hands in his.

3 *nm* **à chacun le s.,** to each his own; **y mettre du s.,** to pull one's weight, to do one's bit; **les siens,** (*famille*) one's (own) family; (*amis, partisans*) one's (own) people; **faire des siennes,** to be up to one's tricks.

Sienne [sjɛn] *n* Siena; *Com* **terre de S. naturelle/brûlée,** raw/burnt sienna.

sierra [sjɛra] *nf Géog* sierra.

Sierra Leone [sjɛraleɔn] *nf* Sierra Leone.

sieste [sjɛst] *nf* siesta, nap (*after lunch*); **faire la s.,** to take *or* have a siesta.

sieur [sjœr] *nm* **le s. Martin,** *Jur & Arch* Mr Martin; *Péj* a certain Mr Martin.

sifflant, -ante [siflɑ̃, -ɑ̃t] **1** *adj* hissing (*noise*); whistling (*note*); wheezing, wheezy (*breath, cough*); sibilant (*consonant*). **2** *nf Ling* **sifflante,** sibilant.

sifflement [sifləmɑ̃] *nm* **(a)** whistling, whistle (*of s.o., wind etc*); hiss(ing) (*of snake, goose, steam etc*); swish(ing) (*of whip*); whizz (*of bullet, arrow*); wheezing (*of asthmatic person*); sizzling (*of food in the frying pan, of arc lamp*); **(b)** *Th etc* hiss(ing), boo(ing), catcall; **(c) s. d'oreilles,** buzzing in the ears.

siffler [sifle] **1** *vi* **(a)** (*of person, bird, train, ship, wind etc*) to whistle; (*of serpent, goose, steam etc*) to hiss; (*of asthmatic person*) to wheeze; (*of food frying, arc lamp*) to sizzle; **(b)** (*avec un sifflet*) to blow a *or* the whistle; *Nau* to pipe. **2** *vt* **(a)** to whistle (*tune*); *Nau* to pipe (*command*); *Sp* **s. une faute/la mi-temps,** to blow the whistle for a foul/for half time; **(b)** to whistle for, to whistle up (*taxi etc*); to whistle for *or* after (*dog etc*); *Aut F* **je me suis fait s. (par la police),** I've been pulled up (by the police); *F* **s. une fille,** to (wolf-)whistle at a girl; **(c)** *Th etc* to hiss, to boo (*actor, play etc*); *Arg* **sifflé!,** rubbish!, boo!; **(d)** *Arg* (*boire*) to knock back (*glass of beer etc*).

sifflet [siflɛ] *nm* **(a)** (*instrument*) whistle; *Nau* pipe; **coup de s.,** blow *or* blast of the whistle; *Mil* call; *Nau* pipe; *Sp* **coup de s. final,** final whistle; **s. à vapeur,** steam whistle; *Nau* **s. de brume,** fog whistle; *Arg* **ça lui a coupé le s.,** that shut him up; *Arg* **serrer le s. à qn,** to throttle *or* strangle s.o.; **attaquer en s.,** (*de rameur*) to catch a crab; **(b)** (*sifflement*) whistle; *Th etc* hiss, boo, catcall.

siffleur, -euse [sifloer, -øz] **1** *n* (*personne*) whistler; *Th* hisser, booer. **2** *nm* (*oiseau*) widgeon. **3** *adj* whistling (*bird*); hissing (*snake*); wheezy (*horse etc*); **canard s.,** widgeon.

siffleux [siflø] *nm Can Zool* groundhog, woodchuck.

sifflotement [siflɔtmɑ̃] *nm* whistling (to oneself).

siffloter [siflɔte] *vt & vi* to whistle (to oneself).

sigillaire [siʒilɛr] *adj* **anneau s.,** signet ring.

sigillé [siʒile] *adj Bot Cér etc* sigillate(d).

sigisbée [siʒisbe] *nm Hum & Litt* gallant.

sigle [sigl] *nm* acronym.

sigma [sigma] *nm* (*lettre grecque*) sigma.

signal, -aux [siɲal, -o] *nm* **(a)** (*signe*) signal; (*indice*) sign; *Psy* **réagir à un s.,** to react to a signal; **faire des signaux,** to signal; **envoyer/lancer un s.,** to send a signal; **donner le s. de qch,** to give the signal for sth; *Fig* (*of event etc*) to be the signal for sth, to signal the start of sth; **le s. d'une crise sociale,** the sign of a social crisis; **s. de départ,** starting signal (*of train, race etc*); **au s. donné, tous se levèrent,** on the given signal *or* when the signal was given, they all stood up; **s. à vue, s. optique,** visible signal, visual signal; **s. à bras,** semaphore signal; *Mil* **s. par fanions,** *Nau* **s. à pavillons,** flag signal; **s. lumineux,** light signal; *Admin* **signaux lumineux,** traffic lights; **s. avertisseur, s. d'avertissement, s. d'alerte,** warning signal; **s. d'alerte,** air-raid warning (signal); **s. de fin d'alerte (aérienne/*etc*),** all-clear (signal); **s. d'alarme,** alarm signal; **s. d'incendie,** fire alarm; *Nau* **s. de brume,** fog signal; **s. de détresse,** distress *or* S.O.S. signal; *Nau Rad* **s. horaire,** time signal; **s. de chemin de fer,** *Br* railway *or Am* railroad signal; *Rail* **s. à distance, s. avancé,** distant (block) signal; *Rail* **s. rapproché, s. d'entrée,** home signal; *Rail* **s. d'arrêt,** danger signal; *Rail* **s. à l'arrêt,** signal at danger; *Rail* **s. d'arrêt absolu,** stop signal; *Aut* **signaux routiers,** (*écriteaux*) road signs;

(b) *Electron Rad* signal; *TV* **s. d'image/s. vidéo,** picture signal/video signal; **signaux parasites,** clutter; *Tél* **s. d'appel,** call(ing) signal; *Ordinat* **s. d'invitation à transmettre,** proceed-to-send signal, *Am* start-dialling signal; **s. de (sortie) lecture,** sense signal;

(c) (*en arpentage*) target (*over a bench mark*).

signalé [siɲale] *adj* **(a)** (*indiqué*) indicated by a warning sign; **(b)** *Litt* signal, outstanding (*service*).

signalement [siɲalmɑ̃] *nm* description, particulars (*of person*).

signaler [siɲale] **1** *vt* **(a)** (*faire remarquer*) to point out, to indicate (*mistake, fact etc*) **(à qn,** to s.o.); **s. à qn que,** to point out to s.o. that; **s. un livre à qn,** to recommend a book to s.o.;

(b) (*reporter*) to notify, to report (*delay, change, theft etc*) **(à qn,** to s.o.); **rien à s.,** nothing to report; *Nau* **date à laquelle un navire a été signalé pour la dernière fois,** date when a ship was last spoken;

(c) (*par un signal*) to signal (*train, ship etc*); *Av* to indicate the position of (*runway*);

(d) *Ordinat* to post;

(e) *Vieilli* (*rendre remarquable*) to make (*sth*) conspicuous.

2 se signaler *vpr* to distinguish oneself **(par,** by); **se s. dans les sciences,** to have a reputation as a scientist; **se s. à l'attention de qn,** to catch s.o.'s eye; *F* **se s. par son absence,** to be conspicuous by one's absence.

signalétique [siɲaletik] *adj Admin* descriptive (*of a person*); **fiche s.,** description (*in police records*).

signaleur [siɲalœr] *nm Mil etc* signaller; *Rail* signalman.

signalisation [siɲalizasjɔ̃] *nf* **(a)** *Aut* (*action*) signposting; (*signaux*) signs; **s. routière internationale,** international (system of) road signs; **panneau de s.,** roadsign; **feux de s.,** traffic lights; **(b)** (*action*) *Rail* installation of signals **(de,** on); *Av* installation of lights **(de,** on); **(c)** *Rail* (*signaux*) signals.

signaliser [siɲalize] *vt Aut* to signpost (*road*); *Rail* to install signals on (*track*); *Av* to install lights on (*runway*).

signataire [siɲatɛr] *n* signatory.

signature [siɲatyr] *nf* **(a)** signature; (*acte*) signing; **apposer sa s. à un acte,** to sign a document; **pour s.,** for signature; *Com* **la s. sociale,** the signature of the firm; **document porté à la s. du directeur,** document given to the director for his *or* her signature; **présenter le courrier à la s.,** to present the mail for signature; **avoir la s.,** to be authorized to sign (*on behalf of the firm etc*); **livre de signatures,** autograph book; **(b)** *Typ* signature.

signe [siɲ] *nm* **(a)** (*indice*) sign, indication (*of rain, impatience etc*); sign (*of illness*); sign, mark, token (*of friendship etc*); **ne donner aucun s. de vie, ne pas donner s. de vie,** to show no sign of life; **elle ne nous a pas fait s. de vie depuis un mois,** we haven't heard from her for a month; **porter du noir en s. de deuil,** to wear black as a sign of mourning; **un s. des temps,** a sign of the times; **signes extérieurs de richesses,** trappings *or* outward signs of wealth; **la réunion a eu lieu sous le s. de la cordialité,** cordiality was the keynote of the proceedings; **elle commence à montrer des signes d'ennui,** she is beginning to show signs of boredom; **c'est bon s./mauvais s.,** it's a good/bad sign; **c'est s. que quelque chose ne va pas,** it's a sign that there's something wrong;

(b) (*symbole*) sign, symbol; (*de rang*) insignia; **s. algébrique,** algebraical sign; **les signes de (la) ponctuation,** the punctuation marks; *Typ* **signes de correction,** proof correction marks; *Mus* **signes constitutifs,** key signature; **s. du zodiaque,** sign of the zodiac; **s. de chance,** lucky sign; *Ordinat* **chiffre de s.,** sign digit;

(c) (*trait physique*) (distinctive) mark (*of person*); *Admin* **signes particuliers,** special peculiarities;

(d) (*geste*) sign, gesture; **parler par signes,** to talk in signs; **s. d'adieu,** farewell wave (of the hand); **s. de l'œil,** wink; **faire s. à qn,** to make a sign to s.o.; (*contacter*) to get in touch with s.o.; **faire s. à qn de faire qch,** to signal to s.o. to do sth; **je lui ai fait s. de venir,** I beckoned him to come; **il fit s. de se taire,** he gave a signal *or* signalled for silence; **faire s. à qn (de la main) de reculer/de s'écarter/de partir,** to wave s.o. back/aside/off *or* away; **faire s. que oui,** to nod (*in agreement*); **faire s. que non,** (*de la tête*) to shake one's head; (*du doigt*) to wag one's finger;

(e) *Rel* **s. de (la) croix,** sign of the cross; **faire le s. de la croix** *ou* **un s. de croix,** to make the sign of the cross, to cross oneself.

signer [siɲe] **1** *vt* **(a)** to sign (*contract, letter, painting etc*); *Can Sp* to sign (up) (*player*); **s. son nom,** to sign one's name; *Nau* **s. l'engagement,** to sign on; *Fig F* **c'est signé,** it's easy to guess who did that; *Fig F* **c'est signé Paul,** it has Paul written all over it, it's just like *or* typical of Paul; **(b)** *Tech* to hallmark (*jewellery*). **2** *vi* to sign; **s. de son nom,** to sign one's name. **3 se signer** *Rel* to cross oneself.

signet [siɲɛ] *nm* bookmark.

signifiant [siɲifjɑ̃] **1** *adj Litt* (*plein de sens*) meaningful, expressive. **2** *nm Ling* signifier.

significatif, -ive [siɲifikatif, -iv] *adj* significant; **s. de,** indicative of.

signification [siɲifikasjɔ̃] *nf* **(a)** meaning, sense (*of word, symbol etc*); significance (*of event, fact etc*); **(b)** *Jur* notification (*of decision*); serving (*of writ*).

signifié [siɲifje] *nm Ling* signified.

signifier [siɲifje] *vt* (*impf & pr sub* **n. signifiions, v. signifiiez) (a)** (*vouloir dire*) to mean, to signify; **s. que,** (*of action etc*) to show *or* mean that; **cela ne signifie rien,** it doesn't mean anything; **des remarques qui ne signifient rien,** meaningless remarks; **qu'est-ce que cela signifie?,** (*indignation*) what's the meaning of this?; **liberté ne signifie pas nécessairement anarchie,** liberty need not mean *or* does not necessarily mean anarchy; **la moindre imprudence signifierait la mort pour eux,** the slightest imprudence would mean death for them; **(b)** (*notifier*) to notify (**qch à qn,** s.o. of sth); **s. son congé à qn,** (*of landlord, employer*) to give s.o. notice; *Jur* **s. un jugement à qn,** to notify s.o. of a decision.

sikh, -e [sik] **1** *adj* Sikh. **2** *n* **S.,** Sikh.

silence [silɑ̃s] *nm* **(a)** silence; (*pause*) pause; **il se fit un s. subit,** there was a sudden silence *or* hush; (*dans une conversation etc*) there was a sudden pause; **dans le s. de la nuit,** in the silence of the night; **un s. de mort,** a deathly silence *or* hush; **s. ému** *ou* **anxieux,** breathless silence; **observer une minute de s.,** to observe a minute's silence; **réduire qn au s.,** to reduce s.o. to silence, to silence s.o.; **rompre le s.,** to break the silence; **garder** *ou* **observer le s.,** to keep silent (**sur,** about); **(du) s.!,** silence!, be quiet!; **souffrir en s.,** to suffer in silence; **passer qch sous s.,** to hush sth up, to keep sth secret; (*par diplomatie*) not to mention sth; **la loi du s.,** the law of silence (*preventing criminals from informing on their fellows*); **écrire à qn après un s. de deux ans,** to write to s.o. after a silence of two years; **préparer qch dans le s.,** to prepare sth in secrecy; **faire jurer le s. à qn,** to swear s.o. to secrecy; *Av* **cône de s.,** cone of silence; *Électron* **zone de s.,** silent zone;

(b) *Mus* rest.

silencieusement [silɑ̃sjøzmɑ̃] *adv* silently.

silencieux, -ieuse [silɑ̃sjø, -jøz] **1** *adj* silent (*person, footsteps etc*); silent, quiet (*street, garden, engine etc*); peaceful, quiet (*evening*); **après la dispute, la reste de la soirée fut s.,** (*plus personne ne parla*) after the quarrel the rest of the evening passed in silence. **2** *nm Aut* silencer, *Am* muffler; (*d'arme*) silencer; *Rad* squelch.

silène [silɛn] *nm Bot* campion.

Silène [silɛn] *nm Myth* Silenus.

Silésie [silezi] *nf* Silesia.

silex [silɛks] *nm inv* (*roche*) flint; **des s.,** (*outils, armes*) flints.

silhouette [silwɛt] *nf* silhouette; *Mil* (*cible*) figure target; **en s.,** silhouetted.

silhouetter [silwete] **1** *vt* (*dessiner*) to outline; *Phot* to block out. **2 se silhouetter** *vpr* to be silhouetted, to be outlined (**sur,** against).

silicate [silikat] *nm Ch* silicate.

silice [silis] *nf Ch* silica, silicon dioxide; **verre de s., s. fondue,** silica (glass).

siliceux, -euse [silisø, -øz] *adj* siliceous.

silicium [silisjɔm] *nm Ch* silicon.

silicone [silikɔn] *nf Ch* silicone.

silicose [silikoz] *nf Méd* silicosis.

silique [silik] *nf Bot* siliqua, silique.

sillage [sijaʒ] *nm* wake (*of ship*); *Av etc* slipstream; *Av* **s. aérodynamique,** aerodynamic drag; *Fig* **marcher dans le s. de qn,** to follow in s.o.'s wake.

sillet [sijɛ] *nm* nut (*of stringed instrument*).

sillon [sijɔ̃] *nm* **(a)** *Agr* furrow; *Fig* (*sur le front*) furrow, line; *Litt* **sillons,** (*champs*) fields, country; **(b)** track (*of wheel*); wake (*of ship*); path (*of projectile*); **s. de lumière/feu,** streak of light/fire (*of rocket etc*); **(c)** (*de disque*) groove.

sillonner [sijɔne] *vt* **(a)** (*creuser*) to furrow; (*traverser*) to cross; **flanc de montagne sillonné par les torrents,** mountainside grooved *or* scored by torrents; **forêt sillonnée de nombreux sentiers,** forest crossed by many paths; **front sillonné de rides,** furrowed brow; **(b)** (*of light, lightning etc*) to streak (*the sky*).

silo [silo] *nm* (*fosse, tour*) silo; **mettre en s.,** to silo; **s. à blé,** grain silo; **s. à ciment,** cement silo; *Mil* **s. (de lancement),** (launching) silo.

silotage [silɔtaʒ] *nm Agr etc* (*action*) ensilage.

silure [silyr] *nm* (*poisson*) silurid.

silurien, -ienne [silyrjɛ̃, -jɛn] *Géol* **1** *adj* Silurian. **2** *nm* Silurian; **s. inférieur,** Ordovician.

simagrée [simagre] *nf* pretence; **simagrées,** affected airs, affectation; **ne fais pas tant de simagrées,** don't make so much fuss.

simien, -ienne [simjɛ̃, -jɛn] *Zool* **1** *adj* simian. **2** *nmpl* **simiens,** simians, *Spéc* Simiidae.

simiesque [simjɛsk] *adj* simian, monkey-like, ape-like (*face, grimace etc*).

similaire [similɛr] *adj* similar (**à** to), of the same kind.

similairement [similɛrmɑ̃] *adv* similarly.

similarité [similarite] *nf* similarity.

simili [simili] **1** *préf* imitation, artificial. **2** *nm F Vieilli* imitation; *Tex* silk-finished cotton; *Phot* half-tone; **bijoux en s.,** imitation *or* costume jewellery. **3** *nf F* = **SIMILIGRAVURE.**

similicuir [similikɥir] *nm* artificial leather, imitation leather, leatherette.

similigravure [similigravyr] *nf* half-tone (engraving, block).

similisage [similizaʒ] *nm Tex* silk-finishing (*of cotton*).

similiser [similize] *vt Tex* to silk-finish (*cotton*).

similitude [similityd] *nf* similarity.

simoniaque [simɔnjak] *Rel* **1** *adj* simoniacal. **2** *nm* simoniac, simonist.

simonie [simɔni] *nf Rel* simony.

simoun [simun] *nm Météo* simoom, simoon.

simple [sɛ̃pl] **1** *adj* **(a)** (*direct*) simple, unaffected (*person*); simple (*dress, food, truth etc*); **modestie s.,** unaffected *or* natural modesty; **réduit à sa plus s. expression,** reduced to its simplest form; **dans le plus s. appareil,** (*nu*) in the altogether, in one's birthday suit;

(b) (*facile*) simple, easy, straightforward (*method etc*); **c'est bien s., il accepte ou on part,** it's quite simple, either he accepts or we go; **c'est s. comme bonjour,** it's as easy as pie *or* as falling off a log;

(c) (*crédule*) simple, ingenuous; **s. d'esprit,** simple-minded;

(d) (*pur*) **condamner qn sur un s. soupçon,** to condemn s.o. on a mere suspicion; **c'est une s. question de temps,** it is simply a matter of time; **c'est de la folie pure et s.,** it's sheer madness; **croire qn sur sa s. parole,** to believe s.o. on his word alone; **la s. prudence veut que ...,** ordinary *or* elementary prudence demands that ...;

(e) (*commun*) ordinary; **un s. particulier,** an ordinary citizen; **s. soldat,** private (soldier); **s. matelot,** ordinary seaman;

(f) (*non multiple*) single (*flower, ticket etc*);

(g) (*non composé*) *Courses de chevaux* **faire un pari s.,** to back a horse to win; *Gram* **passé s.,** past historic (tense), simple past; *Ch* **corps s.,** element; *Math* **équation s.,** simple equation.

2 *nm* **(a)** *Tennis* **jouer un s.,** to play a singles match; **s. messieurs/dames,** men's/ladies' singles;

(b) un s. d'esprit, a simpleton;

(c) varier du s. au double, to vary by twice as much.

3 *nmpl Bot* **simples,** medicinal herbs.

simplement [sɛ̃pləmɑ̃] *adv* **(a)** (*vivre etc*) simply; **habillé s.,** simply *or* plainly *or* quietly dressed; **(b)** (*avec naturel*) simply, naturally, unaffectedly; **le plus s. du monde,** without any fuss; **il faut prendre les choses s.,** you have to take things as they come; **(c)** (*uniquement*) simply, just, merely; **purement et s.,** purely and simply; **je voulais s. te dire que ...,** I simply *or* just *or* merely wanted to tell you that ... .

simplet, -ette [sɛ̃plɛ, -ɛt] *adj* simple, ingenuous (*person*); simplistic (*idea, theory, book etc*).

simplex [sɛ̃plɛks] *nm Ordinat* simplex.

simplicité [sɛ̃plisite] *nf* **(a)** simplicity (*of dress, manners etc*); **elle manque de s.,** she makes too much of a fuss; **en toute s.,** without affectation, simply, naturally; **venez en toute s.,** come as you are; (*pour manger*) come and take pot luck; **vivre avec s.,** to live simply; **(b)** *Phys* elementary nature (*of atoms etc*); **(c)** (*facilité*) simplicity; **c'est d'une s. enfantine,** it's child's play, a child could do it.

simplifiable [sɛ̃plifjabl] *adj* that can be simplified, capable of simplification; *Math* reducible (*fraction*).

simplificateur, -trice [sɛ̃plifikatœr, -tris] **1** *adj* simplifying (*method etc*). **2** *nm* simplifier.

simplification [sɛ̃plifikɑsjɔ̃] *nf* simplification; *Math* reduction, cancellation.

simplifier [sɛ̃plifje] *v* (*impf & pr sub* **n. simplifiions, v. simplifiiez**) **1** *vt* to simplify; **s. une fraction,** to simplify a fraction; **cela me simplifie la vie,** that simplifies my life, that makes life *or* things easier for me; **trop s.,** to oversimplify. **2 se simplifier** *vpr* to become simplified.

simplisme [sɛ̃plism] *nm* oversimplification.

simpliste [sɛ̃plist] *Péj* **1** *adj* simplistic, over-simple (*theory, explanation etc*); simplistic, superficial (*mind*). **2** *n* simplistic person.

simulacre [simylakr] *nm* semblance, show, pretence; **s. de résistance,** semblance *or* show of resistance; *Mil* **s. de combat,** sham fight; **son procès ne fut qu'un s.,** his trial was a travesty of justice *or* a mere mockery.

simulateur, -trice [simylatœr, -tris] **1** *n* pretender; *Méd* malingerer. **2** *nm Tech* simulator; *Av* **s. de vol,** flight simulator.

simulation [simylɑsjɔ̃] *nf* **(a)** (*action*) simulation, feigning; *Méd* malingering; **(b)** *Av Électron Ordinat etc* simulation; **formation en s. de vol,** simulated flight training.

simulé [simyle] *adj* feigned (*illness*); sham (*fight*); feigned, sham, bogus (*feeling, anger etc*); simulated (*situation, con-*

ditions etc); bogus (*sale*); simulated (*ivory, wood etc*).
simuler [simyle] *vt* to simulate (*ivory, wood etc*); to feign, to simulate, to sham (*feeling, anger etc*); to simulate (*situation, conditions etc*); **s. une maladie,** to pretend to be ill, to feign (an) illness, to malinger.
simultané [simyltane] *adj* simultaneous.
simultanéité [simyltaneite] *nf* simultaneousness, simultaneity.
simultanément [simyltanemɑ̃] *adv* simultaneously.
Sinaï [sinai] *nm* Sinai; **le mont S.,** Mount Sinai.
sinapisé [sinapize] *adj* **bain/cataplasme s.,** mustard bath/poultice *or* plaster.
sinapisme [sinapism] *nm Méd* mustard poultice *or* plaster, *Spéc* sinapism.
sincère [sɛ̃sɛr] *adj* **(a)** (*franc*) sincere, frank, candid (*person*); candid (*opinion*); **être s. avec soi-même,** to be frank with oneself; **(b)** (*véritable*) genuine (*supporter etc*); genuine, sincere (*joy, love, sorrow etc*); sincere, earnest (*effort*); sincere (*words etc*); **vœux/remerciements sincères,** sincere *or* heartfelt wishes/thanks; **agréez mes sincères salutations,** yours sincerely; **(c)** (*authentique*) genuine, authentic (*document etc*).
sincèrement [sɛ̃sɛrmɑ̃] *adv* **(a)** (*franchement*) sincerely, frankly, candidly; **(b)** (*vraiment*) genuinely, sincerely (*glad etc*).
sincérité [sɛ̃serite] *nf* **(a)** (*franchise*) sincerity, frankness, *Br* candour, *US* candor; **en toute s.,** in all sincerity; **(b)** sincerity, genuineness (*of regret, love etc*); sincerity (*of words etc*).
sinécure [sinekyr] *nf* sinecure; *F* **ce n'est pas une s.,** it's not exactly a rest cure.
sine die [sinedje] *adv* sine die.
sine qua non [sinekwanɔn] *adj* **condition s. q. n.,** sine qua non.
Singapour [sɛ̃gapur] *nm* Singapore.
singe [sɛ̃ʒ] *nm* **(a)** (*animal*) monkey, ape; (*enfant espiègle*) monkey; *F* (*imitateur*) ape, imitator; *F* (*personne laide*) ugly devil; **laid comme un s.,** as ugly as sin; **malin/adroit comme un s.,** as crafty/clever as a monkey; *Prov* **on n'apprend pas à un vieux s. à faire des grimaces,** don't teach your grandmother to suck eggs; **(b)** *Culin Arg* **du s.,** bully beef; **(c)** *Arg* **le s.,** (*patron*) the boss.
singer [sɛ̃ʒe] *vt* (**je singeai(s), n. singeons**) to ape, to mimic, to take (*s.o.*) off; to feign (*passion etc*).
singerie [sɛ̃ʒri] *nf* **(a) singeries,** (*grimaces, gestes*) antics, monkey tricks; **(b)** (*imitation*) (grotesque) imitation; **(c)** (*cage*) monkey *or* ape house.
single [siŋgəl] *nm* **(a)** *Tennis* singles (game); **(b)** *Rail* single-berth compartment; **(c)** (*dans un hôtel*) single room.
singulariser [sɛ̃gylarize] **1** *vt* to make (*s.o.*) conspicuous. **2 se singulariser** *vpr* to attract attention, to make oneself conspicuous.
singularité [sɛ̃gylarite] *nf* **(a)** (*particularité*) peculiarity; **cette maison a la s. d'être solaire,** the house is unusual in that it is solar-heated; **(b)** (*caractère remarquable*) remarkableness; (*caractère étrange*) strangeness, oddness, peculiarity; **esprit de s.,** desire to be different.
singulier, -ière [sɛ̃gylje, -jɛr] **1** *adj* **(a)** *Gram* singular; **(b) combat s.,** single combat; **(c)** (*remarquable*) remarkable, *Fml* singular; (*étrange*) strange, odd, peculiar, *Fml* singular; **il est s. qu'il ne soit pas encore arrivé,** it is strange *or* odd *or* peculiar that he has not arrived yet. **2** *nm Gram* singular; **au s.,** in the singular.
singulièrement [sɛ̃gyljɛrmɑ̃] *adv* **(a)** (*étrangement*) in a peculiar manner, oddly, strangely, *Fml* singularly; **(b)** (*en particulier*) specially, in particular, particularly, *Fml* singularly; **(c)** (*très, beaucoup*) remarkably, extremely, *Fml* singularly.
sinistre [sinistr] **1** *adj* **(a)** (*effrayant*) sinister; **un s. individu,** a sinister character; **événement s.,** fatal event; **un s. individu,** a sinister character; **(b)** (*emploi intensif*) awful, terrible; **un s. menteur,** an awful *or* a terrible liar. **2** *nm* (*catastrophe*) disaster, catastrophe; *Jur* (*dommage*) damage (*through disaster*); **bonification pour non-s.,** no-claims bonus.
sinistré, -ée [sinistre] **1** *adj* **population sinistrée,** stricken population; **bâtiment s.,** damaged building; **région** *ou* **zone sinistrée,** disaster area. **2** *n* disaster victim.
sinistrement [sinistrəmɑ̃] *adv* sinisterly.
sinistrose [sinistroz] *nf* (excessive) pessimism.
sino- [sinɔ] *préf* Sino-; **s.-japonais,** Sino-Japanese.
sinologue [sinɔlɔg] *n* Sinologist, Sinologue.
sinon [sinɔ̃] *conj* **(a)** (*autrement*) otherwise, or else; **donne-moi la clef, s. je me fâche,** give me the key otherwise *or* or (else) I'll get angry; **un jus d'orange, s. rien,** an orange juice, otherwise nothing, an orange juice or, failing that, nothing; **(b)** (*excepté*) except, but; **il ne fait rien s. manger et boire,** he does nothing except *or* but eat and drink; **s. que,** except that; **(c)** (*si ce n'est*) if not; **c'est un des meilleurs, s. le meilleur,** it's one of the best, if not the best.
sinoque [sinɔk] *adj Arg* (*fou*) crackers, crazy, nuts.
sinueux, -euse [sinɥø, -øz] *adj* sinuous (*line*); winding, meandering (*path, stream etc*); *Fig* tortuous (*reasoning*).
sinuosité [sinɥozite] *nf* winding, meandering, curve (*of path, stream etc*); *Fig* tortuousness (*of reasoning*).
sinus¹ [sinys] *nm Anat* sinus.
sinus² *nm Math* sine.
sinusite [sinyzit] *nf Méd* sinusitis; **avoir de la s.,** to have sinusitis.
sinusoïdal, -aux [sinyzɔidal, -o] *adj Math* sinusoidal.
sinusoïde [sinyzɔid] *nf Math* sinusoid, sine curve.
Sion [sjɔ̃] *n* Zion.
sionisme [sjɔnism] *nm* Zionism.
sioniste [sjɔnist] *adj & n* Zionist.
sioux [sju] **1** *adj & inv* Sioux. **2** *n inv* **S.,** Sioux; *Fig* **ruses de S.,** crafty *or* cunning tricks.
siphon [sifɔ̃] *nm* **(a)** *Phys etc* (*tube*) siphon; **(b)** (*bouteille*) (soda-water) siphon; **(c)** *Constr etc* trap (*of sink pipe, drain etc*); **(d)** *Géol* siphon; **(e)** *Zool* siphon.
siphonné [sifɔne] *adj F* (*fou*) crackers, crazy, nuts.
siphonner [sifɔne] *vt* to siphon.
sire [sir] *nm* **(a)** lord, sir; **beau s.,** fair sir; *Péj* **un triste s.,** a sad specimen (of humanity); **(b) S.,** (*à un souverain*) Sire.
sirène [sirɛn] *nf* **(a)** *Myth* siren, mermaid; *Fig* (*femme*) siren; **chant de s.,** siren song; **(b)** (*appareil*) siren; (*d'usine*) hooter, siren; (*de brume*) foghorn; **s. d'alarme,** fire alarm; (*en temps de guerre*) air-raid siren.
siroc(c)o [sirɔko] *nm* (*vent*) sirocco.
sirop [siro] *nm* syrup, (fruit) cordial; *Pharm* syrup; **s. de sucre,** golden syrup; **s. contre la toux,** cough mixture *or* syrup *or Br* linctus.
siroter [sirɔte] *vt F* to sip (*one's wine, coffee etc*).
sirupeux, -euse [sirypø, -øz] *adj* syrupy (*liquid, Péj music*).
sis [si] *adj Jur & Litt* situated, located; **maison sise rue Saint-Honoré,** house situated *or* located in the Rue Saint-Honoré.
sisal [sizal] *nm Bot* sisal.
sismal, -aux [sismal, -o] *adj* **ligne sismale,** line of an *or* the earthquake.
sismicité [sismisite] *nf* seismicity.
sismique [sismik] *adj* seismic.
sismogramme [sismɔgram] *nm* seismogram.
sismographe [sismɔgraf] *nm* seismograph.
sismographie [sismɔgrafi] *nf* seismography.
sismologie [sismɔlɔʒi] *nf* seismology.
sismomètre [sismɔmɛtr] *nm* seismometer.
Sisyphe [sizif] *nm* Sisyphus.
sitar [sitar] *nm Mus* sitar.
sitcom [sitkɔm] *nm TV* sitcom.
site [sit] *nm* **(a)** (*pittoresque*) beauty spot; **s. (touristique),** (*monument etc*) place of interest; **s. classé,** conservation area; **s. historique,** historic site; **(b)** *Archéol Ind* (*lieu*) site; **(c)** (*configuration d'un lieu*) setting, site; **(d)** *Mil etc* **ligne de s.,** line of sight.
sit-in [sitin] *nm inv* sit-in; **faire un s.-in,** to have *or* hold a sit-in.
sitôt [sito] *adv* **(a)** (*aussitôt*) **s. le soleil couché,** as soon as the sun was set; **s. dit s. fait,** no sooner said than done; **s. que** + *ind*, as soon as; **s. après,** immediately after; **(b)** (*with nég*) **vous ne la reverrez pas de s.,** it will be some time *or* a good while before you see her again.
sittelle [sitɛl] *nf* (*oiseau*) nuthatch.
situation [sitɥasjɔ̃] *nf* **(a)** (*emplacement*) situation, position, location (*of town, building etc*); *Nau* bearing;

(b) (*circonstances*) situation, position; **je lui ai exposé ma s.,** I explained my situation *or* position to him, I explained to him how I was placed *or* how I stood; **quelle est votre s. de famille?,** what is your marital status?; **être en s. de faire qch,** to be in a position to do sth; **se trouver devant une s. de fait,** to be faced with a fait accompli; *F* **elle est dans une s. intéressante,** (*enceinte*) she is in an interesting condition *or* in the family way; **l'homme de la s.,** the right man in the right place; **mettre qn en s.,** to try s.o. out in a real-life situation;

(c) *Admin Mil etc* report, return; **s. de la banque,** bank statement;

(d) (*emploi*) position; **il a une belle s.,** he has a good position; **se faire une belle s.,** to work one's way up into a

good position; *Journ* **situations vacantes,** job vacancies, *Br* situations vacant.
situé [sitɥe] *adj* situated, located; **bien/mal s.,** well/badly situated *or* located.
situer [sitɥe] *vt* to situate, to locate (*house etc*); *Fig* to place (*sth in its context*); *F* **s. qn,** to make s.o. out, to size s.o. up; *Th etc* **l'action se situe à Rome en 1516,** the action takes place *or* is situated in Rome in 1516; **ce parti se situe à droite,** this party is on the right.
six (*before noun beginning with consonant* [si]; *before noun beginning with vowel sound* [siz]; *otherwise* [sis]) **1** *adj inv* six; **le s. mai,** (on) the sixth of May, (on) May the sixth, *Am* (on) May sixth; **Charles S.,** Charles the Sixth; *Aut* **une s. chevaux,** a six-horsepower car; **les s. jours,** (*course cycliste*) = six-day cycle race. **2** *nm inv* six; **habiter au s.,** to live at number six; **lettre datée du s.,** letter dated the sixth; *Cartes* **le s. de cœur,** the six of hearts.
sixain [sizɛ̃] *nm* = **SIZAIN**.
six-huit [sisɥit] *nm inv Mus* six-eight time.
sixième [sizjɛm] **1** *adj num* sixth; **au s. étage,** on the sixth *or Am* seventh floor. **2** *n* (*personne, objet, événement etc*) sixth (one); **habiter au s.,** to live on the sixth *or Am* seventh floor; *Sp etc* **arriver le** *ou* **la s.,** to come (in) sixth. **3** *nm* sixth (part); **cinq sixièmes,** five sixths. **4** *nf Scol Br* ≈ first form, *Am* ≈ sixth grade (*of secondary school*); **entrer en s.,** to go into the *Br* first form *or Am* sixth grade.
sixièmement [sizjɛmmɑ̃] *adv* in the sixth place, sixthly.
six-quatre-deux (à la) [alasiskatdø] *adv F Vieilli* **faire qch à la s.-q.-d.,** to do sth in a slapdash manner.
sixte [sikst] *nf* **(a)** *Mus* sixth; **(b)** *Escrime* sixte.
Sixtine [sikstin] *adj f* **la chapelle S.,** the Sistine Chapel.
sizain [sizɛ̃] *nm* **(a)** *Littér* six-line stanza; **(b)** *Cartes* set of six packs *or Am* decks of playing cards.
Skai ® [skaj] *nm* leatherette.
skate(-board) [skɛtbɔrd] *nm* skateboard; **faire du s.(-b),** to skateboard; (*pl skate-boards, skates*).
sketch [skɛtʃ] *nm Th* sketch; (*pl sketches*).
ski [ski] *nm* **(a)** (*objet*) ski; **descendre à** *ou* **en skis,** to ski down; **(b)** (*activité*) skiing; **s. alpin,** downhill (skiing); **s. de fond, s. de randonnée,** cross-country (skiing), langlauf; **faire du s.,** to ski; **chaussures de s.,** ski boots; **(c) s. nautique,** water-skiing; **faire du s. nautique,** to water-ski.
skiable [skjabl] *adj* skiable, fit for skiing.
ski-bob [skibɔb] *nm* skibob; (*pl ski-bobs*).
skier [skje] *vi* to ski.
skieur, -euse [skjœr, -øz] *n* skier; **s. nautique,** water-skier; **s. de fond,** cross-country *or* langlauf skier; *Mil* **éclaireurs skieurs,** ski troops.
skif(f) [skif] *nm Nau* skiff.
skin(head) [skin(ɛd)] *nm* skin(head).
skip [skip] *nm Ind* skip.
skippé [skipe] *adj Nau* **s. par,** skippered by.
skipper [skipœr] *nm Nau* (*barreur*) skipper.
slacker [slake] *vi Can* (*relâcher*) to ease up; **s. d'une coche,** to ease up a bit.
slalom [slalɔm] *nm Ski* slalom; **descente en s.,** slalom descent; **s. géant,** giant slalom; *Fig* **faire du s. entre les voitures/***etc*, to dodge in and out among the cars/*etc*.
slalomer [slalɔme] *vi Ski* to slalom; *Fig* to dodge in and out.
slalomeur, -euse [slalɔmœr, -øz] *n Ski* slalom skier.
slave [slav] **1** *adj* Slav(onic). **2** *nm Ling* Slavonic. **3** *n* **S.,** Slav.
slavisant, -ante [slavizɑ̃, -ɑ̃t], **slaviste** [slavist] *n* Slavist.
sleeping [slipiŋ] *nm Rail F Vieilli* (*wagon*) sleeping car; (*couchette*) berth.
slip [slip] *nm* **(a)** (*d'homme*) briefs, underpants; (*de femme*) briefs, panties, pants; **s. de bain,** (*d'homme*) swimming trunks; (*de femme*) bikini bottoms; **s. de soutien (pour sportifs),** athletic support, *F* jockstrap; **(b)** *Nau* slipway.
slogan [slɔgɑ̃] *nm Com Pol* slogan; **s. publicitaire,** advertising slogan.
sloop [slup] *nm Nau* sloop; **s. à tape-cul,** yawl.
sloughi [slugi] *nm* (*chien*) Saluki.
slovaque [slɔvak] **1** *adj* Slovak. **2** *nm Ling* Slovak. **3** *n* **S.,** Slovak.
Slovaquie [slɔvaki] *nf* Slovakia.
slovène [slɔvɛn] **1** *adj* Slovene, Slovenian. **2** *nm Ling* Slovene, Slovenian. **3** *n* Slovene, Slovenian.
Slovénie [slɔveni] *nf* Slovenia.
slow [slo] *nm* (*danse, musique*) slow dance.
S.-lt *Mil abrév* **sous-lieutenant.**
S.M. [ɛsɛm] (*abrév* **Sa Majesté**) HM.
smala(h) [smala] *nf* (*de chef arabe*) retinue; *F* (*famille etc*) tribe; *F* **toute la s.,** the whole tribe.
smart [smart] *adj inv F Vieilli* (*élégant*) smart.
smash [smaʃ] *nm Tennis etc* smash.
smasher [smaʃe] *Tennis* **1** *vt* to smash (*ball*). **2** *vi* to smash (the ball).
S.M.E. [ɛsɛmə] *nm CE* (*abrév* **Système monétaire européen**) EMS.
smectique [smɛktik] *adj* **argile s.,** fuller's earth.
S.M.I.C. [smic] *nm abrév* **salaire minimum interprofessionnel de croissance**.
smicard, -arde [smikar, -ard] *n F* worker on minimum wage, minimum wage earner.
smocks [smɔk] *nmpl Couture* smocking.
smog [smɔg] *nm* smog.
smoking [smɔkiŋ] *nm* (*veston*) dinner jacket, *Am* tuxedo; (*costume*) dinner *or* evening suit.
smurf [smœrf] *nm* break dance; **danser le s.,** to break-dance.
snack(-bar) [snak(bar)] *nm F* snack bar; (*pl snack-bars, snacks*).
SNCF [ɛsɛnseɛf] *nf* (*abrév* **Société nationale des chemins de fer français**) = (French) national railway company.
snif [snif] *int F* sniff; **s., s. il me l'a pris!,** boohoo, he's taken it from me!
sniffer¹ [snifœr] *nm Arg* glue-sniffer.
sniffer² [snife] *vt Arg* **s. de la colle,** to sniff glue.
snob [snɔb] **1** *n* snob. **2** *adj* (*inv in f sing*) snobbish, snobby (*person, restaurant etc*).
snober [snɔbe] *vt* (*mépriser*) to look down on (*s.o.*); (*éviter*) to snub (*s.o.*).
snobinard, -arde [snɔbinar, -ard] *F Péj* **1** *adj* stuck-up, snobbish. **2** *n* stuck-up *or* snobbish type.
snobisme [snɔbism] *nm* snobbery, snobbishness; **s. à rebours,** inverted snobbery.
snow-boot [snobut] *nm* snow boot; (*pl snow-boots*).
sobre [sɔbr] *adj* **(a)** sober, temperate, abstemious (*person*); moderate (*meal*); **s. comme un chameau,** as sober as a judge; **(b) s. de paroles/louanges,** sparing of words/praise; **(c)** restrained (*drawing, style*).
sobrement [sɔbrəmɑ̃] *adv* **(a)** (*manger, boire*) in moderation; **(b)** (*s'habiller etc*) soberly.
sobriété [sɔbrijete] *nf* temperateness, abstemiousness (*in food and drink*); moderation (*in speech etc*); sobriety, restraint (*in style*); **manger et boire avec s.,** to eat and drink in moderation.
sobriquet [sɔbrikɛ] *nm* nickname.
soc [sɔk] *nm* ploughshare, *US* plowshare.
sociabilité [sɔsjabilite] *nf* sociability, sociableness.
sociable [sɔsjabl] *adj* sociable; **peu s.,** unsociable.
social, -aux [sɔsjal, -o] **1** *adj* **(a)** social; **l'homme est un animal s.,** man is a social animal; **l'ordre s.,** the social order; **science sociale,** social science; **œuvres sociales,** welfare activities; **guerre sociale,** class war; **assistante sociale,** social worker; **aide sociale,** social welfare; **l'échelle sociale,** the social ladder; **couche sociale,** social stratum; *Zool* **animal s.,** social animal; **(b)** *Com* **nom s., raison sociale,** company name; **siège s.,** head office. **2** *nm* *Écon etc* social questions; *Journ* (*rubrique*) society column; *F* **faire du s.,** to do one's good turn for the day.
social-démocrate [sɔsjaldemɔkrat] *adj & n Pol* social democrat; (*pl sociaux-démocrates*).
social-démocratie [sɔsjaldemɔkrasi] *nf Pol* social democracy; (*pl sociaux-démocraties*).
socialement [sɔsjalmɑ̃] *adv* socially.
socialisant, -ante [sɔsjalizɑ̃, -ɑ̃t] *Pol* **1** *adj* with socialist tendencies. **2** *n* socialist sympathiser.
socialisation [sɔsjalizasjɔ̃] *nf* **(a)** *Écon* socialization, collectivization (*of capital, industries*); **(b)** socialization (*of person*).
socialiser [sɔsjalize] *vt* **(a)** *Écon* to socialize, to collectivize (*property etc*); **(b)** to socialize (*person*).
socialisme [sɔsjalism] *nm* socialism; **s. d'État,** State socialism; **s. chrétien,** Christian socialism.
socialiste [sɔsjalist] *adj & n* socialist.
sociétaire [sɔsjetɛr] *n* **(a)** (*membre*) member; **(b)** (*actionnaire*) shareholder.
société [sɔsjete] *nf* **(a)** (*communauté*) society; **dans notre s.,** in our society; **problème de s.,** social problem; **s. de consommation,** consumer society; **s. d'abondance,** affluent society; **devoirs envers la s.,** duty to society *or* to the community; **ça ne se fait pas dans la bonne s.,** that is not done in the best society; **animaux qui vivent en s.,** social animals;

(b) (*association*) society, association; *Sp* club; *Hist* **la S. des Nations,** the League of Nations; **s. de secours aux blessés,** first-aid association;

(c) *Com Ind* company, firm; **s. par actions,** *Br* joint-stock company, *US* incorporated company; **s. anonyme,** public company; **s. à responsabilité limitée,** = limited (liability) company; **s. d'utilité publique,** public utility company, *Am* utility; **la S. Martin,** the Martin Company; **s. de crédit mutuel,** friendly society; *Fin* **s. à portefeuille,** holding company; **s. de placement,** investment trust;

(d) (*compagnie*) company, companionship, *Fml* society; **il aime la s.,** he likes company; **la s. des personnes de son âge,** the company *or Fml* society of people his own age;

(e) (*beau monde*) (*fashionable*) society; **la haute s.,** high society; **femmes de s.,** society women;

(f) **jeux de s.,** board games; *Vieilli Br* parlour *or US* parlor games.

socio [sɔsjo] *nf F* = **SOCIOLOGIE**.

socio- [sɔsjɔ] *préf* socio-.

socioculturel, -elle [sɔsjɔkyltyrɛl] *adj* sociocultural; **centre s.-c.,** social and cultural centre.

sociodrame [sɔsjɔdram] *nm Psy* sociodrama.

socio-économique [sɔsjɔekɔnɔmik] *adj* socioeconomic; (*pl socio-économiques*).

sociogramme [sɔsjɔgram] *nm Psy* sociogram.

sociolinguistique [sɔsjɔlɛ̃gɥistik] **1** *adj* sociolinguistic. **2** *nf* sociolinguistics.

sociologie [sɔsjɔlɔʒi] *nf* sociology.

sociologique [sɔsjɔlɔʒik] *adj* sociological.

sociologiquement [sɔsjɔlɔʒikmɑ̃] *adv* sociologically.

sociologisme [sɔsjɔlɔʒism] *nm* sociologism.

sociologue [sɔsjɔlɔg] *n* sociologist.

sociométrie [sɔsjɔmetri] *nf* sociometry.

socioprofessionnel, -elle [sɔsjɔprɔfɛsjɔnɛl] *adj* socio-professional.

socle [sɔkl] *nm* base, pedestal, plinth (*for statue, column*); base (*for vase, clock*); stand (*for apparatus*); base, socket (*for mast etc*); bed plate (*of engine*); *Géol* insular shelf; *Constr* **s. de lambris,** skirting board.

socque [sɔk] *nm* (*sabot*) clog; *Th Antiq* sock.

socquette [sɔkɛt] *nf* ankle sock, *Am* bobby sock.

Socrate [sɔkrat] *nm* Socrates.

socratique [sɔkratik] *adj* Socratic.

soda [sɔda] *nm* fizzy drink, *Am* soda (pop); **s. à l'orange,** orangeade; **whisky s.,** whisky and soda.

sodique [sɔdik] *adj Ch* sodic.

sodium [sɔdjɔm] *nm Ch* sodium.

Sodome [sɔdɔm] *n* Sodom.

sodomie [sɔdɔmi] *nf* sodomy, buggery.

sodomiser [sɔdɔmize] *vt* to sodomize, to bugger.

sodomite [sɔdɔmit] *nm* sodomite.

sœur [sœr] *nf* **(a)** sister; **s. jumelle,** twin sister; **s. de lait,** foster sister; **baiser de s.,** sisterly kiss; *Arg* **et ta s.!,** tell that to the marines!; *Fig* **ces deux théories sont sœurs,** these two theories are akin; *Fig* **rencontrer l'âme s.,** to find a soul mate; **(b)** *Rel* sister, nun; **entrez, ma s.,** come in, sister; **S. Thérèse,** Sister Theresa.

sœurette [sœrɛt] *nf F* little sister.

sofa [sɔfa] *nm* sofa, settee.

soffite [sɔfit] *nm Archit* soffit.

Sofia [sɔfja] *nm* Sofia.

SOFRES [sɔfrɛs] *nf* (*abrév* **Société française d'enquêtes et de sondages**) *Br* ≈ MORI.

software [sɔftwɛr] *nm Ordinat* software.

soi [swa] *pron pers* (*stressed referring to an indef subject*) **(a)** (*reflexive or reciprocal*) oneself, one; (*referring to 'il', 'elle'*) himself, herself, itself; **parler de s.,** to talk about oneself; **avoir de l'argent/ses papiers sur s.,** to have some money/one's papers on one; **prendre sur s.,** to get *or* take a grip on oneself; **chacun pour s.,** every man for himself; **en s.,** in itself, per se; **il va de s. que ...,** it goes without saying that ...; *F* **ça va de s.!,** it goes without saying!; **avoir la loi pour s.,** to have the law on one's side; **content/fier de s.,** pleased with/proud of oneself; **il n'est plus maître de s.,** he is no longer in control of himself; **se parler à s.-même,** to talk to oneself; **difficile de rester s.-même,** difficult to remain (true to) oneself; **petits services qu'on se rend entre s.,** small mutual services;

(b) (*emphatic*) **pour s'assurer qu'une chose sera bien faite, il faut la faire s.-même,** if you want a thing well done, (you must) do it yourself.

soi-disant [swadizɑ̃] **1** *adj inv* **(a)** (*qui se prétend*) self-styled, would-be (*novelist, artist etc*); **une s.-d. comtesse,** a self-styled countess; **(b)** (*appelé*) so-called; **les arts s.-d. libéraux,** the so-called liberal arts. **2** *adv* supposedly, ostensibly; **il est parti s.-d. pour réfléchir,** he went away, supposedly *or* ostensibly to think it over; *F* **s.-d., qu'il serait parti,** he's gone apparently.

soie¹ [swa] *nf* **(a)** *Tex* silk; **robe de s.,** silk dress; **papier de s.,** tissue paper; **(b)** bristle (*of wild boar, caterpillar etc*); **couvert de soies,** bristly, covered with bristles.

soie² *nf Tech* tang (*of file, blade etc*).

soierie [swari] *nf* (*tissu*) silk; (*commerce*) silk trade.

soif [swaf] *nf* thirst; *Fig* (*désir*) thirst, craving (**de,** for; **de faire,** to do); **avoir s.,** to be thirsty; **boire à sa s.,** *F* **boire jusqu'à plus s.,** to drink one's fill; **cela me donne s.,** it makes me thirsty; *Fig* **rester sur sa s.,** to remain unsatisfied; **avoir s. de,** to be thirsty *or* thirst for; **avoir s. de sang,** to be bloodthirsty, to be thirsty *or* thirsting for blood.

soiffard, -arde [swafar, -ard] *Arg* **1** *adj* boozy (*person*). **2** *n* boozer.

soignant [swaɲɑ̃] *adj Méd* **aide soignant(e),** nursing auxiliary, auxiliary nurse; **personnel s.,** auxiliary nursing staff.

soigné [swaɲe] *adj* **(a)** neat, well-groomed (*person, appearance*); careful (*work*); carefully prepared (*meal*); neat, tidy (*garment*); polished (*style*); groomed (*horse*); well-kept (*hands, nails, garden*); **elle est très soignée (de sa personne),** she is very careful *or* particular about her appearance; **peu s.,** untidy (*person, appearance, garment*); **(b)** *Arg* **une raclée soignée,** a sound thrashing; **un rhume s.,** a hell *or* a stinker of a cold.

soigner [swaɲe] **1** *vt* **(a)** (*maintenir en bon état*) to look after, to take care of (*furniture, books, hands, appearance etc*); (*apporter du soin à*) to take care over (*work, meal, details etc*); **s. une maladie,** to treat an illness; **s. sa ligne,** to watch one's figure; **s. sa popularité,** to nurse one's public; *F* **s. l'addition,** (*dans un restaurant etc*) to bump up the bill;

(b) **s. qn,** (*of host etc*) to look after s.o., to take care of s.o.; *Méd* (*of nurse etc*) to look after s.o., to take care of s.o., to tend s.o.; (*of doctor*) to treat s.o.; **il faut te faire s.,** *Méd* you should have (medical) treatment *or* see a doctor; *F* (*tu es fou*) you need your head examined; *F* **ils nous ont soignés,** (*dans un restaurant etc*) they've ripped us off.

2 se soigner *vpr* (*of person*) to take care of *or* look after oneself; **cette maladie ne se soigne pas bien,** the disease is difficult to treat; *F* **ça se soigne!,** you need your head examined!

soigneur [swaɲœr] *nm Sp* trainer; *Boxe* second.

soigneusement [swaɲøzmɑ̃] *adv* carefully.

soigneux, -euse [swaɲø, -øz] *adj* careful (**de,** with); (*propre*) tidy, neat (*person, work etc*).

soi-même [swamɛm] *pron pers voir* **SOI, MÊME**.

soin [swɛ̃] *nm* **(a)** (*charge*) care; **le s. des enfants,** the care of children, looking after children; **avoir** *ou* **prendre s. de qn/de qch,** to look after *or* take care of s.o./sth; **confier qch aux soins de qn,** to place sth in s.o.'s care, to entrust s.o. with sth; **aux (bons) soins de ...,** (*sur une lettre etc*) care of ..., c/o ...; **par les soins de ...,** by courtesy of ..., thanks to ...; **les soins du ménage,** housekeeping; **il prend peu de s. de sa personne,** he is very careless *or* slovenly about his appearance;

(b) (*effort*) care; **avoir (grand) s. de faire qch,** to take (particular) care to do sth, to make a (particular) point of doing sth; **avoir s. que** + *sub*, to see that (*sth is done etc*); to make a point of (*doing sth etc*); **mettre tous ses soins à faire qch/à ce que qch soit fait,** to go to a great deal of trouble *or* take great pains to do sth/to see that sth is done;

(c) (*tâche*) **on lui a confié le s. de les recevoir,** he was entrusted with the task *or* job of receiving them; **je vous laisse le s. de décider,** I leave it to you to decide;

(d) **avoir beaucoup de s.,** to be very tidy *or* orderly; **avec s.,** carefully, with care; **avec beaucoup de s.,** very carefully, with great care; **sans s.,** (*adj*) careless; (*pas propre*) untidy; (*adv*) carelessly; (*pas proprement*) untidily; **manque de s.,** carelessness;

(e) **soins,** (*attention*) care, attention; **soins de beauté,** beauty care; **soins médicaux,** medical care; **premiers soins, soins d'urgence,** first aid; **les soins dont il entoure sa femme/son jardin,** the care he lavishes on his wife/his garden; **être aux petits soins pour** *ou* **avec qn,** to fuss over s.o., to wait hand and foot on s.o.;

(f) *Arch* (*souci*) anxiety, worry.

soir [swar] *nm* evening; **ce s.,** this evening, tonight; **à ce s.!,** see you tonight *or* this evening!; **il fait frais le s.,** it's cool in the evening; **que faites-vous le s.?,** what do you do in the evening(s)?; **à dix heures du s.,** at ten (o'clock) in the evening; **lundi/demain/hier (au) s.,** Monday/

tomorrow/yesterday evening; **tous les lundis s.,** every Monday evening; **le lendemain s.,** the next evening; **la veille au s.,** the evening before, on the previous evening; **travailler du matin au s.,** to work from morning till night; **robe du s.,** evening dress; **presse du s.,** evening newspapers; **journal du s.,** evening newspaper; *TV* evening news; **être du s.,** to be a night owl.

soirée [sware] *nf* **(a)** (*durée du soir*) evening; **passer la s. chez un ami,** to spend the evening at a friend's house; **toute la s.,** all evening, the whole evening; **les longues soirées d'hiver,** the long winter evenings; **en fin de s.,** late in the evening, towards the end of the evening; **bonne s.!,** have a good evening (out)!, enjoy your evening!; **tard dans la s.,** late in the evening; *F* **faire une s. télévision,** to spend an evening in front of the television; **(b)** (*fête*) party; **s. dansante,** dance; **s. musicale,** musical evening; **tenue de s.,** evening dress; **(c)** *Th Cin etc* **(représentation de) s., représentation donnée en s.,** evening performance; **projecter un film en s.,** to show a film in the evening, to have an evening showing of a film.

soit [swa; *before a vowel or as adv* swat] (*third person of pr sub of* **être**) **1** *adv* all right!, *Fml* so be it!; **s., allez,** all right then, go.

2 *conj* **(a)** (*supposons*) **s. trois multiplié par six,** if three is multiplied by six; **s. ABC un triangle,** let ABC be a triangle, given a triangle ABC;

(b) (*à savoir*) that is to say; **trois objets à dix francs, s. trente francs,** three articles at ten francs, that is to say thirty francs;

(c) s. ... s. ..., s. ... ou ..., either ... or ..., whether ... or ...; **s. l'un s. l'autre,** (either) one or the other; **s. maintenant ou demain, cela arrivera sûrement,** whether it happens today or tomorrow, it is bound to happen; **s. modestie, s. paresse, il n'a jamais rien écrit,** whether it's from modesty or laziness, he has never written anything;

(d) s. qu'il vienne ou qu'il ne vienne pas, whether he comes or not.

soixantaine [swasɑ̃tɛn] *nf* **(a)** (*nombre*) **une s.,** about sixty; **une s. de,** about sixty (*cars, people, years etc*); **la s. de livres qu'elle a,** the sixty (or so) books she has; **(b)** (*âge*) **la s.,** (the age of) sixty; **elle approche de la s.,** she's getting on for sixty; **avoir dépassé la s.,** to be in one's sixties, to be over sixty.

soixante [swasɑ̃t] **1** *adj inv* sixty; **page s.,** page sixty; **s. et un,** sixty-one; **s. et onze,** seventy-one; **s. et onzième,** seventy-first. **2** *nm inv* sixty; **habiter au s.,** to live at number sixty.

soixante-dix [swasɑ̃tdis] *adj & nm inv* seventy.

soixante-dixième [swasɑ̃tdizjɛm] **1** *adj* seventieth. **2** *n* seventieth. **3** *nm* (*fraction*) seventieth (part).

soixante-huitard, -arde [swasɑ̃tɥitar, -ard] *Pol* **1** *adj* relating to the events of May 1968. **2** *n* participant in *or* supporter of the events of May 1968.

soixantième [swasɑ̃tjɛm] **1** *adj* sixtieth. **2** *n* sixtieth. **3** *nm* (*fraction*) sixtieth (part).

soja [sɔja] *nm* (*plante*) soya (bean); *Culin* **germes de s.,** bean sprouts.

sol[1] [sɔl] *nm* **(a)** (*surface de la terre*) ground; (*territoire*) soil; **le s. natal,** one's native soil; **au s.,** at ground level; **interdit sur le s. français,** prohibited on French soil; *Él* **relier un fil au s.,** *Br* to earth *or Am* ground a wire; **conducteur au s.,** *Br* earthed *or Am* grounded conductor; **cloué au s.,** *Av* grounded; *Fig* rooted to the spot; **position s.,** ground position; *Av* **personnel au s.,** ground staff; **tapis de s.,** groundsheet; **(b)** *Géol Agr* (*matière*) soil; **(c)** (*plancher*) floor; **revêtement de s.,** floor covering.

sol[2] *nm inv Mus* (*note*) G; (*en chantant la gamme*) so(h), sol; **morceau en s.,** piece in G.

sol-air [sɔlɛr] *adj inv* ground-to-air (*missile*).

solaire [sɔlɛr] *adj* solar; **système s.,** solar system; **cadran s.,** sundial; **lunettes solaires,** sunglasses; **crème s.,** sun lotion; **moteur/four s.,** solar engine/furnace; **chauffage s.,** solar heating; **maison s.,** solar-heated house; *Méd* **traitement s.,** sunray treatment; *Astron* **taches solaires,** sunspots; *Anat* **plexus s.,** solar plexus.

solarium [sɔlarjɔm] *nm* **(a)** *Méd* (*établissement*) solarium (*for sun-bathing*); **(b)** (*terrasse*) sun terrace.

soldat, -ate [sɔlda, -at] **1** *nm* **(a)** soldier; **s. du génie,** engineer; **s. de marine,** marine; **s. Dubois!,** Private Dubois!; **s. de 2e classe, simple s.,** private; **les simples soldats,** the rank and file; **le S. inconnu,** the Unknown Soldier *or* Warrior; **se faire s.,** to go into *or* join the army; **s. de fortune,** soldier of fortune; *Fig* **c'est un vrai petit s.,** he's a real trooper; *Av* **s. de 2e classe/de première classe,** aircraftman second-class/first-class; **s. de plomb,** tin soldier; **(b) s. des bois,** soldier (ant); **s. marin,** (*crustacé*) soldier (crab). **2** *nf* **soldate,** (woman *or* female) soldier; **à la soldate,** in a soldierly *or* soldier-like way *or* fashion.

soldatesque [sɔldatɛsk] *Péj* **1** *adj* barrackroom (*language, manners etc*). **2** *nf* army rabble.

solde[1] [sɔld] *nf Mil etc* (*rémunération*) pay; *Mil Ind* **feuille de s.,** payroll; **soldes et indemnités,** ordinary pay and allowances; **officier en demi-s.,** officer on half pay; **cahier de s.,** ledger; *Péj* **être à la s. de qn,** to be in s.o.'s pay; *Péj* **avoir qn à sa s.,** to have s.o. in one's pay.

solde[2] *nm Com* **(a)** (*somme*) balance; **s. de compte,** balance of account; **s. débiteur** *ou* **déficitaire,** debit balance; **s. créditeur,** credit balance, balance in hand; **paiement pour s.,** payment of balance; **pour s. (de tout compte),** in (full) settlement; **(b) soldes,** (*articles*) sale goods; **(vente de) soldes,** (clearance) sale; **courir** *ou* **faire les soldes,** to go round the sales; **saison des soldes,** sales season; **ce magasin fait des soldes,** this shop is having a sale; **s. d'édition,** (*livre*) remainder; **(en) s.,** to clear; **je l'ai eu en s.,** I got it in *or* at a sale *or* the sales; **prix de s.,** bargain prices.

solder [sɔlde] **1** *vt* **(a)** *Fin* (*arrêter*) to balance (*an account*); (*pour acquitter*) to settle, to discharge, to pay (off) (*an account*); **s. l'arriéré,** to make up back payments; **(b)** *Com* to sell off, to clear (*surplus stock*); to remainder (*book*). **2 se solder** *vpr* **(a)** *Fin* **les comptes se soldent par un bénéfice net de ...,** the accounts show a net profit of ...; **(b)** *Fig* **se s. par,** to end in (*failure etc*).

soldeur, -euse [sɔldœr, -øz] *n Com* buyer and seller of clearance lines.

sole[1] [sɔl] *nf* sole (*of animal's hoof*).

sole[2] *nf* **(a)** *Tech Métal* bed plate; *Min Constr* sill; **(b)** *Nau* flat bottom (*of vessel*).

sole[3] *nf* (*poisson*) sole.

sole[4] *nf Agr* field (*under crop rotation*).

solécisme [sɔlesism] *nm Ling* solecism.

soleil [sɔlɛj] *nm* **(a)** (*astre*) sun; **lever/coucher du s.,** sunrise/sunset; **s. de minuit,** midnight sun; **se lever avec le s.,** to rise with the sun; **il n'y a rien de nouveau sous le s.,** there is nothing new under the sun; *Hist Fr* **le Roi S.,** the Sun King, Louis XIV; *Couture* **plissé s.,** sunray pleats; *Astron* **faux s.,** parhelion, mock sun, sundog;

(b) (*lumière, chaleur*) sun, sunshine; **il fait du s.,** the sun is shining, it's sunny; **dans le s.,** against the sun; **au (grand) s.,** in the sunshine, (full) in the sun; **il y fait un s. de plomb,** the sun is scorching hot there; *Fig* **avoir sa/se faire une place au s.,** to have one's/find oneself a place in the sun; **lunettes/chapeau de s.,** sunglasses/sunhat; **prendre des bains de s.,** to sunbathe; **jour de s.,** sunny day; **avoir du bien au s.,** to own property; *F* **cette petite est mon rayon de s.!,** this little girl is my ray of sunshine!; **sans s.,** sunless; **coup de s.,** sunburn; (*plus fort*) touch of sunstroke; *F* **piquer un s.,** to blush; **ôte-toi de mon s.!,** get out of my light!;

(c) *Bot* sunflower;

(d) *Gym* **grand s.,** grand circle;

(e) (*feu d'artifice*) Catherine wheel, pinwheel.

solennel, -elle [sɔlanɛl] *adj* **(a)** solemn (*oath, declaration etc*); solemn, formal (*occasion etc*); **(b)** solemn, grave (*tone*); solemn, impressive (*silence*); **(c)** *Rel* **communion solennelle,** solemn communion.

solennellement [sɔlanɛlmɑ̃] *adv* solemnly; (*inaugurer etc*) formally.

solenniser [sɔlanize] *vt* to solemnize.

solennité [sɔlanite] *nf* **(a)** (*caractère*) solemnity; **avec s.,** solemnly; **(b)** (*fête*) solemn ceremony.

solenoïde [sɔlenɔid] *nm Él* solenoid.

soleret [sɔlrɛ] *nm* (*partie d'armure*) solleret.

solex ® [sɔlɛks] *nm* moped.

solfatare [sɔlfatar] *nf Géol* solfatara, sulphur spring.

solfège [sɔlfɛʒ] *nm Mus* (tonic) sol-fa; **apprendre le s.,** to learn the rudiments of music.

solfier [sɔlfje] *vt Mus* to sol-fa (*tune*).

solidaire [sɔlidɛr] *adj* **(a)** *Jur* jointly liable *or* responsible **(de,** for); **obligation s.,** obligation binding on all parties; **(b)** (*lié*) interdependent (*gearwheel etc*); **nous sommes tous solidaires,** we all stand *or* stick together; **ses intérêts sont solidaires des nôtres,** his interests are bound up with ours; **être s. de qn,** to stand by s.o., to support s.o.; *Tech* **roue s. d'une autre,** wheel integral with another.

solidairement [sɔlidɛrmɑ̃] *adv* jointly.

solidariser [sɔlidarize] **1** *vt* **(a)** *Jur* to render jointly liable *or* jointly responsible; **(b)** *Tech* **mécanisme à action solidarisée,** interlocking gear. **2 se solidariser** *vpr* to

make common cause, to show solidarity (**avec,** with).
solidarité [sɔlidarite] *nf* **(a)** *Jur* joint liability *or* responsibility; **(b)** *Tech* interdependence (*of parts*); **(c)** (*entre personnes*) solidarity; **faire appel à la s. nationale,** to make a call for national solidarity; **grève de s.,** sympathy strike; **débrayer par s. (avec),** to come out (on strike) in sympathy (with).
solide [sɔlid] **1** *adj* **(a)** (*non liquide*) solid (*body, food, earth*); *Math* **angle s.,** solid angle;
(b) (*résistant*) solid, strong (*wall, cloth*); solid, secure (*foundation*); solid, sturdy (*person*); solid, hearty (*meal*); hearty (*appetite*); solid, sound (*evidence*); sound (*argument, education*); fast (*colour*); *Com* sound, solvent (*person*); well established (*position, business*); **s. sur ses jambes,** steady on one's legs; **peu s.,** (*personne*) weak; (*meuble*) flimsy; **un coup de poing s.,** a hefty blow; **qualités solides,** solid *or* sterling qualities; **garantie s.,** solid *or* reliable guarantee; **ami s.,** staunch *or* reliable *or* trusty friend; **de solides liens nous unissent,** strong *or* close ties unite us; **avoir la tête s.,** to have a strong head, to have a good head for drink; **j'ai de solides raisons pour croire que ...,** I have good *or* sound reasons for believing that ...; *Fig* **ça ne repose sur rien de s.,** there is no sound *or* solid basis for that; **être encore s. (comme un chêne** *ou* **un roc),** to be still hale and hearty.
2 *nm* **(a)** *Géom Phys* solid (body); *Géom* **s. de révolution,** solid of revolution;
(b) *F* **ça, c'est du s.!,** that's pretty solid!
solidement [sɔlidmɑ̃] *adv* (*construire etc*) solidly; (*attacher, tenir, établir etc*) firmly, securely; **homme s. bâti,** solidly *or* sturdily built man; *F* **elle s'est fait s. reprendre,** she got a good telling-off.
solidification [sɔlidifikɑsjɔ̃] *nf* solidification.
solidifier [sɔlidifje] *v* (*impf & pr sub* **n. solidifiions, v. solidifiiez**) **1** *vt* to solidify. **2 se solidifier** *vpr* to solidify.
solidité [sɔlidite] *nf* solidity; strength (*of building, material*); soundness (*of a company, of judgment*); strength, stability (*of friendship*); fastness (*of colour*); **c'est d'une s. à toute épreuve,** it stands up to anything.
soliloque [sɔlilɔk] *nm* soliloquy.
soliloquer [sɔlilɔke] *vi* to soliloquize.
solin [sɔlɛ̃] *nm Constr* (*espace*) space; (*plâtre*) plaster filling (*between joists*).
solipède [sɔlipɛd] *Zool adj & nm* solidungulate.
solipsisme [sɔlipsism] *nm Phil* solipsism.
soliste [sɔlist] *n* soloist.
solitaire [sɔlitɛr] **1** *adj* **(a)** (*qui vit seul*) solitary; (*involontairement*) lonely, *Am* lonesome (*person*); **vivre s.,** to live on one's own *or* alone; **avoir l'humour s.,** to like to be on one's own *or* alone, to like one's own company; **(b)** (*séparé des autres*) solitary, lone (*traveller, tree, house etc*); **(c)** (*désert*) lonely, deserted (*road, place etc*); **(d) vers s.,** tapeworm. **2** *n* (*personne*) loner, lone wolf; (*ermite*) hermit, recluse; **en s.,** on one's own, alone; *Nau* **voyage en s.,** solo voyage. **3** *nm* **(a)** (*jeu*) solitaire, pegboard; **(b)** (*diamant*) solitaire; **(c)** (*sanglier*) old boar (*living apart from its fellows*).
solitairement [sɔlitɛrmɑ̃] *adv* on one's own, alone.
solitude [sɔlityd] *nf* **(a)** (*de personne*) solitude; (*involontaire*) loneliness; **j'aime la s.,** I like being alone *or* on my own; **vivre dans la s.,** to live alone *or* on one's own; **(b)** (*de lieu*) loneliness; **dans la s. de la nuit/campagne,** in the loneliness of the night/countryside; **(c)** *Litt* (*endroit*) lonely spot.
solive [sɔliv] *nf Constr* joist.
sollicitation [sɔlisitɑsjɔ̃] *nf* **(a)** (*demande*) request; (*avec instance*) entreaty; **(b) les sollicitations de la faim/de l'ambition,** gnawing hunger/ambition.
solliciter [sɔlisite] *vt* **(a)** to request (*interview etc*); **s. un emploi (de qn),** to apply (to s.o.) for a job; **s. des voix,** to canvass for votes; **s. qn,** to appeal to s.o.; **s. qn de faire qch,** to appeal to s.o. to do sth; **il est sollicité de toutes parts,** he is very much in demand; **(b)** to attract (*attention*); to appeal to (*curiosity*).
solliciteur, -euse [sɔlisitœr, -øz] *n* petitioner, supplicant (**de,** for).
sollicitude [sɔlisityd] *nf* (*soin*) solicitude; (*inquiétude*) solicitude, concern, anxiety (**pour,** for).
solo [sɔlo] **1** *nm* solo; **s. de violon,** violin solo; **jouer en s.,** to play solo. **2** *adj inv* solo; **violon s.,** solo violin.
sol-sol [sɔlsɔl] *adj inv* ground-to-ground (*missile*).
solstice [sɔlstis] *nm* solstice; **s. d'été/d'hiver,** summer/winter solstice.
solubiliser [sɔlybilize] *vt* to make (*sth*) soluble.
solubilité [sɔlybilite] *nf* **(a)** solubility (*of a body*); **(b)** solvability (*of a problem*).
soluble [sɔlybl] *adj* **(a)** soluble (*substance*); **café s.,** instant coffee; **(b)** solvable (*problem*).
soluté [sɔlyte] *nm Pharm Ch* solution.
solution [sɔlysjɔ̃] *nf* **(a)** (*de problème, situation, d'équation etc*) solution, answer (**de,** to); **s. de paresse** *ou* **de facilité,** easy way out; **ce n'est pas une s.!,** that's no answer *or* solution!; **brusquer la s. d'une crise,** to find a quick way to end a crisis; **(b)** *Ch Phys etc* (*action, liquide*) solution (*of solid in liquid*); **sel en s. (dans l'eau),** salt in solution (in water); **s. détergente,** cleaning solution *or* fluid; **(c) s. de continuité,** solution of continuity; *Él etc* break of continuity.
solutionner [sɔlysjɔne] *vt* to solve (*problem, difficulty*).
solvabilité [sɔlvabilite] *nf* solvency.
solvable [sɔlvabl] *adj* (financially) solvent.
solvant [sɔlvɑ̃] *nm Ch* solvent.
soma [sɔma] *nm Biol* soma.
somali, -ie [sɔmali] **1** *adj* Somali. **2** *nm Ling* Somali. **3** *n* **S.,** Somali; **les Somalis,** the Somali(s).
Somalie [sɔmali] *nf Hist* **S. britannique/italienne,** British/Italian Somaliland.
somatique [sɔmatik] *adj Biol Psy* somatic.
somatotrope [sɔmatɔtrɔp] *adj* somatotropic.
sombre [sɔ̃br] *adj* **(a) des robes bleu s.,** dark blue dresses; **(b)** (*obscur*) dark, dim (*forest, room, light etc*); dull, overcast (*sky*); **il fait s.,** (*temps*) it is dull (weather); **il faisait très s. dans la pièce,** it was very dark in the room; **(c)** (*triste*) gloomy, sombre, *US* somber, dismal (*face, thoughts, character etc*); dark (*despair*); **l'avenir est s. pour ces jeunes-là,** the future is gloomy for these young people; **une s. histoire de s. assassinat,** a sinister tale of foul murder; **(d)** *F* **un s. imbécile,** a first-class imbecile *or* idiot.
sombrement [sɔ̃brəmɑ̃] *adv* (*tristement*) gloomily, sombrely, *US* somberly; **s'habiller s.,** to wear dark clothes.
sombrer [sɔ̃bre] *vi* (*of ship*) to sink; (*of empire*) to founder; (*of business*) to come to grief; (*of person*) to sink (*into sleep, despair etc*); **s. dans l'alcool/la misère,** to sink into alcoholism/poverty; **il vit s. sa fortune,** he saw his fortune swallowed up; **elle vit s. ses espérances,** she saw her hopes dashed; **sa raison sombra,** his mind *or* his reason gave way; **le bateau a sombré corps et biens,** the boat went down with all hands.
sombrero [sɔ̃brero] *nm* sombrero.
sommaire [sɔmɛr] **1** *adj* **(a)** summary, succinct, concise (*account*); **tenue s.,** scant attire; **(b)** (*rudimentaire*) hasty, improvised (*meal, examination*); **(c)** *Jur* summary (*proceedings, execution*). **2** *nm* summary, synopsis.
sommairement [sɔmɛrmɑ̃] *adv* **(a)** (*expliquer etc*) in summary; *Jur* (*juger*) summarily; **vêtu s.,** scantily clad *or* dressed; **(b) s. organisé,** hastily improvised.
sommation[1] [sɔmɑsjɔ̃] *nf* **(a)** *Jur* (*injonction*) notice, demand; (*de paraître en justice*) summons; **avoir s. de payer une dette,** to receive notice *or* a demand to pay a debt; **(b)** *Mil* (*de sentinelle*) challenge.
sommation[2] *nf Math* summation (*of a series*).
somme[1] [sɔm] *nf* **bête de s.,** beast of burden; *Fig* drudge; **travailler comme une bête de s.,** to work like a slave, to slave away.
somme[2] *nf* **(a)** *Math* sum, total; **faire la s. de dix nombres,** to add (up) ten numbers; **s. générale/totale,** general total/total sum; **la s. des trois angles d'un triangle vaut deux angles droits,** the sum of the three angles of a triangle is two right angles; **(b)** (*quantité*) number (*of things*); amount (*of sth*); **en s.,** (*tout compte fait*) on the whole, all things considered; (*en bref*) in short; **s. toute,** when all is said and done; **(c) s. (d'argent),** sum (of money); **payer une s. de 200 francs,** to pay (a sum of) 200 francs; **dépenser des sommes folles,** to spend vast sums *or* amounts (of money); **être mis à l'amende pour la s. de 500 francs,** to be fined (a total of) 500 francs; **un million! c'est une s.!,** a million! that's a lot of money!; **(d)** (*d'une œuvre*) outline, survey.
somme[3] *nm* nap, short sleep; **faire un (petit) s.,** to have *or* take a nap, *F* to have forty winks.
sommeil [sɔmɛj] *nm* **(a)** (*de dormeur*) sleep, *Litt* slumber; **s. de mort** *ou* **de plomb,** heavy *or* deep sleep; **dormir d'un s. de plomb,** to sleep like a log; **avoir le s. léger/profond,** to be a light/a heavy sleeper; **avoir le s. dur,** to be hard to wake; **chercher le s.,** to try to sleep; **faire une cure de s.,** to undergo sleep therapy; *Fig* **s. éternel,** eternal rest; **j'en perds le s.,** I'm losing sleep over it; *Bot* **en s.,** (lying) dormant; *Fig* **laisser une affaire en s.,** to put a matter aside, *Fml* to leave a matter in abeyance; *Zool* **s.**

hibernal, winter sleep; **(b)** (*somnolence*) sleepiness, drowsiness; **avoir s.,** to be *or* feel sleepy *or* drowsy; **le s. me gagne,** I'm beginning to fall asleep; **je tombe** *ou* **je meurs de s.,** I can't keep awake, I'm ready to drop (with sleep); **maladie du s.,** sleeping sickness.

sommeiller [sɔmeje] *vi* **(a)** to sleep lightly, to doze; **(b)** *Fig* to lie dormant (*within s.o.*).

sommelier [sɔməlje] *nm* wine waiter.

sommellerie [sɔmɛlri] *nf* **(a)** wine waiter's job; **(b)** (*cave*) wine cellar.

sommer¹ [sɔme] *vt Math* to sum.

sommer² *vt* (*demander à*) **s. qn de faire qch,** to call on s.o. to do sth; *Jur* **s. qn de comparaître,** to summon s.o. to appear.

sommet [sɔmɛ] *nm* top, summit (*of roof, mountain, hill*); top (*of tree, tower, hierarchy*); vertex (*of angle, curve, trajectory, cone*); crest (*of wave*); crown (*of arch, of the head*); *Fig* pinnacle (*of power, fame*); *Fig* **être au s. de l'échelle,** to be at the top of the ladder; *Pol* **conférence** *ou* **réunion** *ou* **rencontre au s.,** summit (meeting *or* conference).

sommier¹ [sɔmje] *nm* **(a)** base (*of bed*); **s. à ressorts/lattes,** spring/slatted base; **(b)** wind chest (*of organ*); string plate (*of piano*); **(c)** *Tech* springer (*of arch*); lintel (*of door etc*); cross beam (*of floor*); stringer (*of bridge*); beam (*of balance*); bed (*of machine*); **(d)** *Rail* bolster.

sommier² *nm* **(a)** *Admin etc* register; *Jur* **sommiers judiciaires,** criminal records; **il n'y a rien sur lui au s.,** he's got a clean record; **(b)** *Com* cash book.

sommier-divan [sɔmjedivɑ̃] *nm* divan base; (*pl sommiers-divans*).

sommité [sɔmite] *nf* **(a)** *Bot* head; **(b)** *Fig* (*personnage*) leading figure *or* light; **sommités de l'art,** leading figures *or* lights in the art world.

somnambule [sɔmnɑ̃byl] **1** *adj* somnambulistic, somnambulant; **il est s.,** he walks in his sleep. **2** *n* sleepwalker, *Spéc* somnambulist; **travailler/parler comme un s.,** to work/speak as if in a trance.

somnambulisme [sɔmnɑ̃bylism] *nm* sleepwalking, *Spéc* somnambulism; **s. provoqué,** hypnotic state.

somnifère [sɔmnifɛr] *Méd* **1** *adj* sleep-inducing, soporific; **comprimé s.,** sleeping tablet *or* pill. **2** *nm* sleeping tablet *or* pill.

somnolence [sɔmnɔlɑ̃s] *nf* sleepiness, drowsiness, *Litt* somnolence.

somnolent [sɔmnɔlɑ̃] *adj* sleepy, drowsy, *Litt* somnolent.

somnoler [sɔmnɔle] *vi* to doze.

somptuaire [sɔ̃ptɥɛr] *adj* **(a)** *Jur* sumptuary (*law*); **(b)** *Fin* **taxes somptuaires,** tax on luxury articles; **dépenses somptuaires,** expenditure on luxuries.

somptueusement [sɔ̃ptɥøzmɑ̃] *adv* sumptuously, magnificently.

somptueux, -euse [sɔ̃ptɥø, -øz] *adj* sumptuous, magnificent.

somptuosité [sɔ̃ptɥozite] *nf* sumptuousness, magnificence.

son¹, sa, *pl* **ses** [sɔ̃, sa, se] *adj poss* (**son** *is used instead of* **sa** *before f nouns beginning with a vowel or* **h** *mute*) (*d'homme etc*) his; (*de femme etc*) her; (*de chose, d'idée, d'insecte etc*) its; (*de bébé*) his, her; (*d'animal*) its, his, her; (*après un sujet indéfini*) one's; (*après 'tout le monde', 'personne', 'chacun' etc*) his, her, their; **s. père, sa mère et ses enfants,** his *or* her father, mother and children; **tirer s. épée,** to draw one's sword; **il tira s. épée,** he drew his sword; **un de ses amis,** a friend of his *or* of hers; **un militaire de ses amis,** a soldier friend of his *or* hers; **s. imbécile de frère,** his *or* her idiot of a brother; **ses père et mère,** his *or* her father and mother; **à sa pensée,** the thought of him *or* her; **à chacun selon ses besoins,** to each according to his (or her) *or* their needs; *F* **elle a fait sa crise,** she threw one of her tantrums; *F* **il fait s. malin,** he's showing off; **elle gagne bien ses dix mille francs par mois,** she certainly earns her ten thousand francs a month.

son² *nm* **(a)** sound (*of voice, instrument, bell etc*); **le s. profond de la cloche,** the deep sound *or* tone of the bell; *Fig* **je n'ai entendu qu'un s. de cloche jusqu'à maintenant,** I've heard only one side of the story up to now; **s. du tambour/de la trompette,** beat of the drum/blare of the trumpet; **danser au s. des accordéons,** to dance to the sound of accordions; **annoncer une nouvelle à s. de trompe,** to shout out a piece of news from the rooftops; *Nau* **s. de sirène** *ou* **de sifflet,** siren blast;

(b) *Phys Mus* sound; **s. pur,** clean tone; **niveau du s.,** sound level; **vitesse du s.,** speed of sound; *Av* **mur du s.,** sound barrier; *Cin etc* **enregistrement du s.,** sound recording; **prise de s.,** sound pick-up; **la prise de s. est bonne,** the recording is good; *Cin etc* **ingénieur du s.,** sound engineer; **(spectacle) s. et lumière,** son et lumière.

son³ *nm* (*de grains*) bran; **s. mouillé,** bran mash; **tache de s.,** freckle; **poupée de s.,** stuffed doll.

sonal, *pl* **-als** [sɔnal] *nm Rad TV* (advertising) jingle.

sonar [sɔnar] *nm Nau* sonar.

sonate [sɔnat] *nf Mus* sonata; **s. pour violon,** violin sonata.

sonatine [sɔnatin] *nf Mus* sonatina.

sondage [sɔ̃daʒ] *nm* **(a) s. (d'opinion),** (opinion) poll; **s. Gallup,** Gallup poll; **faire un s.,** to carry out a poll; **s. aléatoire,** random sampling; **sondages de paix,** peace feelers; **(b)** *Nau Av etc* sounding, probe; **faire des sondages,** to take soundings; **ballon de s.,** pilot balloon, sounding balloon; **(c)** *Min* boring; **appareil de s.,** drilling rig; **(d)** *Métal* **essai de s.,** probe test; **(e)** *Méd* probing (*of wound*).

sonde [sɔ̃d] *nf* **(a)** *Nau* (sounding) lead, sounding line, plummet; **naviguer à la s.,** to navigate by soundings; **être sur la s.,** to be in soundings, to have struck soundings; **(b)** sounding rod (*for pump, well etc*); **(c) faire la s.,** (*of whale*) to sound; **(d)** *Météo Av* **s. aérienne,** sounding balloon; **s. spatiale,** space probe; *Av* **s. de réservoir,** tank probe; **s. à fil chaud,** hot-wire anemometer; **(e)** *Méd* probe; **s. (creuse),** catheter; **nourri à la s.,** tube-fed; **(f)** taster (*for cheese etc*); **(g)** *Min* borer, drill.

sonder [sɔ̃de] **1** *vt* **(a)** *Nau* to sound; *Fig* to fathom (*a mystery*); **(b) s. l'atmosphère,** to make soundings in the atmosphere; **(c)** *Min* **s. un terrain,** to make borings; **(d)** (*examiner*) to taste (*cheese*); to examine (*beam*); to scan (*the horizon*); to go into (*the statements of a witness*); to sound (*s.o.*) out; **je l'ai sondée là-dessus,** I sounded her out on the matter; **s. l'opinion,** to sound public opinion, to make a survey of public opinion; *Fig* **s. le terrain,** to feel one's way, to see how the land lies; **(e)** *Méd* to probe (*wound*); to sound (*patient*); (*avec une sonde creuse*) to catheterize (*patient*). **2** *vi* **(a)** (*of whale*) to sound; **(b)** *Min* to make borings.

sondeur, -euse [sɔ̃dœr, -øz] **1** *nm* **(a)** *Nau* (*personne*) leadsman; (*machine*) sounder; **(b)** *Min* (*personne*) borer, driller. **2** *nf Min* **sondeuse,** borer, drill.

songe [sɔ̃ʒ] *nm Litt* dream; **faire un s.,** to have a dream; **en s.,** in a dream.

songe-creux [sɔ̃ʒkrø] *nm inv Litt* dreamer.

songer [sɔ̃ʒe] *vi* (**je songeai(s); n. songeons**) **(a) s. à qch,** (*penser à*) to think of sth; (*considérer*) to consider sth, to think sth over; **il ne faut pas y s.,** that's quite out of the question; **s. au mariage,** to contemplate marriage; **sans s. à mal,** without meaning any harm; **s. à faire qch,** to think of doing sth, to contemplate doing sth; **il ne songe qu'à gagner de l'argent,** making money is all he thinks about; **s. à l'avenir,** to think about the future; **sans y s.,** without thinking; **songez à ce que vous faites!,** think what you're doing!;

(b) (*imaginer*) to imagine (**que,** that); **songez si j'étais furieux,** you can imagine how angry I was; **je ne songeais guère que ...,** little did I think *or* imagine that ...; **songez donc!,** just think!, just imagine!;

(c) s. à, (*se souvenir de*) to remember; **songez à lui,** keep *or* bear him in mind, remember him; **songez que ...,** remember *or* bear in mind that ...; **je ne songeais pas que ...,** I had forgotten that ...; **cela m'a fait s. que ...,** that reminded me that ...;

(d) *Arch* (*rêver*) to dream.

songerie [sɔ̃ʒri] *nf Litt* reverie.

songeur, -euse [sɔ̃ʒœr, -øz] *adj* (*rêveur*) dreamy (*person, nature*); (*pensif*) pensive, thoughtful (*person*).

sonique [sɔnik] *adj* sonic; **bang s.,** sonic boom.

sonnaille [sɔnaj] *nf* (cow)bell.

sonnant [sɔnɑ̃] *adj* **(a)** striking (*clock*); **arriver à dix heures sonnant(es),** to arrive on the stroke of ten; **(b) monnaie sonnante et trébuchante,** hard cash.

sonné [sɔne] *adj* **(a) il est dix heures sonnées,** it is past ten, it's gone ten; **il a quarante ans (bien) sonnés,** he's on the wrong side of forty; **(b)** *F Boxe etc* (*groggy*) groggy, punch-drunk; (*fou*) crazy, cracked.

sonner [sɔne] **1** *vi* (*of clocks*) to strike; (*of bells, telephone, alarm clock*) to ring; **le glas sonne,** the bell is tolling; **s. creux,** to sound hollow; *Fig* to ring hollow; **sa réponse a sonné faux,** his answer did not ring true; *Fig* **s. bien/mal,** to sound good/bad; **l'italien sonne bien à l'oreille,** Italian is a pleasant-sounding language; **adresse qui sonne bien,** good address; **l'r sonne dans 'mer',** the r is sounded in 'mer'; **faire s. les r.,** to roll one's r's; **faire s.**

un mot, to emphasize a word; **faire s. son argent/ses clefs,** to jingle one's money/one's keys; *F* **il va se faire s.!,** he'll catch it!; **six heures sonnèrent,** the clock struck six; **midi vient de s.,** it has just struck twelve; **les vêpres sonnent,** the bells are ringing for vespers; **on sonne,** there's a ring at the door; **on a sonné,** that was the doorbell, there's someone ringing at the door; **s. avant d'entrer,** (*sur panneau*) ring before entering; **s. pour les morts,** to toll for the dead; **s. du clairon,** to sound the bugle; *Th* **s. pour faire lever le rideau/pour faire baisser le rideau,** to ring up/ring down the curtain; **son heure a sonné,** his last hour has come; **la trompette sonne,** the trumpet sounds; **les oreilles lui sonnaient,** his ears were buzzing.

2 *vt* **(a)** to sound (*trumpet etc*); **s. la cloche,** to ring the bell; *F* **il va se faire s. les cloches!,** he'll catch it!; **horloge qui sonne les heures,** clock that strikes the hours; **l'horloge a sonné dix heures,** the clock struck ten; **ne (pas) s. mot,** not to utter a word; **s. la messe/l'office,** to ring the bell for mass/for church; **s. le dîner,** to ring the dinner bell; *Mil* **s. la charge/la retraite,** to sound the charge/the retreat;

(b) (*appeler*) to ring for (*servant, nurse etc*); *Arg* **on ne vous a pas sonné!,** mind your own business!;

(c) *Arg* (*assommer*) to knock (*s.o.*) out;

(d) *Tech* to sound (*metal for cracks*); to ring, to test (*coin*);

(e) s. le creux, to have a hollow ring.

sonnerie [sɔnri] *nf* **(a)** (*son*) ringing (*of bells, telephone*); (*cloches*) (set of) bells *or* chimes; **(b)** (*mécanisme*) striking mechanism (*of clock*); (*sonnette*) bell; **pendule à s.,** striking clock; **bouton de s.,** bell push; **fil à s.,** bell wire; **(c)** *Mil* (*de clairon etc*) call.

sonnet [sɔnɛ] *nm* sonnet.

sonnette [sɔnɛt] *nf* **(a)** (*de maison etc*) bell; (*clochette*) (small) bell; (*à main*) handbell; **cordon de s.,** bell pull; **s. d'alarme,** alarm bell; **coup de s.,** ring; **personne ne répondit à mon coup de s.,** no one answered the bell; **as-tu entendu la s.?,** did you hear the bell?; **(b)** *Constr* pile driver; **(c) serpent à s.,** rattlesnake.

sonneur, -euse [sɔnœr, -øz] **1** *n* bellringer; *F* **dormir comme un s.,** to sleep like a log. **2** *nm Constr* pile-driver operator.

sono [sɔno] *nf F* (= **sonorisation**) P.A. (system); (*de discothèque etc*) sound system.

sonore [sɔnɔr] **1** *adj* **(a)** (*relatif au son*) sound; **onde s.,** soundwave; *Cin* **film s.,** sound film; **effets sonores,** sound effects; **bande** *ou* **piste s.,** sound track; **bip s.,** beep; **pollution s.,** noise pollution; **église s.,** church with good acoustics; **vibrations sonores,** acoustic resonance; **(b)** ringing, sonorous (*voice*); clear-toned (*bell*); resounding (*laughter*); *Péj* high-sounding, sonorous (*phrases*); resonant, echoing (*vault etc*); *Ling* **consonne s.,** voiced consonant; **niveau (d'intensité) s.,** sound (intensity) level. **2** *nf Ling* voiced consonant.

sonorisation [sɔnɔrizasjɔ̃] *nf* **(a)** *Ling* voicing (*of consonant*); **(b)** *Cin* addition of the soundtrack (**de,** to); **(c)** wiring (*of room*) for sound; (*équipement*) public address system; (*de discothèque etc*) sound system.

sonoriser [sɔnɔrize] **1** *vt* **(a)** *Ling* to voice (*consonant*); **(b) s. un film,** to add the soundtrack to a film; **(c) s. une salle,** to wire a hall for sound. **2 se sonoriser** *vpr Ling* (*of consonant*) to be voiced.

sonorité [sɔnɔrite] *nf* **(a)** (*qualité de son*) tone; **(b)** (*résonance*) resonance; (*de salle etc*) acoustics.

sonothèque [sɔnɔtɛk] *nf* sound effects library.

sonotone ® [sɔnɔtɔn] *nm* miniature hearing aid.

sont [sɔ̃] *voir* **ÊTRE²**.

sophisme [sɔfism] *nm* sophism.

sophiste [sɔfist] *n* sophist.

sophistication [sɔfistikasjɔ̃] *nf* **(a)** sophistication (*of person, equipment*); **(b)** *Vieilli* adulteration (*of wine etc*).

sophistique [sɔfistik] **1** *adj* sophistic(al). **2** *nf* sophistry.

sophistiqué [sɔfistike] *adj* **(a)** sophisticated (*person*); sophisticated, advanced (*equipment etc*); **(b)** *Vieilli* (*frelaté*) adulterated (*wine etc*).

Sophocle [sɔfɔkl] *nm* Sophocles.

soporifique [sɔpɔrifik] **1** *adj* soporific, sleep-inducing (*drug*); *F* (*ennuyeux*) soporific, boring. **2** *nm* (*drogue*) sleeping drug, soporific; *F* (*livre*) soporific book.

sopraniste [sɔpranist] *nm Mus* male soprano.

soprano [sɔprano] *Mus* **1** *nm* soprano (voice). **2** *n* (*person*) soprano. **3** *adj* **saxophone s.,** soprano saxophone.

sorbe [sɔrb] *nf Bot* sorb (apple).

sorbet [sɔrbɛ] *nm Culin* sorbet, water ice; **s. au cassis,** blackcurrant sorbet *or* water ice.

sorbetière [sɔrbətjɛr] *nf* ice-cream maker.

sorbier [sɔrbje] *nm Bot* sorb (tree), service (tree).

sorbique [sɔrbik] *adj Ch* sorbic (*acid*).

sorbonnard, -arde [sɔrbɔnar, -ard] *F Péj* **1** *n* (*étudiant, professeur*) student *or* lecturer at the Sorbonne. **2** *adj* pedantic.

Sorbonne (la) [lasɔrbɔn] *nf* the Sorbonne.

sorcellerie [sɔrsɛlri] *nf* witchcraft, sorcery, magic.

sorcier [sɔrsje] **1** *nm* sorcerer, wizard, **s. guérisseur,** witch doctor, medicine man. **2** *adj F* **ce n'est pas bien s.,** there's no magic about that, you couldn't call that difficult.

sorcière [sɔrsjɛr] *nf* sorceress, witch; *F Péj* **vieille s.,** old hag, old witch; **chasse aux sorcières,** witch hunt; **cercle** *ou* **rond de sorcières,** fairy ring.

sordide [sɔrdid] *adj* **(a)** filthy (*clothes*); sordid, squalid (*room, district etc*); **(b)** sordid (*crime, greed etc*).

sordidement [sɔrdidmɑ̃] *adv* sordidly; **vivre s.,** to live in squalor.

sordidité [sɔrdidite] *nf* sordidness.

sorgho [sɔrgo] *nm Bot* sorghum.

Sorlingues (les) [lesɔrlɛ̃g] *nfpl* the Isles of Scilly, the Scilly Isles.

sornettes [sɔrnɛt] *nfpl* twaddle, rubbish.

sort [sɔr] *nm* **(a)** (*situation*) **assurer le s. de ses enfants/des réfugiés/***etc*, to provide for one's children/refugees/*etc*; **faire un s. à,** to dispose of (*sth*); *F* (*ne rien laisser de*) to polish off (*the bottle, a whole chicken etc*); **il fait un s. à chaque phrase,** he emphasizes each sentence; **(b)** (*destin*) fate, destiny; **notre s. est décidé,** our fate is sealed; **l'artillerie fit le s. de la bataille,** the artillery decided the battle; **coup/ironie du s.,** stroke/irony of fate; **(c)** (*hasard*) chance, fortune; **tirer au s.,** to draw lots; (*faire pile ou face*) to toss *or* spin a coin; **tirer une place/***etc* **au s.,** to draw lots for a place/*etc*; **tirage au s.,** drawing of lots; *Fb etc* toss; **le s. en est jeté,** the die is cast; **(d)** (*magique*) spell, charm; **jeter un s. à qn,** to cast a spell on *or* over s.o..

sortable [sɔrtabl] *adj F* presentable (*person*); **tu n'es pas s.!,** I can't take you anywhere!

sortant, -ante [sɔrtɑ̃, -ɑ̃t] **1** *adj* winning (*number in lottery*); outgoing, retiring (*members of committee etc*); **élèves sortants,** pupils in their last term; *Mil* cadets passing out. **2** *n* **les sortants,** those going *or* coming out.

sorte [sɔrt] *nf* **(a)** (*manière*) way; **ne parlez pas de la s.,** don't talk like that *or* in that way *or* in that fashion; **en quelque s.,** as it were, in a way; **il est sorti sans pardessus, de s. qu'il a attrapé un rhume,** he went out without his overcoat, so that *or* with the result that he caught cold; **de s. à faire,** so as to do; **parlez de (telle) s. qu'on vous comprenne,** speak so *or* in such a way as to be understood; **faites en s. que tout soit prêt à temps,** see to it that everything is ready in time;

(b) (*genre*) sort, kind; **toute(s) sorte(s) de choses, des choses de toute(s) sorte(s),** all sorts *or* kinds of things; **un homme de la s.,** a man of that sort *or* kind; **une s. de ragoût,** a *or* some sort *or* kind of stew; **je n'ai rien dit/rien fait de la s.,** I said/did no such thing *or* nothing of the kind *or* sort; **j'ai une s. d'impression qu'il viendra,** I have a sort of feeling he'll come.

sortie [sɔrti] *nf* **(a)** (*action de quitter un lieu*) going out, coming out, leaving; *Th* exit; **faire une s. pour prendre l'air,** to go out for a breath of (fresh) air; **c'était ma première s. depuis mon accident,** it was the first time I had been out since my accident, it was my first outing after my accident; **à la s. du théâtre,** at the end of the performance; **à la s. des classes,** when the children come *or* came out of school, after school;

(b) *Com* appearance (*of book*); release (*of film, record*); appearance, launch(ing) (*of model*);

(c) (*écoulement*) outflow, flowing out (*of liquid*); **tuyaux de s.,** outlet pipes;

(d) *Él Électron* output;

(e) *Ordinat* exit; (*information*) output; **dispositif de s.,** output device;

(f) *Tech* delivery (*of sheets from printing press etc*); **table de s.,** delivery table;

(g) *Com* export (*of goods*); **sorties de fonds,** outgoings, expenses;

(h) *Fin* **les sorties or,** the gold withdrawals; **s. de devises/de capitaux,** currency/capital outflow;

(i) (*excursion*) trip, excursion, outing; (*congé*) leave; **priver qn de s.,** to keep s.o. in; **faire une s. en mer,** to go for a short sea trip; **jour de s.,** day out, holiday; **avoir un jour de s. par semaine,** to have one free day a week; **nous**

sommes de s. aujourd'hui, we're going out today; **quelles sont vos sorties?,** when you go out where do you go?; *Nau* **s. à terre,** shore leave; **l'année dernière les canots de sauvetage ont fait cinquante sorties,** last year the lifeboats went out fifty times;

(j) *Mil* sally, sortie; *Fb* run out (*by goalkeeper*);

(k) *F* (*verbale*) outburst, tirade; **faire une s. à** *ou* **contre qn,** to lash out at s.o.; **elle est capable de n'importe quelle s. devant les gens,** she is capable of saying anything in front of people;

(l) (*issue*) exit, way out; **porte de s.,** exit door; *Fig* **se ménager une porte de s.,** to make sure one has a way out *or* an escape route; **s. de secours,** emergency exit; **il y a une s. sur la ruelle,** there is a way out into the lane; **à la s. de la gare,** at the station exit; **par ici la s.,** this way out;

(m) (*pour l'eau, la vapeur*) outlet;

(n) s. de bain, bathrobe; *Vieilli* **s. de bal,** evening wrap, opera cloak.

sortilège [sɔrtilɛʒ] *nm* spell, charm.

sortir[1] [sɔrtir] *v* (*prp* **sortant;** *pp* **sorti;** *pr ind* **je sors, il sort, n. sortons, ils sortent;** *pr sub* **je sorte;** *impf* **je sortais;** *p hist* **je sortis;** *fu* **je sortirai**) **1** *vi* (*aux* **être**) **(a)** (*à pied*) (*aller*) to go out, to leave; (*venir*) to come out, to leave; **s. de la salle,** to go out of *or* come out of *or* leave the room; **sortez (d'ici)!,** get out (of here)!; **faire s. qn,** (*en promenade etc*) to take s.o. out; (*mettre à la porte*) to make s.o. leave, to show s.o. the door; **il ne sort pas de chez moi,** he practically lives at my place; *Fig F* **nous ne sommes pas sortis de l'auberge!,** we're not out of the wood(s) yet; **cela ne doit pas s. d'ici,** (*cela doit rester secret*) it must go no further; **entrer par une porte et s. par l'autre,** to go in at one door and out at the other; **s. de son lit,** to get out of bed; *Méd* to leave one's bed; (*of river*) to overflow its banks; *F* **s. faire des courses,** to go out shopping; *Th* **Macbeth sort,** exit Macbeth; *F* **d'où sortez-vous?,** where have you been all this time (that you don't know that)?; **s. du port,** (*of ship*) to leave harbour; **s. d'un emploi,** to leave a job; **s. de la vie,** to depart this life; **cela m'est sorti de la mémoire** *ou* **de la tête,** it has slipped my mind *or* gone out of my head; **il ne sortira pas grand-chose de tout cela,** not much will come of all this; *Ordinat* **s. (d'un système),** to exit (from a system); *Ordinat* **s. sans sauvegarder,** to exit without saving; *Ind* **s. de la chaîne de fabrication,** to come off the production line; **le premier numéro de cette revue sortira le 8 mars,** the first number of the review will come out on the 8th of March; *Scol F* **est-ce que je peux s.?,** may I be excused?; *Fin* **s. au tirage,** (*of bonds*) to be drawn; *Cartes* **le dix de carreau est sorti,** the ten of diamonds turned up;

(b) (*of horseman*) to ride out; (*of driver or vehicle*) to drive out; (*of captain or ship*) to sail out;

(c) s. en courant/en dansant, to run/dance out; **s. précipitamment** *ou* **à la hâte** *ou* **en toute hâte,** to hurry out; **s. furtivement** *ou* **à pas de loup,** to steal *or* creep out; **parvenir à s.,** to (manage to) get out;

(d) (*of flowers*) to come out; (*of plant*) to come up, to spring up; **ses dents commencent à s.,** (*of baby*) his teeth are beginnng to come through; *Scol* **cette question est sortie (à l'examen),** this question came up (in the examination);

(e) (*quitter*) **je sors du collège/de table,** I have just left school/the table; **s. de l'enfance,** to emerge from childhood; **je sors d'une typhoïde,** I am just recovering from typhoid; **s. vainqueur d'un tournoi,** to come out on top *or* emerge the winner in a tournament; **s. indemne d'un accident,** to come out of an accident unscathed; **sortira-t-elle blanchie de ce scandale?,** will she come out of this scandal with her name cleared?; **on sortait de l'hiver,** winter was just over; **il sort d'ici,** he has just left;

(f) *Arch & F* **s. de faire qch,** to have just done sth; *Arg* **merci bien! je sors d'en prendre,** no thank you! once is enough;

(g) s. de, (*s'écarter de*) to swerve *or* deviate from (*one's duty etc*); **s. de son sujet,** to deviate *or* depart *or* wander from one's subject; **cela sort de ma compétence,** that doesn't come within my scope; **s. des bornes de la bienséance,** to overstep the bounds of decency; **s. d'une règle,** to ignore *or* depart from a rule; (*transgresser*) to break a rule; **s. des rails,** (*of train*) to jump the rails; **il ne sort pas de là, il n'en sort pas,** he is sticking to his guns; **ça sort de l'ordinaire,** that's out of the ordinary; **s. de cadence,** (*of dancer*) to be *or* get out of step; *Mus* **s. de mesure,** to be *or* get out of time; **s. du ton,** to be *or* get out of tune;

(h) (*quitter la maison*) to go out; **Madame Dupont est sortie — elle est sortie à trois heures,** Mrs Dupont is out *or* has gone out — she went out at three o'clock; **s. à cheval/à pied,** to go out riding/walking; **ils sortent tous les samedis soir,** they go out every Saturday evening; **elle sort avec lui,** she is going out with him;

(i) s. de, (*échapper à*) to get out of, to extricate oneself from (*difficulty, danger*); **aider qn à s. d'une difficulté,** to help s.o. out (of a difficulty); **il n'y a pas à s. de là,** there is no way out (of it); **soyez plus précis ou nous n'en sortirons pas,** be more precise or we shall never get to the end of it; **on n'en sort pas!,** there's no end to it!; **j'ai trop à faire, je n'en sors pas,** I've too much to do, I shall never get through it *or* to the end of it;

(j) s. de, (*être issu de*) to come from (*a good family etc*); **ce livre sort de ma plume,** this book is one of mine; **s. de l'université,** to graduate (from university); **cheval sorti d'un bon haras,** horse (that comes) from a good stud *or* stable;

(k) (*en relief*) to stand out, to stick out, to protrude, to project (**de,** from); **s. de la brume,** to emerge from the mist; *Fig* **s. de l'obscurité,** to emerge from obscurity; **yeux qui sortent de la tête,** protruding *or* bulging eyes; **les yeux lui sortaient de la tête,** his eyes were popping out of his head;

(l) (*of figure in picture, thought, characteristic etc*) to stand out, to be prominent; **faire s. un trait de caractère/un rôle,** to emphasize a characteristic/a part.

2 *vt* (*aux* **avoir**) **(a)** (*mener dehors*) to take out (*child, dog etc*); to throw out (*intruder*); **s. la voiture,** to get the car out; **sortez-la!,** get her out (of here)!; **cela nous sortira de l'ordinaire,** that will make a change; **sortez-moi de cette affaire/de ce mauvais pas,** get me out of this business/out of this fix; **on doit le s. de là,** we must get him out of it;

(b) (*retirer*) to take out (*object*); **s. les mains de ses poches,** to take one's hands out of one's pockets; **il sortit sa pipe,** he brought out *or* took out *or* got out his pipe; **l'escargot sort ses cornes,** the snail puts out its horns; **s. un ouvrage,** to publish *or* bring out a book; **s. un livre de la bibliothèque,** to take a book out of the library; **s. un disque/film,** to bring out *or* release a record/film; *F* **il nous en a sorti une bien bonne,** he came out with a good one; *Typ* **s. une ligne,** to run out a line (*into the margin*);

(c) *Ordinat* to output.

3 se sortir *vpr* **se s. d'une situation difficile,** to get out of *or* extricate oneself from a difficult situation; **le malade s'en sortira,** the patient will pull through.

sortir[2] *nm* **au s. du cinéma,** on coming out of the cinema; **au s. de l'école,** when school ends *or* ended, when they *or* we *etc* come *or* came out of school; (*pour toujours*) on leaving school; **au s. de la table,** at the end of the meal, when we *or* they *etc* got up *or* get up from the table; **au s. de l'hiver/de la réunion,** at the end of the winter/the meeting.

sortir[3] *vt* (*conj like* **finir**; *used only in third person*) *Jur* **cette sentence sortira son plein (et entier) effet,** this decision shall have full effect.

S.O.S. [ɛsoɛs] *nm Av Nau & Fig* SOS; **envoyer ou lancer un S.O.S.,** to send (out) an SOS (**à,** to).

sosie [sɔzi] *nm* (*personne*) double.

sot, sotte [so, sɔt] **1** *adj* **(a)** (*idiot*) silly, stupid, foolish (*person, answer, plan etc*); **(b)** (*confus*) confused (*person*). **2** *n* fool, idiot, ass; *Hist Th* fool.

sotie [sɔti] *nf Hist Th* (medieval) farce.

sot-l'y-laisse [solilɛs] *nm inv Culin* oyster (*of poultry*).

sotte [sɔt] *adj voir* **SOT**.

sottement [sɔtmɑ̃] *adv* stupidly, foolishly.

sottise [sɔtiz] *nf* **(a)** (*stupidité*) stupidity, silliness, foolishness; **(b)** (*action stupide*) foolish *or* stupid act; (*parole stupide*) foolish *or* stupid remark; **faire des sottises,** to do foolish *or* stupid things; (*of child*) to be naughty; **dire des sottises,** to say foolish *or* stupid things, to talk nonsense; **ai-je dit une s.?,** have I said something stupid?; **(c)** (*parole injurieuse*) offensive remark, insult; **dire des sottises à qn,** to abuse s.o..

sottisier [sɔtizje] *nm* collection of howlers.

sou [su] *nm* **(a) des gens à gros sous,** (very) rich people; **il y a une question de gros sous,** there's big money involved; **être près de ses sous,** to count every penny; **amasser une fortune s. par s.,** to scrape a fortune together; **un s. est un s.,** every penny counts; **payer s. à s.,** to pay in small instalments; **ne pas avoir** *ou* **être sans le s.,** to be penniless; **appareil** *ou* **machine à sous,** slot machine; (*jeu*) one-armed bandit, *Br* fruit machine; *F* **s'ennuyer à cent sous de l'heure,** to be bored stiff *or* bored out of one's mind; **cela vaut cent mille francs comme un s.,** it's worth a hundred thousand francs if it's worth a penny; **affaire de quatre sous,** *Br* twopenny-halfpenny business, *Am* nickel-and-dime business; **pas ambitieux pour deux sous** *ou* **pour un s.,** not in the least ambitious; **il n'a pas pour deux sous de courage,** he hasn't a scrap of courage;

(b) *Can* (*cent*) cent;

(c) *Hist* (*pièce de cinq centimes*) sou; *F Arch* **pièce de cent sous,** five-franc piece.

souahéli [swaheli] **, souahili** [swahili] **1** *adj* Swahili. **2** *nm Ling* Swahili.

soubassement [subɑsmɑ̃] *nm* **(a)** *Archit* base, basement (*of building*); *Fig* **le s. social,** the social substructure; **(b)** *Tech* base (plate) (*of machine tool etc*); **(c)** *Géol* bedrock; **(d)** *Aut* sub-frame; **s. de châssis,** underframe.

soubresaut [subrəso] *nm* jolt (*of vehicle*); **avoir un s.,** to give a start; **cette nouvelle m'a donné un s.,** the news gave me a start.

soubrette [subrɛt] *nf Th* soubrette, maidservant; *F* (*servante coquette*) soubrette.

souche [suʃ] *nf* **(a)** stump (*of tree*); root stock (*of iris etc*); stock (*of vine*); *F* **rester (là) comme une s.,** to stand stock still; **dormir comme une s.,** to sleep like a log; **(b)** founder (*of family*); **faire s.,** to found a family; **il vient de bonne s.,** he comes of sound stock; **famille de vieille s.,** an old family; **(c)** strain (*of virus etc*); **(d)** *Com* counterfoil, stub (*of cheque, Am check, ticket etc*); **carnet de tickets à s.,** book of tickets with counterfoils; **(e)** stack (*of chimney*); **(f)** *Ling* root; **mot s.,** root word.

souci[1] [susi] *nm Bot* marigold; **s. d'eau,** marsh marigold.

souci[2] *nm* **(a)** (*soin*) concern (**de,** for); **avoir le s. de plaire,** to be anxious to please; **avoir le s. de la vérité/de l'exactitude,** to be meticulously truthful/accurate; **ne prendre nul s. des conseils de qn,** to take no notice of s.o.'s advice; **il ne prend s. de rien,** he doesn't care about anything; **c'est le moindre** *ou* **le dernier** *ou* **le cadet de mes soucis,** that's the least of my worries; **(b)** (*inquiétude*) worry, anxiety; **sans s., libre de soucis,** carefree, free from worry *or* anxiety; **cet enfant est un perpétuel s.,** this child is a perpetual (source of) worry; *F* **il nous fait bien de s.,** he worries us a lot, he gives us a lot of worry; **se faire du s.,** to worry (**pour qch,** about sth); **soucis d'argent, soucis financiers,** money *or* financial troubles *or* worries.

soucier [susje] *v* (*impf & pr sub* **n. souciions, v. souciiez**) **1** *vt Arch* (*of thing*) to trouble, to worry (*s.o.*). **2 se soucier** *vpr* **se s. de qn/de qch,** to worry *or* be concerned about s.o./sth; **se s. de faire qch,** to worry *or* be concerned about doing sth; **il se soucie toujours des autres,** he is always worrying about other people; **ne se s. de rien,** not to worry about anything; *F* **je m'en soucie comme de l'an quarante** *ou* **de ma première chemise,** I don't give *or* care a damn (about it), I don't give a monkey's.

soucieux, -ieuse [susjø, -jøz] *adj* **(a)** (*attentif*) anxious, concerned (**de,** about); **être s. de faire qch,** to be anxious to do sth; **peu s.,** unconcerned (**de,** about); **peu s. de se rencontrer avec elle,** not very anxious to meet her; **(b)** (*inquiète*) anxious, worried, concerned; **avoir un air s.,** to look anxious *or* worried *or* concerned.

soucoupe [sukup] *nf* saucer; *Fig F* **elle a ouvert** *ou* **fait des yeux comme des soucoupes,** her eyes were as big as saucers; *F* **s. volante,** flying saucer.

soudage [sudaʒ] *nm* soldering; **s. (autogène),** welding (*of metal pieces etc*).

soudain [sudɛ̃] **1** *adj* sudden. **2** *adv* suddenly, all of a sudden.

soudainement [sudɛnmɑ̃] *adv* suddenly.

soudaineté [sudɛnte] *nf* suddenness.

Soudan (le) [ləsudɑ̃] *nm* the Sudan.

soudanais, -aise [sudanɛ, -ɛz] **1** *adj* Sudanese. **2** *n* **S.,** Sudanese.

soudant [sudɑ̃] *adj Métal* **blanc s.,** welding heat.

soudard [sudar] *nm Litt Péj* brutish soldier.

soude [sud] *nf* **(a)** *Bot* saltwort, (prickly) glasswort; **(b)** *Ch Ind* soda; **(carbonate de) s., cristaux de s., s. ordinaire,** washing soda, common soda; **bicarbonate de s.,** bicarbonate of soda; **s. caustique,** caustic soda.

souder [sude] **1** *vt* **(a)** (*avec de la soudure*) to solder; **s. au cuivre/au laiton,** to braze/to hard-solder; **s. à l'étain,** to soft-solder; **(b)** (*autogène*) to weld; **s. à l'arc (électrique),** to arc-weld; **machine à s.,** welding machine, welder; **s. par points,** to spot-weld; **(c)** (*unir*) to knit, to join (*fractured bone*); to unite (*groups etc*). **2 se souder** *vpr* (*of bones*) to knit (together), to join; (*of group*) to unite.

soudeur, -euse [sudœr, -øz] **1** *n* (*personne*) solderer; (*autogène*) welder; **s. par points,** spot-welder; **s. au chalumeau,** lamp *or* torch welder. **2** *nf* **soudeuse,** (*machine*) welder, welding machine; **s. par points,** spot-welder.

soudoyer [sudwaje] *vt* (**je soudoie, n. soudoyons; je soudoierai**) **(a)** *Péj* to bribe, to buy (*s.o.*); **s. un assassin,** to hire a killer; **(b)** *Mil Arch* to pay (*mercenary*).

soudure [sudyr] *nf* **(a)** (*opération*) soldering; (*autogène*) welding; **s. au cuivre/au laiton,** brazing/hard- soldering; **s. à l'étain,** soft-soldering; **(b)** (*lieu*) soldered joint; (*autogène*) weld; **s. à nœud,** wipe(d) joint; **sans soudure(s),** seamless; **(c)** (*alliage*) solder; **(d)** (*d'os*) join; **(e)** *Écon* **faire la s.,** to bridge the gap; *Fig* **faire la s. entre deux directeurs/systèmes,** to bridge the gap between two directors/systems.

soufflage [suflaʒ] *nm* **(a)** (*de verre*) glass blowing; **(b)** *Nau* sheathing (*of ship's bottom*); **(c)** *Métal* blowing.

soufflant, -ante [suflɑ̃, -ɑ̃t] **1** *adj* **(a)** *Tech* blowing; **machine soufflante,** blowing engine, blast engine; **(b)** *Ling* fricative (*consonant*); **(c)** *F* (*étonnant*) breathtaking. **2** *nf Tech* **soufflante,** blower, fan; **soufflante de sustentation,** lift fan (*of hovercraft*); *Aut etc* **soufflante de suralimentation,** supercharger.

soufflard [suflar] *nm Géol* fumarole.

souffle [sufl] *nm* **(a)** breath, puff (*of air, wind*); **pas un s. de vent,** not a breath of air;

(b) blast (*of exploding shell*);

(c) *Av* slipstream, wash (*of propeller*);

(d) (*respiration*) breathing; (*de coureur etc*) breath, wind; (*air respiré*) breath; (*air expiré*) blow, puff; **retenir son s.,** to hold one's breath; **éteindre une chandelle d'un (seul) s.,** to blow out a candle; **on la renverserait d'un s.,** you could knock her over with a feather; **couper le s. à qn,** to take s.o.'s breath away; **le s. vital** *ou* **de la vie,** the breath of life; **être à bout de s.,** to be winded *or* out of breath *or F* puffed; *Fig* to be unable to go on, *F* to have run out of steam; **manquer de s., avoir le s. court,** to be short of breath *or* short-winded; **reprendre son s.,** to get one's breath back; **exhaler son dernier s.,** to breathe one's last; **n'avoir plus de s.,** to be out of breath; **sa vie ne tient qu'à un s.,** his life hangs by a thread; *Fig* **second s. de l'économie,** new lease of life for the economy; *F* **c'est à vous couper le s.,** it's breathtaking; *F* **il ne manque pas de s.!,** (*culot*) he's got a cheek *or* a nerve!;

(e) *Méd* **(bruit de) s.,** murmur; **s. au cœur,** heart murmur;

(f) (*force créatrice*) inspiration; **s. poétique,** poetic inspiration.

soufflé [sufle] **1** *adj* puffed up (*face*); *Culin* soufflé (*omelette, potatoes*); *F* (*ahuri*) flabbergasted, taken aback. **2** *nm Culin* soufflé; **moule à soufflés,** soufflé dish.

soufflement [sufləmɑ̃] *nm* blowing.

souffler [sufle] **1** *vi* **(a)** (*en expulsant de l'air*) to blow; (*of cat etc*) to spit; (*of buffalo*) to snort; **s. dans ses doigts,** to blow on one's fingers; **s. dans une trompette,** to blow a trumpet; *F* **tu peux s. dessus,** you can whistle for it!; *F* **s. aux oreilles de qn,** to have a quiet *or* private word with s.o.;

(b) (*reprendre son souffle*) to get one's breath back; **laisser s. un cheval,** to let a horse get its wind, to give a horse a breather; **elle ne nous a pas laissé s.,** she didn't give us time to get our breath back;

(c) (*respirer avec peine*) to pant, to puff; **suant et soufflant,** puffing and blowing; *Fig F* **s. comme un bœuf,** to puff *or* wheeze like a grampus;

(d) (*of the wind etc*) to blow; *Fig* **regarder** *ou* **voir d'où vient** *ou* **de quel côté souffle le vent,** to see which way the wind is blowing; *Fig* **un vent de révolte soufflait,** there was a spirit of revolt in the air.

2 *vt* **(a)** to blow (*glass*); to blow up (*balloon etc*);

(b) to blow (*smoke, dust etc*) (**dans,** into); to blow (*organ*); to blow out (*candle*);

(c) (*chuchoter*) to whisper (**à qn,** to s.o.); **ne pas s. un mot,** not to breathe a word; **s. (son rôle à) un acteur,** to prompt an actor;

(d) *F* (*prendre*) to pinch (**à qn,** from s.o.); **s. un pion,** (*aux dames*) to huff a man;

(e) *Nau* to sheathe (*ship's bottom*);

(f) (*of explosion*) to blast (*building etc*);

(g) *F* (*ahurir*) to flabbergast (*s.o.*), to take (*s.o.*) aback; **son culot nous a soufflés,** his cheek took our breath away.

soufflerie [sufləri] *nf* **(a)** bellows (*of organ, forge*); **(b)** *Ind* blower; **(c)** *Av Phys* wind tunnel; **essais en s.,** wind-tunnel tests.

soufflet [suflɛ] *nm* **(a)** (*instrument*) (pair of) bellows; **(b)** **valise à soufflets,** expanding suitcase; **(c)** *Rail* concertina vestibule (*joining coaches*); **(d)** *Couture* gusset; **(e)** *Mus* swell (*of organ*); **(f)** *Litt* (*gifle*) slap (in the face); (*insulte*) insult.
souffleter [sufləte] *vt* (**je soufflette, n. souffletons; je souffletterai**) *Litt* **s. qn,** (*gifler*) to slap s.o.'s face; (*insulter*) to insult s.o..
souffleur, -euse [suflœr, -øz] **1** *n* **(a)** **s. de verre,** glass blower; **(b)** *Th* prompter. **2** *nf* **souffleuse** **(a)** *Can* (*chasse-neige*) snowblower; **(b)** *Agr* blower container (*for seeds etc*).
soufflure [suflyr] *nf* blister, bubble, flaw (*in paint, glass, metal*); bulge (*in Br tyre, Am tire*).
souffrance [sufrɑ̃s] *nf* **(a)** **en s.,** (*of work*) pending; (*of candidates*) on the waiting list; (*of bills*) overdue, outstanding; (*of parcels*) held up in transit, awaiting delivery; **(b)** (*douleur*) suffering, pain; **s. physique/morale,** physical/mental suffering *or* pain.
souffrant [sufrɑ̃] *adj* **(a)** (*un peu malade*) unwell, poorly, indisposed; **il a l'air s.,** he doesn't look well; **(b)** *Litt* (*qui souffre*) suffering; **l'humanité souffrante,** suffering humanity.
souffre-douleur [sufrədulœr] *nm inv* scapegoat.
souffreteux, -euse [sufrətø, -øz] *adj* sickly (*child etc*).
souffrir [sufrir] *v* (*prp* **souffrant**; *pp* **souffert**; *pr ind* **je souffre, il souffre, n. souffrons, ils souffrent**; *impf* **je souffrais**; *p hist* **je souffris**; *fu* **je souffrirai**) **1** *vt* **(a)** (*supporter*) to suffer, to endure (*pain, fatigue, cold, loss, insult etc*); **je ne peux pas s. qu'on vienne me déranger,** I cannot bear to be disturbed, I cannot stand being disturbed; *F* **je ne peux pas s. cet homme/cette odeur,** I can't bear *or* stand that man/smell;

(b) (*permettre*) to permit, to allow; **je ne saurais s. cela,** I cannot permit *or* allow that; **souffrez que je vous dise la vérité,** allow *or* permit me to tell you the truth; **situation qui ne souffre aucun retard,** situation that admits of *or* brooks no delay; **s. l'étalon,** (*of mare*) to take the stallion.

2 *vi* **(a)** (*physiquement*) to be in pain, to suffer; (*moralement*) to suffer; **mon bras me fait s.,** my arm is hurting (me) *or* giving me pain; **s. du froid/des maux de tête/***etc*, to suffer from the cold/from headaches/*etc*; **s. de la jambe/***etc*, to have trouble with one's leg/*etc*; **je souffre de le voir si changé,** it pains *or* grieves me *or* I am very sorry to see him so changed; **je souffre à marcher,** I find walking painful; **avoir cessé de s.,** to be out of pain;

(b) (*pâtir*) to suffer (**de,** from); **les vignes ont souffert de la gelée,** the vines have suffered from the frost; **nous avons beaucoup souffert de la guerre,** we suffered a lot in the war, we were hard hit by the war.

3 se souffrir *vpr F* (*se supporter*) **ils ne peuvent pas se s.,** they can't stand each other.
soufi [sufi] *Rel* **1** *adj inv* Sufic. **2** *nm* Sufi.
soufisme [sufism] *nm Rel* Sufism.
soufrage [sufraʒ] *nf* sulphuring, *US* sulfuring (*of matches, plants etc*); *Tex* sulphuration, *US* sulfuration.
soufre [sufr] **1** *nm* sulphur, *US* sulfur; *Fig* **ces écrits sentent le s.,** these writings reek of heresy. **2** *adj inv* **s. (jaune),** sulphur *or US* sulfur yellow.
soufré [sufre] *nm* (*papillon*) brimstone.
soufrer [sufre] *vt* to sulphur, *US* to sulfur (*matches, plants etc*); *Tex* to sulphurate, *US* to sulfurate.
souhait [swɛ] *nm* wish; **présenter ses souhaits à qn,** to offer s.o. one's good wishes; **présenter ses souhaits de bonne année,** to wish s.o. a Happy New Year; **à s.,** to one's liking; **avoir tout à s.,** to have everything one could wish for; **réussir à s.,** to succeed to perfection; **à vos souhaits!,** (*à qn qui éternue*) bless you!
souhaitable [swɛtabl] *adj* desirable; **il est s. que** + *sub*, it is to be hoped that ...; **ce n'est guère s.,** one can hardly wish for that; **il serait s. que ...,** it would be desirable if ... .
souhaiter [swete] *vt* to wish for (*success etc*); **s. les richesses,** to wish for wealth, to want to be rich; **je souhaite qu'on me tienne au courant,** I wish to be kept informed; **je souhaite que vous réussissiez, je vous souhaite de réussir,** I hope you will succeed; **s. la réussite/***etc* **à qn,** to wish s.o. success/*etc*; **je vous souhaite une bonne année,** I wish you a Happy New Year; **s. bon voyage à qn,** to wish s.o. a good journey; *F Iron* **je vous en souhaite!,** you'll be lucky!; **cela n'est pas à s.,** that is not very desirable; **il est à s. que** + *sub*, it is to be hoped that ... .
souiller [suje] *vt* **(a)** to soil, to dirty (*garments etc*) (**de,** with); **vêtements souillés de boue,** mudstained clothes; **(b)** *Fig* (*contaminer*) to taint; **s. ses mains de sang,** to stain one's hands with blood; **(c)** *Litt* to tarnish (*reputation, s.o.'s memory etc*).
souillon [sujɔ̃] *nf Litt* slut, sloven; (*servante*) slovenly maid.
souillure [sujyr] *nf* stain (*on garment etc*); *Litt* blot, blemish (*on one's reputation*).
souk [suk] *nm* (*marché*) souk; *Arg* (*lieu en désordre*) shambles.
soul [sul] *adj inv & nf Mus* soul.
soûl [su] **1** *adj* **(a)** *F* (*ivre*) drunk; **s. comme un Polonais** *ou* **comme un cochon** *ou* **comme une bourrique,** drunk as a lord; **s. perdu,** blind drunk; **(b)** *Arch* (*rassasié*) replete; *Litt* **être s. de plaisir/de musique,** to have had a surfeit of pleasure/music, to be sated with pleasure/music. **2** *nm* **rire/chanter/fumer/***etc* **tout son s.,** to laugh/sing/smoke/*etc* to one's heart's content; **manger/boire tout son s.,** to eat/drink one's fill *or* to one's heart's content.
soulagement [sulaʒmɑ̃] *nm* relief.
soulager [sulaʒe] *v* (**je soulageai(s); n. soulageons**) **1** *vt* to ease (*pressure, pain*); to relieve, to alleviate (*pain, grief*); to soothe, to comfort (*s.o.'s mind, sorrow*); to relieve (*s.o.*); **s. les pauvres,** to relieve the poor; **je suis soulagé de l'apprendre,** I'm relieved to hear it; **on soulage ses maux à les raconter,** it is a relief *or* a comfort *or* it helps to talk about one's troubles; **s. une poutre,** to ease the strain on a beam; **s. les soupapes,** to blow off steam; **cela me soulage l'esprit d'un grand poids,** that's a great weight off my mind; *F* **s. qn de son portefeuille,** to relieve s.o. of his wallet. **2 se soulager** *vpr* **(a)** (*en parlant etc*) to ease one's mind; **(b)** *F* (*satisfaire un besoin naturel*) to relieve oneself.
soûlant [sulɑ̃] *adj F* boring, tiresome (*person*).
soûlard [sular] **, soûlaud** [sulo] *n Arg* boozer, soak, *Br* piss artist.
soûler [sule] **1** *vt* **(a)** *F* (*enivrer*) to get *or* make (*s.o.*) drunk; *Fig* **s. qn,** (*of perfume, success, ideas etc*) to go to s.o.'s head; **(b)** *F* (*ennuyer*) to bore (*s.o.*) silly. **2 se soûler** *vpr F* (*s'enivrer*) to get drunk; *Arg* **se s. la gueule,** to get blind drunk; *Fig* **se s. de paroles,** to get drunk on *or* with the sound of one's own voice.
soûlerie [sulri] *nf Arg* **(a)** (*beuverie*) drinking bout, booze-up, binge; **(b)** (*ivresse*) drunkenness.
soulèvement [sulɛvmɑ̃] *nm* **(a)** rising, heaving (*of the ground, stomach*); **s. de cœur,** nausea; **(b)** *Géol* upheaval, upthrust; **(c)** (*révolte*) revolt, uprising.
soulever [sulve] *v* (**je soulève, n. soulevons; je soulèverai**) **1** *vt* **(a)** to lift (up), to raise (*load, patient, lid etc*); **la marée soulèvera le bateau,** the tide will float the boat off; **s. le porte-monnaie de qn,** to steal *or F* lift s.o.'s purse; *Fig* **cette odeur me soulève le cœur,** this smell makes me feel sick *or* turns my stomach; **la voiture soulevait de la poussière,** the car raised *or* threw up dust; **(b)** to raise (*doubts, question, objection*); **(c)** to rouse, to stir up (*people to revolt*); **(d)** to excite, to provoke, to arouse (*passion, enthusiasm, indignation*). **2 se soulever** *vpr* **(a)** (*être levé*) to rise; (*of sea, stomach*) to heave; **(b)** (*se lever*) to raise *or* lift oneself up; **(c)** (*se révolter*) to revolt, to rise up.
soulier [sulje] *nm* shoe; **souliers de marche,** walking shoes; *F* **être dans ses petits souliers,** to be in an awkward situation.
soulignage [suliɲaʒ] **, soulignement** [suliɲmɑ̃] *nm* underlining.
souligner [suliɲe] *vt* **(a)** (*d'un trait*) to underline (*word, passage etc*); **s. ses yeux d'un trait de noir,** to accentuate one's eyes with black eye-liner; **(b)** *Fig* to emphasize (*word, fact etc*); to underline, to emphasize (*importance etc*); **s. que ...,** to emphasize that ... .
soûlographie [sulɔgrafi] *nf F* drunkenness.
soumettre [sumɛtr] *v* (*conj like* **mettre**) **1** *vt* **(a)** to subdue (*people, country, passions*); **(b)** to refer, to submit (*question, request*) (**à qn,** to s.o.); **s. ses projets à qn,** to lay *or* put one's plans before s.o.; **(c)** (*à un examen etc*) to subject (**à,** to); **s. qn à une épreuve,** to put s.o. through a test; **être soumis à des règles strictes,** to be bound by strict rules. **2 se soumettre** *vpr* (*obéir*) to submit; **se s. à,** to submit to (*authority*); to comply with (*s.o.'s wishes*); to abide by (*law, s.o.'s decision*).
soumis [sumi] *adj* **(a)** (*docile*) submissive, obedient; **(b)** (*à une loi, une autorité etc*) subject (**à,** to); (*à un impôt*) liable, subject (**à,** to); **non s.,** unconquered; *Arch* **fille soumise,** registered prostitute.
soumission [sumisjɔ̃] *nf* **(a)** (*à une loi, une autorité etc*) submission (**à,** to); **faire (sa) s.,** to surrender, yield; **(b)** (*docilité*) obedience, submissiveness (**à,** to); **(c)** *Com* tender; **faire une s. pour un travail,** to tender for a job.

soumissionnaire [sumisjɔnɛr] *nm Com* tenderer.
soumissionner [sumisjɔne] *vt Com* to tender for (*a job*).
soupape [supap] *nf Tech* valve; *Tech & Fig* **s. de sûreté,** safety valve; **s. d'admission** *ou* **d'arrivée,** inlet valve, induction valve; **s. d'échappement** *ou* **de décharge,** outlet valve, exhaust valve, escape valve; **s. à flotteur,** ballcock; *Aut* **soupapes en tête** *ou* **en chandelle,** overhead valves; *Aut* **soupapes latérales** *ou* **en chapelle,** side valves.
soupçon [supsɔ̃] *nm* **(a)** (*suspicion*) suspicion; **s'exposer aux soupçons,** to lay oneself open to suspicion; **devenir l'objet des soupçons,** to fall under suspicion; **éveiller/endormir les soupçons,** to arouse/allay suspicion; **avoir des soupçons sur qn,** to feel *or* be suspicious about s.o.; **j'en avais le s.!,** I thought so *or* as much!, I suspected as much!; **il est au-dessus de tout s.,** he is above suspicion; **arrêter qn sur un s.,** to arrest s.o. on suspicion; **(b)** (*idée*) suspicion; **je n'en avais pas le moindre s.,** I didn't have the slightest suspicion, I never suspected it for a moment; **(c)** (*faible quantité*) dash, hint, soupçon (*of vinegar, garlic etc*); touch (*of fever, rouge, irony etc*); drop (*of wine*).
soupçonnable [supsɔnabl] *adj* open to suspicion.
soupçonner [supsɔne] *vt* **(a)** (*suspecter*) to suspect; **s. qn de qch/d'avoir fait qch,** to suspect s.o. of sth/of having done sth; **(b)** (*deviner*) to suspect; **je ne soupçonnais pas que ...,** I had no suspicion *or* no idea that ..., I did not suspect that ...; **je soupçonne de la jalousie dans ses paroles,** I suspect jealousy in what he says.
soupçonneusement [supsɔnøzmɑ̃] *adv* suspiciously.
soupçonneux, -euse [supsɔnø, -øz] *adj* suspicious.
soupe [sup] *nf* **(a)** *Culin* soup; **s. aux pois/à l'oignon,** pea/onion soup; *F* **cracher dans la s.,** to bite the hand that feeds you; *F* **gros plein de s.!,** fatso!; *F* **il mange la s. à la grimace,** he's in the doghouse; *Arg* **par ici la bonne s.!,** that's the way to make money!; *F* **il monte comme une s. au lait, il est très s. au lait,** he flares up very easily, he's always flying off the handle; **(b)** (*repas*) meal; *F* **à la s.!,** grub's up!; **s. populaire,** (*lieu*) soup kitchen; **(c)** *Ski F* soft snow; **(d)** *Arch* (*tranche de pain*) sop, soaked slice of bread.
soupente [supɑ̃t] *nf* closet, cupboard (*usu under the stairs*).
souper[1] [supe] *nm* **(a)** *Belg Suisse Can & Arch* (*dîner*) dinner, supper, evening meal; **(b)** (*après le spectacle*) (late) supper.
souper[2] [supe] *vi* **(a)** *Belg Suisse Can & Arch* (*dîner*) to have dinner *or* supper *or* the evening meal; **(b)** (*après le spectacle*) to have a late supper; *F* **j'en ai soupé,** I've had enough of it, I'm fed up with it.
soupeser [supəze] *vt* (**je soupèse, n. soupesons; je soupèserai**) to feel the weight of (*sth*), to weigh (*sth*) in one's hand; *Fig* to weigh up (*problem, argument etc*).
soupière [supjɛr] *nf* soup tureen.
soupir [supir] *nm* **(a)** sigh; **pousser un s.,** to (heave a) sigh; **s. de soulagement,** sigh of relief; **un gros s.,** a heavy sigh; *Hum* **l'objet de ses soupirs,** the object of his affections; **rendre le dernier s.,** to breathe one's last; **s. du vent,** sighing of the wind; **(b)** *Mus Br* crotchet rest, *Am* quarter rest; **quart de s.,** *Br* semiquaver rest, *Am* sixteenth rest.
soupirail, -aux [supiraj, -o] *nm* **(a)** (*de cave*) (cellar) ventilator; **(b)** (*d'appartement en contre-bas*) (small) basement window.
soupirant [supirɑ̃] *nm Hum* suitor, admirer.
soupirer [supire] *vi* to sigh; **en soupirant,** with a sigh; **s. après** *ou* **pour qch,** to long *or* yearn *or* sigh for sth.
souple [supl] *adj* supple, flexible (*branch etc*); supple, lithe (*body, dancer etc*); limp (*binding*); soft, supple (*leather*); manageable (*hair*); *Fig* flexible (*system, rule etc*); *Fig* flexible, adaptable (*person*); **esprit s.,** adaptable *or* versatile mind; *Aut* **moteur s.,** flexible engine.
souplesse [suplɛs] *nf* (*de branche*) suppleness, flexibility; (*de corps, danseur etc*) suppleness, litheness; *Fig* (*de système, règle etc*) flexibility; (*de personne*) flexibility, adaptability; (*d'esprit*) adaptability, versatility; **en s.,** (*travailler, démarrer etc*) smoothly; **transition en s.,** smooth transition (**entre,** between).
souquenille [suknij] *nf Vieilli* smock.
souquer [suke] *Nau* **1** *vt* to haul (*rope*) taut. **2** *vi* **s. (dur) sur les avirons,** to pull (hard) at the oars.
source [surs] *nf* **(a)** (*eau*) spring; (*lieu*) source (*of a river*); **eau de s.,** spring water; **s. d'eau minérale,** mineral spring; **s. thermale,** hot spring; **le fleuve prend sa s. dans le Massif Central,** the river has its source *or* rises in the Massif Central; *F* **ça coule de s.,** it's obvious; (*c'est naturel*) it's inevitable *or* natural; **s. jaillissante,** gusher; **s. boueuse,** mud geyser, mud volcano; *Opt etc* **s. lumineuse,** light source; **s. de chaleur,** heat source; *Él* **s. d'énergie** *ou* **d'alimentation,** power supply; *Ordinat* **s. de données,** data source; *Ordinat* **code s.,** source code; *Ling* **langue s.,** source language; **(b)** *Fig* source, origin (*of evil, wealth, news etc*); **puiser aux sources,** (*dans une étude etc*) to draw on the sources *or* source material; *Fin* **imposé à la s.,** taxed at source; **aller à la s. du mal,** to get to the root of the evil; **informations de s. américaine,** information from an American source; **citer ses sources,** to cite one's sources; **je le tiens de bonne s.,** I have it on good authority *or* from a good source.
sourcier, -ière [sursje, -jɛr] *n* water diviner, dowser; **baguette de s.,** divining rod, dowsing rod.
sourcil [sursi] *nm* eyebrow; **aux sourcils épais,** beetle-browed, with shaggy eyebrows.
sourcilier, -ière [sursilje, -jɛr] *adj Anat* superciliary.
sourciller [sursije] *vi* **sans s.,** without batting an eyelid, without turning a hair; **elle n'a pas sourcillé,** she didn't bat an eyelid *or* turn a hair.
sourcilleux, -euse [sursijø, -øz] *adj* **(a)** (*pointilleux*) fussy, finicky; **(b)** *Litt* (*hautain*) haughty, supercilious.
sourd, sourde [sur, surd] **1** *adj* **(a)** deaf (*person*); **s. d'une oreille,** deaf in one ear; *F* **s. comme un pot,** deaf as a post; *Fig* **rester s. aux prières,** to turn a deaf ear *or* to be deaf to entreaties; **(b)** dull (*tint, pain*); dull, muffled (*noise*); muted (*string*); hollow (*voice*); secret (*desire*); veiled (*hostility*); underhand (*incitement*); *Ling* **consonne sourde,** voiceless consonant. **2** *n* (*personne*) deaf person; **les sourds,** the deaf, deaf people; **crier comme un s.,** to yell; **frapper** *ou* **taper comme un s.,** to hit out wildly; **autant vaut parler à un s.,** you might as well talk to a brick wall; **un dialogue de sourds,** a dialogue of the deaf. **3** *nf Ling* **sourde,** voiceless consonant.
sourdement [surdəmɑ̃] *adv* **(a)** (*avec un bruit sourd*) dully, with a dull *or* hollow sound; **(b)** (*au secret*) secretly.
sourdine [surdin] *nf* **(a)** *Mus* mute; **en s.,** softly, quietly; *Fig* (*en secret*) in secret, on the sly; **violons en s.,** muted violins; **mettre une s. à ses plaintes,** to tone down one's complaints; **(b)** *Rad etc* damper.
sourdingue [surdɛ̃g] *Arg Péj* **1** *adj* deaf. **2** *n* deaf person.
sourd-muet, sourde-muette [surmɥɛ, surdmɥɛt] (*pl sourds-muets, sourdes-muettes*) **1** *adj* deaf-and-dumb. **2** *n* deaf mute.
sourdre [surdr] *vi* (*used only in third person* **il sourd, ils sourdent,** *and in inf; the past tenses are rare*) *Arch & Litt* (*of water*) to spring, to rise (up); *Fig* (*of emotion*) to well up.
souriant [surjɑ̃] *adj* smiling (*person*); pleasant (*climate, surroundings*).
souriceau, -eaux [suriso] *nm* young mouse.
souricier [surisje] *adj m & nm* **(chat) s.,** mouser.
souricière [surisjɛr] *nf* mousetrap; *Fig* (*piège*) trap; (*tendu par la police*) police trap.
sourire[1] [surir] *vi* (*conj like* **rire**) **(a)** to smile (**à qn,** at s.o.); **on peut difficilement en s.,** it's hardly a laughing matter; **faire s.,** to provoke a smile; **(b)** (*plaire*) to appeal (**à qn,** to s.o.); **tout lui sourit,** he makes a success of everything; **la chance lui sourit,** Fortune smiles on him.
sourire[2] *nm* smile; **large s.,** broad smile, grin; **le s. aux lèvres,** with a smile on his lips; **adresser** *ou* **faire un s. à qn,** to give s.o. a smile, to smile at s.o.; **avoir le s.,** to have a smile on one's face; **garder le s.,** to keep smiling.
souris [suri] **1** *nf* **(a)** mouse, *pl* mice; **s. de terre,** field mouse; **s. d'eau,** water shrew; **s. sauteuse, s. de montagne,** jerboa, jumping mouse; **s. blanche,** white mouse; **on aurait entendu trotter une s.,** you could have heard a pin drop; **trou de s.,** mousehole; *Fig* **il serait bien rentré dans un trou de s.,** he would have liked the ground to open up and swallow him; **(b)** *Ordinat* mouse, *pl* mice; **(c)** *Arg* (*femme*) *Br* bird, *Am* dame; **s. d'hôtel,** (female) hotel thief; **(d)** *Culin* knuckle end (*of leg of mutton*). **2** *adj inv* **(couleur) gris (de) s.,** mouse grey *or US* gray.
sournois, -oise [surnwa, -waz] **1** *adj* sly, crafty, underhand (*person*); sly, cunning, shifty (*look*); sly, underhand (*method etc*). **2** *n* sly *or* crafty *or* underhand person.
sournoisement [surnwazmɑ̃] *adv* slyly.
sournoiserie [surnwazri] *nf* **(a)** (*caractère*) slyness, craftiness; **(b)** (*acte*) underhand trick.
sous [su] *prép* **(a)** (*position*) under(neath), beneath; (*rang*) under; **s'asseoir s. un arbre,** to sit down under(neath) *or* beneath a tree; **s. terre,** underground, below ground; **s. clef,** under lock and key; **nager s. l'eau,** to swim underwater; **lettre s. enveloppe,** letter in an envelope; **s. le sceau du secret,** under pledge of secrecy; **s. nos**

propres yeux, before our very eyes; **chercher un mot s. la lettre S,** to look up a word under (the letter) S; **connu s. le nom de ...,** known as *or* by the name of ...; **enfant s. la responsabilité du père,** child who is the responsibility of his father; **accord passé s. conditions,** conditional agreement; **s. la pluie,** in the rain; *Mil* **s. les armes,** under arms, fighting; *Nau* **s. pavillon anglais,** flying the English flag; **s. le vent,** under the lee; **s. les tropiques,** in the tropics; **s. l'équateur,** at the equator; **s. Louis XIV,** under Louis XIV, in the reign of Louis XIV; **s. peine de mort,** on *or* under pain of death; **s. cet angle,** from that angle *or* point of view; **s. un prétexte,** under a pretext; **(b)** (*avant*) within; **s. trois jours,** within three days; **s. huitaine,** within the week; **s. peu,** shortly, before long.

sous- [su] (*before vowel sound* [suz]) *préf* **(a)** (*subordination, subdivision*) sub-; **s.-préfet,** subprefect; **s.-entrepreneur,** subcontractor; **s.-catégorie,** subcategory; **(b)** (*insuffisance*) under-; **s.-productif,** underproductive; **s.-informer,** to underinform; **(c)** (*infériorité*) pseudo-; **s.-littérature,** pseudo-literature. (NOTE *in the plural of hyphenated words of which the first element is* **sous-, sous-** *remains invariable and the second element takes the pl form*).

sous-affréter [suzafrete] *vt* (*conj like* **fréter**) to sub-charter (*ship etc*).

sous-aide [suzɛd] *n* junior assistant.

sous-alimentation [suzalimɑ̃tasjɔ̃] *nf* malnutrition, undernourishment.

sous-alimenté [suzalimɑ̃te] *adj* underfed, undernourished (*person*).

sous-arrondissement [suzarɔ̃dismɑ̃] *nm* subdistrict (*of naval administration*).

sous-bail [subaj] *nm* sublease; (*pl sous-baux*).

sous-bibliothécaire [subiblijɔtekɛr] *n* sublibrarian, assistant librarian.

sous-bock [subɔk] *nm* beer mat.

sous-bois [subwa] *nm inv* **(a)** undergrowth, underwood; **(b)** *Beaux-Arts* picture of a forest interior.

sous-brigadier [subrigadje] *nm* = deputy sergeant (*of excise officers, of police*).

sous-calibré [sukalibre] *adj Mil etc* subcalibre (*projectile*).

sous-chef [suʃɛf] *nm* **(a)** (*de bureau*) deputy chief clerk; **(b)** (*d'entreprise*) assistant manager; **s.-c. de gare,** deputy stationmaster; **(c)** *Mus* deputy conductor.

sous-classe [suklas] *nf Biol* subclass.

sous-comité [sukɔmite] *nm* subcommittee.

sous-commission [sukɔmisjɔ̃] *nf* subcommittee.

sous-consommation [sukɔ̃sɔmasjɔ̃] *nf inv Pol Écon* underconsumption.

sous-continent [sukɔ̃tinɑ̃] *nm Géog* subcontinent.

sous-couche [sukuʃ] *nf* (*de peinture*) undercoat.

souscripteur, -trice [suskriptœr, -tris] *n* (*de journal etc*) subscriber (**de,** to); (*de chèque etc*) drawer.

souscription [suskripsjɔ̃] *nf* **(a)** (*à un journal etc*) subscription; **(b)** *Fin* subscription, application (**à des actions,** for shares); **(c)** subscription, contribution (*of sum of money*); **lancer une s.,** to start a fund.

souscrire [suskrir] *v* (*conj like* **écrire**) **1** *vt Vieilli* to sign (*Br cheque, Am check etc*); to subscribe (*money to a charity*); to take out (*subscription, policy*); *Fin* to subscribe for *or* apply for (*shares*). **2** *vi* **s. à,** to subscribe to (*publication etc*); *Fig* to subscribe to, to endorse (*opinion, plan etc*); *Fin* **s. à une émission,** to apply for *or* subscribe to an issue; **s. à des actions,** to take up shares; **s. pour (la somme de) mille francs,** to subscribe a thousand francs; **s. pour une œuvre de bienfaisance,** to subscribe to a charity.

sous-critique [sukritik] *adj Phys Nucl etc* subcritical.

sous-cutané [sukytane] *adj* subcutaneous.

sous-développé [sudevlɔpe] *adj* **(a)** *Écon* underdeveloped (*country etc*); **(b)** underequipped (*factory etc*).

sous-développement [sudevlɔpmɑ̃] *nm Écon* underdevelopment.

sous-diacre [sudjakr] *nm* subdeacon.

sous-directeur, -trice [sudirɛktœr, -tris] *n* **(a)** (*de société*) assistant manager, *f* assistant manageress; **(b)** *Scol* deputy head.

sous-diviser [sudivize] *vt* to subdivide.

sous-division [sudivizjɔ̃] *nf* subdivision.

sous-dominante [sudɔminɑ̃t] *nf Mus* subdominant.

sous-économe [suzekɔnɔm] *n* assistant treasurer, assistant bursar.

sous-embranchement [suzɑ̃brɑ̃ʃmɑ̃] *nf Biol* subphylum.

sous-emploi [suzɑ̃plwa] *nm inv Écon* underemployment.

sous-employé [suzɑ̃plwaje] *adj Écon* underemployed.

sous-ensemble [suzɑ̃sɑ̃bl] *nm Math* subset.

sous-entendre [suzɑ̃tɑ̃dr] *vt* to imply; *Gram* **on s.-entend 'pendant',** 'pendant' is understood; **il est s.-entendu que ...,** it is understood that ... .

sous-entendu [suzɑ̃tɑ̃dy] *nm* implication, *Péj* insinuation.

sous-entrepreneur [suzɑ̃trəprənœr] *nm Constr* subcontractor.

sous-équipé [suzekipe] *adj Écon* underequipped.

sous-équipement [suzekipmɑ̃] *nm Écon* under-equipment.

sous-espace [suzɛspas] *nm Math* subspace.

sous-espèce [suzɛspɛs] *nf Biol* subspecies.

sous-estimation [suzɛstimasjɔ̃] *nf* underestimation.

sous-estimer [suzɛstime] *vt* to underestimate.

sous-évaluation [suzevalyasjɔ̃] *nf* undervaluation.

sous-évaluer [suzevalye] *vt* to undervalue.

sous-exposer [suzɛkspoze] *vt Phot* to underexpose.

sous-exposition [suzɛkspozisjɔ̃] *nf Phot* underexposure.

sous-famille [sufamij] *nf Biol* subfamily.

sous-fifre [sufifr] *nm F* underling, dogsbody.

sous-garde [sugard] *nf* trigger guard.

sous-genre [suʒɑ̃r] *nm Biol* subgenus.

sous-gouverneur [suguvɛrnœr] *nm* deputy governor, vice-governor.

sous-groupe [sugrup] *nm Biol Math* subgroup.

sous-homme [suzɔm] *nm* subhuman person.

sous-humanité [suzymanite] *nf* (*sous-hommes*) subhuman race; (*état*) subhuman condition.

sous-ingénieur [suzɛ̃ʒenjœr] *nm Ind etc* assistant engineer.

sous-inspecteur, -trice [suzɛ̃spɛktœr, -tris] *n* assistant inspector.

sous-jacent [suʒasɑ̃] *adj* underlying.

Sous-le-Vent [sulvɑ̃] *n* **les îles S.-le-V.,** the Leeward Islands.

sous-lieutenant [suljøtnɑ̃] *nm Mil* second lieutenant; *Nau* sub-lieutenant; *Av* **s.-l. (aviateur),** *Br* pilot officer, *Am* second lieutenant.

sous-locataire [sulɔkatɛr] *n* subtenant.

sous-location [sulɔkasjɔ̃] *nf* **(a)** (*par le propriétaire*) subletting; (*contrat*) sublease; **(b)** (*par le locataire*) subrenting; (*contrat*) subtenancy.

sous-louer [sulwe] *vt* **(a)** (*of landlord*) to sublet (*house*); **(b)** (*of tenant*) to subrent (*house*).

sous-main [sumɛ̃] *nm inv* desk blotter, blotting pad; *Fig* **en s.-m.,** secretly.

sous-maître, -maîtresse [sumɛtr, -mɛtrɛs] *Arch* **1** *n Scol* teacher's assistant. **2** *nf* **s.-maîtresse,** brothel-keeper's assistant.

sous-marin [sumarɛ̃] **1** *adj* submarine (*vessel, volcano etc*); submerged (*reef*); **chasse** *ou* **pêche s.-marine,** underwater fishing; **masque s.-m.,** frogman's mask. **2** *nm* submarine; **s.-m. nucléaire,** nuclear(-powered) submarine; **s.-m. de poche,** pocket submarine.

sous-marinier [sumarinje] *nm* submariner.

sous-maxillaire [sumaksilɛr] *adj Anat* submaxillary (*glands etc*).

sous-médiante [sumedjɑ̃t] *nf Mus* supertonic.

sous-menu [suməny] *nm Ordinat* submenu.

Sous-ministre [suministr] *nm Can Admin* Deputy Minister; **S.-m. adjoint,** Assistant Deputy Minister.

sous-multiple [sumyltipl] *adj & nm Math* submultiple (**de,** of).

sous-nappe [sunap] *nf* underlay (*for tablecloth*).

sous-œuvre (en) [ɑ̃suzœvr] *adv Constr* **reprise en s.-o.,** underpinning.

sous-off [suzɔf] *nm Mil F* N.C.O., non-com.

sous-officier [suzɔfisje] *nm Mil* non-commissioned officer.

sous-ordre [suzɔrdr] *nm* **(a)** *Péj* (*employé*) subordinate, underling; **(b)** *Biol* suborder.

sous-palan (en) [ɑ̃supalɑ̃] *adv Com Nau* **livraison en s.-p.,** delivery ready for shipping.

sous-payer [supeje] *vt* (*conj like* **payer**) to underpay.

sous-pied [supje] *nm* (*de pantalon*) footstrap.

sous-préfectoral, -aux [suprefɛktɔral, -o] *adj* sub-prefectorial.

sous-préfecture [suprefɛktyr] *nf* subprefecture.

sous-préfet [suprefe] *nm Admin* subprefect.

sous-préfète [suprefɛt] *nf Admin* (*female*) subprefect.

sous-principal, -aux [suprɛ̃sipal, -o] *nm Scol* vice-principal.

sous-production [suprɔdyksjɔ̃] *nf Econ* underproduction.

sous-produit [suprɔdɥi] *nm Ind etc* by-product; *Fig* poor imitation.

sous-programme [suprɔgram] *nm Ordinat* subroutine, subprogram.

sous-prolétaire [syprɔletɛr] *n* member of the underclass.

sous-prolétariat [suprɔletarja] *nm* underclass.

sous-pull [supyl] *nm* thin sweater *(for wearing under a thicker one)*.

sous-race [suras] *nf Zool* subrace.

sous-refroidissement [surəfrwadismɑ̃] *nm Phys* supercooling.

sous-répertoire [surepɛrtwar] *nm Ordinat* subdirectory.

sous-secrétaire [susəkretɛr] *n* undersecretary; **s.-s. (d'État)**, undersecretary (of state).

sous-secrétariat [susəkretarja] *nm* undersecretaryship.

sous-seing [susɛ̃] *nm Jur* private agreement *or* contract.

soussigné, -ée [susiɲe] *adj & n* undersigned; **je soussigné(e)**, I the undersigned.

sous-sol [susɔl] *nm* **(a)** *Géol* subsoil, substratum; **(b)** *Constr* basement.

sous-station [sustasjɔ̃] *nf Él* substation.

sous-tasse [sutas] *nf* saucer.

sous-tendre [sutɑ̃dr] *vt Géom* to subtend; *Fig* to underlie.

sous-tension [sutɑ̃sjɔ̃] *nf El* undervoltage.

sous-titrage [sutitraʒ] *nm Cin* subtitling.

sous-titre [sutitr] *nm (de livre etc) & Cin* subtitle.

sous-titrer [sutitre] *vt Cin* to subtitle; **film s.-titré en anglais**, film with English subtitles.

soustractif, -ive [sustraktif, -iv] *adj Math Phot* subtractive.

soustraction [sustraksjɔ̃] *nf* removal; *Math* subtraction.

soustraire [sustrɛr] *v (conj like* **traire**) **1** *vt (enlever)* to take away, to remove *(sth)* (**à qn,** from s.o.); *Fig* to protect, to shield *(s.o.)* (**à qch,** from sth); *Math* to subtract (**de,** from). **2 se soustraire** *vpr* **se s. à qch,** to avoid *or* elude sth; **se s. à une obligation,** to back out of an obligation.

sous-traitance [sutrɛtɑ̃s] *nf* subcontracting; **faire de la s.-t.,** to subcontact.

sous-traitant [sutrɛtɑ̃] *nm* subcontractor.

sous-traité [sutrete] *nm* subcontract.

sous-traiter [sutrete] *vt & vi* to subcontract.

sous-variété [suvarjete] *nf Biol* subvariety.

sous-ventrière [suvɑ̃trijɛr] *nf* bellyband; *(avec selle)* (saddle)girth; *Arg* **manger à s'en faire péter la s.-v.,** to eat till one is fit to burst.

sous-verre [suvɛr] *nm inv* glass mount(ing); *(photo, image)* photograph *or* picture mounted under glass.

sous-vêtement [suvɛtmɑ̃] *nm* undergarment; **s.-vêtements,** underwear, undergarments.

sous-virer [suvire] *vi Aut* to understeer.

soutache [sutaʃ] *nf Couture* braid.

soutacher [sutaʃe] *vt Couture* to braid.

soutane [sutan] *nf* cassock, soutane; **prendre la s.,** to take (holy) orders; **la s.,** *(prêtres)* the cloth.

soute [sut] *nf Nau* store (room); **s. à charbon,** coal bunker; **s. à munitions,** magazine; **s. aux bagages,** *Nau* baggage room; *Av* baggage compartment; **s. à mazout,** oil tank; **s. à valeurs,** strongroom; *Av* **s. à essence,** refuelling point; *Av* **s. à bombes,** bomb bay.

soutenable [sutnabl] *adj* **(a)** bearable, supportable *(burden, existence etc)*; **(b)** tenable *(opinion, position)*; tenable, arguable *(theory)*; **peu s.,** untenable.

soutenance [sutnɑ̃s] *nf Univ* **s. (de thèse),** defence of one's thesis, *Br* viva voce (examination) *(to obtain doctorate)*.

soutènement [sutɛnmɑ̃] *nm Constr* support; **mur de s.,** retaining *or* supporting wall.

souteneur, -euse [sutnœr, -øz] **1** *n* upholder *(of system etc)*. **2** *nm (proxénète)* pimp.

soutenir [sutnir] *v (conj like* **tenir**) **1** *vt* **(a)** *(tenir debout etc)* to support *(s.o., sth)*, to hold *(s.o., sth)* up;

(b) *(fortifier) (of medicine, love etc)* to sustain *(s.o.)*, to keep *(s.o.)* going;

(c) *(aider)* to back (up), to support *(undertaking, cause, troops, person etc)*;

(d) *(faire valoir)* to maintain, to uphold *(opinion, theory, one's character etc)*; to assert, to affirm *(fact)*; *Univ* to defend *(thesis)*;

(e) *(faire durer)* to keep up, to maintain *(conversation, speed, struggle, one's rank, one's credit etc)*; **il ne soutient pas la boisson,** he can't hold his drink;

(f) *(résister à)* to bear *(slight, reproach, comparison etc)*; to hold out against, to stand up to *(siege, attack etc)*.

2 se soutenir *vpr* **(a) se s. sur ses pieds,** to stand on one's feet; **je ne me soutiens plus,** I'm ready to drop;

(b) *(of fashion, friendship etc)* to last, to continue; **l'intérêt se soutient,** the interest is kept up *or* is maintained *or* does not flag;

(c) *(s'aider)* to support *or* back (up) each other;

(d) *(se défendre)* **ça se soutient/ne se soutient pas,** that's tenable/untenable; **se s. difficilement/facilement,** *(of theory etc)* to be hard/easy to maintain.

soutenu [sutny] *adj* **(a)** sustained *(attention, effort)*; sustained, unflagging, constant *(interest)*; steady *(trot, market)*; **(b)** elevated *(style of writing, language etc)*; **(c)** firm *(outline)*; solid, strong *(colour)*.

souterrain [sutɛrɛ̃] **1** *adj* **(a)** underground, subterranean *(water, explosion etc)*; **passage s.,** subway; **chemin de fer s.,** *Br* underground (railway), *Am* subway; **(b)** *Fig* underhand *(person, methods)*. **2** *nm* underground passage, tunnel.

soutien [sutjɛ̃] *nm* **(a)** *Pol Mil etc (aide)* support; **apporter son s. à,** to lend one's support to; **en s.,** in support; *Mil* **unité de s.,** support unit; **(b)** *(personne, groupe)* support; *Admin* **s. de famille,** breadwinner.

soutien-gorge [sutjɛ̃gɔrʒ] *nm* bra, *Fml & Am* brassière; *(pl soutiens-gorge)*.

soutirage [sutiraʒ] *nm* drawing off, racking *(of wine etc)*.

soutirer [sutire] *vt* **(a)** to draw off, to rack *(wine etc)*; **(b)** to extract *(money, information, promise etc)* (**à qn,** from s.o.).

souvenance [suvnɑ̃s] *nf Arch & Litt* recollection; **avoir s. de,** to recollect.

souvenir¹ [suvnir] *v (conj like* **venir**; *aux* **être**) **1** *v impers Litt* **il me souvient d'avoir lu que …,** I recall *or* remember reading *or* having read that … . **2 se souvenir** *vpr* **se s. de qch/de qn,** to remember *or* recall sth/s.o.; **nous nous souviendrons de lui,** we shall remember him; **je m'en souviens,** I remember; **autant que je m'en souviens** *ou* **que je m'en souvienne,** as far as I can remember *or* recall, to the best of my recollection; **on s'en souviendra,** we won't forget it; **souviens-toi de prendre un pull!,** remember *or* don't forget to take a sweater! **3** *vi* **faire s. qn de qch,** to remind s.o. of sth.

souvenir² *nm* **(a)** recollection, memory; **avoir garde un bon s. de qch,** to have a pleasant recollection *or* memory of sth; **je n'en ai pas s.,** I have no recollection *or* memory of it; **ce n'est plus qu'un mauvais s.,** it's just a bad memory now; **si mes souvenirs sont exacts,** if my memory serves me well; **souvenirs de ma jeunesse,** memories of my youth; **souvenirs d'enfance,** childhood memories, **veuillez me rappeler à son bon s.,** please remember me to him; **ma mère vous envoie son affectueux s.,** my mother sends her love; **en s. de qn,** in remembrance of s.o.; **en s. du passé,** for old times' sake; **(b)** *(objet, cadeau)* keepsake, souvenir, memento *(of person, place)*; *(de touriste)* souvenir; **offrir un s. à qn,** to make a presentation to s.o. *(on retirement etc)*; **magasin de souvenirs,** souvenir shop.

souvent [suvɑ̃] *adv* often; **peu s.,** not often, seldom, infrequently; **il ne vient pas s. nous voir,** he doesn't often come and see us, he seldom comes to see us; **il est malade plus s. qu'à son tour,** he has more than his share of illness; **le plus s.,** usually, as often as not, more often than not; *Arg* **plus s.!,** no fear!, not likely!

souverain, -aine [suvrɛ̃, -ɛn] **1** *adj* sovereign *(power, prince, state, beauty, remedy etc)*; supreme *(happiness, contempt, Jur court)*. **2** *n* sovereign. **3** *nm Hist (monnaie)* sovereign.

souverainement [suvrɛnmɑ̃] *adv* **(a)** *(extrêmement)* supremely, intensely. **(b)** *Jur* **juger s.,** to judge without appeal.

souveraineté [suvrɛnte] *nf* sovereignty.

soviet [sɔvjɛt] *nm* soviet.

soviétique [sɔvjetik] **1** *adj* Soviet. **2** *n* **S.,** Soviet (citizen).

soviétiser [sɔvjetize] *vt* to sovietize.

sovétologue [sɔvjetɔlɔg] *n* Sovietologist, expert on Soviet affairs.

soya [sɔja] *nm* soya.

soyeux, -euse [swajø, -øz] **1** *adj* silky. **2** *nm (industriel)* silk merchant.

spacieux, -euse [spasjø, -øz] *adj* spacious *(room, house etc)*; roomy *(car)*.

spadassin [spadasɛ̃] *nm* **(a)** *Arch* swordsman; **(b)** *Litt (assassin)* hired assassin.

spadice [spadis] *nm Bot* spadix.

spaghetti(s) [spageti] *nmpl Culin* spaghetti; *Fig* **western s.,** spaghetti western.

spahi [spai] *nm Mil* spahi.
spalax [spalaks] *nm Zool* mole rat.
spallation [spalɑsjɔ̃] *nf Phys Nucl* spallation.
sparadrap [sparadra] *nm Br* (adhesive *or* sticking) plaster, *Am* Band-Aid®.
spart(e) [spart] *nm Bot* esparto (grass).
Sparte [spart] *nf* Sparta.
spartiate [sparsjat] **1** *adj Hist & Fig* Spartan. **2** *n Hist* **S.**, Spartan. **3** *nf* leather sandal.
spasme [spasm] *nm* spasm.
spasmodique [spasmɔdik] *adj Méd* spasmodic.
spasmodiquement [spasmɔdikmɑ̃] *adv Méd* spasmodically.
spasmophilie [spasmɔfili] *nf Méd* spasmophilia.
spath [spat] *nm Minér* spar.
spathique [spatik] *adj Minér* spathic, sparry.
spatial, -aux [spasjal, -o] *adj* spatial; *Astronaut* space; **engin s.,** spacecraft; **voyage s.,** space flight; **combinaison spatiale,** spacesuit; **guerre spatiale,** space warfare; **station spatiale,** space station; *Électron* **charge spatiale,** space charge.
spatialisation [spasjalizɑsjɔ̃] *nf* spatialization.
spatialiser [spasjalize] *vt* **(a)** (*donner un caractère spatial à*) to spatialize; **(b)** (*lancer*) to send into space.
spationaute [spasjɔnot] *n* astronaut.
spationef [spasjɔnɛf] *nm* spaceship, spacecraft.
spatio-temporel, -elle [spasjɔtɑ̃pɔrɛl] *adj* space-time, spatiotemporal; (*pl spatio-temporel(le)s*).
spatule [spatyl] *nf* **(a)** spatula; **en s.,** spatulate; **(b)** (*de ski*) (ski) tip; **(c)** (*oiseau*) spoonbill.
spatulé [spatyle] *adj* spatulate.
speaker [spikœr] *nm Rad TV* announcer; (*qui donne les nouvelles*) newsreader.
speakerine [spikrin] *nf Rad TV* (woman) announcer; (*qui donne les nouvelles*) (woman) newsreader.
spécial, -aux [spesjal, -o] **1** *adj* special; special, specialized (*knowledge*); **privilège s. aux militaires,** privilege reserved for *or* restricted to military men; **savon s. peaux grasses,** special soap for greasy skin; *Journ* **envoyé s.,** special correspondent; **édition spéciale,** special edition; *F* **c'est/il est un peu s.,** (*bizarre*) it's/he's rather odd *or* peculiar; **mœurs spéciales,** homosexuality. **2** *nm Can* **(a)** (*plat du jour*) special; **(b)** *Can* **en s.,**(*en solde*) on special.
spécialement [spesjalmɑ̃] *adv* (e)specially, particularly; (*exprès*) specially.
spécialisation [spesjalizɑsjɔ̃] *nf* specialization.
spécialisé [spesjalize] *adj* specialized (*work, materials etc*); **ouvrier s.,** semi-skilled worker; **école/hôpital spécialisé(e),** special school/hospital; **aciers spécialisés,** speciality *or Am* specialty steels.
spécialiser [spesjalize] **1** *vt* **(a)** to make *or* turn (*s.o.*) into a specialist; **(b)** *Arch* (*spécifier*) to specify. **2 se spécialiser** *vpr* **se s. dans** *ou* **en qch,** to specialize *or* be a specialist in sth.
spécialiste [spesjalist] **1** *n* specialist (**de, en,** in); *Méd* **s. du cœur,** heart specialist; **s. du vol à voile,** gliding specialist *or* expert. **2** *adj* specialist; **médecin s.,** specialist (doctor); *Iron F* **elle est s. de ce genre de gaffes,** she specializes in that sort of blunder.
spécialité [spesjalite] *nf* **(a)** speciality, *Am* specialty; *Culin* **s. de la maison,** speciality of the house; **faire sa s. de qch,** to specialize in *or* make a special study of sth; **s. budgétaire,** budgetary restriction (*limiting use of funds to designated purpose*); **il a la s. de me taper sur les nerfs,** he has a knack of *or* a talent for getting on my nerves; **(b) spécialités pharmaceutiques,** patent medicines.
spécieusement [spesjøzmɑ̃] *adv Litt* speciously.
spécieux, -euse [spesjø, -øz] *adj Litt* specious.
spécification [spesifikɑsjɔ̃] *nf* (*action, définition*) specification.
spécificité [spesifisite] *nf Méd etc* specificity.
spécifier [spesifje] *vt* (*impf & pr sub* **n. spécifiions, v. spécifiiez**) to specify, to state definitely (**que,** that); **compte spécifié,** detailed account, itemized account.
spécifique [spesifik] **1** *adj* specific. **2** *nm Méd* specific (remedy) (**contre,** for).
spécifiquement [spesifikmɑ̃] *adv* specifically.
spécimen [spesimɛn] *nm* specimen; (*livre, fascicule*) specimen *or* inspection copy; **page s.,** specimen page.
spectacle [spɛktakl] *nm* **(a)** (*choses vues*) sight, scene, spectacle; **au s. de,** at the sight of; **se donner en s.,** to make an exhibition *or* spectacle of oneself; **(b)** *Th Cin etc* (*représentation*) show; **le s.,** (*industrie*) show business; **s. solo,** one-man show; **aller au s.,** to go to a show; **salle de s.,** hall; *Th* theatre, *US* theater; *Cin* cinema, *US* movie theater; *Th* **pièce à grand s.,** lavish production; *Cin* **film à grand s.,** epic (film).
spectaculaire [spɛktakylɛr] *adj* spectacular.
spectateur, -trice [spɛktatœr, -tris] *n* **(a)** (*témoin*) spectator, onlooker; (*d'accident*) witness; **s. de,** witness of; **(b)** *Sp* spectator; *Th* member of the audience; *Th* **spectateurs,** audience.
spectral, -aux [spɛktral, -o] *adj* **(a)** (*de fantôme*) ghostly, spectral; **(b)** *Opt* spectral.
spectre [spɛktr] *nm* **(a)** (*de fantôme*) ghost, apparition; *Fig* spectre, *US* specter (*of war etc*); **(b)** *Phys etc* spectrum; **s. solaire,** solar spectrum.
spectrogramme [spɛktrɔgram] *nm* spectrogram.
spectrographe [spɛktrɔgraf] *nm* spectrograph.
spectroscope [spɛktrɔskɔp] *nm Opt* spectroscope.
spectroscopie [spɛktrɔskɔpi] *nf* spectroscopy.
spéculaire [spekylɛr] *adj* **(a)** specular (*mineral*); **(b)** *Méd* **écriture s.,** mirror writing.
spéculateur, -trice [spekylatœr, -tris] *n Fin* speculator; **s. sur devises,** currency speculator.
spéculatif, -ive [spekylatif, -iv] *adj Phil Fin* speculative.
spéculation [spekylɑsjɔ̃] *nf* **(a)** *Phil* speculation (**sur,** on); **(b)** *Fin* speculation.
spéculer [spekyle] *vi* **(a)** *Phil* to speculate (**sur,** on, about); **(b)** *Fin* to speculate (**sur,** in; **à,** for); *Fig* **s. sur qch,** to count *or* bank on sth.
speculum, spéculum [spekylɔm] *nm Méd* speculum.
speech [spitʃ] *nm* speech (*in reply to a toast etc*); (*pl speeches*).
speedé [spide] *adj F* **(a)** (*hyperactif*) hyped up, *Am* hyper; **(b)** (*drogué*) high.
spéléologie [speleɔlɔʒi] *nf* caving, potholing, *Am* spelunking; (*étude*) spel(a)eology.
spéléologique [speleɔlɔʒik] *adj* spel(a)eological.
spéléologue [speleɔlɔg] *n* caver, potholer, *Am* spelunker; (*étudiant*) spel(a)eologist.
spencer [spɛ̃sɛr] *nm* **(a)** (*d'homme*) *Nau* monkey jacket; *Mil* mess jacket; **(b)** (*de femme*) short jacket, *Arch* spencer.
spermaceti [spɛrmaseti] *nm* spermaceti.
spermatique [spɛrmatik] *adj Anat* spermatic.
spermatogénèse [spɛrmatɔʒenɛz] *nf Biol* spermatogenesis.
spermatozoïde [spɛrmatɔzɔid] *nm Biol* spermatozoon; (*pl spermatozoa*).
sperme [spɛrm] *nm* **(a)** *Physiol* sperm, semen; **(b) s. de baleine,** spermaceti.
spermicide [spɛrmisid] *adj Méd* **1** *adj* spermicidal. **2** *nm* spermicide.
spermophile [spɛrmɔfil] *nm Zool* gopher, *Spéc* spermophile.
sphaigne [sfɛɲ] *nf Bot* sphagnum (moss), peat moss.
sphénoïde [sfenɔid] *adj & nm Anat* sphenoid.
sphère [sfɛr] *nf* **(a)** *Astron* sphere; *Géog* **s. terrestre,** globe; **s. céleste,** celestial sphere; **(b)** *Fig* sphere (*of activity, influence etc*); **les hautes sphères de la politique,** the higher reaches *or* realms of politics.
sphéricité [sferisite] *nf* sphericity.
sphérique [sferik] *adj* spherical.
sphéroïde [sferɔid] *nm* spheroid.
sphéromètre [sferɔmɛtr] *nm* spherometer.
sphincter [sfɛ̃ktɛr] *nm Anat* sphincter.
sphinx [sfɛ̃ks] *nm* **(a)** *Myth & Fig* sphinx; **sourire de s.,** sphinx-like smile; **(b)** *Ent* hawk moth, *Am* sphinx moth.
sphygmomanomètre [sfigmɔmanɔmɛtr] *nm Méd* sphygmomanometer.
spi [spi] *nm Nau F* = **SPINNAKER**.
spic [spik] *nm Bot* spike lavender.
spicule [spikyl] *nm Zool Astron* spicule.
spider [spidɛr] *nm Aut Br* dick(e)y, *Am* rumble seat.
spin [spin] *nm Phys Nucl* spin.
spina-bifida [spinabifida] *nm Méd* spina bifida.
spinal, -aux [spinal, -o] *adj Anat* spinal.
spinelle [spinɛl] *nm Minér* spinel.
spinnaker [spinakɛr] *nm Nau* spinnaker.
spiracle [spirakl] *nm* spiracle (*of tadpole*).
spiral, -ale, -aux [spiral, -o] **1** *adj* spiral. **2** *nm* hairspring (*of watch*). **3** *nf* **spirale,** spiral, *Spéc* helix; **en spirale,** (*adv*) in a spiral, spirally; (*adj*) spiral; **descendre/monter en spirale,** to spiral down/up.
spirant, -ante [spirɑ̃, -ɑ̃t] *Ling* **1** *adj* spirant. **2** *nf* **spirante,** spirant.
spire [spir] *nf* (single) turn (*of spiral, Él of coil*); whorl (*of seashell*).
spirée [spire] *nf Bot* spiraea, *US* spirea.

spirille [spiril] *nm Biol* spirillum.
spirite [spirit] *adj & n* spiritualist.
spiritisme [spiritism] *nm* spiritualism.
spiritualiser [spiritɥalize] *vt* to spiritualize.
spiritualisme [spiritɥalism] *nm Phil* spiritualism.
spiritualiste [spiritɥalist] *Phil* **1** *adj* spiritualist(ic). **2** *n* spiritualist.
spiritualité [spiritɥalite] *nf Phil* spirituality.
spirituel, -elle [spiritɥɛl] **1** *adj* **(a)** *Phil Rel etc* spiritual (*being, power, life etc*); sacred (*music*); **père s.,** spiritual father; **(b)** (*fin*) witty (*person, answer etc*). **2** *nm* **le s.,** things spiritual; (*pouvoir*) spiritual power.
spirituellement [spiritɥɛlmɑ̃] *adv* **(a)** (*de l'esprit*) spiritually; **(b)** (*finement*) wittily.
spiritueux, -euse [spiritɥø, -øz] **1** *adj Admin* spirituous (*drink*). **2** *nm* (*liqueur*) spirit, *Admin* spirituous liquor.
spiroïdal, -aux [spirɔidal, -o] *adj* spiroid.
splanchnique [splɑ̃knik] *adj Anat* splanchnic.
spleen [splin] *nm Litt* (*mélancolie*) spleen, melancholy; **avoir le s.,** to be melancholic.
spleenétique [splinetik] *adj Litt* splenetic, melancholy.
splendeur [splɑ̃dœr] *nf* **(a)** (*somptuosité*) splendour, *US* splendor, magnificence; *Litt* (*éclat*) radiance, brightness; (*gloire*) splendour, grandeur, glory; **dans toute sa s.,** in all his splendour; **(b)** (*chose*) **splendeurs,** splendours, *US* splendors; **c'est une s.,** it's splendid.
splendide [splɑ̃did] *adj* splendid (*day, weather*); brilliant (*sun*); splendid, magnificent (*palace, victory, meal*); splendid, glorious (*sunset*); splendid-looking (*person*).
splendidement [splɑ̃didmɑ̃] *adv* splendidly.
splénectomie [splenɛktɔmi] *nf Chir* splenectomy.
splénétique [splenetik] *adj Litt* splenetic, melancholy.
splénique [splenik] *adj* splenic (*artery, disease*).
spoliateur, -trice [spɔljatœr, -tris] **1** *n* despoiler. **2** *adj* spoliatory (*law etc*).
spoliation [spɔljɑsjɔ̃] *nf* despoiling, robbing (*of s.o.*).
spolier [spɔlje] *vt* (*impf & pr sub* **n. spoliions, v. spoliiez**) to despoil, to rob (*s.o.*) (**de,** of).
spondée [spɔ̃de] *nm Littér* spondee.
spondylarthrite [spɔ̃dilartrit] *nf Méd* spondylarthritis; **s. ankylosante,** ankylosing spondylitis.
spondylite [spɔ̃dilit] *nf Méd* spondylitis; **s. tuberculeuse,** Pott's disease.
spongieux, -ieuse [spɔ̃ʒjø, -jøz] *adj* spongy.
sponsor [spɔ̃sɔr] *nm* sponsor.
sponsoriser [spɔ̃sɔrize] *vt* to sponsor.
spontané [spɔ̃tane] *adj* spontaneous (*action, person, combustion, Biol generation etc*).
spontanéité [spɔ̃taneite] *nf* spontaneity.
spontanément [spɔ̃tanemɑ̃] *adv* spontaneously.
sporadique [spɔradik] *adj* sporadic.
sporadiquement [spɔradikmɑ̃] *adv* sporadically.
sporange [spɔrɑ̃ʒ] *nm Bot* sporangium, spore case.
spore [spɔr] *nf Bot* spore.
sporozoaire [spɔrɔzɔɛr] *nm Zool* sporozoan.
sport [spɔr] **1** *nm* sport; **faire du s.,** to do sport; **sports d'hiver,** winter sports; **s. d'équipe/de combat,** team/combat sports; **chaussures de s.,** sports shoes; *F* **vous allez voir du s.,** now you're going to see some fun. **2** *adj inv* **(a) vêtements s., costume s.,** casual clothes; **voiture s.,** sports car; **(b)** sporting, fair (*person*).
sportif, -ive [spɔrtif, -iv] **1** *adj* **(a)** sports (*results, edition, club etc*); **réunion sportive,** sports *or* athletics meeting; **(b)** (*fair-play*) sporting, fair (*person*); **esprit s.,** sporting spirit, sportsmanship; **(c)** (*qui aime le sport*) fond of sport, *F* sporty; **allure sportive,** sporty *or* athletic look. **2** *n* sportsman, *f* sportswoman.
sportivement [spɔrtivmɑ̃] *adv* sportingly, in a sporting spirit.
sportivité [spɔrtivite] *nf* sportsmanship; **elle eut la s. de ...,** she was sporting enough to ... .
sport(s)wear [spɔrt(s)wɛr] **1** *nm* sportswear, casual wear. **2** *adj* casual (*style etc*).
sporuler [spɔryle] *vi Biol* to sporulate.
spot [spɔt] *nm* **(a)** *TV Electron etc* (*point*) spot; *Rad* blip; **(b)** *Th* (*lampe*) spot(light); **(c)** *Rad TV* **s. (publicitaire),** commercial.
spouler [spule] *vt Ordinat* to spool.
spoutnik [sputnik] *nm* sputnik.
sprat [sprat] *nm* (*poisson*) sprat.
spray [sprɛ] *nm* spray, aerosol (spray); **peinture en s.,** spray *or* aerosol paint.
springbok [spriŋbɔk] *nm* springbok.
springer [spriŋœr] *nm* (*chien*) springer (spaniel).
sprint [sprint] *nm Sp* (final) sprint (*at end of race*); (*course*) sprint; *F* **piquer un s.,** to sprint; **être bon au s.,** to have a good sprint finish.
sprinter¹ [sprintœr] *nm Sp* sprinter.
sprinter² [sprinte] *vi Sp* to sprint.
sprue [spry] *nf Méd* sprue.
squale [skwal] *nm* (*roussette*) dogfish; (*requin*) shark.
squame [skwam] *nf Méd* scale, *Spéc* squama.
squameux, -euse [skwamø, -øz] *adj Méd* scaly, *Spéc* squamous.
square [skwar] *nm* (public) square (*with garden*).
squash [skwaʃ] *nm Sp* squash.
squat [skwat] *nm* (*action, lieu*) squat.
squatter¹ [skwatœr] *nm* squatter.
squatter² [skwate], **squatteriser** [skwaterize] *vt* to squat in (*empty building*).
squaw [skwo] *nf* (Indian) squaw.
squelette [skəlɛt] *nm* **(a)** skeleton; **c'est un vrai s.,** he's a bag of bones; **(b)** *Fig* skeleton, framework (*of ship, novel etc*).
squelettique [skəletik] *adj* **(a)** *Anat* skeletal; **(b)** (*maigre*) skeleton-like (*person, arms etc*); **(c)** (*réduit*) skeleton (*staff, army etc*).
squille [skij] *nf* (*crustacé*) squill.
squirr(h)e [skir] *nm Méd* scirrhus.
Sri Lanka [srilɑ̃ka] *nf* Sri Lanka.
sri lankais, -aise [srilɑ̃kɛ, -ɛz] **1** *adj* Sri Lankan. **2** *n* **S.,** Sri Lankan.
S.R.P.J. [ɛsɛrpeʒi] *nm abrév* **Service régional de la police judiciaire.**
S.S. [ɛsɛs] **1** *nm Hist* member of the SS; **les S.S.,** the SS. **2** *nf Admin abrév* **Sécurite Sociale.**
stabilisant [stabilizɑ̃] *nm Ch* stabilizing agent.
stabilisateur, -trice [stabilizatœr, -tris] **1** *adj* stabilizing; **appareil s.,** stabilizing device. **2** *nm* **(a)** (*de vélo*) & *Nau* stabilizer; *Av* tailplane, *US* horizontal stabilizer; (*vertical*) fin, *US* vertical stabilizer; **(b)** *Ch* stabilizer.
stabilisation [stabilizɑsjɔ̃] *nf* stabilization.
stabilisé [stabilize] *adj Ch Econ etc* stabilized; *Biol* balanced.
stabiliser [stabilize] **1** *vt* to stabilize. **2 se stabiliser** *vpr* to stabilize.
stabilité [stabilite] *nf* stability.
stable [stabl] *adj* stable (*substance, equilibrium, ladder, character etc*); stable, lasting (*peace*).
stabulation [stabylɑsjɔ̃] *nf* **(a)** keeping (*of cattle*) in sheds; stabling (*of horses*); **(b)** storing (*of fish*) in tanks.
staccato [stakato] *adv & nm Mus* staccato.
stade [stad] *nm* **(a)** (*de sport*) stadium; **(b)** (*étape*) stage (*of evolution, development, disease etc*); *Psy* **s. anal/oral/génital,** anal/oral/genital stage; **(c)** *Ent* instar (*of caterpillars etc*).
staff [staf] *nm* **(a)** *Constr* (*matériau*) staff; **(b)** (*personnel*) staff.
stage [staʒ] *nm* (*période*) period of instruction *or* training; (*cours*) training course; (*pédagogique*) teaching practice; **faire un s. de musique/de poterie,** (*en vacances*) to do a music/pottery course; **être en s.,** to be undergoing training *or* under instruction.
stagflation [stagflɑsjɔ̃] *nf Econ* stagflation.
stagiaire [staʒjɛr] **1** *adj* trainee; **interprète s.,** trainee interpreter. **2** *n* trainee.
stagnant [stagnɑ̃] *adj* stagnant (*water, Fig sales etc*).
stagnation [stagnɑsjɔ̃] *nf* stagnation (*of water, Fig sales etc*); *Fig* **en s.,** at a standstill, stagnant.
stagner [stagne] *vi* (*of water, Fig trade etc*) to stagnate.
stakhanovisme [stakanɔvism] *nm* Stakhanovism.
stalactite [stalaktit] *nf Géol* stalactite.
stalag [stalag] *nm* stalag.
stalagmite [stalagmit] *nf Géol* stalagmite.
stalinien, -ienne [stalinjɛ̃, -jɛn] *adj & n* Stalinist.
stalinisme [stalinism] *nm* Stalinism.
stalle [stal] *nf* **(a)** stall (*in cathedral*); **(b)** stall, box (*in stable*).
stance [stɑ̃s] *nf* (*strophe*) stanza.
stand [stɑ̃d] *nm* **(a)** stand (*on racecourse, at exhibition etc*); stall (*at fete*); *Sp Aut* **les stands de ravitaillement,** the pits; **(b) s. (de tir),** rifle range; **(c)** stand, rest (*for typewriter etc*).
standard [stɑ̃dar] **1** *nm* **(a)** (*norme*) standard; **s. de vie,** standard of living; **(b)** *Tél* switchboard. **2** *adj inv* standard; *Péj* **sourire s.,** forced smile.
standardisation [stɑ̃dardizɑsjɔ̃] *nf* standardization.
standardiser [stɑ̃dardize] *vt* to standardize.
standardiste [stɑ̃dardist] *n Tél* (switchboard) operator.
stand-by [stɑ̃dbaj] *Av* **1** *adj inv* stand-by. **2** *nm* **ticket/**

passager en s.-by, stand-by ticket/passenger.

standing [stɑ̃diŋ] *nm F* status, (*social*) standing; **appartement de grand s.,** luxury *Br* flat *or Am* apartment; **quartier de grand s.,** select district.

stanneux, -euse [stanø, -øz] *adj Ch* stannous (*oxide*).

stannique [stanik] *adj Ch* stannic (*acid*).

staphylin [stafilɛ̃] *nm Ent* staphylinid, rove beetle, *F* devil's coach horse.

staphylocoque [stafilɔkɔk] *nm* (*bactérie*) staphylococcus.

star [star] *nf* (*vedette de cinéma, chanteur, sportif etc*) star.

stariser [starize] *vt F* to turn (*s.o.*) into a star.

starlette [starlɛt] *nf Cin* starlet.

star-system [starsistɛm] *nm Cin Th etc* star system; (*pl star-systems*).

starter [startɛr] *nm* **(a)** *Sp* starter (*who gives the signal*); **(b)** *Aut* choke; **mettre/enlever le s.,** to pull out/push in the choke.

starting-block [startiŋblɔk] *nm Sp* starting block; (*pl starting-blocks*).

starting-gate [startiŋgɛt] *nm Courses de chevaux* starting gate; (*pl starting-gates*).

stase [staz] *nf Méd* stasis.

statice [statis] *nm Bot* statice, sea lavender.

station [stɑsjɔ̃] *nf* **(a)** (*position*) position; **s. debout,** standing position; **cela me fatigue de faire des stations debout,** standing tires me; **s. horizontale/verticale,** horizontal/vertical position; **mise en s.,** setting up (*of instrument etc*);
(b) (*halte*) halt, stop; **faire une s. à ...,** to halt *or* stop at ...;
(c) *Rel* station (*of the Cross*);
(d) (*lieu d'arrêt*) (*d'autobus*) (bus) stop; (*de métro*) station; (*de train*) halt; (*de taxis*) (taxi) rank; *Aut* **s. de lavage,** car wash;
(e) (*lieu de séjour*) resort; **s. de ski,** ski resort;
(f) (*centre de recherches*) station; **s. météorologique,** weather *or* meteorological station; **s. orbitale/spatiale,** orbiting/space station;
(g) s. radio, radio station; **s. de télévision,** television station;
(h) *El* **s. centrale,** power station; **s. pompage,** pumping station.

stationnaire [stasjɔnɛr] **1** *adj* stationary; steady (*barometer*). **2** *nm Nau* guardship, station ship.

stationné [stasjɔne] *adj* parked.

stationnement [stasjɔnmɑ̃] *nm* **(a)** parking (*of cars etc*); **en s.,** parked; **s. interdit,** (*sur panneau*) no parking; (*devant la gare etc*) no waiting; **s. gênant,** no parking; **(b)** *Can* (*parking*) *Br* car park, *Am* parking lot; **(c)** *Av* **aire de s.,** apron.

stationner [stasjɔne] *vi* (*of car, driver etc*) to park; **défense de s.,** (*sur panneau*) no parking; (*devant la gare etc*) no waiting.

station-service [stɑsjɔ̃sɛrvis] *nf Aut* service station, filling station, *Br* petrol *or Am* gas station; (*pl stations-service*).

statique [statik] **1** *adj* static (*electricity, character etc*). **2** *nf* statics.

statiquement [statikmɑ̃] *adv* statically.

statisticien, -ienne [statistisjɛ̃, -jɛn] *n* statistician.

statistique [statistik] **1** *adj* statistical. **2** *nf* **(a)** (*science*) statistics; **(b)** (*donnée*) statistic.

statistiquement [statistikmɑ̃] *adv* statistically.

statoréacteur [statɔreaktœr] *nm Av* ramjet.

statuaire [statɥɛr] **1** *adj* statuary (*art, marble etc*). **2** *nm* sculptor. **3** *nf* **(a)** (*art of*) statuary; **(b)** (*sculpteur*) sculptress.

statue [staty] *nf* statue; **immobile comme une s.,** stock-still.

statuer [statɥe] *vi* to give a decision *or* a ruling (**sur,** on).

statuette [statɥɛt] *nf* statuette.

statufier [statyfje] *vt* (*impf & pr sub* **n. statufiions, v. statufiiez**) *F* to erect a statue to (*s.o.*).

statu quo [statykwo] *nm* status quo.

stature [statyr] *nf* stature; **de haute s.,** very tall; *Fig* of (great) stature.

statut [staty] *nm* **(a)** (*état*) status; **s. social,** social status; **avoir le s. de cadre,** to have executive status; **(b) statuts,** (*de société, d'association*) statutes, regulations.

statutaire [statytɛr] *adj* statutory.

statutairement [statytɛrmɑ̃] *adv* in accordance with the statutes *or* regulations.

stayer [stɛjœr] *nm Cyclisme* long-distance cyclist (*behind motorcycle*); *Courses de chevaux* stayer.

St(e) (*abrév* **Saint(e)**) St.

Sté (*abrév* **Société**) Co.

steak [stɛk] *nm Culin* steak; **s. au poivre,** pepper steak, steak au poivre; **s. frites,** steak and chips.

stéarine [stearin] *nf Ch* stearin.

stéarique [stearik] *adj Ch* stearic (acid).

stéatite [steatit] *nf Minér* steatite, soapstone.

stéatose [steatoz] *nf Méd* steatosis.

steeple(chase) [stipl, stipəltʃɛs] *nm Sp* steeplechase; (*pl steeple-chases*).

stèle [stɛl] *nf* stele.

stellaire [stelɛr] **1** *adj* stellar (*light etc*). **2** *nf Bot* starwort.

stem(m) [stɛm] *nm Ski* stem turn.

stencil [stɛnsil] *nm* (*à polycopier*) stencil.

sténo [steno] **1** *nf* (= **sténographie**) shorthand, stenography; **prendre une lettre en s.,** to take down a letter in shorthand. **2** *n* (= **sténographe**) stenographer.

sténodactylo [stenɔdaktilo] **1** *n* shorthand typist, *Am* stenographer. **2** *nf* (= **sténodactylographie**) shorthand typing.

sténodactylographie [stenɔdaktilɔgrafi] *nf* shorthand typing.

sténographe [stenɔgraf] *n* stenographer.

sténographie [stenɔgrafi] *nf* shorthand, stenography.

sténographier [stenɔgrafje] *vt* (*pr sub & impf* **n. sténographiions, v. sténographiiez**) to take (*letter etc*) down in shorthand.

sténographique [stenɔgrafik] *adj* shorthand (*writing etc*).

sténotype [stenɔtip] *nf* stenotype.

sténotyper [stenɔtipe] *vt* to stenotype.

sténotypie [stenɔtipi] *nf* stenotypy.

sténotypiste [stenɔtipist] *n* stenotypist.

stentor [stɑ̃tɔr] *nm* **(a) voix de s.,** stentorian voice; **(b)** *Zool* stentor.

stéphanois, -oise [stefanwa, -waz] **1** *adj* of *or* from Saint-Étienne. **2** *n* **S.,** native *or* inhabitant of Saint-Étienne.

steppe [stɛp] *nf Géog* steppe.

stercoraire [stɛrkɔrɛr] **1** *adj Méd* stercoraceous. **2** *nm* (*oiseau*) skua.

stère [stɛr] *nm* (*unité de mesure*) stere.

stéréo [stereo] **1** *adj inv* stereo. **2** *nf* **(a)** (*abrév* **stéréophonie**) stereo; **en s.,** in stereo; **(b)** (*radio*) stereo radio.

stéréogramme [stereɔgram] *nm Opt Phot* stereogram, stereograph.

stéréographie [stereɔgrafi] *nf Opt* stereography.

stéréométrie [stereɔmetri] *nf* stereometry.

stéréophonie [stereɔfɔni] *nf* stereophony.

stéréophonique [stereɔfɔnik] *adj* stereophonic.

stéréoscope [stereɔskɔp] *nm Opt* stereoscope.

stéréoscopie [stereɔskɔpi] *nf* stereoscopy.

stéréoscopique [stereɔskɔpik] *adj* stereoscopic.

stéréotype [stereɔtip] *nm Typ & Fig* stereotype.

stéréotypé [stereɔtipe] *adj* stereotype(d) (*ideas, phrases etc*).

stéréotypie [stereɔtipi] *nf Typ Psy* stereotypy.

stérile [steril] *adj* sterile (*man, woman, animal*); childless (*marriage*); sterile, barren, unproductive (*land*); unprofitable (*work*); sterile, fruitless (*discussion, efforts etc*); *Méd etc* **instruments stériles,** sterile *or* sterilized instruments.

stérilement [sterilmɑ̃] *adv* (*discuter etc*) fruitlessly.

stérilet [sterilɛ] *nm* (*contraceptif*) coil, loop, IUD.

stérilisant [sterilizɑ̃] *adj* sterilizing (*agent etc*).

stérilisateur [sterilizatœr] *nm* sterilizer.

stérilisation [sterilizɑsjɔ̃] *nf* sterilization.

stériliser [sterilize] *vt* to sterilize (*milk, instrument, person etc*).

stérilité [sterilite] *nf* sterility (*of person*); barrenness (*of land*); *Fig* fruitlessness (*of discussion, efforts etc*).

sterling [stɛrliŋ] **1** *adj inv* sterling; **dix livres s.,** ten pounds sterling. **2** *nm inv* sterling.

sterne [stɛrn] *nf* (*oiseau*) tern.

sternum [stɛrnɔm] *nm Anat* breastbone, *Spéc* sternum.

sternutatoire [stɛrnytatwar] *adj* sternutatory; **poudre s.,** sneezing powder.

stéroïde [sterɔid] *nm Biol Méd* steroid; **stéroïdes anabolisants,** anabolic steroids.

stérol [sterɔl] *nm Ch Physiol* sterol.

stertoreux, -euse [stɛrtɔrø, -øz] *adj Méd* stertorous (*breathing*).

stéthoscope [stetɔskɔp] *nm Méd* stethoscope.

steward [stiwart] *nm Nau Av* steward.

stick [stik] *nm* **(a)** *Mil Sp Av etc* stick; (*de cavalier*) riding whip *or* crop; **(b)** (*de colle etc*) stick; **un s. de rouge à lèvres,** a lipstick; **déodorant en s.,** stick deodorant.

stigmate [stigmat] *nm* **(a)** *Méd* stigma; **(b)** *Hist* (*châtiment*) brand; *Fig* mark, brand (*of vice etc*); **(c)** *Hist Rel* **stigmates,** stigmata; **(d)** *Bot Ent* stigma.
stigmatisation [stigmatizɑsjɔ̃] *nf* (*condamnation*) *& Rel* stigmatization.
stigmatisé, -ée [stigmatize] **1** *adj* stigmatized. **2** *n Hist Rel* stigmatist, stigmatic.
stigmatiser [stigmatize] *vt* **(a)** (*condamner*) to stigmatize, to condemn (*s.o.*); **(b)** *Hist* (*marquer*) to brand (*convict*); **(c)** *Méd* to pockmark (*s.o.*).
stillation [stilɑsjɔ̃] *nf* (*en sciences*) dripping.
stimulant [stimylɑ̃] **1** *adj* stimulating. **2** *nm* **(a)** *Méd etc* stimulant; **(b)** *Fig* stimulus, spur, incentive.
stimulateur [stimylatœr] *nm Méd* **s. cardiaque,** pacemaker.
stimulation [stimylɑsjɔ̃] *nf* stimulation.
stimuler [stimyle] *vt* **(a)** to stimulate, to spur (*s.o.*) on; to stimulate (*enthusiasm, the digestion*); **(b)** to whet (*the appetite*); to stimulate, encourage (*friendship, trade etc*).
stimulus [stimylys] *nm* stimulus; (*pl stimulus ou stimuli*).
stipendiaire [stipɑ̃djɛr] **, stipendié, -ée** [stipɑ̃dje] *Litt Péj* **1** *adj* hired (*soldier etc*); **2** *n* hireling.
stipendier [stipɑ̃dje] *vt* (*pr sub & impf* **n. stipendiions, v. stipendiiez**) *Litt Péj* to hire (*soldiers, politicians etc*).
stipulation [stipylɑsjɔ̃] *nf* stipulation, condition.
stipuler [stipyle] *vt* to stipulate; **il est stipulé dans le contrat que ...,** it is stipulated in the contract that ... .
stock [stɔk] *nm Com* stock (*of goods*); **stocks,** (*en comptabilité*) stock, *Am* inventory; **en s.,** in stock; **rupture de s.,** stock outage; **être en rupture de s.,** to be out of stock; *F* **tout un s., un vrai s.,** a whole stock, plenty (*of sth*); **dans la limite des stocks disponibles,** while stocks last, subject to availability.
stockage [stɔkaʒ] *nm* **(a)** stocking (*of goods*); *Ordinat* storage; **(b)** (*en grande quantité*) stockpiling, building up of stocks.
stock-car [stɔkkar] *nm Sp* (*voiture*) stock car; (*sport*) stock-car racing; (*pl stock-cars*).
stocker [stɔke] *vt* **(a)** to stock (*goods*); **(b)** (*en grande quantité*) to stockpile; **(c)** *Ordinat* to store (*data*).
stockfish [stɔkfiʃ] *nm inv* stockfish.
stockiste [stɔkist] *nm Com* stockist, *Am* dealer; *Aut* agent.
stoïcien, -ienne [stɔisjɛ̃, -jɛn] **1** *adj* stoical, stoic; *Hist Phil* Stoic. **2** *n* stoic; *Hist Phil* Stoic.
stoïcisme [stɔisism] *nm* stoicism; *Hist Phil* Stoicism; **avec s.,** stoically, with stoicism.
stoïque [stɔik] **1** *adj* stoic, stoical. **2** *n* stoic.
stoïquement [stɔikmɑ̃] *adv* stoically.
stolon [stɔlɔ̃] *nm Bot* stolon, runner.
stomacal, -aux [stɔmakal, -o] *adj* stomach (*spasm etc*).
stomachique [stɔmaʃik] *adj & nm Pharm* stomachic.
stomatite [stɔmatit] *nf Méd* stomatitis.
stomatologie [stɔmatɔlɔʒi] *nf* stomatology.
stomatologiste [stɔmatɔlɔʒist] **stomatologue** [stɔmatɔlɔg] *n* stomatologist.
stop [stɔp] **1** *int* stop!; (*dans un télégramme*) stop. **2** *nm Aut* (*feu arrière*) brake light; (*panneau*) stop sign. **3** *nm F* (*abrév* **auto-stop**) hitchhiking; **faire du s.,** to hitch(hike); **aller à Paris en s.,** to hitch(hike) to Paris.
stoppage *nm Couture* invisible mending (*of garment*).
stopper¹ [stɔpe] *vt & vi* to stop.
stopper² *vt Couture* to repair by invisible mending.
stoppeur, -euse [stɔpœr, -øz] *n F* **(a)** (= **auto-stoppeur**) hitcher, hitchhiker; **(b)** *Sp* fullback.
store [stɔr] *nm* blind, shade; (*devant un magasin*) awning; **s. vénitien,** Venetian blind.
strabisme [strabism] *nm* strabismus, squint(ing).
stradivarius [stradivarjys] *nm Mus* Stradivarius.
stramonium [stramɔnjɔm] *nm Bot* stramonium.
strangulation [strɑ̃gylɑsjɔ̃] *nf* strangulation.
strapontin [strapɔ̃tɛ̃] *nm* **(a)** *Aut Th etc* folding seat, tip-up seat; **(b)** *Fig* (*fonction secondaire*) minor role.
Strasbourg [strazbur] *nm ou f* Strasbourg.
strasbourgeois, -oise [strazburʒwa, -waz] **1** *adj* of *or* from Strasbourg. **2** *n* **S.,** native *or* inhabitant of Strasbourg.
stras(s) [stras] *nm* (*clinquant*) paste, strass.
stratagème [strataʒɛm] *nm* stratagem.
strate [strat] *nf Géol* stratum, layer.
stratège [stratɛʒ] *nm* strategist.
stratégie [strateʒi] *nf* strategy.
stratégique [strateʒik] *adj* strategic.
stratégiquement [strateʒikmɑ̃] *adv* strategically.
stratification [stratifikɑsjɔ̃] *nf* stratification.
stratifié [stratifje] **1** *adj* stratified; *Tech* laminated (*paper, cloth etc*). **2** *nm* laminate.
stratifier [stratifje] *vt* to stratify.
strato-cumulus [stratɔkymylys] *nm inv Météo* stratocumulus.
stratosphère [stratɔsfɛr] *nf Météo* stratosphere.
stratosphérique [stratɔsferik] *adj* stratospheric.
stratus [stratys] *nm inv Météo* stratus.
streptocoque [strɛptɔkɔk] *nm* (*bactérie*) streptococcus.
streptomycine [strɛptɔmisin] *nf Méd* streptomycin.
stress [strɛs] *nm Méd & Fig* stress.
stressant [strɛsɑ̃] *adj* stressful.
stresser [strɛse] *vt* to put (*s.o.*) under stress; **être stressé,** to be under stress.
stretch ® [strɛtʃ] *nm* (*tissu*) stretch material.
striation [strijɑsjɔ̃] *nf* striation.
strict [strikt] *adj* **(a)** strict (*obligation, principles etc*); bare (*essentials, minimum*); **au sens s.,** in the strict sense; **dans la plus stricte intimité,** strictly in private; **c'est la stricte vérité,** it's the simple or absolute truth; **(b)** strict (*person*) (**sur,** about); **(c)** severe (*suit, hairstyle*).
strictement [striktəmɑ̃] *adv* **(a)** (*rigoureusement*) strictly; **(b)** (*sévèrement*) severely (*dressed etc*).
striction [striksjɔ̃] *nf Méd* constriction.
stricto sensu [striktosɛ̃sy] *adj* in the strict sense.
strident [stridɑ̃] *adj* strident, shrill.
stridulation [stridylɑsjɔ̃] *nf* stridulation.
strie [stri] *nf* **(a)** (*sillon*) groove; (*en relief*) ridge; *Anat Bot Géol* stria; **(b)** streak (*of colour*).
strié [strije] *adj* **(a)** (*sillonné*) grooved; (*en relief*) ridged; *Anat Bot Géol* striated; **(b)** (*rayé*) streaked (*marble etc*).
strier [strije] *vt* (*impf & pr sub* **n. striions, v. striiez**) **(a)** (*sillonner*) to groove; (*en relief*) to ridge; **(b)** (*rayer*) to streak.
string [striŋ] *nm* (*maillot de bain*) tanga.
strioscopie [strijɔskɔpi] *nf Opt* schlieren photography.
stripper [stripɛr] *nm Chir* (*instrument*) stripper.
stripping [stripiŋ] *nm Phys Nucl* stripping.
strip-tease [striptiz] *nm* striptease; *Fig* soul-baring; (*pl strip-teases*).
strip-teaseur [striptizœr] *nm* male stripper.
strip-teaseuse [striptizøz] *nf* stripper, striptease artiste; (*pl strip-teaseuses*).
striure [strijyr] *nf* striation.
stroboscope [strɔbɔskɔp] *nm Opt* stroboscope.
stroboscopique [strɔbɔskɔpik] *adj* stroboscopic, strobe.
strontium [strɔ̃sjɔm] *nm Ch* strontium.
strophe [strɔf] *nf Littér* stanza.
structural, -aux [stryktyral, -o] *adj* structural; *Ling* **analyse structurale,** structural analysis.
structuralement [stryktyralmɑ̃] *adv* structurally.
structuralisme [stryktyralism] *nm* structuralism.
structuraliste [stryktyralist] *adj & n* structuralist.
structurant [stryktyrɑ̃] *adj* structuring.
structuration [stryktyrɑsjɔ̃] *nf* structuring.
structure [stryktyr] *nf* structure; **s. d'acceuil,** reception facilities (*for disadvantaged groups*); *Ordinat* **s. en arbre,** tree structure.
structurel, -elle [stryktyrɛl] *adj* structural; **chômage s.,** structural unemployment.
structurellement [stryktyrɛlmɑ̃] *adv* structurally.
structurer [stryktyre] *vt* to structure.
strume [strym] *nf Méd Arch* **(a)** (*goitre*) goitre; **(b)** (*scrofule*) scrofula.
strychnine [striknin] *nf Ch Pharm* strychnine.
stuc [styk] *nm Constr* stucco; **décoration en s.,** stucco decoration.
stucage [stykaʒ] *nm Constr* stucco work.
stucateur [stykatœr] *nm* stucco worker.
studieusement [stydjøzmɑ̃] *adv* studiously.
studieux, -ieuse [stydjø, -jøz] *adj* studious (*person*); study (*vacation etc*).
studio [stydjo] *nm* **(a)** *Cin Phot TV Beaux-Arts etc* studio; **s. de danse,** dance studio; **(b)** (*logement*) studio *or* one-roomed flat *or Am* apartment.
stupéfaction [stypefaksjɔ̃] *nf* stupefaction, amazement.
stupéfait [stypefɛ] *adj* stupefied, stunned, amazed (**de,** by).
stupéfiant [stypefjɑ̃] **1** *adj* **(a)** *Méd* stupefying, *Spéc* stupefacient (*drug*); **(b)** astounding, amazing (*news*). **2** *nm Méd* drug, narcotic, *Spéc* stupefacient; **brigade des stupéfiants,** drug squad.
stupéfier [stypefje] *vt* (*impf & pr sub* **n. stupéfiions, v. stupéfiiez**) to stupefy, to stun, to amaze.
stupeur [stypœr] *nf* **(a)** *Méd* stupor; **(b)** (*étonnement*) amazement; **muet de s.,** dumbfounded.

stupide [stypid] *adj* **(a)** *(idiot)* stupid, silly, foolish; **accident/morte s.**, stupid *or* silly accident/death; **(b)** *Litt (stupéfait)* stunned.
stupidement [stypidmɑ̃] *adv* stupidly.
stupidité [stypidite] *nf* **(a)** *(caractère)* stupidity, foolishness; **(b)** *(parole, acte)* stupid thing (to say *or* do); **répondre par une s.**, to give a silly answer.
stupre [stypr] *nm Litt* debauchery.
stups [styp] *nmpl F* (= **stupéfiants**) *voir* **STUPÉFIANT**.
stuquer [styke] *vt Constr* to stucco.
style [stil] *nm* **(a)** *Littér Archit etc* style; **tourner ses phrases avec s.**, to have a stylish turn of phrase; **s. de vie,** lifestyle; **ce skieur a un beau s.**, this skier has (a) good style; **ce chapeau est tout à fait ton s.**, this hat is just your style; *F Péj* **ça serait bien son s.!**, that would be just like him!; **dans le s. de,** in the style of; **meubles/robe de s.**, period furniture/dress; **vieux/nouveau s.**, Old/New style *(of calendar)*; **(b)** *Antiq (pour écrire)* stylus, style; **(c)** *(pour enregistrer un disque)* record cutter; *(d'appareil enregistreur)* (recording) needle; **(d)** style, pin, gnomon *(of sundial)*; hand *(of barometer)*; **(e)** *Bot* style.
stylé¹ [stile] *adj Biol* stylate.
stylé² *adj* trained *(servant etc)*.
styler [stile] *vt* to train *(servant etc)*.
stylet [stilɛ] *nm* **(a)** *(poignard)* stiletto; **(b)** *Chir* stylet, probe; **(c)** *Zool* stylet; **(d)** *Ordinat* **s. lumineux,** light pen.
stylisation [stilizasjɔ̃] *nf* stylization.
styliser [stilize] *vt Beaux-Arts etc* to stylize.
stylisme [stilism] *nm* **(a)** *Littér* attention to style; **(b)** *Com Ind* designing.
styliste [stilist] *n* **(a)** *Littér* stylist; **(b)** *Com Ind* designer.
stylisticien, -ienne [stilistisjɛ̃, -jɛn] *n* expert in stylistics.
stylistique [stilistik] **1** *adj* stylistic. **2** *nf* stylistics.
stylite [stilit] *nm Hist Rel* stylite.
stylo [stilo] *nm* pen; **s. à encre,** fountain pen; **s.-bille, s.-bic** ®, ballpoint (pen), *Br* Biro ®; **s.-feutre,** felt-tip (pen).
stylographe [stilɔgraf] *nm Arch* fountain pen.
Stylomine ® [stilomin] *nm* propelling pencil.
styptique [stiptik] *adj & nm Méd* styptic.
styrax [stiraks] *nm Bot* styrax.
styrène [stirɛn] *nm Ch* styrene.
Styx [stiks] *nm* **le S.**, the Styx.
su [sy] *nm* **au su de,** to the knowledge of; **à mon (vu et) su,** to my (certain) knowledge.
suage¹ [sɥaʒ] *nm* sweating, oozing *(of timber etc)*.
suage² *nm* fillet (border) *(of candlestick, of silver plate etc)*.
suaire [sɥɛr] *nm* **(a)** *Litt (linceul)* winding sheet, shroud; **(b)** *Rel* **le saint s.**, the holy shroud.
suant [sɥɑ̃] *adj* **(a)** *F* sweating, sweaty; **(b)** *Arg (ennuyeux)* boring.
suave [sɥav] *adj* **(a)** sweet, pleasant *(music, scent etc)*; soft *(shade)*; mild *(cigar)*; **(b)** *Fig* suave, smooth *(tone, manner)*.
suavement [sɥavmɑ̃] *adv (voir adj)* **(a)** pleasantly; **(b)** suavely.
suavité [sɥavite] *nf* **(a)** sweetness *(of perfume, melody)*; **(b)** suavity *(of manner)*.
subaigu, -uë [sybegy] *adj Méd* subacute.
subalpin [sybalpɛ̃] *adj* subalpine.
subalterne [sybaltɛrn] **1** *adj* subordinate, minor *(official, position, role)*; inferior *(mind)*; junior *(employee)*. **2** *nm* **(a)** subordinate; **(b)** *Mil* subaltern (officer).
subaquatique [sybakwatik] *adj* subaquatic, underwater.
subatomique [sybatɔmik] *adj* subatomic.
subconscient [sybkɔ̃sjɑ̃] *adj & nm* subconscious.
subdiviser [sybdivize] **1** *vt* to subdivide. **2 se subdiviser** *vpr* to be subdivided.
subdivision [sybdivizjɔ̃] *nf* subdivision.
subéquatorial, -aux [sybekwatɔrjal, -o] *adj Géog* subequatorial.
subéreux, -euse [syberø, -øz] *adj Bot* suberose, corky.
subir [sybir] *vt* to undergo *(trial, examination, operation, torture, change etc)*; to suffer *(death, violence, consequences)*; to serve *(one's sentence)*; to come *or* be under *(an influence)*; to suffer, to sustain *(defeat, casualties, loss)*; to submit to, to suffer, to put up with *(punishment, events, one's fate)*; **s. qn,** to put up with s.o.; **faire s. qch à qn,** to subject s.o. to sth.
subit [sybi] *adj* sudden, unexpected *(death, change)*.
subitement [sybitmɑ̃] *adv* suddenly, all of a sudden.
subito [sybito] *adv F* all of a sudden; *(immédiatement)* at once.
subjectif, -ive [sybʒɛktif, -iv] *adj* subjective; *Gram* **cas s.**, nominative case.
subjectivement [sybʒɛktivmɑ̃] *adv* subjectively.
subjectivisme [sybʒɛktivism] *nm Phil* subjectivism.
subjectivité [sybʒɛktivite] *nf* subjectivity.
subjonctif, -ive [sybʒɔ̃ktif, -iv] *Gram* **1** *adj* subjunctive *(mood)*; **2** *nm* subjunctive; **au s.**, in the subjunctive.
subjugation [sybʒygasjɔ̃] *nf* subjugation.
subjuguer [sybʒyge] *vt* to subjugate, to subdue *(people, nation)*; to subdue, to master *(horse)*; *Fig* to captivate *(audience, hearts etc)*.
sublimation [syblimasjɔ̃] *nf Ch Psy* sublimation.
sublime [syblim] **1** *adj* sublime; *F* **ça n'a rien de s.**, it's nothing to write home about. **2** *nm* **le s.**, the sublime.
sublimé [syblime] **1** *adj* sublimated. **2** *nm Ch* sublimate.
sublimement [syblimmɑ̃] *adv* sublimely.
sublimer [syblime] *vt Ch Psy* to sublimate.
subliminaire [sybliminɛr], **subliminal, -aux** [sybliminal, -o] *adj* subliminal.
sublimité [syblimite] *nf Litt* sublimeness.
sublingual, -aux [syblɛ̃gwal, -o] *adj Anat* sublingual *(gland etc)*; *Pharm* **comprimé s.**, tablet to be placed under the tongue.
submerger [sybmɛrʒe] *vt* **(je submergeai(s); n. submergeons) (a)** to submerge, to flood *(meadow etc)*; to submerge, to swamp *(boat)*; to submerge *(object)*; **ville submergée par les touristes,** town inundated with *or* overrun by tourists; **(b)** *Fig* to overwhelm *(s.o.)*; **submergé de travail,** snowed under *or* overwhelmed with work.
submersible [sybmɛrsibl] **1** *adj* **(a)** submersible *(boat)*; **(b)** *Bot* submerged *(plant)*; **(c)** *(ground)* liable to flooding. **2** *nm Nau* submarine.
submersion [sybmɛrsjɔ̃] *nf* submersion, flooding; **mort par s.**, death by drowning.
subodorer [sybɔdɔre] *vt F* to suspect, to scent *(danger, plot etc)*; **il a subodoré quelque chose,** he smelt a rat.
subordination [sybɔrdinasjɔ̃] *nf* subordination.
subordonnant [sybɔrdɔnɑ̃] *adj Gram* subordinating *(conjunction etc)*.
subordonné, -ée [sybɔrdɔne] **1** *adj* **(a)** *Gram* subordinate *(clause)*; **(b)** *(dépendant)* subordinate (**à**, to). **2** *n (personne)* subordinate. **3** *nf Gram* **subordonnée,** subordinate clause.
subordonner [sybɔrdɔne] **1** *vt* to subordinate (**à**, to); *Fig* **s. ses dépenses à son revenu,** to cut one's coat according to one's cloth; **le service est subordonné au nombre des voyageurs,** the service depends on the number of travellers. **2 se subordonner** *vpr* **se s. à qn,** to subordinate oneself to s.o..
subornation [sybɔrnasjɔ̃] *nf Jur* subornation, bribing.
suborner [sybɔrne] *vt* **(a)** *Jur* to suborn, to bribe *(witness)*; **(b)** *Litt (séduire)* to seduce *(woman)*.
suborneur, -euse [sybɔrnœr, -øz] **1** *n Jur* suborner, briber *(of witness)*. **2** *nm Litt (séducteur)* seducer.
subreptice [sybrɛptis] *adj* surreptitious.
subrepticement [sybrɛptismɑ̃] *adv* surreptitiously.
subrogation [sybrɔgasjɔ̃] *nf Jur* subrogation, substitution.
subrogé, -ée [sybrɔʒe] **1** *adj* subrogated; deputy, surrogate *(guardian)*. **2** *n Rel Jur* surrogate, deputy.
subroger [sybrɔʒe] *vt* **(je subrogeai(s); n. subrogeons)** *Jur* to subrogate, to substitute.
subséquemment [sypsekamɑ̃] *adv Jur & Litt* subsequently.
subséquent [sypsekɑ̃] *adj Jur Géog & Litt* subsequent.
subside [sypsid] *nm* subsidy, allowance.
subsidence [sypsidɑ̃s, sybz-] *nf Géol* subsidence.
subsidiaire [sypsidjɛr, sybz-] *adj* subsidiary.
subsidiairement [sypsidjɛrmɑ̃, sybz-] *adv* subsidiarily; **s. à,** in addition to.
subsistance [sybzistɑ̃s] *nf* **(a)** *(survie)* subsistence; **pourvoir à la s. de sa famille,** to keep *or* support one's family; **moyen de s.**, means of subsistence; **(b) subsistances,** *(vivres)* provisions; *Mil* supplies.
subsistant [sybzistɑ̃] *adj* remaining, existing.
subsister [sybziste] *vi* **(a)** *(of thing)* to (continue to) exist, to remain; **(b)** *(of person)* to live, *Fml* to subsist (**de,** on); **moyens de s.**, means of subsistence.
subsonique [sypsɔnik] *adj Av* subsonic.
substance [sypstɑ̃s] *nf* **(a)** *(essentiel)* substance, gist *(of an article etc)*; **sans s.**, insubstantial *(arguments etc)*; **en s.**, in substance; **(b)** *(matière)* substance, matter; **s. étrangère,** extraneous substance; **plaie avec perte de s.**, wound with loss of tissue; *Anat* **s. grise,** grey matter.
substantialité [sypstɑ̃sjalite] *nf Phil* substantiality.
substantiel, -ielle [sypstɑ̃sjɛl] *adj* substantial.
substantiellement [sypstɑ̃sjɛlmɑ̃] *adv* substantially.

substantif, -ive [sypstɑ̃tif, -iv] *Gram* **1** *adj* substantive. **2** *nm* substantive, noun.

substantifique [sypstɑ̃tifik] *adj* **la s. moelle,** the essence, the pith (*of a text etc*).

substantivement [sypstɑ̃tivmɑ̃] *adj Gram* substantively, as a noun.

substantiver [sypstɑ̃tive] *Gram* **1** *vt* to use (*word, phrase etc*) substantively *or* as a noun. **2 se substantiver** *vpr* to be used substantively *or* as a noun.

substituer [sypstitɥe] **1** *vt* **(a)** (*remplacer*) to substitute (**à** for); **(b)** *Jur* **s. un héritier,** to appoint an heir in succession to another *or* failing another; **s. un héritage,** to entail an estate. **2 se substituer** *vpr* **se s. à qn/à qch,** to substitute for s.o./sth, to take the place of s.o./sth.

substitut [sypstity] *nm* substitute (**de,** for); *Jur* deputy public prosecutor.

substitution [sypstitysj̃ɔ] *nf* **(a)** (*remplacement*) substitution (**à,** for); **(b)** *Jur* entail (*to grandchildren etc*).

substrat [sypstra] *nm Géol Ling Phil* substratum; *Phot Biol Ordinat* substrate.

subterfuge [syptɛrfyʒ] *nm* subterfuge.

subtil [syptil] *adj* **(a)** (*fin*) subtle; discerning, shrewd (*mind, leader etc*); *Arch* acute, keen (*senses*); **(b)** (*ténu*) delicate, fine (*distinction etc*); **(c)** (*ingénieux*) ingenious (*argument, remark etc*); **(d)** *Arch* tenuous, thin (*fluid*); fine (*dust*); **(e)** (*qui pénètre*) pervasive (*poison, scent etc*).

subtilement [syptilmɑ̃] *adv* subtly.

subtiliser [syptilize] **1** *vt* **(a)** *F* (*dérober*) to pinch, *Br* to nick (**à,** from); **(b)** *Arch* to refine (*substance*). **2** *vi* (*en raisonnant*) to split hairs, to be too subtle.

subtilité [syptilite] *nf* **(a)** subtlety, shrewdness (*of mind*); **(b)** subtlety, fineness (*of distinction*); **(c)** subtlety (*of argument*); **(d)** (*argument, distinction*) subtlety.

subtropical, -aux [syptrɔpikal, -o] *adj* subtropical.

suburbain [sybyrbɛ̃] *adj* suburban.

subvenir [sybvənir] *vi* (*conj like* **venir**) (*aux* **avoir**) **s. à,** to provide for (*s.o.'s needs*); to meet (*expenses*); to relieve (*distress*).

subvention [sybvɑ̃sj̃ɔ] *nf* subsidy, grant; **s. aux entreprises,** development grant.

subventionner [sybvɑ̃sjɔne] *vt* to subsidize, to grant (financial) aid to (*undertaking, institution etc*); **subventionné,** subsidized (*industry, theatre etc*); maintained, grant-aided (*school*); grant-aided (*student*).

subversif, -ive [sybvɛrsif, -iv] *adj* subversive.

subversion [sybvɛrsj̃ɔ] *nf* subversion.

subversivement [sybvɛrsivmɑ̃] *adv* subversively.

subvertir [sybvɛrtir] *vt Litt* to subvert.

suc [syk] *nm* **(a)** (*de fruit, viande*) juice; *Bot* sap; *Physiol* juice; **s. gastrique,** gastric juice; **(b)** *Fig* essence, pith (*of text etc*).

succédané [syksedane] *adj & nm* substitute (**de,** for).

succéder [syksede] *v* (**je succède, n. succédons; je succéderai**) **1** *vi* **s. à qn/qch,** to succeed s.o./sth; **un sentiment de pitié succéda à sa rage,** his anger gave way to a feeling of pity; **les champs succèdent aux bois,** (the) fields give way to woods; **s. au trône,** to succeed to the throne; **s. à une fortune,** to inherit a fortune. **2 se succéder** *vpr* **les révolutions se succédèrent,** the revolutions followed one another, revolution followed revolution, there was a succession of revolutions.

succès [syksɛ] *nm* success; **avoir du s.,** to be successful; **elle a un grand s. auprès des hommes,** she is very successful *or* has great success with men; **remporter de grands s.,** to achieve great success; **sans s.,** (*used adjectivally*) unsuccessful; (*used adverbially*) unsuccessfully; **une seconde tentative n'eut pas plus de s.,** a second attempt met with no more success *or* was no more successful; **je n'ai pas eu de s. avec ma proposition,** I was unsuccessful *or* had no success with my proposal; **remporter un beau s.,** to have (a) great success; *Sp* **le plus beau s. de l'équipe,** the team's greatest success; **livre à s., s. de librairie,** bestseller; **auteur à s.,** bestselling author, bestseller; **avoir grand s.,** (*of play etc*) to be a great *or* a huge success; **le public a fait un s. à ce livre/cette pièce/ce film,** the book/play/film has been well received (by the public); **s. fou,** great success, *Th* smash hit; **pièce à s.,** hit.

successeur [syksesœr] *nm* successor (**de,** to, of).

successif, -ive [syksesif, -iv] *adj* successive.

succession [syksesj̃ɔ] *nf* **(a)** (*série*) succession (*of visitors, ideas, sounds, days etc*); *Cin TV* **par ordre de s.,** in order of appearance; **(b)** (*au trône, au pouvoir etc*) succession (**à,** to); **prendre la s. d'une maison de commerce,** to take over a business; **(c)** *Jur* (*par héritage*) succession; (*biens*) inheritance; **droits de s.,** death duties.

successivement [syksesivmɑ̃] *adv* successively.

succinct [syksɛ̃, syksɛ̃kt] *adj* **(a)** succinct, brief, concise; *F* **repas s.,** scanty meal; **sois s.,** be brief, keep it brief; **(b)** *Ordinat* **résumé s.,** compendium.

succinctement [syksɛ̃tmɑ̃, -ɛktəmɑ̃] *adv* succinctly, briefly; *F* (*manger*) frugally.

succion [syksj̃ɔ] *nf* suction; **bruit de s.,** sucking noise.

succomber [sykɔ̃be] *vi* **(a)** (*tomber*) to succumb, to sink (under the weight); **je succombe au sommeil,** I can't stay awake; **(b)** to be overpowered (**sous le nombre,** by numbers); **(c) s. à,** to succumb to, to yield to, to give way to (*grief, temptation etc*); to be overcome by (*emotion*); **(d)** (*mourir*) to die, to succumb.

succube [sykyb] *nm* succubus, succuba.

succulence [sykylɑ̃s] *nf Litt* succulence.

succulent [sykylɑ̃] *adj* succulent (*food*); *Bot* fleshy (*leaf*); **plante succulente,** succulent.

succursale [sykyrsal] *nf Com* branch.

sucer [syse] *v* (**je suçai(s); n. suçons**) **1** *vt* to suck (*milk, orange, bone etc*); **s. son pouce,** to suck one's thumb; *F* **s. qn jusqu'au dernier sou** *ou* **jusqu'à la moelle des os,** to suck s.o. dry, to bleed s.o. white; *Arg* **s. la poire à qn,** to kiss s.o.. **2 se sucer** *vpr* **(a) se s. les doigts,** to suck one's fingers; *Arg* **se s. la poire,** to kiss; **(b) ces cachets se sucent,** these tablets are (meant) to be sucked *or* are for sucking.

sucette [sysɛt] *nf* **(a)** (*de bébé*) dummy, *US* pacifier; **(b)** (*confiserie*) lollipop, *F* lolly; **s. glacée,** ice lolly, *US* popsicle ®.

suceur, -euse [sysœr, -øz] **1** *n Péj* **s. de sang,** (*personne*) bloodsucker. **2** *nm* **(a)** (*poisson*) sucker, sucking fish; **(b)** nozzle (*of vacuum cleaner*). **3** *nf* **suceuse,** (*drague*) suction dredger.

suçon [syś̃ɔ] *nm F* lovebite; **faire un s. à qn,** to give s.o. a lovebite.

suçoter [sysɔte] *vt F* to suck (away) at (*sth*).

sucrage [sykraʒ] *nm* sugaring (*of wine*).

sucrant [sykrɑ̃] *adj* sweetening; **le miel est très s.,** honey makes things very sweet.

sucrase [sykraz] *nf Ch* sucrase.

sucre [sykr] *nm* sugar; **s. de canne,** cane sugar; **s. de betterave,** beet sugar; **s. en pains,** loaf sugar; **pain de s.,** sugar loaf; **montagne en pain de s.,** sugar-loaf mountain; **s. en poudre, s. semoule,** caster sugar; **s. cristallisé,** granulated sugar; **s. glace, s. à glacer,** icing sugar; **s. en morceaux,** lump sugar, sugar lumps; **s. brut,** crude sugar; **s. d'orge,** barley sugar; **s. roux,** brown sugar; *F* **s. noir,** liquorice; **un s. dans mon café,** one sugar in my coffee; **fruit au s.,** fruit sprinkled with sugar; **décorations en s.,** sugar decorations; *F* **il a été tout s. tout miel,** he was all sweetness and light; *Fig* **elle n'est pas en s.!,** she's pretty resilient!; *F* **mon bébé en s.,** my sugar baby; *Arg* **c'est un vrai s.,** he's a honey; *Can* **partie de s.,** sugaring party; *Ch* **s. de lait,** lactose; **s. de fruit,** fructose.

sucré [sykre] *adj* **(a)** sugared, sweetened (*coffee etc*); sweet (*fruits etc*); **mon thé est trop s.,** my tea is too sweet; **eau sucrée,** sugar and water; **(b)** *Fig* sugary (*words, manner, smile*); **elle fait la sucrée,** butter wouldn't melt in her mouth.

sucrer [sykre] **1** *vt* **(a)** to sugar, to sweeten; **(b)** *Fig F* **on lui a sucré sa prime,** he has had his bonus taken away; **(c)** *Fig F* **s. les fraises,** (*trembler*) to shake; (*être gâteux*) to be an old dodderer. **2** *vi* (*of honey etc*) to sweeten. **3 se sucrer** *vpr* **(a)** *F* (*prendre du sucre*) to help oneself to sugar; **(b)** *Arg* (*faire des bénéfices*) to line one's pockets.

sucrerie [sykrəri] *nf* **(a)** (*usine*) sugar refinery; **(b) sucreries,** (*friandises*) confectionery, sweets, *surtout US* candy; **aimer les sucreries,** to have a sweet tooth; **(c)** *Can* (*forêt*) maple tree grove.

sucrette [sykrɛt] *nf* artificial sweetener.

sucrier, -ière [sykrije, -jɛr] **1** *adj* sugar; **industrie sucrière,** sugar industry. **2** *n* (*fabricant*) sugar manufacturer. **3** *nm* (*récipient*) sugar bowl *or* basin; **s. verseur,** sugar shaker.

sud [syd] **1** *nm no pl* **(a)** south; **un vent du s.,** a southerly wind, a wind from the south; **le vent du s.,** the south wind; **maison exposée au s.,** house that faces south; **dans le S. (de l'Angleterre),** in the South (of England); **au s.,** in the south; **au s. de Paris,** (to the) south of Paris; **l'Amérique du S.,** South America; **l'Afrique du S.,** South Africa; **vers le s.,** southward; **(b)** *Nau* **le s.,** (*vent*) the south wind. **2** *adj inv* south, southerly (*wind*); southern (*part, latitude etc*); **le Pôle S.,** the South Pole; **Pacifique S.,** South Pacific; **le côté s.,** the south side (*of house, wall etc*).

sud-africain, -aine [sydafrikɛ̃, -ɛn] (*pl sud-africain(e)s*) **1** *adj* South African; **la République s.-africaine,** the Republic of South Africa. **2** *n* **S.-A.,** South African.
sud-américain, -aine [sydamerikɛ̃, -ɛn] (*pl sud-américain(e)s*) **1** *adj* South American. **2** *n* **S.-A.,** South American.
sudation [sydasjɔ̃] *nf Méd etc* sudation, sweating.
sud-coréen, -enne [sydkɔreɛ̃, -ɛn] (*pl sud-coréen(ne)s*) **1** *adj* South Korean. **2** *n* **S.-C.,** South Korean.
sud-est [sydɛst] **1** *nm no pl* southeast; **vers le s.-e.,** southeastward, toward(s) the southeast. **2** *adj inv* southeast, south-easterly (*wind*); southeastern (*region*).
sudiste [sydist] *Hist Am* **1** *n* Southerner (*in the Civil War*). **2** *adj* Southern.
sudorifère [sydɔrifɛr] *adj* = **SUDORIPARE**.
sudorifique [sydɔrifik] *adj & nm Pharm* sudorific.
sudoripare [sydɔripar] *adj Anat* sudoriferous; **glande s.,** sweat gland.
sud-ouest [sydwɛst] **1** *nm no pl* southwest; **vers le s.-o.,** southwestward, toward(s) the southwest. **2** *adj inv* southwesterly (*wind*); southwestern (*region*).
Sud-Ouest Africain [sydwɛstafrikɛ̃] *nm Hist* South West Africa.
sud-vietnamien, -ienne [sydvjɛtnamjɛ̃, -jɛn] (*pl sud-vietnamien(ne)s*) **1** *adj* South Vietnamese. **2** *n* **S.-V.,** South Vietnamese.
Suède [sɥɛd] *nf* Sweden.
suédé [sɥede] *adj & nm* suede.
suédine [sɥedin] *nf Tex* suedette.
suédois, -oise [sɥedwa, -az] **1** *adj* Swedish; *Gym* **la gymnastique suédoise,** Swedish gymnastics *or* exercises. **2** *nm Ling* Swedish. **3** *n* **S.,** Swede. **4** *nf Gym* **suédoise,** Swedish gymnastics *or* exercises.
suée [sɥe] *nf F* **(a)** (*transpiration*) sweating, sweat; (*sous l'effet de la peur*) (cold) sweat; **prendre une s.,** to get up *or* work up a sweat; **une bonne s.,** a good sweat; **(b)** *Arg* (*travail dur*) sweat.
suer [sɥe] **1** *vi* **(a)** (*of person*) to sweat, to perspire; *F* **s. comme un phoque,** to sweat like a pig; **faire s. qn,** to make s.o. sweat; *F* (*embêter*) to annoy *or* sicken s.o.; **tu me fais s.!,** you make me sick!; **(b)** (*of walls etc*) to ooze; **(c)** (*travailler*) to labour, *US* to labor, to sweat; *F* **faire s. le burnous,** to use sweated labour. **2** *vt* to sweat (*blood*); to ooze (*piety, boredom, hypocrisy etc*); **maison qui sue le crime,** house that reeks of crime.
sueur [sɥœr] *nf* sweat, perspiration; **être en s.,** to be sweating *or* in a sweat; **avoir des sueurs froides,** to be in a cold sweat; **à la s. de son front,** by the sweat of one's brow; **le fruit de mes sueurs,** the fruits of my labour *or US* labor.
Suez [sɥɛz] *n* Suez; **le canal de S.,** the Suez Canal.
suffire [syfir] *v* (*prp* **suffisant**; *pp* **suffi**; *pr ind* **je suffis, n. suffisons, ils suffisent**; *pr sub* **je suffise**; *impf* **je suffisais**; *p hist* **je suffis**; *fu* **je suffirai**) **1** *vi* to suffice, to be enough; **cela ne me suffit pas (pour vivre),** that is not enough for me (to live on); **votre promesse me suffit,** your promise is enough for me; *Prov* **à chaque jour suffit sa peine,** sufficient unto the day is the evil thereof; **s. à qch/à faire qch,** to be equal to sth/to doing sth; **s. à la tâche,** to be up to *or* equal to the job; **cela suffit à mes besoins,** that's enough for my needs; **je n'y suffis plus,** it's too much for me, I can't cope.

2 se suffire *vpr* **il s'est toujours suffi,** he has always supported himself *or* earned his own living; **pays qui se suffisent (à eux-mêmes),** self-supporting countries.

3 *v impers* **il a suffi de quelques mots pour le persuader,** a few words were enough to persuade him; **il suffit de l'écouter pour ...,** one only has to *or* one need only listen to him to ...; **il suffit qu'il le dise,** (it is) enough for him to say so; **ça ne lui suffit pas,** that's not enough for him; **il suffisait que tu passes un coup de téléphone,** all you had to do was phone; *F* **(il) suffit!, ça suffit!,** that's enough!, that'll do!; **il suffit d'une heure pour ...,** it only takes an hour to ... .
suffisamment [syfizamɑ̃] *adv* sufficiently, enough; **agir sans avoir s. réfléchi,** to act without sufficient thought; **s. de,** sufficient, enough.
suffisance [syfizɑ̃s] *nf* **(a) avoir s. de,** to have sufficient *or* enough; **manger à sa s.,** to eat one's fill; **avoir de qch à s.** *ou* **en s.,** to have sth in abundance, to have plenty of sth; **(b)** (*vanité*) complacency, self-importance; **il est d'une s. insupportable,** he is unbearably conceited; **(c)** *Arch* (*capacité*) competence; **homme de s.,** competent man.
suffisant, -ante [syfizɑ̃, -ɑ̃t] **1** *adj* **(a)** sufficient, enough; **c'est plus que s.,** that is more than sufficient *or* enough; **(b)** (*vaniteux*) self-satisfied, self-important, conceited (*air, tone*). **2** *n* **faire le s.,** to give oneself airs.
suffixe [syfiks] *nm Gram Ordinat* suffix.
suffixer [syfikse] *vt Gram Ordinat* to suffix, to add a suffix to; **mot suffixé,** word with *or* that has a suffix.
suffocant [syfɔkɑ̃] *adj* **(a)** suffocating, stifling (*heat etc*); **(b)** *Fig* staggering, incredible (*news, reply etc*).
suffocation [syfɔkasjɔ̃] *nf* suffocation; (*crise*) choking fit.
suffoquer [syfɔke] **1** *vt* **(a)** (*of smell, smoke etc*) to suffocate, to stifle; (*of news etc*) to stagger (*s.o.*); **les sanglots la suffoquaient,** she was choking with sobs; **(b)** *Arch* (*tuer*) to suffocate (*s.o.*). **2** *vi* to suffocate, to choke; **s. de colère/d'indignation,** to choke with anger/indignation.
suffragant [syfragɑ̃] *Rel* **1** *adj* suffragan (*bishop*). **2** *nm* suffragan (bishop).
suffrage [syfraʒ] *nm Pol* (*voix*) vote; (*système*) suffrage; **dix mille suffrages,** ten thousand votes; **s. universel,** universal franchise *or* suffrage; **s. universel pur et simple,** one-man-one-vote; **ce nouveau modèle remporte tous les suffrages,** this new model wins everyone's approval *or* is universally liked.
suffragette [syfraʒɛt] *nf Hist Pol* suffragette.
suffusion [syfyzjɔ̃] *nf Med* suffusion.
suggérer [sygʒere] *vt* (**je suggère, n. suggérons; je suggérerai**) to suggest (**à,** to); **s. de faire qch,** to suggest doing sth; **s. à qn de faire qch,** to suggest to s.o. that he should do sth; **s. que,** to suggest that; **cette expression suggère la lumière/la vitesse,** this expression suggests light/speed.
suggestibilité [sygʒɛstibilite] *nf* suggestibility.
suggestible [sygʒɛstibl] *adj* suggestible.
suggestif, -ive [sygʒɛstif, -iv] *adj* **(a)** (*évocateur*) evocative, suggestive; **(b)** (*impudique*) suggestive (*joke, gesture etc*).
suggestion [sygʒɛstjɔ̃] *nf* suggestion; **suggestions en vue d'une amélioration,** suggestions for improvement; **agir sur la s. de qn,** to act on s.o.'s suggestion; **pas la moindre s. de ...,** not the slightest hint *or* suggestion of ... .
suggestionner [sygʒɛstjɔne] *vt* **s. qn,** to put an idea *or* ideas into s.o.'s head; **se laisser s.,** to allow ideas to be put into one's head (**par,** by).
suicidaire [sɥisidɛr] **1** *adj* suicidal (*tendencies, person, Fig undertaking etc*). **2** *n* suicidal person.
suicide [sɥisid] *nm* (*acte*) suicide; **faux s.,** attempted suicide; **tentative de s.,** suicide attempt; *Fig* **le s. économique d'un pays,** the economic suicide of a country; **attentat-s.,** suicide attack; **avion-s.,** suicide plane.
suicidé, -ée [sɥiside] **1** *adj* who has committed suicide. **2** *n* (*personne*) suicide.
suicider (se) [səsɥiside] *vpr* to commit suicide; *Fig* **se s. politiquement,** to commit political suicide.
suie [sɥi] *nf* soot.
suif [sɥif] *nm* **(a)** tallow; **s. de mouton,** mutton fat; **chandelle de s.,** tallow candle; **(b)** *Arg* **recevoir un s.,** to get a dressing down; **faire du s.,** to kick up a row; **chercher du s.,** to be looking for a fight.
suifer [sɥife] *vt* to tallow (*leather etc*); to grease (*hinge*).
sui generis [sɥiʒeneris] *adj* sui generis; *Euph* **odeur s. g.,** (*mauvaise*) distinctive smell.
suint [sɥɛ̃] *nm* suint (*of wool*).
suintant [sɥɛ̃tɑ̃] *adj* oozing, dripping (*wall etc*).
suintement [sɥɛ̃tmɑ̃] *nm* oozing, dripping (*of rock, wall etc*); running, weeping (*of wound*).
suinter [sɥɛ̃te] **1** *vi* **(a)** (*of rock, wall etc*) to ooze, to drip; **(b)** (*of vessel*) to leak; (*of wound*) to run, to weep. **2** *vt* to exude, to ooze (*hatred etc*).
suisse [sɥis] **1** *adj* Swiss. **2** *n* **S.,** Swiss; **les Suisses,** the Swiss. **3** *nm* **(a)** *Hist Mil* Swiss mercenary; (*au Vatican*) Swiss guard; *F* **boire en s.,** to drink on one's own; **(b)** *Rel* verger (*in full regalia*); **(c) petit s.,** petit suisse (= *small cream cheese*); **(d)** *Can Zool* **s. (rayé),** chipmunk.
Suisse [sɥis] *nf* Switzerland; **la S. alémanique/romande/italienne,** German-/French-/Italian-speaking Switzerland.
Suissesse [sɥisɛs] *nf Péj* Swiss (woman).
suite [sɥit] *nf* **(a)** (*action de poursuivre*) pursuit; **être à la s. de qn,** to be in pursuit of s.o. *or F* after s.o.;

(b) (*continuation*) continuation, what follows; (*au restaurant*) the next course; **j'oublie la s. de l'air,** I forget how the tune goes on; **faire s. à,** to be a continuation of (*sth*); (*of room*) to lead out of (*another room*); **comme s. à notre lettre d'hier,** further to our letter of yesterday; **à la s. de votre demande,** with reference to your request; *Com* **donner s. à,** to deal with, to carry out (*order*); to give effect to (*decision*); **pour s. à donner,** (passed to you) for action; *Com* **sans s.,** discontinued (*article*); **prendre la s. des affaires d'une maison,** to take over a business; **à la s. les uns des autres,** one after the other; **il a avalé deux gâteaux à la s.,** he swallowed two cakes one after the other; **à la s. de cette discussion,** following (on) this discussion; **les historiens venus à sa s.,** the historians who came after him; **les maux que la guerre traîne à sa s.,** the evils that war brings in its wake *or* train; **se mettre à la s.,** to join (the back of) the queue *or Am* the line;

(c) de s., (*à la suite*) in a row, in succession; **dix heures de s.,** ten hours on end; **dix jours de s.,** ten days running; **pendant plusieurs semaines de s.,** for several weeks at a time *or* running; **et ainsi de s.,** and so on;

(d) tout de s., *F* **de s.,** at once, immediately; **dans la s.,** subsequently; **par la s.,** later on, afterwards;

(e) (*nouveau roman, film etc*) sequel; (*nouvel episode*) continuation; **je ne connais pas la s. de l'histoire,** I don't know the rest of the story; *Journ* **s. à la page 30,** continued on page 30; **s. et fin,** concluded; **la s. au prochain numéro,** continued in the next issue;

(f) (*de raisonnement*) coherence, consistency; **sans s.,** (*used adjectivally*) incoherent, disconnected (*words, thoughts etc*); (*used adverbially*) disconnectedly, incoherently; **s. dans les idées,** single-mindedness; **elle a de la s. dans les idées!,** she is very single-minded!; **manquer (d'esprit) de s.,** to lack application *or* perseverance; (*méthode*) to lack method;

(g) (*escorte*) suite, retinue, train (*of monarch etc*);

(h) (*série*) series, succession (*of events etc*); line (*of ancestors*); set (*of prints*); **s. de malheurs,** run of misfortunes, chapter *or* series of accidents; **dans la s. des siècles,** in the course of time *or* of the centuries;

(i) *Math* series;

(j) *Mus* suite;

(k) (*conséquence*) consequence, result; (*de maladie etc*) aftereffects; **mourir des suites d'une blessure,** to die (as the result) of a wound; **par s.,** consequently; **par s. de,** in consequence of, through, on account of; **par s. de maladie,** owing to illness; **par s. d'une erreur,** by *or* through an error; **par s. de sa blessure,** as a result of his wound;

(l) (*dans un hôtel*) suite.

suivant[1] [sɥivɑ̃] **1** *prép* **(a)** (*direction*) in the direction of, along (*line etc*); **(b)** (*selon*) according to, in accordance with (*one's means, instructions etc*); **s. le jour/etc,** according to *or* depending on the day/*etc*; **s. lui,** in his opinion, according to him. **2** *conj* **s. que** + *ind*, depending on whether, according to whether.

suivant[2], -ante [sɥivɑ̃, -ɑ̃t] **1** *adj* **(a)** next, following (*page, day etc*); **voir page 6 et suivantes,** see page 6 and following; **les trois jours suivants,** the next three days; **pas dimanche prochain mais le dimanche s.,** not this Sunday but the next (one) *or* the one after; **notre méthode est la suivante,** our method is as follows; **(b)** *Ordinat* **caractère de mise en début de ligne suivante,** new line character. **2** *n* (*prochain*) **le s., la suivante,** the next (one); **les suivant(e)s,** the next (ones); **au s.!,** next (person) please! **3** *nm* (*accompagnateur*) attendant. **4** *nf Th* **suivante,** attendant.

suiveur, -euse [sɥivœr, øz] **1** *nm* follower (**de,** of). **2** *adj* **voiture suiveuse,** = car following a cycle race *etc*.

suivi [sɥivi] **1** *adj* **(a)** connected (*speech*); sustained, coherent (*reasoning*); regular (*correspondence*); consistent (*work, effort, quality, story*); steadfast, unwavering (*policy*); *Com* steady, persistent (*demand*); **article s.,** stock item; **(b)** well attended, popular (*course of lectures etc*). **2** *nm* follow-up; **faire le s. de qch,** to keep track of sth, to follow sth up; **assurer le s. d'un projet,** to follow a project through.

suivisme [sɥivism] *nm Pol etc* tagging-along attitude.

suivre [sɥivr] *v* (*prp* **suivant**; *pp* **suivi**; *pr ind* **je suis, il suit, n. suivons, ils suivent**; *pr sub* **je suive**; *impf* **je suivais**; *p hist* **je suivis**; *fu* **je suivrai**) **1** *vt* **(a)** (*aller derrière*) to follow (*s.o., sth*); **s. qn de près,** to follow close on s.o.'s heels; **partez, je vous suis,** you go on, I'll follow (on); **elle le suivit des yeux** *ou* **du regard,** she followed him with her eyes; *Com* **s. une affaire,** to follow up business; *Com* **nous n'avons pas suivi cet article,** we have discontinued this line; *Tennis etc* **s. la balle,** to follow through;

(b) (*comprendre*) to follow, to understand; **je ne vous suis pas,** I don't follow you; (*je ne suis pas d'accord*) I don't agree with you; **s. une conversation dans une langue étrangère,** to follow a conversation in a foreign language;

(c) (*escorter*) to escort, to attend, to accompany (*s.o.*);

(d) (*poursuivre*) to follow, to pursue (*animal, enemy etc*); **nous sommes suivis,** we're being followed;

(e) (*porter son attention sur*) to follow, to be attentive to (*sth*); **il parle si vite que je ne peux pas le s.,** he talks so quickly that I cannot follow him; **suivez attentivement,** follow closely;

(f) (*observer*) to follow, to watch, to observe (*s.o.'s progress, course of events etc*); **s. l'actualité à la télévision/à la radio,** to follow events on the television/radio; **affaire à s.,** affair worth following;

(g) (*enquêter sur*) to follow up (*clue*);

(h) to follow, to succeed, to come after (*sth*); **le printemps suit l'hiver,** spring follows winter, winter is succeeded by spring; **conjonction suivie du subjonctif,** conjunction followed by the subjunctive;

(i) (*longer*) to go along, to follow (*road, Fig train of thought etc*); **s. son chemin,** to go on one's way; **la rivière suit son cours,** the river follows its course; **la justice suivra son cours,** justice will take its course;

(j) (*obéir à*) to obey, to conform to (*fashion, law etc*); to follow (*fashion*); to follow, to act upon (*advice*); to follow, to pursue (*line of conduct*); **s. son intuition,** to follow one's intuition; **son exemple n'est pas à s.,** his example is not to be followed; **voici la marche à s.,** this is the procedure, this is what you have to do; **s. son penchant,** to follow one's bent;

(k) (*être présent à*) to attend (*series of concerts, lectures etc*) (regularly); *Méd* to follow (*course of treatment*); **s. un régime,** to follow *or* be on a diet; **s. un cours,** to follow *or* take a course (of study);

(l) (*exercer*) to practise, to exercise (*profession, calling*);

(m) (*en disciple*) to follow (*s.o.*);

(n) s. son temps, to keep abreast of the times.

2 *vi* **(a)** (*venir après*) to follow; **le reste du repas suit,** the rest of the meal is coming; **avoir du mal à s.,** (*pendant la marche*) to have trouble keeping up; **les personnes dont les noms suivent,** the following persons; **faire s. une lettre,** to forward *or* redirect a letter; **(prière de) faire s.,** (*sur une enveloppe*) please forward; *Typ* **(faire) s.,** run on; **à s.,** (*à la fin d'un feuilleton*) to be continued;

(b) *Scol* **elle ne suit plus,** she can't keep up any more; (*elle rêve*) she doesn't pay attention any more.

3 se suivre *vpr* **arguments qui se suivent bien,** arguments that are connected *or* coherent; **ces deux mots se suivent,** these two words follow each other *or* are consecutive; **événements qui se suivent de près,** events that follow each other in quick succession.

4 *v impers* **il suit de là que ...,** it follows (from this) that ...; **que s'en est-il suivi?,** what came of it?; **conditions ainsi qu'il suit,** terms as follows.

sujet[1], -ette [syʒɛ, -ɛt] **1** *adj* **(a) s. à,** (*exposé à*) subject to, liable to, prone to (*illness etc*); **s. à la mort,** mortal; **s. à caution,** unconfirmed (*news etc*); **s. à oublier/mentir,** apt *or* liable to forget/given to lying; **(b)** *Jur* **s. à,** liable to, subject to (*tax etc*); **(c)** *Arch* (*soumis*) dependent. **2** *n* (*d'un État, d'un souverain*) subject.

sujet[2] *nm* **(a)** (*cause*) cause, reason, grounds (**de qch,** for sth; **de faire,** for doing); **un s. de pitié,** an object of pity; **le Déluge avait été le s. de ses études,** the Flood had been the object of his studies; **je n'ai pas eu s. de me plaindre,** I had no cause *or* reason *or* grounds for complaint *or* complaining; **si je me plains c'est que j'en ai s.,** if I complain I have good cause *or* reason; **se mettre en colère sans s.,** to lose one's temper without *or* for no good reason *or* cause; **agir avec s.,** to act with good reason *or* cause;

(b) au s. de qn/de qch, relating to *or* concerning *or* about s.o./sth; **au s. de votre lettre,** with reference to your letter; **éprouver des craintes au s. de qch,** to have fears about sth;

(c) (*question*) subject (matter), theme (*of speech, book, play, picture, discussion etc*); subject, topic (*of conversation*); *Mus* subject (*of fugue etc*); **un beau s. de roman,** a fine subject for a novel; *Scol* **une dissertation hors (du) s., un hors s.,** a dissertation that doesn't deal with the subject;

(d) *Gram* **s. du verbe,** subject of the verb; **inversion du s.,** inversion of the subject;

(e) *Psy Méd etc* subject (*of an experiment*), *F* guinea pig;

(f) (*individu*) individual, fellow; *Vieilli* **mauvais s.,** bad lot, ne'er-do-well; *Vieilli* **bon s.,** steady *or* reliable person; *Scol* **brilliant s.,** brilliant pupil;

(g) (*en horticulture*) stock;

(h) (*en logique*) & *Ling* subject; **le s. parlant/pensant,** the speaker/thinker.

sujétion [syʒesjɔ̃] *nf* **(a)** (*servitude*) subjection (**à,** to); **s.**

aux lois, subservience to the laws; **une habitude devient vite une s.,** we soon become slaves to a habit; **(b)** (*contrainte*) constraint; **emploi d'une grande s.,** job that keeps one tied down.

sulfamide [sylfamid] *nm Ch Br* sulphonamide, *US* sulfonamide; *Méd* sulpha *or US* sulfa drug.

sulfatage [sylfataʒ] *nm* **(a)** *Ch Ind* sulphating, *US* sulfating; *Él* corrosion (*on battery terminals*); **(b)** treating (*of vines*) with copper sulphate *or US* sulfate.

sulfate [sylfat] *nm Ch* sulphate, *US* sulfate.

sulfaté [sylfate] *adj Ch* sulphated, *US* sulfated (*lime etc*).

sulfater [sylfate] *vt Agr Ind* to sulphate, *US* to sulfate.

sulfateuse [sylfatøz] *nf* **(a)** (*pour la vigne*) sulphate *or US* sulfate sprayer; **(b)** *Arg* (*mitraillette*) submachine-gun.

sulfhydrique [sylfidrik] *adj Ch* **acide s.,** hydrogen sulphide *or US* sulfide.

sulfite [sylfit] *nm Ch* sulphite, *US* sulfite.

sulfurage [sylfyraʒ] *nm Agr etc* sulphurizing, *US* sulfurizing.

sulfuration [sylfyrasjɔ̃] *nf Ch* sulphur(iz)ation, *US* sulfurization.

sulfure [sylfyr] *nm Ch* sulphide, *US* sulfide; **s. de fer,** iron pyrites.

sulfuré [sylfyre] *adj Ch* sulphuretted, *US* sulfuretted; **hydrogène s.,** hydrogen sulphide *or US* sulfide, sulphuretted *or US* sulfuretted hydrogen; *Minér* **fer s.,** iron pyrites.

sulfurer [sylfyre] *vt Agr etc* to sulphurize, *US* to sulfurize.

sulfureux, -euse [sylfyrø, -øz] *adj Ch* sulphurous, *US* sulfurous; sulphur, *US* sulfur (*water, spring*).

sulfurique [sylfyrik] *adj Ch* sulphuric, *US* sulfuric.

sulfurisé [sylfyrize] *adj* sulphurized, *US* sulfurized; **papier s.,** greaseproof paper.

sulky [sylki] *nm Courses de chevaux* sulky; (*pl sulkies*).

sultan [syltɑ̃] *nm* sultan.

sultanat [syltana] *nm* sultanate.

sultane [syltan] *nf* (*épouse d'un sultan*) sultana, sultaness.

sumac [symak] *nm Bot* sumac(h).

sumérien, -ienne [symerjɛ̃, -jɛn] **1** *adj* Sumerian. **2** *nm Ling* Sumerian. **3** *n* **S.,** Sumerian.

summum [sɔmɔm] *nm* acme, summit; **au s. de la gloire,** at the height of glory.

sunlight [sœnlait] *nm Cin* sun lamp.

sunnite [synit] *adj & n Rel* Sunni.

super[1] [sypɛr] *F* **1** *adj* (*bon*) super, great, terrific. **2** *nm Aut* (= **supercarburant**) *Br* four-star petrol, *Am* premium *or* hi-test gas.

super[2] [sype] **1** *vt Nau* (*of pump*) to suck. **2** *vi* **(a)** (*of pipe etc*) to get blocked; **(b) navire supé,** ship stuck in the mud.

super- [sypɛr] *préf F* (*hors de commun*) (*avant nom*) super-; (*avant adj*) ultra-; **s.-professeur/bombe,** superteacher/bomb; **s.-chic,** ultra-chic.

superbe [sypɛrb] **1** *adj* **(a)** (*magnifique, remarquable*) superb, magnificent (*building, weather, show, horse etc*); **il fait des affaires superbes,** he is doing splendid *or* excellent business; **(b)** (*beau*) (very) beautiful. **2** *nf Arch & Litt* pride, haughtiness.

superbement [sypɛrbəmɑ̃] *adv* **(a)** superbly, magnificently; **(b)** *Arch* (*orgueilleusement*) proudly, haughtily.

supercagnotte [sypɛrkaɲɔt] *nf F* (*de loterie etc*) grand jackpot.

supercarburant [sypɛrkarbyrɑ̃] *nm Aut* high-octane petrol *or Am* gasoline.

supercherie [sypɛrʃəri] *nf* deception.

superciment [sypɛrsimɑ̃] *nm Constr* rapid-hardening (Portland) cement.

supérette [syperɛt] *nf* mini-market, (small) supermarket.

superfétation [sypɛrfetasjɔ̃] *nf Litt* superfluity (*of words etc*).

superfétatoire [sypɛrfetatwar] *adj* superfluous.

superficialité [sypɛrfisjalite] *nf* superficiality.

superficie [sypɛrfisi] *nf* **(a)** (*surface*) surface; **(b)** (*étendue*) (surface) area (*of field, triangle etc*); **(c)** *Fig* **tout en s.,** all on the surface, entirely superficial.

superficiel, -ielle [sypɛrfisjɛl] *adj* superficial (*area, wound, knowledge, reply, observer etc*); superficial, skin-deep (*beauty*); superficial, shallow (*mind*); *Géog* **eau superficielle,** surface water; *Phys* **tension superficielle,** surface tension.

superficiellement [sypɛrfisjɛlmɑ̃] *adv* superficially.

superfin [sypɛrfɛ̃] *adj Com* superfine.

superflu [sypɛrfly] **1** *adj* **(a)** superfluous (*weight, explanation etc*); vain, useless (*regrets*); **(b)** *Ordinat* redundant. **2** *nm* (*caractère*) superfluity; (*ce qui est superflu*) surplus.

superfluité [sypɛrflyite] *nf Litt* superfluity.

super-grand [sypɛrgrɑ̃] *nm* superpower; **s.-g. de la presse,** press baron *or* tycoon; (*pl super-grands*).

supérieur, -ieure [syperjœr] **1** *adj* **(a)** (*plus haut*) upper (*storey, limb, province etc*);

(b) (*d'une valeur plus grande*) superior (**à,** to); **s. à la moyenne,** above *or* better than average; **être s. en poids/en nombre,** to be superior in weight/numbers; **lutter** *ou* **combattre contre des forces supérieures,** to fight against superior odds *or* forces; **se montrer s. aux événements,** to rise above events; **être s. à la tâche,** to be more than equal to the task; **un esprit s.,** superior mind; **nommer qn à un emploi s.,** to appoint s.o. to a higher post; **il se croit s. à tout le monde,** he thinks he's above everyone else, he thinks he's superior;

(c) (*dans une hiérarchie*) higher, upper; *Scol* advanced (*course*); *Mil etc* **un commandement s.,** a senior command; **classes supérieures,** upper classes (*of society*); *Scol* upper forms; **enseignement s.,** higher education; **offre supérieure,** higher bid; **les animaux supérieurs,** the higher animals; *Jur* **cour supérieure,** higher court;

(d) *Com* **de qualité supérieure,** of superior quality;

(e) (*hautain*) superior, condescending (*manner, tone*).

2 *n* **(a)** *Admin etc* superior; **il est mon s. hiérarchique,** he is my senior;

(b) *Rel* superior; **la Mère supérieure, la Supérieure,** the Mother Superior.

supérieurement [syperjœrmɑ̃] *adv* exceptionally.

supériorité [syperjɔrite] *nf* superiority (**de, in**); **s. d'âge,** seniority; **un air de s.,** an air of superiority; **s. numérique/intellectuelle,** numerical/intellectual superiority; **s. sur les marchés mondiaux,** command of the world markets; **lutter contre une s. écrasante,** to fight against overwhelming odds.

superlatif, -ive [sypɛrlatif, -iv] **1** *adj* superlative. **2** *nm Gram* superlative; **s. relatif/absolu,** relative/absolute superlative; **laid au s.,** superlatively ugly.

superlativement [sypɛrlativmɑ̃] *adv F* superlatively.

super-léger [sypɛrleʒe] *nm Boxe* (*boxeur, catégorie*) light welterweight; (*pl super-légers*).

superman [sypɛrman] *nm F* superman; **jouer les supermen,** to act the superman; (*pl supermen*).

supermarché [sypɛrmarʃe] *nm* supermarket.

supernova [sypɛrnɔva] *nf Astron* supernova.

superpétrolier [sypɛrpetrɔlje] *nm* supertanker.

superphosphate [sypɛrfɔsfat] *nm Agr* superphosphate.

superposable [sypɛrpozabl] *adj* superimposable (*images etc*); **chaise/table s.,** stacking chair/table.

superposé [sypɛrpoze] *adj* superimposed (*images etc*); *Él Électron* superposed; **lits superposés,** bunk beds.

superposer [sypɛrpoze] **1** *vt* to superpose, to pile (*boxes etc*) (**à,** (up)on); to stack (*chairs, tables etc*); to superimpose (*images etc*). **2 se superposer** *vpr* (*of pictures etc*) to be superimposed.

superposition [sypɛrpozisjɔ̃] *nf* superposition (*of triangles, geological strata etc*); *Phot Cin* superimposition; *Ordinat* **mode de s. d'écriture,** overwrite mode.

superproduction [sypɛrprɔdyksjɔ̃] *nf Cin Th* spectacular.

superprofit [sypɛrprɔfi] *nm* huge profit.

superpuissance [sypɛrpɥisɑ̃s] *nf Pol* superpower.

supersonique [sypɛrsɔnik] *adj* supersonic.

superstar [sypɛrstar] *nf* superstar.

superstitieusement [sypɛrstisjøzmɑ̃] *adv* superstitiously.

superstitieux, -euse [sypɛrstisjø, -øz] *adj* superstitious.

superstition [sypɛrstisjɔ̃] *nf* superstition; **avoir la s. du passé,** to be foolishly attached to the past.

superstrat [sypɛrstra] *nm Ling* superstratum.

superstructure [sypɛrstryktyr] *nf* superstructure.

supertanker [sypɛrtɑ̃kœr] *nm* supertanker.

superviser [sypɛrvize] *vt* to supervise; *Ordinat* to control.

superviseur [sypɛrvizœr] *nm* supervisor.

supervision [sypɛrvizjɔ̃] *nf* supervision.

supin [sypɛ̃] *nm Gram* supine.

supplanter [syplɑ̃te] *vt* to supplant, to supersede.

suppléance [sypleɑ̃s] *nf* (*fonction*) temporary *or* supply post; (*action*) temporary replacement; **remplir une s.,** to deputize for *or* stand in for someone.

suppléant [sypleɑ̃] **1** *n* substitute (**de,** for); (*professeur*) supply teacher; *Méd* locum; *Th* understudy. **2** *adj* **(a)** acting, temporary (*official etc*); surrogate (*judge*); **professeur s.,** (assistant) lecturer; (*remplaçant*) supply teacher; **(b)** *Gram* substitute (*verb etc*).

suppléer [syplee] **1** *vt Arch & Litt* **(a)** (*remplacer*) to supply, to make up (for) (*what is lacking*); to take the place of, to deputize for (*s.o.*); **se faire s.,** to find a substitute *or* a deputy for oneself; **(b)** (*ajouter*) to supply. **2** *vi* **s. à qch,** to make up *or* compensate for sth; **s. au vin par le cidre,** to eke out the wine with cider; **s. à un poste vacant,** to fill a vacant post.

supplément [syplemɑ̃] *nm* **(a)** (*surcroît*) **un s. de,** additional, extra (*information, work etc*); **en s.,** extra; **(b)** (*somme*) extra *or* additional charge; *Rail* excess fare, supplement; **s. de prix,** extra charge; **s. de solde,** extra pay; **s. d'imposition,** additional tax; *Rail* **train à s.,** = train in which an excess fare or a supplement is charged; **(c)** supplement (*book, magazine etc*); **(d)** (*plat de restaurant*) extra (dish); **(e)** *Math* supplement (*of an angle*).

supplémentaire [syplemɑ̃tɛr] *adj* additional, extra, further; *Ind* **une heure s.,** an hour's overtime; **faire des heures supplémentaires,** to do *or* work overtime; *Rail* **train s.,** relief train; *Math* **angles supplémentaires,** supplementary angles; *Mus* **lignes supplémentaires,** ledger lines, added lines.

supplémenter [syplemɑ̃te] *vt* **s. un billet,** to issue a supplementary ticket for an excess fare.

supplétif, -ive [sypletif, -iv] *adj & nm Mil* auxiliary.

suppliant [syplijɑ̃] **1** *adj* imploring, pleading (*look etc*); **d'un air s.,** imploringly. **2** *n* suppliant, supplicant.

supplication [syplikasjɔ̃] *nf* entreaty, plea; *Rel* supplication.

supplice [syplis] *nm* **(a)** (*torture*) torture; **le s. du fouet,** the penalty of the lash; **le dernier s.,** capital punishment, the extreme penalty; **(b)** (*tourment*) torment, agony; *Fig* **la goutte est un s.,** gout is agony *or* a real torture; **être au s.,** to be in agonies; **mettre qn au s.,** to torment *or* torture s.o..

supplicié [syplisje] *n* victim of torture.

supplicier [syplisje] *vt* (*impf & pr sub* **n. suppliciions, v. suppliciiez**) to torture (*s.o.*).

supplier [syplije] *vt* (*impf & pr sub* **n. suppliions, v. suppliiez**) to beseech, to beg, to implore; **s. qn pour obtenir qch,** to beg s.o. for sth; **s. qn de faire qch,** to implore *or* entreat *or* beg s.o. to do sth; **ne dites rien, je vous en supplie,** say nothing, I beg you.

supplique [syplik] *nf* petition.

support [sypɔr] *nm* **(a)** (*étai*) support, prop, stay; *Menuis* strut; **(b)** *Hér* supporter (*of shield*); **(c)** *Tech* rest (*for tools etc*); stand (*for lamp, test tube etc*); holder (*for memo block etc*); mount (*of photograph*); *Archit Constr* support (*of structure, arch etc*); **s. de bicyclette,** bicycle stand; **s. pour bicyclettes,** bicycle rack; **s. plantaire,** arch support; **(d)** bearer, bracket, support (*of machine part*); **(e)** *Nau* bracket, crutch (*of spar, appliances*); **(f)** *Él* (electrode) support; **(g)** *Phot Cin* backing (*of emulsion*); **s. audio-visuel,** audio-visual aids; *Com* **s. publicitaire,** publicity *or* advertising medium; **(h)** *Ordinat* **s. (d'information),** medium.

supportable [sypɔrtabl] *adj* **(a)** (*tolérable*) bearable, endurable (*pain etc*); tolerable (*behaviour*); **pas s.,** unbearable (*pain etc*); intolerable (*behaviour*); **(b)** (*correct*) tolerably good, fair.

supportablement [sypɔrtabləmɑ̃] *adv* fairly well, tolerably well.

supporter¹ [sypɔrtɛr] *nm Sp* supporter.

supporter² [sypɔrte] **1** *vt* **(a)** (*soutenir*) to support, to prop, to hold up (*ceiling, arch etc*); to support, to back up (*person, policy, theory etc*); to bear (*cost of sth*); *Sp F* to support (*team*);

(b) to endure, to withstand (*heat, misfortune etc*); to be equal to (*test*); to stand up to (*investigation*); to take, to carry (*one's drink*); *Nau* to weather (*storm*); **s. de lourdes responsabilités,** to shoulder great responsibilities; **s. les conséquences d'un acte,** to bear the consequences of an action; **il ne supporte plus de se coucher tard,** he can't take staying up late any longer;

(c) (*tolérer*) to tolerate, to put up with, to stand (*rudeness etc*); **je ne peux pas le s.,** I can't stand him; **ne pouvoir s. que qn fasse qch,** to be unable to stand s.o. doing sth.

2 se supporter *vpr* **ils ne peuvent pas se s.,** they can't stand each other; **cela ne peut pas se s.,** that is intolerable.

supporteur, -trice [sypɔrtœr, -tris] *n Sp* supporter.

supposé [sypoze] *adj* **(a)** supposed, alleged (*thief etc*); supposed (*author*); **(b)** assumed, false, fictitious (*name etc*); forged (*will*).

supposer [sypoze] **1** *vt* **(a)** (*imaginer*) to suppose, to assume; **l'auteur suppose tout et ne prouve rien,** the author assumes everything and proves nothing; **s. vrai ce qui est en question,** to beg the question; **en supposant que** *+sub*, **à s. que** *+sub*, **supposons que** *+sub*, suppose that; **on suppose que ...** *+ind*, it is thought *or* inferred that...; **suppose qu'il revienne,** suppose (that) he comes back; **elle lui supposait une grande fortune,** she assumed he had *or* credited him with a large fortune; **tu es supposé le savoir,** you are supposed to know it; **on le suppose à Paris, on suppose qu'il est à Paris,** he is supposed to be in Paris; **supposez-vous à Paris,** imagine yourself in Paris;

(b) (*impliquer*) to presuppose, to imply; **cela lui suppose du courage,** it implies courage on his part;

(c) *Jur* to put forward (*impostor*); to present (*forged will*).

2 *vi* **vous avez supposé juste,** you guessed right; **tu as raison, je suppose,** you are right, I suppose.

supposition [sypozisjɔ̃] *nf* supposition, conjecture, assumption; **si par s. il revenait,** supposing (that) he came back; *F* **une s. qu'elle soit en retard,** supposing she's late.

suppositoire [sypozitwar] *nm Méd* suppository.

suppôt [sypo] *nm* henchman; **s. de Satan** *ou* **du diable,** hellhound, fiend.

suppression [sypresjɔ̃] *nf* **(a)** abolition (*of law, tax etc*); suppression (*of newspaper etc*); discontinuance (*of service etc*); removal (*of difficulty*); **s. d'un emploi,** axing of a job; **la Commission pour la s. du bruit,** the Noise Abatement Commission; **(b)** *Jur* suppression (*of document, fact*); **(c)** *Ordinat* deletion.

supprimable [syprimabl] *adj* suppressible.

supprimer [syprime] **1** *vt* **(a)** to suppress (*newspaper, document etc*); to abolish, to do away with (*law, tax etc*); to discontinue (*service etc*); to put an end to, to withdraw (*credit*); to omit, to leave out (*word, sentence*); to cancel (*train etc*); to axe (*job*); to remove (*difficulty*); to dispose of (*objections*); to quell (*revolt*); *Ordinat* to delete; **l'avion supprime les distances,** air travel makes distance irrelevant; **vous devez s. le sucre de votre alimentation,** you must cut sugar out of your diet; *F* **s. qn,** to kill s.o., to bump s.o. off; *Typ* **à s.,** delete; **la première partie du concert a été supprimée,** the first part of the concert was cancelled;

(b) *Jur* to suppress, to withhold (*document, fact*);

(c) **s. qch à qn,** to deprive s.o. of sth.

2 se supprimer *vpr F* **se s.,** to commit suicide, *F* to top oneself.

suppurant [sypyrɑ̃] *adj Méd* suppurating.

suppuration [sypyrasjɔ̃] *nf* suppuration.

suppurer [sypyre] *vi* (*of wound, sore*) to suppurate.

supputation [sypytasjɔ̃] *nf* computation, calculation.

supputer [sypyte] *vt* to compute, to calculate; **s. ses chances,** to calculate one's chances.

supra [sypra] *adv* (*renvoi*) supra.

supra- [sypra] *préf* supra-.

supraconducteur [syprakɔ̃dyktœr] *nm Phys Él* superconductor.

supraconductivité [syprakɔ̃dyktivite] *nf Phys Él* superconductivity.

supranational, -aux [sypranasjɔnal, -o] *adj* supranational.

supraterrestre [sypratɛrɛstr] *adj* superterrestrial.

suprématie [sypremasi] *nf* supremacy.

suprême [syprɛm] **1** *adj* **(a)** supreme (*effort, happiness etc*); highest (*degree*); **le pouvoir s.,** sovereignty; **(b)** last (*requests, moments*). **2** *nm Culin* suprême; **s. de volaille,** chicken suprême.

suprêmement [syprɛmmɑ̃] *adv* supremely.

sur¹ [syr] *prép* **(a)** on, upon; (*avec mouvement*) on (to); **assis s. une chaise,** sitting on a chair; **'virages s. 2 kilomètres',** 'bends for 2 kilometres'; **ville s. la Seine,** town on the Seine; **se promener s. l'avenue,** to walk in the avenue; **je suis venu s. le bateau,** I came by boat; *F* **la clef est s. la porte,** the key is in the door; **je n'ai pas d'argent s. moi,** I have no money on me; **fenêtre qui donne s. le jardin,** window which looks on to the garden; **la police a tiré s. la foule,** the police fired on *or* at the crowd; **tu es tombé s. la tête?,** are you mad?; **tirage photo s. papier brillant,** print on glossy paper; **page s. page,** page after page; **juger qn s. la mine,** to judge s.o. by appearances; **s. sa bonne réputation,** on the strength of his good reputation; **s. un ton de reproche,** in a reproachful tone; **chanter qch s. un certain air,** to sing sth to a certain tune; **vente s. catalogue,** mail order; **s. une fausse accusation,** on a false charge;

(b) **marcher** *ou* **fonctionner s.,** to work *or* operate on *or* off;

(c) (*vers*) towards; **avancer s. qn,** to advance on s.o.; **s. votre gauche,** on *or* to your left; **les trains s. Orléans,** the trains for Orleans;

(d) (*au-dessus de*) over, above; **les astres s. nos têtes,** the stars above our heads; **dormir s. son travail,** to go to sleep over one's work; **être s. un travail,** to be engaged in *or* on a piece of work; **avoir autorité s. qn,** to have authority over s.o.; **s. toute(s) chose(s),** above all (things); **un pont s. une rivière,** a bridge across a river;

(e) (*à propos de*) on, about, concerning; **s. ce point,** on this point;

(f) (*temps*) about (*midday*); towards (*evening*); **s. mes dix-huit ans,** when I was about eighteen;

(g) s. ce, s. quoi, whereupon; **s. ce, je vous quitte,** and now I must leave you; **il est s. son départ,** he is about to leave;

(h) (*parmi*) out of; **un professeur s. cinq,** one teacher in *or* out of five; **huit s. dix,** (*note*) eight out of ten; **une fois s. deux,** every other time; **on paie les pompiers s. les fonds de la ville,** the firemen are paid out of the municipal coffers;

(i) (*mesure*) by; **huit mètres s. six,** eight metres by six.

sur² *adj* sour, tart (*fruit etc*).

sur- [syr] *préf* over-; **surévaluer,** to overvalue; **suremploi,** overemployment.

sûr [syr] **1** *adj* **(a)** (*sans danger*) safe (*locality, shelter, beach etc*); **peu s.,** unsafe; **en lieu s.,** in a safe place;

(b) (*digne de confiance*) trustworthy, reliable (*person, memory*); trusty, true, staunch (*friend*); reliable (*information, firm*); **temps s.,** settled weather; **avoir le coup d'œil s.,** to have an accurate eye; **goût s.,** discerning taste; **avoir la main sûre/le pied s.,** to have a steady hand/to be surefooted; **frapper un coup s.** *ou* **à coup s.,** to strike an unerring blow; **mettre son argent en mains sûres,** to put one's money into safe hands;

(c) (*certain*) certain, sure; **il l'a oublié, c'est s.,** he has forgotten it, that's for certain *or* sure; **c'est une affaire sûre,** it's a certainty *or* a sure thing *or F* a dead cert; **être s. de réussir,** to be sure of success; **être s. de qch,** to be sure *or* certain of sth; **je suis s. de lui,** I can depend on him; **s. de soi,** self-assured; *F* **j'en suis s. et certain,** I'm absolutely certain *or* sure of it; **parier à coup s.,** to bet on a certainty; **à coup s.,** for certain, without fail.

2 *nm* **jouer au plus s.,** to play for safety; **le plus s. serait de ...,** the safest course *or* thing would be to ...; **pour le plus s.,** to be on the safe side.

3 *adv F* surely; **s.!,** of course!, *Am* sure!; **pas s.!,** perhaps not!; *F* **bien s.!, pour s.!,** of course!, *Am* sure!; *F* **bien s.?,** you really mean it?; **bien s. que non!,** of course not!

surabondance [syrabɔ̃dɑ̃s] *nf* superabundance, overabundance; *Com* glut.

surabondant [syrabɔ̃dɑ̃] *adj* superabundant, overabundant.

surabonder [syrabɔ̃de] *vi* to be overabundant *or* superabundant; **s. de** *ou* **en qch,** to have an overabundance *or* superabundance of sth.

suractivité [syraktivite] *nf Physiol* overactivity.

surah [syra] *nm Tex* syrah.

suraigu, -uë [syregy] *adj* high-pitched.

surajouter [syraʒute] **1** *vt* to add on top. **2 se surajouter** *vpr* to be added on top.

suralimentation [syralimɑ̃tɑsjɔ̃] *nf* **(a)** (*de personne*) overfeeding; *Méd* feeding up; **(b)** *Aut* (*de moteur*) supercharging.

suralimenter [syralimɑ̃te] *vt* **(a)** to overfeed; *Méd* to feed up (*person*); **(b)** to supercharge (*engine*).

suranné [syrane] *adj* **(a)** (*vieilli*) outdated, old-fashioned; **beauté surannée,** faded beauty; **(b)** *Arch* (*qui a expiré*) expired (*passport etc*).

surarmement [syrarməmɑ̃] *nm Mil* excessive build-up of arms.

surbaissé [syrbese] *adj* **(a)** *Archit* depressed, flattened (*arch, vault*); **(b)** *Aut etc* dropped (*axle, frame etc*); (extra-)low, underslung (*chassis*); **taille surbaissée,** (*d'une robe*) drop waist.

surbaissement [syrbɛsmɑ̃] *nm Archit* surbasement.

surbaisser [syrbese] *vt* **(a)** *Archit* to surbase, to flatten, to depress (*arch, vault*); **(b)** *Aut etc* to drop, to undersling (*frame etc*).

surboum [syrbum] *nf F Vieilli* party.

surcapacité [syrkapasite] *nf Ind etc* overcapacity, surplus production capacity.

surcapitalisation [syrkapitalizɑsjɔ̃] *nf* overcapitalization.

surcharge [syrʃarʒ] *nf* **(a)** *Tech* overload, *Él* overcharge (*of accumulator*); *Fig* **une s. de travail/de responsabilités/de soucis,** extra work/responsibilities/worries; **(b)** excess load (*in vehicle*); excess weight (*of luggage*); **prendre des passagers en s.,** to take on excess passengers; **(c)** weight handicap (*of racehorse*); **(d)** (*à payer*) surcharge; **(e)** (*dans un contrat etc*) alteration; (*imprimée sur une timbre-poste*) surcharge.

surcharger [syrʃarʒe] *vt* (**je surchargeai(s); n. surchargeons**) **(a)** to overload (*vehicle, horse, one's stomach etc*); *Él* to overcharge (*accumulator*); *Fig* **s. ses employés de travail,** to overwork one's employees; *Fin* **s. le marché,** to overload *or* glut the market; **(b)** *Typ* to write over (*other words*); to surcharge, to overprint (*postage stamp*).

surchauffe [syrʃof] *nf* **(a)** overheating (*of oven*); **(b)** superheating (*of steam*); **(c)** superheat (*in steam*); **(d) s. (économique),** overheating (*of the economy*).

surchauffer [syrʃofe] *vt* **(a)** to overheat (*oven etc*); **salle surchauffée,** overheated room; **(b)** to superheat (*steam*).

surchoix [syrʃwa] *Com* **1** *nm* finest quality. **2** *adj inv* top quality (*product*).

surclasser [syrklase] *vt* to outclass.

surcompensation [syrkɔ̃pɑ̃sɑsjɔ̃] *nf Psy* overcompensation.

surcomposé [syrkɔ̃poze] *adj Gram* double-compound (*tense*).

surcompression [syrkɔ̃presjɔ̃] *nf Tech* supercharging.

surcomprimer [syrkɔ̃prime] *vt Tech* to supercharge.

surconsommation [syrkɔ̃sɔmɑsjɔ̃] *nf Écon* overconsumption.

surcontrer [syrkɔ̃tre] *vt Cartes* to redouble.

surcouper [syrkupe] *vt Cartes* to overtrump.

surcroît [syrkrwa] *nm* **un s. de,** extra; **avoir un grand s. de travail,** to have a great deal of extra work; **un s. d'effort,** an extra effort; **pour donner un s. d'effet à ...,** to give an added effect to ...; **par s., de s.,** in addition, moreover; **par s. de besogne,** to add to my work; **pour s. de malheur,** to make matters worse.

surdéveloppé [syrdevlɔpe] *adj Écon* highly developed; (*excessivement*) overdeveloped.

surdéveloppement [syrdevlɔpmɑ̃] *nm Écon* high state of development; (*excessif*) overdevelopment.

surdi-mutité [syrdimytite] *nf* deaf-muteness.

surdité [syrdite] *nf* deafness; **s. musicale,** tone deafness.

surdosage [syrdozaʒ] *nm Méd* overdosage.

surdoué, -ée [syrdwe] *adj & n* exceptionally gifted (child).

sureau, -eaux [syro] *nm* elder (tree); **baie de s.,** elderberry.

sureffectif [syrefektif] *nm* excessive numbers; **personnel en s.,** excessive numbers of staff.

surélévation [syrelevɑsjɔ̃] *nf* (*action*) raising; (*augmentation de hauteur*) increase in height.

surélevé [syrɛlve] *adj* **(a)** elevated (*railway*); **(b)** *Archit* raised (*arch etc*).

surélever [syrɛlve] *vt* (*conj like* **élever**) *Constr etc* to heighten, to raise.

sûrement [syrmɑ̃] *adv* **(a)** (*sans hésiter*) steadily, unhesitatingly, confidently; **(b)** (*certainement*) surely, certainly; **s.!,** certainly!; **s. pas!,** certainly not!; **il va s. y avoir des changements,** there are sure to be (some) changes; **(c)** (*sans risques*) safely; **(d) frapper s.,** to strike an unerring blow.

surémission [syremisjɔ̃] *nf Fin* overissue.

suremploi [syrɑ̃plwa] *nm* overemployment.

surenchère [syrɑ̃ʃɛr] *nf* **(a)** *Com* higher bid; **faire une s. sur qn,** to outbid s.o.; **(b)** *Fig* **une s. de violence,** ever-increasing violence; **faire de la s.,** to try to go one better than *or* outdo one's rivals; **faire de la s. électorale,** to make more extravagant promises to catch the votes.

surenchérir [syrɑ̃ʃerir] *vi* **(a)** *Com* to bid higher; *Fig* to try to outdo each other; **s. sur qn,** to outbid s.o., to bid higher than s.o.; *Fig* to try to outdo s.o. *or* go one better than s.o.; **(b)** (*devenir plus cher*) to rise in price.

surencombré [syrɑ̃kɔ̃bre] *adj* (*severely*) congested (*street etc*) (**de,** with).

surencombrement [syrɑ̃kɔ̃brəmɑ̃] *nm* (severe) congestion.

surentraînement [syrɑ̃trɛnmɑ̃] *nm Sp* overtraining.

surentraîner [syrɑ̃trene] *vt Sp* to overtrain.

suréquipement [syrekipmɑ̃] *nm Écon* overequipment.

suréquiper [syrekipe] *vt Écon* to overequip.

surestimation [syrɛstimɑsjɔ̃] *nf* overestimate, overvaluation.

surestimer [syrɛstime] **1** *vt* to overestimate (*importance, ability, price etc*); to overvalue (*work of art etc*); **s. qn,** to overrate s.o.. **2 se surestimer** *vpr* to think too highly of oneself.

suret, -ette [syrɛ, -ɛt] *adj* sour(ish), tart (*fruit, taste etc*).
sûreté [syrte] *nf* **(a)** (*absence de danger*) safety; **lieu de s.,** place of safety; **être en s.,** to be safe *or* in a safe place *or* out of harm's way; **mettre qn en (lieu de) s.,** (*en prison*) to put s.o. in prison; (*à l'abri*) to put s.o. in a safe place *or* out of harm's way; **pour plus de s.,** for greater safety; **rasoir/serrure de s.,** safety razor/lock; **(b)** *Pol etc* security; **la s. de l'État,** state security; **la S. (nationale),** the (French) criminal investigation department, *Br* ≈ the CID, *US* ≈ the FBI; **agent de la S.,** detective; **(c)** sureness (*of hand, foot*); soundness (*of vision, taste, judgment*); unerringness (*of blow, stroke*); **s. de soi,** self-confidence, self-assurance; **(d)** *Com* (*garantie*) surety, guarantee.
surévaluer [syrevalɥe] *vt* to overvalue.
surexcitable [syrɛksitabl] *adj* overexcitable, easily excited.
surexcitation [syrɛksitɑsjɔ̃] *nf* overexcitement.
surexciter [syrɛksite] *vt* to overexcite.
surexploitation [syrɛksplwatɑsjɔ̃] *nf* overexploitation.
surexploiter [syrɛksplwate] *vt* to overexploit (*land, workers etc*).
surexposer [syrɛkspoze] *vt Phot* to overexpose.
surexposition [syrɛkspozisjɔ̃] *nf Phot* overexposure.
surf [sœrf] *nm Sp* **(a)** (*sport*) surfing; **faire du s.,** to go surfing, to surf; **(b)** (*planche*) surfboard.
surface [syrfas] *nf* **(a)** surface; **eau de s.,** surface water; *Phys* **tension de s.,** surface tension (*of liquid*); **bruit de s.,** surface noise; **vitesse en s.,** (*de sous-marin*) surface speed; **nager en s.,** to swim near the surface; **faire s., revenir en s.,** (*of submarine*) to (break) surface; *F* (*of person*) to surface; **en s.,** (*travailler etc*) superficially; **tout en s.,** superficial; **(b)** *Géom* surface; **s. de révolution** *ou* **de rotation,** surface of revolution; **s. plane,** plane surface; **(c)** (*étendue etc*) (surface) area; **s. d'appui, s. de portée, s. portante,** bearing area *or* surface; **s. utile,** useful *or* working surface; *Constr* **s. couverte, s. au sol,** floor area; **s. de voilure,** sail area; *F* **il présente une s. financière suffisante,** his financial standing is satisfactory; **(magasin à) grande s.,** hypermarket; **grande s. de bricolage,** DIY centre.
surfaceuse [syrfasøz] *nf Tech* surfacer, planing machine.
surfaire [syrfɛr] *vt* (*conj like* **faire**) *Litt* **(a)** to ask too much for (*goods etc*); **(b)** to overestimate, to overrate (*person, talent etc*).
surfait [syrfɛ] *adj* excessive (*prices*); overrated (*person, reputation etc*).
surfilage [syrfilaʒ] *nm Couture* overcasting, oversewing.
surfiler [syrfile] *vt* **(a)** *Couture* to overcast, to oversew; **(b)** *Tex* to give an extra twist to (*thread*).
surfin [syrfɛ̃] *adj Com* superfine (*product*).
surgélateur [syrʒelatœr] *nm* freezer.
surgélation [syrʒelɑsjɔ̃] *nf* deep freezing, quick freezing.
surgelé [syrʒəle] **1** *adj* deep-frozen, quick-frozen. **2** *nmpl* **surgelés,** deep-frozen *or* quick-frozen foods.
surgeler [syrʒəle] *vt* (*conj like* **geler**) to deep-freeze, to quick-freeze.
surgénérateur [syrʒeneratœr] *adj & nm Phys Nucl* **(réacteur) s.,** breeder reactor.
surgeon [syrʒɔ̃] *nm* (*de plante*) sucker.
surgir [syrʒir] *vi* (*aux* **avoir,** *parfois* **être**) to appear suddenly; (*of plant*) to spring up; (*of difficulty*) to crop up; **faire s. de nouveaux problèmes,** to throw up new problems.
surgissement [syrʒismɑ̃] *nm Litt* sudden appearance.
surhaussé [syrose] *adj Archit* raised.
surhaussement [syrosmɑ̃] *nm Archit* raising; (*différence de hauteur*) increase in height.
surhausser [syrose] *vt Archit* to raise (*wall etc*).
surhomme [syrɔm] *nm* superman.
surhumain [syrymɛ̃] *adj* superhuman.
surimposer [syrɛ̃poze] *vt* (*par l'impôt*) to overtax.
surimposition [syrɛ̃pozisjɔ̃] *nf* **(a)** (*par l'impôt*) overtaxation; **(b)** *Géol* pseudomorphism.
surimpression [syrɛ̃presjɔ̃] *nf Phot Cin* superimposition.
surin [syrɛ̃] *nm Arg Vieilli* knife, dagger.
Surinam [syrinam] *nm* Surinam.
suriner [syrine] *vt Arg Vieilli* to knife (*s.o.*).
surinfection [syrɛ̃fɛksjɔ̃] *nf Méd* secondary infection.
surinformation [syrɛ̃fɔrmɑsjɔ̃] *nf* overinformation.
surinformé [syrɛ̃fɔrme] *adj* overinformed.
surintendance [syrɛ̃tɑ̃dɑ̃s] *nf Hist* superintendence.
surintendant [syrɛ̃tɑ̃dɑ̃] *nm Hist* superintendent.
surir [syrir] *vi* (*of wine, soup etc*) to turn sour.
surjet [syrʒɛ] *nm Couture* overcasting, whipping (*of seams*).
surjeter [syrʒəte] *vt* (*conj like* **jeter**) *Couture* to overcast, to whip (*seam*).
sur-le-champ [syrləʃɑ̃] *adv* at once, immediately.
surlendemain [syrlɑ̃dmɛ̃] *nm* **le s.,** the day after the next, two days later; **le s. de leur départ,** two days after their departure.
surligner [syrliɲe] *vt* to highlight.
surligneur [syrliɲœr] *nm* highlighter (pen).
surmenage [syrmənaʒ] *nm* **(a)** (*état*) overwork; **s. intellectuel,** mental fatigue; **(b)** (*action*) overworking.
surmenant [syrmənɑ̃] *adj* exhausting (*work etc*).
surmené [syrməne] *adj* overworked.
surmener [syrməne] *v* (*conj like* **mener**) **1** *vt* to overwork, to work (*employees, pupils etc*) too hard. **2 se surmener** *vpr* to overwork, to work too hard, *F* to overdo it.
sur-moi [syrmwa] *nm no pl Psy* superego.
surmontable [syrmɔ̃tabl] *adj* surmountable.
surmonter [syrmɔ̃te] **1** *vt* **(a)** (*être placé sur*) to surmount; **colonne surmontée d'une croix,** column surmounted *or* topped by a cross; **(b)** *Fig* to overcome, to surmount (*obstacle, difficulty*); to master, to get the better of (*one's anger, grief*); *Litt* to overcome (*one's enemies*). **2 se surmonter** *vpr* to master *or* control one's feelings.
surmortalité [syrmɔrtalite] *nf* excessively high death rate.
surmultiplication [syrmyltiplikɑsjɔ̃] *nf Aut* overdrive (system).
surmultiplié, -ée [syrmyltiplije] *adj & nf Aut* **(vitesse) surmultipliée,** overdrive.
surnager [syrnaʒe] *vi* (**je surnageai(s); n. surnageons**) **(a)** to float on the surface; **(b)** *Fig* to survive, to remain.
surnatalité [syrnatalite] *nf* excessively high birth rate.
surnaturel, -elle [syrnatyrɛl] **1** *adj* supernatural. **2** *nm* **le s.,** the supernatural.
surnom [syrnɔ̃] *nm* nickname.
surnombre [syrnɔ̃br] *nm* **en s.,** too many; **les exemplaires/passagers en s.,** the excess copies/passengers; **ils étaient en s.,** there were too many of them.
surnommer [syrnɔme] *vt* to nickname; **s. qn 'le Tigre',** to nickname s.o. 'The Tiger'.
surnuméraire [syrnymerɛr] *adj & n* supernumerary.
suroffre [syrɔfr] *nf* better offer, better bid.
suroît [syrwa] *nm* (*vent, chapeau*) sou'wester.
suroxygéner [syrɔksiʒene] *vt* (**je suroxygène, n. suroxygénons; je suroxygénerai**) *Ch* to superoxygenate.
surpaie [syrpɛj, -pɛ] *nf* overpaying, overpayment.
surpasser [syrpɑse] **1** *vt* to surpass, to exceed (*one's hopes*); to surpass, to outdo (*rival*); **dépense qui surpasse mes moyens,** expense beyond my means; **s. qn en éclat,** to outshine s.o.; **s. une armée en nombre,** to outnumber an army; *F* **cela me surpasse,** that beats me. **2 se surpasser** *vpr* to surpass oneself.
surpatte [syrpat] *nf F Vieilli* (*surprise-party*) party.
surpaye [syrpɛj, -pɛ] *nf* overpaying, overpayment.
surpayer [syrpeje] *vt* (*conj like* **payer**) to overpay (*s.o.*); to pay too much for (*sth*).
surpeuplé [syrpœple] *adj* overpopulated (*country, region etc*); overcrowded (*house etc*).
surpeuplement [syrpœpləmɑ̃] *nm* (*de pays etc*) overpopulation; (*de maison etc*) overcrowding.
sur(-)place [syrplas] *nm* balance (*of cyclist before starting a race*); *Aut F* **faire du s.(-)p.,** to crawl.
surplis [syrpli] *nm Rel* surplice.
surplomb [syrplɔ̃] *nm* overhang; **en s.,** overhanging.
surplombant [syrplɔ̃bɑ̃] *adj* overhanging.
surplomber [syrplɔ̃be] *vi & vt* to overhang.
surplus [syrply] *nm* surplus; **le s.,** the surplus, what is left (over); **le s. de marchandises,** the surplus goods, the goods that are left (over); **payer le s.,** to pay the difference; **au s.,** besides, what is more; **les s. du gouvernement,** government surplus (stock).
surpopulation [syrpɔpylɑsjɔ̃] *nf* overpopulation.
surprenant [syrprənɑ̃] *adj* amazing, astonishing; **chose surprenante,** strange to say; **rien de s. si ...,** I shouldn't be surprised if ...; **il est s. que vous le sachiez,** it is surprising that you should know of it.
surprendre [syrprɑ̃dr] *v* (*conj like* **prendre**) **1** *vt* **(a)** (*prendre sur le fait*) to surprise (*s.o.*); **aller s. un ami chez lui,** to drop in unexpectedly on a friend; **la nuit nous surprit,** night overtook us; **être surpris par la pluie,** to be caught in the rain; **s. qn à faire qch,** to catch s.o. (in the act of) doing sth; **(b)** (*découvrir*) to intercept (*letter, glance*); to overhear (*conversation etc*); **s. le secret de qn,** to find out s.o.'s secret; **(c)** (*étonner*) to surprise, to astonish; **ce qui me surprend c'est que ...,** what surprises

or astonishes me is that ...; **cela me surprendrait qu'il revienne** *ou* **s'il revenait,** I should be surprised *or* astonished if he came back; **ça a l'air de vous s.,** you seem surprised; **ce n'est pas pour me s.,** it doesn't surprise me in the least. **2 se surprendre** *vpr* **se s. à faire qch,** to find oneself doing sth.

surpression [syrpresjɔ̃] *nf Tech* overpressure, excessive pressure.

surprime [syrprim] *nf (d'assurance)* extra premium.

surpris [syrpri] *adj* surprised (*de*, at); **je m'arrêtai, s.,** I paused in surprise; **s., je les regardais,** I watched them in surprise; **s. que** + *sub*/**si** + *ind*, surprised that/if; **je ne serais pas s. qu'il revienne** *ou* **s'il revenait,** I should not *or* wouldn't be surprised if he came back.

surprise [syrpriz] *nf (étonnement, cadeau)* surprise; **à sa grande s.,** to his great surprise, much to his surprise; **à la s. générale,** to everyone's surprise; **s'emparer d'une ville par s.** *ou* **par un coup de s.,** to capture a town by surprise; **il m'a fait sa demande par s.,** he surprised me with his request, he sprang his request on me; **expédition/voyage sans s.,** uneventful expedition/journey; **craindre une s.,** to fear a sudden attack; **quelle bonne s.!,** what a pleasant surprise!; **attendez-vous à une drôle de s.,** be prepared for a shock; **boîte à s.,** Jack-in-the-box; **pochette s.,** lucky bag.

surprise-partie [syrprizparti] *nf* party; (*pl surprises-parties*).

surproduction [syrprɔdyksjɔ̃] *nf* overproduction.

surproduire [syrprɔdɥir] *vt & vi* to overproduce.

surpuissant [syrpɥisɑ̃] *adj* extremely powerful (*engine, country etc*).

surréalisme [syrealism] *nm* surrealism.

surréaliste [syrealist] *adj & n* surrealist.

surréel, -elle [syreɛl] **1** *adj* surreal(istic). **2** *nm* **le s.,** the surreal.

surrégénérateur, -trice [syreʒeneratœr, -tris] *adj & nm Phys Nucl* **(réacteur) s.,** breeder reactor.

surrénal, -aux [syrenal, -o] *adj Anat* suprarenal (*artery, ganglion*); adrenal (*gland*).

sursalaire [syrsalɛr] *nm* bonus.

sursaturé [syrsatyre] *adj* supersaturated (*solution*); *Fig* **s. de,** overwhelmed with.

sursaut [syrso] *nm* start, jump; **avoir** *ou* **faire un s.,** to (give a) start, to (give a) jump; **en s.,** with a start; **se lever en s.,** to start up; **dans un s. d'énergie,** with a (sudden) burst of energy; **un s. de terrorisme,** a new outbreak of terrorism.

sursauter [syrsote] *vi* to (give a) start, to (give a) jump; **faire s. qn,** to startle s.o.; **s. d'indignation,** to leap up in indignation.

surseoir [syrswar] *vi* (*prp* **sursoyant**; *pp* **sursis**; *pr ind* **je sursois, n. sursoyons**; *pr sub* **je sursoie**; *impf* **je sursoyais**; *p hist* **je sursis**; *fu* **je surseoirai**) *Jur* **s. à un jugement,** to suspend a judgement; **s. à l'exécution d'un condamné,** to reprieve a condemned man; **ordonnance de s. (à un jugement),** stay of execution.

sursis [syrsi] *nm Jur* stay of execution; (*de condamné à mort*) *& Fig* reprieve; **condamné à un an de prison avec s.,** given a suspended (prison) sentence of one year; *Mil* **s. d'appel,** deferment (of call-up); *Fig* **mort en s.,** condemned man.

sursitaire [syrsitɛr] *Mil* **1** *adj* provisionally exempted. **2** *nm* provisionally exempted conscript.

surtaux [syrto] *nm* overassessment.

surtaxe [syrtaks] *nf* **(a)** supertax, surtax, extra tax; (*de lettre etc*) surcharge; **(b)** (*excessive*) excessive tax.

surtaxer [syrtakse] *vt* **(a)** *Admin* to surtax; **(b)** to surcharge (*letter etc*).

surtension [syrtɑ̃sjɔ̃] *nf Él* overvoltage.

surtout[1] [syrtu] *adv* particularly, especially; (*avant tout*) above all; **ayez s. soin de ...,** be especially *or* particularly careful to ...; **s. n'oubliez pas de ...,** above all, do not forget to ...; **non, s. pas!,** no, certainly not!; *F* **s. que ...,** especially as ... .

surtout[2] *nm* **(a)** centrepiece, *US* centerpiece (*on dinner table*); **(b)** *Arch* (*manteau*) overcoat.

surveillance [syrvɛjɑ̃s] *nf* (*contrôle*) supervision; *Scol* invigilation; *Mil* observation, surveillance; *Rad* monitoring; (*en prenant soin de qn ou qch*) watch; **exercer une s. discrète sur qn/qch,** to keep a discreet watch on s.o./sth; **être sous la s. de la police,** to be under police observation *or* surveillance; *Mil* **avion/navire de s.,** surveillance plane/ship; **s. médicale,** medical supervision.

surveillant, -ante [syrvɛjɑ̃, -ɑ̃t] **1** *n Ind Admin etc* supervisor; (*de prison*) *Br* warder, *Am* guard; *Rail* inspector; *Scol* (*d'examen*) invigilator; (*chargé de la discipline*) supervisor. **2** *nf Méd* **surveillante,** head nurse, *Br* = (ward) sister.

surveiller [syrveje] **1** *vt* **(a)** (*contrôler*) to supervise (*work, workers etc*); to man (*machine*); *Scol* to invigilate (*exam*); *Mil* to observe; **(b)** (*prendre soin de*) to watch (over) (*s.o.*); **s. les enfants,** to watch (over) *or* keep an eye on the children; **s. la situation de près,** to keep a close eye on the situation; **s. son langage,** to watch *or* mind one's language; **s. sa ligne,** to watch one's figure; *Jur* **en liberté surveillée,** on probation; **le français parlé surveillé,** careful French speech; **(c)** *Rad* to monitor. **2 se surveiller** *vpr* to keep a watch on oneself.

survenir [syrvənir] *v* (*conj like* **venir**; *aux* **être**) **1** *vi* (*of events*) to happen, to occur; (*of crisis, difficulty*) to arise; (*of person*) to arrive unexpectedly. **2** *v impers* **s'il ne survient pas de complications,** if no complications arise *or* occur; **s'il survient un visiteur,** if a visitor happens to come.

survenue [syrvəny] *nf Litt* unexpected arrival, supervention.

survêt [syrvɛt] *nm F* = **SURVÊTEMENT**.

survêtement [syrvɛtmɑ̃] *nm* tracksuit.

survie [syrvi] *nf* survival; *Rel* afterlife; *Astronaut etc* **équipement de s.,** life support equipment; **une s. de quelques jours, quelques jours de s.,** a few more days of life.

survirer [syrvire] *vi Aut* to oversteer.

survivance [syrvivɑ̃s] *nf* **(a)** survival (*of the soul*); **(b)** (*vestige*) survival, relic (*of the past etc*).

survivant, -ante [syrvivɑ̃, -ɑ̃t] **1** *adj* surviving. **2** *n* survivor.

survivre [syrvivr] *v* (*conj like* **vivre**; *aux* **avoir**) **1** *vi* to survive; **s. à,** to survive, to outlive (*s.o.*); to outlive (*period, theory etc*); to survive (*accident, illness etc*); **va-t-il s.?,** will he live *or* survive? **2 se survivre** *vpr* **(a)** (*dans ses enfants, son œuvre etc*) to live on; **(b)** *Péj* (*of person who has become mediocre*) to outlive one's day.

survol [syrvɔl] *nm* **(a)** *Av* **le s. d'un lieu,** flying over a place; **(b)** *Fig* (*d'un problème etc*) cursory glance (**de,** at).

survoler [syrvɔle] *vt* **(a)** *Av* to fly over (*mountain, locality etc*); **(b)** *Fig* to get a general view of (*problem etc*).

survoltage [syrvɔltaʒ] *nm Él* boosting.

survolté [syrvɔlte] *adj* **(a)** *Él* boosted; **(b)** *F* (*surexcité*) excited, worked up.

survolteur [syrvɔltœr] *nm Él* booster.

sus [sy(s)] **1** *adv* **courir s. à son adversaire,** to rush upon *or* at one's opponent, to charge one's opponent; **en s. de,** in addition to, over and above (*sum of money*). **2** *int* **s. à l'ennemi!,** at them!

susceptibilité [sysɛptibilite] *nf* **(a)** touchiness, sensitiveness; **ménager la s. de qn,** to tread carefully where s.o. is concerned; **blesser les susceptibilités de qn,** to wound s.o.'s feelings; **(b)** (*en magnétisme*) susceptibility.

susceptible [sysɛptibl] *adj* **(a) s. de,** susceptible of (*proof, interpretation etc*); open to (*improvement*); **s. de faire qch,** (*capacité*) capable of doing sth; (*probabilité*) liable *or* likely to do sth; **(b)** (*facilement offensé*) touchy, sensitive, thin-skinned.

susciter [sysite] *vt* to give rise to (*difficulties*); to cause (*astonishment*); to arouse (*hostility, admiration, interest etc*); **s. des ennuis à qn,** to cause *or* create trouble for s.o..

suscription [syskripsjɔ̃] *nf Admin* address (*on letter*).

susdit, -ite [sysdi, -it] *adj & n Jur* aforesaid, above-mentioned.

sus-dominante [sysdɔminɑ̃t] *nf Mus* submediant; (*pl sus-dominantes*).

susmentionné, -ée [sysmɑ̃sjɔne] *adj & n Jur* above-mentioned, aforesaid.

susnommé, -ée [sysnɔme] *adj & n Jur* above-named.

suspect, -ecte [syspɛ(kt), -ɛkt(ə)] **1** *adj* suspicious, suspect (*person, action etc*); suspect (*ideas, evidence etc*); **s. de,** suspected of, under suspicion of; **cela m'est s.,** it looks suspicious *or* suspect to me, I don't like the look of it; **tenir qn pour s.,** to be suspicious of s.o.; **devenir s. (à qn),** to arouse (s.o.'s) suspicion. **2** *n* suspect.

suspecter [syspɛkte] *vt* to suspect (*s.o.*) (**de qch,** of sth; **de faire,** of doing); to suspect, to question, to doubt (*s.o.'s good faith etc*).

suspendre [syspɑ̃dr] **1** *vt* **(a)** to suspend; to hang up (*clothes, painting, lamp etc*); to hang up, to sling (*hammock*); **(b)** to suspend (*hostilities, inquiry etc*); to suspend, to stop (*payment, work*); **s. une séance,** to adjourn a meeting; **s. son jugement,** to suspend judgement; **la séance est suspendue,** we will now adjourn; **les abonnements sont suspendus pour ce soir,** season tickets are not valid tonight; **s. un journal/une émission,** to suspend a newspaper/a programme; *Aut* **s. un permis de conduire,** to suspend a driving licence; **(c)** to suspend (*official etc*). **2 se suspendre** *vpr* to hang (**à,** from; **par,** by).

suspendu [syspɑ̃dy] *adj* **(a)** hanging, suspended; **les jardins suspendus de Babylone,** the hanging gardens of Babylon; **pont s.,** suspension bridge; *Aut* **voiture bien suspendue,** car with good suspension; *Fig* **enfant toujours s. aux jupes de sa mère,** child always tied to his mother's apron strings; **lampe suspendue au plafond,** lamp hanging *or* suspended from the ceiling; **être s. aux lèvres de qn,** to be hanging on s.o.'s every word; **(b)** (*arrêté*) suspended; **l'enquête est suspendue,** the inquiry is suspended.

suspens [syspɑ̃] *nm* **(a) en s.,** (*of person*) in suspense; (*of work, matter etc*) in abeyance; (*of problem*) that has been shelved *or* has still to be solved; **tenir qn en s.,** to keep s.o. in suspense; **(b)** *Litt* (*suspense*) suspense.

suspense [syspɛns] *nm Cin Littér etc* suspense; **film à s.,** suspense movie, thriller.

suspensif, -ive [syspɑ̃sif, -iv] *adj Jur* suspensive (*veto etc*).

suspension [syspɑ̃sjɔ̃] *nf* **(a)** (*en haut*) suspension, hanging (up); **(b)** *Ch* **en s.,** in suspension, suspended; **(c)** suspension (*of hostilities, work, inquiry, payment etc*); stoppage (*of traffic*); abeyance (*of law*); *Gram* **points de s.,** suspension points, dots; *Mil* **s. d'armes,** suspension of fighting; *Aut* **s. pour un an du permis de conduire,** a year's driving ban; *Jur* **arrêt de s.,** injunction; **(d)** suspension (*of official etc*); **(e)** (*lampe*) light pendant, ceiling lamp; **(f)** *Aut* suspension.

suspicieux, -euse [syspisjø, -øz] *adj* suspicious.

suspicion [syspisjɔ̃] *nf* suspicion; **avoir de la s. à l'égard de qn,** to have one's suspicions about s.o..

sustentateur, -trice [systɑ̃tatœr, -tris] *Av* **1** *adj* lifting (*force etc*); **effort s.,** lift; **surface sustentatrice,** aerofoil, *US* airfoil. **2** *nm* **s. rotatif,** rotor (*of helicopter*).

sustentation [systɑ̃tasjɔ̃] *nf* **(a) base** *ou* **polygone de s.,** *Géom* basis of support; **(b)** *Av* lift.

sustenter [systɑ̃te] **1** *vt Arch* (*nourrir*) to sustain, to nourish. **2 se sustenir** *vpr F* to take nourishment, to keep up one's strength.

sus-tonique [systɔnik] *nf Mus* supertonic; (*pl sus-toniques*).

susurrement [sysyrmɑ̃] *nm Litt* murmuring, *Litt* susurration.

susurrer [sysyre] *vi & vt Litt* to murmur, *Litt* to susurrate.

suture [sytyr] *nf Anat Chir* suture; **(point de) s.,** stitch.

suturer [sytyre] *vt Chir* to stitch, to suture.

suzerain, -aine [syzrɛ̃, -ɛn] *adj & n* suzerain.

suzeraineté [syzrɛnte] *nf* suzerainty.

svastika [svastika] *nm* swastika.

svelte [svɛlt] *adj* slender, svelte, slim (*person, body etc*).

sveltesse [svɛltɛs] *nf* slenderness, slimness.

S.V.P. [ɛsvepe] (*abrév* **s'il vous plaît**) please.

swap [swap] *nm Fin* swap.

sweater [switœr] *nm* sweater.

sweat-shirt [switʃœrt] *nm* sweat shirt; (*pl sweat-shirts*).

sweepstake [swipstɛk] *nm Courses de chevaux* sweepstake.

swing [swiŋ] *nm* **(a)** *Boxe Golf* swing; **(b)** *Mus* swing.

swinger [swiŋge] *vi Mus F* to swing.

sybarite [sibarit] *adj & n* sybarite.

sybaritique [sibaritik] *adj* sybaritic.

sybaritisme [sibaritism] *nm* sybaritism.

sycomore [sikɔmɔr] *nm* sycamore (tree).

sycophante [sikɔfɑ̃t] *nm* informer.

syllabe [silab] *nf* syllable; *Fig* **ne pas prononcer** *ou* **dire une s.,** not to say a word.

syllabique [silabik] *adj* syllabic.

syllogisme [silɔʒism] *nm* syllogism.

syllogistique [silɔʒistik] *adj* syllogistic.

sylphe [silf] *nm,* **sylphide** [silfid] *nf* sylph; **taille de sylphide,** sylphlike waist.

sylvestre [silvɛstr] *adj Bot* woodland (*tree etc*).

sylviculteur [silvikyltœr] *nm* sylviculturist.

sylviculture [silvikyltyr] *nf* forestry, *Spéc* sylviculture.

symbiose [sɛ̃bjoz] *nf Biol* symbiosis.

symbole [sɛ̃bɔl] *nm* **(a)** symbol; **(b)** *Rel* (*formule*) creed.

symbolique [sɛ̃bɔlik] **1** *adj* **(a)** symbolic; (*qui signifie une intention*) token (*payment, gesture etc*); **payer le franc s.,** to make a token payment; **(b)** *Ordinat* symbolic. **2** *nf* **(a)** (*science*) symbolics; **(b)** (*système de symboles*) system of symbols; **(c) la s. des rêves,** the interpretation of dreams.

symboliquement [sɛ̃bɔlikmɑ̃] *adv* symbolically.

symbolisation [sɛ̃bɔlizasjɔ̃] *nf* symbolization.

symboliser [sɛ̃bɔlize] *vt* to symbolize.

symbolisme [sɛ̃bɔlism] *nm* symbolism; *Littér Beaux-Arts* Symbolism.

symboliste [sɛ̃bɔlist] *adj & n Littér Beaux-Arts* Symbolist.

symétrie [simetri] *nf* symmetry.

symétrique [simetrik] *adj* symmetrical (**par rapport à,** about); *Électron* balanced (*circuit*).

symétriquement [simetrikmɑ̃] *adv* symmetrically.

sympa [sɛ̃pa] *adj F* = **SYMPATHIQUE (a)**.

sympathicectomie [sɛ̃patisɛktɔmi] *nf,* **sympathectomie** [sɛ̃patɛktɔmi] *nf Chir* sympathectomy.

sympathie [sɛ̃pati] *nf* **(a)** (*affinité*) sympathy; (*amitié*) liking; **avoir de la s. pour qn,** to have a liking for s.o.; **concevoir de la s.** *ou* **se prendre de s. pour qn,** to take (a liking) to s.o.; **sympathies et antipathies,** likes and dislikes; **(b)** (*condoléances*) sympathy; **(c) idées qui ne sont pas en s.,** conflicting ideas.

sympathique [sɛ̃patik] **1** *adj* **(a)** (*agréable*) likeable, nice (*person, personality*); friendly (*meeting etc*); nice, pleasant (*surroundings etc*); pleasant (*holiday*); **personnalité peu s.,** unattractive personality; **il m'a été tout de suite s.,** I took to him at once; **il m'est devenu s.,** I came to like him; **Paul est fort s. à ma mère,** my mother is very fond of Paul; **(b) encre s.,** invisible ink; **(c)** *Anat Physiol etc* sympathetic (*nerve etc*). **2** *nm Anat* sympathetic nervous system.

sympathiquement [sɛ̃patikmɑ̃] *adv* (*accueillir etc*) in a friendly way, warmly; (*offrir etc*) kindly.

sympathisant [sɛ̃patizɑ̃] **1** *adj* sympathizing. **2** *n Pol etc* sympathizer.

sympathiser [sɛ̃patize] *vi* to get on well (together); **s. avec qn,** to get on well with s.o..

symphonie [sɛ̃fɔni] *nf Mus & Fig* symphony.

symphonique [sɛ̃fɔnik] *adj Mus* symphonic (*form, poem etc*); symphony (*orchestra*).

symphoniste [sɛ̃fɔnist] *n* **(a)** (*auteur*) symphonist; **(b)** (*musicien*) orchestral player.

symphyse [sɛ̃fiz] *nf Anat* symphysis.

symposium [sɛ̃pozjɔm] *nm* symposium.

symptomatique [sɛ̃ptɔmatik] *adj Méd & Fig* symptomatic (**de,** of).

symptomatiquement [sɛ̃ptɔmatikmɑ̃] *adv* symptomatically.

symptôme [sɛ̃ptom] *nm Méd & Fig* symptom.

synagogue [sinagɔg] *nf* synagogue.

synapse [sinaps] *nf* **(a)** *Anat* synapse; **(b)** *Biol* synapsis.

synchrone [sɛ̃kron] *adj* synchronous (**de,** with).

synchronie [sɛ̃krɔni] *nf Ling etc* synchrony.

synchronique [sɛ̃krɔnik] *adj* synchronic.

synchronisation [sɛ̃krɔnizasjɔ̃] *nf* synchronization.

synchronisé [sɛ̃krɔnize] *adj* synchronized.

synchroniser [sɛ̃krɔnize] *vt* to synchronize (**avec,** with).

synchroniseur, -euse [sɛ̃krɔnizœr, -øz] **1** *nm* **(a)** *Él etc* synchronizer; **(b)** *Aut* synchromesh device. **2** *nf Cin* **synchroniseuse,** film synchronizer.

synchronisme [sɛ̃krɔnism] *nm* synchronism; **en s.,** in synchronism; **hors de s.,** out of synchronism, *Cin F* out of sync(h).

synchrotron [sɛ̃krɔtrɔ̃] *nm Phys Nucl* synchrotron.

synclinal, -aux [sɛ̃klinal, -o] *adj Géog* synclinal.

syncope [sɛ̃kɔp] *nf* **(a)** *Méd* fainting fit, *Spéc* syncope; **tomber en s.,** to faint; **(b)** *Gram* syncope; **(c)** *Mus* syncopation.

syncopé [sɛ̃kɔpe] *adj Mus* syncopated.

syncrétisme [sɛ̃kretism] *nm Phil* syncretism.

syndic [sɛ̃dik] *nm Hist* syndic; **s. (de copropriété),** association representative (*of co-owners in block of flats or Am apartments*); **s. de faillite,** = official receiver.

syndical, -aux [sɛ̃dikal, -o] *adj* (*de salariés, d'ouvriers*) (trade-)union (*movement, leader, claim etc*).

syndicalisation [sɛ̃dikalizasjɔ̃] *nf* (*action*) unionization; (*appartenance à un syndicat*) union membership.

syndicalisme [sɛ̃dikalism] *nm* trade unionism; **faire du s.,** to be involved in (trade-)union activities.

syndicaliste [sɛ̃dikalist] **1** *adj* (trade-)union (*doctrine, leader etc*). **2** *n* trade unionist.

syndicat [sɛ̃dika] *nm* **(a)** (*de salariés, d'ouvriers*) (trade) union; **s. ouvrier,** trade union; **(b)** (*d'employeurs*) federation; (*de producteurs, propriétaires*) association; (*de financiers*) syndicate; **s. d'initiative,** tourist (information) office *or* bureau.

syndicataire [sɛ̃dikatɛr] *Fin* **1** *adj* of a syndicate. **2** *n* member of a syndicate.

syndiqué, -ée [sɛ̃dike] **1** *adj* belonging to a (trade) union; **ouvriers syndiqués,** union members; **ouvriers non syndiqués,** non-union workers. **2** *n* union member.
syndiquer [sɛ̃dike] **1** *vt* to unionize, to form (*workers etc*) into a (trade) union. **2 se syndiquer** *vpr* to form a (trade) union, to organize; (*adhérer à un syndicat*) to join a (trade) union.
syndrome [sɛ̃drom] *nm Méd* syndrome.
synérèse [sinerɛz] *nf Phys Ling* synaeresis, *US* syneresis.
synergie [sinɛrʒi] *nf* synergy.
synesthésie [sinɛstezi] *nf Psy* synaesthesia, *US* synesthesia.
syngnathe [sɛ̃gnat] *nm* pipefish.
synode [sinɔd] *nm Rel* synod.
synodique [sinɔdik] *adj* **(a)** *Astron* synodic(al); **(b)** *Rel* synodal.
synonyme [sinɔnim] **1** *adj* synonymous (**de,** with). **2** *nm* synonym.
synonymie [sinɔnimi] *nf* synonymy, synonymity.
synopse [sinɔps] *nf* synoptic table of the Gospels.
synopsis [sinɔpsis] *nf* synopsis.
synoptique [sinɔptik] *adj* synoptic; **les Évangiles synoptiques,** the Synoptic Gospels; **tableau s.,** conspectus (*of a science etc*).
synovial, -iaux [sinɔvjal, -jo] *adj Anat* synovial.
synovie [sinɔvi] *nf Anat Physiol* synovia; *Méd* **épanchement de s.,** water on the knee.
synovite [sinɔvit] *nf Méd* synovitis.
syntacticien, -ienne [sɛ̃taktisjɛ̃, -jɛn] *n Gram* syntactician.
syntactique [sɛ̃taktik] *adj Gram* syntactic(al).
syntagmatique [sɛ̃tagmatik] *adj Gram* syntagmatic.
syntagme [sɛ̃tagm] *nm Gram* syntagm(a).
syntaxe [sɛ̃taks] *nf Gram Ordinat* syntax; **erreur de s.,** syntax error.
syntaxique [sɛ̃taksik] *adj Gram* syntactic(al).
synthèse [sɛ̃tɛz] *nf* synthesis; **de s.,** synthetic.
synthétique [sɛ̃tetik] **1** *adj* synthetic. **2** *nm Tex* synthetic material.
synthétiquement [sɛ̃tetikmɑ̃] *adv* synthetically.
synthétiser [sɛ̃tetize] *vt* to synthesize.
synthétiseur [sɛ̃tetizœr] *nm Électron Mus* synthesizer; **s. de paroles,** speech synthesizer.
syntoniseur [sɛ̃tɔnizœr] *nm Rad* tuner.
syphilis [sifilis] *nf Méd* syphilis.
syphilitique [sifilitik] *adj & n Méd* syphilitic.
Syrie [siri] *nf* Syria.
syrien, -ienne [sirjɛ̃, -jɛn] **1** *adj* Syrian. **2** *n* **S.,** Syrian.
syringe [sirɛ̃ʒ] *nf Archéol* syrinx.
systématique [sistematik] **1** *adj* **(a)** (*méthodique*) systematic; *F* **c'est s.,** it's automatic; **(b)** *Péj* (*dogmatique*) hide-bound (*opinions, person*); **(c)** (*absolu*) absolute (*support*). **2** *nf* systematics.
systématiquement [sistematikmɑ̃] *adv* systematically.
systématisation [sistematizasjɔ̃] *nf* system(at)ization.
systématiser [sistematize] *vt* to system(at)ize.
système [sistɛm] *nm* **(a)** (*méthode, moyen etc*) system; **le s.,** (*la société etc*) the system; *Ordinat* **s. d'exploitation,** operating system; **s. expert,** expert system; **agir par s.,** to stick to a system; **avoir l'esprit de s.,** to have a systematic mind; *Péj* to refuse to deviate from the (established) system; **le s. D,** resourcefulness; **(b)** system, set (*of wheels, of valves etc*); system, network (*of roads*); *Physiol* system; **s. solaire,** solar system; *F* **il me tape sur le s.,** he gets on my nerves; **(c) fusils de divers systèmes,** rifles of various makes *or* types; **cravate à s.,** clip-on tie.
systémique [sistemik] *adj* systemic (*insecticide etc*).
systole [sistɔl] *nf Physiol* systole.
syzygie [siziʒi] *nf Astron* syzygy; **marées de s.,** spring tides.

T

T, t [te] *nm inv* **(a)** (the letter) T, t; **(b) t euphonique,** *forms a link between verbal endings* **-a, -e** *and the pronouns* **il, elle, on — va-t-il? ira-t-elle? donne-t-on?; (c) en T,** T-shaped.

t (a) (*abrév* **tonne(s)**) t; **(b)** (*abrév* **tome**) vol.

t' [t] *voir* **TE, TU.**

ta [ta] *adj poss voir* **TON¹.**

tabac¹ [taba] **1** *nm* **(a)** *Bot* tobacco (plant); **(b)** (*produit*) tobacco; **t. à chiquer** *ou* **à mâcher/à fumer,** chewing/smoking tobacco; **(débit** *ou* **bureau de) t.,** tobacconist's (shop), *Am* tobacco store; *F* **c'est toujours le même t.,** it's always the same thing; **(c) t. à priser, t. râpé,** snuff; **prendre du t.,** to take snuff; **(d)** *Hist Admin* **les Tabacs,** the Tobacco Department. **2** *adj inv* buff (-coloured).

tabac² *nm F* **passer qn à t.,** (*of police etc*) to handle s.o. roughly, to beat s.o. up; **passage à t.,** rough handling, beating up; **il y a du t.,** we're up against it, we're for it; *Fig* **son spectacle a fait un sacré t.,** his show was a huge success *or* a big hit.

tabagie [tabaʒi] *nf* **(a)** *F* = place reeking of stale tobacco smoke; **(b)** *Can* (*bureau de tabac*) tobacconist's (shop), *Am* tobacco store.

tabagique [tabaʒik] *adj* nicotine (*poisoning etc*).

tabagisme [tabaʒism] *nm* nicotine addiction.

tabar(d) [tabar] *nm Hist* (*manteau*) tabard.

tabassée [tabase] *nf F* beating, (good) thrashing.

tabasser [tabase] *F* **1** *vt* to beat (*s.o.*) up. **2 se tabasser** *vpr* to beat each other up.

tabatière [tabatjɛr] *nf* **(a)** (*boîte*) snuffbox; **(b)** (*lucarne*) (hinged) skylight.

tabellion [tabeljɔ̃] *nm F Hum* lawyer.

tabernacle [tabɛrnakl] *nm* tabernacle.

tabes, tabès [tabɛs] *nm Méd* tabes.

tablature [tablatyr] *nf Mus* tablature.

table [tabl] *nf* **(a)** (*meuble*) table; **t. de salle à manger/de jeu/de billard,** dining/card/billiard table; **t. (à thé) roulante,** tea trolley; **t. de nuit, t. de chevet,** bedside table; **t. de toilette,** dressing table; **t. à rallonges,** extending table; **t. basse,** coffee table; **t. à dessiner,** draughtsman's *or US* draftsman's table *or* board; **t. d'opération,** operating table; *Littér* **la T. ronde,** the Round Table; *Pol Ind* **t. ronde,** round-table conference; **tables frappantes,** (*en spiritisme*) table rapping; *Fig* **jouer cartes sur t.,** to put one's cards on the table;

(b) (*tablée, nourriture*) table; **t. d'honneur,** high table (*at a college*); top table (*at a banquet etc*); **mettre/débarrasser la t.,** to lay *or* set/clear the table; **aimer la t.,** to be fond of good food; **avoir une bonne t.,** to keep a good table; **la t. est bonne,** the food is good; **se mettre à t.,** to sit down at the table *or* to dinner *etc*; *Arg Fig* to confess, to come clean; **à t.!,** dinner *or* lunch *etc* is ready!; **être à t.,** to be at the table *or* at dinner *etc*; **(service de) petites tables,** separate tables (*at a restaurant*); *Mil* **t. d'officiers,** officers' mess; *F* **sous la t.,** secretly; *Rel* **la Sainte T.,** the Communion table;

(c) t. de cuisson, hob (unit), boiling ring unit; **t. à repasser,** ironing board; **t. de travail,** work(ing) surface, worktop;

(d) table (*of gem*);

(e) *Mus* **t. (d'harmonie),** sounding board, belly (*of violin etc*);

(f) *Hér* **t. d'attente,** field;

(g) *Tech* face (*of hammer, valve etc*); flange (*of girder*); *Rail* **t. de roulement,** tread (*of rail*);

(h) *Tél* switchboard; **t. interurbaine,** trunk switchboard; **nous étions sur t. d'écoute,** our phone was being tapped, we were being listened into;

(i) *Électron* table, board;

(j) slab (*of stone etc*); cap stone (*of a dolmen*); *Bible* **les tables de la loi,** the Tables of the Law; *Phil* **t. rase,** tabula rasa; *Fig* **faire t. rase,** to make a clean sweep **(de,** of);

(k) (*liste*) table; **t. de multiplication,** multiplication table; **t. des matières,** (table of) contents; *Mil etc* **t. de tir,** firing table, range table.

tableau, -eaux [tablo] *nm* **(a)** (*panneau, support*) board; **t. d'affichage,** notice board, *Am* bulletin board; *Scol* **t. (noir),** (black)board; *Scol* **aller au t.,** to come out *or* go out to the board; **t. blanc,** whiteboard; *Él Tél* **t. de distribution, t. commutateur,** switchboard, distribution board *or* panel; **t. de contrôle,** *Tech* control panel; *Tél* monitoring board; *Él etc* **t. d'éclairage,** lighting panel; **t. de manœuvre,** instrument board *or* panel; **t. de bord,** *Aut* dashboard; *Av* instrument panel; *Ordinat* **t. de connexions,** plugboard;

(b) (*pour les clefs*) key rack *or* board;

(c) *Beaux-Arts* picture; (*peinture*) painting; **t. de maître,** old master; *F* **tu imagines le t.!,** you can picture *or* imagine the scene!; **de la colline se découvre un magnifique t.,** there is a beautiful view from the hill; *Fig* **faire le t. de la situation,** to give a picture of the situation; *F* **vieux t.,** (*vieille coquette*) (painted) old hag;

(d) *Th* scene; **t. vivant,** tableau (vivant);

(e) (*liste*) list, table; (*graphique*) chart; *Rail* **t. horaire,** timetable; *Gram* **t. de conjugaison,** conjugation table; *Pharm* **produit de t. A/B/C,** A-/B-/C-list product; *Méd* **t. clinique,** clinical picture; **mettre sous forme de t.,** to tabulate; *F* **gagner sur tous les** *ou* **sur les deux tableaux,** to win all along the line *or* on all counts;

(f) *Jur* roll (*of lawyers*); panel (*of jurymen, doctors etc*); **être rayé du t.,** to be struck off the rolls; **se faire inscrire au t.,** to be called to the bar;

(g) *Scol* **t. d'honneur,** honours *or US* honors board;

(h) *Typ* table;

(i) t. de chasse, (*animaux abattus*) bag; *Fig* (*avions abattus, conquêtes amoureuses*) tally of successes.

tableautin [tablotɛ̃] *nm Beaux-Arts* small picture.

tablée [table] *nf* (*personnes à table*) table.

tabler [table] *vi* **t. sur qch,** to count *or* bank on sth.

tablette [tablɛt] *nf* **(a)** shelf (*of bookcase etc*); **t. à coulisse,** pull-out flap (*of desk*); **(b)** flat top (*of piece of furniture etc*); **t. de fenêtre,** window sill; **t. de piano,** music rest; *Él* **t. à bornes,** terminal plate; **(c)** *Hist* **tablettes,** (*pour écrire*) (writing) tablets; *Fig* **mettre qch sur ses tablettes,** to make a note of sth; **(d)** bar (*of chocolate*); slab (*of butter*); stick (*of chewing gum*); *Pharm* tablet.

tableur [tablœr] *nm Ordinat* spreadsheet.

tablier [tablije] *nm* **(a)** (*vêtement*) apron, *Br F* pinny; (*d'écolier*) smock; **t. blouse,** (woman's) overall; *F* **rendre son t.,** (*of servant*) to give notice; **(b)** *Mil* footboard (*of limber*); footrest (*of motor scooter*); **(c)** hood (*of fireplace*); **(d)** (steel) shutter (*of shop etc*); **(e)** deck, road(way) (*of bridge*); footplate (*of locomotive*); **(f)** table (*of rolling mill*); apron (*of lathe*); *Ind* **t. sans fin,** apron feed; **(g)** hearth (*of forge*).

tabloïd(e) [tablɔid] **1** *nm* **(a)** *Journ* tabloid (newspaper); **(b)** *Pharm* tablet. **2** *adj* **format t.,** tabloid format.

tabou [tabu] *adj & nm* taboo.

tabou(is)er [tabw(iz)e] *vt* to taboo (*sth*).

taboulé [tabule] *nm Culin* tabbouleh.

tabouret [tabure] *nm* stool; (*pour les pieds*) footstool; **t. de bar/piano,** bar/piano stool.

tabulaire [tabylɛr] *adj* tabular.

tabulateur [tabylatœr] *nm* (*de machine à écrire*) tabulator.

tabulation [tabylasjɔ̃] *nf* tabulation, tabbing; (*colonne*) tab.

tabulatrice [tabylatris] *nf* tabulator (*in punched-card system*).

tabuler [tabyle] *vt* to tabulate, to tab.

tac [tak] *nm* click (*of steel etc*); **t. t. t.,** rattle (*of machine gun*); **le t. t. du pivert,** the ratatat of the woodpecker; **riposter** *ou* **répondre du t. au t.,** to give tit for tat, to make a lightning retort.

tacet [tasɛt] *nm Mus* tacet.

tachant [taʃɑ̃] *adj* staining.

tache [taʃ] *nf* **(a)** stain, spot (*of grease, mud etc*); blob, splash (*of paint*); flaw, blemish (*in precious stone, work of art, fruit*); blot (*of ink*); *Fig* blot, stain (*on reputation etc*); **t. de suie,** fleck of soot, smut; **t. solaire, t. du soleil,** sunspot; **t. de lumière,** *Th Cin* hot spot; *TV* shading; **sans t.,** spotless; **sa réputation était sans t.,** he had a spotless *or* blameless reputation; *Fig* **faire t.,** (*of decoration, person etc*) to stick out like a sore thumb; **(b)** (*sur la peau*) mark; **t. de rousseur,** freckle; **t. de vin,** strawberry mark; **chien blanc à taches feu,** white dog with reddish markings *or* patches *or* spots; *Anat* **t. jaune (de la rétine),** yellow spot; **t. de Mariotte,** blind spot (*of the eye*).

tâche [tɑʃ] *nf* task, job; **travail à la t.,** *Ind* piecework; (*intermittent*) jobbing (work); **ouvrier à la t.,** *Ind* pieceworker; (*par intermittence*) jobbing workman; **prendre à t. de faire qch,** to undertake to do sth, to make a point of doing sth.

taché [taʃe] *adj* **(a)** *Biol* spotted; **(b)** bruised (*fruit*).

tachéomètre [takeɔmɛtr] *nm* tacheometer, tachymeter.

tachéométrie [takeɔmetri] *nf* tacheometry, tachymetry.

tacher [taʃe] **1** *vt* to stain (*garment etc*); to sully, to tarnish (*reputation etc*); **taché d'encre,** ink-stained. **2** *vi* (*of ink, wine etc*) to stain. **3 se tacher** *vpr* (*of person*) to get dirty, to get one's clothes dirty; (*of cloth, garment etc*) to stain.

tâcher [tɑʃe] *vi* **t. de faire qch,** to try *or* attempt to do sth; **tâchez de ne pas oublier,** try not to forget; **tâchons que cela ne se reproduise plus,** let's make sure it doesn't happen again.

tâcheron [tɑʃrɔ̃] *nm* **(a)** *Péj* drudge; **(b)** *Agr* pieceworker; **(c)** *Constr etc* subcontractor, jobber.

tacheté [taʃte] *adj* spotted, speckled, mottled (*paper, skin etc*); tabby (*cat*).

tacheter [taʃte] *vt* to spot, to speckle.

tacheture [taʃtyr] *nf* spot, speckle.

tachisme [taʃism] *nm Beaux-Arts* Tachisme.

tachiste [taʃist] *adj & n Beaux-Arts* Tachiste.

tachycardie [takikardi] *nf Méd* tachycardia.

tachygraphe [takigraf] *nm* tachograph.

tachymètre [takimɛtr] *nm* tachometer.

tachymétrie [takimetri] *nf* tachometry.

tachyon [takjɔ̃] *nm Phys Nucl* tachyon.

tacite [tasit] *adj* tacit (*consent etc*); *Jur* **t. reconduction,** tacit renewal.

Tacite [tasit] *nm* Tacitus.

tacitement [tasitmɑ̃] *adv* tacitly.

taciturne [tasityrn] *adj* taciturn, silent.

tacle [takl] *nm Fb* tackle; **t. glissé,** sliding tackle.

tacler [takle] *vt & vi Fb* to tackle.

tacot [tako] *nm F Péj* (*voiture*) (old) jalopy, *Br* (old) banger.

tact [takt] *nm* **(a)** (*délicatesse etc*) tact; **avoir du t., être plein de t.,** to be tactful; **manquer de t.,** to be tactless, to lack tact; **avec t.,** tactfully, with tact; **sans t.,** (*adj*) tactless; (*adv*) tactlessly; **(b)** *Vieilli* (*toucher*) (sense of) touch.

tacticien, -ienne [taktisjɛ̃, -jɛn] *n* tactician.

tactile [taktil] *adj* tactile.

tactique [taktik] **1** *adj* tactical. **2** *nf* tactics; **une t. nouvelle,** new tactics.

tadorne [tadɔrn] *nm Orn* shelduck.

tænia [tenja] *nm Méd* tapeworm, *Spéc Br* taenia, *Am* tenia.

taffetas [tafta] *nm* **(a)** *Tex* taffeta; **(b)** *Méd* **t. anglais** *ou* **gommé,** *Br* sticking plaster, *Am* Band-Aid ®.

tagliatelles [taljatɛl] *nfpl Culin* tagliatelle.

Tahiti [taiti] *nf* Tahiti.

tahitien, -ienne [taisjɛ̃, -jɛn] **1** *adj* Tahitian. **2** *n* **T.,** Tahitian.

taïaut [tajo] *int* tally-ho!

taie [tɛ] *nf* **(a) t. (d'oreiller),** pillowcase, pillowslip; **(b)** *Méd* leucoma; *Fig* **avoir une t. sur l'œil,** to be blinkered.

taïga [taiga] *nf Géog* taiga.

taillable [tajabl] *adj* **t. et corvéable (à merci),** (*of servant etc*) ready to do one's master's bidding; *Hist* (*of serf etc*) liable to tallage.

taillade [tɑjad] *nf* slash, gash.

taillader [tɑjade] *vt* to slash, to gash; *Couture* **tailladé,** slashed.

taillandier [tɑjɑ̃dje] *nm* maker of edge-tools.

taille [tɑj] *nf* **(a)** (*action*) cutting (*of stone, gems, garments, hair etc*); pruning, trimming (*of shrubs*); trimming, clipping (*of hedge*); milling (*of gearwheels*); (*en marches*) step cutting;

(b) *Chir* lithotomy;

(c) (*manière d'être taillé*) **à t. double,** double-cut (*file*); **grosse t.,** rough cut; **t. douce,** smooth cut; **t. brute/plane,** (*de pierre*) rough/smooth dressing;

(d) (*tranchant*) edge (*of sword etc*);

(e) (*taillis*) **jeune t.,** coppice;

(f) *Min* gallery;

(g) (*hauteur*) height (*of person*); **t. debout,** full height (*of s.o.*); **de grande t./t. moyenne,** very tall/of medium height; **de petite t.,** short;

(h) (*grandeur*) *& Com* size; **de petite t.,** small; **une lettre de la t. d'une affiche,** a letter the size of a poster, a poster-sized letter; **quelle est votre t.?,** what size are you *or* do you take?; **avez-vous la t. en dessus/dessous?,** do you have the next size up/down?; **pour les tailles exceptionnelles, pour les grandes tailles,** outsize;

(i) être à la t. de qn, (*of subject etc*) to be within s.o.'s capabilities; (*of adversary etc*) to be a match for s.o.; **il est de t. à vous battre,** he is big enough *or* strong enough to beat you; **il n'est pas de t. à être chef,** he is not cut out to be a leader; **il n'est pas de t. à lutter contre vous,** he is no match for you, he stands no chance against you; **rien à craindre, il n'est pas de t.,** have no fear, he is not up to it; **le mensonge est de t.,** it's a thumping lie; **une erreur, et de t.!,** a mistake and how!;

(j) (*partie du corps*) waist; (*de vêtement*) waist, waistline; **tour de t.,** waist (measurement); **elle a une t. de guêpe,** she is wasp-waisted; **avoir la t. bien prise,** to have a slim waist; **prendre qn par la t.,** to seize s.o. round the waist; (*d'un bras*) to put an arm round s.o.'s waist; *Couture* **t. normale,** natural waistline; **pantalon à t. haute/basse,** trousers with a high/low waist(line), high-/low-waisted trousers; **pardessus à t.,** fitted overcoat; **en t.,** with no (over)coat on;

(k) *Hist* (*redevance*) tallage.

taillé [tɑje] *adj* **bien t.,** well-built (*person*); **t. pour commander,** cut out to be a leader; **cheveux taillés en brosse,** crew cut.

taille-crayon(s) [tɑjkrɛjɔ̃] *nm inv* pencil sharpener.

taille-douce [tɑjdus] *nf* (*technique, estampe*) copper-plate engraving; (*pl tailles-douces*).

tailler [tɑje] **1** *vt* **(a)** to cut (*stone, diamond, grass, hair etc*); to mill (*gearwheels*); to prune, to trim (*tree*); to trim, to clip (*hedge, beard etc*); to dress (*vine*); to sharpen (*pencil*); to cut, to slice (*bread*); **t. une armée en pièces,** to cut an army to pieces; **lion taillé dans le roc,** lion carved in the stone; *Fig F* **t. une bavette,** to have a chat *or* *Br* natter;

(b) *Couture* **t. un vêtement,** to cut out a garment; **bien taillé,** well cut; **t. une robe d'après** *ou* **sur un patron,** to cut out a dress from a pattern; *Prov* **il faut t. la robe selon le corps,** you must cut your coat according to your cloth.

2 *vi* **(a)** *Chir* to make an incision; **t. dans la chair,** to cut into the flesh;

(b) (*en marches*) to cut steps.

3 se tailler *vpr* **(a)** (*se couper*) **se t. la barbe,** to trim one's beard; **se t. un chemin à travers ...,** to carve one's way through ...; **se t. un beau succès,** to be very successful;

(b) *Arg* (*partir*) to split, to beat it.

tailleur [tɑjœr] *nm* **(a)** cutter (*of stone, gems, trees, files etc*); **(b)** *Couture* tailor; **s'asseoir en t.,** to sit cross-legged; **(c)** (*costume*) (lady's) suit.

tailleur-pantalon [tɑjœrpɑ̃talɔ̃] *nm* trouser suit, *Am* pant suit; (*pl tailleurs-pantalons*).

taillis [taji] **1** *nm* copse, coppice; **dans les t.,** in the copse *or* coppice. **2** *adj* **bois t.,** copsewood, brushwood.

tain [tɛ̃] *nm* **(a)** silvering (*for mirrors*); **glace** *ou* **miroir sans t.,** two-way mirror; **(b)** *Ind* tin bath (*for tinning iron*).

taire [tɛr] *v* (*prp* **taisant**; *pp* **tu**; *pr ind* **je tais, il tait, n. taisons, ils taisent**; *pr sub* **je taise**; *impf* **je taisais**; *p hist* **je tus**; *fu* **je tairai**) **1** *vt* to say nothing about, not to mention (*sth*); (*cacher*) to suppress (*sth*), to hush (*sth*) up; **une dame dont je tairai le nom,** a lady who shall be nameless; **t. qch à qn,** to keep *or* hide *or* conceal sth from s.o.. **2 se taire** *vpr* (*être silencieux, cesser de parler etc*) to be quiet, to be silent; (*décider de ne rien dire*) to keep quiet, to keep silent; (*of sound*) to cease; **tais-toi!,** be quiet!, *F* shut up!; **faire t.,** to silence (*talkative person, opposition etc*), *F* to shut (*talkative person, opposition etc*) up; to keep (*child*) quiet; **faire t. sa douleur,** to stifle one's grief; **savoir se t.,** to know how to keep a secret; **elle a perdu une occasion de se t.,** she would have done better to have said nothing.

Taiwan [tajwan] *n* Taiwan.

taiwanais, -aise [tajwanɛ, -ɛz] **1** *adj* Taiwanese. **2** *n* **T.,**

Taiwanese.

tajine [taʒin] *nm Culin* = (pot for cooking) North African stew.

take-off [tekɔf] *nm inv Écon* takeoff.

talc [talk] *nm Minér* talc; (*produit*) talc(um powder).

talé [tale] *adj* bruised (*fruit*).

talent [talɑ̃] *nm* **(a)** (*don*) talent; **avoir du t.**, to be talented; **homme/musicien de t.,** talented man/musician; **avoir le t. des langues,** to have a talent *or* gift for languages; **elle n'a aucun t. pour faire la cuisine,** she has no talent for cooking; **son t. de pianiste,** his talent as a pianist; **il a le t. de se faire des amis,** he has a gift for making friends; *Iron* **elle a le t. de m'agacer/de se faire des ennemis,** she has a *or* the knack of irritating me/ making enemies; **faire appel à tous les talents,** to call in the best brains *or* all the available talent; **éditeur à la recherche de nouveaux talents,** publisher in search of new talent; **(b)** *Antiq* (*monnaie*) talent.

talentueusement [talɑ̃tyøzmɑ̃] *adv* with talent.

talentueux, -euse [talɑ̃tɥø, -øz] *adj* talented.

taler [tale] *vt* **(a)** to bruise (*fruit etc*); **(b)** *Fig* (*énerver*) to annoy.

taleth [talɛt] *nm Rel* tallith.

talion [taljɔ̃] *nm* retaliation; **la loi du t.**, the law of retaliation, tit for tat.

talisman [talismɑ̃] *nm* talisman.

talitre [talitr] *nm (crustacé)* sand flea, sand hopper.

talkie-walkie [tɔkiwɔki] *nm* walkie-talkie; (*pl talkies-walkies*).

Talmud [talmyd] *nm Rel* **le T.,** the Talmud.

talmudique [talmydik] *adj* Talmudic(al).

talmudiste [talmydist] *nm* Talmudist.

taloche [talɔʃ] *nf* **(a)** *F* (*gifle*) clout, cuff; **(b)** *Constr* (plasterer's) hawk.

talocher [talɔʃe] *vt F* to clout, to cuff (*s.o.*).

talon [talɔ̃] *nm* **(a)** heel (*of foot, shoe, stocking etc*); **chaussures à talons hauts/bas,** high-/low-heeled shoes; **elle ne porte que des talons hauts,** she only wears high heels; **marcher sur les talons de qn,** to follow close *or* hard on s.o.'s heels; **être toujours sur les talons de qn,** to dog s.o.'s footsteps; **la police est sur ses talons depuis quinze jours,** the police have been on his heels for two weeks; **donner du t. à son cheval,** to give one's horse the spur; **montrer** *ou* **tourner les talons, jouer des talons,** to take to one's heels; **t. d'Achille,** Achilles' heel; **t. minute,** heel (repair) bar;

(b) *Tech* heel (*of tool, mast, golf club, rifle butt, keel*); heel, nut (*of violin, bow*); butt (*of billiard cue*); shoulder (*of sword blade, bayonet, pulley block, axle*);

(c) *Cartes* stock, reserve, talon;

(d) (*bout*) heel (*of loaf, cheese, ham, sausage*);

(e) counterfoil, stub (*of cheque etc*);

(f) *Archit* ogee (moulding), talon.

talonnage [talɔnaʒ] *nm Rugby* heeling (out).

talonnement [talɔnmɑ̃] *nm* spurring on (*of horse*); *Fig* (*harcèlement*) hounding (*of s.o.*).

talonner [talɔne] **1** *vt* **(a)** (*suivre*) to follow on the heels of (*s.o.*); **(b)** (*harceler*) **t. qn,** (*of person*) to breathe down s.o.'s neck, to hound s.o.; (*of thirst, death etc*) to hound s.o.; **(c)** (*presser du talon*) to spur on (*horse, Fig pupil*); **(d)** *Rugby* to heel. **2** *vi* **(a)** *Nau* (*of ship, boat*) to touch, to bump; **(b)** *Rugby* to heel.

talonnette [talɔnɛt] *nf* **(a)** heelpiece (*of shoe*); **(b)** lift (*inside shoe*); **(c)** binding (*inside trouser bottoms*).

talonneur [talɔnœr] *nm Rugby* hooker.

talquer [talke] *vt* to sprinkle with talc *or* talcum powder.

talqueux, -euse [talkø, -øz] *adj Minér* talcose.

talure [talyr] *nf* bruise (*on fruit*).

talus [taly] *nm* **(a)** (*pente*) slope; **en t.,** sloping; **(b)** (*construit*) embankment, slope, ramp; **(c)** *Géol* talus, scree (*slope*).

talweg [talvɛg] *nm Géog* t(h)alweg.

tamanoir [tamanwar] *nm Zool* great anteater, ant bear.

tamarin¹ [tamarɛ̃] *nm* **(a)** (*fruit*) tamarind; **(b)** (*tamaris*) tamarisk.

tamarin² *nm Zool* tamarin.

tamarinier [tamarinje] *nm* tamarind (tree).

tamaris [tamaris] *nm Bot* tamarisk.

tambouille [tɑ̃buj] *nf Arg* **(a)** (*cuisine*) cooking; **faire la t.,** to do the cooking; **(b)** (*plat etc*) grub, nosh.

tambour [tɑ̃bur] *nm* **(a)** (*instrument de musique*) drum; **battre du t.,** to play the drum, to drum; **bruit de t.,** drumming; **chasser un soldat au son du t.,** to drum a soldier out; **peau de t.,** drum-head; **t. de basque,** tambourine; **coup de t.,** beat *or* roll on the drum; *F* **raisonner comme un t.,** to talk through one's hat; **sans t. ni trompette,** quietly, without (any) fuss, *F* without a song and dance;

(b) (*personne*) drummer; **t. de ville,** town crier;

(c) *Tech* drum (*of turbine, washing machine, recording instrument etc*); *El* cylinder (*of coil*); *Nau* drum (*of capstan*); *Typ* **t. d'impression,** print drum; **t. de frein,** brake drum; **freins à t.,** drum brakes; **t. de câble,** cable drum;

(d) (*entrée*) vestibule (*of church etc*); (*tourniquet*) revolving door;

(e) (*à broder*) tambour, (embroidery) frame;

(f) *Archit* drum (*of column etc*).

tambourin [tɑ̃burɛ̃] *nm* **(a)** (*tambour long et étroit*) tambourin (*of Provence*); **(b)** (*tambour de basque*) tambourine.

tambourinage [tɑ̃burinaʒ] *nm* drumming.

tambourinaire [tɑ̃burinɛr] *nm* **(a)** (*musicien*) tambourin player; **(b)** (*annonceur*) town crier.

tambourinement [tɑ̃burinmɑ̃] *nm* drumming.

tambouriner [tɑ̃burine] **1** *vi* (*avec ses doigts, des objets etc*) to drum; **la pluie tambourine sur le toit,** the rain is drumming on the roof. **2** *vt* **(a)** to drum (out) (*rhythm etc*); **(b)** *Arch* to announce (*piece of news*).

tambour-major [tɑ̃burmaʒɔr] *nm Mil* drum major; (*pl tambours-majors*).

Tamerlan [tamɛrlɑ̃] *nm* Tamburlaine.

tamil, -ile [tamil] **1** *adj* Tamil. **2** *nm Ling* Tamil. **3** *n* **T.,** Tamil.

tamis [tami] *nm* sieve; (*pour le sable etc*) sifter; (*pour les liquides*) strainer; *Ind* riddle, screen; **passer qch au t.,** to sieve (*flour etc*); to sift (*sand etc*); to strain (*liquid*); *Ind* to riddle, to screen; *Fig* to sift, to examine (*evidence etc*) thoroughly.

tamisage [tamizaʒ] *nm* sieving (*of flour etc*); sifting (*of sand etc*); straining (*of liquid*); *Ind* riddling, screening.

Tamise [tamiz] *nf* **la T.,** the Thames.

tamiser [tamize] **1** *vt* to sieve (*flour etc*); to sift (*sand etc*); to strain (*liquid*); *Ind* to riddle, to screen; **rideaux qui tamisent la lumière,** curtains that filter the light. **2** *vi* (*of dust, light etc*) to filter through.

tamoul, -oule [tamul] **1** *adj* Tamil. **2** *nm Ling* Tamil. **3** *n* **T.,** Tamil.

tampon [tɑ̃pɔ̃] *nm* **(a)** (*bouchon*) plug, stopper, bung (*of cask*); **(b)** *Constr* wall plug; **(c)** *Méd* swab; *Chir* pad, plug, tampon; **t. hygiénique** *ou* **périodique,** tampon; **(d)** pad (*of flute key etc*); **(e) t. encreur,** ink(ing); **(f)** (*cachet, instrument*) stamp; (*de la poste*) postmark; **coup de t.,** stamp; **(g) t. buvard,** blotter; **(h)** (*pour polir*) pad; **t. à récurer,** scourer, scouring pad; **(i) t. (de choc),** buffer (*of train*); **coup de t.,** collision (*between buffers*); *Pol* **etat/ zone t.,** buffer state/zone; *F* **servir de t. (entre deux personnes),** to act as a buffer (between two people).

tamponnage [tɑ̃pɔnaʒ] *nm Ch* neutralizing.

tamponnement [tɑ̃pɔnmɑ̃] *nm* **(a)** (*bouchage*) plugging (*of wound etc*); **(b)** (*essuyage*) dabbing (*with pad*); **(c)** *Aut Rail* collision.

tamponner [tɑ̃pɔne] **1** *vt* **(a)** (*boucher*) to plug, to stop (up); *Méd* to put a wad over, to plug (*wound*); **(b)** *Constr* to plug (*wall*); **(c)** (*essuyer*) to dab (*with pad*); *Méd* to swab (*wound*); *Typ* to ink up (*type, metal plate*); **(d)** (*timbrer*) to stamp (*document etc*); **(e)** (*polir*) to French-polish (*furniture*); **(f)** *Métal* to dust (*mould*); **(g)** *Ch* to neutralize; **(h)** to run into, to collide with (*another car or train etc*). **2 se tamponner** *vpr* **(a)** (*of cars, trains etc*) to run into each other, to collide (*with each other*); **(b) se t. le front,** to mop one's brow; **se t. les yeux,** to dab one's eyes; *Arg* **s'en t. (le coquillard),** not to give a damn.

tamponneur, -euse [tɑ̃pɔnœr, -øz] **1** *adj* **train t.,** train that ran into another; **autos tamponneuses,** dodgems, bumper cars. **2** *n* official (*who stamps documents etc*).

tamponnoir [tɑ̃pɔnwar] *nm* wall drill.

tam-tam [tamtam] *nm* (*pl tam-tams*) **(a)** (*tambour*) tom-tom; **(b)** *F Péj* (*tapage*) fuss, ballyhoo; **faire du t.-t. autour de qch,** to make a great fuss *or* great ballyhoo about sth; **(c)** (*gong*) gong.

tan [tɑ̃] *nm* tan, (tanner's) bark.

tanaisie [tanezi] *nf Bot* tansy.

tancer [tɑ̃se] *vt* (**je tançai(s); n. tançons**) *Litt* to berate, to scold.

tanche [tɑ̃ʃ] *nf* (*poisson*) tench.

tandem [tɑ̃dɛm] *nm* **(a) chevaux attelés en t.,** horses driven tandem; **(b)** (*bicyclette*) tandem; **(c)** (*deux personnes ou groupes*) twosome, duo; **travailler en t.,** to work in tandem; **(d)** *Tech* **cylindres en t.,** tandem cylinders; **(e)** *Ordinat* **central t.,** tandem exchange, tandem central office.

tandis que [tɑ̃di(s)kə] *conj* **(a)** (*alors que*) whereas, while; **lui s'amuse, t. que nous, nous travaillons,** he plays, whereas *or* while we have to work; **(b)** (*pendant que*) while, *Fml* whilst; **il s'amuse t. que nous travaillons,** he plays while *or Fml* whilst we work.
tangage [tɑ̃gaʒ] *nm Nau Av* pitching; *Fig* reeling, swaying.
tangara [tɑ̃gara] *nm Orn* tanager.
tangence [tɑ̃ʒɑ̃s] *nf Géom* tangency; **point de t.,** point of contact.
tangent, -ente [tɑ̃ʒɑ̃, -ɑ̃t] **1** *adj Géom* tangential, tangent (**à,** to); *F* **c'est t.,** it's as near as dammit; (*critique*) it's touch and go. **2** *nf* **tangente,** tangent; *F* **s'échapper par la tangente, prendre la tangente,** to dodge the question; (*partir*) to slip away.
tangentiel, -ielle [tɑ̃ʒɑ̃sjɛl] *adj Géom* tangential.
Tanger [tɑ̃ʒe] *n* Tangier(s).
tangible [tɑ̃ʒibl] *adj* tangible.
tangiblement [tɑ̃ʒibləmɑ̃] *adv* tangibly.
tango [tɑ̃go] **1** *nm* (*danse, musique*) tango. **2** *adj inv* (*couleur*) tangerine.
tangon [tɑ̃gɔ̃] *nm Nau* (*mobile*) swinging boom; (*de spi*) spinnaker boom.
tanguer [tɑ̃ge] *vi* **(a)** *Av Nau* to pitch; **(b)** *Fig* to reel, to sway.
tanière [tanjɛr] *nf* **(a)** (*d'animal*) den, lair; **(b)** (*habitation sordide*) hovel; **(c)** (*retraite*) retreat.
tanin [tanɛ̃] *nm Ch Ind* tannin.
tank [tɑ̃k] *nm* **(a)** *Mil* tank; **(b)** *Nau* tank (*of oil tanker*); **(c)** *F* (*grande voiture*) tank.
tanker [tɑ̃kɛr] *nm Nau* tanker.
tankiste [tɑ̃kist] *nm Mil* soldier with a *or* the tank unit.
tannage [tanaʒ] *nm Tech* tanning (*of hides*).
tannant [tanɑ̃] *adj* **(a)** *Arg* (*ennuyeux*) annoying; **il est t.!,** he's a drag!; **(b)** *Tech* tanning.
tanne [tan] *nf* spot (*on leather*); blackhead (*on face*).
tanné, -ée [tane] **1** *adj* tanned (*hide, face etc*). **2** *nm* **(a)** (*couleur*) tan (colour); **(b) gants en t.,** tan(ned) leather gloves. **3** *nf F* **tannée,** thrashing, good hiding.
tanner [tane] *vt* **(a)** *Tech* to tan (*hides*); **(b)** *Arg* (*ennuyer*) to annoy (*s.o.*); (*harceler*) to pester (*s.o.*); **elle m'a tanné pour que je le lui dise,** she pestered me to tell her; **(c)** *Arg* **t. (le cuir à) qn,** to thrash s.o., to tan s.o.'s hide.
tannerie [tanri] *nf* (*établissement*) tannery; (*industrie*) tanning.
tanneur [tanœr] *nm* tanner (*of hides*).
tannin [tanɛ̃] *nm Ch Ind* tannin.
tannique [tanik] *adj Ch* tannic (*acid*).
tanrec [tɑ̃rɛk] *nm Zool* tenrec.
tan-sad [tɑ̃sad] *nm* pillion(-seat); (*pl tan-sads*).
tant [tɑ̃] *adv* **(a)** (*quantité*) so much; **t. de bonté,** so much *or* such kindness; **il a t. bu que ...,** he has drunk so much that ...; **ce n'est pas la peine de t. vous presser,** you needn't be in such a hurry; **elle s'est donné t. de mal,** she went to such a lot of *or* so much trouble; **pour t. faire** *ou* **à t. faire** *ou F* **t. qu'à faire, j'aimerais autant ...,** while I'm at it *or* about it, I would just as soon ...; *F* **tu m'en diras t.!,** you don't say!, really?; **t. pour cent,** so much per cent; **être t. à t.,** to be even (*at play*); **onze cent et t.,** eleven hundred and something; **votre lettre du t.,** your letter of such and such a date; **il a t. et plus d'argent,** he has any amount of money; **ils tiraient t. et plus,** they were pulling for all they were worth; **je me suis ennuyé t. et plus,** I was bored to tears *or* to death; **faire t. (et si bien) que ...,** to work to such good purpose that ...; **j'ai crié t. et t. qu'il est parti,** I shouted so much that he went (away); **t. s'en faut,** far from it; **t. soit peu,** a little, somewhat; **il y a une école dans tout village t. soit peu considérable,** there is a school in every village of any importance; **ils sont t. soit peu cousins,** they are more or less cousins; **il est t. soit peu avare,** he's a bit of a miser; **si t. est qu'il soit mort,** if he really is dead; **il y en a peu, si t. est qu'il y en ait du tout,** there is little *or* there are few, if any;

(b) (*nombre*) so many; **t. de fois,** so many times, so often; **t. d'amis,** so many friends; **il a t. et plus d'amis,** he has plenty of friends;

(c) (*tellement*) so, to such a degree; **il ne peut pas se lever, t. il est malade,** he cannot get up, he is so ill; **t. était grande sa discrétion que ...,** so great was his discretion that ...; **t. il est vrai que ...,** so true is it that ...; **elle est t. aimée,** she is loved so (much); **elle n'est pas t. sotte!** she is not so stupid!; **n'aimer rien t. que ...,** to like nothing so much as ...;

(d) en t. que, in so far as; **je suis Russe en t. que je suis né en Russie,** I am a Russian in so far as I was born in Russia; **l'homme en t. qu'il diffère des animaux,** man, as distinct from animals; **en t. que vieil ami de votre père,** as a very old friend of your father('s);

(e) (*quelque*) however; **t. aimable qu'il soit,** however pleasant he may be;

(f) t. mieux, so much the better, that's all to the good!; **t. pis!,** too bad!, it can't be helped!, what a pity!, never mind!; **t. pis pour toi!,** (that's) too bad for you!;

(g) t. que, (*autant que*) as much as; **j'ai couru t. que j'ai pu,** I ran as hard as I could; *F* **il pleut t. qu'il peut,** it's raining like anything; **t. aux Indes qu'ailleurs,** both in India and elsewhere; **t. pour vous que pour moi,** as much for your sake as mine; **t. avec la maison qu'avec le bureau,** what with the house and the office; **t. bien que mal,** somehow or other, after a fashion;

(h) t. que, (*aussi longtemps que*) as long as; (*pendant que*) while; **t. que je vivrai,** as long as I live; **t. que la vue s'étend,** as far as the eye can see; **t. que vous y êtes,** while you're about *or* at it; **il n'y a rien à faire t. qu'il ne sera pas là,** there is nothing to be done so long as he isn't there;

(i) *Arg* **t. qu'à,** = **quant à,** *voir* **QUANT**.
tantale [tɑ̃tal] *nm Ch* tantalum.
Tantale [tɑ̃tal] *nm* Tantalus.
tante [tɑ̃t] *nf* **(a)** aunt; **t. à la mode de Bretagne,** first cousin once removed; (*très éloigné*) very distant relative; **(b)** *Vulg Péj* (*homosexuel*) queer, *Br* poof(ter); **(c)** *Arg* **ma t.,** (*mont-de-piété*) uncle's, the pawnbroker's (shop).
tantième [tɑ̃tjɛm] *nm Com* percentage, quota (*of profits etc*).
tantine [tɑ̃tin] *nf F* auntie, aunty.
tantinet [tɑ̃tinɛ] *nm F* tiny bit (**de,** of); **un t. plus long,** a tiny bit *or* shade *or* a fraction longer.
tantôt [tɑ̃to] *adv* **(a)** (*parfois*) **t. triste, t. gai,** now sad, now gay; **t. je suis à Paris, t. à Londres,** sometimes I am in Paris, sometimes in London; **(b)** *Arch* (*bientôt*) soon, presently; (*il y a peu de temps*) just now, a little while ago; **(c)** (*cet après-midi*) this afternoon; **il pleuvra/il a plu t.,** it will rain/it rained this afternoon.
tantouse [tɑ̃tuz] *nf Vulg Péj* (*homosexuel*) queer, *Br* poof(ter).
Tanzanie [tɑ̃zani] *nf* Tanzania.
tanzanien, -ienne [tɑ̃zanjɛ̃, -jɛn] **1** *adj* Tanzanian. **2** *n* **T.,** Tanzanian.
Tao [tao] *nm* Tao.
taôisme, taoïsme [taɔism] *nm Rel* Taoism.
taôiste, taoïste [taɔist] *adj & n Rel* Taoist.
taon [tɑ̃] *nm* gadfly, horsefly, cleg.
tapage [tapaʒ] *nm* **(a)** (*bruit*) din, uproar, *F* racket, row; **faire du t.,** to kick up a din *or* racket *or* row; **(b)** (*publicité*) fuss, ballyhoo; **faire du t. autour de qch,** to make a great fuss *or* ballyhoo about sth.
tapageur, -euse [tapaʒœr, -øz] **1** *adj* **(a)** noisy (*child etc*); noisy, rowdy, uproarious (*party etc*); **(b)** loud, flashy (*clothes etc*); obtrusive (*publicity*). **2** *n* rowdy; **petit t., petite tapageuse,** noisy little brat.
tapageusement [tapaʒœzmɑ̃] *adv* (*s'habiller etc*) flashily.
tapant [tapɑ̃] *adj* **à sept heures tapant(es),** on the stroke of seven, at seven sharp *or* on the dot.
tape [tap] *nf* slap; **il m'a donné une t. sur l'épaule/une petite t. sur la joue,** he gave me a slap on the shoulder/a pat on the cheek.
tapé [tape] *adj* **(a)** (*séché*) dried (*fruit*); (*abîmé*) damaged (*fruit*); **(b)** *Arg* **réponse tapée,** smart answer; **(c)** *F (fou)* nuts, cracked.
tape-à-l'œil [tapalœj] **1** *adj inv* loud, gaudy, flashy. **2** *nm inv* gaudy *or* flashy rubbish.
tape(-)cul [tapky] *nm* (*pl tape(-)culs*) **(a)** (*bascule*) seesaw; **(b)** (*barrière*) counterpoise barrier; **(c)** *Nau* jigger (sail); **(d)** (*véhicule*) rattletrap, boneshaker.
tapée [tape] *nf F* **une t.** *ou* **des tapées de ...,** masses *or* heaps *or* loads of ... .
taper¹ [tape] **1** *vt* **(a)** (*frapper*) to slap (*child, thigh etc*); to bang (*table etc*); **t. du tambour,** to beat the drum; **t. la porte,** to slam the door; **t. un coup/deux coups à la porte,** to knock/knock twice at the door; **t. une lettre (à la machine),** to type a letter; **t. un air (au piano),** to thump out a tune (on the piano); *F* **t. la carte,** to play cards;

(b) *F* **t. qn de mille francs,** to touch s.o. for a thousand francs.

2 *vi* **(a)** (*frapper*) to bang (**sur,** on); **t. sur le piano,** to thump *or* plonk away on the piano; **t. à la porte,** to bang on the door; *F* **t. sur le ventre à qn,** to give s.o. a dig in the ribs (*as a mark of familiarity*); **le soleil nous tapait sur la**

tête, the sun was beating down on us; *F* **ça tape,** (*il fait chaud*) it's scorching; **t. sur qn,** to hit s.o.; *F* (*critiquer*) to knock s.o., to have a go at s.o.; **t. dans,** to help oneself to, to dig into (*food etc*); *F* **t. dans l'œil à qn,** to take s.o.'s fancy; **t. dans un ballon,** to knock *or* kick a ball around; **t. du pied,** to stamp one's foot; *Mil F* **t. sur un objectif,** to strafe a target; **t. à côté,** to miss the target; **t. à la tête,** (*of wine*) to go to one's head;

(b) t. (à la machine), to type; **t. au toucher,** to touch-type;

(c) *Arg* (*puer*) to stink.

3 se taper *vpr* **(a)** (*se frapper*) to knock each other about; **se t. les cheveux,** to pat one's hair; **se t. sur la cuisse,** to slap one's thigh; *Fig* **se t. le derrière par terre,** to split one's sides laughing;

(b) *Arg* **se t. qch,** (*manger, boire*) to put sth away; (*avoir à supporter*) to let oneself in for sth;

(c) *Arg* **s'en t.,** not to give a damn (**de,** about);

(d) *Arg* **tu peux te t.!,** you'll be lucky!, nothing doing!

taper² *vt* (*boucher*) to plug, to stop up (*hole etc*).

tapette [tapɛt] *nf* **(a)** (*petit marteau*) mallet; **(b)** (*à tapis*) carpet beater; **(c)** (*de graveur*) (engraver's) pad; **(d)** (*à mouches*) fly swatter; **(e)** *Arg* (*langue*) **quelle t.!,** what a chatterer *or* chatterbox!; **il a une fière t.,** he CAN talk!; **(f)** (*petite tape*) (gentle) slap; **(g)** *Vulg* (*homosexuel*) queer, *Br* poof(ter).

tapeur, -euse [tapœr, -øz] *n F* cadger.

tapin [tapɛ̃] *nm* **(a)** *Arg* **faire le t.,** (*of prostitute*) to be on the game, to walk the streets; **(b)** *F Arch* drummer.

tapinois (en) [ɑ̃tapinwa] *adv* stealthily, on the sly.

tapioca [tapjɔka] *nm* tapioca; (*soupe*) tapioca soup.

tapir¹ [tapir] *nm* **(a)** *Zool* tapir; **(b)** *Scol F* = pupil who takes private lessons.

tapir² (se) [sətapir] *vpr* to crouch; (*se cacher*) to cower, to hide; **maison tapie dans un bois,** house nestling in a wood; **peur tapie en lui,** fear lurking within him.

tapis [tapi] *nm* **(a)** (*recouvrant un meuble*) cloth, cover; **t. de sol,** groundsheet; **t. de table,** table cover; **t. de selle,** saddlecloth; **t. de billard,** billard cloth; **t. vert,** gaming table; (*de conseil*) conference table; **le t. brûle!,** put down your stakes!; **mettre qch sur le t.,** to bring sth up for consideration *or* for discussion; **ce genre de discussion revient toujours sur le t.,** this sort of discussion is always coming up;

(b) (*de sol*) carpet; (*petit*) ring; **t. de haute laine/de laine rase,** long-pile/short pile carpet; **dérouler le t. rouge,** to roll out the red carpet; **t. à prière,** prayer mat; **t. d'Orient,** oriental carpet; **marchand de t.,** carpet dealer; **recouvrir le plancher d'un t.,** to carpet the floor; **t. de pied,** rug; **t. de gym,** gym mat; **t. de salle de bain,** bathroom carpet; **terrain recouvert d'un t. de gazon/de neige,** ground carpeted with turf/snow;

(c) t. roulant, *Ind etc* conveyor belt; (*pour piétons*) moving walkway, travelator;

(d) *Boxe etc* canvas; **aller au t.,** to be knocked down; *Fig* **entreprise française mise au t. par la concurrence,** French company knocked for six by the competition.

tapis-brosse [tapibrɔs] *nm* doormat; (*pl tapis-brosses*).

tapisser [tapise] *vt* **(a)** (*de papier paint*) to (wall)paper (*room etc*); **les murs sont tapissés de jaune,** the walls are papered in yellow; **mur tapissé d'affiches,** wall covered *or* plastered with posters; **(b)** (*de tentures ou tapisseries*) to cover (*room etc*) with hangings *or* tapestries; **(c)** (*of wallpaper, tapestries etc*) to line, to cover; **une membrane tapisse l'estomac,** the stomach is lined with a membrane; **mur tapissé de lierre,** wall covered with ivy, ivy-clad wall.

tapisserie [tapisri] *nf* **(a)** (*papier peint*) wallpaper; **(b)** (*tissage*) tapestry making *or* weaving; **(c)** (*tenture*) tapestry; **chaise en t.,** chair upholstered with tapestry; **faire t.,** (*of dancer at a ball*) to be a wallflower; **(d)** (*broderie*) **t. (au** *ou* **sur canevas),** tapestry work, crewel work; **pantoufles en t.,** carpet slippers.

tapissier, -ière [tapisje, -jɛr] *n* **(a)** (*décorateur*) (interior) decorator; **(b)** (*de tissage*) tapestry maker; **(c)** (*de broderie*) crewel worker; **(d)** (*de meubles*) upholsterer.

tapon [tapɔ̃] *nm Vieilli* ball (*of material, paper etc*); **en t.,** (*of clothes etc*) in a ball, bundled up; (*of hair*) screwed up into a ball *or* a bun.

tapotement [tapɔtmɑ̃] *nm* tapping; (*de piano*) plonking.

tapoter [tapɔte] **1** *vt* to tap; to pat (*child's cheek etc*); **t. un air (au piano),** to thump out a tune (on the piano). **2** *vi* **t. sur,** to tap on.

tapuscrit [tapyskri] *nm* typescript.

taquet [takɛ] *nm* **(a)** *Menuis etc* (*support*) angle block; (*cale*) wedge; **(b)** (*butée*) stop; **t. de sûreté,** safety stop; **(c)** (*de machine à écrire*) stop; **poser un t. (de tabulateur),** to set a tab(ulator stop); **(d)** (*d'arpenteur*) *& Agr* (small) picket, peg; **(e)** *Nau* **t. (de tournage),** (belaying) cleat.

taquin, -ine [takɛ̃, -in] **1** *adj* (*personne, tempérament*) (given to) teasing; (*sourire*) teasing. **2** *n* (*personne*) tease(r).

taquiner [takine] *vt* **(a)** (*of person*) to tease (*s.o.*); *F* **t. le goujon,** to do a bit of fishing; *F* **t. la muse,** to write the odd bit of verse; **(b)** (*of thing*) to bother, to worry (*s.o.*).

taquinerie [takinri] *nf* teasing.

tarabiscoté [tarabiskɔte] *adj* over-elaborate (*style, furniture etc*).

tarabuster [tarabyste] *vt* **(a)** (*of person*) to pester (*s.o.*); **(b)** (*of thing*) to bother, to worry (*s.o.*).

tarage [taraʒ] *nm Com* allowance for tare.

tarama [tarama] *nm Culin* taramasalata.

taratata [taratata] *int* rubbish!

taraud [taro] *nm* (screw) tap.

taraudage [tarodaʒ] *nm* screw cutting, tapping.

tarauder [tarode] *vt* **(a)** *Tech* to tap, to cut, to screw, to thread (*rod, nut etc*); **(b)** (*of insect*) to bore into (*wood*); **(c)** *Litt Fig* (*of remorse, scruples etc*) to gnaw (*s.o.*).

taraudeuse [tarodøz] *nf* (*machine*) tapper, thread cutter.

tarbouch(e) [tarbuʃ] *nm* tarboosh.

tard [tar] **1** *adv* late; **plus t.,** later, later on; **au plus t.,** at the latest; **tôt ou t.,** sooner or later; **il est t.,** it's late; **il se fait t.,** it's getting late; **je ne pensais pas qu'il fût si t.,** I did not think it was so late; **je me suis couché t.,** I went to bed late, I was late (in) going to bed; **trop t., il fallait te décider plus vite,** (it's) too late, you should have decided sooner; **il se maria t.,** he married late (in life); **deux minutes plus t. et je manquais le bateau,** another two minutes and I would have missed the boat; *Prov* **mieux vaut t. que jamais,** better late than never; **il est t. dans la nuit,** it is late (at night); **remettre qch à plus t.,** to put sth off until later; **je le ferai et pas plus t. que ce soir,** I'll do it this very evening; **pas plus t. qu'hier,** only yesterday. **2** *nm* **sur le t.,** (*dans la vie*) late in life; *Arch* (*dans la journée*) late in the day.

tarder [tarde] **1** *vi* to delay; **pourquoi tarde-t-il?,** why is he (taking) so long?; **il ne tardera pas maintenant,** he won't be long now; **t. en chemin,** to loiter on the way; **t. à faire qch,** to put off *or* delay doing sth; **ça tarde à commencer/venir,** it's a long time starting/coming; **sans t.,** without delay; **nous ne tarderons pas à le voir venir,** it won't be long before he appears; **cela n'a pas tardé,** it wasn't long coming. **2** *v impers* **il lui tarde de partir/qu'elle revienne,** he is longing to get away/for her to return.

tardif, -ive [tardif, -iv] *adj* belated (*regrets etc*); late (*hour, fruit etc*).

tardivement [tardivmɑ̃] *adv* belatedly; (*rentrer etc*) late.

tare [tar] *nf* **(a)** (*défaut*) defect; **(b)** *Com* (*pour calculer le poids net*) tare; **faire la t.,** to allow for the tare.

taré [tare] *adj* **(a)** *Com* spoilt (*fruit etc*); damaged (*goods*); **(b)** (*corrumpu*) depraved, corrupt (*régime etc*); **(c)** (*dégénéré*) degenerate; **(d)** *F* (*idiot*) cretinous.

tarentelle [tarɑ̃tɛl] *nf* (*danse, musique*) tarantella.

tarentule [tarɑ̃tyl] *nf* (*araignée*) tarantula.

tarer [tare] *vt Com* to tare (*packing case etc*).

taret [tarɛ] *nm* (*mollusque*) teredo, shipworm.

targette [tarʒɛt] *nf* (flat door) bolt.

targuer (se) [sətarge] *vpr* **se t. de qch/de faire qch,** to pride oneself on sth/on doing sth; **se t. de ce que ...,** to pride oneself on the fact that ... .

targui, -ie, *pl* **touareg** [targi, twarɛg] **1** *adj* Tuareg. **2** *n* **T.,** Tuareg.

tarière [tarjɛr] *nf* **(a)** (*pour le bois*) auger; **(b)** (*de forage*) drill; *Min* borer; **(c)** *Ent* terebra.

tarif [tarif] *nm* (*tableau des prix*) tariff, price list; (*prix*) rate; **t. douanier,** customs tariff; **tarifs postaux,** postal *or* postage rates; **t. (des) lettres,** letter rate; **t. intérieur,** inland rate; **t. d'urgence,** = first-class rate; **plein t.,** full fare (*for passengers*); full tariff (*for goods etc*); *F* maximum penalty (*for crime etc*); **voyager à plein t./à t. réduit,** to travel at full/reduced rate; **billet (à) plein t.,** full-fare ticket; *F* **trois mots de prison, c'est le t.,** three months' prison is what it'll cost you.

tarifaire [tarifɛr] *adj* tariff (*laws etc*).

tarifer [tarife] *vt* to tariff, to fix the rate for (*duties, price of goods etc*).

tarification [tarifikasjɔ̃] *nf* tariffing (**de,** of), fixing of rates (**de,** for).

tarin [tarɛ̃] *nm* **(a)** (*oiseau*) siskin; **(b)** *Arg* (*nez*) beak, *Br*

conk.
tarir [tarir] **1** *vt* to dry up (*spring, river, tears*). **2 se tarir** *vpr* (*of river, milk, inspiration etc*) to dry up. **3** *vi* **(a)** (*of waters*) to dry up, to run dry; **la source a tari,** the spring has dried up; **la source est tarie,** the spring is dry; **(b)** *Fig* (*of conversation, tears, resources, inspiration etc*) to dry up; **la discussion n'a pas tari pendant deux heures,** the discussion has been flowing freely for two hours; **ne pas t. d'éloges sur qch,** to be for ever praising sth; **une fois lancé sur ce sujet, il ne tarit pas,** once he is on this subject he never stops.
tarissement [tarismɑ̃] *nm* drying up.
tarlatane [tarlatan] *nf Tex* tarlatan.
tarmacadam [tarmakadam] *nm Constr Arch* tarmacadam.
tarot [taro] *nm Cartes* **(jeu de) tarot(s),** tarot (pack).
tarse [tars] *nm Anat Zool* tarsus.
Tarse [tars] *n* Tarsus.
tarsien, -ienne [tarsjɛ̃, -jɛn] *adj Anat* tarsal (*bone*).
tarsier [tarsje] *nm Zool* tarsier.
tartan [tartɑ̃] *nm* (*tissu, vêtement*) tartan.
tartane [tartan] *nf* (*bateau*) tartan (*of the Mediterranean*).
tartare [tartar] **1** *adj* **(a)** *Hist* Ta(r)tar; **(b)** *Culin* **sauce t.,** tartar(e) sauce; **steak t.,** steak tartare. **2** *n Hist* **T.,** Ta(r)tar. **3** *nm Culin* steak tartare.
tarte [tart] **1** *nf* **(a)** *Culin* tart, *Am* (open) pie; **t. aux pommes,** apple tart *or Am* pie; **t. à la crème,** custard tart *or Am* pie; *Cin F* custard pie (*thrown at s.o.*); *F* **c'est de la t.,** it's easy *or* a piece of cake; **ce n'est pas de la t.,** it's no easy thing; **(b)** *Arg* (*gifle*) slap. **2** *adj F* **(a)** (*ridicule*) ridiculous; **(b)** (*laid*) ugly.
tartelette [tartəlɛt] *nf Culin* tartlet.
tartempion [tartɑ̃pjɔ̃] *nm F Péj* so-and-so; **entreprise T.,** Company So-and-so; **un quelconque t.,** some fellow *or* other.
tartignole [tartiɲɔl] *adj F* ridiculous.
tartine [tartin] *nf* **(a)** (*beurrée*) slice of bread and butter; (*pas encore beurrée*) slice of bread; **t. de confiture,** slice of bread and jam; **t. grillée,** slice *or* piece of toast; **faire des tartines,** to butter (some) bread; **(b)** *F* (*tirade*) long-winded speech; (*dans un journal, une lettre etc*) screed; **pourquoi en mettre toute une t.?,** why go on about it at such length?
tartiner [tartine] *vt* to spread (*butter*); to spread (*bread*) (**de,** with); **t. du pain (de beurre),** to butter bread, to spread bread with butter; **fromage à t.,** cheese spread.
tartre [tartr] *nm* tartar (*on teeth, in wine bottle etc*); fur, scale (*in boiler, kettle*).
tartrique [tartrik] *adj Ch* tartaric (*acid*).
tartuf(f)e [tartyf] **1** *nm* tartuf(f)e, (sanctimonious) hypocrite. **2** *adj* hypocritical.
tartuf(f)erie [tartyfri] *nf* hypocrisy.
tas [ta] *nm* **(a)** (*amas*) heap, pile (*of stones, mud, wood etc*); stook, shock (*of corn*); **t. de fumier,** manure heap; **mettre en t.,** to heap up, to pile up; *Min* **t. de déblais,** dump;
(b) (*grand nombre, grande quantité*) mass (**de,** of); **un t. de mensonges,** a pack of lies; *F* **il y en a des t. (et des t.),** there are heaps of them; **elle a fait un t. de choses dans sa vie,** she has done masses of things *or* lots (of things) in her life; **des t. de fois,** lots of times; *F Péj* **tout un t. de gens,** a whole gang (of people), a whole load of people; **t. d'imbéciles!,** bunch of idiots!;
(c) tirer dans le t., to fire into the crowd; *F* **dans le t., il doit y en avoir un ou deux que tu connais,** there must be one or two out of that lot that you know;
(d) *Métal* stake (anvil);
(e) (*construction*) building under construction; (*chantier*) building site; **être sur le t.,** to be at work *or* on the job; *Ind etc* **formation sur le t.,** on-the-job training; **apprendre sur le t.,** to learn on the job; **grève sur le t.,** sit-down strike;
(f) *Archit Constr* **t. de charge,** tas-de-charge, springing stones (*on pier*).
Tasmanie [tasmani] *nf* Tasmania.
tasmanien, -ienne [tasmanjɛ̃, -jɛn] **1** *adj* Tasmanian. **2** *n* **T.,** Tasmanian.
tassage [tasaʒ] *nm Sp* crowding (*of opponent*).
tasse [tas] *nf* **(a)** cup; **t. à café,** coffee cup; **t. de café,** cup of coffee; **t. en métal,** tin mug; **boire dans une t.,** to drink out of a cup; **(b) boire une** *ou* **la t.,** to get a mouthful (*when swimming*).
tassé [tase] *adj* **(a)** (*serré*) huddled up (*prisoners, passengers etc*); **t. par l'âge,** shrunk with age; **(b)** *F* **1 500 pages bien tassées,** a good 1500 pages; **un verre bien t.,** a good glassful; **(c)** *F* **bien t.,** stiff (*whisky*); strong (*coffee*).
tasseau, -eaux [taso] *nm* batten (*supporting shelf etc*).
tassement [tasmɑ̃] *nm* **(a)** packing (down) (*of earth, snow etc*); **(b)** settling, sinking, subsidence (*of foundations etc*); *Méd* **t. de vertèbres,** spinal compression; **(c)** *Écon* slowing down (**de,** in).
tasser [tase] **1** *vt* **(a)** to cram, to squeeze (*objects etc*) (**dans,** into); to pack (down), to tamp (down) (*earth, snow etc*); to cram, to pack (*passengers etc*) (**dans,** into); **(b)** *Sp* to crowd (*opponent*). **2** *vi* (*of plants*) to grow thick(ly). **3 se tasser** *vpr* **(a)** (*of foundations etc*) to settle, to sink, to subside; **les opinions se sont tassées,** opinions have consolidated; *F* **ça se tassera,** things will settle down; **il commence à se t.,** (*se voûter*) he is beginning to shrink (with age); **(b)** (*se serrer*) to crowd (up) together, to huddle up; **tassez-vous un peu,** squeeze up a bit.
taste-vin [tastəvɛ̃] *nm inv* (*tasse*) wine taster.
tata [tata] *nf* **(a)** *Enf* auntie, aunty; **(b)** *Arg* (*homosexuel*) queer, *Br* poof(ter).
tatane [tatan] *nf F* shoe.
tatar, -are [tatar] **1** *adj Hist* Ta(r)tar. **2** *nm Ling* Ta(r)tar. **3** *n Hist* **T.,** Ta(r)tar.
tâter [tɑte] **1** *vt* **(a)** (*toucher*) to feel; **t. le pouls à qn,** to feel s.o.'s pulse; **avancer en tâtant,** to grope one's way forward; **t. la porte pour trouver la poignée,** to feel for the door handle; **(b)** *Fig* (*sonder*) to sound (*s.o.*) out; **t. l'opinion,** to sound out opinion; **t. le terrain,** to see how the land lies. **2** *vi* **(a)** *Litt* **t. d'un mets,** to taste a dish; **(b) t. d'un métier,** to try one's hand at a trade; *F* **il a tâté de la prison,** he's done time. **3 se tâter** *vpr* **(a)** to feel oneself (*for injuries*); **(b)** (*hésiter*) to think it over.
tâte-vin [tɑtvɛ̃] *nm inv* (*tasse*) wine taster.
tatillon, -onne [tatijɔ̃, -ɔn] *adj & n* finicky, fussy (person).
tâtonnant [tɑtɔnɑ̃] *adj* tentative, hesitant (*efforts, progress etc*).
tâtonnement [tɑtɔnmɑ̃] *nm* **(a)** (*d'aveugle etc*) groping; **(b)** (*essai*) trial and error; **procéder par tâtonnements,** to proceed by trial and error.
tâtonner [tɑtɔne] *vi* **(a)** to grope about; **se diriger en tâtonnant vers qch,** to grope *or* feel one's way towards sth; **(b)** *Fig* to proceed by trial and error; (*involontairement*) to grope about.
tâtons (à) [atɑtɔ̃] *adv* **avancer/entrer/sortir à t.,** to grope *or* feel one's way along/in/out; **chercher qch à t.,** to grope *or* feel for sth.
tatou [tatu] *nm Zool* armadillo.
tatouage [tatwaʒ] *nm* (*action*) tattooing; (*motif*) tattoo.
tatouer [tatwe] *vt* to tattoo; **se faire t. le bras,** to have one's arm tattooed.
tatoueur [tatwœr] *nm* tattooist, tattooer.
tau [to] *nm inv* (*lettre grecque*) tau.
taud [to] *nm Nau* rain awning, boat cover.
taudis [todi] *nm* slum.
taulard, -arde [tolar, -ard] *n Arg* convict; **vieux t.,** old lag.
taule [tol] *nf Arg* **(a)** (*prison*) clink, *Br* nick; *Mil F* glasshouse; **faire de la t.,** to do time *or* a stretch; **sortir de t.,** to come out of the clink *or Br* the nick; **faire dix ans de t.,** to do a ten-year stretch; **(b)** (*chambre*) room.
taulier, -ière [tolje, -jɛr] *n Arg* (*propriétaire*) (hotel) owner; (*gérant*) (hotel) keeper.
taupe [top] *nf* **(a)** *Zool* mole; **t. de mer,** porbeagle; **myope comme une t.,** blind as a bat; **noir comme une t.,** black as pitch; **(b)** (*fourrure*) moleskin; **(c)** *Scol F* special maths *or Am* math class; **(d)** *Arg Péj* **vieille t.,** (*femme*) old crone, old hag; **(e)** (*espion*) mole.
taupier [topje] *nm* mole catcher.
taupin [topɛ̃] *nm* **(a)** *Scol F* = student in special maths *or Am* math class; **(b)** *Mil Arch* sapper.
taupinière [topinjɛr] *nf* molehill; (*galeries*) mole tunnel.
taureau, -eaux [tɔro] *nm* **(a)** bull; **au cou de t.,** bull-necked; **course** *ou* **combat de taureaux,** bullfight; *F* **prendre le t. par les cornes,** to take the bull by the horns; **fort comme un t.,** as strong as an ox; **(b) le T.,** (*constellation, signe du zodiaque*) Taurus, the Bull; **être (du) T.,** to be (a) Taurus.
taurillon [tɔrijɔ̃] *nm* bull calf.
taurin [tɔrɛ̃] *adj* **jeux taurins,** bullfights.
tauromachie [tɔromaʃi] *nf* bullfighting, *Spéc* tauromachy.
tauromachique [tɔromaʃik] *adj* (*art, rules etc*) of bullfighting.
tautologie [tɔtɔlɔʒi] *nf* tautology.
tautologique [tɔtɔlɔʒik] *adj* tautological.
taux [to] *nm* **(a)** (*montant*) rate (*of wages, tax etc*); **t. de change,** exchange rate, rate of exchange; **(b)** (*proportion*) proportion, ratio; *Mil* scale (*of rations*); *Tech Ind* **t. de**

rendement, coefficient of efficiency, utilization factor; **t. de compression,** (*de moteur*) compression ratio; **(c)** (*pourcentage*) rate; **t. d'intérêt,** interest rate, rate of interest; **t. de huit pour cent,** rate of eight per cent; **t. interbancaire offert à Paris,** ≈ *Br* London Inter-Bank Offer Rate; *Can Banque* **t. préférentiel,** prime rate; **t. des naissances,** birth rate; *Mil* **t. de pertes,** casualty rate; *Méd* **t. d'invalidité,** degree of disablement; *Rail etc* **t. de pente,** rate of grade *or* gradient; **(d)** *Ordinat* ratio, rate.

tavelé [tavle] *adj* spotted, speckled (*face etc*) (**de,** with); marked (*fruit*).

taveler [tavle] *v* (**il tavelle; il tavellera**) **1** *vt* to spot, to speckle (*face etc*); to mark (*fruit*). **2 se taveler** *vpr* (*of fruit*) to become marked.

tavelure [tavlyr] *nf* **(a)** spot, speckle; (*de fruit*) mark; **(b)** *Agr* (*maladie*) scab.

taverne [tavɛrn] *nf* **(a)** (*restaurant*) café-restaurant; **(b)** *Can* beer parlour; **(c)** *Hist* (*auberge*) tavern.

tavernier, -ière [tavɛrnje, -jɛr] *n Hist* innkeeper.

taxable [taksabl] *adj* taxable.

taxateur [taksatœr] **1** *nm* taxer, assessor. **2** *adj* taxing (*official etc*).

taxation [taksɑsjɔ̃] *nf* **(a)** (*fixation des prix*) fixing of prices (**de,** for); *Jur* taxing (*of costs*); **(b)** (*par l'impôt*) taxation; (*contrôle*) assessment; **(c)** *Tél* **zone de t.,** charging area; *Ordinat* **période de t.,** charging period.

taxe [taks] *nf* **(a)** (*prix fixé*) fixed price, official price; **(b)** (*redevance*) charge (*for service*); **t. postale** *ou* **des lettres,** postage; **(c)** (*impôt*) tax, duty; **t. à la production** *ou* **à l'achat** *ou* **de consommation,** purchase tax; **t. à la valeur ajoutée,** *Br* value added tax, *US* processing tax; **t. sur les chiens,** dog tax; **t. de séjour,** tourist tax; **t. d'habitation,** inhabited house duty; **t. foncière,** land tax; **t. locale,** local tax; **t. officielle,** assessment; *Th etc* **t. sur les spectacles,** entertainment tax; **(d) t. de port,** harbour *or US* harbor dues; **(e)** *Jur* taxing, taxation (*of costs*).

taxer [takse] *vt* **(a)** (*fixer le prix de*) to fix the price of (*bread etc*); **(b)** to surcharge (*letter*); **(c)** *Tél* to charge for (*call*); **(d)** (*soumettre à l'impôt*) to tax (*s.o., sth*); **(e)** *Jur* to tax (*costs*); **(f)** to tax (**de,** with); (*accuser*) to accuse (**de,** of); (*qualifier*) to denounce (**de,** as).

taxi [taksi] *nm* **(a)** (*voiture*) taxi (cab), cab; **chauffeur de t.,** taxi driver; **avion-t., t. aérien,** taxiplane; **station de taxis,** taxi rank, *Am* taxi stand; **(b)** *F* (*chauffeur*) cabby, taxi driver.

taxidermie [taksidɛrmi] *nf* taxidermy.

taxidermiste [taksidɛrmist] *n* taxidermist.

taxi-girl [taksigœrl] *nf* (*danseuse*) taxi dancer; (*pl taxi-girls*).

taximètre [taksimɛtr] *nm* taximeter.

taxinomie [taksinɔmi] *nf Biol* taxonomy.

taxinomique [taksinɔmik] *adj* taxonomic(al).

taxiphone [taksifɔn] *nm* pay phone.

taxiway [taksiwɛ] *nm Av* taxiway.

taxonomie [taksɔnɔmi] *nf Biol* taxonomy.

taylorisme [telɔrism] *nm Econ* Taylorism.

Tchad [tʃad] *nm* Chad; **le lac T.,** Lake Chad.

tchadien, -ienne [tʃadjɛ̃, -jɛn] **1** *adj* Chadian. **2** *n* **T.,** Chadian.

tchador [tʃadɔr] *nm* (*voile*) chador, chuddar.

tchécoslovaque [tʃekɔslɔvak] **1** *adj* Czechoslovak, Czechoslovakian. **2** *n* **T.,** Czechoslovak, Czechoslovakian.

Tchécoslovaquie [tʃekɔslɔvaki] *nf* Czechoslovakia.

tchèque [tʃɛk] **1** *adj* Czech. **2** *nm Ling* Czech. **3** *n* **T.,** Czech.

tchin-tchin [tʃintʃin] *int F* cheers!, *Br* chin-chin!

te, *before a vowel sound or mute h* **t'** [t(ə)] *pron pers* **(a)** (*objet direct*) you; **il t'adore,** he adores you; **te voilà,** there you are; **(b)** (*objet indirect*) (to) you; **il t'a écrit,** he wrote to you; **il te l'a dit,** he told you so; **ça te servira,** it will be of use to you; **(c)** (*reflexive*) **tu te fatigues,** you are tiring yourself; **tu vas te faire mal,** you will hurt yourself; **à quelle heure t'es-tu levé(e)?,** (at) what time did you get up?; **va-t'en,** go away; **(d)** (*en s'adressant à Dieu*) Thee, You.

té [te] *nm* **(a) en té,** T-shaped; **(b) (équerre en) té,** T-square.

tec [tɛk] *nm inv abrév* **tonne-équivalent-charbon.**

technétium [tɛknesjɔm] *nm Ch* technetium.

technicien, -ienne [tɛknisjɛ̃, -jɛn] *n* technician; (*expert*) expert (**de,** in).

technicité [tɛknisite] *nf* technical nature.

technico-commercial, -iaux [tɛknikokɔmɛrsjal, -jo] *adj* **agent t.-c.,** sales engineer.

technicolor ® [tɛknikɔlɔr] *nm Cin* Technicolor ®; *Fig* **souvenirs en t.,** vivid memories.

technique [tɛknik] **1** *adj* technical. **2** *nf* **(a)** (*science*) technology; **t. de l'ingénieur,** engineering; **t. électrique,** electrical engineering; **t. des ultrasons,** ultrasonics; **(b)** (*méthode*) technique (*of artist, specialist etc*); **ce pianiste a une bonne t./manque de t.,** this pianist has good technique/lacks technique; *F* **tu n'a pas la t.!,** you haven't got the knack!

techniquement [tɛknikmɑ̃] *adv* technically.

technocrate [tɛknɔkrat] *n* technocrat.

technocratie [tɛknɔkrasi] *nf* technocracy.

technocratique [tɛknɔkratik] *adj* technocratic.

technologie [tɛknɔlɔʒi] *nf* technology; **haute t.,** high technology; **appareil de haute t.,** high-tech apparatus.

technologique [tɛknɔlɔʒik] *adj* technological.

technologiste [tɛknɔlɔʒist], **technologue** [tɛknɔlɔg] *n* technologist.

teck [tɛk] *nm* (*bois*) teak.

teckel [tɛkɛl] *nm* dachshund.

tectonique [tɛktɔnik] **1** *adj* tectonic. **2** *nf* tectonics.

teddy-bear [tedibɛr] *nm* teddy bear; (*pl teddy-bears*).

Te Deum [tedeɔm] *nm inv Mus Rel* Te Deum.

tee [ti] *nm Golf* tee.

teenager [tinedʒœr] *nm* teenager.

tee(-)shirt [tiʃœrt] *nm* teeshirt; (*pl tee(-)shirts*).

téflon ® [teflɔ̃] *nm* Teflon ®.

téflonisé ® [teflɔnize] *adj* Teflon ® (*saucepan etc*).

tégument [tegymɑ̃] *nm Biol* (in)tegument.

Téhéran [teerɑ̃] *n* Teh(e)ran.

teigne [tɛɲ] *nf* **(a)** (*papillon*) moth; **t. des draps,** clothes moth; **(b)** *Arg* (*personne méchante*) rat, *Br* nasty piece of work; **méchant** *ou* **mauvais comme la t.,** as nasty as they come; **(c)** *Méd* ringworm, *Spéc* tinea.

teigneux, -euse [tɛɲø, -øz] **1** *adj Méd* suffering from ringworm. **2** *n* **(a)** *Méd* ringworm sufferer; **(b)** *Arg* (*personne méchante*) rat, *Br* nasty piece of work.

teindre [tɛ̃dr] *v* (*prp* **teignant**; *pp* **teint**; *pr ind* **je teins, il teint, n. teignons**; *pr sub* **je teigne**; *impf* **je teignais**; *p hist* **je teignis**; *fu* **je teindrai**) **1** *vt* **(a)** to dye (*garment, hair etc*); **t. qch en rouge,** to dye sth red; **faire t. une robe,** to have a dress dyed; **(b)** to stain (*hands etc*). **2 se teindre** *vpr* **(a)** to dye one's hair; **(b)** *Litt* (*se colorer*) to be tinged (**de,** with).

teint [tɛ̃] *nm* **(a)** *Tex* (*couleur*) colour, *US* color; **bon t., grand t.,** fast colour; **tissu bon** *ou* **grand t.,** colourfast material; *Fig* **bon t.,** dyed-in-the-wool, staunch (*Catholic, Communist etc*); **(b)** (*du visage*) complexion, colour, *US* color; **au t. frais,** fresh-complexioned; **au t. jaune,** sallow; **avoir le t. pâle/bilieux,** to have a pale/bilious complexion.

teinte [tɛ̃t] *nf* **(a)** (*couleur nuancée*) tint, shade; **(b)** *Fig* touch, tinge, hint (*of irony, melancholy etc*).

teinter [tɛ̃te] **1** *vt* **(a)** to tint; **(lunettes à) verres teintés,** tinted glasses; **(b)** *Fig* **t. (légèrement),** to tinge (**de,** with). **2 se teinter** *vpr* (*se colorer*) *& Fig* to be tinged (**de,** with).

teinture [tɛ̃tyr] *nf* **(a)** (*action*) dyeing (*of cloth, hair etc*); tinting (*of drawing etc*); **(b)** (*produit*) dye; **tissu qui prend bien la t.,** material that dyes well; **couvertures sans t.,** undyed blankets; **(c)** *Fig* (*connaissance superficielle*) smattering (**d'histoire/d'anglais/***etc*, of history/English/*etc*); **(d)** *Pharm* tincture; **t. d'iode,** tincture of iodine.

teinturerie [tɛ̃tyr(ə)ri] *nf* **(a)** (*industrie*) dyeing; **(b)** (*pressing*) dry cleaner's.

teinturier, -ière [tɛ̃tyrje, -jɛr] *n* **(a)** *Ind* dyer; **(b)** (*qui tient un pressing*) dry cleaner.

tek [tɛk] *nm* (*bois*) teak.

tel, telle [tɛl] **1** *adj* **(a)** such; **un t. homme,** such a man; **de telles choses,** such things; **en t. lieu,** in such and such a place; **dans telle et telle rue,** in such and such a street; **selon que telle ou telle méthode est choisie,** depending on whether this or that method is chosen; **inutile de demander si t. ouvrage remplit son but mieux que t. autre,** it is useless to ask whether one book achieves its aim better than another; **dans telles circonstances qu'on le jugera convenable,** under such conditions as may be deemed suitable; **vous amènerez telle personne que vous voudrez,** you may bring any person you like; **sa bonté est telle que ...,** so great is his kindness that ...; **elle n'en a pas un besoin t. qu'il faille de lui rendre aujourd'hui,** she doesn't need it so badly that we have to give it to her today; **t. charlatan qu'il puisse être,** no matter how much of a quack he may be; **à t. point,** to such an extent, to such a pitch; **de telle sorte que** + *ind* (*result*) *ou* + *sub* (*purpose*), in such a way that; **il parle de telle sorte que je ne le comprends pas,** he speaks in such a way that I don't understand him; **je m'arrangerai de telle**

sorte qu'elle puisse partir dimanche, I will arrange things in such a way that *or* so that she can leave on Sunday;
(b) t. père, t. fils, like father like son;
(c) t. que, (*comme*) such as, like; **un homme t. que lui,** a man like him; **une lassitude telle qu'on en éprouve par un jour orageux,** a tiredness such as one feels on a stormy day; **des gens connus tel(s) qu'Elvis Presley,** well-known people such as *or* like Elvis Presley; **la clause telle qu'elle est,** the clause as it stands; **voir les hommes tels qu'ils sont,** to see men as they are; *F* **elle me l'a dit t. que!,** she told me straight out!;
(d) t. fut son langage, such were his words; **il n'est pas beau mais il se prend pour t.,** he is not handsome but he thinks he is *or* he thinks himself so;
(e) rien de t. qu'un bon cigare, there's nothing like *or* you can't beat a good cigar; **il n'est rien de t. que d'être jeune,** there's nothing like being young;
(f) *Litt* **il allait et venait t.** *ou* **telle une bête en cage,** he paced to and fro like a caged animal;
(g) t. quel, *Arg* **t. que,** (*chose*) (just) as it is *or* was; (*personne*) (just) as he is *or* was; **je vous achète la maison telle quelle,** I'll buy the house from you (just) as it is *or* stands; **j'ai retrouvé la maison telle quelle,** I found the house just as I had left it.
2 *pron* **t. l'en blâmait, t. l'en excusait,** one would blame him, another would excuse him; **t. admire le père qui blâme le fils,** some who blame the son admire the father; *Prov* **t. est pris qui croyait prendre,** it's a case of the biter bit; *Prov* **t. qui rit vendredi, dimanche pleurera,** laugh today, cry tomorrow; **t. ou t. vous dira que ...,** some people will tell you that ...; **je serais incapable d'attribuer l'article à t. ou t.,** I cannot attribute the article to any particular person.
3 *n* **un t., une telle,** so-and-so; **Monsieur un t.** *ou* **un T.,** Mr So-and-so.

télé [tele] *nf F* **(a)** TV, *Br* telly, tube; **regarder la t.,** to watch TV *or Br* the telly *or Br* the box *or* the tube; **(b) la t.,** (*organisme, technique, émissions*) TV.
télébenne [telebɛn] *nf* (*dispositif, cabine*) cable car.
téléboutique [telebutik] *nf* telephone shop (*of the French PTT*).
télécabine [telekabin] *nf* (*dispositif, cabine*) cable car.
télécarte [telekart] *nf* phonecard.
téléchargeable [teleʃarʒabl] *adj Ordinat* downloadable.
téléchargement [teleʃarʒəmɑ̃] *nm Ordinat* downloading; **effectuer un t.,** to download.
télécharger [teleʃarʒe] *vt Ordinat* to download.
télécinéma [telesinema] *nm* (*appareil*) telecine.
télécommande [telekɔmɑ̃d] *nf* remote control.
télécommander [telekɔmɑ̃de] *vt* **(a)** *Tech* to operate by remote control; **télécommandé,** remote-controlled; **(b)** *Fig* to control (*plot, decision etc*) from a distance.
télécommunication [telekɔmynikɑsjɔ̃] *nf* telecommunication.
téléconférence [telekɔ̃ferɑ̃s] *nf* teleconference.
télécopie [telekɔpi] *nf* (*procédé*) fax, facsimile transmission; (*message*) fax; **envoyer une t. à qn,** to send s.o. a fax, to fax s.o.; **numéro de t.,** fax number.
télécopieur [telekɔpjœr] *nm* fax (machine).
télécran [telekrɑ̃] *nm* large-sized television screen (*for an auditorium*).
télédétection [teledetɛksjɔ̃] *nf* remote detection.
télédiffusé [teledifyze] *adj* televised (*programme*).
télédiffuser [teledifyze] *vt* to televise.
télédiffusion [teledifyzjɔ̃] *nf* televising.
télédistribution [teledistribysjɔ̃] *nf* cable television.
télé(-)enseignement [teleɑ̃sɛɲəmɑ̃] *nm* distance learning.
téléférique [teleferik] **1** *adj Tech* telpher (*cable etc*). **2** *nm* (*dispositif, cabine*) cable car.
téléfilm [telefilm] *nm* television film, TV film.
télégénique [teleʒenik] *adj* telegenic.
télégestion [teleʒɛstjɔ̃] *nf Ordinat* teleprocessing, remote processing.
télégramme [telegram] *nm* telegram, cable, wire.
télégraphe [telegraf] *nm* telegraph.
télégraphie [telegrafi] *nf* telegraphy; *Vieilli* **t. sans fil,** wireless (telegraphy).
télégraphier [telegrafje] *v* (*impf & pr sub* **n. télégraphiions, v. télégraphiiez**) **1** *vt* to wire, to cable, to telegraph (*message*). **2** *vi* **t. à qn,** to wire *or* cable s.o..
télégraphique [telegrafik] *adj* telegraphic; **fil/poteau t.,** telegraph wire/pole; **dépêche t.,** telegram; **style t.,** telegraphic style, *F* telegraphese.
télégraphiquement [telegrafikmɑ̃] *adv* by telegram, by cable, by wire.
télégraphiste [telegrafist] *n* (*technicien*) telegraphist, telegraph operator; **(petit) t.,** (*porteur de dépêches*) telegraph boy.
téléguidage [telegidaʒ] *nm* remote control.
téléguidé [telegide] *adj* remote-controlled; **engin t.,** guided missile.
téléguider [telegide] *vt* **(a)** *Tech* to operate by remote control; **(b)** *Fig* to control (*plot, decision etc*) from a distance.
téléimprimeur [teleɛ̃primœr] *nm* teleprinter, *Am* teletypewriter.
téléinformatique [teleɛ̃fɔrmatik] *adj* teleprocessing, remote data processing.
télékinésie [telekinezi] *nf* telekinesis.
télémaintenance [telemɛ̃tnɑ̃s] *nf Astronaut* housekeeping.
télémanipulateur [telemanipylatœr] *nm Phys Nucl* remote manipulator.
Télémaque [telemak] *nm* Telemachus.
télémark [telemark] *nm Ski* telemark.
télématique [telematik] *nf* telematics.
télémesure [teleməzyr] *nf Électron etc* telemetering, telemetry.
télémètre [telemɛtr] *nm* telemeter; *Mil Phot* rangefinder.
télémétrie [telemetri] *nf* telemetry; *Mil Phot* range finding.
téléobjectif [teleɔbʒɛktif] *nm Phot* telephoto lens; **photographie au t.,** telephotography.
téléologie [teleɔlɔʒi] *nf Phil* teleology.
téléologique [teleɔlɔʒik] *adj* teleologic(al).
téléostéen [teleɔsteɛ̃] *nm* (*poisson*) teleost.
télépathe [telepat] **1** *adj* telepathic. **2** *n* telepathist, telepath.
télépathie [telepati] *nf* telepathy.
télépathique [telepatik] *adj* telepathic.
téléphérage [teleferaʒ] *nm Tech* telpherage, overhead cable transport.
téléphérique [teleferik] *adj & nm* = **TÉLÉFÉRIQUE**.
téléphonage [telefɔnaʒ] *nm* telephoning (*of telegram*).
téléphone [telefɔn] *nm* (*appareil*) telephone, phone; (*système*) telephone; **t. sans fil,** cordless (tele)phone; **t. cellulaire,** cellular phone; **t. de voiture,** car phone; **t. à carte,** cardphone; **t. bâtiment-terre,** ship to shore (tele)phone; *Pol* **t. rouge,** hot line; **t. vert,** hot line (*Élysée to Kremlin*); *F* **t. arabe,** bush telegraph, grapevine; *F* **par le t. arabe,** on the grapevine; **être abonné au t., avoir le t.,** to be on the phone; **numéro de t.,** (tele)phone number; **coup de t.,** (tele)phone call; **appeler qn au t., donner un coup de t. à qn,** to ring s.o. (up), to (tele)phone s.o., to call s.o. (up); **parler à qn au** *ou* **par t.,** to speak to s.o. on the phone; **apprendre qch par t.,** to learn of sth by phone; **demander qch par t.,** to phone for sth.
téléphoner [telefɔne] **1** *vt* **(a)** to (tele)phone (*piece of news etc*); **(b)** *Sp etc Fig* to telegraph (*one's punches, strokes etc*); *Pol etc* **une manœuvre téléphonée,** an obvious manoeuvre *or US* maneuver. **2** *vi* to (tele)phone; **t. à qn,** to ring s.o. (up), to (tele)phone s.o., to call s.o. (up); **t. à qn de venir,** to (tele)phone for s.o.. **3 se téléphoner** *vpr* to ring each other (up), to (tele)phone each other, to call each other (up).
téléphonie [telefɔni] *nf* telephony; **t. sans fil,** wireless telephony, radiotelephony.
téléphonique [telefɔnik] *adj* telephone (*booth, call, line, network etc*); **commande t.,** order by telephone, telephone order.
téléphoniste [telefɔnist] *n* (telephone) operator, *Br* telephonist.
téléphotographie [telefɔtɔgrafi] *nf* **(a)** *Télécom* phototelegraphy; **(b)** *Phot* telephotography; (*cliché*) telephotograph.
téléreportage [telerəpɔrtaʒ] *nm* (*activité*) television reporting; (*commentaire*) television report.
télescopage [telɛskɔpaʒ] *nm* telescoping (*of parts, trains etc*); *Aut* **t. (en série),** pile-up.
télescope [telɛskɔp] *nm* telescope.
télescoper [telɛskɔpe] **1** *vt* **(a)** *Aut Rail* to crash into (*vehicle, train etc*); **(b)** *Ling* to telescope (*words*). **2 se télescoper** *vpr* **(a)** (*of vehicles, trains*) to concertina; **(b)** *Fig* (*of memories, images etc*) to overlap.
télescopique [telɛskɔpik] *adj* telescopic.
téléscripteur [teleskriptœr] *nm* teleprinter, *Am* teletypewriter.
télésecrétariat [telesəkretarja] *nm* remote secretarial

services.
télésiège [telesjɛʒ] *nm* chair lift.
téléski [teleski] *nm* ski lift *or* tow.
télésouffleur [telesuflœr] *nm* teleprompter.
téléspectateur, -trice [telespɛktatœr, -tris] *n* (television) viewer.
télésurveillance [telesyrvɛjɑ̃s] *nf* remote surveillance.
télétex [teletɛks] *nm Ordinat* teletex.
télétexte [teletɛkst] *nm TV* teletext.
téléthèque [teletɛk] *nf* television film library.
télétraitement [teletrɛtmɑ̃] *nm Ordinat* teleprocessing, remote data processing.
télétransmission [teletrɑ̃smisjɔ̃] *nf* remote transmission.
Télétype ® [teletip] *nm* Teletype ®, teleprinter.
téléviser [televize] *vt* to televise; **journal télévisé,** television news.
téléviseur [televizœr] *nm* television (set).
télévision [televizjɔ̃] *nf* **(a)** (*organisme, technique, émissions*) television; **t. en couleur(s),** colour *or US* color television; **t. par câble,** cable television; **t. à péage** *ou* **payante,** pay television; **t. en circuit fermé,** closed-circuit television; **t. scolaire,** schools television, television for schools; **à la t.,** on television; **travailler à la t.,** to work in television; **(b)** (*poste*) television (set); **regarder la t.,** to watch television; **écran de t.,** television screen; **(c) (chaîne de) t.,** television channel; **t. généraliste,** general-interest television channel.
télévisuel, -elle [televizɥɛl] *adj* televisual; television (*version of play etc*).
télex [telɛks] *nm* (*service, message*) telex; **envoyer par t.,** to send by telex, to telex.
télexer [telɛkse] *vt* to telex.
télexiste [teleksist] *n* telex operator.
tellement [tɛlmɑ̃] *adv* **(a)** (*si*) so; (+ *comp*) so much; **elle en parle t. souvent,** she talks about it so often; **c'est t. facile,** it's so (very) easy; **ce serait t. plus simple,** it would be so much simpler; **il est t. sourd qu'il faut crier,** he is so deaf that one has to shout; **ce n'est pas t. beau,** it's not all that beautiful; **ça te plaît? — pas t.,** do you like it? – not all that much; **(b)** *F* **t. de,** (*nombre*) so many; (*quantité*) so much; **t. de choses à faire,** so many things to do, **ça demande t. de courage,** it requires so much courage; **(c)** (*tant*) so; **elle ne peut pas se lever, t. elle est malade,** she cannot get up, she is so ill.
tellure [telyr] *nm Ch* tellurium.
tellurique[1] [telyrik] *adj Ch* telluric (*acid*).
tellurique[2] *adj* telluric (*fever, currents*); **secousse t.,** earth tremor.
téméraire [temerɛr] *adj* rash, reckless (*person, undertaking*); rash (*judgment, statement*).
témérairement [temerɛrmɑ̃] *adv* rashly, recklessly.
témérité [temerite] *nf* rashness, recklessness.
témoignage [temwaɲaʒ] *nm* **(a)** (*attestation*) testimony, evidence; **recueillir des témoignages,** to collect evidence; **porter t.,** to bear witness, to give evidence; **rendre t. de qch,** to give evidence about sth, to bear testimony to sth; **rendre t. à** *ou* **pour qn,** to testify in s.o.'s favour *or US* favor; **appeler qn en t.,** to call s.o. as (a) witness; **invoquer le t. de qn,** to call s.o. to witness; **faux t.,** false witness, false evidence; (*délit*) perjury; **(b)** (*déclaration*) evidence, statement; **d'après son t.,** according to his statement; **t. des sens,** evidence of the senses; **(c)** (*démonstration*) token, sign (*of friendship, admiration etc*); **en t. de,** as a token *or* sign of.
témoigner [temwaɲe] **1** *vi* **(a)** to testify (**en faveur de/contre qn,** in s.o.'s favour *or US* favor/against s.o.); to give evidence (**en faveur de/contre qn,** for/against s.o.); **(b) t. de,** (*montrer*) to show, to give evidence of (*gratitude, good will, courage etc*); (*confirmer*) to testify to (*s.o.'s good faith etc*); **t. d'un goût pour ...,** to show *or* display a taste for ...; **t. de l'intérêt à qn,** to show an interest in s.o.; **t. du dédain à qn,** to show contempt for s.o.. **2** *vt* **(a)** (*attester*) **t. que,** to testify that; **(b)** (*montrer*) to show (*one's feelings, gratitude etc*) (**à qn,** to s.o.); **cela témoigne que/combien ...,** that shows that/how much ...; **t. que ...,** to show that ... .
témoin [temwɛ̃] *nm* **(a)** (*spectateur*) witness; **être t. de qch,** to witness sth, to be a witness to sth; **t. à un acte/d'un mariage,** witness to a signature/at a marriage; *Rel* **T. de Jéhovah,** Jehovah's Witness; **parler à qn sans témoins,** to speak to s.o. in private; **mes yeux en sont témoins,** I saw it with my own eyes;
(b) *Jur* witness; **t. à charge/à décharge,** witness for the prosecution/for the defence; **faux t.,** lying *or* untruthful witness; **barre des témoins,** witness box, *US* (witness) stand; **à la barre des témoins,** in the witness box, *US* on the stand; **t. oculaire,** eyewitness; **citer qn comme t.,** to call s.o. as (a) witness; **je vous prends tous à t. que ...,** I call on you all to witness that ...; **Dieu m'est t. que ...,** God is my witness that ...;
(c) (*dans un duel*) second;
(d) (*trace*) evidence; **les témoins d'une civilisation perdue,** the evidence of a lost civilization; **t. les coups que j'ai reçus,** witness the blows which I received;
(e) (*borne*) boundary mark;
(f) (*échantillon*) sample; *Ch* reference solution; **animal/plante/***etc* **t.,** (*dans un essai*) control animal/plant/*etc*; *Phot* **plaque t., épreuve t.,** pilot print; **denrée t.,** basic commodity; **appartement t.,** *Br* show flat, *Am* model apartment;
(g) *El Ind etc* **(lampe) t.,** pilot light, warning light;
(h) *Typ* dog's ear (*showing size before trimming*);
(i) *Sp* baton (*in relay race*).
tempe [tɑ̃p] *nf Anat* temple; **aux tempes grisonnantes,** (going) grey at the temples.
tempera (a) [atɑ̃pera] *Beaux-Arts* **1** *adj* **peinture a t.,** tempera painting. **2** *adv* **peindre a t.,** to paint in tempera.
tempérament [tɑ̃peramɑ̃] *nm* **(a)** (*physique*) constitution; **t. de fer,** iron constitution; *F* **se tuer le t.,** to ruin one's health; **(b)** (*moral*) temperament, disposition; **être d'un** *ou* **avoir un t. violent,** to have a violent disposition; **c'est un t.,** he has character; **avoir du t.,** to have character; (*sexuel*) to be highly sexed; **(c)** *Arch* (*modération*) moderation, restraint; **(d)** *Mus* temperament; **(e)** *Com* **à t.,** by instalments; **vente** *ou* **achat à t.,** *Br* hire purchase, *Am* installment plan.
tempéramental, -aux [tɑ̃peramɑ̃tal, -o] *adj* (*moral*) temperamental; (*physique*) constitutional.
tempérance [tɑ̃perɑ̃s] *nf* **(a)** (*modération*) temperance, moderation; **(b)** (*sobriété*) temperance; **société de t.,** temperance society.
tempérant [tɑ̃perɑ̃] *adj* temperate (*person*).
température [tɑ̃peratyr] *nf* temperature (*of person, liquid, region etc*); **t. du corps humain,** temperature of the human body, blood heat; *Méd F* **avoir** *ou* **faire de la t.,** to have a (high) temperature; *Phys* **t. d'ébullition,** boiling point; **prendre la t. d'un malade,** to take a patient's temperature; *Fig* **prendre la t. de l'auditoire/***etc*, to gauge the temperature of the audience/*etc*.
tempéré [tɑ̃pere] *adj* **(a)** temperate, moderate (*climate, speech*); restrained, sober (*style*); constitutional (*monarchy*); **(b)** *Mus* tempered.
tempérer [tɑ̃pere] *vt* (**je tempère, n. tempérons; je tempérerai**) to temper, to moderate (*heat, passions etc*).
tempête [tɑ̃pɛt] *nf Météo & Fig* storm; **t.,** (*sur un baromètre*) stormy; **t. de neige,** blizzard, snowstorm; **il faisait une t.,** a storm was raging; **une t. dans un verre d'eau,** a storm in a teacup; **t. d'injures/d'applaudissements,** storm of abuse/of applause.
tempêter [tɑ̃pete] *vi* (*of person*) to storm, to rage.
tempétueux, -euse [tɑ̃petɥø, -øz] *adj* tempestuous, stormy (*wind, sea etc*); boisterous (*welcome*); turbulent, stormy (*life*).
temple [tɑ̃pl] *nm* temple; (*protestant*) church, chapel; *Hist* **les chevaliers du T.,** the Knights Templar(s).
templier [tɑ̃plije] *nm Hist* (Knight) Templar.
tempo [tɛ̃po, tɛmpo] *nm Mus & Fig* tempo.
temporaire [tɑ̃pɔrɛr] *adj* **(a)** (*provisoire*) temporary; **agence de travail t.,** temporary employment agency; **emploi t.,** temporary job; **employé t.,** temporary employee; **(b)** *Mus* **valeur t. d'une note,** time value of a note.
temporairement [tɑ̃pɔrɛrmɑ̃] *adv* temporarily.
temporal, -ale, -aux [tɑ̃pɔral, -o] *Anat* **1** *adj* temporal (*bone, artery*). **2** *nm* **(a)** (*os*) temporal bone; **(b)** (*muscle*) temporal muscle, *Spéc* temporalis. **3** *nf* **temporale,** temporal (artery).
temporalité [tɑ̃pɔralite] *nf Rel Phil Gram* temporality.
temporel, -elle [tɑ̃pɔrɛl] *adj* **(a)** (*terrestre*) temporal, worldly; **déroulement t. de la vie,** the temporal progression of life; **(b)** *Gram* temporal (*clause etc*); **(c)** (*qui concerne le temps*) time; **sur une échelle temporelle de l'ordre de trois ans,** on a timescale of about three years.
temporellement [tɑ̃pɔrɛlmɑ̃] *adv* temporally.
temporisateur, -trice [tɑ̃pɔrizatœr, -tris] **1** *adj* temporizing. **2** *n* (*personne*) temporizer. **3** *nm El* (automatic) time switch.
temporisation [tɑ̃pɔrizasjɔ̃] *nf* temporizing, playing for time.
temporiser [tɑ̃pɔrize] *vi* to temporize, to play for time.

temps [tɑ̃] *nm* **(a)** (*durée*) time; **mettre beaucoup de t. à faire qch,** to take a long time doing sth; **tuer le t.,** to kill time; **pour passer le t.,** to pass *or* while away the time; **vous avez bien le t., vous avez tout le t.,** you have plenty of time; **cela prend du t.,** it takes *or* requires time; **prendre (tout) son t.,** to take one's time; **(donnez-moi) le t. de signer** *ou* **que je signe et je suis à vous,** just give me time *or* a minute to sign this and I'll be with you; **je trouve le t. long,** time is dragging; **nous n'avons pas le t. à présent,** there's no time *or* we don't have time now; **nous n'avons que le t. de ...,** we have just time to ...; **combien de t. faut-il pour ...?,** how long does it take to ...?; **gagner du t.,** to gain time; (*temporiser*) to temporize, to play for time; **perdre du t.,** to waste time; (*à cause d'un imprévu*) to lose time; **dans le cours du t., dans la suite du t., avec le t.,** in (the course of) time, with time; **de t. en t., de t. à autre,** now and then, from time to time; **en d'autres t.,** at any other time; **en tout t.,** at all times; **en même t.,** at the same time; **en même t. mère et sœur,** both mother and sister, mother and sister at the same time; **travailler à plein t./à t. partiel/à mi-t.,** to work full time/ part time/half time; **prendre/se donner du bon t.,** to have a good time, to enjoy oneself; *Prov* **le t., c'est de l'argent,** time is money; *Myth etc* **le T.,** (Father) Time;

(b) (*moment*) time; **un (certain) t., quelque t.,** for a while, for a time; **cela ne durera qu'un t.,** it will only last for a while, it won't last for ever; **tout n'a qu'un t.,** there is an end to everything; **t. mort,** period of inactivity; idle time *or* period (*of machine etc*); *Sp* stoppage; *Av* **t. mort au sol,** turn-round time; **le t. de la moisson,** harvest time; **le t. des cerises,** the cherry season; **T. de l'Ascension,** Ascensiontide; **les t. forts de l'actualité/de l'année 1991,** the main points of the news/main events of 1991; **il y a peu de t.,** a little while ago, not long ago; **peu de t. après,** not long after; **d'ici quelque t.,** in a short time; **au bout de très peu de t.,** in a very short space of time; **entre t.,** meanwhile, in the meantime; **tout le t.,** all the time; **il est beau t. qu'il est parti,** he left a long time ago; **faire un t. de galop,** to have a short gallop, to gallop for a time *or* a while; **t. d'arrêt,** pause, halt; **marquer un t.,** to pause;

(c) term (*of service etc*); **faire son t.,** to serve one's time; (*of convict*) to serve one's sentence, *F* to do one's time; **cette théorie a fait son t.,** this theory is out of date *or* out-dated *or* outmoded;

(d) *Tech* **t. à vide,** off-load period (*of machine etc*); **t. de fonctionnement,** running time (*of machine*); *Ind* **étude des t. et ordonnancements,** time and motion study; *Él Électron* **t. d'ouverture,** on period; *Ordinat* **utilisation (d'un ordinateur) en t. partagé,** time sharing; *Ordinat* **t. machine,** computer time; *Ordinat* **t. réel,** real time; *Ordinat* **horloge t. réel,** real-time clock; *Ordinat* **en t. réel,** in real time; *Ordinat* **base de t.,** time base; *Ordinat* **t. d'attente,** wait state;

(e) (*période, époque*) time(s), days; **les t. préhistoriques,** prehistoric times; **les hauts t.,** remote antiquity; **en t. normal,** in normal times, normally; **le bon vieux t.,** the good old days; **l'Angleterre des t. passés,** the England of the past; **dans le t., au t. jadis,** in times past, in the old days; **dans la suite des t.,** in the course of time; **en d'autres t.,** (*dans le passé*) formerly, in other times; (*dans le futur*) in times to come; **dans ce t.-là,** at that time; **ces t.-ci,** these days; **ce fut un grand homme dans son t.,** he was a great man in his day; **elle a eu son t. de beauté,** she was a beauty in her day; **du t.** *ou* **au t. de Napoléon,** in Napoleon's time;

(f) du t. de ma jeunesse, du t. où j'étais jeune, when I was young, in my youth; **les t. sont durs,** times are hard; **il fut un t. où ...,** there was a time when ...; **signe des t.,** sign of the times; **par le t. qui court, par les t. qui courent,** as things are at present; **être de son t., vivre avec son t.,** to move with the times, to be up to date; **vous n'êtes pas de votre t.,** you're behind the times; **de notre t.,** nowadays; **il n'en était pas ainsi de mon t.,** it wasn't so in my day; **cela est arrivé de mon t.,** it happened in my time; **de tout t., en tout t.,** at all times, always;

(g) (*heure*) **arriver à t.,** to arrive in time; **arriver juste à t.,** to arrive just in time *or* in the nick of time; **en t. voulu** *ou* **utile,** in due time; **je serai de retour en t. voulu,** I shall be back in *or* on time; **il est t. qu'elle descende,** it is time she came down; **il est grand t. que ...,** it's high time *or* about time that ...; **il serait t.!,** it's about time!; **il n'est plus t.,** it is too late; **il n'était que t.,** it was only just in time; **il n'est que t. de faire cela,** it's high time to do this; **il était t.!,** it was a narrow escape!; **venir en son t.,** (*of event*) to be timely;

(h) *Astron* **t. apparent,** apparent time; **t. vrai,** true time; **t. moyen local,** local mean time; **t. astronomique,** astronomical time;

(i) (*occasion*) opportunity; **il y a t. pour tout,** there is a time for everything; **chaque chose en son t.,** everything in good time; **en t. et lieu,** in the proper time and place; **je le ferai à mon t.,** I shall do it in my own time *or* when it suits me;

(j) *Météo* weather; **par tous les t.,** in all weathers; **vous sortez par un pareil t.** *ou* **par le t. qu'il fait!,** you're going out in weather like this *or* in this weather!; **quel t. fait-il?,** what's the weather like?; **quelque t. qu'il fasse,** whatever the weather (is like); **si le t. le permet,** weather permitting; **beau t.,** fine weather; **il fait beau/mauvais t.,** the weather's fine/bad; *F* **il fera beau t. quand je ferai cela,** it'll be a long time before I do that; *Nau* **gros t.,** heavy weather; **le t. est à la pluie,** it looks like rain, we're going to have rain; **prévision du t.,** weather forecast; **une robe couleur du t.,** a sky-blue dress;

(k) *Gram* tense; **t. primitifs,** principal parts (*of a verb*); **adverbes de t.,** adverbs of time;

(l) *Mus* beat; **mesure à trois t.,** three-four time;

(m) *Mil etc* **exercice en trois t.,** exercise in three motions; **au t.!,** as you were!; **au t. pour moi,** my mistake!; *Escrime* **coup de t.,** time thrust;

(n) *Tech* **moteur à deux/à quatre t.,** two-stroke/four-stroke engine;

(o) *Chir etc* stage (*of operation, of labour*);

(p) *Sp* time (*of runner etc*).

tenable [tənabl] *adj* (*often with negation*) **(a)** *Mil etc* tenable, defensible (*position*); **(b)** bearable (*state of affairs*); **par cette chaleur, le bureau n'est pas t.,** in this heat the office is unbearable; **ce n'est plus t., je pars,** it has become unbearable *or* I can't bear it any longer, I'm going.

tenace [tənas] *adj* tenacious, stubborn (*person*); clinging (*smell, perfume*); fast (*colour, resistance*); dogged, stubborn (*will, purpose*); retentive (*memory*); persistent (*prejudice, illness, pain*); **espoir t.,** fond hope; **les vieilles habitudes sont tenaces,** old habits die hard.

tenacement [tənasmɑ̃] *adv* stubbornly, tenaciously.

ténacité [tenasite] *nf* tenacity, stubbornness (*of person*); clinging nature (*of smell*); doggedness (*of resistance*); persistance (*of prejudice, illness*).

tenaillant [tənajɑ̃] *adj* gnawing (*hunger*); tormenting (*remorse*).

tenaille [tənaj] *nf* **(a)** (*pour saisir*) tongs; **t. à vis,** hand vice; **t. de cordonnier,** shoemaker's nippers; **(b) tenailles,** pincers (*for drawing nails*); *Mil* **manœuvre en tenailles,** pincer movement.

tenailler [tənaje] *vt Hist & Fig* to torture; **tenaillé par la faim/par le remords,** gnawed by hunger/tortured *or* tormented by remorse.

tenancier, -ière [tənɑ̃sje, -jɛr] *n* **(a)** manager (*of hotel etc*); keeper (*of brothel, gambling house*); **(b)** *Arch* holder (*of land*); **(c)** (*fermier*) tenant farmer.

tenant, -ante [tənɑ̃, -ɑ̃t] **1** *adj* **(a) séance tenante,** there and then, then and there, on the spot; **(b) chemise à col t.,** shirt with collar attached. **2** *n* **(a)** (*partisan*) champion, defender (*of s.o., an opinion etc*); **(b)** *Sp* holder (*of title, cup*). **3** *nm* **(a)** *Hér* supporter (*of shield*); **(b) tout d'un (seul) t.,** (*of landed property*) continuous, all in one block, lying together; **tenants et aboutissants,** adjacent parts (*of estate*); *Fig* ins and outs, full details (*of an affair*).

tendance [tɑ̃dɑ̃s] *nf* tendency, inclination; (*de l'opinion, de l'art moderne, du cinéma etc*) trend; (*d'un livre, discours etc*) tenor; **tendance(s) vers le communisme,** communist leanings *or* tendencies; **avoir (une) t. à qch/à faire qch,** to be inclined to sth/to do sth, to have a tendency to sth/to do sth; *Bourse* **t. générale à la hausse/baisse,** general upward/downward trend.

tendancieusement [tɑ̃dɑ̃sjøzmɑ̃] *adv* tendentiously.

tendancieux, -ieuse [tɑ̃dɑ̃sjø, -jøz] *adj* tendentious; *Jur* leading (*question*).

tender [tɑ̃dɛr] *nm Rail Nau* tender.

tendeur, -euse [tɑ̃dœr, -øz] **1** *n* (*personne*) hanger (*of tapestries*); setter, layer (*of traps, snares*). **2** *nm* **(a)** *Tech* (*de fil métallique*) (wire) strainer; (*de corde de tente*) runner; **t. de chaîne,** (*de bicyclette*) chain adjuster *or* tightener; **t. à vis,** turnbuckle; **(b)** (*de machine à coudre*) tension (device); **(c) t. pour chaussures,** shoe tree; **(d)** (*courroie élastique*) elastic strap.

tendineux, -euse [tɑ̃dinø, -øz] *adj Anat* tendinous; **viande tendineuse,** stringy meat.

tendinite [tɑ̃dinit] *nf Méd* tendinitis.

tendon [tɑ̃dɔ̃] *nm Anat* tendon, sinew; **t. d'Achille,** Achilles tendon; **t. du jarret,** hamstring.

tendre¹ [tɑ̃dr] **1** *adj* **(a)** soft (*stone, porcelain, wood, metal, grass, pencil etc*); delicate, soft (*colour* etc); new, fresh (*bread*); **viande t.,** tender meat; **peau t.,** sensitive *or* tender *or* soft skin; *Fig* **avoir la peau t.,** to be thin-skinned *or* touchy; *Equitation* **cheval t. à l'éperon,** horse tender to the spur; **(b)** early (*age, childhood*); **dès ma plus t. enfance,** from my earliest youth; **(c)** (*affectueux*) fond, tender, affectionate, loving (*person, look etc*); tender (*heart*); **ne pas être t. (pour** *ou* **avec qn),** to be hard *or* severe (on s.o.); **il a le vin t.,** drink makes him sentimental. **2** *nm* **(a)** *F* **avoir un t. pour qn,** to have a soft spot for s.o.; **(b)** *Culin* **t. de tranche,** topside (of beef). **3** *n* (*personne*) softhearted person.

tendre² **1** *vt* **(a)** (*raidir*) to stretch, to tighten (*a belt*); to tighten (*violin string etc*); to bend, to draw (*bow*); to set (*spring, trap*);

(b) (*poser*) to fix up (*tent, net, ropes etc*); to spread (*sail, net etc*); to stretch (*material, canvas*); to hang (*wallpaper, tapestry*); **t. un piège à qn,** to set a trap for s.o.;

(c) (*porter en avant*) to stretch out, to hold out (*arm, foot etc*); **t. la main,** to hold out *or* stretch out one's hand; (*mendier*) to beg; *Fig* **t. l'oreille,** to prick up one's ears; **t. le cou,** to crane one's neck; **t. un briquet/***etc* **à qn,** to hold out a lighter/*etc* to s.o..

2 *vi* to tend, to lead (**à,** to); **vos paroles ne tendent qu'à le fâcher,** your words only tend to annoy him; **t. vers le même résultat,** to tend *or* lead towards the same result; **où tendent ces questions?,** where are these questions leading?; **nez tendant à l'aquilin,** nose inclined to be aquiline; **t. à sa fin,** (*of thing*) to be near(ing) its end; **cela tendrait à confirmer la première hypothèse,** that would tend to confirm the original hypothesis; **les voyelles faibles tendent à disparaître,** weak vowels tend to disappear, there is a tendency for weak vowels to disappear; *Math* **la valeur de n tend vers zéro,** the value of n tends towards zero.

3 se tendre *vpr* to become taut; (*of relations*) to become strained; (*of prices etc*) to harden; **pas une main ne s'est tendue vers moi,** no hand stretched out towards me.

tendrement [tɑ̃drəmɑ̃] *adv* tenderly, fondly, affectionately; **ménage t. uni,** loving couple.

tendresse [tɑ̃drɛs] *nf* **(a)** (*affection*) tenderness, fondness; **t. maternelle,** maternal affection *or* love; **avoir de la t. pour qn,** to feel tenderness *or* affection for s.o., to be fond of s.o.; **avec t.,** fondly, tenderly, lovingly; **(b) tendresses,** (*témoignages d'affection*) tokens of affection, caresses; **mille tendresses,** (*en fin de lettre*) (with) lots of love, all my love; **(c) tendresses royalistes,** royalist sympathies.

tendreté [tɑ̃drəte] *nf* tenderness (*of food*).

tendron [tɑ̃drɔ̃] *nm* **(a)** *Bot* tender shoot; **(b)** *Culin* tendron, gristle (*of veal*); **(c)** *F* (*jeune fille*) very young and innocent girl.

tendu [tɑ̃dy] *adj* **(a)** taut, tight (*string, canvas etc*); flat (*trajectory*); strained (*relations*); tense (*situation, atmosphere*); distended (*stomach*); **corde tendue,** taut *or* tight rope; *Gym* tightrope; **chaîne mal tendue,** slack chain; **elle est tendue** *ou* **elle a les nerfs tendus en ce moment,** she is tense *or* strung up *or* strained at the moment; **style t.,** strained *or* stilted style; *Bourse* **prix tendus,** hard *or* firm prices; **(b)** *Ling* strong (*sound*); voiceless (*consonant*); **(c)** outstretched (*hand*); **tenir qch à bras tendus,** to hold sth at arm's length; **politique de la main tendue,** policy of making friendly overtures; **(d) t. de,** (*tapissé*) hung with (*tapestries, material*); covered with (*wallpaper*).

ténèbres [tenɛbr] *nfpl* darkness, gloom; **les t. de la nuit,** the shades of night; **le Prince des T.,** the Prince of Darkness; **t. de l'ignorance/de l'inconscient,** darkness of ignorance/of the unconscious.

ténébreux, -euse [tenebrø, -øz] **1** *adj* **(a)** (*obscur*) gloomy, dark (*wood, prison etc*); **(b)** (*mystérieux*) mysterious, sinister, dark (*affair etc*); obscure (*style, period of history*). **2** *nm Hum* **beau t.,** mean and moody beau.

teneur¹, -euse [tənœr, -øz] *n* **(a)** *Typ* **t. de copie,** copy holder; **(b) t. de livres,** book-keeper.

teneur² *nf* **(a)** terms (*of document, letter etc*); **(b)** tenor (*of life*); **(c)** *Tech Ind etc* (*quantité*) content; **t. en eau/or,** water/gold content; **(d)** *Minér etc* (*qualité*) grade (*of ore, metal etc*); **minerai/acier de haute t.,** high-grade ore/steel; **(e)** *Ch* (standard) strength, titration (standard) (*of solution*); **(f)** *Phys Nucl* **t. isotopique,** isotopic abundance.

ténia [tenja] *nm Méd* tapeworm, *Spéc Br* taenia, *US* tenia.

tenir [tənir] *v* (*prp* **tenant**; *pp* **tenu**; *pr ind* **je tiens, il tient, n. tenons, v. tenez, ils tiennent**; *pr sub* **je tienne, n. tenions**; *impf* **je tenais**; *p hist* **je tins, n. tînmes, v. tîntes, ils tinrent**; *p sub* **je tinsse, il tînt, n. tinssions**; *fu* **je tiendrai**) **1** *vt* **(a)** to hold; **t. qch à la main/sur ses genoux,** to hold sth in one's hand/in one's lap; **t. qn par la taille,** to hold s.o. round the waist; *F* **t. un bon rhume,** to have a stinking cold; **je tiens mon homme,** I've got my man; **t. tout dans un coup d'œil,** to take in everything at a glance; **t. qn de près,** to keep s.o. under strict control; *Prov* **un 'tiens' vaut mieux que deux 'tu l'auras', mieux vaut t. que courir,** a bird in the hand is worth two in the bush; **tiens!, tenez!,** look!, look here!; **tenez, mon chien à moi ...,** now, that dog of mine ...; **tenez! (ceci est pour vous),** here you are!; **tiens, ça ne m'étonne pas,** well, that doesn't surprise me; **tiens, voilà Paul!,** hullo *or* hello, here's Paul!; **tenez, ôtez-moi cela,** here, take this away;

(b) (*contenir*) to hold; **voiture qui tient six personnes,** car that holds *or* takes six; **baril qui tient l'eau,** barrel that holds water *or* that is watertight;

(c) t. de, (*recevoir*) to have *or* get (*sth*) from; **j'en suis sûr, je le tiens de mon médecin,** I am sure of it, I have it from my doctor; **il tient sa timidité de sa mère,** he gets his shy nature from his mother;

(d) (*stocker*) to keep, to stock (*groceries etc*);

(e) elle en tient, (*of partridge etc*) she's winged; *F* **il en tient,** (*of person*) he's had a nasty blow; *Arg* **en t. une,** to be gloriously drunk;

(f) (*gérer*) to keep, to run (*shop, hotel, school etc*); to have charge of (*the cash*); **chambre bien tenue,** well-kept *or* tidy room; **Mlle Martin tenait le piano,** Miss Martin was at the piano;

(g) to hold, to maintain (*opinion, certain line of conduct*); to keep (*one's word, promise*); **t. un rôle difficile/important,** to have a difficult/important role;

(h) (*dire*) to deliver (*speech etc*); **t. des propos ambigus,** to use ambiguous words, to speak ambiguously;

(i) t. qn en mépris/en grand respect, to hold s.o. in contempt/in great esteem;

(j) (*maîtriser*) to hold back, to restrain (*one's impatience*); to hold (*one's tongue*); to control (*children, horse*); **t. son sérieux,** to keep a straight face; **t. qn par le chantage/la pitié,** to have a hold over s.o. by using blackmail/pity;

(k) (*dans une certaine position*) to hold, to keep; (*dans un certain état*) to keep; **cette poutre tient le plafond,** that beam holds up the ceiling; **mon rhume me tient à la maison,** my cold is keeping me indoors; **t. son chien en laisse,** to keep one's dog on a lead; **il nous a tenus debout pendant deux heures,** he kept us standing for two hours; **t. les yeux fermés,** to keep one's eyes shut; **t. qn captif,** to keep *or* hold s.o. prisoner; **t. qch en état** *ou* **en bon état,** to keep sth in good order; **t. qn à l'œil,** to keep an eye on s.o.; **cette visite m'a tenu longtemps,** this visit kept *or* delayed me a long time; **tenez votre gauche/votre droite,** keep to the left/to the right;

(l) (*ne pas pouvoir sortir de*) to be confined to (*one's room, one's bed*);

(m) t. la mer, (*of ship*) to keep the sea; (*of country*) to be master *or* mistress of the seas; *Aut* **t. la route,** to hold the road; **capable/incapable de t. la mer,** seaworthy/unseaworthy (*ship*);

(n) (*occuper*) to occupy, to take up (*space*); **vous tenez trop de place,** you are taking up too much room; **la table tient la moitié de la pièce,** the table occupies *or* takes up half the room; **t. toute la route,** (*of car, driver*) to hog the road; **les soucis/enfants tiennent trop de place dans ta vie,** worries/children take up *or* occupy too much of your life;

(o) (*considérer*) **t. qn pour habile/***etc*, to think *or* consider s.o. clever/*etc*; **t. qch comme établi,** to assume sth; **t. une information comme incertaine,** to treat a piece of information as doubtful; **tenez cela pour fait,** consider it done.

2 *vi* **(a)** to hold; (*of knot, rope etc*) to hold up, to stay up; (*of unstable construction etc*) to hold up, to stay up; **clou qui tient bien,** nail that holds well; **la porte tient,** the door won't open; **ça tient au mur par des clous,** it's kept on the wall with nails; **vêtements qui ne tiennent plus (ensemble),** garments that won't hold together *or* that are falling to pieces; *Fig* **leur succès ne tient qu'à un fil,** their success is hanging by a thread; *F* **cela tient comme poix,** it sticks like pitch; *F* **ses pieds ne tiennent pas à terre,** he is never still for a minute; **il ne tient plus sur ses jambes,** he is ready to drop (with fatigue); **elle ne pouvait t. en place,** she couldn't keep still;

(b) (*border*) to border on, to adjoin; **sa terre tient à la**

mienne, his estate borders on *or* adjoins mine;

(c) (*résister*) **t. (bon** *ou* **ferme),** to hold out, to stand fast *or* firm, to hold one's own; (*of cable etc*) to stand the strain, to hold; **tenez bon!,** hold on!; **tenez bon** *ou* **ferme!,** hold tight!; *Nau* (a)vast!; *Fig* never say die!; **t. le coup,** to hold out; **je n'ai pas pu t. une heure,** I couldn't hold out for an hour; **votre argument ne tient pas debout/guère,** your argument doesn't stand/hardly stands up; **il n'y a pas de raisons qui tiennent,** there are no valid reasons; **je n'y tiens plus,** I can't stand it any longer; **n'y tenant plus, elle a tout avoué,** unable to stand it any longer, she confessed everything;

(d) (*durer*) to last; **ma mise en plis n'a pas tenu deux jours,** my set didn't last *or* stay in two days; **le vent va t.,** the wind will last; **son commerce ne tiendra pas,** his business won't last; **couleur qui tient bien,** fast colour; **mon offre/le pari tient toujours,** my offer/the bet still stands; **ça tient toujours pour dimanche?,** is it still on for Sunday;

(e) (*être contenu*) **voiture où l'on tient à six,** car that takes *or* holds six; **on tient douze à cette table,** this table seats twelve; **tous ces livres tiendront dans cette caisse,** all these books will easily fit *or* go into this box; **tout ça tient en deux mots,** all that can be said in a couple of words;

(f) *Arg* **qu'est-ce qu'il tient!,** (*il est ivre*) he's completely sozzled; (*il est idiot*) what an idiot!;

(g) (*avoir lieu*) be held, to take place; **le marché tient tous les samedis,** the market is held *or* takes place on Saturdays;

(h) t. pour, (être partisan de) to be for, to be in favour *or US* favor of (*s.o., sth*); **en t. pour qn,** to be fond of s.o.; **en t. pour son idée,** to stick to one's idea;

(i) t. à, (*aimer*) to value, to prize (*liberty etc*); **elle tient beaucoup à cette amie/ce vase,** she is very fond of this friend/this vase; **t. à la vie,** to value one's life, to care about living; **cette idée me tient à cœur,** this idea is close *or* dear to my heart, I am keen on the idea; **tu en veux? — je n'y tiens pas,** do you want some? — not particularly *or* I'm not bothered; *F* **je n'y tiens pas plus que cela,** I'm not that keen on it; **t. à faire qch,** to be anxious *or* keen to do sth; **je tiens à vous le dire,** I am anxious to tell you, I am making a point of telling you; **t. à ce qu'on fasse qch,** to be anxious that sth should be done; **je tiens beaucoup à ce qu'il vienne,** I am very anxious that he should come *or* for him to come; **puisque vous y tenez,** since you are set *or* keen on it;

(j) t. à , (*venir de*) to be the result of, to be due to; **cela tient à son éducation,** that's the result of *or* due to his education; **à quoi cela tient-il?,** what's the reason for it?, what is it due to?; **cela tient à ce que vous êtes écossais,** that comes of your being Scottish, that's because you're Scottish;

(k) t. de, (*ressembler à*) to take after (*s.o.*); **cela tient du miracle/du délire/du génie,** there is something miraculous/mad/of the genius about it; **cela tient de (la) famille,** it runs in the family; **il a de qui t.,** it runs in his family.

3 *v impers* **il tient qu'à vous de le faire,** it rests *or* lies entirely with you to do it; **il ne tient qu'à vous que cela se fasse,** it depends entirely on you whether it is done; **qu'à cela ne tienne,** never mind that, that need be no obstacle; **s'il ne tient qu'à cela,** if that is all (the difficulty); **il n'a tenu à rien qu'il ne se noyât,** he was as near as could be to drowning;

4 se tenir *vpr* **(a)** (*dans un certain état, dans une certaine position*) to keep; (*dans un certain lieu*) to stay, to remain; **se t. chez soi,** to stay *or* remain at home; **tenez-vous là,** stay where you are!, don't move!; **tenez-vous droit,** (*assis*) sit (up) straight, sit up; (*debout*) stand (up) straight; **se t. tranquille,** to keep quiet; **se t. bien/mal,** (*à cheval*) to sit well/badly, to have a good/a poor seat; **ce tissu se tient bien,** this material keeps its shape well; **se t. debout,** to be standing, to stand; **se t. auprès de qn,** to be standing *or* stand next to s.o.; **tenez-vous bien, la voiture a disparu,** prepare yourself for a shock *or* brace yourself, the car has disappeared; **et alors, tiens-toi bien, il n'était pas là non plus!,** well, you won't believe it, but he wasn't there either!;

(b) se t. à qch, to hold on to sth; **tenez-vous bien!,** (*dans un autobus etc*) hold tight!; **ils se tenaient par la main,** they were holding hands; **se t. les côtes de rire,** to hold one's sides laughing;

(c) la boisson, la misère, le crime, tout cela se tient, drink, poverty, crime, all these go together; **ses arguments se tiennent (bien),** his arguments hold together;

(d) (*se conduire*) to behave; **on sait se t. avec les femmes,** I *or* we know how to behave in the presence of ladies; **tenez-vous bien!, vous n'avez qu'à vous bien t.!,** you'd better behave yourself;

(e) (*se retenir*) **il ne se tient pas de joie,** he cannot contain his joy *or* himself for joy; **je ne pouvais me t. de rire,** I couldn't help laughing; **je ne pus me t. de l'embrasser/de tout lui avouer,** I couldn't resist giving him a kiss/confessing everything to him;

(f) s'en t. à, (*se borner à*) to keep to, to confine oneself to (*pleasantries, generalities etc*); to adhere to, to abide by (*decision, a treaty*); **s'en t. à ce qu'on a décidé,** to stick to *or* abide by what was decided; **il ne s'en tint pas là,** he did not stop at that; **tenons-nous-en là,** let it go at that; **je ne sais pas à quoi m'en t.,** I don't know what to believe, I don't know how I stand;

(g) (*avoir lieu*) to be held, to take place; **la conférence se tiendra à l'université,** the lecture will be held *or* will take place at the university;

(h) tiens-le-toi pour dit!. (*avertissement*) I'm telling you once and for all *or* for the last time!

tennis [tenis] *nm* **(a)** (*sport*) tennis; **t. de table,** table tennis; **(b) (court de) t.,** tennis court; **(c)** (*chaussure*) tennis shoe.

tennisman, *pl* **tennismen** [tenisman, tenismen] *nm F* tennis player.

tenon [tənɔ̃] *nm* **(a)** *Menuis* tenon; **(b)** pivot (*of crowned tooth*).

ténor [tenɔr] **1** *nm* **(a)** *Mus* tenor; **(b)** *Pol Sp etc F* star performer. **2** *adj Mus* **saxophone t.,** tenor saxophone.

tenrec [tɑ̃rɛk] *nm Zool* tenrec.

tenseur [tɑ̃sœr] **1** *adj Anat* **muscle t.,** tensor. **2** *nm* **(a)** *Anat* tensor; **(b)** *Math* tensor; **(c)** *Tech* = **TENDEUR 2 (a)** .

tensioactif, -ive [tɑ̃sjɔaktif, -iv] *Ch* **1** *adj* surface-active, wetting (*agent*). **2** *nm* surface-active *or* wetting agent, surfactant.

tension [tɑ̃sjɔ̃] *nf* **(a)** tension (*of muscles, violin string, Fig between people etc*); **écrou à t.,** tightening nut; **t. de rupture,** breaking strain *or* stress; **t. de cisaillement,** shear stress; *Phys* **t. superficielle,** surface tension; *Tech* **t. de courroie,** belt tension; **acier à haute t.,** high-tensile steel; **période de t. internationale,** period of international tension; **t. des esprits,** tension, tense atmosphere; **t. intellectuelle,** mental stress; **état de t. nerveuse,** state of nervous tension; **la guerre nous met sous t.,** the war is putting us under stress *or* strain;

(b) *Bourse* hardness, firmness (*of prices*);

(c) pressure (*of steam etc*); *Méd* **t. artérielle, t. du sang,** blood pressure; *F* **avoir** *ou* **faire de la t.,** to suffer from *or* have high blood pressure; **prendre la t. de qn,** to take s.o.'s blood pressure;

(d) *Él Électron* voltage, tension; **basse/haute t.,** low/high voltage *or* tension; **t. nulle,** zero voltage, zero potential; **t. de 2 000 volts,** tension of 2000 volts; **sans t.,** dead; **mettre sous t.,** to apply the voltage to, to switch on (*circuit etc*); **fil sous t.,** live *or* charged wire; **montage de piles en t.,** connection of batteries in series.

tensoriel, -ielle [tɑ̃sɔrjɛl] *adj Math* tensorial.

tentaculaire [tɑ̃takylɛr] *adj Zool* tentacular; *Fig* **ville tentaculaire,** sprawling town.

tentacule [tɑ̃takyl] *nm Zool & Fig* tentacle.

tentant [tɑ̃tɑ̃] *adj* tempting, enticing (*meal etc*); attractive, tempting (*offer*).

tentateur, -trice [tɑ̃tatœr, -tris] **1** *adj* tempting. **2** *nm* tempter; *Rel* **le T.,** the Tempter. **3** *nf* **tentatrice,** temptress.

tentation [tɑ̃tasjɔ̃] *nf* temptation (**de faire qch,** to do sth); **la t. de saint Antoine,** the temptation of Saint Anthony; **je n'ai pas pu résister à la t. de lui faire la grimace,** I couldn't resist the temptation to make a face at him; **et si vous aviez la t. de nous rejoindre ...,** and if you felt tempted to join us ... .

tentative [tɑ̃tativ] *nf* attempt, endeavour, *US* endeavor, bid; **t. d'évasion,** attempt to escape, escape bid; **t. de suicide,** suicide attempt, attempted suicide; **t. d'assassinat,** murder attempt, attempted murder; **t. de résistance,** attempt to resist.

tente [tɑ̃t] *nf* **(a)** tent; **t. conique,** bell tent; **t. igloo,** igloo tent; *Méd* **t. à oxygène,** oxygen tent; **coucher sous la t.,** to sleep under canvas; *Fig* **se retirer dans** *ou* **sous sa t.,** to sulk in one's corner; **(b)** *Nau* awning.

tente-abri [tɑ̃tabri] *nf* shelter tent; (*pl tentes-abris*).

tenter [tɑ̃te] *vt* **(a)** *Bible & Arch* (*éprouver*) to tempt, to put (*s.o.*) to the test; *Fig* **t. le diable,** to tempt fate;

(b) t. la chance *ou* **la fortune,** to try one's luck; *F* **t. le**

coup, to give it *or* have a try *or* go; **t. la Providence,** to tempt Providence;

(c) (*faire envie à, essayer de séduire*) to tempt (*s.o.*); **se laisser t.,** to allow oneself to be tempted, to yield to temptation; **je serais tenté de croire qu'il est responsable, lui aussi,** I'm tempted to believe that he is responsible too; **je fus tenté d'essayer,** I was tempted to try;

(d) (*essayer*) to attempt, to try; **t. d'inutiles efforts pour ...,** to make useless attempts to ...; **t. une expérience,** to try an experiment; **il faut tout t. pour le convaincre,** we must try everything to convince him; **t. de faire qch,** to attempt *or* try to do sth; **t. de se suicider,** to attempt *or* try to commit suicide, to make a suicide attempt.

tenture [tɑ̃tyr] *nf* **(a)** (*tapisserie*) hanging; (*de porte*) curtain; (*de cérémonie funèbre*) funeral drape; **(b)** (*ensemble de tapisseries*) hangings.

tenu [təny] **1** *adj* **(a) bien t.,** well kept, tidy (*house etc*); neat, trim (*garden etc*); neatly turned out (*child*); **mal t.,** neglected, uncared for (*child, garden etc*); poorly kept, untidy (*house etc*); **(b) être t. de** *ou* **à faire qch,** to be obliged to do sth; **les passants sont tenus de marcher sur le trottoir,** pedestrians must walk on the pavement; **le médecin est t. au secret professionnel,** the doctor is bound by professional secrecy; **(c)** *Bourse* firm, hard (*prices*); **(d)** (*pari*) **t.!,** done!, you're on!; **(e)** *Mus* held (*note*). **2** *nm Sp* (*faute*) holding (*of the ball*); *Boxe* holding.

ténu [teny] *adj* slender, fine (*thread etc*); fine (*sand etc*); light (*mist*); thin, reedy (*voice*); tenuous, subtle, fine (*distinction*); thin, watery (*liquid etc*); flimsy (*hope, reason*).

tenue [təny] *nf* **(a)** keeping, holding (*of position etc*);

(b) sitting, session (*of an assembly etc*);

(c) keeping, running (*of shop, hotel, house etc*); **t. des livres,** book-keeping; *Tech* **t. des chaudières,** care of the boilers;

(d) (*conduite*) (good) behaviour, *US* behavior; **Paul, de la t.!,** Paul, behave yourself!; **un peu de t.!,** (mind your) manners!; **elle manque de t.,** she lacks (good) manners, she doesn't know how to behave; **la haute t. de ce périodique,** the high standard maintained by this periodical;

(e) (*maintien*) posture; *Équitation* **bonne/mauvaise t.,** good/poor seat;

(f) *Av* **t. en l'air, t. aéronautique,** behaviour in the air; *Av* **t. en vol,** attitude of flight; *Aut* **t. en côte,** climbing ability; **t. de route,** road-holding (qualities);

(g) (*habillement*) dress, clothes; (*aspect*) appearance; **quelle t.!,** what an outfit!; **t. de soirée,** (*smoking*) evening dress; *Mil etc* mess dress; **t. de ville,** (*de femme*) town clothes; (*d'homme*) lounge suit; **elle était en t. de ville,** she was dressed for going out; **t. de loisirs** *ou* **de tous les jours,** casual clothes *or* dress; *Mil etc* **en t.,** in uniform; **en t. légère,** lightly dressed; *F* **je vais me mettre en t.,** I'm going to change; *F* **en petite t.,** scantily dressed; *Mil* **t. de combat,** battledress; *Mil etc* **t. civile** *ou* **bourgeoise,** plain clothes, civilian clothes, *F* civvies, mufti;

(h) *Mus* holding note, sustained note;

(i) *Bourse* steadiness, firmness (*of prices*); tone (*of the market*).

ténuité [tenɥite] *nf* slenderness, fineness (*of thread etc*); fineness (*of sand etc*); tenuousness, subtlety, fineness (*of distinction*); thinness, wateriness (*of liquid*).

tenure [tənyr] *nf Hist Jur* tenure; (*terre*) holding.

tep [tɛp] *nm inv* (*abrév* **tonne-équivalent-pétrole**) TOE.

tequila [tekila] *nf* tequila.

ter [tɛr] **1** *adv Mus* ter. **2** *adj* **numéro 5 t.,** (*adresse*) No. 5b.

tératogène [teratɔʒɛn] *adj Méd* teratogenic.

tératologie [teratɔlɔʒi] *nf* teratology.

terbium [tɛrbjɔm] *nm Ch* terbium.

tercet [tɛrsɛ] *nm Littér* tercet, triplet.

térébenthine [terebɑ̃tin] *nf* turpentine.

térébinthe [terebɛ̃t] *nm Bot* terebinth, turpentine tree.

térébrant [terebrɑ̃] *adj* **(a)** boring, *Spéc* terebrant (*insect etc*); **(b)** *Méd* probing, boring (*pain*); deep (*ulceration*).

tergal¹, -aux [tɛrgal, -o] *adj Zool* tergal.

tergal² ® *nm Tex Br* Terylene ®, *Am* Dacron ®.

tergiversations [tɛrʒivɛrsasjɔ̃] *nfpl* equivocation, beating about the bush, evasiveness; **assez de t.!,** stop beating about the bush *or* being evasive!

tergiverser [tɛrʒivɛrse] *vi* to equivocate, to be evasive, to beat about the bush; **agir sans t.,** to act without equivocation.

terme¹ [tɛrm] *nm* **(a)** (*fin*) end, *Litt* term (*of life, journey, race etc*); **au t. de sa vie/de sa règne,** at the end of his life/of his reign; **toucher à son t.,** (*d'un projet*) to be near completion *or* an end; (*d'une période*) to be nearing an end *or* drawing to a close; **t. d'un mandat,** date of completion of a mandate; **mettre un t. à qch,** to put an end *or* a stop to sth; **il y a t. à tout,** there is an end to everything; **mener qch à bon t.,** to bring sth to a successful conclusion, to carry sth through;

(b) (*date limite*) time (limit), date; **être à t.,** (*of pregnant woman*) to have reached her term; **avant t.,** prematurely; **accouchement avant t.,** premature birth; *Mil etc* **engagement à long t.,** long(-term) service; **dans le t. de trois mois,** within three months; **t. de rigueur,** latest time, latest date; **marché à t.,** forward futures *or* market; **avance à long t.,** long-term advance; **à court/long t.,** short-/long-dated (*bills*); short-/long-term (*project etc*); **argent à court t.,** money at short notice *or* at call; *Bourse* **le t.,** the settlement; **valeurs à t.,** securities dealt in for the account; **acheter à t.,** *Com* to buy on credit; *Bourse* to buy for the settlement *or* for the account; *Ind etc* **prévisions à court t./à long t.,** short-range/long-range forecasts; **voir les choses à long/court t.,** to see things in the long/short term, to take a long-/short-term view (of things);

(c) (*délai*) delay (for payment); **demander un t. de grâce,** to ask for time to pay;

(d) (*versement*) instalment, *US* installment; **payable à deux termes,** payable in two instalments;

(e) (*loyer*) rent; (*jour*) rent day; (*période*) rental period; **je suis un t. en retard,** I'm one payment behind (with my rent);

(f) (*sculpture*) term, terminus.

terme² *nm* **(a)** (*mot*) term; **t. de métier, t. technique,** technical term; **t. de médecine/de droit,** medical/legal term; **employer les termes propres,** to use the appropriate terms; **en d'autres termes,** in other words; **elle n'a pas ménagé ses termes,** she didn't mince her words; **il m'a parlé de vous en très bons termes,** he spoke very well *or* favourably *or* *US* favorably of you; **termes contradictoires,** contradiction in terms; *Math* **t. d'une progression,** term of a progression; **termes d'une équation,** terms of an equation; *Écon* **termes de l'échange,** terms of trade;

(b) termes, terms (*of contract etc*);

(c) termes, (*relations*) terms; **être en bons/mauvais termes avec qn,** to be on good *or* friendly terms/bad terms with s.o.; **en quels termes l'a-t-il quittée,** what terms were they on when he left her?;

(d) moyen t., (*solution*) middle course.

terminaison [tɛrminɛzɔ̃] *nf* **(a)** *Gram* ending; **t. en 'ion',** ending in 'ion'; **(b)** *Anat* **t. nerveuse,** nerve ending; **(c)** (*action*) termination (*of trial, illness etc*).

terminal, -ale, -aux [tɛrminal, -o] **1** *adj* final; (*à l'extrémité de qch*) terminal; *Méd* terminal (*phase*); *Méd* **être cancéreux en phase terminale,** to have terminal cancer; *Scol* **classe terminale,** final year; *Br* ≈ upper sixth (form); *Am* ≈ twelfth grade; *Ordinat* **marque terminale,** end mark. **2** *nm* **(a)** *Ordinat* terminal; **(b)** *Pétr* (pipeline) terminal; **t. maritime,** shipping terminal; **(c)** *Av* (*gare*) (air) terminal. **3** *nf Scol* **terminale,** = **classe terminale.**

terminer [tɛrmine] **1** *vt* to end, to finish, to terminate (*war, speech, letter, meal etc*); to settle, to conclude (*bargain etc*); to complete, to finish (off) (*piece of work*); to end, to finish, to terminate, to conclude (*meeting etc*) (**par,** with); to end (*one's days*); **t. la soirée autour de la cheminée,** to end the evening by the fireside; **la phrase qui termine le poème,** the phrase that ends the poem; **il faut en t.,** we must end *or* finish; **nous en avons terminé avec ça,** we have finally finished with it.

2 *vi* to end, to finish; **t. court,** to end abruptly, to come to an abrupt ending; *Rad* **terminé!,** out!

3 se terminer *vpr* to end; **le concert s'est terminé par une chanson,** the concert ended with a song; **la rue se termine par une place,** the street ends in a square; **la guerre venait de se t.,** the war was just over *or* had just ended; **mot qui se termine par une voyelle,** word that ends in a vowel; **la veste se termine en pointe,** the jacket ends in *or* comes to a point; **l'année s'est terminée en beauté,** the year ended with a flourish.

terminologie [tɛrminɔlɔʒi] *nf* terminology.

terminologue [tɛrminɔlɔg] *n* terminologist.

terminus [tɛrminys] **1** *nm* (*de train, de l'autobus etc*) terminus; **t.!,** all change! **2** *adj inv* **gare t.,** terminus.

termite [tɛrmit] *nm Ent* termite, white ant; *Fig* **faire un travail de t.,** to work secretly and destructively.

termitière [tɛrmitjɛr] *nf Ent* termite nest, termitarium.

ternaire [tɛrnɛr] *adj Math Ch* ternary; *Mus* **mesure t.**, triple time.

terne [tɛrn] *adj* dull, lustreless, *US* lusterless (*metal*); drab, dull (*clothes, existence*); dull, lifeless (*eyes*); flat (*voice*); dull, flat, drab (*style, conversation*); dull, drab (*person*).

ternir [tɛrnir] **1** *vt* to tarnish (*metal*); *Fig* to stain, to tarnish (*reputation*). **2 se ternir** *vpr* (*of metal, Fig reputation*) to become tarnished.

ternissure [tɛrnisyr] *nf* (*aspect*) tarnished appearance (*of metal*); (*tache*) tarnished spot; *Fig* blemish, stain (*on reputation etc*).

terrafungine [tɛrafɔ̃ʒin] *nf Pharm* oxytetracycline, Terramycin ®.

terrain [tɛrɛ̃] *nm* **(a)** (*étendue*) land; **un t.**, a piece *or* plot of land; **terrains à bâtir,** development site, building land; **terrains vagues,** waste ground;

(b) *Géog etc* ground, terrain; **relief du t.**, relief; **véhicule tout(-)t.** *ou* **tous(-)terrains,** all-terrain vehicle, ATV, off-road vehicle; **vélo tout(-)t.**, mountain bike;

(c) (*sol*) soil, ground; **t. gras,** rich soil;

(d) (*destiné à une activité*) *Fb Rugby* pitch, field; *Golf* course; *Mil* terrain; *Cin* **t. (de studio),** (studio) lot; **t. de sport,** sports ground; **t. de camping,** campsite; **t. de jeu,** (*pour les sports*) recreation ground, *Br* playing field; (*pour les enfants*) playground; *Av* **t. d'aviation,** airfield; **t. d'atterrissage,** landing strip, airstrip; **t. de manœuvres,** drill ground, parade ground; **aller sur le t.**, (*se battre en duel*) to fight a duel; *Fig* **les journalistes sont tenus d'aller sur le t.**, journalists are obliged to go out in the field; *Ind etc* **sur le t.**, in the field; **travaux sur le t.**, fieldwork, work in the field; **rester sur le t.**, to be killed (*in a duel*); *Fig* (*être battu*) to be defeated; *Mil etc & Fig* **gagner du t.**, to gain ground; *Mil etc & Fig* **perdre** *ou* **céder du t.**, to lose ground; *Fig* **sonder** *ou* **tâter le t.**, to see how the land lies; *Fig* **être sur son t.**, to be on familiar ground; *Fig* **je ne suis plus sur mon t.**, I'm out of my depth; *Fig* **chercher un t. d'entente,** to look for (some) common ground; **homme de t.**, man with practical experience; *Fig* **préparer le t.**, to prepare the ground, to pave the way;

(e) *Géol* (rock) formation.

terrarium [tɛrarjɔm] *nm* terrarium.

terrasse [tɛras] *nf* **(a)** (*levée de terre*) terrace; **jardin en t.**, terraced garden; **cultures en terrasses,** terrace cultivation; **(b)** (*de café*) **nous étions assis à la t.**, we were sitting outside (the café); **prix des consommations en t.**, price of drinks served outside; **(c)** (*d'appartement*) terrace; **nous étions assis sur la t.**, we were sitting on the terrace; **(toit en) t.**, terrace (roof), flat roof.

terrassement [tɛrasmɑ̃] *nm* **(a)** (*action*) banking, digging (*of earth*); **(b)** (*remblai*) earthwork, embankment.

terrasser [tɛrase] *vt* **(a)** *Agr* to work the soil of (*vineyard etc*); **(b)** (*abattre*) to bring down, to floor (*opponent*); *Fig* (*of emotion, tiredness etc*) to overwhelm, to overcome (*s.o.*); (*of illness*) to lay (*s.o.*) low; **terrassé par le chagrin,** prostrate(d) *or* overcome with grief.

terrassier [tɛrasje] *nm Constr* labourer, *US* laborer, *Br F* navvy.

terre [tɛr] *nf* **(a)** (*monde*) world; **la T.**, (*planète*) (the) Earth; **être encore sur t.**, to be still in the land of the living; **elle vient de quitter cette t.**, she has just left this world; **revenir sur t.**, to come down to earth; **qui a les pieds sur t.**, down-to-earth;

(b) (*sol*) ground; (*étendue*) land; **armée** *ou* **forces de t.**, land forces; **pénétrer dans les terres,** to go inland; **village dans les terres,** inland village; **basses terres,** lowlands; **hautes terres,** highlands; **tremblement de t.**, earthquake; *Av* **toucher t.**, to touch down, to land; **à t., par t.**, on the ground, to the ground; **frapper qn à t.**, to strike s.o. when he is down; **tomber par t.**, to fall down (*from standing position*); **tomber à t.**, to fall down (*from height*); **être assis/couché par t.**, to be sitting/lying on the ground; *Fig* **tous nos projets sont tombés par t.**, all our plans have fallen through; *F* **ça va tout ficher par t.**, that'll mess everything up; **mettre pied à t.**, to dismount (*from horse*); **attaquer une ville par t. et par mer,** to attack a town by land and sea; **tactique** *ou* **politique de la t. brûlée,** scorched earth policy; **appuyer son oreille contre t.**, to put one's ear to the ground; **sous t.**, underground; **être sous t.** *ou* **en t.**, to be in one's grave, *F* to be six foot under, to be dead and buried;

(c) *Él Br* earth, *Am* ground; **mettre** *ou* **relier** *ou* **raccorder à la t.**, *Br* to earth, *Am* to ground;

(d) (*opposé à mer*) land; **mettre qn à t.**, to land s.o., to put s.o. ashore; **descendre à t., prendre t.**, to land, to go ashore; **perdre t.**, to lose sight of land; **t. (en vue)!**, land ho!; **être à t.**, (*of ship*) to be aground *or* ashore; **t. ferme,** (dry) land, terra firma; (*opposé à l'espace*) earth, terra firma;

(e) t. à t., matter-of-fact, down-to-earth;

(f) *Agr* (*matière*) soil, earth; **cultiver la t.**, to cultivate the soil; **chemin de t.**, dirt track; **sol en t. battue,** mud floor; *Tennis* **jouer sur la t. battue,** to play on clay; *Tennis* **jouer bien sur la t. battue,** to be good on clay, to be a good clay court player; *Tennis* **court en t. battue,** clay court; **t. grasse,** rich soil; **hutte de t. séchée,** mud hut;

(g) (*propriété*) estate, land; **elle a une t. en Normandie,** she has some land *or* an estate in Normandy; **vivre de ses terres,** to live off one's land(s) *or* estates;

(h) (*territoire*) land, country; **terres étrangères,** foreign countries *or* lands; **terres australes,** southern lands; **la T. Sainte,** the Holy Land; **La T. de Feu,** Tierra del Fuego; **revenir à la t. natale,** to return to one's native soil *or* the land *or* country of one's birth;

(i) (*argile etc*) clay; **t. végétale** *ou* **franche** *ou* **naturelle,** mould, *US* mold; **t. à potier,** potter's clay; **t. de pipe,** pipeclay; **pipe en t.**, clay pipe; **t. cuite,** baked clay; *Beaux-Arts* terracotta; *Beaux-Arts* **une t. cuite,** a terracotta; **cruche de** *ou* **en t.**, earthenware jar; **t. de Chine** *ou* **à porcelaine,** kaolin; **t. à poêle,** fireclay;

(j) *Ch* **terres rares,** rare earths;

(k) (*colorant*) **t. de Sienne/d'ombre,** sienna/umber.

terreau, -eaux [tɛro] *nm* compost.

Terre-Neuve [tɛrnœv] **1** *nf* Newfoundland. **2** *nm inv* **t.-n.**, Newfoundland (dog).

terre-neuvien, -ienne [tɛrnœvjɛ̃, -jɛn] (*pl terre-neuviens*) **1** *adj* Newfoundland. **2** *n* **T.-N.**, Newfoundlander.

terre-neuvier, -ière [tɛrnœvje, -jɛr] (*pl terre-neuviers*) **1** *adj* Newfoundland (*fisherman etc*). **2** *nm* **(a)** (*pêcheur*) Newfoundland fisherman; **(b)** (*bateau*) banker, Newfoundland fishing vessel.

terre-plein [tɛrplɛ̃] *nm* (*pl terre-pleins*) **(a)** *Constr* earth platform, raised strip (*of ground*); **(b)** *Aut* **t.-p. central,** central reservation, *Am* median strip; **t.-p. circulaire,** central island (*of roundabout*).

terrer [tɛre] **1** *vt* **(a)** to earth up (*tree, plant*); **(b)** to spread earth over (*ground*); **(c)** *Tex* to full (*cloth*). **2 se terrer** *vpr* (*of animal*) to go to earth; *Mil* to entrench oneself; *Fig* to go to earth, to hole up; **être terré dans,** (*of animal*) to have gone to earth in; *Mil* to be entrenched in; *Fig* to be holed up in.

terrestre [tɛrɛstr] *adj* **(a)** ground (*plant*); land (*animal*); **(b) rotation t.**, rotation of the earth; **(c)** *Fig* earthly, worldly (*thoughts, pleasures etc*); **paradis t.**, earthly paradise; **(d)** *Mil* **effectifs terrestres,** land forces.

terreur [tɛrœr] *nf* **(a)** (*effroi*) terror, dread; **fou de t.**, wild with fear; **être dans la t.**, to be in terror; **t. du noir,** fear of the dark; **(b)** (*emploi de la violence etc*) terror; **gouverner par la t.**, to rule by terror; *Hist Fr* **la T.**, the (Reign of) Terror (*1793*); **(c)** *Fig* (*personne*) terror (*of the town, school etc*); **il est la t. de ses ennemis,** he is an object of dread to his enemies; **jouer les terreurs,** to play the tough guy.

terreux, -euse [tɛrø, -øz] *adj* **(a)** earthy (*matter, taste, smell*); **(b)** grubby (*hands*); muddy (*complexion, sky, grey etc*); sickly (*face*); gritty (*lettuce*).

terrible [tɛribl] **1** *adj* **(a)** terrible, appalling (*catastrophe, accident etc*); dreadful (*cold, noise*); terrific (*thunderstorm*); awful, terrible (*weather, temper*); **d'une humeur t.**, in an awful *or* a terrible mood; **enfant t.**, enfant terrible; *F* **ce n'est pas bien t., cette coupure,** this cut is nothing much; **(b)** *F* (*formidable*) terrific, great (*person, film, effect etc*); **ce n'est pas t.**, it's nothing special *or* much. **2** *adv F* **ça marche t.!**, it's going great!

terriblement [tɛribləmɑ̃] *adv* (*extrêmement*) terribly, dreadfully, awfully.

terrien, -ienne [tɛrjɛ̃, -jɛn] **1** *adj* **(a)** landed (*proprietor etc*); **(b)** (*rural*) country, rural; **(c)** (*de la Terre*) of the Earth. **2** *n* **(a)** (*propriétaire*) landowner, landed proprietor; **(b)** *Nau* landsman, landswoman; **(c)** (*paysan*) countryman, countrywoman; **(d)** (*habitant de la Terre*) earthling, earthman, earthwoman.

terrier[1] [tɛrje] *nm* burrow, hole (*of rabbit, mole etc*); earth (*of fox*); set (*of badger*).

terrier[2], -ière [tɛrje, -jɛr] *n* (*chien*) terrier.

terrifiant [tɛrifjɑ̃] *adj* **(a)** (*effrayant*) terrifying; **(b)** (*extraordinaire*) incredible.

terrifier [tɛrifje] *vt* (*impf & pr sub* **n. terrifiions, v.**

terrifiiez) to terrify.
terril [tɛril] *nm Min* slag heap.
terrine [tɛrin] *nf Culin* **(a)** (*pâté*) pâté, terrine; **t. de canard/de foie de volaille,** duck/chicken-liver pâté; **(b)** (*récipient*) terrine.
terrir [tɛrir] *vi Pêche* **poissons qui terrissent,** fish living in coastal waters.
territoire [tɛritwar] *nm* territory (*of state, bird, animal*); (*de juge, d'évêque*) jurisdiction; (*de commune, d'arrondissement etc*) area; **t. d'outre-mer,** (*French*) overseas territory; **aménagement du t.,** regional planning *or* development.
territorial, -aux [tɛritɔrjal, -o] **1** *adj* territorial (*tax, army, waters etc*). **2** *nm Hist Mil* territorial (soldier). **3** *nf Hist Mil* **la territoriale,** the territorial army.
territorialité [tɛritɔrjalite] *nf* territoriality.
terroir [tɛrwar] *nm Agr* soil; **goût de t.,** (*of wine*) tang of the soil, native tang; **accent du t.,** local brogue.
terrorisant [tɛrɔrizɑ] *adj* terrifying (*experience etc*).
terroriser [tɛrɔrize] *vt* to terrorize.
terrorisme [tɛrɔrism] *nm* terrorism; *Fig* **faire du t.,** (*of small child etc*) to be a terror.
terroriste [tɛrɔrist] *adj & n* terrorist.
tertiaire [tɛrsjɛr] **1** *adj* tertiary; *Écon* **secteur t.,** tertiary sector *or* industries. **2** *nm* **(a)** *Écon* tertiary sector *or* industries; **(b)** *Géol* Tertiary. **3** *n Cathol* tertiary.
tertiairisation [tɛrsjɛrizɑsjɔ̃] *nf*, **tertiarisation** [tɛrsjarizɑsjɔ̃] *nf Écon* development of the tertiary sector *or* service industries.
tertio [tɛrsjo] *adv* thirdly.
tertre [tɛrtr] *nm* hillock, mound, knoll; *Archéol* **t. funéraire,** barrow, tumulus.
tes [te] *adj poss voir* **TON¹**.
tessiture [tesityr] *nf Mus* tessitura, range (*of voice*); range (*of instrument*).
tesson [tesɔ̃] *nm* shard; **t. de bouteille,** fragment of broken bottle.
test¹ [tɛst] *nm Zool* test (*of echinoderm etc*).
test² *nm Méd Psy Scol etc* test; **t. professionnel,** vocational *or* occupational test; **passer/réussir un t.,** to take/pass a test; *Can* **t. aveugle,** blind test; **c'est le t. de sa bonne foi,** it is a test of his good faith.
testament [tɛstamɑ̃] *nm* **(a)** *Jur* will, testament; **absence de t.,** intestacy; **ceci est mon t.,** this is my last will and testament; **elle l'a mis** *ou* **couché sur son t.,** she put him in her will; **mourir sans t.,** to die intestate; *F* **il peut faire son t.,** (*menace*) he may as well make his will; **(b)** *Fig* (*artistique, politique*) legacy.
Testament [tɛstamɑ̃] *nm Bible* **Ancien/Nouveau T.,** Old/New Testament.
testamentaire [tɛstamɑ̃tɛr] *adj* **disposition t.,** clause (*of a will*); **exécuteur/-trice t.,** executor/executrix.
testateur [tɛstatœr] *nm Jur* testator.
testatrice [tɛstatris] *nf Jur* testatrix.
tester¹ [tɛste] *vi Jur* to make one's will.
tester² *vt* to test (*pupil, product etc*).
testiculaire [tɛstikylɛr] *adj Anat* testicular.
testicule [tɛstikyl] *nm Anat* testicle, *Spéc* testis.
testimonial, -iaux [tɛstimɔnjal, -jo] *adj Jur* **preuve testimoniale,** evidence of witnesses.
testostérone [tɛstɔsterɔn] *nf Biol Physiol* testosterone.
têt [tɛ] *nm Ch* **t. à gaz,** beehive shelf; **t. à rôtir,** roasting crucible.
tétanie [tetani] *nf Méd* tetany.
tétanique [tetanik] *Méd* **1** *adj* tetanic; **malade t.,** tetanus sufferer. **2** *n* tetanus sufferer.
tétaniser [tetanize] *Méd* **1** *vt* to tetanize (*muscle*). **2 se tétaniser** *vpr* (*of muscle*) to become tetanized.
tétanos [tetanos, -ɔs] *nm Méd* (*maladie*) tetanus, lockjaw; (*contraction de muscle*) tetanus.
têtard [tɛtar] *nm* **(a)** *Zool* tadpole; **(b)** *Arg* (*enfant*) kid; **(c)** (*arbre taillé*) pollard.
tête [tɛt] *nf* **(a)** *Anat* head; **de la t. aux pieds,** from head to foot, from top to toe; **dépasser qn de la t.,** to stand head and shoulders above s.o.; **il a une t. de plus que sa mère,** he is a head taller than his mother; **t. nue,** bare-headed; **voix de t.,** head voice; **vieillard à t. grise,** grey-headed old man; **t. de mort,** = **TÊTE-DE-MORT**; *F* **une grosse t.,** (*intellectuel*) a highbrow, an intellectual; **monstre à deux têtes,** two-headed monster; **corps sans t.,** headless body; *F* **faire la t.,** to sulk; *F* **faire sa t.,** to give oneself airs; **faire t.,** (*of hunted animal*) to stand at bay; **faire** *ou* **tenir t. à qn,** to stand up to s.o.; **faire** *ou* **tenir t. au malheur,** to bear up in the face of misfortune; **tenir t. à l'orage,** to confront the storm; *Fig F* to face the music; **les nuages qui flottent sur nos têtes,** the clouds overhead; **endetté par-dessus la t.,** up to the eyes in debt; **j'en ai par-dessus la t.,** I've had it up to here, I can't stand it any longer; **la t. en bas,** head down(wards), upside down; (*thing*) upside down; **marcher la t. haute,** to walk with (one's) head held high; **la t. la première,** head first; **tomber sur la t.,** to fall on one's face; *Arg* (*devenir fou*) to go crackers; **ne (pas) savoir où donner de la t.,** not to know which way to turn; *Fig* **donner t. baissée dans un piège,** to rush headlong into a trap; **t. couronnée,** (*souverain*) crowned head; **payer tant par t.** *ou F* **par t. de pipe,** to pay so much a head; **t. à t.,** = **TÊTE-A-TÊTE**; **mettre tous ses biens sur la t. de sa femme,** to settle all one's property on one's wife; **il y va de votre t.,** your life is at stake; **ça va lui en coûter la t.,** it is going to cost him his life; **j'en donnerais ma t. à couper que ...,** I'll bet anything you like *or* I'd stake my life that ...; **signe de t.,** nod (of the head); **faire un signe de t. à qn,** to nod to s.o.; **mal de t.,** headache; **avoir mal à la t.,** to have a headache; **la t. lui tourne** *ou* **il a la t. qui tourne,** his head is spinning; **t. chauve,** bald head; **t. ronde,** bullet head, round head; *Hist* Roundhead; **à t. ronde,** bullet-headed, round-headed; *Fb* **faire une t.,** to head the ball; *Natation* **piquer une t.,** to take a header, to dive; *Gym Mil* **t. (à) droite!,** eyes right!; **t. d'une médaille,** obverse of a medal; *Arch* **t. ou pile?,** heads or tails?;

(b) (*cheveux*) hair; **se laver la t.,** to wash one's hair;

(c) (*visage*) face; *Th* **se faire la t. d'un rôle,** to make up for a part; *F* **faire une t.,** to pull a (long) face, to look glum; **je ne sais pas quelle t. il fera,** I don't know how he will take it; **faire la t. à qn,** to frown at s.o.; (*bouder*) to be sulky with s.o.; **faire une t. de circonstance,** to put on an expression to suit the occasion; **je connais cette t.-là,** I know that face; *Arg* **t. d'imbécile!,** you idiot!, *Br* you clot!, you thickhead!;

(d) head (*of animal, fish, bird etc*); *Vét* **t. noire,** blackhead;

(e) *Nau* **faire t. sur son ancre,** (*of ship*) to be brought up by its anchor;

(f) (*esprit*) mind; (*cerveau*) brains; **il n'a rien dans la t., il a une petite t.,** he is empty-headed, he has no brains; **une pareille idée ne me serait jamais passée par la t.,** such an idea would never have entered my mind *or* head; **se creuser la t.,** to rack one's brains; **avoir de la t.,** to have a good head on one's shoulders; **c'est une femme de t.,** she's a capable woman; **elle n'a pas de t.,** she is not very capable, *F* she's not with it; **avoir la t. légère,** to be irresponsible *or* featherbrained; **avoir la t. dure,** to be stupid *or F* thick; (*têtu*) to be pigheaded; **c'est une t. de mule** *ou F* **de pioche** *ou F* **de cochon** *ou Arg* **de lard,** he's pig-headed, he's as stubborn as a mule; **être une t. de linotte,** to be bird-brained, to be a bird-brain; *F* **c'est une t. à gifles** *ou* **à claques,** he just asks for it; *Vulg* **t. de nœud!,** *Br* dickhead!, *Am* asshole!; **mettre qch dans la t. de qn,** to get sth into s.o.'s head; **il s'est mis dans la t. d'écrire un roman,** he has got *or* taken it into his head to write a novel; **n'avoir qu'une idée en t.,** to have a one-track mind; **il n'a que ça en t.,** he's got that on the brain; **je l'ai en t.,** I'm bearing it in mind; **avoir toutes les informations en t.,** to have all the information in one's head; **ça m'est sorti de la t.,** I've forgotten, it's gone clean out of my head *or* mind; **il a quelque chose en t.,** he's planning something, *F* he's up to something; **forte t.,** (*personne*) strong-minded person; **mauvaise t.,** (*personne*) awkward *or* difficult person; **faire la mauvaise t.,** to be awkward *or* difficult; **t. chaude,** hothead; **c'est une t. brûlée,** he has a bit of the devil in him; **travail de t.,** brainwork; **calculer de t.,** to reckon in one's head; **calcul de t.,** (*discipline*) mental arithmetic; (*opération*) mental calculation; **en faire à sa t.,** to do as one pleases, to go one's own way; **il n'en fait qu'à sa t.,** he does exactly what he pleases; **avoir sa petite t. à soi,** to have a mind of one's own; **avoir une idée derrière la t.,** to have an idea at the back of one's mind; **idée de derrière la t.,** idea at the back of one's mind; **où ai-je la t.!,** what am I thinking of!; **conserver sa t.,** to keep one's head, to remain calm; **est-ce que vous perdez la t.?,** have you taken leave of your senses?; **ne perdez pas la t.!,** keep *or* don't lose your head!, keep calm!; **faire perdre la t. à un candidat,** to fluster a candidate; **c'était à perdre la t.,** it was bewildering; **avoir toute sa t.,** to have one's wits about one; **il a la t. montée,** his blood is up; **il faut ne rien faire qu'à t. reposée,** we must do nothing without thinking it out carefully;

(g) (*chef*) head (*of company, establishment etc*);

(h) summit, crown, top (*of volcano, tree etc*); head, top (*of book*); *Nau* **t. de roche,** rock summit; *Aut* **soupapes en t.**, overhead valves; *Typ* **blanc de t.**, margin at the head of a book; **ligne de t.**, headline; **t. de chapitre,** chapter heading;

(i) head (*of cabbage, garlic etc*);

(j) *Anat* apophysis (*of the femur*); head (*of the humerus*); **t. du condyle,** condyle head;

(k) *Tech* head (*of violin, mast, hammer, nail, pin, rivet, screw etc*); butt (*of plank*); **t. de lit,** bed head; **t. ronde** *ou* **cylindrique** *ou* **plate,** cheese-head (*of rivet*); **t. hémisphérique,** cup head (*of rivet*); **t. de hache,** axe head; **t. de benne,** grab head; **t. de cabestan,** drum head; **t. de flèche,** jib head (*of crane*); **t. porte-outil,** tool head; **t. porte-foret, t. de perçage,** drill(ing) head; **t. porte-fraise, t. de fraisage,** cutter head, milling head; **t. porte-segments,** grinding attachment (*of grinding machine*); **t. filière,** die head (*of threading machine*); *Min* **t. de sonde,** casing head; *Pétr* **t. d'injection,** swivel; **t. inclinable,** tilting head (*of machine tool, of camera or instrument stand*); **t. mobile,** bolt head (*of rifle*); **t. d'électrode,** electrode tip; **t. de câble,** cable terminal; *Électron* **t. d'effacement,** erase head (*of tape recorder etc*); **t. d'enregistrement, t. enregistreuse,** record(ing) head (*of computer, tape recorder, record player*); **t. d'impression,** print head; **t. de lecture,** *Cin* sound head; *Ordinat* read(ing) head; (*de magnétophone*) tape reader, play-back head; **t. magnétique,** magnetic head; **t. sonore,** sound head; *Ordinat* **t. d'écriture,** writing *or* write head; **t. (de fusée),** warhead; **t. nucléaire,** nuclear warhead; **t. chercheuse,** homing device (*of missile etc*);

(l) head (*of procession, column etc*); front (*of train*); **colonne de t.**, leading column; **taxi en t. de file,** taxi at the head of the rank; *Journ* **article de t.**, feature (article), *Am* leading article; *Rail* **voiture de t.**, front carriage *or Am* car; **en t. du train,** at the front of the train; **à la t. du régiment,** at the head of the regiment; **marcher en t.**, to lead the way; **marcher à la t.** *ou* **en t. du cortège,** to walk at the head of the procession, to lead *or* head the procession; **venir tout en t.**, to come first and foremost; **venir en t. du scrutin,** to head the poll; **se trouver à la t. d'une fortune,** to find oneself with a fortune; **prendre la t. d'une entreprise,** to take over as the head of a company; **être à la t. d'une entreprise,** to be (at) the head of a company, to head a company; **être à la t. de la classe,** to be at the top of the class; *Th Cin* **t. d'affiche,** top of the bill (**de,** in); *Tennis* **têtes de série,** seeded players, seeds; *Sp etc* **prendre la t.**, to take the lead; *Mil* **t. de pont,** bridgehead; *Rail etc* **t. de ligne,** starting point, terminus.

tête-à-queue [tɛtakø] *nm inv Aut* spin; *Équitation* (sudden) turn; **faire (un) t.-à-q.**, *Aut* to spin *or* slew round; (*of horse*) to whip round.

tête-à-tête [tɛtatɛt] *nm inv* **(a)** (*à deux*) private interview, tête-à-tête; **en t.-à-t.**, in private; **en t.-à t. avec,** alone with; **un dîner t.-à-t.**, a(n intimate) dinner for two; **(b)** (*canapé*) tête-à-tête, (two-seater) sofa; **(c)** tea *or* coffee *or* breakfast set (for two).

tête-bêche [tɛtbɛʃ] *adv* (*of two persons*) head to foot (*alongside one another*); (*of two things*) top to bottom.

tête-de-loup [tɛtdəlu] *nf* ceiling brush; (*pl têtes-de-loup*).

tête(-)de(-)maure [tɛtdəmɔr] *nf* Dutch cheese; (*pl têtes-de-maure*).

tête-de-mort [tɛtdəmɔr] *nf* (*pl têtes-de-mort*) **(a)** (*emblème*) death's-head; **pavillon à t.-de-m.**, skull-and-crossbones (flag), Jolly Roger; **(b)** *Ent* death's-head moth; **(c)** (*fromage*) Dutch cheese.

tête-de-nègre [tɛtdənɛgr] *adj inv & nm inv* dark brown.

tétée [tete] *nf* **(a)** (*repas de nourrisson*) feed; **(b)** (*action*) sucking.

téter [tete] *vt* (**il tète; il tètera**) **(a)** (*of baby, young animal*) to suck; **t. sa mère,** to suck at one's mother's breast, to feed; **donner à t. à un enfant,** to feed a child (at the breast), to suckle a child; **(b)** *F* to suck (on) (*cigar, pipe etc*); **enfant qui tète son pouce,** child who sucks his thumb.

têtière [tɛtjɛr] *nf* **(a)** (*de harnais*) headstall; **(b)** (*de fauteuil*) antimacassar.

tétin [tetɛ̃] *nm Arch* nipple (*of person*); dug (*of cow, sow etc*).

tétine [tetin] *nf* **(a)** dug (*of sow etc*); udder (*of cow*); **(b)** nipple, teat (*of feeding bottle*); **t. (sur anneau),** (*sucette*) comforter, *Br* dummy, *Am* pacifier.

téton [tetɔ̃] *nm F* (*sein de femme*) boob, tit.

tétrachlorure [tetraklɔryr] *nm Ch* tetrachloride; **t. de carbone,** carbon tetrachloride.

tétracorde [tetrakɔrd] *nm Hist Mus* tetrachord.

tétraèdre [tetraɛdr] *Géom* **1** *adj* tetrahedral. **2** *nm* tetrahedron.

tétraédrique [tetraedrik] *adj Géom* tetrahedral.

tétralogie [tetralɔʒi] *nf Littér Th* tetralogy; *Mus* **la T. (de Wagner),** The Ring, Wagner's Ring.

tétramètre [tetramɛtr] *nm Littér* tetrameter.

tétraplégie [tetrapleʒi] *nf Méd* tetraplegia.

tétrapode [tetrapɔd] *nm Zool* tetrapod.

tétrarque [tetrark] *nm* tetrarch.

tétras [tetra] *nm* (*oiseau*) grouse; **grand t.**, capercaillie.

tétrasyllabe [tetrasilab], **tétrasyllabique** [tetrasilabik] *adj Gram* tetrasyllabic; **mot t.**, tetrasyllable.

têtu, -ue [tety] **1** *adj* stubborn, obstinate, *F* pigheaded; *F* **t. comme un mulet** *ou* **comme une mule,** as stubborn *or* obstinate as a mule. **2** *n* stubborn *or* obstinate person.

teuf-teuf [tøftøf] *nm inv Aut F* (*voiture*) jalopy, rattletrap; (*bruit*) chug-chug.

teuton, -onne [tøtɔ̃, -ɔn] **1** *adj* Teuton(ic). **2** *nm Ling* Germanic, Teutonic. **3** *n* **T.**, Teuton.

teutonique [tøtɔnik] *adj* Teutonic.

texan, -ane [tɛksɑ̃, -an] **1** *adj* Texan. **2** *n* **T.**, Texan.

texte [tɛkst] *nm* **(a)** text (*of author, book, contract etc*); *Th* lines (*of actor*); *Scol* (*de devoir*) subject; **erreur de t.**, textual error; **critique des textes,** textual criticism; **gravure hors t.**, plate, full-page engraving; **lire Goethe dans le t.**, to read Goethe in the original; *Scol* **cahier de textes,** homework book (*listing work to be done*); **textes choisis,** selected passages (**de,** from); **(b)** *Ordinat* text.

textile [tɛkstil] **1** *adj* textile. **2** *nm* **(a)** textile; **textiles artificiels,** synthetic *or* man-made textiles, synthetics; **(b) le t.**, (*industrie*) the textile industry.

texto [tɛksto] *adj F* word for word.

textuel, -elle [tɛkstɥɛl] *adj* **(a)** textual (*analysis etc*); **(b)** (*conforme au texte*) word-for-word, literal (*translation, quotation etc*); *F* **c'est t.!**, those were his *or* their *etc* exact words!

textuellement [tɛkstɥɛlmɑ̃] *adv* **(a)** textually; **(b)** (*conformément au texte*) word for word, literally.

texture [tɛkstyr] *nf* texture.

texturer [tɛkstyre], **texturiser** [tɛkstyrize] *vt Tech* to texturize.

TF1 [teɛfœ̃] *nf* (*abrév* **Télévision française 1**) *Br* ≈ BBC1.

T.G.V. [teʒeve] *nm abrév* **train à grande vitesse.**

thaï, -ïe [tai] **1** *adj* Thai. **2** *nm Ling* Thai. **3** *n* **T.**, Thai.

thaïlandais, -aise [tailɑ̃dɛ, -ɛz] **1** *adj* Thai. **2** *n* **T.**, Thai.

Thaïlande [tailɑ̃d] *nf* Thailand.

thalamus [talamys] *nm Anat* thalamus.

thalassémie [talasemi] *nf Méd* thalassaemia, *US* thalassemia.

thalidomide [talidɔmid] *nf Pharm* thalidomide.

thalle [tal] *nm Bot* thallus.

thallium [taljɔm] *nm Ch* thallium.

thalweg [talvɛg] *nm Géol* t(h)alweg.

thaumaturge [tomatyrʒ] **1** *adj* miracle-working, *Spéc* thaumaturgic. **2** *nm* miracle worker, *Spéc* thaumaturge, thaumaturgist.

thé [te] **1** *nm* **(a)** (*boisson, feuilles*) tea; (*arbrisseau*) tea plant; **t. de Ceylan,** Ceylon tea; **t. indien, de l'Inde,** Indian tea; **t. de Chine,** China tea; **t. nature/au lait,** tea without milk/with milk; **t. au citron,** lemon tea; **t. en sachet,** tea bags; **t. en vrac,** loose tea; **négociant en t.**, tea merchant; **boule à t.**, tea ball; **c'est l'heure du t.**, it's tea time; **t. de bœuf,** beef tea; **(b)** (*goûter*) tea party; **t. dansant,** tea dance, thé dansant; **(c) salon de t.**, teashop, tearoom(s). **2** *adj inv* **rose t.**, tea rose.

théâtral, -aux [teatral, -o] *adj* theatrical; dramatic (*effect*); stage (*performance*); *Péj* (*artificiel*) theatrical, stagy.

théâtralement [teatralmɑ̃] *adv* theatrically.

théâtraliser [teatralize] *vt Th* to dramatize (*novel etc*).

théâtralité [teatralite] *nf* theatricality.

théâtre [teatr] *nm* **(a)** (*salle*) theatre, *US* theater; **t. de verdure,** open-air theatre; **t. en rond,** theatre-in-the-round;

(b) (*scène*) stage; **mettre une pièce au t.**, to stage *or* put on a play; **adapté pour le t.**, adapted for the stage; **se retirer du t.**, to give up the stage;

(c) (*art, métier*) theatre, *US* theater; **t. d'ombres/de marionnettes,** shadow/puppet theatre; **pièce de t.**, play; **costumier de t.**, theatrical costumier; **faire du t.**, to be an actor *or* actress, to be on the stage; **homme/femme de t.**, man/woman of the theatre; **école/cours de t.**, theatre *or* stage school/course; **coup de t.**, *Th & Fig* coup de théâtre; *Fig* dramatic *or* sensational turn of events;

(d) (*œuvres*) plays, dramatic works (*of writer*); (*genre*) theatre, *US* theater; **le t. anglais,** British theatre *or* drama;

t. de boulevard, light comedies; **(e)** *Fig* (*de crime, d'accident etc*) scene; *Mil* **t. d'opérations,** theatre of operations; **(f)** (*attitude artificielle*) play-acting, histrionics.
théâtreuse [teatrøz] *nf F Péj* actress (of sorts).
thébaïsme [tebaism] *nm Méd* opium poisoning.
théier, -ière [teje, -jɛr] **1** *adj* tea (*industry etc*). **2** *nm Bot* tea (plant). **3** *nf* **théière,** teapot.
théine [tein] *nf* theine, caffeine; **thé sans t.,** caffeine-free tea.
théisme¹ [teism] *nm Méd* tea poisoning.
théisme² *nm Rel* theism.
théiste [teist] *Rel* **1** *adj* theistic. **2** *n* theist.
thématique [tematik] **1** *adj* thematic. **2** *nf* (set of) themes.
thème [tɛm] *nm* **(a)** (*sujet*) theme (*of discourse, debate, musical composition etc*); **(b)** *Scol* (*traduction*) prose (composition), translation; **t. latin,** Latin prose (composition), translation into Latin; *F* **un fort en t.,** a good and hard-working pupil; **(c)** *Gram* stem, theme (*of verb, noun*); **(d)** *Astrol* **t. (astral),** birth chart; **faire son t. à qn,** to draw up s.o.'s birth chart.
théocratie [teɔkrasi] *nf* theocracy.
théocratique [teɔkratik] *adj* theocratic.
théodicée [teɔdise] *nf Phil* theodicy.
théodolite [teɔdɔlit] *nm* theodolite.
théologal, -aux [teɔlɔgal, -o] *adj* **les trois vertus théologales,** the three theological virtues.
théologie [teɔlɔʒi] *nf* theology; **docteur en t.,** doctor of divinity, D.D..
théologien [teɔlɔʒjɛ̃] *nm* theologian.
théologique [teɔlɔʒik] *adj* theological.
théologiquement [teɔlɔʒikmɑ̃] *adv* theologically.
théophylline [teɔfilin] *nf Ch* theophylline.
théorbe [teɔrb] *nm Hist Mus* theorbo.
théorème [teɔrɛm] *nm* theorem; **le t. de Newton,** the binomial theorem.
théorétique [teɔretik] *Phil* **1** *adj* theoretic(al). **2** *nf* theoretics.
théoricien, -ienne [teɔrisjɛ̃, -jɛn] *n* theoretician, theorist.
théorie¹ [teɔri] *nf* **(a)** (*doctrine*) theory; **en t.,** in theory; **bâtir une t.,** to construct *or* build up a theory; *Math Ordinat* **t. des probabilités,** theory of probability; **t. de la rélativité,** theory of relativity; **la t. et la pratique,** theory and practice; **(b)** *Mil* theoretical instruction.
théorie² *nf Litt* (*défilé*) procession.
théorique [teɔrik] *adj* theoretic(al).
théoriquement [teɔrikmɑ̃] *adv* theoretically.
théoriser [teɔrize] **1** *vi* to theorize. **2** *vt* to theorize about.
théosophe [teɔzɔf] *n* theosophist.
théosophie [teɔzɔfi] *nf* theosophy.
thèque [tɛk] *nf Anat Bot* theca.
thérapeute [terapøt] *n Méd* therapist.
thérapeutique [terapøtik] **1** *adj* therapeutic. **2** *nf* (*science*) therapeutics; (*traitement*) therapy.
thérapie [terapi] *nf Méd* therapy; *Psy* **t. de groupe,** group therapy.
thermal, -aux [tɛrmal, -o] *adj* thermal; **eaux thermales,** thermal springs, hot springs; **établissement t.,** hydropathic establishment, *Br* hydro; **station thermale,** spa; **cure thermale,** water cure; **faire une cure thermale,** to take the waters.
thermalisme [tɛrmalism] *nm* **(a)** (*organisation*) organization of spas; **(b)** (*thérapie*) hydrotherapy; **(c)** (*science*) balneology.
thermes [tɛrm] *nmpl* **(a)** *Antiq* thermae, public baths; **(b)** *Méd* thermal baths.
thermicien, -ienne [tɛrmisjɛ̃, -jɛn] *n* heat engineer.
thermidor [tɛrmidɔr] *nm Hist* = eleventh month of the French Republican calendar (*July-August*).
thermie [tɛrmi] *nf Phys* = thermal unit (= *1000 large calories*).
thermique [tɛrmik] **1** *adj Phys* thermal; heat (*engine, screen, treatment*); *El* **centrale t.,** thermal power station; *Av* **courant t.,** thermal (current); *Électron* **relais t.,** thermorelay; *Ch* **analyse t.,** thermoanalysis; **science t.,** science of heat; *Géog* **régime t.,** temperature regime *or* pattern; *Physiol* **sensibilité t.,** temperature sense. **2** *nm Av* (*courant*) thermal. **3** *nf* science of heat.
thermisteur [tɛrmistœr] *nm*, **thermistor** [tɛrmistɔr] *nm* *El* thermistor.
thermocautère [tɛrmɔkotɛr] *nm Chir* (*instrument*) thermocautery.
thermochimie [tɛrmɔʃimi] *nf* thermochemistry.
thermocollage [tɛrmɔkɔlaʒ] *nm* heat sealing.
thermocouple [tɛrmɔkupl] *nm Él* thermocouple.
thermodynamique [tɛrmɔdinamik] **1** *adj* thermodynamic. **2** *nf* thermodynamics.
thermoélectricité [tɛrmɔelɛktrisite] *nf* thermoelectricity.
thermoélectrique [tɛrmɔelɛktrik] *adj* thermoelectric(al); **pince t.,** thermocouple; **couple t.,** thermoelectric couple; **pile t.,** thermopile.
thermoélectronique [tɛrmɔelɛktrɔnik] *adj* thermoelectronic.
thermoformage [tɛrmɔfɔrmaʒ] *nm Tech* thermoforming.
thermogène [tɛrmɔʒɛn] *adj Physiol* thermogenetic, heat-producing.
thermographe [tɛrmɔgraf] *nm Phys* thermograph.
thermomagnétisme [tɛrmɔmaɲetism] *nm Phys* thermomagnetism.
thermomètre [tɛrmɔmɛtr] *nm* thermometer; **t. médical ou de clinique,** clinical thermometer; **t. à maxima et minima,** maximum and minimum thermometer; **le t. monte/baisse,** the temperature is rising/falling; *Fig* **le t. de l'opinion,** the barometer of public opinion.
thermométrie [tɛrmɔmetri] *nf Phys* thermometry.
thermométrique [tɛrmɔmetrik] *adj* thermometric(al).
thermonucléaire [tɛrmɔnykleɛr] *adj Phys Nucl & Mil* thermonuclear.
thermopile [tɛrmɔpil] *nf Él* thermopile.
thermoplastique [tɛrmɔplastik] *adj & nm* thermoplastic.
thermoplongeur [tɛrmɔplɔ̃ʒœr] *nm* (portable) immersion heater.
thermopompe [tɛrmɔpɔ̃p] *nf* heat pump.
thermopropulsion [tɛrmɔprɔpylsjɔ̃] *nf Av* thermopropulsion.
thermorégulateur [tɛrmɔregylatœr] *nm* thermoregulator, thermostat.
thermorégulation [tɛrmɔregylasjɔ̃] *nf* thermoregulation.
thermorésistant [tɛrmɔrezistɑ̃] *adj* heat-resistant.
thermos ® [tɛrmɔs] *nm ou f inv* **(bouteille) t.,** Thermos ® (flask *or Am* bottle).
thermoscope [tɛrmɔskɔp] *nm Phys* thermoscope.
thermosphère [tɛrmɔsfɛr] *nf* thermosphere.
thermostable [tɛrmɔstabl] *adj Ch Méd* thermostable.
thermostat [tɛrmɔsta] *nm* thermostat; **réglage par t.,** thermostatic control.
thermothérapie [tɛrmɔterapi] *nf* heat treatment, thermotherapy.
thésard, -arde [tezar, -ard] *n Univ F* PhD student.
thésaurisation [tezɔrizasjɔ̃] *nf* hoarding (of money); *Écon* building up of capital.
thésauriser [tezɔrize] **1** *vi* to hoard (money). **2** *vt* to hoard (*money*).
thésauriseur, -euse [tezɔrizœr, -øz] *n* hoarder (*of money*).
thesaurus [tezɔrys] *nm* thesaurus.
thèse [tɛz] *nf* **(a)** (*doctrine*) thesis, proposition, argument; **pièce à t.,** problem play, drama of ideas; **roman/littérature à t.,** novel/literature of ideas; **(b)** *Univ* thesis (*submitted for degree*); **soutenir sa t.,** to have one's viva (voce); *F* **inviter qn à sa t.,** to invite s.o. to one's viva (voce); **(c)** *Phil* thesis; **t., antithèse, synthèse,** thesis, antithesis, synthesis.
Thésée [teze] *nm* Theseus.
Thessalonique [tesalɔnik] *nf* Thessalonica.
thêta [tɛta] *nm* (*lettre grecque*) theta.
thiamine [tjamin] *nf Biol Ch* thiamin(e), aneurin.
thibaude [tibod] *nf* carpet felt, (felt) underlay.
Thierry [tjɛri] *nm* Terry.
thioalcool [tjɔalkɔl] *nm Ch* thioalcohol.
thionate [tjɔnat] *nm Ch* thionate.
thionine [tjɔnin] *nf Ch* thionine.
thionique [tjɔnik] *adj Ch* thionic.
thiosulfate [tjɔsylfat] *nm Ch* thiosulphate, *US* thiosulfate.
thiosulfurique [tjɔsylfyrik] *adj Ch* thiosulphuric, *US* thiosulfuric.
thio-urée [tjɔyre] *nf Ch* thiourea; (*pl thio-urées*).
thixotropie [tiksɔtrɔpi] *nf Ch Phys* thixotropy.
tholos [tɔlɔs] *nf Archéol* (*tombe*) tholos.
Thomas [tɔmɑ] *nm* **(a)** Thomas; **Saint T. d'Aquin,** St Thomas Aquinas; **(b)** *Arg Vieilli* (*pot de chambre*) chamberpot, *Br* jerry.
thomisme [tɔmism] *nm Rel* Thomism.
thomiste [tɔmist] *adj & n Rel* Thomist.

thon [tɔ̃] *nm* tuna, tunny; *Culin* tuna (fish); **t. au naturel/à l'huile,** tuna (fish) in brine/in oil.
thonaire [tɔnɛr] *nf Pêche* tuna *or* tunny net.
thonier [tɔnje] *nm* tuna *or* tunny boat.
Thor [tɔr] *nm* Thor.
Thora [tɔra] *nf Rel* Torah.
thoracique [tɔrasik] *adj Anat* thoracic; **cage t.,** ribcage.
thoracoplastie [tɔrakɔplasti] *nf Chir* thoracoplasty.
thorax [tɔraks] *nm* thorax.
thorium [tɔrjɔm] *nm Ch* thorium.
thoron [tɔrɔ̃] *nm Phys Nucl* thoron.
Thrace [tras] *nf* Thrace.
thrène [trɛn] *nm Antiq* threnody.
thriller [srilœr] *nm Cin Littér* thriller.
thrips [trips] *nm Ent* thrips, thysanopter.
thrombine [trɔ̃bin] *nf Biol Ch* thrombin.
thrombocyte [trɔ̃bɔsit] *nm Physiol* thrombocyte.
thrombophlébite [trɔ̃bɔflebit] *nf Méd* thrombophlebitis.
thrombose [trɔ̃boz] *nf Méd* thrombosis.
thrombus [trɔ̃bys] *nm Méd* thrombus.
Thucydide [tysidid] *nm* Thucydides.
thulium [tyljɔm] *nm Ch* thulium.
thune [tyn] *nf Arg* **(a)** (*argent*) dough, bread; **sans une t.,** without a penny; **(b)** *Arch* (*pièce*) five-franc piece.
thuriféraire [tyriferɛr] *nm* **(a)** *Rel* thurifer, incense bearer; **(b)** *Litt* (*flatteur*) flatterer.
thuya [tyja] *nm Bot* thuja, thuya, arbor vitae.
thylacine [tilasin] *nm* thylacine, Tasmanian wolf.
thym [tɛ̃] *nm Bot Culin* thyme; **t. sauvage,** wild thyme.
thymique [timik] *adj Anat Méd* thymic (*asthma etc*).
thymol [timɔl] *nm Pharm* thymol.
thymus [timys] *nm Anat* thymus, thymus gland.
thyroglobuline [tirɔglɔbylin] *nf Biol Ch* thyroglobulin.
thyroïde [tirɔid] *adj & nf Anat* **(glande) t.,** thyroid (gland).
thyroïdectomie [tirɔidɛktɔmi] *nf Chir* thyroidectomy.
thyroïdien, -ienne [tirɔidjɛ̃, -jɛn] *adj Anat Méd* thyroid (*hormone, artery etc*).
thyroïdisme [tirɔidism] *nm Méd* thyroidism.
thyroïdite [tirɔidit] *nf Méd* thyroiditis.
thyrse [tirs] *nm Antiq Bot* thyrsus.
tiare [tjar] *nf* (*du pape*) tiara.
Tibère [tibɛr] *nm* Tiberius.
Tibet [tibɛ] *nm* Tibet; **dogue du T.,** Tibetan mastiff; **griffon du T.,** Tibetan terrier, chrysanthemum dog.
tibétain, -aine [tibetɛ̃, -ɛn] **1** *adj* Tibetan. **2** *nm Ling* Tibetan. **3** *n* **T.,** Tibetan.
tibia [tibja] *nm* **(a)** *Anat* tibia, shinbone; **s'érafler le t.,** to bark one's shin; **(b)** *Ent* tibia.
tibial, -iaux [tibjal, -jo] *adj Anat* tibial.
Tibre [tibr] *nm* **le T.,** the Tiber.
tic [tik] *nm* **(a)** *Méd* tic, twitch; **il a un t.,** he has a twitch *or* a tic, his face twitches; **t. douloureux,** tic douloureux, facial neuralgia; **(b)** *Vét* vicious habit (*of horse*); **(c)** *Fig* (*habitude*) habit, mannerism; **t. de langage,** verbal tic *or* mannerism.
ticket [tikɛ] *nm* **(a)** (*billet*) ticket; *Rail* **t. de quai,** platform ticket; *Admin Arch* **t. de pain,** bread coupon; **t. modérateur,** = portion of the cost of treatment paid by the insured; **(b)** *Ordinat* tag; **(c)** *Arg* (*billet de dix francs*) ten-franc note; **(d)** *Arg* **avoir un t. avec qn,** to be popular *or* to click with s.o..
ticket-repas [tikɛrəpɑ] *nm*, **ticket-restaurant** [tikɛrɛstɔrɑ̃] *nm* luncheon voucher; (*pl tickets-repas, tickets-restaurant*).
tickson [tiksɔ̃] *nm Arg* ticket.
tic(-)tac [tiktak] **1** *nm inv* tick-tock, tick, ticking (*of clock*); **faire t.-t.,** to tick. **2** *int* tick-tock!
tictaquer [tiktake] *vi* (*of clock*) to tick; (*of heart*) to go pit-a-pat.
tie-break [tajbrɛk] *nm Tennis* tie break; (*pl tie-breaks*).
tiédasse [tjedas] *adj Péj* lukewarm, tepid.
tiède [tjɛd] **1** *adj* tepid, lukewarm (*bath, drink, Fig friendship etc*); mild (*air, climate*); half-hearted (*faith, welcome, supporter etc*). **2** *adv* **il fait t.,** it's mild (*weather*). **3** *n* half-hearted person.
tièdement [tjɛdmɑ̃] *adv* half-heartedly.
tiédeur [tjedœr] *nf* tepidness, lukewarmness (*of water, Fig friendship etc*); mildness (*of climate etc*); half-heartedness (*of welcome, supporter etc*); **avec t.,** half-heartedly.
tiédir [tjedir] **1** *vi* (*devenir plus chaud*) to warm up; (*devenir moins chaud*) to cool down; (*of friendship, ardour etc*) to cool off. **2** *vt* (*rechauffer*) to take the chill off, to warm (up); (*refroidir*) to cool (down).
tiédissement [tjedismɑ̃] *nm* (*refroidissement*) cooling (off); (*réchauffement*) warming (up).
tien, tienne [tjɛ̃, tjɛn] **1** *pron poss* **le t., la tienne, les tiens, les tiennes,** yours; *Bible & Arch* thine; **ce cadeau n'est pas le t.,** this gift is not yours, this is not your gift; **leurs enfants ressemblent aux tiens,** their children are like yours; **les deux tiens,** your two, the two of yours; *F* **le t. de bébé est plus intelligent,** YOUR baby is cleverer; *F* **à la tienne!,** cheers!, your health!

2 *adj poss Litt* (of) yours; **ce chapeau est t.,** this hat is yours; **un t. parent,** a relative of yours; **tu as fait tiennes mes théories,** you've adapted my theories as yours *or* as your own.

3 *nm* **(a) si tu veux du mien, donne-moi du t.,** if you want some of mine, give me some of yours; **le t. et le mien,** questions *or* arguments about property; **y mettre du t.,** to do your fair share, to help out; **(b) les tiens,** (*parents*) your (own) family; (*amis, partisans etc*) your own people; *F* **tu as encore fait des tiennes,** you've been up to your usual (stupid) tricks again.
tiens, tient [tjɛ̃] *voir* **TENIR.**
tierce [tjɛrs] *nf* **(a)** *Astron Math* = sixtieth part of a second; **(b)** *Escrime* tierce; **(c)** *Rel* terce, tierce; **(d)** *Mus* third; **(e)** *Typ* final revise, press proof; **(f)** *Cartes* tierce.
tiercé [tjɛrse] **1** *adj* **(a)** *Agr* ploughed *or US* plowed for the third time; **(b)** *Hér* tierced, tiercé; **(c) rimes tiercées,** terza rima; **(d)** *Courses de chevaux* **pari t.,** = forecast of the first three horses. **2** *nm Courses de chevaux* = **pari t.; un beau t.,** a good win on the tiercé.
tiercelet [tjɛrsəlɛ] *nm* tercel, male falcon.
tiercer [tjɛrse] *vt* **(je tierçai(s); n. tierçons)** *Agr* to plough *or US* plow (*land*) for the third time.
tierceron [tjɛrs(ə)rɔ̃] *nm Archit* tierceron (rib).
tiers, tierce [tjɛr, tjɛrs] **1** *adj Arch* third (*power etc*); **une tierce personne,** a third party; *Hist* **le t. état,** the third estate, the commonalty; *Pol* **le t. monde,** the Third World; *Rel* **t. ordre,** Third Order; *Jur* **en main tierce,** in the hands of a third party; **t. porteur,** second endorser (*of bill*).

2 *nm* **(a)** (*fraction*) third (part); **une remise d'un t. (du prix),** a discount of a third, *F* a third off; *Fin* **t. provisionnel,** interim (tax) payment (= *one third of previous year's tax*); **perdre le t./les deux t. de son argent,** to lose a third/two thirds of one's money;

(b) (*personne*) third party; **être en t.,** to be present as a third party, to make a third; *F* **le t. et le quart,** everybody, anybody; *F* **se moquer du t. comme du quart,** not to give a damn about anybody or anything; **prendre le parapluie d'un t.,** to take a perfect stranger's umbrella; **assurance au t.,** third party insurance; *Admin* **t. payant,** = system of direct payment for medical treatment by the insurer.
tiers-arbitre [tjɛrarbitr] *nm Jur* (independent) arbitrator; (*pl tiers-arbitres*).
tiers-monde [tjɛrmɔ̃d] *nm Pol* **le t.-m.,** the Third World; **pays du t.-m.,** Third World countries; (*pl tiers-mondes*).
tiers-mondiste [tjɛrmɔ̃dist] *Pol* **1** *adj* Third World. **2** *n* supporter of the Third World.
tiers-point [tjɛrpwɛ̃] *nm* (*pl tiers-points*) **(a)** *Archit* **arc en t.-p.,** pointed equilateral arch; **(b)** (*outil*) triangular file.
tifoso [tifozo] *nm* fan; (*pl tifosi*).
tifs, tiffes [tif] *nmpl Arg* hair, thatch.
tige [tiʒ] *nf* **(a)** stem, stalk (*of plant*); scape (*of feather*); **(b)** stem (*of tree*); **(arbre de) haute/basse t.,** (tall) standard/half standard; **(c)** *Fig Litt* stock (*of family*); **faire t.,** to found a line; **(d)** shaft (*of column*); stem (*of valve, candlestick etc*); shank (*of rivet, key, anchor, Typ letter*); stick (*of violin bow*); leg (*of pedestal table*); **t. à caractères,** type bar; **(e)** *Tech* rod (*of pump, piston etc*); *Pétr* **t. de forage,** drill(ing) pipe; *Aut etc* **t. de jauge,** dipstick; **t. de paratonnerre,** lightning rod; **t. de selle,** (*de bicyclette*) saddle pillar; **t. de frein,** brake rod; **t. à vis du frein,** brake screw; **(f)** leg (*of stocking*); leg, upper (*of boot*); **bottes à tiges,** top boots; **(g)** *Arg* (*cigarette*) cig(gy), *Br* fag; **(h)** *Av Arg* **les Vieilles Tiges,** the very first pilots.
tiglon [tiglɔ̃] *nm* tigon.
tignasse [tiɲas] *nf* mop (of tousled hair).
tigre [tigr] *n* tiger; **t. du Bengale** *ou* **royal,** Bengal tiger; **jaloux comme un t.,** madly *or* wildly jealous.
Tigre [tigr] *nm* **le T.,** the Tigris.
tigré [tigre] *adj* **(a)** (*rayé*) striped; **chat t.,** tabby (cat); **lis t.,** tiger lily; **(b)** (*tacheté*) spotted **(de,** with).
tigresse [tigrɛs] *nf* tigress; *Fig* (*femme jalouse*) jealous cat; **jalouse comme une t.,** madly *or* wildly jealous.
tigron [tigrɔ̃] *nm* tigon.
tilbury [tilbyri] *nm* (*voiture à cheval*) tilbury, gig.
tilde [tild(e)] *nm Typ etc* tilde.

tillac [tijak] *nm Hist Nau* upper deck.
tilleul [tijœl] **1** *nm* **(a)** lime (tree); **(b) (infusion de) t.,** lime-blossom tea. **2** *adj inv & nm* **(vert) t.,** lime green.
tilt [tilt] *nm* (*au billard électrique*) tilt signal; **faire t.,** to signal the end of the game; *Fig* (*of idea, word etc*) to ring a bell.
timbale [tɛ̃bal] *nf* **(a)** *Mus* kettledrum; **les timbales,** (*dans un orchestre*) the timpani; **(b)** (*gobelet*) (metal) drinking cup; **t. en argent,** (*donnée aux enfants baptisés*) silver christening cup; *Fig F* **décrocher la t.,** to hit the jackpot; **(c)** *Culin* (*moule*) timbale (mould, *US* mold); (*plat*) timbale; **t. de langouste,** lobster timbale.
timbalier [tɛ̃balje] *nm Mus* timpanist.
timbrage [tɛ̃braʒ] *nm* stamping (*of passport, letter etc*).
timbre [tɛ̃br] *nm* **(a)** (*sonnette*) bell (*with striking hammer*); **t. de bicyclette,** bicycle bell; **t. électrique,** electric bell; **presser le t.,** to press *or* ring the bell; *F Arch* **avoir le t. fêlé,** to be cracked *or* daft, to have a screw loose;
(b) *Mus* snare (*of drum*);
(c) (*son*) timbre, tone (*of voice, instrument*); **voix sans t.,** toneless voice;
(d) (*marque, cachet*) stamp (*on document etc*); **t. (de la poste),** postmark; **t. sec,** embossed stamp;
(e) (*vignette*) stamp; **t.(-poste),** (postage) stamp; **t. antituberculeux,** TB research stamp; **t. fiscal,** excise stamp; **t. de quittance,** receipt stamp; **album de timbres,** stamp album;
(f) (*tampon*) stamp; **t. sec,** embossing press; **t. humide,** rubber stamp; **t. à date, t. dateur,** date stamp; **t. à encrage automatique,** self-inking stamp;
(g) *Fin* (*droit*) stamp duty.
timbré [tɛ̃bre] *adj* **(a)** sonorous (*voice*); **(b)** (*fou*) cracked, screwy; **(c)** stamped (*paper, document, envelope etc*).
timbre-épargne [tɛ̃breparɲ] *nm* savings-bank stamp; (*pl timbres-épargne*).
timbre-poste [tɛ̃br(ə)pɔst] *nm* postage stamp; (*pl timbres-poste*).
timbre-prime [tɛ̃br(ə)prim] *nm Com* trading stamp; (*pl timbres-prime*).
timbre-quittance [tɛ̃br(ə)kitɑ̃s] *nm* receipt stamp; (*pl timbres-quittance*).
timbrer [tɛ̃bre] *vt* **(a)** (*avec un tampon*) to stamp (*passport, document etc*); to postmark (*letter, parcel etc*); **lettre timbrée de Paris,** letter with a Paris postmark; **(b) papier timbré au chiffre de qn,** paper stamped with s.o.'s arms; **(c)** (*coller un timbre sur*) to stamp, to put *or* stick a stamp *or* stamps on (*letter etc*).
timbre-taxe [tɛ̃br(ə)taks] *nm* postage-due stamp; (*pl timbres-taxe*).
timide [timid] **1** *adj* **(a)** (*gêné*) shy, timid (*person, smile etc*); **(b)** (*timoré*) timid, timorous, apprehensive (*person*); **critique/protestation t.,** timid criticism/protest. **2** *n* **c'est un grand t.,** he's very shy.
timidement [timidmɑ̃] *adv* **(a)** (*d'une manière gênée*) shyly, timidly, diffidently; **(b)** (*d'une manière timorée*) timidly.
timidité [timidite] *nf* **(a)** (*gêne*) shyness, timidity, diffidence; **(b)** (*manque d'audace*) timidity.
timing [tajmiŋ] *nm* timing.
timon [timɔ̃] *nm* **(a)** shaft, pole (*of horse-drawn vehicle etc*); beam (*of plough*); **(b)** *Nau Arch* tiller.
timonerie [timɔnri] *nf* **(a)** *Nau* **(kiosque de) t.,** wheelhouse, pilot house; **(b)** *Nau* (*fonction*) (naval) signalling; **(c)** *Aut* steering gear; (*freins*) brake gear.
timonier [timɔnje] *nm* **(a)** *Nau* (*à la barre*) helmsman, man at the wheel; (*aux signaux*) signalman; **(b)** (*cheval*) wheelhorse, wheeler.
timoré [timɔre] *adj* timorous, fearful; **conscience timorée,** overscrupulous conscience.
Timothée [timɔte] *nm* Timothy.
tins [tɛ̃] *nmpl Nau* keel blocks (*in dry dock*); stocks (*on slip*).
tinctorial, -iaux [tɛ̃ktɔrjal, -jo] *adj* tinctorial, dyeing (*plant, product, process etc*).
tinette [tinɛt] *nf* **(a)** (*baquet*) (sanitary) soil tub; **(b)** *F* **tinettes,** (*toilettes*) latrines.
tintamarre [tɛ̃tamar] *nm F* (*bruit*) din, racket; **faire du t.,** to make *or* kick up a din *or* racket.
tintement [tɛ̃t(ə)mɑ̃] *nm* **(a)** ringing (*of large bell*); **t. funèbre,** tolling; **(b)** tinkling, tinkle (*of small bells etc*); jingling, jingle (*of sleigh bells, coins, keys*); chink(ing) (*of coins, glasses*); **(c) t. d'oreilles,** ringing *or* buzzing in the ears, *Spéc* tinnitus.
tinter [tɛ̃te] **1** *vt* to ring (*bell*); **t. la messe,** to ring for mass. **2** *vi* **(a)** (*of large bell*) to ring; (*of small bells etc*) to tinkle; (*of coins, glasses etc*) to chink; (*of sleigh bells, coins, keys*) to jingle; **faire t. les verres,** to chink glasses; **(b)** (*of the ears*) to ring, to buzz; **les oreilles me tintaient,** my ears were ringing *or* buzzing; *Fig* **les oreilles ont dû vous t. hier soir,** (*on a parlé de vous*) your ears must have been burning last night.
tintin [tɛ̃tɛ̃] *int F* no go!, nothing doing!; **faire t.,** to go without.
tintinnabuler [tɛ̃tinabyle] *vi Litt* (*of bells*) to tintinnabulate, to tinkle.
Tintoret (le) [lətɛ̃tɔrɛ] *nm* Tintoretto.
tintouin [tɛ̃twɛ̃] *nm F* **(a)** (*bruit*) din, racket; **(b)** (*souci*) trouble, worry; **se donner du t.,** to go to a lot of trouble.
TIOP [tiɔp] *nm Banque* (*abrév* **taux interbancaire offert à Paris**) *Br* ≈ LIBOR.
tipule [tipyl] *nf Ent* crane fly.
tique [tik] *nf Ent* tick.
tiquer [tike] *vi* **(a)** *F* to wince; **il n'a pas tiqué,** he didn't turn a hair *or* bat an eyelid; **(b)** *Vét* (*of horse*) to suck wind, to crib(-bite).
tiqueté [tikte] *adj* speckled, mottled, variegated.
tir [tir] *nm* **(a)** (*activité*) shooting; **t. aux pigeons,** pigeon shooting; **(b)** (*action de tirer*) firing; (*feu*) fire; **champ de t.,** (*lieu*) firing range; (*d'arme*) field of fire; **t. au but,** precision firing; **t. au fusil** *ou* **à la carabine,** rifle shooting; **t. automatique,** automatic fire; **habileté au t.,** marksmanship; **cadence** *ou* **régime** *ou* **vitesse du t.,** rate of fire; **allonger/raccourcir le t.,** to increase/reduce the range; **t. d'artillerie,** artillery fire; **t. de batterie,** battery fire; *Nau* **t. en chasse/en retraite,** bow/stern fire; **(c)** *Min* blasting; **(d)** (*concours*) shooting match *or* competition; **(e)** *Fb* **t. (au but),** shot (at goal); **(f)** (*stand*) rifle range; **t. (forain),** shooting gallery.
tirade [tirad] *nf* **(a)** *Péj* tirade; **(b)** *Th* monologue.
tirage [tiraʒ] *nm* **(a)** pulling, hauling (*of carriages etc*); **cheval de t.,** draught *or US* draft horse; *Él* **interrupteur à t.,** pull-and-push switch;
(b) *F* (*difficultés*) trouble, difficulty; **il y a du t. entre eux,** there's friction between them, they don't get on together;
(c) towing (*of barges*); (*chemin*) towpath;
(d) *Métal* wire drawing;
(e) quarrying, extraction (*of stone*); **t. à la poudre,** blasting;
(f) *Phot* (*distance*) extension, *Arch* focal length (*of camera*);
(g) draught (*of flue*); **t. renversé** *ou* **inverti,** back draught; *Aut* **carburateur à t. en bas,** down-draught carburettor;
(h) drawing (*of lottery, bonds etc*); **t. du numéro gagnant,** drawing of the winning number;
(i) *Typ Phot etc* (*action*) printing; (*objet*) print; (*quantité*) number printed, edition (*of book, engraving etc*); edition (*of recording*); *Typ* **un mille de t.,** run *or* printing of a thousand; **journal à gros** *ou* **grand t.,** paper with a wide circulation; **t. de luxe,** de luxe edition; **t. numéroté,** numbered edition; **t. à part,** offprinting; **édition à t. limité,** limited edition;
(j) *Typ* **t. héliographique,** arc print; *Cin* **t. en surimpression,** overprint;
(k) *Banque etc* drawing, emission (*of cheque, bill of exchange*); **t. en blanc** *ou* **en l'air,** drawing *or* emission of a dud cheque *etc*.
tiraillement [tirajmɑ̃] *nm* **(a)** tugging, pulling (*on rope etc*); **(b) t. d'estomac,** gnawing at *or* of the stomach, pangs of hunger; **(c)** (*friction*) friction, wrangling; (*entre deux choses contradictoires*) conflict (**entre,** between).
tirailler [tiraje] **1** *vt* to pull at, to tug at, to pull about; *Fig* **tiraillé entre deux émotions,** torn between two opposing feelings. **2** *vi Mil* to shoot wildly; (*pour harceler*) to fire in skirmishing order. **3 se tirailler** *vpr* to get on badly (**avec qn,** with s.o.).
tiraillerie [tirajri] *nf* **(a)** *Mil* wild firing; **(b)** (*friction*) wrangling, friction.
tirailleur [tirajœr] *nm* **(a)** *Mil* skirmisher, sharpshooter; *Hist* **tirailleurs algériens/sénégalais,** native Algerian/Senegalese infantry; **en tirailleurs,** in skirmishing order; **(b)** *Journ F* freelance (journalist).
tirant [tirɑ̃] *nm* **(a)** (*de bourse*) (draw)string; **(b)** (*de botte*) boot strap; **(c)** *Constr* tie beam (*of roof*); **(d)** *Tech* stay, brace; **t. de frein,** brake rod; **(e)** *Nau* **t. d'eau,** (ship's) draught, *US* draft; **avoir dix pieds de t. d'eau,** to draw ten feet of water; **navire à faible t. d'eau,** shallow-draught ship; **échelle de t. d'eau,** draught marks *or* numbers; **(f)** *Constr etc* **t. d'air,** head room.

tirasse [tiras] *nm* **(a)** (*filet de chasse*) draw net; **(b)** *Mus* pedal coupler (*of organ*).

tire [tir] *nf* **(a) voleur à la t.,** pickpocket; **(vol à) la t.,** pickpocketing; **(b)** *Can* (*confiserie*) molasses toffee, *Am* molasses candy, taffy; **t. d'érable,** maple toffee *or Am* taffy; **(c)** *Arg* (*voiture*) car.

tiré, -ée [tire] **1** *adj* **(a)** drawn, haggard (*features*); **il avait les traits tirés,** his face was drawn *or* haggard, he looked drawn *or* haggard; **aux cheveux tirés,** with her hair drawn back; **(b)** *Fig* **t. par les cheveux,** far-fetched; **(c)** *Golf* **coup t.**, pulled shot, pull; **(d) broderie à fils tirés,** drawn-thread work; **(e)** *Banque* **chèque t. sur qn,** cheque drawn on s.o.; **personne tirée,** drawee. **2** *n Com* drawee. **3** *nm* **(a)** (*chasse*) shoot; **(b)** *Typ* **t. à part,** offprint. **4** *nf* **tirée (a)** *F* (*trajet*) long haul; **il y a encore toute une tirée,** there's still a long haul ahead; **(b)** *F* **une tirée de qch,** (*grande quantité*) loads of sth.

tire-au-cul [tiroky] *nm inv Arg* = **TIRE-AU-FLANC.**

tire-au-flanc [tiroflɑ̃] *nm inv F* shirker, *Br* skiver.

tire-botte [tirbɔt] *nm* (*crochet*) boothook; (*planchette*) bootjack; (*pl tire-bottes*).

tire-bouchon [tirbuʃɔn] *nm* (*pl tire-bouchons*) **(a)** (*pour bouteille*) corkscrew; **en t.-b.**, in a spiral, in corkscrews; **(b)** (*mèche*) corkscrew curl.

tire(-)bouchonné [tirbuʃɔne] *adj* (*pl tire(-)bouchonnés*) twisted; crumpled (*trousers*).

tire-bouton [tirbutɔ̃] *nm Vieilli* buttonhook; (*pl tire-boutons*).

tire-clous [tirklu] *nm inv* nail puller.

tire-d'aile (à) [atirdɛl] *adv* **s'envoler à t.-d'a.,** to fly swiftly away; *Fig* **partir à t.-d'a.,** to fly off, to be up and away.

tire-fesses [tirfɛs] *nm inv F* T-bar.

tire-filet [tirfilɛ] *nm* screw-cutting *or* thread-cutting tool, threader; (*pl tire-filets*).

tire-fond [tirfɔ̃] *nm inv* **(a)** (*longue vis*) long bolt, screw spike; *Rail* sleeper screw; **(b)** (*avec un anneau*) eye bolt.

tire-jus [tirʒy] *nm inv Arg* (*mouchoir*) nosewipe, snot rag.

tire-lait [tirlɛ] *nm inv* breast pump.

tire-larigot (à) [atirlarigo] *adv F* **boire à t.-l.,** to drink to one's heart's content *or* like a fish; **il y en a à t.-l.,** there is *or* are enough to keep anyone happy.

tire-ligne [tirliɲ] *nm* drawing pen; (*pl tire-lignes*).

tirelire [tirlir] *nf* **(a)** (*pour économiser*) money box; *Fig* **il a dû casser sa t. pour s'offrir ce livre,** he had to break into his piggy bank to buy himself this book; **(b)** *Arg* (*figure*) mug; (*tête*) nut; (*ventre*) belly.

tire-pognon [tirpɔɲɔ̃] *nm F Vieilli* one-arm(ed) bandit, fruit machine; (*pl tire-pognons*).

tirer [tire] **1** *vt* **(a)** (*étendre*) to pull out, to lengthen (out), to stretch; to draw (*wire*); to pull up (*socks*); **t. une affaire en longueur,** to spin out a piece of business; *F* **encore une heure à t. d'ici le déjeuner!,** still another hour to get through before lunch!; *Arg* **t. cinq ans,** (*de prison*) to get five years *or* a five-year stretch;

(b) (*traire*) to milk (*cow etc*);

(c) (*dans une direction*) to pull; **t. qn par la manche,** to tug at s.o.'s sleeve; **t. les cheveux à qn,** to pull s.o.'s hair; **je vais te t. les oreilles!,** I'll give you what for!; **t. la jambe,** *F* **t. la patte,** to limp; (*traîner*) to lag behind; **t. les rideaux,** to draw the curtains; **t. le verrou,** to shoot the bolt; (*pour ouvrir*) to draw the bolt; **t. qch à soi,** to pull sth to *or* towards one; *F* **t. la couverture à soi,** to want more than one's share; **t. un auteur à soi.,** to put a personal interpretation on an author's words; *Fig* **tableau qui tire l'œil** *ou* **le regard** *ou* **l'attention,** eye-catching picture; *Hist* **t. un criminel à quatre (chevaux),** to (hang,) draw and quarter a criminal; *Mus* **tire!,** (*à un violiniste*) down bow!;

(d) t. son chapeau à qn, to raise *or* lift one's hat to s.o.;

(e) (*extraire*) to pull out, to draw out, to take out, to extract; to draw (*water, wine etc*); **t. un journal de sa poche,** to pull *or* take a newspaper out of one's pocket; **t. une dent à qn,** to pull (out) *or* draw s.o.'s tooth; **t. les cartes,** to tell fortunes with cards; *Cartes* **t. pour la donne,** to cut for deal; **t. plaisir de qch,** to derive pleasure from sth; **t. vanité de qch,** to pride oneself on sth; **je n'ai rien pu t. de lui,** I couldn't get anything *or* a word out of him; **t. de l'argent de qn,** to get money out of s.o., to extract money from s.o.; **t. de l'huile des olives,** to extract oil from olives; **ce mot tire son origine de ...,** this word has its origin(s) in ...; **mot tiré du latin,** word derived from Latin; **t. la racine carrée d'un nombre,** to extract the square root of a number; **t. qn d'un mauvais pas** *ou* **d'embarras,** to get s.o. out of a tight spot *or* a difficulty; **t. qn de son lit,** to drag *or* pull s.o. out of bed; **t. qn du sommeil,** to drag s.o. from his sleep; **t. qn du doute,** to remove s.o.'s doubts; **t. qn de l'erreur,** to show s.o. his mistake;

(f) (*tracer*) to draw (*line*); **t. des plans,** to draw up *or* prepare plans;

(g) *Typ* to pull, to print (off), to strike off (*engraving, proof*); **t. un livre à cinq mille exemplaires,** to print five thousand copies of a book; **donner le bon à t. d'un volume,** to pass a book for press; **t. une épreuve d'un cliché,** to take a print from a negative; **t. à part,** to off-print;

(h) *Com* to draw (*bill of exchange, cheque*); **t. un chèque sur une banque,** to draw a cheque on a bank;

(i) (*avec une arme*) to fire (*shot*); to shoot (*arrow*); to let off (*fireworks*); **t. un coup de revolver sur qn,** to fire *or* shoot at s.o. with a revolver; **t. un lièvre,** to shoot a hare;

(j) *Nau* **navire qui tire vingt pieds,** ship that draws twenty feet (of water).

2 *vi* **(a)** (*of marksman etc*) to shoot; (*of firearm*) to go off; **t. au hasard,** to fire at random; **t. à couvert,** to fire from behind cover; **t. à la carabine,** to shoot with a rifle; **t. dans le tas** *ou* **la foule,** to fire *or* shoot into the crowd; **t. sur qn/sur qch,** to shoot *or* fire at s.o./at sth; **t. dans le dos à qn,** to shoot s.o. in the back; *Fig* to gossip behind s.o.'s back;

(b) (*sur une corde etc*) to pull (**sur,** on, at); **j'ai la peau qui tire,** my skin feels tight; **t. sur sa pipe,** to have a pull at one's pipe;

(c) *Fb* to shoot; **t. au but,** to shoot at goal;

(d) (*aux boules*) to throw;

(e) *Fig* **bleu tirant sur le vert,** blue verging on green; **le jour tire à sa fin,** the day is drawing to its close; **le bonhomme tire à sa fin,** the old man's life is drawing to a close; **nos provisions tirent à leur fin,** our stores are running low *or* are giving out; **cela ne tire pas à conséquence,** it is of no consequence; **ça pourrait t. à conséquence pour ta carrière,** it could be of consequence for your career; *F* **t. à la ligne,** to pad out an article; **t. sur la soixantaine,** to be getting on for sixty;

(f) t. sur la gauche, to pull to the left; **t. au large,** *Nau* to stand out to sea; *F* (*partir*) to scram, to beat it;

(g) (*of chimney etc*) to draw.

3 se tirer *vpr* **(a) se t. d'un mauvais pas,** to extricate oneself from a difficulty, to get out of a fix *or* tight spot; **vous ne vous en tirerez pas avec cette excuse-là,** you won't get away with that excuse; **s'en t. sans aucun mal,** to escape uninjured; **s'en t. tout juste,** to escape by the skin of one's teeth; **on s'en tire, voilà tout!,** we just manage to make both ends meet, we just get by;

(b) *F* (*finir*) to come to an end; **ça se tire,** it'll soon be done now; **ça s'est bien tiré?,** I hope it went well?;

(c) (*partir*) to be off, to make tracks, to beat it.

tiret [tirɛ] *nm Typ* (*trait d'union*) hyphen; (*petit trait*) dash; **ligne de tirets,** broken line.

tirette [tirɛt] *nf* **(a)** writing slide (*of desk*); leaf (*of table*); **(b)** *Tech* pull handle, pull knob; flue damper (*of furnace etc*); *Aut etc* (pull-out) knob; **(c)** *Belg* (*fermeture éclair*) zip, *Am* zipper.

tireur, -euse [tirœr, -øz] **1** *n* **(a)** *Com* drawer (*of cheque, bill of exchange etc*); **(b) t. de cartes,** fortune teller; **(c)** *Mil etc Arg* **t. au flanc,** shirker, *Br* skiver; **(d)** (*photographe*) printer; **(e)** (*d'arme*) shooter, firer; **c'est un bon/mauvais t.,** he's a good/bad shot; **t. d'élite,** marksman, sharpshooter; **t. embusqué** *ou* **isolé,** sniper; **(f) t. d'armes,** fencer; **(g)** (*voleur*) pickpocket; **(h)** (*aux boules*) thrower. **2** *nf* **tireuse (a)** *Phot* (*appareil*) printer; **(b)** (*pour remplir les bouteilles*) bottle-filling machine, bottle filler.

tiroir [tirwar] *nm* **(a)** drawer (*of table etc*); **fonds de t.,** (*petite monnaie*) small change; **râcler ses fonds de t.,** to scrape one's pennies together; **publier ses fonds de t.,** to publish things from one's bottom drawer; *Littér* **roman/comédie à tiroir(s),** episodic novel/play; **nom à tiroir(s),** double-barrelled name; **(b)** *Tech* slide, slide valve (*of steam engine*); **t. de soutirage,** weirbox; **(c) t. à papier,** paper tray.

tiroir-caisse [tirwarkɛs] *nm Com* till, cash register; (*pl tiroirs-caisses*).

tisane [tizan] *nf* **(a)** (*infusion*) herb(al) tea; **t. de camomille,** camomile tea; **t. d'orge,** barley water; **(b) t. de champagne,** light champagne; **(c)** *Arg* (*coups*) thrashing, hiding.

tisanière [tizanjɛr] *nf* = pot for preparing herb(al) tea.

tison [tizɔ̃] *nf* **(a)** (*de bois*) (fire)brand; **garder les tisons,** to stay by the fire; **(b) allumette t.,** fusee (match).

tisonné [tizɔne] *adj* (*horse's coat*) with black spots.

tisonner [tizɔne] *vt* to poke (*fire*).
tisonnier [tizɔnje] *nm* poker.
tissage [tisaʒ] *nm Tex* **(a)** (*activité*) weaving; **t. à la main** *ou* **à bras,** handloom weaving; **t. mécanique,** power-loom weaving; **(b)** (*installation*) cloth mill *or* works.
tisser [tise] *vt* **(a)** *Tex* to weave; **l'araignée tisse sa toile,** the spider spins its web; **(b)** *Fig* to weave (*lies, plot etc*).
tisserand, -ande [tisrɑ̃, -ɑ̃d] *n* weaver.
tisserin [tisrɛ̃] *nm Orn* weaver(bird).
tisseur, -euse [tisœr, -øz] *n* weaver.
tissu[1] [tisy] *nm* **(a)** *Tex* material, fabric, cloth; **t. métallique,** wiregauze; *Fig* **t. de mensonges/d'absurdités/***etc*, string *or* tissue of lies/of absurdities *etc*; **(b)** *Biol* tissue; **(c) le t. urbain/social/industriel,** the urban/social/industrial fabric.
tissu[2] *adj Litt* **t. de,** shot through with (*absurdities, complications etc*).
tissu-éponge [tisyepɔ̃ʒ] *nm Tex* (terry) towelling; (*pl tissus-éponges*).
tissulaire [tisylɛr] *adj Biol* (of) tissue.
Titan [titɑ̃] *nm Myth Astron* Titan; **travail de T.,** titanic work; *Ind* **grue T.,** giant crane.
titane [titan] *nm Ch* titanium.
titanesque [titanɛsk] *adj* titanic (*undertaking etc*); colossal (*pride*).
Tite [tit] *nm* Titus; **T.-Live,** Livy.
titi [titi] *nm F* (*gavroche*) cheeky (Parisian) urchin.
Titien [tisjɛ̃] *nm* Titian.
titillation [titilɑsjɔ̃] *nf* titillation.
titiller [titile] *vt* (*chatouiller*) *& Fig* to titillate.
titisme [titism] *nm Pol* Titoism.
titiste [titist] *adj & n Pol* Titoist.
titrage [titraʒ] *nm* **(a)** *Ch Ind* titration, titrating (*of solution*); assaying (*of ore etc*); determination of the strength (*of alcohol, wine etc*); **(b)** *Cin* titling.
titre [titr] *nm* **(a)** (*de noblesse, fonction etc*) title; **porter le t. de duc,** to bear the title of duke; **se donner le t. de ...,** to style oneself ...;
(b) (*qualification*) title; **avoir le t. d'avocat,** to have the title of lawyer; **sans t. officiel,** without any official status; **en t.,** titular, on the regular staff; *F* **la maîtresse en t. du roi,** the King's acknowledged mistress; **elle ne mérite plus son t. d'amie,** she no longer deserves the title *or* name of friend *or* to be called a friend; *Jur* **propriétaire en t.,** legal owner;
(c) *Sp* title; *Boxe* **combat comptant/ne comptant pas pour le t.,** title/non-title fight; **tenant du t.,** titleholder;
(d) (*diplôme etc*) qualification; **pourvu de tous ses titres,** fully qualified;
(e) (*certificat*) voucher; *Jur* **t. de propriété,** title deed; **t. de transport,** ticket; *Mil* **t. de permission,** pass (for leave); **t. universel de paiement,** payment form (*attached to invoice*);
(f) *Fin Com* warrant, bond, certificate; **titres,** stocks and shares, securities; **t. au porteur,** bearer bond, negotiable instrument;
(g) (*droit*) title, claim, right; **t. juridique à qch,** legal claim to sth; **à t. de,** as a; **à t. d'office,** ex officio; **à t. de précaution,** just in case; **à t. d'ami,** as a friend; **à t. d'essai,** as a trial measure, experimentally; **à t. de faveur,** as a favour *or US* favor; **à bon t., à juste t.,** fairly, rightly; **à quel t.?,** by what right?, on what grounds?; **au même t.,** for the same reason; **à t. gratuit,** free of charge; **à ce t.,** (*pour cette raison*) therefore; (*en cette qualité*) as such;
(h) (*de livre, chanson, film etc*) title;
(i) (*de chapitre, page*) heading; **(page de) t.,** title page; **faux t.,** half-title; *Typ* **t. courant,** running head(line) *or* title; **les gros titres,** the large headlines;
(j) (*subdivision*) part, section (*of regulations etc*);
(k) titre, *US* titer (*of solution, gold*); grade, content (*of ore*); fineness (*of coinage*); **t. d'eau,** degree of humidity;
(l) size, number (*of cotton, wire*).
titré [titre] *adj* **(a)** titled (*person*); **(b)** *Ch* titrated, standard (*solution*).
titrer [titre] **1** *vt* **(a)** to give a title to (*s.o., sth*); *Cin* to title (*film*); **(b)** *Ch Ind* to titrate, to standardize (*solution*); to assay (*ore etc*); to determine the strength of (*alcohol, wine etc*); **(c)** *Tech* to size, to number (*cotton, wire etc*); to determine the blend of (*textile material*); **(d) t. tant pour cent métal,** (*of ore etc*) to assay so much percent of metal. **2** *vi* **la presse titrait en énormes manchettes,** the press printed enormous headlines.
titreuse [titrøz] *nf Cin* (*appareil*) titler.
titubant [titybɑ̃] *adj* reeling, lurching, staggering.
tituber [titybe] *vi* to reel (about), to lurch, to stagger, to totter; **marcher/entrer/sortir en titubant,** to stagger *or* lurch along/in/out; **t. de fatigue,** to stagger *or* totter with exhaustion.
titulaire [titylɛr] **1** *adj* titular (*bishop, professor etc*). **2** *n* holder (*of right, title, certificate etc*); bearer (*of passport*); occupant (*of office*); *Rel* incumbent (*of parish*).
titularisation [titylarizɑsjɔ̃] *nf Admin* establishment (*of civil servants etc*).
titulariser [titylarize] *vt Admin etc* to confirm (*s.o.*) in his post *or* appointment, to establish (*s.o.*).
T.M.G. [teɛmʒe] *nm* (*abrév* **temps moyen de Greenwich**) GMT.
toast [tost] *nm* **(a)** (*tranche de pain grillé*) piece *or* slice of toast; **t. beurré,** piece *or* slice of buttered toast; **(b)** (*allocution*) toast; **porter un t. à qn,** to drink *or* propose a toast to s.o., to toast s.o..
toasteur [tostœr] *nm* toaster.
toboggan [tɔbɔgɑ̃] *nm* **(a)** (*traîneau*) toboggan; **piste de t.,** toboggan run; **(b)** (*de piscine*) chute; (*de terrain de jeu etc*) slide; **(c)** *Com etc* (*pour marchandises*) chute; **(d)** *Aut* flyover, *Am* overpass.
toc [tɔk] **1** *int* tap! **2** *nm* **(a)** tap, rap (*on door etc*); **(b)** *F* **bijoux en t.,** imitation jewellery; **c'est du t.,** it's imitation *or* fake. **3** *adj inv* **être un peu t.,** (*fou*) to be a bit crazy *or* cracked.
tocante [tɔkɑ̃t] *nf F* (*montre*) watch, ticker.
tocard, -arde [tɔkar, -ard] *Arg* **1** *adj* worthless, trashy. **2** *nm Courses de chevaux* (rank) outsider. **3** *n Péj* (*person*) hopeless case, dead loss.
toccata [tɔkata] *nf Mus* toccata.
tocsin [tɔksɛ̃] *nm* alarm bell, tocsin; **faire sonner le t.,** to sound the alarm (bell) *or* tocsin.
toc-toc [tɔktɔk] *adj inv F* (*fou*) crazy, cracked.
toge [tɔʒ] *nf* **(a)** *Antiq* toga; **(b)** *Jur Scol* gown.
Togo [togo] *nm* Togo.
tohu-bohu [tɔybɔy] *nm* (*désordre*) chaos, confusion; (*bruit*) hubbub.
toi [twa] *pron pers* **(a)** you; *Bible & Arch* thou; (*complément direct*) you; *Bible & Arch* thee; **c'est t.,** it's you; **t. et moi nous irons ensemble,** you and I will go together; **il est plus âgé que t.,** he is older than you; **il n'aime que t.,** he loves only you; **tu as raison, t.,** you are right; **avec t.,** with you; **ce livre est à t.,** this book is yours *or* belongs to you; **moi, je reste, et t., tu pars,** I'll stay and you go; **t. parti, que vais-je faire?,** once you've gone *or* with you gone, what am I going to do?; **(b)** (*reflexive*) **dépêche-t.!,** hurry up!; **tais-t.!,** be quiet!; **assieds-t.!,** sit down!; **maîtrise-t.!,** control yourself!
toile [twal] *nf* **(a)** (*de lin*) linen, linen cloth; **t. à matelas,** tick, ticking; **drap de t.,** linen sheet; *F* **se mettre dans les toiles,** to hit the sack, to go to bed; **pantalon de t.,** duck trousers; **marchand de t.,** linen draper;
(b) cloth; (*morceau*) piece of cloth; **t. de crin,** horsehair cloth; **t. de coton,** calico; **t. peinte,** print; **t. cirée,** American cloth, oilcloth; *Nau* oilskin; **t. vernie,** oilskin; **t. à voiles,** canvas, sailcloth; **t. à bâches,** tarpaulin; **reliure en t.,** cloth binding; **t. de sauvetage,** jumping sheet, life net;
(c) (*plus grossière*) canvas; **t. de tailleur,** tailor's canvas; *F* **coucher sous la t.,** to sleep under canvas; **sac en t.,** canvas bag; **collé sur t.,** mounted on canvas; **papier collé sur t.,** linen-backed paper;
(d) t. métallique, wire gauze; **t. (d')émeri,** emery cloth; **t. d'amiante,** asbestos;
(e) t. d'araignée, cobweb, spider's web;
(f) *Beaux-Arts* (*œuvre, support*) canvas;
(g) *Th* **t. de fond,** backdrop, backcloth; *Fig* **avec la guerre en t. de fond,** with the war as a backdrop, against the backdrop of the war; **derrière la t.,** behind, off;
(h) *Nau* (*voiles*) sails; **à sec de t.,** under bare poles;
(i) toiles, (*de moulin*) sails;
(j) *F* (*film*) film.
toilerie [twalri] *nf* (*commerce*) cotton, linen and hemp industry *or* trade; (*fabrique*) cotton, linen and hemp mill.
toilettage [twalɛtaʒ] *nm* grooming (*of pet*).
toilette [twalɛt] *nf* **(a)** (*action de se laver etc*) washing (and dressing), *Litt* toilet; **faire sa t.,** to wash and dress; **faire un bout** *ou* **un brin de t.,** to have a wash and brush up, to freshen up; **le chat fait sa t.,** the cat is washing; **faire la t. d'une voiture,** to clean a car; **cabinet de t.,** washroom, bathroom, lavatory; **table de t.,** washstand; **trousse** *ou* **sac de t.,** sponge bag, toilet bag; **gant de t.,** = facecloth, *Br* (face) flannel, *US* washcloth; **savon de t.,** toilet soap; **(b) toilettes,** (*W.-C.*) toilets; (*publiques*) public conveniences *or* lavatory; **(c)** (*vêtements de femme*) dress, clothes; (*costume*) outfit; **être en (grande) t.,** to be in

formal dress; **t. de bal,** ball dress; **changer de t.,** to change one's clothes.

toiletter [twalete] *vt* to groom (*pet*).

toi-même [twamɛm] *pron pers* yourself; *Bible & Arch* thyself; *voir* **MÊME**.

toise [twaz] *nf* (*règle*) height gauge; **passer à** *ou* **sous la t.,** to have one's height measured; to measure the height of (*s.o.*); **je mesure 1 m 78 à** *ou* **sous la t.,** my official height is 1 m 78.

toisé [twaze] *nm Tech* measuring (up), measurement.

toiser [twaze] **1** *vt* to eye (*s.o.*) up (contemptuously). **2 se toiser** *vpr* to eye each other up (contemptuously).

toison [twazɔ̃] *nf* (*de mouton*) fleece; (*de lion, de cheval*) mane; (*d'homme*) (*chevelure*) mane (of hair); (*poils*) thick body hair; *Myth* **la T. d'or,** the Golden Fleece.

toit [twa] *nm* **(a)** (*de maison, voiture etc*) roof; *Fig* (*habitation*) home (of one's own); **t. d'ardoises/de tuiles/de chaume,** slate/tiled/thatched roof; *Beaux-Arts* **paysage de toits,** roofscape; **des ruines sans toits,** roofless ruins; **sous son t.,** under one's (own) roof; **être sans t.,** to have no roof over one's head, to be homeless; **habiter sous les toits,** to live in a garret; *Fig* **publier** *ou* **crier qch sur les toits,** to proclaim sth from the rooftops *or* housetops; *Aut* **t. ouvrant,** sun roof; **double t.,** (*de tente*) flysheet; **le t. paternel,** the home, the paternal roof; **(b)** *Min* top, roof (*of mine*); hanging wall (*of lode*).

toiture [twatyr] *nf* roofing, roof.

tokai, tokay [tɔkɛ] *nm* (*vin*) Tokay.

tôle¹ [tol] *nf* **(a)** (*matériau*) sheet metal; (*de fer*) sheet iron; **t. d'acier,** sheet steel; **t. ondulée,** corrugated iron; **t. de cuivre,** copper sheeting; **(b)** (*feuille*) metal sheet; (*de fer*) iron sheet; (*d'acier*) steel sheet.

tôle² *nf Arg* (*prison*) = **TAULE**.

tôlé [tole] *adj & nf Ski* **(neige) tôlée,** crusted snow.

tolérable [tɔlerabl] *adj* (*supportable*) bearable, tolerable; (*admissible*) permissible.

tolérance [tɔlerɑ̃s] *nf* **(a)** (*compréhension*) tolerance; *Rel* toleration; **faire preuve de t.,** to be tolerant; **par t.,** on sufferance; *Can Jur* **chemin de t.,** right of way; *Arch* **maison de t.,** licensed brothel; **(b)** (*concession*) concession; **t. orthographique,** acceptable variation in spelling; **(c)** *Tech* tolerance, margin; **t. nulle,** zero allowance; **t. sur l'épaisseur/la longueur,** thickness/length margin; **t. de fonctionnement,** operational tolerance; *Électron* **t. de fréquence,** frequency tolerance; **(d)** (*à la douane*) **t. (permise),** allowance; **il y a une t. d'un demi-litre,** you are allowed to bring in half a litre free of duty; **(e)** *Méd* tolerance; **t. immunitaire,** immune tolerance.

tolérant, -ante [tɔlerɑ̃, -ɑ̃t] *adj & nm* tolerant (person).

tolérantisme [tɔlerɑ̃tism] *nm Rel* tolerationism.

tolérer [tɔlere] *v* **(je tolère, n. tolérons; je tolérerai) 1** *vt* **(a)** (*être indulgent pour*) to tolerate (*opinions, religions etc*); (*supporter*) to put up with, to tolerate (*s.o., sth*); **je ne tolère pas qu'on dise ça,** I cannot tolerate people saying that (kind of thing); **(b)** *Méd* to tolerate (*drug*). **2 se tolérer** *vpr* to put up with *or* tolerate each other.

tôlerie [tolri] *nf* **(a)** (*commerce*) steel-metal trade; **(b)** (*atelier*) sheet-metal workshop; *Aut* body shop; **(c)** (*tôles*) metal sheets *or* plates; *Aut* panels, bodywork.

tolet [tɔlɛ] *nm Nau* thole pin.

tôlier¹ [tolje] *nm* **(a)** (*marchand*) sheet-iron merchant; **(b)** (*ouvrier*) sheet-metal worker; *Aut* panel beater.

tôlier², -ière [tolje, -jɛr] *n Arg* = **TAULIER**.

tollé [tɔle] *nm* (indignant) outcry.

toluène [tɔlɥɛn] *nm Ch* toluene, methyl benzene.

T.O.M. [tɔm] *nm abrév* **territoire d'outre-mer**.

tomahawk [tɔmaok] *nm* tomahawk.

tomaison [tɔmɛzɔ̃] *nf Typ* volume numbering.

tomate [tɔmat] *nf* **(a)** *Bot Culin* tomato; **sauce t.,** tomato sauce; **concentré de tomates,** tomato concentrate *or* purée; *F* **être (rouge) comme une t.,** to be as red as a beetroot; **(b)** *F* (*boisson*) pastis with grenadine.

tombal, -aux [tɔ̃bal, -o] *adj* **pierre tombale,** tombstone, gravestone; **inscription tombale,** tombstone *or* gravestone inscription.

tombant [tɔ̃bɑ̃] *adj* **(a) à la nuit tombante,** at nightfall; **(b)** hanging (*drapery etc*); flowing (*hair, lines of dress*); drooping (*branch, ears of animal, moustache*); **épaules tombantes,** sloping shoulders.

tombe [tɔ̃b] *nf* **(a)** (*sépulture*) grave; (*avec un monument*) tomb; **t. collective,** mass grave; **être dans la t.,** to be dead; **avoir un pied dans la t.,** to have one foot in the grave; **suivre qn dans la t.,** to follow s.o. to the grave; **se retourner dans sa t.,** to turn in one's grave; **(b)** (*pierre tombale*) tombstone, gravestone.

tombé [tɔ̃be] *adj* fallen; **roi t.,** fallen king; *Rugby Fb* **coup de pied t.,** drop kick.

tombeau, -eaux [tɔ̃bo] *nm* tomb; *Fig* **le t.,** (*la mort*) the grave; **t. de famille,** family vault; **descendre au t.,** to go to one's grave; **être aux portes du t.,** to have one foot in the grave; **mettre au t.,** to entomb; **mise au t.,** entombment; *F* **il me mettra** *ou* **conduira au t.,** he will outlive me; (*il me tuera*) he'll be the death of me; *Fig* **à t. ouvert,** at breakneck speed.

tombée [tɔ̃be] *nf* fall (*of rain, snow, night etc*); **t. du jour** *ou* **de la nuit,** nightfall.

tomber¹ [tɔ̃be] *nm* **(a) au t. du jour,** at nightfall; **(b)** (*de lutte*) fall.

tomber² **1** *vi* (*aux* **être**) **(a)** (*of person, object*) to fall (down); (*of aircraft, leaves etc*) to fall; *Fig* (*of government, Mil town etc*) to fall; **le plafond est tombé,** the ceiling has come down *or* fallen in; **tout tombe en poussière,** everything is crumbling to dust; **la neige tombe,** snow is falling; **t. à bas d'une échelle,** to fall off a ladder; **t. de cheval,** to fall off one's horse; **t. la tête la première,** to fall head first; **t. sur ses pieds,** to fall on one's feet; *F* **t. dans les pommes,** to pass out, to faint; **je tombe de fatigue** *ou* **de sommeil,** I'm ready to drop; **faire t.,** to knock *or* push over; *Fig* to bring down (*government etc*); **laisser t. qch,** to drop sth; *F* **laisser t. qn,** to drop s.o.; (*lui faire faux bond*) to let s.o. down; *F* **laisse t., ça ne vaut pas la peine,** forget it *or* leave it, it's not worth it; **se laisser t. dans un fauteuil,** to drop *or* sink *or F* flop into an armchair; **mes cheveux commencent à t.,** I'm beginning to lose my hair, my hair is beginning to fall out; **t. à l'eau,** to fall in (the water); *Fig* (*of plan etc*) to fall through, to come to nothing; *Journ* **le journal est tombé,** the paper has gone to press *or* bed; *TV Rad* **la nouvelle est tombée ce matin — c'est la guerre!,** the news came through this morning — it's war!; *F* **les bras m'en tombent,** I can't believe it; **fruits tombés,** windfalls; **la lumière qui tombe dans la chambre,** the light that is falling into the room;

(b) (*of wind, anger, fever etc*) to drop, to abate, to subside, to die down; (*of conversation*) to flag; **laisser t. sa voix,** to drop one's voice; **la nuit** *ou* **le jour tombe,** night is falling; **une fois la nuit tombée,** after dark;

(c) t. entre les mains *ou* **aux mains** *ou* **sous la main de qn,** to fall into s.o.'s hands *or* clutches; **t. dans un piège,** to fall into a trap; **t. en disgrâce/en ruine,** to fall into disgrace/ruin(s); **faut-il être tombé bien bas,** he must have hit rock bottom; *Nau* **t. sous le vent,** to fall off, to fall to leeward;

(d) t. sur l'ennemi, to attack *or* fall on the enemy; *F* **t. sur qn,** (*attaquer*) to pitch into *or* fall on s.o.;

(e) t. sur qn/qch, (*traverser*) to come across *or* upon s.o./sth; **ce livre m'est tombé sous la main,** I came across this book; **il va nous t. sur le dos d'un moment à l'autre,** he'll be bursting in on us any moment; **Noël tombe un jeudi cette année,** Christmas falls *or* is on a Thursday this year; **ça tombe sous le sens,** it stands to reason, it's obvious; **t. pile** *ou* **à pic** *ou* **à propos,** to come at (just) the right moment *or* time; **vous tombez bien,** you've come at the right moment; **avec tous ces ennuis qui me tombent dessus,** with all these worries that come my way; **il fallait que ça tombe sur moi!,** it had to happen to me!; **comme ça tombe!,** what a coincidence!; **t. juste,** to come at the right moment *or* time; *Math* to come out exactly; **cet argent lui tombe du ciel,** this money is a godsend to him; *F* **ça tombe comme un cheveu sur la soupe,** it has come at an awkward moment *or* time;

(f) (*échouer*) to fail; *Th* **la pièce est tombée (à plat),** the play flopped *or* was a failure; **sa proposition/plaisanterie est tombée à plat,** his suggestion/joke fell flat *or* went down like a lead balloon;

(g) (*pendre*) (*of hair, drapery etc*) to fall, to hang (down); **ses cheveux lui tombent dans le dos,** her hair hangs down her back; **jupe qui tombe bien,** skirt that hangs well;

(h) t. amoureux de qn, to fall in love with s.o.; **t. malade,** to fall ill; **t. mort,** to drop (down) dead; *F* **t. enceinte,** to get pregnant.

2 *vt* (*aux* **avoir**) **(a)** *Sp* **t. un adversaire,** to throw an opponent; *Arg* **t. une femme,** to have *or* lay a woman;

(b) *Métal* to flange;

(c) *F* **t. la veste,** to take off one's jacket.

3 *v impers* **il tombe de la pluie/de la grêle,** it is raining/hailing.

tombereau, -eaux [tɔ̃bro] *nm* **(a)** (*charrette*) tip-cart; (*contenu*) cartload (**de,** of); **(b)** (*camion*) dumper; **t. à ordures,** *Br* dustcart, *Am* garbage truck.

tombeur [tɔ̃bœr] *nm* **t. (de femmes),** ladykiller, womanizer.
tombola [tɔ̃bɔla] *nf* tombola, raffle.
Tombouctou [tɔ̃buktu] *n* Timbuktu.
tome [tɔm] *nm* (*volume*) volume; (*division*) part (*of book*).
tomer [tɔme] *vt Typ* (*diviser*) to divide into parts; (*marquer*) to mark with volume numbers.
tomette [tɔmɛt] *nf* (small red hexagonal) floor tile.
tomme [tɔm] *nf* = cheese made in Savoie and Dauphiné.
tom-pouce [tɔmpus] *nm* (*pl tom-pouces*) **(a)** *F* dwarf, midget; **(b)** (*petit parapluie*) stumpy umbrella.
ton[1], ta, *pl* **tes** [tɔ̃, ta, te] *adj poss* (**ton** *is used instead of* **ta** *before f words beginning with a vowel or* **h** *mute*) your; *Bible & Arch* thy; **t. ami, t. amie,** your friend; **un de tes amis,** a friend of yours, one of your friends; **ta propre fille,** your own daughter; **c'est t. affaire à toi,** that's YOUR business; *Litt* **tes père et mère,** your father and mother; *Rel* **que ta volonté soit faite,** Thy will be done.
ton[2] *nm* **(a)** (*qualité de voix*) tone; (*hauteur*) pitch; **parler d'un t. doux/sur un t. amical,** to speak gently *or* in a gentle tone/in a friendly tone; **hausser le t.,** to raise one's voice; **forcer le t.,** to speak more loudly and more urgently; **parler d'un t. bas,** to speak in a low key; **entre deux tons,** in an undertone; **les employés prennent le t. du chef,** the employees take their tone from the boss; *Fig* **changer de t.,** to change one's tune; *F* **faire baisser le t. à qn,** to take s.o. down a peg or two; **écrire sur un t. de plaisanterie,** to write in a humorous tone *or* style; **elle le prend sur ce t.?,** is that how she speaks to you?;
(b) (*goût*) tone, manners; **le bon t.,** good form *or* manners; **c'est de mauvais t.,** it is bad form *or* bad manners *or* vulgar; **remarques de bon t.,** remarks in good taste;
(c) *Mus* **(hauteur du) t.,** pitch; **donner le t.,** to give the tuning A; *Fig* to set the fashion; **sortir du t.,** to be out of tune; **se mettre dans le t.,** to tune up;
(d) *Mus* (*tonalité*) key; **le t. d'ut,** the key of C; **t. d'église,** church mode; *Fig F* **chanter sur un autre t.,** to change one's tune;
(e) *Mus* **tons et demi-tons,** tones and semitones; **t. entier,** whole tone;
(f) *Ling* tone;
(g) *Beaux-Arts Phot etc* (*couleur*) tone, shade; **tons chauds,** warm tones *or* shades; **tapis dans le t. des rideaux,** carpet toning (in) with the curtains; **peinture/voiture deux tons,** two-tone paint/car;
(h) *Méd Arch* tone;
(i) t. de chasse, hunting call (*to hounds*).
tonal, -als [tɔnal] *adj Mus* tonal.
tonalité [tɔnalite] *nf* **(a)** *Beaux-Arts Phot Mus* tonality; **paysage d'une t. claire,** landscape in a light key; **(b)** *Tél* **t. (continue),** dialling tone; **t. d'appel,** ringing tone; **(c)** (*de poste de radio etc*) tone.
tondeur, -euse [tɔ̃dœr, -øz] **1** *n* shearer (*of cloth, sheep*); **t. de moutons,** sheepshearer. **2** *nf* **tondeuse (a)** shears (*for cloth, sheep*); clippers (*for human hair, for animal's coat*); **(b) tondeuse (à gazon),** (lawn) mower; **tondeuse électrique/mécanique,** electric/hand mower.
tondre [tɔ̃dr] *vt* **(a)** to shear (*cloth, sheep*); to clip (*hair, dog, horse, hedge*); to mow (*lawn*); **(b)** *F* (*dépouiller*) to fleece (*s.o.*).
tondu [tɔ̃dy] **1** *adj* mown (*grass*); clipped (*hedge*); shorn (*sheep*); cropped (*hair, head*); (*person*) with cropped hair. **2** *nm Rel* monk; *Hist F* **le petit t.,** Napoleon (Bonaparte).
tong [tɔ̃g] *nf* (*chaussure de plage*) *Br* flip-flop, *Am* thong.
tonicardiaque [tɔnikardjak] *adj & nm Méd* cardiotonic.
tonicité [tɔnisite] *nf Méd* tonicity, tonus (*of the muscles etc*); *Fig* bracing *or* tonic effect (*of sea air etc*).
tonifiant [tɔnifjɑ̃] *adj* bracing, tonic (*air, walk etc*); tonic (*lotion*).
tonifier [tɔnifje] *vt* (*impf & pr sub* **n. tonifiions, v. tonifiiez**) to tone up (*muscles, skin, nervous system, patient etc*); *Fig* to invigorate.
tonique [tɔnik] **1** *adj* **(a)** tonic (*medicine, lotion etc*); **(b)** *Méd* **convulstion t.,** tonic spasm; **(c)** *Fig* bracing, tonic (*sea air, climate etc*); invigorating (*cold*); stimulating (*idea etc*); **(d)** *Ling* tonic (*accent*); accented, stressed (*syllable*); **l'accent t. tombe sur ...,** the stress falls on ...; **(e)** *Mus* **note t.,** tonic, keynote. **2** *nm Méd* tonic; (*lotion*) tonic lotion. **3** *nf Mus* tonic, keynote.
tonitruant [tɔnitryɑ̃] *adj* like thunder, thundering, resounding (*voice*).
tonitruer [tɔnitrye] *vi* to thunder, resound.
tonka [tɔ̃ka] **1** *nm Bot* tonka bean (plant); **fève t.,** tonka bean. **2** *nf* tonka bean.
tonnage [tɔnaʒ] *nm Nau* **(a)** tonnage (*of ship*); **t. brut,** gross tonnage; **t. net,** register tonnage; displacement (*of warship*); **(b)** tonnage (*of a port*); **(c) (droit de) t.,** (duty based on) tonnage.
tonnant [tɔnɑ̃] *adj* thundering; **voix tonnante,** voice of thunder.
tonne [tɔn] *nf* **(a)** (*unité de poids*) (metric) ton, tonne (= *1000 kg*); **t. courte,** short ton (= *907.185 kg*); **t. forte,** long ton, gross ton (= *1016.06 kg*); **t. kilométrique,** ton kilometre *or US* kilometer; **t. équivalent charbon/pétrole,** ton coal/oil equivalent; *F* **des tonnes de,** tons of; **(b)** *Nau* **t. de déplacement,** ton of displacement; **t. de jauge,** gross ton, register ton; **(c)** (*récipient*) tun, (large) cask.
tonneau, -eaux [tɔno] *nm* **(a)** barrel, cask; **un t. de vin,** a barrel *or* a cask of wine; **bière au t.,** beer from the barrel; draught *or US* draft beer; *Fig* **du même t.,** of the same kind, alike; **petit t.,** keg; **t. à mortier,** mortar mixer; *Hist* **le t. de Diogène,** Diogenes' tub; **t. d'arrosage,** water cart; **(b)** *Nau* (*unité de volume*) ton; **navire de 500 tonneaux,** 500-tonner, ship of 500 tons burden; **(c)** *Hist* (*voiture à cheval*) governess cart; **(d)** *Av Aut* roll; **faire un t.,** to flip *or* roll over; **la voiture a fait trois tonneaux,** the car flipped *or* rolled over three times.
tonnelet [tɔnlɛ] *nm* (small) cask, keg.
tonnelier [tɔnəlje] *nm* cooper.
tonnelle [tɔnɛl] *nf* **(a)** (*charmille*) arbour, *US* arbor, *Br* bower; **(b)** *Archit* barrel *or* tunnel vault.
tonnellerie [tɔnɛlri] *nf* cooperage.
tonner [tɔne] **1** *vi* **(a)** (*de canons etc*) to thunder, to boom; **(b)** (*fulminer*) to thunder (**contre,** against). **2** *v impers* **il tonne,** it is thundering.
tonnerre [tɔnɛr] *nm* **(a)** (*bruit*) thunder; **coup de t.,** clap *or* peal of thunder, thunderclap; *Fig* bombshell; **roulement de t.,** roll of thunder; **t. d'applaudissements,** thunderous applause; **voix de t.,** voice of *or* like thunder; **(b)** (*foudre*) **le t. est tombé sur une maison,** a house was struck by lightning; **(c)** *F* **du t.,** wonderful, terrific; **t. (de Dieu** *ou* **de Brest)!,** heavens above!; **il fera un marin du t. de Dieu,** he'll make a thundering good *or* a hell of a good sailor; **un dîner du t. de Dieu,** a stupendous dinner.
tonométrie [tɔnɔmetri] *nf* tonometry.
tonsure [tɔ̃syr] *nf* **(a)** *Rel* tonsure; **(b)** *F* (*calvitie*) bald patch.
tonsuré [tɔ̃syre] *Rel* **1** *adj* tonsured; **tête tonsurée,** shaven head. **2** *nm* cleric.
tonsurer [tɔ̃syre] *vt* to tonsure (*a cleric*).
tonte [tɔ̃t] *nf* **(a)** (*des moutons*) shearing; (*laine*) clip; (*saison*) shearing times; **(b)** (*du gazon*) mowing.
tontine[1] [tɔ̃tin] *nf Jur* tontine.
tontine[2] *nf* protective sacking (*round roots of trees to be transplanted*).
tonton [tɔ̃tɔ̃] *nm F* uncle; **T. Jules,** Uncle Jules.
tonus [tɔnys] *nm* **(a)** *Méd* tonicity, tonus, tone (*of muscle*); **(b)** *Fig* (*énergie*) energy, dynamism.
top [tɔp] **1** *nm Rad TV* time signal; **les tops,** the pips; **au quatrième t. il sera exactement dix heures,** at the fourth stroke it will be exactly ten o'clock; *Électron* **t. d'écho,** blip, *US* pip; **t. de synchronisation,** synchronizing signal; **donner le t. départ,** to give the starting signal. **2** *int* **un, deux, trois, t.!,** one, two, three, now!
topaze [tɔpaz] *nf* topaz.
toper [tɔpe] *vi F* to agree (**à qch,** to sth); **tope (là)!,** done!, agreed!
tophus [tɔfys] *nm Méd* tophus.
topinambour [tɔpinɑ̃bur] *nm Bot Culin* Jerusalem artichoke.
topique [tɔpik] **1** *adj* **(a)** *Méd* topical, local (*remedy etc*); **(b) lieu t.,** commonplace. **2** *nm Méd* topical *or* local remedy. **3** *nf Phil* **la t.,** topics.
top niveau [tɔpnivo] *nm F* top level; **être au t. n.,** to be a top-level *or* top-flight scientist *or* player *etc*.
topo [tɔpo] *nm F* **(a)** *Journ* article; **(b)** (*discours*) lecture; (*exposé*) rundown; **faire le t. de la situation,** to give a rundown on the situation; **c'est toujours le même t.,** it's always the same old story.
topographe [tɔpɔgraf] *n* topographer.
topographie [tɔpɔgrafi] *nf* **(a)** (*technique, relief*) topography; **(b)** (*représentation*) map, plan.
topographique [tɔpɔgrafik] *adj* topographic(al).
topographiquement [tɔpɔgrafikmɑ̃] *adv* topographically.
topologie [tɔpɔlɔʒi] *nf* topology.
topologique [tɔpɔlɔʒik] *adj* topologic(al).
toponyme [tɔpɔnim] *nm* toponym, place name.
toponymie [tɔpɔnimi] *nf* toponymy.

toponymique [tɔpɔnimik] *adj* toponymic(al).
top secret [tɔpsəkrɛ] *adj inv* top secret.
toquade [tɔkad] *nf F* craze (**pour qch,** for sth); infatuation (**pour qn,** with s.o.); **avoir une t. pour qn,** to be infatuated with s.o..
toquante [tɔkɑ̃t] *nf F* (*montre*) watch, ticker.
toquard, -arde [tɔkar, -ard] = **TOCARD.**
toque [tɔk] *nf* (*de fourrure*) fur hat; (*de jockey, juge*) cap; (*de cuisinier*) hat.
toqué, -ée [tɔke] *F* **1** *adj* **(a)** (*fou*) crazy, nuts; **(b)** (*amoureux*) infatuated, madly in love (**de,** with). **2** *n* (*fou*) nut, *Br* nutter.
toquer [tɔke] **1** *vi F* to knock, to rap (*at door etc*). **2 se toquer** *vpr F* **se t. de qn,** to fall for s.o., to go crazy over s.o..
Torah [tɔra] *nf Rel* Torah.
torche [tɔrʃ] *nf* (*flambeau*) torch; **t. électrique,** (electric) torch, *Am* flashlight; **procession à la t.,** torchlight procession.
torché [tɔrʃe] *adj F* **(a) bien t.,** well done, (pretty) good; **(b)** (*bâclé*) botched (*work etc*).
torche-cul [tɔrʃky] *nm inv Vulg Arch* (*papier*) toilet paper, *Br* loo paper; *Vulg Péj* (*texte*) (piece of) trash.
torchée [tɔrʃe] *nf Arg* (*coups*) (good) thrashing.
torcher [tɔrʃe] **1** *vt* **(a)** *F* (*nettoyer*) to wipe (*sth*) clean; *Arg* to wipe (*child's bottom, child etc*); **(b)** (*bâcler*) to botch, to do in a hurry (*work etc*). **2 se torcher** *vpr Arg* **se t. (le derrière),** to wipe one's bottom *or* oneself; *Fig* **je m'en torche!,** I don't give a damn!
torchère [tɔrʃɛr] *nf* (*candélabre*) candelabra.
torchis [tɔrʃi] *nm Constr* cob, daub.
torchon [tɔrʃɔ̃] **1** *nm* **(a)** cloth; (*pour essuyer la vaisselle*) tea towel; (*pour épousseter*) duster; *F* **le t. brûle chez eux,** they lead a cat and dog life; **il ne faut pas mélanger les torchons et les serviettes,** we mustn't get our values mixed; **(b)** *Fig F* (*texte sans soin*) mess; (*texte sans valeur*) trash; (*journal*) rag. **2** *adj inv Beaux-Arts* **papier t.,** torchon paper.
torchonner [tɔrʃɔne] *vt F* to botch (*piece of work etc*).
torcol [tɔrkɔl] *nm Orn* **t. (fourmilier),** wryneck.
tordant [tɔrdɑ̃] *adj F* screamingly funny, hilarious.
tord-boyaux [tɔrbwajo] *nm Arg Péj* (*eau-de-vie*) rotgut; (*fabriqué maison*) jungle juice.
tordeur, -euse [tɔrdœr, -øz] **1** *n Tex* (*ouvrier*) twister. **2** *nf* **tordeuse (a)** (*machine*) cable-twisting machine; **(b)** (*papillon*) leaf roller.
tordre [tɔrdr] **1** *vt* to twist (*wool, wire etc*); to wring (*clothes etc*); to twist (*one's hair into a bun etc*); **t. le cou à un poulet/***F* **à qn,** to wring a chicken's/s.o.'s neck; **t. l'estomac à qn,** (*of fear etc*) to churn up s.o.'s insides; (*of brandy etc*) to rot s.o.'s insides; **t. la bouche,** to pull a face. **2 se tordre** *vpr* to writhe, to twist (*with pain etc*); **se t. le pied,** to twist one's ankle; *F* **se t. (de rire), rire à se t.,** to split one's sides laughing; **il y a de quoi se t.,** it's screamingly funny.
tordu, -ue [tɔrdy] **1** *adj* **(a)** twisted, distorted (*limbs, features*); bent, buckled (*chassis etc*); *Arg* **avoir la gueule tordue,** to be as ugly as sin; **(b)** warped (*mind*); **(c)** *F* (*fou*) cracked, nutty. **2** *n F* (*fou*) nut, *Br* nutter.
tore [tɔr] *nm Archit Géom* torus; *Ordinat* (magnetic) core.
toréador [tɔreadɔr] *nm* toreador, bullfighter.
toréer [tɔree] *vi* to fight (in the bullring).
torero [tɔrero] *nm* bullfighter, torero.
torgnole [tɔrɲɔl] *nf Arg* (*coup*) clout.
toril [tɔril] *nm* bull pen.
torique [tɔrik] *adj Géom Opt etc* toric.
tormentille [tɔrmɑ̃tij] *nf Bot* tormentil.
tornade [tɔrnad] *nf* tornado; *Fig* hurricane (*of abuse etc*); **entrer comme une t.,** to come in like a whirlwind.
toron [tɔrɔ̃] *nm* strand (*of rope*).
torpédo [tɔrpedo] *nf Hist Aut* (open) tourer, *Am* touring car.
torpeur [tɔrpœr] *nf* torpor; **je voulus le faire sortir de sa t.,** I tried to rouse him from his torpor.
torpide [tɔrpid] *adj* torpid.
torpillage [tɔrpijaʒ] *nm* torpedoing.
torpille [tɔrpij] *nf* **(a)** (*poisson*) torpedo (ray), electric ray; **(b)** *Nau Mil* torpedo; (*mine*) mine; **t. d'avion,** aerial torpedo.
torpiller [tɔrpije] *vt* to torpedo (*ship, oil well, Fig project*).
torpilleur [tɔrpijœr] *nm* torpedo boat.
torque [tɔrk] **1** *nm* (*collier*) torque. **2** *nf Tech* coil of wire.
torréfacteur [tɔrefaktœr] *nm* **(a)** (*appareil*) roaster; **t. à café,** coffee roaster; **(b)** (*marchand*) roast coffee merchant.
torréfaction [tɔrefaksjɔ̃] *nf* roasting (*of coffee, tobacco*).
torréfier [tɔrefje] *vt* (*impf & pr sub* **n. torréfiions, v. torréfiiez**) to roast (*coffee, maize etc*).
torrent [tɔrɑ̃] *nm* (*cours d'eau*) torrent; **il pleut à torrents,** it's raining in torrents; **t. de larmes/de lumière,** flood of tears/of light; **t. d'injures,** torrent of abuse.
torrentiel, -ielle [tɔrɑ̃sjɛl] *adj* torrential.
torrentueux, -euse [tɔrɑ̃tɥø, -øz] *adj Litt* torrent-like (*river etc*); stormy, tempestuous (*life etc*).
torride [tɔrid] *adj* torrid (*zone, climate etc*); torrid, scorching (*heat, day etc*); **érotisme t.,** torrid eroticism.
tors, torse[1] [tɔr, tɔrs] **1** *adj* twisted. **2** *nm* (*torsion*) twist (*of rope etc*).
torsade [tɔrsad] *nf* **(a)** twisted cord; *Tricot* cable; **t. de cheveux,** twist *or* coil of hair; *Tricot* **(point) t.,** cable stitch; *Tricot* **aiguille à t.,** cable needle; **(b)** *Archit* rope *or* cable moulding *or US* molding.
torsadé [tɔrsade] *adj El Tél* **paire torsadée,** twisted pair; **raccord t.,** twist joint.
torsader [tɔrsade] *vt* **(a)** to twist (*rope, wire etc*); to twist, to coil (*hair*); **(b)** (*mettre ensemble*) to twist (*wires etc*) together.
torse[2] [tɔrs] *nm* (*poitrine*) chest, torso, trunk; *Beaux-Arts* torso; **le t. nu,** stripped to the waist; **se mettre t. nu,** to strip to the waist; **bomber le t.,** to stick out one's chest; *Fig* to be swollen with pride.
torseur [tɔrsœr] *nm Phys* torque.
torsion [tɔrsjɔ̃] *nf* twisting; *Tech Phys* torsion.
tort [tɔr] *nm* **(a)** (*faute*) fault; **avoir t.,** to be wrong (**de faire,** to do); **il a eu le t. de ne pas demander de reçu,** he made the mistake of not asking for a receipt; **donner t. à qn,** to lay the blame on s.o.; (*d'un résultat, d'une preuve etc*) to prove s.o. wrong; **avoir des torts envers qn,** to have treated s.o. badly; **être en t.** *ou* **dans son t.,** to be in the wrong *or* at fault; **c'est son seul t.,** it is his own fault; **il a tous les torts,** he is entirely to blame; **à t.,** wrongly; **à t. ou à raison,** rightly or wrongly; **à t. et à travers,** at random, without rhyme or reason; **(b)** (*dommage*) harm; **un t.,** a wrong; **la grêle a fait beaucoup de t.,** the hail has done a great deal of harm *or* damage; **faire du t. à qn,** to wrong s.o., to do s.o. an injustice; **quel t. cela peut-il vous faire?,** what harm can it do you?
torticolis [tɔrtikɔli] *nm Méd* stiff neck, *Spéc* torticollis; **avoir/attraper un t.,** to have/get a stiff neck.
tortillard [tɔrtijar] *nm* local train.
tortillement [tɔrtijmɑ̃] *nm* wriggling; (*des hanches*) wiggling.
tortiller [tɔrtije] **1** *vt* **(a)** (*tordre*) to twist (up) (*paper, ribbon, hair etc*); to twirl (*moustache*); (*tripoter*) to twiddle; **(b)** *Arg* (*manger*) to wolf down, to make short work of (*food*). **2** *vi* **(a) t. des hanches,** to wiggle one's hips; **(b)** *F* **il n'y a pas à t.,** it's no good trying to wriggle out of it. **3 se tortiller** *vpr* to wriggle; (*en dansant, des hanches*) to wiggle.
tortillon [tɔrtijɔ̃] *nm* **(a)** twist (*of paper etc*); **(b)** (*sur la tête*) pad (*for carrying loads*).
tortillonner [tɔrtijɔne] **1** *vt* to twist and turn. **2** *vi F* to quibble, to hedge.
tortionnaire [tɔrsjɔnɛr] *nm* torturer.
tortorer [tɔrtɔre] *vt Arg* (*manger*) to wolf down, to gobble up.
tortu [tɔrty] *adj Litt* crooked.
tortue [tɔrty] *nf* **(a)** (*reptile*) tortoise; **t. de mer,** turtle; **à pas de t.,** at a snail's pace; **(b)** *Fig* (*personne lente*) tortoise, *Br* slowcoach, *Am* slowpoke; **(c)** *Hist Mil* testudo, tortoise; **(d)** (*papillon*) tortoiseshell (butterfly).
tortueusement [tɔrtɥøzmɑ̃] *adv* tortuously; (*se conduire etc*) deviously.
tortueux, -euse [tɔrtɥø, -øz] *adj* tortuous, winding, meandering (*river, street etc*); devious (*conduct, person*); tortuous (*argument, speech etc*).
torturant [tɔrtyrɑ̃] *adj* tormenting (*thoughts etc*).
torture [tɔrtyr] *nf* torture; *Fig* torment, torture; *Fig* **mettre qn à la t.,** to torment *or* torture s.o..
torturer [tɔrtyre] **1** *vt* to torture (*prisoner etc*); **la jalousie le torturait,** he was tortured by jealousy. **2 se torturer** *vpr* **se t. l'esprit,** to rack one's brains.
torve [tɔrv] *adj* grim, menacing (*look etc*).
toscan, -ane [tɔskɑ̃, -an] **1** *adj* Tuscan. **2** *nm Ling* Tuscan. **3** *n* **T.,** Tuscan.
Toscane [tɔskan] *nf* Tuscany.
tôt [to] *adv* **(a)** (*bientôt, vite*) soon, early; **le plus t. possible,** as soon *or* as early as possible; **mardi au plus t.,** (on) Tuesday at the earliest; **vous auriez dû me le dire plus t.,** you should have told me sooner *or* earlier *or* before; **le plus t. sera le mieux,** the sooner *or* earlier the better; *F*

c'est pas trop t.!, and about time too!; **t. après,** soon after; **t. ou tard,** sooner or later; **nous n'étions pas plus t. rentrés que ...,** we had no sooner returned than ...; **on ne le reverra pas de si t.,** we won't see him again in a hurry; **revenez au plus t.,** come back as soon *or* quick(ly) as possible; **elle a eu t. fait de changer d'avis,** she soon changed her mind, it wasn't long before she changed her mind;

(b) (*de bonne heure*) early; **se lever t.,** to get up early; **t. dans l'après-midi/dans l'année/dans sa vie,** early in the afternoon/in the year/in his life; **il est trop t. pour manger,** it's too early to eat.

total, -ale, -aux [tɔtal, -o] **1** *adj* total (*sum, war, destruction, eclipse, silence etc*). **2** *nm* total; **le t. de la population,** the total population; **faire le t.,** to work out the total; **faire le t. de,** to add up, to total; **au t.,** (all) in all, in total; (*tout compte fait*) all in all; *F* **et t., on l'a sacqué,** and, to cut a long story short, he got the sack. **3** *nf Chir F* **totale,** hysterectomy.

totalement [tɔtalmɑ̃] *adv* totally, completely.

totalisateur, -trice [tɔtalizatœr, -tris] **1** *adj* adding (*machine etc*). **2** *nm* adding machine; *Ordinat* accumulator; *Courses de chevaux Br* totalizer, totalizator, *F* tote, *Am* pari-mutuel.

totalisation [tɔtalizasjɔ̃] *nf* totalling, adding up.

totaliser [tɔtalize] *vt* **(a)** (*additionner*) to total, add up; **(b)** (*compter en tout*) to total, to have a total of.

totalitaire [tɔtalitɛr] *adj Pol* totalitarian.

totalitarisme [tɔtalitarism] *nm Pol* totalitarianism.

totalité [tɔtalite] *nf* **la (presque) t. de,** (almost) all of; **pris dans sa t.,** taken as a whole; **en t.,** entirely, totally, wholly.

totem [tɔtɛm] *nm* totem.

totémique [tɔtemik] *adj* totemic.

totémisme [tɔtemism] *nm* totemism.

toto [toto] *nm Arg* (*pou*) louse, *Am* cootie.

toton [tɔtɔ̃] *nm* (*toupie*) teetotum.

touage [twaʒ] *nm Nau* (*avec point fixe*) warp; (*avec ancre*) hedging.

touareg [twarɛg] **1** *adj inv* Tuareg. **2** *nm Ling* Tuareg. **3** *n inv* **T.,** Tuareg.

toubib [tubib] *nm F* doctor, quack.

toucan [tukɑ̃] *nm* (*oiseau*) toucan.

touchant [tuʃɑ̃] **1** *adj* touching, moving (*sight, speech etc*); touching (*gratitude etc*); **elle est touchante d'humilité,** she is touchingly humble. **2** *prép* (*au sujet de*) touching, concerning, about.

touche [tuʃ] *nf* **(a)** (*style*) touch, manner (*of painter*); style (*of writer*);

(b) key (*of piano, typewriter, computer etc*); **t. contrôle,** control key; **t. de tabulation,** tab key; **t. (de) fonction,** function key; **t. (à) flèche,** arrow key;

(c) pierre de t., touchstone;

(d) *Billard Escrime* hit;

(e) *Pêche* bite, nibble; *F* **avoir** *ou* **faire une t. avec qn,** to make a hit with s.o.;

(f) *Sp* (*ligne*) touchline; (*remise en jeu*) *Fb Rugby* throw-in; *Rugby* line-out; (*au hockey*) roll-in; *Rugby* **trouver la t.,** to find touch; **sortir en t.,** to go into touch; **rester sur la t.,** to stay on the sidelines *or* touchlines; *Fig* to stay on the sidelines;

(g) *Arg* (*aspect*) appearance, look; **avoir une drôle de t.,** to be weird-looking;

(h) *Arg* shot, jab (*of narcotic etc*);

(i) *Beaux-Arts* (*tache de couleur*) (brush)stroke; **comme t. finale,** as a finishing touch;

(j) *Mus* finger board (*of violin*); **touches,** frets (*of guitar etc*).

touche-à-tout [tuʃatu] *F* **1** *adj inv* meddling, meddlesome. **2** *n inv* **(a)** meddler; **(b)** (*personne qui a plusieurs occupations*) Jack-of-all-trades.

toucher¹ [tuʃe] *nm* **(a)** (*sens, action*) touch; (*qualité*) feel; **reconnaître qch au t.,** to know sth by touch, to know sth by the feel of it; **le mur était chaud au t.,** the wall was hot to the touch *or* felt hot; **(b)** *Méd* examination; **t. vaginal,** vaginal examination; **(c)** *Mus* touch (*of pianist*).

toucher² **1** *vt* **(a)** (*du doigt, avec un objet etc*) to touch (*sth, s.o. on the shoulder etc*); *Fb* to handle (*the ball*); to hit (*target, Billard ball, Escrime one's opponent*); *F* **touche du bois!,** touch wood!; *F* **pas touche!,** (*à un enfant*) don't touch!; **t. ses appointements/sa paie,** to draw *or* receive one's salary/one's pay; **t. un chèque,** to cash a cheque *or US* check; *Rugby* **t. dans les buts,** to touch down;

(b) (*émouvoir*) to move, to touch (*s.o.*); **t. qn jusqu'aux larmes,** to move s.o. to tears; **être touché au vif,** to be cut *or* stung to the quick;

(c) (*concerner*) to concern, to affect; **en ce qui vous touche,** as far as you are concerned;

(d) *Nau* to touch (*land*);

(e) *Min* **t. le pétrole,** to strike oil;

(f) *Nau* **t. le fond,** to strike, to touch (bottom); (*être à sec*) to be aground; *Fig* (*déprimer*) to touch (rock) bottom;

(g) (*contacter*) to get in touch with, to get hold of, to reach (*s.o.*); (*of letter*) to reach (*s.o.*);

(h) (*être tout proche de*) to adjoin; **la bibliothèque touche l'église,** the library adjoins the church;

(i) je lui en toucherai un mot *ou* **deux mots,** I'll mention it to him.

2 *vi* **(a) t. à un port,** (*of ship*) to touch *or* call at a port;

(b) (*être payé*) to be paid;

(c) t. à., (*entrer en contact avec*) to touch; *Fig* (*en modifiant*) to touch, to meddle with, to tamper with; **si tu touches au chat, je te quitte!,** if you touch *or* lay a finger on the cat, I'll leave you!; **n'y touchez pas!,** (keep your) hands off!; **on ne touche pas!,** hands off!; **il n'avait pas touché à la nourriture,** he hadn't touched the food, he had left the food untouched; **avoir l'air de ne pas y t.,** to look as if butter wouldn't melt in one's mouth;

(d) t. à, (*être en contact avec*) to touch (*sth*); to border on (*a country*); to adjoin (*house, garden etc*); **économie qui touche à l'avarice,** thrift that borders on avarice; **l'année touche à sa fin,** the year is drawing to a close; **il touche à la quarantaine,** he is getting on for *or* nearing forty;

(e) t. à, (*concerner*) to concern, to affect;

(f) palmes qui touchent au plafond, palms that touch *or* reach the ceiling; **t. à terre,** to touch the ground;

(g) t. du piano, to play the piano.

3 se toucher *vpr* (*of lines etc*) to touch; **nos deux maisons se touchent,** our two houses adjoin *or* are adjoining.

touchette [tuʃɛt] *nf* fret (*of mandolin, guitar*).

toucheur, -euse [tuʃœr, -øz] *n* (cattle) drover.

touée [twe] *nf Nau* **(a)** (*câble*) warp, (warping) cable; **(b)** (*longueur*) scope.

touer [twe] *vt* **(a)** *Nau* (*avec point fixe*) to warp; **(b)** (*avec ancre*) to kedge.

toueur [twœr] *nm Nau* tug.

touffe [tuf] *nf* tuft (*of hair, grass etc*); clump (*of trees*).

touffeur [tufœr] *nf Arch & Litt* suffocating heat.

touffu [tufy] *adj* bushy (*beard, hair etc*); thick (*wood, vegetation*); dense (*book*).

touillage [tujaʒ] *nm F* stirring; (*de salade*) mixing; (*de cartes*) shuffling.

touiller [tuje] *vt F* to stir (*washing, liquid etc*), to mix, to toss (*salad*); to shuffle (*cards*).

toujours [tuʒur] *adv* **(a)** (*continuité, répétition*) always; **t. plus nombreux,** more and more numerous; **comme t.,** as always, as ever; **presque t.,** almost *or* nearly always; **un ami de t.,** a lifelong friend; **pour t. à t.,** for ever; **(b)** (*encore*) still; **il fait t. aussi chaud,** it is as hot as ever; **cherchez t.,** go on looking; **allez t.!,** go ahead!, go on!; **(c)** (*concession*) anyhow, always; **je peux t. essayer,** I can always *or* at least try; **elle peut t. attendre!,** she'll be lucky!, she'll have a long wait!; **entrez t.,** come in anyhow; **t. est-il que ...,** the fact remains that ..., anyhow ...; **c'est t. ça,** it's better than nothing at any rate, it's something at least.

toulousain, -aine [tuluzɛ̃, -ɛn] **1** *adj* of *or* from Toulouse. **2** *n* **T.,** native *or* inhabitant of Toulouse.

toundra [tundra] *nf Géog* tundra.

toupet [tupɛ] *nm* **(a)** (*de cheveux*) tuft of hair, *Br* quiff; **(faux) t.,** toupee, toupet; **(b)** *F* (*culot*) cheek, nerve; **quel t.!,** what a cheek *or* a nerve!; **avoir du t.,** to have a cheek *or* a nerve; **il a eu le t. de ...,** he had the cheek *or* the nerve to ...; **elle ne manque pas de t.!,** she's got a cheek *or* a nerve!

toupie [tupi] *nf* **(a)** (*jouet*) (spinning) top; **(b)** *Menuis etc* moulding *or US* molding machine; **(c)** (*de meuble*) moulded *or US* molded foot (*Louis XVI style*); **(d)** *F* **vieille t.,** (*femme*) old trout.

tour¹ [tur] *nf* **(a)** (*bâtiment*) tower; **(immeuble) t., grande t.,** tower block; **t. d'un moulin à vent,** tower of a windmill; **t. d'observation,** watchtower, observation tower; *Fig* **se retirer dans sa t. d'ivoire,** to withdraw to one's ivory tower; **la T. Eiffel,** the Eiffel Tower; **(b)** *Av* **t. de contrôle,** control tower; **t. de remplissage,** umbilical tower (*for rocket fuelling*); **t. de lancement,** launch tower; **(c)** *Ind Ch* **t. de fractionnement,** fractionating tower; **t. de réfrigération,** cooling tower; **t. de sondage** *ou* **de forage,**

derrick, rig; **(d)** *F* (*personne*) massively built person; **(e)** *Échecs* castle, rook.

tour² *nm* **(a)** *Tech* (*machine-outil*) (turning) lathe; **fait au t.**, machine-turned; *F* shapely (*leg etc*); **atelier des tours,** turning shop;
(b) *Cér* (potter's) wheel;
(c) (*circonférence*) circumference; (*de partie du corps*) measurement; (*de visage, d'yeux etc*) contour, outline; **ville qui a dix kilomètres de t.**, town ten kilometres *or US* kilometers in circumference; **faire le t. du monde,** to go round the world; *Fig* **faire un t. d'horizon, faire le t. de la situation,** to make a general survey of the situation; **faire un t. de table,** (*pendant un débat*) to go round the table; *Sp* **t. de piste** *ou* **de circuit,** lap; **T. de France (cycliste),** Tour de France (cycle race); *Rad* **t. de page,** jingle; **faire le t. du cadran,** to sleep the clock round; **faire le grand t.**, to take the longest way round; **avoir 75 cm de t. de taille,** to have a waist measurement of 75 cm, to measure 75 cm round the waist; **t. de cou,** collar size *or* measurement; **arbre qui a deux mètres de t.**, tree with a girth of two metres *or US* meters;
(d) t. de lit, bed valance;
(e) *Nau* turn (*round the bitt*); **prendre un t.**, to take a turn; **avoir des tours,** to have a foul hawse;
(f) tours et retours d'un chemin, twists and turns of a road;
(g) (*tournure*) turn (*of phrase*); course, direction (*of business affair*); turn (*of situation*); **l'affaire prend un mauvais t.**, the matter is taking a bad turn; **donner un autre t. à la conversation,** to turn the conversation; **t. d'esprit,** turn of mind;
(h) se donner un t. de reins, to strain *or* rick one's back;
(i) (*rotation*) round, revolution, turn (*of wheel, engine etc*); **donner un t. de clef à la porte,** to turn the key in the door; **frapper à t. de bras,** to strike with all one's might; *F* **le sang ne m'a fait qu'un t.**, my heart seemed to stop beating; **partir au quart de t.**, (*of car*) to start first time; *Fig* (*of person*) to fly off the handle; **(disque à) 45/33 tours,** single/LP;
(j) (*balade*) stroll; **faire un t. de** *ou* **dans le jardin,** to have *or* take a turn *or* a stroll round the garden; *Euph* **faire un petit t.**, to go and spend a penny;
(k) (*petit voyage*) trip, tour; **faire un t.**, to go for a tour;
(l) *Tricot* row;
(m) (*de participation*) rotation, turn; **à qui le t.?**, whose turn is it?; **t. de service,** spell of duty; **chacun (à) son t.**, each one in his turn; **chacun son t.!**, wait your turn!; **t. à t.**, in turn, by turns, turn and turn about; **s'emporter et se calmer t. à t.**, to flare up one moment and calm down the next;
(n) *Cartes* (*partie*) round;
(o) *Th etc* turn, number; **t. de chant,** vocal number;
(p) *Pol* **t. de scrutin,** ballot;
(q) (*sale coup*) trick; **faire** *ou* **jouer un mauvais t. à qn,** to play a nasty trick on s.o., to play s.o. a nasty trick; **cela te jouera des tours,** you'll (live to) regret it; *F* **un t. de cochon,** a lousy *or* rotten trick; *F* **avoir plus d'un t. dans son sac,** to have more than one trick up one's sleeve;
(r) (*d'adresse*) feat; (*de prestidigitateur*) trick; **t. de cartes,** card trick; **un t. de main,** a flick of the wrist; *F* **il peut faire ça en un t. de main,** he can do it standing on his head; **je n'ai pas le t. de main,** I haven't the knack of it; **c'est un t. à prendre,** it's a knack you learn; **t. de force,** feat of strength.

Touraine [turɛn] *nf* Touraine.

tourangeau, -elle [turɑ̃ʒo, -ɛl] **1** *adj* of *or* from Touraine *or* Tours. **2** *n* **T.**, native *or* inhabitant of Touraine *or* Tours.

tourbe [turb] *nf* peat, turf.

tourbeux, -euse [turbø, -øz] *adj* peaty (*soil etc*).

tourbière [turbjɛr] *nf* peat bog.

tourbillon [turbijɔ̃] *nm* **(a)** whirlwind; **monter en tourbillons,** (*of dust*) to swirl *or* whirl up; **t. de neige,** flurry of snow; **(b)** (*remous*) whirlpool; **(c)** *Phys Astron Phil* vortex; **(d)** *Fig* whirl (*of life, business, pleasures etc*).

tourbillonnaire [turbijɔnɛr] *adj* swirling.

tourbillonnant [turbijɔnɑ̃] *adj* whirling (*wheels, senses, skirts etc*).

tourbillonnement [turbijɔnmɑ̃] *nm* whirl(ing).

tourbillonner [turbijɔne] *vi* to whirl (round).

tourelle [turɛl] *nf* **(a)** *Archit* turret; **(b)** *Mil Nau* (*fortification*) (gun) turret; **(c)** *Opt Phot* **t. à objectifs,** lens turret; **(d)** *Tech* capstan (head), turret (head) (*of lathe*).

tourier, -ière [turje, -jɛr] *adj & n Rel* extern.

tourillon [turijɔ̃] *nm* **(a)** (*d'axe*) journal; (*axe*) (wheel) spindle; **(b)** (*de canon etc*) trunnion; **(c)** (*pivot*) pivot (pin).

tourisme [turism] *nm* tourism; (*industrie*) tourism, tourist trade; **faire du t.**, to go *or* do some touring; **office du** *ou* **de t.**, tourist office; **agence** *ou* **bureau de t.**, travel agency, tourist agency; **centre** *ou* **ville de t.**, tourist centre *or US* center; **t. de masse,** mass tourism.

touriste [turist] **1** *n* tourist; *Fig Péj* **faire qch en t.**, to do sth amateurishly. **2** *adj Nau Av* **classe t.**, tourist class.

touristique [turistik] *adj* tourist (*guide, information, region etc*).

tourmaline [turmalin] *nf Minér* tourmaline.

tourment [turmɑ̃] *nm* **(a)** torture, torment, anguish; **tourments,** pangs (*of hunger, jealousy*); torment (*of uncertainty*); **(b)** (*cause de souci*) torment; **(c)** *Arch & Litt* (*physique*) torture (*of prisoner etc*).

tourmente [turmɑ̃t] *nf* **(a)** gale, tempest; **t. de neige,** blizzard; **t. en mer,** sea storm; **(b)** *Fig* upheaval.

tourmenté [turmɑ̃te] *adj* **(a)** jagged (*coastline*); wild (*landscape*); **(b)** tortured (*conscience, person, face*); **(c)** turbulent (*sea, life, period, mind*); **(d)** *Beaux-Arts Archit etc* unnatural, overelaborate.

tourmenter [turmɑ̃te] **1** *vt* **(a)** (*of jealousy, hunger etc*) to torment, to torture (*s.o.*); **l'ambition tourmente l'homme,** man is tormented by ambition; **il est tourmenté par la goutte,** he is racked *or* tormented *or* tortured with gout; **(b)** (*of person*) to torment, to harass, to plague (*s.o.*); **(c)** *Arch* (*physiquement*) to torture (*prisoner etc*). **2 se tourmenter** *vpr* to be anxious *or* uneasy, to worry; **ne vous tourmentez pas!**, don't worry!

tourmentin [turmɑ̃tɛ̃] *nm* **(a)** *Nau* storm jib; **(b)** *Orn* petrel.

tournage [turnaʒ] *nm* **(a)** turning (*on the lathe*); **(b)** *Cér* turning, shaping (*on the wheel*); **(c)** *Nau* belaying; **(d)** *Cin* shooting.

tournailler [turnaje] *vi F* to keep wandering round and round, to prowl (around).

tournant [turnɑ̃] **1** *adj* **(a)** turning; revolving (*bookcase, stage etc*); live (*axle*); **fauteuil/siège t.**, swivel chair/ seat; **pont t.**, swing bridge; *Rail etc* **plaque tournante,** turntable; **plateau t.**, turntable (*of record player*); **(b)** winding (*road etc*); spiral (*staircase*); **(c)** *Mil* encircling (*movement*). **2** *nm* **(a)** bend (*in road, river*); corner (*of street*); *F* **savoir prendre le t.**, to know how to adapt oneself to a situation; *F* **je l'aurai** *ou* **l'attendrai au t.!**, I'll get him yet!; **(b)** (*changement*) turning point (**de,** in); **marquer un t.**, to mark a turning point; **au t. de sa carrière,** at the turning point in his career.

tourne [turn] *nf* **(a)** turning, going sour (*of milk*); souring (*of wine*); **(b)** *Journ* continuation (*of article on another page*).

tourné [turne] *adj* **(a)** turned (*on a lathe*); **bien t.**, well made; **une petite brune bien tournée,** a little brunette with a lovely figure; **phrase bien tournée,** neatly turned sentence; **mal t.**, badly made; (*laid*) ugly, unattractive; **avoir l'esprit mal t.**, to have an unpleasant turn of mind; **(b)** sour (*milk, wine etc*); **(c) t. le coin c'est la deuxième maison,** when you have turned the corner it's the second house.

tourne-à-gauche [turnagoʃ] *nm inv* (*outil*) wrench.

tournebouler [turnəbule] *vt F* (*bouleverser*) to bowl (*s.o.*) over.

tournebroche [turnəbrɔʃ] *nm Culin* (*appareil*) roasting jack; *Arch* (*garçon, chien*) turnspit.

tourne-disque [turnədisk] *nm* record player; (*pl tourne-disques*).

tournedos [turnədo] *nm Culin* tournedos, fillet steak.

tournée [turne] *nf* **(a)** (*de médecin, facteur, d'inspecteur etc*) round; *Th* tour; *Th* **en t.**, on tour; **faire la t. des musées,** to go round *or F* to do the art galleries; *F* **faire la t. des grands-chics,** to go out on the town; **faire une t. en France,** to go on a trip round *or* through France; **faire une t. électorale,** to canvass a constituency; **t. de golf,** round of golf; **(b)** *F* (*consommations*) round (of drinks); **payer une t.**, to pay for *or* stand a round (of drinks), to pay for *or* stand drinks all round; **c'est ma t.**, it's my round; **(c)** *Arg* (*raclée*) thrashing; **flanquer une t. à qn,** to thrash s.o..

tournemain (en un) [ɑ̃nœturnəmɛ̃] *adv* in an instant, in the twinkling of an eye.

tourner [turne] **1** *vt* **(a)** *Tech* to turn (*sth*) (*on a lathe*); *Fig* to turn (*a phrase*); *Cér* to throw (*pot*);
(b) to turn (*wheel, key in lock etc*); *F* **t. qn à son gré,** to twist s.o. round one's little finger; **t. qch autour de qch,** to wind sth round sth; **t. la tête/les yeux vers qn,** to turn one's head/one's eyes towards s.o.; **t. le dos à qn/à qch,** to

turn one's back on s.o./on sth, to turn away from s.o./sth; (*en étant statique*) to have one's back turned to s.o./to sth; **t. les talons,** (*partir*) to turn and leave; (*s'enfuir*) to take to one's heels; **t. les pieds en dedans/en dehors,** to turn in/turn out one's toes; *Cin* **t. un film,** to make a film; **t. une scène/un roman,** to film a scene/a novel; *Culin* **t. une crème,** to stir a custard;

(c) (*changer*) to turn (**en,** into); **t. tout en bien/en mal,** to put a good/a bad interpretation on everything; **t. qch à la plaisanterie,** to turn sth into a joke, to laugh sth off; **t. qn en ridicule,** to hold s.o. up to ridicule, to poke fun at s.o.;

(d) to turn (over) (*page etc*); to turn up (*card*); **t. et retourner qch,** to turn sth over and over; **t. une affaire en tous sens,** to turn a matter over and over (in one's mind); *Fig* **il faut t. la page,** it's time to make a fresh start;

(e) (*contourner*) to get round (*corner, obstacle etc*); to outflank, to circumvent (*enemy*); to evade, to get round (*difficulty, the law*); **vous trouverez l'épicerie en tournant le coin,** you will find the grocer round the corner; *Nau* **t. un promontoire,** to weather a headland;

(f) *Fig* **il lui a tourné la tête,** he has turned her head, she has become infatuated with him; **les honneurs ne lui ont pas tourné la tête,** success hasn't turned his head *or* gone to his head; **cela m'a tourné l'estomac,** it turned my stomach.

2 *vi* **(a)** (*of wheel, planet, clock, hand etc*) to turn, to go round; (*of machine*) to run; (*of top*) to spin; **t. autour de qn/de qch,** to move *or* turn round s.o./sth; *F* **t. autour du pot,** to beat about the bush; **t. de l'œil,** to pass out, to faint; **tout tourne autour de lui, la tête lui tourne,** he feels giddy, his head is swimming *or* spinning; **l'heure tourne,** time passes; **le sentier tourne autour de la pelouse,** the path winds round the lawn; **faire t. la machine,** to set the machinery going; **faire t. une entreprise,** to run a company; **faire t. la clef dans la serrure,** to turn the key in the lock; *F* **ça ne tourne pas rond (chez lui),** he's not all there; *Fig F* **avoir l'impression de t. en rond,** to feel that one is going round in circles;

(b) (*obliquer*) **tournez à gauche,** turn left; **t. court,** to turn sharply; (*finir*) to end suddenly; **ne savoir de quel côté t.,** not to know which way to turn, to be at one's wits' end; **le vent a tourné à l'ouest,** the wind has changed *or* shifted to the west; **le temps tourne au froid,** it is turning cold; **sa chance a tourné,** his luck has turned; **il a tourné contre moi,** he has turned against me;

(c) (*of fruit etc*) to colour, *US* to color, to ripen;

(d) (*évoluer*) to turn out; **les choses tournent bien/mal,** things are turning out well/badly; **mal t.,** (*of person*) to turn out badly, to go to the bad; **cela tournait mal,** things were taking a bad turn; **cela tournera mal,** no good will come of it; **portraits qui tournent à la caricature,** portraits that are almost caricatures; **l'affaire tournait au tragique,** the matter was taking a tragic turn *or* was turning to tragedy; **son amour a tourné en haine,** his love has turned *or* changed to hatred; **t. au vinaigre,** (*of wine*) to turn acid; **lait qui tourne à l'aigre** *ou* **qui tourne,** milk that is turning (sour);

(e) *Cin* **t. dans un film,** to act in a film.

3 *v impers Cartes* **il tourne carreau,** the turn-up is diamonds.

4 se tourner *vpr* **(a)** (*se retourner*) to turn round; **se t. vers qn,** to turn towards s.o.; **ses yeux se tournèrent vers la porte,** his eyes turned to the door; *F* **se t. les pouces,** to twiddle one's thumbs;

(b) se t. contre qn, to turn against s.o.; **c'est sa femme qui l'a fait t. contre vous,** it was his wife who turned him against you; **se t. du côté du peuple,** to side with the people;

(c) son amour se tourna en haine, his love turned to hate; **se t. en vinaigre,** (*of wine*) to turn into vinegar.

tournesol [turnəsɔl] *nm* **(a)** *Bot* sunflower; **(b)** *Ch* litmus; **papier (de) t.,** litmus paper.

tournette [turnɛt] *nf* **(a)** (*pour couper*) circular glass cutter; **(b)** *Th* revolve.

tourneur [turnœr] **1** *adj* whirling (*dervish*). **2** *nm Tech* turner; *Cér* thrower; **t. de vis,** screwcutter.

tournevis [turnəvis] *nm* screwdriver.

tournicoter [turnikɔte], **tourniquer** [turnike] *vi F* to wander round and round, to hover (round).

tourniquet [turnikɛ] *nm* **(a)** (*barrière*) turnstile; *Mil Arg* **passer au t.,** to be court-martialled; **(b)** (*présentoir*) revolving display stand; **(c)** roller (*for ropes etc to pass over*); **(d)** fastener (*on shutter etc*); **(e)** (*de jardin*) sprinkler; **(f)** *Méd* tourniquet.

tournis [turni] *nm* **(a)** *Vét* staggers, gid; **(b)** *F* (*vertige*) giddiness, dizziness; **donner le t. à qn,** to make s.o. giddy *or* dizzy.

tournoi [turnwa] *nm Hist Sp Cartes etc* tournament; **t. d'éloquence,** contest of eloquence.

tournoiement [turnwamɑ̃] *nm* **(a)** whirling; spinning (*of suspended object*); wheeling (*of birds*); eddying, swirling (*of water*); **(b)** (*vertige*) giddiness, dizziness.

tournoyant [turnwajɑ̃] *adj* whirling; wheeling (*birds*); eddying, swirling (*water*).

tournoyer [turnwaje] *vi* (**je tournoie, n. tournoyons; je tournoierai**) to whirl, to turn round and round; (*of suspended object*) to spin, to whirl; (*of birds*) to wheel; (*of water*) to eddy, to swirl; **descendre en tournoyant,** to come whirling down; **faire t. qch,** to twirl *or* whirl sth.

tournure [turnyr] *nf* **(a)** (*direction*) turn; (*of events*) **les affaires prennent (une) meilleure/une mauvaise t.,** things are taking a turn for the better/the worse; **donner une t. agréable à la conversation,** to give a pleasant turn to the conversation; **(b)** (*aspect*) appearance (*of object, building etc*); form (*of story etc*); *Vieilli* (*maintien*) bearing (*of person*); **t. (de phrase),** turn of phrase; **t. d'esprit,** turn of mind; **prendre t.,** to take shape.

tour-opérateur [turɔperatœr] *nm* tour operator; (*pl tour-opérateurs*).

tourte [turt] *nf* **(a)** *Culin* pie; **t. aux pommes/à la viande,** apple/meat pie; **(b)** *F* (*idiot*) idiot, clot.

tourteau, -eaux [turto] *nm* **(a)** *Agr* cattle cake; **(b)** (*crustacé*) **t. (dormeur),** edible crab.

tourtereau, -eaux [turtəro] *nm* **(a)** (*oiseau*) young turtledove; **(b)** *Fig* **tourtereaux,** (*amoureux*) lovebirds.

tourterelle [turtərɛl] *nf* (*oiseau*) turtledove.

tourtière [turtjɛr] *nf* **(a)** (*pour tourte*) pie dish; (*pour tarte*) flan dish; **(b)** *Can* (*tourte*) = (minced) pork pie.

tous [tu(s)] *adj & pron voir* **TOUT.**

touselle [tuzɛl] *nf Bot* beardless wheat.

toussailler [tusaje] *vi* to have a little cough.

Toussaint (la) [latusɛ̃] *nf* All Saints' day, Allhallows; **la veille de la T.,** Hallowe'en.

tousser [tuse] *vi* **(a)** to cough; **il toussa pour m'avertir,** he coughed *or* gave a cough to warn me; **(b) moteur qui tousse,** spluttering engine.

tousseur, -euse [tusœr, -øz] *n F* cougher.

toussotement [tusɔtmɑ̃] *nm* slight cough(ing).

toussoter [tusɔte] *vi* **(a)** to cough slightly; **(b)** (*avoir un léger rhume*) to have a slight cough.

tous-temps [tutɑ̃] *adj inv* all-weather.

tout, toute, *pl* **tous, toutes** [tu, tut, tu, tut] (*when* **tous** *is a pron it is pronounced* [tus]) **1** *adj* **(a)** (*n'importe quel*) any, every, all; **t. travail lui est interdit,** he is forbidden to do any work; **pour toute arme il avait une canne,** his only weapon was a walking stick; **pour toute réponse il éclata de rire,** his only answer was to burst out laughing; **t. autre que vous,** anybody but you; **toute liberté d'agir,** full liberty to act; **j'ai toute raison de croire que ...,** I have every reason to believe that ...; **repas à toute heure,** meals served at any time;

(b) (*emploi intensif*) **dans sa toute jeunesse,** when he was quite a child, in his early youth; **à la toute dernière minute,** at the very last minute; **des arbres de toute beauté,** most beautiful trees; **à toute vitesse,** at full speed; **t.** *ou* **toute à vous,** entirely yours; **de toute importance,** of the utmost importance, all-important; **il est de toute importance que ... +** *sub*, it is of the utmost importance that ...; *Nau* **la barre toute!,** hard over!;

(c) (*complet*) **t. le, toute la,** all (the), the whole; **t. le monde,** everybody, everyone; **toute la famille,** the whole family, all the family; **t. mon argent,** all my money; **t. le jour, toute la journée,** the whole day, all day long; **pendant t. l'hiver,** throughout the (whole) winter, all through the winter, all winter long; **répéter t. le temps la même chose,** to keep on saying the same thing; **au milieu de t. ça ...,** in the midst of all that *or* it all ...; **tout cet été,** that whole summer, all that summer; **t. Paris est en danger,** the whole of Paris *or* all Paris is in danger; **t. La Haye se trouvait dans les rues,** the whole population of the Hague was in the streets; **lire t. Joyce,** to read all of *or* the whole of Joyce; **t. mars se passa sans nouvelles,** the whole of March went by without news;

(d) tous, toutes, (*la totalité de*) all, every; **tous les, toutes les,** (*chaque*) every; **tous les invités,** all the guests; **tous ces livres,** all these books; **tous les jours,** every day; **tous les quarts d'heure,** every quarter of an hour; **toutes les fois que ...,** whenever ..., each time that ...; **au-dessus de toutes choses,** above all; **de tous (les) côtés, de toutes parts,** on all sides; (from) everywhere;

de toutes (les) couleurs, of every (possible) colour *or US* color; **champion toutes catégories,** overall champion; **meubles tous budgets,** furniture to suit all pockets; **toute(s) proportion(s) gardée(s),** making due allowance;

(e) (*avec des nombres*) **tous (les) deux,** both; **tous (les) trois/(les) dix,** all three/ten; **tous les deux jours,** every other *or* second day; **tous les trois jours,** every third day; *F* **tous les combien?,** how often?;

(f) t. un, toute une, a whole; **t. un quartier de la ville,** a whole district of the town; **passer toute une année à voyager,** to spend a whole year travelling; **c'est toute une histoire,** it's a long story; (*c'est difficile*) it's quite a job; **pas la peine d'en faire toute une histoire,** there's no point in making a big thing *or* a big fuss about it.

2 *pron* **(a)** everything, all; **l'argent n'est pas t.,** money isn't everything; **il faut t. lui montrer,** we must show him everything; **je crois que c'est t.,** I think that's (about) all; *F* **et t. et t.,** and all the rest of it; *Prov* **t. est bien qui finit bien,** all's well that ends well; **voilà t. ce que je sais,** that's all I know; **j'aime t. ce qui est français,** I love anything *or* everything French; **t. ce qui vous plaira,** whatever you like, anything you like; **c'est t. ce qu'il y a de plus beau/de plus drôle,** it is most beautiful/nothing could be funnier; **il a t. mangé,** he has eaten everything *or* the whole lot; **il mange de tout,** he eats anything (and everything); **on trouve de t. à Paris,** you find all sorts of things in Paris; **depuis lors j'ai fait de t.,** since then I've done all sorts of things; **il est capable de t.,** he is capable of anything; *F* **il a t. du fonctionnaire,** he's the typical *or* complete civil servant; **c'est t. dire,** I needn't say more; **c'est t. un,** it's all one; **homme à t. faire,** (*bon en tout*) all-rounder; (*qui touche à tout*) Jack-of-all-trades; (*factotum*) odd-job man; **à t. prendre ...,** on the whole ..., taking it all in all ...; *F* **drôle comme t.,** awfully funny; **rire comme t.,** to laugh like anything;

(b) tous, toutes, all; **une (bonne) fois pour toutes,** once (and) for all; **venez tous** [tus] **!,** come along all of you!; **ils sont tous là** [tusla], they are all there; **il faut tous faire votre devoir,** all of you must do your duty; **le meilleur de tous,** the best of (them) all; **il est impossible de les nommer tous,** it is impossible to name them all *or* all of them; **on nous en offrit un verre à tous,** we were all offered a glass; **leur bonheur à tous,** the happiness of all of them *or* them all; **tous à la fois,** all together; *F* **on l'aimait bien tous,** we were all very fond of him; **nous/ vous/eux tous,** all of us/of you/of them; **combien d'argent ont-ils à eux tous?** how much money do they have between them?

3 *nm* **(a) le t.,** the whole, the lot; **le t. est de réussir,** the main thing is to succeed; **jouer le t. pour le t.,** to stake everything; **son fils est son t.,** her son is everything to her; *F* **ce n'est pas le t., ça!,** that's not getting us very far!;

(b) du t. au t., entirely; **en t.,** (*au total*) in all; (*complètement*) entirely, wholly; **(pas) du t.,** not at all;

(c) *Math* (*pl* **touts**) total; **mon t.,** (*dans une charade*) my whole.

4 *adv* (*before a f adj beginning with a consonant or* **h** *aspirate* **tout** *becomes* **toute**) **(a)** (*complètement*) quite, entirely, completely, very; **t. nouveau(x), toute(s) nouvelle(s),** quite new; **ils sont t. seuls, elles sont toutes seules,** they are (quite) alone; **elle était encore toute jeune,** she was still quite young; **hommes t. bon(s) ou t. mauvais,** men entirely good or entirely bad; **toute vêtue de noir,** dressed all in black; **elle était toute honteuse,** she was utterly ashamed; **des lutteurs de t. premier ordre,** wrestlers of the very first order; **t. enfant,** when still a child; **une t. autre personne,** an entirely different person; **t. droit,** bolt upright; **t. neuf,** brand new; **t. nu,** stark naked; **t. éveillé,** wide awake; **vêtement t. fait,** ready-made garment; **viande toute cuite,** ready-cooked meat; **t. au bout,** right at the end, at the very end; **t. là-bas,** right over there; **t. contre le mur,** right against the wall; **mains t. en sang,** hands (all) covered with blood; **c'est t. comme chez nous!,** it's just like home!; **il est t. à son commerce,** he is entirely absorbed in *or* taken up with his business; **t. doux!,** gently!;

(b) t. à fait, quite, entirely, altogether; **cela me va t. à fait,** it suits me perfectly *or* down to the ground; **il lui ressemble t. à fait,** he is just like him; *F* **il y a t. plein de livres/de neige,** there are loads of books/is loads of snow; **à t. va,** anyhow; **t. au plus,** at the very most; **t. au moins, t. le moins,** at the very least; **t. à vous,** (*dans une lettre*) yours ever;

(c) t. en parlant/*etc*, while speaking/*etc*;

(d) (*aussi*) **t. ignorant qu'il soit** *ou* **qu'il est,** however ignorant he is, ignorant though *or* as he is, ignorant though he may be; **t. père/toute mère que je suis,** although I am a father/a mother;

(e) être t. oreilles, to be all ears; **il était toute crainte et toute haine,** he was all fear and hate; **elle était t. attention,** she was all attention; **elle est t. le portrait de sa mère,** she is the living *or* spitting image of her mother.

tout-à-l'égout [tutalegu] *nm inv* mains drainage; **avoir le t.-à-l'é.,** to have mains drainage.

Toutankhamon [tutɑ̃kamɔ̃] *nm* Tutankhamen.

toute-épice [tutepis] *nf Bot Culin* allspice; (*pl toutes-épices*).

toutefois [tutfwa] *adv* nevertheless, however.

toute-puissance [tutpɥisɑ̃s] *nf* **(a)** *Rel* omnipotence; **(b)** *Pol etc* absolute power.

tout-fou [tufu] *F* **1** *adj* crazy. **2** *nm* idiot, nut; (*pl tout-fous*).

toutou [tutu] *nm Enf* doggie; **filer comme un t.,** to let oneself be led.

tout-petit [tupəti] *nm* (tiny) tot, toddler.

tout-puissant, toute-puissante [tupɥisɑ̃, tutpɥisɑ̃t] (*pl tout(es)-puissant(e)s*) **1** *adj* almighty, omnipotent; *Fig* overwhelming (*desire*). **2** *nm Rel* **le T.-P.,** the Almighty.

tout-terrain [tutɛrɛ̃] *adj* **véhicule t.-t.,** all-terrain vehicle, off-road vehicle, ATV; **vélo t.-t.,** mountain bike; (*pl tous-terrains*).

tout-venant [tuvnɑ̃] *nm Com* ungraded product; (*houille*) unsorted coal; *Fig* **le t.-v.,** (*gens*) the ragtag and bobtail.

toux [tu] *nf* cough; **accès de t.,** coughing fit, fit of coughing; **t. sèche/grasse,** dry/loose cough.

toxémie [tɔksemi] *nf Méd* toxaemia, *US* toxemia, blood-poisoning.

toxicité [tɔksisite] *nf* toxicity.

toxico [tɔksiko] *n F* drug addict.

toxicodépendance [tɔksikɔdepɑ̃dɑ̃s] *nf* drug dependence.

toxicologie [tɔksikɔlɔʒi] *nf* toxicology.

toxicologique [tɔksikɔlɔʒik] *adj* toxicological.

toxicologue [tɔksikɔlɔg] *n* toxicologist.

toxicomane [tɔksikɔman] **1** *adj* addicted to drugs. **2** *n* drug addict.

toxicomanie [tɔksikɔmani] *nf* drug addiction.

toxine [tɔksin] *nf Physiol* toxin.

toxique [tɔksik] **1** *adj* toxic; **gaz t.,** poison gas. **2** *nm* poison.

T.P. [tepe] *nmpl Scol* (*abrév* **travaux pratiques**) practical work; **avoir un T.P. de chimie,** to have a practical chemistry lesson.

t.p.m. [tepeɛm] *MecE* (*abrév* **tours par minute**) rpm.

trac¹ [trak] *nm F* fright, funk; *Th* stage fright; **il a le t.,** he's got the wind up; *Th* he's got stage fright.

trac² *nm* **tout à t.,** out of the blue.

traçage [trasaʒ] *nm* drawing (*of diagrams etc*); laying out (*of roads, gardens etc*).

traçant [trasɑ̃] *adj* **(a)** *Bot* running, creeping (*root*); **(b) obus t.,** tracer shell; **balle traçante,** tracer bullet.

tracas [traka] *nm* worry, trouble, bother.

tracasser [trakase] **1** *vt* (*of problem etc*) to worry, to bother (*s.o.*); (*of person, organization etc*) to harass, to pester (*s.o.*). **2 se tracasser** *vpr* to worry.

tracasserie [trakasri] *nf* **tracasserie(s),** harassment; **tracasseries administratives,** administrative worries.

tracassier, -ière [trakasje, -jɛr] *adj* pestering, interfering (*person etc*).

trace [tras] *nf* **(a)** trail, track, spoor (*of beast*); tracks, trail (*of person*); (wheel) track (*of vehicle*); **t. de lumière,** trail of light; *Ski etc* **faire la t.,** to break trail; *Ski* **t. directe,** direct descent; **être sur la t. de qn/qch,** to be on the track of s.o./sth; **retrouver la t.,** to pick up the scent *or* the trail; *Fig* **il marche sur** *ou* **il suit les traces de son père,** he's following in his father's footsteps; **laisser une t. profonde,** to leave a deep impression (behind); **retrouver la t. de qn/de qch,** to find a trace of s.o./sth; **on n'a plus retrouvé t. des explorateurs,** no trace was ever found of the explorers; **cette musicienne n'a pas laissé beaucoup de t.,** this musician didn't leave much of a mark; *Électron* **t. du spot,** trace (*in cathode ray tube*);

(b) (*marque*) mark; scar, mark (*of wound, burn etc*); marks (*of suffering, exhaustion*); **traces de peinture,** paint marks;

(c) (*petite quantité*) (slight) trace (*of poison, Fig regret, foreign blood etc*);

(d) traces, (*vestiges*) traces (*of ancient civilization etc*);

(e) *Géom* trace (*of plane etc*).
tracé [trase] *nm* (a) (*plan*) layout (*of road, railway, town etc*); **faire le t. de,** to lay out; (b) (*ligne, contour*) line (*of graph, coast etc*).
tracer [trase] *v* (**je traçai(s); n. traçons**) 1 *vt* (a) (*indiquer*) to lay out (*road, railway etc*); to map out (*route, policy*); (b) (*dessiner*) to draw (*line, plan, pattern etc*); to plot (*curve, graph*), to write (*letter, word etc*). 2 *vi* (a) (*of root*) to run out, to creep; (b) *Arg* (*aller vite*) to move quickly, to get a move on.
traceret [trasrɛ] *nm* (*outil*) scriber, tracing awl.
traceur, -euse [trasœr, -øz] 1 *nm* (a) **t. (radioactif),** tracer; (b) *Ordinat* **t. (de courbes),** plotter. 2 *adj* tracer (*substance, shell, bullet*).
trachéal, -aux [trakeal, -o] *adj Anat* tracheal.
trachée [traʃe] *nf* (a) *Anat Zool* windpipe, *Spéc* trachea; (b) *Bot* trachea, vessel, duct.
trachée-artère [traʃeartɛr] *nf Anat Zool Vieilli* windpipe, *Spéc* trachea; (*pl trachées-artères*).
trachéite [trakeit] *nf Méd* tracheitis.
trachéo-bronchite [trakeɔbrɔ̃ʃit] *nf Méd* tracheobronchitis.
trachéotomie [trakeɔtɔmi] *nf Chir* tracheotomy.
trachome [trakom] *nm Méd* trachoma.
trachyte [trakit] *nm Minér* trachyte.
traçoir [traswar] *nm* (*outil*) scriber, tracing awl.
tract [trakt] *nm Pol Rel* tract, pamphlet; *Com etc* leaflet.
tractable [traktabl] *adj* towable.
tractation [traktɑsjɔ̃] *nf Péj* deal; **tractations,** dealings, bargaining.
tracté [trakte] *adj* tractor-drawn.
tracter [trakte] *vt* to tow.
tracteur, -trice [traktœr, -tris] 1 *nm* tractor; **t. et semi-remorque,** articulated vehicle. 2 *adj* (a) (*qui remorque*) towing; (b) *Géog* **force tractrice,** transport capacity (*of a current*).
traction [traksjɔ̃] *nf* (a) *Phys etc* traction, pulling; **effort de t.,** tractive effort, pull; **t. magnétique,** magnetic pull; **résistance à la t.,** tensile strength; *Gym* **faire des tractions,** (*en tirant*) to do pull-ups; (*en poussant*) to do press-ups *or Am* push-ups; (b) (*remorque*) traction, haulage; *Aut* **t. avant/arrière,** front-wheel/rear wheel drive.
tractoriste [traktɔrist] *n* tractor driver.
tractus [traktys] *nm Anat* tract, system.
tradescantia [tradɛskɑ̃sja] *nm Bot* tradescantia.
tradition [tradisjɔ̃] *nf* (a) tradition; **de t.,** traditional; (b) *Jur* delivery, handing over (*of property etc*).
traditionalisme [tradisjɔnalism] *nm* traditionalism.
traditionaliste [tradisjɔnalist] *adj & n* traditionalist.
traditionnel, -elle [tradisjɔnɛl] *adj* (*fondé sur la tradition*) traditional; (*habituel*) usual, habitual; standard (*excuse, equipment etc*); standing (*joke*).
traditionnellement [tradisjɔnɛlmɑ̃] *adv* traditionally.
traducteur, -trice [tradyktœr, -tris] 1 *n* translator. 2 *nm Ordinat* translator.
traduction [tradyksjɔ̃] *nf* (a) (*action*) translation, translating; **t. automatique/simultanée,** machine/simultaneous translation; *Ordinat* **t. des informations,** data reduction; (b) (*texte*) translation.
traduire [tradɥir] *v* (*prp* **traduisant**; *pp* **traduit**; *pr ind* **je traduis, il traduit, n. traduisons, ils traduisent**; *impf* **je traduisais**; *p hist* **je traduisis**; *fu* **je traduirai**) 1 *vt* (a) *Jur* **t. qn en justice,** to sue *or* prosecute *or* indict s.o.; (b) to translate (**de,** from; **en,** into); (c) *Ordinat* to interpret (*card*); (d) *Fig* (*exprimer*) to represent, to express (*feeling, idea etc*); **vous traduisez mal ma pensée,** you're misinterpreting me *or* my thoughts. 2 *vi Ling* to translate; **t. mot à mot,** to translate word for word. 3 **se traduire** *vpr* (a) *Ling* to be translated; (b) **sa douleur se traduisit par des larmes,** his grief found expression in tears; *Com* **les comptes se traduisent par une perte de 5 000 francs,** the accounts show a loss of 5,000 francs.
traduisible [tradɥizibl] *adj* (a) *Jur* **t. en justice,** liable to prosecution; (b) *Ling* translatable; **ce jeu de mots n'est pas t.,** this play on words is untranslatable.
Trafalgar [trafalgar] *nm* Trafalgar; *Fig* **coup de T.,** underhand trick.
trafic [trafik] *nm* (a) (*circulation*) traffic; **t. aérien/routier,** air/road traffic; (b) (*commerce illégal*) **t. des stupéfiants,** drug traffic; **t. des armes,** gunrunning, traffic in arms; *F* **faire t. de ses charmes,** (*of prostitute*) to sell one's body; *F* **un drôle de t.,** a queer sort of business; (c) *Électron* traffic; (d) *Vieilli* (*commerce*) trading, trade.
traficoter [trafikɔte] 1 *vi F Péj* (*trafiquer*) to do a bit of trafficking. 2 *vt F* (*manigancer*) **je me demande ce qu'il traficote,** I wonder what he's up to.
trafiquant, -ante [trafikɑ̃, -ɑ̃t] *n Péj* trafficker; **t. de** *ou* **en stupéfiants,** drug trafficker; **t. d'armes,** gunrunner; **t. du marché noir,** black marketeer.
trafiquer [trafike] 1 *vi Péj* to traffic (**de, en,** in); **t. de sa conscience,** to sell one's conscience. 2 *vt F* (a) (*modifier*) to doctor (*wine, car engine etc*); (b) (*manigancer*) **qu'est-ce qu'il trafique?,** what's he up to?
trafiqueur, -euse [trafikœr, -øz] *n Péj* trafficker (**de, en,** in).
tragédie [traʒedi] *nf Th & Fig* tragedy; *F* **jouer la t.,** to put on a tragic act; *Fig* **ce n'est pas une t.!,** it's not the end of the world!
tragédien, -ienne [traʒedjɛ̃, -jɛn] *n* tragic actor *or* actress, tragedian.
tragi-comédie [traʒikɔmedi] *nf Th & Fig* tragi-comedy; (*pl tragi-comédies*).
tragi-comique [traʒikɔmik] *adj Th & Fig* tragi-comic; (*pl tragi-comiques*).
tragique [traʒik] 1 *adj* tragic (*writer, play, role, Fig event etc*). 2 *nm* (a) tragedy, tragic side (*of an event*); **cela tourne au t.,** the thing is becoming tragic; **prendre qch au t.,** to make a tragedy of sth; **ne le prenez pas si au t.,** don't take it so much to heart; (b) *Th* **le t.,** tragedy. 3 *n* (*auteur*) writer of tragedies.
tragiquement [traʒikmɑ̃] *adv* tragically.
trahir [trair] 1 *vt* (a) (*divulguer*) to reveal, to give away (*secret*); **je fus trahi par les aboiements d'un chien,** I was betrayed by a dog barking; **t. sa pensée,** to give oneself away; (b) (*cesser d'être fidèle à*) to betray (*person, one's country, s.o.'s confidence, s.o.'s interests*); **t. ses serments,** to go back on one's word; **au premier pas ses jambes le trahirent,** at the first step his legs failed him; (c) *Arch* **t. qch/qn à qn,** to betray sth/s.o. to s.o. 2 **se trahir** *vpr* (*of person*) to give oneself away; (*of feeling etc*) to betray itself.
trahison [traizɔ̃] *nf* (a) (*défection*) treachery; *Jur* treason; **haute t.,** high treason; (b) (*parjure*) betrayal.
traille [traj] *nf* (a) (*câble*) ferry cable; (b) (*bac*) ferry.
train [trɛ̃] *nm* (a) *Rail* train; **t. de voyageurs,** passenger train; **t. de marchandises,** goods train, *Am* freight train; **t. supplémentaire,** relief train; **t. à grande vitesse,** high-speed train; **t. de neige,** winter sports train; **t. électrique,** electric train; **t. militaire,** troop train; **voyager en t.** *ou* **par le t.,** to travel by train; **être dans un t.,** to be on a train; **comme une vache qui regarde passer un t.,** like a cow at a five-bar gate; **t. autos-couchettes,** car-sleeper train; *Fig* **prendre le t. en marche,** to jump *or* climb on the bandwagon;
(b) *Mil* train (*of transport*); **le t.,** *Br* = transport branch of Army Service Corps, *US* = transportation company;
(c) (*file*) train, string, line (*of pack animals, vehicles etc*); series, set (*of wheels etc*); **t. de bois,** timber raft, float; **t. spatial,** space train; *Phys* **t. d'ondes,** wavetrain; **t. de réformes,** series *or* set of reforms; **t. de pensées,** train of thought;
(d) *Aut* **t. avant,** front axle (assembly);
(e) *Arch* (*escorte*) suite, attendants; train (*of servants etc*);
(f) quarters (*of horse*); **t. de derrière/de devant,** hindquarters/forequarters;
(g) *Arg* (*derrière*) backside, rear (*of person*); **se manier le t.,** to get a move on;
(h) **t. de roulement,** undercarriage (*of wheeled vehicle*); suspension and tracks (*of tracked vehicle*); *Av* **t. (d'atterrissage),** landing gear, undercarriage; *Av* **t. avant,** nose gear, nose wheel;
(i) *Typ* (*press*) carriage;
(j) (*allure*) **aller bon t.,** to go at a good pace; **aller son petit t.,** to jog along; **à fond de t.,** at full *or* top speed, at full tilt, all out; **au t. où il va,** at the rate he's going; **à ce t.-là,** at that rate; **tout d'un t.,** without stopping; *Sp* **meneur de t.,** pacemaker; **mener le t.,** to set the pace; **mise en t.,** warming-up; **faire tout le t.,** to make all the running; **gagner au t.,** to win at a steady pace;
(k) **il y a quelque chose en t.,** there's something afoot *or* in the wind; **mettre qch en t.,** to start sth, to set sth going; *Typ* **mettre en t.,** to make ready; *F* **mettre qn en t.,** to get s.o. going; *F* **ils ont un petit en t.,** they've got a little one on the way; **c'est lui qui met tout en t.,** he's the life and soul of the party; *F* **il était un peu en t.,** he'd had a drop (too much); **l'affaire est mal en t.,** the business is hanging fire *or* has had a bad start; **être en bon t.,** to be making good progress; **être en t. de faire qch,** to be (busy) doing sth; **il était en t. de travailler,** he was (busy)

working; **elle est en t. de chanter,** she is singing; **ta chemise est en t. de sécher,** your shirt is drying; **le t. ordinaire des jours,** the daily routine; **les choses vont leur t.,** things are proceeding *or* going along as usual; **dans le t.,** up to date;

(l) **t. de vie,** way of life; **t. de maison,** style of living; **mener grand t.,** to live on a grand scale; **mener un t. d'enfer,** to live it up;

(m) *F* (*tapage*) noise, row; **faire du t., faire un t. de tous les diables,** to kick up (a hell of) a row;

(n) (*humeur*) **être en t.,** to be in good spirits *or* in good form; **il n'était pas en t. ce jour-là,** he wasn't at his best that day; **être mal en t.,** to be out of sorts, to feel unwell; **je ne suis pas en t. pour travailler,** I'm not in a working mood.

traînage [trɛnaʒ] *nm* **(a)** *Min* haulage (*of trains*); **câble de t.,** haulage rope; **(b)** (*transport par traîneaux*) sleigh transport.

traînailler [trɛnaje] *vi F* = **TRAÎNASSER**.

traînant [trɛnɑ̃] *adj* **(a)** trailing (*dress etc*); **(b)** languid, listless (*life*); drawling (*voice*); dawdling (*walk*).

traînard, -arde [trɛnar, -ard] *n* (*en arrière d'un groupe*) straggler; (*dans son travail*) dawdler, *Br F* slowcoach, *Am F* slowpoke.

traînasser [trɛnase] *vi F* **(a)** (*errer*) to trail around, to loaf around; **(b)** (*être lent*) to dawdle.

traîne [trɛn] *nf* **(a)** *Nau* **à la t.,** in tow; *Fig F* **être à la t.,** to lag behind; **(b)** train (*of dress*); **(c)** *Pêche* seine (net), drag net; **(d)** *Can* **t. sauvage,** toboggan.

traîneau, -eaux [trɛno] *nm* **(a)** sleigh, sledge, *US* sled; **faire une promenade en t.,** to go for a sleigh ride; **chien de t.,** husky; **attelage de chiens de t.,** dog team; **(b)** *Pêche* seine (net), drag net.

traîne-bûches [trɛnbyʃ] *nm inv Pêche F* caddis worm, bait.

traîne-buisson [trɛnbɥisɔ̃] *nm Orn* dunnock, hedge sparrow; (*pl traîne-buissons*).

traînée [trɛne] *nf* **(a)** trail (*of smoke, blood, light etc*); train (*of gunpowder*); trail (*of snail*); *Av* contrail, vapour *or US* vapor trail; **semer une t. de persil,** to sow a row of parsley; **se répandre comme une t. de poudre,** to spread like wildfire; **(b)** *Av etc* (*force*) drag; **(c)** *Arg* (*prostituée*) tart.

traînement [trɛnmɑ̃] *nm* dragging, trailing; drawling (*of voice*).

traîne-misère [trɛnmizɛr] *nm inv F* miserable wretch.

traîner [trɛne] **1** *vt* to drag, to trail (*s.o., sth*) along; *Rail* to pull, to haul (*coaches etc*); to tow (*barges*); to drag out (*one's existence*); to spin out, to drag out (*speech, business etc*); to drawl (*one's words*); **elle traînait cinq enfants après elle,** she was trailing five children after her; **t. la jambe,** to limp; **t. les pieds,** to shuffle; *Fig* **t. le pied,** to lag behind; **la perdrix traînait l'aile** *ou* **traînait de l'aile,** the partridge was dragging a wing; **t. qn en prison,** to drag s.o. off to prison; *Fig* **t. qn dans la boue,** to drag s.o. *or* s.o.'s name through the mud; *F* **t. ses bottes quelque part,** to drag oneself somewhere.

2 *vi* **(a)** to trail (*in the dust etc*); **votre robe traîne,** your dress is trailing;

(b) (*rester en arrière*) to lag *or* trail (behind); **une voix qui traîne,** a drawling voice;

(c) (*errer*) to hang around, to loaf around; **t. dans la rue** *ou* **par les rues,** to hang *or* loaf around the streets; **il y a un virus qui traîne,** there's a virus going around;

(d) (*être lent*) to dawdle;

(e) (*en désordre*) to lie around; **laisser t. son argent,** to leave one's money lying around; **des vêtements qui traînent sur le plancher,** clothes littering the floor;

(f) (*of illness, conversation etc*) to drag on; **l'affaire traîne,** the matter is dragging on; **intrigue qui traîne,** plot that drags; **t. en longueur,** (*of lawsuit etc*) to drag (on); **les choses ne traînent pas avec vous,** you don't let the grass grow under your feet; *F*... **et que ça ne traîne pas!,** ... and don't take forever about it!; **laisser t. un compte,** to leave an account unpaid.

3 se traîner *vpr* **(a)** (*of person*) to drag oneself; **il se traîna jusqu'au fossé,** he dragged himself *or* crawled to the ditch; **se t. aux genoux de qn,** to go on one's knees to s.o.; **il se traînait à peine,** he could hardly drag himself along;

(b) (*of conversation, evening etc*) to drag on; **les heures se traînent lourdement,** time hangs heavy.

traîne-savates [trɛnsavat] *nm inv F* layabout, loafer.

traîneur, -euse [trɛnœr, -øz] *n* **(a)** dragger, hauler (*of sth*); *F* **t. de sabre,** swashbuckler; **(b)** *F* **t. de cafés,** pub crawler.

training [trɛniŋ] *nm* **(a)** *Sp* (*entraînement*) training; **(b)** *Psy* **t. autogène,** relaxation by autosuggestion; **(c)** (*survêtement*) tracksuit; **(d)** (*chaussure*) trainer.

train-poste [trɛ̃pɔst] *nm* mail train; (*pl trains-poste*).

train-train [trɛ̃trɛ̃] *nm F* routine, daily round; **rien qui sort du t.-t. des événements ordinaires,** nothing to break the humdrum routine.

traire [trɛr] *vt* (*prp* **trayant**; *pp* **trait**; *pr ind* **je trais, n. trayons, ils traient**; *impf* **je trayais**; *fu* **je trairai**; *no p hist*) to milk (*cow etc*); to draw (*milk*); **machine à t.,** milking machine.

trait [trɛ] *nm* **(a)** pulling, pull (*of cord, weight*); *Échecs etc* **avoir le t.,** to have first move; **tout d'un t.,** at one stretch; **cheval de (gros) t.,** (heavy) draught *or US* draft horse;

(b) trace (*of harness*);

(c) (*flèche*) arrow; **partir comme un t.,** to be off like an arrow *or* like a shot; **t. de médisance,** piece of slander; *Fig* **envoyer** *ou* **lancer un t. à qn,** to have a dig at s.o.;

(d) beam (*of light*);

(e) **t. d'esprit,** flash *or* stroke of wit, witticism;

(f) *Mus* brilliant passage;

(g) (*de boisson*) gulp, draught; **boire à longs traits,** to gulp down (*beer etc*); **d'un (seul) t.,** at one gulp; *Fig F* at one go;

(h) (*ligne etc*) stroke, line; **d'un t. de plume,** with a stroke of the pen; **t. plein/discontinu,** continuous/broken line; **dessin au t.,** outline drawing; **copier qch t. pour t.,** to copy sth line by line; *Fig* **c'est sa sœur t. pour t.,** she is her sister to a T; **gravure au t.,** line engraving; **les grands traits de qch,** the main outlines *or* main features of sth; *Télécom* **points et traits,** dots and dashes;

(i) **t. d'union,** hyphen; *Fig* link (*between two people, two towns etc*);

(j) **t. de scie,** cut(ting) line;

(k) feature (*of face*); **traits réguliers,** regular features; **traits fins/grossiers,** fine/coarse features;

(l) trait (*of character*); characteristic touch (*of writer etc*);

(m) act, deed (*of courage, kindness etc*); stroke (*of genius*); **ce sont là de ses traits,** those are some of his tricks;

(n) **avoir t. à qch,** to be connected with sth, to relate to sth.

traitable [trɛtabl] *adj* **(a)** *Litt* tractable, accommodating (*person*); **(b)** treatable, manageable (*subject etc*).

traitant [trɛtɑ̃] *adj* **(a)** medicated (*shampoo, beauty cream etc*); **(b)** **mon médecin t.,** my (usual) doctor; **nom du médecin t.,** name of the doctor in attendance.

traite [trɛt] *nf* **(a)** stretch (*of road etc*); **j'ai fait une longue t.,** I have come a long way; **(tout) d'une t.,** in one go, without interruption; **boire qch d'une (seule) traite,** to drink sth at one gulp; **(b)** *Arch* transport (*of goods*); **(c)** **t. des Noires,** slave trade; **t. des Blanches,** white slave trade; **(d)** *Fin* (*billet*) (banker's) draft, bill (of exchange); **(e)** (*des vaches*) milking.

traité [trete] *nm* **(a)** (*ouvrage*) treatise (**de, sur,** on); **(b)** *Pol* (*accord*) treaty; **t. d'alliance,** treaty of alliance; **t. de paix,** peace treaty; **t. de commerce,** commercial treaty.

traitement [trɛtmɑ̃] *nm* **(a)** (*comportement*) *& Méd* treatment; **mauvais t.,** ill-treatment, maltreatment; *Méd* **premier t.,** initial treatment; **t. chirurgical,** surgery; **malade en t.,** patient under(going) treatment; **t. de choc/de fond,** shock/long-term treatment;

(b) *Tech* processing, treatment (*of raw materials*); treatment (*of water*); **t. anodique,** anodising (*in electrolysis*); *Constr etc* **t. superficiel,** surfacing (*of road etc*); *Ind* **capacité de t.,** processing *or* handling capacity;

(c) *Ordinat* processing; **t. (automatique) de l'information,** (automatic) data processing; **t. de texte,** word processing, WP; **(machine à** *ou* **de) t. de texte,** word processor; **logiciel de t. de texte,** word processor, word processing software; **réaliser qch par t. de texte,** to word process sth; **données en t., capacité** *ou* **débit de t.,** throughput; **unité de t.,** task, job; **t. à distance,** teleprocessing;

(d) (*rémunération*) salary; **sans t.,** honorary (*secretary*); unsalaried (*magistrate*).

traiter [trete] **1** *vt* **(a)** (*se conduire envers*) to treat (*s.o.*); **t. qn bien/mal,** to treat s.o. well/badly; **t. qn en ami/en enfant,** to treat s.o. like *or* as a friend/a child; **t. qn d'égal (à égal),** to treat s.o. as an *or* one's equal; **t. qn durement/comme un chien,** to treat s.o. harshly/like a dog;

(b) (*qualifier*) to call; **t. qn de lâche/***etc*, to call s.o. a coward/*etc*; **elle l'a traité de tous les noms,** she called him all the names under the sun;

(c) *Méd* to treat (*a patient, disease*); **se faire t. d'un cancer,** to undergo *or* have treatment for cancer;

(d) *Tech* to process; to coat (*lens*); to treat, to spray (*vines etc*); **oranges non traitées,** unsprayed oranges;

(e) *Ordinat* to process (*data*); **données non traitées,** raw data;

(f) *Litt* (*régaler*) to entertain (*s.o.*);

(g) *Com* to negotiate (*deal etc*); to handle, to transact (*business*);

(h) (*s'occuper de*) to treat, to deal with (*subject, problem etc*); **comment Paris-Match traite-t-il cet évènement?,** how does Paris-Match treat *or* deal with this event?; **t. une accusation avec mépris,** to treat an accusation with scorn.

2 *vi* **(a)** (*négocier*) to negotiate, to deal (**avec,** with); **t. avec ses créanciers,** to treat *or* negotiate with one's creditors;

(b) t. d'un sujet, (*of book, writer etc*) to deal with a subject.

3 se traiter *vpr* **(a)** (*réciproque*) to treat each other; **elles se traitent de tous les noms,** they call each other all the names under the sun;

(b) (*se négocier*) to be dealt with; **les affaires se traitent dans le plus grand secret,** matters are dealt with in the greatest secrecy;

(c) (*of subject, problem etc*) to be dealt with; **cela se traite facilement,** that can be easily dealt with.

traiteur [trɛtœr] *nm* **(a)** *Com* caterer; **(b)** *Arch* (*restaurateur*) restaurateur.

traître, traîtresse [trɛtr, trɛtrɛs] **1** *adj* treacherous (*person, look, words etc*); vicious (*animal*); dangerous, treacherous (*stair, crevasse etc*); deceptively strong (*wine etc*); *F* **pas un t. mot,** not a single word. **2** *n* **(a)** (*homme*) traitor; (*femme*) traitress; **en t.,** treacherously; **(b)** *Th* **le t.,** the villain.

traîtreusement [trɛtrøzmɑ̃] *adv* treacherously.

traîtrise [trɛtriz] *nf* **(a)** (*comportement*) treachery, treacherousness; **(b)** (*action*) (piece of) treachery.

trajectoire [traʒɛktwar] *nf* path (*of star, aircraft, electron, Météo depression*); trajectory (*of comet, satellite, missile*); *Av* **t. de vol,** flight path; **t. de collision,** collision course.

trajet [traʒɛ] *nm* **(a)** (*voyage*) journey; (*distance*) distance; (*itinéraire*) route; **t. de mer** *ou* **par mer,** voyage; **j'ai fait une partie du t. en avion,** I flew part of the way; **faire le t. en voiture,** to do the journey by car; **(b)** course (*of artery, nerve etc*); path (*of projectile, Él current*).

tralala [tralala] **1** *nm inv F* **en grand t.,** with a lot of fuss, with all the trimmings; (*en tenue de soirée*) all dressed up; **pas la peine d'en faire tout un t.,** there's no point making a great fuss about it. **2** *int* **j'ai gagné, t.!,** ha-ha, I've won!

tram [tram] *nm F* = **TRAMWAY.**

tramail, -ails [tramaj] *nm Pêche* trammel (net).

trame [tram] *nf* **(a)** *Tex* woof, weft; *Fig* thread (*of existence*); **pull/tapis usé jusqu'à la t.,** threadbare sweater/carpet; *Fig* **la t. du récit,** the framework of the story; **(b)** *Arch* (*complot*) plot, conspiracy; **(c)** *Phot Typ* (*écran*) (half-tone) screen; **(d)** *TV* raster; **t. (double),** frame.

tramer [trame] **1** *vt* **(a)** *Tex* to weave; *Fig* to weave (*plot of novel*); **(b)** (*combiner*) to hatch (*plot*); **(c)** *Phot* **t. un cliché,** to take a negative through a screen. **2 se tramer** *vpr* **il se trame quelque chose,** there's something in the wind *or* something afoot.

traminot [tramino] *nm* tram *or Am* streetcar worker.

tramontane [tramɔ̃tan] *nf* **(a)** (*vent*) tramontana; **(b)** *Arch* (*étoile*) north star; *Fig* **perdre la t.,** to lose one's bearings; (*devenir fou*) to go off one's head.

tramp [trɑ̃p] *nm Nau* tramp (steamer).

trampoline [trɑ̃pɔlin] *nm* (*toile*) trampoline; (*sport*) trampolining; **faire du t.,** to go *or* do trampolining.

tramway [tramwɛ] *nm* **(a)** (*ligne*) tramway, *Am* streetcar line; **(b)** (*voiture*) tram, *Am* streetcar.

tranchant [trɑ̃ʃɑ̃] **1** *adj* **(a)** sharp (*tool, sword etc*); keen, sharp (*edge*); **(b)** *Fig* trenchant, decisive (*words, opinion*); sharp, peremptory (*tone*); (self-)assertive (*person*). **2** *nm* **(a)** (cutting) edge (*of knife, sword etc*); thin end (*of wedge*); edge (*of hand*); **mettre le t. à une lame,** to put an edge on a blade; *Fig* **le t. d'une remarque,** the force of a remark; **épée à double t.,** two-edged sword; **argument à deux tranchants,** argument that cuts both ways; **(b)** (*de tanneur*) fleshing knife.

tranche [trɑ̃ʃ] *nf* **(a)** (*morceau coupé*) slice (*of bread, melon, meat etc*); rasher (*of bacon*); **en tranches,** in slices, sliced; *Fig* **une t. de vie,** a slice *or* cross-section of life; *F* **s'en payer une t.,** to have the time of one's life;

(b) (*partie*) block, portion (*of an issue of shares etc*); instalment, *US* installment (*of loan*); tranche (*of international financial assistance*); *Rail* **t. de voitures,** portion (*of train*); *Rad TV* **t. horaire,** (time) slot; **t. d'âge,** age bracket *or* group; **t. d'imposition,** tax band *or* bracket; **t. des salariés moyens,** middle-income bracket;

(c) slab (*of marble, stone*); *Culin* **t. napolitaine,** Neapolitan ice (cream); *Culin* **t. grasse,** (*morceau de bœuf*) round, top rump;

(d) face (*of wheel, gun muzzle etc*); edge (*of coin, plank*); (cut) edge (*of book*); *Tech* (*coupe*) section; **t. verticale,** vertical section;

(e) t. cellulaire, cellular compartment (*of ship*);

(f) (*outil*) set, chisel.

tranché [trɑ̃ʃe] *adj* distinct (*colour, pattern etc*); clear-cut (*opinion*); blunt (*refusal*).

tranchée [trɑ̃ʃe] *nf* **(a)** (*fossé*) trench; *Agr* drain; *Rail* cutting; *Mil* **guerre de tranchées,** trench warfare; **(b)** (*dans une forêt*) cutting; **t. garde-feu,** firebreak; **(c)** *Méd* **tranchées,** colic, griping pains.

tranchefile [trɑ̃ʃfil] *nf* headband (*of bound book*).

trancher [trɑ̃ʃe] **1** *vt* **(a)** to cut (*rope etc*); **t. la gorge à qn,** to slit *or* cut s.o.'s throat; **t. la tête à qn,** to cut off s.o.'s head; **(b)** to cut short (*discussion, s.o.'s career*); to settle (*question*) once and for all; to make short work of (*problem, difficulty*); **t. le mot,** to speak plainly. **2** *vi* **(a) t. dans le vif,** *Chir* to operate; *Fig* to adopt drastic measures; **pour t. net,** to cut it short; **tranchons là,** let us say no more; **il tranche sur tout,** he's always laying down the law; **(b)** (*of colours, characteristics etc*) to contrast strongly (**sur,** with), to stand out (**sur,** against).

tranchet [trɑ̃ʃɛ] *nm* **(a)** (*de serrurier etc*) anvil cutter; **(b)** (*de tanneur*) paring knife.

trancheur, -euse [trɑ̃ʃœr, -øz] **1** *nm* **(a)** *Tech Min* cutter; **(b)** *Pêche* cod gutter. **2** *nf* **trancheuse,** stone saw.

tranchoir [trɑ̃ʃwar] *nm* (*planche*) chopping board.

tranquille [trɑ̃kil] *adj* **(a)** calm, still, *Litt* tranquil (*sea, night etc*); steady (*compass*); **se tenir t.,** to keep still; (*ne rien dire*) to keep quiet; *Com* **marché t.,** easy market, dull market;

(b) quiet, peaceful (*town, person, life etc*); *F* **un père t.,** a placid sort of man;

(c) untroubled, easy (*conscience, mind etc*); untroubled, peaceful (*sleep*); **vous pouvez dormir t.,** you can sleep in peace *or* rest easy; **ne pas avoir l'esprit t.,** to be uneasy *or* uncomfortable in one's mind (**au sujet de,** about); **laissez-moi t.,** leave me alone; *F* **laisse ce vase t.!,** leave that vase alone!; **soyez t.,** set your mind at rest *or* at ease; **elle ne m'a pas rappelé, je ne suis pas t.,** she hasn't phoned me back, I'm anxious; **soyez t., il reviendra,** he'll come back, don't (you) worry *or* rest assured!; *F* **il avait pris une décision, je suis t.,** he had made up his mind, I'm sure.

tranquillement [trɑ̃kilmɑ̃] *adv* (*répondre, examiner etc*) calmly; (*vivre*) quietly, peacefully; (*travailler*) calmly; (*dormir*) peacefully.

tranquillisant [trɑ̃kilizɑ̃] **1** *adj* reassuring (*news etc*); soothing, calming (*effect*). **2** *nm Méd* tranquillizer.

tranquilliser [trɑ̃kilize] **1** *vt* **t. qn,** to reassure s.o., to set s.o.'s mind at rest. **2 se tranquilliser** *vpr* **(a)** (*of sea etc*) to become calm; **(b) tranquillisez-vous,** set your mind at rest.

tranquillité [trɑ̃kilite] *nf* **(a)** calmness, stillness (*of sea, night etc*); **(b)** peace and quiet (*of person*); peacefulness (*of sleep*); **t. d'esprit,** peace of mind; **troubler la t. publique,** to disturb the peace; **en toute t.,** without being disturbed; (*sans souci*) with an easy mind.

trans- [trɑ̃s, trɑ̃z] *préf* trans-.

transaction [trɑ̃zaksjɔ̃] *nf* **(a)** *Com* transaction; **transactions,** transactions, dealings, deals; **(b)** (*arrangement*) compromise.

transactionnel, -elle [trɑ̃zaksjɔnɛl] *adj Psy* **analyse transactionnelle,** transactional analysis; **solution transactionnelle,** compromise.

transalpin [trɑ̃zalpɛ̃] *adj* transalpine.

transat [trɑ̃zat] *nm F* = **TRANSATLANTIQUE 2.**

transatlantique [trɑ̃zatlɑ̃tik] **1** *adj* transatlantic. **2** *nm* **(a)** (*paquebot*) (transatlantic) liner; **(b)** (*chaise longue*) deck chair.

transbahuter [trɑ̃sbayte] *F* **1** *vt* to shift, to lug. **2 se transbahuter** *vpr* to shift.

transbordement [trɑ̃sbɔrdəmɑ̃] *nm Nau* transhipment; *Rail* transfer.

transborder [trɑ̃sbɔrde] *vt Nau* to tranship; *Rail* to transfer (*passengers, goods*).

transbordeur [trɑ̃sbɔrdœr] *adj & nm* (**pont**) **t.**, transporter bridge.

transcanadien, -ienne [trɑ̃skanadjɛ̃, -jɛn] **1** *adj* trans-Canada. **2** *nf* **la Transcanadienne,** (*autoroute*) the Trans-Canada Highway.

transcendance [trɑ̃sɑ̃dɑ̃s] *nf Phil Rel etc* transcendence.

transcendant [trɑ̃sɑ̃dɑ̃] *adj* **(a)** *Phil Rel etc* transcendent; *F* **il n'a rien de t.,** he's not much to write home about; **(b)** *Math* transcendental.

transcendantal, -aux [trɑ̃sɑ̃dɑ̃tal, -o] *adj Phil* transcendental.

transcendantalisme [trɑ̃sɑ̃dɑ̃talism] *nm Phil* transcendentalism.

transcender [trɑ̃sɑ̃de] **1** *vt* to transcend. **2 se transcender** *vpr* to surpass oneself.

transcodage [trɑ̃skɔdaʒ] *nm Ordinat* transcribing.

transcoder [trɑ̃skɔde] *vt Ordinat* to transcribe.

transcontinental, -aux [trɑ̃skɔ̃tinɑ̃tal, -o] *adj* transcontinental.

transcripteur [trɑ̃skriptœr] *nm* transcriber.

transcription [trɑ̃skripsjɔ̃] *nf* **(a)** (*action*) transcription, transcribing; (*dans un autre alphabet*) transliteration; **t. phonétique,** phonetic transcription; **(b)** (*texte*) transcript; *Mus* transcription; **t. à l'état civil,** = certified copy of registry office document.

transcrire [trɑ̃skrir] *vt* (*conj like* **écrire**) **(a)** (*recopier*) to transcribe; **t. une lettre à la machine,** to type a letter; **(b)** *Jur* to register (*divorce etc*); *Com* to post (*the journal into the ledger*); **(c)** (*dans un autre alphabet*) to transliterate (*a text etc*); **t. un mot arabe en caractères grecs,** to transliterate an Arabic word into Greek letters.

transdisciplinaire [trɑ̃sdisipliner] *adj* interdisciplinary.

transducteur [trɑ̃sdyktœr] *nm Phys Électron* transducer.

transe [trɑ̃s] *nf* **(a) transes,** (*anxiété*) fear; **être dans les transes,** to be on tenterhooks; **(b)** (*hypnose*) (hypnotic) trance; **médium en t.,** medium in a trance; **entrer en t.,** to go into a trance; *Fig Iron* (*se mettre en colère*) to be beside oneself.

transept [trɑ̃sɛpt] *nm Archit* transept.

transférable [trɑ̃sferabl] *adj* transferable.

transfèrement [trɑ̃sfɛrmɑ̃] *nm* transfer(ring) (*of prisoner etc*); **t. cellulaire,** transfer(ring) by police van.

transférer [trɑ̃sfere] *vt* (**je transfère, n. transférons; je transfererai**) **(a)** to transfer; **t. un évêque,** to translate a bishop; **(b)** to transfer, to make over, to assign (*goods etc*); to convey (*estate*) (**à**, to); **t. de l'argent d'un compte à un autre,** to transfer money from one account to another; **(c)** *Psy* to transfer (*one's affections etc*) (**à**, to).

transfert [trɑ̃sfɛr] *nm* **(a)** transfer(ring) (*of prisoner, headquarters etc*); resettlement (*of population*); **(b)** *Ordinat* **t. de magnétisation,** magnetic printing; **clavier à t.,** storage keyboard; **(c)** making over, transfer, assignment (*of stock, rights etc*); conveyance (*of estate*); **(d)** *Psy* transference.

transfiguration [trɑ̃sfigyrɑsjɔ̃] *nf* transfiguration.

transfigurer [trɑ̃sfigyre] *vt* to transfigure.

transfiler [trɑ̃sfile] *vt Nau* **(a)** to lace (*sails etc*); **(b)** to snub (*rope*).

transfo [trɑ̃sfo] *nm Él F* transformer.

transformable [trɑ̃sfɔrmabl] *adj* convertible (*sofa etc*).

transformateur, -trice [trɑ̃sfɔrmatœr, -tris] *Él* **1** *adj* transforming; transformer (*station*). **2** *nm* transformer.

transformation [trɑ̃sfɔrmɑsjɔ̃] *nf* **(a)** transformation (**en,** into); **acteur à transformations,** quick-change artist(e); **industrie de t.,** processing industry; *Math* **t. algébrique,** algebraic transformation; **(b)** *Él* **rapport de t.,** transformer ratio; *Électron* **t. de signaux,** signal transformation; **(c)** *Rugby* conversion (*of try*); **faire une t.,** to convert a try.

transformer [trɑ̃sfɔrme] **1** *vt* **(a)** to transform, to change; **t. en,** to turn *or* change *or* transform into; **t. du plomb en or,** to turn *or* change *or* transform lead into gold; **son mariage l'a transformé,** his marriage has transformed *or* changed him; **(b)** *Math* to transform (*equation*); **(c)** *Rugby* to convert (*try*); **(d)** *Électron* to transform, to map; **(e)** (*en logique*) to convert (*proposition*). **2 se transformer** *vpr* to be transformed, to change; **se t. en monstre/papillon/***etc*, to be transformed *or* change *or* turn into a monster/butterfly/*etc*.

transformisme [trɑ̃sfɔrmism] *nm Phil etc* transformism.

transformiste [trɑ̃sfɔrmist] *adj & n Phil etc* transformist.

transfuge [trɑ̃sfyʒ] *n* renegade, defector; *Mil* defector, deserter to the other side.

transfuser [trɑ̃sfyze] *vt* **(a)** to transfuse (*blood*); **(b)** *Fig* to instil (**à**, into).

transfusion [trɑ̃sfyzjɔ̃] *nf* (blood) tranfusion; **faire une t. à un malade,** to give a patient a transfusion; **centre de t. sanguine,** blood transfusion centre.

transgresser [trɑ̃sgrese] *vt* to infringe, *Fml* to transgress (*rule, law*); to disobey (*orders*).

transgresseur [trɑ̃sgresœr] *nm Litt* transgressor.

transgression [trɑ̃sgrɛsjɔ̃] *nf* infringement, *Fml* transgression (*of rule, law*); disobeying (*of orders*).

transhumance [trɑ̃zymɑ̃s] *nf* transhumance.

transhumant [trɑ̃zymɑ̃] *adj* transhumant.

transhumer [trɑ̃zyme] *vt & vi* to move to *or* from mountain pastures.

transi [trɑ̃zi] *adj* perished (**de froid**, with cold); paralysed (**de peur**, with fear); *Iron* **un amoureux t.,** a bashful lover.

transiger [trɑ̃ziʒe] *vi* (**je transigeai(s); n. transigeons**) **(a)** to compromise (**avec,** with; **sur,** on); **(b)** *Can* (*faire des transactions*) to carry out transactions.

Transilvanie [trɑ̃silvani] *nf* Transylvania.

transir [trɑ̃sir, -zir] **1** *vt* (*of wind etc*) to chill to the bone; (*of fear*) to paralyse. **2** *vi Arch* (*de froid*) to be paralysed with cold; (*de peur*) to be paralysed with fear.

transistor [trɑ̃zistɔr] *nm Électron* **(a)** (*dispositif*) transistor; **à transistors,** transistorized; **(b)** (*poste de radio*) transistor (radio).

transistorisé [trɑ̃zistɔrize] *adj Électron* transistorized.

transistoriser [trɑ̃zistɔrize] *vt Électron* to transistorize.

transit [trɑ̃zit] *nm* **(a)** transit; **en t.,** in transit; **marchandises de t.,** goods for transit; **maison de t.,** forwarding agency; **(b)** *Électron* **t. par bande perforée,** tape relay; **(c)** *Méd* **t. intestinal,** intestinal transit.

transitaire [trɑ̃zitɛr] **1** *adj* **pays t.,** country of transit; **commerce t.,** transit trade. **2** *nm* forwarding agent, transport agent.

transiter [trɑ̃zite] **1** *vt* to forward (*goods*). **2** *vi* (*of goods, travellers*) to pass in transit (**par**, through).

transitif, -ive [trɑ̃zitif, -iv] *adj Gram Math* transitive.

transition [trɑ̃zisjɔ̃] *nf* transition; **sans t.,** abruptly; **l'art de la t.,** (*d'orateur*) the art of making connections; *Archit* **style de t.,** transition style; *Géol* **terrain de t.,** transitional stratum.

transitivement [trɑ̃zitivmɑ̃] *adv Gram* transitively.

transitivité [trɑ̃zitivite] *nf Gram Math* transitivity.

transitoire [trɑ̃zitwar] *adj* **(a)** (*fugitif*) transitory, transient; **(b)** (*provisoire*) transitional (*period*); transitional, temporary (*measure, solution*).

transitoirement [trɑ̃zitwarmɑ̃] *adv* (*d'une manière fugitive*) transitorily; (*d'une manière provisoire*) transitionally.

Transjordanie [trɑ̃sʒɔrdani] *nf Hist* Trans-Jordan.

translation [trɑ̃slɑsjɔ̃] *nf* **(a)** (*transfer*) transfer(ring) (*of prisoner, court etc*); *Télécom* retransmission, relaying (*of message*); **(b)** *Tech* **mouvement de t.,** translatory motion; **(c)** *Jur* **t. de propriété,** transfer of property.

transli(t)tération [trɑ̃sliterɑsjɔ̃] *nf* transliteration.

translit(t)érer [trɑ̃slitere] *vt* to transliterate.

translucide [trɑ̃slysid] *adj* translucent.

translucidité [trɑ̃slysidite] *nf* translucence, translucency.

transmetteur [trɑ̃smɛtœr] *nm* **(a)** *Télécom Ordinat Biol* transmitter; **(b)** *Nau* **t. d'ordres,** (turret) telegraph, transmitter.

transmettre [trɑ̃smɛtr] *v* (*conj like* **mettre**) **1** *vt* **(a)** to transmit (*light, heat*); to pass on, to convey (*message, order etc*); to pass on, to transmit (*disease, virus*); to pass on (*recipe etc*); to impart (*the truth, energy*); to hand (*tradition etc*) down; *Télécom Rad* to send, to transmit (*information*); *Rad TV* to broadcast (*programme etc*); **transmettez mon amitié à vos parents,** pass on *or* give my best wishes to your parents; **(b)** *Jur* to transfer (*property, right etc*); to assign (*shares etc*). **2 se transmettre** *vpr* (*of message, disease etc*) to be passed on.

transmigration [trɑ̃smigrɑsjɔ̃] *nf* transmigration.

transmigrer [trɑ̃smigre] *vi* to transmigrate.

transmissible [trɑ̃smisibl] *adj* **(a)** transmissible (*disease*); **sexuellement t.,** sexually transmitted; **(b)** *Jur* transferable (*right etc*).

transmission [trɑ̃smisjɔ̃] *nf* **(a)** transmission (*of heat etc*); passing on (*of message, order*); imparting (*of truth*); handing down (*of tradition etc*); *Méd* transmission (*of disease, virus*); *Télécom Rad* transmission, sending (*of message, image etc*); *Rad TV* broadcasting (*of programme etc*); *Rad etc* **antenne de t.,** transmitting aerial; *Rad TV* **t. directe** *ou* **en direct,** live broadcast *or* programme; **t. différée** *ou* **en différé,** recorded broadcast *or* programme; *Com* **fiche de t.,** routing slip; *Tech* **t. du mouvement,**

transmission of movement; **arbre de t.**, driving shaft; **courroie de t.**, driving belt; **engrenage(s) de t.**, driving gear; *Fb* **t. du ballon,** passing; **t. de pensée,** thought transference; *Fig* **c'est de la t. de pensée!,** we *or* they *or* you can read each other's mind!; **(b)** *Nau Mil* **les transmissions,** signals; **officier de transmissions,** signal(s) officer; **centre de transmissions,** signal centre; **(c)** *Aut Tech* **la t.**, the transmission (gear); *Aut* **t. automatique,** automatic transmission; *Tech* **t. flexible,** flexible shaft(ing); **(d)** *Ordinat* **voie de t.**, transmission channel; **t. de données,** data transmission; **(e)** *Jur* transfer(ence) (*of property, right etc*); assignment (*of shares etc*); *Admin* **t. des pouvoirs,** handing over.

transmodulation [trɑ̃smɔdylɑsjɔ̃] *nf Rad etc* cross modulation.

transmuer [trɑ̃smɥe] *vt* to transmute (**en,** into).

transmutation [trɑ̃smytɑsjɔ̃] *nf* transmutation (**en,** into).

transmuter [trɑ̃smyte] *vt* to transmute (**en,** into).

transnational, -aux [trɑ̃snasjɔnal, -o] *adj* transnational.

transocéanien, -ienne [trɑ̃zɔseanjɛ̃, -jɛn], **transocéanique** [trɑ̃zɔseanik] *adj* transoceanic.

transpacifique [trɑ̃spasifik] *adj* transpacific.

transpalette [trɑ̃spalɛt] *nm* pallet truck.

transparaître [trɑ̃sparɛtr] *vi* (*conj like* **paraître**) to show (through); **le doute transparaît sous son calme,** doubt is showing (through) beneath his calm.

transparence [trɑ̃sparɑ̃s] *nf* **(a)** transparency; *Fig* transparency, obviousness (*of allusion etc*); **(b)** *Cin* back projection.

transparent [trɑ̃sparɑ̃] **1** *adj* transparent; *Fig* transparent, clear, obvious (*intention, allusion*); **c'était un homme t.**, he was a man whose thoughts were easy to read; **c'est t., elle est vexée,** it's transparent *or* clear *or* obvious, she's upset. **2** *nm* **(a)** transparency (*picture, print etc illuminated from behind*); **(b)** guide (*for writing pad*).

transpercer [trɑ̃spɛrse] *vt* (**je transperçai(s); n. transperçons**) to pierce; (*of bullet*) to go through; (*of cold, damp etc*) to go *or* come through; **t. qn (d'un coup d'épée),** to run s.o. through (with a sword); **transpercé d'une balle,** shot through; **t. qn du regard,** to give s.o. a piercing look; **son attitude me transperce le cœur,** his attitude is breaking my heart.

transpirant [trɑ̃spirɑ̃] *adj* perspiring, sweating.

transpiration [trɑ̃spirɑsjɔ̃] *nf* **(a)** (*sueur*) perspiration, sweat; **en t.**, perspiring, sweating; **humide de t.**, sweaty (*garment etc*); **(b)** (*action*) perspiration, sweating; *Bot* transpiration.

transpirer [trɑ̃spire] *vi* **(a)** (*of person*) to perspire, to sweat; *F* **t. sur,** (*travailler à*) to sweat over; **(b)** *Bot* to transpire; **(c)** *Fig* (*of secret, news etc*) to come to light, to come out.

transplant [trɑ̃splɑ̃] *nm Chir* (*organe, tissu*) transplant.

transplantable [trɑ̃splɑ̃tabl] *adj* transplantable.

transplantation [trɑ̃splɑ̃tɑsjɔ̃] *nf* transplantation, transplanting (*of trees, people etc*); *Chir* transplant; **t. cardiaque,** heart transplant.

transplanter [trɑ̃splɑ̃te] **1** *vt* to transplant (*trees, people etc*); *Chir* **t. un cœur,** to perform a heart transplant (operation). **2 se transplanter** *vpr* (*dans un autre milieu*) to resettle.

transplantoir [trɑ̃splɑ̃twar] *nm* trowel.

transpolaire [trɑ̃spɔlɛr] *adj* transpolar.

transport [trɑ̃spɔr] *nm* **(a)** transport, *Fml* carriage (*of goods, passengers*); **les transports,** transport; **capacité de t.**, transport capacity; **travailler dans le t.**, to work in transport; **compagnie de t.**, transport company; *Com* carrying *or* forwarding company; **entrepreneur de t.**, haulage contractor; **frais de t.**, freight charges, carriage; **moyen de t.**, means of transport; **les transports en commun,** public transport; **t. urbain,** urban transport; **t. aérien/maritime,** air/sea transport; *Ind* **courroie de t.**, conveyor belt; *Mil* **véhicule de t. de personnel,** personnel carrier; **t. par (chemin de) fer** *ou* **par voie ferrée,** rail transport; **t. par canalisations,** piping (*of oil*); **avion de t.**, transport aircraft; **avion de t. de passagers,** passenger aircraft; **avion de t. de frêt,** cargo aircraft; **cela permet de faire les transports urgents par avion,** this enables urgent freight to be sent by air; *El* **t. d'énergie,** power transmission; **t. de force,** high-voltage power transmission; **(b)** *Jur* **t. sur les lieux,** visit to the scene of the accident *or* crime *etc*; **(c)** (*navire*) transport (ship); **t. de troupes,** troopship; **(d)** *Jur* **t.(-cession),** transfer, conveyance (*of property, rights etc*); **(e)** (*en lithographie*) transfer (*on to the stone*); **papier à t.**, transfer paper; **(f)** *Litt* (*émotion*) rapture; **transports de joie,** transports of joy; **transports de colère,** outbursts *or* fits of anger; **avec t.**, rapturously.

transportable [trɑ̃spɔrtabl] *adj* transportable; *Méd* fit to be moved (*patient etc*).

transportation [trɑ̃spɔrtɑsjɔ̃] *nf Jur* (penal) transportation.

transporté, -ée [trɑ̃spɔrte] **1** *n* transported convict, transport. **2** *adj Fig* beside oneself (**de,** with), carried away.

transporter [trɑ̃spɔrte] **1** *vt* **(a)** to transport, to carry (*goods, troops etc*); **t. qn à l'hôpital,** to take s.o. to hospital; **produits transportés par mer/air,** products transported *or* carried by sea/air; **l'intrigue nous transporte à Moscou/dans les années 50,** the plot transports us to Moscow/to the 1950s; **(b)** *Jur* to transport (*convict*); **(c)** *Jur* to transfer (*property, rights etc*) (**à,** to); **(d)** (*ravir*) to transport, to carry away; **cette bonne nouvelle l'a transporté,** he was overjoyed by the good news. **2 se transporter** *vpr* **(a)** *Jur* **se t. sur les lieux,** (*of police*) to visit the scene of the crime *or* accident; **(b)** *Com* **se t. mal/facilement,** to be difficult/easy to transport.

transporteur, -euse [trɑ̃spɔrtœr, -øz] **1** *nm* **(a)** (*entrepreneur*) carrier, haulage contractor; *Av* carrier; **t.-roulier,** road haulage contractor; **(b)** *Ind* (*appareil*) conveyor; **(chariot) t.**, travelling crane, travelling platform; **t. élévateur,** elevator; **(c)** *Mil* feeder, feed mechanism. **2** *adj* **hélice/courroie transporteuse,** spiral/belt conveyor.

transposable [trɑ̃spozabl] *adj* transposable.

transposer [trɑ̃spoze] *vt* to transpose; **t. un roman à l'écran,** to adapt a novel for the screen.

transposition [trɑ̃spɔzisjɔ̃] *nf Anat Chir Mus etc* transposition; **t. d'un roman à l'écran,** adapting of a novel for the screen.

transputer ® [trɑ̃spytœr] *nm Ordinat* transputer.

transpyrénéen [trɑ̃spireneɛ̃, -ɛn] *adj* transpyrenean.

transsaharien, -ienne [trɑ̃ssaarjɛ̃, -jɛn] *adj* trans-saharan.

transsexualisme [trɑ̃ssɛksɥalism] *nm* transsexualism.

transsexuel, -elle [trɑ̃ssɛksɥɛl] *adj & n* transsexual.

transsibérien, -ienne [trɑ̃ssiberjɛ̃, -jɛn] **1** *adj* Trans-Siberian. **2** *nm* **le T.**, the Trans-Siberian Railway.

transsubstantiation [trɑ̃ssypstɑ̃sjɑsjɔ̃] *nf Rel* transubstantiation.

transsuder [trɑ̃ssyde] *vi* to transude.

Transvaal (le) [lətrɑ̃sval] *nm* the Transvaal.

transvasement [trɑ̃svɑzmɑ̃] *nm* decanting (*of liquid*).

transvaser [trɑ̃svɑze] **1** *vt* to decant (*wine etc*). **2 se transvaser** *vpr* (*of water*) to siphon.

transversal, -aux [trɑ̃svɛrsal, -o] **1** *adj* transverse, transversal; cross (*section, gallery, street, girder, artery etc*); *Constr* **mur t.**, partition (wall); *Anat* **muscle t.**, transverse (muscle); *Nau* **dans le sens t.**, athwartship; *Nau* **soutes transversales,** cross bunkers; *Tech* **avance transversale,** cross feed; *Géog* **vallée transversale,** transverse valley. **2** *nm Anat* transverse (muscle).

transversalement [trɑ̃svɛrsalmɑ̃] *adv* transversely, crosswise, across.

transverse [trɑ̃svɛrs] **1** *adj Math Anat etc* transverse. **2** *nm Anat* transverse (muscle).

transvestisme [trɑ̃svɛstism] *nm* transvestism.

transvider [trɑ̃svide] *vt* to pour; (*transvaser*) to decant.

Transylvanie [trɑ̃silvani] *nf* Transylvania.

trapèze [trapɛz] **1** *nm* **(a)** *Géom Br* trapezium, *Am* trapezoid; **(b)** *Anat* trapezius; **(c)** *Gym* trapeze; **t. volant,** flying trapeze; **faire du t.**, to perform on the trapeze. **2** *adj Anat* trapezius (*muscle*); trapezium (*bone*).

trapéziste [trapezist] *n* trapeze artist.

trapézoïdal, -aux [trapezɔidal, -o] *adj Géom Br* trapezial, *Am* trapezoidal.

trapézoïde [trapezɔid] *adj & nm Anat* **(os) t.**, trapezoid.

trapillon [trapijɔ̃] *nm* **(a)** catch, lock (*of trap door*); **(b)** *Th* slot (*for scenery, rising from below the stage*).

trappe [trap] *nf* **(a)** (*dans le plancher*) *& Th* trap (door); *Tech* hatch; **t. de visites,** inspection hatch; **t. de la soute aux bombes,** bomb door; **(b)** (*piège à animaux*) trap, pitfall.

Trappe [trap] *nf Rel* **(a)** (*monastère*) Trappist monastery; **(b)** (*order*) Trappist order.

trappeur [trapœr] *nm* trapper (*of wild animals*).

trappillon [trapijɔ̃] *nm* = **TRAPILLON**.

trappiste [trapist] *nm Rel* Trappist (monk).

trapu [trapy] *adj* **(a)** thickset, stocky (*man, horse*); squat (*building etc*); **(b)** *Scol F* (*fort*) bright (**en,** at); (*difficile*) tough, sticky (*problem*).
traquenard [traknar] *nm* (*piège*) trap; *Fig* (*de langue etc*) pitfall, trap.
traquer [trake] **1** *vt* to hunt down, to track down (*game, criminal etc*); **bête traquée,** hunted animal. **2** *vi F* to get stage fright.
traquet [trakɛ] *nm* **(a)** (*battant*) (mill) clapper *or* clack; **(b)** *Orn* **t. (motteux),** wheatear.
trauma [troma] *nm Méd Psy* trauma.
traumatique [tromatik] *adj Méd* traumatic.
traumatisant [tromatizɑ̃] *adj* traumatizing.
traumatiser [tromatize] *vt* to traumatize.
traumatisme [tromatism] *nm Méd Psy* traumatism; **t. crânien,** cranial traumatism.
traumatologie [tromatɔlɔʒi] *nf Méd* traumatology.
travail[1], -ails [travaj] *nm Vét* sling, frame.
travail[2], -aux [travaj, -o] *nm* **(a)** (*activité*) work; **dur t.,** hard work; **division du t.,** division of labour; **se mettre au t.,** to begin *or* start *or* set to *or* get down to work; **allons, au t.!,** come on, let's get (down) to work!; **cesser le t.,** to stop work; (*à la fin de la journée*) to stop work, to knock off; **fournir un t. utile,** to do useful work; **à t. égal, salaire égal,** equal pay for equal work; **arrêt de t.,** (*pour grève*) stoppage; (*pour maladie*) sick leave; **accident de t.,** industrial accident; **carte de t.,** work permit; **code du t.,** code of work; **contrat de t.,** work contract, contract of work; **vêtements de t.,** working clothes; **groupe de t.,** working party; **méthode de t.,** working method; **homme de grand t.,** hardworking man; **ça demande beaucoup de t.,** that requires a lot of work; *Péj* **ça sent le t.,** it's rather laborious *or* laboured; **séance de t.,** business meeting (*of an association etc*); **le monde du t.,** the world of work; *Admin* **admission des enfants au t.,** employment of children; **Ministère du T.,** = Department of Employment; *Jur* **t. disciplinaire,** hard labour; **condamné aux travaux forcés,** sentenced to hard labour; *Myth* **les douze travaux d'Hercule,** the twelve labours of Hercules; *Hum* **inspecteur des travaux finis,** idler, *Br* skiver (*who arrives after the work has been done*); **t. de tête, t. intellectuel,** intellectual work, brainwork; **t. manuel,** manual labour; *Scol* **travaux manuels,** arts and crafts; **c'est du t. à la main,** it's handmade; **travaux des champs,** agricultural labour; *Ind* **t. mécanique,** machine work; **t. à mi-temps/à plein t.,** part-time/full-time work; **t. à domicile,** work done at home; **t. à l'entreprise,** contract work; **t. en série,** mass production; **t. (au) noir,** moonlighting; **t. à l'aiguille,** needlework; *Min* **t. à ciel ouvert,** opencast mining; *Min* **vieux travaux,** old workings; **t. au tour,** lathe work; **t. du bois/du fer,** working of wood/iron; **travaux pratiques,** *Scol* practical work; *Méd* tutorials;
(b) *Ordinat* job;
(c) *Tech etc* working (*of the digestion*); working, fermenting (*of wine*); action (*of water on banks of stream etc*); **t. musculaire,** muscular effort; **t. mécanique, t. moteur,** mechanical energy; **t. à la tension,** tension stress; **pression de t.,** working pressure;
(d) (*emploi*) work, job, employment; **donner du t. à qn,** to give s.o. work *or* a job; **être sans t.,** to be out of work *or* unemployed *or F* jobless; **chercher du t.,** to look for work *or* a job;
(e) (*lieu*) work; **il est à son t.,** he's at work; **je l'ai rencontré au t.,** I met him at work;
(f) (*tâche*) (piece of) work, job; **montre-moi ton t.,** show me your work;
(g) (*écrit*) work; **auteur d'un t. sur les métaux,** author of a work on metals;
(h) *Admin* **travaux publics,** public works; **travaux attention,** road works ahead; *Mil* **travaux de défense,** defensive works, outworks;
(i) (*exécution*) **c'est du beau t.,** it's a fine piece of work, it's fine work; *F Iron* that's very clever; **c'est du t. d'amateur,** it's an amateurish piece of work, it's amateurish work;
(j) *Méd* **femme en t.,** woman in labour; **salle de t.,** (*d'hôpital*) labour room.
travaillé [travaje] *adj* **(a)** worked (*iron, wood, stone*); **(b)** laboured, *US* labored (*style etc*).
travailler [travaje] **1** *vi* **(a)** to work; **t. ferme pour nourrir sa famille,** to work hard to keep one's family; **t. à la terre,** to work on the land; **t. dur,** to work hard; **t. à la pièce,** to do piecework; **t. au noir,** to moonlight; **t. en free-lance,** to work as a freelance, to do freelance work; *F* **t. comme un nègre** *ou* **comme quatre** *ou* **comme un cheval,** to work like a slave *or* a Trojan *or* a horse; *Arg* **t. du chapeau,** to have a screw loose; **son imagination travaille,** his imagination is working overtime; **le temps travaille pour nous,** time is on our side; **cela risque de t. contre lui,** there's a danger that it will work against him; **t. pour qn,** to work for s.o.; *Fig* **t. pour le roi de Prusse;** to get nothing out of it; **se rendre malade à force de t.,** to make oneself ill with work; **elle travaille trop,** she works too much, she overworks; **t. à l'aiguille,** to do needlework; **t. pour soi-même, t. pour** *ou* **à son compte,** to work for oneself *or* on one's own account, to be self-employed; **t. à la perte de qn** *ou* **à perdre qn,** to aim at ruining s.o.; **t. à un roman,** to work at *or* on a novel; **t. à faire qch,** to make an effort *or* exert oneself to do sth;
(b) (*s'entraîner*) to practise; (*of performing animals etc*) to go through their performance; **t. sans filet,** (*of trapeze artist*) to work without a net; *Fig* to be out on a limb;
(c) (*of ship, cable etc*) to strain; (*of wine*) to ferment, to work; (*of the mind*) to be in a ferment; (*of wood*) to warp, to shrink; (*of walls*) to crack;
(d) faire t. une machine, to work *or* run an engine; **faire t. son argent,** to make one's money work for one.
2 *vt* **(a)** (*façonner*) to work, to fashion, to shape (*wood, iron etc*); **t. la terre,** to work the land; *Tennis* **t. son revers,** to work on one's backhand; *Tennis* **t. une balle,** to spin a ball; **t. un cheval,** to work a horse; **t. la pâte,** to knead the dough; **t. son style,** to work on *or* polish one's style;
(b) (*étudier*) to work at, to study (*one's part, a subject etc*); **t. le piano,** to practise the piano;
(c) *Litt* (*inquiéter*) to torment, to worry, to obsess; **un désir le travaillait,** he was tormented *or* obsessed with a desire; **être travaillé de** *ou* **par la goutte,** to be a martyr to gout;
(d) (*influer sur*) to work (up)on (*s.o., the feelings, public opinion etc*).
3 se travailler *vpr* **se t. l'esprit,** to worry.
travailleur, -euse [travajœr, -øz] **1** *adj* industrious, hard-working; **les masses travailleuses,** the workers, the working classes. **2** *n* worker; **bon t.,** good *or* hard worker; **t. manuel/intellectuel,** manual/non-manual worker; **t. indépendant,** self-employed worker; **t. en bâtiment,** building worker; **les travailleurs,** the workers, the working people. **3** *nf* **travailleuse,** (*table à ouvrage*) (lady's) work table.
travaillisme [travajism] *nm Pol* (British) socialism, doctrine of the Labour Party.
travailliste [travajist] *Pol* **1** *nm* member of the Labour Party; **les travaillistes,** the Labour Party, Labour. **2** *adj* Labour (*Party, member etc*).
travailloter [travajɔte] *vi* to do just a bit of work.
travée [trave] *nf* **(a)** *Constr Archit* bay; **(b)** (*de pont*) span; (*séparée*) independent girder; **(c)** *Av* rib (*of wing*); **(d)** bank (*of seats, machines etc*).
traveller's check, traveller's chèque [travlœr(s)-ʃɛk] *nm* traveller's cheque, *US* traveler's check.
travelling [travəliŋ] *nm Cin* **(a)** (*dispositif*) dolly, travelling platform (*for the camera*); **(b)** (*déplacement*) tracking.
travelo [travlo] *nm F* (*travesti*) drag queen.
travers [travɛr] *nm* **(a) en t.,** across, crosswise; **autobus avec places disposées en t.,** bus with seats arranged crosswise; **profil en t.,** cross section; **en t. de,** across; **se mettre en t. du chemin de qn,** to stand in s.o.'s way; **il ne faut pas que des problèmes personnels se mettent en t. du travail,** personal problems must not get in the way of work;
(b) à t. qch, au t. de qch, through sth; **à t. le monde,** throughout the world; *Fig* **elle n'a pas réussi à passer au t.,** she didn't manage to escape;
(c) *Nau* **de t., par le t.,** on the beam, abeam; **vent de t.,** wind on the beam; **collision par le t.,** collision broadside on; *F* **prendre par le t.,** to take a short cut; **en t. (du navire),** athwart (ships);
(d) *Ordinat* **correction de mise en t.,** deskew;
(e) (*locutions*) **marcher de t.,** (*of drunkard etc*) to stagger (along); **la machine marche de t.,** the machine is not working properly; **tout va de t.,** everything goes wrong; **comprendre de t.,** to misunderstand; **regarder qn de t.,** to look askance *or* to scowl at s.o.; **votre chapeau est de t.,** your hat is (on) crooked; **il a la bouche/le nez de t.,** his mouth/nose is crooked; **j'ai avalé de t.,** it went down the wrong way; **les tableaux pendaient de t.,** the pictures were hung crooked; **il a des idées tout(es) de t.,** his ideas are all wrong; **il a répondu de t.,** he gave a

ridiculous answer; **prendre tout de t.**, to take everything the wrong way;

(f) *(défaut)* failing, shortcoming, fault; *Arch* **t. (d'esprit)**, eccentricity;

(g) *(largeur)* breadth; **un t. de doigt**, a finger's breadth.

traversable [travɛrsabl] *adj (desert, river etc)* that can be crossed.

traverse [travɛrs] *nf* **(a) (chemin de) t.**, short cut; **(b) (barre de) t.**, cross bar, cross piece; *(d'échelle)* rung; *Constr* transom; *Rail* sleeper, *US* tie; *Aut etc* cross member *(of frame)*; **(c)** *Litt (obstacle)* setback.

traversée [travɛrse] *nf* **(a)** crossing *(of sea, desert, street etc)*; going *or* passing through, crossing *(of town etc)*; going *or* passing through *(forest, crowd etc)*; *Nau* **t. agitée**, rough crossing; **faire la t. d'une ville**, to go through *or* pass through *or* cross a town; **la t. en voiture (de)**, driving through; **la t. en avion (de)**, flying across; **(b)** *Pol Fig* **t. du désert**, period spent in the wilderness.

traverser [travɛrse] *vt* **(a)** to cross, to go across *(street, bridge etc)*; to go through, to pass through, to cross *(town etc)*; to cross *(sea, river etc)*; to go through, to pass through *(forest etc)*; *Fig* to go *or* pass through *(danger, crisis etc)*; **t. la foule**, to make one's way *or* go *or* pass through the crowd; **il est arrivé à t. la rivière**, he got across the river; **t. la rivière à la nage/en bateau**, to swim/row across the river; **pont/route qui traverse la rivière**, bridge/road that crosses *or* goes across the river; **une planche traverse le ruisseau**, there is a plank across the stream; **t. une forêt à cheval/à bicyclette/en auto**, to ride/cycle/drive through a forest; **t. un désert en avion**, to fly across a desert; **la balle lui traversa le bras**, the bullet went through his arm; **la pluie avait traversé mon pardessus**, the rain had gone *or* come *or* got through my overcoat; **son nom n'a pas traversé les siècles**, his name has not come down through the ages; **elle traverse une mauvaise période**, she is going through a bad period; **l'idée me traversa l'esprit comme un éclair**, the idea flashed through my mind;

(b) *Arch (contrarier)* to cross, to thwart *(s.o., s.o.'s plans)*.

traversier, -ière [travɛrsje, -jɛr] **1** *adj* **rue traversière**, cross street; *Mus* **flûte traversière**, (transverse) flute. **2** *nm Can (bac)* ferry (boat).

traversin [travɛrsɛ̃] *nm* **(a)** bolster *(for bed)*; **(b)** *Menuis etc* crosspiece; **(c)** *Nau* crosstree.

travesti [travɛsti] **1** *adj* disguised; **bal t.**, fancy-dress ball, costume ball; *Th* **acteur t.**, actor playing a female part; **rôle t.**, female part (for an actor). **2** *nm* **(a)** *Th (acteur)* actor playing a female part; *(rôle)* female part (for an actor); **(b)** *(homosexuel)* transvestite; **(c)** *(déguisement)* fancy dress.

travestir [travɛstir] **1** *vt* **(a)** *(déguiser)* to disguise *(s.o.)* **(en**, as); **(b)** *Littér* to travesty, to parody, to burlesque *(play, poem etc)*; **(c)** *(déformer)* to distort, to misrepresent *(truth, thought etc)*. **2 se travestir** *vpr (pour un bal)* to put on fancy dress; *(en femme)* to dress (up) as a woman.

travestisme [travɛstism] *nm* transvestism.

travestissement [travɛstismɑ̃] *nm* **(a)** *(action)* disguising; **(b)** *(déguisement)* disguise; *Th* **rôle à travestissements**, quick-change part; **(c)** *Littér* travesty *(of play etc)*; **(d)** misrepresentation *(of truth, facts etc)*; **(e)** *(travestisme)* transvestism.

traviole (de) [dətravjɔl] *adv F* crooked; **avec sa cravate de t.**, with his tie crooked; **il comprend tout de t.**, he always gets hold of the wrong end of the stick.

trayeur, -euse [trɛjœr, -øz] **1** *n (personne)* milker. **2** *nf* **trayeuse**, *(machine)* milking machine.

trayon [trɛjɔ̃] *nm* dug, teat *(of cow etc)*.

trébuchant [trebyʃɑ̃] *adj* staggering, stumbling *(gait, drunkard etc)*; stumbling, halting *(diction)*.

trébucher [trebyʃe] **1** *vi* to stumble **(sur**, over; **contre**, against); **marcher en trébuchant**, to stumble *or* stagger along; **faire t. qn**, to trip s.o. up; *Fig* **t. sur les mots étrangers**, to stumble over foreign words. **2** *vt Tech* to test *(coin)* for weight.

trébuchet [trebyʃɛ] *nm* **(a)** *(piège)* bird trap; **(b)** *(petite balance)* assay balance.

tréfilage [trefilaʒ] *nm* wiredrawing.

tréfiler [trefile] *vt* to (wire)draw *(metal)*.

tréfilerie [trefilri] *nf* wireworks.

trèfle [trɛfl] *nm* **(a)** *Bot* clover; **t. blanc**, wild white clover; **t. rouge**, red clover; **t. à quatre feuilles**, four-leaf *or* four-leaved clover; **(b)** *Archit Hér (motif)* trefoil; *Aut* **croisement en t.**, clover-leaf intersection; **(c)** *Cartes (couleur)* clubs; *(carte)* club; **jouer (du) t.**, to play clubs *or* a club; **as/dix de t.**, ace/ten of clubs; **avez-vous du t.?**, do you have any clubs?

tréfonds [trefɔ̃] *nm* **(a)** *Jur* **t. (d'un immeuble)**, ground underneath (a building); **(b)** *Litt* **dans le t. de mon cœur/âme**, in my heart of hearts/in the depths of my soul; **atteint jusqu'au t.**, very deeply hurt.

treillage [trɛjaʒ] *nm* **(a)** trellis (work), lattice work; **(b)** *(clôture)* trellis fencing; **t. métallique** *ou* **en fil de fer**, wire fencing.

treillager [trɛjaʒe] *vt* **(je treillageai(s); n. treillageons)** to trellis *(wall etc)*; to lattice *(window)*; **fenêtre treillagée**, lattice window.

treille [trɛj] *nf* **(a)** *(sur support)* vine arbour, trellised vines; **(b)** *(grimpante)* (climbing) vine; *F* **le jus de la t.**, *(vin)* the juice of the grape.

treillis [trɛji] *nm* **(a)** *(treillage)* trellis (work), lattice; **t. métallique**, wire mesh; **(b)** *Tex* (coarse) canvas; **(c)** *Mil* combat uniform.

treize [trɛz] **1** *adj inv* thirteen; *Com* **t. à la douzaine**, a baker's dozen; **le numéro t.**, number thirteen; **le t. mai**, (on) the thirteenth of May, (on) May the thirteenth, *Am* (on) May thirteenth; **Louis T.**, Louis the Thirteenth; *Sp* **jeu** *ou* **rugby à t.**, Rugby League football. **2** *nm inv* thirteen; **le t. gagne**, number thirteen is the winner; **habiter au t.**, to live at number thirteen.

treizième [trɛzjɛm] **1** *adj & n* thirteenth. **2** *nm (fraction)* thirteenth (part). **3** *nf Mus* thirteenth.

treizièmement [trɛzjɛmmɑ̃] *adv* in the thirteenth place.

trekking [trɛkiŋ] *nm* trek; **faire un t.**, to go on a trek.

tréma [trema] *Ling* **1** *nm* di(a)eresis, *pl* di(a)ereses. **2** *adj inv* **e/i tréma**, e/i di(a)eresis.

trémail [tremaj] *nm Pêche* trammel (net).

tremblant [trɑ̃blɑ̃] *adj* trembling *(knees, hand)*; quivering *(face)*; shaky *(bridge)*; quaking *(ground)*; flickering *(light)*; tremulous *(voice)*; **t. (de peur)**, trembling *or* shaking with fear; **t. de froid**, shivering *or* trembling with cold.

tremble [trɑ̃bl] *nm Bot* aspen.

tremblé [trɑ̃ble] *adj* **(a)** shaky *(handwriting etc)*; wavy *(line)*; **(b)** tremulous, shaky *(voice)*; *Mus* tremolo *(notes)*.

tremblement [trɑ̃bləmɑ̃] *nm* **(a)** trembling, quiver(ing), shaking *(of body, hand, bridge etc)*; tremulousness, quavering *(of voice)*; shuddering *(with horror)*; **(b)** tremor *(of fear, joy, anger)*; **t. de fièvre**, fit of (feverish) shivering; **t. de froid**, shiver(ing); **t. de terre**, earth tremor, *(plus fort)* earthquake; *F* **et tout le t.**, and the whole lot; **(c)** *Mus* tremolo.

trembler [trɑ̃ble] *vi* **(a)** to tremble; *(de froid)* to shiver; *(de colère)* to shake; *(of earth)* to shake, to quake; *(of light)* to flicker; *(of voice)* to tremble, to shake, to quaver; **le pont tremble**, the bridge is shaking; **faire t. les vitres**, to make the windows shake *or* rattle; **la main lui tremblait**, his hand was shaking; **(b)** *(de peur)* to tremble; **t. de tout son corps**, to shake all over; *F* **t. dans sa peau**, to quake *or* shake in one's shoes; **t. devant qn**, to stand in fear of s.o.; **en tremblant**, tremblingly, tremulously; **je tremble de le rencontrer**, I tremble *or* I am terrified at the thought of meeting him; **je tremblais de le réveiller**, I was fearful of awakening him; *Fig* **elle tremble qu'il ne s'en rende compte**, she fears he may not realize it.

trembleur [trɑ̃blœr] *nm Él* trembler, vibrator; *Télécom Tél* buzzer.

tremblotant [trɑ̃blɔtɑ̃] *adj* trembling (slightly); quivering, shivering *(body)*; tremulous *(smile, voice)*; flickering *(light)*.

tremblote [trɑ̃blɔt] *nf F* **avoir la t.**, *(de vieillesse)* to have the shakes; *(de peur)* to have the jitters; *(de froid)* to have the shivers.

tremblotement [trɑ̃blɔtmɑ̃] *nm* trembling; quavering *(of voice)*; flickering *(of light)*.

trembloter [trɑ̃blɔte] *vi* to tremble (slightly); *(of voice)* to quaver, to shake; *(of light)* to flicker; *(of wings)* to flutter.

trémie [tremi] *nf* **(a)** *Ind etc (entonnoir)* hopper; **(b)** *(mangeoire)* feeding box *(for chickens)*; **(c)** *Constr (pour cheminée)* hearth cavity.

trémière [tremjɛr] *adj Bot* **rose t.**, hollyhock.

tremolo, trémolo [tremɔlo] *nm Mus* **(a)** tremolo; *Fig* **avec des trémolos dans la voix**, with a tremor *or* quaver in one's voice; **(b)** tremolo stop *(of organ)*.

trémoussement [tremusmɑ̃] *nm* jigging up and down; *(en se dandinant)* wiggling.

trémousser (se) [sətremuse] *vpr* **(a)** *(remuer)* to jig up and down; **(b)** *(se dandiner)* to wiggle; **marcher en se trémoussant**, to walk with a wiggle; **se t. du derrière**, to wiggle one's behind; **(c)** *(of birds)* to flutter (about).

trempage [trɑ̃paʒ] *nm* soaking.

trempe [trɑ̃p] *nf* **(a)** (*immersion*) soaking, steeping; *Typ* damping (*of paper*); **mettre qch en t.,** to put sth to soak; **(b)** *Métal* (*traitement*) hardening, quench(ing); **t. et revenu,** quenching and hardening; **acier/atelier/***etc* **de t.,** hardening steel/plant/*etc*; **t. à l'air,** air hardening; **t. à l'eau/à l'huile,** water/oil quenching; **t. par cémentation, t. de** *ou* **en surface,** case hardening; **bain de t.,** hardening *or* quenching bath; **(c)** (*dureté*) temper, hardness (*of steel*); **(d)** (*qualité*) calibre; **un homme de sa t.,** a man of his calibre; **(e)** *F* (*volée de coups*) thrashing, hiding.

trempé [trɑ̃pe] *adj* **(a)** (*mouillé*) soaked, drenched; **t. de larmes,** bathed in tears, wet with tears; **t. jusqu'aux os** *ou F* **comme une soupe,** wet through, soaked to the skin; **(b)** *Tech* hardened (*glass*); hardened, tempered (*steel*); *Fig* **bien t.,** resolute (*mind*); *Sp* with plenty of stamina; **(c) vin t.,** wine diluted with water.

tremper [trɑ̃pe] **1** *vt* **(a)** (*mouiller*) to soak, to steep (*in a liquid*); (*plonger*) to dip, to dunk (*bread in soup*); **t. un pied dans l'eau,** to dip a foot in the water; **t. la soupe,** to pour the soup on the bread; **t. sa plume dans l'encre,** to dip one's pen in the ink; **t. ses lèvres dans son verre,** to put one's lips to one's glass; *Typ* **t. le papier,** to wet *or* damp the paper;

(b) *Métal* to harden, to quench (*steel*); to chill (*cast iron*); *Fig* **t. les muscles,** to harden the muscles;

(c) (*diluer*) to mix *or* dilute (*wine*) with water.

2 *vi* (*du linge sale etc*) to (lie in) soak; **mettre les lentilles à t.,** to soak the lentils; **votre ceinture trempe dans la flaque,** your belt is trailing in the puddle; *Fig* **t. dans un complot/une affaire,** to have a hand in *or* to be involved in a plot/an affair.

3 se tremper *vpr* (*se baigner*) to have a quick dip *or Br* bathe; **se t. dans l'eau,** to plunge into the water; **se t. dans l'atmosphère du moyen âge,** to steep oneself in the atmosphere of the Middle Ages.

trempette [trɑ̃pɛt] *nf* **(a) faire t.,** *Culin* to dip *or* dunk one's bread *etc* (*in coffee, wine etc*); (*se baigner*) to have a quick dip *or Br* bathe; **(b)** *Culin Can* dip.

tremplin [trɑ̃plɛ̃] *nm Natation Gym & Fig* springboard; *Ski* ski jump.

trémulation [tremylasjɔ̃] *nf Méd* tremor.

trémuler [tremyle] **1** *vi* to tremble. **2** *vt* **t. les doigts,** to twiddle one's fingers.

trench(-coat) [trɛnʃ(kot)] *nm* trench coat; (*pl trench (-coat)s*).

trentaine [trɑ̃tɛn] *nf* **(a)** (*nombre*) **une t.,** about thirty; **une t. de voitures/d'années/***etc*, about thirty cars/years/*etc*; **une bonne t. (de),** a good thirty; **la t. de livres qu'elle a,** the thirty (or so) books she has; **(b)** (*âge*) **la t.,** (the age of) thirty; **il approche de la t.,** he's getting on for thirty.

trente [trɑ̃t] **1** *adj inv* thirty; **t. jours,** thirty days; **le t. juin,** (on) the thirtieth of June, (on) June the thirtieth, *Am* (on) June thirtieth; **les années t.,** the thirties; *Hist* **la Guerre de T. Ans,** the Thirty Years' War; **t. et un,** thirty-one; *Cartes* (*jeu*) trente et un; *Tennis* **t. à,** thirty all. **2** *nm inv* thirty; **habiter au t.,** to live at number thirty; *F* **se mettre sur son t. et un,** to get dressed *or* dolled up.

trente-six [trɑ̃tsi, -sis, -siz] (*for rules of pronunciation see* **SIX**) **1** *adj inv* thirty-six; *F* (*beaucoup*) umpteen; **voir t.-s. chandelles,** to see stars (*after a blow on the head*); **il n'y va pas par t.-s. chemins,** he doesn't beat about the bush; **il n'y a pas t.-s. façons de le faire,** there are no two ways of doing it. **2** *nm inv* thirty-six; *Fig* **tous les t.-s. du mois,** once in a blue moon.

trente-trois tours [trɑ̃ttrwatur] *nm inv* (*disque*) LP.

trentième [trɑ̃tjɛm] **1** *adj* thirtieth. **2** *n inv* thirtieth. **3** *nm* (*fraction*) thirtieth (part).

trépan [trepɑ̃] *nm Chir Tech* trepan.

trépanation [trepanasjɔ̃] *nf Chir* trepanning.

trépaner [trepane] *vt Chir* to trepan.

trépas [trepɑ] *nm Litt* death; **passer de vie à t.,** to depart this life.

trépassé, -ée [trepɑse] *Litt* **1** *adj* deceased (*person*). **2** *n* deceased person; **les trépassés,** the departed, the deceased; **la fête des Trépassés,** All Souls' Day.

trépasser [trepɑse] *vi Arch & Litt* to die, to depart this life.

trépidant [trepidɑ̃] *adj* vibrating (*machine etc*); hectic (*life*); **vivre à un rythme t.,** to live at a hectic pace.

trépidation [trepidasjɔ̃] *nf* **(a)** vibration (*of machinery, floor etc*); **(b)** trembling (*of limbs*); **(c)** bustle, flurry (*of life etc*).

trépider [trepide] *vi* (*of machine, floor etc*) to vibrate.

trépied [trepje] *nm* **(a)** (*tabouret*) three-legged stool; **(b)** *Culin* trivet; **(c)** (*support*) tripod, three-legged stand.

trépignement [trepiɲmɑ̃] *nm* stamping (of feet).

trépigner [trepiɲe] **1** *vi* to stamp (one's feet); **t. de colère/d'enthousiasme,** to stamp (one's feet) with rage/enthusiasm; *Fig* **il trépignait de partir,** he was itching to start. **2** *vt* to trample *or* stamp on.

trépointe [trepwɛ̃t] *nf* welt (*of shoe*).

tréponème [trepɔnɛm] *nm Biol* treponema.

très [trɛ] ([trɛz] *before vowel or mute h*) *adv* very, most; **t. bon,** very good; (*généreux*) very *or* most kind; **t. connu,** very well known; **t. différent,** very different; **t. estimé,** much *or* highly esteemed; **t. aimé,** much *or* greatly liked; **t. vite,** very quickly; **elle est t. femme,** she is very feminine; **prendre qch t. au sérieux,** to take sth very seriously; *F* **avoir t. faim/soif/peur,** to be very hungry/thirsty/scared *or* very much afraid; **ces robes sont t. portées,** these dresses are very fashionable *or* very much in fashion; **content?— oui, t.!,** satisfied? — yes, very (much)!; **ça t'a plu? — non, pas t.,** did you like it? — no, not (very) much.

trésor [trezɔr] *nm* **(a)** (*choses précieuses*) treasure; *Jur* treasure-trove; *F* **ma bonne est un t.,** my maid is a treasure; *F* **mon t.,** darling; **(b)** *Rel* (collection of) relics and ornaments; **(c)** (*endroit*) treasure house; **(d) trésors,** (*richesses*) treasures; *Fig Hum* (*jouets, bibelots etc*) treasures; *Fig* **déployer des trésors d'imagination,** to display limitless *or* a wealth of imagination; **(e) le T. (public),** (*service*) public revenue (department); (*finances*) public funds; **(f) ce livre est un t. de faits,** the book is a treasure house *or* mine of information.

trésorerie [trezɔrri] *nf* **(a)** (*fonction*) treasurership; **(b)** (*bureau*) accounts department, treasurer's office; **(c)** (*fonds*) funds, finances; **(d)** (*gestion*) accounting.

trésorier, -ière [trezɔrje, -jɛr] *n* treasurer; *Admin* **t. (-payeur) général,** chief treasurer and paymaster (*of a département*); **commis t.,** treasury clerk; *Mil* **officier t.,** paymaster.

tressage [trɛsaʒ] *nm* plaiting (*of hair, straw etc*); weaving (*of basket, garland*).

tressaillement [tresajmɑ̃] *nm* start (*of surprise*); shudder (*of fear*); wince (*of pain*).

tressaillir [tresajir] *vi* (*prp* **tressaillant**; *pp* **tressailli**; *pr ind* **je tressaille, n. tressaillons, ils tressaillent**; *impf* **je tressaillais**; *p hist* **je tressaillis**; *fu* **je tressaillirai**) to start (*from surprise*); to shudder (*with fear*); to leap (*with joy*); (*of heart*) to flutter; **t. (de douleur),** to wince.

tressautement [tresotmɑ̃] *nm* **(a)** start, jump (*of fear, surprise etc*); **(b)** (*secousse*) jolt.

tressauter [tresote] *vi* **(a)** to start, to jump (*with fear, surprise etc*); **(b)** (*être secoué*) to be jolted about.

tresse [trɛs] *nf* **(a)** plait (*of hair*); braid (*of yarn etc*); **t. de coton,** cotton tape; *Él* **fil conducteur sous t.,** braided conductor wire; **(b)** *Archit* (*motif*) strap work.

tressé [trese] *adj Minér* having interlaced fibres.

tresser [trese] *vt* to plait (*hair, straw etc*); to weave (*basket, garland*); *Fig* **t. des couronnes à qn,** to praise s.o. to the skies.

tréteau, -eaux [treto] *nm* **(a)** (*support*) trestle; **table à tréteaux,** trestle table; **(b)** *Th* **les tréteaux,** the boards, the stage; *Fig* **monter sur les tréteaux,** to tread the boards, to go on the stage.

treuil [trœj] *nm Tech* winch, windlass, winding drum; (*d'ascenseur*) winding gear; **t. à chaîne,** chain hoist.

treuillage [trœjaʒ] *nm* winching (up).

treuiller [trœje] *vt* to winch (up).

trêve [trɛv] *nf* **(a)** (*amnistie*) truce; *Hist* **la t. de Dieu,** the truce of God; *Pol F* **t. des confiseurs,** Christmas *or* New Year truce; **(b)** *Fig* (*pause, arrêt*) respite, rest; *F* **t. de bêtises** *ou* **de plaisanteries!,** that's enough *or* no more of your nonsense!; **il ne me laisse pas de t.,** he doesn't give me a moment's peace; **sans t.,** unceasingly.

tri [tri] *nm* sorting (out); sorting (*of letters*); classifying (*of skills etc*); selection (*of candidates etc*); *Ordinat* sort; **faire le t. de,** to sort out; **on ne peut pas tous les garder, il va falloir faire le t.,** we can't keep them all, we'll have to sort some *or* them out; *Rail etc* **bureau de t.,** sorting office; *Ordinat* **effectuer un t.,** to do a sort.

triacide [triasid] *nm Ch* triacid.

triade [trijad] *nf* triad.

triage [trijaʒ] *nm* **(a)** sorting (*of coal, letters, ores etc*); *Rail* marshalling; *Rail* **gare de t.,** marshalling yard; *Rail* **voie de t.,** siding; *Mil* **hôpital de t.,** clearing hospital; **(b)** (*en choisissant*) selecting, picking out, sorting.

trial [trijal] *nm* (*pl trials*) *Sp* **(a)** (*épreuve*) motocross, *Br* (*motorcycle*) scrambling; **(b)** (*moto*) motocross *or Br* scrambling bike.

triangle [trijɑ̃gl] *nm* **(a)** *Géom* triangle; **en t.,** triangular (*face, scarf etc*); *F* **l'éternel t.,** the eternal triangle; **(b)** *Nau* (*pavillon*) triangular flag; **(c)** *Mus* triangle.
triangulaire [trijɑ̃gylɛr] *adj* triangular; *Pol* three-cornered (*election, fight*); **relation t.,** triangular relationship.
triangulation [trijɑ̃gylɑsjɔ̃] *nf* (*en arpentage*) triangulation.
trianguler [trijɑ̃gyle] *vt* (*en arpentage*) to triangulate.
trias [trijɑs] *nm Géol* (*période*) Trias, Triassic.
triasique [trijazik] *adj Géol* Triassic.
triathlon [tr(j)atlɔ̃] *nm Sp* triathlon.
triatomique [triatɔmik] *adj Ch* triatomic.
tribal, -aux [tribal, -o] *adj* tribal.
tribalisme [tribalism] *nm* tribalism.
tribo-électricité [tribelɛktrisite] *nf* triboelectricity.
tribo-électrique [tribɔelɛktrik] *adj* triboelectric.
tribologie [tribɔlɔʒi] *nf* tribology.
tribord [tribɔr] *nm Nau* starboard (side); **à t.,** on the starboard side, to starboard.
tribu [triby] *nf* tribe; *Fig F* (*famille, groupe etc*) tribe.
tribulations [tribylɑsjɔ̃] *nfpl* tribulations, troubles.
tribun [tribœ̃] *nm* **(a)** *Antiq* (*officier*) tribune; **(b)** (*orateur*) popular orator.
tribunal, -aux [tribynal, -o] *nm Jur* court; **en plein t.,** in open court; **t. civil/criminel,** civil/criminal court; **t. d'instance,** = trial court, court of first instance; *Eng* ≈ magistrates' court, *Scot & US* ≈ district court; **t. de grande instance,** = court presided over by three judges, authorized to try more serious cases; *Eng* ≈ Crown court; **t. pour enfants et adolescents,** juvenile court; **t. militaire,** military tribunal; **porter une affaire devant le t.,** to bring a case before the court; **prendre la voie des tribunaux,** to take legal action; *Fig* **le t. de l'opinion publique,** the bar of public opinion; *Nau* **t. de prise,** prize court.
tribunat [tribyna] *nm Hist* tribunate.
tribune [tribyn] *nf* **(a)** (*débat*) forum, discussion, debate; **t. libre d'un journal,** opinion column of a newspaper; **(b)** (*d'orateur*) tribune, rostrum, (speaker's) platform; *Parl* **monter à la t.,** to address the House; **(c)** (*galerie*) gallery; **t. de la presse,** press gallery; **(d)** *Sp* **t. (d'honneur),** (grand)stand; **(e)** *Mus* **t. d'orgues,** organ loft.
tribut [triby] *nm* **(a)** *Hist* (*contribution*) tribute, tribute-money; **payer t.,** to pay tribute; **(b)** *Arch & Litt* (*impôt*) duty, tax; **(c)** *Fig* **apporter son t. d'éloges,** to bring *or* offer one's tribute of praise; **t. légitime,** fair reward (*for one's labour*).
tributaire [tribytɛr] *adj* **(a)** *Hist* (*qui paie tribut*) tributary; **(b)** (*dépendant*) **être t. de,** to be dependent (up)on (*foreign supplies etc*); **(c) rivière t.,** tributary.
tric [trik] *nm* (*au bridge*) odd trick.
tricentenaire [trisɑ̃tnɛr] *nm* tercentenary, tricentennial.
tricéphale [trisefal] *adj* three-headed (*monster*).
triceps [trisɛps] *adj & nm Anat* **(muscle) t.,** triceps (muscle).
triche [triʃ] *nf F* cheating.
tricher [triʃe] *vi* to cheat (**sur,** over); (*mentir*) to lie (**sur,** about); (*pour dissimuler un défaut*) to cheat a bit, to fiddle it; **elle triche aux cartes,** she cheats at cards; **t. à un examen,** to cheat in an exam.
tricherie [triʃri] *nf* cheating.
tricheur, -euse [triʃœr, -øz] *n* cheat.
trichine [trikin] *nf* (*ver*) trichina, threadworm.
trichinose [trikinoz] *nf Méd* trichinosis.
trichloréthylène [triklɔretilɛn] *nm* trichlorethlyene.
trichoma [trikɔma] *nm,* **trichome** [trikom] *nm Méd* plica.
trichrome [trikrom] *adj Br* three-colour, *US* -color, trichromatic (*photography etc*).
trichromie [trikrɔmi] *nf Phot etc* three-colour *or US* -color process.
trick [trik] *nm* (*au bridge*) odd trick.
tricolore [trikɔlɔr] **1** *adj* three-coloured, *US* three-colored; (*bleu, blanc et rouge*) red, white and blue; **le drapeau t.,** the French flag, the Tricolour, *US* the Tricolor; *Admin* **feux tricolores,** traffic lights *or* signals; *Sp* **l'équipe t.,** the French team. **2** *nmpl Sp* **les tricolores,** the French team.
tricorne [trikɔrn] *nm* three-cornered hat, tricorn.
tricot [triko] *nm* **(a)** (*activité*) knitting; **faire du t.,** to do some knitting; **(b)** (*ouvrage*) knitting; *Com* knitwear; **un t.,** a piece of knitting; **(c)** (*chandail*) sweater, *Br* jumper, *F* woolly; **t. de corps,** *Br* vest, *Am* undershirt; **(d)** (*tissu*) knitted fabric; **jupe en t.,** knitted shirt.
tricotage [trikɔtaʒ] *nm* knitting.
tricoter [trikɔte] **1** *vt* to knit; **aiguilles à t.,** knitting needles; **machine à t.,** knitting machine; **tricoté main,** hand-knitted. **2** *vi* to knit; *Arg* **t. des jambes,** (*s'enfuir*) to make off, to scram; (*pédaler*) to pedal like mad.
tricoteur, -euse [trikɔtœr, -øz] **1** *n* (*personne*) knitter. **2** *nf* **tricoteuse,** (*machine*) knitting machine.
trictrac [triktrak] *nm* (*jeu*) backgammon; (*partie*) game of backgammon; (*damier*) backgammon board.
tricuspide [trikyspid] *adj Anat* tricuspid (*valve*).
tricycle [trisikl] **1** *adj Av* three-wheeled (*undercarriage*). **2** *nm* tricycle.
trident [tridɑ̃] *nm* **(a)** *Myth* trident; **(b)** *Pêche* fish spear; **(c)** *Agr* three-pronged (pitch)fork.
tridimensionnel, -elle [tridimɑ̃sjɔnɛl] *adj* three-dimensional.
trièdre [triɛdr] *Géom* **1** *adj* trihedral. **2** *nm* trihedron.
triennal, -aux [triɛnal, -o] *adj* triennial, three-yearly (*festival, election etc*); appointed for three years (*president etc*); three-year (*plan, appointment, Agr rotation*).
triennat [triɛna] *nm* three-year period of office.
trier [trije] *vt* (*impf & pr sub* **n. triions, v. triiez**) **(a)** (*classer*) to sort (*letters, ore etc*); to go through (*one's wardrobe*); *Tex* to pick (*wool*); *Ordinat* to sort; *Rail* to marshall; **(b)** (*en choisissant*) to sort out, to pick out, to select; **t. à la main,** to hand-pick; **candidats triés sur le volet,** hand-picked candidates.
trière [trijɛr] *nf Hist Nau* trireme.
trieur, -euse [trijœr, -øz] **1** *n* (*personne*) sorter (*of letters etc*); *Tex* picker (*of wool*). **2** *nm Ind* (*appareil*) grader. **3** *nf* **trieuse,** (*machine*) sorter, sorting machine.
trieur-calibreur [trijœrkalibrœr] *nm Ind* grading machine; (*pl trieurs-calibreurs*).
trifolié [trifɔlje] *adj Bot* trifoliate, three-leaved.
trifouiller [trifuje] *F* **1** *vt* to rummage (around) in (*s.o.'s papers etc*). **2** *vi* to rummage (around) (**dans,** in).
trigonométrie [trigɔnɔmetri] *nf* trigonometry.
trigonométrique [trigɔnɔmetrik] *adj* trigonometric(al).
trijumeau [triʒymo] *adj m & nm Anat* **(nerf) t.,** trigeminal nerve.
trilingue [trilɛ̃g] *adj* trilingual (*person, dictionary etc*).
trille [trij] *nm Mus* trill.
triller [trije] *vt & vi Mus* to trill.
trillion [triljɔ̃] *nm* (10^{18}) trillion, *Am* quintillion.
trilobé [trilɔbe] *adj* **(a)** *Archit* trefoil (*arch etc*); **(b)** *Bot* trilobate.
trilobite [trilɔbit] *nm* (*fossile*) trilobite.
trilogie [trilɔʒi] *nf Littér* trilogy.
trimaran [trimarɑ̃] *nm Nau* trimaran.
trimarder [trimarde] *vi Arg* to be on the road.
trimardeur [trimardœr] *nm Arg* tramp, *US* hobo.
trimbal(l)age [trɛ̃balaʒ] *nm,* **trimbal(l)ement** [trɛ̃balmɑ̃] *nm F* lugging *or* carting around (*of parcels etc*); trailing around (*of children etc*).
trimbal(l)er [trɛ̃bale] *F* **1** *vt* to lug *or* cart (*parcels etc*) around; to trail (*children etc*) around; *Arg* **qu'est ce qu'il trimbale!,** (*qu'est-ce qu'il est bête*) what an idiot (he is)! **2 se trimballer** *vpr* **se t. jusqu'à la gare,** to trail *or US Sl* schlep over to the station; **je ne vais pas me t. en ville,** I'm not trailing *or US Sl* schlepping into town.
trimer [trime] *vi F* (*travailler dur*) to slave away; **faire t. qn,** to keep s.o. at it.
trimestre [trimɛstr] *nm* **(a)** (*trois mois*) quarter; *Scol* term; **par t.,** quarterly; *Scol* every term; **(b)** (*salaire*) quarter's salary; (*loyer*) quarter's rent; *Scol* (*frais*) term fees.
trimestriel, -elle [trimɛstrijɛl] *adj* quarterly; *Scol* end-of-term (*report*); **fonction trimestrielle,** position lasting for three months.
trimestriellement [trimɛstrijɛlmɑ̃] *adv* quarterly; *Scol* once a term.
trimètre [trimɛtr] *nm* (*vers*) trimeter.
trimoteur [trimɔtœr] *nm* three-engined plane.
tringle [trɛ̃gl] *nf* **(a)** (*barre*) rod; **t. à rideau,** curtain rod; **t. d'escalier,** stair rod; **(b)** (*de commande*) control rod; *Rail* switch bar (*of points*); **(c)** *Archit* (*moulure*) square moulding.
tringler [trɛ̃gle] *vt* **(a)** *Tech* to mark with a line (*using chalked string*); **(b)** *Vulg* (*sexuellement*) to screw, to lay (*woman*); **se faire t.,** to get laid.
trinitaire [trinitɛr] *adj & n Rel* Trinitarian.
trinité [trinite] *nf* **(a)** *Rel* **la (Sainte) T.,** the (Holy) Trinity; **la T.,** (*fête*) Trinity Sunday; **(b) (île de) la T.,** Trinidad; **(c)** (*groupe de trois éléments*) trinity.
trinitrotoluène [trinitrɔtɔlyɛn] *nm* trinitrotoluene, T.N.T..
trinôme [trinom] *nm Math* trinomial.

trinquer [trɛ̃ke] *vi* **(a)** (*porter un toast*) to clink glasses; **t. à qn/qch,** to drink to s.o./sth; **(b)** *F* (*boire avec excès*) to booze; **(c)** (*se cogner*) to bang about, to knock together; **(d)** *F* (*subir un désagrément*) to get the worst of it.
trinquet [trɛ̃kɛ] *nm Nau* foremast.
trinquette [trɛ̃kɛt] *nf Nau* storm jib.
trio [trijo] *nm* threesome, trio; *Mus* trio.
triode [triɔd] *adj & nf Electron Rad* triode.
triolet [trijɔlɛ] *nm* **(a)** *Mus* triplet; **(b)** *Littér* triolet.
triomphal, -aux [trijɔ̃fal, -ol] *adj* triumphal.
triomphalement [trijɔ̃falmɑ̃] *adv* triumphantly.
triomphalisme [trijɔ̃falism] *nm* triumphalism.
triomphaliste [trijɔ̃falist] *adj & n* (person) certain of victory.
triomphant [trijɔ̃fɑ̃] *adj* triumphant (*general, air etc*).
triomphateur, -trice [trijɔ̃fatœr, -tris] **1** *adj* triumphant, victorious. **2** *n* (*vainqueur*) victor. **3** *nm Antiq* conquering hero.
triomphe [trijɔ̃f] *nm* triumph (**sur,** over) **le t. de la justice,** the triumph of justice; **faire un t. à qn,** to give s.o. an ovation; **arc de t.,** triumphal arch; **porter qn en t.,** to carry s.o. in trumph; **sourire/cri de t.,** smile/cry of triumph, triumphant smile/cry; **(d)** (*succès*) triumph.
triompher [trijɔ̃fe] *vi* **(a)** (*l'emporter*) to triumph (**de,** over); **(b)** (*exceller*) to excel (**dans,** in); (*avoir un grand succès*) to triumph; **(c)** (*exulter*) to rejoice, to exult.
trioxyde [triɔksid] *nm Ch* trioxide.
trip [trip] *nm* **(a)** (*de drogue*) trip; **t. d'acide,** acid trip; **(b)** *F* **c'est pas mon t.,** (*ça ne m'intéresse pas*) it's not my thing; **son t., c'est le jazz,** jazz is his thing; **il est dans son t. d'écolo,** he's on his environmental kick.
tripaille [tripaj] *nf F* (*intestins*) guts.
triparti [triparti] *adj* tripartite.
tripartisme [tripartism] *nm* three-party government.
tripartite [tripartit] *adj* tripartite.
tripatouillage [tripatujaʒ] *nm F* tampering *or* fiddling with (*text, accounts*).
tripatouiller [tripatuje] *vt F* to tamper *or* fiddle with (*text, accounts etc*).
tripatouilleur, -euse [tripatujœr, -øz] *n F* fiddler, tamperer.
tripe [trip] *nf* **(a) tripes,** entrails (*of animal*); *Culin* tripe; *Arg* guts (*of person*); **une histoire qui vous prend aux tripes,** a story that gets you in the guts; **parler avec ses tripes,** to speak from the heart; **rendre tripes et boyaux,** to spew one's guts out; **elle a des tripes,** she's got guts; **(b)** *Fig F* **avoir la t. républicaine,** to be an out-and-out republican; **(c)** core, filling (*of cigar*); **(d) peau en t.,** pelt.
triperie [tripri] *nf* **(a)** (*boutique*) tripe shop; **(b)** (*commerce*) tripe trade.
tripette [tripɛt] *nf F* **ne pas valoir t.,** to be utterly worthless.
triphasé [trifaze] *Él* **1** *adj* three-phase. **2** *nm* three-phase current; **installation en t.,** three-phase wiring.
triphtongue [triftɔ̃g] *nf Ling* triphthong.
tripier, -ière [tripje, -jɛr] *n* tripe butcher.
triplace [triplas] *adj Av* three-seater.
triplan [triplɑ̃] *nm Av* triplane.
triple [tripl] **1** *adj* **(a)** triple; (*trois fois plus grand*) treble, triple, threefold; **t. menton,** triple chin; **plié en t.,** folded in three; **en t. exemplaire,** in triplicate; **au t. galop,** at breakneck speed; *Mus* **t. croche,** demisemiquaver, *Am* thirty-second note; *Ch* **sel t.,** triple salt; *Astron* **étoile t.,** triple star; **(b)** (*emploi intensif*) **un t. sot,** a prize idiot. **2** *nm* **le t.,** three times as much (**de,** as); **douze est le t. de quatre,** twelve is three times four.
triplé, -ée [triple] **1** *n* triplet. **2** *nm Sp* (*triple succès*) triple success; *Courses de chevaux* (*pari*) = bet on winning horses in three races.
triplement¹ [tripləmɑ̃] *adv* trebly, triply, threefold; **elle a t. raison,** she is right in three ways.
triplement² *nm* trebling, tripling.
tripler [triple] *vt & vi* to treble, to triple, to increase threefold.
triplette [triplɛt] *nf* (*aux boules*) threesome, team of three.
triplex ® [triplɛks] *nm* (*verre*) laminated safety glass, *Br* Triplex ®.
tripode [tripɔd] *adj Nau* tripod (*mast*).
triporteur [tripɔrtœr] *nm* delivery tricycle.
tripot [tripo] *nm* gambling-den.
tripotage [tripɔtaʒ] *nm F* **(a)** fiddling (around) (**de,** with); **(b) tripotages,** (*magouilles*) shady dealings; **tripotages électoraux,** election fiddles.
tripotée [tripɔte] *nf Arg* **(a)** (*râclée*) thrashing, hiding; **(b)** (*grand nombre*) **une t. de,** loads of, lots of.
tripoter [tripɔte] *F* **1** *vi* **(a)** to mess about (*in the water*); to rummage (*in a drawer etc*); **(b)** (*magouiller*) to engage in shady business; **t. dans la caisse,** to tamper with the cash. **2** *vt* **(a)** to fiddle (around) with (*object, one's hair etc*); *Péj* **t. qn,** to paw *or* grope s.o., to touch s.o. up; **(b)** to deal shadily with (*money etc*).
tripoteur,-euse [tripɔtœr,-øz] **1** *n* (*magouilleur*) shady dealer. **2** *adj* groping (*hands*).
triptyque [triptik] *nm* **(a)** *Beaux-Arts Littér Mus* triptych; **(b)** *Aut Admin* triptyque.
trique [trik] *nf F* cudgel, heavy stick; **avoir recours à la t.,** to use the big stick; **maigre comme une t.,** as thin as a rake.
triquet [trikɛ] *nm* (*échelle*) pair of steps.
trirème [trirɛm] *nf Hist Nau* trireme.
trisaïeul, -euls *ou* **eux** [trizajœl, -ø] *nm* great-great-grandfather; **trisaïeuls, trisaïeux,** great-great-grand-parents.
trisaïeule [trizajœl] *nf* great-great-grandmother.
trisannuel, -elle [trizanɥɛl] *adj* triennial.
trisection [trisɛksjɔ̃] *nf Géom* trisection.
trisomie [trizɔmi] *nf Méd* trisomy; **t. 21,** trisomy 21.
trisser (se) [sətrise] *vpr Arg* (*s'enfuir*) to scram, to beat it.
trissyllabe [trisilab] **1** *nm* trisyllable. **2** *adj* trisyllabic.
triste [trist] **1** *adj* **(a)** (*malheureux*) sad (*person*); sad, sorrowful (*face, news etc*); **tout t.,** (very) dejected, in low spirits; **sourire t.,** sad *or* wan smile; **je fus (bien) t. d'apprendre que ...,** I was (very) sorry to hear that ...; **avoir le vin t.,** not to be a happy drunk; *F* **c'est tout de même t.!,** isn't it pathetic!; *F* **c'était vraiment pas t.,** it was really funny;

(b) dreary, dismal, gloomy (*life, weather, colour, room etc*); bleak, depressing (*countryside*); gloomy, miserable (*person*); **faire t. mine à qn,** to receive s.o. without enthusiasm;

(c) (*douloureux*) sad, unfortunate, painful (*news, duty, state*); sad (*occasion*); **c'est la t. réalité,** it is a sad *or* painful reality; **c'est une t. affaire,** it's a sorry *or* bad business;

(d) (*before noun*) (*médiocre*) poor, sorry, wretched (*meal, excuse etc*); **(quelle) t. époque!,** what terrible times we live in!

2 *n* (*personne sombre*) gloomy *or* miserable person.
tristement [tristəmɑ̃] *adv* **(a)** (*avec tristesse*) sadly, sorrowfully; **(b)** (*d'une façon sombre*) gloomily; **(c)** (*cruellement*) sadly (*true etc*); **t. célèbre,** notorious.
tristesse [tristɛs] *nf* **(a)** sadness (*of person*); **joie mêlée de t.,** joy tinged with sadness; **avec t.,** sadly; **(b)** dreariness, gloominess (*of a room etc*); bleakness (*of landscape*); **(c) tristesses,** (*moments*) sorrows (*of life etc*).
tristounet, -ette [tristunɛ, -ɛt] *adj F* dreary, gloomy (*room, colour etc*); gloomy (*person*).
trisyllabe [trisilab] **1** *nm* trisyllable. **2** *adj* trisyllabic.
tritium [tritjɔm] *nm Ch* tritium.
triton¹ [tritɔ̃] *nm* **(a)** *Myth* **T.,** Triton; **(b)** (*amphibien*) triton newt; **(c)** (*mollusque*) trumpet shell, triton.
triton² *nm Mus* tritone, augmented fourth.
trituration [trityrasjɔ̃] *nf* (*broyage*) grinding, *Spéc* trituration.
triturer [trityre] **1** *vt* **(a)** (*broyer*) to grind, *Spéc* to triturate; **(b)** (*mastiquer*) to masticate; **(c)** (*manier*) to manipulate. **2 se triturer** *vpr F* **se t. la cervelle** *ou* **les méninges,** to rack one's brains.
triumvir [trijɔmvir] *nm Antiq* triumvir.
triumvirat [trijɔmvira] *nm Antiq* triumvirate.
trivalent [trivalɑ̃] *adj Ch* trivalent.
trivalve [trivalv] *adj Biol* trivalvular, trivalve.
trivial, -iaux [trivjal, -jo] *adj* **(a)** (*vulgaire*) vulgar, coarse (*expression etc*); **(b)** (*commun*) trite, mundane; *Math etc* self-evident, obvious (*solution*).
trivialement [trivjalmɑ̃] *adv* (*vulgairement*) vulgarly, coarsely.
trivialité [trivjalite] *nf* **(a)** (*vulgarité*) vulgarity, coarseness; **(b)** (*expression*) vulgar *or* coarse expression.
troc [trɔk] *nm* exchange (in kind); (*système économique*) barter; **économie de t.,** barter economy; **faire du t.,** to barter; **faire un t.,** to make an exchange (**avec qn,** with s.o.).
trochaïque [trɔkaik] *adj & nm Littér* trochaic.
trochée [trɔʃe] *nm Littér* trochee.
troène [trɔɛn] *nm Bot* privet.
troglodyte [trɔglɔdit] *nm* **(a)** (*personne*) troglodyte, cave dweller; **(b)** (*oiseau*) wren.
troglodytique [trɔglɔditik] *adj* **habitation t.,** cave

dwelling.

trogne [trɔɲ] *nf F* (boozy) face.

trognon [trɔɲɔ̃] **1** *nm* **(a)** core (*of apple etc*); stump (*of cabbage etc*); *F* **jusqu'au t.,** (*jusqu'au bout*) to the (bitter) end; (*complètement*) completely; **(b)** *F* (*terme d'affection*) poppet, sweetie. **2** *adj inv F* (*mignon*) sweet.

Troie [trwa] *n* Troy; **guerre/cheval de T.,** Trojan War/horse.

troïka [trɔika] *nf* (*traîneau, triumvirat*) troika.

trois [trwa] ([trwaz] *before a vowel sound or mute h in the same word group*) **1** *adj inv* three; **à t. heures,** at three o'clock; **les t. quarts du temps,** most of the time; **couper** *ou* **diviser une ligne/un angle en t.,** to trisect a line/an angle; **partager la somme en t.,** to divide the sum into three; **entrer par t.,** to come in in threes *or* three at a time; **ménage à t.,** ménage à trois; **Henri T.,** Henry the Third. **2** *nm inv* three; **le t. août,** (on) the third of August, (on) August the third, *Am* (on) August third; **t. de carreau,** three of diamonds; **j'habite au t.,** I live at number three.

trois étoiles [trwazetwal] *nm inv* three-star hotel.

trois-huit [trwaɥit] *nm inv* **(a)** *Mus* three-eight time; **(b)** *Ind* **régime des t.-h.,** three-shift working; **faire les t.-h.,** to operate three shifts (*of eight hours each*).

troisième [trwazjɛm] **1** *adj* third; **au t. étage,** on the third *or Am* fourth floor; **de t. ordre,** third-rate; *Écon* **personnes du t. âge,** senior citizens. **2** *n* (*personne, chose etc*) third; **habiter au t.,** to live on the third *or Am* fourth floor. **3** *nm* (*fraction*) **deux troisièmes,** two thirds. **4** *nf* **(a)** *Scol* **(classe de) t.,** *Br* ≈ fourth form, *Am* ≈ eighth grade; **(b)** *Aut* third (gear); **en t.,** in third (gear); **passer la t.,** to go (up *or* down) into third (gear).

troisièmement [trwazjɛmmɑ̃] *adv* thirdly, in the third place.

trois-mâts [trwamɑ] *nm inv Nau* three-masted ship, three-master.

trois-pièces [trwapjɛs] *nm inv* **(a)** (*appartement*) three-room(ed) *Br* flat *or Am* apartment; **(b)** (*costume*) three-piece suit.

trois-quarts [trwakar] *nm inv* **(a)** (*violon*) three-quarter violin; **(b)** *Rugby* three-quarter; **t.-q. aile/centre,** wing/centre three-quarter; **t.-q. arrière,** three quarter back; **(c)** (*manteau*) three-quarter-length coat.

trois-quatre [trwakatr] *nm inv Mus* three-four time.

trois-six [trwasis] *nm* proof spirit.

troll [trɔl] *nm Myth* troll.

trolley [trɔlɛ] *nm* **(a)** (*caténaire*) trolley pole and wheel; **perche de t.,** trolley pole; **(b)** (*véhicule*) trolleybus.

trolleybus [trɔlɛbys] *nm* trolleybus.

trombe [trɔ̃b] *nf* **(a)** (*cyclone*) waterspout; **(b) t. de vent,** whirlwind; **t. d'eau,** cloudburst; **(c)** *F* **entrer/sortir en t.,** to burst in/out (like a whirlwind).

trombine [trɔ̃bin] *nf Arg* **(a)** (*tête*) nut; **(b)** (*visage*) mug.

tromblon [trɔ̃blɔ̃] *nm* **(a)** *Hist* (*fusil*) blunderbuss; **(b)** *Mil* grenade sleeve (*fitted to rifle*).

trombone [trɔ̃bɔn] *nm* **(a)** *Mus* (*instrument*) trombone; (*instrumentiste*) trombone (player); **(b)** (*agrafe*) paper clip.

trompe [trɔ̃p] *nf* **(a)** *Mus* horn; **t. de brume/chasse,** fog/hunting horn; *Fig* **publier qch à son de t.,** to trumpet sth abroad; **(b)** *Zool* proboscis (*of animal, insect*); trunk (*of elephant*); **(c)** *Anat* **t. d'Eustache/de Fallope,** Eustachian/Fallopian tube; **(d)** *Archit* pendentive, squinch; **(e)** *Tech* pump; *Métal* blast pump, trompe.

trompe-la-mort [trɔ̃plamɔr] *n inv F* death dodger; (*volontaire*) daredevil.

trompe-l'œil [trɔ̃plœj] *nm inv* **(a)** *Beaux-Arts* trompe l'œil (painting); **en t.-l'o.,** trompe l'œil (*painting, scenery etc*); **(b)** *Fig Péj* bluff, window-dressing.

tromper [trɔ̃pe] **1** *vt* **(a)** (*abuser*) to deceive, to take in (*s.o.*); **il est incapable de t.,** he is incapable of deception;

(b) (*être infidèle à*) to deceive, to be unfaithful to (*wife, husband*); **t. une jeune fille,** to ruin a girl;

(c) (*induire en erreur*) to mislead (*s.o.*) (**sur,** as to); to disappoint (*s.o.'s hopes*);

(d) (*échapper à*) to outwit, to elude (*s.o.*); **t. la vigilance de ses gardiens,** to elude the vigilance of one's guards;

(e) *Fig* to relieve (*tedium*); to while away (*the time*); **t. la faim,** to stave off (one's) hunger.

2 se tromper *vpr* (*faire une erreur*) to be mistaken, to be wrong, to make a mistake; **si je ne me trompe,** if I am not mistaken; **ou je me trompe,** or I'm much mistaken; **se t. dans son calcul,** to be out in one's reckoning; *Tél* **vous devez vous t. de numéro,** you must have the wrong number; **je me suis trompé de direction/de maison,** I went the wrong way/to the wrong house; **se t. d'heure/de jour,** to mistake the time/day; **elle ressemble à sa sœur à s'y t.,** you can't tell her and her sister apart; **il n'y a pas à s'y t.,** there is no mistake about it; **que l'on ne s'y trompe pas,** let there be no misunderstanding about it; **vous m'avez fait (me) t.,** you made me make a mistake.

tromperie [trɔ̃pri] *nf* deceit, deception, fraud.

trompeter [trɔ̃p(ə)te] *vt* (**je trompette, je trompetterai**) to trumpet abroad, to shout (*news*) from the rooftops.

trompette [trɔ̃pɛt] **1** *nf* **(a)** *Mus* trumpet; *Mil* **jouer/sonner de la t.,** to play/sound the trumpet; **t. de jazz,** jazz trumpet; **à la t., Louis Armstrong!,** on the trumpet, Louis Armstrong!; *Litt* **la t. du jugement dernier,** the last trump; **nez en t.,** turned-up nose; **(b)** (*coquillage*) trumpet shell; **(c)** (*poisson*) pipe fish. **2** *nm* trumpet (player), trumpeter.

trompette-de-la-mort [trɔ̃pɛtdəlamɔr] *nf* (*champignon*) horn of plenty; (*pl trompettes-de-la-mort*).

trompettiste [trɔ̃pɛtist] *n Mus* trumpet (player), trumpeter.

trompeur, -euse [trɔ̃pœr, -øz] **1** *adj* **(a)** deceitful (*person, words etc*); **(b)** deceptive, misleading (*appearance, symptom etc*). **2** *n* deceiver.

trompeusement [trɔ̃pøzmɑ̃] *adv* deceptively.

tronc [trɔ̃] *nm* **(a)** trunk (*of tree, body*); *Archit* drum (*of column*); *Anat* trunk, main stem (*of artery etc*); **homme/femme-t.,** armless and legless man/woman; **(b)** parent stock (*of family*); **(c) t. pour les pauvres,** poor-box, almsbox; **(d)** *Math* **t. de cône,** truncated cone; **(e)** *Univ etc* **t. commun,** foundation course.

tronche [trɔ̃ʃ] *nf* **(a)** (*arbre*) stem-pruned tree; **(b)** *Arg* (*tête*) nut; (*visage*) mug.

tronçon [trɔ̃sɔ̃] *nm* **(a)** section, length (*of pipe etc*); (broken) stump (*of sword, lance, mast etc*); **t. de bois,** log; **(b)** section (*of railway etc*); **(c)** part, fragment (*of sentence, a text etc*).

tronconique [trɔ̃kɔnik] *adj* **segment t.,** truncated segment.

tronçonnage [trɔ̃sɔnaʒ] *nm*, **tronçonnement** [trɔ̃sɔnmɑ̃] *nm* cutting into lengths *or* pieces.

tronçonner [trɔ̃sɔne] *vt* to cut into lengths *or* pieces.

tronçonneuse [trɔ̃sɔnøz] *nf* (*à chaîne*) chain saw; (*circulaire*) circular saw.

trône [tron] *nm* **(a)** (*de roi, pape etc*) throne; **placer** *ou* **mettre qn sur le t.,** to put s.o. on the throne; *Pol* **discours du t.,** king's *or* queen's speech; **(b)** *F Hum* (*siège des cabinets*) throne; **(c)** *Rel* **les Trônes,** (*anges*) the Thrones.

trôner [trone] *vi* **(a)** (*of monarch, Fig person*) to sit enthroned; **(b)** (*of things*) to occupy a place of honour *or US* honor; **son diplôme trône sur la cheminée,** his diploma occupies a place of honour on the mantelpiece; **(c)** *Péj* (*faire l'important*) to lord it.

tronqué [trɔ̃ke] *adj* truncated; stub (*mast*); curtailed (*text*).

tronquer [trɔ̃ke] *vt* to truncate; *Péj* to curtail (*novel etc*).

trop [tro] **1** *adv* **(a)** (*with adj*) too, over-; (*with adv*) too; **c'est t. difficile,** it's too difficult; **un travail t. difficile,** too difficult a job; **t. aimable** [tropɛmabl]**,** too *or* very kind; **vous êtes t. aimable de ...,** it is most *or* very kind of you to ...; **il est t. gentil pour le renvoyer,** he is too kind to sack him; **aliments t. riches,** over-rich food; **vous n'êtes que t. généreux,** you are all too generous; **elle est t. belle pour toi,** she is too beautiful for you; **t. fatigué,** too tired (**pour,** to), overtired; *Litt* **par t. généreux/***etc*, far too generous/*etc*; **t. beau pour être vrai,** too good to be true; **vous n'êtes pas t. en avance,** you are none too early; **c'était t. drôle,** it was too funny for words *or* just too funny; **le trou était t. étroit pour qu'un rat entrât par là,** the hole was too narrow for a rat to get in by; *F* **il est vraiment t.!,** he's really too much!;

(b) (*with verb*) too much, over-; **t. travailler,** to overwork, to work too much *or* hard; **boire t., t. boire,** to drink to excess *or* too much; **je l'ai t. aimé** [tropɛme], I loved him too much; **il n'y tient pas t.,** he is not too bothered (about it); *F* **ça te plaît?, — pas t.,** do you like it? — not (very) much; **ne vous y fiez pas t., il ne faut pas t. vous y fier,** don't count on it too much; **on ne saurait t. le répéter,** it cannot be repeated too often; **je ne sais t. que dire/penser,** I hardly know *or* I don't quite know what to say/think.

2 *nm* (*quantité*) too much; (*nombre*) too many; **t. de,** too much; too many; **il allait t. en dire** *ou* **en dire t.,** he was going to say too much; **je n'aurai pas t. d'une heure pour le faire,** it will take me a good hour; **t. de bruit,** too much noise; **t. d'amis,** too many friends; **elle n'a fait preuve que de t. de patience,** she has shown far too much patience; **je ne l'ai que t. dit, je ne l'ai dit que t.,** I've said it too many times already; **j'ai une carte de t.** *ou* **en**

t., I have one card too many; **c'est une fois de t.**, that is once too often; **quand j'ai du temps de t.**, when I have time to spare; **payer en t.**, to pay too much; **être/se sentir de t.**, to be/feel in the way *or* unwelcome *or* de trop; *F* **travailler/boire de t.**, to work too hard *or* much/drink too much; **t., c'est t.!**, enough is enough!; **c'en est t.!**, this really is the limit!

trope [trɔp] *nm Littér* trope.

trophée [trɔfe] *nm* trophy.

tropical, -aux [trɔpikal, -o] *adj* tropical (*plant, temperature etc*).

tropicaliser [trɔpikalize] *vt* to tropicalize (*material etc*).

tropique [trɔpik] **1** *adj* tropical (*year*). **2** *nm* **(a)** *Astron Géog* (*cercle*) tropic; **(b) les tropiques,** (*région*) the tropics; **sous les tropiques,** in the tropics.

tropisme [trɔpism] *nm Biol* tropism.

troposphère [trɔpɔsfɛr] *nf Météo* troposphere.

trop-perçu [trɔpɛrsy] *nm Fin* over-payment (*of taxes*); (*pl trop-perçus*).

trop-plein [trɔplɛ̃] *nm* (*réservoir, excédent*) overflow; **(tuyau de) t.-p.**, waste pipe, overflow pipe; **t.-p. d'énergie/de tendresse,** overabundance of energy/affection; (*pl trop-pleins*).

troque [trɔk] *nm* (*mollusque*) top shell.

troquer [trɔke] *vt Com* to exchange, to barter, to swap (*sth*); *Fig* (*remplacer*) to swap, to exchange (*sth*) (**contre qch,** for sth).

troquet [trɔkɛ] *nm F* (small) café.

trot [tro] *nm* (*de cheval*) trot; **t. assis,** sitting trot; **faire du t. assis,** to trot close; **t. enlevé,** rising trot, *US* posting trot; **au petit/au grand t.**, at a gentle/brisk trot; **prendre le t.**, to break into a trot; **aller le t.** *ou* **au t.**, to trot; *Fig F* **allez-y, et au t.!**, go on, and be quick about it!; **course de t.**, trotting race.

Trotski [trɔtski] *nm* Trotsky.

trotskisme, trotskysme [trɔtskism] *nm* Trotskyism.

Trotskiste, Trotskyste [trɔtskist] *adj & n* Trotskyist, Trotskyite.

trotte [trɔt] *nf F* (*longue distance*) (long) stretch; **il y a une bonne t. d'ici là,** it is a good step *or* way from here; **tout d'une t.**, without stopping, at a stretch.

trotte-menu [trɔtmәny] *adj inv* pattering, scampering (*steps of mice etc*).

trotter [trɔte] *vi* (*of horse, rider*) to trot; (*of person*) to trot (around *or* along); (*of mice*) to scamper; *F* **toujours à t.**, always on the go; **on entendrait t. une souris,** you could hear a pin drop; *Fig* **cette chanson me trotte dans la tête,** that song keeps running through my head.

trotteur, -euse [trɔtœr, -øz] **1** *adj* **talons trotteurs,** flat *or* low heels. **2** *n* (*cheval*) trotter. **3** *nm* (*chaussure*) flat(-heeled) *or* low-heeled shoe. **4** *nf* **trotteuse,** second hand (*of watch*).

trottinement [trɔtinmɑ̃] *nm* scampering (*of mouse*); trotting (*of person*).

trottiner [trɔtine] *vi* **(a)** (*of horse etc*) to trot short; **(b)** (*of mouse*) to scamper (around *or* along); (*of person*) to trot (around *or* along).

trottinette [trɔtinɛt] *nf* **(a)** (*jouet*) scooter; **(b)** *F* small car.

trottoir [trɔtwar] *nm* **(a)** pavement, *Am* sidewalk; *Aut* **heurter le t.**, to hit the kerb; **artiste de t.**, pavement artist; **faire le t.**, to walk the streets; **(b) t. roulant,** travelator, moving pavement *or Am* sidewalk.

trou [tru] *nm* **(a)** (*ouverture*) hole; (*d'aiguille*) eye; **avoir des trous à ses chaussettes,** to have holes in one's socks; **t. de clef,** keyhole (*of clock, watch*); **t. de serrure,** keyhole (*of lock*); **le t. de la couche d'ozone,** the hole in the ozone layer; **faire son t.**, to settle down; *Nau* **t. du chat,** lubber's hole; *Av Arg* **il a fait un t. dans l'eau,** he's gone for a Burton; *F* **boire comme un t., avoir un t. sous le nez,** to drink like a fish; **faire le t. normand,** to have a (glass of) Calvados (*between courses of meal*); *Astron* **t. noir,** black hole; *Fig* **c'est le t. noir,** I am *or* she is *etc* extremely depressed;

(b) gap (*in hedge, in memory, in explanation, in accounts, in timetable, between players etc*); **un t. dans mes économies,** a hole in my savings; **j'ai eu un t. (de mémoire),** my mind went blank; *Sp & Fig* **faire le t.**, to break away from the field;

(c) *Anat* foramen; *F* **trous de nez,** nostrils; *F* **ne pas avoir les yeux en face des trous,** to be still fast asleep; *Méd F* **t. dans le cœur,** hole in the heart; *F* **t. de balle,** *Vulg* **t. du cul,** arsehole, *Am* asshole; **espèce de t. du cul!**, you bloody little fool!;

(d) (*creusé etc*) hole; *Aut* (pot)hole; **t. de souris,** mouse-hole; *Av* **t. d'air,** air pocket; *Th* **t. du souffleur,** prompter's box; *Agr* **t. au fumier,** manure pit;

(e) *F Péj* (*village etc*) hole; **elle n'est jamais sortie de son t.**, she has never been out of her own backyard; **habiter un petit t. (perdu),** to live at the back of beyond;

(f) *Golf* hole; **envoyer la balle dans le t.**, to hole out; **partie par trous,** match play;

(g) *Arg* (*tombe*) grave; (*prison*) prison; **on l'a mis dans le t.**, (*au tombeau*) they buried him; **on l'a mis au t.**, (*en prison*) he was jailed;

(h) *Tech* **t. d'homme,** manhole; **t. de graissage,** oil hole; **t. d'aération,** air vent; *Min* **t. de mine,** blast hole, drill hole; *Min Constr* **t. de sondage** *ou* **de sonde,** borehole; *Constr* **t. d'écoulement,** weep hole;

(i) *Phys Électron* hole, aperture.

troubadour [trubadur] *nm Hist Littér* troubadour.

troublant [trublɑ̃] *adj* **(a)** (*déconcertant*) disconcerting, disturbing, unsettling; **(b)** (*sensuel*) disturbing, provocative.

trouble¹ [trubl] **1** *adj* **(a)** cloudy (*liquid*); dim (*light, eyes*); murky, overcast (*sky*); confused (*situation*); blurred, fuzzy (*picture, photograph*); **avoir la vue t.**, to have blurred vision; **aux yeux troubles,** bleary-eyed; **(b)** *Fig* **avoir une vue t. de qch,** to have a blurred vision of sth; **(c)** confused (*mind*); uneasy (*conscience*); mixed, uneasy (*emotion*); **période t. de l'histoire,** murky period of history; **il y a du t. dans cette affaire,** there's something shady about this business. **2** *adv* **voir t.**, to see things through a mist.

trouble² *nm* **(a)** (*confusion*) confusion, disorder; **jeter le t. dans une famille,** to cause trouble in a family; *Méd* **troubles de digestion/de vision,** digestive troubles/eye trouble; **(b)** (*agitation*) agitation, uneasiness; (*gêne*) confusion, embarrassment; (*amoureux*) agitation; **cause de t.**, disturbing factor; **jeter le t. dans l'esprit de qn,** to perturb s.o.; **(c) troubles,** (public) disturbances, unrest; **fauteur de troubles,** agitator, troublemaker; **troubles sociaux,** social unrest; **(d)** *Jur* **t. de jouissance,** disturbance of possession.

trouble³ *nf Pêche* hoop net.

trouble-fête [trubləfɛt] *nm inv* spoilsport, wet blanket, killjoy.

troubler [truble] **1** *vt* **(a)** to make (*liquid etc*) cloudy *or* muddy; to cloud (*s.o.'s mind*); to dim (*s.o.'s eyes*);

(b) to disturb (*meeting, sleep, silence etc*); to interfere with, to disrupt (*operations, plans, activities*); to impede (*progress*); to spoil (*happiness*); to upset (*digestion*); **période troublée par la guerre,** period disrupted by war; **un vent léger troubla l'eau,** a slight wind ruffled the water; **t. le repos** *ou* **l'ordre public,** to create a disturbance; *Jur* to disturb the peace; **l'ordre public n'a été nullement troublé,** there has been no breach of the peace; **imagination troublée,** disordered imagination;

(c) (*déconcerter*) to disturb, to disconcert, to make (*s.o.*) uneasy; (*gêner*) to confuse (*s.o.*);

(d) (*sensuellement*) to excite, to thrill (*s.o.*); to stir (*senses, emotions*);

(e) (*émouvoir*) to move (*s.o.*);

(f) *Jur* **t. qn dans la jouissance d'un bien,** to disturb s.o.'s enjoyment of possession.

2 se troubler *vpr* **(a)** (*of wine etc*) to get cloudy; (*of sky*) to become overcast; (*of vision*) to become blurred; (*of voice*) to break (with emotion);

(b) (*se déconcerter*) to become confused *or* flustered; **sans se t.**, (*répondre etc*) unruffled, without turning a hair.

trouée [true] *nf* gap, opening (**de,** in).

trouer [true] **1** *vt* to make a hole *or* holes in (*wall etc*); to breach (*enemy lines etc*); to wear *or* make a hole in (*garment*); *Tech* to perforate (*zinc etc*); **avoir les bas troués,** to have holes in one's stockings. **2 se trouer** *vpr* (*of sock etc*) to get holes; **les nuages commencent à se t.**, the clouds are beginning to break; *Arg* **se faire t. la peau,** to be pumped full of lead.

troufignon [trufiɲɔ̃] *nm Arg* (*derrière*) arse, *Am* ass.

troufion [trufjɔ̃] *nm Arg* soldier, private.

trouillard, -arde [trujar, -ard] *Arg* **1** *adj* yellow-bellied, cowardly. **2** *n* yellow-belly, coward.

trouille [truj] *nf Arg* (*peur*) **avoir la t.**, to have *or* get the wind up; **ficher** *ou* **flanquer la t. à qn,** to put the wind up s.o.; *Iron* **tu n'as pas la t.!**, you've got a nerve!

trouillomètre [trujɔmɛtr] *nm Arg* **avoir le t. à zéro,** to be scared stiff *or Br* in a blue funk.

troupe [trup] *nf* **(a)** troop, band, group (*of people*); gang, set (*of thieves etc*); (*de scouts*) troop; **(b)** *Th* troupe, company; **t. d'amateurs,** amateur troupe *or* company; **(c)** herd, drove (*of cattle, deer*); pride (*of lions*); flock (*of birds*); **ces animaux vivent en t.**, these animals herd together *or* are gregarious; **(d)** *Mil* troop; **troupes,** (*armée*) troops, forces; **officier de t.,** regimental officer; **officiers et t.,** officers and other ranks; *Vieilli* **enfant de t.,** army child; **cigarettes de t.,** army issue cigarettes; *F* **en route, mauvaise t.!,** come on, let's be moving!

troupeau, -aux [trupo] *nm* herd, drove (*of cattle*); flock (*of sheep, geese etc*); flock, herd, *Péj* horde (*of people*).

troupier [trupje] *nm Mil F* private, soldier; **jurer comme un t.,** to swear like a trooper; **fumer comme un t.,** to smoke like a chimney.

troussage [trusaʒ] *nm Culin* trussing (*of fowl*).

trousse [trus] *nf* **(a) être aux trousses de qn,** to be after s.o. *or* (hot) on s.o.'s heels; **avoir la police aux trousses,** to have the police after one *or* (hot) on one's heels; **(b)** (*étui*) kit; (*de médecin etc*) (instrument) case; **t. de toilette,** dressing case, toilet case; **t. d'écolier,** pencil case; **t. à ongles,** manicure kit.

troussé [truse] *adj F* **bien t.,** neat (*object, compliment*).

trousseau, -eaux [truso] *nm* **(a)** bunch (*of keys*); **(b)** outfit (*of clothing*); **(c)** (*de fiancée*) trousseau, bottom drawer, *US* hope chest.

trousser [truse] **1** *vt* **(a)** *Culin* to truss (*fowl*); **(b)** *F* (*faire rapidement*) to polish off (*work, meal*); **(c)** *Vieilli* (*retrousser*) to tuck up (*skirt etc*); *F* **il est toujours à t. les filles,** he's always chasing women. **2 se trousser** *vpr* to tuck up one's clothes.

trousseur [trusœr] *nm F Vieilli* **t. de jupons,** skirt chaser.

trouvaille [truvaj] *nf* **(a)** (*chose trouvée*) (lucky) find; **(b)** (*bonne idée*) brainwave.

trouver [truve] **1** *vt* **(a)** (*en cherchant*) to find; **je ne trouve pas mes clefs,** I can't find my keys; **où est-ce qu'on trouve cela?,** where is that to be found?, where can you *or* one find that?; **aller t. qn,** to go and see s.o.;

(b) (*inventer*) to discover, to invent (*process etc*);

(c) t. (par hasard), to find (by chance), to discover, to come upon, to come across; to hit upon (*an idea*); **on l'a trouvé mort,** he was found dead; **t. qn en faute,** to catch s.o. out; **t. qn en train de dormir,** to find s.o. sleeping *or* asleep; **je lui trouve du charme/mauvaise mine,** I think he has charm/looks ill; **qu'est-ce qu'elle lui trouve?,** what does she see in him?; **bureau des objets trouvés,** lost-property office; **c'est bien trouvé!,** good idea!; **exemple bien/mal trouvé,** well-chosen/badly chosen example; **je n'ai pas trouvé le temps de le faire,** I didn't find time to do it; *Fig* **il a trouvé à qui parler,** he has met his match; **il trouva la mort à ...,** he met his death at ...; **il trouve du plaisir à lire,** he finds pleasure in reading, he enjoys reading; **il va bien t. qch à redire,** he's sure to find fault; **elle trouve au malin plaisir à me faire attendre,** she takes malicious pleasure in making me wait;

(d) (*juger*) to find; (*penser*) to think; **je la trouve jolie,** I find *or* consider her pretty, I think she's pretty; **vous trouvez?,** you think so?; **comment as-tu trouvé ce livre?,** how did you find *or* like the book?; **je la trouve mauvaise** *ou* **saumâtre,** (*action*) I think it's a bit much *or* a bit thick; **il trouve bon/mauvais de vous en parler,** he thinks it a good/bad idea to talk to you about it; **je trouve mieux de ne pas ...,** I think it better not to ...; **je trouve qu'il exagère,** I think (that) he is overdoing it;

(e) (*obtenir*) to find, to get (*job, husband, house etc*); **t. le sommeil,** to get to sleep.

2 se trouver *vpr* **(a)** to be, to find oneself (*in a situation*); (*of thing*) to be; (*sentir*) to feel; **ce moment-là, je me suis trouvé bien bête,** at that moment I felt really stupid; **ces plantes se trouvent partout,** these plants are to be found everywhere; **je me trouve très bien ici,** I'm very comfortable here; **comment vous êtes-vous trouvé de ce traitement?,** how did the treatment work?; **je me trouve trop grosse,** I think I'm too fat; **se t. bien de qch/d'avoir fait qch,** to feel all the better for sth/having done sth; **je me trouve mieux,** I feel better; **elle se trouve mal,** she feels faint;

(b) (*arriver*) to happen, to turn out; **je me trouve avoir** *ou* **il se trouve que j'ai une heure de libre,** I happen to have *or* it so happens that I have an hour to spare; **la dame se trouva être sa propre femme,** the lady turned out to be his own wife; *F* **si cela se trouve, il est déjà rentré,** maybe he's back;

(c) (*se réaliser*) to find oneself.

trouvère [truvɛr] *nm Hist Littér* trouvère.

troyen¹, -enne [trwajɛ̃, -ɛn] **1** *adj* (*de Troie*) Trojan. **2** *n* **T.,** Trojan.

troyen², -enne 1 *adj* (*de Troyes*) of *or* from Troyes. **2** *n* **T.,** native *or* inhabitant of Troyes.

truand, -ande [tryɑ̃, -ɑ̃d] *n* **(a)** *F* (*escroc*) crook; (*gangster*) gangster; **(b)** *Arch* (*mendiant*) beggar.

truander [tryɑ̃de] **1** *vt F* to swindle (*s.o.*); **se faire t.,** to be swindled. **2** *vi F* to cheat; **t. à un examen,** to cheat in an exam.

truble [trybl] *nf Pêche* hoop net, shove net.

trublion [tryblijɔ̃] *nm* troublemaker.

truc¹ [tryk] *nm F* **(a)** (*moyen*) trick; **connaître les trucs du métier,** to know the tricks of the trade; *Th* **pièce à trucs,** play with elaborate stage effects; **t. d'optique,** optical illusion; **il y a un t.!,** there's a trick in it!; **un t. pour enlever les taches,** a trick for removing stains; **(b) (Monsieur) T.,** (Mr) what's-his-name; **(c)** (*chose*) thing; (*machin*) thingummy, thingy; **des trucs comme ça,** things like that; **(d) ce n'est pas son t.,** (*ce qui l'intéresse*) it's not his thing, he's not into that.

truc² *nm Rail* truck, *Am* freight car.

trucage [trykaʒ] *nm* **(a)** *Cin* special effect; **(b)** faking (*of antiques, photograph etc*); fixing, rigging (*of match, election etc*).

truchement [tryʃmɑ̃] *nm* **(a)** (*intermédiaire*) go-between, intermediary; **par le t. de ...,** through ...; **(b)** *Arch* (*interprète*) interpreter.

trucider [tryside] *vt F* (*tuer*) to bump off.

truck [tryk] *nm Rail* truck, *Am* freight car.

trucmuche [trykmyʃ] *nm* **(a)** (*chose*) thingummy, thingy; **(b) T.,** (*personne*) Whatsit.

truculence [trykylɑ̃s] *nf* colourfulness, *US* colorfulness (*of character, language etc*).

truculent [trykylɑ̃] *adj* colourful, *US* colorful (*character, language etc*).

truelle [tryɛl] *nf* **(a)** (*outil*) trowel; **(b)** *Culin* **t. à poisson,** fish slice.

truffe [tryf] *nf* **(a)** (*champignon*) truffle; **omelette aux truffes,** truffle omelet(te); **(b)** (*au chocolat*) truffle; **(c)** (*nez*) nose (*of a dog*); *Arg* bulbous nose (*of person*).

truffer [tryfe] *vt* **(a)** *Culin* to flavour *or* lard (*sth*) with truffles; **dinde truffée,** truffled turkey; **(b)** *Fig* **truffé de,** riddled with (*bullets, mistakes*); peppered with (*quotations*).

truffier, -ière [tryfje, -jɛr] *adj* truffle(-producing) (*ground*); **chien t.,** truffle hound.

truie [trɥi] *nf* sow.

truisme [tryism] *nm* truism.

truite [trɥit] *nf* trout; **t. de rivière,** brown trout; **t. arc-en-ciel,** rainbow trout; *Culin* **t. meunière,** = trout sautéed in butter and served with parsley and lemon juice.

truité [trɥite] *adj* speckled; spotted (*dog, horse*); crackled (*china*).

truiticulture [trɥitikyltyr] *nf* trout breeding.

trumeau, -eaux [trymo] *nm* **(a)** *Archit* pier; **(b)** (*miroir*) pier glass; **(c)** *Culin* leg of beef.

truquage [trykaʒ] *nm* = **TRUCAGE**.

truquer [tryke] *vt* **(a)** to fake (*antiques, photograph, experiment etc*); to fix, to rig (*match, fight, election etc*); *F* to cook (*accounts*); **t. les dés,** to fix the dice; **(b)** *Cin* **scène truquée,** scene with special effects; **(c)** *Min* to salt (*mine, mineral sample*).

truqueur, -euse [trykœr, -øz] *n* **(a)** faker (*of jewellery, antiques etc*); (*qui triche*) cheat; **(b)** *Cin* special effects person.

truquiste [trykist] *n Cin* special effects person.

trusquin [tryskɛ̃] *nm Menuis Tech* marking gauge.

trust [trœst] *nm Fin Com* trust; **t. de l'acier/du pétrole,** steel/oil trust.

truster [trœste] *vt* **(a)** *Fin Com* to group into a trust; **(b)** *Fig F* to monopolize.

trypanosome [tripanozom] *nm* trypanosome.

trypanosomiase [tripanozɔmjɑz] *nf Méd Vét* trypanosomiasis.

tsar [tsar, dzar] *nm* tsar, czar.

tsarévitch [tsarevitʃ, dz-] *nm* tsarevitch, czarevitch.

tsarine [tsarin, dz-] *nf* tsarina, czarina.

tsarisme [tsarism, dz-] *nm Hist* tsarism.

tsariste [tsarist, dz-] *adj & n Hist* tsarist.

tsé-tsé [tsetse] *nf Ent* tsetse (fly).

t-shirt [tiʃœrt] *nm* T-shirt, tee shirt; (*pl t-shirts*).

tsigane [tsigan] *adj & n* tzigane, Hungarian gypsy.

T.S.V.P. [teesvepe] (*abrév* **tournez s'il vous plaît**) PTO.

T.T.C. [tetese] (*abrév* **toutes taxes comprises**) inclusive of tax.

tu [ty] *pron pers* **(a)** (*usual form of address to relations, close friends, children and animals*) you; **tu as raison,** you are right; **qui es-tu?,** who are you?; **à tu et à toi,** on terms of close friendship (**avec qn,** with s.o.); **être à tu et à toi avec tout le monde,** to be hail-fellow-well-met with everybody; **elle lui dit tu,** she says 'tu' to him; **(b)** *Rel* thou; (*à Dieu*) Thou; *Bible* **tu ne tueras point,** thou shalt not kill; **(c)** *Arg* (*elided to* **t'** *before vowel or* **h** *mute*) **qu'est-ce que t'as?,** what's up (with you)?

tuant [tɥɑ̃] *adj F* **(a)** killing, back-breaking (*work*); **(b)** (*insupportable*) exasperating.

tub [tœb] *nm Vieilli* (*cuvette*) tub, bath; (*bain*) bath; **prendre un t.,** to take *or* have a bath.

tuba [tyba] *nm* **(a)** *Mus* tuba; **(b)** (*de plongée*) snorkel.

tubage [tybaʒ] *nm Constr Min Chir Vét* tubing.

tubaire [tybɛr] *adj Méd* tubal.

tubard, -arde [tybar, -ard] *n Méd F* T.B. case.

tube [tyb] *nm* **(a)** (*tuyau*) tube; (*de canalisation*) pipe; *Métal* **t. étiré/laminé,** drawn/rolled tube; *Constr* **bâti en tubes d'acier,** tubular steel frame; **clef à t.,** tubular spanner;

(b) t. de graissage, oil duct *or* way; **t. raccord,** pipe connection; **t. à flamme,** flame tube (*of jet engine*); *Aut* **t. de direction,** steering column; **t. d'alimentation,** feed pipe; **t. de chaudière,** boiler tube; **chaudière à tubes,** tubular boiler; *F* **à pleins tubes,** all out, at full blast; **t. de condenseur, t. à condensation,** condenser tube; **t. de niveau d'eau,** water-gauge column; *Min* **t. carrottier,** core barrel; **tubes d'exploitation** *ou* **de pompage,** tubing; *Él* **t. guide-fils,** race track, race way (*in building*);

(c) (*de canon*) barrel; *Nau* **t. lance-torpille(s),** torpedo tube;

(d) *Chir Vét* tube;

(e) *Anat* tube, duct; **t. digestif,** digestive tract, alimentary canal; **t. bronchique,** bronchial tube; *Anat Phys* **t. capillaire,** capillary tube;

(f) *Bot* tube (*of corolla, calyx*);

(g) *Courses de chevaux Arg* (*indication*) tip;

(h) *F* (*chanson, disque*) hit; *Th* (smash) hit, smash;

(i) (*emballage*) tube (*of toothpaste, colour*); **t. de rouge à lèvres,** (stick of) lipstick; **moutarde en t.,** mustard in a tube;

(j) *Ch* **t. pour dosage, t. doseur,** measuring tube; **t. à essais,** test tube;

(k) *El Électron* tube; *Él* **t. au néon,** neon tube; **t. fluorescent,** fluorescent tube; *Électron Rad* **t. cathodique,** cathode-ray tube; **t. électronique,** electron tube; **t. à gaz,** gas-filled tube *or* valve; **t. à vide,** vacuum tube *or* valve; **t. amplificateur,** amplifier tube *or* valve; **t. de balayage,** scanning tube; **t. d'affichage,** (*de radar*) display tube; **t. phare,** lighthouse.

tuber [tybe] *vt Constr* to tube, to case (*borehole, well*); to case (*shaft, well*).

tubercule [tybɛrkyl] *nm* **(a)** *Bot* tuber; **(b)** *Méd* tubercle.

tuberculeux, -euse [tybɛrkylø, -øz] **1** *adj* **(a)** *Bot* tubercular (*root*); **(b)** *Méd* tubercular. **2** *n* tubercular patient, T.B. case.

tuberculine [tybɛrkylin] *nf Méd* tuberculin.

tuberculiser (se) [sətybɛrkylize] *vpr Méd* to become tubercular.

tuberculose [tybɛrkyloz] *nf Méd* tuberculosis; **t. pulmonaire,** pulmonary tuberculosis.

tubéreux, -euse [tyberø, -øz] *Bot* **1** *adj* tuberous. **2** *nf* **tubéreuse,** tuberose.

tubulaire [tybylɛr] **1** *adj* tubular. **2** *nm Zool* tubularia.

tubulé [tybyle] *adj* tubulate (*flower*); tubulated (*retort etc*); tubular (*boiler*).

tubuleux, -euse [tybylø, -øz] *adj* tubulous.

tubulure [tybylyr] *nf* **(a)** *Tech* (*ouverture*) tubulure, pipe(-run), neck; *Aut* manifold; *Av* **t. d'évacuation,** tailpipe (*of jet engine*); **(b)** (*tube*) pipe; (*ensemble de tubes*) piping, pipes.

TUC [tyk] **1** *nmpl* (*abrév* **Travaux d'utilité collective**) *Br* ≈ YTS. **2** *n F* (*employé(e)*) *Br* ≈ YTS.

tue-mouches [tymuʃ] **1** *nm inv* **(a)** (*champignon*) fly agaric; **(b)** (*tapette*) fly swatter; (*insecticide*) fly killer. **2** *adj inv* **papier** *ou* **ruban t.-m.,** fly paper.

tuer [tɥe] **1** *vt* **(a)** to kill (*person, animal*); **t. qn d'un coup de couteau** *ou* **de poignard,** to stab s.o. to death; **t. qn d'un coup de revolver,** to shoot s.o. (dead) with a revolver; **un coup à t. un bœuf,** a blow to fell an ox; **se faire t.,** to get killed; **ils se firent t. en braves,** they died like heroes; **les tués et les blessés,** the dead and wounded; *Fig* **tu veux te faire t.!,** you're asking for it!; **le froid a tué les oliviers,** the cold has killed the olive trees; *Fig* **t. le temps,** to kill time;

(b) *Pétr* to kill (*oil well, gas well*);

(c) *Tennis* to kill (*the ball*);

(d) *Fig* **l'ennui le tue,** he's bored to death; **ces escaliers me tuent,** these stairs will be the death of me; **l'habitude tue la passion,** habit kills passion;

(e) *Fig F* **ça me tue, qu'il se comporte comme ça,** it staggers me that he behaves like that; **ça m'a tué d'apprendre qu'il se remariait,** I was staggered to hear that he was going to remarry.

2 se tuer *vpr* **(a)** (*se suicider*) to kill oneself, to commit suicide;

(b) (*mourir dans un accident etc*) to get killed;

(c) (*s'entre-tuer*) to kill one another;

(d) se t. au travail *ou* **à travailler/à force de boire,** to work/drink oneself to death; **je me tue à vous le dire,** I am sick and tired of telling you.

tuerie [tyri] *nf* slaughter, butchery.

tue-tête (à) [atytɛt] *adv* at the top of one's voice.

tueur, -euse [tɥœr, -øz] **1** *n* (*assassin*) killer; **t. de lions,** lion killer; **t. à gages,** hired killer *or* assassin. **2** *nm* (*dans un abattoir*) butcher, slaughterman.

tuf [tyf] *nm* **(a)** *Géol* **t. volcanique,** tuff; (*calcaire*) tufa; **(b)** *Fig Litt* bedrock, foundation.

tuile [tɥil] *nf* **(a)** *Constr* (roof) tile; **(b)** *Culin* **tuiles aux amandes,** almond biscuits; **(c)** *F* (*malchance*) (piece of) bad luck, blow; **il lui est arrivé une (sale) t.,** he has had a terrible blow *or* piece of bad luck.

tuilerie [tɥilri] *nf* **(a)** (*fabrique*) tile works; (*four*) tile kiln; **(b) les Tuileries,** the Tuileries.

tulipe [tylip] *nf* **(a)** *Bot* tulip; **(b)** (*lampe*) tulip-shaped lamp; (*verre*) tulip glass.

tulipier [tylipje] *nm Bot* tulip tree.

tulle [tyl] *nm Tex* tulle, net (fabric); *Méd* **t. gras,** tulle gras.

tuméfaction [tymefaksjɔ̃] *nf Méd* tumefaction, swelling.

tuméfier [tymefje] **1** *vt* to tumefy, to cause (*joint etc*) to swell. **2 se tuméfier** *vpr* to swell (up).

tumescence [tymesɑ̃s] *nf* tumescence; swelling.

tumescent [tymesɑ̃] *adj* tumescent, swelling.

tumeur [tymœr] *nf Méd* **(a)** tumour, *US* tumor, growth; **t. dure,** indurated tumour; **t. bénigne/maligne,** benign/malignant tumour; **(b)** (*gonflement*) swelling.

tumulaire [tymylɛr] *adj* **pierre t.,** tombstone.

tumulte [tymylt] *nm* tumult, hubbub, uproar, commotion; thunder (*of applause*); clash (*of arms*); turmoil (*of politics, passions*); hustle and bustle (*of business*); **dans le t.,** in an uproar, in confusion; **il y eut des tumultes,** there were riots.

tumultueusement [tymyltɥøzmɑ̃] *adv* tumultuously.

tumultueux, -euse [tymyltɥø, -øz] *adj* tumultuous, riotous (*gathering etc*); noisy (*streets*); tumultuous (*life, period etc*); noisy (*debate*).

tumulus [tymylys] *nm* tumulus, barrow; (*pl tumulus ou tumuli*).

tuner [tjunœr] *nm Rad* tuner.

tungstène [tœ̃gstɛn] *nm Métal* tungsten.

tunique [tynik] *nf* **(a)** (*vêtement*) tunic; *Rel* tunicle; **(b)** *Biol* tunic, envelope, membrane (*of an organ*); *Bot* coat (*of bulb*); skin (*of seed*).

Tunisie [tynizi] *nf* Tunisia.

tunisien, -ienne [tynizjɛ̃, -jɛn] **1** *adj* Tunisian. **2** *n* **T.,** Tunisian.

tunnel [tynɛl] *nm* tunnel; **t. routier,** road tunnel; **le t. sous la Manche,** the Channel Tunnel, *F* the Chunnel; *Fig* **arriver au bout du t.,** to come to the end of the tunnel; *Av* **t. aérodynamique,** wind tunnel; *Él etc* **t. de câbles,** cable subway.

tuque [tyk] *nf Can* tuque, *F* pompom hat, bobble cap.

turban [tyrbɑ̃] *nm* **(a)** (*coiffure*) turban; **(b)** (*mollusque*) turban shell.

turbide [tyrbid] *adj* turbid, muddy (*liquid etc*).

turbidité [tyrbidite] *nf* turbidity, cloudiness.

turbin [tyrbɛ̃] *nm Arg* (*travail*) work, grind, slog; (*emploi*) job.

turbine [tyrbin] *nf* turbine; **t. à air,** air *or* wind turbine; **t. à eau, t. hydraulique,** water turbine, water wheel; **t. à gaz/à vapeur,** gas/steam turbine.

turbiner [tyrbine] *vi Arg* (*travailler*) to slog; *Scol* to swot.

turbo[1] [tyrbo] *nm* (*mollusque*) turbo, turban shell.

turbo[2] *F* **1** *nm* (*turbocompresseur*) turbo. **2** *adj* turbocharged.

turbo-alternateur [tyrbɔaltɛrnatœr] *nm Él* turbo-alternator; (*pl turbo-alternateurs*).

turbocompresseur [tyrbɔkɔ̃prɛsœr] *nm Tech Av* turbocompressor; *Aut* turbosupercharger, turbocharger.

turbomoteur [tyrbɔmɔtœr] *nm* turbomotor, turboshaft engine.

turbopompe [tyrbɔpɔ̃p] *nf* turbo pump, turbine pump.

turbopropulseur [tyrbɔprɔpylsœr] *nm* turboprop(eller);

avion à t., turboprop aircraft.
turboréacteur [tyrbɔreaktœr] *nm* turbojet (engine).
turbot [tyrbo] *nm* (*poisson*) turbot.
turbotière [tyrbɔtjɛr] *nf Culin* (*récipient*) flatfish dish.
turbotrain [tyrbɔtrɛ̃] *nm Rail* turbotrain.
turbulence [tyrbylɑ̃s] *nf* turbulence; boisterousness (*of child, wind, sea*); *Av* **il y aura des turbulences,** there will be some turbulence.
turbulent [tyrbylɑ̃] *adj* **(a)** restless, unruly (*population*); **(b)** boisterous (*child*); boisterous, stormy (*wind, sea*); **(c)** *Phys* **régime t.,** turbulent flow.
turc, turque [tyrk] **1** *adj* Turkish; **café t.,** Turkish coffee; **être assis à la turque,** to sit cross-legged; **WC** *ou* **cabinets à la turque,** seatless lavatory. **2** *nm Ling* Turkish. **3** *n* **T.,** Turk; *Pol* **jeune T.,** Young Turk; *F* **fort comme un T.,** as strong as an ox; **tête de T.,** whipping-boy; *Nau* Turk's head (knot).
turf [tyrf] *nm* **(a)** (*terrain*) racecourse; **(b) le t.,** (*activité*) racing, the turf; **habitué du t.,** racegoer.
turfiste [tyrfist] *n* racegoer.
turgescence [tyrʒesɑ̃s] *nf Méd Bot* turgescence.
turgescent [tyrgesɑ̃] *adj* turgescent.
turgide [tyrʒid] *adj Litt* turgid, swollen.
turista [turista] *nf Méd F* holiday tummy.
turlupiner [tyrlypine] *vt F* to worry, to bother (*s.o.*).
turluter [tyrlyte] *vi Can F* to trill, to sing tra-la-la.
turlututu [tyrlytyty] *int* fiddlesticks!
turne [tyrn] *nf* **(a)** *Arg Péj* (*chambre, maison*) dump, hole; **(b)** *Scol Arg* (student's) room.
turnep(s) [tyrnɛp(s)] *nm Agr* kohlrabi.
turpitude [tyrpityd] *nf* **(a)** (*caractère*) turpitude, depravity; **(b)** (*action*) act; **(c)** (*parole*) depraved remark.
turque [turk] *adj & nf voir* **TURC**.
turquerie [tyrk(ə)ri] *nf* work of art in an Oriental style.
Turquie [tyrki] *nf* Turkey; **tapis de T.,** Turkish carpet.
turquoise [tyrkwaz] **1** *nf* (*pierre*) turquoise. **2** *adj inv & nm inv* (*couleur*) turquoise (blue).
tussor(e) [tysɔr] *nm Tex* tussore (silk).
tutélaire [tytelɛr] *adj* tutelary (*divinity etc*); guardian (*angel etc*); *Jur* **gestion t.,** guardianship.
tutelle [tytɛl] *nf* **(a)** *Jur* guardianship, tutelage; **enfant en t.,** child under guardianship; **(b)** *Pol* **territoires sous t.,** trust territories; **(c)** (*protection*) protection; **sous la t. de,** under the protection of (*family, law etc*); **prendre qn sous sa t.,** to take s.o. under one's wing; **(d) t. administrative,** administrative supervision (*established over mismanaged public body*).
tuteur, -trice [tytœr, -tris] **1** *n* **(a)** *Jur* guardian; **t. légal,** legal guardian; **(b)** (*protecteur*) protector. **2** *nm* (*pour plante*) support, stake.
tutoiement [tytwamɑ̃] *nm* use of the familiar 'tu' (*instead of the more formal 'vous'*).
tutoyer [tytwaje] *v* (**je tutoie, n. tutoyons; je tutoierai**) **1** *vt* to address (*s.o.*) as 'tu' (*instead of 'vous'*); *Fig* to be on familiar terms with (*s.o.*). **2 se tutoyer** *vpr* to address each other as 'tu'; *Fig* to be on familiar terms (with each other).
tutti [tyti] *nm inv Mus* tutti.
tutti frutti [tutifruti] *nm inv* (*glace*) tutti-frutti.
tutti quanti [tutikwɑ̃ti] *nmpl* **et t. q.,** and all the rest of them.
tutu [tyty] *nm* tutu, ballet skirt.
tuyau, -aux [tɥijo] *nm* **(a)** (*canalisation etc*) pipe; (*flexible*) tube; **t. d'eau/de gaz,** water/gas pipe; **t. vertical, t. de chute,** standpipe; **t. flexible, t. en caoutchouc,** rubber tube *or* tubing; **t. d'incendie,** fire hose; **t. d'arrosage,** garden hose; **t. de cheminée,** (chimney) flue; **t. de poêle,** stove pipe, flue pipe; *Aut* **t. d'échappement,** exhaust (pipe); **t. acoustique,** speaking tube; *Mus* **t. d'orgue,** organ pipe; *F* **dire qch à qn dans le t. de l'oreille,** to whisper sth in s.o.'s ear; **(b)** stem (*of tobacco pipe*); **(c)** stalk (*of corn, grass etc*); **(d)** (*pli*) flute, goffer, quill; **(e)** *F* (*conseil*) tip; **je vais te filer un t.,** I'll give you a tip; **un t. crevé,** a rotten tip; **avoir des tuyaux,** to be in the know; **c'est un t. increvable,** it's straight from the horse's mouth.
tuyautage [tɥijotaʒ] *nm* **(a)** fluting, goffering (*of linen*); **(b)** *F* (*action de donner des conseils*) giving of tips.
tuyauter [tɥijote] *vt* **(a)** to flute, to goffer (linen); **fer à t.,** goffering tongs; **(b)** (*conseiller*) to give (*s.o.*) a tip; (*mettre au courant*) to put (*s.o.*) in the know.
tuyauterie [tɥijotri] *nf* (*tuyaux*) piping, pipes.
tuyauteur, -euse [tɥijotœr, -øz] *n F* tipster.
tuyère [tɥijɛr] *nf Tech Métal* nozzle; *Av etc* **t. d'échappement,** jet pipe; **t. de propulsion,** thrust nozzle.
T.V. [teve] *nf* (*abrév* **télévision**) TV.
T.V.A. [tevea] *nf* (*abrév* **taxe à la valeur ajoutée**) VAT; **exempt de T.V.A.,** zero-rated.
tweed [twid] *nm Tex* tweed; **veste de t.,** tweed jacket.
twin-set [twinsɛt] *nm* matching pullover and cardigan, *Br* twinset; (*pl twin-sets*).
twist [twist] *nm* (*danse*) twist.
twister [twiste] *vi* to twist.
tympan [tɛ̃pɑ̃] *nm* **(a)** *Anat* eardrum, *Spéc* tympanum; **bruit à briser** *ou* **crever** *ou* **déchirer** *ou* **rompre les tympans,** ear-splitting noise; **(b)** *Typ* tympan; **(c)** *Archit* tympanum; **(d)** *Tech* pinion (*mounted on shaft*).
tympanal, -aux [tɛ̃panal, -o] *adj & nm Anat* **(os) t.,** tympanic bone.
tympanique [tɛ̃panik] *adj* **(a)** *Anat* tympanic; **(b)** *Méd* tympanitic.
tympanon [tɛ̃panɔ̃] *nm Mus* dulcimer.
type [tip] *nm* **(a)** (*modèle*) type; (*chose ou personne typique*) classic example (**de,** of); *Zool* type, phylum; *Biol* **genre t.,** type genus; **arbre t.,** sample tree; **t. de la beauté italienne,** typical Italian beauty; **avoir le t. latin/nordique,** to have Latin/Nordic looks; **il n'est pas du tout mon t.,** (*sexuel*) he is not at all my type; **c'est un problème t.,** it's a typical problem, it's a standard type of problem; **maison t.,** show house; **motocyclette t.,** motor bicycle of standard design; **c'est le t. même de la femme d'affaires,** she is the classic example of a businesswoman, she is a *or* the classic businesswoman; **des ennuis techniques (du) t. (de la) panne,** breakdown problems;
(b) *F* (*bonhomme*) fellow, guy, *Br* bloke; **un drôle de t.,** a queer sort of fellow *or* guy; **un t. à barbe,** a fellow *or* guy with a beard; **t'es un chic t.!,** you're a good sort!; **un sale t.,** a bastard, a swine; *Péj* **pauvre t.!,** swine!, bastard!;
(c) *Arg* (*amant*) boyfriend, man;
(d) (*personnage*) *F* character; **c'est un vrai t.,** he's quite a character;
(e) *Typ* type.
typé [tipe] *adj* **il est bien** *ou* **très t.,** he has all the characteristic features.
typer [tipe] *vt Tech* to stamp, to mark (*sth*).
typesse [tipɛs] *nf Arg Péj* (*femme, fille*) female.
typhique [tifik] *Méd* **1** *adj* (*du typhus*) typhous; (*de la typhoïde*) typhoidal. **2** *n* typhus *or* typhoid sufferer.
typhoïde [tifɔid] *adj Méd* typhoid (fever).
typhoïdique [tifɔidik] *adj* typhoidal; **bacille t.,** typhoid bacillus.
typhon [tifɔ̃] *nm Météo* typhoon.
typhus [tifys] *nm Méd* typhus (fever); *Vét* **t. du chat,** (infectious) feline gastroenteritis.
typique [tipik] *adj* **(a)** (*caractéristique*) typical; **t. de l'époque romantique,** typical of the Romantic period; **ça ne m'étonne pas, c'est t. (d'elle)!,** that doesn't surprise me, it's typical (of her)!; **(b)** *Biol* typical.
typiquement [tipikmɑ̃] *adv* typically.
typo [tipo] *F* **1** *nf* = **TYPOGRAPHIE**. **2** *nm* (= **typographe**) typo.
typographe [tipɔgraf] *n* typographer.
typographie [tipɔgrafi] *nf* (*art, procédé*) typography, letterpress printing; (*présentation d'un texte*) typography.
typographique [tipɔgrafik] *adj* typographic(al); **erreur t.,** typographic(al) error, misprint.
typographiquement [tipɔgrafikmɑ̃] *adv* typographically.
typolithographie [tipɔlitɔgrafi] *nf* typolithography.
typologie [tipɔlɔʒi] *nf* typology.
typologique [tipɔlɔʒik] *adj* typological.
typote [tipɔt] *nf F* (= **typographe**) typo.
Tyr [tir] *n* Tyre.
tyran [tirɑ̃] *nm Pol & Fig* tyrant; **se conduire en t.,** to act tyrannically; **faire le t.,** to play the tyrant; **il est le t. de sa famille,** he tyrannizes his family.
tyranneau, -eaux [tirano] *nm Litt* petty tyrant.
tyrannie [tirani] *nf Pol & Fig* tyranny.
tyrannique [tiranik] *adj* tyrannical.
tyranniquement [tiranikmɑ̃] *adv* tyrannically.
tyranniser [tiranize] *vt* to tyrannize (*s.o.*).
tyrannosaure [tiranɔzɔr] *nm* tyrannosaurus.
Tyrol (le) [lətirɔl] *nm* the Tyrol.
tyrolien, -ienne [tirɔljɛ̃, -jɛn] **1** *adj* Tyrolean, Tyrolese. **2** *n* **T.,** Tyrolean, Tyrolese. **3** *nf Mus* **tyrolienne,** Tyrolienne.
tzar [tsar, dzar] *nm* tsar, czar.
tzarévitch [tsarevitʃ, dz-] *nm* tsarevitch, czarevitch.
tzarine [tsarin, -dz] *nf* tsarina, czarina.
tzigane [tsigan, dz-] *adj & n* tzigane, Hungarian gypsy.

U

U, u [y] *nm* **(a)** (the letter) U, u; **fer en U,** channel iron; *Géog* **vallée (à profil) en U,** U-shaped valley; **tables (disposées) en U,** tables arranged in a horseshoe; **(b)** *Univ F* (= **universitaire**) **resto/cité U,** student refectory/residence *or* hall(s) of residence.
ubiquité [ybikɥite] *nf* ubiquity; **avoir le don d'u.,** to be ubiquitous, to be in several places at the same time.
U.E.R. [yəɛr] *nf Univ* (*abrév* **unité d'enseignement et de recherche**) = university department.
ufologie [yfɔlɔʒi] *nf* ufology.
ukase [ykɑz] *nm* ukase; **u. paternel,** paternal fiat.
ukrainien, -ienne [ykrɛnjɛ̃, -jɛn] **1** *adj* Ukranian. **2** *nm Ling* Ukranian. **3** *n* **U.,** Ukranian.
ulcération [ylserɑsjɔ̃] *nf* ulceration.
ulcère [ylsɛr] *nm* ulcer; **avoir un u. à l'estomac,** to have a stomach ulcer.
ulcéré [ylsere] *adj* **(a)** *Méd* ulcerated; **(b) avoir une conscience ulcérée,** to suffer pangs of conscience; **cœur u.,** embittered heart; **elle en était ulcérée,** it rankled with her.
ulcérer [ylsere] *v* (**il ulcère; il ulcérera**) **1** *vt* **(a)** *Méd* to ulcerate; **(b)** to wound, to embitter (*s.o.*). **2 s'ulcérer** *vpr Méd* to ulcerate, to fester.
ulcéreux, -euse [ylserø, -øz] *adj Méd* ulcerous; ulcerated, festering (*wound etc*).
U.L.M. [yɛlɛm] *nm inv Av* (*abrév* **Ultra-Léger Motorisé**) microlight.
ulmaire [ylmɛr] *nf Bot* meadowsweet.
ulnaire [ylnɛr] *adj Anat* ulnar.
ultérieur [ylterjœr] *adj* ulterior; subsequent (**à,** to); later (*news, date etc*); *Com* **ordres ultérieurs,** further orders.
ultérieurement [ylterjœrmɑ̃] *adv* later (on), subsequently.
ultimatum [yltimatɔm] *nm* ultimatum; **adresser un u. à un pays,** to present a country with an ultimatum; **c'est un u.?,** is that an ultimatum?
ultime [yltim] *adj* ultimate, final, last.
ultimo [yltimo] *adv* lastly, finally.
ultra [yltra] *n Pol* extremist.
ultra-chic [yltraʃik] *adj F* ultra-fashionable.
ultra-confidentiel, -elle [yltrakɔ̃fidɑ̃sjɛl] *adj* top-secret.
ultra-court [yltrakur] *adj Phys* **ondes ultra-courtes,** ultra-short waves.
ultramicroscope [yltramikrɔskɔp] *nm* ultra-microscope.
ultramoderne [yltramɔdɛrn] *adj* ultramodern, state-of-the-art, high-tech (*equipment*).
ultramontain, -aine [yltramɔ̃tɛ̃, -ɛn] **1** *adj* **(a)** *Rel Pol* ultramontane; **(b)** beyond the Alps (*from France*). **2** *n Rel Pol* ultramontanist.
ultra-royaliste [yltrarwajalist] *adj & n Hist* ultraroyalist; (*pl ultra-royalistes*).
ultra-sensible [yltrasɑ̃sibl] *adj* ultra-sensitive; **pellicule/film u.-s.,** ultra-sensitive *or* high-speed film; *F* **elle est u.-s.,** she's hyper-sensitive.
ultra(-)son [yltrasɔ̃] *nm Phys* ultrasound; **ultra(-)sons,** ultrasonic waves; **science des ultra(-)sons,** ultrasonics.
ultrasonique [yltrasɔnik] *adj* ultrasonic, supersonic.
ultra(-)violet, -ette [yltravjɔlɛ, -ɛt] *adj & nm* ultraviolet.
ululation [ylylɑsjɔ̃] *nf*, **ululement** [ylylmɑ̃] *nm* ululation; hoot(ing) (*of owl*).
ululer [ylyle] *vi* to ululate; (*d'un hibou*) to hoot.
Ulysse [ylis] *nm* Ulysses.
un, une [œ̃, yn] **1** *adj* **(a)** one; **deux brioches et un pain,** two buns and a loaf (of bread); **il n'en reste qu'un,** there's only one left; **il vient un jour sur deux,** he comes every other *or* second day; **un à un** [œ̃aœ̃], **un par un,** one by one; **prendre les difficultés une à une,** to tackle the problems one by one *or* one at a time; **il est une heure,** it's one o'clock; *F* **je viendrai entre une et deux,** I'll come between one and two (o'clock); **page un,** page one, the first page; **numéro un,** number one;

(b) (*uni*) one (and indivisible); **Dieu est un,** God is one; **c'est tout un** [sɛtutœ̃], it's the same thing *or* all one *or* all the same; **ils ne font qu'un,** (*ils sont très proches*) they are as one.

2 *n* **un et un** [œ̃eœ̃] **font deux,** one and one are two; *Journ* **la une** [layn], the front page (*of newspaper*); **la guerre fait la une,** the war is front-page news *or* in the headlines; *F* **en savoir plus d'une,** to know a thing *or* two; *F* **il était moins une,** it was a close thing *or* a close shave; **un(e), deux, trois, partez!,** one, two, three, go!; **il n'a fait ni une ni deux,** he didn't hesitate (for a moment), he made no bones about it; **et d'un! et d'une!,** well, that's that! so much for that!

3 *pron* one; **un de ces jours,** one of these days; **un qui a de la chance,** a lucky one, a lucky man; **un que je plains, c'est ...,** someone I do pity is ...; *F* **menteur comme pas un,** a dreadful liar; *F* **il fait du bruit comme pas un,** he's unbelievably noisy; **(l')un de nous, (l')un d'entre nous,** one of us; **ni l'un ni l'autre,** neither (of them), neither one nor the other; **les uns et les autres,** some people; **l'un dans l'autre,** all in all, by and large; **(l')un des danceurs les plus célèbres du monde,** one of the most famous dancers in the world; **les uns disent que ...,** some say that ...; **il n'y en a pas un qui parle anglais,** there's no-one who speaks English.

4 *art indéf* (*pl* **des,** *see* **DE**) **(a)** a; (*devant voyelle ou* **h** *muet*) an; (*pl* some); **un jour/une pomme/une heure,** a day/an apple/an hour; **un père et une mère,** a father and mother; **un père de famille,** the father of a family; **venez me voir un lundi,** come and see me one Monday *or* some Monday; **un jour de la semaine dernière,** one day last week; *F* **un de ces quatre, il faudra que j'aille lui parler,** one of these days I'll have to have a word with him; **pour une raison** *ou* **pour une autre,** for some reason or other;
(b) such a one as; **ce sera un Einstein,** he'll be another Einstein;
(c) (*intensif*) **j'ai eu un monde aujourd'hui!,** I've had such a lot of visitors today!; **il a fait une de ces têtes!,** you should have seen his face; **tu m'as fait une peur!,** you gave me such a fright!, you DID give me a fright!; **tu en as une belle montre,** what a nice watch you've got.
unanime [ynanim] *adj* unanimous; **ils sont unanimes à vous accuser,** they are unanimous in accusing you.
unanimement [ynanimmɑ̃] *adv* unanimously.
unanimité [ynanimite] *nf* unanimity; **à l'u.,** unanimously; **élu à l'u.,** unanimously elected; **l'u. d'une réponse/réaction,** the unanimity of a response/reaction; **la proposition a fait l'u.,** the proposal was accepted unanimously.
underground [œdɛrgrawnd] *adj & nm* underground.
une [yn] *voir* **UN.**
U.N.E.F. [ynɛf] *nf Univ* (*abrév* **Union nationale des étudiants de France**) *Br* ≈ NUS.
Unesco [ynɛsko] *nf* Unesco.
uni [yni] **1** *adj* **(a)** united, harmonious (*family etc*); **(b) le Royaume-U.,** the United Kingdom; **les États-Unis,** the United States; **(c)** smooth, level, even (*ground etc*); smooth, calm, unruffled (*sea etc*); **(d)** plain (*material, colour etc*); self-coloured (*material*). **2** *nm Tex* self-coloured material.
uniate [ynjat] *adj & n Rel* Uniat(e).
unicellulaire [ynisɛlylɛr] *adj Biol* unicellular.
unicité [ynisite] *nf Phil etc* uniqueness.
unicolore [ynikɔlɔr] *adj* one-coloured *or US* -colored, self-coloured, plain (*material etc*).
unicorne [ynikɔrn] *nm Myth* unicorn.
unidirectionnel, -elle [ynidirɛksjɔnɛl] *adj* unidirectional.
unième [ynjɛm] *adj* (*used only in compounds*) first; **trente et u.,** thirty-first.
unièmement [ynjɛmmɑ̃] *adv* (*used only in compounds*) firstly; **vingt et u.,** in twenty-first place.
unificateur, -trice [ynifikatœr, -tris] *adj* unifying.

unification [ynifikɑsjɔ̃] *nf* unification (*of country etc*); consolidation (*of loans etc*); standardization (*of weights and measures etc*).
unifier [ynifje] *vt* (*impf & pr sub* **n. unifiions, v. unifiiez**) to unify (*ideas, political party etc*); to consolidate (*loans etc*); to standardize (*weights and measures etc*).
uniforme [ynifɔrm] **1** *adj* uniform; regular, unvarying (*life etc*); even (*pace* etc); **taux u.,** flat rate (*of interest etc*). **2** *nm* uniform; *Mil etc* **grand u.,** full-dress uniform; **endosser l'u.,** to join the forces; **prestige de l'u.,** the appeal of the uniform; **quitter l'u.,** to leave the service.
uniformément [ynifɔrmemɑ̃] *adv* uniformly, unvaryingly.
uniformisation [ynifɔrmizɑsjɔ̃] *nf* standardization.
uniformiser [ynifɔrmize] *vt* to standardize, to make uniform.
uniformité [ynifɔrmite] *nf* uniformity.
unijambiste [yniʒɑb~ist] *adj & n* one-legged (person).
unilatéral, -aux [ynilateral, -o] *adj* unilateral (*decision, disarmament etc*); one-sided (*contract etc*); **stationnement u.,** parking on one side only.
unilingue [ynilɛ̃g] *adj* monolingual, unilingual (*dictionary etc*).
uniment [ynimɑ̃] *adv* smoothly, evenly; *Litt* **tout u.,** (*simplement*) plainly, simply.
uninominal, -aux [yninɔminal, -o] *adj Pol* **scrutin u.,** voting for a single member *or* for one member only.
union [ynjɔ̃] *nf* **(a)** union; combination (*of two or more things etc*); *Beaux-Arts etc* blending (*of colours etc*); **(b)** (*association*) union, society, association; **l'U. des républiques socialistes soviétiques,** the Union of Soviet Socialist Republics; **l'U. soviétique,** the Soviet Union; **U. Nationale des Étudiants de France,** French National Union of Students; **u. douanière,** customs union; **(c)** (*marriage*) marriage; **u. conjugale,** marriage; **u. libre,** cohabitation (*of unmarried couple*); **(d)** (*accord, entente*) unity, agreement; **resserrer l'u. entre deux personnes,** to strengthen the links *or* bond between two people; *Prov* **l'u. fait la force,** unity is strength, strength through unity.
unioniste [ynjɔnist] *n* unionist.
unipare [ynipar] *adj Biol* uniparous.
unipolaire [ynipɔlɛr] *adj Él* unipolar, single-pole (*switch etc*); *Biol* unipolar (*cell etc*).
unique [ynik] *adj* **(a)** (*seul*) sole, only, single; **fils u.,** only son; **(rue à) sens u.,** one-way street; **voie u.,** single-line traffic; **exemplaire u.,** sole copy; **c'est son u. souci,** it's his only *or* sole concern; **ne rate pas cette occasion u.,** don't miss this unique opportunity; **u. en son genre,** one of a kind; **seul et u.,** one and only; **le seul, l'u. et l'irremplaçable Depardieu,** the one and only Depardieu; **(b)** (*incomparable*) unique, unrivalled, unparalleled; *F* **il est u.,** he's priceless!, he's the limit!
uniquement [ynikmɑ̃] *adv* solely; **je viens u. pour vous voir,** I've come especially *or* just to see you; **vous faites des dictionnaires? — pas u., nous faisons des traductions aussi,** you compile dictionaries, don't you? — not only that, we do translation(s) as well.
unir [ynir] **1** *vt* **(a)** to unite, to join, to link; **faits étroitement unis,** closely related facts, facts closely linked together *or* closely bound together; **u. un territoire à un autre,** to unite one territory with another; **le Tunnel sous la Manche unit Londres à Paris,** the Channel Tunnel links London and Paris; **être uni par le mariage à ...,** to be joined in wedlock to ...; **(b)** to smooth, to level (*ground etc*). **2 s'unir** *vpr* to unite, to join (together); **s'u. à qn,** to join forces with s.o.; (*se marier*) to marry s.o..
unisexe [ynisɛks] *adj* unisex (*clothes etc*).
unisexué [ynisɛksɥe] *adj Biol* unisexual.
unisson [ynisɔ̃] *nm Mus* unison; **à l'u.,** in unison; *Fig* **nos pensées sont à l'u.,** we think as one; **ses idées ne sont pas à l'u. avec celles de la maison,** his ideas are not in keeping with the company's.
unitaire [ynitɛr] **1** *adj* **(a)** unitary (*system etc*); *Com* **prix u.,** unit price; **(b)** *Rel* Unitarian. **2** *n Rel* Unitarian.
unitarien, -ienne [ynitarjɛ̃, -jɛn] *adj & n Pol* unitarian; *Rel* Unitarian.
unité [ynite] *nf* **(a)** *Math etc* unity, one; **10 F l'unité,** 10 francs each; *Com* **prix de l'u.,** unit price;
(b) unit (*of measure etc*); **u. de temps/de longueur,** unit of time/length; **u. monétaire,** unit of currency;
(c) u. d'intervention chirurgicale, field surgical unit; **u. de production,** production unit; *Ordinat* **u. centrale,** central processing unit, CPU; **u. de traitement,** processing unit; **u. de visualisation,** visual display unit, VDU; *Univ* **u. de valeur,** ≈ credit;
(d) *Mil* unit; *Nau* ship; **grosse u.,** capital ship; **u. de choc,** shock unit; *Pétr* **u. de craquage,** cracking unit;
(e) (*caractère de ce qui forme un tout*) unity; oneness (*of God etc*); uniformity (*of plan, action etc*); consistency (*of style etc*); *Littér* **les trois unités,** the three unities;
(f) *F* (*million d'anciens francs*) ten thousand francs; **ça lui a coûté plus de trois unités,** it cost him over thirty thousand francs.
univalent [ynivalɑ̃] *adj Ch* univalent.
univers [ynivɛr] *nm* universe; **l'u. mathématique,** the field of mathematics; **l'u. du rêve,** the world *or* realm of dreams; **les voitures ne sont pas vraiment mon u.,** cars are not really my thing *or* line, I'm not into cars.
universalisation [ynivɛrsalizɑsjɔ̃] *nf* universalization.
universaliser [ynivɛrsalize] *vt* to universalize, to make (*sth*) universal.
universalité [ynivɛrsalite] *nf* universality; **l'u. d'une théorie,** the universal nature of a theory.
universaux [ynivɛrso] *nmpl Phil* universals.
universel, -elle [ynivɛrsɛl] **1** *adj* universal; all-purpose (*device*); **réputation universelle,** worldwide reputation; **paix universelle,** universal peace; **suffrage u.,** universal suffrage, one man one vote; **savoir u.,** all-embracing knowledge; *MecE* **joint u.,** universal joint; **proposition universelle,** universal (proposition); *Jur* **légataire u.,** sole legatee; *Jur* **légataire à titre u.,** residuary legatee. **2** *nm* (*en logique*) universal.
universellement [ynivɛrsɛlmɑ̃] *adv* universally.
universitaire [ynivɛrsitɛr] **1** *adj* **ville u.,** university town; **études universitaires,** university studies; **honneurs universitaires,** academic honours; **cité u.,** ≈ (students') residence, hall(s) of residence; **restaurant u.,** student refectory. **2** *n* academic.
université [ynivɛrsite] *nf* **(a)** university; **aller à l'u.,** to go to university; **u. d'été,** summer school; **u. du troisième âge,** = university for mature students; **(b) l'U. (de France),** the teaching profession (*including university staff, schoolmasters, inspectors etc*).
univoque [ynivɔk] *adj* (*paroles*) univocal; *Math* (*correspondance*) one-to-one.
Untel [œ̃tɛl] *nm* **Monsieur U.,** Mr So-and-So.
uranifère [uranifɛr] *adj Géol* uranium-bearing.
uranium [yranjɔm] *nm* uranium.
urbain [yrbɛ̃] *adj* **(a)** (*de la ville*) urban; **la population urbaine,** city dwellers; **architecture urbaine,** town planning; **transport u.,** urban transport; *Tél* **communication urbaine,** local call; **vivre en milieu u.,** to live in an urban environment; **(b)** (*raffiné*) urbane.
urbanisable [yrbanizabl] *adj* **zone difficilement u.,** an area which would be difficult to develop.
urbanisation [yrbanizɑsjɔ̃] *nf* urbanization; **plan d'u.,** urban development plan.
urbaniser [yrbanize] *vt* to urbanize (*rural district etc*); **zone urbanisée,** built-up area.
urbanisme [yrbanism] *nm* town planning, urban development; **cabinet d'u.,** firm of town-planning consultants.
urbaniste [yrbanist] **1** *adj* urban; **architecture u.,** urban architecture. **2** *n* town planner.
urbanistique [yrbanistik] *adj* **politique u.,** town-planning *or* urban development policy.
urbanité [yrbanite] *nf Litt* urbanity; **avec u.,** urbanely.
urbi et orbi [yrbiɛtɔrbi] *adv* urbi et orbi; *Fig* far and wide, to all and sundry.
urée [yre] *nf Ch* urea.
urémie [yremi] *nf Méd* uraemia.
uretère [yrtɛr] *nm Anat* ureter.
urètre [yrɛtr] *nm Anat* urethra.
urgence [yrʒɑ̃s] *nf* **(a)** urgency; **il y a u.,** it's a matter of urgency, it's an emergency; **y a-t-il u. à ce qu'il parte?,** does he have to leave right *or* straight away?; **faire qch en toute u.,** to do sth as a priority; **transporter qn d'u. à l'hôpital,** to rush s.o. to hospital; **opérer d'u.,** to perform an emergency operation; **en cas d'u.,** in an emergency; **état d'u.,** state of emergency; **à envoyer d'u.,** to be sent immediately; **convoquer d'u. les actionnaires,** to call an extraordinary meeting of the shareholders; **il a été appelé d'u.,** he received an urgent call; **(b)** *Méd* **une u.,** an emergency; **salle des urgences,** emergency ward.
urgent [yrʒɑ̃] *adj* urgent, pressing; **rien d'u. ne l'obligeait à sortir,** there was nothing urgent to force him to go out; **cas u.,** urgent case, emergency; **il devient u. de trouver une solution,** a solution must be found urgently, a solution is urgently required; **avoir un besoin u. d'argent,** to be in urgent need *or* to be urgently in need of money.

urger [yrʒe] *vi F* to be urgent; **rien n'urge,** there's no desperate hurry; **vite, ça urge!,** quick, it's urgent!
urinaire [yrinɛr] *adj Anat* urinary.
urinal, -aux [yrinal, -o] *nm Méd* bed-pan, urinal.
urine [yrin] *nf* urine; **évacuer l'u.,** to pass water; **analyses d'urines,** urine tests.
uriner [yrine] *vi* to urinate, to pass water.
urinoir [yrinwar] *nm* (public) urinal.
urique [yrik] *adj* uric (*acid etc*).
urne [yrn] *nf* **(a)** (*pour voter*) ballot box; **aller aux urnes,** to go to the polls; **(b)** (*vase*) urn.
urogénital, -aux [yrɔʒenital, -o] *adj Méd* urogenital.
urologue [yrɔlɔg] *n* urologist.
U.R.S.S. [yɛrɛsɛs, *parfois* yrs] *nf* (*abrév* **Union des républiques socialistes soviétiques**) USSR.
urticacées [yrtikase] *nfpl Bot* Urticaceae.
urticaire [yrtikɛr] *nf Méd* nettlerash, hives, *Spéc* urticaria; **crise d'u.,** attack of hives; *Fig F* **sa présence me donne de l'u.,** he irritates me, he sets my teeth on edge.
urticant [yrtikɑ̃] *adj* stinging.
urtication [yrtikɑsjɔ̃] *nf Méd* stinging.
Uruguay [yrygwɛ] *nm* Uruguay.
uruguayen, -enne [yrygwɛjɛ̃, -ɛn] **1** *adj* Uruguayan. **2** *n* **U.,** Uruguayan.
urus [yrys] *nm Zool* urus, aurochs.
us [ys] *nmpl* **les us et coutumes d'un pays,** the ways and customs of a country.
usage [yzaʒ] *nm* **(a)** (*utilisation*) use; **mettre un article en u.,** to put an article into use; **mot en u.,** word in use; *Gram* **les règles de l'u. anglais,** the rules of English usage; **les mots se modifient par l'u.,** words are changed by *or* through use; **mot sorti de l'u.,** word which has fallen into disuse *or* is no longer in use; **faute d'u.,** (*d'un mot*) misuse; **faire u. de qch,** to make use of sth; **faire u. de la force,** to use *or* employ force; **faire bon u. de qch,** to make good use of sth, to put sth to good use; **faire mauvais u. de qch,** to make bad use of sth, to misuse sth; **je n'en aurai pas l'u.,** I won't be needing it, I won't have any use for it; *Pharm* **à u. externe/interne,** for external/internal use; **servir à plusieurs usages,** to have various uses; **article à mon u.,** article for my personal use; **à l'u. des écoles,** for use in schools; **réservé à son u. personnel,** reserved for his personal use; **article d'u.,** article for everyday use; **à usages multiples,** multi-purpose (*equipment etc*); **s'améliorer à l'u.,** to improve with use; **tu t'y habitueras à l'u.,** you'll get used to it once you start *or* with practice; **avoir l'u. de,** to have the use of; **hors d'u.,** out of service, out of use; (*usé*) worn out; (*démodé*) obsolete (*word etc*); **faire un u. immodéré de l'alcool,** to drink too much *or* to excess; **le bon u.,** *Arch* **le bel u.,** correct French; *Br* ≈ the Queen's English;
(b) wear, service (*of garments etc*); **faire de l'u.** *ou* **beaucoup d'u.,** to wear well; **ce manteau vous fera de l'u.,** you'll get a lot of wear out of this coat; **garanti à l'u.,** guaranteed to wear well;
(c) *Jur* **droit d'u. continu,** (right of) use;
(d) (*coutume*) custom, practice; **conforme/contraire aux usages,** in keeping with/contrary to common practice; **usages locaux,** local customs; **d'u. courant,** in common *or* everyday use; **c'est l'u.,** it's the usual practice, it's the done thing; **les conditions d'u.,** the usual terms; **comme il est d'u. en Algérie,** as is customary in Algeria; **selon** *ou* **suivant l'u.,** according to custom; **il est d'u. de** + *inf*, it is usual *or* customary to ...;
(e) (*expérience*) practice, experience; **avoir l'u. de qch,** to be used to sth; **l'u. du monde,** good breeding; **avoir de l'u., avoir l'u. du monde,** to have a knowledge of the ways of society; **manquer d'u.,** to lack breeding.
usagé [yzaʒe] *adj* used, worn; (*d'occasion*) secondhand; **non u.,** unused, new; **plaisanteries usagées,** tired jokes.
usager, -ère [yzaʒe, -ɛr] *n* user (*of sth*); **les usagers de la route/du téléphone/du train,** road users/telephone users/rail travellers; **les usagers du français/de l'anglais,** French language/English language users.
usant [yzɑ̃] *adj* wearing, exhausting (*life, work*); **il est u.,** he wears you out.
usé [yze] *adj* (*métal, pierre etc*) worn; (*vêtements*) worn(-out), threadbare; (*corde*) frayed; **u. par le temps,** timeworn; **u. par le travail,** worn out by work; **sujet u.,** hackneyed *or* stale *or* trite subject; **c'est u.!,** that's an old one!; **argument u. jusqu'à la corde,** well-worn *or* threadbare argument; **terre usée,** exhausted land; *Ind* **eaux usées,** waste water.
user [yze] **1** *vi* **u. de qch,** to use sth, to make use of sth; **u. de son droit,** to exercise one's right; **u. de violence/de ruse,** to use *or* resort to violence/cunning; **u. qn de douceur,** to deal gently with s.o.; **u. de son influence,** to use one's influence; **u. d'une pièce pour répéter,** to use a room for rehearsals, to use a room to rehearse in; *Litt* **en u. bien/mal avec qn,** to treat s.o. well/badly.
2 *vt* **(a)** to use (up), to consume (*sth*); **u. du charbon,** to use *or* burn coal;
(b) to wear (*sth*) (out, away, down); to ruin (*health etc*); **u. ses vêtements,** to wear out one's clothes; **u. un pull aux coudes,** to wear out a pullover at the elbows; **usé par le frottement,** worn (out) by rubbing; **l'érosion use la roche,** erosion wears *or* eats away the rock; **l'habitude use la passion,** habit is the enemy of passion; **u. ses forces à essayer de convaincre qn,** to wear oneself out trying to convince s.o.; *Fig* **tu use tes yeux à lire dans le noir,** you'll ruin your eyesight reading in the dark; *F* **tais-toi, tu m'uses,** shut up, you're wearing *or* tiring me out.
3 s'user *vpr* to wear (out, away, down); **ce tissu s'use vite,** this material wears (out) quickly; **sa résistance s'usera à la fin,** his resistance will wear down *or* break down in due course; **il s'est usé à ce travail,** he's worn himself out with this work; **je me suis usé à le lui dire,** I'm worn out telling him, I've told him till I'm blue in the face.
usinage [yzinaʒ] *nm Métal* machining, tooling (*of castings etc*); machine finishing (*of parts*).
usine [yzin] *nf* factory, plant; **navire-u.,** factory ship; **u. pilote,** pilot plant; **u. à gaz,** gasworks; **u. à papier,** paper mill; **u. de construction automobiles,** car factory *or* plant; **ouvrier d'u.,** factory worker; *Fig F* **ce restaurant est une u.,** this restaurant is like a works canteen.
usiner [yzine] **1** *vt* **(a)** *Métal* to machine, to tool (*castings etc*); to machine-finish (*parts*); **parties usinées,** bright parts; **(b)** (*fabriquer*) to manufacture. **2** *vi F* **ça usine là-dedans,** they're hard at it in there.
usinier, -ière [yzinje, -jɛr] *adj* factory (*life, industry etc*); **faubourg u.,** industrial suburb.
usité [yzite] *adj* in common *or* current use; **mot très u.,** word in common *or* current use; **mot peu u.,** little used word.
ustensile [ystɑ̃sil] *nm* implement, tool; **u. de cuisine,** kitchen utensil.
usuel, -elle [yzɥɛl] *adj* usual, common, ordinary; **l'anglais u.,** everyday English; **dénomination usuelle,** common name (*for plant etc*).
usuellement [yzɥɛlmɑ̃] *adv* usually, ordinarily.
usufruit [yzyfrɥi] *nm Jur* usufruct.
usufruitier, -ière [yzyfrɥitje, -jɛr] **1** *adj Jur* usufructuary. **2** *n* **(a)** *Jur* usufructuary; **(b)** (*d'un bien immobilier*) tenant for life.
usuraire [yzyrɛr] *adj* usurious (*interest etc*).
usure¹ [yzyr] *nf* usury; **pratiquer l'u.,** to practise usury; **rendre un bienfait avec u.,** to repay a service with interest.
usure² *nf* **(a)** wear (and tear); **tissu qui résiste à l'u.,** material that wears well; **u. par frottement,** abrasion; **guerre d'u.,** war of attrition; *Tech* **surface d'u.,** wearing surface; **organes sujets à l'u.,** wearing parts (*of a machine*); *F* **je l'aurai à l'u.,** I'll wear him down; **(b)** (*érosion*) wearing away, erosion.
usurier, -ière [yzyrje, -jɛr] *n* usurer.
usurpateur, -trice [yzyrpatœr, -tris] *n* usurper.
usurpation [yzyrpɑsjɔ̃] *nf* **(a)** *Jur* usurpation; **u. de titre,** usurpation of title; **u. de pouvoir,** usurping *or* usurpation of power; **(b)** (*empiètement*) encroachment.
usurper [yzyrpe] **1** *vt* **(a)** *Jur* to usurp (**sur,** from); **(b)** to encroach (up)on, to usurp (*s.o.'s rights etc*). **2** *vi* **u. sur les droits/le domaine de qn,** to encroach (up)on s.o.'s rights/territory *or F* patch.
ut [yt] *nm inv Mus* (the note) C; **ut dièse,** C sharp; **clef d'ut,** C clef; **clef d'ut quatrième ligne,** tenor clef.
utérin [yterɛ̃] *adj* uterine; **frère u.,** half brother on the mother's side.
utérus [yterys] *nm* uterus, womb.
utile [ytil] **1** *adj* useful; useful, helpful (*advice, knowledge, person etc*); **si je puis vous être u.,** if I can be of any use *or* help *or* service *or* assistance to you; **en quoi puis-je vous être u.?,** what can I do for you?, how can I help you?; **se rendre u.,** to make oneself useful; **cela m'a été bien u.,** it came in very handy; **en temps u.,** in (good) time, duly, in due course; **prendre toutes dispositions utiles,** to make all necessary arrangements; **est-il u. d'y aller?,** is there any use *or* any point in going?; **dictionnaire u. à consulter,** useful *or* helpful dictionary to consult; *Tech* **effet u.,** effective power; **charge u. d'un véhicule,** payload of a

vehicle. **2** *nm* **joindre l'u. à l'agréable,** to combine *or* mix business with pleasure.

utilement [ytilmɑ̃] *adv* usefully; **conseiller u. qn,** to give s.o. useful advice.

utilisable [ytilizabl] *adj* usable, fit for use; **billet u. pour tous les trains,** ticket which is valid *or* can be used on all trains.

utilisateur, -trice [ytilizatœr, -tris] *n* user.

utilisation [ytilizɑsjɔ̃] *nf* use, utilization (*of sth*); **u. réduite à certaines périodes,** use restricted to certain periods.

utiliser [ytilize] *vt* to use, *Fml & US* to utilize; (*profiter de*) to make use of (*sth*); *Ordinat* to run; **pouvez-vous u. ce logiciel sur votre ordinateur?,** can you run this software on your computer?; *Ordinat* **il peut être utilisé sur ...,** it can run on ...; *Péj* **avoir l'impression qu'on vous utilise,** to have the feeling you're being used.

utilitaire [ytilitɛr] **1** *adj* utilitarian; *Aut* **véhicule u.,** commercial vehicle; *Ordinat* **programme u.,** utility (program). **2** *n* utilitarian.

utilitarisme [ytilitarism] *nm* utilitarianism.

utilité [ytilite] *nf* **(a)** (*fonction*) utility, use(fulness); **être d'une grande u.,** to be of great use, to be very useful; **cela ne m'est d'aucune u.,** it's absolutely no use to me, it's no earthly use to me; **sans u.,** useless(ly); **s'entremettre sans grande u.,** to intervene to little purpose; **association d'u. publique,** public utility; (*charitable*) registered charity; **(b)** *Th* **jouer les utilités,** to play small *or* bit parts; *Fig* to play second fiddle.

utopie [ytɔpi] *nf* utopia; *Fig Péj* **c'est une u.!,** it's nothing but a pipedream.

utopique [ytɔpik] *adj* utopian.

utopiste [ytɔpist] *n* Utopian.

utriculaire [ytrikylɛr] *nf Bot* utricularia, bladderwort.

U.V.[1] [yve] *nf inv Univ abrév* **unité de valeur.**

U.V.[2] *nm inv* (*abrév* **ultra-violet**) U.V.; **se faire faire des U.V.,** to go on a sunbed.

uval, -aux [yval, -o] *adj* of grapes.

uvulaire [yvylɛr] *adj* uvular.

uvule [yvyl] *nf Anat* uvula.

V

V, v [ve] *nm* **(a)** (the letter) V, v; **double v,** W, w; **moteur (à cylindres) en V,** V (type) engine; *Geog* **vallée (à profil) en V,** V-shaped valley; **col en v,** V-neck; **(b)** *F* (*abrév* **vitesse**) **à la vitesse grand v,** at a rate of knots, *Br* like the clappers; **(c)** (*abrév* **voir**) see.

vacance [vakɑ̃s] *nf* **(a) vacances,** holiday(s), *surtout Am* vacation; (*of parliament*) recess; **départ/retour de vacances,** going away on/coming back from holiday; **les grandes vacances,** *Scol* the summer holidays; *Univ* the long vacation; **être en vacances,** to be on holiday; (*of school*) to break up; (*of parliament*) to rise; **partir en vacances,** to go away on holiday; **vacances de neige** *ou* **d'hiver/d'été,** winter/summer holiday; **prendre ses vacances en août,** to take one's holiday in August; **un jour de vacance(s),** a (day's) holiday; **colonie de vacances,** holiday camp; **village v.,** holiday village; **vacances judiciaires,** vacation, recess (*of law courts*); **(b)** (*poste*) vacancy; **(c)** *Jur* abeyance (*of succession*).

vacancier, -ière [vakɑ̃sje, -jɛr] *n* holiday-maker, *Am* vacationer, vacationist; **l'afflux des vacanciers,** the influx of holiday-makers.

vacant [vakɑ̃] *adj* **(a)** vacant, unoccupied (*house etc*); **poste v.,** vacancy; **(b)** *Jur* **succession vacante,** estate in abeyance.

vacarme [vakarm] *nm* uproar, din, racket; **faire du v.,** to create *or* make an uproar, *F* to kick up a row.

vacataire [vakatɛr] *n* short-term replacement, stand-in; **c'est une v.,** she's on a short-term *or* temporary contract.

vacation [vakɑsjɔ̃] *nf Jur* **(a)** attendance, sitting (*of officials*); day's sale (*at auction*); **(b) vacations,** (*tarif*) fees (*of lawyer etc*); (*arrêt*) vacation, recess (*of lawcourts*).

vaccin [vaksɛ̃] *nm* vaccine; **injection du v.,** vaccine injection; **v. antivariolique/contre la coqueluche,** smallpox/whooping-cough vaccine; *Fig* **le meilleur v. contre la paresse,** the best antidote to laziness.

vaccinable [vaksinabl] *adj* able to be vaccinated *or* inoculated.

vaccinal, -aux [vaksinal, -o] *adj* vaccinal.

vaccination [vaksinɑsjɔ̃] *nf* vaccination, inoculation; **v. préventive,** protective inoculation; **v. obligatoire,** compulsory vaccination; **v. contre la coqueluche,** vaccination against whooping cough.

vaccine [vaksin] *nf* **(a)** *Vét* cowpox, *Spéc* vaccinia; **(b)** *Méd* inoculated cowpox.

vacciner [vaksine] *vt Méd* to vaccinate, to inoculate; **v. contre la diphtérie,** to vaccinate *or* inoculate *or* immunize against diphtheria; **v. un enfant,** to vaccinate *or* inoculate a child; **se faire v.,** to get vaccinated *or* inoculated **(contre,** against); *Fig* **être vacciné contre les désagréments du métier/les voyages organisés,** to be immune to the drawbacks of the job/package holidays.

vache [vaʃ] **1** *nf* **(a)** cow; *Agr* **v. laitière,** *Agr & Fig* **v. à lait,** milch cow; *F* **le plancher des vaches,** dry land, terra firma; *Fig F* **finies, les vaches grasses!,** the good days are over!; *Fig* **connaître une période de vaches maigres,** to go through a lean period; *F* **parler français comme une v. espagnole,** to murder *or* torture the French language; *F* **manger de la v. enragée,** to have a hard time of it; **coup de pied en v.,** stab in the back; **nœud de v.,** granny knot; *Prov* **chacun son métier, les vaches seront bien gardées,** cobbler, stick to your last; *F* **il pleut comme v. qui pisse,** it's bucketing (down), *Vulg* it's pissing down; *Zool* **v. marine,** sea cow;

(b) *F* swine, sod, *f* cow, bitch; **ah la v.!,** the swine!;

(c) *Arg* policeman; **les vaches,** the cops, the fuzz, the filth;

(d) (*cuir*) cowhide; **valise en v.,** leather suitcase;

(e) v. à eau, (canvas) water carrier.

2 *adj F* rotten, nasty; **elle a été v. avec lui,** she was rotten to him; **ça serait v.,** that would be rotten.

3 *n F* **un v. de mec!,** a *or* one hell of a guy; **une v. de surprise,** a hell of a surprise.

vachement [vaʃmɑ̃] *adv F* **c'est v. difficile,** it's damned *or* bloody difficult; **c'est v. bien,** it's bloody good; **il a v. vieilli,** he's got a helluva lot older-looking.

vacher, -ère [vaʃe, -ɛr] *n* cowherd, *f* cowgirl.

vacherie [vaʃri] *nf F* (*action*) dirty trick; (*remarque*) nasty remark; **elle lui a fait/dit une sale v.,** she played a dirty trick on him/made a nasty remark to him; **il est d'une v. terrible,** he's a really nasty customer, he's rotten to the core.

vacherin [vaʃrɛ̃] *nm Culin* **(a)** (*fromage*) vacherin cheese; **(b)** = meringue with cream, ice cream and fruit.

vachette [vaʃɛt] *nf* **(a)** (*animal*) calf; **(b)** (*cuir*) calfskin.

vacillant [vasijɑ̃] *adj* **(a)** unsteady, wobbly (*table etc*); flickering (*flame etc*); unsteady, wobbly, shaky (*hand*); uncertain, staggering (*gait etc*); **(b)** wavering, indecisive, vacillating (*mind etc*); failing (*health*).

vacillation [vasijɑsjɔ̃] *nf*, **vacillement** [vasijmɑ̃] *nm* **(a)** unsteadiness, shakiness; wobbling (*of table etc*); flickering (*of flame etc*); **(b)** (*hésitation*) vacillation, shilly-shallying.

vaciller [vasije] *vi* **(a)** to be unsteady (on one's feet), to sway, to wobble; **il vacille sur ses jambes,** (*parce qu'il est vieux*) he's shaky on his legs; (*parce qu'il est ivre, blessé*) he's staggering; **(b)** (*d'une flamme, lumière*) to flicker; **(c)** (*faiblir*) to vacillate, to waver, to falter.

va-comme-je-te-pousse (à la) [alavakɔmʃtəpus] *adv* haphazardly, (in a) slapdash (manner *or* way), any old how *or* way; **élever ses enfants à la va-c.-je-te-p.,** to bring up one's children any old how.

vacuité [vakɥite] *nf* vacuity, vacuousness; (*de paroles*) emptiness.

vacuum [vakɥɔm] *nm* vacuum.

vade-mecum [vademekɔm] *nm* vade-mecum, pocketbook.

vadrouille [vadruj] *nf* **(a)** *F* (*balade*) ramble, stroll; **partir** *ou* **aller en v.,** = **VADROUILLER**; **(b)** *Can* mop, floorcloth; **(c)** *Nau* (deck) swab.

vadrouiller [vadruje] *vi F* to roam *or* rove *or* wander about.

vadrouilleur, -euse [vadrujœr, -øz] *n F* rover, wanderer.

va-et-vient [vaevjɛ̃] *nm inv* **(a)** (*mouvement*) backward and forward motion; **faire le va-et-v. entre,** to go to and fro between; (*d'un bateau*) to go to and fro between, to ply between; **faire le va-et-v. entre Paris et Lyon,** to go to and fro between Paris and Lyons, to make regular journeys between Paris and Lyons; **(porte) va-et-v.,** swing door; **(b)** coming(s) and going(s), toing(s) and froing(s) (*of people etc*); **(c)** *El* two-way wiring (system); **(commutateur) va-et-v.,** two-way switch; **installer un va-et-v.,** to put in a two-way switch; **(d)** *MecE* reciprocation; **(e)** *Nau* backstay traveller.

vagabond, -onde [vagabɔ̃, -ɔ̃d] **1** *adj* wandering, roving, roaming (*life etc*); *Fig* **avoir l'humeur vagabonde,** to be changeable. **2** *n Péj* vagabond, vagrant, tramp; *Litt* (*voyageur*) wanderer.

vagabondage [vagabɔ̃daʒ] *nm* (*d'un clochard etc*) wandering(s); *Péj* vagrancy; **arrêté pour v.,** arrested for vagrancy; *Admin* **v. spécial,** living on immoral earnings.

vagabonder [vagabɔ̃de] *vi* to rove, to roam, to wander (about); *Fig* **ses pensées vagabondent,** his thoughts wander.

vagin [vaʒɛ̃] *nm* vagina.

vaginal, -aux [vaʒinal, -o] *adj* vaginal.

vagir [vaʒir] *vi* (*d'un nouveau-né*) to cry, to wail; (*d'un animal*) to squeak, to whimper.

vagissant [vaʒisɑ̃] *adj* crying, wailing (*baby*).

vagissement [vaʒismɑ̃] *nm* cry, wail(ing) (*of baby*); squeak(ing), whimper(ing) (*of animal*).

vague[1] [vag] *nf* wave; **une v. a balayé le pont,** a wave washed over the deck; **plonger dans les vagues,** to dive into the waves; **canot renversé par les vagues,** canoe capsized *or* overturned by the waves; **v. de fond,** ground swell, (blind) roller; *Fig* ground swell (of opinion); **cette épidémie frappe comme une v. de fond,** this epidemic strikes everyone in its path; **v. de chaleur/froid,** heat wave/cold spell *or* snap; **v. d'enthousiasme/de tendresse,** wave of enthusiasm/of tenderness; **v. de colère/*Él* de courant,** surge of anger/*El* of current; *Fig* **faire des vagues,** to make waves, to rock the boat; **être dans le creux de la v.,** to be down in the dumps, to be in the doldrums; **première v. de départs/d'immigrants,** first wave of departures/immigrants; *Littér etc* **nouvelle v.,** new wave.

vague² **1** *adj* **(a)** vague, sketchy, hazy (*knowledge etc*); vague, dim, indistinct (*memory*); **geste v.,** vague gesture; **quelque v. écrivain,** some writer or other; **(b)** *Anat* **nerf v.,** vagus (nerve). **2** *nm* vagueness, indefiniteness; **avoir du v. à l'âme,** to have vague yearnings.

vague³ **1** *adj* **regarder qn d'un air v.,** to look vacantly at s.o.; **terrain v.,** waste ground. **2** *nm* space; **fixer les yeux dans le v.,** to gaze into space; **regard perdu dans le v.,** faraway *or* far-off *or* distant look.

vaguelette [vaglɛt] *nf* wavelet.

vaguement [vagmɑ̃] *adv* vaguely; **on la reconnaît v. sur la photo,** you can just make her out in the photo; **c'est ce que j'ai v. compris,** that's what I had more or less understood.

vaguemestre [vagmɛstr] *nm Mil* post orderly; *Nau* postman.

vaguer [vage] *vi Litt* to wander, to roam (about); **laisser v. ses pensées,** to let one's thoughts wander.

vahiné [vaine] *nf* Tahitian woman.

vaigrage [vɛgraʒ] *nm Nau* inner planking, inner plating.

vaigre [vɛgr] *nf Nau* ceiling plate, inner plank; bottom-board (*of small boat*).

vaillamment [vajamɑ̃] *adv* valiantly, bravely, courageously; **s'attaquer v. à qch,** to tackle sth courageously.

vaillance [vajɑ̃s] *nf* valour, *US* valor, bravery, courage; *Mil* gallantry; **supporter une épreuve avec v.,** to face an ordeal with courage.

vaillant [vajɑ̃] *adj* **(a) être v.,** to be in good health; **je ne suis pas v.,** I'm not up to the mark, I feel under the weather; **(b) n'avoir pas un sou v.,** to be stony broke; **(c)** (*courageux*) valiant, brave, courageous; stout (*heart*); *Mil* gallant.

vain [vɛ̃] *adj* **(a)** vain, useless, fruitless, futile (*efforts etc*); **en v.,** in vain, vainly; **c'est en v. qu'elle le lui a demandé,** she asked him for it in vain *or* but to no avail; **(b)** (*vide de sens*) sham, unreal, empty (*title etc*); **ce n'étaient pas là de vaines paroles,** these were no empty words *or* no idle words; **vaines promesses,** hollow promises; **je te dis qu'elle est dangereuse, et ce n'est pas un v. mot!,** I tell you she's dangerous, and it's no empty claim *or* and I know what I'm talking about; **(c) vaine pâture,** common (land); **(d)** *Litt* vain, conceited.

vaincre [vɛ̃kr] *v* (*prp* **vainquant;** *pp* **vaincu;** *pr ind* **je vaincs, il vainc, n. vainquons;** *impf* **je vainquais;** *p hist* **je vainquis;** *fu* **je vaincrai**) **1** *vt* **(a)** (*écraser*) to conquer, to defeat, *surtout Litt* to vanquish (*adversary*); **(b)** *Sp etc* to beat (*rival*); **v. qn aux échecs,** to beat s.o. at chess; **(c)** *Fig* to overcome, to master, to conquer (*disease, difficulties etc*); **v. ses complexes,** to overcome one's complexes; **v. une résistance,** to overcome resistance. **2** *vi* **il faut v. ou mourir,** we must do or die.

vaincu [vɛ̃ky] *adj* beaten, defeated; **(être) v. d'avance,** (to be) beaten before one starts; **s'avouer v.,** to admit defeat; **attitude/comportement de v.,** defeatist attitude/behaviour.

vainement [vɛnmɑ̃] *adv* vainly, in vain.

vainqueur [vɛ̃kœr] **1** *nm* **(a)** *Sp etc* winner; **le v. de la course,** the winner of the race; **le v. de l'Anapurna,** the conqueror of Annapurna; **(b)** *Mil* victor, conqueror, *surtout Litt* vanquisher. **2** *adj* conquering, victorious, *surtout Litt* vanquishing; **air/sourire v.,** triumphant look/smile.

vair [vɛr] *nm* **(a)** vair; **pantoufle de v.,** glass slipper; **(b)** *Hér* vair.

vairon [vɛrɔ̃] **1** *adj* **aux yeux vairons,** wall-eyed. **2** *nm* (*poisson*) minnow.

vaisseau, -eaux [vɛso] *nm* **(a)** *Anat Bot* vessel, canal, duct; **v. sanguin,** blood vessel; **(b)** *Arch* nave (*of church*); body, hall (*of building*); **(c)** *Nau Vieilli* ship, vessel; **v. à voiles,** sailing vessel; **v. de guerre,** warship; **v. amiral,** flagship; **brûler ses vaisseaux,** to burn one's boats; **v. spatial,** spaceship; **(d)** *Arch* vessel, receptacle; *Bible* **v. d'élection,** chosen vessel.

vaisselier [vɛsəlje] *nm* (*meuble*) dresser.

vaisselle [vɛsɛl] *nf* dishes, crockery; (*de céramique, de porcelaine*) china; **v. de porcelaine,** porcelain; **v. plate,** (gold, silver) plate; **faire** *ou* **laver la v.,** to wash up, to do the washing up, to do the dishes; *F* **je dois finir ma v.,** I must finish washing up; **machine à laver la v.,** dishwasher; **liquide (de) v.,** washing-up liquid; **eau de v.,** dishwater; *Fig F Péj* **cette bière/soupe, c'est de l'eau de v.,** this beer/soup is like dishwater.

val [val] *nm Géog* (narrow) valley; (*pl often* **vals** *except in the phrase*) **par monts et par vaux** [vo], up hill and down dale.

valable [valabl] *adj* valid, legitimate (*title, excuse*); **billet v. pour deux mois,** ticket valid for two months; **votre titre de transport n'est pas v.,** your ticket is not valid; **cette excuse n'est pas v.,** this is not a valid *or* legitimate *or* good excuse; **c'est un argument tout à fait v.,** this is a perfectly valid *or* acceptable argument; **promesse toujours v.,** promise that still holds good; *Pol* **pouvoir s'adresser à un interlocuteur v.,** to be able to speak to an authorized representative; **devenir un partenaire v. dans la CEE,** to become a fully-fledged partner in the EEC; **un roman v.,** a good novel; *F* **c'est v.!,** it's great! it's brill!

valablement [valabləmɑ̃] *adv* validly; **être v. autorisé à qch/à faire qch,** to have the necessary authority for sth/to do sth; **c'est ce qu'on lui a reproché v.,** this is what he was accused of, and rightly so.

valdinguer [valdɛ̃ge] *vi F* to fall flat on one's face; **envoyer v. ses affaires,** to send everything flying; *Fig* **tout envoyer v.,** to pack *or* jack it all in.

valence [valɑ̃s] *nf Ch* valency, *Am* valence.

Valence [valɑ̃s] *nf* **(a)** (*ville d'Espagne*) Valencia; **(b)** (*ville de France*) Valence.

valenciennes [valɑ̃sjɛn] *nf* Valenciennes lace.

valériane [valerjan] *nf Bot* valerian.

valet [valɛ] *nm* **(a)** *Cartes* jack, knave; **jouer son v. de cœur,** to play one's jack of hearts; **(b)** (*domestique*) **v. (de chambre),** manservant; **elle a fait de son fils un v.,** she treats her son like a servant; **v. de pied,** footman; **v. d'écurie,** groom, stableboy; **v. de ferme,** farmhand; (*chasse*) **v. de chiens,** (*à la chasse*) whipper-in; *Prov* **tel maître, tel v.,** like master, like man; **(c)** *Menuis etc* clamp, holdfast; **(d)** support, rest, stand (*of mirror etc*); **v. de nuit,** valet; **(e)** *Arch* varlet, page.

valetaille [valtaj] *nf F Péj* the servants.

valétudinaire [valetydinɛr] *adj & n* valetudinarian.

valeur [valœr] *nf* **(a)** value, worth; **cela n'a pas grande v.,** it's not worth much; **homme de v.,** (*doué*) man of real ability, talented man; (*de mérite*) man of merit; **estimer qn à sa juste v.,** to judge s.o. at his true value *or* worth; **ne pas avoir conscience de sa propre v.,** to be unaware of one's own worth; **mettre une terre en v.,** to develop a piece of land; **mise en v. d'un terrain,** development of a site; *Econ* **taxe à la v. ajoutée,** value-added tax, VAT; **v. d'échange,** exchange value; **v.-or du dollar/du franc,** gold value of the dollar/franc; **v. d'usage,** value as a going concern; **v. marchande,** market(able) value; **article de v.,** article of value, valuable article; **objets de v.,** valuables; **bijou de grande v.,** jewel of great value, very valuable jewel; **livre de grande v.,** book of considerable merit; **il ne cesse de prendre de la v.,** it keeps going up in value, its value is constantly increasing; **sans v.,** worthless, valueless; **colis chargé avec v. déclarée cent francs,** parcel insured for one hundred francs;

(b) merit, worth, value; **votre argument n'est pas sans v.,** there's something in what you say; **renseignements sans v.,** worthless information; **v. des mots,** value of words; **mettre qch en v.,** to show sth to advantage; **mettre un mot en v.,** to emphasize *or* give importance to a word; **elle était très en v. avec sa robe bleue,** her blue dress was very flattering; **savoir se mettre en v.,** (*physiquement*) to present oneself well; (*par son attitude*) to use one's abilities to advantage;

(c) *Fin* asset; **valeurs,** bills, shares, securities, stocks; **valeurs vedettes,** glamour stock; **valeurs mobilières,** stocks and shares, transferable securities; **valeurs passives,** liabilities;

(d) *Mus* time (value), length (*of a note*); *Math* value;

(e) boire la v. d'un verre de vin, to drink the equivalent of a glass of wine;

(f) (*morale*) value; **jugement de v.,** value judgment; **avoir le sens des valeurs,** to have a sense of values; **selon son échelle de valeurs,** according to his scale of values; **les valeurs chrétiennes,** Christian values;

(g) *Litt* (*courage*) valour, *US* valor; **homme de v.,** man of courage; **v. militaire,** gallantry.

valeureusement [valœrøzmɑ̃] *adv Litt* valorously, gallantly.
valeureux, -euse [valœrø, -øz] *adj Litt* valorous, gallant (*in battle*).
validation [validɑsjɔ̃] *nf* validation (*of election, marriage etc*); ratifying (*of law*); authentication (*of document etc*).
valide [valid] *adj* **(a)** valid (*contract, reason etc*); **(b)** (*personne*) fit, able-bodied.
validement [validmɑ̃] *adv* validly.
valider [valide] *vt* to validate (*election, marriage*); to ratify (*contract etc*); to authenticate (*document*); **(faire) v. son titre de transport,** to have one's ticket stamped.
validité [validite] *nf* validity (*of contract, passport etc*); **durée de v. d'un billet,** period of validity of a ticket; **établir la v. d'un testament,** to prove a will.
valise [valiz] *nf* (suit)case; **faire sa v.** *ou* **ses valises,** to pack (one's bag(s)); **la v. diplomatique,** the diplomatic bag.
vallée [vale] *nf* valley; **remonter une v.,** to go up a valley; **v. sèche** *ou* **morte,** dried-up valley; **gens de la v.,** (*pour les montagnards*) lowlanders; *Litt* **cette v. de larmes,** this vale of tears.
vallon [valɔ̃] *nm* small valley; (*écossais*) glen.
vallonné [valɔne] *adj* undulating (*country*).
valoche [valɔʃ] *nf F* case, bag.
valoir [valwar] *v* (*prp* **valant;** *pp* **valu;** *pr ind* **je vaux, il vaut, n. valons, ils valent;** *pr sub* **je vaille, n. valions, ils vaillent;** *impf* **je valais;** *p hist* **je valus;** *fu* **je vaudrai**) **1** *vi* **(a)** (*coûter*) to be worth; **maison qui vaut deux cent mille francs,** house worth two hundred thousand francs; **ça vaut cher,** it's expensive; **c'est tout ce que ça vaut,** that's all it's worth; **à v. sur (une somme),** on account of (a sum); **à v. sur qn,** on *or* for account of s.o.; **payer dix francs à v.,** to pay ten francs on account; **ne pas v. grand-chose,** not to be worth much; **son explication ne vaut rien,** his explanation is worthless *or* useless; **il ne vaut pas grand-chose, il ne vaut pas cher,** he's not much good *or* up to much; **prends mon avis pour ce qu'il vaut,** take my advice for what it's worth; **cela ne vaut rien,** that's no good; **ce climat ne vous vaut rien,** this climate is bad for you *or* doesn't suit you; **ce n'est rien qui vaille,** it isn't worth having, it isn't of any value; **cela ne me dit rien qui vaille,** that doesn't sound good to me; **rien ne vaut un bon petit déjeuner,** there's nothing like a good breakfast;
(b) (*correspondre à*) to be equivalent to; **un franc vaut cent centimes,** a franc is equal to a hundred centimes; **une livre vaut dix francs,** a pound is worth *or* equal to ten francs; **c'est une façon qui en vaut une autre,** it's as good a way as any (other); **l'un vaut (bien) l'autre,** one is (just) as good *or* as bad as the other, there's nothing to choose between them; **il ne vaut pas mieux que son frère,** he's no better than his brother; **il ne vaut pas son frère,** he can't compare with *or F* isn't a patch on his brother;
(c) faire v. qch, to make the most of sth; **monture qui fait v. la pierre,** setting that shows off the stone (to (good) advantage); **faire v. ses opinions,** to command respect for one's opinions; **faire v. ses droits,** to assert *or* enforce one's claims; **faire v. son bon droit,** to vindicate one's rights; **faire v. ses raisons,** to put forward one's reasons; **j'ai fait v. que ...,** I pointed out *or* urged that ...; **faire v. son argent,** to invest one's money profitably *or* to good account; **faire v. une terre,** to farm an estate;
(d) (*mériter*) to be worth, to deserve, to merit (*sth*); **un service en vaut un autre,** one good turn deserves another; **le livre vaut d'être lu,** the book is worth reading; **cela vaut la peine de faire le voyage,** it's worth making the journey; **cela vaut le voyage,** it's worth the journey, it's worth a special trip; **je viendrai si cela en vaut la peine,** I'll come if it's worth (my) while *or* worth the trouble *or* worth it; **cela ne vaut pas la peine d'y penser,** it's not worth a moment's thought; *F* **ça vaut le coup,** it's worth a try; *F* **ça ne vaut pas le coup,** it isn't worth the trouble.
2 *v impers* **il vaut mieux** *ou* **il vaudrait mieux rester à la maison,** it's *or* it would be better to stay at home; **mieux vaudrait ne pas vous en mêler,** you'd better not interfere, it would be better if you didn't interfere; **il vaut mieux qu'il en soit ainsi,** it is better that way; **il vaut mieux que vous restiez,** you had better stay, it would be better if you stayed; **il vaut mieux** *ou* **mieux vaut partir que de rester,** it's better to go away than to stay; *Prov* **mieux vaut tard que jamais,** better late than never; **autant vaut rester ici,** we may as well stay here; **choses qu'il vaut autant ne pas rappeler,** things best forgotten; **il ne vaut pas la peine de les mentionner,** they're not worth mentioning.
3 se valoir *vpr* **tous les métiers se valent,** one job is as good as another; **ils se valent,** one is (just) as good *or* as bad as the other, there's nothing to choose between them; *F* **ça se vaut,** it's the same either way, it's six of one and half a dozen of the other.
4 *vt* **(a) v. qch à qn,** to earn s.o. sth; **cette action lui a valu d'être décoré,** this act won him a decoration; **qu'est-ce qui me vaut cet honneur?,** to what do I owe this honour?; **les facilités que lui a valu son succès,** the opportunities his success has brought him;
(b) vaille que vaille, at all costs, come what may.
valorisation [valɔrizɑsjɔ̃] *nf Com Fin* valorization.
valoriser [valɔrize] *Com Fin etc* **1** *vt* to valorize. **2 se valoriser** *vpr* to increase in value; **région/secteur qui se valorise,** region/industry which is going through a period of growth, up-and-coming region/industry.
valse [vals] *nf* waltz; **faire un tour de v.,** to waltz round the room; *Fig F* **la v. du personnel/des ministres,** constant changes of staff/the ministerial merry-go-round; *Com* **v. des étiquettes,** constant price rises; *Fig* **v.-hésitation,** pussyfooting, shillyshallying.
valser [valse] *vi* to waltz; **faire v. qn,** to waltz with s.o.; *Fig F* to keep s.o. on the hop; *Fig F* **envoyer v. qn,** to send s.o. packing, to show s.o. the door; *Fig F* **envoyer v. qch,** to send sth flying; *Fig* **faire v. l'argent,** to spend money like water.
valseur, -euse [valsœr, -øz] *n* waltzer.
valve [valv] *nf* valve; **v. de chambre à air,** tyre valve; *Électron* **v. redresseuse,** rectifying valve.
valvulaire [valvylɛr] *adj* valvular.
valvule [valvyl] *nf Biol* valvule; *Anat* valve, valvule.
vamp [vɑ̃p] **1** *nf* vamp; **prendre des airs de v.,** to put on a vampish look. **2** *adj* vampish; **habillée très v.,** dressed very vampishly.
vamper [vɑ̃pe] *vt F* to vamp, to seduce; **elle veut le v.,** she wants to vamp *or* seduce him.
vampire [vɑ̃pir] *nm* **(a)** *Myth* vampire; **(b)** *Fig Vieilli* vampire, extortionist, bloodsucker; (*assassin*) mass murderer; **(c)** *Zool* vampire bat.
vampiriser [vɑ̃pirize] *vt* to dominate (psychologically); **v. un enfant,** to dominate a child.
vampirisme [vɑ̃pirism] *nm* vampirism.
van¹ [vɑ̃] *nm Agr* winnowing basket.
van² *nm* (*fourgon à chevaux*) horsebox.
van³ [van] *nm* (*camionnette*) van.
vanadium [vanadjɔm] *nm Ch* vanadium.
vandale [vɑ̃dal] *n* vandal.
vandalisme [vɑ̃dalism] *nm* vandalism.
vandoise [vɑ̃dwaz] *nf* (*poisson*) dace.
vanesse [vanɛs] *nf* **v. tortue,** tortoiseshell butterfly.
vanille [vanij] *nf* vanilla; **gousse de v.,** vanilla pod; **glace à la v.,** vanilla ice cream.
vanillé [vanije] *adj* vanilla(-flavoured, *US* -flavored); **crème vanillée,** vanilla custard; **sucre v.,** vanilla sugar.
vanillier [vanije] *nm* vanilla plant.
vanité [vanite] *nf* **(a)** (*orgueil*) vanity, conceit; **tirer v. de qch,** to pride oneself on sth; **flatter la v. de qn,** to flatter s.o.'s vanity; **agir par v.,** to act out of vanity; **(b)** futility, emptiness, hollowness, *Litt* vanity (*of wordly pleasures etc*).
vaniteusement [vanitøzmɑ̃] *adv* conceitedly.
vaniteux, -euse [vanitø, -øz] **1** *adj* vain, conceited. **2** *n* **c'est un v.,** he's (very) conceited.
vanity-case [vanitikɛs] *nm* vanity case.
vannage¹ [vanaʒ] *nm* winnowing (*of grain*).
vannage² *nm HydE* **(a)** sluicing (*of water gate*); **(b)** (*vannes*) (system of) sluice gates.
vanne¹ [van] *nf* **(a)** *HydE* sluice (gate), floodgate, water gate; **v. de décharge,** overflow weir; **lever les vannes,** to open the floodgates; **mettre les vannes,** to close the floodgates; **(b)** *Tech etc* valve; **(c)** *Nau* cock.
vanne² *nf F* dig, jibe; **lancer** *ou* **faire des vannes,** to make snide remarks.
vanneau, -eaux [vano] *nm* (*oiseau*) lapwing, peewit; *Culin* **œufs de v.,** plovers' eggs.
vanner [vane] *vt* **(a)** *F* to wear out, to exhaust; **être (complètement) vanné,** to be dead beat *or* all in; **(b)** to winnow (*grain*).
vannerie [vanri] *nf* **(a)** (*activité*) basket making, basketry; **(b)** (*objet*) basketwork, wickerwork.
vanneur, -euse [vanœr, -øz] *n* winnower.
vannier [vanje] *nm* basket worker *or* maker.
vantail, -aux [vɑ̃taj, -o] *nm* leaf (*of door, shutter, sluice gate*); **porte à deux vantaux,** folding door.
vantard, -arde [vɑ̃tar, -ard] **1** *adj* boasting, boastful, bragging, *F* loudmouthed. **2** *n* braggart, boaster, *F*

loudmouth.
vantardise [vɑ̃tardiz] *nf* (*caractère*) bragging, boastfulness; (*parole*) boast.
vanter [vɑ̃te] **1** *vt* to praise, to speak highly of; *Litt* to vaunt; **magazine qui vante les charmes de l'Écosse,** magazine which sings the praises of Scotland. **2 se vanter** *vpr* to boast, to brag; **il n'y a pas de quoi se v.,** there's nothing to boast about; **tu ne t'en es pas vanté!,** you kept that quiet *or* under your hat!; **se v. de qch/d'être ...,** to pride oneself on sth/on being ... .
va-nu-pieds [vanypje] *n inv* tramp, beggar; (*enfant*) (street) urchin, ragamuffin.
vapes [vap] *nfpl F* **être dans les v.,** to be groggy; (*rêver*) to have one's head in the clouds; **tomber dans les v.,** to pass out, to faint.
vapeur¹ [vapœr] *nf* **(a) v. (d'eau),** steam, (water) vapour, *US* vapor; **machine à v.,** steam engine; **bateau à v.,** steamer, steamship; **mettre la v.,** to put steam on; **navire sous v.,** ship under steam; **à toute v.,** (at) full steam *or* speed, full steam ahead; **(b) v. d'éther/d'alcool,** ether/alcoholic vapour; **(c)** (*brume*) haze, vapour; **(d)** *Culin* **cuire (des légumes/***etc***) à la v.,** to steam (vegetables/*etc*); **(e) vapeurs,** fumes (*of wine, petrol etc*); *Arch Méd* vapours; **avoir ses vapeurs,** to have the vapours.
vapeur² *nm Nau* steamer, steamship.
vaporeux, -euse [vapɔrø, -øz] *adj* vaporous, steamy (*atmosphere*); filmy, hazy (*ideas etc*); *Fig* **femme vaporeuse,** sylphlike woman.
vaporisateur [vapɔrizatœr] *nm* spray, atomizer (*for perfume etc*); *Tech* vaporizer; (*de jardinage*) spray(er).
vaporisation [vapɔrizɑsjɔ̃] *nf* (*de parfum, engrais etc*) spraying; *Tech* vaporization.
vaporiser [vapɔrize] **1** *vt* **(a)** (*gazéifier*) to vaporize; **(b)** to spray, to atomize (*liquid*). **2 se vaporiser** *vpr* to become vaporized, to vaporize.
vaquer [vake] *vi* **(a) v. à qch,** to attend to sth; **v. aux soins du ménage,** to see to the housework; **v. à ses affaires,** to go about *or* see to one's business; **(b)** (*de parlement, tribunal*) to be on vacation *or* in recess, not to be sitting; **les classes vaqueront la semaine prochaine,** there will be no school next week; **(c)** *Vieilli* (*d'un poste*) to be vacant.
varangue [varɑ̃g] *nf Nau* floor timber, floor frame.
varappe [varap] *nf* rock climbing; **faire de la v.,** to rock-climb, to go rock climbing.
varapper [varape] *vi* to rock-climb.
varappeur, -euse [varapœr, -øz] *nm* rock climber.
varech [varɛk] *nm* wrack, seaweed, kelp, varec.
vareuse [varøz] *nf* **(a)** (*de marin*) pea jacket *or* coat, reefing jacket *or* reefer; **(b)** *Mil* tunic; **(c)** (*veste large*) loose-fitting jacket.
variabilité [varjabilite] *nf* **(a)** *Biol Gram etc* variability; **(b)** changeableness (*of mood, weather*).
variable [varjabl] **1** *adj* **(a)** *Biol Gram Math* variable; **(b)** changeable, altering (*mood etc*); unsteady (*barometer*); varying (*speed*); changeable, unsettled (*weather*); **le baromètre est au v.,** the barometer is at change; **être v.,** to vary; **c'est très v.,** it's very variable, it varies a lot. **2** *nf Math Ordinat* variable; *Ordinat* **v. de mémoire,** memory variable.
variance [varjɑ̃s] *nf* variance.
variant, -ante [varjɑ̃, -ɑ̃t] **1** *adj* variable, fickle. **2** *nf* **variante,** variant, variation (*reading of text, spelling of word*).
variateur [varjatœr] *nm* **v. d'intensité,** dimmer switch (*of electric light*).
variation [varjɑsjɔ̃] *nf* **(a) v. du temps,** change in the weather; **v. des températures/des prix,** variation in temperature/prices; **v. du compas,** compass error; **(b)** *Mus* **air avec variations,** theme with variations.
varice [varis] *nf Méd* varicose vein; **avoir des varices,** to have varicose veins; **bas anti-varices,** support stockings.
varicelle [varisɛl] *nf Méd* chickenpox; **avoir la v.,** to have chickenpox.
varié [varje] *adj* varied; varying, various (*types etc*); miscellaneous (*news*); variegated (*leaf etc*); varied, chequered (*life*); *Mus* **air v.,** air with variations; **mouvement v.,** variable motion; **terrain v.,** uneven *or* irregular terrain; *Culin* **entrées variées,** selection of starters.
varier [varje] *v* (*impf & pr sub* **n. variions, v. variiez**) **1** *vt* to vary; to vary, to diversify (*occupations etc*); to variegate (*leaves*); **v. son alimentation,** to vary one's diet; *Fig Iron* **pour v. les plaisirs,** by way of a pleasant change. **2** *vi* to vary, to change; *Fin* (*des marchés*) to fluctuate; **v. dans ses réponses,** to be inconsistent in one's replies; **les auteurs varient souvent,** authors often differ *or* vary; **les prix peuvent v. du simple au double,** prices can vary by a factor of two; **leurs opinions varient sur ce point,** they differ *or* they don't see eye to eye on this point; **v. de méthode,** to vary one's methods; *Math* **y varie dans le même sens que et proportionnellement à x,** y varies as x.
variété [varjete] *nf* **(a)** variety (**de,** of); diversity, range (*of opinions etc*); **la v. des paysages,** the varying nature of the landscapes; *Com* **grande v. de rayons,** wide range of departments; **donner de la v. au menu,** to vary the menu; **(spectacle de) variétés,** variety show; *TV* **regarder les variétés à la télévision,** to watch variety shows on TV; **(b)** *Biol* variety (*of flower etc*).
variole [varjɔl] *nf Méd* smallpox; **avoir la v.,** to have smallpox; *Vét* **v. des vaches,** cowpox.
variolé [varjɔle] *adj* pockmarked.
varioleux, -euse [varjɔlø, -øz] *Méd* **1** *adj* variolous (*pustules etc*). **2** *n* smallpox victim.
variqueux, -euse [varikø, -øz] *adj* varicose (*vein etc*).
varlet [varlɛ] *nm Arch* varlet, page.
varlope [varlɔp] *nf Menuis* trying plane.
Varsovie [varsɔvi] *nf* Warsaw; **pays du Pacte de V.,** Warsaw Pact countries.
vasculaire [vaskylɛr] *adj* vascular.
vase¹ [vɑz] *nm* vase; **v. à fleurs,** flower vase; **v. à pied,** vase with a stem, stemmed vase; **v. en cristal,** crystal vase; **v. de nuit,** chamber pot; **vivre en v. clos,** to live in isolation *or* a vacuum; *Phys* **vases communicants,** communicating vessels; *El* **v. d'un élément de pile,** battery jar; **v. poreux,** porous cell.
vase² *nf* mud, silt, ooze, sludge; **banc de v.,** mudbank.
vasectomie [vazɛktɔmi] *nf Chir* vasectomy.
vaseline [vazlin] *nf* Vaseline ®, petroleum jelly; *Pharm* **huile de v.,** liquid paraffin.
vaseux, -euse [vɑzø, -øz] *adj* **(a)** *F* (*personne*) off-colour, *US* -color; **il a l'air v.,** he looks a bit off-colour *or* under the weather; **des idées vaseuses,** woolly ideas; **explication vaseuse,** confused *or* muddled explanation; **plaisanterie vaseuse,** off-colour *or* unsavoury joke; **(b)** (*rivière*) muddy, silty, sludgy.
vasistas [vazistɑs] *nm* fanlight (*over a door or window*).
vaso(-)constricteur, -trice [vazɔkɔ̃striktœr, -tris] *adj & nm Anat* vasoconstrictor; (*pl vaso(-)constricteurs, -trices*).
vaso(-)dilatateur, -trice [vazɔdilatatœr, -tris] *adj & nm Anat* vasodilator; (*pl vaso(-)dilatateurs, -trices*).
vaso(-)moteur, -trice [vazɔmɔtœr, -tris] *adj Anat* vasomotor (*nerve centre*); (*pl vaso(-)moteurs, -trices*).
vasouillard [vazujar] *adj F* dopy, muddleheaded.
vasouiller [vazuje] *vi F* to struggle, to flounder; **ça vasouille depuis hier,** things haven't been going well since yesterday.
vasque [vask] *nf* **(a)** basin (*of fountain*); **(b)** (*coupe décorative*) (ornamental) bowl.
vassal, -ale, -aux [vasal, -o] *n* vassal.
vassalité [vasalite] *nf,* **vasselage** [vaslaʒ] *nm* vassalage; *Fig* (*soumission*) vassalage, bondage.
vaste [vast] *adj* vast, immense, huge; *F* big, great (*joke etc*); **v. étendue,** vast *or* broad expanse; **le v. monde,** the wide world; **v. érudition,** vast *or* comprehensive learning; **quelle v. plaisanterie!,** it's a complete *or* total con!
vastement [vastəmɑ̃] *adv* vastly.
Vatican (le) [ləvatikɑ̃] *nm* the Vatican.
vaticane [vatikan] *adj & nf* **la (Bibliothèque) V.,** the Vatican Library.
vaticination [vatisinɑsjɔ̃] *nf Litt* vaticination.
vaticiner [vatisine] *vi Litt* to vaticinate.
va-tout [vatu] *nm inv* (*au jeu*) *& Fig* **jouer son va-t.,** to stake one's all.
vau (à) [avo] *adv* **à v.-l'eau,** downstream, with the stream; **tout va à v.-l'eau,** everything's going to rack and ruin *or* to the dogs.
vaudeville [vodvil] *nm* **(a)** *Th* vaudeville, light comedy (*with occasional song*); *Fig* **cette histoire est un vrai v.,** this story is a real farce; **(b)** *Vieilli* (*chanson*) topical *or* satirical song (*with refrain*).
vaudevillesque [vodvilɛsk] *adj* comical, farcical.
vaudevilliste [vodvilist] *nm Th* vaudeville writer.
vaudois, -oise [vodwa, -waz] **1** *adj* **(a)** Vaudois, of *or* from Vaud (*Swiss canton*); **(b)** *Hist Rel* Waldensian. **2** *n* **(a) V.,** Vaudois, native *or* inhabitant of Vaud; **(b)** *Hist Rel* **V.,** Waldensian.
vaudou [vodu] **1** *nm* voodoo. **2** *adj* **culte v.,** voodoo cult.
vaurien, -ienne [vorjɛ̃, -jɛn] *n* good-for-nothing, *F* layabout, *Br Sl* yob; **petit v.!,** you little scamp!, you little

rascal!

vautour [votur] *nm* vulture.

vautrer (se) [səvotre] *vpr* (*d'un cochon*) to wallow (*in mud*); (*d'une personne*) to sprawl (*on grass, a sofa*); *Fig* **se v. dans le vice,** to wallow in vice.

vauvert [vovɛr] *adj* **c'est au diable v.,** it's miles from anywhere, it's out in the wilds *or* a long way away.

va-vite (à la) [alavavit] *adv* in a rush, in a hurry; **travail fait à la va-v.,** rushed work *or* job.

veau, -eaux [vo] *nm* **(a)** calf; **v. marin,** seal; **le v. gras,** the fatted calf; **le v. d'or,** the golden calf; *F* **pleurer comme un v.,** to cry one's eyes out, to blubber; **(b)** *Culin* veal; **côtelette de v.,** veal cutlet; **tête de v.,** calf's head; **gelée de pied de v.,** calf's *or* calves' foot jelly; **(c)** *F* (*idiot*) fool, clot; (*abruti*) lump, lout; **(d)** (*cuir*) calf leather, calfskin; **(e)** *F* (*mauvaise voiture*) jalopy, old banger.

vecteur, -trice [vɛktœr, -tris] **1** *adj Math* **rayon v.,** radius vector. **2** *nm* **(a)** *Math Méd* vector; *Fig* **v. d'information/de progrès,** vehicle for information/for progress; **(b)** vehicle (*of atomic warhead etc*).

vectoriel, -ielle [vɛktɔrjɛl] *adj Math* vectorial.

vécu [veky] **1** *adj* **(a) choses vécues,** things which have been lived through, actual experiences; **(b)** (*pièce, roman*) true to life, founded on fact. **2** *nm* real-life experience.

vedettariat [vədɛtarja] *nm Cin etc* stardom.

vedette [vədɛt] *nf* **(a)** *Th Cin etc* star; **une grande v. de la politique,** a leading light in politics; **(b) avoir la v. (sur l'affiche),** (*d'un acteur*) to head *or* top the bill, to have star billing; **cette question a la v. dans tous les journaux,** this issue is making the headlines in all the newspapers; **être en v.,** to be in the limelight, to (have) hit the headlines; **mettre qn/qch en v.,** to highlight *or* spotlight s.o./sth; **mettre qch en v.,** to write *or* print sth in a line by itself; **mots en v.,** words in bold type; **(c)** *Nau* small motorboat, launch; (*de police etc*) patrol boat; **(d)** *Mil Arch* vedette, mounted sentry; **en v.,** on vedette duty.

végétal, -aux [veʒetal, -o] **1** *adj* **vie végétale,** plant life; **sol v.,** humus; **huile végétale,** vegetable oil. **2** *nm* vegetable, plant.

végétalien, -ienne [veʒetaljɛ̃, -jɛn] *adj & n* vegan.

végétalisme [veʒetalism] *nm* veganism.

végétarien, -ienne [veʒetarjɛ̃, -jɛn] *adj & n* vegetarian.

végétarisme [veʒetarism] *nm* vegetarianism.

végétatif, -ive [veʒetatif, -iv] *adj* vegetative; *Fig Péj* vegetable-like (*existence*).

végétation [veʒetasjɔ̃] *nf* **(a)** (*flore*) vegetation; **(b)** *Méd* **végétations,** vegetations; **végétations (adénoïdes),** adenoid growths, *F* adenoids; **opérer un enfant des végétations,** to have a child's adenoids taken out.

végéter [veʒete] *vi* **(je végète; je végéterai) (a)** *Fig Péj* (*d'une personne*) to vegetate; **il végète dans ce bureau,** he's just vegetating in that office; **(b)** *Arch* (*d'une plante*) to vegetate, to grow.

véhémence [veemɑ̃s] *nf Litt* vehemence; **avec v.,** vehemently.

véhément [veemɑ̃] *adj Litt* vehement, violent.

véhémentement [veemɑ̃tmɑ̃] *adv Litt* vehemently.

véhiculaire [veikylɛr] *adj* **langue v.,** common language.

véhicule [veikyl] *nm* vehicle; **v. utilitaire/de tourisme,** commercial/private vehicle; **v. spatial,** spacecraft; **l'air est le v. du son,** air is the medium *or* the vehicle of sound; *Fig* **la radio est un v. de l'information,** radio is a vehicle for information *or* is a news medium.

véhiculer [veikyle] *vt* to transport, to convey, to carry.

veille [vɛj] *nf* **(a)** (*jour qui précède*) preceding day, previous day; **je l'avais vu la v.,** I'd seen him the day before; **la v. au soir,** the evening before; **la v. de Noël,** Christmas Eve; **la v. du jour de l'an,** New Year's Eve; **la v. de la bataille,** the day before *or* the eve of the battle; *Fig* **être à la v. de la ruine/d'une guerre,** to be on the brink *or* verge of ruin/of a war; **être à la v. de se marier,** to be on the point of getting married, to be about to get married; **à la v. de la réunion,** just before the meeting; *F* **ce n'est pas demain la v.,** it's not going to happen tomorrow; **(b)** (*absence de sommeil*) wakefulness; **entre la v. et le sommeil,** between waking and sleeping; **(c)** sitting up, staying up (*at night*); watching (*by night*); **(d)** *Mil* (night) watch; *Nau* lookout; *Nau* **homme de v.,** lookout (man); *Nau* **chambre de v.,** chart house; **ancre de v.,** sheet anchor.

veillée [veje] *nf* **(a)** (*soirée*) evening (*spent in company*); **v. au coin du feu,** evening spent round the fire; **faire la v. chez qn,** to spend the evening at s.o.'s house; **(b)** night nursing (*of the sick*); watch, vigil (*by dead body*); *Arch* **v. d'armes,** vigil of arms.

veiller [veje] **1** *vi* **(a)** (*ne pas dormir*) to sit up, to stay up, to keep awake; **je n'ai pas l'habitude de v.,** I'm not used to staying up late; **v. fort avant dans la nuit,** to burn the midnight oil; **(b) v. à qch,** to watch over *or* see to sth; **v. aux intérêts de qn,** to attend to *or* look after *or* watch over s.o.'s interests; **v. à la besogne,** to keep an eye on the work; **v. à ce que qch se fasse,** to see (to it) that sth is done; *Fig* **v. au grain,** to keep an eye open for trouble; **(c) v. sur qn,** to watch over *or* look after s.o., to take care of s.o.; **(d)** *Mil etc* to watch, to be on (the) lookout. **2** *vt* to sit up with, to look after, to watch over, to attend to (*sick person etc*); **v. un mort,** to keep vigil over a dead body.

veilleur, -euse [vɛjœr, -øz] **1** *nm* watcher (*by night*); *Mil etc* lookout; **v. de nuit,** night watchman. **2** *nf* **veilleuse (a)** (*lampe*) night light; (*sur TV etc*) standby; **mettre la lampe en veilleuse,** to dim the light; *Fig* **mettre une entreprise en veilleuse,** to reduce output to a minimum; *Fig* **mettre un projet en veilleuse,** to shelve a project, to put a project on the back burner; *Fig F* **s'il pouvait la mettre en veilleuse!,** I wish he'd cool it *or* put a sock in it!; **(b)** *Aut* sidelight; **(c)** pilot light (*on gas cooker etc*); **(d)** *Bot* meadow saffron.

veinard, -arde [vɛnar, -ard] *F* **1** *adj* lucky, *Br Sl* jammy (*person*). **2** *n* lucky devil, *Br Sl* jammy so-and-so; **c'est un v.,** he has all the luck; **v.!,** lucky *or Br Sl* jammy devil!

veine [vɛn] *nf* **(a)** *Anat Bot etc* vein; *Anat* **v. cave,** vena cava; **elle menace de s'ouvrir les veines,** she's threatening to slash *or* slit *or* cut her wrists; *Fig* **il a du sang dans les veines,** he's got guts; **montre-nous si tu as du sang dans les veines!,** show us what you're made of, show us your mettle, show us whether you're a man or a mouse!; **(b)** *Géol* vein; lode (*of ore*); seam (*of coal*); **(c)** (*inspiration*) vein; **la v. poétique,** the poetic vein; **en v. de plaisanterie,** in humorous vein; **être en v. de faire qch,** to be in the mood to do sth *or* for doing sth; **être en v. de générosité,** to be in a generous mood, to be feeling generous; **(d)** *F* (*chance*) luck; **avoir de la v.,** to be in luck, to be lucky; **coup de v.,** stroke of luck, fluke; **pas de v.!,** rotten luck!; **c'est bien ma v.!,** just my (rotten) luck!; **quelle v.!,** talk about lucky!

veiné [vene] *adj* **(a)** *Anat* **bras v.,** arm where the veins are very close to the surface; **(b)** grained (*wood etc*).

veiner [vene] *vt* to vein, to grain (*door etc*).

veineux, -euse [vɛnø, -øz] *adj* **(a)** venous (*system, blood*); **(b)** veined (*wood etc*).

veinure [venyr] *nf* graining (*of wood etc*).

vêlage [vɛlaʒ] *nm* (*d'une vache*) calving.

vélaire [velɛr] *adj & nf Ling* velar.

velcro ® [vɛlkro] *nm* **(fermeture) v.,** Velcro ® (fastening).

vêlement [vɛlmɑ̃] *nm* = **VÊLAGE.**

vêler [vele] *vi* (*d'une vache*) to calve.

vélin [velɛ̃] *nm* vellum (parchment); **(papier) v.,** vellum (paper).

véliplanchiste [veliplɑ̃ʃist] *n* windsurfer.

velléitaire [veleitɛr] *adj & n* indecisive (person).

velléité [veleite] *nf* slight desire *or* inclination, stray impulse; **faire qch par v.,** to do sth on a whim; **avoir des velléités de travail,** to toy with the idea of work.

vélo [velo] *nm* bicycle, bike; **aller à** *ou* **en v.,** to cycle, to ride a bike; **v. de course,** racing cycle, *F* racer; **v. d'appartement,** exercise bike; **v. tout-terrain,** mountain bike; **aimez-vous faire du v.?,** do you like cycling?

vélocipède [velɔsipɛd] *nm Arch* velocipede; *Hum* bike.

vélocité [velɔsite] *nf* speed, swiftness; *Tech* velocity.

vélodrome [velɔdrɔm] *nm* velodrome.

vélomoteur [velɔmɔtœr] *nm* lightweight motorcycle.

velours [v(ə)lur] *nm* **(a)** *Tex* velvet; **v. uni,** plain velvet; **v. façonné,** figured velvet; **v. bouclé,** uncut velvet; **v. côtelé** *ou* **à côtes,** ribbed velvet, corduroy (velvet); **v. de coton,** cotton velvet, velveteen; **v. de laine,** velour(s); *Fig* **jouer sur le v.,** to be on velvet; **goûte ce vin, c'est du v.,** taste this wine, it's sheer velvet; **elle lui fait ses yeux de v.,** she is making (sheep's) eyes at him; **(b)** (*liaison incorrecte*) incorrect liaison (e.g. **j'ai été** [ʒezete]).

velouté [vəlute] **1** *adj* velvety, velvet-soft (*cheeks*); velvety, downy (*peach*); velvety, smooth, mellow (*wine*). **2** *nm* **(a)** velvetiness, softness (*of material, voice etc*); bloom (*of peach etc*); **(b)** *Culin* thick *or* cream soup *or* sauce; **v. de champignons,** cream of mushroom soup.

velouter [vəlute] *vt* to give a velvety appearance to (*sth*); (*d'une ombre*) to soften (*contour*).

velouteux, -euse [vəlutø, -øz] *adj* velvety, soft.

Velpeau ® [vɛlpo] *nm Méd* **bande V.** ®, crêpe bandage.

velu [vəly] *adj* hairy.

vélum, velum [velɔm] *nm* awning.

venaison [vənɛzɔ̃] *nf* venison.

vénal, -aux [venal, -o] *adj* **(a)** venal, purchasable (*privilege, right etc*); *Com* **valeur vénale,** market value; **(b)** *Péj* venal, mercenary, corruptible (*person*); corrupt (*press*).

vénalement [venalmɑ̃] *adv* venally.

vénalité [venalite] *nf* venality.

venant [vənɑ̃] *nm* **à tout v., à tous venants,** to all comers, to all and sundry; **s'occuper du tout v.,** to deal with the everyday *or* run-of-the-mill stuff.

vendable [vɑ̃dabl] *adj* saleable, marketable.

vendange [vɑ̃dɑ̃ʒ] *nf* **(a) vendanges,** vintage (season); **(b)** (*récolte*) grape gathering *or* picking, wine harvest, grape harvest, vintage; **(c)** (*raisin récolté*) grapes (harvested).

vendanger [vɑ̃dɑ̃ʒe] *vt & vi* **(je vendangeai(s); n. vendangeons)** to harvest, to pick, to gather, to vintage (*the grapes*).

vendangeur, -euse [vɑ̃dɑ̃ʒœr, -øz] **1** *n* grape picker, vintager. **2** *nf Bot* **vendangeuse,** aster.

vendéen, -enne [vɑ̃deɛ̃, -ɛn] **1** *adj* of *or* from the Vendée. **2** *n* **V.,** inhabitant *or* native of the Vendée.

vendémiaire [vɑ̃demjɛr] *nm Hist Fr* = first month of the French Republican calendar (*Sep. 22nd - October 21st*).

vendetta [vɑ̃deta] *nf* vendetta.

vendeur, -euse [vɑ̃dœr, -øz] *n* (*dans un magasin*) salesperson, salesman, saleswoman, salesgirl, (shop) assistant, *Am* (sales)clerk; *Bourse* seller; *Jur* vendor; **v. ambulant,** travelling salesman; *Fig* **les vendeurs d'évasion,** dream merchants, the dream industry; **j'allais vendre ma voiture mais je ne suis plus v.,** I was going to sell my car but I've decided not to; **un très bon/mauvais v.,** a very good/bad salesman.

vendre [vɑ̃dr] **1** *vt* **(a)** to sell; **v. qch à qn,** to sell s.o. sth, to sell sth to s.o.; **v. à terme,** to sell on credit; **v. comptant,** to sell for cash; **v. moins cher que qn,** to undersell s.o.; **v. chèrement sa vie,** to sell one's life dearly; **v. un objet (à) 50 francs,** to sell an object for 50 francs; **maison à v.,** house for sale; **l'art de v.,** salesmanship; *Écon* **pays qui vend du pétrole/du café,** oil-/coffee-selling country; *Fin* **v. des valeurs,** to sell stocks and shares; *Fig* **v. de l'évasion** *ou* **du rêve,** to sell dreams; **v. son âme au Diable,** to sell one's soul to the Devil; **(b) v. qn,** to sell s.o. up (*for debt*); **(c)** to betray, to give away (*s.o., a secret*). **2 se vendre** *vpr* **(a) cela se vend comme des petits pains,** it's selling like hot cakes; **(b)** to sell oneself; *Péj* **se v. à un parti,** to sell oneself to a party.

vendredi [vɑ̃drədi] *nm* Friday; **le v. saint,** Good Friday.

vendu, -ue [vɑ̃dy] *Péj* **1** *n* traitor. **2** *adj* bribed.

venelle [vənɛl] *nf* alley.

vénéneux, -euse [venenø, -øz] *adj* poisonous; **champignon v.,** toadstool.

vénérable [venerabl] **1** *adj* venerable. **2** *nm* worshipful master (*of masonic lodge*).

vénération [venerɑsjɔ̃] *nf* veneration, reverence; **avoir de la v. pour qn,** to hold s.o. in veneration, to revere s.o..

vénérer [venere] *vt* **(je vénère, n. vénérons; je vénérerai) (a)** (*admirer*) to venerate, to revere; **(b)** to worship (*saint etc*).

vénerie [vɛnri] *nf* hunting, *Spéc* venery; **petite/grande v.,** small/big game hunting.

vénérien, -ienne [venerjɛ̃, -jɛn] *adj Méd* venereal; **maladie vénérienne,** venereal disease, VD.

veneur [vənœr] *nm* huntsman; *Hist* **le Grand V.,** the Master of the Royal Hunt.

Vénézuéla (le) [ləvenezɥela] *nm* Venezuela.

vénézuélien, -ienne [venezɥeljɛ̃, -jɛn] **1** *adj* Venezuelan. **2** *n* **V.,** Venezuelan.

vengeance [vɑ̃ʒɑ̃s] *nf* revenge, vengeance; **par v.,** out of revenge; **tirer v. d'une injure,** to be revenged for an insult; *Prov* **la v. est un plat qui se mange froid,** revenge bides its time; **v. sanglante,** bloodthirsty revenge; **exercer sa v. sur qn,** to have one's revenge *or* vengeance on s.o.; **crime qui crie v.,** crime that cries out for vengeance; *Rel* **v. divine,** divine retribution.

venger [vɑ̃ʒe] *v* **(je vengeai(s); n. vengeons) 1** *vt* to avenge; **v. qn d'une injure,** to avenge s.o. for an insult. **2 se venger** *vpr* to be revenged, to have *or* get one's revenge; **se v. sur qn (de qch),** to take (one's) revenge on s.o. (for sth); *F* **pas la peine de te v. sur moi!,** there's no point in taking it out on me!

vengeur, -eresse [vɑ̃ʒœr, -ərɛs] *Litt* **1** *n* avenger. **2** *adj* avenging, (re)vengeful.

véniel, -ielle [venjɛl] *adj* venial (*sin*).

venimeux, -euse [vənimø, -øz] *adj* **(a)** venomous (*snake*); poisonous (*bite, snake*); **(b)** *Fig* spiteful, malicious.

venin [vənɛ̃] *nm* **(a)** venom, poison (*of snake etc*); **(b)** *Fig* spite, malice; **jeter** *ou* **cracher son v.,** to vent one's spleen.

venir [v(ə)nir] *v* (*prp* **venant**; *pp* **venu**; *pr ind* **je viens, il vient, n. venons, ils viennent**; *pr sub* **je vienne**; *impf* **je venais**; *p hist* **je vins, n. vînmes, v. vîntes, ils vinrent**; *p sub* **je vinsse**; *fu* **je viendrai**; *aux* **être**) **1** *vi* **(a)** to come; **je viens!,** I'm coming!; **je ne ferai qu'aller et v.,** I'll come straight back; **je n'ai fait qu'aller et v. entre la maison et le bureau,** I just went to and fro *or* back and forth between the house and the office; **il va et vient dans sa chambre,** he's pacing up and down (in) his room; **mais venez donc!,** do come along!; **d'où venez-vous?,** (*par où êtes-vous passé?*) where have you come from?; **il est venu à** *ou* **vers moi,** he came up to me; **il est venu sur moi,** he advanced on me (threateningly); **v. au monde,** to be born, to come into the world; **l'année qui vient,** the coming year, next year; **ses succès à v.,** his future successes; **dans les temps à v.,** in the days to come; **faire v. qn,** to send for *or* call in *or* fetch s.o.; **faire v. ses robes de Paris,** to get one's dresses from Paris; **voir v. qn,** to see s.o. coming; *Fig* **je vous vois v.!,** I can see you coming a mile off; **je préfère voir v.,** I'd rather wait and see; **le voici v.** *ou* **le voici qui vient,** here he comes; **être bien/mal venu,** to be welcome/unwelcome; **il serait mal venu de le lui faire remarquer,** it would be a bit out of place *or F* a bit off to point it out to him; *Nau* **v. dans le vent,** to come round; **v. sur bâbord/tribord,** to alter course to port/to starboard; **il est venu tomber à mes pieds,** he fell at my feet; **venez me trouver à quatre heures,** come (round) and see me at four o'clock; **je viens vous voir,** I've come to see you; **v. chercher, v. prendre (qch, qn),** to come for, to come to collect (sth, s.o.); **il vient d'Amérique,** he's from *or* he comes from America; **d'où venez-vous?,** where do you come *or Litt* hail from?, where are you from?; **mot qui vient du latin,** word which comes *or* is derived from Latin; **ce bien lui est venu de famille,** he inherited this property from his family; **tout cela vient de ce que ...,** all this is the result of ...;

(b) (*pr & impf only*) **v. de faire qch,** to have (only) just done sth; **il vient/venait de sortir,** he has/had just gone out;

(c) (*apparaître, arriver*) to occur; **le premier exemple venu,** the first example that comes to mind; *F* **alors ce steak, ça vient?,** is my steak coming *or* not?, how much longer do I have to wait for that steak?; **les idées ne viennent pas,** I just can't come up with anything; **il lui est venu une idée géniale,** he had *or* hit on a brillant idea; **l'idée me vient que ..., il me vient à l'esprit que ..., il me vient l'idée que ...,** the thought comes to my mind *or* it occurs to me that ...; **il ne m'est pas venu à l'idée que ...,** it never entered my head that ...; **il ne me viendrait pas à l'esprit de (penser) que ...,** it would never occur to me (to think) that ...; **ça ne me viendrait pas à l'esprit,** that would never occur *or* have occurred to me;

(d) en v. à qch/à faire qch, to come to sth/to the point of doing sth; **en v. aux coups** *ou* **aux mains,** to come to blows; **les choses en sont-elles venues là?,** have things come to such a point?; **je comprends où vous voulez en v.,** I see what you're getting at *or* driving at; **j'en suis venu à votre manière de penser,** I've come round to your way of thinking;

(e) (*atteindre*) to attain, to reach; **l'eau leur venait aux genoux,** the water came up to their knees; **les cheveux lui viennent aux épaules,** he has shoulder-length hair; **elle lui vient au menton,** she comes up to his chin;

(f) v. à faire qch, to happen *or* chance to do sth;

(g) (*grandir, pousser*) to come on *or* along; **bien v.,** (*d'une plante*) to thrive; (*d'une photo*) to come out well; **faire v. du blé,** to grow wheat; **il lui est venu une tumeur,** he developed a tumour;

(h) (*avoir un orgasme*) to come.

2 *v impers* **d'où vient(-il) que ...?,** how is it that ...?

3 se venir *vpr Arch & Région* **s'en venir,** to come along.

Venise [vəniz] *nf* Venice; **point de V.,** Venetian lace.

vénitien, -ienne [venisjɛ̃, -jɛn] **1** *adj* Venetian; **store v.,** Venetian blind. **2** *n* **V.,** Venetian.

vent [vɑ̃] *nm* **(a)** wind; **le v. du nord/sud,** the north/south wind; *Nau* **v. frais,** strong breeze; **grand v., v. fort,** high wind, gale; **journée de grand v.,** windy day; **coup de v.,** gust of wind, squall; *Fig* **entrer/sortir en coup de v.,** to dash in/out; **elle courait les cheveux au v.,** she ran with her hair streaming in the wind; **à l'abri du v.,** sheltered from the wind; *Mus* **instrument à v.,** wind instrument; **il fait du v.,** it's windy (weather); **aller comme le v.,** to go like the wind; **bon v.!,** God speed!; *Iron* good riddance!; **avoir le v. en poupe,** to have the wind right aft *or* dead aft; *Fig* **il a le v. en poupe,** he's on the road to success, he's riding high, he has the wind in his sails; *Fig* **avoir du v. dans les voiles,** to be three sheets in the wind, to be drunk; *Péj* **ce n'est que du v.,** it's just hot air; *Fig* **prendre le v., regarder de quel côté vient le v.,** to see which way the wind blows, to see how the land lies; **tourner à tous les vents,** to be a weathercock; **quel bon v. vous amène?,** what lucky chance brings you here?; *Prov* **qui sème le v. récolte la tempête,** he who sows the wind shall reap the whirlwind; *F* **être dans le v.,** to be up-to-date *or* with it; **les îles du V.,** the Windward Islands; *Nau* **v. arrière,** following wind; *Av* tail wind; **aller v. arrière,** to sail *or* run before the wind; **v. debout,** head wind; **contre le v.,** against the wind, into the wind; *Nau* **sous le v.,** alee, (to) leeward; **avoir bon v.,** to have a fair wind; **au v.,** a-weather, (to) windward; **mettre la barre au v.,** to put the helm up; **côté du v.,** weather side; **côté sous le v.,** lee side; **avoir l'avantage du v.,** to have the weather gauge; **aire de v.,** point of the compass; **logé aux quatre vents,** exposed to the four winds;

(b) *(air)* air; **marché/assemblée en plein v.,** open-air market/meeting; **mettre qch au v.,** to hang sth out to dry;

(c) blast *(of bellows, gun)*; *Av* **v. de l'hélice,** propeller slipstream;

(d) *(flatulence)* flatulence, wind; **lâcher un v.,** to break wind; **avoir des vents,** to have wind;

(e) *(à la chasse)* scent; **avoir le v. de son gibier,** to have the wind of one's game; *Fig* **avoir v. de qch,** to get wind of sth .

vente [vɑ̃t] *nf* **(a)** *(action)* sale; **v. au détail/en magasin/ en semi-gros/en gros,** retail/counter/small wholesale/ wholesale sales; **v. aux enchères,** (sale by) auction; **v. par correspondance,** mail order; **v. à crédit,** hire purchase, HP; **salle des ventes,** auction rooms, saleroom(s), salesroom; **v. de charité,** (charity) bazaar; **v. judiciaire,** sale by order of the court; **v. publique,** public sale, auction; **bureau de v.,** sales agency; **acte de v.,** bill of sale; **promotion des ventes,** sales promotion; **en v.,** for sale, on sale; **mettre qch en v.,** to put sth up for sale, to offer sth for sale; **médicament en v. libre,** medicine available over the counter *or* without prescription; **en v. dans toutes les bonnes librairies,** on sale in all good bookshops; **(livre) retiré de la v.,** (book) withdrawn from sale; **faire une forte v.,** *(d'un livre)* to be a best seller; **de v. difficile,** difficult to sell;

(b) *Can* **v. d'hiver,** winter sales;

(c) *(action de couper)* felling *(of timber)*; *(clairière)* clearing *(in forest)*; **jeune(s) vente(s),** new undergrowth.

venté [vɑ̃te] *adj* windswept, windblown, windy *(area)*.

venter [vɑ̃te] *v impers* to blow, to be windy; **il vente fort,** it's blowing hard, it's very windy.

venteux, -euse [vɑ̃tø, -øz] *adj* windy *(weather)*; windswept *(country)*.

ventilateur [vɑ̃tilatœr] *nm* ventilator; **v. rotatif,** fan; **v. électrique,** electric fan.

ventilation [vɑ̃tilɑsjɔ̃] *nf* **(a)** *(aération)* ventilation; **mettre la v. (en marche),** to switch on the ventilation; **(b)** *Jur* separate valuation *(of parts of estate etc)*; **(c)** breakdown *(of expenses etc)*.

ventiler [vɑ̃tile] *vt* **(a)** to ventilate, to air *(room etc)*; **mal ventilé,** poorly *or* badly ventilated, stuffy; **(b)** *Jur* to value separately *(parts of estate etc)*; **(c)** to break down *(expenses etc)*.

ventilo [vɑ̃tilo] *nm F* fan.

ventôse [vɑ̃toz] *nm Hist Fr* = sixth month of the French Republican calendar *(Feb 19th or 21st - March 19th or 21st)*.

ventouse [vɑ̃tuz] *nf* **(a)** *Méd* cupping glass; **poser des ventouses à qn,** to cup s.o.; **(b)** *Zool* sucker *(of leech etc)*; **(c)** *(de plastique etc)* suction cup *or* disc; **flèchettes/ cendrier à v.,** rubber-tipped darts/suction-grip ashtray; **faire v.,** to adhere by suction; **mine v.,** limpet mine; **voiture v.,** illegally parked car, abandoned car; **(d)** *(aération)* airhole, vent(hole).

ventral, -aux [vɑ̃tral, -o] *adj* ventral; **parachute v.,** lap pack (parachute).

ventre [vɑ̃tr] *nm* **(a)** *(estomac)* stomach, *F* tummy; *(d'animal, F de qn)* belly; **danse du v.,** belly dance; **se coucher à plat v.,** to lie flat on one's stomach *or* belly *or F* tummy; *Fig* **se mettre à plat v. devant qn,** to grovel to s.o.; **v. à terre,** *(cheval)* at full speed; **avoir du v.,** to have a paunch, to be potbellied; **prendre du v.,** to be getting a paunch *or F* a tummy; **se serrer le v.,** to tighten *or* pull in one's belt; **avoir le v. creux,** to have an empty stomach; **avoir mal au v.,** to have stomach *or F* tummy ache; *Fig* **ça fait mal au v. de voir ça,** it makes me sick to see that; **ne rien avoir dans le v.,** to have nothing in one's stomach; *Fig* to have no guts; **ne bois pas si tu n'as rien dans le ventre,** don't drink on an empty stomach; **je savais bien qu'il avait quelque chose dans le v.,** I was sure he had it in him; **donner du cœur au v. à qn,** *F* to buck s.o. up; *Prov* **v. affamé n'a point d'oreilles,** it's no use reasoning with a hungry man; **tu as les yeux plus grands que le v.,** your eyes are bigger than your belly;

(b) *(utérus)* womb; **dès le v. de sa mère,** since before he was born;

(c) underbelly *(of animal)*;

(d) *Tech* bulge, swell *(of bottle, girder)*; belly, sag *(of sail)*; belly *(of ship)*; **faire v.,** to bulge (out), to belly out; *(pendre)* to sag;

(e) *Phys* antinode, ventral segment *(of wave)*; **v. de tension,** potential loop, voltage loop.

ventrebleu [vɑ̃trəblø] *int Arch* gadzooks!, zounds!

ventrée [vɑ̃tre] *nf* bellyful *(of food)*.

ventricule [vɑ̃trikyl] *nm Anat* ventricle.

ventrière [vɑ̃trijɛr] *nf* **(a)** *(harnais)* girth; sling *(for hoisting animal)*; **(b)** *Constr* purlin; **(c)** *Nau Arch* bilge block.

ventriloque [vɑ̃trilɔk] **1** *adj* ventriloqu(i)al. **2** *n* ventriloquist.

ventriloquie [vɑ̃trilɔki] *nf* ventriloquy, ventriloquism.

ventru [vɑ̃try] *adj* **(a)** *(gros)* potbellied, portly; **(b)** bulbous *(column)*; bulging, swelling *(sail)*.

venu, -ue [v(ə)ny] **1** *adj* **(a)** *(bien développé)* well developed; **plante bien venue,** sturdy *or* healthy plant; **photographie bien venue,** photograph that has come out well; **enfant mal v.,** stunted *or* puny child; **(b)** *(approprié)* **bien v.,** appropriate; **mal v.,** inappropriate; **je serais mal v. de,** it's not for me to ...; **il serait mal v. d'insister,** it would be ill-mannered to insist. **2** *n* **le premier v.,** the first to arrive; *(n'importe qui)* anybody; **le premier v. vous le dira,** anybody *or* anyone will tell you that; **à la portée du premier v.,** easy to use, user-friendly; **ce n'est pas le premier v.,** he's not just anybody; **le dernier v.,** the last to arrive; **les nouveaux venus, les nouvelles venues,** the newcomers.

venue [v(ə)ny] *nf* **(a)** coming, arrival; coming, advent, approach *(of spring etc)*; advent *(of computers, air travel etc)*; *rush (of water)*; **allées et venues,** comings and goings; **(b)** growth *(of tree etc)*; **d'une belle v., tout d'une v.,** well grown *(tree)*.

Vénus [venys] *nf Myth Astron* Venus; *Bot* **cheveu de V.,** maidenhair fern; *Anat* **mont de V.,** mons veneris, mound of Venus.

vêpres [vɛpr] *nfpl Rel* vespers.

ver [vɛr] *nm* **(a) v. (de terre),** (earth)worm; **v. de sable, v. des pêcheurs,** lug(worm); **nu comme un v.,** stark naked; *Méd* **v. solitaire,** tapeworm; *F* **tirer les vers du nez à qn,** to worm *or* winkle information out of s.o.; **(b)** *(asticot, larve)* grub, larva; **v. blanc,** cockchafer grub; **v. de viande,** maggot; **v. de farine,** mealworm; **v. du bois,** woodworm; **rongé** *ou* **piqué des vers,** worm-eaten; **fruit plein de vers,** worm-eaten fruit; **mangé aux vers,** *(vêtement)* moth-eaten; **rose rongée de vers,** cankered rose; **v. à soie,** silkworm; **v. luisant,** glow worm; **v. rongeur,** canker(worm).

véracité [verasite] *nf* truth, truthfulness, *Fml* veracity.

véranda [verɑ̃da] *nf* veranda(h).

verbal, -aux [vɛrbal, -o] *adj* **(a)** *(promesse)* verbal; **la violence verbale d'une description,** the violence of the language used in a description; **(b)** *Gram* verbal; **locution verbale,** verbal phrase.

verbalement [vɛrbalmɑ̃] *adv* verbally, by word of mouth.

verbalisation [vɛrbalizasjɔ̃] *nf* **(a)** *(expression)* verbalisation; **v. des angoisses,** putting (one's) anxieties into words; **(b)** *Jur* entry of charge *(by policeman for minor offence)*.

verbaliser [vɛrbalize] *vi* **(a)** *(exprimer)* to verbalise; **v. ses fantasmes,** to put one's fantasies into words, to verbalise one's fantasies; **(b)** *(d'un policier)* to charge s.o..

verbe [vɛrb] *nm* **(a)** *Gram* verb; **v. pronominal/transitif/ intransitif,** reflexive/transitive/intransitive verb; **v. composé,** compound verb; **v. composé** *ou* **à particule,** *(en anglais)* phrasal verb; **(b)** *(langage)* language, word(s); **la magie du v.,** the magic of words *or* language; **avoir le v. haut,** to speak loudly; *Fig* to be dictatorial; **(c)** *Rel* **le V.,** the Word; **le V. s'est fait chair,** the Word was made flesh.

verbeux, -euse [vɛrbø -øz] *adj* verbose, long-winded *(orator etc)*; wordy, long-winded, verbose *(explanation etc)*.

verbiage [vɛrbjaʒ] *nm* verbiage; **se lancer dans un v. creux,** to launch oneself into a meaningless torrent of words.

verbosité [vɛrbozite] *nf* verbosity, wordiness.

ver-coquin [vɛrkɔkɛ̃] *nm* *(parasite)* vine grub; *Vét*

stagger worm; (*pl vers-coquins*).
verdâtre [vɛrdɑtr] *adj* greenish.
verdeur [vɛrdœr] *nf* **(a)** tartness, acidity (*of fruit, wine*); **(b)** crudeness (*of speech*); **(c)** (*vitalité*) vigour, *US* vigor, vitality.
verdict [vɛrdik(t)] *nm Jur* verdict, finding (*of the jury*); **prononcer** *ou* **rendre un v.**, to return *or* bring in a verdict; **prononcer** *ou* **rendre un v. pour/contre qn,** to find for/against s.o.; **v. de culpabilité** *ou* **positif/d'acquittement** *ou* **négatif,** verdict of 'guilty'/'not guilty'; **attendre le v. du médecin,** to await the doctor's verdict; **quel est votre v.?,** what is your verdict?
verdier [vɛrdje] *nm* (*oiseau*) greenfinch.
verdir [vɛrdir] **1** *vt* to make *or* paint (*sth*) green. **2** *vi* (*de végétation etc*) to grow *or* become *or* turn green; *Fig* **v. (de jalousie),** to go *or* turn green with envy; **v. de peur,** to go *or* turn white with fear.
verdissage [vɛrdisaʒ] *nm* dyeing *or* colouring *or US* coloring (*sth*) green.
verdissement [vɛrdismɑ̃] *nm* growing *or* becoming *or* turning green.
verdoiement [vɛrdwamɑ̃] *nm* **(a)** turning *or* becoming green; **(b)** greenness (*of fields*).
verdoyant [vɛrdwajɑ̃] *adj* green, *Litt* verdant (*meadow etc*).
verdoyer [vɛrdwaje] *vi* (**il verdoie; il verdoiera**) (*de végétation etc*) to turn *or* become green.
verdure [vɛrdyr] *nf* **(a)** (*couleur*) greenness; **(b)** (*végétation*) greenery, *Litt* verdure; **rideau de v.,** curtain of greenery; **salle de v.,** green arbour; **tapis de v.,** greensward; **(c)** *Culin* lettuce; (*autres légumes verts*) greens.
véreux, -euse [verø, -øz] *adj* **(a)** wormy, maggoty (*fruit*); **(b)** *Péj* dubious, shady, *F* fishy (*dealings*); **financier v.,** shady financier; **dettes véreuses,** bad debts; **tremper dans une affaire véreuse,** to be involved in a shady business.
verge [vɛrʒ] *nf* **(a)** *Anat* penis; **(b)** (*baguette*) rod, cane, switch; **v. d'huissier, (poignée de) verges,** birch (rod); **battre de verges un enfant,** to birch a child; **(c)** shank (*of anchor*); **(d)** *Bot* **v. d'or,** golden rod, Aaron's rod; **(e)** *Can* (*mesure*) yard.
vergé [vɛrʒe] **1** *adj* **(a)** *Tex* badly dyed, streaky; **(b) papier v.,** laid paper. **2** *nm* laid paper.
vergeoise [vɛrʒwaz] *nf* = low-grade beet sugar.
verger [vɛrʒe] *nm* orchard.
vergeté [vɛrʒəte] *adj* streaky, streaked.
vergette [vɛrʒɛt] *nf* small cane, switch.
vergeture [vɛrʒətyr] *nf* **(a)** *Obst* stretch mark; **avoir des vergetures,** to have stretch marks; **crème contre les vergetures,** cream to prevent stretch marks; **(b)** weal, red mark (*caused by lash of whip etc*).
vergeure [vɛrʒyr] *nf* wire mark (*on laid paper*).
verglacé [vɛrglase] *adj* icy (*road*); *Can* **pluie verglacée,** freezing rain.
verglas [vɛrgla] *nm* (*sur la route*) (black) ice, *US* glaze; **il y a du v.,** it's icy *or* slippery.
vergogne [vɛrgɔɲ] *nf* **sans v.,** shameless(ly).
vergue [vɛrg] *nf Nau* yard; **grande v.,** main yard; **v. de misaine,** foretop yard; **v. de hunier,** topsail yard; **bout de v.,** yardarm.
véridique [veridik] *adj* truthful, *Litt* veracious.
véridiquement [veridikmɑ̃] *adv* truthfully, *Litt* veraciously.
vérifiable [verifjabl] *adj* verifiable; (*statement etc*) that can be checked.
vérificateur, -trice [verifikatœr, -tris] **1** *n* (*personne*) inspector, examiner, checker; **v. de comptes,** auditor. **2** *adj* **appareil v.,** testing machine; **instrument v.,** gauge, calipers.
vérification [verifikasjɔ̃] *nf* checking, verification (*of statements etc*); inspection, examination, checking (*of work etc*); scrutiny (*of votes*); *Aut etc* **v. sur place,** spot check; **v. de comptes** *ou* **d'écritures,** audit(ing) of accounts.
vérifier [verifje] *v* (*impf & pr sub* **n. vérifiions, v. vérifiez**) **1** *vt* to verify; to inspect, to examine, to check (*work etc*); to verify, to check, to confirm (*statement*); to overhaul (*machinery etc*); to audit (*accounts*); to scrutinize (*votes*); **vérifié et revérifié,** checked and double-checked; **v. des références,** to take up references; **v. que tous les robinets sont fermés,** to check that all the taps have been turned off; **v. si qch est vrai,** to check whether sth is true. **2 se vérifier** *vpr* (*d'une affirmation etc*) to prove correct, to be confirmed; **mes soupçons se sont vérifiés par la suite,** my suspicions were subsequently confirmed.
vérin [verɛ̃] *nm Tech* jack; **v. à vis,** screw jack; **v. hydraulique/pneumatique,** hydraulic/pneumatic jack.
véritable [veritabl] *adj* **(a)** true (*story etc*); **(b)** (*réel*) real, genuine, true, *Fml* veritable; **un v. ami,** a real *or* genuine *or* true friend; **c'est un v. coquin,** he's a downright *or* an absolute *or* an out-and-out rogue; **c'est un v. épouvantail,** he's a perfect fright; **c'était une v. surprise,** it was a real surprise.
véritablement [veritabləmɑ̃] *adv* **(a)** truly, *Fml* veritably; **(b)** (*réellement*) really, genuinely; **nous nous sommes v. compris,** we understood each other perfectly.
vérité [verite] *nf* **(a)** truth, *Fml* verity (*of statement etc*); **dire la v.,** to tell *or* speak the truth; **la v. finit toujours par se découvrir,** truth will out; **à la v.,** to tell the truth, as a matter of fact; **en v.,** really, actually; **heure de v.,** moment of truth; *Jur* **la v., toute la v., rien que la v.,** the truth, the whole truth and nothing but the truth; **c'est la v.,** it's true, it's a fact; *F* **c'est la v. vraie,** it's an actual fact, it's the honest truth, *F* it's gospel; **la v. d'un personnage,** the trueness to life of a character; *Cin* **cinéma-v.,** cinéma vérité; **dire à qn (toutes) ses vérités** *ou* **ses quatre vérités,** to tell s.o. a few home truths; **(b)** (*sincérité*) sincerity, truthfulness; **accent/intonation de v.,** truthful note/tone.
verjus [vɛrʒy] *nm* verjuice.
verlan [vɛrlɑ̃] *nm Ling* back slang; **parler en v.,** to speak in back slang.
vermeil, -eille [vɛrmɛj] **1** *adj* vermilion, bright red; ruby(-red), bright red (*lips*); rosy, bright red (*cheeks*). **2** *nm* silver gilt.
vermicelle [vɛrmisɛl] *nm Culin* vermicelli, noodles; **v. chinois,** Chinese noodles.
vermiculaire [vɛrmikylɛr] *adj* vermicular, worm-shaped; *Anat* **appendice v.,** vermiform appendix.
vermiculé [vɛrmikyle] *adj* **(a)** *Archit* vermiculated (*stonework etc*); **(b)** engine-turned (*watchcase etc*); **(c)** *Biol* vermiculate (*markings*).
vermiculure [vɛrmikylyr] *nf Archit etc* vermiculation.
vermiforme [vɛrmifɔrm] *adj* vermiform.
vermifuge [vɛrmifyʒ] *adj & nm Pharm* vermifuge; **(poudre) v.,** worming powder.
vermillon [vɛrmijɔ̃] **1** *nm* **(a)** (*couleur*) vermilion; **(b)** (*poudre*) vermilion, cinnabar. **2** *adj inv* vermilion, bright red.
vermine [vɛrmin] *nf* **(a)** vermin; **couvert** *ou* **grouillant de v.,** verminous, crawling with vermin; **(b)** *Fig Péj* **fréquenté par la v.,** frequented by lowlife characters *or* members of the underworld; **quelle v.!,** what a rat!
vermisseau, -eaux [vɛrmiso] *nm* small (earth) worm.
vermoulu [vɛrmuly] *adj* worm-eaten (*wood etc*); *Fig* decrepit.
vermoulure [vɛrmulyr] *nf* **(a)** wormhole (*in wood*); **(b)** (*poussière*) worm dust (*from wormhole*).
vermout(h) [vɛrmut] *nm* vermouth.
vernaculaire [vɛrnakylɛr] *adj* vernacular; **la langue vernaculaire,** the vernacular.
vernal, -aux [vɛrnal, -o] *adj* vernal.
verni [vɛrni] *adj* **(a)** varnished; French-polished (*mahogany*); **cuir v.,** patent leather; **chaussures vernies,** patent(-leather) shoes; **(b)** *F* **être v.,** to be lucky *or Br Sl* jammy; **(c)** *Cér* glazed, vitrified (*tile etc*).
vernier [vɛrnje] *nm* vernier, sliding gauge.
vernir [vɛrnir] *vt* **(a)** to varnish (*picture etc*); to French-polish (*mahogany*); to japan (*iron, leather*); **v. au tampon,** to French-polish; **(b)** *Cér* to glaze.
vernis [vɛrni] *nm* **(a)** varnish; **v. à ongles,** nail varnish *or* polish; **v. à l'alcool,** spirit varnish; **v. à l'essence,** turpentine varnish; **v. cellulosique,** cellulose varnish; **v. japonais,** japan; **v. au tampon,** French polish; *Cér* **v. (luisant),** glaze; **v. de plomb,** lead glaze; **(b)** *Fig* veneer; **dès qu'on gratte le v. on se rend compte qu'il n'est pas compétent,** as soon as you scratch the surface, you realize he's incompetent; **ce n'est qu'un v.,** it's nothing but a veneer; **v. de politesse,** veneer of politeness; **(c)** *Bot* **v. du Japon,** varnish tree, lacquer tree, tree of heaven.
vernissage [vɛrnisaʒ] *nm* **(a)** varnishing; *Cér* glazing; **(b)** private view (*at art exhibition*).
vernissé [vɛrnise] *adj* **(a)** *Cér* glazed; **(b)** (*brillant*) glossy.
vernisser [vɛrnise] *vt* to glaze (*pottery*).
vernisseur, -euse [vɛrnisœr, -øz] *n* **(a)** (*de bois etc*) varnisher; **v. au tampon,** French polisher; **(b)** *Cér* glazer.
vérole [verɔl] *nf Méd* **(a) petite v.,** smallpox; **avoir la petite v.,** to have smallpox; **(b)** *Arg* syphilis, (the) pox.
vérolé [verɔle] *adj Arg* syphilitic; **il est v.,** he's got the pox.
véronal ® [verɔnal] *nm Pharm* Veronal ®, barbitone.
Véronique [verɔnik] *nf* **(a)** Veronica; **(b)** *Bot* **v.,**

speedwell, veronica.

verrat [vɛra] *nm* boar.

verre [vɛr] *nm* **(a)** (*matière*) glass; **v. blanc,** white glass; **v. à vitres,** window glass; **v. moulé,** pressed glass; **v. à glaces,** plate glass; **v. armé** *ou* **grillagé,** wire(d) glass; **v. de sécurité,** safety glass; **v. trempé,** toughened glass; **v. pare-balles,** bulletproof glass; **v. dépoli,** frosted glass; **v. coloré,** stained glass; **v. filé,** spun glass; **laine de v.,** glass wool; **papier de v.,** glasspaper, sand paper; **passer qch au papier de v.,** to sand(paper) sth; **coton de v.,** fibreglass, *US* fiberglass, glass fibre; **articles de v.,** glassware; **œil de v.,** glass eye; **peintre sur v.,** artist in stained glass; **sous v.,** under glass; **se casser** *ou* **se briser comme du v.,** to be as brittle as glass;

(b) (*récipient*) **v. (à boire),** (drinking) glass; **v. gobelet,** tumbler; **v. à moutarde,** cheap glass; **v. à pied,** stemmed glass; **v. à vin,** wineglass; **v. gradué,** graduated measure; **v. à dents,** tooth glass; **lever son v. à qn,** to raise one's glass to s.o.;

(c) (*contenu*) glass(ful); **v. de vin,** glass of wine; *F* **boire un petit v.,** to have a drink (*of alcohol*); **prendre un v. de trop,** to have (had) one too many, to have (had) a drop too much; **avoir un v. dans le nez,** to have (had) one too many *or* one over the eight, to have (had) a drop too much; **tempête dans un v. d'eau,** storm in a teacup;

(d) (*objet en verre*) glass; lens (*of spectacles*); **il porte des verres,** he wears glasses; (*de contact*) he wears contact lenses *or F* contacts; **verres de contact,** contact lenses; **v. grossissant,** magnifying glass; **v. de montre/de vitrine,** watch-glass/window pane; **verres dalles,** pavement lights;

(e) v. soluble, water glass.

verrerie [vɛr(ə)ri] *nf* **(a)** (*fabrication*) glass-making, glasswork; **(b)** (*atelier*) glassworks; **(c)** (*marchandise*) glassware, glasswork.

verrier [vɛrje] **1** *nm* **(a)** (*artisan*) glass-maker, glass-blower, glass-worker; **(b)** (*casier*) glass rack. **2** *adj* **peintre v.,** artist in stained glass.

verrière [vɛrjɛr] *nf* **(a)** glass roof *or* wall (*of railway station etc*); **(b)** glass casing (*to protect picture etc*); **(c)** (*vitre*) stained glass window; **(d)** *Av* canopy.

verroterie [vɛrɔtri] *nf* (*bijoux*) glass jewellery; **collier de v.,** string of glass beads, glass necklace.

verrou [vɛru] *nm* **(a)** bolt; **fermer une porte à** *ou* **au v.,** to bolt a door; **s'enfermer au v.,** to bolt oneself in; **pousser** *ou* **mettre le(s) verrou(s),** to bolt the door; **tirer le(s) verrou(s),** to unbolt the door; **sous les verrous,** under lock and key; **(b)** *F* **verrous,** (*prison*) prison, *Br Sl* nick; **il est sous les verrous depuis 5 ans,** he's been inside *or* behind bars *or Br Sl* in the nick for 5 years; **mettre qn sous les verrous,** to put s.o. inside *or* behind bars; **(c)** breech bolt (*of shotgun*).

verrouillage [vɛrujaʒ] *nm* bolting, locking; (*mécanisme*) locking mechanism; *Aut* **v. central,** central locking.

verrouiller [vɛruje] **1** *vt* **(a)** to bolt (*door*); *Ordinat* to lock on (*capitals*); **v. qn,** to bolt s.o. in, to lock s.o. up; **(b)** *Mil* to lock (*breech*). **2 se verrouiller** *vpr* to bolt oneself in.

verrue [vɛry] *nf* wart; (*surtout au pied*) verruca; *Fig* **ce musée est une v. dans la ville,** this museum is a real eyesore in the town, the museum is a carbuncle on the face of the town.

vers¹ [vɛr] *nm* verse, line (*of poetry*); **v. blancs,** blank verse; **v. libres,** free verse; **écrire** *ou* **faire des v.,** to write verse *or* poetry.

vers² *prép* **(a)** (*dans l'espace*) toward(s), to; **façade qui regarde v. la forêt/le nord,** façade facing the forest/(the) north, north-facing façade; **le lieu v. où nous allons,** the place we're heading for *or* toward(s) *or* to; **un pas v. la démocratie,** a step towards democracy; **v. Pau,** in the neighbourhood *or US* neighborhood of Pau; **(b)** (*dans le temps*) toward(s); (*autour de*) about; **v. la fin du siècle/de sa vie,** towards the end of the century/his life; **venez v. (les) trois heures,** come (at) about three (o'clock).

versant [vɛrsɑ̃] *nm* slope, side (*of mountain*); bank (*of canal etc*); **v. de colline,** hillside.

versatile [vɛrsatil] *adj* **(a)** changeable, fickle (*disposition etc*); **(b)** *Biol* versatile.

versatilité [vɛrsatilite] *nf* **(a)** changeability, fickleness; **(b)** *Biol* versatility.

verse [vɛrs] *nf* **(a)** laying, beating down (*of crops by wind etc*); **(b) à v.,** in torrents; **il pleut à v.,** it's pouring (down).

versé [vɛrse] *adj* experienced, practised, skilled, (well) versed (**dans,** in); conversant (**dans,** with).

Verseau (le) [ləvɛrso] *nm Astron* Aquarius, the Water Carrier; **être (du signe du) V.,** to be (an) Aquarius *or* an Aquarian.

versement [vɛrsəmɑ̃] *nm* payment; **en plusieurs versements, par versements échelonnés,** by *or* in instalments *or US* installments; **premier v.,** down payment; *Banque* **bulletin de v.,** paying in slip, *Am* deposit slip.

verser [vɛrse] **1** *vt* **(a)** to pour (out) (*liquid etc*); **v. à boire à qn,** to pour s.o. a drink, to pour a drink for s.o.; *Litt* **v. ses chagrins,** to pour out one's troubles;

(b) (*renverser*) to overturn (*vehicle*); (*du vent*) to lay, to beat down (*crops*);

(c) to shed (*tears, light*); to spill, to shed (*blood*);

(d) to pay (in), to deposit (*money*); **v. de l'argent sur son compte,** to pay money into one's account; **capitaux versés,** paid-up capital;

(e) v. un document au dossier, to add a document to the file;

(f) *Mil* **v. des hommes à un régiment/dans une armée,** to draft *or* assign *or* transfer men to a regiment/to an army;

(g) *Mil* to issue (*stores*).

2 *vi* **(a)** (*d'un véhicule*) to overturn; (*des cultures*) to be beaten down, to be laid flat;

(b) v. dans ..., to fall *or* drift into ...; **v. dans le snobisme,** to be a snob, to be snobbish.

verset [vɛrsɛ] *nm* verse (*of Bible etc*).

verseur, -euse [vɛrsœr, -øz] **1** *n* pourer (*of liquids*); *Min* tipper. **2** *nf* **verseuse,** (*de cafetière*) jug, (coffee)pot. **3** *adj* **bec v.,** spout.

versicolore [vɛrsikɔlɔr] *adj* particoloured, *US* particolored, variegated.

versificateur [vɛrsifikatœr] *nm* versifier.

versification [vɛrsifikɑsjɔ̃] *nf* versification.

versifier [vɛrsifje] *v* (*impf & pr sub* **n. versifiions, v. versifiiez**) *Littér* **1** *vi* to write verse. **2** *vt* to put (*prose*) into verse.

version [vɛrsjɔ̃] *nf* **(a)** translation (*into mother tongue*); *Scol* unseen (translation); **v. latine,** Latin translation, translation from Latin; **(b)** *Cin* **film en v. originale,** original language version; **film américain en v. française,** American film dubbed into French; **(c)** version, account (*of event etc*); **chacun a sa v. des faits,** everyone has their own version of the facts *or* events.

verso [vɛrso] *nm* verso, back, reverse (*of sheet of paper*); **voir au v.,** see over(leaf).

versoir [vɛrswar] *nm Agr* mouldboard (*of plough*), *US* moldboard (*of plow*).

vert, -te [vɛr, -ɛrt] **1** *adj* **(a)** green; **légumes verts,** green vegetables, *F* greens; **plantes vertes,** house *or* pot plants; *Aut etc* **feu v.,** green light; **attendre le feu v.,** to wait for the green light; *Fig* **donner son feu v. (à qch),** to give the green light (for sth);

(b) (*écologique*) green; **produit v.,** green *or* environmentally friendly product; **candidat v.,** green candidate;

(c) (*agricole*) **pouvoir v.,** power of the farming lobby; **l'Europe verte,** European agriculture; **encourager les vacances vertes,** to encourage holidays in the country; **partir en classe verte,** to go on a school trip to the countryside; **la ceinture verte qui entoure Paris,** the green belt around Paris;

(d) green (*wood*); unripe (*fruit*); young (*wine*); **chêne v.,** holm oak, ilex; **cuir v.,** rawhide;

(e) *Tel* **téléphone v.,** *Br* ≈ Freefone ®; *Can* ≈ Zenith; *US* ≈ 800 number;

(f) (*vieillard*) spry, sprightly; **verte vieillesse,** green old age;

(g) spicy, risqué (*story etc*);

(h) langue verte, slang;

(i) *Vieilli* sharp, tart (*reprimand etc*).

2 *nm* **(a)** (*couleur*) green; **v. bouteille/olive/cendré,** bottle/olive/sage green; **v. d'eau,** sea green; **v. pomme,** apple green; **v. tendre,** soft green;

(b) mettre un cheval au v., to put a horse out to pasture *or* to grass; *F* **se mettre au v.,** to go to the country to recuperate; (*pour se cacher*) to hide out, to lie low, to hole up (*in the country, abroad etc*);

(c) *Pol* Green; **la montée des Verts,** the rise of the Greens.

3 *nfpl F* **en dire de vertes,** to tell spicy *or* risqué stories; **il en a vu des vertes et des pas mûres,** he's been through a lot.

vert-de-gris [vɛrdəgri] *nm inv* verdigris.

vert-de-grisé [vɛrdəgrize] *adj* coated with verdigris; (*pl vert-de grisé(e)s*).

vertébral, -aux [vɛrtebral, -o] *adj Anat* vertebral; **colonne vertébrale,** spinal *or* vertebral column, spine,

backbone.
vertèbre [vɛrtɛbr] *nf Anat* vertebra.
vertébré [vɛrtebre] *adj & nm Zool* vertebrate.
vertement [vɛrtəmɑ̃] *adv* **réprimander v. qn,** to reprimand s.o. sharply *or* severely, *F* to give s.o. a good telling off *or* ticking off.
vertical, -ale, -aux [vɛrtikal, -o] **1** *adj* vertical, upright; (*organisation, structuration*) vertical; **éclairage v.,** overhead lighting; *Ordinat* **boîtier v.,** tower; *Écon* **concentration verticale,** vertical integration. **2** *nf* **verticale,** vertical; **à la verticale,** straight up; (*monter*) vertically, straight up; **falaise à la verticale,** sheer cliff.
verticalement [vɛrtikalmɑ̃] *adv* vertically; (*avec mouvement vers le haut*) straight up; (*avec mouvement vers le bas*) straight down; (*dans les mots croisés*) down.
verticalité [vɛrtikalite] *nf* verticality.
verticille [vɛrtisil] *nm Bot* whorl.
vertige [vɛrtiʒ] *nm* vertigo, fear of heights; (*étourdissement*) dizziness, giddiness; **cela me donne le v.,** it gives me vertigo, it makes me feel dizzy *or* giddy, it makes my head swim; **avoir facilement le v.,** to have a bad head for heights; **avoir des vertiges,** to have fits of giddiness, to have dizzy spells; *Fig* **les vertiges du succès,** the intoxication of success.
vertigineusement [vɛrtiʒinøzmɑ̃] *adv* vertiginously, dizzily.
vertigineux, -euse [vɛrtiʒinø, -øz] *adj* dizzy, giddy (*height etc*); *Fml* vertiginous (*person, height etc*); breakneck, breathtaking (*speed*); **hausse vertigineuse des prix,** staggering rise in prices.
vertigo [vɛrtigo] *nm Vét* (blind) staggers.
vertiport [vɛrtipɔr] *nm Av* heliport.
vertu [vɛrty] *nf* **(a)** quality, property, virtue (*of remedy etc*); **plantes qui ont la v. de guérir,** plants that have healing properties; **en v. de,** by virtue of; *Jur* in pursuance of; **en v. de cet arrangement,** under this agreement; **et en v. de quoi se le permet-il?,** and what gives him the right to do that?; **(b)** (*morale*) virtue; **faire de nécessité v.,** to make a virtue (out) of necessity; **l'honnêteté est une v.,** honesty is a virtue; **il a de la v. à la supporter,** I admire his courage in putting up with her; **elle le pare de toutes les vertus,** she's forever singing his praises; **femme de petite v.,** woman of easy virtue.
vertueusement [vɛrtɥøzmɑ̃] *adv* virtuously.
vertueux, -euse [vɛrtɥø, -øz] *adj* virtuous; **intentions vertueuses,** honourable intentions; *Arch* **femme vertueuse,** virtuous *or* chaste woman.
verve [vɛrv] *nf* verve, vigour, *US* vigor, *F* go; **être en v.,** to be in top form; **jouer avec v.,** to give a spirited performance.
verveine [vɛrvɛn] *nf Bot* vervain, verbena.
verveux[1], -euse [vɛrvø, -øz] *adj Litt* animated, lively, spirited.
verveux[2] *nm* (*filet*) hoop net.
vesce [vɛs] *nf Bot* vetch, tare.
vésical, -aux [vezikal, -o] *adj Anat* vesical.
vésicant [vezikɑ̃] *adj & nm Méd* vesicatory; **gaz v.,** blister gas.
vésicatoire [vezikatwar] *adj & nm Méd* vesicatory; **appliquer un v. à qn,** to blister s.o..
vésicule [vezikyl] *nf* **(a)** *Anat* vesicle; *Bot* air cell; *Anat* **v. biliaire,** gall bladder; **(b)** blister (*on the skin*).
vespasienne [vɛspazjɛn] *nf* street urinal.
vesse-de-loup [vɛsdəlu] *nf* puffball; (*pl vesses-de-loup*).
vessie [vesi] *nf Anat etc* bladder; **v. natatoire,** (*de poisson*) air bladder, swim bladder; *Méd* **v. à glace,** ice bag; *Fig* **prendre des vessies pour des lanternes,** to believe that the moon is made of green cheese.
vestale [vɛstal] *nf Antiq* vestal (virgin).
veste [vɛst] *nf* jacket; **v. d'intérieur,** smoking jacket; **v. croisée,** double-breasted jacket; **v. matelassée,** quilted jacket; *F* **tomber la v.,** to take off one's jacket; *Fig* **retourner sa v.,** to be a turncoat; *Fig F* **ramasser** *ou* **prendre une v.,** to come a cropper (*in business, love etc*).
vestiaire [vɛstjɛr] *nm* **(a)** (*dans un théâtre etc*) cloakroom; *Sp etc* changing room, locker room; *Jur* robing room; *F* **mon v., s'il vous plaît,** could I have my (hat and) coat, please?; *Th F* **au v.!,** off!, off!; **(b)** (*vêtements*) **renouveler son v.,** to renew one's wardrobe; **(c)** (*meuble*) (hat and) coat stand, rack; (*dans une usine etc*) locker.
vestibule [vɛstibyl] *nm* vestibule, (entrance) hall, lobby.
vestige [vɛstiʒ] *nm* vestige, trace (*of former habitations etc*); **derniers vestiges de ...,** last remnants of ...; **vestiges du passé,** relics of the past.
vestimentaire [vɛstimɑ̃tɛr] *adj* clothing (*trade*); **détails vestimentaires,** accessories.
veston [vɛstɔ̃] *nm* (*man's*) jacket; *Nau* monkey jacket; **complet v.,** lounge suit.
Vésuve [vezyv] *nm* Vesuvius.
vêtement [vɛtmɑ̃] *nm* garment, article *or* item of clothing; **vêtements,** clothes, clothing; **industrie du v.,** clothing trade, *F* rag trade; **tissus pour vêtements,** dress material; **mettre ses vêtements du dimanche,** to put on *or* dress in one's Sunday best; **vêtements de dessous,** underwear, underclothes, underclothing; **vêtements de plage/de pluie,** beachwear/rainwear; *Rel* **vêtements sacerdotaux,** vestments; **tu devrais mettre** *ou* **passer un v.,** you should put something on.
vétéran [veterɑ̃] *nm Mil etc* veteran, old campaigner; *Sp* veteran; *Fig* old hand; *Pol* elder statesman.
vétérinaire [veterinɛr] **1** *adj* veterinary. **2** *n* veterinary surgeon, *F* vet, *Am* veterinarian.
vétille [vetij] *nf* (mere) trifle, triviality; **vétilles,** trivia.
vétilleux, -euse [vetijø, -øz] *adj Litt* captious, finicky, fastidious.
vêtir [vetir] *v* (*prp* **vêtant**; *pp* **vêtu**; *pr ind* **je vêts, n. vêtons**; *impf* **je vêtais**; *p hist* **je vêtis**; *fu* **je vêtirai**) **1** *vt* to clothe, to dress (*s.o.*) **(de,** in); **tout de noir vêtu,** dressed *or Fml* clad all in black. **2 se vêtir** *vpr* to dress (oneself) **(de,** in).
veto [veto] *nm* veto; **mettre son v. à qch,** to veto sth; **droit de v.,** right of veto.
vêtu [vety] *adj* dressed; **être v. chaudement** *ou* **chaudement v.,** to be warmly dressed; **v. légèrement,** lightly dressed; **professeurs vêtus de leurs toges,** professors wearing *or* in their gowns; **à demi-v.,** half-dressed; *Litt* **mur v. de lierre,** ivy-clad wall, wall covered in ivy.
vétuste [vetyst] *adj* decayed, decrepit.
vétusté [vetyste] *nf* decay, decrepitude.
veuf, veuve [vœf, vœv] **1** *adj* widowed (*man, woman*); *Fig* **v. de qch,** bereft of sth. **2** *n* widower, *f* widow. **3** *nf F Arch* **la Veuve,** the guillotine.
veule [vøl] *adj* weak, feeble (*person etc*); **un air v.,** a listless look.
veulerie [vølri] *nf* inertia, listlessness.
veuvage [vœvaʒ] *nm* widowhood.
vexant [vɛksɑ̃] *adj* **(a)** (*contrariant*) vexing, provoking, annoying; **(b)** hurtful (*remark etc*).
vexation [vɛksasjɔ̃] *nf* **(a)** (*humiliation*) mortification; **être en proie aux vexations de qn,** to be constantly being put down by s.o.; **(b)** vexation, harassing.
vexatoire [vɛksatwar] *adj* vexatious.
vexer [vɛkse] **1** *vt* **(a)** to humiliate, to mortify (*s.o.*). **2 se vexer** *vpr* to get upset *or* offended; **elle se vexe facilement,** she gets upset very easily; **se v. de qch,** to feel humiliated.
V.H.F. [veaʃɛf] *nf* VHF.
via [vja] *prép* via, by way of; **Paris, v. Calais,** Paris, via Calais.
viabilisé [vjabilize] *adj Admin* **terrain v.,** serviced site, site with services.
viabiliser [vjabilize] *vt* to service; **v. un terrain/un lotissement,** to service a site/a plot.
viabilité[1] [vjabilite] *nf* viability (*of fœtus, plan etc*).
viabilité[2] *nf* **(a)** (*de chemin etc*) practicability; **(b)** *Constr* development (*of site ready for building*).
viable [vjabl] *adj* viable (*fœtus, plan etc*).
viaduc [vjadyk] *nm* viaduct.
viager, -ère [vjaʒe, -ɛr] **1** *adj* (for) life; **rente viagère,** life annuity. **2** *nm* life interest; **placer son argent en v.,** to invest one's money in *or* buy an annuity.
viande [vjɑ̃d] *nf* **(a)** meat; **v. de boucherie,** butcher meat, fresh meat; **v. blanche/rouge,** white/red meat; **jus de v.,** meat juices; **v. hachée,** minced *or Am* ground meat, *Br* mince; **ne pas manger de v.,** not to eat meat; **v. de cheval,** horsemeat, horseflesh; **(b)** *Arg* **amène ta v.!,** come on! move your carcass!
viatique [vjatik] *nm* **(a)** money *or* provisions for a journey; **on lui a donné un v. de 200 livres pour son voyage,** we gave him £200 for his trip; *Fig* **il n'a que ce diplôme pour v.,** this diploma is his only meal ticket; **(b)** *Rel* last sacrament.
vibrant [vibrɑ̃] *adj* **(a)** (*corde etc*) vibrating; **(b)** resonant, vibrant (*voice*); rousing, stirring (*speech*); vibrant (*personality etc*); **v. et réceptif,** (*personne*) eager and receptive; **c'est une nature vibrante,** he is very sensitive *or* highly strung.
vibraphone [vibrafɔn] *nm Mus* vibraphone.
vibraphoniste [vibrafɔnist] *n Mus* vibraphone player.
vibrateur [vibratœr] *nm* vibrator.

vibration [vibrɑsjɔ̃] *nf* **(a)** vibration; **(b)** resonance (*of voice*); *Phys* **v. de la lumière,** vibration of light; *Fig F* **ça me donne de bonnes vibrations,** it gives me good vibrations *or F* vibes.

vibrato [vibrato] *nm Mus* vibrato.

vibratoire [vibratwar] *adj* vibratory.

vibrer [vibre] *vi* to vibrate; *Fig* **faire v. le cœur de qn,** to stir *or* thrill s.o. *or* s.o.'s heart; *Fig* **v. d'enthousiasme,** to be quivering with excitement; *Fig* **c'est la seule chose qui le fait v.,** it's the only thing that gets him going *or* brings him to life.

vibreur [vibrœr] *nm Tech* vibrator.

vibrion [vibrijɔ̃] *nm* **(a)** (*bactérie*) vibrio(n); *Méd* **v. septique,** gas bacillus; **(b)** (*personne agitée*) fidget.

vibromasseur [vibrɔmasœr] *nm* (*electric*) vibrator (*for massage*).

vicaire [vikɛr] *nm Rel* **(a) v. apostolique,** vicar apostolic; **grand v., v. général,** vicar-general; **(b)** *Église anglicane* curate; *Cathol* (assistant) priest.

vicariat [vikarja] *nm Rel* curacy.

vice [vis] *nm* **(a)** (*défaut moral*) vice; **il a tous les vices,** he has all the vices; **l'alcool, c'est mon seul v.,** drink(ing) is my only vice; **v. contre nature,** unnatural vice; *Fig* **mais c'est un v.!,** it's an obsession, he is totally obsessed; **(b)** (*défaut*) fault, defect, flaw; **v. de fabrication,** manufacturing defect; *Vét etc* **v. de conformation,** (congenital) malformation, physical defect; **v. de prononciation,** faulty pronunciation; *Jur* **v. de forme,** flaw (*in a deed etc*); **v. propre,** inherent defect; **(c)** (*corruption etc*) vice; **vivre dans le v.,** to lead a life of vice.

vice-amiral [visamiral] *nm* vice admiral; (*pl vice-amiraux*).

vice-chancelier [visʃɑ̃səlje] *nm* vice chancellor; (*pl vice-chanceliers*).

vice-consul [viskɔ̃syl] *nm* vice consul; (*pl vice-consuls*).

vice-consulat [viskɔ̃syla] *nm* vice consulate; (*pl vice-consulats*).

vice-gérant, -ante [visʒerɑ̃, -ɑ̃t] *n* deputy manager *or* manageress; (*pl vice-gérant(e)s*).

vicennal, -aux [visenal, -o] *adj* vicennial.

vice-présidence [visprezidɑ̃s] *nf* (*d'état, d'organisation*) vice-presidency; (*d'entreprise*) vice-chairmanship; (*pl vice-présidences*).

vice-président, -ente [visprezidɑ̃, -ɑ̃t] *n* (*d'état, d'organisation*) vice president; (*d'entreprise*) vice-chairman; (*pl vice-président(e)s*).

vice-roi [visrwa] *nm* viceroy; (*pl vice-rois*).

vice-versa [visevɛrsa] *adv* vice versa.

vichy [viʃi] *nm* **(a)** *Tex* **jupe en v. rouge et blanc,** red and white checked cotton skirt; **(b)** (*eau minérale*) vichy water; **v. fraise,** strawberry syrup in vichy water; **(c) V.,** Vichy; *Hist* **la France de V.,** Vichy France.

viciateur, -trice [visjatœr, -tris] *adj* vitiating, contaminating.

viciation [visjɑsjɔ̃] *nf* vitiation; corruption (*of morals etc*); pollution, contamination (*of the air etc*); poverty (*of blood*).

vicié [visje] *adj* vitiated, corrupt; tainted (*food etc*); poor, thin (*blood*); **air v.,** (*par des émanations*) stale *or* foul air.

vicier [visje] *vt* (*impf & pr sub* **n. viciions, v. viciiez**) **(a)** to vitiate, to corrupt, to spoil; to pollute, to contaminate (*air*); **(b)** *Jur* to vitiate, to invalidate (*deed*).

vicieux, -ieuse [visjø, -jøz] *adj* **(a)** (*corrompu*) depraved, corrupt (*person*); **(b)** (*incorrecte*) faulty, wrong, incorrect (*pronunciation*); **cercle v.,** vicious circle; **c'est un cercle v.,** it's a vicious circle, it's a catch-22 (situation); **(c)** (*rétif*) restive, bad-tempered (*horse*).

vicinal, -aux [visinal, -o] *adj* **chemin v.,** local road.

vicissitude [visisityd] *nf* vicissitude (*of fortune etc*); **les vicissitudes de la vie,** the ups and downs *or* trials and tribulations of life.

vicomte [vikɔ̃t] *nm* viscount.

vicomté [vikɔ̃te] *nf* **(a)** (*titre*) viscountcy; **(b)** (*terrain*) viscounty.

vicomtesse [vikɔ̃tɛs] *nf* viscountess.

victime [viktim] *nf* **(a)** victim; **être (la) v. de qn,** to be the victim of s.o., to be s.o.'s victim; **j'ai été (la) v. d'un escroc,** I've been had by a conman; **les victimes du désastre,** the victims *or* casualties of the disaster; **les victimes de la route,** road victims; **être (la) v. d'un système d'imposition,** to be badly hit by a system of taxation; **être (la) v. d'une illusion/d'un malentendu,** to labour *or US* labor under an illusion/a misconception; **j'ai été v. de la grippe,** I've been down with flu; **être v. de la fourberie/négligence,** to be the victim of s.o.'s deceit/negligence; **(b)** victim (*of sacrifice*).

victoire [viktwar] *nf* **(a)** victory; *Sp* win, victory; **remporter la v.,** to gain a victory (**sur,** over); to carry *or* win the day; **remporter une v. sur soi-même,** to overcome *or* conquer one's fears *etc*; **chanter** *ou* **crier v.,** to claim victory; **v. à la Pyrrhus,** Pyrrhic victory; **(b) V.,** Victoria.

Victoria [viktɔrja] *nf* **(a)** Victoria; **la reine V.,** Queen Victoria; **(b) v.,** (*voiture*) victoria.

victorien, -ienne [viktɔrjɛ̃, -jɛn] *adj* Victorian.

victorieusement [viktɔrjøzmɑ̃] *adv* victoriously.

victorieux, -ieuse [viktɔrjø, -jøz] *adj* victorious; triumphant (*air*); *Sp* **sortir v. d'une épreuve/d'un match,** to emerge the winner of a heat/a match; **être v.,** to win (the day).

victuailles [viktɥaj] *nfpl Vieilli* food provisions, *Fml* victuals.

vidage [vidaʒ] *nm* **(a)** gutting, cleaning (*of fish*); drawing (*of fowl*); **(b)** *F* throwing out, chucking out (*from pub etc*); **(c)** *Ordinat* dump.

vidange [vidɑ̃ʒ] *nf* **(a)** *Aut* oil change; **faire la v.,** to change the oil; **v.-graissage,** oil change and lubrication; **bouchon de v.,** sump plug; (*de radiateur*) draining plug **robinet de v.,** draincock; **tuyau de v.,** waste pipe; **tonneau en v.,** broached cask; **(b)** draining, emptying (*of cesspool, sump etc*); blowing off (*of boiler*); **(c) vidanges,** sewage.

vidanger [vidɑ̃ʒe] *vt* (**je vidangeai(s); n. vidangeons**) to empty, to drain (*cesspool, radiator, engine sump etc*); to blow off (*boiler*).

vidangeur [vidɑ̃ʒœr] *nm* cesspit clearer *or* emptier.

vide [vid] **1** *adj* empty (*glass, room etc*); blank (*space in document etc*); unoccupied, vacant, empty (*seat*); **l'appartement est encore très v.,** (*pas meublé*) the flat is still very bare; **bouteilles vides,** empty bottles, *F* empties; **revenir les mains vides,** to return empty-handed; **je suis rentré de vacances les poches vides,** I came back from holiday penniless; **avoir l'estomac v.,** to have an empty stomach; **j'ai l'estomac v.,** my stomach is empty; **j'ai la tête v.,** my mind's a blank; **ma vie est v.,** my life is empty; **v. de sens,** devoid of meaning, meaningless; **phrases vides,** empty words; **avoir le regard v.,** to have a blank look.

2 *nm* empty space, gap; blank (*in document*); *Phys* vacuum; *Fig* (*néant*) emptiness, void; **combler les vides,** to fill (up) the gaps; **v. sanitaire,** crawl space; *Fig* **son départ laisse un v.,** his departure has left a gap *or* void; **faire le v.,** to create a vacuum; **la nature a horreur du v.,** nature abhors a vacuum; *Fig* **il faut faire le v.,** (*tout oublier*) you'll have to put it out of your mind; *Fig* **ça me permet de faire le v.,** it helps me (to) switch off *or* blank everything out; **nettoyage par le v.,** vacuum cleaning; *Fig* **faire le nettoyage par le v.,** to throw everything out, *F* to gut the place; **le v. dans sa vie,** the void in his life; **emballé sous v.,** vacuum- packed; **taper dans le v.,** to (hit out and) miss the mark; **regarder dans le v.,** to stare into space; **avoir peur du v.,** to be afraid of *or* to have no head for heights; **j'étais attiré par le v.,** I felt an urge to jump; **camion revenant à v.,** lorry *or Am* truck returning empty; **poids à v.,** unladen weight; **marcher à v.,** (*d'une machine*) to run light *or* without load; **le train est parti à v.,** the train left empty; **le mécanisme tourne à v.,** the engine is in neutral; *Mus* **corde à v.,** open string.

vidé [vide] *adj* **(a)** (*poisson*) gutted; (*volaille*) drawn; **(b)** *F* (*personne*) tired out, worn out, all in, dead beat; **c'est un homme v.,** he's played out.

vidéo [video] **1** *adj inv* video; **caméra/cassette v.,** video camera/cassette. **2** *nf inv* (*média*) video; (*cassette*) video (-tape); **la dernière v. de Madonna,** Madonna's latest *or* new video.

vidéocassette [videɔkasɛt] *nf* video cassette.

vidéoclip [videɔklip] *nm TV* video (*of rock group etc*).

vidéodisque [videɔdisk] *nm Électron* videodisc, *surtout Am* videodisk.

vidéofréquence [videɔfrekɑ̃s] *nf Rad* video frequency.

vidéophone [videɔfɔn] *nm Électron* videophone.

vide-ordures [vidɔrdyr] *nm inv* rubbish chute.

vide-poches [vidpɔʃ] *nm inv* **(a)** (*de voiture*) glove compartment; **(b)** (*de table*) (dressing table) tidy.

vide-pomme [vidpɔm] *nm* apple corer; (*pl vide-pommes*).

vider [vide] **1** *vt* **(a)** to empty; to empty, to clear out (*room, drawer*); to empty, to drain (*cask, one's glass, pond etc*); to blow off (*boilers*); to blow (*an egg*); *Ordinat* **v. l'écran,** to clear the screen; **videz vos verres!,** drink up!; **v. les lieux,** to vacate the premises; **le juge a ordonné de faire v. la salle,** the judge ordered the court (to be) cleared; **v.**

une chambre de ses meubles, to clear the furniture from a room; *F* **v. qn,** to drain s.o. (of energy), to exhaust s.o., to wear s.o. out; **partir en vidant la caisse,** to make off with the takings; **v. les poches de qn,** to empty s.o.'s pockets; (*d'un voleur*) to pick s.o.'s pockets; *F* **v. son sac,** to get sth off one's chest; **v. son cœur,** to pour out one's feelings;

(b) *F* to throw (*s.o.*) out (*of a bar etc*); to sack (*s.o.*); *Équitation* to throw (*rider*); *Équitation* **v. les arçons** *ou* **les étriers,** to be thrown (from one's horse); **se faire v.,** to be thrown (*from horse*); *F* to be sent out (*of the room*); to be chucked *or* thrown out (*of bar etc*); to be expelled (*from college*); (*être renvoyé*) to get the sack;

(c) to eviscerate (*carcass*); to gut, to clean (*fish*); to draw (*fowl*); to core (*apple*); to stone, *surtout Am* to pit (*fruit*);

(d) to settle (*question*); **v. une querelle,** to settle a quarrel *or* difference.

2 se vider *vpr* to (become) empty.

vide-tasses [vidtas] *nm inv* slop basin.

videur, -euse [vidœr, -øz] *n* (*dans un club etc*) bouncer.

vie [vi] *nf* **(a)** life; **v. végétative/animale,** vegetable/animal life; **être en v.,** to be alive; **donner la v. à un enfant,** to give birth to a child; **avoir la v. dure,** to be hard to kill; **il est entre la v. et la mort,** he is (hovering) between life and death; **question de v. ou de mort,** question of life and death; **il y va de la v.,** it's a case of life and death; **sauver la v. à qn,** to save s.o.'s life; **rappeler qn à la v.,** to bring s.o. back to life; *Fig* **revenir à la v.,** to come back to life, to be back in the land of the living; **assurance-v.,** life assurance *or* insurance; **sans v.,** lifeless; **donner de la v. à une conversation/une réunion,** to liven up *or* enliven *or* animate a conversation/a meeting; **elle déborde de v.,** she's full of *or* brimming with life; **la v. des idées/des volcans,** the evolution of ideas/volcanoes; **musique pleine de v.,** lively *or* animated music;

(b) (*existence*) life, lifetime; **pour la v.,** for life; **une fois dans la v.,** once in a lifetime; **plus tard dans la v.,** later (on) in life; **de toute ma v. je n'ai jamais entendu chose pareille!,** I've never heard such a thing in all my life!; **jamais de la v.!,** never!, not on your life!; **pension à v., pension la v. durant,** life pension; **nommé à v.,** appointed for life;

(c) (*biographie*) biography, life story; **écrire la v. de qn,** to write s.o.'s biography *or* life (story); *F* **tu nous racontes ta v.!,** we don't want your life story!;

(d) (*façon de vivre*) existence, way of life, life style; **ainsi va la v.!, c'est la v.!,** that's life!, such is life!; **je connais la v.,** I've seen something of life; **regarder la v. en face,** to look life in the face; **v. sédentaire,** sedentary life; **changer de v.,** to change one's (way of) life; (*faire amende honorable*) to mend one's ways, to turn over a new leaf, **elle veut mener sa v. comme elle l'entend,** she wants to lead her life as she sees fit; **rendre la v. dure à qn,** to make life hard *or* a misery for s.o.; **avoir une v. dure,** to have a hard life; **la v. à l'américaine,** the American way of life; **la v. nocturne,** nightlife; **femme de mauvaise v.,** loose woman; *F* **faire la v.,** to lead a riotous life; **faire tout une v.,** to kick up a fuss *or* a row;

(e) *Écon* living, livelihood; **niveau de v.,** standard of living; **coût de la v.,** cost of living; **indemnité de v. chère** *ou* **de cherté de v.,** cost of living allowance; **gagner sa v.,** to earn one's living *or Sl* crust; **bien gagner sa v.,** to earn a good living *or* wage; **comment gagne-t-elle sa v.?,** what does she do for a living?, how does she earn a living?

vieil, vieille *voir* **VIEUX**.

vieillard [vjɛjar] *nm* (*f often* **vieille**, *see* **VIEUX**) old man; **les vieillards,** old people, the elderly, the aged; **hospice de vieillards,** old people's *or F* old folk's home.

vieillerie [vjɛjri] *nf* (*souvent pl*) **vieilleries,** old(-fashioned) *or* out-of-date things; (*idées*) old(-fashioned) *or* out-of- date *or* outdated ideas.

vieillesse [vjɛjɛs] *nf* (old) age; **bâton de v.,** support *or* prop of old age; **ma fille est mon bâton de v.,** my daughter gives me support in my old age; **la v.,** old people, the elderly, the aged; **aide à la v.,** help for the aged.

vieilli [vjeji] *adj* **(a)** obsolescent (*word etc*); old-fashioned, out-of-date (*style etc*); **(b)** (*vieux*) (grown) old, aged.

vieillir [vjejir] **1** *vi* **(a)** to grow old, to age; to age (*in appearance*); **il a vieilli, il est vieilli,** he looks older, he's aged; **(b)** (*d'un usage, d'un mot*) to become obsolete *or* antiquated *or* out of date; **ce mot a vieilli,** this word is obsolescent; **(c)** (*d'un fromage, d'un vin*) to mature. **2** *vt* **(a)** to age (*s.o.*), to make (*s.o.*) look older; **ce chapeau la vieillit,** that hat makes her look old(er); **(b)** to distress (*furniture*). **3 se vieillir** *vpr* **(a)** (*par l'apparence*) to make oneself look old(er); **(b)** (*en mentant*) to pretend to be older (than one is).

vieillissant [vjejisɑ̃] *adj* ageing.

vieillissement [vjejismɑ̃] *nm* **(a)** ageing, growing old; **v. général de la population,** general ageing of the population; **(b)** (*d'un mot etc*) becoming obsolete, obsolescence; **(c)** ageing, maturing (*of cheese, wine etc*); **(d)** distressing (*of furniture*).

vieillot, -otte [vjɛjo, -ɔt] *adj* antiquated, old-fashioned.

vielle [vjɛl] *nf Mus* hurdy-gurdy.

Vienne [vjɛn] *nf* Vienna.

viennois, -oise [vjɛnwa, -waz] **1** *adj* Viennese. **2** *n* **V.,** Viennese.

vierge [vjɛrʒ] **1** *nf* **(a)** virgin; **la (Sainte) V.,** the Blessed Virgin (Mary); **chapelle de la V.,** Lady chapel; **(b)** *Astron* **la V.,** Virgo; **les natifs de la V.,** Virgos, those born under (the sign of) Virgo. **2** *adj* **(a)** (*personne*) virgin, virginal; virgin (*soil, forest, oil etc*); **laine v.,** virgin wool; **(b)** blank (*page, tape etc*); pure (*white etc*); *Phot* unexposed (*plate*); **cahier v.,** new *or* blank jotter; **réputation v.,** untarnished reputation.

Viêt-cong [vjɛtkɔ̃g] *nm* Vietcong, Viet Cong.

Viêt(-)nam (le) [ləvjɛtnam] *nm* Vietnam.

vietnamien, -ienne [vjɛtnamjɛ̃, -ɛn] **1** *adj* Vietnamese. **2** *nm Ling* Vietnamese. **3** *n* **V.,** Vietnamese.

vieux, vieil, *f* **vieille** [vjø, vjɛj] **1** *adj* (*the form* **vieil** *is used before masc nouns beginning with a vowel or* **h** *mute, but* **vieux** *also occurs in this position*) **(a)** (*personne*) old; **se faire v.,** to be getting old, to be getting on (in years); **il est plus v. que moi,** he's older than me; **vivre v.,** to live to a ripe old age; **se sentir v.,** to feel old; **il n'est pas bien v.,** he's not very old, he's still young;

(b) old, longstanding (*friendship etc*); **un vieil ami,** an old friend, a friend of long standing; **il est v. dans ce métier,** he's an old hand at this job; **v. garçon,** bachelor; **vieille fille,** old maid, spinster; *F* **v. crétin!,** old fool!; *F* **salut vieille noix** *ou* **branche!,** hullo old stick; **c'est un v. marin,** he's an old salt; **c'est un homme/une femme de la vieille école,** he's/she's one of the old school;

(c) (*objet*) old, ancient (*building etc*); old, stale (*bread, news etc*); old, worn, shabby (*hat etc*); **v. papiers,** waste paper; **mes vieilles mains tremblent,** my old hands are shaking; **elle ne va pas faire de v. os,** she won't make old bones, she won't live long; *Fig* **je ne vais pas faire de v. os ici,** I'm not going to hang around here for long; **c'est v. comme Hérode** *ou* **comme le Pont-Neuf** *ou* **le monde,** it's as old as the hills, it goes back to the year dot; **le bon v. temps,** the good old days; **il est très vieille France,** he's very much one of the old school; **c'est une vieille histoire,** it's an old story; **elle est vieille, celle-là!,** that's a real oldie *or* an old one!; **de v. souvenirs,** old memories;

(d) *inv* **v. jeu,** old-fashioned, antiquated, out of date; **ça, c'est v. jeu,** that's old hat; **s'habiller/être v. jeu,** to be old-fashioned in one's dress/to be old-fashioned; **des rubans vieil or/v. rose,** old-gold/old-rose ribbons.

2 *adv* **elle s'habille plus v. que son âge,** she dresses too old for *or* older than her age;

3 *n* **un v./une vieille,** an old man/an old woman; **les v.,** old people, the old *or* elderly *or* aged; *F* **mes v.,** my parents *or F* folks; **mon v./ma vieille,** (*père/mère*) my old man/my old woman; *F* **mon v.,** (*mon ami*) mate, chum; **comment ça va ma vieille?,** (*mon ami(e)*) how are you?; **viens, ma vieille!,** come on, old girl!

4 *nm F* **prendre un coup de v.,** to age, to look (a lot) older.

5 *nf* **vieille,** (*poisson*) wrasse, seawife.

vif, vive [vif, viv] **1** *adj* **(a)** alive, living; **être brûlé v.,** to be burnt alive; **prendre de vive force,** to take by storm *or* by force; **de vive voix,** by word of mouth, *Litt* viva voce; **haie vive,** quickset hedge; **eau vive,** running water, spring water; **marée de vive eau,** spring tide; **chaux vive,** quicklime; *Ordinat* **mémoire vive,** random access memory, RAM;

(b) lively, animated, brisk (*action, discussion etc*); vivacious, lively, animated (*person*); **vive allure, allure vive,** brisk pace; **être v., avoir l'humeur un peu vive,** to be quick-tempered; **il y avait un échange de paroles vives,** there was a sharp exchange of words; **v. à répondre,** quick to answer *or* reply, quick in answering; **avec mes plus vives félicitations,** with my warmest *or* most heartfelt congratulations; **une flambée vive brûlait dans la cheminée,** a fire was blazing away merrily in the hearth; **cheval v.,** high-spirited horse;

(c) sharp (*wind, reprimand etc*); acute, sharp (*pain etc*); **l'air est v.,** there's a nip in the air; **arête vive,** sharp edge;

(d) keen, quick (*wit etc*); vivid (*imagination etc*); *Euph* **il n'est pas très v.,** he's not very bright *or* quick (-witted); **v. plaisir,** keen *or* great pleasure; **vive satisfaction,** keen *or* great satisfaction; **écouter avec un v. intérêt,** to listen with keen *or* deep *or* great interest;
(e) bright, vivid, intense (*colour*).
2 *nm* **(a) peindre sur le v.,** to paint from life; *Fig* **être pris sur le v.,** to be caught red-handed *or* in the act; *Fig* **un photo pris sur le v.,** an action shot *or* photo;
(b) blessé *ou* **piqué au v.,** cut *or* stung to the quick; **j'ai les nerfs à v.,** my nerves are on edge; **entrer dans le v. de la question,** to get to the heart of the matter; **couper** *ou* **trancher dans le v.,** to take drastic measures;
(c) pêcher au v., to fish with live bait;
(d) *Jur* living person; **donation entre vifs,** donation inter vivos.

vif-argent [vifarʒɑ̃] *nm* **(a)** *Fig* **il a du v.-a. dans les veines, c'est du v.-a.,** he's never still (for a minute); **(b)** *Arch* quicksilver, mercury.

vigie [viʒi] *nf* **(a)** (*garde, gardien*) lookout (man); **être de v.** *ou* **en v.,** to be on the lookout; **(b)** (*poste*) watchtower; *Rail* (observation) box (*on van*); *Rail* **v. de signaux,** signal cabin; *Rail* **v. de frein,** brake cabin.

vigilance [viʒilɑ̃s] *nf* vigilance, watchfulness; **surprendre la v. de qn,** to catch s.o. napping; **redoubler de v.,** to increase one's vigilance.

vigilant [viʒilɑ̃] *adj* vigilant, watchful, alert.

vigile[1] [viʒil] *nf Rel* vigil (*of feast day*).

vigile[2] *nm* (night)watchman.

vigne [viɲ] *nf* **(a)** (*arbre*) vine; **feuille de v.,** vine-leaf; **(b)** (*vignoble*) vineyard; *Fig* **être dans les vignes du Seigneur,** to be drunk, to be in one's cups; **(c)** *Bot* **v. vierge,** Virginia creeper.

vigneau, -eaux [viɲo] *nm (mollusque)* periwinkle.

vigneron, -onne [viɲ(ə)rɔ̃, -ɔn] *n* wine grower.

vignette [viɲɛt] *nf* **(a)** *Com* label, ticket (*on packets of tobacco etc*); *Aut* **v. automobile,** (road) tax disc; **(b)** *Beaux-Arts* vignette; *Typ Arch* text illustration.

vignettiste [viɲetist] *n Typ Arch* vignettist.

vignoble [viɲɔbl] **1** *nm* vineyard. **2** *adj* **région v.,** wine (growing) region.

vignot [viɲo] *nm* (*mollusque*) periwinkle.

vigogne [vigɔɲ] *nf Zool* vicuña, vicuna; *Tex* vicuña, vicuna (wool, cloth).

vigoureusement [vigurøzmɑ̃] *adv* vigorously.

vigoureux, -euse [vigurø, -øz] *adj* vigorous, robust, sturdy; **elle est encore vigoureuse pour son âge,** she's still hale and hearty for her age; **coup v.,** powerful blow; **faire une opposition vigoureuse à un projet,** to vigorously oppose a plan.

vigueur [vigœr] *nf* **(a)** vigour, *US* vigor, strength, sturdiness; **donner de la v. à qn,** to invigorate s.o., to brace s.o. up; **sans v.,** (*personne*) exhausted, washed out; (*style etc*) flat, lifeless; **avec v.,** vigorously; **(b) en v.,** (*décret etc*) in force, in effect; **entrer en v.,** to come into force *or* effect *or* operation; **cesser d'être en v.,** to lapse; **mettre un règlement en v.,** to enforce a regulation.

viking [vikiŋ] *Hist* **1** *adj* Viking. **2** *n* **V.,** Viking.

vil [vil] *adj* **(a) vendre qch à v. prix,** to sell sth at a low price, *F* to sell sth dirt cheap; **(b)** *Litt & Arch* vile, base (*person, motive etc*); *Arch* low(ly) (*origin, condition etc*); **vile calomnie,** foul calumny; **(c)** base (*metal*).

vilain, -aine [vilɛ̃, -ɛn] **1** *n* **(a)** *F* **oh, le v.!/la vilaine!,** (*à un enfant*) you naughty boy!, you little villain!/you naughty girl!, you little villain!; **(b)** *F* **il y aura du v.,** there's going to be trouble; **il y a du v. dans l'air,** there's something (nasty) brewing; **(c)** *Hist* villain, villein. **2** *adj* **(a)** nasty, bad, unpleasant; **c'est un v. monsieur,** he's a nasty piece of work; **ce sont de vilaines gens,** they're a bad *or* nasty lot; **v. tour,** mean *or* dirty trick; **c'est une vilaine histoire,** it's not a nice story, it's an ugly story; **une vilaine blessure,** a nasty *or* an ugly wound; **(b)** ugly, shabby (*hat etc*); ugly, sordid, wretched (*street etc*); **elle n'est pas vilaine,** she's not bad looking, she's not what you'd call ugly.

vilainement [vilɛnmɑ̃] *adv* in an unpleasant *or* a nasty way.

vilebrequin [vilbrəkɛ̃] *nm* **(a)** (*outil*) (bit) brace, brace and bit; **v. à cliquet,** ratchet brace; **(b)** (*dans moteur*) crankshaft.

vilement [vilmɑ̃] *adv Vieilli* vilely, basely.

vilenie [vil(ə)ni] *nf* **(a)** (*caractère*) vileness, baseness; **(b)** *Litt* mean *or* vile *or* low action, foul deed.

villa [vila] *nf* **(a)** villa, detached house; **(b)** *Antiq* villa.

village [vilaʒ] *nm* village; **il est bien de son v.,** you can tell that he comes from the country; **v. de vacances,** holiday village.

villageois, -oise [vilaʒwa, -waz] **1** *n* villager; (*campagnard*) countryman, *f* countrywoman. **2** *adj* rustic; **traditions villageoises,** country *or* village customs.

ville [vil] *nf* town; (*plus grande*) city; **grande v.,** city; **centre v.,** town centre, *Am* downtown; (*plus grande*) city centre, *Am* downtown; **v. d'eaux,** spa; **v. champignon,** boom town; **v. satellite,** satellite town; **la seconde v. de France,** France's second city; **v. nouvelle,** new town; **gens de la v.,** townspeople, townsfolk, citydwellers, *F* townies; **la V. éternelle,** the Eternal City, Rome; **en v.,** in (the) town; (*au centre ville*) in the town *or* city centre, *Am* downtown; **dîner en v.,** to dine out; **en v.,** (*sur enveloppe*) local; **aller à la v.,** to go into town, *Am* to go downtown; **habiter à la v.,** to live in a town (*as opposed to the country*); **tenue de v.,** town clothes; (*sur une invitation*) lounge suit; **financé par la v.,** financed by the local authority; **hôtel de v.,** town hall, *surtout Am* city hall.

villégiature [vileʒjatyr] *nf* **(a)** holiday, *Am* vacation; **être en v.,** to be on holiday *or Am* vacation; **(b)** (*station*) (holiday) resort.

villeux, -euse [vilø, -øz] *adj Biol* villous, villose, hairy.

villosité [vilozite] *nf* **(a)** hairiness; **(b)** *Anat etc* villosity, villus.

vin [vɛ̃] *nm* wine; **les grands vins,** vintage wines; **v. ordinaire, v. de table,** table wine; **v. de pays** *ou* **du cru,** regional wine (*not from recognized vineyard*); **v. d'appellation contrôlée,** wine of guaranteed vintage; **v. délimité de qualité contrôlée,** medium quality wine; **v. de Bordeaux,** claret; **v. du Rhin,** hock; **v. de Bourgogne,** burgundy; **v. rosé,** rosé wine; **v. mousseux,** sparkling wine; **v. de fruits,** fruit wine; *Rel* **v. de messe,** altar wine; **marchand de v.,** (retail) wine merchant; **négociant en vins,** (wholesale) wine merchant; **offrir un v. d'honneur à qn,** to hold a reception in honour *or US* honor of s.o.; **être pris de v.,** to be the worse for drink; *F* **cuver son v.,** to sleep it off; **avoir le v. gai/triste,** to be/not to be a happy drunk; **entre deux vins,** tipsy, merry; *Prov* **quand le v. est tiré, il faut le boire,** there's no turning back now, you've made your bed and you must lie in it; **mettre de l'eau dans son v.,** to water (down) one's wine; *Fig* to cut down expenses, to draw in one's horns.

vinaigre [vinɛgr] *nm* **(a)** vinegar; **v. de vin,** wine vinegar; **v. à l'estragon,** tarragon vinegar; *Prov* **on ne prend pas les mouches avec du v.,** harsh treatment pays no dividends; **(b)** (*au jeu*) **donner du v.,** to turn (*the skipping rope*) quickly; **(c)** *F* **faire v.,** to hurry, to get a move on.

vinaigrer [vinegre] *vt* to season with vinegar.

vinaigrerie [vinɛgrəri] *nf* (*fabrique*) vinegar factory; (*fabrication*) vinegar making; *Com* vinegar trade.

vinaigrette [vinɛgrɛt] *nf Culin* vinaigrette, French dressing; **poireaux v.,** leaks (in) vinaigrette.

vinaigrier [vinɛgrije] *nm* **(a)** (*flacon*) vinegar bottle; **(b)** (*fabricant*) vinegar manufacturer; (*marchand*) vinegar merchant.

vinasse [vinas] *nf F* (cheap and nasty) wine, *Br* plonk.

vindicatif, -ive [vɛ̃dikatif, -iv] *adj* vindictive, spiteful, revengeful.

vindicte [vɛ̃dikt] *nf Jur* prosecution (*of crime*); **v. publique,** vindication of public morality; *Litt* **désigner qn à la v. publique,** to expose s.o. to public condemnation.

vineux, -euse [vinø, -øz] *adj* **(a)** *Spéc* (*vin*) full-bodied; **(b)** vinous (*taste*); wine-flavoured, *US* -flavored (*peach etc*); **(c)** (*couleur*) wine-coloured, *US* -colored; *F* **nez v.,** ruby *or* winy *or* bibulous nose.

vingt [vɛ̃] **1** *adj num inv* twenty; **v. et un** [vɛ̃teœ̃], twenty-one; **v.-deux** [vɛ̃tdø], twenty-two; *Arg* **v.-deux!,** watch it!, look out!; **le v. juin** [ləvɛ̃ʒyɛ̃] , (on) the twentieth of June, (on) June (the) twentieth; **ouvert v.-quatre heures sur v.-quatre,** open all day *or* round the clock *or* twenty-four hours (a day); **les années v.,** the twenties; **il n'a pas encore v. ans,** he's not yet twenty, he's still in his teens; **je n'ai plus mon cœur de v. ans,** I'm no youngster any more; **les moins de v. ans,** teenagers; **je te l'ai dit v. fois,** I've told you a hundred times *or* time and time again; **quatre-vingts,** eighty; **quatre-v. deux,** eighty-two. **2** *nm inv* (number) twenty; *Cartes* **v.-et-un,** pontoon, *Am* blackjack, *US* twenty-one; **habiter au v. de l'avenue,** to live at number twenty in the avenue.

vingtaine [vɛ̃tɛn] *nf* (about) twenty, a score; **une v. de personnes,** twenty or so people; **d'une v. d'années,** about twenty years old.

vingtième [vɛ̃tjɛm] **1** *adj* twentieth. **2** *n* twentieth. **3** *nm* twentieth (part).

vingtièmement [vɛ̃tjɛmmɑ̃] *adv* in (the) twentieth place.

vinicole [vinikɔl] *adj* wine(-growing) (*area etc*).
vinifère [vinifɛr] *adj* wine-producing (*soil etc*).
Vintimille [vɛ̃timij] *n* Ventimiglia.
vinyle [vinil] *nm Ch* vinyl.
viol [vjɔl] *nm* **(a)** rape; **(b)** violation (*of a sanctuary etc*).
violacé, -ée [vjɔlase] **1** *adj* purplish-blue; **prendre un teint v.,** (*d'une personne*) to go blue (*with cold*). **2** *nfpl Bot* **violacées,** Violaceae.
violacer [vjɔlase] *v* (**je violaçai(s); n. violaçons**) **1** *vt* to turn (*sth*) blue *or* purplish. **2 se violacer** *vpr* to turn blue *or* purplish.
violateur, -trice [vjɔlatœr, -tris] *n* violator; transgressor (*of laws etc*).
violation [vjɔlasjɔ̃] *nf* violation, infringement, transgression, breach (*of law etc*); desecration (*of grave*); **v. des règles,** breaking of rules; **agir en v. d'une règle,** to act in contravention of a rule; **v. de domicile,** illegal entry.
violâtre [vjɔlɑtr] *adj* purplish.
viole [vjɔl] *nf Mus* viol; **v. d'amour,** viol(a) d'amore.
violemment [vjɔlamɑ̃] *adv* violently; **il me dégoûtait v.,** I found him deeply offensive.
violence [vjɔlɑ̃s] *nf* violence, force; fierceness (*of encounter etc*); **faire v. à qn/qch,** to do violence to s.o./sth; **j'ai dû me faire v. pour me lever tôt,** I had to force myself to get up early; **se faire une douce v.,** to force oneself (*to do sth pleasant*); **faire v. à un texte,** to distort a text; **subir des violences physiques/morales,** to suffer *or* be subjected to physical violence/mental cruelty; *Vieilli* **faire v. à une femme,** to violate *or* rape a woman.
violent, -ente [vjɔlɑ̃, -ɑ̃t] **1** *adj* violent; high, fierce (*wind*); fierce, violent (*exchange of words*); drastic (*measures etc*); pungent (*smell*); **homme v.,** violent man; **mourir de mort violente,** to die a violent death; **choc très v.,** a tremendous impact; **une violente opposition,** violent opposition; *F* **c'est par trop v.!,** it really is too much!, that really is the limit! **2** *n* violent person.
violenter [vjɔlɑ̃te] *vt* **(a)** to rape (*a woman*); **(b)** *Litt* to do violence to (*s.o., sth*).
violer [vjɔle] *vt* **(a)** to rape (*a woman*); **se faire v.,** to be raped; **(b)** (*transgresser*) to violate (*truce, law*); to transgress, to infringe (*law*); to break (*law, treaty, faith*); **v. un secret,** to divulge a secret; **v. une sépulture,** to desecrate a grave; **v. le domicile de qn,** to break into s.o.'s house.
violet, -ette [vjɔlɛ, -ɛt] *adj* **1** violet, purple (-coloured, *US* -colored); **elle était violette de fureur,** she was livid *or* purple with rage; **mains violettes de froid,** hands blue with the cold. **2** *nm* (the colour, *US* color) violet, purple.
violette [vjɔlɛt] *nf Bot* violet; **v. de Parme,** Parma violet.
violeur [vjɔlœr] *nm* rapist.
violier [vjɔlje] *nm Bot* stock; **v. jaune,** wallflower.
violine [vjɔlin] *adj* purple-violet.
violon [vjɔlɔ̃] *nm Mus* **(a)** (*instrument*) violin, *F* fiddle; **jouer du v.,** to play the violin *or F* fiddle; **c'est son v. d'Ingres,** it's his hobby; *F* **accordez vos violons,** make sure you all tell the same story, make sure you get your stories straight; **(b)** violin (player); **premier v.,** first violin, leader (*of the orchestra*); *Fig* **payer les violons,** to pay the piper; **(c)** *Arg* **le v.,** the cells, the lockup; **au v.,** in the lockup; **(d)** *Tech* **(poulie à) v.,** fiddle block; **(e)** *Nau* **violons de mer,** fiddles (*for the tables*).
violoncelle [vjɔlɔ̃sɛl] *nm Mus* **(a)** (*instrument*) cello, *Fml* violoncello; **(b)** (*musicien*) cello (player), cellist.
violoncelliste [vjɔlɔ̃selist] *n* cellist.
violoneux [vjɔlɔnø] *nm* fiddler; *Péj* second-rate *or US* two-bit musician.
violoniste [vjɔlɔnist] *n* violinist, violin player.
viorne [vjɔrn] *nf Bot* viburnum.
vipère [vipɛr] *nf* viper, adder; *Fig* (*personne*) viper; **v. aspic,** asp; **v. heurtante,** puff adder; *Fig* **langue de v.,** spiteful *or* viperish *or* venomous tongue; *Fig* **nid de vipères,** nest of vipers, snake pit.
viperau, -eaux [vipro] *nm* young viper.
vipérin, -ine [viperɛ̃, -in] **1** *adj* viperine. **2** *nf* **vipérine (a)** *Bot* viper's bugloss; **(b)** (*reptile*) viperine snake.
virage [viraʒ] *nm* **(a)** (*mouvement*) turn, turning (round); turning *or* swinging *or* slewing round (*of crane etc*); *Nau* tacking, going about; *Av* **v. (incliné), v. sur l'aile,** bank(ing); **angle de v.,** angle of bank;
(b) (*tournant*) (sharp) turn, bend, corner (*in road*); **v. sans visibilité,** blind corner; **v. en épingle à cheveux,** hairpin bend; **v. à la corde,** sharp turn; **virages sur 5 km.,** (*sur panneau*) bends for 5 kms; **prendre** *ou* **aborder un v.,** to take a bend, to corner;
(c) banked corner, bank (*of racing track*);
(d) (*changement*) change (in direction); **le parti amorce** *ou* **prend un v.,** the party is changing direction *or* shifting ground; **cela marque un v. net dans la vie politique du pays,** this marks a U-turn in the political life of the country;
(e) *Ch* changing of colour *or US* color; **v. au rouge,** turning red;
(f) *Phot* toning (*of proofs*).
virago [virago] *nf* virago, termagant.
viral, -aux [viral, -o] *adj Méd* viral.
virée [vire] *nf F* trip, run, outing (*in a car etc*); (*dans les cafés, pubs*) *Br* ≈ pub crawl, *Am* ≈ bar hop; **faire une v.,** to go for an outing *or* a run (*in a car etc*); (*dans les cafés, pubs*) *Br* to go on a pub crawl, *Am* to bar hop.
virement [virmɑ̃] *nm* **(a)** *Banque* (credit) transfer; **banque de v.,** clearing bank; **v. automatique,** automatic transfer; **(b)** *Nau* **v. de bord,** tacking, going about.
virer [vire] **1** *vi* **(a)** (*tourner*) (*of wind*) to veer; *Aut etc* to take a bend *or* a corner, to corner; *Av* to bank; (*of crane etc*) to slew round, to swing round; *Aut* **v. court,** to corner sharply; *Aut* **v. sur place,** to turn in one's own length; **la discussion a viré à l'aigre,** the discussion took an acrimonious turn; *Nau* **v. de bord,** to tack, to go about; (*of steamship*) to turn; *Nau* **v. vent arrière,** to wear (*ship*); *Nau* **v. vent devant** *ou* **vent avant,** to go about in stays, to stay; *Nau* **pare à v.!,** ready about!; *Nau* **v. au cabestan,** to heave (at the capstan);
(b) to change colour *or US* color; *Phot* (*of print*) to tone; **encre qui vire au noir en séchant,** ink that dries black.
2 *vt* **(a)** *Banque* to transfer (*a sum*); to clear (*cheques etc*);
(b) *Phot* to tone (print);
(c) *F* to throw *or* kick *or* chuck (*s.o.*) out; **il faudrait v. ces étagères,** we should throw *or* chuck these shelves out, we should get rid of these shelves.
3 se virer *vpr F* **vire-toi!,** move!
vireux, -euse [virø, -øz] *adj* poisonous, noxious.
virevolte [virvɔlt] *nf* **(a)** (*changement*) volte-face; **v. de la fortune,** sudden change of fortune; **je m'attends à une v. de sa part,** I expect he'll change his mind; **(b)** *Équitation Arch* quick circling (*of horse*); **(c)** half-turn (*of dancer etc*).
virevolter [virvɔlte] *vi* (*of horse*) to circle; (*of person*) to spin round; *Fig* to make a U-turn.
Virgile [virʒil] *nm Littér* Virgil, Vergil.
virginal, -aux [virʒinal, -o] **1** *adj* virginal; **blanc v.,** pure *or* virginal white. **2** *nm Mus* virginal, (pair of) virginals.
Virginie [virʒini] *nf* Virginia.
virginité [virʒinite] *nf* virginity; **perdre sa v.,** to lose one's virginity.
virgule [virgyl] *nf* **(a)** *Gram* comma; **point v.,** semicolon; *Fig* **sans changer une v.,** without changing one *or* a single iota; **(b)** *Math* decimal point; **trois v. cinq (3,5),** three point five (3.5); *Ordinat* **v. flottante,** floating point; **arithmétique à v. flottante,** floating point arithmetic.
viril [viril] *adj* **(a)** male (*sex etc*); *Anat* **membre v.,** male member *or* organ; **toge virile,** toga virilis; **(b)** manly (*action etc*); **l'âge v.,** manhood; **qualité virile,** male characteristic.
virilement [virilmɑ̃] *adv* like a man, in a manly way.
virilisant [virilizɑ̃] *adj Méd* (*drug etc*) which gives male characteristics.
viriliser [virilize] *vt* **(a)** to make more virile *or* manly; to make (*woman*) appear masculine; **(b)** *Biol* to give male characteristics to (*an organism etc*).
virilité [virilite] *nf* virility, manhood; **se sentir menacé/attaqué dans sa v.,** to feel that one's manhood is being threatened/attacked.
virole [virɔl] *nf* ferrule (*of walking stick etc*); *MecE* collar, hoop, sleeve.
viroler [virɔle] *vt* to fit (*tool handle etc*) with a ferrule.
virologie [virɔlɔʒi] *nf Méd* virology.
virologiste [virɔlɔʒist], **virologue** [virɔlɔg] *n Méd* virologist.
virtualité [virtɥalite] *nf* potentiality.
virtuel, -elle [virtɥɛl] *adj* potential; *Opt Phil* virtual (*image etc*).
virtuellement [virtɥɛlmɑ̃] *adv* virtually.
virtuose [virtɥoz] *n* virtuoso.
virtuosité [virtɥozite] *nf* virtuosity.
virulence [virylɑ̃s] *nf* (*d'un poison etc*) virulence.
virulent [virylɑ̃] *adj* virulent (*poison, satire etc*); **diatribe virulente,** scathing diatribe.
virure [viryr] *nf Nau* strake.
virus [virys] *nm Méd Ordinat etc* virus; **maladie à v.,** viral disease; *F* **il y a un v. qui traîne** *ou* **dans l'air,** there's a virus going around; *F* **avoir le v. du ski,** to have a craze for skiing, to have been bitten by the skiing bug.

vis [vis] *nf* screw; **v. à bois,** wood screw; **v. à métaux,** metal screw; **v. à tête cylindrique,** cheese-head(ed) screw; **v. à tête fraisée,** countersunk (head) screw; **v. à tête ronde,** roundhead(ed) screw; **v. à oreilles** *ou* **à ailettes,** wing screw; **v. autotaraudeuse,** self-tapping screw; **v. à droite/à gauche,** righthanded/lefthanded screw *or* thread; **tige à v.,** screwed *or* threaded rod; **escalier à v.,** spiral staircase; *Fig* **serrer la v. à qn,** to be very hard *or* crack down on s.o.; **v. sans fin,** endless screw, worm (screw); *HydE* **v. d'Archimède,** Archimedean screw; *Ind* **v. de transport,** spiral conveyor; *F* **v. platinées,** (contact) points.

visa [viza] *nm* **(a)** (*pour passeport*) visa; **demander/ obtenir un v.,** to apply for/obtain a visa; **apposer un v. à un passeport,** to stamp *or* visa a passport; **(b)** (*signature*) signature (*on document etc*); (*paraphe*) initials (*of supervisor etc*); (*sceau*) stamp (*on document*); *Cin* **v. de censure,** censor's certificate.

visage [vizaʒ] *nm* face; **homme au v. agréable,** pleasant-faced man; **v. ouvert,** open *or* honest face; **il a un v. d'enfant,** he's baby faced, he's a baby-face; **elle a changé de v.,** her face *or* expression changed; **à deux visages,** two-faced; **il a deux visages,** he's two-faced; **avoir bon v.,** to look well; **faire bon v.,** to put a brave face on things; **faire bon v. à qn,** to be outwardly friendly to s.o.; **sans v.,** faceless; **à v. découvert,** (*ouvertement*) openly; **faire v. de bois à qn,** to shut the door in s.o.'s face; **socialisme à v. humain,** socialism with a human face; **je n'arrive pas à mettre un nom sur ce v.,** I can't put a name to that face; **il y a des visages qui frappent,** some faces are very striking; **rencontrer de nouveaux visages,** to meet new faces; **présenter un pays sous un autre** *ou* **nouveau v.,** to present a country in a new light; **visages pâles,** palefaces.

visagiste [vizaʒist] *n* beautician.

vis-à-vis [vizavi] **1** *prép* **(a)** (*en face*) **v.-à-v. de (qn, qch),** opposite, facing (s.o., sth); **(b)** (*pour etc*) **v.-à-v. de (qn, qch),** towards, in relation to, vis-à-vis (s.o., sth); **ses sentiments v.-à-v. de moi,** his feelings towards me; **être sincère v.-à-v. de soi-même,** to be truthful with oneself. **2** *nm* **(a)** person opposite (*at table etc*); *Cartes* partner; (*à un entretien*) tête-à-tête, meeting; **mon v.-à-v.,** the person sitting opposite me; **un long v.-à-v.,** a long tête-à-tête; **faire v.à-v.** *ou* **être en v.-à-v. à qn,** to be *or* stand *or* sit opposite s.o., to face s.o.; **nous avons le lac pour v.-à-v.,** we look out on to *or* face the lake; **(b)** (*meuble*) vis-à-vis, S-shaped couch.

viscéral, -aux [viseral, -o] *adj* **(a)** *Anat* visceral; **(b)** *Fig* deep-seated (*hatred etc*); innermost (*thoughts etc*).

viscères [visɛr] *nmpl Anat* viscera, internal organs.

viscose [viskoz] *nf Ch Ind* viscose.

viscosité [viskozite] *nf* viscosity, stickiness.

visée [vize] *nf* **(a)** aim; *Mil etc* aiming, sighting; **ligne de v.,** line of sight; **point de v.,** target; **(b)** *Fig* **visées,** aims, designs; **avoir de grandes visées** *ou* **des visées ambitieuses,** to have big *or* ambitious plans, to have great ambitions, to aim high; **il a des visées sur ce poste,** he has designs on this job.

viser[1] [vize] **1** *vi* to aim, to take aim (**à,** at, for); *Fig* **v. à un but précis,** to have a specific purpose; **v. à faire qch,** to aim at doing sth *or* to do sth; **v. haut,** to aim high; **v. juste,** to aim straight; **v. plus haut,** to aim higher, to set one's sights higher.

2 *vt* **(a)** to aim *or* take aim at (*s.o., sth*); to set one's sights on (*sth*); (*d'un arpenteur*) to sight, to take a sight on (*sth*); (*chercher à obtenir*) to have (*sth*) in view; (*concerner*) to relate to (*sth*); **il vise ce poste depuis longtemps,** he's had his eye on this job for a long time; **accusation visant qn,** accusation aimed *or* directed at s.o.; **les denrées alimentaires ne sont pas visées par ce décret,** articles of food are not affected by this order; **je ne vise personne,** I am not alluding *or* referring to anybody in particular; *Golf* **v. la balle,** to address the ball;

(b) *Arg* (*regarder*) to (have a) look at (*s.o., sth*).

viser[2] *vt Admin* to visa (*passport*); to countersign, to initial, to stamp (*document*).

viseur, -euse [vizœr, -øz] **1** *n* aimer. **2** *nm Phot* viewfinder; eyepiece, sighting tube (*of surveying instrument etc*); *Av* **v. de lancement,** bomb sight(s).

visibilité [vizibilite] *nf* visibility; **v. nulle,** zero visibility; **bonne/mauvaise v.,** good/poor visibility; *Av* **vol sans v.,** instrument flying.

visible [vizibl] *adj* **(a)** visible; **v. à l'œil nu/au microscope,** visible to the naked eye/under a microscope; **c'est à peine v.,** it's scarcely visible, you can hardly see it; **très v.,** highly visible, conspicuous; **il n'y avait personne de v.,** there was nobody in sight; **(b)** (*à qui l'on peut rendre visite*) ready to receive company; **je ne suis pas v.,** I am not at home, I am not in; **je ne serai pas v. avant trois heures,** I can't see anybody before three o'clock; *F* **n'entre pas, je ne suis pas v.,** don't come in, I'm not decent; **cette collection n'est pas v.,** the collection is not open to the public.

visiblement [viziblǝmɑ̃] *adv* visibly.

visière [vizjɛr] *nf* peak (*of cap*); (*pour protéger les yeux*) eyeshade; visor, vizor (*of helmet*); **mettre sa main en v.,** to shade one's eyes with one's hand; *Litt* **rompre en v. à** *ou* **avec qn,** (*se quereller*) to quarrel openly with s.o.; (*être d'avis contraire*) to take up a diametrically opposite view to that of s.o..

vision [vizjɔ̃] *nf* **(a)** (*sens*) (eye)sight; (*vue*) sight, view; **trouble de la v.,** eye disease; **v. momentanée de qch,** momentary glimpse of sth; **nous n'avons pas la même v. des choses,** we don't see things the same way; **v. réaliste/ simpliste,** realistic/simplistic view; *Cin* **première v.,** premiere; **(b)** vision, imagination (*of poet etc*); **(c)** (*hallucination*) vision; **avoir des visions,** (*hallucinations*) to have visions; *F* (*rêver*) to fantasize.

visionnaire [vizjɔnɛr] **1** *adj* visionary. **2** *n* visionary, dreamer.

visionner [vizjɔne] *vt Cin* to screen; (*pour analyser*) to view.

visionneuse [vizjɔnøz] *nf Cin Phot* viewer.

visiophone [vizjɔfɔn] *nm* viewphone.

visitandine [vizitɑ̃din] *nf Cathol* nun of the Order of the Visitation.

visitation [vizitɑsjɔ̃] *nf Rel* visitation (*of the Virgin to St Elizabeth*).

visite [vizit] *nf* **(a)** visit, (social) call; (*visiteur*) visitor, caller; **faire (une) v.** *ou* **rendre v. à qn,** to visit s.o., to call on s.o., to pay s.o. a visit *or* a call; **rendre une v.** *ou* **sa v. à qn,** to return s.o.'s visit *or* call; **il nous fait une petite v. tous les soirs,** he drops in on us every evening; **être en v. chez qn,** to be visiting *or* on a visit to s.o.; **nous avons eu la v. de Marc,** Marc called in to see us; **v. de politesse,** courtesy call, duty visit; **v. officielle,** official visit; **carte de v.,** visiting card; *Com* **recevoir les visites d'un représentant,** to be called on by a representative; *Sp* **équipe en v.,** visiting team; **heures de v.,** (*at hospital etc*) visiting hours; **nous attendons des visites** *ou* **de la v.,** we're expecting visitors *or* guests; **visites à domicile,** (*d'un médecin*) house calls; **le docteur ne fait pas de visites,** the doctor doesn't make house calls; *Jur* **droit de v. aux enfants,** right of access to the children;

(b) (*inspection*) inspection, examination, survey (*of building, ship etc*); *Méd* (medical) examination; search (*of house, ship etc*); visit (*to place of interest*); **faire la v.,** to go on one's round of inspection; **passer (à) une v. médicale,** to have a medical examination; *Mil etc* **passer la v.,** to come before the medical officer *or* the medical board; *Mil* **v. des malades,** sick parade; *Rel* **v. pastorale** *ou* **de l'évêque,** pastoral visit, visitation (by bishop); **trou de v.,** inspection hole, manhole (*of sewer etc*); *Nau* **droit de v.,** right of search; **v. de douane,** customs examination; **v. dirigée** *ou* **guidée,** guided *or* conducted tour.

visiter [vizite] **1** *vt* **(a)** to visit (*as a tourist*); **v. une cathédrale,** to visit *or* tour a cathedral; **on nous a fait v. l'usine,** we were shown round *or* over the factory, we were given a tour of the factory; **(b)** (*inspecter*) to inspect, to examine (*building, machinery etc*); to survey (*ship*); to view, to go over (*house for sale*); (*de la police etc*) to search (*house etc*); to inspect, to examine (*luggage*); **je vais te faire v. les lieux/la maison,** I'll show you round the premises/the house; **(c)** to visit (*the sick etc*); to visit (*a patient*); *Com* to call on (*a client*). **2 se visiter** *vpr* to be open to visitors; **la chapelle ne se visite pas,** the chapel is not open to visitors.

visiteur, -euse [vizitœr, -øz] *n* **(a)** (*touriste*) visitor (*to a museum etc*); **ouvert aux visiteurs à partir de quinze heures,** open to visitors *or* to the public from 3 pm; **(b)** (*hôte etc*) visitor, caller; (*dans une prison*) visitor; **nous avons eu de nombreux visiteurs,** we had a large number of visitors; **infirmière visiteuse,** community *or* district nurse; (*for babies*) health visitor; *Sp* **les visiteurs,** the visitors, the visiting team; *Com* **v. en soies,** representative *or* traveller in silks; **v. médical** *ou* **pharmaceutique,** representative in pharmaceutical products; **(c)** (*inspecteur*) inspector; **v. des douanes,** customs officer.

vison [vizɔ̃] *nm* **(a)** (American) mink; **(b)** (*fourrure*) mink; *F* (*manteau*) mink coat.

visonnière [vizɔnjɛr] *nf Can* mink farm.
visqueux, -euse [viskø, -øz] *adj* viscous, gluey, sticky; thick, viscous (*oil*); slimy (*secretion etc*); *Fig* **sourire v.,** smarmy smile.
vissage [visaʒ] *nm* screwing (on, in, down, up).
visser [vise] **1** *vt* **(a)** to screw (on, in, down, up); **v. un écrou à bloc,** to screw a nut tight; *F* **être vissé sur sa chaise,** to be glued to one's chair; **(b)** *F* to treat (*s.o.*) severely, to be very hard *or* crack down on (*s.o.*). **2 se visser** *vpr* to screw on; **la lance se visse au bout du tuyau,** the nozzle screws on to the end of the hose.
visualisation [vizɥalizɑsjɔ̃] *nf* visualization; *Ordinat* **console** *ou* **unité** *ou* **écran de v.,** (visual) display unit; *Ordinat* **v. de la page à l'écran,** page preview.
visualiser [vizɥalize] *vt* (*imaginer*) to visualize; (*rendre visible*) to make (*sth*) visible to the eye; *Ordinat* to display.
visuel, -elle [vizɥɛl] **1** *adj* visual; **champ v.,** field of vision. **2** *nm Ordinat* visual display unit, VDU.
visuellement [vizɥɛlmɑ̃] *adv* visually.
vital, -aux [vital, -o] *adj* vital; **centres vitaux,** vital organs; **question vitale,** vital question; *F* **il faut que tu viennes, c'est v.!,** you must come, it's vital!, you absolutely must come!; *F* **ne t'en fais pas, ce n'est pas v.,** don't worry, it isn't the end of the world.
vitalisme [vitalism] *nm Biol* vitalism.
vitalité [vitalite] *nf* vitality.
vitamine [vitamin] *nf Biol Ch* vitamin; **alimentation riche/pauvre en vitamines,** food with a high/low vitamin content, food that is high/low in vitamins; **enfant qui manque de v.,** child with a vitamin deficiency; **as-tu pris tes vitamines?,** have you taken your vitamins?
vitaminé [vitamine] *adj* enriched with vitamins, vitamin-enriched.
vitaminique [vitaminik] *adj Méd* **carence v.,** vitamin deficiency.
vite [vit] **1** *adj Sp* fast, quick, speedy (*cars etc*).
2 *adv* quickly, fast, rapidly, swiftly, speedily; **plus v.!,** faster!; *Nau* increase speed!; **le temps passe v.,** time goes quickly, time flies; **manger trop v.,** to eat too fast *or* too quickly; **tu as parlé trop v.,** you spoke too soon; **ne va pas si v.!,** (*en voiture*) not so fast!, slow down a bit!; **vous allez v. en besogne,** you're a fast *or* quick worker, that's fast *or* quick work; **ça ne va pas v.,** it's slow work; **vous serez v. guéri,** you'll soon be better; **(faites) v.!,** quick!, hurry up!, be quick (about it)!; **allons, et plus v. que cela!,** now then, get a move on!; **au plus v.,** as quickly as possible; **je me suis v. rendu compte que ...,** I soon *or* quickly realized that ...; **avoir v. fait de faire qch,** to be quick (about) doing sth; **il eut v. fait de s'habiller,** he was dresssed in no time; *F* **on a tout rangé v. fait (bien fait),** we tidied everything away in no time; **on a v. fait de dire ...,** it's easy to say ... .
vitellus [vitelys] *nm Biol* vitellus, yolk.
vitesse [vitɛs] *nf* **(a)** speed, rapidity, quickness, swiftness; *Ordinat* **v. d'impression,** print speed; **à la v. de ...,** at the rate of ...; *Aut* at a speed of ...; **v. folle,** breakneck speed; **faire de la v.,** to move *or* go quickly *or* at (high) speed, to speed along; *Aut etc* **excès de v.,** exceeding *or* breaking the speed limit, speeding; **elle a été arrêtée pour excès de v.,** she was arrested for speeding; *Aut* **limitation de v.,** speed limit; *F* **en v.,** quickly, at speed; *F* **sors, et en v.!,** get out – pronto! *or* now!; **partir en v.,** to rush away *or* off; **un petit mot en v. pour vous dire ...,** just a quick line to let you know ...; **lutter de v. avec qn,** to race s.o.; **gagner** *ou* **prendre qn de v.,** to outrun *or* outstrip s.o.; *Sp* to overtake *or* pass s.o.; (*l'anticiper*) to steal a march on s.o.; **prendre de la v.,** to pick up *or* gather *or* increase speed; *Pol* **ce parti est en perte de v.,** the party is losing ground *or* popularity; *Av* **se mettre en perte de v.,** to stall; *Aut etc* **compteur** *ou* **indicateur de v.,** speedometer; **aller à toute v.,** to go at full *or* top speed, to rush along, *F* to go all out; *Nau* **en avant à toute v.,** full speed ahead; **v. de croisière,** cruising speed (*of ship, aircraft, car*); *Fig* **adopter la v. de croisière,** to get into the swing of things; *Rail Arch* **grande/petite v.,** fast/slow goods service;
(b) *Phys* velocity; **v. initiale,** initial velocity; (*en ballistique*) muzzle speed *or* velocity; **v. du son,** speed of sound; **v. acquise,** impetus, momentum;
(c) *Aut* gear; **changer de v.,** to change gear; **boîte de vitesses,** gearbox; **passer en deuxième v.,** to go *or* move into second (gear); **filer en quatrième v.,** to drive in top (gear); *F* to disappear at top speed.
viticole [vitikɔl] *adj* wine-producing, wine-growing (*area, region etc*); **industrie v.,** wine industry.
viticulteur, -trice [vitikyltœr, -tris] *n* vine grower, wine grower.
viticulture [vitikyltyr] *nf* vine growing, wine growing; *Spéc* viticulture.
vitrage [vitraʒ] *nm* **(a)** glazing (*of greenhouse* etc); **double v.,** double glazing; **(b)** windows (*of building etc*); **(c)** (*cloison*) glass partition *or* door; **(d)** (*rideau*) net curtain.
vitrail, -aux [vitraj, -o] *nm* leaded glass window; *surtout* stained glass (window); **l'art du v.,** the art of making stained-glass windows *or* stained glass; **les vitraux sont superbes,** the stained glass is superb.
vitre [vitr] *nf* window (pane); pane (*of glass*); *F* **casser les vitres,** to get angry, to kick up a fuss; *F* **ça ne casse pas les vitres,** it's pretty ordinary *or* run-of-the-mill, it's nothing to write home about.
vitré [vitre] *adj* **(a)** glazed (*door etc*); **baie vitrée,** picture window; **bibliothèque vitrée,** glass-fronted bookcase; **porte vitrée,** glass door; **(b)** vitreous, glassy (*substance etc*).
vitrer [vitre] *vt* to glaze (*window etc*).
vitrerie [vitrəri] *nf* glaziery; (*industrie*) glass industry.
vitreux, -euse [vitrø, -øz] *adj* vitreous (*mass, rock etc*); glassy (*appearance etc*); glazed (*eyes etc*); **porcelaine vitreuse,** vitreous china.
vitrier [vitrije] *nm* glazier.
vitrification [vitrifikɑsjɔ̃] *nf* vitrification; (*du parquet*) varnishing, sealing.
vitrifier [vitrifje] *vt* (*impf & pr sub* **n. vitrifiions, v. vitrifiiez**) to vitrify (*sand etc*); **brique vitrifiée,** glazed brick; **v. un parquet,** to varnish *or* seal a parquet floor.
vitrine [vitrin] *nf* **(a)** shop window; **faire une v.,** to do *or* dress a window; **refaire la v.,** to change the window display; **articles en v.,** articles (on show) in the window; **regarder** *ou* **lécher les vitrines,** to go window shopping; **(b)** (*de musée*) glass case, cabinet, showcase; (*armoire*) display cabinet.
vitriol [vitrijɔl] *nm Ch Arch* vitriol; **(huile de) v.,** oil of vitriol; *Fig* **critique au v.,** vitriolic criticism.
vitriolage [vitrijɔlaʒ] *nm* **(a)** (*sur qn*) vitriol throwing; **(b)** *Tex* souring (*of material*).
vitrioler [vitrijɔle] *vt* **(a)** to throw vitriol at (*s.o.*); **se faire v.,** to be the victim of an acid attack; **(b)** *Tex* to sour (*material*).
vitrioleur, -euse [vitrijɔlœr, -øz] *n* vitriol thrower.
vitro-céramique [vitrɔseramik] *adj* ceramic; **plaque v.-c.,** ceramic hob.
vitupération [vityperɑsjɔ̃] *nf Litt* vituperation.
vitupérer [vitypere] *v* (**je vitupère, n. vitupérons; je vitupérerai**) **1** *vt Litt* to abuse (*s.o., sth*). **2** *vi* to vituperate, to protest, to storm (**contre qn/qch,** against s.o./sth).
vivable [vivabl] *adj F* (*person*) livable with; (*house etc*) livable (in); **cette situation n'est plus v.,** this situation is intolerable; **il n'est pas v.,** he's just impossible (to live with).
vivace[1] [vivas] *adj* (*résistant*) long-lived; *Biol* hardy, robust; *Bot* perennial; *Fig* undying, inveterate (*hatred etc*); *Fig* **souvenirs encore vivaces,** memories that are still fresh; *Bot* **pois v.,** everlasting pea.
vivace[2] [vivatʃe] *adj inv & adv Mus* vivace.
vivacité [vivasite] *nf* **(a)** vivacity, vivaciousness, liveliness; (*enthousiasme*) keenness; (*rapidité*) briskness, quickness; **v. d'esprit,** quick- wittedness; (*humour*) sparkling wit; **avoir de la v.,** to be vivacious *or* full of life; (*malgré son âge*) to be sprightly; **avec v.,** vivaciously; **(b)** acuteness (*of feeling*); heat (*of a discussion*); fire, intensity (*of passion*); **(c)** hastiness (*of temper*); **avec v.,** hastily.
vivandier, -ière [vivɑ̃dje, -jɛr] *n Arch* sutler, *f* vivandière.
vivant [vivɑ̃] **1** *adj* **(a)** alive, living; **il est encore v.,** he is still alive; **être enterré v.,** to be buried alive; **cadavre v.,** (*très malade*) walking corpse; (*très fatigué*) zombie; **être v.,** living creature; **un poisson v.,** a live fish; **pas une âme vivante,** not a living soul; **portrait v.,** lifelike portrait; **être le portrait v. de qn,** to be the living *or* spitting image of s.o.; **langue vivante,** modern language; *F* **c'est une bibliothèque vivante,** he's a walking encyclopaedia; *Th* **tableau v.,** tableau (vivant);
(b) lively, animated (*street, scene, conversation etc*) lively (*child*); **image vivante de ...,** vivid picture of ... .
2 *nm* **(a)** (*personne*) living being; **les vivants et les morts,** the living and the dead; **bon v.,** man who enjoys (the pleasures of) life;
(b) de son v., during his lifetime, in his day; **du v. de votre père,** when your father was alive, in your father's (life)time.
vivarium [vivarjɔm] *nm* vivarium.

vivat [viva] **1** *int Arch* hurrah! bravo! **2** *nmpl* **vivats,** cheers (*of audience etc*).

vive [viv] *nf* (*poisson*) weever, stingfish.

vivement [vivmɑ̃] *adv* **(a)** briskly, sharply; **se tourner v.,** to turn round quickly; *F* **v. les vacances!,** roll on the holidays!; **v. qu'il parte!,** I'll be glad when he's gone!, he can't leave soon enough!; **réprimander v. qn,** to give s.o. a sharp rebuke, to rebuke s.o. sharply; **répondre v.,** to answer sharply *or* brusquely; **(b)** (*de couleurs*) vividly (coloured, *US* colored); **v. peint/décoré,** painted/decorated in vivid colours *or US* colors; **(c)** (*intensément*) keenly, deeply, acutely; **s'intéresser v. à qch,** to take a keen interest in sth; **remercier qn v.,** to thank s.o. warmly; **être v. ému,** to be deeply moved.

viveur [vivœr] *nm Péj* pleasure seeker, *F* fast liver.

vivier [vivje] *nm* fishpond; (*dans un restaurant*) fish tank; (*de bateau*) fish well; *Fig* breeding ground (**de,** for).

vivifiant [vivifjɑ̃] *adj* enlivening; (*air, climat etc*) invigorating, bracing.

vivifier [vivifje] *vt* (*impf & pr sub* **n. vivifiions, v. vivifiiez**) to enliven, to (re)vitalize; (*of air etc*) to invigorate; **v. l'industrie d'un pays,** to revive *or* give fresh life to a country's industry.

vivipare [vivipar] *adj Biol* viviparous.

viviparité [viviparite] *nf Biol* viviparity.

vivisection [vivisɛksjɔ̃] *nf* vivisection.

vivoir [vivwar] *nm Can* living room.

vivoter [vivɔte] *vi* to live frugally, to keep body and soul together, to rub along; **usine qui vivote,** factory that is just managing to keep going *or* is just keeping its head above water.

vivre¹ [vivr] *nm* **(a) vivres,** provisions, supplies; *Mil* rations; **vivres de réserve,** iron rations; **couper les vivres à qn,** to stop s.o.'s allowance; **(b)** *Arch* food; **le v. et le couvert,** bed and board, board and lodging.

vivre² *v* (*prp* **vivant**; *pp* **vécu**; *pr ind* **je vis, il vit, n. vivons, ils vivent**; *pr sub* **je vive**; *impf* **je vivais**; *p hist* **je vécus**; *fu* **je vivrai**) **1** *vi* **(a)** to live, to be alive; **elle vit encore,** she's still alive; **v. longtemps,** to live a long time, to be long-lived; **cesser de v.,** to die; *Litt* **il a vécu,** he is dead; **le Front populaire a vécu,** the Popular Front has had its day *or* is finished; **ne v. que pour son travail,** to live (only) for one's work; **être las de v.,** to be tired of living *or* of life; **vive le roi!,** long live the King!; **vive l'armée,** three cheers for the army!; *Mil etc* **qui vive?,** who goes there?; **ne rencontrer âme qui vive,** to meet no one *or* not a living soul; *Prov* **qui vivra verra,** live and learn, time will show; **il vécut vieux,** he lived to be an old man; **ouvrage qui vivra,** work that will endure; **traditions qui vivent encore,** traditions that are still alive; **v. au vingt et unième siècle,** to live in the twenty-first century;

(b) (*d'une certaine façon*) to live; **v. dans une maison/un appartement,** to live in a house/flat; **v. à Paris/en province/à la campagne/à l'étranger,** to live in Paris/in the provinces/in the country/abroad *or* overseas; **elle a (beaucoup) vécu,** she's seen (a lot of) life; **v. en honnête homme,** to lead an honest life; **v. saintement,** to live a saintly life; **v. chez ses parents,** to live with one's parents; **v. avec qn,** to live with s.o.; **être facile à v.,** to be easy to live with *or* to get on with; **savoir v.,** to know how to behave, to be well-bred; **v. heureux,** to live happily; **v. dans le présent/au jour le jour,** to live in the present/one day at a time; **apprendre à v. à qn,** to teach s.o. good *or* better manners; *F* **je vais t'apprendre à v.!,** I'll teach you some manners!; **se laisser v.,** to take life easily *or* as it comes; **il fait bon v. ici,** life is pleasant here; **le plaisir de v.,** the joy of living; **prendre le temps de v.,** to take the time to enjoy life;

(c) (*économiquement*) to live; **on vivait bien juste,** we could just manage *or* just rub along; **v. bien,** to live in comfort, to live well; **travailler pour v.,** to work for one's living; **il fait cher v. ici,** life *or* living is expensive here, the cost of living is high here; **faire v. sa famille,** to support *or* keep one's family; **v. au jour le jour,** (*avec ce qu'on a*) to live from hand to mouth *or* from day to day; **v. de poisson,** to live on fish; **v. de sa plume/de ses rentes,** to live by one's pen/on one's (private) income; **v. d'amour et d'eau fraîche,** to live on fresh air; **v. d'espérances,** to live on hope; **l'espoir fait v.,** where there's life there's hope; *Iron* what a hope!, you're *or* he's *etc* optimistic!; **de quoi vit-il?,** what does he live on?; (*que fait-il dans la vie?*) what does he do for a living?; **avoir de quoi v.,** to have enough to live on; **ils n'ont que de quoi v.,** they've just enough to live on.

2 *vt* **v. sa vie,** to live one's (own) life; **les événements que nous avons vécu(s),** the events we('ve) experienced *or* lived through; **elle a vécu la guerre,** she lived *or* went through the war; **v. des moments difficiles,** to be going through *or* having *or* experiencing a difficult time; **v. une passion,** to live out a passion; **v. sa foi,** to live one's faith.

3 se vivre *vpr* **ça se vit mal quand on est seul,** it's difficult when you're on your own; **la maladie, ça se vit mal quand on est seul,** it's difficult being ill when you're on your own.

vivrier, -ière [vivrije, -jɛr] *adj* **cultures vivrières,** food crops.

vizir [vizir] *nm* vizier.

vlan, v'lan [vlɑ̃] *int* slap(-bang)!, whack!, wham!; **et v.! il est tombé,** and bang he fell over!

vlimeux [vlimø] *nm Can Arg* **(a)** (*chanceux*) lucky person; **le petit v.!,** (the) lucky devil; **(b)** (*intrigant*) crafty person, cunning person.

V.O. [veo] *nf Cin* (*abrév* **version originale**) original (language) version; **voir un film en V.O.,** to see a film in the original (language) version; **la V.O. est meilleure que la version doublée,** the original version is better than the dubbed one.

vocable [vɔkabl] *nm* **(a)** (*mot*) word, *Spéc* vocable; **(b)** *Rel* name, patronage (*of saint*); **église sous le v. de saint Pierre,** church dedicated to Saint Peter.

vocabulaire [vɔkabylɛr] *nm* **(a)** (*liste*) vocabulary, word list; **(b)** (*of person etc*) vocabulary; **enrichir son v.,** to enlarge one's vocabulary; **le v. d'un enfant de six ans,** the vocabulary of a six-year old (child); **ce mot n'est pas dans mon v.,** it's not a word that I use; *Péj* **quel v.!,** what an expression!, what a thing to say!; **(c)** (*jargon*) vocabulary; **v. administratif/juridique/technique,** administrative/legal/technical vocabulary; **employer le v. à la mode,** to use all the in words.

vocal, -aux [vɔkal, -o] *adj* vocal; **musique vocale,** vocal music.

vocalement [vɔkalmɑ̃] *adv* vocally.

vocalique [vɔkalik] *adj Ling* vocalic; **son v.,** vocalic *or* vowel sound.

vocalisation [vɔkalizasjɔ̃] *nf Ling Mus* vocalization.

vocalise [vɔkaliz] *nf Mus* exercise in vocalization; **faire des vocalises,** to do singing exercises.

vocaliser [vɔkalize] *vt* to vocalize (*melody, consonant*).

vocalisme [vɔkalism] *nm Ling Mus* vocalism.

vocatif [vɔkatif] *nm Gram* vocative (case).

vocation[vɔkasjɔ̃] *nf* **(a)** vocation, calling, bent, inclination; **manquer/suivre sa v.,** to miss/follow one's vocation; **avoir la v. du professorat,** to have a vocation for teaching, *F* to be cut out for teaching; **avoir la v. du commerce,** to have an aptitude for business; **la v. industrielle de l'Allemagne,** Germany's long industrial tradition; *F* **il faut avoir la v.,** you really need to be dedicated; **faire qch par v.,** to do sth as a labour of love; **(b)** (*religieuse*) vocation, call; **je ne me sens pas la v. de la prêtrise,** I feel no call to the Church *or* no calling for the Church.

vociférateur, -trice [vɔsiferatœr, -tris] *n Litt* vociferator.

vocifération [vɔsiferasjɔ̃] *nf* outcry, *Fml* vociferation; **vociférations,** shouts, yells; **pousser des vociférations,** to shout and bawl.

vociférer [vɔsifere] *v* (**je vocifère, n. vociférons; je vociférerai**) **1** *vi* to shout, to yell, to bawl, *Fml* to vociferate (**contre,** against). **2** *vt* **v. des injures,** to shout *or* hurl insults (**contre,** at).

vodka [vɔdka] *nf* vodka; **v. orange,** (*verre*) vodka and orange.

vœu, -x [vø] *nm* **(a)** (*souhait*) wish; **faire un v.,** to make a wish, to wish; **émettre un v.,** to express a wish *or* a desire; **former le v. que qch se réalise,** to express a *or* the wish that sth should be done; **j'ai fait le v. de ne plus y retourner,** I vowed never to go back (there again); **je fais des vœux pour qu'il ne pleuve pas dimanche,** I'm praying it won't rain on Sunday; **tous mes** *ou* **nos vœux!, avec mes** *ou* **nos meilleurs vœux,** best wishes, with all good wishes; **tous mes vœux de bonheur,** best wishes for your future happiness; **vœux de bonne** *ou* **de nouvelle année,** New Year greetings; **carte de vœux,** greetings card; **envoyer ses vœux à qn,** to send s.o. one's best wishes; *Pol* **si c'est le v. de la nation,** if it is the people's wish; **agir en conséquence du v. de la nation,** to act in accordance with the people's wishes;

(b) *Rel* (*promesse*) vow; **faire v. de pauvreté,** to take a vow of poverty; **prononcer ses vœux,** to take one's vows; **les vœux de baptême,** the baptismal vows.

vogue [vɔg] *nf* fashion, vogue; **en v.,** fashionable, in vogue; **musique/artiste en v.,** fashionable music/artist; **connaître une v., être en v.,** to be popular *or* fashionable, to be in fashion *or* in vogue; **entrer en v.,** to come into vogue *or* fashion, to come in; **mettre qch en v.,** to bring sth into vogue; **c'est la grande v.,** it's all the rage.

voguer [vɔge] *vi Litt* to sail; **les nuages voguant dans le ciel,** the clouds sailing *or* floating by, the drifting clouds; **vogue la galère!,** let's chance it!, come what may!

voici [vwasi] *prép* **(a)** here is *or* are; **v. Henri,** here's Henry; **v. mes neveux,** (*en les présentant*) these are my nephews; (*ils arrivent*) here are my nephews; **me/les v.,** here I am/they are; **nous v. arrivés!,** here we are!; **nous v. à Paris,** here we are in Paris; **nous v. riches,** we're rich!; **du pain? en v.,** bread? here's some *or* here you are; **la v. qui vient,** here she comes, that's her coming now; **v. qu'il se met à pleuvoir,** and now it's started raining; **v. venir Jeanne,** here comes Jeanne; **mon ami que v. vous le dira,** my friend here will tell you; **Monsieur que v.,** this gentleman; **la petite histoire que v.,** the following little story; **la bague que v.,** this ring; **v. ce dont il s'agit,** this is *or* here's what it's all about; **v. ce qu'il m'a dit,** this is *or* here's what he told me; **v. ce que tu dois faire,** this is *or* here's what you have to do; **je le ferai et v. comment,** I'll do it and here's how, *Fml* I shall do it in the following manner; **v. pourquoi,** this is why; **et v. pour toi,** and this is for you; **v. l'automne,** autumn is coming; **v. Noël!,** Christmas is here!;

(b) (*il y a*) **je l'ai vu v. trois ans,** I saw him three years ago; **v. trois mois que j'habite ici,** I have been living here for (the last) three months.

voie [vwa] *nf* **(a)** way, road, route, track; *Admin Aut* traffic lane; **v. publique,** public thoroughfare, public highway; **v. privée,** private road; **v. sans issue,** dead end, cul-de-sac; **v. express** *ou* **rapide,** expressway; **route à quatre voies,** four-lane road *or Am* highway; **v. romaine,** Roman road; *Astron* **la V. lactée,** the Milky Way; *Fig* **être par voies et par chemins,** to be always on the move; **v. de communication,** road, thoroughfare; (*avion, bateau, train*) means of transport; **grande v. de communication,** main artery, arterial road; **v. fluviale, v. navigable,** waterway; **la V. maritime du Saint-Laurent,** the St Lawrence Seaway; **par v. de terre,** by land, overland; **par v. de mer,** by sea; **par la v. des airs,** by air; *Min* **v. d'aérage,** airway;

(b) (*à la chasse*) **voies,** tracks (*of game*); slot (*of deer etc*); **mettre les chiens sur la v.,** to put the dogs on the scent; *Fig* **mettre qn sur la v.,** to put s.o. on the right track; **être sur la bonne v.,** to be on the right track;

(c) *Rail* **v. ferrée,** railway, *US* railroad (track, line); **v. de service** *ou* **de garage,** siding; *Fig* **mettre un projet sur une v. de garage,** to shelve a plan; **on l'a mis sur une v. de garage,** he's been side-lined; **v. impaire, v. descendante,** down line; **v. paire, v. montante,** up line; **ligne à une v./à deux voies,** single-/double-track line; **v. étroite,** narrow-gauge line; **sur quelle v. arrive le train?,** what platform does the train come in at?;

(d) *Ordinat* **v. d'entrée,** input channel; **v. de transmission de données,** data link;

(e) (*moyen*) way; **voies et moyens,** ways and means; **préparer la v.,** to prepare *or* pave the way; **il finira par trouver sa v.,** he'll find his way in the end; **la v. des armes,** recourse to arms; **par la v. diplomatique,** through diplomatic channels; **la v. la plus simple/rapide,** the easiest/quickest way; **une v. dangereuse,** a dangerous course; **les voies de Dieu,** the ways of God; **la v. étroite,** the straight and narrow; **affaire en bonne v.,** business that is going well; **en v. d'achèvement,** nearing completion; **en v. de construction,** under construction; **en v. de formation,** in the process of formation; **pays en v. de développement,** developing country *or* countries; **en v. de réparation,** under *or* undergoing repair; **il est en v. de guérir** *ou* **de guérison,** he's on the mend, he's recovering; **être en bonne v. de guérir,** to be well on the road *or* way to recovery; **être en v. de faire qch,** to be (well) on the way to doing sth; **être en (bonne) v. de réussir,** to be (well) on the way *or* road to success; *Jur* **voies de droit,** recourse to legal proceedings; *Jur* **voies de fait,** assault and battery; **en venir aux voies de fait,** to come to blows, to exchange blows; *Ch etc* **v. sèche/humide,** dry/wet process; **essai par la v. sèche,** dry test;

(f) gauge (*of wheels of vehicle*); kerf, clearance (*of a tool*); set (*of a saw*); **donner de la v. à une scie,** to set a saw;

(g) *Nau* **v. d'eau,** leak; **faire une v. d'eau,** to spring a leak;

(h) *Anat* passage, duct; **les voies digestives,** the digestive tract(s); **par v. buccale,** orally.

voilà [vwala] *prép* **(a)** there is *or* are; **v. Henri,** (*qu'on cherche*) there's Henri; (*qui arrive*) there's Henri (now), that's Henri (now); (*dont je te parlais*) that's Henri; **v. Paul et Henri,** (*en les présentant*) this is Paul and this is Henri; (*sur une photo*) this is Paul and this *or* that is Henri; **la/les v.,** there she is/they are; **la pendule que v.,** that clock (there); **la petite histoire que v.,** the following little story; **v. où il demeure,** that's where he lives; **en v. assez!,** that's enough!, that will do!; **en v. une idée!,** what an idea!, there's an idea!; **en v. de la reconnaissance!,** there's gratitude for you!; **en v. un qui fera son chemin!,** there's a man who will get on!; **v. tout,** that's all; **le v. qui entre, v. qu'il entre,** there he is coming in; **v. (ce) qui s'appelle danser!/un homme!/***etc*, that's what I call dancing!/a man!/*etc*; **v. qui est curieux!,** that's curious!; **v. ce qu'il m'a dit,** that's what he told me; **v. comme elle est, la v. bien!,** that's just like her!; **v. qu'il se remarie,** and now he's getting married again; **v.!,** there you are!; **et v.!,** and that's that!; **v., monsieur!,** (*in restaurant*) coming, sir!;

(b) (*voici*) **me v.!,** here I am!; **le v.!,** here he is!, here he comes!;

(c) (*il y a*) **en juin v. trois ans,** three years ago in June; **v. dix ans que je le connais,** I've known him (for) ten years.

voilage [vwalaʒ] *nm* **(a)** net (*on hat etc*); **(b) voilages,** net curtains.

voile [vwal] **1** *nf* sail; **v. carrée,** square sail; **déployer** *ou* **établir une v.,** to set a sail; **bateau à voiles,** sailing boat; **aller à la v.,** to sail; **vaisseau sous voile(s),** ship under sail; **faire v., mettre à la v.,** to get under sail, to set sail (**pour,** for); **faire force de voiles,** to crowd on *or* cram on all sail; **toutes voiles dehors,** in full sail, all sail(s) set, with every stitch of canvas spread; **faire de la v.,** to sail; *F* **mettre les voiles,** (*partir*) to scram, to do a bunk; **marcher à v. et à vapeur,** (*être bisexuel*) to be AC/DC.

2 *nm* **(a)** veil; **les femmes qui portent le v.,** women who wear the veil; *Rel* **prendre le v.,** to take the veil; **sous le v. de la religion,** under the cloak *or* mask of religion;

(b) film, mist (*before one's eyes*); *Méd F* **v. noir,** black-out; *Méd* **avoir un v. au poumon,** to have a shadow on one's lung; **v. de larmes,** blur of tears;

(c) *Tex* voile;

(d) *Anat* **v. du palais,** soft palate, velum;

(e) *Phot* fog (*on negative*).

voilé [vwale] *adj* **(a)** veiled, dim (*light*); veiled, obscure (*meaning*); muffled (*drum*); husky (*voice*); *Phot* fogged (*print*); **femme voilée,** woman wearing the veil; **des yeux voilés de larmes,** eyes dimmed *or* blurred with tears; **allusion peu voilée,** broad hint; **en termes peu voilés,** in thinly veiled terms; **(b)** (*wheel, rod etc*) buckled, out of true.

voiler [vwale] **1** *vt* **(a)** to veil; to veil, to obscure, to dim, to cloud (*light etc*); to muffle (*sound, drum etc*); to shade (*light*); *Phot* to fog (*plate, print*); **v. une statue/sa nudité,** to cover a statue/one's nakedness; **v. ses sentiments/la vérité,** to conceal one's feelings/the truth; **(b)** to buckle (*wheel etc*); **(c)** *Nau* to rig (*ship*) with sails. **2 se voiler** *vpr* **(a) se v. (le visage),** to wear a veil; **les femmes doivent se v.,** women must wear the veil; *Fig* **se v. la face,** to hide *or* bury one's head in the sand; **sa voix se voile (d'émotion),** his voice is husky (with emotion); **(b)** (*of sky etc*) to become overcast, to cloud over; (*of eyes*) to mist over; **(c)** (*of wheel etc*) to buckle.

voilerie [vwalri] *nf Nau* sail loft.

voilette [vwalɛt] *nf* (hat) veil.

voilier [vwalje] *nm* **(a)** *Nau* (*de plaisance*) yacht; **faire du v.,** to go yachting; **un v. de 15 mètres,** a 15 metre yacht; **(b) navire bon/mauvais v.,** good/bad sailer; **(c)** (*fabricant*) sailmaker; **(d)** (*oiseau*) **grand v.,** long-flight bird.

voilure[1] [vwalyr] *nf* **(a)** sails (*of ship*); **réduire la v.,** to shorten *or* reduce sail; **(b)** *Av* wing(s), flying surface, aerofoil, *US* airfoil; **appareil à v. fixe/tournant,** fixed/rotary wing aircraft.

voilure[2] *nf* buckling (*of metal, wheel*).

voir [vwar] *v* (*prp* **voyant**; *pp* **vu**; *pr ind* **je vois, il voit, n. voyons, ils voient**; *pr sub* **je voie**; *impf* **je voyais**; *p hist* **je vis**; *fu* **je verrai**) **1** *vt* **(a)** to see (*s.o., sth*); *Nau* to sight (*ship*); **il n'y a rien à v.,** there's nothing to see *or* to be seen; **as-tu vu 'Highlander'?,** have you seen 'Highlander'?; **hôtel vu de face,** front view of the hotel; **(détail) vu de près,** close-up (detail); *F* **on aura tout vu!,** now we've seen everything!, wonders will never cease!; **il faut le v. pour le croire,** it has to be seen to be believed; **je l'ai vu de mes (propres) yeux,** I saw it with my own eyes; **c'est à v.,** it's worth seeing; **je le vois qui arrive,** I can see him coming; **à le v. on dirait ...,** by the look of him *or* to judge by his looks one would say ...; **on voit son jupon,** her (under)slip is showing; **mon fils, voyez-vous, est mort,** my son is dead, you see; *Litt* **que vois-je?,** what is this (that I see)?; **faire v. qch à qn,** to show sth to s.o.; **laisser v. qch à qn,** to let s.o. see sth; **laisser v. son ignorance,** to show *or* reveal *or* betray one's ignorance;

(b) (+ *inf*) **v. venir qn,** to see s.o. coming; **je l'ai vu tomber,** I saw him fall; **quels acteurs avez-vous vus jouer ce rôle?,** what actors have you seen in this part?; **quelles pièces avez-vous vu jouer?,** what plays have you seen (acted)?; **v. faire qch,** to see sth done; **v. faire qch à qn,** to see s.o. do sth;

(c) (*rendre visite à*) to visit (*s.o., sth*); **aller v. qn,** to go to see s.o., to go and see s.o.; **venez me v. quand vous serez à Paris,** come and see me when you're in Paris; **nous avons vu les musées,** we visited the museums; **je n'ai jamais vu Venise,** I've never seen Venice; **v. du pays,** to travel;

(d) (*avoir la visite de*) to see; **il ne voit personne,** he sees no one; **nous le voyons beaucoup,** we see a lot of him; **v. qn,** to receive a visit from s.o.; **on ne vous voit plus!,** you're quite a stranger!; **nous ne les voyons plus,** we don't see them any more; **je ne peux pas le v. (en peinture),** I can't stand (the sight of) him;

(e) (*comprendre*) to see, to understand; **je vois où vous voulez en venir,** I see *or* understand what you're driving at; **ah oui, je vois,** oh yes I see; **on voit bien qu'il est incompétent/jeune/innocent,** you can see *or* it's obvious that he's incompetent/young/innocent; **je vois que vous m'avez attendu,** I see you've waited for me; *F* **ni vu, ni connu,** without anyone being any the wiser for it; *F* **vu?,** understood?, all right?, O.K.?; **c'est tout vu!,** that's all there is to it; **comment voyez-vous l'avenir?,** how do you see *or* view the future?;

(f) (*observer*) to see, to notice, to observe (*sth*); **je vois que vous avez compris,** I see you have understood; **à ce que je vois,** from what I can see; **vous voyez ça d'ici,** you can guess what it was *or* is *or* would be like; **je vois ça d'ici,** I can see it coming;

(g) (*examiner, étudier*) to look after, to see to, to see about (*sth*); **v. une affaire à fond,** to look into *or* examine a matter thoroughly; **c'est ce que nous verrons!,** we shall see!, that remains to be seen!; *F* **va-t'en v. si j'y suis!,** get lost!, clear out!, scram!, **il n'a rien à v. là-dedans** *ou* **à y voir,** it's nothing to do with him, it's no business *or* concern of his, it's none of his business; **cela n'a rien à v. avec l'affaire,** that's beside the point, that has nothing to do with it; **ceci est à v., c'est à v.,** it remains to be seen; **juste pour v. si ça marche,** just to see if it works;

(h) **(v. à** + *inf*) **il va v. à nous loger,** he will see that we have somewhere to stay, he'll take care of our accommodation;

(i) **(v. que** + *sub*) **c'est à vous de v. que rien ne nous manque,** it's up to you to see that we have everything we need;

(j) (*considérer*) to see, to look at, to consider, to regard (*sth in a particular way*); **je ne le vois pas marié,** I can't see *or* imagine him married; **elle a tendance à v. tout en noir,** she tends to look on the gloomy side of things; **v. la vie en rose,** to see life through rose-coloured spectacles; **sa façon de v. les choses,** his way of looking at things, his outlook; **elle voit en lui un père,** she looks on him as a father; **v. les choses telles qu'elles sont,** to see things as they are; **je ne vois pas cela comme ça,** I don't see *or* look at it like that; **elle y voit un seul inconvénient,** she can see only one drawback; **si tu n'y vois pas d'inconvénient,** if that's alright *or* OK with you; **c'est un café où il faut se faire v.,** it's THE café to go to *or* be seen in; **se faire bien v. de qn,** to gain s.o.'s favour, to get into s.o.'s good books; **se faire mal v. de qn,** to get into s.o.'s bad books; **être bien vu de tous,** to be highly esteemed *or* well thought of by everyone; **elle est mal vue de tous,** everyone has a low opinion of her; **il est mal vu de manger avec la main gauche,** eating with the left hand is frowned (up)on.

2 *vi* to see; **elle ne voit plus,** she can't see any more; **v. double,** to see double; **v. mal,** to have poor eyesight; **v. loin,** to be farsighted; **il ne voit pas plus loin que le bout de son nez,** he can't see further than the end of his nose; *Fig* **v. grand,** to think big; **v. c'est croire,** seeing is believing; **je n'y vois plus,** I can't see any more; **on n'y voit rien,** (*il fait noir*) you can't see a thing; **v. rouge,** to see red; **il faut y aller v.,** we must go and see; **regarder sans v.,** to look without seeing, to look and not see; **voyez vous-même!,** see for yourself!; **voyez un peu!,** just look at him; **faites v.!,** let me see it!, let's have a look!; **en faire v. (de toutes les couleurs) à qn,** to make s.o.'s life a misery; (*le faire tourner en bourrique*) to lead s.o. a merry dance; *Arg* **voyons v.,** let's see, let me see, let's have a look, show it to me; **montrez v.,** just let me see it; **dites v. ...,** tell me ...; **essayez v.,** just have a try; (*menace*) just you try it; **regardez v.,** just have a look; **faire qch seulement pour v.,** to do sth to see what happens *or* just as an experiment; **eh bien, je verrai,** well, I'll see *or* think about it; **tu peux toujours essayer pour v.,** you can always try just to see; **voyons!,** let's see; (*allons!*) come (on) now!, come, come!

3 se voir *vpr* to be seen; **cela se voit tous les jours,** you see things like that all the time, that kind of thing happens every day; **ça se voit,** that's obvious; *F* **cela se voit comme le nez au milieu de la figure,** it's as plain as the nose on your face; **monument qui se voit de loin,** monument that can be seen from far away *or* a distance; **il se voyait déjà perdu,** he already imagined himself lost.

voire [vwar] *adv* indeed; **v. (même),** and even; (*alternativement*) or even; **j'en suis ahuri, v. révolté,** I'm astounded, indeed disgusted.

voirie [vwari] *nf* **(a)** *Admin* = administration of public thoroughfares; **service de v.,** roads department; **travaux de v.,** road works; **employé de la v.,** street sweeper; **(b)** (*routes etc*) road system; **la grande v.,** the main roads; **(c)** refuse dump, *surtout Am* garbage heap; **jeter les ordures à la v.,** to dump the rubbish.

voisin, -ine [vwazɛ̃, -in] **1** *adj* neighbouring, *US* neighboring; (*mitoyen*) adjoining; bordering (**de,** on); **la chambre voisine,** the next room; **deux maisons voisines,** two houses next to each other, two adjoining houses; **il habite dans la maison voisine,** he lives (in the house) next door; **pays voisins,** neighbouring countries; *Biol* **espèces voisines,** closely allied *or* related species; **être v. de qn/qch,** to be next to s.o./sth; *Fig* **émotion voisine de la terreur,** emotion akin to terror *or* bordering on terror; **v. de la mort,** at death's door. **2** *n* neighbour, *US* neighbor; **v. d'à côté** *ou* **de porte** *ou* **de palier,** next-door neighbour; **mon v. de table,** the person I was sitting next to (at table), my neighbour at table; **agir en bon v.,** to act in a neighbourly *or US* neighborly way.

voisinage [vwazinaʒ] *nm* **(a)** (*proximité*) vicinity, proximity, nearness; **les maisons dans le v. des montagnes,** the houses in the vicinity of *or* near the mountains; **le v. de la gare est un avantage,** proximity *or* being close to the station is an advantage; **(b)** (*entourage*) vicinity, neighbourhood, *US* neighborhood; **il n'y avait personne dans le v.,** there was nobody in the vicinity, there was nobody about; **relations de bon v.,** (good) neighbourliness, *US* neighborliness; **être en bon v. avec qn, entretenir des relations de bon v. avec qn,** to be on good terms with s.o..

voisiner [vwazine] *vi* **(a)** *Litt* to visit one's neighbours *or US* neighbors; **à Paris on voisine peu,** in Paris you don't see much of your neighbours; **(b) v. avec qn,** to be (placed) side by side with s.o.; **v. avec qch,** to be (placed) side by side with sth; (*être mitoyen de)* to adjoin sth.

voiturage [vwatyraʒ] *nm* carriage, conveyance, cartage (*of goods etc*).

voiture [vwatyr] *nf* **(a)** car, *Am aussi* automobile; **v. de tourisme,** private car; **v. de sport,** sports car; **location de voitures,** car hire *or* rental; **prendre sa v.,** to take the car; **aller à Paris en v.,** to go to Paris by car; **(b)** *Rail* coach, carriage, *Am* car; **en v.!,** take your seats!; *surtout Am* all aboard!; **(c) v. d'enfant** *ou* **de bébé,** pram, perambulator, *Am* baby carriage; **v. à bras,** barrow, handcart; **v. d'infirme, petite v.,** invalid carriage; *Vieilli* **v. de malade,** Bath chair; **(d)** *Arch* conveyance, transport; **(e)** *Com* **lettre de v.,** waybill, consignment note; **(f)** (horse-drawn) vehicle; (*for people*) carriage, coach; (*for goods*) cart; **v. à deux chevaux,** carriage and pair; **v. de place,** hackney (carriage, cab).

voiture-bar [vwatyrbar] *nf Rail* buffet car, refreshment car; (*pl voitures-bars*).

voiturée [vwatyre] *nf Vieilli* carriageful (*of people*); cartload (*of goods etc*).

voiture-lit [vwatyrli] *nf Rail* sleeping car, *F* sleeper; (*pl voitures-lits*).

voiturer [vwatyre] *vt Vieilli* to convey, to transport, to carry, to cart (*goods etc*); *F* **je vais te v.,** I'll drive you (in, there).

voiture-restaurant [vwatyrrɛstɔrɑ̃] *nf Rail* restaurant car, dining car; (*pl voitures-restaurants*).

voiturette [vwatyrɛt] *nf* trap; *Aut* small car.

voiturier [vwatyrje] *nm Arch & Jur* carrier, carter.

voix [vwa] *nf* **(a)** voice; **parler à v. haute** *ou* **à haute v.,** to speak in a loud voice; (*clairement*) to speak out loud *or* aloud; **parler à v. basse,** to speak in a low voice *or* under one's breath *or* in a whisper *or* in an undertone; **faire la grosse v.,** to speak sternly *or* in a severe tone; **élever la v.,** to speak up; (*se mettre en colère*) to raise one's voice; **à portée de (la) v.,** within earshot; **hors de portée de (la) v.,** out of hearing, out of earshot; **donner de la v.,** (*of dogs*) to bark; (*of bloodhound*) to give tongue, to bay; *Mus* **v. de basse/de ténor,** bass/tenor voice; **v. de poitrine,** chest voice; **v. de tête,** head voice; **v. de fausset,** falsetto (voice); **avoir une belle v.,** (*en chantant*) to have a fine voice; (*en parlant*) to have a pleasant voice; **v. claire/gaie/enjouée,** clear/cheerful/lively voice; **avoir une v. grave/chaude,** to have a deep/warm voice; **chanter à plusieurs v.,** to sing in parts; **je ne suis pas en v.,** I'm not in voice; **v. humaine,** vox humana (*stop of organ*);

(b) *Fig* **rester sans v.,** to remain speechless; **de vive v.,** by word of mouth, viva voce; **la v. de la conscience,** the voice *or* the dictates of conscience; **la v. de la nature,** the call of nature; **'arrêtez', dit une v.,** 'stop', said a voice; *Cin* **v. off,** voice over; **la v. du peuple,** the voice of the people, public opinion, vox populi; **d'une commune v.,** by common consent, with one voice; **donner sa v. à qn,** to vote for s.o.; **gagner/perdre des v.,** to win/lose votes; **mettre une question aux v.,** to put a question to the vote; **la Chambre alla aux v.,** the House divided; **avoir v. consultative/délibératrice,** to have a consultative role/voting rights; **avoir v. au chapitre,** to have a say in the matter;

(c) *Gram* **à la v. active/passive,** in the active voice/in the passive (voice).

vol¹ [vɔl] *nm* **(a)** flying, flight; **prendre son v.,** (*d'un oiseau*) to take wing, to take off; *Fig* (*prendre son essor*) to take off; **tirer un oiseau au v.,** to shoot a bird on the wing; **saisir l'occasion au v.,** to grasp *or* leap at the opportunity; **à v. d'oiseau,** as the crow flies; **à v. d'oiseau, il y a cinq kilomètres,** it's five kilometres as the crow flies; **vue à v. d'oiseau,** bird's-eye view; **oiseau de haut v.,** high-flying bird; **de haut v.,** (*personne*) high-class, top-flight; (*par ses aptitudes, ambitions*) high-flying; **être de haut v.,** to be a high-flier;

(b) *Av* flight; **heures de v.,** flying time; **à trois heures de v. de Paris,** three hours flying time from Paris; **numéro de v.,** flight number; **v. 944 pour Glasgow,** flight 944 to Glasgow; **tous les vols sont annulés,** all flights are cancelled; **avion en v.,** aircraft in flight; **v. de nuit,** night flying; **v. à voile,** gliding; **v. libre,** hang-gliding;

(c) flock, flight (*of birds flying together*); covey (*of game birds*); swarm (*of locusts*);

(d) *Arch* **(chasse au) v.,** hawking.

vol² *nm* theft, stealing, robbery; **commettre un v.,** to commit a theft *or* robbery; *Jur* **v. qualifié,** aggravated theft, robbery; **v. avec effraction,** breaking and entering, housebreaking; **v. à la tire,** pickpocketing, pocket picking; **être victime d'un v. à la tire,** to have one's pocket picked; **v. à l'étalage,** shoplifting; **v. à l'américaine,** confidence trick; **v. de grand chemin,** highway robbery; **v. à main armée,** armed robbery; *F* **c'est du v.!,** it's a rip-off!, it's daylight robbery!; **commettre plusieurs vols,** to commit several thefts.

volage [vɔlaʒ] *adj* fickle, inconstant, flighty.

volaille [vɔlaj] *nf* **(a)** poultry; **une v.,** a fowl; **marchand de v.,** poulterer; **(b)** *Culin* poultry, *surtout* chicken; **foies de v.,** chicken livers.

volailler [vɔlaje] *nm* poulterer.

volant [vɔlɑ̃] **1** *adj* **(a)** flying; fluttering (*ribbons etc*); **objet v. non identifié,** unidentified flying object, UFO; *F* **soucoupe volante,** flying saucer; **poisson v.,** flying fish; *Av* **personnel v.,** flight crew; *Mil* air crew; *Nau* **escadre volante,** flying squadron;

(b) loose (*cable etc*); movable (*partition etc*); **feuille volante,** loose leaf (*of paper*); **table volante,** occasional table; *Nau* **cabestan v.,** portable winch; **pont v.,** spar deck; *Constr* flying bridge.

2 *nm* **(a)** *Aut* (steering) wheel; **prendre le v.,** to take the wheel; **un violent coup de v.,** a violent swerve *or* turn of the wheel;

(b) (*de badminton*) shuttlecock; **jeu de v.,** (game of) battledore and shuttlecock;

(c) *Couture* flounce; (*panneau*) shaped panel; **volants froncés,** gathered flounces; **jupe à volants,** flounced skirt;

(d) flywheel (*of engine*); (*d'horloge*) fly;

(e) handwheel (*of engine etc*);

(f) (*in book of tickets*) **talon et v.,** counterfoil and leaf.

volatil [vɔlatil] *adj* volatile.

volatile [vɔlatil] *nm Hum* winged creature, bird.

volatilisable [vɔlatilizabl] *adj* volatilizable.

volatilisation [vɔlatilizɑsjɔ̃] *nf* volatilization.

volatiliser [vɔlatilize] **1** *vt* **(a)** *Ch* to volatilize; **(b)** to make (*sth*) disappear. **2 se volatiliser** *vpr* to fade away, to vanish (into thin air); *Hum* **quand on a besoin de lui, il se volatilise,** he vanishes into thin air *or* he's never there when you need him.

volatilité [vɔlatilite] *nf* volatility.

vol-au-vent [vɔlovɑ̃] *nm inv Culin* vol-au-vent.

volcan [vɔlkɑ̃] *nm* **(a)** volcano; **v. actif/dormant/éteint,** active/dormant/extinct volcano; **v. en activité,** active volcano; **(b)** *Fig* fiery *or* impetuous person; (*situation*) volcano; **danser sur un v.,** to be sitting on a powder keg *or* a time bomb; **son imagination est un v.,** he has a vivid imagination.

volcanique [vɔlkanik] *adj* volcanic (*rock etc*); *Fig* fiery, ardent (*passion*); *Fig* vivid (*imagination*).

volcanologie [vɔlkanɔlɔʒi] *nf* vulcanology.

volcanologue [vɔlkanɔlɔg] *n* vulcanologist.

vole [vɔl] *nf Cartes* vole, all the tricks.

volée [vɔle] *nf* **(a)** flight (*of bird, projectile etc*); *Tennis* volley; **prendre sa v.,** to take wing; *Fig* to take off; **tirer à toute v.,** to fire (*a gun*) at maximum elevation; **lancer qch à toute v.,** to hurl sth, to send sth flying; **coup de v.,** *Rugby* punt; *Fb* volley; *Tennis* **relancer une balle à la v.,** to volley a return; *Tennis* **v. amortie,** drop volley; **attraper une balle à la v.,** to catch a ball in mid air; *Fig* **saisir une allusion à la v.,** to catch an allusion promptly *or* instantly; *Agr* **semer à la v.,** to broadcast;

(b) flock, flight (*of crows etc*); covey (*of partridges*); band, bevy (*of girls etc*);

(c) rank, high standing; **de haute v.,** (*personne*) high-class, top-flight; (*par ses aptitudes*) high-flying;

(d) volley (*of missiles*); shower (*of blows*); **recevoir une bonne v.,** to get a sound thrashing; **sonner à toute v.,** to set all the bells ringing; (*of bells*) to ring a full peal, to be in full peal;

(e) v. d'escalier, flight of stairs;

(f) *Tech* jib (*of crane*); chase (*of gun*).

voler¹ [vɔle] *vi* **(a)** to fly; *Fig* **v. de ses propres ailes,** to stand on one's own two feet, to fend for oneself; **on aurait entendu v. une mouche,** you could have heard a pin drop; **nous volons à une vitesse de ...,** we are flying at a speed of ...; **v. en éclats,** to fly into pieces; **faire v. un cerf-volant,** to fly a kite; *Fig* **elle lui a volé dans les plumes,** she went for him, she flew at him; **(b)** *Litt* to travel fast, to move with speed; **le temps vole,** time flies; **il vola revoir ses amis,** he flew back *or* rushed back *or* sped back to his friends; **faire v. une nouvelle,** to spread a piece of news.

voler² *vt* **(a)** to steal; **v. qch à qn,** to steal sth from s.o., to rob s.o. of sth; **elle lui a volé cette idée,** she stole the idea from him; **je me suis fait v. mon pardessus,** I've had my overcoat stolen; *Prov* **qui vole un œuf vole un bœuf,** it's the thin end of the wedge; *F* **il ne l'a pas volé,** it serves him right; **(b)** (*dépouiller*) to rob (*s.o.*); (*rouler*) to swindle, to cheat (*s.o.*); **on s'est fait v.,** (*dans ce restaurant*) we were ripped off, we were really stung.

volet [vɔlɛ] *nm* **(a)** (inside) shutter (*of window*); (= **contrevent**) (outside) shutter; (*de magasin*) (shop) shutter; **ouvrir/fermer les volets,** to open/close the shutters; **mettre/enlever les volets,** to put up/take down the shutters; **volets d'un triptyque,** volets of a triptych; **(b)** throttle valve, butterfly valve (*of carburettor*); *El* **indicateur à volets,** drop indicator (*of annunciator board etc*); *Tél* **v. d'appel,** call indicator, disc, drop; **carte à v.,** stub card; **(c) trié sur le v.,** hand-picked; **(d)** *Av* flap; **v. de courbure,** camber changing flap; **v.-d'intrados,** split flap; **sortir/rentrer les volets,** to lower/raise flaps; **(e)** flatboard, paddle (*of waterwheel*); **(f)** *Arch* sorting board (*for seeds etc*).

voleter [vɔlte] *vi* (**il volette; il volettera**) (*of bird*) to flutter; **v. d'arbre en arbre,** to flit from tree to tree.

voleur, -euse [vɔlœr, -øz] **1** *n* thief, *pl* thieves; (*cambrioleur*) robber, burglar; **v. à la tire,** pickpocket; **v. à l'étalage,** shoplifter; **v. d'enfants,** kidnapper; **au v.!,** stop thief!; **ce commerçant est un v.,** this shopkeeper is a swindler *or* a shark; *Hist* **v. de grand chemin,** highwayman, footpad; **v. d'idées,** stealer of ideas; **v. de moutons,** sheep stealer. **2** *adj* thieving, thievish; *Fml* rapacious (*tradesman etc*); pilfering (*child*); **elle est voleuse comme une pie,** she has sticky fingers.

volière [vɔljɛr] *nf* aviary.

volige [vɔliʒ] *nf Constr* scantling, batten; (*pour tuiles*) slate lath; **caisse en voliges,** crate.

voligeage [vɔliʒaʒ] *nm Constr* battening; (*pour tuiles*) lathing.

voliger [vɔliʒe] *vt* (**je voligeai(s); n. voligeons**) *Constr* to batten; (*pour tuiles*) to lath.
volis [vɔli] *nm* broken tree top.
volitif, -ive [vɔlitif, -iv] *adj* volitional.
volition [vɔlisjɔ̃] *nf* volition.
volley-ball [vɔlɛbol] *nm Sp* volleyball; **jouer au v.-b.,** to play volleyball.
volleyeur, -euse [vɔlɛjœr, -øz] *n Sp* **(a)** volleyball player; **(b)** *Tennis* volleyer.
volontaire [vɔlɔ̃tɛr] **1** *adj* **(a)** voluntary; **homicide v.,** wilful murder, voluntary homicide; **acte v.,** wilful act; *Mil* **engagé v.,** volunteer; **(b)** *(person)* self-willed, wilful, headstrong, obstinate; **menton v.,** firm *or* determined chin. **2** *n* volunteer.
volontairement [vɔlɔ̃tɛrmɑ̃] *adv* **(a)** voluntarily, willingly; **(b)** (*délibérément*) deliberately, intentionally.
volontariat [vɔlɔ̃tarja] *nm Mil etc* voluntary service.
volonté [vɔlɔ̃te] *nf* **(a)** will; **la v. de vaincre/de puissance,** the will to win/for power; **v. de fer,** will of iron, iron will; **avoir une v. de fer,** to be iron-willed, to have a will of iron *or* an iron will; **cause indépendante de la v. de qn,** cause beyond s.o.'s control; **par un effort de la v.,** by an effort of will; **manque de v.,** lack of will(power); **ne pas avoir de v.,** to have no will of one's own; **avec la meilleure v. du monde,** with the best will in the world; **arriver à qch à coups** *ou* **à force de v.,** to achieve sth by sheer willpower; **bonne v.,** willingness; **mauvaise v.,** unwillingness; **montrer de la bonne/de la mauvaise v.,** to do sth willingly/unwillingly, to do sth with good/bad grace; **elle montre toujours de la bonne v.,** she always shows willing; **faire qch de bonne v.,** to do sth willingly *or* with good grace; **elle y met de la mauvaise v.,** she's doing it with very bad grace; **homme de bonne v.,** volunteer (*for dangerous enterprise etc*); **en faire à sa v.,** to have one's own way; **à v.,** at will; **vin à v.,** (*in restaurant*) (drink) as much wine as you like; *Culin* **ajouter du sucre à v.,** add sugar to taste; **billet payable à v.,** promissory note payable on demand; *Mil* **feu à v.,** fire at will; **de sa propre v.,** of one's own accord, spontaneously;
(b) (*souhait*) wish; **les dernières volontés (de qn),** (s.o.'s) last will and testament; **ses dernières volontés,** his last wishes; **dire sa v. de réussir/progresser,** to express a wish to succeed/advance; **il fait ses quatre volontés,** he does just what he pleases; **elle lui fait faire ses quatre volontés,** she can twist him round her little finger.
volontiers [vɔlɔ̃tje] *adv* **(a)** willingly, gladly, with pleasure; **très v.,** I'd be glad to, I'd love to; **je prendrais v. un verre de vin,** I could do with *or* I'd love a glass of wine; **il cause v.,** he is fond of talking; **vous venez? — (oui,) v.,** are you coming?–yes, I'd love to; **je le ferai le plus v. du monde,** I'll be absolutely delighted *or* it'll give me the greatest pleasure to do so; **(b)** (*facilement*) readily; **on croit v. que ...,** we are apt to think that ...; **elle serait v. solitaire,** she's a loner by nature.
volt [vɔlt] *nm El* volt.
voltage [vɔltaʒ] *nm El* voltage.
voltaïque [vɔltaik] *adj El* voltaic (*cell, pile*).
voltairien, -ienne [vɔltɛrjɛ̃, -jɛn] *adj & n* Voltairian.
voltampère [vɔltɑ̃pɛr] *nm El* voltampere.
volte [vɔlt] *nf* **(a)** *Équitation Escrime* volt; **(b)** *Nau* turn (*to alter course*).
volte-face [vɔltəfas] *nf inv* **(a)** about-turn, *Am* about-face; **faire v.-f.,** to turn round; **(b)** *Fig* about-turn, U-turn, *Litt* volte-face, *Am* about-face; **faire v.-f.,** to do a U-turn *or* an about-turn *or Am* about-face.
volter [vɔlte] *vi Équitation* **faire v. un cheval,** to make a horse circle.
voltige [vɔltiʒ] *nf* **(a)** *Équitation* mounted gymnastics; **haute v.,** trick riding; **(b)** (*au cirque*) acrobatics; (*sur trapèze*) flying-trapeze exercises; *Av* aerobatics; *Av* **pilote de v.,** stunt pilot; *Fig* **c'est de la haute v. intellectuelle,** it's intellectual acrobatics *or* gymnastics.
voltiger [vɔltiʒe] *vi* (**je voltigeai(s); n. voltigeons**) **(a)** to do acrobatics; (*sur trapèze*) to perform on the flying trapeze; (*sur cheval*) to perform on horseback; **(b)** (*of bird, insect*) to fly about, to flutter (about); (*of curtain, flag etc*) to flutter, to flap.
voltigeur, -euse [vɔltiʒœr, -øz] **1** *n (au cirque)* acrobat; (*sur trapèze*) trapeze artist; (*sur cheval*) performer on horseback. **2** *nm Mil Arch* light infantryman, rifleman.
voltmètre [vɔltmɛtr] *nm El* voltmeter.
volubile [vɔlybil] *adj* **(a)** *Bot* voluble; twining (*stalk*); **(b)** (*person*) voluble.
volubilis [vɔlybilis] *nm Bot* convolvulus; **v. des jardins,** morning glory.
volubilité [vɔlybilite] *nf* volubility; **parler avec v.,** to be a voluble talker, to talk volubly.
volucompteur [vɔlykɔ̃tœr] *nm* volume indicator.
volume [vɔlym] *nm* **(a)** (*livre*) volume; **il faudrait des volumes pour raconter ...,** it would take volumes to relate ...; **(b)** volume, bulk, mass (*of solid, fluid*); **v. excessif,** bulkiness (*of parcel etc*); *Nau* **chargé en v.,** laden in bulk; **faire du v.,** (*of thing*) to take up a lot of space; *F* (*of person*) to show off, to throw one's weight about; **(c)** volume (*of sound, voice*); **(d)** capacity (*of bunkers etc*).
volumétrique [vɔlymetrik] *adj* volumetric.
volumineux, -euse [vɔlyminø, -øz] *adj* voluminous, bulky, large; **dossier v.,** bulky file.
volupté [vɔlypte] *nf* (sensual) pleasure, delight; **toutes les voluptés,** every pleasurable sensation; **la v. de la revanche accomplie,** the sweet taste of revenge.
voluptueusement [vɔlyptɥøzmɑ̃] *adv* voluptuously.
voluptueux, -euse [vɔlyptɥø, -øz] **1** *adj* voluptuous. **2** *n* voluptuary, sensualist.
volute [vɔlyt] *nf* **(a)** *Archit etc* helix; scroll (*of violin*); curl, spiral, wreath (*of smoke*); **ressort en v.,** helical spring; **(b)** *(de coquillage)* whorl.
vomer [vɔmɛr] *nm Anat* vomer.
vomi [vɔmi] *nm* vomit, *F* sick.
vomique [vɔmik] *adj Bot Pharm* **noix v.,** nux vomica.
vomiquier [vɔmikje] *nm Bot* nux vomica (tree).
vomir [vɔmir] **1** *vt* **(a)** to vomit, to bring up, to spew up (*food*); **(b)** (*of chimney, volcano etc*) to vomit, to belch forth, to spew out (*smoke, flames etc*); **v. des insultes ou des injures (sur qn),** to heap insults *or* abuse (on s.o.); **(c)** *Fig* to loathe, *Fml* to abhor (*s.o.*). **2** *vi* to be sick, *Am & F* to throw up; **avoir envie de v.,** to feel sick *or Am* nauseous; **c'est à (faire) v.,** it's enough to make you sick.
vomissement [vɔmismɑ̃] *nm* **(a)** (*action*) vomiting; **il fut pris de vomissements,** he started vomiting *or* to vomit; **(b)** (*matière*) vomit, *F* sick.
vomissure [vɔmisyr] *nf* vomit, *F* sick.
vomitif, -ive [vɔmitif, -iv] *adj & nm Méd* emetic, vomitory.
vorace [vɔras] *adj* voracious; (*appétit*) voracious, ravenous; **plante v.,** plant that exhausts the soil.
voracement [vɔrasmɑ̃] *adv* voraciously.
voracité [vɔrasite] *nf* voracity, voraciousness.
vortex [vɔrtɛks] *nm* vortex.
vos [vo] *voir* **VOTRE**.
vosgien, -ienne [voʒjɛ̃, -jɛn] **1** *adj* (of the) Vosges. **2** *n* **V.,** native *or* inhabitant of the Vosges.
votant, -ante [vɔtɑ̃, -ɑ̃t] *n* voter.
vote [vɔt] *nm* **(a)** vote; (*action*) voting, ballot(ing), poll; **droit de v.,** right to vote, franchise; **accorder le droit de v. aux femmes,** to give women the vote; **prendre part au v.,** to go to the polls, to vote; **bulletin de v.,** ballot paper; **section de v.,** polling district *or* station; **v. direct/indirect,** direct/indirect vote; **v. par procuration,** vote by proxy; **(b)** *Parl* **v. d'une loi,** passing of a bill; **provoquer un v.,** to challenge a division; **v. de confiance,** vote of confidence.
voter [vɔte] **1** *vi* to vote; **v. à main levée,** to vote by (a) show of hands; **v. pour/contre un projet de loi,** to vote for/against a bill; **v. communiste,** to vote communist; **v. (pour) Thomas!,** vote for Thomas! **2** *vt* **(a)** *Parl* to pass, to carry (*a bill*); **(b)** to vote (*money etc*); **v. des remerciements à qn,** to offer s.o. a vote of thanks.
votif, -ive [vɔtif, -iv] *adj* votive (*offering, mass*).
votre, *pl* **vos** [vɔtr, vo] *adj poss* your; **un de vos amis,** one of your friends, a friend of yours; **v. père et v. mère,** *Litt* **vos père et mère,** your father and mother.
vôtre [votr] **1** *pron poss* **le v., la v., les vôtres,** yours; **sa mère et la v.,** his mother and yours; **mes enfants ressemblent plutôt aux vôtres,** my children are rather like yours; *F* **à la v.!,** cheers!, (your) good health! **2** *nm* **(a) il faut y mettre du v.,** you must do your share *or* bit; **(b) les vôtres,** your family, *Am* your folks; **je bois à vous et aux vôtres,** I drink to you and yours; **je serai des vôtres ce soir,** I'll be with you *or* joining you tonight; **(c)** *F* **vous avez encore fait des vôtres,** you've been up to your old tricks again. **3** *adj poss Arch & Litt* yours; **je suis tout v.,** I am entirely at your service.
vouer [vwe] **1** *vt* to dedicate, to consecrate; **v. obéissance au roi,** to pledge allegiance to the king; **v. sa vie à l'étude,** to devote *or* dedicate *or* give up one's life to study; **voué à l'échec,** doomed to failure. **2 se vouer** *vpr* **se v. à l'étude,** to devote oneself to study; *F* **il ne sait (pas) à quel saint se v.,** he's at his wits' end, he doesn't know which way to turn.

vouloir¹ [vulwar] *nm* will; **bon/mauvais v.,** goodwill/ill will (**pour, envers,** towards); **cela dépendra de son bon v.,** it will depend on how he feels.

vouloir² *v* (*prp* **voulant**; *pp* **voulu**; *pr ind* **je veux, il veut, n. voulons, ils veulent**; *pr sub* **je veuille, n. voulions, ils veuillent**; *imp in* **voulez**, *otherwise* **veuille, veuillez**; *impf* **je voulais**; *p hist* **je voulus**; *fu* **je voudrai**) **1** *vt* **(a)** (*désirer*) to want, to wish (for), to desire (*sth*); **elle sait ce qu'elle veut,** she knows what she wants, she knows her own mind, she has a mind of her own; **faites comme vous voudrez,** do as you please *or* like *or* wish; **c'est comme vous voudrez,** just as you like; **vous le ferez, je le veux!,** you SHALL do it; **qu'il le veuille ou non,** whether he likes it or not; **je ne le veux pas!,** I will not have it!; **que voulez-vous?, qu'est-ce que vous voulez?,** what do you want?; (*qu'est ce que vous croyez?*) what do you expect?; **que voulez-vous que j'y fasse?,** what do you want me to do about it?; **v. qch de qn,** to want sth from s.o.; **que lui voulez-vous?,** what do you want from him?; (*pourquoi le cherchez-vous?*) what do you want him for?; **combien en voulez-vous?,** how much are you asking *or* do you want for it?; **voulez-vous du thé?,** would you like some tea?; **v. de qch,** to want (some of) sth; **je ne veux pas de cela,** I'll have none of that; **ils ne veulent pas de moi,** they won't have me; **en voulez-vous?,** do you want any?, will you have some?, would you like some?; **ils ont de l'argent en veux-tu (en voilà),** they're not short or money, they've got money to spare; **v. qn pour roi,** to want s.o. for (a) king *or* as king; **je te veux heureux,** I want you to be happy; **v. du bien à qn,** to wish s.o. well; **je ne lui veux pas de mal,** I mean him no harm; **en v. à qn,** to bear s.o. a grudge; **ne m'en veuillez pas,** don't be cross with me, don't hold it against me; **en v. à qn de qch/ d'avoir fait qch,** to have a grudge against s.o. for sth/for doing sth; **à qui en voulez-vous?,** what's the trouble now?; **pourquoi lui en veux-tu?,** what have you got against him?;

(b) to will (*sth*); **ce que Dieu veut,** the will of God; **Dieu le veuille!,** please God!; **vous l'avez voulu!,** you have only yourself to blame!, you asked for it!; **nous n'avons pas voulu cela,** we didn't expect that;

(c) v. + *inf* (*expressed or understood*), **v. que** + *sub*, to require, to demand, to will; (*avoir envie de*) to want, to wish; (*essayer de*) to try to (*do sth*); (*avoir l'intention de*) to intend, to mean; **le sort voulut qu'il mourût,** fate willed *or* ordained that he should die; **le mauvais sort voulut qu'il arrivât trop tard,** as ill luck would have it he arrived too late; **je veux être obéi,** I intend *or* mean to be obeyed, I WILL be obeyed; **v. absolument** *ou* **à toute force faire qch,** to insist on doing sth, to be determined to do sth; **je veux absolument que vous veniez,** I insist on your coming; **le moteur ne veut pas démarrer,** the engine won't start; **il voulait me frapper,** he wanted to hit me; **elle voulut me frapper,** she made as if to strike me; **elle ne voulait pas s'en aller,** she didn't want to go; **je fais de lui ce que je veux,** I can do as I like with him; **j'aurais tant voulu le voir,** I should so much like to have seen him; **j'aurais voulu y rester toujours,** I would *or* could have stayed there for ever; **je voudrais bien être à votre place,** I wish I were in your place; **voulez-vous que j'ouvre la fenêtre?,** shall I *or* should I open the window?, would you like me to *or* do you want me to open the window?; **je veux que vous sachiez que ...,** I should like you to know that ...; **j'aurais voulu qu'elle le sache,** I wish she had been told; **je voudrais le voir me parler sur ce ton,** I'd like to see him speak to me in that tone of voice; **je veux que vous soyez heureux,** I want you to be happy; **que voulez-vous que je fasse?,** what do you expect *or* want me to do?; **rentrons, voulez-vous?,** let's go in, shall we?; **quand j'ai voulu l'embrasser,** when I tried to kiss him; **nous n'avons jamais su ce qu'elle voulait faire,** we never knew what she meant to do; **faire qch sans le v.,** to do sth unintentionally *or* without meaning to *or* it;

(d) v. (bien) faire qch, to consent *or* be willing to do sth; **je veux bien que vous veniez,** I'm quite willing for you to come; **voulez-vous bien attendre un instant?,** would you (please) wait *or* would you care to wait a moment?; **veuillez (bien) vous asseoir,** please sit down; (*plus poli*) do (please) sit down, won't you sit down?; **je veux bien attendre,** I'm quite happy *or* quite willing to wait; **si vous voulez,** if you like, if you wish; **je viens quand je veux,** I come when I choose *or* when I like *or* please; **si vous (le) voulez bien,** if you don't mind;

(e) (**bien** *used as an intensive*) **voulez-vous bien vous taire!,** WILL you be quiet!, *F* do shut up!;

(f) (*admettre*) to admit, to allow (*sth for the sake of argument*); **je veux bien que vous ayez raison,** (I grant that) you may be right; **vous n'avez rien à vous reprocher, je le veux bien, mais ...,** you are in no way to blame; I am ready to admit *or* I grant you, but ...;

(g) (*être convaincu de*) to be convinced, to maintain; **il veut absolument que je me sois trompé,** he insists that I was mistaken;

(h) (*of thing*) to require, to need, to demand (*sth*); **la vigne veut un terrain crayeux,** vines need *or* require a chalky soil; **ce verbe veut l'accusatif,** this verb takes the accusative.

2 se vouloir *vpr* **(a) elle se veut différente,** she thinks she's different;

(b) s'en v., to be angry *or* annoyed with oneself (**de qch,** about sth).

3 *vi* to want; **il ne suffit pas de v.,** it's not enough just to want something; *Prov* **v., c'est pouvoir,** where there's a will there's a way.

voulu [vuly] *adj* **(a)** required, requisite (*formalities etc*); **cela se fera à l'heure voulue,** it will be done in due course; **(b)** (*délibéré*) deliberate, intentional.

vous [vu] *pers pron sing & pl* **(a)** (*subject*) you; **v. et votre femme,** you and your wife; **v. deux/v. tous,** you two, the two of you, you both, both of you/you all, all of you; **v. autres Anglais,** you English; **c'est v. qui êtes arrivé le premier, c'est v. qui êtes arrivés les premiers,** it was you who arrived first, you arrived first; **c'était v.-même qui me l'avez dit,** you told me so yourself; **v., v. avez raison** *ou* **v. avez raison, v.,** you're the one who's right;

(b) (*object*) you; to you; **il ne v. connaît pas,** he doesn't know you; **je v. en ai parlé,** I've spoken to you about it; **c'est à v. que je parle,** it's you I'm talking to; **c'est à v. de jouer,** it's your turn (to play); **ces gants sont à v.,** these gloves are yours; **c'est un ami à v.,** it's a friend of yours; **voilà une photo de v.,** here's a photo of you; **j'ai confiance en v.,** I trust you;

(c) (*reflexive*) **v. êtes-v. bien amusé(e)/amusé(e)s?,** did you enjoy yourself/yourselves?; **v. allez v. faire du mal,** you're going to hurt yourself *or* yourselves; **taisez-v.!,** be quiet!; **v. les avez rassemblés autour de v.,** you gathered them round you; **v. ne pensez qu'à v.(-même),** you think only of yourself;

(d) (*reciprocal*) **est-ce que v. v. connaissez?,** do you know each other *or* one another?;

(e) (*object case of* **on**) you, *surtout Fml* one; **ça v. frappe quand on voit ...,** it strikes you *or surtout Fml* one when you see *or* one sees ... .

vous-même(s) [vumɛm] *pers pron* yourself, *pl* yourselves; *voir* **VOUS, MÊME**.

vousseau, -eaux [vuso] *nm*, **voussoir** [vuswar] *nm Archit* voussoir, archstone.

voussure [vusyr] *nf Archit* curve (*of arch*); arch moulding.

voûte [vut] *nf Archit* vault, arch; **v. d'arête,** groined vault; **v. en berceau,** barrel vault; **v. d'ogives,** ribbed vault; **v. en plein cintre,** semicircular vault; **voûte(s) en éventail,** fan vaulting; **en v.,** vaulted; *Litt* **la v. céleste,** the vault *or* canopy of heaven; *Anat* **v. crânienne,** dome of the skull; **v. palatine** *ou* **du palais,** roof of the mouth.

voûté [vute] *adj* vaulted, arched (*roof etc*); stooping, round-shouldered (*person*); bent (*back*).

voûter [vute] **1** *vt* to arch, to vault (*roof etc*); **l'âge voûte la taille,** age bows the back *or* makes you stoop. **2 se voûter** *vpr* to become bent *or* bowed *or* round-shouldered, to begin to stoop.

vouvoiement [vuvwamɑ̃] *nm* addressing s.o. as 'vous' (*as opposed to 'tu'*).

vouvoyer [vuvwaje] *vt* (**je vouvoie, n. vouvoyons; je vouvoierai**) to address (*s.o.*) as 'vous' (*as opposed to 'tu'*).

voyage [vwajaʒ] *nm* journey, trip, tour; **v. en chemin de fer,** rail(way) journey; **v. (sur mer),** (sea) voyage; **v. (touristique) accompagné,** conducted *or* guided tour; **v. d'information,** fact-finding mission *or* tour; **v. d'affaires,** business trip; **aimer les voyages,** to be fond of travel *or* of travelling; **v. d'agrément,** pleasure trip; **v. de noces,** honeymoon; **récit/livre de v.,** travelogue/travel book; **v. autour du monde,** world tour, round-the-world trip; **elle est en v.,** she is travelling; **est-il toujours en v.?,** is he still away, is he still on his travels?; **partir en v.,** to set off on a journey; **bateau engagé au v.,** ship hired by the run; **frais de v.,** travelling expenses; **compagnon de v.,** travelling companion; (*dans voiture etc*) fellow passenger; **bon v.!,** have a good trip!; **ça va t'obliger à faire deux voyages,** that way you'll need to make two trips; **je n'aurai**

pas fait le v. pour rien, I haven't made the trip for nothing, it hasn't been a wasted journey; *Litt* **faire le grand v.,** to go on one's last journey.

voyager [vwajaʒe] *vi* **(je voyageai(s); n. voyageons) (a)** to travel; **v. par mer/par chemin de fer,** to travel by sea/by rail; **(b)** *Com* to travel, *F* to be on the road; **v. pour les vins,** to travel in wine; **(c)** (*of goods etc*) to be transported; **vin qui ne peut pas v.,** wine that does not travel.

voyageur, -euse [vwajaʒœr, -øz] **1** *n* **(a)** traveller, *US* traveler; (*in train etc*) passenger; (*in taxi*) fare; **(b)** *surtout Hist* voyager, explorer; **(c) v. (de commerce),** (commercial) traveller. **2** *adj* **(a)** travelling; **commis v.,** commercial traveller; **(b) pigeon v.,** carrier pigeon, homing pigeon.

voyagiste [vwajaʒist] *n* tour operator.

voyance [vwajɑ̃s] *nf* clairvoyance.

voyant, -ante [vwajɑ̃, -ɑ̃t] **1** *n* **(a)** sighted (person) (*as opposed to blind*); **(b)** *Arch* seer, prophet. **2** *adj* gaudy, loud, garish (*colour*); showy, conspicuous (*monument etc*). **3** *nm* **(a)** (*signal*) mark, signal; (*pour arpenteur*) sighting board, slide vane, sight (*of levelling rod*); *Nau* sphere (*of lightship*); **(b)** sighting slit, aperture (*of scientific instrument*); **(c)** *Aut* **v. d'huile/d'essence,** oil/petrol indicator light. **4** *nf* **voyante extra-lucide,** clairvoyant.

voyelle [vwajɛl] *nf Ling* vowel.

voyeur, -euse [vwajœr, -øz] *n* voyeur, voyeuse, *F* Peeping Tom.

voyeurisme [vwajœrism] *nm Psy* voyeurism.

voyou [vwaju] **1** *nm* (*délinquant*) (young) lout, hooligan, *Br Sl* yob(bo); (*enfant*) (cheeky) street urchin, guttersnipe. **2** *adj* (*souvent inv in f, parfois* **voyoute**) crude, loutish.

vrac [vrak] *nm* **en v.,** loose, in bulk; **charger en v.,** to load in bulk; **marchandises en v.,** loose goods (*not packed*); **outils jetés en v. sur le plancher,** tools thrown higgledy piggledy on the floor; **elle a déposé ses affaires en v. sur la table,** she dumped her things on the table.

vrai, -aie [vrɛ] **1** *adj* **(a)** true; **c'est (bien) v.!,** it's true!, that's right!; *F* **pour de v.,** really, seriously, *surtout Am* for real; **c'est pour de v.,** I'm serious, I (really) mean it;

(b) (*réel*) true, real, genuine; **le v. Dieu,** the true God; **un v. ami,** a real *or* true friend; **un v. Anglais d'Angleterre,** a real Englishman, an Englishman born and bred; **un v. Matisse,** a genuine Matisse; **un v. diamant,** a real *or* genuine diamond; **couleurs vraies,** lifelike *or* realistic colours; **un homme v.,** a genuine man; *Astron* **temps v.,** true time;

(c) real, downright, regular; **c'est un v. clown,** he's a real clown; **c'est une vraie menteuse,** she's a real *or* a downright liar.

2 *adv* truly, really, indeed; **dire v.,** to tell the truth; **à v. dire, à dire v.,** as a matter of fact, to tell the truth; **faire v.,** to write *or* paint etc realistically; **tu m'aimes (pas) v.?,** you DO love me, don't you?; **v. de v.!,** really and truly!; **pas v.?,** I'm right, aren't I?, isn't that so?; *F* **c'est pas v.!,** really?, oh, no!, I don't believe it!, you're joking!

3 *nm* **distinguer le v. du faux,** to distinguish truth from falsehood; **être dans le v.,** to be right; **il y a du v. là-dedans,** there's some truth in it.

4 *n* **un homme, un v.,** a real man.

vraiment [vrɛmɑ̃] *adv* really; **vous êtes v. trop bon,** you are really too kind; **v.?,** really?; **ils voyagent v. beaucoup,** they really travel a lot; **oui v.,** yes indeed.

vraisemblable [vrɛsɑ̃blabl] **1** *adj* probable, likely; (*crédible*) credible; (*plausible*) plausible; **il n'est pas v. que** + *sub*, it is hardly likely that; **excuse peu v.,** implausible *or* unconvincing excuse. **2** *nm* **le v.,** what is probable *or* likely.

vraisemblablement [vrɛsɑ̃blabləmɑ̃] *adv* probably, very likely, in all likelihood.

vraisemblance [vrɛsɑ̃blɑ̃s] *nf* probability, likelihood; **selon toute v.,** in all probability.

vrille [vrij] *nf* **(a)** *Bot* tendril; **(b)** (*outil*) gimlet, borer, piercer; **yeux percés en v.,** gimlet eyes, beady eyes; **(c)** *Av* spin; **descente en v.,** spinning dive; **faire la v., se mettre en v., tomber en v.,** to go into a spin; **monter en v.,** to corkscrew; **v. à plat,** flat spin; **v. serrée,** steep spin; **v. sur le dos,** inverted spin.

vrillé [vrije] *adj* **(a)** spiral; twisted, kinked (*thread*); **(b)** *Bot* with tendrils, tendrilled.

vrillée [vrije] *nf Bot F* bindweed.

vriller [vrije] **1** *vt* to bore (*with a gimlet*). **2** *vi* **(a)** (*of aircraft etc*) to spiral, to spin (up *or* down); **(b)** (*of thread, rope*) to twist, to kink.

vrillette [vrijɛt] *nf* deathwatch (beetle).

vrombir [vrɔ̃bir] *vi* (*of flies etc*) to buzz; (*of top, aircraft etc*) to hum; (*of engine*) to roar.

vrombissement [vrɔ̃bismɑ̃] *nm* buzz(ing) (*of insects*); hum(ming) (*of top, aircraft etc*); roar(ing) (*of engine*).

V.R.P. [veɛrpe] *nm* (*abrév* **Voyageur, représentant, placier**), commercial traveller, sales representative, *F* rep.

VTT [vetete] *nm* (*abrév* **vélo tout-terrain**) mountain bike.

vu [vy] **1** *nm* **(a) au vu de tous,** openly, publicly; **au vu et au su de tous,** openly and publicly; **c'est du déjà vu,** that's nothing new; *Com* **sur le vu de la facture,** on sight of the invoice; **(b)** *Jur* preamble (*of a decree*). **2** *prép* in view of, considering, seeing; **vu la chaleur je voyagerai de nuit,** in view of *or* because of the heat, I'll travel by night; *F* **vu que** + *ind*, seeing that ...; *Jur* whereas ... .

vue [vy] *nf* **(a)** (eye)sight; **perdre la v.,** to lose one's sight; **avoir la v. courte** *ou* **basse,** to be shortsighted; **jeter** *ou* **porter la v. sur qch,** to take a look at sth; **tourner la v. du côté de la maison,** to look towards the house; **connaître qn de v.,** to know s.o. by sight; **perdre qn de v.,** to lose sight of s.o.; (*perdre contact*) to lose touch with s.o.; **à perte de v.,** as far as the eye can see; **parler à perte de v.,** to talk endlessly, to keep on talking; **personnes les plus en v.,** people most in the public eye; **une personnalité en v.,** a prominent *or* conspicuous personality; **mettre qch (bien) en v.,** to display sth (conspicuously); *F* **en mettre plein la v. à qn,** to impress *or* dazzle s.o.; **faire qch à la v. de tous,** to do sth in sight *or* in full view of everybody; **se tenir hors de v.,** to keep out of sight; *F* **à v. de nez,** at a rough guess *or* estimate; **à v. d'œil,** visibly; *Av Nau* **navigation à v.,** visual navigation; *Av* **voler à v.,** to fly visually;

(b) (*d'extra-lucide*) **seconde v.,** second sight;

(c) (*opinion*) view; **échange de vues,** exchange of views; *Péj* **c'est une v. de l'esprit,** that's a very academic point of view; **vues saines,** sound views;

(d) à la v. de qn/qch, at the sight of s.o./sth; **à première v.,** at first sight; *Mus* **jouer un morceau à v.,** to play a piece at sight; **à v.** *ou* **en v. de terre,** (with)in sight of land; *Com* **payable à v.,** payable at sight;

(e) (*panorama*) view, outlook; **chambre qui a v. sur le jardin,** room that looks out on(to) the garden; **v. de face/de côté,** (*d'objet, de personne*) front/side view; **v. en coupe,** cross section; **vues de Paris,** views of Paris;

(f) *Jur* window, light (*of house*); **droit de vues,** ancient lights; **condamner les vues,** to block up the windows;

(g) (*intention*) intention, purpose, design; **avoir des vues sur qn/qch,** to have plans for *or* designs on s.o./sth; **elle a des vues sur mon frère,** she has designs on my brother; **avoir qch en v.,** to have sth in view *or* in mind; **je crois qu'il a déjà quelqu'un en v.,** I think he's already got someone in mind; **en v. de,** with a view to; **travailler en v. de l'avenir,** to work with an eye to the future.

Vulcain [vylkɛ̃] *nm* **(a)** *Myth Astron* Vulcan; **(b)** *Ent* **v.,** red admiral (butterfly).

vulcanisation [vylkanizɑsjɔ̃] *nf Ind* vulcanization.

vulcaniser [vylkanize] *vt Ind* to vulcanize, to cure (*rubber*).

vulgaire [vylgɛr] **1** *adj* **(a)** *Péj* vulgar, common; **tenue v.,** tarty *or* common outfit; **plaisanterie v.,** vulgar joke; **cela la rend v.,** it makes her look common; **(b)** (*courant*) common, everyday (*custom etc*); **l'opinion v.,** the common *or* general opinion; **langue v.,** vernacular; **le latin v.,** vulgar Latin; **nom v. (d'une plante),** common name (for a plant); **expression v.,** common *or* widely used expression. **2** *nm* **(a) le v.,** (*les gens*) the common people *or* herd; **(b) donner dans le v.,** to be vulgar.

vulgairement [vylgɛrmɑ̃] *adv* **(a)** *Péj* vulgarly; **parler v.,** to be vulgar in one's speech; **(b)** (*en général*) generally, commonly.

vulgarisateur, -trice [vylgarizatœr, -tris] *n* popularizer.

vulgarisation [vylgarizɑsjɔ̃] *nf* popularization (*of knowledge*); **ouvrage de v.,** popular work, popular treatise.

vulgariser [vylgarize] *vt* to popularize (*knowledge*).

vulgarisme [vylgarism] *nm* vulgarism.

vulgarité [vylgarite] *nf* vulgarity.

Vulgate (la) [lavylgat] *nf* the Vulgate (version of the Bible).

vulgum pecus [vylgɔmpekys] *nm F* **le v. p.,** the hoi polloi, the rabble.

vulnérabilité [vylnerabilite] *nf* vulnerability.

vulnérable [vylnerabl] *adj* vulnerable.

vulnéraire [vylnerɛr] *nf Bot* kidney vetch, lady's finger, woundwort.

vulpin [vylpɛ̃] *nm Bot* foxtail (grass).

vulvaire[1] [vylvɛr] *adj Anat* vulvar.

vulvaire[2] *nf Bot* stinking goosefoot.

vulve [vylv] *nf Anat* vulva.

vumètre [vymɛtr] *nm Electron* modulation meter.

W

W, w [dubləve] *nm inv* (the letter) W, w.
W (a) (*abrév* **ouest**) w; **(b)** *El* (*abrév* **watt**) w.
wagnérien, -ienne [vagnerjɛ̃, -jɛn] *adj & n Mus* Wagnerian.
wagon [vagɔ̃] *nm Rail* **(a)** (*véhicule*) *Br* carriage, coach, *Am* car (*for passengers*); *Br* truck, wagon, *Am* car (*for goods*); **monter en w.,** to get into *or* onto *or* to board the train; **w. à bagages,** *Br* luggage van, *Am* baggage car; **w. à bestiaux,** *Br* cattle truck, *Am* stock car; **w. frigorifique,** refrigerated *Br* van *or Am* car; **(b)** (*contenu*) *Br* truckload, wagonload, *Am* carload (**de,** of); *Fig F* **il y en a des wagons,** (*d'objets*) there are loads of them; (*de sable, vin etc*) there is loads of it.
wagon-bar [vagɔ̃bar] *nm Rail* buffet car; (*pl wagons-bars*).
wagon-citerne [vagɔ̃sitɛrn] *nm Rail Br* tank wagon, *Am* tank car; (*pl wagons-citernes*).
wagon-couloir [vagɔ̃kulwar] *nm Rail Br* corridor carriage *or* coach, *Am* corridor car; (*pl wagons-couloirs*).
wagon-foudre [vagɔ̃fudr] *nm Rail Br* tank wagon, *Am* tank car; (*pl wagons-foudres*).
wagon-lit [vagɔ̃li] *nm Rail* sleeping car, sleeper; **voyager en w.-l.,** to take a sleeper; (*pl wagons-lits*).
wagonnet [vagɔnɛ] *nm* tip truck.
wagonnier [vagɔnje] *nm Rail Br* truck *or Am* car shunter.
wagon-poste [vagɔ̃pɔst] *nm Rail Br* mail van, *Am* mail car; (*pl wagons-poste*).
wagon-réservoir [vagɔ̃rezɛrvwar] *nm Rail Br* tank wagon, *Am* tank car; (*pl wagons-réservoirs*).
wagon-restaurant [vagɔ̃restɔrɑ̃] *nm Rail* dining car, *Br* restaurant car; (*pl wagons-restaurants*).
wahhabite [waabit] *adj & n* Wahhabi.
Walhalla [valala] *nm Myth* Valhalla.
walkie-talkie [wɔkitɔki] *nm* walkie-talkie; (*pl walkies-talkies*).
walkman ® [wɔkman] *nm* Walkman ®.
Walkyrie [valkiri] *nf Myth* Valkyrie, Walkyrie.
wallaby [walabi] *nm* wallaby; (*pl wallabies*).
wallingant, -ante [walɛ̃gɑ̃, -ɑ̃t] *n Péj* Walloon separatist.
wallon, -onne [walɔ̃, -ɔn] **1** *adj* Walloon. **2** *nm Ling* Walloon. **3** *n* **W.,** Walloon.
wapiti [wapiti] *nm Zool* wapiti, American elk.
warrant [warɑ̃t, va-] *nm Com Jur* (*warehouse*) warrant; **w. en marchandises,** produce warrant.
warranté [warɑ̃te, va-] *adj* **marchandises warrantées,** goods covered by a warehouse warrant.
wassingue [wasɛ̃g] *nf* (*dans le Nord de la France*) floor-cloth.
water-closet [waterklɔzɛt] *nm* lavatory, toilet; (*pl water-closets*).
watergang [watɛrgɑ̃g] *nm* (*dans le Nord de la France, en Belgique*) polder channel.
wateringue [watərɛ̃g] *nf* (*dans le Nord de la France, en Belgique*) draining works.
water-polo [waterpɔlo] *nm Sp* water polo.
waterproof [watɛrpruf] *adj inv* waterproof.
waters [watɛr, va-] *nmpl* lavatory, toilet; **où sont les w.?,** where is the lavatory *or* toilet?
watt [wat] *nm Él* watt.
watt-heure [watœr] *nm Él* watt-hour; (*pl watts-heures*).
wattman [watman] *nm Vieilli* driver (*of electric tram*); (*pl wattmen* [watmɛn]).
wattmètre [watmɛtr] *nm Él* wattmeter.
W.-C. [vese, dubləvese] *nmpl* lavatory, toilet.
week-end [wikɛnd] *nm* weekend; **partir en w.,** to go away for the weekend; (*pl week-ends*).
western [wɛstɛrn] *nm Cin* western; **w.-spaghetti,** spaghetti western.
Westphalie [ves(t)fali] *nf* Westphalia.
wharf [warf] *nm* wharf.
whisky [wiski] *nm* whisky; (*irlandais, américain*) whiskey; **un w. sans glace,** a whisky without ice; **verre à w.,** whisky glass; (*pl whiskies*).
whist [wist] *nm* whist; **w. de Gand,** solo (whist).
white-spirit [wajtspirit] *nm* white spirit; (*pl white-spirits*).
wigwam [wigwam] *nm* wigwam.
winch [wintʃ] *nm Nau* winch.
wishbone [wiʃbon] *nm* (*de planche à voile*) wishbone boom.
wisigoth, -othe [vizigo, -ɔt] *Hist* **1** *adj* Visigothic. **2** *n* **W.,** Visigoth.
wolfram [vɔlfram] *nm Minér* wolfram.
wombat [vɔ̃ba] *nm* wombat.
woofer [wufœr] *nm* (*haut-parleur*) woofer.
wurtembergeois, -oise [vyrtɛ̃bɛrʒwa, -waz] **1** *adj* of *or* from Würtemberg. **2** *n* **W.,** Würtemberger.

X

X, x [iks] *nm inv* (the letter) X, x; **Monsieur X,** Mr X; **rayons X,** x-rays; *Univ F* **l'X,** the École polytechnique; *Univ F* **un X,** a student at the École polytechnique; **je vous l'ai dit x fois,** I've told you n times *or* a thousand times; **film classé X,** adults-only *or* X film.
xanthome [gzɑ̃tom] *nm Méd* xanthome.
xanthophylle [gzɑ̃tofil] *nf Bot* xanothophyll.
Xavier [gzavje] *nm* Xavier.
xénon [ksenɔ̃] *nm Ch* xenon.
xénophobe [ksenɔfɔb] **1** *adj* xenophobic. **2** *n* xenophobe.
xénophobie [ksenɔfɔbi] *nf* xenophobia.
Xénophon [gzenɔfɔ̃] *nm* Xenophon.
xéranthème [kserɑ̃tɛm] *nm Bot* xeranthemum.
xérès [kserɛs, gzerɛs] **1** *nm* (*vin*) sherry. **2** *n* **X.,** (*ville*) Jerez.
xérodermie [kserɔdɛrmi] *nf Méd* xeroderm(i)a.
xérophile [kserɔfil] *adj Bot* xerophilous.
xérophyte [kserɔfit] *nf Bot* xerophyte.
Xerxès [gzɛrsɛs] *nm* Xerxes.
xi [ksi] *nm* xi.
xiphoïde [ksifɔid] *adj Anat* **l'appendice x.,** the xiphoid process.
xiphophore [ksifɔfɔr] *nm (poisson)* sword-tail.
xylène [ksilɛn] *nm Ch* xylene.
xylographe [ksilɔgraf] *n* xylographer, wood engraver.
xylographie [ksilɔgrafi] *nf* **(a)** (*technique*) xylography, wood engraving; **(b)** (*gravure*) xylograph, woodcut.
xylophone [ksilɔfɔn, gz-] *nm Mus* xylophone.

Y

An asterisk (*) before a noun indicates that the definite article is **le** *or* **la** *not* **l'**.
Y, y¹ [igrɛk] *nm inv* (*the letter*) Y, y.
y² [i] **1** *adv* (*lieu*) there; **est-il à Paris? — ou, il y est,** is he in Paris? – yes, he is (there); **j'y suis, j'y reste!,** here I am and here I stay; **je n'y suis pour personne,** I am not at home to anybody; **en quittant la table j'y ai laissé ma lettre,** when I got up from the table I left my letter on it; *F* **ah, j'y suis!,** ah, now I understand *or* I've got it *or* I'm with you!; **vous n'y êtes pas du tout,** you're wide of the mark; **pendant que vous y êtes,** while you are about *or* at it.

2 *pron inv* **(a) j'y pense sans cesse,** I am always thinking of *or* about it; **j'y gagnerai,** I shall gain by it; **n'y compte pas,** don't count on it; **je m'y attendais,** I expected as much; **venez nous voir — je n'y manquerai pas,** come and see us – I certainly shall *or* I'll be there!;

(b) (*standing for person just mentioned*) **pensez-vous à lui? — oui, j'y pense,** do you think of him? – yes I do; **les femmes?, je n'y comprends rien,** women? I can't understand them.

3 (*indeterminate uses*) **je vous y prends!,** I have caught you (at it)!; **ça y est** [sajɛ], that's it!; (*je comprends*) I knew it!; **j'y suis pour un tiers,** I'm in for a third share; **elle n'y est pour rien,** she has got nothing to do with it *or* got no hand in it; **il y est pour quelque chose,** he's got a hand in it *or* got something to do with it; **prix, y compris le port,** price, including carriage.

4 (*imperative form preceding y takes s for liaison*) **vas-y** [vazi], go there; (*agis*) get on with it!, go on!; **penses-y** [pɑ̃szi], think of it.
y³ *pron pers F* = **IL(S)**.
***yacht** [jɔt] *nm* yacht; **croisière en y.,** yachting cruise.
***yachting** [jɔtiŋ] *nm* yachting; **faire du y.,** to go yachting.
***yacht(s)man** [jɔtman] *nm* yachtsman; (*pl yacht(s)men* [jɔtmɛn]).
***ya(c)k** [jak] *nm Zool* yak.
***yang** [jɑ̃g] *nm* yang.
***yankee** [jɑ̃ki] **1** *adj* Yankee. **2** *n* **Y.,** Yankee.
***yaourt** [jaur(t)] *nm* yog(h)urt; **y. nature/aux fruits/aromatisé,** natural/fruit/flavoured yog(h)urt.
***yaourtière** [jaurtjɛr] *nf* (*appareil*) yog(h)urt maker.
***yatagan** [jatagɑ̃] *nm (sabre)* yataghan.
***yearling** [jɛrliŋ] *nm* yearling (colt).
***Yémen** [jemɛn] *nm* Yemen.
***yéménite** [jemenit] **1** *adj* Yemeni. **2** *n* **Y.,** Yemeni.
***yen** [jɛn] *nm* (*monnaie japonaise*) yen.
***yeti** [jeti] *nm* yeti.
yeuse [jøz] *nf Bot* ilex, holm oak, holly oak.
yeux [jœ] *nmpl voir* **ŒIL**.
***yé-yé** [jeje] *Vieilli* **1** *adj inv* pop; **chanteur yé-yé,** pop singer. **2** *n* pop fan.
***yiddish** [jidiʃ] *adj inv & nm* Yiddish.
***yin** [jin] *nm* yin.
***yod** [jɔd] *nm Ling* yod.
***yoga** [jɔga] *nm* yoga; **faire du y.,** to do yoga.
***yog(h)ourt** [jogurt] *nm* = **YAOURT**.
***yogi** [jɔgi] *nm* yogi.
***yole** [jɔl] *nf Nau* gig, skiff.
Yom Kippour [jɔmkipur] *nm Rel* Yom Kippur.
***yorkshire** [jɔrkʃir] *nm* Yorkshire terrier.
***yougoslave** [jugɔslav] **1** *adj* Yugoslav, Yugoslavian. **2** *n* **Y.,** Yugoslav, Yugoslavian.
***Yougoslavie** [jugɔslavi] *nf* Yugoslavia.
youp [jup] *int* hup!
youpi [jupi] *int* yippee!
***youpin, -ine** [jupɛ̃, -in] *n Arg* (*terme injurieux*) (*juif*) yid.
***youyou** [juju] *nm Nau* dinghy.
***yo-yo** [jojo] *nm inv* yo-yo.
ypérite [iperit] *nf Mil* mustard gas, yperite.
ypréau, -aux [ipreo] *nm Bot* **(a)** (*orme*) wych elm; **(b)** (*peuplier blanc*) white poplar.
ytterbium [itɛrbjɔm] *nm Ch* ytterbium.
yttrium [itrijɔm] *nm Ch* yttrium.
***yucca** [juka] *nm Bot* yucca.
***yuppie** [jœpi, jupi] *n* yuppie.

Z

Z, z [zɛd] *nm inv* (the letter) Z, z.
Z.A.C. [zak] *nf abrév* **zone d'aménagement concerté.**
Zacharie [zakari] *nm* Zachariah, Zechariah.
Z.A.D. [zad] *nf abrév* **zone d'aménagement différé.**
zagaie [sagɛ] *nf* (*javelot*) assegai.
Zaïre [zair] *nm* Zaire.
zaïrois, -oise [zairwa, -waz] **1** *adj* Zairean. **2** *n* **Z.,** Zairean.
zakouski [zakusi] *nmpl Culin* zak(o)uski.
Zambèze [zɑ̃bɛz] *nm* **le Z.,** the Zambezi.
Zambie [zɑ̃bi] *nf Geog* Zambia.
zambien, -ienne [zɑ̃bjɛ̃, -jɛn] **1** *adj* Zambian. **2** *n* **Z.,** Zambian.
zanzi(bar) [zɑ̃zi(bar)] *nm* = sort of dice game (*played for drinks*).
Zanzibar [zɑ̃zibar] *nm* Zanzibar.
zapper [zape] *vi TV* to zap.
zappeur [zapœr] *nm TV* zapper.
zapping [zapiŋ] *nm TV* zapping; **faire du z.,** to zap.
Zarathoustra [zaratustra] *nm* Zarathustra.
zazou, -oue [zazu] *F Vieilli* **1** *adj* hep. **2** *n* hepcat.
zèbre [zɛbr] *nm* **(a)** *Zool* zebra; *F* **courir comme un z.,** to run like a hare; **(b)** *F* (*individu*) individual, guy, *Br* bod.
zébré [zebre] *adj* striped (**de,** with), stripy.
zébrer [zebre] *vt* (**je zébre; je zébrerai**) to stripe, to streak.
zébrure [zebryr] *nf* stripes.
zébu [zeby] *nm Zool* zebu, humped ox.
zée [ze] *nm* (*poisson*) John Dory.
zélateur, -trice [zelatœr, -tris] *n* zealot, zealous supporter.
zèle [zɛl] *nm* zeal, ardour, *US* ardor (**pour,** for); **avec z.,** zealously; **brûler de z. pour qch,** to be fired with enthusiasm for sth; **faux z.,** misguided zeal; **grève du z.,** work-to-rule; **faire du z.,** to be over-zealous, to overdo it; **pas de z.!,** don't overdo it!
zélé, -ée [zele] **1** *adj* zealous (*person*); **peu z.,** slack, remiss. **2** *n* zealous person.
zélote [zelɔt] *nm Hist* Zealot.
zen [zɛn] **1** *nm inv* Zen. **2** *adj inv* Zen; *F Hum* **décoration/alimentation z.,** Spartan decoration/diet.
zénith [zenit] *nm* zenith; *Astron & Fig* **être à son z.,** to have reached one's zenith.
zénithal, -aux [zenital, -o] *adj Astron* zenithal.
Zénon [zenɔ̃] *nm* Zeno.
zéolit(h)e [zeɔlit] *nf Minér* zeolite.
zéphyr [zefir] *nm* **(a)** *Litt* (*vent*) zephyr, balmy breeze; **(b)** *Tex* zephyr (cotton).
zéro [zero] **1** *nm* **(a)** (*chiffre*) zero, *Br* nought; *Tél Br* nought, *Am* zero; *Scol* (*note*) zero, *Br* nought; **c'est un z.,** (*personne*) he's a nonentity; *Sp* **trois à z.,** three nil; *Tennis* **quinze à z.,** fifteen love; *Pol* **option z.,** zero option; **(b)** (*d'échelle de graduation*) zero; **point z.,** zero point; *Él* 'off' (*on electric stove etc*); *Nau* **z. (la barre)!,** helm amidships!; *F* **être** *ou* **avoir le moral à z.,** to be feeling down (in the dumps) *or* low; **partir de z.,** to start from scratch; **il faut tout reprendre à z.,** you *or* we *etc* will have to start all over again *or* to start from scratch. **2** *adj* **z. faute,** no mistakes; **z. heure cinq,** five past twelve (midnight).
zérotage [zerɔtaʒ] *nm* calibration, fixing of the zero point (*of thermometer*).
zest [zɛst] *nm Arch* **être entre le zist et le z.,** to be neither one thing nor the other, to be betwixt and between; (*hésiter*) to shillyshally, to waver.
zeste [zɛst] *nm Culin* peel, zest (*of citrus fruit*); **un z. de citron,** a piece of lemon peel; **z. confit, z. d'Italie,** candied peel.
zêta [dzɛta] *nm* (*lettre grecque*) zeta.
zeugma [zøgma] *nm Littér* zeugma.
Zeus [zœs] *nm Myth* Zeus.
zézaiement [zezɛmɑ̃] *nm* lisping, lisp.
zézayer [zezeje] *vi* (**je zézaie, je zézaye, n. zézayons; je zézaierai, je zézayerai**) to lisp.
Z.I. [zɛdi] *nf abrév* **zone industrielle.**
zibeline [ziblin] *nf* **(a)** *Zool* **(martre) z.,** sable; **(b)** (*fourrure*) sable (fur).
zieuter [zjœte] *vt Arg* = **ZYEUTER.**
zig [zig] *nm* fellow, *F* guy, *Br* chap; **un bon z.,** a decent type, a good sort; **c'est un drôle de z.,** he's a queer customer.
ziggourat [zigurat] *nf Archéol* (*temple*) ziggurat.
zigoteau, -eaux, zigoto [zigɔto] *nm F* = **ZIG.**
zigouiller [ziguje] *vt F* (*tuer*) to do in.
zigue [zig] *nm F* = **ZIG.**
zigzag [zigzag] *nm* zigzag; **éclair en z.,** forked lightning; **tranchées en z.,** zigzag trenches; **faire des zigzags,** (*of road, car*) to zigzag; (*of drunk person etc*) to stagger *or* zigzag along; *Nau* **faire route en z.,** to steer a zigzag course; **rivers disposés en z.,** staggered rivets.
zigzaguer [zigzage] *vi* to zigzag; (*of drunk person etc*) to stagger *or* zigzag along.
Zimbabwe [zimbabwe] *nm* Zimbabwe.
zimbabwéen, -enne [zimbabweɛ̃, -ɛn] **1** *adj* Zimbabwean. **2** *n* **Z.,** Zimbabwean.
zinc [zɛ̃g] *nm* **(a)** (*métal*) zinc; *Com* spelter; **z. à souder,** spelter solder; **galvanisation au gris de z.,** sherardizing; **pommade à l'oxyde de z.,** zinc ointment; **gravure sur z.,** zincograph; **(b)** *F* (*comptoir*) counter, bar; **prendre un verre sur le z.,** to have a drink at the counter *or* bar; **(c)** *F* (*avion*) plane.
zincographie [zɛ̃kɔgrafi] *nf* zincography.
zingage [zɛ̃gaʒ] *nm* **(a)** covering (*of roof etc*) with zinc; **(b)** *Métal* coating with zinc; galvanizing (*of iron*).
zingaro [dzingaro] *nm Arch* gipsy; (*pl zingari*).
zinguer [zɛ̃ge] *vt* **(a)** to cover (*roof etc*) with zinc; **(b)** *Métal* to coat with zinc; to galvanize (*iron*).
zingueur [zɛ̃gœr] *nm* **(a)** zinc worker; **(b)** *Constr* zinc roofer.
zinnia [zinja] *nm Bot* zinnia.
zinzin [zɛ̃zɛ̃] *F* **1** *adj* (*inv in sing*) (*fou*) screwy, cracked. **2** *nm* (*truc*) thingummy, whatsit.
zinzolin, -ine [zɛ̃zɔlɛ̃, -in] *adj & nm* reddish purple.
zip [zip] *nm* zip.
zircon [zirkɔ̃] *nm Minér* zircon.
zist [zist] *nm voir* **ZEST.**
zizanie [zizani] *nf* **(a)** discord; **semer la z. entre les familles,** to sow discord between families; **perpétuellement en z.,** perpetually at loggerheads; **(b)** *Bible* (*ivraie*) tare.
zizi [zizi] *nm Enf* (*pénis*) thing(y), *Br* willy; (*sexe féminin*) hole.
zloty [zlɔti] *nm* (*monnaie polonaise*) zloty.
zodiacal, -aux [zɔdjakal, -o] *adj* zodiacal (*star, light*); **signes zodiacaux,** signs of the zodiac.
zodiaque [zɔdjak] *nm* **le z.,** the zodiac; **signe du z.,** sign of the zodiac.
Zoé [zoe] *nf* Zoe.
zombi(e) [zɔ̃bi] *nm* (*revenant*) *& Fig F* zombie.
zona [zona] *nm Méd* shingles, *Spéc* (herpes) zoster; **avoir le z.,** to have shingles.
zonage [zɔnaʒ] *nm* (*en urbanisme*) zoning.
zonal, -aux [zɔnal, -o] *adj* zonal.
zonard, -arde [zɔnar, -ard] *n F* (*marginal*) drifter.
zone [zon] *nf* **(a)** *Géom* zone; **z. sphérique,** spherical zone; **la z. du zodiaque,** (the belt of) the zodiac; *Minér* **les zones de l'onyx,** the zones *or* bands of onyx; *Géog* **z. tempérée,** temperate zone; **z. des alizés,** trade-wind belt; **z. houillère,** coal belt; *Météo* **z. de dépression,** trough (of low pressure);
(b) *Admin* **z. frontière,** frontier zone; **z. verte,** green belt; **z. d'aménagement différé,** area designated for future development; **z. d'aménagement concerté,** area

developed through cooperation between public and private sectors; **z. à urbaniser en priorité,** priority development area; **z. industrielle,** industrial estate *or* park; *Aut* **z. bleue,** meter zone; **z. postale,** postal area; **la z.,** (*bidonville*) the slum area (*on outskirts of city*); *F Péj* **c'est la z.!,** it's the pits!; *Hist Fr* **z. occupée/libre,** occupied/unoccupied France; *Écon* **z. franche,** free zone; **z. franc,** franc area; **z. d'influence,** sphere of influence; **z. des armées,** war zone, zone of operations; **z. dangereuse,** danger zone; **z. interdite,** prohibited *or* restricted area.
zoné [zone] *adj Minér* zoned, zonate.
zoner [zone] *vi F* (*ne pas travailler etc*) to drift.
zoo [zo, zoo] *nm* zoo.
zoogéographie [zɔɔʒeɔgrafi] *nf* zoogeography.
zoolâtrie [zɔɔlatri] *nf* zoolatry.
zoologie [zɔɔlɔʒi] *nf* zoology.
zoologique [zɔɔlɔʒik] *adj* zoological; **jardin z.,** zoological garden(s), zoo.
zoologiste [zɔɔlɔʒist] *n*, **zoologue** [zɔɔlɔg] *n* zoologist.
zoom [zum] *nm Cin* (*effet*) zoom; (*objectif*) zoom (lens).
zoomorphe [zɔɔmɔrf], **zoomorphique** [zɔɔmɔrfik] *adj* zoomorphic.
zoospore [zɔɔspɔr] *nf Biol* zoospore.
zootechnie [zɔɔtɛkni] *nf* zootechnics.
Zoroastre [zɔrɔastr] *nm* Zoroaster, Zarathustra.
zoroastrien, -ienne [zɔrastrijɛ̃ -jɛn] *adj & n* Zoroastrian.
zoroastrisme [zɔrɔastrism] *nm* Zoroastrianism.
zostère [zɔstɛr] *nf Bot* zostera, eel grass.
zou [zu] *int F* **(allez) z!.,** off with you!, off you go!
zouave [zwav] *nm Mil* Zouave; *F* **faire le z.,** to play the fool, to fool about.
zoulou, -oue [zulu] **1** *adj* Zulu. **2** *n* **Z.,** Zulu.
zozo [zɔzɔ] *nm F* nitwit, *Br* twit.
zozoter [zɔzɔte] *vi F* to lisp.
Z.U.P. [zyp] *nf abrév* **zone à urbaniser en priorité.**
zut [zyt] *int F* damn!, hang it all!; **z. pour vous!,** go to hell!; **avoir un œil qui dit z. à l'autre,** to squint, to be cross-eyed.
zyeuter [zjøte] *vt Arg* to have a look *or Br* a dekko at.
zygomatique [zigɔmatik] *adj Anat* zygomatic.
zygomorphe [zigɔmɔrf] *adj Bot* zygomorphous, zygomorphic.
zygote [zigɔt] *nm Biol* zygote.
zymase [zimɑz] *nf Ch* zymase.
zymotique [zimɔtik] *adj* zymotic.

French grammar

French conversation guide

Weights and measures

Grammaire française

Guide pratique de conversation française

Poids et mesures

CONTENTS

1. GLOSSARY OF GRAMMATICAL TERMS

ADJECTIVE A describing word, which adds information about a noun, telling us what something is like (eg *a* ***small*** *house, a* ***red*** *car, an* ***interesting*** pastime).

ADVERB Adverbs are normally used with a verb to add extra information by indicating **how** the action is done (adverbs of manner), **when, where** and **with how much intensity** the action is done (adverbs of time, place and intensity), or **to what extent** the action is done (adverbs of quantity). Adverbs may also be used with an adjective or another adverb (eg *a* ***very*** *attractive girl,* ***very*** *well*).

AGREEMENT In French, words such as adjectives, articles and pronouns are said to agree in number and gender with the noun or pronoun they refer to. This means that their spelling changes according to the **number** of the noun (singular or plural) and according to its **gender** (masculine or feminine).

ANTECEDENT The antecedent of a relative pronoun is the word or words to which the relative pronoun refers. The antecedent is usually found directly before the relative pronoun (eg in the sentence *I know* ***the man*** *who did this, the man* is the antecedent of *who*).

APPOSITION A word or a clause is said to be in apposition to another when it is placed directly after it without any joining word (eg *Mr Jones,* ***our bank manager****, rang today*).

ARTICLE See DEFINITE ARTICLE, INDEFINITE ARTICLE and PARTITIVE ARTICLE.

AUXILIARY The French auxiliary verbs, or 'helping' verbs, are **avoir** (*to have*) and **être** (*to be*). They are used to make up the first part of compound tenses, the second part being a past participle (eg ***I have*** *eaten*).

CARDINAL Cardinal numbers are numbers such as *one, two, ten, fourteen*, as opposed to **ordinal** numbers (eg *first, second*).

CLAUSE A clause is a group of words which contains at least a subject and a verb: *he said* is a clause. A clause often contains more than this basic information, eg *he said this to her yesterday*. Sentences can be made up of several clauses, eg *he said/ he'd call me / if he were free*. See SENTENCE.

COMPARATIVE The comparative forms of adjectives and adverbs allow us to compare two things, persons or actions. In English, *more ... than, ...er than, less ... than* and *as ... as* are used for comparison.

COMPOUND Compound tenses are verb tenses consisting of more than one element. In French, the compound tenses of a verb are formed by the **auxiliary** verb and the **past participle**: *j'ai visité, il est venu.*

CONDITIONAL This mood is used to describe what someone would do, or something that would happen if a condition were fulfilled (eg ***I would come*** *if I were well; the chair* ***would have broken*** *if he had sat on it*).

CONJUGATION The conjugation of a verb is the set of different forms taken in the particular tenses of that verb.

CONJUNCTION Conjunctions are linking words. They may be coordinating or subordinating. Coordinating conjunctions are words like *and, but, or*; subordinating conjunctions are words like *because, after, although.*

DEFINITE ARTICLE The definite article is *the* in English and *le, la* and *les* in French.

DEMONSTRATIVE Demonstrative adjectives (eg *this, that, these*) and pronouns (eg *this one, that one*) are used to point out a particular person or object.

DIRECT OBJECT A noun or a pronoun which in English follows a verb without any linking preposition, eg *I met* ***a friend.***

ELISION Elision consists in replacing the last letter of certain words (*le, la, je, me, te, se, de, que*) with an apostrophe (**'**) before a word starting with a **vowel** or a **silent h** (eg *l'eau, l'homme, j'aime*).

ENDING The ending of a verb is determined by the **person** (1st/2nd/3rd) and **number** (singular/plural) of its subject. In French, most tenses have six different endings. See PERSON and NUMBER.

EXCLAMATION Words or sentences used to express surprise, wonder (eg *what!, how!, how lucky!, what a nice day!*).

FEMININE See GENDER.

GENDER The gender of a noun indicates whether the noun is **masculine** or **feminine** (all French nouns are either masculine or feminine).

IDIOMATIC Idiomatic expressions (or idioms), are expressions which cannot normally be translated word for word. For example, *it's raining cats and dogs* is translated by *il pleut des cordes.*

IMPERATIVE A mood used for giving orders (eg *eat!, don't go!*).

INDEFINITE Indefinite pronouns and adjectives are words that do not refer to a definite person or object (eg *each, someone, every*).

INDEFINITE ARTICLE The indefinite article is *a* in English and *un, une* and *des* in French.

INDICATIVE The normal form of a verb as in *I like, he came, we are trying*. It is opposed to the subjunctive, conditional and imperative.

INDIRECT OBJECT A pronoun or noun which follows a verb indirectly, with a linking preposition (usually **to**), eg *I spoke to* ***my friend/him.***

INFINITIVE The infinitive is the basic form of the verb as found in dictionaries. Thus *to eat, to finish, to take* are infinitives. In French, the infinitive is recognized by its ending: *mang**er**, fin**ir**, prend**re**.*

INTERROGATIVE Interrogative words are used to ask a question. This may be a direct question (***when*** *will you arrive?*) or an indirect question (*I don't know* ***when*** *he'll arrive*). See QUESTION.

MASCULINE See GENDER.

MOOD The name given to the four main areas within which a verb is conjugated. See INDICATIVE, SUBJUNCTIVE, CONDITIONAL, IMPERATIVE.

NOUN A naming word, which can refer to living creatures, things, places or abstract ideas, eg *postman, cat, shop, passport, life.*

NUMBER The number of a noun indicates whether the noun is **singular** or **plural**. A singular noun refers to one single thing or person (eg *boy, train*) and a plural noun to several (eg *boys, trains*).

ORDINAL Ordinal numbers are *first, second, third, fourth* and all other numbers which end in **-th**. In French, all ordinal numbers, except for *premier* (first) and *second* (second), end in **-ième**.

PARTITIVE ARTICLE The partitive articles are *some* and *any* in English and *du, de la* and *des* (as in *du pain, de la confiture, des bananes*) in French.

PASSIVE A verb is used in the passive when the subject of the verb does not perform the action but is subjected to it. The passive is formed with the verb **to be** and the past participle of the verb, eg *he was rewarded.*

PAST PARTICIPLE The past participle of a verb is the form which is used after **to have** in English, eg *I have* ***eaten****, I have* ***said****, you have* ***tried.***

PERSON In any tense, there are three persons in the singular (1st: *I* ..., 2nd: *you* ..., 3rd: *he/she* ...), and three in the plural (1st: *we* ..., 2nd: *you* ..., 3rd: *they* ...). See also ENDING.

PERSONAL PRONOUNS Personal pronouns stand for a noun. They usually accompany a verb and can be either the subject (*I, you, he/she/it, we, they*) or the object of the verb (*me, you, him/her/it, us, them*).

PLURAL See NUMBER.

POSSESSIVE Possessive adjectives and pronouns are used to indicate possession or ownership. They are words like *my/mine, your/yours, our/ours.*

PREPOSITION Prepositions are words such as *with, in, to, at*. They are followed by a noun or a pronoun.

PRESENT PARTICIPLE The present participle is the verb form which ends in **-ing** in English (**-ant** in French).

PRONOUN A word which stands for a noun. The main categories of pronouns are:
★ **Relative pronouns** (eg *who, which, that*)
★ **Interrogative pronouns** (eg *who?, what?, which?*)
★ **Demonstrative pronouns** (eg *this, that, these*)
★ **Possessive pronouns** (eg *mine, yours, his*)
★ **Personal pronouns** (eg *you, him, us*)
★ **Reflexive pronouns** (eg *myself, himself*)
★ **Indefinite pronouns** (eg *something, all*)

QUESTION There are two question forms: **direct** questions stand on their own and require a question mark at the end (eg *when will he come?*); **indirect** questions are introduced by a clause and require no question mark (eg *I wonder when he will come*).

REFLEXIVE Reflexive verbs 'reflect' the action back onto the subject (eg *I dressed myself*). They are always found with a reflexive pronoun and are much more common in French than in English.

SENTENCE A sentence is a group of words made up of one or more clauses (see CLAUSE). The end of a sentence is indicated by a punctuation mark (usually a full stop, a question mark or an exclamation mark).

SILENT H The name 'silent **h**' is actually misleading since an **h** is never pronounced in French. The point is that, when a silent **h** occurs, any preceding vowel is not pronounced either. For example, the **h** in *j'habite* is silent (note the *j'*). The **h** in *je hurle* is not silent (note the **je**).

SIMPLE TENSE Simple tenses are tenses in which the verb consists of one word only, eg *j'habite, Maurice partira*.

SINGULAR See NUMBER

SUBJECT The subject of a verb is the noun or pronoun which performs the action. In the sentences *the train left early* and *she bought a record, the train* and *she* are the subjects.

SUBJUNCTIVE The subjunctive is a verb form which is rarely used in English (eg *if I were you, God save the Queen*), but common in French.

SUPERLATIVE The form of an adjective or an adverb which, in English, is marked by *the most ..., the ...est* or *the least ...*.

TENSE Verbs are used in tenses, which tell us when an action takes place, eg in the present, the imperfect, the future.

VERB A 'doing' word, which usually describes an action (eg *to sing, to work, to watch*). Some verbs describe a state (eg *to be, to have, to hope*).

2. ARTICLES

A. THE DEFINITE ARTICLE

1. Forms

In English, there is only one form of the definite article: **the.** In French, there are three forms, depending on the gender and number of the noun following the article:

– with a masculine singular noun:	**le**	
– with a feminine singular noun:	**la**	the
– with a plural noun (masc or fem):	**les**	

MASC SING	FEM SING	PLURAL
le chauffeur the driver	**la secrétaire** the secretary	**les étudiants** the students
le salon the lounge	**la cuisine** the kitchen	**les chambres** the bedrooms

Note: **le** and **la** both change to **l'** before a vowel or a silent **h**:

	MASCULINE	FEMININE
BEFORE VOWEL	**l'avion** the plane	**l'odeur** the smell
BEFORE SILENT H	**l'homme** the man	**l'hôtesse** the hostess

Pronunciation: the **s** of **les** is pronounced **z** when the noun following it begins with a vowel or a silent **h.**

2. Forms with the prepositions 'à' and 'de'

When the definite article is used with **à** or **de**, the following spelling changes take place:

a) *with* ***à*** *(to, at)*

à + le → **au**
à + les → **aux**

à + la and **à + l'** do not change

au restaurant at/to the restaurant	**aux enfants** to the children
à la plage at/to the beach	**à l'aéroport** at/to the airport

Pronunciation: the **x** of **aux** is pronounced **z** when the noun following it begins with a vowel or a silent **h.**

b) *with* ***de*** *(of, from)*

de + le → **du**
de + les → **des**

de + la and **de + l'** do not change

du directeur of/from the manager	**des chômeurs** of/from the unemployed
de la région of/from the area	**de l'usine** of/from the factory

Pronunciation: the **s** of **des** is pronounced **z** when the noun following it begins with a vowel or a silent **h.**

3. Use

As in English, the definite article is used when referring to a particular person or thing, or particular persons or things:

les amis dont je t'ai parlé the friends I told you about	**le café est prêt** the coffee is ready

However, the definite article is used far more frequently in French than in English. It is used in particular in the following cases where English uses no article:

a) *when the noun is used in a general sense*

i) to refer to all things of a kind:

vous acceptez les chèques ?
do you accept cheques?

le sucre est mauvais pour les dents
sugar is bad for the teeth

ii) to refer to abstract things:

le travail et les loisirs — work and leisure
la musique classique — classical music

iii) when stating likes and dislikes:

j'aime la viande, mais je préfère le poisson
I like meat, but I prefer fish

je déteste les tomates
I hate tomatoes

b) *with geographical names*

i) continents, countries and areas:

le Canada	**la France**	**l'Europe**
Canada	France	Europe
la Bretagne	**l'Afrique**	**les Etats-Unis**
Brittany	Africa	the United States

But: the article **la** is omitted with the prepositions **en** (to, in) and **de** (from):

j'habite en France — I live in France
il vient d'Italie — he comes from Italy

ii) mountains, lakes and rivers:

le mont Everest — Mount Everest
le lac de Genève — Lake Geneva

c) *with names of seasons*

l'automne	autumn
l'hiver	winter
le printemps	spring
l'été	summer

But: **en automne/ été/ hiver**
in autumn/ summer/ winter

au printemps — in spring
un jour d'été — a summer's day

d) *with names of languages*

j'apprends le français
I'm learning French

But: **ce film est en anglais**
this film is in English

e) *with parts of the body*

j'ai les cheveux roux — I've got red hair
ouvrez la bouche — open your mouth
les mains en l'air ! — hands up!
l'homme à la barbe noire — the man with the black beard

f) *with names following an adjective*

le petit Pierre — little Peter
la pauvre Isabelle — poor Isabelle

g) *with titles*

le docteur Coste — Doctor Coste
le commandant Cousteau — Captain Cousteau

h) *with days of the week to express regular occurrences*

que fais-tu le samedi ?
what do you do on Saturdays?

i) *with names of subjects or leisure activities*

les maths — maths
l'histoire et la géographie — history and geography

la natation, la lecture, le football
swimming, reading, football

j) *in expressions of price, quantity etc*

c'est combien le kilo/ la douzaine/ la bouteille ?
how much is it for a kilo/ dozen/ bottle?

B. THE INDEFINITE ARTICLE

1. Forms

In French, there are three forms of the indefinite article, depending on the number and gender of the noun it accompanies:

– with a masculine singular noun:	**un**	a
– with a feminine singular noun:	**une**	a
– with a plural noun (masc or fem):	**des**	some

Note: **des** is often not translated in English:

il y a des nuages dans le ciel
there are clouds in the sky

2. Use

a) On the whole, the French indefinite article is used in the same way as its English equivalent:

un homme	**une femme**	**des hommes/femmes**
a man	a woman	(some) men/women
un livre	**une tasse**	**des livres/ tasses**
a book	a cup	(some) books/ cups

b) However, the English indefinite article is not always translated in French:

i) when stating someone's profession or occupation:

mon père est architecte
my father is an architect

elle est médecin
she is a doctor

But: the article is used after **c'est**, **c'était** etc:

c'est un acteur célèbre
he's a famous actor

ce sont des fraises
these are strawberries

ii) with nouns in apposition:

Madame Leclerc, employée de bureau
Mrs Leclerc, an office worker

iii) after **quel** in exclamations:

quel dommage ! — what a pity!
quelle surprise ! — what a surprise!

c) In negative sentences, **de** (or **d'**) is used instead of **un**, **une**, **des**:

je n'ai pas d'amis — I don't have any friends
je n'ai plus de voiture — I don't have a car any more

d) In French (but not in English), the indefinite article is used with abstract nouns followed by an adjective:

avec une patience remarquable
with remarkable patience

elle a fait des progrès étonnants
she's made amazing progress

But: the article is not used when there is no adjective:

avec plaisir — with pleasure
sans hésitation — without hesitation

C. THE PARTITIVE ARTICLE

1. Forms

There are three forms of the French partitive article, which corresponds to 'some'/ 'any' in English:

– with a masculine singular noun:	**du**
– with a feminine singular noun:	**de la**
– with plural nouns (masc or fem):	**des**

du vin	**de la bière**	**des fruits**
some wine	some beer	some fruit

Note: **de l'** is used in front of masculine or feminine singular nouns beginning with a vowel or a silent **h**:

de l'argent — some money
de l'eau — some water

2. Use

a) On the whole, the French partitive article is used as in English. However, English tends to omit the partitive article where French does not:

achète du pain — buy (some) bread
vous avez du beurre ? — do you have (any) butter?
je voudrais de la viande — I'd like some meat
tu veux de la soupe ? — do you want (any) soup?
tu dois manger des légumes — you must eat (some) vegetables
as-tu acheté des poires ? — did you buy any pears?

b) The partitive article is replaced by **de** (or **d'**) in the following cases:

i) in negative expressions:

il n'y a plus de café — there isn't any coffee left
je n'ai pas de verres — I don't have any glasses

But: **ce n'est pas du cuir, c'est du plastique** — it's not leather, it's plastic
je n'ai que de l'argent français — I have only French money

ii) after expressions of quantity (see also p C57):

il boit trop de café — he drinks too much coffee
il gagne assez d'argent — he earns enough money

iii) after **avoir besoin de**:

j'ai besoin d'argent — I need (some) money
tu as besoin de timbres ? — do you need (any) stamps?

iv) where an adjective is followed by a plural noun:

de grands enfants — (some) tall children
de petites villes — (some) small towns

But: if the adjective comes after the noun, **des** does not change:

des résultats encourageants — encouraging results

3. Partitive or definite article?

When no article is used in English, be careful to use the right article in French: **le/ la/ les** or **du/ de la/ des**?

If **some/ any** can be inserted before the English noun, the French partitive article should be used. But if the noun is used in a general sense and inserting **some/ any** in front of the English noun does not make sense, the definite article must be used:

did you buy fish? (*ie any fish*)
tu as acheté *du* poisson ?

yes, I did; I like fish (*ie fish in general*)
oui ; j'aime *le* poisson

3. NOUNS

Nouns are naming words, which refer to persons, animals, things, places or abstract ideas.

A. GENDER

All French nouns are either masculine or feminine; there is no neuter as in English. Though no absolute rule can be stated, the gender can often be determined either by the meaning or the ending of the noun.

1. Masculine

a) *by meaning*

i) names of people and animals:

un homme a man	**le boucher** the butcher	**le tigre** the tiger

ii) names of common trees and shrubs:

le chêne the oak	**le sapin** the fir tree	**le laurier** the laurel
But: **une aubépine** a hawthorn	**la bruyère** the heather	

iii) days, months, seasons:

lundi Monday	**mars** March	**le printemps** spring

iv) languages:

le français French	**le polonais** Polish	**le russe** Russian

v) rivers and countries not ending in a silent **e**:

le Nil the Nile	**le Portugal** Portugal	**le Danemark** Denmark
But: **le Danube** the Danube	**le Rhône** the Rhone	**le Mexique** Mexico

b) *by ending*

-acle	**le spectacle** (show) *But:* **une débâcle** (shambles)
-age	**le fromage** (cheese) *But:* **la cage** (cage), **une image** (picture), **la nage** (swimming), **la page** (page), **la plage** (beach), **la rage** (rage, rabies)
-é	**le marché** (market) *But:* nouns ending in **-té** and **-tié** (see p C6)
-eau	**le chapeau** (hat) *But:* **l'eau** (water), **la peau** (skin)
-ège	**le piège** (trap), **le collège** (secondary school)
-ème	**le thème** (theme, topic) *But:* **la crème** (the cream)
-isme, -asme	**le communisme** (communism), **le tourisme** (tourism), **l'enthousiasme** (enthusiasm)
-o	**le numéro** (the number) *But:* **la dynamo** (dynamo) and most abbreviated expressions: **une auto** (car), **la météo** (weather forecast), **la photo** (photograph), **la radio** (radio), **la sténo** (shorthand), **la stéréo** (stereo)

Nouns ending in a *consonant* are usually *masculine*. *Notable exceptions* are:

i) most nouns ending in **-tion, -sion, -ation, -aison, -ison**

ii) most abstract nouns ending in **-eur** (see p C6)

iii) the following nouns ending in a consonant:

la clef (key)	**la nef** (nave)
la soif (thirst)	**la faim** (hunger)
la fin (end)	**la façon** (manner)
la leçon (lesson)	**la boisson** (drink)
la moisson (harvest)	**la rançon** (ransom)
la mer (sea)	**la cuiller** (spoon)
la chair (flesh)	**la basse-cour** (farmyard)
la cour (yard)	**la tour** (tower)
la brebis (ewe)	**une fois** (once)
la vis (screw)	**la souris** (mouse)
la part (share)	**la plupart** (majority, most)
la dent (tooth)	**la dot** (dowry)
la forêt (forest)	**la jument** (mare)
la mort (death)	**la nuit** (night)
la croix (cross)	**la noix** (nut)
la paix (peace)	**la perdrix** (partridge)
la toux (cough)	**la voix** (voice)

2. Feminine

a) *by meaning*

i) names of females (people and animals):

la mère	**la bonne**	**la génisse**
the mother	the maid	the heifer

ii) names of rivers and countries ending in a silent **e**:

la Seine	**la Russie**	**la Belgique**
the Seine	Russia	Belgium

iii) saints days and festivals:

la Toussaint	**la Pentecôte**
All Saints' Day	Whitsun

But: **Noël** (Christmas) is masculine except with the definite article: **à la Noël** (at Christmas)

b) *by ending*

-ace	**la place** (square, seat) *But:* **un espace** (space)
-ade	**la salade** (salad) *But:* **le grade** (degree, rank), **le stade** (stadium)
-ance, -anse	**la puissance** (power), **la danse** (dancing)
-ée	**la soirée** (evening) *But:* **le musée** (museum), **le lycée** (secondary school)
-ence, -ense	**une évidence** (evidence), **la défense** (defence) *But:* **le silence** (silence)
-ère	**la lumière** (light) *But:* **le mystère** (mystery), **le caractère** (character)
-eur	**la peur** (fear) *But:* **le bonheur** (happiness), **le chœur** (choir), **le cœur** (heart), **un honneur** (honour), **le labeur** (toil), **le malheur** (misfortune)
-ie	**la pluie** (rain) *But:* **le génie** (genius), **un incendie** (fire), **le parapluie** (umbrella)
-ière	**la bière** (beer) *But:* **le cimetière** (cemetery)
-oire	**la gloire** (glory) *But:* **le laboratoire** (laboratory), **le pourboire** (tip)
-tion, -sion, -ation, -aison, -ison	**la fiction** (fiction), **la nation** (nation), **la raison** (reason), **la prison** (prison)
-té	**la bonté** (goodness) *But:* **le côté** (side), **le comté** (county), **le traité** (treaty), **le pâté** (pâté)
-tié	**la moitié** (half), **la pitié** (pity)

Most nouns ending in a silent **e** following two consonants:

la botte (boot), **la couronne** (crown), **la terre** (earth), **la masse** (mass), **la lutte** (struggle)

But: **le verre** (glass), **le parterre** (flower-bed), **le tonnerre** (thunder), **un intervalle** (interval), **le carosse** (carriage)

3. Difficulties

a) some nouns may have either gender depending on the sex of the person to whom they refer:

un artiste	**une artiste**
a (male) artist	a (female) artist
le Russe	**la Russe**
the Russian (man)	the Russian (woman)

similarly:

un aide/une aide	an assistant
un camarade/ une camarade	a friend
un domestique/une domestique	a servant
un enfant/une enfant	a child
un malade/une malade	a patient
un propriétaire/ une propriétaire	an owner

b) others have only one gender for both sexes:

un ange	**un amateur**	**un auteur**
an angel	an amateur	an author(ess)
une connaissance	**la dupe**	**un écrivain**
an acquaintance	the dupe	a writer
Sa Majesté	**le médecin**	**le peintre**
His/Her Majesty	the doctor	the painter
une personne	**le poète**	**le professeur**
a person	the poet(ess)	the teacher
la recrue	**le sculpteur**	**la sentinelle**
the recruit	the sculptor (sculptress)	the sentry
le témoin	**la victime**	**la vedette**
the witness	the victim	the (film) star

c) the following nouns change meaning according to gender:

	MASCULINE	FEMININE
aide	male assistant	assistance, female assistant
crêpe	mourning band	pancake
critique	critic	criticism
faux	forgery	scythe
livre	book	pound
manche	handle	sleeve
manœuvre	labourer	manoeuvre
mémoire	memorandum	memory
mode	method, way	fashion
mort	dead man	death
moule	mould	mussel
page	pageboy	page
pendule	pendulum	clock
physique	physique	physics
poêle	stove	frying pan
poste	post (*job*), set	post office
somme	nap	sum
tour	trick, tour	tower
trompette	trumpeter	trumpet
vapeur	steamer	steam
vase	vase	silt
voile	veil	sail

d) **gens** is regarded as feminine when it follows an adjective, and masculine when it precedes it:

de bonnes gens	**des gens ennuyeux**
good people	bores

B. THE FORMATION OF FEMININES

The feminine of nouns may be formed in the following ways:

1. Add an 'e' to the masculine

un ami	**une amie**
a (male) friend	a (female) friend
un Hollandais	**une Hollandaise**
a Dutchman	a Dutch woman

a) nouns which end in **e** in the masculine do not change:

un élève	**une élève**
a (male) pupil	a (female) pupil

b) the addition of **e** often entails an alteration of the masculine form:

i) nouns ending in **t** and **n** double the final consonant:

le chien **la chienne** (dog/ bitch)

le chat **la chatte** (cat)

ii) nouns ending in **-er** add a grave accent to the **e** before the silent **e**:

un ouvrier **une ouvrière** (workman/ female worker)

iii) nouns ending in **-eur** change into **-euse**:

le vendeur **la vendeuse** (male/female shop assistant)

a few nouns ending in **-eur** change into **-eresse**:

le pécheur **la pécheresse** (sinner)

iv) nouns ending in **-teur** change into **-teuse** or **-trice** according to the following guidelines:

if the stem of the word is also that of a present participle the feminine form is in **-euse**:

le chanteur **la chanteuse** (male/female singer)

but if the stem is not that of a present participle, the feminine form is in **-trice**:

le lecteur **la lectrice** (male/female reader)

v) nouns ending in **f** change to **-ve**:

le veuf **la veuve** (widower/widow)

vi) nouns ending in **x** change to **-se**:

un époux **une épouse** (husband/wife)

vii) nouns ending in **-eau** change to **-elle**:

le jumeau **la jumelle** (male/female twin)

2. Use a different word (as in English)

le beau-fils	**la belle-fille** (son/daughter-in-law)
le beau-père	**la belle-mère** (father/mother-in- law)
le bélier	**la brebis** (ram/ewe)
le bœuf	**la vache** (ox/cow)
le canard	**la cane** (drake/duck)
le cheval	**la jument** (horse/mare)
le cerf	**la biche** (stag/hind)
le coq	**la poule** (cock/hen)
le fils	**la fille** (son/daughter)
le frère	**la sœur** (brother/sister)
un homme	**une femme** (man/woman)
un jars	**une oie** (gander/goose)
le mâle	**la femelle** (male/female)
le neveu	**la nièce** (nephew/niece)
un oncle	**une tante** (uncle/aunt)
le parrain	**la marraine** (godfather/godmother)
le père	**la mère** (father/mother)
le porc	**la truie** (pig/sow)
le roi	**la reine** (king/queen)

3. Add the word '**femme**' (or '**femelle**' for animals)

une femme poète (poetess)
un perroquet femelle (female parrot)

4. Irregular feminines

un abbé	**une abbesse** (abbot/abbess)
un âne	**une ânesse** (donkey)
le comte	**la comtesse** (count/countess)
le dieu	**la déesse** (god/goddess)
le duc	**la duchesse** (duke/duchess)
un Esquimau	**une Esquimaude** (Eskimo)
le fou	**la folle** (madman/mad woman)
un héros	**une héroïne** (hero/heroine)
un hôte	**une hôtesse** (host/hostess)
le maître	**la maîtresse** (master/mistress)
le prêtre	**la prêtresse** (priest/priestess)
le prince	**la princesse** (prince/princess)
le tigre	**la tigresse** (tiger/tigress)
le Turc	**la Turque** (Turk)
le vieux	**la vieille** (old man/ old woman)

C. THE FORMATION OF PLURALS

1. Most nouns form their plural by adding **s** to the singular:

le vin	**les vins**	wine
un étudiant	**des étudiants**	student

2. Nouns ending in 's', 'x' or 'z' remain unchanged:

le bras	**les bras**	arm
la voix	**les voix**	voice
le nez	**les nez**	nose

3. Nouns ending in **-au**, **-eau** and **-eu** add **x** to the singular:

	le tuyau	**les tuyaux**	drain-pipe
	le bateau	**les bateaux**	boat
	le jeu	**les jeux**	game
But:	**le landau**	**les landaus**	pram
	le bleu	**les bleus**	bruise
	le pneu	**les pneus**	tyre

4. Nouns ending in **-al** change to **-aux**:

	le journal	**les journaux**	newspaper
But:	**le bal**	**les bals**	dance
	le carnaval	**les carnavals**	carnival
	le festival	**les festivals**	festival

5. Nouns ending in **-ail** change to **-aux**:

le bail	**les baux**	lease
le travail	**les travaux**	work
le vitrail	**les vitraux**	stained-glass window

Common exceptions in which the plural is formed in **-ail**:

le chandail	**les chandails**	sweater
le détail	**les détails**	detail
l'épouvantail	**les épouvantails**	scarecrow
l'éventail	**les éventails**	fan
le rail	**les rails**	rail

6. Nouns ending in *-ou*:

a) seven nouns ending in **-ou** add **x** in the plural:

le bijou	**les bijoux**	jewel
le caillou	**les cailloux**	pebble
le chou	**les choux**	cabbage
le genou	**les genoux**	knee
le hibou	**les hiboux**	owl
le joujou	**les joujoux**	toy
le pou	**les poux**	louse

b) other nouns ending in **-ou** add **s**:

le clou	**les clous**	nail

7. Plural of compound nouns

Each noun ought to be checked individually in a dictionary:

eg	**le chou-fleur**	**les choux-fleurs**	cauliflower
	le beau-père	**les beaux-pères**	father-in-law
But:	**un essuie-glace**	**des essuie-glaces**	windscreen wiper
	le tire-bouchon	**les tire-bouchons**	corkscrew

8. Irregular plurals:

un œil	**des yeux**	eye
le ciel	**les cieux**	sky
Monsieur	**Messieurs**	Mr
Madame	**Mesdames**	Mrs
Mademoiselle	**Mesdemoiselles**	Miss

9. Collective nouns

a) *singular in French but plural in English*

le bétail	cattle
la famille	family
la police	police

la police *a* arrêté certains grévistes
the police *have* arrested some strikers

b) *plural in French but singular in English*

les nouvelles sont bonnes
the news is good

10. Proper nouns

a) Ordinary family names are invariable:

j'ai rencontré les Leblanc
I met the Leblancs

b) Historical names add - **s**:

les Stuarts	**les Bourbons**	**les Tudors**
the Stuarts	the Bourbons	the Tudors

4. ADJECTIVES

Adjectives are describing words which usually accompany a noun (or a pronoun) and tell us what someone or something is like:

une *grande* ville a *large* city	**un passe-temps *intéressant*** an *interesting* pastime
elle est *espagnole* she is *Spanish*	**c'était *ennuyeux*** it was *boring*

A. AGREEMENT OF ADJECTIVES

In French, adjectives agree in number and gender with the noun or pronoun they refer to. This means that, unlike English adjectives, which don't change, French adjectives have four different forms which are determined by the noun they go with:

- **masculine singular** for masculine singular words (basic form, found in the dictionary)
- **feminine singular** for feminine singular words
- **masculine plural** for masculine plural words
- **feminine plural** for feminine plural words

un passeport *vert* a green passport	**une voiture *verte*** a green car
des gants *verts* green gloves	**des chaussettes *vertes*** green socks

Note: If two singular words share the same adjective, the adjective will be in the plural:

un foulard et un bonnet *rouges*
a red scarf and (a red) hat

If one of these words is feminine, one masculine, the adjective will be masculine plural:

une robe et un manteau *noirs*
a black dress and (a black) coat

B. FEMININE FORMS OF ADJECTIVES

1. General rule

Add the letter **e** to the masculine singular form:

MASCULINE	FEMININE
grand	**grande**
amusant	**amusante**
anglais	**anglaise**
bronzé	**bronzée**
un livre amusant an amusing book	**une histoire amusante** an amusing story
il est bronzé he is suntanned	**elle est bronzée** she is suntanned

2. Adjectives already ending in 'e'

These do not change:

MASCULINE	FEMININE
rouge	**rouge**
jeune	**jeune**
malade	**malade**
mon père est malade my father is ill	**ma mère est malade** my mother is ill

3. Others

The spelling of some adjectives changes when the **e** is added:

a) The following masculine endings generally double the final consonant before adding **e**:

MASCULINE ENDING	FEMININE ENDING
-el	**-elle**
-eil	**-eille**
-en	**-enne**
-on	**-onne**
-as	**-asse**
-et	**-ette**

MASCULINE		FEMININE
réel	(real)	**réelle**
cruel	(cruel)	**cruelle**
pareil	(similar)	**pareille**
ancien	(old)	**ancienne**
italien	(Italian)	**italienne**
bon	(good)	**bonne**
gras	(greasy)	**grasse**
bas	(low)	**basse**
muet	(dumb)	**muette**
net	(clear)	**nette**

un problème actuel — a topical problem
la vie actuelle — present-day life

un bon conseil — good advice
c'est une bonne recette — it's a good recipe

But: the feminine ending of some common adjectives in **-et** is **-ète** instead of **-ette**:

MASCULINE		FEMININE
complet	(complete)	**complète**
incomplet	(incomplete)	**incomplète**
concret	(concrete)	**concrète**
discret	(discreet)	**discrète**
inquiet	(worried)	**inquiète**
secret	(secret)	**secrète**

b)

MASCULINE IN -er		FEMININE IN -ère
cher	(dear)	**chère**
fier	(proud)	**fière**
dernier	(last)	**dernière**

c)

MASCULINE IN -x		FEMININE IN -se
heureux	(happy)	**heureuse**
malheureux	(unhappy)	**malheureuse**
sérieux	(serious)	**sérieuse**
jaloux	(jealous)	**jalouse**

But:

doux	(soft)	**douce**
faux	(false)	**fausse**
roux	(red-haired)	**rousse**
vieux	(old)	**vieille**

d)

MASCULINE IN -eur		FEMININE IN -euse
menteur	(lying)	**menteuse**
trompeur	(deceitful)	**trompeuse**

But: This rule applies only when the stem of the adjective is also the stem of a present participle (eg **mentant**, **trompant**). The following five adjectives simply add an **e** to the feminine, **-eur** becoming **-eure**:

MASCULINE		FEMININE
extérieur	(external)	**extérieure**
intérieur	(internal)	**intérieure**
inférieur	(inferior)	**inférieure**
supérieur	(superior)	**supérieure**
meilleur	(better)	**meilleure**

The feminine ending of the remaining adjectives in **-teur** is **-trice**:

MASCULINE		FEMININE
protecteur	(protective)	**protectrice**
destructeur	(destructive)	**destructrice**

e)

MASCULINE IN -f		FEMININE IN -ve
neuf	(new)	**neuve**
vif	(lively)	**vive**
naïf	(naive)	**naïve**
actif	(active)	**active**
passif	(passive)	**passive**
positif	(positive)	**positive**
bref	(brief)	**brève** (note the **è**!)

f)

MASCULINE IN -c		FEMININE IN **-che** or **-que**
blanc	(white)	**blanche**
franc	(frank)	**franche**
sec	(dry)	**sèche** (note the **è**!)
public	(public)	**publique**
turc	(Turkish)	**turque**
grec	(Greek)	**grecque** (note the **c**!)

g) The following five common adjectives have an irregular feminine form and two forms for the masculine singular; the second masculine form, based on the feminine form, is used before words starting with a vowel or a silent **h**:

MASCULINE	FEMININE	MASCULINE 2
beau (beautiful)	**belle**	**bel**
nouveau (new)	**nouvelle**	**nouvel**
vieux (old)	**vieille**	**vieil**
fou (mad)	**folle**	**fol**
mou (soft)	**molle**	**mol**

un beau lac a beautiful lake	**une belle vue** a beautiful view	**un bel enfant** a beautiful child
un nouveau disque a new record	**la nouvelle année** the new year	**un nouvel ami** a new friend
un vieux tableau an old painting	**la vieille ville** the old town	**un vieil homme** an old man

h) Other irregular feminines:

MASCULINE		FEMININE
favori	(favourite)	**favorite**
gentil	(nice)	**gentille**
nul	(no)	**nulle**
frais	(fresh)	**fraîche**
malin	(shrewd)	**maligne**
sot	(foolish)	**sotte**
long	(long)	**longue**
aigu	(sharp)	**aiguë**
ambigu	(ambiguous)	**ambiguë**
chic	(elegant)	**chic**
châtain	(chestnut)	**châtain**

C. PLURALS OF ADJECTIVES

1. General rule

The masculine and feminine plural of adjectives is formed by adding an **s** to the singular form:

un vélo neuf — a new bike
des vélos neufs — new bikes

une belle fleur — a beautiful flower
de belles fleurs — beautiful flowers

2. Adjectives ending in '*s*' or '*x*'

If the masculine singular ends in **s** or **x**, there is obviously no need to add the **s**:

il est heureux — he's happy
ils sont heureux — they are happy

un touriste anglais an English tourist	**des touristes anglais** English tourists

3. **Others**

A few masculine plurals are irregular (the feminine plurals are all regular):

a) SINGULAR IN -al — PLURAL IN -aux

normal	(normal)	**normaux**
brutal	(brutal)	**brutaux**
loyal	(loyal)	**loyaux**
But: **fatal**	(fatal)	**fatals**
final	(final)	**finals**
natal	(native)	**natals**
naval	(naval)	**navals**

b) SINGULAR IN -eau — PLURAL IN -eaux

beau	(beautiful)	**beaux**
nouveau	(new)	**nouveaux**

D. POSITION OF ADJECTIVES

1. Unlike English adjectives, French adjectives usually follow the noun:

un métier intéressant an interesting job	**des parents modernes** modern parents

Adjectives of colour and nationality always follow the noun:

des chaussures rouges red shoes	**le drapeau britannique** the British flag

2. However the following common adjectives generally come before the noun:

beau	beautiful
bon	good
court	short
gentil	nice
grand	big, tall
gros	fat
haut	high
jeune	young
joli	pretty
long	long
mauvais	bad
méchant	nasty, naughty (*child*)
meilleur	better
moindre	lesser, least
petit	small
pire	worse
vieux	old
vilain	nasty, ugly

3. Some adjectives have a different meaning according to their position:

	BEFORE NOUN	AFTER NOUN
ancien	former	ancient
brave	good	brave
certain	some	sure
cher	dear	expensive
dernier	last	last (= *latest*)
grand	great (*people only*)	big, tall
même	same	very
pauvre	poor (*pitiable*)	poor (*not rich*)
propre	own	clean
seul	single, only	alone, lonely
simple	mere	simple
vrai	real	true

mon ancien métier my former job	**un tableau ancien** an old painting
un brave type a nice fellow	**un homme brave** a brave man
un certain charme a certain charm	**un fait certain** a definite fact
chère Brigitte dear Brigitte	**un cadeau cher** an expensive present
la dernière séance the last performance	**le mois dernier** last month
une grande vedette a great star	**un homme assez grand** a fairly tall man
le même endroit the same place	**la vérité même** the truth itself
mon pauvre ami ! my poor friend!	**des gens pauvres** poor people
mon propre frère my own brother	**une chambre propre** a clean room
mon seul espoir my only hope	**un homme seul** a lonely man
un simple employé an ordinary employee	**des goûts simples** simple tastes
un vrai casse-pieds a real bore	**une histoire vraie** a true story

4. If a noun is accompanied by several adjectives, the same rules apply to each of them:

le bon vieux temps
the good old days

un joli foulard rouge
a pretty red scarf

E. COMPARATIVE AND SUPERLATIVE OF ADJECTIVES

Persons or things can be compared by using:

1. *the comparative form of the adjective:*

more ... than, ...er than, less ... than, as ... as

2. *the superlative form of the adjective:*

the most ... , the ...est, the least ...

1. **The comparative**

The comparative is formed as follows:

plus ... (que) more ..., ...er (than)	**plus long** longer	**plus cher** more expensive
moins ... (que) less ... than	**moins long** less long	**moins récent** less recent
aussi ... (que) as ... (as)	**aussi bon** as good	**aussi important** as important

une plus grande maison a larger house	**un village plus ancien** an older village

le football est-il plus populaire que le rugby ?
is football more popular than rugby?

ces gants sont moins chauds que les autres
these gloves are less warm than the other ones

elle est beaucoup/bien moins patiente que lui
she's far less patient than he is

le problème de la pollution est tout aussi grave
the pollution problem is just as serious

2. **The superlative**

a) *Formation*

le/la/les plus ...	the most ..., the ...est
le/la/les moins ...	the least ...

le plus grand pays the largest country	**la plus grande ville** the largest city
les plus grands acteurs the greatest actors	**les plus grandes voitures** the largest cars

b) *Word order*

i) The normal rules governing word order of adjectives apply. When a superlative adjective comes after the noun, the article is used twice, before the noun and before the adjective:

le plat le plus délicieux	**l'histoire la plus passionnante**
the most delicious dish	the most exciting story

ii) When a possessive adjective is used, there are two possible constructions, depending on the position of the adjective:

ma plus forte matière
my best subject

or:

son besoin le plus urgent est de trouver un emploi
his most urgent need is to find a job

c) *'in' is normally translated by* ***de:***

la plus jolie maison du quartier/de la ville
the prettiest house in the area/town

le restaurant le plus cher de France
the most expensive restaurant in France

Note: Verbs following the superlative usually take the subjunctive (see p C31).

3. Irregular comparatives and superlatives

ADJECTIVE	COMPARATIVE	SUPERLATIVE
bon good	**meilleur** better	**le meilleur** best
mauvais bad **mauvais**	**pire** **plus mauvais** worse	**le pire** **le plus** the worst
petit **small**	**moindre** **plus petit** smaller, lesser	**le moindre** **le plus petit** the smallest, the least

Note: – **plus mauvais** is used in the sense of worse in quality, taste etc
– **moindre** usually means 'less in importance', and **plus petit** means 'less in size':

le moindre de mes soucis
the least of my worries

elle est plus petite que moi
she is smaller than I (am)

5. ADVERBS

Adverbs are normally used with a verb to express:

		ADVERBS OF
how		manner
when		time
where	an action is done	place
with how much intensity		intensity
to what extent		quantity

A. ADVERBS OF MANNER

These are usually formed by adding **-ment** to the adjective (like **-ly** in English):

1. If the adjective ends in a consonant, **-ment** is added to its feminine form:

ADJECTIVE (masc, fem)	ADVERB
doux, douce (soft)	**doucement** (softly)
franc, franche (frank)	**franchement** (frankly)
final, finale (final)	**finalement** (finally)

2. If the adjective ends in a vowel, **-ment** is added to its masculine form:

	ADJECTIVE	ADVERB
	absolu (absolute)	**absolument** (absolutely)
	désespéré (desperate)	**désespérément** (desperately)
	vrai (true)	**vraiment** (truly)
	simple (simple)	**simplement** (simply)
But:	**gai** (cheerful)	**gaiement** *or* **gaîment** (cheerfully)
	nouveau (new)	**nouvellement** (newly)
	fou (mad)	**follement** (madly)

3. Many adverbs have irregular forms:

a) Some change the **e** of the feminine form of the adjective to **é** before adding **-ment:**

ADJECTIVE	ADVERB
commun (common)	**communément** (commonly)
précis (precise)	**précisément** (precisely)
profond (deep)	**profondément** (deeply)
énorme (enormous)	**énormément** (enormously)
aveugle (blind)	**aveuglément** (blindly)

b) Adjectives which end in **-ent** and **-ant** change to **-emment** and **-amment** (*Note:* both endings are pronounced **-amant**):

	ADJECTIVE	ADVERB
	prudent (careful)	**prudemment** (carefully)
	évident (obvious)	**évidemment** (obviously)
	brillant (brilliant)	**brillamment** (brilliantly)
But:	**lent** (slow)	**lentement** (slowly)

4. Some adverbs are completely irregular, including some of the most commonly used ones:

ADJECTIVE	ADVERB
bon (good)	**bien** (well)
bref (brief)	**brièvement** (briefly)
gentil (kind)	**gentiment** (kindly)
mauvais (bad)	**mal** (badly)
meilleur (better)	**mieux** (better)

5. Some adjectives are also used as adverbs in certain set expressions, eg:

parler bas/ haut *or* **fort** to speak softly/ loudly

coûter/ payer cher	to cost/ pay a lot
s'arrêter court	to stop short
couper court	to cut short
voir clair	to see clearly
marcher droit	to walk straight
travailler dur	to work hard
chanter faux/ juste	to sing off key/ in tune
sentir mauvais/ bon	to smell bad/ good
refuser net	to refuse point blank

6. After verbs of saying and looking in French an adverbial phrase is often preferred to an adverb, eg:

"tu m'écriras ?" dit-il *d'une voix triste*
"will you write to me?" he said *sadly*

elle nous a regardés *d'un air dédaigneux*
she looked at us *disdainfully*

7. English adverbs may be expressed in French by a preposition followed by a noun, eg:

sans soin	carelessly
avec fierté	proudly
avec amour	lovingly

B. ADVERBS OF TIME

These are not usually formed from adjectives. Here are the commonest ones:

alors	then
après	afterwards
aujourd'hui	today
aussitôt	at once
bientôt	soon
d'abord	first
déjà	already
demain	tomorrow
encore	still, again
pas encore	not yet
enfin	at last, finally
hier	yesterday
parfois	sometimes
rarement	seldom
souvent	often
tard	late
tôt	early
toujours	always
tout de suite	immediately

c'est déjà Noël !
it's Christmas already!

tu as déjà essayé ?
have you tried before?

il mange encore !
he's still eating!

elle n'est pas encore arrivée
she hasn't arrived yet

C. ADVERBS OF PLACE

Here are the commonest ones:

ailleurs	somewhere else
ici	here
là	there
loin	far away
dessus	on top, on it
au-dessus	over, above
dessous	underneath
au-dessous	below
dedans	inside
dehors	outside
devant	in front, ahead
derrière	behind
partout	everywhere

ne restez pas dehors !
don't stay outside!

mon nom est marqué dessus
my name is written on it

qu'est-ce qu'il y a dedans ?
what's inside?

passez devant
go in front

D. ADVERBS OF INTENSITY AND QUANTITY

These may be used with a verb, an adjective or another adverb. Here are the commonest ones:

à peine	hardly
assez	enough, quite
autant	as much/ many
beaucoup	a lot, much/ many
combien	how much/ many
comme	how
moins	less
plus	more
presque	nearly
peu	little
seulement	only
si	so
tant	so much/ many
tellement	so much/ many
très	very
trop	too, too much/ many
un peu	a little

vous avez assez bu !
you've had enough to drink!

il ne fait pas assez chaud
it's not warm enough

nous avons beaucoup ri
we laughed a lot

comme c'est amusant !
how funny!

je vais un peu mieux
I'm feeling a little better

c'est si fatigant !
it's so tiring!

elle parle trop
she talks too much

il est très timide
he's very shy

Note: All of these adverbs, except **à peine**, **comme**, **presque**, **si**, **très**, **seulement**, may be followed by **de** and a noun to express a quantity (see p C57).

E. POSITION OF ADVERBS

1. Adverbs usually follow verbs:

je vais rarement au théâtre
I seldom go to the theatre

comme vous conduisez prudemment !
you do drive carefully!

2. With compound tenses, shorter adverbs usually come between the auxiliary and the past participle:

j'ai enfin terminé
I have finished at last

nous y sommes souvent allés
we've often gone there

il me l'a déjà dit
he's already told me

elle avait beaucoup souffert
she had suffered a lot

3. But adverbs of place and many adverbs of time follow the past participle:

je l'ai rencontré hier
I met him yesterday

elle avait cherché partout
she had looked everywhere

mettez-le dehors
put it outside

tu t'es couché tard ?
did you go to bed late?

4. Adverbs usually come before adjectives or other adverbs:

très rarement
very seldom

trop vite
too quickly

elle est vraiment belle
she is really beautiful

F. COMPARATIVE AND SUPERLATIVE OF ADVERBS

1. The comparative and superlative of adverbs are formed in the same way as adjectives:

ADVERB	COMPARATIVE	SUPERLATIVE
souvent	**plus souvent (que)**	**le plus souvent**

often	more often (than)	(the) most often
	moins souvent (que)	**le moins souvent**
	less often (than)	(the) least often
	aussi souvent (que)	
	as often (as)	

Note: The superlative of the adverb always takes the masculine singular article **le**:

je le vois plus souvent qu'avant
I see him more often than I used to

il conduit moins prudemment que moi
he drives less carefully than I do

c'est lui qui conduit le moins prudemment
he's the one who drives the least carefully

je sais cuisiner aussi bien que toi !
I can cook as well as you!

Note:

a) **as ... as possible** is translated either by **aussi ... que possible** or by **le plus ... possible:**

as far as possible — **aussi loin que possible** / **le plus loin possible**

b) after a negative, **aussi** is often replaced by **si**:

pas si vite !
not so fast!

c) In French, the idea of **not so, not as** is often expressed by **moins** (less):

parle moins fort !
don't talk so loud!

2. Irregular comparatives and superlatives

ADVERB	COMPARATIVE	SUPERLATIVE
beaucoup	**plus**	**le plus**
much, a lot	more	(the) most
bien	**mieux**	**le mieux**
well	better	(the) best
mal	**pis** *or* **plus mal**	**le pis** *or* **le plus mal**
badly	worse	(the) worst
peu	**moins**	**le moins**
little	less	(the) least

Note:

i) **mieux/le mieux** must not be confused with **meilleur/le meilleur**, which are adjectives, used in front of a noun.

ii) **pis/le pis** are only found in certain set expressions:

tant pis — so much the worse, too bad
de mal en pis — from bad to worse

6. PRONOUNS AND CORRESPONDING ADJECTIVES

A. DEMONSTRATIVES

1. Demonstrative adjectives

a) *CE*

ce is often used to point out a particular person or thing, or persons or things. It is followed by the noun it refers to and agrees in number and gender with that noun.

– with a masculine singular noun:	**ce (cet)**	this/that
– with a feminine singular noun:	**cette**	this/that
– with a plural noun (masc or fem):	**ces**	these/ those

ce roman m'a beaucoup plu
I really liked this novel

il a neigé ce matin
it snowed this morning

cette chanson m'énerve
that song gets on my nerves

cette fois, c'est fini !
this time, it's over!

tu trouves que ces lunettes me vont bien ?
do you think these glasses suit me?

cet is used instead of **ce** in front of a word that begins with a vowel or a silent **h**:

cet après-midi
this afternoon

cet hôtel
that hotel

b) *-CI and -LA*

French does not have separate words to distinguish between 'this' and 'that'. However, when a particular emphasis is being placed on a person or object, or when a contrast is being made between persons or objects, **-ci** and **-là** are added to the noun:

-ci translates the idea of — this/these
-là translates the idea of — that/those

je suis très occupé ces jours-ci
I'm very busy these days

que faisiez-vous ce soir-là ?
what were you doing that evening?

d'où vient ce fromage-là ? – ce fromage-ci, Monsieur ?
where does that cheese come from? – this cheese, sir?

2. Demonstrative pronouns

Demonstrative pronouns are used instead of a noun with **ce/cette/ces**. They are:

a) **celui, celle, ceux, celles**
b) **ce**
c) **ceci, cela, ça**

a) *CELUI*

i) **celui** agrees in number and gender with the noun it refers to. It has four different forms:

	MASCULINE	FEMININE
SINGULAR	**celui**	**celle**
PLURAL	**ceux**	**celles**

ii) use of **celui**

celui, celle, ceux and **celles** cannot be used on their own. They are used:

★with **-ci** or **-là**, for emphasis or for contrast:

celui-ci	**celle-ci**	this (one)
celui-là	**celle-là**	that (one)
ceux-ci	**celles-ci**	these (ones)
ceux-là	**celles-là**	those (ones)

j'aime bien ce maillot, mais celui-là est moins cher

I like this swimsuit, but that one is cheaper

je voudrais ces fleurs – lesquelles ? celles-ci ou celles-là ?
I'd like these flowers – which ones? these or those?

★with **de** + noun, to express possession:

je préfère mon ordinateur à celui de Jean-Claude
I prefer my computer to Jean-Claude's

range ta chambre plutôt que celle de ta sœur
tidy your own bedroom rather than your sister's

mes parents sont moins sévères que ceux de Nicole
my parents aren't as strict as Nicole's

les douches municipales sont mieux que celles du camping
the public showers are better than those at the campsite

★ with the relative pronouns **qui**, **que**, **dont** to introduce a relative clause (for use of these relative pronouns, see pp C20-2).

celui/celle/ ceux/ celles qui	the one(s) who/which
celui/ celle/ ceux/ celles que	the one(s) whom/which
celui/ celle/ ceux/ celles dont	the one(s) of which/ whose

lequel est ton père ? celui qui a une moustache ?
which one is your father? the one with the moustache?

regarde cette voiture ! celle qui est garée au coin
look at that car! the one which is parked at the corner

deux filles, celles qu'il avait rencontrées la veille
two girls, the ones he had met the day before

voilà mon copain, celui dont je t'ai parlé l'autre jour
here's my friend, the one I told you about the other day

b) ***CE***

i) **ce** (meaning 'it', 'that') is mostly found with the verb **être**:

c'est	**ce serait**	**c'était**
it's/that's	it/that would be	it/that was

Note: **ce** changes to **c'** before an **e** or an **é**.

ii) use of **ce**

★ with a noun or pronoun, **ce** is used to identify people or things, or to emphasize them; it is translated in a variety of ways:

qu'est-ce que c'est ? – c'est mon billet d'avion
what's that? – it's my plane ticket

qui est-ce ? – c'est moi who is it? – it's me	**ce doit être lui** that must be him
c'est un artiste bien connu he's a well-known artist	**c'était une bonne idée** it was a good idea
ce sont mes amis they're my friends	**c'est la dernière fois !** it's the last time!
c'est elle qui l'a fait she's the one who did it	**c'est celui que j'ai vu** he's the one I saw

★ before an adjective, **ce** is used to refer to an idea, an event or a fact which has already been mentioned; it does not refer to any specific noun:

c'était formidable it was great	**ce serait amusant** it would be funny
oui, c'est vrai yes, that's true	**c'est sûr ?** is that definite?
ce n'est pas grave it doesn't matter *or* it's not serious	**c'est bon à entendre** that's good to hear

Note: the translation of **it** is an area of some difficulty for students of French, as it is sometimes translated by **ce** and sometimes by **il/elle**; see the section on p C63.

3. CECI, CELA, ÇA

ceci (this), **cela** (that) and **ça** (that) are used to refer to an idea, an event, a fact or an object. They never refer to a particular noun already mentioned.

non, je n'aime pas ça ! no, I don't like that!	**ah, bon ? cela m'étonne** really? that surprises me
ça, c'est un acteur ! that's what I call an actor!	**souvenez-vous de ceci** remember this
ça m'est égal I don't mind	**cela ne vous regarde pas** that's none of your business
buvez ceci, ça vous fera du bien drink this, it'll do you good	**ça alors !** well, really!

cela s'appelle comment, en anglais ?
what do you call this in English?

Note: **ceci** is not very common in French; **cela** and **ça** are often used to translate 'this' as well as 'that'; **ça** is used far more frequently than **cela** in spoken French.

B. INDEFINITE ADJECTIVES AND PRONOUNS

1. Indefinite adjectives

They are:

MASCULINE	FEMININE	
autre(s)	**autre(s)**	other
certain(s)	**certaine(s)**	certain
chaque	**chaque**	each, every
même(s)	**même(s)**	same
plusieurs	**plusieurs**	several
quelque(s)	**quelque(s)**	some
tel(s)	**telle(s)**	such
tout (tous)	**toute(s)**	all, every

a) ***CHAQUE and PLUSIEURS***

chaque (each) is always singular, **plusieurs** (several) always plural; the feminine form is the same as the masculine form:

j'y vais chaque jour I go there every day	**chaque personne** each person
plusieurs années several years	**il a plusieurs amis** he's got several friends

b) ***AUTRE, MEME and QUELQUE***

autre (other), **même** (same) and **quelque** (some) agree in number with the noun that follows; the feminine is the same as the masculine:

je voudrais un autre café I'd like another coffee	**d'autres couleurs** other colours
la même taille the same size	**les mêmes touristes** the same tourists
quelque temps après some time later	**à quelques kilomètres** a few kilometres away

Note: **même** has a different meaning when placed after the noun (see p C10).

c) ***CERTAIN, TEL and TOUT***

certain (certain, some), **tel** (such) and **tout** (all) agree in number and gender with the noun; they have four different forms:

un certain charme a certain charm	**une certaine dame** a certain lady
à certains moments at (certain) times	**certaines personnes** some people
un tel homme such a man	**une telle aventure** such an adventure
de tels avantages such advantages	**de telles difficultés** such difficulties

quoi ! tu as mangé tout le fromage et tous les fruits ?
what! you've eaten all the cheese and all the fruit?

toute la journée all day long	**toutes mes matières** all my subjects

Note:

i) **tel**: the position of the article **un/une** with **tel** is not the same as in English: **un tel homme** = such a man.

ii) **tel** cannot qualify another adjective; when it is used as an adverb, 'such' is translated by **si** or **tellement** (so):

c'était un si bon repas/ un repas tellement bon !
it was such a good meal!

iii) **tous les/ toutes les** are often translated by 'every':

tous les jours every day	**toutes les places** all seats, every seat

2. Indefinite pronouns

a) These are:

MASC	FEM	
aucun	**aucune**	none, not any
autre(s)	**autre(s)**	another one, other ones
certains	**certaine(s)**	certain, some
chacun	**chacune**	each one, everyone
on		one, someone, you, they, people, we
personne		nobody
plusieurs	**plusieurs**	several (ones)
quelque chose		something, anything
quelqu'un		someone
quelques-uns	**quelques-unes**	some, a few
rien		nothing
tout (tous)	**toute(s)**	everything, every one, all

pas celui-là, l'autre not that one, the other one	**où sont les autres ?** where are the others?
certains disent que ... some say that...	**personne n'est venu** no one came
qui est là ? – personne who's there? – nobody	**qu'as-tu ? – rien** what's wrong? – nothing
plusieurs d'entre eux several of them	**chacun pour soi !** every man for himself!
il manque quelque chose ? is anything missing?	**dis quelque chose !** say something!
quelqu'un l'a averti someone warned him	**il y a quelqu'un ?** is anyone in?
j'ai tout oublié I've forgotten everything	**c'est tout, merci** that's all, thanks
elles sont toutes arrivées they've all arrived	**allons-y tous ensemble** let's all go together

b) *Points to note*

i) **aucun(e)**, **personne** and **rien**: these can be used on their own, but they are more often used with a verb and the negative word **ne** (see negative expressions, p C60).

personne n'habite ici no one lives here	**il n'y a rien à manger** there's nothing to eat

ii) **aucun(e), un(e) autre, d'autres, certain(e)s, plusieurs** and **quelques-un(e)s**: when these pronouns are used as direct objects, the pronoun **en** must be used before the verb:

je n'en ai lu aucun I haven't read any (of them)	**donne-m'en une autre** give me another one

j'en ai vu d'autres qui étaient moins chers
I saw other ones which were cheaper

j'en connais certains I know some of them	**il y en a plusieurs** there are several
tu m'en donnes quelques-uns will you give me a few?	**achètes-en quelques-unes** buy a few

iii) **personne, quelque chose, rien, plusieurs**: when these are followed by an adjective, the preposition **de (d')** must be used in front of the adjective:

il n'y a personne de libre there's no one available	**quelque chose de mieux** something better
il y en avait plusieurs de cassés several of them were broken	**rien de grave** nothing serious

iv) **autre** is commonly used in the following expressions:

quelqu'un d'autre someone else	**quelque chose d'autre** something else	**rien d'autre** nothing else

c) *ON*

This pronoun is used in a variety of ways in French. It can mean:

i) *one/you/they/people* in a general sense:

en France, on roule à droite
in France, they drive on the right

on ne sait jamais you/one never know(s)	**on ne doit pas mentir** you shouldn't lie

ii) *someone* (an undefined person)

In this sense, **on** is often translated by the passive (see p C36):

on me l'a déjà dit someone's already told me I've already been told	**on vous l'apportera** someone will bring you it it will be brought to you

iii) *we*

In spoken French, **on** is increasingly used instead of **nous**; although it refers to a plural subject, it is followed by the third person singular:

qu'est-ce qu'on fait ? what shall we do?	**fais vite, on t'attend !** hurry up, we're waiting for you!

Note: in compound tenses with the auxiliary **être**, the agreement of the past participle with **on** is optional:

on est allé au cinéma **on est allés au cinéma** we went to the pictures	**on est rentré en taxi** **on est rentrées en taxi** we got home by taxi

C. INTERROGATIVE AND EXCLAMATORY ADJECTIVES AND PRONOUNS

1. The interrogative adjective QUEL ?

a) *Forms*

quel (which, what) agrees in number and gender with the noun it refers to. It has four forms:

– with a masc sing noun:	**quel ?**
– with a fem sing noun:	**quelle ?**
– with a masc plur noun:	**quels ?**
– with a fem plur noun:	**quelles ?**

b) *Direct questions*

quel est votre passe-temps favori ?
what's your favourite pastime?

quelle heure est-il ? what time is it?	**quels jours as-tu de libres ?** which days have you got free?

quelles affaires comptes-tu prendre avec toi ?
what/which things do you intend to take with you?

c) *Indirect questions:*

je ne sais pas quel disque choisir
I don't know which record to choose

il se demande quelle veste lui va le mieux
he's wondering which jacket suits him best

2. The exclamatory adjective QUEL !

quel ! has the same forms as the interrogative adjective **quel ?**:

quel dommage ! what a pity!	**quelle belle maison !** what a beautiful house!

quels imbéciles !
what idiots!

3. Interrogative pronouns

These are:

lequel/ laquelle/ lesquel(le)s ?	which (one)?
qui ?	who?, whom?
que ?	what?
quoi ?	what?
ce qui	what
ce que	what

ce qui and **ce que** are used only in indirect questions; all other interrogative pronouns can be used both in direct and indirect questions.

a) ***LEQUEL ?***

i) forms

lequel (which., which one?) agrees in gender and in number with the noun it stands for:

– with a masc sing noun:	**lequel ?**	which (one)?
– with a fem sing noun:	**laquelle ?**	which (one)?
– with a masc plur noun:	**lesquels ?**	which (ones)?
– with a fem plur noun:	**lesquelles ?**	which (ones)?

after the prepositions **à** and **de**, the following changes occur:

à + lequel ?	→	**auquel ?**
à + lesquels ?	→	**auxquels ?**
à + lesquelles ?	→	**auxquelles ?**
de + lequel ?	→	**duquel ?**
de + lesquels ?	→	**desquels ?**
de + lesquelles ?	→	**desquelles ?**

à/de + laquelle? do not change

ii) direct questions:

je cherche un hôtel; lequel recommandez-vous ?
I'm looking for a hotel; which one do you recommend?

nous avons plusieurs couleurs; vous préférez laquelle ?
we have several colours; which one do you prefer?

lesquels de ces livres sont à toi ?
which of these books are yours?

je voudrais essayer ces chaussures – lesquelles ?
I would like to try these shoes on – which ones?

iii) indirect questions

demande-lui lequel de ces ordinateurs est le moins cher
ask him which (one) of these computers is the cheapest

c'est dans une de ces rues, mais je ne sais plus laquelle
it's in one of these streets, but I can't remember which one

b) ***QUI ?***

qui (who?, whom?) is used to refer to people; it can be both subject and object and can be used after a preposition:

qui t'a accompagné ?
who accompanied you?

qui as-tu appelé ?
who did you call?

tu y vas avec qui ?
who are you going with?

c'est pour qui ?
who is it for?

pour qui vous prenez-vous ?
who do you think you are?

à qui l'as-tu donné ?
who did you give it to?

Note: **que** (not **qui**!) changes to **qu'** before a vowel or a silent **h**:

qui est-ce qu'elle attend ?
who is she waiting for?

qui ? can be replaced by **qui est-ce qui ?** (subject) or **qui est-ce que ?** (object) in direct questions:

qui est-ce qui veut du café ?
who wants coffee?

qui est-ce que tu as vu ?
who did you see?

avec qui est-ce que tu sors ce soir ?
who are you going out with tonight?

But: **qui** cannot be replaced by **qui est-ce qui** or **qui est-ce que** in indirect questions:

j'aimerais savoir qui vous a dit ça
I'd like to know who told you that

elle se demandait de qui étaient les fleurs
she was wondering who the flowers were from

For more details on the use of **qui/que** as relative pronouns, see p C20.

c) ***QUE ?***

que (what?) is used to refer to things; it is only used in direct questions; it is always a direct object and cannot be used after prepositions:

que désirez-vous ?
what do you wish?

qu'a-t-il dit ?
what did he say?

que ? is rather formal and is usually replaced by **qu'est-ce qui ?** or **qu'est-ce que ?** in spoken French.

Note: **que** becomes **qu'** before a vowel or a silent **h**.

d) ***QU'EST-CE QUI ?***

qu'est-ce qui ? (what?) is used as the subject of a verb; it cannot refer to a person:

qu'est-ce qui lui est arrivé ?
what happened to him?

qu'est-ce qui la fait rire ?
what makes her laugh?

e) ***QU'EST-CE QUE ?***

qu'est-ce que ? (what?) replaces **que ?** as the object of a verb; it becomes **qu'est-ce qu'** before a vowel or a silent **h**:

qu'est-ce que tu aimes lire ?
what do you like reading?

qu'est-ce qu'il va faire pendant les vacances ?
what's he going to do during the holidays?

f) ***QUOI ?***

quoi ? (what?) refers to things; it is used:

i) instead of **que** or **qu'est-ce que** after a preposition:

à quoi penses-tu ?
what are you thinking about?

dans quoi l'as-tu mis ?
what did you put it in?

ii) in indirect questions:

demandez-lui de quoi il a besoin
ask him what he needs

je ne sais pas à quoi ça sert
I don't know what it's for

g) ***CE QUI, CE QUE***

ce qui and **ce que** (what) are only used in indirect questions; they replace **qu'est-ce qui** and **(qu'est- ce) que**. They are used in the same way as the relative pronouns **ce qui** and **ce que** (see p C21).

i) **ce qui** is used as the subject of the verb in the indirect question (**ce qui** is the subject of **s'est passé** in the following example):

nous ne saurons jamais ce qui s'est passé
we'll never know what happened

ii) **ce que**

ce que (**ce qu'** before a vowel or a silent **h**) is used as the object of the verb in the indirect question (**ce que** is the object of **il faisait** in the following example):

je n'ai pas remarqué ce qu'il faisait
I didn't notice what he was doing

D. PERSONAL PRONOUNS

There are four categories of personal pronouns:

- **subject** pronouns
- **object** pronouns
- **disjunctive** pronouns
- **reflexive** pronouns

For reflexive pronouns, see p C26.

1. Subject pronouns

PERSON	SINGULAR		PLURAL	
1st	**je (j')**	I	**nous**	we
2nd	**tu**	you	**vous**	you
3rd	**il**	he, it	**ils**	they
	elle	she, it	**elles**	they
	on	one, we, they		

Note:

a) **je** changes to **j'** before a vowel or a silent **h**:

j'ai honte — I'm ashamed
j'adore les frites — I love chips
j'habite en Ecosse — I live in Scotland

b) **tu** and **vous**

vous can be plural or singular; it is used when speaking to more than one person (plural), or to a stranger or an older person (singular):

vous venez, les gars ? — are you coming, lads?
vous parlez l'anglais, Monsieur ? — do you speak English(, sir)?

tu is used when speaking to a friend, a relative, a younger person, or someone you know well:

tu viens, Marc ? — are you coming, Marc?

c) **il/ils, elle/elles** may refer to people, animals or things, and must be of the same gender as the noun they replace:

ton stylo ? *il* est là — your pen? there *it* is
ta montre ? *elle* est là — your watch? there *it* is
tes gants ? *ils* sont là — your gloves? there *they* are
tes lunettes ? *elles* sont là — your glasses? there *they* are

When referring to several nouns of different genders, French uses the masculine plural **ils**:

tu as vu *le* stylo et *la* montre de Marie. – oui, *ils* sont dans son sac
have you seen Marie's pen and watch. – yes, *they*'re in her bag

d) **on**: see p C15.

2. Object pronouns

These include:
- direct object pronouns
- indirect object pronouns
- the pronouns **en** and **y**

a) *Forms*

	PERSON	DIRECT	INDIRECT
SING	1st	**me (m')** me	**me (m')** (to) me
	2nd	**te (t')** you	**te (t')** (to) you
	3rd	**le (l')** him, it	**lui** (to) him
		la (l') her, it	**lui** (to) her
PLUR	1st	**nous** us	**nous** (to) us
	2nd	**vous** you	**vous** (to) you
	3rd	**les** them	**leur** (to) them

Note:

i) **me, te, le** and **la** change to **m', t'** and **l'** before a vowel or a silent **h**:

il m'énerve ! — he gets on my nerves!
je m'habituerai à lui — I'll get used to him

ii) **te** and **vous**: the same distinction should be made as between the subject pronouns **tu** and **vous** (see section **1. b**).

iii) **le**: is sometimes used in an impersonal sense, when it refers to a fact, a statement or an idea which has already been expressed; it is usually not translated in English:

j'irai en Amérique un jour ; en tout cas je *l'*espère
I'll go to America one day; I hope so anyway

elle a eu un bébé – je *le* sais, elle me *l'*a dit
she's had a baby – I know, she told me

iv) **moi** and **toi** are used instead of **me** and **te**, except when **en** follows:

écris-*moi* bientôt — write to me soon
donne *m'*en — give me some

b) *Position*

In French, object pronouns come immediately before the verb they refer to. With a compound tense, they come before the auxiliary:

on *t'*attendra ici — we'll wait for you here
je *l'*ai rencontrée en ville — I met her in town

Note: When there are two verbs, the pronoun comes immediately before the verb it refers to:

j'aimerais lui demander — I'd like to ask him
tu l'as entendu chanter ? — have you heard him sing?

In positive commands (affirmative imperative) the pronoun follows the verb and is joined to it by a hyphen:

regarde-*les* ! — look at them!
parle-*lui* ! — speak to him!
dis-*nous* ce qui s'est passé — tell us what happened

c) *Direct pronouns and indirect pronouns*

i) Direct object pronouns replace a noun which follows the verb directly. They answer the question 'who(m)?' or 'what'?

WHO(M) did you see? — I saw *my friend*; I saw *him*
qui as-tu vu ? — **j'ai vu *mon ami* ; je *l'*ai vu**

tu *me* connais — you know *me*
j'aime *le* voir danser — I like to see *him* dance
je *les* ai trouvés — I found *them*
ne *nous* ennuie pas ! — don't bother *us!*

ii) Indirect object pronouns replace a noun which follows the verb with a linking preposition (usually **à** = 'to'). They answer the question 'who(m) to?':

WHO did you speak to? — I spoke *to Marc*; I spoke *to him*
à qui as-tu parlé ? — **j'ai parlé *à Marc* ; je *lui* ai parlé**

elle *lui* a menti — she lied *to him*
je *te* donne ce disque — I'm giving this record *to you*
je ne *leur* parle plus — I'm not talking *to them* any more

iii) **le/la/les** or **lui/leur**?

Direct pronouns differ from indirect pronouns only in the 3rd person and great care must be taken here:

★ English indirect object pronouns often look like direct objects; this becomes obvious when the object is placed at the end of the sentence:

I showed him your photo = I showed your photo to him
je *lui* ai montré ta photo

This is particularly the case with the following verbs:

acheter	to buy	**offrir**	to offer
donner	to give	**prêter**	to lend
montrer	to show	**vendre**	to sell

je *lui* ai acheté un livre — I bought him a book = I bought a book *for him*
ne *leur* prête pas mes affaires — don't lend them my things = don't lend my things *to them*

★ Some verbs take a direct object in English and an indirect object in French (see p C50):

je ne *lui* ai rien dit — I didn't tell *him* anything
je *leur* demanderai — I'll ask *them*
tu *lui* ressembles — you look like *him*
téléphone-*leur* — phone *them*

★ Some verbs take a direct object in French and an indirect object in English (see pp C49-50):

je *l'*attends — I'm waiting *for him*
écoutez-*les* ! — listen *to them*!

d) *Order of object pronouns*

When several object pronouns are used together, they come in the following order:

i) Before the verb:

1	**me**	**te**	**nous**	**vous**
2	**le**	**la**	**les**	
3	**lui**	**leur**		

il *me l'*a donné — he gave me it
je vais *vous les* envoyer — I'll send them to you
ne *la leur* vends pas — don't sell it to them
je *le lui* ai acheté — I bought it for him

ii) After the verb:

With a positive command (affirmative imperative), the order is as follows:

1	**le**	**la**	**les**	
2	**moi (m')**	**toi (t')**	**nous**	**vous**
3	**lui**	**leur**		

apporte-*les-moi* ! — bring them to me!
prête-*la-nous* ! — lend us it!
dites-*le lui* ! — tell him!
rends-*la leur* ! — give it back to them!

3. The pronoun *EN*

a) *Use*

en is used instead of **de** + noun. Since **de** has a variety of meanings, **en** can be used in a number of ways:

i) It means 'of it/them', but also 'with it/them', 'about it/them', 'from it/there', 'out of it/there':

tu es sûr *du prix* ? – j'*en* suis sûr
are you sure of the price? – I'm sure *of it*

je suis content *de ce cadeau* ; j'*en* suis content
I'm pleased with this present; I'm pleased *with it*

elle est folle *des animaux* ; elle *en* est folle
she's crazy about animals; she's crazy *about them*

il est descendu *du train* ; il *en* est descendu
he got off the train; he got *off it*

il revient *de Paris* ; il *en* revient
he's coming back from Paris; he's coming *from there*

ii) Verb constructions

Particular care should be taken with verbs and expressions which are followed by **de** + noun. Since **de** is not always translated in the same way, **en** may have a number of meanings:

il a envie *de ce livre* ; il *en* a envie
he wants this book; he wants *it*

je te remercie *de ta carte* ; je t'*en* remercie
I thank you for your card; I thank you *for it*

tu as besoin *de ces papiers* ? tu *en* as besoin ?
do you need these papers? do you need *them?*

elle a peur des chiens ; elle *en* a peur
she's afraid of dogs; she's afraid *of them*

tu te souviens de ce film ? tu t'*en* souviens ?
do you remember this film? do you remember *it*?

iii) 'some'/'any'

en replaces the partitive article **(du, de la, des)** + noun; it means 'some'/'any':

tu veux *du café* ? – non, je n'*en* veux pas
do you want (any) coffee? – no, I don't want *any*

j'achète *des fruits* ? – non, j'*en* ai chez moi
shall I buy fruit. – no, I've got *some* at home

il y a *de la place* ? – *en* voilà là-bas
is there any room? – there's some over there

iv) Expressions of quantity

en must be used with expressions of quantity not followed by a noun. It replaces **de** + noun and means 'of it/them', but is seldom translated in English:

tu as pris assez *d'argent* ? tu *en* as pris assez ?
did you take enough money? did you take enough?
vous avez *combien de frères* ? – j'*en* ai deux
how many brothers do you have? – I've got two

j'ai fini *mes cigarettes* ; je vais *en* acheter un paquet
I've finished my cigarettes; I'm going to buy a packet

b) *Position*

Like object pronouns, **en** comes immediately before the verb, except with positive commands (affirmative imperative), where it comes after the verb and is linked to it by a hyphen:

j'en veux un kilo — I want a kilo (of it/them)
j'en ai marre ! — I'm fed up (with it)!
prends-en assez ! — take enough (of it/them)!
laisses-en aux autres ! — leave some for the others!

When used in conjunction with other object pronouns, it always comes last:

ne *m'en* parlez pas ! — don't tell me about it!
je *vous en* donnerai — I'll give you some
prête-*lui-en* ! — lend him some!
gardez-*nous-en* ! — keep some for us!

4. The pronoun Y

a) *Use*

y is used instead of **à** + noun (not referring to a person). It is used:

i) As the indirect object of a verb. Since the preposition **à** is translated in a variety of ways in English, **y** may have various meanings (it, of it/them, about it/them etc):

tu joues *au tennis* ? – non, j'*y* joue rarement
do you play tennis? – no, I seldom play (*it*)

je pense *à mes examens* ; j'*y* pense souvent
I'm thinking *about* my exams; I often think *about them*

il s'intéresse *à la photo* ; il s'*y* intéresse
he's interested in photography; he's interested *in it*

ii) Meaning 'there':

j'ai passé deux jours *à Londres* ; j'*y* ai passé deux jours
I spent two days in London; I spent two days there

il est allé *en Grèce* ; il *y* est allé
he went to Greece; he went there

Note: **y** must always be used with the verb **aller** (to go) when the place is not mentioned in the clause. It is often not translated in English:

comment vas-tu *à l'école* ? – j'*y* vais en bus
how do you go to school? – I go (there) by bus

allons-y! — let's go!
on *y* va demain — we're going (there) tomorrow

iii) Replacing the prepositions **en**, **dans**, **sur** + noun; **y** then means 'there', 'in it/them', 'on it/them':

je voudrais vivre *en France* ; je voudrais *y* vivre
I'd like to live in France; I'd like to live *there*

je les ai mis *dans ma poche* ; je les *y* ai mis
I put them in my pocket; I put them *there*

***sur la table* ? non, je ne l'*y* vois pas**
on the table? no, I don't see it *there*

b) *Position*

Like other object pronouns, **y** comes immediately before the verb, except with a positive command (affirmative imperative), where it must follow the verb:

j'*y* réfléchirai — I'll think about it
il s'*y* est habitué — he got used to it

pensez-*y* !	**n'*y* allez pas !**
think about it!	don't go!

When used with other object pronouns, **y** comes last:

il va *nous y* rencontrer	**je *l'y* ai vu hier**
he'll meet us there	I saw him there yesterday

5. Disjunctive pronouns

a) *Forms*

PERSON	SINGULAR	PLURAL
1st	**moi** me	**nous** us
2nd	**toi** you	**vous** you
3rd (masc)	**lui** him	**eux** them
(fem)	**elle** her	**elles** them
(impersonal)	**soi** oneself	

Note:

i) **toi/vous**: the same difference should be made as between **tu** and **vous** (see p C17).

ii) **soi** is used in an impersonal, general sense to refer to indefinite pronouns and adjectives (**on, chacun, tout le monde, personne, chaque** etc); it is mainly found in set phrases, such as:

chacun pour soi
every man for himself

b) *Use*

Disjunctive pronouns, also called emphatic pronouns, are used instead of object pronouns (only when referring to persons) in the following cases:

i) In answer to a question, alone or in a phrase without a verb:

qui est là ? – moi	**j'aime les pommes ; et toi ?**
who's there? – me	I like apples; do you?

qui préfères-tu, lui ou elle ? – elle, bien sûr
who do you prefer, him or her? – her, of course

ii) After **c'est/ce sont, c'était/étaient** etc:

ouvrez, c'est moi !	**non, ce n'était pas lui**
open up, it's me!	no, it wasn't him

iii) After a preposition:

vous allez chez lui ?	**tu y vas avec elle ?**
are you going to his place?	are you going with her?
regarde devant toi !	**oh, c'est pour moi ?**
look in front of you!	oh, is that for me?

iv) Verb constructions: special care should be taken with verbs followed by a preposition:

tu peux compter sur moi	**quoi ! tu as peur de lui ?**
you can count on me	what! you're afraid of him?
il m'a parlé de toi	**je pense souvent à vous**
he told me about you	I often think about you

Note: Emphatic pronouns are only used when referring to persons. Otherwise, use **y** or **en**.

v) For emphasis, particularly when two pronouns are contrasted. The unstressed subject pronoun is usually included:

vous, vous m'énervez !	**lui, il joue bien ; elle, non**
you get on my nerves!	*he* plays well; *she* doesn't
moi, je n'aime pas l'hiver	**eux, ils sont partis**
I don't like winter	*they*'ve left

vi) In the case of multiple subjects (two pronouns or one pronoun and one noun):

lui et son frère sont dans l'équipe
he and his brother are in the team

ma famille et moi allons très bien
my family and I are very well

vii) As the second term of comparisons:

il est plus sympa que toi	**elle chante mieux que lui**
he is nicer than you	she sings better than he does

viii) Before a relative pronoun:

c'est lui que j'aime	**c'est toi qui l'as dit**
he's the one I love	you're the one who said it

lui qui n'aime pas le vin blanc en a bu six verres
he, who doesn't like white wine, had six glasses

ix) With **-même(s)** (-self, -selves), **aussi** (too), **seul** (alone):

faites-le vous-mêmes	**j'irai moi-même**
do it yourselves	I'll go myself
lui aussi est parti	**elle seule le sait**
he too went away	she alone knows

x) To replace a possessive pronoun (see p C20):

c'est *le mien* ; il est à moi
it's mine; it belongs to me

E. POSSESSIVE ADJECTIVES AND PRONOUNS

1. Possessive adjectives

a) *Forms*

Possessive adjectives always come before a noun. Like other adjectives, they agree in gender and number with the noun; the masculine and feminine plural are identical:

SINGULAR MASC	FEM	PLURAL	
mon	**ma**	**mes**	my
ton	**ta**	**tes**	your
son	**sa**	**ses**	his/her its/one's
notre	**notre**	**nos**	our
votre	**votre**	**vos**	your
leur	**leur**	**leurs**	their

j'ai mis mon argent et mes affaires dans mon sac
I've put my money and my things in my bag

comment va ton frère ? et ta sœur ? et tes parents ?
how's your brother? and your sister? and your parents?

notre rue est assez calme	**ce sont vos amis**
our street is fairly quiet	they're your friends

Note: **mon/ton/son** are used instead of **ma/ta/sa** when the next word starts with a vowel or silent **h**:

mon ancienne maison	**ton amie Christine**
my old house	your friend Christine

son haleine sentait l'alcool
his breath smelled of alcohol

b) *Use*

i) The possessive adjective is repeated before each noun and agrees with it:

mon père et ma mère sont sortis
my mother and father have gone out

ii) **son/sa/ses**

son, sa and **ses** can all mean 'his', 'her' or 'its'. In French, the form of the adjective is determined by the gender and number of the noun that follows, and not by the possessor:

il m'a prêté sa mobylette et son casque
he lent me his moped and his helmet

elle s'entend bien avec sa mère, mais pas avec son père
she gets on well with her mother, but not with her father

il cire ses chaussures ; elle repasse ses chemisiers
he's polishing his shoes; she's ironing her shirts

iii) **ton/ta/tes** and **votre/vos**

The two sets of words for 'your', **ton/ta/tes** and **votre/vos**, correspond to the two different forms **tu** and **vous**; they must not be used together with the same person:

Papa, tu as parlé à ton patron ?
have you spoken to your boss, Dad?

Monsieur ! votre brochure ! vous ne la prenez pas ?
Sir! your brochure! aren't you taking it?

iv) In French, the possessive adjective is replaced by the definite article (**le/la/les**) with the following:

★ parts of the body:

il s'est essuyé les mains	**elle a haussé les épaules**
he wiped his hands	she shrugged (her shoulders)

★ descriptive phrases tagged on to the end of a clause, where English adds 'with':

il marchait lentement, les mains dans les poches
he was walking slowly, with his hands in his pockets

elle l'a regardé partir les larmes aux yeux
she watched him leave with tears in her eyes

2. Possessive pronouns

MASC	FEM	PLURAL (MASC AND FEM)	
le mien	**la mienne**	**les mien(ne)s**	mine
le tien	**la tienne**	**les tien(ne)s**	yours
le sien	**la sienne**	**les sien(ne)s**	his/hers/its
le nôtre	**la nôtre**	**les nôtres**	ours
le vôtre	**la vôtre**	**les vôtres**	yours
le leur	**la leur**	**les leurs**	theirs

Possessive pronouns are used intead of a possessive adjective + noun. They agree in gender and in number with the noun they stand for, and not with the possessor (it is particularly important to remember this when translating 'his' and 'hers'):

j'aime bien ton chapeau, mais je préfère le mien
I quite like your hat, but I prefer mine

on prend quelle voiture ? la mienne ou la tienne ?
which car shall we take? mine or yours?

comment sont vos profs ? les nôtres sont sympas
what are your teachers like? ours are nice

j'ai pris mon passeport, mais Brigitte a oublié le sien
I brought my passport, but Brigitte forgot hers

j'ai gardé ma moto, mais Paul a vendu la sienne
I've kept my motorbike but Paul has sold his

à or **de** + possessive pronoun

The prepositions **à** or **de** combine with the articles **le** and **les** in the usual way:

à + le mien	→	**au mien**
à + les miens	→	**aux miens**
à + les miennes	→	**aux miennes**
de + le mien	→	**du mien**
de + les miens	→	**des miens**
de + les miennes	→	**des miennes**

demande à tes parents, j'ai déjà parlé aux miens
ask your parents, I've already spoken to mine

leur appartement ressemble beaucoup au nôtre
their flat is very similar to ours

j'aime bien les chiens, mais j'ai peur du tien
I like dogs, but I'm afraid of yours

Note: after the verb **être**, the possessive pronoun is often replaced by **à** + emphatic (disjunctive) pronoun (see p C19):

à qui est cette écharpe ? – elle est à moi
whose scarf is this? – it's mine

ce livre est à toi ? – non, il est à elle
is this book yours? – no, it's hers

c'est à qui ? à vous ou à lui ?
whose is this? yours or his?

F. RELATIVE PRONOUNS

1. Definition

Relative pronouns are words which introduce a relative clause. In the following sentence:

I bought the book which you recommended

'which' is the relative pronoun, 'which you recommended' is the relative clause and 'the book' is the antecedent (ie the noun the relative pronoun refers to).

2. Forms

Relative pronouns are:

qui	who, which	**lequel**	which
que	who(m), which	**dont**	of which, whose
quoi	what	**ce qui**	what
où	where	**ce que**	what

qui, **que**, **quoi**, **lequel**, **ce qui** and **ce que** can also be used as interrogative pronouns (see p C16) and must not be confused with them.

3. Use

a) ***QUI***

qui is used as the subject of a relative clause; it means:

i) 'who', 'that' (referring to people):

connaissez-vous le monsieur qui habite ici ?
do you know the man who lives here?

ce n'est pas lui qui a menti
he's not the one who lied

ii) 'which', 'that' (referring to things):

tu as pris le journal qui était sur la télé ?
did you take the paper which/that was on the telly?

b) ***QUE***

que (written **qu'** before a vowel or a silent **h**) is used as the object of a relative clause; it is often not translated and means:

i) 'who(m)', 'that' (referring to people):

la fille que j'aime ne m'aime pas
the girl (that) I love doesn't love me

ii) 'which', 'that' (referring to things):

j'ai perdu le briquet qu'il m'a offert
I've lost the lighter (which/that) he gave me

c) ***qui or que?***

qui (subject) and **que** (object) are translated by the same words in English (who, which, that). To use the correct pronoun in French, it is essential to know whether a relative pronoun is the object or the subject of the relative clause:

i) when the verb of the relative clause has its own subject, the object pronoun **que** must be used:

c'est un passe-temps que *j*'adore
it's a pastime (that) *I* love (*the subject of 'adore' is 'je'*)

ii) otherwise the relative pronoun is the subject of the verb in the relative clause and the subject pronoun **qui** must be used:

j'ai trouvé un manteau qui me plaît
I found a coat that I like (*the subject of 'plaît' is 'qui'*)

d) ***LEQUEL***

i) forms

lequel (which) has four different forms, as it must agree with the noun it refers to:

	SINGULAR	PLURAL	
MASCULINE	**lequel**	**lesquels**	which
FEMININE	**laquelle**	**lesquelles**	

lequel etc combines with the prepositions **à** and **de** as follows:

à + lequel	→	**auquel**
à + lesquels	→	**auxquels**
à + lesquelles	→	**auxquelles**

de + lequel → **duquel**
de + lesquels → **desquels**
de + lesquelles → **desquelles**

à + laquelle and **de** + laquelle do not change.

quels sont les sports auxquels tu t'intéresses ?
what are the sports (which) you are interested *in*?

voilà le village près duquel on campait
here's the village near which we camped

ii) **qui** or **lequel** with a preposition?

When a relative pronoun follows a preposition, the pronoun used is either **qui** or **lequel**. In English, the relative pronoun is seldom used and the preposition is frequently placed after the verb or at the end of the sentence.

qui is generally used after a preposition when referring to people:

où est la fille *avec* qui je dansais ?
where's the girl I was dancing *with*?

montre-moi la personne *à* qui tu as vendu ton vélo
show me the person you sold your bike *to*

lequel is often used after a preposition when referring to things:

l'immeuble *dans* lequel j'habite est très moderne
the building (which) I live *in* is very modern

je ne reconnais pas la voiture *avec* laquelle il est venu
I don't recognize the car (which) he came *in*

lequel is also used when referring to persons after the prepositions **entre** (between) and **parmi** (among):

des touristes, parmi lesquels il y avait des Japonais
tourists, among whom were (some) Japanese people

il aimait deux filles, entre lesquelles il hésitait
he loved two girls, between whom he was torn

e) ***DONT***

dont (of which, of whom, whose) is frequently used instead of **de qui**, **duquel** etc. It means:

i) *of which, of whom:*

un métier dont il est fier
a job (which) he is proud of

Care must be taken with verbs that are normally followed by **de** + object: **de** is not always translated by 'of' in English, and is sometimes not translated at all (see section on verb constructions p C50):

voilà les choses *dont* j'ai besoin
here are the things (*which*) I need

les gens *dont* tu parles ne m'intéressent pas
I'm not interested in the people you're talking about

l'enfant *dont* elle s'occupe n'est pas le sien
the child she is looking *after* is not hers

ii) *whose*

dont is also used to translate the English pronoun 'whose'. In French, the construction of the clause that follows **dont** differs from English in two ways:

★ the noun which follows **dont** is used with the definite article (**le, la, les, l'**):

mon copain, dont *le* père a eu un accident
my friend, whose father had an accident

★ the word order in French is **dont** + subject + verb + object:

je te présente Hélène, dont tu connais déjà le frère
this is Helen, whose brother you already know

c'était dans une petite rue dont j'ai oublié le nom
it was in a small street the name of which I've forgotten

Note: **dont** cannot be used after a preposition:

une jolie maison, *près* de laquelle il y a un petit lac
a pretty house, *next* to which there is a small lake

f) ***OU***

i) **où** generally means 'where':

l'hôtel où on a logé était très confortable
the hotel where we stayed was very comfortable

ii) **où** often replaces a preposition + **lequel**, meaning 'in/to/on/at which' etc:

c'est la maison où je suis né
that's the house in which/where I was born

une surprise-partie où il a invité tous ses amis
a party to which he invited all his friends

iii) **où** is also used to translate 'when' after a noun referring to time:

le jour où	**la fois où**	**le moment où**
the day when	the time when	the moment when

tu te rappelles le soir où on a raté le dernier métro ?
do you remember the evening when we missed the last train?

g) ***CE QUI, CE QUE***

ce is used before **qui** and **que** when the relative pronoun does not refer to a specific noun. Both **ce qui** and **ce que** mean 'that which', 'the thing which', and are usually translated by 'what':

i) **ce qui**

ce qui is followed by a verb without a subject (**qui** is the subject):

ce qui s'est passé ne vous regarde pas
what happened is none of your business

ce qui m'étonne, c'est sa patience
what surprises me is his patience

Note the comma and the **c'**

ii) ***ce que***

ce que (**ce qu'** before a vowel or a silent **h**) is followed by a verb with its own subject (**que** is the object):

fais ce que tu veux
do what you want

c'est ce qu'il a dit?
is that what he said?

ce que vous me demandez est impossible
what you're asking me is impossible

iii) **tout ce qui/que**

tout is used in front of **ce qui/que** in the sense of 'all that', 'everything that':

c'est tout ce que je veux
that's all I want

tout ce que tu as fait
everything you did

tu n'as pas eu de mal ; c'est tout ce qui compte
you weren't hurt; that's all that matters

iv) **ce qui/que** are often used in indirect questions (see p C16):

je ne sais pas ce qu'ils vont dire
I don't know what they'll say

v) when referring to a previous clause, **ce qui** and **ce que** are translated by 'which':

elle est en retard, ce qui arrive souvent
she's late, which happens often

vi) **ce que**/**qui** are used with a preposition (when the preposition refers to **ce**):

ce n'est pas étonnant, après ce qui lui est arrivé
it's not surprising, after what happened to him

il y a du vrai dans ce que vous dites
there is some truth in what you say

But: **QUOI** is used instead of **ce que** after a preposition when the preposition refers to **que**, and not to **ce**:

c'est ce à quoi je pensais
that's what I was thinking about

vii) **ce que** is used with the preposition **de** when **de** refers to **ce**:

je suis fier de ce qu'il a fait
I'm proud of what he did

But: **ce dont** is used instead of **de** + ce que when **de** refers to **que**, and not to **ce**:

c'est ce dont j'avais peur
that's what I was afraid of

tu as trouvé ce dont tu avais besoin ?
did you find what you needed?

7. VERBS

A. REGULAR CONJUGATIONS

1. Conjugations

There are three main conjugations in French, which are determined by the infinitive endings. The first conjugation verbs, by far the largest category, end in **-er** (eg aim**er**) and will be referred to as **-er** verbs; the second conjugation verbs end in **-ir** (eg fin**ir**) and will be referred to as **-ir** verbs; the third conjugation verbs, the smallest category, end in **-re** (eg vend**re**) and will be referred to as **-re** verbs.

2. Simple tenses

The simple tenses in French are:

a) present
b) imperfect
c) future
d) conditional
e) past historic
f) present subjunctive
e) imperfect subjunctive

For the use of the different tenses, see pp C28-32.

3. Formation of tenses

The tenses are formed by adding the following endings to the stem of the verb (mainly the stem of the infinitive) as set out in the following section:

a) *PRESENT:* stem of the infinitive + the following endings:

-er VERBS	**-ir** VERBS	**-re** VERBS
-e, -es, -e, -ons, -ez, -ent	**-is, -is, -it, -issons, -issez, -issent**	**-s, -s, -, -ons, -ez, -ent**
AIMER	FINIR	VENDRE
j'aim**e**	je fin**is**	je vend**s**
tu aim**es**	tu fin**is**	tu vend**s**
il aim**e**	il fin**it**	il vend
elle aim**e**	elle fin**it**	elle vend
nous aim**ons**	nous fin**issons**	nous vend**ons**
vous aim**ez**	vous fin**issez**	vous vend**ez**
ils aim**ent**	ils fin**issent**	ils vend**ent**
elles aim**ent**	elles fin**issent**	elles vend**ent**

b) *IMPERFECT:* stem of the first person plural of the present tense (ie the '**nous**' form minus **-ons**) + the following endings: **-ais, -ais, -ait, -ions, -iez, -aient**

j'aim**ais**	je finiss**ais**	je vend**ais**
tu aim**ais**	tu finiss**ais**	tu vend**ais**
il aim**ait**	il finiss**ait**	il vend**ait**
elle aim**ait**	elle finiss**ait**	elle vend**ait**
nous aim**ions**	nous finiss**ions**	nous vend**ions**
vous aim**iez**	vous finiss**iez**	vous vend**iez**
ils aim**aient**	ils finiss**aient**	ils vend**aient**
elles aim**aient**	elles finiss**aient**	elles vend**aient**

Note: the only irregular imperfect is **être: j'étais** etc.

c) *FUTURE:* infinitive + the following endings:

-ai, -as, -a, -ons, -ez, -ont

Note: Verbs ending in **-re** drop the final **e** of the infinitive

j'aimer**ai**	je finir**ai**	je vendr**ai**
tu aimer**as**	tu finir**as**	tu vendr**as**
il aimer**a**	il finir**a**	il vendr**a**
elle aimer**a**	elle finir**a**	elle vendr**a**
nous aimer**ons**	nous finir**ons**	nous vendr**ons**
vous aimer**ez**	vous finir**ez**	vous vendr**ez**
ils aimer**ont**	ils finir**ont**	ils vendr**ont**
elles aimer**ont**	elles finir**ont**	elles vendr**ont**

d) *CONDITIONAL:* infinitive + the following endings:

-ais, -ais, -ait, -ions, -iez, -aient

Note: Verbs ending in **-re** drop the final **e** of the infinitive

j'aimer**ais**	je finir**ais**	je vendr**ais**
tu aimer**ais**	tu finir**ais**	tu vendr**ais**
il aimer**ait**	il finir**ait**	il vendr**ait**
elle aimer**ait**	elle finir**ait**	elle vendr**ait**
nous aimer**ions**	nous finir**ions**	nous vendr**ions**
vous aimer**iez**	vous finir**iez**	vous vendr**iez**
ils aimer**aient**	ils finir**aient**	ils vendr**aient**
elles aimer**aient**	elles finir**aient**	elles vendr**aient**

e) *PAST HISTORIC:* stem of the infinitive + the following endings:

-er VERBS	**-ir** VERBS	**-re** VERBS
-ai, -as, -a, -âmes, -âtes, -èrent	**-is, -is, -it, -îmes, -îtes, -irent**	**-is, -is, -it, -îmes, -îtes, -irent**
j'aim**ai**	je fin**is**	je vend**is**
tu aim**as**	tu fin**is**	tu vend**is**
il aim**a**	il fin**it**	il vend**it**
elle aim**a**	elle fin**it**	elle vend**it**
nous aim**âmes**	nous fin**îmes**	nous vend**îmes**
vous aim**âtes**	vous fin**îtes**	vous vend**îtes**
ils aim**èrent**	ils fin**irent**	ils vend**irent**
elles aim**èrent**	elles fin**irent**	elles vend**irent**

f) *PRESENT SUBJUNCTIVE:* stem of the first person plural of the present indicative + the following endings:

-e, -es, -e, -ions, -iez, -ent

j'aim**e**	je finiss**e**	je vend**e**
tu aim**es**	tu finiss**es**	tu vend**es**
il aim**e**	il finiss**e**	il vend**e**
elle aim**e**	elle finiss**e**	elle vend**e**
nous aim**ions**	nous finiss**ions**	nous vend**ions**
vous aim**iez**	vous finiss**iez**	vous vend**iez**
ils aim**ent**	ils finiss**ent**	ils vend**ent**
elles aim**ent**	elles finiss**ent**	elles vend**ent**

g) *IMPERFECT SUBJUNCTIVE:* stem of the first person singular of the past historic + the following endings:

-er VERBS	**-ir** VERBS	**-re** VERBS
-asse, -asses, -ât, -assions, -assiez, -assent	**-isse, -isses, -ît, -issions, -issiez, -issent**	**-isse, -isses, -ît, -issions, -issiez, -issent**
j'aim**asse**	je fin**isse**	je vend**isse**
tu aim**asses**	tu fin**isses**	tu vend**isses**
il aim**ât**	il fin**ît**	il vend**ît**
elle aim**ât**	elle fin**ît**	elle vend**ît**
nous aim**assions**	nous fin**issions**	nous vend**issions**
vous aim**assiez**	vous fin**issiez**	vous vend**issiez**
ils aim**assent**	ils fin**issent**	ils vend**issent**
elles aim**assent**	elles fin**issent**	elles vend**issent**

B. STANDARD SPELLING IRREGULARITIES

Spelling irregularities only affect **-er** verbs.

1. Verbs ending in *-cer* and *-ger*

a) Verbs ending in **-cer** require a cedilla under the **c** (**ç**) before an **a** or an **o** to preserve the soft sound of the **c**: eg **commencer** (to begin).

b) Verbs ending in **-ger** require an **-e** after the **g** before an **a** or an **o** to preserve the soft sound of the **g**: eg **manger** (to eat).

Changes to **-cer** and **-ger** verbs occur in the following tenses: present, imperfect, past historic, imperfect subjunctive and present participle.

COMMENCER	MANGER
PRESENT	
je commence	je mange
tu commences	tu manges
il commence	il mange
elle commence	elle mange
nous **commençons**	nous **mangeons**
vous commencez	vous mangez
ils commencent	ils mangent
elles commencent	elles mangent
IMPERFECT	
je **commençais**	je **mangeais**
tu **commençais**	tu **mangeais**
il **commençait**	il **mangeait**
elle **commençait**	elle **mangeait**
nous commencions	nous mangions
vous commenciez	vous mangiez
ils **commençaient**	ils **mangeaient**
elles **commençaient**	elles **mangeaient**
PAST HISTORIC	
je **commençai**	je **mangeai**
tu **commenças**	tu **mangeas**
il **commença**	il **mangea**
elle **commença**	elle **mangea**
nous **commençâmes**	nous **mangeâmes**
vous **commençâtes**	vous **mangeâtes**
ils commencèrent	ils mangèrent
elles commencèrent	elles mangèrent
IMPERFECT SUBJUNCTIVE	
je **commençasse**	je **mangeasse**
tu **commençasses**	tu **mangeasses**
il **commençât**	il **mangeât**
elle **commençât**	elle **mangeât**
nous **commençassions**	nous **mangeassions**
vous **commençassiez**	vous **mangeassiez**
ils **commençassent**	ils **mangeassent**
elles **commençassent**	elles **mangeassent**
PRESENT PARTICIPLE	
commençant	**mangeant**

2. Verbs ending in *-eler* and *-eter*

a) Verbs ending in **-eler**

Verbs ending in **-eler** double the **l** before a silent **e** (ie before **-e**, **-es**, **-ent** of the present indicative and subjunctive, and throughout the future and conditional): eg **appeler** (to call).

PRESENT INDICATIVE	*PRESENT SUBJUNCTIVE*
j'**appelle**	j'**appelle**
tu **appelles**	tu **appelles**
il **appelle**	il **appelle**
elle **appelle**	elle **appelle**
nous appelons	nous appelions
vous appelez	vous appeliez
ils **appellent**	ils **appellent**
elles **appellent**	elles **appellent**
FUTURE	*CONDITIONAL*
j'**appellerai**	j'**appellerais**
tu **appelleras**	tu **appellerais**
il **appellera**	il **appellerait**
elle **appellera**	elle **appellerait**
nous **appellerons**	nous **appellerions**
vous **appellerez**	vous **appelleriez**
ils **appelleront**	ils **appelleraient**
elles **appelleront**	elles **appelleraient**

But: some verbs in **-eler** including the following are conjugated like **acheter** (see p C24):

celer	to conceal
congeler	to (deep-)freeze
déceler	to detect, reveal
dégeler	to defrost
geler	to freeze

harceler	to harass
marteler	to hammer
modeler	to model
peler	to peel

b) Verbs ending in **-eter**

Verbs ending in **-eter** double the **t** before a silent **e** (ie before **-e**, **-es**, **-ent** of the present indicative and subjunctive, and throughout the future and conditional): eg **jeter** (to throw).

PRESENT INDICATIVE	*PRESENT SUBJUNCTIVE*
je **jette**	je **jette**
tu **jettes**	tu **jettes**
il **jette**	il **jette**
elle **jette**	elle **jette**
nous jetons	nous jetions
vous jetez	vous jetiez
ils **jettent**	ils **jettent**
elles **jettent**	elles **jettent**
FUTURE	*CONDITIONAL*
je **jetterai**	je **jetterais**
tu **jetteras**	tu **jetterais**
il **jettera**	il **jetterait**
elle **jettera**	elle **jetterait**
nous **jetterons**	nous **jetterions**
vous **jetterez**	vous **jetteriez**
ils **jetteront**	ils **jetteraient**
elles **jetteront**	elles **jetteraient**

But: some verbs in **-eter** including the following are conjugated like **acheter** (see section **e**):

crocheter	to pick (*lock*)
fureter	to ferret about
haleter	to pant
racheter	to buy back

c) Verbs ending in **-oyer** and **-uyer**

In verbs ending in **-oyer** and **-uyer** the **y** changes to **i** before a silent **e** (ie before **-e**, **-es**, **-ent** of the present indicative and subjunctive, and throughout the future and conditional): eg **employer** (to use) and **ennuyer** (to bore).

PRESENT INDICATIVE	*PRESENT SUBJUNCTIVE*
j'**emploie**	j'**emploie**
tu **emploies**	tu **emploies**
il **emploie**	il **emploie**
elle **emploie**	elle **emploie**
nous employons	nous employions
vous employez	vous employiez
ils **emploient**	ils **emploient**
elles **emploient**	elles **emploient**
FUTURE	*CONDITIONAL*
j'**emploierai**	j'**emploierais**
tu **emploieras**	tu **emploierais**
il **emploiera**	il **emploierait**
elle **emploiera**	elle **emploierait**
nous **emploierons**	nous **emploierions**
vous **emploierez**	vous **emploieriez**
ils **emploieront**	ils **emploieraient**
elles **emploieront**	elles **emploieraient**

Note: **envoyer** (to send) and **renvoyer** (to dismiss) have an irregular future and conditional: **j'enverrai**, **j'enverrais**; **je renverrai**, **je renverrais**.

d) Verbs ending in **-ayer**

In verbs ending in **-ayer**, eg **balayer** (to sweep), **payer** (to pay), **essayer** (to try), the change from **y** to **i** is optional:

eg je **balaie**	*or*	je **balaye**
je **paie**	*or*	je **paye**
j'**essaie**	*or*	j'**essaye**

e) Verbs in **e** + consonant + **er**

Verbs like **acheter**, **enlever**, **mener**, **peser** change the (last) **e** of the stem to **è** before a silent **e** (ie before **-e**, **-es**, **-ent** of the present indicative and subjunctive and throughout the future and conditional):

PRESENT INDICATIVE	*PRESENT SUBJUNCTIVE*
j'**achète**	j'**achète**
tu **achètes**	tu **achètes**
il **achète**	il **achète**
elle **achète**	elle **achète**
nous achetons	nous achetions
vous achetez	vous achetiez
ils **achètent**	ils **achètent**
elles **achètent**	elles **achètent**
FUTURE	*CONDITIONAL*
j'**achèterai**	j'**achèterais**
tu **achèteras**	tu **achèterais**
il **achètera**	il **achèterait**
elle **achètera**	elle **achèterait**
nous **achèterons**	nous **achèterions**
vous **achèterez**	vous **achèteriez**
ils **achèteront**	ils **achèteraient**
elles **achèteront**	elles **achèteraient**

Verbs conjugated like **acheter** include:

achever to complete	**haleter** to pant
amener to bring	**harceler** to harass
celer to conceal	**lever** to lift
crever to burst	**marteler** to hammer
crocheter to pick (*lock*)	**mener** to lead
élever to raise	**modeler** to model
emmener to take away	**peler** to peel
enlever to remove	**peser** to weigh
étiqueter to label	**se promener** to go for a walk
fureter to ferret about	**semer** to sow
geler to freeze	**soulever** to lift

f) Verbs in **é** + consonant + **er**

Verbs like **espérer** (to hope) change **é** to **è** before a silent **e** in the present indicative and subjunctive. BUT in the future and conditional **é** is retained.

PRESENT INDICATIVE	*PRESENT SUBJUNCTIVE*
j'**espère**	j'**espère**
tu **espères**	tu **espères**
il **espère**	il **espère**
elle **espère**	elle **espère**
nous espérons	nous espérions
vous espérez	vous espériez
ils **espèrent**	ils **espèrent**
elles **espèrent**	elles **espèrent**
FUTURE	*CONDITIONAL*
j'**espérerai**	j'**espérerais**
tu **espéreras**	tu **espérerais**
il **espérera**	il **espérerait**
elle **espérera**	elle **espérerait**
nous **espérerons**	nous **espérerions**
vous **espérerez**	vous **espéreriez**
ils **espéreront**	ils **espéreraient**
elles **espéreront**	elles **espéreraient**

Verbs conjugated like **espérer** include verbs in **-éder**, **-érer**, **-éter** etc:

accéder	to accede to
céder	to yield
célébrer	to celebrate
compléter	to complete
considérer	to consider
décéder	to die
digérer	to digest
gérer	to manage
inquiéter	to worry
libérer	to free
opérer	to operate
pénétrer	to penetrate
persévérer	to persevere
posséder	to possess
précéder	to precede
préférer	to prefer
protéger	to protect
récupérer	to recover
refréner	to curb

régler	to rule
régner	to reign
répéter	to repeat, to rehearse
révéler	to reveal
sécher	to dry
succéder	to succeed
suggérer	to suggest
tolérer	to tolerate

C. AUXILIARIES AND THE FORMATION OF COMPOUND TENSES

1. Formation

a) The two auxiliary verbs **AVOIR** and **ETRE** are used with the past participle of a verb to form compound tenses.

b) *The past participle*

The regular past participle is formed by taking the stem of the infinitive and adding the following endings:

-er	**-ir**	**-re**
aim(**er**) + **é**	fin(**ir**) + **i**	vend(**re**) + **u**
aimé	fini	vendu

For the agreement of past participles see pp C35-6.

c) *Compound tenses*

In French there are seven compound tenses: perfect, pluperfect, future perfect, past conditional (conditional perfect), past anterior, perfect subjunctive, pluperfect subjunctive.

2. Verbs conjugated with AVOIR

a) *PERFECT*	b) *PLUPERFECT*
present of **avoir** + past participle	imperfect of **avoir** + past participle
j'ai aimé	**j'avais aimé**
tu as aimé	**tu avais aimé**
il a aimé	**il avait aimé**
elle a aimé	**elle avait aimé**
nous avons aimé	**nous avions aimé**
vous avez aimé	**vous aviez aimé**
ils ont aimé	**ils avaient aimé**
elles ont aimé	**elles avaient aimé**

c) *FUTURE PERFECT*	d) *PAST CONDITIONAL*
future of **avoir** + past participle	conditional of **avoir** + past participle
j'aurai aimé	**j' aurais aimé**
tu auras aimé	**tu aurais aimé**
il aura aimé	**il aurait aimé**
elle aura aimé	**elle aurait aimé**
nous aurons aimé	**nous aurions aimé**
vous aurez aimé	**vous auriez aimé**
ils auront aimé	**ils auraient aimé**
elles auront aimé	**elles auraient aimé**

e) *PAST ANTERIOR*

past historic of **avoir** + past participle

j'eus aimé
tu eus aimé
il eut aimé
elle eut aimé
nous eûmes aimé
vous eûtes aimé
ils eurent aimé
elles eurent aimé

f) *PERFECT SUBJUNCTIVE*	g) *PLUPERFECT SUBJUNCTIVE*
present subjunctive of **avoir** + past participle	present pluperfect of **avoir** + past participle
j'aie aimé	**j'eusse aimé**
tu aies aimé	**tu eusses aimé**
il ait aimé	**il eût aimé**
elle ait aimé	**elle eût aimé**
nous ayons aimé	**nous eussions aimé**
vous ayez aimé	**vous eussiez aimé**
ils aient aimé	**ils eussent aimé**
elles aient aimé	**elles eussent aimé**

3. Verbs conjugated with *ETRE*

a) *PERFECT*	b) *PLUPERFECT*
present of **être** + past participle	imperfect of **être** + past participle
je suis arrivé(e)	**j'étais arrivé(e)**
tu es arrivé(e)	**tu étais arrivé(e)**
il est arrivé	**il était arrivé**
elle est arrivée	**elle était arrivée**
nous sommes arrivé(e)s	**nous étions arrivé(e)s**
vous êtes arrivé(e)(s)	**vous étiez arrivé(e)(s)**
ils sont arrivés	**ils étaient arrivés**
elles sont arrivées	**elles étaient arrivées**

c) *FUTURE PERFECT CONDITIONAL*	d) *PAST*
future of **être** + past participle	conditional of **être** + past participle
je serai arrivé(e)	**je serais arrivé(e)**
tu seras arrivé(e)	**tu serais arrivé(e)**
il sera arrivé	**il serait arrivé**
elle sera arrivée	**elle serait arrivée**
nous serons arrivé(e)s	**nous serions arrivé(e)s**
vous serez arrivé(e)(s)	**vous seriez arrivé(e)(s)**
ils seront arrivés	**ils seraient arrivés**
elles seront arrivées	**elles seraient arrivées**

e) *PAST ANTERIOR*

past historic of **être** + past participle

je fus arrivé(e)
tu fus arrivé(e)
il fut arrivé
elle fut arrivée
nous fûmes arrivé(e)s
vous fûtes arrivé(e)(s)
ils furent arrivés
elles furent arrivées

f) *PERFECT SUBJUNCTIVE*	g) *PLUPERFECT SUBJUNCTIVE*
present subjunctive of **être** + past participle	imperfect subjunctive of **être** + past participle
je sois arrivé(e)	**je fusse arrivé(e)**
tu sois arrivé(e)	**tu fusses arrivé(e)**
il soit arrivé	**il fût arrivé**
elle soit arrivée	**elle fût arrivée**
nous soyons arrivé(e)s	**nous fussions arrivé(e)s**
vous soyez arrivé(e)(s)	**vous fussiez arrivé(e)(s)**
ils soient arrivés	**ils fussent arrivés**
elles soient arrivées	**elles fussent arrivées**

4. AVOIR or ETRE?

a) *Verbs conjugated with* ***avoir***

The compound tenses of most verbs are formed with **avoir.**

j'ai marqué un but	**elle a dansé toute la nuit**
I scored a goal	she danced all night

b) *Verbs conjugated with* ***être***

i) all reflexive verbs (see p C26):

je me suis baigné
I had a bath

ii) the following verbs (mainly of motion):

aller	to go
arriver	to arrive
descendre	to go/come down
entrer	to go/come in
monter	to go/come up
mourir	to die

naître	to be born
partir	to leave
passer	to go through, to drop in
rester	to remain
retourner	to return
sortir	to go/come out
tomber	to fall
venir	to come

and most of their compounds:

revenir	to come back
devenir	to become
parvenir	to reach, to manage to
rentrer	to return home
remonter	to go up again
redescendre	to go down again

But: **prévenir** (to warn) and **subvenir** (to provide for) take a direct object and are conjugated with **avoir**.

Note: **passer** can also be conjugated with **avoir**:

il a passé par Paris
he went via Paris

Some of the verbs listed above can take a direct object. In such cases they are conjugated with **avoir** and can take on a different meaning:

descendre	to take/bring down, to go down (*the stairs, a slope*)
monter	to take/bring up, to go up (*the stairs, a slope*)
rentrer	to take/bring/put in
retourner	to turn over
sortir	to take/bring out

les élèves sont sortis à midi	**les élèves ont sorti leurs livres**
the pupils came out at midday	the pupils took out their books

elle n'est pas encore descendue
she hasn't come down yet

elle a descendu un vieux tableau de l'atelier
she brought an old painting down from the loft

elle a descendu l'escalier
she came down the stairs

les prisonniers sont montés sur le toit
the prisoners climbed on to the roof

le garçon a monté les bouteilles de vin de la cave
the waiter brought the bottles of wine up from the cellar

nous sommes rentrés tard	**j'ai rentré la voiture dans le garage**
we returned home late	I put the car in the garage
je serais retourné à Paris	**le jardinier a retourné le sol**
I would have returned to Paris	the gardener turned over the soil

ils sont sortis de la piscine
they got out of the swimming pool

le gangster a sorti un revolver
the gangster pulled out a revolver

D. REFLEXIVE VERBS

1. Definition

Reflexive verbs are so called because they 'reflect' the action back onto the subject. Reflexive verbs are always accompanied by a reflexive pronoun; eg in the following sentence:

I looked at myself in the mirror

'myself' is the reflexive pronoun.

je lave la voiture	**je *me* lave**
I'm washing the car	I'm washing *myself*
j'ai couché le bébé	**je *me* suis couché**
I put the baby to bed	I went to bed (I put *myself* to bed)

2. Reflexive pronouns

They are:

PERSON	SINGULAR	PLURAL
1st	**me (m')** myself	**nous** ourselves
2nd	**te (t')** yourself	**vous** yourself/selves
3rd	**se (s')** himself, herself, itself, oneself	**se (s')** themselves

Note:

a) **m', t'** and **s'** are used instead of **me, te** and **se** in front of a vowel or a silent **h**:

tu t'amuses ? – non, je m'ennuie
are you enjoying yourself? – no, I'm bored

il s'habille à la salle de bain
he gets dressed in the bathroom

b) French reflexive pronouns are often not translated in English:

je me demande si ...	**ils se moquent de moi**
I wonder if ...	they're making fun of me

c) Plural reflexive pronouns can also be used to express reciprocal actions; in this case they are translated by 'each other' or 'one another':

nous nous détestons	**ils ne se parlent pas**
we hate one another	they're not talking to each other

d) **se** can mean 'ourselves' or 'each other' when it is used with the pronoun **on** meaning 'we' (see p C15):

on s'est perdu	**on se connaît**
we got lost	we know each other

3. Position of reflexive pronouns

Reflexive pronouns are placed immediately before the verb, except in positive commands, where they follow the verb and are linked to it by a hyphen:

tu te dépêches ?	**dépêchons-nous !**
will you hurry up?	let's hurry!
ne t'inquiète pas	**ne vous fiez pas à lui**
don't worry	don't trust him

Note: reflexive pronouns change to emphatic (disjunctive) pronouns in positive commands:

elle doit se reposer	**repose-toi**
she needs to rest	have a rest

4. Conjugation of reflexive verbs

a) *Simple tenses*

These are formed in the same way as for non-reflexive verbs, except that a reflexive pronoun is used.

b) *Compound tenses*

These are formed with the auxiliary **être** followed by the past participle of the verb.

A full conjugation table is given on p C44.

5. Agreement of the past participle

a) In most cases, the reflexive pronoun is a direct object and the past participle of the verb agrees in number and in gender with the reflexive pronoun:

il s'est trompé	**elle s'est endormie**
he made a mistake	she fell asleep
ils se sont excusés	**elles se sont assises**
they apologised	they sat down

b) When the reflexive pronoun is used as an indirect object, the past participle does not change:

nous nous sommes écrit	**elle se l'est achetée**
we wrote to each other	she bought it for herself

When the reflexive verb has a direct object, the reflexive pronoun is the indirect object of the reflexive verb and the past participle does not agree with it:

Caroline s'est tordu la cheville
Caroline sprained her ankle

vous vous êtes lavé les mains, les filles ?
did you wash your hands, girls?

6. Common reflexive verbs

s'en aller to go away	**s'éloigner (de)** to move away (from)	**se moquer de** to laugh at
s'amuser to have fun	**s'endormir** to fall asleep	**s'occuper de** to take care of
s'appeler to be called	**s'ennuyer** to be bored	**se passer** to happen
s'approcher (de) to come near	**s'étonner (de)** to be surprised (at)	**se passer de** to do without
s'arrêter to stop	**s'excuser (de)** to apologize (for)	**se promener** to go for a walk
s'asseoir to sit down	**se fâcher** to get angry/ fall out	**se rappeler** to remember
s'attendre à to expect	**s'écrier** to cry out/exclaim	**se raser** to shave
se baigner to have a bath	**s'habiller** to get dressed	**se renseigner** to make enquiries
se battre to fight	**se hâter** to hurry	**se ressembler** to look alike
se blesser to hurt oneself	**s'inquiéter** to worry	**se retourner** to turn round
se coucher to go to bed	**s'installer** to settle down	**se réveiller** to wake up
se débarrasser de to get rid of	**se laver** to wash	**se sauver** to run away
se demander to wonder	**se lever** to get up	**se souvenir (de)** to remember
se dépêcher to hurry	**se mêler de** to meddle with	**se taire** to be/keep quiet
se déshabiller to undress	**se mettre à** to start	**se tromper** to be mistaken
se diriger vers to move towards	**se mettre en route** to set off	**se trouver** to be (situated)

E. IMPERSONAL VERBS

1. Conjugation

Impersonal verbs are used only in the third person singular and in the infinitive. The subject is always the impersonal pronoun **il** = it.

il neige it's snowing	**il y a du brouillard** it's foggy

2. List of impersonal verbs

a) *verbs describing the weather:*

i) **faire** + adjective:

il fait beau/chaud it's fine/warm	**il fait frais/froid** it's cool/cold
il fera beau demain the weather will be good tomorrow	**il va faire très froid** it will be very cold

ii) **faire** + noun:

il fait beau temps the weather is nice	**il fait mauvais temps** the weather is bad

Note:

il fait jour it's day(light)	**il fait nuit** it's dark

iii) other impersonal verbs and verbs used impersonally to describe the weather:

il gèle	**(geler)**	it's freezing
il grêle	**(grêler)**	it's hailing
il neige	**(neiger)**	it's snowing
il pleut	**(pleuvoir)**	it's raining
il tonne	**(tonner)**	it's thundering

Note: some of these verbs may be used personally:

je gèle — I am freezing

iv) **il y a** + noun:

il y a des nuages	it's cloudy
il y a du brouillard	it's foggy
il y a du verglas	it's icy

b) ***être***

i) **il est** + noun:

il est cinq heures	it's five o'clock
il était une fois un géant	there was once a giant

ii) **il est** + adjective + **de** + infinitive:

il est difficile de	it's difficult to
il est facile de	it's easy to
il est nécessaire de	it's necessary to
il est inutile de	it's useless to
il est possible de	it's possible to

il est difficile d'en parler
it is difficult to speak about it

Note: the indirect object pronoun in French corresponds to the English 'for me, for him' etc:

il m'est difficile d'en parler
it is difficult for me to speak about it

iii) **il est** + adjective + **que**:

il est douteux que	it's doubtful that
il est évident que	it's clear that
il est possible que	it's possible that
il est probable que	it's probable that
il est peu probable que	it's unlikely that
il est vrai que	it's true that

Note: **que** may be followed by the indicative or the subjunctive (see p C30):

il est probable qu'il ne viendra pas he probably won't come	**il est peu probable qu'il vienne** it's unlikely that he'll come

c) ***arriver, se passer*** *(to happen)*

il est arrivé une chose curieuse a strange thing happened	**que se passe-t-il ?** what's happening

d) ***existter*** *(to exist)*, ***rester*** *(to remain)*, ***manquer*** *(to be missing)*

il existe trois exemplaires de ce livre
there are three copies of this book

il me restait six francs I had six francs left	**il me manque vingt francs** I am twenty francs short

e) ***paraître, sembler*** *(to seem)*

il paraîtrait/semblerait qu'il ait changé d'avis
it would appear that he has changed his mind

il paraît qu'il va se marier
it seems he's going to get married

il me semble que le professeur s'est trompé
it seems to me that the teacher has made a mistake

f) *other common impersonal verbs*

i) **s'agir** (to be a matter of):

may be followed by a noun, a pronoun or an infinitive:

il s'agit de ton avenir it's about your future	**de quoi s'agit-il ?** what is it about?

il s'agit de trouver le coupable
we must find the culprit

ii) **falloir** (to be necessary):

may be followed by a noun, an infinitive or the subjunctive:

il faut deux heures pour aller à Paris
it takes two hours to get to Paris

il me faut plus de temps
I need more time

il faudra rentrer plus tôt ce soir
we'll have to come home earlier tonight

il faut que tu parles à Papa
you'll have to speak to your Dad

iii) **suffire** (to be enough):

may be followed by a noun, an infinitive or the subjunctive:

il suffit de peu de chose pour être heureux
it takes little to be happy

il suffit de passer le pont
you only have to cross the bridge

il suffira qu'ils te donnent le numéro de téléphone
they will only have to give you the telephone number

iv) **valoir mieux** (to be better):

may be followed by an infinitive or the subjunctive:

il vaudrait mieux prendre le car
it would be better to take the coach

il vaut mieux que vous ne sortiez pas seule le soir
you'd better not go out alone at night

F. TENSES

For the formation of the different tenses, see pp C22-3 and C25.

Note: French has no continuous tenses (as in 'I am eating', 'I was going', 'I will be arriving'). The 'be' and '-ing' parts of English continuous tenses are not translated as separate words. Instead, the equivalent tense is used in French:

ENGLISH	FRENCH
I am eating	**je mange**
I will be eating	**je mangerai**

1. PRESENT

The present is used to describe what someone does/ something that happens regularly, or what someone is doing/ something that is happening at the time of speaking.

a) *regular actions*

il travaille dans un bureau
he works in an office

je lis rarement le journal
I seldom read the paper

b) *continuous actions*

ne le dérangez pas, il travaille
don't disturb him, he's working

je ne peux pas venir, je garde mon petit frère
I can't come, I'm looking after my little brother

Note: the continuous nature of the action can also be expressed by using the phrase **être en train de** (to be in the process of) + infinitive:

je suis en train de cuisiner
I'm (busy) cooking

c) *immediate future*

je pars demain
I'm leaving tomorrow

But: the present cannot be used after **quand** and other conjunctions of time when the future is implied (see pp C29-30):

je le ferai quand j'aurai le temps
I'll do it when I have the time

d) *general truths*

la vie est dure
life is hard

2. IMPERFECT

The imperfect is a past tense used to express what someone was doing or what someone used to do or to describe something in the past. The imperfect refers particularly to something that *continued* over a period of time, as opposed to something that happened at a specific point in time.

a) *continuous actions*

the imperfect describes an action that was happening eg when something else took place (imperfect means unfinished):

il prenait un bain quand le téléphone a sonné
he was having a bath when the phone rang
excuse-moi, je pensais à autre chose
I'm sorry, I was thinking of something else

Note: the continuous nature of the action can be emphasised by using **être en train de** + infinitive:

j'étais en train de faire le ménage
I was (busy) doing the housework

b) *regular actions in the past*

je le voyais souvent quand il habitait dans le quartier
I used to see him often when he lived in this area

quand il était plus jeune il voyageait beaucoup
when he was younger he used to travel a lot

c) *description in the past*

il faisait beau ce jour-là
the weather was fine that day

c'était formidable !
it was great!

elle portait une robe bleue
she wore a blue dress

elle donnait sur la rue
it looked onto the street

3. PERFECT

The perfect tense is a compound past tense, used to express *single* actions which have been completed, ie what someone did or what someone has done/has been doing or something that has happened or has been happening:

je l'ai envoyé lundi
I sent it on Monday

on est sorti hier soir
we went out last night

tu t'es bien amusé ?
did you have a good time

je ne l'ai pas vu
I didn't see him

j'ai lu toute la journée
I've been reading all day

tu as déjà mangé ?
have you eaten?

Note: Perfect or imperfect?

In English, the simple past ('did', 'went', 'prepared') is used to describe both single and repeated actions in the past. In French, the perfect only describes single actions in the past, while repeated actions are expressed by the imperfect (they are sometimes signposted by 'used to'). Thus 'I went' should be translated 'j'allais' or 'je suis allé' depending on the nature of the action:

après dîner, je suis allé en ville
after dinner I went to town

l'an dernier, j'allais plus souvent au théâtre
last year, I went to the theatre more often

4. PAST HISTORIC

This tense is used in the same way as the perfect tense, to describe a single, completed action in the past (what someone did or something that happened). It is a literary tense, not common in everyday spoken French; it is found mainly as a narrative tense in written form:

le piéton ne vit pas arriver la voiture
the pedestrian didn't see the car coming

5. PLUPERFECT

This compound tense is used to express what someone had done/had been doing or something that had happened or had been happening:

il n'avait pas voulu aller avec eux
he hadn't wanted to go with them

elle était essoufflée parce qu'elle avait couru
she was out of breath because she'd been running

However, the pluperfect is not used as in English with **depuis** (for, since), or with **venir de** + infinitive (to have just done something). For details see sections **9.** and **10.**

il neigeait depuis une semaine
it had been snowing for a week

les pompiers venaient d'arriver
the firemen had just arrived

6. FUTURE

This tense is used to express what someone will do or will be doing or something that will happen or will be happening:

je ferai la vaisselle demain — I'll do the dishes tomorrow
j'arriverai tard — I'll be arriving late

Note: the future and not the present as in English is used in time clauses introduced by **quand** (when) or other conjunctions of time where the future is implied (see section **11.**):

il viendra quand il le pourra
he'll come when he can

French makes frequent use of **aller** + infinitive (to be about to do something) to express the immediate future:

je vais vous expliquer ce qui s'est passé
I'll explain (to you) what happened

il va déménager la semaine prochaine
he's moving house next week

7. FUTURE PERFECT

This compound tense is used to describe what someone will have done/will have been doing in the future or to describe something that will have happened in the future:

j'aurai bientôt fini
I will soon have finished

In particular, it is used instead of the English perfect in time clauses introduced by **quand** or other conjunctions of time where the future is implied (see section **11.**):

appelle-moi quand tu auras fini
call me when you've finished

on rentrera dès qu'on aura fait les courses
we'll come back as soon as we've done our shopping

8. PAST ANTERIOR

This tense is used instead of the pluperfect to express an action that preceded another action in the past (ie a past in the past). It is usually introduced by a conjunction of time (translated by 'when', 'as soon as', 'after' etc) and the main verb is in the past historic:

il se coucha dès qu'ils furent partis
he went to bed as soon as they'd left

à peine eut-elle raccroché que le téléphone sonna
she'd hardly hung up when the telephone rang

9. Use of tenses with 'depuis' (for, since)

a) The present must be used instead of the perfect to describe actions which started in the past and have continued until the present:

il habite ici depuis trois ans
he's been living here for three years

elle l'attend depuis ce matin
she's been waiting for him since this morning

But: The perfect, not the present, is used when the clause is negative or when the action has been completed:

il n'a pas pris de vacances depuis longtemps
he hasn't taken any holidays for a long time

j'ai fini depuis un bon moment
I've been finished for quite a while

Note:

i) **il y a ... que** or **voilà ... que** are also used with the present tense to translate 'for':

it's been ringing for ten minutes
ça sonne depuis dix minutes
il y a dix minutes que ça sonne
voilà dix minutes que ça sonne

ii) **depuis que** is used when 'since' introduces a clause, ie when there is a verb following **depuis**:

elle dort depuis que vous êtes partis
she's been sleeping since you left

iii) do not confuse **depuis** (for, since) and **pendant** (for, during): **depuis** refers to the starting point of an action which is still going on and **pendant** refers to the duration of an action which is over and is used with the perfect:

il vit ici depuis deux mois
he's been living here for two months

il a vécu ici pendant deux mois
he lived here for two months

b) the imperfect must be used instead of the pluperfect to describe an action which had started in the past and was still going on at a given time:

elle le connaissait depuis son enfance
she had known him since her childhood

il attendait depuis trois heures quand on est arrivé
he had been waiting for three hours when we arrived

But: if the sentence is negative or if the action has been completed, the pluperfect and not the imperfect is used:

je n'étais pas allé au théâtre depuis des années
I hadn't been to the theatre for years

il était parti depuis peu
he'd been gone for a short while

Note:

i) **il y avait ... que** + imperfect is also used to translate 'for':

she'd been living alone for a long time
elle habitait seule depuis longtemps
il y avait longtemps qu'elle habitait seule

ii) **depuis que** is used when 'since' introduces a clause; if it describes an action which was still going on at the time, it can be followed by the imperfect, otherwise it is followed by the pluperfect:

il pleuvait depuis que nous étions en vacances
it had been raining since we had been on holiday

il pleuvait depuis que nous étions arrivés
it had been raining since we arrived

iii) do not confuse **depuis** and **pendant**: **depuis** refers to the starting point of an action which is still going on and **pendant** refers to the duration of an action which is over; **pendant** is used with the pluperfect:

j'y travaillais depuis un an
I had been working there for a year

j'y avais travaillé pendant un an
I had worked there for a year

10. Use of tenses with 'venir de'

venir de + infinitive means 'to have just done'.

a) if it describes something that has just happened, it is used in the present instead of the perfect:

l'avion vient d'arriver — the plane has just arrived
je viens de te le dire ! — I've just told you!

b) if it describes something that had just happened, it is used in the imperfect instead of the pluperfect:

le film venait de commencer — the film had just started
je venais de rentrer — I'd just got home

11. Use of tenses after conjunctions of time

quand	when
tant que	as long as
dès/aussitôt que	as soon as
lorsque	when
pendant que	while

Verbs which follow these conjunctions must be used in the following tenses:

a) *future instead of present:*

je te téléphonerai quand je serai prêt
I'll phone you when I am ready

on ira dès qu'il fera beau
we'll go as soon as the weather is fine

b) *future perfect instead of perfect* when the future is implied:

on rentrera dès qu'on aura fini les courses
we'll come back as soon as we've done our shopping
je t'appellerai dès qu'il sera arrivé
I'll call you as soon as he has arrived

c) *conditional present/perfect instead of perfect/pluperfect* in indirect speech:

il a dit qu'il sortirait quand il aurait fini
he said that he would come out when he had finished

For the tenses of the subjunctive and conditional, see below and p C31.

G. MOODS

1. THE SUBJUNCTIVE

In spoken everyday French, the only two subjunctive tenses that are used are the present and the perfect. The imperfect and the pluperfect subjunctive are found mainly in literature or in texts of a formal nature.

The subjunctive is always preceded by the conjunction **que** and is used in subordinate clauses when the subject of the subordinate clause is different from the subject of the main verb.

Some clauses introduced by **que** take the indicative. But the subjunctive must be used after the following:

a) *Verbs of emotion*

être content que	to be pleased that
être déçu que	to be disappointed that
être désolé que	to be sorry that
être étonné que	to be surprised that
être fâché que	to be annoyed that
être heureux que	to be happy that
être surpris que	to be surprised that
être triste que	to be sad that
avoir peur que ... ne	to be afraid/to fear that
craindre que ... ne	to be afraid/to fear that
regretter que	to be sorry that

ils étaient contents que j'aille les voir
they were pleased (that) I went to visit them

je serais très étonné qu'il mente
I would be very surprised if he was lying

on regrette beaucoup que tu n'aies pas pu vendre ta voiture
we're very sorry (that) you couldn't sell your car

Note: **ne** is used after **craindre que** or **avoir peur que**, but does not have a negative meaning in itself and is not translated in English:

je crains que l'avion *ne* soit en retard
I'm afraid (that) the plane will be late

b) *Verbs of wishing and willing:*

aimer que	to like
désirer que	to wish (that)
préférer que	to prefer (that)
souhaiter que	to wish (that)
vouloir que	to want

Note: In English, such verbs are often used in the following type of construction: verb of willing + object + infinitive (eg I'd like you to listen); this type of construction is impossible in French, where a subjunctive clause has to be used:

je souhaite que tu réussisses
I hope you will succeed

il aimerait que je lui écrive plus souvent
he'd like me to write to him more often

voulez-vous que je vous y amène en voiture ?
would you like me to drive you there?

préférez-vous que je rappelle demain ?
would you rather I called back tomorrow?

c) *Impersonal constructions* (expressing necessity, possibility, doubt, denial, preference):

il faut que	it is necessary (that) (*must*)
il est nécessaire que	it is necessary that (*must*)
il est important que	it is important (that)
il est possible que	it is possible that (*may*)
il se peut que	it is possible that (*may*)
il est impossible que	it is impossible (that) (*can't*)
il est douteux que	it is doubtful whether
il est peu probable que	it is unlikely that
il semble que	it seems (that)
il est préférable que	it is preferable (that)
il vaut mieux que	it is better (that) (*had better*)
c'est dommage que	it is a pity (that)

Note: these expressions may be used in any appropriate tense:

il faut qu'on se dépêche
we must hurry

il était important que tu le saches
it was important that you should know

il se pourrait qu'elle change d'avis
she might change her mind

il est peu probable qu'ils s'y intéressent
they're unlikely to be interested in that

il semble qu'elle ait raison
she appears to be right

il vaudrait mieux que tu ne promettes rien
you'd better not promise anything

c'est dommage que vous vous soyez manqués
it's a pity you missed each other

d) *Some verbs and impersonal constructions expressing doubt or uncertainty* (mainly used negatively or interrogatively):

douter que	to doubt (that)
(ne pas) croire que	(not) to believe (that)
(ne pas) penser que	(not) to think (that)
(ne pas) être sûr que	(not) to be sure that
il n'est pas certain que	it isn't certain that
il n'est pas évident que	it isn't obvious that
il n'est pas sûr que	it isn't certain that
il n'est pas vrai que	it isn't true that

je doute fort qu'il veuille t'aider
I very much doubt whether he'll want to help you

croyez-vous qu'il y ait des places de libres ?
do you think there are any seats available?

on n'était pas sûr que ce soit le bon endroit
we weren't sure that it was the right place

il n'était pas certain qu'elle puisse gagner
it wasn't certain whether she could win

e) ***attendre que*** (to wait until, to wait for someone to do something):

attendons qu'il revienne
let's wait until he comes back

f) *Some subordinating conjunctions:*

bien que	although
quoique	although
sans que	without
pour que	so that
afin que	so that
à condition que	provided that
pourvu que	provided that
jusqu'à ce que	until
en attendant que	until
avant que ... (ne)	before
à moins que ... (ne)	unless
de peur que ... ne	for fear that
de crainte que ... ne	for fear that
de sorte que	so that
de façon que	so that
de manière que	so that

Note: When **ne** is shown in brackets, it may follow the conjunction, although it is seldom used in spoken French;

it does not have a negative meaning, and is not translated in English.

il est allé travailler bien qu'il soit malade
he went to work although he was ill

elle est entrée sans que je la voie
she came in without me seeing her

voilà de l'argent pour que tu puisses aller au cinéma
here's some money so that you can go to the pictures

d'accord, pourvu que tu me promettes de ne pas le répéter
all right, as long as you promise not to tell anyone

tu l'as revu avant qu'il (ne) parte ?
did you see him again before he left?

je le ferai demain, à moins que ce (ne) soit urgent
I'll do it tomorrow, unless it's urgent

elle n'a pas fait de bruit de peur qu'il ne se réveille
she didn't make any noise, in case he would wake up

parle moins fort de sorte qu'elle ne nous entende pas
talk more quietly so that she doesn't hear us

Note: when **de façon/manière que** (so that) express a result, as opposed to a purpose, the indicative is used instead of the subjunctive:

il a fait du bruit, de sorte qu'elle l'*a entendu*
he made some noise, so that she heard him

g) *A superlative or adjectives like **premier** (first), **dernier** (last), **seul** (only) followed by **qui** or **que**:*

c'était le coureur le plus rapide que j'aie jamais vu
he was the fastest runner I ever saw

But: the indicative is used with a statement of fact rather than the expression of an opinion:

c'est le coureur le plus rapide qui a gagné
it was the fastest runner who won

h) *Negative and indefinite pronouns (eg **rien**, **personne**, **quelqu'un**) followed by **qui** or **que**:*

je ne connais personne qui sache aussi bien chanter
I don't know anyone who can sing so well

il n'y a aucune chance qu'il réussisse
he hasn't got a chance of succeeding

ils cherchent quelqu'un qui puisse garder le bébé
they're looking for someone who can look after the baby

2. Avoiding the subjunctive

The subjunctive can be avoided, as is the tendency with modern spoken French, provided that both verbs in the sentence have the same subject. It is replaced by an infinitive introduced by the preposition **de**, the preposition **à** or by no preposition at all (see pp C32-3).

a) ***de** + infinitive replaces the subjunctive after:*

i) verbs of emotion:

j'ai été étonné d'apprendre la nouvelle
I was surprised to hear the news

il regrette de ne pas avoir vu cette émission
he's sorry he didn't see this programme

tu as peur de ne pas avoir assez d'argent ?
are you worried you won't have enough money?

ii) **attendre** (to wait) and **douter** (to doubt):

j'attendrai d'avoir bu mon café
I'll wait until I've drunk my coffee

iii) most impersonal constructions:

il serait préférable de déclarer ces objets
it would be better to declare these things

il est important de garder votre billet
it's important that you should keep your ticket

iv) most conjunctions:

il est resté dans la voiture afin de ne pas se mouiller
he stayed in the car so as not to get wet

j'ai lu avant de m'endormir
I read before falling asleep

tu peux sortir, à condition de rentrer avant minuit
you can go out, as long as you're back before midnight

b) ***à** + infinitive replaces the subjunctive after:*

i) **de façon/manière**

mets la liste sur la table, de manière à ne pas l'oublier
put the list on the table so that you won't forget it

ii) **premier, seul, dernier**

il a été le seul à s'excuser
he was the only one who apologised

c) the infinitive without any linking preposition replaces the subjunctive after:

i) verbs of wishing and willing:

je voudrais sortir avec toi
I'd like to go out with you

ii) **il faut, il vaut mieux**:

il vous faudra prendre des chèques de voyage
you'll have to take some traveller's cheques

il lui a fallu recommencer à zéro
he had to start all over again

il vaudrait mieux lui apporter des fleurs que des bonbons
it would be better to take her flowers than sweets

Note: an indirect object pronoun is often used with **il faut** to indicate the subject (who has to do something)

iii) verbs of thinking:

je ne crois pas le connaître
I don't think I know him

tu penses être chez toi à cinq heures ?
do you think you'll be home at five?

iv) **pour** and **sans**:

le car est reparti sans nous attendre
the coach left without waiting for us

j'économise pour pouvoir acheter une moto
I'm saving up to buy a motorbike

3. THE CONDITIONAL

a) *The conditional present*

i) The conditional present is used to describe what someone would do or would be doing or what would happen (if something else were to happen):

si j'étais riche, j'*achèterais* un château
if I were rich, I *would buy* a castle

Note: when the main verb is in the conditional present, the verb after **si** is in the imperfect.

ii) It is also used in indirect questions or reported speech instead of the future:

il ne m'a pas dit s'il *viendrait*
he didn't tell me whether he *would come*

b) *The conditional perfect (or past conditional)*

The conditional perfect or past conditional is used to express what someone would have done or would have been doing or what would have happened:

si j'avais su, je n'aurais rien dit
if I had known, I wouldn't have said anything

qu'aurais-je fait sans toi ?
what would I have done without you?

Note: if the main verb is in the conditional perfect, the verb introduced by **si** is in the pluperfect.

c) *Tenses after si:*

The tense of the verb introduced by **si** is determined by the tense of the verb in the main clause:

MAIN VERB		VERB FOLLOWING 'SI'
conditional present	→	imperfect
conditional perfect	→	pluperfect

je te le dirais si je le savais
I would tell you if I knew

je te l'aurais dit si je l'avais su
I would have told you if I had known

Note: never use the conditional (or the future) with **si** unless **si** means whether (ie when it introduces an indirect question):

je me demande si j'y serais arrivé sans toi
I wonder if (= *whether*) I would have managed without you

4. THE IMPERATIVE

a) *Definition*

The imperative is used to give commands, or polite instructions, or to make requests or suggestions; these can be positive (affirmative imperative: 'do!') or negative ('don't!'):

mange ta soupe !
eat your soup

n'aie pas peur !
don't be afraid!

partons !
let's go!

entrez !
come in!

faites attention !
be careful!

n'hésitez pas !
don't hesitate!

tournez à droite à la poste
turn right at the post office

b) *Forms*

The imperative has only three forms, which are the same as the **tu, nous** and **vous** forms of the present tense, but without the subject pronoun:

	-ER VERBS	-IR VERBS	-RE VERBS
'TU' FORM:	**regarde** watch	**choisis** choose	**attends** wait
'NOUS' FORM:	**regardons** let's watch	**choisissons** let's choose	**attendons** let's wait
'VOUS' FORM:	**regardez** watch	**choisissez** choose	**attendez** wait

Note:

i) the **-s** of the **tu** form of **-er** verbs is dropped, except when **y** or **en** follow the verb:

parle-lui !
speak to him!
But **parles-en avec lui**
speak to him about it

achète du sucre !
buy some sugar!
But **achètes-en un kilo**
buy a kilo (of it)

ii) the distinction between the subject pronouns **tu** and **vous** (see p C17) applies to the **tu** and **vous** forms of the imperative:

prends ta sœur avec toi, Alain
take your sister with you, Alain

prenez le plat du jour, Monsieur ; c'est du poulet rôti
have today's set menu, sir; it's roast chicken

les enfants, prenez vos imperméables ; il va pleuvoir
take your raincoats, children; it's going to rain

c) *Negative commands*

In negative commands, the verb is placed between **ne** and **pas** (or the second part of other negative expressions):

ne fais pas ça !
don't do that!

ne dites rien !
don't say anything!

d) *Imperative with object pronouns*

In positive commands, object pronouns come after the verb and are attached to it by a hyphen. In negative commands, they come before the verb (see pp C17 and C18):

dites-moi ce qui s'est passé
tell me what happened

attendons-les !
let's wait for them

prends-en bien soin, ne l'abîme pas !
take good care of it, don't damage it!

ne le leur dis pas !
don't tell them (that)!

ne les écoutez pas
don't listen to them

e) *Imperative of reflexive verbs*

The position of the reflexive pronoun of reflexive verbs is the same as that of object pronouns:

tais-toi !
be quiet!

levez-vous !
get up!

méfiez-vous de lui
don't trust him

arrêtons-nous ici
let's stop here

ne nous plaignons pas
let's not complain

ne t'approche pas plus !
don't come any closer!

f) *Alternatives to the imperative*

i) infinitive

the infinitive is often used instead of the imperative in written instructions and in recipes:

s'adresser au concierge
see the caretaker

ne pas fumer
no smoking

verser le lait et bien mélanger
pour in the milk and stir well

ii) subjunctive

as the imperative has no third person (singular or plural), **que** + subjunctive is used for giving orders in the third person:

que personne ne me dérange !
don't let anyone disturb me!

qu'il entre !
let him (come) in!

qu'elle parte, je m'en fiche !
I don't care if she goes!

g) *Idiomatic usage*

The imperative is used in spoken French in many set phrases. Here are some of the most common ones:

allons donc !
you don't say!

dis/ dites donc !
by the way!
hey! (*protest*)

tiens/tenez !
here you are!

tiens ! voilà le facteur
ah! here comes the postman

tiens (donc) !
(oh) really?

tiens ! tiens !
well, well! (fancy that!)

voyons !
come (on) now!

voyons donc !
let's see now

H. THE INFINITIVE

1. The infinitive is the basic form of the verb. It is recognized by its ending, which is found in three forms corresponding to the three conjugations: **-er, -ir, -re.**

These endings give the verb the meaning 'to ...':

acheter
to buy

choisir
to choose

vendre
to sell

Note: although this applies as a general rule, the French infinitive will often be translated by a verb form in *-ing* (see p C62).

2. Uses of the infinitive

The infinitive can follow a preposition, a verb, a noun, a pronoun, an adverb or an adjective.

a) *After a preposition*

The infinitive can be used after some prepositions (**pour, avant de, sans, au lieu de, afin de** etc):

sans attendre
without waiting

avant de partir
before leaving

b) *After a verb*

There are three main constructions when a verb is followed by an infinitive:

i) with no linking preposition
ii) with the linking preposition **à**
iii) with the linking preposition **de**

i) Verbs followed by the infinitive with no linking preposition:

★ verbs of wishing and willing, eg:

vouloir	to want
souhaiter	to wish
désirer	to wish, to want
espérer	to hope

voulez-vous manger maintenant ou plus tard ?
do you want to eat now or later?

je souhaite parler au directeur
I wish to speak to the manager

★ verbs of seeing, hearing and feeling, eg:

voir	to see
écouter	to listen to
regarder	to watch
sentir	to feel, to smell
entendre	to hear

je l'ai vu jouer	**tu m'as regardé danser ?**
I've seen him play	did you watch me dance?

j'ai entendu quelqu'un crier
I heard someone shout

★ verbs of motion, eg:

aller	to go
monter	to go/come up
venir	to come
entrer	to go/come in
rentrer	to go/come home
sortir	to go/come out
descendre	to go/come down

je viendrai te voir demain
I'll come and see you tomorrow

il est descendu laver la voiture
he went down to wash the car

va acheter le journal
go and buy the paper

Note: in English, 'to come' and 'to go' may be linked to the verb that follows by 'and'; 'and' is not translated in French.

aller + infinitive can be used to express a future action, eg what someone is going to do:

qu'est-ce que tu vas faire demain ?
what are you going to do tomorrow?

★ modal auxiliary verbs (see pp C36-7)

★ verbs of liking and disliking, eg:

aimer	to like
adorer	to love
aimer mieux	to prefer
détester	to hate
préférer	to prefer

tu aimes voyager ?	**j'aime mieux attendre**
do you like travelling?	I'd rather wait

je déteste aller à la campagne
I hate going to the country

j'adore faire la grasse matinée
I love having a long lie in

★ some impersonal verbs (see pp C27)

★ a few other verbs, eg:

compter	to intend to
sembler	to seem
laisser	to let, to allow
faillir	'to nearly' (do)
oser	to dare

ils l'ont laissé partir
they let him go

je n'ose pas le lui demander
I daren't ask him

tu sembles être malade
you seem to be ill

je compte partir demain
I intend to leave tomorrow

j'ai failli manquer l'avion
I nearly missed the plane

★ in the following set expressions:

aller chercher	to go and get, to fetch
envoyer chercher	to send for
entendre dire (que)	to hear (that)
entendre parler de	to hear about
laisser tomber	to drop
venir chercher	to come and get
vouloir dire	to mean

va chercher ton argent
go and get your money

j'ai entendu dire qu'il était journaliste
I've heard that he is a journalist

tu as entendu parler de ce film ?
have you heard about this film?

ne le laisse pas tomber !
don't drop it!

ça veut dire "demain"
it means 'tomorrow'

ii) Verbs followed by **à** + infinitive:

A list of these is given on p C49:

je dois aider ma mère à préparer le déjeuner
I must help my mother prepare lunch

il commence à faire nuit
it's beginning to get dark

alors, tu t'es décidé à y aller ?
so you've made up your mind to go?

je t'invite à venir chez moi pour les vacances de Noël
I invite you to come to my house for the Christmas holidays

je passe mon temps à lire et à regarder la télé
I spend my time reading and watching TV

cela sert à nettoyer les disques
this is used for cleaning records

iii) Verbs followed by **de** + infinitive:

A list of these is given on p C49:

je crois qu'il s'est arrêté de pleuvoir
I think it's stopped raining

tu as envie de sortir ?
do you feel like going out?

le médecin a conseillé à Serge de rester au lit
the doctor advised Serge to stay in bed

j'ai décidé de rester chez moi
I decided to stay at home

essayons de faire du stop
let's try and hitch-hike

tu as fini de m'ennuyer ?
will you stop annoying me?

demande à Papa de t'aider
ask your Dad to help you

je t'interdis d'y aller
I forbid you to go

n'oublie pas d'en acheter !
don't forget to buy some!

j'ai refusé de le faire
I refused to do it

je vous prie de m'excuser
please forgive me

il vient de téléphoner
he's just phoned

c) *After a noun, a pronoun, an adverb or an adjective*

There are two possible constructions: with **à** or with **de**.

i) with the linking preposition **à**:

il avait plusieurs clients à voir
he had several customers to see

c'est difficile à dire
it's difficult to say

ii) with the linking preposition **de**:

je suis content de te voir
I am pleased to see you

iii) **à** or **de** with pronouns, adverbs or nouns?

★ **à** conveys the idea of something to do or to be done after the following:

beaucoup	a lot
plus	more
tant	so much
trop	too much
assez	enough
moins	less
rien	nothing
tout	everything
quelque chose	something

une maison à vendre — a house for sale
j'ai des examens à préparer — I've got exams to prepare

il nous a indiqué la route à suivre
he showed us the road to follow

il y a trop de livres à lire
there are too many books to read

il n'y a pas de temps à perdre
there's no time to lose

c'était une occasion à ne pas manquer
it was an opportunity not to be missed

★ **de** is used after nouns of an abstract nature, usually with the definite article, eg:

l'habitude de	the habit of
l'occasion de	the opportunity to
le temps de	the time to
le courage de	the courage to
l'envie de	the desire to
le besoin de	the need to
le plaisir de	the pleasure of
le moment de	the time to

il n'avait pas l'habitude d'être seul
he wasn't used to being alone

je n'ai pas le temps de lui parler
I don't have time to talk to him

avez-vous eu l'occasion de la rencontrer ?
did you have the opportunity to meet her?

ce n'est pas le moment de le déranger
now is not the time to disturb him

je n'ai pas eu le courage de le lui dire
I didn't have the courage to tell him

iv) **à** or **de** with adjectives?

★ **à** is used in a passive sense (something to be done) and after **c'est**:

un livre agréable à lire
a pleasant book to read

il est facile à satisfaire
he is easily satisfied

c'est intéressant à savoir
that's interesting to know

c'était impossible à faire
it was impossible to do

★ **de** is used after **il est** in an impersonal sense (see p C27):

il est intéressant de savoir que ...
it is interesting to know that ...

Note: for the use of **c'est** and **il est**, see p C63.

★ **de** is used after many adjectives, in particular those where the idea of 'of' is present in English, eg:

certain/sûr de	certain of/to
capable de	capable of
incapable de	incapable of
coupable de	guilty of

j'étais sûr de réussir
I was sure of succeeding

il est incapable d'y arriver seul
he is incapable of managing on his own

de is also used with adjectives of emotion, feeling and generally with adjectives denoting a state of mind, eg:

content de	pleased/happy to
surpris/étonné de	surprised to
fier de	proud to
heureux de	happy to
fâché de	annoyed to/at
triste de	sad to
gêné de	embarrassed to
désolé de	sorry for/to

j'ai été très content de recevoir ta lettre
I was very pleased to get your letter

elle sera surprise de vous voir
she will be surprised to see you

nous avons été très tristes d'apprendre la nouvelle
we were very sad to hear the news

But: **à** is used with **prêt à** (ready to) and **disposé à** (willing to):

es-tu prête à partir ?
are you ready to go?

je suis tout disposé à vous aider
I'm very willing to help you

d) *faire* + infinitive

faire is followed by an infinitive without any linking preposition to express the sense of 'having someone do something' or 'having something done'; two constructions are possible:

i) with one object
ii) with two objects

i) when only one object is used, it is a direct object:

je dois le faire réparer
I must have it fixed

il veut faire repeindre sa voiture
he wants to have his car resprayed

je ferai nettoyer cette veste ; je la ferai nettoyer
I'll have this jacket cleaned; I'll have it cleaned

tu m'as fait attendre ! — you made me wait!
je le ferai parler — I'll make him talk

Note: the following set expressions:

faire entrer	to show in
faire venir	to send for

faites entrer ce monsieur — show this gentleman in
je vais faire venir le docteur — I'll send for the doctor

ii) when both **faire** and the following infinitive have an object, the object of **faire** is indirect:

elle lui a fait prendre une douche
she made him take a shower

je leur ai fait ranger leur chambre
I made them tidy their room

e) *Infinitive used as subject of another verb:*

trouver un emploi n'est pas facile
finding a job isn't easy

3. The perfect infinitive

a) *Form*

The perfect or past infinitive is formed with the infinitive of the auxiliary **avoir** or **être** as appropriate (see pp C25-6), followed by the past participle of the verb, eg:

avoir mangé	**être allé**	**s'être levé**
to have eaten	to have gone	to have got up

b) *Use*

i) after the preposition **après** (after):

après avoir attendu une heure, il est rentré chez lui
after waiting for an hour, he went back home

il s'en est souvenu après s'être couché
he remembered after going to bed

ii) after certain verbs:

se souvenir de	to remember
remercier de	to thank for
regretter de	to regret, to be sorry for
être désolé de	to be sorry for

je vous remercie de m'avoir invité
I thank you for inviting me

il regrettait de leur avoir menti
he was sorry for lying to them

tu te souviens d'avoir fait cela ?
do you remember doing this?

I. PARTICIPLES

1. The present participle

a) *Formation*

Like the imperfect, the present participle is formed by using the stem of the first person plural of the present tense (the **nous** form less the **-ons** ending):

-ons is replaced by **-ant** (= English *-ing*)

Exceptions:

INFINITIVE	PRESENT PARTICIPLE
avoir to have	**ayant** having
être to be	**étant** being
savoir to know	**sachant** knowing

b) *Used as an adjective*

Used as an adjective, the present participle agrees in number and in gender with its noun or pronoun:

un travail fatigant tiring work	**la semaine suivante** the following week
ils sont très exigeants they're very demanding	**des nouvelles surprenantes** surprising news

c) *Use as a verb*

The present participle is used far less frequently in French than in English, and English present participles in *-ing* are often not translated by a participle in French (see p C62).

i) used on its own, the present participle corresponds to the English present participle:

ne voulant plus attendre, ils sont partis sans moi
not wanting to wait any longer, they left without me

pensant bien faire, j'ai insisté
thinking I was doing the right thing, I insisted

ii) **en** + present participle

When the subject of the present participle is the same as that of the main verb, this structure is often used to express simultaneity (ie 'while doing something'), manner (ie 'by doing something') or to translate English phrasal verbs.

★ simultaneous actions

In English this structure is translated by:

- while/when/on + present participle (eg 'on arriving')
- while/when/as + subject + verb (eg 'as he arrived')

il est tombé en descendant l'escalier
he fell as he was going down the stairs

en le voyant, j'ai éclaté de rire
when I saw him, I burst out laughing

elle lisait le journal en attendant l'autobus
she was reading the paper while waiting for the bus

Note: the adverb **tout** is often used before **en** to emphasize the fact that both actions are simultaneous, especially when there is an element of contradiction:

elle écoutait la radio tout en faisant ses devoirs
she was listening to the radio while doing her homework

tout en protestant, je les ai suivis
under protest, I followed them

★ manner

when expressing how an action is done, **en** + participle is translated by: 'by' + participle, eg:

il gagne sa vie en vendant des voitures d'occasion
he earns his living (by) selling second-hand cars

j'ai trouvé du travail en lisant les petites annonces
I found a job by reading the classified ads

★ phrasal verbs of motion

en + present participle is often used to translate English phrasal verbs expressing motion, where the verb expresses the means of motion and a preposition expresses the direction of movement (eg 'to run out', 'to swim across'). In French, the English preposition is translated by a verb, while the English verb is translated by **en** + present participle:

il est sorti du magasin *en courant*
he *ran* out of the shop

elle a traversé la route *en titubant*
she *staggered* across the road

2. The past participle

a) *Forms*

For the formation of the past participle see p C25.

b) *Use*

The past participle is mostly used as a verb in compound tenses or in the passive, but it can also be used as an adjective. In either case, there are strict rules of agreement to be followed.

c) *Rules of agreement of the past participle*

i) When it is used as an adjective, the past participle always agrees with the noun or pronoun it refers to:

un pneu crevé a burst tyre	**une pomme pourrie** a rotten apple
ils étaient épuisés they were exhausted	**trois assiettes cassées !** three broken plates!

Note: in French, the past participle is used as an adjective to describe postures or attitudes of the body, where English uses the present participle. The most common of these are:

accoudé	leaning on one's elbows
accroupi	squatting
agenouillé	kneeling
allongé	lying (down)
appuyé (contre)	leaning (against)
couché	lying (down)
étendu	lying (down)
penché	leaning (over)
(sus)pendu	hanging

il est allongé sur le lit he's lying on the bed	**une femme assise devant moi** a woman sitting in front of me

ii) In compound tenses:

★ with the auxiliary **avoir:**

the past participle only agrees in number and gender with the direct object when the direct object comes before the participle, ie in the following cases:

– in a clause introduced by the relative pronoun **que**:

le jeu-vidéo que j'ai acheté the video-game I bought	**la valise qu'il a perdue** the suitcase he lost

– with a direct object pronoun:

ta carte ? je l'ai reçue hier
your card? I got it yesterday

zut, mes lunettes ! je les ai laissées chez moi
blast, my glasses! I've left them at home

– in a clause introduced by **combien de**, **quel (quelle, quels, quelles)** or **lequel (laquelle, lesquels, lesquelles)**:

combien de pays as-tu visités ?
how many countries have you visited?

laquelle avez-vous choisie ?
which one did you choose?

Note: if the direct object comes after the past participle, the participle remains in the masculine singular form:

on a rencontré des gens très sympathiques
we met some very nice people

★ with the auxiliary **être**

– the past participle agrees with the subject of the verb:

quand est-elle revenue ?
when did she come back?

elle était déjà partie
she'd already left

ils sont passés te voir ?
did they come to see you?

elles sont restées là
they stayed here

Note: this rule also applies when the verb is in the passive:

elle a été arrêtée
she's been arrested

– reflexive verbs

in most cases, the past participle of reflexive verbs agrees with the reflexive pronoun if the pronoun is a direct object; since the reflexive pronoun refers to the subject, the number and gender of the past participle are determined by the subject:

Jacques s'est trompé
Jacques made a mistake

Marie s'était levée tard
Marie had got up late

ils se sont disputés ?
did they have an argument?

elles se sont vues
they saw each other

Michèle et Marie, vous vous êtes habillées?
Michèle and Marie, have you got dressed yet?

But: the past participle does not agree when the reflexive pronoun is an indirect object:

elles se sont écrit
they wrote *to* each other

This is the case in particular where parts of the body are mentioned:

elle s'est lavé les cheveux
she washed her hair

ils se sont serré la main
they shook hands

J. THE PASSIVE

1. Formation

The passive is used when the subject does not perform the action, but is subjected to it, eg:

the house has been sold

he was made redundant

Passive tenses are formed with the corresponding tense of the verb '**être**' ('to be', as in English), followed by the past participle of the verb, eg:

j'ai été invité
I was invited

The past participle must agree with its subject, eg:

elle a été renvoyée
she has been dismissed

ils seront déçus
they will be disappointed

elles ont été vues
they were seen

2. Avoidance of the passive

The passive is far less common in French than in English. In particular, an indirect object cannot become the subject of a sentence in French, ie the following sentence where 'he' is an indirect object has no equivalent in French:

he was given a book (*ie a book was given to him*)

In general, French tries to avoid the passive wherever possible. This can be done in several ways:

a) *Use of the pronoun* **on**:

on m'a volé mon portefeuille
my wallet has been stolen

on construit une nouvelle piscine
a new swimming pool is being built

en France, on boit beaucoup de vin
a lot of wine is drunk in France

b) *Agent becomes subject of the verb*

If the agent, ie the real subject, is mentioned in English, it can become the subject of the French verb:

la nouvelle va les surprendre
they will be surprised by ***the news***
mon correspondent m'a invité
I've been invited by *my penfriend*

mon cadeau te plaît ?
are you pleased with *my present?*

c) *Use of a reflexive verb*

Reflexive forms can be created for a large number of verbs, particularly in the third person:

elle s'appelle Anne
she is called Anne

ton absence va se remarquer
your absence will be noticed

ce plat se mange froid
this dish is eaten cold

cela ne se fait pas ici
that isn't done here

d) *Use of **se faire*** + infinitive (when the subject is a person):

il s'est fait renverser par une voiture
he was run over by a car

je me suis fait voler (tout mon argent)
I've been robbed (of all my money)

3. Conjugation

For a complete conjugation table of a verb in the passive, see **être aimé** (to be loved) p C38.

K. MODAL AUXILIARY VERBS

The modal auxiliary verbs are always followed by the infinitive. They express an obligation, a probability, an intention, a possibility or a wish rather than a fact.

The five modal auxiliary verbs are: **DEVOIR, POUVOIR, SAVOIR, VOULOIR** and **FALLOIR.**

1. Devoir (conjugation see p C41)

Expresses:
a) obligation, necessity
b) probability
c) intention, expectation

a) *obligation*

nous devons arriver à temps
we must arrive in time

demain tu devras prendre le bus
tomorrow you'll have to take the bus

nous avions dû partir
we had (had) to go

j'ai dû avouer que j'avais tort
I had to admit that I was wrong

In the conditional, **devoir** may be used for advice, ie to express what should be done (conditional present) or should have been done (past conditional):

vous devriez travailler davantage
you ought to/should work harder

tu ne devrais pas marcher sur l'herbe
you shouldn't walk on the grass

tu aurais dû tout avouer
you should have admitted everything

tu n'aurais pas dû manger ces champignons
you shouldn't have eaten those mushrooms

Note: the French infinitive is translated by a past participle in English: **mang*er*** = eat*en*.

b) *probability*

il doit être en train de dormir
he must be sleeping (he's probably sleeping)

j'ai dû me tromper de chemin
I must have taken the wrong road

Note: in a past narrative sequence in the distant past 'must have' is translated by a pluperfect in French:

il dit qu'il avait dû se tromper de chemin
he said he must have taken the wrong road

c) *intention, expectation*

je dois aller chez le dentiste
I am supposed to go to the dentist's

le train doit arriver à 19h30
the train is due to arrive at 7.30 p.m.

2. Pouvoir (conjugation see p C45)

Expresses: a) capacity, ability
b) permission
c) possibility

a) *capacity/ability*

Superman peut soulever une maison
Superman can lift a house

cette voiture peut faire du 150
this car can go up to 93 mph

il était si faible qu'il ne pouvait pas sortir de son lit
he was so weak that he couldn't get out of bed

b) *permission*

puis-je entrer ? may I come in?

puis-je vous offrir du thé ? may I offer you some tea?

c) *possibility*

cela peut arriver
it can happen

Note: **pouvoir** + the infinitive is usually replaced by **peut-être** and the finite tense: eg **il s'est peut-être trompé de livres** (he may have taken the wrong books).

In the conditional, **pouvoir** is used to express something that could or might be (conditional present) or that could or might have been (past conditional):

tu pourrais t'excuser
you might apologize

j'aurais pu vous prêter mon magnétophone
I could have lent you my tape-recorder

Note: with verbs of perception (eg **entendre** to hear, **sentir** to feel, to smell, **voir** to see), **pouvoir** is often omitted:

j'entendais le bruit des vagues
I could hear the sound of the waves

3. Savoir (conjugation see p C46)

Means: 'to know how to'

je sais/savais conduire une moto
I can/used to be able to ride a motorbike

4. Vouloir (conjugation see p C48)

Expresses: a) desire
b) wish
c) intention

a) *desire*

je veux partir I want to go

voulez-vous danser avec moi ? will you dance with me?

b) *wish*

je voudrais être un lapin
I wish I were a rabbit

je voudrais trouver un travail intéressant
I should like to find an interesting job

j'aurais voulu lui donner un coup de poing
I would have liked to punch him

c) *intention*

il a voulu sauter par la fenêtre
he tried to jump out of the window

Note: **veuillez**, the imperative of **vouloir**, is used as a polite form to express a request ('would you please'):

veuillez ne pas déranger
please do not disturb

5. Falloir (conjugation see p C43)

Expresses: necessity

il faut manger pour vivre
you must eat to live

il faudrait manger plus tôt ce soir
we should eat earlier tonight

il aurait fallu apporter des sandwichs
we should have brought sandwiches

Note: some of the above verbs can also be used without infinitive constructions. They then take on a different meaning (eg **devoir** = to owe, **savoir** = to know).

L. CONJUGATION TABLES

The following verbs provided the main patterns of conjugation including the conjugation of the most common irregular verbs. They are arranged in alphabetical order.

-er verb (*see p C22*)	AIMER
-ir verb (*see p C22*)	FINIR
-re verb (*see p C22*)	VENDRE
Reflexive verb (*see pp C26-7*)	SE MEFIER
Verb with auxiliary **être** (*see pp C25-6*)	ARRIVER
Verb in the passive (*see p C36*)	ETRE AIME
Auxiliaries (*see pp C25-6*)	AVOIR ETRE
Verb in **-eler/-eter** (*see pp C23-4*)	APPELER
Verb in **e** + consonant + **er** (*see p C24*)	ACHETER
Verb in **é** + consonant + **er** (*see p C24*)	ESPERER
Modal auxiliaries (*see pp C36-7*)	DEVOIR POUVOIR SAVOIR VOULOIR FALLOIR

Irregular verbs	ALLER	METTRE
	CONDUIRE	OUVRIR
	CONNAITRE	PRENDRE
	CROIRE	RECEVOIR
	DIRE	TENIR
	DORMIR	VENIR
	ECRIRE	VIVRE
	FAIRE	VOIR

ACHETER to buy

PRESENT
j'achète
tu achètes
il achète
nous achetons
vous achetez
ils achètent

IMPERFECT
j'achetais
tu achetais
il achetait
nous achetions
vous achetiez
ils achetaient

FUTURE
j'achèterai
tu achèteras
il achètera
nous achèterons
vous achèterez
ils achèteront

PAST HISTORIC
j'achetai
tu achetas
il acheta
nous achetâmes
vous achetâtes
ils achetèrent

PERFECT
j'ai acheté
tu as acheté
il a acheté
nous avons acheté
vous avez acheté
ils ont acheté

PLUPERFECT
j'avais acheté
tu avais acheté
il avait acheté
nous avions acheté
vous aviez acheté
ils avaient acheté

PAST ANTERIOR
j'eus acheté etc

FUTURE PERFECT
j'aurai acheté etc

CONDITIONAL

PRESENT
j'achèterais
tu achèterais
il achèterait
nous achèterions
vous achèteriez
ils achèteraient

PAST
j'aurais acheté
tu aurais acheté
il aurait acheté
nous aurions acheté
vous auriez acheté
ils auraient acheté

SUBJUNCTIVE

PRESENT
j'achète
tu achètes
il achète
nous achetions
vous achetiez
ils achètent

IMPERFECT
j'achetasse
tu achetasses
il achetât
nous achetassions
vous achetiez
ils achetassent

PERFECT
j'aie acheté
tu aies acheté
il ait acheté
nous ayons acheté
vous ayez acheté
ils aient acheté

IMPERATIVE
achète
achetons
achetez
avoir acheté

INFINITIVE

PRESENT
acheter

PAST
acheté

PARTICIPLE

PRESENT
achetant

PAST
acheté

AIMER to like, to love

PRESENT
j'aime
tu aimes
il aime
nous aimons
vous aimez
ils aiment

IMPERFECT
j'aimais
tu aimais
il aimait
nous aimions
vous aimiez
ils aimaient

FUTURE
j'aimerai
tu aimeras
il aimera
nous aimerons
vous aimerez
ils aimeront

PAST HISTORIC
j'aimai
tu aimas
il aima
nous aimâmes
vous aimâtes
ils aimèrent

PERFECT
j'ai aimé
tu as aimé
il a aimé
nous avons aimé
vous avez aimé
ils ont aimé

PLUPERFECT
j'avais aimé
tu avais aimé
il avait aimé
nous avions aimé
vous aviez aimé
ils avaient aimé

PAST ANTERIOR
j'eus aimé etc

FUTURE PERFECT
j'aurai aimé etc

CONDITIONAL

PRESENT
j'aimerais
tu aimerais
il aimerait
nous aimerions
vous aimeriez
ils aimeraient

PAST
j'aurais aimé
tu aurais aimé
il aurait aimé
nous aurions aimé
vous auriez aimé
ils auraient aimé

SUBJUNCTIVE

PRESENT
j'aime
tu aimes
il aime
nous aimions
vous aimiez
ils aiment

IMPERFECT
j'aimasse
tu aimasses
il aimât
nous aimassions
vous aimassiez
ils aimassent

PERFECT
j'aie aimé
tu aies aimé
il ait aimé
nous ayons aimé
vous ayez aimé
ils aient aimé

IMPERATIVE
aime
aimons
aimez

INFINITIVE

PRESENT
aimer

PAST
avoir aimé

PARTICIPLE

PRESENT
aimant

PAST
aimé

ETRE AIME to be loved

PRESENT
je suis aimé(e)
tu es aimé(e)
il (elle) est aimé(e)
nous sommes aimé(e)s
vous êtes aimé(e)(s)
ils (elles) sont aimé(e)s

IMPERFECT
j'étais aimé(e)
tu étais aimé(e)
il (elle) était aimé(e)
nous étions aimé(e)s
vous étiez aimé(e)(s)
ils (elles) étaient aimé(e)s

FUTURE
je serai aimé(e)
tu seras aimé(e)
il (elle) sera aimé(e)
nous serons aimé(e)s
vous serez aimé(e)(s)
ils (elles) seront aimé(e)s

PAST HISTORIC
je fus aimé(e)
tu fus aimé(e)
il (elle) fut aimé(e)
nous fûmes aimé(e)s
vous fûtes aimé(e)(s)
ils (elles) furent aimé(e)s

PERFECT
j'ai été aimé(e)
tu as été aimé(e)
il a (elle) été aimé(e)
nous avons été aimé(e)s
vous avez été aimé(e)(s)
ils (elles) ont été aimé(e)s

PLUPERFECT
j'avais été aimé(e)
tu avais été aimé(e)
il (elle) avait été aimé(e)
nous avions été aimé(e)s
vous aviez été aimé(e)(s)
ils (elles) avaient été aimé(e)s

PAST ANTERIOR
j'eus été etc aimé(e)

FUTURE PERFECT
j'aurai été aimé(e) etc

CONDITIONAL

PRESENT
je serais aimé(e)
tu serais aimé(e)
il (elle) serait aimé(e)
nous serions aimé(e)s
vous seriez aimé(e)(s)
ils (elles) seraient aimé(e)s

PAST
j'aurais été aimé(e)
tu aurais été aimé(e)
il (elle) aurait été aimé(e)
nous aurions été aimé(e)s
vous auriez été aimé(e)(s)
ils (elles) auraient été aimé(e)s

SUBJUNCTIVE

PRESENT
je sois aimé(e)
tu sois aimé(e)
il (elle) soit aimé(e)
nous soyons aimé(e)s
vous soyez aimé(e)(s)
ils (elles) soient aimé(e)s

IMPERFECT
je fusse aimé(e)
tu fusses aimé(e)
il (elle) fût aimé(e)
nous fussions aimé(e)s
vous fussiez aimé(e)(s)
ils (elles) fussent aimé(e)s

PERFECT
j'aie été aimé(e)
tu aies été aimé(e)
il (elle) ait été aimé(e)
nous ayons été aimé(e)s
vous ayez été aimé(e)(s)
ils (elles) aient été aimé(e)s

IMPERATIVE
sois aimé(e)
soyons aimé(e)s
soyez aimé(e)(s)

INFINITIVE

PRESENT
être aimé(e)(s)

PAST
avoir été aimé(e)(s)

PARTICIPLE

PRESENT
étant aimé(e)(s)

PAST
été aimé(e)(s)

ALLER to go

PRESENT
je vais
tu vas
il va
nous allons
vous allez
ils vont

IMPERFECT
j'allais
tu allais
il allait
nous allions
vous alliez
ils allaient

FUTURE
j'irai
tu iras
il ira
nous irons
vous irez
ils iront

PAST HISTORIC
j'allai
tu allas
il alla
nous allâmes
vous allâtes
ils allèrent

PERFECT
je suis allé(e)
tu es allé(e)
il (elle) est allé(e)
nous sommes allé(e)s
vous êtes allé(e)(s)
ils (elles) sont allé(e)s

PLUPERFECT
j'étais allé(e)
tu étais allé(e)
il (elle) était allé(e)
nous étiez allé(e)s
vous étiez allé(e)(s)
ils (elles) étaient allé(e)s

PAST ANTERIOR
je fus allé(e) etc

FUTURE PERFECT
je serai allé(e) etc

CONDITIONAL

PRESENT
j'irais
tu irais
il irait
nous irions
vous iriez
ils iraient

PAST
je serais allé(e)
tu serais allé(e)
il (elle) serait allé(e)
nous serions allé(e)s
vous seriez allé(e)(s)
ils (elles) seraient allé(e)s

SUBJUNCTIVE

PRESENT
j'aille
tu ailles
il aille
nous allions
vous alliez
ils aillent

IMPERFECT
j'allasse
tu allasses
il allât
nous allassions
vous allassiez
ils allassent

PERFECT
je sois allé(e)
tu sois allé(e)
il il (elle) soit allé(e)
nous soyons allé(e)s
vous soyez allé(e)(s)
ils (elles) soient allé(e)s

IMPERATIVE
va
allons
allez

INFINITIVE

PRESENT
aller

PAST
être allé(e)(s)

PARTICIPLE

PRESENT
allant

PAST
allé

APPELER to call

PRESENT
j'appelle
tu appelles
il appelle
nous appelons
vous appelez
ils appellent

IMPERFECT
j'appelais
tu appelais
il appelait
nous appelions
vous appeliez
ils appelaient

FUTURE
j'appellerai
tu appelleras
il appellera
nous appellerons
vous appellerez
ils appelleront

PAST HISTORIC
j'appelai
tu appelas
il appela
nous appelâmes
vous appelâtes
ils appelèrent

PERFECT
j'ai appelé
tu as appelé
il a appelé
nous avons appelé
vous avez appelé
ils ont appelé

PLUPERFECT
j'avais appelé
tu avais appelé
il avait appelé
nous avions appelé
vous aviez appelé
ils avaient appelé

PAST ANTERIOR
j'eus appelé etc

FUTURE PERFECT
j'aurai appelé etc

CONDITIONAL

PRESENT
j'appellerais
tu appellerais
il appellerait
nous appellerions
vous appelleriez
ils appelleraient

PAST
j'aurais appelé
tu aurais appelé
il aurait appelé
nous aurions appelé
vous auriez appelé
ils auraient appelé

SUBJUNCTIVE

PRESENT
j'appelle
tu appelles
il appelle
nous appelions
vous appeliez
ils appellent

IMPERFECT
j'appelasse
tu appelasses
il appelât
nous appelassions
vous appelassiez
ils appelassent

PERFECT
j'aie appelé
tu aies appelé
il ait appelé
nous ayons appelé
vous ayez appelé
ils aient appelé

IMPERATIVE
appelle
appelons
appelez

INFINITIVE

PRESENT
appeler

PAST
avoir appelé

PARTICIPLE

PRESENT
appelant

PAST
appelé

ARRIVER to arrive, to happen

PRESENT
j'arrive
tu arrives
il arrive
nous arrivons
vous arrivez
ils arrivent

IMPERFECT
j'arrivais
tu arrivais
il arrivait
nous arrivions
vous arriviez
ils arrivaient

FUTURE
j'arriverai
tu arriveras
il arrivera
nous arriverons
vous arriverez
ils arriveront

PAST HISTORIC
j'arrivai
tu arrivas
il arriva
nous arrivâmes
vous arrivâtes
ils arrivèrent

PERFECT
je suis arrivé(e)
tu es arrivé(e)
il (elle) est arrivé(e)
nous sommes arrivé(e)s
vous êtes arrivé(e)(s)
ils (elles) sont arrivé(e)s

PLUPERFECT
j'étais arrivé(e)
tu étais arrivé(e)
il (elle) était arrivé(e)
nous étiez arrivé(e)s
vous étiez arrivé(e)(s)
ils (elles) étaient arrivé(e)s

PAST ANTERIOR
je fus arrivé(e) etc

FUTURE PERFECT
je serai arrivé(e) etc

CONDITIONAL

PRESENT
j'arriverais
tu arriverais
il arriverait
nous arriverions
vous arriveriez
ils arriveraient

PAST
je serais arrivé(e)
tu serais arrivé(e)
il (elle) serait arrivé(e)
nous serions arrivé(e)s
vous seriez arrivé(e)(s)
ils (elles) seraient arrivé(e)s

SUBJUNCTIVE

PRESENT
j'arrive
tu arrives
il arrive
nous arrivions
vous arriviez
ils arrivent

IMPERFECT
j'arrivasse
tu arrivasses
il arrivât
nous arrivassions
vous arrivassiez
ils arrivassent

PERFECT
je sois arrivé(e)
tu sois arrivé(e)
il (elle) soit arrivé(e)
nous soyons arrivé(e)s
vous soyez arrivé(e)(s)
ils (elles) soient arrivé(e)s

IMPERATIVE
arrive
arrivons
arrivez

INFINITIVE

PRESENT
arriver

PAST
avoir arrivé

PARTICIPLE

PRESENT
arrivant

PAST
arrivé

AVOIR to have

PRESENT
j'ai
tu as
il a
nous avons
vous avez
ils ont

IMPERFECT
j'avais
tu avais
il avait
nous avions
vous aviez
ils avaient

FUTURE
j'aurai
tu auras
il aura
nous aurons
vous aurez
ils auront

PAST HISTORIC
j'eus
tu eus
il eut
nous eûmes
vous eûtes
ils eurent

PERFECT
j'ai eu
tu as eu
il a eu
nous avons eu
vous avez eu
ils ont eu

PLUPERFECT
j'avais eu
tu avais eu
il avait eu
nous avions eu
vous aviez eu
ils avaient eu

PAST ANTERIOR
j'eus eu etc

FUTURE PERFECT
j'aurai eu etc

CONDITIONAL

PRESENT
j'aurais
tu aurais
il aurait
nous aurions
vous auriez
ils auraient

PAST
j'aurais eu
tu aurais eu
il aurait eu
nous aurions eu
vous auriez eu
ils auraient eu

SUBJUNCTIVE

PRESENT
j'aie
tu aies
il ait
nous ayons
vous ayez
ils aient

IMPERFECT
je eusse
tu eusses
il eût
nous eussions
vous eussiez
ils eussent

PERFECT
j'aie eu
tu aies eu
il ait eu
nous ayons eu
vous ayez eu
ils aient eu

IMPERATIVE
aie
ayons
ayez

INFINITIVE

PRESENT
avoir

PAST
avoir eu

PARTICIPLE

PRESENT
ayant

PAST
eu

CONDUIRE to lead, to drive

PRESENT
je conduis
tu conduis
il conduit
nous conduisons
vous conduisez
ils conduisent

IMPERFECT
je conduisais
tu conduisais
il conduisait
nous conduisions
vous conduisiez
ils conduisaient

FUTURE
je conduirai
tu conduiras
il conduira
nous conduirons
vous conduirez
ils conduiront

PAST HISTORIC
je conduisis
tu conduisis
il conduisit
nous conduisîmes
vous conduisîtes
ils conduisirent

PERFECT
j'ai conduit
tu as conduit
il a conduit
nous avons conduit
vous avez conduit
ils ont conduit

PLUPERFECT
j'avais conduit
tu avais conduit
il avait conduit
nous avions conduit
vous aviez conduit
ils avaient conduit

PAST ANTERIOR
j'eus conduit etc

FUTURE PERFECT
j'aurai conduit etc

CONDITIONAL

PRESENT
je conduirais
tu conduirais
il conduirait
nous conduirions
vous conduiriez
ils conduiraient

PAST
j'aurais conduit
tu aurais conduit
il aurait conduit
nous aurions conduit
vous auriez conduit
ils auraient conduit

SUBJUNCTIVE

PRESENT
je conduise
tu conduises
il conduise
nous conduisions
vous conduisiez
ils conduisent

IMPERFECT
je conduisisse
tu conduisisses
il conduisit
nous conduisissions
vous conduisissiez
ils conduisissent

PERFECT
j'aie conduit
tu aies conduit
il ait conduit
nous ayons conduit
vous ayez conduit
ils aient conduit

IMPERATIVE
conduise
conduisons
conduisez

INFINITIVE

PRESENT
conduire

PAST
avoir conduit

PARTICIPLE

PRESENT
conduisant

PAST
conduit

CONNAITRE to know

PRESENT
je connais
tu connais
il connait
nous connaissons
vous connaissez
ils connaissent

IMPERFECT
je connaissais
tu connaissais
il connaissait
nous connaissions
vous connaissiez
ils connaissaient

FUTURE
je connaîtrai
tu connaîtras
il connaîtra
nous connaîtrons
vous connaîtrez
ils connaîtront

PAST HISTORIC
je connus
tu connus
il connut
nous connûmes
vous connûtes
ils connurent

PERFECT
j'ai connu
tu as connu
il a connu
nous avons connu
vous avez connu
ils ont connu

PLUPERFECT
j'avais connu
tu avais connu
il avait connu
nous avions connu
vous aviez connu
ils avaient connu

PAST ANTERIOR
j'eus connu etc

FUTURE PERFECT
j'aurai connu etc

CONDITIONAL

PRESENT
je connaîtrais
tu connaîtrais
il connaîtrait
nous connaîtrions
vous connaîtriez
ils connaîtraient

PAST
j'aurais connu
tu aurais connu
il aurait connu
nous aurions connu
vous auriez connu
ils auraient connu

SUBJUNCTIVE

PRESENT
je connaisse
tu connaisses
il connaisse
nous connaissions
vous connaissiez
ils connaissent

IMPERFECT
je connusse
tu connusses
il connût
nous connussions
vous connussiez
ils connussent

PERFECT
j'aie connu
tu aies connu
il ait connu
nous ayons connu
vous ayez connu
ils aient connu

IMPERATIVE
connais
connaissons
connaissez

INFINITIVE

PRESENT
connaître

PAST
avoir connu

PARTICIPLE

PRESENT
connaissant

PAST
connu

CROIRE to believe

PRESENT
je crois
tu crois
il croit
nous croyons
vous croyez
ils croient

PAST HISTORIC
je crus
tu crus
il crut
nous crûmes
vous crûtes
ils crurent

IMPERFECT
je croyais
tu croyais
il croyait
nous croyions
vous croyiez
ils croyaient

PERFECT
j'ai cru
tu as cru
il a cru
nous avons cru
vous avez cru
ils ont cru

FUTURE
je croirai
tu croiras
il croira
nous croirons
vous croirez
ils croiront

PLUPERFECT
j'avais cru
tu avais cru
il avait cru
nous aviez cru
vous aviez cru
ils avaient cru

CONDITIONAL

PAST ANTERIOR
j'eus cru etc

FUTURE PERFECT
j'aurai cru etc

PRESENT
je croirais
tu croirais
il croirait
nous croirions
vous croiriez
ils croiraient

PAST
j'aurais cru
tu aurais cru
il aurait cru
nous aurions cru
vous auriez cru
ils auraient cru

SUBJUNCTIVE

PRESENT
je croie
tu croies
il croie
nous croyions
vous croyiez
ils croient

IMPERFECT
je crusse
tu crusses
il crût
nous crussions
vous crussiez
ils crussent

PERFECT
j'aie cru
tu aies cru
il ait cru
nous ayons cru
vous ayez cru
ils aient cru

IMPERATIVE
crois
croyons
croyez

INFINITIVE

PRESENT
croire

PAST
avoir cru

PARTICIPLE

PRESENT
croyant

PAST
cru

DEVOIR to have to

PRESENT
je dois
tu dois
il doit
nous devons
vous devez
ils doivent

PAST HISTORIC
je dus
tu dus
il dut
nous dûmes
vous dûtes
ils durent

IMPERFECT
je devais
tu devais
il devait
nous devions
vous deviez
ils devaient

PERFECT
j'ai dû
tu as dû
il a dû
nous avons dû
vous avez dû
ils ont dû

FUTURE
je devrai
tu devras
il devra
nous devrons
vous devrez
ils devront

PLUPERFECT
j'avais dû
tu avais dû
il avait dû
nous avions dû
vous aviez dû
ils avaient dû

CONDITIONAL

PAST ANTERIOR
j'eus dû etc

FUTURE PERFECT
j'aurai dû etc

PRESENT
je devrais
tu devrais
il devrait
nous devrions
vous devriez
ils devraient

PAST
j'aurais dû
tu aurais dû
il aurait dû
nous aurions dû
vous auriez dû
ils auraient dû

SUBJUNCTIVE

PRESENT
je doive
tu doives
il doive
nous devions
vous deviez
ils doivent

IMPERFECT
je dusse
tu dusses
il dût
nous dussions
vous dussiez
ils dussent

PERFECT
j'aie dû
tu aies dû
il ait dû
nous ayons dû
vous ayez dû
ils aient dû

IMPERATIVE
dois
devons
devez

INFINITIVE

PRESENT
devoir

PAST
avoir dû

PARTICIPLE

PRESENT
devant

PAST
dû

DIRE to say

PRESENT
je dis
tu dis
il dit
nous disons
vous dites
ils disent

PAST HISTORIC
je dis
tu dis
il dit
nous dîmes
vous dîtes
ils dirent

IMPERFECT
je disais
tu disais
il disait
nous disions
vous disiez
ils disaient

PERFECT
j'ai dit
tu as dit
il a dit
nous avons dit
vous avez dit
ils ont dit

FUTURE
je dirai
tu diras
il dira
nous dirons
vous direz
ils diront

PLUPERFECT
j'avais dit
tu avais dit
il avait dit
nous avions dit
vous aviez dit
ils avaient dit

CONDITIONAL

PAST ANTERIOR
j'eus dit etc

FUTURE PERFECT
j'aurai dit etc

PRESENT
je dirais
tu dirais
il dirait
nous dirions
vous diriez
ils diraient

PAST
j'aurais dit
tu aurais dit
il aurait dit
nous aurions dit
vous auriez dit
ils auraient dit

SUBJUNCTIVE

PRESENT
je dise
tu dises
il dise
nous disions
vous disiez
ils disent

IMPERFECT
je disse
tu disses
il dît
nous dissions
vous dissiez
ils dissent

PERFECT
j'aie dit
tu aies dit
il ait dit
nous ayons dit
vous ayez dit
ils aient dit

IMPERATIVE
dis
disons
dites

INFINITIVE

PRESENT
dire

PAST
avoir dit

PARTICIPLE

PRESENT
disant

PAST
dit

DORMIR to sleep

PRESENT
je dors
tu dors
il dort
nous dormons
vous dormez
ils dorment

IMPERFECT
je dormais
tu dormais
il dormait
nous dormions
vous dormiez
ils dormaient

FUTURE
je dormirai
tu dormiras
il dormira
nous dormirons
vous dormirez
ils dormiront

PAST HISTORIC
je dormis
tu dormis
il dormit
nous dormîmes
vous dormîtes
ils dormirent

PERFECT
j'ai dormi
tu as dormi
il a dormi
nous avons dormi
vous avez dormi
ils ont dormi

PLUPERFECT
j'avais dormi
tu avais dormi
il avait dormi
nous avions dormi
vous aviez dormi
ils avaient dormi

CONDITIONAL

PAST ANTERIOR
j'eus dormi etc

FUTURE PERFECT
j'aurai dormi etc

PRESENT
je dormirais
tu dormirais
il dormirait
nous dormirions
vous dormiriez
ils dormiraient

PAST
j'aurais dormi
tu aurais dormi
il aurait dormi
nous aurions dormi
vous auriez dormi
ils auraient dormi

SUBJUNCTIVE

PRESENT
je dorme
tu dormes
il dorme
nous dormions
vous dormiez
ils dorment

IMPERFECT
je dormisse
tu dormisses
il dormît
nous dormissions
vous dormissiez
ils dormissent

PERFECT
j'aie dormi
tu aies dormi
il ait dormi
nous ayons dormi
vous ayez dormi
ils aient dormi

IMPERATIVE
dors
dormons
dormez

INFINITIVE

PRESENT
dormir

PAST
avoir dormi

PARTICIPLE

PRESENT
dormant

PAST
dormi

ECRIRE to write

PRESENT
j'écris
tu écris
il écrit
nous écrivons
vous écrivez
ils écrivent

IMPERFECT
j'écrivais
tu écrivais
il écrivait
nous écrivions
vous écriviez
ils écrivaient

FUTURE
j'écrirai
tu écriras
il écrira
nous écrirons
vous écrirez
ils écriront

PAST HISTORIC
j'écrivis
tu écrivis
il écrivit
nous écrivîmes
vous écrivîtes
ils écrivirent

PERFECT
j'ai écrit
tu as écrit
il a écrit
nous avons écrit
vous avez écrit
ils ont écrit

PLUPERFECT
j'avais écrit
tu avais écrit
il avait écrit
nous avions écrit
vous aviez écrit
ils avaient écrit

CONDITIONAL

PAST ANTERIOR
j'eus écrit etc

FUTURE PERFECT
j'aurai écrit etc

PRESENT
j'écrirais
tu écrirais
il écrirait
nous écririons
vous écririez
ils écriraient

PAST
j'aurais écrit
tu aurais écrit
il aurait écrit
nous aurions écrit
vous auriez écrit
ils auraient écrit

SUBJUNCTIVE

PRESENT
j'écrive
tu écrives
il écrive
nous écrivions
vous écriviez
ils écrivent

IMPERFECT
j'écrivisse
tu écrivisses
il écrivît
nous écrivissions
vous écrivissiez
ils écrivissent

PERFECT
j'aie écrit
tu aies écrit
il ait écrit
nous ayons écrit
vous ayez écrit
ils aient écrit

IMPERATIVE
écris
écrivons
écrivez

INFINITIVE

PRESENT
écrire

PAST
avoir écrit

PARTICIPLE

PRESENT
écrivant

PAST
écrit

ESPERER to hope

PRESENT
j'espère
tu espères
il espère
nous espérons
vous espérez
ils espèrent

IMPERFECT
j'espérais
tu espérais
il espérait
nous espérions
vous espériez
ils espéraient

FUTURE
j'espérerai
tu espéreras
il espérera
nous espérerons
vous espérerez
ils espéreront

PAST HISTORIC
j'espérai
tu espéras
il espéra
nous espérâmes
vous espérâtes
ils espérèrent

PERFECT
j'ai espéré
tu as espéré
il a espéré
nous avons espéré
vous avez espéré
ils ont espéré

PLUPERFECT
j'avais espéré
tu avais espéré
il avait espéré
nous avions espéré
vous aviez espéré
ils avaient espéré

CONDITIONAL

PAST ANTERIOR
j'eus espéré etc

FUTURE PERFECT
j'aurai espéré etc

PRESENT
j'espérerais
tu espérerais
il espérerait
nous espérerions
vous espéreriez
ils espéreraient

PAST
j'aurais espéré
tu aurais espéré
il aurait espéré
nous aurions espéré
vous auriez espéré
ils auraient espéré

SUBJUNCTIVE

PRESENT
j'espère
tu espères
il espère
nous espérions
vous espériez
ils espèrent

IMPERFECT
j'espérasse
tu espérasses
il espérât
nous espérassions
vous espérassiez
ils espérassent

PERFECT
j'aie espéré
tu aies espéré
il ait espéré
nous ayons espéré
vous ayez espéré
ils aient espéré

IMPERATIVE
espère
espérons
espérez

INFINITIVE

PRESENT
espérer

PAST
avoir espéré

PARTICIPLE

PRESENT
espérant

PAST
espéré

ETRE to be

PRESENT
je suis
tu es
il est
nous sommes
vous êtes
ils sont

IMPERFECT
j'étais
tu étais
il était
nous étions
vous étiez
ils étaient

FUTURE
je serai
tu seras
il sera
nous serons
vous serez
ils seront

PAST HISTORIC
je fus
tu fus
il fut
nous fûmes
vous fûtes
ils furent

PERFECT
j'ai été
tu as été
il a été
nous avons été
vous avez été
ils ont été

PLUPERFECT
j'avais été
tu avais été
il avait été
nous avions été
vous aviez été
ils avaient été

CONDITIONAL

PAST ANTERIOR
j'eus été etc

FUTURE PERFECT
j'aurai été etc

PRESENT
je serais
tu serais
il serait
nous serions
vous seriez
ils seraient

PAST
j'aurais été
tu aurais été
il aurait été
nous aurions été
vous auriez été
ils auraient été

SUBJUNCTIVE

PRESENT
je sois
tu sois
il soit
nous soyons
vous soyez
ils soient

IMPERFECT
je fusse
tu fusses
il fût
nous fussions
vous fussiez
ils fussent

PERFECT
j'aie été
tu aies été
il ait été
nous ayons été
vous ayez été
ils aient été

IMPERATIVE
sois
soyons
soyez

INFINITIVE

PRESENT
être

PAST
avoir été

PARTICIPLE

PRESENT
étant

PAST
été

FAIRE to do, to make

PRESENT
je fais
tu fais
il fait
nous faisons
vous faites
ils font

IMPERFECT
je faisais
tu faisais
il faisait
nous faisions
vous faisiez
ils faisaient

FUTURE
je ferai
tu feras
il fera
nous ferons
vous ferez
ils feront

PAST HISTORIC
je fis
tu fis
il fit
nous fîmes
vous fîtes
ils firent

PERFECT
j'ai fait
tu as fait
il a fait
nous avons fait
vous avez fait
ils ont fait

PLUPERFECT
j'avais fait
tu avais fait
il avait fait
nous avions fait
vous aviez fait
ils avaient fait

CONDITIONAL

PAST ANTERIOR
j'eus fait etc

FUTURE PERFECT
j'aurai fait etc

PRESENT
je ferais
tu ferais
il ferait
nous ferions
vous feriez
ils feraient

PAST
j'aurais fait
tu aurais fait
il aurait fait
nous aurions fait
vous auriez fait
ils auraient fait

SUBJUNCTIVE

PRESENT
je fasse
tu fasses
il fasse
nous fassions
vous fassiez
ils fassent

IMPERFECT
je fisse
tu fisses
il fît
nous fissions
vous fissiez
ils fissent

PERFECT
j'aie fait
tu aies fait
il ait fait
nous ayons fait
vous ayez fait
ils aient fait

IMPERATIVE
fais
faisons
faites

INFINITIVE

PRESENT
faire

PAST
avoir fait

PARTICIPLE

PRESENT
faisant

PAST
fait

FALLOIR to be necessary

PRESENT
il faut

IMPERFECT
il fallait

FUTURE
il faudra

PAST HISTORIC
il fallut

PERFECT
il a fallu

PLUPERFECT
il avait fallu

CONDITIONAL

PAST ANTERIOR
il eut fallu

FUTURE PERFECT
il aura fallu

PRESENT
il faudrait

PAST
il aurait fallu

SUBJUNCTIVE

PRESENT
il faille

IMPERFECT
il fallût

PERFECT
il ait fallu

IMPERATIVE

INFINITIVE

PRESENT
falloir

PAST
avoir fallu

PARTICIPLE

PRESENT

PAST
fallu

FINIR to finish

PRESENT
je finis
tu finis
il finit
nous finissons
vous finissez
ils finissent

IMPERFECT
je finissais
tu finissais
il finissait
nous finissions
vous finissiez
ils finissaient

FUTURE
je finirai
tu finiras
il finira
nous finirons
vous finirez
ils finiront

PAST HISTORIC
je finis
tu finis
il finit
nous finîmes
vous finîtes
ils finirent

PERFECT
j'ai fini
tu as fini
il a fini
nous avons fini
vous avez fini
ils ont fini

PLUPERFECT
j'avais fini
tu avais fini
il avait fini
nous avions fini
vous aviez fini
ils avaient fini

PAST ANTERIOR
j'eus fini etc

FUTURE PERFECT
j'aurai fini etc

CONDITIONAL

PRESENT
je finirais
tu finirais
il finirait
nous finirions
vous finiriez
ils finiraient

PAST
j'aurais fini
tu aurais fini
il aurait fini
nous aurions fini
vous auriez fini
ils auraient fini

SUBJUNCTIVE

PRESENT
je finisse
tu finisses
il finisse
nous finissions
vous finissiez
ils finissent

IMPERFECT
je finisse
tu finisses
il finît
nous finissions
vous finissiez
ils finissent

PERFECT
j'aie fini
tu aies fini
il ait fini
nous ayons fini
vous ayez fini
ils aient fini

IMPERATIVE
finis
finissons
finissez

INFINITIVE

PRESENT
finir

PAST
avoir fini

PARTICIPLE

PRESENT
finissant

PAST
fini

SE MEFIER to be suspicious

PRESENT
je me méfie
tu te méfies
il se méfie
nous nous méfions
vous vous méfiez
ils se méfient

IMPERFECT
je me méfiais
tu te méfiais
il se méfiait
nous nous méfiions
vous vous méfiiez
ils se méfiaient

FUTURE
je me méfierai
tu te méfieras
il se méfiera
nous nous méfierons
vous vous méfierez
ils se méfieront

PAST HISTORIC
je me méfiai
tu te méfias
il se méfia
nous nous méfiâmes
vous vous méfiâtes
ils se méfièrent

PERFECT
je me suis méfié(e)
tu t'es méfié(e)
il (elle) s'est méfié(e)
nous nous sommes méfié(e)s
vous vous êtes méfié(e)(s)
ils (elles) se sont méfié(e)s

PLUPERFECT
je m'étais méfié(e)
tu t'étais méfié(e)
il (elle) s'était méfié(e)
nous nous étions méfié(e)s
vous vous étiez méfié(e)(s)
ils (elles) s'étaient méfié(e)s

PAST ANTERIOR
je me fus méfié(e) etc

FUTURE PERFECT
je me serai méfié(e) etc

CONDITIONAL

PRESENT
je me méfierais
tu te méfierais
il se méfierait
nous nous méfierions
vous vous méfieriez
ils (elles) se méfieraient

PAST
je me serais méfié(e)
tu te serais méfié(e)
il (elle) se serait méfié(e)
nous nous serions méfié(e)s
vous vous seriez méfié(e)(s)
ils (elles) se seraient méfié(e)s

SUBJUNCTIVE

PRESENT
je me méfie
tu te méfies
il se méfie
nous nous méfiions
vous vous méfiiez
ils se méfient

IMPERFECT
je me méfiasse
tu te méfiasses
il se méfiât
nous nous méfiassions
vous vous méfiassiez
ils se méfiassent

PERFECT
je me sois méfié(e)
tu te sois méfié(e)
il (elle) se soit méfié(e)
nous nous soyons méfié(e)s
vous vous soyez méfié(e)(s)
ils (elles) se soient méfié(e)s

IMPERATIVE
méfie-toi
méfions-nous
méfiez-vous

INFINITIVE

PRESENT
s'être méfié(e)(s)

PAST
méfié

PARTICIPLE

PRESENT
se méfiant

PAST
méfié

METTRE to put

PRESENT
je mets
tu mets
il met
nous mettons
vous mettez
ils mettent

IMPERFECT
je mettais
tu mettais
il mettait
nous mettions
vous mettiez
ils mettaient

FUTURE
je mettrai
tu mettras
il mettra
nous mettrons
vous mettrez
ils mettront

PAST HISTORIC
je mis
tu mis
il mit
nous mîmes
vous mîtes
ils mirent

PERFECT
j'ai mis
tu as mis
il a mis
nous avons mis
vous avez mis
ils ont mis

PLUPERFECT
j'avais mis
tu avais mis
il avait mis
nous avions mis
vous aviez mis
ils avaient mis

PAST ANTERIOR
j'eus mis etc

FUTURE PERFECT
j'aurai mis etc

CONDITIONAL

PRESENT
je mettrais
tu mettrais
il mettrait
nous mettrions
vous mettriez
ils mettraient

PAST
j'aurais mis
tu aurais mis
il aurait mis
nous aurions mis
vous auriez mis
ils auraient mis

SUBJUNCTIVE

PRESENT
je mette
tu mettes
il mette
nous mettions
vous mettiez
ils mettent

IMPERFECT
je misse
tu misses
il mît
nous missions
vous missiez
ils missent

PERFECT
j'aie mis
tu aies mis
il ait mis
nous ayons mis
vous ayez mis
ils aient mis

IMPERATIVE
mets
mettons
mettez

INFINITIVE

PRESENT
mettre

PAST
avoir mis

PARTICIPLE

PRESENT
mettant

PAST
mis

OUVRIR to open

PRESENT
j'ouvre
tu ouvres
il ouvre
nous ouvrons
vous ouvrez
ils ouvrent

IMPERFECT
j'ouvrais
tu ouvrais
il ouvrait
nous ouvrions
vous ouvriez
ils ouvraient

FUTURE
j'ouvrirai
tu ouvriras
il ouvrira
nous ouvrirons
vous ouvrirez
ils ouvriront

PAST HISTORIC
j'ouvris
tu ouvris
il ouvrit
nous ouvrîmes
vous ouvrîtes
ils ouvrirent

PERFECT
j'ai ouvert
tu as ouvert
il a ouvert
nous avons ouvert
vous avez ouvert
ils ont ouvert

PLUPERFECT
j'avais ouvert
tu avais ouvert
il avait ouvert
nous avions ouvert
vous aviez ouvert
ils avaient ouvert

CONDITIONAL

PAST ANTERIOR
j'eus ouvert etc

FUTURE PERFECT
j'aurai ouvert etc

PRESENT
j'ouvrirais
tu ouvrirais
il ouvrirait
nous ouvririons
vous ouvririez
ils ouvriraient

PAST
j'aurais ouvert
tu aurais ouvert
il aurait ouvert
nous aurions ouvert
vous auriez ouvert
ils auraient ouvert

SUBJUNCTIVE

PRESENT
j'ouvre
tu ouvres
il ouvre
nous ouvrions
vous ouvriez
ils ouvrent

IMPERFECT
j'ouvrisse
tu ouvrisses
il ouvrît
nous ouvrissions
vous ouvrissiez
ils ouvrissent

PERFECT
j'aie ouvert
tu aies ouvert
il ait ouvert
nous ayons ouvert
vous ayez ouvert
ils aient ouvert

IMPERATIVE
ouvre
ouvrons
ouvrez

INFINITIVE

PRESENT
ouvrir

PAST
avoir ouvert

PARTICIPLE

PRESENT
ouvrant

PAST
ouvert

POUVOIR to be able to

PRESENT
je peux
tu peux
il peut
nous pouvons
vous pouvez
ils peuvent

IMPERFECT
je pouvais
tu pouvais
il pouvait
nous pouvions
vous pouviez
ils pouvaient

FUTURE
je pourrai
tu pourras
il pourra
nous pourrons
vous pourrez
ils pourront

PAST HISTORIC
je pus
tu pus
il put
nous pûmes
vous pûtes
ils purent

PERFECT
j'ai pu
tu as pu
il a pu
nous avons pu
vous avez pu
ils ont pu

PLUPERFECT
j'avais pu
tu avais pu
il avait pu
nous avions pu
vous aviez pu
ils avaient pu

CONDITIONAL

PAST ANTERIOR
j'eus pu etc

FUTURE PERFECT
j'aurai pu etc

PRESENT
je pourrais
tu pourrais
il pourrait
nous pourrions
vous pourriez
ils pourraient

PAST
j'aurais pu
tu aurais pu
il aurait pu
nous aurions pu
vous auriez pu
ils auraient pu

SUBJUNCTIVE

PRESENT
je puisse
tu puisses
il puisse
nous puissions
vous puissiez
ils puissent

IMPERFECT
je pusse
tu pusses
il pût
nous pussions
vous pussiez
ils pussent

PERFECT
j'aie pu
tu aies pu
il ait pu
nous ayons pu
vous ayez pu
ils aient pu

IMPERATIVE

INFINITIVE

PRESENT
pouvoir

PAST
avoir pu

PARTICIPLE

PRESENT
pouvant

PAST
pu

PRENDRE to take

PRESENT
je prends
tu prends
il prend
nous prenons
vous prenez
ils prennent

IMPERFECT
je prenais
tu prenais
il prenait
nous prenions
vous preniez
ils prenaient

FUTURE
je prendrai
tu prendras
il prendra
nous prendrons
vous prendrez
ils prendront

PAST HISTORIC
je pris
tu pris
il prit
nous prîmes
vous prîtes
ils prirent

PERFECT
j'ai pris
tu as pris
il a pris
nous avons pris
vous avez pris
ils ont pris

PLUPERFECT
j'avais pris
tu avais pris
il avait pris
nous avions pris
vous aviez pris
ils avaient pris

CONDITIONAL

PAST ANTERIOR
j'eus pris etc

FUTURE PERFECT
j'aurai pris etc

PRESENT
je prendrais
tu prendrais
il prendrait
nous prendrions
vous prendriez
ils prendraient

PAST
j'aurais pris
tu aurais pris
il aurait pris
nous aurions pris
vous auriez pris
ils auraient pris

SUBJUNCTIVE

PRESENT
je prenne
tu prennes
il prenne
nous prenions
vous preniez
ils prennent

IMPERFECT
je prisse
tu prisses
il prît
nous prissions
vous prissiez
ils prissent

PERFECT
j'aie pris
tu aies pris
il ait pris
nous ayons pris
vous ayez pris
ils aient pris

IMPERATIVE
prends
prenons
prenez

INFINITIVE

PRESENT
prendre

PAST
avoir pris

PARTICIPLE

PRESENT
prenant

PAST
pris

RECEVOIR to receive

PRESENT
je reçois
tu reçois
il reçoit
nous recevons
vous recevez
ils reçoivent

IMPERFECT
je recevais
tu recevais
il recevait
nous recevions
vous receviez
ils recevaient

FUTURE
je recevrai
tu recevras
il recevra
nous recevrons
vous recevrez
ils recevront

PAST HISTORIC
je reçus
tu reçus
il reçut
nous reçûmes
vous reçûtes
ils reçurent

PERFECT
j'ai reçu
tu as reçu
il a reçu
nous avons reçu
vous avez reçu
ils ont reçu

PLUPERFECT
j'avais reçu
tu avais reçu
il avait reçu
nous avions reçu
vous aviez reçu
ils avaient reçu

CONDITIONAL

PAST ANTERIOR
j'eus reçu etc

FUTURE PERFECT
j'aurai reçu etc

PRESENT
je recevrais
tu recevrais
il recevrait
nous recevrions
vous recevriez
ils recevraient

PAST
j'aurais reçu
tu aurais reçu
il aurait reçu
nous aurions reçu
vous auriez reçu
ils auraient reçu

SUBJUNCTIVE

PRESENT
je reçoive
tu reçoives
il reçoive
nous recevions
vous receviez
ils reçoivent

IMPERFECT
je reçusse
tu reçusses
il reçût
nous reçussions
vous reçussiez
ils reçussent

PERFECT
j'aie reçu
tu aies reçu
il ait reçu
nous ayons reçu
vous ayez reçu
ils aient reçu

IMPERATIVE
reçois
recevons
recevez

INFINITIVE

PRESENT
recevoir

PAST
avoir reçu

PARTICIPLE

PRESENT
recevant

PAST
reçu

SAVOIR to know

PRESENT
je sais
tu sais
il sait
nous savons
vous savez
ils savent

IMPERFECT
je savais
tu savais
il savait
nous savions
vous saviez
ils savaient

FUTURE
je saurai
tu sauras
il saura
nous saurons
vous saurez
ils sauront

PAST HISTORIC
je sus
tu sus
il sut
nous sûmes
vous sûtes
ils surent

PERFECT
j'ai su
tu as su
il a su
nous avons su
vous avez su
ils ont su

PLUPERFECT
j'avais su
tu avais su
il avait su
nous avions su
vous aviez su
ils avaient su

CONDITIONAL

PAST ANTERIOR
j'eus su etc

FUTURE PERFECT
j'aurai su etc

PRESENT
je saurais
tu saurais
il saurait
nous saurions
vous sauriez
ils sauraient

PAST
j'aurais su
tu aurais su
il aurait su
nous aurions su
vous auriez su
ils auraient su

SUBJUNCTIVE

PRESENT
je sache
tu saches
il sache
nous sachions
vous sachiez
ils sachent

IMPERFECT
je susse
tu susses
il sût
nous sussions
vous sussiez
ils sussent

PERFECT
j'aie su
tu aies su
il ait su
nous ayons su
vous ayez su
ils aient su

IMPERATIVE
sache
sachons
sachez

INFINITIVE

PRESENT
savoir

PAST
avoir su

PARTICIPLE

PRESENT
sachant

PAST
su

TENIR to hold

PRESENT
je tiens
tu tiens
il tient
nous tenons
vous tenez
ils tiennent

IMPERFECT
je tenais
tu tenais
il tenait
nous tenions
vous teniez
ils tenaient

FUTURE
je tiendrai
tu tiendras
il tiendra
nous tiendrons
vous tiendrez
ils tiendront

PAST HISTORIC
je tins
tu tins
il tint
nous tînmes
vous tîntes
ils tinrent

PERFECT
j'ai tenu
tu as tenu
il a tenu
nous avons tenu
vous avez tenu
ils ont tenu

PLUPERFECT
j'avais tenu
tu avais tenu
il avait tenu
nous avions tenu
vous aviez tenu
ils avaient tenu

CONDITIONAL

PAST ANTERIOR
j'eus tenu etc

FUTURE PERFECT
j'aurai tenu etc

PRESENT
je tiendrais
tu tiendrais
il tiendrait
nous tiendrions
vous tiendriez
ils tiendraient

PAST
j'aurais tenu
tu aurais tenu
il aurait tenu
nous aurions tenu
vous auriez tenu
ils auraient tenu

SUBJUNCTIVE

PRESENT
je tienne
tu tiennes
il tienne
nous tenions
vous teniez
ils tiennent

IMPERFECT
je tinsse
tu tinsses
il tînt
nous tinssions
vous tinssiez
ils tinssent

PERFECT
j'aie tenu
tu aies tenu
il ait tenu
nous ayons tenu
vous ayez tenu
ils aient tenu

IMPERATIVE
tiens
tenons
tenez

INFINITIVE

PRESENT
tenir

PAST
avoir tenu

PARTICIPLE

PRESENT
tenant

PAST
tenu

VENDRE to sell

PRESENT
je vends
tu vends
il vend
nous vendons
vous vendez
ils vendent

IMPERFECT
je vendais
tu vendais
il vendait
nous vendions
vous vendiez
ils vendaient

FUTURE
je vendrai
tu vendras
il vendra
nous vendrons
vous vendrez
ils vendront

PAST HISTORIC
je vendis
tu vendis
il vendit
nous vendîmes
vous vendîtes
ils vendirent

PERFECT
j'ai vendu
tu as vendu
il a vendu
nous avons vendu
vous avez vendu
ils ont vendu

PLUPERFECT
j'avais vendu
tu avais vendu
il avait vendu
nous avions vendu
vous aviez vendu
ils avaient vendu

PAST ANTERIOR
j'eus vendu etc

FUTURE PERFECT
j'aurai vendu etc

CONDITIONAL

PRESENT
je vendrais
tu vendrais
il vendrait
nous vendrions
vous vendriez
ils vendraient

PAST
j'aurais vendu
tu aurais vendu
il aurait vendu
nous aurions vendu
vous auriez vendu
ils auraient vendu

SUBJUNCTIVE

PRESENT
je vende
tu vendes
il vende
nous vendions
vous vendiez
ils vendent

IMPERFECT
je vendisse
tu vendisses
il vendît
nous vendissions
vous vendissiez
ils vendissent

PERFECT
j'aie vendu
tu aies vendu
il ait vendu
nous ayons vendu
vous ayez vendu
ils aient vendu

IMPERATIVE

vends
vendons
vendez

INFINITIVE

PRESENT
vendre

PAST
avoir vendu

PARTICIPLE

PRESENT
vendant

PAST
vendu

VENIR to come

PRESENT
je viens
tu viens
il vient
nous venons
vous venez
ils viennent

IMPERFECT
je venais
tu venais
il venait
nous venions
vous veniez
ils venaient

FUTURE
je viendrai
tu viendras
il viendra
nous viendrons
vous viendrez
ils viendront

PAST HISTORIC
je vins
tu vins
il vint
nous vînmes
vous vîntes
ils vinrent

PERFECT
je suis venu(e)
tu es venu(e)
il (elle) est venu(e)
nous sommes venu(e)s
vous êtes venu(e)(s)
ils (elles) sont venu(e)s

PLUPERFECT
j'étais venu(e)
tu étais venu(e)
il (elle) était venu(e)
nous étions venu(e)s
vous étiez venu(e)(s)
ils (elles) étaient venu(e)s

PAST ANTERIOR
je fus venu(e) etc

FUTURE PERFECT
je serai venu(e) etc

CONDITIONAL

PRESENT
je viendrais
tu viendrais
il viendrait
nous viendrions
vous viendriez
ils viendraient

PAST
je serais venu(e)
tu serais venu(e)
il (elle) serait venu(e)
nous serions venu(e)s
vous seriez venu(e)(s)
ils (elles) seraient venu(e)s

SUBJUNCTIVE

PRESENT
je vienne
tu viennes
il vienne
nous venions
vous veniez
ils viennent

IMPERFECT
je vinsse
tu vinsses
il vînt
nous vinssions
vous vinssiez
ils vinssent

PERFECT
je sois venu(e)
tu sois venu(e)
il (elle) soit venu(e)
nous soyons venu(e)s
vous soyez venu(e)(s)
ils (elles) soient venu(e)s

IMPERATIVE

viens
venons
venez

INFINITIVE

PRESENT
venir

PAST
être venu(e)(s)

PARTICIPLE

PRESENT
venant

PAST
venu

VIVRE to live

PRESENT
je vis
tu vis
il vit
nous vivons
vous vivez
ils vivent

IMPERFECT
je vivais
tu vivais
il vivait
nous vivions
vous viviez
ils vivaient

FUTURE
je vivrai
tu vivras
il vivra
nous vivrons
vous vivrez
ils vivront

PAST HISTORIC
je vécus
tu vécus
il vécut
nous vécûmes
vous vécûtes
ils vécurent

PERFECT
j'ai vécu
tu as vécu
il a vécu
nous avons vécu
vous avez vécu
ils ont vécu

PLUPERFECT
j'avais vécu
tu avais vécu
il avait vécu
nous avions vécu
vous aviez vécu
ils avaient vécu

PAST ANTERIOR
j'eus vécu etc

FUTURE PERFECT
j'aurai vécu etc

CONDITIONAL

PRESENT
je vivrais
tu vivrais
il vivrait
nous vivrions
vous vivriez
ils vivraient

PAST
j'aurais vécu
tu aurais vécu
il aurait vécu
nous aurions vécu
vous auriez vécu
ils auraient vécu

SUBJUNCTIVE

PRESENT
je vive
tu vives
il vive
nous vivions
vous viviez
ils vivent

IMPERFECT
je vécusse
tu vécusses
il vécût
nous vécussions
vous vécussiez
ils vécussent

PERFECT
j'aie vécu
tu aies vécu
il ait vécu
nous ayons vécu
vous ayez vécu
ils aient vécu

IMPERATIVE

vis
vivons
vivez

INFINITIVE

PRESENT
vivre

PAST
avoir vécu

PARTICIPLE

PRESENT
vivant

PAST
vécu

VOIR to see

PRESENT
je vois
tu vois
il voit
nous voyons
vous voyez
ils voient

PAST HISTORIC
je vis
tu vis
il vit
nous vîmes
vous vîtes
ils virent

IMPERFECT
je voyais
tu voyais
il voyait
nous voyions
vous voyiez
ils voyaient

PERFECT
j'ai vu
tu as vu
il a vu
nous avons vu
vous avez vu
ils ont vu

FUTURE
je verrai
tu verras
il verra
nous verrons
vous verrez
ils verront

PLUPERFECT
j'avais vu
tu avais vu
il avait vu
nous avions vu
vous aviez vu
ils avaient vu

CONDITIONAL

PAST ANTERIOR
j'eus vu etc

FUTURE PERFECT
j'aurai vu etc

PRESENT
je verrais
tu verrais
il verrait
nous verrions
vous verriez
ils verraient

PAST
j'aurais vu
tu aurais vu
il aurait vu
nous aurions vu
vous auriez vu
ils auraient vu

SUBJUNCTIVE

PRESENT
je voie
tu voies
il voie
nous voyions
vous voyiez
ils voient

IMPERFECT
je visse
tu visses
il vît
nous vissions
vous vissiez
ils vissent

PERFECT
j'aie vu
tu aies vu
il ait vu
nous ayons vu
vous ayez vu
ils aient vu

IMPERATIVE
vois
voyons
voyez

INFINITIVE

PRESENT
voir

PAST
avoir vu

PARTICIPLE

PRESENT
voyant

PAST
vu

VOULOIR to want

PRESENT
je veux
tu veux
il veut
nous voulons
vous voulez
ils veulent

PAST HISTORIC
je voulus
tu voulus
il voulut
nous voulûmes
vous voulûtes
ils voulurent

IMPERFECT
je voulais
tu voulais
il voulait
nous voulions
vous vouliez
ils voulaient

PERFECT
j'ai voulu
tu as voulu
il a voulu
nous avons voulu
vous avez voulu
ils ont voulu

FUTURE
je voudrai
tu voudras
il voudra
nous voudrons
vous voudrez
ils voudront

PLUPERFECT
j'avais voulu
tu avais voulu
il avait voulu
nous avions voulu
vous aviez voulu
ils avaient voulu

CONDITIONAL

PAST ANTERIOR
j'eus voulu etc

FUTURE PERFECT
j'aurai voulu etc

PRESENT
je voudrais
tu voudrais
il voudrait
nous voudrions
vous voudriez
ils voudraient

PAST
j'aurais voulu
tu aurais voulu
il aurait voulu
nous aurions voulu
vous auriez voulu
ils auraient voulu

SUBJUNCTIVE

PRESENT
je veuille
tu veuilles
il veuille
nous voulions
vous vouliez
ils veuillent

IMPERFECT
je voulusse
tu voulusses
il voulût
nous voulussions
vous voulussiez
ils voulussent

PERFECT
j'aie voulu
tu aies voulu
il ait voulu
nous ayons voulu
vous ayez voulu
ils aient voulu

IMPERATIVE
veuille
veuillons
veuillez

INFINITIVE

PRESENT
vouloir

PAST
avoir voulu

PARTICIPLE

PRESENT
voulant

PAST
voulu

M. VERB CONSTRUCTIONS

There are two main types of verb constructions: verbs can be followed:

1. by another verb in the infinitive
2. by an object (a noun or a pronoun)

1. Verbs followed by an infinitive

There are three main constructions when a verb is followed by an infinitive:
a) verb + infinitive (without any linking preposition)
b) verb + **à** + infinitive
c) verb + **de** + infinitive

For examples of these three types of constructions, see pp C32-3 and C34-5.

a) *Verbs followed by an infinitive without preposition*

These include verbs of wishing and willing, of movement and of perception:

adorer to love	**aimer** to like	**aimer mieux** to prefer
aller to go (and)	**compter** to intend to	**descendre** to go down (and)
désirer to wish	**détester** to hate	**devoir** to have to
écouter to listen to	**entendre** to hear	**entrer** to go in (and)
envoyer to send	**espérer** to hope to	**faire** to make
falloir to have to	**laisser** to let	**monter** to go up (and)
oser to dare	**pouvoir** to be able to	**préférer** to prefer to
regarder to watch	**rentrer** to go in/back (and)	**savoir** to know how to
sembler to seem to	**sentir** to feel	**sortir** to go out (and)
souhaiter to wish to	**valoir mieux** to be better to	**venir** to come (and)
voir to see	**vouloir** to want to	

c) *Verbs followed by **à*** + infinitive

aider à	to help (to do)
s'amuser à	to enjoy (doing)
apprendre à	to learn (to do)
s'apprêter à	to get ready (to do)
arriver à	to manage (to do)
s'attendre à	to expect (to do)
autoriser à	to allow (to do)
chercher à	to try (to do)
commencer à	to start (doing)
consentir à	to agree (to do)
consister à	to consist in (doing)
continuer à	to continue (to do)
se décider à	to make up one's mind (to do)
encourager à	to encourage (to do)
enseigner à	to teach how (to do)
forcer à	to force (to do)
s'habituer à	to get used (to doing)
hésiter à	to hesitate (to do)
inciter à	to prompt (to do)
s'intéresser à	to be interested in (doing)
inviter à	to invite (to do)
se mettre à	to start (doing)
obliger à	to force (to do)
parvenir à	to succeed (in doing)
passer son temps à	to spend one's time (doing)
perdre son temps à	to waste one's time (doing)
persister à	to persist in (doing)
pousser à	to urge (to do)
se préparer à	to get ready (to do)
renoncer à	to give up (doing)
rester à	to be left (to do)
réussir à	to manage (to do)
servir à	to be used for (doing)
songer à	to think of (doing)
tarder à	to delay/be late in (doing)
tenir à	to be keen (to do)

c) *Verbs followed by **de*** + infinitive:

accepter de	to agree (to do)
accuser de	to accuse of (doing)
achever de	to finish (doing)
s'arrêter de	to stop (doing)
avoir besoin de	to need (to do)
avoir envie de	to feel like (doing)
avoir peur de	to be afraid (to do)
cesser de	to stop (doing)
se charger de	to undertake (to do)
commander de	to order (to do)
conseiller de	to advise (to do)
se contenter de	to make do with (doing)
craindre de	to be afraid (to do)
décider de	to decide (to do)
déconseiller de	to advise against (doing)
défendre de	to forbid (to do)
demander de	to ask (to do)
se dépêcher de	to hasten (to do)
dire de	to tell (to do)
dissuader de	to dissuade from (doing)
s'efforcer de	to strive (to do)
empêcher de	to prevent (from doing)
s'empresser de	to hasten (to do)
entreprendre de	to undertake (to do)
essayer de	to try (to do)
s'étonner de	to be surprised (at doing)
éviter de	to avoid (doing)
s'excuser de	to apologize for (doing)
faire semblant de	to pretend (to do)
feindre de	to pretend (to do)
finir de	to finish (doing)
se garder de	to be careful not to (do)
se hâter de	to hasten (to do)
interdire de	to forbid (to do)
jurer de	to swear (to do)
manquer de	'to nearly' (do)
menacer de	to threaten (to do)
mériter de	to deserve (to do)
négliger de	to fail (to do)
s'occuper de	to undertake (to do)
offrir de	to offer (to do)
omettre de	to omit (to do)
ordonner de	to order (to do)
oublier de	to forget (to do)
permettre de	to allow (to do)
persuader de	to persuade (to do)
prier de	to ask (to do)
promettre de	to promise (to do)
proposer de	to offer (to do)
recommander de	to recommend (to do)
refuser de	to refuse (to do)
regretter de	to be sorry (to do)
remercier de	to thank for (doing)
résoudre de	to resolve (to do)
risquer de	to risk (doing)
se souvenir de	to remember (doing)
suggérer de	to suggest (doing)
supplier de	to implore (to do)
tâcher de	to try (to do)
tenter de	to try (to do)
venir de	to have just (done)

2. Verbs followed by an object

In general, verbs which take a direct object in French also take a direct object in English, and verbs which take an indirect object in French (ie verb + preposition + object) also take an indirect object in English.

There are however some exceptions:

a) *Verbs followed by an indirect object in English but not in French* (the English preposition is not translated):

attendre	to wait for

chercher	to look for
demander	to ask for
écouter	to listen to
espérer	to hope for
payer	to pay for
regarder	to look at
reprocher	to blame for

on a demandé l'addition — we asked for the bill

j'attendais l'autobus — I was waiting for the bus

je cherche mon frère — I'm looking for my brother

tu écoutes la radio ? — are you listening to the radio?

b) *Verbs which take a direct object in English, but an indirect object in French:*

convenir à	to suit
se fier à	to trust
jouer à	to play (*game, sport*)
jouer de	to play (*musical instrument*)
obéir à	to obey
désobéir à	to disobey
pardonner à	to forgive
renoncer à	to give up
répondre à	to answer
résister à	to resist
ressembler à	to resemble (to look like)
téléphoner à	to phone

tu peux te fier à moi — you can trust me

tu joues souvent au tennis ? — do you often play tennis?

il joue bien de la guitare — he plays the guitar well

tu as répondu à sa lettre ? — did you answer his letter?

téléphonons au médecin — let's phone the doctor

obéis à ton père ! — obey your father!

c) *Verbs which take a direct object in English but* **de** *+ indirect object in French:*

s'apercevoir de	to notice
s'approcher de	to come near
avoir besoin de	to need
changer de	to change
douter de	to doubt
se douter de	to suspect
s'emparer de	to seize, to grab
jouir de	to enjoy
manquer de	to lack, to miss
se méfier de	to mistrust
se servir de	to use
se souvenir de	to remember
se tromper de ...	to get the wrong ...

je dois changer de train ? — do I have to change trains?

il ne s'est aperçu de rien — he didn't notice anything

méfiez-vous de lui — don't trust him

je me servirai de ton vélo — I'll use your bike

tu te souviens de Jean ? — do you remember Jean?

il s'est trompé de numéro — he got the wrong number

d) *Some verbs take* **à** *or* **de** *before an object, whereas their English equivalent uses a different preposition:*

i) Verb + à + object:

croire à	to believe in
s'intéresser à	to be interested in
penser à	to think of/about
songer à	to think of
rêver à	to dream of/about
servir à	to be used for

je m'intéresse au football et à la course automobile
I'm interested in football and in motor-racing

à quoi penses-tu ? — what are you thinking about?

ça sert à quoi ? — what is this used for?

ii) Verb + de + object:

dépendre de	to depend on
être fâché de	to be annoyed at
féliciter de	to congratulate for
parler de	to speak of/about
remercier de	to thank for
rire de	to laugh at
traiter de	to deal with, to be about
vivre de	to live on

cela dépendra du temps — it'll depend on the weather

il m'a parlé de toi — he told me about you

tu l'as remercié du cadeau qu'il t'a fait ?
did you thank him for the present he gave you?

3. Verbs followed by one direct object and one indirect object

a) In general, these are verbs of giving or lending, and their English equivalents are constructed in the same way, eg:

donner quelque chose à quelqu'un
to give something to someone

il a vendu son ordinateur à son voisin
he sold his computer to his neighbour

Note: After such verbs, the preposition 'to' is often omitted in English but **à** cannot be omitted in French, and particular care must be taken when object pronouns are used with these verbs (see p C17).

b) With verbs expressing 'taking away', **à** is translated by 'from' (**qn** stands for 'quelqu'un' and **sb** for 'somebody'):

acheter à qn	to buy from sb
cacher à qn	to hide from sb
demander à qn	to ask sb for
emprunter à qn	to borrow from sb
enlever à qn	to take away from sb
ôter à qn	to take away from sb
prendre à qn	to take from sb
voler à qn	to steal from sb

à qui as-tu emprunté cela ? — who did you borrow this from?

il l'a volé à son frère — he stole it from his brother

4. Verb + indirect object + *de* + infinitive

Some verbs which take a direct object in English are followed by **à** + object + **de** + infinitive in French (**qn** stands for 'quelqu'un' and **sb** for 'somebody'):

commander à qn de faire	to order sb to do
conseiller à qn de faire	to advise sb to do
défendre à qn de faire	to forbid sb to do
demander à qn de faire	to ask sb to do
dire à qn de faire	to tell sb to do
ordonner à qn de faire	to order sb to do
permettre à qn de faire	to allow sb to do
promettre à qn de faire	to promise sb to do
proposer à qn de faire	to offer to do for sb, to suggest to sb to do

je lui ai conseillé de ne pas essayer
I advised him not to try

demande à ton fils de t'aider
ask your son to help you

j'ai promis à mes parents de ne jamais recommencer
I promised my parents never to do this again

8. PREPOSITIONS

Prepositions in both French and English can have many different meanings, which presents considerable difficulties for the translator. The following guide to the most common prepositions sets out the generally accepted meanings on the left, with a description of their use in brackets, and an illustration. The main meanings are given first. Prepositions are listed in alphabetical order.

à

at	(place)	**au troisième arrêt** at the third stop
	(date)	**à Noël** at Christmas
	(time)	**à trois heures** at three o'clock
	(idiom)	**au hasard, au travail** at random, at work
in	(place)	**à Montmartre** in Montmartre **à Lyon** in Lyons **au supermarché** in the supermarket **à la campagne** in the country **au lit** in bed **au loin** in the distance
	(manner)	**à la française** in the French way **à ma façon** (in) my way
to	(place)	**aller au théâtre** to go to the theatre **aller à Londres** to go to London
	(+ infinitive)	**c'est facile à faire** it is easy to do (*see p C33*)
away from	(distance)	**à 3 km d'ici** three kms away
by	(means)	**aller à bicyclette/ à vélo** to go by bike **je l'ai reconnu à ses habits** I recognized him by his clothing
	(manner)	**fait à la main** made by hand
	(rate)	**à la centaine** by the hundred **100 km à l'heure** 60 mph
for/ up to	(+ pronoun)	**c'est à vous de jouer** it's your turn **c'est à nous de le lui dire** it's up to us to tell him
	(purpose)	**une tasse à café** a coffee cup
his/her/my etc	(possessive)	**son sac à elle** her bag
on	(means)	**aller à cheval/ à pied** to go on horseback/ on foot
	(place)	**à la page 12** on page 12 **à droite/à gauche** on/to the right/left
	(time)	**à cette occasion** on this occasion
with	(descriptive)	**une maison à cinq pièces** a house with five rooms **un homme aux cheveux blonds** a man with blond hair **l'homme à la valise** the man with the case
	(idiom)	**à bras ouverts** with open arms

*For the use of the preposition **à** with the infinitive see verb constructions p C49.*

après

after	(time)	**après votre arrivée** after your arrival
	(sequence)	**24 ans après la mort du président** 24 years after the death of the President **après avoir/être** *(see pp C34-5)*

auprès de

near		**assieds-toi auprès de moi** sit down near me
compared to		**ce n'est rien auprès de ce que tu as fait** it's nothing compared to what you've done

avant

before	(time)	**avant cet après-midi** before this afternoon **avant ce soir** before tonight **avant de s'asseoir** before sitting down
	(preference)	**la famille avant tout** the family first (before everything)

avec

with	(association)	**aller avec lui** to go with him
	(means)	**il a tondu le gazon avec une tondeuse** he cut the lawn with a lawnmower

chez

at	(place)	**chez moi/toi** at/to my/your house **chez mon oncle** at my uncle's **chez le pharmacien** at the chemist's
among		**chez les Ecossais** among the Scots
about		**ce qui m'énerve chez toi, c'est ...** what annoys me about you is ...

in		**chez Sartre** in Sartre's work

contre

against	(place)	**contre le mur** against the wall
with	(after verb)	**je suis fâché contre elle** I'm angry with her
for		**échanger des gants contre un foulard** to exchange gloves for a scarf

dans

in	(position)	**dans ma serviette** in my briefcase
	(time)	**je pars dans deux jours** I'm leaving in two days' time
	(idiom)	**dans l'attente de vous voir** looking forward to seeing you
from	(idiom)	**prendre quelque chose dans l'armoire** to take something from the cupboard
on	(idiom)	**dans le train** on the train
out of	(idiom)	**boire dans un verre** to drink out of a glass

de

from	(place)	**je suis venu de Glasgow** I have come from Glasgow
	(date)	**du 5 février au 10 mars** from February 5th to March 10th **d'un weekend à l'autre** from one weekend to another
of	(adjectival)	**un cri de triomphe** a shout of triumph
	(contents)	**une tasse de café** a cup of coffee
	(cause)	**mourir de faim** to die of hunger
	(measurement)	**long de 3 mètres** 3 metres long
	(time)	**ma montre retarde de 10 minutes** my watch is 10 minutes slow
	(price)	**le montant est de 200 francs** the total is 200 francs
	(possessive)	**la mini-jupe de ma sœur** my sister's miniskirt
	(adjectival)	**les vacances de Pâques** the Easter holidays
	(after 'quelque chose')	**quelque chose de bon** something good
	(after 'rien')	**rien de nouveau** nothing new
	(after 'personne')	**personne d'autre** nobody else
	(quantity)	**beaucoup de, peu de** many, few
by	(idiom)	**je le connais de vue** I know him by sight
in	(manner)	**de cette façon** in this way
	(after superlatives)	**la plus haute montagne d'Ecosse** the highest mountain in Scotland
on		**de ce côté** on this side
than	(comparative)	**moins de 5 francs** less than 5 francs **plus de trois litres** more than three litres
to	(after adjectives)	**ravi de vous voir** delighted to see you **il est facile de le faire** it is easy to do it
	(after verbs)	**s'efforcer de** to try to
with	(cause)	**tomber de fatigue** to drop with exhaustion

depuis

for	(time)	**j'étudie le français depuis 3 ans** I have been studying French for 3 years **j'étudiais le français depuis 3 ans** I had been studying French for 3 years **je n'ai pas vu de lapins depuis des années** I haven't seen a rabbit for years
from	(place)	**depuis ma fenêtre, je vois la mer** from my window I can see the sea
	(time)	**depuis le matin jusqu'au soir** from morning till evening
since		**depuis dimanche** since Sunday

derrière

behind	(place)	**derrière la maison** behind the house

dès

from	(time)	**dès six heures** from six o'clock onwards **dès 1934** as far back as 1934 **dès le début** from the beginning **dès maintenant** from now on
	(place)	**dès Edimbourg** from (the moment of leaving) Edinburgh

devant

before/in front of	(place)	**devant l'école** in front of the school

en

in	(place)	**être en ville** to be in town **en Angleterre** in England
	(colour)	**un mur peint en jaune** a wall painted yellow
	(material)	**une montre en or** a gold watch
	(dates etc)	**en quelle année ?** in what year? **en 1986** in 1986 **en été, en juillet** in the summer, in July
	(dress)	**en bikini** in a bikini
	(language)	**en chinois** in Chinese
	(time)	**j'ai fait mes devoirs en 20 minutes** I did my homework in 20 minutes
by	(means)	**en auto/en avion** by car/by plane
like, as		**il s'est habillé en femme** he dressed as a woman
on	(idiom)	**en vacances** on holiday **en moyenne** on average
	(+ present participle)	**en faisant** on/while/by doing

Note: ***en** is not used with the definite article except in certain expressions: **en l'an 2000** (in the year 2000), **en l'honneur de** (in honour of) and **en la présence de** (in the presence of).*

en tant que

as/in (my) capacity as		**en tant que professeur** as a teacher

entre

among		**être entre amis** to be among friends
between	(place)	**entre Londres et Douvres** between London and Dover
	(time)	**entre 6 et 10 heures** between 6 and 10
	(idiom)	**entre toi et moi** between you and me
in	(punctuation)	**entre guillemets** in inverted commas **entre parenthèses** in brackets

d'entre

of/from among		**certains d'entre eux** some of them

envers

to/towards		**être bien disposé envers quelqu'un** to be well-disposed towards someone

hors de

out of		**hors de danger** out of danger

jusque

up to/ as far as	(place)	**jusqu'à la frontière espagnole** as far as the Spanish border
	(time)	**jusqu'ici/ jusque-là** up to now/up till then
till		**jusqu'à demain** till tomorrow

malgré

in spite of		**malgré la chaleur** in spite of the heat

par

by	(agent)	**la lettre a été envoyée par mon ami** the letter was sent by my friend
	(means of transport)	**par le train** by train
	(distributive)	**trois fois par semaine** three times a week
by		**deux par deux** two by two
	(place)	**par ici/là** this/that way
in/on	(weather)	**par un temps pareil** in such weather **par un beau jour d'hiver** on a beautiful winter's day
out of	(place)	**regarder par la fenêtre** to look out of the window **jeter du pain par la fenêtre** to throw bread out of the window
to/on		**tomber par terre** to fall to the ground **étendu par terre** lying on the ground
	(+ infinitive)	**commencer/finir par faire** to begin/end by doing

parmi

among		**parmi ses ennemis** among his enemies

pendant

for	(time)	**il l'avait fait pendant 5 années** he had done it for 5 years
during		**pendant l'été** during the summer

pour

for		**ce livre est pour vous** this book is for you **mourir pour la patrie** to die for one's country

	(purpose)	**c'est pour cela que je suis venu** that's why I have come
	(emphatic)	**pour moi, je crois que** personally, I think that
	(time)	**j'en ai pour une heure** it'll take me an hour **je serai là pour 2 semaines** I'll be here for 2 weeks

(**pour** stresses intention and future time: see **depuis** and **pendant** pp C52 and C53)

	(idiom)	**c'est bon pour la santé** it's good for your health
to	(+ infinitive)	**il était trop paresseux pour réussir aux examens** he was too lazy to pass the exams

près de

near	(place)	**près du marché** near the market
nearly	(time)	**il est près de minuit** it's nearly midnight
	(quantity)	**près de cinquante** nearly fifty

quant à

as for		**quant à moi** as for me

sans

without	(+ noun)	**sans espoir** without hope
	(+ pronoun)	**je n'irai pas sans vous** I'll not go without you
	(+ infinitive)	**sans parler** without speaking **sans s'arrêter** without stopping

sauf

except for		**ils sont tous partis, sauf John** everyone left except John
barring		**sauf accidents/ sauf imprévu** barring accidents/ the unexpected

selon

according to		**selon le président** according to the President **selon moi** in my opinion

sous

under	(physical)	**sous la table** under the table
	(historical)	**sous Elisabeth II** under Elizabeth II
in	(weather)	**sous la pluie** in the rain
	(idiom)	**sous peu** shortly/before long **sous la main** to hand **sous tous les rapports** in all respects **sous mes yeux** before my eyes

sur

on/upon	(place)	**le bol est sur la table** the bowl is on the table
off		**prendre sur le rayon** to take off the shelf
out of	(proportion)	**neuf sur dix** nine out of ten **une semaine sur trois** one week in three
over	(place)	**le pont sur la Loire** the bridge over the Loire
about	(idiom)	**une enquête sur …** an enquiry about …
at		**sur ces paroles** at these words **sur ce, il est sorti** at this /whereupon he went out
by		**quatre mètres sur cinq** four metres by five
in		**sur un ton amer** in a bitter tone (of voice)
over		**l'emporter sur quelqu'un** to prevail over someone

vers

towards	(place)	**vers le nord** towards the north
	(time)	**vers la fin du match** towards the end of the match
about	(time)	**vers 10 heures** about 10 o'clock

voici/voilà

here	(is)	**le voici qui vient** here he comes
there	(is)	**voilà où il demeure** that is where he lives

9. CONJUNCTIONS

Conjunctions are words or expressions which link words, phrases or clauses. They fall into two categories:

A. coordinating
B. subordinating

A. COORDINATING CONJUNCTIONS

1. Definition

These link two similar words or groups of words (eg nouns, pronouns, adjectives, adverbs, prepositions, phrases or clauses). The principal coordinating conjunctions (or adverbs used as conjunctions) are:

et and	**mais** but	**ou** or
ou bien or (else)	**soit** or (either)	**ni** neither
alors then	**aussi** therefore	**donc** then, therefore
puis then (next)	**car** for (because)	**or** now
cependant however	**néanmoins** nevertheless	**pourtant** yet, however
toutefois however		

il est malade, mais il ne veut pas aller au lit
he's ill but he won't go to bed

il faisait beau, alors il est allé se promener
it was fine so he went for a walk

2. Repetition

a) Some co-ordinating conjunctions are repeated:

soit ... soit either ... or

prenez soit l'un soit l'autre
take one or the other

ni ... ni neither ... nor

le vieillard n'avait ni amis ni argent
the old man had neither friends nor money

b) **et** and **ou** can be repeated in texts of a literary nature:

et ... et both ... and
ou ... ou whether ... or

3. aussi

aussi means 'therefore' only when placed before the verb. The subject pronoun is placed after the verb (see p C59).

il pleuvait, aussi Pascal n'est-il pas sorti
it was raining, so Pascal didn't go out

when **aussi** follows the verb it means 'also':

j'ai aussi mis mon imperméable
I also put my raincoat on

B. SUBORDINATING CONJUNCTIONS

These join a subordinate clause to another clause, usually a main clause. The principal subordinating conjunctions are:

comme	as	**parce que**	because
puisque	since	**ainsi que**	(just) as
à mesure que	as	**tant que**	as long as
avant que	before	**après que**	after
jusqu'à ce que	until	**depuis que**	since
si	if	**à moins que**	unless
pourvu que	provided that	**quoique**	although
bien que	although	**quand**	when
lorsque	when	**dès que**	as soon as
aussitôt que	as soon as	**pour que**	in order that
afin que	so that	**de sorte que**	so that
de façon que	so that	**de peur que** (+ ne)	for fear that, lest

Note: some subordinating conjunctions require the subjunctive (see pp C30-1).

C. QUE

que can be coordinating or subordinating

1. coordinating in comparisons (see pp C10 and C12-13)

il est plus fort que moi
he is stronger than I

2. subordinating

a) *meaning 'that'*:

elle dit qu'elle l'a vu
she says she has seen him

je pense que tu as raison
I think you're right

il faut que tu viennes
you'll have to come

b) *replacing another conjunction:*

When a conjunction introduces more than one verb, **que** usually replaces the second (and subsequent) subordinating conjunctions to avoid repetition:

comme il était tard et que j'étais fatigué, je suis rentré
as it was late and I was tired, I went home

Note: the mood after **que** is the same as that taken by the conjunction it replaces, except in the case of **si** in which **que** requires the subjunctive:

s'il fait beau et que tu sois libre, nous irons à la piscine
if it's fine, and you are free, we'll go to the swimming pool

10. NUMBERS AND QUANTITY

A. CARDINAL NUMBERS

0	**zéro**	40	**quarante**
1	**un (une)**	50	**cinquante**
2	**deux**	60	**soixante**
3	**trois**	70	**soixante-dix**
4	**quatre**	71	**soixante et onze**
5	**cinq**	72	**soixante-douze**
6	**six**	80	**quatre-vingt(s)**
7	**sept**	90	**quatre-vingt-dix**
8	**huit**	99	**quatre-vingt-dix-neuf**
9	**neuf**	100	**cent**
10	**dix**	101	**cent un(e)**
11	**onze**	102	**cent deux**
12	**douze**	121	**cent vingt et un(e)**
13	**treize**	122	**cent vingt-deux**
14	**quatorze**	200	**deux cents**
15	**quinze**	201	**deux cent un(e)**
16	**seize**	1000	**mille**
17	**dix-sept**	1988	**mille neuf cent quatre-vingt-huit**
18	**dix-huit**		
19	**dix-neuf**	2000	**deux mille**
20	**vingt**	10,000	**dix mille**
30	**trente**	1,000,000	**un million**

Note:

a) **un** is the only cardinal number which agrees with the noun in gender:

un kilo	**une pomme**
a kilo	an apple

b) hyphens are used in compound numbers between 17 and 99 except where **et** is used (this also applies to compound numbers after 100: **cent vingt-trois** 123).

c) **cent** and **mille** are not preceded by **un** as in English (one hundred).

d) **vingt** and **cent** multiplied by a number take an **s** when they are not followed by another number.

e) **mille** is invariable.

B. ORDINAL NUMBERS

		abbreviation
1st	**premier/ première**	**1er/1ère**
2nd	**deuxième/ second**	**2e**
3rd	**troisième**	**3e**
4th	**quatrième**	**4e**
5th	**cinquième**	**5e**
6th	**sixième**	**6e**
7th	**septième**	**7e**
8th	**huitième**	**8e**
9th	**neuvième**	**9e**
10th	**dixième**	**10e**
11th	**onzième**	**11e**
12th	**douzième**	**12e**
13th	**treizième**	**13e**
14th	**quatorzième**	**14e**
15th	**quinzième**	**15e**
16th	**seizième**	**16e**
17th	**dix-septième**	**17e**
18th	**dix-huitième**	**18e**
19th	**dix-neuvième**	**19e**
20th	**vingtième**	**20e**
21st	**vingt et unième**	**21e**
22nd	**vingt-deuxième**	**22e**
30th	**trentième**	**30e**
100th	**centième**	**100e**
101st	**cent unième**	**101e**
200th	**deux centième**	**200e**
1000th	**millième**	**1000e**
10,000th	**dix millième**	**10 000e**

Note:

a) ordinal numbers are formed by adding **-ième** to cardinal numbers, except for **premier** and **second**; **cinq**, **neuf** and numbers ending in **e** undergo slight changes: **cinq*u*ième**, **neu*v*ième**, **onzième**, **douzième** etc.

b) ordinal numbers agree with the noun in gender and number:

le premier ministre	**la première fleur du printemps**
the Prime Minister	the first flower of spring

c) there is no elision with **huitième** and **onzième**:

le huitième jour	**du onzième candidat**
the eightth day	of the eleventh candidate

d) cardinal numbers are used for monarchs, except for 'first':

Charles deux	**Charles premier**
Charles II	Charles I

C. FRACTIONS AND PROPORTIONS

1. Fractions

Fractions are expressed as in English: cardinal followed by ordinal:

deux cinquièmes
two fifths

But: ¼ **un quart** ½ **un demi, une demie; la moitié**
⅓ **un tiers** ¾ **trois quarts**

2. Decimals

The English decimal point is conveyed by a comma in French:

un virgule huit (1,8)
one point eight (1.8)

3. Approximate numbers

une huitaine	**une dizaine**
about eight	about ten
une trentaine	**une centaine**
some thirty	about a hundred

But: **un millier**
about a thousand

Note: **de** is used when the approximate number is followed by a noun:

une vingtaine d'enfants
about twenty children

4. Arithmetic

Addition	**deux plus quatre**	$2+4$
Subtraction	**cinq moins deux**	$5-2$
Multiplication	**trois fois cinq**	3×5
Division	**six divisé par deux**	$6\div 2$
Square	**deux au carré**	2^2

D. MEASUREMENTS AND PRICES

1. Measurements

a) *Dimensions*

la salle de classe est longue de 12 mètres
la salle de classe a/fait 12 mètres de longueur/de long
the classroom is 12 metres long

Similarly:

profond(e)/de profondeur/de profond deep
épais(se)/d'épaisseur thick
haut(e)/de hauteur/de haut high

ma chambre fait quatre mètres sur trois
my bedroom is about 4 metres by three

b) *Distance*

à quelle distance sommes-nous du lycée ?
how far are we from the secondary school?

nous sommes à deux kilomètres du lycée
we are 2 kilometres from the secondary school

combien y a-t-il d'ici à Blois ?
how far is it to Blois?

2. Price

ce chandail m'a coûté 110 francs
this sweater cost me 110 francs

j'ai payé ce chandail 110 francs
I paid 110 francs for this sweater

des pommes à 10 francs le kilo
apples at 10 francs a kilo

du vin blanc à 12 francs la bouteille
white wine at 12 francs a bottle

cela fait/revient à 42 francs
that comes to 42 francs

ils coûtent 25 francs pièce
they cost 25 francs each

E. EXPRESSIONS OF QUANTITY

Quantity may be expressed by an adverb of quantity (eg 'a lot', 'too much') or by a noun which names the actual quantity involved (eg 'a bottle', 'a dozen').

1. Expression of quantity + 'de' + noun

Before a noun, expressions of quantity are followed by **de** (**d'** before a vowel or a silent **h**) and never by **du**, **de la** or **des**, except for **bien des** and **la plupart du/des**:

assez de
enough

autant de
as much/many

beaucoup de
a lot of, much, many

combien de
how much/many

moins de
less, fewer

plus de
more

peu de
little, few

un peu de
a little

tant de
so much/many

tellement de
so much/many

trop de
too much/many

bien du/de la/des
many, a lot of

la plupart du/de la/des
most

il y a assez de fromage ?
is there enough cheese?

j'ai beaucoup d'amis
I've got a lot of friends

je n'ai pas beaucoup de temps
I haven't got much time

il y a combien de pièces ?
how many rooms are there?

tu as combien d'argent ?
how much money have you got?

mange plus de légumes !
eat more vegetables!

il y avait peu de choix
there was little choice

peu de gens le savent
not many people know that

tu veux un peu de pain ?
would you like a little bread?

il y a tant d'années
so many years ago

j'ai trop de travail
I've got too much work

il y a trop de voitures
there are too many cars

bien des gens
a good many people

la plupart des Français
most French people

2. Noun expressing quantity + 'de' + noun

une boîte de
a box/tin/jar of

une bouteille de
a bottle of

une bouchée de
a mouthful of (*food*)

une cuillerée de
a spoonful of

une douzaine de
a dozen

une gorgée de
a mouthful of (*drink*)

un kilo de
a kilo of

un litre de
a litre of

une livre de
a pound of

un morceau de
a piece of

un paquet de
a packet of

une paire de
a pair of

une part de
a share/helping of

une tasse de
a cup of

une tranche de
a slice of

un verre de
a glass of

je voudrais une boîte de thon et un litre de lait
I'd like a tin of tuna fish and a litre of milk

il a mangé une douzaine d'œufs et six morceaux de poulet
he ate a dozen eggs and six pieces of chicken

3. Expressions of quantity used without a noun

When an expression of quantity is not followed by a noun, **de** is replaced by the pronoun **en** (see p C18):

il y avait beaucoup de neige ; il y en avait beaucoup
there was a lot of snow; there was a lot (of it)

elle a mangé trop de chocolats ; elle en a trop mangé
she's eaten too many chocolates; she's eaten too many (of them)

11. EXPRESSIONS OF TIME

A. THE TIME

quelle heure est-il?	what time is it?

a) *full hours*

il est midi/minuit it is 12 noon midday/midnight	**il est une heure** it is 1 o'clock

b) *half-hours*

il est minuit et demi(e) it is 12.30 a.m.	**il est midi et demi(e)** it is 12.30 p.m.
il est une heure et demie it is 1.30	

c) *quarter-hours*

il est deux heures un/et quart it is a quarter past two	**il est deux heures moins le/un quart** it is a quarter to two

d) *minutes*

il est quatre heures vingt-trois it 23 minutes past 4	**il est cinq heures moins vingt** it is 20 to 5

Note: **minutes** is usually omitted; **heures** is never omitted.

e) *a.m. and p.m.*

du matin a.m.	**de l'après-midi/du soir** p.m.
il est sept heures moins dix du matin it is 6.50 a.m.	**il est sept heures dix du soir** it is 7.10 p.m.

The 24 hour clock is commonly used:

dix heures trente 10.30 a.m.	**quatorze heures trente-cinq** 2.35 p.m.
dix-neuf heures dix 7.10 p.m.	

Note: times are often abbreviated as follows:

dix-neuf heures dix	**19h10**

B. THE DATE

1. Names of months, days and seasons

a) *Months* (***les mois***)

janvier	January
février	February
mars	March
avril	April
mai	May
juin	June
juillet	July
août	August
septembre	September
octobre	October
novembre	November
décembre	December

b) *Days of the week* (***les jours de la semaine***)

dimanche	Sunday
lundi	Monday
mardi	Tuesday
mercredi	Wednesday
jeudi	Thursday
vendredi	Friday
samedi	Saturday
dimanche	Sunday

c) *Seasons (**les saisons**)*

le printemp (spring)	**l'été** (summer)
l'automne (autumn)	**l'hiver** (winter)

For prepositions used with the seasons see p C4.

Note: in French the months and days are masculine and do not have a capital letter, unless they begin a sentence.

2. Dates

a) cardinals (eg **deux, trois**) are used for the dates of the month except the first:

le quatorze juillet the fourteenth of July	**le deux novembre** the second of November

But: **le premier février**
the first of February

The definite article is used as in English; French does not use prepositions ('on' and 'of' in English):

je vous ai écrit le trois mars
I wrote to you on the third of March

b) **mil** (a thousand) is used instead of **mille** in dates from 1001 onwards:

mil neuf cent quatre-vingt sept
nineteen hundred and eighty-seven

3. Année, journée, matinée, soirée

Année, journée, matinée, soirée (the feminine forms of **an, jour, matin** and **soir**) are usually found in the following cases:

a) *when duration is implied* (eg the whole day):

pendant une année	for a (whole) year
toute la journée	all day long
dans la matinée	in the (course of the) morning
passer une soirée	to spend an evening
l'année scolaire/universitaire	the school/academic year

b) *with an ordinal number (eg **première**) or an indefinite expression*

la deuxième année	the second year
dans sa vingtième année	in his twentieth year
plusieurs/quleques années	several/a few years
bien des/de nombreuses années	many years
environ une année	about a year

c) *with an adjective:*

de bonnes/mauvaises années	good/bad years

C. IDIOMATIC EXPRESSIONS

à cinq heures	at 5 o'clock
à onze heures environ	about 11 o'clock
vers minuit	about midnight
vers (les) dix heures	about 10 o'clock
il est six heures passées	it is past 6 o'clock
à quatre heures précises/pile	at exactly 4 o'clock
il est neuf heures sonnées	it has struck nine
sur le coup de trois heures	on the stroke of three
à partir de neuf heures	from 9 o'clock onwards
peu avant sept heures	shortly before seven
peu après sept heures	shortly after seven
tôt ou tard	sooner or later
au plus tôt	at the earliest
au plus tard	at the latest
il est tard	it is late
il est en retard	he is late
il se lève tard	he gets up late

il est arrivé en retard	he arrived late
le train a vingt minutes de retard	the train is twenty minutes late
ma montre retarde de six minutes	my watch is six minutes slow
ma montre avance de six minutes	my watch is six minutes fast
ce soir	tonight
demain soir	tomorrow night
hier soir	yesterday evening, last night
demain matin	tomorrow morning
demain en huit	tomorrow week
le lendemain	the next day
le lendemain matin	the next morning
hier matin	yesterday morning
la semaine dernière	last week
la semaine prochaine	next week
lundi	on Monday
le lundi	on Mondays
il y a trois semaines	three weeks ago
une demi-heure	a half-hour, half an hour
un quart d'heure	a quarter of an hour
trois quarts d'heure	three quarters of an hour
passer son temps (à faire)	to spend one's time (doing)
perdre son temps	to waste one's time
de temps en temps	from time to time
tous les samedis	every Saturday
tous les samedis soirs	every Saturday evening/night
le combien sommes-nous aujourd'hui	what's the date today?
nous sommes/c'est le trois avril	it is the third of April
le vendredi treize juillet	Friday the thirteenth of July
en février/au mois de février	in February/in the month of February
en 1970	in 1970
dans les années soixante	in the sixties
au dix-septième siècle	in the seventeenth century
au XVIIe	in the 17th Century
le jour de l'An	New Year's Day
avoir treize ans	to be thirteen years old
être âgé de quatorze ans	to be fourteen years old
elle fête ses vingt ans	she's celebrating her twentieth birthday
un plan quinquennal	a five-year plan
une année bissextile	a leap year
une année civile	a calendar year
une année-lumière	a light year

12. THE SENTENCE

A. WORD ORDER

Word order is usually the same in French as in English, except in the following cases:

1. Adjectives

Many French adjectives follow the noun (see p C10):

de l'argent *italien*	**j'ai les yeux *bleus***
(some) *Italian* money	I've got *blue* eyes

2. Adverbs

In simple tenses, adverbs usually follow the verb (see p C12):

j'y vais *rarement*	**il fera *bientôt* nuit**
I *seldom* go there	it will *soon* be dark

3. Object pronouns

Object pronouns usually come before the verb (see p C17):

je *t'*attendrai	**il *la* lui a vendue**
I'll wait *for you*	he sold *it* to him

4. Noun phrases

Noun phrases are formed differently in French (see p C64):

une chemise en coton	**le père de mon copain**
a cotton shirt	my friend's father

5. Exclamations

The word order is not affected after **que** or **comme** (unlike after 'how' in English):

que tu es bête !	**qu'il fait froid !**
you are silly! (how silly you are!)	it's so cold!
comme il chante mal !	**comme c'est beau !**
he sings so badly!	that's so beautiful!

6. DONT

dont must be followed by the subject of the clause it introduces; compare:

l'agence d'emploi dont j'ai perdu la lettre
the employment agency whose letter I lost

l'agence d'emploi dont la lettre est arrivée hier
the employment agency whose letter arrived yesterday

7. Inversion

In certain cases, the subject of a French clause is placed after the verb. Word order is effectively that of an interrogative sentence (see p C61). This occurs:

a) *after the following, but only when they start a clause:*

à peine	**aussi**	**peut-être**
hardly	therefore	maybe, perhaps

à peine Alain était-il sorti qu'il a commencé à pleuvoir
Alain had hardly gone out when it started raining

il y avait une grève du métro, aussi a-t-il pris un taxi
there was an underground strike, so he took a taxi

peut-être vont-ils téléphoner plus tard
maybe they'll phone later

But: **Alain était à peine sorti qu'il a commencé à pleuvoir**

ils vont peut-être téléphoner plus tard

b) *when a verb of saying follows direct speech:*

"si tu veux", a répondu Marie 'if you want', Marie replied	**"attention !" a-t-elle crié** 'watch out!', she shouted
"j'espère que non", dit-il 'I hope not', he said	**"répondez !" ordonna-t-il** 'answer!', he ordered

B. NEGATIVE EXPRESSIONS

1. Main negative words

a)

ne ... pas	not
ne ... point	not (*literary*)
ne ... plus	no more/longer, not ... any more
ne ... jamais	never
ne ... rien	nothing, not ... anything
ne ... guère	hardly

b)

ne ... personne	nobody, no one, not ... anyone
ne ... que	only
ne ... ni (ni ... ni)	neither ... nor
ne ... aucun(e)	no, not any, none
ne ... nul(le)	no
ne ... nulle part	nowhere, not ... anywhere

Note:

i) **ne** becomes **n'** before a vowel or a silent **h**

ii) **aucun** and **nul**, like other adjectives and pronouns, agree with the word they refer to; they are only used in the singular.

2. Position of negative expressions

a) *with simple tenses and with the imperative*

negative words enclose the verb: **ne** comes before the verb, and the second part of the negative expression comes after the verb:

je ne la connais pas I don't know her	**n'insistez pas !** don't insist!
je n'ai plus d'argent I haven't any money left	**tu ne le sauras jamais** you'll never know
ne dis rien don't say anything	**il n'y a personne** no one's here
je n'avais que dix francs I only had ten francs	**il n'est nulle part** it isn't anywhere

tu n'as aucun sens de l'humour
you have no sense of humour

ce n'est ni noir ni bleu
it's neither black nor blue

b) *with compound tenses*

with **ne ... pas** and the other expressions in list **1a**, the word order is: **ne** + auxiliary + **pas** + past participle:

il n'est pas revenu he didn't come back	**je n'ai plus essayé** I didn't try any more
je n'avais jamais vu Paris I had never seen Paris	**on n'a rien fait** we haven't done anything

with **ne ... personne** and the other expressions in list **1b**, the word order is: **ne** + auxiliary + past participle + **personne/que/ni** etc:

il ne l'a dit à personne he didn't tell anyone	**tu n'en as acheté qu'un ?** did you only buy one?
je n'en ai aimé aucun I didn't like any of them	**il n'est allé nulle part** he hasn't gone anywhere

c) *with the infinitive*

i) **ne ... pas** and the other expressions in list **1a** are placed together before the verb:

je préfère ne pas y aller I'd rather not go	**essaye de ne rien perdre** try not to lose anything

ii) **ne ... personne** and the other expressions in list (**1b**) enclose the infinitive:

il a été surpris de ne voir personne
he was surprised not to see anybody

j'ai décidé de n'en acheter aucun
I decided not to buy any of them

d) *at the beginning of a sentence*

when **personne**, **rien**, **aucun** and **ni ... ni** begin a sentence, they are followed by **ne**:

personne ne le sait nobody knows	**rien n'a changé** nothing has changed

ni Paul ni Simone ne sont venus
neither Paul nor Simon came

aucun secours n'est arrivé
no help arrived

3. Combination of negative expressions

Negative expressions can be combined:

ne ... plus jamais	
ne ... plus rien	**ne ... jamais rien**
ne ... plus personne	**ne ... jamais personne**
ne ... plus ni ... ni	**ne ... jamais ni... ni**
ne ... plus que	**ne ... jamais que**

on ne l'a plus jamais revu we never saw him again	**il n'y a plus rien** there isn't anything left
plus personne ne viendra no one will come any more	**tu ne dis jamais rien** you never say anything
je ne bois jamais que de l'eau I only ever drink water	**je ne vois jamais personne** I never see anybody

4. Negative expressions without a verb

a) *PAS*

pas (not) is the most common of all negatives; it is frequently used without a verb:

tu l'aimes ? – pas beaucoup do you like it? – not much	**ah non, pas lui !** oh no, not him!
non merci, pas pour moi no thanks, not for me	**un roman pas très long** not a very long novel
lui, il viendra, mais pas moi he will come, but I won't	**j'aime ça ; pas toi ?** I like that; don't you?

b) *NE*

ne is not used when there is no verb:

qui a crié ? – personne who shouted? – nobody	**jamais de la vie !** not on your life!
rien ! je ne veux rien ! nothing! I want nothing!	**rien du tout** nothing at all

c) *NON*

non (no) is always used without a verb:

tu aimes la natation ? – non, pas du tout
do you like swimming? – no, no at all

tu viens, oui ou non ? are you coming, yes or no?	**je crois que non** I don't think so

Note: **non plus** = 'neither':

je ne le crois pas – moi non plus
I don't believe him – neither do I

je n'ai rien mangé – nous non plus
I haven't eaten anything – neither have we

C. DIRECT AND INDIRECT QUESTIONS

1. Direct questions

There are three ways of forming direct questions in French:

a) subject + verb (+ question word)
b) (question word) + **est-ce que** + subject + verb
c) (question word) + verb + subject = inversion

a) *subject + verb (+ question word)*

The word order remains the same as in statements (subject + verb) but the intonation changes: the voice is raised at the end of the sentence. This is by far the most common question form in conversational French:

tu l'as acheté où ?
where did you buy it?

je peux téléphoner d'ici ?
can I phone from here?

vous prendrez quel train ?
which train will you take?

tu lui fais confiance ?
do you trust him?

c'était comment ?
what was it like?

la gare est près d'ici ?
is the station near here?

le train part à quelle heure ?
what time does the train leave?

cette robe me va ?
does this dress suit me?

b) *(question word) + **est-ce que** + subject + verb*

This question form is also very common in conversation:

qu'est-ce que tu as ?
what's the matter with you?

est-ce qu'il est là ?
is he in?

est-ce que ton ami s'est amusé ?
did your friend have a good time?

où est-ce que vous avez mal ?
where does it hurt?

c) *inversion*

This question form is the most formal of the three, and the least commonly used in conversation.

i) if the subject is a pronoun, word order is as follows:

(question word) + verb + hyphen + subject

où allez-vous ?
where are you going?

voulez-vous commander ?
do you wish to order?

quand est-il arrivé ?
when did he arrive?

avez-vous bien dormi ?
did you sleep well?

ii) if the subject is a noun, a pronoun referring to the noun is inserted after the verb, and linked to it with a hyphen:

(question word) + noun subject + verb + hyphen + pronoun

où ton père travaillait-il ?
where did your father work?

Nicole en veut-elle ?
does Nicole want any?

iii) **-t-** is inserted before **il** and **elle** when the verb ends in a vowel:

comment va-t-il voyager ?
how will he travel?

aime-t-elle le café ?
does she like coffee?

pourquoi a-t-il refusé ?
why did he refuse?

Marie viendra-t-elle ?
will Marie be coming?

Note: when a question word is used, modern French will often just invert verb and noun subject, without adding a pronoun; no hyphen is then necessary:

où travaille ton père ?
where does your father work?

2. Indirect questions

a) *Definition*

Indirect questions follow a verb and are introduced by an interrogative (question) word, eg:

ask him when he will arrive
I don't know why he did it

b) *Word order*

i) The word order is usually the same as in statements: question word + subject + verb:

je ne sais pas s'il voudra
I don't know if he'll want to

dis-moi où tu l'as mis
tell me where you put it

il n'a pas dit quand il appellerait
he didn't say when he would phone

ii) If the subject is a noun, verb and subject are sometimes inverted:

demande-leur où est le camping
ask them where the campsite is

But: **je ne comprends pas comment l'accident s'est produit**
I don't understand how the accident happened

il ne savait pas pourquoi les magasins étaient fermés
he didn't know why the shops were closed

3. Translation of English question tags

a) Examples of question tags are: isn't it? aren't you? doesn't he? won't they? haven't you? is it? did you? etc.

b) French doesn't use question tags as often as English. Some of them can however be translated in the following ways:

i) **n'est-ce pas ?**

n'est-ce pas ? is used at the end of a sentence when confirmation of a statement is expected:

c'était très intéressant, n'est-ce pas ?
it was very interesting, wasn't it?

tu voudrais trouver un emploi stable, n'est-ce pas ?
you would like to find a secure job, wouldn't you?

vous n'arriverez pas trop tard, n'est-ce pas ?
you won't be arriving too late, will you?

ii) **hein ?** and **non ?**

In conversation **hein ?** and **non ?** are often used after affirmative statements instead of **n'est-ce pas** :

il fait beau, hein ?
it's nice weather, isn't it?

il est amusant, non ?
he's funny, isn't he?

D. ANSWERS ('YES' AND 'NO')

1. OUI, SI and NON

a) **oui** and **si** mean 'yes' and are equivalent to longer positive answers such as: 'yes, it is', 'yes, I will', 'yes, he has' etc:

tu m'écriras ? – oui, bien sûr !
will you write to me? – (yes) of course I will

b) **non** means 'no' and is equivalent to longer negative answers such as: 'no, it isn't', 'no, I didn't' etc:

c'était bien ? – non, on s'est ennuyé(s)
was it good? – no, it wasn't; we were bored

2. OUI or SI ?

oui and **si** both mean 'yes', but **oui** is used to answer an affirmative question, and **si** to contradict a negative question:

cette place est libre ? – oui
is this seat free? – yes (it is)

tu n'aimes pas lire ? – si, bien sûr !
don't you like reading? – yes, of course (I do)

13. TRANSLATION PROBLEMS

A. GENERAL TRANSLATION PROBLEMS

1. French words not translated in English

Some French words are not translated in English, particularly:

a) *Articles*

Definite and indefinite articles are not always translated (see pp C3-4):

dans *la* société moderne, *les* prix sont élevés
in modern society, prices are high

ah non ! encore *du* riz ! je déteste *le* riz !
oh no! rice again! I hate rice!

b) ***que***

que meaning 'that' as a conjunction (see p C55) or 'that'/'which'/'whom' as a relative pronoun (see p C20) cannot be omitted in French:

j'espère *que* tu vas mieux I hope you're better	**elle pense *que* c'est vrai** she thinks it's true
celui *que* j'ai vu the one I saw	**c'est un pays *que* j'aime** it's a country I like

c) *Prepositions*

Some French verbs are followed by a preposition (+ indirect object) when their English equivalent takes a direct object (without preposition) (see p C50):

elle a téléphoné *au* médecin she phoned the doctor	**tu l'as dit *à* ton père ?** did you tell your father?

d) ***le***

When **le** (it) is used in an impersonal sense (see p C17), it is not translated:

oui, je *le* sais yes, I know	**dis-*le*-lui** tell him

2. English words not translated in French

Some English words are not translated in French, for example:

a) *Prepositions*

i) with verbs which take an indirect object in English, but a direct object in French (see pp C49-50):

tu l'as payé combien ? how much did you pay *for* it?	**écoutez cette chanson** listen *to* this song

ii) in certain expressions (see pp C58-9):

je viendrai te voir lundi soir
I'll come and see you *on* Monday night

b) *'can'*

'can' + verb of hearing or seeing (see p C37):

je ne vois rien ! I can't see anything	**tu entends la musique ?** can you hear the music?

3. Other differences

a) *English phrasal verbs*

Phrasal verbs are verbs which, when followed by a preposition, take on a different meaning, eg 'to give up', 'to walk out'. They do not exist in French and are translated by simple verbs or by expressions:

to give up **abandonner**	to run away **s'enfuir**	to run across **traverser en courant**

b) *English possessive adjectives*

English possessive adjectives (my, your etc) are translated by the French definite article (**le/la/les**) when parts of the body are mentioned (see p C20):

brush *your* teeth **brosse-toi *les* dents**	he hurt *his* foot **il s'est fait mal *au* pied**

c) *'from'*

'from' is translated by **à** with verbs of 'taking away' (see p C50):

he hid it *from* his parents **il l'a caché *à* ses parents**	borrow some *from* your dad **empruntes-en *à* ton père**

B. SPECIFIC TRANSLATION PROBLEMS

1. Words in -ing

The English verb form ending in **-ing** is translated in a number of ways in French:

a) *by the appropriate French tense (see p C28):*

he's speaking (present tense)	**il parle**
he was speaking (imperfect)	**il parlait**
he will be speaking (future)	**il parlera**
he has been speaking (perfect)	**il a parlé**
he had been speaking (pluperfect)	**il avait parlé**
he would be speaking (conditional)	**il parlerait**

b) *by a French present participle (see p C35)*

i) as an adjective:

un livre amusant a funny book	**c'est effrayant** it's frightening

ii) as a verb, with **en** (while/on/by doing something; see p C35):

"ça ne fait rien", dit-il en souriant
'it doesn't matter', he said smiling

j'ai vu mes copains en sortant du lycée
I saw my friends while (I was) coming out of school

But: **en** + present participle cannot be used when the two verbs have different subjects, eg:

I saw my brother coming out of school
j'ai vu mon frère sortir du lycée/qui sortait du lycée

c) *by a present infinitive (see pp C32-4):*

i) after a preposition:

au lieu de rire instead of laughing	**avant de traverser** before crossing

ii) after verbs of perception:

je l'ai entendu appeler I heard him calling	**je l'ai vue entrer** I saw her going in

iii) after verbs of liking and disliking:

j'adore faire du camping I love camping	**tu aimes lire ?** do you like reading?

iv) after verbs followed by **à** or **de**:

tu passes tout ton temps à ne rien faire
you spend all your time doing nothing

il a commencé à neiger it started snowing	**continuez à travailler** go on working
tu as envie de sortir ? do you feel like going out?	**il doit finir de manger** he must finish eating

v) when an English verb in **-ing** is the subject of another verb:

attendre serait inutile waiting would be pointless	**écrire est une corvée !** writing is a real chore!

vi) when an English verb in **-ing** follows 'is' or 'was' etc:

mon passe-temps favori, c'est d'aller à la discothèque
my favourite pastime is going to the disco

d) *by a perfect infinitive (see pp C34-5)*

i) after **après** (after):

j'ai pris une douche après avoir nettoyé ma chambre
I had a shower after cleaning my room

ii) after certain verbs:

regretter to regret	**remercier de** to thank for	**se souvenir de** to remember

e) *by a noun*

particularly when referring to sports, activities, hobbies etc:

le ski skiing	**la natation** swimming	**l'équitation** horse-riding
la voile sailing	**le patinage** skating	**le canoë** canoeing
la lecture reading	**la planche à voile** wind-surfing	**la cuisine** cooking
la boxe boxing	**la lutte** wrestling	**la marche à pied** walking

2. IT IS (IT'S)

'it is' (it's) can be translated in three ways in French:

a) il/elle + être
b) ce + être
c) il + être

a) ***il*** *or* ***elle*** *(see p C17)*

il or **elle** are used with the verb **être** to translate 'it is', 'it was' etc (+ adjective) when referring to a particular masculine or feminine noun (a thing, a place etc):

merci de ta carte ; elle était très amusante
thanks for your card; it was very funny

regarde ce blouson ; il n'est vraiment pas cher
look at that bomber jacket; it really isn't expensive

b) ***ce*** *(see p C14)*

ce (c' before a vowel) is used with the verb **être** to translate 'it is', 'it was' etc in two cases:

i) if **être** is followed by a word which is not an adjective on its own, ie by a noun, a pronoun, an expression of place etc:

c'était sa voix it was his voice	**c'est une grande maison** it's a big house
c'est moi ! c'est Claude ! it's me! it's Claude!	**c'est le tien ?** is it yours?
c'est en France que tu vas ? is it France you're going to?	**c'est pour lundi** it's for Monday

ii) if **être** is followed by an adjective which refers to something previously mentioned, an idea, an event, a fact, but not to a specific noun:

l'homme n'ira jamais sur Saturne ; ce n'est pas possible
man will never go to Saturn; it's not possible

j'ai passé mes vacances en Italie ; c'était formidable !
I spent my holidays in Italy; it was great!

oh, je m'excuse ! – ce n'est pas grave
oh, I'm sorry! – it's all right

c) ***il*** *(see pp C27-8)*

il is used to translate 'it is', 'it was' etc in three cases:

i) with **être** followed by an adjective + **de** or **que** (ie referring to something that follows, but not to a specific noun):

il est impossible de connaître l'avenir
it's impossible to know the future

il est évident que tu ne me crois pas
it's obvious you don't believe me

ii) to describe the weather (see p C27):

il y a du vent it's windy	**il faisait très froid** it was very cold

iii) with **être** to tell the time and in phrases relating to the time of day, or in such expressions as **il est temps de** (it's time to):

il est deux heures du matin it's two a.m.	**ah bon ! il est tard !** really! it's late!
il est temps de partir it's time to go	

Note: with other expressions of time, **c'est** is used:

c'est lundi ou mardi ? is it Monday or Tuesday?	**c'était l'été** it was summer

3. TO BE

Although 'to be' is usually translated by **être**, it can also be translated in the following ways:

a) ***avoir***

i) **avoir** is used instead of **être** in many set expressions:

avoir faim/soif	to be hungry/thirsty
avoir chaud/froid	to be warm/cold
avoir peur/honte	to be afraid/ashamed
avoir tort/raison	to be right/wrong

ii) **avoir** is also used for age:

quel âge as-tu ? how old are you?	**j'ai vingt- cinq ans** I'm twenty five

b) ***aller***

aller is used for describing health:

je vais mieux I am/feel better	**tout le monde va bien** everyone's fine

c) ***faire***

faire is used in many expressions to describe the weather (see p C27):

il fait beau it's fine	**il fera chaud** it will be hot

Note: **il y a** can also be used to describe the weather, but only before **du/de la/des**:

il y a du vent/des nuages/de la tempête
it's windy/cloudy/stormy

d) *untranslated*

"to be" is not translated when it is the first part of an English continuous tense; instead, the appropriate tense is used in French (see p C28):

I'm having a bath **je prends un bain**	he was driving slowly **il conduisait lentement**

4. ANY

'any' can be translated in three different ways:

a) ***du/de la/des*** *or* ***de*** *(see pp C4-5)*

the partitive article is used with a noun in negative and interrogative sentences:

il ne mange jamais de viande he never eats any meat	**tu veux du pain ?** do you want any bread?

b) ***en*** *(see p C18)*

en is used to translate 'any' without a noun in negative and interrogative sentences:

je n'en ai pas I haven't got any	**il en reste ?** is there any left?

c) ***n'importe quel(le)/quel(le)s*** *or* ***tout(e)/tou(te)s***

these are used to translate "any" (and "every") when they mean "no matter which":

il pourrait arriver à n'importe quel moment
he could be arriving any time

prends n'importe quelle couleur, je les aime toutes
take any colour, I like them all

5. ANYONE, ANYTHING, ANYWHERE

Like 'any', these can be translated in different ways:

a) *in interrogative sentences:*

il y a quelqu'un ?
is anyone in?

tu l'as vu quelque part ?
did you see it anywhere?

il a dit quelque chose ?
did he say anything?

b) *in negative sentences:*

il n'y a personne
there isn't anyone

je ne le vois nulle part
I can't see it anywhere

je n'ai rien fait
I didn't do anything

c) *in the sense of 'any' (and 'every'), 'no matter which':*

n'importe qui peut le faire
anyone can do that

il croit n'importe quoi
he believes anything

j'irai n'importe où
I'll go anywhere

n'importe quand
anytime

6. YOU, YOUR, YOURS, YOURSELF

French has two separate sets of words to translate 'you', 'your', 'yours', 'yourself':

a) tu, te (t'), toi, ton/ta/tes, le tien etc
b) vous, votre/vos, le vôtre etc

For their respective meanings and uses, see pp C17, C19, C20.

a) ***tu** etc*

tu, te, ton etc correspond to the **tu** form of the verb (second person singular) and are used when speaking to one person you know well (a friend, a relative) or to someone younger. They represent the familiar form of address:

***tu* viens au concert avec *ton* copain, Annie ? alors, je *t'*achète deux places : une pour *toi* et une pour lui**
are *you* coming to the concert with *your* boyfriend, Annie? well, then, I'll get *you* two seats: one for *you* and one for him

b) ***vous** etc*

vous, vos etc correspond to the **vous** form of the verb (second person plural) and are used:

i) when speaking to more than one person:

dépêchez-*vous*, les gars ! *vous* allez manquer le train
hurry up, boys! *you*'ll miss the train

ii) when speaking to one person you do not know well or to someone older. They represent the formal or polite form of address:

je regrette, Monsieur, mais *vous* ne pouvez pas garder *votre* chien avec *vous* dans ce restaurant
I'm sorry, sir, but *you* can't keep *your* dog with you in this restaurant

c) when speaking or writing to one person, you must not mix words from both sets, but decide whether you are being formal or familiar, and use the same form of address throughout:

Cher Michel,
Merci de *ta* lettre. Comment vas-*tu* ?...
Dear Michel,
Thanks for *your* letter. How are *you*? ...

Monsieur,
Pourriez-*vous* me réserver une chambre dans *votre* hôtel pour le huit juin ?
Dear Sir,
Could *you* book a room for me in *your* hotel for the eighth of June?

vous etc and **tu** etc can only be used together when **vous** is plural (ie when it refers to more than one person):

***tu* sais, Jean, *toi* et *ta* sœur, *vous vous* ressemblez**
you know, Jean, *you* and *your* sister look like *each other*

7. Noun phrases

A noun phrase is a combination of two nouns used together to name things or people. In English, the first of these nouns is used to describe the second one, eg 'a love story'. In French, however, the position of the two nouns is reversed, so that the describing noun comes second and is linked to the first one by the preposition **de** (or **d'**):

une histoire d'amour
a love story

un magasin de disques
a record shop

un acteur de cinéma
a film actor

un arrêt d'autobus
a bus stop

un film d'aventure
an adventure film

un coup de soleil
sunstroke

une boule de neige
a snowball

un roman de science-fiction
a science fiction novel

un match de football
a football game

le château d'Edimbourg
Edinburgh castle

un conte de fées
a fairy tale

un joueur de rugby
a rugby player

un employé de bureau
an office clerk

Note: when the describing noun refers to a material, the preposition **en** is often used instead of **de**:

un pull en laine
a woollen jumper

un pantalon en cuir
leather trousers

une bague en or
a gold ring

un sac en plastique
a plastic bag

8. Possession

In English, possession is often expressed by using a noun phrase and tagging **'s** at the end of the first word, eg:

my friend's cat

This is translated in French by: object + **de** + possessor:

le chat de mon ami

Note the use of the article **le/la/les**.

le fiancé de ma sœur
my sister's fiancé

les amis de Chantal
Chantal's friends

les événements de la semaine dernière
last week's events

When **'s** is used in the sense of "someone's house" or "shop" etc, it is translated by the preposition **chez**:

je téléphone de chez Paul
I'm telephoning from Paul's

chez le dentiste
at/to the dentist's

Compiled by LEXUS
with Raymond Perrez, Noël Peacock
and Sabine Citron.

Practical conversation guide

Compiled by Fabrice Antoine and Michael Janes.

Comment s'excuser

On utilise d'ordinaire
(Je suis) désolé
Excusez-moi
Je m'excuse

On pourra dire de quoi on s'excuse
(Je suis) désolé de vous déranger/d'être en retard/de ce contretemps
Désolé, je suis en retard/je ne veux *ou* voulais pas vous déranger
Excusez-moi d'être en retard/de vous déranger
Excusez mon retard/excusez-moi si je vous dérange
Je m'excuse de ce retard/de vous déranger

On s'excusera d'un oubli, d'une erreur, d'une faute etc passés
(Je suis) désolé d'avoir interrompu la conversation
Excusez-moi de n'avoir pu prévenir de mon retard/d'avoir fait du bruit hier soir
J'ai fait du bruit hier soir, j'en suis désolé
Vous m'excuserez si je n'ai pas pu prévenir de mon retard

Excuses écrites ou formelles
Veuillez accepter/Je vous prie d'accepter toutes mes excuses (pour mon retard/pour cette erreur)
Je vous prie de croire que je suis sincèrement désolé (de l'attitude de mon collègue/d'avoir manqué ce rendez-vous)
Je tiens absolument à m'excuser (de cette erreur)
Je suis vraiment navré

On se justifiera ainsi :
Désolé, mais (je ne vous avais pas vu/je n'ai pas pu me libérer)
Désolé, je ne peux pas (,j'ai énormément de travail)
Désolé, vous ne pouvez pas (utiliser le téléphone, il est en panne)

On répondra à des excuses ainsi :
Ce n'est rien
Mais pas du tout
Il n'y a pas de mal
Cela n'a pas d'importance
Ne vous tracassez pas pour cela
Vous êtes tout excusé

A la réception

Pour attirer l'attention de l'employé
S'il vous plaît !
Pourriez-vous me renseigner, s'il vous plaît ?
Vous pouvez me renseigner ?

Pour demander à voir quelqu'un
Je voudrais *ou* j'aimerais voir (Mlle/Mme/M. Dupont), s'il vous plaît
Où se trouve le bureau de (Mlle/Mme/M. Dupont) ?
J'ai rendez-vous avec (le docteur Durand)
Je dois le/la rencontrer à (10 heures)
Pourrais-je rencontrer *ou* voir (le chef de service) ?

On pourra vous répondre
Vous attendez *ou* Vous voulez bien attendre un instant, s'il vous plaît ?
Asseyez-vous un instant, je vais l'appeler
Je vais le/la prévenir (de votre arrivée/que vous êtes là)
Vous êtes M. .../Mme ... ?

En cas de difficultés
Il n'y a personne d'autre (qui puisse me renseigner/recevoir) ?
Est-ce que je pourrais voir quelqu'un d'autre du même service ?
Puis-je téléphoner, s'il vous plaît ?
Puis-je (lui) laisser un message ?

Pour trouver un service, un rayon etc
Où se trouve le service (radiologie)/le rayon (jouets)/le guichet (de change) ?
A qui dois-je m'adresser pour (une commande) ?
Je voudrais voir quelqu'un pour (une réclamation)

On pourra vous répondre
C'est au rez-de-chaussée/au premier/deuxième (étage)
Prenez l'ascenseur/l'escalier jusqu'au (premier)
Porte numéro (27)
Passez la porte et c'est sur votre droite/gauche

On se présentera ainsi :
Je suis Mlle/Mme/M. (Legras) de (la Maison Dupont/l'entreprise Durand/chez Duval)
Je viens de la part de (M. Martin)
C'est (M. Martin) qui m'envoie (chez vous)

Comment s'excuser
désolé (de faire/d'être) *sorry (for doing/being)*
:désolé de ce contretemps *sorry for the slight mishap*
:j'en suis désolé *I'm sorry (about that)*
excuser *to excuse*
:excusez-moi (d'être/de faire) *excuse me (for being/doing)*
:excusez mon retard *excuse me for being late*
:vous êtes tout excusé *no apology needed*
s'excuser (de qch/de faire) *to apologize (for sth/for doing)*
:je m'excuse *excuse me, sorry*
importance : cela n'a pas d'importance *it doesn't matter*
mal : il n'y a pas de mal *that's all right, no harm done*
navré *awfully sorry*
oubli *omission, oversight*
pas du tout *not at all, that's quite all right*
pouvoir : je ne peux pas/vous ne pouvez pas *I can't/you can't*
prévenir: je n'ai pas pu prévenir de . . . *I didn't warn you about . . .*
prier : je vous prie d'accepter *kindly accept*
rien : ce n'est rien *it doesn't matter*
tracasser : ne vous tracassez pas pour cela *don't worry about that*

A la réception
aimer : j'aimerais voir . . . *I would like to see*
chef de service *head of department*
d'autre : quelqu'un/personne d'autre *somebody/nobody else*
devoir : je dois le rencontrer à . . . *I'm supposed to* or *I have to meet him at . . .*
:à qui dois-je m'adresser pour . . . ? *who do I* or *should I see about . . .?*
guichet *counter, window*
part : je viens de la part de *I've come from . . .*
passez la porte *go through the door*
plaire : s'il vous plaît ! *excuse me!, hello!* (attracting s.o.'s attention)
:s'il vous plaît *please*
pouvoir : pourriez-vous/vous pouvez me renseigner ? *could you/can you help me?*
: puis-je téléphoner ? *may I use your phone?*
rayon *department*
réception *reception desk*
rendez-vous *appointment*
service *department*
vouloir : je voudrais voir *I would like to see*
:vous voulez bien attendre *please wait, will you (kindly) wait*

Comment prendre rendez-vous

On propose un rendez-vous
Pourrions-nous nous rencontrer ?
Pourrais-je vous rencontrer *ou* venir vous voir ?
Pourriez-vous venir me voir ?
Prenons rendez-vous
Convenons d'un rendez-vous/d'une date (pour nous rencontrer)

On fixe une date
Quel jour vous convient le mieux ?
Que dites-vous de (jeudi) ?
(Jeudi,) ça vous va *ou* convient ?
(Jeudi/Assez rapidement,) si c'est possible
Je suis libre (le jeudi)
(Vendredi) prochain me conviendrait tout à fait
(D'accord pour) lundi/mardi/mercredi
Le 25 mars
Demain/Après-demain
Demain/Lundi en huit/en quinze
Dans les jours à venir/Dans quelques jours

On fixe une heure
Quelle heure voulez-vous *ou* vous conviendrait *ou* vous convient ?
A quelle heure êtes-vous libre *ou* pouvez-vous venir ?
(En début/fin d'après-midi,) cela vous convient *ou* va ?
Je suis libre l'après-midi
Vers (dix) heures, si c'est possible
(Treize heures trente) me conviendrait tout à fait
Dans l'après-midi
En matinée/soirée
Avant/Après déjeuner
Vers/A onze heures/onze heures trente

On convient d'un endroit
Où nous rencontrerons-nous ?
Où voulez-vous ?
Retrouvons-nous (à la gare), d'accord ?
Convenons d'un endroit
(Chez moi/A la gare,) si cela vous convient ?
Disons (chez moi/à la gare)
A votre bureau/hôtel
Chez moi/vous
Ici/Là-bas/À Paris

Comment demander son chemin

Pour aborder quelqu'un
Excusez-moi
S'il vous plaît

Pour demander sa route
Où se trouve (le commissariat) ?
Savez-vous où se trouve (la gare) ?
Suis-je loin de (la station de métro Porte d'Orléans) ?
Comment fait-on pour rejoindre (la rue de Rennes)/pour se rendre à (la gare du Nord) ?
Connaissez-vous (la rue Fromentin) ?
Pouvez-vous *ou* Pourriez-vous m'indiquer le chemin le plus court pour aller à (la poste) ?
Quelle est la façon la plus rapide d'aller (au centre) ?

En voiture
Comment rejoint-on (la route de Montpellier) ?
Peut-on (se) garer facilement (dans le centre) ?
Est-ce que cela roule bien par là ?

Pour se renseigner sur la distance
Est-ce que c'est loin ?
Combien de temps faut-il pour y aller (en bus/à pied/en voiture) ?
Cela me prendra-t-il plus de (dix minutes) ?
Est-ce qu'il vaut mieux prendre (un taxi) ?

Pour renseigner quelqu'un
C'est près de (l'église)
Allez tout droit
Prenez la première/deuxième à gauche/droite
Prenez la direction de (Rouen) puis tournez à droite
Laissez (la poste) derrière vous/Dépassez (la poste)
C'est la première/deuxième (rue) sur votre droite/gauche
C'est sur la gauche/droite

Pour donner une idée de la distance
C'est assez loin/Ce n'est pas très loin
C'est trop loin (pour y aller à pied)
C'est tout près d'ici
C'est à environ (deux kilomètres) d'ici
C'est à (dix minutes) à pied/en bus/en voiture
C'est à (une heure) de marche
Il faut compter (une demi-heure)
Il vaudrait mieux prendre (un taxi)

Comment prendre rendez-vous
après-demain *the day after tomorrow*
convenir : convenons d'un rendez-vous *let's arrange an appointment*
:convenons d'un endroit *let's agree on* or *arrange a place*
:convenir à qn *to suit s.o.*
:ça vous convient ? *is that suitable* or *agreeable?*
:. . . me conviendrait tout à fait *. . . would suit me perfectly*
d'accord (pour . . .) *O.K. (for . . .)*
déjeuner *lunch*
dire : que dites-vous de . . . ? *what do you say to . . .?*
en : demain/lundi en huit/en quinze *a week/two weeks (from) tomorrow/Monday*
prendre rendez-vous *to make an appointment*
proposer *to suggest*
(se) rencontrer *to meet*
(se) retrouver *to meet*
venir : dans les jours à venir *in the coming days, in the next few days*

Comment demander son chemin
à : c'est à deux kilomètres d'ici *it's two kilometres away*
:c'est à dix minutes à pied *it's ten minutes away on foot, it's a ten-minute walk away*
aborder *to approach*
chemin : demander son chemin *to ask the* or *one's way*
:indiquer le chemin (à) *to point out the way (to)*
commissariat *police station*
compter : il faut compter . . . *you should allow . . .*
dépassez la poste *go past the post office*
faire : comment fait-on pour se rendre à . . . ? *how do I* or *we get to . . .?*
(se) garer *to park*
laissez la poste derrière vous *go past the post office*
pouvoir : pouvez-vous ?/pourriez-vous ? *can you?/could you?*
prenez la direction de . . . *go in the direction of . . .*
rejoindre *to get to*
se renseigner sur *to inquire about*
rouler : est-ce que ça roule bien ? *is the traffic moving?*
temps : combien de temps faut-il pour y aller ? *how long does it take to get there?*
trouver : où se trouve . . . ? *where is . . .?*
valoir : il vaut/vaudrait mieux . . . *it is/would be better to . . .*

Comment faire appel à un avocat, un médecin etc

Comment demander un avocat
Pour avoir un avocat
Je veux voir un/mon avocat
Je veux parler à un/mon avocat
Je veux une assistance juridique
Pour insister
Je ne dirai rien avant d'avoir vu un/mon avocat
Je ne ferai rien avant d'avoir consulté un/mon avocat
J'exige de voir un/mon avocat
Pour s'adresser à l'avocat
J'ai besoin de vos conseils/votre assistance
J'aimerais que vous me représentiez/vous agissiez en mon nom (dans cette affaire)
J'ai besoin de vos conseils (dans cette affaire)
Pourriez-vous m'éclairer (dans cette affaire) ?
A votre avis, quelle est la meilleure solution pour (régler ce problème) ?

Comment demander un médecin
Pour avoir un médecin
Je veux voir un médecin/Il me faut un médecin
J'ai besoin des conseils d'un médecin
Il faut que je consulte un médecin
Pour insister
Je ne bougerai pas avant d'avoir vu un médecin
Je ne ferai rien avant d'avoir consulté un médecin
Pour s'adresser au médecin
Je voudrais passer une visite médicale
J'aimerais que vous m'examiniez
J'ai besoin de vos conseils à ce sujet/au sujet de ...
Comment recueillir un second point de vue
Pourrais-je consulter quelqu'un d'autre ?
J'aimerais avoir le point de vue de quelqu'un d'autre/un second point de vue
Je veux consulter un expert/un spécialiste à ce sujet/au sujet de ...
Qui d'autre puis-je consulter (à ce sujet) ?

Comment demander son consul
Je veux contacter mon consulat
Il faut que je contacte *ou* joigne le consul de (Grande-Bretagne)
Je souhaite contacter mon consul
J'exige que mon consulat soit prévenu *ou* informé

Les toilettes, la salle de bain, la laverie

Comment demander où se trouvent les toilettes
Chez un particulier
Où sont les toilettes ?
Où est le petit coin ?
Dans un lieu public
Y a-t-il des toilettes quelque part ?
Les toilettes, s'il vous plaît ?
Où sont les toilettes (messieurs/dames) ?
Où sont les W.-C. *ou* les waters ?

Comment demander où se trouve la salle de bain
Chez un particulier
Puis-je me laver/me débarbouiller ?
Je ne suis pas très propre
Puis-je utiliser la salle de bain/passer dans la salle de bain ?
J'aimerais me laver les mains
Puis-je faire un brin de toilette ?
Dans un lieu public
Les lavabos, s'il vous plaît ?
Y a-t-il des lavabos quelque part ?
Est-ce que je peux me débarbouiller/me laver les mains quelque part ?
Je voudrais me laver les mains
Peut-on se laver les mains quelque part ?
Dans un hôtel ou une pension
Où est la douche ?
Où est la salle de bain ?
Puis-je *ou* peut-on prendre une douche/un bain ?

Nettoyage de vêtements
Pour savoir où l'on peut nettoyer des vêtements
Y a-t-il une laverie automatique dans le quartier ?
Où se trouve la laverie la plus proche ?
Il faudrait que je lave des vêtements/je fasse nettoyer des vêtements à sec
Pour faire nettoyer son linge
Y a-t-il un service blanchisserie ?
J'ai du linge à faire laver
J'ai des vêtements à faire porter au pressing
Peut-on faire laver du linge ?
Quelqu'un peut-il porter ce costume/ces vêtements au pressing ?

Comment faire appel à un avocat, un médecin etc
s'adresser à *to speak to*
affaire : dans cette affaire *in this matter*
agir au nom de qn *to act for s.o.*
assistance (juridique) *(legal) help*
avis : à votre avis *in your opinion*
avocat *lawyer*
bouger : je ne bougerai pas avant d'avoir vu ... *I'm not moving until I see ...*
conseils *advice*
consul *consul*
consulat *consulate*
d'autre : quelqu'un d'autre/qui d'autre ? *somebody else/who else?*
éclairer *to advise*
exiger : j'exige de voir *I insist on seeing*
faire appel à *to call upon the services of*
joindre : il faut que je joigne ... *I must get in touch with ...*
médecin *doctor*
passer une visite médicale *to have a medical (examination)*
point de vue *opinion*
prévenu *informed*
recueillir un second point de vue *to get a second opinion*
sujet : à ce sujet/au sujet de ... *on* or *about this/on* or *about ...*

Les toilettes, la salle de bain, la laverie
bain *bath*
blanchisserie : service blanchisserie *laundry service*
brin : faire un brin de toilette *to have a quick wash*
costume *suit*
se débarbouiller *to wash one's face*
douche *shower*
faire : à faire porter à ... *to be taken to ...*
lavabos *toilets*
laverie (automatique) Br *launderette*, Am *laundromat*
linge : du linge à faire laver *washing to be done*
nettoyer à sec *to dry-clean*
particulier : chez un particulier *in a private house*
pension *boarding house*
petit coin Br *loo*, Am *john*
pressing *dry-cleaner's*
salle de bain *bathroom*
:utiliser/passer dans la salle de bain *to use/go to the bathroom*
toilettes (messieurs/dames) *(men's/women's) toilets*
waters, W.-C. *toilets*

Les bagages

L'enregistrement
Où se trouve le guichet d'enregistrement ?
Où enregistre-t-on/doit-on enregistrer les bagages ?
Expressions utiles
C'est lourd
Porteur !
Y a-t-il des porteurs ?
J'ai besoin d'un porteur
Où prend-on un chariot à bagages ?
Y a-t-il des chariots libres ?

Les formalités d'enregistrement
Je voudrais enregistrer ces bagages, s'il vous plaît
Il y en a (trois)/J'en ai (trois)
Je garde (ceci) en bagage à main
Je n'enregistre pas (celui-ci/celle-ci)
Je garde (ceci) avec moi
Y a-t-il un supplément (à payer) ?

La récupération des bagages
Où récupère-t-on les bagages ?
Où se trouve la salle des bagages ?
Faut-il récupérer ses bagages avant ou après les formalités de police ?

Incidents
A qui s'adresse-t-on/doit-on s'adresser pour les bagages égarés ?
J'ai enregistré mes bagages à (Paris) et ils ne sont pas arrivés
Je n'ai pas encore récupéré mes bagages
J'étais sur le vol en provenance de (Miami)
Je ne trouve pas mes bagages
Mes bagages (se) sont perdus
Mes bagages sont endommagés *ou* abîmés/en mauvais état
Il me manque (quelque chose)

Comment décrire ses bagages
C'est une valise/un sac de voyage/un sac à dos/une caisse
Il/Elle est bleu(e)/vert(e)/jaune/marron
Il/Elle a à peu près la même taille que celui-ci/celle-là
Il/Elle est en plastique/en cuir
Il/Elle a des sangles *ou* des courroies en cuir
Il y a mon nom et mon adresse dessus

La consigne

Pour trouver la consigne
Puis-je laisser *ou* déposer mes bagages quelque part ?
Y a-t-il une consigne ?
Y a-t-il un endroit où laisser *ou* déposer les bagages ?
Où se trouve la consigne automatique ?
J'aimerais mieux ne pas être obligé de garder (cela) avec moi

A la consigne
Puis-je déposer (ces bagages) ici (jusqu'à quatre heures) ?
Serez-vous *ou* Etes-vous ouvert après (six heures) ?
Faites attention, le sac marron est fragile

A la consigne automatique
Pour demander de la monnaie à quelqu'un
Excusez-moi, auriez-vous la monnaie de (dix/cinquante francs) ?
Auriez-vous de la monnaie ?
Pourriez-vous me faire de la monnaie ?
Pour demander de l'aide à quelqu'un
Savez-vous *ou* Vous savez comment ça marche ?
Pourriez-vous m'aider ?

Incidents
Excusez-moi, est-ce vous qui vous occupez de la consigne automatique ?
Ma (valise) est trop grande. (Elle) ne rentrera pas
J'ai mis les pièces/mes bagages dedans
Je n'arrive pas à ouvrir/à la faire marcher
Je ne peux pas récupérer mes bagages
Je n'arrive pas à récupérer mes pièces

A l'hôtel
Pour laisser des bagages
Est-ce que je pourrais laisser (mes bagages/ma valise) ici pour (une heure) ?
Est-ce que je peux laisser ça ici (jusqu'à six heures) ?
Pourriez-vous me garder (ceci), s'il vous plaît ?
Je viendrai le/la/les chercher vers six heures
Je serai de retour dans (quelques heures)
Pour récupérer ses bagages
C'est le/la vert(e)
Le mien/La mienne est marron
Je vous ai laissé (deux valises)

Les bagages
abîmé *damaged*
s'adresser : à qui s'adresse-t-on/doit-on s'adresser pour . . . ? *who do/should I* or *we see about . . .?*
bagages *luggage, baggage*
(en) bagage à main *(as) hand luggage*
caisse *box*
chariot (à bagages) *(luggage* or *baggage)* Br *trolley* or Am *cart*
courroies *straps*
égaré *lost, gone astray*
endommagé *damaged*
enregistrement *checking in*
: guichet d'enregistrement *check-in desk*
enregistrer *to check in*
manquer : il me manque (quelque chose) *(something) is missing* or *gone*
provenance : en provenance de . . . *from . . .*
récupération des bagages *baggage reclaim*
récupérer *to reclaim*
sac à dos *rucksack*
sac de voyage *(travelling) bag*
salle des bagages *baggage reclaim area*
sangles *straps*
supplément : un supplément (à payer) *extra (to pay)*
taille *size*
valise *(suit)case*

La consigne
arriver : je n'arrive pas à . . . *I can't . . .*
consigne Br *left-luggage office*, Am *baggage check-room*
consigne automatique *(baggage) lockers*
déposer *ou* laisser ses bagages *to leave one's luggage*
faites attention *be careful*
marcher *to work*
marron *brown*
mettre les pièces/ses bagages dedans *to put the money/one's luggage in*
monnaie *change*
:auriez-vous de la monnaie (de. . .) ? *would you have change (for* or *of. . .)?*
:pourriez-vous me faire de la monnaie ? *could you give me some change?*
s'occuper de : est-ce vous qui vous occupez de . . . ? *are you the person in charge of . . .?*
récupérer : récupérer ses bagages *to get one's luggage out* (from the lockers); *to ask for one's luggage back* (from the hotel)
: récupérer ses pièces *to get one's money back*
rentrer *to fit in*
retour : être de retour *to be back*
valise *(suit)case*

Au garage

Pour expliquer que l'on a un problème
Elle ne marche pas (correctement *ou* normalement)
Elle est en panne
Elle ne veut pas démarrer
Il y a quelque chose qui cloche dans (l'embrayage)
J'ai des problèmes avec (les freins/le clignotant)

Pour décrire la cause probable de la panne
Je crois que c'est (le démarreur)
C'est peut-être (les câbles électriques/les bougies)
J'ai déjà eu des problèmes de (batterie/carburateur)
La batterie est à plat *ou* déchargée
Le pneu est dégonflé *ou* à plat/J'ai un pneu dégonflé *ou* à plat
C'est le (clignotant droit/démarreur) qui ne marche pas

Pour se renseigner auprès du garagiste
Est-ce que vous réparez cette marque ?
Avez-vous des pièces détachées pour cette marque ?
Vous pouvez faire quelque chose ?
Vous pouvez jeter un coup d'œil ?

Pour se renseigner d'un garage
Est-ce qu'il y a un garage dans les environs qui pourrait me dépanner ?
Y a-t-il un concessionnaire (de cette marque/Rover) par ici ?
Vous pouvez peut-être m'indiquer un bon garage/garagiste ?
Connaissez-vous un garage/garagiste par ici ?

Pour demander un devis
Quand pouvez-vous vous en occuper ?
Quand sera-t-elle prête ?
Vous pouvez me donner une idée de ce que cela va coûter ?
Vous pouvez me faire un devis ?
Cela va coûter dans les combien ?
Cela va vous prendre combien de temps ?
Vous pouvez me donner une idée du prix/du délai ?

Pour fixer un délai
Pouvez-vous vous en occuper tout de suite ?
Il me la faut demain/pour le week-end
J'aimerais bien la récupérer *ou* la reprendre demain

Location de voitures

Pour savoir où s'adresser
Peut-on louer une voiture par ici ?
Où peut-on louer une voiture pour pas trop cher ?
Où faut-il s'adresser pour une location de voiture ?

Pour indiquer ce que l'on désire
J'ai besoin d'une petite/grosse voiture pour (une semaine)
J'aurai besoin d'une voiture (mardi prochain)
Pouvez-vous me réserver une voiture pour la semaine prochaine ?
Je voudrais quelque chose de pas trop cher/de confortable
Il me faut une voiture à quatre places
Il me la faut (à neuf heures demain matin)
Il me faut une voiture tout de suite
J'en ai besoin pour (le week-end)
Je vais aller à Turin
Pouvez-vous me l'amener ?
Est-ce que je peux venir la chercher ?
Est-ce que je peux la prendre à l'aéroport ?
Je veux une assurance tous-risques

Pour se renseigner des tarifs
A combien cela me reviendra-t-il ?
Quels sont les/vos prix ?
Vous pouvez m'indiquer votre tarif ?
Puis-je voir votre tarif ?
Combien faut-il compter pour (une quatre/cinq portes) ?
Le prix est-il indépendant du kilométrage ?
Quel est le prix du kilomètre/à la journée ?
Y a-t-il des suppléments à prévoir ?

Les formalités
J'ai un permis (international)
Un permis américain suffit *ou* suffira ?
Voulez-vous une pièce d'identité ?
Quel est le montant du dépôt de garantie ?
Acceptez-vous (la carte Diners Club) ?
Le passeport est-il nécessaire ?
Quel type d'assurance est compris dans le prix ?
Puis-je avoir une facture, s'il vous plaît ?
Où dois-je signer ?
Dois-je signer quelque part ?

Au garage
batterie à plat *ou* déchargée *flat battery*
bougies Br *sparking plugs* or Am *spark plugs*
câbles électriques *electric wiring*
carburateur Br *carburettor*, Am *carburetor*
clignotant *indicator*
clocher : quelque chose qui cloche (dans) *something wrong (with)*
concessionnaire (d'une marque) *dealer (for a make)*
coûter : cela va coûter dans les combien ? *roughly how much will it cost?*
délai : fixer un délai *to fix a deadline*
démarrer *to start*
démarreur *starter*
dépanner qn *to fix s.o.'s car*
devis : faire un devis à qn *to give s.o. an estimate*
embrayage *clutch*
garagiste *garage mechanic*
marcher *to work*
panne *breakdown*
: être en panne *to have broken down*
pièces détachées *spare parts*
pneu dégonflé *ou* à plat *flat* Br *tyre or* Am *tire*
récupérer *to get back*
se renseigner auprès de *to get information from*
se renseigner de *to inquire about*

Location de voitures
s'adresser : où faut-il s'adresser pour . . .? *where do I* or *we inquire about . . .?*
assurance tous-risques *comprehensive insurance*
cher : pas trop cher *fairly cheap*
: louer une voiture pour pas trop cher *to rent* or Br *to hire a car fairly cheaply*
combien : à combien cela me reviendra-t-il ? *how much will it cost me?*
compter : combien faut-il compter pour . . . ? *how much is . . .?*
dépôt de garantie *deposit*
kilométrage *mileage*
location de voiture(s) *car rental*, Br *hiring a car*, Br *car hire*
louer *to rent*, Br *to hire*
permis (international) *international* Br *driving licence* or Am *driver's license*
pièce d'identité *proof of identity*
prix au kilomètre/à la journée *charge per kilometre/per day*
se renseigner de *to inquire about*
supplément : des suppléments (à prévoir) ? *any extras (to be anticipated)?*
tarif *rate(s)*

Les services d'urgence

Pour expliquer qu'il s'agit d'une urgence
C'est *ou* Il y a une urgence
C'est (très) grave/Ça a l'air (très) grave
Nous avons besoin d'aide de toute urgence

Pour préciser l'aide requise
Envoyez une voiture de police/une ambulance immédiatement
Appelez les pompiers/l'hôpital tout de suite
Faites venir un médecin/un policier tout de suite
Il nous faut une embarcation de secours/une ambulance de toute urgence

Pour préciser le type d'urgence dont il s'agit
Il y a eu un accident
Il y a un incendie/un blessé grave
Il y a quelqu'un de très malade/de gravement blessé
Il y a (deux) personnes à l'eau
Quelqu'un a été sérieusement blessé
En cas d'incendie, contactez :
les pompiers
En cas d'accident de la route, de vol, etc contactez :
la police, la gendarmerie
En cas d'urgence médicale, appelez :
une ambulance, le SAMU (service d'aide médicale d'urgence), SOS médecins, l'hôpital
En cas d'accident en mer, contactez :
les garde-côtes, la SNSM (société nationale de secours en mer)

Au téléphone
Composez le 17 pour la police, le 18 pour les pompiers. Il faut être prêt à répondre aux questions suivantes :
Qui êtes-vous ?/Où vous trouvez-vous ?
Que se passe-t-il ?/Où cela s'est-il passé ?
Réponses :
Je suis Monsieur/Madame/Mademoiselle Durand
Je vous appelle de (la rue Rimbaud)
Je me trouve (au 22, rue Rimbaud/à l'angle du boulevard Dupleix et de la rue Rimbaud)
Ça c'est passé (sur la nationale 19)
C'est à environ cinq kilomètres de (Provins) en allant vers (Troyes)
Il y a eu un accident/Il y a un incendie *ou* le feu
Il y a (plusieurs) blessés

Achat de vêtements

Pour avoir un vendeur
S'il vous plaît !
Vous pouvez me renseigner, s'il vous plaît ?
Je pourrais avoir un vendeur ?

Pour refuser un vendeur
Non merci, je regarde, c'est tout

Pour expliquer ce que l'on cherche
Je cherche le/la même *ou* la même chose (que cela) en (vert)
Je cherche *ou* voudrais (une veste)
Je voudrais voir (un pantalon/une chemise)
Je voudrais quelque chose dans les 300 F
Pouvez-vous me montrer ce que vous avez comme foulards/pantalons ?

Le choix des couleurs
L'avez-vous d'une autre couleur ?
Est-ce qu'il/elle existe dans une autre couleur ?
Celui-ci/Celle-ci est trop foncé(e)/clair(e)
J'aime bien/Je n'aime pas (cette couleur/ce bleu)

Le prix
C'est combien ?
Celui-ci/Celle-ci fait combien *ou* est à combien ?
Avez-vous un modèle plus cher/moins cher ?
Ce n'est pas très cher/C'est cher. C'est trop/un peu cher

Les tailles
Quelle est la taille de celui-ci/celle-ci ?
Est-ce que ça m'irait/m'ira ?
Avez-vous la taille au-dessus/au-dessous ?
L'avez-vous en plus grand/plus petit ?
C'est trop petit/grand
Il/Elle est trop long(ue)/court(e)
Je suis trop serré dedans/Je flotte trop dedans
Non, ça ne m'ira pas/ce n'est pas ma taille

L'essayage et les retouches
Je voudrais essayer ceci/Peut-on essayer ?
Où sont les cabines d'essayage ?
Où peut-on essayer ?
Faites-vous des retouches ?
Pourriez-vous le raccourcir/rallonger ?

Les services d'urgence
s'agir : il s'agit de . . . *it is . . .*
air : ça a l'air (grave) *it looks (serious)*
angle : à l'angle *at the corner*
blessé : gravement *ou* sérieusement blessé *seriously injured*
:un blessé grave *a seriously injured person*
composer *to dial*
embarcation de secours *rescue boat*
en cas d'incendie/de vol/*etc* *in the event of a fire/a robbery/*etc
falloir : il nous faut . . . *we need . . .*
: il faut être . . . *we have to be . . .*
garde-côtes *coastguards*
médecin *doctor*
nationale Br *trunk road,* Am *highway*
se passer *to happen*
policier *police officer*
pompiers *fire services*
préciser *to specify*
tout de suite *at once*
urgence *emergency*
:de toute urgence *very urgently, as an emergency*
:services d'urgence *emergency services*

Achat de vêtements
aller : est-ce que ça m'irait/m'ira ? *would this/will this fit me?*
cher *expensive*
clair *light*
combien ? *how much?*
:celui-ci fait combien *ou* est à combien ? *how much is this one?*
couleur : d'une/dans une autre couleur ? *in another colour?*
en : l'avez-vous en plus grand/plus petit ? *do you have it in a bigger/smaller size?*
essayage *trying on*
:cabines d'essayage *fitting* or *changing rooms*
essayer *to try on*
flotter : je flotte dedans *it's loose on me*
foncé *dark*
plaire : s'il vous plaît ! *excuse me!*
:s'il vous plaît ? *please?*
quelque chose dans les . . . *something around . . .*
raccourcir *to shorten*
rallonger *to lengthen*
renseigner qn *to help s.o.*
retouches *alterations*
taille *size*
:la taille au-dessus/au-dessous *the next size (up/down)*
(trop) serré *(too) tight*
vendeur Br *sales assistant,* Am *sales clerk*

Les réclamations (concernant un achat)

Pour obtenir un interlocuteur
J'aimerais parler au (gérant/chef de rayon/directeur)
Je veux voir le responsable
Je ne suis pas satisfait (d'une chemise) et je voudrais voir quelqu'un

Au téléphone
Passez-moi/Pouvez-vous me passer (le gérant/le chef de rayon/le directeur), s'il vous plaît (?)
Je ne suis pas satisfait (d'une radio que j'ai achetée chez vous). Pouvez-vous me passer la personne qui s'occupe de cela ?

Pour exposer la situation
Je vous ai acheté (ces marchandises) (la semaine dernière)
Vous m'avez envoyé (ceci) hier
Je vous ai commandé (un appareil photo)
J'ai un reçu/Je n'ai pas de reçu
J'ai/Je n'ai pas le bon de garantie

Pour exposer le motif de la réclamation
Il/Elle ne marche pas *ou* ne fonctionne pas
Il/Elle est cassé(e)/défectueux (-euse)/a un défaut
Ce n'est pas le modèle que je voulais/que j'ai commandé/que j'avais vu
Ce n'est pas la bonne taille/couleur/Ce n'est pas le bon modèle
On m'avait dit que c'était (en cuir)
On ne m'a pas donné/envoyé/livré ce que je voulais
Je n'en ai pas l'usage
Il/Elle n'a marché que deux jours

Pour demander que quelque chose soit fait
Je veux qu'on me rembourse/Je veux être remboursé
Je veux que ce soit réparé (immédiatement)
Je veux un échange (immédiat)
Allez-vous me l'échanger ?
Je veux soit un échange soit un remboursement

Pour indiquer ce que l'on compte faire
Je vous l'ai retourné/Je vais vous le retourner
Je vais écrire à (votre directeur)
Je vais consulter (mon avocat)
Je vous envoie la facture

Les réclamations (concernant un service)

Pour obtenir un interlocuteur
J'aimerais parler (au gérant/au chef de service/au directeur)
Je veux voir (le responsable des expéditions)
Je ne suis pas satisfait de (la livraison) et je voudrais voir quelqu'un/celui qui s'en occupe

Au téléphone
Passez-moi/Pouvez-vous me passer (le gérant/le chef de service/le directeur), s'il vous plaît (?)
Je ne suis pas satisfait (d'une réparation effectuée chez vous). Pouvez-vous me passer la personne qui s'occupe de cela ?

Pour exposer la situation
Je me suis rendu chez vous/à vos bureaux/à votre agence/dans votre magasin aujourd'hui
Je vous ai donné ma voiture/une paire de chaussures/ma montre à réparer
Je vous ai donné une pellicule à développer

Pour exposer le motif de la réclamation
On m'a dit que ce/qu'il/qu'elle serait prêt(e) (jeudi) et (j'attends toujours)
On m'avait dit que cela prendrait une demi-heure
La viande n'était pas assez cuite/Les légumes n'étaient pas assez cuits
La réparation a été mal faite
La chambre n'était pas propre
Le service était très lent/laissait (beaucoup) à désirer
Le personnel a été incapable de me renseigner
On m'a accueilli de façon très discourtoise/désinvolte
On m'a fait attendre
On s'est trompé/On m'a trop compté dans ma facture/mon addition/ma note

Pour demander que quelque chose soit fait
Vous allez régler ce problème, j'espère
J'espère que vous veillerez à ce que (cela ne se reproduise pas)
J'espère bien que vous allez (me faire une réduction)

Pour indiquer ce que l'on compte faire
Je vais écrire à (votre directeur)
Je vais en informer (les services municipaux)

Les réclamations (concernant un achat)
bon de garantie *guarantee*
le chef de rayon *the manager of the department*
commander *to order*
défaut : avoir un défaut *to be faulty*
défectueux *faulty*
directeur *(company) manager*
échange *exchange*
échanger *to exchange*
exposer *to explain*
facture *bill, invoice*
gérant *(shop) manager*
interlocuteur : obtenir un interlocuteur *to get the correct person to speak to*
livrer *to deliver*
marchandises *goods*
s'occuper de *to deal with*
réclamation *complaint*
reçu *receipt*
remboursement *refund*
rembourser *to refund*
réparer *to repair*
responsable *person in charge*
satisfait de *satisfied with*
taille *size*
usage : je n'en ai pas l'usage *I can't use it*

Les réclamations (concernant un service)
accueillir : on m'a accueilli de façon très discourtoise/désinvolte *I was received with great rudeness/in a very offhand manner*
attendre : on m'a fait attendre *I was kept waiting*
chef de service *department head*
compter : on m'a trop compté dans ma facture *I was overcharged (on my bill)*
directeur *(company) manager*
expéditions : le responsable des expéditions *the person in charge of dispatch*
gérant *(shop) manager*
interlocuteur : obtenir un interlocuteur *to get the correct person to speak to*
laisser (beaucoup) à désirer *to leave a lot to be desired*
livraison *delivery*
s'occuper de *to deal with*
pellicule (à développer) *film (to be developed)*
réclamation *complaint*
renseigner *to help, to give information to*
réparation *repair*
réparer *to repair*
se reproduire *to happen again*
satisfait de *satisfied with*
services municipaux *local government*
veiller à ce que . . . + *sub* *to see to it that . . .*

Formules de politesse

Avec les gens que l'on connaît
On utilise le prénom des personnes que l'on connaît très bien et on les tutoiera. Avant d'avoir recours au tutoiement ou d'utiliser le prénom, on dira :
Puis-je vous appeler par votre prénom ?
Ça ne vous dérange pas que je vous tutoie ?
On pourrait se tutoyer ?
On peut utiliser le prénom et le vouvoiement :
Bernard, vous reprendrez bien un verre ?
On sera plus formel en utilisant, avec le vouvoiement :
Monsieur/Madame/Mademoiselle Dupont

Pour attirer l'attention de quelqu'un ou l'interpeller
On utilise généralement :
Excusez-moi !/S'il vous plaît !
Monsieur/Madame/Mademoiselle, s'il vous plaît !
De façon plus abrupte et moins polie :
Hep !/Hé !
Pour s'adresser à un adolescent :
Jeune homme/Monsieur/Mademoiselle
Pour s'adresser à un enfant :
Mon petit/Fiston/Ma petite
Pour s'adresser à un policier :
Excusez-moi (Monsieur)
Pour appeler un serveur :
Garçon !/Barman !/S'il vous plaît !
Pour appeler une serveuse :
Mademoiselle !/S'il vous plaît !
Pour appeler un infirmier ou un médecin :
Infirmier !/Infirmière !/Docteur !
Pour appeler un avocat :
Maître !

Dans la correspondance
Sur l'enveloppe
M. Alain Dupont/Mme Jeanne Durand/Mlle Claire Dubois
M. A. Dupont/Mme J. Durand/Mlle C. Dubois
Pour commencer une lettre
A quelqu'un que l'on ne connaît pas :
Monsieur/Madame/Mademoiselle
A quelqu'un que l'on connaît un peu :
Cher Monsieur/Chère Madame/Chère Mademoiselle
A un(e) ami(e) :
Cher Jean/Chère Claire
Mon cher Jean/Ma chère Claire

Comment insister

Au téléphone
Lorsqu'on ne peut obtenir son correspondant
Je vais attendre/Je reste en ligne
Quand puis-je (le/la) rappeler ?
Ça vous dérangerait de vous renseigner pour savoir où il/elle est ?
Ça vous dérangerait de lui demander de venir au téléphone ?
Ça vous dérangerait de lui dire que je la/le demande au téléphone ?
Vous ne manquerez pas de lui dire de me rappeler, n'est-ce pas ?
Savez-vous où il/elle est *ou* se trouve ?
Savez-vous quand il/elle rentrera ?
Savez-vous où je peux le/la joindre *ou* toucher ?

A une réception, un secrétariat etc
Lorsqu'on ne veut pas vous recevoir
J'attendrai
Je vais attendre ici, si vous n'y voyez pas d'inconvénient
Il faut absolument que je voie (le directeur)
J'insiste pour le/la voir/lui parler
Je ne partirai pas avant de l'avoir vu(e)

Pour expliquer pourquoi l'on insiste
J'ai déjà appelé/essayé de la/le joindre quatre fois
Je suis déjà venu/J'ai déjà écrit plusieurs fois
C'est la (troisième) fois que j'essaie de la/le joindre cette semaine !
C'est à propos de ...
C'est extrêmement important
Il faut absolument que je la/le voie pour régler (ce problème/cette affaire de facture)

Pour persuader quelqu'un
Je vous assure que c'est (important)
Croyez-moi, c'est ce que (vous devriez faire)
Je peux vous prouver que (c'est vrai)
Laissez-moi au moins (vous expliquer jusqu'au bout)
Je propose que l'on recommence au début/que l'on reprenne tout cela
De façon plus familière
Allons !/Voyons !
Soyez plus accommodant/sympa !
Mettez-vous à ma place !

Formules de politesse
s'adresser à *to speak to*
attirer *to attract*
avocat *lawyer*
déranger : ça ne vous dérange pas si . . .? *do you mind if . . .?, you don't mind if . . .?*
excusez-moi ! *excuse me!*
fiston *son*
formule *(set) phrase* or *term*
: formule de politesse *polite phrase, term of politeness*
garçon ! *waiter!*
hé !, hep ! *hey!*
infirmier, infirmière *nurse*
interpeller qn *to shout (out) to s.o.*
médecin *doctor*
petit : mon petit *son, little one, young man*
:ma petite *little one, young lady*
plaire : s'il vous plaît ! *excuse me!*
poli *polite*
policier *police officer*
prénom *first name*
recours : avoir recours à *to resort to*
serveur *waiter; barman*
serveuse *waitress; barmaid*
tutoiement *familiar address (*using *tu)*
tutoyer qn *to address s.o. familiarly*
utiliser *to use*
vouvoiement *formal address (*using *vous)*

Comment insister
allons ! *come on!*
assurer qn que . . . *to assure s.o. that . . .*
correspondant : obtenir son correspondant *to get through to the person one is calling*
déranger : ça vous dérangerait de faire ? *would you mind doing?*
falloir : il faut absolument que je voie . . . *I* ***must*** *see . . .*
inconvénient : si vous n'y voyez pas d'inconvénient *if you don't mind*
insister (pour faire) *to insist (on doing)*
joindre qn *to reach s.o.*
ligne : rester en ligne *to hang on*
manquer : vous ne manquerez pas de . . . *you won't forget to . . .*
propos : à propos de . . . *about . . .*
proposer que . . . + *sub* *to suggest that . . .*
rappeler (qn) *to call (s.o.) back*
réception *reception desk*
régler *to solve* (a problem); *to settle* (a matter)
se renseigner *to inquire*
reprendre *to go back over*
secrétariat *secretary's office*
toucher qn *to get in touch with s.o.*
voyons ! *come on!*

Descriptions

Dimensions
C'est/Ils sont petit(s)/gros
Ça a la taille (d'un ballon de football)
Ça a *ou* fait environ 10 (centimètres) de long et *ou* sur 5 de large
Ça a 20 (mètres) de haut
C'est grand *ou* gros comme un (ballon de football)
Pour se renseigner sur des dimensions
Quelle taille cela a-t-il ?/De quelle taille est-ce ?
Quelle hauteur/longueur/largeur cela fait-il *ou* a-t-il ?
Cela a combien de haut/long/large ?
Cela a quelle hauteur/longueur/largeur ?
C'est grand comment ?

Forme, aspect général
C'est rond/carré/rectangulaire
Cela a la forme d'un cercle/carré/rectangle
Cela a une forme circulaire/carrée/rectangulaire
C'est pointu
Ça a la forme d'une banane/d'un S/d'un L
C'est en S/en L
Ça ressemble à une banane/à un œuf
Pour se renseigner sur la forme
C'est rond ou carré ?/Est-ce que c'est rond ou carré ?
Quelle forme cela a-t-il ?/Ça a quelle forme ?
Pour décrire la texture
C'est lisse/rugueux
Pour décrire l'aspect
C'est vert/bleu/bleu foncé
Ça a des rayures/C'est moucheté
Ça a (une surface brillante)
Pour se renseigner sur l'aspect
C'est de quelle couleur ?/De quelle couleur est-ce ?
Cela ressemble à quoi ?/A quoi cela ressemble-t-il ?

Destination
Pour décrire à quoi quelque chose sert
Cela sert à (ouvrir les bouteilles)
On s'en sert pour (allumer la lumière)/quand (on fait la lessive)
C'est utilisé *ou* utile pour (ouvrir les portes)
Pour se renseigner sur la destination de quelque chose
A quoi cela sert-il ?
Ça sert à quoi ?
On s'en sert pour quoi ?
Quand s'en sert-on ?

Comment donner et obtenir des explications

Pour se faire expliquer un mot, une expression etc
Qu'est-ce que (cela) veut dire *ou* signifie ?
Que veut dire *ou* signifie (ce mot) ?/Quel est le sens de (ce mot) ?
Est-ce que cela signifie *ou* veut dire (oui) ou (non) ?
Demandes indirectes
Je crois que je ne comprends pas/que je n'ai pas compris *ou* saisi
Pourriez-vous expliquer (le début), s'il vous plaît ?
Lorsque l'on a compris
Je vois/Ça y est/J'y suis/J'ai compris
Merci, j'ai compris/j'y suis maintenant
Si l'on n'a toujours pas compris
Je ne comprends *ou* ne vois toujours pas
Je crois bien que je ne comprends toujours pas/que je ne vous suis toujours pas

Pour expliquer ce que l'on veut dire
Ce que je veux dire, c'est (cela/que ...)
En d'autres termes,/Autrement dit,/C'est à dire, (jeudi)
Pour s'assurer que l'on se fait comprendre
Vous comprenez/avez compris ?/Vous me suivez ?
C'est (bien) le mot exact/ce que l'on dit ?
Est-ce que je me fais bien comprendre ?
Suis-je clair ?
Pour reformuler quelque chose, changer l'ordre des mots
Il y a quelque chose qui cloche dans ma voiture
C'est à dire, ma voiture a quelque chose qui ne marche pas
Je serai absent vendredi
En d'autres termes, vendredi, je ne serai pas là

Pour expliquer des causes, des raisons
Nous opérons ainsi parce que (c'est plus rapide)
C'est parce que (nous étions en retard)
C'est pour (empêcher les gens de se garer ici)
Ce qui motive tout cela, c'est (l'argent)
La cause de tout cela, c'est (la chaleur)
Pour connaître une cause
Pourquoi ?
Pourquoi a-t-il/-elle fait cela ?
Quelle est la raison de cela ?
Quelle en est la raison ?
Pouvez-vous m'expliquer cela ?

Descriptions
aspect *appearance*
ballon de football *football*
bleu foncé *dark blue*
ça a *ou* fait . . . *it is . . .*
couleur : c'est de quelle couleur ? *what colour is it?*
de : . . . centimètres/mètres de long/de large/de haut *. . . centimetres/metres long/wide/high*
en : en S/en L *S-shaped/L-shaped*
grand : c'est grand comment ? *how big is it?*
lisse *smooth*
moucheté *spotted*
pointu *pointed, pointy*
quelle hauteur/longueur/largeur cela fait-il *ou* a-t-il ? *how high/long/wide is it?*
rayures *stripes*
se renseigner sur *to inquire about*
ressembler : cela ressemble à quoi ? *what does it look like?*
rugueux *rough*
servir : cela sert à faire *it's (used) for doing*
:ça sert à quoi ? *what's it (used) for?*
:on s'en sert pour faire *people use it for doing or to do*
:on s'en sert pour quoi ? *what do people use it for?*
taille *size*
:quelle taille cela a-t-il ? *what size is it?*

Comment donner et obtenir des explications
s'assurer que . . . *to make sure that . . .*
autrement dit *in other words*
ça y est *I've got it*
c'est à dire . . . *that is . . .*
clocher : il y a quelque chose qui cloche *there's something not quite right*
comprendre *to understand*
croire : je crois (bien) que . . . + *ind I'm afraid that . . .*
explications *explanations*
faire : se faire comprendre *to be understood*
:se faire expliquer un mot *to get someone to explain a word*
j'y suis (maintenant) *(now) I get it*
marcher *to work*
motiver : ce qui motive tout cela, c'est . . . *the motivation for all of that is . . .*
pouvoir : pouvez-vous ?/pourriez-vous ? *can you?/could you?*
reformuler *to rephrase*
saisir *to understand*
sens *meaning*
signifier *to mean*
suivre *to follow*
termes : en d'autres termes *in other words*
vouloir dire *to mean*

Les présentations

Pour présenter quelqu'un à quelqu'un d'autre
(Bernard), voici *ou* je vous présente (M. Durand)
(M. Durand), voici *ou* je vous présente (mon ami Bernard Dubois)
De façon plus formelle
Puis-je vous présenter (M. Durand) ?
Permettez-moi de vous présenter (M. Durand)
J'aimerais vous présenter (M. Durand)
Pour présenter quelqu'un à un groupe
J'ai le (grand) plaisir de vous présenter (M. Durand)
J'ai l'honneur de vous présenter (M. Durand)
De façon familière
(Bernard), (Marie)
Vous vous connaissez ?
Vous vous êtes déjà rencontrés ?
Vous ne vous connaissez pas, je crois ? (Marie), (Jean)

Pour se renseigner du nom de quelqu'un
Je ne connais pas votre nom
Je ne crois pas connaître votre nom
Dites-moi votre nom que je vous présente à (mes amis)
De façon plus formelle
Puis-je vous demander votre nom ?
Je n'ai pas le plaisir de vous connaître
Je ne crois pas vous avoir déjà rencontré
De façon familière
Qui êtes-vous ?/Vous êtes ... ?
Votre nom, c'est ... ?
On ne se connaît pas, je crois
Pour s'assurer du nom de quelqu'un
Comment l'écrivez-vous ?/Comment cela s'écrit-il ?
(Durand), c'est (bien) cela ?
Je n'ai pas entendu/retenu votre nom/prénom
Puis-je vous appeler par votre prénom ?
Puis-je vous appeler (Bernard) ?
De façon familière
Vous êtes (bien) (Bernard), c'est cela ?
Votre prénom, c'est (bien) (Bernard), non ?

Pour situer quelqu'un
Il/Elle vient de/habite à (Lille)
Il/Elle travaille à (l'hôtel)
C'est un(e) ami(e) à moi
C'est le patron/la patronne de mon frère
C'est mon/ma collègue

Les salutations

Comment saluer quelqu'un
Ne pas oublier qu'on se serre souvent la main pour se saluer
Bonjour !
Réponse :
Bonjour !
De façon très familière
Salut !
Réponse :
Salut !
On pourra réserver 'Bonjour !' pour le matin et l'après-midi et utiliser 'Bonsoir !' à partir de la fin de l'après-midi. On répondra 'Bonsoir' à 'Bonsoir'.
De façon formelle
Bonjour, enchanté *ou* ravi de vous rencontrer/de faire votre connaissance
Réponse :
Enchanté/Le plaisir est pour moi
Moi de même

Formules de politesse
Après avoir salué quelqu'un, on pourra dire :
Comment allez-vous ?
Réponse :
Bien/Très bien, merci (et vous ?)
Je vais bien, merci (et vous-même ?)
Ça va, merci (et vous ?)
De façon familière :
Vous allez bien ?
Comment va ?/Comment ça va ?/Ça va ?
Réponse :
Ça va !/Bien !/Pas mal !
Pas trop mal, et vous ?/Ça peut aller !/On fait aller !

Pour dire au revoir
On se serre également la main pour dire au revoir
Au revoir !/A bientôt !
Réponse :
Au revoir !/A bientôt !
Familièrement
Salut !/A la prochaine !/Ciao !
Au coucher
Bonne nuit !
Réponse :
Bonne nuit !

Les présentations
collègue *colleague*
se connaître *to know each other*
croire : je ne crois pas connaître . . . *I don't believe I know . . ., I'm afraid I don't know . . .*
d'autre : quelqu'un d'autre *somebody else*
écrire *to spell*
s'écrire *to be spelt* or *spelled*
nom : s'assurer du nom de qn *to make sure one gets s.o.'s name right*
:se renseigner du nom de qn *to inquire about s.o.'s name*
:votre nom, c'est . . . ? *what's your name ?*
:je n'ai pas retenu votre nom *I didn't catch your name*
patron, patronne *boss*
permettez-moi de . . . *allow me to . . .*
prénom *first name*
présentations *introductions*
présenter *to introduce*
:. . . que je vous présente à . . . *. . . so that I can introduce you to . . .*
se rencontrer *to meet (each other)*
situer *to place*
vous êtes (bien) . . ., c'est cela ? *you're . . ., aren't you ?*

Les salutations
à bientôt ! *see you (again) soon!*
à la prochaine ! *see you (again) soon!*
aller : ça peut aller !/on fait aller ! *so so!/can't complain!*
:(comment) ça va ?/comment va ? *how are things?/how's things?*
:ça va ! *O.K.!, all right!*
:comment allez-vous ? *how are you?*
au coucher *at bedtime*
au revoir *goodbye*
bonjour ! *hello!*
bonne nuit ! *good night!*
bonsoir ! *hello!, good evening!*
enchanté *ou* ravi de vous rencontrer/de faire votre connaissance *how do you do?, pleased to meet you/make your acquaintance*
enchanté *how do you do?* (as reply)
formules de politesse *polite phrases, terms of politeness*
moi de même *likewise*
pas (trop) mal *not (too) bad*
le plaisir est pour moi *the pleasure is mine*
saluer *to greet*
se saluer *to greet each other*
salut ! *hi ! ;* (when taking leave of someone) *bye !*
salutations *greetings*
serrer : se serrer la main *to shake hands*

La conversation courante

Avec des gens que l'on ne connaît pas
On peut parler de l'endroit où l'on se trouve
Cet endroit est agréable/intéressant, non ?
C'est tranquille ici, non *ou* vous ne trouvez pas ?
Il y a beaucoup de monde/de bruit ici, non ?
On est bien *ou* pas mal ici, vous ne trouvez pas ?
On peut parler du temps
Belle journée, vous ne trouvez pas ?
Quel beau/sale temps aujourd'hui, non ?
Il fait meilleur *ou* plus beau aujourd'hui, vous ne trouvez pas ?
Ça se rafraîchit/va tourner à la pluie/sent la pluie, vous ne croyez pas ?
On peut parler de soi
C'est la première fois que je viens ici, et vous ?
Je viens/J'arrive d'Espagne, et vous ?
On peut faire des commentaires
Le service laisse vraiment à désirer/est vraiment très lent, vous ne trouvez pas ?
Il fait toujours chaud dans ce genre d'endroit, non ?

Avec des gens que l'on connaît un peu
Au bureau, dans une soirée, on posera des questions
Vous habitez/travaillez dans le coin ?
Vous êtes du coin/de la région ?
Vous êtes dans quoi *ou* dans quel secteur ?
On parlera de l'endroit où l'on se trouve
C'est tranquille/agréable/gentil ici, non ?
On est bien ici (en été), non ?
On parlera de soi
Je ne connais pas beaucoup (cette région), et vous ?
J'ai eu un mal fou à trouver à (me) garer, pas vous ?
Pour parler de soi
J'habite à (Exeter)
Je suis (étudiant)
Je travaille dans (un bureau)
Je viens de/J'arrive de (Munich)
Ma famille est à/est (originaire) de (Leeds)
Pour inviter quelqu'un à parler de soi
Où habitez-vous ?
Que faites-vous (dans la vie) ?/Vous faites quoi ?
Vous venez d'où ?/D'où venez-vous ?
Où est/D'où vient votre famille ?
Quel genre de musique/travail/cuisine aimez-vous ?
Ça vous plaît (d'habiter ici) ?
Vous aimez cette région ?

Expression d'un point de vue

Ce que l'on aime ou n'aime pas
J'adore cela
J'aime beaucoup cela
C'est superbe/sensationnel/super
Je trouve que c'est/qu'il est/qu'elle est sensationnel(le)/génial(e)
J'ai horreur de cela
Je déteste cela
Je ne supporte pas cela
C'est horrible/affreux/répugnant/imbuvable
Je trouve que c'est/qu'il est/qu'elle est insupportable/horrible/affreux (-euse)

Ce que l'on croit
Je crois vraiment/Je crois absolument (que c'est vrai)
Absolument !
C'est exactement ce que je pense/crois
Je suis tout à fait sûr *ou* certain de cela

Pour marquer son accord
Avec une opinion
C'est tout à fait vrai
Exactement !/Parfaitement !
Je suis tout à fait d'accord
On ne pourrait pas être plus d'accord (avec cela) que moi
Avec une suggestion
C'est une très bonne idée
C'est exactement ce que je proposerais/ce que j'allais proposer/ce qu'il faut faire

Pour marquer son désaccord
Avec une opinion
Je ne suis pas du tout d'accord
Absolument pas !/Pas du tout !
C'est absolument faux !
N'importe quoi !
Vous n'y êtes pas du tout !
Avec une suggestion
Ce n'est vraiment pas une bonne idée (du tout)
Certainement pas !

Pour marquer que l'on dit quelque chose sérieusement
Je veux que cela soit bien clair
Je dis cela tout à fait sérieusement
Je veux que vous compreniez bien cela

La conversation courante
agréable *pleasant*
bien : on est bien ici *it's nice here*
coin : dans le coin *locally*
:être du coin *to be local*
conversation courante *everyday conversation*
dans : vous êtes dans quoi *ou* dans quel secteur ? *what (job) do you do?, what line are you in?*
d'où : vous venez d'où ? *where do you come from?*
(se) garer *to park*
gentil *nice, pleasant*
il fait meilleur *ou* plus beau *it's better* or *nicer*
laisser à désirer *to leave something to be desired*
mal : avoir un mal fou à faire *to have an awful lot of trouble doing*
non ? *isn't it?/aren't you?*/etc
originaire : être originaire de *to originate from*
pas mal *not bad*
pluie : ça va tourner à la pluie *it's beginning to turn to rain*
:ça sent la pluie *it feels like rain*
rafraîchir : ça se rafraîchit *it's getting cooler*
sale temps *nasty* or *awful weather*
soirée *party*
vous ne trouvez pas ? *don't you think?, isn't it?/aren't you?*/etc

Expression d'un point de vue
absolument (pas) ! *absolutely (not) !*
d'accord : être d'accord (avec) *to agree (with)*
affreux *dreadful, hideous*
avoir horreur de *to loathe*
certain de *certain about* or *of*
exactement *exactly, precisely*
faux *wrong*
génial *brilliant*
imbuvable *insufferable*
insupportable *unbearable*
marquer *to indicate*
n'importe quoi ! *nonsense !*
parfaitement *certainly*
pas du tout ! *certainly not !, not at all !*
répugnant *disgusting, revolting*
sensationnel *terrific*
super *fantastic*
supporter : je ne supporte pas . . . *I can't stand . . .*
sûr de *sure about* or *of*
tout à fait *completely, entirely*
trouver : je trouve que . . . *I think that . . .*
vous n'y êtes pas du tout ! *you're completely missing the point!*

Les compliments

Pour féliciter quelqu'un
d'une naissance, de fiançailles etc :
Félicitations !/Toutes mes félicitations !
d'une réussite à un examen, d'une victoire etc :
Félicitations !/Toutes mes félicitations !/Bravo !
Je suis (très) heureux pour vous
au cours d'un travail etc :
Bien !/Très bien !/Bravo !

Pour complimenter quelqu'un
un inférieur ou un égal:
Bravo !/Bien !
C'était/C'est très bien !
Ce (plat) est/était très bon/excellent/fameux
Je suis très satisfait *ou* content de (votre travail)
un supérieur :
Bravo !
J'ai trouvé (ce travail excellent)
Je suis admiratif devant ce (travail)
De façon familière
Super !/Génial !
C'est super/génial/vachement bien
Tu as été super/génial/vachement bon *ou* bien

Pour consoler quelqu'un
d'un échec :
Pas de chance !
Allez, ne vous en faites pas !
Ça ira mieux la prochaine fois, allez !
de mauvaises nouvelles :
J'ai appris *ou* su pour (votre père), je suis désolé pour vous
Cela m'a fait de la peine de savoir pour (votre père)
J'ai su, pour (votre voiture), quelle déveine !
De façon plus formelle
J'ai été (très) navré d'apprendre que (vous avez eu un accident)
J'ai appris (la mauvaise nouvelle) avec tristesse

Pour transmettre ses compliments
Transmettez-lui toutes mes félicitations
Dites-lui bien que j'ai beaucoup aimé cela
Vous lui direz (bien) que je l'ai trouvé(e) épatant(e)/très bien *ou* bon(ne)
Félicitez-le/-la pour moi *ou* de ma part

Comment refuser

Pour refuser une invitation
De plus en plus poliment
Désolé, je ne peux/pourrai pas
C'est dommage, mais je (ne serai pas là)
Je crois que je ne pourrai pas (être des vôtres)
Cela me ferait très plaisir, mais j'ai (énormément de travail)
J'accepterais volontiers (votre aimable invitation) mais je me vois malheureusement obligé de refuser
De façon plus abrupte
Non, je ne peux pas
Non, merci, j'ai du travail/j'ai autre chose à faire/je suis déjà pris

Pour refuser une offre
De plus en plus poliment
Non, merci/Non, je vous remercie
Merci, ce n'est pas la peine
Non merci, je n'ai pas besoin de (votre aide)
Merci, je ne prendrai pas de (café)
Ça va, merci, je vais (me débrouiller tout seul)
Je vous remercie, mais je n'aurai pas besoin de (votre aide)
C'est gentil à vous, mais ce n'est pas la peine, merci
Je vous remercie de me le proposer, mais je n'en aurai pas besoin
Je vous remercie beaucoup (de votre aimable proposition), mais je n'aurai pas à faire appel à (vos services)
De façon plus abrupte
Non
Merci
Je n'en veux pas

En face de quelqu'un qui insiste
Non, vraiment
Je vous assure que je n'en ai pas besoin/que c'est inutile
Je ne tiens pas du tout à (sortir)
Je ne peux vraiment pas (prendre un autre verre)
Je n'ai pas l'intention de changer d'avis
Vous ne me ferez pas changer d'avis
Vous n'arriverez pas à me convaincre
Ce n'est pas la peine d'insister
Je vous ai dit non, c'est non !
Je ne veux rien vous acheter, un point c'est tout !

Les compliments
admiratif : être admiratif devant *to admire greatly*
allez ! *come on!*
apprendre : j'ai appris pour *I heard about*
bravo ! *well done!*
chance : pas de chance ! *bad luck!*
content de *happy with* or *about*
désolé : je suis désolé pour vous *I sympathize with you*
déveine *bad luck*
épatant *marvellous*
faire : ne vous en faites pas ! *don't worry!*
fameux *first-class*
félicitations : (toutes mes) félicitations ! *(many) congratulations!*
féliciter *to congratulate*
génial *brilliant*
heureux : je suis heureux pour vous *I'm pleased* or *happy for you*
navré (de) *sorry (to)*
part : de ma part *on my behalf*
peine : faire de la peine à qn *to distress s.o.*
satisfait de *happy with* or *about*
savoir : j'ai su pour . . . *I heard about . . .*
super *fantastic*
transmettre à qn *to convey* or *pass on to s.o.*
vachement bien *damn good*

Comment refuser
appel : faire appel à *to resort to*
arriver à faire *to manage to do*
autre chose *something else*
ça va *it's O.K.*
. . .c'est non ! *. . .and I mean no!*
se débrouiller (tout seul) *to manage*
désolé *sorry*
dommage : c'est dommage *it's a pity*
énormément de *an enormous amount of*
gentil à vous *kind of you*
inutile *pointless*
peine : ce n'est pas la peine (de faire) *don't bother (to do)*
plaisir : cela me ferait très plaisir *I'd be delighted*
point : un point c'est tout ! *and that's that!*
pouvoir : je ne peux/pourrai pas *I can't/won't be able to*
pris : je suis déjà pris *I'm busy (doing something else)*
proposer *to suggest*
tenir à faire *to be keen on doing*
voir : je me vois obligé de . . . *I have to . . .*
volontiers : j'accepterais volontiers *I'd love to accept*
vôtre : être des vôtres *to be one of your party*
vouloir : je n'en veux pas *I don't want it*

Comment dire qu'on n'a pas compris

Pour faire répéter quelque chose qu'on n'a pas entendu
De plus familier au plus poli
Quoi ?/Hein ?
Pardon ?/Comment ?
Qu'avez-vous dit ?
Que disiez-vous ?
Vous pouvez répéter, s'il vous plaît ?
Je n'ai pas entendu *ou* saisi ce que vous avez dit
Excusez-moi, je crois que je n'ai pas entendu
Désolé, je ne vous ai pas bien entendu
Pouvez-vous/Pourriez-vous répéter ce que vous venez de dire ?

Pour indiquer qu'on n'a pas compris quelque chose
Que signifie *ou* veut dire (cette expression) ?
Je ne comprends pas (le sens de) (ce mot)
Je ne connais pas (ce mot/cette expression)
(Ce mot/Cette expression) m'est inconnu(e)
J'ai compris (le début) mais pas (la fin)
Vous avez dit (ceci) ou (cela) ?
Désolé, je crois que je ne comprends pas (cela)
Excusez-moi, mon français n'est pas très bon
Je crois bien que le sens de ce que vous avez dit m'échappe/m'a échappé
Pourriez-vous épeler (ce mot) ?
Pourriez-vous me l'écrire ?

Lorsqu'on ne vous comprend pas
Ce n'est peut-être pas ce que l'on dit
J'ai peut-être utilisé le mauvais mot/la mauvaise expression
Je n'ai peut-être pas utilisé le bon mot/la bonne expression
Je me trompe peut-être de mot/d'expression
Peut-être que ma prononciation n'est pas correcte
Je vais essayer de dire cela autrement

Lorsqu'on a du mal à comprendre quelqu'un
Pourriez-vous parler plus lentement *ou* moins vite ?
Pas si vite, s'il vous plaît
Je ne vous comprends pas
Vous parlez trop vite pour moi
Je ne comprends pas (ce que vous dites)
Pourriez-vous me traduire cela ?
Parlez-vous (une autre langue) ?

Comment dire aux gens qu'ils se trompent

Pour indiquer à quelqu'un une erreur de méthode, de direction etc
Les sept premières expressions peuvent être précédées de 'il me semble que . . . + *ind' pour les rendre moins abruptes.*
Vous vous trompez (de façon/de route/de direction)
Vous êtes *ou* allez dans la mauvaise direction
Vous le/la tenez (à l'envers)
C'est dans l'autre sens
Vous ne l'avez pas allumé(e)/mis(e) en marche
Vous devriez aller vers (le nord) et pas vers (le sud)
Vous devriez vous trouver (là-bas), pas (ici)
Ne faites pas cela comme ça, mais comme ceci
Je vais vous montrer (comment faire/vous y prendre)
Voulez-vous que je vous montre/que je le fasse ?

Pour indiquer à quelqu'un une erreur de raisonnement, d'analyse etc
Les sept premières expressions peuvent être précédées de 'il me semble que . . . + *ind' pour les rendre moins abruptes.*
Ce n'est pas juste *ou* exact/C'est faux *ou* inexact
Ce n'est pas le bon nom/la date exacte/la bonne orthographe
Ce n'est pas cela/lui/elle
Il y a une erreur/un malentendu quelque part
Il y a quelque chose de faux quelque part/là-dedans
Vous avez fait une erreur ici
Vous vous êtes trompé
Vous êtes sûr ? C'est vraiment (aujourd'hui) ?
Non, en fait, c'est (le contraire)
Je suis pratiquement sûr que c'est (mardi)
Je ne suis pas d'accord avec vous
Non, ce n'est pas vrai/c'est inexact
Non, ce n'est pas (dangereux), c'est tout à fait (sûr)

Pour interrompre quelqu'un
Attendez (voir)
Arrêtez (un instant)
Attendez (une seconde/une minute/un instant)
Puis-je vous interrompre une minute ?
Je peux (vous) dire quelque chose ?
Vous permettez ?
Vous permettez que je dise quelque chose/que je vous montre ?

Comment dire qu'on n'a pas compris
autrement *in a different way*
bon (mot) *right (word)*
comment ? *pardon?, what?*
désolé *sorry*
échapper : le sens de . . . m'échappe/m'a échappé *I haven't got/didn't get the gist of . . .*
écrire *to spell*
épeler *to spell*
excusez-moi *excuse me*
hein ? *what?, eh?*
inconnu (à qn) *unknown (to s.o.)*
mal : avoir du mal à faire *to have trouble doing*
mauvais (mot) *wrong (word)*
pardon ? *sorry?, pardon?*
pouvoir : pouvez-vous ?/pourriez-vous ? *can you?/could you?*
quoi ? *what?*
répéter *to repeat*
saisir *to catch, to understand*
sens *meaning*
signifier *to mean*
se tromper de mot/d'expression *to use the wrong word/expression*
utiliser *to use*
vouloir dire *to mean*

Comment dire aux gens qu'ils se trompent
attendez (voir) *wait (a moment)*
bon (nom) *right (name)*
comment faire/s'y prendre *how to do it/go about it*
contraire : le contraire *the opposite*
envers : à l'envers *upside down*
exact *right*
faux *wrong*
inexact *wrong*
juste *right*
malentendu *misunderstanding*
mauvaise (direction) *wrong (direction)*
orthographe *spelling*
permettre : vous permettez ? *may I?, excuse me!*
:vous permettez que je dise . . . ? *may I say . . .?, do you mind if I say . . .?*
raisonnement : erreur de raisonnement *error in one's reasoning*
sens : dans l'autre sens *in the opposite direction*
sûr : c'est tout à fait sûr *it's quite safe*
sûr (que) . . . *sure (that) . . .*
se tromper *to make a mistake, to be wrong*
:se tromper de façon *to do things in the wrong way*
:se tromper de direction *to go in the wrong direction*

Le coût de la vie

Pour parler de l'évolution des prix
A la hausse
Le prix/Ça a augmenté (le mois dernier)
Ça a augmenté d'un seul coup/petit à petit
Les prix (de . . .) sont en hausse *ou* augmentent
Il y a eu une augmentation (des prix)
A la baisse
En (été), les prix devraient baisser *ou* être en baisse
Les prix de (cet article) ont baissé (l'année dernière)
Les prix (du pétrole) vont peut-être baisser
Nous avons enregistré une baisse (des coûts de main-d'œuvre)
Les prix ont dégringolé/baissé petit à petit
Il y a eu une baisse brutale/progressive
Il y a eu une chute des prix
Stabilité des prix
Les prix n'ont pas bougé
Le coût de la vie ne bougera pas *ou* ne changera pas
Les prix sont au même niveau (que l'an dernier)

Pour parler du coût de la vie
(Le logement) est cher/bon marché
Ça revient cher de (se loger à Paris)
On peut acheter (un magnétoscope)
On ne peut pas acheter (de magnétoscope)
La vie est dure/facile
Il y a des gens qui ont du mal (à joindre les deux bouts)
Ce n'est pas facile pour (ceux qui vivent sur une retraite)
Notre situation s'est améliorée/s'est détériorée
Et dans votre pays *ou* chez vous, c'est comment ?
Et votre situation à vous ?

Pour parler des impôts
L'Etat prend (30%) des revenus en impôts
On doit payer un impôt sur le revenu/la TVA/des impôts indirects
Je laisse (un tiers de mon salaire) aux impôts
Les impôts m'enlèvent *ou* me mangent (un tiers de mon salaire)
On paie (10% de son salaire) pour la Sécurité Sociale
Les cotisations sociales représentent (10% du salaire)
Les impôts sont élevés/peu élevés
On a une bonne couverture sociale
On peut toucher sa retraite à (60 ans)
Et chez vous, vous payez beaucoup d'impôts ?
Les impôts sont élevés chez vous ?

Comment corriger quelqu'un

Pour corriger une erreur de fait, de date etc
En fait, mon nom est (Duval), pas (Durand)
Ce n'est pas exact/C'est inexact
Ce n'est pas la date exacte/le nom exact/la bonne orthographe
Ce que vous dites n'est pas exact/est inexact
Ce n'est pas (cela)
Je ne suis pas/Il n'est pas (ingénieur)
Il y a erreur sur la personne. Je ne suis pas M. Dupont
Il y a quelque chose qui ne va pas là-dedans
Vous vous êtes trompé/Vous vous trompez
Je crains que ce ne soit inexact
Il semble qu'il y ait une erreur/un malentendu
Vous êtes sûr ? Il serait (français) ?
En réalité, nous sommes (vendredi) aujourd'hui
Je suis pratiquement sûr (qu'ils sont suisses)
A vrai dire, je crois que vous faites erreur

Pour corriger un jugement, une analyse
Non, ce n'est pas vrai/c'est faux
Non, ce n'est pas (politique), c'est (économique)
Non, vous vous trompez/Vous faites erreur
Vous faites fausse route
Vous avez une fausse impression
C'est ce que vous pensez vraiment ?
Je n'ai pas cette impression
Je ne pense pas comme vous
Vraiment ? Je l'ai toujours trouvé(e) (charmant(e))
Je crois que vous n'avez pas bien compris (la situation)
Je crains fort que vous ne voyiez pas les choses comme il faut
Il me semble que votre impression n'est pas la bonne
Très familièrement
N'importe quoi !/Vous n'y êtes pas du tout !/Quelle idée !

Pour répondre lorsqu'on vous corrige
Vraiment ?
Ah, excusez-moi
Excusez-moi, je croyais que vous vous appeliez (Durand)
On m'avait dit (quelque chose d'autre)
J'ai été mal renseigné *ou* informé
J'ai dû être mal renseigné *ou* informé
Je vous remercie de cette précision
Merci de m'avoir donné l'information exacte

Le coût de la vie
augmentation *increase*
augmenter *to go up, to increase*
baisse *fall, drop*
:à la baisse *downwards*
:être en baisse *to be falling*
baisser *to fall, to drop*
chute des prix *fall in prices*
cotisations sociales *Social Security contributions*
coup : d'un seul coup *in one go*
coût de la vie *cost of living*
couverture sociale *Social Security cover*
dégringoler *to fall, to tumble*
élevé *high*
enregistrer *to record*
évolution des prix *price changes*
hausse *rise*
:à la hausse *upwards*
:être en hausse *to be rising*
impôt sur le revenu *income tax*
joindre les deux bouts *to make ends meet*
magnétoscope *video (recorder)*
mal : avoir du mal *to have a lot of trouble*
retraite *pension*
:toucher sa retraite *to get one's pension*
revenir : ça revient cher de *it's expensive to*
revenus *income*
TVA *VAT*

Comment corriger quelqu'un
bonne (orthographe) *right (spelling)*
comme il faut *properly*
craindre : je crains fort que . . . + *sub* *I'm (very) afraid that . . .*
en fait *in fact*
en réalité *in fact*
erreur *mistake, error*
:erreur de fait *factual error*
:erreur de date *mistake* or *error in the date*
:faire erreur *to make a mistake*
:il y a erreur sur la personne *you've made a mistake, you've got the wrong person*
exact *right*
faux *wrong*
inexact *wrong*
malentendu *misunderstanding*
mal renseigné *ou* informé *misinformed*
n'importe quoi ! *nonsense!*
nous sommes (vendredi) *it's (Friday)*
précision *clarification, explanation*
quelle idée ! *the (very) idea of it!*
route : vous faites fausse route *you're on the wrong track*
se tromper *to be mistaken*
vous n'y êtes pas du tout ! *you're completely missing the point!*

Les pièces d'identité et autres documents

Pour savoir quels documents posséder
Quels documents sont nécessaires ?
De quels documents aurai-je besoin ?
Quelles sont les formalités ?
(Une pièce d'identité) est-elle obligatoire ?
Faut-il (un visa) ?
Mon permis de conduire suffit-il ?
Est-ce qu'ils acceptent *ou* prennent (la carte bancaire) ?

Pour parler de ses documents officiels
Voici mon (permis de conduire/extrait d'acte de naissance)
C'est (un passeport américain/une carte d'identité française)
Voici (un chéquier/une carte de crédit)
Ça, ce sont *ou* c'est mes papiers
Voici le certificat d'assurance
On ne peut se faire embaucher sans ce document
Il faut avoir (cela)
Il/Elle est valable jusqu'en (juin)
Il/Elle expire au mois de (juin)
Tout est en règle
Ce passeport/Cette carte d'identité est périmé(e) *ou* n'est plus valable
Tout est à jour

Les démarches pour obtenir des documents
Je voudrais un imprimé de demande de visa *ou* une demande de visa
Je voudrais demander (une carte de travail)
Je voudrais déposer une demande de (carte de travail)
Il me faudrait un imprimé de déclaration de revenus
Je voudrais renouveler/prolonger mon assurance
Je voudrais (faire) renouveler mon visa
J'ai deux photos d'identité
Voici une photocopie de mon (extrait d'acte de naissance)
Il en faut combien d'exemplaires ?
Il le/la faut en combien d'exemplaires ?
J'ai/Je n'ai pas signé
Pourriez-vous m'indiquer comment remplir cet imprimé, s'il vous plaît ?
Pouvez-vous m'aider (à remplir cet imprimé) ?
Je ne comprends pas cette question
Que faut-il mettre dans cette case/sur cette ligne ?

L'apprentissage du français

Pour situer son niveau et ses motivations
Je voudrais apprendre le français
Je ne parle pas beaucoup/bien le français
J'apprends à parler français/Je prends des cours de français
Cela fait (trois ans) que j'ai commencé à l'apprendre
J'en ai fait un peu à l'école/à l'université
J'en ai besoin pour mon (travail)
Je vais faire un séjour dans une famille française
Je crois que la connaissance du français est importante/indispensable/utile

Pour parler de ce que l'on trouve facile/difficile
C'est facile/Ce n'est pas facile de le parler/de l'écrire
Le vocabulaire/La grammaire est simple/difficile à retenir/à utiliser
Je n'ai pas de/J'ai pas mal de problèmes à comprendre le français parlé/écrit
J'ai des problèmes avec (les conjugaisons/les accords)

Pour parler des méthodes d'apprentissage
Quelle est la meilleure méthode pour apprendre ?
Comment pourrais-je enrichir mon vocabulaire/améliorer mon accent ?
Quelle méthode me conseilleriez-vous ?
Pour donner son opinion sur cette question
Je crois que le mieux, c'est de lire beaucoup/d'écouter des Français parler
Vous devriez essayer de parler avec des Français
Il faut s'entraîner (à parler)

Pour expliquer ses attentes à un professeur
Je veux pouvoir parler de façon plus naturelle
Je veux améliorer (ma prononciation/grammaire)
Je voudrais pouvoir lire du français plus facilement
Pour (lire), ça va *ou* je n'ai pas de problèmes, c'est (mon accent) qui est mauvais
J'ai trop peu de vocabulaire

Pour savoir quand employer une expression
Est-ce que c'est du français correct/familier ?
C'est (trop) familier/emprunté ?
Cela s'emploie dans la conversation familière ?
Est-ce que je peux utiliser cela dans une conversation avec (un client) ?

Les pièces d'identité et autres documents
à jour *up-to-date*
carte bancaire *bank* or *banker's card*
carte de crédit *credit card*
carte d'identité *identity card*
case *space, square*
certificat d'assurance *insurance certificate*
chéquier Br *cheque* or Am *check book*
déclaration de revenus *(income) tax return*
demande (de visa) *application (for a visa)*
démarches (pour) *required steps* or *procedures (to)*
déposer *to lodge, to make*
embaucher : se faire embaucher *to get hired*
en règle *in order*
exemplaires *copies*
expirer *to expire*
extrait d'acte de naissance *birth certificate*
imprimé (de) *(printed) form (for)*
obligatoire *compulsory*
périmé *expired*
permis de conduire Br *driving licence*, Am *driver's license*
pièce d'identité *identity document, ID, proof of identity*
prolonger *to extend*
renouveler *to renew*
valable (jusqu'en) *valid (till)*

L'apprentissage du français
accords *agreements*
améliorer *to improve*
apprendre *to learn*
apprentissage *learning*
attentes *expectations*
ça va *that's O.K.*
client *customer, client*
conjugaisons *conjugations*
conseiller qch à qn *to recommend s.o. sth*
cours de français *French lessons*
écrit *written*
employer *to use*
s'employer *to be used*
emprunté *formal, awkward*
enrichir *to enrich*
s'entraîner (à parler) *to practise (speaking)*
familier *informal, colloquial*
mieux : le mieux, c'est de . . . *the best thing is to . . .*
niveau *level*
parlé *spoken*
problèmes avec /à comprendre . . . *problems with/(in) understanding . . .*
séjour : faire un séjour (dans) *to stay (with)*
situer *to situate*
vocabulaire : trop peu de vocabulaire *not (too) much vocabulary*

A table avec des francophones

Au début du repas
Pour dire que l'on peut passer à table
C'est prêt !/A table !
Prenez place !/Passons à table/On peut passer à table
(Le dîner) est servi
Avant de commencer, on dira :
Bon appétit !
Réponse :
Merci (vous aussi)
Ça a l'air (très) bon/délicieux/très appétissant
Cela sent (très) bon
Avant de boire, on pourra dire :
A votre santé !
Réponse :
Santé !
A la (bonne) vôtre !
Réponse :
A la vôtre !

Au cours du repas
Passez-moi (le sel), s'il vous plaît
Vous pouvez me passer (le sel), s'il vous plaît ?
Puis-je avoir (du sel), s'il vous plaît ?
Puis-je reprendre (des pommes de terre), s'il vous plaît ?
C'est délicieux/très bon
Comment appelez-vous ce plat ?
Comment s'appelle ce plat ?
L'hôte(sse) dira :
Vous reprendrez bien (des pommes de terre) ?
Voulez-vous encore (des pommes de terre) ?
Il ne vous manque rien ?
Vous préférez (le blanc) ou (le rouge) ?
Voulez-vous un peu d'eau/de vin/de pain ?
Réponse :
Volontiers, merci
Un tout petit peu (mais c'est par gourmandise)
Non, merci

Après le repas
L'invité dira :
Je vous remercie de (ce déjeuner/ce délicieux repas)
Tout était délicieux/très bon
Je me suis (vraiment) régalé
L'hôte(sse) dira :
Je suis ravi(e) que cela vous ait plu
Vous me flattez !

Comment proposer à boire et à manger

Pour proposer à boire
Qu'est-ce que je vous sers ?/Que puis-je vous servir ?
Qu'est-ce que je vous offre ?/Que voulez-vous boire ?
Vous boirez bien quelque chose ?
Que diriez-vous d'un whisky/apéritif ?
Voulez-vous un (café) ?
Prenez-vous du (sucre) ? Combien de morceaux ?
Café ? Avec du sucre ?
Whisky ? Avec ou sans glace ?
Servez-vous !
Pour accepter
Oui, merci/Merci beaucoup
Pourquoi pas ?/Bien sûr
Pour refuser
Non, merci/Merci, non
Je ne prendrai rien (pour le moment), merci
Je n'ai pas soif (pour le moment), merci

Pour proposer à manger
Je vous sers quelque chose à manger ?
Que voulez-vous manger ?/Vous mangerez bien quelque chose ?
Prendrez-vous/Reprendrez-vous de (cette entrée) ?
Je vous remets un peu de ce plat ?
Pour accepter
Oui, merci/Merci beaucoup
Pourquoi pas ?/Bien sûr
Pour refuser
Non, merci/Merci, non
Je n'en (re)prendrai pas, merci
Je n'ai pas/plus faim, merci

Pour conseiller un mets ou une boisson
Connaissez-vous/Avez-vous déjà goûté (cela) ?
Je vous recommande ce plat/ce vin
Pour demander conseil
Vous me conseillez quoi ?/Que me conseillez-vous ?

Pour savoir ce que préfère un invité
Vous préférez (du thé) ou (du café) ?
Voulez-vous autre chose à la place ?
Cela ne vous dérange pas si (ce n'est pas salé) ?
Pour indiquer ce que l'on préfère
Je préférerais quelque chose (de froid), en fait
Je peux l'avoir avec (de l'eau gazeuse) ?

A table avec des francophones
appétissant *appetizing*
bon appétit ! *enjoy your meal!*
gourmandise : mais c'est par gourmandise *because it's so tempting*
hôte, hôtesse *host, hostess*
invité *guest*
manquer : il ne vous manque rien ? *would you like anything else?*
passer qch à qn *to pass s.o. sth*
prenez place ! *take your seats!*
ravi que . . . + *sub* *delighted that . . .*
se régaler *to have a real treat*
reprendre (des pommes de terre) *to have some more (potatoes)*
santé : à votre santé ! *(to your) good health!, cheers!*
:santé ! *good health!, cheers!*
:à la (bonne) vôtre ! *(to your) (very) good health!*
:à la vôtre *good health!, and to you!*
table : à table (avec) *eating (with)*
:à table ! *(food is) ready!*
:passer à table *to go and eat, to go and sit down*
volontiers *I'd love to*

Comment proposer à boire et à manger
autre chose *something else*
bien sûr *of course*
boire : vous boirez bien quelque chose ? *would you care for a drink?*
conseil : demander conseil *to ask for a recommendation*
conseiller qch (à) *to recommend sth (to)*
déranger : cela ne vous dérange pas si . . . ? *I hope you don't mind if . . .?*
dire : que diriez-vous de . . . ? *what would you say to . . .?*
eau gazeuse *soda water*
goûter *to taste*
invité *guest*
manger : vous mangerez bien quelque chose ? *would you care for something to eat?*
mets *dish*
place : à la place *instead*
plat *dish*
prendre *to have*
:prendre de . . . *to have some of . . .*
proposer à boire/à manger *to offer s.o. a drink/(some) food*
recommander qch (à) *to recommend sth (to)*
remettre de qch à qn *to give s.o. some more of sth*
reprendre de . . . *to have some more of . . .*
servir *to serve*
:servez-vous *help* or *serve yourself*

Au restaurant

Avant de passer la commande
Auriez-vous *ou* Avez-vous une table pour (trois) ?
Je voudrais/nous voudrions déjeuner/dîner
Peut-on déjeuner/dîner ?
Vous me donnerez la carte/la carte des vins
Puis-je avoir la carte ?
Pour appeler le serveur ou *la serveuse*
S'il vous plaît !
Monsieur !/Mademoiselle !

Au moment de passer la commande
Pour demander conseil
Que me/nous conseillez-vous ?
(Le poisson) est bien ?
Quel vin conseilleriez-vous avec (ce plat) ?
Pour savoir ce qu'est un plat
Cela, qu'est-ce que c'est ?
Est-ce que c'est (du poisson) ?
Qu'est-ce qu'il y a dedans ?
Pour passer la commande
Je prendrai (une *ou* la soupe)
Je ne prendrai pas de (hors-d'œuvre/dessert)
Je ne prendrai que (le plat du jour)
Ce sera (un steak), mais sans (frites), s'il vous plaît
Je ne veux plus rien, merci/J'ai terminé, merci
(Une bière) pour Monsieur/Madame, s'il vous plaît
Vous nous apporterez (deux cafés), s'il vous plaît ?
Pour moi ce sera un steak bleu/saignant/à point/bien cuit

Au moment de régler l'addition
Pour demander l'addition
L'addition, s'il vous plaît/Peut-on avoir l'addition ?
Vous me donnerez l'addition, s'il vous plaît
Pour demander des précisions sur l'addition
Le service est-il compris ?
La TVA est-elle comprise ?
Ce total est-il tout compris ?
A quoi correspond ce montant ?
Vous êtes sûr de ne pas vous être trompé ?
Il y a une erreur dans l'addition
Vous m'avez compté (deux bouteilles de vin)
Pour payer
Acceptez-vous les chèques/la carte bleue/les cartes de crédit ?
Je peux vous faire un chèque ?

La cuisine

Pour décrire un mets
C'est sucré/salé
C'est servi froid/chaud
C'est un plat de viande/poisson
C'est cuit dans une sauce au vin/à la moutarde/à la crème
C'est assez relevé/fade
C'est très bon
Pour savoir comment est préparé un mets
Est-ce que c'est (frit) ?
Comment le fait-on cuire ?
Ça a quel goût ?
Cela se cuit au four *ou* en cocotte ?

Pour donner une recette
C'est assez simple/compliqué à faire
Il faut (un poulet d'un kilo/un (bon) kilo de bœuf)
On le fait mijoter environ (quarante) minutes
La cuisson prend environ une heure
On le passe au réfrigérateur/au four
On le fait revenir *ou* dorer/frire dans un peu d'huile *ou* de beurre
Après, on ajoute (la crème)
Dans le recette, ils disent (deux verres de vin)
Il vaut mieux (saler et poivrer en fin de cuisson)
Pour demander une recette
Quelle est la recette ?
Comment fait-on (cela) ?
Il faut le faire cuire pendant combien de temps ?
Est-ce qu'on (y) met du lait ?
Est-ce que cela se sert froid ou chaud ?

Les spécialités culinaires
C'est un plat français/italien
C'est un plat typique (d'Inde)
C'est une recette (mexicaine)
C'est un plat de quel pays ?
Est-ce que c'est une spécialité espagnole ?
Vous aimez la cuisine (indienne) ?
La cuisine (marocaine), c'est comment ?
Qu'est-ce qu'il y a comme plat typique de la cuisine (chinoise) ?
J'aime/Je n'aime pas la cuisine (japonaise)
Je préfère la cuisine (européenne) à la cuisine (orientale)
Mon plat préféré, c'est (les lasagnes)
Je ne cours pas après (les plats relevés)

Au restaurant
addition   Br *bill*, Am *check*
bien : (le poisson) est bien ?   *is (the fish) good?*
carte   *menu*
  :carte des vins   *wine list*
carte bleue   *Visa* ® *card*
cartes de crédit   *credit cards*
chèque : faire un chèque à qn   *to give s.o. a* Br *cheque* or Am *check*
commande : passer la commande   *to order*
compris   *included*
compter qch à qn   *to charge s.o. for sth*
conseil : demander conseil   *to ask for a recommendation*
plaire : s'il vous plaît   *please*
  :s'il vous plaît !   *excuse me!* (when calling someone)
plat   *dish*
plat du jour   *today's set menu*
précisions (sur)   *information (about)*
prendre   *to have*
  :je ne prendrai pas de   *I won't have any*
serveur, -euse   *waiter, waitress; barman, barmaid*
steak bleu/saignant/à point/bien cuit   *(very) rare/rare/medium (rare)/well done steak*
total : ce total est-il tout compris ?   *does this total include everything?*
se tromper   *to make a mistake*
TVA   *VAT*

La cuisine
cocotte   *casserole*
comment : c'est comment ?   *what's it like?*
courir : je ne cours pas après   *I'm not keen on*
cuire : faire cuire   *to cook*
cuisine   *cooking*
cuisson   *cooking*
culinaire   *culinary*
dorer : faire dorer   *to brown*
fade   *bland*
frire : faire frire   *to fry*
lasagnes   *lasagna*
mijoter : faire mijoter   *to simmer*
mets   *dish*
passer qch à . . .   *to put sth in . . .*
plat   *dish*
poivrer   *to pepper*
recette   *recipe*
relevé   *spicy*
revenir : faire revenir   *to brown*
salé   *savoury*
saler   *to salt*
sauce au vin/à la moutarde/à la crème   *wine/mustard/cream sauce*
sucré   *sweet*

La nourriture et les régimes

Pour demander à quelqu'un ce qu'il mange habituellement
Mangez-vous (des œufs) ?
Que prenez-vous au (petit déjeuner) ?
Que mangez-vous au (déjeuner) ?
Qu'est-ce que vous faites (d'ordinaire) pour le (dîner) ?
Mangez-vous beaucoup de (pâtes) ?
Faites-vous de gros repas ?
Consommez-vous beaucoup de (viande rouge) ?

Pour dire ce que l'on mange habituellement
Nous faisons toujours (trois) repas par jour
Nous prenons souvent/rarement (des œufs) (au petit déjeuner)
Nous mangeons légèrement (le midi)
Je déjeune souvent sur le pouce
Nous mangeons peu dehors
Ils mangent beaucoup de plats à base (d'œufs)
Je ne mange pas beaucoup de (viande)
Ils consomment beaucoup de (fruits)
Ils (ne) mangent (pas) beaucoup (le soir)
Ce sont de gros consommateurs de (légumes verts)

Pour savoir si quelqu'un suit un régime
Vous suivez un régime (particulier) ?
Y a-t-il des choses qui vous sont interdites ?
Y a-t-il des choses que vous ne pouvez pas manger ?
Pouvez-vous manger de tout ?
Mangez-vous de tout ?
Que pouvez-vous manger ?

Pour indiquer qu'on suit un régime
Je suis au régime/végétarien
Le médecin me fait suivre un régime
Je suis un régime
J'essaie de maigrir
Je dois faire attention à ce que je mange
Je ne dois pas manger de (pain)
(Le pain) m'est interdit par mon médecin
Le médecin m'a interdit (les féculents)
Je ne peux pas boire de café
Je ne dois pas dépasser les (600) calories par jour
Savez-vous combien il y a de calories dans (cela) ?
Y a-t-il du sel dans (cela) ?
Le sel m'est interdit
Est-ce que (cela) contient de l'alcool ?

La santé

Pour parler de sa santé
Je suis/Je ne suis pas en bonne santé/forme
Je n'ai pas de problèmes de santé
J'ai des problèmes (de dos/d'estomac/de digestion)
J'ai le cœur plutôt/très/assez fragile
J'ai le cœur en parfaite santé
J'ai des (comprimés) à prendre/un traitement à suivre
Je suis sous traitement
Je dois suivre un régime/éviter certains aliments
Je suis allergique à (la pénicilline)
J'ai trop/Je n'ai pas assez de tension
Je fais de l'hypertension
J'ai eu (un accident l'année dernière)
Je n'ai jamais/J'ai déjà été hospitalisé

Pour décrire des symptômes
Je ne me sens pas très bien
Je me sens fatigué/nerveux (depuis un moment)
Je ne dors pas très bien/Je ne dors plus
Je n'ai pas beaucoup d'appétit
J'ai des maux de tête/d'estomac
J'ai des sifflements/bourdonnements dans les oreilles
J'ai les yeux qui me tirent
J'ai mal à (l'épaule/la cheville)
J'ai une douleur (dans les reins/au genou)
Pour évoquer une cause possible
J'ai l'impression que c'est (la grippe)
C'est peut-être parce que (je fais du tennis)
Ça serait bien (quelque chose que j'ai mangé)
C'est probablement dû à ...
Pour décrire une évolution
Je me sens mieux/Je ne me sens pas mieux
C'est de pire en pire/J'ai encore plus mal
J'ai toujours aussi mal/Rien n'a changé
Les médicaments/cachets m'ont fait du bien/ne m'ont rien fait

Pour s'enquérir de la santé de quelqu'un
Comment vous sentez-vous aujourd'hui ?
Comment va votre (jambe) ?
Ça va mieux ?
Vous vous sentez mieux ?
Qu'a dit le médecin ?
Vous avez des médicaments à prendre ?
Vous êtes-vous fait examiner ?
Etes-vous allé voir un/le médecin ?

La nourriture et les régimes
au petit déjeuner/déjeuner *for* or *at breakfast/lunch*
consommateur *eater*
consommer *to eat*
déjeuner sur le pouce *to have a snack*
dépasser les (600) calories *to have more than (600) calories*
d'ordinaire *usually*
faire un repas *to have* or *eat a meal*
féculents *starchy foods*
habituellement *usually*
interdit : le pain/le sel m'est interdit *I'm not allowed to have bread/salt*
:le pain/le sel m'est interdit par mon médecin *my doctor doesn't allow me to have bread/salt*
maigrir *to lose weight*
manger (de tout) *to eat (everything)*
manger légèrement *to have a light meal*
pâtes *pasta*
prendre *to have*
régime *diet*
:être au régime *to be on a diet*
:suivre un régime *to be on* or *follow a diet*
:faire suivre un régime à *to put on a diet*
savoir : pour savoir si . . . *to find out if . . .*

La santé
allergique (à) *allergic (to)*
cachets *tablets*
ça serait bien . . . *it could well be . . .*
cœur fragile *weak heart*
comprimés *tablets*
évolution *change*
faire : faire du bien à qn *to do s.o. some good*
:ne rien faire à qn *to do s.o. no good*
forme : en bonne forme *fit, in good shape*
hypertension : faire de l'hypertension *to have high blood pressure*
mal : j'ai mal à (l'épaule) *my (shoulder) hurts*
:j'ai plus mal *it hurts more* or *worse*
:j'ai aussi mal *it hurts the same*
maux de tête/d'estomac *headaches/stomach aches*
médicaments *medicines*
oreilles : sifflements/bourdonnements dans les oreilles *whistling/buzzing in one's ears*
régime *diet*
santé: en bonne/parfaite santé *in good/perfect health*
tension : trop de/pas assez de tension *high/low blood pressure*
traitement *treatment*
:sous traitement *undergoing treatment*
yeux : j'ai les yeux qui me tirent *I've got eyestrain*

Chez le médecin

Les questions qu'il posera
Qu'est-ce qui vous amène ?
Qu'est-ce qui ne va pas ?
Pourquoi venez-vous me voir ?
Où avez-vous mal ?
Ça vous fait mal (là) ?
Pouvez-vous (toucher vos orteils du bout des doigts) ?
Faites-vous des allergies ?
Etes-vous allergique à quoi que ce soit ?
Suivez-vous déjà un traitement ?
Vous a-t-on déjà suivi/soigné pour cela ?
Avez-vous déjà consulté pour la même chose ?
Questions plus générales
Est-ce que vous dormez bien ?
Avez-vous bon appétit ?
Quand avez-vous vu un médecin pour la dernière fois ?
Vous faites beaucoup/assez d'exercice ?
Est-ce que vous fumez ? Combien par jour ?
Est-ce que vous buvez de l'alcool ? En quelle quantité ?
Vous avez beaucoup travaillé ces derniers temps ?
Est-ce que vous digérez bien ?/Pas de problèmes de digestion ?
Est-ce que vous vous sentez stressé ?
Avez-vous quelquefois des maux de tête/des vertiges ?

Les ordres qu'il donnera
Enlevez votre veste/chemise/chemisier
Asseyez-vous/Allongez-vous
Déshabillez-vous/Défaites-vous
Passez (à côté/de l'autre côté)
Relevez votre manche (gauche/droite)
Respirez profondément/Ne respirez plus
Inspirez/Soufflez
Ouvrez la bouche/Tirez la langue
Toussez
Montrez-moi votre langue
Voyons cette jambe/cet œil
Pliez (le bras gauche)
Mettez (les mains sur les hanches)
Penchez-vous (un peu)
Je vais vous ausculter/contrôler vos réflexes
Je vais vous prendre votre tension
Dites-moi si cela vous fait mal
Dites-moi si c'est douloureux
Cela va (peut-être) être un peu douloureux
Cela ne vous fera pas mal

Chez le médecin : conseils et traitement

Le médecin indique ce qu'il faut faire
Gardez le lit *ou* la chambre pendant quelques jours
Prenez du repos/Reposez-vous/Ne vous fatiguez pas
Ne travaillez pas trop
Revenez me voir (mardi prochain)
Revenez me voir si ça ne va pas mieux *ou* si ça ne s'améliore pas
Revenez me voir à la fin du traitement
Vous vous êtes surmené
Il faut arrêter de (fumer)
N'interrompez pas le traitement

Il prescrit un traitement
Vous irez chercher cela chez votre pharmacien
Je vous prescris (une pommade)
Le pharmacien vous préparera (cette pommade)
Je vous mets (cela) pour (les maux de tête)
Ce médicament devrait faire disparaître (la douleur)
Vous prendrez (deux) comprimés/cuillerées de ce sirop (quatre) fois par jour
Vous le/les prendrez après/avant chaque repas
Ne prenez pas le volant après avoir pris (cela)
Vous ne boirez pas d'alcool avec ces médicaments
Vous finirez le flacon/la boîte
Ne prenez pas d'aspirine
Vous appliquerez la pommade sur (le genou) et vous masserez

Il conseille d'aller voir quelqu'un d'autre
Je vais vous envoyer chez un spécialiste/Il faut voir un spécialiste
Vous allez passer une radio
Je vais vous faire faire des analyses (de sang/d'urine)
Je crois qu'il serait préférable de vous faire entrer à la clinique/à l'hôpital
Je m'occupe du rendez-vous
Vous donnerez cette lettre au (Docteur Guy)
Je vous fais une lettre pour l'hôpital
A la clinique ou à l'hôpital
Nous allons vous garder en observation
Nous voulons faire quelques analyses/vous faire passer une radio
Vous avez (un virus)
Il n'y a rien de cassé/de grave/Ce n'est pas grave
Vous allez devoir rester ici (quelques jours)

Chez le médecin
allergies : faire des allergies *to have allergies*
allergique à *allergic to*
allongez-vous *lie down*
amener *to bring*
ausculter qn *to listen to s.o.'s chest*
chemisier *blouse*
consulter : avez-vous consulté (pour . . .) ? *have you consulted a doctor (about . . .)?*
contrôler *to check*
défaites-vous *undo your shirt* or *blouse* etc
digérer bien *to have good digestion*
douloureux *painful*
inspirez *breathe in*
mal : où avez-vous mal ? *where does it hurt ?*
 :ça vous fait mal ? does that hurt (you) ?
maux de tête *headaches*
se pencher *to lean forward*
qu'est-ce qui ne va pas ? *what's the matter?*
relever *to roll up*
soigné (pour qch) *treated (for sth)*
soufflez *breathe out*
stressé *under stress*
suivi (pour qch) *treated (for sth)*
tension *blood pressure*
tirer la langue *to put one's tongue out*
vertiges *dizzy spells*

Chez le médecin : conseils et traitement
aller mieux *to get better*
s'améliorer *to improve*
analyses (de sang/d'urine) *(blood/urine) tests*
 :faire faire des analyses à qn *to have some tests done on s.o.*
clinique *(private) clinic*
comprimés *tablets*
cuillerées *spoonfuls*
flacon *bottle*
garder la chambre *to stay indoors*
garder le lit *to stay in bed*
garder (qn) en observation *to keep (s.o.) under observation*
interrompre *to stop*
masser *to massage*
médicament *medicine*
mettre : je vous mets (cela) pour . . . *I'll give you (this) for . . .*
pharmacien Br *chemist*, Am *druggist*
pommade *ointment, cream*
prendre le volant *to drive*
prescrire *to prescribe*
radio : passer une radio *to have an X-ray*
 :faire passer une radio à qn *to give s.o. an X-ray*
sirop *cough mixture*
se surmener *to overwork*

Les vacances

Les projets de vacances
Ceux des autres
Vous prenez des vacances (cette année) ?
Vous partez (en vacances) cette année/cet été ?
Avez-vous projeté de partir cette année/cet été ?
Avez-vous décidé de l'endroit où vous irez ?
Vous avez (déjà) des projets de vacances (pour cette année/cet été) ?
Ceux que l'on a envisagés
Nous prendrons des/Nous ne prendrons pas de vacances (cette année/cet été)
Je vais/pars en vacances (en août)
Nous avons (quatre semaines) de vacances par an
Je pars/Nous partons un peu (en hiver)

Les lieux de séjour
Nous irons à l'hôtel/chez des amis
Nous irons à la mer/à la neige
Nous partons faire du ski/du camping
Nous (ne) partons (pas) à l'étranger
Je m'en vais (au Kenya)

Après les vacances
Celles des autres
Où avez-vous passé vos vacances ?
Vous êtes allé(s) où pour vos vacances ?
C'est bien ?/C'était bien ?/Ça s'est bien passé ?
Comment était la nourriture/l'hôtel ?
Quel temps avez-vous eu ?
Celles que l'on a prises
Je suis allé/Nous sommes allés (en Suisse)
Je me suis/Nous nous sommes ennuyé(s)/bien amusé(s)
Ça m'a/nous a fait une coupure/un changement/voir quelque chose de nouveau
J'ai/Nous avons eu du très beau temps/un temps atroce
Il a fait chaud/trop chaud
J'ai bien aimé/Je n'ai pas aimé la nourriture/le cadre

Les jours fériés
On a (quatre) ponts chaque année
Il y a (six) jours fériés chaque année
(Demain) est férié
Est-ce que c'est férié aujourd'hui ?/Est-ce qu'aujourd'hui est férié ?
Pourquoi est-ce férié ?

Comment parler de chez soi

Pour dire où l'on habite
C'est en ville/à la campagne/en banlieue/au bord de la mer
Ça se trouve près de (Lille)
Ce n'est pas très loin de (Rouen)
J'habite à moins de (deux heures) de (Paris)
Plus précisément
C'est situé dans un quartier calme/très fréquenté
J'habite (tout) près d'un parc/dans une rue bourgeoise
C'est (tout) près du centre(-ville)
C'est à (cinq) minutes de la gare
C'est à côté du stade
Pour savoir où habite quelqu'un
Où habitez-vous ?
Comment est le quartier ?/C'est quel genre de quartier ?
Est-ce que c'est proche de (Nancy) ?

Pour décrire sa maison
J'ai/Nous avons un appartement/une maison/un studio
C'est un appartement (trois) pièces *ou* de (trois) pièces
Mon appartement est au (troisième) (étage)
J'ai un balcon/une terrasse
Nous sommes locataires/propriétaires (de notre maison)
Nous avons (trois) chambres
C'est une maison sur (trois) étages
Nous avons un jardin/une cour(ette)
Il y a un garage
Notez que le mot 'appartement' est souvent réduit à 'appart' [apart] *dans la langue familière :*
C'est un petit appart dans un vieil immeuble
Pour demander à quelqu'un des détails sur sa maison
Vous habitez en appartement ou en maison ?
Vous êtes locataire ?
Vous l'avez acheté(e) ?/C'est à vous ?
C'est grand ?/Vous avez combien de pièces ?

Pour parler de ceux qui vivent sous le même toit
Je suis marié(e)/Je vis avec quelqu'un
Nous avons/J'ai (deux) enfants
Nous avons/J'ai (un) fils et (deux) filles
J'habite chez mes parents
Vous habitez seul(e) dans cette maison ?
Vous vivez seul(e) ?
Vous êtes marié(e) ?/Vous avez des enfants ?

Les vacances
à l'étranger *abroad*
aller à la mer/à la neige *to go to the coast/on a skiing* Br *holiday* or Am *vacation*
s'amuser bien *to have a (very) good time*
ça s'est bien passé ? *was it good?, did it go off well?*
cadre *setting*
changement *change*
comment: comment était (la nourriture) ? *what was (the food) like?*
coupure *break*
s'ennuyer *to get bored*
faire du ski/du camping *to go skiing/camping*
férié : jours fériés *public holidays*
:c'est férié *it's a public holiday*
lieux de séjour *places to stay*
nourriture *food*
partir un peu *to take a (short) break*
ponts *long weekends*
projeter de faire *to plan to do*
vacances Br *holiday(s)*, Am *vacation*
:projets de vacances Br *holiday* or Am *vacation plans*
:aller/partir en vacances *to go/go away on* Br *holiday* or Am *vacation*

Comment parler de chez soi
à la campagne *in the country*
appartement Br *flat*, Am *apartment*
:en appartement *in a* Br *flat* or Am *apartment*
au bord de la mer *on the coast, by the sea*
balcon *balcony*
bourgeois *middle-class*
centre(-ville) *(city) centre*
chez soi *one's home*
comment est le quartier ? *what's the neighbourhood like?*
cour(ette) *(little) courtyard*
en banlieue *in the suburbs, in suburbia*
en ville *in town*
étage *floor*
fréquenté *busy*
habiter *to live*
immeuble *building*
locataire (de) *tenant (of)*
maison *house*
:en maison *in a house*
moins : à moins de (deux heures) de . . . *less than (two hours) from . . .*
pièce *room*
propriétaire (de) *owner (of)*
situé *situated*
stade *stadium*
studio *studio* Br *flat* or Am *apartment*
terrasse *terrace*

Les réservations d'hôtel

Pour indiquer le type d'hôtel désiré
Je veux quelque chose (de bon marché/de pas trop cher)
Je veux un (deux ou trois) étoiles
Quel genre d'hôtel est-ce ?
Combien d'étoiles a-t-il ?
Est-il bien situé ?
Je veux quelque chose près de (la gare)
Je voudrais une pension de famille
Est-ce qu'il y a des chambres d'hôtes ?
Peut-on loger chez l'habitant ?

La réservation
Une chambre pour une personne avec (salle de) bains, s'il vous plaît
Je voudrais/Il me faudrait une (chambre pour une personne)
Je voudrais réserver une (chambre pour deux personnes)
Je voudrais (une chambre à deux lits)
Il me faudrait une chambre à trois lits
Auriez-vous deux chambres qui communiquent ?
Je voudrais une chambre avec (douche)
Avez-vous une chambre avec balcon ?
Je voudrais avoir (la télévision) dans ma chambre
Y a-t-il une chambre avec salle de bains de libre ?
Pour indiquer les dates
Je voudrais une chambre pour (une) nuit
Pour (trois) nuits
Pour la nuit du (jeudi) et celle du (vendredi)
Du (3) au soir au (10) au matin
Cela fait (huit) nuits
J'arriverai (dans la soirée du 15) et partirai (le 22 au matin)
Réservez-la-moi pour la nuit de (jeudi à vendredi)

Pour se renseigner des prix
Ce sera une chambre avec/sans petit déjeuner
Faites-vous la demi-pension ?
Je prendrai la pension complète
Quels sont vos tarifs ?
Cela fera combien par personne/la chambre ?
Cela inclut-il le petit déjeuner ?
Quel est le tarif de la demi-pension/la pension complète ?
La TVA et le service sont-ils compris ?
Ce prix est-il TTC ?
Une chambre avec bains est plus chère de combien ?

Comment préparer une excursion

Pour dire ...
Où l'on veut aller
Nous aimerions aller à (Chambord)
J'aimerais faire des réservations pour une excursion à (Fontainebleau)
Nous aimerions visiter (la Vallée de la Loire)
Quand on veut partir
Nous aimerions y aller (jeudi)
Je voudrais réserver pour (dimanche prochain)
Organisez-vous une excursion (dans les jours à venir) ?
Quelle est la date de votre prochaine excursion à (Blois) ?
Nous aimerions faire une excursion (vendredi).
Qu'avez-vous d'intéressant à nous proposer ?
Combien on sera
Nous serons (quatre)/Ce sera un groupe de (quatre)
Nous serons/Il y aura (douze) adultes et (huit) enfants
Je voudrais des places pour (huit) personnes

Pour se faire conseiller
Est-ce que (ce voyage) est bien *ou* vaut le coup ?
Vous nous le conseillez vraiment ?
C'est intéressant ?/Il y a des choses (intéressantes) à voir ?
Est-ce que c'est un voyage fatigant/long/agréable ?
Cela convient-il à (une famille avec des enfants) ?

Pour se renseigner des prix
Combien cela coûte-t-il ?
Tout est-il compris dans le prix ?
C'est un prix tout compris ?
Combien cela coûterait-il de (prendre un taxi) ?
Avez-vous des tarifs de groupe ?
Faites-vous un tarif spécial pour un groupe de (douze) personnes/des tarifs spéciaux pour les groupes importants ?

Pour se renseigner des détails pratiques
Où se retrouve-t-on ?
Où prend-on le car ?
A quelle heure faut-il être là ?
Combien de temps dure le voyage ?
A quelle heure arrive-t-on là-bas ?
A quelle heure sera-t-on de retour ?

Les réservations d'hôtel
bains : avec (salle de) bains *with bath(room)*
bon marché *cheap*
chambre *room*
:chambre pour une personne *single room*
:chambre pour deux personnes *double room*
:chambre à deux/trois lits *room with twin* or *two/three beds*
:chambres d'hôtes *rooms in a private house*
:chambres qui communiquent *adjoining rooms*
cher : pas trop cher *inexpensive, fairly cheap*
combien : cela fera combien ? *how much will that be?*
demi-pension : faites-vous la demi-pension ? *do you do* Br *half board* or Am *demi-pension?*
douche *shower*
étoile *star*
:un deux/trois étoiles *a two/three star (hotel)*
loger chez l'habitant *to stay with a local person*
pension complète Br *full board*, Am *American plan*
pension de famille *guesthouse*
se renseigner de *to inquire about*
réservations *bookings*
réserver *to book*
tarif (de) *rate (for)*
TTC *inclusive of tax*
TVA *VAT*

Comment préparer une excursion
avoir : qu'avez-vous d'intéressant à nous proposer ? *do you have anything interesting to suggest?*
bien : est-ce que (ce voyage) est bien ? *is this (trip) good?*
car *bus*, Br *coach*
compris *included*
conseiller : conseiller à *to recommend to*
:se faire conseiller *to get a recommendation*
convenir : cela convient-il à . . . ? *is it suitable for . . .?*
être : nous serons (quatre) *there will be (four) of us*
important : groupes importants *large groups*
jours à venir *next few days, coming days*
prix tout compris *(all) inclusive price*
se renseigner de *to inquire about*
réservations *bookings*
réserver pour . . . *to book for . . .*
se retrouver *to meet*
tarif *price, rate*
:tarif de groupe *group price* or *rate*
valoir : . . . vaut le coup *. . . is worth it*

Les poids et les mesures

Dimensions
Cela fait combien de large/long/haut ?
Cela a combien de largeur/longueur/hauteur ?
Réponse :
Cela fait (3 mètres) de large/long/haut
Cela a (3 mètres) de largeur/longueur/hauteur
Cette (pièce) fait (3 mètres) sur (2)/(6 mètres) carrés
Equivalences approximatives
1 centimètre (10 millimètres) = environ 0.4 inch
1 mètre (100 centimètres) = environ 40 inches *ou* 3.3 feet *ou* 1.1 yards
1 kilomètre (1 000 mètres) = environ 1 100 yards *ou* 0.6 mile
Il mesure 1.80 m (1 mètre 80) (= environ 6 feet)
Pour demander une équivalence
Savez-vous ce que ça fait en pouces/pieds/yards/miles ?
Cela représente à peu près combien de pouces/pieds/*etc* ?

Poids
Combien cela pèse-t-il ?/Quel poids cela fait-il ?
Combien pèse-t-il/-elle ?/Quel poids fait-il/-elle ?
Combien pesez-vous ?/Quel poids faites-vous ?
Réponse :
Cela/Il/Elle pèse *ou* fait (45 kilos)
Cela pèse quelques grammes
Cela pèse *ou* fait dans les (60) kilos
Equivalences approximatives
1 gramme = environ 0.04 ounce
1 kilogramme (1 000 grammes) = environ 2.2 pounds
Donnez-moi un kilo et demi *ou* 3 livres de pommes
Pour demander une équivalence
Savez-vous ce que cela fait en livres anglaises ?
Cela représente à peu près combien de livres anglaises ?

Volumes
Quel volume cela fait-il ?/Cela contient combien ?
Réponse :
Cela fait (un litre)
Equivalence approximative
1 litre (100 centilitres) = environ 1.8 pints (GB) *ou* 2.1 pints (US)
Ajoutez un demi-litre de lait
Pour demander une équivalence
Savez-vous ce que cela fait en pintes (anglaises) ?
Cela représente à peu près combien de pintes (anglaises) ?

Comment donner des ordres

Pour avoir l'attention de quelqu'un
Ecoutez (s'il vous plaît)
Regardez
Ecoutez bien (s'il vous plaît)
Je vais vous expliquer (ce qu'il faut faire)

Pour donner un ordre
Expédiez-le/-la chez moi, s'il vous plaît
Appelez-moi quand vous aurez fini
Donnez-moi un coup de fil dès que vous serez prêt
Passez-moi ma valise, s'il vous plaît
Posez-le/-la là
Pour justifier un ordre
Tournez à gauche, sinon on va se perdre
Posez-le/-la, autrement vous allez le/la casser
Si vous ne tournez pas ce bouton, ça ne marchera pas
Pour exprimer une interdiction
Ne m'appelez pas chez moi, d'accord ?
Surtout, ne débranchez pas l'appareil
Ne faites pas l'enfant
Ne posez pas ça là, s'il vous plaît
De façon moins abrupte
Pourriez-vous me réveiller à 7 heures, s'il vous plaît ?
Pouvez-vous le faire livrer chez moi ?
Est-ce que vous pourriez me passer ma valise ?
Cela vous dérangerait de ne pas m'appeler chez moi ?

Pour expliquer une marche à suivre
D'abord, (mettez-le/-la en marche)
Tout d'abord, (vérifiez la tension)
La première chose à faire est de (le/la brancher)
Ensuite/Deuxièmement, (tournez le bouton rouge)
Après, (appelez-moi)
Avant de faire (cela), faites (ceci)
Après avoir fait (cela), faites (ceci)
Si rien ne se passe (venez me voir)

Pour commander à boire ou à manger
Deux cafés, s'il vous plaît !
Je prendrai (un whisky)
Ce sera (deux jus d'orange)
Je voudrais (un sandwich), s'il vous plaît
Peut-on avoir (deux cafés) ?
Donnez-moi (un croque-monsieur)
Vous ferez monter le petit déjeuner à ma chambre

Les poids et les mesures
avoir *to be*
:cela a combien de largeur/longueur/hauteur ? *what width/length/height is it?*
:cela a . . . de largeur/longueur/hauteur *it's . . . in width/length/height*
carrés : (6 mètres) carrés *(6) square (metres)*
contenir *to contain*
dans les . . . *about . . .*
faire *to be*
:cela fait combien de large/long/haut ? *how wide/long/high is it?*
:cela fait . . . de large/long/haut *it's . . . wide/long/high*
: . . . fait (3 mètres) sur (2) *. . . is (3 metres) by (2)*
:quel poids/volume cela fait-il ? *what weight/volume is it?*
mesurer 1,80 *to be six feet tall* (person); *to be six feet long* or *high* (thing)
mesures *measures*
peser *to weigh*
pieds *feet*
poids *weight(s)*
pouces *inches*

Comment donner des ordres
appareil *appliance*
autrement *or else*
brancher *to plug in*
ce sera . . . *that will be . . .*
commander à boire/à manger *to order something to drink/eat*
coup de fil : donner un coup de fil à qn *to ring* or *phone* or *call s.o.*
croque-monsieur *toasted cheese and ham sandwich*
d'accord ? *O.K.?*
débrancher *to unplug*
déranger : cela vous dérangerait de ne pas faire ? *would you mind not doing?*
dès que vous serez prêt *as soon as you're ready*
écoutez (bien) *listen (carefully)*
expédiez-le *send it*
faire : faire l'enfant *to be silly* or *childish*
:faire livrer/monter qch *to have sth delivered/brought up*
interdiction *negative order*
marche à suivre *procedure (to be followed)*
posez-le *put it down*
pouvoir : pourriez-vous/pouvez-vous ? *could you?/can you?*
regardez *look, watch*
sinon *or else*
tension *voltage*

Les enfants

Leur âge
Quel âge a-t-il/-elle ?/Il/Elle a quel âge ?
Il/Elle a à peu près (six) ans
C'est encore un bébé
Il/Elle va (déjà) à l'école
Ce sont des adolescents *ou* des ados
C'est un(e) adolescent(e)
L'aîné a (vingt) ans et le plus jeune a (cinq) ans
(Ma fille) a (trois) ans de plus que (mon fils)

Leur scolarité
Où va-t-il/-elle à l'école ?/A quelle école va-t-il/-elle ?
Il/Elle aime l'école ?
Ça va à l'école ?/Ça marche (bien) à l'école ?
Il/Elle va à l'école (du quartier)
Il/Elle est en primaire/au collège/au lycée
Ils aiment bien/Ils n'aiment pas (beaucoup) l'école
Ça marche bien/Tout se passe bien
Il/Elle marche bien à l'école
Il/Elle marche bien en (mathématiques)/Il/Elle a de bons résultats en (mathématiques)
Il/elle va à l'université

Leurs loisirs
A quoi s'intéresse-t-il/-elle ?
A-t-il/-elle un passe-temps favori ?
Il/Elle aime bien dessiner/faire du volley
Elle adore (le modélisme)
C'est un mordu de (foot)
Elle aime/adore (la musique)
Il/Elle fait énormément de (tennis/marche)

Leur avenir
Que veut-il/-elle faire plus tard ?
Il/Elle sait (déjà) ce qu'il/qu'elle veut faire (plus tard) ?
Quel métier veut-il/-elle faire (plus tard) ?
Est-ce qu'il/qu'elle va faire comme ses parents ?
Est-ce qu'il/qu'elle veut aller à l'université ?
Compte-t-il/-elle poursuivre ses études ?
Il veut arrêter ses études à (16) ans
(Je crois qu')il veut devenir (pharmacien)
Elle veut être (vétérinaire)
Ils voudraient bien faire des études supérieures
Elle fait des études pour devenir (enseignante)
Il/Elle prépare un diplôme (d'ingénieur)

Les hommes

Le physique et l'apparence
Comment est-il ?
A-t-il (une forte carrure) ?
Que porte-t-il ?/Comment est-il habillé ?
Il est assez grand/de taille moyenne
Il est plutôt mince/gros
C'est le plus (âgé)
C'est celui qui a (les cheveux blonds)
C'est un grand barbu à lunettes
Il a (les cheveux bouclés)
Il ne lui reste plus beaucoup de cheveux/Il est chauve
Il a une moustache/barbe
Il s'habille assez (jeune/sport)
Il porte *ou* a (une veste marron)
D'habitude, il a (un chapeau)
Il est beau/Il n'est pas mal
Il est assez laid

Le caractère
Quel genre d'homme est-ce ?/C'est quel genre d'homme ?
Il est comment avec les gens ?
Il est (très) (chaleureux)/C'est quelqu'un de (très) (chaleureux)
Il est assez (taciturne)/C'est quelqu'un d'assez (taciturne)
C'est le genre (calme)
C'est quelqu'un qui sait (écouter les gens)
Sa principale qualité, c'est (la franchise)
Le défaut chez lui, c'est qu'il (parle trop)

La position sociale
Est-il marié ?
A-t-il des enfants ?
Que fait-il ?/Il fait quoi ?
Sa femme est (médecin)
Il habite (dans la même rue que nous)
Il est marié/célibataire
Il a (deux) enfants
Il n'a pas d'enfants
Il travaille au (garage) comme (mécanicien)/Il est (mécanicien) au (garage)
Il est (chef des ventes)
Il travaille sous mes ordres
C'est mon supérieur hiérarchique
Il fait quelque chose dans (la publicité)

Les enfants
âge *age*
:quel âge a-t-il/-elle ? *how old is he/she?*
aîné *eldest, oldest*
avoir six/vingt ans *to be six/twenty (years old)*
collège Br *secondary school*, Am *high school*
compter faire *to expect to do*
enseignant, -ante *teacher*
études : faire des études *to study*
:faire des études supérieures *to study at university*
foot *football*
loisirs *free time, leisure time*
lycée Br *secondary school*, Am *high school*
marcher : ça marche bien *things are going well*
:il/elle marche bien à l'école/en mathématiques *he/she is getting on well at school/in mathematics*
métier *occupation, job*
modélisme *model-making*
mordu : être un mordu de *to be very keen on*
se passer : tout se passe bien *everything's going well*
passe-temps *hobby*
pharmacien Br *chemist*, Am *druggist*
primaire : en primaire *in primary school*
scolarité *schooling*
vétérinaire Br *vet(erinary surgeon)*, Am *veterinarian*

Les hommes
âgé : le plus âgé *the eldest* or *oldest*
barbu *man with a beard*
carrure : une forte carrure *a big build*
célibataire *single*
chaleureux *warm*
chauve *bald*
chef des ventes *sales manager*
cheveux blonds/bouclés *fair* or *blond/curly hair*
comment est-il ? *what is he like?*
s'entendre facilement (avec) *to get along easily (with)*
défaut : le défaut chez lui, c'est *his failing is*
franchise *honesty, candour*
genre : quel genre d'homme est-ce ? *what sort of man is he?*
mécanicien *mechanic*
mince *slim, thin*
ordres : sous mes ordres *under me*
pas mal *not bad*
supérieur : c'est mon supérieur hiérarchique *he's over me*
taciturne *quiet*
taille : de taille moyenne *(of) average height*

Les femmes

Le physique et l'apparence
Comment est-elle ?
A-t-elle (les cheveux gris) ?
Que porte-t-elle ?/Comment est-elle habillée ?
Elle est (assez) grande/mince
C'est la (plus jeune)
C'est celle qui a (les cheveux bruns/raides)
Elle s'habille assez (jeune/sport)
Elle porte (un manteau vert)
D'habitude, elle a (un chapeau)
Elle est jolie/Elle n'est pas mal
Elle est assez laide

Le caractère
Quel genre de femme est-ce ?/C'est quel genre de femme ?
Elle est (très) (sociable)/C'est quelqu'un de (très) (sociable)
Elle est assez (calme)/C'est quelqun'un d'assez (calme)
C'est le genre exubérante/très calme
C'est quelqu'un avec qui on peut/on ne peut pas s'entendre facilement
Sa principale qualité, c'est (son ouverture d'esprit)
Le défaut chez elle, c'est qu'elle (parle trop)

La position sociale
Est-elle mariée ?
A-t-elle des enfants ?
Que fait-elle ?/Elle fait quoi ?
Elle est mariée/célibataire
Son mari est (ingénieur)
Elle a (deux) enfants
Elle n'a pas d'enfants
Elle travaille à (la banque) comme (caissière)/Elle est (caissière) à (la banque)
Elle est (chef des ventes)

Pour parler de la libération de la femme
(Je pense que) les femmes sont/ne sont pas opprimées/exploitées
Les femmes sont mal/bien traitées
Je suis d'accord/Je ne suis pas d'accord avec les féministes
Il faudrait/Il ne faudrait pas que les femmes aient plus de pouvoirs/de responsabilités

Le temps qu'il fait

Les prévisions météorologiques
Pour les connaître
Quel temps va-t-il faire (demain) ?/Quel est le temps prévu pour (demain) ?
Vous avez entendu/vu le bulletin météo *ou* la météo ?
Savez-vous quel (genre de) temps il va faire ?
Pour en parler
On va avoir du soleil/de la pluie (demain)
(Demain), soleil/pluie !
Je crois qu'il va (pleuvoir)
On dirait que ça va (se réchauffer)
Ça sent la pluie/neige
Ils ont dit qu'il y aurait (du vent) (demain)/Ils ont annoncé (du vent) pour (demain)
On prévoit (des gelées) pour après
Ça ne devrait pas tarder à (se dégager)
Je ne crois pas que ce soit parti pour (s'améliorer)
Le baromètre est (haut)/La pression est (élevée)
La pluie arrive par (l'ouest)

Les types de temps
Questions :
Quel temps fait-il (là-bas) au (printemps) ?/Le (printemps) est comment là-bas ?
Le mois de juin est-il chaud/froid ?
Est-ce qu'il y a souvent (du brouillard) ?
Faut-il prévoir des vêtements chauds/légers ?
(L'automne) est-il (pluvieux) ?/Vous avez beaucoup de (pluie) en (automne) ?
Quel temps avez-vous eu (pendant vos vacances) ?
Réponses :
En général, c'est plutôt (froid et pluvieux)
D'habitude, il fait (doux) à cette époque-ci
C'est très agréable (à cette époque de l'année)
On a souvent de la (sécheresse)
Il a fait très (chaud) (l'année dernière)
Nous avons eu pas mal de (pluie) (le mois dernier)
Jusqu'à présent, nous n'avons eu que du froid/du vent cette année

Pour échanger ses impressions sur le temps
Belle journée, aujourd'hui, vous ne trouvez pas ?
Vilain temps, non ?
Il fait (meilleur) que la semaine dernière, non ?
On ne peut pas trop se plaindre du temps pour cette époque de l'année, vous ne croyez pas ?

Les femmes
caissière *cashier*
célibataire *single*
chef des ventes *sales manageress*
cheveux bruns/raides *brown/straight hair*
comment est-elle ? *what is she like?*
d'accord : être d'accord avec *to agree with*
d'habitude *usually*
défaut : le défaut chez elle, c'est ... *her failing is ...*
s'entendre facilement (avec) *to get along easily (with)*
falloir : il faudrait/ne faudrait pas que les femmes ... + *sub* *women should/shouldn't ...*
genre : quel genre de femme est-ce ? *what sort of woman is she?*
grande *tall*
ingénieur *engineer*
mariée *married*
mince *slim, thin*
opprimées *oppressed*
ouverture d'esprit *openness*
pas mal *not bad*
pouvoirs *power*
quelqu'un de très/d'assez ... *somebody very/fairly ...*

Le temps qu'il fait
arriver : arriver par (l'ouest) *to come from (the west)*
bulletin météo *weather report*
ça sent la pluie/neige *it feels like rain/snow*
se dégager *to clear (up)*
doux *mild*
élevée *high*
haut : le baromètre est haut *the barometer is showing high pressure*
météo *weather report*
partir : ... que ce soit parti pour (s'améliorer) *... that it's about to (improve)*
pluvieux *rainy*
prévisions météorologiques *weather forecast*
prévoir : on prévoit (des gelées) *(frosts) are forecast*
:faut-il prévoir des vêtements chauds/légers ? *should we reckon on warm/light clothes?*
:prévu pour ... *forecast for ...*
se réchauffer *to get warmer*
sécheresse *drought*
tarder : ça ne devrait pas tarder à ... *it shouldn't take (too) long to ...*
temps *weather*
:le temps qu'il fait *the weather*
:quel temps va-t-il faire ? *what is the weather going to be (like)?*
vilain *nasty*

Déclaration de perte

Pour dire ce que l'on a perdu
J'ai perdu (mon passeport/un appareil photo)
Je ne trouve plus (mon portefeuille)
Je crois que j'ai perdu (mon permis de conduire)
(Mon caméscope) a disparu !
Pour savoir ce que quelqu'un a perdu
Qu'avez-vous perdu ?
Etes-vous sûr que vous l'aviez ?
Il/Elle était comment ?
Pouvez-vous le/la décrire ?/Pouvez-vous dire comment il/elle était ?
Essayez de vous rappeler quand vous vous en êtes servi pour la dernière fois

Quand l'a-t-on perdu ?
Je suis sûr que je l'avais (ce matin)
J'ai dû le/la perdre (hier soir)
La dernière fois que je l'ai vu(e), c'était (hier matin)
Pour interroger quelqu'un
Quand vous êtes-vous rendu compte que vous ne l'aviez plus ?
Quand l'avez-vous vu(e) pour la dernière fois ?

Où l'a-t-on perdu ?
Je l'ai perdu(e) (sur la plage)
Je l'ai oublié(e) (dans le train)
Ça a dû se passer (dans ma chambre)
Je l'ai peut-être laissé(e) (à la banque)
J'ai dû le/la perdre (au théâtre)
Pour interroger quelqu'un
Où l'avez-vous vu(e) pour la dernière fois ?
Où avez-vous pu le/la perdre ?

Pour laisser ses coordonnées
Mon nom est ...
Voici mon adresse/ma carte
Je vais vous donner mon nom et mon adresse
Pouvez-vous m'appeler (à ce numéro) si vous le/la trouvez ?
Pourriez-vous m'écrire (à cette adresse) si quelqu'un le/la rapporte ?
Je compte sur vous pour me l'envoyer à cette adresse
Pour demander ses coordonnées à quelqu'un
Laissez-moi votre nom et votre adresse
Pouvez-vous me laisser votre nom et votre adresse ?

Déclarations à la police

Pour signaler quelque chose à la police
Je viens/Je vous appelle pour signaler un accident/un cambriolage/une agression
Je voudrais faire une déclaration de perte pour (mon passeport)
J'ai perdu (mes bagages)
Ma femme s'est fait voler ses papiers/s'est fait agresser
On m'a volé ma voiture/mes papiers
Il y a eu un accident/Un accident vient de se produire
Je viens de me faire voler (mon portefeuille)

Pour exposer les circonstances
Nous descendions la rue
Nous étions en train de dormir
J'étais occupé/à table
Je faisais mes courses
J'allais entrer à la banque
Il était environ (dix) heures
Cela s'est passé hier soir/la nuit dernière
Cela s'est passé à l'hôtel/dans la rue
Deux hommes ont arraché (le sac à main de ma femme)
Un homme/Une femme m'a abordé
On m'a vidé les poches/J'ai été la victime de pickpockets
Ils sont partis en courant
Ils ont pris la fuite en voiture
Je n'ai vu personne (entrer/sortir)
Je n'ai rien vu/entendu/remarqué (d'anormal/de bizarre)

Pour décrire les coupables
C'était quelqu'un de (barbu/blond)
Il/Elle avait dans les (25 ans)
Ils étaient plutôt jeunes/minces/grands
Il/Elle avait les cheveux (courts/longs)
Ils étaient au volant d'une (Renault 5)
Il avait un (blouson à fermeture éclair)
Elle portait (un manteau gris)
Je n'ai pas très bien vu leurs visages

Pour décrire ce qui a été volé
C'est une (Renault 19 bleue)
Il/Elle/Ça vaut dans les (4 000 F)
J'avais (500 F et mes papiers) dedans
Mon nom est inscrit dedans
C'était dans (un sac bleu/une pochette en cuir)

Déclaration de perte
caméscope *camcorder*
comment : il/elle était comment ? *what was it like?*
compter sur qn pour faire *to trust s.o. will do*
coordonnées *particulars, details*
déclaration de perte *notification of a loss*
devoir : j'ai dû le/la perdre *I must have lost it*
:ça a dû se passer . . . *it must have happened . . .*
interroger *to question*
permis de conduire Br *driving licence*, Am *driver's license*
plage *beach*
portefeuille Br *wallet*, Am *billfold*
pouvoir : pouvez-vous ?/pourriez-vous ? *can you?/ could you?*
:où avez-vous pu le perdre ? *where could you have lost it?*
se rappeler *to remember*
rapporter *to bring back*
se rendre compte que . . . + *ind* *to realize that . . .*
savoir : pour savoir . . . *to find out . . .*
se servir de *to use*
sûr que . . . *sure that . . .*
trouver : je ne trouve plus . . . *I can't find . . .*

Déclarations à la police
aborder qn *to come up to s.o., to approach s.o.*
agresser : se faire agresser *to get mugged*
agression *mugging*
arracher *to snatch*
blouson Br *windcheater*, Am *windbreaker*
cambriolage *burglary*
courses : faire ses courses *to do one's shopping*
déclaration : faire une déclaration de perte pour . . . *to notify* or *report the loss of . . .*
:déclarations à . . . *statements to . . .*
exposer *to explain*
fermeture éclair Br *zip*, Am *zipper*
inscrit dedans *written inside*
mince *slim, thin*
partir en courant *to run off*
se passer *to happen, to take place*
pochette *(clutch) bag*
prendre la fuite en voiture *to drive off, to get away by car*
se produire *to happen*
sac à main *handbag*
signaler (à) *to report (to)*
valoir : ça vaut dans les *it's worth about*
vider les poches à qn *to pick s.o.'s pockets*
volant : être au volant de . . . *to be driving . . .*
voler : se faire voler qch *to have sth stolen*

A la poste

Pour savoir où se trouve la poste
Y a-t-il un bureau de poste près d'ici ?
Où se trouve la poste (la plus proche) ?
Où y a-t-il une boîte aux lettres ?
Où puis-je poster une lettre ?

L'envoi d'un objet par la poste
Pour se renseigner des tarifs
Combien faut-il mettre sur une lettre pour (les Etats-Unis) ?/A combien faut-il affranchir une lettre pour (les Etats-Unis) ?
Il faut (mettre) un timbre à combien pour (le Japon) ?
Y a-t-il un tarif particulier pour (les cartes postales) ?
Combien faut-il mettre pour envoyer (ceci) par avion (au Canada) ?
Pour acheter des timbres
(Trois) timbres au tarif ordinaire/lent, s'il vous plaît
Je voudrais affranchir cette lettre pour (l'Allemagne)
Je voudrais envoyer ce paquet en urgent/en ordinaire/en recommandé
Donnez-moi (six) timbres pour (des cartes postales)
Pour se renseigner des délais
Est-ce que cela part aujourd'hui ?
Quand cela arrivera-t-il à (Athènes) ?
Cela prendra combien de temps pour arriver ?

Incidents
J'ai envoyé une lettre à (Edimbourg) il y a six jours et elle n'est pas encore arrivée
Ceci m'est parvenu déchiré/ouvert/éventré
J'attends un colis posté il y a (deux semaines)
Pouvez-vous vous renseigner/faire des recherches ?

Autres services
J'aimerais envoyer un télégramme/un mandat/une télécopie
Quelle est la façon la plus rapide/la plus sûre d'expédier cela ?
Je voudrais expédier ceci en exprès (au Caire)
Je voudrais que cela parte en recommandé (avec accusé de réception)/en valeur déclarée
Puis-je avoir un reçu *ou* un récépissé ?
Puis-je avoir un formulaire/une étiquette de douane ?
Puis-je avoir un formulaire de recommandé/de mandat/de télégramme ?

Au téléphone

Pour appeler quelqu'un
Lorsque le correspondant a décroché
Allô ? Je suis (bien) à (la banque Dupont) ?
Allô ? (La banque Dupont) ?
Pour demander à parler à quelqu'un
Puis-je parler au (directeur), s'il vous plaît ?
Pouvez-vous me passer (le directeur), s'il vous plaît ?
(Le directeur) est là ?

Pour répondre au téléphone
Après avoir décroché
Allô (oui) !
(Maison Durand,) bonjour ?
Pour identifier le correspondant
Qui est à l'appareil ?
Si l'on est la personne demandée
C'est moi(-même)
C'est lui/elle qui vous parle
Si le correspondant demande quelqu'un d'autre
Ne quittez pas/Restez en ligne
C'est de la part de qui ?
Je vais l'appeler/Je vous le/la passe
Je vous mets en communication avec lui/elle

Incidents
On se trompe de numéro
Excusez-moi, j'ai dû faire un mauvais numéro
J'ai fait un faux numéro, désolé (de vous avoir dérangé)
On vous a appelé par erreur
Vous avez fait un faux numéro
Vous vous êtes trompé de numéro
Vous vous êtes trompé sur (un) chiffre
Votre correspondant est sorti
Puis-je laisser un message ?/Pouvez-vous noter un message ?
Je rappellerai. Vers quelle heure ai-je une chance de le/la joindre ?
Pouvez-vous lui demander de me rappeler ?
Votre correspondant veut parler à quelqu'un qui est sorti
Puis-je prendre un message ?
Pourriez-vous rappeler (dans une demi-heure) ?
Voulez-vous qu'il/qu'elle vous rappelle ?
Pour s'adresser à l'opérateur ou à l'opératrice
J'essaie d'avoir le (45 67 89 00)
Cela sonne occupé sans arrêt
J'ai été coupé

A la poste
accusé de réception *acknowledgement of receipt*
affranchir (une lettre) *to put postage on (a letter)*
bureau de poste *post office*
combien ? *how much?*
:il faut (mettre) un timbre à combien pour . . . ? *what's the stamp for . . .?*
:à combien faut-il affranchir une lettre pour . . . ? *what's the letter rate for . . .?*
:combien faut-il mettre pour envoyer . . . ? *how much should I put on to send . . .?*
envoyer en urgent/en ordinaire/en recommandé *to send by first-class/by second-class/by registered mail*
expédier en exprès *to send express*
mandat *money order*
poste *post office*
recherches : faire des recherches *to make inquiries*
reçu *receipt*
renseigner qn *to help s.o.*
se renseigner (de) *to inquire (about)*
télécopie *fax*
tarif (particulier) *(special) rate*
:tarif ordinaire/lent *first-class/second-class (rate)*
valeur : en valeur déclarée *insured*

Au téléphone
s'adresser à *to speak to*
allô ? *hello?*
cela sonne occupé *it's the* Br *engaged tone* or Am *busy signal*
(votre) correspondant *the person making the call (to you), your caller; the person you are calling* or *you have called*
couper qn *to cut s.o. off*
décrocher *to pick up the receiver* or *phone*
désolé (de) *sorry (for)*
être : je suis (bien) à . . . ? *is this . . .?*
faire un mauvais *ou* un faux numéro *to dial the wrong number*
joindre *to reach*
mettre qn en communication avec qn *to put s.o. through to s.o.*
part : c'est de la part de qui ? *who's speaking?*
qui est à l'appareil ? *who's speaking?*
ne quittez pas *hold on*
opérateur, -trice *operator*
passer qn à qn *to put s.o. through to s.o.*
rappeler *to call back*
restez en ligne *hold the line*
se tromper de numéro/sur (un) chiffre *to get the wrong number/(one) figure wrong*

Dans une cabine téléphonique

On trouve en France deux types de cabines téléphoniques : à cartes (Télécarte) ou à pièces. Les instructions sont affichées sur la paroi, et, pour les cabines à cartes, s'inscrivent sur un petit écran. On trouve des 'Point-Phone' dans des lieux publics ; ils fonctionnent avec des pièces de monnaie.
Marche à suivre
1 – Décrochez
2 – Introduire votre carte/vos pièces de monnaie
3 – Composez le numéro demandé
4 – Lorsque votre correspondant décroche, parlez
Instructions usuelles
Décrochez (le combiné)
Introduisez votre carte/les pièces de monnaie
Introduisez un minimum de (1 F)
Attendez la tonalité
Composez le numéro demandé/l'indicatif du pays
De Paris, composez le 16 pour avoir la province
De province, composez le 16 puis le 1 pour avoir la région parisienne
Ne raccrochez pas
Pour ne pas être coupé lorsque le voyant clignote, introduisez de nouvelles pièces
Vous allez être coupé
Pour les renseignements, composez le 12
Pour les renseignements internationaux, composez le 19 suivi du 33 et du 12 et de l'indicatif du pays
Pour l'international, composez le 19 puis l'indicatif du pays après la deuxième tonalité
Pour signaler un dérangement, composez le 13

Les tonalités
On peut entendre différents sons :
un bourdonnement continu (la tonalité)
un bourdonnement continu un peu moins aigu (la tonalité du 16 ou du 19)
une série de bips aigus (avant la sonnerie chez votre correspondant)
des bips aigus (en composant un numéro sur un téléphone à touches)
une tonalité prolongée à intervalles réguliers (la sonnerie chez le correspondant)
une série ininterrompue de tonalités assez aiguës (sonnerie 'occupé')
trois notes aiguës (suivies d'un message enregistré, en cas d'encombrement des lignes ou de numéro non attribué)

Les spectacles

Pour se renseigner du programme et des horaires
Quel est le programme de (samedi) ?
Que donnez-vous (mercredi soir) ?
Peut-on réserver (des places) pour (le film) de (dimanche soir) ?
Je voudrais voir (Carmen) (jeudi)
Y a-t-il une représentation de (Rigoletto) (vendredi soir) ?
A quelle heure est la représentation/le film ce soir ?
Quels sont les horaires de (demain) ?
A quelle heure commence le spectacle/le film *ou* la séance/la représentation ?

Pour réserver des places
Je voudrais (réserver) (deux) places
Il me faudrait (deux) places
Vous reste-t-il (deux) places pour (demain) ?
Avez-vous encore des places pour la représentation de (ce soir) ?
Y a-t-il encore de bonnes places disponibles ?
Je voudrais (une) place pour la séance/la représentation de (20 heures)
(Deux) places pour celle de 19 heures 30, s'il vous plaît
Pour choisir ses places
Deux/Des fauteuils (d'orchestre)
Des loges
En haut/bas
Dans les premiers rangs/Vers le fond
Au (premier) rang
Dans le milieu de la salle
Dans les cinq derniers rangs
Sur le côté
C'est une bonne place ?/Elle est bien située ?
Est-ce qu'on voit/entend bien (de cette place) ?

Demandes de précisions
Doit-on arriver en avance ?
A quelle heure doit-on se présenter ?
Me garderez-vous les billets jusqu'à (19 heures 30)
A quelle heure se termine la représentation/la séance/le spectacle ?
Cela finit à quelle heure ?
Combien de temps dure la représentation/la séance/le spectacle ?
Y a-t-il un entracte/des entractes ?

Dans une cabine téléphonique
bips *pips*
bourdonnement *hum*
cabine téléphonique *phone booth*
clignoter *to flash*
composer *to dial*
correspondant *person one is calling*
couper qn *to cut s.o. off*
décrocher (le combiné) *to pick up the receiver* or *the phone*
encombrement : en cas d'encombrement des lignes *in the event of all lines being busy*
indicatif *code*
introduire *to insert, to put in*
marche à suivre *instructions*
message enregistré *recorded message*
numéro non attribué *unobtainable number*
occupé Br *engaged*, Am *busy*
pièces (de monnaie) *coins*
raccrocher *to hang up*
signaler un dérangement *to report a phone out of order*
sonnerie *ringing tone*
télécarte *phone card*
téléphone à touches *push-button phone*
tonalité *tone* ; (before dialling) Br *dialling* or Am *dial tone*
voyant *light signal*

Les spectacles
côté : sur le côté *on the side*
demandes de précisions *requesting further details*
disponible *available*
donner : que donnez-vous ? *what are you showing?, what's on?*
en avance *early*
entracte *intermission*, Br *interval*
falloir : il me faudrait deux places *I should like* or *I need two seats*
fauteuils (d'orchestre) *seats in the stalls*
fond : vers le fond *towards the back*
horaires *times*
loges : des loges *seats in the dress circle*
place *seat*
se présenter *to turn up*
rang *row*
se renseigner de *to inquire about*
représentation *performance*
réserver *to book, to reserve*
rester : vous reste-t-il deux places (pour . . .) ? *do you have two seats left (for . . .)?*
salle *auditorium*
séance *performance, showing* (of film)
spectacle *show*
:les spectacles *entertainment* (at theatre, cinema *etc*)

Achats de billets (transports)

Pour savoir où s'adresser
Où peut-on acheter un billet ?
Où s'achètent les billets ?
Y a-t-il un guichet (près d'ici) ?
Où dois-je m'adresser pour acheter un billet d'avion pour (Berlin) ?
Où se trouve l'agence de voyages la plus proche ?
Réponse
Vous pouvez/On peut acheter des billets à deux pas d'ici
Vous trouverez un guichet sur votre droite/gauche
On achète son billet dans le car/à l'aéroport

Pour acheter un billet
Pour savoir quel type de billet prendre
Dois-je prendre un aller simple/un aller-retour ?
Quel type de billet me faut-il ?
Pour demander son billet
Un billet, s'il vous plaît
Deux allers simples pour (Paris)
Un aller-retour pour (Londres)
Un aller-retour (Paris-Lyon), s'il vous plaît
Je voudrais une place dans le bus/sur l'avion de 14 heures, s'il vous plaît
Donnez-moi un aller-retour pour (Brest), s'il vous plaît
Les tarifs
C'est combien ?
Combien cela fait-il ?
Combien coûte l'aller-retour ?
Y a-t-il une réduction (pour) (étudiants) ?
Y a-t-il un tarif réduit ?
Acceptez-vous les chèques/les cartes de crédit ?
Demandes de précisions
Ce billet me permet-il d'aller jusqu'à (l'aéroport) ?
Est-ce que je peux aller jusqu'à (Grenoble) en première classe avec ce billet ?
Puis-je prendre ce train avec ce billet ?
Y a-t-il un supplément à payer pour (le train de midi) ?
Ce billet est valable pendant combien de temps ?
Autres services
Faut-il réserver sa place ?
Puis-je réserver (une couchette) ?
Je voudrais que mes bagages partent avant moi
Je voudrais réserver une place en compartiment (non-)fumeurs
Où puis-je me faire rembourser un billet inutilisé ?

Organisation de voyages

Pour se renseigner des moyens de transport
A quelle heure part le prochain (train) pour (Paris) ?
Y a-t-il un avion pour (Turin) (demain soir) ?
Les trains/avions pour (Lyon) partent tous les combien ?
Est-ce que c'est bien desservi (par le train/l'avion) ?
Les départs ont lieu tous les combien ?
Le voyage prend combien de temps ?
A quelle heure arrive-t-on/est prévue l'arrivée ?
A quelle heure est le départ ?
D'où part-il ?
Est-ce que l'on passe par (Calais) ?

Pour se renseigner des routes
Quel est l'itinéraire le plus court pour aller à (Lyon) ?
Quelle route prendriez-vous/faut-il prendre pour aller à (Dijon) ?
Par où faut-il passer pour aller à (Dijon) ?
Combien de temps faut-il (compter) pour aller à (Caen) en voiture ?
Combien de kilomètres cela fait-il ?/Cela fait combien de kilomètres ?
C'est une bonne route
Combien de temps faut-il prévoir *ou* compter ?
Il y a combien de kilomètres pour aller à (Rouen) en voiture/par la route ?
Les routes sont bonnes pour aller à (Toulouse) ?

L'organisation : suggestions
Prenons l'avion du matin
Je propose qu'on passe par (Meaux)
Nous pourrons déjeuner sur la route
On pourra s'arrêter en cours de route/à (Aix)
Et si on passait par (Bruxelles) ?
Ce serait plus rapide/moins cher en (train)
Nous y serions plus vite en (train)
Je crois que (la route de la côte) est mieux
Je dirais que c'est mieux de passer par (la Belgique)
Je crois qu'il faudrait partir à (neuf heures)
Je n'ai pas envie de/Je ne tiens pas à (traverser Paris)
Je préférerais être rendu *ou* arriver (avant la nuit)
Si je pars à (sept heures), j'y serai avant (midi)
Si nous arrivons à prendre celui de (15h), nous y serons à temps
En passant par (Bordeaux), on peut y être pour midi
Qu'en dites-vous ?
Qu'est-ce que vous en pensez ?

Achats de billets (transports)
achats de billets *buying tickets*
à deux pas d'ici *very close by*
s'adresser (pour acheter) *to go (to buy)*
:savoir où s'adresser *to find out where to go*
agence de voyages *travel agency*
aller-retour (pour . . .) Br *return (ticket)* or Am *round-trip (ticket) (to . . .)*
aller simple (pour . . .) *one-way (ticket)* or Br *single (ticket) (to . . .)*
car Br *coach*, Am *bus*
carte de crédit *credit card*
combien ? *how much?*
:combien cela fait-il ? *how much is that?*
compartiment (non-)fumeurs *(non-)smoking compartment*
couchette *sleeper, sleeping berth*
coûter *to cost*
guichet *ticket office*
inutilisé *unused*
permettre (de) *to allow (to)*
place *seat*
première classe *first class*
rembourser *to refund*
réserver *to reserve*
savoir : pour savoir . . . *to find out . . .*
supplément : supplément à payer *extra to pay*
tarif réduit *reduced rate*

Organisation de voyages
arriver à faire *to manage to do*
avoir lieu *to take place*
combien : tous les combien ? *how often?*
:combien de kilomètres cela fait-il ? *how many kilometres is it?*
:combien de temps faut-il prévoir *ou* compter ? *how much time should we allow?*
côte *coast*
desservir : c'est bien desservi (par le train/l'avion) *there's a frequent (train/air) service*
dire : qu'en dites-vous ? *what do you say?*
itinéraire *route, itinerary*
moyens de transport *means of transport*
passer par . . . *to go through . . .*
:par où faut-il passer pour aller à . . .? *which way do you have to go to get to . . .?*
prévu *expected, planned*
proposer que . . . + *sub* *to suggest that . . .*
rendu : être rendu *to have arrived*
se renseigner de *to inquire about*
route *road*
:en cours de route *on the way*
:par la route *by road*
tenir à faire *to be keen on doing*

Dans l'autobus

Pour savoir où prendre le bus
Y a-t-il un arrêt de bus pas loin d'ici ?
Où se trouve l'arrêt de bus le plus proche ?
L'arrêt (de bus) pour le (32), c'est bien ici ?
On prend (bien) le bus ici pour aller (en ville) ?
Où se trouve la gare routière, s'il vous plaît ?
D'où partent les bus pour (Orly) ?

Les horaires et les lignes
Savez-vous à quelle heure passe/part le prochain bus (pour le centre-ville) ?
Ces bus passent tous les combien ?
A quelle heure est le prochain bus (pour l'aéroport) ?
Quel bus va (au parc) ?/Quel est le bus qui va (au parc) ?
Quel bus faut-il prendre pour aller (à l'université) ?
Quelle est la ligne qui va (en ville) ?
Il faut prendre quel bus *ou* quel numéro pour aller (en ville) ?
C'est bien ce bus qui va (à la gare) ?
Pour renseigner quelqu'un
Vous pouvez prendre un *ou* le (42) pour aller en ville/Le (42) va en ville
Il s'arrête ici
Il passe toutes les (dix minutes)
Prenez un *ou* le (17) jusqu'à (la gare)
(Là,) vous changerez pour prendre le bus (28) qui passe à (l'université)
Ça prend environ une demi-heure

Une fois dans l'autobus
C'est bien ce bus qui va à (l'aéroport) ?
Vous allez à (la gare) ?
Pour acheter un billet
Pour aller (en ville), c'est combien ?
Je voudrais un billet, s'il vous plaît. C'est combien ?
Peut-on acheter un aller-retour ?
Autres renseignements
Est-ce que c'est direct pour (la gare) ?
Faut-il changer ?
Il y a combien d'arrêts avant le mien ?
Combien de temps cela prend-il ?
Vous pouvez me dire où je dois descendre, s'il vous plaît ?
A quel arrêt dois-je descendre ?
Y a-t-il une correspondance pour (l'hôpital) ?

Dans le métro

Pour savoir où prendre le métro
Y a-t-il une station de métro pas loin d'ici ?
Où se trouve la station de métro la plus proche ?
Comment fait-on pour trouver une station de métro ?
Est-ce qu'il y a une ligne de métro qui passe pas loin d'ici ?
Peut-on prendre le métro près d'ici ?

Les horaires et les lignes
Savez-vous à quelle heure passe/part le prochain métro (en direction de Créteil) ?
Ce métro passe tous les combien ?
A quelle heure est le prochain métro ?
Quelle ligne va (au bois de Boulogne) ?
Quelle ligne faut-il prendre pour aller à (l'aéroport) ?
Quel est le numéro de la ligne qui va à (Clichy) ?
Est-ce qu'il y a une ligne qui dessert (Saint-Denis) ?
C'est bien ce métro qui va à (Saint-Lazare) ?
Pour renseigner quelqu'un
Vous prenez un ticket (à la machine *ou* au distributeur)
La ligne qui va (au nord de Paris), c'est la (13), direction (Porte de Clichy)
Vous changerez à (Saint-Lazare)
Il y a des trains toutes les (cinq minutes) (pour aller à Montparnasse)
Il faut prendre la ligne (10)/la ligne (Nation-Dauphine)

A la station
C'est bien cette ligne/la ligne (13) qui va à (Clichy) ?
Cette ligne/La ligne (9) mène bien à (Saint-Lazare) ?
Pour acheter un ticket
Un ticket pour (Saint-Germain-en-Laye), s'il vous plaît
Je voudrais un ticket, s'il vous plaît. C'est combien ?
Un carnet (de tickets) (première/deuxième classe), s'il vous plaît
Un coupon hebdomadaire/mensuel, s'il vous plaît
Autres renseignements
Est-ce que c'est direct ?
Faut il changer ?
Il y a combien de stations avant la mienne/jusqu'à (Invalides) ?
A quelle station faut-il descendre ?
Est-ce que je vais jusqu'au terminus ?
Quelle direction faut-il prendre ?
Où est la correspondance pour la ligne (12) ?

Dans l'autobus
acheter *to buy*
aller-retour Br *return (ticket)*, Am *round-trip (ticket)*
arrêt (de bus) *(bus) stop*
s'arrêter *to stop*
autobus *bus*
billet *ticket*
centre-ville *town centre*
changer (pour prendre . . .) *to change (onto . . .)*
correspondance *connection*
descendre *to get off*
gare routière Br *coach* or Am *bus station*
horaires *times*
ligne *service*
où se trouve . . . ? *where is . . . ?*
passer : à quelle heure passe le bus ? *what time does the bus come?*
: . . . le bus qui passe à (l'université) *. . . the bus that goes to (the university)*
prendre (un bus) *to catch (a bus)*
prendre (une demi-heure) *to take (a half-hour)*
renseigner qn *to give s.o. information*
savoir : pour savoir . . . *to find out . . .*
tous les combien ? *how often?*
toutes les (dix minutes) *every (ten minutes)*

Dans le métro
carnet (de tickets) *book (of tickets)*
classe : première/deuxième classe *first/second class*
comment fait-on pour trouver . . . ? *how do I* or *we find . . .?*
correspondance *connection*
descendre *to get off*
desservir : une ligne qui dessert . . . *a line that goes to . . .*
distributeur *ticket machine*
en direction de . . . *for . . ., to . . .*
hebdomadaire *weekly*
horaires *times*
ligne *line*
mensuel *monthly*
métro Br *underground*, Am *subway*
:station/ligne de métro Br *underground* or Am *subway station/line*
:peut-on prendre le métro . . . ? *can I* or *we get the* Br *underground* or Am *subway . . .?*
:le prochain métro *the next train*
passer : à quelle heure passe le métro ? *what time does the train come?*
renseigner qn *to give s.o. information*
renseignements *information*
savoir : pour savoir . . . *to find out . . .*
tous les combien ? *how often?*

Le travail

Emploi et situation
Pour dire ce que l'on fait
Je suis (stagiaire)
Je travaille chez Bordas/pour une maison d'édition/dans une banque
Je m'occupe de (la comptabilité)
Je suis à la comptabilité/au service clientèle
Je travaille là depuis (six ans)/J'y suis depuis (six ans)
J'aime bien/Je n'aime pas ce que je fais
C'est un bon emploi *ou* boulot
C'est intéressant/bien payé
Pour savoir ce que quelqu'un fait
Que faites-vous (dans la vie) ?
Vous travaillez où/dans quoi/chez qui ?
Vous avez un emploi ?
Vous êtes dans quoi *ou* quelle branche ?
C'est intéressant/bien payé ?
Est-ce que c'est très prenant ?

Pour expliquer ce que l'on fait
On commence à (8 heures 30) et on finit à (17 heures)
On travaille de (9 à 5)
On travaille/ne travaille pas le (samedi)
On a (une heure) pour déjeuner
Je fais beaucoup de déplacements
J'ai beaucoup de tâches administratives/de paperasseries à faire
On a énormément de travail (à la fin du mois)
On a (six semaines) de congé par an

Les collègues de travail
Mon chef, c'est (le responsable des ventes)
Je suis sous les ordres de ...
Nous sommes (six) dans mon service
Les autres sont (des femmes) pour la plupart
Mes collègues sont pour la plupart (des femmes)
C'est un service où tout le monde s'entend bien
Il y a (600) employés au total chez nous
L'entreprise *ou* La boîte emploie (600) personnes

Le chômage
Il est au chômage/Il a perdu son emploi
Il est à la recherche d'un emploi/Il cherche du travail
Il y a beaucoup de chômeurs par ici
Le chômage touche beaucoup de gens

L'école

Le système éducatif
L'école que l'on fréquente
C'est un établissement (technique)/C'est un établissement spécialisé dans (les métiers du bois)
Il y a (400) élèves
C'est/Ce n'est pas un (très) grand établissement
L'organisation
L'année est divisée en (trois trimestres)
L'école *ou* La scolarité n'est plus obligatoire après (16) ans
On peut entrer à l'université dès qu'on a le baccalauréat
Les cours commencent à (8 heures 30) et se terminent à (17 heures)
Il n'y a pas (de) cours le (mercredi)
On n'a cours que le matin le (samedi)
Les cours durent (une) heure
Nous devons fournir beaucoup de travail
Nous (n')avons (pas) assez de sport *ou* d'EPS
Nous avons beaucoup/peu de travail à faire chez nous *ou* à la maison

Les examens
Il passe un/son/l'examen en (juin)
Nous préparons l'examen (de fin d'année)/le baccalauréat
Les examens sont difficiles/faciles
J'ai réussi/échoué *ou* été collé l'an dernier
Il faut réussir ses examens pour (trouver un bon emploi)

Les matières
On fait de (la physique)
Je trouve les mathématiques compliquées/faciles
Elle (n')est (pas) bonne en (langues)
Nous n'avons pas de cours (d'arts plastiques)
La matière que je préfère, c'est l'histoire
J'aime/J'aimais bien (la chimie)
Nous avons de nouvelles matières cette année
On manque d'équipements sportifs

Les professeurs
C'est un(e) bon(ne)/mauvais(e) prof
Elle est prof de (géographie)/Elle enseigne (la géographie)
Elle nous fait (cours de) géographie
Elle est sévère/Elle n'est pas très sévère

Le travail
boîte *firm*
boulot *job*
chef *boss*
chez : travailler chez . . . *to work at* or *for . . .*
chômage *unemployment*
:au chômage *unemployed*
chômeur *unemployed person*
comptabilité *accounts*
congé : (six semaines) de congé *(six weeks) off*
emploi *job*
s'entendre bien *to get along well*
entreprise *company*
faire des déplacements *to travel*
maison d'édition *publishing company*
s'occuper de *to take care of*
paperasseries (à faire) *paperwork (to do)*
prenant *absorbing*
quoi : vous travaillez *ou* vous êtes dans quoi ? *what's your line of work?*
responsable des ventes *sales manager*
savoir : pour savoir . . . *to find out . . .*
service *department*
situation *position*
sous les ordres de qn *under s.o.*
stagiaire *trainee*
toucher *to affect*

L'école
baccalauréat *school leaving certificate*
bon en . . . *good at . . .*
chimie *chemistry*
collé : être collé *to fail*
cours *lessons*
:avoir cours *to have lessons*
dès qu'on a . . . *as soon as you have . . .*
échouer *to fail*
école *school*
élève *pupil, student*
enseigner *to teach*
EPS Br *PE*, Am *Phys Ed*
établissement *school*
fournir beaucoup de travail *to put in a lot of work*
fréquenter une école *to attend a school*
matière *subject*
obligatoire *compulsory*
passer un examen *to take an exam*
prof(esseur) *teacher*
:être prof de . . . *to be a teacher of . . .*
réussir (un examen) *to pass (an exam)*
scolarité *schooling*
sévère *strict*
système éducatif *education system*
technique *technical*
trimestre *term*

Weights and measures
Conversion tables

Poids et mesures
Tables de conversion

Length / Longueur

Length GB & US			Système Métrique		Metric System
1 inch	=	25,4 millimètres 2,54 centimètres	1 millimètre	=	0.03937 inch
1 foot (= 12 inches)	=	30,48 centimètres 0,3048 mètre	1 centimètre (= 10 millimètres)	=	0.3937 inch
1 yard (= 3 feet or 36 inches)	=	91,44 centimètres 0,9144 mètre	1 mètre (= 100 centimètres)	=	39.37 inches 3.2808 feet 1.0936 yards
1 furlong (= 220 yards)	=	201,17 mètre 0,20117 kilomètre	1 kilomètre (= 1 000 mètres)	=	1093.6 yards 4.97 furlongs 0.62137 mile
1 mile (= 1760 yards or 8 furlongs)	=	1609,3 mètres 1,6093 kilomètres			

Area / Surface

Area GB & US			Système Métrique		Metric System
1 square inch	=	645,16 millimètres carrés 6,4516 centimètres carrés	1 millimètre carré	=	0.00155 square inch
1 square foot (= 144 square inches)	=	929,03 centimètres carrés 0,092903 mètre carré	1 centimètre carré	=	0.155 square inch
1 square yard (= 9 square feet)	=	0,83613 mètre carré	1 mètre carré	=	1.196 square yards
1 acre (= 4840 square yards)	=	0,405 hectare	1 are (= 100 mètres carrés)	=	0.025 acre 119.6 square yards
1 square mile (= 640 acres)	=	2,59 kilomètres carrés 259 hectares	1 hectare (= 100 ares)	=	2.471 acres
			1 kilomètre carré	=	0.38608 square mile

Capacity / Capacité

Capacity GB & US			Système Métrique		Metric System
1 fluid ounce (GB) (= 0.9608 fluid ounce (US))	=	28,41 millilitres 0,02841 litre	1 millilitre	=	0.0352 fluid ounce (GB) 0.0338 fluid ounce (US)
1 fluid ounce (US) (= 1.0408 fluid ounces (GB))	=	29,57 millilitres 0,02957 litre	1 centilitre (= 10 millilitres)	=	0.352 fluid ounce (GB) 0.338 fluid ounce (US)
1 pint (GB) (= 20 fluid ounces) (= 1.201 pints (US))	=	0,5683 litre	1 litre (= 100 centilitres)	=	1.76 pints (GB) 0.22 gallon (GB)
1 pint (US) (= 16 fluid ounces) (= 0.8327 pint (GB))	=	0,4732 litre		=	2.113 pints (US) 0.264 gallon (US)
1 quart (GB) (= 2 pints) (= 1.201 quarts (US))	=	1,1365 litre			
1 quart (US) (= 2 pints) (= 0.8327 quart (GB))	=	0,9464 litre			
1 gallon (GB) (= 4 quarts or 8 pints) (= 1.201 gallons (US))	=	4,5461 litres			
1 gallon (US) (= 4 quarts or 8 pints) (= 0.8327 gallon (GB))	=	3,7854 litres			

Weights GB & US: Avoirdupois			Poids Système Métrique		Metric System
1 ounce	=	28,35 grammes	1 gramme	=	0.03527 ounce
1 pound (= 16 ounces)	=	453,59 grammes 0,45359 kilogramme	1 kilogramme (= 1 000 grammes)	=	2.2046 pounds
1 stone (GB) (= 14 pounds)	=	6,35026 kilogrammes	1 tonne (= 1 000 kilogrammes)	=	19.6841 hundredweight (GB) 22.046 hundredweight (US) 0.9842 ton (GB) 1.1023 tons (US)
1 (long) hundredweight (GB) (= 112 pounds)	=	50,8 kilogrammes			
1 (short) hundredweight (US) (= 100 pounds)	=	45,36 kilogrammes			
1 (long) ton (GB) (= 20 (long) hundredweight or 2240 pounds)	=	1 016,04 kilogrammes 1,01604 tonnes			
1 (short) ton (US) (= 20 (short) hundredweight or 2000 pounds)	=	907,18 kilogrammes 0,90718 tonne			

Abréviations usuelles des mesures du système GB et US

Longueur et surface

inch(es)	in/in(s)
foot (feet)	ft
yard(s)	yd/yds
mile(s)	m
square	sq (eg. 10 sq ft)

Capacité et poids

fluid ounce(s)	fl oz
pint(s)	pt/pts
quart(s)	qt/qts
ounce(s)	oz
pound(s)	lb/lb(s)
stone	st
hundredweight	cwt/cwts

Common abbreviations of metric measures

Length and area

millimètre(s)	mm
centimètre(s)	cm
mètre(s)	m
kilomètre(s)	km
hectare(s)	ha

Capacity and weights

millilitre(s)	ml
centilitre(s)	cl
litre(s)	l
gramme(s)	g
kilogramme(s)	kg
tonne(s)	t

How to use the dictionary

- plurals of compound words
- masculine and feminine noun
- slashes indicate non-equivalent alternatives
- examples in secondary bold; translations in roman; glosses in italics
- headwords in primary bold
- British and American alternative translations
- extensive illustrative examples
- gender of French nouns
- field labels in italics
- irregular verb conjugations indicated with tenses in italics
- letters indicate sense divisions
- Canadian usage
- explanatory glosses in italics
- colloquial usage
- technical terms
- alternative headwords
- specialized terms

best-seller [bɛstsɛlœr] *nm* best-seller; (*pl best-sellers*).
bêta[1], -asse [bɛta, -ɑs] *F* **1** *adj* silly, stupid. **2** *n* idiot, nit(wit); **oh le gros b.!,** (*à un enfant*) silly billy!
bêta[2] [bɛta] *nm* **(a)** (*lettre de l'alphabet grec*) beta; **(b)** *Nucl* **particules/rayons b.,** beta particles/rays.
bêtabloquant [betablɔkɑ̃] *nm Pharm* beta-blocker.
bétail [betaj] *nm* livestock, cattle; **gros b.,** livestock (*including cattle, horses, asses, mules*); **menu** *ou* **petit b.,** smaller livestock; *Fig* **on était traité comme du b.,** we were treated like cattle.
bêtatron [bɛtatrɔ̃] *nm Nucl* betatron.
bête [bɛt] **1** *nf* **(a)** animal, beast; **b. à quatre pieds,** four-legged animal *or* beast; **b. à cornes,** horned animal *or* beast; **b. de trait,** draught animal; **les bêtes,** (*on farm*) the livestock; **donner aux bêtes,** to feed the animals; *F* **reprendre du poil de la b.,** (*reprendre le dessus*) to perk up, to pick up; **les bêtes féroces,** wild animals; **une b. sauvage,** a wild animal; **nos amies les bêtes,** our four-legged friends; *Fig* **c'est sa b. noire,** he's *or* it's *etc* his pet hate; **travailler comme une b.,** to work like a slave; *Fig Péj* **b. à concours,** *Br* swot, *Am* grind; **c'est une belle b., ce cheval,** that horse is a fine animal; *F* **tu as vu sa moto, c'est une belle b.!,** have you seen his motorbike?, it's a beauty!; **tu as vu son nouveau mec, c'est une belle b.!,** have you seen her new man?, he's absolutely gorgeous!; **elle m'a regardé comme une b. curieuse,** she looked at me as if I was from another planet;
(b) (*insecte*) insect, *Am* bug; **petites bêtes,** insects; (*nocives*) vermin; **b. à bon Dieu,** *Br* ladybird, *Am* ladybug; **il y a une b. dans ma pomme,** there's a maggot in my apple; *Fig* **chercher la petite b.,** to be over-critical, *F* to nitpick;
(c) (*l'homme*) **la b. humaine,** the old Adam;
(d) (*idiot*) fool, idiot, nit(wit); **faire la b.,** to pretend to be stupid; (*sans le vouloir*) to act foolishly *or* stupidly.
2 *adj* stupid, silly, foolish; **que je suis b.!,** how silly *or* stupid of me!; **pas si b.!,** I'm *or* she's *etc* not such a fool (as all that)!, not likely!; **c'est vraiment b., j'ai oublié mes clés,** how stupid, I've forgotten my keys; **il n'est pas si b. qu'il en a l'air,** he's not as stupid *or* as silly as he looks; **elle est b. comme un âne** *ou* **comme ses pieds,** she's a real idiot *or* fool; **mon Dieu qu'il est b.!,** God he's stupid!; **l'âge b.,** the difficult age; **b. et méchant,** stupid and nasty; **c'est b. comme chou,** it's as easy as pie *or* as anything; *Can* **rester tout b.,** (*décontenancé*) to be stupefied; **une mort b.,** a stupid *or* senseless death.
bétel [betɛl] *nm* (*plante*) betel.
bêtement [bɛtmɑ̃] *adv* stupidly, foolishly, idiotically; **mourir b.,** to die senselessly; **tout b.,** purely and simply.
Bethléem [bɛtleɛm] *nm Bible* Bethlehem.
bêtifiant [betifjɑ̃] *adj* idiotic.
bêtifier [betifje] *v* (*pr sub & impf* **n. bêtifiions, v. bêtifiiez**) **1** *vt* to make (*s.o.*) stupid. **2** *vi* to talk nonsense; (*faire l'idiot*) to play the fool; **quand il parle à un enfant, il bêtifie,** he uses baby-talk to children.
bêtise [betiz] *nf* **(a)** (*imbécillité*) stupidity, silliness; **être d'une b. extrême,** to be exceedingly stupid;
(b) (*chose idiote*) nonsense, absurdity; **dire des bêtises,** to talk nonsense *or Br* rubbish; **quelle b.!,** what nonsense!, how ridiculous!; **se disputer pour des bêtises,** to argue over nothing; **perdre son temps à des bêtises,** to waste one's time on idiotic things; **dépenser tout son argent en bêtises,** to fritter away one's money;
(c) (*gaffe*) blunder, silly *or* stupid mistake; **faire des bêtises,** to play the fool; **faire une grande b.,** to do something extremely stupid *or* silly; **ça, c'est une grosse b.,** that is *or* was very stupid; **une b.,** a stupid move; **il ne faudrait pas qu'elle fasse une b.,** we don't want her to do anything silly;
(d) *Can* **bêtises,** (*injures*) insults;
(e) bêtises de Cambrai, ≈ *Br* mint humbugs (*hard mint Br sweets or Am candies*).
béton [betɔ̃] *nm* **(a)** *Constr* concrete; **b. armé,** reinforced concrete; *Fig* **des muscles en b.,** rock-hard muscles; *F* **un alibi en b.,** a cast-iron alibi; **(b)** *Fb* **faire le b.,** to pack the defence; **(c)** *F* **laisse b.,** let it drop!, drop it!
bétonnage [betɔnaʒ] *nm* **(a)** *Constr* concreting; **(b)** *Fb* packing the defence.
bétonner [betɔne] *vt* **(a)** to build with concrete; (*couler du béton sur*) to concrete; **(b)** *Fb* to pack the defence.
bétonneuse [betɔnøz] *nf*, **bétonnière** [betɔnjɛr] *nf* concrete mixer, cement mixer.
bette [bɛt] *nf* (spinach) beet; **b. à carde (blanche), b. à côtes,** seakale beet, Swiss chard.

- pluriels des mots composés
- nom masculin et féminin
- les barres obliques évitent la répétition d'un même élément de phrase
- exemples en caractères mi-gras; traductions en caractères maigres; explications en italiques
- mots d'entrée en caractères gras
- variantes de l'anglais britannique ou de l'anglais américain
- de très nombreux exemples mettent le mot en situation
- genre des noms communs
- indications de champs sémantiques en italiques
- conjugaisons des verbes irréguliers (les temps sont indiqués en italiques)
- les lettres repèrent les différentes catégories sémantiques
- termes canadiens
- gloses en italiques
- langue familière
- termes techniques
- variantes lexicales
- termes spécialisés